W9-BDD-094

Britannica Book of the Year

Encyclopædia Britannica, Inc.
Chicago • London • Paris • Rome • Seoul • Sydney • Tokyo

1998 Britannica Book of the Year

Library of Congress Catalog Card Number: 38-12082
International Standard Book Number: 0-85229-675-4
International Standard Serial Number: 0068-1156

BRITANNICA BOOK OF THE YEAR

Britannica Online may be accessed on the Internet at http://www.eb.com.

(Trademark Reg. U.S. Pat. Off.) Printed in U.S.A.

FOREWORD

The staff of the *Britannica Book of the Year* is pleased to present its review of the events, developments, and trends that have shaped 1997. In many ways the year was a good one, marked by peace and prosperity throughout a large part of the world and by few major natural disasters. Conflict and violence continued in central Africa, and the high-flying economies of East and Southeast Asia suffered setbacks late in the year. Great Britain experienced a particularly eventful 12 months with the election of the first Labour Party government since 1979 and the handover to China of Hong Kong, one of the last vestiges of the British Empire. The year's notable births included the cloned sheep Dolly and the first set of septuplets to be born alive in the United States. The world mourned the loss of Diana, princess of Wales, and Mother Teresa, among many others.

Special features in the yearbook discuss many of these developments. Ian Wilmut, the lead scientist in the group that produced Dolly, writes about both the science of cloning and the ethical issues that are involved. Paris-based correspondent David Buchan describes how the changing role of the French in Africa is affecting political stability on that continent, and Steven Levine of Boulder Run Research recounts the Hong Kong handover and views its implications for the future. The increasing dominance of the English language throughout the world is discussed by Gerald Knowles of Britain's University of Lancaster. Providing an overview of the year in a personal commentary is Gro Harlem Brundtland, the first woman to become prime minister of Norway and a leading figure in the political life of Europe.

In a special report Martin Marty, a prominent theologian, places the mass suicide of the Heaven's Gate followers within the general context of doomsday cults. Other features discuss the growth of gambling as a business in the United States, the increasing popularity of such "fringe" sports as snowboarding and in-line skating, the International Year of the Reef, the ongoing conflict over water rights in the Middle East and North Africa, and the 50th anniversary of Jackie Robinson's first year in major league baseball.

Children's literature receives extended coverage in this volume, and the Beanie Baby phenomenon is noted. Three photo essays reveal the worldwide popularity of tattooing, efforts by zoos to protect the Earth's most endangered animals, and the turmoil in Albania after the collapse of the nation's widespread pyramid schemes.

In addition to these special features there are, of course, the regular articles in *Britannica Book of the Year* and the rich lode of facts and figures, photos, and graphics. For the first time, the book is illustrated predominantly in full colour. I hope you find the yearbook a valuable addition to your library. If you have suggestions on how to improve it, please let us know.

David R. Calhoun, Editor

CONTENTS

Page 138

Page 286

Page 94

Page 22

Page 418

Page 218
DAN LECCA

Page 241

Page 229

Page 290

Page 42
MIKE SEGAR—REUTERS

Page 321

Page 212

Page 474

Page 65

Page 266

Page 367

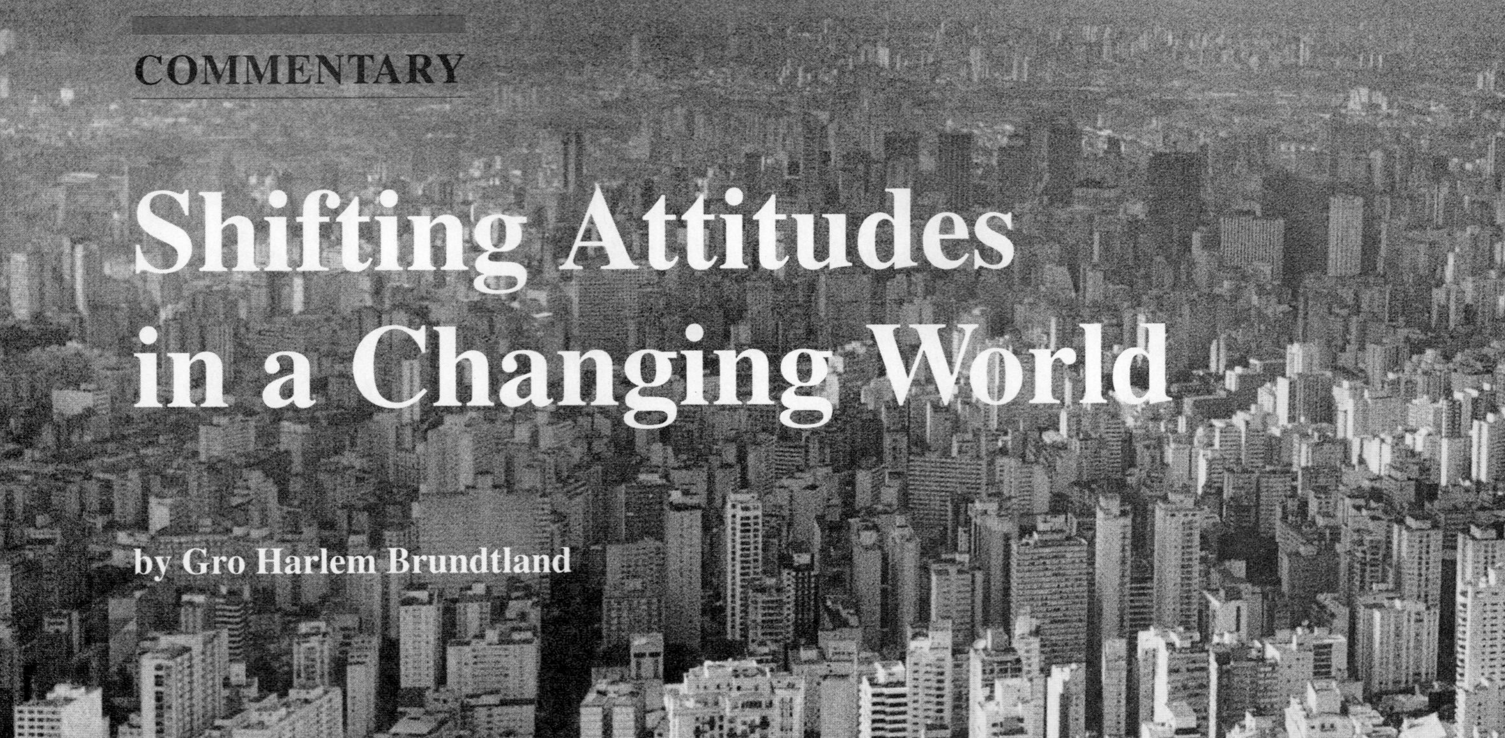

COMMENTARY

Shifting Attitudes in a Changing World

by Gro Harlem Brundtland

Gro Harlem Brundtland is a physician who left medicine to launch a career in politics. During the time she served as prime minister of Norway (February–October 1981, 1986–89, and 1990–96), she was the dominant figure in domestic politics. She is a tireless crusader for such issues as preventive medicine, the environment, and school health. She served as chair of the 1987 UN World Commission on Environment and Development and has been the recipient of numerous awards, including the 1989 Third World Prize for Work on Environmental Issues, the 1990 Indira Gandhi Prize, and the 1992 Onassis Foundation Award. She is currently working on her memoirs.

It was once said that "almost everything in history almost never happened"—a feeling, perhaps, that many of us have had about our own lives. When we look back, we often find an awkward chain of events that escapes logic, and only by willful disregard of such complicating factors as facts will we succeed in finding anything resembling a pattern or a plan guiding us. In westernized societies, rife with information, it has become increasingly difficult to define and describe the time in which we live. We cannot possibly relate to all of the information competing for our attention, claiming to be relevant, important, and even essential. To the question, "What happened yesterday?" there would be millions of different answers.

Having spent more than 20 years in public life, 10 of them as prime minister of Norway, I have often been called upon both to pinpoint the challenges we as a society face and to provide solutions for the best ways of tackling them. These occasions have often vied for attention with other events. There is a reason why politicians do not address the nation on the day that those in the Christian world celebrate Christmas or why American politicians do not try to compete for attention with the Super Bowl, the championship game in football. There has to be space for political messages, and there is a time and a place for everything.

During my formative years, I was accustomed to an orderly progression of events, when topics under discussion seemed much more predictable. That was several decades ago, and the discussion among family, friends, fellow students, and colleagues would be the day's most topical issues—the headline news. At that time the perception was that everyone more or less talked about the same issues. In addition, the media covered the same events, and often the news was shared worldwide. During the 1962 Cuban missile crisis, the 1967 and 1973 Middle East crises, and the frostiest years of the Cold War, eyes and ears were on alert whenever a newspaper headline was viewed or a radio heard. As the old East-West divide largely crumbled, so did the parts of the framework that defined our lives. The welcoming of formerly communist countries seeking membership in NATO and the European

São Paulo, Braz.
SEBASTIÃO SALGADO—CONTACT PRESS IMAGES

Union has become less astonishing, with each step toward integration no longer necessarily a headline news item. Nowadays, international politics seems to attract less serious and sustained attention. Instead, the larger parts of populations concentrate on such events as the Olympic Games, the Super Bowl, or the World Cup in football (soccer). This phenomenon is not limited to the West, however; the British soccer team Manchester United has been virtually adopted as the home team of Singapore. In addition, more countries are establishing sports teams. Although there is nothing inherently wrong with this new focus, it has resulted in a fragmentation of the world's attention.

This was never truer than in 1997, when the rapid growth of the information industry and the number of Internet connections and E-mail subscriptions all provided us with a 24-hour-a-day avalanche of views and news, and the commercial part of that flow and overflow was growing, inspired and financed by global sales of products. As a result of this information overload, threats to the environment and public health were now perceived as common and not important enough to generate action on the national level. Threats to the environment no longer gathered the widespread attention that prompted proposals for policy changes that would enjoy sustained support over a long period of time.

Changes in our immediate physical environment were increasingly driven by anonymous processes. "In my next life I want to be the stock market," quipped James Carville, the prime strategist of U.S. Pres. Bill Clinton's 1992 election campaign. We can find people to blame for the smaller accidents and even the somewhat larger accidents, but no one seems to take responsibility for the increasingly more complex forces that gradually change the configuration of our natural surroundings.

The year 1997 marked the 10th anniversary of the independent commission that I had been called upon to lead—the UN World Commission on Environment and Development, which had released the report "Our Common Future"; the fifth anniversary of the 1992 UN "Earth Summit" in Rio de Janeiro; and the summer that the UN again took stock of world developments. The latter meeting went largely unnoticed, compared with the widespread public attention devoted to the December 1997 conference of the UN Framework Convention on Climate Change in Kyoto, Japan.

At the Kyoto conference on global warming, it became abundantly clear how complex it has become to work out international agreements relating to the environment because of the economic concerns unique to each country. It is no longer enough to try to prohibit certain activities or to reduce emissions of certain substances. The global challenges of the interlink between the environment and development increasingly bring us to the core of the economic life of states. During the late 1980s we were able, through international agreements, to make deep cuts in emissions harmful to the ozone layer.

These reductions were made possible because substitutions had been found for many of the harmful chemicals and, more important, because the harmful substances could be replaced without negative effects on employment and the economies of states.

Drawing up solutions to environmental problems has become ever more difficult because of the way that everything is connected—investment with employment and fiscal measures with wages. The globalized economy means that even measures applied to one sector in one country could affect global competition. This complexity has also posed a challenge to the way we cooperate internationally.

Although the threat of global warming has been known to the world for decades and all countries and leaders agree that we need to deal with the problem, we also know that the effects of measures, especially harsh measures taken in some countries, would be nullified if other countries pursued laissez-faire policies. That is the intrinsic nature of global warming. We find ourselves in a prisoner's dilemma. In essence, as demonstrated at Kyoto, the issue of global warming challenges how our political systems work. The foremost challenge for democracies is to gather support for policies that might require immediate sacrifices in order to avoid negative effects for future generations.

Whereas the UN panel on climate change has found that the emissions of carbon dioxide would have to be cut globally by 60% to stabilize the content of CO_2 in the atmosphere, this path is not feasible for several reasons. Such deep cuts would, in the short-term perspective, cause a breakdown of the world economy. Important and populous low- or medium-income countries are not yet willing to undertake legal commitments about their energy uses. In addition, the state of world technology would not yet permit us to make such a quantum leap.

We must, however, approach a sustainable energy use and find a solution to the threat of global warming early in the 21st century. Such a commitment would require a degree of shared vision and common responsibilities new to humanity. Success lies in the force of imaginations, among those who can forcefully reject the notion of benign neglect by envisioning what would happen if we fail to act. Although many would welcome the global-warming effect of a warmer summer, few would cheer the arrival of the resultant tropical diseases, especially where there had been none.

The positive news is that societies have managed to handle and even eliminate a series of grave threats to the human environment and human health. With that perspective, we must conclude that the 20th century has seen enormous gains in human progress, particularly when we look at the combined effect of increased educational opportunities and improved health care, hygiene, and sanitation. As we approach the millennium, we are likely to hear doomsday prophesies about how low we as a species have plunged and why the present is an uncomfortable time in which to live. Although there are hundreds of millions of poor and unfortunate people in all countries of the world, the overall global trend is one of immense human progress.

Those who have shown special interest in the environment have for a long time encountered a low level of concern among the general public. This malaise changed about 1987—the year that the Earth was voted Planet of the Year and was featured on the front page of *Time* magazine. During the late 1980s and early '90s, it seemed possible to gather high-profile attention to such long-term and complex issues as global warming, desertification, the vanishing rain forests, and the exponential growth of megacities.

The Rio "Earth Summit" was the first to be broadcast live on CNN; other networks and media also devoted widespread coverage to the event. Many perceived a growing public awareness and held higher hopes that it would be possible to explain complex issues, gather political support for long-term goals, and implement internationally agreed-upon measures that would be viewed by the public at large as short-term sacrifices. Many single issues gained symbolic effect and brought many people in contact with the environmental movement. The spotted owl controversy in the U.S. was one such issue that led to heated debate between logging interests and biodiversity groups. Thereafter, public interest seemed to fade.

Unfortunately, catastrophes have frequently catapulted the environment to the centre of world attention, notably the 1978 *Amoco Cadiz* and 1989 *Exxon Valdez* oil spills and the chemical tragedies in Bhopal, India (the 1984 leakage of methyl isocyanate from a pesticide plant), and Schweizerhalle, Switz. (the 1986 explosion and fire at the Sandoz AG chemical warehouse), which had disastrous effects and led to serious legal consequences. The 1986 accident at the Chernobyl nuclear power station in the Soviet Union—the gravest of all these industrial calamities—probably contributed significantly to the collapse of the Soviet political system.

Fortunately, there were few such industrial accidents in 1997—ones that could be traced to imperfections in the development or neglect in the use of technology. A hallmark of the year was, in a sense, what did not happen, and this was a graphic illustration of the present state of development, more so than any actual and highly visible negative event. Although the great forest fires in Indonesia, where burning is an accepted practice for clearing land, attracted worldwide attention and worry, they seemed to be atypical of the problems of our time.

More important, in the future how will public issues be able to compete for attention with the private sector? Perhaps on the basis of quality. Let us hope that there is a limit to what the average person would like to know about blue jeans or a new face cream. The position of news networks to provide increased coverage of public issues offers some hope in sustaining the public interest in them.

A decade earlier the word *solidarity* was avoided by Scandinavians traveling in other industrialized countries because they feared that it might sound like a word with communist overtones and thus offend people. *Solidarity* in present-day terms means that we all stand to gain if societies are able to harness the collective resources of people regardless of economic position, family background, gender, or race. In addition, by pursuing the common interest, we often also pursue our own self-interest. Solidarity implies reciprocity; during some phases in our life, we might be in need of help and support, whereas at other times we might be in a position to offer support and help to others.

Solidarity—with the present and with future generations—is at the very core of the concept of sustainable development. We must meet the needs of our own generation without compromising the ability of future generations to meet theirs. We must consider our planet to be on loan from our successors rather than being a gift from our predecessors.

When David Halberstam wrote *The Best and the Brightest* in the 1970s, the group described by the title sought to serve in the public sector or in public office attained by election or appointment. During my December 1997 visit to the United States, I was astonished to hear that by a large majority the best and brightest of today were aiming to join the private sector to make individual fortunes. Besides the possibility of wealth, why has there been such a dramatic change? Is there perhaps a sense that many of the public challenges have been resolved? If so, why is the present perceived in this way?

Never before in history have so many enjoyed such a high standard of living. In addition, general health has improved dramatically, especially in less-developed countries, where in the past 30 years life expectancy has increased by more than one-third and the infant mortality rate has been reduced by more than one-half.

We have forgotten about the terrible living conditions of a majority of people at the dawn of the 20th century, especially in those cities and countries that today are known for their riches and splendour. Terrible diseases, hunger, and malnutrition blighted countries that are now finding overweight and high cholesterol to be their major health problems.

What then, besides environmental issues, are the main challenges we face today? On a global scale, underdevelopment, poverty, and health care capture centre stage. The vast majority of human suffering and premature death in the world is poverty-related; the cure is economic and social development.

Increased globalization has provided new opportunities for growth and progress but at the same time has posed new threats to public health. While the scourge of illegal drugs has been spreading worldwide, new infectious diseases are emerging—among them Ebola hemorrhagic fever, hantavirus, and in late December 1997 bird-to-human influenza in China—and such old diseases as cholera, anthrax, plague, and dengue, once apparently eliminated, have reemerged. In our global society there is no health sanctuary. Solutions, like the problems, have to be global in scope.

Another primary goal is to make costly treatment available on an equitable basis. There are always people who can pay their way and people who cannot. We are in deep trouble if health is increasingly viewed as a benefit for the rich and unnecessary for the needy.

The issue of AIDS is particularly relevant. Its prevalence in some parts of Africa is astounding. While traveling through several African countries in October, I was updated on the newest data on the prognosis of that pandemic. The costs and availability of medicines, however, can make AIDS treatment affordable only to the wealthy.

CAROL GUZY—THE WASHINGTON POST

A nun aids an elderly woman in a facility founded by Mother Teresa. Making health care available to all is one of many public challenges.

We must be conscious of the dangers that threaten to widen the health gaps that already exist between the rich and the poor, males and females, and the educated and the uneducated. UN statistics reveal that in some regions of the world, boys receive more calories and vitamins than girls and fewer girls than boys live past adolescence. The education columns of these statistical compendiums reveal that fewer girls than boys enroll in secondary schools and that this gap has increased by graduation. The narrowing of gaps—within as well as between countries—must be our goal.

The 20th century has been called the century of extremes, one in which human vices reached unfathomable depths—the century of dictators and torture, the Holocaust, ethnic cleansing in Bosnia and Herzegovina, and the bombings of Pearl Harbor and Hiroshima. It was, however, also a century of great progress. Many countries experienced unprecedented economic growth. In the West population growth was stabilized, which allowed social and educational systems to accommodate demands. The situation, however, was different in the countries where population growth exceeded 3% and where it was difficult to see how a cycle of declining living standards and deteriorating environments could be averted.

Poverty, population growth, inadequate development of human resources, and insufficient public services were linked to a vicious circle in too many parts of the world. Regardless of social and economic conditions, health care for all should be available and affordable. There are no insurmountable obstacles to establishing acceptable standards throughout the world. The obstacles are located in the minds of those people who have the power to set new priorities but fail to do so and the people who can influence national budgets but shirk their duties to humankind.

During the 1990s a number of UN conferences and other international meetings addressed the environment, health, population, women, and development. These events reinforced the notion that many of our health problems are global in nature and closely linked to the economy and the environment. Such concerns, therefore, can be overcome only by intensified global cooperation and by strong, efficient, and forward-looking international institutions underpinning our common efforts.

By the turn of the century, almost one-half of humanity will live in urban areas. A failure to manage the urban infrastructure will lead to further mushrooming of settlements having insufficient access to essential facilities such as clean water, sanitation, food supplies, transportation, education, health care, and other public services. We know what that means: overcrowding and a disease pattern linked to poverty and an unhealthy environment.

The scale and scope of these health care challenges call for societal management and a change to an extremely sophisticated and forward-looking manner. Analyses across sectors are called for—and public health must be the basis for our thinking. The costs of making the wrong decisions or of not making any decisions, with the hope that the invisible hand will straighten things out, will be enormous. Presently, in all countries, successful public-health management is perhaps the most rewarding business.

Think of it. The greatest profits to society will not come from playing the stock market or downsizing the microchip. The greater good is in devising optimal solutions to problems plaguing the environment, public health, and education and in harnessing the very best of human energies.

The statement that 1997 was a year of progress might be perceived as an affront to the person who lost his or her job or who suffered for another reason, but humankind made some headway during the year—at least in education. It will never make the headlines that more millions of children went to school this morning than in 1996—but it is the most important thing that happened today.

Israelis protest the signing of the Hebron Agreement at the Western (Wailing) Wall: January 15

1

Ghanaian Kofi Annan replaces Egyptian Boutros Boutros-Ghali in the position of United Nations secretary-general.

•

Among those knighted by Queen Elizabeth II in the annual New Year's Day ceremony is pop musician and former Beatle Paul McCartney (*see* October 14).

•

Texaco Inc. begins paying a 10% salary increase to African-American employees in response to charges of past racial discrimination in the company.

2

Singapore's Prime Minister Goh Chok Tong leads his People's Action Party to a resounding 81–2 electoral victory over the opposition.

•

The *Nakhodka,* a Russian-owned tanker carrying 19 million litres (119,000 bbl) of fuel oil, breaks in two off the coast of Japan.

•

The Serbian Orthodox Church issues a statement supporting the opposition Zajedno group and condemning Serbian leader Slobodan Milosevic; the church earlier endorsed Milosevic.

3

The Assembly of the Union, the new parliament of Bosnia and Herzegovina, meets under the cochairmanship of Haris Silajdzic (a Muslim) and Boro Bosic (a Serb) and approves a Cabinet.

•

At the town of Sodere, representatives of 26 Somali factions meet and agree to form a National Salvation Council, a step on the road to a national government.

•

Two Hutu, Deogratias Bizimana and Egide Gatanazi, become the first persons in Rwanda to be found guilty of having committed genocide during the 1994 massacres; they are sentenced to death.

•

Bryant Gumbel completes his last "Today" show on NBC television.

4

Der Spiegel, the German weekly news magazine, celebrates its 50th anniversary.

•

Storms in Minas Gerais and Rio de Janeiro states of Brazil on January 4–5 kill at least 65 people and leave hundreds of thousands homeless.

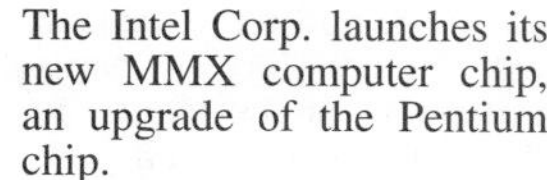

GILLES PERESS—MAGNUM

Henk Angenent triumphs over 16,000 other entrants in the 15th Elfstedentocht (Eleven Cities Tour), a grueling 200-km (125-mi) ice-skating race on the frozen canals in The Netherlands.

5

French soldiers kill at least 10 army mutineers and capture dozens of others as violence continues in the aftermath of the mutiny that began in Bangui, the capital of the Central African Republic, late in 1996.

•

It is reported that the government of Greek Cyprus has ordered a number of Russian surface-to-air missiles; there is great concern that this could alter the delicate balance of power between the Greek and Turkish entities that divide the island.

6

The Canadian government and the Royal Canadian Mounted Police issue a formal apology to former prime minister Brian Mulroney and acknowledge that their allegations that he had received bribes were unjustified.

•

Widespread strikes resume in South Korea, largely in protest against the imposition of a new labour law (*see* January 21).

•

Pakistan establishes a Council for Defence and National Security, chaired by the president; the action gives the military a formal role in Pakistani politics for the first time in recent years.

7

The U.S. Congress begins its 105th session; Newt Gingrich is reelected speaker of the House of Representatives in a close vote following allegations of ethical improprieties by Gingrich.

•

Apple Computer, Inc., unveils its plans for a new operating system incorporating technology from NeXT Software, Inc.

8

The ruling Grimaldi family of Monaco celebrates its 700th anniversary; the tiny principality in the western Mediterranean begins a yearlong celebration.

•

The Intel Corp. launches its new MMX computer chip, an upgrade of the Pentium chip.

•

The U.S. Supreme Court begins hearing appeals from states seeking to overturn lower court rulings that would prohibit physician-assisted suicide.

9

The U.S. electoral college formally votes for the president and vice president.

•

Pres. Hosni Mubarak of Egypt inaugurates an $810 million project to irrigate a large area of desert from Lake Nasser on the Nile in Upper Egypt.

•

A full-page letter signed by 34 cultural and entertainment personalities protesting the German government's "organized persecution" of members of the Church of Scientology is published in the *International Herald Tribune* (*see* January 29).

•

Acknowledging the "possibility of illegal activities," Volkswagen A.G. agrees to

COR MULDER—EPA/ANP/AFP

The 15th Elfstedentocht (Eleven Cities Tour) in The Netherlands: January 4

pay $100 million to the General Motors Corp. in partial settlement of the latter's industrial espionage suit.

10

Police in Brazil's Mato Grosso state begin a two-week program to remove 8,000–12,000 miners and loggers who are threatening the environment and the culture of the small indigenous Kathitaullu tribe.

•

Ethnic unrest continues in Burundi; in Muyinga province the Tutsi-dominated army shoots dead 126 Hutu refugees returning from Tanzania.

11

Hans Werner Henze's opera *Venus and Adonis* receives its world premiere at the Bavarian State Opera, Munich.

12

HAL (in full, HAL 9000, production number 3), the computer featured in Stanley Kubrick's 1968 motion picture *2001: A Space Odyssey,* is born, according to the film script, in Urbana, Ill.

•

Two of the four female cadets enrolled at the Citadel withdraw, saying that they have been subjected to harassment and hazing.

13

Pres. Abdala Bucaram of Ecuador visits Pres. Alberto Fujimori of Peru—the first official visit by an Ecuadorian president in 150 years.

•

Vernon Baker becomes the first living African-American to be awarded the Medal of Honor for service in World War II.

DIANA WALKER—GAMMA LIAISON

Medal of Honor recipient Vernon Baker: January 13

14

Imata Kabua is elected president of the Marshall Islands by the Nitijela (legislature).

•

Greek archaeologists announce that they have discovered an ancient site in Athens that may have been Aristotle's Lyceum.

•

The U.S. space shuttle *Atlantis,* with a crew of six, docks with the Russian space station *Mir,* which has a crew of two.

15

Representatives of Israel and Palestine sign the Hebron agreement, which provides for the redeployment of Israeli troops in that West Bank city; in less than two months, however, the two sides are at odds again.

•

ChinaByte, an Internet service sponsored jointly by Rupert Murdoch's News Corp. and the Communist Party of China's newspaper, *People's Daily,* is launched.

16

Raytheon purchases Hughes Aircraft in a new round of consolidation of American defense companies.

•

The Sundance Film Festival opens in Salt Lake City, Utah; on January 26 the Grand Jury Prize for a dramatic film goes to Jonathan Nossiter's *Sunday.*

17

Friedrich St. Florian's design for a World War II memorial on the National Mall in Washington, D.C., is selected as the winner in a nationwide contest.

•

The report of a formal investigation confirms allegations of sexual harassment and inappropriate conduct on the part of Canadian military personnel in Bosnia and Herzegovina in 1993.

18

Norwegian Børge Ousland becomes the first person to ski solo across Antarctica; the 2,695-km (1,675-mi) trek, during which he pulled a 180-kg (400-lb) sled, took 64 days.

•

An international hot air balloon festival begins at Château-d'Oex, Switz.

19

Petar Stoyanov of the Union of Democratic Forces is inaugurated as Bulgarian president; he takes office on January 22.

•

Thousands of Albanians demonstrate in Tiranë's Skanderbeg Square after a pyramid investment scheme collapses; pyramid schemes are banned by the government on January 23.

•

Evita is the top film in the 54th annual Golden Globe Awards ceremony in Beverly Hills, Calif., winning in three categories.

20

U.S. celebrates Martin Luther King, Jr., Holiday, honouring the birth (Jan. 25, 1929, Atlanta, Ga.) of the civil rights leader.

•

Inauguration Day: Bill Clinton is inaugurated as U.S. president for a second term in Washington, D.C.

•

Near Sultanpur, India, Steve Fossett abandons his effort to become the first person to fly nonstop around the world in a hot air balloon after having traveled more than 16,000 km (9,900 mi); this distance is still almost twice the previous distance record, which Fossett, a former securities broker, held.

•

Edith Haisman, 100, the oldest survivor of the sinking of the *Titanic* on April 14–15, 1912, dies in Southampton, Eng.; only 7 of the 705 survivors are still living (*see* December 19).

21

German and Czech leaders sign a joint reconciliation agreement in which both sides express regret over what happened during World War II.

•

South Korean Pres. Kim Young Sam meets with leaders of the main political parties and agrees to revise the controversial labour law; on January 23 the Organisation for Economic Co-operation and Development takes the unusual step of censuring the law (*see* January 6, 23).

•

The Swedish central Riksbank announces it will look into its wartime financial transactions with an eye to finding possible receipt of looted Nazi gold (*see* January 23).

22

Seven cows, the first in Germany to be discovered with "mad cow" disease, are destroyed.

•

Humane Society International announces a five-year, $1 million plan for the protection of the elephant population in South Africa's Kruger National Park.

•

In Rio de Janeiro the Association of Coffee Producing Countries begins a two-day meeting and agrees to cut back exports for the first half of the year.

23

This is the dawning of the Age of Aquarius for many astrologers: for the first time since 1475, a number of planets, the Sun, and the Moon are aligned in a perfect six-pointed star in the first degrees of Aquarius.

•

Madeleine Albright is sworn in as U.S. secretary of state, the first woman to hold the job.

•

The Hanbo Business Group, South Korea's 14th largest conglomerate, which includes the huge Hanbo Iron and Steel Co., collapses under its debts, and bankruptcy proceedings begin (*see* January 21, October 22).

The government and the banking community in Switzerland agree to establish a fund to aid victims of the Holocaust and their families (*see* January 21).

24

Tung Chee-hwa, chief executive of the Hong Kong special administrative region, announces the membership of the Executive Council; the HKSAR assembly convenes for the first time on January 25 and elects Rita Fan as speaker.

•

Materials posted on the World Wide Web by researchers at Yale University prove that Pol Pot's Khmer Rouge regime in Cambodia orchestrated killings of very large numbers of people in the 1970s.

25

Hong Kong postage stamps bearing the likeness of Queen Elizabeth II are withdrawn from sale, to be replaced by a new 16-stamp set with a view of the Hong Kong waterfront.

•

Martina Hingis of Switzerland wins the women's competition in the Australian Open in Melbourne (at 16, the youngest woman to win a grand-slam tennis tournament in 110 years); Pete Sampras wins the men's competition on January 26.

26

The Green Bay Packers defeat the New England Patriots by a score of 35–21 in Superbowl XXXI in New Orleans.

•

Jacob William Pasaye of Palatine, Ill., is born 92 days after his twin brother, Joshua; the span between births of twins is believed to be a record.

27

The Russian republic of Chechnya holds presidential and parliamentary elections; Aslan Maskhadov is elected president.

•

Physical Review Letters reports that a team of researchers at the Massachusetts Institute of Technology led by Wolfgang Ketterle has developed an atom laser, which is similar to an optical laser but emits atoms rather than light.

•

Engineers begin working on a spectacular new rail tunnel under Berlin's future government quarter.

28

South Africa's Truth and Reconciliation Commission announces that former police officers have confessed to political killings in the apartheid era and have requested amnesty from the state.

•

Demonstrations take place in Brussels against the Belgian government's decision to cut expenditures in order to qualify for the European single currency.

29

The Supreme Court of Pakistan rules that the dismissal of Prime Minister Benazir Bhutto by the president on charges of corruption will stand.

•

The U.S. Department of State releases its annual survey of human rights; included in the listing of countries that have committed human rights abuses is Germany for its treatment of members of the Church of Scientology (*see* January 9).

30

As fighting continues between Zairean rebel forces and loyal troops, the central government accuses Uganda of having invaded its territory by sending in some 2,000 troops.

•

Panama and Colombia sign an agreement to establish a 600,000-sq km (230,000-sq mi) park in the Darien jungle region that will span the border of the two countries.

•

A tiny portrait by Rembrandt, only 11 × 6.5 cm (4.25 × 2.5 in), is sold by Sotheby's for $2.9 million, probably the most ever paid for a painting on a per-square-centimetre basis.

31

Marc Dutroux, already charged with serious crimes in connection with the exposure of a pedophile ring in Belgium, is charged with the murder of two children.

•

The journal *Science* reports that researchers in the U.S. and Australia have discovered a gene linked to the most common form of glaucoma.

THE EVERETT COLLECTION

Antonio Banderas and Madonna in *Evita:* January 19

1

The new government of Gabon, headed by Prime Minister Paulin Obame-Nguéma and comprising mainly ministers from his Gabonese Democratic Party, is confirmed; the ministers had been named on January 28.

•

The Sixth World Winter Games open in Toronto, drawing 2,000 mentally handicapped athletes from more than 80 countries.

2

In protest over the closing of the Forges de Clabecq, the bankrupt steelworks, some 80,000 people demonstrate in Wallonia, Belg.

•

Jeremy Sonnenfeld, a student at the University of Nebraska, becomes the first person ever to bowl a perfect 900 (in a three-game series) sanctioned by the American Bowling Congress.

•

"Sculpture of Angkor and Ancient Cambodia: Millennium of Glory" opens at the Grand Palais in Paris; the exhibition will later travel to Washington, D.C., Tokyo, and Osaka, Japan.

Funeral for Deng Xiaoping, who died on February 19

3

Nawaz Sharif and his Pakistan Muslim League (134 seats) decisively defeat recently ousted Prime Minister Benazir Bhutto and her Pakistan People's Party (18 seats) in legislative elections (*see* February 17).

The Netherlands, which has one of the most liberal drug policies in the world, signs an agreement with France aimed at plugging drug-smuggling routes between the two countries.

CHIP HIRES—GAMMA LIAISON

A triumphant Nawaz Sharif: February 3

4

Pres. Bill Clinton delivers the annual state of the union address to the U.S. Congress; he promises more federal support for education and a balanced budget by the year 2002 (*see* February 6).

•

A jury in Santa Monica, Calif., finds O.J. Simpson liable in the wrongful death of Nicole Brown Simpson and Ron Goldman and instructs him to pay $8.5 million in compensation (*see* February 10).

•

Two Israeli army helicopters collide over northern Israel, killing 73 military personnel; the air disaster is the country's worst ever.

FEB

SYGMA

Cigar is named North America's Horse of the Year (1996) for the second straight year at the Eclipse Awards in Bal Harbour, Fla.; he is the first horse to receive the award in two successive years since Affirmed did so in 1978 and 1979.

5

The government of Switzerland approves the establishment of a fund to compensate victims of the Holocaust.

•

Morgan Stanley, a large U.S. investment bank, and Dean Witter, a retail broker that owns the Discover credit card, announce that they will merge to form a company valued at $24 billion.

•

With a pair of T-shirts, Stephen Hawking settles a bet he lost with fellow physicists John Preskill and Kip Thorne after it is proved to the satisfaction of all three that the laws of physics do allow for the existence of a naked singularity.

6

President Clinton submits the 1998 U.S. budget to Congress; it outlines a balanced budget by 2002.

•

Riots break out in the southern suburbs of Johannesburg, S.Af., mostly involving the country's Coloured (*i.e.,* mixed-race) population.

•

The German government announces that unemployment in the country has reached a seasonally unadjusted rate of 12.2%, the highest figure since 1933.

7

Haitian Pres. René Préval distributes some 1,000 ha (2,500 ac) of land to 1,600 peasant farmers, a rare occurrence in Haitian history.

•

The U.S. Immigration and Naturalization Service reports that the number of illegal immigrants in the U.S. had reached five million by October 1996.

8

The Panamanian-flag tanker *San Jorge* runs aground 32 km (20 mi) south of Punta del Este, Uruguay, spilling much of its cargo into the sea; by mid-March some 1,500 sea lions have died as a result of the spill.

•

With a victory over the Boston Bruins, Detroit Red Wings coach Scotty Bowman becomes the first National Hockey League coach to win 1,000 games.

9

Vice Pres. Rosalia Arteaga of Ecuador is sworn in as president—the first woman to hold the position—following the dismissal from office of Abdalá Bucaram Ortíz, called "El Loco" for his unorthodox behavior; she resigns two days later (*see* February 12).

•

For the first time, France's far-right National Front wins a municipal election with an absolute majority, and its candidate, Catherine Mégret, becomes mayor of Vitrolles, near Marseille (*see* March 29).

10

The jury in the civil trial of O.J. Simpson calls for him to pay punitive damages of $25 million in addition to the compensatory damages of $8.5 million (*see* February 4).

•

Jury selection for the retrial of Heidi Fleiss, "the Hollywood madam," begins in Los Angeles.

•

At the annual Milia multimedia fair in Cannes, France

DANIEL STAPFF—REUTERS

One of hundreds of sea lions affected by an oil spill in Uruguay: February 8

(February 8–12), Peter Gabriel's CD *Eve* is awarded the Milia d'Or grand prize.

11

The Media Research Center concludes its survey of the new American television rating system and judges it a failure in providing guidance to parents about suitability of programming for children.

•

Parsifal Di Casa Netzer ("Pa"), a champion standard schnauzer owned by Rita Holloway and Gabrio Del Torre, wins the best-in-show honours at the 121st annual Westminster Kennel Club Show in New York City.

•

Diane Wood, a nurse from Shrewsbury, Mass., wins $1 million, the largest payout from a bingo game in history.

12

Fabián Alarcón Rivera is sworn in as interim president of Ecuador following the dismissal of President Bucaram and a week of constitutional chaos (*see* February 9).

•

A proposal for a constitutional amendment setting term limits for members of the U.S. Congress is defeated in the House of Representatives, which effectively ends a movement that had begun in the 1980s.

•

The reward being offered by Iran's 15th Khordad Foundation for the assassination of author Salman Rushdie is raised another $500,000 to a total of $2,500,000.

•

Japan's Institute of Space and Astronautical Science launches the MUSES-B (renamed HALCA) satellite radio telescope, described as one million times more powerful than the U.S.'s Hubble telescope and the largest astronomical "instrument" ever created.

•

Moroccan runner Hicham al-Guerrouj breaks the indoor record for the mile with a time of 3:48.45; the previous record of 3:49.28, set by Irishman Eamonn Coghlan, had stood for 14 years and was the sport's oldest record.

13

Sinqobili Mabhena, a 23-year-old native of Bulawayo, Zimb., is elected *nduna* (chief) of the Ndebele tribe, the first women to hold that position.

•

Former representative Bill Richardson from New Mexico is sworn in as U.S. ambassador to the UN.

•

The Dow Jones industrial average, continuing its fastest rise ever, tops 7,000 points for the first time.

The New England Journal of Medicine reports that a study by two University of Toronto researchers indicates that the risk of a traffic accident is four to five times greater for persons who use car phones—virtually the same risk as driving drunk.

14

A chain of 220,000 people extending more than 96 km (60 mi) in Germany protests planned reductions in government coal subsidies.

•

It is announced in Sydney that an Australian farmer accidentally discovered a 220 million-year-old fossil of what is believed to be a new type of amphibian on a rock that he was using to landscape his garden.

15

At a conference in Geneva, 67 countries agree to open their telecommunications markets to all competition.

•

Tara Lipinski, 14, in competition in Nashville, Tenn., becomes the youngest American figure-skating champion in history; in Lausanne, Switz., on March 22, she goes on to become the youngest woman to win a world championship.

16

Jeff Gordon, driving a Chevrolet sponsored by DuPont Refinishes, wins the 39th annual running of the Daytona 500 NASCAR auto race in Florida.

The Laurence Olivier Theatre Awards for the 1996 season are announced in London; *Tommy* (outstanding musical production) and *Stanley* (best new play) take many of the top prizes.

17

Sharif is formally elected and sworn in as Pakistan's prime minister (*see* February 3).

•

Christophe Auguin, a former high-school teacher from Normandy, wins the Vendée Globe sailing race and sets a record for a solo round-the-world sail: 105 days 20 hours 31 minutes.

•

The Virginia House of Delegates votes unanimously to retire the state's official song, "Carry Me Back to Old Virginny" (written by James A. Bland, a black composer and minstrel), which has been criticized for text that glorifies slavery.

•

Blackjack (also known as variety QA 194), the darkest tulip ever bred, is presented by its developers in Bovenkarspel, Neth.

18

Author E.L. Konigsberg wins the Newbery Medal and illustrator David Wisniewski receives the Caldecott Medal in the annual awards for children's literature from the Association for Library Service to Children.

•

A mud slide strikes two mountain villages southeast of Lima, Peru; at least 300 people are feared dead.

•

The outlawed Confederation of Trade Unions begins a series of nationwide strikes in South Korea.

19

China's paramount leader, Deng Xiaoping, who introduced market-opening econimic reforms in 1978, dies in Beijing.

•

Gen. Jesús Gutiérrez Rebollo, the head of Mexico's National Drug Agency, is arrested on charges of being in the pay of a leading drug trafficker; Oscar Malherbe de León, leader of the "Gulf Cartel" is arrested on February 26.

•

DESY, the German Electron Synchrotron in Hamburg, Ger., reports that two teams may have discovered the hybrid "leptoquark," which possesses the characteristics of both leptons and quarks and would be the heaviest known subatomic particle.

20

Frank Williams, a Formula One team chief, and five others go on trial for manslaughter in the 1994 death of Brazilian driver Ayrton Senna.

•

The spacecraft Galileo makes its closest pass to Jupiter's moon Europa; photos taken seem to show large blocks of ice and suggest a large subsurface ocean.

•

An eight-member panel convened by the U.S. National Institutes of Health reports that some seriously ill patients may derive therapeutic benefits from smoking marijuana.

21

Serbian Democratic Party leader Zoran Djindjic takes over as mayor of Belgrade; this is the highest post to be won by the opposition to Serbian Pres. Slobodan Milosevic and his Socialist Party.

•

Jeanne Calment of Arles, France, believed to be the world's oldest person, celebrates her 122nd birthday; she dies in August 1997, and the *Guinness Book of Records* finds that Marie-Louise Febronie Meilleur, 116, of Quebec is now the oldest person.

22

Brasil Raça ("Brazil Race"), a new magazine for that country's blacks, is launched; the 250,000 copies of the first issue sell out in two days.

•

The third annual Screen Actors Guild Awards ceremony takes place in Los Angeles;

ALASTAIR MUIR

Antony Sher in *Stanley:* February 16

winners include Geoffrey Rush, Frances McDormand, Dennis Franz, and Gillian Anderson.

23

Palestinian Ali Abu Kamak opens fire on the observation deck of the Empire State Building in New York City, killing one tourist and wounding six before taking his own life.

•

A fire rages through temporary structures erected for the followers of Swami Nigamananda near Baripada, Orissa state, India, and kills more than 110 people.

•

It is announced that Ian Wilmut and colleagues at the Roslin Institute, near Edinburgh, have accomplished the first successful cloning of an adult mammal; the result is a sheep named Dolly.

24

Qatar's emir inaugurates Ras Laffan, one of the world's largest gas-exporting facilities, comprising an industrial port and the Persian Gulf state's first gas-liquefaction plant.

•

U.S. Robotics announces that it has begun shipping its new 56,000-bits-per-second (56K) modems, the fastest on the market.

•

The Whitbread Book of the Year Award is given to Irish poet Seamus Heaney's *The Spirit Level.*

•

The Golden Berlin Bear award of the Berlin International Film Festival goes to Milos Forman's *The People vs. Larry Flynt;* the festival opened on February 13.

25

South Korean Pres. Kim Young Sam makes a public apology on television for the scandal surrounding the collapse of the Hanbo Group; Kim's own son has been implicated in the affair (*see* January 23).

•

The fourth International Non-Governmental Organization Conference on Land Mines opens in Maputo, Mozambique (through February 28).

26

Amid controversy and condemnation from several quarters, the Israeli government approves the establishment of a Jewish settlement at Har Homa, a hill in East Jerusalem that links the West Bank with East Jerusalem, an area claimed by the Palestinians.

•

The 39th annual Grammy awards are presented in New York City; among the winners are Eric Clapton, LeAnn Rimes, Celine Dion, Kenneth ("Babyface") Edmunds, Toni Braxton, Hillary Clinton, and Pete Seeger.

27

Ireland officially lifts the ban on divorce.

•

Nature magazine reports that archaeologists excavating in a coal mine near Hannover, Ger., have discovered wooden spears believed to be the oldest intact hunting weapons used by humans.

•

Anna Lelkes, a harpist who had played with the Vienna Philharmonic for 26 years, becomes the first official female member after the orchestra votes to end its all-male policy.

28

New regulations to cut down smoking among teenagers—requiring that persons up to age 27 prove that they are at least 18 years old when purchasing tobacco products—go into effect in the U.S.

•

Science magazine reports that scientists have dated stone tools found near Yakutsk, Siberia, to 300,000 years—a much earlier date than had been thought possible for primitive humans to have lived that close to the Arctic Circle.

•

The federal Republic of Yugoslavia and the Republika Srpska, the entity formed by the Bosnian Serbs, sign an agreement to establish "special ties."

1

The Albanian People's Assembly declares a state of emergency because of continuing violence in the southern regions of the country; Sali Berisha (who is reelected president on March 3) orders the government of Prime Minister Aleksander Meksi to resign.

•

Some 5,000 skinheads in Munich, Ger., protest an art exhibit that links the German army with atrocities during World War II.

•

The 15th biannual Pan-African Film and Television Festival of Ouagadougou (FESPACO) concludes in the Burkina Faso capital; the winner of the Grand Prize-Etalon de Yennenga is the film by Gaston Kaboré, *Buud Yam.*

2

Stock and other financial trading is suspended in Thailand as several financial institutions teeter on the brink of collapse (*see* August 11).

•

The Nordic world skiing championships close in Norway (they began on February 20); Yelena Vyalbe of Russia is the first ever to sweep the five gold medals in women's cross-country events.

3

U.S. Pres. Bill Clinton announces a ban on federal funds for human cloning research pending a report from the National Bioethics Advisory Committee (*see* February 23).

The discovery of remnants off Beaufort Inlet, N.C., presumedly of *Queen Anne's Revenge,* the flagship of the English pirate Blackbeard, which foundered in 1718, is announced by a team of marine archaeologists.

•

In its annual rating of the restaurants of France, the Guide Michelin awards its top honours—three stars—to 18 establishments, the same number as last year; Alain Ducasse becomes the first chef ever to win five stars (for two restaurants).

4

In a U.S. federal court, Harold J. Nicholson pleads guilty to charges of spying for Russia, the highest-ranking U.S. CIA official ever to do so; his trial begins in Alexandria, Va., on March 10.

The flooding Ohio River rises to its highest crest in 30 years; floods affect several states, with at least 30 persons dead and property damage exceeding $500 million.

•

The Svobodny cosmodrome, 100 km (60 mi) north of the city of Blagoveshchensk, is inaugurated as Russia's new space launch facility with the liftoff of a satellite-bearing rocket.

5

The charter establishing the Indian Ocean Rim Association for Regional Cooperation (IORAEC) is signed by representatives of Australia and 13 countries of Africa and Asia meeting in Port Louis, Mauritius.

•

It is announced that Pandurang Shastri Athavale of

Ralph Fiennes and Kristin Scott Thomas in *The English Patient:* March 24

Bombay (Mumbai) will receive the 1997 John M. Templeton Prize for Progress in Religion, valued at $1.2 million.

•

President Clinton signs a directive requiring that legal immigrants wishing to purchase a handgun prove residence of 90 days in the state of purchase.

6

It is announced that Great Western Financial, a large savings institution, will be acquired by Washington Mutual in a $6.6 billion deal that creates the largest savings and loan institution in the U.S.

•

Queen Elizabeth II of England inaugurates the Royal Web site (http://www.royal.gov.uk) with a message to students at the Nakina (Ont.) Public School.

PHIL BRAY—THE EVERETT COLLECTION

7

Pres. Boris Yeltsin appoints Anatoly B. Chubais, who is widely disliked among Russian government officials, first deputy prime minister to oversee the country's economic reform program (*see* February 9).

•

Using mitochondrial DNA analysis techniques, scientists in Great Britain prove a genetic link between a 9,000-year-old skeleton known as Cheddar Man and a schoolteacher who lives in the same neighbourhood where the remains were found.

8

The first international conference on maternal mortality attracts some 2,500 researchers to Marrakech, Mor.

•

James N. Burmeister is sentenced to two life terms in the penitentiary without possibility of parole after being convicted in February of the random murder of a black couple as part of a racist skinhead initiation.

9

The world indoor athletic (track and field) championships end in Paris (began March 7); Wilson Kipketer, who was born in Kenya but is running for Denmark, sets a world record of 1:42.67 in the 800 m.

10

The Progressive Citizens' Party of Liechtenstein withdraws from the coalition that has governed the Alpine principality since 1938, and the government collapses (*see* April 9).

11

Bashkim Fino, a member of the opposition Socialist Party of Albania and former mayor of the southern city of Gjirokastër, is appointed prime minister; the popular Socialist leader Fatos Nano is released from prison on March 13 (*see* March 1, April 12).

•

Strikes by miners in Germany reach a peak when about 20,000 workers besiege Bonn and paralyze the city for one day; steelworkers in the industrial Ruhr area strike on March 18 and 24.

•

A fire and explosion at the Tokaimura nuclear-waste-reprocessing plant in Japan exposes 37 workers to low-level radioactivity.

•

The Columbus Quest defeats the Richmond Rage 77–64 to win the first-ever championship of the women's professional American Basketball League in Columbus, Ohio.

•

Martin Buser wins the 1,770-km (1,100-mi) Iditarod Trail Sled Dog Race from Anchorage to Nome, Alaska, in 9 days 8 hours 31.75 minutes; five dogs die in the competition, which refuels protests from animal rights groups.

SAURABH DAS—ASSOCIATED PRESS

Sister Nirmala (left) and Mother Teresa: March 13

12

A court in Lagos, Nigeria, accuses Wole Soyinka, the Nobel Prize-winning novelist, and 14 others of high treason; two days earlier Soyinka had publicly criticized the regime of Gen. Sani Abacha.

•

Two large insurance brokers, Marsh & McLennan Companies and Johnson & Higgins, announce that they are merging in a $1.8 billion deal that will form the largest insurance brokerage in the world.

13

French police announce that they have arrested more than 250 people and confiscated thousands of videocassettes in connection with a crackdown on child pornography.

•

Sister Nirmala, a 63-year-old Indian-born nun, is selected to take over the Order of Missionaries of Charity, the mission established by Mother Teresa (*see* September 5).

14

President Clinton undergoes surgery on a knee after having sustained an injury in the early hours of the morning when he missed a step and stumbled at a friend's home in Florida.

•

The journal *Genome Research* reports that David Schlessinger and a team of scientists at the Washington University School of Medicine, St. Louis, Mo., have completed a high-resolution map of the X chromosome, one of the major goals of the Human Genome Project.

•

Sprinter Michael Johnson, world record holder in the 200-m dash, wins the Sullivan Award as the best amateur athlete of 1996.

15

The strategically important city of Kisangani, Zaire, falls to rebel forces (*see* March 24).

•

In Canada Giles Duceppe is elected leader of the Bloc Québecois, succeeding Michel Gauthier.

•

Dean Smith, coach of the University of North Carolina basketball team, wins his 877th game, a new record for a college coach.

16

Demonstrations in Brussels bring out tens of thousands of workers disgruntled with job losses and what they consider inhumane conditions at their companies and an uncaring government.

17

Anthony Lake, who had been nominated by President Clinton to become director of central intelligence, withdraws his candidacy, calling the process of confirmation by the U.S. Senate a "political circus."

•

The Ford Motor Co announces that after 43 years it will stop production of the Thunderbird.

18

Israel begins construction of 6,500 houses for Jewish settlers at Jabal Abu Ghaneim in East Jerusalem, defying international opposition and precipitating weeks of demonstrations in the area.

•

"Henry Dreyfuss Directing Design," a major show of the late American industrial designer, opens at New York City's Cooper-Hewitt National Design Museum.

19

Greek Foreign Minister Theodoros Pangalos visits Macedonia, the first Cabinet-level official to do so; Greece has resisted the use of the name Macedonia and other manifestations of sovereignty by the former Yugoslav republic.

•

Mansoor Sarfarazi of the University of Connecticut Health Center and his coworkers report that they have identified the major gene responsible for primary congenital glaucoma.

20

Presidents Yeltsin and Clinton begin a two-day summit meeting in Helsinki, Fin.; the top item on the agenda is the expansion of the NATO alliance to include countries of Eastern Europe.

•

Liggett Group Inc., one of the top five American tobacco manufacturers, breaks ranks with the other leading companies and admits that smoking is addictive and that it causes lung cancer, heart disease, and emphysema.

•

Archaeologists excavating in eastern Dominican Republic discover a city of the Taino, the indigenous people who met Columbus in 1492; the city may be the same one whose destruction was described by the early missionary Bartolomé de Las Casas.

21

A U.S. district judge approves a record $176 million settlement of the race-discrimination lawsuit reached between Texaco Inc. and its African-American employees (*see* January 1).

•

The discovery of tiny fragments of the Spanish flu virus that killed 20 million people around the world in 1918 is announced in the journal *Science;* scientists hope to determine what made the virus so deadly.

•

The Royal Museum of Fine Arts in Brussels marks its centennial until July 27; a special exhibit of 250 works by Belgian artist Paul Delvaux opens.

22

The Dalai Lama begins his first visit ever to Taiwan (through March 27); following the visit, the Tibetan government in exile opens a liaison office in Taipei.

•

Sunset Boulevard, the musical by Andrew Lloyd Webber, closes on Broadway after nearly a two-and-a-half-

Buddhist monks in Taiwan: March 22

CHIEN-CHI CHANG—MAGNUM

year, 977-performance run; the elaborately staged production did not make a profit.

23

Comet Hale-Bopp makes its closest approach, about 193 million km (120 million mi) from Earth.

•

Belarus expels a U.S. diplomat who was monitoring an antigovernment rally in the capital, Minsk; the U.S. recalls Ambassador Kenneth Yalowitz and expels a Belarusian diplomat on March 26 in retaliation.

•

Bunny, Bunny, a play based upon the life of popular American television personality Gilda Radner, opens on Broadway; Radner died in 1989.

24

Prime Minister Léon Kengo wa Dondo of Zaire resigns under pressure; Pres. Mobutu Sese Seko returns to the limelight after months of absence from the country to undergo cancer treatment and begins consultations to form a new government (*see* March 15, April 2).

•

The English Patient wins nine awards, including those for best picture and best director, at the 69th annual Academy Awards ceremonies in Hollywood.

25

Former U.S. president George Bush, 72, fulfills a pledge that he made to himself when he first parachuted out of an airplane (in that case, a burning bomber in the Pacific Ocean during World War II) by repeating the feat at the Yuma (Ariz.) Proving Ground.

•

An international arrest warrant is issued for Gen. Leopoldo Galtieri, a president of Argentina in the 1980s, for the murder of three people and the "disappearance" of several hundred others.

•

Sofia Figueroa, a three-year-old Peruvian girl, sets a record of some sort by swimming about 915 m (1,000 yd) in 48 minutes without stopping.

26

In Rancho Santa Fe, Calif., the bodies of 39 members of the Heaven's Gate cult are discovered, the largest incident of mass suicide in U.S. history.

•

Sir Julius Chan, prime minister of Papua New Guinea, resigns; he is accused of having hired foreign mercenaries to put down the rebellion on the island of Bougainville; a caretaker government is appointed on March 27.

•

The U.S. Army announces it will appoint its first female three-star general; Maj. Gen. Claudia Kennedy is promoted to lieutenant general.

27

Russia experiences the largest strikes since the dissolution of the Soviet Union, as millions of trade union workers take to the streets.

•

A district court in Sapporo, Japan, rules against the central government and in favour of the Ainu people, the first time that the Ainu, the aboriginal people of Hokkaido, have been officially recognized in Japan.

•

Quaker Oats Co. agrees to sell the Snapple beverages business to Triarc Companies Inc. for $300 million; Quaker acquired Snapple in 1994 for $1.7 billion.

28

The Commonwealth of Independent States holds its fifth summit meeting in Moscow and reelects Russian President Yeltsin chairman of its Council of Heads of State.

•

President Clinton announces new guidelines to prevent the U.S. government from conducting medical experiments on humans using dangerous substances without their informed consent.

•

Dexter Scott King, the son of Martin Luther King, Jr., tells a court in Nashville, Tenn., that the family of the assassinated civil rights leader believes that James Earl Ray, who is in prison for the crime, is innocent (*see* February 20).

•

Robert Pinsky is named poet laureate of the U.S.

29

The far-right National Front opens its 10th congress in Strasbourg, France; tens of thousands of protesters demonstrate against the party (*see* February 9).

•

Cambridge beats Oxford by two lengths in the 143rd annual rowing race on the River Thames, their fifth win in a row.

WALLY PACHOLKA

Comet Hale-Bopp: March 23

30

Pope John Paul II delivers his annual Easter address in the Vatican City and calls for the world to find the "courage of forgiveness and reconciliation."

•

Ascend Communications Inc. announces it will acquire Cascade Communications Corp. for $3.7 billion in stocks.

•

Canadian Jacques Villeneuve, driving a Williams-Renault, wins the Brazilian Grand Prix auto race at São Paolo.

31

The trial of Timothy J. McVeigh, accused of the bombing of the federal office building in Oklahoma City, Okla., in 1995, opens in Denver, Colo. (*see* April 24).

•

President Clinton names U.S. Army Gen. Wesley K. Clark commander of NATO and all U.S. forces in Europe.

•

Soprano Michele Crider makes her Metropolitan Opera debut as Cio-Cio-San in Giacomo Puccini's opera *Madama Butterfly.*

•

NASA shuts off the power on the Pioneer 10 spacecraft, which has traveled 10 billion km (6.2 billion mi) from Earth since its launch on March 2, 1972.

PHOTOS, (TOP) EPITACIO PESSOA—ASSOCIATED PRESS (BOTTOM) REUTERS

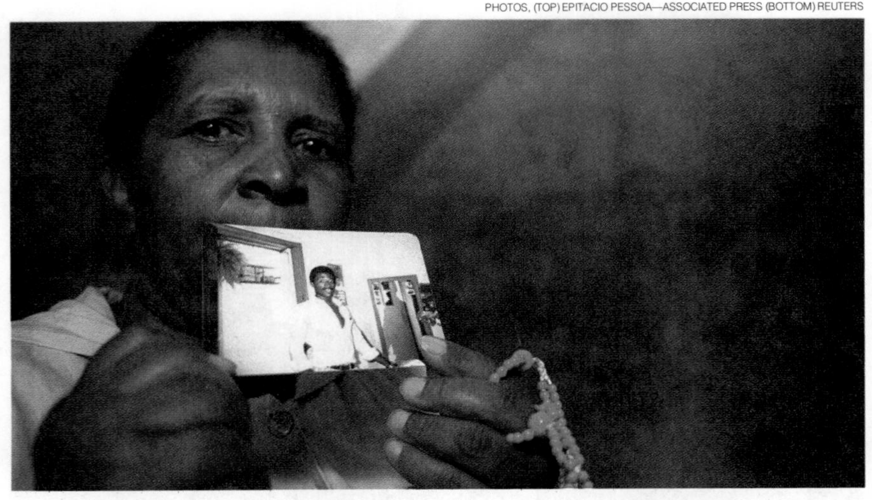

A Brazilian woman holding a photograph of a victim of police brutality: April 7

1

Étienne Tshisekedi, a longtime political enemy of Zaire's president, Mobutu Sese Seko, is elected prime minister by the parliament (*see* March 24).

•

An arbitrator appointed by the U.S. Supreme Court recommends that historic Ellis Island be divided between the states of New Jersey and New York.

2

The presidents of Russia and Belarus sign a charter leading in the direction of the unification of the two states (*see* June 10).

•

Capt. Craig Button breaks formation in his A-10 Thunderbolt fighter airplane, carrying four bombs, over Arizona, flies off toward the Rocky Mountains, and crashes into a mountainside in Colorado.

•

The state of Michigan reports 153 cases of hepatitis traced to strawberries imported from Mexico; several other states are also at risk.

•

Gary Sheffield signs the largest deal in baseball history—a $61 million six-year extension of his contract with the Florida Marlins.

3

Helmut Kohl announces that he will seek a record fifth four-year term as chancellor of Germany.

•

Swiss police reveal that the government is preparing to seize $100 million held in bank accounts by Raúl Salinas de Gortari, brother of the former president of Mexico, who has been implicated in drug trafficking (*see* April 9).

•

The Dubayy World Cup horse race, with a prize of $4 million, is won by Singspiel, owned by Sheikh Muhammad and ridden by American Jerry Bailey.

4

The U.S. space shuttle *Columbia,* with a crew of seven, lifts off from Cape Canaveral, Florida, on a planned 16-day mission to research the effects of lack of gravity.

5

American poet Allen Ginsberg dies in New York City.

•

The running of the Grand National steeplechase at Aintree, Eng., is postponed because of a bomb threat from the Irish Republican Army.

6

A parcel bomb explodes at the home of Lieut. Gen. Tin Oo, a top official of the ruling junta in Myanmar (Burma), killing Tin Oo's daughter.

•

The *Nicorette,* a 24.4-m (80-ft) yacht, skippered by Finnish captain Ludde Ingvall, breaks the record for Atlantic crossing by nonmotorized monohull vessels that had stood since 1905; the time is 11 days 13 hours 22 minutes from Sandy Hook, N.Y., to Lizard Point, Cornwall, Eng.

7

Under heavy pressure because of mounting evidence of police brutality against civilians, the Brazilian government adopts legislation classifying torture as a crime and establishes an official Human Rights Secretariat to monitor police conduct.

The Pulitzer Prizes are announced in New York City; among the winners are Lisel Mueller's *Alive Together: New and Selected Poems* for poetry and Wynton Marsalis's jazz opera *Blood on the Fields,* the first jazz composition to win a Pulitzer Prize for music.

•

Pres. Hashemi Rafsanjani of Iran formally opens the $1.1 billion Tabriz petrochemical complex.

•

French Polynesia reports a 46% growth in the sale of black pearls in 1996; pearl sales contribute 90% of the territory's import revenues.

8

President Mobutu declares an emergency situation in Zaire and imposes military rule as forces led by rebel leader Laurent Kabila consolidate and expand their control in the east of the country (*see* May 16).

•

Roman Catholic Archbishop Francis E. George of Portland, Ore., is named archbishop of Chicago, replacing Joseph Cardinal Bernardin, who died in November 1996; he is formally installed on May 7.

9

A new government under Prime Minister Mario Frick is announced in Liechtenstein (*see* March 10).

•

Prosecutors in Mexico City present evidence suggesting that former president Carlos Salinas de Gortari covered up the role of his brother Raúl in a 1994 political assassination (*see* April 3).

•

Lockheed Martin rolls out its new F-22 fighter jet for the U.S. Air Force in Marietta, Ga.

10

A German court announces its findings that the highest circles in Iran ordered the killing of exiled Iranian Kurdish leaders in Berlin in 1992; all European Union nations withdraw their ambassadors from Tehran in protest.

•

A report published by the World Wildlife Fund warns that apes are under such environmental pressure, especially from war and deforestation, that they could become extinct.

Heavy flooding in North Dakota: April 27

11

In India the government of Prime Minister H.D. Deve Gowda resigns after losing a vote of confidence in the Lok Sabha, the lower house of Parliament.

•

The San Giovanni Cathedral in Turin, Italy, is gutted by fire, but the most famous relic housed in its Guarini Chapel, the Shroud of Turin, is not damaged.

•

The journal *Science* publishes a report that suggests that life began on Earth around a volcano, where the chemical and thermal conditions for the first biochemical compounds exist.

12

Pope John Paul II arrives in Sarajevo, Bosnia and Herzegovina, for a two-day visit during which he meets separately with representatives of the three ruling factions and conducts mass in a football stadium on April 13.

•

The Museum of African American History opens in Detroit.

13

Tiger Woods breaks multiple records when he shoots a 270—18 under par—in the Masters golf tournament in Augusta, Ga.

•

Jacques Villeneuve, driving a Williams-Renault, wins the Argentine Grand Prix auto race at Buenos Aires.

14

James McDougal, a former business associate of Pres. Bill Clinton, is sentenced to a three-year prison term plus $4.3 million in fines for having illegally obtained federal loans for the Whitewater land-development project.

•

Sverre Fehn, whose work is little known outside his native Norway, is named the recipient of the Pritzker Architecture Prize for 1997.

•

The Indigenous Parliament of the Americas, an institution pledged to promote the interests of the native populations of Latin-American countries, opens its 12th congress in Guatemala City, Guat.

15

In Belgium the parliamentary committee set up to investigate the murders by pedophiles of a number of children accuses the police and judicial system of gross incompetence in handling the affair.

•

The inspector general of the U.S. Department of Justice reports "extremely serious and significant problems" with the research conducted in the crime labs of the FBI, including laboratory results used in some very prominent recent trials.

16

Rolf Bloch, head of the Swiss Federation of Hebrew Congregations, is named by the Swiss government to oversee a fund for Holocaust victims (*see* January 23).

17

About 50,000 people, including many landless peasants who marched 1,000 km (600 mi) in 70 days across the country, demonstrate in Brasília, the Brazilian capital, against the land policies of Pres. Fernando Henrique Cardoso.

•

Hundreds of demonstrators gather in Cayenne, French Guiana, to protest the arrest of eight pro-independence militants and clash with police; the actions continues on April 22–23.

•

Two paleontologists report in the journal *Nature* that they have discovered fossil remains of a very primitive snake that has short but well-developed hind legs; the creature lived in a shallow sea in present-day Israel about 95 million years ago.

KEVIN HORAN

The Museum of African American History: April 12

18

A diplomatic impasse between the U.S. and Russia develops in Washington, D.C., over an exhibit of Tsarist jewels that was to have been shown in Houston, Texas, but has been recalled to Moscow for the celebration of its 850th anniversary (*see* September 5).

•

Researchers at the Whitehead Institute for Biomedical Research, Cambridge, Mass., report that they have discovered the harpoonlike mechanism by which the AIDS virus penetrates cells.

•

The Newseum, a museum dedicated to the news in all forms, opens in Arlington, Va.

19

Bulgaria holds a general election in which the centre-right United Democratic Forces coalition wins decisively; the UDF nominates its chairman, Ivan Kostov, for prime minister.

•

American actress Brooke Shields and American tennis player Andre Agassi are married in Monterey, Calif.

20

Citing lack of evidence, state prosecutors in Israel drop charges against Prime Minister Benjamin Netanyahu that he improperly appointed Attorney General Roni Bar-On.

•

Sweden defeats Germany to win the men's crown in the world curling championships in Bern, Switz.; Canada defeated Norway in the women's event on April 19.

21

Bomb threats from the Irish Republican Army paralyze London during the morning rush hour; terrorist activity has increased during the run-up to the May 1 British general elections.

•

A 40-man contingent of the People's Liberation Army from China quietly assumes its post in Hong Kong, the

SILVIA IZQUIERDO—REUTERS

An end to the hostage crisis in Peru: April 22

first deployment of an expected 10,000-man PLA force to be stationed there.

•

In accord with the wishes of "Star Trek" creator Gene Roddenberry and counterculture guru Timothy Leary, their ashes, as well as those of 22 others, are launched into orbit aboard the Spanish MiniSat research satellite.

22

Peruvian government commandos free 72 hostages held for four months in the Japanese ambassador's residence in Lima; one hostage is wounded and later dies of a heart attack, and all 14 rebels from the Túpac Amaru Revolutionary Movement perish in the action.

•

The Armed Islamic Group is blamed for the brutal massacre of 93 villagers 19 km (12 mi) south of Algiers, the Algerian capital.

•

Chinese Pres. Jiang Zemin begins a four-day visit in Russia; on April 24 the presidents of China, Russia, Kazakstan, Kyrgyzstan, and Tajikistan sign an agreement to reduce the number of troops stationed along the former Sino-Soviet border.

•

The Ontario government votes to merge the six municipalities of Metropolitan Toronto as of Jan. 1, 1998.

23

The city of Gdansk, Pol., begins the celebration of its 1,000th anniversary on the Feast Day of Swiaty Wojciech (St. Adalbert), who was martyred in 997.

•

After 145 years of spirited in-person trading, the floor of the Toronto Stock Exchange closes; trading will henceforth be conducted on the TSE electronically.

24

The prosecution opens its case against Timothy J. McVeigh, accused of the bombing of the federal office building in Oklahoma City, Okla., in 1995 (*see* March 31, June 2).

•

A group of paleontologists announces the discovery of a trove containing a large number of fossilized dinosaurs in northeastern China.

25

District Judge William Osteen of North Carolina rules that the U.S. Food and Drug Administration has the authority to regulate tobacco as a drug although it lacks the authority to regulate tobacco advertising and promotion.

26

In South Africa Winnie Madikizela-Mandela wins reelection as president of the African National Congress Women's League (*see* December 17).

•

The Super National Scholastic Chess Championships open in Knoxville, Tenn., drawing some 4,300 junior chess players to the largest chess tournament ever held in the U.S.

27

The crest of the flooding Red River, which caused heavy damage in the north-central U.S., especially North Dakota, crosses the border into Manitoba (*see* August 9).

•

The Lantau Link, comprising the Tsing Ma suspension bridge and the Kap Shui Mun cable bridge, officially opens part of a chain of projects linking Hong Kong and the new Chep Lap Kok airport, which is now under construction.

•

Arceli Keh, a woman in southern California, reveals that she had given birth to a baby girl in 1996 at the age of 63; she is believed to be the oldest woman ever to give birth.

28

Russia's Pres. Boris Yeltsin signs a series of economic decrees designed by his new team of aides and intended to restrict the energy and transport monopolies.

•

Richard L. McLaren and members of his secessionist Republic of Texas movement free two hostages after police deliver a member who had been jailed (*see* May 3).

29

The worldwide Chemical Weapons Convention takes effect after ratification by 88 countries; the U.S. ratified the treaty on April 24, but Russia and a number of other states known to possess such weapons have failed to do so.

•

U.S. astronaut Jerry M. Linenger and Russian cosmonaut Vasily Tsibliyev complete the first-ever Russo-American space walk, a five-hour excursion from the Russian space station *Mir* (*see* January 14).

•

Sgt. Delmar Simpson, the first of 12 U.S. Army drill instructors at Aberdeen Proving Ground, Maryland, to stand trial for sexual misconduct, is convicted on 18 of 19 counts of rape.

30

The so-called Mothers of Plaza de Mayo gather in Buenos Aires to commemorate the 20th anniversary of their protest of the disappearance of their children, the *desaparecidos,* at the hand of Argentina's military government.

•

Alexis Herman is confirmed by the U.S. Senate as secretary of labour after her nomination was delayed by concerns about her fund-raising activities in 1996, when she held a high political post.

•

Ellen Morgan, the character played by Ellen DeGeneres on the television sitcom "Ellen," announces that she is a lesbian, the first openly homosexual lead character in an American prime-time television series.

1

Tony Blair and his Labour Party rout the Conservatives in the British elections, winning a majority of some 177 seats in Parliament.

•

Two British astronomers, Simon Goodwin and John Gribbin, announce their conclusion, based on interpretation of data from the Hubble Space Telescope, that the universe is at least 13 billion years old.

•

U.S. Secretary of Energy Federico Peña announces that he is revoking the contract of Associated Universities, Inc., to run Brookhaven National Laboratory, Upton, N.Y., and calls for a major environmental-safety inspection.

•

Mongolia becomes the only country in the world to impose no taxes on trade; the radical decision to abolish these taxes was taken in a session of the Great Hural (parliament) on April 18.

2

A large (3-ha [7.5-ac]) monument to former U.S. president Franklin D. Roosevelt is dedicated in Washington, D.C., amid controversy over the appropriateness of not depicting FDR, who was partially paralyzed by poliomyelitis in 1921, in his customary wheelchair.

3

Georgian Pres. Eduard Shevardnadze ends his first official visit to neighbouring Armenia; during his two-day stay, a number of cooperative agreements are signed.

•

Richard McLaren and his militant separatist Republic of Texas movement surrender to police near Fort Davis, Texas; two members of the group escape into the woods.

•

Silver Charm, ridden by jockey Gary Stevens, wins the 123rd running of the Kentucky Derby horse race at Churchill Downs, Louisville, Ky., in a photofinish.

•

Katrina and the Waves, representing the United Kingdom, win the annual Eurovision Song Contest in Dublin with their entry "Love Shine a Light."

LUC DELAHAYE—MAGNUM

Rebel soldiers in Kinshasa: May 16

4

Ceferino Jiménez Malla, known as "El Pele," a horse trader who was shot by a Republican forces firing squad during the Spanish Civil War, is beatified by Pope John Paul II, the first Roma (Gypsy) to be so honoured.

5

The Wajay Free Trade Zone, near Havana's international airport, the first of four planned zones to open in Cuba, is formally inaugurated.

•

A gold-speculation bubble begins to burst when it is revealed that gold samples from the Busang mine in East Kalimantan province, Borneo, Indon., collected by Bre-X Minerals, a Canadian mining concern, had been tampered with and their gold content enhanced.

•

A court in Florida rules in favour of the R.J. Reynolds Tobacco Co. in a suit brought by a relative of a lifelong smoker who had not tried to quit smoking and who had died of lung cancer.

•

Pat Henry of Bloomington, Ill., becomes the first American woman to sail solo around the world; she began the 43,000-km (27,000-mi) trip on May 4, 1989, from Acapulco, Mex.

6

U.S. Pres. Bill Clinton begins an official visit in Mexico, the first by an American head of state in almost 20 years.

7

In The Hague the UN International Criminal Tribunal for the Former Yugoslavia convicts Dusan Tadic, a Bosnian Serb, of killing two police officers and torturing and persecuting Muslim civilians in 1992; he is the first person to be tried by an international tribunal since the war-crimes trials after World War II.

•

Intel Corp. launches the Pentium II processor chip for personal computers; the chip runs at clock speeds up to 300 MHz.

•

The U.S. Food and Drug Administration approves the first laser device for hard-tissue dental procedures such as repairing cavities in teeth.

8

Top government officials of six Central American countries, the Dominican Republic, and the U.S. meet in San José, Costa Rica, for a summit entitled "Bridge into the 21st Century."

•

In Moscow Moldovan Prime Minister Petru Lucinschi and Ivan Smirnov, leader of Moldova's secessionist Trans-Dniester region, sign an agreement they reached on April 10 to normalize relations.

UNIVERSAL STUDIOS, INC/SHOOTING STAR

9

Douglas ("Pete") Peterson, a Vietnam War veteran, arrives in Hanoi to begin his duties as U.S. ambassador to Vietnam, the first person to hold that post since the end of the Vietnam War.

•

More than 100 corporate and government leaders from 25 countries, including U.S. Vice Pres. Al Gore, attend the "CEO Summit" convened in Seattle, Wash., by the Microsoft Corp. and discuss applications of technology in business.

10

An earthquake of magnitude 7.1 strikes the northeastern region of Iran; at least 1,560 people perish.

•

Pope John Paul II arrives in Lebanon, his first visit to the Middle East; on May 11 he celebrates mass for a crowd of about 300,000 in Beirut.

•

Fourteen heads of state of Caricom, the Caribbean community, as well as those of the U.S. and Haiti hold a summit meeting in Barbados on economic and trade issues.

•

Queen Beatrix of The Netherlands formally inaugurates the Storm Surge Barrier across the Meuse-Rhine estuary, the last link in the elaborate system the country has built to prevent disastrous flooding from North Sea storms.

11

Alpha Oumar Konaré wins reelection as president of Mali in the first round of voting with over 95% of the vote; the planned second round of the election is canceled.

In the general elections in Burkina Faso, Pres. Blaise Compaoré's party, the Congress for Democracy and Progress, wins 97 of the total of 111 seats in the National Assembly.

•

Hundreds of thousands of Muslims demonstrate in Istanbul in protest against the secular military government's plans to close Islamic schools.

•

World chess champion Garry Kasparov concedes defeat after 19 moves of his game with Deep Blue, a computer program developed by a team of engineers and chess experts assembled by the IBM Corp., losing the match by 3½ to 2½ games.

12

Presidents Boris Yeltsin of Russia and Aslan Maskhadov of Chechnya sign an agreement aimed at ending violence while avoiding the key question of whether Chechnya will eventually become independent of Russia.

•

The U.S. Supreme Court rules that employers may not release employees and "outsource" services as a way to reduce the financial burden of employee benefits.

13

Representatives of Afghanistan, Azerbaijan, Iran, Kazakstan, Kyrgyzstan, Pakistan, Tajikistan, Turkey, Turkmenistan, and Uzbekistan—members of the Economic Cooperation Organization—gather in Ashgabat (formerly Ashkhabad), Turkmenistan, for a two-day summit meeting.

•

It is reported that seven climbers have died in storms in the past few days on Mt. Everest.

A record opening for *The Lost World: Jurassic Park:* May 22

14

Following the April 27 elections in Yemen, the first since the 1994 civil war, Pres. Ali Abdallah Salih names Faraj Said ibn Ghanem prime minister; Ghanem's government is formed on May 15.

•

The government of Turkey launches a major military campaign against the forces of the Kurdistan Workers' Party and their bases in northern Iraq.

•

Canada defeats Sweden two games to one in the Pool A final at the 61st world ice hockey championship in Helsinki, Fin.

15

German Finance Minister Theo Waigel raises a storm of protest by proposing a reevaluation of the country's currency reserves in order to support public finances and conform to plans for European economic and monetary union; calls for Waigel's resignation continue past the month's end.

•

Dirk Coetzee, the South African police officer who first called attention to the covert war against antiapartheid activists conducted by the former South African government, is convicted of murder in Durban.

16

Pres. Mobutu Sese Seko of Zaire relinquishes power and flees the capital, Kinshasa, as rebel forces led by Laurent Kabila take the city (*see* April 8, May 17).

•

A bipartisan agreement to balance the U.S. budget by the year 2002 is announced; a series of budget resolution bills pass through Congress in the days that follow.

•

President Clinton formally apologizes to the participants in the "Tuskegee experiment," a group of African-American men whom the U.S. government used as subjects, without their knowledge or consent, in 1932–72 in studies of the effects of untreated syphilis.

17

Zairean rebel leader Laurent Kabila declares himself head of state and changes the name of the country to the Democratic Republic of the Congo; deposed Pres. Mobutu Sese Seko had renamed the country Zaire in 1971 (*see* May 16).

•

Kim Hyung Chul, the second son of South Korean Pres. Kim Young Sam, is arrested on charges of bribery and tax evasion.

18

Natsagiyn Bagabandi, leader of the opposition Mongolian People's Revolutionary Party, emerges victorious in the presidential elections, easily defeating incumbent Punsalmaagiyn Ochirbat and his Democratic Alliance coalition.

•

New York City's news zipper, which flashed headlines to viewers in Times Square, is closed down and taken to a museum, to be replaced by a high-tech electronic version a few weeks later.

•

A box of 25 Cohiba cigars that once belonged to Cuban Pres. Fidel Castro brings $11,500 in a sale at Christie's auction house.

19

In Malaysia Mahathir bin Mohamad begins a two-month leave of absence as prime minister, reportedly to rest, travel, and finish writing a book.

•

The U.S. Department of Defense completes its quadrennial defense review and publishes a report that calls for further military base closings and reductions of service personnel into the 21st century.

ABBAS—MAGNUM

New Iranian president Mohammad Khatami: May 23

The American Medical Association publishes a report that supports the proposed federal ban on "partial-birth" abortions; the U.S. Senate approves the ban on May 20.

•

Joan Kroc, the heiress to the McDonald's restaurant chain, is revealed as the "Angel of Grand Forks," the person who anonymously donated $15 million to flood victims in that North Dakota city.

20

A group of Chinese fishermen is arrested by a Philippines naval vessel off the Spratly Islands in the South China Sea; six nations in the area have claimed the uninhabited island group.

Fernando Novas of the Museum of Natural History in Buenos Aires, Arg., announces that 20 fossil bones of a 90 million-year-old lizard suggest that the animal, though flightless, had flappable wings.

21

Ivan Kostov is formally elected prime minister in Bulgaria and his Cabinet is approved by the National Assembly.

•

The American Academy of Arts and Letters in New York City inducts six new members: writers Daniel Aaron, Philip Levine, Albert Murray, and Studs Terkel and composers John Adams and Ornette Coleman.

•

A two-day auction at Sotheby's of the contents of the homes of Pamela Harriman, U.S. ambassador to France, who died in February, brings in $8.7 million.

22

President Yeltsin dismisses two top Russian military leaders, Defense Minister Igor N. Rodionov and Chief of General Staff Gen. Viktor N. Samsonov, for their unresponsiveness to the president's reforms and moves to economize.

•

The Lost World: Jurassic Park, the sequel to the 1993 hit film *Jurassic Park,* opens in 3,000 theatres (5,000 screens) across the U.S. and sets new four-day opening records for attendance.

23

A moderate cleric, Mohammad Khatami, is elected president of Iran despite the opposition to his candidacy by the ruling ayatollahs; he takes office on August 3.

•

The Eritrean Constitutional Assembly completes deliberations and votes to accept the country's first constitution.

•

In the American Tour de Sol race in Portland, Maine, a converted Geo Metro auto sets a distance record for an electric vehicle by traveling

ALASTAIR MUIR

Shakespeare's Globe Theatre in London: May 27

398 km (249 mi) without recharging.

24

The far northern stronghold of Mazar-e Sharif in Afghanistan falls to the Taliban religious fighters, which virtually completes their drive to reunite the country under conservative Muslim law.

25

Sierra Leone's Pres. Ahmad Tejan Kabbah flees the country in the wake of a military coup by junior army officers; Maj. Johnny Paul Koroma declares himself head of state.

•

Poland holds a national referendum and approves a new constitution by a narrow margin; the Roman Catholic Church in Poland has opposed the draft constitution principally because it lacks a ban on abortion.

•

Strom Thurmond, 94, a Republican from South Carolina, breaks the record for the longest tenure—41 years and 10 months—in the U.S. Senate; the previous record holder was Carl Hayden of Arizona.

•

Jacques Villeneuve, driving a Williams-Renault, wins the Spanish Grand Prix auto race at Barcelona.

26

Kenny Anthony takes over as prime minister of St. Lucia after his centre-left St. Lucia Labour Party handily defeated the incumbent United Workers' Party in elections on May 23.

•

Swiss pharmaceutical company Roche Holding Ltd. announces plans to acquire Boehringer Mannheim GmbH., a German manufacturer of drugs and diagnostic equipment, for about $11 billion.

27

In Paris leaders of NATO nations and President Yeltsin of Russia sign the Founding Act on Mutual Relations, Cooperation and Security, an agreement that establishes a new basis for the relationship between the former adversaries.

•

Twenty-two British women on a relay expedition reach the North Pole, the first all-female group to do so.

•

The season opens at Shakespeare's Globe Theatre; the new facility opened near the original site of the Globe Theatre in London.

28

The first medfly (Mediterranean fruit fly) is discovered in Tampa, Fla., triggering a pitched assault on the insect, which could devastate the state's citrus fruit and other crops.

•

Linda Finch, a businesswoman from Texas, lands at Oakland, Calif., after having re-created the flight planned by famed aviator Amelia Earhart 60 years earlier; Earhart and her navigator disappeared over the Pacific Ocean.

29

Not unexpectedly, in elections in Indonesia the Golkar alliance of President Suharto increases its legislative majority.

30

Science magazine reports that investigators from institutions in Madrid and Tarragona, Spain, have identified what is believed to be the last common ancestor of humans and Neanderthals; the new hominid species is named *Homo antecessor.*

31

In Kiev on his first official visit to Ukraine in seven years, Russian President Yeltsin signs a 10-year treaty of friendship and cooperation with Pres. Leonid Kuchma; on May 28 agreement was reached on the disposition of the Black Sea Fleet, which had been a bone of contention since the breakup of the U.S.S.R.

•

Confederation Bridge, the 13-km (8-mi) span that joins Prince Edward Island to the Canadian mainland, is officially opened.

•

A new U.S. national park in the Flint Hills area of Kansas, Tallgrass Prairie National Preserve, is formally dedicated.

1

Betty Shabazz, the widow of Black Muslim leader Malcolm X, is severely burned (and later dies) in a fire in her New York City apartment believed to have been set by her emotionally disturbed grandson.

•

The 1997 Antoinette Perry (Tony) Awards are given out in New York City: *The Last Night of Ballyhoo* wins the best play award, and *Titanic,* which wins a total of five awards, is chosen the best musical.

2

In Denver, Colo., Timothy J. McVeigh is found guilty of the April 1995 bombing of the Alfred P. Murrah Federal Building in Oklahoma City, Okla.; on August 14 the judge sentences him to death by lethal injection (*see* April 24).

•

The Canadian general election returns Prime Minister Jean Chrétien to power; it is the first overall majority for the Liberal Party in two successive elections in more than 40 years.

•

Amid continuing uncertainty following the military coup in Sierra Leone (*see* May 25), vessels of the Nigerian navy shell Freetown, the capital, and Nigerian ground forces battle troops loyal to coup leader Maj. Johnny Paul Koroma.

3

Lionel Jospin, leader of France's Socialist Party, is sworn in as prime minister following his party's narrow victory in the legislative elections held on May 25 and June 1.

•

Ehud Baraq is elected to lead the Israeli opposition Labour Party, replacing Shimon Peres.

4

The report of an Italian parliamentary constitutional reform commission calls for the direct election of the president and enhanced powers for that office.

•

The Bulgarian National Assembly approves a government plan to peg the Bulgarian monetary unit, the lev, to the Deutsche Mark at a rate of 1,000 to one.

•

A panel of the Institute of Medicine reports that Americans are not being provided adequate care and sympathetic treatment of their needs when their lives are nearing an end and when death has become unavoidable; the study calls for improved palliative health care.

5

Elections held in Algeria for a new National Assembly result in a victory for the National Democratic Rally but are tainted by reports of irregularities; Prime Minister Ahmed Ouyahia announces the new government on June 25.

•

In a significant personal political victory, Pres. Fernando Henrique Cardoso of Brazil signs into law a constitutional amendment that allows the president and certain other key officials to run for a second term.

•

Harold J. Nicholson, the highest-ranking U.S. intelligence officer ever tried for espionage, is sentenced to 23 years 7 months in prison for selling secrets to Russia (*see* March 4).

•

The F.W. Olin Foundation announces what is believed to be the largest gift ever—$200 million—to an American institution of higher education for the establishment of a new college of engineering near Boston.

6

Germany imposes a yearlong nationwide watch by the police and counterintelligence units on the Church of Scientology because of the government's suspicions of the group's antidemocratic intent.

7

It is reported that the Eye of the Needle, a natural stone arch in the federally administered Upper Missouri National Wild and Scenic River in Montana, has been destroyed by vandals.

•

Touch Gold inches past Silver Charm in the Belmont Stakes to deprive the latter horse, which had already won the Kentucky Derby and the Preakness Stakes, of thoroughbred racing's Triple Crown.

8

In a nationwide referendum Swiss voters reject by a three-to-one margin a proposal that would ban the export of arms.

•

Brazil makes its mark in another international sport as unseeded Gustavo Kuerten wins the men's competition in the French Open tennis tournament; ninth-seeded Iva Majoli of Croatia had defeated Martina Hingis in the women's final June 7.

LES STONE—SYGMA

BEBETO MATTHEWS—ASSOCIATED PRESS

Flowers for the funeral of Betty Shabazz, who died from severe burns suffered on June 1

Destruction in Montserrat: June 25

9

Haitian Prime Minister Rosny Smarth resigns under criticism of doing too little for the poor in the country.

•

Pol Pot, head of the Khmer Rouge organization in Cambodia, orders a purge of the top leadership; Son Sen, a key official, is murdered shortly thereafter (*see* January 24, July 25).

10

Russia and Belarus sign a treaty of union that brings the two countries closer together in some vague ways; the treaty is welcomed on the Belarusian side and among Russian conservative groups concerned about Russia's loss of influence in recent years.

•

At a meeting of the American Astronomical Society in Winston-Salem, N.C., a team of astrophysicists led by William Blair of Johns Hopkins University, Baltimore, Md., presents unique images of colliding supernovas taken by the Hubble Space Telescope.

11

Russian Pres. Boris Yeltsin announces his intention to remove Yevgeny I. Nazdratenko as governor of Primorsky *kray* in the extreme southeastern part of the country for his autocratic mismanagement of the region.

•

Sweden's Riksdag (parliament) votes to begin closing down the country's 12 nuclear power plants; a referendum approving the move had passed in 1980.

•

Media executive Rupert Murdoch, who owns the Fox television network, announces that he plans to purchase International Family Entertainment Inc., the holding company for religious leader Pat Robertson's Family Channel, for $1.9 billion.

•

The U.S. Army's Mobile Army Surgical Hospital at Camp Humphreys, South Korea, which inspired the motion picture and television series M*A*S*H, is closed.

•

The British House of Commons votes a total ban on handguns of all calibres; the new law will be one of the strongest in the world.

12

The U.S. Congress approves an $8.6 billion disaster relief bill; the vote by the Republican-dominated Congress is seen as a victory for Pres. Bill Clinton.

•

Secretary-General Kofi Annan names Mary Robinson, the president of Ireland, as United Nations High Commissioner for Human Rights; she is approved by the UN General Assembly on June 17.

•

The U.S. Treasury issues a redesigned $50 bill with new technology designed to deter forgery.

13

Russia announces that it will close the Molodyozhnaya station, its main research base in Antarctica, in two or three years as an economic move.

•

The Chicago Bulls win their fifth National Basketball Association championship in

seven years with a 90–86 victory over the Utah Jazz.

14

Pres. Ibrahim Baré Maïnassara of Niger names a new government under Prime Minister Amadou Boubacar Cissé.

•

The Microsoft Corp. announces that it will spend some $80 million to establish a research laboratory in Cambridge, Eng., to be headed by a University of Cambridge professor, Roger Needham.

15

Officials from the world's eight largest Muslim states—Bangladesh, Egypt, Indonesia, Iran, Malaysia, Nigeria, Pakistan, and Turkey—meet to form the "D8" group to promote economic and political cooperation.

•

Franjo Tudjman, leader of the nationalist Croatian Democratic Union, wins a second five-year term as president of Croatia with over 60% of the vote.

•

The Venice Biennale officially opens after three days of previews; the U.S. is represented by artist Robert Colescott, the first African-American to be so honoured.

16

Heads of government of the European Union nations convene for a two-day summit meeting in Amsterdam; observers remark on the optimism about EU projects by Great Britain's Labour-led government and the unusual restraint by German Chancellor Helmut Kohl.

•

Genesis Health Ventures Inc. announces that it will acquire Multicare Companies Inc. for $1,060,000,000 in cash; the resulting venture becomes a major provider of health care and outpatient services for the elderly in the northeast and mid-Atlantic areas.

•

The new edition of James Joyce's classic *Ulysses,* heavily revised by Danis Rose, is published on the 75th anniversary of the original and is greeted with a storm of controversy.

17

Two giants in telecommunications, Lucent Technologies and Philips Electronics NV, announce that they plan to combine their production of wireless telephones to form a new venture with $2.5 billion in anticipated revenue.

•

In South Africa, Afrikaner Resistance Movement leader Eugene Terreblanche is sentenced to six years in prison for two instances of assault against black men in 1996.

•

U.S. Army Maj. Gen. Claudia Kennedy becomes the first woman to hold the rank of lieutenant general (three-stars); she is the highest-ranking officer in U.S. Army Intelligence.

18

Prime Minister Necmettin Erbakan of Turkey resigns amid growing political unrest and rumours of a possible military coup; a new government with Mesut Yilmaz of the Motherland Party as prime minister is approved on June 30.

•

The Southern Baptist Convention, meeting in Dallas, Texas, votes to boycott the Walt Disney Co., which controls a wide variety of popular media and entertainment enterprises, for what the church group calls its "anti-Christian and anti-family" direction.

19

William Hague is elected leader of the British Conservative Party to replace John Major; at 36, Hague is the youngest person to become leader of a major British political party in 214 years.

•

Hideo Sakamaki, former president of Nomura Securities Co., the largest brokerage firm in Japan, is indicted for allegedly having made payments to an organized crime syndicate and other irregular financial dealings.

•

The long-standing worldwide ban on trading in elephant ivory enacted by a UN environmental committee is loosened to permit Namibia, Botswana, and Zimbabwe to sell a total of 58 tons of stockpiled ivory to Japan.

•

With its 6,138th performance, Lord Lloyd-Webber's musical *Cats* becomes the longest-running Broadway production, passing *A Chorus Line.*

20

The Summit of the Eight leading industrial nations, comprising the former Group of Seven plus new

Lord Lloyd-Webber's *Cats:* June 19

CAROL ROSEGG

KEVORK DJANSEZIAN—ASSOCIATED PRESS

member Russia, convenes for a summit meeting in Denver.

•

American tobacco companies agree to pay a total of $368.5 billion over 25 years and institute major changes in their marketing practices; the companies, in turn, will be free from liability for past wrongdoing.

21

The "Treasures from Mount Athos" exhibit opens at the Museum of Byzantine Culture in Thessaloniki, Greece, which has been designated the culture capital of Europe for 1997.

•

The eight-team Women's National Basketball Association debuts; the rival American Basketball League had completed its first season in March (*see* March 11).

22

Ernie Els wins his second major golf tournament in as many weeks, outshooting Jeff Maggert by two strokes in the Buick Classic in Harrison, N.Y.

23

The UN Conference on Environment and Development, a follow-up to the 1992 "Earth Summit" in Rio de Janeiro, convenes in New York City; delegates mostly bemoan the lack of progress on environmental initiatives begun in Rio and the continuing differences of approach between developed and less-developed countries.

•

Representatives of India and Pakistan meeting in Islamabad, Pak., agree to negotiate the future of Kashmir, an area that has been disputed between the two countries since they gained independence 50 years ago.

•

The Russian Duma (legislature) approves a bill that severely limits the activities of religious groups that have not practiced in the country for at least 50 years and that do not operate in at least half the regions.

•

Private companies begin operations in Lake Superior to recover some of the hundreds of thousands of sunken logs lost during logging operations in the 19th century; the old-growth logs have been preserved well in the cold waters of the lake.

24

A court in Egypt overturns a year-old law by the Ministry of Health banning, in state and private clinics, the ritual cutting of female genitals; the practice is favoured by some Islamic leaders and opposed by feminists and human rights advocates.

•

The Matthew, a replica of the ship in which explorer John Cabot sailed from Bristol, Eng., in 1497, arrives at Bonavista, Nfd., in celebration of the 500th anniversary of the voyage.

25

The Russian space station *Mir* is damaged when the unmanned cargo ship Progress rams into it in space; three astronauts—two Russians and a British-born American—are aboard *Mir.*

•

Soufrière Hills, a volcano on Montserrat, begins to expel large amounts of superheated gas, rock, and ash, killing at least 19 people and causing evacuation of several villages (*see* July 31).

•

At Christie's in New York City, cocktail and evening dresses culled from the closet of Diana, princess of Wales, are sold at an auction for the benefit of cancer and AIDS charities; the 79 dresses bring in $3,250,000.

26

Bertie Ahern of the Fianna Fail becomes prime minister of Ireland as head of a minority coalition government; the FF won 77 of the 166 seats in the Dail (parliament) in the June 6 election.

•

Tensions between Congolese Pres. Laurent Kabila and chief opposition leader Étienne Tshisekedi peak as Tshisekedi is arrested in his home by government troops (*see* May 17).

•

The U.S. Supreme Court votes to overturn the 1996 Communications Decency Act, which had sought to restrict indecency on the Internet, on the grounds that all provisions of the law violate the First Amendment to the Constitution.

27

In Moscow Pres. Imomali Rakhmonov of Tajikistan, United Tajik Opposition leader Sayed Abdullo Nuri, and the UN special envoy to Tajikistan, Gerd Merrem, sign a peace treaty that could end the civil war in that country.

•

The U.S. Supreme Court rules that a provision of the 1993 Brady Handgun Violence Protection Act that compels local law-enforcement agencies to run full background checks of prospective handgun buyers is unconstitutional.

28

The World Boxing Association heavyweight title fight in Las Vegas, Nev., is ended by the referee as challenger Mike Tyson is disqualified after he twice bites the ears of titleholder Evander Holyfield (*see* July 9).

29

Elections in Albania result in a victory for the opposition Socialist Party.

•

Michael Schumacher, driving a Ferrari, wins the French Grand Prix auto race at Magny-Cours.

30

The U.S. Court of Appeals for the Federal Circuit upholds a lower court finding that the General Electric Co. had violated the patents of Raymond V. Damadian, the inventor of technology used in magnetic resonance imaging machines.

Women's National Basketball Association debut: June 21

1

Hong Kong reverts to Chinese sovereignty, and the former colony becomes a special region of China; Prince Charles and Gov. Chris Patten leave aboard the royal yacht *Britannia.*

•

Luxembourg assumes the six-month European Union presidency.

2

The *Diamond Grace,* a Panamanian-registered supertanker, runs against a reef in Tokyo Bay and spills an estimated 13,400 tons of crude oil; it is called the worst oil spill in Japanese history.

•

The U.S. cruise line Royal Caribbean International announces that it will buy Celebrity Cruise Lines Inc. in a cash, stock, and debt-assumption deal worth $1,315,000,000.

3

Four American tobacco companies agree to settle a lawsuit with the state of Mississippi over the costs of health care programs associated with smoking.

•

Aerospace industry giant Lockheed Martin Corp. announces that it will buy Northrop Grumman Corp. for $8.3 billion in stock and will assume an additional $3.3 billion in debt.

4

The U.S. spacecraft Mars Pathfinder reaches Mars and lands on the surface successfully; it is the first spacecraft to land on the red planet in 21 years.

•

Haile Gebrselassie of Ethiopia runs the 10,000-m race in 26 min 31.32 sec, a world record, in the Bislett Games Grand Prix in Oslo.

5

The Lilith Fair, a concert tour featuring women singers, musicians, and songwriters, opens in George, Wash.

•

On this day 50 years ago, a ranch hand discovers remains of an unidentified flying object that crashed 280 km (75 mi) north of Roswell, N.M.; the U.S. Army Air Force announces that the fragments are those of a flying saucer but later retracts that statement.

6

In parliamentary elections in Mexico, the Institutional Revolutionary Party loses its absolute majority in the Chamber of Deputies; residents of Mexico City vote for a mayor for the first time, and opposition leader

Hong Kong handover: July 1

CHRISTOPHER MORRIS—BLACK STAR

CORRINE DUFKA—REUTERS

Protesters in Kenya: July 7

Cuauhtémoc Cárdenas Solórzano wins in a landslide.

•

Hun Sen, second prime minister of Cambodia, declares victory over the forces of his rival, First Prime Minister Prince Norodom Ranariddh, after two days of civil violence in the capital, Phnom Penh (*see* July 16).

•

American Pete Sampras wins the men's competition for the fourth time in the All England Championships in tennis at Wimbledon; on July 5 Martina Hingis, 16, of Switzerland had won the women's, the youngest winner in 110 years.

7

The government of Kenya reacts sharply to protesters calling for constitutional reforms, and at least seven people are killed; two days later violence breaks out at the University of Nairobi.

Montgomery Ward & Co., the ninth largest retail chain in the U.S., files for bankruptcy.

8

Formal invitations to join NATO in April 1999 are extended to Poland, the Czech Republic, and Hungary.

9

Two large financial firms in Russia, the Renaissance Capital Group and the International Company for Finance and Investment, announce that they will merge, forming the largest investment bank in the country, with total assets of more than $2 billion.

•

Gilbert F. Amelio, chairman and chief executive officer of troubled Apple Computer, Inc., resigns unexpectedly.

The Nevada Athletic Commission votes to revoke the boxing license of Mike Tyson and impose a $2,980,000 fine for his conduct during a heavyweight title fight 11 days earlier (*see* June 28).

10

It is announced that Joe Camel, the flashy and popular advertising symbol launched in 1988 by the RJ Reynolds Tobacco Co., will be retired.

•

The crew of the French research submersible *Nautile* discovers a large volcanic vent field in the Atlantic Ocean southwest of the Azores.

11

The journal *Cell* reports that Svante Paabo of the University of Munich, Ger., and associates, working on the basis of DNA analysis, have determined that Neanderthal man should not be placed in the direct evolutionary lineage of humans.

•

Scientists in Gainesville, Fla., for the first time transplant fetal tissue into the spine of a person suffering from syringomyelia, a rare degenerative spinal cord condition.

12

The remains of Cuban revolutionary leader Ernesto ("Che") Guevara are returned to his adopted homeland for burial after having been discovered at an airstrip in south-central Bolivia; Guevara was killed in 1967 (*see* October 17).

•

The murder of Miguel Angel Blanco, a town official, apparently by the Basque guerrilla group ETA, touches off several days of street demonstrations across Spain—some over a million strong—against ETA.

13

To commemorate Capt. Baron Georg von Trapp, who died in 1947, a service that includes representatives of the Austrian government is held in Stowe, Vt.; the Trapp family's flight from Austria is the subject of the stage musical and film *The Sound of Music.*

•

Jacques Villeneuve, driving a Williams-Renault, wins the British Grand Prix auto race at Silverstone.

14

Indian national and state legislatures vote for a new president and elect K.R. Narayanan; for the first time, the Indian president is a member of the Dalits, the lowest Hindu caste; he assumes office on July 25.

•

To accommodate a two-year renovation project, the historic Main Reading Room of the New York Public Library is closed for the first time.

15

In a secret kept remarkably well for a week, South African Pres. Nelson Mandela, on a visit to Jakarta, persuades his host, Indonesian Pres. Suharto, to convene a meeting with Mandela and José Alexandre ("Xanana") Gusmão, the imprisoned leader of the East Timorese Fretilin resistance group, in an attempt to find a resolution to the continuing problem in East Timor, a former Portuguese colony.

•

Italian fashion designer Gianni Versace is shot and killed in front of his mansion in Miami Beach, Fla. (*see* July 23).

16

Foreign Minister Ung Huot is selected to replace ousted Ranariddh as first prime minister of Cambodia (*see* July 6).

•

Russian Pres. Boris Yeltsin signs a decree reducing the Russian armed forces by nearly one-third, to 1.2 million.

17

U.S. Army Gen. Henry Shelton is selected to become the

next chairman of the Joint Chiefs of Staff.

•

The Woolworth Corp. announces plans to close more than 400 of its five-and-dime stores, the last in the United States; Woolworth's first store opened in Lancaster, Pa., in 1879.

•

The first World Congress on Breast Cancer concludes its five-day session in Kingston, Ont.

•

The Georgia O'Keeffe Museum opens in Santa Fe, N.M.; more than 80 pieces of O'Keeffe's art are on display in the adobe structure, a converted Spanish Baptist church.

18

The Monona Terrace Community and Convention Center, designed by architect Frank Lloyd Wright, opens in Madison, Wis.; Wright died in 1959.

19

Liberia holds presidential and parliamentary elections that are judged fair, partly owing to the presence of Ghanaian and Nigerian troops; guerrilla leader Charles G. Taylor wins comfortably.

•

Bosnian Serbs expel Pres. Biljana Plavsic as leader of the Serb Democratic Party and demand, unsuccessfully, that she resign as president of Republika Srpska, the Serb part of Bosnia and Herzegovina.

•

At odds over salmon fishing rights with their counterparts in the United States, Canadian fishermen begin a blockade of an American ferry and prevent it from leaving the British Columbia port of Prince Rupert.

20

Vietnam holds elections for the 450-seat National Assembly.

•

First Union Corp. of Virginia says it will buy Signet Banking Corp. of Richmond, Va., in a $3.3 billion deal (*see* November 19).

•

American Justin Leonard wins the British Open golf tournament at the Royal Troon Golf Club in Troon, Scot., with a score of 272, 12 under par.

21

The two largest banks in Bavaria (the fourth and fifth largest in Germany), Bayerische Vereinsbank AG and Bayerische Hypotheken und Wechselbank, announce plans to merge in a $10 billion deal that will create Europe's second largest bank.

•

Bishop Frank T. Griswold III of Chicago is elected presiding bishop of the Episcopal Church at that body's triennial General Convention in Philadelphia.

22

President Yeltsin vetoes the bill on religion that would have protected the Russian Orthodox Church but that was opposed by religious and human rights organizations and governments outside Russia (*see* June 23).

•

The Mormon Pioneer Trail wagon train, a reenactment of the 1,770-km (1,100-mi) trek made by Brigham Young and his followers 150 years ago from Omaha, Neb., arrives at Salt Lake City, Utah.

•

Maidenform Worldwide Inc., manufacturer of women's undergarments, files for Chapter 11 bankruptcy.

23

Slobodan Milosevic assumes the presidency of the Yugoslav federation, heretofore a symbolic post, resigning as president of Serbia, one of the two constituent republics in the federation (*see* October 19).

•

Pres. Alberto Fujimori, under strong political pressure in recent weeks, receives another blow when the opposition makes public documents that show that Fujimori may not have been born in Peru, a requirement for the president.

•

The body of a suicide victim found aboard a houseboat in Miami Beach, Fla., is identified as that of Andrew Cunanan, who was being sought throughout the United States for five murders, including that of Versace a few days earlier (*see* July 15).

•

British Prime Minister Tony Blair announces that, beginning in 1998, the government will no longer support free university education in the U.K.

24

The Scottish scientists who cloned a sheep (*see* February 23) announce that they have made a lamb, named Polly, all of whose cells contain a human gene, an important step in the production of biological products for use on or in humans.

Manhunt for Andrew Cunanan: July 23

BILL COOKE—ASSOCIATED PRESS

PHOTOS, (BELOW) REUTERS; (BOTTOM) ROBERT BALLARD—INSTITUTE FOR EXPLORATION

Pol Pot on trial: July 25

25

In Cambodia leaders of the Khmer Rouge revolutionary movement under Gen. Ta Mok hold a "people's tribunal" for the movement's longtime leader, Pol Pot, and sentence him to life imprisonment; he disappears shortly thereafter (*see* June 9).

26

The Pro Football Hall of Fame inducts four new members: Don Shula, Baltimore Colts and Miami Dolphins coach; center Mike Webster of the Pittsburgh Steelers; cornerback Mike Haynes of the New England Patriots and the Los Angeles Raiders; and New York Giants owner Wellington Mara.

27

National Airport in Washington, D.C., reopens after extensive renovations that cost approximately $1 billion; the complex features a dramatic new main terminal building designed by architect Cesar Pelli, as well as works by 30 American artists.

•

Jan Ullrich of Germany wins the Tour de France bicycle race with a commanding lead of 9 min 9 sec.

Gerhard Berger, driving a Benetton, wins the German Grand Prix auto race at Hockenheim; Alex Zanardi in a Reynard-Honda wins the U.S. 500 race in Brooklyn, Mich.

28

Latvian Prime Minister Andris Skele resigns amid deepening political and economic problems in the Baltic land.

•

The International Youth Festival, the first such left-wing celebration since the fall of the Soviet Union, is opened in Havana by Pres. Fidel Castro; although in violation of U.S. law, the 740-person American delegation is the largest national group attending.

29

Gen. Ronald R. Fogelman, U.S. Air Force chief of staff, announces his retirement, which is linked in the press to the likelihood that high-ranking air force officers will be held responsible for the bomb attack on a U.S. base in Saudi Arabia in 1996.

•

Yatsushiro Bay, off the Japanese industrial city of Minamata, is declared free of mercury, and a 40-year ban on consuming fish from the bay is lifted.

30

Two bombs explode in a market in Jerusalem, killing at least 15 people, including the bombers; the militant Islamist organization Hamas acknowledges responsibility.

•

Lebanon's Baalbek Festival opens; the cultural festival had not been held since 1974 because of civil unrest.

•

Oceanographer and undersea explorer Robert Ballard announces the discovery of eight ancient vessels, five from Roman times, sunk in deep water between Sicily and Sardinia; this is the largest find of old vessels in deep water ever.

31

Montserrat's Soufrière Hills volcano begins erupting, and by mid-August a succession of small eruptions has devastated the southern part of the island (*see* June 25, September 15).

•

Scientists at the University of California, Berkeley, report in *Nature* that they have discovered "quantum vibrations," a fundamental property of superfluids analogous to the Josephson effect in superconductors.

An artifact from one of eight ancient vessels discovered by Robert Ballard: July 30

1

Two aerospace giants, the Boeing Co. and McDonnell Douglas Corp., merge in a $16.3 billion deal, creating the world's largest aerospace group.

•

The United States lifts a ban on the sale of high-tech weapons to Latin-American countries; the prohibition on sales dates from 1977.

•

Queen Elizabeth II dedicates the American Air Museum in Duxford, Cambridgeshire, Eng., a memorial to American air power in the 20th century, especially the U.S. 8th Air Force, which flew bombing missions against Nazi Germany from Great Britain.

2

Charles G. Taylor is inaugurated as president of Liberia; he led one of the military factions in the protracted civil war and is the first elected president of Liberia in 12 years.

•

William S. Burroughs, American author who helped to define the Beat movement, dies in Lawrence, Kan., aged 83.

3

Separatists on the Indian Ocean island of Anjouan declare the island's independence from Comoros; two days later they name Abdallah Ibrahim president (*see* September 3).

•

China announces the discovery of a previously unknown colony of some 30 pandas in Gansu province; reportedly fewer than 1,000 pandas in about 20 discrete groups survive in the wild in China.

4

Negotiations in Washington, D.C., break down between the International Brotherhood of Teamsters and United Parcel Service, and the union goes on strike; UPS handles 80% of the parcels delivered in the U.S. (*see* August 19).

For the first time since the Korean War, a telephone link between North Korea and South Korea is opened.

•

It is reported that a U.S. government advisory panel recommends dismantling the Immigration and Naturalization Service and spreading its responsibilities among the Departments of Justice, State, and Labor.

5

The Bolivian Congress confirms Gen. Hugo Bánzer Suárez as president; he had served in that office once previously.

•

The budget bill signed by U.S. Pres. Bill Clinton includes a radical reduction of "home rule," the governmental autonomy of the District of Columbia, for at least four years but provides for an infusion of about $1 billion into the capital's treasury.

6

A Korean Airlines Boeing 747-300 crashes on the island of Guam, killing at least 225.

•

The Cambodian National Assembly confirms the appointment of Foreign Minister Ung Huot as first prime minister without, however, having formally dismissed the ousted incumbent, Prince Norodom Ranariddh (*see* July 16).

•

In a development that stuns the crowd at the Macworld Expo in Boston, it is announced that the Microsoft Corp., seen as a key rival, will purchase a $150 million nonvoting share in Apple Computer, Inc.

7

Four of the five former presidents of Central American countries who 10 years earlier signed the Esquipulas (Guat.) peace agreement to end the series of civil wars and unrest that were raging in the region—Oscar Arias of Costa Rica, Vinicio Cerezo of Guatemala, José Azcona of Honduras, and Daniel Ortega of Nicaragua (the fifth, José Napoleon Duarte was deceased)—reunite for the anniversary in the small Guatemalan town.

•

On the Roman Catholic Feast Day of Saint Cajetan of Thiene, more than one million people stream through San Cayetano church in Buenos Aires, Arg., to pray to the patron of bread and work; the extraordinary turnout is seen as a protest against high unemployment and declining salaries in the country.

•

Jean-François Tomb and scientists at the Institute for Genomic Research in Rockville, Md., report in the journal *Nature* that they have mapped the genes of the bacterium *Helicobacter pylori,* which is instrumental in causing ulcers and other stomach diseases.

•

A consortium led by the Nova Corp. of Canada formally opens a $325 million natural gas pipeline across the Andes on a 465-km (290-mi) route from Argentina to Chile.

8

In order to avoid international trade conflicts with the European Union, the U.S. agrees to change a law that required a country's identification on the label of clothes made from cloth woven in that country; the law would have affected European houses that make fine apparel from silk imported from China.

•

The journal *Cell* publishes two articles (and a third appears in *Neuron* in August) that report the discovery of the cause of cell death in Huntington's disease and several related disorders; the finding is considered a major medical breakthrough.

•

The government of Greece announces that archaeologists have discovered the Demosion Sima, a cemetery in Athens dating to Greece's Golden Age, which may contain the graves of many classical figures.

9

Ground is broken for a levee to contain flooding from the Mississippi River at the historical city of Sainte Genevieve, Mo.; three days earlier $201 million in federal funds had been promised for recovery from the spring flooding in North Dakota (*see* April 27).

KAMAL KISHORE—REUTERS

10

At the sixth world track and field championships in Athens, Sergey Bubka of Ukraine wins his sixth straight world pole vault championship, double the total of anyone else in a single event.

•

Greg Maddux, a pitcher for the Atlanta Braves, signs a five-year contract for $57.5 million, the highest ever in baseball.

The 50th anniversary of Indian independence: August 15

The U.S. wins the Walker Cup, defeating the British-Irish team by 18–6 at the Quaker Ridge Golf Club in Scarsdale, N.Y.

•

Jacques Villeneuve wins the Hungarian Grand Prix auto race at Budapest.

11

Eliminating three relatively minor provisions in a budget bill, President Clinton makes the first use of the line-item veto, a power the president was granted by Congress in 1996.

•

The International Monetary Fund, Japan, and a group of other Asian countries offer a package that is eventually worth $17.2 billion to stabilize the tottering economy of Thailand.

•

Crédit Suisse, Switzerland's second largest bank, announces plans to buy the Winterthur Group for about $9 billion in stock.

12

Hudson Foods, Inc., producers of beef for hamburgers, recalls 9,070 kg (20,000 lb) of ground beef patties after 20 cases of illness are reported, apparently caused by contamination of some of the company's products by *Escherichia coli* bacteria; on August 21 an additional 11,340,000 kg (25 million 1b) of beef are recalled and the company announces it will close its plant in Nebraska.

•

It is announced that the Lin Television Corp. of Providence, R.I., will be bought by Hicks, Muse, Tate & Furst Inc. in a deal worth more than $1.7 billion.

13

Violence breaks out in and near Mombasa, Kenya, as elections approach; several dozen persons die in weeks of clashes principally involving youths and police.

•

The government of Ontario announces that it plans to close seven nuclear power plants near the U.S. border, primarily out of concern for the safety of the facilities.

•

The United States defeats defending champion Italy to win the Champagne Mumm Admiral's Cup yachting race at Cowes, Isle of Wight, Eng.; this is the first American win since 1969.

•

At the Weltklasse track and field meet in Zürich, Switz., three world records are broken: Kenyan-born Wilson Kipketer betters the 16-year-old time for the 800 m at 1 min 41.24 sec; another runner, Wilson Boit Kipketer of Kenya, runs the 3,000-m steeplechase in 7 min 59.08 sec; and Haile Gebrselassie of Ethiopia improves on his own record by running the 5,000-m race in 12 min 41.86 sec.

14

Several days of violence that result in the deaths of at least 70 people precede the 50th anniversary of the founding of the country of Pakistan from part of British India.

•

Sony Corp., Philips Electronics NV, and the Hewlett-Packard Co. announce that they will not support the proposed standards for the rerecordable DVD-RAM disc technology, which threatens further instability in the home electronics market.

•

The W.R. Grace Co. announces that it will divest itself of its packaging business, most of which will be eventually purchased by the Sealed Air Corp. for about $5 billion.

•

Lee Berger of the University of the Witwatersrand, Johannesburg, S.Af., announces that his team has discovered footprints of an anatomically modern human on the shore of a lagoon in South Africa in sandstone dated at 117,000 years old, the oldest such record known.

15

The 50th anniversary of India's declaration of independence from British rule is marked.

•

Pres. Eduard Shevardnadze of Georgia and Vladislav Ardzinba of the breakaway territory of Abkhazia issue statements renouncing violence in the settlement of the Caucasian territories' dispute.

16

The Turkish Grand National Assembly passes a law that would require attendance at secular schools for eight years, rather than the former five, an attempt to limit the influence of Muslim religious schools.

•

An estimated 50,000 fans congregate in Memphis, Tenn., to commemorate the 20th anniversary of the death of rock idol Elvis Presley, who would have been 62 in 1997.

17

Golfer Davis Love III wins the Professional Golfers' Association of America championship with an 11-under-par score of 269 at the Winged Foot Golf Club in Mamaroneck, N.Y.

18

The Churchwide Assembly of the Evangelical Lutheran Church in America, meeting in Philadelphia, votes to draw closer to three other Protestant churches—the Presbyterian Church (U.S.A.), the United Church of Christ, and the Reformed Church in America—and offer full communion among them.

•

In the shadow of the Brooklyn Bridge in New York City, the durable Rolling Stones announce a new 35-city tour in the U.S., Canada, and Mexico to begin in September.

JOE TRAVER—GAMMA LIAISON

Announcement of a new Rolling Stones tour: August 18

CHRIS STEELE-PERKINS—MAGNUM

The 50th anniversary of the birth of Pakistan: August 14

19

The two-week strike by the Teamsters Union against UPS ends (*see* August 4).

•

President Clinton spends his 51st birthday on the Massachusetts resort island of Martha's Vineyard.

•

The world target championships begins in Victoria, B.C.

20

Without opposition, NATO troops in Banja Luka, Bosnia and Herzegovina, take over police buildings in the city and find caches of arms believed to have been assembled for a possible coup against Pres. Biljana Plavsic.

In Iran the legislature approves the Cabinet of Pres. Mohammad Khatami.

•

Illinois Gov. Jim Edgar suddenly and unexpectedly announces that he will not again seek public office.

21

The sporting-goods manufacturer Speedo releases a new mask for swimming competitions that reduces drag around the head and goggles of the swimmer and is expected to become standard equipment in top competitions.

•

The General Motors Corp. celebrates the 100th anniversary of the Oldsmobile; the company was established by Ranson E. Olds in Lansing, Mich., in 1897.

J.B. RUSSELL—SYGMA

NATO troops in Bosnia and Herzegovina: August 20

22

A federal judge in Little Rock, Ark., sets a date in May 1998 for jury selection to begin in the sexual harassment suit brought by Paula Jones against President Clinton.

23

The new Arthur Ashe Stadium, part of the renovation and expansion of the U.S. Tennis Association National Tennis Center at Flushing Meadows, Queens, N.Y., opens; it is officially dedicated on August 25, during the U.S. Open tournament (*see* September 7).

•

In the 1997 Little League Baseball World Series, Linda Vista from Guadalupe, Nuevo León, Mex. (Latin America region), defeats South Mission Viejo from Mission Viejo, Calif. (U.S. West region), 5–4.

24

Egon Krenz, the last leader of the former East Germany, is found guilty of manslaughter for his complicity in the shooting deaths by border policemen of persons trying to escape the country; on August 25 he is sentenced to prison for six and a half years.

•

Cardinal Health Inc. agrees to buy the Bergen Brunswig Corp. for more than $2.4 billion plus $386 million in debt; the resulting company will be the largest drug wholesaler in the U.S.

•

Michael Schumacher, driving a Ferrari, wins the Belgian Grand Prix auto race at Spa-Francorchamps.

25

Five major American cigarette manufacturers agree to pay $11.3 billion to settle a lawsuit by the state of Florida over the cost of health care due to smoking-related illnesses.

•

North Korea's ambassador to Egypt, Chang Sung Gil, and his brother, Chang Sung Ho, the country's chief trade official in France, defect to the U.S.

26

F.W. de Klerk, former president of South Africa and corecipient with Nelson Mandela of the 1993 Nobel Peace Prize, announces his resignation as head of the National Party and his retirement from politics.

27

Two gangs engage in battle in the El Dorado penal centre in Venezuela, killing 29 and injuring 13; the prison system in the country has been plagued by overcrowding and poor conditions for some years.

•

The Asatru, a Nordic pagan sect, holds a consecration ceremony on the banks of the Columbia River at Kennewick, Wash., where in June 1996 an ancient skull—called the Kennewick Man—was discovered; the skull and its future are contested by the U.S. Corps of Engineers, custodians of the land on which the skull was discovered, Native American groups that assert the Kennewick man is an ancestor, scientists who believe the remains are of a Caucasoid man, and the pagans.

28

In California the first state law in the U.S. reversing affirmative action (legal encouragement to hire and promote the welfare of women and minorities) takes effect as thousands demonstrate against the new situation.

•

The freestyle wrestling world championships begin in Krasnoyarsk, Russia.

29

Islamist terrorists wreak havoc in the village of Rais, Alg., brutally killing dozens of people and abducting at least 20 women.

•

The oldest nuclear power plant in the U.S., the Big Rock Point facility near Charlevoix, Mich., is closed because it is no longer economical to run.

•

A U.S. federal judge reduces the punitive damages awarded by a lower court in a controversial case by Food Lion supermarkets against the ABC television network and others from $5,500,000 to $315,000; two TV reporters had falsified their applications to get jobs in a supermarket in order to report on unsanitary handling of food products.

•

New guidelines for handling doctrinal differences within the Roman Catholic Church are made public in Rome.

30

The names of chemical elements 101–109 become official as the Council of the International Union of Pure and Applied Chemistry ends a long selection procedure.

•

The World Amazigh Congress, dedicated to the promotion of Berber identity throughout North Africa, completes its inaugural four-day meeting in Tafira, Canary Islands.

•

The Houston Comets defeat the New York Liberty 65-51 in the inaugural Women's National Basketball Association championship in Houston, Texas; Cynthia Cooper of the Comets is chosen Most Valuable Player (*see* March 11).

31

Diana, princess of Wales, her friend Emad Mohamed al-Fayed, and their driver are killed in an automobile crash in a Paris highway tunnel.

•

Indigenous leaders from Venezuela, Brazil, and Guyana end a five-day meeting in Boa Vista, Braz., with a statement urging their native peoples to be more vocal in discussing large-scale development projects that affect their lives and welfare.

•

A five-day celebration of the 100th anniversary of the Zionist movement ends in Basel, Switz., where on Aug. 29, 1897, Thedor Herzl convened the first Zionist congress to work for a Jewish homeland in Palestine.

1

Physicists at Brookhaven National Laboratory, Upton, N.Y., and other facilities in the U.S. and Russia announce that they have discovered a new particle, which they call the "exotic meson"; the team speculated that the exotic meson might comprise four quarks, unlike all other known particles, which have three.

2

At a summit meeting of Central American presidents in Managua, Nic., it is decided to create an economic union on the model of the European Community in order to improve economic conditions within the region and trade status with other countries.

3

Troops from Comoros land on the island of Anjouan in an attempt to put down the secessionist movement; both sides suffer many casualties (*see* August 3).

•

Gov. Fife Symington of Arizona resigns, effective September 5, after he is convicted of seven counts of fraud dating from the time, before he was elected governor, that he was a real-estate developer.

•

The Rev. Henry J. Lyons retains the presidency of the National Baptist Convention, USA, Inc., after his supporters thwart a strong move to unseat him because of allegations that he had misappropriated church funds.

•

Citizens in Newfoundland vote overwhelmingly to end church control of public schools in the Canadian province; local Roman Catholic organizations are expected to appeal the vote in court.

•

Philanthropist George Soros closes the offices of the Soros Foundation in Minsk, Belarus, under pressure from the government.

4

Three suicide bombers set off explosions in a shopping area in Jerusalem; at least 4 persons are killed, and at least 180 are wounded.

5

Mother Teresa, Nobel Peace Prize winner, dies in Calcutta at age 87; in a break with tradition, the Indian government gives her a state funeral on September 13.

Flowers for Diana, princess of Wales: September 6

PHOTOGRAPHS (BELOW) PETER TURNLEY—BLACK STAR;
(BOTTOM) PETER MARLOW—MAGNUM; (INSET) DAVID LEVENSON—BLACK STAR

The International Olympic Committee chooses Athens as the host city of the 2004 Summer Olympic Games; other contenders were Buenos Aires, Arg., Cape Town, Rome, and Stockholm.

•

Following a meeting of the Southern African Development Community in Blantyre, Malawi, ministers from several countries in the region warn that bovine pleuropneumonia, a cattle disease, has reached epidemic proportions and could soon affect local economies, which rely heavily on livestock breeding and farming.

•

The National University of Samoa is officially opened in the capital, Apia.

•

The city of Moscow celebrates its 850th anniversary with a three-day gala that includes parades, concerts, and pageantry throughout the city.

6

Diana, princess of Wales, is buried at her family's estate in Northamptonshire following a formal funeral at Westminster Abbey (*see* August 31).

•

An American astronaut and a Russian cosmonaut venture outside the *Mir* space station to repair damage incurred in a collision with a cargo ship on June 25; a succession of computer failures and other problems have plagued the space station during the year.

7

Australian Patrick Rafter defeats Briton Greg Rusedski to win the men's competition in the U.S. Open tennis tournament in Flushing Meadows, N.Y.; Martina Hingis (Switz.) beats Venus Williams (U.S.) to win the women's title.

•

David Coulthard, driving a McLaren-Mercedes, wins the Italian Grand Prix auto race at Monza.

8

A ferry sinks off the west coast of Haiti, and at least 172 persons are killed.

•

WorldCom, Inc., announces that it will buy CompuServe Inc. for $1.2 billion and then sell CompuServe's on-line services, which include about 2.6 million customers, to industry leader America Online, Inc.

9

In anticipation of the peace talks for Northern Ireland on September 15, Sinn Fein, the political wing of the Irish Republican Army, formally renounces violence and agrees, in the words of the party's leader, Gerry Adams, "to take all the guns out of Irish politics."

•

At a time when figures in Pres. Bill Clinton's administration are undergoing close political scrutiny for allegedly having used U.S. government facilities for party fund-raising activities, Donald L. Fowler, national chairman of the Democratic National Committee during the 1996 election, admits that he assisted in arranging meetings between key party supporters and high U.S. government officials.

10

Maj. Gen. Robert D. Shadley, former director of the Aberdeen Ordnance Center and School, Maryland, the site of alleged incidents of sexual harassment that racked the U.S. Army earlier in the year, receives a reprimand; on September 11 the army announces that its investigation has confirmed reports of widespread sexual harassment in the organization.

11

In a referendum Scotland votes overwhelmingly in favour of establishing a parliament independent of the British government in London to oversee domestic affairs in the country (*see* September 18).

•

In a follow-up to the spacecraft Mars Pathfinder's mission, NASA-led Mars Global Surveyor enters the planet's orbit; it will spend two years mapping the surface of the red planet (*see* July 4).

(From left) Earl Spencer, Prince William, and Prince Harry at Diana's funeral: September 6

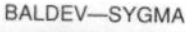

The death of Mother Teresa: September 5

Film actor and vice president of the National Rifle Association Charlton Heston, speaking at the National Press Club in Washington, D.C., comes out forcefully in favour of private citizens' right to own guns, calling that right the "first among equals" in the U.S.

12

In a radical departure from the socialist form of centralized control of industry but studiously avoiding the word *privatization,* the Chinese government announces an agreement to sell off 10,000 of the country's 13,000 large and medium-sized state enterprises.

•

Mary Robinson steps down as president of Ireland in order to accept the position of UN High Commissioner for Human Rights (*see* June 17).

13

Two days of municipal elections begin in Bosnia and Herzegovina.

•

Oscar de la Hoya defeats Hector ("Macho") Camacho in a World Boxing Council welterweight title fight in Las Vegas, Nev.

•

The first annual World Air Games opens in Ankara, Tur.; included are events for powered and nonpowered aircraft, ballooning, model airplanes, and parachuting.

•

The Toronto International Film Festival closes; *In & Out* and *FairyTale: A True Story* receive their world premieres during the festival.

14

The government of New Zealand formally returns the 1,150-ha (2,842-ac) Onewhero Forest on North Island to the Maori people; this land, along with other tracts, had been seized from the Maoris during the British colonial period.

•

A train derailment on a bridge in Madyah Pradesh, India, kills at least 80 persons and injures hundreds.

•

Television's Emmy awards are given out in ceremonies at Pasadena, Calif.; "Law & Order" wins for best drama, and "Frasier" takes the Emmy for best comedy.

•

The Washington Redskins professional football team plays its first game in the new Jack Kent Cooke Stadium, the largest open-air facility in the National Football League.

15

Former Massachusetts governor William F. Weld, who had been nominated by President Clinton to be U.S. ambassador to Mexico, withdraws his candidacy after encountering withering opposition from Sen. Jesse Helms, chairman of the Senate Foreign Relations Committee.

•

Two popular diet drugs, fenfluramine and dexfenfluramine, are withdrawn from the market by their manufacturers after the U.S. Food and Drug Administration (FDA) establishes a possible link between the preparations—often used in combination with another appetite suppressant, phentermine—and heart-valve damage.

•

The Museum of Jewish Heritage, located in New York City near Battery Park, is opened to the public; included are items of Jewish culture from Europe, North America, and Israel, as well as exhibits on the Holocaust.

16

The German sportswear company adidas AG announces plans to buy Salomon SA, a French sports-equipment manufacturer, for $1.4 billion.

•

A report presented by scientists from the U.S. National Cancer Institute and the FDA and based on a review of medical studies finds no link between silicone breast implants and incidence of breast cancer.

•

In a report in the *Proceedings of the National Academy of Sciences,* scientists at the Johns Hopkins University School of medicine, Baltimore, Md., report that broccoli sprouts contain 30–50 times the amount of chemicals that stimulate the growth of antitoxic enzymes that fight cancer as are found in mature broccoli plants.

17

In Oslo representatives of 100 nations sign the draft treaty banning the use, sale, stockpiling, and production of antipersonnel land mines (*see* December 3).

•

Tran Duc Luong, a mining engineer from Quang Ngai province, is elected president of Vietnam by the Vietnamese Communist Party; Phan Van Kai replaces Vo Van Kiet as prime minister on September 25 (*see* December 30).

•

The World Health Organization reports that Cambodia is suffering the highest infection rate from HIV in Southeast Asia and that 40,000 deaths from related causes are expected in that country by the year 2000.

•

Japanese and Peruvian archaeologists uncover a royal tomb in northern Peru that contains a number of gold ornaments believed to be the oldest known items in the Americas.

18

Media mogul Ted Turner announces that he will establish a foundation and through it donate $1 billion—$100 million a year for 10 years—to programs that are approved by the United Nations.

•

A referendum held in Wales on the question of establishing an assembly passes narrowly, unlike the enthusiastic support a similar proposal received earlier in Scotland (*see* September 11).

•

A bomb attack on a tourist bus in downtown Cairo kills 10, mostly German tourists.

•

Two accounting firms, Coopers & Lybrand and Price Waterhouse, announce plans to merge; the resulting company will be the world's largest accounting firm, with some $11.8 billion in annual revenue (*see* October 20).

19

The American Medical Association announces that three of its top executives are leaving; on December 4, P. John Seward, the AMA's chief executive, resigns, acknowledging that a serious mistake was made when the influential organization agreed to a commercial endorsement agreement with the Sunbeam Corp.

•

The 40th Monterey (Calif.) Jazz Festival opens; it is the longest-running jazz festival in the U.S.

20

The 28th meeting of the South Pacific Forum concludes in Rarotonga, Cook Islands.; among a variety of issues discussed is the effort to bring peace to the island of Bougainville, Papua New Guinea, where a violent secessionist movement continues.

21

In the Polish elections the centre-right Solidarity coalition regains power from the Socialists after four years.

•

In Yugoslavia the Socialist Party of Serbia of Pres. Slobodan Milosevic wins legislative elections but loses a number of seats such that for the first time it will have to form a coalition government.

•

The Whitbread Round the World race begins as 10 yachts from six countries depart on the first leg from Southampton, Eng., for Cape Town; the full race will take eight months.

22

The exchange rate for the Malaysian ringgit reaches a 26-year low, falling to 3.122 to the U.S. dollar.

•

The computer aboard the *Mir* space station fails again; two other failures had crippled the ship in recent weeks.

•

The 52nd annual Albert Lasker Medical Research Awards go to Mark S. Ptashne of Memorial Sloan-Kettering Cancer Center in New York City and Victor A. McKusick and Alfred Sommer, both of Johns Hopkins University.

•

The Seagram Co. Ltd. announces it will buy the remainder of the USA Network—the 50% share it does not already own—from Viacom Inc. for $1.7 billion.

23

A massacre in which at least 85 people are slaughtered takes place on the outskirts of Algiers and is attributed by the government to the Armed Islamic Group, which was also held responsible for a similar incident on August 29 (*q.v.*).

•

Students hold an illegal demonstration in Mongolia to protest rising costs of tuition and lodging in universities; Prime Minister Mendsaikhan Enkhsaikhan orders universities to lower these fees on September 24.

•

Elton John's recording of his "Candle in the Wind 1997," the song he rewrote and performed at the funeral of Diana, princess of Wales, goes on sale in New York City; 37 days later the single compact disc becomes the best-selling single recording ever (almost 32 million copies).

24

The Travelers Group of financial companies announces that it will buy Salomon Inc. for $9 billion, creating a new giant corporation on the New York City financial scene.

25

Andy Green, a British fighter pilot, breaks the world land-speed record that had stood since 1983 in the jet Thrust SuperSonic Car, attaining an average speed of 1,149.3 km/h (714.14 mph) on the required two runs on a course in Black Rock Desert, Nevada; on October 15 he becomes the first driver to exceed the speed of sound in a land vehicle.

•

The International Court of Justice in The Hague finds both Hungary and Slovakia at fault in their squabble over the diversion of water from the Danube River at the Gabcikovo-Nagymaros Project.

26

Two earthquakes shake central Italy, killing 11 people and causing heavy damage to the priceless 13th- and 14th-century frescoes in the vaulted ceiling of the Basilica of St. Francis of Assisi.

•

Salvatore Riina and 23 other officials of the Sicilian Mafia are sentenced to life in prison for the murder in 1992 of Giovanni Falcone, the courageous prosecutor of organized crime in Italy.

•

Southcom, the headquarters for all U.S. military operations in Latin America south of Mexico, closes its base at Quarry Heights, Pan., and moves to Miami, Fla.; the base at Quarry Heights had opened in 1916.

27

Taliban leaders seize Kabul, the capital, and declare Afghanistan a "complete" Islamic state.

•

The Adelaide Crows defeat St. Kilda by a score of 19.11 (125) to 13.16 (94) in the grand final of the Australian Football League in Melbourne.

28

The 400th anniversary of the dedication of the Mimizuka, or "Ear Mound," in Kyoto, Japan, which contains the noses and ears taken as trophies from tens of thousands of Koreans by invading Japanese samurai, is commemorated.

•

By a score of 14½ to 13½ Europe defeats the U.S. to win the Ryder Cup at Valderrama Golf Club, Sotogrande, Spain, the first time the biennial golf tournament has been held outside the U.S. or the U.K.

•

Jacques Villeneuve, driving a Williams-Renault, wins the Luxembourg Grand Prix auto race at Nürburgring.

29

Combivir, a medication that combines AZT and 3TC, two common AIDS-therapy preparations, becomes the first combination drug for AIDS to win approval by the U.S. FDA.

•

Little, Brown & Co., Inc., which had planned to publish a book by the 13th-century Italian-Jewish merchant Jacob d'Ancona, who purportedly visited China four years before the voyage of Marco Polo, announces it will postpone publication because it is suspected of being a hoax.

30

The Roman Catholic Church of France apologizes to the Jewish people for not having spoken up against the repression of Jews during the period of French collaboration with Nazi Germany.

•

Toys "Я" Us, Inc., the leading U.S. toy retailer, is found guilty of colluding with manufacturers to control the distribution of popular items, such as Barbie and GI Joe dolls, and keep prices artificially high.

OCT

1

The month of October has been dedicated by Pres. Islam Karimov of Uzbekistan to the celebration of the 2,500th anniversary of the city of Khiva.

•

Leland's auction house in New York City opens the largest-ever sale of memorabilia from the television show "Howdy Doody"; the marionette figure, beloved by millions of young viewers, also celebrates his 50th birthday in 1997.

2

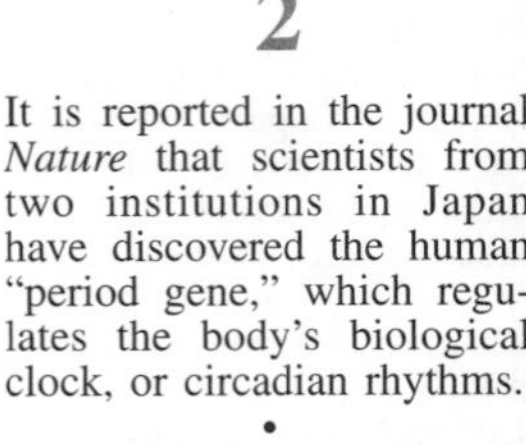

It is reported in the journal *Nature* that scientists from two institutions in Japan have discovered the human "period gene," which regulates the body's biological clock, or circadian rhythms.

•

The Ford Motor Co. announces plans to build a new factory in southern Brazil that could cost up to $1 billion.

3

The Guggenheim Museum, housed in a spectacular titanium-clad building designed by American architect Frank Gehry, is inaugurated in the Basque city of Bilbao, Spain; it opens to the public on October 19.

•

U.S. Attorney General Janet Reno rejects allegations made by Republican representatives of misdeeds on the part of Pres. Bill Clinton in connection with campaign financing.

The new Solomon R. Guggenheim Museum of European and American Art, Bilbao, Spain: October 3

4

In a spate of attacks in three separate Algerian villages by rival Islamist organizations, more than 100 civilians, many of them children, are brutally massacred (*see* April 22).

•

Hundreds of thousands of Promise Keepers, evangelical Christian men dedicated to making themselves better husbands and fathers, convene on the Mall in Washington, D.C., in what is believed to be the largest religious gathering in U.S. history.

•

Princess Cristina Federica de Borbón y Grecia, daughter of King Juan Carlos I of Spain, and Iñaki Urdangarín, a commoner and professional team handball player from the Basque Country in northwestern Spain, are married in Barcelona.

5

French jockey Olivier Peslier rides Peintre Celebre to victory in the Prix de l'Arc de Triomphe horse race at Longchamp, Paris.

•

The 50th anniversary of the death of German physicist Max Planck (Oct. 4, 1947) is commemorated with a special exhibition about his life and work, sponsored by the Max Planck Society and the German Physical Society at Magnus House, Berlin.

6

Ten Bosnian Croats accused of war crimes, including Dario Kordic, especially sought for his role in the ethnic cleansing in Bosnia and Herzegovina, turn themselves in to the international war crimes tribunal in The Hague; Croatia has come under criticism and international pressure for its lack of cooperation in helping bring Croat war criminals to justice.

•

Stanley B. Prusiner is awarded the Nobel Prize for Physiology or Medicine for his discovery and study of prions, a previously unknown type of disease-causing agent.

TIMOTHY HURSLEY

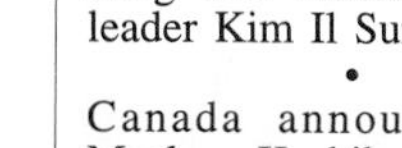

7

Sun Microsystems, Inc., owner and inventor of the Java Internet application development language, brings suit in San Jose, Calif., accusing the Microsoft Corp., which has developed its own, incompatible version of Java, of trademark infringement and breach of contract, among other wrongful practices.

•

A team of astronomers from the Space Telescope Science Institute in Baltimore, Md., and the University of California, Los Angeles, reports finding the Pistol Star, perhaps the brightest and most massive (up to 450.6 million km [280 million mi] in diameter) body ever observed, near the centre of the Milky Way Galaxy in the direction of the constellation Sagittarius.

•

The National Academy of Engineering announces that Vladimir Haensel, inventor of "platforming" (platinum reforming), a catalytic process for producing clean and efficient high-performance fuels from petroleum, has been awarded the biennial Charles Stark Draper Prize; the award is valued at $450,000.

8

Kim Jong Il assumes the post of general secretary of the Korean Workers' (Communist) Party; the post, as well as that of president of North Korea, have been unfilled since the death more than three years ago of Kim Jong Il's father, longtime leader Kim Il Sung.

•

Canada announces that Muskwa-Kechika, a one million-hectare (2.5 million-ac) area of wilderness in northern British Columbia, will be set aside and protected from development; in addition, the area is to be surrounded by a buffer zone, where only limited economic exploitation will be permitted.

9

Dario Fo, Italian playwright and performer, wins the Nobel Prize for Literature.

•

Unexpectedly, the German Bundesbank raises its repo rate for the first time in five years, which puts pressure on other European countries and prompts increases also in France, The Netherlands, and Belgium.

•

A hurricane rakes the Mexican coastline at Acapulco, killing hundreds and leaving thousands of people homeless, mostly those who were living in poorly built structures on the hillsides above the popular resort town.

10

The Nobel Prize for Peace is awarded to the International Campaign to Ban Landmines and to its coordinator, American Jody Williams.

•

Pres. Nursultan Nazarbayev of Kazakstan removes from office Prime Minister Akezhan Kazhegeldin, a reformist, who left the country for medical treatment, and replaces him with a tractable, low-key ally, Nurlan Balgimbayev.

•

Prime Minister Lionel Jospin presents a proposal to cut the workweek in France from 39 to 35 hours, without any corresponding drop in pay, in order to stimulate job growth.

•

An Argentine DC-9 airliner crashes and explodes in Uruguay, killing all 75 people aboard.

•

Actress and animal rights activist Brigitte Bardot is fined $1,600 by a French court for protesting the sacrificial slaughter of sheep by Muslims.

11

Meeting in Strasbourg, France, the Council of Europe adopts an agreement that would create a common social model for all of Europe that emphasizes human rights, civil rights, and protection from crime.

•

Following $140 million in renovations, the Teatro Real, Madrid's 19th-century opera house, is formally reopened to opera performances after a lapse of 72 years; the world premiere of Antón García Abril's opera *Divinas Palabras,* with the lead role sung by Spanish tenor Plácido Domingo, takes place on October 18.

12

Paul Biya easily wins reelection as president of Cameroon with about 80% of the vote in an election that was carefully controlled by his government and that the main opposition parties boycotted.

•

Laurent Brochard of France wins the 256.5-km (159-mi) world road championship bicycle race in San Sebastián, Spain, with a time of 6 hr 16 min 48 sec.

13

The Christian Democratic Union, Chancellor Helmut Kohl's party, begins its annual party congress in Leipzig, Ger.

•

The women's World Open squash championship begins in Sydney, Australia, and is dominated by the home team.

14

The Nobel Memorial Prize in Economic Science is awarded to Robert C. Merton and Myron Samuel Scholes for their work on devising a formula to evaluate stock options.

•

Queen Elizabeth II of England, on a visit to celebrate

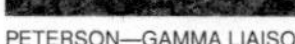

PETERSON—GAMMA LIAISON

Massacres in Algeria: October 4

MEALAND ADRIAN—GAMMA LIAISON

Hurricane Pauline: October 9

the 50th anniversary of Indian independence, lays a wreath at a memorial dedicated to the nearly 400 unarmed Indian civilians massacred by British soldiers in 1919 at Amritsar.

•

The five delegates who constitute the legislature of the Caribbean island of Nevis vote unanimously to leave the federation with St. Kitts; a referendum on the issue is required.

•

The Booker Prize is awarded in London to Indian writer Arundhati Roy for her novel *The God of Small Things.*

•

Sir Paul McCartney's (*see* January 1) full-length symphonic poem *Standing Stone* receives its world premiere at the Royal Albert Hall, London, with Lawrence Foster leading the London Symphony Orchestra; the piece was recorded earlier and tops the U.S. classical music charts.

15

The Nobel Prize for Physics is awarded to Steven Chu, William D. Phillips, and Claude Cohen-Tannoudji for having developed a method to slow down atoms for study; winners of the Nobel Prize for Chemistry are Paul D. Boyer, John E. Walker, and Jens C. Skou for their studies of adenosine triphosphate (ATP), a molecule that stores energy.

•

Brazzaville, the capital, and Pointe-Noir, the second largest city of the Republic of Congo, fall to advancing rebel forces; on October 19 Pres. Pascal Lissouba flees the country.

•

A truck bomb in Colombo, the Sri Lankan capital, kills 18 people and wounds approximately 100, many of them foreign tourists; at least 2 members of the Liberation Tigers of Tamil Eelam, a Tamil-speaking separatist group in Sri Lanka, are killed by police following the bombing.

•

Amid concerns about the possible danger of launching the vehicle because its reactor uses plutonium, the Cassini spacecraft is launched from Cape Canaveral, Florida, and begins a seven-year trek to the planet Saturn.

16

The U.S. Federal Maritime Commission orders the Coast Guard to prohibit the entry of Japanese ships into American ports and to prohibit Japanese ships already in port from leaving, the latest round in a trade dispute between the two countries.

•

A clinic in Atlanta, Ga., reports success in freezing human eggs, thawing them, fertilizing them, and bringing the resultant set of twins to full-term pregnancy and birth; the procedure opens the possibility that young women could preserve their eggs for fertilization later in their lives.

•

The 1997 Dorothy and Lillian Gish Prize, which honours outstanding contributors to the arts, is presented to singer-songwriter Bob Dylan at a ceremony in New York City; the 1996 award went to theatre director Robert Wilson.

17

Jerzy Buzek is named prime minister of Poland; his right-wing Solidarity-linked government takes over after four years of rule by the former communists.

•

The remains of Argentine-born revolutionary Ernesto ("Che") Guevara are buried at the base of a monument to the leader of the Cuban Revolution in Santa Clara, Cuba; Pres. Fidel Castro Ruz speaks in homage to his former comrade-in-arms (*see* July 12).

18

The Women in Military Service for America Memorial on the grounds of the Arlington (Va.) National Cemetery outside Washington, D.C., is dedicated; some 1.8 million women have served in the U.S. armed forces.

19

Milo Djukanovic, a political opponent of Serbian strongman Slobodan Milosevic, is elected president of Montenegro, one of the two constituent republics of the rump Yugoslav state.

•

Ecumenical Patriarch Bartholomew I of Constantinople, spiritual leader of the world's Eastern Orthodox churches, arrives in Washington, D.C., for a month-long pastoral visit that will take him to 16 cities in the U.S.

20

The U.S. government files a petition in a federal court, stating that the Microsoft Corp., by requiring personal computer manufacturers to install its Internet browser software together with the predominant Microsoft Windows operating system, is in violation of an antitrust agreement that the two parties had reached earlier; on December 11 a federal judge rules in favour of the government.

•

KPMG Peat Marwick LLP and Ernst & Young LLP, two of the world's largest accounting firms, announce plans to merge, creating the largest such company in the world, even after the Coopers & Lybrand/Price Waterhouse union (*see* September 18).

•

Starwood Lodging Trust of Phoenix, Ariz., becomes the largest hotel corporation in the world when it acquires the Sheraton chain from its owner, ITT Corp., for $9.8 billion.

•

"Sue," the fossilized skeleton of a 65 million-year-old *Tyrannosaurus rex* that was sold at auction on October 4 in New York City for $8,360,000, arrives at the facilities of the high bidder, Chicago's Field Museum of Natural History.

21

A nurse and a doctor in Copenhagen are charged with having administered lethal injections—on the grounds of euthanasia—to 22 patients in a nursing home over a four-year period; the week before, on October 14, the U.S. Supreme Court had elected not to review the constitutionality of an Oregon law that

permits terminally ill persons to seek the assistance of a physician to end their own lives.

22

The government of South Korea announces that it will take over the Kia Motors Corp., the country's third largest auto manufacturer.

•

Two young American conductors, Alan Gilbert and David Robertson, are awarded the $100,000 Seaver/National Endowment for the Arts Conductors Award.

•

Nike, the manufacturer of sports footwear, announces that it has signed a sponsorship deal with the professional U.S. Soccer Federation, agreeing to pay a $120 million subsidy over an eight-year period.

23

After the Hong Kong Monetary Authority nearly doubles the overnight lending rate to 20% in order to stop widespread foreign sell-offs of the Hong Kong dollar, stocks fall sharply; the Hang Seng index is down 765.33, and a ripple effect is set off in the Japanese and other Asian markets, European bourses, and the U.S. exchanges throughout the day; the U.S. Dow Jones industrial average (DJIA) finishes down 2.3%.

24

The nomination of Hershel Gober to the top post in the United States Department of Veterans Affairs is withdrawn by the White House when it becomes clear that the Senate Committee on Veterans Affairs will not approve Gober, who was accused of sexual misconduct in 1993.

•

Biologists at the University of North Carolina at Chapel Hill, reporting in the journal *Science,* present evidence, based on the development of the wing structures of embryonic birds, that modern birds are not evolved from dinosaurs, as is widely believed.

25

Continuing the recent American trend of mass rallies that had begun with the Million Man March in October 1995 and had continued with the convocation of the Promise Keepers (*see* October 4), the Million Woman March attracts several hundred thousand African-American women from throughout the U.S. to Philadelphia to listen to speeches on aspects of "repentance, resurrection and restoration."

26

Mika Hakkinen of Finland, driving a McLaren-Mercedes, wins the European Grand Prix in Jerez de la Frontera, Spain; with his third-place finish in this race—and after having collided with German driver Michael Schumacher, who did not finish the race—Canadian driver Jacques Villeneuve accrues enough points to edge past Schumacher, a two-time winner, for the Formula One world title.

27

Stock prices fall worldwide, and trading on the New York Stock Exchange is halted under a rarely used procedure to decelerate price falls; the DJIA is down some 554 points, and markets in Asia also close sharply down.

•

In the 11th inning of the 7th game (which extended past midnight) in Miami, Fla., the Florida Marlins, a team barely five years old, defeats the Cleveland Indians in professional baseball's World Series.

NASA

The launch of the Cassini spacecraft: October 15

28

The roller-coaster stock market in the United States, jittery over the instabilities in the Asian markets, lurches sharply upward, and the DJIA registers a 337-point gain, the greatest single-day rise in history.

•

Pres. Frederick Chiluba of Zambia announces that a brief coup attempt has been put down and the mid-level officers responsible have been arrested.

29

Presidents Jiang Zemin of China and Clinton meet in the White House and arrive at a number of commercial agreements but disagree on many human rights and social issues; Jiang arrives in Hawaii on October 26 and concludes his highly publicized trip to the U.S. on November 3.

30

The government of Iraq refuses to admit into the country three citizens of the United States who are part of United Nations weapons-inspection teams, causing yet another standoff between Iraq and the U.S. to be precipitated.

•

In a court in Cambridge, Mass., Louise Woodward, a 19-year-old British au pair, is found guilty of the second-degree murder of an eight-month-old child in her care; the case arouses intense controversy in Great Britain as well as in U.S. legal circles (*see* November 10).

•

The Juilliard String Quartet, itself newly renovated with Joel Smirnoff in the role of first violinist and Ronald Copes as second, plays a public concert to reopen the refurbished Coolidge Auditorium at the Library of Congress in Washington, D.C.

31

Mary McAleese becomes the second woman in a row to be elected president of Ireland; she enjoys the additional distinction of being the first person from Northern Ireland to win this position.

•

The U.S. offers $3 billion in funds to help stabilize the economy of Indonesia, which, like other countries in Southeast Asia, is coming under financial pressure; the International Monetary Fund is also providing $15 billion in emergency aid loans.

1

Martin Luther King III, the eldest son of the Rev. Dr. Martin Luther King, Jr., is elected president of the Southern Christian Leadership Conference, a prominent American civil rights organization.

•

McLain Ward of Brewster, N.Y., riding Amity, wins the Budweiser Grand Prix equestrian jumping event during the 114th National Horse Show at Madison Square Garden in New York City.

•

At the end of the world team bridge championships in Hammamet, Tunisia, France is awarded the Bermuda Bowl for open teams for its victory over the U.S., and an American team beats the Chinese for the Venice Cup for women's teams.

2

Brazil's maiden space launch from the facility at Alcântara, Maranhão state, is aborted about a minute after liftoff because one of the four engines does not fire; the booster rocket carries an environmental research satellite.

•

David Duval wins the Professional Golfers Association Tour championship in Houston, Texas, the final event of the PGA Tour; Duval's posting of three wins in PGA Tour events in 1997 is second only to Tiger Woods's four.

•

Canadian figure skater Elvis Stojko wins the Nations Cup title at Gelsenkirchen, Ger.

•

John Kagwe of Kenya wins the New York Marathon with a time of 2 hr 8 min 12 sec; the fastest woman is Franczsika Rochat-Moser of Switzerland, with a time of 2 hr 28 min 43 sec.

3

Chavalit Yongchaiyudh, prime minister of Thailand, resigns after having proved unable to bring order to a fractious coalition government or stability to the faltering economy.

Truckers in France go on strike and set up blockades on a number of arterial highways throughout the country, disrupting international as well as local freight traffic.

•

Ellen Highstein is appointed director of the Tanglewood Music Center in the Berkshire Mountains of western Massachusetts, the summer home of the Boston Symphony Orchestra and an important training facility for musicians; relations between Tanglewood management and Seiji Ozawa, music director of the Boston Symphony, which owns the facility, have been strained for more than a year.

4

New York City Mayor Rudolph W. Giuliani is decisively elected to a second term; he will be sworn in on New Year's Day 1998.

•

Might and Power, a four-year-old gelding ridden by jockey Greg Hall, wins the Melbourne Cup in a photo finish over the 1995 winner, Doriemus.

5

An expert panel convened by the U.S. National Institutes of Health concludes that acupuncture is an effective therapy for certain medical conditions, especially those that involve pain and nausea, and recommends that it be considered when a treatment is being selected.

6

The George Bush Library, the 11th presidential library in the U.S., is inaugurated at Texas A & M University; except for ailing Ronald Reagan, all current and past presidents and their wives are present for the dedication ceremonies.

•

After American best-selling author Stephen King decides to leave Viking, his longtime publishing house, and search for a new deal with another publisher, Simon & Schuster announces that they have offered an unusual three-book deal that will give King a smaller advance but a greater percentage of the profits on his books.

7

Fred Meyer Inc., a large retail grocery company, announces that it will acquire Quality Food Centers Inc. and the Ralphs Grocery Co. for a total of $2 billion, creating the fourth largest supermarket chain in the United States.

•

It is announced that a judge in Tampa, Fla., has granted asylum to a member of the Church of Scientology on the grounds that she would be subjected to religious persecution if she returned home to Germany (*see* June 6).

•

Deutsche Guggenheim Berlin, a new museum of modern art on Berlin's famed Unter den Linden, opens to the public.

8

Engineers at the site of the Three Gorges Dam in China divert the waters of the Chang Jiang (Yangtze River) from its normal channel in order to begin construction work; the controversial dam will be the largest in the world.

•

The capital of Kazakstan is formally transferred from Almaty (formerly Alma-Ata) in the southeast to Akmola in the north-central part of the country.

•

American heavyweight boxer Evander Holyfield strips the International Boxing Federation title from

PHOTOS, (TOP) TIMOTHY HURSLEY; (BOTTOM) JOAN MARCUS

Michael Moorer, knocking him down five times in the process; Holyfield also retains his World Boxing Association title in the eight-round technical knockout in Las Vegas, Nev.

•

The Breeder's Cup Classic race at Hollywood Park racetrack in Inglewood, Calif., is won by Skip Away, ridden by jockey Mike Smith; Countess Diana, with Shane Sellers in the saddle, wins the Juvenile Fillies race.

•

The Miho Museum, designed by Chinese-born American architect I.M. Pei on a commission from Shinji Shumeikai, a small Japanese religious order, opens near Kyoto, Japan; the museum, approximately 80% of which is located underground, houses works of East and West Asian art.

The opening of the Miho Museum in Japan: November 8

The Lion King opens on Broadway: November 8

9

The U.S. Congress, at the end of its term, approves a new charter for the Food and Drug Administration (FDA) that will allow this powerful body to streamline and speed up its procedures for approving new drugs.

•

Fortovase, a new, stronger version of the widely prescribed protease inhibitor saquinavir, a drug used in the treatment of AIDS, is approved by the FDA; the drug goes on sale on November 17.

•

The British Broadcasting Corporation begins News 24, a 24-hour news channel in Great Britain; an international news service, BBC World, has been in operation for three years.

•

Rodney Eyles of Australia defeats Peter Nicol of Scotland to win the men's world open squash championship in Petalan Jaya, Malaysia.

10

Meeting in Beijing, Russian and Chinese leaders sign an agreement regulating the 4,300-km (2,580-mi) border between the two countries and another agreement to build a 3,000-km (1,800-mi) pipeline between Siberia and northeastern China.

•

MCI Communications, the second largest long-distance telephone company in the U.S., agrees to be acquired by Worldcom Inc. for $36.5 billion in cash and stock; the transaction will be the largest merger ever in the United States, and the resulting company, MCI WorldCom, with $30 billion in annual revenues, will be the world's second largest international voice carrier.

•

In Cambridge, Mass., Judge Hiller B. Zobel abruptly changes the second-degree murder conviction of British au pair Louise Woodward in the death of her eight-month-old charge to involuntary manslaughter and sentences her to prison time already served (*see* October 30).

•

A record for a single-owner sale is set at Christie's auction house in New York City as the Victor and Sally Ganz collection of modern art brings a total of $206.5 million; the top price, $48 million, is brought by Pablo Picasso's "The Dream."

11

Roger Clemens of the Toronto Blue Jays wins the American League Cy Young Award as the best pitcher in the league for the fourth time; he is the first American League player and only the third major league player to win the award four times.

12

Two defendants, Ramzi Ahmed Yousef and Eyad Ismoil, are found guilty of involvement in the 1993 bombing of the World Trade Center in New York City; four other men were convicted in 1994.

The U.S. Federal Bureau of Investigation informally announces that it has concluded its investigation into the crash of TWA Flight 800 in 1996, finding "absolutely no evidence" of a criminal act; the FBI's formal announcement follows on December 18.

•

Oil begins to flow from the oil fields in the Caspian Sea off the Azerbaijani capital of Baku by pipeline to the Russian Black Sea port of Novorossiysk for the first time since the dissolution of the Soviet Union and the independence of Azerbaijan; the obstructions have been political and strategic, since the pipeline runs through the breakaway Russian republic of Chechnya (*see* December 29).

13

Iraq expels the American members of the UN team that had been dispatched by the international organization to verify Iraq's compliance with UN directives.

•

The U.S. Congress rules that the National Academy of Sciences is exempt from the Federal Advisory Committee Act and may conduct its advisory committee deliberations in closed session but that it must make procedures for selection of committee members less confidential.

•

With much fanfare and large advance-ticket sales, *The Lion King,* a stage adaptation of the 1994 hit movie designed and directed by Julie Taymor, opens in the restored New Amsterdam Theatre on Broadway.

14

Sara E. Lister, the assistant secretary of the army for manpower and reserve affairs, resigns after apologizing for having spoken of the U.S. Marine Corps as "extremists."

15

The 19th CableAce awards, American cable television's annual awards ceremony, is telecast from the Wiltern Theatre in Los Angeles; voted best dramatic series was "Oz" on HBO, best comedy series was "The Larry Sanders Show" (HBO), best miniseries was "George Wallace" (TNT), and best movie was *Miss Evers' Boys* (HBO).

16

In a referendum the citizens of Hungary vote overwhelmingly (85% of the vote) in favour of joining NATO.

•

Meeting in Hanoi, representatives of 50 Francophone countries agree to form a loose political bloc; former UN secretary-general Boutros Boutros-Ghali is appointed its first spokesman.

•

The Toronto Argonauts defeat the Saskatchewan Roughriders by a score of 47–23 to win their second successive Grey Cup championship of the Canadian Football League in Edmonton, Alta.

•

Finishing only 17th in the Napa 500 auto race at the Atlanta (Ga.) Motor Speedway, Jeff Gordon barely wins Nascar's $1.5 million Winston Cup; Gordon needed to finish 18th or better to accrue enough points for the title.

17

Six Islamist militants open fire on a group of tourists, mostly from Switzerland, Germany, and Japan, at Luxor, Egypt, killing 60; 10 additional fatalities, including the gunmen, are reported after a three-hour gunfight.

•

Hokkaido Takushoku Bank Ltd., the 10th largest bank in Japan, announces it will close because of bad debts; one other large Japanese bank has already received heavy government subsidies, and other large national and local banks are believed to be at risk.

18

Five persons believed to have been working under the direction of Libyan intelligence go on trial in Berlin for the 1996 bombing of a nightclub in which three persons were killed.

•

The National Book Awards are announced at a ceremony in New York City; the winners were Charles Frazier's *Cold Mountain* for fiction, Joseph Ellis's *American Sphinx: The Character of Thomas Jefferson* for nonfiction, William Meredith's *Effort at Speech: New and Selected Poems* for poetry, and Han Nolan's *Dancing on the Edge* for young people's literature.

19

Bobbi McCaughey gives birth to septuplets in Des Moines, Iowa, the first time in the U.S. that seven babies have been born and survived.

20

In Frankfurt, Ger., 29 leading industrial nations working under the auspices of the Organisation for Economic Co-operation and Development formally agree to outlaw the practice of bribing officials of foreign governments.

•

Over resistance from the right-wing deputies, the Socialist government of France passes a law granting automatic right to citizenship to children who were born in France of non-French parents and who have lived in France for at least five of the past seven years.

•

The New England Journal of Medicine publishes a study that finds that consumption of *trans* fatty acids correlates strongly with increased risk of heart disease and that these lipids, found principally in stick margarine and hardened vegetable fats, are actually worse in this regard than saturated fats such as those found in animal products.

•

The Mauritius Ball Envelope, which includes a penny postage stamp issued on the British Indian Ocean colony 150 years ago, brings Sw F 2 million at auction in Switzerland.

21

The government of South Korea announces that it will seek \$20 billion–\$60 billion in assistance from the International Monetary Fund to help stabilize its economy (*see* November 17); an IMF loan valued at \$55 billion is announced on December 3.

•

Pres. Boris Yeltsin replaces Anatoly B. Chubais, the top planning official in Russia who has been implicated in an influence-peddling scandal, as finance minister; Chubais retains his position as first deputy prime minister, however.

22

Amistad, a new opera by Anthony Davis, receives its world premiere at the Lyric Opera of Chicago to mixed reviews; Steven Spielberg's film of the same name on the same subject, a revolt by African slaves aboard a 19th-century Spanish slave ship and the ensuing legal battles and moral decisions, opens in U.S. theatres on December 10.

•

New Zealanders Robert Hamill and Phil Stubbs arrive in Barbados from the Canary Islands in their 23-foot fibreglass boat, *Kiwi Challenge*, after 41 days 1 hr 55 min, a new record for rowing across the Atlantic.

23

Avigdor Lieberman, the chief of Israeli Prime Minister Benjamin Netanyahu's staff, resigns.

•

Former prime minister John Major is appointed by Prince Charles as the legal and financial protector of Princes William and Harry in the settlement of the estate of Diana, princess of Wales; some £8.4 million in inheritance taxes is believed to be at stake from Diana's estate, variously estimated to be worth £20 million to £40 million.

24

The large old Japanese brokerage firm Yamaichi Securities Co. declares bankruptcy and announces it will close; it is called the largest business failure in postwar Japanese history.

•

The Williams Companies, a large natural gas pipeline company, announces it will acquire Mapco Inc., a butane and propane pipeline company, for \$2,650,000,000 in stock and another \$750,000,000 in Mapco debts.

25

The annual three-day Asia Pacific summit meeting ends in Vancouver, B.C.; most of the talk has centred on the precarious situation of several Asian economies and the recent slide in value of the Japanese yen.

•

Ron Carey, the president of the powerful International Brotherhood of Teamsters labour union, resigns his office; Carey's management of union funds has been under close scrutiny by labour and U.S. government officials, and on November 17 he is barred from seeking reelection as Teamsters president.

•

Popular ballerina Merrill Ashley gives her last performance with the New York City Ballet, with which she has been associated for 30 years.

YUN JAI-HYOUNG—ASSOCIATED PRESS

One of many South Koreans worried by an unstable economy: November 21

26

The international price of gold in New York City falls to \$298 per ounce, the lowest level in 12 years.

•

UNAIDS, part of the United Nations medical office in Paris, reports that the spread of HIV, the virus linked with AIDS, is proceeding much faster than they had earlier thought, with as many as 16,000 new infections worldwide each day.

27

Tens of thousands of students fill the streets of Bonn to protest the decline of Germany's higher education system and the inattention of the government that has led to overcrowded classrooms and outdated textbooks.

28

Play begins in tennis's Davis Cup tournament in Göteborg, Swed.; the resounding Swedish victory, a clean sweep, is already clear on November 29 after the American team has lost the first two singles matches as well as the doubles competition.

29

Prime Minister I.K. Gujral, leader of India's fourth government in a year and a half, resigns.

•

In a ceremony that is broadcast around the world by satellite, some 28,000 couples gather in Washington, D.C.'s RFK Stadium for a "wedding" by the Rev. Sun Myung Moon of the Unification Church.

30

The government of Prime Minister Vaclav Klaus of the Czech Republic resigns; Klaus's Civic Democratic Party has been accused of having accepted contributions from foreign sources that may have affected the government's privatization decisions.

Smog in Paris; protocol approved to reduce industrial emissions: December 11

1

Two banks in the U.S. Midwest, National City Corp. of Cleveland, Ohio, and the First of America Bank Corp. of Kalamazoo, Mich., announce a $6.7 billion merger that creates the 13th largest bank in the U.S.

•

It is announced that the Walt Disney Co. will donate $25 million to Los Angeles for the construction of the Walt Disney Concert Hall, a major new facility for the city centre.

2

In London, representatives of 41 countries convene to discuss the whereabouts of gold and other valuable assets that were seized by the Nazi government from Jews in Germany and occupied countries before and during World War II and to plan for their restitution to the survivors of the Holocaust.

•

Government spokesmen announce in Tegucigalpa that Carlos Flores Facussé of the centre-right Liberal Party has won the presidential election in Honduras; he defeated Nora de Melgar of the National Party and is scheduled to take office in January 1998.

•

The annual Turner Prize, which is given to a British artist under the age of 50, is awarded to Gillian Wearing in ceremonies at the Tate Gallery in London.

3

In Ottawa, delegates from 131 countries meet to begin signing the Convention on the Prohibition, Use, Stockpiling, Production and Transfer of Anti-Personnel Mines; 123 nations, not including China, Russia, or the U.S., sign within a few days (*see* September 17).

•

Authorities in South Korea agree to a $55 billion international package of aid to fund the retooling of the country's economy; meanwhile, activities are suspended at nine banks; five others are affected on December 10 as the Korean currency, the won, continues to fall on world markets (*see* December 6).

4

Eight groups of four national teams each constitute the draw for the 1998 World Cup football (soccer) finals in Marseille, France; favoured Brazil is placed in Group A with Morocco, Norway, and Scotland.

•

Top health officials in Europe vote to ban most forms of advertising of tobacco beginning in four to five years.

5

The submission by Yoshio Taniguchi, a Japanese architect little known in the U.S., is chosen in the design competition for the expansion

TIM ZIELENBACH—CONTACT PRESS IMAGES

and remodeling of New York City's Museum of Modern Art.

6

Halla Group, a large South Korean *chaebol* (conglomerate), collapses, the sixth such failure in 1997 (*see* December 3, 18). It provides further evidence that the collapse of the East Asian economies that began in Thailand is now widespread.

•

The Kamchatka Peninsula in Russia's Far East is hit with one of the largest earthquakes ever recorded, measuring a magnitude of 8.5 to 9; Kamchatka is sparsely settled, and, consequently, there are no reports of loss of life.

7

At a gala celebration, the John F. Kennedy Center for the Performing Arts in Washington, D.C., issues its annual awards to Jessye Norman, soprano; Lauren Bacall, actress; Bob Dylan, singer-songwriter; Charlton Heston, actor; and Edward Villella, dancer.

8

The Union Bank of Switzerland and the Swiss Bank Corp. announce plans to merge, creating the world's second largest bank (after the Bank of Tokyo-Mitsubishi), with assets of some $600 billion.

•

Jenny Shipley is sworn in as prime minister of New Zealand; the first woman to occupy the post, Shipley upset Jim Bolger in elections in November.

9

Gold prices on the London exchange fall $4.80 per troy ounce to a 19-year low of $282.90 (*see* November 26).

•

In Madrid it is announced that Guillermo Cabrera Infante, a Cuban-born writer resident in London, has been awarded the Cervantes Prize, considered the top honour in Spanish-language literature.

10

The Swiss high court rules that $100 million of the money that had been salted away in banks by former dictator Ferdinand Marcos will be returned to the government of the Philippines; another $400 million in Swiss banks is expected to be returned later as well.

•

Yugoslav and Bosnian Serb delegates walk out of a meeting of the Peace Implementation Council, the consultative mechanism set up after the Dayton peace accords in 1995, in protest against the council's reference to the Serbian area of Kosovo, over which, the Serbs say, the council has no mandate.

The Palestinian Authority begins the first census of the West Bank and the Gaza Strip.

11

Delegates from more than 150 countries meeting at the United Nations Framework Convention on Climate Change in Kyoto, Japan, approve the Kyoto Protocol, which calls for the industrial countries to reduce emissions of industrial gases into the Earth's atmosphere; the ratification procedure is to begin in March 1998.

•

A federal judge in Washington, D.C., rules that the Microsoft Corp. may not bundle Microsoft Internet Explorer, its Internet browser software, with the Windows 95 operating system; Windows software dominates the market worldwide.

12

Secretary of State Madeleine Albright, on a visit to Kinshasa, Democratic Republic of the Congo, expresses the support of the U.S. government for the fledgling country and its leader, Laurent Kabila, despite some concerns about reported violations of human rights and democratic principles (*see* June 26).

13

International trade receives a boost as the members of the World Trade Organization sign an agreement to liberalize financial services in banking, insurance, asset management, and brokerage around the world.

•

The Getty Center, a monumental $1 billion new museum complex designed by architect Richard Meier and built on a hilltop overlooking Los Angeles, is officially opened; it opens to the public on December 16.

14

With an eye to the planned visit to Cuba by Pope John Paul II in early 1998, Pres. Fidel Castro announces that Christmas will be an official holiday for the first time since 1968.

•

The 1997 National Finals Rodeo concludes (began on December 5) at the University of Nevada at Las Vegas; Dan Mortensen of Manhattan, Mont., wins the world champion all-around cowboy award for his season earnings of $184,559.

15

The U.S. Department of Defense orders that all 1.4 million men and women in uniform be inoculated against anthrax, a virulent biological agent; about a dozen countries are believed to have biological warfare capabilities that include delivery of anthrax.

•

A Tajik charter airline crashes in the United Arab Emirates, killing 85 persons aboard.

16

More than 700 children in Japan are admitted to hospitals having lost consciousness, complaining of convulsions, or vomiting blood after a televised cartoon (and later a videotape version) triggers a condition called "light epilepsy" or "Nintendo epilepsy," which is caused by intense intermittent flashes of light viewed from close to the source.

•

Czech Pres. Vaclav Havel appoints Josef Tosovsky, director of the central bank, to the post of prime minister (*see* November 30).

•

The highest wind speed ever measured—380 km/h (236 mph)—is recorded by an anemometer at Anderson Air Force Base on Guam as Typhoon Paka slams into the Pacific island.

17

Reeling from a series of recent political reversals and seeing her support in the party much reduced, Winnie Madikizela-Mandela announces that she will not run for the position of deputy president of the African Na-

©PARAMOUNT PICTURES/20TH CENTURY FOX/KOBAL COLLECTION

A scene from the hit movie *Titanic:* December 19

tional Congress; the post is filled by Jacob Zuma, and South African Pres. Nelson Mandela's right-hand man, Deputy Pres. Thabo Mbeki, is elected party leader.

•

As New Jersey becomes the first state in the United States to permit homosexual couples to adopt children, Jon Holden and Michael Galluccio legally adopt Adam, a two-year-old former ward of the state, who has been in their care since he was three months old.

18

South Koreans elect longtime leftist opposition leader Kim Dae Jung president; it is the first time in the nations's history that a member of the opposition has defeated the candidate of the tightly knit New Korea Party and its predecessors.

•

The 10-km (6-mi) Tokyo Bay tunnel connecting the cities of Kawasaki and Kisarazu is opened; the project took eight and a half years to complete and cost $17 billion.

•

Katja Seizinger of Germany ties skier Jean-Claude Killy's 1967 record of six consecutive wins in downhill ski races when she claims the top spot in the super G race at the World Cup competition in Val d'Isère, France.

19

The UN General Assembly acts positively on a suggestion by Secretary-General Kofi Annan and votes to create the post of deputy secretary-general.

•

Te motion picture *Titanic,* directed by James Cameron, opens in U.S. theatres to generally favourable reviews (*see* January 20).

20

American figure skater Tara Lipinski wins the Champions Series Final in Munich, Ger.; Ilya Kulik of Russia wins the men's competition.

21

A disastrous fire sweeps through Tokyo's Tsukiji wholesale fish market, destroying more than a hundred shops and stores.

•

The Louvre Museum in Paris reopens its Egyptian galleries, which have been closed for restoration.

22

Members of a pro-government militia attack the village of Chenalhó in Chiapas state, Mex., and kill 45 people, including a number of children; violence between pro-government and antigovernment Indian groups has simmered in the state since January 1994.

23

Milan Milutinovic, a Socialist ally of Slobodan Milosevic, easily defeats ultranationalist Vojislav Seselj in elections for the presidency of Serbia. In this position Milutinovic replaces Milosevic, who was elected president of Yugoslavia; Serbia is one of the two parts of Yugoslavia (*see* July 23).

Terry Nichols, the second defendant in the Oklahoma City, Okla., bombing trials to stand trial, is found guilty of conspiracy and involuntary manslaughter—but not first-degree murder—by a jury in Denver, Colo.

•

A court in Germany convicts financier Jürgen Schneider of fraud and sentences him to six years and nine months in prison in connection with the collapse of his commercial empire at the end of the reunification building boom.

24

Ilich Ramírez Sánchez, the terrorist and international assassin known as Carlos, is convicted of the murder of three men in Paris in 1975 and sentenced to life in prison by a French court.

•

Earlybird 1, the first privately owned spy satellite, is placed in Earth orbit from a Russian launch rocket at an altitude of 471 km (293 mi); photos from the satellite are for sale by Earthwatch, Inc., the American company that built the craft.

25

Pope John Paul II delivers his annual Christmas message; the pontiff calls for the well-off in the world not to neglect the "new poor" and to hear "the imploring calls for freedom and harmony"

ELIZABETH DALZIEL—ASSOCIATED PRESS

Survivors of a massacre in Chiapas state, Mexico: December 22

in places beset by ethnic and political violence.

•

Queen Elizabeth II gives her annual holiday address; observers note the changed tone from previous addresses as she speaks personally of a year of "joy and woe"—*i.e.,* the 50th anniversary of her marriage and the death of Diana, princess of Wales, respectively.

•

Comedian Jerry Seinfeld announces that his popular television show, "Seinfeld," will cease production at the end of the season.

26

Jean-Marie Le Pen, leader of France's far-right-wing National Front, is convicted of the crime of denying that Nazi war crimes took place, an offense he has been convicted of on previous occasions; he is ordered to pay about $50,000.

27

Billy Wright, a prominent Protestant guerrilla leader from Northern Ireland, is shot and killed in a maximum-security prison in Belfast by other inmates loyal to a splinter group of the Irish Republican Army.

•

Windsor Castle is reopened to the public after £36.5 million in restoration work is completed under budget and six months before the target date; 100 rooms in the royal palace were damaged in a fire in 1992.

28

Local officials in Hong Kong announce that all chickens in the territory will be destroyed in an attempt to eradicate carriers of the avian flu, which has already killed several people; more than a million chickens, ducks, and geese are involved.

29

Pres. Saparmurad Niyazov of Turkmenistan and visiting Pres. Mohammad Khatami of Iran formally open a 200-km (125-mi) gas pipeline between the two countries, the first facility to move gas from the Caspian Sea area bypassing Russia; a few days earlier the Royal Dutch Shell petroleum company had concluded a contract with those two countries and Turkey for the construction of a $1.6 billion pipeline to transport gas from Turkmenistan to European markets (*see* November 12).

•

The European Union elects not to renew trade benefits to Yugoslavia beyond the end of 1997; EU officials cite concerns about human rights and democratic practices in the country.

30

Gen. Le Kha Phieu, a hardliner formerly responsible for maintaining political discipline in the military, is named to lead the Vietnamese Communist Party (*see* September 17).

•

Pamela C. Rasmussen of the United States National Museum of Natural History in Washington, D.C., announces that she and two associates have recently sighted the Indian forest owlet (*Athene blewitti*), which has not been seen since 1884 and had been thought extinct.

31

Muslims celebrate the beginning of Ramadan, the holy month of fasting; as in past years, Islamist terrorists in Algeria pick up the pace of the massacres of innocents; 80 are killed in the villages of Shari and Sidi al-Antar on December 23, another 59 in Algiers and Tiaret on December 24, and 27 more in Zouabria on December 25.

•

Mohammed Rafiq Tarar, a supporter of Prime Minister Nawaz Sharif, is chosen by Pakistan's electoral college to be the next president of the country.

•

Former Zambian president Kenneth Kaunda is released from jail, where he had been sent on December 25 on suspicion of involvement in an abortive coup attempt.

•

Beginning at midnight tonight in the state of California, it is illegal to smoke in all bars and nightclubs (as well as restaurants and cafés, which were already included in the ban).

VINCENT VU—ASSOCIATED PRESS

Avian flu in Hong Kong: December 28

Disasters

The loss of life and property from disaster in 1997 included the following:

Aviation

January 9, Near Detroit. A twin-engine commuter airplane with 29 persons aboard crashed during a snowstorm; there were no survivors.

February 1, Tambacounda, Senegal. An airliner carrying 52 persons, most of them French tourists, crashed on takeoff and burned, apparently after an engine malfunctioned; 23 persons died, including the plane's two pilots, one of whom was the son of Pres. João Bernardo Vieira of Guinea-Bissau.

February 4, Sha'ar Yishuv, Israel. While ferrying troops to the Israeli security zone in southern Lebanon, two army helicopters collided in heavy fog, killing all 65 soldiers and 8 airmen aboard the two craft; it was the worst military air disaster in Israel's history.

March 13, Near Neyshabur, Iran. A military cargo plane crashed in the mountains of northeastern Iran after the pilot had reported technical difficulties; the wreckage was discovered one week later; all 88 persons aboard the craft were killed.

March 18, Near Cherkessk, Russia. An explosion aboard an airliner en route to Turkey caused the plane to plunge into a wooded area; 41 passengers and 9 crew members died.

March 18, Near Sipitang, Sabah, Malaysia. Two Malaysian air force helicopters flying in adverse weather slammed into a hillside in a remote jungle on the island of Borneo; all 11 servicemen aboard the two craft were killed.

April 19, Billiton, Indon. A passenger plane exploded in midair and crashed on a palm plantation; of the 52 persons aboard, at least 15 died.

May 8, Shenzhen, Guangdong province, China. A Boeing 737 attempted to touch down twice during a heavy rainstorm before slamming onto the runway and bursting into flames; at least 35 persons died, including 2 crew members.

May 18, Lajes, Braz. A midair collision between two small planes claimed the lives of all 12 persons aboard the two craft; one woman on the ground, who was hit by falling debris, also died after suffering a heart attack.

July 11, Off the coast of southeastern Cuba. About three minutes after taking off from Santiago de Cuba, a Havana-bound airliner plummeted into the Caribbean Sea; all 39 passengers and 5 crew members aboard the plane were killed.

July 17, Bandung, Indon. A commuter airplane en route to Jakarta lost power soon after takeoff and crashed near a housing complex; at least 29 persons, including all 5 crew members, perished; 3 persons on the ground were injured.

August 6, Near Agana, Guam. A Boeing 747-300 flying through heavy rain plowed into a jungle ravine a few kilometres short of Guam International Airport, apparently after the crew misjudged the location of the runway; a software error had crippled an airport radar system that might have aided the pilot in landing the plane safely; of the 254 persons aboard, 27 survived.

August 10, Matsu Island, Taiwan. A small passenger plane with 16 persons aboard slammed into a mountain while preparing to land; there were no survivors.

August 30, Nazca, Peru. A collision between two small planes over the Nazca Lines, a group of huge animal figures and geometric forms etched into the ground before the 12th century, claimed the lives of the two pilots and 10 tourists aboard the two craft.

September 3, Phnom Penh, Cambodia. An airliner attempting to land in a monsoonal downpour crashed and burned in a rice paddy just short of the single runway at Pochentong International Airport; 65 persons, including 6 crew members, were killed; one young boy survived.

September 6, Near Miri, Sarawak, Malaysia. A passenger plane crashed in a jungle in Lambir Hills National Park; all 10 persons aboard the craft were killed.

September 13, Off the coast of Namibia. A collision between a German military jet and a U.S. Air Force cargo plane claimed the lives of all 33 persons aboard the two craft.

September 17, Near Bugojno, Bosnia and Herzegovina. An Mi-8 helicopter carrying members of a United Nations delegation slammed into a fog-covered mountainside about 72 km (45 mi) northwest of Sarajevo; all 12 passengers aboard the craft, including senior German diplomat Gerd Wagner, were killed; the four crew members survived the crash.

September 26, Near Medan, Indon. An airliner went down about 32 km (20 mi) from Polonia International Airport in an area clouded with smoke from regional forest fires; according to witnesses, the plane was flying low in a haze when it struck a tree and exploded into pieces in a ravine; all 234 persons aboard were killed; it was Indonesia's worst aviation disaster.

October 3, Off the coast of Azerbaijan. A helicopter transporting oil workers to an offshore oil field crashed into the Caspian Sea; 22 persons were killed.

October 10, Near Nuevo Berlín, Uruguay. A DC-9 en route to Buenos Aires with 75 persons aboard crashed while trying to avoid a heavy rainstorm; there were no survivors.

December 6, Near Irkutsk, Russia. A military cargo plane, carrying two fighter jets, smashed into an apartment complex just after takeoff, clipping an orphanage with its wing and demolishing one end of the five-story apartment building; more than 60 persons were killed, including 17 crew members and 6 passengers; it was reported that two of the plane's four engines had failed, possibly owing to poor fuel.

December 15, Near Sharjah, U.A.E. A Tajik airliner with 86 persons aboard went down in a desert area when an explosion rocked the plane as it started to land; one person survived.

December 17, Near Katerini, Greece. A Ukrainian airliner crashed on a snowy mountainside about 80 km (50 mi) southwest of Salonika, apparently after the pilot became disoriented and believed he had cleared the mountains; all 70 persons aboard the craft were killed.

December 19, Near Palembang, Indon. A Boeing 737 en route to Singapore and carrying 104 persons crashed in the Musi River; there were no survivors.

December 31, Near San Blas, Panama. A small plane slammed into a mountain while flying in foggy weather; 10 persons were killed.

DAN GROSHONG—SYGMA

The site of the worst aviation disaster in Indonesia's history: September 26

Fires and Explosions

February 4, Xichong, Sichuan province, China. An explosion at a storehouse for materials used in making fireworks claimed the lives of 21 persons and injured 26; more than 20 houses were destroyed by the blast.

February 23, Baripada, India. A fire that swept through an encampment of thatched-roof huts where scores of Hindu worshippers had gathered killed more than 110 persons and injured at least 165; many of the victims may have died in a stampede as they tried to escape the flames; the cause of the fire was unknown.

March 19, Jalalabad, Afg. A powerful explosion at a police department where the Islamic Taliban militia stored weapons and ammunition killed at least 40 persons and injured 150; the blast created a crater 50 m (165 ft) in diameter and 10 m (33 ft) deep; the Taliban insisted that the explosion was accidental and not the result of sabotage.

April 15, Mina, Saudi Arabia. A raging fire and an ensuing stampede in a crowded tent compound claimed the lives of at least 300 Muslims who were making the annual pilgrimage to Mecca, and about 1,300 persons were injured; the fire began when a gas cylinder used for cooking exploded.

April 26, Cotabato, Phil. A hotel fire that started in a prayer room on the third floor raced through the upper stories of the structure, killing at least 25 persons and injuring 9.

April 30, Burrel, Alb. Antigovernment rebels inadvertently set off an explosion at an underground ammunition depot they were attempting to plunder; 27 rebels were killed.

May 23, Banjarmasin, Indon. On the final day of a parliamentary election campaign that had been marred by numerous riots, at least 130 persons died in a shopping complex that rioters had looted and then set ablaze; according to police, all of the victims were looters who had been trapped in the complex after the fire began in a ground-floor bank.

June 7, Thanjavur, India. A fire at an 11th-century Hindu temple claimed the lives of 41 persons.

June 13, New Delhi. An explosion of an electrical transformer started a fire that engulfed a crowded movie theatre, killing 60 persons and injuring more than 200; four theatre managers were subsequently arrested for suspected criminal negligence after survivors reported that their escape had been hampered by locked doors.

July 3, Valencia, Spain. A ship caught fire as it was being loaded with fuel; at least 19 shipyard workers died in the blaze.

July 9, Craiova, Rom. A bomb exploded while being loaded onto a plane at a military airfield, killing at least 16 military engineers and defense industry workers.

July 11, Pattaya, Thai. A hotel fire, which erupted when a gas oven exploded in a first-floor coffee shop, swept through the 17-story building and claimed the lives of 90 persons; many victims died next to exits that were chained shut to keep guests from skipping out on their bills; 64 persons were injured.

August 20, Blaye, France. A grain silo exploded and collapsed onto the offices of a storage company, burying 12 persons under tons of grain and concrete; a buildup of dust and static electricity inside the silo was suspected of having caused the blast.

September 8, Casablanca, Mor. A fire engulfed a wing of a jail and killed 28 prisoners; an electrical fault may have started the blaze.

September 14, Vishakhapatnam, India. Four gas tanks exploded in a petroleum refinery, causing six buildings to collapse and igniting a fire that blazed for several days; an estimated 60,000 persons were forced to flee their homes after electricity was cut and dense smoke blanketed the city; at least 60 persons were killed.

September 29, Santiago, Chile. An electrical short circuit started a fire that swept through a home for the mentally impaired; 30 residents of the home were killed, including several who did not recognize the danger and walked back into the burning building after being rescued.

October 24, Jiangxi province, China. A fire engulfed a seven-story hotel and claimed the lives of 22 persons.

October 31, Milan. Flames ignited by an electrical fault swept through a high-pressure treatment chamber at a hospital, killing 10 patients and a nurse.

November 10, Kaduna, Nigeria. At least eight inmates at a police station were burned to death and three persons killed in a stampede caused by a fire in Kaduna's central market.

November 26, Maracaibo, Venez. A blaze sparked by a short circuit in a cellblock of a prison claimed the lives of at least 16 persons and injured more than 30.

December 8, Jakarta, Indon. Flames engulfed the top floors of an office tower of Bank Indonesia, killing 15 persons; the fire was thought to have been started by a short circuit in the building's air-conditioning system.

Marine

February 12, Lake Victoria, Kenya. A boat overloaded with passengers capsized during a storm and sank near the island of Sukuru; 34 persons lost their lives; 6 men survived the disaster by clinging to pieces of wood and other debris.

Mid-February, Off the coast of Norway. A freighter registered in Cyprus sank after its captain had radioed that the ship was taking on water; all 20 crewmen aboard were killed.

February 20, Off the northern coast of Sri Lanka. A boat carrying Tamil refugees to India overturned after leaving the port of Nachchikuddah; 165 persons were presumed drowned.

March 13, Congo (Zaire) River, Zaire. A storm hit boats carrying hundreds of Rwandan refugees, mostly Hutu, who were fleeing advancing Tutsi rebels; at least 200 persons drowned.

March 15, Irrawaddy River, Myanmar (Burma). A ship with 537 passengers aboard capsized in a sudden storm; 35 persons died.

March 28, Off the coast of Brindisi, Italy. A boat carrying between 120 and 130 Albanian refugees sank after colliding with an Italian naval vessel; over 80 refugees were killed; although survivors claimed that the warship purposely rammed their craft to prevent it from landing, the Italian navy denied the charges.

July 13, Sumatra, Indonesia. More than 75 persons were killed when an overcrowded boat, carrying about 200 passengers from Tomok who were returning from a cultural festival in Parapat, sank in Lake Toba.

July 18, Kosi River, India. A crowded boat capsized in a river swollen by monsoonal rains; at least 35 persons drowned.

August 15, Central Philippines. A predawn storm overturned a ferry in the Visayan Sea; 13 persons drowned, and 15 were missing.

August 26, Bonny River, Nigeria. Two riverboats transporting passengers and cargo collided during conditions of poor visibility; 100 persons were feared dead.

September 8, Port-au-Prince Bay, Haiti. An overcrowded ferry that was carrying at least 700 passengers, more than twice its capacity, capsized near the port of Montrouis when passengers rushed to one side of the vessel; more than 172 persons drowned.

September 26, Strait of Malacca, at Port Dickson, Malaysia. A supertanker collided with a cargo ship in conditions of low visibility possibly created by thick smoke from regional forest fires; 29 crew members from the cargo ship were missing and feared dead.

October 10, Eastern India. An overcrowded boat capsized in Bihar, killing at least 15 persons.

November 14, Northwestern Uganda. One of two boats carrying teachers and pupils of a primary school capsized off the shore of Lake Albert, where the group had been having a picnic; 18 persons drowned.

December 12, Mano River, between Sierra Leone and Liberia. At least 60 civilians fleeing renewed fighting in eastern Sierra Leone were feared drowned after their canoe capsized.

December 15, Port-au-Prince Bay. A ferry headed to the Haitian island of La Gonave sank after leaving Port-au-Prince; 18 people were killed, and more than 20 were missing and feared dead.

Mining and Tunneling

March 4, Henan province, China. A series of explosions in underground shafts that connected three privately run coal mines claimed the lives of 86 miners and injured 12.

May 28, Fushun, Liaoning province, China. A gas explosion at a coal mine killed 68 miners.

June 23, Northern Iran. Part of a tunnel collapsed in a coal mine after a gas explosion; 18 miners were killed, and 32 were injured.

July, Hartbeesfontein, S.Af. A sudden rupture of rock in a gold mine entombed 18 miners.

July 26, Guangdong province. Workers were trapped in a coal mine after water rushed into a shaft; 10 miners were feared dead.

September 3, Near Tarkwa, Ghana. A landslide killed 12 gold miners who were digging in a pit illegally after the regular workers at the mine had left for the day.

September 18, Spitsbergen Island, Svalbard, Nor. A powerful methane explosion claimed the lives of 26 miners in a Russian-operated coal mine.

Late September, Central Vietnam. Flooding triggered by Typhoon Fritz collapsed tunnels and caused landslides at two gold mines; some 54 miners were killed.

October 17, Northeastern Colombia. A buildup of methane gas was the apparent cause of an explosion at a coal mine; 16 miners lost their lives.

November 4, Guizhou province, China. An explosion at a coal mine claimed the lives of 43 miners.

November 13, Anhui province, China. A gas explosion ripped through a coal mine in the city of Huainan; 87 miners and 2 rescue workers died.

November 27, Anhui province. A gas explosion at a coal mine killed 45 miners; at another mine on the same day, a gas explosion claimed the lives of 28.

December 2, Southern Siberia, Russia. A massive methane gas explosion ripped through a deep shaft in a coal mine, killing at least 61 miners.

Natural

Early January, California, Idaho, Nevada, Oregon, and Washington. Heavy rains and snowstorms triggered widespread flooding during the last week of December and the first days of January; at least 125,000 persons were forced from their homes, and a state of emergency was declared in more than 90 counties; at least 29 deaths were attributed to the floods.

Early January, Europe. An intense cold wave that began in late December claimed the lives of at least 228 persons across the continent; it was the worst freeze in Europe in a decade.

January 21, Xinjiang Uygur, China. Two strong earthquakes, one of magnitude 6.4 and another of magnitude 6.3, occurred one minute apart and caused more than 500 buildings to collapse; at least 12 persons died.

February 4–5, Northeastern Iran. An earthquake of magnitude 5.4 was followed by another of magnitude 6.1 less than an hour later; an aftershock of magnitude 5.7 further jolted the region the following day; 72 persons were killed, and 200 were injured.

February 18, Southern Peru. A massive mud slide caused by heavy rains buried the Andean villages of Cocha and Pumaranra; as many as 300 persons were killed.

Destruction in Vietnam caused by Typhoon Linda: Early November

RICHARD VOGEL—ASSOCIATED PRESS

February 28, Balochistan, Pak. A powerful earthquake of magnitude 7.3 claimed the lives of more than 100 persons and left hundreds homeless.

February 28 and March 2, Northwestern Iran. An earthquake of magnitude 6.1 damaged or destroyed 83 villages; another quake, of magnitude 5.2, struck two days later; at least 965 persons died, and more than 2,600 were injured.

Late February–early March, Bolivia. The heaviest rains in Bolivia in nearly three decades caused massive flooding in the country's tropical lowlands; the crops of some 100,000 farmers were destroyed, and at least 16 persons were killed.

Late February–early March, Indiana, Kentucky, Ohio, Tennessee, and West Virginia. Torrential rains triggered extensive flooding along portions of the Ohio River; thousands of residents were forced to leave their homes as floodwaters inundated many small towns; at least 30 persons were killed.

Early March, Arkansas. Tornadoes swept across the state, flattening buildings, uprooting trees, and destroying houses and trailer homes; at least 25 persons lost their lives.

Early March, Fiji. Cyclone Gavin wreaked havoc on the nation, causing extensive damage and claiming the lives of at least 26 persons, including 10 who were lost at sea when their fishing trawler sank about 72 km (45 mi) southwest of Suva.

March 26, Northern Afghanistan. An avalanche roared down onto the Salang Highway, burying at least 100 persons who were walking toward a tunnel to catch a bus.

Late March, Saudi Arabia. Strong winds and heavy rains were responsible for killing 21 persons.

Late April, Pohnpei Island, Federated States of Micronesia. Landslides brought on by heavy rains and flooding were blamed for the deaths of 13 persons.

May 2, Northern Egypt. A sandstorm claimed the lives of 12 persons and injured 50.

May 10, Northeastern Iran. An earthquake of magnitude 7.1 accompanied by aftershocks as strong as 5.5 wrecked 200 villages and left some 50,000 residents homeless; at least 1,560 persons died.

Mid-May, Guangdong province. Floods caused by torrential rains inundated 177 villages; at least 110 persons were killed, and more than 1,300 were injured.

May 19, Southeastern Bangladesh. A cyclone devastated the coastal region, destroying or damaging more than 600,000 homes; at least 100 persons were killed, and nearly 10,000 were injured.

May 22, Central India. An earthquake of magnitude 6.1 struck near Jabalpur; at least 30 persons perished.

May 27, Central Texas. Several tornadoes ripped through the state from Waco to Austin, ravaging about 400 ha (1,000 ac) of farmland and destroying some 60 homes; 30 persons were killed, 27 in the small town of Jarrell, 64 km (40 mi) north of Austin.

Late May, Philippines. Widespread flooding brought on by three days of rain claimed the lives of at least 29 persons.

June, Central Chile. Three weeks of incessant rain left at least 18 persons dead and at least 45,000 homeless.

June–August, India. Torrential rains during the monsoon season caused floods and landslides throughout the country; at least 945 persons were killed, and crops covering an area of 1,550,000 ha (3,800,000 ac) were damaged.

June–December, Indonesia and Papua New Guinea. Drought and frosts brought on by the El Niño weather phenomenon destroyed crops, contributed to the spread of regional forest fires, and produced a devastating famine; by year's end more than 500 persons in the Indonesian province of Irian Jaya and at least 70 persons in Papua New Guinea had died.

June 23, Western Ukraine and western Belarus. Severe storms claimed the lives of 11 persons.

Late June, Northern Pakistan. During a thunderstorm lightning struck a huge rock, causing the rock to break and tumble down a slope onto houses in a village; 25 persons were killed.

Late June, Montserrat. A major eruption of the Soufrière Hills volcano on June 25 devastated the southern two-thirds of the island and killed at least 19 persons; some 8,000 of Montserrat's 12,000 residents were evacuated, and the island's only airport was forced to close; an eruption of the Chances Peak volcano on June 30 compounded the disaster. Both volcanoes had been active since 1995.

Late June–early August, Central Europe. Torrential rains triggered the worst flooding in the region in 200 years; more than 100 persons were killed in western Poland and the northern third of the Czech Republic as the Oder River and smaller rivers overflowed, inundating hundreds of towns and forcing hundreds of thousands of residents to evacuate their homes; floods also hit the lowlands of eastern Germany in late July, causing extensive damage but no deaths.

Early July–late August, Myanmar. Heavy rains spawned widespread flooding; at least 13 persons were killed, and thousands were left homeless.

July 2, Southern Michigan. Thunderstorms and tornadoes knocked down trees, interrupted electricity, and destroyed 339 homes and businesses; 16 persons lost their lives, and more than 100 were injured.

July 9, Eastern Venezuela. A strong earthquake of magnitude 6.9 jolted the coastal region east of Caracas, leaving at least 79 persons dead, more than 500 injured, and some 3,000 homeless.

July 10, Izumi, Japan. Torrential rains set off a mud slide that crashed through a concrete barrier 14 m (45 ft) high and destroyed 16 houses; 19 persons were killed.

July 13, Southeastern Bangladesh. Massive flooding killed at least 57 persons and left some 250,000 homeless.

July 18, Guizhou province. More than 30 persons were killed by a landslide that occurred after days of heavy rain.

July 30, Thredbo, Australia. Part of a road collapsed on a steep mountainside above a popular ski resort, setting off a massive landslide that buried two lodges; 18 persons perished; rescuers pulled one survivor from the rubble on August 2.

Early August, Southern China. Typhoon Victor battered the provinces of Guangdong and Fujian, destroying 10,000 homes and claiming the lives of 49 persons; millions of residents were affected by the storm and related flooding.

August 12, Northern Arizona. A flash flood scoured the narrow Antelope Canyon, sweeping 11 hikers to their death; the wall of water had entered the canyon after a thunderstorm struck near Page.

Mid-August, Central Chile. A four-day storm claimed the lives of at least 10 persons and destroyed bridges and roads in the region.

August 18–19, Taiwan, eastern China, and the Philippines. Typhoon Winnie swept across the Taiwan Strait and the East China Sea, creating winds of up to 148 km/h (92 mph) and producing heavy rain; at least 37 persons died in Taiwan, where low-lying areas suffered severe flooding; at least 140 persons were killed and tens of thousands of homes were destroyed in the Chinese provinces of Zhejiang and Jiangsu; the typhoon also spawned flooding in the Philippines, where 16 persons died and 60,000 residents were forced to abandon their homes.

Late August, Southern Thailand. Storms from the South China Sea and Indian Ocean caused massive flooding; 28 persons were killed.

September 11, Andhra Pradesh, India. Lightning killed 19 persons and injured 6.

Late September–October, Central Italy. Repeated earthquakes wreaked havoc on the region for weeks, displacing an estimated 38,000 persons; on September 26 two quakes, one of magnitude 5.5 and another of magnitude 5.6, struck nine hours apart, severely damaging the Basilica of St. Francis of Assisi and killing 11 persons.

September 27, Southeastern Bangladesh. A cyclone ravaged the coastal region, killing at least 60 persons and injuring hundreds.

September 28, Sulawesi, Indon. A magnitude-6 earthquake followed by more than 300 aftershocks claimed the lives of at least 17 persons and destroyed or damaged hundreds of homes.

October 8–10, Southern Mexico. Hurricane Pauline devastated the resort city of Acapulco and pummeled numerous villages along the Pacific coast in the states of Oaxaca and Guerrero; winds of up to 185 km/h (115 mph) and waves as high as 9 m (30 ft) were reported; 217 persons were killed, and 20,000 were left homeless.

October 12, Tongi, Bangladesh. A tornado claimed the lives of at least 25 Muslim worshippers who had gathered on the banks of the Turag River for a prayer ceremony; thousands were injured.

Mid-October–late November, Somalia, Ethiopia, and Kenya. Torrential rains and the worst flooding in eastern Africa in more than three decades destroyed crops and prompted fears of widespread famine; more than 2,000 persons were killed, and an estimated 800,000 were displaced.

Late October, Colorado, Kansas, Nebraska, Missouri, Iowa, Wisconsin, and Michigan. Early snowstorms blanketed many areas, closed roads and airports, and caused widespread electrical power outages; at least 16 persons were killed.

October 31, Azores, Portugal. Heavy rains that fell on the Azores, roughly 1,600 km (1,000 mi) west of Portugal in the North Atlantic Ocean, triggered mud slides that buried houses in Ribeira Quente on the island of São Miguel; 18 persons were killed, and at least 12 were missing and feared dead.

Early November, Cook Islands. Cyclone Martin roared through the Polynesian state, wreaking havoc on the islands of Pukapuka, Manihiki, and Rakahanga; the storm claimed the lives of 9 persons and left 10 missing.

Early November, Vietnam, Cambodia, and Thailand. Typhoon Linda pummeled the southern regions of the three countries, flattening thousands of homes and sinking hundreds of fishing boats; nearly two weeks after the storm hit, an official tally of casualties in Vietnam listed 464 persons dead and 3,218 missing; more than 20 persons were killed in Cambodia and Thailand.

November, Ecuador. Torrential rains and mud slides caused severe damage throughout the country; 25 persons were killed, and some 10,000 were left homeless.

November 23, Eastern Uganda. Landslides and floods triggered by heavy rains claimed the lives of at least 29 persons.

December 1, Northern India. A powerful storm struck approximately 35 villages; at least 44 persons died, and 100 were injured.

Late December, Ambar, Peru. A strong storm attributed to the El Niño triggered a mud slide that washed three makeshift homes into a river in the Andes Mountains; 13 persons, all members of the same family, were believed dead.

Railroad

February 3, Radissiyah, Egypt. A cargo train rear-ended a passenger train stopped at the station; 11 persons lost their lives.

February 10, Near Ciego de Ávila, Cuba. A train carrying military conscripts collided with a locomotive, killing 13 persons and injuring 65.

March 3, Near Khanewal, Pak. At least 125 persons were killed and 175 injured when a train derailed after an apparent brake failure.

March 31, Huarte Arakil, Spain. A speeding passenger train derailed as it entered the station; 22 persons were killed, and 89 were injured.

April 29, Hunan province, China. A cross-country passenger train plowed into the rear of a local train; at least 58 persons lost their lives.

May 5, Near Szczecin, Pol. A passenger train jumped the tracks and slammed into a stationary freight train; at least 11 persons died.

July 27, Faridabad, India. A crowded express train sped past a stop signal and rear-ended a passenger train that was pulling out of the station; at least 12 persons perished.

September 8, Near Bordeaux, France. A train struck a fuel truck at a railroad crossing and caused the truck to explode into flames; 12 persons died, including the truck's driver.

September 14, Near Champa, Madhya Pradesh, India. A train derailed when its driver applied the emergency brakes after spotting a red flag just 100 m (328 ft) before a bridge; no one had informed the driver that the bridge was under repair; five railroad cars plunged into a river; at least 82 persons were killed, and more than 200 were injured.

November 5, Near Kotabumi, Indon. An express train slammed into a bus at an unguarded level crossing, killing at least 26 persons.

November 6, Eastern Cuba. A collision between a 12-coach passenger train and a bus at a railroad crossing claimed the lives of 56 persons and seriously injured 6.

December 24, Eastern Pakistan. A passenger train slammed into a second train stopped at a station; at least 20 persons were killed.

Traffic

January 14, Cairo. A speeding bus crashed through a fence and plunged off a bridge into the Nile River; at least 39 persons were killed, and at least 24 were injured.

January 19, Punjab, India. A bus transporting a wedding party plummeted into a rain-swollen river after the driver lost control of the vehicle on a sharp curve; 29 persons lost their lives, and 12 were injured.

January 19, Near Huancayo, Peru. A bus carrying people to a religious festival hurtled off the side of a cliff and fell about 80 m (265 ft); at least 20 persons were killed.

March 10, Guatemala City, Guat. A passenger bus exploded when canisters of paint thinner were accidentally ignited by a cigarette; 11 persons burned to death, and 24 were injured.

March 17, Western Azerbaijan. A bus smashed through a safety barrier on a bridge and dropped 15 m (50 ft) into a river; at least 46 persons died.

April 21, Nakhon Ratchasima, Thai. A truck went out of control and hit the rear of one bus before crashing into another; at least 16 persons were killed, and more than 80 were injured.

July 21, Near Rio de Janeiro. A multiple pileup involving two trucks, two buses, and a car occurred on the busy Via Dutra highway after the driver of the car slammed on his brakes to avoid hitting a truck in front of him; 14 persons lost their lives, and 22 were injured.

July 29, Concord, Mich. A pickup truck collided with a dump truck at a rural intersection; 11 persons in the pickup, including 9 children, were killed.

July 30, Plymouth, N.C. A sport utility vehicle carrying 10 high-school students tried to pass in a no-passing zone on a rain-slickened road and collided with a tractor trailer; all 10 students perished.

Early August, Peru. Three major bus crashes took place in a week; near Trujillo a collision between a bus and a minibus claimed the lives of 23 persons and injured 40; in northern Peru a minibus collision killed 17 persons and injured 40; between Cuzco and Nazca a bus overturned, killing 23 persons and injuring 50.

August 8, Erzincan, Tur. A bus attempting to round a curve veered off a road and fell into a ravine; 25 persons were killed, and 17 were injured, 7 seriously.

August 27, Near Sargodha, Pak. A head-on collision between two buses during a rain shower claimed the lives of 14 persons and injured 45.

September 4, Northwestern Turkey. Two buses collided on the main highway between Ankara and Istanbul, apparently after one of the drivers fell asleep at the wheel; 33 persons were killed, and at least 40 were injured.

September 4, Near Dese, Eth. An overcrowded bus plunged 130 m (425 ft) into a ravine; 36 persons lost their lives, and 13 were injured.

September 9, Southern California. A pickup truck veered across the centre line on Highway 1 and collided head-on with a crowded van; 11 persons were killed in the fiery crash.

September 15, Jakarta. A head-on collision between a bus and a truck on a busy toll road claimed the lives of 36 persons.

September 16, Maseer, Egypt. A truck transporting a group of child labourers overturned on a narrow, unpaved road and fell into a canal; 29 children drowned, and more than 50 were injured.

STEPHEN FERRY—GAMMA LIAISON

An overcrowded train in the Democratic Republic of the Congo: the scene of a disaster on May 4

September 21, Jammu and Kashmir, India. A bus skidded off a highway and plunged 150 m (490 ft) into a river; 22 persons were killed, and 14 were seriously injured.

October 2, Southern France. The driver of a bus lost control of his vehicle, possibly because of a blown-out tire; the bus smashed through the security rails of an overpass and dropped 15 m (50 ft) onto a road below; at least 12 persons died.

October 2, Southern India. An overcrowded bus fell from a bridge into a river; at least 43 persons were killed, and 20 were missing.

October 3, Northwestern India. A collision between a four-wheel-drive vehicle and a truck claimed the lives of at least 14 persons and injured 6.

October 11, Northeastern Zimbabwe. A bus and a truck collided, killing at least 22 persons.

October 13, Central Quebec. A tourist bus carrying senior citizens to view the autumn foliage plunged about 20 m (65 ft) into a ravine; 43 persons lost their lives.

October 15, Central Bangladesh. A bus fell into a ditch while trying to avoid a collision with another vehicle; 58 persons perished.

October 19, Near Freetown, Sierra Leone. At least 67 Sierra Leoneans fleeing air raids by Nigerian warplanes were killed when the truck in which they were traveling somersaulted on a bridge and plunged into a ravine.

November 9, Western Bangladesh. The driver of a speeding bus swerved into a river to avoid hitting two buffalo; at least 11 persons died, and 30 were injured.

November 16, Near Mendota, Calif. A van collided with a tractor trailer in foggy conditions on a rural highway; 11 persons were killed, 10 of whom were farmworkers.

November 18, Near New Delhi. An overcrowded school bus skidded off a bridge and dropped 12 m (40 ft) into the Yamuna River; at least 25 children were killed, and some 60 were injured.

November 24, Northern Thailand. A head-on collision between two packed buses killed at least 20 persons and injured more than 30.

December 26, Near Huancayo. A bus loaded with passengers careened off a highway in the Andes after striking a large rock and tumbled 150 m (500 ft) into a ravine; 27 persons died, and 36 were injured.

Miscellaneous

January 8, Lahore, Pak. Toxic gas leaked from the cylinders of a truck that had broken down in a densely populated neighbourhood; at least 32 persons were killed.

January 20, Hyderabad, Pak. At least 32 persons died after drinking a poisonous brew of homemade liquor.

May 4, Near Kisangani, Democratic Republic of the Congo. More than 100 Rwandan Hutu refugees suffocated or were crushed to death on a severely overcrowded train; 6,000 refugees had swarmed onto the six-car train to travel to Kisangani, where they were hoping to join a United Nations airlift to Rwanda.

June–August, France, Italy, and Switzerland. Heavy snowfall in the Alps followed by unusually hot weather created treacherous conditions for mountain climbers during the summer; at least 92 climbers perished, most in avalanches and rockfalls triggered by melting snow.

June–August, Yunnan province, China. At least 76 persons died after eating poisonous mushrooms they had collected.

June 12, Enugu, Nigeria. An unfinished three-story building collapsed, killing 20 persons; the cause of the collapse was unknown.

July 12, Zhejiang province. A housing complex that had been converted into a textile factory collapsed, killing 36 persons.

July 17, Tomsk, Russia. A barracks at a military academy collapsed a few minutes before reveille; 11 cadets were killed and 37 injured; the barracks, a 19th-century monastery that the military had converted, had been badly in need of repairs.

August 24, San Pedro Sula, Honduras. A rat chewed through an electrical cable at a state-run hospital and caused a power outage; at least 14 persons on life-support machines, including 4 newborn infants, were killed.

August 31, Nsele, Democratic Republic of the Congo. As troops were trying to impose order at a crowded swimming pool where boys were attempting to undress girls, 21 children fell into the pool and drowned.

September 4, Ciudad del Este, Paraguay. Strong winds caused part of a sports stadium to collapse while the ruling Colorado Party held a political rally; at least 33 persons were killed, and more than 100 were injured.

September 11, Northwestern Estonia. While crossing a strait on foot as part of a training exercise, a platoon of 22 soldiers was swept into deep waters when strong winds arose; 14 soldiers drowned.

November 16, Bombay (Mumbai). At least 18 persons, mostly farmers, died after drinking contaminated liquor at a pub.

People of 1997

NOBEL PRIZES

Prize for Peace

The banning of antipersonnel land mines took only six years—from November 1991, when American activist Jody Williams helped found the International Campaign to Ban Landmines (ICBL), to December 1997, when 131 nations met in Ottawa and 123 signed or indicated that they would sign the historic treaty. On December 10, six days after the closing of the Ottawa conference, Williams and ICBL were honoured in Oslo with the Nobel Prize for Peace; Williams and ICBL were awarded equal shares in the prize.

Inexpensive to manufacture (about $5 apiece) but costly to detect and defuse (about $1,000 for each one), antipersonnel mines, which were more compact and more prevalent than antitank mines, were considered especially advantageous for their ease of placement and indiscriminate element of terror. According to Williams and ICBL, in some 68 countries there were an estimated 110 million antipersonnel land mines that maimed or killed at the rate of 26,000 persons—most of them civilians—each year. Because minefields were more likely to be found in less-developed countries recovering from recent wars—such as Angola, Bosnia and Herzegovina, and Cambodia—resulting deaths and injuries took a tremendous toll on overburdened health services, and land mine removal drained national finances and rendered land unusable.

The treaty signed in December mandated an absolute ban on land mine production, export, and use, as well as the destruction of existing stockpiles and the removal of active mines. Despite major signatory holdouts—such as the United States and China—the campaign to ban land mines received worldwide support, and the efforts of ICBL were supported by such figures as Diana, princess of Wales (*see* OBITUARIES), U.S. Sen. Patrick Leahy, and Canadian Foreign Minister Lloyd Axworthy. Accepting the Nobel Prize on behalf of ICBL was Cambodian Tun Channareth, who had lost his legs to a land mine in 1982.

Jody Williams and land mine victim Tun Channareth

POOL—NTB/IPOL

Williams was born on Oct. 9, 1950, and earned (1984) a master's degree in international studies from Johns Hopkins University, Washington, D.C. For more than a decade, she worked to influence U.S. foreign policy in Central America as coordinator of the Nicaragua-Honduras Education Project and as associate director of Medical Aid to El Salvador.

By November 1991 these interests had brought her into contact with the Vietnam Veterans of America Foundation (VVAF), which, along with the German-based group Medico International, formed ICBL, with Williams as campaign coordinator. The campaign built upon the failures of the 1980 Geneva Convention on Inhumane Weapons, which was unable to achieve an absolute ban on antipersonnel land mines—although attending nations, reconvening later in the mid-1990s, agreed to standardize some specifications for producing the weapons.

Under Williams, ICBL expanded into a coalition of about 1,000 nongovernmental humanitarian, medical, and developmental groups from more than 50 nations. Its steering committee, under the leadership of the VVAF, was made up of nine international organizations. Williams was coauthor, with Shawn Roberts, of *After the Guns Fall Silent: The Enduring Legacy of Landmines* (1995).

(TOM MICHAEL)

Prize for Economics

The stereotype that the Nobel Memorial Prize in Economic Science is usually awarded for dry academic concepts with only theoretical rather than applied value was far from the truth in 1997. Not only had the prizewinners, American Robert C. Merton and Canadian-born Myron Samuel Scholes, seen their ideas put to use, but they also had profited from them. The pair shared the award for providing an answer to the fundamental question of how to measure the value of stock options and other derivatives, an answer that had helped fuel the growth of world financial markets for 20 years. They had also put their money where their mouths were by becoming principals in Long-Term Capital Management, a $6 billion firm that invested primarily in fixed-income securities and derivatives of those securities; Merton was even one of the firm's cofounders.

Scholes's greatest contribution to the field of economics was the formula that bore his name: the Black-Scholes option-valuation formula, developed in tandem with Fischer Black, whose death in 1995 made him ineligible for the Nobel Prize (which is not awarded posthumously). Despite some early difficulty in finding a publisher, Scholes and Black were able to present their landmark formula in the *Journal of Political Economy* in 1973. Prior to this time, it had been difficult for people to determine the value of stock options (purchased agreements that give investors or traders the right to either buy or sell an asset at a fixed time in the future). Although investors could calculate a risk premium to hedge against major financial losses, they lacked the means to predict such a premium accurately.

The Black-Scholes formula, though mathematically complex, was based on a series of rather straightforward variables: the current share price, the future strike price, the time to maturity, the time to expiry, and the interest rate on alternative, risk-free investments. The formula helped lessen the high risk inherent in the derivatives market by demonstrating that risk premiums are not necessary for investment in stock options because they already are factored into the price of the stock. The implication was that options should be priced as a type of insurance, or hedging device, so that they mirrored risk-free investment alternatives, such as treasury bills. This made the trading of options and other derivatives more attractive to investors, and soon the Black-Scholes formula was adopted by traders worldwide as the main method for valuing stock options. By the mid-1970s traders at the Chicago Board Options Exchange were able to compute instantly the value of options on hand-held electronic calculators. Merton used his background in mathematics to build on the Black-Scholes formula by demonstrating how certain restrictions, such as the assumption that a stock will pay no dividends, could be relaxed. By altering the formula, he showed how it could be applied to financial matters other than options, including home mortgages and student loans, and to risk management in general.

Scholes was born on Jan. 7, 1941, in Timmins, Ont., and educated at McMaster University, Hamilton, Ont. (B.A., 1961), and the University of Chicago (M.B.A., 1964; Ph.D., 1970), where he studied under Nobel laureate Merton H. Miller. Scholes taught at the Massachusetts Institute of Technology (MIT; 1968–73) and the University of Chicago (1973–83) before joining (1983) Stanford University as a professor of both law and finance.

Merton, whose father was a noted sociologist, was born in New York City on July 31, 1944. He studied engineering mathematics at Columbia University, New York City (B.S., 1966), applied mathematics at the California Institute of Technology (M.S., 1967), and economics at MIT (Ph.D., 1970). He taught at MIT's Sloan School of Management from 1970 until 1988, when he joined the Harvard Business School. Merton, who sat on the boards of several economic journals and mutual fund companies, wrote economic treatises on corporate finance, as well as the book *Continuous-Time Finance* (1990). (TOM MICHAEL)

Prize for Literature

Soon after being named winner of the 1997 Nobel Prize for Literature in October, Italian actor-playwright Dario Fo demonstrated to the world how he had secured his reputation as a social agitator. He announced that his $1 million Nobel award would be donated to the legal defense of three former radicals who were imprisoned for a murder associated with an incident that formed the centrepiece of one of his best-known satires, *Morte accidentale di un anarchico* (1974; *Accidental Death of an Anarchist*). The play tells of an anarchist who was unjustly blamed for terrorist bombings and during police interrogation was thrown from a fifth-story window to his death—a death that was ruled accidental. The police interrogators, led by the main character, Il Matto ("The Maniac"), beat the suspect and brought him to the window "and made him lean out for a bit of cool night air to revive him…Apparently, there was a misunderstanding between the two officers supporting him as often happens in these cases, each of them thought the other one was holding him—'You got him Gianni?' 'You got him Luigi?' and bump, down he went." In the real-life 1969 case, the government destroyed evidence relating to the bombing, and the three radicals for whom Fo lent his celebrity support were convicted of the 1972 assassination of the chief interrogator. They were demanding a new trial, however.

The selection of the avant-garde dramatist and performer came as a surprise to many Nobel Prize watchers, including Fo himself, and the international literary establishment reacted somewhat coolly to the news. Partially blinded by a stroke in 1996, Fo brought characteristic levity to the staid Nobel ceremony in December by handing out colourful drawings and delivering an improvised speech. His risky theatrical caricatures lampooned what he viewed as hypocrisy in government, society, and religion and were occasionally the subject of official condemnation. The Vatican, for example, censured his popular one-man show, *Mistero Buffo* (1973) as "the most blasphemous show in the history of television" for such irreverent scenes as the one in which Jesus Christ transforms the wedding at Cana into a drunken bacchanal. Based on medieval mystery plays, *Mistero Buffo* remained topical, changing with every audience. Fo's biting brand of comedy was perhaps best described in a monologue from the same work: "I am the jongleur…I make fun of those in power, and I show you how puffed up and conceited are the big shots who go around making wars in which we are the ones who get slaughtered. I reveal them for what they are. I pull out the plug, and pssss they deflate."

Fo was born on March 24, 1926, in Leggiuno-Sangiamo, a fishing village north of Milan, the city where he later settled. By the early 1950s he was creating satirical revues for small theatres, often appearing with the actress Franca Rame, whom he married in 1954. Their agitprop theatre of leftist politics was rooted in the traditions of commedia dell'arte and court jesters, and when their clownish sketches on the television show "Canzonissima" lasted only seven weeks in 1962, their notoriety was fueled. In 1968 Fo and Rame founded the acting troupe Nuova Scena, which was financed by the Italian Communist Party. They left the party in 1970, however, to establish the touring company Collettivo Teatrale La Comune.

Fo wrote about 70 plays, coauthoring some of them with Rame, notably *Female Parts* (1981). Fo's other works include *Non si paga, non si paga!* (1974; *We Can't Pay? We Won't Pay!*), *Tutta casa, letto e chiesa* (1978; *Adult Orgasm Escapes from the Zoo*), *Il papa e la strega* (1989; *The Pope and the Witch*), and *Il diavolo con le zinne* (1997). (TOM MICHAEL)

Prize for Chemistry

A Dane, a Briton, and an American shared the 1997 Nobel Prize for Chemistry for discoveries about ATP synthase, an enzyme responsible for making adenosine triphosphate (ATP), the universal energy carrier in living cells. By means of energy-rich chemical bonds, the molecule ATP captures the chemical energy released from food and makes it available to cells for muscle contraction, transmission of nerve impulses, construction of cell components, and other processes. It serves this critical function, often described as the energy currency of cells, in living things ranging from microbes to humans.

The Royal Swedish Academy of Sciences awarded half of the $1 million prize to Paul D. Boyer of the University of California, Los Angeles (UCLA), and John E. Walker of the Medical Research Council (MRC) Laboratory of Molecular Biology, Cambridge, Eng. They were honoured for research conducted independently that explained the way ATP synthase works as a catalyst in cells to promote the synthesis of ATP. The other half of the prize went to Jens C. Skou of Aarhus University, Århus, Den., for discovery of the first molecular pump in cells. Powered by ATP, molecular pumps are protein molecules that transport ions, or electrically charged atoms, through cell membranes. Skou discovered sodium, potassium-ATPase, a special enzyme that functions as such a pump by degrading ATP and using the released energy to power the transport process.

When Boyer began his research on ATP formation in the early 1950s, scientists knew that it was the energy carrier in living cells. ATP consists of a molecule of adenosine linked to a chain of three phosphate groups by high-energy bonds. Removal of a phosphate group releases the stored energy for use by cells. In the process ATP becomes adenosine diphosphate (ADP). With help from chemical energy in food, a phosphate can be added to ADP, producing more ATP. In the late 1970s Boyer proposed the "binding-change hypothesis," a detailed elucidation of the mechanism by which ATPase catalyzes synthesis of ATP from ADP and phosphate.

"Walker's work complements Boyer's in a remarkable manner," the Swedish Academy stated. Walker, who began studies on ATP synthase in the early 1980s, verified that the mechanism proposed by Boyer was valid. In the 1980s Walker deciphered the sequence, or linear arrangement, of the amino-acid building blocks of ATP synthase. He added further evidence in the 1990s by obtaining the first high-resolution crystal structure of the active part of ATP synthase. All of Walker's structural clarifications were consistent with Boyer's mechanism.

Skou was honoured for research that he had done in the late 1950s. He established sodium, potassium ATPase as the first enzyme known to promote transport of ions through cell membranes. Such transport maintains normal concentrations of sodium, potassium, and other chemicals in cells. Sodium concentration inside cells is lower than outside, and potassium concentration is higher inside than out. When, for example, a nerve cell transmits an impulse, sodium ions pour into the cell, increasing their internal concentration. They must be transported out of the cell for it to fire again. That transport requires energy, which sodium, potassium-ATPase acquires by detaching phosphate groups from ATP molecules.

Other researchers later discovered more ion pumps with similar structures and functions. A calcium pump, for instance, helps to control muscle contraction, and a hydrogen pump produces hydrochloric acid in the stomach. Popular drugs used to treat stomach ulcers and gastritis work by inhibiting action of the pump enzyme.

Boyer was born in 1918 in Provo, Utah, and received a doctoral degree in biochemistry from the University of Wisconsin at Madison. After joining UCLA in 1963, he directed the institution's Molecular Biology Institute (1965–83) and became professor emeritus of chemistry and biochemistry (1990). Walker was born in 1941 in Halifax, Eng., and received a Ph.D. from the University of Oxford. In 1982 he became senior scientist at the MRC Laboratory of Molecular Biology. Skou, born in 1918 in Denmark, trained in medicine at the University of Copenhagen and earned a Ph.D. from Aarhus University, where he became professor of physiology (1963). In 1977 he was made professor of biophysics at Aarhus. (MICHAEL WOODS)

Prize for Physics

The 1997 Nobel Prize for Physics was awarded to two American scientists and a French colleague for developing techniques for using laser light to cool and trap atoms so that they can be studied in detail. Other scientists extended the methods in 1995 to achieve a new state of matter termed a Bose-Einstein condensate and in 1997 to make an atom laser. (*See* MATHEMATICS AND PHYSICAL SCIENCES: *Physics*.)

Additional applications "are just around the corner," stated the Royal Swedish Academy of Sciences, which awarded the prize. It cited superior atomic clocks for more accurate determinations of position on Earth and in space and new ways of making very small electronic components. "The new methods…have contributed greatly to increasing our knowledge of the interplay between radiation and matter," the Nobel citation added.

The prize was shared by Steven Chu of Stanford University, William D. Phillips of the National Institute of Standards and Technology, Gaithersburg, Md., and Claude Cohen-Tannoudji of the Collège de France and the École Normale Supérieure, Paris. Chu was born in 1948 in St. Louis, Mo., and received a doctoral degree from the University of California, Berkeley. In 1990 he became a professor at Stanford. Phillips, born in 1948 in Wilkes-Barre, Pa., received a doctoral degree from the Massachusetts Institute of Technology. Cohen-Tannoudji was born in 1933 in Constantine, Alg., and received a doctoral degree from the École Normale.

The three physicists worked independently, each moving the technology farther ahead. In 1985 Chu and his co-workers at Bell Laboratories,

PATRICK DURAND—SYGMA

Claude Cohen-Tannoudji

Holmdel, N.J., developed the original method for cooling atoms. The techniques were needed because atoms and molecules in gases move so fast—*e.g.,* 4,000 km/h (2,500 mph) for atoms and molecules in air at room temperature—that detailed observations are difficult. Scientists knew that lowering the temperature could reduce the speed of the particles. To slow atomic and molecular motion enough for detailed study, intense chilling to temperatures near absolute zero (0 K, or −273.15° C, or −459.67° F) was needed. At such cold temperatures, however, gases normally condense and freeze.

Chu and associates made an apparatus that allowed gases to be chilled to within a fraction of a degree of absolute zero without freezing. It consisted of six laser beams that bombard the gas's constituent particles from all directions, slowing their motion. The laser light acts much like an extremely thick liquid, which has been dubbed optical molasses, that slows movement of the particles. Individual atoms thus can be studied in great detail, and scientists can get glimpses of their inner structure, the Royal Academy observed.

The apparatus created a glowing pea-sized cloud containing about one million chilled atoms. In the initial experiments Chu's group cooled atoms to a temperature of about 240 microkelvins (μK), or 240 millionths of a degree above absolute zero. Atoms at that temperature were slowed to a speed of about 30 cm (12 in) per second. Subsequent addition of magnetic coils to Chu's device allowed scientists to trap the atoms so that they could be studied or used for experiments.

Phillips and his associates designed a similar experiment, developing several new methods for measuring temperature. By 1988 his group had achieved temperatures of 40 μK. Between 1988 and 1995 Cohen-Tannoudji and his colleagues made further advances, finally cooling atoms to a temperature within 1 μK, which corresponded to a speed of only 2 cm (0.8 in) per second.

"Intensive development is in progress concerning laser cooling and the capture of neutral atoms," the Academy noted. "Among other things, Chu has constructed an atomic fountain, in which laser-cooled atoms are sprayed up from a trap like jets of water." Chu visualized the device as the basis of a new generation of ultraprecise atomic clocks. Existing atomic clocks are accurate to about one second in 32 million years. Chu's work could make them accurate to one second in three billion years. (MICHAEL WOODS)

Prize for Physiology or Medicine

An American scientist who discovered an entirely new kind of disease-causing agent, called a prion, won the 1997 Nobel Prize for Physiology or Medicine. Prions are believed to cause a number of degenerative brain diseases in humans and other animals. They include bovine spongiform encephalopathy (BSE), or "mad cow" disease, which forced wide destruction of cattle herds in the U.K. beginning in the late 1980s, and Creutzfeldt-Jakob disease (CJD) in humans. Recent evidence suggested that a newly discovered variant of CJD can be transmitted from cows with BSE to humans.

The Nobel Assembly of the Karolinska Institute, Stockholm, awarded the prize to Stanley B. Prusiner of the University of California, San Francisco. It was the first time since 1987, and only the 10th time in the last 50 years, that the prize had gone to a single scientist. Nobel Prizes often have recognized originators of unpopular theories who were finally vindicated after years of struggle against opposition from colleagues. As of 1997, however, the prion controversy showed little sign of ending, with skeptics questioning whether prions exist and with some insisting that BSE, CJD, and other diseases actually are caused by still-undiscovered viruses.

"Stanley Prusiner has added prions to the list of well known infectious agents including bacteria, viruses, fungi and parasites," the Nobel Assembly stated. "[His] discovery provides important insights that may furnish the basis to understand the biological mechanisms underlying other types of dementia-related diseases, for example Alzheimer's disease, and establishes a foundation for drug development and new types of medical treatment strategies."

Prusiner began his research in 1972 after a patient died of CJD, a rare brain disease that results in dementia. Other scientists had established that CJD, and related conditions termed kuru and scrapie, could be transmitted in brain tissue. Kuru occurred among cannibalistic people in Papua New Guinea who ate the brains of tribesmen who had been infected with kuru. Scrapie is a brain disease in sheep that causes the animals to scratch and scrape off their skin. Nevertheless, no conventional agent could be isolated from infected tissue. Furthermore, the tissue remained infectious despite treatment that would have destroyed the DNA or RNA of any viruses or bacteria present.

Scientists had proposed several theories about the agent responsible for these diseases. Some blamed an unusual, slow-acting virus. In the 1960s British scientists Tikvah Alper and J.S. Griffith proposed that an infectious agent lacking nucleic acid could cause scrapie. "[It was] a sensational hypothesis since at the time all known infectious agents contained the hereditary material DNA or RNA," the Nobel Assembly explained.

Prusiner and his associates embraced this idea. By 1982 they had announced discovery of an unusual protein in the brains of scrapie-infected hamsters that was not present in healthy animals. To describe this "proteinaceous infectious particle" Prusiner coined the term *prion.* Whereas "the scientific community greeted this discovery with great skepticism," the Assembly stated, "an unwavering Prusiner continued the arduous task to define the precise nature of this novel infectious agent."

Prusiner's group later showed that humans and other animals have a gene that specifies the production of prion protein. The protein's amino acid chain can fold into two distinct forms with different three-dimensional structures. One is a tightly coiled, unstable, normal form that does not cause disease. The other is an unwound, more stable, abnormal form. Prusiner's research indicated that the abnormal protein causes CJD, scrapie, and other prion diseases by a catalytic process in which it, on contact with the normal protein, causes the latter to change its structure and become abnormal. In a chain reaction ever more of the abnormal protein is produced, and after months or years it finally accumulates to levels that cause obvious brain damage.

Prusiner's work could help scientists understand Alzheimer's disease and other more common brain disorders. For example, some researchers believed that Alzheimer's disease is caused by a structural change in certain nonprion proteins, which leads to the accumulation of abnormal deposits in the brain. His research also suggested possible ways of treating and preventing prion diseases in humans and animals. Prusiner's group, for instance, was trying to develop drugs that attach to normal prion protein and stabilize it, so that the protein resists unwinding. Prusiner also suggested breeding sheep and cows that lack the prion gene, which did not seem essential for normal life. (MICHAEL WOODS)

Stanley Prusiner

KERMANI—GAMMA LIAISON

BIOGRAPHIES

Abacha, Sani
Many found it downright curious how in 1997 Gen. Sani Abacha, who had ruthlessly seized power in Nigeria in a coup four years earlier, was sending troops to Sierra Leone in an effort to defend democracy there. Earlier he had assisted peacekeeping forces in Liberia, and it was thought that Abacha was also providing economic aid to support democracy in that country. At home, however, Abacha oversaw a dictatorial regime that suppressed political parties, gagged the press, violated human rights, and pushed the country in the direction of economic and ecological ruin.

Abacha was born on Sept. 20, 1943, in Kano, the major city in Muslim-dominated northern Nigeria. A career military man, he was commissioned a second lieutenant in 1963 after attending Nigerian Military Training College in Kaduna and Mons Defence Officers' Cadet Training College in England. He rose through the ranks of the military and was serving as a brigadier when he assisted (1983) Ibrahim Babangida in overthrowing elected Pres. Alhaji Shehu Shagari. Two years later Babangida staged another military coup against Muhammadu Buhari and installed himself as leader of the nation. Abacha served as army chief of staff and later, in the post of defense minister, as second in command to Babangida. General elections were held in 1993 and were apparently won by the Social Democratic candidate, Moshood ("MKO") Abiola, a Yoruba businessman from the southwest, but the military government soon annulled the election results. Abacha managed to weather the political and civil upheaval that ensued, and in November 1993 he declared himself president.

Though Abacha promised a return to civilian rule by 1995, he dismantled democratic institutions, banned political activity of any kind, and shut down several independent publications, stating in an address, "Any attempt to test our will will be decisively dealt with." In June 1994 Abiola tested that will by publicly declaring himself the rightful elected ruler of Nigeria. He was promptly jailed and charged with treason. Unfavourable attention came to Abacha again in November 1995 when writer Ken Saro-Wiwa and a number of other ecological activists from the oil-rich Ogoniland area in the southeast, were executed for treason. In March 1997 Wole Soyinka, self-exiled Nobel laureate and Nigeria's best-known writer, was also formally charged with treason.

In October 1995 Abacha had again promised national elections, this time for 1998, and said that he would step down at that time. In early 1997, however, as new political parties were being formed under the government's careful scrutiny, Abacha even hinted that he might want to run for president himself. (ANTHONY L. GREEN)

Adams, John Coolidge
American composer John Adams, whose works were among the most performed of contemporary composers, was elected to the American Academy of Arts and Letters in 1997. He had already won a number of honours, including a Guggenheim fellowship in 1982 and the Grawemeyer Award for Music Composition in 1995. The latest honour, however, set an official seal of approval on his work.

Adams was born on Feb. 15, 1947, in Worcester, Mass. He became proficient on the clarinet at an early age (sometimes free-lancing with the Boston Symphony Orchestra and performing with other groups) and by his teenage years was composing. His teachers at Harvard University (A.B., 1969; M.A., 1971) included Leon Kirchner and Roger Sessions. Adams was the first person in the history of the university to be allowed to submit a musical composition as a senior honours thesis. After graduation he moved to California, where from 1972 to 1982 he taught at the San Francisco Conservatory of Music. In 1978 he founded and directed the San Francisco Symphony Orchestra's series "New and Unusual Music," and he was composer in residence with the orchestra from 1982 to 1985.

Although his early compositions were in an academic style, Adams soon began drawing on much broader sources, including pop, jazz, electronic music, and minimalism. His use of minimalist techniques—characterized by repetition and simplicity—came to be tempered by expressive, even neo-Romantic, elements. His works encompassed a wide range of genres and included *Shaker Loops* (1978), chamber music for string septet; *Harmonium* (1980), a cantata for chorus and orchestra using the poetry of John Donne and Emily Dickinson; *Grand Pianola Music* (1981–82), a reworking of early-20th-century American popular music for instrumental ensemble, three sopranos, and two pianos; *Harmonielehre* (1984–85), an homage to Arnold Schoenberg, whose music was the antithesis of minimalism, for orchestra; *Fearful Symmetries* (1988), for orchestra; and *Wound-Dresser* (1988), for baritone and orchestra. One of his especially popular orchestral works was *Short Ride in a Fast Machine* (1986).

Adams's most ambitious works, however, were two operas, both created in collaboration with director Peter Sellars, poet Alice Goodman, and choreographer Mark Morris. The first, *Nixon in China* (1987), took as its subject the visit of U.S. Pres. Richard M. Nixon to China in 1972. The second, *The Death of Klinghoffer* (1991), was based on the hijacking by Palestinian terrorists of the cruise ship *Achille Lauro* in 1985 and the killing of a disabled Jewish passenger. Both operas received a number of performances, and both were recorded, with *Nixon in China* winning a Grammy in 1989. Both works also had their detractors, but a number of critics found them to be among the most significant of contemporary operas, arguing that they succeeded in melding the communicative and expressive requirements of the form with eclectic musical styles and minimalist techniques. Meanwhile, *The Chairman Dances*, subtitled "Foxtrot for Orchestra," which was written for *Nixon in China* but dropped from the final score, became one of Adams's most often played orchestral works. (ROBERT RAUCH)

Albright, Madeleine
On Jan. 23, 1997, Czech-born American diplomat Madeleine Albright, known for her tough-mindedness, was sworn in as the first woman to hold the post of U.S. secretary of state. She was not yet two years old when Nazi Germany occupied Czechoslovakia. The betrayal of that nation through the appeasement policies of British Prime Minister Neville Chamberlain at the 1938 Munich Conference proved an enduring influence that shaped her political life. Considerably more hawkish than her predecessor, Warren Christopher, Albright was a strong advocate of the use of U.S. military and political power to accomplish foreign policy goals, stating "My mind-set is Munich. Most of my generation's is Vietnam."

Albright, the daughter of a Czech diplomat, was born Marie Jana Korbel on May 15, 1937, in Prague. Following the Nazi occupation of Czechoslovakia in 1939, her family fled to England. Although she spent most of her life believing that they had fled for political reasons, in 1997 she learned that her family was Jewish and that three of her grandparents had died in German concentration camps. The family returned to Czechoslovakia after World War II, but the Soviet-sponsored communist coup made the family refugees again, and by 1948 they had settled in the United States.

In 1959 Albright graduated from Wellesley (Mass.) College and married Joseph Albright, a member of the Medill newspaper-publishing family. After earning (1968) a master's degree from Columbia University, New York City, she worked as a Democratic fund-raiser for Sen. Edmund Muskie's failed 1972 presidential campaign, and she later served as Muskie's chief legislative assistant. By 1976 she had received a Ph.D. from Columbia and was working for Zbigniew Brzezinski, Pres. Jimmy Carter's national security adviser.

MARTIN SIMON—SABA

Madeleine Albright

During the Republican administrations of Presidents Ronald Reagan and George Bush in the 1980s and early 1990s, Albright worked for several nonprofit organizations, and her Washington, D.C., home became a salon for influential Democratic politicians and policy makers. She also served (1982–93) as professor of international affairs at Georgetown University, Washington, D.C. After the election of Pres. Bill Clinton, a Democrat, in 1992, Albright's political star began rising, and Clinton named her ambassador to the United Nations in 1993. At the UN she gained a reputation as a fierce advocate for American interests while promoting an increased role for the United States in UN operations, particularly those with a military component.

Following her unanimous confirmation by the Senate in 1997, the new secretary of state faced a number of volatile international situations. The Middle East peace process had collapsed in a welter of bloodshed; an increasingly bellicose North Korea was facing famine; and the expansion of NATO was meeting with vociferous opposition from Russia. By the year's end, Albright had visited Africa, Russia, China, Latin America, and the Middle East. Some critics charged her with emphasizing style over substance, suggesting that she lacked the vision necessary for the post. Others pointed out that it was Albright's job to implement foreign policy, not create it, and that she was not to blame for the somewhat confused vision that emerged from an administration focused on domestic issues. (JOHN H. MATHEWS)

Annan, Kofi Atta
When he moved into the office of UN secretary-general on Jan. 1, 1997, Kofi Annan of Ghana knew exactly what was expected from him by the organization's member nations. He was to clean house. The UN had become a sprawling bureaucracy—inefficient, costly, and misunderstood by many of the nations it was meant to aid.

The affable and intelligent Annan, the first person from sub-Saharan Africa to serve as secretary-general, was elected to the post during stormy times at the UN. His predecessor, Boutros Boutros-Ghali of Egypt, was determined to keep the top post at the organization, though many member nations, most notably the United States, were put off by his independent and aloof style. The U.S., concerned about the UN's operation costs and its activities under Boutros-Ghali, had been deliberately withholding its contributions and was more than $1.5 billion in arrears to the organization at the time Boutros-Ghali's term was ending. The U.S. used its veto power as a member of the Security Council to block his reelection and to stall the entire process until a suitable candidate was found. After some heated bickering between the U.S. and France, the nomination of Annan was finally approved.

Annan was a surprisingly popular choice to become the seventh secretary-general of the UN. At a time when the UN was in desperate need of bureaucratic reform and new thinking regarding its role in peacekeeping operations, he was the first secretary-general to rise through the ranks of the organization (since 1962 he had spent all but two years of his life working for the UN); he also had been deeply involved in the peacekeeping missions of the 1990s. His wide range of experience and his gentle manner made him a particularly desirable candidate. He joined the UN in 1962 as a budget officer for the World Health Organization in Geneva. With the exception of 1974–76 (spent as director of the Ghana Tourist Development Co.), Annan rose through the administrative ranks of the UN, reaching the positions of assistant secretary-general and controller for program planning, budget, and finance in 1990. During this time he established a reputation as an effective and approachable manager. On March 1, 1993, he was elevated to under-secretary-general of peacekeeping operations. In that position he distinguished himself during the civil war in Bosnia and Herzegovina, particularly in his graceful handling of the transition of peacekeeping operations from UN forces to NATO troops.

Kofi Atta Annan was born on April 8, 1938, in Kumasi, Gold Coast (now Ghana). His father was the governor of Ashanti province and a hereditary chief of the Fanti people. Annan studied at the University of Science and Technology in Kumasi before traveling to the U.S. There, in 1961, he completed his undergraduate studies in economics at Macalester College in St. Paul, Minn. He continued his education at the Institute for Advanced International Studies in Geneva (1961–62). Ten years later he earned a master's degree in management while a Sloan Fellow at the Massachusetts Institute of Technology (1972).

In July 1997 Annan proposed a plan to reform the bureaucracy of the UN that included consolidating some offices. He also called for revisions of the UN charter that would allow for further streamlining. His proposals aimed not only to improve the efficacy of the UN but also to help mend relations with the U.S., the host nation of the UN headquarters. (JAMES HENNELLY)

Armani, Giorgio

In 1997 Italian designer Giorgio Armani, for years a fashion trendsetter, launched Giorgio Armani Exclusive, a limited-edition line of handmade couture dresses that were available only by order and to select clients. In addition, his signature style, which included both relaxed yet luxurious ready-to-wear and elegant, intricately beaded chiffon evening wear, was reinvented by other designers on numerous international catwalks.

The death of colleague and countryman Gianni Versace allowed Armani to pay tribute to his archrival. Although each had pioneered a different approach to style (Armani's designs were minimalist, whereas Versace's ensembles were flamboyant), Armani attended the debut of Donatella Versace's (Gianni's sister's) collection for the house of Versace and then at the close of the show led the standing ovation that hailed her first collection a success.

Armani was born on July 11, 1934, in Piacenza, Italy, and was the son of a shipping manager. Rising from humble origins, he intended to become a doctor but left medical school and worked as a buyer, beginning in 1957, for the Milan department store La Rinascente. In 1964, after a seven-year stint in that position, Armani pursued

FOTEX/IPOL

Giorgio Armani

a career in fashion design, training in the atelier of Nino Cerruti. About 10 years later, with the help of his friend and business partner Sergio Galeotti, Armani launched his own label of ready-to-wear for men and women. Each year he added new offerings to his company—introducing perfume, accessories, a jeans line, the lower-priced diffusion line Emporio Armani, and sportswear.

Armani, a perfectionist who always wore the same shade of midnight blue, best described his approach to fashion as follows: "I was the first to soften the image of men, and harden the image of women. I dressed men in women's fabrics, and stole from men what women wanted and needed—the power suit." His androgynous approach rarely disappointed fashion critics, who dutifully appeared each season at shows staged at his 17th-century palazzo on Via Borgonuovo in central Milan. Meanwhile, the public developed an insatiable demand for his minimalist style, and such Hollywood leading ladies as Jodie Foster, Michelle Pfeiffer, and Annette Bening became torchbearers for the Armani look at the Academy Awards ceremonies. The measure of his success was staggering—in 1996 his company, Giorgio Armani SpA, enjoyed stratospheric sales totaling 1,870,000,000 lira, an astounding 10% increase from the previous year. (BRONWYN COSGRAVE)

Arnault, Bernard

During much of 1997 French businessman Bernard Arnault, the president and chairman of the French conglomerate LVMH Moët Hennessy Louis Vuitton, the largest luxury-products company in the world, attempted to quash the proposed $38 billion merger of Guinness PLC and Grand Metropolitan PLC (Grand Met)—two British spirits and food firms in which he was a major shareholder. Despite his efforts the deal, which created Diageo PLC—the world's largest spirits company—went through. In May Arnault, who had issued a legal challenge, complained, "I do not see any logic combining hamburgers, food, wine, and spirits; I think there are better ideas."

Arnault's better idea had been to become the leading shareholder in a new company. He proposed that the beverage businesses of Guinness, Grand Met, and LVMH be merged and that the new firm divest itself of the Guinness breweries and such food entities as Burger King Corp. and Pillsbury Co. Although his grand plan did not succeed, his worries were, according to *The Economist,* "assuaged by a promise of £250m when the [GMG] deal goes through."

Arnault was born on March 5, 1949, in Roubaix, France. He graduated from the École Polytechnique in Paris with a degree in engineering but left France in the early 1980s to pursue a career in real estate in New York City. Four years later he was back in France on the cusp of his first big fashion deal and armed with American business know-how and skills at playing hardball.

With $15 million of his own money, Arnault and Antoine Bernheim, a managing partner of the French bank Lazard Frères and Co., raised the $80 million necessary to purchase Boussac, a bankrupt textile company that owned the fashion house of Christian Dior. Then, in 1987, Arnault was invited to invest in LVMH by the company's chairman, Henri Racamier. Investing through a joint venture with Guinness, Arnault soon ousted Racamier and started to sweep a slew of fashion companies into the LVMH fold: Christian Lacroix, Givenchy, Kenzo, the leather goods companies Loewe, Céline, and Berluti, the jeweler Fred Joailler, the DFS group (the world's biggest duty-free chain), and Sephora, a chain of perfume shops.

Although Arnault was not a household name in the U.S., he was known in Europe as the man who revitalized French couture in 1995 by appointing British fashion designer John Galliano to replace the venerable Hubert de Givenchy at the latter's Paris fashion house. The "Pope of Fashion," as Arnault was dubbed by *Women's Wear Daily,* a year later moved Galliano to Christian Dior and appointed the brash British fashion designer Alexander McQueen to replace him. Arnault then hired Marc Jacobs, a young American designer, to the post of creative director at Louis Vuitton, the maker of luxury leather goods.

Even though his fashion foresight had revived interest in these traditional fashion houses, Arnault was both loathed and respected by his countrymen. He was unrepentant in his approach. "I am not interested in anything else but the youngest, the brightest and the very, very talented." (BRONWYN COSGRAVE)

Arzú Irigoyen, Alvaro

As Alvaro Arzú neared the end of his second full year as president of Guatemala in 1997, he helped the country take the first steps toward recovery from its long civil war. During 1996 the president had achieved a number of agreements with guerrilla forces, culminating in the signing of a peace accord, and benefits from his actions began to appear in 1997.

Arzú was born on March 14, 1946, in Guatemala City. Descended from Basque immigrants, he was a member of the country's small but powerful European elite. As a young man he tried boxing and bullfighting, and he was successful in business. From 1985 to 1990 Arzú served as mayor of Guatemala City. He made an unsuccessful run for the presidency in 1990 and in 1991 was appointed minister of foreign affairs. He resigned the post that same year, however, to become secretary-general of the conservative National Advancement Party. Advocating various social reforms, as well as peace with Guatemala's guerrillas, he ran for president again in 1995 and, with strong support from voters in Guatemala City, narrowly won the office in a runoff election held on Jan. 7, 1996.

Although peace talks had begun in 1990 and the fighting had waned, during 1996 Arzú moved swiftly to bring the civil war to an end. His efforts involved reaching accords with the leftist Guatemalan National Revolutionary Unity (URNG), including plans to demobilize the guerrillas and reintegrate them into society, reduce the size of the armed forces, and create a civilian force to take over police duties. The government also signed an international agreement outlining the rights of indigenous peoples. In March the government and the URNG agreed to a temporary cease-fire. On December 4 they signed a permanent cease-fire in Oslo, and on December 29, in Guatemala City, they signed the Accord for a Firm and Lasting Peace, which thus ended a conflict that had lasted more than 35 years.

The task of implementing the agreements was among Arzú's principal concerns in 1997. In January he traveled to Brussels, where he met with representatives of the United Nations and major lending countries to secure financial aid. Overcoming diplomatic objections from China, he then won agreement by the UN to station observers in Guatemala. By late 1997 the URNG had taken steps to transform itself into a political party. It was clear, however, that not all the country's problems would be solved easily. Human rights groups had criticized legislative action in late 1996 that granted pardons to both government and guerrilla officials and soldiers for political and common crimes, and they complained of difficulties in gaining access to the records needed to trace victims of the civil war.

(ROBERT RAUCH)

Ashley, Merrill

Ballerina Merrill Ashley's farewell performance on Nov. 25, 1997, not only marked her retirement from a 30-year career with the New York City Ballet (NYCB); it also represented a good-bye to one of the few remaining direct links to George Balanchine, the company's legendary founder. Ashley was the only NYCB ballerina who was still performing a ballet that Balanchine had created especially for her. *Ballo della regina,* choreographed in 1978, showcased the virtuoso aspects of her technique—her speed, clarity, and precision—and was featured frequently throughout her final season.

Ashley, born Linda Michelle Merrill on Dec. 2, 1950, in St. Paul, Minn., and raised in Rutland, Vt., began studying ballet when she was seven. In 1964, when she was 13, she received a Ford Foundation scholarship and began to study full time at the School of American Ballet, the official school of NYCB. In 1967 she joined NYCB's corps de ballet—and changed her name because the company already had a member named Linda Merrill—and before long she was dancing solo roles in addition to appearing with the corps. Ashley officially became a soloist in 1974 and began adding such demanding choreography as the "Sanguinic" movement in *The Four Temperaments,* the "Rubies" section of *Jewels,* and the lead role in *Square Dance* to her repertoire. She was promoted to the rank of principal dancer in 1977. Balanchine began casting Ashley in more lyrical ballets—the "Emeralds" section of *Jewels,* his one-act *Swan Lake,* and *In the Night* among them—to broaden her range, and in 1980 he created the second of the two ballets he choreographed for her, *Ballade,* to display this softer, more romantic side. Other Balanchine ballets that especially demonstrated her artistry included *Concerto barocco, Donizetti Variations, Gounod Symphony,* and *Chaconne.*

Besides dancing with NYCB, Ashley formed her own group, Merrill Ashley and Dancers, which toured in 1980 and 1981. She also performed as a guest artist with a number of companies. Her autobiography, *Dancing for Balanchine,* was published in 1984. Ashley's departure from the stage did not mean she was abandoning ballet; she planned to teach dance.

(BARBARA WHITNEY)

Ballard, Robert Duane

In 1997 American oceanographer Robert Ballard inaugurated a new era in archaeology with the discovery of eight ancient ships, including one that dated to 200 BC, 760 m (2,500 ft) below an old trade route in the Mediterranean Sea. Whereas previous maritime explorations had largely been limited to depths of 60 m (200 ft), Ballard and a team of archaeologists, oceanographers, and deep-sea specialists were able to locate the wreckage by using a nuclear-powered submarine equipped with long-range sonar. Robot vessels then photographed the site and retrieved artifacts. Found in deep water, the ships were well preserved, not subjected to the looting and coral layering that occured in shallow-water sites. The finding introduced deep-sea archaeology and established Ballard, already noted for his discovery of the *Titanic,* as "curator of the world's underwater museum."

Born on June 30, 1942, in Wichita, Kan., Ballard grew up in San Diego, Calif., where he developed a fascination with the ocean. He attended the University of California, Santa Barbara, earning degrees in chemistry and geology in 1965. As a member of the Reserve Officers Training Corps, he entered the army following graduation, serving a two-year tour before requesting a transfer to the navy. In 1967 he was assigned to the Woods Hole (Mass.) Oceanographic Research Institution, becoming a full-time marine scientist in 1974 after completing his doctoral degrees in marine geology and geophysics at the University of Rhode Island. At Woods Hole he was involved in more than 65 expeditions. For Project FAMOUS (French-American Mid-Ocean Undersea Study), Ballard helped develop *Alvin,* a three-person submersible equipped with a mechanical arm, which was used to map the Mid-Atlantic Ridge, an underwater mountain chain in the Atlantic Ocean. In 1977 he was part of an expedition that uncovered thermal vents in the Galapagos Rift. The presence of plant and animal life within these deep-sea warm springs led to the discovery of chemosynthesis, the chemical synthesis of food energy.

To advance deepwater exploration, Ballard designed a series of high-tech vessels, most notably the *Argo-Jason,* an automated system that enabled a remote-controlled camera to explore the ocean depths while transmitting live images to a monitor; scientists thus could survey the site and maneuver the camera. It was used to locate the *Titanic* and numerous other shipwrecks, including the *Lusitania* and *Bismarck.* Ballard, a commander in the navy, left Woods Hole in 1997 to head the Institute for Exploration, Mystic, Conn., a centre for deep-sea archaeology.

(AMY TIKKANEN)

Binoche, Juliette

The French actress Juliette Binoche had a face that was mesmerizing, not only because of its obvious beauty—dark hair and eyes, pale complexion, and pink cheeks—but also because of a countenance that conveyed an innocence and mystery reminiscent of the heroines of Edgar Allan Poe's poetry. Without speaking, Binoche could relate a range of emotions—despair, surprise, loneliness, contentment, in a direct way, without falling into cliché. Her performances in *The English Patient* (1996), *Trois couleurs: Bleu* (1993; *Blue*), and *The Unbearable Lightness of Being* (1988) were notable for their complex characterizations that were both illuminating and shaded. She was able to hold the attention of audiences by revealing her characters while being careful not to reveal too much. In 1997 Binoche's hold on audiences won her the Academy Award for best supporting actress for her role in *The English Patient* and a place in the first rank of international cinema stars.

In *The English Patient* Binoche played Hana, a French-Canadian nurse stationed in Italy during World War II. To prepare for the role, she talked with a number of nurses who had served during the war. Inspired by the experiences of those women, Binoche was able to present Hana as a strong, caring woman emotionally devastated by the loss and suffering around her. Through the course of the film, she revealed Hana's resiliency and her struggle to regain her faith in life and love. In addition to her Oscar, Binoche received the Silver Berlin Bear for best actress at the 1997 Berlin International Film Festival for her memorable portrayal of Hana.

Binoche was born on March 9, 1964, in Paris. Her father was a sculptor and a theatre director; her mother was a teacher and actress. Her parents divorced when she was two years old, and she remained in the custody of her mother, who encouraged her to try acting. After she completed her general education, Binoche studied acting at the Paris Conservatoire and received private instruction from Vera Gregh, a renowned teacher of film acting. She appeared on the stages of Paris in the late 1970s, performing in works by Molière, Eugène Ionesco, and Luigi Pirandello among others. In the first half of the 1980s, she appeared in small film roles and on French television. Her first important break came in 1984 when she auditioned for a role in Jean-Luc Godard's *Je vous salue, Marie* (1985; *Hail Mary*). Though she was initially rejected, she left such an impression on Godard that he wrote a new part into the screenplay expressly for her.

JOYCE SILVERSTEIN—IPOL

Juliette Binoche

The same year Binoche landed one of the lead roles in André Téchiné's *Rendez-vous* (1985), which won broad acclaim at the Cannes Film Festival. Her portrayal of Nina, a provincial woman aspiring to be an actress in Paris, garnered much attention from critics and earned her the 1986 Romy-Schneider Prize, awarded by French journalists to the outstanding actress of the year. The next year she became romantically involved with the French director Léos Carax, with whom she made two films—*Mauvais sang* (1986; *Bad Blood*) and *Les Amants du Pont-Neuf* (1991; *Lovers on the Pont-Neuf*). *The Unbearable Lightness of Being* was her first English-language film and the first film to bring her talents effectively to the attention of the international public.

(JAMES HENNELLY)

Blair, Tony

On May 1, 1997, Tony Blair led Britain's Labour Party to its biggest-ever election victory. The following day he became the U.K.'s youngest prime minister since William Pitt the Younger at the end of the 18th century. Blair was just 43.

Anthony Charles Lynton Blair was born in Edinburgh on May 6, 1953. After graduating from the University of Oxford in 1975, he became a barrister. He was elected to the House of Commons for the safe Labour constituency of Sedgefield, in the county of Durham, in the general election of 1983, when Labour sustained its heaviest defeat since 1935. Blair belonged to a generation of young, open-minded Labour MPs who wanted the party to abandon its traditional devotion to state socialism. Pro-European unity and pro-NATO, he was one of the keenest supporters of Neil Kinnock, who, as party leader from 1983 to 1992, sought to modernize Labour. Blair was elected to the shadow cabinet by his fellow Labour MPs in 1988, when he was just 35. In 1992, after Labour's fourth successive election defeat, Kinnock resigned and John Smith became party leader. As shadow home secretary, Blair sought to jettison Labour's image of being "soft" on criminals. He employed the phrase "tough on crime, tough on the causes of crime" to summarize Labour's policies and attacked the Conservatives for their failure to tackle the underlying social causes of rising crime. While bolstering his public image, Blair sought to speed up the process of party modernization and was frustrated at what he felt was Smith's unwillingness to bring the party's constitution and economic and industrial policies up-to-date.

In May 1994 Smith died suddenly of a heart attack. There was little doubt who would win the contest to succeed him, and on July 21 Blair became party leader. About two months later he told Labour's annual conference that he wished to rewrite the party's constitution and abandon its commitment to "the common ownership of the means of production, distribution, and exchange." At a special conference in April 1995, he secured agreement to a new set of party objectives that explicitly acknowledged the virtues of market competition. Blair also sought to woo the middle classes by promising not to increase the standard rate or higher rates of the income tax. Within the Labour Party he acted to make it a more effective election-fighting force. He borrowed a number of techniques developed in U.S. Pres. Bill Clinton's 1992 and 1996 election campaigns; for example, he established a "rapid rebuttal" unit, employing the most up-to-date information technology, to respond swiftly to statements made by Labour's rivals. Blair summed up his reforms by describing his party not as Labour but as New Labour.

On the morning of May 2, following his landslide election victory, Blair said, "We were elected as New Labour; we will govern as New Labour." Fears that the party might break its pre-election promises, especially on taxation, were quickly quelled. Labour, and Blair personally, entered an extended honeymoon period with an electorate mostly delighted to see the end of the Conservative regime. Blair's opinion-poll ratings during the second half of 1997 were the highest for any prime minister since Winston Churchill, though late in the year his support was somewhat eroded by cuts in welfare benefits and reports of a tax haven for wealthy government ministers.

(PETER KELLNER)

Bowman, William Scott

In 1997 Scotty Bowman demonstrated why many considered him the greatest coach in the history of the National Hockey League as he posted his 1,000th regular-season victory, an NHL record, en route to guiding the Detroit Red Wings to the Stanley Cup championship, the team's first in 42 years. With the title—Bowman's seventh behind the bench—he became the only coach to win the Cup with three different teams, and he moved within one championship of Hector ("Toe") Blake's record (eight). Already a member of the Hockey Hall of Fame (1991), Bowman had rewritten the NHL record books during his 30 years in the league. Amid speculation that he would retire after the 1996–97 season, he signed a two-year contract extension to stay on as Detroit's coach.

Born on Sept. 18, 1933, in Montreal, Bowman dreamed of skating in the NHL, but a severe head injury sustained in junior hockey ended his playing career. He began coaching, working the bench for numerous youth, junior, and minor league teams until 1967, when he took over the reins of the St. Louis Blues, an NHL expansion team. He led the club to three Stanley Cup finals before signing with the Montreal Canadiens in 1971. Bowman quickly established Montreal as the NHL's dominant team of the 1970s, guiding it to five championships (1973 and 1976–79). In 1977 he won the Jack Adams Award as the NHL's coach of the year. After a stint with the Buffalo Sabres as general manager and, at times, coach (1979–87), Bowman joined the Canadian Broadcasting Corporation's "Hockey Night in Canada" as a television commentator. In 1990 he returned to the NHL as a member of the Pittsburgh Penguins' front office. As director of player development, he helped the club win the 1991 championship. When the team's coach, Bob Johnson, became ill during the 1991–92 season, Bowman assumed the responsibilities behind the bench, and the Penguins repeated as Stanley Cup champions.

By the time he joined the Detroit Red Wings in 1993, Bowman had become as known for his mind games as for his line changes, often switching players' positions and threatening trades to motivate his athletes. Controlling and uncompromising, he often drew the ire of players and fans. His methods, however, produced results. Under his leadership the Wings finished the regular season first overall in 1995 and 1996, reached the 1995 Stanley Cup finals, and set an NHL record for most wins (62) in a season (1995–96). During the 1995–96 campaign, Bowman broke Al Arbour's record of games coached (1,606) and received his second Jack Adams Award. After Detroit swept the Philadelphia Flyers to win the 1997 championship, Bowman donned a pair of skates to take a victory lap with hockey's Holy Grail. The move was unprecedented, as were most of Bowman's achievements. (AMY TIKKANEN)

Cárdenas Solórzano, Cuauhtémoc

In December 1997 Mexican leftist-opposition leader Cuauhtémoc Cárdenas of the Democratic Revolutionary Party (PRD) was sworn in as mayor of Mexico City, the first-ever elected mayor of North America's largest city. Previously, the president of Mexico had appointed the mayor. Having won the July 6 election in a landslide, with 47% of the vote, he had the largest margin of victory by an opposition leader since 1929. The governing Institutional Revolutionary Party (PRI) polled 26% of the vote, followed by the right-wing National Action Party, which registered 16%. His election represented an opportunity for change, especially to dispel the criminal reputation that the ruling PRI government had acquired for alleged drug trafficking, bribery, and political assassination.

KEITH DANNEMILLER—SABA

Cuauhtémoc Cárdenas

Cárdenas was born on May 1, 1934, the year that his father, Gen. Lázaro Cárdenas del Río, became president of Mexico. Raised within the confines of Los Pinos, the presidential palace, he led a privileged life. Later, after having worked almost 20 years in engineering, Cárdenas launched a political career and was elected (1976) to the Senate. In 1980, as a member of the PRI, he began a six-year term as governor of Michoacán, his father's native state.

Disillusioned with PRI maneuvers to undo reforms instituted by his father, Cárdenas split with the party in 1987. The following year he headed a coalition comprising Socialists and former Communists and made a bid for the presidency. In what Cárdenas believed to be an act of intimidation, his top campaign aide was murdered shortly before the election. While ballots were being tabulated, the government abruptly ended the count, declaring PRI candidate Carlos Salinas de Gortari president. Cárdenas continued to campaign during Gortari's six-year presidency, however, but ran third in the 1994 presidential election. In retaliation for Cárdenas's outspoken stand against government privatization and the North American Free Trade Agreement, Salinas's government targeted Cárdenas and his supporters. From 1988 to 1994 approximately 500 activists affiliated with the PRD were murdered.

Cárdenas returned, however, to clinch the 1997 Mexico City race for mayor. Promising to tackle problems never before addressed by PRI leaders, he campaigned against poverty, corruption, crime, and pollution—issues that had plagued Mexico City for years. His campaign trips into some of the poorest districts in Mexico City gained him favour in the eyes of the poor and middle class, who were discouraged by the lack of progress within the city and the criminal allegations surrounding the PRI. (HEATHER A. BLACKMORE)

Carrey, Jim

In 1997 comedian Jim Carrey again hit it big, this time with the film *Liar Liar,* in which he played a fast-talking lawyer forced—by a magic spell invoked by his young son by means of a birthday wish—to tell the truth for one day. It was an important turnaround for Carrey after the public's less-than-enthusiastic reception for his $20 million performance as an obnoxious cable television installer in the 1996 black comedy *The Cable Guy.*

Known for his racing energy level and frenetic improvisation, Carrey had a comic appeal that was mainly visual. With absolute control over his rubbery face, he was a technically brilliant mimic and boasted over 100 characterizations, with a repertoire ranging from Humphrey Bogart to Kermit the Frog. Carrey, who began his career as a stand-up comic, specialized in simple look-and-laugh escapist comedy routines. His success as the star of the film *Ace Ventura: Pet Detective* (1994) enabled him to command large salaries for subsequent movies. In 1995 he was nominated for a Golden Globe Award for his role in *The Mask* (1994), a variation of the Jekyll and Hyde story based on a popular comic-book character. In this film Carrey played a timid bank clerk who becomes a hip, wisecracking (albeit green-faced) dandy when he dons a magical mask.

Born on Jan. 17, 1962, in New Market, Ont., James Eugene Carrey grew up in and around Toronto. At age eight he began making faces before a mirror and discovered a talent for doing impressions. After leaving school in 1978 to help support his family, Carrey worked for two years as a janitor in a factory. He made his professional debut as a stand-up comedian in a Toronto club at the age of 15 and by 1979 had found that he was able to make a living as a comedian. He wrote most of his own material as an opening act for such comics as Buddy Hackett and Rodney Dangerfield.

At the age of 19 he moved to Hollywood, where he acted in films and on television. In 1983 Carrey played a role in the Canadian television film *Introducing…Janet,* for which he was nominated for an ACTRA Award. In the television series "The Duck Factory," Carrey played a young cartoonist who worked in a Hollywood animation studio. His first TV special, "Jim Carrey's Unnatural Act," (1991) received rave reviews and led to a regular role in the TV series "In Living Color." He made his film debut in *Finders Keepers* (1984). After the success of the first Ace Ventura film, he made several more comedies in rapid succession, notably *Dumb and Dumber* (1994), *The Mask,* and the second Ace Ventura film, *Ace Ventura: When Nature Calls* (1995). He also played the Riddler in the film *Batman Forever* (1995).

Although Carrey was best known for his comic roles, he occasionally took on more serious parts, as in *The Cable Guy* and *Introducing…Janet,* in which he played an unfunny would-be comedian. It was reported that he was venturing in that direction again with *The Truman Show,* the tale of a man who discovers that his apparently ordinary life is really a popular TV show; it was due for release in 1998. (DIANE LOIS WAY)

Carter, Chris

"The truth is out there." This enigmatic mantra appeared in the opening credits and was silently implied throughout each episode of Chris Carter's Emmy award-winning science-fiction television series "The X-Files." The series, which was filmed in Vancouver, B.C., debuted in 1993, and by 1997 it had become an international sensation. The story line followed two FBI agents who investigated paranormal activity and other bizarre phenomena. Fox Mulder (played by David Duchovny) was the believer, haunted by childhood memories of his sister's abduction by aliens and driven to find what he believed to be the truth. His partner, Dana Scully (Gillian Anderson), was a doctor and pathologist whose practical, scientific approach usually led her to play the devil's advocate and keep Mulder terrestrially grounded.

The program won immediate cult status, and many of the series' fans were tireless in their attempts to decode every detail—such as the meaning of some cryptic episode titles or the significance of Mulder's apartment number (42)—in an effort to piece together the ultimate truth behind the mystery that lingered on at the end of each episode. Although critics of the show expressed concern over its unhealthy effect on impressionable minds, Carter, the program's creator and executive producer, said that by bringing together those things that haunt the minds of the paranoid—conspiracy theories, alien abductions, government cover-ups, espionage, murder—he was able to "scare you in a smart way that makes you think and question."

Carter was born on Oct. 13, 1957, in Bellflower, Calif., a blue-collar suburb of Los Angeles. In 1979 he graduated from California State University at Long Beach with a degree in journalism and took a job as associate editor for *Surfing* magazine. During his five years there, Carter tried his hand at screenwriting. A script about three young men going off to Vietnam never made it to the big screen, but it encouraged him to write a second script—this time a comedy. Although that too was a failure, it brought him to the attention of Jeffrey Katzenberg, who was then chairman of Walt Disney Studios. Katzenberg hired him as a writer for "The Disney Sunday Movie," and Carter's interests switched from movies to television.

In 1995 Carter received an Emmy nomination for outstanding writing in a dramatic series for "The X-Files" episode "Duane Barry." In 1996 he created another series, "Millennium," in which a member of the mysterious Millennium Group investigated more earthly, yet still frightening, crimes and other weird phenomena supposedly arising as the world approached the new millennium.

At year-end 1997, fans could access the official X-Files Web site or read *The X-Files Official Magazine.* Finally, they could anticipate the 1998 release of *The X-Files* film, which promised to shed some light on at least a few of Carter's mysteries. "The truth is out there." "Trust no one."

(MARIA OTTOLINO RENGERS)

Charles, prince of Wales

During the 1990s Great Britain's monarchy was subject to more criticism—and more doubts about its future survival—than at any other time during the 20th century. In the eye of the storm was Charles, prince of Wales, eldest son of Queen Elizabeth II and heir to her throne. In particular, 1997 proved to be a turbulent year, in which he struggled with the aftermath of a difficult divorce, the death of his former wife, Diana, princess of Wales, and his attempts to secure public acceptance of his long-standing relationship with Camilla Parker Bowles.

Prince Charles Philip Arthur George was born at Buckingham Palace, London, on Nov. 14, 1948. He was the first heir to the British throne to go to school, as distinct from being educated by private tutors. Following five years of enduring the rigours of the Gordonstoun School in Scotland (1962–67), he entered Trinity College, Cambridge, graduating in 1970 with an honours degree in history. From 1971 to 1976 he served in the Royal Navy. On July 29, 1981, he married Lady Diana Frances Spencer. Their elder son, Prince William of Wales, became second in line to the British throne at his birth on June 21, 1982; Prince Henry, third in succession, was born on Sept. 15, 1984.

For a time Charles's marriage to Diana seemed the perfect match for a modern royal family, and the princess's glamour appeared to complement the prince's seriousness. Charles sought to widen the limits imposed by royal protocol, involving himself in those public debates in which he could participate without being seen as politically partisan. As president of the charity Business in the Community, he spent time in some of Britain's most deprived urban areas, coaxing companies into activities that would help to solve local problems. He also established a charitable foundation, the Prince's Youth Business Trust, to support mainly young people with the kind of entrepreneurial ideas that the banks seldom backed.

By the late 1980s strains in the marriage had become apparent, and they were increasingly widely reported in the media. In December 1992 Prime Minister John Major announced that Charles and Diana would separate. In February 1996 the couple agreed to divorce; their marriage formally ended on Aug. 28, 1996, with the decree absolute. By this time both Charles and Diana had admitted, in separate television interviews, that they had committed adultery during their marriage, in Charles's case with Parker Bowles.

The death of Diana in a car crash in Paris on Aug. 31, 1997, brought intense new pressures to bear on Charles. Opinion polls showed his reputation to be at a low ebb, with a majority of the British people wanting the crown to pass straight to Prince William when the reign of Elizabeth II came to an end. Charles, however, proved resilient in adversity. His dignity following Diana's death and his sensitive handling of her funeral, as well as a successful and widely publicized trip to southern Africa in November (accompanied by Prince Harry on his first overseas tour), helped to begin the process of restoring his appeal. By the end of the year, opinion polls were showing that Charles's standing in the U.K. had begun to improve.

(PETER KELLNER)

Cruz, Celia

By 1997 brash and sassy Cuban singer Celia Cruz, the "Queen of Salsa Music," had performed for more than 40 years, becoming the best-selling artist of that genre and an idol in the United States' Hispanic community. She was awarded the National Medal of Arts by U.S. Pres. Bill Clinton in 1994 for her contributions to the musical arts.

Cruz was born on Oct. 21, *c.* 1929, in Havana. She did not divulge the year of her birth. She grew up in Santos Suárez, a district of Havana, in an extended family of 14. After high school she attended the Escuela Normal para Maestros (Havana), intending to become a literature teacher. After winning a talent show, however, in which she interpreted the tango piece "Nostalgia" in a bolero tempo, Cruz interrupted her studies to pursue a singing career. Despite the misgivings of her father—who felt that music was a disreputable career—Cruz sang in amateur venues and on the radio. She also attended voice and theory classes at Havana's Conservatory of Music.

Her musical breakthrough came in 1950 when she replaced lead singer Myrta Silva of the popular orchestra La Sonora Matancera. Cruz sang regularly with the ensemble on radio and television, toured extensively, and appeared with it in five films produced in Mexico. She also headlined Havana's Tropicana nightclub in the 1950s.

After Fidel Castro's 1959 revolution, Havana's nightlife all but disappeared along with many of

Celia Cruz

GRANT LEDUC—CORBIS

Cuba's most talented performers. La Sonora Matancera left Cuba in 1960, working in Mexico for some 18 months before immigrating to the United States. In 1962 Cruz married the orchestra's first trumpet player, Pedro Knight, who became her musical director and manager after she became a solo artist. During the 1960s, however, Cruz did not experience in the U.S. the success she had enjoyed in Cuba, despite recording 20 albums for Seeco Records and several for Tico Records, including 7 with bandleader Tito Puente.

That success came after she became identified with salsa, a dance music that evolved from the musical experimentation of various Hispanic musicians with Caribbean sounds during the late 1960s. Cruz re-created herself for a younger generation of Hispanics by singing in the Latin opera *Hommy* (a version of the Who's *Tommy*) in Carnegie Hall and by recording updated, contemporary Latin music for Johnny Pacheco's Vaya record label (*Celia & Johnny,* 1974). With a voice described as operatic, she moved through high and low pitches with an ease that belied her age, and her style of improvising rhymed lyrics added a distinctive flavour to salsa.

In recent years Cruz earned renown in a wider circle. She was the subject of a BBC documentary, *My Name Is Celia Cruz* (1988), and appeared in the films *The Mambo Kings* (1992) and *The Perez Family* (1995). Her many honours ranged from an honorary doctorate of music from Yale University to a star on the Hollywood Walk of Fame and a 1990 Grammy award for her album *Ritmo en el corazón.* (SUSAN DOLL)

DeGeneres, Ellen

One of the most eagerly awaited events on television during the 1996–97 season was an episode of the sitcom "Ellen," in which the title character, portrayed by comedian Ellen DeGeneres, would reveal her sexuality. The groundbreaking story line came at the end of a long series of innuendo-riddled trailers and interviews and articles that speculated that both "Ellens" were gay. During that particular show, the rumour was confirmed, and "Ellen" became the first prime-time show to feature an openly gay lead character. In a *Time* magazine cover story, DeGeneres addressed her own sexuality by quipping, "Yep, I'm gay."

DeGeneres was born Jan. 26, 1958, in Metairie, La. There she and her older brother, Vance, were reared as Christian Scientists. When she was 13, her parents divorced, and DeGeneres moved with her mother to Texas. After graduating from high school, she briefly attended the University of New Orleans, where she majored in communications. Dissatisfied with university life, she left to work in a law firm. She then held a string of jobs, including waitress, bartender, house painter, and oyster shucker, before realizing that she wanted to be her own boss.

After putting together a comedy routine for a group of friends, DeGeneres was asked to perform in local coffeehouses. She was soon traveling through the United States on the comedy-club circuit, earning applause with her quirky, naive stories that were punctuated with her loose-limbed gestures. Her style was compared to those of Mary Tyler Moore and Lucille Ball. DeGeneres's act also caught the attention of HBO, and the cable network named her Funniest Person of the Year in 1982. Her career hit a high note in 1986 after she was invited to perform on "The Tonight Show Starring Johnny Carson." Following her side-splitting rendition of "Phone Call to God," Carson motioned DeGeneres to come and chat—the first time a female comedian had been given that honour.

Besides appearing on TV in stand-up comedy routines, DeGeneres had parts in such TV shows as "One Night Stand" (1989), "Open House" (1989–90), and "Laurie Hill" (1992) before starring (1994) as Ellen Morgan in "These Friends of Mine." The show's name was changed to "Ellen" the following season, and the anything-to-please bookstore owner and her friends soon became obligatory watching for millions of viewers. The show earned DeGeneres the 1995 People's Choice Favorite Female Performer in a New TV Series award and nominations for Golden Globe, American Comedy, and Emmy awards. In 1995 she was honoured with an American Comedy Award for her role as cohost of the "46th Annual Primetime Emmy Awards," to which she wore a dress, reportedly for the first time in 15 years. In 1997 "Ellen" was nominated for five Emmy awards.

DeGeneres, who appeared in such films as *Coneheads* (1993) and *Mr. Wrong* (1996), also published a book—*My Point—and I Do Have One* (1995). (LESLEY EDMONDSON)

Duany, Andres, and Plater-Zyberk, Elizabeth

In 1980 a Florida developer hired Andres Duany and Elizabeth Plater-Zyberk to design a resort called Seaside on 30 ha (80 ac) of Gulf Coast scrubland. By 1997 the Miami-based husband-and-wife team of architects and planners were transforming urban landscapes around the world with their pioneering design movement known as New Urbanism. "Without question," said urban critic Philip Langdon, "Duany and Plater-Zyberk have emerged as the masters and the most prolific practitioners of this new-old form of design."

Their rise to prominence began with their revolutionary scheme for Seaside. Instead of replicating the fortresslike condominium towers commonly found along the Florida coast, Duany and Plater-Zyberk turned to 19th-century town planning for their design cues, including the compact, picturesque streets of such cities as New Orleans and Charleston, S.C. One of their most radical prescriptions called for reserving the town's choicest real estate, the beachfront overlook, as the centrepiece of the community and site of its public square and marketplace. Clustered along gridded streets radiating from the town centre were low-rise houses designed with traditional roof lines and featuring picket fences. Housing densities were increased, which enabled residents to live within easy walking distance of shopping, the post office, and the beach. To promote spontaneous neighbourly interactions, the detailed building code mandated front porches in close proximity to the sidewalk and pedestrian paths.

Seaside caused an immediate sensation, and Duany and Plater-Zyberk's New Urbanism became as prominent in the popular press as in professional design journals. Whereas critics derided New Urbanist principles as an exercise in irrelevant nostalgia, supporters hailed them as an antidote to the anonymous, automobile-dependent suburban sprawl overtaking the U.S. Herbert Muschamp, architecture critic for the *New York Times,* called the movement the "most important phenomenon to emerge in American architecture in the post-Cold War era."

Following the development of Seaside, Duany Plater-Zyberk & Co. (DPZ), the pair's architecture and planning firm, designed more than 80 new towns and community-revitalization projects and drafted nearly a dozen development proposals for existing communities around the world. Projects ranged from plans for the town of Bamberton, a 880-ha (2,170-ac) site on the coast of Vancouver Island, British Columbia, that was intended as a model of ecological sustainability, to communities as humble as a 30-ha mobile-home park near Phoenix, Ariz. Moreover, DPZ's concepts inspired scores of neotraditionalist projects by others.

Duany and Plater-Zyberk's early success was rare in a profession in which critical acclaim often was not achieved until late in a career. Duany was born Sept. 7, 1949, in New York City and was raised in Cuba and Spain, the son of refugees who fled the Cuban revolution in 1960. Plater-Zyberk, the daughter of émigrés who escaped communist Poland in the late 1940s, was born Dec. 20, 1950, in Bryn Mawr, Pa. They both earned undergraduate degrees in architecture and urban planning from Princeton University and graduate degrees in architecture from the Yale School of Architecture. They moved to southern Florida in 1975, establishing DPZ in Miami in 1980. In 1995 Plater-Zyberk became dean of the University of Miami School of Architecture.

(ADELHEID FISCHER)

Atom Egoyan
PHM LOVINO—M.P.A./GAMMA LIAISON

Egoyan, Atom

Canadian film director Atom Egoyan, no stranger to the awards podium, cemented his reputation in 1997 when his latest movie, *The Sweet Hereafter,* won the Grand Jury Prize, the International Film Critics Award, and the Ecumenical Prize at the Cannes (France) International Film Festival. In December it won Canada's Genie Award as the year's best movie, and Egoyan won as best director. The film, which was based on a novel by Russell Banks, was a chilling depiction of characters in a small town divided by grief and greed following a tragic school bus accident. The movie, unlike Egoyan's earlier films, was the first to be based on another's work. Previously, Egoyan had written, produced, directed, and, in one instance, starred in his movies. The story line was also a departure from earlier ones, which had focused on an individual in extreme circumstances and had recurring themes of emotional detachment and sexual obsession.

Egoyan was born to Armenian parents on July 19, 1960, in Cairo, and from the age of three was reared in Victoria, B.C. Although he received a B.A. (1982) in international studies from the University of Toronto, his abiding interest in the arts prompted him to look toward a career in theatre. He had written his first play at age 13 and found a creative outlet in writing. At the university he immersed himself in artistic activity, writing plays and making short films.

In his first short film, *Howard in Particular* (1979), an aging employee is ushered into retirement by a tape recorder. That film's theme, an examination of the impact of technology on experience, recurred in such later films as *Peep Show* (1981) and *Family Viewing* (1987). In *Speaking Parts* (1989) a hotel employee is given the chance to play the lead in a film, and *Exotica* (1994), which won the International Film Critics Award at Cannes and eight Genie Awards in

Canada, depicted the patrons of an exotic strip club.

Egoyan drew upon his Armenian background and family experiences for such films as *Next of Kin* (1984), in which a young man masquerades as a lost son of an Armenian family; *Family Viewing,* a story about a man estranged from his Armenian wife; and *Calendar* (1993), in which Egoyan starred as a Canadian photographer taking snapshots of Armenian churches for a calendar. The premise for *The Adjuster* (1991) took shape as Egoyan studied the insurance agent who came to assess the damage to his family's business when it was destroyed by fire. Egoyan first gained widespread recognition when *Next of Kin* was chosen in 1984 to be shown at the Toronto International Film Festival.

Egoyan also worked in television, directing *Gross Misconduct* (1992), a TV movie about the life of hockey player Brian ("Spinner") Spencer, and episodes of "Alfred Hitchcock Presents" and "The Twilight Zone." In 1996 he mounted a production of the opera *Salome* for the Canadian Opera Company, and in 1997 he wrote the libretto for Rodney Sharman's opera *Elsewhereless.*

(DIANE LOIS WAY)

Favre, Brett Lorenzo

On Jan. 26, 1997, American professional football player Brett Favre proved himself leader of the pack as he guided the National Football League's (NFL's) Green Bay Packers to the team's first Super Bowl title in 29 years. En route to the Packers' 35–21 victory over the New England Patriots, the quarterback set a Super Bowl record for longest pass completion with an 81-yd touchdown throw. The win capped a season in which Favre won his second consecutive NFL Most Valuable Player (MVP) award and established himself as one of the league's dominant players. At the end of the 1997 season, he was again voted MVP, the first NFL player to win the award three years in a row. He again led his team to the Super Bowl, but the Packers lost 31–24 to the Denver Broncos in a contest that was not decided until the final seconds. In 1997 Favre released his autobiography, *Favre: For the Record,* which recounted his journey to the top.

Born Oct. 10, 1969, Favre grew up in Kiln, Miss., and was encouraged to play football by his father, who later coached his son in high school. Not heavily recruited by colleges, Brett ended up at the University of Southern Mississippi as the eighth-team quarterback. Armed with confidence and a powerful throw, however, he became the starter during his freshman year. After recovering from a serious car accident before his senior season, Favre was named MVP in the All-American Bowl and was selected by the Atlanta Falcons in the 1991 NFL draft. Following a rookie season spent mostly on the bench, he was traded in 1992 to the Green Bay Packers, where he quickly developed into one of the league's premier players. Originally the backup quarterback, he started for an injured teammate in the third game of the 1992 season and never relinquished the position. That year he was named to the National Football Conference (NFC) Pro Bowl team, the first of his four appearances (1992, '93, '95, and '96). In 1993 Favre proved his durability as he started in all 16 games and was first among NFC quarterbacks in completions (318). Known for his agility, competitiveness, and field presence, he was named MVP in 1995 as he led the NFC in passer rating (99.5) and touchdown throws (38) and posted the most passing yards (4,413) in the NFL. He also tied an NFL record for longest pass completion (99 yd).

The 1996 season proved a personal and professional triumph for Favre. He overcame an addiction to painkillers, won his second consecutive MVP award, set NFC and team records for most touchdown throws in a season (39), and led the NFC with 3,899 passing yards; it was his fifth consecutive year of throwing more than 3,000 yd.

(AMY TIKKANEN)

Fayed, Mohamed al-

Although frustrated in his efforts to be accepted as a British citizen, Egyptian-born billionaire Mohamed al-Fayed continued to play an influential—and highly controversial—role in Great Britain in 1997. Fayed's public feuds with the British establishment were credited with helping secure the election victory of Tony Blair's Labour Party and wrecking the careers of several Conservative politicians. Even the British royalty was entangled with Fayed when it was reported on August 31 that Diana, princess of Wales, had died in a car crash alongside Fayed's son Emad ("Dodi"), with whom she had been romantically linked; that evening the couple had dined at the Fayed-owned Ritz Hotel in Paris. The controversy sparked by the incident had not quieted by year's end. In December it was reported that Fayed was launching an investigation into the crash and had hired a former French police chief to head it. Days later Diana's family announced plans to sue Fayed for at least $13.3 million over the princess's death, since the car in which she died was driven by a Ritz employee, Henri Paul, who also was killed. Tests confirmed that Paul had been drunk at the time of the accident.

Fayed was born on Jan. 27, 1933, in Alexandria, where he founded his own company in 1956. From the 1960s he lived primarily in the United Kingdom. Among the vast holdings he had acquired were the famous Harrods department store, the venerable humour magazine *Punch,* and the Parisian villa of the late duke and duchess of Windsor, the contents of which were slated for auction in 1998.

Fayed's contentious relationship with the British establishment was well documented. In a rancorous takeover in 1985, he beat out mining giant Lonrho to purchase the House of Fraser, the holding company that controlled Harrods. Spurred on by Lonrho owner Roland ("Tiny") Rowland, the government accused Fayed of having misrepresented his ability to finance the takeover. Though Fayed proved his solvency, his wealth continued to be suspect in some quarters, and his name did not appear on *The Sunday Times* annual list of the wealthiest people in Britain until 1997. Fayed's relationship with the establishment was further strained by his involvement in the "cash-for-questions" scandal that arose in 1994 after Fayed named ministers who had accepted money from him in return for tabling parliamentary questions on his behalf. After the disclosures were made, two junior ministers resigned and a new committee was established to monitor standards at Westminster. Fayed's 1995 attempt to buy London News Radio and his 1996 bid to buy *The Observer* also attracted considerable publicity.

Though fallout from the deaths of Diana and Dodi Fayed was sure to continue in 1998, one bright spot could emerge on the horizon for Fayed in the form of a coveted British passport. Fayed's longtime hopes to become a British citizen were revived in December when the government announced that it would withdraw its appeal against a 1995 court decision that nullified earlier refusals of citizenship that had gone unexplained. This paved the way for Fayed to reapply for citizenship and to be given reasons for any rejection.

(TOM MICHAEL)

Fehn, Sverre

In 1997 the Pritzker Architecture Prize was awarded by the Hyatt Foundation to Norwegian architect Sverre Fehn, who for nearly half a century toiled both in the shadows of the great modern architects and, especially, in the long shadows, low light, and regional vernacular of Scandinavia, outside of which he remained little known. His corpus of completed works, largely museums and private houses, numbered about a dozen and seemed to meld elements of international influence—Mies van der Rohe, Le Corbusier, Louis Kahn, and Frank Lloyd Wright—with decidedly Scandinavian materials and designs. The design of his Glacier Museum (1991) in Fjaerland, Nor.—a long, low-lying, white-and-gray concrete structure with sloping ends—echoed the steep glaciers that surrounded it. Broad panels of green glass in the centre and two towering staircases at one end afforded views of the rocky, snow-covered mountain and bathed the museum in low, dusky light. The Hedmark Cathedral Museum (1979) in Hamar, Nor., was built astride the historic ruins of a 14th-century cathedral and manor house. The ancient building's rough fieldstone walls were juxtaposed with sleek, molded concrete ramps, pillars, and bridges.

Fehn was born on Aug. 14, 1924, in Kongsberg, Nor. Graduating from the Oslo School of Architecture in 1948, he became associated with the school's post-World War II graduates, which included architecture theorist Christian Norberg-Schulz. He received mentoring from Arne Korsmo, who designed the house in which Fehn lived and who introduced him to another mentor, French engineer Jean Prouvé. One of Fehn's first ongoing projects was the Handicraft Museum in Lillehammer, Nor. (1949–56). He first gained international acclaim in 1958 at the World Exhibition in Brussels, where his Norwegian Pavilion captured first prize in the design competition. Built in the International style, the low wooden building made a horizontal statement with its wide, overhanging, segmented eves. Fehn again received widespread notice with his Nordic Pavilion at the Venice Biennale in 1962, which also won first prize. The spaced rectangular forms—concrete inlaid with marble—were built around large, leafy trees, which created the effect of Venetian blinds by diffusing the strong Mediterranean light that entered the building through the latticed roof.

With Per Olaf Fjeld, Fehn wrote *Sverre Fehn: The Thought of Construction* (1983). From 1971 to 1993 he was a professor at the Oslo School of Architecture, and he lectured elsewhere in Europe and in the U.S. In 1997 he was working on an expansion for the Royal Theatre in Copenhagen.

(TOM MICHAEL)

Flatley, Michael

At the 1994 Eurovision Song Contest, held at the Point Theatre in Dublin, the most successful act was not even entered in the competition. An intermission entertainment entitled *Riverdance,* starring American dancer Michael Flatley, captivated the audience with a modern interpretation of traditional Irish dancing. His arms flying, Flatley leapt across the stage, transforming Irish dance from a rigid, tradition-bound art form that placed a premium on discipline and control into an expressive, buoyant celebration. The jubilant response to the seven-minute performance was overwhelming, and the producers of *Riverdance* soon expanded it into a feature-length spectacle that thrilled audiences in London and Dublin. Following a bitter creative dispute with the show's producers, however, Flatley was fired in October 1995. His response was to develop *Lord of the Dance,* a spectacular Las Vegas-style Celtic dance show that featured Flatley at his most flamboyant.

Flatley was born on July 16, 1958, in Chicago to Irish immigrant parents. Flatley, whose grandmother was a champion Irish dancer, began taking dancing lessons at the age of 11. His first teacher told him he had started too late to achieve real success, but Flatley persevered. When he was 17, he became the first American to win the all-world championship in Irish dancing. Flatley was also a Golden Gloves boxer and a champion flute player. None of these skills, however, seemed likely to help him earn a living, so he went to work for his father's contracting business and performed with local Irish dance groups in his spare time.

In the early 1980s Flatley was invited to tour with the traditional Irish musical group the Chieftains. It was on these tours that he developed and refined the progressive style of dance that became his trademark. He was soon recognized as a rising talent, and many awards and honours came his way, including a National Heritage fellowship and recognition by the National Endowment for the Arts for his contribution to dance. By the 1990s Flatley's reputation as a performer with incredible tap-dancing skills was firmly established.

Though *Riverdance* had established Flatley as a star, *Lord of the Dance* turned him into a one-man entertainment empire. In the spring of 1997, the show opened its U.S. tour in New York City with 13 sold-out performances at Radio City Music Hall. Although some critics considered *Lord of the Dance* to be an overblown exercise in self-indulgence, and dance purists cringed at the sequined jackets and tight pants that Flatley favoured, his talent and stage presence were undeniable. The public response was overwhelmingly positive, and by 1997 international sales of his live video, *Lord of the Dance,* had passed three million copies, and sales of the soundtrack CD that featured the music from the show approached 500,000 copies. Flatley also performed at the 1997 Academy Awards, a fitting stage for a performer who, having conquered the dance world, was now setting his sights on Hollywood and film stardom. (JOHN H. MATHEWS)

Ford, Harrison

In 1997 moviegoers were able to trace the path to stardom of versatile American actor Harrison Ford, whose brand-new blockbusters were screened alongside rereleased versions of the films that had begun his rise to fame two decades earlier. The *Star Wars* trilogy—*Star Wars* (1977), *The Empire Strikes Back* (1980), and *Return of the Jedi* (1983)—was reprised in early 1997 with Ford portraying maverick freedom-fighter Han Solo in the wildly popular space fantasies. In the spring he played a good-hearted American policeman at odds with a boarder (who unbeknownst to Ford is a member of the Irish Republican Army) in *The Devil's Own.* By July he was starring as the president of the United States in the action-thriller *Air Force One,* one of the summer's box-office smash hits. No stranger to popular success, he had appeared in 6 of the 30 highest-grossing films of all-time. Ford, a sturdy leading man, infused his characters with a stoicism and wry charm that recalled the likes of film star Gary Cooper. In May his rugged good looks won him inclusion in *People* magazine's cover story of the 50 most beautiful people in the world.

Ford was born on July 13, 1942, in Chicago and was raised in the city's suburbs. After attending Ripon (Wis.) College, he took minor acting roles in movies and television for Columbia and Universal studios but soon fell back on a sideline career in carpentry. His film career began in earnest with a bit part in the successful *American Graffiti* (1973), the first major work of director George Lucas. The movie was produced by Francis Ford Coppola, who later directed Ford in *The Conversation* (1974) and *Apocalypse Now* (1979). Ford struck pay dirt with Lucas's *Star Wars,* which became the highest-grossing motion picture ever. He followed with a series of small films but was unable to find true stardom until the 1980s.

His fame was cemented in two *Star Wars* sequels and, in another trilogy, as adventurer-archaeologist Indiana Jones. Produced by Lucas and directed by Steven Spielberg, *Raiders of the Lost Ark* (1981) and its two sequels (1984, 1989) featured Ford as a swashbuckling 1930s action hero whose larger-than-life qualities were tempered with a charming vulnerability. He expanded his repertoire in the science-fiction classic *Blade Runner* (1982), the drama *The Mosquito Coast* (1986), the thriller *Frantic* (1988), and the comedy *Working Girl* (1988). His performance in *Witness* (1985)—as an urban homicide detective hiding out in an Amish community—earned him an Academy Award nomination for best actor.

In the 1990s Ford accepted dramatic leading roles in *Presumed Innocent* (1990) and *Regarding Henry* (1991) and returned to romantic comedy with *Sabrina* (1995), but his fame rested with action-adventure movies. He portrayed CIA agent Jack Ryan in two popular films adapted from Tom Clancy novels—*Patriot Games* (1992) and *Clear and Present Danger* (1994). In *The Fugitive* (1993) he was the beleaguered Dr. Richard Kimble, on the lam after having been wrongly convicted of murdering his wife.

(TOM MICHAEL)

Freeman, Cathy

In 1997 Australian sprinter Cathy Freeman gained international renown not only for how she carried herself on the track but also for what she carried on the track. Exhausted after winning the 400-m event at the world track and field championships in Athens in August, she staggered through a victory lap under the weight of two flags: the Australian national flag and the native Aboriginal flag. As the first Australian Aborigine to win a world track title, she beamed, "I'm so glad of what I am. Australian and Aboriginal. They're two and the same." Some Australians, however, did not share her pride and viewed her flag-waving as an act of defiance, particularly in light of recent contention over land-rights issues between the government and the Aborigines, a tiny indigenous minority that had historically encountered discrimination. In spite of the controversy, Freeman remained an international celebrity, a role model to young women, an Aborigine heroine, and one of track and field's most exciting world champions.

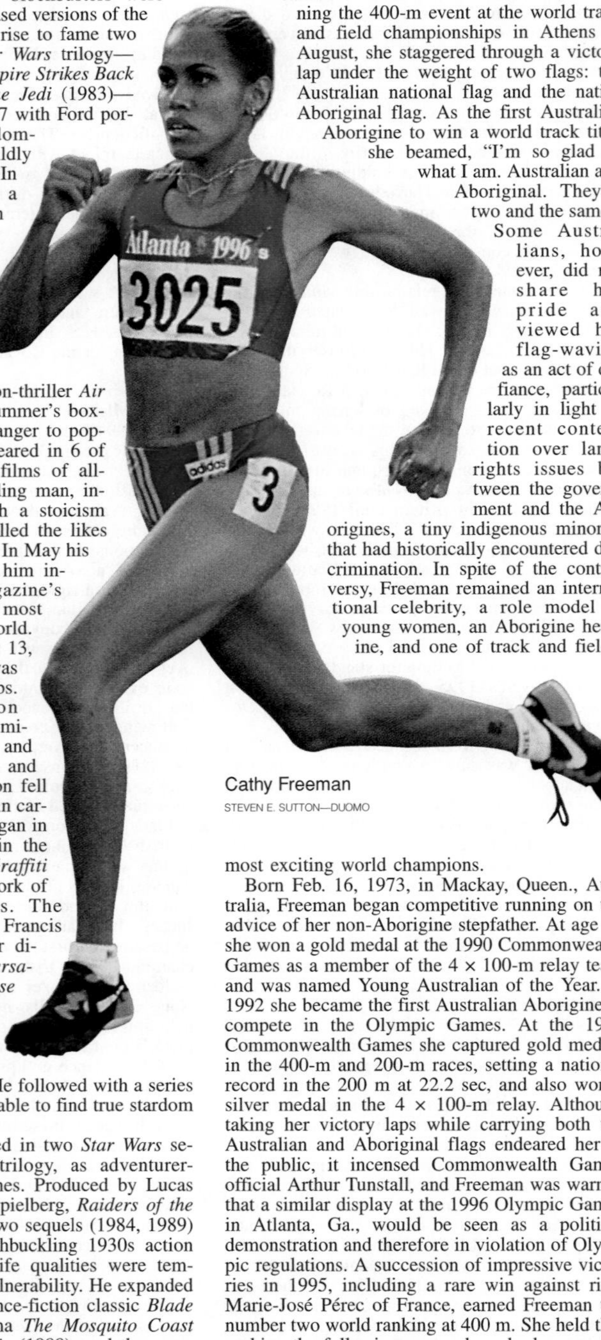

Cathy Freeman
STEVEN E. SUTTON—DUOMO

Born Feb. 16, 1973, in Mackay, Queen., Australia, Freeman began competitive running on the advice of her non-Aborigine stepfather. At age 17 she won a gold medal at the 1990 Commonwealth Games as a member of the 4 × 100-m relay team and was named Young Australian of the Year. In 1992 she became the first Australian Aborigine to compete in the Olympic Games. At the 1994 Commonwealth Games she captured gold medals in the 400-m and 200-m races, setting a national record in the 200 m at 22.2 sec, and also won a silver medal in the 4 × 100-m relay. Although taking her victory laps while carrying both the Australian and Aboriginal flags endeared her to the public, it incensed Commonwealth Games official Arthur Tunstall, and Freeman was warned that a similar display at the 1996 Olympic Games in Atlanta, Ga., would be seen as a political demonstration and therefore in violation of Olympic regulations. A succession of impressive victories in 1995, including a rare win against rival Marie-José Pérec of France, earned Freeman the number two world ranking at 400 m. She held that ranking the following year, when she became the first Australian woman to break 50 seconds at 400 m, which she did seven times in race finals.

At the 1996 Olympic Games, in what was considered one of the greatest 400-m matches, Freeman and Pérec led the field and were neck and neck down the final straightaway until Pérec outkicked Freeman, leaving her with a silver medal. Freeman finished the 1996 season with a string of Grand Prix victories at 400 m, and after a brief layoff, during which she shaved off her long hair, she returned to form in 1997 with the year's fastest 400-m time when she clocked 49.39 sec at Oslo in July. At the world championships, with Pérec a no-show, she won the 400-m gold in 49.77 sec, beating her training partner, Sandie Richards of Jamaica, to retain her number one world ranking. (TOM MICHAEL)

Fujimori, Alberto

In 1997 Peruvian Pres. Alberto Fujimori faced some of the most formidable challenges of his seven years in office. Peru had been stunned in December 1996 when left-wing guerrillas stormed the residence of the Japanese ambassador during a party and took hundreds of people hostage. As the ordeal continued into 1997, many of the hostages were released, and by April only 72 people were still being held. The standoff ended on April 22 when government troops attacked the building; all of the guerrillas were killed, and all but one of the hostages were freed without serious injury. Fujimori's popularity rose as he was credited with the successful resolution of the crisis.

A few short months later, however, the tide had turned and public support for him had reached an all-time low. His government was implicated in a phone-tapping scandal, and there was concern that he might have lost control to military and intelligence forces. After announcing his intention to seek a third term in the year 2000, Fujimori dismissed three Supreme Court justices, who had ruled that move unconstitutional. These actions led to the largest antigovernment demonstrations of his tenure and the resignation of several Cabinet ministers. Even potentially more ruinous, the political opposition alleged that Fujimori, a first-generation Peruvian of Japanese descent, had actually been born in Japan and therefore was ineligible to hold the office of president.

That accusation was vehemently denied by his family, who had emigrated from Japan in 1934 and insisted that Fujimori was born on July 28, 1938, in Lima, Peru. After earning (1961) an agronomic engineering degree from the National Agrarian University in Lima, he did postgraduate studies at the University of Strasbourg, France, and at the University of Wisconsin. Prior to his bid for the presidency, he held teaching and administrative posts at the university level, and he also served as host of the television program "Getting Together."

When Fujimori launched his 1990 presidential campaign, Peru's resources had been depleted by a decade of guerrilla war, and the country suffered from an unstable economy. Although a political outsider up to that time, Fujimori formed the political party Cambio (Change) 90 and mounted a grassroots campaign that involved selling his truck and tractor to secure campaign funds. To the surprise of many, he was elected president of Peru in a runoff election on June 10, 1990. Owing in part to his progress in checking both inflation and guerrilla activity, he won a second term in the 1995 election, securing almost two-thirds of the popular vote. Although the country's economy had greatly improved by 1997 and inflation was at its lowest rate in over two decades, Fujimori's prospect for a third term remained uncertain.

(SANDRA LANGENECKERT)

Gordon, Jeff

U.S. race-car driver Jeff Gordon sped into the history books in 1997, winning the National Association for Stock Car Auto Racing's (NASCAR's) Winston Cup season points championship for the second time, an unprecedented feat for a 26-year-old. He also became the first driver to win NASCAR's oldest race, the Southern 500, three years in a row. A handsome Californian whose clean-cut image differed sharply from the rough-and-tumble persona of the traditional stock-car driver, Gordon was disliked by many of his sport's fans. His rare misfortunes, such as a crash that put his Winston Cup hopes in doubt the day before the last race of the season, invariably drew loud cheers from the crowds who witnessed them. Still, Gordon, known popularly as "the Kid," had abundant talent, an aggressive driving style, and a knack for publicity, all of which were credited with drawing new fans to the fastest-growing sport in the U.S.

Gordon was born on Aug. 4, 1971, in Vallejo, Calif. As a child he raced BMX bicycles until his stepfather, a machinist, bought him a quarter-midget go-cart. Gordon won the national quarter-midget championship at age eight and again two years later. Racing more powerful go-carts, he routinely beat boys nearly twice his age. When Gordon was 13, his stepfather moved his family to Pittsboro, Ind., so that Gordon could legally drive a 650-hp sprint car in a race circuit that did not have a minimum-age requirement. By the time he was 18, Gordon had decided to take up stock-car racing. During the next two years, he gained invaluable experience at a number of driving schools, including that run by the National Motorsports Press Association's Hall of Fame race-car driver Buck Baker.

Racing in NASCAR's Busch Grand National Series (a level below Winston Cup competition), Gordon was named Rookie of the Year in 1991. In March 1992 Rick Hendrick, owner of a Winston Cup team, saw Gordon perform in a race in Atlanta, Ga., and signed him to a contract two days later. In 1993, his first full year of racing on the Winston Cup circuit, Gordon won no major races but did earn Rookie of the Year honours. He turned heads in 1994 when he won the inaugural Brickyard 400, the first major stock-car race held at the Indianapolis (Ind.) Motor Speedway. By 1995 he was winning at a steady clip, claiming his first season points championship that year while earning a record $4,347,343. To open the 1997 season, Gordon became the youngest driver in history to win the sport's premier event, the Daytona 500. Later he became the first driver since Bill Elliott in 1985 to win the Winston Million, a prize awarded to any driver who can win three of the sport's four most difficult races in one season. At the season's end Gordon led all drivers with a total of 10 victories and a record $6.5 million in earnings. (ANTHONY G. CRAINE)

Grove, Andrew S.

In January 1997 Intel Corp., the world's largest manufacturer of microprocessor chips used to control personal computers (PCs), announced record 1996 earnings of $5.2 billion from total sales that reached nearly $21 billion. For the company, which was founded in 1968, this was a far cry from its first-year revenues of $2,672. Much of Intel's success was credited to its CEO and chairman, Andrew Grove, whose own total 1996 earnings were estimated at more than $97 million. Grove, who had been with the Santa Clara, Calif.-based company since it was established, became CEO in early 1987. From that time the average annual return to Intel's investors was a lucrative 44%. Grove's advancement to the top at Intel was an impressive ascent for a young man who had arrived in the U.S. with reportedly only $20 in his pocket and limited English-language skills.

Grove was born Andras Grof in Budapest on Sept. 2, 1936, the son of a dairyman, and immigrated to the U.S. shortly after the suppression of the Hungarian revolt by the Soviet Union in 1956. He attended the City College of New York while working as a waiter, obtaining his B.S. degree in 1960. In 1963 Grove received a Ph.D. in chemical engineering from the University of California, Berkeley, and five years later he joined a new company that became known as Intel (a contraction for integrated electronics). The company introduced the world's first microprocessor in 1971, and the 8088 microchip, which Intel introduced in 1978, was chosen by IBM for use in its first personal computer. By 1997 Intel controlled 85% of the world's PC chip market, and it was estimated that in 1997 alone the company would ship over 80 million Pentium and Pentium Pro microprocessors.

Although the feisty Grove was one of the most respected managers in the industry, he was reported to occupy a simple work cubicle at Intel, eschewing the office trappings normally bestowed upon one of his business stature. It was a reflection of his open style of management, a style that had proved to be highly successful at Intel. In 1995 Grove underwent treatment for prostate cancer. By 1997, however, Grove's radiation treatments had been successful, and some analysts predicted that Intel was on its way to becoming the world's most profitable company.

(SANDRA LANGENECKERT)

Gwynn, Tony

U.S. athlete Tony Gwynn declared 1997 his best year in major league baseball. Few would argue with him. The San Diego Padres right fielder won his 8th batting crown, tying Honus Wagner for the National League record (Ty Cobb held the major league mark with 12), and recorded his 5th consecutive season batting .350 or better with an average of .372; his career average (.340) placed him 14th on the all-time list, tied with Lou Gehrig and George Sisler. In addition, Gwynn set personal highs during 1997 in home runs (17), runs batted in (119), extra-base hits (68), and total bases (324).

Born May 9, 1960, in Los Angeles, Anthony Keith Gwynn first attracted attention as a basketball player. He attended San Diego (Calif.) State University on a basketball scholarship and, as the Aztecs' point guard, set the school record for assists. Gwynn also played on the university's baseball team, and in 1981 he was selected in both the major league baseball and National Basketball Association (NBA) drafts. He turned down the NBA San Diego Clippers (later Los Angeles Clippers) to sign with the Padres. In 1983, his second year in the league, Gwynn batted .309; since then, he had not ended a season with an average below .300, and his current streak of 15 such seasons set a major league record. In 1984 he won the first of his eight batting titles (1987–89, 1994–97). His .394 average in 1994 was the highest finish in the major leagues since Ted Williams's .406 in 1941. Gwynn's success at the plate was due to outstanding hand-eye coordination, instinct for pitch selection, and a batting technique that was refined through countless hours of video analysis. While not a power hitter, he developed one of the sport's most efficient swings, reaching base on line drives and sharply hit grounders. Though best known for his offense, Gwynn also developed into a solid defensive player after initially struggling in the outfield; he was a five-time Golden Glove recipient (1986–87, 1989–91).

Possibly the only accolade missing from Gwynn's credits was a World Series title. The Padres' lone appearance in the championships came during the 1984 season, when they lost to the Detroit Tigers. Nonetheless, the 13-time all-star remained loyal to the Padres, forgoing free agency and signing for less money to stay with the franchise. In an era when professional players regularly changed teams, he proved a rarity.

(AMY TIKKANEN)

Hague, William Jefferson

On June 19, 1997, 36-year-old William Hague became the youngest leader of a major political party in the United Kingdom in 200 years. As the new leader of the Conservative Party, he embarked immediately on radical changes designed to reverse the fortunes of a party that had just suffered its worst election defeat since 1906.

Hague was born on March 26, 1961, at Rotherham, Yorkshire, into a family that ran a small soft-drink business. He attended local schools—like John Major, his immediate predecessor as Conservative leader, but unlike most prominent Tories. At the age of 12, Hague sold his collection of toy soldiers and began devoting his attention to politics. Four years later he spoke at his first Conservative Party conference. The confident attack on the then Labour government by a 16-year-old schoolboy with a pronounced northern accent captivated the media and impressed the Conservative leader, Margaret Thatcher.

Hague attended the University of Oxford, was elected president of the Oxford Union debating society, and obtained a first-class honours degree in philosophy, politics, and economics. After graduation he joined the Shell Oil Co. as a management trainee, but a year later he was recruited by the management consultants McKinsey and Co. In February 1989 he was selected to contest a by-election in the "safe" Conservative seat of Richmond, North Yorkshire, and within two years he had become parliamentary private secretary to the chancellor of the Exchequer, Norman Lamont. When Major, by then prime minister, appointed him secretary of state for Wales in 1995, the 34-year-old Hague became Britain's youngest Cabinet minister since Harold Wilson in 1947. Despite having no previous connections with Wales, Hague won the respect of his new constituents for his sympathy, good humour, and intelligence.

In May 1997, following the party's heavy defeat by the revived Labour Party under Tony Blair (*q.v.*), Major announced his resignation as Conservative Party leader. One of the men widely expected to take over, Michael Portillo, had lost his seat in the election and was out of the running, while other contenders from the party's right wing had their detractors. Hague stood on a centre-right, Euroskeptic platform and finally won on the third ballot.

Andrew Grove

LEIMDORFER—REA/SABA

Hague then set about reviving his party's fortunes. He announced a series of reforms, similar to those implemented by Labour in the 1980s and early '90s, to bring greater internal democracy to his party, including giving local party members a say in future leadership elections. In October, at his first party conference as Conservative leader, Hague sought to soften the party's image by declaring his support for more compassionate policies. He also advocated "understanding and tolerance of people making their own decisions about how they lead their lives," including accepting the rights of people to have gay relationships or to bear and raise children outside marriage. Hague's speech marked a clear break with the strictly pro-family ethos of the Thatcher years.

(PETER KELLNER)

Hanson, Pauline Lee

In April 1997 a new political party, One Nation, was formed in Australia by controversial independent MP Pauline Hanson, who in her short political career had become well known throughout the country for her extremist racist and anti-immigrant views. Despite harsh attacks on Hanson and her political opinions, she had developed a large following among some groups of Australians, and membership in and support for One Nation grew rapidly.

Hanson, born May 27, 1954, in Brisbane, Queen., was the mother of four, when her second marriage ended in the late 1980s. She settled in Ipswich, Queen., and opened a fish-and-chips shop, which she sold in early 1997. She was elected to the Ipswich City Council in 1994 but was defeated the following year. A member of the Liberal Party, she was forced out of the party in 1996 for her extremist views and ran successfully for Parliament as an independent in the March 1996 general election.

Hanson shocked Australia in September 1996 with her maiden speech to Parliament, in which she blamed Aborigines, Asian immigrants, and public policy regarding them for many of the country's problems, particularly its high unemployment rate (8.7% overall, with some areas as high as 30%). She stated that Australia was in danger of being overrun by Asians—who took jobs needed by Australian citizens and made no effort to assimilate into Australian society—and called for a short-term halt to Asian immigration. She also demanded that foreign aid be abolished and the money used to create jobs at home. On the subject of Aborigines, she said, "I am fed up with being told, 'This is our land.' Well, where the hell do I go? I was born here, and so were my parents and children. I will work beside anyone and they will be my equal but I draw the line when told I must pay and continue paying for something that happened over 200 years ago."

In August the Australian Electoral Commission redrew federal electoral boundaries in Queensland in order to create another seat for the growing population. Hanson's electorate, Oxley, was redistributed, which made it more difficult for her to be reelected—the newly drawn district contained a significant population of Asian immigrants. By September membership in One Nation and support for Hanson appeared to be declining.

(WENDY TANNER)

Helms, Jesse

Widely recognized as an icon of Republican conservatism, U.S. Sen. Jesse Helms of North Carolina exerted considerable influence over foreign policy in 1997 as chairman of the Senate Foreign Relations Committee. Portrayed by his critics as a demagogue and an extremist, Helms nevertheless displayed formidable skills as a politician, utilizing the power of his chairmanship to influence debate on foreign-policy issues and to stall the confirmation of White House nominees. In a well-publicized round of political hardball, Helms refused to schedule a confirmation hearing for Pres. Bill Clinton's nominee for the ambassadorship to Mexico, William F. Weld, a moderate Republican who was a two-term governor of Massachusetts. Eventually forced to hold a committee meeting on the subject in September, Helms invoked his right to set the meeting's agenda, which consisted only of a Helms monologue lambasting his opponents. Weld withdrew his name from consideration for the post the following week. Earlier in the year, Helms had flexed his political muscles by delaying a Senate vote on the Chemical Weapons Convention, a disarmament treaty that he opposed. The treaty was ratified, but not until Helms won key concessions from Clinton on another issue, the reorganization of foreign-policy agencies.

Helms was born in Monroe, N.C., on Oct. 18, 1921. After attending Wingate (N.C.) Junior College and Wake Forest College, Winston-Salem, N.C., he served in the U.S. Navy (1942–45). He worked as a journalist, congressional aide, and banking executive before embarking on a career as a political commentator for WRAL-TV (1960–72) in Raleigh, N.C. Originally a Democrat, Helms left the Democratic Party in 1970 and two years later won a Senate seat as a Republican. Having won every subsequent election, including a notoriously expensive race in 1984 against Gov. James B. Hunt, Jr., Helms was serving his fifth consecutive term in 1997.

As senator, Helms maintained a staunchly conservative stance on social issues, leading crusades against abortion and homosexuality, supporting prayer in public schools, and opposing the busing of students for racial integration. When the tobacco industry came under attack in 1997, he remained loyal to tobacco interests, as North Carolina was the country's leading tobacco producer.

Helms's installation as chairman of the Senate Foreign Relations Committee in 1994 assured him of a powerful voice in foreign affairs. With Republican Rep. Dan Burton of Indiana, he cosponsored the Helms-Burton Act (1996), which punished certain foreign companies that did business with Cuba. A longtime critic of the United Nations, Helms was the driving force behind budget cuts that forestalled payment of debts to the UN.

(AFRODITE MANTZAVRAKOS)

Hingis, Martina

Martina Hingis dominated women's tennis in 1997, winning three of the four major tournaments and replacing Steffi Graf as the world's top-ranked player. The latest teen sensation in women's tennis, Hingis was named after the legendary Martina Navratilova. The outstanding performance of the Swiss right-hander during the first three years of her professional career suggested that she would build a legacy equal to that of her namesake.

Hingis was born Sept. 30, 1980, in Kosice, Czech. (now Slovakia). Her mother, Melanie Molitor, a former top tennis player in Czechoslovakia, and her father, a tennis coach, wasted little time before introducing their daughter to sports. Hingis could ski and play tennis at three, and she began entering tennis tournaments at five. Following her parents' divorce, she moved with her mother to Trübbach, Switz., at seven. Molitor then began coaching her daughter in tennis intensively, and Hingis improved rapidly. She defeated older opponents regularly and at 12 became the youngest-ever Grand Slam junior titlist when she won the 1993 junior French Open. In 1994 she won in France again and then became the youngest junior Wimbledon champion weeks later. In October of the same year, shortly after her 14th birthday, Hingis turned professional. Three months later she became the youngest player to win a match at a Grand Slam event when she advanced to the second round of the 1995 Australian Open. Partnered with Helena Sukova, Hingis became the youngest player ever to win at Wimbledon when the pair took the doubles title in 1996.

Hingis's decision to turn pro at such a young age was controversial. Navratilova spoke out publicly against it and refused to watch Hingis play during the early stages of her pro career. Many of the age-related records broken by Hingis had been set by Tracy Austin, Jennifer Capriati, and Andrea Jaeger, all three of whom had seen similarly promising young careers come to an untimely end. Soon after Hingis's pro debut, the Women's Tennis Association instituted new rules that prohibited 14-year-olds from regular tour events and allowed 15–17-year-olds gradual exposure to major tournaments. Hingis, however, seemed immune to the pressures of pro tennis. Her victories appeared effortless, and she displayed a casual, confident demeanour when being interviewed by reporters.

She opened 1997 ranked fourth in the world and won six straight tournaments, including the Australian Open, and 40 consecutive matches. Along the way she gained the top ranking after defeating Monica Seles in the final of the Lipton Championships. A knee injury suffered in April while horseback riding sidelined Hingis only briefly. Her winning streak was halted when she was upset by Iva Majoli in the French Open final, but she rebounded to win at Wimbledon and the U.S. Open.

(ANTHONY G. CRAINE)

Holyfield, Evander

In one of the strangest boxing matches in history, Evander Holyfield successfully defended his World Boxing Association (WBA) heavyweight title against Mike Tyson on June 28, 1997, in Las Vegas, Nev. Holyfield was in clear control of the bout when Tyson, while in a clinch with Holyfield in the third round, suddenly bit a chunk out of the champion's right ear. The referee gave Tyson a warning, but when the fight resumed after a doctor indicated that Holyfield could continue, Tyson unaccountably bit the champion on the left ear and was disqualified. A riot nearly erupted when members of both corners, photographers, and police officers rushed into the ring. Tyson's bizarre behaviour—and the gruesome scene it engendered—created a furor that overshadowed Holyfield's second victory over a fighter once thought to be invincible. Holyfield cemented his position as boxing's best heavyweight later in the year when he defeated International Boxing Federation (IBF) titleholder Michael Moorer by technical knockout on November 8.

Holyfield was born on Oct. 19, 1962, in Atmore, Ala. He began boxing competitively at the age of eight and eventually compiled an amateur record of 160–14. At the 1984 Olympic Games in Los Angeles, he fought as a light heavyweight and was awarded the bronze medal after being disqualified on a controversial call in the semifinal bout. He soon turned professional, and in July 1986 he won the junior heavyweight title by upsetting WBA champion Dwight Muhammad Qawi in a grueling 15-round battle.

In April 1988, with an eighth-round knockout of Carlos DeLeon, Holyfield became boxing's first undisputed cruiserweight champion. He became a heavyweight later that year. At 1.89 m (6 ft 2½ in) and 97.5 kg (215 lb), Holyfield was smaller than most of his opponents, but his quickness and his ability to take a punch helped to make up for his lack of size. A devout Christian, he credited his faith for also giving him extraordinary willpower and courage. On Oct. 25, 1990, Holyfield scored a third-round knockout of James ("Buster") Douglas to win the undisputed heavyweight title of the WBA, the IBF, and the World Boxing Council.

Holyfield held the title until November 1992, when he dropped a 12-round decision to Riddick Bowe. In a rematch with Bowe one year later, he recaptured the WBA and IBF titles in another decision. After losing the championship belts once again when Moorer earned a decision against him in April 1994, Holyfield was diagnosed with a heart defect and announced his retirement. Though the diagnosis was later reversed and Holyfield returned to the ring, his career was thought to be on the ropes after he turned in a string of lacklustre performances. On Nov. 9, 1996, Holyfield had his first clash with Tyson in a much-anticipated WBA title bout. Despite being a 25–1 underdog, Holyfield shocked the boxing world when he scored a technical knockout of Tyson in the 11th round. The victory made Holyfield the only fighter besides Muhammad Ali to have won the heavyweight championship three separate times.

(ANTHONY G. CRAINE)

Hughes, Robert Studley Forrest

Following three years of work, respected Australian art critic and writer Robert Hughes launched

WALLY SANTANA—SYGMA

Hun Sen

in May 1997 an eight-part television series for PBS—*American Visions: The Epic History of Art in America.* Like the richly illustrated companion book of the same title, the highly acclaimed series explored the emergence of art in the United States as a reflection of the political and social events of the times. Hughes, who had a distinctive style of criticism—characterized by a dynamic, accessible, and succinct writing style—narrated the TV series and provided the text for the companion book.

Hughes was born on July 28, 1938, in Sydney. After graduating (1956) from St. Ignatius College, a Jesuit school in Sydney, he entered the University of Sydney. Though initially drawn to law and architecture, he abandoned his studies when, though not formally trained, he began painting and drawing political cartoons for local newspapers. He turned to art criticism when he covered an art show for a newspaper that had fired its critic. His lifelong interest in modern art inspired him to continue writing criticism for such Australian journals as the *Observer* and the *Nation.* In 1961 he was hired to write an exhibition catalog and contracted by Penguin Books to write a history of Australian art. Though he completed his studies in architecture in 1962, he had already found his niche in art criticism.

Hughes moved to Italy in 1964, traveling extensively to study firsthand the painting and architecture of Europe. The result was a second book, *Heaven and Hell in Western Art* (1968). By that time he had settled in London and had established himself as a freelance writer for *The Observer* and the *Sunday Times* newspapers. He also produced dozens of art documentaries for BBC-TV. On the basis of his growing reputation, he was hired in 1970 by *Time* magazine to serve as its art critic.

Hughes's television initiation in the United States came in 1978 when he was named cohost of the ABC-TV magazine series *20/20.* His debut was a failure, but he rebounded nicely with the eight-part television series *The Shock of the New,* an exploration of the impact of modern art and architecture. Appearing on PBS in 1981, the series showcased his prickly, critical style, his refreshingly frank viewpoint, and his penetrating appraisals.

Other books followed, including *The Fatal Shore* (1987), an epic history of his native Australia, as well as *Barcelona* (1992) and *The Culture of Complaint* (1993). Hughes, the only critic to twice receive the Frank Jewett Mather Award (1982 and 1985), also was given an honorary doctorate (1995) from the University of Melbourne and elected (1993) to the American Academy of Arts and Letters.

(SUSAN DOLL)

Hun Sen

On July 5, 1997, Hun Sen, the second prime minister of Cambodia, ordered troops to attack the stronghold of Prince Norodom Ranariddh, the first prime minister and the son of King Norodom Sihanouk. The attack signaled the collapse of Cambodia's four-year-old coalition government, which had been mandated by UN-organized elections after nearly two decades of civil war ended in 1993. Relations between the ministers, uneasy at best, had become increasingly bitter as Prince Ranariddh tried to forge an alliance with Khmer Rouge party members who had defected to the government during the preceding year.

Born in 1950 or 1952 in Kompang, Cambodia, Hun Sen was educated in Phnom Penh at the Buddhist monastery Wat Tuk La'ak. In the late 1960s he joined the resistance Communist Party of Kampuchea. He soon became a courier for the local communist leader and in 1970 joined the Khmer Rouge movement, rising to the position of commandant. During Pol Pot's regime, when the Khmer Rouge killed more than one million people (1975–79), Hun Sen fled to Vietnam, joining pro-Vietnamese troops against the Khmer Rouge. He returned to Cambodia after the Vietnam-backed takeover and was eventually installed as chairman of the Council of Ministers, having previously served as minister of foreign affairs and deputy prime minister. He led the country until the 1993 elections.

Although Prince Ranariddh's royalist Funcinpec Party (FP) had garnered more votes than Hun Sen's Cambodian People's Party, Hun Sen refused to cede power, and the international community eventually agreed to the compromise partnership between the two leaders. Under a new constitution, the Cambodian people began to rebuild their country. With general elections scheduled for 1998, however, both Hun Sen and the prince jockeyed for support from smaller parties, and Hun Sen feared that the defecting Khmer Rouge leaders might distance themselves from their past and successfully realign with Prince Ranariddh. A deal signed by a Khmer Rouge faction with the FP on July 4 was said to have provoked Hun Sen's violent coup d'état on July 5.

In the days immediately following the coup, government troops reportedly conducted door-to-door searches to locate FP members, at least 40 of whom were executed. Fighting, which had started in Phnom Penh, advanced northward through the summer and fall to other royalist holdouts, as well as to villages held by former Khmer Rouge guerrilla fighters. Thousands of Cambodians fled to Thailand to escape the violence. While Prince Ranariddh sought international support, Hun Sen told foreign governments and the Association of Southeast Asian Nations not to interfere in what was merely a law-enforcement issue. He and his party named a token FP official to replace the prince as first prime minister, but Hun Sen continued his tactics of domination and intimidation through the end of the year. Some believed that because of his age and unpredictability, Hun Sen had generally been underestimated by outsiders.

(REBECCA RUNDALL)

Jospin, Lionel

On June 1, 1997, the people of France elected a Socialist Party (PS) majority to the National Assembly, and two days later party leader Lionel Jospin assumed the office of prime minister, sending a clear message to Gaullist Pres. Jacques Chirac: his austere plan to guide France into the European Union (EU) was not acceptable. Jospin offered a perfect tonic to Chirac and Prime Minister Alain Juppé, who had angered many French voters with their stern, rather condescending style and their hard-edged policies to privatize industries and cut back entitlements at a rapid pace. During his campaign Jospin showed a ready smile and a clear respect for working people as he argued for a shortened workweek, reduced unemployment, and a more thoughtful transition into the EU. During the first months of his term, however, he surprised many in the business world with his pragmatic leadership. Whereas he often clashed with the conservative Chirac, he also pursued moderate policies of privatization and fiscal restraint that would put France more in step with the global economic environment.

Born July 12, 1937, in the Parisian suburb of Meudon, Jospin inherited many of his Socialist beliefs from his schoolteacher father. After two years of obligatory military service, he entered (1963) the École Nationale d'Administration, the training ground for nearly all of France's governing elite. He graduated near the top of his class and joined the Foreign Ministry. Amid the protests against Gaullist leadership in the late 1960s, Jospin became restless with his place in the government bureaucracy, and he was sent to the U.S. to study. In 1970 he returned to France and took a position at the University Institute of Technology of Paris-Sceaux, where he taught economics until 1981.

Jospin joined the PS in 1971 and won his first parliamentary seat six years later. He soon became a favourite of party leader François Mitterrand, and when Mitterrand became president in 1981, Jospin was promoted to the head of the party. As minister of education during Mitterrand's second term, Jospin developed a plan to build new class-

Lionel Jospin

ALAIN BUU—GAMMA LIAISON

rooms throughout the country, as well as seven new universities, but he also encountered problems. In 1989 he made the decision to allow Muslim female students to wear the veil in public schools, a violation of the principle of separation of church and state in the view of many French people.

In the early 1990s Jospin's political career was in severe decline. He lost his Cabinet post in 1992 and his parliamentary seat in 1993. In 1995, with Mitterrand dying of prostate cancer and many of the other PS leaders reeling from revelations of financial improprieties, the party turned to Jospin as its candidate for president. Although Jospin ran with no platform and little fanfare, he astonished everyone by winning the preliminary round of the vote. In the runoff he earned an impressive 47% of the vote but came in second to Chirac. When scandal again haunted the PS leaders in 1997, Jospin was asked to be the party's candidate for prime minister. This time he won.

(JAMES HENNELLY)

Kabila, Laurent Desire

After having dropped out of sight for nearly a decade, Zairean opposition leader Laurent Kabila reemerged in October 1996 as leader of the newly formed Alliance of Democratic Forces for the Liberation of Congo-Zaire. Supported by a nation outraged by the dictatorial leadership of Mobutu Sese Seko, Kabila rallied forces consisting mostly of Tutsi from eastern Zaire and marched west toward the capital city of Kinshasa, forcing Mobutu to flee the country before their arrival. On May 17, 1997, Kabila installed himself as head of state. He also rejected the name Zaire, which Mobutu had given the country in 1971, and reverted its name to the Democratic Republic of the Congo. In September Mobutu died in Morocco after having squandered the country's mineral-rich resources and having left it poorer than it had been since before independence in 1960. As the country's leader, Kabila inherited an economy that by 1994 had shrunk to 1958 levels, although the population had tripled. By 1997 commercial banks had recorded only about 8,000 accounts from a population of more than 46 million.

Kabila was born in 1939 into the Luba tribe in Jadotville, a city in the Belgian Congo's southern province of Katanga. He studied political philosophy at a French university and attended the University of Dar es Salaam, Tanz., where he met and formed a friendship with Ugandan Yoweri Museveni (*q.v.*). In 1960 Kabila became a youth leader in a political party allied to Congo's first postindependence prime minister, Marxist-Maoist Patrice Lumumba. Lumumba was deposed in 1961 by Mobutu and later killed. Assisted for a time in 1964 by guerrilla leader Che Guevara, Kabila helped Lumumba supporters lead a revolt that was eventually suppressed in 1965 by the Congolese army led by Mobutu. Mobutu seized power that same year. Kabila then founded (1967) the People's Revolutionary Party, which established a Marxist territory in the Kivu region of eastern Zaire and managed to sustain itself through gold mining and ivory trading. When that enterprise came to an end during the 1980s, he ran a business selling gold in Dar es Salaam until he resurfaced in Zaire.

Kabila charged that under Mobutu's rule the country had been sold out to international capitalists who sought to plunder Zaire's resources. In August 1997 he pledged, "We came to rebuild the country. We will...halt the intolerable interference of foreign powers in our internal affairs." Kabila publicly stated that his model for Congo's future was the one fashioned by Museveni, who as president of Uganda had turned around the economy by embracing capitalism. Regional support was swelling for the new Kabila government, but international bodies raised several reservations. Reportedly, Kabila's troops had been responsible for the murders of thousands of Hutu refugees who had fled Rwanda into Zaire in 1994. In addition, many international aid agencies had been denied access into the country to assess the needs of the people. Although it was too soon to be certain what direction the Kabila government would eventually take, the United States government offered aid and believed that Kabila could be encouraged to accept elections soon.

(ANTHONY L. GREEN)

PHOTO NEWS/GAMMA LIAISON

Laurent Kabila

Kadare, Ismail

Albanian poet and novelist Ismail Kadare, a resident of Paris since 1990, was hard at work in 1997 revising his collected works, which were being published—some for the first time—in both French and Albanian. His 1978 historical novel *Ura me tri harqe* was translated into English as *The Three-Arched Bridge* (1991) and received critical acclaim. Kadare's self-imposed exile brought him a freedom to publish and speak that he had rarely, if ever, experienced in his native country. These newfound freedoms came years after he had alternately sought an official relationship with Albania's pro-Stalinist leader Enver Hoxha (they were born in the same town) and yet criticized Hoxha's dictatorial rule. The contradictory actions made Kadare a somewhat controversial and suspect figure. Some of his works had been banned or had remained unpublished, but others seemed a dutiful knuckling under to the party line and as such were artistically undistinguished. Although attitudes toward his works remained mixed, most reviewers believed that Kadare had done much to shape Albanian literature and to bring Albanian letters into the 20th century.

Kadare was born in Gjirokastër on Jan. 28, 1936, at a time of great turmoil in Albania. He attended the University of Tiranë and, until Soviet-Albanian ties became strained, the Gorky Institute of World Literature in Moscow. Upon his return to Albania in 1960, Kadare became a journalist and also initiated his literary career. He first won recognition in his native country with his poetry, but the work that brought him international attention was *Gjenerali i ushtërisë së vdekur* (1963; *The General of the Dead Army,* 1971), a perceptive evaluation of postwar Albania. In *Kështjella* (1970; *The Castle,* 1974), his next significant work, Kadare explored Albanian nationalism by examining the time during the 15th century when Skanderbeg became an Albanian hero. Both this novel and *Kronikë në gur* (1971; *Chronicle in Stone,* 1987), a powerful portrait of the historic city of Gjirokastër under occupation, captured the hearts of the Albanian people. In 1973, however, a political purge of several intellectuals prompted Kadare to cover himself by writing a politically expedient novel, *Nëntori i një kryeqyteti* (1975; "November of a Capital City"). This was followed by *Dimri i madh* (1977; "The Great Winter"), which, despite its unrealistically rosy view of Hoxha, depicted the fascinating story of Albania's break from the Soviet sphere.

Many of Kadare's later works, including *Komisioni i festës* (1977; "The Celebration Commission"), *Pashallëqet e mëdha* (1978; "The Great Pashalics"), and *Krushqit janë të ngrirë* (1986; "The Wedding Procession Turned to Ice") presented views of critical times in Albanian history. His *Nëpunësi i pallatit të ëndrrave* (1981; *The Palace of Dreams,* 1993), set in the time of the Ottoman Empire, was perhaps his masterpiece.

(KATHLEEN KUIPER)

Kawamoto, Nobuhiko

When Nobuhiko Kawamoto, president of Honda Motor Co., Ltd., visited Soichiro Honda a few months before the legendary industrialist's death in 1991, he said to the old man, "You left behind lots of good things but also things that are not right for the present." Honda responded, "Times change. You should do things the way you want to." Kawamoto took Honda's advice to heart and immediately set about not only reviving a slumping corporate giant but radically transforming its management structure. With a hands-on, dictatorial style that differed sharply from that of his predecessors, Kawamoto forced engineers to heed marketing studies and cut new-car-development costs. He also frequently bypassed top executives to communicate directly with employees at all levels of the company. The results were spectacular. Net profit for 1996 zoomed to a record $1,780,000,000. In 1997 Honda passed Mitsubishi Motors Corp. to become the third-leading automaker in Japan, and the company's North American sales, buoyed by sporty new models, were expected to jump 9% and top one million units for the first time.

Kawamoto was born on March 3, 1936, in Tokyo. He developed a passion for cars early in life, and as an engineering student at Tohoku University, he organized a club that fixed up automobiles left behind by U.S. occupation forces. Kawamoto idolized Soichiro Honda for his maverick spirit and interest in racing cars, and he went to work for the research-and-development wing of Honda after earning a master's degree in 1963. He quickly gained a reputation as a talented engineer, excelling as a designer of Honda's racing-car engines. Kawamoto became a director of Honda in 1981, a senior managing director in 1989, and president in 1990.

As president, Kawamoto eschewed traditional consensus-style management and held himself accountable for the decisions he made. Though he often came across as abrasive and admittedly preferred tinkering with car engines to thinking about running a company, he showed an undoubtedly keen sense for business. After the burst of Japan's vulnerable asset-inflated "bubble" economy in the early 1990s, Kawamoto decided to place more emphasis on marketing.

(TEIJI SHIMIZU)

Khatami, Mohammad

With strong support from the young and from women and intellectuals, the charismatic Mohammad Khatami took nearly 70% of the vote in Iran's presidential elections on May 23, 1997. He was one of only four persons approved by the Council of Guardians to run for the office and of the four decidedly the most moderate, particularly on questions of social policy. His victory, in what was called the first freely contested presidential election under the current Islamic regime, raised questions both within Iran and throughout the world about possible changes in policy in that Islamic republic.

Khatami was born in 1943 in Ardakan in central Iran and was the son of a well-known religious teacher. He studied theology at schools in Qom and in Esfahan and later took university degrees in philosophy and education. In addition to Farsi, he spoke Arabic, English, and German. During the 1960s and '70s, he wrote pamphlets against the rule of Mohammad Reza Shah Pahlavi. In 1978 Khatami was appointed head of the Hamburg Islamic Center in Germany, and in 1979 he was elected to the national assembly and appointed head of a group of pro-government newspapers. For a decade, beginning in 1982, he was Iran's minister of culture and Islamic guidance, but he was forced to resign in 1992 on charges that he was too permissive in allowing books, magazines, and films that some considered subversive. He then became the director of the National Library and a teacher and adviser to the government. Khatami held the title Hojatolislam, signifying his position as a midlevel cleric, and as a direct descendant of the Prophet Muhammad, he wore a black turban.

Although Khatami had the support of the outgoing moderate, president Hojatolislam Ali Akbar Hashemi Rafsanjani, Khatami's principal opponent, Ali Akbar Nateq-Nouri, the speaker of the assembly, had the tacit support of Iran's political and religious leader, Ayatollah Sayyed Ali Khamenei. Voters, nonetheless, overwhelmingly chose Khatami, apparently both for his more tolerant social views and for his promise to deal with the country's high inflation and unemployment. He took office on August 3. Among his Cabinet appointments were two controversial nominees—Ataollah Mohajerani, who had advocated talks with the United States, as minister of culture and Islamic guidance (Khatami's former position) and Abdollah Nouri as interior minister, a moderate who would help determine policy on social mores. There also were objections to his choice for foreign minister, Iran's ambassador to the United Nations, Kamal Kharrazi, who had studied in the U.S., but the conservative assembly approved all nominees. In December Khatami stated that he hoped to achieve "a thoughtful dialogue with the American people." Observers noted, however, that the power of the Iranian president to formulate policy was strictly limited and that foreign policy particularly remained in the hands of spiritual leader Khamenei. (ROBERT RAUCH)

Kim Dae Jung

On Dec. 18, 1997, Kim Dae Jung became the first opposition leader to be elected president of South Korea. During his campaign Kim had called for a "horizontal change of power" between the ruling and opposition parties, contending that such a change was necessary for further development of Korean democracy. He also sharply criticized the economic policies of the ruling party candidate, Lee Hoi Chang.

Kim's strategy paid off at the polls. In a hotly contested race, he managed to eke out a victory by a narrow 1.6% margin, earning 40.3% of the vote to Lee's 38.7% and third-party candidate Rhee In Je's 19.2%. Despite being a native of one of the southwestern Cholla provinces, which were disdained by many people elsewhere in South Korea, Kim won surprising support from the midwestern and southeastern regions. He accomplished this in part by allying his party, the National Congress for New Politics (NCNP), with the United Liberal Democrats (ULD), whose leaders were influential in those regions. In return for their support in the presidential election, Kim promised to establish a coalition government with the ULD once he had taken office.

Only six months before the election, a victory for Kim seemed impossible, as Lee enjoyed the support of more than 50% of those polled. Lee's reputation for integrity was damaged in August, however, when both of his sons were accused of having intentionally lost weight in an effort to evade compulsory military service. Moreover, Lee lost much of his support in the southeastern regions to Rhee, who ran independently after failing to capture the ruling party's presidential nomination.

The 1997 election was marked by the emergence of televised debates between the candidates, the neutrality of the outgoing administration, and a high level of political participation among South Koreans. All of these factors greatly aided Kim, a talented public speaker and veteran politician.

Kim was born on Dec. 3, 1925, in Mokp'o, South Cholla province and was the son of a farmer. He graduated from the Mokp'o School of Commerce at the top of his class in 1943. After a brief stint in business, he became an ardent pro-democracy activist in the 1950s. He was elected to the National Assembly in 1960, the first of six terms he would serve over the next 35 years.

In 1971 Kim ran for president against Park Chung Hee, a race many believed Kim would have won had the election been fairly conducted. In 1973 Kim was abducted in Tokyo by Park's agents; he was spared execution only after South Korea relented under intense diplomatic pressure from the U.S. and Japan. Kim later served a total of six years in prison for his pro-democracy activism. Released from prison in 1982, he was exiled to the U.S., where he spent 26 months.

Allowed to return to South Korea, Kim re-entered politics but failed in his presidential bids in 1987 and 1992. He formed the NCNP in 1995, stressing the need for a strong opposition party in a country dominated by one-party rule. In his speeches as well as in numerous books and articles, Kim expressed his long-held conviction that Western-style democracy was quite compatible with East Asian values and economic development. (JUNGBOCK LEE)

Lawless, Lucy, and Sorbo, Kevin

Playing ancient warriors on the television shows "Hercules: The Legendary Journeys" and its spin-off, "Xena: Warrior Princess," actors Kevin Sorbo and Lucy Lawless conquered their toughest opponent in 1997—the fickle TV viewer—to become king and queen of the syndicated small screen. The well-oiled hero and the leather-bustier-clad heroine outmuscled their competition with a combination of high camp and moral storylines that appealed to a diverse audience. The shows' phenomenal success spawned Xena and Hercules clothing, action figures, trading cards, conventions, and hundreds of Web sites and catapulted Sorbo and Lawless into stardom. As fans clamoured to see more of the actors in 1997, Sorbo appeared as a legendary barbarian in the feature film *Kull the Conqueror,* and Lawless made her Broadway debut as Rizzo in *Grease!*

Born on Sept. 24, 1958, in Mound, Minn., Sorbo left the University of Minnesota one semester short of graduation to pursue a career in acting. Following a small role in an episode of the television series "Dallas" in 1983, he headed to Europe, where he began modeling and acting in TV commercials. Sorbo, who appeared in more than 150 television spots, moved to Los Angeles in 1986. After a number of auditions and small parts on television, he won the lead role of the Greek demigod Hercules in a series of made-for-TV movies, beginning with *Hercules and the Amazon Women* (1994). Their huge success led to the creation of the weekly hour-long show "Hercules: The Legendary Journeys," which debuted in 1995. The program—filmed in Auckland, N.Z.—combined, to great effect, computerized special effects, elaborate fight scenes, contemporary references, and a vocabulary filled with modern American slang. Sorbo's tongue-in-cheek portrayal of the brawny but sensitive hero—accompanied by his faithful sidekick, Iolaus (played by New Zealand actor Michael Hurst)—helped make the show an instant hit. The Xena spin-off soon followed, with a third show, "Young Hercules," in the works.

Lawless, who was born Lucy Ryan on March 28, 1968, in Mount Albert, N.Z., first acted in school drama productions. After traveling throughout Europe and Australia, working at times as a grape picker and a gold miner, she married Garth Lawless (they were later divorced) and moved back to New Zealand. While rearing her daughter, Daisy, she returned to acting, performing in commercials and in small parts on television and in movies. Her breakthrough came with a guest appearance on "Hercules" as Xena, a female warrior whose punch was as fierce as her banshee-like battle cry: "Yi yi yi yi yi!" In 1995 a separate program was created for her character. As the statuesque warrior who vanquished evil and broke hearts, Lawless combined toughness and femininity to redefine television's version of the female action hero. Strong images of women, mixed with humour, special effects, and lesbian undertones between the warrior and her sidekick, Gabrielle (American actress Renee O'Connor), attracted a widespread audience that soon rivaled that of "Hercules" in number and made Lawless the centre of a cultlike following.

The growing popularity of Sorbo and Lawless, however, may have signaled the end of their work as the ancient warriors. Although "Xena" and "Hercules" were renewed through the 1999–2000 season, both actors suggested that they might leave the show at the turn of the century to pursue other projects. (AMY TIKKANEN)

LeBow, Bennett S.

On March 20, 1997, the Liggett Group, the fifth largest tobacco company in the United States, took an unprecedented step in the controversy over the dangers of smoking. Bennett S. LeBow, chairman, president, and CEO of Liggett's owner, Brooke Group Ltd., admitted in a settlement with 22 states that cigarette smoking is addictive and causes cancer.

Liggett, whose brands included Chesterfield, Eve, Lark, and L&M, held only 2% of the U.S. tobacco market and continued to lose business. The company had a negative net worth and was unable to pay its debts. LeBow's move was seen by many as a strictly financial one, intended both to prevent Liggett from sliding into bankruptcy and to make it attractive to potential buyers; the settlement would limit the amount of money Liggett had to pay in other tobacco industry legal settlements and thereby protect new owners from financial backlash. LeBow called Liggett's agreement "a business, a moral, and a personal decision."

LeBow was born in Philadelphia in 1938. He received an engineering degree from Drexel University, Philadelphia, and did postgraduate work at Princeton University. In 1961 he formed a computer company, DSI Systems, Inc. During the 1970s and 1980s, he was successful as a financial speculator. In one notable venture he made a profit of $30 million on sales of stock in cigarette maker American Brands. LeBow acquired Liggett in 1986, 20 years after he himself had quit smoking. As recently as 1993 in a lawsuit, he maintained solidarity with the heads of the other big tobacco companies by refusing to admit any knowledge of the dangers of smoking. In early 1996, however, Liggett became the first tobacco company to arrange a monetary settlement in a class-action lawsuit, although the amount was small. Some said LeBow's plan at the time was to merge Liggett with the much larger firm RJR Nabisco, which would participate in the settlement and be free from future litigation. LeBow then hoped to profit by splitting RJR into two parts, food and tobacco.

The statement signed by LeBow in March included frank admissions about the hazards of smoking. In it he affirmed that "we at Liggett know and acknowledge that, as the Surgeon General and respected medical researchers have found, cigarette smoking causes health problems, including lung cancer, heart and vascular disease and emphysema. We at Liggett also know and acknowledge that...nicotine is addictive." Later in the document he also admitted that "the tobacco industry markets to 'youth,' which means those under 18 years of age." The statement also promised that Liggett would turn over pertinent documents to plaintiffs' lawyers in tobacco lawsuits. LeBow's settlement was immediately attacked by larger tobacco companies such as Philip Morris, which claimed it was made simply as a business ploy and had no basis in fact.

By mid-1997 Liggett had begun labeling its cigarette packages with the warning "Smoking is addictive." In June LeBow announced the company's intent to list all ingredients, including nicotine levels, on all cartons of cigarettes. Liggett was the first company to take such a step.

(WENDY TANNER)

Lemper, Ute

With the release in 1997 of the recording *Berlin Cabaret Songs,* Ute Lemper confirmed her standing as the foremost modern interpreter of the music of 1920s Germany. Including songs by a number of composers banished from the country by the government of Adolf Hitler, the recording was a vivid re-creation of the German cabaret music of the period. The release by Decca/London was part of its *Entartete Musik* ("Degenerate Music") series, documenting works that had been banned by Nazi Germany and, as a consequence, sometimes forgotten. As a way of reaching a larger audience, Lemper recorded each song in both German and English, with the versions in the two languages being released separately.

Lemper was born on July 4, 1963, in Münster, W.Ger. Her mother was an opera singer, and the girl began piano, voice, and ballet lessons at an early age. She took children's parts in operettas and plays, sang in jazz and piano bars as a teenager, and later studied acting and theatre in Stuttgart, W.Ger., and in Vienna. In 1983 she appeared in a Viennese production of *Cats,* and she later took the title role in *Peter Pan* and the role of Sally Bowles in *Cabaret.* After several years away from the musical theatre, she returned in 1997 in a starring role in the London revival of *Chicago.* Her first recording (1988) of the music of Kurt Weill rose to number one on *Billboard* magazine's crossover chart. Lemper later released a second recording of the music of Weill—also a best-seller—as well as recordings of *The Threepenny Opera* (1988) and *Mahagonny-Songspeil* (1989), among Weill's best-known collaborations with Bertolt Brecht. Other recordings include *Illusions,* an homage to Marlene Dietrich and Edith Piaf that was another best-seller and that led to Lemper's being named the Crossover Artist of the Year in 1993.

During the late 1980s and the early '90s, Lemper appeared in a review of Weill's music and wrote the script for a musical biography of him, danced in the ballet *La Morte subite,* created for her by Maurice Béjart, and took the role of Lola in a stage production of *The Blue Angel.* She appeared in films, including Peter Greenaway's *Prospero's Books* (1991) and Robert Altman's *Ready to Wear* (1994). Her paintings were shown in Hamburg, Ger., and Paris, and a collection of essays and reminiscences was published as *Unzensiert* in 1995. She received a number of awards, including the French Culture Prize in 1993.

It was as a songstress, however, and particularly as an exponent of the popular music of the Weimar Republic, that Lemper achieved renown. Critics agreed that she brought the right kind of theatricality to the music, an ironic and sardonic art of political and social satire and one that was unusually frank in matters of sex. She was sometimes called its best interpreter since Dietrich and Lotte Lenya. Through her recordings Lemper helped audiences become acquainted with a music that, although banished two generations earlier, continued to speak to the human condition.

(ROBERT RAUCH)

Lomax, Alan

A monument of sorts was partially unveiled in 1997—*The Alan Lomax Collection: Southern Journey,* a set of six compact discs that included blues, hymns, and spirituals. Over the next five years, Rounder Records was to continue to issue in segments the complete collection of over 100 hour-long CDs from the Lomax Archive at Hunter College, New York City. These recordings formed the core of a truly monumental folk music archive built up over 60 years by Lomax. Prolific writer, tireless collector, and avid promoter of folk music from the American South and around the world, Lomax helped shape the musical landscape of the 20th century.

Lomax was born Jan. 15, 1915, in Austin, Texas. His father, John Lomax, was a pioneer in folklore studies, one of the first to focus on contemporary folk music and to transcribe it. In 1933 Alan and his father lugged a 160-kg (350-lb) recording machine through the South in pursuit of folk music for the Library of Congress. For about a decade the Lomaxes traveled through small towns, farms, and prisons, making thousands of recordings. One early discovery was Huddie Ledbetter ("Leadbelly"), a remarkable singer and guitar player who was serving a sentence for murder in a Louisiana prison. After his release in 1934, Leadbelly went with the Lomaxes to New York City, where the "sweet-singing convict" caused a minor sensation with such now-classic songs as "Goodnight, Irene" and "The Midnight Special."

Alan Lomax went on to record numerous hitherto-unknown folk, blues, and jazz musicians. In 1938 he recorded jazz pianist Jelly Roll Morton, later writing a biography, *Mr. Jelly Roll* (1950). He was the first to record blues singer Muddy Waters. Lomax introduced the world to bluesmen such as Fred McDowell and folk singers Woody Guthrie and Pete Seeger. During the 1950s Lomax embarked on a project to collect folk music from around the world, including the Caribbean, the British Isles, Spain, Japan, and Italy. "Before Alan came along," said the British folklorist Peter Kennedy, "we really only knew American folk song. We didn't know we had anything in our own country."

In the 1960s Lomax helped lead the American folk music boom and wrote many popular and academic books, such as *The Penguin Book of American Folk Songs* (1964) and *Folk Song Style and Culture* (1968). He went on to develop (with Victor Grauer) "cantometrics," a statistical method for comparing singing styles and anthropological data. In 1990 he produced the critically acclaimed television documentary series *American Patchwork,* and in 1993 he released his book *The Land Where the Blues Began.* Most recently Lomax was working on a "Global Jukebox," a multimedia database of song and dance styles, representing more than 600 cultures. Lomax's work earned him the National Medal of Arts and a MacArthur Foundation grant.

(BENJAMIN SCHALET)

Lubich, Chiara

More than 50 years ago, amid the rubble of an Italian town ravaged by heavy bombing during World War II, Chiara Lubich and a few close friends ministered to the needs of their homeless and devastated neighbours. From the ashes of destruction arose a group dedicated to healing the rifts that divide humans—the Focolare Movement. Since founding the organization in 1943, Lubich had worked tirelessly to promote religious dialogue between people of disparate faiths, and the Focolare Movement, which was rooted in Roman Catholicism but extended its ties to other religions, had spread throughout the world. For her contribution to the cause of peace and inter-religious understanding, Lubich was awarded the UNESCO Prize for Peace Education in December

Ute Lemper

O. ABOLAFIA—GAMMA LIAISON

MARCELLO CASUBOLO—CENTRO S. CHIARA AUDIOVISIVI

Chiara Lubich

1996. On a trip to the U.S. in 1997, she led an international convention in New York, visited and spoke at a Harlem mosque, and received an honorary doctorate from Sacred Heart University, Fairfield, Conn., for her efforts to promote Christian-Jewish dialogue.

Lubich was born on Jan. 22, 1920, in Trento, Italy. She was training to be a teacher when World War II broke out. Living in fear in war-torn Trento, she and her companions often gathered in underground shelters to read the Gospels. The stark contrast between the message of love they found in their readings and the hatred they saw in the war spurred them to action. Soon after the group began to offer assistance to the needy, 500 people from various walks of life joined their cause. The residents of Trento named the community Focolare ("fireplace") to indicate the warmth and closeness of home that the members of the group engendered. After the war numerous Focolare centres were formed, first throughout Italy and then across Europe and other continents. Eventually the movement expanded to include 2.2 million adherents in 198 countries worldwide.

In 1962 the Focolare Movement was approved by Pope John XXIII as an association of the faithful. In the following years Lubich was heavily involved in both ecumenical and interfaith work, for which she was awarded the Templeton Prize for Progress in Religion in 1977.

In her travels around the world, Lubich rarely let any opportunity to spread her message of "love and unity" escape. Invited to Tokyo to speak to Buddhists of the Rissho Kosei-kai movement in 1981, she became aware during her trip that members of Asian Focolare communities needed help in developing a better understanding of indigenous Eastern religions. To address this need, she founded the School for Oriental Religions in Tagaytay, Phil. The horrors of poverty Lubich witnessed on a trip to Brazil inspired her in 1991 to found the Economy of Communion project, through which businesses committed a share of profits to alleviating poverty and creating jobs.

In 1994 Lubich was named honorary president of the World Conference on Religion and Peace. The recipient of many additional awards and honours, she was also the author of a number of books, including *On the Holy Journey* (1988).

(MARY JANE FRIEDRICH)

Luzhkov, Yury Mikhaylovich

In September 1997 Moscow Mayor Yury Luzhkov was host of a lavish birthday party for his native city. The three-day extravaganza, which cost at least $60 million, was intended not only to celebrate Moscow's rich 850-year history but to show the world that the Russian capital, already home to two-thirds of the country's foreign investment, was eager to maintain its rapid pace of development. Since becoming mayor in 1992, Luzhkov had transformed Moscow into the engine of post-Soviet state capitalism, overseeing a wave of entrepreneurialism and a building boom that pushed office rents higher than those of New York City. The birthday bash over which Luzhkov presided also marked his unofficial entry into the race to succeed Russian Pres. Boris Yeltsin, who indicated that he would not seek a third term in 2000. Even though he had not announced his candidacy, Luzhkov was cited as the front-runner in a poll published in October. His June unveiling of a regional television network owned and operated by the city was further testimony to the mayor's desire to reach a wider audience.

Popular and powerful, Luzhkov was the quintessential *khozyain* ("boss"), a strong-willed, at times bullying, leader who had harnessed his loyal team to the single goal of remaking the city of Moscow. Through careful manipulation of post-Soviet privatization, the city owned about 1,500 businesses outright and had a financial stake in some 300 more. Luzhkov took a personal interest in these enterprises, from regular visits of construction sites to approving the menu and logo of Russkoye Bistro, a fast-food chain created to compete with McDonald's. Though cognizant of mafia influence in some new businesses, his administration was untainted by any major scandals. Outlying provinces harboured suspicions of Moscow's newfound wealth, but Luzhkov was praised by his constituents, nearly 90% of whom reelected him over a communist challenger in June 1996.

Often appearing in public in an open collar and peaked leather cap, the mayor affected a populist stance in his public battles with the Kremlin. Although he had backed Yeltsin in times of crisis—the coup attempt of August 1991, the parliamentary revolt of October 1993, and the presidential elections of June and July 1996—Luzhkov was often critical of the president and his young reform-minded advisers, particularly First Deputy Prime Minister Anatoly Chubais. Luzhkov frequently squared off against Chubais over the handling of the privatization process in Moscow. In 1994 Luzhkov persuaded Yeltsin to give him control over the city's vast inventory of state holdings, and in 1996 Moscow took in $1 billion in privatization revenues.

Luzhkov was born into a poor Muscovite family on Sept. 21, 1936. He studied mechanical engineering at Gubkin Academy of Oil and Gas in Moscow and worked as a technical manager until 1987, when he became first deputy chairman of the Moscow government. In 1990 he rose to the position of executive committee leader under Mayor Gavril Popov, and he became deputy mayor when Popov was reelected in 1991. Popov's resignation in June 1992 prompted Yeltsin to name Luzhkov the new mayor.

(TOM MICHAEL)

McTeer, Janet

In 1997 British actress Janet McTeer, little known to U.S. audiences, took New York City by storm after making her Broadway debut in Anthony Page's revival of Henrik Ibsen's *A Doll's House.* With a commanding stage presence (she stood 1.85 m [6 ft 1 in]), the striking blonde delivered what was described as a "perfect" performance as the childlike Nora. She evoked a gamut of emotions, ranging from sensitivity to sensuality and from vulnerability to boldness. For her portrayal she won a Tony award for best actress in a play.

McTeer was born on May 8, 1961, in Newcastle, Eng. At the age of 17, she left her hometown to enter the Royal Academy of Dramatic Art in London. In 1984 she made her stage debut at the Nottingham (Eng.) Playhouse in *Mother Courage and Her Children.* Following that performance she worked steadily either on stage, in film, or on television. It was her work as a classically trained stage actress, however, that defined her career.

Among her theatre credits were roles in plays by Shakespeare and Chekhov and performances

SONIA MOSKOWITZ—GLOBE PHOTOS

Janet McTeer

with the Royal Shakespeare Company, Queen's Theatre, Manchester Royal Exchange, and the Royal National Theatre. McTeer was nominated for Olivier awards for her leading roles as Mary in Timberlake Wertenbaker's *The Grace of Mary Traverse* (1985) and as Yelena in Chekhov's *Uncle Vanya* (1992). On U.S. television she appeared in such "Masterpiece Theater" productions as "102 Boulevard Haussman," "Precious Bane," and "Portrait of a Marriage," in which she starred as British novelist Victoria ("Vita") Sackville-West. McTeer also was the voice of Sackville-West for the 1996 audio book *In Your Garden.* McTeer's British TV performances included roles in the miniseries "The Governor" (1996), and such made-for-TV films as *A Masculine Ending* (1992), and *Dead Romantic* (1993), and she also appeared in motion pictures, among them *Half Moon Street* (1986) and *Carrington* (1995).

McTeer believed that "you can [touch people] via a camera but it's good to have direct contact with an audience." She accomplished that while perfecting the role of Nora in Britain, first on radio and then at the Playhouse Theatre in London. For her performances there she was the recipient of an *Evening Standard* and an Olivier award. (ANTHONY L. GREEN)

Manning, Preston

In the Canadian general election held on June 2, 1997, Preston Manning's Reform Party of Canada received 19% of the popular vote and won 60 seats in the House of Commons. Thus, barely 10 years after its founding in 1987, the Reform Party had risen from a western fringe party to become the official opposition, with Manning becoming leader of the opposition. He had not even held elected office until 1993, when he was voted into Parliament for the riding of Calgary Southwest.

Manning was born on June 10, 1942, in Edmonton, Alta., into a family deeply involved in politics. His father, Ernest, was leader of the Alberta Social Credit Party, premier of Alberta (1943–68), and a Canadian senator (1970–83). After graduating from the University of Alberta with a degree in economics (1964), the younger

Manning spent three years working on projects for his father. He followed in his father's footsteps as a populist and an evangelical Christian fundamentalist and gave sermons on the elder's radio program, the "Back to the Bible Hour." After running unsuccessfully as a candidate for the Social Credit Party in the 1965 federal election, he helped his father write *Political Realignment* (1967), a book that outlined a social conservative agenda for Canadian politics and was a synthesis of marketplace economics and humanitarian socialism. After his father retired from provincial politics, Manning launched a career as a management consultant in the energy industry.

In 1987, however, he returned to the political arena and founded the Reform Party in an effort to gain economic and political power for the western provinces. Four years later the party voted to expand its regional base and become a national force. A new party mission was also outlined in Manning's book, *The New Canada* (1992), and later was adopted. Its goals were to work for a balanced, democratic federation of provinces and to recognize that all provinces and citizens were equal. As the first and only leader of the party, Manning formed its name, its statement of principles, and many of its policies, and it came to represent a mixture of his populist views and the conservatism of most party members. Manning saw populism as the "common sense of the common people" and espoused policies that would allow the populace to have more say in the development of public policy. Some, however, voiced fears that Manning was trading popularity for principles. After the 1993 election he underwent a physical transformation that included eye surgery, hair colouring, a sleek new wardrobe, and voice training. He also rescinded an earlier vow not to live in Stornoway, the official residence of the opposition leader, and in September 1997 he supported the Calgary declaration that recognized Quebec's "unique" character, an action that made traditional party members uneasy.

Although the Reform Party was disappointed that in the 1997 election no party candidates were elected outside the western provinces, it expected that the strong showing of the party would give the Canadian West a greater voice in the federal government. (DIANE LOIS WAY)

Mueller, Lisel

Throughout a long-established career as a poet, Lisel Mueller had been honoured with a number of literary awards, ranging from the National Book Award in 1981 for *The Need to Hold Still* (1980) to the Illinois Poet Laureate Award in 1987, but in 1997 she found herself celebrating an unexpected honour. With a body of work heralded as quiet and powerful, enchanting and warm, Mueller won the 1997 Pulitzer Prize for Poetry for her collection *Alive Together: New and Selected Poems.*

Lisel Neumann, the daughter of schoolteachers, was born on Feb. 8, 1924, in Hamburg, Ger. During the mid- and late 1930s, she and her family moved often and abruptly to places such as Italy and France to evade Nazi persecution. In 1939, at the age of 15, she fled Europe with her mother and sister. Her father, Fritz Neumann, had already acquired a professorship at Evansville (Ind.) College (now the University of Evansville), and the family established a residence there. It was those experiences in particular that inspired themes pertaining to a cultural and family history in poems that were often dour and explicit yet sensuously palpable.

The death of her mother in 1953 prompted Mueller to begin writing in earnest. In "When I Am Asked" she says, "I sat on a gray stone bench ringed with the ingenue faces of pink and white impatiens and placed my grief in the mouth of language, the only thing that would grieve with me."

Drawn to the modernist school of writing, Mueller was highly influenced by such poets as W.H. Auden, T.S. Eliot, and Edna St. Vincent Millay. Mueller's lyrical poetry bent toward the mythological, depicting fantastic characters and dreamlike milieus with the sturdy, accessible diction often found in folklore. In "Paul Delvaux: The Village of the Mermaids" she wrote:

The mermaids, if that is what they are
under their full-length skirts,
sit facing each other
all down the street, more of an alley,
in front of their gray row houses.
They all look the same, like a fair-haired
order of nuns, or like prostitutes
with chaste identical faces.
How calm they are, with their vacant eyes,
their hands in laps that betray nothing.
Only one has scales on her dusky dress.

Prior to achieving universal acclaim as a poet, Mueller wrote prose. Her first major publication was a book of essays printed in 1965. She also worked as a book reviewer for the *Chicago Daily News* before becoming a founding member of the Poetry Center of Chicago. Later Mueller frequently taught and gave lectures on creative writing at the University of Chicago, Elmhurst (Ill.) College, and Goddard College, Plainfield, Vt.. Some of her other volumes of poetry include *The Private Life* (1976), *Waving from Shore* (1989), and *Learning to Play by Ear* (1990).

Mueller, the mother of two daughters, resided in Lake Forest, Ill., with her husband of 53 years. Although she was nearly blind, suffering from the degenerative eye disease glaucoma as well as cataracts, she continued to render poems with strength in the midst of grief and tragedy, fantasy within the vivid harshness of reality.
(JACKIE ORIHILL)

Murdock, Richard D.

In 1997 Rick Murdock, CEO of CellPro, Inc., a small biotechnology firm based in Bothell, Wash., was in the midst of a battle for the company that had saved his life. In late 1995 the then 48-year-old Murdock, a successful executive with no family history of cancer, found lumps in his neck and groin. He was eventually diagnosed with advanced mantle cell lymphoma, a rare and deadly form of cancer. Murdock needed to find a treatment, and fast—the average life expectancy following such a diagnosis was only about 30 months. Fortunately, he had an advantage not afforded others in his position; his best hope for a cure was right in his own backyard.

At the time Murdock announced his condition, CellPro, founded in 1989, was working on cell separation technology that it hoped would improve the outcome of bone marrow transplants, which were used to treat a variety of cancers, including mantle cell lymphoma. Because Murdock's cancer was so advanced, the project was given top priority, and within a couple of months his researchers believed that they had found a viable treatment. The U.S. Food and Drug Administration granted CellPro a "compassionate use exemption," which allowed the company to test the new treatment on Murdock in June 1996. It was a success; within a month after Murdock completed the procedure, test results revealed that he was free of cancer.

During 1997 it was too soon for Murdock's doctors to consider him cured, but his prognosis appeared good. The future of CellPro, however, was less certain. The company was involved in an ongoing patent-infringement lawsuit brought by Johns Hopkins University, Baltimore, Md.; Baxter International, Inc.; and Becton Dickinson & Co. concerning an antibody used in the treatment that had given Murdock his second chance. In March 1997 a federal district court jury ruled in favour of the plaintiffs, and CellPro was ordered to pay $2.3 million in damages. The company was hit even harder in July 1997 when a judge upheld the jury's decision and increased the amount of the damages to some $7 million.

Murdock was born March 21, 1947, in Martinez, Calif. In 1969 he received a bachelor's degree in zoology from the University of California, Berkeley. Following graduation he held positions in sales and marketing, and from 1989 to 1991 he was European vice president of the Fenwal Division of Baxter Healthcare Corp. He began at CellPro as vice president of marketing and corporate development in September 1991, and by 1992 he had become president of the company. From June 1992 he also held the positions of CEO and director. (SANDRA LANGENECKERT)

Museveni, Yoweri Kaguta

Political developments in 1997 helped focus attention once again on Yoweri Museveni of Uganda, touted by many observers as a new kind of African leader. The Ugandan president could boast of a revitalized country that was enjoying political stability, a growing economy, and improving infrastructure. Uganda also was said to be the only African nation having success in battling AIDS. The president, whom some called an African Bismarck, had achieved success with a mixture of one-party rule and private enterprise, coupled with a willingness to interfere in the conflicts of neighbouring countries, especially when doing so improved Uganda's security and furthered his goal of regional integration.

Museveni was born to cattle farmers in 1944 in the Mbarara district of southern Uganda. He attended missionary schools and graduated from the Ntara School in 1966. He then studied political science and economics at the University of Dar es Salaam, Tanz. (B.A., 1970), where he was chairman of a leftist student group allied with African liberation movements. When Idi Amin came to power in Uganda in 1971, Museveni returned to Tanzania, this time in exile. There he

CHRISTOPHER MORRIS—TIME/BLACK STAR

Yoweri Museveni

founded the Front for National Salvation, which in 1979 helped topple Amin. Museveni held posts in transitional governments and ran for president of Uganda in 1980. When the elections, widely believed to have been rigged, were won by Milton Obote, Museveni formed the National Resistance Movement. The resistance eventually prevailed, and on Jan. 26, 1986, Museveni became president of Uganda. He won election to the post on May 9, 1996, and in legislative elections a month later, backers won control of the National Assembly.

Although as a young man he had espoused Marxism, Museveni came to believe that free enterprise was necessary for economic development. On the other hand, he rejected multiparty democracy, arguing that such an arrangement in a poor African country degenerated into tribal politics. At the same time, he allowed a free press, even though it was frequently critical of his policies. Museveni also advocated that Africans look to themselves, not to the West, for solutions to their problems, arguing that their principal conflict was no longer with colonists but rather with corrupt rulers. Perhaps his most controversial policy was to support rebels in other African countries, including Laurent Kabila (*q.v.*), who deposed Mobutu Sese Seko (*see* OBITUARIES) in neighbouring Zaire in 1997. Museveni also supported Tutsi exiles fighting against the government of Rwanda and a Sudanese group, headed by a former schoolmate, fighting the Islamic fundamentalist rulers of that country. Museveni's goal, he proclaimed, was to achieve regional integration in both politics and economics, and he justified his support for opponents of corrupt regimes as necessary to bring about such a union.

(ROBERT RAUCH)

Narayanan, Kocheril Raman

A remarkable moment in history occurred on July 25, 1997, when Indian Vice Pres. Kocheril Raman Narayanan was sworn in as the country's 10th president and thus became the first untouchable (a member of India's lowest social caste as determined by heredity) to occupy the post. Supported by nearly all of the main political parties, Narayanan won the vote of 95% of the mainly upper-caste federal and state lawmakers and defeated former chief election commissioner T.N. Seshan in the election. The occasion held even greater significance because Narayanan's installment preceded the 50th anniversary of India's independence from Great Britain by only a few weeks. Although caste discrimination had not been completely eliminated in the intervening 50 years and had, in fact, led to recent violent eruptions, his election was viewed as a harbinger of social and political change that could lead to a more democratic India.

Narayanan was born on Feb. 4, 1921, in the town of Uzhavoor, now in Kerala state. Although he faced difficulties as a result of his family's poverty and social status, he possessed a keen intellect and thus qualified for a government-sponsored college scholarship. After earning a B.A. in English from the University of Travancore (now the University of Kerala) and graduating with top honours, Narayanan launched a career as a journalist for the *Hindu* (1944–45) and the *Times of India* (1945). He then won a Tata scholarship to the London School of Economics. While studying abroad (1945–48), he received top academic honours and also served as a foreign correspondent for *Social Welfare Weekly.*

Upon his return to India, Narayanan was aided by a letter of recommendation written by a professor, the distinguished British political scientist Harold Laski, and addressed to Indian Prime Minister Jawaharlal Nehru. This glowing introduction inspired Nehru to help Narayanan enter foreign service, despite opposition from upper-caste officials. During a long and distinguished career as a diplomat (1949–83), Narayanan held posts in numerous countries but was especially effective while serving (1976–78) in China, where he helped mend relations following a 15-year rift in diplomacy. He was also ambassador to the U.S. at a time (1980–83) of strained relations between the two countries. In 1979 he was named vice-chancellor of Jawaharlal Nehru University. An intellectual and scholar, Narayanan was the author or coauthor of works on Indian politics and international relations, notably *India and America—Essays in Understanding* (1984) and *Non-Alignment in Contemporary International Relations* (1981).

After 1984 Narayanan became active in politics, serving in the Lok Sabha (People's Assembly), as a Cabinet minister, and as vice president from 1992. Although his role as president was largely ceremonial, many predicted that Narayanan would have an opportunity to play a key role in forming and stabilizing the government because he had the power to appoint the prime minister when the government was made up of a coalition. During his confirmation address, he expressed concern over violence, corruption, international relations, and the disadvantaged in society, as well as emphasizing that he intended to be a president for all Indians.

(AFRODITE MANTZAVRAKOS)

O'Donnell, Rosie

Rosie O'Donnell rattled daytime television in 1997, threatening to dethrone the top-rated, feel-good talk show, "The Oprah Winfrey Show," with her own celebrity-studded talk-variety program. In the midst of sexually suggestive talk shows and soap operas, "The Rosie O'Donnell Show" exploded onto the daytime scene with fresh humour and optimism, debuting on June 10, 1996, with the highest premiere ratings of any talk show of the past decade. The spunky comedienne-of-the-people endeared herself to audiences with her frisky frankness, neighbourly chatter, and unabashed love for popular culture, namely television theme songs, commercial jingles, and actor Tom Cruise. Polls revealed that she was second to Winfrey in popularity among the most dominant daytime television viewing group, women. Rewarded with a four-year, $4 million renewal contract, O'Donnell capped her show's first season with the Daytime Emmy award for best talk show host.

Roseanne O'Donnell, the third of five children, was born March 21, 1962, in Commack, N.Y. Her mother died when O'Donnell was 10 years old. Left to be raised by an emotionally reserved father, she used humour to contend with her own emotions. Throughout her youth her sense of humour also gained her popularity, as demonstrated by her elections as homecoming queen, senior class president, and prom queen while in high school. After graduating from high school, O'Donnell attempted to earn a college degree, first as a prelaw student at Dickinson College, Carlisle, Pa., in 1980 and then a year later as a drama student at Boston University. While doing so, she sporadically toured comedy clubs throughout the U.S. from 1979 to 1984. Show business beckoned, and so O'Donnell left college without a degree in order to develop her professional stand-up comedy career. After touring in less-than-extravagant circumstances, she finally earned enough as a five-time comedy champion on the television show "Star Search" to pursue a movie acting career in Los Angeles. She honed her comedy skills as host and executive producer of the comedy show "Stand-Up Spotlight" on the cable television channel VH-1. In 1992 O'Donnell relinquished her duties as host in order to launch a movie career. She usually got parts as the comic sidekick and/or best friend in such feature films as *A League of Their Own* (1992), *Sleepless in Seattle* (1993), and *The Flintstones* (1994), the movie version of the classic cartoon. In her first starring role, she attempted to broaden her image by playing a police-woman-turned-leather-clad dominatrix in *Exit to Eden* (1994), but the movie and O'Donnell's performance were generally panned by critics. She then moved to the New York stage and achieved critical acclaim in the part of Rizzo in the Broadway revival of *Grease!* in 1994. Soon afterward she returned to film, again as the comical confidant, in *Now and Then* (1995) and *Beautiful Girls* (1996). She returned to theatre only to be host of the 1997 Tony awards.

(JACKIE ORIHILL)

Paik, Nam June

Throughout his career Korean-born contemporary artist Nam June Paik had been variously described by critics as a sculptor, a performance artist, and the father of video art. Some preferred to call him a visionary world traveler. What almost every critic agreed on, however, was that since the early 1960s Paik consistently had been one of Postmodern art's most provocative and innovative figures.

Nam June Paik

COURTESY OF THE ARTIST AND HOLLY SOLOMON GALLERY, PHOTOGRAPH: ADAM REICH

Because he had performed infrequently in recent years, Paik's video opera performance *Coyote 3* at the Anthology Film Archives in New York City aroused considerable interest in 1997. Typical of Paik's shows, *Coyote 3* featured a disconcerting mixture of multiple television screens, laser lights, and smoke. Accompanied by two fellow performers, Paik played piano and sang fragments of songs from the diverse places to which he had traveled. The overall effect, as one reviewer put it, was that of a world in which the "irrational is given as much importance as the rational."

Paik was born on July 20, 1932, in Seoul. He studied art and music history at the University of Tokyo before moving to West Germany, where he continued his studies at the University of Munich (1956–58). In the late 1950s, while working in the studio for *elektronische Musik* in Cologne, Paik met American avante-garde composer John Cage, whose inventive compositions and unorthodox ideas would prove to be a major influence on Paik.

Paik's 1963 exhibition *Exposition of Music/ Electronic Television*, held in Wuppertal, W.Ger., marked the first time anyone had used video as an artistic medium. The next year Paik moved to New York City and began a fruitful collaboration with avant-garde cellist Charlotte Moorman. In a well-publicized incident, Moorman, playing topless, and Paik were arrested for public indecency at the opening of his four-part *Opera Sextronique* in 1967.

In the following years Paik made art-quality videos, including *Global Groove* (1973), and produced video sculptures and installations. The most notable of these were *TV Buddha* (1974), *TV Garden* (1974–78), and *Family of Robot* (1986).

Paik was honoured by a large-scale retrospective of his work at the Whitney Museum of American Art in 1982. Starting with *Good Morning Mr. Orwell* (1984), he produced a number of groundbreaking live satellite-broadcast shows, emphasizing the need for communication between the East and West through the exchange of art and culture.

From the late 1970s Paik divided his time between the U.S. and Germany, teaching at the Düsseldorf State Academy of Art. He was the recipient of numerous awards, including the American Film Institute's Maya Deren Award for Independent Film and Video Artists, South Korea's Ho-Am Prize, and most recently the Goethe Medal, an award given to non-German artists for outstanding creative achievement. (TAEHI KANG)

Pugacheva, Alla Borisovna

By 1997 Russian pop idol Alla Pugacheva had reportedly sold as many as 250 million records—perhaps more than the amount sold by U.S. pop star Michael Jackson—but they were nearly all in Russia and the other countries of the former Soviet Union. Widely admired at home, she was still little known elsewhere.

Pugacheva was born in Moscow on April 15, 1949, and, like most Russian young people, was reared on classical music. She studied at the A.V. Lunacharsky State Institute of Theatre Art, Moscow, in the department of variety music and launched her career in 1965 with "Robot," a rock song that proved a modest success. Disappointed with similarly styled songs that were written for her, Pugacheva toured the Soviet Union in search of a singing style that would move audiences and make use of her vocal finesse and expressive stage presence. While performing in obscurity over the next decade, she developed a versatile pop style that was coloured by Western influences but quintessentially Slavic in its dramatic and emotional appeal.

In 1975 Pugacheva won the grand prize at the Golden Orpheus Song Festival in Bulgaria with her interpretation of "Arlekino" ("The Harlequin"). Her performance of the song, which was broadcast on Soviet television and recorded a short time later by Melodiya, the Soviet record monopoly, finally brought her success and public recognition. Thereafter, hit followed hit, her concerts were sellouts, and she rapidly became every Russian's favourite performer. A major fixture at European song festivals during the late 1970s and early '80s, the flamboyant strawberry-blonde Pugacheva also turned her talents to motion pictures and television. She appeared in such films as *Jenschina, Kotoraya poet* (1977; "The Woman Who Sings") and *Prishla i govoryo* (1985; "Came to Say") and in television productions throughout Europe. In 1988 she was named artistic director of a studio theatre, the Theatre of Song, in Moscow, and that same year she toured the U.S. for the first time. Pugacheva was proclaimed National Artist of the U.S.S.R. in 1991 by Pres. Mikhail Gorbachev.

As the country's leading—perhaps only—pop superstar, she had an uninhibited and extravagant lifestyle that included a white stretch limousine, a chic apartment in the centre of Moscow, and four husbands (the latest, Filipp Kirkorov, was himself a rock star and 18 years younger than Pugacheva) and drew much attention in the tabloid press. In 1997 she won the dubious honour of becoming the subject of the first unauthorized biography published in Russia, Aleksey Belyakov's *Alka, Allochka, Alla Borisovna.* The year also saw the release of a 13-CD set of her recordings entitled *Kollektsiya* ("Collection").

Nonetheless, Pugacheva still had difficulty finding an audience for her music outside the Russian-speaking area, and she was clearly out of her element at the Eurovision Song Contest in Dublin in May 1997, where she finished in 15th place. Amid speculation that her retirement from the stage loomed in the near future, the versatile Pugacheva seemed to be finding new ways to keep her name before her public. Having already launched a line of clothing and a perfume, in Moscow in April she showed her spring and autumn collection of shoes, which was received positively by the press and enthusiastically by her legions of fans. (SUSAN DOLL)

Rimes, LeAnn

On Feb. 26, 1997, 14-year-old country music vocalist LeAnn Rimes won Grammy awards in two categories: best female country vocal performer and best new artist. She gained the honours less than a year after the release of her hit single "Blue" took her from relative anonymity to the top of the country music charts. Written some 35 years earlier by Dallas, Texas, disc jockey Bill Mack, the ballad was intended for country music legend Patsy Cline. Cline, however, died in a plane crash in 1963 without ever having recorded it, and Rimes's rich, smoky rendition of the number led to frequent comparisons between the two. When "Blue" reached the airwaves in May 1996, radio stations across the U.S. were inundated with calls requesting the tune. Shortly thereafter Rimes released an album with the same title, which sold more than 123,000 copies in its first week. Her ability to sing about the heartache of love gone wrong, songs that typify the country music genre, went far beyond her years. When Rimes crooned "Now that it's over, I realized/ Those weak words you whispered, were nothing but lies," it was difficult to believe that at the time it was recorded, she had never been on a date.

Rimes was born Aug. 28, 1982, in Jackson, Miss. She began singing before the age of two and won her first competition at age five. When Rimes was 8, she appeared for two weeks as a champion on television's "Star Search," and at 11 she recorded her first album, which was locally released on an independent label. Curb Records signed the young artist after Mike Curb heard her music and immediately recognized her ability. "Someone sent me her CD," said Curb. "I put it on, and everyone just turned their heads and said, 'Who is that?'"

In early 1997 Rimes released her second nationally distributed album, *Unchained Melody/The Early Years,* a collection of songs recorded prior to *Blue,* when she was 11 and 12 years old. The album included versions of the Beatles' "Yesterday" and the title track, the Righteous Brothers' "Unchained Melody." In April she received three Academy of Country Music awards, including the honour for best new female vocalist. During the remainder of the year, Rimes's career showed no signs of slowing down. She signed a reported six-figure contract to collaborate on a book entitled *Holiday in Your Heart* and was the subject of at least two paperback biographies. Her third album, *You Light Up My Life,* was released early in the fall and in the first six weeks sold more than one million copies. (SANDRA LANGENECKERT)

Ronaldo

What was perhaps the most noteworthy battle in association football (soccer) in 1997 took place off the field. The Spanish club FC Barcelona wrangled with Internazionale of Italy over the rights to a mild-mannered young Brazilian striker, who—in 1996 at just 20 years of age—had been declared the best player in the world by the Fédération Internationale de Football Association (FIFA), the sport's governing body. In the end Internazionale won out, and as the club led in the standings near year's end, Italian soccer fans had come to refer to the player with the shaved head and a knack for scoring goals as "Il Fenomeno."

SHAUN BOTTERILL—ALLSPORT

Ronaldo

The rest of the world, however, knew him simply as Ronaldo.

Ronaldo Luiz Nazario da Lima was born Sept. 22, 1976, in Bento Ribeiro, near Rio de Janeiro, and was raised in poverty. Displaying soccer prowess at a young age, he began playing in Brazilian leagues as a teenager in 1990. After scoring 102 goals in 126 matches, Ronaldo left for Europe, where he joined PSV Eindhoven of The Netherlands in 1994. He scored 55 goals in 56 games from 1994 to 1996 before Barcelona paid a $20 million transfer fee to obtain his services. He scored 34 goals in 37 matches while leading that club to the Spanish League Cup and victory in the 1996–97 European Cup–Winners' Cup. Italian powerhouse Internazionale came calling next, paying the young superstar $27 million so that he could buy out his contract with Barcelona and move on to Italy. Barcelona petitioned FIFA to block the deal, claiming the buyout violated international rules for player transfers. Near the end of July, FIFA ruled that the buyout was legitimate and that Ronaldo could join Internazionale. Ronaldo also played with Brazil as it triumphed in the Copa America during the summer, but the youngster still had at least one challenge left: the World Cup. He had been a part of the Brazilian squad that won the World Cup in 1994, but he was just 17 years old at the time and saw no action.

Rather than being lucky and scoring goals at opportune times, Ronaldo was said to have earned nearly every goal he scored. Tall, strong, and fast, he was an excellent dribbler and could work his way past defenders. But observers noted that Ronaldo had room to improve: He was not terribly effective with the ball inside the goalkeeper's box, and his ability to hit headers in traffic needed work. Ronaldo himself admitted that while he considered himself an accomplished player, he was still not a "complete" player and would not become one until he had matured further. This left the rest of the soccer world to contemplate just what it might be like when the world's best player got even better. (ANTHONY G. CRAINE)

Salgado, Sebastião

In 1997 Sebastião Salgado solidified his reputation as one of the world's preeminent photojournalists with the publication of *Terra: Struggle of the Landless.* A collection of 100 black-and-white photographs taken between 1980 and 1996, *Terra* documented the plight of impoverished migrants in Salgado's native Brazil, where vast tracts of arable land, concentrated in the hands of a few owners, were only moderately cultivated or lay idle for the sake of profit. An impassioned work that included a preface by Portuguese novelist José Saramago and poems by Brazilian singer-songwriter Chico Buarque, *Terra* was a signal achievement for a man who had devoted his career to portraying the lives of the homeless and the downtrodden. As in his widely praised earlier collection, *Workers: An Archaeology of the Industrial Age* (1993), the images in *Terra* demonstrated Salgado's unique ability to express the suffering of his subjects in photographs of great formal beauty.

Salgado was born on Feb. 8, 1944, in Aimorés, Braz. The only son of a cattle rancher who wanted him to become a lawyer, Salgado instead studied economics at São Paulo University. After earning a master's degree, he worked as an economist for the Ministry of Finance (1968–69) and joined the popular movement against Brazil's military government. Seen as a political radical, Salgado was exiled in August 1969. He and his wife fled to France, where he continued his studies at the University of Paris. In 1971, on an assignment in Rwanda while working as an economist for the International Coffee Organization, he took his first photographs and soon decided to teach himself the craft. He became a freelance photojournalist in 1973.

Over the next decade Salgado photographed a wide variety of stories, including the famine in Niger and the civil war in Mozambique. In 1979 he joined the prestigious Magnum cooperative for photojournalists, and two years later he gained prominence in the U.S. with a riveting photograph that captured John Hinckley's attempt to assassinate U.S. Pres. Ronald Reagan. By the mid-1980s Salgado had begun to devote himself almost entirely to long-term projects. He won the City of Paris/Kodak Award for his first photographic book, *Other Americas* (1986), which recorded the everyday lives of Latin-American peasants. This was followed by *Sahel: Man in Distress* (1986), a book on the 1984–85 famine in the Sahel region of Africa, and *An Uncertain Grace* (1990), which included a remarkable group of photographs of mud-covered workers at the Serra Pelada gold mine in Brazil.

In 1993 Salgado's international stature was confirmed when his retrospective exhibition "In Human Effort" was shown at the Tokyo National Museum of Modern Art; it was the first time in the history of Japan's national museums that the works of an individual photographer had been displayed. That same year the Arles International Festival awarded him its prize for the Best Photography Book of the Year for *Workers,* Salgado's epic portrait of the working class. After the publication of *Terra,* Salgado concentrated his attention on a six-year project he had started in 1994, documenting migration throughout the world. (SHERMAN HOLLAR)

Schweitzer, Louis

In February 1997 Renault SA, the French automobile-making giant, demonstrating the impact of decreased government control over business in a multinational economy, announced plans to close a plant in Vilvoorde, Belg., and eliminate more than 3,000 jobs. Thus, Louis Schweitzer, the chairman of Renault, was suddenly cast into the public eye, vilified by those who saw his actions as an expression of the human cost of unrestrained capitalism and praised by others for making difficult choices in an effort to increase the company's competitiveness. For decades following World War II, French industry and the French government had been closely entwined. In addition to being the majority shareholder in many of the nation's largest corporations, the government had set national economic policy in coordination with business and frequently intervened in disputes between companies and the powerful French labour unions. In the 1980s and '90s, however, as the booming global economy created a more competitive business environment, the government relaxed much of its control over industry. Although French companies became more competitive internationally, pleasing both company executives and shareholders, this increased competitiveness had a price, and Schweitzer appeared to be paying it.

Schweitzer was born in Geneva on July 8, 1942. He was educated mainly in France and graduated (1970) from the École Nationale d'Administration (ENA), the elite school that produced the majority of that nation's government and corporate leaders. Following his graduation Schweitzer began a career in government, gaining a reputation for efficiency and honesty. By the 1980s he was a high-level government administrator, holding important positions in the Ministry of the Budget and in the Ministry of Industry and Research. He had also become a leading adviser to Laurent Fabius, a rising Socialist Party political figure.

In 1984 French Pres. François Mitterrand appointed Fabius prime minister. Schweitzer became his chief of staff, a position he held until Fabius's resignation in 1986. Schweitzer left government service that same year, taking a position at Renault as vice president for finance and planning. His rise through the ranks of the corporate world was as rapid and assured as his ascent in government. He was Renault's chief financial officer by 1988, executive vice president by the following year, and president and chief operating officer by 1990. In 1992 he was made chairman and chief executive officer.

Schweitzer inherited a troubled company. Outdated manufacturing facilities, increased competition, and reduced consumer demand had cut into Renault's profits, which plummeted 41% in 1995 alone. The closing of the Belgian plant was justified by Schweitzer as a hard but necessary decision designed to restore Renault's competitiveness. He also stated that Renault expected to cut some 2,700 jobs in France. Some observers felt that the government, fearful of a political backlash from French voters frightened for their jobs, would use Schweitzer's actions as justification to return to the interventionist policies of the past. In the end, however, the situation was defused and some jobs were saved. (JOHN H. MATHEWS)

ALAIN BUU—GAMMA LIAISON

Louis Schweitzer

Sharif, Mohammed Nawaz

In the seesaw world of Pakistani politics, Mohammed Nawaz Sharif once again vaulted to the top of the political heap in 1997 when his party, the Pakistan Muslim League (PML), won a landslide victory in the parliamentary elections on February 3. The victory, which secured for Sharif the office of prime minister and gave the PML 134 of the 217 seats in the National Assembly, may have marked the end of the political career of Sharif's chief rival, Benazir Bhutto. The first woman to lead a Muslim nation, Bhutto was Pakistan's prime minister from late 1988 until her government was sacked for alleged corruption in August 1990. She was replaced by Sharif, who held the prime ministership until he himself was dismissed on corruption charges in 1993. In the October 1993 elections Bhutto resumed power, which she held until her government was ousted again in November 1996. Because of widespread discontent with Bhutto's government, a victory for Sharif in 1997 had been expected, though his stunning performance at the polls surprised even the most ardent of his supporters.

Sharif was born on Dec. 25, 1949, in Lahore, Pak. After earning an L.L.B. from the University of the Punjab, Lahore, he joined his family's influential House of Ittefaq (Ittefaq Group), an industrial conglomerate with interests in sugar, steel, and textiles. Entering politics, he became the finance minister of Punjab in 1981 and the chief minister of Punjab in 1985. As leader of the PML, the primary party of the coalition Islamic Democratic Alliance, he was first elected prime minister in October 1990. He became known both for his efforts to revitalize the country economically and for his headstrong and controversial personality. He continued as a vocal opponent to Bhutto until his 1997 victory.

Despite a strong mandate, Sharif's government faced severe problems. A harsh fiscal diet imposed by the International Monetary Fund was strangling spending at a time when about half of the country's money was being allocated to servicing the debt. Tax evasion was rife, corruption was widespread, and sectarian tensions were hot. Relations with India remained thorny, although

Sharif announced that he would renew efforts to improve them.

Soon after taking office, Sharif set about trimming the powers of the president and the military. His attempt to block the appointment of five additional judges to the Supreme Court late in the year, however, sparked a constitutional crisis. Chief Justice Sajjad Ali Shah, another of Sharif's rivals, was later suspended from the court on a technicality. Rather than appoint a replacement for the chief justice, Pres. Farooq Ahmed Leghari unexpectedly resigned from his post in December after bitterly accusing Sharif of attempting to grab sole power. The twin exits of the president and the chief justice appeared to be another major triumph for Sharif. (ANN M. BELASKI)

Shiva, Vandana

In recent years biotechnology and pharmaceutical companies had begun to probe the farthest reaches of the Earth in search of plants and animals that may yield benefits for humans. This research had already paid off in the development of products ranging from new medicines and cosmetics to agricultural goods. According to Indian scientist Vandana Shiva, however, the biological wealth of poorer countries too often was appropriated by global corporations that neither sought their hosts' consent nor shared the profits. These practices were tantamount to biological theft, she charged in her 1997 book *Biopiracy: The Plunder of Nature and Knowledge.* In addition, Shiva believed that the power of multinational companies to patent life-forms—and therefore maintain exclusive control over their use—deprived indigenous people of the right to benefit from the natural resources in their own backyards.

This was not the first time that Shiva, who had a master's degree in particle physics and a Ph.D. in the philosophy of science, had spoken out in defense of protecting biodiversity and the rights of people in less-developed countries. The author of 11 books, she had emerged as an internationally renowned advocate of sustainable development and an authority on women's issues. In 1993 she was the recipient of the Right Livelihood Award, often regarded as the alternative Nobel Prize and bestowed to "honour and support those offering practical and exemplary answers to the most urgent challenges facing us today."

As founder and director of the Research Foundation for Science, Technology, and Natural Resource Policy in New Delhi, Shiva had worked on grassroots campaigns to prevent clear-cut logging and the construction of large dams. She was perhaps best known, however, as a longtime critic of Asia's Green Revolution, an international effort that began in the 1960s to increase food production in less-developed countries through higher-yielding seed stocks and the increased use of pesticides and fertilizers. The Green Revolution, she maintained, had led to pollution, a loss of indigenous seed diversity and traditional agricultural know-how, and a troubling dependence of poor farmers on costly chemical inputs. In response, Research Foundation scientists established seed banks throughout India to preserve the country's agricultural heritage while training farmers in sustainable agricultural practices.

Born in 1952 in India, Shiva became interested in environmental issues as a college student after she returned to a favourite childhood place in the Himalayan mountains only to find that the forest had been cleared and a stream drained so that an apple orchard could be planted. "I think there's nothing as exhilarating as protecting that which you find precious," she said in a 1997 interview in *The Progressive* magazine. "To me, fighting for people's rights, protecting nature, protecting diversity is a constant reminder of that which is so valuable in life." (ADELHEID FISCHER)

Simon of Highbury, Lord

When the Labour Party returned to power in Great Britain in May 1997, one of the most surprising and significant appointments to the new government was that of David Simon as the minister for trade and competitiveness in Europe. As chairman of British Petroleum (BP), Simon was one of Britain's leading industrialists. He had never been a politician, nor had he expressed any sympathy for a political party, and his only declared political passion was for the unity of Europe. In a country where it was rare for nonpoliticians to become ministers, Simon's appointment sent a clear message that the new Labour government would be more sympathetic to the European Union (EU) than the previous Conservative administration. Upon his appointment, Simon was immediately made a life peer, taking the title Lord Simon of Highbury, so that he could be a minister in the House of Lords.

David Alec Gwyn Simon was born in London on July 24, 1939. Until he joined Prime Minister Tony Blair's (*q.v.*) government, his life story had been that of a conventional high-flying business executive. After graduating (1961) from the University of Cambridge (where he had studied modern languages), he joined BP as a management trainee and spent the next three decades climbing steadily through the company's ranks. His career was interrupted only by his time at INSEAD, the European Institute of Business Administration at Fontainebleau, near Paris. Simon's linguistic skills and European connections made him one of BP's leading figures in its strategy of expanding into Europe. He was promoted to chief executive of BP Oil International in 1982 and to BP Group managing director in 1986. Simon's devotion to the cause of European unity set him apart from the prevailing anti-European mood of those close to Margaret Thatcher, then Britain's prime minister. Despite his position as one of the country's leading industrialists, he was excluded from the informal network of business leaders close to Thatcher.

In 1992 Simon became BP's chief executive. His slogan for running the company—"Purpose, Process, People"—reflected a belief that effective management should be inclusive rather than autocratic, persuading staff to work for a common cause rather than simply issuing orders and expecting them to be blindly obeyed. Simon's approach, which was similar to the co-determination philosophy of modern German business management, reflected his experience serving on the advisory boards of the Deutsche Bank and Allianz Group insurance company in Frankfurt. He also advised Jacques Santer, the president of the European Commission, on competitiveness policy. Through the early and mid-1990s, Simon was one of Britain's most outspoken advocates of European integration, including the EU's controversial plans to establish a single currency. He was made a CBE in 1991 and was knighted in 1995. His appointment as "minister for Europe" (the widely used contraction of his full title) made him one of the key players in Blair's strategy of transforming Britain's relations with the rest of Europe. (PETER KELLNER)

Smith, Dean Edwards

The 1982 Atlantic Coast Conference (ACC) championship game between the University of North Carolina and the University of Virginia featured some of the greatest players in college basketball—among them North Carolina guard Michael Jordan and Virginia centre Ralph Sampson. As a national television audience watched, however, Dean Smith, the North Carolina coach, instructed his players to stall en route to a 47–45 victory. Smith's name had become synonymous with the low-scoring style of play known as the four-corner offense. Opponents of Smith's strategy, craving the high-scoring game played in the National Basketball Association (NBA), pointed to that ACC championship contest as proof that changes were in order. The outcry was loud enough to effect two rules changes that would significantly alter the college game: the 45-second shot clock and the three-point basket. Smith guided his team to the National Collegiate Athletic Association (NCAA) championship that year, but observers predicted that his mastery would fade as the game changed.

On March 15, 1997, Smith made a mockery of those predictions, earning his 877th career win to surpass Kentucky's Adolph Rupp as the NCAA basketball coach with the most victories. Not only had Smith adapted to the new up-tempo game; he had thrived, achieving unprecedented runs of 27 seasons with at least 20 wins and 23 straight NCAA tournament appearances, including another championship in 1993. He had amassed more wins (65) in the tournament than any other coach. Successfully recruiting and coaching some of the game's most notable players (Jordan, James Worthy, Sam Perkins, Billy Cunningham, Bobby Jones, Phil Ford, Walter Davis, Eric Montross, Jerry Stackhouse, Rasheed Wallace), Smith guided his team to no worse than a third-place finish in the highly competitive ACC regular season for an astonishing 33 consecutive seasons.

Smith was born Feb. 28, 1931, in Emporia, Kan. After a standout athletic career at Topeka (Kan.) High School, he attended the University of Kansas, where he played basketball under the lengendary F.C. ("Phog") Allen. With Smith serving as a reserve guard, Kansas won the NCAA title in 1952. After his graduation in 1953, Smith joined Allen's staff as an assistant coach before joining the U.S. Air Force in 1954. After a stint as an assistant coach at the United States Air Force Academy, Colorado Springs, Colo., Smith was hired in 1958 as an assistant on the staff of Frank McGuire at North Carolina. When that program was penalized by the NCAA for recruiting violations, McGuire left to take a job in the NBA, and Smith replaced him in 1961. Smith coached the 1976 U.S. Olympic team and was elected to the Naismith Memorial Basketball Hall of Fame in 1982. (ANTHONY G. CRAINE)

Spice Girls

The British pop phenomenon Spice Girls made music history in 1997 by becoming the first group to have its first four singles hit the number one spot on the British charts. The group (sometimes referred to as a cross between Madonna and the Monkees) took Great Britain, North America, and the Far East by storm in a way not seen since the Beatles, and their contrived but catchy dance-bop songs reached number one on the music charts in more than 30 countries.

Responding to a 1994 advertisement in *The Stage* for a "manufactured" female pop group, wannabe singers Geri Halliwell, Mel Brown, Mel Chisholm, Victoria Aadams, and Michelle Stephenson won the open audition and worked so well together that they became housemates. Their talent scout-managers reportedly wanted them to look, dress, and act alike, but the girls' shared credo of "Girl Power," along with their boundless energy and more than a modicum of talent, led them to fire their original managers and hire a new manager, who signed them up with Virgin Records. Stephenson was replaced by Emma Bunton, and when the Spice Girls were teamed with songwriter-producers Richard Stannard and Mathew Rowe, the resulting album, *Spice,* and the songs "Wannabe," "2 Become 1," and "Mama" propelled them into pop music mythology. In 1997 the group won two BRIT Awards for best single ("Wannabe") and best video ("Say You'll Be There"), a World Music Award as best newcomer, and the MTV music television award for best dance video ("Wannabe"). They also signed a lucrative deal to appear in a Pepsi Cola ad campaign and released a book, *Girl Power!,* and a new album, *Spiceworld.* The motion picture *Spiceworld* was filmed during the summer for release at Christmas. In all, it was estimated that the group earned more than £30 million in 1997.

Each girl established a unique style and persona, and the group's millions of fans worldwide eagerly gleaned every fact about their idols from Web sites, fan clubs, and the thousands of articles in publications ranging from the frivolous to the serious. Geraldine Estelle Halliwell (b. Aug. 6, 1972, Watford, Eng.), known as Ginger Spice because of her hair colour, was a former aerobics instructor and TV game-show host. Melanie Jayne Chisholm (b. Jan. 12, 1974, Liverpool, Eng.), who answered to Mel C. or Sporty Spice, had a dance background and a penchant for association football (soccer) and sports gear. Cool, unsmiling Posh Spice was Victoria Aadams (b. April 7, 1975, Hertfordshire, Eng.), a former dancer and actress. Melanie Janine Brown (b. May 29, 1975, Yorkshire, Eng.), or Mel B., was a drummer,

ALL ACTION/ IPOL

Spice Girls members include (l–r) Baby Spice, Scary Spice, Sporty Spice, Posh Spice, and Ginger Spice.

dancer, and actress whose unusual clothing, supercurly hair, and body piercings prompted the moniker Scary Spice. Aptly named Baby Spice, Emma Lee Bunton (b. Jan. 21, 1976, London), was the youngest, renowned for her perilously high platform shoes and blonde babydoll looks.

(LESLEY EDMONDSON)

Stern, Howard

Labeled by some as a racist, misogynist, and homophobe for his controversial humour and uncensored commentary, American radio "shock jock" Howard Stern named himself "King of All Media," and in 1997 he staked his claim to the entertainment throne. Already a best-selling author and host of a radio show that boasted some 20 million listeners, he added movie star to his credentials with the screen adaptation of his autobiography, *Private Parts.* The film was a box-office success, and Stern earned praise for his self-portrayal. Not content to conquer the American public, he then invaded Canada as "The Howard Stern Show" was heard for the first time on radio stations outside the U.S.

Born on Jan. 12, 1954, in Roosevelt, N.Y., Stern was introduced to radio by his father, a sound engineer. The younger Stern, an awkward and shy child, found an outlet in the medium and began producing his own show on a tape recorder. As a student at Boston College, he worked at the school's radio station; he graduated in 1976 with a degree in communications. After a series of unmemorable on-the-air jobs in Hartford, Conn., and Detroit, he landed in Washington, D.C. There, teamed with Robin Quivers, who became his sidekick, he developed a highly popular format. With its mix of Stern's self-deprecating jokes; provocative interviews with lesbians; commentary on sex, celebrities, and bodily functions; and in-studio visits by naked women, the radio program shot to number one in the D.C. area. In 1982, however, the duo were fired following a dispute with station management, and they moved to New York City, signing on with WNBC-AM. Though Stern produced another top-rated show, continuous arguments over program content led to his dismissal. In 1985 "The Howard Stern Show" found its home at WXRK-FM. Attracting national attention, it was syndicated the following year and by 1997 was heard in some 40 U.S. cities. Stern's outrageous humour, however, did not have everyone laughing. The Federal Communications Commission levied over $2 million in fines against the program because of its often lewd content, and various groups called for its boycott. Stern, a vocal supporter of the First Amendment, refused to change his highly inflammatory act.

In the early 1990s Stern began to build his media empire. He produced a cable-television program that evolved in 1992 into the weekly "The Howard Stern Interview." His graphic autobiography, *Private Parts* (1993), became the quickest-selling book in Simon & Schuster's publishing history. Reaching number one on the *New York Times* best-seller list, it was followed by *Miss America* (1995), an account of his radio show and his opinions on a wide range of topics. Stern also appeared on the Internet as loyal fans dedicated hundreds of Web sites to the entertainer.

(AMY TIKKANEN)

Stojko, Elvis

In the countdown to the 1998 Winter Olympics, many eyes were on Canada's latest superjumping ice skater, Elvis Stojko. At the 1997 Champions Series Final, he put his name in the record books by landing the first quadruple toe–triple toe loop combination in competition. His repeat of that feat at the world championships helped him add the 1997 world title to his list of accomplishments, which already included winning gold medals at the 1994 and '95 world championships and a silver at the 1994 Olympic Winter Games in Lillehammer, Nor. Although this would seem to give him an edge on his rivals for Olympic gold, Stojko knew that his competitors were formidable, and he was taking nothing for granted. Nonetheless, he was hoping to become the first Canadian man to capture that prize.

Stojko was born on March 22, 1972, in Newmarket, Ont., and by the time he was two and a half, he knew he wanted to skate. By 1986 he had come in third in the Canadian novice national championships; two years later he was Canadian junior national champion; and in 1990 he finished ninth in the world championships. His improvement in the standings continued the following year with a second-place finish at the Canadian nationals and a sixth at the world championships, where he made history for the first time by landing a quadruple toe–double toe loop combination. He was seventh at his Olympic debut in 1992 but followed that with a bronze medal at the '92 world championships the following month and a silver at the world meet the next year. His 1994 Olympic silver medal and '94 and '95 world golds made him a favourite for capturing Olympic gold in 1998, but a fall on the triple axel of a required jump combination at the 1996 world championships left him in only seventh place after the short program. Stojko rose to the challenge, however, skated a powerful long program, and moved up to fourth place on the strength of a quadruple toe combination and a triple axel–triple toe loop combination, missing the bronze medal by only a narrow margin. In taking back the world crown in 1997, he became one of a very small number of skaters to regain a world championship after having missed medaling the year before.

When he was not competing, Stojko performed with the Tour of World Figure Skating Champions and with his own tour. He also enjoyed such recreational activities as motorcycle riding, dirt biking, and snowmobiling, and he had gained a black belt in karate. Stojko was Canadian Male Athlete of the Year in 1994, and in 1996 he was honoured with the Governor-General's Meritorious Service Medal. In late 1997 his first book, *Heart and Soul: Elvis Stojko in His Own Words,* was published.

(BARBARA WHITNEY)

Stoppard, Sir Thomas

Few playwrights had been as celebrated for their virtuoso command of the English language as Czech-born dramatist Tom Stoppard. A master of the "serious comedy," he had captivated theatregoers for more than 30 years with his plays of ideas. When *The Invention of Love* captured the London *Evening Standard* award for best play in November 1997, it marked the seventh time that Stoppard—also a three-time Tony award winner—had been presented with the honour and was the culmination of a year in which he had received (in June) the personal honour of a knighthood.

Born July 3, 1937, in Zlin, Czech. (now Czech Republic), Tomas Straussler was the youngest son of a company physician who was transferred to Singapore in 1939. When the Japanese attacked Singapore in 1941, Straussler remained there and was killed, whereas his wife and two sons fled to India. In 1946 his widow married a British army officer, who moved the family to Bristol, Eng. At age 17, after taking his stepfather's name, Stoppard launched a career in journalism. Working first in Bristol (1954–60) and later in London, he wrote theatre and film criticism among other assignments. In the 1960s Stoppard wrote his first play, *A Walk on the Water,* as well as several short radio plays and short stories. A novel, *Lord Malquist and Mr. Moon,* was published in 1966. His big break came the following year when a National Theatre production of his play *Rosencrantz and Guildenstern Are Dead* enjoyed wide acclaim. Based on two minor characters in Shakespeare's *Hamlet, Rosencrantz and Guilden-*

stern became a classic of modern theatre and established a pattern of borrowing from history and literature that would become one of Stoppard's trademarks.

Unlike the works of many of his British contemporaries, Stoppard's early plays were not concerned with politics or class conflict. Instead, he became a master of witty wordplay and comic invention, through which he examined the myriad contradictions of experience and philosophy. Even as he was occasionally criticized for writing plays that lacked emotion or creating characters that existed primarily as mouthpieces for the his wide-ranging intellectual preoccupations, Stoppard created an astounding body of work that was as entertaining as it was enlightening. Outstanding works included *Jumpers* (1972), a metaphysical whodunnit; *Travesties* (1974), one man's account of V.I. Lenin, James Joyce, and Dadaist poet Tristan Tzara in 1917 Zürich, Switz.; *Every Good Boy Deserves Favour* (1977), his first political play; *The Real Thing* (1982), a romantic comedy about art and marriage; and *Arcadia* (1993), which brought together Fermat's Last Theorem, chaos theory, landscape architecture, and Lord Byron. Stoppard also wrote screenplays, notably for *Brazil* (1986) and *Empire of the Sun* (1987), and wrote and directed the 1991 film version of *Rosencrantz and Guildenstern Are Dead.* It was the plays, however—the mounting of which had become national cultural occasions in Britain—for which he would be remembered.

(JEFF WALLENFELDT)

Suo, Masayuki

Japanese film director Masayuki Suo made his professional debut in the U.S. in 1997 with the highly successful comedy *Shall We Dansu?* (*Shall We Dance?*). The movie, about a disillusioned middle-aged businessman who finds escape from his tedious routine by surreptitiously taking ballroom dancing classes at night, was a box-office hit in Japan in 1996 and gave a much-needed shot in the arm to the Japanese motion picture industry, which had been in the doldrums for decades. A favourite with audiences at the 1996 Cannes Film Festival, *Shall We Dance?* also succeeded in dispelling some of the prejudice that Japanese people held against ballroom dancing, which, as a voice-over in the film explained, "is considered shameful in a country where married people never embrace or say 'I love you.'"

Suo was born on Oct. 29, 1956, in Tokyo. After graduating from Tokyo's Rikkyo (St. Paul's) University, he established a movie-production company, Unit 5, in 1982 and served as an assistant director of 60 mosaically blurred X-rated films. He made his directorial debut in 1983 with the soft-porn movie *Hentai kazoku: Aniki no yomesan* ("Abnormal Family: My Brother's Wife"). In 1989 Suo advanced into the field of mainstream cinema with *Fanshii dansu* ("Fancy Dance"). Based on a comic book, *Fanshii dansu* told the story of a musician in a big city band who learns he must succeed his father as a Buddhist priest and encounters joy and sorrow in undergoing training at a Zen temple.

One of the major influences on Suo was the late Japanese film director Yasujiro Ozu, whose works drew international acclaim. Suo emulated Ozu's style through the use of such techniques as setting cameras at ground level and giving actors and actresses long pauses in conversation. In the 1990s Suo concentrated his energy and efforts on providing film lovers with entertaining movies showing persons or subject matters that were not very well known in society. A surprise hit at the Cannes Film Festival in 1993 was *Shiko Funjatta* ("Sumo Do, Sumo Don't"), which Suo wrote and directed. An amusing tale about a young man forced to play on his university's lamentably bad sumo wrestling team, *Shiko funjatta* won the Japanese Academy Award for best film in 1992.

Tamiyo Kusakari, the leading lady of *Shall We Dance?,* soon became Suo's leading lady off-screen as well. The foremost prima ballerina in Japan, Kusakari won rave reviews as the dance instructor whose grace and beauty entrance the film's hero. Soon after *Shall We Dance?* was released, Suo and Kusakari celebrated by tying the knot. In 1997 the newlyweds toured cities across the U.S. to promote the movie.

(TEIJI SHIMIZU)

Masayuki Suo, with wife, Tamiyo Kusakari

JOHN MARK SORUM—COURTESY MIRAMAX FILMS/KRT

Taylor, Charles Ghankay

In an ironic twist of fate, in 1997 Liberians elected as president the very man who had sparked the civil war that ravaged the country for nearly a decade. On July 19 former guerrilla leader Charles Taylor won an overwhelming 75.3% of the vote, with the runner-up, Harvard-educated former UN official Ellen Johnson-Sirleaf, garnering a mere 9.6% in the balloting. Taylor's monopoly of the formerly state-owned national radio station (on which he was referred to as "His Excellency") and his handouts to the largely illiterate and impoverished electorate were some of the resources he used to win the election. There was also the fear that if Taylor did not win, he would again resort to force.

Taylor was born on Jan. 27, 1948, in Liberia. He was a member of the elite Americo-Liberian ethnic group descended from the freed American slaves who colonized the region in the early 19th century. After receiving a degree in economics in 1977 from Bentley College, Waltham, Mass., he became director of Liberia's General Services Administration under Pres. Samuel K. Doe, a military leader who had gained power in a bloody 1980 coup. In 1983 Doe accused Taylor of having embezzled nearly $1 million in federal funds, and Taylor fled to the U.S., where he was jailed when U.S. officials found evidence to support the charges. Before he could be extradited, however, Taylor escaped from a Massachusetts jail and emerged in Libya to form the National Patriotic Front of Liberia (NPFL), a militia that invaded Liberia in late 1989. His forces advanced on the Liberian capital of Monrovia in 1990, but Taylor's bid for power was checked by rival factions; in the fray, Doe was killed. For the next seven years, the armed factions fought a bitter war, in which over 150,000 people were killed and more than one-half of the country's population were made refugees or were internally displaced. Although Taylor's dominant NPFL faction never took control of the capital, it controlled the countryside and plundered Liberia's rich natural resources. A 1996 peace pact led to the 1997 election.

Taylor's administration faced tough challenges. Years of civil war had ruined the country's civil and economic infrastructure, leaving most citizens without running water, electricity, or access to health or educational facilities. The national treasury was empty, and there was little chance that Liberia's businessmen would return. Sixty thousand former fighters were growing restless while unemployed; hostilities lingered after years of ethnic rivalry; and some $2 billion–$3 billion was owed in foreign debt. In addition, more than 750,000 people, many of them orphans, had been left homeless after years of fighting.

(ANN M. BELASKI)

Terfel, Bryn

The recording *Something Wonderful,* an album of the music of Richard Rodgers and Oscar Hammerstein II as sung by the Welsh bass-baritone Bryn Terfel, won accolades from both critics and listeners in 1997. The success of the recording, which included such favourites as "There Is Nothin' like a Dame" and "The Surrey with the Fringe on Top," no doubt won the singer an even wider audience, but it was not news to aficionados of opera and the art song that Terfel was one of the best young singers of the 1990s. With a rich, warm, vibrant voice that was capable of expressive pianissimos as well as roaring fortissimos, he continued to stand out in the world of classical singing.

Bryn Terfel Jones was born on Nov. 9, 1965, near Pant Glas in North Wales. His parents were cattle and sheep farmers, and his family was a musical one. In school the boy excelled in athletics and sang in choirs. He was trained at the Guildhall School of Music and Drama in London, and by the early 1990s he was already established in a professional career. In 1992 *Gramophone* magazine named him Young Singer of the Year, and in 1993 Terfel was proclaimed Newcomer of

BEATRIZ SCHILLER

Bryn Terfel

the Year in the International Classical Music Awards.

Among Terfel's most prominent operatic roles were the title characters in Mozart's *The Marriage of Figaro* and *Don Giovanni,* both of which he recorded. When he sang Figaro at the Metropolitan Opera in New York City in 1994, the *New York Times* put him on the front page, a rare tribute in the United States for an opera singer. Terfel also became especially identified with the role of Jokanaan in Richard Strauss's *Salome,* which he performed in productions with a number of companies and recorded twice. He took on roles in Strauss's *Die Frau ohne Schatten* and in works by Richard Wagner and others. He was perhaps as well known for lieder and songs and for choral works, however, as for opera. He performed and recorded lieder by Franz Schubert, in addition to *Kindertotenlieder* by Gustav Mahler. Terfel became especially known for recordings of songs by British compatriots such as Frederick Delius, Ralph Vaughan Williams, Gerald Finzi, and George Butterworth. He also recorded choral works by George Frideric Handel, Edward Elgar, and John Ireland, among others.

Standing 1.92 m (6 ft 3½ in) tall, Terfel created an imposing and virile presence on both operatic and the concert stages. His ability as a dramatic actor, coupled with a virtuosic command over his dark, resonant voice, made him one of the most highly sought-after of modern singers.

(ROBERT RAUCH)

Tung Chee-hwa

Few of Hong Kong's 6.3 million people were sleeping as midnight approached on June 30, 1997. Those celebrating in the streets and those watching television at home were all waiting for the historic moment when the Union Jack would be furled and the flag of China hoisted over what had been a British colony for 156 years. Most eyes, however, were on Tung Chee-hwa, the wealthy businessman Beijing had picked to serve for the next five years as chief executive of the new special administrative region of Hong Kong.

Tung Chee-hwa was born in Shanghai on May 29, 1937 (a date derived from the Chinese lunar calendar). He was educated in Great Britain, became fluent in English, and spent six years in the U.S. studying business practices. In numerous interviews the unassuming millionaire had spoken confidently of his ability to persuade China's rulers, if it ever became necessary, to adhere to the provisions of the Joint Declaration signed by China and Britain in 1984 and officially registered at the United Nations as an international treaty. The principles of the document, which were incorporated into Hong Kong's miniconstitution known as the Basic Law, guaranteed that Hong Kong's traditional way of life would remain essentially unchanged for 50 years.

Tung's supporters as well as pro-democracy activists conceded that the new chief executive would have to exhibit exceptional diplomatic skills to keep Hong Kong on an even keel in the months ahead. The people of Hong Kong had been promised, and expected to continue enjoying, substantial economic and political freedoms unknown in the rest of China. The ultimate authority, however, would reside in Beijing, and "one country, two systems" would come to mean what Beijing said it meant.

Those who viewed Tung as China's man in Hong Kong rather than as a protector of Hong Kong's rights noted that his wealth was derived from the Orient Overseas shipping company founded by his father, who died in 1982. At that time the company owed more than $2.7 billion to some 200 banks and was on the verge of bankruptcy. Tung Chee-hwa worked tirelessly to save the company and in 1986 obtained a $120 million loan, $50 million of which came from the state-owned Bank of China. Additional millions were provided by China Merchants, the Hong Kong branch of China's Transport Industry. This alone, critics charged, made Tung beholden to China and involved a conflict of interests. Tung also came under fire for supporting Beijing's decision to abolish Hong Kong's legislature, which had been elected in 1995, and to replace it with an appointed provisional legislature the moment Hong Kong reverted to Chinese sovereignty.

(ARTHUR LATHAM)

Vogelstein, Bert

When American cancer researcher Bert Vogelstein graduated from medical school in 1974, the underlying causes of cancer were not well understood. Although scientists knew that cancer cells were once-normal cells transformed into unruly mavericks, the reasons for the transformation were unclear—until Vogelstein took on the task of elucidating the life history of a tumour cell. For his groundbreaking work on the genetics of cancer, he was awarded the 1997 William Beaumont Prize.

Vogelstein's decision to study cancer stemmed from his curiosity about the molecular basis of the disease as well as from his experiences working with young cancer patients during his residency in pediatrics at Johns Hopkins Hospital, Baltimore, Md. He then spent two years (1976–78) as a research associate at the National Cancer Institute. In 1982 Vogelstein set out to apply his laboratory expertise to the study of colon cancer. His goal was to identify the genes that, when damaged or defective, give rise to the disease. Analyzing DNA (the genetic material) from the cells of colon cancer tumours, he and colleagues found that a particular gene was present in a mutated form in more than one-half of all the tumours they studied. The gene in question, called K-*ras,* belongs to the class known as oncogenes (*i.e.,* cancer-inducing genes). In their normal form, as proto-oncogenes, these genes stimulate cells to replicate when necessary. When damaged, however, they may signal the cell to divide ceaselessly. Could a single mutated gene then trigger the development of cancer? Evidence suggested that this was not the case, and Vogelstein suspected that a defect in another class of growth regulators—called tumour-suppressor genes for their role in preventing uncontrolled cell proliferation—might also be involved. Again studying DNA from colon cancer cells, Vogelstein eventually identified three tumour-suppressor genes, *APC, DCC,* and *p53,* mutated forms of which were found in the tumour cells. Further research on *p53* showed that mutations in this gene were involved not only in colon cancer but in a host of other malignancies; in fact, *p53* was implicated in more than 50% of all cancerous tumours. More recent data from Vogelstein's laboratory provided evidence of still another class of cancer-causing genes, called mismatch repair genes, whose normal function is to identify and repair defective DNA segments. Vogelstein's research made it clear that tumours develop as a result of the sequential accumulation of mutations in proto-oncogenes, tumour-suppressor genes, and mismatch repair genes. On a practical level, his work led to the development of diagnostic tests for colon cancer that promised to greatly reduce deaths from the disease.

Vogelstein was born on June 2, 1949, in Baltimore, Md., and attended the University of Pennsylvania (B.S., 1970) and Johns Hopkins University School of Medicine (M.D., 1974). He was coauthor (with Kenneth Kinzler) of the book *The Genetics of Cancer* (1997) and had published more than 200 research papers in professional journals. Although Vogelstein was a driven scientist who spent most of his time in his laboratory, he relaxed by playing keyboards for Wild Type, a band made up of a number of scientists from Johns Hopkins University.

(MARY JANE FRIEDRICH)

Vyalbe, Yelena

As 1997 came to a close and the 1998 Winter Olympics drew near, Russian cross-country skier Yelena Vyalbe had one colour in mind: gold. She had excelled in her sport at every other level, turning in a record-setting performance at the 1997 Nordic world championships, but an individual Olympic gold medal had thus far eluded her.

Vyalbe was born on April 20, 1968, in Magadan, a city in far northeastern Russia. Heading into 1997 she had won a total of six Olympic medals, 12 world championship medals, four World Cup overall titles, and 35 World Cup individual events. Skiing in her familiar pink hat, Vyalbe stole the show at the Nordic world championships at Trondheim, Nor., in March. She won gold medals in her first two races, the 10-km and 15-km events, and then finished second in the 5-km race to teammate Lyubov Yegorova. Later, however, Yegorova tested positive for performance-enhancing drugs and was subsequently banned from further competition. Because Yegorova was also stripped of her title, Vyalbe was named the winner of the race and received a third gold medal. In a move not often seen in sports, Vyalbe then stepped forward as the leader of the Russian team and, speaking in German, addressed the crowd just before her team competed in the 4 × 5-km relay, assuring those in attendance that Yegorova had acted alone. Vyalbe anchored the Russian team as it triumphed in the relay. In the 30-km race two days later, she led from start to finish, beating Stefania Belmondo of Italy by 28.3 seconds to take an unprecedented fifth gold medal and wrap up her fifth World Cup crown. By the end of the 1996–97 season, Vyalbe had won 44 World Cup races in her career, a record for both men and women.

It seemed that the only challenge left for Vyalbe was the 1998 Winter Olympics at Nagano, Japan. She had competed in two previous Winter Games. At Albertville, France, in 1992, she won a gold medal as a member of the Unified Team's 4 × 5-km relay squad and gained bronze medals in the 5-km classical, the combined pursuit, the 15-km classical, and the 30-km freestyle. Vyalbe's performance marked the first time in the history of the Winter Games that a woman had collected four bronze medals. At

SHAUN BOTTERILL—ALLSPORT

Yelena Vyalbe

Lillehammer, Nor., in 1994, she won another gold medal as a member of the relay team, but she failed to finish among the top three in any of the individual events and thus was left to wait until 1998 to try to add the ultimate prize to her crowded trophy case. (ANTHONY G. CRAINE)

Waugh, Mark Edward and Stephen Rodger
In the second of the three cricket Tests in South Africa in March 1997, S.R. and M.E. Waugh, the twins from the western suburbs of Sydney, Australia, became the most capped set of brothers in Test history. It was their 44th Test together. The irony was that Mark, the younger of the two by four minutes—hence his nickname "Junior"—made his Test debut in Adelaide as a replacement for Steve, who had been pushed into the Australian side five years earlier after just nine first-class matches. By general consent, Mark was the more gifted of the two, an inventive strokemaker blessed with natural timing. Yet ask any Test bowler his most feared foe, and the answer would be Steve Waugh, a tough competitor who by sheer hard work and dedication turned himself into the best batsman in the world. Steve was more intense than Mark, an avid student of the game, captain of the Australian one-day side, and a candidate for the Test captaincy. The nonidentical twins, who were born on June 2, 1965, did not seem close on the surface and did not share a room on tour. "We shared a room together for 20 years as kids" was their stock reply to questions about the perceived coolness of their relationship. Together, however, they were at the heart of Australia's revival as the world's best team.

Steve made his debut at the age of 20 against India in 1985–86 and did not score a century in his first 26 Tests. His breakthrough came in England in 1989 when he made 177 not out and 152 not out in the first two Tests and finished the series with an average of 126. Despite another successful Ashes tour four years later, it was not until the tour to the West Indies in 1995 that Steve fully matured into the complete Test batsman. His 200 at Sabina Park against a strong West Indian attack was a masterpiece and answered the critics who had consistently questioned his technique against short-pitched bowling. Against England at Old Trafford in 1997, he became only the third Australian to score two centuries in the same Test.

Once Mark had broken into the Australian team, making 138 on his debut in 1990–91, he rarely looked back. He was out too often when well set, however, to be considered a great batsman. A classic innings of 116 made in 5½ hours against South Africa in Port Elizabeth seemed to herald a new stage in Mark's career, but a lean spell followed—notably on the Ashes tour to England—and an inevitable loss of confidence. Surprisingly, given that they batted at numbers four and five, the Waughs' record of partnerships together was fairly thin, though they once made double hundreds in an unbeaten 464 for New South Wales. Both were also excellent fielders—Steve in the gully and Mark at slip—and occasional, though curiously effective, medium-pace bowlers. (ANDREW LONGMORE)

Weil, Andrew Thomas
Once described as a practitioner of integrative medicine, an ethnobotanist, an educator, and a writer, Andrew Weil by 1997 had become more commonly viewed as a guru of alternative medicine. A strong proponent of the body's potential to generate its own healing, he emphasized this belief in two best-selling books, *Spontaneous Healing* (1995) and *8 Weeks to Optimum Health* (1997). His directives for achieving this harmony were, however, often met with trepidation.

Andrew Weil

CLAUS GUGLBERGER—BLACK STAR

Weil was born on June 8, 1942, in Philadelphia, the only child of parents who owned a millinery supply store. As a child, he developed a strong interest in plants, which he said he inherited from his mother and grandmother. After graduating from high school in 1959, Weil, on a full scholarship from the American Association for the United Nations, traveled around the world learning about other cultures and their practices. He then entered Harvard University, majoring in biology with a concentration on the ethnobotany of medicinal plants and graduating cum laude in 1964. He entered Harvard Medical School, not with the intention of becoming a physician but rather simply to obtain a medical education. In 1968 he received his medical degree, although the Harvard faculty had threatened to withhold it because of a controversial marijuana study Weil had helped conduct in his senior year. In 1969 he worked briefly at the drug studies division of the National Institute of Mental Health but resigned in order to pursue personal research ambitions and to write his first book, *The Natural Mind: A New Way of Looking at Drugs and the Higher Consciousness* (1972). In this book Weil suggested that altered states of consciousness could be achieved without the use of drugs, later stating, "Highs come from within; they are simply triggered by external agents in the right conditions."

In a subsequent coauthored book entitled *Chocolate to Morphine: Understanding Mind-Active Drugs* (1983), Weil aroused the ire of a Florida senator, who demanded that the book, a veritable encyclopedia of various drugs and their effects on humans, be removed from schools and libraries. In *Health and Healing: Understanding Conventional and Alternative Medicine,* also published in 1983, Weil contended that current medical practices were more curative than preventive, too expensive, and too reliant upon drugs, surgery, and technology. In his vision of health care in the future, Weil saw a shift to preventive therapies, to the understanding of the benefits of using natural drugs in diluted forms, and to a better understanding of the mind-body connection. In *Spontaneous Healing* and *8 Weeks to Optimum Health,* he advocated a mix of herbal medicine, good nutrition, and a healthful lifestyle. This information was parlayed into television specials and also was incorporated into Weil's Internet site. (ANTHONY L. GREEN)

Williams, Walter Ray, Jr.
In the summer of 1997, bowling champion Walter Ray Williams, Jr., said, "This year might be the best year I've ever had"; considering his accomplishments, it appeared that he was correct. Ranked the number one bowler in the world, Williams in June became the first professional bowler to reach the $2 million mark in career earnings when he beat Pete Weber, his closest competitor for the title. By the year's end he had increased his winnings to $240,544, and for the second year in a row and the fourth time in his career, he was voted bowling's Player of the Year.

Williams was born Oct. 6, 1959, in San Jose, Calif., and grew up in Eureka and Auburn, Calif. Citing horseshoes as his favourite sport, at age 11 he became the youngest junior world horseshoe champion just two years after he was introduced to the game by his father. He went on to amass six world horseshoe-pitching titles by 1997. It was when he reached his teen years and wanted to pay his way through college that he began bowling in tournaments. Williams later earned a B.S. degree in physics from California State Polytechnic University, where he also studied mathematics. For his senior thesis Williams wrote about the physical behaviour of a bowling ball being thrust down a lane. In 1980, his first year on the Professional Bowlers Association (PBA) tour, he won only $641. He won his first PBA tournament in 1986, and in 1993, after 13 years of professional bowling, he joined only about 15 others who had earned $1 million in tournament winnings. His second million came only four years later.

By the end of 1996, Williams had bowled 39 perfect games and earned 21 career titles, including the PBA Player of the Year title in 1986, 1993, 1996, and 1997. In 1993 he set PBA records for bowling a perfect score (300) four times in a tournament, for most games bowled in a year, and for bowling the most games with a score of at least 200 in succession. In 1995 he was inducted into the PBA Hall of Fame. Although an accomplished bowler and one of the few athletes ever to hold national titles simultaneously in two different sports, Williams lamented that he did not get as much media coverage as more mainstream athletes. "I'm in the same class as Michael Jordan," he said. "The only difference is everyone knows who he is and not many people know who I am." Williams's wife, Paige, however, summed it all up by saying, "It would be great to have Tiger Woods's or Michael Jordan's money, but I wouldn't want to be in the position they're in. We still like to go to...dinner without being mobbed."

(ANTHONY L. GREEN)

Wilson, William Julius

In August 1997, just one year after signing a sweeping welfare-reform bill, U.S. Pres. Bill Clinton declared, "The debate is over. We know now that welfare reform works." American sociologist William Julius Wilson, however, would be one of the first to disagree, even though he had helped shape much of Clinton's social policy since 1992 as his unofficial adviser. Regarded as one of the leading national authorities on race and poverty, Wilson found that Clinton's welfare-reform legislation failed to address what Wilson considered a main issue—the lack of job opportunities in the inner cities. Clinton's program coincided with the publication of Wilson's book, *When Work Disappears: The World of the New Urban Poor* (1996), which stated that in the past generation or so, the disappearance of low-skilled manufacturing jobs and the flight of the urban middle class to the suburbs had become a greater detriment to the ghetto poor than had racism and other cultural pathologies.

The much-debated book added to the confusion over the author's standing along the political spectrum. An African-American scholar and self-described social democrat, Wilson continued to find himself under attack both from conservatives—who opposed his call for programs of national health care, education reform, and government-financed jobs—and from liberals, who were uncomfortable with his de-emphasis of race and with his consideration of the behavioral problems associated with poverty.

Although considered a dispassionate writer and a longtime critic of partisanship in academia, Wilson was no stranger to public policy and had been a consultant to such Democratic politicians as Chicago Mayor Richard M. Daley, former New York governor Mario Cuomo, and retired U.S. senator Bill Bradley. In fact, his much-publicized decision in 1996 to leave his 25-year professorship at the University of Chicago for the halls of Harvard University put him in a better position to affect government policy. It also placed him among the elite of black intellectuals, including Henry Louis Gates, Jr., and Cornel West, whom he joined in the department of Afro-American studies. In addition, his influence was felt in his main role as professor of social policy in the John F. Kennedy School of Government.

Wilson was born on Dec. 20, 1935, in Derry township, Westmoreland county, Pa., and was educated at Wilberforce (Ohio) University (B.A., 1958), Bowling Green (Ohio) State University (M.A., 1961), and Washington State University (Ph.D., 1966). He taught at the University of Massachusetts at Amherst from 1965 to 1971 before joining the sociology department at the University of Chicago, where he became a full professor (1975) and department chairman (1978). In this capacity he assumed leadership of the "Chicago School" of sociology and used Chicago's "Black Belt"—the South and West sides of the city—as his laboratory. It was there that he

MARTHA STEWART

William Julius Wilson

sent legions of graduate students and other researchers on fact-finding fieldwork.

Wilson's first major book, *The Declining Significance of Race: Blacks and Changing American Institutions* (1978), caused a sensation in the academic community because of its assertion that class divisions were more damaging than racial ones. In *The Truly Disadvantaged: The Inner City, the Underclass, and Public Policy* (1987), he suggested that civil rights legislation and affirmative action served the educated black middle class well but left the poor unaffected. His intensive ethnographic study of Chicago ghettos in the late 1980s led to the establishment in 1993 of the Center for the Study of Urban Inequality, an important research and policy-making foundation.

(TOM MICHAEL)

Woods, Tiger

Although it seemed impossible for him to do it, U.S. golfer Tiger Woods exceeded expectations in 1997. The 21-year-old sensation, who had won three consecutive U.S. Amateur championships, continued his remarkable success as a professional. His stardom seemed inevitable when two companies signed him to endorsement deals totaling $60 million before he turned pro in August 1996. When he began playing on the Professional Golfers' Association of America (PGA) tour, Woods won two of the tournaments he entered—an impressive feat for a rookie. So it was not a complete surprise when, in April 1997, Woods won the 61st Masters Tournament. What was astonishing was his domination of the grueling tourney. His 18-under-par 270 set a record for the event, and his 12-stroke margin of victory was the largest ever. Adding to the drama was the fact that Woods, of mixed racial descent, was the first nonwhite golfer in history to win a major tournament. His dynamic presence on the PGA tour attracted a larger, younger, and more ethnically diverse following to the game.

Eldrick ("Tiger") Woods was born on Dec. 30, 1975, in Cypress, Calif. His parents, who nicknamed him after a soldier his father had fought with in Vietnam, recognized his golfing talent early on. At age two Woods was seen putting with comedian Bob Hope on a nationally televised talk show, and at age five he was featured in a golf magazine. He won his first U.S. Junior Amateur title in 1991, in 1992 became the first golfer to win the title twice, and in 1993 won it again. In 1994 he won the first of his three U.S. Amateur titles, and he was also a member of the U.S. amateur team that won the world championship. In 1996 Woods, a student at Stanford University, won the National Collegiate Athletic Association championship.

At the end of the 1997 PGA season, Woods led the tour in earnings with a single-season record $2,066,833. He had won four tournaments (the Masters, the Mercedes championship, the GTE Byron Nelson Classic, and the Motorola Western Open) and finished in the top 10 nine times. The year did have its rough spots, however, and Woods's fame only served to magnify them. After a disappointing performance at the U.S. Open, he refused to talk to reporters and then threw a tantrum in the dressing room. Late in the season he related that he had been the subject of persistent death threats. Observers also noted that the rigours of Woods's first year on the tour seemed to catch up with him, since he did not win a tournament after July 6. After the season Woods vowed to cut back on his schedule in 1998.

(ANTHONY G. CRAINE)

Yu Miri

A writer of Korean ancestry living in Japan, Yu Miri won the Akutagawa Prize in 1997 for her novel *Kazoku shinema* (1996; "Family Cinema"), about a broken family modeled after her own. A narrative Möbius strip, *Kazoku shinema* told the story of a young woman's reuniting with long-estranged relatives to film a semifictional documentary about themselves. Written in clear and simple language, the novel alternated briskly between real-life scenes and those being filmed for the movie. Yu believed that many people hold their families together by acting out prescribed roles within the social unit. By having her characters play familial roles within their own film, she deftly underscored both the reality and the fiction of family life.

Yu was born in Yokohama, Japan, on June 22, 1968. Her family was extremely dysfunctional. Her father was a compulsive gambler who physically abused his wife and children, and her mother was a bar hostess who frequently took the teenaged Yu along to parties, where Yu was occasionally molested. One of Yu's sisters became an actress in pornographic films. As a child, Yu became so confused about languages—when to use Japanese or Korean—that she developed a stutter.

Because she was Korean and because of her difficult home life, Yu was often ostracized and victimized by other children at school. Her parents separated when she was a teenager; she repeatedly tried to commit suicide and was eventually expelled from high school.

While working as an actress, Yu turned to writing plays and found that distilling her past through writing could help her come to terms with her pain. Besides *Kazoku shinema* her publications included nine plays, an autobiography, and an additional novel. Each of her works was unsparing in its depiction of destructive family relationships in which individuals were unable to communicate or connect with others.

Even after receiving a top Japanese literary prize, Yu continued to feel uncomfortable as a non-Japanese in Japan. Though *Kazoku shinema* was written in Japanese, Yu was enthusiastically embraced in South Korea after her novel was translated into Korean. The book's publication turned up the heat on the simmering Korean-Japanese ethnic stew, however. *Kazoku shinema* became a best-seller in Japan but was vehemently attacked by members of the conservative press, who felt that Yu had portrayed the Japanese as fools in her novel. Her defenders argued that such critics did not like Yu simply because she was Korean. Yu then began receiving death threats. In February as she prepared to hold a book signing in Japan, a right-wing terrorist threatened to bomb the event. Although her writing was not overtly political, Yu felt that the threat to her freedom of speech forced her to take a political stand by proceeding with the book signing, which was eventually held in Tokyo in June with 24 police officers and security guards to protect her.

(REBECCA RUNDALL)

OBITUARIES

Aguilar Manzo, Luis ("THE WILD ROOSTER"), Mexican singer and actor whose career spanned half a century and included some 150 movies, most notably the comedy *Full Steam Ahead* (1951), in which he played a motorcycle policeman seeking romance and adventure (b. Jan. 29, 1918—d. Oct. 24, 1997).

Akii-Bua, John, Ugandan athlete who in 1972 became the first, and thus far the only, Ugandan to win an Olympic gold medal when he triumphed in the 400-m hurdles in 47.82 seconds, a world record (b. Dec. 3, 1949—d. June 20, 1997).

Allchurch, Ivor John, Welsh association football (soccer) player who was the "Golden Boy" of Welsh soccer from 1949 to 1968. Allchurch, an inside forward known for his superb ball control, scored 251 goals in 694 league matches, mainly for Swansea Town, Newcastle United, and Cardiff City, made a then-record 23 goals in 68 appearances for Wales, and was instrumental in guiding Wales in 1958 to its only appearance in a World Cup final, where it narrowly lost to Brazil in a semifinal match (b. Dec. 16, 1929—d. July 9, 1997).

Allison, Luther, American blues singer and guitarist who during a 30-year career appeared with almost all of the leading blues performers and also served as an influence on rock and roll; although he was especially popular in Europe and had moved to Paris in 1983, recent American albums had brought new life to his career in the U.S. (b. Aug. 17, 1939—d. Aug. 12, 1997).

JACK VARTOOGIAN

Luther Allison

Amin, Mustafa, outspoken Egyptian journalist and publisher who was sentenced to life imprisonment under Pres. Gamal Abdel Nasser as an American spy in 1965, allegedly because he promoted Western-style democracy and closer ties to the U.S.; he was released by Pres. Anwar as-Sadat in 1974 (b. Feb. 21, 1914—d. April 13, 1997).

Arcaro, George Edward ("EDDIE"), American jockey (b. Feb. 19, 1916, Cincinnati, Ohio—d. Nov. 14, 1997, Miami, Fla.), was one of the greatest riders in the history of thoroughbred horse racing and the only jockey ever to win the Triple Crown twice, riding Whirlaway to victory in the Kentucky Derby, the Preakness Stakes, and the Belmont Stakes in 1941 and repeating the feat in 1948 on Citation. Known as "the Master," Arcaro chalked up 4,779 wins and more than $30 million in earnings during a 31-year career. He began exercising horses at the Latonia Race Course in northern Kentucky after dropping out of school at the age of 13, and he rode in his first race in 1931. Although his first win did not come until a year later, Arcaro soon rose to become one of the most illustrious jockeys of all time, and his mounts were some of the most famous race horses of the mid-20th century. His record-breaking achievements include winning both the Preakness and Belmont Stakes six times—more than any other jockey—and the Kentucky Derby five times, a record he shared with Bill Hartack. He also captured the Jockey Club Gold Cup 10 times. Arcaro's fierce and competitive nature got him into trouble in 1942 when interference with another jockey during a race caused him to be suspended for a year. He returned to the sport a more mature and well-tempered athlete, however, and resumed his spectacular career in the saddle. Arcaro was a founding member and president (1949–61) of the Jockeys' Guild, an organization devoted to the welfare of jockeys. He was inducted into the Racing Hall of Fame in 1958. After his retirement in 1961, he worked as a racing analyst for network television and spent his free time perfecting his golf game.

Eddie Arcaro

ASSOCIATED PRESS

Ashburn, Rich ("RICHIE"; "WHITEY"), American baseball player whose 15-year major league career included two National League batting championships, five All-Star honours, and membership in the 1950 pennant-winning Philadelphia Phillies' "Whiz Kids" lineup. Following his playing career, he was a broadcaster with the Phillies for 35 years, and he was voted into the Hall of Fame in 1995 (b. March 19, 1927—d. Sept. 9, 1997).

Auerbach, Oscar, American pathologist whose research showing that cigarette smoking was causally related to lung cancer, based on his examination of thousands of lung tissue samples, gained national prominence in the first Surgeon General's Report on Smoking and Health in 1964 (b. Jan. 1, 1905—d. Jan. 15, 1997).

Awdry, Wilbert Vere, British clergyman and author who created the enormously popular children's series *Thomas the Tank Engine;* between 1945 and 1972 he wrote 26 stories about the mischievous locomotive, selling more than 50 million books and spawning some 500 products, including videos, toys, and clothing (b. June 15, 1911—d. March 21, 1997).

Azcárraga Milmo, Emilio ("EL TIGRE"), Mexican billionaire who created the Spanish-speaking world's largest media empire by building up his family's radio and television network; his fortune was estimated at $2 billion (b. Sept. 6, 1930—d. April 16, 1997).

Baker, La Vern (DELORES WILLIAMS), American rhythm-and-blues singer who achieved her greatest success in the 1950s and '60s with such hits as "Tweedle Dee" and "I Cried a Tear"; in 1991 she became the second woman inducted into the Rock and Roll Hall of Fame (b. Nov. 11, 1929—d. March 10, 1997).

Banda, Hastings Kamuzu, Malawian politician (b. *c.* 1902, near Kasungu, British Central Africa protectorate [now Malawi]—d. Nov. 25, 1997, Johannesburg, S.Af.), was the founder and first president of Malawi. An autocratic leader, Banda was criticized by many other African rulers for his pro-Western policies and his friendly relationship with white-ruled South Africa. His early education was in Scottish missionary schools, and he went to work at the South African gold mines at an early age. He saved enough money to travel to the United States, where he studied at a number of universities and became a physician. He then moved to Scotland, continued to study medicine there, and was made an elder of the Church of Scotland. Banda practiced medicine in Great Britain for a number of years, building a successful practice. Much of his time, however, was devoted to the burgeoning anticolonial movement. By the mid-1950s he had moved back to Africa and become involved in the independence campaign in Nyasaland, the colonial name of Malawi. In 1964 Malawi was granted its independence, and Banda became prime minister. In 1966 Malawi declared itself a republic, and Banda was proclaimed president. His political opponents were killed, imprisoned, or sent into exile, and in 1971 he had himself made president for life. A leader with Victorian social views, Banda outlawed short skirts and pants on women, forbade male tourists with long hair to enter the country, and banned television. By the 1990s his excesses had angered the Malawian people, and in elections in 1994 they voted him out of office. He was then tried for the 1983 murder of four political opponents but was eventually acquitted. Banda was given a state funeral.

Bao Dai (NGUYEN VINH THUY), Vietnamese ruler (b. Oct. 22, 1913, Hue, Vietnam—d. July 31, 1997, Paris, France), was the last reigning emperor of Vietnam from 1926 until his exile in 1945 but exerted little influence over his domain. The son of Emperor Khai Dinh, Thuy was raised and educated in France. After his father died in 1925, he succeeded him to the throne in January 1926 and adopted the name Bao Dai ("Keeper of Greatness"). His duties were ceremonial, however, since the French firmly governed Vietnam. In March 1945 the Japanese staged a *coup de force* but maintained Bao Dai as a puppet. When the Viet Minh (communists), led by Ho Chi Minh, expelled the Japanese in August of that year, they allowed Bao Dai to remain in an honorary position. In 1946, however, Bao Dai, unhappy with his powerless position, fled to Hong Kong. He returned in 1949 after French control had been reestablished, became temporary premier of the newly independent Vietnam, and was reinstated as sovereign. Known as the "Playboy Emperor," he neglected his few government duties, preferring instead to hunt tigers and collect mistresses. With the end of French rule in 1954, Bao Dai tried to align himself with Premier Ngo Dinh Diem, who was backed by the United States. In 1955, when Diem used his military power and a questionable referendum to declare himself head of state, Bao Dai left Vietnam. In exile on the French Riviera, he lived idly off the wealth he had appropriated during his reign but spent his latter years in more modest circumstances in Paris.

Baquero y Díaz, Gastón, Cuban poet who left his homeland after the 1959 revolution and spent the rest of his life in exile in Spain; only in 1994 did his poems begin to be published once again in Cuba (b. May 4, 1918—d. May 15, 1997).

Barakat, Henri Antoine, Egyptian filmmaker who made 112 motion pictures during his 55-year career and was known for the "poetic realism" of his works (b. June 11, 1914—d. May 27, 1997).

Barbara (MONIQUE SERF), French singer and composer who specialized in singing the songs of Jacques Brel and Georges Brassens in Belgium before she found stardom in France singing many of her own compositions, notably "L'Aigle noir" ("Black Eagle"), "Ma plus belle histoire d'amour, c'est vous" ("You Are My Most Beautiful Love Story"), and "Il pleut sur Nantes" ("It's Raining in Nantes"); her melancholy songs, although poetic, defied translation and made her a celebrity mainly in French-speaking countries. She was also an ardent AIDS activist, dispensing condoms at her series of Paris concerts in 1987, 1990, and 1993 (b. June 9, 1930—d. Nov. 24, 1997).

Barbosa de Rosario, Pilar, Puerto Rican historian and political adviser who in 1921 became the first woman to teach at the University of Puerto Rico; she was named the commonwealth's official historian in 1993 and served as mentor to generations of politicians, notably from the ruling New Progressive Party (b. July 4, 1897—d. Jan. 22, 1997).

Barco Vargas, Virgilio, Colombian politician (b. Sept. 17, 1921, Cúcuta, Colom.—d. May 20, 1997, Bogotá, Colom.), served as president of Colombia from 1986 to 1990 after having won the election by the largest margin in the country's history. During his term his ambitious plans for social reform were interrupted when he was forced to combat the powerful Medellín-based drug cartel, which was waging terror on public officials. Born to a wealthy oil family, Barco attended the National University of Colombia in Bogotá and graduated (1943) from the Massachusetts Institute of Technology (MIT) with a degree in civil engineering. He earned (1952) a master's degree in social sciences from Boston University and a doctorate in economics from MIT. His political career began in 1943 when he became a Liberal councillor in the town of Durania, and he later was elected to the lower house of Congress. During a volatile period in the late 1940s and early 1950s, known as *La Violencia,* in which the Liberal and Conservative factions waged a brutal war against one another and in which hundreds of thousands of people died, Barco was forced into exile in the U.S. He returned to Colombia in 1954 and was instrumental in negotiating an agreement that led to interparty peace. Over the next 40 years, he held a variety of ministerial and diplomatic offices, enjoyed two terms in the Senate (1958–66), and served as ambassador to Britain (1961–62 and 1990–92) and the United States (1977). Barco was appointed mayor of Bogotá in 1966 and served as a director of the World Bank from 1969 to 1974. His career peaked in 1986, when he was elected to the presidency. Barco campaigned for social reform, but violence—first by leftist guerrilla groups and then by drug lords—plagued his term as president. Barco had marginal success at controlling guerrilla violence, but his efforts to combat "narcoterrorism," including extradition of drug criminals to the U.S. and seizure of their estates, escalated the violence. Though lauded by the international community for his actions, he was denounced in Colombia. Barco retired from political life in 1992.

Barwick, Sir Garfield Edward John, Australian barrister who was highly regarded for his service to the Australian government as attorney general, foreign minister, and chief justice of the High Court but whose reputation was clouded by the controversy that ensued when his advice led the governor-general to dismiss the Labor government of Gough Whitlam in 1975 (b. June 22, 1903—d. July 13, 1997).

Baseley, (Cyril) Godfrey, British radio executive and actor who created the country life radio show "The Archers," the world's longest-running daily serial, and for more than 20 years served as the program's script editor (b. Oct. 2, 1904—d. Feb. 2, 1997).

Bauby, Jean-Dominique, French journalist whose struggle with "locked-in syndrome," a state of almost total paralysis, was recounted in his critically acclaimed memoir, *The Diving Bell and the Butterfly* (1997), which he dictated by blinking his left eyelid (b. 1952—d. March 9, 1997).

Bell, Bob Lewis, American performer who starred (1959–84) as the original fiery-red-haired Bozo the Clown on WGN-TV's "Bozo's Circus," a Chicago program that attracted more than 30 million viewers when the show was aired over cable stations; his side-splitting antics earned Bell induction into the International Clown Hall of Fame in 1996 (b. 1922?—d. Dec. 8, 1997).

Bellou, Sotiria, Greek singer who was the first woman to have a career performing *rebetika* songs, Greek urban folk music, which she made her trademark for some 40 years (b. Aug. 29, 1921—d. Aug. 27, 1997).

Berlin, Sir Isaiah, British lecturer and essayist (b. June 6, 1909, Riga, Latvia [then part of the Russian Empire]—d. Nov. 5, 1997, Oxford, Eng.), produced essays on historical, philosophical, political, and cultural topics; was noted for his support of traditional liberalism; and was credited with founding the discipline of intellectual history. In 1915 his family moved from his birthplace to Russia; they resided in St. Petersburg during the 1917 Revolution and in 1920 settled in England. Berlin studied philosophy at Corpus Christi College, Oxford, and remained connected with Oxford for the remainder of his life. During World War II he worked for the British government in Washington, D.C., reporting on U.S. opinion. In 1956 he married the French golf champion Aline de Gunzbourg. Berlin's early years at Oxford were marked by the pursuit of analytic or "pure" philosophy, but after World War II his concerns shifted to political science, political theory, and what came to be classified as intellectual history. Rejecting determinism—the idea that events are determined by prior conditions—Berlin found some value in Carlyle's "great man" theory of history, which holds that the course of history is determined by a few individuals. Berlin's 1957 lecture "Two Concepts of Liberty" introduced his concepts of "negative liberty" (freedom from restraint) and "positive liberty" (freedom viewed as producing a positive good), arguing that society should restrict itself to the former and leave individuals free to pursue the latter on their own. A pluralist, he rejected the idea that there could be a "single solution" to the problem of organizing society. Berlin's best-known essay, *The Hedgehog and the Fox* (1953), compared "foxes" such as Aristotle and Shakespeare, who "knew many things," with "hedgehogs such as Plato and Dante, who "knew one big thing." Politically, he was an unwavering supporter of Israel and Zionism and was a doctrinaire anticommunist, and his book *Karl Marx: His Life and Environment* (1939) was one of the first attempts in the noncommunist world to treat the subject objectively. Besides numerous collections of essays, Berlin published such books as *The Age of Enlightenment* (1956), *Four Essays on Liberty* (1969), *Vico and Herder* (1976), and *The Magus of the North: J.G. Hamann and the Origins of Modern Irrationalism* (1993). He was also celebrated as a brilliant raconteur and admired for his wide-ranging interests. He was honoured in his lifetime as few intellectuals had been, receiving countless awards and prizes, including 23 honorary doctorates.

Bernard, Jeffrey Joseph, British journalist whose life as a heavy-drinking habitué of London's Soho hangouts was reflected in his weekly "Low Life" column in *The Spectator* magazine; a play named for the line that often ran when his column failed to appear, *Jeffrey Bernard Is Unwell,* was a West End hit (b. May 27, 1932—d. Sept. 4, 1997).

Berry, Richard, American musician who wrote "Louie Louie," a simple rock song that reached the number two spot on American charts, became the second most recorded pop song in history, and was investigated by the FBI on suspicion of having lewd lyrics; he sold the publishing rights for $750 in 1959 but regained them in 1986 (b. April 11, 1935—d. Jan. 23, 1997).

Bertil, Prince (PRINCE BERTIL GUSTAF OSCAR CARL EUGEN, DUKE OF HALLAND), third son of King Gustaf VI Adolph of Sweden and uncle of King Carl XVI Gustav, was heir presumptive to the Swedish throne from 1973 until 1979, when a change in the laws of succession enabled King Carl Gustav's daughter, Princess Victoria, to be named heir. Prince Bertil was also president of the Swedish Olympic Committee and was chairman of the national sports federation for more than four decades (b. Feb. 28, 1912—d. Jan. 5, 1997).

Bertone, Giuseppe ("NUCCIO"), Italian car-body designer and head of the influential family-owned automobile-design company that produced models for such notable manufacturers as Fiat, Alfa Romeo, and Lamborghini (b. July 4, 1914—d. Feb. 26, 1997).

Bing, Sir Rudolf Franz Joseph, British operatic impresario (b. Jan. 9, 1902, Vienna, Austria—d. Sept. 2, 1997, New York, N.Y.), directed the Metropolitan Opera through one of its most turbulent periods (1950–72). The son of a Viennese industrialist, Bing grew up in a musical household. Although he studied voice in his teens, he soon started working for a bookstore that expanded its business into concert and opera management. He moved to Berlin in 1927 and became assistant manager of the Darmstadt Opera a year later. He followed opera director Carl Ebert first to the Charlottenburg (Berlin) Opera in 1931 and then, as the Nazi era dawned, to Glyndebourne, Eng. During World War II Bing worked in a department store; he later claimed that his experiences soothing hysterical women gave him insight into how to deal with sopranos. After cofounding (1946) the Edinburgh Festival, Bing moved (1949) to New York City. Following a year of observation, he assumed full control of the Metropolitan Opera and revolutionized opera production, in part, by hiring eminent directors from theatre and film, such as Peter Brook, Tyrone Guthrie, and Alfred Lunt. Though Bing became notorious for his quarrels with American soprano Maria Callas and Danish tenor Lauritz Melchior, he engaged such great international stars as Renata Tebaldi, Jussi Björling, and Franco Corelli. In 1955 Bing hired Marian Anderson to sing Ulrica in *Un ballo in maschera,* the first time that a black singer had appeared at the Met in a major role. Besides contending with the crippling strikes of 1961 and 1969, he supervised the Met's move in 1966 from its theatre on 39th Street to Lincoln Center. One year before he retired, Bing hired James Levine as the company's artistic director. Some critics held that Bing relied too heavily upon Italian Romantic operas. Renowned for his autocratic methods as well as his wit, Bing reportedly remarked, "Don't be misled; beneath that cold, austere, severe exterior, there beats a heart of stone." He was knighted in 1971 and wrote two memoirs, *5,000 Nights at the Opera* (1972) and *A Knight at the Opera* (1981). In later years he suffered from Alzheimer's disease.

Blos, Peter, German-born American child psychoanalyst who was known as "Mr. Adolescence" as a result of his research into the problems of teenagers and his theories describing their struggles between wanting to break free of their parents and desiring to remain dependent (b. Feb. 2, 1904—d. June 12, 1997).

Bremner, William J. ("BILLY"), Scottish association football (soccer) player whose skill, inspiring leadership (usually as captain), and fierce determination made him vital to the success of Leeds United (1959–76), Hull City (1976–78), and Scotland (54 caps, 1965–75); as tough off the field as on, in 1975 he was banned from international play for life after an altercation in a night club. He later became manager of Leeds (1985–88) and Doncaster Rovers (1978–85, 1989–92) (b. Dec. 9, 1942—d. Dec. 7, 1997).

Brennan, William Joseph, Jr., U.S. Supreme Court justice (b. April 25, 1906, Newark, N.J.—d. July 24, 1997, Arlington, Va.), was considered the prototypical liberal interpreter of the Constitution during his tenure (1956–90) with the tribunal. Brennan was the author of some 1,350 Supreme Court decisions, second only to Justice William O. Douglas. The son of an Irish laborer and union activist, Brennan adopted his father's social vision. At Harvard Law School he studied under Felix Frankfurter (associate justice, 1939–62), who was a proponent of judicial self-restraint and with whom he came to bitterly disagree over political redistricting. After law school Brennan became a highly successful labour lawyer. In 1942 he joined the army; he was awarded the Legion of Merit for resolving labour disputes in the military. Returning to his law firm in 1946, he became an advocate of court reform. In 1949 he was appointed to the Superior Court, and he quickly advanced to the New Jersey Supreme Court. Brennan was widely praised for improving the flow of court cases, and he caught the attention of U.S. Pres. Dwight Eisenhower, who appointed him to the U.S. Supreme Court in 1956. Brennan quickly rose to the occasion. In *Baker* v. *Carr* (1962), he wrote the majority opinion that the federal courts would thereafter supervise fair apportionment of legislative seats. Chief Justice Earl Warren later called this "the most vital decision" of his tenure. In the landmark 1964 ruling *New York Times Co.* v. *Sullivan,* Brennan considerably expanded the freedom of the press by ruling that public figures could collect damages for publication of false statements only if "actual malice" could be shown. In *Goldberg* v. *Kelly* (1970), Brennan broadened the right of due process by ruling that a state violates the 14th Amendment if it cuts off an individual's welfare benefits without a hearing. Citing the right to privacy, Brennan ruled in *Eisenstadt* v. *Baird* (1972) that a state could not criminalize the distribution of contraceptives to unmarried individuals. A champion of minority causes, Brennan ruled in 1979 that private affirmative action programs did not violate the 1964 Civil Rights Act. Though he considered the death penalty "cruel and unusual," he was never able to achieve a majority on this issue. In 1990 he authored *United States* v. *Eichman,* which held that flag burning is protected speech under the First Amendment. After suffering a stroke, he retired that same year.

Bristol, Horace, American photojournalist whose idea for a collaboration with John Steinbeck on a chronicle of the life of migrant workers led to Steinbeck's novel *The Grapes of Wrath;* Bristol's photos were used as an aid in the casting of the 1940 film version of the novel (b. Nov. 16, 1908—d. Aug. 4, 1997).

Bryce, Robert Broughton, Canadian public servant who served three prime ministers as secretary to the Cabinet and was influential in the formation of economic policy for some three decades (b. Feb. 27, 1910—d. July 30, 1997).

Buckley, Jeffrey Scott ("JEFF"), American folk, rock, and pop singer and songwriter whose multi-octave voice was compared to that of his father, the late Tim Buckley; through his one full album, *Grace,* two minialbums, and performances on other artists' albums as well as in concert, he attracted a devoted international following (b. Nov. 17, 1966—d. May 29, 1997).

Burhoe, Ralph Wendell, American educator and writer who was both a theologian and a scientist and spent his career attempting to merge those fields; he founded several organizations toward that end, and in 1980 he was the first American to win the Templeton Prize for Progress in Religion (b. June 21, 1911—d. May 8, 1997).

Burnum, Burnum (HENRY JAMES PENRITH), Australian Aboriginal political activist who often conducted his battle for Aboriginal rights by performing flamboyant stunts; his best-known one involved claiming England for Aborigines by planting an Aboriginal flag atop the white cliffs of Dover (b. January 1936—d. Aug. 17, 1997).

Burroughs, William Seward, American writer (b. Feb. 5, 1914, St. Louis, Mo.—d. Aug. 2, 1997, Lawrence, Kan.), was the author of the notorious avant-garde novel *Naked Lunch (1959).* After graduating from Harvard University in 1936, Burroughs moved to New York City, where in the early 1940s he associated with Jack Kerouac, Allen Ginsberg (*q.v.*), Neal Cassady, and others with whom he would be identified as a member of the Beat Generation. During this period Burroughs developed a heroin addiction that lasted into the 1960s. Despite his open homosexuality, he entered into a common-law marriage with Joan Vollmer in 1946; five years later, attempting a drunken stunt during a party in Mexico City, he shot and killed her. He fled Mexico and was never tried for the offense. Though ostensibly an accident, Burroughs was tormented by the idea that subconsciously he had desired her death; his remorse spurred him to devote himself to writing. His most famous novel, *Naked Lunch*, simulates nightmarish heroin-induced hallucinations through a variety of experimental techniques, including lack of narrative, stream of consciousness, and random ordering of story parts. The book was acclaimed (and also condemned) as a disturbing representation of existential alienation. Though *Naked Lunch* features explicit depictions of sex and violence, a legal attempt to ban it in the United States for obscenity failed, which cleared the way for more open treatment of such subject matter in literature. His next novels—*The Soft Machine* (1961), *The Ticket That Exploded* (1962), and *Nova Express* (1964)—employed his "cut-up" technique, in which quotations from unrelated sources were cut and randomly inserted into his own text. Few of his subsequent writings attracted significant attention. In later life Burroughs became an all-purpose avant-garde icon, appearing with rock musicians and in television advertisements and movies.

K. SIMON—SYGMA

William S. Burroughs

Caen, Herbert Eugene ("HERB"), American newspaper columnist for the *San Francisco Chronicle,* 1938–50 and 1958–97, and *San Francisco Examiner,* 1950–58; his longtime encomiums on San Francisco, characterized by pithy wordplay and, later, nostalgia, earned him a Pulitzer Prize in 1996 (b. April 3, 1916—d. Feb. 1, 1997).

Callado, Antônio, Brazilian novelist and leading journalist whose masterpiece, *Quarup* (1967), tells the story of an idealistic priest who undergoes a religious and political transformation in light of events in Brazil, notably the advent of liberation theology and the 1964 military coup (b. Jan. 26, 1917—d. Jan. 28, 1997).

Calvin, Melvin, American biochemist (b. April 8, 1911, St. Paul, Minn.—d. Jan. 8, 1997, Berkeley, Calif.), studied the structure and behaviour of organic molecules and was awarded the 1961 Nobel Prize for Chemistry for having determined the steps by which carbon is converted to carbohydrates, an important mechanism in the process of photosynthesis. Calvin, who earned his Ph.D. at the University of Minnesota in 1935, began investigating the photosynthetic process in the late 1940s while serving as director of the bioorganic chemistry group at the Lawrence Radiation Laboratory at the University of California, Berkeley. Taking advantage of newly developed tools—chromatography and the radioactive isotope carbon-14—to carry out his experiments, he fed radioactive carbon dioxide to the green alga *Chlorella* and followed its path through a cycle of reactions, now called the Calvin cycle. After devoting almost 15 years to elucidating this pathway, Calvin served as director of the Laboratory of Chemical Biodynamics at Berkeley (1960–80), where he turned his attention to conjectures such as the origins of life on Earth and the possibility of life elsewhere in the universe. He also conducted research into the development of alternative fuels. In addition to the Nobel Prize, Calvin received the National Medal of Science (1989) and the Priestley Medal of the American Chemical Society (1978), and he was elected to the National Academy of Sciences (1954). Over the years he was the author of more than 500 papers and a number of books, including *The Path of Carbon in Photosynthesis* (1957; with J.A. Bassham) and *Following the Trail of Light: A Scientific Odyssey* (1992).

Carcani, Adil, Albanian politician who served (1981–91) as the last communist prime minister of Albania during a political career that spanned nearly five decades and included numerous offices; in 1994 he was placed under house arrest for abuse of power (b. May 4, 1922—d. Oct. 13, 1997).

Carpenter, Thelma, American performer who was a big-band singer during the 1930s and '40s and performed on Broadway in the '40s and '50s but then disappeared from show business until 1968, when she became Pearl Bailey's understudy in *Hello, Dolly!;* she subsequently went on for Bailey more than 100 times and thereafter had a successful stage, film, and television career (b. Jan. 15, 1920—d. May 15, 1997).

Castillo Martínez, Heberto, Mexican political leader of the leftist opposition to the long-entrenched Institutional Revolutionary Party; he was imprisoned for more than two years for his support of the 1968 student movement and was one of the founders of the Party of the Democratic Revolution (b. Aug. 23, 1928—d. April 5, 1997).

Cato, (Robert) Milton, Caribbean politician who served, 1979–84, as the first prime minister of St. Vincent and the Grenadines after the country achieved independence (b. June 3, 1915—d. Feb. 10, 1997).

Chambers, George, Trinidadian politician who served (1981–86) as prime minister of Trinidad and Tobago and was faced with the difficult task of diversifying the economy following the oil boom of the 1970s. Although his policies were unpopular, many credited him with the country's continuing economic success (b. Oct. 4, 1928—d. Nov. 4, 1997).

Chaplin, Saul (Saul Caplan), American songwriter and Hollywood musical director who won three Academy Awards for best scoring of a musical picture for *An American in Paris, West Side Story,* and *Seven Brides for Seven Brothers;* Chaplin collaborated with Sammy Cahn before striking out on his own and composing such hits as "The Anniversary Song," "Until the Real Thing Comes Along," and "Bei Mir Bist du Schoen," a mainstay of the Andrews Sisters' repertoire (b. Feb. 19, 1912—d. Nov. 15, 1997).

Cheatham, Adolphus Anthony ("Doc"), American jazz trumpeter whose 70-year international career took him from playing in bands—working with such notables as Cab Calloway, Benny Goodman, and Eddie Heywood—and backing such singers as Ma Rainey, Bessie Smith, and Billie Holiday to a solo career, begun when he was in his 60s, that brought him his greatest popularity (b. June 13, 1905—d. June 2, 1997).

Cioaba, Ion, Romanian self-proclaimed king of all Roma (Gypsies) everywhere and a champion of their rights (b. 1935?—d. Feb. 23, 1997).

Clarke, Shirley Brimberg, American motion picture director of independent films whose gritty cinema verité works in the 1950s and '60s, including *The Connection, The Cool World,* and *Portrait of Jason,* tackled such controversial topics as heroin addiction, gang membership, and male prostitution (b. Oct. 2, 1925—d. Sept. 23, 1997).

Coffin, Tristram, American journalist who had a nearly 50-year career that encompassed reporting for a newspaper and on radio, writing books, penning a syndicated column, and, from 1968, publishing the newsletter that went on to become the *Washington Spectator* (b. July 25, 1912—d. May 28, 1997).

Compton, Denis Charles Scott, British cricketer (b. May 23, 1918, Hendon, Middlesex, Eng.—d. April 23, 1997, Windsor, Berkshire, Eng.), was one of the 20th century's most gifted and audacious batsmen, admired for his mastery of the sweeping stroke and his "cheeky schoolboy" spirit both on and off the field. In a first-class career that spanned almost three decades (1936–64), Compton scored 38,942 runs (average, 51.85) and 123 centuries, including 5,807 runs (avg. 50.06) and 17 centuries in 78 Test matches. Although he batted right-handed, as an occasionally devastating left-arm spin bowler he took 622 first-class wickets (avg. 32.27), including 25 in Tests. "Compo" made his first-class debut for Middlesex in 1936, and the next season he was selected for his first Test appearance, in which he scored a 65 against New Zealand. He played in international sports matches while serving in the military in India during World War II and returned home with a boyish enthusiasm that delighted war-weary English fans. In 1947, at the pinnacle of his career, he scored 3,816 runs (avg. 90.85) and 18 centuries, both single-season records that still stood at the time of his death. In 1948–49, playing for the Marylebone Cricket Club against North-Eastern Transvaal in South Africa, he scored 300 runs in 181 minutes, the fastest-ever triple-hundred in first-class cricket. An outstanding all-around athlete, he also played association football (soccer) for Arsenal from 1936 until 1950, when knee surgery ended his football career shortly after Arsenal won the FA Cup. Compton was cricket correspondent for the *Sunday Express* from 1950, a sports commentator for BBC television from 1958, and the author of numerous books. He made his last Test appearance in 1956 and was made C.B.E. in 1958. A celebrated series of postwar Brylcreem hair-dressing advertisements made the dashing Compton a familiar face, even outside sporting circles.

Cooke, Jack Kent, Canadian-born American businessman and sports team owner who amassed a fortune through ownership of broadcast media companies, newspapers, and real estate, created the closed-circuit television megabroadcast, and went on to own such properties as New York City's Chrysler Building and the Los Angeles Lakers and the Washington Redskins sports teams (b. Oct. 25, 1912—d. April 6, 1997).

Copeland, Johnny Clyde, American blues singer and guitarist who performed for over 25 years before becoming nationally and internationally known in the 1980s; his performance on the album *Showdown!* won a Grammy award in 1986 (b. March 27, 1937—d. July 3, 1997).

Cousteau, Jacques-Yves, French oceanographer, filmmaker, and inventor (b. June 11, 1910, Saint-André-de-Cubzac, France—d. June 25, 1997, Paris, France), popularized the study of marine environments through numerous books, films, and television programs that chronicled his undersea investigations. Cousteau, not formally trained as a scientist, was drawn to undersea exploration by his love both of the ocean and of diving. After graduating from France's naval academy in 1933, he was commissioned a second lieutenant. His plans to become a navy pilot were undermined by an almost fatal automobile accident in which both of his arms were broken. During his convalescence he discovered goggle diving, and his fascination with the sport inspired him to design, with Émile Gagnan, the aqualung, also known as scuba (self-contained underwater breathing apparatus), which became commercially available in 1946. Cousteau helped to invent many other tools useful to oceanographers, including the diving saucer, a small, easily maneuverable submarine for seafloor exploration, and a number of underwater cameras. He served in World War II as a gunnery officer in France and was also a member of the French Resistance. He later was awarded the Legion of Honour for his espionage work. Cousteau's experiments with underwater filmmaking began during the war, and when the war ended, he continued this work by founding and heading the French navy's Undersea Research Group. To expand his work in marine exploration, he founded numerous marketing, manufacturing, engineering, and research organizations, which were incorporated (1973) as the Cousteau Group. In 1950 Cousteau converted a British minesweeper into the *Calypso,* an oceanographic research ship aboard which he and his crew carried out numerous expeditions. He gained international recognition with the publication of *The Silent World* (1953), the first of many books. Two years later he adapted the book into a documentary film that won both the Palm d'Or at the 1956 Cannes International Film Festival and an Academy Award in 1957, one of three Oscars his films received. Retiring from the navy in 1956 with the rank of captain, Cousteau served as director of the Oceanographic Institute and Museum, Monaco. In the early 1960s he conducted experiments in underwater living in undersea laboratories called Conshelf I, II, and III. Cousteau produced and starred in many television programs, including the U.S. series

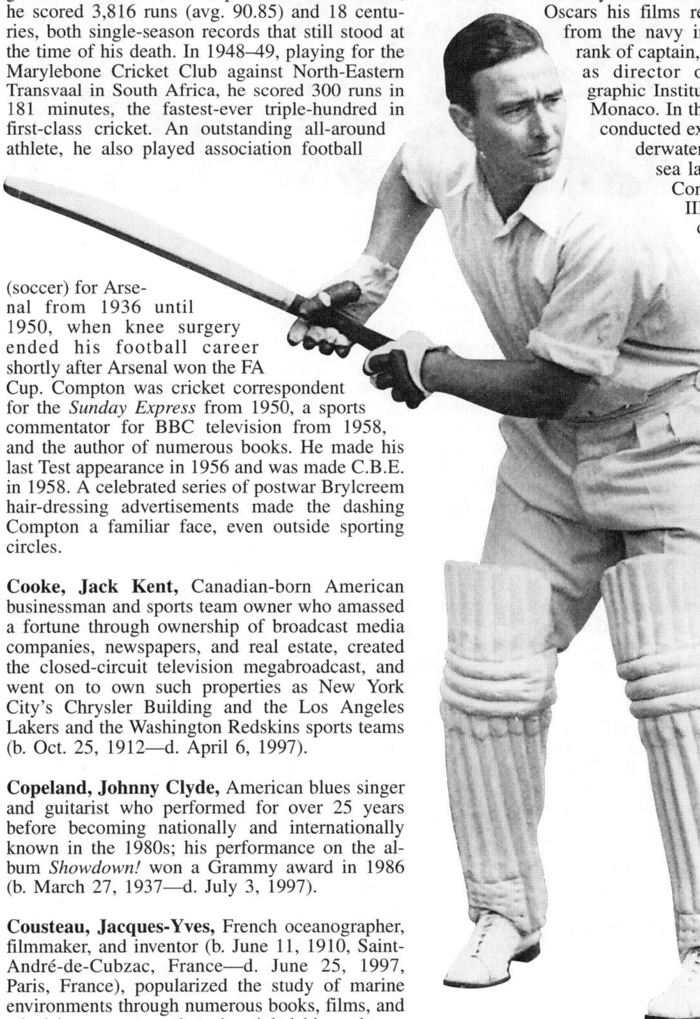

Denis Compton
COLORSPORT

STEPHANE SPEISER—GAMMA LIAISON

Jacques Cousteau

CULVER PICTURES

Alexandra Danilova, with Leon Danielian

"The Undersea World of Jacques Cousteau" (1968–76). In 1974 he formed the Cousteau Society, a nonprofit environmental group dedicated to marine conservation. His last book, *Man, the Octopus, and the Orchid,* was published posthumously.

Crowe, Dame Sylvia, British landscape architect who created designs for gardens at nuclear power stations, colleges, churchyards, reservoirs, office buildings, and new towns and wrote a number of books on the subject; she was created C.B.E. in 1967 and advanced to D.B.E. in 1973 (b. Sept. 15, 1901—d. June 30, 1997).

Crump, Neville Franklin, British racehorse trainer and one of the most successful steeplechase trainers after World War II; he logged three victories in the Grand National and won five Scottish Grand Nationals, two Welsh Nationals, and three Whitbread Gold Cups, among others (b. Dec. 27, 1910—d. Jan. 18, 1997).

Damião, Frei (PIO GIANOTTI), Italian-born Brazilian Roman Catholic monk who walked from town to town in northeastern Brazil preaching to poor villagers, who considered him a saint capable of performing miracles (b. Nov. 5, 1898—d. May 31, 1997).

Danielian, Leon, American ballet dancer who had an inimitable stage presence and masterful technique and achieved his greatest fame with the Ballet Russe de Monte Carlo during the 1940s and '50s; in the '60s he became a highly respected teacher (b. Oct. 31, 1920—d. March 8, 1997).

Danilova, Alexandra (ALEKSANDRA DIONISYEVNA DANILOVA; "CHOURA"), Russian-born American ballerina and teacher (b. Nov. 20, 1903, Peterhof [now Petrodvorets], Russia—d. July 13, 1997, New York, N.Y.), possessed charm, vivacity, and flair, attributes that enhanced her excellent balletic technique and versatility. She captivated audiences while starring in such signature roles as Odette in *Swan Lake,* Swanilda in *Coppélia,* the cancan dancer in *La Boutique fantasque,* the street dancer in *Le Beau Danube,* and the glove seller in *Gaîté Parisienne.* Danilova was trained in St. Petersburg at the Imperial Ballet and the Soviet State Ballet schools and joined the Mariinsky Ballet (later renamed the Kirov Ballet), becoming soloist in 1922. In the summer of 1924, she joined a small ensemble led by George Balanchine for a tour of Western Europe. The group did not return to Russia, and in December they joined Sergey Diaghilev's Ballets Russes. Danilova performed with that company until it disbanded following Diaghilev's death (1929). After dancing in operas and appearing (1931–32) in the stage musical *Waltzes from Vienna* in London's West End, she joined (1933) Les Ballets Russes de Monte-Carlo and made her American debut. During the following years Danilova toured extensively with that company and the various successive Ballets Russes, as well as such companies as Sadler's Wells Ballet and, in 1954–56, her own Great Moments of Ballet. After her final ballet performance, in 1957 at a gala honouring her at New York City's Metropolitan Opera House, she returned to the stage for the Broadway musical *Oh, Captain!* In addition, Danilova choreographed for operas and made lecture tours, and in 1964 she joined the faculty of the School of American Ballet, where she became a highly respected and beloved teacher. She remained there until 1989, staging ballet excerpts for the school's workshop productions and full-length ballets for such companies as the New York City Ballet. Danilova appeared in the motion picture *The Turning Point* (1977) in a role based largely on herself and, with Holly Brubach, published her memoirs, *Choura* (1986). In 1989 she was a recipient of the Kennedy Center Honors.

Davis, Kingsley, American sociologist and demographer (b. Aug. 20, 1908, Tuxedo, Texas—d. Feb. 27, 1997, Stanford, Calif.), was a world-renowned expert on population trends; he coined the terms population explosion and zero population growth and promoted methods of bringing the latter about. Later, however, he came to be concerned about low birthrates in developed countries, fearing a shortage of educated leaders. Davis was educated at the University of Texas (B.A., 1930; M.A., 1933) and Harvard University (Ph.D., 1936). He spent the early years of his career teaching at Smith College, Northampton, Mass. (1934–36), Clark University, Worcester, Mass. (1936–37), Pennsylvania State University (1937–42), and Princeton University (1942–48). The publication of *Human Society* (1949) led to Davis's appointment to the directorship (1949–55) of the Bureau of Applied Social Research at Columbia University, New York City, and he followed that with 22 years (1955–77) at the University of California, Berkeley. From 1977 until his retirement in 1992, he was a professor of sociology at the University of Southern California, and from 1981 he was also a fellow of the Hoover Institution at Stanford University. Davis conducted studies in Europe, Latin America, and less-developed countries such as India, Nepal, and Bahrain and was a much-sought-after consultant and analyst. Among his books were *A Crowding Hemisphere: Population Change in the Americas* (1958) and *World Urbanization 1950–70* (2 vol., 1969–72). In 1966 Davis was elected to the National Academy of Sciences, the first sociologist to be so honoured.

de Kooning, Willem, Dutch-born American artist (b. April 24, 1904, Rotterdam, Neth.—d. March 19, 1997, East Hampton, N.Y.), became one of the most important painters of the 20th century as a leading practitioner of Abstract Expressionism, the dominant movement in art following World War II. He was one of the last surviving giants of the postwar period and, as such, formed a historical link between the early modern legacy of Pablo Picasso and Joan Miró and the subsequent movements of Minimalism, Deconstruction, Op art, and Pop art. Along with contemporaries of the New York School—Jackson Pollock, Mark Rothko, Robert Motherwell, and others—de Kooning catapulted American art to the forefront of the international scene. His finest work, often classified as Action painting, included the "Woman" paintings of the early 1950s, a series of constantly reworked pieces in which the female figure was executed in a ferocious, slashing style. These paintings became famous not just for their ruthless dynamism and sexual themes but also because de Kooning reintroduced the human figure into an art community that emphasized abstraction. De Kooning studied art in Rotterdam before arriving (1926) in the U.S. as a stowaway; he eventually settled in New York City. He began painting full-time after working (1935–37) on the Federal Arts Project of the Works Progress Administration. His early paintings, influenced by Arshile Gorky, alternated between both figurative and abstract and black-and-white and colour. In the period following his first one-man exhibition, mounted in 1948 at the Charles Egan Gallery in New York City, de Kooning gained international celebrity for such large-scale abstractions as "Attic" (1949) and "Excavation" (1950). Other major paintings of this period include "Woman and Bicycle" (1952–53) and "Gotham News" (1955). The freneticism of these works eventually gave way to roomy, colourful landscapes, notably "Door to the River" (1960). After permanently settling in East Hampton in 1963, he returned to the female form in such works as "Woman Acabonic" (1966), "Woman and Child" (1967), and "The Visit" (1967). In 1978 his estranged wife, accomplished painter Elaine Fried, returned to help him recover from alcoholism and manage his affairs; during the 1980s he was diagnosed with Alzheimer's disease. Though later works—quiet, flowing abstractions—were considered spare and undeveloped, his estate increased with the record-setting sales of such paintings as "Pink Lady" (1944) for $3.6 million in 1987 and "Interchange" (1955) for $20.6 million in 1989.

De Santis, Giuseppe, Italian film director whose *Riso amaro (Bitter Rice)* was considered the first successful Neorealist film and established his career; in 1995 he was honoured with a Lifetime Achievement Award at the Berlin Film Festival (b. Feb. 11, 1917—d. May 16, 1997).

De Souza, Ivo, Jamaican diplomat who served as a Royal Air Force pilot during World War II and in 1953 founded the British Caribbean Welfare Service, which he headed until 1962, when he joined the diplomatic service of the newly independent Jamaica and helped foster international relations, notably in promoting free trade among other less-developed nations (b. Aug. 24, 1918—d. Jan. 19, 1997).

Deng Xiaoping, Chinese revolutionary (b. Aug. 22, 1904, Sichuan province, China—d. Feb. 19, 1997, Beijing, China), transformed China's drab and listless society into a dynamic industrial workforce by compromising traditional communist doctrines and adopting a free-enterprise system "with Chinese characteristics." While studying (1921–24) in France, he joined the fledgling communist movement and then returned to China to indoctrinate and train groups of communist military and political cadres. He joined the historic 10,000-km (6,000-mi) Long March (1934–35), a massive migration of communist forces fleeing to northwestern China to avoid direct confrontation with Chiang Kai-shek's more powerful Nationalist army. Following World War II, Mao Zedong's communist forces launched an all-out war against the Nationalist government and took over the country.

Three years after Chairman Mao proclaimed the establishment of the People's Republic of China, Deng was named a vice-premier. He became secretary-general of the Communist Party of China (CPC) in 1954 and a member of the party's powerful Political Bureau in 1955. His deep conviction that China's future development depended on well-educated managers and highly skilled technicians brought him into conflict with Mao and led to his political downfall during the early years of the Cultural Revolution (1966–76). He was rehabilitated in 1973 and two years later was appointed vice-chairman of the party's Central Committee, a member of the Political Bureau, and chief of the general staff.

After the death of Premier Zhou Enlai in January 1976, the Gang of Four, led by Mao's wife, succeeded in ousting Deng from his leadership posts for the second time. Following Mao's death in September, a momentous power struggle ensued. Mao's widow and her three associates were arrested, and Deng was rehabilitated for the second time. By 1981 Premier Hua Guofeng, realizing that he had been outmaneuvered by Deng, yielded the premiership to Zhao Ziyang and the leadership of the CPC to Hu Yaobang. Both willingly embraced Deng's program of reforms, which included long-term economic planning, individual responsibility, material incentives for efficient managers and workers, and advanced training for those needed to direct China's economic development. Deng urged his countrymen to be more concerned about economic progress and less concerned about ideology. His 1979 visit to the United States underscored his determination to forge economic and cultural ties with the West in order to foster trade and encourage foreign investment in China.

In 1987, satisfied that China would never revert to its old ways, Deng resigned his post on the Central Committee and thereby forced many veteran party members who had opposed or resisted his reforms to follow his example and relinquish their posts of influence. Deng's willingness to experiment and to "seek truth from facts" brought dire warnings from old comrades that the freedoms already granted would spark demands for even greater freedom. The warnings proved prophetic. When political activists gathered peacefully in Beijing's Tiananmen Square in July 1989 to plead for greater democracy, Deng, who was determined that no one ever be allowed to challenge the authority of the CPC, ordered the army to crush "the rebellion." The ensuing bloody massacre, filmed by foreign reporters and shown on television worldwide, permanently tarnished the image of a man who had won wide acclaim at home and abroad for having transformed China into a major force on the world stage by the sheer power of his vision and determination. Despite serious infirmities, Deng remained China's paramount and unchallenged leader until his death.

Denver, John (Henry John Deutschendorf, Jr.), American singer and songwriter (b. Dec. 31, 1943, Roswell, N.M.—d. Oct. 12, 1997, Monterey Bay, Calif.), was identified by his wholesome, sentimental music that extolled nature's and life's simple pleasures. He began playing folk songs on the 1910 Gibson guitar that his grandmother gave him when he was 12. In the mid-1960s Denver moved to Los Angeles, where he adopted the name of the capital of Colorado, a state whose natural beauty he especially loved, and began performing with the Chad Mitchell Trio. His first songwriting effort, "Leaving on a Jet Plane," was recorded in 1967 by Peter, Paul, and Mary and became a number one hit in 1969. His first solo album, *Rhymes and Reasons,* was released that same year. In 1971 he recorded the million-selling single "Take Me Home, Country Roads," and that was followed by the evocative "Rocky Mountain High" (1972) and the smash hit "Sunshine on My Shoulders" (1974). Playing an acoustic guitar, Denver gained an international following with his clear tenor voice and homegrown lyrics. Along with 14 gold and 8 platinum albums, he received

Deng Xiaoping

PICTURES/MAGNUM

honours ranging from poet laureate of Colorado (1974) to the Country Music Association's Entertainer of the Year (1975). Although Denver had reached his commercial peak in the mid-1970s, with such albums as *Greatest Hits* (1973), *Back Home Again* (1974), and *Windsong* (1975), he continued to record and perform, starring in a number of television specials and in the motion picture *Oh, God!* (1977). A tireless advocate for wildlife and land conservation, Denver cofounded (1976) the Windstar Foundation, and his 20 years with UNICEF reflected his commitment to eradicating hunger and poverty. His wholesome image suffered in the 1990s, however, when he was twice arrested for drunk driving in Aspen, Colo., where he resided for many years. Although he was an experienced pilot trained by his father, an air force officer, Denver died when the handmade experimental airplane he was flying crashed off the coast of California.

Diana, princess of Wales (LADY DIANA FRANCES SPENCER), British royal (b. July 1, 1961, Sandringham, Norfolk, Eng.—d. Aug. 31, 1997, Paris, France), during a 17-year period in the public eye was transformed from "Shy Di," the naive fiancée of the heir to the British throne, to "Princess Di," the most photographed woman in the world, to the "Queen of People's Hearts" cherished by millions. Diana was the youngest child of Viscount Althorp (later Earl Spencer) and his first wife, Frances. Her parents' troubled marriage ended in divorce when Diana was a child, and she, along with her brother and two sisters, remained with her father. She attended boarding school in Norfolk and finishing school in Switzerland before taking a part-time job teaching kindergarten at the Young England school in Pimlico.

Diana's engagement to Charles, prince of Wales, a longtime family friend, was announced on Feb. 24, 1981, and her beauty and shy demeanour made her an instant sensation with the media and the public. The couple was married on July 29, 1981, in a "fairy-tale" wedding broadcast worldwide on live television; soon afterward Prince William of Wales was born (June 21, 1982), followed by Prince Henry (called Harry) on Sept. 15, 1984. "Princess Di" rapidly evolved into an icon of grace, elegance, and glamour. Exuding natural charm and charisma, she used her celebrity status to aid numerous charitable causes, including those of needy children and AIDS patients. Adoring crowds followed her everywhere, and her changing hairstyles and increasingly expensive wardrobe made her a fashion trendsetter. Meanwhile, publishers, who paid exorbitant amounts to aggressive freelance photographers known as paparazzi, who stalked her every move, plastered pictures of her face on hundreds of newspapers and magazine covers.

Behind the scenes, however, marital difficulties between the princess and prince were growing. Diana struggled with severe postnatal depression, low self-esteem, eating disorders, and the mounting strain of being constantly pursued by both the official media royal-watchers and the intrusive tabloid press, particularly the paparazzi. The marital breakdown became increasingly apparent amid mutual recriminations, tell-all biographies, and admissions of infidelity on both sides, and the couple formally separated in 1992. Diana presented her side in Andrew Morton's controversial book *Diana: Her True Story* (1992) and in an unusually candid television interview in 1995. After prolonged negotiations that left Diana with a substantial financial settlement but without the title Her Royal Highness, the couple's divorce became final in August 1996. Although the newly independent Diana cut back on her charity work, she remained a humanitarian figure, notably in her highly visible campaign against antipersonnel land mines. In 1997 she became romantically linked with "Dodi" al-Fayed (*q.v.*), with whom she was killed in a car crash in Paris after a high-speed pursuit by paparazzi. The royal family, apparently caught off guard by the extraordinary public outpouring of grief for the "People's Princess" and by the criticism of their emotional reticence, broke with tradition in arranging the internationally televised royal funeral, and the government formed a committee to plan a permanent memorial.

Even after her death the princess remained front-page news. As the French police revealed that Fayed's driver had been legally drunk and sought to establish the exact cause of the crash, controversy still raged about Diana's legacy. Whereas her detractors condemned her as an insecure and shallow publicity seeker, her admirers extolled her generous spirit and her ability to bring a breath of fresh air into a stuffy monarchy. Everyone agreed, however, that Princess Di, who had been the wife of one future king and was the mother of another, had changed forever the British monarchy and that she would go down as one of the most beloved figures in the latter half of the 20th century.

Dicke, Robert Henry, American physicist (b. May 6, 1916, St. Louis, Mo.—d. March 4, 1997, Princeton, N.J.), worked in such wide-ranging fields as microwave physics, cosmology, and relativity and was noted as both an inspired theorist and a successful experimentalist. Dicke earned an A.B. (1939) from Princeton University and a Ph.D. in physics (1941) from the University of Rochester, N.Y. After graduation he joined the Radiation Laboratory at the Massachusetts Institute of Technology, where during World War II he made significant contributions to radar technology and microwave-circuit systems. Through high-precision gravitational experiments, Dicke confirmed a concept integral to Einstein's general theory of relativity, the equivalence principle, which states that the gravitational mass of a body is equal to its inertial mass. Dicke was an early proponent of the big-bang theory of the origin of the universe, and in the 1960s he and several colleagues proposed that a remnant of that explosive origin should pervade the universe in the form of detectable radiation of microwave wavelengths. Before Dicke was able to confirm this hypothesis through observation, two other investigators, Robert Wilson and Arno Penzias, detected the microwave background radiation, a discovery for which they eventually were awarded the Nobel Prize for Physics in 1978. Dicke joined the faculty of Princeton in 1946, rose to full professor in 1957, and was appointed Albert Einstein professor of science in 1975, becoming professor emeritus in 1984. Dicke was elected to the National Academy of Sciences in 1967 and received its Comstock Prize in 1973. Among other numerous awards he received in recognition of his scientific achievements were the National Medal of Science (1971) and NASA's Exceptional Scientific Achievement Medal (1973). His writings include *Principles of Microwave Circuits* (1948; with Carol G. Montgomery and Edward M. Purcell) and *Gravitation and the Universe* (1970).

Dickerson, Nancy, American journalist and author who was a pioneer in television reporting, serving as the first female news correspondent at CBS (1960) and producing award-winning documentaries; her autobiography, *Among Those*

Diana, princess of Wales

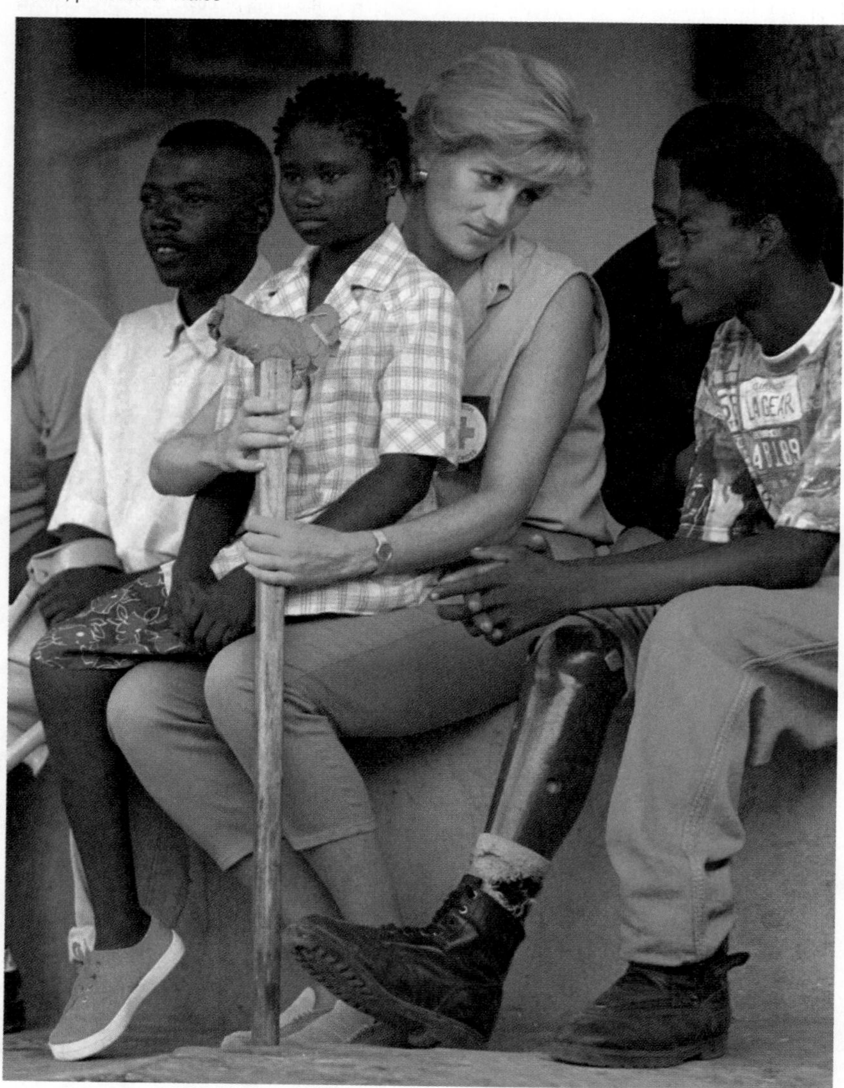

JOAO SILVA—ASSOCIATED PRESS

Present (1976), attributed part of her success to contacts she established as one of Washington, D.C.'s most popular party hostesses (b. Jan. 27, 1927—d. Oct. 18, 1997).

Dickey, James Lafayette, American novelist and poet (b. Feb. 2, 1923, Atlanta, Ga.—d. Jan. 19, 1997, Columbia, S.C.), produced some 20 volumes of poetry combining themes of nature, religion, and history but perhaps was best known to the general public for his powerful novel *Deliverance* (1970), the story of a male-bonding canoe trip that ends in violence. For the 1972 motion picture of the same name, which was nominated for an Academy Award, he wrote the screenplay and appeared as a sheriff. Dickey attended Clemson (S.C.) College for a year before enlisting (1942) in the U.S. Army Air Forces; he served as a fighter-bomber pilot and flew over 100 missions in World War II, and at about that same time he began writing poetry. After the war he earned B.A. (1949) and M.A. (1950) degrees from Vanderbilt University, Nashville, Tenn. Dickey returned to the military for service in the Korean War, was a university teacher and lecturer, and worked in advertising before publishing (1960) his first book of poems, *Into the Stone.* After spending the following year in Europe on a Guggenheim fellowship, he served as teacher and poet in residence at several colleges and universities and in 1968 finally settled at the University of South Carolina. During those years Dickey also produced such poetry collections as *Drowning with Others* (1962), *Helmets* (1964), and *Buckdancer's Choice* (1965), which won the 1966 National Book Award for poetry. From 1966 to 1968 he was poetry consultant to the Library of Congress. Later collections include *The Zodiac* (1976) and *The Whole Motion* (1992), and he published such notable nonfiction prose as *Babel to Byzantium: Poets & Poetry Now* (1968), the autobiographical *Self-Interviews* (1970), and *Jericho: The South Beheld* (1974) and the novels *Alnilam* (1987) and *To the White Sea* (1993). In 1977 Dickey was honoured with an invitation to read the poem "The Strength of Fields," which he wrote for the occasion, at the inauguration of Pres. Jimmy Carter.

Dixon, Jeane L. Pinckert, U.S. astrologer who gained renown as a psychic when it was revealed in 1963 that in 1956 she seemingly had predicted the death of U.S. Pres. John F. Kennedy (b. Jan. 5, 1918—d. Jan. 25, 1997).

Dorris, Michael Anthony, American writer whose best-known book, the 1989 National Book Award-winning *The Broken Cord,* chronicled the struggle his adopted son faced as a result of fetal alcohol syndrome; suffering from chronic depression, separated from his wife, writer Louise Erdrich, and facing legal difficulties, Dorris took his own life (b. Jan 30, 1945—found dead April 11, 1997).

Dungkar Lobsang Trinley, Tibetan historian and Buddhist scholar who at the age of four was recognized as the eighth reincarnation of the Lama of the Dungkar monastery—Dungkar Rinpoche; later, however, he left the monastic life and, after years of forced labour during the Cultural Revolution, became a leading advocate of education in the Tibetan language (b. 1927—d. July 21, 1997).

Duvalier, Simone (SIMONE OVIDE), Haitian political figure who presided as first lady of the country as the wife ("Mama Doc") of Haitian dictator François ("Papa Doc") Duvalier, the brutal and corrupt leader of Haiti from 1957 to 1971, and as the mother of Jean-Claude, who was a teenager when he succeeded to the throne after his father's death; she wielded considerable power during her son's reign (1971–86) but lost her status as first lady when he married in 1981. When Jean-Claude was ousted in a 1986 coup, she fled with her son and daughter-in-law and eventually settled in France, where she and Jean-Claude (who was later divorced) lived in greatly reduced circumstances (b. *c.* 1913—d. Dec. 26, 1997).

Eccles, Sir John Carew, Australian neurophysiologist (b. Jan. 27, 1903, Melbourne, Australia—d. May 2, 1997, Contra, Switz.), discovered many aspects of the vertebrate nervous system, notably how nerve impulses are transmitted between neurons, or nerve cells, work for which he shared the 1963 Nobel Prize for Physiology or Medicine with Alan L. Hodgkin and Andrew F. Huxley. Eccles's prizewinning research showed that one neuron communicates with a closely adjacent neuron by releasing chemicals into the synapse, the narrow space between the two cells. The chemicals, called neurotransmitters, cross the synapse and bind to the second cell, either activating or inhibiting it. His findings resolved a long-standing debate over whether nerve cell communication occurs through chemical or electrical means. Eccles studied biology and medicine at Melbourne University (M.B. and B.S; 1925), where he qualified for a Rhodes scholarship. At the University of Oxford, he studied with leading neurophysiologist Sir Charles Scott Sherrington. After graduating (1929; Ph.D) Eccles taught and conducted research at Oxford until 1937, when he returned to Australia to become director of the Kanematsu Memorial Institute of Pathology, Sydney. During World War II he was a medical consultant to the Australian army. Eccles then served (1944–51) as professor of physiology at the University of Otago, Dunedin, N.Z., before heading (1952–66) the physiology department at the Australian National University, Canberra. Facing mandatory retirement, he left Australia and continued his work (1966–68) at the Institute for Biomedical Research, Chicago, and the State University of New York at Buffalo, where he was distinguished professor of physiology (1968–75). He was elected (1941) to the Royal Society of London and received (1962) the Royal Medal. He served as president of the Australian Academy of Science (1957–61) and was knighted in 1958. In addition to the more than 500 scientific papers that he published, Eccles was the author of a number of books, including the purely scientific *The Physiology of Nerve Cells* (1957) and the philosophical *Facing Reality: Philosophical Adventures by a Brain Scientist* (1970).

Edel, (Joseph) Leon, American biographer and critic (b. Sept. 9, 1907, Pittsburgh, Pa.—d. Sept. 5, 1997, Honolulu, Hawaii), established a reputation as the first and foremost authority on the life and works of American novelist Henry James. Edel was reared in Canada and earned (1928) a master's degree from McGill University, Montreal. He had entered the university at the age of 16, and it was there that his interest in James was sparked. Edel attended the University of Paris on a scholarship and was awarded a doctorate (1932) for his dissertation on James's years as a playwright. In Paris he met American author Edith Wharton, a close friend of James's, who provided him with information that gave him a scholarly advantage over later Jamesian biographers and ultimately a deeper insight into how his subject's personality related to his art. After returning to Montreal, he taught (1932–34) English at Sir George Williams University, but he soon returned to Europe, where he worked as a freelance writer in London and Paris and pursued research on James until serving in the U.S. Army during World War II. In 1949 he published *The Complete Plays of Henry James,* and the following year he joined the faculty at New York University. In 1963 he won a Pulitzer Prize and a National Book Award for the second and third volumes (*Henry James: The Conquest of London, 1870–1881* and *Henry James: The Middle Years, 1882–1895,* both published in 1962) of a five-volume definitive James biography, completed in 1972. Edel was named Henry James professor of English and American letters in 1966. Besides teaching during the 1970s at the University of Hawaii, he lectured in later years. Edel's four-volume *Henry James Letters* (1974–84), while not exhaustive, served to round out James's biography. He also completed critical biographies of two other literary figures, Willa Cather and Henry David Thoreau, and edited the papers and diaries of influential critic Edmund Wilson.

Elizalde, Manuel, Philippine official and amateur anthropologist who in 1971 announced the discovery in Mindanao of the Tasaday, a tiny, primitive tribe living in isolation in the rain forest in such harmony there was no word for "war"; he was later accused of having perpetrated a hoax, and the controversy was never completely settled (b. 1937?—d. May 3, 1997).

Engen, Alf, Norwegian-born American skier who won eight national ski-jumping and eight combined-competition championships and set a number of world records between 1931 and 1947 after having won the 1931 world pro championship; he went on to teach, coach, and run a ski school that he founded (b. 1909—d. July 20, 1997).

Erikson, Joan Mowat Serson, Canadian-born American psychologist, writer, and craftsperson who, in addition to pursuing her own arts and crafts interests, collaborated with her husband, Erik Erikson, on a human-development theory that proposed that there are eight cycles through which a person's sense of identity progresses; she later added a ninth cycle (b. 1902?—d. Aug. 3, 1997).

Essen, Louis, British physicist (b. Sept. 6, 1908, Nottingham, Nottinghamshire, Eng.—d. Aug. 24, 1997, Great Bookham, Surrey, Eng.), built the cesium-beam atomic clock, a device that ultimately changed the way time is measured. Atomic clocks measure the passage of time by using a device that counts the extremely regular waves of electromagnetic radiation emitted from atoms. This new method of timekeeping generated a more accurate time scale than was previously possible and eventually, in 1967, replaced the astronomical methods used until then to determine the international time standard. Essen developed the clock in 1955 with his collaborator J.V.L. Parry at the National Physical Laboratory in Teddington, Middlesex, Eng. Essen began working at the laboratory in 1929, not long after receiving his B.Sc. in physics (1928) from the University of London, where he also earned a Ph.D. (1941) and D.Sc. (1948). There he began his career-long focus on the physics of frequency generation and measurement. In 1938 he developed the Essen quartz ring clock, a highly stable timepiece that allowed measurement of the seasonal variations in the Earth's rate of rotation. During World War II Essen devised a number of instruments to measure radio waves, such as the cavity resonance wavemeter, and after the war he used these devices to measure the velocity of light. In 1946 his measurements, carried out with A.C. Gordon-Smith, showed that light travels 16 km (10 mi) per second faster than the value accepted at the time. Essen's expertise in measuring time and velocity led him to question some aspects of Einstein's theories, criticisms he detailed in his paper *The Special Theory of Relativity: A Critical Analysis.* Essen received numerous honours, including the A.S. Popov Gold Medal from the U.S.S.R. Academy of Sciences in 1959, the same year he was made an O.B.E. In 1960 he was elected a fellow of the Royal Society of London.

Eysenck, Hans Jürgen, German-born British psychologist best known for espousing controversial views; he held that genetic makeup might be responsible for IQ differences between whites and blacks and that smoking had not been shown to cause lung cancer (b. March 4, 1916—d. Sept. 4, 1997).

Farley, Chris, American comedian whose larger-than-life performances (1990–95) on television's "Saturday Night Live" often parodied his own problems with alcohol, drugs, and obesity and who turned his physical brand of humour into a movie career, notably in *Beverly Hills Ninja;* he died of a drug overdose (b. Feb. 15, 1964—d. Dec. 18, 1997).

Fassi, Carlo, Italian-born American figure-skating coach (b. Dec. 20, 1929, Milan, Italy—d. March 20, 1997, Lausanne, Switz.), was one of the most successful coaches in the history of singles ice skating. He guided athletes to numerous championships, including four Olympic gold medals. An accomplished skater in his own right, Fassi won 2 European titles, 10 Italian national championships, and 8 Italian pairs-skating titles before turning professional in 1954 to pursue a career in coaching. In 1961 he was asked to rebuild the American skating program after a plane crash claimed much of the country's talent. Seven years later he produced his first Olympic champion, Peggy Fleming. Other skaters under his tutelage to earn Olympic gold were Dorothy Hamill (1976) and the British skaters John Curry (1976) and Robin Cousins (1980). In addition, he guided athletes to 4 world championships and to national titles in 15 countries, including Canada, Italy, and the United States. Fassi, who coached with his wife, Christa, was known for encouraging the individual personalities of his pupils rather than imposing a style upon them. He also wrote a textbook, *Figure Skating with Carlo Fassi* (1980), that described his teaching techniques. In recent years he had worried about the direction of women's figure skating, arguing that the elimination of the compulsory figures and the emphasis on triple jumps would diminish the artistry of the sport and cause injuries to skaters.

Fayed, Emad Mohamed al- ("DODI"), Egyptian-born producer of motion pictures, including *The World According to Garp* and the Oscar-winning *Chariots of Fire,* and playboy son of multimillionnaire Mohamed al-Fayed, the owner of Harrods department stores. Fayed was killed in an automobile crash with Diana, princess of Wales (*q.v.*), with whom he was romantically linked (b. April 15, 1955—d. Aug. 31, 1997).

Feder, Abraham Hyman, American lighting designer who provided illumination for both buildings and theatrical productions for over 50 years; his trademark, Lighting by Feder, came to represent the highest standards in theatrical lighting (b. June 27, 1909—d. April 24, 1997).

Fela (FELA ANIKULAPO KUTI), Nigerian musician and activist (b. Oct. 15, 1938, Abeokuta, Nigeria—d. Aug. 2, 1997, Lagos, Nigeria), launched a modern African-based music called afro-beat, which fuses American blues, jazz, and funk with traditional Yoruba music. From the late 1960s he used his music as a vehicle to protest oppression by Nigeria's military governments and became one of the most celebrated stars of Africa. The firebrand singer, who gyrated over the keyboard as he sang in "broken English" and Yoruba, struck a chord among the unemployed, disadvantaged, and oppressed. Born Fela Ransome Kuti, he was the son of feminist and labour activist Funmilayo Kuti. As a youth he took lessons in piano and percussion before studying (1959) classical music at Trinity College, London, where he encountered various musical styles by playing piano in jazz and rock bands. Returning to Nigeria in the mid-1960s, he formed the band from which the afro-beat sound evolved. Following his 1969 tour of the United States, where he was influenced by the politics of Malcolm X, the Black Panthers, and other militants, he used his music to enact political change in such songs of social protest as "Zombie," "Monkey Banana," "Beasts of No Nation," and "Upside Down." Fela and Egypt 80, his 27-member band, performed for packed houses at the early-morning concerts they staged at Fela's often-raided nightclub in Lagos. His politically charged songs prompted authorities to routinely raid his club, looking for reasons to jail Fela. Near there he also set up a communal compound, which he proclaimed the independent Kalakuta Republic. As head of the commune, he often provoked controversy and attracted attention by promoting indulgence in sex, polygamy (he married his harem of 27 women), and drugs, especially marijuana. A 1977 raid on the complex by Nigerian authorities resulted in his brief incarceration and the death of his mother from a fall. In exile in Ghana in 1978, he changed his name from Ransome to the tribal Anikulapo. In 1979 Fela formed a political party, the Movement of the People, and ran unsuccessfully for the presidency

EBET ROBERTS

Fela

of Nigeria. Five years later he was jailed for 20 months on charges of currency smuggling. Upon his release, he turned away from active political protest and left his son, Femi, to carry the torch of afro-beat music. Fela was jailed again in 1993 for murder, but the charges were eventually dropped.

Fenneman, George, American entertainer who was best known for his role as announcer and straight-man sidekick to Groucho Marx on the quiz show "You Bet Your Life" on radio for 3 years and then, from 1950, on television for 11 years (b. Nov. 10, 1919—d. May 29, 1997).

Ferreri, Marco, Italian director whose bizarre, outrageous, and satiric motion pictures expressed his bleak and derisive view of society; in his best-known film, *La Grande Bouffe,* 1973, a group of men purposely gorge themselves to death (b. May 11, 1928—d. May 9, 1997).

Figueroa Mateos, Gabriel, Mexican cinematographer (b. April 24, 1907, Mexico City, Mex.—d. April 27, 1997, Mexico City), was internationally celebrated for the visually stunning use he made of the Mexican landscape, clouds, shadows, and starkly contrasting light and shade in some 200 films. He worked with such notable directors as John Ford, Luis Buñuel, John Huston, and, during what was considered the golden age of Mexican cinema, Emilio Fernández. Figueroa was orphaned at a young age and as a teenager took up still photography to earn a living. Working on motion picture sets, he soon progressed to the movie camera, and in the mid-1930s he spent a year in Hollywood studying with and assisting the noted cinematographer Gregg Toland. The first film to gain Figueroa attention was *Allá en el rancho grande* (1936), but it was his films with Fernández, beginning with *Flor silvestre* (1943), that secured his reputation. Their second collaboration, *María Candelaria* (1943), won the 1946 Cannes Film Festival's best photography award. Another of their most highly regarded joint efforts was *La perla* (1948), whose script John Steinbeck based on his own novel *The Pearl* (1947). Figueroa worked with Ford on *The Fugitive* (1947); with Buñuel on such well-known films as *Los olvidados* (1950; *The Young and the Damned*) and *El ángel exterminador* (1962; *The Exterminating Angel*); and with Huston on *The Night of the Iguana* (1964), for which Figueroa was nominated for an Academy Award, and *Under the Volcano* (1984), his last film. Among Figueroa's honours were Mexico's National Arts Prize in 1977 and, in 1995, the American Society of Cinematographers' lifetime achievement award, only the third such award in that society's history.

Flood, Curtis Charles ("CURT"), American baseball player (b. Jan. 18, 1938, Houston, Texas—d. Jan. 20, 1997, Los Angeles, Calif.), challenged the major league player reserve system in court and, though he lost his suit, paved the way for players to become free agents in baseball and other professional sports. The reserve system that had existed in big league baseball since 1879 gave the clubs complete ownership of their players, who had no say over trades and no leverage in contract negotiations except the threat of retirement. Flood, traded by the St. Louis Cardinals to the Philadelphia Phillies after the 1969 season, refused to report to his new team and, with the help of the players union, decided to fight the reserve system, asserting that he was "the rightful proprietor of my own person and my own talents." The ensuing court battle lasted more than two years and ended when the U.S. Supreme Court upheld a lower court decision in favour of major league baseball. Though Flood and the union lost, their arguments resulted in a legal decision that clearly perceived problems in the business operations of baseball. Flood was signed by the Cincinnati Reds in 1956 and spent two years in the minor leagues before being traded in 1958 to the Cardinals. For the next 12 years, he played centre field for them, earning seven gold gloves for his defensive artistry and helping the team capture three National League pennants and two World Series championships. He sat out the 1970 season in order to pursue his lawsuit, returning to the game in 1971 with the Washington Senators. Advancing age, the year off, and the emotional drain of his legal battles had led to the deterioration of his skills, and he retired from baseball after appearing in only 13 games with the Senators. He achieved a career batting average of .293, accumulating 1,861 hits and 851 runs, and gained a reputation as one of the finest defensive players ever to patrol centre field. Flood, an accomplished painter, then moved to Majorca. In 1976 he returned to the U.S., where he became a broadcaster for the Oakland Athletics and later worked as commissioner of a youth baseball league.

Curt Flood

ASSOCIATED PRESS

Foccart, Jacques, French businessman and politician who served as an adviser to several French presidents, including Charles de Gaulle; Foccart shaped France's African policy with behind-the-scenes maneuvers that enabled the country to maintain influence in its former colonies (b. Aug. 31, 1913—d. March 19, 1997).

Fonseca, Gonzalo, Uruguayan-born artist whose stone sculptures reflected architectural and archaeological influences; after leaving his homeland, he settled in Paris and then lived alternately in Italy and in the U.S. (b. July 2, 1922—d. June 11, 1997).

Forrest, Leon, U.S. novelist, journalist, and educator (b. Jan. 8, 1937, Chicago, Ill.—d. Nov. 6, 1997, Evanston, Ill.), used folklore, history, legend, and realism to create epic novels that explored African-American life and teemed with richly drawn characters. In his works, set in Chicago, Forrest County was the fictional name he used for the city where he was reared and educated—at Roosevelt University and the University of Chicago. After U.S. Army service he returned to his hometown, wrote for and edited neighbourhood newspapers, and served (1969–73) as a reporter and then editor of *Muhammad Speaks,* the Nation of Islam's popular national weekly newspaper. Meanwhile, he was writing the novel *There Is a Tree More Ancient than Eden,* in which he drew on his upbringing in Baptist and Roman Catholic churches, on jazz and blues music, and on works by authors as diverse as Ralph Ellison, William Faulkner, and James Joyce. It was published in 1973, the year he began teaching at Northwestern University, Evanston; in 1985 he became chairman of the university's African-American studies department. Between the publication of his next two novels, *The Bloodworth Orphans* (1977) and *Two Wings to Veil My Face* (1983), in which a former slave relates her life story to her great grandson, Forrest wrote the libretto for T.J. Anderson's opera *Soldier Boy, Soldier* (1982). His final novel, *Divine Days* (1992), was his largest and most ambitious work, weaving together bawdy comedy and tragedy in a playwright's search for a charismatic, manipulative evangelist; a slaveholder's tangled relationships with his black consort and mulatto children; the suicide of a brilliant young woman artist; and the doings of the denizens of a neighbourhood tavern. In a collection of essays, *Relocations of the Spirit* (1994), Forrest examined literary and jazz figures, wrote lyrically about African-American churches, and showed acute insight into Elijah Muhammad and the Nation of Islam.

Frankl, Viktor, Austrian psychiatrist and psychotherapist (b. March 26, 1905, Vienna, Austria—d. Sept. 2, 1997, Vienna), developed the psychological approach known as logotherapy, widely recognized as the "third school" of Viennese psychotherapy after the "first school" of Sigmund Freud and the "second school" of Alfred Adler. The basis of Frankl's theory was that the primary motivation of an individual is the search for meaning in life and that the primary purpose of psychotherapy should be to help the individual find that meaning. As a teenager he entered into a correspondence with Freud, who asked permission to publish one of his papers. After graduating from the University of Vienna Medical School in 1930, Frankl joined the staff of the Am Steinhof psychiatric hospital in Vienna. By 1938 he had become chief of neurology at Vienna's Rothschild Hospital. Anti-Semitism was on the rise, however, and in 1942 Frankl and his family were sent to the concentration camps, where his mother, father, and wife perished. As he observed the brutality and degradation around him, Frankl theorized that those inmates who had some meaning in their lives were more likely to survive. Following liberation, Frankl returned to Vienna, where he became head of the neurological department at the Polyclinic Hospital. He also produced the classic book *Man's Search for Meaning* (1946), which he dictated to a team of assistants in nine days and which went on to sell some nine million copies in 26 languages. Frankl also taught at the University of Vienna until 1990 and held chairs at a number of American universities. A few months before his death, he published *Man's Search for Ultimate Meaning* and *Recollections: An Autobiography.*

Franquin, André, Belgian cartoonist and creator of the popular comic-book characters Gaston Lagaffe, a humorous misfit office boy, and the frenetic leopardlike creature Marsupilami, both of which first appeared in the weekly comic book *Spirou* (b. Jan. 3, 1924—d. Jan. 5, 1997).

Fratellini, Annie, French performer who was the first female circus clown in France, was a founder of the country's first circus school, and went on to a successful stage and motion picture career (b. Nov. 14, 1932—d. July 1, 1997).

Freire, Paulo, Brazilian educator and author (b. Sept. 19, 1921, Recife, Braz.—d. May 2, 1997, São Paulo, Braz.), sought to empower the world's oppressed through literacy programs that encouraged social and political awareness. In his seminal work, *Pedagogia do oprimido* (1970; *Pedagogy of the Oppressed,* 1972), Freire argued that the passive nature of traditional education promoted repression; it was a system he likened to a bank, wherein a teacher deposited information—which Freire believed was largely false—and the student was simply the collector. Freire favoured a "pedagogy of liberation" that encouraged dialogue between teacher and student, enabling the pupil to ask questions and to challenge the status quo. He began refining his methods during the 1950s, when he taught literacy to peasants. The use of everyday words and ideas in his lessons proved highly effective—many of Freire's students needed only 30 hours of instruction before being able to read and write. In 1963 he was appointed director of the Brazilian National Literacy Program, and in this post he outlined a plan to educate five million Brazilians. Following a military coup in 1964, however, Freire was jailed for subversion. After his release he went into exile, traveling around the world to assist in the establishment of literacy programs and to teach at a number of universities. In 1979 he returned to Brazil, where he cofounded the left-wing Workers Party. He was made education secretary of São Paulo in 1988 but resigned several years later. Freire wrote more than 20 books, many considered classics in the field of education.

Frey, Roger, French politician (b. June 11, 1913, Nouméa, New Caledonia—d. Sept. 13, 1997, Neuilly-sur-Seine, France), was a close adviser to French president Charles de Gaulle and a leading figure in the Algerian independence crisis of the early 1960s. Frey, a native of the French Pacific territory of New Caledonia, joined with the Free French Forces after the outbreak of World War II, serving as an infantryman in Africa, Italy, and France. Following the war, he was a leading member of the Gaullist Rally of the French People. After de Gaulle's fall in 1947, Frey organized the Union for the New Republic, which restored de Gaulle to power in 1958. Appointed minister of the interior in 1961, Frey was immediately faced with the problem of Algerian independence and the possibility of civil war. The anti-independence forces formed the Secret Army Organization (OAS), a terrorist group composed of French Algerian settlers and deserters from Foreign Legion and paratroop regiments. Frey spearheaded the government's war against the OAS, fighting terror with terror, and brutality on both sides was common. He was also responsible for containing the pro-independence Algerian nationalists, who had been waging a bombing campaign in France since the late 1950s. He crushed the OAS, and Algeria was granted independence in 1962. Frey served as minister of the interior until 1967, when he left to become minister of state. In 1974 he was appointed president of the Constitutional Council, a post he held until 1983.

Fuchs, Joseph, American violinist and educator who toured the world and gave performances that were noted for their vigorous style, assured technique, and rich, warm tone; a highly regarded teacher, he taught at the Juilliard School in New York City from 1946 until his death (b. April 26, 1900—d. March 14, 1997).

Fuller, Samuel, American motion picture director, screenwriter, and producer (b. Aug. 12, 1911, Worcester, Mass.—d. Oct. 30, 1997, Los Angeles, Calif.), was considered a master of the low-budget B-film. His works, with their sensational plots and grounded in dark emotion, gained him a cult following and the respect of many important European directors and critics. At a young age, Fuller became enamoured of the newspaper world, and by his teens he was a copyboy at the *New York Journal.* At 17 he became New York City's youngest crime reporter, and during the 1920s and '30s he worked at a number of American papers. He also began writing short stories for magazines and published a few pulp novels, and the 1938 film *Gangs of New York* carried his first screenwriting credit. For his service in the infantry in North Africa and Europe during World War II, Fuller was awarded the Purple Heart and the Bronze and Silver stars. His directorial debut came with *I Shot Jesse James* (1949), for which he also wrote the script, and he followed it with such other westerns as *The Baron of Arizona* (1950), *Forty Guns* (1957), and *Run of the Arrow* (1957). His first war films, *The Steel Helmet* and *Fixed Bayonets* (both 1951), were also the first Hollywood films to be concerned with the Korean War. Other war films included *China Gate* (1957), *Merrill's Marauders* (1962), and *The Big Red One* (1980). He also made such thrillers as *Pickup on South Street* (1953), *House of Bamboo* (1955), *Shock Corridor* (1963), and *The Naked Kiss* (1964). Fuller's antiracist *White Dog* (1982), which focused on an attempt to retrain a dog that attacked blacks, was considered too controversial and received only limited release in 1992. From the early 1980s Fuller lived in Paris, continuing to work on his own projects and appearing in the works of directors who still held him in high esteem.

Furet, François, French historian whose reinterpretation of the French Revolution challenged the then-prevailing Marxist viewpoint and reshaped the country's perception of its history; he was elected to the French Academy in 1997 (b. March 27, 1927—d. July 12/13, 1997).

Samuel Fuller

NOEL QUIDU—GAMMA LIAISON

Gairy, Sir Eric Matthew, Grenadan politician (b. Feb. 18, 1922, St. Andrew's Parish, Grenada—d. Aug. 23, 1997, Grand Anse, Grenada), served as the first prime minister of Grenada after it gained independence from Britain in 1974. Although he was initially viewed as a champion of the working class, he turned into a ruthless dictator who silenced critics by dispatching the "Mongoose Gang," his unique security group. Born near Grenville to a peasant family, Gairy was educated at a Catholic parish school. He left Grenada during the early 1940s to seek employment, first at an American military base in Trinidad and then at an oil refinery in Aruba. After running afoul of Dutch authorities in Aruba because of his union activities, Gairy returned to Grenada in 1949. The following year he formed the Grenada Manual, Maritime and Intellectual Workers' Union and later the Grenada United Labour Party (GULP). His political efforts against the planter aristocracy won him the support of the island's poor and launched his political career in 1951, when he was elected to the Legislative Council. He became minister of trade and production in 1956 and chief minister and minister of finance in 1961. Charges of petty corruption led to his dismissal in 1962, but he and the GULP came back in 1967, and in 1974 he was elected prime minister. As prime minister, he had a tenure marred by accusations of election tampering and his eccentric claim to being divinely appointed. In 1979, while addressing the United Nations in New York City on the subject of UFOs, Gairy was ousted by the left-wing New Jewel Movement (NJM). He went into exile (1979–83) in the U.S., and though he returned home, his party failed to return to power in the elections of 1984, 1990, and 1995.

Geneen, Harold, American business executive who built the International Telephone and Telegraph Corp. (ITT) into a worldwide business conglomerate. During Geneen's tenure (1959–77) as president and CEO of ITT, the company came to exemplify the modern international corporation, with business interests in bakeries, hotels, and insurance (b. Jan. 22, 1910—d. Nov. 21, 1997).

Geva, Tamara (TAMARA GEVERGEYEV), Russian-born American actress and ballerina who performed with the Soviet State Dancers and Diaghilev's Ballets Russes before introducing (1927) the works of choreographer George Balanchine, to whom she was briefly married, to the New York City stage; she later hung up her ballet slippers to appear in Broadway musicals, notably *Three's a Crowd* and *Flying Colors,* and such films as *Their Big Moment* and *Manhattan Merry-Go-Round* (b. March 17, 1906?—d. Dec. 9, 1997).

Gill, Brendan, American man of letters whose luminous writings graced *The New Yorker* magazine for more than 60 years, beginning in 1936, when he joined the staff as a regular contributor; an urban sophisticate, he later took up the mantles of film critic (1960–67), drama critic (1968–87), and writer (1987–97) of the "Sky Line" column, an architectural forum for his views on historic preservation. He also penned biographies of Cole Porter, Frank Lloyd Wright, and Charles Lindbergh and was the author of the 1975 best-seller *Here at The New Yorker* (b. Oct. 4, 1914—d. Dec. 27, 1997).

Ginsberg, (Irwin) Allen, American poet (b. June 3, 1926, Newark, N.J.—d. April 5, 1997, New York, N.Y.), was the poet laureate of the cultural movement in the 1950s whose members were known as the Beat Generation, disaffected anti-establishment writers whose lifestyle embraced alienation, nonconformity, and, often, drug use. His influence on art, music, and politics lasted throughout the following four decades, and such varied individuals as Abbie Hoffman, Vaclav Havel, Bob Dylan, and Yoko Ono were said to have considered him a guru. While attending Columbia University, New York City, with the intention of becoming a lawyer, Ginsberg switched to a major in literature and came under the influence of Jack Kerouac, William S. Burroughs (*q.v.*), and Neal Cassady. Together they became the leaders of the Beats. Ginsberg's springboard to renown was his poem "Howl," an explicit rage against mainstream society and a celebration of his politically radical upbringing and his homosexuality. Lawrence Ferlinghetti's City Lights Books published the poem in *Howl and Other Poems* (1956), and Ferlinghetti was tried on obscenity charges. He was acquitted, and the case became a landmark in the anticensorship crusade. Perhaps Ginsberg's best and most highly regarded poem was "Kaddish for Naomi Ginsberg (1894–1956)," published in *Kaddish and Other Poems* (1961); it honoured his mother and dealt with both his relationship with her and her death in a mental hospital. As beatniks gave way to hippies in the 1960s, Ginsberg remained firmly ensconced in the counterculture. He adopted Buddhist religious beliefs, was an organizer of the first "be-in," coined the term flower power, advocated the legalization of drugs, campaigned against the Vietnam War, and in 1968 demonstrated—and was teargassed—at the Democratic national convention in Chicago. The following decades found him both traveling throughout the world and continuing his political protesting in the U.S. A one-volume anthology of Ginsberg's works, *Collected Poems, 1947–80,* was published in 1984. Among his many honours and awards were the National Book Award for *The Fall of America: Poems of These States, 1965–1971* (1972) and an American Book Award (1990), and he was a 1995 Pulitzer Prize finalist for *Cosmopolitan Greetings: Poems 1986–1992.*

Goizueta, Roberto Crispulo, American businessman (b. Nov. 18, 1931, Havana, Cuba—d. Oct. 18, 1997, Atlanta, Ga.), served as chairman and CEO of the Coca-Cola Co. and during his 16-year tenure at the helm increased Coke's market value from $4 billion in 1981 to some $150 billion at the time of his death. Born into a prosperous family with interests in the sugar industry, Goizueta was educated at a Jesuit school in Havana and

Allen Ginsberg

SOPHIE BASSOULS—SYGMA

a private preparatory school in New Haven, Conn. After receiving (1953) a bachelor's degree in chemical engineering from Yale University, he began a 43-year career with Coca-Cola as a chemist for a company subsidiary in Havana. After Cuban leader Fidel Castro nationalized Coca-Cola in 1960, Goizueta and his family immigrated in 1961 to the U.S., arriving in Miami with $40 and 100 shares of Coca-Cola stock. Goizueta maintained that this experience developed his self-assurance, which enabled him to turn the conservative, risk-avoiding, disorganized company of the late 1970s into the purveyor of two of the four top-selling soft drinks in the world. Revising the firm's financial strategy to focus more attention on shareholder returns, he sold off unrelated and unprofitable parts of the business, developed new products, and launched global advertising and distribution campaigns that would leave Coca-Cola's chief competitor, PepsiCo, trailing in worldwide market share. The company's goal was to place Coke "within an arm's reach of desire" anywhere in the world. The introduction of Diet Coke in 1982 was a stroke of marketing genius; the 1985 introduction of New Coke and the simultaneous withdrawal of original Coke seemed to be a marketing disaster. Following massive consumer protest, Goizueta remarketed the original formula as Classic Coke; 10 years after the "blunder," Coca-Cola's volume of cola sales had increased by 29%. Goizueta was praised for his integrity and a legacy of philanthropy to the city of Atlanta, including endowments to Emory University, which in 1994 renamed its business school in his honour. He was listed by *Forbes* magazine as having an estimated wealth of $1.3 billion, which made him the richest Hispanic in the U.S. Goizueta died of complications from lung cancer within six weeks of having been diagnosed with the disease.

Goldberg, Bertrand, American architect (b. July 17, 1913, Chicago, Ill.—d. Oct. 8, 1997, Chicago), changed the shape of Chicago's modern skyline with his pioneering design for Marina City, the twin concrete corncob-shaped cylindrical towers built in the mid-1960s. Conceived as a mixed-use complex that integrated housing with parking, restaurants, shops, recreation, and offices in a downtown setting, Marina City reflected Goldberg's vision that architecture could inspire a sense of community among inhabitants of the urban landscape. During the early 1930s he studied in Germany under Ludwig Mies van der Rohe at the Bauhaus, but he eventually departed from the steel and glass skyscrapers of the Miesian tradition, which he increasingly found dehumanizing. Instead, he strove to evoke a more naturalistic effect through the use of a cylindrical form, a design concept he used for the Raymond M. Hilliard Homes, a public housing project in Chicago. Goldberg designed other Chicago buildings, such as the Astor Tower Hotel and a residential complex called River City, and many hospitals throughout the United States.

Goldsmith, Sir James Michael, British-French financier (b. Feb. 26, 1933, Paris, France—d. July 18, 1997, Benahavis, Spain), amassed a fortune by buying and selling companies. Goldsmith's father, Maj. Frank Goldsmith, owned luxury hotels in France and the U.K. and served as a Conservative member of Parliament. Goldsmith was educated at Eton College but left at age 16 after winning a sizable amount of money by betting on horse races. This penchant for gambling became his trademark in later business ventures. After building up a small pharmaceutical company, he acquired food companies in the 1960s to create the conglomerate Cavenham Foods. He was also the founder and chairman of the French company Générale Occidentale from 1969 until he sold out in 1987. Goldsmith was often the target of journalists and filed numerous libel suits against the satirical magazine *Private Eye,* yet he sought to be a press magnate himself. In the 1970s he briefly owned the news magazine *L'Express* in France and launched the British magazine *NOW!,* which failed in less than two years. In the 1980s he was a corporate raider in the U.S., where his bid to control the Goodyear Tire and Rubber Co. in 1986 (deflected by Goodyear, which paid Goldsmith millions of dollars for his shares) was an issue in U.S. congressional hearings on corporate takeovers. He also pulled off the difficult feat of anticipating the October 1987 stock market crash and liquidating most of his assets in time. Although Goldsmith was elected to represent France in the European Parliament in 1994, he had become convinced that federalism in Europe would prove disastrous. In 1995 he established the Referendum Party, with the sole mission of granting the British people the right to vote on their country's relationship with the European Union, but his party failed to win even one seat in the 1997 British election. Goldsmith was knighted by Britain in 1976, and two years later he was made a knight of the French Legion of Honour.

Graham, Robert Andrew, American Roman Catholic priest and historian who researched the career of Pope Pius XII in the Vatican archives to disprove allegations, made by Rolf Hochhuth in his play *The Deputy,* about the pope's failure to speak out against Nazi atrocities. Graham's report, eventually 11 volumes long, revealed that the pope had helped rescue over 800,000 Jews (b. March 11, 1912—d. Feb. 10, 1997).

Grappelli, Stéphane, French violinist (b. Jan. 26, 1908, Paris, France—d. Dec. 1, 1997, Paris), was one of the few notable jazz improvisers on violin and one of the first popular European jazz musicians; he played with a lilting swing and quick wit that made him an international favourite for over 60 years. With the great Gypsy guitarist Django Reinhardt, he formed (1934) the first Quintette du Hot Club de France, a Paris-based group with a unique instrumentation—violin, three guitars, and bass—and a style that continued to influence jazz and popular musicians in Europe and the U.S. for decades. Grappelli's graceful, highly decorated solos contrasted with Reinhardt's dramatic intensity, and Reinhardt's antics complemented Grappelli's urbanity. The quintet disbanded in 1939, and Grappelli spent the World War II years in England, playing with pianist George Shearing and others. He went on to tour the world, performed five years at the Paris Hilton, and made his American debut in 1969, inventing romantic solos with groups that emulated the Hot Club style. Recordings, concerts, and television programs enhanced his popularity in the 1970s and '80s, when he teamed with Oscar Peterson and other leading jazz pianists, fellow jazz violinists Jean-Luc Ponty and Joe Venuti, and classical violinist Yehudi Menuhin, who likened Grappelli's improvisations to "the juggler who throws his pots and plates to the wind and yet retrieves them every time." In New York City at a Carnegie Hall tribute concert in 1988, he was joined by jazz musicians, the Juilliard String Quartet, and cellist Yo-Yo Ma. Although confined to a wheelchair, he continued concert touring into the mid-1990s.

Green, Charles ("CHUCK"), American tap dancer whose lithe and humorous style made him one of the premier old-time hoofers; his career spanned more than 70 years and included appearances on Broadway and in films (b. Nov. 6, 1918—d. March 6/7, 1997).

Green, Hugh Hughes ("HUGHIE"), British entertainer who at 15 was the highest-paid child star in Great Britain; he went on to create and star as host of the popular television game shows "Double Your Money" and "The Sky's the Limit" and the talent show "Opportunity Knocks" (b. Feb. 2, 1920—d. May 3, 1997).

Guétary, Georges (LAMBROS WORLOOU), Egyptian-born French singer whose career of over 50 years on the musical theatre stage, in cabarets, on recordings, on television, and in films included a notable role as the man who lost Leslie Caron to Gene Kelly in *An American in Paris* (b. Feb. 8, 1915—d. Sept. 13, 1997).

Harriman, Pamela Beryl Digby Churchill Hayward, British-born socialite and American political figure (b. March 20, 1920, Farnborough, Hampshire, Eng.—d. Feb. 5, 1997, Paris, France), made a name for herself first as the wife or lover of a succession of prominent wealthy and powerful men and later as a doyenne of the Democratic Party. She was a successful fund-raiser for the party in the 1980s and for Bill Clinton's 1992 presidential election campaign and in 1993 was rewarded with the ambassadorship to France. The vivacious daughter of a British aristocrat, Pamela Digby saw that her chance of attaining prominence lay in influencing prominent men. In 1939, shortly after World War II broke out, she accepted the marriage proposal of Randolph Churchill, who was expecting to be killed in the fighting. He was not killed, and the marriage ended in 1946, but not before she had acted as confidante and hostess for her father-in-law, Winston Churchill, and given birth to a son—also named Winston and later a Conservative MP. She had also had liaisons with diplomat W. Averell Harriman and broadcast journalist Edward R. Murrow, both of whom were married at the time. Following her divorce from Churchill, she moved to Paris, where her lovers

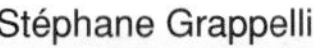

Stéphane Grappelli

GUY LE QUERREC—MAGNUM

MICHEL LIPCHITZ—ASSOCIATED PRESS

Pamela Harriman

included Prince Aly Khan, the Fiat automobile heir Gianni Agnelli, and Baron Elie de Rothschild. Moving to New York City in 1960, she married Broadway producer Leland Hayward. After his death 11 years later, she again took up with the very wealthy Harriman, who also had recently been widowed. They were married a month later, and she became a U.S. citizen. With her husband's encouragement and support, Harriman formed a political action committee and became a valuable asset to the Democrats. Her death in 1986 left her with a huge fortune, but a court battle with other heirs diminished it considerably. France made Harriman a Commander of the Legion of Honour's Order of Arts and Letters in 1996, and she was posthumously given the Legion's Grand Cross.

Harshaw, Margaret, American opera singer celebrated especially for her Wagnerian performances at the Metropolitan Opera in New York City for 22 seasons beginning in November 1942; singing both soprano and mezzo-soprano roles, she performed in more Wagner operas than any other singer in the history of the Met (b. 1909—d. Nov. 7, 1997).

Hassan, Sir Joshua Abraham, Gibraltarian politician who spent more than 40 years in government; he was especially noted for his leadership in resisting Spain's claims to the British colony and for instilling a sense of Gibraltarian identity in the colony's inhabitants (b. Aug. 21, 1915—d. July 1, 1997).

Helmsley, Harry Brakmann, American real-estate investor and property developer whose New York holdings, which included the Empire State Building, were valued at their height at about $5 billion but who came to be overshadowed by his second wife, Leona, who was dubbed "the Queen of Mean"; when in 1988 the Helmsleys were charged with tax evasion, Leona was convicted and spent time in prison, but Harry was found mentally unfit to stand trial (b. March 4, 1909—d. Jan. 4, 1997).

Hempel, Carl Gustav, German-born American philosopher who was a part of the logical positivist movement, an approach to scientific logic that argued for the superiority of verifiable experience over abstract thought (b. Jan. 8, 1905—d. Nov. 9, 1997).

Henry, Aaron E., American civil rights leader who was head of the Mississippi branch of the National Association for the Advancement of Colored People from 1960 to 1993; he persevered in the fight against racism through some 38 arrests, the firebombing of his home and business, and an unsuccessful attempt in 1964 to unseat a segregationist delegation at the Democratic national convention. In 1980 he was elected to a seat in Mississippi's state legislature (b. July 2, 1922—d. May 19, 1997).

Henry, Marguerite, American author of some 50 children's books that featured tales about animals, notably the classic novel *Misty of Chincoteague* (1947), a story about a wild horse and one of the most popular children's books of all time; Henry received numerous awards, including the Newbery Medal (b. April 13, 1902—d. Nov. 26, 1997).

Hershey, Alfred Day, American biochemist (b. Dec. 4, 1908, Owosso, Mich.—d. May 22, 1997, Syosset, N.Y.), was recognized as one of the founders of molecular genetics and shared the 1969 Nobel Prize for Physiology or Medicine with Salvador Luria and Max Delbrück, two other giants in the field. The three were honoured for their enormous contributions to the understanding of genetic processes and of the fundamental role of nucleic acid in the transmission of inherited characteristics. Hershey carried out experiments primarily on bacteriophages or phages, viruses that infect bacteria. In the early 1940s Hershey, Luria, and Delbrück formed the core of the "phage group," an informal association of scientists from a variety of laboratories who collaborated in the study of bacteriophages. Hershey's research demonstrated the occurrence of such basic viral phenomena as the spontaneous mutation of genetic, heritable factors and the ability of genetic material from different viral particles to recombine—discoveries that helped other investigators devise methods to combat major disease-causing viruses. This work also led to a greater understanding of the molecular mechanisms by which all organisms, including humans, inherit genetic information. Hershey's best-known experiment was carried out in 1952 with his assistant Martha Chase at Cold Spring Harbor (N.Y.) Laboratory. Their work, often referred to as the "blender experiment" in deference to the common household appliance they employed, demonstrated that DNA alone, and not protein, is the stuff of which genes are made. That discovery, together with James Watson and Francis Crick's elucidation of the structure of DNA the next year, paved the way for scientists to study the molecular basis of inheritance. After earning (1934) a doctorate in chemistry from Michigan State College, Hershey taught at Washington University School of Medicine, St. Louis, Mo., where he remained until 1950. That year he joined the research staff of the department of genetics (later renamed the Genetics Research Unit) of the Carnegie Institution of Washington at Cold Spring Harbor. He was named director of the unit in 1962 and retired in 1974. In addition to the Nobel Prize, Hershey was awarded the Albert Lasker Award (1958) and the Kimber Genetics Award (1965). Hershey was also elected (1958) a member of the U.S. National Academy of Sciences.

Herzog, Chaim, Irish-born Israeli politician, soldier, lawyer, and author (b. Sept. 17, 1918, Belfast, Ire.—d. April 17, 1997, Tel Aviv, Israel), was an eloquent and passionate spokesman for the Zionist cause and was instrumental in the development of Israel, both as a soldier and as the country's longest-serving president (1983–93). The son of Rabbi Isaac Halevi Herzog, Chaim grew up in Dublin before immigrating with his family to Palestine in 1935. The following year he joined the Haganah, an organization that sought to create a separate Jewish state. Herzog returned to Britain, studying law at the University of London, and served in the British army during World War II. In 1947 he rejoined the Haganah, and with the formation of Israel in 1948, Herzog fought against neighbouring Arab countries in the war of independence and was named head of the country's military intelligence, a position he held until 1950 and again from 1959 to 1962. He rose to the rank of major general before retiring from the army in 1962 to practice law and pursue business ventures. With a series of radio broadcasts during the Arab-Israeli Six-Day War (1967), Herzog became one of the country's foremost political and military commentators. As ambassador to the United Nations (1975–78), he drew international attention for his passionate, though unsuccessful, campaign to defeat the resolution that equated Zionism with racism. In 1981, as a member of the Israeli Labour Party, Herzog was elected to the Knesset (parliament). Two years later he was nominated for president, a largely ceremonial post. Though the rival Likud Party controlled the Knesset, Herzog's widespread popularity led to his narrow victory. Once in office, he increased the role of the president. Herzog traveled abroad and spoke before numerous foreign governments, improving Israel's international

Chaim Herzog

MICHA BAR'AM—MAGNUM

image. He stressed tolerance, supporting greater rights for the Druze and Arabs, and was an outspoken critic of the country's electoral system. In 1988 he ran unopposed in his bid for reelection, winning a second term, the maximum allowed under Israeli law. A noted author, Herzog wrote extensively on Israeli history. His autobiography, *Living History: A Memoir,* was published in 1996.

Hines, the Right Rev. John Elbridge, American religious leader who, as the presiding bishop of the Episcopal Church from 1965 to 1974, pursued a socially progressive and activist agenda, supporting such issues as the ordination of women as priests and bishops and the withdrawal of investments from South Africa in protest against apartheid (b. Oct. 3, 1910—d. July 19, 1997).

Hogan, William Benjamin ("BEN"), American professional golfer (b. Aug. 13, 1912, Dublin, Texas—d. July 25, 1997, Fort Worth, Texas), was one of the greatest golfers of all time. Born to a poor family in rural Texas, the left-handed Hogan had to learn to play right-handed, since left-handed clubs were not available. Turning professional in 1931, he was hampered early in his career by a severe right-to-left hook. After years of frustration, a swing adjustment that he called his "secret" allowed him to use a controlled left-to-right fade as his basic shot. He became the dominant golfer of his era, winning his second Professional Golfers' Association of America championship and the first of four United States Open championships in 1948. In February 1949, however, an automobile crash nearly killed him; he suffered multiple injuries that seemed certain to end his career. In the tireless fashion that characterized everything he did, Hogan rebounded and returned to tournament competition in 1950. His win at the U.S. Open that year capped his comeback, inspiring the Hollywood film biography *Follow the Sun.* Although never again able to walk without pain and limited to an abbreviated schedule, Hogan played his greatest golf after the accident. His dramatic final-round 67 at the 1951 U.S. Open, played at Oakland Hills Country Club near Detroit on perhaps the most difficult course in Open history, was often considered the finest round of golf ever played. In 1953 he won the British Open—the only time he entered it—despite never having played before on a Scottish link-style course. That victory completed Hogan's "Triple Crown," victories that year in the Masters, the U.S. Open, and the British Open—the only time a player had won all three in the same year. He won nine major championships and 63 professional tournaments in all. Slight of frame and not blessed with a classically beautiful swing, Hogan developed his game through endless practice. He was dubbed "the Hawk" because of his single-minded determination and habitual expressionless stare, which became as familiar to fans as his white shirt, gray trousers, and trademark white cap. His 1957 instruction book, *The Modern Fundamentals of Golf,* was probably the best-known and mostly highly praised work of its kind.

Hrabal, Bohumil, Czech writer (b. March 28, 1914, Brünn, Moravia, Austria-Hungary [now Brno, Czech Rep.]—d. Feb. 3, 1997, Prague, Czech Rep.), was the author of wry, imaginative, and slightly surreal comic stories about a variety of nonconformist people. His works gained attention in the West when the film *Closely Watched Trains* (1966), the screenplay of which he had based on his novel *Ostře sledované vlaky* (1965), won the Academy Award for best foreign film. Hrabal's law studies at Charles University, Prague, were interrupted by World War II, when he worked on the railway. Though he received a doctorate in 1946, he never practiced law and instead took jobs as a traveling salesman, steelworker, warehouse worker, and stagehand until the early 1960s, when he devoted himself to writing. A volume of Hrabal's short stories, *Perlička na dně* (1963; "A Pearl at the Bottom"), brought him instant popularity and was soon followed by another short-story collection, *Pábitelé* (1964; "Palaverers"); a 90-page book about an elderly man's life story, told in a single sentence, *Taneční hodiny pro starší a pokročilé* (1964; *Dancing Lessons for the Advanced in Age,* 1995); and a third short-story collection, *Automat svět* (1966; *The Death of Mr. Baltisberger,* 1975). He had published several more short-story collections by the time of the Prague Spring of 1968, but then the Warsaw Pact forces invaded and put an end to the democracy movement, and Hrabal was forced to publish his works clandestinely. With the end of Soviet domination in 1989, however, his works from the 1970s could finally be published in his homeland. Among these were Hrabal's autobiographical trilogy *Městečko, kde se zstavil čas* (1989; *The Little Town Where Time Stood Still,* 1993), *Příliš hlučná samota* (1989; *Too Loud a Solitude,* 1990), and *Obsluhoval jsem anglického krále* (1990; *I Served the King of England,* 1989).

Huggins, Charles Brenton, Canadian-born American surgeon and medical researcher (b. Sept. 22, 1901, Halifax, N.S.—d. Jan. 12, 1997, Chicago, Ill.), specialized in the surgical and therapeutic treatment of cancer of the prostate and mammary glands and shared (with Peyton Rous) the 1966 Nobel Prize for Physiology or Medicine for discovering the influence that hormones have on the onset and growth of certain forms of human cancer. His work demonstrated that cancer cells are not necessarily autonomous and self-perpetuating and that some depend on chemical signals such as hormones to survive. This insight led to the development of hormone therapy as a treatment for endocrine-dependent tumours. Huggins graduated from Harvard Medical School (M.D., 1924) and began his career as a surgeon at the University of Michigan. In 1927 he joined the faculty of the University of Chicago, where he founded and served as director (1951–69) of the university's Ben May Laboratory for Cancer Research. Although initially involved in urology research, in the early 1930s Huggins became intrigued by discoveries being made in the field of cancer research by the German biochemist Otto Warburg, who won a Nobel Prize in 1931. Through his own research, Huggins discovered that the growth of prostate cancer could be stemmed by lowering levels of androgens, the male sex hormones, either by removal of the testes or by administration of real or synthetic female sex hormones. In 1944, recognizing that the adrenal glands were compensating for the loss of androgens in some treated patients whose prostate cancer recurred, Huggins performed the first complete removal of the adrenal glands, although this was considered a radical treatment to be used only as a last resort. Huggins turned his attention to breast cancer in the 1950s and showed that removal of the ovaries and adrenal glands combined with cortisone-replacement therapy was beneficial to 30–40% of women who were treated. His work led to the development of a test to distinguish between two types of breast cancer—one that was hormone-dependent and the other not—that helped determine which patients would benefit from this treatment. Huggins became involved in the 1960s controversy over whether birth control pills stimulated the growth of cancer of the breast and reproductive organs, and he maintained that data collected from thousands of patients did not support this link. Huggins received a number of honours, including the Lasker Award for Clinical Research in 1963. He was also the author of several books, notably *Experimental Leukemia and Mammary Cancer: Induction, Prevention, Cure* (1979).

Hughes, (George) Patrick ("PAT"), British tennis player, who was the only Englishman to become the singles titleholder at the Italian Open and also was considered one of his generation's best doubles players (b. Dec. 21, 1902—d. May 8, 1997).

Humphrey, William, American writer who featured small-town Texan family life in his works; his first and best-known novel, *Home from the Hill,* was published in 1957 and filmed in 1960 (b. June 18, 1924—d. Aug. 20, 1997).

Hutchence, Michael, Australian rock star and lead singer for INXS, one of the most popular bands of the late 1980s and early '90s. He began his career on the Australian pub circuit in the 1970s and founded INXS in 1978. By 1990 the band was one of the top-selling acts in the world, although its popularity had diminished at the time of Hutchence's death, by suicide. (b. Jan. 22, 1960—d. Nov. 22, 1997).

Huxley, Elspeth Josceline Grant, British writer (b. July 23, 1907, London, Eng.—d. Jan. 10, 1997, Tetbury, Gloucestershire, Eng.), was the versatile, prolific author of more than 30 books and hundreds of newspaper and magazine articles. Her wit and sharp insights were evident in works that included biographies, crime novels, memoirs, and travel books. When Huxley was five, her family moved to Kenya, and Africa figured largely in most of her writings. Her best-known work, the autobiographical novel *The Flame Trees of Thika* (1959), was based on her early years in Kenya. It was a best-seller and was adapted for television in the early 1980s. Much of Huxley's early schooling was done at home, though during World War I she attended boarding school in England. When she was 14, an East African newspaper published an article of hers on polo and made her its polo correspondent. By the age of 17 she had had 65 articles published and had illustrated some of them with her own photographs. Huxley earned (1927) a degree in agriculture from the University of Reading, Eng., and attended (1928–29) Cornell University, Ithaca, N.Y. She then became an assistant press officer for the Empire Marketing Board in London. It was there that she met Gervas Huxley, and in 1931 they were married. He was appointed head of the Ceylon Tea Propaganda Board, and they traveled around the world for five years as he encouraged the drinking of tea. Huxley established her reputation with her first book, *White Man's Country: Lord Delamere and the Making of Kenya* (1935), and other works soon followed, among them *Murder at Government House* (1937), *Murder on Safari* (1938), and *Red Strangers* (1939). Huxley returned to England with her husband during World War II and worked for the BBC's propaganda office and then as a liaison between the BBC and the Colonial Office. She served from 1952 to 1959 on the BBC's General Advisory Council and from 1959 to 1960 on the Moncton Advisory Commission on Central Africa. Huxley was appointed C.B.E. in 1962. Among her later books were three other autobiographical novels—*On the Edge of the Rift* (1962), *Love Among the Daughters* (1968), *Out in the Midday Sun* (1985)—and a collection of excerpts from her mother's letters prefaced by a memoir, *Nellie: Letters from Africa* (1980).

Ibuka, Masaru, Japanese businessman (b. April 11, 1908, Nikko, Japan—d. Dec. 19, 1997, Tokyo), was the cofounder and leading engineer of the Sony Corp. His development of the tape recorder, transistor radio, and many other products put Sony at the forefront of technological innovation for more than three decades and made it the world's most successful and recognized electronics company. In 1933 Ibuka earned a degree in engineering from Waseda University, Tokyo, and also won a prize at a Paris exhibit for an invention—a modulated-light transmission system. Ibuka worked for several scientific companies before founding Tokyo Tsushin Kogyo K.K. (Tokyo Telecommunications Engineering Corp.) with Akio Morita in 1946; the company was renamed the Sony Corp. in 1958. Combining Ibuka's technical innovations with the flamboyant Morita's marketing savvy, Sony soon dominated the electronics industry in Japan. Ibuka developed magnetic recording tape in 1949 and that led to the introduction of the first tape recorder in Japan a year later. He guided the development of Japan's first transistor radio (introduced in 1955), the world's first transistor television (1960), and the Trinitron colour television (1967). He served as president of Sony from 1950 to 1971, when he became chairman. In 1976 he retired from active involvement with the company and became honorary chairman. Ibuka was interested in education, writing books on the subject and chairing the

JIJI PRESS/AFP

Masaru Ibuka

Early Development Association. He also served as chairman of the Boy Scouts of Japan.

Itami, Juzo (Yoshihiro Ikeuchi), Japanese film director (b. May 15, 1933, Kyoto, Japan—d. Dec. 20, 1997, Tokyo, Japan), created satiric comedies that challenged authority and satirized social conventions and that gained him renown as one of Japan's greatest film directors. After a successful 20-year career as an actor, Itami directed (1984) his first film, *Ososhiki* (*The Funeral*), a black comedy about a family's squabbles at a funeral; among the film's targets were the Buddhist monks who exploited the bereaved for financial gain. Itami's refusal to hold anything sacred was a novelty in Japanese cinema, and the film won great critical and popular acclaim. Next came *Tampopo* (1986), his best-known film abroad, about the culinary and financial struggles of a noodle-shop proprietor. His other credits include *Masura no onna* (1987; *A Taxing Woman*) and *Minbo no onna* (1992; *The Gentle Art of Japanese Extortion*). In response to the latter film's harsh portrayal of the *yakuza,* Japan's powerful crime syndicate, five gangsters armed with knives attacked Itami in the street shortly after its release. He was nearly killed and was badly scarred on his face and neck. Itami's unique films were noted for their contemporary settings and unsentimental comic realism. Most of his films starred his wife, the actress Nobuko Miyamoto. Itami's death was by suicide; he jumped from the roof of the eight-story building in which his office was located. His suicide was apparently in anticipation of the publication of a tabloid magazine's story alleging an extramarital affair between himself and a young woman. Itami denied the affair to the magazine's reporters and again in his suicide note.

Jackson, Raymond Allen ("Jak"), British political cartoonist whose irreverent *Evening Standard* drawings entertained Londoners for some 30 years; he claimed he was the first to produce a caricature of Queen Elizabeth II, and one of his cartoons nearly caused the paper's pressmen to walk out (b. March 11, 1927—d. July 27, 1997).

Jacobs, Helen Hull, American tennis player and author (b. Aug. 6, 1908, Globe, Ariz.—d. June 2, 1997, East Hampton, N.Y.), was noted for her on-court rivalry with compatriot Helen Wills Moody in the 1920s and '30s. The "Battle of the Helens," as it was dubbed by the press, began in 1923 when Moody defeated Jacobs in a practice set. For more than a decade, Moody dominated their matches, but Jacobs's charisma and pluck—a sharp contrast to Moody's reserved demeanour—made her a crowd favourite. Jacobs's only victory over her rival came by default at the finals of the 1933 U.S. nationals when Moody, who was trailing in the match, withdrew because of a back injury. Though often in Moody's shadow, Jacobs posted an impressive tennis record, including U.S. singles (1932–35), doubles (1932 and 1934–35), and mixed doubles (1934) championships. She made six appearances at the Wimbledon finals, winning the title in 1936. Jacobs was ranked in the world's top 10 from 1928 to 1940 and was also a member of the U.S. Wightman Cup team (1927–39). In 1933 she became the first woman to break with tradition by wearing man-tailored shorts at Wimbledon. Jacobs enlisted in the U.S. Navy during World War II, serving in the intelligence unit, where she was one of only five women to earn the rank of commander. She wrote many books mostly on tennis and fitness. She retired from competitive play in 1947 and in 1962 was inducted into the International Tennis Hall of Fame.

Jaeckel, Richard, American baby-faced tough-guy actor whose 54-year career took him from roles mainly as stereotypical characters in war films and westerns to parts in television series, most recently "Baywatch"; he received an Academy Award nomination for his supporting role in the 1971 film *Sometimes a Great Notion* (b. Oct. 10, 1926—d. June 14, 1997).

Jagan, Cheddi Berret, Guyanese politician (b. March 22, 1918, Plantation Port Mourant, British Guiana [now Guyana]—d. March 6, 1997, Washington, D.C.), played a major role in Guyanese politics for half a century and was a leader in the country's quest for independence from Great Britain, which it achieved in 1966. In 1953 he became the first popularly elected prime minister of British Guiana, and though his Marxist beliefs led the British, with U.S. support, to dismiss him from office later that year, he subsequently headed the government from 1957 to 1964 and from 1992 until his death. Jagan was educated at Howard University, Washington, D.C., and the Northwestern University Dental School, Chicago, and qualified as a dentist in 1942. He returned to British Guiana the next year and set up a dental practice. He also became active in political and labour union activities and in 1947 was elected to the legislature. Jagan and his American-born wife founded (1950) the People's Progressive Party (PPP), and in elections in 1953 the party was victorious. Following his ouster after 133 days as prime minister, Jagan practiced dentistry and continued his political activities; he was jailed for some six months for defying a restriction order. The PPP was victorious in the 1957 election, and Jagan pursued economic reform policies. He became prime minister after the party's victory in 1961 and had hopes of leading the country to independence, but strikes, rioting, and ethnic conflict caused the British to intervene once again. In 1964 the British instituted a new system of proportional representation, and the PPP lost the election. Jagan became the leader of the opposition and served through nearly three decades in which elections were rigged to favour the ruling party. In the 1992 elections, however, the PPP won, and Jagan, now more moderate and supported by the U.S., became president.

Helen Hull Jacobs

ASSOCIATED PRESS

BOB HENRIQUES—MAGNUM

Cheddi Jagan

Jamali, Muhammad Fadhil al- ("Mohd"), Iraqi statesman who was the last survivor of the signatories to the UN Charter, was prime minister of Iraq twice, and—following the overthrow of the monarchy in 1958—was sentenced to be hanged; his sentence was later commuted, and he spent the remainder of his life in exile (b. April 20, 1903—d. May 24, 1997).

Jamalzadeh, Mohammad Ali, Iranian writer (b. Jan. 13, 1892, Esfahan, Iran—d. Nov. 8, 1997, Geneva, Switz.), was viewed as the father of modern Persian literature. In his writings about the nation's peasants and the poor, he used colloquial Persian rather than the ornate Turkish-style prose favoured at that time by Iranian authors. Although Jamalzadeh's father was a Muslim cleric, he sent his son to be educated by Jesuits in Beirut, Lebanon. Jamalzadeh then studied in Paris, where he earned a law degree from the University of Dijon. Returning to Iran in 1915, he briefly fought with a Kurdish force against the Allies in World War I but soon returned to Europe. He settled in Germany, where there was a significant expatriate Iranian community, and embarked on his literary career. He published a collection of short stories in the 1920s entitled *Yakī būd yakī nabūd* (*Once Upon a Time,* 1985), which was viewed as the first truly modern Persian literary work. Jamalzadeh's output slowed for a time while he served as the Iranian representative to the International Labour Organisation in Geneva and as a Persian literature and language instructor. By the 1940s he was again writing in earnest and produced some of his greatest novels, including *Dār al-majānīn* (1942; "The Madhouse") and *Qultashan-e dīvān* (1946; "The Custodian of the Divan"). Both of these works were highly critical of Iranian society and culture and were roundly condemned by conservative Iranians. In addition to his fiction, Jamalzadeh wrote a number of historical and political works and translated from English, German, and French.

James, Dennis (DEMIE JAMES SPOSA), American television personality who for nearly 60 years worked as game show and variety show host, sports commentator, actor, commercial spokesman, and charity fund-raising telethon host (b. Aug. 24, 1917—d. June 3, 1997).

Jarrico, Paul (ISRAEL SHAPIRO), American screenwriter who was blacklisted in the 1950s after being labeled "subversive" by the House Committee on Un-American Activities; his credits include *Salt of the Earth* (1953) and *Tom, Dick, and Harry* (1941), nominated for an Academy Award (b. Jan. 12, 1915—d. Oct. 28, 1997).

Jawahiri, Muhammad Mahdi al-, Iraqi poet considered one of the Arab world's all-time finest poets and said to be the last neoclassic Arab bard (b. July 26, 1899?—d. July 27, 1997).

Jepson, Helen, American singer and stunning blond beauty whose career as a lyric soprano at the Metropolitan Opera and other companies in the 1930s and '40s was launched by radio performances (b. Nov. 28, 1904—d. Sept. 16, 1997).

Johnson, Leon William, general (ret.), U.S. Air Force (b. Sept. 13, 1904, Columbia, Mo.—d. Nov. 10, 1997, Fairfax, Va.), was awarded (1943) the Medal of Honor, the U.S. military's highest decoration, for his World War II heroic role in the attack on the oil fields at Ploesti, Rom., an action that effectively destroyed enemy fuel supplies. Following graduation (1926) from the U.S. Military Academy at West Point, N.Y., he served in the infantry before transferring in 1930 to the Army Air Corps. In January 1943 he became commander of the 44th Bomb Group, and later that year his unit was part of a larger crew of B-24 bombers that took off from North Africa on a mission that was to take them nearly 4,000 km (2,400 mi) to the strategically significant Romanian oil fields and back. En route, however, while flying in difficult conditions, Johnson's group became separated from the others. He later reestablished contact, but when he arrived at Ploesti, he found that the oil fields were damaged and in flames, having already been struck by an earlier wave of bombers. Although their target was readied, they faced decreased visibility, owing to smoke, and the risk of explosions; he led his team of bombers in low, however, and destroyed the target. Johnson's plane was the only one from his squad to survive the mission. He continued to serve in combat until the end of the war and received a number of other commendations during a military career that spanned some four decades.

Johnson, U(ral) Alexis, American diplomat who sat at numerous negotiating tables during his 42-year career in the Foreign Service, culminating in his role as chief U.S. negotiator at the Strategic Arms Limitation Talks (b. Oct. 17, 1908—d. March 24, 1997).

Jones, Bob, Jr., American clergyman and educator (b. Oct. 19, 1911, Montgomery, Ala.—d. Nov. 12, 1997, Greenville, S.C.), was board chairman and chancellor of Bob Jones University, a fundamentalist Christian institution that gained attention in the 1970s when it opted to lose its federal tax-exempt status rather than allow interracial dating among its students. Bob Jones College was founded in College Point, Fla., in 1927 by Jones's father, evangelist Bob Jones, Sr. The school later relocated to Cleveland, Tenn., and then to Greenville in 1947, when it became known as Bob Jones University. Jones graduated from the college in 1930 and later taught a number of classes there. The nondenominational university, which in 1997 had an enrollment of about 5,000, enforced strict rules for students: a ban on interracial dating and a dress code that dictated ties for men and skirts for women. Jones held the posts of acting president (1932–47) and president (1947–71). In 1971 he was elected chancellor, and his son, Bob Jones III, succeeded him as president; in addition, Jones had held the post of chairman since 1964. He wrote a number of books, notably the autobiographical *Cornbread and Caviar* (1985).

Katsu, Shintaro (TOSHIO OKUMURA), Japanese actor whose portrayal of Zatoichi, a blind master swordsman, in a series of motion pictures and on television brought him tremendous popularity throughout Southeast Asia and influenced similar action films in Hong Kong and Taiwan (b. Nov. 29, 1931—d. June 21, 1997).

Katz, Amron Harry, American physicist whose studies in aerial reconnaissance made possible the use of space satellites for collecting military intelligence as well as information to be used in conserving resources and aiding disaster victims (b. Aug. 15, 1915—d. Feb. 10, 1997).

Kaye, Stubby, American comedian and singer who electrified audiences with his showstopping rendition of "Sit Down, You're Rockin' the Boat" in the Broadway production of *Guys and Dolls* (1950); the portly performer also appeared on such television series as "Love and Marriage" and "My Sister Eileen" and in films, notably as Nat King Cole's banjo-strumming balladeer partner in *Cat Ballou* (b. Nov. 11, 1918—d. Dec. 14, 1997).

Keith, (Robert) Brian, Jr., American actor who appeared in over 100 films, including *The Parent Trap* and *The Russians Are Coming! The Russians Are Coming!* but achieved more fame on television, especially as the crusty bachelor guardian of three children on "Family Affair" from 1966 to 1971 (b. Nov. 14, 1921—d. June 24, 1997).

Kelley, Clarence Marion, American law-enforcement official who in 1973 became the first permanent director of the FBI after the 49-year reign of J. Edgar Hoover; he served until 1978 and in that time brought modern techniques for crime fighting to the bureau and changed its focus to white-collar and organized crime (b. Oct. 24, 1911—d. Aug. 5, 1997).

Kempton, (James) Murray, American journalist whose columns championing the underdog—and featuring ultracomplex sentences—in such publications as the *New York Post* and *Newsday* made him a literary presence for some five decades and whose bicycle made him a familiar figure on Manhattan streets; he won the Pulitzer Prize in 1985 (b. Dec. 16, 1917—d. May 5, 1997).

Kendrew, Sir John Cowdery, British biochemist (b. March 24, 1917, Oxford, Eng.—d. Aug. 23, 1997, Cambridge, Eng.), deduced the structure of the muscle protein myoglobin, and for this work he was awarded the 1962 Nobel Prize for Chemistry along with colleague Max Perutz, who worked out the structure of the related protein, hemoglobin. Kendrew's work was groundbreaking because it was the first time that the three-dimensional conformation of a protein had been solved, and this knowledge led to the understanding of how myoglobin binds and transports oxygen in muscles. He studied physical chemistry at Trinity College, Cambridge (B.A.; 1939), but his studies were interrupted by World War II. Kendrew joined the Air Ministry to work on airborne radar and then served as scientific adviser to the Allied Air Command, eventually finishing his wartime service in Southeast Asia. There he met the physicist and X-ray crystallographer J.D. Bernal, who stimulated his interest in the study of proteins. Kendrew began working at the Cavendish Laboratory in Cambridge with Perutz, who was using X-ray crystallographic techniques to unravel protein structure. Kendrew received a doctorate in physics in 1949, whereupon he turned his attention to myoglobin. By 1959, as the result of laborious studies of the patterns into which crystallized samples of myoglobin diffracted X-ray beams, he had elucidated the protein's structure. After receiving the Nobel Prize, Kendrew shifted from laboratory work to administration. He served as deputy chairman of the department at Cambridge that he and Perutz created, the Medical Research Council Unit for Molecular Biology (now called the Laboratory of Molecular Biology). His influence led to the creation of the European Molecular Biology Laboratory in Heidelberg, Ger., where he served (1975–82) as director. In 1981 he was appointed president of St. John's College, Oxford. Kendrew became a fellow of the Royal Society in 1960, was knighted in 1963, and received the Royal Medal in 1965. He founded the *Journal of Molecular Biology* in 1959 and served as its editor in chief until 1987. He was the author of *The Thread of Life: An Introduction to Molecular Biology* (1966).

Khaldey, Yevgeny, Ukrainian photographer best known for his World War II images, most notably one of Soviet soldiers raising the hammer-and-sickle flag over the Reichstag during Berlin's fall in 1945 (b. March 10, 1917—d. Oct. 7, 1997).

Khan, Nusrat Fateh Ali, Pakistani singer considered one of the greatest performers of the Sufi Muslim devotional music known as *qawwali;* he was heard on the sound tracks of such films as *Natural Born Killers* and *Dead Man Walking* (b. Oct. 13, 1948—d. Aug. 16, 1997).

Kingsley, Dorothy, American screenwriter who began by writing radio comedy routines for Bob Hope and Edgar Bergen and went on to write, co-write, or collaborate on a series of Esther Williams movies and film versions of such Broadway musicals as *Pal Joey, Kiss Me, Kate,* and *Seven Brides for Seven Brothers* (b. Oct. 14, 1909—d. Sept. 26, 1997).

Kirk, Grayson, American academic who as president (1953–68) of Columbia University, New York City, gained national notoriety for using over 1,000 riot police officers to suppress a student disturbance there in 1968. An able administrator and fund-raiser, he was forced to resign following student protests against his heavy-handed tactics (b. Oct. 12, 1903—d. Nov. 21, 1997).

Knie, Rodolphe ("ROLF"), Swiss elephant trainer who was director of the highly respected family-owned Swiss National Circus for 50 years (b. Nov. 23, 1921—d. Aug. 18, 1997).

Knowles, Stanley Howard, American-born Canadian politician (b. June 18, 1908, Los Angeles, Calif.—d. June 9, 1997, Ottawa, Ont.), was an eloquent defender of social justice during the four decades he served in Parliament. He fought relentlessly for a number of causes, including better pensions for the elderly, improved housing, and women's rights. Knowles received a B.A. (1930) from Brandon College, formerly a part of the University of Manitoba and now Brandon University, and later studied theology at the University of Manitoba. He served for a number of years as a United Church minister in the Winnipeg area but left the ministry when he concluded that he could make a stronger impact in the political arena. As a member of the Co-operative Commonwealth Federation, which later merged with the New Democratic Party (NDP), Knowles ran unsuccessfully for Parliament in 1935 and 1940. In 1942 he won the seat of Winnipeg North Centre in a by-election, and he won reelection 12 times, losing only once, in 1958. In 1961 Knowles was involved in the founding of the NDP. He declined offers to become speaker of the Commons, preferring to remain on the floor of the House. After having suffered a stroke in 1981, he decided in 1984 to leave politics. After retirement he was given an honorary seat for life at the clerk's table, an unprecedented honour. He was awarded the Order of Canada and in 1979 was made a member of the Privy Council.

Kodaira, Kunihiko, Japanese mathematician who made important contributions to harmonic analysis, algebraic geometry, complex analytic manifolds, and other areas of mathematical research and significantly influenced a number of younger mathematicians through his work and teaching in the U.S. and Japan. He received a Fields Medal in 1954 and the Order of Culture from the emperor of Japan in 1957 (b. March 16, 1915—d. July 26, 1997).

Kopelev, Lev Zinoviyevich, Russian-born writer and human rights activist who was imprisoned in a Soviet labour camp after he objected to Soviet troops' brutality against German civilians in occupied territory following World War II and was considered the model for a character, Lev Rubin, in Aleksandr Solzhenitsyn's *The First Circle*; further dissident activities led to the stripping of his citizenship in 1981, and he spent the rest of his life in Germany (b. April 9, 1912—d. June 18, 1997).

Krainik, Ardis Joan, American arts executive (b. March 8, 1929, Manitowoc, Wis.—d. Jan. 18, 1997, Chicago, Ill.), was the general director of the Lyric Opera of Chicago for 15 years. Only the second person to hold that position, she guided the company out of financial difficulty and into worldwide renown. Krainik was educated at Northwestern University, Evanston, Ill. (B.S., 1951), taught drama and public speaking in Wisconsin (1951–53), and returned to Northwestern for postgraduate studies before joining (1954) the fledgling Lyric Theatre as secretary to the company's founder, Carol Fox, and as a singer. She performed in supporting roles in some 11 operas, but in 1960, having become assistant manager of what was by then the Lyric Opera, she chose to concentrate on administration and gave up her stage career. She was named artistic administrator in 1975. By 1980, however, the Lyric had become seriously unstable financially, and Krainik saw her future there as uncertain. When she was offered the leadership of the Australian Opera in Sydney, she made plans to take that position. Fox left the Lyric in early 1981, though, and Krainik agreed to stay on and take her place. She quickly returned the company to financial health and went on to raise enough money to renovate the Civic Opera House, the company's home. Krainik also made her mark artistically, presenting contemporary works, commissioning new works, and instituting a composer-in-residence program. In addition she staged (1996) the company's first complete Wagner *Ring* cycle. Krainik made headlines in 1989 when she announced that because of his numerous cancellations Luciano Pavarotti was no longer welcome at the Lyric. In June 1996 she announced her impending retirement because of deteriorating health. The Civic's main auditorium was named the Ardis Krainik Theatre.

Krüss, James, German writer of children's literature whose abundant stories and poems were highly regarded for their wordplay as well as for the fun of their plots (b. May 31, 1926—d. Aug. 2, 1997).

Kuralt, Charles, American broadcast journalist and author (b. Sept. 10, 1934, Wilmington, N.C.—d. July 4, 1997, New York, N.Y.), chronicled everyday life in the "On the Road" television segments that appeared for some 13 years during the "CBS Evening News." Each year from 1967 to 1980, he traveled in a motor home roughly 80,000 km (50,000 mi) throughout the 50 states, roaming off the beaten path in search of stories that otherwise might have gone unreported. His travels led him to a variety of engaging subjects, among them a beer-can collector, a 93-year-old brickmaker, and a high-school basketball team on a losing streak that had lasted 127 games. Kuralt was educated at the University of North Carolina at Chapel Hill, where he was editor of the student newspaper. After graduation (1955) he spent two years at the *Charlotte* (N.C.) *News* before joining CBS in 1957. In 1959 he became a correspondent—the network's youngest ever—and he later reported from Africa, Latin America, and Asia. In 1967 Kuralt, who later confessed that he had "always had the travel itch," persuaded executives to let him take a look at the lighter side of the news, the result of which was "On the Road." During a career that spanned some four decades, he made a number of documentaries, special broadcasts, and other cable and network programs. He anchored "CBS News Sunday Morning" from 1979. His work received widespread recognition, earning him 12 Emmy and 3 Peabody awards. After retiring from CBS in 1994, he spent "a perfect year" revisiting his favourite places. The trip was recorded in his final book, *Charles Kuralt's America* (1995).

DAVID ALLEN—CORBIS

Charles Kuralt

Lane, Burton (Burton Levy), American composer (b. Feb. 2, 1912, New York, N.Y.—d. Jan. 5, 1997, New York), created melodies for musical stage shows and motion pictures for more than 50 years. Though he was not the best known of show business composers, his songs graced a number of popular and highly respected shows, and he collaborated with such well-known lyricists as Ira Gershwin, Alan Jay Lerner, Frank Loesser, and E.Y. ("Yip") Harburg. Lane, a high-school dropout, was a song plugger in Tin Pan Alley when he came to the attention of George Gershwin, who became his mentor. By the early 1930s Lane's songs were being featured in Broadway revues, and in 1933 his first song for a Hollywood musical—"Everything I Have Is Yours"—was featured in *Dancing Lady.* Of the numerous motion pictures that followed, another success was the Judy Garland film *Babes on Broadway* (1942), whose hit song "How About You?" was nominated for an Academy Award. Lane had launched Garland's career in 1934 when he heard the 11-year-old sing in an act with her sisters and arranged for an audition at a Hollywood studio. His Broadway career also continued, and in 1947 his greatest success, the classic *Finian's Rainbow,* opened. With such memorable songs as "How Are Things in Glocca Morra?" and "Old Devil Moon," it ran for 725 performances. It was filmed in 1968. Lane's first collaboration with Lerner, the motion picture *Royal Wedding* (1951), resulted in another Oscar nomination—for "Too Late Now"—and brought to the silver screen the unforgettable scene in which Fred Astaire dances on the walls and ceiling. Until the mid-1960s Lane's work gained less attention. Another joint effort with Lerner, however, gave him his last notable success. *On a Clear Day You Can See Forever* opened on Broadway in 1965 and was filmed in 1970. A revival of *Finian's Rainbow* opened at the Goodspeed Opera House, East Haddam, Conn., in April 1997, a half century after its Broadway premiere.

Lane, Ronald ("Ronnie"), British rock bass guitarist, singer, and songwriter who was cofounder of the influential 1960s band the Small Faces (later the Faces), which gave a boost to the careers of a number of musicians, including Ron Wood and Rod Stewart; in 1983 Lane organized a concert featuring many top rock stars at London's Royal Albert Hall to raise money for research in multiple sclerosis, the disease that ultimately caused his death (b. April 1, 1946—d. June 4, 1997).

Latsis, Mary Jane ("M.J."), American crime-fiction writer who, with collaborator Martha Henissart, wrote under the pseudonym Emma Lathen; the two turned out over two dozen mysteries, most notably the series featuring John Putnam Thatcher, a Wall Street banker turned amateur detective (b. 1927—d. Nov. 3, 1997).

Laughlin, James, American publishing executive (b. Oct. 30, 1914, Pittsburgh, Pa.—d. Nov. 12, 1997, Norfolk, Conn.), was the founder of the

New Directions publishing house, which introduced the works of such important writers as Ezra Pound, Dylan Thomas, Tennessee Williams, William Carlos Williams, and Henry Miller. Laughlin was Vladimir Nabokov's first American publisher, and he also was known for aiding writers financially. Born into a wealthy family whose fortune was made in iron and steel, Laughlin attended the Choate School, Wallingford, Conn., where he edited the school's literary magazine, and then went on to Harvard University. On a leave of absence during his sophomore year, he went first to France, where he met Gertrude Stein and Alice B. Toklas, and then to Italy, where he studied with Pound for six months. Pound suggested that Laughlin be a publisher rather than a poet, and when he returned to Harvard, Laughlin, aided by money from his father, began New Directions. The company's first book, the experimental-writing anthology *New Directions in Prose and Poetry,* appeared in 1936 and became the first volume of a series that eventually numbered at least 45. Laughlin graduated from Harvard in 1939 and during the 1940s began the Five Young American Poets series. He went on to add a New Classics series, in which he reprinted works other publishers would not. Although New Directions was subsidized by Laughlin family money for many years, with the aid of such best-sellers as Lawrence Ferlinghetti's *A Coney Island of the Mind* and reprints of Herman Hesse's *Siddhartha,* it eventually became financially successful. Laughlin also continued writing, and a number of collections of his works were published, among them *The Pig* (1970), *The House of Light* (1986), *Selected Poems, 1935–1985* (1986), *Pound as Wuz: Essays and Lectures on Ezra Pound* (1987), *Random Essays: Recollections of a Publisher* (1989), and *Random Stories* (1990). His *Poems, New and Selected* was to be published posthumously. Among Laughlin's numerous honours was the 1992 National Book Foundation Medal for Distinguished Contribution to American Letters.

Launder, Frank, British motion picture director and screenwriter who was best known for his long collaboration with Sidney Gilliat on the screenplays for such films as *The Lady Vanishes* and *Night Train to Munich* and on the series of "St. Trinian's" farces (b. January 1906—d. Feb. 23, 1997).

Leach, Janet Darnell, American-born British potter who ran Leach Pottery, the business of her more famous husband, Bernard Leach, but who also was successful with her own distinctive style of crockery; because they were both thrown on the wheel and hand-built, her creations had irregular shapes, and they were accentuated by the glazes she used to produce an innovative effect (b. March 15, 1918—d. Sept. 12, 1997).

Leburton, Edmond Jules Isidore, Belgian politician who served as prime minister for a year, January 1973–January 1974, during which the government was scandal-ridden; he was the last holder of that office to be a Socialist and a native French speaker (b. April 18, 1915—d. June 15, 1997).

Lee, Laurie, British poet and prose writer (b. June 26, 1914, Slad, near Stroud, Gloucestershire, Eng.—d. May 13, 1997, Slad), was best known for his book *Cider with Rosie* (1959; U.S. title *The Edge of Day*), a memoir of his boyhood in the Cotswold countryside. The later volumes of what proved to be his autobiographical trilogy were *As I Walked Out One Midsummer Morning* (1969), a description of his trip to London and Spain, and *A Moment of War* (1991), an account of his experiences in Spain during the Spanish Civil War (1936–39). Lee's father abandoned the family in 1917, when Lee was three. At age 19 Lee headed to London and then to Spain. There he traveled and began to feel some sympathy for the Republican cause. He returned to England and during World War II worked for various government departments. In the war's aftermath he published three volumes of poetry and several prose works, not making much of a reputation until Leonard Woolf reluctantly published *Cider with Rosie.* It was an instant classic and soon a regular part of the educational curriculum. Awakening in its public a deep-seated longing for the simplicity and innocence of a joyous youth in a bygone era, the book essentially recorded daily life and the unique personalities that made life in a small village memorable. It sold so many copies that Lee was able to purchase his boyhood home, and it was there that he died.

Leonard, Buck (Walter Fenner Leonard), American baseball player who was widely considered the finest first baseman in the history of the Negro Leagues. Leonard starred for the legendary Homestead (Pa.) Grays, playing alongside Josh Gibson. The Grays were the dominant Negro Leagues team throughout the 1930s and '40s, and the combination of Gibson and Leonard was compared by many to the New York Yankees duo of Babe Ruth and Lou Gehrig. In 1972 Leonard was elected to the Baseball Hall of Fame (b. Sept. 8, 1907—d. Nov. 27, 1997).

Leonard, Sheldon (Sheldon Leonard Bershad), American performer, producer, and director whose career ranged from playing roles as rogues on Jack Benny's radio show and in such films as *Guys and Dolls* and *It's a Wonderful Life* to producing and directing a number of popular television shows, among them "I Spy" and "The Dick Van Dyke Show" (b. Feb. 22, 1907—d. Jan. 10, 1997).

Levertov, Denise, British-born American poet (b. Oct. 24, 1923, Ilford, Essex, Eng.—d. Dec. 20, 1997, Seattle, Wash.), delved into the depths of her political convictions in emotion-charged verse that reflected her role as an activist and propounded her pacifist views, especially her opposition to the Vietnam War. Levertov, who was schooled exclusively at home, served as a civilian nurse in London during World War II and published her first book of poetry, *The Double Image,* in 1946. That volume, and her second, *Here and Now* (1957), were regarded by many as overly sentimental accounts of the war. After moving (1948) to the U.S. and marrying American writer Mitchell Goodman, she began developing an American voice that bore hallmarks of the familiar and everyday traditions of William Carlos Williams. She also found inspiration in the works of Wallace Stevens, Ezra Pound, and Black Mountain poets such as Robert Duncan. Some poems and essays extolled the beauties of nature, whereas *Relearning the Alphabet* (1970), *The Sorrow Dance* (1967), and *To Stay Alive* (1971) addressed her social concerns. The prolific writer of more than 35 books, she also wrote of riots, nuclear disarmament, and ecological issues. She cofounded the Writers and Artists Protest Against the War in Vietnam and was jailed a number of times for civil disobedience.

Lewenstein, Oscar, British theatre impresario and film producer who was a central figure in London's Royal Court Theatre for over 20 years, formed the English Stage Company, and helped produce such notable films as *Tom Jones* (b. Jan. 18, 1917—d. Feb. 23, 1997).

Lewis, Robert, American actor, drama teacher, and theatre director who cofounded, directed, and performed in the 1930s with the Group Theatre in such plays as *Waiting for Lefty* and *Golden Boy* before helping to found (1947) the Actors Studio, where for one year he tutored such future stars as Marlon Brando and Karl Malden; he eventually went on to Broadway, where he directed *Brigadoon, Teahouse of the August Moon,* and *Witness for the Prosecution.* Lewis taught (1941–76) at the Yale School of Drama and later established his own theatre workshop in New York City (b. March 16, 1909—d. Nov. 23, 1997).

Lichtenstein, Roy, American artist (b. Oct. 27, 1923, New York, N.Y.—d. Sept. 29, 1997, New York), was one of the founders and foremost practitioners of Pop art, a movement that used pop-culture icons such as comic-strip and advertisement images to counter Abstract Expressionism's tactile technique and deep personal involvement with abstruse concepts. At the age of 16, Lichtenstein took summer classes at the Art Students League in New York City under realist Reginald Marsh. After serving in World War II, he earned a master's degree (1949) from Ohio State University, where he also served on the faculty (1946–51). At the beginning of his artistic career, he produced modern images of cowboys and Indians and even dabbled (1957) in Abstract Expressionism before finding his inspiration in a painting he made for his children. His 1961 landmark "Look Mickey, I've Hooked a Big One!!," was a scaled-up representation of a comic-strip panel featuring Mickey Mouse and Donald Duck, an image that he found on a bubblegum wrapper. Although he was at first dissatisfied with his technique and such direct appropriation, he found deep satisfaction in presenting a comic image as fine art. He increased the size of his canvases to rival any produced by Abstract Expressionists and began to extract and adapt for his own purposes the graphic and linguistic conventions of romantic, science-fiction, and war comic strips. He used words to express sound effects such as in "Whaam!" (1963), a diptych in which one jet fighter shoots another over the separation between the canvases. He used commonplace images and developed a detached and taut mass-produced effect by outlining areas of primary colours in thick black lines and by using a benday technique (a dot pattern used by engravers). He achieved this effect by stippling with a toothbrush through a metal screen. Following the huge commercial success of his first one-man show in 1962, his unusual work found an international audience and he became (1966) the first American to exhibit at the Tate Gallery, London. Some of his other trademarks included speeches encompassed in balloons and landscapes made in the comic-book vein. When he began producing (1967) sculptures, they evoked the glass and curved-chrome styles of the 1930s. During the 1970s and '80s, his studio became a kind of factory, where assistants helped him to produce one variation after another. His

Roy Lichtenstein

RICHARD SCHULMAN—GAMMA LIAISON

creations during this period, especially of landscapes and still lifes, were a dramatic departure from earlier works that had used little brushwork.

Liman, Arthur, American lawyer (b. Nov. 5, 1932, New York, N.Y.—d. July 17, 1997, New York), served as chief counsel on many high-profile cases, including the congressional investigation of the Iran-Contra arms-for-hostages scheme. Unglamorous and often disheveled in appearance, Liman was considered one of the top trial lawyers of his generation. After graduating magna cum laude from Harvard University (1954) and finishing first in his class at Yale Law School (1957), Liman joined the prestigious New York City law firm Paul, Weiss, Rifkind, Wharton & Garrison. In 1985 he won his biggest corporate case, in which he represented Pennzoil against Texaco as the two oil companies were vying for control of Getty Oil. In the 1980s he handled cases involving white-collar crimes, working for such clients as junk-bond mogul Michael Milken and fugitive financier Robert Vesco. From 1961 to 1963 he was employed by the U.S. attorney's office, often taking cases that no one else wanted. In 1971 he served as chief counsel on the New York state commission investigating the bloody Attica prison riot. The commission, which determined that the police assault had been excessively harsh, published its conclusions in a 470-page report that was nominated for a National Book Award. Liman came into the national spotlight in 1987 when he served as chief counsel to the U.S. Senate committee probing the Iran-Contra scandal. Although he was criticized by some for not following leads to determine Pres. Ronald Reagan's possible involvement and for not being aggressive enough in his questioning of Lieut. Col. Oliver North, Liman defended his decisions throughout the trial.

Lorant, Stefan (ISTVAN LORANT), Hungarian-born American editor, writer, and photojournalist (b. Feb. 22, 1901, Budapest, Austria-Hungary—d. Nov. 14, 1997, Rochester, Minn.), expressed himself through visual images, an ability he first realized as a maker of silent films, to become a pioneer in the development of modern photojournalism. He believed that events should be recorded as they happened—as they appeared to ordinary people—instead of being manipulated for staged, posed photographs, and he arranged pictures in layouts that allowed the story to unfold. Lorant graduated (1919) from the Academy of Economics in Budapest and then worked for a time in the silent-film industry in Vienna and Berlin. He had been serving as editor of the *Münchner Illustrierte Presse* in Munich when Adolf Hitler became (1933) chancellor of Germany, and he was imprisoned for more than six months before Hungarian journalists were successful in gaining his freedom. He spent the next few months in Budapest editing the Sunday pictorial magazine of the newspaper *Pesti Naplo* before moving to Great Britain. There he published his diary, *I Was Hitler's Prisoner* (1935), and created and edited the picture magazines *Weekly Illustrated* (1934), *Lilliput* (1937–40), and *Picture Post* (1938–40). Lorant disliked Britain's treatment of him as a wartime enemy alien, however, and in 1940 moved to the U.S. He thereafter was noted especially for historical works, such as the pictorial biographies *Lincoln: His Life in Photographs* (1941; rev. ed. 1957) and *Lincoln: A Picture Story of His Life* (1952; rev. ed. 1969) and the German history *Sieg Heil!* (1974). At the time of his death, Lorant was working on a multivolume autobiography, *I Dared.*

Louis, Jean (JEAN-LOUIS BERTHAULT), French-born costume designer (b. Oct. 5, 1907, Paris, France—d. April 20, 1997, Palm Springs, Calif.), designed fashions and costumes during the 1940s, '50s, and '60s for some 200 of Hollywood's most glamorous stars, among them Lana Turner, Marlene Dietrich, Betty Grable, Judy Garland, Kim Novak, and Doris Day. Of the numerous designs he created for about 60 films, as well as for television productions and personal collections, two were especially memorable: the black satin strapless gown Rita Hayworth wore when she sang "Put the Blame on Mame" in *Gilda* (1946) and the shimmering form-fitting dress Marilyn Monroe wore in 1962 for her breathy rendition of "Happy Birthday" for Pres. John F. Kennedy at New York City's Madison Square Garden. Louis was trained in Paris and, while visiting New York City, submitted some designs to the Hattie Carnegie firm and was given a job. His creations were soon being worn by many of the most fashionable American women. In 1944 Joan Cohn—the wife of Columbia Pictures head Harry Cohn—persuaded her husband to make Louis the studio's chief designer, and screen credits began to carry the notation "Gowns by Jean Louis." In the years that followed, he received 14 nominations for Academy Awards and won one—for the Judy Holliday film *The Solid Gold Cadillac* (1956). From 1953 to 1961 his ensembles were featured on the weekly television program "The Loretta Young Show"; Young made 52 of her legendary grand entrances twirling through a doorway in Jean Louis gowns. In 1958 Louis moved to Universal Pictures, and in the early 1960s he opened a salon and began costuming motion pictures on a freelance basis. He retired in 1988. Louis, widowed in 1987, married Young in 1993.

Loynaz, Dulce María, Cuban poet who wrote of personal matters and avoided political themes and thus was long out of favour; her only novel, *Jardín*—written in the late 1920s and early '30s but not published until 1951—was considered a precursor of magic realism. Only late in life did she achieve recognition, winning the 1987 Cuban National Prize for Literature and the 1992 Cervantes Prize (b. Dec. 10, 1902—d. April 27, 1997).

Lukas, J(ay) Anthony, American journalist and author (b. April 25, 1933, New York, N.Y.—d. June 5, 1997, New York), wrote meticulous examinations of the societal and racial fissures in the U.S. He was known and highly regarded for his tenacity, perfectionism, and painstaking research and won a number of the country's top literature and journalism awards, including two Pulitzer Prizes. Lukas was educated at Harvard University and served on the staff of the *Crimson,* the campus newspaper. He graduated magna cum laude (B.A., 1955) and studied further at the Free University of Berlin. After service in the U.S. Army, he worked (1958–62) for the *Baltimore* (Md.) *Sun* and then (1962–71) for the *New York Times.* Lukas's first Pulitzer was awarded in 1968 for the *Times* article "The Two Worlds of Linda Fitzpatrick," which detailed the double life a teenage murder victim had led with her wealthy Connecticut family and—unbeknownst to that family—in the counterculture of New York City's East Village. He included her story in his book about the generation gap, *Don't Shoot—We Are Your Children!* (1971). His second Pulitzer was for his book *Common Ground: A Turbulent Decade in the Lives of Three American Families* (1985), generally considered his masterpiece. The culmination of seven years of work, it probed the effect of court-ordered school desegration on three Boston families—one upper-middle-class white, one working-class black, and one working-class Irish Catholic. Besides the Pulitzer, it won the 1985 National Book Award and the 1986 National Book Critics Circle Award. Lukas, long a sufferer from depression and in despair because of what he saw as the shortcomings of his recently finished book, *Big Trouble,* took his own life.

Maar, Dora (HENRIETTE THÉODORA MARKOVITCH), French photographer and painter who was one of Pablo Picasso's mistresses for eight years in the 1930s and '40s and was the subject of many of his portraits (b. Nov. 22, 1907—d. July 16, 1997).

Macapagal, Diosdado, Philippine politician who was president of the country from 1961 until his defeat by Ferdinand Marcos in 1965; during his term Macapagal instituted land reform policies, but they were largely ineffectual (b. Sept. 28, 1910—d. April 21, 1997).

McCormick, Kenneth Dale, American editor who served as editor in chief at Doubleday and Co., Inc., from 1942 to 1971 and then as senior consulting editor until 1987; during that time he worked with such famous and varied authors as Daphne du Maurier, Richard Nixon, Noël Coward, Earl Warren, and Hedda Hopper (b. Feb. 25, 1906—d. June 27, 1997).

Mallary, Robert W., American Neo-Dadaist, or junk, artist who was best known for his use of urban detritus in his sculptures and who pioneered the use of the computer in the creation of art (b. Dec. 2, 1917—d. Feb. 10, 1997).

Manley, Michael Norman, Jamaican politician (b. Dec. 10, 1924, St. Andrew, Jam.—d. March 6, 1997, Kingston, Jam.), was a popular leader—nicknamed "Joshua" for the biblical prophet—who served three terms (1972–80 and 1989–92) as prime minister and was a powerful champion of Third World issues. Though he initially espoused hard-line socialism and defied U.S. policy, especially toward Cuba, in later years he embraced a capitalistic outlook and sought close

Michael Manley

ALEX WEBB—MAGNUM

relations with the U.S. Manley was the son of the noted sculptor Edna Swithenbank Manley and Norman Manley, a national hero, the founder of the People's National Party (PNP), and Jamaica's prime minister from 1959 to 1962. He was educated at Jamaica College and, following service in the Royal Canadian Air Force during World War II, at the London School of Economics, where he came under the influence of the socialist Harold Laski. After working as a freelance journalist in London, Manley returned (1951) to Jamaica and went to work for *Public Opinion,* a leftist weekly newspaper. He soon became active in the trade-union movement, attaining positions of union leadership and gaining recognition as a skilled negotiator. In 1962 he was appointed to Jamaica's Senate, and in 1967 he was elected to the House of Representatives. Two years later Manley succeeded his father as president of the PNP, and when the party won the election of 1972, he became prime minister. He set about instituting policies for redistributing wealth and became a champion of the less-developed nations' nonaligned movement. In 1973 he was one of the founders of the Caribbean Community and Common Market (Caricom), and he cultivated close relationships with Cuba and the socialist countries of Eastern Europe and the Far East. Though Manley was reelected in 1976, his policies eventually proved to be financially disastrous. Violence between the left and the right escalated, and he lost the 1980 election to the conservative Edward Seaga. In 1989, however, having adopted a more moderate outlook, Manley was returned to the prime ministership. Still claiming to be a socialist, he nonetheless pursued free-market policies and privatized many state-owned enterprises. In 1992 ill health forced Manley to resign from office.

Maples, William Ross, American forensic anthropologist who examined and identified the skeletons of a number of historical figures, including Tsar Nicholas II and other members of the Romanov family killed in 1918 by the Bolsheviks, and in 1994 helped convict Byron De La Beckwith of the 1963 murder of civil rights leader Medgar Evers (b. Aug. 7, 1937—d. Feb. 27, 1997).

Marchais, Georges-René-Louis, French political leader (b. June 7, 1920, La Hoguette, France—d. Nov. 16, 1997, Paris, France), was the secretary-general of the French Communist Party from 1972 to 1994. During that time the party's importance steadily diminished, in no small part because of his support of the Soviet Union and his defense of such actions as its invasion of Afghanistan. Marchais left school in 1934 and went to work in the aeronautical industry. His World War II years were surrounded by controversy; although he claimed to have been forced to work in a German aircraft factory, it was rumoured that he had volunteered. In 1946 Marchais became active in the metalworkers union, and the following year he joined the Communist Party. He rose rapidly through the ranks, becoming a Central Committee member in 1956 and ultimately secretary-general. Marchais helped form an alliance of French leftist parties and in 1973 was elected to the National Assembly, to which he continually won reelection. The alliance disintegrated in 1977. Marchais ran for president in 1981 but dropped out after the first round; he had garnered only a little over 15% of the vote. The winner, François Mitterrand, included four communists in his government, but they pulled out in 1984. Although the breakup of the Soviet Union in 1991 left Marchais politically isolated, he remained committed to communism.

Mark, J. Carson, Canadian-born American scientist who, as head of the theoretical division at the Los Alamos (N.M.) Scientific Laboratory, was instrumental in the development of the hydrogen bomb (b. July 6, 1913—d. March 2, 1997).

Marshall, Lois Catherine, Canadian soprano (b. Jan. 29, 1924, Toronto, Ont.—d. Feb. 20, 1997, Toronto), was considered one of Canada's greatest singers. Even though paralysis resulting from a bout of polio she suffered at the age of two largely prevented her from performing in staged opera productions, she enjoyed an international concert career for over 25 years, singing operatic arias, lieder, oratorios, and folk songs in appearances with such conductors as Arturo Toscanini, Leonard Bernstein, Sir Thomas Beecham, and Sir Ernest MacMillan. In 1938, when she was 12, Marshall began studying voice with Weldon Kilburn; they performed together for many years and were married in 1968. A performance of Bach's *St. Matthew's Passion* in Toronto in the late 1940s brought her to national attention, and she made her New York debut in 1952. That led the following year to a recording of Beethoven's *Missa Solemnis* with Toscanini that established her reputation. Marshall was made a Companion of the Order of Canada in 1968. She gave her farewell concert in 1982 but continued to teach voice at the University of Toronto, a job she had begun in 1976. Following her death, the Lois Marshall Memorial Scholarships were created there, and on March 19 a memorial tribute was held.

Mas Canosa, Jorge, Cuban exile leader (b. Sept. 21, 1939, Santiago de Cuba—d. Nov. 23, 1997, Miami, Fla.), headed an anti-Castro organization that became one of the most powerful lobbying groups in the United States. The son of an officer in the Cuban army, Mas was an early opponent of the Cuban dictator Fulgencio Batista and was arrested at the age of 14 for his role in an anti-Batista radio broadcast. Sent by his father to study in the United States, Mas returned to Cuba in 1959, shortly after Fidel Castro gained power. His initial admiration for Castro soon turned to disenchantment, however, and Mas was again implicated in antigovernment activities. He fled in 1960 to the U.S., where he trained with the exile force that undertook the disastrous Bay of Pigs invasion, although he did not take part in the operation. Following a stint in the U.S. Army, Mas worked in a variety of jobs while devoting much of his time to the anti-Castro cause. By the 1970s he was the owner of a telecommunications company and was on his way to becoming one of the wealthiest Hispanic businessmen in the U.S. After turning away from advocating a violent overthrow of Castro, Mas concentrated on political advocacy, forming the Cuban-American National Foundation, a powerful and wealthy lobbying group that had considerable influence over politicians from both parties. He was also instrumental in founding Radio Marti, the U.S. government-financed station broadcasting to Cuba, and in promoting legislation that tightened the economic embargo on Cuba.

Mascolo, Dionys, French writer, intellectual, and political activist who was known both for his protests in support of various causes, such as opposition to the torture of prisoners, and for his love affair with novelist Marguerite Duras, during which he fathered her only child (b. 1916—d. Aug. 20, 1997).

Matthews, Drummond Hoyle, British geophysicist whose work, with student Fred Vine, led to the discovery that magnetic stripes on the sides of ridges on the ocean floor were the result of seafloor spreading; the finding was critical to the theory of plate tectonics (b. Feb. 5, 1931—d. July 20, 1997).

Matthews, William Procter, III, American poet and university English professor who was awarded the 1996 National Book Critics Circle Award for his book *Time & Money: New Poems* (b. Nov. 11, 1942—d. Nov. 12, 1997).

Mayuzumi, Toshiro, Japanese composer (b. Feb. 20, 1929, Yokohama, Japan—d. April 10, 1997, Kawasaki, Japan), combined avant-garde Western instrumentation and techniques with traditional Japanese music and established a long-standing reputation for experimentation and eclecticism. Mayuzumi studied at what is now the Tokyo National University of Fine Arts and Music from 1945 to 1951, a period when Western music was widespread and accessible because of the American occupation. His early works revealed a number of influences, ranging from jazz rhythms in *Hors d'oeuvre* (1947) to Balinese music in *Sphenogrammes* (1951), which received international acclaim after it was performed in Frankfurt, W.Ger. In 1951 he studied briefly with Tony Aubin at the Paris Conservatoire National Supérieur de Musique. Upon his return to Tokyo in 1952, he introduced into Japanese music modern musical trends and techniques, notably those of John Cage. Mayuzumi's *Shusaku I* (1955; *Study I*) represented the first Japanese example of synthetic electronic music, and *X,Y,Z* (1955) became the first Japanese work to use *musique concrète,* a modernist technique consisting of a recorded montage of electronically altered natural sounds. A significant change occurred in Mayuzumi's career in the late 1950s when he turned back to traditional Japanese music to find models for his work. *Nirvana Symphony* (1958) was based on the sounds made by Buddhist temple bells, and *Bugaku* (1962) imitated the sounds and rhythms of the court dance that was part of traditional gagaku music. Along with other artists, including novelist Yukio Mishima, he became an outspoken critic of the Westernization of his country and attempted to redefine a Japanese cultural identity by nurturing unique Japanese qualities in his art. Mayuzumi also composed for the symphony and the ballet as well as for theatre and films.

Meisner, Sanford, American drama instructor, original member of the Group Theater (founded 1931), and director (1936–59; 1964–89) of the Neighborhood Playhouse School of the Theater in New York City, where he taught such students as Gregory Peck, Joanne Woodward, and Grace Kelly; he was the subject of the documentary film *The Theater's Best-Kept Secret,* 1985, and coauthor of *Sanford Meisner on Acting,* 1987 (b. Aug. 31, 1905—d. Feb. 2, 1997).

Melvin, Harold James, American singer who founded the Blue Notes, a rhythm-and-blues band that was fronted for a few years by singer Teddy Pendergrass and popularized the "Philly sound" in the 1970s with such hits as "The Love I Lost" and "If You Don't Know Me by Now" (b. June 25, 1939—d. March 24, 1997).

Meredith, (Oliver) Burgess, American actor, director, and writer whose performing career, which spanned nearly seven decades, included a notable film debut in *Winterset* after a Broadway success in the same vehicle, the role of George in the 1939 film *Of Mice and Men,* a television run as the Penguin in the 1960s "Batman" series, and the role of Mickey the fight trainer in the film *Rocky* and several of its sequels (b. Nov. 16, 1907—d. Sept. 9, 1997).

Merril, Judith (JOSEPHINE JULIET GROSSMAN), American-born Canadian science-fiction writer whose highly regarded works, which reflected a feminist stance, were among the first of the genre to be published by a woman; she was considered most important, however, for having compiled influential science-fiction anthologies (b. Jan. 21, 1923—d. Sept. 12, 1997).

Michener, James Albert, American novelist (b. Feb. 3, 1907, New York, N.Y.—d. Oct. 16, 1997, Austin, Texas), launched a 50-year literary career with *Tales of the South Pacific* (1947), a book that won the 1948 Pulitzer Prize for literature. It was later adapted for Broadway and became the Rodgers and Hammerstein hit *South Pacific* (1949), and in 1958 it became a motion picture of the same title. Michener's ability to weave epic fictional narratives of people and places with a touch of history placed him atop best-seller lists and in 1992 made him one of eight authors who had produced six or more number one best-sellers. It was not until after the 1959 publication of *Hawaii,* however, that his work became a common fixture on American bookshelves. His nomadic lifestyle carried him around the globe, and his temporary addresses served as titles for many of his more than 20 books, among them *Iberia* (1968), *Chesapeake* (1978), *Poland* (1983), and

JIJI PRESS/AFP

Toshiro Mifune (right)

Mexico (1992). Michener also explored such topics as sports, Japanese prints, politics, archaeology, and the sonnet. Abandoned at birth, he was raised in an adoptive Quaker home in Doylestown, Pa., and never discovered his origins. Michener spent the largest part of his last two decades in Austin, Texas, where he wrote *Texas* (1985), his longest novel (1,096 pages). Over the years he donated more than $100 million to schools and charities and became the single-largest benefactor of the University of Texas, with gifts topping $37 million.

Mifune, Toshiro, Japanese actor (b. April 1, 1920, Qingdao province, China—d. Dec. 24, 1997, near Tokyo, Japan), was the archetypal samurai sword-wielding warrior in a series of period films by director Akira Kurosawa and became a screen idol with his magnetic screen persona, which he could quickly transform for dramatic, tragic, and comedic roles. Mifune was born to Japanese parents in China and served during World War II in the Japanese Imperial Air Force. He appeared in small film roles shortly before starring in Kurosawa's *Drunken Angel* (1948) as an angry gangster, a role that established his powerful screen presence. In *Rashomon* (1950) he secured his reputation as a lightning-quick samurai hero and linked his rising star with that of Kurosawa; the two made 16 films together between 1948 and 1965, including such masterpieces as *The Seven Samurai* (1954) and *Yojimbo* (1961), which were remade as Hollywood westerns called, respectively, *The Magnificent Seven* and *A Fistful of Dollars.* Although he appeared as a samurai in about half of his more than 120 films, he also appeared in Kurosawa's adaptations of Fyodor Dostoyevsky's *The Idiot* (1951), Maksim Gorky's *The Lower Depths* (1957), and *Throne of Blood* (1957), modeled after Shakespeare's *Macbeth.* He portrayed Adm. Isoroku Yamamoto, the architect of the attack on Pearl Harbor, in *Storm over the Pacific* (1960) and reprised the role for the American-made *Midway* (1976). In the U.S., however, he was perhaps best known as the warlord Toranaga in the 1980 television miniseries *Shogun,* an adaptation of James Clavell's novel. Mifune also established (1963) his own company, Mifune Productions, and directed one film before seizing his sword onscreen once again.

Milburn, Rodney, Jr., American track and field star who won the 1972 Olympic gold medal in the 110-m hurdles. The winner of numerous collegiate, national, and international races, Milburn later was a track coach at Southern University, Baton Rouge, La. (b. May 18, 1950—d. Nov. 11, 1997).

Mills, Victor, American chemical engineer who, while working for the Procter & Gamble Co., revolutionized child care with the invention of the disposable diaper; he began work on that product in the 1950s, using his grandchildren as test subjects (b. 1897—d. Nov. 1, 1997).

Miró Romero, Pilar, Spanish motion-picture and television director who shaped Spain's entertainment industry; in addition to making award-winning movies, she advanced the careers of aspiring filmmakers while a member (1982–86) of the Ministry of Culture and, as head (1986–89) of the state television, brought bold programming to the small screen before controversy surrounding misuse of funds led to her resignation (b. April 20, 1940—d. Oct. 19, 1997).

Mitchum, Robert Charles Duran, American actor (b. Aug. 6, 1917, Bridgeport, Conn.—d. July 1, 1997, Santa Barbara, Calif.), portrayed roles in a series of movies in the late 1940s that constructed an image for him as Hollywood's ultimate tough guy. His notorious offscreen exploits nourished this persona until the real-life Mitchum and the Hollywood movie star merged into one screen legend. During the Depression Mitchum attended Haaren High School in New York City's Hell's Kitchen but was expelled. Around age 15 he took to the open road to roam the country, experiencing a series of misadventures that included serving time on a Georgia chain gang. He became interested in the theatrical arts in 1936 after his sister, Julie, suggested he join her as part of the Long Beach (Calif.) Theatre Guild. His Hollywood career began in 1943 when he landed a bit part in the Hopalong Cassidy western movie *Hoppy Serves a Writ.* Other small parts followed, and RKO Radio Pictures, Inc., signed him to a contract in 1944. A career highlight was his Academy Award-nominated performance in *The Story of G.I. Joe* (1945). In 1948 he was arrested for marijuana possession. What could have been a career-destroying scandal turned into a boon for Mitchum, who evoked sympathy from the press and public by handling the situation with dignity and honesty. The conviction was later overturned and stricken from his record. Mitchum, an insomniac who developed a trademark sleepy-eyed appearance, was a fixture in films and television for over 50 years. He often was cast in offbeat or villainous roles, notably in *The Night of the Hunter* (1955), *Thunder Road* (1958), and *Cape Fear* (1962). He also starred as a cynical, unlucky private eye in a series of gritty films noirs, including *Out of the Past* (1947), and portrayed Raymond Chandler's Philip Marlowe in *Farewell, My Lovely* (1975) and *The Big Sleep* (1978). Some of

Robert Mitchum

UNITED ARTISTS/ARCHIVE PHOTOS

his other film credits include *Heaven Knows, Mr. Allison* (1957), *El Dorado* (1967), and *Mr. North* (1988). Besides acting in motion pictures, Mitchum also composed and recorded the 1958 hit song "The Ballad of Thunder Road" and starred in the television miniseries "The Winds of War."

Mlynar, Zdenek, Czech politician who sought to institute reforms during the Prague Spring of 1968. In the years after the 1968 Soviet-led invasion of Czechoslovakia, Mlynar helped to found the dissident group Charter 77 and went into exile in Austria (b. June 22, 1930—d. April 15, 1997).

Mobutu Sese Seko Koko Ngbendu wa za Banga (JOSEPH-DÉSIRÉ MOBUTU), Zairean politician (b. Oct. 14, 1930, Lisala, Belgian Congo—d. Sept. 7, 1997, Rabat, Mor.), as president of Zaire for nearly 32 years, ruled with absolute power. During his reign he took full advantage of the backing he received from the West, which viewed him during the Cold War as a guardian against communism. He amassed a personal fortune worth billions of dollars at the expense of the country's treasury and natural resources. The term *kleptocracy* was coined to define his despotic regime, which left the country in a shambles. Mobutu's education in missionary schools was followed by military service; he rose to the rank of sergeant major while working as a clerk and a journalist. Discharged in 1956, he found work as a journalist, first for the newspaper *L'Avenir* in Léopoldville (now Kinshasa) and then for the radical weekly *Actualités Africaines,* where he served as editor. In 1958 Mobutu joined Patrice Lumumba's Congolese National Movement, and when Lumumba became (1960) prime minister of the newly independent Congo in a coalition government with Pres. Joseph Kasavubu, Mobutu was named secretary of state for national defense. During a power struggle between Lumumba and Kasavubu at a time that the copper-rich Katanga (now Shaba) province was attempting to secede, Mobutu took over the government for a few months but then returned control to Kasavubu and was named commander in chief of the armed forces. Lumumba was killed during this time. In 1965 Mobutu staged a coup, installed himself as president, and set about consolidating his power. He nationalized businesses and industries, outlawed all political parties but his Popular Movement of the Revolution, and Africanized place names, including changing the country's name to Zaire. Over the following years, as neglect, mismanagement, and corruption caused the country's infrastructure to collapse, Mobutu was able to survive attempted coups, invasions, and other challenges to his rule with the aid of Western powers. In 1990, however, with the Cold War over and those powers' support waning, he was forced to allow multiparty elections. Though he was able to remain in power, opposition grew, and ethnic violence in Rwanda and a resultant influx of refugees further undermined his government. In 1996 Mobutu underwent cancer treatment in Switzerland, and in his absence the rebel forces of Laurent Kabila were able to seize ever-larger amounts of territory. In May 1997 Mobutu abandoned the country to Kabila and went into exile in Morocco.

WALTER DHLADHLA—ASSOCIATED PRESS

Mobutu Sese Seko

Mosbacher, Emil, Jr. ("BUS"), American yachtsman and government official who won the America's Cup in 1962 and 1967; served as the State Department's chief of protocol from 1969 to 1972, during the Richard Nixon administration; and organized the Operation Sail tall-ship processions that participated in celebrations of the U.S. bicentennial in 1976, the 100th anniversary of the Statue of Liberty in 1986, and the 500th anniversary of Christopher Columbus's arrival in the New World in 1992 (b. April 1, 1922—d. Aug. 13, 1997).

Moss, Carlton, American filmmaker who, excluded from a career at the Hollywood motion picture studios because he was African-American, made industrial, training, and educational films; his army documentary *The Negro Soldier,* filmed in the 1940s and depicting black soldiers' heroism, served as an inspiration both to future black participants in the film industry and to people seeking an end to segregation (b. 1909?—d. Aug. 10, 1997).

Moss, John Emerson, American politician who served (1953–79) as a Democratic representative from California; he championed consumer rights, was instrumental in dismantling government secrecy as the architect of the 1966 Freedom of Information Act, and played a leading role in the passage of acts on toy safety, poison packaging control, consumer product safety, and the 1974 automobile "lemon law" (b. April 13, 1915—d. Dec. 5, 1997).

Mulhare, Edward, Irish-born American actor who was best known for his portrayal of roles first made famous by Rex Harrison; on Broadway he followed Harrison as Henry Higgins in *My Fair Lady,* and on television he played the ghost of Captain Gregg in "The Ghost and Mrs. Muir," Harrison's role in the film of the same name. Mulhare followed that with a costarring role in the TV series "Knight Rider" (b. April 8, 1923—d. May 24, 1997).

Murison, David Donald, Scottish lexicographer who was editor of the 10-volume *Scottish National Dictionary* from 1946 until it was completed in 1976; his work was credited with having given the language respectability and having helped form Scotland's 20th-century cultural identity (b. April 28, 1913—d. Feb. 17, 1997).

Nabrit, James M., Jr., American lawyer and academic who while practicing law (1930–36) in Houston, Texas, and serving as a teacher and administrator (1936–60) at Howard University, Washington, D.C., was involved in a number of important civil rights cases; he successfully argued before the U.S. Supreme Court in *Bolling* v. *Sharpe* that school segregation was unconstitutional. Nabrit later presided as dean (1958–60) of the Howard Law School before serving as president (1960–69) of Howard University at a time when the rise of "black power" created campus unrest (b. Sept. 4, 1900—d. Dec. 27, 1997).

Najdorf, Mieczyslaw ("MIGUEL"), Polish-born Argentine chess grandmaster who was active in the sport for nearly 70 years, during which he won 52 international tournaments, was for a time ranked in the top-10 players in the world, and had his name given to a popular variation of the Sicilian defense (b. April 15, 1910—d. July 4, 1997).

Namias, Jerome, American meteorological researcher most noted for having pioneered the development of extended weather forecasts and who also studied the Dust Bowl of the 1930s and the El Niño phenomenon (b. March 19, 1910—d. Feb. 10, 1997).

Nikulin, Yury, Russian circus clown and comic actor (b. Dec. 18, 1921, Smolensk, Russian S.F.S.R.—d. Aug. 21, 1997, Moscow, Russia), captured the hearts of millions around the globe, but especially in his native land, with his portrayal of a deceptively simple character who appeared slow of speech and action but was quick-witted enough to cope with the absurdities and misfortunes of life. Although his humour provided some relief for those contending with the rigours of life in the Soviet Union, it also had a universal appeal. Nikulin, affectionately called Uncle Yury by Russian children, was known as a "brainy" clown because he relied upon his wits. The natural dolefulness of his face needed little makeup, which he applied sparingly. After a long military service (1939–46), during which his comedic talents were put to use providing entertainment for the troops, and following an unsuccessful attempt to earn admission to a drama school, Nikulin entered the clown studio of the Moscow Circus school. He joined (1950) the circus as an assistant to the leading clown and later formed a duo with another assistant. He improved his act, gained popularity, and attracted an audience of his own before eventually realizing his dream of becoming a movie star in 1958. His film credits during the 1960s and '70s included about a dozen feature films and a series of shorts in which he portrayed a fool as part of a trio that included a coward and an ex-con. He also appeared on television as the host of "The White Parrot Club," a venue for comics. His heart, however, remained in the big top. He returned (1982) to the Moscow Circus to serve as its artistic director, and in 1984 he became its general director, a post he still held at the time of his death.

Nkubito, Alphonse Marie, Rwandan Hutu politician who was a longtime campaigner for human rights, founded the Association for the Defense of Human Rights, and was minister of justice in the Tutsi-dominated government from July 1994 to August 1995 (b. 1954—d. Feb. 13, 1997).

Notorious B.I.G. (CHRISTOPHER WALLACE; "BIGGIE SMALLS"), American rap singer whose transformation from drug dealer and street hustler to one of hip-hop's premier artists was chronicled in his platinum-selling debut album, *Ready to Die* (1994); weeks before the release of his second album, *Life After Death,* he was killed during a drive-by shooting (b. May 21, 1973—d. March 9, 1997).

Nyro, Laura (LAURA NIGRO), American singer and songwriter (b. Oct. 18, 1947, New York, N.Y.—d. April 8, 1997, Danbury, Conn.), made solo recordings of her emotional, confessional songs, had a cult following, and influenced a number of other songwriters but made her biggest impact when her songs were recorded by other popular artists. Among those were "Stoned Soul Picnic" and "Wedding Bell Blues," recorded by the Fifth Dimension; "And When I Die," by Peter, Paul & Mary and later by Blood, Sweat & Tears; and "Stoney End" by Barbra Streisand. Nyro began writing songs when she was 8 years old, and by the time she was 18, she had released her first album, *More than a New Discovery* (1966). She was invited to perform at the 1967 Monterey Pop

DAVID GAHR

Laura Nyro

Festival, but her perception that her soulful style and appearance had not been to the rock-oriented audience's taste caused her to avoid public appearances for several years. Nyro continued making albums, though, and other singers began making hit recordings of her songs. *Eli and the Thirteenth Confession* was released in 1968, and *New York Tendaberry* (1969), *Christmas and the Beads of Sweat* (1970), and *Gonna Take a Miracle* (1971) followed. Nyro then left the music business for a while, married, and had a child. After her marriage ended, she began recording again—beginning with *Smile* (1976) and following that with *Nested* (1978), *Mother's Spiritual* (1984), *Live at the Bottom Line* (1989), and *Walk the Dog and Light the Light* (1993)—and occasionally performed. The retrospective album *The Best of Laura Nyro: Stoned Soul Picnic* was released shortly before Nyro's death; a tribute concert was held in New York City in October 1997; and work on a tribute album was under way.

Oku, Mumeo, Japanese feminist politician who served three terms in the Diet (parliament) after having been a leader in the fight for women's suffrage; she also founded the Housewives Association, Japan's first consumer organization (b. Oct. 24, 1895—d. July 7, 1997).

Okudzhava, Bulat Shalvovich, Russian poet, writer, and folksinger who was able to conceal enough of his political message within his works, which often dealt with love and longing, that he was never officially branded a dissident; he had a cult following, and in 1994 he won the Russian Booker Prize (b. May 9, 1924—d. June 12, 1997).

Panter-Downes, Mollie Patricia, British writer who, although virtually unknown in her homeland, was well respected in the United States for her longtime column in *The New Yorker*, "Letters from London" (1939–84), which earned immediate acclaim on its debut during World War II; her best-known novel was *One Fine Day,* 1947 (b. Aug. 25, 1906—d. Jan. 22, 1997).

Parker, "Colonel" Tom (ANDREAS CORNELIUS VAN KUIJK), Dutch-born American show business promoter who was best known for managing the career of Elvis Presley (b. June 26, 1909—d. Jan. 21, 1997).

Parker, Frank (FRANCISZEK A. PAJKOWSKI), American tennis player who in the 1940s was U.S. singles champion twice, Wimbledon doubles champion—with Pancho Gonzales—once, and French singles champion twice; he spent 17 years in the top-10 ranks (b. Feb. 13, 1916—d. July 24, 1997).

Pastrana Borrero, Misael, Colombian politician who served as president of Colombia from 1970 to 1974, heading a progressive National Front coalition that failed in its attempt to bring an end to the violence and turmoil that was engulfing the country and had killed some 200,000 people (b. Nov. 14, 1923—d. Aug. 21, 1997).

Patnaik, Bijoyananda ("BIJU"), Indian politician who parlayed his fame as a World War II aviator, anti-British freedom fighter, and commercial airline entrepreneur into a political career, notably as chief minister of Orissa state, 1961–63 and 1990–95 (b. March 5, 1916—d. April 17, 1997).

Paulsen, Patrick L. ("PAT"), American comedian whose doleful countenance was introduced to the public on "The Smothers Brothers Comedy Hour," from which in 1968 he launched the first of his five tongue-in-cheek campaigns for the presidency of the U.S. (b. July 6, 1927—d. April 24, 1997).

Payton, Lawrence, American singer who for more than 40 years was a member of the Motown group the Four Tops, which sold over 50 million records and had almost 30 singles, including "Baby I Need Your Loving," and "Reach Out I'll Be There," on the pop charts (b. 1938—d. June 20, 1997).

Péladeau, Pierre, Canadian press baron who parlayed a $1,500 loan from his mother into a media empire; although he probably was most renowned as the tabloid publisher of *Le Journal de Montréal,* Canada's third largest newspaper, his holding company, Quebecor Inc., also owned three other Canadian newspapers, several magazines, a multimedia company, and Donohue Inc., a forestry concern; the outspoken Péladeau supported Quebec separatism, was candid about his bouts with alcoholism and depression, and professed an admiration for Beethoven (b. April 11, 1925—d. Dec. 24, 1997).

Pelletier, Gérard, Canadian politician, journalist, and activist (b. June 21, 1919, Victoriaville, Que.—d. June 22, 1997, Montreal, Que.), was hailed, along with Pierre Trudeau and Jean Marchand, as one of Quebec's "three wise men." The trio was recruited by Liberal Prime Minister Lester Pearson to help derail the rising Quebec separatist movement. Pelletier received a B.A. from the University of Montreal, where he met Trudeau, a fellow student. While working as a labour reporter for the newspaper *Le Devoir,* he covered the epic asbestos strike of 1949. Seeking a forum for the expression of their liberal views, Pelletier and Trudeau were involved in the founding of the monthly social and political journal *Cité libre* in 1950. Pelletier became editor in chief of the newspaper *La Presse* in 1961 but was dismissed in 1965 because of his radical opinions. Following the 1965 election he served (1965–69) in Pearson's Cabinet. After Trudeau succeeded Pearson, Pelletier served as secretary of state for external affairs (1968–72) and as communications minister (1972–75). He was instrumental in the passage of the Official Languages Act of 1969, which stated that English and French were to share equal status in all areas of the government. From 1975 to 1981 he lived in Paris as the Canadian ambassador to France, and from 1981 to 1984 he served as ambassador to the United Nations. His memoir, *Years of Impatience, 1950–1960,* appeared in 1984.

Peng Zhen, Chinese political leader (b. Oct. 12, 1902, Quwo county, Shanxi province, China—d. April 26, 1997, Beijing, China), was a hard-line elder of the Communist Party and one of the "Eight Immortals," the veterans of China's 1949 revolution who helped the Communist Party set policy well into the 1980s. Though born to a peasant family, Peng attended middle school, where he joined the underground Communist Youth League. He became a member of the Communist Party in 1923. Arrested in 1929, Peng served six years in prison for organizing antigovernment activities. He led guerrilla resistance in the north during the Japanese invasion of China, later joining Mao Zedong and his forces in Yan'an. When Mao's Communists ousted Chiang Kai-shek's Nationalists in 1949, Peng was appointed Beijing's first party chief and, two years later, its mayor. In the 1960s Peng's relationship with Mao soured after the Great Leap Forward, a disastrous plan to accelerate the pace of development, resulted in mass starvation. Peng sided with Deng Xiaoping (*q.v.*) in blaming the famine on Mao. In 1966 Mao exiled Peng to the countryside, making him the first high-ranking victim of the Cultural Revolution, Mao's campaign to oust opponents and create an egalitarian society. In 1978, two years after Mao's death, Peng returned from exile to help rebuild an authoritarian legal system that included a harsh criminal code but, more important, reaffirmed Communist Party control. In 1983 he was appointed chairman of the legislative National People's Congress. He retired in 1988 but remained a force in politics, supporting the removal of reform-minded party leaders Hu Yaobang and Zhao Ziyang and the suppression of the 1989 pro-democracy demonstrations.

Peralta y Díaz Ceballos, Alejo, Mexican entrepreneur who used his skills at both building business enterprises and forging friendships with powerful politicians in the governing Institutional Revolutionary Party to promote industrialization and to create a conglomerate comprising over 100 companies; his family's fortune was estimated at some $2.5 billion (b. May 5, 1916—d. April 8, 1997).

Peralta Azurdia, Enrique, Guatemalan military dictator (1963–66) who was known for his brutal disregard for human rights (b. June 17, 1908—d. Feb. 19, 1997).

Piaget, Gérald, Swiss watchmaker who turned a small family business into a fashion phenomenon known for its high-quality but unusually expensive jeweled and ultrathin women's watches (b. 1918—d. April 19, 1997).

Pickersgill, John Whitney, Canadian politician who was one of the most influential members of the Liberal Party; he held a number of government appointments but was most noted for his role as political adviser and chief of staff to Prime Ministers Mackenzie King and Louis St. Laurent (b. June 23, 1905—d. Nov. 14, 1997).

Pinget, Robert, prolific Swiss-born French novelist and playwright who was associated with the *nouveau roman* movement and was best known for his plays, which showcased his mastery of the use of dialogue (b. July 19, 1919—d. Aug. 25, 1997).

Piper, Myfanwy, British art critic, founder and editor (1935–37) of the abstract art journal *Axis*, creative assistant to her husband, the painter John Piper, and, perhaps most notably, librettist for three operas by Benjamin Britten—*The Turn of the Screw* (1954), *Owen Wingrave* (1970), and *Death in Venice* (1973) (b. March 28, 1911—d. Jan. 18, 1997).

Pirie, Norman Wingate, British biochemist and virologist who, with his long-time collaborator, Frederick Bawden, demonstrated that the genetic material found in viruses is RNA. In later years Pirie championed the use of extracted leaf protein as a dietary supplement (b. July 1, 1907—d. March 29, 1997).

Porter, Keith Roberts, Canadian-born American cell biologist (b. June 11, 1912, Yarmouth, N.S.—d. May 2, 1997, Bryn Mawr, Pa.), was one of the founding fathers of modern cell biology and pioneered the use of the electron microscope to observe biological cells and the fine structures within them. While working in the 1940s at the Rockefeller Institute (later Rockefeller University), New York City, Porter developed a technique called whole-mount electron microscopy, by which images of single, complete cells, magnified about 100,000 times, were produced. The procedure provided a window through which scientists were able to view the internal organization of the cell in detail for the first time. As an undergraduate, Porter studied biology at Acadia University, Wolfville, N.S., and went on to receive a doctorate in biology (1938) from Harvard University. After graduation he moved (1939) to the Rockefeller Institute, where during the 1940s and '50s he and colleague George Palade, along with other scientists, made many significant contributions to the study of cell structure, including the understanding that cells are divided and, in large part, organized by highly convoluted networks of skeletal-like microtubules and membranous sacs. In 1961 Porter returned to Harvard, and he later (1965–67) served as chairman of the biology department. He moved on in 1968 to establish and head the department of molecular, cellular, and developmental biology at the University of Colorado at Boulder. After relinquishing the chairmanship in 1975, Porter worked for several years as part-time director of the Marine Biological Laboratory at Woods Hole, Mass. He helped organize the American Society for Cell Biology and the Tissue Culture Association and also was instrumental in starting the *Journal of Biophysical and Biochemical Cytology,* now the *Journal of Cell Biology.* Porter was elected to the U.S. National Academy of Sciences in 1964 and received a number of prestigious awards, including the National Medal of Science (1977). In addition to writing more than 200 scientific papers, he published several books, notably *An Introduction to the Fine Structure of Cells and Tissues* (1963; with Mary Bonneville).

Pritchett, Sir Victor Sawdon ("V.S."), British writer (b. Dec. 16, 1900, Ipswich, Suffolk, Eng.—d. March 20, 1997, London, Eng.), was especially appreciated for his dozens of short stories, though for some six decades he also wrote prolifically in a number of other genres—novels, essays, travelogues, biographies, and literary criticism. His powers of observation inspired stories that examined people leading ordinary lives and revealed their uniqueness, their aspirations, and the extraordinary circumstances in which they often found themselves. Pritchett's family was not well-off, and as he recounted in his first volume of autobiography, *A Cab at the Door* (1968), his father's business failures caused them to move frequently around the London area to stay ahead of creditors. His education was therefore haphazard, though he read voraciously and had an aptitude for languages. When Pritchett was 15, he had to leave school and take a clerical job, but when he was 20, he moved to Paris. He worked there at a variety of jobs, traveled, and began writing. *The Christian Science Monitor* published some of his essays and then hired him as a foreign correspondent, sending him first to Ireland and then to Spain, which caught his imagination—Pritchett's first book, *Marching Spain* (1928), recounted a walking trip, and his first book of short stories was *The Spanish Virgin and Other Stories* (1930). Returning to London, he became (1926) a literary critic for the *New Statesman*, an association that lasted some four decades. He also contributed to such periodicals as *The Nation* and *The New Yorker.* Pritchett's novels include *Dead Man Leading* (1937) and—his last and best-known— *Mr. Beluncle* (1951). His second volume of autobiography, *Midnight Oil,* was published in 1971. Among his books of essays are *In My Good Books* (1942), *Books in General* (1953), *The Myth Makers* (1979), and *Complete Collected Essays* (1997), and short stories were collected in such volumes as *You Make Your Own Life* (1938), *When My Girl Comes Home* (1961), and *On the Edge of the Cliff* (1979). *The Complete Short Stories* appeared in 1990. Pritchett was appointed C.B.E. in 1968 and knighted in 1975.

V.S. Pritchett

JERRY BAUER

Purcell, Edward Mills, American physicist (b. Aug. 30, 1912, Taylorville, Ill.—d. March 7, 1997, Cambridge, Mass.), shared the 1952 Nobel Prize for Physics with Felix Bloch for independently developing nuclear magnetic resonance (NMR), a method used to detect and measure the magnetic fields of atomic nuclei and a powerful tool for investigating molecular structures and chemical interactions. Purcell's work formed the basis of spectroscopic and imaging techniques with applications ranging from chemical analysis and radio astronomy to medical diagnosis. He studied electrical engineering as an undergraduate at Purdue University, West Lafayette, Ind., during which time he developed an interest in physics. After graduation (B.S., 1933) he spent a year at the Technische Hochschule in Karlsruhe, Ger., studying physics as an international exchange student. On returning to the United States, he enrolled at Harvard University, receiving a master's degree (1935) and doctorate (1938) in physics. Purcell, who spent most of his career at Harvard, served as an instructor there until 1941 and as a full professor from 1949 until his retirement in 1980. He took a brief leave of absence from the university during World War II, however, when he contributed to the war effort as a member of a research team investigating shortwave radar at the Massachusetts Institute of Technology. He returned to Harvard in 1946 and soon thereafter developed NMR methodology for measuring magnetic fields in atomic nuclei. In 1951 Purcell applied the principles of this discovery to detecting the wavelengths of radiation emitted from neutral hydrogen clouds in space. His research proved useful to astronomers attempting to map galactic structures in the universe. Purcell wrote a number of classic books on microwaves, electricity, and magnetism, including *Physics: For Science and Engineering Students* (1952), which he coauthored, and *Electricity and Magnetism* (1965). He was elected to the National Academy of Sciences in 1951 and received the National Medal of Science from the National Science Foundation in 1978.

Rata, Matiu, New Zealand Maori politician who spent 33 years in Parliament fighting to resolve historic Maori grievances; he set up the Waitangi Tribunal, which dealt with Maori land claims (b. March 26, 1934—d. July 25, 1997).

Remer, Otto Ernst Fritz Adolf, German military officer and political activist who was instrumental in thwarting a 1944 military coup against Adolf Hitler; active in neo-Nazi organizations, he went into exile in 1994 to avoid a jail sentence stemming from his public denial of the Holocaust (b. Dec. 18, 1912—d. Oct. 5, 1997).

Reynolds, Marjorie (Marjorie Goodspeed), American actress whose career was highlighted by her portrayal of both Bing Crosby's and Fred Astaire's love interest in the 1942 film classic *Holiday Inn;* other notable roles included the Viennese refugee in Fritz Lang's 1944 film of Graham Greene's *Ministry of Fear* and Peg Riley in the 1953–58 TV series "The Life of Riley" (b. Aug. 12, 1921—d. Feb. 1, 1997).

Ricard, Paul-Louis-Marius, French business executive who created the fashionable Ricard pastis, an anise-flavoured liquor that became the third largest-selling alcoholic beverage in the world. The son of a Marseille wine merchant, Ricard built his family business into an international beverage conglomerate (b. July 9, 1909—d. Nov. 6, 1997).

Richey, Charles Robert, American federal judge whose influential rulings during his 25 years on the bench advanced women's rights and checked presidential powers; he presided over several Watergate cases and strongly supported the people's right to know the actions of government (b. Oct. 16, 1923—d. March 19, 1997).

Richter, Sviatoslav (Svyatoslav Teofilovich Rikhter), Russian pianist (b. March 20, 1915, Zhitomir, Ukraine, Russian Empire—d. Aug. 1, 1997, Moscow, Russia), was considered one of the preeminent pianists of the 20th century. Richter's distinctive playing managed to balance technical virtuosity with subtle introspection. Though his repertoire was enormous, he was especially praised for his interpretations of Bach, Schumann, Liszt, Prokofiev, and Mussorgsky. Richter's father, an organist and composer, taught his son musical rudiments at an early age—the young Richter largely taught himself piano on the side. As a teenager he became a coach at the Odessa (Ukraine) Opera, where he astounded others with his sight-reading ability. Though initially a composer, by age 20 Richter had decided to devote himself to piano. In 1937 he became a pupil of Heinrich Neuhaus at the Moscow Conservatory. Having met Prokofiev that year, Richter went on to premiere the composer's Sixth Sonata in 1940, as well as the Seventh and Ninth sonatas in later years. In 1945 Richter won the U.S.S.R. Music Competition. During the 1950s he toured Eastern Europe and China. Meanwhile, the West eagerly awaited Richter's appearance. "Every musician in town was present," reported the *New York Times,* for his 1960 debut at Carnegie Hall. To great acclaim, he subsequently toured Western Europe, Japan, and elsewhere. In 1970 Richter made his last appearance in North America. He favoured intimate venues, such as the Aldeburgh festival in England, where he played Schubert duets with his friend Benjamin Britten. In 1964 Richter started a lifelong association with the French Fêtes Musicales near Tours. Because he detested the artificiality of the studio, more than half of his recordings were of live performances. Among Richter's distinguished recorded works are his superb performance of Mussorgsky's *Pictures at an Exhibition,* as well as his controversial interpretation of Schubert's *Sonata in B Flat Major,* which features an unusually slow, hypnotic first movement. Though Richter always considered himself to be "a mirror" to the composer, his independent style drew some dissent. Critics took him to task for overpowering Schubert or, alternatively, being inappropriately introspective with Beethoven. Eccentric, though never flamboyant, Richter was indifferent to his audience; "I play above all for myself," he once said.

Rippon of Hexham, Aubrey Geoffrey Frederick Rippon, Baron, British politician, Conservative member of Parliament (1955–64, 1966–87), and

Cabinet member (1963–64), who negotiated Great Britain's 1973 entrance into the European Economic Community (b. May 28, 1924—d. Jan. 28, 1997).

Robbins, Harold, American novelist (b. May 21, 1916, New York, N.Y.—d. Oct. 14, 1997, Palm Springs, Calif.), created gossipy-style formulaic works that featured the triple themes of sex, money, and power and made him one of the best-selling authors of all time. He once bragged that he had experienced firsthand all the vices he presented in his novels. Orphaned at birth, Robbins was placed in a Roman Catholic orphanage and was given the name Francis Kane. He was raised in several foster homes and assumed the last name Rubins from a Jewish foster family, but he changed it when his writing career took off. At the age of 19, he began speculating on crop futures; he became a millionaire the following year but lost his fortune after speculating unsuccessfully in sugar. After filing for bankruptcy, Robbins took a job with Universal Pictures. Dissatisfied with the films that the studio was producing, he bet the head of production $100 that he could write a better story. *Never Love a Stranger* (1948), his first novel, made him a best-selling author. *The Dream Merchants* (1949) and *A Stone for Danny Fisher* (1952) followed. In 1961 Robbins realized international fame when *The Carpetbaggers,* a blockbuster novel based on the life of millionaire Howard Hughes, was released. It sold millions of copies and became the fourth most-read book in history. His 23 books—all currently in print—were distributed in more than 40 countries and sold 750 million copies; many of his works were also adapted for motion pictures.

Rodríguez Pedotti, Andrés, Paraguayan politician (b. June 19, 1923, Borja, Paraguay—d. April 21, 1997, New York, N.Y.), served (1989–93) as president of Paraguay after leading the coup that overthrew the nearly 35-year-old dictatorship of Gen. Alfredo Stroessner. He succeeded in establishing a democracy and restoring civil liberties and conducted the first truly free elections in Paraguay's history as an independent nation. Rodríguez's army career began (1942) with his entrance into the country's military academy, from which he graduated four years later. A captain when Stroessner became president in 1954, Rodríguez began rising in the ranks with his promotion (1961) to colonel and assumption of command of the important 1st Cavalry Division. He became brigadier general in 1967 and general in 1970, by then second in command only to Stroessner himself. He became wealthy in this post through the ownership of a number of businesses, and it was rumoured, though never proved, that he was also involved in drug smuggling. Nonetheless, despite his powerful position, in 1989 Rodríguez, who had become commander of the 1st Army Corps, staged a bloody coup, declared himself acting president, and three months later was elected to a four-year term. In 1993 he kept his promise to give up power to the civilian winner of a democratic election and turned the office over to Juan Carlos Wasmosy. Rodríguez then retired from the army and was named a senator for life.

Rogers, Jimmy (JAMES LANE), American blues musician who played rhythm guitar in the Muddy Waters band of the 1950s, considered the finest electric blues band, and achieved renown with his own '50s recordings, including "Walking by Myself," "Chicago Bound," and "Sloppy Drunk," in which his genial singing was usually accompanied by the Waters band; he left the music business in the '60s only to return in the '70s, playing in Chicago, his hometown, and on international tours (b. June 3, 1924—d. Dec. 19, 1997).

Rosario, Edwin ("CHAPO"), Puerto Rican boxer who won the world lightweight championship three times and the junior welterweight once but was hindered by drug-abuse problems. He died of acute pulmonary edema that was thought to have been caused by drugs. His career record stood at 43 wins, 37 of them by knockout, and 6 losses (b. March 19, 1963—d. Dec. 1, 1997).

Rossi, Aldo, Italian architect (b. May 3, 1931, Milan, Italy—d. Sept. 4, 1997, Milan), created simple yet powerful works by using such geometric shapes as cones, cylinders, and squares and by making skillful use of light and shadow. Rossi was educated at the Milan Polytechnic and following graduation (1959) went to work for the design magazine *Casabella,* becoming its editor in 1964. In 1966 he set forth his architecture theories in *L'architettura della città* (*The Architecture of the City,* 1982), which established his reputation as a theorist and became an influential classic. He later published the manifesto *Architettura razionale* (1973) and *A Scientific Autobiography* (1981). Considered Rossi's most famous design was the Cemetery of San Cataldo in Modena, Italy (1971–77), in which a simple cube-shaped ossuary is surrounded by an apparently unending colonnade. Other well-known works were the Teatro del Mondo, created for the 1980 Venice Biennale; the Museum of Maastricht, Neth.; and the Hotel Il Palazzo in Fukuoka, Japan. In 1990 Rossi was honoured with the Pritzker Prize, architecture's highest award.

Rosten, Leo Calvin, Polish-born American writer (b. April 11, 1908, Lodz, Pol.—d. Feb. 19, 1997, New York, N.Y.), had a six-decade-long career during which he wrote numerous works, both fiction and nonfiction, that celebrated the culture, humour, and language of the Jewish people. He was best known for two books: *The Education of H*Y*M*A*N K*A*P*L*A*N* (1937), which was based on the language struggles of an immigrant student in one of his night English classes and first appeared in *The New Yorker* as a series of short stories written under the name Leonard Q. Ross; and *The Joys of Yiddish* (1968), a lighthearted reference work of commonly used Yiddish expressions. Rosten moved to the U.S. with his family when he was three, and they settled in Chicago. He was educated at the University of Chicago (Ph.B., 1930; Ph.D., 1937) and the London School of Economics and Political Science. To help pay for his studies, Rosten taught the evening classes that inspired some of his stories, and he later taught at the University of Chicago, Columbia University, New York City, Yale University, and the University of California, Berkeley, among others. During World War II he worked for the U.S. government in such capacities as chief of the Motion Pictures Division of the Office of Facts and Figures and deputy director of the Office of War Information. As a consultant to the secretary of war, he was sent to France, Germany, and England on a special mission, and from 1947 to 1949 he worked for the RAND Corporation. Among Rosten's other works were *Hollywood: The Movie Colony, the Movie Makers* (1941), a sociological study of the film industry; six screenplays; and sequels to the Kaplan book, *The Return of H*Y*M*A*N K*A*P*L*A*N* (1959) and *O K*A*P*L*A*N! My K*A*P*L*A*N!* (1976).

Rothschild, Edmond Adolphe Maurice Jules Jacques de, French banker and businessman who was one of the wealthiest members of the Rothschild family and a major contributor to Israel. He also had a hand in his family's traditional wine business, owning the Château Clarke and the Savour Club, one of the first mail-order wine services (b. Sept. 30, 1926—d. Nov. 2/3, 1997).

Royko, Michael ("MIKE"), American journalist (b. Sept. 19, 1932, Chicago, Ill.—d. April 29, 1997, Chicago), was the sometimes irreverent, sometimes cantankerous or controversial, sometimes funny or satiric, and sometimes poignant—but always interesting—champion of the "little guy" in columns published in Chicago's major newspapers and syndicated to hundreds of others. Five days a week for most of his 30-plus years as a columnist, he fearlessly expounded on the issues of the day and came to the rescue of the downtrodden, occasionally using the voice of his working-class alter ego Slats Grobnik or "expert" psychiatrist Dr. I.M. Kookie. In 1972 his efforts won him a Pulitzer Prize. In later years what were perceived as slurs against minority groups gave rise to several protests, but Royko, though unhappy that his satire was not being understood as such, did not change his style. He grew up over his father's tavern, a vantage point that helped form his view of life in Chicago. He cut short his college education to join the U.S. Air Force during the Korean War and eventually fibbed his way into a job on the base's newspaper, where he appropriated space for his own column. Upon Royko's return to civilian life, he became (1956) a reporter for the *Lincoln-Belmont Booster* and then (1956–59) worked at the City News Bureau. In 1959 he started at the *Chicago Daily News,* and in 1964 he became a full-time columnist. Royko's favourite targets included corrupt officials, bigots, and politicians misusing their power. He did not hesitate to take on Chicago's mayor at the time, Richard J. Daley, and Royko's best-selling book

Mike Royko

KRT

Boss (1971) was an especially thorough look at the Daley political machine. With the closing down (1978) of the *Daily News,* Royko moved to the *Chicago Sun-Times.* It was for that paper that he wrote perhaps the most memorable and moving of his columns, about the death (1979) of his first wife, Carol, with whom he had fallen in love when he was nine years old. When Rupert Murdoch's conglomerate bought (1984) the *Sun-Times,* Royko moved to the *Chicago Tribune,* where he remained for the rest of his career.

Rudolph, Paul, American architect (b. Oct. 23, 1918, Elkton, Ky.—d. Aug. 8, 1997, New York, N.Y.), became one of the most eminent postwar Modernist architects in the U.S. before fading into relative obscurity in the 1970s. Rudolph studied with German Modernist Walter Gropius at the Harvard Graduate School of Design, where he earned (1947) a master's degree in architecture. One year later he established his own architectural firm in Sarasota, Fla. His designs for a series of spare, airy houses in the Siesta Key area earned him a reputation as a virtuoso composer of space, form, and light. His renown quickly spread, and in 1957 Rudolph was named chairman of Yale University's prestigious architecture school, a position he held until 1965. During his tenure he completed one of the most defining commissions of his career—the 10-story Art and Architecture Building on the Yale campus. Never simply a slavish disciple of European Modernism, Rudolph, it was said, "broke the Atlantic sound barrier, creating designs that were more than the sum of their European influences." Anchored by poured-in-place concrete towers, the Yale building's exterior formed a lively collage of interlocking geometric shapes. In contrast to this monumental street presence, the interior appeared seamless, flowing, and shot with light, an illusion Rudolph created by using a complex assemblage of 37 different levels divided by glass walls. The building, however, became the target of student protesters who set fire to it in 1969. By then, Rudolph's reputation had begun to decline in the United States, and his abstract Modernist aesthetic was soon eclipsed by the growing popularity of Postmodernism's revival of historical styles and ornamentation. He continued, however, to find an audience for his work in Asia. Working from his historic brownstone on Beekman Place in New York City, famous in design circles for the architect's controversial Modernist renovation in the 1960s, Rudolph drafted monolithic high-rise projects for such cities as Hong Kong, Singapore, and Jakarta, Indon.

Sager, Ruth, American geneticist (b. Feb. 7, 1918, Chicago, Ill.—d. March 29, 1997, Brookline, Mass.), conducted groundbreaking research on where genetic material is found in cells; her findings changed the way that biologists view cell heredity. Later in her career she studied the genetic mechanisms related to cancer. Sager entered the University of Chicago at age 16, sampling the liberal arts before a chance encounter with a survey course on biology ignited her interest in the field. She graduated with a B.S. in 1938. Graduate work in plant physiology followed at Rutgers University, New Brunswick, N.J., where she received an M.S. in 1944. She continued graduate studies in genetics at Columbia University, New York City, earning a doctorate in 1948. Sager joined the research staff at the Rockefeller Institute (now Rockefeller University), New York City, as an assistant in 1951. There she challenged the prevailing theory that inherited characteristics are transmitted exclusively by the genes in the chromosomes, which are found in a cell's nucleus. In studying heredity in *Chlamydomonas* alga, she discovered that a gene located outside the chromosomes also transmits inherited characteristics. Nonchromosomal genes were later shown to be ubiquitous in living organisms. In 1955 Sager joined Columbia University's zoology department, where she expanded her understanding of how nonchromosomal genes work. She served as a professor of biology at Hunter College, New York City, from 1966 through 1975, when she was appointed professor of cellular genetics at Harvard University and head of Harvard's Dana-Farber Cancer Institute. Sager's extensive research into the mechanisms associated with cancer involved tumour suppressor genes, breast cancer, and the genetic means by which cancer multiplies. Her numerous prizes included the Gilbert Morgan Smith Medal, the National Cancer Institute's Outstanding Investigator Award, and a Guggenheim fellowship.

Salkind, Alexander, German-born film producer best known for the popular *Superman* movies that featured Christopher Reeve as the superhero (b. June 2, 1921—d. March 8, 1997).

Sánchez Vilella, Roberto, Puerto Rican politician who, as governor of Puerto Rico (1964–69), helped modernize the U.S. commonwealth (b. 1913—d. March 25, 1997).

Santi, Gino P., American engineer whose long career with the U.S. Air Force was most notable for his development of the pilot ejection system (b. 1916/17?—d. April 3, 1997).

Sarlos, Andrew, Hungarian-born Canadian investor and philanthropist who both made and lost fortunes and came to be known as the "Buddha of Bay Street" because of his expertise and daring in deal making and playing the stock market; he shared his knowledge and his money, and he was awarded the Order of Canada in recognition of the contributions he made to charities (b. Nov. 24, 1931—d. April 28, 1997).

Saw Maung, Burmese general and politician who led the junta that took over the Burmese government in a bloody coup in 1988; he served as head of the repressive regime until 1992 (b. December 1928—d. July 24, 1997).

MATTHEW GILSON—ASSOCIATED PRESS

David Schramm

Schramm, David N., American theoretical astrophysicist who was an international leader in the field of cosmology and a distinguished professor (1974–97) at the University of Chicago; by making a cosmic inventory of the material making up the universe, he helped determine that most of the universe consists of unseen and as-yet-unknown forms of matter. He was killed when the plane he was piloting crashed near Denver (b. Oct. 25, 1945—d. Dec. 19, 1997).

Schwarzschild, Martin, German-born American astronomer who in 1957 introduced the use of high-altitude hot-air balloons to carry scientific instruments and photographic equipment into the stratosphere for solar research (b. May 31, 1912—d. April 10, 1997).

Sengstacke, John H., American editor and longtime influential publisher, notably of the *Chicago Defender,* the national voice of African-Americans; he used his formidable role to champion civil rights, including the integration of the armed forces, the breaking of the colour barrier in major league baseball, and the coverage of a presidential press conference by a black reporter (b. Nov. 25, 1912—d. May 28, 1997).

Seni Pramoj, Mom Rajawong, Thai diplomat and politician whose refusal to honour Japanese demands that he deliver a Thai declaration of war against the U.S. and the U.K. during World War II kept the U.S. from attacking Thailand and gained U.S. aid in organizing resistance forces (b. May 26, 1905—d. July 28, 1997).

Shabazz, Betty (BETTY SANDERS), American educator and civil rights activist who was the widow of assassinated black nationalist leader Malcolm X and from 1976 served on the faculty of Medgar Evers College, Brooklyn, N.Y., most recently as director of institutional advancement; she died from burns suffered in a fire set by her emotionally troubled grandson (b. May 28, 1936—d. June 23, 1997).

Shanker, Albert, American union official best remembered as the leader of New York City's United Federation of Teachers in 1968 during a bitter series of strikes over decentralization that became racially and religiously divisive; later, as president of the American Federation of Teachers, he was known as a champion of high standards in education (b. Sept. 14, 1928—d. Feb. 22, 1997).

Shoemaker, Eugene Merle ("GENE"), American planetary geologist (b. April 28, 1928, Los Angeles, Calif.—d. July 18, 1997, Alice Springs, Australia), was hailed as one of the chief founders of planetary geology and considered by many scientists to be the consummate sky gazer of the 20th century. Throughout much of his long career, Shoemaker worked closely with his wife and colleague, Carolyn Spellman Shoemaker. Between them they identified 32 comets and 1,125 asteroids, missing by only 5 the world comet record set by 19th-century astronomer Jean-Louis Pons. Their most spectacular find, Comet Shoemaker-Levy 9, was discovered with amateur astronomer David Levy. The comet dazzled the world in July 1994 as its 21 glowing fragments tore into Jupiter's southern hemisphere, the largest chunks exploding with a force comparable to several million megatons of TNT. This was not the first time that Shoemaker had made headlines. In 1948 after graduating at age 20 with a master's degree in geology from the California Institute of Technology (Caltech), he surveyed craters in the landscape of the American Southwest. The young geologist rocked the scientific world in the late 1950s by supplying confirmation of the origin of Meteor Crater near Winslow, Ariz. Following his discovery of coesite, a form of silica created under the high pressure of meteoric impacts, Shoemaker theorized that the 1,200-m (4,000-ft)-wide bowl-shaped pit was formed when a meteorite crashed into the Earth's surface more than 50,000 years ago. His research lent credence to the theory that the bombardment of the Earth and other planets with celestial debris played an important role in the history of planetary evolution. He later supported the hypothesis that an object from outer space may have been responsible for the cataclysmic changes on Earth that led to the extinction of the dinosaurs and other life forms 65 million years ago. Shoemaker warned of the possibility of other such devastating encounters with the Earth and favoured the development of technology that would intercept threatening astral projectiles before impact. During his tenure with the U.S. Geological Survey from 1948 to his retirement in 1993, he established the agency's Center of Astrogeology in Flagstaff, Ariz., where he served as chief scientist. While also teaching at Caltech from 1962 to 1985, Shoemaker found time to pursue one of his life long interests—the geologic history of the Moon. As principal investigator for

NASA's Apollo Moon project in the 1960s, he used a telescope to map lunar craters and studied rock specimens retrieved from the Moon's surface, as well as helping to train NASA astronauts in lunar geology, a discipline that he was credited with inventing. Shoemaker received the U.S. National Medal of Science in 1992.

Simjian, Luther, Turkish-born American inventor who held patents on more than 200 inventions, including the Teleprompter, the flight simulator, and the automated teller machine (b. 1905—d. Oct. 23, 1997).

Singh, Ganesh Man, Nepalese political activist who during some 50 years of struggle against Nepal's monarchy was a leader in the fight for democracy (b. November 1915—d. Sept. 18, 1997).

Sinyavsky, Andrey Donatovich, Russian writer and dissident (b. Oct. 8, 1925, Moscow, U.S.S.R.—d. Feb. 25, 1997, Fontenay-aux-Roses, near Paris, France), was imprisoned (1966) after having been convicted along with another writer, Yuly Daniel, of having published anti-Soviet works. His trial attracted worldwide attention and sparked a new wave of dissent nationwide. Following service in the Red Army during World War II, Sinyavsky attended Moscow M.V. Lomonov State University, graduating in 1949 and receiving a doctorate in 1952. He later joined the faculty of the A.M. Gorky Institute of World Literature, Moscow, and in the early 1960s he began contributing criticism in the literary journal *Novy Mir* and wrote an incisive introduction to a volume of Boris Pasternak's poetry. In the late 1950s, however, writing under the pseudonym Abram Tertz, Sinyavsky began having his works smuggled to the West and published there. First was the essay "Chto takoe sotsialistichesky realizm" (*On Socialist Realism,* 1960). This was followed by such novels as *Sud idyot* (1959; *The Trial Begins,* 1960) and *Lyubimov* (1964; *The Makepeace Experiment,* 1965) and the short-story collection *Fantasticheskiye povesti* (1961; *Fantastic Stories,* 1963) as the literary world speculated about the true name of the author. His identity was revealed when Sinyavsky and Daniel were arrested in 1965. Sinyavsky was sentenced to seven years' hard labour and Daniel five. Sinyavsky was released after five and a half years, in 1971, and two years later moved to Paris to teach Russian literature at the Sorbonne. Soon thereafter he published *Golos iz khora* (1973; *A Voice from the Chorus,* 1976), based on letters he sent to his wife, Maria Rozanova, from the labour camp, and in 1978 he and Rozanova founded the literary journal *Sintaksis.* After Daniel's death in 1988, Sinyavsky made his first return visit to Moscow.

Skelton, Richard Bernard ("Red"), American comic actor (b. July 18, 1913, Vincennes, Ind.—d. Sept. 17, 1997, Rancho Mirage, Calif.), was a favourite clown of many generations of Americans. A rubber-faced master of the pratfall, he used his talents as a mime to create such memorable characters as Clem Kaddiddlehopper, Freddie the Freeloader, the cross-eyed seagulls Gertrude and Heathcliffe, and the Mean Widdle Kid, whose catchphrase "I dood it" was soon heard all over the country and was later (1943) the title of one of his films. Because his family was destitute, Skelton went to work when he was seven, both delivering newspapers and entertaining on the street. At 10 he joined a traveling medicine show. It was at auditions for that show, when he accidentally fell off the stage, that he discovered his talent for making people laugh by means of physical comedy. After performing on showboats, in burlesque houses, and on the vaudeville circuit, Skelton appeared (1937) on Broadway, thanks to a doughnut-dunking-and-eating pantomime routine he had developed. Radio appearances and a role in the film *Having Wonderful Time* (1938) followed and led to such other films as *Whistling in the Dark* (1941), *Bathing Beauty* (1944), *The Fuller Brush Man* (1948), *Neptune's Daughter* (1949), and *Three Little Words* (1950) and the popular radio program "Red Skelton's Scrapbook of Satire." A notable later motion picture appearance came at the beginning of *Those Magnificent Men in Their Flying Machines* (1965), his last film, in which he portrayed a Neanderthal attempting to fly. Television proved to be Skelton's best medium, however. For some 20 years in the 1950s and '60s, "The Red Skelton Hour" showcased his stable of hilarious characters and made him one of the country's most well-known and well-liked entertainers. In 1970, though, despite the fact that the show was consistently in the top 20 in the ratings, CBS canceled it, considering it irrelevant to younger audience members. It aired for one more year on NBC. Skelton then returned to performing live and made 75 or more appearances a year. He also took up the painting of clowns, earning an estimated $2.5 million a year from the sale of his creations, and wrote children's books, short stories, and symphonies. Skelton was given the Governors Award of the Academy of Television Arts and Sciences at the 1986 Emmy awards ceremony and in 1989 was inducted into the academy's Hall of Fame.

STEVE LISSAU—GAMMA LIAISON

Red Skelton

Skelton, Robin, British-born Canadian poet, scholar, and witch who published scores of books, founded the creative writing department at the University of Victoria, B.C., cofounded the *Malahat Review* literary journal, and publicly promoted his belief in witchcraft (b. Oct. 12, 1925—d. Aug. 27, 1997).

Smith, Julia, British television producer and director who was one of the creators of the long-running BBC soap opera "EastEnders," which from its first airing in 1985 was one of the most popular television programs in Great Britain (b. June 1927—d. June 19, 1997).

Snow, Helen Foster, American writer who produced some 40 works, mostly about China, that were less well known than those of her husband, Edgar Snow, but came to be considered superior; she was also instrumental in the creation of industrial cooperatives known as the Gung-Ho—from the Chinese *gonghe,* "working together"—movement and was proud of having added that term to the American vocabulary (b. Sept. 21, 1907—d. Jan. 11, 1997).

Soloukhin, Vladimir Alekseyevich, Soviet writer who penned nonfiction and nostalgic novels, poetry, and short stories but was perhaps best known for his campaign to preserve prerevolutionary Russian art and architecture, most notably historic Russian Orthodox churches and icons (b. June 14, 1924—d. April 4, 1997).

Solti, Sir Georg (Gyorgy Stern), Hungarian-born British conductor and pianist (b. Oct. 21, 1912, Budapest, Austria-Hungary—d. Sept. 5, 1997, Antibes, France), was the longtime music director (1969–91) of the Chicago Symphony Orchestra (CSO), which he reestablished as a world-class ensemble. His conducting career began in the 1930s when he became a rehearsal leader for the Budapest State Opera, and in 1937 Arturo Toscanini gave him the same job at the Salzburg (Austria) Festival. In 1938 he made his conducting debut at the Budapest State Opera. Solti, who was Jewish, was just beginning to receive his own engagements when his career was interrupted by World War II; he spent the war in Switzerland, giving piano lessons and coaching singers. After the war the removal of Nazi-affiliated conductors from their posts created opportunities for many non-German maestros. Solti was among those to benefit, serving as the music director of the Bavarian State Opera in Munich from 1946 to 1952 and of the Frankfurt Opera from 1952 to 1961. More notable, however, was his tenure as music director of the Royal Opera at Covent Garden, London (1961–71). Solti came to international prominence as the conductor of the first complete recording of Richard Wagner's opera cycle *The Ring of the Nibelung.* This immense seven-year project, concluded in 1966, was considered by many to have been one of the landmark recordings of the 20th century.

Solti's ambitions as an orchestral conductor were most fully realized, however, during his tenure with the CSO, which he distinguished with energy and discipline. He also held directorships with the Orchestre de Paris (1972–75) and the London Philharmonic Orchestra (1979–83). As an opera conductor he was acclaimed as a superb Wagnerian and was probably the greatest interpreter of Richard Strauss. Solti was also described as highly excitable, especially by musicians, some of whom referred to him as "the screaming skull.'' In orchestral music Solti conducted everything from Mozart to Sir Michael Tippett, but he was most at home with the mammoth late-Romantic symphonies of Anton Bruckner and Gustav Mahler. Nearly all of Solti's readings were characterized by rhythmic discipline, high energy, and

KLAUS TITZER—GAMMA LIAISON

Sir Georg Solti

dynamic impact, especially from the brass instruments. He recorded prolifically, both as a conductor and as a solo pianist, and he won more Grammy awards (32) than any other classical or pop music artist. He was knighted in 1971 but did not use the title until he took British citizenship the following year.

Son Sen, Cambodian Khmer Rouge official who supervised some of the worst brutality perpetrated while the radical Khmer Rouge movement held power from 1975 to 1979; factional infighting led to his execution by movement leader Pol Pot's loyalists, and Pol Pot was himself arrested shortly thereafter (b. June 12, 1930—d. June 10, 1997).

Sopinka, John, Canadian judge (b. March 19, 1933, Broderick, Sask.—d. Nov. 24, 1997, Ottawa, Ont.), served as a member of the Supreme Court of Canada from 1988 until his death. He was widely respected as one of the court's most able members, a legal generalist who could bring his formidable intelligence to bear on a wide variety of legal issues. Sopinka attended the University of Toronto, where he gained recognition as a star football player on a national championship team. He played football professionally with the Toronto Argonauts and Montreal Alouettes of the Canadian Football League until 1959. In 1960 he was called to the bar and soon gained a reputation as a talented litigator. Sopinka served on a number of royal commissions and taught law at the Osgoode Hall Law School and the University of Toronto. In 1981 he gained nationwide fame when he represented accused murderer Susan Nelles in her action against the Ontario attorney general and the Toronto police for malicious prosecution; he won the case and thereby established that the attorney general was not immune from such lawsuits. Sopinka's appointment to the Supreme Court raised some eyebrows among the legal community, as he had no background as a judge. He proved, however, to be a successful jurist, combining an expertise in procedural issues with a firm understanding of legal theory. Sopinka wrote many of the court's opinions and won a reputation as a strong defender of individual liberties and of protections for accused criminals.

Sorell, Walter, Austrian-born American writer who was the author of more than 25 books, including *The Dance Through the Ages* (1967) and *Dance in Its Time* (1981); contributed to a number of dance publications; and taught theatre and dance history at several colleges and universities (b. May 2, 1905—d. Feb. 21, 1997).

Soriano, Osvaldo, Argentine journalist and author of best-selling novels characterized by action and humour, notably *No habrá más penas ni olvido*, about internecine squabbles among Peronists in the early 1970s (b. Jan. 6, 1943—d. Jan. 29, 1997).

Souza, Herbert José de ("BETINHO"), Brazilian social activist (b. Nov. 13, 1935, Bocaiúva, Braz.—d. Aug. 9, 1997, Rio de Janeiro, Braz.), was an outspoken champion of the poor and was nominated in 1994 for the Nobel Prize for Peace for his efforts to improve their living standards and to combat hunger. Souza was in his 20s when he helped to found the Acao Popular, a Marxist group that arose from a radical branch of the Roman Catholic Church. A 1964 military coup in Brazil drove him into exile, first to Chile and then to Canada, Sweden, and France. He returned to Brazil under a general amnesty in 1979 and founded an institute for economic and social studies—one of the country's first nongovernmental organizations—which performed research on a wide range of social issues. Souza came to national prominence in 1992 when his Movement to Restore Ethics to Politics helped unseat the corrupt Pres. Fernando Collor de Mello. Souza then launched his campaign against hunger, a broad-based effort to donate food to the poor; it became a cause célèbre, and many of Brazil's most prominent citizens participated. Souza also worked to raise AIDS consciousness. A hemophiliac, in 1986 he was infected with HIV through a contaminated blood transfusion; he was one of the first Brazilians to reveal publicly that he was HIV-positive. In 1993 Souza's image was tarnished, however, when it was learned that he had knowingly allowed his AIDS advocacy group to accept a $58,000 donation from racketeers. Souza developed AIDS in 1995, which severely eroded his frail health.

Spitzer, Lyman, Jr., American astrophysicist (b. June 26, 1914, Toledo, Ohio—d. March 31, 1997, Princeton, N.J.), advanced knowledge of the physical processes occurring in interstellar space and pioneered efforts to harness nuclear fusion as a source of clean energy. After Spitzer earned a B.A. from Yale University in 1935, he spent a year at the University of Cambridge. He received a Ph.D. in astrophysics from Princeton University in 1938 and shortly thereafter began teaching at Yale. During World War II he was recruited by the U.S. Navy for the Division of War Research at Columbia University, New York City, where he assisted in the development of sonar. Spitzer's interest in the study of star formation took him in 1947 to Princeton as a professor of astronomy and the director of the observatory there. In 1946 he had begun urging the United States government to launch an orbiting space telescope to record astronomical phenomena without interference from the Earth's atmospheric effects. His efforts resulted in the construction and launch in 1990 of the Hubble Space Telescope in addition to other orbiting observatories. In the early 1950s his study of the ionized gases (plasmas) that are crucial to aspects of stellar formation and energy production led to the organized study of plasma physics. Hoping to find a new source of power for peaceful applications, he persuaded the U.S. Atomic Energy Commission in 1951 to fund the development of his "stellarator," a device that theoretically could achieve controlled thermonuclear fusion in ionized gas contained in a magnetic field. Despite decades of experimentation at Princeton's Plasma Physics Laboratory, the device and later fusion machines at Princeton were never completely successful. Funds for the project were cut off by Congress just days before Spitzer's death. Among Spitzer's numerous awards was the National Medal of Science, bestowed in 1979.

Steel, Dawn, American business executive who became the first woman to head a major Hollywood film studio when she became (1987) president of Columbia Pictures; the intrepid Steel had shown her mettle while serving at Paramount Pictures as director of merchandising and both vice president and president of production. When Columbia was purchased by the Sony Corp. in 1990, Steel left and formed Atlas Entertainment, which produced *Fallen* and *City of Angels,* both scheduled to be released in 1998 (b. Aug. 19, 1946—d. Dec. 20, 1997).

Sterne, Max, research veterinarian born in Trieste, Austria-Hungary (now in Italy), who developed an effective, safe, and reproducible vaccine against anthrax that succeeded in virtually eliminating the disease (b. June 1, 1905—d. Feb. 26, 1997).

Stewart, James Maitland ("JIMMY"), American actor (b. May 20, 1908, Indiana, Pa.—d. July 2, 1997, Beverly Hills, Calif.), performed in some 80 motion pictures during a 57-year-long career and became one of Hollywood's most beloved stars. With an unpretentious manner, he came to personify a decent everyman, struggling to overcome difficult circumstances while rising to heroic stature in the process. After graduating (1932) from Princeton University with a degree in architecture, Stewart joined the University Players, a summer stock company in Falmouth, Mass. There he met Henry Fonda, and the two became lifelong best friends. Stewart made his Broadway debut in *Carrie Nation* (1932), and by 1935 he was in Hollywood under contract to Metro-Goldwyn-Mayer. Over the next five years, he made about two dozen movies, including *Born to Dance* (1936), *The Shop Around the Corner* (1940), and two of the three he made for director Frank Capra, *You Can't Take It with You* (1938) and *Mr. Smith Goes to Washington* (1939), in which he played a young idealist fighting corruption. He portrayed a likable reporter in *The Philadelphia Story* (1940), a role for which he won an Academy Award. Early in 1941 Stewart enlisted in the army—gaining weight in order to meet minimum requirements. He became a pilot and led more than 20 bombing missions; for this he was awarded the Distinguished Flying Cross, the Air Medal, and the Croix de Guerre. Stewart rose to colonel by the end of the war, remained in the reserves, and

CULVER PICTURES

James Stewart

in 1959 was promoted to brigadier general. He retired from the service in 1968. After the war Stewart starred in his third Capra film, *It's a Wonderful Life* (1946), memorably as George Bailey, an honest banker beset by personal and financial woes. Although the movie was a disappointment at the box office, it went on to become an enduring classic. Other quintessential Stewart roles were Elwood P. Dowd in *Harvey*—in which he starred on Broadway (1947), in the motion picture (1950), and in the stage revival (1970)—and Charles Lindbergh in *The Spirit of St. Louis* (1957). The 1950s also found him in a number of westerns directed by Anthony Mann, the Alfred Hitchcock thrillers *Rear Window* (1954), *The Man Who Knew Too Much* (1956), and *Vertigo* (1958), and Otto Preminger's *Anatomy of a Murder* (1959). Later films include *The Man Who Shot Liberty Valance* (1962), *The Flight of the Phoenix* (1966), and *The Shootist* (1976). Among Stewart's honours were an honorary Oscar and the Presidential Medal of Freedom, both presented in 1985.

Strehler, Giorgio, Italian theatre director and actor who was a preeminent figure in post-World War II European theatre as cofounder and artistic director (1947–68, 1972–97) of the Piccolo Teatro di Milano, Italy's first important modern regional theatre; founding director (1968–72) of the Gruppo Teatro e Azione; and artistic director (1983–90) of the Paris-based Théâtre de l'Europe. A passionate and innovative director, he staged some 250 plays, most notably works by Shakespeare, Bertolt Brecht, and Carlo Goldoni. He also directed operas at La Scala, Milan, played the title role in his own epic production of Goethe's *Faust,* and served one term (1987–92) in the Italian Senate (b. Aug. 14, 1921—d. Dec. 25, 1997).

Sumii, Sue, Japanese social reformer and writer (b. Jan. 7, 1902, near Nara, Japan—d. June 16, 1997, Ushiku City, Japan), was an outspoken advocate for victims of discrimination, notably the *burakumin* (an underclass composed of gravediggers, leatherworkers, and butchers who are in Buddhist eyes unclean). The first volume of her popular seven-volume book, published under the title *Hashi no nai kawa* (*The River with No Bridge*), appeared serially in a magazine called *Buraku* and was published as a book in 1961. The story, which follows the fortunes of a *burakumin* family in the first decades of the 20th century, was filmed twice in Japan. Though born in Nara prefecture, home to many *burakumin* communities, Sumii was not herself a member of the group of occupational outcasts she later came to champion. She graduated from Haramoto Women's School, and in her late teens she worked briefly for Kodansha publishers but quit over their ill treatment of women. She then married an activist in the proletarian agrarian movement and moved with him to a rural area. There she bore four children, worked on the farm, and published a number of "peasant literature" genre novels and stories for young people, eventually winning a literary award (the now defunct Mainichi Newspaper Prize) for her writing. In 1958, the year after her husband's death, she began to compose her most famous work. Opposed to discrimination in any form, Sumii continued to fight many causes throughout her long life. She built a lecture and discussion hall and a movie theatre for Ushiku City with royalties from her novels. Sumii was at work on an eighth volume of *River with No Bridge* when she died.

Surinach, Carlos, Spanish-born American composer whose classical compositions were strongly influenced by traditional Spanish flamenco rhythms; he was best known for composing ballet scores for Martha Graham (b. March 1915—d. Nov. 12, 1997).

Tanaka, Tomoyuki, Japanese film producer who was best known for his series of motion pictures featuring the dragonlike monster Godzilla (b. April 26, 1910—d. April 2, 1997).

Tartikoff, Brandon, American television executive (b. Jan. 13, 1949, New York, N.Y.—d. Aug. 27, 1997, Los Angeles, Calif.), was a programming wizard who selected shows that became the highest-rated television series during the 1980s and propelled NBC, which had trailed behind the other major networks for a decade, into first place in the TV ratings. He graduated (1970) from Yale University with a B.A. in English before landing (1972) his first job in the television industry as the director of advertising and promotion for an ABC affiliate in New Haven, Conn. The following year he was hired by WLS-TV in Chicago in a similar capacity. After boosting the station's afternoon ratings by offering viewers old horror movies, he attracted the attention of Fred Silverman, ABC's head of programming. Silverman hired him as ABC's director of dramatic development in 1976, beginning an association that spanned several years and two networks. Silverman and Tartikoff joined forces in 1978 to lift NBC from third place in the ratings. In 1980 he became the youngest division chief in network history when Silverman named him president of NBC entertainment, a position he retained even after Silverman left. Tartikoff's formula for success involved combining critically acclaimed dramatic series such as "St. Elsewhere" and "Hill Street Blues" with popular sitcoms such as "Family Ties," "The Cosby Show," and "Cheers." Under his direction NBC became the top-rated network in 1986. He moved to film production in 1991 when he became chairman of Paramount Pictures. Tartikoff resigned in 1992 to devote more time to one of his daughters, who had been seriously injured in a 1991 car accident. His success came in spite of recurring bouts of Hodgkin's disease (1974 and 1982), which eventually caused his death.

Taylor, Charles Plunket Bourchier, Canadian journalist, author of five books, and horseman whose career with the Toronto-based *Globe and Mail* took him to East Asia, where he was responsible for negotiating the reopening of the paper's Beijing bureau, and also to England, Africa, the Middle East, and Southeast Asia; he later took over the operation of Windfields Farm from his father and became an internationally important figure in thoroughbred racing (b. Feb. 13, 1935—d. July 8, 1997).

Taylor of Gosforth, Peter Murray Taylor, BARON, British jurist who was an eloquent critic of flaws in the British criminal justice system, even while he served as lord chief justice of the Court of Appeal, 1992–96 (b. May 1, 1930—d. April 28, 1997).

Teresa, Mother (AGNES GONXHA BOJAXHIU), Albanian-born Indian nun (baptized Aug. 27, 1910, Shkup, Albania, Ottoman Empire [now Skopje, Macedonia]—d. Sept. 5, 1997, Calcutta, India), was the venerated founder and superior general (1950–97) of the Roman Catholic Order of the Missionaries of Charity and the recipient of the 1979 Nobel Prize for Peace. Born into a working-class Albanian family, she joined the Institute of the Blessed Virgin Mary in Rathfarnham, Ire., in 1928. She soon sailed for India, however, where she became a nun in the Congregation of Loreto and taught history and geography at a girls' school in Entally, Bengal. She later became an Indian citizen. In 1946, having obtained permission to leave the convent, she studied nursing and ministered among the poor of Calcutta. In 1948 she founded the Missionaries of Charity, which received canonical sanction from Pope Pius XII two years later. The order was raised in 1965 to the status of pontifical congregation, which made it responsible only to the Vatican. Despite many obstacles, including resistance from Indian officials who considered her an outsider and conservative Roman Catholics who felt that a nun belonged inside a convent, the diminutive and deceptively mild Mother Teresa tenaciously expanded the order's work to provide compassionate aid to the dying, lepers, abandoned children, and the elderly. Over the years, she established missions (with varying degrees of success) among the needy in other parts of South Asia, Europe, Africa, Australia, Latin America, and the Middle East. In 1971 the order opened its first house in New York City.

After receiving the first Pope John XXIII Peace Prize (1971) and the Nobel Prize, Mother Teresa gained a wider international platform for her passionate advocacy of the poor and needy. In later years she also publicly voiced her opposition to working women, divorce, contraception, and abortion, often becoming quietly involved in political debates outside her usual sphere of influence. In 1990 Mother Teresa, who suffered from increasing heart problems, officially resigned as superior general, but she was forced to stay on until a suitable successor, Indian-born Sister Nirmala, was finally named in March 1997. The Indian government, which had initially been skeptical of the modest little nun, granted her a national award in 1963 and honoured her with an elaborate, hours-long state funeral, the grandeur of which was in marked contrast to the simple life of India's "saint of the gutter."

Thimann, Kenneth Vivian, British-born plant physiologist (b. Aug. 5, 1904, Ashford, Kent, Eng.—d. Jan. 15, 1997, Haverford, Pa.), isolated and purified the plant hormone auxin and identified it as a chemical messenger with principal roles in regulating plant growth. After receiving (1928) a doctorate in biochemistry from Imperial College, University of London, Thimann joined the faculty of the California Institute of Technology in 1930 and began conducting research to isolate the universal growth substance that was known to control plant growth toward light and against the force of gravity. A few years earlier Dutch plant physiologist Frits Went had extracted the growth-stimulating substance from seedlings. Thimann demonstrated that auxin not only stimulated cell growth but also exerted an inhibitory effect on it. He identified the three main functions of auxin—cell elongation (with James Bonner), root formation (with Went), and bud growth (with Folke Skoog). Thimann's elucidation of the chemical structure of auxin allowed the hormone to be synthetically manufactured and put to use for a variety of purposes in farming and horticulture. For example, by spraying fruit trees with auxin

DAVID BINDER—CONTACT PRESS IMAGES

Mother Teresa

prior to harvest, growers could prevent the premature falling of fruit (especially apples). Auxin was also found useful in promoting the joining of grafts and, in high concentrations, in controlling weeds. Thimann also investigated other aspects of plant physiology such as the formation of pigments in plants, the role of various wavelengths of light in photosynthesis, and the mechanisms involved in plant aging. He continued his research at Harvard University (1935–65) and moved to the University of California, Santa Cruz, where he served (1965–72) as the founding provost of Crown College. He was a member of the U.S. National Academy of Sciences and the American Academy of Arts and Sciences and published more than 300 research papers and a number of influential books, including *Phytohormones* (1937; with Went) and *Hormone Action in the Whole Life of Plants* (1977).

Tikhonov, Nikolay Aleksandrovich, Soviet politician (b. May 14, 1905, Kharkov, Ukraine, Russian Empire—d. June 1, 1997, Moscow, Russia), served as premier of the Soviet Union from 1980 to 1985 and was aided in his career by his longstanding friendship and political association with Soviet leader Leonid Brezhnev. Tikhonov, who was raised in a middle-class Ukrainian family, became an assistant train driver in 1924. After graduating (1930) as a metallurgical engineer from Dnipropetrovsk (Ukraine) Metallurgical Institute, he began working in heavy industry, rising from engineer to plant manager. Tikhonov met Brezhnev in the 1930s and joined the Communist Party in 1940. Though he was only 35 at the time, it was an advanced age for someone hoping to achieve high political rank. Between 1947 and 1950 he was a manager at a pipe factory located in the same area where Brezhnev was serving as regional party secretary. Tikhonov entered government administration in 1950 when he joined the Ministry of Ferrous Metallurgy; he became a deputy minister five years later. In the early 1960s Tikhonov worked for Gosplan, the state planning committee. He became deputy chairman of the Council of Ministers in 1965, and in 1976 he was named first deputy chairman to Aleksey Kosygin. Tikhonov was made a full (voting) member of the Politburo in 1979, and the following year he succeeded Kosygin as premier. He was primarily responsible for the economy but was not particularly effective in that role. He retired in September 1985, just a few months after Mikhail Gorbachev's election, and was replaced by the younger, reform-minded Nikolay Ryzhkov—a changing of the guard that symbolized the ushering in of perestroika, the policy of economic restructuring.

Todd of Trumpington, Alexander Robertus Todd, Baron, Scottish organic chemist (b. Oct. 2, 1907, Glasgow, Scot.—d. Jan. 10, 1997, Cambridge, Eng.), studied the chemistry of a variety of chemicals involved in life processes and was awarded the 1957 Nobel Prize for Chemistry for his discovery of the structure and synthesis of the nucleotides that are subunits of nucleic acids—the hereditary material of cells. His work provided the foundation for further studies into the physical structure and biological function of nucleic acids, particularly the discovery of the double-helical structure of DNA by James Watson, Francis Crick, and Maurice Wilkins. Todd received doctorates from the Johann Wolfgang Goethe University of Frankfurt, Ger. (1931), and the University of Oxford (1933). He held posts at the University of Edinburgh, where he was one of the first chemists to study the structure of vitamin B_1 (thiamine). Although his method for synthesizing the vitamin was not the first, it proved the best suited to industrial application and continued to be used in manufacturing. From 1938 to 1944 he continued his research at the University of Manchester, Eng., studying the chemistry of a variety of compounds, including vitamin E, substances found in marijuana and hashish, and nucleosides and nucleotides. Todd temporarily interrupted his research during World War II to develop and produce gases to be used in chemical warfare. He accepted the chair in organic chemistry at the University of Cambridge, where he spent the greater part of his career (1944–71) and carried out his most important work. During this time Todd synthesized the nucleoside adenosine as well as adenosine diphosphate and triphosphate (ADP and ATP), nucleotides that are not subunits of nucleic acids but are responsible for energy production and energy storage in plant and animal cells. He also established the structure of the coenzyme flavin adenine dinucleotide (FAD) and was involved in working out the structure of vitamin B_{12}. Todd was knighted in 1954, created a life peer in 1962, and made a member of the Royal Order of Merit in 1977. His autobiography, *A Time to Remember: The Autobiography of a Chemist,* was published in 1983.

Tombaugh, Clyde William, American astronomer (b. Feb. 4, 1906, Streator, Ill.—d. Jan. 17, 1997, Las Cruces, N.M.), discovered the planet Pluto, the ninth planet in the solar system and the only one found in the 20th century. Tombaugh was 24 years of age when he made the discovery in 1930 at Lowell Observatory in Flagstaff, Ariz. At that time he had had no formal training in astronomy, only a keen interest that had been sharpened by his first glimpse of the heavens through his uncle's telescope. After finishing high school, Tombaugh built his own telescope according to specifications published in a 1925 issue of *Popular Astronomy.* Using this instrument, he made observations of Jupiter and Mars and sent sketches of these planets to Lowell Observatory, hoping to receive advice about his work. Instead, he received a job offer. Tombaugh's assignment was to locate the ninth planet, a search instigated in 1905 by astronomer Percival Lowell. To carry out this task Tombaugh used a 33-cm (13-in) telescope to photograph the sky and an instrument called a blink comparator to examine the plates for signs of moving celestial bodies. On Feb. 18, 1930, Tombaugh pinpointed Pluto, and on March 13 Lowell Observatory announced the discovery of the new planet. After his discovery Tombaugh attended the University of Kansas on a scholarship, returning each summer to the observatory until completing (1939) his M.A. in astronomy. Upon graduating he returned to the observatory and continued his patrol of the skies, cataloging more than 30,000 celestial objects before he left in 1946. His observations of Mars led him to conclude in 1950 that the surface of the planet would be pitted with craters as a result of its proximity to the asteroid belt, a prediction borne out by images taken by the Mariner 4 space probe in the 1960s. Tombaugh also taught at Arizona State College and at the University of California, Los Angeles, and he worked as an astronomer and optical physicist at White Sands Missile Range near Las Cruces, N.M., where he helped set up an optical tracking system to follow ballistic missiles. He joined the faculty of New Mexico State University in 1955 and there instituted a major program of planetary research. He retired in 1973 but remained involved as an observer and adviser at the university. In 1980 he published, with

Patrick Moore, *Out of the Darkness: The Planet Pluto.*

Tsongas, Paul Efthemios, American politician (b. Feb. 14, 1941, Lowell, Mass.—d. Jan. 18, 1997, Boston, Mass.), came to national attention when he campaigned for the Democratic Party's presidential nomination in 1992. Making a strong case for politically dangerous, painful measures to ensure reduction of the federal budget deficit, he won the New Hampshire primary and thereby nudged the party toward a policy of heightened fiscal responsibility. Following losses to Bill Clinton in a number of other important primaries, though, he withdrew from the race. Tsongas graduated (1962) from Dartmouth College, Hanover, N.H., spent two years in the Peace Corps, and then attended Yale Law School, receiving his degree in 1967. He began his career in politics with election to the Lowell City Council in 1968, and in 1974 he was elected his district's first Democratic representative to the U.S. Congress in some 90 years. He won election to the Senate four years later. After being diagnosed with non-Hodgkin's lymphoma in 1983, Tsongas chose not to run for reelection, and upon leaving the Senate, he joined a Boston law firm. His cancer treatment, which included an experimental bone marrow transplant in 1986, was successful, and in 1991 he declared his candidacy for president. After withdrawing from that campaign, Tsongas helped found the Concord Coalition, a group formed to focus on economic problems. Late in 1992 Tsongas was diagnosed with a different type of lymphoma, which was also successfully treated, but in 1996 he underwent another bone marrow transplant to treat a disorder caused by his earlier treatment. Tsongas died after developing pneumonia following surgery to treat liver problems that also had resulted from the cancer treatments.

Turkes, Alpaslan, Cypriot-born Turkish army officer and politician who was a leader of the military overthrow of the Turkish government in 1960; he later formed the right-wing Nationalist Action Party and served as deputy prime minister (b. Nov. 25, 1917—d. April 4, 1997).

Tutuola, Amos, Nigerian author (b. 1920, Abeokuta, Nigeria—d. June 8, 1997, Ibadan, Nigeria), was celebrated for his first novel, *The Palm-Wine Drinkard and His Dead Palm-Wine Tapster in the Dead's Town* (1952), the first Nigerian book to achieve international fame. The story is a classic quest tale in which the hero, a lazy boy who likes to spend his days drinking palm wine, gains wisdom, confronts death, and overcomes many perils in the course of his journey. Tutuola, who had only six years of schooling, was inspired by the earlier Yoruba tales of D.O. Fagunwa. Tutuola utilized both Yoruba themes and storytelling methods in *The Palm-Wine Drinkard,* but scholars also noted thematic links to such works as *The Thousand and One Nights* and John Bunyan's *The Pilgrim's Progress.* His charming and unconventional language, vivid presentation of Yoruba mythology and religion, and grasp of literary form made him a great success with African, British, and American audiences. From 1939 Tutuola worked as a blacksmith and at other jobs until his first novel was published. He followed it with two more quest novels, *My Life in the Bush of Ghosts* (1954), the experiences of a boy who, in trying to escape from slave traders, finds himself in strange company, and *Simbi and the Satyr of the Dark Jungle* (1955), the tale of a rich and beautiful girl who leaves home and experiences poverty and starvation. In these and books that followed—*The Brave African Huntress* (1958), *Feather Woman of the Jungle* (1962), *Ajaiyi and His Inherited Poverty* (1967), and *The Witch-Herbalist of the Remote Town* (1981)—Tutuola's rich vision imposed unity on relatively random events. His better-known later works include *Yoruba Folktales* (1986), *Pauper, Brawler, and Slanderer* (1987), and *The Village Witch Doctor and Other Stories* (1990).

van den Bergh, Hendrik Johan, South African police official who created and headed the much-feared Bureau of State Security, which acted ruthlessly to suppress antiapartheid activity, and reportedly employed political murder and torture among his oppressive methods (b. Nov. 27, 1914—d. Aug. 16, 1997).

Van Zandt, Townes, American country and folk musician whose public obscurity was countered by the high esteem with which he was held by the musicians who transformed his haunting ballads into such hits as "Pancho and Lefty" (Willie Nelson and Merle Haggard) and "If I Needed You" (Emmylou Harris and Don Williams). His songs inspired a new generation of songwriters including Nanci Griffith, who recorded a well-known version of Van Zandt's "Tecumseh Valley" (b. March 7, 1944—d. Jan. 1, 1997).

Vander Meer, Johnny, American professional baseball player who, as a member of the Cincinnati Reds in 1938, became the only pitcher in major league history to throw no-hitters in consecutive starts (b. Nov. 2, 1914—d. Oct. 6, 1997).

Vasarely, Victor (GYOZO VASARHELYI), Hungarian-born French artist (b. April 9, 1908, Pecs, Austria-Hungary—d. March 15, 1997, Paris, France), was one of the leaders of the movement known as Op art—brightly coloured geometric abstraction that suggests movement through optical illusion—which reached its peak of popularity in the 1960s. He was considered the "grandfather" of the movement, and his works were exhibited internationally into the 1980s. Vasarely initially studied medicine in Budapest but in 1927 quit to concentrate on art, supporting himself by working as a clerk. In 1930 he moved to Paris and became a commercial graphic artist while continuing his studies. Vasarely began painting again in the mid-1940s and had his first one-man show in 1944 in Paris. By 1947 he was emphasizing geometric abstractions, and by the mid-1950s he had developed the style of visual trickery that exemplifies Op art. In the 1970s Vasarely established a foundation in Aix-en-Provence, France, and museums in Budapest, Pecs, New York City, and Gordes, France. He was made a Chevalier of the Legion of Honour in 1970.

Vegh, Sandor, Hungarian violinist, conductor, and music teacher noted for his chamber music performances (he left the Hungarian String Quartet in 1940 to form the Vegh Quartet) and his influence among younger musicians, especially as founder in 1972 of the International Musicians Seminar (b. May 17, 1905—d. Jan. 7, 1997).

Velázquez Sánchez, Fidel ("DON FIDEL"), Mexican labour leader (b. May 12?, 1900, San Pedro Azcapotzaltongo [now Villa Nicolás Romero], Mex.—d. June 21, 1997, Mexico City, Mex.), was leader of the Confederation of Mexican Workers (CTM), Mexico's largest labour union, for more than half a century. The CTM was closely affiliated with the ruling Institutional Revolutionary Party (PRI), which had been in power since 1929, and was deemed essential to the party's political domination. Velázquez, who received no formal education beyond the sixth grade, worked as a field labourer and a milkman and in 1921 helped found the Union of Milk Workers. The CTM was formed in 1936, and within five years he was at its helm. He used his charisma and innate leadership ability to control the union, and during his tenure it grew to boast some six million members. In the early years the relationship between the CTM and the PRI was mutually beneficial; the government provided favours to those belonging to the union, and in return the union provided the PRI with political support and a stable workforce. Velázquez was credited with having played a key role in gaining for employees the legal right to strike, and during the 1950s and '60s he helped to secure significant wage increases. In recent years, however, Velázquez was criticized for going along with the government's plan to keep wages down to help fuel the country's economic recovery, which caused the workers' standard of living to suffer. He also served two terms (1946–52 and 1958–64) in the Mexican Senate.

EVAN AGOSTINI—GAMMA LIAISON

Gianni Versace, with his sister Donatella

Versace, Gianni, Italian fashion designer (b. Dec. 2, 1946, Reggio di Calabria, Italy—d. July 15, 1997, Miami Beach, Fla.), was the first designer to recognize that fashion was just like any other form of popular culture—it had entertainment value. His seasonal fashion shows at his lavish design headquarters in Milan were staged like rock concerts, with groupies and paparazzi awaiting the arrival of both celebrity guests like Elton John and Madonna and Versace's troupe of models, who were paid such high salaries that the press dubbed them "supermodels." Though his glittering shows featured strobe lights, TV screens flashing colour images, and loud pop music, his designs were rarely upstaged by the excessive atmosphere. Versace built an empire by producing "prostitute-style" ensembles that oozed sensuality and sexuality. His most famous designs, notably sophisticated bondage gear, polyvinyl chloride baby-doll dresses, and silver-metal mesh togas, gained him worldwide celebrity. Versace's mother, Francesca, was a dressmaker, and it was from her that he learned the fine art of cutting and stitching. He left his hometown in the early 1970s to pursue a design career in Milan and found work in the ateliers of Genny, Complice, Mario Valentino, and Callaghan. Backed by the Girombellis, an Italian fashion family, Versace established (1978) his own company, Gianni Versace SpA. In the '80s his then family-run business thrived. His brother, Santo, served as CEO, and his sister, Donatella, was a designer and vice president. At the time of his death, his company produced clothing for men, women, and children as well as handbags, precious jewelry, perfume, and items for the home. In addition, many fashion aficionados believed that his 25-year design career was at its peak. Versace had tempered his garish early work, as evidenced by the increasingly refined yet colourful and sexy ensembles he created, especially those worn by Diana, princess of Wales (*q.v.*). Versace was shot and killed, allegedly by spree killer Andrew Cunanan, outside Casa Casaurina, his Miami Beach estate.

Villoresi, Luigi ("GIGI"), Italian race-car driver for Maserati, Ferrari, and Lancia teams during the 1930s, '40s, and '50s who was considered the most elegant racer of his time (b. May 16, 1909—d. Aug. 24, 1997).

Wald, George, American biologist and biochemist (b. Nov. 18, 1906, New York, N.Y.—d. April 12, 1997, Cambridge, Mass.), was a co-winner, with Haldan K. Hartline of the U.S. and Ragnar Granit of Sweden, of the 1967 Nobel Prize for Physiology or Medicine for the research he carried out on the chemistry of vision. He was also outspoken in his opposition to the Vietnam War, nuclear weapons proliferation, and human rights abuses and was proud of the fact that his name had been included on Pres. Richard M. Nixon's "enemies list." Wald, who received a bachelor's degree (1927) in zoology from Washington Square College, New York University, and a doctorate (1932) from Columbia University, New York City, was conducting research in Berlin on a National Research Council fellowship (1932–33) when he identified the presence of Vitamin A in the pigments in the retina and thus its importance to the maintenance of vision. He continued his research in Heidelberg, Ger., and the Universities of Zürich, Switz., and Chicago before joining (1934) the faculty of Harvard University, where he spent the following 43 years, becoming professor emeritus in 1977. At Harvard, often in collaboration with Ruth Hubbard—whom he married in 1958—and Paul Brown, he made further discoveries regarding the means by which images are transmitted from the eye to the brain and the role of vitamin A in this process. Besides the Nobel, Wald's many awards included the Eli Lilly Award of the American Chemical Society (1939), the Lasker Award of the American Public Health Association (1953), and the Rumford Medal of the American Academy of Arts and Sciences (1959).

Wannūs, Sàdallāh, Syrian playwright, producer, and critic (b. 1941, Hosain al-Bahr [near Tartus], Syria—d. May 15, 1997, Damascus, Syria), was widely regarded as one of the leading innovators in Arab drama. He reportedly invented *masrah at-tasyīs,* or "political theatre," largely in response to his profound shock following Israel's victory over the Arabs in the 1967 Six-Day War. His best plays effectively combined traditional Arabic elements, including the use of a storyteller, with modern Western dramatic techniques, such as employing Bertolt Brecht's *Verfremdungseffekt,* or alienation effect. After graduating with a degree in journalism from Cairo University, Wannūs studied in France, where he was influenced by the works of such playwrights as Jean Anouilh, Brecht, Eugène Ionesco, and Erwin Piscator. He returned to Syria and worked as an editor and critic for the Syrian Ministry of Education and, later, taught at the Institute of Drama, Damascus. Like many Arabs, Wannūs was deeply shaken by the outcome of the Arab-Israeli wars. In his short stories and one-act plays, he examined the subjects of power and corruption and the need for personal involvement in political life. His best-known works include *Ḥaflat samar min ajl khamsa Huzayran* ("An Evening's Entertainment for the 5th of June"; produced 1968), in which cast members were planted in the audience to heckle the onstage actors and involve the audience in dialogue; and *Al-Fil yā malik az-zamān* ("The Elephant, O King of All Ages"; produced 1969; published 1971), a dramatization of the effects of despotic rule. Two other notable plays were *Al-Malik huwa al-malik* (1977; *The King Is the King*) and *Mughāmarat ra's al-mamlūk Jābir* ("The Adventure of the Slave Jabir's Head"; produced 1969). Both plays were derived from stories in the collection known as *Arabian Nights,* or *The Thousand and One Nights.* Wannūs resigned from the Writers Union in support of writer Adonis (or Adūnis, pseudonym of 'Ali Āhmad Sa'īd), who was expelled from the organization for his liberal attitude toward Israel. In 1993 Wannūs was diagnosed with cancer, and, despite his antiauthoritarian work, his medical treatment was financed by Syrian Pres. Hafez al-Assad.

Wedgwood, Dame (Cicely) Veronica ("C.V."), British historian (b. July 20, 1910, Stocksfield, Northumberland, Eng.—d. March 9, 1997, London. Eng.), was one of Great Britain's most distinguished and celebrated historians. Her biographies and historical works, especially those on the English Civil Wars, provided a clear, entertaining middle ground between popular and scholarly works; she used a narrative approach, preferring to explain the "how" of events rather than presuming to interpret the "why." Wedgwood—a descendant of Josiah Wedgwood, founder of the famous pottery firm—graduated (1931) from Lady Margaret Hall, Oxford, with first-class honours. In 1935 she published her first historical work, *Strafford, 1593–1641;* she revised and rewrote it as *Thomas Wentworth, First Earl of Strafford, 1593–1641: A Revaluation* (1961) after family papers were made available. Among Wedgwood's most acclaimed books were *The Thirty Years War* (1938), which became a standard history text, and the biography *William the Silent* (1944). Other notable works include the first two volumes of *The Great Rebellion,* which was to have been a trilogy on the civil wars: *The King's Peace, 1637–1641* (1955) and *The King's War, 1641–1647* (1958). Wedgwood was appointed C.B.E. in 1956 and advanced to D.B.E. in 1968; in 1969 she was awarded membership in the Order of Merit, a rare honour for a writer.

Weisgall, Hugo David, Czech-born American composer and educator (b. Oct. 13, 1912, Eibenschutz, Moravia [now Ivancice, Czech Republic]—d. March 11, 1997, Manhasset, N.Y.), was considered one of the most influential opera composers in the U.S.; his works were praised for their literary merit, psychological drama, and strong vocal line. Born into a musical family that had produced several generations of composers and cantors, Weisgall immigrated with his parents to the United States in 1920. He studied (1927–32) at the Peabody Conservatory, Baltimore, Md., and later attended the Curtis Institute, Philadelphia, where he earned diplomas in conducting (1938) and composition (1939). Following service in the U.S. Army (1941–48), he began a career in teaching, holding positions at Johns Hopkins University, Baltimore, and the Juilliard School, New York City, among others. Weisgall, who had begun writing operas in the 1930s, premiered two one-act operas in 1952—*The Tenor* and *The Stronger*—which established his reputation in the genre. The latter, a monologue for sopranos, was considered one of his finest works. In 1956 he completed his first full-length opera, *Six Characters in Search of an Author,* an adaptation of Luigi Pirandello's play. His next opera, *Purgatory* (1958), based on William Butler Yeats's poem, marked Weisgall's first attempt at the 12-note method, an atonal style that characterized much of his later work. Altogether he wrote 10 operas, including *Jenny, or the Hundred Nights* (1976) and *Esther* (1993). In addition, he also composed song cycles, ballets, and chamber music. Weisgall was awarded three Guggenheim fellowships along with numerous grants and commissions.

Wethered, Joyce (LADY HEATHCOAT-AMORY), British golfer (b. Nov. 17, 1907, Brook, Surrey, Eng.—d. Nov. 18, 1997, London, Eng.), dominated women's golf in the 1920s and was considered one of the best female players in the history of the sport. Wethered, who took up golf as a child, received only one formal lesson. Instead, she studied the play of others, including her brother Roger, himself an accomplished golfer, to improve her game. In 1920 she won her first major tournament, the English native championship, a title she would retain for the next four years. Winner of the British Women's Open (1922, 1924–25, 1929), she also had success on the international circuit and in mixed-foursome events. In 1932 she was captain of the Curtis Cup team against the U.S., and three years later she toured that country as a professional, defeating, among others, Babe Didrikson Zaharias. Known for her intense concentration and calm demeanour, Wethered, who stood 1.78 m (5 ft 10 in), had a powerful swing that often produced

ASSOCIATED PRESS

Joyce Wethered

drives longer than those of her male counterparts. She would have won more championships had not her career been shortened by several retirements and the loss of her amateur status due to work as a golf adviser. In 1937 she married Sir John Heathcoat-Amory, and she competed infrequently thereafter. An avid gardener, Wethered created one of Great Britain's leading botanical collections at her home at Knighthayes Court, near Tiverton, Devon.

Widerberg, Bo, Swedish film director whose works generally stressed themes of social consciousness; his best-known film, *Elvira Madigan,* 1967, which made a popular hit of Mozart's *Piano Concerto No. 21,* portrays young lovers whose disregard for society's rules dooms them to life on the run and eventual murder-suicide (b. June 8, 1930—d. May 1, 1997).

Williams, Anthony ("TONY"), American musician (b. Dec. 12, 1945, Chicago, Ill.—d. Feb. 23, 1997, Daly City, Calif.), exploded onto the national jazz scene shortly after his 17th birthday to become a major innovator in jazz percussion. A drummer from age eight, he was already a well-known musician in Boston in 1962 when alto saxophonist Jackie McLean invited him to New York City to perform during Christmas week. He played on McLean's noted modal jazz album *One Step Beyond* before joining Miles Davis the following May, and he also played on Eric Dolphy's groundbreaking album *Out to Lunch.* Williams made his major impact with Davis's 1963–69 quintet, creating rhythmic tension in the band with his accompaniments. Joined by guitarist John McLaughlin, Williams then formed the Tony Williams Lifetime, one of the first and most-praised jazz-rock groups. After a few years of inactivity (1973–75), he formed a second Lifetime but spent most of the rest of his career with straightforward jazz groups, including V.S.O.P., a reunion band of former Davis sidemen, with the Great Jazz Trio, and with his own combos. Always an aggressive, dramatic player, he accompanied with powerful arrhythmic accenting and dynamic contrasts, altering tempo and metre at will, then soloed without reference to metre; in later years he emphasized virtuoso technique and dense layers of cross-rhythms. Studies in classical composition at the University of California, Berkeley, in the

1980s led to his composing *Rituals.* The piece was performed by the Kronos (string) Quartet together with Williams and pianist Herbie Hancock. Williams contributed to *A Tribute to Miles* (1994), which won a Grammy award, and joined fusion and classical music in *Wilderness,* his last album.

Witherspoon, James ("JIMMY"; "SPOON"), American blues singer who was one of the great blues shouters—those whose loud delivery could be heard above the band; his 1949 recording of "Ain't Nobody's Business" topped the rhythm and blues charts for 34 weeks (b. Aug. 8, 1923—d. Sept. 18, 1997).

Wolpe, Joseph, South African-born American psychotherapist who helped usher in cognitive behavioral therapy during the 1960s; he devised a treatment to help desensitize patients with phobias by exposing them to their fears incrementally. Besides founding the Association for Advancement of Behaviour Therapy and the *Journal of Behavior Therapy and Experimental Psychiatry,* Wolpe helped develop "assertiveness training" (b. April 20, 1915—d. Dec. 4, 1997).

Woodhull, Nancy Jane, American journalist who began as a reporter and worked her way up to become one of the founding editors of *USA Today,* president of the Gannett News Service, and editor in chief of Time Warner's Southern Progress Corp.; an avid champion of equal rights for women, she was a founding chairwoman of Women, Men and Media, which monitored media coverage given to women (b. March 1, 1945—d. April 1, 1997).

Wooller, Wilfred ("WILF"), Welsh all-around athlete who played international rugby for Wales 18 times between 1933 and 1939, scored 13,593 runs (average 22.57) and took 958 wickets for the Glamorgan cricket side, and served as a cricket Test selector (1955–61). After he retired as Glamorgan's captain in 1960, he became a popular sports journalist (b. Nov. 20, 1912—d. March 10, 1997).

Wu, Chien-Shiung, Chinese-born American experimental physicist (b. May 29, 1912, Liuhe, Jiangsu province, China—d. Feb. 16, 1997, New York, N.Y.), gained international acclaim for her research in nuclear and particle physics, especially on the process of radioactive beta decay. In 1956 she designed and conducted experiments that disproved what had been thought to be a universal symmetry law of nature: the principle of the conservation of parity. The principle held that the interactions of fundamental particles, such as the interactions that take place in decaying atomic nuclei, do not distinguish between mirror-image cases—that is, between right and left or clockwise and counterclockwise. Tsung-Dao Lee and Chen Ning Yang (Nobel laureates in 1957) believed that the principle of parity conservation does not hold for interactions between subatomic particles involving the weak force, one of the four basic forces of nature. They encouraged Wu to find experimental evidence that this was so. Working with a sample of the radioactive isotope cobalt-60 at an extremely low temperature, Wu found that in undergoing beta decay, a weak force interaction, the cobalt nuclei ejected electrons whose spins were predominantly left-handed; *i.e.,* the spin rotation of the electrons was that of a left-handed screw. She thus confirmed the Lee-Yang hypothesis and caused a reformulation of the principle of parity conservation. In the early 1960s Wu and her associates conducted other experiments that confirmed a theory of vector-current conservation in nuclear beta decay that had been put forth by Murray Gell-Mann and Richard Feynman. After completing undergraduate studies in Nanjing, Wu traveled to the U.S., where she earned (1940) a Ph.D. in physics from the University of California, Berkeley. She taught at Smith College, Northampton, Mass., and Princeton University before joining the secret Manhattan Project, which produced the atomic bomb during World War II. Wu continued her research and taught at Columbia University, New York City, where she spent 37 years before retiring in 1980. Her book *Beta Decay* (1966) became a standard reference book. Wu's honours include the National Medal of Science and the Wolf Prize in physics. She also served as president of the American Physical Society.

Wynne-Edwards, Vero, British zoologist who espoused a theory of evolution known as group selection, the view that animals behave altruistically to control population growth. His theory supported the claim that natural selection operates not only at the level of the individual, as Darwin's theory of natural selection contends, but at the level of the group as well; his theories, published in *Animal Dispersion in Relation to Social Behaviour* (1962), ignited intense debate between proponents of group selection and those of individual selection, and although the view of individual selection came to be generally accepted, Wynne-Edwards's thinking sparked the development of more sophisticated models of how natural selection operates (b. July 4, 1906—d. Jan. 5, 1997).

Coleman Young

THE DETROIT NEWS/REUTERS

Yamashina, Naoharu, Japanese entrepreneur who founded the Bandai Co., a trendsetting toy manufacturer that produced the highly popular action figures Mighty Morphin Power Rangers and the virtual pet Tamagotchi (b. 1918?—d. Oct. 28, 1997).

Yar'Adua, Shehu Musa, Nigerian major general (ret.) and former vice president in Gen. Olusegun Obasanjo's military government (1976–79) who, amid international protests, was convicted in 1995 of conspiring to overthrow Gen. Sani Abacha's Provisional Ruling Council and reestablish civilian rule. Yar'Adua died while serving a 25-year prison term (b. March 5, 1943—d. Dec. 8, 1997).

Yepes, Narciso García, Spanish classical guitarist and composer who was known for both his brilliant technique and his interpretations and who designed a 10-string guitar to aid him in arranging music; his arrangements, compositions, and performance for the 1952 film *Jeux interdits* brought him especially wide acclaim (b. Nov. 14, 1927—d. May 3, 1997).

Yokoi, Gumpei, Japanese inventor and entrepreneur who was best known as the chief designer of Game Boy, an electronic toy that sold nearly 60 million units and established the Nintendo Co. as one of the world's leading computer game developers (b. September 1941—d. Oct. 4, 1997).

Young, Coleman, American politician who served (1973–93) as the first African-American mayor of Detroit and helped build biracial coalitions within the Democratic Party. Reelected to office an unprecedented four times, he ran the city during difficult economic and racially divisive times (b. May 24, 1918—d. Nov. 29, 1997).

Zale, Tony (ANTHONY FLORIAN ZALESKI), American world middleweight boxing champion (1941–46, 1948), known as the "Man of Steel," whose intense and brutal title matches against Rocky Graziano in the late 1940s were legendary (b. May 29, 1913—d. March 20, 1997).

Zinnemann, Fred, Austrian-born American motion picture director (b. April 29, 1907, Vienna, Austria—d. March 14, 1997, London, Eng.), made films in a variety of genres, paying meticulous attention to both performance and atmosphere and often featuring characters facing a crisis of conscience and a challenge to their moral integrity. Among his masterpieces are *High Noon* (1952), *From Here to Eternity* (1953), and *A Man for All Seasons* (1966); the latter two won Academy Awards for best picture. Zinnemann studied (1925–27) law at the University of Vienna but abandoned that field to pursue a career in cinema. He studied film in Paris and worked as an assistant cameraman on silent films in Berlin before moving (1929) to the U.S. at the advent of sound pictures. Zinnemann's first Hollywood job was as an extra in *All Quiet on the Western Front* (1930), and in 1934 he co-directed his first feature, *The Wave.* Over the following several years, he made mostly documentaries and short subjects; *That Mothers Might Live* (1938) and *Benjy* (1951) both won Oscars. From early on, he was noted for boosting the careers of performers whose talent he had recognized. *The Search* (1948), which established Zinnemann as an important feature director, also marked the debut of Montgomery Clift, and Marlon Brando was introduced to film audiences in *The Men* (1950). In casting Deborah Kerr and Donna Reed against type in *From Here to Eternity* and Audrey Hepburn in *The Nun's Story* (1959), he allowed them to demonstrate their versatility. Other Zinnemann motion pictures include *The Member of the Wedding* (1953), *Oklahoma!* (1955), and *The Day of the Jackal* (1973). His last film was *Five Days One Summer* (1982).

Zivotic, Miladin, Serbian philosopher and political activist who, as leader of a group of intellectuals known as the Belgrade Circle, opposed Serbian nationalism, especially the country's involvement in the Balkan wars (b. Aug. 14, 1930—d. Feb. 27, 1997).

THE EVENTS OF 1997

Agriculture and Food Supplies

INTERNATIONAL ISSUES

World agricultural production in 1997 was 1% above the previous high recorded in 1996, according to statistics compiled by the Food and Agriculture Organization (FAO) of the United Nations. Crop production remained about the same as in 1996, but livestock production increased nearly 2%. Food products accounted for the increase in agricultural output; production of nonfood agricultural products such as fibres and industrial products remained the same as in 1996. The increase in food production in 1997 kept pace with world population growth. Since 1990, world agricultural production per capita had increased 4%.

Farmers in industrial countries expanded their production at the modest pace of about 1% per year between 1990 and 1997. Their crop output expanded at twice the rate of livestock production. Farm production of fibres, industrial products, and other nonfood items declined slightly from 1990. Total agricultural production in the United States grew at a vigorous rate of over 2% per year, whereas in the European Union (EU) there was no obvious trend. The growth in U.S. agricultural production was boosted in 1996 and 1997 by a change in federal farm policy that relaxed restrictions on the area planted to crops and allowed farmers more freedom in allocating their land among crops. The lack of growth in agriculture in the EU reflected an agricultural policy that gradually removed financial incentives for farmers to increase output.

Since 1990, food production in less-developed African countries had been expanding about 2% per year. In 1997, however, grain production was down nearly 10% from the record 1996 harvest, which more than offset increases in production of other crops and livestock products. Growth in food production did not keep up with population growth. On average, per capita production in 1997 was down about 3% from 1990.

China demonstrated amazing ability to expand agricultural production in the 1990s. At something over 3%, production expansion in 1997 was modest, relative to recent years, owing to a poor grain harvest. Between 1990 and 1997, however, total agricultural output grew well over 50%, recording a 35% increase in crop production and a 115% increase in livestock products. Per capita food production in China increased 50% during the seven years; per capita production of animal products doubled.

Experts on Chinese agriculture accurately predicted China's rapid expansion of production and consumption of livestock products. They also predicted that China would not be able to expand feed production enough to meet the needs of the livestock and would have to greatly increase imports of coarse grains (corn, sorghum, oats, and barley). By year-end 1997, however, that had not happened. During the 1990s production of domestic feeds—along with the near elimination of coarse grain exports—enabled the domestic feed supply to keep pace with livestock production. Domestic production of high-protein meal, an important source of animal feed obtained from processed oilseeds, increased more than 300% between 1990 and 1997. Grain production increased about 15% from 1990, with most of that increase being used to feed livestock rather than people. In addition, inventories of grain reached a record high by the end of the 1996–97 crop year. In 1997 coarse grain production fell about 4%, but feed requirements were expected to be maintained through the 1997–98 feeding year by drawing down year-end stocks by about 50%.

The countries of Eastern Europe and the former Soviet republics presented an entirely different picture of agricultural well-being. Production from their farms peaked in 1990. During the following years of political and economic restructuring, agricultural output in those countries declined by more than one-fourth. Crop production fell 18%, owing primarily to lower crop yields, and livestock products were down 34%. The hardest-hit countries—Azerbaijan, Bulgaria, Estonia, and Latvia—experienced declines in agricultural production of between 40%

Table I. Selected Indexes of World Agricultural and Food Production

(1989–91 = 100)

	Total agricultural production					Total food production					Per capita food production				
Region or country	1993	1994	1995	1996	1997	1993	1994	1995	1996	1997	1993	1994	1995	1996	1997
Developed countries	**95.4**	**96.6**	**94.7**	**97.7**	**97.2**	**95.7**	**96.7**	**95.0**	**98.3**	**97.9**	**94.1**	**94.7**	**92.6**	**95.4**	**94.7**
Canada	102.5	107.0	111.1	115.2	111.2	102.7	106.7	110.6	115.2	110.6	99.1	101.9	104.5	107.9	102.7
European Union	98.7	97.3	97.2	101.8	99.6	98.7	97.2	97.1	101.9	99.6	97.6	95.9	95.4	99.8	97.4
Japan	94.7	99.9	97.9	96.1	95.7	95.0	100.3	98.4	96.5	96.1	94.2	99.3	97.1	95.1	94.5
Russia	86.3	74.3	67.3	69.3	69.8	86.6	74.6	67.7	69.8	70.2	86.2	74.3	67.5	69.8	70.4
South Africa	95.6	99.2	86.4	102.4	98.5	97.3	101.4	88.3	104.9	100.7	90.9	92.7	78.9	91.7	86.1
United States	100.4	116.3	109.4	114.7	116.8	100.1	115.9	109.3	114.5	117.6	97.1	111.3	104.0	108.0	110.0
Less-developed countries	**111.2**	**116.3**	**122.6**	**128.0**	**130.0**	**112.1**	**117.8**	**124.0**	**129.6**	**131.8**	**106.2**	**109.7**	**113.5**	**116.6**	**116.7**
Argentina	102.0	109.5	116.0	119.4	118.6	103.8	111.7	117.8	121.0	120.7	99.8	105.9	110.3	111.8	110.1
Bangladesh	103.2	100.5	103.4	106.2	110.2	103.5	99.9	103.8	105.9	110.1	98.9	94.1	96.3	96.8	99.0
Brazil	106.1	110.8	114.1	118.6	122.3	107.1	112.3	116.9	121.4	125.2	102.3	105.9	108.8	111.5	113.6
China	120.0	129.8	141.8	152.3	157.3	121.9	133.0	145.5	156.6	162.1	117.7	127.1	137.8	146.8	152.0
Congo, Dem. Rep. of the	104.0	105.6	104.2	103.7	102.7	104.4	106.1	105.5	105.1	104.1	92.5	90.5	87.0	84.1	81.2
Egypt	114.8	111.0	119.2	119.7	118.8	113.6	112.6	121.6	119.7	119.7	107.0	104.1	110.3	106.5	104.6
Ethiopia	106.4	107.2	118.2	127.1	128.1	107.7	107.7	118.8	128.5	129.1	98.0	94.9	101.4	106.2	103.4
India	108.7	112.2	116.0	117.4	118.0	108.6	111.8	115.2	116.5	117.4	102.9	104.1	105.5	104.9	104.0
Indonesia	112.8	113.1	119.6	124.2	123.7	112.7	113.0	119.7	124.3	124.7	107.5	106.2	110.8	113.3	112.0
Malaysia	112.1	113.2	114.4	116.9	119.0	118.6	119.7	121.1	124.1	126.7	110.3	108.8	107.6	108.0	107.9
Mexico	108.4	113.3	117.2	117.8	123.0	110.6	115.0	118.3	117.3	122.9	104.7	106.9	108.1	105.3	108.5
Nigeria	124.7	128.9	132.1	134.2	134.9	124.9	129.4	132.5	134.6	135.7	114.3	114.8	114.2	112.7	110.4
Philippines	111.2	114.2	115.2	116.3	120.9	111.7	115.2	116.2	117.4	122.4	104.6	105.5	104.1	103.1	105.2
Turkey	103.5	103.0	104.6	107.0	104.1	103.5	104.0	104.2	106.8	104.0	98.5	97.4	96.1	96.9	93.0
Venezuela	110.9	113.2	110.5	115.9	117.4	112.3	114.4	111.7	116.7	117.9	104.7	104.3	99.7	101.9	101.0
Vietnam	116.6	122.9	129.4	135.2	136.1	116.1	121.7	127.7	133.2	134.0	109.1	112.1	115.4	118.1	116.8
World	**104.0**	**107.4**	**109.9**	**114.3**	**115.2**	**104.5**	**108.1**	**110.6**	**115.1**	**116.2**	**99.9**	**101.8**	**102.7**	**105.4**	**104.9**

Source: World Wide Web site for the Food and Agriculture Organization: http://apps.fao.org (Nov. 5, 1997).

and 50%. In 1997, however, there were signs that the decline had hit bottom. A large increase in cereal production, due to higher yields, offset small declines in production of other crops and livestock.

Food Emergencies. A study by the U.S. Department of Agriculture's (USDA's) Economic Research Service showed that 9 million–11 million tons of food aid in the form of cereals were estimated to be needed during the 1996–97 crop year to raise food consumption in hard-hit less-developed countries to target levels. The target was the average of their food consumption in the previous five years—a figure that was still far short of their minimal nutritional needs. Food needs in those countries were less than in previous years because of their improved harvests and increased commercial food purchases. The FAO reported that aid shipments of cereals by donors, principally the U.S. and the EU, during the 1996–97 reporting year totaled slightly under five million tons—which was far short of food-aid needs. (*See* TABLE II.)

In general, food production in 1997 continued to improve in countries defined by the FAO as "low-income food-deficit," increasing 2% over 1996. Food emergencies continued to exist, however. The FAO identified food emergencies in 31 countries in 1997, up from 25 the previous year. Most were in Africa.

Even so, the African situation eased somewhat in 1997. The FAO estimated that food production in the continent declined slightly in 1997 from the record-high level of the previous year, and overall there was somewhat less civil strife. Emergencies did, however, exist. The FAO reported that Ethiopia and Uganda suffered crop failures and food shortages as a result of adverse weather and civil disorder. Food production was also seriously reduced in Somalia, Tanzania, Burkina Faso, The Gambia, Senegal, Cape Verde, and Malawi. The ravages of war continued to cut food production in The Sudan, Rwanda, and Burundi, but some recovery was evident in 1997 in the latter two countries. Food emergencies also continued in Sierra Leone and Liberia. Civil strife in the Republic of Congo seriously disrupted food production and distribution in 1997.

The food crisis continued in North Korea during the year. A typhoon and severe drought in 1997 followed two years of destructive flooding of farmland in the nation. The disruptions of the Persian Gulf War and the resulting trade embargo continued to greatly restrict food supplies to Iraq. As a consequence, malnutrition was widespread. The UN-brokered food-for-oil trade agreement eased the food situation somewhat in 1997, but malnutrition persisted. The FAO reported that Mongolia continued to have food shortages. Papua New Guinea and Haiti suffered from very poor harvests due to prolonged droughts. In addition, four of the former Soviet republics—Armenia, Azerbaijan, Georgia, and Tajikistan—suffered food shortages as a result of poor weather and the disruptions of the transition to new civil and economic conditions.

Food-Aid Supplies. Food-aid shipments in 1996–97 sharply declined, continuing the downward trend of the 1990s. (*See* TABLE II.) Cereals, primarily wheat, accounted for about 85% of the volume of food aid. The FAO estimated that cereal shipments in 1996–97 fell 37% from the previous year; noncereal shipments (meat, fish, dried fruit, fats, oil, skim milk) fell 28%. Virtually all aid shipments came from developed countries. In 1996–97, however, China became a significant donor of cereals. Most of the food-aid shipments in 1996–97 went to low-income food-deficit countries in Asia and Africa. The remainder went to countries in Eastern Europe, the former Soviet republics, Latin America, and the Caribbean.

Nearly three-fourths of cereal aid historically had been provided by the U.S. and the EU. Over the years, their aid shipments were high when domestic stocks—especially government-controlled stocks—were abundant and cereal prices were low. Shipments dropped in years when cereal surpluses disappeared and prices increased. High cereal prices and tight global supplies thus helped explain the sharp drop in cereal-aid shipments by all donor countries in 1995–96. Although prices dropped in 1996–97, cereal stocks in the U.S. and the EU remained at very low levels. A combination of low cereal stocks and government fiscal constraints helped restrict food-aid shipments in 1996–97. Food-aid shipments were forecast by the FAO to decline further in

Table II. Shipment of Food Aid in Cereals

In 000-metric ton grain equivalent

Region and country	Average 1992–93 to 1994–95	1995–96	1996–97	1997–98[1]
Australia	238	238	272	250
Canada	674	463	349	300
China	6	0	111	100
European Union	3,740	2,730	1,596	1,500
By individual countries	1,145	940	717	...
By the Union	2,595	1,790	879	...
Japan	375	845	238	300
Norway	41	19	25	20
Switzerland	58	47	31	30
United States	6,976	3,094	2,019	2,300
Others	420	307	186	200
Total	12,528	7,743	4,872	5,000
To LIFDC[2]	8,638	6,700	4,116	4,200
Sub-Saharan Africa	4,176	2,402	1,641	1,700
To other countries	3,890	1,043	756	800

[1]Estimate partly based on minimum commitments under the Food Aid Convention of 1995 and budgetary allocations.
[2]Low-income food-deficit countries with per capita incomes under U.S. $1,395 in 1994.
Source: FAO, November 1997.

Table III. World Cereal Supply and Distribution

In 000,000 metric tons

	1994–95	1995–96	1996–97[1]	1997–98[2]
Production				
Wheat	525	537	582	605
Coarse grains	874	802	906	886
Rice, milled	365	371	379	383
Total	1,763	1,710	1,867	1,874
Utilization				
Wheat	548	550	579	584
Coarse grains	861	843	882	900
Rice, milled	367	370	376	381
Total	1,776	1,763	1,837	1,865
Feed use	676	640	680	698
Food and other uses	1,100	1,123	1,157	1,167
Exports				
Wheat	111	114	117	114
Coarse grains	103	108	102	104
Rice, milled	22	20	19	20
Total	236	243	238	238
Ending stocks[3]				
Wheat	118	105	109	129
Coarse grains	136	95	120	106
Rice, milled	49	50	53	55
Total	304	251	281	290
Stocks as % of utilization				
Wheat	22	19	19	22
Coarse grains	16	11	14	12
Rice, milled	13	14	14	14
Total	17	14	15	16
Stocks held by U.S. in %				
Wheat	12	10	11	14
Coarse grains	33	15	23	27
Stocks held by EU in %				
Wheat	11	10	13	11
Coarse grains	14	10	11	16

[1]Estimated. [2]Forecast. [3]Data not available for all countries.
Source: USDA, December 1997.

Table IV. World Production of Major Oilseeds and Products
In 000,000 metric tons

	1995–96	1996–97[1]	1997–98[2]
Total production of oilseeds	**256.4**	**258.7**	**279.9**
Soybeans	**125.0**	**131.2**	**149.2**
U.S.	59.2	64.8	74.5
China	3.5	13.2	13.5
Argentina	12.4	11.2	14.5
Brazil	24.2	26.5	29.0
Cottonseed	**35.2**	**34.3**	**35.0**
U.S.	6.2	6.5	6.6
Former Soviet republics	3.3	2.8	3.4
China	8.6	7.6	7.0
Peanuts	**25.9**	**28.2**	**26.0**
U.S.	1.6	1.7	1.6
China	10.2	10.1	8.0
India	7.4	8.2	8.0
Sunflower seed	**25.8**	**23.7**	**25.2**
U.S.	1.8	1.6	1.7
Former Soviet republics	7.4	5.2	6.1
Argentina	5.6	5.2	6.0
European Union	3.2	3.9	3.7
Rapeseed	**34.5**	**30.6**	**33.6**
Canada	6.4	5.1	6.1
China	9.8	9.2	9.4
European Union	8.3	7.1	8.4
India	6.2	6.3	6.2
Copra	**5.0**	**5.4**	**5.5**
Palm kernel	**5.0**	**5.3**	**5.4**
Oilseeds crushed	**218.8**	**219.7**	**227.0**
Soybeans	112.1	116.3	122.5
Oilseed ending stocks	**22.0**	**16.2**	**22.0**
Soybeans	17.4	12.8	18.5
World production[3]			
Total fats and oils	**85.7**	**87.6**	**89.3**
Edible vegetable oils	72.0	73.8	75.6
Soybean oil	20.2	20.8	22.0
Palm oil	16.0	17.2	17.6
Animal fats	12.3	12.3	12.3
Marine oils	1.4	1.4	1.4
High-protein meals[4]	**140.4**	**143.0**	**147.5**
Soybean meal	89.2	92.6	97.5
Fish meal	9.2	9.7	9.2

[1]Preliminary. [2]Forecast. [3]Processing potential from crops in year indicated. [4]Converted, on the basis of product's protein content, to weight equivalent of soybeans of 44% protein content.
Source: USDA, November 1997.

1997–98, mainly because of expected reductions in noncereal shipments.

El Niño. Every two to seven years, the weather in much of the world is disturbed by increases in water temperatures in the equatorial Pacific Ocean, beginning off the coasts of Peru and Ecuador. The disturbance tends to build during the year, peak around Christmas (the name El Niño means "the Child" and refers to the Christ child), and then gradually dissipate. Strong El Niño disturbances were observed in 1982–83 and 1991–92. They created severe drought in some regions of the world and flooding in other areas. The associated changes in ocean currents and water temperature also had an impact on fish supplies. (*See also* EARTH SCIENCES: *Meteorology.*)

Scientists found that the impacts of El Niño on weather and the ocean ecosystem were somewhat predictable. Consequently, private markets and governments had some early warnings in 1997 of potential food production problems. For example, the FAO and World Food Program took steps to monitor food-supply conditions in regions of the world where people were most vulnerable.

In early 1997 the signs of a new El Niño began to appear. Drought developed in Indonesia, Papua New Guinea, and Australia. Heavy rain hit California and parts of South America. Drought in much of Southeast Asia reduced coconut and palm yields. Crops in other parts of the world also were damaged by drought and floods, but it was more difficult to link those weather disturbances to El Niño.

El Niño-related weather disturbances caused some severe localized crop damage, but the impact on world food supplies was minimal in 1997. Greater damage was expected to occur in 1998, especially to Southern Hemisphere crops planted in late 1997 and harvested in 1998, including tropical products as coffee, tea, cocoa, and fruits.

The effects of El Niño on cereal production in 1997 were minor. Drought had put the Australian wheat crop on the brink of disaster, but rains came just in time to prevent major damage. Because of the low stocks of grain expected to be carried over from the 1997 crop, weather conditions in 1998 could have a major impact on world grain prices. The FAO observed that the largest impact of El Niño in late 1997 and 1998 likely would be on supplies of oil and meal (a high-protein feed for livestock). A contributing problem was expected to be the decline in meal and oil processed from fish caught off the Pacific coast of South America because of the reduced fish population there.

Low Grain Stocks. At the end of the 1995–96 crop year, grain stocks were only 14% of world grain consumption—the lowest in decades. Nine years earlier, stocks had been 28% of consumption. In addition, considerable quantities of stocks were located in countries such as China, where they were not available to world markets. As a result, there was virtually no grain safety net to protect the world's consumers from a poor grain harvest in 1996–97. Because of the rapidly increasing livestock numbers in the less-developed countries, the world demand for grain was rapidly expanding. Fortunately, a record world grain harvest in 1996–97 and an expected record harvest in 1997–98 were able to satisfy demand and provide a small recovery in world stock levels. Even so, grain stock levels at the end of the 1997–98 crop year were expected to be slightly below the minimum recommended by the FAO to provide protection against the possibility of a poor harvest in 1998. Another record grain harvest would be needed in 1998–99 to replenish stocks.

Dolly. In February a team of scientists at the Roslin Institute near Edinburgh announced that they had cloned an adult sheep. The seven-month-old clone, Dolly, grew from an altered embryo placed in a surrogate mother. The embryo was created from an egg cell whose nucleus had been replaced by the nucleus of a cell from an adult sheep.

The world's first clone of an adult animal was a milestone in science and could have a significant impact on livestock production. It also sparked an international debate on the ethics of research that could possibly lead to the cloning of humans. A team of Danish researchers stopped research on cloning cattle, pending public debate. (*See* LIFE SCIENCES: *Special Report.*)

AGRICULTURAL COMMODITIES

Grains. The poor grain harvest in 1995–96 drove up prices on world grain markets. High prices stimulated many of the world's farmers to plant additional land to grains. As a result, world production in 1996–97 increased 9%. (*See* TABLE III.) Much of the increase came from wheat and coarse grains produced in China and in grain-exporting countries such as the U.S., the EU, Canada, Australia, and Argentina. World production of coarse grains increased 104 million tons (13%) in 1996–97, with most of the increase coming from the U.S., China, and the EU. The coarse grain harvest in the former Soviet republics declined 7% and offset their gain in wheat production.

Global stocks of coarse grains had declined to a record low stock-to-use ratio just before the 1996–97 harvest. There were virtually no stocks available to protect against a poor crop. Fortunately, the bountiful 1996–97 harvest was adequate to feed the world's expanding livestock herd and still leave 25 million tons to add to carryover stocks. World rice production in 1996–97 continued its modest upward trend, and wheat production increased 8%.

The world's 1997–98 grain crop was forecast to exceed slightly the previous year's record. China was expected to enjoy a 9% larger wheat harvest, but the nation's coarse grain production would likely be down 16%. China's livestock production could be maintained, however, by drastically reducing year-end stocks. The former Soviet republics, on the other hand, were forecast to experience their first major increase in ce-

Table V. Livestock Inventories and Meat Production in Major Producing Countries

In 000,000 head and 000,000 metric tons (carcass weight)

Region and country	1996[1]	1997[2]	1996	1997[1]
	Cattle and buffalo[3]		Beef and veal	
World total	...	...	**56.9**	**57.6**
Canada	13	13	1.0	1.0
United States	101	99	11.6	11.5
Mexico	27	26	1.8	1.8
Argentina	52	50	2.6	2.6
Brazil	144	146	6.2	6.0
European Union	83	82	7.8	7.6
Eastern Europe[4]	13	13	1.0	1.0
Russia	36	34	2.6	2.3
Ukraine	15	14	1.2	0.9
Australia	26	26	1.6	1.7
India	277	279	1.3	1.3
China	140	147	4.9	5.4
	Hogs		Pork	
World total	...	...	**86.9**	**91.4**
Canada	12	12	1.2	1.3
United States	56	60	7.8	7.7
Mexico	10	10	0.9	0.9
European Union	117	113	16.2	16.0
Eastern Europe[5]	37	37	3.5	3.4
Russia	19	17	1.7	1.5
Ukraine	11	10	0.8	0.8
Japan	10	10	1.3	1.3
China	457	475	40.4	42.5
Taiwan	11	7	1.3	1.0
			Poultry meat	
World total	...	...	**58.4**	**62.6**
United States	...	...	14.5	15.0
Mexico	...	...	1.6	1.7
Brazil	...	...	4.3	4.4
European Union	...	...	8.1	8.3
Eastern Europe[6]	...	...	1.1	1.1
Russia	...	...	0.7	0.7
Ukraine	...	...	0.2	0.2
Japan	...	...	1.2	1.2
China	...	...	10.7	12.5
			Sheep, goat meat	
World total	...	...	**11.1**	**11.5**
			All meat	
Total	...	...	**217.3**	**227.2**

[1]Preliminary. [2]Forecast. [3]Livestock numbers at year's end. [4]Bulgaria, Czech Republic, Poland, and Romania. [5]Bulgaria, Czech Republic, Hungary, Poland, and Romania. [6]Hungary, Poland, and Romania.
Sources: Country data: USDA, November 1997; world totals: FAO, July–September 1997.

real grain output (about 25%) since 1990. As a result, abundant feed and food would be available, and carryover stocks would likely double. Production of wheat rose in the U.S., and the EU harvested a larger coarse grain crop, but most other countries were expected to have smaller harvests.

Oilseeds. Most oilseeds were crushed to produce meal and vegetable oil. The near-record world harvest of oilseeds in 1996–97 still fell short of the rapidly growing demand for oilseed products. As a result, the prices of oilseed products increased on world markets, and year-end global stocks of oilseeds fell to their lowest level in recent years. The USDA forecast an 8% increase in world oilseed production for 1997–98. (*See* TABLE IV.) That increase was expected to exceed the growth in world consumption of oilseed products and to replenish world year-end stocks. On the other hand, fishmeal production (7% of world meal production) was expected to decline in 1997–98.

Soybeans accounted for more than half of the world production of oilseeds. The U.S. (with 50% of world production), Brazil (20%), and Argentina (9%) were the world's three largest producers and exporters of soybeans and their products. In 1996–97 they experienced a profitable export market. The USDA forecast that each would set new production records in 1997–98, with output exceeding the previous year's level by 15% in the U.S., 9% in Brazil, and nearly 30% in Argentina.

The 1997–98 forecast was for robust exports of soybeans and products. Because of its rapidly expanding livestock industry, China was expected to need a major increase in imports of soybeans and meal. The EU, the largest importer, was expected to maintain a high level of imports in 1997–98. On the other hand, East Asian countries other than China showed no signs of growth in imports owing to the downturn in their economies.

Though not revealed in the numbers in TABLE IV, evidence was accumulating by December 1997 that world oil production in 1997–98 would fall short of expectations. Drought in Southeast Asia was affecting tropical oil production there. In addition, El Niño's negative impact on the fish catch off the coast of Chile was expected to lower that nation's production of fish oil.

Livestock and Meat. The FAO estimated that world meat production in 1997 increased nearly 5% over 1996 because of strong demand and lower feed prices. (*See* TABLE V.) Most of the meat expansion occurred in the production of pork and poultry in less-developed countries. The rapid increase in meat production in China in recent years made it by far the world's leading producer, followed by the U.S. and the EU. Per capita consumption of meat was estimated by the FAO to increase 6% in less-developed countries but remain the same in developed countries.

Beef production was estimated by the FAO and the USDA to be down marginally in most regions of the world. In the EU food-safety issues plagued the beef industry. In China, however, beef production was expected to increase 9%. Overall, a small increase in world beef trade was expected. The world's beef herd marginally decreased in 1997. The herds in the U.S. and the former Soviet republics declined 2% and 8%, respectively. China's herd increased about 5%. These changes in China and the former Soviet republics in 1997 were continuations of trends that existed throughout the 1990s.

World pork production in 1997 was estimated to increase 5% over 1996, including 9% growth across the less-developed countries. Production was down in the EU and Russia. World trade of pork, which represented less than 3% of production, was not expected to change significantly from 1996. The global inventory of hog numbers increased about 1% in 1997. Growth of hog inventories in the U.S. and in the less-developed countries—especially China—slightly exceeded drops in numbers in the EU and the former Soviet republics.

As with beef and pork, the less-developed countries led the way in poultry expansion in 1997. Production was estimated to increase nearly 10% in those nations, whereas the largest producer, the U.S., registered a 3% gain. World trade volume increased in 1997, with the U.S. showing an increase of about 8%.

Dairy. According to FAO estimates, world milk production from cattle, buffalo, camels, sheep, and goats was expected to increase 1% in 1997, with most of the increase coming from the less-developed countries. (*See* TABLE VI.) Domestic demand for milk products in most developed countries remained relatively static in recent years. In contrast, higher incomes in many less-developed countries in Asia and Latin America stimulated their demand for milk products, and production increased rapidly. As a group, less-developed countries had increased milk production by one-third since 1990.

The multiyear decline in milk production in Eastern Europe and the former Soviet republics showed evidence of bottoming out in 1997. Between 1990 and 1996 it dropped over 50%, but FAO estimates revealed no further decline in 1997. Russia purchased large quantities of butter from the world market in 1997, strengthening world prices. Near the end of 1997, there were concerns in world markets about the possible drought-induced effects of El Niño on the dairy industry in New Zealand and Australia—two major exporters. The impact of El Niño on 1997 milk production was surprisingly small.

Sugar. The USDA forecast that world sugar production in 1997–98 would remain essentially the same as in the previous two

Table VI. World Production of Milk[1]
In 000,000 metric tons

Region and country	1995	1996[2]	1997[3]
Developed countries	**342**	**336**	**338**
United States	70	70	71
Canada	8	8	8
Europe	160	159	160
European Union	125	125	124
France	26	26	26
Germany	29	29	29
Italy	11	12	11
Netherlands, The	11	11	11
United Kingdom	15	15	15
Eastern Europe	29	29	30
Poland	12	12	11
Romania	5	5	6
Former Soviet republics	78	71	70
Russia	39	36	34
Ukraine	17	16	16
Australia/New Zealand[4]	18	19	20
Japan	8	9	9
Less-developed countries	**195**	**202**	**206**
Latin America	50	52	55
Brazil	17	18	19
Africa	22	23	23
Asia	123	127	128
China	9	10	10
India[5]	66	69	69
World total	**537**	**538**	**544**

[1]Includes milk from cattle, buffalo, camels, sheep, and goats. [2]Preliminary. [3]Forecast. [4]Year ended June 30 of year shown for Australia and May 31 for New Zealand. [5]Year begun April 1 of year shown.
Source: FAO, November 1997.

Table VII. World Production of Centrifugal (Freed from Liquid) Sugar
In 000,000 metric tons raw value

Region and country	1995–96	1996–97	1997–98[1]
North America	**11.5**	**11.5**	**12.1**
United States	6.7	6.6	7.0
Mexico	4.7	4.8	5.0
Caribbean	**5.5**	**5.4**	**4.9**
Cuba	4.4	4.2	3.9
Central America	**2.8**	**3.2**	**3.4**
Guatemala	1.3	1.6	1.6
South America	**20.2**	**21.0**	**21.8**
Argentina	1.6	1.4	1.7
Brazil	13.7	14.6	15.2
Colombia	2.0	2.1	2.0
Europe	**20.7**	**23.1**	**23.1**
Western Europe	17.3	18.5	18.9
European Union	17.2	18.3	18.7
Eastern Europe	3.4	4.6	4.2
Poland	1.7	2.5	2.3
Former Soviet republics[2]	**6.4**	**5.2**	**4.3**
Russia	2.1	1.8	1.6
Ukraine	3.8	2.9	2.2
Africa and Middle East	**9.8**	**10.8**	**11.7**
South Africa	1.8	2.4	2.6
Turkey	1.4	2.0	2.3
Asia	**40.0**	**36.5**	**34.5**
China	6.7	7.3	7.5
India	18.2	14.6	13.4
Indonesia	2.1	2.1	2.0
Pakistan	2.6	2.6	3.0
Philippines	1.8	1.8	1.8
Thailand	6.2	6.0	4.6
Oceania	**5.6**	**6.2**	**6.3**
Australia	5.0	5.7	5.9
Totals			
Beginning stocks	22.5	26.6	26.1
As % of consumption	19.0	21.6	20.9
Production	122.3	122.8	122.2
Consumption	118.3	123.2	124.8
Exports	34.7	35.8	35.9

[1]Preliminary. [2]Includes Estonia, Latvia, and Lithuania.
Source: USDA, November 1997.

years. (*See* TABLE VII.) About 70% of the world's sugar was produced from cane, and the remaining 30% came from beets. Global consumption just matched production in 1996–97, but it was forecast to exceed production slightly in 1997–98 and draw down global sugar stocks. Little change in world trade of sugar was forecast.

In 1997–98 Brazil was forecast to displace India as the world's leading sugar producer. Since 1991–92 Brazil's production had more than doubled, with most of the growth going into exports. India's production dropped one-fourth from the previous two years because farmers took land out of sugar and used it for more profitable crops. Production in the U.S. and the EU was forecast to increase 5% and 2%, respectively.

On the other hand, the USDA forecast a continued decline of production in the former Soviet republics and in Cuba. Cuba's sugar harvest suffered from a combination of poor weather and shortages of production inputs. Sugar production in the countries of Eastern Europe was forecast to decrease slightly in 1997–98 after the large increase in 1996–97. Thailand was forecast to have a sharp reduction in 1997–98 because of the drought. Sugar consumption was expected to continue its upward trend in the less-developed countries as a result of population growth and higher incomes. The demand for beverages accounted for much of the growth in the consumption of sugar. In the developed countries, a combination of slow population growth and the substitution of other sweeteners for sugar accounted for their lack of growth in demand for sugar.

Coffee. World green coffee stocks were at a 16-year low at the beginning of the 1996–97 crop year because of a poor crop the previous year. Fortunately, the coffee harvest in 1996–97 was very good. USDA data revealed that Brazil, with a 64% increase in production, provided the main source of recovery. (*See* TABLE VIII.) A combination of record-high domestic use in producing countries plus record-high exports, however, exhausted the world's 1996–97 coffee crop and further depleted year-end stocks. In exporting countries total coffee exports were up 11% from 1995–96; domestic consumption increased 3%.

A tight world coffee market was expected during the 1997–98 crop year. Beginning stocks were very low, and coffee demand was expected to exceed the previous year's record. June 1997 estimates by the USDA indicated that the 1997–98 coffee harvest worldwide would be about 3% above 1996–97. Vietnam became the fifth largest producer and was expected to account for the most growth. Nonetheless, the growth in world production was expected to fall short of the predicted demand, which would lead to even lower levels of year-end stocks. As a result, coffee prices sharply increased.

After the June production estimates were reported, El Niño entered the picture. It was blamed for bringing additional uncertainty to the world coffee market. Drought hurt the coffee crop in Indonesia and Kenya, and Tropical Storm Pauline destroyed several thousand hectares of coffee in Mexico. Additional weather damage from El Niño was expected in early 1998. As a result, estimates made by the FAO in late 1997 indicated that world coffee production in 1997–98 would be down about 8% rather than increasing, as previously forecast by the USDA.

Cocoa. World cocoa production in 1996–97 declined 8% from the record crop harvested the previous year. (*See* TABLE IX.) The two largest producers, Côte d'Ivoire and Ghana, accounted for most of the increase in 1995–96 and most of the decline in 1996–97. The 1997–98 world cocoa crop was expected to be marginally larger.

Farmers in Côte d'Ivoire, which accounted for more than 40% of world cocoa production, had expanded production by cutting into virgin forests. The government, however, planned to prohibit this practice and thus sharply reduce the potential for future growth in production. Ghana was expected to increase production 8% in 1997–98 owing to cyclical production patterns and favourable weather. An increase in the cocoa tree population in Ghana continued, spurred by a jump in government-set producer prices for the beans. Indonesia was expected to have a record harvest of cocoa beans in 1997–98 in spite of the drought. Production had increased by one-fourth since 1992–93 as a result of an aggressive government-industry program of research and farmer assistance.

By contrast, Brazil and Malaysia exhibited downward production trends. Brazil, where production had declined 50% in five years, suffered from serious disease problems and seemed slow to overcome them. In Malaysia more profitable oil palm trees and other crops were replacing cocoa trees.

Cotton. The USDA estimated that world cotton production in 1996–97 declined 4% from the previous year, but production in 1997–98 was forecast to increase slightly. (*See* TABLE X.) During the past four decades, cotton yield per hectare had increased about 1.8% per year. Harvested area and yield were forecast to increase slightly in 1997–98.

Africa experienced a healthy increase in cotton production, 10% in 1996–97 and a forecast of 9% in 1997–98. In the former Soviet republics, cotton production was forecast to increase 17% in 1997 after eight years of decline, during which production was cut in half. On the other hand, China's cotton harvest shrank in both 1996 and 1997.

World consumption of cotton was expected to continue its upward trend of between 1% and 2% per year. In South Korea, Thailand, Indonesia, and other Southeast Asian countries, however, economic disruptions in 1997 were expected to reduce imports and consumption of cotton. Domestic cotton use in the former Soviet republics in 1996–97 was 70% below its peak of seven years earlier, but consumption was forecast to increase in 1997–98.

World cotton stocks at the beginning of 1997–98 rose 7% from the previous year and were equivalent to about 40% of annual world consumption. The USDA forecast year-end stocks to be about the same as beginning stocks. China, which held 40% of the world's cotton stocks, was forecast to reduce its huge stockpile during 1997–98 in order to fill the growing gap between domestic production and consumption and also to reduce imports. (JERRY A. SHARPLES)

See also Business and Industry Review: *Textiles;* Earth Sciences: *Meteorology.*

This article updates the *Macropædia* article The History of AGRICULTURE.

Table VIII. World Green Coffee Production
In 000,000 60-kg bags

Region and country	1995–96	1996–97[1]	1997–98[2]
North America	**19.5**	**19.8**	**20.7**
Costa Rica	2.6	2.3	2.4
El Salvador	2.3	2.4	2.6
Guatemala	3.8	4.1	4.2
Honduras	2.3	2.4	2.6
Mexico	5.5	5.6	5.7
South America	**34.7**	**42.2**	**44.3**
Brazil	16.8	27.5	28.0
Colombia	12.9	0.3	11.3
Ecuador	1.9	1.8	1.9
Peru	1.8	1.5	1.8
Africa	**18.2**	**19.8**	**19.5**
Cameroon	1.0	1.0	1.0
Côte d'Ivoire	2.9	4.7	3.8
Ethiopia	3.8	4.0	4.0
Kenya	1.6	1.3	1.7
Uganda	4.2	4.0	4.0
Zaire	1.0	0.9	1.0
Asia and Oceania	**16.8**	**19.0**	**19.2**
India	3.7	3.4	3.8
Indonesia	5.8	7.6	6.8
Thailand	1.3	1.3	1.2
Vietnam	3.6	4.2	5.0
Total production	**89.2**	**100.7**	**103.7**
Exportable	65.5	76.3	78.1
Beginning stocks	40.8	32.1	26.0
Exports[3]	74.7	82.9	84.4

[1]Preliminary. [2]Forecast. [3]By exporting countries.
Source: USDA, June 1997.

Table IX. World Cocoa Bean Production
In 000 metric tons

Region and country	1995–96	1996–97	1997–98[1]
North and Central America	**118**	**115**	**118**
South America	**411**	**346**	**333**
Brazil	221	145	152
Africa	**1,920**	**1,756**	**1,822**
Cameroon	130	120	120
Côte d'Ivoire[2]	1,219	1,130	1,180
Ghana	403	324	350
Nigeria[3]	140	155	145
Asia and Oceania	**485**	**497**	**487**
Indonesia	305	322	325
Malaysia	127	120	115
Total production	**2,935**	**2,714**	**2,759**

[1]Forecast. [2]Includes some cocoa marketed between Ghana and Côte d'Ivoire. [3]Includes cocoa marketed through Benin.
Source: USDA, November 1997.

Table X. World Cotton Production and Consumption
In 000,000 480-lb bales

Region and country	1995–96	1996–97[1]	1997–98[2]
Production	**93.0**	**89.1**	**90.2**
Western Hemisphere	24.1	23.9	24.8
United States	17.9	18.9	18.8
Brazil	1.8	1.3	1.8
Europe	2.2	1.8	2.1
Former Soviet republics	8.3	6.5	7.6
Uzbekistan	5.7	4.8	5.5
Africa	6.7	7.4	8.1
Asia and Oceania	51.7	49.5	47.6
China	21.9	19.3	18.0
India	13.2	13.8	12.9
Pakistan	8.2	7.3	7.7
Consumption	**86.9**	**88.4**	**89.8**
United States	10.6	11.1	11.4
China	20.6	21.0	21.5
India	11.9	11.9	13.2
Pakistan	7.2	7.0	7.0
European Union	5.1	5.2	5.2
Southeast Asia	4.5	4.5	4.3
Turkey	4.4	4.6	4.7

[1]Estimated. [2]Forecast.
Source: USDA, October and November 1997.

FISHERIES

According to the latest figures released by the UN Food and Agriculture Organization (FAO), 1995 provided yet another increase in the world catch of fish. The total of 112.9 million metric tons represented a gain of 3.3 million metric tons over 1994. The increase was due exclusively to a higher level of aquaculture production. Indeed, the FAO reported a slight fall in the total wild catch from 92.1 million metric tons in 1994 to just under 92 million in 1995. The top 20 producing countries accounted for about 80% of total world production, and the top 10 accounted for almost 70%.

China again dominated the producing nations with a total output of 24.4 million metric tons of fish caught or raised. This was approximately 15.5 million metric tons ahead of the second-place nation, Peru, which recorded just over 8.9 million metric tons, a drop from 11.6 million in 1994. Of Peru's 8.9 million metric tons, only 51,508 were produced through aquaculture, whereas in China 10.8 million metric tons of the 15.5 million total were derived from aquaculture. Third-place Chile with 7.6 million metric tons, fourth-place Japan with 6.8 million, and fifth-place U.S. with 5.6 million showed decreases in catch in 1995. In contrast, sixth-place India continued to show a steady increase in production, with a rise to 4.9 million metric tons from 4.5 million in 1994.

Despite a drop from 12,520,000 metric tons in 1994 to 8,640,000 in 1995, South American anchoveta (tropical anchovy) again topped the leading species caught. Alaska pollock lost the number two spot to Chilean jack mackerel, which rose from 4,260,000 metric tons to more than 4,960,000. Also increasing in quantity in 1995 were Alaska pollock, from 4,300,000 to 4,690,000 metric tons; Atlantic herring, from 1,900,000 to 2,240,000 metric tons; and skipjack tuna, from 1,490,000 to 1,560,000 metric tons. The Atlantic cod and European pilchard also registered slight increases. The Japanese pilchard catch, however, continued to decline, with just 733,000 metric tons caught in 1995, compared with as many as 3,770,000 as recently as 1991.

Of the total fishery production in 1995, approximately 31.5 million metric tons were used for reduction to fish meal, and the total available for human consumption was estimated at 80 million metric tons, 3.4 million more than 1994. This represented a greater increase than the estimated population growth rate for the same year and resulted in an increase in the average per capita availability of food fish to 14 kg (31 lb). Most of the production increase occurred in Asia, particularly China.

The trend of growth in the value of the international trade in fish continued in 1995. In 1985 the value of international fish exports was $17 billion; five years later it had risen to $35.8 billion, and by 1995 it had reached $52 billion. The overall trend in the value of the trade, however, was one of slower growth in recent years. In 1995 Japan, with some 30% of the world's total, continued to be the largest importer of fishery products. In value terms developed countries accounted for about 85% of total fish imports.

The U.S. was the world's second biggest importer of fishery products but was also the world's second biggest exporter. The European Union increased its dependence on imports for its fish supply.

For many less-developed countries the fish trade represented a significant source of earnings. The increase in net receipts of foreign exchange in those countries—deducting their imports from the total value of their exports—was impressive, rising from $5.1 billion in 1985 to $16 billion in 1994; a further increase to $18 billion was recorded in 1995.

During 1995 the Japanese government, with technical assistance from the FAO, convened the International Conference on the Sustainable Contribution of Fisheries to Food Security. The conference adopted the Kyoto Declaration and Plan of Action on the Sustainable Contribution of Fisheries to Food Security. The Kyoto Declaration was a comprehensive document that took into account previous decisions that had undermined sustainable resource use, which in turn constrained the fisheries sector's contribution to food security. Both the Kyoto Declaration and the Plan of Action were a major contribution to the 1996 FAO World Food Summit. (MARTIN GILL)

This article updates the *Macropædia* article Commercial FISHING.

Top 20 Species Landed, 1995
In order of tonnage

Species	Metric tons
Anchoveta	8,644,576
Chilean jack mackerel	4,955,186
Alaska pollock	4,687,718
Silver carp	2,556,981
Atlantic herring	2,235,781
Grass carp	2,107,932
Common carp	1,901,837
Skipjack tuna	1,559,650
Chub mackerel	1,556,888
South American pilchard	1,503,131
Yesso scallop	1,423,811
Atlantic cod	1,264,105
Bighead carp	1,259,340
Largehead hairtail	1,237,240
European pilchard (sardine)	1,207,128
Yellowfin tuna	1,052,192
Pacific cupped oyster	1,020,969
Japanese anchovy	972,008
Atlantic mackerel	789,733
Capelin	748,796

World Fisheries, 1995[1]

	Catch in metric tons		Trade in $000	
Country	Total	Inland	Imports	Exports
China	24,433,321	10,780,500	941,293	2,854,373
Peru	8,943,208	51,508	4,002	869,727
Chile	7,590,947	2,630	45,887	1,704,260
Japan	6,757,570	166,204	17,853,481	713,219
United States	5,634,419	311,406	7,141,428	3,383,589
India	4,903,659	2,204,109	7,055	1,240,603
Russia	4,373,827	272,954	346,172	1,628,204
Indonesia	4,118,000	821,390	101,104	1,666,752
Thailand	3,501,772	279,672	825,606	4,449,457
Norway	2,807,549	413	490,383	3,122,662
South Korea	2,688,024	30,011	824,817	1,564,878
Philippines	2,269,234	536,344	134,789	502,201
Denmark	2,041,133	35,669	1,573,732	2,459,629
North Korea	1,850,000	118,500	2,336	77,430
Iceland	1,616,033	1,599	40,306	1,342,552
Mexico	1,358,353	147,735	89,832	707,748
Spain	1,320,000	33,353	3,105,684	1,190,676
Taiwan	1,288,406	175,561	589,723	2,328,105
Malaysia	1,239,755	19,457	323,619	334,873
Vietnam	1,200,000	300,000	2,506	512,937
Bangladesh	1,170,365	906,475	199	220,229
Argentina	1,148,761	13,287	70,072	917,580
United Kingdom	1,003,740	18,763	1,910,091	1,195,477
Canada	901,225	43,020	1,034,070	2,314,413
Morocco	846,201	2,200	7,905	786,487
Myanmar (Burma)	832,469	225,998	0	79,743
Brazil	800,000	210,000	397,574	160,133
France	793,413	64,029	3,221,298	993,364
Turkey	652,193	61,089	50,857	14,196
New Zealand	612,243	1,334	57,537	813,912
World Total	**112,910,300**	**21,005,400**	**56,028,539**	**52,048,539**

[1]Excludes aquatic mammals, crocodiles and alligators, pearls, corals, sponges, and aquatic plants.
Source: United Nations Food and Agriculture Organization, *Yearbook of Fishery Statistics,* vol. 80 and 81.

FOOD PROCESSING

Consumption of fast foods and convenient meals increased considerably throughout the world in 1997. Americans and Japanese ate away from home most often. In Europe the chilled-foods sector rose more than 8% over 1996, the U.K. taking first place with a 42% share. Some 90% of Americans turned to low-fat and low-calorie foods on a regular basis. Dietary fibre was back in favour as a healthful food, but, as the term meant different things to different people, nutritionists called for a definition of it. Confusion existed on what constituted a healthful diet; research by the U.S. Department of Agriculture found that throughout the world the foods that people were advised to eat and those they actually ate were different. The fear of "mad cow" disease continued to stimulate demand for meats other than beef, especially in Europe, where more than 4% of the population had become vegetarians. Gaining in popularity in many parts of the world were exotic meats, such as kangaroo, emu, and crocodile.

Consumption of nonalcoholic beverages increased worldwide, most strongly in less-developed countries. Flower-flavoured beverages found favour in Asia, especially in China. Low-calorie beverages remained a popular trend in Japan. The market for iced tea grew fastest in Asia, taking 16% of the continent's soft-drink market; 80% of that market was in Japan, Indonesia, and Taiwan. In Europe iced tea was most popular in Switzerland and Austria and least so in the U.K. Bottled water took the highest share of the soft-drink market in Europe. Clear sparkling drinks were past their peak in the U.S. but increased in popularity in Europe. Sales of alcoholic fruit drinks, known as alcopops, soared. The main markets were in Australia and the U.K., where sales rose to $375 million, but there was also much activity throughout Europe. Public concern that such beverages encouraged underage drinking caused sales bans in some British supermarket chains and the withdrawal of some brands by manufacturers and the relabeling of others.

Food-borne disease increased to record levels throughout the world and remained a serious public health problem. Infected fruit juice in the U.S. hospitalized 60 people and shut down the California plant of the largest American juice processor, which had to recall juice nationwide. In the U.K. the death toll believed to result from beef infected by "mad cow" disease rose to 21, and in December the British government announced that beginning in 1998 it would ban the sale of beef on the bone.

Food adulteration became more prevalent. Some unscrupulous European suppliers sent large quantities of adulterated fruit juice to the U.S. market, and a fraud involving adulterated concentrated juices was uncovered in Germany. Honey, coffee, and cheese, yogurt, and other milk products were also involved.

Business Trends. Latin America was identified as a major area for expansion for international food companies. McCain Foods of Canada announced plans to invest $25 million in a plant in Buenos Aires, Arg., to produce frozen french fries. Pavan Mapimpianti of Italy teamed with Molinos Rio de la Plata to inaugurate a $14 million plant, also in Buenos Aires, to produce 100 million tons per year of pasta products.

Able to supply only 46% of its total food requirements, Japan remained the world's largest net food importer in 1997. The nation spent more than $60 billion on food imports, of which the U.S. accounted for 30%. Japan's food and drink spending, at more than $3,000 per person, was the highest in the world and was growing the fastest. In China demand grew for snacks, many from Japan. India's several large food companies predicted high growth rates.

The European chilled-foods market, worth more than $10 billion annually, grew by 8.6% in 1997. The U.K. had the largest share with 42%, followed by France with 21%. In Europe sales of own-label products, at more than $30 billion, grew at a rate higher than the general market growth; the U.K. led with a 40% share.

Beer sales in Europe continued their 1% annual growth. Germany remained the most important national beer market, with a consumption per head of about 140 litres (One litre=0.264 gal). The European market for herbal teas grew strongly, mint flavours becoming the most popular.

Company Developments. Quaker Oats Co. of the U.S. wrote off $1.4 billion after selling for $300 million the Snapple soft drinks company acquired for $1.7 billion in December 1994. H.J. Heinz Co. of the U.S. announced the biggest reorganization in its history, involving a $650 million restructuring charge, the loss of 2,500 jobs (a cut in its worldwide workforce of 43,000 by about 6%), and the closing of 25 factories in Europe, North America, and Asia. With the acquisition of Coca-Cola Bottlers Philippines Inc for about $2.5 billion, Coca-Cola Amatil Ltd., the Australian Coca-Cola franchisee, became the largest Coca-Cola bottling group outside the U.S.

The U.K.'s Trade and Industry Department blocked the acquisition of the nation's third largest brewer, Carlsberg-Tetley PLC, by the second largest, Bass PLC, because it would reduce competition. Both the European Commission and the U.S. Federal Trade Commission said they would investigate the proposed merger of the two British alcoholic beverage firms Grand Metropolitan PLC and Guinness PLC. The combined sales of the two companies would give them 40% of the Scotch whisky market in some countries.

Nestlé SA of Switzerland remained the top world food and drink company, with a sales total in 1996 of $39 billion. It was followed by Philip Morris Companies Inc. (U.S., $33 billion) and Unilever PLC (U.K./Neth., $27 billion).

New Products and Ingredients. Iceland Frozen Foods of the U.K. launched a range of flavoured vegetables for children that included chocolate-flavoured carrots and pizza-flavoured sweet corn. In Italy La Faraona introduced a low-fat ostrich meat, and in the U.K. the retail chain Tesco PLC launched its own brand of ostrich steaks and kangaroo products from Australia.

In the U.S. Kerry Ingredients developed KerryBits, flavoured pieces to add the flavour, texture, and appearance of real fruit to bakery products economically. Yoghurtesse of San Francisco introduced a fat replacer made from skim milk protein containing no fat or cholesterol and only one-tenth the calories of ordinary fat. Archer- Daniels-Midland Co. in the U.S. launched NutriBev, a vegetarian alternative to milk based on soya protein that could be made into a drink. New snack foods that were quickly prepared and easy to eat abounded. Bacon Pizza Bakes from Tulip International in the U.K. used breadcrumb-coated bacon instead of bread as a pizza base, and a similar product from Soviplus in France used a breaded poultry slice as a base.

Despite adverse publicity for alcopops, the British market for these beverages continued to grow. Fruit-flavoured tea drinks containing 4% alcohol appeared in Japan under the name Fantasy Time Cocktail. Whitbread & Co. Ltd. of the U.K. launched beers containing vodka and whiskey, which again caused concern among antialcohol groups.

Technology. Interest in electronic aroma-sensing instruments grew, and several became commercially available. They were used for such purposes as detecting rancidity in fats, distinguishing between blends of tea, predicting the shelf life of dairy products, detecting product adulteration, and checking food-grade packaging materials. GEC Alsthom of Nantes, France, unveiled the Hyperbar high-pressure processing machine for nonthermal sterilization of food. Two such machines were in operation in France.

The U.S. became the world leader in the processing of spices by irradiation. Steri-Genics of California extended its spice-irradiation activities to fresh fruit and vegetables. The number of countries that approved the use of irradiation for one or more food items reached 39, and 29 were using the technology.

Packaging. Edible protein-based water-soluble packaging films, which were made from carrageenan (a colloid extracted from red algae and used as a stabilizing or thickening agent) and became part of the food they wrapped, were being developed by Watson Foods Co. in the U.S. in partnership with Polymer Films and the British companies Cambridge Consultants and Enak. The Coca-Cola Co. introduced a 12-oz contoured can, in the shape of the original Coca-Cola bottle, in Terre Haute, Ind., birthplace of the original bottle in 1915, and in four southwestern U.S. markets.

Successful launches of Quaker Oats's and Kellogg Co.'s cereals in microwavable stand-up pouches, in the U.S. and Canada, respectively, marked the first packaging changes in 90 years in the breakfast cereal industry. Flexible packaging also was gaining in popularity for microwavable full meals, soups, snacks, cake mixes, and milk.

Government Action. European Union (EU) regulations effective as of May 1997 required special labeling for novel foods and ingredients and for those containing genetically modified organisms. EU regulations effective from March 1997 required companies that were involved in any packaging activity valued at more than $7.5 million a year (falling to $1.5 million in 2000) and handled more than 50 tons per year of packaging materials to recover and recycle specific tonnages of packaging waste. The new British government, elected in May, announced the establishment of an independent food standards agency, consisting of 10 food experts, to oversee food safety.

In the U.S. the government established new rules requiring seafood processors to take steps to prevent contamination of their products and also proposed new regulations for organic foods. The Clinton administration also proposed an increase in government spending for food inspection and safety research.

(ANTHONY WOOLLEN)

See also Business and Industry Review: *Beverages; Tobacco;* The Environment; Health and Disease.

This article updates the *Macropaedia* article FOOD PROCESSING.

Anthropology and Archaeology

ANTHROPOLOGY

Physical Anthropology. In 1997 science fiction became science fact when ancient DNA, believed to be between 30,000 and 100,000 years old, was extracted from a Neanderthal specimen originally discovered in 1856 in the Feldhofer Cave of the Neander Valley near Düsseldorf, Ger. In a technically brilliant tour de force, Matthias Krings, working in Svante Pääbo's laboratory at the University of Munich, Ger., succeeded in piecing together a nucleotide sequence for 379 base pairs of maternally inherited mitochondrial DNA preserved in a 3.5-g (0.11-oz) section of the specimen's right humerus. What made this claim so convincing was that the results were meticulously replicated by Anne Stone, working in Mark Stoneking's laboratory at Pennsylvania State University. When the Neanderthal DNA sequence was compared with the corresponding region in modern humans and chimpanzees, the overall Neanderthal-human difference was approximately three times greater than the average difference among modern humans but only about half as large as the human-chimpanzee difference. Because the Neanderthal sequence was so unlike any modern human sequence, many experts thought it highly unlikely that Neanderthals contributed to the human mitochondrial DNA pool. These data strengthened the case for the separate-species status of the Neanderthals initially advocated by William King in 1864, whereby the taxonomic designation *Homo neanderthalensis* is preferred to membership in *H. sapiens.* It should be noted, however, that no biparental nuclear DNA was recovered from the Neanderthal humerus, and, thus, at present there is no way to refute the hypothesis that some Neanderthal genes still exist in the human nuclear gene pool or the conjecture that genetic differences between human and Neanderthal nuclear DNA are not as large as those exhibited by the faster-evolving mitochondrial DNA molecule.

Fossil remains recovered from the cave site of Gran Dolina, Sierra de Atapuerca, Spain, were placed in the new species, *H. antecessor,* by a team of Spanish investigators from Madrid and Tarragona. The nearly 80 bones and teeth belonged to a minimum of six individuals who lived more than 780,000 years ago. The specimens exhibited a unique combination of cranial, mandibular, and dental traits along with a fully modern midfacial morphology. The researchers suggested that *H. antecessor* may represent the last common ancestor of both Neanderthals and modern humans and tentatively proposed an evolutionary link to the earlier Early Pleistocene species, *H. ergaster.*

The topic of early human migrations received great attention during the year. Multiple out-of-Africa expansion events were championed by both paleoanthroplogists and human geneticists. These dispersals involved numerous extinct species of the genus *Homo* as well as modern humans. In South Africa human footprints dated to 117,000 years ago were discovered in a sand dune, the oldest such imprints attributable to *H. sapiens.* Analyses of the B-globin gene and human Y chromosomes led two different research teams to propose that some of the genetic variants they studied actually arose in Asia and were carried back to Africa. The implications of these discoveries were that some of the substantial genetic diversity found in today's African populations had non-African roots and that migrations between Africa and the rest of the Old World may have been bidirectional for a much longer time than experts had previously thought. A new set of controversial dates also led to the extension of the temporal span of *H. erectus* in Southeast Asia to as recently as 27,000 to 53,000 years ago, which thereby implied the coexistence of these specimens from Ngandong and Sambungmacan in Java, Indonesia, with modern humans who had already reached Australia approximately 50,000 to 60,000 years ago. The discovery called into question the theory that *H. erectus* was among the ancestors of modern Australians and lent additional support to those favouring the out-of-Africa explanation.

New mitochondrial genetic data reported by Brazilian investigators reinforced a recent interpretation of previous mitochondrial DNA data sets concerning the number and timing of early migrations to the Americas. Specifically, these maternal-specific data supported the hypothesis that Native Americans, as well as the Chukchi of northeastern Siberia, originated from a single migration across the Bering Sea land bridge, probably from east-central Asia, at least 30,000 years ago. This interpretation was at variance with the three-migration hypothesis for the peopling of the New World, which was based on linguistic, dental, and nuclear genetic data, as well as with recently proposed two- and four-migration scenarios. This chronological framework also conflicted with the opinion of the majority of American archaeologists, who viewed with great skepticism any hypothesized date for the initial colonization of the Americas older than about 13,000 years ago.

A milestone event in the ongoing debate about the peopling of the Americas was the announcement of a consensus that the Monte Verde site in Chile was both authentic and at least 12,500 years old and thus the oldest authenticated human occupation in the New World. Discovery of evidence of human occupation from the continental shelf edge of British Columbia dated to more than 10,000 years ago led to the suggestion that the exposed shelf edge may have served as a coastal migration route to the Americas during times of lowered sea levels between 13,500 and 9,500 years ago.

The finds from the Gona River region of Ethiopia pushed the dates for the earliest known stone-tool manufacturing back to between 2.5 million and 2.6 million years ago. Although it was not known which hominid group was responsible for the several thousand tools at Gona, two principal candidates were put forward: members of the genus

University of Munich, Ger., researcher Matthias Krings poses with part of the skull from a Neanderthal skeleton discovered in 1856 near Düsseldorf, Ger. Analysis of data from DNA extracted from the bones suggested that Neanderthals did not contribute to the modern human gene pool.

PETER BLICK—ASSOCIATED PRESS

Scientists make a cast of fossilized footprints discovered in 117,000-year-old sandstone on the shore of a lagoon about 97 km (60 mi) north of Cape Town, S.Af. The footprints are among the oldest known fossilized traces of anatomically modern humans.
KENNETH GARRETT—NATIONAL GEOGRAPHIC

Homo and of the robust australopithecine genus, *Paranthropus.* The tools were so similar to the later Early Pleistocene Oldowan tools that they were placed in the Oldowan industry, which thereby extended the temporal range of that industrial complex to include a variety of Plio-Pleistocene assemblages dated between 1.5 million and 2.6 million years ago.

(STEPHEN L. ZEGURA)

Cultural Anthropology. Cultural anthropologists continued to reexamine and reevaluate the goals, roles, and objects of their discipline in 1997. Many ethnologists questioned whether their field was most properly a humanistic project that critically interpreted culture or a scientific enterprise devoted to the discovery of the basic laws governing human behaviour. Others debated whether dwindling public and private research resources were most effectively expended upon basic theoretical scholarship or in applied research programs that directly addressed practical issues and problems. Many investigators reflected on whether other cultures or their own were the most appropriate objects of study. All pondered the theoretical, methodological, and physical limitations that influence what anthropologists can and cannot learn about the human condition.

These concerns were mirrored in the 340 articles published in the four-volume *Encyclopedia of Cultural Anthropology* (1996), edited by David Levinson and Melvin Ember, anthropologists associated with Human Relations Area Files at Yale University. The first comprehensive survey of the discipline, the encyclopedia contained articles addressing economic anthropology, initiation rites, oral tradition, and other traditional anthropological concerns. Other article topics, such as altruism, colonialism, feminist anthropology, and Postmodernism, reflected more recent developments and interests.

Long accustomed to carrying on scholarly discourse in the printed pages of academic publications, growing numbers of ethnologists in 1997 were communicating with one another via World Wide Web pages, Internet chat rooms, and other electronic media. Because of the strongly conflicting views expressed in many of these exchanges, cultural anthropology appeared to be a discipline in disarray. Dismayed by the occasional sharp tones punctuating their disputations, most anthropologists nevertheless regarded energetic debate as the mark of a discipline in creative ferment. This view was not fully accepted beyond disciplinary boundaries, and as contacts with colleagues in disciplines that traditionally shared ideas and information with anthropology diminished, anthropologists were alarmed by decreasing public interest in their research. Aware that the health of the discipline depended upon closer communication with the widest-possible audience, past American Anthropological Association president James L. Peacock challenged anthropologists to increase efforts to reach out to associates in other fields and to the general public.

Whatever their differences, most ethnologists agreed that cultural anthropology continued to possess the ability to make unique contributions to human understanding. Although colleagues in history, literature, women's studies, and other fields employed such anthropological concepts as culture, holism, and participant observation, none had yet adopted the broad comparative, observation-based perspective necessary to fully understand cultural similarities and diversities. People coping with the stresses of an increasingly diverse multicultural world needed this perspective more and more.

It was also difficult in 1997 to find ethnologists who regarded themselves as detached neutral observers or their subjects as pristine objects unaffected by time, space, or sociopolitical context. In contrast to widespread public perceptions of anthropologists as field workers among exotic tribal peoples, most ethnographers worked with people in complex modern societies. For example, in *Golden Arches East,* a collection of articles edited by Harvard University anthropologist James L. Watson, field ethnographers examined the ways in which people in several East Asian countries creatively utilized McDonald's American-style fast-food restaurants as important family and community centres and meeting places. Half a world away, the results of a 15-year study among poor Hispanic residents on New York City's Lower East Side, coordinated by City College of New York ethnographer Jagna Wojcicka Sharff, were reported in *King*

Kong on 4th Street. Assessing the impacts of large-scale socioeconomic processes on families, especially children, Sharff and her colleagues found that in the group studied, violence and other behaviour that the wider society regarded as deviant represented "survival strategies in a situation of great economic distress."

Although many ethnologists focused attention upon problems facing people in developed nations, others continued working with indigenous people who were coping with the expansion of modern civilization onto their lands. Findings of ethnographers who had been working with such people to affirm the precision and exactitude of native traditions played an important role in the December 11 Canadian Supreme Court decision recognizing oral histories as valid evidence in native land and resource claims. By raising public awareness of those problems and coordinating projects that directly benefited native communities, other anthropologists working with international support groups such as the Cambridge, Mass.-based Cultural Survival assisted indigenous people and ethnic minorities who were struggling to preserve their traditional ways of life.

Field workers involved in issues affecting the lives of those they studied struggled to balance advocacy with a level of detachment essential to both establish scholarly credibility and maintain the comparative perspective necessary to place their data within the broadest possible context. Anthropologists in 1997 increasingly recognized the need to expand the scope of their studies from small, marginal, or disenfranchised groups to broader groups encompassing entire cultures and societies. The ethical dilemmas and methodological innovations accompanying such a shift promised to challenge ethnologists well into the coming millennium.

(ROBERT S. GRUMET)

ARCHAEOLOGY

Eastern Hemisphere. In 1997 stone tools from Ethiopia's Gona River were dated to between 2,600,000 and 2,520,000 years ago, which made them the oldest in the world by at least 120,000 years. Three wooden spears from Schöningen, Ger., were dated to between 400,000 and 380,000 years ago. According to a report in *Archaeology,* "the spears show design and construction skills previously attributed only to modern humans"; at the time, archaic *Homo sapiens* inhabited Europe. Flints and grooved wooden tools, which probably served as handles, found at the site may be remains of the oldest composite tools in the world.

Chlorine-36 dating revealed that the spectacular petroglyphs in Portugal's Côa Valley, brought to public attention in 1994, were at least 16,000 years old. The new results settled a debate between scholars who dated the artworks to the Upper Paleolithic (35,000 to 10,000 years ago) on the basis of their style and others who argued that stylistic dating was unreliable and that the petroglyphs were no older than 3,000 years.

Diring Yuriakh, a site with stone tools in central Siberia, was thermoluminescence-dated to between 370,000 and 260,000 years ago, long before the date of 30,000 years ago that had been generally accepted for the settlement of the area. Some experts, however, questioned whether the tools were actually man-made, while others sought confirmation of the dates by the use of another method.

In Oceania stone tools from the Indonesian island of Flores were dated to just after 730,000 years ago, which suggested that *H. erectus* could cross open sea; the controversial claim awaited verification. Optical-luminescense dates from several sites suggested that Australia had been colonized by 60,000 years ago, instead of the usual 40,000 to 30,000.

A 13,000-year-old burial from San Teodoro Cave in Sicily yielded the first evidence of Paleolithic archery—a fragment of flint, probably part of an arrowhead, embedded in a human pelvis. A 7,000-year-old skull found at Ensisheim, France, provided the earliest unequivocal evidence of trepanning, a surgical procedure, in which a small disk or square of bone is removed from the cranium.

As the British Museum reopened its "Celtic Europe" halls, scholars argued over the widely accepted link between the Keltoi described by classical authors and the predominant style of late Iron Age European art, La Tène (*c.* 450–55 BC). Some pointed out that ancient descriptions, confusing and often contradictory, did not attest the existence of a coherent pan-European Celtic ethnic group that could be identified with La Tène. Furthermore, La Tène itself displayed substantial regional variations, and there was no La Tène in Spain, where there were known to have been Celts. Defenders of the Celtic ethnicity of people across Iron Age Europe noted the overarching similarity of cultures across the continent. The argument highlighted the caution necessary to avoid what John Collis of the University of Sheffield, Eng., called "simplistic correlations between material culture and ethnic groups."

COURTESY NATURE

A 400,000-year-old wooden spear was one of three discovered by archaeologist Hartmut Thieme in 1994 near Hannover, Ger. Thieme's study of these oldest complete hunting weapons ever found appeared in 1997.

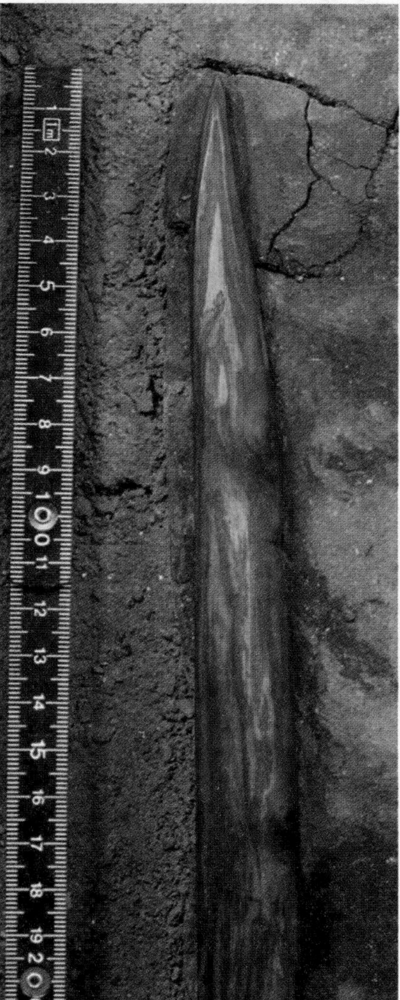

Excavations at Pompeii questioned much of the site's traditional chronology, in which each historical period was thought to have a distinctive type of masonry, suggesting that many structures there and elsewhere in Italy would have to be redated. The finding also emphasized the importance of dating buildings by materials found in construction layers rather than by wall fabric, which often varied according to structural or financial considerations.

An Israeli archaeologist argued that skeletons found at Masada in the 1960s were those of Roman soldiers, not Jewish patriots who fought the Romans in AD 70. Bones of pigs, which the zealots would have regarded as unclean but which Romans sacrificed at burials, were found with the skeletons. The authorship of the Dead Sea Scrolls was also debated. Arguments against their usual ascription to the Essenes, a Jewish sect living at Qumran, were based on differences of doctrine and lifestyle between the texts on the scrolls and descriptions of the sect by classical authors.

In China discoveries from more than 100 sites along the Chang Jiang (Yangtze River) showed that rice cultivation began 11,500 years ago rather than 8,000. Archaeologists also identified a site in Hebei province, long under excavation, as Zhongdu, one of three capitals of the Yuan dynasty (1260–1368). In Japan the Imperial Household Agency for the first time permitted archaeologists to map two imperial tombs of the 5th century AD, but it continued to prohibit the excavation of such mounds.

Preservation of archaeological sites threatened by construction projects continued to a be a problem. China's Three Gorges Dam moved forward, even though its completion would spell doom for many important sites along the Chang Jiang. (*See* ARCHITECTURE AND CIVIL ENGINEERING: *Sidebar.*) The fate of possibly the largest Roman villa in Great Britain, found during the summer near Swindon, remained uncertain, as the local council and the developer who owned the land debated its future.

At Pompeii the superintendent, Pietro Giovanni Guzzo, opposed the renewal of contracts for large excavations like that at the Villa of the Papyri in Herculaneum, arguing that the money would be better spent on restoration and maintenance of decaying buildings already unearthed. The Italian Parliament approved a measure granting Pompeii administrative and fiscal autonomy, which would allow the underfunded superintendency to keep all of its ticket revenues (most of which had been turned over to the Ministry of Culture), thereby tripling its annual budget.

Looting of archaeological sites was also a problem. Additional artifacts from Iraqi

PATRICK E. TYLER—THE NEW YORK TIMES

During construction of China's Three Gorges Dam and subsequent flooding of the Chang Jiang (Yangtze River) valley, many archaeological and historic sites would be destroyed. A man standing at the Stone Precious Stockade temple complex, built during the time of the Ming Dynasty, points to the eventual water level.

sites, including Nineveh, Khorsabad, and Nimrud, appeared on the world market. The museum at Butrint, Alb., was reported to have been looted, and further excavation at that major Roman site was postponed.

Working partly from documents furnished by an insider, British journalist Peter Watson wrote a book pillorying the auction firm Sotheby's for participating knowingly in smuggling and selling looted and stolen works of art. Among the antiquities cited were a goat-headed goddess from a shrine at Lokhari, India, which had been photographed in place before 1986, and an Apulian vase that had been described in an Italian magazine as having been looted. In response, Sotheby's closed its London antiquities and Indian and Islamic art departments and moved all regular sales of such material to New York City, where tighter U.S. laws would limit what it could sell.

In January Swiss and Italian authorities announced the largest seizure ever of looted antiquities—$40 million worth of Roman and Etruscan artifacts discovered in four warehouses in Geneva. Thirteen sculptures stolen from Angkor Wat and found in 1990 in a Bangkok gallery were returned to Cambodia in September 1996, the first time that Thailand, much criticized for its complicity in the illegal antiquities trade, had returned stolen works of art.

The U.S. Customs Service returned several stolen medieval manuscript pages to Spain under a provision of the U.S. Archaeological Resources Protection Act of 1979 that prohibits interstate or international trafficking in antiquities. It was the first time that the act had been invoked in a case involving artifacts of foreign origin.

(ANDREW SLAYMAN)

Western Hemisphere. For more than a century, archaeologists have argued over the date of the first human settlement of the Americas. Most scholars now believe Native Americans arrived from Siberia across the Bering Strait about 15,000 years ago. Recently, new accelerator mass spectrometer (AMS) radiocarbon dates obtained by University of Kentucky professor of anthropology Tom Dillehay from the Monte Verde site in Chile's Llanquihue province shed new light on early settlement in the extreme south of the Americas. Monte Verde is an open-air wetland residential site with bone and wooden artifacts, hut foundations, and ecological data preserved under a peat layer. Dillehay identified hearths, braziers, refuse pits, and footprints. Wooden artifacts included basins, bow drills for making fires, and, possibly, tool handles. Twelve wood-framed houses mantled with hides form rows of dwellings, perhaps a tentlike residential complex. Dillehay compared them to dwellings used by the Tehuelche Indians of southern Argentina, which comprised hides smeared with grease and red ocher drawn over wooden poles. AMS samples from the main occupation layer yielded dates between 10,300 and 10,800 BC, some of the earliest-known dates for human settlement in the Americas.

Far to the north, in Alaska, new archaeological finds were being used to date early settlements on the eastern side of the Bering Strait. East of Kotzebue, Smithsonian Institution paleoanthropologist Dennis Stanford studied undated stone projectile points found near a glacial lake at the Sluiceway site. He believed the style of the points indicated that they were more than 10,500 years old. On-Your-Knees Cave on Prince of Wales Island in the middle of Alaska's Tongass National Forest yielded human bone fragments radiocarbon-dated to about 7800 BC, some of the earliest ever found in North America. Stable isotope analysis of the remains (a comparison of chemical isotopes of food absorbed by bone) revealed a predominantly marine diet. Farther south, in Washington state, archaeologist James Chatters dug a complete human skeleton of a man between 45 and 50 years old, radiocarbon-dated to about 7300 BC, from the banks of the Columbia River near Kennewick. Fierce controversy surrounded this find, a male with an elongated skull more characteristic of Caucasians than Native Americans. Research stalled while the U.S. Army Corps of Engineers and the local Umatilla Indians worked to settle the ownership of the skeleton.

Some of the earliest human-worked wood came from the newly excavated Page-Ladson site on Florida's Aucilla River. The earliest occupation there dated to about 8000 BC, when that part of Florida, now only 8 km (5 mi) from Tallahassee, was more than 160 km (100 mi) from the ocean and situated in open savanna. Within a century, rising sea levels at the end of the Ice Age flooded the site and sealed the occupation layers. The Page-Ladson people used stone projectile points and gouges made of local stone, worked with antler flakers found at the site. They also made spherical stones that were attached to leather cords and used to bring small animals to the ground. Three wooden stakes driven into the ground and a burned and slightly hollowed-out log were the earliest-known wooden objects found in the Americas. On the other side of the continent, a sandal fragment from a cave on southern California's Channel Islands was dated to approximately 7000 BC, the earliest such find on the Pacific coast.

AMS radiocarbon-dating was revolutionizing archaeologists' knowledge of early Native American agriculture. AMS dating, which counts actual carbon-14 atoms, uses tiny organic samples such as individual seeds, which thereby removed such potential

An archaeological team conducts research at the Monte Verde excavation site in Llanquihue province, Chile. Traces of human habitation unearthed at the site, including the remains of huts, fireplaces, and tools, were widely accepted as being 12,500 years old.

KENNETH GARRETT—NATIONAL GEOGRAPHIC

sources of dating error as specimens' being trampled from one level into a lower one. On the basis of this method, Austin Long of the University of Arizona redated early diminutive corncobs from Mexico's Tehuacán Valley—once estimated at 5000 BC—to no older than about 3500 BC. Experts now believed that corn (maize) was first domesticated from wild teosinte grass in southwestern Mexico perhaps as early as 4000 to 3500 BC. Such plant cultivation was not, however, a novelty. For example, Smithsonian Institution archaeologist Bruce Smith recently dated squash seeds from Guilá Naquitz cave in Mexico's Valley of Oaxaca to at least 8000 BC, which showed that some form of simple agriculture was practiced in Central America at the same time food production and village life began in southwestern Asia. Whereas Chinese and southwestern Asian villagers shifted rapidly to diversified agricultural economies, it was generally believed that Native Americans continued to forage rather than plant for several thousand more years; future discoveries and AMS dates could change this scenario dramatically. The new dates for corn domestication, for example, shortened the gestation period for the development of corn agriculture in Mayan and other Native American civilizations by at least 1,500 years.

Many long-known sites were being reinterpreted as a result of modern archaeological technology. The Serpent Mound, a spectacular earthwork depicting a serpent with gaping jaws devouring a burial mound (one of various interpretations), twists along a low ridge in south-central Ohio. The earthwork was originally dated by Frederick Putnam of Harvard University's Peabody Museum to the Adena culture (800 BC–AD 100), but readings taken from wood obtained by core borings put the date at about AD 1070. Consequently, archaeologists Bradley Lepper and Dee Anne Wymer assigned the earthwork to the Fort Ancient culture (900 to 1600), a much later Mississippian group.

Art historian Mary Miller of Yale University used infrared photography to produce computer reconstructions of the faded images on Mexico's Bonampak murals, painted by Mayan artists in the late 8th century. Her research team scanned colour photographs of the images into a computer and then added details based on infrared photographs and study of the murals at the site. The new approach allowed Miller and her colleagues to record previously invisible inscriptions, to distinguish one group of Mayan nobles from another by their regalia and insignia, and to read their titles, such as regional governor or dancers. They then began "stitching" together the digitized images into seamless webs of paintings in order to create a digital restoration of the Mayan Lord Chaan Muan's life and deeds, including scenes of battle and human sacrifice that occurred during his reign, AD 776–795.

The first James Fort, built in 1607 on what is now Jamestown Island, Virginia, was long assumed to have eroded into the nearby James River. During the past few years archaeologist William Kelso delved into contemporary accounts of the settlement and searched for telltale postholes and palisades in the sandy soil. His sophisticated excavations recovered traces of the fortifications and interior buildings and also more than 90,000 artifacts, including 12 coins, none earlier than 1603. Kelso recovered many ceramic fragments, a full breastplate and helmet made before 1610, bullet molds, and cast-iron shot. A skeleton of a male colonist in his 20s found on site revealed bullet wounds to a leg and shoulder. Signs of glassmaking suggested that a special building to fabricate beads to trade with Chief Powhatan lay outside the palisade. This trade was vital, for the Indians supplied corn for the fledgling settlement. Satellite photographs confirmed the position of the fort, which was recorded on an early 17th-century Dutch chart of the James River that was discovered in 1995 in the Dutch National Archives.

(BRIAN FAGAN)

This article updates the *Macropædia* articles Human EVOLUTION; THE STUDY OF HISTORY: *Archaeology*; THE SOCIAL SCIENCES: *Cultural Anthropology*.

CARL C. HANSEN—NATIONAL MUSEUM OF NATURAL HISTORY, SMITHSONIAN INSTITUTION

Archaeologist Bruce Smith of the Smithsonian Institution, Washington, D.C., used an improved radiocarbon-dating technique to confirm that this squash seed, excavated from a cave in Oaxaca, Mex., in 1966, was at least 8,000 years old.

PHOTOS, (LEFT) TIMOTHY HURSLEY, (RIGHT) RICHARD BRYANT—ARCAID

Kohn Pedersen Fox designed the new federal courthouse (left) in Portland, Ore., one example of efforts by the U.S. government to improve the architecture of public buildings. Frank Gehry turned heads with an office building (right) in Prague, nicknamed "Fred and Ginger" for its resemblance to a dancing couple.

Architecture and Civil Engineering

ARCHITECTURE

With many national economies booming, the year 1997 was a good one for architecture in much of the world. It was also a year of increasing internationalism. Several of the most prominent American firms were doing as much as half their work overseas. At the same time, when the Museum of Modern Art in New York City chose 10 finalists to compete for the job of expanding its facilities, 6 of the firms were either European or East Asian. The biggest news, however, was the formal opening of two long-anticipated art museums, one in Los Angeles and the other in Bilbao, Spain. Each was designed by one of the world's most prominent architects, both winners of the Pritzker Prize. The two buildings seemed to define a watershed between an older and a newer kind of architecture.

The first of the two to be completed, a branch of New York City's Guggenheim Museum, opened in October in Bilbao. The architect, Frank O. Gehry of the U.S., created an amazing swirling pile of angled and curving free forms with an exterior surface of shining titanium. It was a building that could have been designed or built only with the aid of a computer. Gehry, in fact, had been a pioneer in adapting computer programs from the world of aircraft design. (See *Buildings,* below). To many observers his museum seemed to be a masterpiece that might inaugurate a new era in architecture. The museum, the cost of which was paid by the people of Bilbao and its province, was also interesting as a demonstration of the way in which a star architect and attention-getting building could put a relatively little-known city on the world's cultural map.

Only two months later, in December, the even larger Getty Center opened in Los Angeles. Bringing together, on a single dramatic site, most of the art-related activities funded by the bequest of wealthy oilman J. Paul Getty, it was undoubtedly the most discussed and anticipated building of its time. With a $1 billion construction budget, it was often called the architectural commission of the century. The architect was Richard Meier, also an American, who had long been known for houses in an elegant, austere Modernist style and for museums in Barcelona, Spain; Frankfurt, Ger.; and Atlanta, Ga. In some ways Meier's museum seemed as much a culmination of traditional modernism as Gehry's seemed a new departure. Its crisply cut white shapes reminded observers of the early modern architecture of the French pioneer Le Corbusier. Dispersed among gardens, courtyards, and water features, the Getty buildings also reminded one of a much older model, the villa built by the Roman Emperor Hadrian outside Rome.

Awards. The Pritzker Prize, often called the architectural equivalent of a Nobel, was won in 1997 by Sverre Fehn of Norway (*see* BIOGRAPHIES), something of a dark horse who was not widely known internationally. Most of his major works were in Scandinavia, including the Glacier Museum in Norway and an extension of the National Theatre in Copenhagen. The Pritzker jury commended Fehn for successfully combining modern architectural form with elements of his Norwegian heritage. Fehn was awarded the prize at a ceremony in May at the site of the Guggenheim in Bilbao.

Tadao Ando of Japan received the Gold Medal of the Royal Institute of British Architects. Best known for his exquisite handling of natural light in chapels in Japan—built, usually, entirely out of smooth concrete—Ando was also named winner of a competition for the design of a new museum of modern art in Fort Worth, Texas, his first U.S. commission. This museum was to be built directly across the street from Louis Kahn's Kimbell Art Museum, one of the most celebrated of 20th-century buildings.

The Gold Medal of the American Institute of Architects was not awarded in 1997. The AIA, however, named 13 U.S. buildings as winners of its annual Honor Awards for architecture. Among the most prominent were a renovation of historic Memorial Hall at Harvard University by Venturi, Scott Brown, with Bruner/Cott and Robert Neiley; the Bass Center for Molecular and Structural Biology at Yale University by Kallmann McKinnell & Wood; and the Neurosciences Institute in San Diego, Calif., by Tod Williams and Billie Tsien. The National Library of France in Paris, by Dominique Perrault, won the Mies van der Rohe award for European buildings "of conceptual and technical merit." The extensive use of glass in the building had outraged bibliophiles because exposure to sunlight makes the preservation of materials problematic.

Civic Buildings. Memorials of various kinds were in the news in the U.S. The Franklin Delano Roosevelt Memorial opened to the public on a site fronting the Potomac River Basin in Washington, D.C.

Designed by landscape architect Lawrence Halprin, it comprised a series of outdoor pools and courtyards with walls of dark basalt stone, on which were engraved quotations and images drawn from the president's four terms in office. As a result of pressure from various interest groups, it was decided not to show Roosevelt with his signature cigarette holder or his wife, Eleanor, in a fur boa. Congress also mandated that the designer add some reference to the fact that the president used a wheelchair.

Opening to general acclaim was the Women in Military Service to America Memorial at the foot of Arlington (Va.) National Cemetery. Designers Marian Weiss and Michael Manfredi carved out new space behind the 1939 semicircular landscape wall by McKim Mead & White, which was also restored as part of the project. The controversial World War II Memorial, planned for a site on the Mall near the Washington Monument, was being revised by Friedrich St. Florian after criticism that his winning design, for a large paved plaza and water feature, might be so intrusive as to interfere with views from the Lincoln Memorial to the Washington Monument.

Also new in Washington was the long-awaited passenger terminal at National Airport by Cesar Pelli. The main concourse was a huge ceremonial space, with a vaulted roof and tall windows overlooking the Potomac River. Washington's other airport, Dulles International, designed by the late Eero Saarinen and regarded as an architectural masterpiece, was doubled in size by architects Skidmore, Owings & Merrill in a manner that seemed only to enhance its power. In Portland, Ore., a new federal courthouse by Kohn Pedersen Fox was an outstanding example of recent efforts by the U.S. government to improve the architecture of public buildings. In Madison, Wis., the Monona Terrace Community and Convention Center, based on a design made more than 50 years earlier by architect Frank Lloyd Wright, opened on a lakefront site in July.

Japan's $1.5 billion Tokyo International Forum, designed by Rafael Viñoly, opened in January. Acclaimed for its elegance and creative use of large space, the forum featured a complex of convention halls and theatres. Viñoly's design was chosen in 1989 from among 395 entries in Japan's first international architectural competition.
TIMOTHY HURSLEY

Cultural Buildings. At the year's end it appeared that the long-stalled Disney Concert Hall in Los Angeles by Gehry would be built. In September it was announced that 83% of its $220 million cost was in hand and that the hall was expected to be completed early in 2001.

In January the Museum of Modern Art in New York City announced that 10 architects had been chosen to make competing proposals for the museum's expansion. The museum avoided many famous names in search of a younger architect. In the spring the 10 proposals went on exhibit in the museum, and in December it was announced that Yoshio Taniguchi of Japan was the winner. Another of the 10 competitors, Stephen Holl of New York City, meanwhile won considerable praise for his Chapel of St. Ignatius at Seattle (Wash.) University.

In Singapore a vast 30-ha (75-ac) technical college, Temasek Polytechnic, was the last building by the late British architect James Stirling, designed with his partner Michael Wilford. In Santa Fe, N.M., a museum for the work of painter Georgia O'Keeffe opened in a former adobe church, renovated and expanded by New York architect Richard Gluckman.

Commercial Buildings. Gehry garnered attention with an office building in Prague known as "Fred and Ginger," named for the dancing pair of Fred Astaire and Ginger Rogers. Its two towers seemed to be locked in a ballroom dance. The RWE AG Hochhaus in Essen, Ger., was seen as the first of a new generation of energy-saving, environmentally responsible office towers, reflecting the great interest in such "green" architecture in Europe. The 30-story tower was cylindrical with small floor areas that allowed maximum daylight for all offices. Exterior walls sandwiched aluminum blinds between two layers of glass. The Commerzbank building in Frankfurt by Norman Foster of Britain was another "green" tower completed in 1997. (See *Buildings*, below).

In Culver City, Calif., architect Eric Moss added two buildings to what had become virtually a town of some 20 commercial structures he had done in a highly personal style. The buildings often looked more like elaborate sculptures than conventional architecture.

Exhibitions. The Metropolitan Museum of Art in New York City staged the largest exhibit ever held of the work of the Scottish designer Charles Rennie Mackintosh. Originating in Glasgow, Scot., the exhibit later traveled to Chicago and Los Angeles. It focused on 250 items, including furniture, watercolours, posters, and other objects by the noted architect, one of the founders of the Art Nouveau style at the turn of the century. At the Canadian Center for Architecture in Montreal, American pop-culture scholar Karal Ann Marling curated an exhibit on the work of the theme-park architecture of the Disney Co. entitled "The Architecture of Reassurance." Mounted at the Vitra Design Museum in Weil am Rhein, Ger., was a major exhibit of the work of American designers Charles and Ray Eames, creators of the "Eames chair" and many other classics of graphic and industrial design.

News Events. Aldo Rossi, one of the most influential architects of his generation, died in Italy in September. Winner of the 1990 Pritzker Prize, Rossi was known for his belief that one purpose of architecture is to embody the memory of a people and a culture and to provide a setting for ritual and everyday drama. His own buildings often seemed to possess a dreamlike familiarity. (*See* OBITUARIES.) Paul Rudolph died in August in New York City of cancer that was thought to date back to his days of working with asbestos in a naval shipyard during World War II. He was best known for a series of monumentally rugged concrete buildings of the 1960s, including the Art and Architecture Building at Yale University. (*See* OBITUARIES.) William Turnbull, much admired as a practitioner of a woody, landscape-sensitive, modest architecture and a collaborator, with Charles Moore and others, on the landmark Sea Ranch condominiums of 1966, died in June.

A political controversy erupted in California over a referendum proposal to award state architectural contracts on the basis purely of low cost rather than quality of the architectural design. It was strongly opposed by architects. Near Chicago the legendary Farnsworth House (1946–50), designed by the architect Ludwig Mies van der Rohe and regarded as one of the great private houses of the Modern movement, was opened for public tours for the first time.

Urban Design. With the runaway commercial success of the Disney new town of Celebration in Florida, the movement known as the New Urbanism continued to gain in strength and popularity. New Urbanists believed in traditional tightly knit, walkable towns rather than the more sprawling, car-oriented suburban developments of recent decades. As the year ended, many New Urbanist communities, sometimes called "neotraditional," were on the drawing boards. Among the largest was Cornell near Toronto, designed to contain 10,000 homes plus a shopping main street and office space. Designed by the Miami, Fla., team of Andres Duany and Elizabeth Plater-Zyberk (*see* BIOGRAPHIES), leaders of the New Urbanism movement, Cornell began selling its first 700 houses in June. The town plan was described by Duany as his firm's "absolutely flawless, best, flagship project." Supported by the U.S. Department of Housing and Urban Development, New Urbanist principles were also beginning to be applied to the renovation of older housing projects in and near the centres of American cities.

Another trend worldwide was the growth of "entertainment retail," in which firms such as Nike, Disney, and Time Warner created stores that were as much theme parks as sales outlets. Their purpose was to advertise their products in key locations.

Controversy surrounded major public spaces in three U.S. cities in 1997. In San Francisco a competition was held in August for the redesign of neglected Union Square, a plaza above an underground garage at the heart of downtown. The winning entry, which the designers described as "one plane that wraps itself over the garage like a piece of origami," was thought too avant-garde by some, and its future was uncertain. In Philadelphia the long-running controversy over Independence Mall, where 500 historic buildings were demolished in the 1960s to create a little-used park, continued. The new proposal, by the National Park Service with landscape architect Laurie Olin, would shrink the park by adding new buildings, including a new shelter for the Liberty Bell. In Boston proposals to shrink and enliven another barren civic space, City Hall Plaza, by adding a new hotel along one edge ran into opposition from the U.S. government on the grounds that the hotel would obstruct views of government workers in a federal building.

RICHARD BRYANT—ARCAID

Temasek Polytechnic, a vast technical college in Singapore, was the last building designed by the renowned late British architect James Stirling and his partner Michael Wilford.

More successful was the ongoing revival of Times Square in New York City, where several deteriorating theatres were restored, two of them into a new Ford Center for the Performing Arts. Plans were also announced for a 16-screen movie theatre complex and for a design by Gehry to wrap the former Times Tower in a "striptease" fabric of see-through mesh and a jazzy new 47-story hotel complex by the Miami design firm Arquitectonica.

(ROBERT CAMPBELL)

See also Business and Industry Review: *Building and Construction.*

This article updates the *Macropædia* article The History of Western ARCHITECTURE.

BRIDGES

Repairs, renovations, and rehabilitations gained prominence in 1997 as bridges throughout the world revealed the need to be strengthened for 21st-century traffic loads and to be upgraded to meet new earthquake-resistant design standards. In regard to the latter, five crossings of the bay area around San Francisco required major upgrades. Some work was under way on the approaches to the Golden Gate Bridge, though funding was still required for the main towers, the main span, and the Fort Point arch. Design and initial construction upgrading work was also under way on the Richmond–San Rafael Bridge, which needed huge new foundations and strengthened steel work. Most problematic was the San Francisco–Oakland Bay Bridge, which needed about $1.5 billion worth of work. The suspension section was to be upgraded to withstand seismic shocks better, but costs for upgrading the viaduct were so high that a $1 billion replacement was to be built. A variety of designs were proposed, including exotic tilting cable-stays and a single-pylon suspension span, though none would be built until after 2000.

On a positive note, 1997 witnessed the resurgence of the suspension bridge, the most suitable design for the longest spans. In Hong Kong the outgoing British administration celebrated the opening in April of the 1,377-m-long central span of the Tsing Ma suspension bridge with fireworks and a speech from Baroness Thatcher (1 m = 3.28 ft). Though second in length to Britain's 1,410-m Humber Bridge, Tsing Ma was the sturdiest of the long suspension bridges, carrying not just a dual three-lane highway to the airport but also a high-speed railway inside its steel deck box. The bridge also had to withstand typhoon-force winds.

Humber's length record would not last much longer. During the year the last deck sections were lifted into place for the 1,624-m central span Great Belt (Store Bælt) East Bridge in Denmark, part of an extended crossing between the islands of Zealand and Funen. The bridge carried a dual two-lane highway.

When completed in 1998, Great Belt East would not hold the world length record for long. In Japan the 1,991-m-long Akashi Kaikyo suspension bridge was nearing the end of its 10-year construction program; it would form the major element of a second crossing to Shikoku Island from Honshu, Japan's main island.

China was pressing ahead with plans for a 28-km (17.4-mi) crossing of the Pearl River Delta to Hong Kong, mainly on a viaduct though including a 1,400-m span, a 900-m span, and a 250-m span. In Bangladesh the 9-km (5.6-mi) Bangabandhu Bridge (until August 28 the Jamuna Multipurpose Bridge) was taking shape; it would cross treacherous and deep soft silts and a riverbed that shifted alignment every year. Huge steel piles up to 100 m long and 7 m in diameter supported the piers for the 99-m-long precast concrete deck spans that were being placed one every 12 days.

Finally, a small cable-stayed bridge completed during the year in Kolding, Den., may have been a portent of the future. Just 40 m long, it could support a five-ton tractor load easily, but the deck weighed only two tons because it was made of reinforced polyester. A normal concrete deck would weigh 30 tons. According to some industry observers, plastic and carbon-fibre bridges might eventually exceed those of steel by a factor of two in length. (ADRIAN LEE GREEMAN)

BUILDINGS

Architects had long dreamed that exterior walls of buildings would protect yet breathe—like human skin. That dream came one step closer to reality in 1997 with the completion of two office towers. The "skin" of the headquarters for RWE AG in Essen, Ger. (Ingenhoven, Overdiek, Kahlen & Partners, architect, Düsseldorf), consisted of two layers sandwiching a 50-cm-wide air space (1 cm=0.39 in). The outer layer of glass incorporated ventilating slots; an inner glass layer slid open as needed. With the outer ventilating slots closed, the air space acted as an insulating layer. When the slots were open, the air space became a cooling chimney; hot, stale air rose and was exhausted, and cooler fresh air was drawn in. The extensive glass usually eliminated the need for daytime electric lights (automated blinds set between the glass layers offered protection from solar heat and glare). The building's exposed concrete slab absorbed heat generated during the day, reradiating it at night for winter heating or summer precooling. These design elements reduced RWE's energy use to well below Germany's strict requirements. At the same time, users had a great deal of discretion in the control of temperature, ventilation, and light.

While many of the same techniques were used by the London-based firm of Sir Norman Foster & Partners in the design of the Commerzbank tower, completed in Frankfurt, Ger., that project took natural ventilation one step farther. Excess heat rose within the full-height open internal shaft, and fresh air was drawn inward through four-story gardens carved into the exterior. Another benefit was that inside offices, which could legally be windowless in some countries but not in Germany, opened onto the gardens.

The Getty Center in Los Angeles opened in December after 14 years of design and construction. At 87,790 sq m (945,000 sq ft), it was among the largest cultural complexes ever constructed at one time. Among its innovations was a louver and skylight system that precisely limited the amount of natural light falling on sensitive paintings.

The Getty Center in Los Angeles opened on December 16. Designed by Richard Meier, the much-anticipated centre was seen as a culmination of traditional Modernism. Its buildings, grounds, and gardens were carefully tailored to provide a wide variety of uses.

THOMAS HOEPKER—MAGNUM

Several large Asian airports were under construction during the year. The first 516,000-sq m (5,554,000-sq ft) terminal area at Chek Lap Kok airport in Hong Kong (Sir Norman Foster & Partners, architect; Ove Arup & Partners, engineer) was roofed in huge 36×36-m vaults supported by a steel lattice set at a diagonal (36 m=118 ft). Seoul, S.Kor.'s vast international airport was divided into a "land side" of ticketing, baggage, and ground-transportation functions linked by an underground automated people mover to several linear "air-side" terminals for boarding and deplaning (Fentress Bradburn, Denver, Colo., with the Korean Architects Collaborative International). Kisho Kurokawa (Japan) designed satellite terminals for Kuala Lumpur, Malaysia's airport that evoked the tropical environment, using tree-form column-trunks that supported inverted double-curved roofs ("branches").

Highly sophisticated computer-modeling software enabled the design of buildings of unprecedented sculptural complexity. Chief among them was the Guggenheim Museum that opened in Bilbao, Spain. CATIA, the computer software used by architect Frank O. Gehry (Santa Monica, Calif.) not only helped realize the museum's sinuous titanium-clad vaults and flowerlike forms; it also analyzed the supporting steel structure, conveying to the fabricator the loads and geometries of the connections and thereby greatly reducing the time needed to calculate their proper strength.

(JAMES S. RUSSELL)

DAMS

More than 1,500 dams were reported to be under construction throughout the world in 1997. The largest numbers were being built in India (650), China (280), Turkey (173), South Korea (131), Japan (126), Iran (49), and Brazil (42). There were 175 dams completed in 1996. The number of new dams on which construction had begun during the past few years varied between 200 and 300. This annual addition of dams was expected ultimately to move upward as population growth stimulated increases in food production, the need for additional municipal water supply and sanitation, and production of hydroelectric power.

Still, dams continued to be a subject of controversy, as some claimed they did more

(continued on page 141)

The Three Gorges Dam

The Three Gorges Dam, on which preliminary construction began in 1993, was the largest engineering project in China. Upon its completion, scheduled for 2009, it would be the largest dam in the world and generate as much hydroelectricity as that produced by 15 coal-burning power stations. The dam, designed to span the Chang Jiang (Yangtze River) just west of the city of Yichang in Hubei province, would also create an immense deep-water reservoir about 600 km (about 400 mi) long that would allow oceangoing 10,000-ton freighters to navigate 2,250 km (1,400 mi) inland from the East China Sea to the city of Chongqing.

First discussed in the 1920s by Chinese Nationalist Party leaders, the idea for the Three Gorges Dam was given new impetus in 1953 when Mao Zedong ordered feasibility studies of a number of sites. Detailed planning for the project began in 1955. Although it would control disastrous flooding along the Chang Jiang, facilitate inland trade, and provide much-needed power for central China, the dam was not without its detractors. Criticisms of the Three Gorges project began as soon as the plans were proposed and continued to the present. Key problems included the danger of dam collapse, the displacement of some 1.2 million people (critics use a figure of 1.9 million) living in nearly 500 cities, towns, and villages along the river, and the destruction of magnificent scenery and countless rare architectural and archaeological sites. There were also fears that human and industrial waste from Chongqing and other cities would pollute the reservoir and even that the huge amount of water impounded in the reservoir could trigger an earthquake. In addition, the project, first estimated at $11 billion, could end up costing $50 billion or more.

Because of these problems, work on the Three Gorges Dam was delayed for nearly 40 years as the Chinese government struggled to reach a decision to carry through with plans for the project. In 1992 Premier Li Peng, who had himself trained as an engineer, was finally able to persuade the National People's Congress to ratify the decision to build the dam, though almost a third of its members abstained or voted against the project—an unprecedented sign of resistance from a normally acquiescent body. Critics within the engineering community were harried into silence, but uneasiness at the scale and unpredictability of the project clearly persisted. Pres. Jiang Zemin did not accompany Premier Li to the official inauguration of the dam in 1994, and the World Bank refused to advance China funds to help with the project, citing major environmental and other concerns.

Chinese and foreign engineers continued to argue that a number of smaller and far-cheaper and less-problematic dams on the Chang Jiang tributaries could generate as much power as the Three Gorges Dam and control flooding equally as well. Construction of those dams, they maintained, would enable the government to meet its main priorities without the terrible risks.

TRYGVE BOLSTAD—PANOS

As of late 1997, however, the Three Gorges project was moving ahead. Workers were beginning to block the river in November, and the forces of opposition seemed to have been successfully bypassed.

(JONATHAN SPENCE)

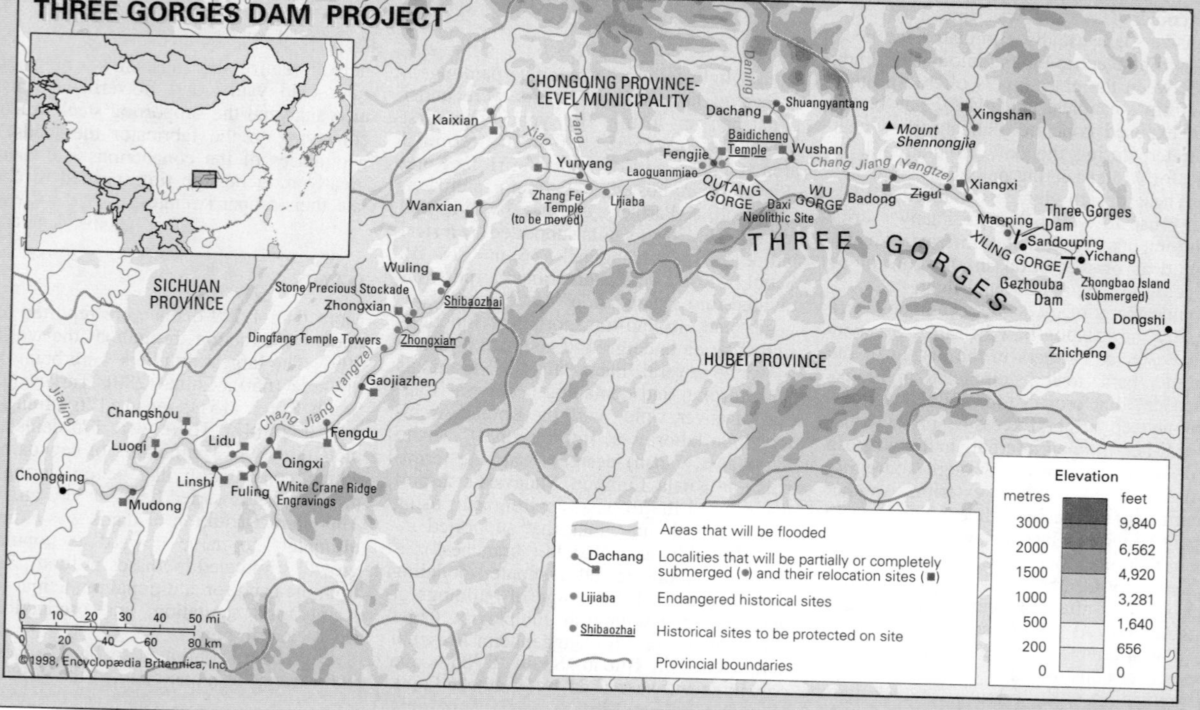

(continued from page 139)
harm than good. Organizations were formed to support both sides. Some called for referees, committees, commissions, and governmental bodies to express the wisdom that should prevail, to identify what was fair, and to discern between right and wrong.

Dam safety continued to command the attention of dam owners and designers. Engineers continued to meet under the auspices of the International Commission on Large Dams, an organization that exchanged views on new developments and experiences and presented technical case studies. Alertness to natural threats was also constantly required. In Nepal, for instance, the Khimti Dam and hydroelectric plant faced the threat of being swept away by the possible failure of a frozen mass of glacial moraine that was holding back 80 million cu m (2.8 trillion cu ft) of water in a lake. Emergency measures were instituted to prevent a disaster. As dams age, modifications to enhance their safety become important design and construction activities.

At the beginning of the year, 40 dams were under construction in the U.S. The highest (168 m [1 m=3.28 ft]), Seven Oaks Dam in California, was designed to be a flood-control project. The Eastside Reservoir Dam, also in California, was being built as a very large water-supply project and would consist of three dams—of 87 m, 56 m, and 40 m in height.

In China the first phase of the Three Gorges Dam on the Chang Jiang (Yangtze River) was scheduled to be completed in 1997. Diversion of the river from its main channel began in November. (*See* Sidebar.)

In Laos the environmental assessment of the Nam Theun 2 Dam was being reviewed. Opponents claimed that the dam would drown 470 sq km (180 sq mi) of remarkable grasslands and forests on the Nakai Plateau, several rare animal species would disappear, and the fisheries that helped feed thousands of people would be wiped out. Supporters, on the other hand, claimed that Nam Theun 2 would help lift Laos from the bottom rung of the poorest nations. In Vietnam the centrepiece of the nation's hydroelectric program was the 3,600-MW Son La Dam (at a cost of $3.5 billion), scheduled to be finished by 2007.

An active dam program in Iran was aided by available foreign money funding. The 1997–98 program called for the completion of six dams already under way and for the start of seven more in 1998. Turkey announced a program to start 19 dams with a combined capacity of 1,534 MW. Work was continuing on the 510-MW, 210-m-high concrete-arch Berke Dam on the Ceyhan River. The biggest project under way in Syria was the Martyr Basil al-Assad storage dam. The 45-m-high dam, with a 4.5-km (2.8-mi) crest length, was being designed to store 600 million cu m (21 trillion cu ft) of water and allow 55,000 ha (135,850 ac) to be irrigated. (T.W. MERMEL)

ROADS

In 1997 the world's first all-electronic toll highway opened in Toronto. Highway 407 was to be a 69-km-long (1 km=0.62 mi) route running east to west around the north of the city, to ease congestion on the existing main artery, Highway 401. The first 36-km section, built at a cost of about $900 million, was opened to traffic in June but initially without its advanced toll-collection system. Under this system, those wishing to use the highway would be required to have a windshield-mounted transponder that would record their journeys and make an automatic charge for the appropriate toll. Vehicles without a transponder would be recorded through an automatic license-plate-recognition system. Drivers could travel at highway speeds, and control gates would not be required.

Difficulties in commissioning the technology led to a series of delays, during which time drivers were allowed free use of the highway. This made the problem worse, as traffic volumes grew rapidly beyond the forecast figures. The installation of additional toll-recording and video-recognition devices finally allowed the technology to be switched on in October, almost a year late.

Many highway developers were watching developments on 407 with great interest. When the technology could be demonstrated to be effective, it would make the construction of new toll roads almost anywhere in the world more attractive to financiers. Because the system did not require large areas of land for a traditional toll-collection plaza, it would also allow existing non-tolled highways to be converted to toll routes with comparative ease.

Throughout the world the movement toward financing road infrastructure by means of private sources and tolls continued to gain popularity, but in one country it went backward. In the late 1980s Mexico had embarked on one of the world's biggest road-building programs, which envisioned the construction of 6,000 km of new high-quality highways. The highways would be built by private companies that would be allowed to operate them and charge tolls for a concession period before ownership reverted to the government (a system known as build-operate-transfer). Economic difficulties and the devaluation of the Mexican peso in 1994–95 resulted in insufficient revenue for servicing the debts. The government was forced to buy back some of the toll roads and assume $5 billion worth of debt.

An alternative system to encourage private-sector financing of highways also was inaugurated in 1997. A bypass around the town of Haltwhistle in northern England was the first "design-build-finance-operate" project to be completed. A private developer built the highway and was to be repaid by the government on the basis of the number of vehicles using the highway, although the drivers themselves would not be required to pay—a system known as "shadow tolling."

A major international conference in October discussed plans to revive the Silk Road, an ancient trading route linking Europe and China. The latter was thought likely to become the largest single market for highway development and was beginning to welcome private-sector investment for its ambitious construction projects.

(RUSS SWAN)

TUNNELS

One of the most shattering events of 1997 occurred in a highway tunnel in Paris when Diana, princess of Wales—along with two of three companions—died following a car crash on August 31. (*See* OBITUARIES.) The car, traveling at a high speed, went out of control and hit a central concrete pillar supporting the roof of the 142-m (465-ft)-long highway underpass built in 1954. Despite steep dips into the tunnel with relatively tight curves close to the portals, there were no crash barriers on either side of the roadway.

There were two other significant accidents in tunnels during the year. In September high concentrations of acrylamide and methylolacrylamide in a chemical grout being used to control heavy water ingress during drill-and-blast excavation of the 8.6-km-long Hallandsås railway tunnel in Sweden (1 km=0.62 mi) drained into a local stream and poisoned a herd of cows. The neurotoxic acrylamide was suspected of having been washed out before the two liquid solutions of the grout had time to polymerize to form the impermeable and inert rubberlike grouting material. An immediate investigation suspended tunneling and initiated an intense testing program of the groundwater wells from which the local rural community drew its drinking water. In July a subway tunnel collapse in São Paulo, Braz., took with it a private home. There were no fatalities or serious injuries, but several residents had to be evacuated.

All, however, was not tragedy and misfortune. London design started on the 26 km of twin-tube soft-ground tunneling on the new 108-km high-speed rail link to the British terminal of the Channel Tunnel. The estimated £3 billion project was scheduled to open in 2003. In Germany work progressed on the 177-km Frankfurt–Cologne high-speed railway, which was to include 27 single-tube, double-track tunnels totaling some 40 km. In Italy excavation of 23 tunnels to house 30 km of the 220-km Rome–Naples high-speed rail line continued, and work started on the 90-km Florence–Bologna line, 71 km of which was to be in a series of tunnels.

In India the last 40 m (130 ft) of difficult soft-ground tunneling marked the successful completion of the 760-km Konkan railway between Bombay (Mumbai) and Mangalore. Some 83 km of the line extended through 92 tunnels along the rugged west coast of the subcontinent, where viaducts across the valleys linked tunnels through the hills.

During the year China received two 8.8-m (28.9-ft)-diameter Wirth TBMs (tunnel boring machines) and their entire support systems from Germany for the 18.5-km Qinling railway tunnel in Shaanxi province. The TBMs were to excavate the east tube of the twin-tube double-track railway tunnel, working toward a mid-tunnel junction, whereas the parallel west tube was to be excavated by a drill-and-blast method.

One of the most significant water-associated tunnels begun in 1997 was the 29-km-long first of the four tunnels on the 70-km Inland Feeder project in southern California. The project would deliver nearly 2.5 billion litres (650 million gal) of water per day from the Colorado River and California State Water Project aqueducts into the new Eastside Reservoir. The new reservoir would secure a six-month emergency storage of drinkable water for Los Angeles should a major earthquake sever the city's vital water-import aqueducts.

(SHANI WALLIS)

This article updates the *Macropædia* articles BUILDING CONSTRUCTION; PUBLIC WORKS.

Name	Location		Year of completion	Notes
Notable Civil Engineering Projects (in work or completed, 1997)				
Airports		Area (ha)		
Chek Lap Kok	ex-Chek Lap Kok Island, Hong Kong	1,248	1997	Artificial island, terminal, bridge, tunnel links
Imam Khomeini International	Tehran, Iran		1997	Located in southern Tehran
Kuala Lumpur (Sepang) International	Sepang, Malaysia	100	end 1997	Includes high-speed rail link to Kuala Lumpur; to open Jan. 1, 1998
Aqueducts		Length (m)		
Great Man-Made River (Phase 2)	Sarir/Tazirbu well fields, Libya	1,670,000	1998	Phase 2: Delivered first water to Tripoli 1996
Lesotho Highlands Water Project	Maluti Mountains, Lesotho–South Africa	82,000	2025?	Original 5-phase plan at risk; social, environmental problems
Bridges		Length (main span; m)		
Akashi Kaikyo	Kobe, Japan	1,991	1998	World record (suspension) upon completion
Great Belt (Storebælt) East	Halsskov–Knudshoved, Den.	1,624	1998	World record (suspension) if completed before Akashi Kaikyo
Jiangyin Yangtze	Jiangsu province, China	1,385	1999	Fourth longest in world (suspension) upon completion
Tsing Ma	Tsing Yi–Ma Wan islands, Hong Kong, China	1,377	1997	Opened by Baroness Thatcher April 1997
High Coast	Västernorrland, Swed.	1,210	1997	Begun 1993; elevation above water 40 m
Tatara (Great)	Honshu–Shikoku, Japan	890	1999	World record (cable-stayed) upon completion
Trans-Tokyo Bay Highway	Kisarazu, Japan	590	1997	Includes 10-km tunnel to Kawasaki
Kobbholet	Magerøy Island, Norway	520	1998	Part of FATIMA project; *see also* "Tunnels"
Øresund	Flinterenden, Denmark-Sweden	492	2000	18-km road, rail tunnel, bridge link
Vasco da Gama (Tagus II)	Lisbon, Port.	420	1998	Total length 17.2 km; planned completion March 1998
Confederation (Northumberland Strait)	New Brunswick–Prince Edward Island, Canada	250	1997	Opened June 1, 1997
Bangabandhu (Jamuna Multipurpose)	Bhuapur, Bangladesh	99	1999	7.7-km road, gas pipeline, flood barrier
Buildings		Height (m)		
World Financial Centre	Shanghai, China	460	2001	World extreme upon completion; groundbreaking Aug. 27, 1997
Jin Mao	Shanghai, China	420	1997	Topped out Aug. 28, 1997
Plaza Rakyat	Kuala Lumpur, Malaysia	382	1999	World record reinforced-concrete structure
T & C Tower	Kaohsiung, Taiwan	347	1997	Completed
Baiyoke Tower II	Bangkok, Thai.	320	1997	Completed
Chek Lap Kok Terminal	Hong Kong, China	516,000 sq m (area)	1998	To replace existing Kai Tak airport
Getty Center	Los Angeles, Calif., U.S.	87,790 sq m (area)	1997	Cultural complex developed over 14 years
City		Area (ha)		
Putrajaya	near Kuala Lumpur, Malaysia	4,400	1998	Planned national capital; government transfer 2000
Dams		Crest length (m)		
Yacyretá-Apipé	Paraná River, Argentina-Paraguay	69,600	1998	Hydroelectric power, navigation, irrigation
Eastside Reservoir East/Domenigoni	Hemet, Calif., U.S.	3,380	1999	Reservoir = 800,000 ac-ft
Eastside Reservoir West/Domenigoni	Hemet, Calif., U.S.	2,736	1999	Reservoir = 800,000 ac-ft
Three Gorges	West of Yichang, China	1,983	2009	Stage 1: 1993–97; 2: 1998–2003; 3: 2004–09
Xiaolangdi	Huang Ho (Yellow River), China	1,667	2001	Flood, ice, silt control; irrigation; power
Seven Oaks	Santa Ana River, Calif., U.S.	802	1999	Flood control
Longtan	Hongshui River, China	800		Pumped storage power facility
Ertan	Yalong River, China	763	1998	Second largest hydroelectric power project in China
Tehri	Bhagirathi River, India	575	2000?	Construction suspended Dec. 1997; environmental controversy
Highway		Length (km)		
Indus	Kotri–Peshawar, Pak.	1,200	1998	Phases 1 & 2 scheduled to be completed by 1997
Pipeline		Length (km)		
Korla–Luoyang	Korla–Luoyang, China	4,200		Petroleum; 482 km completed by late 1997
Railways		Length (km)		
South Xinjiang	Kashi–Korla, China	975	2000	Completes 1,470-km Turpan–Kashi Railway; 200 km built by mid-1997
Nanning–Kunming Electric Railway	Nanning–Kunming, China	898.7	1997	258 tunnels, 447 bridges; opened Dec. 1, 1997
Seoul–Pusan	Seoul–Pusan, S.Kor.	426.2	2005	High-speed; controversy over location of Kyongju segment
Subways		Length (m)		
Seoul Metro (extensions)	Seoul, S.Kor.	61,500	1997	Lines 6, 7, 8
Bangkok: MRTA Red Line (BERTS)	Bangkok, Thai.	60,000	1998	Bangkok Elevated Road and Train System
Taegu Metro: Line 1	Taegu, S.Kor.	27,600	1997	Phase 1 (of 6): 29 stations; partially opened Nov. 26, 1997
Guangzhou (Canton) Subway: Line 1	Guangzhou, China	18,200	1997	Line 1 (of 3): 16 stations; partially opened June 28, 1997
London Metro (Jubilee Extension)	London, Eng.	15,980	1998	Twin 12,390-m tunnels
Chongqing Metro: Line 1	Chongqing, China	15,000	1998	Line 2 planned 1996–2000
Tower		Height (m)		
Millennium Freedom Tower	Newport, Ky., U.S.	330	end 1999	Bell tower to ring in millennium
Tunnels		Length (m)		
Pinglin Highway	near Taipei, Taiwan	12,900	1999	Twin 11.8-m tunnels under Sheuhshan Range
Aqualine Expressway	Kawasaki–Kisarazu, Japan	9,300	1997	Opened Dec. 18, 1997
FATIMA (Magerøy)	Norway	6,820	1998	World's longest subsea road tunnel
Øresund	Copenhagen–Malmö, Denmark–Sweden	3,750	2000	Twin tunnels; world-record immersed tube
Orelle	east of Frejus tunnel, France	3,600	1998	Due to be completed October 1998
Cheung Ching	Hong Kong, China	1,600	1997	17.2 x 10 m
Central Artery/Tunnel	Boston, Mass., U.S.	330	2004	"One of the most complex construction challenges of this century"
Urban Development		Area (sq m)		
Potsdamer Platz	Berlin, Ger.	620,000	2000	19 buildings

1 m = 3.28 ft; 1 km = 0.62 mi; 1 ha = 2.47 ac

Art, Antiques, and Collections

Dubious art transactions, alleged price-fixing, subpoenas, tell-all books, and news about celebrities' lives and deaths—all provided tabloid fodder and embarrassing imbroglios for the art world in 1997. Bad publicity did not seem to affect the market, however, and a strong U.S. economy was reflected in healthy sales from the leading auction houses. Financial results from the first half of the year put Christie's in the lead with $908 million in sales, ahead of arch-rival Sotheby's, which posted sales of $857.9 million.

In February Sotheby's launched an in-house investigation following allegations that the firm's Old Masters specialist in Milan, Roeland Kollewijn, had smuggled a painting by Giuseppe Nogari out of Italy. Later that month Kollewijn resigned. The release of Peter Watson's book *Sotheby's: Inside Story* cast a spotlight on this and other questionable, if not fraudulent, activities at the auction house. Once the word spread, the FBI, news organizations, and other investigators began circling the formerly sacrosanct realm of highbrow art, antiques dealers, collectors, and auction houses. During May some of New York City's leading art dealers and auction houses were subpoenaed as part of a U.S. federal investigation into possible price-fixing. Nevertheless, the art market enjoyed its strongest sales in more than six years. During Christie's Contemporary, Impressionist, and Modern sales in May, the auction house brought in $265 million, up dramatically from 1996 May sales of $119 million.

In October an exhibition 10 years in the planning, "A Grand Design: The Art of the Victoria and Albert Museum," finally made the trip from London to Baltimore, Md., for its debut. The monumental show was scheduled to be mounted at five North American venues through 1999, when it would return to London.

The Cold War seemed likely to reemerge during an East-West squabble over "Jewels of the Romanovs," an exhibition of imperial Russian jewels that was to leave the Corcoran Gallery of Art in Washington, D.C., for a May opening at the Museum of Fine Arts in Houston, Texas. Before the national treasures could be shipped, however, Russians blockaded the museum and demanded that the jewels be returned to Moscow for the city's 850th anniversary celebration. The crisis was defused, however, and the jewels were transported to Texas. The issue of Russia returning artworks and historical documents taken from European countries during World War II was addressed in May when the Russian Duma (parliament) voted to retain the treasures for Russia.

In Spain the Guggenheim Museum Bilbao opened as planned in October, in a new Frank Gehry-designed building. Portugal's first public museum devoted to late-20th-century international art opened in May, thanks to the largesse of Portuguese financier José Berardo, who reportedly spent upward of $100 million on artwork during the 1990s.

In March, Willem de Kooning, the Abstract Expressionist master, died after a long battle with Alzheimer's disease. (*See* Obituaries.)

(REBECCA KNAPP)

PAINTING AND SCULPTURE

In 1997 contemporary art was distinguished by a plurality of styles and by a blurring of the boundaries of traditional artistic media so that the realms of painting and sculpture were expanded and transgressed, displaced and transformed. Foremost among those challenging traditional definitions were young artists, who satisfied an insatiable fascination with the new and were featured internationally in an increasing number of museum and commercial exhibitions.

Geographically, artists continued to gravitate to such established international art centres as New York City and London, but an increasing number of new artists were found in Los Angeles and Germany. In Los Angeles such leaders in the field as Mike Kelley, Chris Burden, Charles Ray, and Lari Pittman trained a new generation of artists, and in Germany painter Gerhard Richter and conceptional photographers Bernd and Hilla Becher trained a new generation of conceptual artists. The contemporary scene in Great Britain was distinguished by the meteoric rise of the so-called young British artists. Among them, Jake and Dinos Chapman established a beachhead in September at the Gagosian Gallery in New York City with their highly controversial sculptures of mutative mannequins.

Another significant worldwide development was the move by young artists to include photography as one medium among many in their repertoires. For some, photography substituted for painting, notably in the strangely futuristic self-portraits of Mariko Mori of Japan, a staged photographic tableau by Sharon Lockhart of the U.S., and photographs by Thomas Demand of Germany of his cardboard reconstructions of images from the media; the photographs revealed a montage of performance art, sculpture, and the formal preoccupations of traditional painting.

Sculpture moved away from the pedestal, and architectural metaphors captured centre stage. Joep van Lieshout of The Netherlands and Stephen Craig of Northern Ireland made their presence felt internationally at such German exhibitions as the Münster Sculpture Project and Documenta in Kassel. Craig's architectural rooms and pavilions were both sculptures in themselves and spaces in which to exhibit other work, while van Lieshout's Pop art-inspired trailers and caravans provided people with living and working environments and thereby redefined the role of the sculptor in society. This blurring of the boundaries of performance art, architecture, and sculpture also was seen in the community-activated sculpture of Rirkrit Tiravanija of Thailand and the U.S., the photos and objects of Gabriel Orozco of Mexico, and the sculptures of Charles Long of the U.S., which doubled as pop music listening stations.

Sculpture also was pushed beyond its traditional definition with the arrivals of film and video as significant sculptural modes. A continuing series of *Cremaster* films by Matthew Barney of the U.S. combined the artist's unique mythological constructions with Busby Berkeley-like dance numbers, operatic narratives, and sculptural installations. Other noteworthy works included video installations by Diana Thater of the U.S. in which a trained chimpanzee performs on a film set, the projection at the Venice Biennale of a couple breaking off their relationship by Sam Taylor-Wood of Great Britain, and a dissonant slow-motion projection of artist Pipilotti Rist of Switzerland happily smashing car windows in Zürich while humming a melody. Often considered the founder of video art, Korean-born Nam June Paik continued his long and productive career, winning a Gold Lion award at the Venice Biennale. (*See* BIOGRAPHIES.)

Also significant during the year was a return to narrative in contemporary art. Kara Walker's disturbing yet beautiful paper silhouette installations of antebellum psychodramas made her one of the most sought-after new artists of the year. Using an 18th-century technique, Walker assembled convoluted visual stories that provided profound and subversive indictments of race relations in the U.S. She also was selected for a MacArthur fellowship in 1997. Narrative characterized the work of such mid-career artists as Robert Gober of the U.S., whose site-specific installation at the Museum of Contemporary Art in Los Angeles combined ideas of baptism, nostalgia, and the theatricality of the Roman Catholic tradition. Figurative painting was reinvigorated by the large-scale allegorical works of Kerry James Marshall of the U.S., which reflected on the African-American experience during the urban-renewal programs in Chicago in the 1960s.

While traditional media were challenged, painting continued to stave off its reported death as artists like Sigmar Polke of Germany, Luc Tuymans of Belgium, and Sue Williams, Elizabeth Peyton, and John Currin of the U.S. made strong showings in worldwide exhibitions. Two towering art figures died during the year, Abstract Expressionist Willem de Kooning and Pop artist Roy Lichtenstein. (*See* OBITUARIES.)

(DOUGLAS FOGLE)

ART EXHIBITIONS

Diversity of theme and work characterized the flavour of art exhibitions in 1997. Shows ranged from knockout blockbusters that included paintings, drawings, and sculptures to those featuring the art of non-Western cultures. Others concentrated on a single artist or a lone painting, and major biographical retrospectives showcased artists in their artistic or cultural niche. Anniversaries, cultural and social phenomena, pop culture, and art itself—all served as themes.

Undoubtedly, the most controversial show of the year was mounted in September at the Royal Academy of Arts in London. "Sensation: Young British Artists from the Saatchi Collection" included 110 graphic works by 46 British neoconceptual artists and opened to a storm of protest and criticism from members of the Royal Academy, art critics, and the public at large. Critics voiced outrage and disgust and asserted that the collection was not art but simply second-rate work meant to shock. The show was also criticized for its apparent official "seal of approval" for the collecting taste of Charles Saatchi, who was the most influential private collector and owned the largest collection of contemporary British art. Others argued, however, that the exhibition was stimulating and challenging, provoking questions and thought about the nature of art and its interaction with the real world. It was the first big radical show of contemporary art at the academy in 16 years. Such young artists as Damien Hirst, Sarah Lucas, and Jake and Dinos Chapman focused on themes that many found repulsive, grisly, and disgusting, including the horror of genetic mutations, disconnected genitalia, and allusions to death and decay. Hirst's piece depicted thousands of flies feeding off the rotting head of a cow. The Chapman brothers' sculpture consisted of representations of dismembered limbs hanging from a tree. Marc Quinn's "Self" was a sculpture of himself made of nine pints of his own frozen blood. Most controversial of all was a portrait by Marcus Harvey of Myra Hindley, a killer of children. The latter, fashioned from palm prints of children, attracted such criticism and outrage that on the opening day it was seriously damaged by vandals, who hurled eggs and ink at the image. As a result, it was temporarily removed for restoration.

A magnificently carved sandstone pediment (*c.* 967) from the temple of Banteay Srei in Angkor, Cambodia, depicts a scene from the *Mahabharata,* one of the two major Sanskrit epics of India. The pediment was one of 66 rarely seen works included in the traveling exhibit "Sculpture of Angkor and Ancient Cambodia: Millennium of Glory."

NATIONAL MUSEUM OF CAMBODIA, PHNOM PENH

Other Royal Academy shows were much less controversial. Shown in the spring was "Braque: The Late Works," the first exhibition in Britain to focus on the last 20 years of the artist's life. Georges Braque was credited with, Pablo Picasso, as a creator of Cubism. Many were surprised by evidence of Braque's long and fruitful artistic life, which endured into the middle of the 20th century, and by the variety and extent of his output. His late works were rich in texture and form and concentrated on the spatial relationships between everyday objects. His use of contrasting textures, such as paint and sand, added variety to surfaces. The exhibition focused on the several major series that he produced during this period—birds, interiors, and studios, notably the ateliers he painted between 1949 and 1956. The show also included some late landscapes, a genre that was rare for the artist and again illustrated his ability to work on both large and small scales and to create variety and interest with a limited palette and low-key subject matter. The show later traveled to the Menil Foundation in Houston, Texas.

In July through September, landscapes were featured in "Hiroshige: Images of Mist, Rain, Moon and Snow" at the Royal Academy. The show celebrated the bicentenary of the birth of Utagawa Hiroshige (1797–1858), a master of the coloured woodcut and one of the Japanese artists whose work had a seminal influence on Western artists and architects of the late 19th century. His landscapes were full of atmosphere and varying lights and included subjects ranging from birds and flowers to moonlit landscapes and wild coastlines.

A number of significant exhibitions were drawn from single collections or explored the collecting activity or philosophy of individuals. The extensive sculpture collection of Raymond D. Nasher of Dallas, Texas, one of the world's finest private collections of 19th- and 20th-century sculpture, was put on view in February and occupied the entire Solomon R. Guggenheim Museum in New York City. "A Century of Sculpture: The Nasher Collection," comprised about 105 sculptures and showcased works by Constantin Brancusi of Romania, Raymond Duchamp-Villon of France, Alberto Giacometti of Switzerland, Picasso of Spain, and David Smith of the U.S., among others. The show included works that represented major art movements such as Cubism, Constructivism, Surrealism, and minimalism.

A slightly different version of the Nasher show was seen at the San Francisco Museum of Fine Arts. The collection, started in the 1960s, boasted more than 300 works, many of them very large in scale. The exhibit contrasted the traditions of abstract and figurative art. The earliest work on view was Auguste Rodin's "Age of Bronze" (*c.* 1876), and Brancusi's "The Kiss" (1907–08) was shown alongside sculptures by Rodin that covered the same subject. There were also seminal works by Picasso, notably "Head" (Fernande, 1909), reportedly the first Cubist sculpture.

The James and Marilynn Alsdorf Collection, probably the largest and finest private collection of Indian, Himalayan, and Southeast Asian art in the United States, was shown at the Art Institute of Chicago from August to October and included about 205 works that had never before been publicly exhibited together. Featured were mainly figurative sculptures, including representations of Hindu and Buddhist deities. Also on view were paintings, jewelry, weapons, and ritual objects. The installation encompassed various themes and included works representing the cultures of Myanmar

TATE GALLERY, LONDON/ART RESOURCE

"Ophelia" was among a number of works by Sir John Everett Millais included in a show devoted to 19th-century English painting that was mounted by the National Gallery of Art, Washington, D.C.

(Burma), Thailand, Cambodia, Vietnam, and India.

Asian sculpture was highlighted at the Grand Palais in Paris with the exhibit "Sculpture of Angkor and Ancient Cambodia: Millennium of Glory." The show of Khmer sculpture surveyed works dating between the 6th and 16th century. The magnificent large-scale objects of stone and bronze were drawn primarily from the collection of the Musée Guimet in Paris and included 66 rarely seen works lent by the National Museum of Cambodia in Phnom Penh. The exhibit later traveled to the National Gallery of Art, Washington, D.C., and became the first show ever in the U.S. devoted to ancient Khmer art. After leaving the U.S., the exhibit traveled to the Japanese cities of Tokyo and Osaka.

A blockbuster exhibition mounted at the Metropolitan Museum of Art in New York City, "The Glory of Byzantium: Art and Culture of the Middle Byzantine Era, AD 843–1261" covered the art of the Byzantine empire's second Golden Age. The show, which boasted more than 350 works from 117 collections in 24 countries, served as a sequel to the 1977 "Age of Spirituality" exhibit, which dealt with late antiquity and early Byzantium. "The Glory of Byzantium"—four years in the planning—was a triumph of organization. Some 107 couriers and foreign dignitaries accompanied national treasures provided by institutions that never before had lent abroad, including the Orthodox monasteries of Iveron on Mt. Athos in Greece and St. Catherine on Mt. Sinai in Egypt. The treasure trove included icons, religious manuscripts, mosaics, carved and inlaid precious objects, textiles, monumental reliefs, and frescoes borrowed from collections throughout the world. Particularly notable were icons lent by the Monastery of St. John the Evangelist on Patmos, Greece, and ivories from the Louvre in Paris and the Fitzwilliam Museum in Cambridge, Eng. The Hermitage in St. Petersburg provided a remarkable diptych, and the Danish government approved the loan of a small enamel Dagmar Cross.

Another blockbuster was devoted to 19th-century English art. The National Gallery of Art mounted "The Victorians: British Painting in the Reign of Queen Victoria, 1837–1901" in an effort to dispel prejudices against Victorian paintings, which were often characterized as repressive and hypocritical. The movement itself was often perceived by "modern" artists as one against which they had to rebel. The 70 paintings, representing 34 artists, included a wide range of works and were not simply defined by the period of Queen Victoria's reign. The centrepiece of the show was devoted to the Pre-Raphaelite period and its immediate aftermath and included such well-known works as Sir John Everett Millais's "Ophelia" and William Holman Hunt's "The Scapegoat." Works by George Frederic Watts, Edward Burne-Jones, and Ford Madox Brown demonstrated the vast impact of this group of artists. The show also depicted many other strands of artistic activity and included works by James Whistler, James Tissot, Edwin Landseer, and J.M.W. Turner.

To mark its 20th anniversary, the Yale Center for British Art in New Haven, Conn., mounted a show with a British theme. "The Human Form Divine" consisted of paintings, watercolours, prints, and books illustrated by William Blake. A complementary show, "The Visionary Company," displayed works by artists closely associated with Blake, such as John Flaxman, Henry Fuseli, and Samuel Palmer.

TATE GALLERY, LONDON/ART RESOURCE

William Hogarth's "The Painter and His Pug" was on display at the Tate Gallery in London in 1997 as part of a special exhibit, "Hogarth the Painter," which commemorated the tercentenary of the birth (Nov. 10, 1697) of the so-called father of British art.

The tercentenary of the birth (Nov. 10, 1697) of William Hogarth, the so-called father of British art, was commemorated in the spring with "Hogarth the Painter," which opened at the Tate Gallery in London and included some notable borrowed items. Included were "Garrick and His Muse," which was lent by the Royal Collection, as well as important works from the Tate's own collection and some new discoveries. Other exhibits included a special showing of "The Rake's Progress" (The Orgy); at Sir John Soane's Museum in London, patrons were able to examine the series of paintings alongside the engravings, the first time that the two had been together since they left Hogarth's atelier. Companion Hogarth shows were held in London at the National Portrait Gallery, the British Museum, and the Victoria and Albert Museum and in Manchester at the Whitworth Art Gallery.

A major exhibition at the Musée d'Art Moderne in Brussels was devoted to the work of Paul Delvaux (1897–1994) and presented a wide-ranging selection of paintings, watercolours, drawings, sketchbooks, and documents. The show commemorated the centenary of his birth and was the first retrospective of his work in that city. The exhibit highlighted both his affinity with the Surrealists, with whom he was usually associated, and the differences he had with that group. Included were early works showing the progression of his strongly independent style. Some early work clearly bordered on Impressionism, and it was only after 1925 that figures began to play an important part. By the late 1930s he had begun placing figures in frequently idealized and disconnected landscapes, as was typified in the "Spitzner Museum" of 1943, in which a self-portrait appears. The contrast between everyday realism and dreamlike unreality rife with symbolism and impact was characteristic of Delvaux's work.

The art connection between France and Belgium in the 19th century was illustrated by a number of exhibitions. The most notable, "Paris-Bruxelles/Brussel-Parijs—An

COLLECTION OF KIYOKO LERNER AND THE NATHAN LERNER LIVING TRUST, COURTESY CARL HAMMER GALLERY, CHICAGO

"Two Spangled Blengins," one of more than 300 fantastic watercolours created by Chicago recluse Henry Darger, was included in an exhibit of Darger's works at the Museum of American Folk Art in New York City. Darger's paintings were among the most notable examples of "outsider art," works by amateurs with no connections to the conventional art world.

Artistic Dialogue Between France and Belgium, 1848–1914," opened at the Grand Palais in Paris and was later shown at the Museum of Fine Arts, Ghent, Belg. The show examined various artistic themes ranging from realism to Art Nouveau and demonstrated that French and Belgian painters were strongly influenced by such themes as Impressionism and pointillism as well as the landscapes of the Barbizon painters. The show highlighted decorative arts and included a powerful display of Art Nouveau objects.

An important exhibition devoted to the works of Sir Anthony Van Dyck was mounted at the Palazzo Ducale in Genoa, Italy, and concentrated on the work he did while living in that city. His sumptuous and elegant Genoese portraits, together with those by his predecessors and disciples, including other Flemish artists in Genoa at that time, formed a rich centrepiece.

At the National Gallery of Canada in Ottawa, the major summer exhibition was devoted to portraits by Pierre-Auguste Renoir and included 65 works, many of them commissioned, from the 1860s to the end of the artist's life. The show later moved to Chicago and Fort Worth, Texas.

Early in the year a series of exhibitions in New York City concentrated on work by Venetian painter Giambattista Tiepolo to commemorate the 300th anniversary of his birth. The Metropolitan Museum of Art displayed 80 of his paintings and oil sketches and 33 etchings and drawings, while the Pierpont Morgan Library showcased his works along with those of his followers and sons Domenico and Lorenzo. Both shows concentrated on placing the artists in context and categorizing their works as characteristic examples of Venetian graphic arts of the 18th century.

The first retrospective devoted to the work of Jasper Johns since 1977 was mounted by the Museum of Modern Art in New York City at the end of 1996. The work of this influential American artist was marked by complexity and personal vision and various shifts in focus. During the '50s he used realistic images, but he turned to abstraction in the '60s before reverting to images in the '70s. The show, which included 225 paintings, drawings, prints, and sculptures, traveled to the Museum Ludwig, Cologne, Ger., and to the Museum of Contemporary Art, Tokyo. A comprehensive retrospective of the work of Ellsworth Kelly was mounted from October 1996 to January 1997 at the Guggenheim Museum and then in Los Angeles at the Museum of Contemporary Art before traveling in the summer to the Tate Gallery and the Haus der Kunst in Munich, Ger., in the fall. Gallerygoers could detect in Kelly's earliest work a tendency toward abstraction, beginning with his 1949 self-portrait. The show contained a wide selection of abstract paintings and sculptures dating from the 1950s as well as some drawings, photographs, and humorous tiny collages. Many of the paintings juxtaposed different painted panels, creating abstract and geometric forms. Although Kelly's work was less varied than that of Johns, it was full of joy and style.

Another thematic exhibition, "Grand Tour: The Lure of Italy in the 18th Century,"

Jasper Johns's "Flag," the painting that launched his career, was featured in a major retrospective of the artist's work at the Museum of Modern Art in New York City. The American flag was a central motif in Johns's paintings for several decades.

PHOTOGRAPH © 1997THE MUSEUM OF MODERN ART, NEW YORK. GIFT OF PHILIP JOHNSON IN HONOUR OF ALFRED H. BARR, JR.

was seen at the end of 1996 at the Tate Gallery and later in Rome at the Palazzo delle Esposizioni. The charming and wide-ranging exhibition demonstrated the crosscurrents between Italian and English art and culture. The diffuse subject was organized around topics such as "travellers and the journey" and "the Antique." Included were maps and guidebooks as well as drawings, portraits, and landscapes, particularly of Rome.

Finally, "It's Only Rock and Roll," an exhibition at the Phoenix (Ariz.) Art Museum, surveyed American art dating from the 1950s to the present and featured works that bore influences of the music. Artists featured included Peter Blake, Andy Warhol, and Robert Rauschenberg.

(SANDRA MILLIKIN)

PHOTOGRAPHY

A diversity of notable exhibitions enriched the photographic gallery scene in 1997, including retrospectives, small but choice one-person shows, and spectacular group collections. The now-famous photographs that launched Cindy Sherman's career as the postmodern superstar of self-portraiture were displayed in "Cindy Sherman: The Complete Untitled Film Stills" at New York City's Museum of Modern Art. The series of 69 black-and-white photographs made from 1977 to 1980 showed Sherman imaginatively posed in female roles that were inspired by the clichés of motion picture publicity stills. With a unique mix of camp and authenticity, she evoked what one reviewer called "the fictional cultures of femininity."

Mathew Brady's reputation for documenting the American Civil War had sometimes obscured his outstanding achievements as a portraitist of celebrated and powerful personalities of his time. "Mathew Brady's Portraits: Images as History, Photography as Art" at the National Portrait Gallery, Washington, D.C., gave a comprehensive view, the first in more than 100 years, of this important aspect of Brady's career. Included were more than 130 daguerreotypes, albumen silver prints, lithographs, oil paintings based on his photographs, and memorabilia.

MARC RIBOUD—MAGNUM

Marc Riboud's 1965 photograph of children sporting straw hats as they walk along a street in Guangxi, China, was part of the International Center of Photography exhibition "Marc Riboud: Forty Years of Photography in China." The exhibition featured pictures of daily life in China from the early Maoist era to the present.

By macabre chance, the "Il Paparazzo/I Paparazzi" exhibition at the Robert Miller Gallery in New York coincided with the fatal crash of the photographer-pursued Mercedes that killed Diana, princess of Wales, in August. The exhibition, planned long in advance of that tragic event, depicted the rise of aggressive photographic celebrity chasers in the 1950s and the infusion of their style and methods into the advertising and fashion media of the '90s. "Marc Riboud: Forty Years of Photography in China" at New York's International Center of Photography used vignettes of daily life to portray the events that transformed China from the early Maoist era to the present. "A Witness to History: Yevgeny Khaldei, Soviet Photojournalist" at New York's Jewish Museum was the first major exhibition of that photographer's work in the U.S. It included his brilliantly staged set piece of a Soviet soldier raising the red flag over Berlin's Reichstag in May 1945 and harrowing images of World War II's impact on civilians. Khaldei died in October. (*See* OBITUARIES.)

Sixty vintage photographs from Paul Strand's early period, including his starkly abstract "White Fence," were shown at the Metropolitan Museum of Art's "Paul Strand, Circa 1916" exhibition in New York. The J. Paul Getty Museum at its recently opened complex in Los Angeles exhibited "The Silver Canvas: The Art of Daguerreotype," a stunning selection from the museum's extensive archives of that early form of photography, whose silvery charm and brilliant detail remained unsurpassed. The Philadelphia Museum of Art's "Robert Capa: Photographs" was a major retrospective including

SYGMA

At a White House party in 1985, Diana, princess of Wales, took to the dance floor with American movie star John Travolta. The dress she wore that evening was later sold at auction for $222,500. Proceeds from the sale of her gowns at a Christie's auction in June benefited AIDS and cancer charities.

about 130 prints, many not before seen, that revealed Capa's skill as a portraitist as well as a war photographer. In Washington, D.C., the Corcoran Gallery of Art's "Half Past Autumn: The Art of Gordon Parks" acknowledged the 84-year-old African-American photographer, documentarian, and modern Renaissance man with a 220-photograph retrospective. Henri Cartier-Bresson, among the greatest masters of 20th-century photography, was internationally honoured in celebration of his 90th birthday.

An extravagant commercial application of photographs was Italian tire manufacturer Pirelli's multimillion-dollar 1997 calendar. Richard Avedon photographed models from 12 countries twice—dressed in designer costumes, they were photographed in colour; nude, in black-and-white. Launched with an exhibit at the Palazzo Grassi in Venice, and with a mere 12,000 copies allocated to the U.S., the calendar was not likely to be found in the usual body-and-fender repair shop.

If one had chosen the right images, fine-arts photography would have performed very well as an investment during the past decade, according to *The Photograph Collector*. In 1987 Robert Mapplethorpe's "X portfolio" sold for $3,500; 10 years later it could easily have brought $50,000 if a set were found. Some Sherman images selling for $1,500 in 1987 brought more than $25,000 each in 1997. Meanwhile, the price for a vintage print by André Kertész reached a new high; "Mondrian's Pipe and Glasses, Paris," sold for $376,000 at Christie's spring auction.

The 1997 Pulitzer Prize for spot news photography went to Annie Wells of the *Press Democrat,* Santa Rosa, Calif., for a dramatic close-up of a firefighter rescuing a young flood victim. Alexander Zemlianichenko of the Associated Press received the Pulitzer for feature photography for his view of an exuberant Russian Pres. Boris Yeltsin dancing the shimmy during a rock concert. At the 54th Annual Pictures of the Year competition sponsored by the National Press Photographers Association and the University of Missouri School of Journalism, Yunghi Kim of Contact Press Images was named Magazine Photographer of the Year and Carol Guzy of the *Washington* (D.C.) *Post* took the title of Newspaper Photographer of the Year. At the 40th Annual World Press Photo Contest, the World Press Photo of the Year award was received by photojournalist Francesco Zizola of Agenzia Contrasto for his photograph of children maimed and traumatized during Angola's civil war.

The primary W. Eugene Smith Grant in Humanistic Photography was awarded to Alain Keler for his documentation of the fate of minorities in the former Eastern European communist bloc. Secondary awards went to Gary Calton for his photographs of England's workingmen's clubs and Nadia Benchallal for her photographs of the world of Muslim women. Susan Grayson received the Howard Chapnick Grant for Leadership in Photojournalism for her book project on the history of New York press photographers. Lori Drinker won the Ernst Haas Award for her photographic essay "After War: Veterans from a World of Conflict."

(ARTHUR GOLDSMITH)

ART AUCTIONS AND SALES

In 1997 the auction market celebrated its strongest year since 1991. The improvement was attributed to strength in the financial markets, particularly those in the United States, which gave consumers a perception of having significant disposable income. Although there were many new buyers in the market, seasoned customers remained active as well. Purchasers continued to pay high prices for quality property that came fresh to the market, particularly works from single-owner collections of distinguished provenance, which, in many cases, performed well beyond expectations. Although record prices were paid for jewelry, objects in the decorative arts, American paintings, and Old Master paintings, the driving force seemed to be Impressionist and Modern art, with single-owner sales of collections of John and Frances L. Loeb, Serge Sabarsky, Evelyn Sharp, and Victor and Sally Ganz making headlines.

The Impressionist and Modern paintings, drawings, and sculpture sale held at Christie's in May earned a total of $119,862,500, with 10 works selling for $3,000,000 or more. "Jeune femme se baignant" by Pierre-Auguste Renoir sold for $12,432,500. This various-owner sale was preceded by the Loeb collection, which achieved $92,794,500, one of the highest totals in auction history for a single-owner collection. Paul Cézanne's "Madame Cézanne au fauteuil jaune" was purchased for $23,102,500, the second highest price paid for his work at auction. The same was true for Édouard Manet, whose "Portrait de Manet par lui-même, en buste" achieved $18,702,500.

Sotheby's May sale of Impressionist and Modern paintings, drawings, and sculpture enjoyed similar success, attaining $81,305,000 in sales. A record was established for the artist Gustav Klimt, whose "Litzlebergerkeller am Attersee" realized $14,742,500. This work was from the Sabarsky single-owner collection, which totaled $19,394,500. A record price for an Edgar Degas pastel was also set at this auction; his "Danseuses" sold for $11,002,500.

The November 1997 sales of Impressionist and Modern art confirmed the vitality in this market and brought the year's sales to an exciting conclusion. The Ganz sale established the record for a single-owner collection sold at auction; it brought $206,516,525. Pablo Picasso's "Le Reve," a portrait of his lover Marie-Thérèse Walter, sold for $48,402,500, the second highest auction price for the artist. Another Picasso, "Les Femmes d'Alger," one of his renditions of the "Women of Algiers" series by Eugène Delacroix, fetched $31,902,500. The top two works at Sotheby's single-owner sale of works from the Sharp collection were also by Picasso, the highest of which, "Nus," brought $6,052,500. The total collection realized $41,213,200. A various-owner sale the following evening commanded a solid $92,717,500 and was highlighted by Renoir's "Baigneuse," which sold for $20,902,500.

Old Master paintings enjoyed one of their strongest years in history. In January Sotheby's in New York offered works from the collection of Saul Steinberg, totaling $10,910.000. One of the highlights was "Plague in an Ancient City" by Michael Sweerts, which set an auction record for the artist, selling for $3,852,500. Paintings from the collection of the British Rail Pension Fund fetched $9,564,625 at auction, with a pair of the works, "Two Views of Venice" by Canaletto, selling together for $4,512,500 and setting an auction record for the artist. Christie's January auction offered El Greco's "Christ on the Cross," which at $3,605,000 set a world record for the artist and for an Old Master picture at auction.

Jewelry continued to rank as the second highest achiever at both auction houses. In May Sotheby's realized a world-record price per carat for a yellow diamond after selling the superb fancy-vivid yellow diamond ring for $3,302,500 in a sale that totaled $25,643,522. Christie's magnificent jewelry sale in October amounted to $28,377,188; the star in that lot was a square-cut diamond that brought $1,927,188. In late October Sotheby's held a sale totaling $36,955,918, of which $10,733,625 came from a private collection of extraordinary jewels.

Another burgeoning market was American paintings, which attracted new buyers and maintained the loyalties of established purchasers. Both Sotheby's and Christie's established records for the top-selling artists in their June sales. Sotheby's sold Andrew Wyeth's "Christina Olson" for $1,707,500, and Christie's hammered "Home Sweet Home" by Winslow Homer for $2,642,075. Sotheby's also set auction records in this same June sale for Norman Rockwell's "Year After Year Only Fine Beer," which realized $354,500, and Thomas Hart Benton's "Politics, Farming and Law in Missouri," which fetched $299,500.

Many of the middle markets were also quite robust, including the furniture and decorative arts categories. There were many world records set in Americana throughout 1997. In January Christie's offered a Chippendale chest-on-chest, which realized $1,212,500 and set a world record for this type of furniture. A Philadelphia high chest of drawers fetched $811,000, setting another world record, and Sotheby's established a record for a Newport highboy, which commanded $910,000. In the October sales of important Americana, Sotheby's achieved a record price for a Massachusetts highboy, which brought $690,000, and a world record price ($233,500) for a Southern open armchair. Christie's set a record with a New York chair that brought $387,500.

The estate of U.S. Ambassador Pamela Harriman, which was offered by Sotheby's, commanded $8,700,568. Other distinguished collections that were auctioned included those of Marlene Dietrich and Leonard Bernstein and the Feiertag collection of fine movie posters, which set a record at $1,337,562. Sotheby's also sold "Sue," the largest and most complete *Tyrannosaurus rex* ever found, to Chicago's Field Museum of Natural History for $8,362,500. The wine cellar of Andrew Lloyd Webber went for $2,308,000. Christie's offered Muhammad Ali memorabilia from the collection of Ron Paloger and sold for $3,258,750 dresses of Diana, princess of Wales, to benefit charities. In October Christie's held its first "Arts of France" sale, which totaled $16,544,435; the top lot was a Louis XIV ormolu-mounted mantel clock that sold for $992,500.

Both auction houses were preparing for the millennium by building new facilities in New York City, a sign of their growing confidence in the auction market. Christie's announced plans to move its entire organization from various New York locations into one consolidated space at Rockefeller Center, and Sotheby's planned to unify its operations by adding six new floors to its current space at 72nd St. and York Ave.

(AMY TODD)

ANTIQUARIAN BOOKS

The 1996–97 market for rare books and manuscripts strengthened. Although prices for Americana manuscripts were low, material new to the market performed above estimated values, and colour-plate books of all kinds, including atlases, sold very well.

Sotheby's New York sold the Victor and Irene Murr Jacobs collection, which included books and letters by Mark Twain, signed presidential books and portraits, and works of literature, notably Shakespeare's first edition of plays printed in 1623; the latter fetched $225,000. At the California Book Auction Galleries, approximately 270 books from Twain's library were sold as a single lot for over $200,000.

Christie's New York sold the "Einstein-Besso" manuscript, an important scientific document from Albert Einstein's early work on relativity, for $350,000, but family correspondence and a parcel of Einstein's love letters brought mixed results. When Sotheby's New York offered the correspondence between cousins Franklin D. Roosevelt and Margaret Suckley, the collection failed to reach its $500,000–$700,000 estimate and was sold privately.

Sotheby's London sold 34 extraordinary illuminated manuscripts from the Beck collection for well over £10 million. Christie's New York botanical-book sale brought $6.5 million in sales, with a complete coloured copy of Caspar Barlaeus's *Rerum in Octennium in Brasilia* (1647) selling for over $330,000. Sotheby's New York offered the library of George M. Pfaumer and fetched a staggering $110,000 for William Birch's early hand-coloured views of Philadelphia.

At Sotheby's London a three-volume set of Robert Estienne's *Dictionarium* (1543) commanded more than $350,000, and Sotheby's New York reached a hammer price of $470,000 for Arthur Conan Doyle's autograph manuscript *Sign of Four.* Publications by John James Audubon soared in value; the folio *Quadrupeds* sold for $189,000 (Sotheby's New York), and Christie's New York sold the second edition of the folio *Birds of America* for $130,000 and an incomplete first edition for $1.5 million. Christie's New York also sold a fine copy of the Kelmscott Chaucer printed on vellum for over $550,000.

Following the exhibition "Let There Be Light: William Tyndale and the Making of the English Bible" at the British Library and other locations, the Württembergische Landesbibliothek in Stuttgart, Ger., announced that it owned a previously unknown third copy of the 1526 Worms New Testament.

(KIMBALL HIGGS)

PHILATELY

Two highly successful stamp exhibitions were held in 1997. In February a huge crowd waited hours in line for admittance to the HONG KONG '97 international exhibition, and in May 170,000 visitors attended PACIFIC '97, an international show held in San Francisco to mark the 150th anniversary of the first U.S. postage stamps. The International Federation of Philately also sponsored exhibitions in Oslo, Moscow, and New Delhi.

In an effort to broaden the public appeal of postage stamps, a number of unusual offerings were made. To publicize PACIFIC '97 the U.S. issued two triangle stamps, the first of that shape in its history. The decision by the U.S. to produce a stamp depicting cartoon character Bugs Bunny, also an official "stamp ambassador," elicited criticism from many traditional collectors but was an immediate hit with the public. New Zealand showcased its most unusual mailboxes in a booklet of six. On the 100th anniversary of the publication of the horror tale bearing his name, Dracula was honoured with images on stamps in Great Britain, Ireland, the U.S., and, of course, Romania. Australia implemented a major change of policy by depicting persons deemed to be living legends. In January Donald Bradman, a famous cricket batsman, became the first Australian so honoured.

Only one new state joined the ranks of stamp-issuing nations in 1997. Mayotte, a French dependency in the Comoros archipelago, resumed issuing stamps on January 1, after having used French stamps since 1975. In Hong Kong, which reverted to Chinese control on July 1, new stamps with pictures of the waterfront were issued to replace the Queen Elizabeth definitives, which were withdrawn from sale on Jan. 25, 1997, but were valid for postage until the handover.

Scott Publishing Co. of Sidney, Ohio, the world's leading producer of stamp catalogs and albums, introduced several changes to its product line. In its 1998 worldwide catalog, the British Commonwealth countries were included—the first time in 65 years that they had not been listed in a separate volume. Scott also began positioning itself for electronic publishing by taking steps in January to prohibit licensees from using its catalog numbers in certain electronic media. The expected CD-ROM version of the Scott Catalog did not appear during the year, however, owing to production difficulties.

Krause Publications of Iola, Wis., pursued an aggressive program of philatelic acquisitions and restructuring after purchasing *Stamp Collector* and *Stamp Wholesaler* in 1996. In January 1997 the company announced that *Stamp Wholesaler,* the world's largest dealer publication, would appear monthly after 60 years as a biweekly. In August Krause announced the purchase of the Minkus line of catalogs and albums.

There was also more experimentation with stamp production. Self-adhesives grew in popularity at a surprising pace in the U.S. The United States Postal Service (USPS) reported that some 60% of the stamps sold in 1996 were self-adhesives, and it estimated that the number would near 80% for 1997. In March the USPS issued two linerless self-adhesive 32-cent coils. Addressing the need for greater printing security, the USPS added a scrambled image of the letters "USAF" across the design of the U.S. Air Force commemorative issued in September. The image could be seen by collectors with the help of a special plastic lens sold through the Philatelic Fulfillment Service Center. Perhaps the most novel philatelic innovation of the year was a sheet of Dutch greeting stamps that featured a hidden message of friendship that could be viewed when a protective coating was scraped away.

Stamp prices showed a steady, though modest, rise during the year. In June, Ivy & Mader of New York City fetched $322,000 for an American Bank Note Co. proof book crammed with rare and valuable proof sheets, including the first two U.S. issues. A unique 1851 unused Baden colour error commanded more than $600,000. A registered 1908 cover with three U.S. 4-cent Grant stamps with perforations from the Joseph Agris private collection was sold by Charles Shreve in September for $220,000, a record for a 20th-century cover.

(ROBERT E. LAMB)

NUMISMATICS

In April 1997 the "king of American coins"—an 1804 U.S. silver dollar—commanded $1,815,000, a record price for a single coin at public auction. The dollar, one of 15 known, was part of a complete collection of U.S. coins that had been assembled by the late Louis E. Eliasberg, Sr., of Baltimore, Md. Eliasberg's 1885 trade dollar sold for $907,500, a record for the series. In all, his collection had brought nearly $44 million at auction since 1982. *Numismatic News* reported that despite record-setting bids for the most valuable old coins, the overall rare-coin market had edged up just over 4% in the 12-month period that ended September 9.

Interest in coin collecting was expected to rebound in 1999, when the U.S. government was scheduled to launch a 10-year program to circulate 50 commemorative quarters, one for each state. The coins would feature state designs on the reverse side, with George Washington's bust remaining on the front.

The U.S. Mint introduced four commemorative coin programs in 1997 amid ongoing complaints that the market for such items was saturated. One of the more popular new coins was a silver dollar honouring Jackie Robinson, who in 1947 became the first African-American to play major league baseball. Many collectors cheered a new law that limited the number of commemorative coin programs to two per year beginning in 1999 and placed caps on mintages. The U.S. Mint was expected to produce about 14 billion coins for circulation in 1997, down from 19.5 billion in 1996 and the record 19.8 billion in 1995. On December 1 U.S. Pres. Bill Clinton signed legislation authorizing production of a gold-coloured dollar coin that eventually would replace the Susan B. Anthony dollar.

In October the U.S. Federal Reserve System began issuing redesigned 50-dollar Federal Reserve notes. Like the 100-dollar notes that made their debut in 1996, they featured several new anticounterfeiting devices, including a watermark and colour-shifting ink. The bills also sported an enlarged numeral 50 on the back to help sight-impaired people, the first U.S. currency to feature such a design element. Several nations, including Australia, Brunei, and Thailand, circulated plastic notes in 1997, and Russia unveiled a 500,000-ruble bill with a variety of anti-counterfeiting devices. Finland put a hologram on its 20-markka note, and Turkey, suffering from high inflation, issued a five million-lira bill to keep up with rising prices.

U.S. Mint workers made the country's first-ever platinum coins, which complemented the American Eagle series of gold and silver pieces sold primarily to precious-metal investors. The new Eagles competed with platinum bullion coins issued by Australia and Canada, among other nations, and came in four sizes ranging from 1 oz ($100 face value) to 0.10 oz ($10 face value). The Austrian Philharmonic was the world's best-selling gold bullion coin in 1995 and 1996, capturing about 40% of the world market both years. Meanwhile, Mexico withdrew ringed bimetallic coins with a .925 fine silver centre that were first issued in 1993. They were believed to be the only circulating silver coins still in use in the world.

Canada changed the composition of its one-cent coin from copper to copper-plated zinc and also sold to collectors a one-dollar coin commemorating the 10th anniversary of the Loon dollar in circulation. The British Royal Mint introduced a five-pound coin commemorating the 50th wedding anniversary of Queen Elizabeth II and Prince Philip on November 20. The return of Hong Kong to China generated several numismatic issues, including a seven-coin set struck by the British Royal Mint and a $1,000 gold commemorative by the Royal Canadian Mint.

(ROGER BOYE)

This article updates the *Macropædia* article COINS AND COINAGE.

COLLECTIBLES

The Pamela Harriman estate auction was the celebrity event of 1997. (*See* OBITUARIES.) Everything was sold, ranging from a worn velvet pillow with ostrich crest ($2,415) to a John Singer Sargent painting, "Staircase in Capri" ($1.4 million). A six-piece suite of Louis XV beechwood furniture fetched $101,500, while a canceled check signed by Winston Churchill brought $9,200.

Dresses worn by Diana, princess of Wales, were sold for charity in June. The highest price, a record $222,500, was paid for the dress she wore while dancing at the White House with John Travolta. Her death on August 31 sent collectors hunting for memorabilia such as commemorative wedding plates ($25–$100), Royal Doulton figurines ($800), and tin biscuit boxes picturing her wedding ($15–$25).

Toy sales also remained strong. At a late 1996 auction of 1950s toy robots, Machine Man went for a record $42,550, Radicon Robot for $21,850, and Musical Drummer Robot R57 for $17,250. An astounding $88,000 was paid in June 1997 for a 24-cm (9½-in) Tipp & Co. (*c.* 1930) Mickey and Minnie Mouse toy motorcycle.

Items related to advertising continued to bring top prices. At a sale of Hires Root Beer memorabilia in Colorado, a record $106,700 was paid for a Mettlach urn dispenser, $15,125 for a straw holder, and $22,000 for a die-cut sign of the Hires boy. At another sale a 1910 tin Coca-Cola sign picturing Hilda Clark brought $82,250.

The only record prices for formal antiques were for Gustav Stickley furniture; a two-door bookcase went for $34,650 and a lady's desk no. 724 for $29,900. An Early American glass Amelung tumbler made about 1788 fetched a record $83,900. A Tiffany Favrile glass and bronze lotus lamp on a mosaic lily-pad base auctioned at $1.1 million, while a Tiffany window made for the 1893 World's Columbian Exposition and picturing parakeets and goldfish commanded $1,047,500.

Prices continued to climb for unusual pieces of pottery and porcelain. A four-tile Grueby frieze of palm trees auctioned for $24,150, and a Marblehead Pottery tile frieze of a lake scene earned $21,850. Rookwood's 1929 vellum glaze plaque showing Venice and ships sold for $49,500, while a Weller vase over 1.8 m (6 ft) high commanded a monumental $112,500. A 122-cm (48-in)-high Mettlach vase with a knight and maiden, signed C. Spindler, brought $46,000.

Very important French silver pieces sold well; in late 1996 $10,287,500 was the price paid for a 1733 Louis XV tureen with vegetables, fish, birds, and reeds, while a pair of wine coolers by Claude Ballin II brought $3,962,500. In April 1997 a record $13,500 was paid for an enameled silver porringer and spoon made by Potter Studios of Cleveland, Ohio, in the early 20th century.

An important sale of American Indian pieces brought six new record prices. Sold were an 18th-century Nootka face mask, $525,000; a wooden spoon carved with a human figure on the handle, $101,500; a Chilkat Tlingit ceremonial coat, $497,500; a Northwest Coast carved wooden pipe with abalone shells, $134,500; a Northwest Coast "bent corner" bowl, $79,500; and a Saltillo (Mex.) serape, $57,500.

Rare sports memorabilia commanded higher prices. A Babe Ruth 1914 rookie card brought $27,114, while a Christy Mathewson signed baseball sold for $21,916. An 1820 brass bait casting reel by George Snyder of Paris, Ky., set a new auction record at $31,350.

(RALPH AND TERRY KOVEL)

Business and Industry Review

The slowdown in world output in 1995–96 raised doubts about the long-term recovery of the economy, but in 1997 they were laid to rest. Although the world economy was some way from firing on all cylinders, 1997 and 1998 seemed likely to register the fastest growth in world output in a decade. Despite their relative longevity, the recoveries in the United States and, to a lesser extent, in Great Britain seemed robust. In continental Europe the deflation imposed by the Treaty on European Union, with its provision for a common currency, was ending now that most of the likely monetary union members had put their fiscal houses in order. In the developed world, only Japan continued to struggle against a chronic lack of confidence in its domestic economy. In the less-developed world, growth continued to be strong, though future prospects in Southeast Asia were threatened by the turbulence of financial markets there; Latin America, however, had emerged from an equivalent crisis in 1995. Finally in the former communist economies, where transition to a market system continued to prove painful, there were increasingly encouraging signs that the process was working.

Nowhere was growth proving more resilient than in the U.S. The recovery that began in 1991, though showing signs of flagging in 1995–96, demonstrated renewed strength in 1997. Commentators began to talk of a "new paradigm" in which an underlying trend of rapid increase in productivity enabled fast growth of gross domestic product (GDP) to be combined with low inflation. With Federal Reserve Board Chairman Alan Greenspan, who seemed to endorse the paradigm, keeping a steady hand on monetary policy, the talk was of a "Goldilocks" economy—neither too hot nor too cold.

In continental Europe, a lagging area in

Table I. Annual Average Rates of Growth of Manufacturing Output, 1980–96

Percent

Area	1980–87	1988–92	1993	1994	1995	1996
World[1]	2.3	0.4	–0.1	5.8	4.7	3.4
Developed countries	1.9	–0.2	–1.1	5.9	4.3	2.9
Less-developed countries	4.5	3.9	4.5	5.1	6.3	5.7

[1]For definition, *see* Table IV.
Source: UN, *Monthly Bulletin of Statistics.*

Table II. Industrial Production in Eastern Europe[1]

1990=100

Country	1992	1993	1994	1995	1996	%[2]
Bulgaria	65	58	63	60	59	–2
Croatia	62	59	57	58	60	3
Czech Republic	72	68	70	76	81	7
Estonia	60	49	47	48	49	2
Hungary	72	75	83	86	89	3
Latvia	65	44	40	38	39	3
Poland	95	101	113	124	134	8
Romania	58	58	60	66	72	9
Slovakia	73	70	74	80	82	2
Slovenia	76	74	79	80	81	1

[1]Former Soviet Union not available.
[2]% change, latest year shown from previous year.
Source: UN, *Monthly Bulletin of Statistics.*

Table III. Pattern of Output, 1993–96

Percent change from previous year

	World[1]				Developed countries				Less-developed countries			
	1993	1994	1995	1996	1993	1994	1995	1996	1993	1994	1995	1996
All manufacturing	0	6	5	3	–1	6	4	3	5	5	6	6
Heavy industries	0	7	6	4	–1	7	6	4	6	6	7	7
Base metals	1	5	3	1	–1	6	3	0	11	4	4	7
Metal products	–2	8	8	6	–2	9	7	5	5	7	11	8
Building materials, etc.	0	5	3	1	–1	5	1	–1	4	6	7	6
Chemicals	1	5	4	3	0	5	4	2	4	5	4	6
Light industries	1	3	2	1	0	3	1	1	3	4	5	4
Food, drink, tobacco	1	3	3	3	1	2	1	2	3	6	7	6
Textiles	–1	2	–1	–1	–3	3	–1	–3	3	1	0	2
Clothing, footwear	0	2	2	2	–2	2	–2	–2	5	1	9	8
Wood products	1	4	1	1	0	4	1	1	2	4	1	2
Paper, printing	2	3	2	0	2	3	1	0	6	4	6	2

[1]Excluding Albania, China, North Korea, Vietnam, former Czechoslovakia, former Soviet Union, and former Yugoslavia.
Source: UN, *Monthly Bulletin of Statistics.*

Table IV. Index Numbers of Production, Employment, and Productivity[1] in Manufacturing Industries

1990 = 100

Area	Production 1995	Production 1996	Employment 1995	Employment 1996	Productivity 1995	Productivity 1996
World[2]	110	113	. . .	. . .	. . .	. . .
Developed countries	107	110	. . .	. . .	. . .	. . .
Less-developed countries	126	133	. . .	. . .	. . .	. . .
North America[3]	119	124	. . .	. . .	. . .	. . .
Canada	110	112	89	93	123	120
United States	115	118	97	97	119	122
Latin America[4]	112	114	. . .	. . .	. . .	. . .
Brazil	111	112	. . .	. . .	. . .	. . .
Mexico	103	117	. . .	. . .	. . .	. . .
Asia[5]	113	119	. . .	. . .	. . .	. . .
India	134	144	. . .	. . .	. . .	. . .
Japan	95	98	100	100	95	98
South Korea	151	163	98	96	154	170
Europe[6]	102	104	. . .	. . .	. . .	. . .
Austria	113	115	. . .	. . .	. . .	. . .
Belgium	104	104	. . .	. . .	. . .	. . .

Area	Production 1995	Production 1996	Employment 1995	Employment 1996	Productivity 1995	Productivity 1996
Denmark	116	117	. . .	. . .	. . .	. . .
Finland	115	118	81	82	142	144
France	97	98	. . .	. . .	. . .	. . .
Germany (1991=100)	96	96	. . .	. . .	. . .	. . .
Greece	98	98	. . .	. . .	. . .	. . .
Ireland	162	176	110	115	147	153
Netherlands, The	105	108	. . .	. . .	. . .	. . .
Norway	112	115	. . .	. . .	. . .	. . .
Portugal	96	97	. . .	. . .	. . .	. . .
Sweden	115	117	. . .	. . .	. . .	. . .
Switzerland	103	103	. . .	. . .	. . .	. . .
United Kingdom	102	102	. . .	. . .	. . .	. . .
Rest of the world[7]	. . .	. . .	. . .	. . .	. . .	. . .
Oceania	104	105	. . .	. . .	. . .	. . .
South Africa	103	103	97	98	106	105

[1]This is 100 times the production index divided by the employment index, giving a rough indication of changes in output per person employed.
[2]Excluding Albania, China, North Korea, Vietnam, former Czechoslovakia, former Soviet Union, and former Yugoslavia.
[3]Canada and the United States.
[4]South and Central America (including Mexico) and the Caribbean islands.
[5]Asian Middle East and East and Southeast Asia, including Japan, Israel, and Turkey.
[6]Excluding Albania, former Czechoslovakia, former Yugoslavia, and European countries of the former Soviet Union.
[7]Africa and Oceania.
Sources: UN, *Monthly Bulletin of Statistics;* ILO, *Yearbook of Labour Statistics.*

the world economy, growth slowed sharply in 1996 as the major economies pursued the fiscal rigour that was required for getting their budget deficits below the 3% necessary to qualify for economic and monetary union (EMU), which was scheduled to be inaugurated on Jan. 1, 1999. In the major economies of the EMU core, especially France and Germany, activity was sluggish; the little growth that took place was derived from the export sector, whose competitiveness was enhanced because of a strong dollar. Even in the face of very low interest rates, domestic demand remained weak.

In the European periphery it was a different story. The British recovery, having started a year later than that in the U.S., was gaining momentum, though for manufacturing the strength of sterling against the European currencies was a significant handicap. The major success story, however, was Ireland, which during the 1990s increased its manufacturing output as fast as any other country and where total GDP was growing annually at rates nearing double figures.

Fueled in part by exports of Japanese capital and in part by an innate dynamism, the economies of the Pacific Rim recorded the fastest rates of growth during the 1990s. Expansion spread from the first phase of "tiger" economies (Hong Kong, Singapore, South Korea, and Taiwan) to other countries around the Pacific Rim and into South Asia. At the same time, growth moved away from the traditional heavy industries to electronic goods, clothing and footwear, and even automobiles. The rate of progress was not without problems, however, and in 1997 concern over rising current-account deficits spread from Thailand across the region. Speculation forced currency devaluation, and interest rates rose, which increased the cost of overseas borrowing and restrained domestic demand. For the rest of the world, the troubles of the region were a mixed blessing. On the one hand, the developed economies enjoyed a continuing stream of consumer goods that were even cheaper in dollar terms than before, whereas on the other, exports to the area were held back by weaker domestic purchasing power.

For the former communist countries taken as a bloc, the process of transition, while undoubtedly painful, was beginning to show results. Progress was uneven, with Poland, Hungary, and the Czech Republic advancing most rapidly. As a general rule, however, those countries that pursued comprehensive stabilization and reform policies were beginning to experience economic growth, which they were combining with reasonable rates of inflation; increasingly, those nations were being rewarded with reintegration into the world financial system. There were backsliders on reform (Belarus and Slovakia) and major problems with inflation (Belarus, Bulgaria, and Romania), but on balance the outlook was good. (GEOFFREY R. DICKS)

ADVERTISING

The buoyant economy and the continued growth in consumer confidence contributed to strong gains in advertising spending in 1997. Worldwide advertising on all media, including direct mail and the Yellow Pages in telephone directories, was expected to climb 6.2% to $411.5 billion in 1997, according to Robert J. Coen, McCann-Erickson Worldwide's senior vice president in charge of forecasting. Total U.S. ad spending in 1997 was expected to reach a record $186 billion, an increase of 6.2% from the 1996 total of $175.2 billion. Coen estimated that expenditure on advertising within the U.S. would rise 6% to $109.2 billion, led by strong growth in television, local radio stations, newspapers, and magazines. Spending on overseas advertising by U.S. firms was forecast by Coen to total $225.5 billion, up 6.3% from $212.1 billion in 1996 and led by strong growth in Brazil, Great Britain, China, Mexico, and South Korea.

By late in the year there were indications that spending by U.S. advertisers in 1998 would increase about 5.6% to $196.5 billion, fueled by interest in advertising during the Winter Olympics in Nagano, Japan. An early indication that spending would continue its robust pace came from advance sales of network television time for the 1997–98 season. Sales hit a record $6 billion, up roughly 6% from $5.6 billion a year earlier, even though the network share of the television viewing audience continued to shrink. One consequence of the brisk sales was that "clutter" on television—the time devoted to commercials and promotions—reached a new high in 1996, according to a report sponsored by the American Association of Advertising Agencies and the Association of National Advertisers. The report found that clutter accounted for one-fourth to one-third of all network television time during all parts of the broadcast day in 1996.

Commercial time on Super Bowl XXXI, broadcast by the Fox network on Jan. 26, 1997, sold at somewhat higher prices than those charged by NBC for Super Bowl XXX. The fifty-six 30-second commercial units that were aired during the game went for a record average price of about $1.2 million each, about $100,000 more than in 1996.

Account change activity reached record levels in 1997 as a wide variety of companies made decisions affecting their advertising. Eastman Kodak Co. dismissed the J. Walter Thompson Co., its agency for over 65 years, and consolidated all its consumer photography accounts, with annual spending of about $300 million, at Ogilvy & Mather Worldwide. McDonald's Corp., after intense creative competition between its two national agencies, selected the Chicago office of DDB Needham Worldwide as its lead domestic agency, relegating the Leo Burnett Co., Chicago, to a secondary role after 15 years. Other major firms changing agencies included Delta Air Lines, which moved its $100 million account to Saatchi & Saatchi Advertising Worldwide from BBDO Worldwide; Taco Bell Corp., which chose TBWA Chiat/Day in Los Angeles to handle the $200 million creative portion of its account; and Saab Cars USA, which selected the Martin Agency in Richmond, Va., to handle its $50 million account.

Despite the many account changes and agency roster realignments, there was during the year a surprisingly strong improvement in the relationship between advertising agencies and clients, according to the results of the 1997 Salz Survey of Advertiser-Agency Relations. In the survey 39% of agencies said there was more teamwork with their clients, a large gain from the 23% that reported that result in the 1996 survey. The percentage of advertisers who said there was more teamwork with their agencies also rose, from 49% in 1996 to 54%, the highest level since the 63% response in 1992.

An annual survey by the American Association of Advertising Agencies reported that the average cost of producing a 30-second national television commercial rose nearly 6% in 1996 to $278,000 from $263,000 in 1995. That increase represented a reversal from the previous year, during which the cost decreased 2% from 1994 to 1995. Advertisers continued to demonstrate their support of television shows that touched on controversial subjects, such as the "coming out" story line in which the character portrayed by Ellen DeGeneres (*see* BIOGRAPHIES) on ABC's sitcom "Ellen" announced that she is gay. Companies that ignored the pressure from conservative groups not to advertise on the show won their bet of taking advantage of the hoopla surrounding the episode, which scored a 23.4 rating, compared with the season's average of 9.6 for the series.

Advertisers aggressively increased their spending in cyberspace during the first half of 1997. According to Cowles/Simba Information, a unit of Cowles Business Media, advertising revenue on the World Wide Web reached $217.3 million through the first six months of 1997, more than triple the $61 million that the company reported was spent in the first six months of 1996. Forrester Research of Cambridge, Mass., estimated that $400 million would be spent on Web advertising in 1997.

Ad pitches on the Web moved during the year beyond simply displaying advertisers' names or products. AT&T introduced Web ads that "talk," incorporating dialogue and motion video. Other sites, including Talk City, a chat site, introduced "intermercials," long-form communications lasting up to four minutes. The name, intermercials, is based on interstitials, a form of Web advertising in which a message automatically pops up in front of a user while the browser is downloading a page within a site. Interstitials generally appear for a certain period of time, usually seconds, and then disappear. Toyota and Sears Roebuck and Co. were among the first to use them.

A landmark settlement between the U.S. Food and Drug Administration and the nation's tobacco marketers pushed such familiar icons as Joe Camel and the Marlboro Man off outdoor billboards. The settlement banned cartoon characters and human images from tobacco advertising and prohibited tobacco signs in outdoor sports arenas and on store signs visible from the outside. Europe's health ministers later agreed on an even stricter ban.

Advertisers were expected to concentrate on promoting their brand names in 1998. A study by Corporate Branding Partnership LLC found that a strong corporate brand may be a public company's best defense against a volatile stock market. The stocks of the 20 U.S. public companies with the strongest brand power gained market value during the October 1997 stock market gyrations, whereas the stocks of the 20 companies with the weakest brand power lost a combined $19.8 billion in market value, the company estimated. "Brand power" was Corporate Branding Partnership's measure of a corporation's reputation and recognition among key audiences. Companies with the strongest brand power included Coca-Cola and Microsoft. (LAURIE FREEMAN)

AEROSPACE

In 1997, after the worst recession in aviation history, most airlines experienced business upturns, some of them vigorous, though often the revenues had to be used to help liquidate debt that had accumulated during the lean years. Pooling arrangements continued to benefit the companies, though the agreement between British Airways and American Airlines caused European Union (EU) officials and smaller airlines to voice fears of monopoly over the North Atlantic. Europe's airline industry began a profound change as deregulation became effective during April, opening competition to smaller operators within a region long dominated by national flag carriers.

Demand for new equipment rose as business improved. Airbus Industrie planned to increase production to 220 aircraft per year in 1998, up from about 185 in 1997 and 126 in 1996. Unlike Airbus, Boeing had already been operating at full capacity and could not immediately meet demand. This was caused partly by the inability of equipment and raw-materials suppliers to meet Boeing's needs. Many such suppliers, cynical because of earlier predictions of an upturn that had failed to materialize and therefore cautious about risking investment, were swamped by the sudden wave of demand. Aircrew hiring was also brisk, and the U.S. Department of Defense became concerned about the drain of expensively qualified military pilots to the airlines.

Encouraged by the upturn, notably around the Pacific Rim, both Boeing and Airbus continued work on their respective "jumbo" designs. Airbus proposed the 550-seat, four-engined A3XX, to be launched in 1999, and Boeing finally abandoned further development of the 747 to concentrate on new, long-range variants of the twin-engined 777. One of these, the 777-300X, would have about the same size and weight as a 747 and was aimed at Pacific Rim operators.

The decision by McDonnell Douglas in 1996 to terminate the Douglas MD-XX trijet airliner, its proposed competitor to the top-of-the-range Boeing and Airbus transports, marked the end of the line for this company as an independent airframe supplier. Boeing and McDonnell Douglas then announced a collaborative deal by which Douglas Aircraft would become a major subcontractor to the Seattle, Wash., firm, and the merger was formally signed in August 1997. Production of the existing MD-11 and MD-90/95 families would continue until demand dried up. With the retreat of Lockheed from the large transport aircraft field in 1983 and the disappearance of Douglas, Boeing remained the sole U.S. supplier.

Boeing again made news when it reached agreement with three airlines to buy its aircraft in return for favourable financial deals. The 20-year agreement with Continental Airlines, finalized in June, followed similar arrangements with Delta Air Lines in March and American Airlines in May and resulted in objections from EU officials, already upset by what they saw as unfair competition by the Boeing-McDonnell Douglas merger.

Consolidation of the aerospace industrial base continued rapidly, most notably in the U.S. European aviation experts criticized the reluctance of their national governments to streamline their still-fragmented industries so that they could compete more effectively with such U.S. companies as Boeing-McDonnell Douglas, Lockheed Martin, Northrop Grumman, and the major electronics giant Raytheon. European efforts to integrate businesses were particularly hampered by the return of a Socialist government in France and the subsequent reversal of a French policy designed to speed both privatization and collaboration with other European partners. The new French government clearly intended to keep aerospace in its own hands and so protect national assets. In particular, an earlier agreement by Airbus consortium partners to restructure the firm into a limited liability company by 1999 was thrown into doubt.

Concern for air safety continued to mount in the face of increasingly crowded skies. Worries were expressed over the lack of adequate—or even any—air traffic control over Africa. A report by the International Federation of Air Line Pilots' Associations describing the situation throughout the region as "critically deficient" noted 77 near collisions involving commercial aircraft in 1996. Fears were justified in September when two large military transports, one German and the other American, collided off Namibia with the loss of all on board.

Poor command of English by many air traffic controllers was also cited as the possible cause of at least two accidents: one in Colombia in December 1995 and the other in Indonesia in September 1997. Meanwhile, detective work continued in an effort to pin down the exact circumstances leading to the TWA Flight 800 disaster off the coast of New York in July 1996, thought to be due to a fuel-tank explosion.

U.S. ambitions to launch a supersonic transport (SST) took a new turn as Boeing teamed with the Russian company Tupolev in a NASA program to refurbish a TU-144 as a flying laboratory. Data returned from the laboratory would help U.S. industry develop a 300-passenger SST with a 12,900-km (8,000-mi) range early in the next century. The 14-strong TU-144 fleet had been abandoned after one crashed at the Paris Air Show in 1973.

In the military field the new Lockheed Martin/Boeing F-22 Raptor made its first flight. This next-generation U.S. Air Force fighter would replace the 1960s-era F-15 Eagle as the top U.S. combat aircraft. Meanwhile, other programs, such as the U.S. Navy's F/A-18E Hornet, the Lockheed Martin/British Aerospace Joint Strike Fighter (JSF), and the Northrop Grumman B-2 stealth bomber, competed for funding. McDonnell Douglas, the longtime leading builder of U.S. fighters, was eliminated from the JSF competition. Consideration was given to a future—unmanned—version of the best-selling U.S./European F-16 fighter.

Europe's Eurofighter 2000 continued in its flight-test program, but German doubts about its cost continued to stall award of a production contract. India stepped up its defense capabilities with the operational deployment of its first squadron of Soviet-designed Sukhoi Su-30 long-range fighters, and plans were made to acquire Russian-made aerial tankers to support them. India also launched a $2.3 billion program to develop and build its own stealth combat aircraft. In the face of a continuing financial crisis, Russian aerospace officials were selling production rights for top-line military planes in order to maintain both a home industry and a national defense capability. Overall, the European aerospace industry reversed five years of decline with a 12% revenue increase in 1996, and an even better result was expected for 1997.

(MICHAEL WILSON)

After abandoning further development of its 747 jetliner, Boeing unveiled the 777-300X, a new, long-range variant of the twin-engined 777 that the company planned to aim at Pacific Rim operators. The 777-300X had about the same size and weight as the 747.

TIM CROSBY—GAMMA LIAISON

APPAREL

Clothing. After several years of lacklustre sales in the apparel-manufacturing industry, there was an upturn in sales and profits in 1997. Whereas many industry experts attributed this positive change to improved consumer confidence, it was also likely that consumers had satisfied their demand for other products, especially electronic ones. Clothing also became a consumer bargain. Efficiencies in production and "quick-response" inventory controls kept apparel prices constant and thereby provided a greater value compared with other goods.

Industry employment in the U.S. continued to decline in 1997, falling to about 800,000 workers. Two factors contributed to the downtrend: low unemployment and increased productivity by U.S. workers, who had twice the capability of workers of the 1970s as a result of new technologies. Unusually low U.S. unemployment forced apparel factories to compete for workers with the service sector and other manufacturing industries. Traditionally, the industry had relied on immigrant labour for assembly work, but tighter immigration laws and a shift to manufacturing in rural communities, where there were usually fewer immigrants, effectively eliminated this resource. A majority of the members of the American Apparel Manufacturers Association, which represented 80% of U.S. production, reported problems in attracting and keeping an adequate workforce.

Owing to labour shortages and price pressures, U.S. apparel companies expanded assembly operations in countries where they could take advantage of lower labour costs and a large workforce. Under the North American Free Trade Agreement (NAFTA), apparel assembly skyrocketed in Mexico. Production also increased in nations in the Caribbean basin, where U.S. legislators considered extending NAFTA-like benefits. Overall, apparel imports into the U.S. increased 17% in the first seven months of 1997.

The globalization of the apparel industry, in both production and sales, prompted the U.S. Federal Trade Commission to test a symbol system for apparel-care labels that was similar to an existing system in Europe. The symbols would appear for 18 months with written care instructions, which would allow consumers time to familiarize themselves with the symbols. The use of symbols would eliminate the multilingual instructions required for products marketed in any of the three NAFTA countries. If the pilot program was successful, the apparel industry would consider switching exclusively to symbols in January 1999.

Criticism of the apparel industry in regard to wage and hour abuses continued. The White House Apparel Industry Partnership, an industry-government-labour task force created by the administration of U.S. Pres. Bill Clinton, attempted to develop recommendations for improving domestic and international labour standards, including the creation of an international monitoring program to inspect apparel factories worldwide. In October U.S. federal investigators found that 63% of the garment companies in New York City that were under suspicion had violated overtime or minimum-wage laws.

Simultaneously, the Smithsonian Institution's National Museum of American History announced plans for an exhibit on "sweatshops" to be centred on the 1995 discovery of an illegal factory in El Monte, Calif. Apparel and retail industry associations criticized the planned exhibit both for its strong bias toward labour and for its focus on one industry.

(ALLISON WHEELER WOLF)

Footwear. It was a year for big deals in 1997 as footwear makers signed licensing agreements, pursued designer alliances, and negotiated endorsement contracts. Stride Rite Corp., owner of the rights to the Tommy Hilfiger and Levi's footwear labels, landed its third licensing deal with Nine West Kids. Meanwhile, Stride Rite sought to reestablish its classic Keds brand by joining forces with high-profile shoe designers Todd Oldham and Cynthia Rowley, who produced modern collections inspired by Keds' 82-year-old Champion Oxford style. Nike, Inc., launched Jordan, a signature brand of basketball footwear and apparel named for superstar Michael Jordan. A midyear downgrade of Nike stock, however, caused industry watchers to worry that the whole athletic category would spiral downward. Nike also came under fire from human rights groups because of its overseas labour practices.

Florsheim Group Inc. reported increased sales and revenues ($28.7 million) in the first quarter, and Steve Madden Ltd. posted higher second-quarter earnings, up $357,000, compared with a $431,000 loss in the first quarter of 1996. Reebok International Ltd.—owner of the Rockport Co. subsidiary and the Ralph Lauren footwear license—had modest growth in the second quarter, and the Timberland Co. returned to profitability after losses in 1996. Wolverine World Wide Inc., maker of Hush Puppies, Caterpillar, and Wolverine Wilderness, reported net earnings up as much as $9.2 million and revenues up $162.2 million.

Action-sports and skate-shoe products were hot sellers. The success of companies like Vans Inc., Airwalk, Etnies, and Reef Brazil was boosted by unprecedented levels of participation in extreme sports, and the ease and casual styling of this footwear took the market by storm.

Wolverine World Wide purchased Merrell Footwear for $17 million and announced the creation of a new outdoor-footwear division. LaCrosse Footwear Inc. paid $6.5 million for Lake of the Woods. Meanwhile, German footwear giant Adidas AG purchased control of Salomon SA in a deal worth almost $1.5 billion.

Payless ShoeSource Inc. acquired the nearly 190-store Parade of Shoes from J. Baker Inc. and proposed an expansion of the chain into locations left open after the 1996 shuttering of J. Baker's 357-store Fayva chain. Payless also opened five stores in the greater Toronto area, its first move into Canada. Nine West Group Inc. closed the deal for about 60 British Shoe Corp. concessions, which brought its total retail units in Great Britain to 180. (BONNIE BABER)

Furs. The winter of 1996–97 was a disappointing season for retail sales of furs, along with other cold-weather apparel. Abnormally mild temperatures throughout much of the Northern Hemisphere contrasted sharply with the previous harsh winter, which had encouraged retailers to prepare for a repeat of that season's brisk business. As a result, stores were left with excess inventory, and there was a decline in fur-skin purchases at the international auction houses in the spring of 1997, which forced a substantial fall in prices. A year earlier there had been strong demand from the new Russia and China, which competed for supplies with South Korea, but reduced pressure from Russia and China coupled with economic problems in South Korea forced buyers to be more conservative.

In the U.S. the price of a mink pelt fell from $53.10 in 1996 to an average of $35.30 in 1997. Nevertheless, world production of ranch-raised mink increased 7% to a total of 26,295,000 pelts that would be earmarked for sale in 1998. Denmark accounted for 14.8 million of that total, or 56.2%. Although the U.S. crop was up 8%, it accounted for only 2.7 million pelts. World production of ranched foxes declined 5% from the previous year, with a total of 4,453,000 pelts. The leading producer was Finland with 2,550,000 pelts.

There was also a sharp upturn in the popularity of fur among leading fashion designers and the media. According to the Fur Information Council of America, about 160 designers incorporated furs into their collections in 1997, either as entire garments or as trimmings or linings to complement textile or leather apparel.

Animal rights activists persisted during the year in their often violent efforts to close down the fur industry. Although the FBI, which had branded the Animal Liberation Front a domestic terrorist organization, stepped up law-enforcement activities, vandals broke into ranches and allowed thousands of pedigreed mink to run free into nearby forests. Although many arrests were made and convictions obtained, the violence continued. (SANDY PARKER)

AUTOMOBILES

The performance of the automobile industry in 1997 very much mirrored the economic performance of the different regions of the world. In the United States a stable economy produced vehicle sales that, though down 1% from 1996, exceeded 15 million units for the fourth year in a row. In Europe, except for occasional bright spots, sluggish economic growth produced a flat market that barely exceeded 13 million units. The Japanese auto market, reeling from a tax increase imposed early in the spring, fell 2% but was off as much as 7% in the later months of the year. The less-developed nations, particularly in Southeast Asia and Latin America, showed strong sales growth through the early part of the year but virtually collapsed when those regions suffered currency and economic crises in the second half.

In Europe automakers worried about the health of the auto market. Weak economic conditions in many countries dampened sales. Analysts pointed out that were it not for tax incentives offered by the Italian government to scrap older, more polluting cars in favour of newer, cleaner ones, the market would have dropped below 13 million units. They forecast that sales would fall below that level in 1998. Nonetheless, certain sectors of the European market performed well. Sales of so-called monocabs—subminivans—were particularly strong, led by the Renault Mégane Scénic. The company had to triple production to meet demand. Mercedes-Benz also unveiled its revolutionary tiny city car called the A-class, which initially enjoyed explosive sales. Mercedes was caught by surprise, however, when a group of Swedish automotive journalists, conducting an emergency swerving maneuver, or what they called the "elk test," managed to flip one over. The ensuing negative publicity forced Mercedes to stop production until it could provide a hasty engineering fix.

In Southeast Asia the collapse of the currency markets in many countries brought car production to a halt. Toyota announced that it would close its plants in Thailand for the year, while other automakers cut back production severely. In South Korea Kia lost a bid with bankers to avoid bankruptcy when it could not cover interest payments on its debts, and the government announced it would nationalize the automaker. At the same time this was happening, Samsung readied plans to jump into the market, which led many auto executives to worry that their fears of excess capacity in the industry were beginning to be realized.

In Japan Suzuki had the best-selling car in the country, the Wagon R, displacing the Toyota Corolla, which had held the position for more than a decade. Honda surpassed Mitsubishi to become Japan's third largest automaker, behind Toyota and Nissan.

In Latin America the repercussions of Southeast Asia's currency problems reverberated through the Brazilian economy. A steep hike in interest rates, combined with a new tax on automobiles designed to shore up the Brazilian currency, brought growth to an end in what had been one of the strongest markets in the world. Because of the sudden drop-off in sales, virtually all automakers there announced immediate production cutbacks to reduce inventories. Brazilians hoped that their strong economic medicine would prove to be an invigorating tonic in the long run, and they pointed to Mexico as a hopeful example. Three years after the collapse of Mexico's peso, the country was able to post solid double-digit increases in sales.

In the United States the market continued its seemingly inexorable swing toward light trucks. Sales of pickup trucks, minivans, and sport utility vehicles reached 45% market share, up from 43% the year before. Many market analysts projected that this share would reach 50% in a few years.

After having lost market share in the U.S. during the previous five years, Japanese automakers were able to regain 1.1 points of share, owing to a weakening yen and new products. The yen, which lost about 13% of its value, allowed Japanese automakers to cut costs on the imported vehicles and parts they brought in from Japan. New designs allowed them to cut costs further. Toyota, for example, introduced an all-new Corolla with a new 1.8-litre engine that, thanks to clever design, used 200 fewer parts than the motor it replaced. These design changes, in conjunction with the weaker yen, allowed Toyota to cut $1,500 from the base price of the Corolla to $11,908. Sales of the subcompact car, by contrast, jumped 6%. Other Japanese automakers also either introduced new models at reduced prices or did not increase the prices of carryover models. American car buyers reacted positively to these alluring prices and pushed up sales figures of most Japanese automakers. Both the Toyota Camry and Honda Accord surpassed the Ford Taurus, which had been the best-selling passenger car in the U.S. for the previous five years. On the other hand, Japanese automakers Nissan, Mazda, and Suzuki saw sales drop 3.5%, 7%, and 21%, respectively.

The European automakers enjoyed impressive increases in sales in the U.S. Mercedes-Benz posted its highest totals ever, surging 27% to more than 100,000 units, thanks largely to the introduction of several new models. The ML320 sport utility vehicle, made at Mercedes-Benz's new assembly plant in Vance, Ala., allowed the prestigious German brand to enter a new segment in the American market, and it scored an instant hit. The first year's production quickly sold out, and the showroom traffic generated by the ML320 carried over to the rest of the Mercedes-Benz line. It was able to capitalize on this momentum and relay that success across its product line.

Audi, BMW, and Porsche also enjoyed solid, double-digit increases in U.S. sales. Market analysts said baby boomers entering their peak earning years were increasingly gravitating to the luxury car market, and most European makes represented the "boutique" type of brands those consumers were after. Even Volkswagen, which competed in the middle part of the market, held its ground as it awaited new replacements for the Golf and Jetta. VW also began laying careful plans for the introduction of the new Beetle, which was first exhibited in early 1998.

While the U.S. Big Three automakers lost more than two points of share to the Japanese and European automakers in passenger cars, they continued to dominate the light truck segment. This strength in trucks, along with various cost-cutting measures, helped General Motors' North American Operations (NAO) to return to profitability for the first time in the 1990s. Even so, GM NAO's performance was hampered by United Automobile Workers of America (UAW) strikes that cost the company more than half a billion dollars in net profits. Future clashes with the union seemed virtually assured when the company announced its goal to shed more than 40,000 hourly workers over the next five years. GM also announced that it would close its Buick City assembly plant in Flint, Mich., in 1999; the plant employed 2,900 workers.

Ford reported record earnings for the year. In North America this was largely due

A welder works at a Toyota plant in Bangkok. The collapse of currency markets in Southeast Asia brought car manufacturers in the region to a halt. Toyota announced it would close its plants in Thailand for the year, and other automakers cut back production severely.

DILIP MEHTA—CONTACT PRESS IMAGES

to the immense popularity and profitability of its large sport utility vehicles and pickup trucks. The company introduced a new full-size sport utility, the Lincoln Navigator, which became an instant sales hit and which analysts estimated earned up to $15,000 per unit in gross profits. To bring its production capacity for passenger cars in line with demand, Ford announced that it would close the assembly plant in Lorain, Ohio, that made the Ford Thunderbird and Mercury Cougar. Unlike the GM announcement to close Buick City that unleashed a torrent of bitter condemnation from the UAW, Ford's announcement to close the Lorain plant provoked no such outcry. To ease the pain of this plant closing, Ford quietly told the UAW that it would invest close to $2 billion for a new paint shop, a new gas tank plant, and a new engine plant at its River Rouge Plant manufacturing complex in Dearborn, Mich. This, Ford told the union, would ensure the viability of the facility and the jobs it provided well into the 21st century.

Chrysler ran into several bumps in the road. After years of speculation, the company announced that it was going to drop its Eagle division, owing to sagging sales. Chrysler was also hit by a strike in the late spring at its Mound Road engine plant in Detroit, Mich., which in turn delayed deliveries of its hot-selling trucks. Sales and profits were additionally reduced owing to the massive retooling of two assembly plants. The Bramalea plant in Brampton, Ont., was shut for months, preparing for the introduction of the all-new Dodge Intrepid and Chrysler Concorde. The Newark, Del., plant was shut to convert to production of the all-new Dodge Durango sport utility vehicle. Production of Chrysler's pickup trucks also slowed as the company readied its plants to produce the Dodge Ram Quad Cab, the first pickup in the American market with four doors. Although the press focused on GM's market-share loss, Chrysler actually lost more share; on a percentage basis it lost nearly twice as much share as GM. Chrysler executives said they expected their new models to regain market share and improve profitability. Analysts agreed with this assessment, pointing out that the Quad Cab pickup alone would likely generate an additional $200 million in revenue.

The large consolidation in the automotive supplier community continued throughout the year. For $625 million Tower Automotive bought A.O. Smith's Automotive Products Co., which specialized in stamping. BREED Technologies, Inc., bought the safety restraints business, including air bags and seat belts, from AlliedSignal for $710 million. Federal Mogul launched a $2.4 billion effort to purchase the British supplier T&N PLC., and Lear Corp. bought the seating component business from ITT Automotive. Rockwell International spun off its automotive operations as a $3.1 billion standalone company that was renamed Meritor.

Ford reorganized its components operations on a global business into a new $16.4 billion business entity called Visteon Automotive Systems, with a goal of quadrupling its non-Ford business to 20% from 5% within five years. Financial analysts predicted Ford would ultimately prepare Visteon for a partial stock spin-off, much as GM planned to do with its Delphi Automotive Systems. GM launched a new program for suppliers to assume more responsibility for warranty expenses, which were estimated to cost the automaker about $600 per vehicle. Previously, GM picked up most of the warranty costs of defective components. Now, it told suppliers, they would have to pay the warranty costs on any defective parts they produced.

The so-called revolution in automotive retailing in the U.S. picked up steam throughout the year. Ford launched a new retail initiative in Indianapolis, Ind., wherein it tried to persuade dealers in that market to join forces. Studies by marketing analysts and automakers alike showed that most new car buyers disliked the treatment they received at dealerships. The company's plan involved buyouts that would reduce its 24 or so dealerships in the Indianapolis market to only 5. Ford reasoned that fewer, but larger, stores would reduce the competition between its dealers, allowing them to obtain better transaction prices. The larger stores would also be expected to provide customers with a better selection of products. Ford also hoped to improve the retail-buying experience of its customers in these new stores. After initial interest, however, the dealers balked at the prices Ford offered for their stores, which they considered too low. Consequently, that effort failed, but Ford launched a new plan in Tulsa, Okla., along the same lines, and the company left little doubt that it wanted to revamp its retail network.

Toyota and Honda fought to almost no avail to prevent Republic Industries, the "megastore" retailer owned by billionaire Wayne Huizenga, from purchasing dealerships in the quantity and time frame it wanted. Soon after Huizenga called a press conference with 25 state's attorneys to state his legal position regarding these purchases, Toyota announced it would drop its legal actions against Republic. By the end of the year, Republic had emerged as the single largest automotive retailer in the U.S., with over 150 stores, more than three times larger than the next largest retailer.

The Internet emerged as a significant source of information for car buyers. Ford's Web site, for example, received more than 650,000 visits a day. Auto-By-Tel, an Internet automotive information service that provided information on new vehicles and where they could be purchased, announced in November that it had reached its millionth request for purchase information.

Automakers and suppliers began to develop the capability for delivering Internet services directly into automobiles. Mercedes-Benz was the first to unveil a prototype to demonstrate the feasibility of such a system. Visteon demonstrated a voice-activated system that would allow drivers to dictate and send E-mail, as well as a speech synthesis system that would allow them to listen to their E-mail. IBM, Delco, Netscape, and Sun Microsystems teamed to produce a similar product. Both these systems allowed for other telecommunications capabilities, such as navigation and emergency services. United Technologies Automotive licensed Microsoft's CE operating system to develop capabilities that would allow consumers to use multimedia products from any company in their cars, instead of just those installed by the factory. Industry observers saw these moves as the first real effort by the consumer electronics industry to break into the auto business.

Honda announced a prototype for a new gasoline engine that could almost meet the zero-emission-vehicle levels proposed by the state of California. While the engine produced some emissions, they were barely higher than the equivalent emissions produced by a plant producing electricity for an electric car. By carefully controlling the combustion in the engine with a more powerful computer, and with a special catalytic converter designed to reduce cold-start emissions drastically, Honda achieved this milestone. Honda also announced its plans to build a five-passenger jet airplane, and it unveiled an anthropomorphic robot designed to cater to the needs of an aging population. As Japan had the oldest average age of any industrialized nation, Honda saw this as a new market opportunity to exploit.

At the end of the year, all automakers were focused on the conference on global warming that took place in Kyoto, Japan. GM, Ford, and Chrysler proposed that the U.S. increase the tax on a gallon of gasoline by 50 cents to steer car buyers into smaller, more fuel-efficient cars. Chrysler chairman Robert Eaton said his company was willing to abandon its full-size pickups and sport utility vehicles in favour of a European-type lineup of smaller vehicles—provided it could charge European-type prices, which were higher than those in the U.S.

With the industry under pressure to produce cleaner cars at lower prices, and with the markets it was relying on for growth sputtering to a stop, the year ended on a far more uncertain note than it started.

(JOHN MCELROY)

BEVERAGES

Beer. A true milestone was achieved in 1997, the year that the United States took Germany's place as having the most breweries in the world. By midyear the U.S. boasted 1,273 breweries, whereas Germany had "only" 1,234. This surge in the American total was directly attributed to the microbrewery boom of the 1990s. All but 23 of the U.S. production sites were classified as craft-beer plants. Although the numbers continued to mount, analysts believed that consumers might be tiring of variety and were likely to veer back toward tried-and-true beers. In terms of consumption, the European nation still set the standard; on a monthly basis the average Bavarian family of four consumed 15 litres (4 gal.) of beer, which was half a litre (one pint) more than they drank in milk. In terms of production, however, it was the U.S.—long looked down upon by Old World brewers as a hopeless neophyte—that led the world.

As craft brewers nervously awaited a shakeout of their suddenly crowded ranks, the largest U.S. brewers showed less interest than in previous years in that segment of the industry. Miller Brewing and Adolph Coors, the number two and three companies, experienced significant growth in 1997 by emphasizing top brands like Miller Genuine Draft and Coors Light to the general exclusion of experimentation with start-up labels. Top market brewer Anheuser-Busch pressured independent distributors to drop micro products and concentrate solely on Anheuser-Busch beers.

Decisions by Anheuser-Busch and Miller to discontinue selling their respective European-pedigreed brands Carlsberg and Löwenbräu represented an opportunity for Labatt to expand its presence across North America. The Toronto-based brewer picked up U.S. rights for both brands, which thereby strengthened the company's position in the "specialty" (craft plus imports) category and raised the profile for those two labels, which were neglected in the houses of Budweiser and Miller Lite. Meanwhile, Anheuser-Busch invested in American Craft Brewing International, a U.S.-based company that built microbreweries in Mexico, Hong Kong, and Ireland and imported on a limited basis some of those beers into the U.S.

Spirits. A new colossus took shape in 1997, creating a force that could dominate the spirits industry well into the 21st century. Guinness PLC and Grand Metropolitan PLC (Grand Met), two gigantic British companies in their own right, in May decided to merge into a single behemoth. The merger, the largest ever by British firms, had an estimated value of $38 billion. Guinness produced such brands as Tanqueray gin and scotch whisky brands Johnnie Walker and Dewar's, and Grand Met, which had the world's largest distilling operation, produced Smirnoff vodka, Bailey's Irish Cream, and J&B Scotch whisky. Other properties in the deal included Guinness beers, Grand Met wines Almaden and Inglenook, and such nonbeverage interests as Pillsbury and Burger King. The deal was held up several months by the French company LVMH Moët Hennessy Louis Vuitton, which held a significant stake in Guinness and was eventually made part of the new organization. The new conglomerate was dubbed Diageo PLC, a combination of the Latin word for "day" and the Greek word for "world."

In the U.S., advertising of all spirit brands continued to infiltrate the television airwaves following the 1996 decision by sellers of distilled spirits to abandon their voluntary 60-year practice of avoiding such advertising. Major TV networks, however, maintained their own prohibition on liquor commercials, and cable and local stations were left as the only outlet for spirits advertising. The Federal Communications Commission (FCC) was petitioned by 10 states to ban spirits advertising, and U.S. Pres. Bill Clinton, in the stated interest of protecting children, implored the industry to restore its previous stance. Corporate heads, however, refused to put the genie back in the whiskey bottle, citing the freedom of beer and wine producers to advertise anywhere they pleased. By year's end the FCC had not taken definitive action on the matter.

The vodka field in particular proved to be fertile territory. France, a noted wine country, jumped into this segment with Grey Goose Vodka; Poland offered a musical tribute with Chopin Vodka; and Canada launched Inferno Pepper Pot Vodka, which was bottled with a pair of fresh, flaming red peppers.

(GREG W. PRINCE)

Wine. Vintage 1997 was generally received with optimism for the quality of the harvest. The quantities, however, were a concern. Italy continued a decline in yield dating back to 1980 with the harvest more than 15% below the average. The only area not suffering from low yields was California, which set records for its volume.

In France the Bordeaux harvest started earlier than it had since 1983, with the picking of the white varietals beginning on August 18 and the reds during the first week of September. In Burgundy the grapes displayed great ripeness, which promised wines of soft fruit. Most of the nation's wine merchants and growers judged the 1997 Beaujolais nouveau, rushed to the market in late November, to be better than the 1996 product. According to Henri Sornin, whose family owned the Domaine des Ronze in the Beaujolais region, "It's nicely fruity; it has very strong violet colour, with a little tart taste of fruit-drop candy."

The Italian harvest promised very good quality despite the low yields. South of the Equator, the story was generally the same. Australia, South Africa, and Chile all harvested smaller-than-average crops. Chile continued its fourth year of drought, which affected the grapes. South Africa experienced a late cool spell that allowed the grapes to hang on the vine longer and develop the fruit. There was some concern about harvesting all the grapes before the rains began, but this turned out not to be a problem.

The entire wine world was shocked and saddened by the sudden death on July 25 of Gerard Jaboulet, of the Rhone firm of Paul Jaboulet. The company would continue to operate, but Jaboulet's guidance, humour, and leadership would be missed. Also dying during the year, on November 3, was Edmond de Rothschild, owner of one of the first mail-order wine services.

Toward the end of the year, financial troubles in Asia caused auction prices to moderate, slowing an almost unbroken upward spiral. Wine publications continued to hold sway over the marketability of the products. One publication declared "co-winners" of its Wine of the Year awards, rating two 1994 Ports equally. (HOWARD HERING)

Soft Drinks. Although Snapple was the soft-drink brand that during the 1990s redefined "New Age" in general and iced tea in particular, the drink lost some of its lustre when it was sold by its entrepreneurial founder in 1994 and became part of the corporate culture at Quaker Oats. In 1997 Quaker lost faith in its $1.7 billion investment and sold the struggling portfolio of ready-to-drink teas and juices to a New York-based upstart conglomerate, Triarc Companies Inc., for the bargain price of $300 million. Many felt that Snapple would revive under the care of a smaller, hungrier company.

Coca-Cola introduced Surge, an energy drink, to about one-half of the U.S. market in an effort to challenge PepsiCo Inc.'s stalwart Mountain Dew, which owned the "heavy citrus" category. Coca-Cola hoped that young consumers would "Feed the Rush" with its "fully loaded citrus soda" (charged with scads of caffeine, sugar, and drink-till-you-drop drive). By far, the top soft-drink brand in the world continued to be Coca-Cola, flagship of an international empire unmatched for reach and recognition in any consumer category. Roberto Goizueta, the company's chairman and chief executive officer and the man responsible for having spurred the company to its greatest heights in its 111-year history, died in October after a brief bout with cancer. (*See* OBITUARIES.) When Goizueta became head of the company in 1981, Coke was valued at $4 billion; at the time of his death, that figure was $145 billion. His successor, M. Douglas Ivester, was expected to continue to steer Coke along its impressive growth curve.

Among the most intriguing newcomers of the year were O2 Water, a "superoxygenated" packaged product that promised to improve athletic performance; Java Juice, a beverage that injected the previous buzz-free domain of orange juice with a shot of caffeine; and Nutz, a sparkling drink available in four nut flavours. (GREG W. PRINCE)

Leading Beer-Consuming Countries in 1995
(in litres per capita)

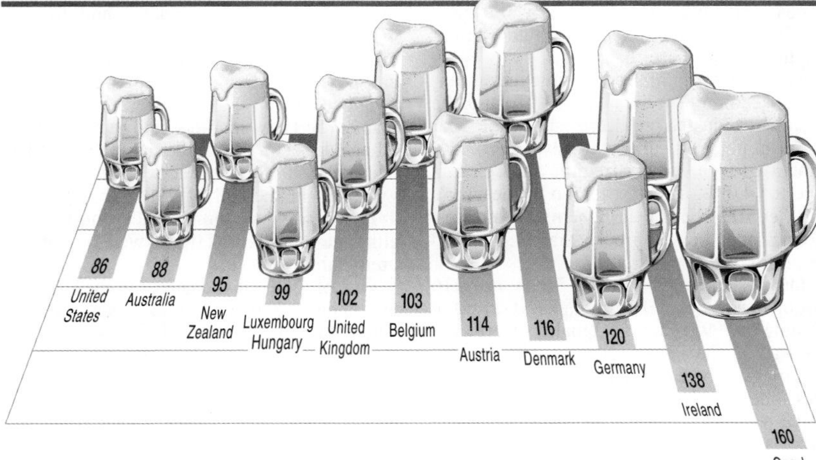

Source: *World Drink Trends*, in association with Produktschap voor Gedistilleerde Dranken, Schiedam, Neth.

BUILDING AND CONSTRUCTION

Construction, fueled by the longest sustained period of U.S. economic expansion since World War II, began to lose momentum in 1997. The National Association of Home Builders reported 1.4 million housing starts for the first three quarters of the year, signaling an annual decline of 2.5% from 1996. In August the U.S. government announced that $601.8 billion of construction had been completed, a 5% increase from the 1996 level. Annual spending on public infrastructure continued to grow at a modest pace of 2.3%.

In California the $1 billion, 5.6-km (3.5-mi)-long Cypress Replacement Project opened to freeway traffic in the San Francisco Bay area. The highway connector replaced a double-decked expressway that had collapsed in the 1989 Loma Prieta earthquake. The six-lane seismically resistant replacement was scheduled for final completion in 1998. The Metropolitan Water District of Southern California continued work on the $1.9 billion Eastside Reservoir Project, which was designed to double surface-storage capacity for a system that supplied water to 16 million residents from Los Angeles to San Diego. A 986,800,000-cu m (800,000-ac-ft) lake would provide a six-month water reserve if an earthquake severed feeder aqueducts from either the Colorado River or northern California. The utility also continued work, begun in 1995 and scheduled for completion in 1999, on three dams to contain water in a valley 145 km (90 mi) southeast of Los Angeles.

U.S. government proposals for tighter emission standards from power plants, coupled with state and federal moves to deregulate the sale of electricity, spawned the construction of more efficient power plants and retrofits to control emissions from existing coal-fired units. A consortium that was building a 520-MW combined-cycle power plant in Bridgeport, Conn., claimed that the natural-gas-fired unit would emit fewer pollutants than the 80-MW coal burner it was replacing.

American architect Frank Gehry's striking $100 million Guggenheim Museum opened in Bilbao, Spain, in October. A cluster of 11 titanium steel-covered building blocks rose in irregular double curves around a 50-m (164-ft)-high glass atrium.

The world's largest public-works project, Hong Kong's Chek Lap Kok Airport, stayed on schedule despite Hong Kong's change in political status in July. The new airport, built on an island, had road and rail links to the city; it was scheduled to open in the spring of 1998. On the Chinese mainland the first phase of the controversial Three Gorges Dam, the largest flood-control and hydropower project in the world, neared completion. (*See* ARCHITECTURE AND CIVIL ENGINEERING: *Sidebar.*) Currency fluctuations imperiled Thailand, which was forced to renegotiate contracts with several international engineering and construction firms for work on Bangkok's massive wastewater-treatment upgrade after the baht went into a tailspin in midyear. Malaysian Prime Minister Dato Seri Mahathir bin Mohamad postponed the start of work on the Bakun Dam, a $5.5 billion hydropower project on the island of Borneo. Critics charged that the structure would have generated 2,400 MW of unneeded power while displacing 10,000 indigenous people and destroying large tracts of rain forest.

In sub-Saharan Africa, where 70% of the population was without running water, several components of the Lesotho Highlands Water Project, a joint multiyear effort by Lesotho and South Africa, neared completion. Botswana embarked upon a $330 million, 30-year effort to bring water to its agrarian-based economy. It completed the Letsibogo Dam in its eastern sector and advanced the North-South Pipeline, an aqueduct that would transport water some 360 km (225 mi) south to Gaborone, the nation's capital.

(ANDREW G. WRIGHT)

PETER MENZEL

A lab assistant checks a flask of plant concentrate in a processing room at Shaman Pharmaceuticals, Inc., in South San Francisco. By studying the treatments of indigenous medicine men in Africa, South America, and Southeast Asia, the company identified more than 3,000 possible sources of new drugs.

CHEMICALS

Even though the world chemical industry increased the value of its output to $1,570,000,000,000 in 1996 and rolled strongly into the next year, 1996 was somewhat disappointing in that the growth from 1995 was only 0.2%—as compared with a 1986–96 average of 6.3%. Much of the slowdown resulted from slumps in several of the major chemical-producing nations, including Japan, Germany, and The Netherlands.

These dips more than offset the slight gains of others in the ranks of the top 10 chemical-producing nations, which were, in order, as tabulated by the U.S.-based Chemical Manufacturers Association (CMA): the United States, Japan, Germany, France, China, Great Britain, Italy, Russia, South Korea, and Spain. Of these, only Italy and possibly China increased the value of their production by more than 4%.

Much of Western Europe enjoyed an excellent economic climate in 1997, and the chemical industry predicted late in the year that it might well surpass the expected 2.5% annual growth for the region and reach a level of 4–5%. The fast tempo at the year's end led the European Chemical Industry Council members to predict that 1998 would be almost as good.

Japan's chemical sales in 1996, at $216 billion, were down 13% compared with the volume in 1995. Chemical makers were cautious about the 1997 prospects. The country was plagued by financial problems, but there was one helpful aspect; the low yen-to-dollar value was viewed as aiding chemical exports.

The U.S. chemical industry, according to a late-1997 survey by the CMA, was estimating a 5.5% rise in revenues (compared with 1% in 1996), with after-tax profits jumping by 10%. Export markets, predicted to rise 12% over the 1996 level, were credited with stimulating the growth, and small companies were particularly optimistic about the future.

Compilations from the CMA showed that sales of chemicals totaled $57.5 billion in 1995 in Central and Eastern Europe, down from $64.9 billion in 1994. Responsible for most of the dip was Russia, estimated to have done a 1994 business of $33.6 billion and just $23.9 billion in 1995. Asian nations with emerging industries had targeted their chemical industries for growth, but the countries' attractiveness to outside investors was limited by their shaky economies and a currency collapse in mid-1997.

National economies were not the only problems of chemical makers in the industrialized nations. The unrelenting pressures applied by the international financial community on every industry pushed chemical companies into trying to find the most immediately profitable products and to trim workforces. It also led to the continued reevaluation of the best mixes of businesses and products. The major companies in 1997 swapped assets, closed plants, opened new plants, tried new markets, and retreated from other markets at the same fast pace that had marked 1996. Despite the wild stock market gyrations in the fall of 1997, the chemical industry was not immediately hurt badly, although long-term effects were not easily predictable.

One of the largest changes in the structure of a chemical company took place in Britain when Imperial Chemical Industries (ICI) purchased the specialty chemical businesses of Unilever for $8 billion. ICI announced in May that it planned to pay for part of this move by reducing its stake in bulk chemicals and selling off $5 billion in assets of this type.

A number of companies were viewing relatively high-priced, low-volume specialty chemicals as important profit boosters. One such specialty area was labeled "life sciences," and many companies were expanding in this arena. As applied by the companies, the term included biotechnology, pharmaceuticals, and new types of agricultural chemicals. In June Rhône-Poulenc of France began a new degree of commitment to life sciences by organizationally and financially separating them from its more conventional chemical businesses and basing an entirely new firm on its Rhône-Poulenc Rorer pharmaceuticals unit. A few months later the U.S.-based Monsanto Co. announced plans to spin off to stockholders its conventional chemical businesses, with annual sales of $3 billion, under the corporate name of Solutia. The Monsanto name was retained for its advanced bioscience products, which included "genetically engineered" forms of molecules that would, for example, stimulate milk production in cows and alter the susceptibility of crops such as corn and cotton to pests or pesticides.

South America and the Middle East continued to strengthen their roles in the chemical industry. Data for 1995—the latest available from the CMA—revealed that South America's domestic sales reached $94 billion, nearly 21% above the 1994 mark of $77.8 billion. Firm figures on the countries of the Middle East were unavailable, but industry experts, noting the continued petrochemical industry expansions there, believed that the region's production was increasing faster than that of Europe.

In Western Europe Germany was the largest producer, with about one-fourth of the region's chemical sales volume. France had 1996 sales of $84.1 billion ($84.6 billion in 1995—although in local currency terms its sales were up) and accounted for more than 17% of Europe's chemical business. Sales in Britain increased to $56 billion in 1996 from $55 billion a year earlier. Italy's sales in 1996 rose 4.3% to $53.1 billion from $50.9 billion in 1995.

World trade in chemicals rose in 1996. Western Europe exported chemicals valued at $294.6 billion and imported $238 billion, with exports up slightly (0.2%) and imports down somewhat more (1.7%). The U.S. in 1996 exported chemicals valued at $48.7 billion (compared with $46.4 billion in 1995) and increased its imports 17%, to $36 billion from $30.7 billion. Japan saw its chemical exports dip to $28.7 billion from $30 billion, and its imports declined to $25.3 billion from $29.5 billion.

(J. ROBERT WARREN)

ELECTRICAL

Sales of electrical power plants, appliances, and lighting fixtures in the Americas and the Asian-Pacific region showed modest growth in 1996 but were offset by a stagnant market in Europe. This sluggish demand cycle continued into 1997, and by late in the year a downturn in sales in East Asia was beginning to be felt by some of the large electrical equipment manufacturers. Competition in all product ranges was so intense that the industry was increasingly dominated by a handful of large multinational firms. To counteract falling profit margins, even the largest multinationals were adopting innovative methods of increasing productivity.

The solution conceived by the General Electric Co. was probably the most speculative. The company introduced a "Six Sigma" quality level, defined as fewer than 3.4 defects per million operations in a manufacturing or service process. Six Sigma was regarded as particularly significant for preserving the reputation of GE's domestic appliances division. In the company's power systems division, 300 people were hired, trained, and certified to lead quality improvement projects. Many smaller manufacturers would consider this to be an unjustifiable expense, but GE claimed that for most U.S. companies defects can cost up to 10–15% of their revenues. Six Sigma was costing GE $90 million in the power division alone, but the division expected to achieve almost $1 billion in cumulative savings over the next four years (the division's 1996 revenue was $7,257,000,000).

Siemens AG, the world's largest electrical equipment manufacturer, had launched a "top" program in 1993 to increase productivity and encourage innovation. In 1996 total productivity gains were up more than 8%, and the cumulative gain over the previous three years was nearly 25%. Gains in 1997 were expected to reach 10%.

Despite its name, GE did not restrict its business to electrical equipment and ranked third in the electrical industry, after Siemens and ABB Asea Brown Boveri Ltd. GE's revenue in 1996 totaled $79,179,000,000, but of that only $28,734,000,000 came from electrical equipment manufacturing. In comparison, total revenue at Siemens in 1996 was $53,817,000,000, and at ABB it was $34,574,000,000.

Innovation appeared to be ABB's top priority to gain competitive advantage. The company stated that it had successfully countered intense price competition in developing power plants through a strategy of utilizing new designs of high-efficiency plants to cut costs and construction times. ABB also found that improvement in production economics was a natural result of its expansion program under way in Asia and Eastern Europe.

Expertise in all aspects of financing was rapidly becoming another important competitive factor. As a result of the privatization and deregulation of the public electricity supply companies in many parts of the world, private investors and operating companies began ordering many new power-generating plants. This was a promising market for those suppliers willing and able to invest in such projects, and beginning in 1995 Siemens invested heavily in power-plant projects in Spain, Portugal, India, Pakistan, Indonesia, and China. In 1996 GE coarranged debt and equity financing for the first large privately funded power project in Mexico and formed a joint venture with Shanghai Power to fund and operate China's first long-term nonguaranteed commercially financed power project.

Maintenance and repair contracts and spare part sales, particularly for power plants, were also becoming increasingly important for the industry. For GE those services brought in $8.4 billion in 1996, an increase of 11% over 1995. The Anglo-French major plant manufacturer, GEC Alsthom, stated that its service and maintenance activity represented about 25% of sales and extended to equipment manufactured by other companies.

One innovation from ABB could have wide sales appeal, as it might make it economically feasible to supply electricity from the public mains to isolated consumers. It could also be viable to connect small isolated generating equipment to the public electric distribution system. Those prospects were based on the development of compact cost-effective equipment to convert alternating current into direct current and vice versa. Such converters would link the consumer and the small generators to the public power networks. Until recently economic considerations had limited direct-current power transmission to the transport of very large amounts of power over long distances, notably in Russia and Canada.

(T.C.J. COGLE)

ENERGY

Petroleum. Crude oil producers continued to benefit from relatively high prices in 1997, as robust economic growth in a number of regions drove global petroleum demand. World oil markets started the year in strong shape when a cold snap in the Northern Hemisphere sent the price of Brent Blend, the North Sea crude that serves as an international price bellwether, as high as $25 a barrel in January. The early price hike caused some industry analysts to predict that the rising price trend evident in 1996—when Brent rose 21% over 1995 to average more than $20 a barrel—would carry over to 1997. With the onset of milder weather, however, spot prices quickly drifted down to an $18–$21-per-barrel range for much of the year.

Iraq continued to be the main wild card in the international oil market. In the summer Iraqi concerns about the slow delivery of food, medicines, and other relief supplies under the United Nations oil-for-food deal resulted in the temporary suspension of Iraqi oil exports. Shipments were later resumed, but a showdown that began in late October with the U.S. and UN over the presence of Americans among UN arms inspectors in Iraq added new uncertainty to oil markets.

The uncertainty surrounding Iraqi exports had a marked influence on world prices, as the amounts were large enough to tip markets into imbalance. Factors that helped underpin prices in 1997 included lower-than-expected output from producers outside OPEC. Continuing delays in bringing new fields into production accounted for much of the problem.

A shortage of skilled workers and key pieces of equipment, including drilling rigs, also plagued the international oil industry during the year. Even with such problems, however, some of the biggest non-OPEC producers remained optimistic about the prospects for production growth. In September Norway, the world's second largest oil exporter, after Saudi Arabia, said its peak output might be higher than the official forecast of 3.7 million bbl per day.

High oil demand from major consuming countries such as the United States also helped support prices. U.S. oil demand grew at an annual rate of approximately 1.5%, a modest level when compared with fast-growing countries such as China, which in September recorded nearly a 15% year-on-year increase. The U.S., however, remained the world's most important oil market in regard to volume, consuming nearly 19 million bbl a day, of which 9.8 million were imported.

World economic growth continued to be a key determinant of overall oil demand, and the financial turmoil that struck a number of Asian countries toward the end of the year added yet another element of uncertainty to petroleum markets. OPEC, which included some of the world's biggest producers, such as Saudi Arabia and Iran, decided in late November to increase by 10% its long-neglected production ceiling of just over 25 million bbl a day. The timing of the decision, in the midst of the Asian economic crisis, was seen as negative for prices, which fell below $18 a barrel shortly after the group concluded its discussions.

The number of OPEC countries that had begun to rely on foreign oil companies to finance ambitious oil expansion plans continued to climb. Venezuela, the only Latin-American member, proved successful in attracting billions of dollars of investment into its oil industry, with much of it coming from U.S. oil companies eager to have a large source of supply only a few days away by ship from the numerous refineries along the U.S. Gulf of Mexico coast.

In November Iran, which had previously offered foreigners only limited access to its oil industry, signaled that it too would be relying more heavily in the future on international investment to boost oil output. For the first time since before the Islamic revolution in 1979, Iran decided to allow foreign companies to explore and develop onshore oil deposits within its borders.

The growing interest of the international oil industry in Iran angered the U.S. government, which imposed unilateral sanctions on foreign companies that invested in oil and gas sectors in Iran, charging the nation with promoting international terrorism. The decision by Total of France, Petronas of Malaysia, and Gazprom of Russia to begin developing Iran's giant offshore South Pars gas field in the Persian Gulf triggered a formal U.S. investigation, which could lead to U.S. sanctions against those companies.

The European Union and other governments objected to the threatened use of unilateral U.S. sanctions. They claimed that oil companies operating in Iran were not breaking any international agreements or domestic laws in their respective home countries.

U.S. oil companies responded to the U.S. government's growing use of unilateral sanctions by mounting a lobbying campaign in Washington. The companies feared they would be increasingly excluded from deals in a number of countries because of the sanctions.

The foreign operations of U.S. oil companies also came under the scrutiny of domestic pressure groups; during the year Texaco decided to withdraw from a controversial gas development in Myanmar (Burma). The Texaco withdrawal allowed Petronas, the Malaysian state oil group, to step into the deal. Petronas exemplified another trend that emerged in 1997, that of state-owned oil groups from less-developed countries competing directly with the established Western firms for new exploration or development rights. The China National Oil Company was similarly successful in using its political influence to win two multibillion-dollar oil-development deals in Kazakstan against fierce competition from Western companies.

During the year a broad commitment to developing the reserves of the Caspian Sea region emerged from the international industry. Some observers believed the area might one day rival the Persian Gulf region in output.

Azerbaijan and Kazakstan signed a series of agreements with international oil groups to open big reserves to development. Many of the deals were in large part politically inspired, as both countries were eager to secure diplomatic support from the U.S., Europe, and China for their independence in a region still dominated by Russia.

Russia remained a priority area for many Western oil companies, which were lured by the country's large number of discovered but undeveloped oil fields. Political opposition within Russia to foreign companies' playing a major role in such a strategic sector and the lack of adequate legal safeguards kept foreign investment levels low, however.

Another region that drew substantial interest from the international oil industry in 1997 was the deep water off the west coast of Africa. Several large discoveries were announced druing the year, especially in Angola.

(ROBERT CORZINE)

Natural Gas. Natural gas in 1997 continued to make inroads into energy markets previously dominated by oil. The fuel received a big boost in December when countries attending the international climate-change conference in Kyoto, Japan, voted to impose legally binding targets for the reduction of greenhouse gases. One of the main ways to reduce such emissions was to replace coal-fired electricity-generation plants with those that used natural gas.

In December European Union energy ministers approved a plan that would open the $1 billion-per-year European natural gas market—presently dominated by national monopolies—to limited competition over a 10-year period. Consequently, many expected European gas prices, which were higher than those in North America and much of Asia, to fall, which would thereby improve the EU's industrial competitiveness.

In the United States, which in 1997 was the world's biggest natural gas market, increasing demand for gas triggered a wave of new proposals to build large-capacity pipelines. Industry figures revealed that U.S. demand for natural gas had risen by almost 3% per year over the past five years.

(ROBERT CORZINE)

Coal. During 1997 the world increased its reliance on an old fuel, coal, to obtain more of its most modern and versatile energy, electric power. Production reached an all-time high of 5.4 billion short tons in 1996, and preliminary statistics for 1997 showed continued strong demand. Coal was the primary fuel for generating electric power, providing almost 40%. Worldwide economic growth raised electricity requirements among nations in all stages of development: industrialized, especially the United States; industrializing; and less-developed, especially China and India. Coal generated more than 55% of the electric power in the U.S. economy, the global economy's largest component, and more than 70% in both China and India, the most populous countries. Preliminary statistics put 1997 U.S. production at a high of about 1.1 billion short tons, the fifth billion-ton year, and consumption for power at about 895 million short tons, another record. Other nations that produced more than 200 million short tons were China, Russia, India, Germany, Australia, South Africa, and Poland.

(RICHARD L. LAWSON)

Nuclear. The International Atomic Energy Agency statistics for 1996, published early in 1997, indicated that there were 442 nuclear units operating in 33 countries at the beginning of the year, a net increase of five over 1995. Total operating capacity was 350,964 MW, an increase of 7,172 MW over the previous year. Worldwide during 1996 nuclear power units produced a total of 2,312.06 TWh, which brought the cumulative total of electrical energy produced by nuclear plants to 29,600.1 TWh (terawatt-hours; 1 TWh = 1 billion kw-h). A total of 36 units were under construction in 14 countries, including 3 new projects on which construction began and 5 that began production. Five units were scheduled to begin production during 1997.

Countries with the largest proportion of the national electricity production from nuclear power in 1996 were Lithuania (83.4%, from 2 nuclear units), France (77.4%, from 57 units), Belgium (57.2%, from 7 units), and Sweden (52.4%, from 12 units). The total number of commercial power reactors permanently shut down throughout the world remained at 71 (Bruce 2 was shut down in Canada but might be restarted).

The second world environmental summit, held in Kyoto, Japan, at the end of the year, provided a platform for countries to renew their pledges to reduce the production of greenhouse gases, made at the 1992 Earth Summit in Rio de Janiero and subsequently largely broken. Thus, in 1997 politics, rather than technology, had been making nuclear power's potential for reducing greenhouse gas production even more difficult to achieve.

Sweden ranked fourth in the world for dependency on nuclear power. Its long-standing political commitment to phasing out nuclear power by 2010 presented the government with several dilemmas. The country was to lose more than 10,000 MW of base load power stations, more than half its generating capacity, which could be replaced only by more expensive, less reliable, and much more environmentally damaging fossil-fuel capacity, including imported electricity. This would result in a dramatic increase in greenhouse gases and other pollution produced by electricity generation and cancel any achievement the country had made toward meeting the commitments made at the Rio conference in 1992.

Ontario, the leading nuclear power province in Canada, continued to suffer the crisis of confidence from the mishaps that had toppled its units from their position of a few years earlier as the world's best-performing nuclear reactors. Ontario Hydro announced that it would shut down 7 of its reactors to allow resources to be concentrated on bringing the remaining 12 back up to the previous levels of excellence.

Progress with nuclear power was still to be found, however, particularly on the eastern Pacific Rim. North Korea became a nuclear energy nation when several protocols signed in New York City cleared the way for construction to start on two reactors at Sinpo, 240 km (150 mi) from Pyongyang. The agreements were between North Korea and the Korean Peninsula Energy Development Organization, a multinational consor-

J.C. TORDAI—PANOS

A woman tends bees in the shadow of Armenia's only nuclear power plant, located in Medzamor. An energy program outlined by the Armenian government in 1995 called for the opening of a second nuclear power plant between 2005 and 2010.

tium formed to implement the earlier agreements between North Korea and the U.S. and to help organize the project.

General Atomics won a $133 million contract from Thailand to design and build a nuclear energy research centre for Thailand's Office of Atomic Energy for Peace. The centre was to include a 10-MW research reactor, an isotope reprocessing facility, and a waste-treatment plant. A Thai government committee was appointed to study the possibility of building that country's first nuclear power plant.

Progress was made with the Shelter Implementation Plan (SIP), the internationally supported effort to finally deal with the deteriorating Chernobyl 4 "sarcophagus." The site of the wrecked reactor was to be rendered environmentally safe in an eight–nine-year project costing about $750 million. Ukraine's minister of environment and nuclear safety, Yury Kostenko, said in early July that the closing of the remaining operating unit at the station would be delayed if the promised financing did not materialize. Further help was needed with the financing of new units at Khmelnitsky and Rivne to replace the Chernobyl generating capacity. Ukraine's contribution was already at the limit of what it could afford; the government had to find $1 billion to deal with the consequences of the accident. The Group of Seven leading industrial countries, meeting at about the same time, set up a new multilateral funding mechanism and agreed upon a $300 million contribution to the SIP.

(RICHARD A. KNOX)

Alternative Energy. The public profile of alternative energy rose in 1997 when two of the world's biggest petroleum companies—the Royal Dutch-Shell Group and British Petroleum (BP)—announced large investments in the sector. Shell designated alternative energy as one of five core businesses for the group, the Western world's largest energy company, and promised to invest $500 million over the next five years to expand its presence in solar energy and sustainable forestry projects.

BP said it aimed to increase its sales of solar panels from $100 million in 1997 to $1 billion over the next decade. The company believed that solar power could compete with conventional power sources to meet peak electricity demand within the next 10 years.

Alternative energy also received a boost from the conference in Kyoto on climate change and global warming, although many experts warned that it would take years, if not decades, before energy sources such as solar, wind, and biomass could make deep inroads into the global energy market. A Shell study predicted that alternative energy could provide 5–10% of the world's energy needs within 25 years and account for half of global energy consumption by the middle of the 21st century.

(ROBERT CORZINE)

See also Architecture and Civil Engineering; Transportation.

This article updates the *Macropædia* articles ENERGY CONVERSION; FOSSIL FUELS.

GAMES AND TOYS

The toy industry in 1997 saw its share of "must-have" items not only during the holiday shopping season but also throughout the year. Tyco Toys, Inc., followed its previous year's holiday success, Tickle Me Elmo, with Sing & Snore Ernie, whose actions included yawning and tummy movements. Similar and also popular was Tyco's Real Talkin' Bubba, a fuzzy bear with a Southern accent. Both disappeared rapidly from store shelves. Elmo remained on the market and was joined by such other Tickle Me toys as Big Bird and Ernie. Another of the year's introductions was the Microsoft Corp.'s interactive ActiMates Barney, which could move, sing, play games, and—with the use of a transmitter plugged into a computer or a videocassette recorder—interact with videotapes or episodes of Barney's TV show. This Barney did not come cheap, however; the basic retail price was at least $100, and additional equipment could raise the cost to as much as $250.

Early in the year electronic "virtual pets" made their entrance into the U.S. First introduced by Bandai Co., Ltd., in Japan in November 1996, Tamagotchi—"cute little egg"—soon was in demand worldwide. Displayed on a tiny liquid-crystal screen, the pet would hatch and then grow up over a period of days. When it needed care—food, medicine, play, sleep, discipline, or cleaning—it would beep, whereupon its owner had to push a button that would attend to its needs. If it was not taken care of, it would "die," though another push of a button would bring forth a new pet. Caring for the pets became an obsession with some owners, and parents, teachers, and even employers were becoming annoyed by the disruptions the toys caused, some going so far as to ban them altogether. Later versions, though, had a pause button that gave owners a break. Bandai received orders for at least 70 million of the cyberpets during the year, and such knockoffs as Tiger Electronics, Inc.'s Giga Pets were also on the market.

Electronic games continued to grow in number and popularity. There was no lack of violent action games aimed mostly at males, but an increasing number of new titles were designed to appeal to young girls. On the Internet, multiplayer games were attracting ever-increasing numbers of participants. Instead of playing against a computer program, users could compete with or against each other. The biggest seller, Ultima Online by Origin Systems, Inc., recorded as many as 9,000 simultaneous players on some occasions. To investigate what computer technology would mean to the future design of toys, the Massachusetts Institute of Technology Media Laboratory in October announced a five-year research project—Toys of Tomorrow.

The perennially popular Barbie—credited with having helped propel Mattel Inc. to the position of world's biggest toy maker—continued to make news in 1997. In May her newest friend, her first one with a disability, was introduced. Share a Smile Becky came equipped with a bright pink wheelchair. Also in May, 16 elegantly costumed limited-edition Chinese Empress Barbies, commemorating the handover of Hong Kong to China, were auctioned, and 5,000 other Chinese Barbies were later offered for sale. Talk With Me Barbie had CD-ROMs and a workstation that could be connected to a real computer; Dentist Barbie had a dentist's chair and instruments; and the 10th annual Happy Holiday Barbie was—for the first, and only, time—a brunette. Perhaps most surprising was the news that one of the 24 new Barbies released in 1998 would have more realistic proportions.

(continued on page 163)

SPECIAL REPORT

Gambling

by William R. Eadington

Gambling in the United States has been experiencing a period of unprecedented growth since the end of the 1980s. Though gambling policy is often controversial, and the activity is still considered a vice in the minds of many, its legal status in many jurisdictions has clearly moved from prohibition to restricted tolerance. Furthermore, increased public acceptance of gambling is reflected both in opinion polls and in the willingness of Americans to allocate considerable time and money to gambling pursuits.

Between 1982 and 1996 revenues from legal gaming industries in the U.S. grew from $10.4 billion to $47.6 billion. By 1997 casinos were operating legally in such diverse places as riverboats, historic mining towns, and Indian reservations. As recently as 1988, true legal casinos could be found only in the deserts of Nevada and at the shore in Atlantic City, N.J. By 1997, however, more than 25 states had operating casinos, and gaming wins of about $25 billion were being generated. This included Indian casinos, operating legally in more than 14 states, which in 1996 brought in more than $5 billion in gaming revenues. Lotteries, which were nonexistent in 1963, were operating in 37 states and the District of Columbia and generated revenues after payment of prizes of $15.4 billion in 1996.

New technologies and product innovations also affected the presence and extent of commercial gaming. Various new games, gambling schemes, or lottery products quickly became major dimensions of the commercial gaming industries in the 1990s. Video lottery terminals (VLTs) first appeared in South Dakota in 1989 and in 1996 were present in five states, where they accounted for nearly $900 million in revenues. Slot machines, VLTs, and/or electronic gaming devices were placed at racetracks in Iowa, Delaware, Rhode Island, West Virginia, and Louisiana, and video poker machines were also in various locations in Montana and Louisiana. These gaming devices accounted for about $750 million in gaming revenues in 1997. Internet gambling, though still in the embryonic stage, quickly became mired in legal controversy, with legislation introduced in Congress in 1997 that would prohibit such activities.

Where casino-style gaming was authorized, especially when there was little or no regional availability beforehand, surprisingly large gaming industries quickly emerged. Billion-dollar casino industries developed from scratch in the 1990s in the states of Mississippi, Illinois, Louisiana, and Connecticut. The casino industries of Missouri, Minnesota, and Indiana all exceeded the $500 million level in 1997, with Colorado and Iowa not far behind. California, which passed statewide regulatory legislation in 1997, had card clubs and technically illegal Indian gaming operations that exceeded $1 billion in gaming revenues.

Between 1994 and 1997 active opposition to the continuing spread of casino-style gambling appeared in the form of the National Coalition Against Legalized Gambling, an activist group that became the most visible opposition to commercial gaming in the country. Partly at their urging and partly as a result of broader concerns regarding the wisdom of such a rapid increase in the presence of gambling, Congress authorized the National Gambling Impact Study Commission in 1996. The commission, which began meeting in 1997, was charged with examining a wide variety of issues linked to gambling, including community impacts and social and economic benefits and costs. It was scheduled to complete its investigations by 1999.

Among those states that introduced casinos for the purpose of economic development in the 1990s, Mississippi was probably the most successful. The city of Biloxi and Tunica county were each becoming major regional casino-based destination resorts, with significant hotel and nongaming development taking place in addition to the casinos. Because of the diminishing political popularity of introducing new casino jurisdictions in the region, it appeared that Mississippi would hold its place as the southern regional casino centre.

Other new jurisdictions have experienced rockier performances. Riverboat casinos expanded operations in various locations in Iowa, Indiana, and Missouri in 1996 and 1997, but competition and market saturation have become issues in many markets, including the metropolitan areas of Kansas City and St. Louis. Riverboats in western Louisiana performed well by catering to the large eastern Texas visitors' market, but casinos in New Orleans continued to disappoint their owners and supporters. The bankrupt land-based casino Harrah's Jazz in New Orleans made no progress toward completion through October 1997, and the last downtown riverboat casino in New Orleans closed in October.

Indian gaming continued its rapid expansion but with some major controversies remaining unresolved. Legal battles involving tribal gaming continued in some states. In New Mexico the legislature finally approved a formula for compacting Indian casinos after previous agreements between tribes and the state's governor were disallowed by the state Supreme Court. In California tribes operated substantial casinos without compacts as legal and political battles raged between various parties, including U.S. attorneys, card clubs, the racing industry, and the governor.

Not every gaming industry has benefited from legal gambling's recent expansion. The pari-mutuel racing industry continued its long-term decline in the face of competition from casinos and lotteries. Gaming revenues generated by wagering on horses and dogs declined by 0.8% in 1996 to about $3.7 billion. More significantly, on-track revenues from live racing fell by 14% in 1996, which reflected a shift in betting activity to offtrack and intertrack wagering. In some states the racing industry has been successful in persuading legislators to allow them to offer slot machines or other electronic gaming. The result has been to make those racetracks de facto casinos.

It seems likely that during the next few years there will be a slowdown in political efforts to expand commercial gaming in America, partly because the general strength of the U.S. economy has reduced the urgency of undertaking significant job-creation and economic-development initiatives. Furthermore, many policy makers will wait until the National Gambling Impact Study Commission has issued its findings before making any future plans.

It is unlikely, however, that the spread of gambling will become totally dormant. Indian gaming will almost certainly continue to become better established and to expand in various locales. The racing industry will continue to lobby to offer casino-style gaming as a means to save racing. Finally, the increasing public acceptance of gambling as a legitimate form of entertainment and the economic benefits to communities in the form of increases in jobs and tax revenues suggest that there will continue to be political efforts to grab the golden ring offered by legal gambling.

William R. Eadington is Professor of Economics and Director of the Institute for the Study of Gambling and Commercial Gaming at the University of Nevada at Reno.

(continued from page 161)

Sales of other traditional toys remained high. The yo-yo was making a big comeback, and Duncan Toy Co. officials thought that 1997 sales figures could match the 1962 record of 25 million. Whereas some of the yo-yos were the basic models of yesteryear and retailed at about $10, others were made of aircraft aluminum, boasted such advanced technology as light-emitting diodes and centrifugal clutches, and sold for as much as $90. Action figures, especially Hasbro, Inc.'s toys tied in with such popular motion pictures as the *Star Wars* and *Batman* series, were popular as both toys and collectibles. The craze surrounding another collectible, the already established Beanie Baby, was heightened by McDonald's distribution of Teenie Beanie Babies in a Happy Meals promotion. (*See* Sidebar.)

Toys "Я" Us Inc., the world's largest toy retailer, made news in September when a federal judge ruled that it had violated U.S. antitrust laws and kept prices of certain popular toys artificially high by pressuring manufacturers to refuse to sell some lines to discounting warehouse clubs if they wanted to keep Toys "Я" Us as a customer. The discounters could obtain selected toys only in combination packages, and consumers thus could not compare prices. Ordered to cease making those deals with toy suppliers, Toys "Я" Us maintained that it had a right to determine what toys it would sell and planned to appeal the ruling.

Hasbro, the maker of such toys as Mr. Potato Head and the board games Monopoly and Trivial Pursuit in addition to its popular action figures, announced in December the biggest restructuring in the company's history. It planned to cut costs, reduce its workforce, and buy back stock in an effort to regain the number one status it had once enjoyed.

GameBoy designer Gumpei Yokoi and Bandai founder Naoharu Yamashina died during the year. (*See* OBITUARIES.)

(BARBARA WHITNEY)

Berserk for Beanie Babies

"Do you have Peace the bear?" To the uninitiated that inquiry might sound peculiar, but to the ever-increasing number of collectors of Beanie Babies—small animal-shaped beanbags filled with polyvinyl chloride pellets—it was one of the most frequently asked questions in shops about one of the most elusive toys in Ty Inc.'s menagerie.

Beanie Babies—each one readily identified by a folded heart-shaped hang tag that inside poetically stated its name and date of birth—were different from past must-have toys, however. They were not advertised on television; they were sold only in small stores such as gift shops, florists, and bakeries; and their retail price was around $5. Furthermore, retailers could not predict when they would receive shipments or just which animals would be included when they did arrive.

Nevertheless, Beanie aficionados were relentless in their search for some of the 135 creatures (not counting a few variations). A secondary market developed for trading, buying, and selling—at inflated prices—those animals that were more difficult to find. New designs came onto the market every few months, at which time a few old-timers would be "retired." Especially sought-after were rare variations of standard characters—a royal blue Peanut the elephant—or those considered to have mistakes—Quackers the duck with no wings, or Spot the dog with no spot. Also desirable were those whose tag, which had to be attached, sported a different character's name. Prices for these could top $2,000.

The first nine Beanies debuted in 1993 at a toy fair and were sold in the Chicago market the following January. Some three dozen designs followed in midyear, and by mid-1995—simply as a result of word-of-mouth advertising—the toys were in demand all over the U.S. Sales in 1996 were estimated at 100 million Beanies, and it was predicted that 1997 sales would be 10 times that figure. Beanies were also spotted in Canada (there was a special Maple the bear), in small shops in England, and at an outdoor market in Beijing.

The proof of the toys' popularity came in April 1997. What began as a simple sales-promotion collaboration between Ty Inc. and the McDonald's Corp., Ty's neighbour in Oak Brook, Ill., became a total frenzy. McDonald's plan was to distribute 100 million Teenie Beanie Babies, miniatures of 10 current designs, in its Happy Meals over a five-week period. The Teenie Beanies were so popular, however, that they virtually disappeared from the market by the end of the second week.

As "children of the '90s," Beanie Babies, along with their parent company, had a Web site that had attracted over a billion visits as of late 1997. At the end of October, that site announced that in December a new Beanie Baby would be introduced—Princess, a purple bear with a rose embroidered on its chest, in memory of Diana, princess of Wales. Profits from its sale would be donated to her memorial fund. (BARBARA WHITNEY)

KAREN WOLLINS

GEMSTONES

Although sales of gemstones increased during 1997, difficulties arising from a currency crisis in some of the leading Asian economies, notably in Thailand, seriously affected some parts of the trade in those countries. Sales of rough diamonds by De Beers Consolidated Mines Ltd. declined 4% from 1996. The crisis in the markets also resulted in lower prices, even for the finest specimens. Thailand, long the cutting and dealing centre for many of the important gem-producing countries, was in short-term danger of losing its role. Reports reaching London indicated that fine blue sapphires and rubies, perhaps the best-known Thai specialties, were in some cases changing hands for half the amount they would have obtained prior to the crisis.

In late October share prices in Hong Kong dropped severely, and the pegging of the Hong Kong dollar to the U.S. dollar appeared under threat. This would affect sales at auction and in particular those of top-quality jadeite jewelry traditionally held by the major auction houses in October–November. Those items were finer and much more plentiful than in previous years; top estimates at Christie's reached HK$5 million for a jadeite cabochon set in a ring.

Christie's was also offering in Asia the largest D-flawless diamond (weighing 22.13 carats) and the largest chrysoberyl cat's-eye (396.59 carats) ever to be sold at auction. At least three "named" diamonds were featured at various auctions; at a Christie's Geneva sale the 26.14-carat cushion-shaped Rajah carried an estimate of $1,500,000, and at Sotheby's New York the Jonker No. 7 diamond (19.74 carats) fetched a top estimate of $1,000,000 and the Presidente Vargas No. 4 diamond (28.03 carats) had a top estimate of $800,000. Christie's Geneva offered probably the finest ruby, an untreated stone of Myanmar (Burmese) origin, weighing 42.98 carats.

The diamond trade in India came under scrutiny after reports of widespread use of child labour in the diamond-cutting factories of Seurat, where some 20,000 children were reportedly working. The employer, De Beers, promised to investigate the matter. In October De Beers agreed to buy at least $550 million in rough-cut diamonds from Russia.

The fine emerald from Zimbabwe (the Sandawana emerald) was again being produced after supplies had long been scarce.

(MICHAEL O'DONOGHUE)

HOME FURNISHINGS

Furniture. While industry watchers were determining whether the furniture industry was undergoing a shake-up or was simply having a shaky period, sales proved that 1997 was not a spectacular business year. Despite an increase of about 5% in the sales of furniture at wholesale and a 7% increase for the top 100 retailers, the industry appeared unsettled. Most notable were the Chapter 11 bankruptcy filings of two retail giants, Levitz and Montgomery Ward, which together owed creditors over $90 million.

On the basis of the 1996 figures compiled by *Furniture/Today,* the top three U.S. manufacturers remained in the same positions as a year earlier. LifeStyle Furnishings International claimed first place ($1,733,300), followed by Furniture Brands International ($1,696,800) and La-Z-Boy ($985,200,000). According to the American Furniture Manufacturers Association, the wholesale total was $19,960,000,000 in 1996 and was projected at $20,978,000,000 for 1997, a 5.1% increase. In retailing, Heilig-Meyers, which placed second a year earlier, moved up into the number one spot nationally. The company was also rated the fastest-growing retailer in the U.S., with 944 stores and sales that amounted to $11,021,500. It replaced the troubled Levitz ($960.7 million), which came in second. Sears HomeLife was third, with $657 million in sales.

The furniture styles were varied. There was a surge in Modern, a newer, more-formal Continentalism, and a smattering of Mediterranean (now called Medi-Mix). The best Mediterranean-style group was Lane's Hearst Castle Collection, which was based on authentic Spanish antiques. As part of the retro movement, Bexley Heath Ltd. reintroduced the Widdicomb Collection designed by T.H. Robsjohn-Gibbings from 1946 to 1960, and Baker reintroduced *c.* 1940 and 1950 pieces by famed Danish Modern designer Finn Juhl. Two new big names entered the market: Bill Blass designed a collection for Pennsylvania House, and Eddie Bauer created a collection for Lane. Bob Timberlake created Timberlake House, using his designs for Lexington. An innovative, complete design program, it consisted of several packages that included house plans, interior designs, furnishings, and landscaping ideas. In addition, leather continued to gain market share, with new distressed textures and engraved patterns. Inducted into the American Furniture Hall of Fame for 1997 were John R. ("Jack") Gerken, Jr., Norwalk Furniture Corp.; Clyde Hooker, Jr., Hooker Furniture; and Albert G. Juilfs, Senco Product, Inc. (ABBY CHAPPLE)

Housewares. During 1996 houseware expenditures decreased by 7.1%, with American consumers spending $54 billion on such items as cookware, cleaning goods, heating and cooling equipment, tabletop appliances, and personal-care products. In 1996 the average U.S. household spent $522 on housewares, a $45 decrease from the previous year. Despite the slight decline in sales, some retail channels for housewares enjoyed high growth levels. Specialty chains expanded rapidly and opened new stores across the country. Virtual stores—those outlets not requiring a physical space (television, catalogs, and direct mail)—contributed to the state of flux. Television shopping networks and infomercials accounted for $4 billion in housewares sales, and consumers purchased $1 billion worth of household merchandise over the Internet. Some predicted that Internet sales of housewares would be five times that amount by the end of the decade.

Most items experienced at least a slight decline in sales. Clocks, hair-care products, and telephones and telephone accessories witnessed the severest decreases, with the latter falling by 62.3%. The 1995 boom in outdoor equipment leveled out and declined, with sales falling by 20.5%.

Expanded sales in safety-related products reflected an increased awareness of home-safety issues by consumers. Much attention was focused on alarms that combined smoke detectors with carbon-monoxide sensors. Smoke-alarm sales increased by an astounding 45.7% in 1996, and purchases of water softeners and filters went up by 18.9%.

(SUSAN DOLL)

INSURANCE

The three "C's"—computers, consolidations, and competition—highlighted the insurance industry in 1997. While companies scrambled to prepare for the "year 2000" computer problem, mergers and acquisitions created more global giants in insurance and financial services. Competition remained intense, particularly in the commercial field. A fourth "C," catastrophes, caused fewer weather-related insured losses, though uninsured losses were high as a result of flooding on the northern U.S. plains, hurricanes in Mexico, and earthquakes in Italy.

In 1996 worldwide insurance sales topped $2 trillion for the first time, with the U.S. accounting for 40% of the total, followed by Japan (14%), Germany (10%), and Great Britain (6%). Emerging Asian markets were relatively stagnant, and uncertainty surrounded the long-term effects of restrictions on competition as Hong Kong was returned to China.

During the first six months of 1997, U.S. property-liability profits were excellent, with net income after taxes up more than 50% to $18 billion. Warmer weather caused by El Niño reduced hurricanes on the Atlantic coast but increased Pacific windstorms. While auto-insurance results were generally favourable, changing demographics, including a declining number of households, hurt life insurers' sales. In the first six months of 1997, however, life-insurance sales increased a strong 6.3%, and annuity sales hit $41 billion, with assets up to $573 billion.

Better communication through E-mail, pagers, faxes, and toll-free telephone numbers brought significant changes. Advanced technology created new opportunities for agent interaction with customers, and the electronic world intensified the search for better methods of administration, asset and document management, claims handling, and underwriting. On-line sales, estimated at $300 million, were generally disappointing, but the Internet was useful for providing consumer information and generating sales leads.

Nearly 60 million people were covered by managed-care plans, and three of every four doctors participated in at least one of these programs. Aggressive pricing by health maintenance organizations raised questions about the relationship of costs to the quality of care and also caused dramatic changes in medical malpractice insurance. Long-term-care insurance received a boost from U.S. Department of the Treasury regulations that permitted taxpayers to deduct the cost of premiums and allowed nontaxable benefits for qualified plans.

Mergers dominated insurance news in 1997. The consolidation trend grew beyond insurance companies and agencies and brokers to encompass the entire financial services business, including banking, securities, accounting, and legal firms. The number of merger transactions was estimated to have been the largest ever in a single year. Large mergers included the acquisition of American States by Safeco Corp. for $2.8 billion, American International Group's purchase of American Bankers Insurance Group for $2.2 billion, and

Lincoln National's buyout of CIGNA Corp.'s life and accident business for $1.4 billion. Smaller mergers included purchases of Colonial Penn Insurance Co. by General Electric Capital Services and Acceleration Life by the Frontier Insurance Group, In Canada, Great-West Lifeco offered to buy the London Insurance Group for $2.1 billion, and in Europe the merger activity heated up, with the Zürich Group's pending acquisition of Scudder, Stevens & Clark for $1.7 billion and its plans to acquire B.A.T. Industries of London. ING Group of The Netherlands purchased Equitable of Iowa for $2.2 billion. Assicurazioni Generali also launched a $15 billion takeover bid for Paris-based AGF. Japan, the leader in the world's life insurance market, suffered its first failed life insurer in 50 years, Nissan Mutual, which lost $1.6 billion.

Lloyd's of London returned as a competitive force in the global insurance market. In January Lloyd's introduced a new internal-monitoring system designed to prevent huge financial reverses like the $12.4 billion it lost between 1988 and 1992. Lloyd's renaissance was spearheaded by new investments from foreign insurers and almost 100 other corporate groups. The company's claims-payment ability remained highly rated.

The U.S. courts handed down several important decisions affecting insurance. National banks would no longer be restricted from selling insurance in places with populations of 5,000 or less. Broadening the banks' authority to write insurance, however, became a federal versus state debate as regulators wrestled with how to limit and oversee this change. In September the House Commerce Committee postponed indefinitely the creation of an omnibus banking bill that would have dismantled many of the industry restrictions.

Several major class-action settlements made big news. The U.S. Supreme Court set aside a landmark $1.3 billion asbestos settlement fund established in 1993, ruling that the agreement did not provide for the legal interests of all the plaintiffs. The fate of the proposed $368.5 billion settlement offered by the tobacco industry to be paid out over 25 years was uncertain; states sought to recover Medicaid costs, and lawmakers put off taking legislative action until 1998. Settlements for deceptive sales practices could cost Prudential Insurance Co. of America up to $2 billion and John Hancock Mutual Life Insurance Co. about $350 million. Consumers could also benefit from the increased spending ($650 million) by insurers for fraud detection and prevention.

(DAVID L. BICKELHAUPT)

MACHINERY AND MACHINE TOOLS

Worldwide sales of machine tools increased 5.4% to about $38 billion during 1996, the last year for which figures were available. Japan was the largest producer, with total production valued at $9.2 billion, followed by Germany ($7.8 billion), the United States ($4.9 billion), Italy ($3.8 billion), and Switzerland ($2.1 billion). Countries with at least $1 billion in production included Taiwan ($1.8 billion), China ($1.8 billion), United Kingdom ($1.3 billion), and South Korea ($1.2 billion).

Metal-cutting machine tools, such as milling machines, drill presses, and lathes, made up the bulk of the machines produced worldwide. In the United States they accounted for about $3.1 billion in shipments. Metal-forming machine tools, such as bending machines, shears, and punch presses, accounted for about $1.4 billion of U.S. production.

The U.S. solidified its position as the largest consumer of machine tools. Sales to the U.S. shot up 7.4%, to $7.2 billion. Germany placed second, with consumption valued at $4.5 billion, and was followed by China ($4 billion), Japan ($3.5 billion), Italy ($3 billion), South Korea ($2.5 billion), France ($1.5 billion), the U.K. ($1.4 billion), Canada ($1.3 billion), and Taiwan ($1.1 billion).

Manufacturers in the U.S. purchased nearly $4 billion in machine tools from other countries. Japan, the major exporter to the U.S., sent $1.8 billion in machinery, and Germany sent $530 million worth of machinery.

The total export market for U.S.-built machine tools grew by nearly 14% in 1996 compared with 1995, reaching a total of over $1.3 billion. The principal export market for U.S.-made machine tools was Canada, which received $320 million in machinery, followed by Mexico with more than $200 million, China with $110 million, and Brazil with $100 million. Exports accounted for 26% of total U. S. production.

(JOHN B. DEAM)

MATERIALS AND METALS

Glass. It appeared in 1997 that between the years 1997 and 2007 the strongest growth within the glass-packaging industry would take place in India and China, where production could increase by over 160%. Production in China at that time would be far higher than in the two largest markets as of 1995—the U.S. (10.3 million metric tons) and Japan (10.2 million metric tons). Strong growth in South America was also forecast, as investment in new machinery and a substantial increase in end-user markets could lead to a near doubling in capacity. In Peru, for example, glass packaging for carbonated soft drinks increased by 180% between 1991 and 1996. By contrast, domestic demand for glass containers in Japan was likely to contract, as growth in the end-user sectors would remain slow because of increased competition from other packaging materials. In the U.S. demand remained static, as it had since 1990.

As predicted, growth in Eastern Europe remained strong, with Poland, Hungary, and the Czech Republic all expected to experience growth in excess of 22%, owing to strong end-user markets, primarily in the beer and soft-drink sectors. The potential for growth in glass packaging was massive in Russia—provided that the political and economic environment remained stable. In comparison, the rate of growth in Western Europe slowed considerably, totaling 6% in 1994, 4% in 1995, and just below 3% in 1996, owing to pressure from competition from other packaging materials. European container-glass producers were heavily involved in cross-border mergers and acquisitions in Western, Central, and Eastern Europe. Following the expansion of the European Union to 15 member states in 1995, the EU accounted for more than 96% of the total Western European production. In the EU container sector, capacity utilization was approximately 92% in 1996, and EU glass recycling was up 2%, just under 150,000 metric tons, from 1995. The total glass collected for recycling in the 17 countries was 7.6 million metric tons. Germany was the clear leader in terms of tonnage, with 2.8 million metric tons. Switzerland had the highest national recycling rate, with a record level of just under 90%, followed by The Netherlands with 81%.

By the year 2000 the countries of the Pacific Rim region should have a significant lead in the worldwide production of flat glass, mainly owing to continued development in the automotive and construction industries. China and India were also expected to experience strong growth. In Japan increased imports from surrounding neighbours signaled a relatively slow growth rate. Flat glass production in Eastern Europe was expected to remain attractive to Western investors as a result of its low cost. The completion of new float glass plants in Saudi Arabia, Turkey, Egypt, and Iran would make the Middle East and North Africa self-sufficient in flat glass manufacture but would add to the global oversupply.

(THERESA GREEN)

Ceramics. The ceramics industry experienced substantial overall growth during 1997, although manufacturing and environmental issues contributed to mixed performances in some sectors. Strong manufacturing economies in the United States, Asia, and parts of Latin America generated double-digit growth rates for some segments, despite financial problems in Asia during late 1997. Growth in Europe mirrored relatively weak economies there. In the U.S., where glass was considered part of the industry, total sales rose to nearly $90 billion; glass accounted for 59%, and the advanced ceramics segment continued to grow in share to 26%.

Persistent economic expansion in the U.S. and other markets drove flat glass production to record levels for both automotive and architectural use. In addition, new product technologies based on surface coatings, tempering, and improved fabrication methods for special shapes were stimulating demand. The glass container market grew modestly on a worldwide basis in 1997, although certain key markets continued to suffer from strong competition from polymer containers. Recycling of glass, long an important technology and practice in Europe, gained momentum in the U.S. Both regions set records for using recycled glass during 1997, and improved melting technology aided glass manufacturers in producing containers from recycled glass.

Production of advanced ceramics grew strongly in 1997, accounting for over a quarter of the ceramics industry. Electronic materials dominated this category (about 75%), and the high growth rate of computers and communication equipment caused electronic ceramics to become the fastest-growing major product sector. Multilayer ceramic capacitors featured reduced thickness and gained market share, and demand for these widely used components outstripped supply. Every new automobile, for example, used 1,000 such capacitors on average. Explosive growth in wireless communication stimulated double-digit growth in most sectors supplying this industry. They included capacitors, piezoelectric crystals, varistors, thermistors, and similar components, many of which were used in mobile phone handsets. On the other hand, the growth of multilayer, multicomponent electronic packages slowed after the fast start in 1996, and the production of conventional ceramic packages for integrated circuits continued to stagnate because of competition from polymer composite packages with improved heat-removal capabilities.

Advanced structural and composite ceramics, historically limited to cost-insensitive aerospace and military applications, continued steady market penetration in industrial sectors owing in part to low costs and high product reliability. Three application markets—silicon nitride ball bearings, certain automotive ceramics, and ceramic composite cutting-tool inserts—showed solid growth during the year. The use of silicon nitride ball bearings increased by more than 10% owing to improved reliability, reduced costs, and greater customer acceptance. Advances in ceramic machining technologies dramatically reduced costs and brought many components in line with traditional materials on a value basis. The most notable examples of commercialized ceramic matrix composite materials were silicon carbide/alumina cutting tools that continued to grow in the markets for machining cast iron, superalloys, and high face-velocity cuts of conventional metals. The production of optical and electro-optical glass and ceramic materials was growing rapidly and became the focus of major capital investments during 1997. The demand for these materials, which included optical fibres, sensors, and planar structures for electronic applications, was expected to increase substantially during the next five years.

Demand in the U.S. for whiteware ceramics—principally floor and wall tile, dinnerware, sanitaryware, artware, and a large miscellaneous group—was relatively flat compared with substantial growth in some global markets such as Mexico and the Pacific Rim nations. Fast firing, a standard part of tile processing, was overcoming technical hurdles in producing sanitaryware and dinnerware and contributed to higher productivity. A principal concern among whiteware manufacturers during the year was the conversion to lead-free glazes and decorations to reduce lead-related workplace risks and to skirt difficult marketplace regulations in some states. Dinnerware and so-called table-top products moved significantly away from heirloom-quality items toward less-formal products for daily use and casual entertaining.

The transition of some manufacturing facilities to low-cost locations in Mexico and Asia had a major effect on many segments of the traditional ceramics industry. The labour-intensive nature of sanitaryware manufacturing, for example, coupled with strong price pressure from bulk retailers, markedly affected U.S. production. With European sanitaryware manufacturers under similar pressure, mergers or proposed mergers between major manufacturers resulted in consolidation during the year.

(CAROL L. ERON; RICHARD L. LEHMAN)

Rubber. The rubber industry, led by a strong growth in the U.S. tire market, continued its worldwide expansion in 1997. Most regions of the world were posting gains, with the exception being portions of Southeast Asia because of currency devaluations there.

In the U.S. a slight decrease in shipments of original-equipment automobile tires was more than offset by strong gains in shipments of replacement and truck tires. Tire shipments were up more than 3.5% in the U.S. and 1.4% in Canada, according to the Rubber Manufacturers Association. Tire-manufacturing capacity increased in the U.S. as Michelin North America Inc. began production at one of its C3M units in Reno, Nev. The Michelin C3M process purportedly reduced overall manufacturing time by 85%, and the Reno facility was the sixth such plant built for the company. Michelin also announced that it would enter the North American agricultural tire market. Bridgestone/Firestone, Inc., said that it would build a new tire plant in South Carolina and chose Aiken, S.C., for a $435 million facility that would be producing 25,000 passenger car and light-truck tires daily by 2000.

Southeast Asia was once again the area of interest for many of the multinational rubber companies and their suppliers. The currency devaluations that were forced on several of the area's economies, coupled with overcapacities in many markets, only slowed the rush to establish manufacturing presence in the region. The combination of an abundant supply of natural rubber and inexpensive labour catapulted Southeast Asia into the position of largest producer of rubber in the world.

The Bridgestone Corp. was especially active in the Asia-Pacific region, announcing plans to build a second tire plant in Indonesia, to double the capacity of its Thailand tire plant, and to enter a joint venture in China; it also purchased the Firestone Tyre & Rubber Co. of New Zealand Ltd. Also in the area, Hankook Tire Mfg. Co., Ltd., announced plans to invest $600 million in China over the next seven years. Hankook would buy an existing plant and modernize it, build a new tire plant, and quadruple capacity at an existing plant. Yunnan Tire Co. opened a tire plant in Kunming, China, with a capacity to produce two million tires per year.

In other major tire industry news Avon Rubber PLC of England was purchased by Cooper Tire and Rubber Co. of the U.S. Italy's Pirelli SpA was spending $170 million to expand its Brazilian tire facility, which would make it the company's largest, and Goodyear Tire & Rubber Co. bought a 60% stake in the Slovenian-based Sava Group and a 75% share in its engineered products operation. Sava had two tire plants with a combined annual output of five million tires.

Synthetic rubber supplier Bayer AG shut down its polychloroprene plant in Houston, Texas, shifting production to its German facility. Bayer also announced plans to expand its polybutadiene rubber and solution styrene-butadiene rubber output at its Orange, Texas, complex, and it was investigating establishing a synthetic rubber plant in India.

Recognition during the year of additional allergies associated with latex products, namely examination gloves and prophylactics, prompted legislation in various parts of the world, especially Europe and the U.S. Natural rubber latex contains antigens to which more than 1% of the people are allergic. In combination with powder, like corn starch, commonly used in the health profession, the possibility that the antigens will spread increases. U.S. health officials estimated that 10–12% of the nation's health care workers were affected by the allergy.

(DONALD SMITH)

Plastics. In 1997 the world used 130 million metric tons of plastic materials. In terms of volume, the most common plastic was high-density polyethylene (HDPE), used mainly in the manufacture of bottles and grocery and trash bags; it accounted for 13%. Industry analysts predicted that the use of plastics was likely to continue to grow at an annual rate of about 5% and that Asian countries would continue to play an important role in plastics manufacturing and imports. In less-developed countries such as China, Malaysia, and Thailand, the growth rate in the production of plastic products in 1997 was more than double that of industrialized countries. Commanding 25% of the total international trade, China was the largest importer of plastic materials.

New developments in 1997 led to many product improvements, especially the protection of plastic materials. Because of its sensitivity to damage by sunlight, nylon had been limited to indoor use. The application of a special hindered-amine light stabilizer (HALS) to nylon materials now provided protection against the harmful rays in sunlight. The outdoor durability of plastic products also was increased by weather-resistant coatings—in particular, pigmented fluoropolymers and acrylics.

In Japan the barrier properties and transparency of food packaging were improved by the addition of a thin silica-glass layer on plastic packaging film. U.S. food packagers were expected to make use of this innovation in the near future. In the meantime, continuing improvements in packaging materials made of metallocene and multilayer linear low-density polyethylene (LLDPE) helped control water and gas transmission in foods and added six to eight weeks to the shelf life of fresh produce. Engineers also developed ethylene–vinyl acetate stoppers to replace corks in wine bottles, an innovation that preserved the taste and odour of wine while controlling its cost.

Several new developments in manufacturing processes lowered the costs and improved the performance of plastic products while minimizing environmental damage. German and Japanese manufacturers showed that halogen heat lamps were faster and more efficient than conventional quartz lamps for preheating plastics for processing. Manufacturers also continued to look for alternatives to ozone-depleting chlorofluorocarbons (CFCs) in the foaming of plastics. Europeans favoured the use of hydrocarbons, whereas U.S. manufacturers leaned toward hydrofluorocarbons and liquid carbon dioxide. Lasers and heat-transfer decals made the printing of information or decorations on the surface of plastic products more efficient and environmentally sound than the conventional wet-ink printing process.

Outlets for recycled plastic materials continued to grow. Sixty companies in North America, for example, were producing millions of board feet of plastic lumber per year. Another growing outlet for recycled plastic was flexible polyurethane foam. The material could be mixed with virgin polyurethane binder and converted into carpet underlay and automobile headrests, armrests, and door liners.

(RUDOLPH D. DEANIN)

Advanced Composites. During 1997 the market for composite materials continued to grow, as indicated by shipments of materials. The Society of the Plastics Industry's Composite Institute estimated that U.S. shipments for composites of all types totaled 1,550,000 metric tons, an increase of about 6% above 1996 levels and 8% above 1995 levels, for the sixth consecutive year of increases. The 1997 gains were most pronounced in the consumer products and transportation sectors, which was reflective of the increased use of composites in sporting goods and of the upturn in the commercial aircraft market.

The market for advanced polymeric composites, primarily carbon fibre-reinforced polymeric composites, had recovered since the early 1990s, a period characterized by a reduced military market due to the end of the Cold War and a worldwide economic recession. From 1992 to 1995 worldwide carbon fibre shipments increased 50% to 8,900 metric tons. In 1996 and 1997 the carbon fibre industry operated at close to capacity. The industry transition from defense applications to higher-volume, lower-cost applications led to an emphasis on the development of cost-effective materials and manufacturing processes. For example, processes that produce low-cost carbon fibres in fibre bundles with an increasing number of filaments were finding applications in high-volume markets.

The industry continued to pursue aggressively two potentially large markets that would make use of lower-cost materials and processing methods—construction and automotive. The applications of advanced composite technology in construction and infrastructure renewal seemed certain to increase. Examples of technologies that were being evaluated included composite bars for reinforcing concrete, composite reinforcement and overwrap for seismic and structural upgrades and repairs, and composite-reinforced wood laminates for beam structures. Composite applications in construction increased significantly in Europe and Japan. Several evaluation programs were under way in the United States, but acceptance of composites continued to be slow.

Composites, especially in the form of sheet molding compounds (SMCs), were becoming increasingly important in the production of automobiles. The amount of SMCs used by the automotive industry had increased more than 70% since 1990. High-performance composites had not, however, found significant application in automotive structures, despite collaborative research and development efforts to develop continuous fibre-reinforced composite structures for lightweight, energy-efficient automobiles. The use of high-performance composites in automotive applications was inhibited by concurrent improvements in strength and toughness of metals (including aluminum alloys, magnesium alloys, and steel alloys), the relatively high cost of composite materials and manufacturing processes, and the difficulty experienced in recycling advanced composites.

(THOMAS E. MUNNS; ROBERT E. SCHAFRIK)

Iron and Steel. World consumption of steel products grew by 30 million metric tons, or 4.5%, to 695 million metric tons in 1997, the fifth consecutive year of growth and 81 million metric tons more than in 1987. During the past five years consumption in the nations that constituted the former Soviet Union had fallen by 42 million tons, but this was more than offset by the increase of 75 million tons in Asia, of which 30 million tons were accounted for by China. Consumption in North America rose 29 million tons.

The continued buoyancy of the U.S. economy, marked by high automobile production and strong growth in residential construction, accounted for a large share of North America's steel use. Consumption in the U.S. plateaued, but at the very high level of 106 million metric tons, and there was double-digit growth in the Canadian and Mexican steel markets. Sixteen million tons of new production capacity came onstream in North America during 1995–97, mainly to make flat steel goods, and all of the new plants used the primarily scrap-based electric furnace process. South American steel use was rising, boosted by automotive demand in Brazil and the construction sector in Argentina.

The strengthening of the dollar and pound sterling against the major European currencies resulted in an export-led revival in the steel industries of the countries of continental Europe, with the automotive and machinery sectors leading the recovery. Construction remained generally weak, depressed by the fiscal and monetary restrictions imposed by governments as they sought to qualify their nations for membership in the European monetary union. Western European steel consumption grew by 10 million tons, or 7.7%, in 1997. The steel consumption of the formerly communist countries of Central and Eastern Europe grew more slowly, at about 5%, whereas that of the former Soviet Union remained in the doldrums.

In Japan steel usage in the construction sector was declining. Steady growth in China's steel consumption took it back above the 100 million-ton threshold, and Taiwan's demand for steel products rose 10%. There was little growth in the other Asian markets, however, owing in part to a currency crisis that affected several countries in the middle of the year. Growth in this region, which accounted for 45% of world steel consumption, was expected to resume in the future, however.

In industry developments the Hanbo Steel Corp., which had planned to become South Korea's second largest steel producer, defaulted on debt payments in January and sought court protection from its creditors. In August steelworkers in the U.S. ended a 10-month strike against the Wheeling-Pittsburgh Steel Corp. The workers received a raise, a signing bonus, and guaranteed pension amounts, and the company was able to implement workplace efficiencies and some job reductions. (ANTHONY TRICKETT)

Light Metals. Light metals are generally those with densities less than five grams per cubic centimeter. Light metals of primary commercial significance include aluminum, magnesium, titanium, and beryllium.

Aluminum. World primary (new metal) aluminum production in 1997 was reported at 19 million tons, a significant increase over the 16 million tons reported for 1996. The apparent increase was, however, a statistical aberration associated with a change in the method of accounting for global production by the reporting agency. Approximately 40 countries produced primary metal, and national production rates varied from the top producer, the United States with 3,600,000 tons, to countries with rates as low as 10,000 tons. Actual world production increased 3%, mostly attributable to the reopening of some plants that had been idled by the industry as a consequence of the 1994 Memorandum of Understanding, an agreement of the major producing countries to curtail production.

The top five primary-metal-producing countries accounted for 60% of world production. In order they were the U.S., Russia, Canada, China, and Australia.

The price of aluminum averaged 73 cents per pound in 1997, but by December it had fallen to 68 cents. It is strongly influenced by the store of the metal in the London Metal Exchange worldwide warehouses. During the year this storage quantity dropped by 300,000 tons to 650,000 tons in December, a trend that countered the decrease in price.

Significant changes were occurring in the U.S. aluminum industry. Reynolds Metals, for 50 years the second largest producer, after Alcoa, ceased making fabricated products and began selling its mills, reclamation facilities, and beverage-can-production plants.

Magnesium. The 1997 production of new magnesium increased 3.5% to 320,000 metric tons. By the end of the year, inventories were depleted, and delivery was tight. Western world production, which excluded Russia, was 240,000 tons. The aluminum industry consumed 42% of the available magnesium for alloying purposes, down from the traditional 50%. This was primarily attributable to the decreasing use of the high-magnesium-content alloy for beverage can ends, which had been redesigned in a smaller diameter. The automotive market increased to 6.4 lb per vehicle, a 15% increase over 1996. The price per pound generally varied between $1.62 and $1.80, though lower prices were sometimes available.

Titanium. The titanium market was bullish in 1997, and some concerns were being expressed by the aerospace industry, which took 60% of production, about the adequacy of future supplies. World production was estimated at 50,000 to 60,000 tons, but the reliability of the figures from sources outside the U.S. was questionable. The successful transition from an overreliance on the defense industry at the beginning of the decade continued, and sports equipment, represented by golf clubs and premium bicycles, was increasing product applications.

Beryllium. Beryllium production remained in the range of 650 to 700 metric tons, with U.S. consumption approximating 230 tons. Base metal price ranged from $165 to $290 per pound, and this confined its usage to niche markets in aerospace, nuclear, and special electric products. Vacuum-cast ingots of greater than 98% beryllium ranged from $290 to $340 per pound, depending on purity.

(GEORGE J. BINCZEWSKI)

Metalworking. Most businesses providing metal parts in 1997 were small or medium-sized companies that specialized in specific markets or metalworking technologies. Because these companies were normally part of a supplier chain for large enterprises, such as automakers or aerospace companies, they reacted to the business needs of the larger companies. During 1997 the dominant need was shortening the time it took to bring both new and existing products to market. One result of that need was an interest in buying parts either cast or pressed to a near-net shape to reduce the number of operations in the manufacturing process. Such near-net-shaped parts required little additional metal removal and assembly.

Consolidating powder metals was an important near-net-shape technology. Worldwide metal powder production exceeded one million tons, and the North American powder metal parts and products industry estimated its sales at more than $3 billion. Shipments of iron- and copper-based powder metal parts, roughly 70% of total U.S. demand, grew an estimated 8%, mostly because of increasing demand from the automobile industry. By 1997 a typical U.S. five- or six-passenger car contained more than 13.5 kg (30 lb) of powder metal parts.

Another business trend in the automobile industry was the use of lightweight materials, such as aluminum and plastic, to reduce a vehicle's overall weight in order to meet government regulations for reduced fuel emissions. The transportation sector was the largest producer of aluminum parts in 1996 and was expected to be the largest consumer of aluminum.

Even with the proliferation of lightweight metals and plastic, the metalworking industries were projected to receive 107 million net tons of iron and steel shipments in 1997, 6% above the previous year. Shipments to the automobile industry, however, fell 1.9% in 1997 to 14.4 million net tons.

Because near-net shapes required the removal of very little material, manufacturers could remove metal from those parts very quickly. Demand for high rates of metal removal and for short times to bring products to market spurred machine-tool builders to increase spindle speeds, sometimes to more than 60,000 rpm, and to add increasingly sophisticated computer technology to their machines. (JAMES KOELSCH)

MICROELECTRONICS

At year-end 1997 the microelectronics industry was commemorating its birth 50 years earlier on Dec. 16, 1947, when Bell Telephone Laboratories, then the research and development arm of AT&T, invented the transistor as an alternative to the vacuum tube. The invention was patented in 1948, and its inventors—William Shockley, John Bardeen, and Walter Brattain—received the Nobel Prize for Physics in 1956. By 1997 microprocessor technology was producing chips containing as many as 7.5 million transistors.

Projected worldwide sales of semiconductors in 1997 rose by 7% to $138 billion, according to the Semiconductor Industry Association (SIA). After a 10.5% drop the previous year, the projected gain was still below 1995's sales of $144.4 billion. Because of the increasing worldwide use of microprocessors in household appliances, cellular phones, and personal computers (PCs), the SIA anticipated an annual growth rate of 20.1% in 1998, 21.9% in 1999, and 21.6% by the millennium, which would result in sales of $245.7 billion in 2000. Microprocessor revenues alone were expected to account for $44.9 billion in sales. In 1997 microprocessor sales exceeded the revenue from dynamic random access memory chips. The metal-oxide semiconductor chip market, including digital signal processors (DSPs) and microprocessors, reached $49.1 billion in 1997 and was projected to reach $89.3 billion in 2000.

The Asia-Pacific region, including India, South Korea, Taiwan, China, and Singapore, remained the fastest-growing market for semiconductors and replaced Europe as the third largest market after the Americas (North and South) and Japan. The Americas represented one-third of the world's market share, a figure that it was predicted to retain through 2000. The Asia-Pacific market was expected to increase its share of the world chip market to 24.3% in 2000, exceeding Japan at 21.5%. Intel Corp., under its aggressive chairman and CEO, Andrew S. Grove (*see* BIOGRAPHIES), controlled 85% of the market for microprocessor chips.

On May 12 rival chip manufacturer Digital Equipment Corp. filed suit accusing Intel of 10 cases of patent infringement. Digital charged that Intel had used designs from Digital's Alpha chips in its Pentium II and Pentium Pro processors. Later that month Intel countersued, and in August it filed a suit accusing Digital of infringing on 14 Intel patents. The two companies eventually settled out of court, with Intel purchasing Digital's semiconductor development and facilities, Digital developing future systems based on Intel's new IA-64, 64-bit architecture, and patent cross-licensing allowed for 10 years.

During the year Intel introduced its new line of Pentium II processors that incorporated the company's new MMX multimedia technology, included 7.5 million transistors, and ran at high speeds of up to 300 MHz. In July the company broke ground on a new $1.3 billion plant in Fort Worth, Texas. Intel also acquired Chips and Technologies of San Jose, Calif., a maker of graphic accelerator chips for mobile PCs. Meanwhile, Intel competitor Cyrix Corp. agreed to be acquired by National Semiconductor for over $500 million. Motorola, Inc., maker of the PowerPC chip used in Apple Computer Inc.'s Macintosh computers, shipped its new PowerPC 750 (or G3) chip, which was comparable to the Pentium II.

In September IBM announced that it would begin using a new manufacturing process that employed copper instead of aluminum in its semiconductor manufacturing. The new process would produce more powerful, lower-cost chips that used less power to operate. One week later Motorola announced a similar process. It was predicted that the design, initially created for large mainframe computers, would find its way into consumer products within two to three years.

By 1997 DSP chips that converted analog signals such as video or sound into compressed digital form had found wide usage in communications devices such as wireless products, modems, and answering machines. Potential uses for DSPs, which were increasing in quantity by about 30% per year, included the new digital versatile (or video) disc and set-top boxes for Internet connections via the television set. It was anticipated that DSPs would replace the microcontrollers used in many modern consumer products.

Also experiencing worldwide growth was the memory- and microprocessor-based smart-card market. It was estimated that over three billion smart cards would be issued by 2000. Already popular in Europe, the smart cards were beginning to be used by companies in the U.S. to track employee travel expenses more accurately. Other potential uses for smart cards included banking transactions, medical history storage, and electronic commerce.

(THOMAS E. KROLL)

An employee of Solectron Corp. inspects a medical imaging device at a 24-hour assembly plant in Fremont, Calif. The Silicon Valley-based corporation, which boasted more than $3.7 billion in annual revenues, provided leading electronics companies with global manufacturing services.

MARK RICHARDS—CONTACT PRESS IMAGES

MINING

For much of 1997 the mining industry benefited from a buoyant world economy, with China and the newly industrializing "tiger" economies of Southeast Asia serving as the dynamo. Ominous signs emerged in the final quarter of the year, however, as a currency crisis spread through Southeast Asia, but it was too early to gauge the extent to which the crisis would slow economies and affect the demand for metals and minerals. The countries of the former Soviet Union

(continued on page 170)

The Bre-X Minerals Scandal

The biggest fraud in the history of mining was exposed in March 1997—the claim by Calgary, Alta.-based Bre-X Minerals Ltd., a small Canadian exploration firm, that it had made one of the world's largest gold discoveries in a remote part of Indonesia.

In August 1993 Bre-X began to explore in Kalimantan (Borneo), and it soon reported significant drilling results at Busang. Assays of the drill samples indicated consistent gold mineralization, extending from the surface to a depth of hundreds of metres, and estimates of the size of the resource steadily grew. By early 1997 it appeared that the deposit could contain some 3–4% of the world's reserves.

By then the value of Bre-X shares had soared from a few cents to give the company a market capitalization higher than that of several major mining companies. Its apparent success contributed to a boom in exploration worldwide, and Indonesia witnessed a gold rush of unprecedented proportions. The Indonesian government, eager to expedite mine development, was criticized, however, for attempting to accelerate proceedings by nominating the Canadian company Barrick Gold as a preferred partner and for allowing members of President Suharto's family to serve as facilitators in some of the negotiations.

Eventually, Bre-X formed a partnership with Freeport-McMoRan, a U.S. company and operator in the Indonesian province of Irian Jaya of the world's largest copper-gold mine. Before making a firm commitment, Freeport insisted on carrying out due diligence and sank some exploratory drill holes to obtain independent data. The results shook the mining industry; Busang contained no significant gold. Overnight the Can$6 billion Bre-X stock was rendered worthless. Curiously, a week before the announcement, Bre-X's chief geologist, Michael de Guzman, had fallen to his death from a helicopter while en route to the exploration site to meet Freeport geologists.

A preliminary report, commissioned by Bre-X and released in October by Forensic Investigative Associates Inc., concluded that de Guzman and a small group of mainly fellow Filipino geologists had salted the drill samples in the field prior to their delivery to the assay laboratories. They substituted mainly gold of alluvial origin purchased from a local gold panner. The salting began in December 1993, after the first two drill holes had revealed no gold and at a time when the company had contemplated ending exploration. The report absolved David Walsh, Bre-X chairman and chief executive officer (he earned Can$35 million trading Bre-X stock in 1996), and two fellow directors of involvement in the swindle. The exploration director's role in the affair was still an open question, however.

After the scam was uncovered, the Bre-X share price crashed, and disgruntled shareholders (who lost about $3 billion) began taking legal action against the company. The affair, which attracted international headlines, seriously undermined investor confidence in small exploration companies, damaged Indonesia's reputation as a country worth exploring, and cast doubt on the effectiveness of the Canadian regulatory authorities. In early November Bre-X declared bankruptcy.

(ROGER ELLIS)

DILIP MEHTA—CONTACT PRESS IMAGES

At this testing area in Busang, Indon., core samples were collected and analyzed by Bre-X geologists. Assays of the samples indicated consistent gold mineralization, but later tests carried out by Freeport-McMoRan, an American company that operated a mine in Indonesia, showed that the Busang site contained no significant gold.

(continued from page 168)
showed some signs of economic improvement in 1997, but domestic consumption of metals and minerals remained far lower than before the Soviet breakup. For the most part, mineral production was also lower because of a lack of investment, but for some commodities, such as aluminum and nickel, output was maintained at a high level.

Exploration throughout the world continued to flourish, and Nova Scotia-based Metals Economics Group, after making a survey of 279 companies, estimated that worldwide spending on the search for nonferrous metals rose 11% in 1997, to about $5.1 billion. Regionally, Latin America accounted for 29% of the total, followed by Australia (17%), Africa (17%), Canada (11%), and the U.S. (9%). In Indonesia the huge gold discovery by Bre-X Minerals Ltd. turned out to be a fraudulent claim. (*See* Sidebar.)

Activity in sub-Saharan Africa was particularly noteworthy. With the exception of South Africa, the continent as a whole had long been regarded as a poor relation, but a number of positive developments occurred in 1997. Angola began to attract greater foreign investment in its diamond sector, and the change of leadership in the Democratic Republic of the Congo (formerly Zaire) triggered considerable interest in that country's huge untapped resource potential. The world-class Tenke-Fungurume copper deposit was being developed, and a $1 billion deal was struck with a U.S. company to revitalize Gécamines, the government-owned copper producer. In neighbouring Zambia, Falconbridge of Canada and Anglo American Corp. of South Africa were involved in a feasibility study for the Konkola Deep mine, and in November an international consortium agreed on terms for the acquisition of Zambia Consolidated Copper Mine's (ZCCM's) Nchanga and Nkana divisions, all key components of the privatization of ZCCM.

A number of new mines came into production. In the copper sector these included Bajo de la Alumbrera in Argentina, Radomiro Tomic in Chile, and Ernest Henry in Australia. There were also major capacity expansions, including at the huge Grasberg mine in Irian Jaya province, Indon., where an eventual expansion to 900,000 metric tons per year of copper and 2,750,000 oz of gold was under consideration. The El Niño weather phenomenon had some impact on copper-mining activities during 1997, with heavy rainfall disrupting some operations in the Andes Mountains and drought conditions in Papua New Guinea precluding the use of vital river transport for the important Ok Tedi mine.

The Australian company BHP had a busy year, developing its new Hartley platinum mine in Zimbabwe, bringing a major new silver mine in Australia onstream, and forging ahead with the development of Canada's first diamond mine. Its Cannington mine in Queensland cost nearly $A 450 million and would contribute about 6% of world silver production. The Lac de Gras diamond mine was estimated to have resources totaling 66 million metric tons at an average grade of 1.09 carats per metric ton and an average value of $84 per carat. The mine would become the largest employer in northern Canada. The final development cost was expected to approach Can$900 million.

More privatizations took place in 1997, notably in Brazil. There the government sold its 42% controlling stake in CVRD, one of the world's largest mining companies, for $3.1 billion.

In general, the mining industry was able to keep pace comfortably with the demand for metals and minerals. Demand for iron ore and steel-alloy metals strengthened in conjunction with the buoyancy in the steel sector; the Organisation for Economic Co-operation and Development forecast that world steel consumption would rise by some 3% to a record 670 million metric tons in 1997 and production by 3.1% to 775 million metric tons. Supply and demand for coal maintained an upward trend, but prices remained highly competitive.

Base metals were characterized by a series of supply squeezes, whereby a metal was deliberately withheld from the market by some participants in order to drive up its price. This activity occurred on the London Metal Exchange (LME), where more than 90% of the world's base-metals trading took place. Aluminum, copper, and zinc were all subject to squeezes, and those short of metal and unable to deliver against their contractual commitments were forced to "borrow" metal and pay a considerable premium to do so. The LME authorities felt obliged to intervene and impose daily limits on the premiums. Describing the squeezes as unwelcome market "aberrations," the LME took action in October when it began to publish, alongside its regular metals stocks figures, the volume of metal held in LME warehouses that was not available for sale.

The copper market was unsettled for much of the year by forecasts that a substantial supply surplus was developing because of increasing mine production. The debate was over the size of the surplus and how soon it would occur. China remained a key player. Its domestic demand for the metal far exceeded its own production capacity, and if it entered the market as a major buyer, the supply-demand balance would be transformed, which would have a major impact on prices. China acted with considerable restraint, but some suspected that its State Reserve Bureau, which held a large copper inventory, was, in effect, operating a buffer stock as a means of limiting price movements.

Nickel had a mediocre year. Despite healthy demand for stainless steel (the main end use for nickel), the market for primary nickel was disappointing, and it appeared that many stainless-steel producers were using up their primary nickel stocks and relying on an abundance of secondary nickel derived from stainless-steel scrap.

Aluminum enjoyed a steady growth in demand, and prices for the metal held up well. Two or three years earlier, the world had been awash with aluminum, stocks were at record levels, and metal prices had slumped. Consequently, under a memorandum of understanding, major producers idled much of their production capacity in order to reduce stocks to manageable proportions.

In the precious metals markets, gold had a dire year. Following sales of gold by central banks from their reserves, the sentiment was that gold was no longer vital for backing currencies. Without this special role, gold became just another commodity. The most publicized sale was by Australia's reserve bank in July, when it sold two-thirds of its total reserves. Australia was one of the world's leading gold producers, and the

Indexes of Production, Mining and Mineral Commodities
(1980 = 100)

	1992	1993	1994	1995	1996	1997 1st qtr.
Mining (total)						
World[1]	101.2	103.0	106.7	108.6	111.3	...
Developed market economies[2]	107.5	108.3	113.7	116.0	119.5	125.0
North America[3]	94.3	93.7	96.5	97.6	99.7	100.8
European Union[4]	92.7	94.6	102.4	105.6	108.3	120.9
Less-developed market economies[5]	96.8	99.4	101.9	103.6	105.7	...
Coal						
World[1]	96.4	91.9	91.3	93.4	94.1	...
Developed market economies[2]	89.1	83.4	82.0	82.3	81.7	80.4
North America[3]	121.8	116.9	127.6	128.3	130.4	130.0
European Union[4]	68.5	60.9	53.1	51.9	49.3	48.0
Less-developed market economies[5]	226.2	242.1	256.0	291.5	313.0	...
Petroleum and natural gas						
World[1]	95.9	99.5	103.8	105.4	107.7	...
Developed market economies[2]	107.1	112.2	122.3	126.2	131.9	144.8
North America[3]	80.6	81.4	83.0	82.9	84.7	86.1
European Union[4]	113.8	125.2	146.7	152.8	161.1	193.6
Less-developed market economies[5]	91.4	94.5	96.5	97.2	98.1	...
Metals						
World[1]	135.3	131.5	131.8	133.8	141.5	...
Developed market economies[2]	144.1	140.7	139.9	137.8	141.7	139.6
North America[3]	145.8	138.5	135.6	142.7	146.1	145.3
European Union[4]	77.8	68.2	72.8	76.4	75.4	65.7
Less-developed market economies[5]	119.9	115.5	117.6	126.8	141.2	...
Manufacturing (total)	125.8	125.7	133.0	139.2	143.9	...

[1]Excluding Albania, China, former Czechoslovakia, North Korea, former U.S.S.R., Vietnam, and former Yugoslavia.
[2]Includes North America (Canada and the United States), Europe (excluding former Czechoslovakia and the European countries of the former U.S.S.R.), Australia, Israel, Japan, New Zealand, and South Africa.
[3]Canada and the United States.
[4]Includes Austria, Belgium, Denmark, France, Germany, Greece, Ireland, Italy, Luxembourg, The Netherlands, Portugal, Spain, Sweden, and the United Kingdom.
[5]Includes Caribbean nations, Central and South America, Africa (excluding South Africa), Asia (excluding China, North Korea, Israel, Japan, Vietnam, and Asian countries of the former U.S.S.R.), and Oceania (excluding Australia and New Zealand).
Source: UN, *Monthly Bulletin of Statistics*, August 1997.

news plunged the gold price to a 12-year low. The market was rocked again in October by a proposal by Swiss gold experts that the country sell more than 50% of its reserves. The price fell to $308 per ounce, $80 less than the 1996 price average, and by year's end the price had fallen below $300. The low prices were putting a number of gold mines at risk, especially some large, high-cost deep mines in South Africa. The industry there employed almost 500,000 people. Although silver demand had exceeded the newly mined supply for several years, above-ground stocks were considerable, and the price remained anchored close to $5 per ounce until December, when investment fund interest pushed the price sharply higher.

The platinum-group metal palladium, an element of growing importance in the manufacture of autocatalysts (used to reduce vehicle exhaust emissions), attracted much interest. This was mainly because the principal supplier, Russia, citing bureaucratic problems, made no shipments during the first half of the year. Russia had more than 70% of the world supply of palladium, and for a time supply shortages drove up prices.

The main interest in diamonds focused on the efforts of De Beers Consolidated Mines to secure a new marketing agreement with Russia (which in 1996–97 accounted for some 16% of world output by value). The previous agreement had expired in 1995. De Beers, through its Central Selling Organisation, dominated the world's rough-diamond market and had continued to purchase Russian rough diamonds on an ad hoc basis, but reportedly Russian diamonds "leaked" onto the market in excess of an official quota. A new agreement was finally made in October. It took effect in December and would run until the end of 1998.

Nongovernmental organizations (NGOs) continued to exert pressure on mining companies to ensure that adequate environmental safeguards were in place, and the NGOs also provided considerable support and publicity for the interests of indigenous groups affected by mining. The industry became more aware that these groups, with their own social-economic culture, were important stakeholders in new mining projects. By the beginning of the year, Rio Tinto of the U.K. had lost patience in its protracted negotiations with local Aboriginal groups regarding plans to develop the Century and Dugald River zinc deposits in Queensland and sold its interest to Pasminco for $A 345 million. The latter managed to secure an agreement to develop what would become the world's largest open-pit zinc mine.

In Canada the Voisey's Bay project in Labrador was scheduled to become the world's richest open-pit nickel mine, but it too ran into problems. The owner of the deposit, Inco Ltd., failed to resolve all the outstanding issues concerning the local Inuit people, who blocked access to the site and forced Inco to concede that project development would be delayed by at least one year. Nevertheless, early in the next decade, Voisey's Bay should be producing copper and cobalt and the equivalent of about 18% of current Western mine output of nickel. The project could pose a serious threat to some of the existing high-cost nickel producers.

The debate about global warming, in anticipation of the UN climate summit in Kyoto, Japan, in December, put coal producers on their mettle. It was widely believed that the carbon dioxide produced by burning fossil fuels was affecting the climate and that emissions of the gas should be curbed. The U.S., which possessed the largest coal reserves, was also the biggest energy consumer. Coal producers in the U.S. were opposed to restrictions on coal use. The U.S. National Mining Association undertook a vigorous lobby, insisting that if global warming was proved, the technology could be developed to burn coal more efficiently without restricting its use. It was doubtful, however, that less-developed countries such as China and India, which relied on coal and where per capita consumption of energy was still very low, would be able to afford such technology. The nuclear industry and uranium miners watched the debate with considerable interest. (ROGER ELLIS)

See also Earth Sciences.

This article updates the *Macropædia* article Extraction and Processing INDUSTRIES.

PAINTS AND VARNISHES

In the paint industry, 1997 seemed certain to be remembered for a technical breakthrough—an acrylic powder coating for automotive topcoats. The first such car, a BMW with a powder-coated clear coat over an aqueous base, was shown at the International Motor Show in Frankfurt, Ger. The feat was all the more astounding because waterborne, rather than powder, systems had been considered the most likely winner for automotive applications. Indeed, Herberts, which had earlier developed a complete water-based paint range—from primer to topcoat—was working on a two-pack waterborne system. In the event, it was Herberts—as well as PPG Industries—that claimed this breakthrough in powder-coating technology. The new system was expected to eliminate 1–1.5 kg (2.2–3.3 lb) of solvent per car. Nonetheless, the competition between waterborne and powder coatings was by no means over; market victory would ultimately be decided by consumers, with the coating's performance as the ultimate arbiter.

For the paint industry, the automobile had always been of critical importance—serving as a technical catalyst, a benchmark for quality, and a source of demand. It was the carmakers who pioneered globalization and forced their paint suppliers to follow the same path; global manufacture of cars required the global production and distribution of car paints. Only a few paint makers could sustain such global strategies, so their number was eventually reduced to just six.

Packaging coatings represented another global market. BASF withdrew from this market during the year by exchanging its $150 million packaging operation for PPG Industries' surfactant business. Dexter Corp. of the U.S. accelerated its push into Europe by adding Kolack of Switzerland and Stolllack of Austria to its existing European packaging business. Dexter also bought Akzo Nobel's can coatings business in Brazil and entered into a 60–40 joint venture with Plascon in South Africa. Earlier Herberts had acquired can coatings producer Plastocoat of Italy.

Economically, the industry experienced variable fortunes. In the U.S. it failed to match the record growth of 1996. Paint shipments during the first half of the year were nearly 5% lower than in 1996. European results were mixed. Germany's building boom in the eastern part of the country ended, which reduced demand there. The U.K., however, proceeded with its recovery, with foreign carmakers contributing to demand.

(HELMA JOTISCHKY)

PHARMACEUTICALS

Direct-to-consumer (DTC) promotion of prescription drugs swept the pharmaceutical industry in the United States in 1997. New, more liberal guidelines from the Food and Drug Administration (FDA) for television advertising opened the floodgates—allowing the airing of commercials that made claims for specific brands along with abbreviated references to side effects. Commercials had to provide a toll-free number or cite a print advertisement where consumers could obtain more information. By the year's end dozens of the new DTC commercials had premiered on U.S. television, and the industry had spent an estimated $1 billion on all forms of DTC promotion, up from $80 million in 1992.

ALLAN TANNENBAUM—SYGMA

A pharmacist packs away bottles of the popular diet drugs Pondimin and Redux, which were pulled from the market after doctors observed heart lesions in 30% of patients using the drugs.

Increased industry involvement with consumers had its pitfalls, however. American Home Products' obesity medicine Pondimin became highly popular as part of the fenfluramine-phentermine ("fen-phen") combination touted by some weight-loss clinics. The company was exposed to widespread litigation, however, when heart-valve problems affected some fen-phen patients. American Home responded by withdrawing the product and related diet pill Redux from the market, promising more studies while attempting to distance itself from the fen-phen controversy.

Despite the FDA's comparatively liberal policies on consumer promotion—and its increasingly faster performance in reviewing new medicines—the agency remained a target of congressional reform attempts. Late in the year Congress linked modest reforms to renewed industry user-fee legislation, and U.S. Pres. Bill Clinton signed it into law.

Managed-care organizations (MCOs) continued to give U.S. pharmaceutical companies a boost in sales, even for high-priced medicines. As the MCOs began to experience the limits of cost containment combined with an influx of patients with serious illnesses, however, they showed impatience with the industry's boost in consumer promotion and newly inflated sales forces. It appeared that if pharmaceutical companies' fortunes continued to rise above those of their customers, the MCOs might return to cutting pharmacy budgets and thus depress sales.

During the year another market shared centre stage with the United States—Asia. With the return of Hong Kong from Great Britain to China, coupled with boom times for other Asian nations such as Singapore and Malaysia, the industry began to concentrate on the fast-developing region as one of tremendous potential growth. Later in the year stock and currency crashes throughout the area made it appear far less attractive for industry investment in the short term. Most global companies, however, remained committed to building their businesses in step with local economies, whatever the difficulties. Meanwhile, Japan began health care reforms that could promote industry growth.

Europe struggled with its own economic woes, and large companies such as Hoechst and Roche finally broke from the old "lifetime employment" tradition, laying off thousands of employees to cut costs. While most European firms turned their attention to the U.S., Asia, and South America for growth opportunities, the European Union continued to remove regulatory impediments to industry innovation and encouraged companies to share more information with patients.

In all, it was a growth year for the industry, especially in the United States. By mid-November U.S. pharmaceutical stocks had withstood a major global upheaval and advanced 44% for the year. Most large companies reported net income growth of 15–19% through the third quarter. Merck registered 19%, Bristol-Myers Squibb 15%, Pfizer, 16%, and Novartis, 12%. Warner-Lambert sales grew 19%. Currency exchanges, restructuring charges, and other costs eroded worldwide corporate earnings for many companies, however.

(WAYNE KOBERSTEIN)

PHOTOGRAPHY

New technologies and marketing opportunities considerably reshaped the photographic industry in 1997. Most dramatic was the rush to participate in the continuing explosive development of digital cameras, along with their accessories, software, and Internet connections, for the mass market and professional applications. Digital cameras, which captured and stored images electronically rather than on film, were introduced by virtually every major camera maker and many electronics manufacturers during the year. Eastman Kodak in particular aggressively attempted to develop and promote digital imaging in all its ramifications, although that heavy commitment failed to generate enough income to offset a substantial loss of market share in conventional film to archrival Fuji.

Kodak's DC120 ZOOM was claimed to be the first point-and-shoot digital camera for less than $1,000 to offer million-pixel (picture element) image quality. The binocular-style camera had a 3× autofocus zoom lens equivalent to 38–114 mm *f*/2.5–3.8 on a 35-mm camera and both an optical viewfinder and a colour liquid-crystal-diode (LCD) monitor for reviewing, reorganizing, or deleting images. Exemplifying modestly priced entry-level digitals was the Agfa ePhoto 307, a simple point-and-shoot camera with a 640×480-pixel resolution, optical viewfinder, automatic flash with red-eye reduction, and fixed-focus 6-mm lens. The Panasonic PV-DC1000 PalmCam, measuring only 9 cm (3.5 in) in its longest dimension, provided a 640×480-pixel resolution, a fixed-focus 5.7-mm *f*/3.8 lens, and a built-in 4.6-cm (1.8-in) colour preview and playback monitor.

After a sluggish start the previous year, the conventional-film, 24-mm-format Advanced Photo System (APS) picked up some speed during 1997. Numerous new second-generation APS point-and-shoot and single-lens-reflex (SLR) models from leading manufacturers filled in or expanded existing lines. Taking advantage of APS's smaller-than-35-mm format, the Pentax IQZoom 2001X was a pocketable camera about the size of a pack of cigarettes. It featured an autofocus 24–48-mm *f*/4.5–8 zoom lens (equivalent to 30–60 mm in 35-mm format), shutter speeds of 1/3–1/300 second, and an easy-to-read dial for flash and exposure modes. Olympus adapted the easy-to-operate noninterchangeable zoom-lens SLR concept of its IS-10 to the APS format for its new Centurion. The camera included a 25–100-mm *f*/4.5–5.6 zoom lens (equivalent to 31–125 mm in 35-mm format), shutter speeds from 4 seconds to 1/2000 second, and a wide variety of flash and exposure modes.

New 35-mm point-and-shoot cameras included a number of attractively styled compact models loaded with useful features. Among them was the Olympus Infinity Stylus Epic. Slightly smaller and lighter than the original ultracompact Stylus, the Epic included a new, faster four-element *f*/2.8 lens that focused down to 36 cm (14 in), a 2–1/1000-second shutter, and automatic red-eye-reducing and fluorescent-compensating flash. The 35-mm SLR cameras introduced in 1997 included no major breakthroughs in design or performance; for the most part they represented refinements or modifications of existing models.

Significant improvements in silver halide film fostered its continuing appeal, vis-à-vis electronic means, as the prime image-capturing medium. Kodak introduced a new family of colour print films: Kodak Gold 400, 200, and 100 and Kodak Gold Max. The last was given no ISO film-speed rating but was said to "self-adjust" to a wide range of lighting conditions. It was actually an ISO 800 film whose extended exposure latitude tolerated meter settings from ISO 25 to 3200, with good results at both extremes. Kodak's T-Max T400CN was a special chromogenic film that produced black-and-white negatives with C-41 processing by any colour photofinisher.

Fujichrome Sensia II 100 established itself as a highly rated ISO 100 colour transparency film in terms of colour saturation, natural skin tones, and resolution. Kodak introduced its Professional Ektachrome E200, claimed to deliver high-quality results even in changing lighting conditions and with push-processing up to ISO 1000. Kodak and Fuji both introduced APS-format colour transparency films: Kodak Advantix Chrome (based on Elite II 100) and Fujichrome 100ix. (ARTHUR GOLDSMITH)

PRINTING

The printing industry reported exceptional expansion during 1997, with growth in all print products, especially advertising and packaging printing. Evidence of the expansion was provided by equipment sales of more than $300 million at the international Print 97 exhibition held in Chicago in September; with about 100,000 visitors, it was the largest such exhibition ever held in North America.

Digital colour printing advanced as the Xerox (U.S. and Japan) DocuColor shipped almost 4,000 systems, and Canon (Japan) shipped more than 3,000 CLC 1000 systems. Xeikon (Belgium) introduced a 50-cm (20-in)-wide toner-based colour printer/press that was competitive with lithographic printing. A major market evolved for personalized colour printing that produces direct mail and marketing materials from databases of text and images.

Presses that integrate platemaking on press by applying Presstek (U.S) technology sold record numbers, as printers worldwide applied totally digital workflows that eliminate graphic arts film, manual assembly, and labour-intensive processes. Scitex (Israel) and KBA Planeta (Germany) joined forces with a new joint venture (Karat Digital Press) to develop and sell new on-press platemaking and press combinations.

Digitally exposed plates and thermal processless (no chemistry) plates gained high levels of acceptance. The result for printers was a reduction in production times for an increasing number of short-run jobs (under 5,000 copies) to meet requirements for on-demand, just-in-time delivery of printed products. The portable document format (PDF; Acrobat software from Adobe Systems) was enhanced by a feature that allowed PDF files to be placed in pages of PageMaker (Adobe Systems, U.S.) and QuarkXPress (Quark, Inc., U.S.) for advertisements to be incorporated into publications electronically.

Mergers and acquisitions continued to create very large printing firms in the U.S. The graphic arts division of Eastman Kodak (U.S.) merged with the Polychrome division of Sun Chemical (owned by Dainippon Ink and Chemicals, Japan) to create Kodak Polychrome Graphics, an independent company. Heidelberger Druckmaschinen (Germany) contracted to build and distribute digital platesetters from Creo Products (Canada), and the Agfa division (Belgium) of Bayer acquired the Du Pont film and plate division. Kodak also partnered with Heidelberger to form a company dedicated to the development of an advanced toner-based press for personalized and customized printing. (FRANK J. ROMANO)

RETAILING

Competitive forces continued to reshape the retailing industry in 1997, a year that marked the passing of one of the oldest, most familiar names in the business. Woolworth Corp. announced the closing of its 400 F.W. Woolworth five-and-dime stores and the layoff of 9,200 workers, ending an era that dated back to 1879. Once a fixture of downtowns across the U.S., the chain had become an anachronism in an industry dominated by giant discount stores and warehouse clubs and was losing money. About 100 of the stores were expected to reopen as sportswear outlets such as Foot Locker. The parent company, Woolworth Corp., remained one of the largest U.S. retailers, nevertheless, operating more than 7,000 stores worldwide.

Consumer spending was generally buoyant, particularly in North America and Great Britain. As consumers flocked to newer and bigger stores, however, many older retailers stumbled. T. Eaton Co. Ltd., one of Canada's largest department-store chains, obtained bankruptcy protection after a string of losses. The 128-year-old company closed unprofitable outlets, reorganized its debts, and hired a new chief executive officer. Britain's largest book retailer, W.H. Smith Group PLC, said it would sell its Waterstone's book chain and a music retailing business in a bid to turn the company around. It had absorbed a loss in 1996—the first in its 204-year history. In the U.S. the 125-year-old Montgomery Ward Holding Corp. filed for Chapter 11 bankruptcy protection, having lost ground for years to nimbler department stores such as Sears, Roebuck & Co.

Wal-Mart Stores Inc., the world's biggest retailer, seemed largely immune to the troubles affecting competitors. The U.S. discount chain paid $1.2 billion for a controlling interest in Cifra SA, Mexico's largest retailer, and in December it announced that it was buying Wertkauf, a chain of 21 large stores in Germany that sold food, clothing, and other general merchandise. These moves underlined Wal-Mart's growing international ambitions. With about 2,800 stores worldwide, it was preparing to add some 200 more in 1998. The firm had a few setbacks, however. In the U.S. it closed 48 of its 61 Bud's Discount City stores, which had not lived up to expectations. The notoriously antiunion company was also faced with its first unionized store, in Windsor, Ont. Although that store's employees had voted against unionization, the Ontario Labour Relations Board, in a controversial decision, overturned the vote. It concluded that management had intimidated employees by creating the impression that the store would close if the union was successful.

Wal-Mart's chief competitor, Kmart Corp., began to see the fruition of its efforts to revive its long-struggling discount chain. The company posted a profit for the first six months of 1997, following back-to-back annual losses. The improvement reflected cost cutting and a new merchandising strategy that featured more high-turnover items such as soft drinks, snacks, and paper towels. Seeking to rid itself of operations that were not core to its business, Kmart sold its Canadian operations and its U.S.-based Builders Square home-improvement stores. Kmart was aiming to remodel 1,600 of its 2,200 stores by 1999 and outfit them with new lights, better layouts, and updated products.

Acquisitions and mergers were common as retailers battled for dominance in an increasingly competitive industry. CVS Corp. acquired rival Revco D.S. Inc. for about $2.9 billion to create the second largest U.S. drugstore chain, one of several big mergers in that field. In France's supermarket industry, Promodès SA offered about $5.5 billion for Casino Guichard-Perrachon SA, the biggest-ever takeover bid in French retailing. The European Commission regarded the proposed merger as being compatible with European Union antitrust rules. The outcome, however, was far from certain because of a competing offer from Rallye SA, which owned a minority stake in Casino. Not all mergers were viewed favourably by competition regulators. Staples Inc. and Office Depot Inc. called off their proposed merger after a U.S. federal judge granted an order blocking the deal. Had the merger been approved, it would have created the largest U.S. office-supplies retailer. The Federal Trade Commission (FTC) had filed suit, charging the merger would reduce competition and lead to higher prices for paper, pencils, and other such items.

In another FTC ruling with broad implications, Toys "Я" Us Inc. was found to have violated U.S. antitrust laws in the late 1980s and early '90s by pressuring manufacturers to keep popular toys off the shelves of competitors. An FTC administrative-law judge ruled that the largest U.S. toy chain, with about 20% of the market, used its clout to demand that manufacturers sell certain toys to warehouse clubs only in more expensive combination formats, which made it impossible for consumers to compare prices. The judge barred Toys "Я" Us from making deals that prevented the sale of products to other retailers, but the company planned to appeal the ruling. (JOHN HEINZL)

SAM FALK—THE NEW YORK TIMES

Women crowd a Woolworth's lunch counter in 1954. Unable to compete with giant discount stores and warehouse clubs, Woolworth Corp. announced the closing of its remaining 400 five-and-dime stores and the layoff of 9,200 workers. The company would retain its footwear divisions.

SHIPBUILDING

There were few surprises in the 1996–97 rankings of the world's principal shipbuilding countries, with Japan and South Korea leading the field again. According to figures released by Lloyd's Register of Shipping for the June quarter of 1997, Japan and South Korea headed the world order book with, respectively, 15,147,000 gt (gross tons) and 14,926,000 gt—30.9% and 30.5%, respectively of the world total. By comparison, Western Europe totaled 8,649,000 gt (17.7%), Eastern Europe 4,565,000 gt (9.5%), and the rest of the world 5,574,000 gt (11.4%). There were 2,548 ships totaling 48,861,000 gt in the world order book (ships currently under construction plus confirmed orders placed but not yet started). The cargo-carrying component of the order book was 2,008 ships of 67.5 million dwt (deadweight tons), with oil tankers leading the way at 24.1 million dwt.

Japanese order books were healthy, and major yards were booked until 1998. The depreciation of the yen from about 90 to the U.S. dollar in 1995 to about 114 in early 1997 helped secure orders. Japan's main rival, South Korea, had to contend with higher inflation and a strong currency. As a result, the 10% price advantage that South Korea had enjoyed in 1993 had been eliminated by 1997. Throughout 1996 South Korean yards invested in extra capacity, which prompted concern over the possible effect of lowering prices for ships. Consequently, Japan and South Korea held negotiations on limiting their shipbuilding.

In the European Union new orders for shipbuilders in 1996 fell by 29%, and some builders faced possible closing. The European Commission voted to maintain through 1997 its 9% subsidy for the construction costs of large ships. The hope was that this would enhance prospects at those yards where competitive, profitable pricing had proved elusive.

The cruise ship market remained buoyant with the delivery of several new vessels, including the 77,000-gt cruise liner *Dawn Princess* delivered from Fincantieri's Monfalcone yard to P&O Princess Cruises. The world's largest cruise ship, P&O's 109,000-gt superliner *Grand Princess*, was floated out of Fincantieri's yard. The 2,600-passenger-capacity ship was to sail from Southampton, Eng., to Istanbul on her maiden voyage in 1998. The 74,140-gt cruise ship *Grandeur of the Seas* was delivered from Kvaerner Masa-Yards in Finland to the Royal Caribbean Cruise Lines. The 2,440-passenger liner was equipped with diesel-electric propulsion having a total output of 50,400 kw. Meyer Werft delivered the 77,713-gt cruise ship *Galaxy* to Celebrity Cruises.

A noticeable building trend was the increasing popularity of floating production, storage, and off-loading units (FPSOs). Demand for FPSOs had grown quickly in recent years, and shipyards and their suppliers responded well. FPSOs in 1997 were dominating the development of new oil fields throughout the world because in many cases an FPSO was much less expensive than a fixed offshore platform, which was burdened with long construction times, inflexibility, and high capital, operating, and abandonment costs. In the North Sea alone, FPSOs were to be used to develop many fields. In other parts of the world, FPSOs were being employed in fields at Terra Nova off the coast of Canada, Zafiro off the coast of Equatorial Guinea, Bayu-Undan and Laminaria/Corallina in the Timor Sea, and Liuhua 11-1 and Lufeng 22-1 in the South China Sea. (EDWARD CROWLEY)

TELECOMMUNICATIONS

At year-end 1997, what was to have been the largest takeover of a U.S. corporation by a foreign company instead became the largest merger in U.S. corporate history. A deal between MCI Communications Corp., the nation's second largest long-distance company, and British Telecommunications PLC (BT) for almost $21 billion fell through after MCI experienced unexpected losses. In the end, the MCI board agreed to be acquired by WorldCom, Inc., the fourth largest long-distance company, for a $51-per-share stock offer worth about $37 billion. In addition, WorldCom, Inc., agreed to a cash buyout of BT's 20% stake in MCI.

Also at the end of the year, a U.S. federal judge struck down sections of the 1996 act that deregulated the telecommunications industry, ruling that the law unfairly prevented the regional Bell companies from entering the long-distance business. In Europe as of Jan. 1, 1998, telephone customers in most countries would for the first time have a choice of service providers, and the U.S. agreed to provide foreign companies with greater access to its markets.

Telecommunications mergers continued in 1997. In April the U.S. Justice Department approved the merger of Bell Atlantic Corp. with the NYNEX Corp. It was followed by Federal Communications Commission (FCC) approval of the deal in August. AT&T Corp. and former Bell operating company SBC Communications, Inc., entered merger discussions that were soon aborted.

Lucent Technologies, Inc., formerly part of AT&T, and Philips Electronics NV combined their consumer products divisions. The joint venture, to be called Philips Consumer Communications, would be 60% owned by Philips to Lucent's 40%. The joint venture would have $2.5 billion in revenue and be the largest provider of both corded and cordless phones.

The Internet and World Wide Web continued to change the face of the on-line access industry. Driven by new high-speed modems, the Web was quickly becoming the interface to information retrieval. America Online, Inc. (AOL), the world's largest on-line access provider, in late 1996 introduced $19.95-per-month flat-rate pricing for unlimited access to the Internet, which resulted in the overtaxing of their network. An electronic-mail (E-mail) outage occurred in April for three days, and other outages were experienced in November, as AOL subscribers expanded to eight million and the amount of time customers spent connected to the services increased. In September WorldCom agreed to buy CompuServe, the second largest service provider, for $1.2 billion in stock; transfer CompuServe's 2.6 million subscribers to AOL; and pay $175 million cash for AOL's ANS networking facilities.

Other Internet glitches occurred when Experian, Inc., provided on-line access to credit histories. Consumers reported receiving other people's reports, and the system was quickly shut down. The International Ad Hoc Committee, an international coalition, proposed adding seven new Internet domains to handle increased demand. In addition to .com, .org, .edu, and .net, new names would include .firm, .store, .web, .arts, .rec, .info, and .nom.

Using the Internet for placing telephone calls, introduced in 1995, by 1997 had led to the formation of the Computer Internet Telephone Industry and to the use of the Internet for video conferencing, faxes, and voice telephone services, with Internet conference software available for under $100. Service providers were able to provide international long distance at prices far below existing long-distance rates for service that used the traditional infrastructure. Although Internet telephony gained the support of Pres. Bill Clinton's administration, several foreign countries moved to ban or severely limit its use. Other companies were using the Internet to transmit both audio and video over their Web sites.

To provide the high-speed data networks needed to transfer information, new telecommunications products and services were being developed. Both Rockwell Semiconductor Systems and U.S. Robotics demonstrated new 56-kbps (kilobits per second) modems. Motorola, Inc., and Lucent soon joined Rockwell in support of their modem technology, which was incompatible with the U.S. Robotics product. Meanwhile, U.S. Robotics was sold to networking hardware manufacturer 3 Com Corp. for $6.6 billion. In October Motorola announced that it was seeking a buyer for its low-end modem business. A standard for 56-kbps modems was expected to be agreed upon by the International Telecommunication Union in 1998. Consumer versions of other high-speed alternatives were also becoming available, including digital subscriber lines, which could download at speeds of up to 256 kbps, and cable modems that connected one's television directly to the Internet and downloaded information at speeds of up to 40 Mbps (megabits per second).

Alliances, where cable and telephone companies eyed one another's traditional business, appeared to have slowed from the 1996 pace until Microsoft Corp. announced in June that it would invest $1 billion in the fourth largest cable company, Comcast Corp. Earlier in the year Microsoft had also purchased WebTV, maker of TV set-top boxes for Internet connections.

In March the U.S. Supreme Court ruled that the federal government has the power to make cable television companies provide access to local stations. According to the 1992 cable TV law, one-third of a provider's capacity must be set aside for local broadcasts.

The FCC set aside 300 MHz of free radio spectrum called the Unlicensed National Information Infrastructure for high-speed wireless local area network applications over distances of less than 4.8 km (3 mi). During the year the FCC tackled access charge reform, universal service to poor and rural customers, the entry of regional Bell operating companies into long-distance service, and phone number portability; in a move that triggered some controversy, it allocated extra spectrum for high-definition television transmission. The FCC also provided more than $2 billion in subsidies to connect schools, libraries, and hospitals to the Internet. Some of the companies that had winning bids for the 1996 FCC auction of wireless spectrum for personal communication services had encountered financial difficulty. The FCC suspended collection of $10 billion from smaller companies until it could decide on four options, three of which would require the reauctioning of some or all of the licenses. The year marked Reed Hundt's last as chairman of the FCC. He was replaced by the FCC general council, William Kennard, its first African-American chairman.

(THOMAS E. KROLL)

TEXTILES

In 1997 the textile industry showed increased confidence in its business prospects but continued to wrestle with environmental and ecological problems, especially concerns about the toxicity of dyes and the breakdown of products. Cone Mills Corp., which had a disappointing 1996, embarked on major cost-cutting programs expected to save $20 million, explored business alliances with manufacturers in Asia and South America, and projected capital expenditures of $40 million. Loom sales in the United States in the first quarter of 1997 increased substantially over the corresponding period in 1996.

In response to projections that the annual demand for spandex fibre would increase by 8% worldwide, Bayer Corp. and the Du Pont Co. each completed major U.S. expansions in production capacity. Burlington Industries, Inc., also invested heavily in its fabric divisions for apparel and expected that its export business would grow and account for more than 10% of production.

The worldwide demand for textile products continued to edge upward, with the greatest rise in less-developed countries (LDCs). Increases in Western developed countries and Japan were much less dramatic. Per capita, however, consumption in LDCs was still only about one-quarter of the level of that in developed nations.

The textile chemical business continued to expand into overseas markets. Monsanto Chemical (now Solutia, Inc.) explored joint ventures in Brazil, South Korea, Argentina, China, Mexico, and Thailand. The Dow

Chemical Co. acquired Sentrachem Ltd. in South Africa, and Exxon was chosen to develop a Chinese refinery and petrochemical installation with the Fujian Petrochemical Co. Hoechst AG announced plans to transfer its European polyester-filament and staple-fibre business and the trademark Trevira to a joint venture with Multikarsa Investama of Jakarta, Indon.

Man-made fibres. During 1997 worldwide demand for man-made fibres increased slightly, with production (excluding olefins [polypropylene]) at about 19.5 billion kg (43 billion lb), compared with 20 billion kg (44 billion lb) in 1996. Business was particularly competitive in the specialty-fibre field. Hoechst phased out its para-aramid Trevar; Lenzing AG ceased production of high-performance fibres in Austria; and Du Pont terminated production of its polyether ether ketone fibre in Europe. Akzo Nobel NV sold its share in Tenax carbon fibre to Toho Rayon. Toyobo's high-performance Zylon, however, seemed to prosper, and the company expanded its carbon-fibre capacity to 5,000 tons per year.

Tencel, the relatively new lyocell fibre by Courtaulds PLC, continued to enjoy strong worldwide demand except in the U.S., the weakest market. Overall, however, the fibre helped boost the company's operating profits by about 14%. Courtaulds announced plans to open a second manufacturing facility in Grimsby, Eng., and several plants in Asia.

Emphasis throughout the world was, however, placed on using traditional rather than exotic new fibre types, with fine-count nylon yarns used for novelty effects and Du Pont's Tactel nylon appearing in evening wear and other apparel. The market for superabsorbent fibres also showed a strong upward trend, with increasing use in disposable hygiene products.

(DENNIS BALMFORTH)

Wool. The world wool clip in 1997–98 was estimated at 1,471,488 metric tons clean, down from 1,476,000 metric tons in 1996–97. Australia reigned as the dominant producer, followed by New Zealand, Eastern Europe, and China; these four accounted for over 60% of world production. As a result of a reduced sheep population, U.S. production was 25,700 metric tons, down slightly from 1996. Global activity (new production and carryover) grew by 3.5% to 1,780,000 metric tons clean, the first increase in five years. Raw wool prices rose an average of 15% owing to an interest in lighter-weight fabrics suitable for spring and autumn wear.

In 1997 U.S. wool-fibre consumption was 61,100 metric tons, down from 64,900 metric tons in 1996. Apparel accounted for 91% of the volume, and carpets made up the remainder. Globally, consumption exceeded production by more than 2.5%, which caused concern about the depletion of merino wool stocks to satisfy demand. Despite the increase in consumption, the wool-fibre share of the apparel market remained low, at slightly over 8%.

A technology was introduced to provide wool carpets with a finish resistant to moths, beetle larvae, and dust mites. In the procedure an insect-resistant agent contained in a low-melt powder was applied during the manufacturing process directly onto the carpet-pile surface. The powder was then fused to the wool fibres at the same time that the backing on the carpet was dried.

Cotton. Worldwide cotton production fell 1.6% in 1997 to 18.9 million metric tons. The five major producers were the U.S., followed by China, India, Pakistan, and Uzbekistan. Production in the U.S. was down owing to a decrease in planted acreage, lower yields, and a change in the 1996 Federal Agricultural Improvement and Reform Act cotton bill that reduced government incentives to plant cotton.

Cotton consumption worldwide was 19.2 million metric tons, up 2.1% from 1996. The largest gains were in China and India, and there was essentially no change in the U.S., Pakistan, Europe, and Asia. In the U.S. cotton continued to claim over 60% of the apparel and home-furnishings market; worldwide, cotton claimed slightly less than the 45.1% share it enjoyed in 1996. The decline was attributed to the inroads into cotton's traditional markets made by man-made fibres, particularly polyester.

The United States continued to dominate the export markets, with exports of 1.5 million metric tons of cotton, primarily to China, Turkey, Mexico, South Korea, and Japan. The volume was up from 1.4 million metric tons in 1996. The other major cotton exporters included Uzbekistan, the countries of French-speaking Africa, Australia, and Argentina.

Genetic engineering played a major role in cotton research. In the U.S. five herbicide-resistant cottons were available for commercial planting, as well as a number of medium- and short-staple cotton varieties that were resistant to butterflies, moths, and certain viruses. (EVERETT E. BACKE)

Silk. World silk production in 1996 was estimated at 81,098 metric tons. China was the leading producer, with 58,000 metric tons, followed by India (12,384), Japan (2,579), and Brazil (2,270). In China the 1997 spring cocoon crop was 20% lower than the 1996 tonnage, which was 40% less than that for 1995. The quality, however, was good. With reduced Chinese production, prices were expected to rise, but the size of the increase was likely to be small and largely the consequence of the introduction of export regulations for raw silk. The quality of Brazilian silk remained excellent, and prices continued to outpace those for Chinese silk.

Worldwide demand remained generally flat, with the exception of India and Great Britain, where much of the silk went into necktie fabric for the U.S. market. Elsewhere, the image of silk was still suffering from the widespread sales of cheap silk garments during the early 1990s. International efforts were made to bolster silk's image, and items made of silk began to reappear in the Paris fashion collections. Spun silk returned to fashion. Unfortunately, several mills in East Asia had to cease production in May and June owing to a shortage of silk waste used for spinning. Operations resumed in July, with noils unaffected and remaining plentiful.

The outlook for the future was uncertain. With production down, a shortage was likely to occur in 1998, but much depended upon demand in such major consuming countries as Japan and India. Much of India's domestically produced silk was unsuitable for use in the warp of machine-woven fabrics. As a result, India was the largest importer of raw silk, at 4,195 metric tons.

(ANTHONY H. GADDUM)

TOBACCO

In spite of a worldwide increase in anti-tobacco sentiment, and a marked rise in legislation designed to curb smoking, global sales of cigarettes rose in 1997 by 0.9% to an estimated 5,370,000,000,000, according to *World Tobacco File.* The continuing decline in consumption in the United States and most Western European countries was more than offset by increased sales of cigarettes in the Middle East, the Asia-Pacific region, and some Eastern European countries, a reflection of rising incomes and an enhanced lifestyle. To meet the demand, output of tobacco leaf rose in almost all the major producing countries to a global figure of 7,513,370 metric tons, the highest total since 1993.

The worldwide trend toward the American-blend type of cigarette, which incorporates Oriental, Burley, and Virginia leaf, continued. It accounted for 25% of global sales in 1990 and about 38% in 1997. The brand leader of this type was Marlboro, made by Philip Morris Inc.; it was the world's best-selling cigarette. Sales of the other most popular type, Virginia blend, grew in the same period but only from 48% to an estimated 52%, primarily because the Chinese, who bought nearly a third of the world's cigarette sales, favoured that variety.

Growing health concerns drove manufacturers in the former Soviet Union and some less-developed countries to produce more filter-tipped cigarettes, which were dominant in the rest of the world. Similarly, sales of light and ultralight cigarettes, with lower tar and nicotine content, rose, particularly in the U.S., Western Europe, and Japan. Meanwhile, Philip Morris and the R.J. Reynolds Tobacco Co. test-marketed new cigarette products designed to eliminate smoke from the burning end of the cigarette.

In the U.S. tobacco manufacturers, led by Philip Morris, R.J. Reynolds, and Brown & Williamson Tobacco Corp. (a subsidiary of B.A.T Industries PLC), sought congressional approval for a landmark settlement, announced on June 20, under which they would gain immunity from costly tobacco liability lawsuits in exchange for payment of $368.5 billion over 25 years and accept restrictions on the way they manufactured, marketed, and sold cigarettes. In October the firms settled a class-action lawsuit concerning the effects of smoking on nonsmokers by agreeing to spend $300 million for the study of tobacco-related diseases.

Ironically, while the cigarette manufacturers were enduring pain, the manufacturers and importers of premium-quality cigars in the U.S. were basking in an unprecedented sales boom, encouraged by two elegant lifestyle magazines focusing on fine cigars.

(LAURENCE RIDGEWAY)

TOURISM

In 1997 the number of international tourist arrivals grew by 5%, reaching 595 million, while revenues from tourism rose 7%, to $425 billion. This steady global expansion continued throughout 1997. The strong U.S. dollar continued to attract North American visitors to overseas destinations, whereas the long-delayed Japanese economic recovery and setbacks in Southeast Asian economies caused the Asia-Pacific region to underperform. A strong pound sterling encouraged the British to visit continental Europe, but the resulting high prices in Great Britain discouraged European visitors from traveling to the U.K.

The hotel sector benefited from tourism's strong 1996–97 recovery. Occupancies in London hotels rose from 82% to 84% as 1996 profits soared by 26%. In New York City occupancy reached 82%, a 5% increase over 1996. Airlines belonging to the International Air Transport Association saw growth of 7.5% in air traffic during 1997. They were concerned, however, about safety issues, fearing that with a projected doubling of air traffic by the year 2010, major jet crashes could increase to an average of one per week.

In Africa the Indian Ocean island of Mauritius had a 12% rise in arrivals, chiefly from Europe, and Tunisia's desert resorts, especially Tawzar, featured prominently in promotions. In Zimbabwe, where tourism accounted for 5% of gross domestic product, the government took initiatives to support indigenous investment by black Zimbabweans. Tanzania emphasized cultural tourism. Tourism in Kenya's popular coastal resorts fell 70% after violence broke out in May prior to elections and continued throughout the summer.

In Volgograd, Russia, tourists gather at the base of "Mother Russia," the 52-m (171-ft)-high statue on Mamayev Hill that commemorates Soviet soldiers in the Battle of Stalingrad.

JASON ESKENAZI—CONTACT PRESS IMAGES

Brazil, which welcomed some 2.2 million tourists each year, launched a campaign to attract more foreign visitors and stepped up security by introducing new tourist-friendly police stations. In Canada the tourism sector employed 500,000 persons, a record level, but the strong Canadian dollar caused foreign expenditure to level off even as domestic demand surged. In Cuba international tourism overtook sugar as the leading currency earner, with the Caribbean island acting as host to 1.2 million foreign visitors. Mexico saw a good summer vacation season, with hotel occupancy 2–4% higher than in 1996; a fall hurricane, however, damaged Acapulco resorts. Eruptions of the Soufrière Hills volcano on the Caribbean island of Montserrat caused thousands to flee and halted tourism. A survey showed that although U.S. residents had doubled their long-distance travel between 1977 and 1995, foreign travel accounted for only 4% of those trips; one-half of those journeys ended in Canada or Mexico.

Australia, looking forward to serving as host for the 2000 Olympic Games in Sydney, saw in that event an outstanding potential for growth and exports. Australia also found that in comparison with other tourists, backpackers spent more, stayed longer, traveled more widely, and thus created more jobs. Among Hong Kong's new projects following its return to China were 40 new hotels, a film city, a virtual-reality theme park, and a new airport at Chek Lap Kok. The 45% devaluation of Thailand's currency, the baht, was welcomed by the nation's tourism industry, which expected to be host to one million Japanese visitors in 1997. In the Philippines tourism soared by 11%, with the U.S. and Japan providing the most visitors. India earned 11% more from foreign tourism in 1997, whereas Indonesia, which welcomed five million tourists in 1996, experienced a decrease of 26% in foreign arrivals owing to a haze problem that emanated from forest fires in the archipelago.

World's Top 20 Tourism Spenders

(International tourism expenditures excluding transportation)

Rank 1985	Rank 1990	Rank 1996	Country	Expenditure ($000,000) 1996	% change 1995–96
1	1	1	United States	52,563	14.6
2	2	2	Germany	49,787	–2.6
4	3	3	Japan	37,040	0.7
3	4	4	United Kingdom	25,445	4.9
5	6	5	France	17,753	8.7
10	5	6	Italy	15,488	24.7
8	8	7	Austria	11,822	1.5
7	9	8	Netherlands, The	11,370	–0.7
6	7	9	Canada	11,090	8.5
—	—	10	Russia	10,597	–8.6
12	13	11	Belgium	9,895	7.4
9	11	12	Switzerland	7,479	1.8
25	19	13	South Korea	6,963	18.0
19	23	14	Brazil	6,825	100.0
17	14	15	Taiwan	6,493	–9.2
14	10	16	Sweden	6,285	15.9
50	46	17	Poland	6,240	13.5
24	22	18	Singapore	6,104	21.1
15	15	19	Australia	5,322	15.6
21	16	20	Spain	4,921	8.4

In Europe, Bulgaria established a visa-free entry for citizens of most nations, and Estonia did so for its Nordic neighbours. Croatia's tourism minister planned to extend both the tourist season and Croatia Airlines' operations to Great Britain and Germany, its main tourism sources. The number of foreign overnight visitors in Croatia rose 72% in 1997. Cyprus expected two million visitors, a 5% increase. On October 26 and Dec. 1, 1997, Italy and Austria, respectively, became members of the Schengen group of border-control-free states for travelers from other European Union countries. Portugal's expected 10.5 million visitors in 1997 were seen as a good omen as preparations were under way for the 1998 Lisbon World Exposition. Spain, the second most popular tourist destination in the world, after France, expected more than 45 million tourists in 1997, with an increase in receipts of 4%. Istanbul was host of the biggest-ever general assembly of the World Tourism Organization; 98 tourism ministers from 131 countries were in attendance. Russia and neighbouring nations continued to develop tourism on market-economy principles, and Silk Road tourism grew as Uzbekistan and its neighbours built new hotels and modernized airports.

Despite bright prospects for business tourism in such Middle East destinations as Dubayy, Abu Dhabi, Egypt, Saudi Arabia, Bahrain, and Kuwait, the menace of terrorism cast a long shadow over the region. Travel to Israel was subdued following suicide bombings in Jerusalem, and the November 17 attack that killed more than 50 German, Japanese, and Swiss tourists in Luxor, Egypt, dealt a severe blow to that nation's tourism industry.

(PETER SHACKLEFORD)

WOOD PRODUCTS

Wood. In 1997 the wood products industry got off to a vigorous start following a surge in prices and demand at the end of 1996. By the middle of the year, however, the market had slowed. U.S. lumber production enjoyed a boost in the first six months of the year owing to the availability of more private timber in the West and record volumes being produced in the South. American timber prices later dropped, however, to an 18-month low as a result of increased production in most supplying regions in North America and increased exports from Scandinavia. Moderate housing starts and reduced export demand, especially from Japan, also contributed to the slump.

The Canada-U.S. lumber quota agreement, which limited duty-free entry of Canadian lumber to the U.S. market, had less impact on the volume of trade between the two countries than was expected but caused uncertainty in the market. Canada, nevertheless, exported a record 42 million cu m (17.8 billion bd ft) of softwood lumber to the U.S. in 1996, the first year under the pact.

In mid-1997 an environmental coalition successfully lobbied a federal judge in California to halt imports of logs and wood chips from Siberia, New Zealand, and Chile by arguing that imported unprocessed wood posed a health risk to U.S. forests. Tropical hardwoods and products from the borders of Canada and Mexico were not included in the order. Although no short-term market impact was expected from this legislation, some exporters in New Zealand, Chile, and Brazil viewed the development with caution.

The use and acceptability of engineered wood products and new wood-based panel products continued to strengthen the main wood products market. Nevertheless, greater production of some goods, such as oriented strand board, was reaching overcapacity, depressing prices and forcing the closing of some older plants in North America.

Europe moved from importing forest products to self-sufficiency after Austria, Finland, and Sweden joined the European Union in 1995. The European lumber market started strong in 1997, but it slowed as the year progressed owing to reduced demand in Europe for saw timber and the near-complete halt of exports to Japan after the first quarter of the year. Although demand in the U.K. did not decline significantly, major markets in Germany, France, and Italy remained sluggish after the middle of the year. In addition, excess production resulting from a strong market at the end of 1996 and the beginning of 1997 coupled with reduced demand later in the year led to oversupply and a drop in prices.

Low demand for wood products in Japan caused oversupply problems for European and North American exporters. This important export market suffered from a weak yen, a sales tax increase, and low housing starts, which dampened consumption. In Japan the supply of and demand for logs, lumber, and panels were not expected to regain a balance until the end of 1997—or, for many items, not until 1998.

By the middle of the year, falling currencies in Southeast Asian countries such as Thailand, Malaysia, and the Philippines had reduced the timber trade for Asia's main exporting countries. There was weak demand from such major consumers as Japan, Taiwan, and South Korea, which also began substituting tropical hardwood species from Southeast Asia with softwood imported from Russia and New Zealand. Competition from African log species and cheaper supplies from South America also hampered the Asian timber trade. Both Japanese and Southeast Asian traders were pessimistic about a price and demand upturn by the end of the year.

(WORLD FOREST INSTITUTE)

Paper and Pulp. Although world paper and board production increased by only 1.3% in 1996, the rise was enough to establish a new world record of 281,960,000 metric tons. It was the 14th consecutive year that output had increased.

Asia was again a star performer, with gains of 5.7% over 1995. Its production, at 82 million metric tons, represented 29% of worldwide paper and board output. Although small mills were closed in China for environmental reasons, production there rose by 2 million, to 26 million metric tons. Japan, with 30 million metric tons, snared the number two position from Europe as the world's second largest producer of paper and board. European production fell by almost 10%, with Russia's output declining 21.1% and accounting for only 3.2 million of Europe's nearly 81 million metric tons.

The United States remained the undisputed leader, with output of 81.8 million metric tons. In North America, which accounted for 35.6% of world output, producers for the first time surpassed 100,000,000 metric tons, reaching 100,260,000.

Pulp continued to lose ground to wastepaper as a raw material. Although pulp represented 62.5% of all basic raw materials used in the paper industry, it had once accounted for 65% and appeared to be in a downward spiral. As a result, total pulp output declined almost 4% in 1996, to 174 million metric tons. Despite decreases from 1995 of 2.4% for the U.S. and 4.1% for Canada, the two nations remained the top producers in 1996, with 58.2 million (U.S.) and 24.3 million metric tons (Canada). Indonesia achieved the sharpest growth, 30.3%, adding more than 600,000 metric tons in output, almost all targeted for export.

Although paper recovery was expected to continue until at least 2005, global demand and supply patterns were changing. By 2005 total paper-recovery levels throughout the world could grow by more than 60% above 1995 levels. The U.S. became the world's leading exporter of surplus recovered paper, whereas fibre-hungry Asia became the world's leading importer.

(H.-CLAUDE LAVALLÉE)

This article updates the *Macropædia* articles BEVERAGE PRODUCTION; BUILDING CONSTRUCTION; DRESS AND ADORNMENT; ELECTRONICS; ENERGY CONVERSION; FORESTRY AND WOOD PRODUCTION; INDUSTRIAL GLASS AND CERAMICS; Chemical Process INDUSTRIES; Extraction and Processing INDUSTRIES; Manufacturing INDUSTRIES; Textile INDUSTRIES; INSURANCE; MARKETING AND MERCHANDISING; PHOTOGRAPHY; PRINTING, TYPOGRAPHY, AND PHOTOENGRAVING; TELECOMMUNICATIONS SYSTEMS; TOOLS.

Logs are loaded along the Tutah River in Sarawak, Malaysia. In 1997 the Southeast Asian currency crisis hampered the timber trade in the region's main exporting countries. Some major consumers of Southeast Asian timber turned to cheaper substitutes from Russia and New Zealand, among other places.

STUART FRANKLIN—MAGNUM PHOTOS

Computers and Information Systems

The year 1997 was one in which the computer industry's financial troubles, government investigations, prominent lawsuits, and business consolidations captured as much attention as advancing technology and the continuing growth of the Internet and on-line services. It also was the year in which the U.S. Supreme Court struck down the Communications Decency Act, an attempt to regulate the content of the Internet. The act had been signed by Pres. Bill Clinton in early 1996 in an attempt to protect children from pornography on the Internet, but opponents had claimed the law was so general it could be used to regulate other, more legitimate types of expression. The legislation made it a crime to publish indecent material on the Internet in a way that would make it available to those under 18; violators could receive up to two years in prison and a $250,000 fine. In June the high court threw out the Communications Decency Act on the grounds that it was too broad, vague, and in violation of the Constitution because it "lacks the precision that the First Amendment requires when a statute regulates the content of speech."

Industry Developments. It was a troubled year for Apple Computer, Inc. Already weakened by declining computer sales, Apple was in turmoil in July when Chairman and CEO Gilbert F. Amelio resigned from the company after some 18 months on the job, during which Apple lost nearly $1.5 billion. Apple's board of directors reportedly was displeased by falling sales of Apple's Macintosh computers. By the first quarter of 1997, Apple's share of the U.S. personal computer (PC) market had fallen sharply to 3.3% as customers continued to favour PCs that ran Microsoft Corp.'s Windows operating system (OS). Though Amelio, who had been welcomed as a corporate turnaround specialist, was unsuccessful, the roots of Apple's troubles ran deep. They were said to include lack of technical innovation, product-handling mistakes, and management upheaval, plus thousands of layoffs.

The year also marked the return of Apple cofounder Steve Jobs, an articulate but temperamental leader who had been pressured to resign as chairman in 1985. Beginning as an unpaid Amelio adviser in December 1996 after his firm, NeXT Software, Inc., was acquired by Apple for more than $400 million, Jobs stepped up his participation in Apple's management as the company tried to find a way back from the brink. In August he announced that Microsoft, a longtime rival of Apple, would buy $150 million in nonvoting Apple stock. Although the Mac OS competed with Windows, it was believed that Microsoft, which sold a substantial amount of applications software to the Macintosh market, had much to gain by helping its competitor remain in business. In September Jobs became interim CEO. During the same month, most of the Apple board of directors resigned, and Apple agreed to buy Power Computing Corp., a Macintosh clone manufacturer, for $100 million, in effect halting the corporate strategy of allowing others to produce clone copies of the Macintosh under license.

Microsoft had no financial problems but ran into difficulty with the federal government. In October it was accused by the U.S. Justice Department of violating the 1995 court order barring it from anticompetitive licensing activities. The Justice Department asked a federal court to impose a $1 million-a-day fine on the software industry leader for requiring PC manufacturers to use Microsoft's World Wide Web browser, Internet Explorer, on their machines when they installed Microsoft's Windows 95 OS. As evidence, the Justice Department said Compaq Computer Corp. claimed that it was threatened with the loss of its license to use Windows 95 if it removed Internet Explorer from some of its PCs. Microsoft said antitrust regulators were mistaken and that it would defend its position; it called the disagreement with Compaq an ordinary dispute over licensing terms.

The Microsoft–Justice Department battle had the potential to have a major impact on the marketing contest between Microsoft and Netscape Communications Corp., both of which were trying to make their own browser the most widely used on the Internet. Justice Department attorneys said they were trying to prevent Microsoft, which had a virtual monopoly in personal computer operating systems, from using that power to take control of the Internet browser market. At issue was the Justice Department's interpretation of a 1995 consent decree with Microsoft that had settled another antitrust dispute. Microsoft said that far from violating the agreement, it was merely making technological improvements to its existing Windows 95 product by adding browser software to it.

Another industry leader, Intel Corp. under Chairman and CEO Andrew Grove (*see* BIOGRAPHIES), also drew the interest of federal government regulators. Intel, the world's leading manufacturer of microprocessor chips for PCs, learned in September that it was being investigated by the Federal Trade Commission (FTC) in connection with its business practices in the PC market. The FTC said it wanted to determine if Intel had tried to monopolize or otherwise restrict price competition in its role as supplier of about 85% of the microprocessors used in PCs. Intel also was the subject of an anti-

A gigantic live video image of Microsoft chief executive Bill Gates dwarfs Apple Computer cofounder Steve Jobs, who stands at the podium at the MacWorld convention in Boston on August 6. It was announced that Microsoft would pay $150 million for a minority nonvoting share in Apple, which had been severely weakened by declining computer sales in recent years.

JULIA MALAKIE—ASSOCIATED PRESS

Electronic Magazines

With the increasing popularity of computers and the Internet, more and more magazines put versions of their material on-line. According to the *Net.Journal Directory,* by 1997 at least 10,000 magazines and journals, out of an estimated 100,000 American and Canadian publications, were available on-line. Some respected magazines—*e.g., Time, Sports Illustrated,* and *National Geographic*—had on-line publications, which often differed from their print siblings. Because the publishers were not constrained by space and printing costs, new topics could be introduced and material that appeared in print could be expanded. Other magazines appeared only on-line—*e.g.,* Microsoft Corp.'s *Slate.* These could focus on one topic or emulate general-interest print magazines.

The most extreme form of electronic magazines, called e-zines or zines, were publications available only electronically—for example, on the Internet. Often of casual design and respect for facts and produced by at most a few people, these magazines tended to be highly personal, irreverent, and/or bizarre. They were usually directed to a small-but-devoted audience and did not take advertisements or seek to make a profit. .

Electronic magazines could trace their deepest roots to 1926, when a writer and small-time publisher, Hugo Gernsback, began a science-fiction magazine called *Amazing Stories.* One section provided readers space for letters, discussing the different stories. Gernsback included addresses of the letter writers so they could contact each other directly. This led to the development of associations and discussion groups where people could write their views on what was being published. Soon other science-fiction magazines were using this approach. In 1930 *Comet* (later renamed *Cosmology*), the first magazine devoted principally to this format of exchanging opinions, was published. Since these magazines were at first put out by the fans themselves, these publications were called fanzines.

The first fanzines were crudely and laboriously produced along a similar pattern: a person would write a personal article on whatever he or she liked, find artwork that would enhance it—either self-drawn or photos found somewhere (the more offbeat, the better), paste it all together, make copies of the work by machine, fold and staple them, and then trade with other fanzine publishers.

With advances in xerography and desktop publishing, the fanzines became slicker and more visually appealing. The next giant step was the move to the Internet and the World Wide Web, which provided fanzine publishers a chance to reach a much larger audience with high-tech zines produced on electronic media. As more user-friendly technology and software appeared, even nontechies could create elaborate, interactive e-zines with frames, sophisticated graphics, animation, and hypertext links.

(STEVEN MONTI)

trust investigation by the FTC from 1991 to 1993 that did not result in any action against the company.

In a surprising move, Digital Equipment Corp. sued Intel in May, alleging that Intel's Pentium microprocessor chips violated as many as 10 Digital patents. Intel denied that it used Digital technology in the Pentium chip, but the suit, which sought unspecified damages, had the potential to cost Intel billions of dollars as well as cripple its ability to use the Pentium technology. The suit also had the potential to disrupt the entire PC industry by forcing Intel to redesign its Pentium chips.

The dispute involved Digital's Alpha microprocessor. Digital claimed that Intel had access to proprietary information about the chip in 1990, when it was evaluating whether to license the Alpha technology from Digital. Intel responded by suing Digital for the return of information about Intel's next-generation Pentium chips. Since many Digital computers depended on Intel chips, Intel's apparent intent was to hurt Digital's computer-development efforts and put Digital at a competitive disadvantage in the PC market. In August Intel filed a counterclaim that alleged Digital had violated 14 Intel patents. Intel claimed that the technologies the patents represented were widely used throughout Digital's product line.

In the end the legal storm passed almost as fast as it began. In October Intel said it would buy Digital's Alpha chip development and manufacturing operations for $700 million as part of an agreement to end their legal wrangling. Digital would keep its Alpha design teams to work on future versions of the chip. The deal also included a series of patent cross-licensing agreements for which Intel would pay Digital an undisclosed sum. Both companies said their lawsuits against each other would be kept on hold, pending government approval of the agreement.

A battle over software standards also escalated into a major lawsuit. Sun Microsystems sued Microsoft in October in a battle for control of Java language software standards. Sun's suit claimed that Microsoft's Internet Explorer 4.0 software contained a variant of Sun's Java programming language that differed from the standard version. Sun accused Microsoft of infringing on Sun's Java trademark, false advertising, breach of contract, unfair competition, and interference. Microsoft denied Sun's allegations and countersued, seeking a dismissal of the Sun suit and asking the court to uphold Microsoft's right to claim that its products were "Java compatible."

There were indications of at least one impending class-action lawsuit against several computer makers for allegedly continuing to sell PCs that could not cope with the "year 2000 problem." This problem, also called the "Millennium Bug," had arisen because old computer systems designed to use a two-digit date to represent the year (*e.g.,* 97 to represent 1997) could fail on Jan. 1, 2000, when faced with the two-digit date 00; they would read this as 1900.

Consolidation continued in the fast-changing computing market. In February 3Com Corp. made the surprise announcement that it would merge with U.S. Robotics Corp., a leading manufacturer of high-speed modems, in a $6.6 billion exchange of stock. The intent was to build one of the largest companies in the rapidly growing field of computer networking. Japanese computer maker NEC Corp. announced in December that it was increasing its stake in Packard Bell NEC, Inc., from 20% to 49%.

In April Microsoft acquired WebTV Networks, which sold units that allowed people to connect to the Internet directly through their television sets, for $425 million. The software company said it wanted to "dramatically accelerate the merger of the Internet and television." In a similar move, Sun Microsystems in July said it would acquire Diba, a maker of Internet set-top boxes that could compete with Microsoft, but terms of that deal were not disclosed. As part of Sun, Diba was to work with consumer electronics companies to provide Internet-ready TVs, set-top boxes, satellite reception boxes, and "smart" telephones.

Compaq's purchase of Tandem Computers for $4 billion in stock was completed in August. Compaq was a major manufacturer of PCs and PC server computers, and Tandem pioneered highly reliable machines called fault-tolerant computer systems. In September America Online Inc. (AOL) agreed to buy its biggest competitor, the CompuServe Inc. on-line service. While CompuServe would continue as a separate operation, it would be operated by AOL, which would then have a combined customer list of more than 11 million subscribers. In a complex deal a third company, telecommunications firm WorldCom, was to buy CompuServe from H&R Block for $1.2 billion in stock and then exchange CompuServe's Interactive Services division for $175 million and AOL's ANS Communications. In the end, WorldCom was to become AOL's largest network service provider.

Technology Developments. New high-speed Internet access technologies for consumers began to appear during the year, including satellite downlinks, cable modems (which transmit signals over cable TV systems), and a group of telephone industry technologies known collectively as digital subscriber line (DSL). Satellite downloads, for example, promised speeds that would be up to 14 times faster than conventional 28,800 bits per second telephone modems. One version of DSL, called asymmetric digital subscriber line, was said to offer speeds of up to six million bits per second over standard telephone lines. At year's end, however, these technologies were in very limited use.

Although digital versatile (or video) disc (DVD) became available to consumers in mid-1997 as a VCR-replacement technology for viewing films, its computer cousin, called DVD-ROM, was in only limited use as a CD-ROM drive replacement for personal computers. A DVD-ROM disc, which could hold about 4.7 billion bytes of information, or about seven times more than a CD-ROM, would enable software companies to offer more complex programs on a single disc. Industry analysts said DVD-ROM drives were held back owing to lack of software, issues of compatibility with the Windows 95 OS, and delays needed to put additional copyright-protection mechanisms in the drives to satisfy Hollywood that DVD-ROM drives would not be used to copy commercially released DVD movies. DVD-ROM was expected to become widely available in PCs in 1998.

IBM said in May that it had developed the highest-capacity hard disk drive for portable PCs, one capable of storing up to five billion bytes of data. That surpassed the previous top capacity of about three billion bytes, although hard drives with one billion to two billion bytes were more common.

Intel and Hewlett-Packard were said to be developing a next-generation microprocessor code-named Merced that could radically change the PC industry because of its design and capabilities. Merced, which was believed to be scheduled for introduction in two years, would use a different set of computer instructions than the line of PC chips Intel had been selling since 1979. Some analysts believed Merced would have a speed of nearly 1,000 MHz, which would more than double the peak performance of the fastest chips in 1997. It also would be a 64-bit microprocessor and therefore able to process data faster than today's 32-bit chips.

The federal government also joined in the development of new technology by moving forward with the Clinton administration's $100 million plan to build a next-generation version of the Internet that would be faster, more reliable, and more secure than one in use in 1997. The government's plan was essential to more than 100 universities throughout the U.S. that were trying to develop new voice, video, and data uses of the Internet that required higher transmission speeds than the present system provided. The planned next-generation Internet would offer the universities, national laboratories, and research institutions 100- to 1,000-times-faster speeds.

Smart cards—credit or other financial cards containing computer memory chips—got a boost in 1997 after a long period of languishing. Industry groups agreed on standards for the cards, and Visa International and Bank of America announced a pilot program under which a small number of people would make purchases over the Internet by using monetary value stored on smart cards.

Computer Crime. Computer crime also continued to gain attention, from the standpoint of both computer sabotage and copyright infringement. The Computer Security Institute, a San Francisco-based association of information security professionals, said that U.S. companies and other organizations it surveyed had reported losing $100 million in the previous 12 months owing to computer security breaches. The institute said the problems included damage from computer viruses, financial fraud, theft of proprietary information, and sabotage. Dataquest, a market-research firm, predicted that corporations around the world would spend $6.3 billion on computer network security in 1997.

In October the Presidential Commission on Critical Infrastructure Protection said that U.S. telephone and banking systems were vulnerable to computer sabotage. The commission recommended that the government increase its spending on computer security research to $1 billion a year from $250 million. The commission also touched on another hot computer security issue—encryption, which involves coding Internet or other computer messages so they cannot be read by anyone who lacks a software "key." The FBI had lobbied hard for a system under which the police would have a software key to unlock all encrypted communications in order to uncover criminal activity. The commission's detailed findings were not made public, but according to some news reports, the commission endorsed some key access by government officials without recommending widespread access to encrypted messages by the police.

Computer crime also involved copyright infringement. A study by accounting firm Price Waterhouse showed that 28% of software sold in North America was pirated, compared with 68% in Latin America, 80% in Eastern Europe, 43% in Western Europe, and 74% in the Middle East. In March Los Angeles police said they had raided one of the biggest software-counterfeiting rings on the West Coast, recovering allegedly pirated Microsoft software and cash valued at about $10 million.

Software, communications, and entertainment companies lobbied heavily in Congress for copyright legislation that would make it illegal to defeat electronic anti-copying protection and could make Internet service providers at least partly liable if people who infringed on copyrights used their networks to do so. The legislation was tied to the ratification of two new international treaties dealing with copyrights. Some library groups, Internet service providers, and telephone companies said the protections sought in the bill were too broad.

The Internet. The Internet continued to grow and attract more attention during the year. While the growth rate slowed somewhat—to about 80% from 100% a year—some experts predicted there might be 200 million computers connected to the Internet by 2000, up from about 16 million in January 1997. The number of people using the Internet via those computers in 1997 was not known precisely but was estimated at about 35 million. The Internet's growing use became clear when NASA landed its Pathfinder space probe on Mars in July. Between the landing on July 4 and July 8, the Mars Pathfinder Web site—where photographs of the mission were made available to the public—recorded nearly 220 million hits, which far exceeded NASA's expectations. The Internet also suffered a major interruption of service in July when a computer technician at the company that handled the Internet's directory of addresses accidentally loaded the wrong information on the network's computers. As a result, E-mail and Web surfing were disrupted on a global scale.

The huge scope of the Internet worried some government officials, who saw unfettered Internet gambling as a threat to society. A report by the National Association of Attorneys General warned that during the previous year widespread Internet gambling had become more technologically feasible—even though Internet gambling was illegal in most states. In October federal legislation that could prohibit states from legalizing such gambling was proposed. One version of the legislation would impose strict fines and prison terms on violators.

Internet use also raised privacy questions. In June FTC hearings produced warnings that Americans were giving out more personal information than they realized and that much of it was available through the Internet. Information was being compiled from people who used the Internet, called toll-free numbers, registered to vote, or sent in product registration cards; more information could be gleaned from federal, state, and county courthouse records that had become available on-line.

The year also marked the first time that a champion chess player was beaten by a champion chess computer in a traditional match. In May world chess champion Garry Kasparov lost his match with the IBM computer Deep Blue. (*See* SPORTS AND GAMES: *Chess.*) The year before, Kasparov had defeated an earlier version of Deep Blue.

(STEVE ALEXANDER)

This article updates the *Macropædia* articles COMPUTERS: INFORMATION PROCESSING AND INFORMATION SYSTEMS.

Earth Sciences

GEOLOGY AND GEOCHEMISTRY

In 1797 James Hutton died and Charles Lyell was born. Their contributions to geology were recounted and celebrated at the Hutton/Lyell Bicentennial Conference, held in London and Edinburgh in 1997. Hutton conceived the imaginative *Theory of the Earth* (published 1788 and 1795). His work is encapsulated in the famous quotation "No vestige of a beginning, no prospect of an end," which introduced a sense of time, or timelessness, to geologic processes. In 1830 Lyell published *Principles of Geology,* which affirmed and consolidated Hutton's ideas. Lyell's work also marked the beginning of a long period in which most geologists concentrated on the mapping and study of rock formations and considered interpretation of the Earth's interior inaccessible and astronomy irrelevant. It was only through the insights provided by the theory of plate tectonics in the 1960s that the relationship of geology to global geophysics and geochemistry became thoroughly appreciated. Don Anderson (California Institute of Technology [Caltech]) presented the paper "A New Theory of the Earth" at the 1997 Edinburgh celebration, in which he demonstrated that essentially all of mantle geochemistry, tectonics, and petrology can be understood in terms of geophysical processes involving the Earth's mantle and crust.

Calibration of the "no-beginning, endless" time of Hutton with respect to observed rock sequences has been a central theme in geology. A quantitative geologic time scale did not become possible until the 1950s, with the application of isotopic studies of minerals. The discovery during the 1960s that the Earth's magnetic field reversed its polarity at intervals, leaving records in magnetized rock that could be calibrated by radiometric methods, provided techniques for dating magnetized sedimentary rocks back through several million years. Many sedimentary rocks display a cyclicity (in which alternating layers differ in chemical characteristics, sediment properties, and fossil communities) that is generally attributed to oscillations in climate. Considerable effort has been directed toward correlating climatic oscillations with perturbations in the Earth's orbit and rotational axis, which affect the solar energy reaching the Earth's surface. In 1997 F.J. Hilgen (University of Utrecht, Neth.), with colleagues W. Krijgsman, C.G. Langereis, and L.J. Lourens, reported a breakthrough in dating of the recent geologic record. They compared cyclic marine sedimentary sequences with curves showing the computed variations in precession (gyration of the rotation axis so as to describe a cone), obliquity (angle between the planes of the Earth's Equator and orbit), and eccentricity of the Earth's axis and orbit and concluded that the alternations reflected precession-controlled variations in regional climate. The sedimentary cycles, dated by the magnetic polarity reversal time scale, were used to calibrate the astronomical time scale, which by 1997 had been established for the past 12 million years and appeared to be more accurate and have higher resolution than the other time scales. Research during the year was directed toward finding a correlation between marine and continental sedimentary sequences and extending the astronomical time scale to earlier times. These findings could lead to a better understanding of paleoclimatology and climate modeling.

Concern about the prospects for and consequences of global warming gave urgency to research in paleoclimatology. Rocks, as well as cores drilled from ice sheets, contain the record of past climatic changes, and evidence confirmed that during the past several hundred thousand years there were significant swings in temperature. In 1997 Sarah J. Fowell (Lamont-Doherty Earth Observatory, Palisades, N.Y.) and John Peck (University of Rhode Island) reported on results obtained from a 1996 reconnaissance in Mongolia to study the climatic variability recorded in sediment cores drilled in lakes. The location was important because its climate is transitional between the Siberian subarctic region and the Asian monsoon belt, and climatic changes should therefore leave high-resolution records in the lake sediments.

Studies of the sediment cores for variations in pollen and spores, magnetic properties, and carbon isotopes were to be correlated with temperature estimates from oxygen isotope measurements of shells and fossilized horse teeth. A sequence of fossil soils indicated that the Gobi Desert in Central Asia expanded and contracted dramatically during the last glacial-interglacial cycle, between 24,000 and 35,000 years ago. An ice core drilled from an old glacier on the Tibetan Plateau also supported the idea of an unstable climate.

The geochemistry of ancient ice layers drilled from the ice sheets of Greenland provided compelling evidence for large temperature increases, many of which appeared to have occurred abruptly. The ice, made up of layers of trapped snow, air, and dust extending back almost 250,000 years, was analyzed for variations in oxygen and hydrogen isotopes (reflecting temperature changes), dust and ash (wind patterns and

Behind a church in the town of Xalitzintla, Mex., rises the Popocatépetl Volcano, which sent a huge ash plume 6.4 km (4 mi) into the air in May before erupting in June. Rain mixed with the ash covered many villages around the volcano's base and deposited a layer of sludge on Mexico City, 72 km (45 mi) away.
RAFAEL DURAN—ASSOCIATED PRESS

volcanic eruptions), ammonia (distant forest fires), and several other variable geochemical tracers.

On the basis of discoveries in the layers, geologists concluded that the end of the last glacial period, 10,000 years ago, did not occur through centuries as previously assumed but probably happened within a few decades—less than a human lifetime. Thus, the evidence suggested that climate change could conceivably occur quite suddenly and be completed within a few years if the current industrial society disturbed the delicate balance of the atmosphere with continued emission of greenhouse gases. The change could involve either global warming or global cooling.

The distribution of glacial rock deposits produced by the latest ice age confirms that the polar ice sheets left uncovered a wide equatorial belt, extending locally well into middle latitudes. D.A. Evans, N.J. Beukes, and J.L. Kirschvink (Caltech, Rand Afrikaans University) published in 1997 a discovery in Africa that indicated the formation of an ice sheet that approached equatorial regions. The only other unequivocally glacial rock deposits known through the 4 billion years of Precambrian history (older than 540 million years) are aged 600 mil-

EL NIÑO CONDITIONS

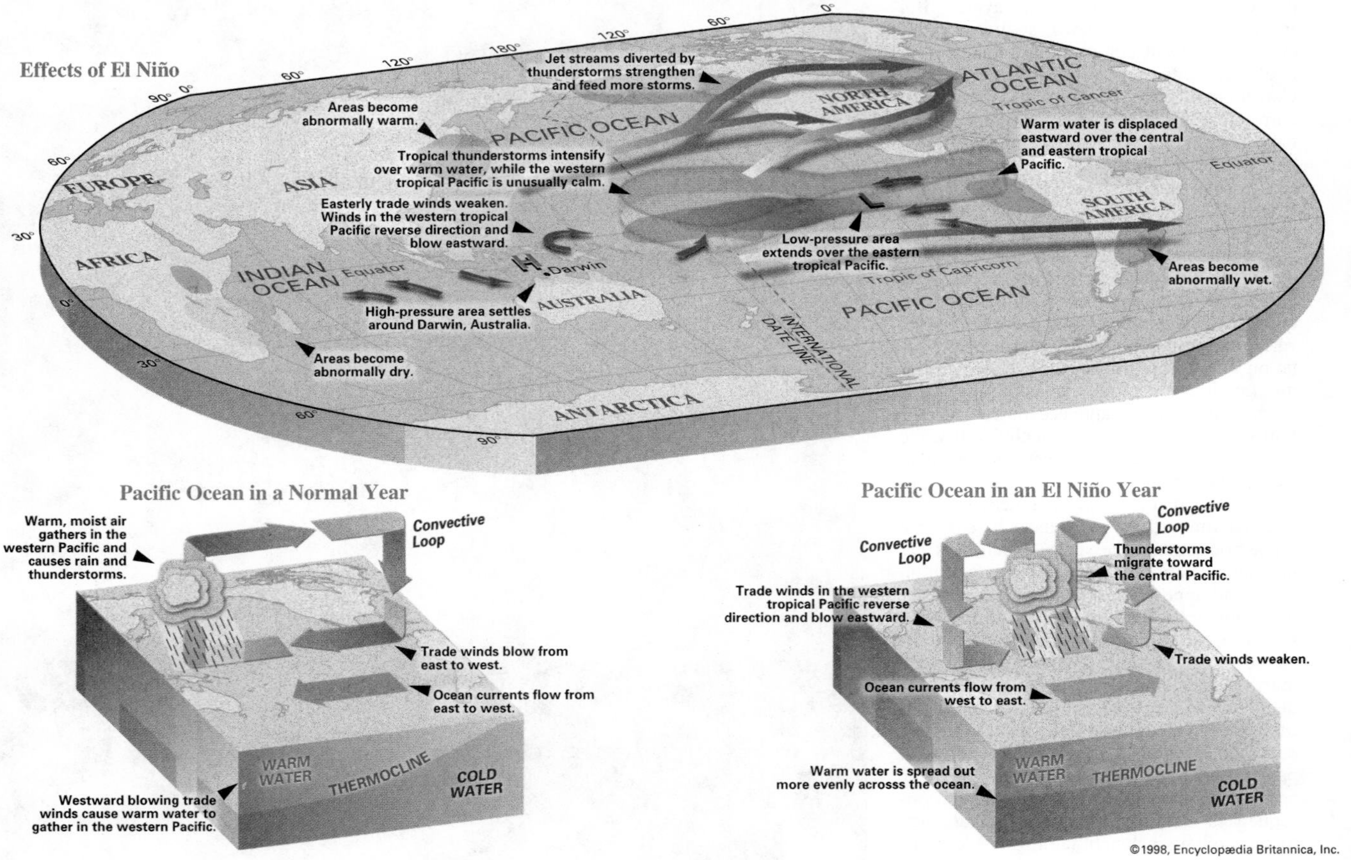

Effects of El Niño

Jet streams diverted by thunderstorms strengthen and feed more storms.
Areas become abnormally warm.
Tropical thunderstorms intensify over warm water, while the western tropical Pacific is unusually calm.
Easterly trade winds weaken. Winds in the western tropical Pacific reverse direction and blow eastward.
High-pressure area settles around Darwin, Australia.
Areas become abnormally dry.
Low-pressure area extends over the eastern tropical Pacific.
Warm water is displaced eastward over the central and eastern tropical Pacific.
Areas become abnormally wet.
EUROPE
ASIA
AFRICA
INDIAN OCEAN
AUSTRALIA
PACIFIC OCEAN
NORTH AMERICA
ATLANTIC OCEAN
SOUTH AMERICA
ANTARCTICA
INTERNATIONAL DATE LINE

Pacific Ocean in a Normal Year

Warm, moist air gathers in the western Pacific and causes rain and thunderstorms.
Convective Loop
Trade winds blow from east to west.
Ocean currents flow from east to west.
WARM WATER
THERMOCLINE
COLD WATER
Westward blowing trade winds cause warm water to gather in the western Pacific.

Pacific Ocean in an El Niño Year

Convective Loop
Convective Loop
Thunderstorms migrate toward the central Pacific.
Trade winds in the western tropical Pacific reverse direction and blow eastward.
Trade winds weaken.
Ocean currents flow from west to east.
Warm water is spread out more evenly acrosss the ocean.
WARM WATER
THERMOCLINE
COLD WATER

lion–800 million years. Some of these rocks are found in Australia, with measurements indicating that they too were formed near the Equator. An interpretation of these two Precambrian events is that they represented severe, globally inclusive ice ages, a model called the "Snowball Earth." Once such a condition is reached, reflection of sunlight should tend to keep the Earth glaciated, and the fact that the Earth recovered both times indicates a resilience to extreme perturbations in climate. Evans suggested that reheating of a Snowball Earth might be caused by carbon dioxide released by the impact of a comet or asteroid or by large volcanic outpourings.

Detailed studies following the 1991 eruption of Mt. Pinatubo in the Philippines confirmed that dust and sulfuric acid aerosols have measurable effects on global temperatures and other climatic factors. The potential effects of volcanoes were demonstrated in 1997 by the devastation caused by the continuing eruptions of the Soufrière Hills volcano on the island of Montserrat, which began in 1995, and the June 30 eruption of the huge volcano Popocatépetl, near Mexico City, which became active in 1994. According to a report by Simon Young of the British Geological Survey and four coauthors, flows of sulfur dioxide from Soufrière Hills monitored by spectrometer observations of the plume ranged from 50 to 500 tons per day—moderate compared with many other volcanoes—but flows up to 1,000 tons per day associated with periods of enhanced dome growth and emissions of lava and ash were observed. Changes in the volume of the volcanic dome were being measured from a helicopter by an innovative technique, using range-finding binoculars and the Global Positioning System. A comparison of the mineralogy and textures of the lavas with the findings from studies on similar compositions was providing estimates of the water content of the magma, rates of magma ascent, and degassing conditions.

The ash plume from Popocatépetl, the largest in 72 years, rose higher than 6.4 km (4 mi) and had a diameter of 55 km (34 mi). Rain mixed with the ash covered many of the 30 villages around the base of the volcano and deposited a layer of sludge on Mexico City, 72 km (45 mi) away. Mexican scientists stressed that there was less than a 10% chance of an imminent major eruption.

Mt. Pinatubo, Soufrière Hills, and Popocatépetl are arc volcanoes, associated with oceanic subduction, the descent of the edge of one oceanic plate beneath another. The explosive eruptions of such volcanoes are caused by the downward transfer of oceanic water and carbon dioxide during subduction and its subsequent transfer back to the surface dissolved in magmas formed at high pressures. The geologic and geochemical processes occurring in this environment constitute a vital link in the recycling of the Earth's crust. An international meeting, State of the Arc, was held in Australia at the University of Adelaide in 1997 to study the impact on the development of models for subduction processes of new geochemical knowledge (from studies of uranium, thorium, and an isotope of beryllium) and techniques (new laser-based methods for the analysis of small inclusions of lavas in minerals. Despite many advances in analytic techniques and computations, the report of the conference by Simon Turner (the Open University, Milton Keynes, Eng.) acknowledged the complexity of the problem with its final statement: "Thus there is still much to be done."

(PETER JOHN WYLLIE)

GEOPHYSICS

There were no great earthquakes in 1997, and of the nine shocks with magnitudes of seven or greater, only one exceeded 7.1. With a magnitude of 7.9, it struck on April 21 in the Santa Cruz Islands, a part of the Solomon Islands, where it generated a tsunami that caused minor damage along the coasts of the Solomon and the Vanuatu islands. The two shocks that caused the most fatalities were those of February 28, magnitude 6.1, in the border region of Armenia, Azerbaijan, and Iran, which resulted in 965 deaths; and of May 10, magnitude 7.1, in northeastern Iran, where some 1,560 died. In all, at least 2,855 people lost their lives as a result of earthquakes.

Though the level of seismic activity was low, this was not necessarily a good thing. Plates continue to move, and stresses continue to grow. It is generally true that the longer the interval since the last quake, the larger the next one is likely to be. One phenomenon, the slow earthquake, may, however, help to reduce this danger in some instances. Slow earthquakes release strain energy very slowly and are difficult to detect. They produce no seismic waves, and their movement is too small to be detected by satellites or other conventional means. They are detected by instruments that measure gradual movement along a fault interface. Research on these quakes has been under way for several years, with the latest work being done on an event recorded in 1992 at the juncture between locked and sliding sections of the San Andreas Fault in central California. Along the sliding sections of a fault, stress is reduced gradually by means of slipping and small earthquakes, whereas stress tends to build over relatively long periods on a locked fault until it is released abruptly by a large earthquake. The 1992 slow event was the slowest ever recorded, having been more than a thousand times slower than an ordinary shock. A series of events with several episodes of varying slip times occurred at depths ranging from 0.1 to 4+ km (1 km=0.62 mi). The surface area of the fault affected was 30 sq km (11.5 sq mi), and the strain release was equal to a normal earthquake of magnitude 4.8. It had a total displacement of only a few centimetres. Current studies seemed to indicate that the amount of slow redistribution of stress is indicative of the size of the next regular shock. The 9.5-magnitude Chilean earthquake of 1960 was preceded by a slow earthquake very large in extent with a cumulative slip of several metres, whereas a 5.8-magnitude shock in Japan in 1978 was preceded by a slow earthquake that produced a slip of about one metre (3.28 ft). Many scientists believe that these slow events are part of the total seismic process and may act as a trigger for the larger shocks.

Russian, Mongolian, and American seismologists were studying a major fault system in Central Asia's Gobi Desert that strongly resembles the San Andreas Fault system in southern California. A point of special interest was the Altai-Gobi earthquake of 1957, during which the strike-slip fault (in which the actual displacement along the fault plane is horizontal) and an adjacent thrust fault (in which displacement occurs vertically) ruptured simultaneously, producing a shock with a magnitude of about 8.0. The team spent two seasons in the field mapping the displacements and found them similar in size and orientation to the Fort Tejon earthquake of 1857, during which approximately 300 km of the San Andreas Fault ruptured with displacements up to 10 m. There was evidence that some movement occurred at the same time on the thrust system on the northeastern side of the nearby Elkhorn Hills. The investigators concluded from this evidence that such a simultaneous concurrence of ruptures could occur along the San Andreas and the large Sierra Madre/Cucamonga thrust fault in the San Gabriel Mountains in the Los Angeles area. Skeptics recognized the similarities between the Gobi and the California geologic structures but held that because of the much faster rate of fault movement in California, the differences outweighed the similarities.

On the basis of their studies of geodetic records from a period surrounding an earthquake of 1868, two geophysicists from Stanford University found evidence that challenged the long-accepted theory that earthquakes are contained within fault segments that limit their spread. Previously known as the San Francisco earthquake, this magnitude-7.0 shock caused damage along 51.5 km of the Hayward Fault in California from south of Fremont north to Berkeley. The ground rupture was thought to have stopped at San Leandro, but the records revealed that it continued 48 km farther to Berkeley and possibly beyond there, though there were no stations to record it farther north. The researchers had to rework the data because the original surveyors did not know that earthquakes distorted the surface. The reworked data showed that there had been a maximum relative movement along the fault interface of two metres and that the rupture had broken through the boundary between what had been assumed to be northern and southern sections of the main fault. Their findings were corroborated by investigators from the U.S. Geological Survey, who found evidence of the rupture in an exploratory trench in Oakland.

(RUTLAGE J. BRAZEE)

METEOROLOGY AND CLIMATE

Early in 1997 atmospheric and oceanic patterns across the tropical Pacific were indicative of a rapidly evolving warm episode, commonly known as El Niño. During the next few months, some of the largest El Niño effects of the 20th century developed. (See *Oceanography,* below.)

In late December 1996 and early January 1997, heavy precipitation and unseasonably mild air caused considerable snowpack melting, which resulted in serious river flooding across the western United States, from central California and northern Nevada northward into Washington and Idaho. In early March severe weather involving tornadoes and torrential rains affected the Ohio, Tennessee, and lower Mississippi valleys. In Arkansas, where tornadoes claimed 26 lives, Arkadelphia was hardest hit when an F4 tornado (wind speeds of 333–418 km/h [207–260 mph]) tore through the town. Severe river flooding developed along the central and lower portions of the Ohio River and middle sections of the Mississippi River. In April flooding in the Northern Plains resulted after unseasonably mild weather had caused rapid melting of the deep snowpack, which led to rapid runoff and ice jams that pushed many streams out of their banks. The Red River at Fargo, N.D., topped the previous flood crest record level observed a century earlier, and Grand Forks, N.D., exceeded its 500-year statistical recurrence level. In early April a change in the jet stream brought unseasonably cool conditions to the eastern two-thirds of the United States until mid-June. Heavy rains, occasionally accompanied by severe weather, affected the south-central and southeastern U.S. throughout the spring. In May an F4 tornado killed 27 people in Jarrell, Texas. Dryness developed across the mid-Atlantic in April, and many areas recorded one of their driest April–August periods. In late October the first major snowstorm of 1997–98 buried the central Rockies and High Plains with 30–130 cm (1–4 ft) of snow.

The 1997 Atlantic hurricane season was rather tranquil, with seven named storms. Only one, Danny, affected the U.S. The eastern Pacific hurricane season, although average in number of storms, was marked by several that were intense. In mid-September Hurricane Linda, packing winds of 300 km/h (185 mph), became the strongest eastern Pacific hurricane on record but never made landfall. At the end of September, however, Hurricane Nora pounded southwestern Baja California, Mex., with 250-km/h (155-mph) wind gusts. As Nora moved northeastward, up to 250 mm (10 in) of rain soaked Mexico's northern Gulf of California coast, and 50–150 mm (2–6 in) of rain deluged much of the U.S. desert Southwest. In early October Hurricane Pauline battered the southwestern coast of Mexico, including the resort town of Acapulco; more than 400 lives were lost.

Above-normal temperatures dominated South America, particularly along the Pacific Coast through late April, where elevated sea-surface temperatures, indicating the strong El Niño event, had a direct influence. During late July, in the middle of the Southern Hemisphere winter, high temperatures in central Argentina reached 34° C (93° F) as far south as lat 32° S.

In Europe the year commenced with bitterly cold weather gripping much of the continent, as temperatures averaged 3° C to 13° C (5° F to 23° F) below normal. Canals in The Netherlands froze over for only the 15th time in 100 years. In late January, however, unusually mild and dry weather developed across the continent and persisted for several weeks. Late in March dryness abruptly abated as copious precipitation fell in western and central Russia, southeastern and north-central Europe, and, especially, central Scandinavia. Farther west, rain soaked much of continental Europe from mid-May through mid-July. Flooding occurred in parts of Poland, the Czech Republic, Slovakia, and Austria. In Poland and the Czech Republic 100 people lost their lives. Unseasonable warmth developed in the Mediterranean basin during late May and overspread much of Europe, especially Scandinavia, throughout the summer.

Warmth covered much of northern Africa during early January, with highs reaching 38° C (100° F) in parts of southeastern Niger and northwestern Senegal. In southern Africa rainfall was above normal the first four months of the year. Late in January Cyclone Gretelle pushed across southeastern Madagascar, dropping 200–250 mm (8–10 in) of rain. A month later two tropical cyclones, Josie and Lisette, fueled torrential downpours in southeastern Africa. After a dry beginning across east-central Africa, heavy rains developed in late March and early April and spread westward to the Gulf of Guinea coast by mid-June. Rainfall deficiencies, however, developed across the western Sahel by early August, and above-normal temperatures in that region and the Gulf of Guinea area aggravated the dryness during September and October.

Unseasonably mild weather covered much of Asia during January. By contrast, temperatures averaged well below normal during March, April, and early May across most of the Indian subcontinent. Tropical Cyclone 01B caused widespread damage as it tracked through southeastern Bangladesh during mid-May. Unofficial reports placed the death toll at some 100 people, with more than a million people homeless. Typhoon Peter dumped torrential rains on South Korea and western Japan in late June, and a month later Typhoon Rosie crossed Japan, raising six-week (mid-June through July) precipitation excesses to 530 mm (21 in).

Two weeks later a fourth typhoon, Tina, brought more heavy rains to western Japan and South Korea. Meanwhile, a sequence of three typhoons (Victor, Winnie, and Zita) doused southern China with excessive rains. As August ended, another pair of tropical systems (Amber and Cass) brought heavy rains and strong winds to eastern China. To the south, heavy rains affected much of western Indonesia, Malaysia, and extreme southern Thailand during May, but as the summer progressed, intense dryness, regarded as an effect of El Niño, overspread Indonesia. The lack of precipitation abetted numerous wildfires through September and October, with heavy smoke affecting health and transportation throughout much of Southeast Asia.

Two tropical cyclones (Phil and Rachel) brought heavy rain and strong winds to northern Australia as the year began. Surplus rains persisted across northern Australia during January, and frequent February precipitation ended dryness across New South Wales and southeastern Queensland. At the end of February, the remnants of Tropical Cyclone Gillian caused locally heavy rains in northeastern Queensland. In March Tropical Cyclone Justin brought strong winds and heavy rain to southeastern Cape York Peninsula, but much drier weather prevailed elsewhere. By early May significant dryness covered northeastern Australia after the rainy season ended early.

(ROBERT S. WINOKUR)

OCEANOGRAPHY

The occurrence of a major El Niño dominated oceanographic research as well as planning for marine and coastal resource management during 1997. The term *El Niño* originally referred to the occurrence of warm southward ocean currents every few years near the coasts of Ecuador and Peru during the Southern Hemisphere summer, when local winds are weakest. This was called El Niño ("the Child") by local inhabitants in reference to the "Christ Child," since it normally occurred around Christmas. It signaled both a shift in local weather and a shift in the biology of the coastal ocean. Occasionally this event is extraordinarily strong, and scientists now recognize that the strong episodes involve climatic anomalies that may begin in the tropics but ultimately extend over the entire Pacific Ocean and even beyond. Such large-scale events are now called El Niño, the common name for El Niño/Southern Oscillation, or ENSO. The most extensive El Niño since 1982–83 began in 1997.

One of the most unusual aspects of this El Niño was the rapidity with which researchers and the public became aware of it. During previous episodes tropical observations had been sparse. They were often not available until moored instruments had been recovered, and even then they were not routinely disseminated rapidly; thus, the onset of an El Niño was recognized only retrospectively. Since late 1994, however, instrumented buoys had spanned the equatorial Pacific, sending observations of surface winds, upper-level ocean currents, and water temperatures via satellite to researchers every day. As a result, governmental agencies had an unprecedented opportunity to plan rationally for the possible effects of the episode.

Under normal circumstances, winds at the Equator are from the east (the southeast trade winds) and are particularly strong in the eastern Pacific. On account of the Earth's rotation, surface waters are forced both northward and southward away from the Equator by these strong winds. Water upwells from depths of many tens of metres to replace the offshore flowing water. This upwelled water is several degrees colder than the surface water it replaces, so that a tongue of cold water extends along the Equator several thousand kilometres westward of South America. During an El Niño, however, the trade winds in the eastern Pacific weaken or even reverse, and equatorial upwelling there ceases so that the entire equatorial eastern Pacific Ocean is anomalously warm by several degrees Celsius. The system of trade winds normally extends well into the western Pacific, but there it is usually weaker than in the eastern Pacific, and the layer of warm surface water is much thicker; consequently, upwelling normally does not bring cold water to the surface. The result is that in the western Pacific, evaporation normally puts water vapour into the atmosphere, and the ocean heats the atmosphere so that the moist air rises. The far western Pacific is, therefore, normally a region of widespread and intense rainfall. During an El Niño, however, the region of rising moist air migrates far eastward into the central tropical Pacific. The normally wet far western Pacific becomes a region of low rainfall and even drought, whereas the rainfall at normally temperate central tropical Pacific islands increases dramatically.

At one time researchers believed that most of the variability in the atmosphere sprang from the processes that generate storms at middle and high latitudes, but now it is clear that much of the variability of weather and climate has its origins in the tropics. El Niño is simply one of the largest and best-studied tropical phenomena; its effects on the atmosphere and the ocean extend far beyond the tropics. The best-known of these effects are profound changes in the marine populations in the rich fisheries of western coastal North and South America. Less well understood but possibly even more important are El Niño effects on sea level and storminess along those coasts, as well as on climate at latitudes far removed from the tropics.

The first indication that something was out of the ordinary came in December 1996, when normally westward-blowing trade winds briefly reversed direction in the far western Pacific. Although this change produced little effect at the ocean surface, it generated a deepening of the equatorial warm-water layer and caused the layer to spread eastward to South America, where it arrived by March 1997. Western Pacific trade winds decisively reversed direction in February 1997, generating another eastward-moving deepening of the equatorial warm-water layer. The region of reversed trade winds began to expand eastward across the Pacific and by December extended as far west as the longitude of California. The combination of deepening warm water pulses and weakening trade winds resulted in a warming of the far eastern tropical Pacific that was first noticeable in May, and by the year's end the warming episode had spread westward with temperatures of several degrees Celsius above normal at the International Date Line and in the eastern tropical Pacific. The plentiful rainfall that accompanies normally strong evaporation in the far western Pacific gave way to drought there, with an unusual incidence of prolonged forest fires.

(MYRL C. HENDERSHOTT)

See also Business and Industry Review: *Energy; Mining; Disasters;* The Environment; Life Sciences.

This article updates the *Macropædia* articles ATMOSPHERE; CLIMATE AND WEATHER; DINOSAURS; The EARTH; The EARTH SCIENCES; EARTHQUAKES; GEOCHRONOLOGY; The HYDROSPHERE; OCEANS; PLATE TECTONICS; RIVERS; VOLCANISM.

PAWEL KOPCZYNSKI—REUTERS

A man rides his bicycle through the flooded village of Stobrawa, Pol. Torrential summer rains triggered the worst flooding in Central Europe in 200 years. More than 100 persons were killed in western Poland and the northern third of the Czech Republic as the Oder River and smaller rivers overflowed.

Economic Affairs

The world economy grew by 4% in 1996 and was expected by the World Bank and the International Monetary Fund (IMF) to grow slightly faster in 1997. Despite the financial and economic crisis in Asia, a reasonably rapid pace looked sustainable into the next decade, as the inflation rate in most countries was low or declining and fiscal deficits had been curtailed. Among the developed economies, growth rates edged up to 3%, compared with 2.7% in 1996. Growth in the U.S. and the U.K. remained robust, and recovery in Western Europe broadened. In Japan, however, overall economic recovery faltered. The rate of growth in the less-developed countries (LDCs) as a group remained high at 6%, double that of the developed countries.

This overall picture masked considerable variations across the world. In the U.S. and Great Britain, growth, at around 3.5%, was strong and long-established, with little spare capacity remaining. The strength of domestic demand was the main engine of growth in both countries. In Western Europe, excluding the U.K., the recovery was still at an early stage, and growth rates remained below long-term trends. Growth stimulus was provided by the previous reductions in interest rates. This was partly countered in many European Union (EU) countries, however, by the continuation of restrictive policies designed to reduce fiscal deficits to ensure compliance with economic and monetary union (EMU) entry criteria of 3% of gross domestic product (GDP). By contrast, appreciation of the dollar and the pound sterling strengthened external demand. Against these developments, GDP in the EU increased an estimated 2.5% from the previous year's 1.7%, with virtually all member countries participating in the upturn. In Japan the economy faltered following a recovery in late 1996 and early 1997. The ending of the stimulatory effects of previous measures, combined with an increase in the consumption tax in April, led to a steep downturn in economic activity. This was exacerbated by the fallout from the financial crisis in Asia, which led to renewed weakness of the Tokyo stock market and Japanese financial institutions. In view of the sharp downturn, GDP growth in Japan was projected to slow to under 1% from 3.6% a year earlier. In Australia and New Zealand, where recovery was well-established, the growth rate moderated somewhat.

The economies of the former centrally planned countries as a whole registered an estimated growth rate of 1.2%—the first increase since the transition began eight years earlier. The Central and Eastern European countries grew much faster than Russia and the Central Asian countries. The long-expected return of economic growth in Russia appeared to be materializing in the second half of the year, but with the exception of Poland, output in this group of countries remained below 1989 levels. The gap was widest in the Commonwealth of Independent States (CIS), including Russia.

Economic performance among the LDCs was also variable. Asia remained the fastest-growing region, even with the slowdown that resulted from the financial crises that engulfed the region in the autumn. It was surprising how fast the July currency crisis and stock market crash in Thailand spread. Malaysia, the Philippines, and Indonesia had been affected by September or October. Rapid devaluation and austerity measures were followed by assistance from the IMF. The crisis then moved on to South Korea and indirectly influenced Japan.

Compared with an estimated 7% GDP growth in Asia, Latin America headed for 4% growth as it continued its recovery from the Mexican crisis of 1995. In the closing months of 1997, Brazil and, to a lesser extent, neighbouring countries in Latin America were adversely influenced by a loss of confidence in the wake of the Asian crisis. Growth rates in Africa and the Middle East, affected by a fall in commodity prices and by civil wars, moderated to around 4%.

As in 1996, unemployment worsened in many Western European countries and Japan but improved in the U.S. and the U.K. To some extent this was attributable to a lack of flexibility in labour markets in continental Europe and to different ideological and practical approaches among EU countries. At the November EU employment summit in Luxembourg, there was some evidence of willingness to try a new approach centred on employability, education, and reduced bureaucracy. Marking a break with previous thinking, the EU leaders showed little enthusiasm for French-style direct interventionist solutions. Instead, they agreed to introduce measures to provide work training for the young unemployed and the long-term jobless, similar to Britain's "new deal" for the unemployed. In the U.K. and the U.S., where there was greater labour market flexibility and economic growth was much faster, the number of unemployed continued to fall rapidly. The unemployment rate dropped to under 5% (about 7 million people) in the U.S. and to 5.2% (1.4 million) in the U.K. near the end of the year. This compared with 18.3 million jobless in the EU, or 11.25% of the workforce. Against the backdrop of a weaker economy, the unemployment rate in Japan edged up to more than 3.5% late in the year, a high level by Japanese standards.

The slowdown in world trade during 1996 was short-lived, and the volume of trade rose by a projected 8% in 1997 (6% in 1996). Much of the acceleration stemmed from the higher volume of imports and exports in the U.S. and the improved export performance of EU countries and Japan.

Table I. Real Gross Domestic Products of Selected OECD Countries

% annual change

Country	1993	1994	1995	1996	1997[1]
United States	2.3	3.5	2.0	2.4	3.6
Japan	0.3	0.6	1.4	3.6	0.9
Germany	−1.1	2.9	1.9	1.4	2.4
France	−1.3	2.8	2.1	1.5	2.3
Italy	−1.2	2.2	2.9	0.7	1.2
Great Britain	2.1	3.8	2.5	2.1	3.5
Canada	2.2	4.1	2.3	1.5	3.5
All developed countries	1.2	2.9	2.2	2.6	3.0
Seven major countries above	1.0	2.8	2.0	2.3	2.9
European Union	−0.5	2.9	2.4	1.6	2.5

[1] Estimated.
Sources: OECD; *The Economist.*

Table II. Consumer Prices in OECD Countries

% change from preceding year

Country	1993	1994	1995	1996	1997[1]
United States	3.0	2.6	2.8	2.9	2.2
Japan	1.2	0.7	−0.1	0.1	1.0
Germany	4.5	2.7	1.8	1.3	1.2
France	2.1	1.7	1.7	1.8	1.0
Italy	4.2	3.9	5.4	3.8	1.8
Great Britain	1.6	2.5	3.4	2.4	2.8
Canada	1.8	0.2	2.2	1.6	1.5
Austria	3.6	3.0	2.2	1.9	1.5
Belgium	2.8	2.4	1.5	2.1	1.6
Denmark	1.3	2.0	2.1	2.1	2.5
Finland	2.2	1.1	1.0	0.6	1.3
Greece	14.4	10.9	8.9	8.2	5.7
Iceland	4.0	1.6	1.7	2.3	2.5
Ireland	1.4	2.3	2.5	1.7	1.7
Luxembourg	3.6	2.2	1.9	1.8	2.0
Netherlands, The	2.6	2.8	1.9	2.1	2.3
Norway	2.3	1.4	2.5	1.3	2.5
Portugal	6.5	5.2	4.1	3.1	2.2
Spain	4.6	4.7	4.7	3.6	2.0
Sweden	4.7	2.4	2.9	0.8	1.0
Switzerland	3.3	0.9	1.8	0.8	0.7
Turkey	66.1	105.1	89.1	80.4	93.5
Australia	1.8	1.9	4.6	2.6	1.1
New Zealand	1.3	1.8	3.8	2.3	1.4
OECD Total	4.4	5.0	5.9	4.2	3.5

[1] Twelve-month rate of change in October 1997.
Sources: OECD; *The Economist.*

There was no significant change in the volume of trade in the LDCs. Regional deficits widened, with Japan and many EU countries running larger current-account balances while the U.S. deficit widened. As a result of an upsurge in imports by some Latin-American countries, the current-account balances of LDCs as a group widened. As in 1996, the LDCs did not experience any problems in funding the current deficits or in servicing existing loans.

In the U.S. and Britain, the primary aim of policy makers was to prevent the emergence of higher inflation rates. In most EU countries, however, the policy continued to be framed mainly by reference to political rather than economic considerations. Thus, in many countries there was a modest rise in interest rates and a continuation of deficit-reduction measures. In the U.S. the Federal Reserve Board (Fed) raised the federal funds rate by 0.25% in March in a precautionary move. As the economy continued to expand at an above-average rate in the autumn, a further rise in interest rates appeared imminent. In the wake of the correction in global stock markets and the financial crisis sweeping Asia, which resulted in a steep devaluation against the dollar, the Fed, however, adopted a wait-and-see policy and refrained from raising the interest rates. By contrast, the Bank of England, with its operational freedom in setting the interest rates to meet the newly elected Labour Party government's inflation target, judged that the economy was expanding at an unsustainable rate. To prevent the economy from overheating, it raised interest rates in five small steps, by a total of 1.25%, to 7.25%. There was a slight tightening in monetary policy in Germany, too, signaling a turning point in the interest rate cycle. Following a 0.3% rise in the Bundesbank's repo rate in October, France and other EU countries that shadowed German monetary policy raised their interest rates by a similar amount. In Japan, against the background of a faltering recovery, interest rates were held steady at their rock-bottom levels. In the crisis-stricken Asian countries and in some Latin-American countries, short-term interest rates rose sharply to defend the depreciating currencies and restore economic stability.

Public-sector deficits continued to shrink rapidly in 1997 as a result of buoyant tax revenues and/or continuing tight control on government spending. In the U.S. and Britain, faster-than-expected reductions in the budget deficits were largely due to higher tax revenues from rapidly growing economies. The budget deficit in the U.S. for the fiscal year ended September 1997 came in at $23 billion, compared with $125 billion forecast a year earlier. In the U.K. the deficit for 1997–98 was revised down to £11.9 billion, compared with a July forecast of £13.4 billion. In France, Germany, and, to a lesser extent, other EU countries, the continuation of existing deficit-reduction measures, supplemented by selective new programs, reduced the budget deficit to close to the 3% of GDP needed to meet the entry criteria for the EMU in 1999. Following years of tax concessions and government spending measures to stimulate the economy, a medium-term fiscal-consolidation plan came into force in Japan in 1997. This program was further extended during the year, and a reduction in government expenditure was envisaged for 1998. Faced with the twin problems of a faltering economy and the crises in the financial institutions, however, the policy was partly reversed as the Bank of Japan bailed out many bankrupt banks and injected liquidity into the system.

NATIONAL ECONOMIC POLICIES

United States. Despite expectations of a slowdown, growth of the U.S. economy accelerated in 1997, and for the year as a whole, GDP was estimated to have expanded by 3.6%—the best annual rate since 1989 and well above 1996's revised growth of 2.8%. With inflation stable and unemployment levels still falling, the economy was in remarkably good shape seven years into the present expansion cycle. Even though there was evidence of some slowdown late in the year, analysts remained concerned about the considerable risks of overheating if the economy continued to expand at this rate.

The economic growth was driven by a combination of strong increases in consumer spending and fixed investment. Consumers spent heavily during most of the year except for a small pause in the spring. Retail sales, which accounted for nearly half of consumer spending, bounced back in the second half of the year and registered an estimated 4% annual growth. Total consumer spending rose by an average of 3.5% during 1997. Rising real-income levels, the continuing strength of labour markets, and booming stock markets buoyed consumer confidence and encouraged higher spending, particularly on durable goods. Business investment continued the uptrend that had been a feature of the current expansion. Investment in machinery and equipment grew by nearly 12%. Investment in computers grew much faster, whereas that in buildings increased by a modest 4.5%. This high level of investment was not surprising, given the rapid expansion in manufacturing production, high rates of capacity utilization, and stable long-term interest rates. The housing market plateaued at a fairly high level despite a small rise in mortgage rates in the spring.

The unemployment rate continued to edge downward and in November stood at 4.7%, compared with the already-low level of 5.2% a year earlier. During the year nearly 700,000 jobs were created. Had it not been for the continued expansion of the labour force, the unemployment rate would have dropped farther and resulted in faster growth in wage rates. The inflation rate remained remarkably stable despite the tightness of the labour market and high rate of capacity utilization. The unadjusted inflation rate, having touched a low of 1.9% in August, rose slightly to 2.2% in October. The strength of the dollar and a drop in oil prices, which translated to a 3% decline in overall import prices, also reduced the inflationary pressures.

Despite the strength of domestic demand and a 15% average appreciation in the value of the dollar (on a trade-weighted basis), the deterioration in the trade balance was relatively small. The value of imports rose by around 16%, but this was largely offset by a 14% growth in exports. As a result, the trade deficit widened by about $10 billion and was projected not to exceed $200 billion. Export markets in Western Europe and the North American Free Trade Agreement members were particularly strong. Demand from the Asian markets was fairly modest and was expected to cool off further in the wake of the sharp depreciations in local currencies against the dollar. The trade deficit with Japan widened during 1997, which reflected the large depreciation of the yen against the dollar, and became a political issue again.

U.S. economic policy was tightened slightly during 1997, but given the maturity of the recovery, the policy stance was best interpreted as fairly neutral. In March the Fed raised the federal funds rate, one of its key interest rates, by 0.25% to counter future inflationary pressures. In early autumn, in the absence of any evidence of a significant economic slowdown, further interest-

Inflation Rate
(percentage change from December to December)

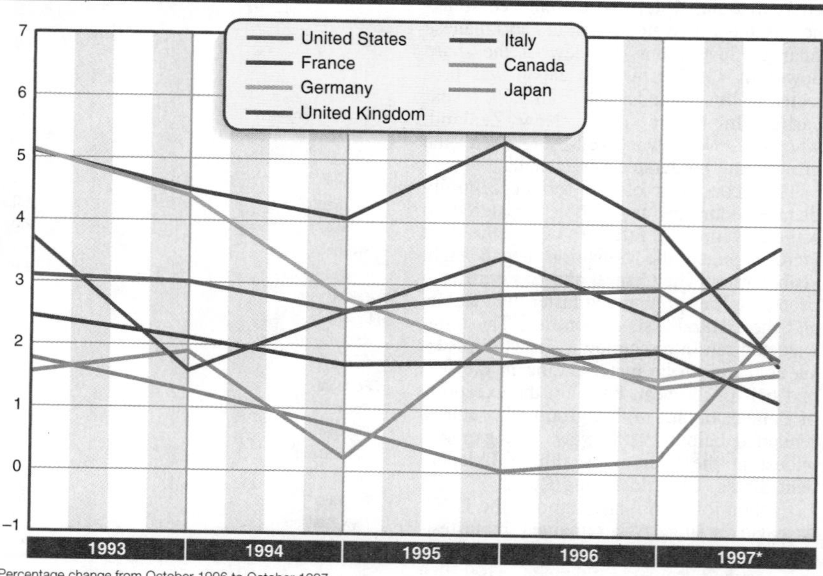

*Percentage change from October 1996 to October 1997.
Source: International Monetary Fund, *International Financial Statistics.*

rate rises were widely expected, but in view of the slide in stock prices and the steep currency devaluations in Asia, the Fed held back from further tightening. Some commentators, however, became pessimistic and claimed that real interest rates (after stripping out inflation) were much higher than historical averages and were too restrictive in any case. Coupled with the sharp appreciation of the dollar and deflationary pressures emanating from Asia, they saw no need for higher interest rates. Other economists remained convinced that in the absence of higher interest rates, growth would continue at an unsustainable rate and the tight labour markets would inevitably lead to an upward pressure on wage rates. At year's end, the odds remained in favour of a small rise in interest rates, intended to take the economy off the inflationary boil.

In February Pres. Bill Clinton's administration forecast that the budget deficit would increase from $107 billion in fiscal year 1996 (ended September 1996) to $125 billion in fiscal 1997. Higher tax revenues from the rapidly growing economy, however, cut the deficit to just $23 billion, the lowest since 1974. In view of this development, the balanced-budget deal agreed to in May, which provided for state spending reductions balanced by tax cuts, looked potentially expansionary even though it was expected to result in a budget surplus in 1998.

United Kingdom. Driven by strong consumer demand and private-sector investment, the British economy raced ahead, ignoring the negative influences of the strong pound and tight public spending. GDP rose by an estimated 3.5% in 1997, compared with 2.4% the year before. Consumer demand was driven by higher real incomes and "windfall" payments. As a result of a continued decline in unemployment, salaries and wages rose by about 6.5% in money terms. Consumer confidence was also boosted by an estimated £30 billion received from the building societies that were converting to banks from "mutual" societies. Unsurprisingly, the volume of retail sales rose by nearly 5% for the year as a whole, despite a temporary dip in most sectors in the weeks immediately following the death of Diana, princess of Wales.

Investment spending also picked up, with most of the 6% growth provided by the private sector. Reflecting the government's spending restrictions, public-sector investment fell by 11%. The manufacturing sector also felt the benefit of rapid economic growth, and industrial production expanded by nearly 2% during the year despite the strong pound. British firms appeared to have protected their share of export markets by reducing their export prices. This led to growth of export volumes at a similar rate as in 1996—nearly 7%. As import volumes rose faster, the balance of payments deficit widened.

Unemployment continued to fall, and toward the close of the year 5.2% of the workforce was without a job, compared with an unemployment rate of 7.3% a year earlier. Although skill shortages emerged in some sectors, pay settlements remained remarkably stable, though at a high level. The inflation rate, having dipped to 2.5% at the time of the general election on May 1, moved up a little to 3.7% as a result of higher interest rates and a rise in food prices during the summer. The underlying inflation rate, which excluded mortgage interest, also rose and remained above the government's target of 2.5%.

Apart from ruling out an entry to the EMU in the first phase (in 1999), the incoming Labour government had an economic policy that was largely unchanged from that of its Conservative predecessor, including the continuation of the tight public-spending plans. As expected, monetary policy was tightened to bring inflation under long-term control. The new chancellor of the Exchequer, Gordon Brown, having reaffirmed the inflation target, provided operational freedom to the Bank of England in setting interest rates to meet it. In keeping with its long-standing view of the need for higher interest rates to prevent inflation from accelerating, the newly formed Monetary Policy Committee raised interest rates four times in as many months by a total of 1%. After a short pause, another 0.25% rise in November took the base rate to 7.25%. Fiscal policy was also subtly tightened in the July budget, the main feature of which was a £3.5 billion windfall tax on privatized corporations to fund the government's program of putting the young unemployed into jobs. Abolition of tax credits on dividends was expected to raise another £2.3 billion annually in future years. Although taxes on gasoline and cigarettes were increased, there was no increase in direct taxation. Even before most of the revenue-raising measures were enacted, the public-sector deficit narrowed sharply, thanks to bumper tax revenues and the Labour government's continuing squeeze on public spending. Ultracautious official figures in Brown's "Green Budget" pointed to a deficit of £11.9 billion, compared with a July forecast of £13.4 billion, excluding the windfall tax. Many independent observers projected a figure of about £6 billion.

Japan. As the stimulatory effect of the measures introduced in 1996 and earlier ended, the economy faltered. The decline in activity was exacerbated by the increase in the consumption tax and lower government spending that came into effect in April. The fallout from the Asian financial crisis and the renewed weakness of the Tokyo stock market, coupled with the crisis in the domestic financial sector, affected business confidence. On the basis of these developments, GDP was estimated to have grown by around 0.9% in 1997 after having expanded by 3.6% in 1996.

The year opened strongly, and GDP surged to an annualized growth rate of 6.6%, largely because of increased demand ahead of the consumption tax increase in April. This lopsided growth was highlighted by the different GDP components; real private consumption rose by nearly 5% over the previous quarter, whereas public investment and housing investment declined. Although export growth was maintained, the role of external demand was less important than in 1996. In the second quarter GDP declined by 2.6% more than the opening quarter increase, more than wiping out the earlier gains. In the second half of the year, the feeble recovery petered out, with consumption, business investment, and housing activity all declining. The new financial initiatives introduced in November, which authorities claimed would add 10 trillion yen to the economy in the next financial year, were seen to be too late and too little to revive the stalled economy.

Despite the uneven GDP trend, industrial production held up reasonably well and rose by nearly 5.5% for the year as a whole. In the first part of the year, production was sluggish, anticipating the decline in domestic demand. In the spring it rebounded as companies started building inventories to

Industrial Production
semiannual averages: 1990 = 100

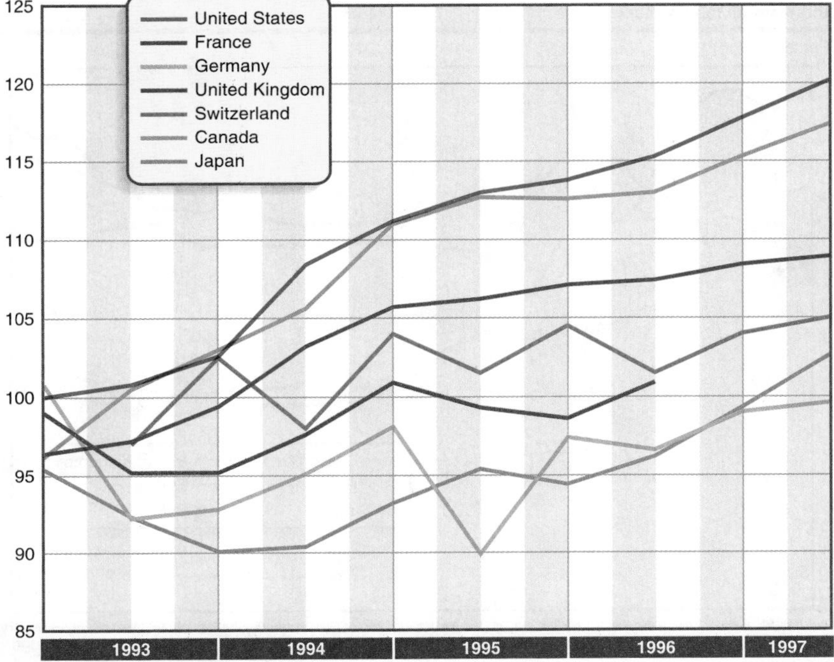

Source: International Monetary Fund, *International Financial Statistics.*

meet stronger foreign demand. The construction industry, however, continued to be adversely affected by falling land prices and declining public-sector building programs. One visible indicator of the misery of the construction sector was the first bankruptcy since 1945 of a contractor with a stock exchange listing.

The recovery in industrial output was not sufficient to prevent unemployment levels from edging upward. In November the unemployment rate stood at 3.5%, compared with 3.3% a year earlier. This level, very high by Japanese standards, was partly due to an increase in the labour force. Against the background of a weak labour market, wages (including summer bonus payments) rose by nearly 3.5% in the first half of the year before slowing down to well under 3% by the year's end.

The trade surplus rose during 1997, despite the higher value of the yen earlier in the year. Exports rose strongly in both volume and value. In the final quarter demand from crisis-ridden Southeast Asia, which normally accounted for 30% of Japan's exports, began to weaken. The trade surplus with the U.S. and Europe increased as the yen depreciated. The fragility of the Japanese economy and the regional financial crisis took their toll and pushed the yen steadily down in the second half of the year, reversing earlier gains. In December it was down to 127.5 yen against the dollar—the year's low.

Fiscal policy became tighter in 1997, extending the budget-deficit measures adopted in 1996. In the early part of the year, measures that came into force included a 2% rise in the sales tax, the ending of the special reductions in income and residential tax, and a large reduction in public-works spending. A medium-term plan adopted in 1997 aimed to reduce the government's fiscal deficit to 3% of GDP by 2003–04 (compared with a 7% deficit in 1996). The new measures, programmed to start in 1998, represented the first overall reduction in government expenditure in 11 years. In the event, as the economy faltered, the government was forced to introduce a package in November to stimulate the economy. Surprisingly, it did not include additional government money but relied largely on private finance initiatives.

To balance the fiscal tightening and avoid pushing the economy into a recession, the monetary policy remained accommodating. The official discount rate was held at its record-low level of 0.5%—unchanged since September 1995. The governor of the Bank of Japan stated that the bank's main priority was to ensure that the economic recovery was nurtured. The currency crisis that sparked a slump in the region's stock markets, including Japan's, led to a renewed weakness among Japanese financial institutions. As share prices fell, many Japanese banks became overexposed. Indeed, Sanyo, a large securities house, fell victim to the crisis in early November, followed by Hokkaido Takushoku, Japan's 10th largest commercial bank. A week later Yamaichi, Japan's fourth largest securities house, collapsed with an estimated $25.5 billion in liabilities. Although this was the largest corporate failure, it may have marked a turning point in Japan's financial institutions crisis. The government and the Bank of Japan moved to protect customers' deposits at Yamaichi and other firms that might run into similar difficulties. Hokkaido Takushoku, however, was allowed to fail.

Germany. After a pause in the last quarter of 1996, economic growth resumed, and GDP expanded by an estimated 2.4% in 1997. The rebound was led principally by exports and business investment, and private consumption lagged behind. Exports grew by nearly 8% for the year as a whole, mainly because of a favourable combination of strong growth in major export markets, a decline in the value of the Deutsche Mark, and improved productivity. By contrast, domestic demand remained weak and expanded by about 1%. Stagnation in real disposable incomes and continuing high unemployment rates, as well as the high savings rate maintained by cautious consumers, dampened domestic demand. The volume of retail sales fell for the second consecutive year.

Led by buoyant export orders, manufacturing output rose by nearly 3%, and investment in machinery and equipment picked up later in the year. Construction orders and output continued to fall as the postunification boom came to an end. Because of budgetary restraints, the sharpest declines were in public construction. Strong exports pushed up the trade surplus, and the current account, which had been in deficit since the unification, headed toward its traditional surplus. The moderate economic recovery, however, failed to be translated to any improvement in the labour market. In November the unemployment rate stood at 11.8% (4.4 million unemployed), compared with 10.6% a year earlier. The other unfavourable development was a gradual rise in the inflation rate. Although it peaked in the summer, inflation at 1.8% late in the year was above the 1.5% in 1996. One reason for the adverse trend was the depreciation of the Deutsche Mark, which induced higher import prices. Other influences included higher prescription charges and vehicle taxes.

The government remained committed to bringing the EMU into operation on time (January 1999), and economic policy focused on reducing the budget deficit to the 3% target. As the midyear projections pointed to a higher deficit than planned, Germany was forced to moderate its plans to reduce the overall tax burden. It still looked as if the deficit would be around 3.2% for 1997, but despite this, it seemed highly unlikely that the start of the EMU would be postponed. The main reason for this was that a postponement might jeopardize the whole EMU project. Furthermore, it might leave the government rudderless, as it would no longer be able to present the much-needed tax- and pension-reform policies to the electorate in a coherent and convincing way. As in France, with a little bit of creative accounting and flexible interpretation of the criteria, this decimal-point dispute was likely to be overcome, which would enable the EMU to start on time. Tighter control on growth of public spending, coupled with higher tax revenue arising from faster economic growth, was projected to lower the deficit to below 3% in 1998. For most of the year, monetary policy remained accommodating as growth in money supply eased to within the target range. Interest rates remained unchanged until October, when the Bundesbank increased the repo rate from 3% to 3.3%, signaling a preemptive tightening in policy to prevent a buildup of further inflationary pressures.

France. Economic growth accelerated in 1997, with GDP growth rising about 2.3% from 1.5% in 1996. This was an encouraging performance against the background of political uncertainty following the spring elections, which resulted in a surprising change in government as well as continuing austerity in anticipation of the EMU.

Much of the growth was provided by foreign demand, whereas domestic demand remained comparatively weak. Consumer spending, excluding automobiles, made a

Interest Rates: Short-term
three-month money market rates

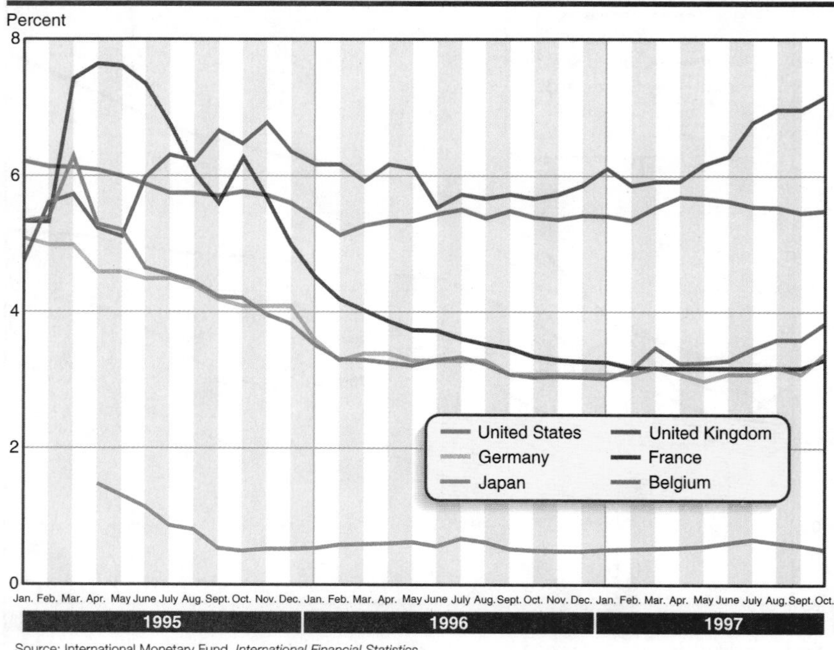

Source: International Monetary Fund, *International Financial Statistics*.

modest recovery, thanks to growth in family incomes outpacing inflation. Business investment rose slightly, reflecting the encouraging outlook. The construction sector remained weak as demand for commercial and private property stagnated. Industrial production gained momentum on the back of a weaker franc and rose by around 3%, in stark contrast to 1996's flat output. Exports grew as a result of the weaker franc and continued growth in the main export-destination countries. By contrast, imports were held back by the weak domestic demand and rose by around 4%, or less than half the increase in exports. As a result, France's trade balance more than doubled to a projected F 27 billion and headed to a record. The economic recovery was not sufficiently strong to improve the unemployment situation. Monthly unemployment peaked in autumn 1996, but a year later the rate, at 12.5%, was almost unchanged. Relatively high unemployment kept wage increases to about 2.4%, above the inflation rate of 1.1%—the lowest for almost three decades. The new Socialist government proposed reducing the working hours to provide work for more people.

As the July audit of the public finances revealed a large fiscal slippage, the new government of Prime Minister Lionel Jospin (*see* BIOGRAPHIES) moderated its opposition to the policies of its predecessors and agreed to introduce new deficit-reducing measures to ensure that France met the EMU entry criteria. Following spending cuts of F 10 billion and corporate tax increases, the 1998 budget deficit was projected at 3% of GDP—the target set for monetary union. Even if the actual deficit, as expected, came in above this figure, France was expected to qualify through a flexible definition of the criteria. Monetary easing continued during 1997, with long-term interest rates dipping to 5.5% and converging with German rates. The central bank raised its intervention rate by 0.2% in late summer, which reflected the interest-rate rise in Germany.

The Former Centrally Planned Economies. The expected increase in economic output of this group of countries had failed to materialize in 1996. After five years of consecutive decline, however, output stabilized and was projected to grow by 1.2% during 1997. The outlook for 1998 was growth of 3–4%. Despite this revival, output remained well below the 1989 levels. According to the European Bank for Reconstruction and Development (EBRD) estimates, Eastern European countries (especially the Baltic states) were within 5% of closing the gap, whereas output in the CIS, including Russia, was at 56% of the 1989 value. In 1997 only Poland, which was one of the first countries to modernize its economy, exceeded its 1989 output, whereas output in Georgia and Moldova remained at 34% of 1989 levels.

Growth in Eastern Europe slowed from around 4% in 1996 to a projected 3% in 1997, largely as a result of economic decline in Albania, Bulgaria, and Romania. Growth in the Czech Republic also slowed, which reflected an austerity program introduced following a financial crisis in the spring. Most of the other countries experienced faster growth rates, though expansion in Poland and Slovakia moderated in 1997. In the CIS the fastest rate of expansion remained in Georgia, Kyrgyzstan, Armenia, and Azerbaijan, whereas negative growth was still the case in Turkmenistan, Ukraine, and Moldova. In Russia it looked as if the long decline was over, and the economy was expected to grow in the second half of 1997.

Despite faster growth, unemployment remained high. In 1996 the number of registered unemployed was 14.4 million, nearly 400,000 more than a year earlier. Although unemployment in the Central and Eastern European countries moderated, it was still rising in the CIS. In view of the contraction in output since 1989, even those unemployment rates suggested overmanning.

According to EBRD estimates, the median inflation rate fell from 32% in 1995 to a projected 14% in 1997. Inflation performance, however, was not uniform. Reflecting financial problems in Bulgaria and Romania, it doubled to 592% and 116%, respectively. In the CIS the average inflation rate was halved to 33%. Lower inflation was expected in most countries—including Russia, where it was projected to decline to 14% from 22%. Relaxation of earlier stabilization efforts, however, led to an upturn in inflation rates in Armenia, Belarus, and Tajikistan. A contributory factor to lower inflation in the CIS was the development of a securities market, which enabled governments to reduce borrowing from the banking system.

Limited progress was made in reducing fiscal deficits, which remained higher in the CIS than in Eastern Europe and the Baltic region. Lack of progress was attributed to poor revenue performance rather than weak expenditure control. In turn, a decline in tax revenues was attributed to policies introduced to reduce the high levels of taxation, as well as to poor economic performance. In the absence of fundamental public-sector reforms, it was thought that many countries would find it difficult to raise sufficient government revenue and implement expenditure controls.

The devaluation, followed by austerity measures in the Czech Republic, highlighted the potential problems of growing trade deficits and deterioration in current-account positions in many countries in the region. In more than half, current-account deficits exceeded 7% of GDP in 1996. This trend was attributable to strong domestic consumption and investment as well as growing capital inflows. It was feared that if unchecked, the growing current-account deficits, in particular the rapid buildup of foreign debt, could lead to economic instability.

Less-Developed Countries. The IMF expected the rate of growth in the LDCs as a group to remain high, at around 6%. A slight downturn was predicted for 1998. Despite expansion's remaining high, many of the poorer countries failed to increase their per capita incomes. Once again, the fastest growth in 1997 was in Asia, with growth projected at around 7%. Spillover from the currency crisis in Thailand engulfed other countries in the region, including the Philippines, Indonesia, and Malaysia. By late November it had spread to South Korea, a much larger and more developed economy. Economic measures taken by those countries to restore stability and standby loans from the IMF ($17 billion for Thailand, $40 billion for Indonesia, and $20 billion for South Korea) led to a widespread slowdown in the final quarter of 1997, but the main effect of these measures was not expected to be evident until 1998. Because China was unaffected by the turmoil, economic growth there remained intact at about 9%.

Interest Rates: Long-term

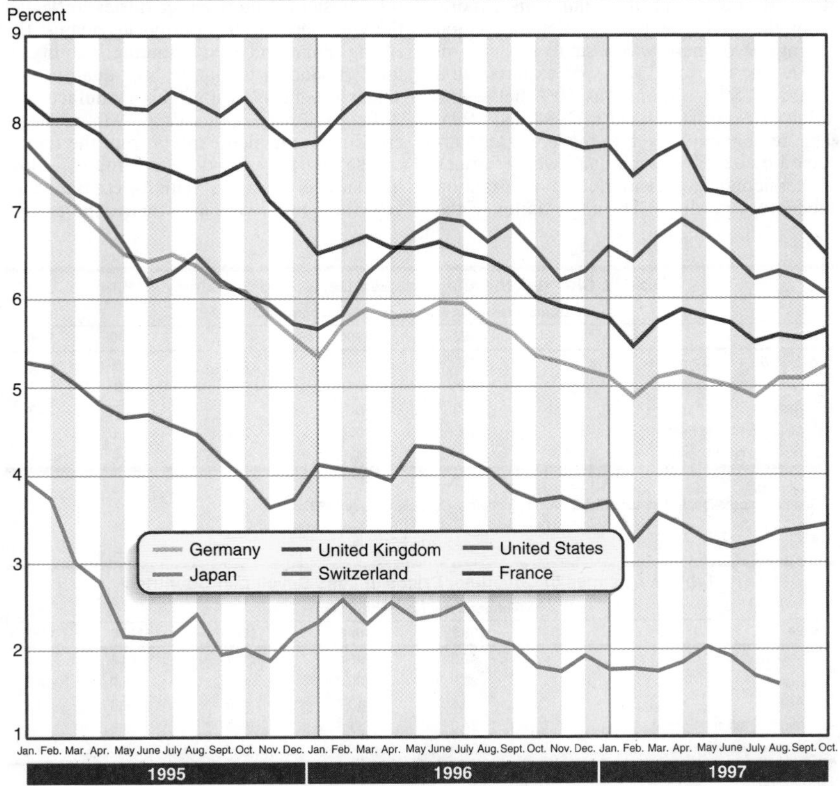

Source: International Monetary Fund, *International Financial Statistics*.

Table III. Standardized Unemployment Rates in Selected Developed Countries

Country	1993	1994	1995	1996	1997[1]
	% of total labour force				
United States	6.9	6.1	5.6	5.4	5.0
Japan	2.5	2.9	3.1	3.3	3.2
Germany	8.9	9.6	9.4	10.3	11.1
France	11.7	12.2	11.5	12.4	12.6
Italy	10.2	11.3	12.0	12.1	12.1
Great Britain	10.2	9.2	8.1	7.4	6.1
Canada	11.2	10.4	9.5	9.7	9.4
All developed countries	8.0	7.9	7.6	7.5	7.3
Seven major countries above	7.3	7.1	6.8	6.9	6.7
European Union	11.1	11.6	11.2	11.3	11.2

[1] Projected.
Sources: OECD; *The Economist.*

The economies of Latin-American countries, having recovered fully from the effects of the 1995 Mexican crisis, grew by an average of 4% in 1997. The buoyancy came to a sudden halt in the wake of the Asian crisis, however, when an unsustainable current-account deficit in Brazil led to similar minicrises in the region, which necessitated widespread austerity measures. Despite lower oil prices, many countries in the Middle East achieved robust economic growth of around 4.6%. Growth in Africa, which declined as a result of civil wars and adverse weather conditions, was projected to moderate to 3.5% from 5% in 1996.

Inflation continued to fall to a projected median rate of 5% (7% in 1996) despite the global economic buoyancy. The highest inflation rates remained in the Middle East and Africa, whereas rates edged down in Latin America. Compared with Latin America's average of 13%, Argentina enjoyed virtually zero inflation. Once again the area with the lowest inflation rate was Asia, with a projected average rate of just under 6%.

The current-account deficits widened in many LDCs. In Asian countries this was largely due to a slowdown in export growth and policies to reduce domestic demand in order to avoid overheating the economy. In Latin America it was primarily because of the resumption of economic growth and capital inflows. (*See* Spotlight: *Latin America's New Investors.*) A decline in commodity prices was the main reason for larger current-account deficits in many African countries. The currency crisis in Thailand highlighted the vulnerability of the LDCs to a sudden reversal of capital inflows and demonstrated how easily it could spill over to neighbouring countries.

INTERNATIONAL TRADE

The slowdown in world trade during 1996 was short-lived, and during 1997 the volume of trade in goods and services was projected by the IMF to have risen by 7.7%. This compared favourably with 6.3% in 1996 but was not as high as the 9% increase registered in 1994 and 1995. In value terms (in U.S. dollars) the rise was much smaller, at about 3%, which reflected the rise in the dollar and weaker prices for some electronic products and commodities. The main source of growth was stronger demand from the developed countries, which accounted for most of world trade. The flow of imports into the developed world rose by an estimated 7% in volume terms, compared with 6% a year earlier. Export growth from the developed countries, at a projected rate of 8%, also expanded at a faster rate than in 1996. Whereas the volume of goods exported from the LDCs rose at a projected rate of 7.4%, import growth accelerated to 8.9% over 7.9% in 1996.

Among developed countries the fastest growth in demand was from the U.S. (up 13%), followed by Canada (11.7%), which reflected the economic buoyancy in North America. Acceleration was fastest in many EU countries—led by Germany, Italy, and France—as a result of a pickup in the economic growth rate. By contrast, the growth in volume of imports into Japan, the world's second largest economy, slumped to a projected 1.4% from 10.5% in 1996, mainly because of faltering domestic demand and the weakness of the yen.

Export volume of goods and services rose, however, at a projected rate of 11%, compared with 2.3% in 1996. Other developed countries to have experienced faster volume growth in exports included Germany and France, which, like Japan, benefited from a combination of weaker local currency against the dollar and stronger global demand. Following the slump in exports from the LDCs in the Asia-Pacific region during 1996, there was a small recovery in 1997, but the total value of exports, at a projected $9.4 billion, was 50% below the value of exports realized in 1994 and 1995. The region continued to be adversely affected by excess capacity and weaker prices of semiconductors and related information technology products. The appreciation of the dollar, to which many of the countries in the region linked their exchange rates, made exports from those countries to Japan and Europe noncompetitive. This was the root cause of the currency crisis that started in Thailand. Reflecting a slowdown in investment in the region, imports into the Asian "tiger" economies (Hong Kong, Taiwan, Singapore, and South Korea) moderated to around 8%, compared with nearly 20% two or three years earlier. As a result of an economic slowdown in China, import inflow remained largely unchanged, whereas exports in dollar terms rose by 24% in the first nine months of 1997, albeit from the previous year's depressed levels. During the remainder of the year, export volumes were expected to moderate, reflecting lower demand from the tigers in the wake of their large currency devaluations.

Liberalization measures and faster economic growth in Latin America stimulated import inflows. During 1997 imports into the region rose by nearly 15%, compared with 11% in 1996. Argentina, Brazil, Mexico, and smaller countries in the region that were experiencing rapid economic growth provided stronger import demand. In Africa import volumes continued to increase, reflecting acceleration in regional economic growth. Both the volume and value of exports from the region grew more slowly than in 1996.

Although comprehensive figures were not available for the former centrally planned economies, current-account balances suggested that import inflow in those countries grew at a faster rate than their exports. An acceleration in the rate of domestic demand and continuing modernization and investment programs sustained import-growth momentum in 1997. Both exports from and imports into Russia were largely unchanged in dollar terms. The higher value of imports into Eastern European countries reflected the weakness of local currencies against the strong dollar and the continuing inability of local producers to supply high-quality consumer products. Despite this manufacturing difficulty, faster economic growth in Western Europe enabled exports from the region to rise modestly. By contrast, import inflow in many of the CIS nations continued to grow at a faster rate than their exports.

Table IV. Changes in Output in Less-Developed Countries

Area	1993	1994	1995	1996	1997[1]
	% annual change in real gross domestic product				
All less-developed countries	6.3	6.6	6.0	6.5	6.2
Africa	0.9	2.9	2.8	5.2	3.7
Asia	8.7	9.1	8.9	8.2	7.5
Middle East and Europe	4.2	0.5	3.5	4.8	4.6
Western Hemisphere	3.2	4.7	1.3	3.4	4.1

[1] Projected.
Source: International Monetary Fund, *World Economic Outlook,* October 1997.

Table V. Changes in Consumer Prices in Less-Developed Countries

Area	1993	1994	1995	1996	1997[1]
	% change from preceding year				
All less-developed countries	42.7	46.8	22.7	13.2	10.0
Africa	29.5	36.8	33.1	25.0	14.8
Asia	9.6	13.4	11.9	6.6	5.8
Middle East and Europe	24.0	31.5	35.9	24.8	22.1
Western Hemisphere	209.5	210.9	41.7	20.5	13.5

[1] Projected.
Source: International Monetary Fund, *World Economic Outlook,* October 1997.

Meanwhile, various trade-liberalization talks continued during 1997. The smaller of these was between South America's two largest trade blocs, the Andean Community and the Southern Cone Common Market (Mercosur), in an effort to form a single free-trade area. The four-nation Mercosur (Argentina, Brazil, Paraguay, and Uruguay) and the five-nation Andean Community (Bolivia, Colombia, Ecuador, Peru, and Venezuela) represented a market of 310 million consumers with a combined GDP of $1.2 trillion. At a summit in Venezuela in October, despite considerable differences on "sensitive products," member countries agreed to aim toward reaching agreement by the end of the year. Apart from replacing bilateral trade agreements, due to expire on December 31, such an agreement would strengthen South America's negotiating position in regard to a 34-nation Free Trade Area of the Americas. As the year drew to a close, however, the talks had not made as much progress as had been hoped, and an agreement before December 31 looked increasingly unlikely. The annual meeting of the Asia-Pacific Economic Cooperation forum in Vancouver, B.C., liberalized trade in nine categories of goods and services. Against the backdrop of financial turmoil in Asian markets, the U.S. increased its efforts to persuade countries in the region to sign a planned World Trade Organization agreement to open their financial markets to international competition.

INTERNATIONAL EXCHANGE AND PAYMENTS

The main developments in international exchange rates during 1997 were the volatile swings in the value of the Japanese yen and a strong advance by the British pound sterling and the U.S. dollar against most currencies. The most spectacular development, however, was the speculative attack against many Asian currencies in the summer and the subsequent slump in many currencies in that region. The yen opened the year on a weak note and had fallen to 127 yen against the dollar by April. This reflected the strength of the U.S. economy as contrasted with concerns for economic recovery in Japan. As the economic outlook improved in Japan and the U.S. economy slowed in the second quarter, the yen strengthened for a short time and reached a high of 110 yen per dollar in June. As the Japanese economy faltered under the weight of the April tax hike and the U.S. economy regained its strength, the yen retraced its steps and fell back to around 120. After the steep fall in Asian currencies in early autumn followed by the decline in the South Korean won, the yen weakened further and settled at the year's low, 127.5 to the dollar. As the Japanese economy became increasingly dependent on exports, no early appreciation was expected.

The dollar's strength against most currencies was a reflection of the continuing rapid economic expansion in the U.S. Although inflationary pressures were subdued for most of the year, expectations of a rise in interest rates boosted the dollar. In November the dollar was almost 10% higher than a year earlier, on a trade-weighted basis. The strength of sterling was largely due to robust economic growth and to rises in interest rates. In the summer the pound was trading against the Deutsche Mark at a level above the trading range prior to Britain's withdrawal from the European exchange-rate mechanism. A late-summer correction inspired by expectations of a long pause in further increases and prospects of an early entry into the EMU was short-lived. Sterling rose again in November when the government ruled out an early entry into the EMU and the Bank of England unexpectedly raised interest rates again. Despite a pickup in German economic recovery and modestly higher interest rates, the Deutsche Mark weakened by about 5% during 1997 on a trade-weighted basis and delivered a boost to the German economy.

The currency crisis in Asia that sparked a slide in share prices around the world started with a speculative run on the Thai baht in mid-May. A large current-account deficit led to concerns about the sustainability of the existing exchange rate pegged to a basket dominated by the strong U.S. dollar, and a series of sharp devaluations of 25–30% followed. By October the Malaysian ringgit was depressed by 25%, the Indonesian rupiah by 33%, and the Philippine peso by 23%, with the Singapore dollar losing 9% of its value. A potentially more serious crisis, however, came in November when South Korea, a much larger economy than the others, could no longer sustain the existing exchange rate and the won fell by over 35% against the dollar. In the spring, against the backdrop of large current-account deficits, there was a similar speculative pressure on the currencies of the Czech Republic and Slovakia, which resulted in a 20% devaluation in the Czech koruna.

The current-account imbalances between some of the developed countries were projected by the IMF to widen but were expected to remain smaller than they had been in the 1980s. The overall current-account surplus of the developed countries was projected to rise modestly to $19 billion from $16 billion. While the current-account balance of the EU was largely unchanged, the British deficit widened, which reflected the appreciation of sterling and the strength of domestic demand. In Germany and France the current-account surpluses widened somewhat against weaker currencies and strong external demand. The Japanese surplus widened significantly and was projected to exceed $100 billion, and the long-standing U.S. deficit was projected to top $200 billion, as strong economic activity and the strength of the dollar increased imports.

In the LDCs the current-account deficit widened significantly to a projected $109 billion, compared with $81 billion a year earlier, according to the IMF. Latin America registered the most significant widening as a result of a strong recovery in domestic demand in countries like Mexico, Argentina, and Brazil. In Africa the current-account deficits widened marginally as a result of a fall in commodity prices. While the deficit in a number of CFA franc zone countries remained largely unchanged in 1997, arrangements for the CFA franc remained uncertain post-1999, pending France's strategy for the region. Deficits in Kenya, South Africa, Tanzania, Uganda, and Zimbabwe also changed little, but oil exporters like Algeria and Nigeria experienced a reduction in their current-account surpluses. In Asia, even before the currency crisis that engulfed the region, both trade and current-account deficits were expected to widen in a number of countries, including Thailand, Malaysia, the Philippines, and South Korea, as a result of a continuing slowdown in exports and policies to contain domestic demand. Current-account deficits in many former centrally planned economies continued to widen. This was particularly evident in some Eastern European countries and many CIS countries, except Russia.

Capital inflow to the LDCs, having reached a high of $207 billion in 1996, was projected by the IMF to remain strong in 1997. In those countries where currencies depreciated following speculative attacks, a decline in net inflows for the year as a whole was a distinct possibility. The IMF projected that the total external financing requirements of the LDCs would moderate to around $200 billion from the previous year's $224 billion. As the proportion of non-debt-creating inflows was projected to continue to increase, the debt burden was likely to have moderated. Even so, reflecting a slowdown in the growth of value exports (both value and volume), debt-servicing ratios—*i.e.,* export earnings as a proportion of interest on total external debt—moved up a little to a projected 9.5%, reversing the decline that began in 1991. (IEIS)

This article updates the *Macropædia* articles ECONOMIC GROWTH AND PLANNING; GOVERNMENT FINANCE; INTERNATIONAL TRADE.

STOCK EXCHANGES

The phenomenal bull run in stock markets around the world during the previous two to three years suffered a setback in October 1997, and for a time share prices experienced a roller-coaster ride. Although this turned out to be a short, sharp downturn in the U.S. and Western European stock exchanges, it was a cataclysmic decline for Japan and many other Asian markets. Even so, the *Financial Times*/Standard & Poor's (FT/S&P) World Index registered a 13.2% gain in dollar terms (19.3% in local currency) for the year. The Dow Jones industrial average (DJIA) ended the year 22.6% higher, and European shares registered a gain of 34%, as measured by the FT/S&P Europe index. Japan, an underperformer since 1989, contracted by another 21.2% (17.3% in local currency), but, as it had started from a lower base, it fell by a smaller percentage than the Pacific region as a whole. (*See* TABLE VI.)

The main influence on the strong global performance was an unusual combination of strong economic growth, stable interest rates, falling unemployment levels, and the absence of inflationary pressures in the U.S. and many other Western nations. In this environment the markets and investors, assuming that corporate profitability would continue to grow at the same rate, drove the markets to dizzying heights and made them vulnerable to external shocks. The crisis began in July with a series of devaluations in Thailand, Indonesia, the Philippines, and Malaysia, which created ripple effects on equity markets. The Hong Kong stock exchange also came off its summer high, but for a while the Western stock exchanges ignored this development. In late October, when interest rates were raised in Hong Kong to defend the Hong Kong dollar, the market there nose-dived and lost a further 30% in a few days. This alarmed world markets and resulted in drops ranging from 7% to 15% in one day. The panic in London and on Wall Street appeared to spread, but soothing remarks from world leaders, including Clinton and Fed Chairman Alan Greenspan, coupled with the underlying strength of the Western economies, encouraged many private investors to see this as a buying opportunity. After a highly volatile week, a period of relative calm returned, only to be shattered when the financial crisis in South Korea deepened and posed a threat to Japanese banks and financial institutions. The government bailout of Yamaichi Securities and the promise of public funds to assist the financial sector restored a sense of relative stability in Japan. Large-scale IMF assistance to Thailand, Indonesia, and South Korea also improved investors' confidence. At the end of the year many Western markets—still nervous but confident that the worst was over—were only slightly below their summer peaks. (IEIS)

Following the busiest day ever on the New York Stock Exchange, traders resume work on the market floor on October 28. They were cheered as the Dow Jones industrial average bounced back strongly from a record drop of 554.26 points. Soothing remarks from world leaders helped encourage many private investors to see the financial crisis as a buying opportunity.
KATHY WILLENS—ASSOCIATED PRESS

Effective Exchange Rates*
average rates, 1990 = 100

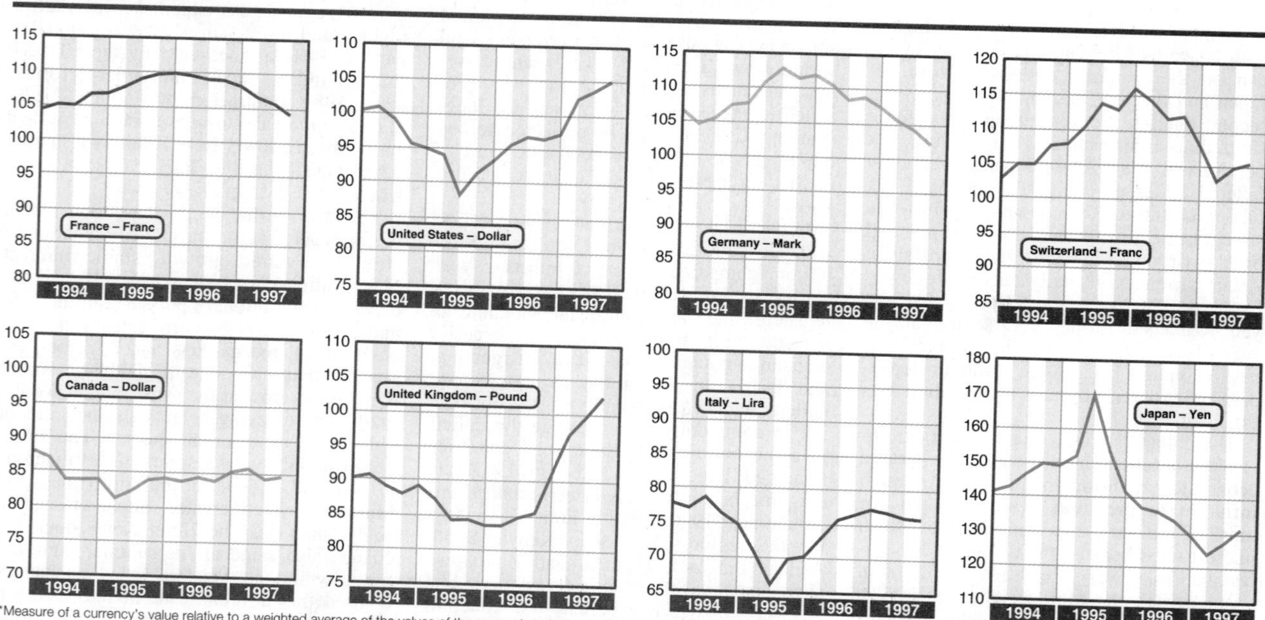

*Measure of a currency's value relative to a weighted average of the values of the currencies of the country's principal trading partners.

Source: International Monetary Fund, *International Financial Statistics.*

United States. The U.S. stock market achieved record levels in 1997 as the bull market maintained its upward momentum in spite of several significant setbacks. The increase of short-term interest rates by the Fed caused a dip in April, but the most traumatic event of the year was the sharp decline on October 27 and the next day's rebound, when record trading volume was achieved on all the exchanges. On October 28, for the first time in history, the New York Stock Exchange (NYSE) had trading volume of 1,200,000,000 shares, shattering the previous one-day record of 684,590,000 shares. Turnover on the over-the-counter market, monitored by the National Association of Securities Dealers automated quotations (Nasdaq) index, was 1,370,000,000 shares, well above its previous record of 970,700,000.

The widely watched DJIA broke 7000 on February 13 and climbed irregularly to a peak of 8259.31 on August 6. The price-earnings ratio of the Dow Jones industrials at the end of September was 21.26, compared with 18.26 a year before. The market jolt on October 27 resulted in the Dow's dropping 554.26 points, or 7.18%, with a next-day recovery of 337.17 points, or 4.71%, the largest point gain ever. During October the Dow slid 7.7%, but for the year the average was up nearly 1,500 points, or 22.64%. Extreme volatility in December, partly as a result of the financial crisis in Asia, pushed the DJIA well down from its August peak before it recovered somewhat to finish the year at 7908.25. The Standard & Poor's index of 500 stocks (S&P 500) achieved a record of 983.12 on October 7, while the Nasdaq index reached a high of 1745.85 on October 9 and the Russell index of 2000 stocks hit 465.21 on October 13. Late in the year investors turned cautious, despite a booming economy, as a number of Asian markets sustained heavy losses. On average, investors achieved stock market returns in excess of 21% during 1997.

The business and economic news throughout 1997 was very positive. The National Association of Purchasing Management index of expected business conditions was more positive than it had been in 1996, and the consumer confidence index published by the Conference Board achieved record levels. The index of industrial production rose steadily in 1997, with the third-quarter jump the biggest in 13 years. The economy was growing at a healthy rate throughout the year. The industry operating rate was 84.4% in September, the highest since February 1995. The U.S. unemployment rate declined below 5%, which raised concerns about inflationary pressures, and the actions of the Fed were closely watched by investors. The national budget deficit fell to $22.6 billion, the lowest since the early 1970s, and most economic signs were encouraging during the year.

Although the market was somewhat volatile on an uptrend, investors placed record sums into mutual funds of all kinds. The stocks of companies with low levels of capitalization (small-cap stocks) underperformed in the first three quarters of 1997 by failing to generate the earnings momentum that large-cap stocks exhibited. Large-cap stocks delivered so well that the price-earnings multiples of the top stocks in the S&P 500 rose from 18 to 25 times earnings. Early in October Greenspan described the reemergence of inflation as without question the greatest threat to the U.S.'s economic expansion. His remarks caused a drop in the Dow that day, and the 30-year Treasury bond yield rose to 6.4% after his remarks provoked fears that interest rates would need to rise. Margin calls were very heavy on October 27. The level of margin credit at major brokerage firms was at an all-time high of almost $125 billion, up more than 25% from the previous year. After Greenspan's warning about "irrational exuberance" in the market, the October crash was viewed as a healthy readjustment of expectations.

More than 40 million U.S. families owned stocks in 1997, a record high. By September 30, there were $86.7 billion in domestic equity issues. Equities as a percentage of household financial assets were 31% at the end of the third quarter of 1997. High-yield ("junk") bonds were only 21% of all corporate debt issued. The largest public corporations, ranked by market capitalization in billions, were: General Electric Co., $224.5; Microsoft Corp., $164.6; Exxon Corp., $160.4; Coca-Cola Co., $148.4; and Intel Corp., $141.6.

Wall Street firms raised $943,900,000,000 in the first three quarters of 1997, slightly below the $967,700,000,000 raised in the same period of 1996 and below the record of $1,050,000,000,000 in 1993. The number of new issues increased by 28% in the first three quarters to 2,721, up from 2,123 a year earlier. By late in the year, 469 initial public offerings of stock had raised $24.2 billion. The leading managing underwriters of corporate securities, ranked by dollar amount raised through new issues, were Merrill Lynch & Co.; Morgan Stanley Dean Witter; Salomon Brothers; J.P. Morgan & Co.; Goldman, Sachs; Lehman Brothers; Bear, Stearns & Co.; Credit Suisse First Boston; and Chase Manhattan Corp.

The top merger and acquisition deal in 1997 was WorldCom, Inc.'s acquisition of MCI Communications Corp. for $37 billion. Other major deals included NationsBank Corp.'s taking over Barnett Banks, Starwood Lodging Trust's acquisition of the Sheraton chain from ITT Corp., First Union Corp.'s taking over CoreStates Financial Corp., and Lockheed Martin Corp.'s acquisition of Northrop Grumman.

Interest rates remained relatively steady in 1997. At the end of October, the prime rate was 8.5%, up from 8.25% a year earlier, while the discount rate at 5% was unchanged. Thirty-year Treasury bonds were 6.14%, down from 6.83% a year earlier. Treasury bills were at 4.97%, down from 5.04% in 1996. The interest rate on three-month Treasury bills ranged from a high of 5.5% in March to a low of 4.8% in June and finished the year at 5.18%.

The NYSE had its busiest week in history in November, with 3,990,000,000 shares changing hands. There were 3,050 companies listed, and 487 brokerage firms were members with trading authority. The average daily volume was 541,000,000 at the end of September. A seat on the NYSE sold for $1,475,000 on July 31; a year earlier a seat had sold for $1,162,000. Market capitalization totaled $8,890,000,000,000 on October 25 but declined to $8,310,000,000,000 on October 27, a drop of $580,000,000,000 in one day. "Circuit

New York Stock Exchange Composite Index, 1997
Stock prices (Dec. 31, 1965 = 50)

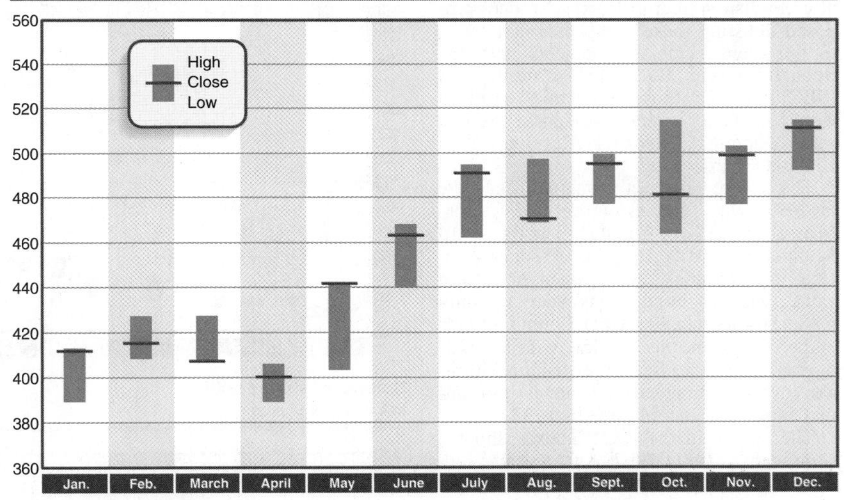

Average daily share volume
In thousands of shares

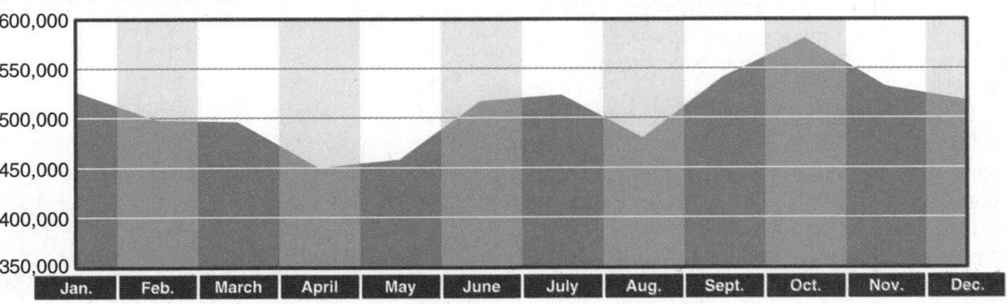

Sources: *Barron's National Business and Financial Weekly; The Wall Street Journal.*

breakers" were activated for the first time in October, halting trading for 30 minutes when the Dow dipped to 350 points below the previous day's close and again for an hour after the market index had dropped a total of 550 points. Of the 4,182 stocks listed on the Big Board (up from 3,895 in 1996), 3,110 advanced, only 975 declined, and 97 remained unchanged for the year. Computer maker Compaq Corp. topped the active list, with more than 1.6 billion shares traded.

Sales volume on the American Stock Exchange (AMEX) rose by slightly more than 1% in 1997. As of October 17, volume was 4,705,524,000 shares, compared with 4,584,983,000 shares in the same period a year earlier. The record volume on October 28 was about 60,600,000 shares, some 40% ahead of the previous record of 43,900,000 shares traded in a single day. Advances exceeded declines by 651 to 329, with only 13 issues unchanged.

Nasdaq volume in 1997 rose 16.9%, with an average daily volume as of September 30 of 699,000,000 shares. Through October 17 the volume was 128,582,754,000 shares, compared with 110,022,495,000 for the corresponding period in 1996. The total market capitalization was $1,930,000,000,000 on October 25, but it dropped $140,000,000,000 on October 27 to $1,790,000,000,000. Nasdaq had 5,500 companies listed (more than half of which advanced for the year), and in October it became the first U.S. stock market to trade more than one billion shares in one day. Intel Corp., headed by Andrew Grove (*see* BIOGRAPHIES), was the most active stock, with more than 3,800,000,000 shares traded. Nasdaq's Bulletin Board, on which some 7,000 very small companies traded, was the subject of concern because there were virtually no listing requirements. Nasdaq proposed delisting those companies that failed to file their financial statements with the Securities and Exchange Commission (SEC). Among those companies affected would be major overseas corporations that traded American Depository Receipts on the Bulletin Board.

There were 6,685 active mutual funds late in 1997, with total assets of $4.2 trillion. Money market mutual funds held $1,046,000,000,000 in assets. Through mid-October U.S. stock funds gained 27.37% in value, whereas bond funds were up only 6.88%. More than 80% of U.S. mutual funds outperformed the S&P index, with technology and small-cap funds the stellar performers. Investors funneled new money into mutual funds at a record pace in 1997.

The stocks in the S&P indexes showed significant gains in 1997. At the year's end, the S&P industrial index was up 28.9% from Dec. 31, 1996; utilities rose 18.61%, financial 45.38%, and the S&P 500 31.01%. The Dow indexes reflected similar gain patterns in 1997. The industrials index was up 22.64%, with transportation up 44.37%, utilities up 17.43%, and the composite index up 28.71%.

U.S. government bond yields declined in 1997, with the bellwether 30-year Treasury bond falling below 6% for the first time since January 1996. The average yields began the year at about 6.8%, rose to 7.3% in April, and then began a steady slide, closing at 5.99% by the middle of December. Treasury prices rose sharply on October 27 in a very active session as panicked investors searched for security. Short-term securities were particularly popular.

Corporate bond yields declined moderately during the year, with AAA bonds (the highest quality) at 6.95% in mid-October, down from 7.4% a year earlier. Private placements of bonds were being done at a record pace, with corporate issuers selling a record $138.5 billion of debt and preferred stock privately by October 1997, according to Securities Data Co.—far outpacing 1996's corresponding figure of $116 billion. These bonds were sold directly only to big institutional investors under the SEC Rule 144a guidelines. These private placements tended to dominate the junk-bond market.

During the year the Chicago Board of Trade and the Chicago Board Options Exchange launched futures and futures options contracts that were pegged to the DJIA. Previous action on indexing had centred on the S&P 500, which had become a benchmark for institutional investors. S&P 500 futures, which were traded on the Chicago Mercantile Exchange (Merc), were among the most heavily traded futures contracts in the world. The panic on October 27 demonstrated the effectiveness of circuit breakers in the trading pits of the Merc, where four separate trading limits were imposed on the S&P 500 contract to slow down the frantic trading.

The SEC was very active in 1997. It urged the marketplaces to move toward decimalization, which advocates contended would make stock prices easier to understand and would probably narrow the spread between bid and ask prices, saving investors money by enabling them to buy at lower and sell at higher prices. The SEC advised regulated companies and funds that they had to keep investors informed about the costs of adapting computer systems to handle the "year 2000 problem," as well as the potential legal liabilities associated with the necessary changes. Prospectuses and registration statements were to be reviewed for disclosure of these risks. The SEC also required disclosures about the policies used to account for derivatives and provide certain quantitative and qualitative information about market risk exposures. The circuit breakers, which were introduced in 1988, worked effectively during the October 27 frenzy, permitting orderly trading in the face of record volume. The SEC, the Commodity Futures Trading Commission, and the Bank of England formally agreed to step up their cooperation and keep one another better informed of regulatory matters involving multinational corporations.

New York Stock Exchange Common Stock Index Closing Prices
Stock prices (Dec. 31, 1965 = 50)

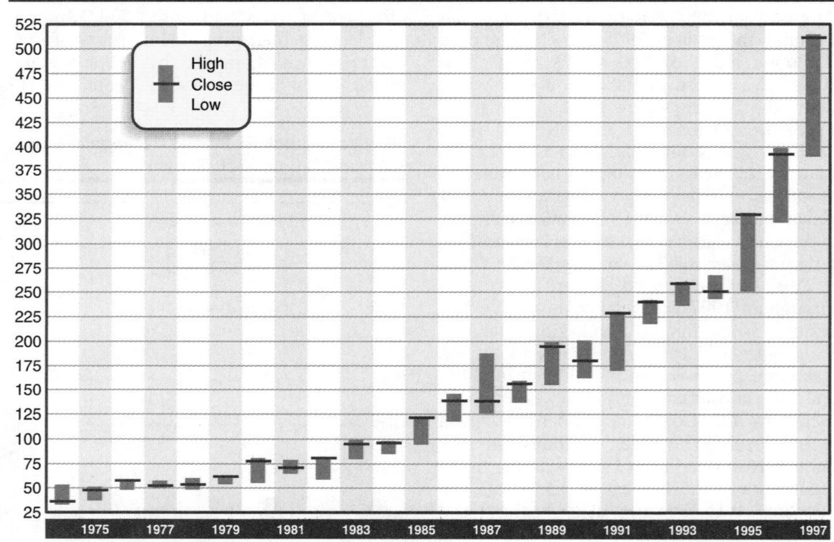

Number of shares sold
In billions of shares

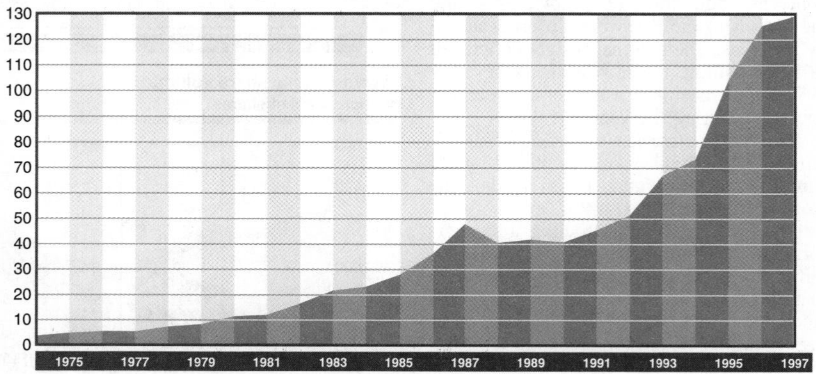

Sources: *Barron's National Business and Financial Weekly; The Wall Street Journal.*

***Financial Times* Industrial Ordinary Share Index**
Annual averages, 1974–97

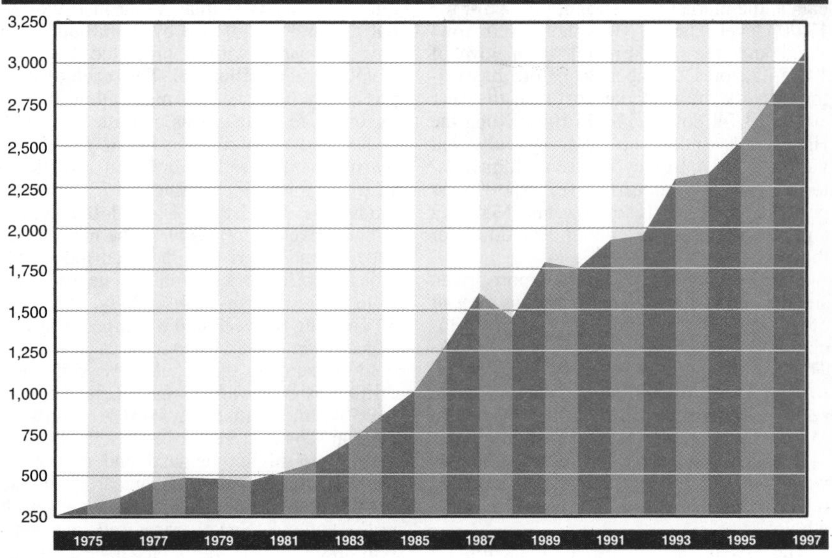

Source: *Financial Times.*

Canada. The Canadian stock market performed well in 1997 as the economy grew at a higher rate than had been forecast. There was an undercurrent of concern in the market because of the inflation threat, but share prices were well above those of the previous year. The weakness of the Canadian dollar led to persistent fears that the Bank of Canada would raise interest rates to protect the declining currency. In December the Canadian dollar fell below U.S. 70 cents for the first time in 11 years as a result of the financial turmoil in Asia and a showdown between currency traders and the Canadian central bank.

The Bank of Canada raised its bank rate to 4% in November, its highest level in a year. Responding to the central bank's action, Canada's commercial banks raised their prime lending rates to 5.5%, up from 5.25%. The bank rate and prime rate were both raised again later to end the year at 4.5% and 6%, respectively. A report by the consulting firm KPMG Peat Marwick, which compared business costs to help companies consider where to locate, found that Canada had significant advantages as a result of low land prices and construction costs. Canada also had among the lowest labour costs, electricity prices, and telecommunications fees. In addition, it had among the lowest corporate income tax rates and interest-rate charges among the seven industrialized countries studied. Canada experienced robust economic growth and low interest rates in 1997 as fiscal and monetary policies promoted reductions in the government's heavy debt-service costs. Canadian corporate profits rose sharply during the year, propelled higher by the country's strong economy. Corporate profits rose by more than 20% compared with the figures for 1996.

Market activity paralleled that of the American market. The leading indexes were up about 13% for the year, and the crash on October 27 resulted in a drop of 7.88%, with the Toronto Stock Exchange being shut down after the composite index of 300 stocks (TSE 300) lost 434.3 points, 6.12% of its value. The collapse of the gold-mining company Bre-X Minerals, which arose from the discovery of massive fraud (*see* BUSINESS AND INDUSTRY: *Mining:* Sidebar), caused the TSE computer system to break down owing to an overload of trading resulting from panic selling of the stock. The market made a speedy recovery, however, and moved on to establish new records. The TSE index of 300 stocks ended the year at 6699.44, up 13%.

Canadian bond markets rallied in line with those of the U.S., even though the Bank of Canada indicated further tightening moves. At the end of September, the 10-year government yield was 5.85%. Interest rates declined steadily after March 1997.

Mutual funds invested heavily in financial services, communications, and consumer stocks to profit from Canada's strong economic growth. There was less emphasis on mining and forestry stocks, but precious-metal and commodity-based stocks remained popular with mutual funds.

(IRVING PFEFFER)

Western Europe. The European markets performed well in 1997, despite the November correction. As continental Europe was at a relatively early stage in the economic-recovery cycle, corporate profits benefited from stable interest rates, low wage increases, and strong export markets. Corporate restructuring and pan-European mergers and acquisitions also drove the European markets during the year. The largest and most important market in Europe, the London Stock Exchange, rose by nearly 20%. The *Financial Times* Stock Exchange 100 (FT-SE 100) index opened the year strongly, buoyed by prospects of an upturn in economic growth and stable interest rates. In May the incoming Labour government was perceived as financially prudent and business-friendly, and the Bank of England, with its newly granted operational freedom in setting interest rates, moved swiftly, raising interest rates by a total of 1.25% in five small successive rises. The market continued to make good progress as the higher interest rates and the strength of sterling failed to dent consumer spending or the outlook for corporate profitability. The FT-SE 100, following Wall Street's lead, rose to 5100 in late summer. Following a consolidation phase related to fears of higher interest rates in the U.S., an autumn surge took the index to a new all-time high of 5330.80, a gain of nearly 30%. A minicrash related to the Asian crisis then took place; at one time the British market was down

Table VI. Selected Major World Stock Market Indexes[1]

Country and index	1997 range[2] High	1997 range[2] Low	Year-end close	Percent change from 12/31/96
Australia, Sydney All Ordinaries	2779	2299	2617	8
Austria, Credit Aktien	474	374	454	19
Belgium, Brussels BEL20	2622	1871	2418	28
Canada, TSE 300 Composite	7210	5679	6699	13
Denmark, Copenhagen Stock Exchange	676	470	676	43
Finland, HEX General	3891	2483	3302	32
France, Paris CAC 40	3094	2257	2999	29
Germany, Frankfurt FAZ Aktien	1481	986	1381	39
Hong Kong, Hang Seng	16,673	9,060	10,723	–20
Ireland, ISEQ Overall	4064	2725	4054	49
Italy, Milan Banca Comm. Ital.	1053	660	1053	58
Japan, Nikkei 225 Average	20,681	14,775	15,259	–21
Mexico, IPC	5369	3359	5206	56
Netherlands, The, CBS All Share	684	429	619	42
Norway, Oslo Stock Exchange	2288	1639	2099	28
Philippines, Manila Composite	3448	1740	1869	–41
Singapore, SES All-Singapore	573	381	426	–21
South Africa, Johannesburg Industrials	9314	7138	7426	–6
South Korea, Stock Price Index	792	351	376	–42
Spain, Madrid Stock Exchange	640	435	633	42
Sweden, Affarsvarlden General	3316	2379	3000	25
Switzerland, SBC General	3898	2506	3898	195
Taiwan, Weighted Price	10,117	6845	8187	18
Thailand, Bangkok SET	859	264	373	–55
United Kingdom, FT-SE 100	5331	4057	5136	25
United States, Dow Jones Industrials	8259	6392	7908	23
World, MS Capital International	982	795	937	13

[1]Index numbers are rounded. [2]Based on daily closing price.
Sources: *Financial Times; Korea Herald.*

457 points (9.3%). A partial recovery in the following days left the FT-SE 100 at 4842, or 128 points down on the week. The worst casualties in London were stocks with a direct link to Hong Kong, such as HSBC, Standard Chartered, and Cable & Wireless. Following the mid-November volatility caused by an unexpected rise in British interest rates and the deepening crisis in the Japanese financial sector, relative optimism returned. In a traditional pre-Christmas rally, the market rose, ending the year up 25% at 5135.5.

The best-performing large market in Europe was Germany, with an annual gain of nearly 40%. An export-driven economic recovery, growing confidence that the budget deficit would meet the EMU criteria, and prospects of economic reforms drove the German bourse. A spring setback that reflected the rise in U.S. interest rates was followed by a strong summer rally that took the FAZ Aktien to 1481 and the DAX index to 4439—a gain of 54%. Following summer profit taking and autumn weakness induced by a precautionary rise in German interest rates, the market rallied before it was hit by the turmoil in the Asian markets. After November the market regained its poise. The liberal market in The Netherlands, with the presence of many international trading companies, staged another year of strong gains, rising 42%.

The Paris Bourse was relatively less rewarding for investors. Early gains were reduced by badly shaken sentiment when the Socialist Party unexpectedly won the French elections in the summer. As concerns about economic reforms and commitment to meeting the entry conditions to the EMU receded, a strong late-summer rally developed and took the CAC 40 Index to a peak of 3094.01, a gain of 33%. Following the autumn correction and volatility, the French market ended the year showing a gain of nearly 30%. The Belgian market, which was closely linked to the French economy, was another laggard and rose by a similar percentage. Although the best gains were seen in southern Europe, where renewed hopes of EMU membership and better-than-expected corporate results drove the markets, Italy, with a gain of 58%, strongly outperformed Spain's 42% rise. With the exception of Denmark, the Nordic countries underperformed much of the continent, but gains of 25–32% represented a good return for investors.

Other Countries. The Asian markets performed disastrously in 1997. The Japanese market, the largest in the region, was overshadowed by the weakness of the nation's economic recovery even before the autumn currency crisis. The market started the year on a weak note, and by April it was down 10%. It rallied strongly, however, when the first-quarter GDP figures came in, and the Nikkei 225 Index average reached a peak of 20,681.07 in June. As the economic recovery faltered and the outlook worsened, the stock market started to retreat. By early October the Nikkei was well below the psychologically important 18,000 level. During the week of the Hong Kong crash, the Nikkei lost about 1,000 points, or 6% of its value, and it then fell by another 623 points the following week. In mid-November the Nikkei dropped again, but as the government stepped in to safeguard the assets of the customers of Yamaichi Securities after its collapse on November 24 and promised public funds to support the other ailing banks, the market rose strongly to above the 17,000 level. The rally was short-lived, however, and the Nikkei fell to a low of 14,775.22 on December 29 before recovering slightly the next day to finish the year at 15,258.74, down 21%. In Hong Kong the Hang Seng Index, up 25% by July, fell victim to the currency upheaval, higher interest rates, and concerns over export prospects in Thailand, Indonesia, and Malaysia and retraced its steps, ending 20% down for the year.

Stock exchanges in many export-driven smaller Asian countries collapsed as a result of unsustainable balance of payments deficits and subsequent currency devaluations. This led to a large-scale sell-off by local and foreign investors. The largest declines were seen in Thailand (down 55%), Malaysia (52%), South Korea (42%), the Philippines (41%), and Indonesia (37%). China and Taiwan managed to stay above the fray and registered modest rises for the year as a whole.

The Asian turmoil also took its toll on other emerging markets. Many Latin-American stock exchanges had risen by 70–80% by the autumn as a result of strong economic growth and encouraging prospects. In the wake of the Asian crisis, however, investors' concerns focused on the growing balance of payments deficit in the region, particularly in Brazil, and a large sell-off resulted. Even so, many markets in the region ended the year with reasonable gains, notably Mexico (56%), Brazil (40%), and Argentina (25%). Some Eastern European markets and Russia (up 86%) registered among the highest gains in 1997.

Commodity Prices. Most commodity prices weakened during 1997 as a result of excess supply as well as low inflation and interest rates throughout the world. In early December *The Economist* Commodities Price Index was 2% below the previous year. The price of crude oil, which was not included in *The Economist* Index, fell by about 16%. For most of the year, prices for North Sea Brent, which served as a global price benchmark, fluctuated around $18 per barrel. In October, at the height of the Iraqi confrontation with the UN, it rose to almost $22 per barrel. During the year demand for oil was reasonably strong, and the supply was ample, despite occasional shortfalls from Russia and the North Sea. The December weakness in oil prices was largely the result of a 10% rise in OPEC production quotas. Analysts estimated that in 1998 global demand would rise by 2 million bbl a day, compared with a projected boost in supply of 2.7 million bbl. This excluded the possibility that the UN might allow Iraq to export more oil than was permitted in 1997.

The two main components of *The Economist* Index moved in different directions, with the food index rising by 7% whereas industrials fell by 11% in dollar terms. Higher beverage prices were the main influence behind the rise in the food index. Although coffee prices fell by nearly 40% from a speculative peak in May, they rose 30% during the year, and a bumper crop was expected in 1988. Cocoa prices could not hold to summer gains of 20% and were drifting as concern over the effect of the El Niño weather pattern on West African production subsided. Tea prices rose by 24% as a result of higher demand and a drop in Kenya's output. After rising earlier in the year, industrial material prices slipped back in the autumn. Nickel prices fell to a four-year low; copper was at its lowest for 17 months, compared with a 11-month low for zinc. These reflected a slowdown in global demand, particularly in Japan. Gold remained on a downward trend and in December fell to a 12½-year low of $292 per troy ounce, a fall of 21%. As a nonproductive asset, gold looked increasingly unattractive in the noninflationary environment of the late 1990s. Record consumption of gold for jewelry was not sufficient to counter the downward pressure exerted by the sale of gold by some central banks and those mines in Australia and South Africa that continued to produce at a loss. (IEIS)

This article updates the *Macropædia* article MARKETS.

BANKING

International. In late 1997 banks and other financial institutions in Southeast and East Asia fell like dominoes—one after another—as currencies and share prices collapsed in many of the much-admired "tiger" economies across the region. Beginning in July with the crash of Thailand's baht, the crisis spread to the Indonesian rupiah, Malaysian ringgit, and Philippine peso, all of which dropped to historic lows against the dollar by mid-December. Many Asian banks that had tied the repayment of short-term

Table VII. Selected U.S. Stock Market Indexes[1]

	1997 range[2] High	Low	Year-end close	Percent change from 12/31/96
Dow Jones Averages				
30 Industrials	8259	6392	7908	23
20 Transportation	3359	2222	3257	44
15 Utilities	272	209	273	17
65 Composite	2643	2015	2607	29
Standard & Poor's				
500 Index	984	737	970	31
Industrials	1147	865	1121	29
Utilities	236	181	236	19
Others				
NYSE Composite	514	389	511	30
Nasdaq Composite	1746	1201	1570	22
Amex Composite	722	541	685	20
Russell 2000	465	336	437	20

[1]Index numbers are rounded. [2]Based on daily closing price.
Sources: *Financial Times; Wall Street Journal.*

foreign debt to the value of Asian currency and other assets found it increasingly difficult to repay the loans, as falling currencies and plummeting stock markets left them short of capital with which to buy the foreign currency needed for repayment. Other banks had made overly large or insufficiently secured loans to companies that were unable to keep up with their payments.

The South Korean won plunged to an 11-year low in December, which forced creditor banks from the Group of Seven industrialized nations in Europe and North America to extend loan repayments and to help arrange new loans, many backed by the International Monetary Fund and the World Bank. In an effort to restore stability, the South Korean government rescued some failing banks, including two of the nation's largest, Korea First Bank and SeoulBank.

The crisis in South Korea and Southeast Asian countries triggered several failures in the already-weakened Japanese financial sector. When Hokkaido Takushoku Bank went under on November 17, the Japanese government allowed the long-troubled bank to collapse. The move was well received, and some analysts speculated that it could be a step by Japanese regulators toward a much-needed restructuring of the entire banking industry. In April the government had merged the failing Hokkaido Bank with the larger Hokkaido Takushoku in an unsuccessful attempt to shore up both.

In 1997 the banking industry in Switzerland, under pressure from the Swiss government, the media, and the international community, finally announced what it called a definitive total of dormant accounts, many opened by German Jews prior to World War II. The Union Bank of Switzerland (UBS), the Swiss Bank Corp. (SBC), and Crédit Suisse—together with the country's central bank—set up a special fund for Holocaust survivors. The fund exceeded $190 million by the end of the year. (*See* WORLD AFFAIRS: *Switzerland:* Sidebar.) In December the UBS and the SBC announced a planned merger that would create the United Bank of Switzerland, with assets of at least $600 billion and more than $900 billion under management. It would be the world's second largest bank, jumping past Germany's Deutsche Bank and exceeded in size only by the Bank of Tokyo-Mitsubishi, Ltd.

The giant Swiss merger overshadowed several previously announced European deals, including the merger of two Bavarian banks, Bayerische Hypotheken- und Wechsel-Bank AG and Bayerische Vereinsbank AG, with combined assets of some $470 billion. The largest financial services company in The Netherlands, ING Group—which had already purchased Barings PLC, Great Britain's oldest merchant bank, and the New York investment bank Furman Selz Inc.—announced the takeover of Banque Bruxelles Lambert in Belgium. The fragmented Belgian banking sector also recorded the sale of the French company Groupe Paribas's Belgian retail-banking business to Belgium's Bacob Bank SC. In Italy another French bank, the state-controlled Crédit Lyonnais, agreed to sell its stake in Credito Bergamasco SpA to the Banca Popolare di Verona. Crédit Lyonnais, which had been the object of a government-backed rescue in 1995, reported a return to profitability in the first half of 1997.

(MELINDA C. SHEPHERD)

United States. Among U.S. commercial bankers, 1997 would be remembered as the year the Great Depression finally ended. Exactly 64 years after Congress passed the Glass-Steagall Act of 1933, which barred commercial banks from underwriting stocks and bonds, U.S. banks once again began reasserting themselves in the securities business. In April Bankers Trust New York Corp., the nation's seventh largest bank, agreed to pay $1.7 billion in stock to acquire the Baltimore, Md.-based Alex. Brown Inc., one of the country's oldest and best-regarded securities firms. Although Glass-Steagall remained technically in place, the deal was made possible by the Fed's little-noticed decision in late 1996 to loosen dramatically the restrictions on the investment-banking work commercial banks could undertake.

Bankers Trust's historic move was followed by a succession of acquisitions of securities firms by banks, including BankAmerica Corp.'s purchase of Robertson, Stephens & Co., NationsBank Corp.'s purchase of Montgomery Securities, First Union Corp.'s purchase of Wheat First Butcher Singer, Inc., Fleet Financial Group, Inc.'s purchase of the Quick & Reilly Group, Inc., and U.S. Bancorp's purchase of the Piper Jaffray Co. Even foreign banks stepped into the fray, with the Canadian Imperial Bank of Commerce agreeing to buy Oppenheimer & Co., Inc., and the Swiss Bank Corp. agreeing to purchase Dillon, Read & Co., Inc.

The deals sent the stock prices of investment banks soaring and left observers wondering when the nation's biggest bank, Chase Manhattan Corp., might make a similar move. Chase officials, under fire from some analysts for dawdling, indicated they were in no hurry. They were willing to wait, they said, until prices came back down to earth. In any case, they had their eyes on a far bigger prize: a blockbuster acquisition along the lines of Merrill Lynch & Co., Inc., the nation's largest securities firm, or Donaldson, Lufkin & Jenrette, Inc. (DLJ), another big investment bank. Merrill Lynch, for its part, rebuffed an initial overture from Chase, while DLJ's French parent, the AXA Group, indicated no eagerness to sell out.

Meanwhile, Wall Street was not exactly sitting idly by, waiting for the commercial bankers to act. In February Morgan Stanley Group Inc. and Dean Witter, Discover & Co. merged in a bid to create a brokerage firm rivaling Merrill Lynch in size and reach. In September Travelers Group Inc., which already owned the Smith Barney brokerage house, added Salomon Inc. to the fold.

In other ways, too, bankers with a case of merger fever sent the walls between various branches of financial services tumbling down. There were bank acquisitions of money-management firms, from Mellon Bank Corp.'s purchase of Founders Asset Management, Inc., to J.P. Morgan & Co.'s purchase of a 45% stake in American Century Companies, a mutual-fund firm. There were bank deals for credit-card issuers, from Banc One Corp.'s acquisition of First USA Inc. to Fleet's acquisition of Advanta Corp. and Citicorp's purchase of the Universal Card business from AT&T Corp. There were also several mergers, including First Bank System's merger with U.S. Bancorp, NationsBank's acquisition of Barnett Banks, Inc., and First Union's purchase of CoreStates Financial Corp.

All the deals were made possible by a red-hot stock market that sent the shares of banks and other financial-services companies soaring and provided them with the currency to strike deals. The market in turn was fueled by a remarkable "Goldilocks economy"—not too hot and not too cold—that combined low unemployment, low inflation, and low interest rates and produced record profits for financial firms. Bankers surveying the landscape realized that if there was ever a time to bulk up and broaden their reach, it was now, before the economy—and their stock prices—cooled off.

Indeed, as year-end approached, there were reasons to worry about the future. The economic turmoil in Asia, driven in part by concerns over the soundness of various big Asian financial institutions, caught several American banks with large overseas operations off guard. Chase Manhattan, J.P. Morgan, and Bankers Trust all acknowledged that they had sustained sizable losses in their emerging-markets trading operations, with Chase alone taking a $160 million bond-trading hit in the last week of October.

The U.S. comptroller of the currency warned U.S. banks that their lending practices to big corporations were becoming too aggressive. Increased competition between bankers to win corporate financing assignments had driven the profit margin on big, multibank corporate loans to record lows, even as the level of such lending soared to record highs. At the same time, banks began taking more risks in their consumer lending, offering home equity loans and unsecured lines of credit to growing numbers of individuals with spotty credit records. Coming at a time when loan losses on credit-card portfolios were already hovering near record levels, the bankers' heightened risk tolerance gave analysts as much reason to worry about 1998 as they had reason to celebrate the historic profits of 1997.

(STEPHEN E. FRANK)

25 Largest U.S. Banks[1]

	Bank	Assets (in U.S. $000,000)
1	Chase Manhattan Corp.	366,574
2	Citicorp	300,381
3	NationsBank Corp.	285,656
4	J.P. Morgan & Co.	269,595
5	BankAmerica Corp.	257,520
6	First Union Corp.	202,766
7	Bankers Trust New York Corp.	140,087
8	Banc One Corp.	122,438
9	First Chicago NBD Corp.	113,306
10	Wells Fargo & Co.	97,655
11	Norwest Corp.	85,252
12	Fleet Financial Group, Inc.	83,575
13	National City Corp.	77,655
14	KeyCorp.	72,077
15	PNC Bank Corp.	71,828
16	U.S. Bancorp	70,174
17	BankBoston Corp.	68,230
18	Bank of New York Co., Inc.	61,429
19	Wachovia Corp.	60,291
20	Republic New York Corp.	57,592
21	SunTrust Banks Inc.	55,454
22	ABN Amro North America, Inc.	51,409
23	Mellon Bank Corp.	43,365
24	Comerica Inc.	35,905
25	State Street Corp.	35,507

[1]Ranked by asset size.
Source: SNL Securities LC.

LABOUR-MANAGEMENT RELATIONS

For the industrialized countries, economic growth in 1997 was generally good. Unemployment was a different story. Though low in the United States, fairly low in the United Kingdom, and low, as usual, in Austria, Japan, Luxembourg, and Switzerland, it averaged more than 10% in the European Union (EU) as a whole. The continuing differences in unemployment and job creation between the U.S. and most continental European countries revived the argument about labour-market flexibility. It was argued that the flexibility of the U.S. labour market favoured efficiency and low unemployment, whereas the more highly regulated practices common in much of Western Europe had led to high labour costs and unemployment. Others maintained that not only did a high degree of regulation afford a level of worker protection that was appropriate in an advanced industrial society but also that there was no strong evidence that it resulted in unemployment or was detrimental to competitiveness.

Europe. In the EU the idea of forming European companies, *i.e.,* companies with establishments in more than one member country incorporated under one (European) law rather than different laws in different countries, had been put forward in 1970 but had made little progress, mainly because of opposing views about the position of workers vis-à-vis the management of these enterprises. In May 1997 an expert group proposed that European companies be required to negotiate, with workers' representation, a "system of written involvement such as workers on the company's board or a works council with specific rights to be informed and consulted about matters of concern to workers. If negotiations proved unsuccessful 'reference rules' for such information and consultation rights, as established by the European Union, would apply." In June the European Commission launched discussions with unions and employers on a proposal that there be a binding EU-wide framework agreement requiring regulations in all member countries for companies to have arrangements for workers to be informed and consulted. An intergovernmental agreement reached in Amsterdam in June proposed new chapters to be added to European treaties dealing with employment and social policy, the latter replacing the Social Policy Protocol agreed upon in Maastricht, Neth., in 1991. An agreement by European unions and employers that intended to remove discrimination in the conditions of part-time workers compared with full-time workers was signed in June and formed the basis of a proposal for a directive to be made by the Council of Ministers.

In Great Britain the major event in 1997 was the sweeping success of the Labour Party in the general election on May 1. In recent years trade union influence had waned, and the party made it clear that Labour would leave in place most of the basic elements of the Conservative Party government's labour laws enacted between 1980 and 1993. There were, however, four matters on which the new government proposed to act immediately. First, it would reverse a ruling by the Conservative government that, on the grounds of national interest, had denied union membership to workers at the Government Communications Headquarters, an intelligence-gathering agency. Second, it would set up a commission on low pay, with a view to establishing some form of national minimum wage. Third, it would end the "opt-out" from certain EU labour proposals, which the Conservatives had negotiated at Maastricht in December 1991. And fourth, it would move toward establishing a means whereby employers could be required to recognize trade unions when a majority of their workers so wished. The government acted quickly on the first three of these matters, but the complicated question of union recognition was seen to need extensive consultation.

In Germany unemployment continued at historically high levels—over 10%. A revision of the Employment Promotion Act in March provided a wide range of modifications aimed at helping the unemployed, with some special sections concerning the long-term unemployed. The new act covered unemployment benefits, training, job creation, liberalization of arrangements governing temporary work, and funding for small businesses. In collective bargaining, wage increases were modest. In April the metal trades union announced that, with the objective of reducing unemployment, it would campaign for a workweek of 32 hours, to start in 1999.

When the unexpected general election in France replaced the right-of-centre government with a Socialist government in June, the new administration quickly announced an ambitious program, including creation of 700,000 jobs for young people in the public and private sectors, reduction of the normal workweek from 39 to 35 hours, financial support for companies making innovative working-time arrangements, strengthening of collective bargaining, a review of unemployment legislation and pension arrangements, and an increase in the national minimum wage. Repeating action taken in 1996, French truck drivers stopped work on November 2, complaining that promises made to them at the end of 1996 had not been honoured. They set up roadblocks, which impeded not only French truck drivers but also those from other countries using French roads. The strike ended after five days, with the truckers gaining an immediate increase in pay of 6%, part of a three-stage rise that would take them up to the year 2000.

In February the Renault car company's Belgian plant at Vilvoorde informed more

Manpower, Inc.

In 1997 Manpower, Inc., a company that provided workers for other employers and by 1997 the largest such firm in the world, was seeking to expand its roster of employees by actively recruiting welfare recipients. As a result of new U.S. legislation, there was increased pressure on business to employ people who had been on the welfare rolls. Manpower's chief executive, Mitchell Fromstein, who sat on the White House panel on welfare reform, believed that the company had the experience in the training and placement of workers to make the reforms work. Earlier, Manpower had collaborated with several not-for-profit organizations to form the Milwaukee (Wis.) Job Center, a program to offer a one-stop employment office for the impoverished people of the inner city. Though the program failed, largely owing to disputes over the roles to be played by each organization, Manpower learned some valuable lessons. The company now better understood the special training needed by some of the people on welfare and was eager to tackle those problems on its own. Manpower's plan to place offices in poor urban neighbourhoods was still in the developmental stages in 1997, but some success had already been achieved in Milwaukee.

This sort of leading role was typical of Manpower, especially under the leadership of Fromstein, who took executive control of the company in the 1970s. The company was founded in 1948 by Elmer Winter and Aaron Scheinfeld, primarily to place workers in industrial positions. When Fromstein took over, he shifted the focus from factory work to office services and instituted an extensive training program to ensure that Manpower could provide competent workers, familiar with the needs and technology of modern offices; in recent years particular emphasis had been placed on computer training by means of a specially devised program called Skillware. Consequently, when the era of corporate downsizing began in the 1980s, Manpower was well prepared to step in and provide skilled workers. During that time the firm signed exclusive national contracts to provide temporary staffing for major corporations (most notably IBM and Hewlett-Packard). The company also expanded rapidly into Europe and by 1997 was operating 2,400 offices in 43 countries and providing work for 1.6 million people. Since 1994 it had been the largest private-sector employer in the United States. In 1996 Manpower formed an alliance with Drake Beam Morin Inc. (DBM), a leading executive job-finding company. The move allowed Manpower to offer highly skilled and experienced businesspeople for temporary work and permitted DBM to return its clients quickly to the workforce while it searched for permanent positions for them.

Manpower often provided valuable training for its workers, and its placements could lead to permanent positions. Also, its many offices allowed employees the opportunity to relocate and work where they pleased. Yet, it had to be recognized that the company had grown and flourished because many workers had been forced to settle for temporary positions rather than the permanent ones they would have preferred.

(JAMES HENNELLY)

than 3,000 employees that the plant would close in July. The European Commission saw Renault's action as having ignored the European Works Council Directive and having raised serious doubts about the adequacy of worker-protection laws. Belgium's National Labour Council opened consideration of stronger legislation concerning substantial layoffs, and tribunals in both Belgium and France ruled that the company had failed to meet its obligation to consult workers. Renault's chairman, Louis Schweitzer (*see* BIOGRAPHIES), confirmed that economic considerations had necessitated the closure, but subsequent discussions with the unions resulted in the introduction of a number of measures to help the Vilvoorde workers.

In Italy a hard-fought agreement reached by the government and unions in 1996 led to legislation in June. The measure adopted concerned the use of temporary employment agencies, training arrangements, encouragement of part-time work (used less in Italy than in other European countries), help for young unemployed workers in the south, employment on socially useful projects, and reduction of the maximum workweek from 48 to 40 hours. A crisis arose in October when the Communist Refoundation Party refused to accept the provisional budget for 1998. Negotiations resulted in agreement that certain of the proposed changes in the pension system would not apply to factory workers and that the government would introduce a measure for the workweek to be reduced to 35 hours by 2001. The package of pension changes was subsequently modified by an agreement that provided for some pension anomalies, such as the right of some public-sector workers to retire after only 19 years' work, to be ended but failed to produce much-needed structural changes.

In Spain unions and employers in April reached agreement on labour-market reform and the strengthening of collective bargaining. The general goal was to reduce the extensive use of short-term contracts and increase competitiveness. In support of the agreement, the government in May promulgated decrees aimed at promoting stable jobs and employment relations and offering reductions in employers' social security costs.

North America. In the United States a nationwide strike by some 185,000 Teamsters Union drivers and package sorters took place at United Parcel Service (UPS). The main point of contention, apart from pay, was union dissatisfaction with the conditions and insecurity of part-time workers, whose numbers had risen to comprise more than one-half of the workforce, and the company's desire to replace the Teamsters' industrywide pension scheme with a company plan. Discussions to settle the strike, which lasted 15 days, went as high as the U.S secretary of labour. A settlement was reached on August 19 on the basis of a wage increase of about 15% for full-time and about 37% for part-time workers over five years. The company undertook to convert 10,000 part-time jobs into full-time jobs, as far as revenue permitted, over the five-year life of the agreement. The company also agreed to maintain its participation in the union's pension plan.

The Teamsters faced additional problems during the year when union president Ron Carey, who was first elected in 1991 as a reform candidate, was found by a court-appointed adjudicator to have engaged in illegal fund-raising during his 1996 reelection campaign. The 1996 vote was declared invalid in August, and Carey was later barred from the rerun called for 1998. Carey's chief opponent, James P. Hoffa (the son of longtime Teamsters leader Jimmy Hoffa), was also under investigation for similar allegations.

Another dispute of interest concerned the more than 9,000 pilots employed by American Airlines. The pilots were concerned about who should fly new jets operated by American Eagle, a subsidiary commuter airline, whose (lower-paid) pilots belonged to a different union with its own collective agreement. When a strike was called in February, Pres. Bill Clinton ordered the union to halt it, invoking his powers under the 1926 Railway Labor Act—the first use of these powers with regard to a commercial airline in 31 years—and set up a Presidential Emergency Board. The settlement of the dispute provided a degree of flexibility in the manning of the airplanes acceptable to American's pilots. In another action the U.S. national minimum wage rose from $4.75 to $5.15 an hour on September 1.

In Mexico an era ended with the death, on June 21, of Fidel Velázquez Sánchez. (*See* OBITUARIES.) His union career spanned 75 years, much of that time as general secretary of the Confederation of Mexican Workers, Mexico's main trade union body, and as a power in the ruling Institutional Revolutionary Party. (R.O. CLARKE)

See also Business and Industry Review.

This article updates the *Macropædia* article WORK AND EMPLOYMENT.

JOHN VINK—MAGNUM

Demonstrators in France march in support of factory workers in Belgium who lost their jobs when the Renault car company decided to close its plant at Vilvoorde. The automaker's decision, which was made without consulting workers' representatives, met with widespread condemnation in Europe.

CONSUMER AFFAIRS

International. Sustainable production and consumption and the privatization of public utilities were the issues that dominated the world consumer movement in 1997. Meeting people's needs without destroying the environment was fast becoming a key concern of consumer organizations both in developed economies and in less-developed countries.

In July a major step forward was achieved when the United Nations Economic and Social Council agreed to set up an expert group to expand consumer protection guidelines into the area of sustainable consumption. The first UN *Guidelines for Consumer Protection* was adopted in 1985 and covered such areas as consumer safety, product standards, education, and information. In 1995 the UN had agreed for the first time to revise and update the guidelines to include more recent areas of consumer concerns, such as how to use purchasing power to reduce the environmental impact of consumption. The 1997 resolution was one of the key steps needed to turn that earlier agreement into a reality. An expert group of government representatives, international organizations, and nongovernmental organizations, coordinated by the UN, would develop the new guidelines—which could cover such areas as eco-labeling, product pricing that takes environmental costs into consideration, education, and the control of misleading "environmentally friendly" advertising—with the aim of having them approved by the summer of 1998.

Consumers International, a federation of 215 member organizations in over 90 countries, celebrated World Consumer Rights Day on March 15 by issuing a booklet, *Consumers and the Environment: Meeting Needs, Changing Lifestyles.* It looked at the enormous problems that face consumers in the areas of water, waste, and energy and used case studies to examine how some organizations were working to make consumers more environmentally responsible. The booklet also focused on advertising and the role it plays in promoting irresponsible consumerism. Consumer organizations campaigned at the World Trade Organization (WTO), which hears international trade disputes, to allow consumer and other nongovernmental groups input in dispute decisions. As of August 1997, the WTO had 100 such disputes in the pipeline.

The concerns from 1996, particularly in the areas of food safety and the genetic manipulation of food products, continued into 1997. Consumers waged a successful battle against a move by the Codex Alimentarius Commission, the international food-standards-setting body, to pass a draft standard that would have allowed the use of a genetically engineered growth hormone to increase milk production in cows. Consumer organizations claimed that use of the hormone could be detrimental in both economic and health terms. Codex delegates agreed to postpone the vote to review new scientific information regarding the hormones. Consumers also lobbied for greater participation by nongovernmental organizations at Codex; in 1997 the approved list of 111 organizations included 104 industry-funded groups, six health and nutrition foundations, and Consumers International.

Western European consumer organizations remained highly concerned about bovine spongiform encephalopathy ("mad cow" disease). A European Union-wide ban on the export of British beef remained in place in 1997. Electronic commerce—including use of the Internet—also became a major consumer issue in Western Europe. The Organisation for Economic Co-operation and Development initiated work on consumer protection guidelines in the areas of fraud, redress, and privacy.

In Eastern and Central Europe and the former Soviet republics, the consumer movement continued to expand, but the emphasis in some parts of the region—particularly in Eastern Europe—was shifting from products to services. In particular, financial services and consumer credit were major issues. The problem of uninformed investing was most clearly demonstrated by the civil unrest in Albania over the collapse of pyramid schemes that had drawn in financially unsophisticated people by promising extremely high rates of return. More than 90% of Albanians participated, with many losing all of their investment. (*See* WORLD AFFAIRS: *Albania:* Sidebar.) Consumer organizations lobbied local and national governments to pass laws protecting investors and worked to educate the public about such schemes. Consumer input into privatization of public utilities remained a high priority for consumer organizations in Eastern and Central Europe.

Privatization was also a key consumer concern in Latin America, where there were renewed efforts to increase consumer representation into the regulatory mechanisms governing utilities. Consumer organizations undertook a series of in-depth studies and initiated a sequence of training seminars in Chile, Brazil, Colombia, Mexico, and Peru aimed at promoting consumer input in the newly privatized electrical, telephone, and water services. In Latin America and the Caribbean region, consumer organizations stepped up activities related to the promotion of sustainable production and consumption. A major initiative in 1997 was the creation of a Regional Environmental Citizen's Forum, which would work with other regional groups to promote awareness of the environmental impact of consumer choices.

Privatization—along with structural adjustment programs and deregulation—meant Asian consumers faced formidable challenges in 1997. In some countries poor monitoring of the privatization process caused waste of resources, while deregulation led to corruption and anticompetitive practices. The consumer movement responded through the promotion of legal reforms, policy formulation, trade practices, and dispute-resolution schemes. Consumers International's Regional Office for Asia and the Pacific (ROAP), together with the Consumer Unity and Trust Society of India, held an international conference in New Delhi in January with the theme "Consumers in the Global Age."

By the end of 1997, five states in the Pacific Islands—Kiribati, Samoa, Cook Islands, Tuvalu, and the Federated States of Micronesia—had passed draft laws and consumer protection regulations. ROAP also instigated a nine-country household consumption survey to examine trends of specific target groups in the region.

In 1990 only seven active consumer organizations existed in five African countries. As of 1997, however, they existed in 45 out of 56 African countries. The French version of the 1996 Model Consumer Protection Law for Africa was launched during the year. In addition, Consumers International's Regional Office for Africa was conducting a survey, funded by the Economic Commission for Africa, intended to halt deterioration of the continent's air transport services. Meanwhile, the head of the National Consumers Movement in Cameroon was jailed for alleging that certain chocolate candies contained pesticides. (ALINA TUGEND)

United States. Consumer safety was an issue on several fronts in the United States in 1997. The year began with the National Highway Traffic Safety Administration (NHTSA) issuing a formal proposal—finalized in November—to allow car owners to have air bag on-off switches installed by auto dealers and repair shops. The NHTSA and the National Transportation Safety Board had reported in 1996 that air bags—mandated for both the driver and the passenger side of all new automobiles and light trucks—actually increased the risk of injury and death for children under 12 riding in the front seat during a frontal crash.

Official data also revealed that despite a positive record overall, air bags showed small, sometimes negative, effectiveness in protecting the elderly and people of short stature. Automakers and the government quickly reached agreement on rules to implement air-bag-design changes for future model years to reduce these risks but stalled over the disconnect policy, which was intended to help affected populations in the more than 56 million air-bag-equipped vehicles already on the road. Opponents of an open disconnection policy feared many people would choose to deactivate air bags unnecessarily and thus increase their risks.

A special White House commission to improve aviation safety and security issued 57 proposals in February following concerns raised in 1996 with the crash of TWA Flight 800 off Long Island, N.Y., and the ValueJet Flight 592 crash into the Florida Everglades. The far-reaching proposals covered aviation safety, air traffic control, airport security, and aviation disaster response. Some safety-regulation experts noted that the costs of certain measures, particularly airport security, would outstrip the benefits to the traveling public by a significant margin, given that the risks of flying were small. Meanwhile, the Federal Aviation Administration reported that publishing airline safety rankings, in the manner of on-time and complaint rankings already provided by the government, would not be helpful because there were "no consistent or persistent distinctions among the major jet carriers."

Ongoing efforts to intensify food-safety oversight were underscored by a string of well-publicized foodborne-illness outbreaks, from tainted raspberries to bad apple cider to hamburger meat processed by the Hudson Foods Co. of Arkansas. (The latter led to Hudson's recall in August of some 11.3 million kg [25 million lb] of hamburger.) Key among several educational and regulatory initiatives were plans to extend the Hazard Analysis and Critical Control Point (HACCP) system of food inspection to cover fruit and vegetable juices. HACCP became fully effective in seafood plants at the end of 1997, and many large meat and poultry plants scheduled to implement HACCP fully by January 1998 already had the system in place. Initiatives also included expansion of the FoodNet monitoring system, which established a national network of "sentinel" sites in the states to provide early warning of food-illness outbreaks. Increased enforcement powers of federal meat and poultry inspectors and increased oversight of imported foods were proposed but eventually bogged down in Congress.

After 10 years of lobbying, broadcasters persuaded the Federal Communications Commission (FCC) to begin the formal transition to the broadcast of digital television signals, which promised to revolutionize the quality of TV. The FCC decided that conventional broadcasts would be phased out by the year 2007. Against their will, however, broadcasters still had to choose precisely the type of digital signals to broadcast and thus were reluctant to choose one format, such as the long-promised "high definition television," over other digital formats until it was clear what competitors would do. This left consumers with the promise of great technological advance, the prospect of having to replace soon-to-be obsolete TV sets (within a year in some markets), and no assurance that near-term purchases would comply with the future standard.

Consumers were more likely to find drug ads on television and radio broadcasts after the Food and Drug Administration issued new guidelines for advertising prescription drugs. Aimed at making such ads more consumer friendly, the guidelines said drugmakers could describe drug benefits without having to post the lengthy, detailed side-effect notices, as was required prior to the August ruling. Drug companies still had to summarize the major risks and include toll-free telephone numbers or Internet addresses for additional consumer information. Nevertheless, the Food and Drug Administration still was vigilant and warned one major drugmaker about misleading ads only a few days after issuing the new rules.

(PETER L. SPENCER)

See also Business and Industry Review: *Advertising; Retailing;* The Environment.

Education

Important educational issues in 1997 included students' mathematics and science achievement, schooling opportunities for girls, values education, adult education, international higher-education coalitions, new university programs, and student protest movements.

In the United States a concerted focus on growth, change, and reform marked the year. Among the major trends were efforts to establish academic standards and tests to assess students' academic progress, a continuing movement for alternative educational arrangements such as charter schools, concerns over the deterioration of schools' physical plants, rising costs of higher education, efforts to infuse information technology into schools, the encouragement of character-education programs, and efforts to devise and implement effective training programs for unemployed and underemployed adults whose skills were obsolete or dated. The focus on change and reform took place in a national educational context in which 66.1 million students were enrolled in schools and colleges, and 4 million persons were employed as elementary and secondary teachers and as college faculty. An additional 4.4 million were employed as administrators and professional staff and support persons.

Primary and Secondary Education. Initial test results were announced for the primary- and middle-school students who participated in the Third International Mathematics and Science Study, sponsored by the International Association for the Evaluation of Educational Achievement (IEA). In the world's largest cross-national testing program, the skills of 500,000 students from 15,000 schools in 45 nations were assessed. For most countries the assessments were done at three levels of the schooling hierarchy: primary grades 3–4, middle-school grades 7–8, and the final year or two of secondary school.

Among the 41 nations in the middle-school study, the five highest in mathematics at the eighth-grade level were, in descending order, Singapore, South Korea, Japan, Hong Kong, and Flemish Belgium. The five lowest were Portugal, Iran, Kuwait, Colombia, and South Africa. France ranked 13th, Canada 18th, Germany 23rd, England 25th, and the United States 28th. The five highest in science were Singapore, the Czech Republic, Japan, South Korea, and Bulgaria. The five lowest were Iran, Cyprus, Kuwait, Colombia, and South Africa. England ranked 10th, the U.S. 17th, Germany 18th, Canada 19th, and France 28th.

In a move toward greater participation in the worldwide educational community, nine former Soviet bloc nations joined the IEA middle-school testing program. In the eighth-grade, 41-nation comparison, the nine Central and Eastern European countries earned the following ranks in mathematics: Czech Republic 6th, Slovakia 7th, Slovenia 10th, Bulgaria 11th, Hungary 14th, Russia 15th, Latvia 30th, Romania 34th, and Lithuania 35th. The ranks in science were: Czech Republic 2nd, Bulgaria 5th, Slovenia 7th, Hungary 9th, Slovakia 13th, Russia 14th, Romania 31st, Latvia 32nd, and Lithuania 35th.

Among the 26 countries that tested fourth-grade students, the top five countries in science were South Korea, Japan, the U.S., Austria, and Australia. The lowest five were Portugal, Cyprus, Thailand, Iran, and Kuwait. England was 8th, Canada 9th, and Singapore 10th. In mathematics the top five nations were Singapore, South Korea, Japan, Hong Kong, and The Netherlands. The lowest five were Thailand, Portugal, Iceland,

JIM HOLMES—PANOS

Junior high students in South Korea ranked near the top in both science and mathematics in a recent study involving 41 nations.

In areas of Afghanistan under the control of the Taliban, an Islamic fundamentalist movement, women are not permitted to go to school. These Afghan girls continue to attend a school in Mazar-e Sharif, where Taliban forces have been expelled.

CHRIS STEELE-PERKINS—MAGNUM

Iran, and Kuwait. The U.S. ranked 12th, Canada 13th, and England 17th. Results of the IEA secondary-school testing were scheduled for release in 1998.

Efforts to promote educational opportunities for girls were expanded in various parts of the world. In Africa UNICEF established a large number of community-operated primary schools in Burkina Faso, Mali, Egypt, and Zambia, offering equal access to schooling for girls and boys. In Kenya teaching and learning materials for the schools were revised to eliminate gender stereotyping. In Zimbabwe courses for parents and school administrators were organized to increase community support for gender equality of educational opportunity. In South Asia Bangladesh introduced part-time study programs for girls who worked, and Pakistan established a mobile teacher-training project. A French Parliament report criticized sexist portrayals of women in school textbooks. Definitions in children's dictionaries associated gentle, passive, and home-based qualities with females and assertive qualities with males. In the nation's official primary-school history book, the only two women studied were Marie Curie and Joan of Arc.

Social activists in India sought to enroll more members of the nation's child labour force (estimated to be as high as 100 million) in mandatory primary education. The goal of the project was to stem the recruitment of poorly educated boys from rural areas into indentured servitude in urban factories. Typical of the reform efforts was the program at the Mufti Ashram rehabilitation centre in New Delhi, where indentured children received three months of training that included basic literacy classes.

Curriculum reforms in India took a more nationalistic turn as a growing number of foundation-sponsored private schools supplemented the government syllabus with studies of Indian culture, music, philosophy, and Sanskrit language. In addition, uniforms in many convent schools were replaced by traditional Indian garb. Hindu nationalists of the Bharatiya Janata Party sought to replace Western science in schools by introducing Vedic mathematics and the ancient science of *vastu shastra*. Party spokesmen charged that Western science was a source of imperialism and rationalism that conflicted with Hindu tradition.

No abrupt changes accompanied the political transfer of Hong Kong from British governance to control by China on July 1. The smooth transition was due to revisions that Hong Kong education officials had gradually introduced over the 13-year period since the transfer date was determined in 1984.

The revisions featured such new subjects in the curriculum as China's national spoken version of Chinese language (*putonghua*) and public-affairs classes that stressed the combined place of China and Hong Kong in world affairs. Existing syllabi were altered to provide a politicized historical framework relevant to Hong Kong's national identity under China, and British colonial history was deleted from the course of study. The number of schools employing English as the medium of instruction was also reduced in favour of Cantonese and *putonghua*. During the first week of July, Tung Chee-hwa (*see* BIOGRAPHIES), Hong Kong's chief executive under its new status as a special administrative district of China, set educational development as a top priority. He committed his administration to upgrading the teaching force so that all teachers in primary and secondary schools would have both a university degree and professional qualifications in education.

The study of values was emphasized in several countries. Israeli Prime Minister Benjamin Netanyahu urged the introduction of new values into the nation's education system, with the approach modeled after religious nationalism. The proposed program would include such topics as sex education and traffic safety. Critics, however, feared the plan would impose a single group's values on the entire school system. The publication of guidelines for sex education in Nigeria officially encouraged the study of sexual behaviour in the health programs for schools and youth groups. In Russia research revealed that young people were increasingly becoming sexually active as a result of liberal attitudes toward sex in the mass media. When public opinion surveys found the majority of Russians in favour of sex education, the government established a project targeted at educating youth.

After three decades of legal delays engineered by Japan's Ministry of Education, the nation's Supreme Court, in a 3–2 decision, found the ministry guilty of having eliminated from a high-school history book an account of World War II atrocities committed by Japan's military forces in northern China. The ruling brought to a successful close the efforts of the textbook author, historian Saburo Ienaga, to have ministry officials censured for having illegally deleted portions of his work that they found politically unsavoury. The disputed passages were restored to Ienaga's textbook.

Agitation by Romania's ethnic Hungarian minority, numbering some two million, for the use of minority languages in education continued. High-school final examinations could now be taken in Romanian. New regulations also provided for teaching in students' mother tongues for a range of subjects that previously had been only in Romanian.

Adult-education efforts progressed in The Sudan and in China. The mobile tent-school program for lower-primary-grade children of nomadic tribes in The Sudan added 126 new schools by early 1997 and expanded the project's offerings to include literacy and self-improvement classes for adults. A special school for divorced couples in China's Jian province completed its fifth year with a record of success in reducing the number of divorces in the region. The school was established to teach divorcing couples constructive methods of handling family disputes by means of a three-month course consisting of classroom instruction, individual counseling, and the analysis of court cases featuring marriage law, the effects of divorce on children, and causes of family disorder.

Between 1985 and 1996, public elementary- and secondary-school enrollments in the U.S. increased 16%. The greatest growth occurred in the elementary grades, where enrollment rose 21% over the same period, from 27 million to a record high of 32.8 million in 1996. Public elementary enrollments were projected at 33.2 million for 1997. After having declined 8% from 1985 to 1990, high-school enrollments rose 15% from 1990 to 1996, for a net increase of 5%. Private-school enrollments grew more slowly, from 5.6 million in 1985 to 5.8 million in 1996.

It was in this context that U.S. Pres. Bill Clinton delivered the 1997 state of the union message to Congress on February 4. In the speech Clinton gave education the highest priority in his second term. His 10-point series of education recommendations included continuing the "America Reads" initiative of tutorial programs to improve children's reading scores so that every eight-year-old is able to read; free access for public schools to the Internet to ensure that every 12-year-old is able to log on; developing and adopting national standards for elementary- and junior-high-school students; developing national tests to improve fourth and eighth graders' achievement in mathematics and reading; establishing standards for teachers based on the National Board for Professional Teaching Standards so that 100,000 teachers can seek certification as "master teachers"; continued support for charter schools, with a goal of establishing 3,000 such schools; continued support for early childhood-education programs, especially expanding enrollment in Head Start to one million children by 2002; emphasis on character education to improve citizenship skills and curb violence and drug abuse; $5 billion for new school construction; tax deduction—up to $10,000 per year—for college students; and continued expansion of worker-training programs. Seeking to avoid charges of federal intrusion into state and local educational prerogatives, Clinton proposed national rather than federal government standards. Clinton's proposals would cost $51 billion, a 20% increase over the current budget and the largest educational funding package in U.S. history.

Spurred by Clinton's recommendation for voluntary national standards, the U.S. Department of Education began developing such yardsticks in reading (for fourth graders) and in mathematics (for eighth graders). The tests were to be based on content frameworks developed for the National Assessment of Educational Progress (NAEP) and were expected to be ready for use in states and local school districts in 1999. Recently released findings from the NAEP 1996 assessment of American students at grades 4, 8, and 12 in mathematics revealed improvements in performance over the 1990 and 1992 assessments.

The charter-school movement gained momentum in the U.S. in 1997, attracting support as an alternative pattern of public-school organization. Though they were public (nonsectarian and publicly funded), charter schools provided an alternative to more conventional institutions. By late 1997, 28 states, the District of Columbia, and Puerto Rico had passed legislation that allowed local districts to issue charters—special agreements—to teachers and other groups to establish schools with innovative programs. Charter schools are characterized as follows: (1) the state authorizes organizations to establish and operate charter schools and issues a waiver freeing them from many public-school regulations; (2) the school is public; (3) the school, through its charter, is responsible for students' academic progress; (4) the school provides choice for educators and parents. As of 1996, approximately

80,000 students were attending 500 charter schools, most of which were elementary schools. Approximately 60% of these schools were small, with enrollments of fewer than 200 students.

Although the momentum for charter schools continued, the movement that would use state vouchers to allow children to attend nonpublic schools received a setback in Wisconsin. A decision by Wisconsin state Judge Paul Higginbotham blocked a plan to expand use of public funds to enable impoverished children in Milwaukee to attend religious schools.

The Board of Education of Oakland, Calif., revised a controversial plan, adopted in 1996, that recognized "Ebonics," a vernacular form of English spoken by some African-Americans, as a language to be used in instruction. The board, on Jan. 15, 1997, removed phrasing that suggested that some students would be taught in Ebonics rather than standard English. In California a ballot referendum seemed likely on an initiative that proposed eliminating bilingual education; in 1997 approximately 1.3 million of California's 5 million students participated in some form of bilingual education.

In curriculum and instruction, constructivism, collaborative learning, and whole-language learning continued to be popular in the U.S., especially in elementary schools. Stressing problem solving, these methods encouraged students to construct their own knowledge base by direct group interaction with materials present in the environment.

On May 2 Paulo Freire, the most prominent figure in literacy training in South America during the 20th century, died at age 75 in São Paulo, Braz. (*See* OBITUARIES.) Over recent decades Freire's best-known book, *Pedagogy of the Oppressed,* had guided literacy movements around the world and inspired a wealth of educational publications by both admirers and critics.

Higher Education. To promote closer cooperation between the chief executives of research universities in the Pacific region, representatives of 20 universities in 11 nations formed an Association of Pacific Rim Universities. Countries included among the charter members were Australia, Canada, China, Indonesia, Mexico, New Zealand, the Philippines, Russia, South Korea, Thailand, and the U.S.

Following six years of planning, an association of 17 private colleges in four Central American countries established an accreditation system to set standards for academic quality and fiscal solvency. The system was administered by the recently established Association of Private Universities of Central America, whose member institutions were located in Costa Rica, El Salvador, Honduras, and Nicaragua. During 1997, 15 of the colleges were accredited, and 18 additional private institutions were considering joining the association.

In China the higher-education system's task of producing the highly trained workers needed to sustain rapid economic growth continued to be hampered by the loss of teachers to industry and research centres, an outdated focus on narrow vocational training, inflexible Confucian and Maoist doctrines, and a low student population. Critics claimed that in order to increase the country's pool of scholars, the nation's universities needed more incentives for students. Hardly one-third of the 260,000 students who left for study abroad in recent years had returned home.

As one step toward addressing this problem, the government began permitting nonreligious foreign groups to establish and manage educational institutions within the nation's borders.

China's State Education Commission announced plans to reduce the number of academic specialties in higher education from 624 to 300 by 1999 because many graduates had been so highly specialized that they could not find jobs. The move marked a retreat from the Soviet model adopted in 1952 that favoured narrow channels of vocational preparation. To reduce the Chinese government's burden of financing higher education, a policy of charging every student an annual tuition fee of approximately $180 was instituted in the nation's 1,032 colleges and universities; this represented a departure from nearly a half century of free education at all levels of the education system. China's official Communist Party newspaper, *People's Daily,* reported a survey in which one-third of the nation's college students said they wanted to join the 57 million-member party. More than 90% of the respondents believed China's political condition was stable, while 80% thought the government had done a good job in opening China to the West.

DANIEL HULSHIZER—ASSOCIATED PRESS

A young girl watches other students arrive at a nonsectarian charter school in New Jersey.

A prizewinning geochemist, Claude Allégre, was appointed France's minister of national education, research, and technology in the new Socialist government of Prime Minister Lionel Jospin. For Allégre the demands of the job were already familiar, for he had served as Jospin's deputy when Jospin was minister of education in the early 1990s. In his new position Allégre hoped to give universities more autonomy, revamp student-aid programs, and improve recruiting at the elite institutions that trained most of France's senior civil servants.

A qualitative comparison of France's 95 universities ranked the Sorbonne at the bottom of the list because only 10% of its students finished the first stage of their studies. Among causes cited for the institution's decline were a lack of entrance examinations and a critical decrease in the funding of state schools. Observers noted that within the French population the Sorbonne's traditional sheen of prestige had become so badly tarnished that the university was currently held in high regard only by foreigners. The private Leonardo da Vinci University in Hauts-de-Seine, recently built with $260 million of local government money to accommodate 5,000 business and engineering students, had attracted only 590, and corporate support to cover operating costs did not materialize. Public university officials and students opposed development of the complex. They claimed that it took resources from the overcrowded public system.

Senior faculty members at the University of Oxford approved the establishment of a business school, whose construction in 1998–99 would be financed largely by a $34 million gift from Wafic Rida Said, a London-based Saudi Arabian businessman. Observers questioned the project because of Said's involvement in British arms sales. The School of Business at Britain's Loughborough University, aided by the Ford Motor Co., introduced a bachelor of science program in automotive management, advertising it as the world's first undergraduate degree for prospective car dealers.

Higher-education costs in the U.S. increased by 5% in 1997–98 at both public and private four-year colleges. The average tuition was $3,111 at public and $13,664 at private four-year colleges. Tuition increased 2% at two-year public colleges, reaching an average cost of $1,501. Private two-year colleges increased their rates 4% to reach an average cost of $6,855.

As another step toward educational autonomy, the Baltic nations of Estonia, Latvia, and Lithuania adopted further changes in higher education. Beginning in 1992, the use of the Russian language in universities was no longer required, as it had been in Soviet times. Instead, students were required to be fluent in their national language in order to graduate. Additional private colleges were established, and an increasing number of state universities charged fees for the first time, particularly for popular programs such as those in law, business, public relations, economics, and foreign languages. In Estonia 3,000 of the year's 8,800 first-year students paid to attend state or private institutions. Plans were laid for every Baltic institution to charge fees in all departments while at the same time providing some financial aid for the most needy and promising students. The three nations also established accreditation procedures designed to prevent the growth of low-quality private institutions.

The Thai government launched a $261 million program to stimulate the production of more engineers and scientists by means of improving teaching, curricula, and laboratories in 21 public universities. The program would be funded with $143 million from the World Bank, $104 million from the

Thai government, and $14 million from the Australian government.

In South Africa, Mamphela Aletta Ramphele, a physician and anthropologist, was installed as vice-chancellor of the University of Cape Town, the first black woman to hold that position in a South African university. She identified the university's mission as that of achieving "excellence with equity." In Japan, where only 10% of the nation's faculty members were women, Masako Niwa of Nara Women's University became the first woman president of a national university. During her period in office, she planned to nurture female scholars who would "produce results that rival men's."

To build the confidence of women students in their ability to excel in computer science, Sweden's northernmost postsecondary institution, the University of Luleá, established a program in computer studies designed exclusively for females. The program was intended to increase the number of women entering technical fields and help overcome the nation's chronic shortage of skilled professionals.

Australia's conservative government under Prime Minister John Howard announced an additional 1% reduction in funding for the country's 36 public universities, a cut to take effect in 2000 following the 5% reduction already scheduled for 1997–99. The measure was designed to help erase the federal deficit by lowering federal grants to universities by more than $900 million by 2001. The government also reduced support for the Australian Research Council by more than $50 million.

Afghanistan's Kabul University reopened in March after having been closed for six months by the Islamic fundamentalist Taliban militia. Because more than half of the university's teaching staff before the shutdown had been women, the conduct of classes upon the school's reopening was seriously crippled by the militia's ban against women's participating at the university as either students or teachers. UNICEF, which ceased all support of Afghanistan's educational establishments in 1995, continued to withhold funds because Taliban law failed to comply with the UN Convention on the Rights of the Child. In contrast, the Swedish Committee for Afghanistan continued to finance education for boys in the region.

In Argentina the University of Buenos Aires's open admissions policy, which entitles all high-school graduates to enter, swelled the enrollment of the Medical College to 18,000. In pressing for stricter admission requirements, the dean noted that a degree in medicine automatically licensed graduates to practice medicine anywhere in the nation. He implied that the quality of the nation's physicians could not be ensured under such enrollment conditions.

Officials curtailed student political activities in several countries. The South Korean government outlawed the nation's largest student organization, Hanchongryon, for having spearheaded nearly a week of antigovernment protests that resulted in two deaths and injuries to 175 participants. The student group not only called for the resignation of South Korea's Pres. Kim Young Sam but also espoused many of the demands of North Korea's communist government, especially the demand that the 37,000 U.S. troops in South Korea be removed.

At the Central University of Venezuela, a campus poll revealed that most students favoured a crackdown on the activists who engaged in periodic violent student protests over such economic conditions as increased bus fares. Stimulated by the poll results, university administrators authorized police to arrest violent demonstrators in the future.

Algerian security forces shot and killed three suspected guerrillas hiding in a dormitory at the University of Science and Technology in Bab Ezzouar, Algiers. Newspapers identified the three as members of an Islamic fundamentalist organization plotting to overthrow the government.

The University of Zambia was closed down for an indefinite period as the result of five days of student riots over the government's delay in paying textbook allowances. At the University of Lausanne, Switz., students ended a two-week strike after officials established a committee to study students' complaints about the government's 10% cut in university funds and about a law to strengthen the power of the university's elected rector. Street demonstrations for 106 consecutive days by students at the University of Belgrade, Yugos., led to the removal of the institution's rector, Dragutin Velickovic, who, the protesters claimed, was a political appointee, academically unqualified for the rectorship. Students throughout Germany went on strike in late November to protest chronic underfunding of higher education by the federal government.

Gender remained an issue in several colleges. In the wake of the U.S. Supreme Court ruling in 1996 that the Virginia Military Institute's all-male enrollment policy was unconstitutional, the Citadel, Charleston, S.C., announced that it would admit women cadets. This ended the all-male policy at the only two public institutions of higher education in the U.S. that did not admit women. In January 1997 the Citadel admitted 24 of 35 female applicants. Two of them left the school, however, alleging that they were victims of illegal hazing and sexual harassment.

(GERALD L. GUTEK; R. MURRAY THOMAS)

See also Libraries and Museums.

This article updates the *Macropædia* articles HISTORY OF EDUCATION; TEACHING.

The Shrinking Ph.D. Job Market

Since the 1980s the market for new Ph.D.'s to fill tenure-track positions in U.S. colleges and universities has decreased significantly. Despite this decrease, the production of new doctorates has increased. Between 1970 and 1993 the number of doctoral degrees awarded annually in the U.S. rose from 29,500 to 39,750. In 1970 approximately 75% of new Ph.D.'s had postgraduation commitments in higher education, either as faculty or in postdoctoral study; by 1993 only 61% had such commitments. According to a National Research Council (NRC) study, the prospects for finding full-time employment as faculty in higher education in 1997 were not bright. In 1970 more than 68% found teaching positions in higher education; since 1980 the figure has declined to a consistent 51%. Ph.D.'s in the social and behavioural sciences experienced the steepest drop in finding employment in higher education, down from 80% in 1970 to 53% in 1993. An exception to the general downward trend was engineering, where employment prospects and salaries remained high.

Despite predicted declines, overall enrollments in higher education remained stable throughout the 1980s and early 1990s. Since the 1970s, however, the general mood in higher education has been one of fiscal retrenchment. Funding decreases in state university systems have caused "downsizing" or "restructuring" in colleges and universities. Some institutions reduced the size of or eliminated whole departments. Some departments, with high percentages of tenured faculty at associate or full professor ranks and with little mobility among faculty, have not been able to hire full-time instructors or assistant professors. Many institutions, relying on attrition to reduce faculty ranks, have not replaced professors when vacancies occur. Between 1991 and 1995, for example, new faculty appointments at public institutions dropped 30%, while those at private institutions declined 12.1%. In addition to institutional retrenchment, the end of the Cold War caused reduced funding for federal government-sponsored research in science and technology, with the result that grants to institutions of higher learning were also reduced. Because of these general trends, the prospects for new hires of Ph.D.'s to fill faculty positions in higher education are severely limited.

While placement prospects for their new Ph.D.'s are discouraging, many graduate programs, in order to maintain their funding and faculty positions, have not reduced the number of students admitted to doctoral programs. Another tendency has been to increase the number of students from other countries in graduate programs. For example, in 1995, 43% of the graduate students in physics programs were not U.S. citizens. The general consequence is that the supply of new Ph.D.'s has outdistanced demand in higher education.

A result of the bleak employment prospects for new Ph.D.'s is what is called the "nomad" in higher education. With fewer tenure-track positions authorized, universities have resorted to using more part-time, nontenured instructors. Nomads are Ph.D.'s who, while searching for full-time positions, move from institution to institution as part-time, non-tenure-track instructors. They receive low pay and few, if any, benefits.

These trends subject the new Ph.D.'s to job searches that are often long and frustrating. They contribute to the underemployment of the nation's most highly educated.

(GERALD LEE GUTEK)

The Environment

INTERNATIONAL ACTIVITIES

United Nations. Earth Summit + 5, a special session of the UN General Assembly, was held in New York City on June 26, 1997, to commemorate the fifth anniversary of the UN Conference on Environment and Development in Rio de Janeiro (more commonly known as the Earth, or Rio, Summit). The conference leader, Malaysian UN Ambassador Ismail Razali, opened the proceedings on a pessimistic note, describing the progress made on environmental problems since the 1992 summit as "paltry."

The session was dominated by public pressure on the United States to join the European Union (EU) in setting specific targets and dates for cutting greenhouse gas emissions, which had continued to rise despite a voluntary agreement among developed countries to reduce emissions to 1990 levels by 2000. Razali also pointed out that ocean fish stocks continued to be depleted and that there had been no progress in curbing deforestation and desertification. He added that the scope of the Global Environment Facility (GEF), an international fund designed to support in less-developed countries environmental projects that would have worldwide benefits, remained too limited to have much effect on these and other environmental problems, in large part because of sharp decreases in aid from rich countries.

Although leaders from the world's major economies addressed participants, the summit ended without agreement on its primary goal—a political statement indicating how the Rio objectives might be met. Instead, the summit became mired in extended negotiations as participants debated the details of a program for implementing Agenda 21, a blueprint for sustainable development drafted during the Rio Summit. Razali called the results "sobering." Environmentalists were even more disappointed, but UN officials claimed that some progress had been made, citing agreements on the universal phaseout of lead in gasoline and global strategies to conserve freshwater and forests.

United Nations Environment Programme. At the annual meeting of the governing council of the United Nations Environment Programme (UNEP), held in Nairobi, Kenya, in February, industrialized countries sharply disagreed with less-developed nations over the agency's purpose. The U.S. and the EU wanted UNEP's permanent representatives, a board composed of diplomats stationed in Nairobi, to relinquish their control of the organization to U.S. and EU representatives, charging that the agency had lost sight of its main task—translating the findings of scientific bodies into policy proposals—in its efforts to oversee local projects in such areas as soil conservation, pest control, and the provision of clean water. Great Britain and the U.S. refused to pay their 1997 subscriptions after several Asian countries blocked the formation of a task force in charge of devising reforms.

World Health Organization. In May the World Health Organization (WHO) published the results of an assessment of 12 toxic organic pollutants conducted by the International Programme on Chemical Safety. The report found sufficient evidence to warrant international action to reduce or -eliminate the discharge of the following chemicals: polychlorinated biphenyls (PCBs), dioxins, furans, aldrin, dieldrin, dichlorodiphenyltrichloroethane (DDT), endrin, chlordane, hexachlorobenzene (HCB), mirex, toxaphene, and heptachlor. All can be transported long distances from their source via air and water.

World Bank. On June 5 the World Bank issued its Green Top 10 Plan, a list of proposed actions to address the world's most pressing environmental problems. The plan pointed out that worldwide energy-related subsidies, amounting to $800 billion annually, rarely benefited the poor and inevitably harmed the environment. According to the authors, carbon dioxide emissions had increased by nearly 25% since the Rio Summit in 1992, and 1.3 billion people were still affected by polluted air. Among the proposed actions were the global phaseout of leaded gasoline and a reduction in the manufacture and use of chlorofluorocarbons (CFCs). The plan also supported the practice of trading greenhouse gas emissions, in which countries that are unable to meet their greenhouse-gas-reduction targets could buy permission to exceed their targets from countries whose emissions were below the established standards.

United Nations Framework Convention on Climate Change. Despite a year of preparatory meetings, signatories to the United Nations Framework Convention on Climate Change entered their December 1997 meeting in Kyoto, Japan, with disagreements, although their differences seemed to be narrowing. The U.S. proposed a scheme to base greenhouse gas reductions on a scale known as Global Warming Potential (GWP), which ranks greenhouse gases according to their levels of destructiveness. (The GWP of carbon dioxide, for example, is 1, compared with a ranking of 11 for methane.) Rather than reduce its carbon dioxide emissions, for example, a country might substitute reductions in methane emissions from its coal mines or curtail its CFC production. Countries also might be allowed to "bank" or "borrow" "credits" years in advance, or they could trade reduction quotas and gain credits by investing in reductions in other countries.

Under a policy known as "differentiation," the U.S. asked for commitments from less-developed countries to reduce greenhouse gas emissions with the proviso that their reductions would be smaller than those of developed nations. The proposal was made in response to a plan agreed to at the Rio Summit that set emissions targets for developed countries but allowed less-developed countries to increase their emissions for several years. The U.S. feared that this policy would drive industries to relocate in countries with less-stringent standards. This differentiation proposal was rejected by China, the EU, the Alliance of Small Island

Dense smoke from forest fires severely reduced road visibility in Indonesia in September and October. The haze presented a major health risk to Southeast Asia as it spread across the region.

JASON REED—REUTERS

States (AoSIS), and some environmental groups. The EU offered to cut its greenhouse gas emissions by 15% by 2010, provided that the U.S. and Japan did so too.

In June The Netherlands, on behalf of the EU, proposed an amendment to the convention that would allow the climate-change treaty to be adopted by a 75–25 majority if achieving consensus proved to be impossible. This proviso would prevent OPEC members and their supporters, the G-77 group of less-developed countries, and some U.S. lobby groups from blocking the signing of the treaty unless it provided them with compensation for lost revenues due to decreased use of fossil fuels.

On July 28 Robert Hill, Australia's environment minister, said his government remained opposed to the EU plan for uniform reduction targets. The next day Warwick Parer, the country's resources and energy minister, added that Australia would accept measures to combat global warming only if the costs of those measures were shared by other countries. Parer emphasized that the government would not accept measures adversely affecting economic growth.

In Japan disagreement between the Environment Agency and the Ministry of Trade and Industry (MITI) delayed the formulation of the nation's greenhouse-gas-reduction policy. MITI favoured per capita reductions, while the Environment Agency preferred a flat-rate cut of more than 5%. Later, in late September, MITI proposed a plan to reduce carbon dioxide emissions to 1990 levels by 2010. The plan called for doubling nuclear-power production and increasing solar power and other alternative energy sources. At the last moment, Japan acceded to the higher—6%—figure for emissions cutbacks.

The treaty, renamed the Kyoto Protocol, was signed on December 11. It committed the industrialized countries to reducing emissions of six gases by an average of 5.2% (below 1990 levels) by 2012. Ratification was to begin in March 1998 and was expected to be rocky in some countries, including Canada and the U.S.

Montreal Protocol on Substances That Deplete the Ozone Layer. Representatives from more than 100 signatory countries met in Montreal in September to celebrate the 10th anniversary of the signing of the Montreal Protocol on Substances That Deplete the Ozone Layer and to discuss ways of improving it. Some of the most important proposals focused on CFCs. Participating nations sought to discourage the illegal trade in CFCs and to seek alternatives to their use in medical products, including asthma inhalers. Governments agreed to adopt a licensing system for the transport of CFCs and to review their procedures for ensuring compliance with the regulations. The decision would give greater power to police and customs officials to intercept cargoes. Participants also agreed to ban most uses of the ozone-depleting pesticide methyl bromide by 2005 in developed countries and by 2015 in less-developed countries. Poorer nations would have access to a fund of $18 million to help farmers convert to alternatives.

International Atomic Energy Agency. On September 5 the 62 member nations of the International Atomic Energy Agency (IAEA) agreed to rules on the handling of nuclear waste and spent fuel. The agreement was formally signed at the IAEA's annual conference in Vienna on September 29.

Ospar Convention. The 12 nations and EU signatories to the Ospar Convention (formerly the Oslo and Paris commissions) convened at an April 14 meeting in The Hague. Representatives from The Netherlands proposed that all defunct steel oil-drilling platforms in less than 150 m (1 m=3.28 ft) of water in the North Sea be removed in their entirety and disposed of onshore. Previously, platforms that weighed more than 4,000 tons and stood in more than 75 m of water could either be sunk or be left floating partially dismantled. British oil companies said the new rule would reduce the number of platforms that could be disposed of on the seafloor from 110 to 8.

On September 2 the signatories of the convention met in Brussels to debate ways to eliminate pollution in the North Sea and northeastern Atlantic Ocean. British Environment Minister Michael Meacher announced that Britain would reverse its previous policy and join the ban on dumping low- and intermediate-level radioactive waste into the Atlantic. Britain also agreed to a virtual halt of the country's discharge of harmful chemicals into the ocean by 2020.

Marpol Convention. At a September 26 meeting in London of parties to the International Convention for the Prevention of Pollution from Ships (MARPOL), the 75 shipping nations belonging to the International Maritime Organization agreed to reduce air pollution from ships by setting a cap of 4.5% on the amount of sulfur permitted in marine fuel oil. This amount was higher than the current 3% average. It was agreed, however, to set lower sulfur limits in designated areas, including the Baltic Sea, where concentrations were limited to 1.5%.

Antarctica and the Arctic. On April 18 the U.S. became the 24th country to ratify the Antarctic Environment Protocol. In Japan and Russia the necessary legislation for signing the document was still pending.

State of the Arctic Environment, a study compiled by 400 scientists from the eight member nations of the Arctic Council, was released in early June at a science symposium at Tromsø, Nor. The authors revealed that concentrations of PCBs, DDT, lindane, and other pesticides from Siberian rivers flowing into the Arctic Ocean were much higher than those in North American and Scandinavian rivers. The main sources of Arctic contamination were said to be the Ob, Yenisey, and Pechora rivers. Although DDT had not been manufactured in Russia since the 1980s, farmers continued to use old stocks to control insect plagues. PCBs were thought to be leaking from ships or from sites on land.

According to the report, the pollutants are carried by winds and ocean currents into the Arctic environment, where they become concentrated in organisms high on the food chain, including humans. One Greenlander in six, for example, was found to have potentially harmful blood levels of mercury, mostly acquired from eating whale and seal meat, and reindeer herders were absorbing radiation doses much higher than those of people in the south, mostly because of persistent fallout from atmospheric testing of nuclear weapons in the 1950s and early 1960s. Later in June the council met at Alta, Nor., to call for a global agreement that would reduce discharges of toxic chemicals.

NATIONAL DEVELOPMENTS

Under the direction of France's new prime minister, Lionel Jospin, the Superphénix nuclear fast-breeder reactor was closed, and the project to widen the Rhine-Rhone Canal was canceled. On February 27 thousands of antinuclear activists began staging a series of demonstrations intended to disrupt the transport of a load of spent reactor fuel from a nuclear power plant in Bavaria to a storage facility at Gorleben, Ger., located 95 km from Hamburg, Ger. (1 km=0.62 mi). Protesters blocked roads and bridges, disrupted traffic signals, temporarily halted trains by throwing grappling hooks onto overhead power lines, and set fire to roads, barricades, and railroad crossings. In what was said to be the largest police deployment since World War II, 30 border-police helicopters and 30,000 police equipped with armoured cars and water cannons were enlisted to guard the cargo, which reached Gorleben on March 6. On September 20 about 500 demonstrators clashed with police near the Krummel nuclear power plant just outside Hamburg. About 250 protesters, demonstrating against the export of spent fuel to other countries for reprocessing, barricaded a rail line and set the barricade on fire.

On the morning of March 11, fire broke out at a nuclear-waste-handling-and-reprocessing plant owned by the state-run Power Reactor and Nuclear Fuel Development Corp. (known as Donen) at Tokai, 115 km northeast of Tokyo. The blaze occurred in a building where low-level waste was mixed with asphalt and then sealed in drums. It was quickly extinguished, but worker carelessness was believed to have created conditions in which volatile asphalt gases accumulated. Ten hours later they caught fire, causing an explosion that blew out a shutter at the entrance, shattered windows, and released smoke. At least 10 of the 50 workers at the plant were reported to have received very small radiation doses in the first fire, and another 27 were exposed in the second blaze. According to officials, 36 minutes after the second fire started, one of the 12 monitoring stations in the 100-ha (1 ha=2.47 ac) compound recorded a small radiation abnormality, but by 9 PM the reading had returned to normal. Scientists at a meteorological station 55 km southwest of the plant, however, reported that cesium levels 10 times above normal had been detected at the station on March 11 and 12.

On March 18 a ship carrying 20 tons of nuclear waste docked at the fishing town of Rokkasho, 565 km northwest of Tokyo. The cargo, taken from the French reprocessing plant at Cap de la Hague, had left France on January 14. The ship was met by about 300 protesters, some of whom chained themselves to gates. Police cleared 50 people who were sitting at the dock gates blocking the road. No arrests were made. The waste was unloaded and taken to a facility outside the town, where it was held until a permanent storage site could be found.

Shortly before midnight on January 8 in the Mughalpura district of Lahore, Pak., a flatbed truck carrying more than 30 poorly sealed cylinders of what officials said was probably chlorine slid into a ditch. Two of the containers leaked, and the resulting toxic cloud killed at least 20 people and injured hundreds more. Nearly 1,000 people had to be evacuated from the area.

Because of declining revenues and membership, Greenpeace USA announced in September that it had closed all 10 of its regional city offices and would concentrate its operations in the organization's Washington, D.C., headquarters. Greenpeace spokespeople attributed the cutbacks to a drop in annual fund-raising. Revenues had fallen from $45 million in 1991 to $25 million in 1997, and the organization had been left with a deficit of $2.6 million. During that same time period, membership also had fallen from 1.2 million to fewer than 400,000.

ENVIRONMENTAL ISSUES

Air Pollution. The worst episode of air pollution in half a century unfolded in mid-September as photochemical smog and a pall of smoke from forest fires settled over parts of Malaysia, Singapore, Brunei, and Indonesia and also spread, although less severely, to Thailand, Hong Kong, and the Philippines. On September 19 officials declared a state of emergency in the state of Sarawak, a major tourist area in the Malaysian part of Borneo, and in adjacent Kalimantan, the Indonesian part of Borneo. At one point Indonesian authorities considered evacuating the city of Rengat, Sumatra, but a change of wind brought some improvement. On October 3 smoke enveloped Jakarta.

Throughout the disaster, officials routinely recorded off-the-chart pollution levels. The Air Pollution Index used in Malaysia (which is slightly different from the one used in the U.S.) registers levels of pollution on a scale of 0–500. A score of more than 500 connotes an "extreme health risk." When the level in Kuching, the capital of Sarawak, reached 635, the authorities closed the airport, ordered schools and shops to close, and advised the 1.9 million residents to stay in their homes. On September 23 the level reached 839. This may have been the highest pollution level ever recorded anywhere in the world. On September 29 heavy rains and a change in the wind direction brought a sharp drop in the Air Pollution Index in Borneo and Malaysia.

By early October, however, four people in Indonesia had died and at least 32,000 had been treated for smoke inhalation. In the worst areas the effect was said to have been the equivalent of smoking 80 cigarettes a day. In Jambi, Sumatra, where fires surrounded the city and smoke alarms had to be turned off to prevent their constant ringing, visibility was never more than 90 m and sometimes as little as 15 m. There, as in many places, drivers were forced to use headlights in the middle of the day. An Indonesian airliner crashed in September near the Sumatran city of Medan in an area clouded by smoke; all 234 persons aboard were killed.

In Kuala Lumpur, Malaysia, the U.S. embassy permitted about 75 staff members and their dependents to leave, although flights were canceled because of poor visibility. In Irian Jaya, the Indonesian half of New Guinea, smoke prevented aircraft from delivering supplies to remote villages where drought had withered crops and dried up rivers. At least 275 villagers died of starvation or waterborne diseases.

Contributing to the degraded air quality was smog created by industrial and traffic emissions in Malaysia, where economic development had been rapid but environmental controls lax. The principal cause, however, was smoke from fires burning in the forests of Indonesia. The blaze was so intense that even underlying peat beds up to nine metres deep also caught fire. Smoke levels in Kalimantan were reported at 7.5 mg per cu m, far exceeding the century's previous record of 4.6 mg per cu m measured during the London smog of 1952, in which 4,000 people died.

Early in September, President Suharto of Indonesia banned the use of fire to clear forests on land destined for conversion to plantation forest or farms, and during the emergency he twice apologized to Malaysia and Singapore for the problems the fires were causing. Despite their devastating effects, more fires continued to be lit, even after the official ban. On September 15 Indonesian Environment Minister Sarwono Kusumaatmadja said at least 300,000 ha had been burned, but Michael Rae of the Australian office of the World Wide Fund for Nature claimed that 485,000–610,000 ha had been incinerated. Conditions were exacerbated by an unusually severe El Niño that caused the worst drought in 50 years. Fires spread out of control in Sumatra, Kalimantan, Java, and Sulawesi. On September 30, forest fires also were reported in Malaysia, affecting 405 ha near Kuantan, 195 km east of Kuala Lumpur.

The bow of the Russian oil tanker *Nakhodka* lies upturned on rocks near Mikuni, Japan. The tanker broke apart during a storm on January 2 while en route from Shanghai to power stations in the Kamchatka Peninsula and spilled an estimated 4.5 million litres of heavy fuel oil into the Sea of Japan. More than 40,000 local volunteers participated in the cleanup, which was completed in late April.

GAMMA LIAISON TOKYO

On September 30, after two weeks of sunshine and no wind, smog pollution in Paris reached stage 3, the highest level on the EU Air Pollution Index. Cars with even-numbered plates were banned from entering the city; speed limits were reduced and strictly enforced; free public transportation was offered; and pupils were told to remain indoors during their breaks. It was the first time such measures had been imposed in Paris. The restrictions were lifted on October 2 after a change in the weather brought an improvement in air quality.

In late June U.S. Pres. Bill Clinton approved new Ambient Air Quality Standards. Under the new regulations, the 24-hour permitted standard for PM2.5 (particles up to 2.5 micrometres in diameter) was set at 65 micrograms per cubic metre of air. Carol Browner, administrator of the Environmental Protection Agency (EPA), said it would take up to five years to establish a monitoring network for PM2.5. In addition, factories that continued to exceed acceptable levels of ozone emissions after their fourth citation would be fined. Municipalities, however, would not have to comply with the new rules for at least seven or eight years.

Following Clinton's approval of the new air-quality standards, a U.S. House of Representatives appropriations subcommittee added $40 million to the $45 million the administration had requested for research into the effects of ozone and particulate matter in 1998. The subcommittee called for the National Institute of Environmental Health to help distribute the money.

Ozone Layer. In September the Environmental Investigation Agency, based in London, reported that between 6,000 and 20,000 tons of ozone-depleting CFCs were being smuggled into the EU each year from factories in Russia and China, often through Britain. Illegal traffickers exploited a loophole in regulations governing the trade in CFCs. Although the manufacture and use of new CFCs were prohibited in developed

(continued on page 210)

SPECIAL REPORT

Coral Reefs: The Forgotten Rain Forests of the Sea

by Clive R. Wilkinson

Because they harbour great concentrations of biodiversity, coral reefs have been called the rain forests of the sea. With hundreds of species of corals and fishes frequently found on a single reef, metre for metre these undersea ecosystems may even exceed tropical rain forests as the most species-rich places on Earth. Ironically, however, reefs have been far less studied—until now. In 1992 scientists at the seventh International Coral Reef Symposium in Guam raised a global alarm. They estimated that 10% of the world's coral reefs were effectively lost, an additional 30% were under immediate threat, and another 30% could be destroyed by 2050. To focus the world's attention on the plight of coral reefs, governments, organizations, and individuals around the world have recognized 1997 as the International Year of the Reef (IYOR).

Even the most concerned researchers agree that coral reefs are remarkably resilient, having withstood such massive forces as periodic temperature fluctuations, ice ages, volcanic eruptions, tropical storms, and flooding for about 35 million years. Recent evidence, however, suggests that while reefs have survived the assaults of nature, they may be succumbing to an unrelenting barrage of human-induced stresses. Steady increases in sediment runoff onto reefs; excessive mining of coral sand and rock for building; increases in pollution, particularly from agriculture and domestic sewage; and chronic overexploitation of reef resources have resulted in widespread reef damage and, in some cases, ecological collapse. The most endangered reefs are located along some of the world's most heavily populated coastlines—Asia, East Africa, and the Caribbean, including the Florida Keys.

Among the most alarming threats to reefs is the increase in destructive fishing practices. The poison cyanide, for example, was being used routinely in the capture of fish for the live fish trade, a billion-dollar business that supplies seafood to Chinese restaurants in Hong Kong and nearby regions, as well as to Taiwan and Singapore. Fishermen liberally douse the reefs with cyanide in concentrations that temporarily stun large fish but indiscriminately kill smaller animals, including the corals themselves. The use of toxins, however, accounts for only part of the damage. With the help of compressed air, fishermen now can dive as deep as 40 m (130 ft), where they are able to flush dazed escapees from reef crevices by demolishing the fishes' refuges with crowbars.

Even more devastating is the wholesale harvesting of fish during critical spawning periods. Particularly targeted are coral trout and other groupers (family Serranidae) and the spectacular humphead wrasse (*Chelinus undulatus*). Once or twice each year, fish from all parts of the reef congregate at a single location, usually a place swept by ocean currents so that their larvae are washed away from the reef's plankton eaters, including the corals, into the relative safety of the open ocean. Intent on spawning and therefore less cautious than normal, the fish are vulnerable to unscrupulous fishermen, who can wipe out all the breeding species on a reef within hours.

Studies conducted on reefs off the coasts of places as far apart as Jamaica, southern Japan, and Kenya have shown that eliminating these large fish can have disastrous consequences. Large fish serve as beneficial grazers, helping to check the growth of algae that threatens to smother the corals. In addition, without a diverse army of fish predators, populations of other marine organisms explode, including sea urchins that wreak havoc by grazing everything in their path, even juvenile corals, and the rampaging crown-of-thorns starfish (*Acanthaster planci*), the scourge of coral colonies throughout the Indo-Pacific.

The effects of black-band disease on brain coral are pictured at left. Caused by blue-green algae, black-band disease kills coral tissue while advancing in a band around the coral and leaving the white coral skeleton behind. Some researchers suspect that rising ocean temperatures and other stresses such as pollution may be causing corals to lose their resistance to once-minor ailments. In the last decade, scientists have also documented new coral diseases.

NORBERT WU

Coral reefs also may be suffering from less-direct, but no-less-damaging, forces. Many scientists suspect that rising ocean temperatures due to global warming are compounding the extent and severity of coral bleaching. Increases in temperature of only one or two degrees can stress corals, causing them to expel the symbiotic algae known as zooxanthellae that they harbour in their stomach cells. The algae not only give corals their brilliant colours (without them corals appear white or "bleached") but also supply them with the surplus energy and nutrients they need to build reefs. Satellite images, especially of the Caribbean and parts of the Pacific, show distinct correlations between large areas of bleaching and increased sea-surface temperatures. In time and under optimal conditions, reefs can recover. Scientists, however, have documented an alarming reef mortality.

Some researchers suspect that these rising temperatures and other stresses such as pollution may be causing corals to lose their resistance to once-minor ailments. In the last decade alone, scientists have documented about eight new diseases of corals. Even very large, century-old corals appear to be succumbing to these previously unknown maladies.

In 1993 concerned scientists realized that it would be necessary to involve the public, particularly communities dependent on reef resources, in rescuing the reefs. In 1994 small-island nations met in Barbados to discuss their concerns about reef destruction and rising sea levels. Many of these countries have few resources other than coral reefs; some are built on coral islands only a few metres above the surrounding reefs. Together they formed the International Coral Reef Initiative, a global effort that has drawn the world's attention to the plight of coral reefs and spawned numerous other monitoring and management initiatives, including the Global Coral Reef Monitoring Network. In one of the projects sponsored by the network, leading coral-reef scientists train personnel in government natural-resource agencies and universities in the basic methods of assessing the health of corals and reef-fish populations.

To highlight reef issues and challenges further, Robert Ginsburg of the University of Miami, Fla., proposed that 1997 be designated the International Year of the Reef. Among the hands-on projects launched under IYOR auspices was Reef Check, coordinated by Gregor Hodgson of the Hong Kong University of Science and Technology. Between June and August hundreds of scientists and recreational divers measured indicators of human activities on 300 reefs in 30 countries. This first global survey of the human impact on coral reefs provided valuable data on reef damage due to blast or cyanide fishing, overharvesting of marine organisms, and boat and anchor collisions.

Preliminary results from the Reef Check reconnaissance were announced at a press conference in Hong Kong on October 16. The report confirmed what recreational divers had been reporting for several years—coral reefs were being abused by people throughout the world. The data showed that although some pristine reefs were found, few were in excellent condition. Even the most remote reefs had been heavily fished for sharks, lobsters, giant clams, and, most troubling, large predator fish such as grouper and snapper. In many of the reefs surveyed in Southeast Asia, these marketable species were completely absent.

IYOR also targeted children by means of interactive educational activities. Coral reef scientists, for example, prepared teaching kits for primary and secondary schools. Children learned about coral reef values and problems through painting, writing, song, and dance competitions. Even a new computer game entitled Murder Under the Microscope was developed, in which players solved problems of reef degradation by enlisting the input of stakeholders in decision making and management of reef resources.

The World Bank helped promote coral reef education and awareness by producing and distributing an award-winning hour-long video, *The Fragile Ring of Life.* The documentary explored reef problems through the eyes of some of the millions of people whose livelihoods depend on ecologically healthy marine environments. Finding solutions will not be easy, but as Charles Birkeland of the University of Guam's Marine Laboratory observed, people "need to develop a new paradigm for the exploitation of coral reefs, a new perspective that might also be a framework for our management of the Earth as a whole."

Clive R. Wilkinson is coordinator of the Global Coral Reef Monitoring Network at the Australian Institute of Marine Science, Townsville, Queen., Australia.

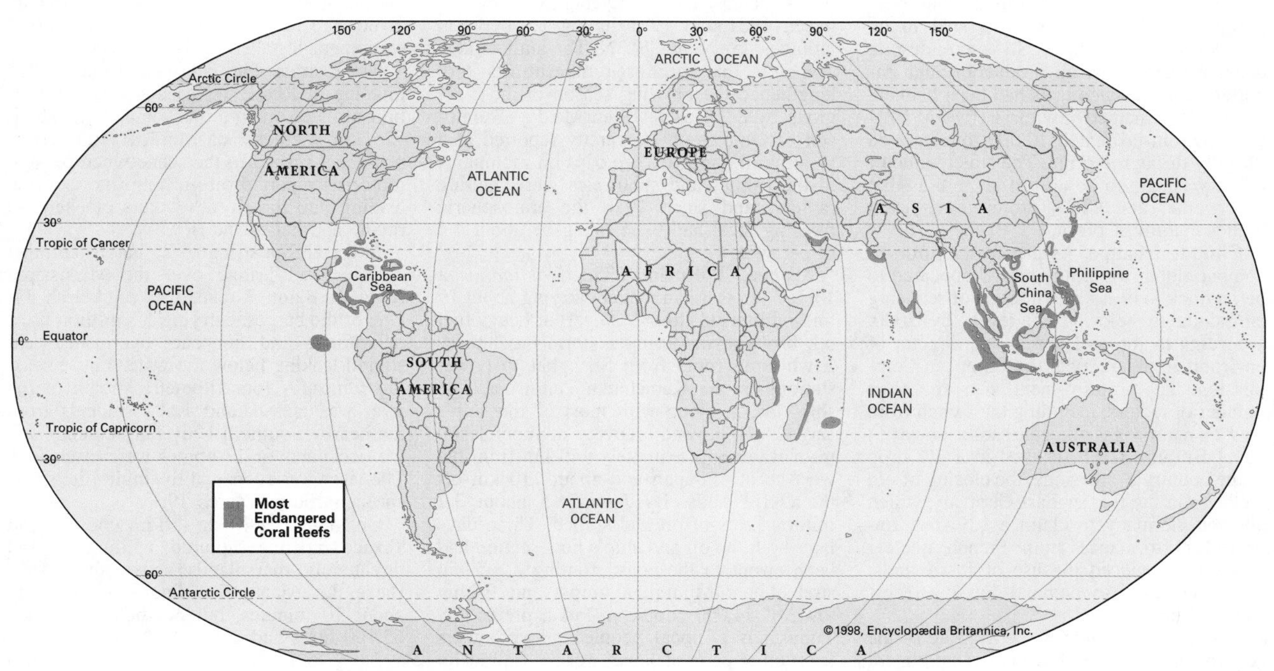

MICHAEL PROBST—ASSOCIATED PRESS

As a smoke grenade explodes, a police officer chases demonstrators near Dannenberg, Ger. For five days in early March, 30,000 policemen battled thousands of protesters who were trying to block delivery of a shipment of nuclear-waste containers to a storage depot in Lower Saxony.

(continued from page 207)
countries, the new chemicals could be imported by these countries provided they were reexported to less-developed countries. Once the chemicals were imported, however, illegal traders often altered their documentation, misrepresenting the new CFCs as reclaimed or recycled chemicals that could be legally sold in developed countries. Smuggling of CFCs also was said to be highly profitable in the U.S., where, despite the fact that almost all production and importation of the chemicals had been banned, their sale remained lawful. Between 1994 and 1996 an estimated 10,000 tons entered illegally through Florida. The street value of CFCs was said to be almost as high as that of cocaine, and CFCs promised an even higher margin of profit.

Climate Change. As part of the effort to combat global warming, the EU appeared to be on track to beat its own target of reducing emissions to below 1990 levels by 2000, according to Jorgen Henningsen, director of environmental quality at the European Commission. The improvement was due to a number of factors, including the switch from coal to natural gas for generating power in Great Britain, which resulted in a 6% drop in the country's emissions; the closing of old factories in the former East Germany, which allowed Germany to claim a 12% cut; improved performance from French nuclear plants that reduced the use of fossil fuels; and reduced energy demand due to a recession in Europe.

A study by William K. de la Mare of the Australian Antarctic Division, Department of the Environment, Sport, and Territories, revealed that the mass of Antarctic sea ice remained constant from 1931 to the mid-1950s and then decreased by about 25% between the mid-1950s and the early 1970s. Since then, sea-ice levels had stabilized.

According to a report released in April, satellite evidence indicated that photosynthesis increased by an average of 10% between 1981 and 1991 in regions between latitudes 45° N and 70° N. The authors also revealed that higher temperatures had lengthened the growing season in those regions by 8–16 days. Ellen Mosley-Thompson of Ohio State University reported at a meeting in April that ice caps on mountains in the tropics and subtropics were melting rapidly, and since 1970 the atmospheric freezing level had been rising by about 4.5 m per year.

Marine Pollution. The *Nakhodka,* a 13,157-ton Russian tanker carrying about 19 million litres (1 litre=0.26 gal) of heavy fuel oil, broke apart during a storm on January 2 while en route from Shanghai to power stations in the Kamchatka Peninsula. The ship's stern, along with most of the ship's cargo, sank beyond recovery in about 1,700 m of water approximately 145 km from the west coast of Japan and about 110 km off the Oki Islands. By January 5 about 3.7 million litres of oil had spilled. Three days later both the oil and ship's bow section had been swept to the coast, fouling a 1.5 km stretch near Mikuni, a tourist and fishing town of 24,000 people in Fukui prefecture. Thousands of local people and volunteers from other parts of Japan worked frantically to clean up the slick with shovels and buckets. By January 29 the bow of the tanker, fragile and filled with oil, rested on rocks near Mikuni, spilling an estimated 4.5 million litres of oil that fouled 800 km of coast. The cleanup was completed on April 27, when more than 40,000 local volunteers participated in a one-day "beach recovery."

On February 8 the Panamanian-registered tanker *San Jorge* ran aground off the coast of Uruguay, releasing an oil slick some 32 km long. Despite attempts to disperse the oil sheet into smaller patches with chemical agents, beaches near José Ignacio and Punta del Este were contaminated.

On August 17 four Greenpeace activists were arrested after having spent a week occupying British Petroleum's (BP's) *Stene Dee* oil rig as it was being towed to the Foinaven field, 180 km west of the Shetland Islands in an area known as the Atlantic Frontier. Later an Edinburgh court froze all Greenpeace UK bank accounts, issued a writ for £1.4 million, and indicted four of the protesters for losses incurred by delays due to the Greenpeace action. After two days BP withdrew its claim and its charges against three of the activists on the condition that Greenpeace cease to harass its operations throughout the Atlantic Frontier. Greenpeace refused. The organization's spokesman, however, suggested that Greenpeace might shift its attention to Schiehallion, the other major oil field in the area.

In July French Environment Minister Dominique Voynet issued a precautionary ban on bathing and fishing in the waters off a public beach near the Cap de la Hague nuclear reprocessing plant in Normandy. The action followed a controversy earlier in the year after seawater and sediment samples that Greenpeace activists collected from the end of one of the plant's waste pipes showed 300 microsieverts of radioactivity escaping every hour. Greenpeace retested the outflow in June and measured 155 million Bq (becquerels) of radioactivity per litre of water, compared with a natural level of 10–20 Bq per litre. There was widespread criticism of Cogema, the company operating the plant, when it was learned that Cogema divers had removed underwater monitoring equipment installed by Greenpeace.

Freshwater. On February 16 a broken pipeline in Russia released nearly 1.3 million litres of oil into the Volga River, about 725 km southeast of Moscow. Emergency personnel rushed to the scene when passing motorists reported oil gushing into a ravine leading into the river. Workers blocked the ravine and halted the flow.

In the U.S. a string of 25 barges collided with a road bridge over the Mississippi River at Baton Rouge, La., on March 17. One of the barges, carrying 1.5 million litres of toluene and benzene, overturned and started leaking below the water line, releasing fumes. A four-kilometre stretch of the river was closed, and 1,600 students from the nearby Southern University campus and the occupants of 17 homes were evacuated. The river was reopened to single-file, slow-speed traffic on March 19.

On May 16 a 40-cm (16-in) underground Texaco pipeline ruptured, spilling oil and threatening marshlands surrounding Lake Barre, Louisiana. The line was sealed in about 10 minutes, but not before 40,000–65,000 litres had escaped.

(MICHAEL ALLABY)

WILDLIFE CONSERVATION

Despite numerous conservation efforts in 1997, evidence pointed to a continued decline in almost all species worldwide. The 1996 Red List of Threatened Animals issued by the International Union for Conservation of Nature and Natural Resources identified 5,205 species in danger of extinction. In tropical forests alone, for example, biologists estimated that three species were being extinguished every hour.

Much of the decline was caused by habitat destruction, especially logging. Only 6% of the Earth's forests were formally protected, which left the remaining 33.6 million sq km (13 million sq mi) vulnerable to exploitation. A study in Africa conducted by the Rainforest Foundation, for example, revealed that most of the forested lands in Cameroon, the Republic of the Congo (Congo [Brazzaville]), and Gabon, including those in conservation areas, had been parceled out to logging firms. In Congo (Brazzaville) a logging concession had been granted along the boundaries of the Nouabale-Ndoki Reserve, one of the last refuges of the bongo (*Tragelaphus euryceros*). In addition to damaging habitat, logging encouraged a trade in bush meat to feed workers in boom towns around sawmills.

Despite these setbacks, critical habitat was reserved in many other parts of the world. In January the Bastak Nature Reserve was declared to protect 910 sq km (350 sq mi) of forest in the Jewish Autonomous Region of the Russian Far East. Other newly established conservation areas included the Hawar Islands in Bahrain, breeding site for the world's largest colony of Socotra cormorants (*Phalacrocorax nigrogularis*), and the Masoala National Park in Madagascar. In January Laos and Vietnam agreed to protect the Northern Truong Son mountain range, home to many new and endangered species, including a new species of muntjac deer found in April.

Scientists reported the discovery of new species in other parts of the world as well, including a tree rat (*Isothrix sinnamariensis*) in French Guiana, the phantom frog (*Eleutherodactylus phasma*) in Costa Rica, and in Brazil a brocket deer (*Mazama bororo*) from the Atlantic rain forest. On the basis of a skull found on Robinson Crusoe Island, Chile, cetologists were able to describe a new species of whale known as the Bahamonde's beaked whale (*Mesoplodon bahamondi*). Scientists also made several important rediscoveries of animals not seen for several decades, including the Borneo river shark (Glyphis species B), previously known only from a specimen taken from an unidentified river in Borneo more than 100 years ago. Taiwan's largest protected animal, the Formosan black bear (*Ursus thibetanus formosanus*), was sighted in Yushan National Park for the first time in 50 years. In Vietnam the orange-necked partridge (*Arborophila davidi*), known only from a single specimen collected in 1927, was rediscovered.

Overexploitation also continued to take its toll on many wild species. Shark populations suffered from the unregulated trade in their fins, cartilage, and liver oil. In some waters the overfishing was so severe that it resulted in the collapse of commercial fisheries, localized species' extinctions, and major disruptions of marine ecosystems. In the absence of aggressive policing, snow leopards (*Panthera uncia*) came under further pressure from poachers, who supplied their bones to the Chinese traditional-medicine trade. The damage to leopard populations was compounded by human encroachment on their habitat as new Chinese settlers joined the millions of others who in the last two decades had relocated in Tibet, the heart of the leopard's territory.

Populations of wild species sustained further damage from such human activities as fishing and farming. A French company was granted a concession to develop 50 ha (125 ac) of fish ponds that would destroy the grasslands that provide forage and display areas for the globally threatened green peafowl (*Pavo muticus*) in Cat Tien National Park, Vietnam. Despite an official ban, industrial fishing fleets from mainland Ecuador, the United States, and the Far East exploited the Galápagos Marine Reserve. Fishermen were implicated in the deaths of hundreds of cetaceans washed ashore by storms on the Atlantic coast of the Bay of Biscay in February and March. More than 74% of the animals showed injuries consistent with being trapped in fishing nets.

Depletion of fish stocks due to commercial overfishing and the effects of climate change forced Magellanic penguins (*Spheniscus magellanicus*) in Argentina's Punta Tombo Reserve to forage record distances. Many animals spent up to three weeks traveling and covered distances of more than 480 km (300 mi) to find food. In Tanzania there was concern that the rise in ostrich farming had led to a decline in populations of wild ostrich (*Struthio camelus massaicus*) after breeders removed young ostriches and eggs from the wild and exported them as farm-bred. Wildlife biologists, on the other hand, successfully reestablished ostriches in the 2,200-sq km (850-sq mi) Mahazat as-Sayd Protected Area in central Saudi Arabia. The hatching of several chicks in February and March marked the first successful breeding by free-ranging ostriches in the Arabian Peninsula since the extinction of the Arabian ostrich in the 1950s.

Scientists continued to investigate the links between pollution and animal abnormalities. Studies found that concentrations of polychlorinated biphenyls (PCBs) and the pesticides DDT and lindane in Siberian rivers flowing into the Arctic Ocean were hundreds of times greater than those found in North American and Scandinavian rivers, which led them to suspect that pollution was responsible for the high death rate of young polar bears on the Svalbard archipelago, located 930 km (580 mi) north of Tromsø, Nor. A study of European otters (*Lutra lutra*) concluded that PCBs had contributed significantly to their decline in Europe. High levels of this contaminant detected in tree swallows (*Tachycineta bicolor*) found along the Hudson River in the northeastern United States were thought to be responsible for the birds' reproductive problems and retarded feather development.

Accidents and disease also affected endangered animal populations around the globe. In May some 150 endangered Mediterranean monk seals (*Monachus monachus*), more than half the existing population, died along the northwestern coast of Africa. Analysis of tissues from the dead animals revealed the presence of more than 20 neurotoxins caused by toxic dinoflagellates (marine plankton) found in the water near the seals' caves. In April press reports claimed that 40 of the last Asiatic lions (*Panthera leo*) in the Gir Lion Sanctuary, India, had been killed in road and rail accidents. About 300 lions remained in the sanctuary, which was crossed by five state highways and a railway line. Poisoning, electrocution, and poaching claimed the lives of 16 additional lions. In May there were unconfirmed reports that at least four mountain gorillas (*Gorilla gorilla beringei*) had been shot dead during a gun battle in the Virunga National Park in the Democratic Republic of the Congo (former Zaire).

The 10th Conference of the Parties to the Convention on International Trade in Endangered Species of Wild Fauna and Flora was held in June in Zimbabwe to discuss problems caused by the wildlife trade. Among the most notable outcomes was the decision to allow Botswana, Namibia, and Zimbabwe to export ivory to Japan, a ruling that reflected a philosophical shift toward balancing species protection with the sustainable use of natural resources, particularly in less-developed countries. (JACQUI MORRIS)

ZOOS

From its conception in 1981, the conservation effort of the American Zoo and Aquarium Association (AZA) had centred on its Species Survival Plans and related programs. In 1997 these programs grew to include 83 Species Survival Plans encompassing 135 species. Studbook programs, the database for which all Species Survival Plans depended, also expanded and by late 1997 exceeded 325 in number. In addition, AZA Taxon Advisory Groups (TAG), the conservation umbrella that oversaw both programs, grew to 45, including 21 TAGs for mammals, 15 for birds, and 9 for reptiles, amphibians, fish, and invertebrates. Finally, the AZA expanded the broadest of its conservation programs by adding two Fauna Interest Groups, the Venezuelan and the North American. The Venezuelan was an effort by the AZA to better coordinate conservation projects sponsored by American zoos within a particular country or region. The latter program was designed to establish a closer relationship between zoos and the U.S. Fish and Wildlife Service at times when zoos had or could develop the expertise to assist in fauna recovery programs and other conservation efforts involving native species.

Coral reefs are among the most beautiful and diverse ecosystems but unfortunately are extremely fragile and have a very narrow tolerance for environmental change. As a result, fewer than one-third of the world's reefs were considered "healthy" and in stable condition. In response to the declaration that 1997 would be the International Year of the Reef (IYOR), many AZA members instituted special programs and exhibits for IYOR. (*See* Special Report: YEAR OF THE CORAL REEFS: THE FORGOTTEN RAIN FORESTS OF THE SEA.)

Few formal standards existed to help regulatory agencies evaluate the conditions of captive wildlife (primates, marine mammals, and domestic animals excepted). To address this problem, the Animal and Plant Health Inspection Service of the U.S. Department of Agriculture invited the AZA to develop

(continued on page 216)

PHOTOS, JAMES BALOG—CONTACT PRESS IMAGES

PHOTO ESSAY

Zoos: The Modern Ark

Owing to problems such as pollution, habitat destruction, and illegal hunting, the numbers of extinct and endangered animals have grown rapidly in recent years. Conservationists have warned that one out of five species of animals living today may disappear within a generation. Although many zoos have traditionally had as their aim not the preservation of wildlife but public entertainment and commercial gain, modern zoos have increasingly become involved in efforts to combat extinction. Around the world, zoos have established endangered species breeding programs in the hope of reintroducing threatened animals into their natural environments.

One of the most effective of these has been the American Zoo and Aquarium Association's (AZA's) Species Survival Plan program. Begun in 1981, this program has given zoos throughout North America the chance to acquire selected wildlife to ensure preservation and to promote public awareness of conservation issues. By 1997 the AZA had placed a total of 135 endangered species in 83 Survival Plans.

These photographs by James Balog show a few of the endangered animals that were on exhibit during the year in zoos in the U.S.

Pygmy loris, San Diego (Calif.) Zoo

Greater one-horned Asian rhinoceros, Oklahoma City (Okla.) Zoological Park

Borneo orangutan, Lincoln Park Zoological Gardens, Chicago

Malayan tapir, San Diego Zoo

Chinese alligators, Bronx Zoo, New York City

Sumatran orangutan, Lincoln Park Zoological Gardens

Western lowland gorilla, Cheyenne Mountain Zoo, Colorado Springs, Colo.

Cheetahs, Binder Park Zoo, Battle Creek, Mich.

(continued from page 211)
minimum husbandry standards for all remaining groups of mammals not regulated by specific requirements. After five years of development, 41 sets of standards were provided to the regulatory agencies to help them evaluate husbandry conditions of federally licensed zoos, dealers, and research facilities.

One of the most complex facilities to open in 1997 was the $12 million Regenstein Small Mammal–Reptile House at the Lincoln Park Zoological Gardens in Chicago. This habitat featured about 200 species of small mammals, reptiles, amphibians, and birds on exhibit in a naturalistic, mixed-species environment. Covered by a 14-m (45-ft)-high glass dome, the Lincoln Park facility had an ecosystem that housed species from Asia, Africa, South America, and Australia. The gallery section featured a 25-seat theatre and a replica of an African baobab tree.

Cat Forest/Lion Overlook, the first major exhibit of cats in nearly 25 years, was opened by the Oklahoma City (Okla.) Zoological Park. Featuring naturalistic habitats, the 1.7-ha (4.2-ac) exhibit complex obtained its $8.7 million funding from a 1/8-cent sales tax that was approved by the citizens of Oklahoma City in 1990. The exhibit featured 10 species of cats plus meerkats (a mongoose) and more than 4,000 plants to help replicate the animals' natural habitat. Aside from the fact that some of the smaller species were seldom seen in captivity (Pallas's cat and black-footed cat), great pains were taken to acquire specimens whose genetic relationship to other specimens in North American zoos was minimal or totally absent, which thereby improved the captive gene pool for AZA management programs.

(ALAN H. SHOEMAKER)

BOTANICAL GARDENS

"Eurogard '97," the first European Botanic Garden Conference, was held in April 1997 at the Royal Botanic Garden in Edinburgh. Attended by 200 delegates from 31 countries, it had as its aims the identification of priorities for botanical gardens in a European Botanic Garden Action Plan for the countries of the European Union and the promotion of closer links and collaboration between botanical gardens throughout Europe. The conference was organized through the Botanic Gardens Conservation International (BGCI)/International Association of Botanic Gardens (IABG) joint advisory European Botanic Gardens Consortium, a body established in 1994 to plan initiatives for botanical gardens throughout Europe.

The secretaries-general of BGCI and IABG also held meetings with the European Commission with a view toward enhancing recognition of the roles of botanical gardens in Europe in conservation, education, science, and culture. This was supported by a motion passed in the European Parliament in June.

A workshop on endangered plants in France was organized by the Conservatoire Botanique National de Brest in October. A new research and education centre at the Chelsea Physic Garden in London was opened, funded by the Heritage Lottery Fund and Glaxo Wellcome PLC. In March the Wellcome Trust awarded a grant of £9.2 million to the Millennium Seed Bank project of the Royal Botanic Gardens, Kew, in London. A new major herbarium building was opened at the Irish National Botanic Gardens at Glasnevin by the Irish prime minister, Bertie Ahern, in October.

New computer software in Russian was released by BGCI for the management of plant collection information. Training workshops in the new software were held at the Petrozavodsk University Botanical Garden in Karelia, Russia, in March and at the M.M. Grishko Central Botanical Garden in Kiev, Ukraine, in October. Development of a Baltic Botanical Gardens Association (Estonia, Latvia, and Lithuania) continued; an annual review of the seven botanical gardens in the region was published, and several meetings were held.

The annual meeting of the American Association of Botanical Gardens and Arboreta was held in May, with the Brooklyn Botanic Garden in New York City as host. The Center for Plant Conservation (CPC) in St. Louis, Mo., was awarded the 1996 Denver Botanic Gardens Medal. This award honours outstanding contributions and leadership in the area of plant stewardship and the environment. CPC linked 28 U.S. botanical gardens and arboretums to maintain a collection of 500 of the nation's rarest plants.

An international symposium on botanical gardens took place in Honolulu, in February, with the Garden Club of Honolulu serving as host. It featured presentations by international delegates and representatives of the seven Hawaiian botanical gardens. The staff of the Harold L. Lyon Arboretum on Oahu Island, Hawaii, reported that they had successfully grown 50 rare native Hawaiian plant species by means of tissue-culture techniques. As of 1997 there were 115 identified Hawaiian plants that were represented by fewer than 10 individuals in the wild. The Fairchild Tropical Garden in Miami, Fla., received a gift of $1 million from the Richard H. Simons Charitable Trust to support the garden's programs in rain-forest research, education, and conservation.

A meeting of the IABG Asia Division was held in Urumqi, China, in August. Also

One of two new bedding and potted-plant introductions that won gold medals from both European and U.S. flower-seed-testing organizations in 1997, *Impatiens walleriana* hybrid Victorian Rose had dark green foilage with rose-pink flowers that contained an extra row of petals.

ALAN AND LINDA DETRICK—PHOTO RESEARCHERS

in China, a regional office for BGCI was opened at the Nanjing Botanical Garden. A new botanical garden was established by the College of Agriculture in Nagpur, India, to serve as a centre of conservation and education in central India. An international workshop on conservation and education was held by the Kebun Raya Bogor (Bogor Botanic Garden) in Indonesia. Work began on a new botanical garden at the Tam Dao National Park, near Hanoi.

A major new conservatory was opened at the Kirstenbosch National Botanical Garden in Cape Town. It enabled the National Botanical Institute in Cape Town to display South African plants that cannot be grown outside in the garden.

(PETER S. WYSE JACKSON)

GARDENING

To the surprise of professional horticulturists, computers had a large impact on the field in 1997. Academics led the way, and numerous universities in industrialized countries converted their reference resources to on-line, searchable form, making them freely available via the World Wide Web. The types of information that were obtained from these sites included low-resolution photographs of many species and cultivars of edible and ornamental garden plants, as well as care recommendations developed for a wide range of climates. Disease and pest identification graphics also became widely available so that gardeners with the necessary equipment could diagnose and treat their own garden problems. Amateur horticulturists also gained much greater access to original research in horticulture and related fields as researchers posted their raw data on the Internet.

Garden encyclopedias and landscape planners on compact disc also became more common, although still not widely distributed, and were regularly reviewed in the garden media. Commercial enterprises also began to establish a presence on the Web, and some entirely new companies became serious players in the dissemination of horticultural product knowledge and a serious threat to established companies in the field.

Interest in heirloom plants continued to increase in the U.S., whereas Australian gardeners lost some of their absorption in historical cultivars. In Europe increased interest from commercial seedsmen considering entry into the market was curbed somewhat by European Union regulations concerning plant-variety protection. In nonindustrial countries the trend continued away from heirlooms and toward more production-oriented hybrids.

Two new bedding and potted-plant introductions, one for sunny conditions and one for shade, won gold medals from both Fleuroselect, the European-based international flower-seed-testing organization, and the U.S.-based All-America Selections (AAS). *Petunia grandiflora* Prism Sunshine's 7.5–8.7-cm-diameter (1 cm=0.4 in) single yellow flowers were borne on prostrate 38–50-cm-high plants. Unlike older yellow cultivars, the flowers did not fade in strong sun or blush pink when stressed by outdoor conditions. *Impatiens walleriana* hybrid Victorian Rose had dark green foliage with rose pink 3.7-cm-diameter flowers that contained an extra row of petals, giving the blossoms a more roselike appearance. Intended for bedding in shady conditions or for use in containers, it grew approximately 20 cm high and had a spread of 35 cm.

Four other new flowers also won gold medals from Fleuroselect. *Campanula medium* Champion Blue and Champion Pink shared a gold medal; these new varieties were the first true annuals in this species. The single 3.7-cm cup-shaped blooms were borne in clusters on 50–60-cm-high stems that could number up to as many as 10.

Another Fleuroselect gold medal was awarded to *Celosia argenta cristata* Bombay Yellow Gold, a sister line to Bombay Purple, the gold medal winner in 1996. The triangular blossoms, borne singly on 1.2–1.5-m (4–5-ft)-high stems, were intended for cut-flower use.

Hybrid *Gazania splendens* Daybreak Red Stripe was awarded a gold medal for its unique colour and abundance of blooms. This drought-tolerant South African native —intended for pots and bedding in sunny spots—was compact at 20 cm high and 30 cm in diameter and had 7.5–8.7-cm golden yellow single daisylike blooms, featuring bronze to red spoked highlights in the centre of each petal.

One vegetable and one herb cultivar won AAS Gold Medals. Sweet Dani was a new Lemon Basil (*Ocimum basilicum*) that was more vigorous than older varieties but had traditional white flowers. The 60-cm-high plants had an enhanced lemon fragrance and were more resistant to transplanting than were older types.

Swiss Chard (*Beta vulgaris*) Bright Lights, an improved form of the Australian heirloom Five Color Silverbeet, won the final AAS Gold Medal for its wide colour range. The 60–91-cm-high plants had broad stems in up to 11 different colours, ranging from bright red and purple to pink, yellow, gold, and even white. Heat tolerance and length of harvest were excellent.

The U.S.-based Perennial Plant Association chose an *Echinacea purpurea* cultivar, Magnus, as its Plant of the Year in 1997 (for the 1998 season). This sturdy North American native had coarse, slightly hairy serrated leaves 10–20 cm long, stiff stems up to 100 cm tall, and purple daisylike flowers 7–10 cm in diameter. Its encircling ray petals were held horizontal, rather than drooping, which was common to the species.

(SHEPHERD OGDEN)

See also Agriculture and Food Supplies; Business and Industry Review; *Energy;* Life Sciences.

This article updates the *Macropædia* articles CONSERVATION OF NATURAL RESOURCES; GARDENING AND HORTICULTURE.

The Blossoming Cut-Flower Industry

In 1997 less-developed countries (LDCs) profited from the lucrative annual $5 billion global cut-flower industry, but importers in Western Europe were scrutinizing their activities and considering boycotting shipments from what they considered "dirty" flower farms—particularly those that used pesticides and inefficiently used water but also those that employed nonunionized workers at low wages. Although a 1995 report on world trade, "The Game of the Rose," concluded that three-fifths of all cut flowers that crossed international borders originated in The Netherlands, by 1997 countries in South America and Africa were entering the market at a rapid pace. An ideal climate, low labour costs, and the availability of direct air flights to markets in industrialized nations contributed to the boom in cut-flower production in such countries as Colombia, Ecuador, Costa Rica, and Guatemala, where much of U.S. production had moved. Airfreight costs were more than offset by lower production costs, and skilled management was readily available in those countries.

European production moved primarily to the African countries of Kenya and Zimbabwe; in the latter country two-thirds of all horticultural export earnings were attributed to cut flowers. South Africa, Zambia, Tanzania, and Côte d'Ivoire also supplied significant amounts for export. In Kenya larger operations were funded by external corporations with direct links to markets, whereas in Zimbabwe producers tended to be farmers who would grow a few hectares of flowers as an additional cash crop and market them through cooperatives. As production rose, consumers in developed countries became more discerning, and producer cooperatives, first in Kenya and then in the rest of Africa, responded by instituting environmentally friendly production methods and hiring independent inspectors to certify and document their practices.

Other countries that were expected to become a major force in both flower production and export included China, which looked to quadruple its current production and revenues from $250 million to $1 billion over the next 10–15 years, and New Zealand, where export business for one company, New Zealand Bloom, had increased eightfold and was expected to continue growing.

In some LDCs major impediments to continued growth included the availability of credit and the development of skilled indigenous management. Most cut-flower operations were dependent on imported management that was hired on relatively short-term contracts. As a result, the quality and yield of flower crops were variable, a situation that could both unsettle bankers and buyers and lead to high volatility in markets. Another obstacle was the reluctance of major flower-breeding companies to release their best new material to LDCs due to what they perceived as insufficient respect for intellectual property rights. Nonetheless, production in LDCs of fresh-cut flowers was expected to increase for the foreseeable future as worldwide consumption grew (mourners purchased some 60 million flowers to honour Diana, princess of Wales, after her death in August), whereas production in developed countries would likely stabilize or decrease.

(SHEPHERD OGDEN)

Fashions

Two opposing themes dominated women's fashion in 1997—minimalism and luxury. Though both styles had served as constant reference points in the '90s, they found new meaning during 1997. Minimalism broadened its definition from a wardrobe based on functionality to include a new sense of sophisticated simplicity. This new form of minimalism became the style preferred by most women, but haute couture's luxurious appeal became fashion's fantasy point.

Couture also found a new sense of energy. Excessively opulent, exotic, and expensive couture designs filled magazine pages as never before. French *Vogue* called the effect "Le Big Bang." It was couture's revitalized approach that carved luxury's new meaning, and designer Christian Lacroix playfully called it "maximalism."

Austrian designer Helmut Lang's seasonal collections of white and off-white severely tailored separates—for both spring-summer and autumn-winter—exemplified the new approach to minimalism, as did the ensembles worn by Carolyn Bessette-Kennedy. The former public-relations officer for designer Calvin Klein had favoured her former employer's pared-down approach to dressing until she married John Kennedy, Jr., and adopted a more individualistic style. She made public appearances in monochromatic ensembles made by other designers, including a Yohji Yamamoto skirt suit, casual clothes by Prada, and classic stilettos by Manolo Blahnik. Her well-groomed appearance—including perfectly applied red lipstick and a long, well-kept mane of shiny-blonde hair—made her simple style look sleek. British *Vogue* included Bessette-Kennedy, along with actress Gwyneth Paltrow and photographer Kelly Klein, as a part of fashion's new "Clean team"—women who always looked so good that they could "turn a white shirt and a pair of [immaculate] black trousers into a style statement." Some women found this approach to minimalism inspirational, whereas others looked to haute couture designs—and the celebrities that wore them—for entertainment.

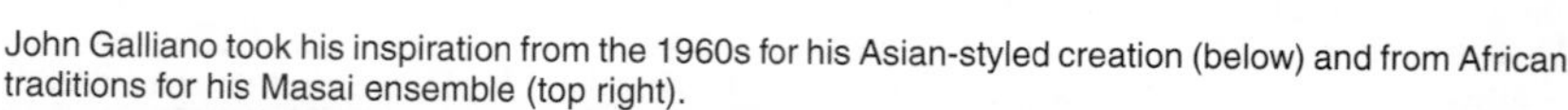

John Galliano took his inspiration from the 1960s for his Asian-styled creation (below) and from African traditions for his Masai ensemble (top right).

PHOTOS, CORINA LECCA

The spring-summer 1997 couture collections—staged in Paris in January—showcased the debut of new British designers at formerly conservative fashion houses: John Galliano at Christian Dior, Alexander McQueen at Givenchy, and Lady Amanda Harlech, a former protégé of Galliano's who became Karl Lagerfeld's collaborator at Chanel. Such other designers as Jean-Paul Gaultier, Thierry Mugler, Adeline Andre, and Dominique Sirop also premiered their first couture collections. Some shows disappointed the critics—particularly McQueen's Givenchy collection of white-and-gold designs, which were irreverently accessorized with nose rings.

After years of producing clothing for an aging and dwindling client base, as well as reporting that couture was a money-losing venture, young designers found a new clientele: Hollywood celebrities such as Demi Moore and Nicole Kidman. Most designers followed the lead of the late Gianni Versace (*see* OBITUARIES), inviting actors to attend their shows as well as to wear their creations at such high-profile events as the Academy Awards and the Cannes Film Festival. Meanwhile, established names like Yves Saint Laurent and Pierre Balmain reported that their couture sales had doubled. The auction house Sotheby's was so convinced of haute couture's marketability and relevance that in February it opened a fashion department that would sell those fashions.

Critics claimed that after years of lagging behind the trendsetting ready-to-wear designs, couture was now setting the pace for fashion. Particularly influential was Galliano's spring-summer Dior couture, which featured several trends coexisting cohesively, including miniskirts, amply tailored trouser suits, 1920s vintage beaded dresses, and feather- and mink-trimmed clothing and accessories. These ideas later became major focal points of other autumn-winter ready-to-wear designs. Meanwhile, Dior's tribal theme, which borrowed traditional African and Asian styles such as Masai-inspired beaded accessories and Chinese embroidery, strengthened the focus on ethnic styles.

With her Asian-inspired spring-summer collection—featuring cheongsams and chunky, Chinese-inspired footwear—Miuccia Prada became the initial purveyor of chinoiserie. Other factors also strengthened the Asian appeal, including the cult status achieved by the London boutique Voyage (whose gemstone-coloured velvet designs became a favourite of models and celebrities), theme parties for Britain's Hong Kong handover in July, and the low cost of assembling an authentic look at a "Chinatown" shop. By summer a look American *Vogue* dubbed "ethnic chic" had become a major street trend.

Fashion's African inspiration focused more on black models than on clothing design. Black African models became fashion's most prominent faces. (The sole exception was model Karen Elson, who with a messy "bad bob" haircut rose to fame, replacing Stella Tennant as the face of Chanel's advertising campaign.) Ralph Lauren chose British model Naomi Campbell to front his Masai-inspired summer ad campaign, while Somalian-born model Iman appeared in Donna Karan's ads. *Vogue Italia*'s July issue included a 16-page couture photo-essay featuring only black models. Among the seven models showcased were Sudanese-born, British-based Alek Wek, whose shapely 1.8-m (6-ft) frame made her a favourite in major fashion editorials, and Ugandan-born Kiara Kabukuru, who grew up in Los Angeles and became the first nonwhite model in three years to appear on the cover of American *Vogue*. Surprisingly, the *New York Times* fashion editor Amy Spindler attacked American *Vogue*—as well as several other fashion publications and designers—for fetishizing black women. Fashion, Spindler claimed, "is once again using people simply as props—one more passing trend."

DAN LECCA

Patrick Cox's 1960s retro look

Fashion's exploitative nature had come under fire in the spring when U.S. Pres. Bill Clinton spoke out against the popularity of "heroin chic." Though the grunge-inspired look had been popular in 1996 and was not a major theme for fashion collections in 1997, Clinton's comments followed the heroin overdose and death in February of 20-year-old New York photographer Davide Sorrenti. Shortly after Sorrenti's death, his mother, Francesca Sorrenti, also a fashion photographer, spoke out against the growing use of heroin by young people (models and aspiring photographers) involved in the fashion industry. Soon to follow were editorials in fashion magazines addressing Sorrenti's cause as well as fashion stories focusing on more positive fashion themes like body-conscious clothing (leggings and miniskirts), athletic gear, and feminine lingerie-inspired dresses.

Negative issues, however, were overshadowed by fashion's positive mood. At the autumn-winter shows, a palate of rich colours like plum, charcoal, olive, and wine replaced black, fashion's perennial shade. Although most designers did not look back for inspiration, there were traces of retro. Designer Randolph Duke presented a collection for Halston, the newly revived 1970s fashion house, and the spring-summer menswear shows sported traces of a '70s lounge-singer flashiness. The look for men, however, was inspired more by the sartorial feel of the 1996 independent film *Swingers*.

Elements of 1980s fashion also emerged with the autumn-winter collections. Gucci revived the black leather suit and high stiletto shoes, and designers in every fashion capital produced sharply tailored trouser and short skirt suits. Some featured jackets with shoulder pads, but rather than replicating the harsh cuts of the '80s "power suit" look, the proportions were softly feminine, roomier, and less structured.

As autumn-winter ready-to-wear styles mimicked ideas from the spring-summer couture collections, it became obvious that trends were not emerging as fast as in previous years. Another group of young designers, however, had moved to more prominent positions, and this made fashion's forecast for original inspiration hopeful. Bernard Arnault (*see* BIOGRAPHIES), the chairman of luxury goods conglomerate LVMH Moët Hennessy Louis Vuitton, appointed New York designer Marc Jacobs artistic director of the French luxury leather-goods house Louis Vuitton. Former Cerrutti designer Narciso Rodriguez assumed the role of women's ready-to-wear designer at the Madrid-based leather house Loewe. Independent British designer Stella McCartney (daughter of musician Sir Paul McCartney) closed her eponymous London fashion label and replaced Karl Lagerfeld at the Paris fashion house Chloé. Meanwhile, after several years of being a minor fashion capital, London reemerged as the world's major style centre. Innovative young London-based designers like husband-and-wife duo Suzanne Clements and Inacio Ribeiro (Clements Ribeiro) and knitwear designers Julien MacDonald and Lainey Keogh made London Fashion Week a major media event. The growing worldwide fame of highly stylized British pop groups such as Oasis, Blur, and the Spice Girls (*see* BIOGRAPHIES) added to what *Women's Wear Daily* called the "London boom."

British fashion was also the main force in menswear. Italian designers Valentino, Dolce & Gabbana, and Giorgio Armani (*see* BIOGRAPHIES) produced autumn-winter menswear collections featuring suits of more ample proportions and traces of classic trademarks of Englishmen's suiting, such as conservative cuts, tweed, and gray flannel. British-made shoes such as Chelsea boots, wing tips, and monkstraps made by London shoemaker John Lobb were popular autumn-winter accessories. More talked-about than the styles seen on the international menswear runways were the custom-made suits designed by a new generation of young British tailors, including Timothy Everest, who created Tom Cruise's wardrobe for *Mission: Impossible*. Though their work was timeless and unadorned in the tradition of London's Savile Row, the suits featured unconventional elements like a colour spectrum including pastels and vibrants, as well as such fabrics as velvets and bold tweeds.

(BRONWYN COSGRAVE)

DAN LECCA

Givenchy's Asian-inspired confection

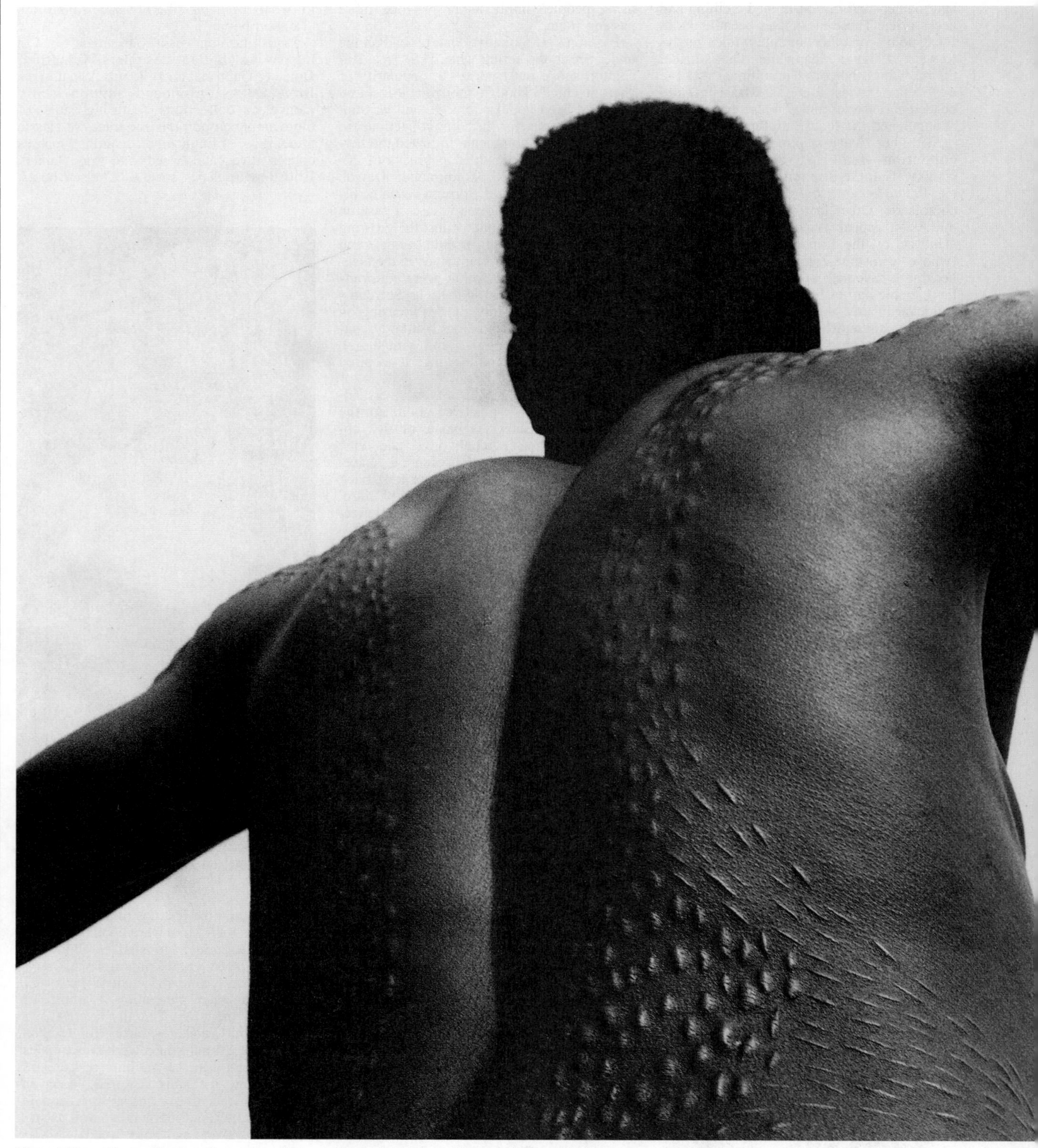

(Above) Man with scarification, Papua New Guinea. (Opposite page, top) Xingu tribesman being tattooed, Brazil. (Opposite page, bottom) A Xingu girl.

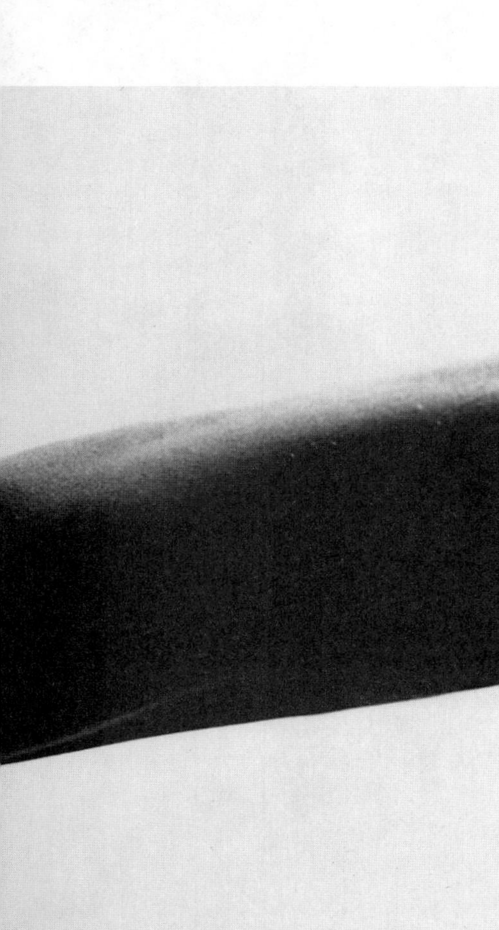

Tattooing: Then and Now

Long popular among seamen, soldiers, labourers, and others who wanted to project a tough, masculine image, tattoos in recent years have moved steadily into the fashion mainstream. Today they are worn by a growing number of young men and women and are likely to be spotted on the bodies of movie stars, fashion models, and professional athletes. Moreover, contemporary tattoos often go beyond small, simple images. Many are elaborate, well-researched designs, and some are full-body imitations of ancient tribal motifs.

The resurgence in tattooing can partly be explained as an attempt to reestablish a sense of belonging to a group. Permanent marks produced by the introduction of pigment through ruptures in the skin, tattoos have in the past served to identify the wearer's rank, status, or membership in a particular group. Sometimes the term tattoo is also loosely applied to the inducement of scars. Pain was and still is today part of the initiation.

Photographer Chris Rainier records aspects of vanishing cultures in the hope of keeping their spirit alive. The following photographs by Rainier, part of his ongoing examination of tattooing in the 20th century, show examples of traditional forms of tattooing found among the peoples of Mali, Brazil, and Papua New Guinea.

PHOTOGRAPHS, CHRIS RAINIER

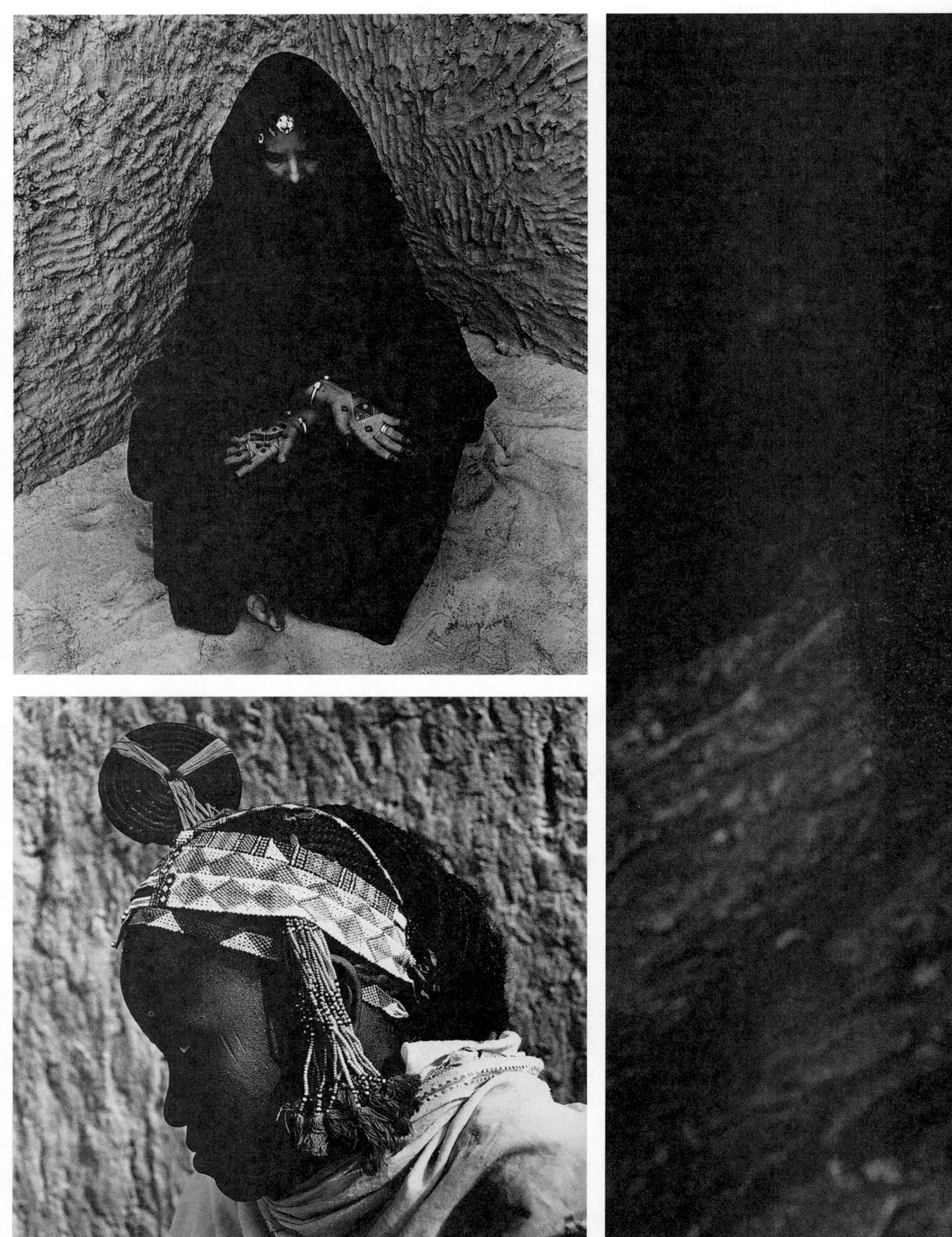

(Top left) Woman with hand tattoos, Mali. (Bottom left) Facial scarification, Mali. (Right) Maisin woman with tattooed face, Papua New Guinea.

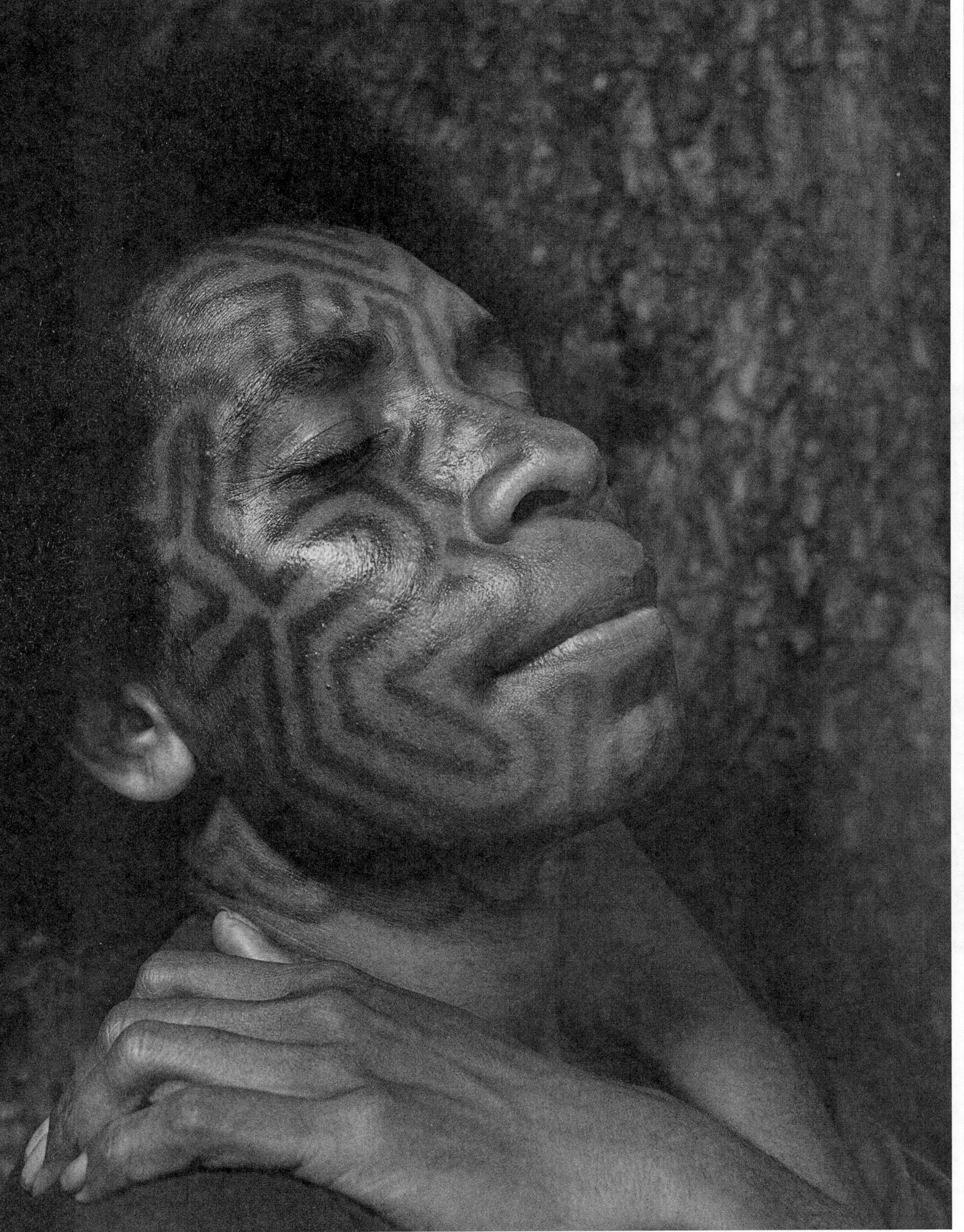

Health and Disease

The degree to which medical and scientific experts should interfere with the natural order of things, in both creating and terminating life, became a major concern in medical science in 1997. In February a startled world said hello to a cloned Scottish sheep named Dolly. The surprising scientific feat stirred moral and legal concerns about the prospect that genetically identical humans could be created as well. *(See* LIFE SCIENCES: Special Report). Meanwhile, medical science was already providing an array of high-tech pregnancy assistance, sometimes with dramatic consequences. In November Bobbi McCaughey, a Carlisle, Iowa, woman who had taken a fertility drug, gave birth to septuplets, four sons and three daughters, the first known case in the United States of seven live human births. A month earlier an Atlanta, Ga., fertility clinic had announced that for the first time in the U.S., two healthy baby boys had been born from eggs that had been frozen and thawed before being fertilized, a technique that was being studied in a number of countries.

DENNIS GRUNDMAN—ASSOCIATED PRESS

In August millions of kilograms of ground beef produced at the Hudson Foods plant in Columbus, Neb., were recalled after tests showed that some of the beef was contaminated.

At the other end of the spectrum, legal debates about how and when it is appropriate to end life confronted the United States Supreme Court, which ruled that terminally ill patients do not have a constitutional right to physician-assisted suicide. The states were left free to take action, however, and in November Oregon voters reaffirmed a controversial Death with Dignity Act allowing doctors to prescribe drugs to help terminally ill people die.

The United States also got a favourable new health report card. An annual report from the federal Centers for Disease Control and Prevention showed a dramatic decline in the AIDS death rate, drops in homicide and suicide rates, and a continuing reduction in the teenage birthrate. American life expectancy achieved an all-time high of 76.1 years in 1996, and infant mortality reached a new low, 7.2 deaths per 1,000 live births. An estimated 15% reduction in mortality rates from sudden infant death syndrome helped account for the continuing infant mortality decline.

Amid growing concern about food safety, the U.S. Food and Drug Administration (FDA) in December approved the use of irradiation to control disease-causing microorganisms in meat products. It said that studies found the procedure to be safe and to have no effect on nutrition, taste, or appearance of fresh and frozen meat, including beef, pork, and lamb. The FDA said that irradiation could help kill dangerous *Escherichia coli* bacteria, which had been traced to undercooked hamburger. In another food-safety initiative, U.S. Pres. Bill Clinton announced in October that the government would be undertaking new steps to ensure the safety of imported as well as domestic fruits and vegetables.

Two major studies of depression in the elderly demonstrated that poor physical and mental health seem to go hand in hand. They found that older patients who suffer from significant signs of depression are far more likely to suffer serious physical illnesses.

Several studies indicated that people living in Europe were receiving insufficient quantities of selenium, which plays a vital role in thyroid hormones and in various bodily processes. Although the element is found in cereals, meat, fish, and poultry, the decline in intake was largely attributed to a fall in imports from North America of selenium-rich, high-protein wheat for bread making. This prompted calls for flour to be supplemented with selenium and for selenium to be more widely used in fertilizers (as had been adopted recently in Finland).

There was progress in the treatment of rheumatoid arthritis. Although the causes of this condition were not fully understood, a role was thought to be played by tumour necrosis factor (TNF), which otherwise has beneficial effects in the body. U.S. researchers therefore developed a protein specifically engineered to interfere with the action of TNF. Given to 180 patients whose rheumatoid arthritis had not responded to conventional treatments, it reduced their symptoms and appeared to be safe and well-tolerated.

Genetics. Medical experts gathered by the U.S. National Institutes of Health (NIH) approved the use of more widespread genetic testing for cystic fibrosis, the most common inherited disorder for people of northern European descent. The independent panel recommended that testing for gene mutations that cause cystic fibrosis be offered to all couples expecting babies and those planning pregnancy, as well as individuals with a family history of the disease and their partners. The debilitating and often deadly lung and digestive disease occurs when a child inherits a defective gene from each parent. Genetic testing can identify healthy adult carriers with only one defective gene—about one in 29 Caucasians—that may be passed on to their offspring.

Significant research progress continued to be made in the Human Genome Project. University of Washington molecular biologists reported in *Science* magazine that by the end of 1997, partial genetic sequences from approximately 40,000 to 50,000 human genes, roughly half of the total, had been recorded in various databases around the world. The detailed sequencing of the three billion base pairs, or genetic building blocks, of the human genome was, however, just beginning, with only about 2% of the total analyzed by the year's end. The genomes of the *E. coli* bacterium, yeast, and 11 other microbes were completely sequenced, which greatly improved the basic understanding of genetics.

During the year the genes responsible for several heritable diseases were found. These included tuberous sclerosis, which causes distinctive tumours in the brain, skin, heart, lungs, and kidneys; Niemann-Pick type C disease, a fatal condition resulting from a failure to process cholesterol; one form of age-related macular degeneration, the most common uncorrectable cause of loss of vision in the elderly; and a type of familial atrial fibrillation, which causes strokes and heart-rhythm abnormalities. Researchers also reported a link between autism and a specific gene, and others found a gene that can suppress the development of tumours in the brain, breast, and prostate. All these discoveries could in time lead to earlier detection and, perhaps, treatment for the conditions concerned.

Cardiovascular Disease. Obesity and efforts to combat obesity continued to pose major health problems, particularly to the heart. In the United States two popular prescription diet drugs—dexfenfluramine and fenfluramine—were withdrawn from the market in September at the recommendation of the FDA. The two drugs were often taken singly or with another drug, phentermine, in a combination known popularly as "fen-phen." In November preliminary studies suggested that as many as one-third of the drugs' users may have suffered heart valve damage. People who had taken either of the diet drugs were urged to consider having a medical checkup. Valve damage can make people more vulnerable to bacterial infection of the heart following dental and medical procedures.

Obesity is a problem that often begins in childhood. New research from a heart study done in Bogalusa, La., found that the children of parents with heart disease were more often overweight than were other children. They also had a higher incidence of obesity—and heart disease risk factors like elevated cholesterol levels—when they became young adults.

In addition to reducing their weight, Americans fighting heart disease needed to double the amount of fibre in their diets to help lower their blood cholesterol and control their body weight, according to a report from an American Heart Association nutrition committee. The committee suggested that a variety of grains, beans, other vegetables, and fruits—important sources of fibre—be included in the diet.

A new Harvard University study found that margarine and other foods made with hardened vegetable oils, including many baked goods, contain a "trans fat" that could increase the risk of heart disease by as much as one-third. Such fats may be even worse than the saturated fats found in meats and cheese, according to the study of more than 80,000 women in the Harvard Nurses' Health Study. University of Washington researchers released a new study that found that lowering the amount of total fat in the diet to about 30% of total intake helped lower cholesterol in people with high levels. This supported national guidelines set by government experts. The study found, however, that more aggressive fat-restriction diets may not help and may even hurt by decreasing levels of high-density lipoprotein, the so-called good form of cholesterol.

In addition to a low-fat diet and exercise, new research evidence suggested that cholesterol-lowering drugs, such as lovastatin, may be valuable in reducing heart attacks in patients with borderline cholesterol levels and no sign of heart disease as well as in patients with high cholesterol and a history of heart disease. Such medication might be important for patients with a family history of heart disease.

U.S. researchers demonstrated the beneficial effect of fish consumption in relation to coronary heart disease. They had a unique opportunity to study a group of 1,800 men who were aged 40 to 55 and free of cardiovascular disease when they were first enrolled in a health study in 1957. Follow-up studies showed that those who were eating 35 g (1.2 oz) or more of fish each day at the outset were much less likely to have suffered a fatal heart attack over the ensuing 30 years than were those who avoided fish altogether.

Cancer. American women in their 40s received conflicting advice about whether to get regular screening mammograms for breast cancer diagnosis. Two major cancer organizations recommended that women aged 40–49 be regularly screened with mammography, a low-dose X-ray test intended to pick up hidden breast tumours. The American Cancer Society, a major voluntary group, urged all women 40 and older to get a mammogram every year, and the government's National Cancer Institute (NCI) said that women 40 and older should be screened every one to two years. Earlier, however, an advisory group convened by the NIH had concluded that the available scientific evidence was not strong enough to warrant a universal recommendation that all women in their 40s get screening mammograms. The panel said women in that age group should decide for themselves, after weighing the risks and benefits. There had long been strong medical agreement that women aged 50 and older should obtain mammograms on a regular basis.

In the treatment of breast cancer, researchers with the U.S. National Surgical Adjuvant Breast and Bowel Project, a federally funded group, recommended that most patients with early-stage disease, regardless of their age, the type of tumour, or the chance that the cancer has spread to nearby lymph nodes, consider undergoing chemotherapy in addition to surgery. The recommendation followed a large new study showing that even lower-risk patients with localized breast cancer that had not spread and who were estrogen-receptor-positive, a sign of a more positive outcome, were more likely to live longer and be disease-free five years after having received a combination of chemotherapy and hormone therapy with tamoxifen.

Evidence from Taiwan showed that the prevention of hepatitis B could also lead to a reduction in the incidence of hepatocellular carcinoma. This type of liver cancer had long been associated with the hepatitis B virus, although the precise relationship was unclear. The Taiwan study revealed that during the decade since the inception of a nationwide immunization program, not only had hepatitis B declined, but hepatocellular carcinoma in children had also fallen to half its original level.

Research in Australia on the effect of diet on cancer suggested that the risk of breast cancer was lower in women who had a high intake of phytoestrogens. These are chemicals, found in many edible plants, whose chemical structures are similar to that of estrogen. One type occurs predominantly in soy products, and another is in grains, fruits, and vegetables.

International collaboration clarified the previously uncertain relationship between breast cancer and hormone replacement therapy (HRT). An analysis showed a slight increase in risk of the disease for every year of use of HRT. The effect is reduced after cessation of the therapy and largely, if not entirely, disappears after five years.

Infectious Diseases. Communicable diseases were the subject of both good and bad news in 1997. Several newly emerging infections provoked concern, as did the spread of strains of bacteria that cause familiar diseases but that have become resistant to the antibiotics routinely used for treatment. There was also evidence, however, that this problem could be ameliorated by more prudent use of antibiotics.

Arguably the most ominous development was the isolation of a resistant strain of *Yersinia pestis,* the organism responsible for bubonic plague, from a patient in Madagascar. It was insensitive to every one of the antibiotics normally administered to combat this life-threatening disease. Because bubonic plague is acquired from fleas that carry the bacterium from infected rats, there was little chance of epidemics in most countries. Nevertheless, the discovery of the multiply-resistant strain was disquieting, especially since the resistance could be passed on to other, initially sensitive strains of *Y. pestis.*

There was dramatic evidence from Finland of how more selective prescribing of antibiotics could lead to a decline in the prevalence of resistant bacteria. This followed anxiety earlier in the 1990s over increasing resistance to erythromycin in streptococci, which cause skin and respiratory infections. National guidelines were instituted so that hospital outpatients received erythromycin only when strictly necessary and only in the required dosage. As a result, the frequency of resistant strains in throat swabs and pus samples fell over four years from 16.5% to 8.6%. Although such a trend might have been predicted, its magnitude was unexpected. It was also the first conclusive demonstration of the benefits of the discriminating deployment of antibiotics.

Federal health statistics documented a dramatic one-year decline in the U.S. death rate for HIV/AIDS, a 26% drop between 1995 and 1996. The latest annual report showed that HIV infection, which had been the leading killer of Americans 25–44, now ranked second in that age group, behind accidents and their adverse effects (largely from car crashes) and just ahead of cancer. Mortality from HIV had increased significantly between 1987 and 1994; the first evidence that mortality was leveling off appeared in 1995.

Nonetheless, there was renewed concern about prevention of new HIV cases, particularly among young people. It was highlighted by an alarming case in which a 20-year-old HIV-infected man may have created a one-man AIDS epidemic. Nushawn Williams, apparently aware of his HIV status, had unprotected sex with numerous young women in a rural area of western New York and in New York City. In an unusual move, health authorities obtained court permission to bypass AIDS confidentiality laws and release the man's name, which led dozens of women to get their blood tested for signs of infection.

On the AIDS treatment front, many patients receiving powerful combination drug therapy remained in good health. Hopes for a permanent cure were put on hold, however, when three teams of researchers reported that the virus could hide out in the body's immune cells even in patients with no signs of the virus in their blood for as long as two years. The research suggested that although the virus can be held at bay, patients may have to stick with the drug treatment indefinitely unless new approaches can be developed.

Scientists found that along with AIDS, other serious infectious diseases, such as tuberculosis, had recently been spread in medical settings by the use of contaminated instruments. Patients in South Carolina and Maryland were found to be infected with TB after they had undergone a common procedure, fibre-optic bronchoscopy, in which a lighted tube is inserted into the lungs for diagnosis or treatment. Researchers were able to prove that the infections were caused by bronchoscopes that had not been properly cleaned. About 460,000 patients undergo fibre-optic bronchoscopy in the U.S. each year.

Stricter hygiene precautions in slaughterhouses and butcher shops were recommended in the report of an inquiry into the previous year's outbreak of food poisoning in Scotland attributed to *E. coli.* Although this bacterium was at one time considered to be entirely innocuous, strain 0157 not only attacks the intestinal tract but also can trigger life-threatening kidney failure. Nearly 500 people became ill and 19 died during the Scottish epidemic—the world's second worst outbreak of disease caused by *E. coli.* Public health authorities in other countries were advised on measures to prevent the organism, which occurs in the feces of infected cattle, from reaching meat for human consumption.

An international team reported that a new drug, zanamavir, reduces the symptoms of influenza A or B if treatment is begun sufficiently early. Trials in 38 centres in North America and Europe indicated that zanamavir is a valuable supplement to vaccines for the treatment of influenza; some vaccines may not be effective against new strains of the virus.

Early in December a new strain of influenza appeared in Hong Kong. By the year's end at least 16 people were known to have been infected, and 4 had died. Researchers determined that the virus was the first ever to have been transmitted directly from birds to humans. More than one million chickens, ducks, and geese were subsequently slaughtered in Hong Kong.

U.S. virologists also reported success in preventing rhinovirus infections by spraying into chimpanzees' noses a substance to prevent the virus from invading their cells. Researchers believed that this method could be used to prevent the 50% of human colds that are caused by rhinoviruses.

There was a major advance in immunization against meningitis and pneumonia produced by *Haemophilus influenzae* type B (Hib). Vaccines had been highly effective in recent years in preventing Hib infections in industrialized countries. There was, however, no comparable evidence of their efficacy in less-developed countries. The success of a new trial, conducted in The Gambia, indicated that a Hib vaccine will substantially reduce childhood deaths due to meningitis and pneumonia in less-developed countries.

Alternative Medicine. Acupuncture, the ancient Chinese practice of using thin needles for treating various ailments, gained an endorsement from American mainstream medicine. An NIH panel concluded that it could be effective in treating nausea and vomiting from surgery, chemotherapy, or pregnancy, as well as postoperative dental pain. The panel said that there was some evidence that acupuncture could also be helpful in treating muscle and skeletal aches, low back pain, headache, drug addiction, arthritis, and asthma. (*See* Special Report.)

Smoking. There was considerable progress in clarifying the effect of smoking, especially passive smoking, on cancer and other conditions. First, a large-scale analysis by London-based epidemiologists, bringing together 19 separate research studies, concluded that marriage to a smoker increased by 26% the chances of a nonsmoking partner's developing lung cancer. There was also a clear dose-response relationship. Those breathing in more tobacco smoke were correspondingly more likely to contract the disease. Another major study, conducted at the Harvard School of Public Health, showed that regular exposure to other peoples' smoke nearly doubled a nonsmoker's risk of contracting coronary artery disease. An analysis by the London group put the increased risk at about 25%.

A new analysis of five major studies of the health effects of cigarettes found that the hazards to women smokers were rising most quickly, with the largest increases occurring in the risks of lung cancer and other smoking-related cancers. The 565-page report released by the NCI found that overall smoking-related mortality rates from all causes, including cancer, heart disease, stroke, and lung disease, had increased among both women and men since the first Surgeon General's report, in 1964, on the health hazards of smoking. For example, a comparison of two long-term studies, one starting in 1959 and the other in 1982, found that lung cancer risks of male smokers doubled between the two studies, whereas the relative risk increased more than fourfold among female smokers. The report noted that cigarettes currently contained smaller amounts of hazardous tar and nicotine than in the past, but the lifetime exposure to cigarette smoke was greater because smokers started earlier, inhaled more deeply, and consumed more cigarettes per day. Another study warned that China, the country with the most smokers in the world, was in the early stages of a smoking epidemic that would likely get much worse. Unless control measures were taken, half of the current 300 million Chinese smokers could die from smoking-related illnesses, according to an estimate by a University of Hong Kong research group. Among China's male smokers, the chief causes of death were cancers of the lung, esophagus, and liver.

Yet another indictment of cigarettes came from a Chinese study showing that children whose fathers smoked faced a higher risk of developing early childhood cancers than those of nonsmoking fathers. The study, conducted in Shanghai by Chinese and American researchers, suggested that the risk occurred before conception from sperm damaged by paternal smoking.

Regarding the effects of active smoking, another analysis in London showed that habitual use of cigarettes also contributed to the loss of bone density. This, in turn, increased the risk of hip fracture by about 50%. Experience reported from the Mayo Clinic in Rochester, Minn., revealed that patients having the operation known as percutaneous coronary revascularization, to increase blood flow to the heart muscle, should be discouraged from smoking. Those who continued to smoke after surgery were much more likely to develop serious irregularities of the heartbeat—and to die—than those who gave up the habit.

(BERNARD DIXON; CRISTINE RUSSELL)

A midwife counsels a pregnant woman in Ethiopia. With only one physician per 30,195 people in Ethiopia, midwives played an important role, though most had little formal training. Since the mid-1980s, the country's infant mortality rate and under-five mortality rate had steadily increased.

CAROL GUZY—THE WASHINGTON POST

MENTAL HEALTH

In 1997 the cause of schizophrenia was clarified as a result of investigations carried out in Iowa City, Iowa, on 17 patients at an early stage in their illness. Prior research had suggested that individuals with schizophrenia have abnormally low metabolic activity in a part of the brain called the prefrontal cortex. Past studies were not conclusive, however, since results may have been affected by medication and by the chronic state of the patients' illness. The 10 young men and 7 young women in the new study had not yet been treated with drugs. Most were experiencing symptoms for the first time and had not been previously admitted to a hospital. The research team used a scanning technique, positron emission tomography, to examine blood flow in various parts of the patients' brains. The brains of 17 healthy volunteers of similar ages were also examined.

Compared with the volunteers who were used as controls, the schizophrenia patients had extensive areas of abnormally low blood flow in several regions of the prefrontal cortex, but other regions showed abnormally high blood flow. This suggested an imbalance between different parts of the brain. The investigators concluded that the dysfunction they observed may impair the normal function of the brain in schizophrenia patients so that the brain cannot process input efficiently or produce output effectively. This impairment leads to hallucinations, delusions, and difficulty in making decisions.

The value of clozapine in treating schizophrenia also became clearer as a result of the first long-term assessment of its use. Clozapine, a relatively expensive drug, was already known to be effective in reducing hallucinations and delusions. Psychiatrists were uncertain as to whether it was more effective than other drugs, especially haloperidol, in dealing with lack of motivation and other symptoms. The new study involved more than 400 patients whose schizophrenia was difficult to manage and who required frequent hospitalization. They were monitored over one year at 15 Veterans Affairs medical centres in the U.S. The results confirmed that clozapine was somewhat more effective than haloperidol. Clozapine also had fewer side effects, and the overall costs were similar for both drugs.

Research conducted in Oxford, Eng., threw new light on the brain chemistry responsible for the relatively common disorder known as depression, greatly strengthening the hypothesis that the condition is associated with reduced activity of serotonin, a neurotransmitter that nerve cells use to communicate with each other. Substances that increase serotonin activity in the brain act as antidepressants; however, there was no direct evidence that depression can be triggered by a low level of serotonin. The Oxford findings provided the most convincing evidence to date.

The subjects in the Oxford study were 15 women who had suffered recurrent episodes of depression but had recovered and were no longer on drug treatment. In laboratory tests they drank a mixture of amino acids that either included or excluded tryptophan, the amino acid that makes up serotonin. Before the tests and seven hours later, the women were evaluated to determine their level of depression. They also rated their own mood. After drinking the tryptophan-free solution (which reduced by 75% the level of tryptophan in their bloodstream), 10 of the 15 women experienced temporary but significant depressive symptoms. The mixture including tryptophan had no such effect. Thus, it seemed that a rapid decrease of tryptophan could precipitate depression in vulnerable individuals, probably by depleting the amount of serotonin in the brain.

There was a major innovation in London in applying a technique—already widely used in the treatment of psychiatric disorders—to help people who are not suffering specific mental health problems. The technique was cognitive behavioural training (CBT), which aimed to modify patients' perceptions of the external and internal reasons for their successes and failures in life. It had been successfully adopted in dealing with depression and compulsive obsessional neurosis. The London researchers felt that the same approach could be helpful for long-term unemployed people. It may help individuals who are free of psychiatric illness but who have developed reduced expectations and self-esteem, which decreases the likelihood of a successful outcome of job hunting and perhaps reduces their motivation to look for work at all.

A total of 200 volunteers took part in the experiment and were divided at random into equal groups to receive either three-hour CBT sessions each week for seven weeks or corresponding sessions that simply emphasized social support. Before and after the program, participants completed questionnaires regarding their mental health and their efforts to find employment. Both groups improved their mental health scores during the training period, but the improvement was significantly greater among those who had received CBT. The groups did not differ in their job-seeking activity during or immediately after training. Four months later, however, 34% of the individuals given CBT had found full-time work, as compared with only 13% of those on the alternative program. The organizers of the study concluded that CBT can improve mental health status and produce tangible results in job hunting, to the benefit of individuals and society at large. (BERNARD DIXON)

This article updates the *Macropædia* article MENTAL DISORDERS and Their Treatment.

VETERINARY MEDICINE

A global overview of animal health problems by the Office International des Epizooties (OIE) in 1997 surveyed progress in controlling major disease threats to the world's livestock population. Rinderpest was restricted to areas of sub-Saharan Africa, the Middle East, and India; a coordinated vaccination program aimed to eradicate the disease completely in the coming decade. Foot-and-mouth disease was eliminated or controlled in North America, southern South America, Europe, Oceania, Japan, and Southeast Asia. An outbreak in Taiwan, however, resulted in the slaughter of three million pigs. Contagious bovine pleuropneumonia remained a serious concern in Africa, where it was spreading to the south of the continent.

Another cause for concern was classical swine fever, which reappeared in Europe. In The Netherlands economic losses resulting from the disease exceeded $250 million. Bovine tuberculosis was again seen in many regions, while the incidence of brucellosis in small ruminants and trypanosomiasis in cattle in Africa and horses in Asia and the Middle East was also creating problems. Rabies was being controlled in Western Europe as a result of an oral-vaccination campaign in foxes, but it continued to represent a growing threat in less-developed countries and in Eastern Europe.

The number of suspected cases of bovine spongiform encephalopathy (BSE; "mad cow" disease) in Great Britain continued to fall. By the middle of 1997, the number of new cases reported each week had dropped to about 100 from a peak of 1,000 in 1993. About 80% of the cases were confirmed. The policy of culling all cattle over 30 months old, introduced in 1996 at the direction of the European Commission, resulted in the slaughter of 1.3 million cattle. A ban on British exports of beef and beef products remained in force, although progress was made toward lifting the ban on certified BSE-free herds where lifetime identity records had been maintained.

Actuarial studies of the life-span expectancy and the causes of mortality in different breeds of dog were in their infancy. The increasing amount of insurance taken out for companion animals was, however, establishing a database from which patterns were beginning to emerge. A study of data on more than 220,000 Swedish dogs enrolled in life insurance programs analyzed rates of mortality and identified 25 breeds that had either consistently high or consistently low mortality. Large breeds generally tended to die earlier, with the Irish wolfhound topping the list; smaller breeds had much lower rates of mortality, with the incidence for the soft-coated wheaten terrier nine times less than for the Irish wolfhound.

At the Roslin Institute, Edinburgh, researchers cloned a lamb from a single cell derived from the mammary gland of an adult sheep. The cell nucleus was implanted into an egg from another sheep and transferred to a third, which carried the embryo to full term and gave birth to a healthy lamb, named Dolly. A similar cloning technique was used to produce a transgenic lamb carrying a human gene for a therapeutic protein. This protein would be harvested from the milk of the adult sheep during lactation. After purification the protein could be used for therapeutic purposes. The technique was expected to facilitate the production of a range of proteins with specific medical applications, such as the treatment of cystic fibrosis. (*See* LIFE SCIENCES: *Special Report.*)

Described as the largest small-animal congress ever held, a joint meeting of the World Small Animal Veterinary Association, the British Small Animal Veterinary Association, and the Federation of European Companion Animal Veterinary Associations at Birmingham, Eng., in April attracted an attendance of more than 6,700. The meeting paid particular attention to the potential of information technology for improving veterinary services. (EDWARD BODEN)

See also Life Sciences: *Molecular Biology.*

This article updates the *Macropædia* articles DIAGNOSIS AND THERAPEUTICS; DISEASE; INFECTIOUS DISEASES; MEDICINE.

SPECIAL REPORT

Alternative Medicine

by Hari M. Sharma and Gerard C. Bodeker

Alternative and complementary medicine covers a broad range of healing philosophies, approaches, and therapies. The Office of Alternative Medicine (OAM) at the U.S. National Institutes of Health (NIH) defines alternative and complementary medicine as "those treatments and health care practices not taught widely in medical schools, not generally used in hospitals, and not usually reimbursed by medical insurance companies." Many of these therapies are holistic, which means that the health care practitioner considers the whole person, including his or her physical, mental, emotional, and spiritual characteristics. Many treatments are also preventive, the practitioner educating and treating the person to prevent health problems from arising rather than treating the patient after disease has already occurred. Some of the commonly used alternative and complementary therapies are acupuncture, Ayurveda, chiropractic, herbal medicine, homeopathy, massage, meditation, naturopathy, prayer, shamanism, therapeutic touch, and yoga.

It is important to note that for large portions of the world's population, nonmainstream approaches to medicine are neither alternative nor complementary. Traditional health care systems constitute the main source of everyday health care for up to 80% of the population of most of the less-developed countries, according to the World Health Organization (WHO). They are also used by ethnic and indigenous populations in industrial countries, such as the U.S., Canada, and Australia. The ratio of traditional health practitioners to population in many places is substantially higher than the ratio of medical personnel trained in mainstream medicine to population and thus represents an irreplaceable health care infrastructure.

International. WHO recently produced reports on training for traditional birth attendants and on evaluating herbal medicines. Its Collaborating Centre for Drug Monitoring announced a new technology for patenting, testing, and approving medicinal plants. While maintaining an official interest in traditional medicine, WHO, however, progressively reduced funding for this sector, and other agencies assumed increased responsibility for work in this field. In 1996 and 1997, for example, the World Bank issued reports on medicinal plants, drawing attention to the need to conserve and cultivate these plants in order to ensure a supply for the $800 billion-per-year medicinal plant market.

In 1996 the Global Initiative for Traditional Systems (GIFTS) of Health, a nongovernment network of traditional medicine research-and-development programs, produced a report on policy in traditional health care. Headquartered in Oxford, Eng., GIFTS recommended formal collaboration between modern and traditional medical sectors. It called for a framework (and adequate budgetary support) for legal recognition of traditional health practitioners and for officially supported training in traditional medicine.

Asia. In India the government became involved in traditional drug production when the Central Drug Research Institute patented two new drugs from ancient Ayurvedic formulas. One, a mixture of black pepper, long pepper, and ginger, allows for the dosage of the antibiotic rifampicin to be halved in the treatment of tuberculosis and other mycobacterial infections. The other is a memory tonic produced from the traditional plant called brahmi. Overseas patenting of turmeric and products of the neem tree caused controversy in India and other nations. In August the U.S. Patent and Trademark Office canceled a U.S. patent on the wound-healing properties of turmeric when the Indian government proved that records had existed for this use for centuries.

Researchers in Thailand and Vietnam reported in the medical journal *The Lancet* in 1996 that artemether, a plant extract from *Artemisia annua* used in Chinese medicine, is effective in treating cerebral malaria. Vietnamese researchers, working in collaboration with colleagues at the University of Oxford, found that traditional Vietnamese treatments for burns and wounds are effective in stimulating tissue growth and reducing scar tissue.

In China, where there is full state support for traditional medicine, almost half of the population uses it on a regular basis. Chinese methods of preventing and treating cardiovascular conditions, cancer, burns, and psoriasis have all been found to be effective in recent studies conducted in China and internationally.

Africa. In many countries of Africa, 80–90% of the people use traditional medicine, often as their only method of health care. A recent study by the African Development Bank and UNICEF found that economic factors, such as devaluation of currencies, result in a substantial shift from modern to traditional medicine, even in urban populations.

In Uganda the government introduced a policy in support of traditional medicine. A group of modern and traditional health practitioners began working together to combat the AIDS epidemic by using herbal remedies to treat opportunistic infections associated with AIDS and by providing culturally relevant emotional support to people with AIDS. In Zambia and Mozambique training courses for traditional healers increased the effectiveness of the AIDS-prevention message being delivered to local communities. Also during the year the new University of the Health Sciences in Tanzania introduced a course in traditional medicine.

Studies in both Ethiopia and Uganda of the plant *Phytolacca dodecandra* found it effective against the snails and larvae that carry schistosomiasis, as well as in controlling larvae of the black fly that carries onchocerciasis. A 1997 issue of the Royal Society of Medicine journal *Tropical Doctor* presented evidence from Uganda of clearance of parasitemia with a local herbal antimalarial mixture.

South and Central America. The Pan-American Health Organization, in a set of guidelines for research with indigenous populations, emphasized the importance of developing research into traditional medicine. A study of the understanding and treatment of gastrointestinal disorders among the Maya of Chiapas state, Mex., presented evidence of the scientific bases of the Maya's large pharmacopeia of local herbal medicines. Faced with a severe malaria epidemic, the Yanomami Indians of northern Brazil identified 82 genera of plants in different parts of their region useful for combating the disease. Antimalarial activity was shown to be linked to a range of compounds, and the plants used by the Yanomami were demonstrated to contain these compounds.

Industrialized Countries. The growth of alternative medicine in the industrialized countries has resulted almost entirely from the efforts of consumers. The Lannoye Report to the European Parliament (1997) revealed that in countries where statistics are available, 20–50% of the population of European countries uses alternative forms of health care.

Current legislation within the European Union is varied. In France a tolerant attitude exists; acupuncture has been recognized by the Académie de Médicine since 1950, and homeopathic remedies are reimbursed by social security when medically prescribed. The northern countries—Great Britain, Ireland, The Netherlands, Germany, Denmark, and

MICHAEL GADOMSKI—PHOTO RESEARCHERS

St. John's Wort (*Hypericum perforatum*) captured the attention of many people in 1997 after a new study indicated that the herb could be effective in treating depression and had fewer side effects than many commonly prescribed antidepressant drugs.

Sweden—have taken a more restrictive position. Although most allow the practice of health care by complementary practitioners, certain activities are reserved for doctors, and policy and supervision of complementary medicine rest in the hands of the biomedical profession.

Clinical research in London revealed that Chinese herbal medicine is an effective means of controlling atopic eczema. The National Health Service programs in Great Britain offer some forms of complementary medicine, such as homeopathy and acupuncture. The Glasgow (Scot.) Homœopathic Hospital established an international data collection network that began collecting information from general practitioners who are using homeopathic remedies. Based on a sample of more than 1,000 cases, the International Data Collection Centres for Integrative Medicine network found that 7 out of 10 patients using homeopathic remedies reported moderate improvement in their condition.

U.S. funding for research on alternative/complementary therapies is increasingly being supplied by the OAM at the NIH. Established by a mandate of Congress in 1992, the OAM awarded grants to six U.S. universities for the study of complementary medicine in relation to cancer, heart disease, women's health, AIDS, pain control, and general medicine. In 1997 Congress allocated $12 million to the OAM, as compared with $7.4 million in 1996.

Because health care in the U.S. is overwhelmingly centred on employer-provided health plans or insurance, it is significant that medical insurance companies in the U.S. have begun to offer coverage for complementary medicine. In January Oxford Health Plans, Inc., of Norwalk, Conn., announced an alternative medicine program that offers patients a network of qualified providers for chiropractic, acupuncture, yoga, massage therapy, and nutrition information. Since 1995 more than one-third of Oxford's 1.8 million members have chosen alternative medical services either alone or in conjunction with conventional medical treatments. Another major American insurer, Mutual of Omaha Companies, began offering coverage for a cardiovascular program that combines a low-fat vegetarian diet; mild exercise, including yoga; and a regime of stress reduction that employs a form of meditation.

U.S. researchers have investigated traditional herbal antioxidants. Studies on an herbal mixture called Maharishi Amrit Kalash from the Maharishi Vedic Approach to Health found it to be an exceptionally potent antioxidant. Other research on this mixture revealed it to have marked anticancer effects and to decrease experimental atherosclerosis.

In a study on Canadians using a stress-reduction program, transcendental meditation (TM), it was found that in a period of up to seven years, government payments to physicians for those patients declined significantly, at a rate of 5–7% annually, as compared with their pre-TM rates. Another study found TM to be efficacious in treating hypertension.

Medical education in the U.S. is beginning to reflect changes in patients' choices of health care. By 1997 more than 30 American medical schools were offering courses in complementary medicine.

Conclusion. Although doubts and opposition remain, it seems inevitable that the momentum of research into traditional, alternative, and complementary health care will continue. While some approaches will likely be found useless or even harmful, others will no doubt be proved effective. They may offer advantages to mainstream medicine by providing treatments in areas where conventional medical approaches have not been successful (such as treatment of chronic disorders), by offering therapies that are cost-effective and free of toxic side effects, and by suggesting new directions for an integrated approach to health care.

Hari M. Sharma is Professor Emeritus and former director, Cancer Prevention and Natural Products Research, Department of Pathology, College of Medicine, Ohio State University; and Fellow, National Academy of Ayurveda, Ministry of Health and Family Welfare, India. He is the author of Freedom from Disease *and* Contemporary Ayurveda: Medicine and Research in Maharishi Ayur-Veda.

Gerard C. Bodeker is a member of the Health Service Research Unit at the University of Oxford, England.

Law, Crime, and Law Enforcement

LAW

The tendency, increasingly visible in previous years, for international law to change from a set of rules governing relations between sovereign nations (and relevant only to those nations) into a framework for joint action on matters that directly affect individual citizens became even more pronounced in 1997. This was reflected in two aspects of the conduct of nations. The first of these was their increasing recourse to international legislation (treaties and multilateral conventions) in order to develop their own laws in collaboration with other nations, and the second was the increasing subordination of national action to international adjudication that was being undertaken by the growing number of international courts and tribunals.

International Courts and Tribunals. During the year nearly all the major international courts set up Web sites on the Internet. In addition, at least two law schools (Cornell in the United States and Düsseldorf in Germany) created Web sites that provided hyperlink access to some or all of those courts. The sites contained information about the court and its activities, usually the full text of recent judgments, and sometimes a calendar of future hearings.

The newest international court, the International Tribunal for the Law of the Sea (ITLOS), spent the year working on its rules of procedure and its internal organization into chambers: the main Seabed Disputes Chamber, a Chamber of Summary Procedure, a Chamber on Fisheries Matters, and a Chamber on the Marine Environment. On November 13 ITLOS received its first case, brought by St.Vincent and the Grenadines against Guinea in relation to the seizure by the latter of a ship off the coast of West Africa.

At the same time as that court became operational, the preparations for yet another reached culmination. The UN General Assembly, by a resolution of Jan. 16, 1997, reapproved the timetable of the Preparatory Committee on the establishment of a permanent international criminal court. Subsequently, the committee met in February, August, and December to prepare the way for a final meeting in March 1998 and a diplomatic conference in Rome in June–July 1998 to adopt a convention. The work of the committee covered the definition of the crimes to be subject to the new court's jurisdiction (within the broad range of genocide, war crimes, and crimes against humanity), the applicable principles of law, the jurisdictional relationship with national courts, procedure, and penalties.

In France on January 16, the Supreme Court produced an important definition of the concept of "crimes against humanity" that was based on Article 6 of the Nürnberg Charter, during the trial of Maurice Papon. The defendant was accused of having participated, as an official in the Vichy government of Nazi-occupied France, in the deportation of some 2,000 Jews between 1942 and 1944.

A third "new" international court was foreshadowed by the entry into force on October 1 of the 11th Protocol to the European Convention on Human Rights. As a result of this protocol, a completely new European Court of Human Rights, resulting from the merger of the existing court and the Commission of Human Rights, would come into existence on Nov. 1, 1998.

The existing courts continued to develop and expand their practices. In December 1996 the World Trade Organization (WTO) Appellate Body adopted Rules of Conduct that supplemented the existing Understanding on Dispute Settlement Procedure and the Working Procedures on Appellate Review. As a result, the Appellate Body had a full set of working texts, and during 1997 it decided several appeals from WTO (formerly the General Agreement on Tariffs and Trade) panel reports. These included the controversial condemnation (upholding the panel report) of the European Union's (EU's) inclusion of bananas in its common agricultural policy (*U.S. and others* v. *EU*), which resulted in discrimination in favour of imports from EU-related countries in the Caribbean.

The bringing before a WTO panel of *EU* v. *U.S.*—a case involving the disputed exercise by the U.S. of extraterritorial jurisdiction against trade with Cuba, Iran, and Libya through the Helms-Burton Act and the Iran and Libya Sanctions Act (ILSA)—was instrumental in settling the dispute. Under an EU-U.S. memorandum of understanding of April 11, the U.S. agreed to continue suspension of Title III of the former and the nonapplication of Title IV and of ILSA to EU nationals in return for EU withdrawal of its complaint from the WTO panel.

The International Court of Justice (ICJ) delivered judgment on a preliminary point in *Iran* v. *U.S.* on Dec. 12, 1996, holding (against the preliminary objection raised by the U.S.) that, on the basis of Article XXI(2) of the Iran/U.S. Treaty of Amity, Economic Relations, and Consular Rights of Aug. 15, 1955, it did have jurisdiction to consider Iran's complaint of breach of the treaty following the destruction by the U.S. Navy of three Iranian oil complexes in the Persian Gulf in 1987 and 1988. Argument on the merits of the case would then follow.

On September 26 the ICJ delivered judgment in *Hungary* v. *Slovakia* concerning the Gabcikovo-Nagymaros Project for the damming and hydroelectric diversion of the Danube River. In this difficult case Hungary had intended in 1989 to terminate a 1977 Hungary-Czechoslovakia treaty because of the adverse environmental consequences of the dam, a consideration that had not applied in 1977; Slovakia thereupon carried out an alternative operation on its territory that affected Hungary's access to Danube waters. The court held that Hungary was not entitled to denounce the treaty or suspend its share of the works under it, that Slovakia was not entitled to operate its own solution, that Slovakia succeeded to Czechoslovakia as party to the 1977 treaty, and that the two parties had to compensate each other for their respective breaches and negotiate in good faith to achieve the objectives of the 1977 treaty in the light of the prevailing situation.

The function of the ICJ, which was the subject of a probing scrutiny by the British Institute of International and Comparative Law in 1996, was considered in a thoughtful and challenging article in April. The article concluded that the court did have the power in certain circumstances to declare UN Security Council decisions invalid, both in advisory opinions and in contentious cases in which a Security Council resolution formed part of the applicable law.

In spite of all the above, press attention concentrated on the two war crimes tribunals: the International Criminal Tribunal for the Former Yugoslavia (ICTY) at The Hague and the International Criminal Tribunal for Rwanda (ICTR) at Arusha, Tanz. Whereas in the previous year there had been some despondency about the ICTY, in view of the seeming difficulty in obtaining physical custody of indicted suspects, 1997 saw the situation change radically. This was illustrated by two developments. First, the ICTY concluded its first contested full trial (a conviction in 1996 had followed a plea of guilty) with the conviction of Dusan Tadic on May 7; the ICTY found him guilty on 10 counts of having beaten Muslim prisoners in various Serb detention camps in Bosnia and Herzegovina and on one count of having participated in the persecution of Muslim civilians; both, according to the ICTY, constituted crimes against humanity (on other counts, including rape and murder, he was found not guilty). In its 301-page judgment of first impression, the ICTY considered for the first time fundamental questions of its jurisdiction and of the laws of war (the existence of an international armed conflict), as well as the nature of a crime against humanity and of individual responsibility.

The second important development was the start of the trial on March 10 of four defendants who were either Croat or Muslim and whose victims were Bosnian Serbs, the defendants being Esad Landzo, Zejnil Delalic, Zdravko Mucic, and Hazim Delic. The multiethnic character of the ICTY was thus established by its second contested case, which also had to consider for the first time fundamental issues of command responsibility (Articles 86 and 87 of Protocol 1 of 1977 additional to the Geneva Conventions) and of rape and sexual assault. It was also the ICTY's first multidefendant trial.

In addition to these two substantive trials, there was a marked, though still slow, increase in the number of accused held in custody by the ICTY as the governments of Croatia and of Bosnia and Herzegovina (but not of Republika Srpska) began to cooperate in extraditing their nationals; for example, 10 Croats were surrendered and charged in October. On May 20 the UN General Assembly elected or reelected the 11 judges of the ICTY to serve for four years beginning November 17.

The sister ICTR, sitting in Arusha, opened its first trial in January, against Jean-Paul Akayesu, charged with genocide, but had to adjourn it almost immediately because witnesses failed to appear. A second trial, against Georges Anderson Rutaganda, was postponed in March at the request of the prosecution. Of the three foreign countries in which accused suspects were being held, two (Cameroon and Switzerland) authorized their transfer to the ICTR's custody in Arusha; the U.S., however, released a suspect, Elizaphan Ntakirutimana, on the order (Dec. 17, 1996) of a federal judge. The judge based his decision on the grounds that extradition must be based on an agreement with another nation and not with an international organization or tribunal. The ICTR's difficulties were highlighted by an internal UN inquiry, which in February issued a severely critical report that resulted soon afterward in the dismissal by the UN secretary-general of two top officials of the ICTR.

International Legislation. Perhaps the most important legislative event of the year was the entry into force of the Chemical Weapons Convention on April 29, by which time it had been ratified by 81 of its 165 signatories. Its implementation was to be supervised by the Organization for the Prohibition of Chemical Weapons, based in The Hague. Of almost equal importance was the adoption in Oslo on September 18 of the UN Convention on the Prohibition of the Use, Stockpiling, Production and Transfer of Anti-personnel Mines and on Their Destruction and its opening for signature in Ottawa on December 3. This treaty had been opposed by powerful military and commercial interests but benefited from an unrelenting worldwide pressure in its behalf.

Other significant legislation, mainly affecting the private sphere, included treaties on private employment agencies, bribery of foreign public officials in business transactions, biomedicine and human rights, human cloning, international digital trade, electronic commerce, model law on cross-border insolvency, telecommunications, trade in information technology products, copyright and performers' rights, and civil liability for nuclear damage. In addition, the UN adopted in May an important convention on nonnavigational uses of international watercourses and agreed in March to establish a relationship with the International Seabed Authority.

(NEVILLE MARCH HUNNINGS)

Court Decisions. During 1997 a number of decisions having jurisprudential or newsworthy importance or both were handed down by the courts of the various countries. In the United States *Clinton* v. *Jones* was a case that attracted national and international attention because it involved the current president of the United States. Jones sued him, alleging that while Clinton was governor of Arkansas he made "abhorrent" sexual advances to her. Clinton urged the district court to defer the action until his presidential term ended, and the court agreed. The U.S. Supreme Court was, however, of a different opinion. It held that the district court had abused its discretion, because nothing in the Constitution requires that civil damages litigation against the president be deferred until his term has ended. It ordered the trial to proceed in a normal manner. *Washington* v. *Glucksberg* sustained the validity of a Washington state statute that provided that a person who knowingly causes or helps another to attempt suicide is guilty of a felony. The Supreme Court said this statute did not violate the due process clause of the Constitution. *Chandler* v. *Miller* held unconstitutional a Georgia statute requiring candidates for designated state offices to certify that they had taken a urinalysis drug test and that the test result was negative. The Supreme Court opined that this statute offended the Constitution's Fourth Amendment, which prohibits the government from undertaking a search or seizure if there is no reasonable suspicion of wrongdoing. *Reno* v. *American Civil Liberties Union* ruled unconstitutional the Communications Decency Act (1996), which prohibited the knowing transmission to minors of indecent or patently offensive communications. The court held that the statute abridged the right to free speech. This case excited national attention and resulted in many newspaper editorials, mostly of a critical nature, because the condemned statute was aimed at Internet pornography.

Another American case of great interest and importance was handed down by a federal appeals court. *Coalition for Economic Equity* v. *Pete Wilson* sustained the validity of an amendment to the constitution of the state of California that provided that the "state shall not discriminate against, or grant preferential treatment to, any individual or group on the basis of race, sex, color, ethnicity or national origin in the operation of public employment, public education or public contracting." This amendment was the result of a referendum, called Proposition 209, that opponents claimed was aimed at ending affirmative action. The U.S. Supreme Court, acting without an opinion or other comment, let stand this decision. Though this action set no national precedent, it was viewed by many to encourage voters in other states to adopt similar measures and thus signaled a possible end to affirmative action in the U.S.

In Australia in *Applicant A* v. *Minister for Immigration and Ethnic Affairs,* the High Court denied asylum to a Chinese couple who claimed that because of China's one-child-only policy, they would be sterilized if forced to return there. The court said the applicants did not fit into any group protected by its laws of asylum.

In Belgium the *Dutroux* case, involving a pedophile who killed several children, attracted worldwide attention and later made headlines when a judge involved in the case was dismissed on the ground that he lacked impartiality because he had accepted a modest token at a fund-raising dinner sponsored by the families of the victims. The judge contended that taking this small token did not violate the rules of the European Convention on Human Rights, but the Cour de Cassation said this fact was irrelevant because Belgium was entitled to apply higher standards. Under those standards the judge was dismissed.

The case of *Illman* v. *The Queen* in Canada clarified the exclusionary rules of sec. 7 (security of the person) and 8 (unreasonable

TED FITZGERALD—REUTERS

British au pair Louise Woodward is consoled by her attorneys on October 30 after being found guilty of second-degree murder in the death of eight-month-old Matthew Eappen. A judge later reduced Woodward's conviction to involuntary manslaughter and her life sentence to time already served. The televised case attracted much attention in Great Britain and the U.S.

seizure) of the Canadian Charter of Rights and Freedoms. In this case the accused was charged with murder. For purposes of DNA testing, samples of his hair and a dental impression were taken from him without his consent and, indeed, despite advice of counsel that he should not consent. The Supreme Court of Canada held that these seizures violated sec. 7 and 8 of the Charter and could not be used in evidence against him. In *R.* v. *Noble* the Supreme Court ruled that a judge cannot draw inferences adverse to a person charged with a crime because of his or her failure to testify. The case seemed to expand the protection of criminally accused persons. Well-established Canadian doctrine precludes the use of statements made involuntarily by one accused of crime, and the presumption of innocence is a constitutional right. The court said these principles should be extended to allow an accused person to remain silent with impunity.

According to newspaper reports, the French public in 1997 was intensely interested in the right of the government to deport "undesirable" aliens and to exclude permanently other "objectionable" persons. Two cases handed down during the year on those matters, therefore, excited much interest. The first, *H.L.R.* v. *France,* was decided by the European Court of Human Rights (ECHR); it involved a Colombian national whom a French court had convicted of drug trafficking and sentenced to permanent exclusion from France. The ECHR sustained this sentence despite the applicant's complaint that he would be subject to treatment forbidden by the European Convention on Human Rights if forced to return to Colombia. The second case was resolved by the Conseil d'État, which held that a foreign national who had committed violent crimes in France could not be expelled. The person involved in the case had been born in France and had lived there all his life, along with his parents and siblings. The court said that expulsion is an extreme remedy aimed at protecting the public order. In this case, the court ruled, expulsion went beyond protecting the public order and interfered with the applicant's right to family and private life, in violation of art. 8 of the European Convention on Human Rights.

In Germany a case of little jurisprudential significance but wide public interest involved Peter Graf, father of the international tennis star Steffi Graf. He was convicted of tax fraud and sentenced to three years and nine months in prison. Another case of interest was the opinion of the Federal Constitutional Court that a federal act requiring the labeling of tobacco products did not violate the free-speech rights of the tobacco companies.

In Britain *The Matter of Serafinowicz* concerned the first war crimes prosecution in that nation. The accused, Szymon Serafinowicz, was the police chief of Belorussia (Belarus) during World War II. He was charged with having played a leading role in the murder of some 2,000 Jews. The case was dismissed after a jury decided that Serafinowicz, who was 86 years old, was unfit to stand trial. In *R.* v. *Shaw* the Court of Appeal held that a defendant who insisted on, and indulged in, sexual intercourse without protection was guilty of rape when the woman did not consent to this activity unless and until the man provided the proper protection. He was sentenced to 12 years in prison by the trial court. Upon appeal and in view of his medical condition, the sentence was reduced to eight years.

In *D.* v. *United Kingdom* the ECHR, on a vote of 11–7, found that the U.K. had violated art. 3 (inhuman activities prohibited) of the European Convention on Human Rights in ordering an applicant deported to St. Kitts. The applicant, domiciled in St. Kitts, was arrested when he arrived in London in possession of a substantial quantity of cocaine. While he was in prison, it was discovered that he had AIDS and that his physical condition was rapidly deteriorating. Under these circumstances the British authorities ordered him deported to the Caribbean island. The applicant contended that he had no family in St. Kitts, no means of support there, and no place to live. The court found that under these circumstances his deportation would amount to inhuman treatment in violation of art. 3.

In *Tsirlis and Kouloumpas* v. *Greece,* the ECHR applied art. 5(1) (liberty of person) and 5(5) (compensation for unlawful detention) to protect two Jehovah's Witnesses' ministers from improper action by the Greek government. The two ministers claimed exemption from military service on religious grounds. The Greek authorities denied the exemption and imprisoned the ministers for refusing to serve in the military. The ministers applied for relief to the ECHR. The court held that the refusal to grant the applicants an exemption from military service violated art. 5(1) of the European Convention on Human Rights and that, under art. 5(5) of the convention, they were entitled to compensation for wrongful imprisonment.

In *M.C. Mehta* v. *Union of India,* the Supreme Court of India ordered that all coke- and coal-consuming industries in the Taj Mahal area, demarcated "Taj Trapezium," be closed because air pollution generated by them was damaging the Taj irreversibly. In *PUCL* v. *Union of India,* the Supreme Court held that telephone tapping violates a citizen's right to privacy. In so ruling the court said that art. 12 of the Universal Declaration of Human Rights 1948 and art. 17 of the International Covenant on Civil and Political Rights 1966 should be read into Indian domestic law.

The Constitutional Court in Italy delivered an important judgment invalidating the use of "reiteration" of government decrees. The Italian constitution allows the government in emergency situations to issue decrees that have immediate effect but become invalid unless converted into legislation within 60 days. In actuality, the government was using this procedure frequently. Under the government's interpretation, when a decree cannot be converted in time, the government can simply "reiterate" it, keeping it in force until the legislature finally acts. The court said the constitution did not authorize this practice.

In *Tala* v. *Sweden* the United Nations Committee Against Torture held that an Iranian political activist opposing the present government of Iran should not be deported to Iran, where, in the opinion of the committee, he was bound to be tortured.

(WILLIAM D. HAWKLAND)

See also World Affairs: *Multinational and Regional Organizations; United Nations.*

This article updates the *Macropædia* articles CONSTITUTIONAL LAW; INTERNATIONAL LAW.

CRIME

Terrorism. On June 2, 1997, a jury in Denver, Colo., did much to restore confidence in a tarnished U.S. criminal justice system when it reached a unanimous finding that Timothy McVeigh was guilty of 11 murder and conspiracy counts relating to the 1995 bombing of a federal government office building in Oklahoma City, Okla. The blast, the worst terrorist attack in U.S. history, had resulted in the loss of 169 lives and had injured some 850 people. A jury-sanctioned penalty of death was imposed on McVeigh in August, but any execution was likely to be delayed for at least five years while he appealed his conviction. Meanwhile, an accused accomplice of McVeigh's in the bombing, Terry Nichols, went on trial in Denver in September on murder and conspiracy charges identical to those laid against McVeigh. In late December Nichols was acquitted of the murder charges but convicted of conspiracy (a capital crime) and involuntary manslaughter. Sentencing was expected early in 1998.

The alleged mastermind behind the terrorist bombing of the World Trade Center in New York City in February 1993, Ramzi Ahmed Yousef, went on trial in New York in August. Yousef, who was arrested in Pakistan in 1995, was said to have admitted to a federal agent that he had hoped that the blast, which killed 6 people and injured more than 1,000, would topple one of the Trade Center towers and kill as many as 250,000 Americans. The attack was conducted in retaliation for U.S. aid to Israel. On November 12 Yousef and Eyad Ismoil, who was accused of having driven the van that carried the bomb into the Trade Center's garage, were found guilty; both faced life in prison.

The U.S. State Department's 1997 report *Patterns of Global Terrorism* said that no international terrorist attacks took place in the U.S. during 1996. Worldwide, 296 acts of international terrorism were recorded, the lowest annual total in 25 years. In contrast, the number of casualties was one of the highest ever, with 311 persons killed and more than 2,600 injured. The report noted that a growing policy of zero tolerance for terrorism had resulted in a decline in state-sponsored acts of terror, although Iran, the primary state sponsor, had not been deterred. Reflecting this situation, American and Saudi Arabian intelligence authorities claimed in April to have linked a senior Iranian government official to a group of Shiʿite Muslims suspected of having bombed a U.S. military compound in Dhahran, Saudi Arabia, in June 1996. That blast killed 19 servicemen and wounded more than 500. Also in April a German court ruled that the highest levels of the Iranian government had ordered the assassination of four people in Berlin in 1992. It was the first time that a Western court had directly implicated Iran's fundamentalist leaders in the killing of Iranian dissidents in Europe. Following the court's ruling, the European Union ordered a mass recall of ambassadors from Tehran and also suspended an ongoing critical dialogue with Iran that had been maintained despite vigorous pressure from the U.S.

On April 22 a 126-day standoff between the Peruvian government and 14 leftist guerrillas holding 72 hostages in the Japanese

ERICH SCHLEGEL—DALLAS MORNING NEWS/KRT

Gatherers outside the Alfred P. Murrah Federal Building in Oklahoma City, Okla., react to news that a jury in Denver, Colo., had found Timothy McVeigh guilty of 11 murder and conspiracy counts in relation to the 1995 bombing of the building that resulted in the loss of 169 lives.

ambassador's residence in Lima came to a violent end. More than 600 hostages, many of them diplomats, had originally been seized on Dec. 17, 1996, when members of the Túpac Amaru Revolutionary Movement stormed a diplomatic reception at the residence. Most of these hostages were subsequently released as protracted negotiations continued in search of a peaceful solution to the international crisis. The guerrillas demanded the release of 400 of their imprisoned comrades—a demand refused by the government, which was prepared only to offer the hostage takers safe passage to asylum in Cuba. After more than four months of discussion, Peruvian Pres. Alberto Fujimori ordered a rescue mission by an elite 140-person military-police team. The team blasted its way into the residence, freeing all of the hostages. One hostage, a Peruvian Supreme Court justice, and two army officers died in the attack, along with all of the guerrillas.

The Israeli government suffered a major embarrassment in September when two suspected members of Mossad, its intelligence agency, were arrested in Amman, Jordan, following an attempt to assassinate Khaled Meshal, a political leader of the Islamic militant movement Hamas. The Israelis sprayed a lethal nerve toxin into Meshal's ear, and only the supply by Israel of an antidote, demanded by Jordanian and U.S. officials after the arrest of the two suspects, saved Meshal's life. The decision to attack Meshal was believed to have been authorized by Israeli Prime Minister Benjamin Netanyahu after two Hamas suicide bombers killed 13 Israelis in the Mahane Yehuda produce market in Jerusalem on July 30. In the wake of the botched assassination attempt, Israel agreed to hand over between 40 and 50 Palestinian and Jordanian prisoners in exchange for their captured agents.

War Crimes. In July the International Criminal Tribunal for the Former Yugoslavia in The Hague sentenced a former Bosnian Serb café owner, Dusan Tadic, to 20 years in prison for his role in the "ethnic cleansing" of Bosnian Muslims and Croats during the conflict in former Yugoslavia. The verdict, which followed a seven-month trial in The Hague, was the first of its kind since the end of World War II. (See *Law,* above.)

Former French official Maurice Papon, charged with complicity in Nazi crimes against humanity during World War II, leaves his hotel for the Palace of Justice in Bordeaux, where his trial began in October. He was first indicted in 1983.

MAX NASH—ASSOCIATED PRESS

Also in Bosnia, NATO-led troops from the Stabilization Force (SFOR), deployed under the terms of the Dayton Peace Agreement in former Yugoslavia, conducted a raid in Prijedor to arrest two Bosnian Serbs secretly indicted by the tribunal as war criminals. Simo Drljaca, the police chief of Prijedor, was shot dead while resisting arrest by the troops, whereas Milan Kovacevic, the director of the Prijedor hospital, was seized and taken to The Hague to face trial by the tribunal. Both men, like Tadic, were said to have been implicated in the savage ill-treatment of prisoners at Omarska and other notorious detention camps that were set up in the Prijedor region during the conflict.

A curious development in the United States had an impact on the working of the International Criminal Tribunal for Rwanda in Arusha, Tanz. A Hutu Seventh-day Adventist clergyman, Elizaphan Ntakirutimana, escaped from Rwanda and made his way to Texas, where he was arrested by federal marshals in 1996 on charges of genocide and crimes against humanity. On Dec. 17, 1997, however, Marcel C. Notzon, a federal magistrate-judge in Laredo, Texas, found the relationship between the U.S. and the tribunal to be unconstitutional, declined to turn Ntakirutimana over to trial, and freed the pastor. He apparently went into hiding.

In October in Bordeaux, France, the trial of 87-year-old Maurice Papon began on charges of complicity in Nazi crimes against humanity by ordering the deportation to death camps of more than 1,500 Jews during World War II. Papon, the highest-ranking official from the period of the German occupation of France to go on trial for such crimes and only the second French citizen to be tried on such charges since the war, had first been indicted in 1983.

Drug Trafficking. The 1997 *World Drug Report,* compiled by the UN International Drug Control Program (UNDCP), estimated that the annual turnover in drugs was $400 billion, or about 8% of total international trade. The UNDCP report said that the world's drug trade, which grew dramatically during the past decade, exceeded the international trade in iron, steel, and motor vehicles. World production of coca leaf, the raw material for cocaine, more than doubled between 1985 and 1996, and opium production more than tripled. Although drug seizures also increased, a drop in the retail price of narcotics indicated that consumers were receiving even more supplies.

In the U.S., the nation with the highest drug-consumption rate, a report published in February by the General Accounting Office (GAO), a research agency for the U.S. Congress, stated that despite a $20 billion prevention effort over a decade, supplies of cocaine and heroin continued to flood into the country at a level more than adequate to meet the demand of American drug users. The GAO report also noted that in 1995 only about 230 of the 780 metric tons of cocaine produced around the world were seized and about 32 of some 300 metric tons of heroin. U.S. antidrug efforts were said to rely heavily on the ability of foreign governments to reduce the amount of drugs by eradication and crop-substitution programs and by prosecuting major traffickers. Regrettably, the antidrug programs of those governments were often corrupted by bribes made possible by the enormous profits generated by the drug trade.

A graphic example of such corruption occurred in February with the arrest by Mexican authorities of that nation's top antidrug official, Gen. Jesus Gutiérrez Rebollo, a 42-year army veteran. Gutiérrez was alleged to have collaborated with one of Mexico's most notorious drug barons, Amado Carrillo Fuentes, who later died while undergoing plastic surgery to change his appearance. The arrest, which U.S Pres. Bill Clinton called "deeply troubling," stunned U.S. law-enforcement officials, who had publicly praised Gutiérrez's appointment and shared with him highly sensitive information about covert measures taken to combat drug trafficking.

Murder and Other Violence. For the fifth consecutive year, the overall rate of serious crime in the U.S. fell in 1996, according to the FBI's annual survey of law-enforcement agencies, with the violent crime rate dropping 6% from the previous year and the murder rate by 9%. The murder rate in 1996, 7.4 incidences for every 100,000 people, was lower than at any other point since the late 1960s. Criminologists and law-enforcement officials believed that the continuing decline in crime could be the result of several converging trends, including the aging of a large segment of the population, improved police efficiency, and more severe prison sentences. This good news was tempered by the release in February of a report by the Centers for Disease Control and Prevention in Atlanta, Ga., which found that the U.S. had the highest rates of childhood homicide, suicide, and firearms-related deaths of any of the world's 26 richest nations. Three-quarters of all the murders of children in the industrialized world occurred in the U.S.

A shooting spree on February 23 by a gunman on the 86th-floor observation deck of the Empire State Building in New York City illustrated how easy it still was to obtain a handgun in the U.S. The gunman, Ali Abu Kamal, killed a Danish tourist and wounded six persons in the attack before taking his own life. Kamal, a Palestinian schoolteacher on a visit to the U.S., had purchased the 14-shot semiautomatic handgun in a Florida gun shop after having established local residency by staying briefly in a motel.

Gun control in the U.S. suffered a setback in June when the nation's Supreme Court found unconstitutional the central part of the Brady Handgun Violence Protection Act, the law, passed by Congress in 1993, requiring checks on the criminal and mental history of gun buyers. The court ruled, in a 5–4 verdict, that it is unlawful for the federal government to require local police to check the backgrounds of people applying to buy guns. Meanwhile, in May Britain's newly elected Labour Party government announced that it would impose an outright prohibition of handguns, toughening what were already some of the most stringent gun-control laws in any Western democracy.

The world of international fashion was shocked on July 15 when Italian designer Gianni Versace was shot to death outside his mansion in Miami Beach, Fla. (*See* OBITUARIES.) The slaying prompted a massive search for his murderer, who was believed to be Andrew Cunanan, a probable spree killer on the FBI's most-wanted list. On July 23, following a five-hour siege, police stormed aboard a houseboat moored just five kilometres (three miles) from the murdered designer's home. Inside the houseboat, police found the body of Cunanan, who had taken his own life. A handgun discovered near the body was later established to be the one that had been used to shoot Versace and two of Cunanan's four other victims.

A contentious verdict in a televised jury trial provoked strong community reactions on both sides of the Atlantic in November when Louise Woodward, a 19-year-old British au pair, was convicted in a Massachusetts court of the second-degree murder of an eight-month-old child in her care. Woodward, who was sentenced to a mandatory term of life imprisonment with no possibility of parole for 15 years, denied the prosecution's charge that she had shaken the infant violently and slammed his head against a hard surface.

The verdict was said to have divided British and Americans almost as deeply as the O.J. Simpson trial had divided whites and blacks. In the U.K. the convicted teenager was portrayed as a naive small-town English girl accused of a vicious crime in a big American city. The murder charge and sentence were also viewed as unduly harsh by European standards. The judge in the case then created further controversy by overturning the jury's verdict, ruling that Woodward was guilty of involuntary manslaughter and sentencing her to the time that she had already served.

In Santa Monica, Calif., in February a civil jury, by unanimous verdict, found O.J. Simpson responsible for the deaths of Nicole Brown Simpson and Ronald Goldman and ordered him to pay a total of $33.5 million in damages to the victims' relatives. The verdict came 16 months after a criminal jury had acquitted Simpson of the murders of his former wife and her friend.

White-Collar Crime, Corruption, and Fraud. In May a study sponsored by the European Commission reported that cross-border fraud in the European Union could cost at least $68 billion a year and fraud within individual countries probably double that total. The study estimated that most of this international fraud, ranging from illegal credit-card use and mobile-phone cloning to passing counterfeit banknotes, had a direct impact on businesses and individual citizens rather than on governments. The study said that with the opening up of Europe's internal frontiers and also because of technological developments, organized criminals were devoting increased attention to fraud.

In September the World Bank unveiled new anticorruption guidelines for its operations. The move reflected a significant change in the attitude taken toward corruption by international lenders. For example, the International Monetary Fund took the unprecedented step on July 31 of suspending $200 million in loans and credits to Kenya because the government of that nation had failed to tackle massive high-level corruption and mismanagement.

In June a court in Seoul, S.Kor., sentenced Chung Tae Soo, the patriarch of one of the nation's largest business conglomerates and a former Cabinet member, together with eight business colleagues and politicians, to prison terms on various bribery charges. Chung received a 15-year sentence relating to payoffs totaling millions of dollars to bankers and senior lawmakers in exchange for loans to support his failing Hanbo business empire. In Japan prosecutors laid a series of charges during the year against the executives of some of the nation's largest brokerage firms and other major corporations, alleging that they had paid gangsters known as *sokaiya* large sums to buy their silence at annual shareholder meetings. *Sokaiya* traditionally extorted these payments by purchasing shares in companies and then threatening to disrupt shareholder meetings and reveal damaging corporate information. As the scandal continued to unfold, it rocked the Japanese financial industry and highlighted the ties between big business and organized crime in Japan.

LAW ENFORCEMENT

In April the U.S. Justice Department's inspector general, Michael Bromwich, re-

Modern-day pirates comb a beach along the South China Sea. In recent years piracy incidents had risen at an alarming rate, with heavily armed buccaneers often making use of high-speed boats and sophisticated technology. The Malaysia-based Regional Piracy Centre reported in July that 224 attacks by pirates occurred worldwide during 1996, more than double the number reported for 1992.

MIKE GOLDWATER—MATRIX

DAVID TURNLEY—THE DETROIT FREE PRESS/BLACK STAR

Dirk Coetzee, a former police officer in South Africa who admitted his involvement in the murders of black activists in the country, applied for amnesty from the Truth and Reconciliation Commission. Because he exposed the illegal activities of the police, he lived in constant fear of being assassinated.

leased the findings of an 18-month investigation into the FBI's crime laboratory. Bromwich announced that he had uncovered "extremely serious and significant problems" at the laboratory, which, since the founding of the bureau by J. Edgar Hoover in 1932, had been one of the symbols of the FBI's leadership in forensic science. The investigation revealed that the laboratory's explosives, chemistry, toxicology, and materials analysis units all demonstrated substandard performance. The findings forced FBI officials to review several hundred past and present cases to determine how many of them might have been prejudiced by the faulty work. The inspector general said he had not found any cases in which laboratory examiners had committed a crime or had intentionally faked forensic evidence, obstructed justice, or lied about their findings in court. Still, the report represented a significant blow to the reputation of the FBI.

Testifying before the U.S. Congress in May, the director of the FBI, Louis Freeh, said that the agency's counterterrorism efforts had been tripled over the past three years and that 2,600 officers were now dedicated to that aspect of law enforcement. The acting director of the CIA, George Tenet, told the same congressional hearings that the CIA had created a new Terrorism Warning Group whose mission it was to ensure that civilian and military leaders were alerted to specific terrorist threats. He said that in cooperation with the FBI and the U.S. State Department, the group had averted bombings at two American embassies. Appearing before another congressional hearing in October, Freeh said that U.S law-enforcement agencies were taking seriously the possibility that nuclear weapons could fall into the hands of Russian criminal gangs. He said that the Russian syndicates were conducting the most sophisticated criminal operations ever seen in the U.S., based on their access to expertise in computer technology, encryption techniques, and money laundering.

The findings of the most comprehensive study ever conducted of U.S. crime-prevention programs were released in April. The study, undertaken by criminologists at the University of Maryland, showed that some of the most favoured programs, including boot camps, midnight basketball, neighbourhood watches, and drug-education classes in schools had little impact. The effectiveness of the huge prison-construction program during the past two decades was also questioned. The study, ordered by Congress in 1996, did find promising results from initiatives such as intensified police patrols in high-crime areas, drug treatment in prisons, and home visits by nurses, social workers, and others for infants in troubled families.

Following a global manhunt, an FBI undercover mission resulted in the arrest in June of Mir Aimal Kansi, who was alleged to have been responsible for the murder of two CIA employees in 1993. Kansi's arrest took place in a small Pakistani town near the border with Afghanistan. To facilitate the arrest and Kansi's immediate transfer back to the United States, the U.S. State Department was said to have negotiated an extraordinary diplomatic agreement with Pakistan that allowed the FBI to operate on foreign soil. On November 10 Kansi was convicted; two days later four American oil company employees were shot and killed in Karachi, Pak., in an apparent revenge attack for the conviction.

Italian law-enforcement officials claimed a major victory in their fight to curb the power of the Mafia when in September a court in Caltanissetta, Sicily, convicted 24 top Mafia leaders and sentenced them to life imprisonment for the 1992 bomb attack in Sicily that killed Italy's top anti-Mafia prosecutor, Giovanni Falcone. The defendants in the trial, which had begun on May 2, 1995, constituted virtually the entire ruling council of the Cosa Nostra.

Police violence and brutality came under strong condemnation in Brazil following the March national television airing of two secretly taped videos that showed police robbing, torturing, and extorting money from citizens. One of the tapes also showed a policeman killing a passenger in a stopped car. Shortly after the release of the videos, Human Rights Watch/Americas published a report on police violence in Brazil that concluded that officers in major urban areas often killed without justification and that the failure to curb these abuses further encouraged the police in their illegal actions. Brazilian Pres. Fernando Henrique Cardoso had sought in 1996 to introduce certain human rights reforms designed to reduce police violence, including stripping military courts of jurisdiction over police killings and allowing federal prosecutions of serious human rights crimes. Few of these proposals had become law, but after the televising of the videos, the legislature passed a law criminalizing torture. (DUNCAN CHAPPELL)

GIGI COHEN—NETWORK/SABA

A woman sits behind bars in the Julia Tutwiler Prison in Montgomery, Ala. Despite seeing a continued drop in its overall crime rate, the U.S. nevertheless had a rate of 615 prisoners per 100,000 population, one of the highest in the world. The proportion of female prisoners in the U.S. was still relatively small, but women were the fastest-growing subset in the overall prison population.

PRISONS AND PENOLOGY

The general toughening of penal policy continued to be evident in many parts of the world during 1997. A consequence of the policy that was of particular concern was the sharp rise in the number of people held within prison systems, often in desperately crowded conditions characterized by violence and disease. A U.S. government study estimated, on the basis of 1991 figures, that one in every 20 persons would serve a sentence in federal or state prison during his or her lifetime. The rate of 615 prisoners per 100,000 of the population in the U.S. was one of the highest in the world. It was, however, exceeded by a rate of 710 in Russia, where in August Pres. Boris Yeltsin urged that there be an amnesty for some 500,000 Russian prisoners (almost half the total) in order to bring prison conditions "in line with universally recognized standards." Comparatively high rates were also reported for several countries that were once part of the Soviet Union, including Belarus (505), Ukraine (390), Latvia (375), Lithuania (360), and Estonia (270). Elsewhere in Europe the highest rates were found in Romania (200), the Czech Republic (190), Poland (170), and Portugal (140).

Confronted by appalling conditions, many governments were nonetheless not acting urgently to remedy them. For example, the first-ever pan-African seminar on prison conditions in Africa noted the low public concern for prisoners, a situation exemplified in Togo, where 50 prisoners died as a result of the extreme heat within their cells. In Pakistan, where fully 70% of the prisoners were awaiting trial, the total number of prisoners was more than double the rated capacity of the prison system, and in some prisons people had to take turns in order to have a place to lie down. About 800 inmates rioted at the vastly overcrowded Sorocaba prison in Brazil on December 28, taking some 600 hostages; at least three people were dead by year's end. Serious prison riots involving fatalities were reported in several other countries as well, including Jessore prison in Bangladesh, Oaxaca prison in Mexico, St. Catherine's prison in Jamaica, El Dorado prison in Venezuela, and Modelo prison in Colombia.

Crowded and dangerous conditions were not confined to prisons in less-developed countries. In Spain there was severe overcrowding at the Modelo prison in Barcelona and at the women's prison in Madrid. Severe levels of crowding continued in Romania, although reform measures were put into effect in some facilities. In Great Britain a ship to house 400 prisoners was purchased from the U.S. The new Labour government also proceeded with contracts for new prisons with the private sector, part of an increasing trend in many nations. At the end of 1996, there were 132 privately operated adult prisons in the U.S., Britain, and Australia.

International agencies and conventions continued to help enhance human rights and improve general conditions within prisons. Much of this activity was generated by the UN, but an especially instructive model for international inspection of places of custody was the Council of Europe's Committee for the Prevention of Torture (CPT), which had jurisdiction within the 33 countries that had ratified the European Convention on Human Rights. For example, in March the Bulgarian government, responding to a CPT visit, stated that efforts were being made to reduce overcrowding and that there had been instructions that verbal or other degrading abuse of prisoners by staff would be dealt with "most severely."

The trends within many prison systems were taking place at a time of generally hardening political climates. In the United States, which continued to exercise enormous influence on penal policy elsewhere, the Supreme Court ruled in June that sex offenders may be held for life in psychiatric hospitals after they have been released from prison. Furthermore, there were legislative proposals to use federal funds as an inducement to states to process increasing numbers of children through adult rather than juvenile courts.

American courts were also turning to a variety of shaming penalties that were intended to draw public attention to the offender and his or her offense. Along with the use of chain gangs in at least six American states, a county in Maryland instead decided to fit prisoners working on outdoor projects with "stun belts." By means of a battery and a receiver with electric prongs, a guard from a distance of up to 90 m (300 ft) would be able to detonate an eight-second burst of 50,000 volts of electricity that would disable an individual for about 10 minutes. Elsewhere, courts in several Caribbean countries reinstated flogging. In July a court in St. Vincent ruled that keeping a prisoner continually in iron leggings and handcuffs and then subjecting him to a whipping was unconstitutional.

Trends counter to these punitive policies were much less discernible. In Greece prisoners, with the exception of those serving life sentences, were granted the right to vote in general elections. A new penal code in Spain reduced maximum sentence lengths to 20 years (up to 30 years in exceptional circumstances) and permitted community service as an option for those convicted of defaulting on fines. An extended use of required community service as an alternative to prison was also under way in several countries, including France, Jamaica, and Zimbabwe.

Death Penalty. Ninety-eight countries had by August 1997 abolished the death penalty in law or practice. Of the 95 countries retaining the penalty, executions were carried out in 39 during 1996. International treaties (global and regional) outlawing the death penalty were playing an increasingly important role in 1997. With the addition of Colombia in August, 30 nations had ratified the appropriate protocol of the UN International Covenant on Civil and Political Rights.

According to Amnesty International, there were at least 5,100 persons executed during 1996, with a small number of countries accounting for the great majority of cases. There were 4,376 reported executions in China, 167 in Ukraine, 140 in Russia, and 110 in Iran. There were unconfirmed reports of 123 executions in Turkmenistan, and, although exact figures were unavailable, numerous cases in Iraq. In the U.S., where 38 of the 50 states provided for the death penalty, there were 45 executions during 1996 and an additional 74 in 1997.

The conditions experienced by many prisoners on death row continued often to be a matter of grave concern. At Hattieville prison in Belize, visiting lawyers found a "total disregard for humanity and basic human rights." In the medieval castle at Minsk, prisoners awaited execution for several months below ground in unfurnished cells that were poorly lit and ventilated. At the Lahore Central prison in Pakistan, some 250 prisoners were being held on death row, four to five to a cell, and were barred from visits or other contact with their families.

(ANDREW RUTHERFORD)

Libraries and Museums

LIBRARIES

Around the globe, libraries captured headlines in 1997 as they were struck by wars or natural disasters and became the subjects of political disputes.

Flooding in Europe during the summer took a heavy toll on some 100 libraries in Poland, where institutions in 23 of the country's 49 administrative districts reported significant damage to collections, buildings, and equipment. At the Academy of Medicine in Wroclaw, some 40% of the library's 300,000 volumes were damaged. Although some 20,000 volumes were destroyed at the University of Wroclaw, the efforts of volunteers saved one of the most outstanding collections of old prints and manuscripts in Europe.

Conflict in Albania resulted in destruction or damage to libraries in Tiranë, where an agricultural library was looted and burned; Sarandë, where the Italian Library was destroyed; and Vlorë, where a public library was heavily damaged. In July police in Purna, India, opened fire on demonstrators who were attempting to burn a college library. The incident was precipitated by the desecration of a statue representing a leader of a lower social caste. Librarians from the United States continued their efforts to rebuild the collection of the war-ravaged National and University Library of Bosnia and Herzegovina.

When libraries made news without mention of destruction or physical violence, censorship was often the issue. Election victories in France by the extreme-right-wing National Front in the cities of Orange, Marignane, Toulon, and Vitrolles resulted both in materials' being removed from library shelves by city officials and in firings and wholesale resignations of librarians who opposed the actions. The library in Orange faced imminent shutdown. French leaders, including Pres. Jacques Chirac and Prime Minister Lionel Jospin (*see* BIOGRAPHIES), condemned the National Front, and the French legislature considered issuing a "library bill of rights," but many observers believed that the situation would worsen before it improved. In response to a suit filed by the American Library Association and other groups, the U.S. Supreme Court struck down the Communications Decency Act, which sought to ban the on-line transmission of "indecent" material. Meanwhile, public libraries across the U.S. faced pressure from politicians and citizens groups to install filtering software to prevent children and other patrons from accessing sexually explicit materials on the Internet.

The provocative design and the staggering cost (some $1.5 billion) of the National Library of France, a part of which opened in December 1996, also caused controversy in France. Wooden shutters were added to the building's four L-shaped glass towers after librarians and scholars warned of the damage that sunlight would inflict on the books. The appearance of the shutters and the building's location in a remote area in Paris drew bitter criticism.

BRIAN K. DIGGS—ASSOCIATED PRESS

Kenneth Lopez was the first director of security at the U.S. Library of Congress in Washington, D.C. Founded in 1800, the Library of Congress was probably the largest national library, currently housing more than 17 million books and 111 million additional items in its special collections.

Other national libraries made more upbeat news. Die Deutsche Bibliotek, a new German national library in Frankfurt, was dedicated in early May. The contemporary building housed some 15 million volumes. The Frankfurt library had an annex in Berlin, where the music collection resided, and another in Leipzig, which duplicated the Frankfurt collection in addition to boasting a few specialized collections of its own. In Nicaragua the Banco Central de Nicaragua had served as a national library since 1964. After the building was destroyed in the devastating earthquake of 1972, however, the library was housed in "temporary" quarters. With a new bank building nearing completion, the library would soon return to a permanent home. In Egypt the government agreed to underwrite the budget of the Library of Alexandria, currently under construction near the site of the original edifice, built around 300 BC. The long-standing process leading to the opening of the new British Library at St. Pancras, London, continued. Some departments were opened, while other collections were still in the process of being moved. On May 1 the U.S. Library of Congress reopened its 1897 Thomas Jefferson Building following a 12-year-long, $102 million restoration and modernization.

In what was hailed as the greatest gift to American libraries since Andrew Carnegie financed the construction of 1,600 libraries at the turn of the 20th century, Microsoft Corp. chairman Bill Gates and his wife, Melinda French Gates, announced in June that they would bestow $200 million to establish the nonprofit Gates Library Foundation to bring computers into public libraries in low-income communities throughout the U.S. and Canada. Microsoft would also match their cash contribution with $200 million in training and software.

The Federal Communications Commission voted in May to provide discounted telecommunications services to U.S. libraries and schools, a measure that would lower the cost of hooking up to the Internet computer network by up to 90%. The plan would limit the amount of discounts to $2,250,000,000 annually, beginning in 1998, and the revenue would be raised by billing homes and businesses with more than one phone line a higher federal monthly charge.

In South Africa two racially separated professional associations of librarians formally united, while in Copenhagen 2,976 librarians from 141 countries attended (August 31 to September 5) the 63rd Council and General Conference of the International Federation of Library Associations and Institutions. Grant support enabled about 140 librarians from less-developed countries to attend that conference. The New York Public Library launched a drive in September to raise $500 million to take the institution into the 21st century. The campaign was reportedly the largest fund-raising effort ever undertaken by an American cultural institution.

(GORDON FLAGG; THOMAS GAUGHAN)

This article updates the *Macropædia* article LIBRARIES AND LIBRARY SCIENCE.

MUSEUMS

Many important new museums opened in 1997, and some old ones were renovated. In South Africa the Robben Island Museum and the Museum of the Freedom Struggle opened on the site of the prison used during the nation's apartheid era to imprison black political activists, including South African Pres. Nelson Mandela. The American Air Museum in Britain, devoted primarily to the U.S.'s cooperation with Great Britain in World War II, was dedicated during the

After being closed nearly 14 years for renovation, the Borghese Gallery, home to one of Italy's greatest art collections, reopened its doors in 1997. Located in Rome, the museum was a fine example of 17th-century architecture and contained works by Raphael, Bernini, and Caravaggio, among others.
EMMANUEL SCORCELLETTI—GAMMA LIAISON

summer in Duxford, Eng. The Famine Museum in Stokestown, Ire., opened 150 years after the Irish potato famine, a subject previously too painful for commemoration, and a historic cemetery used to bury famine victims was restored. In Egypt a new museum devoted to mummies and the process of mummification was inaugurated.

Striking architecture characterized several new museum structures. Perhaps the most stunning was the $100 million Guggenheim Museum building in Bilbao, Spain. Designed by Frank Gehry, it was being heralded as the most creative work of architecture of its time and was to play a central part in a plan to transform this industrial city, which had been plagued by Basque separatist violence. Another architectural wonder, newMetropolis, a science and technology centre, opened in Amsterdam's historic harbour front.

The Georges Pompidou National Art and Cultural Centre in Paris closed for two years for renovations that would allow it to handle its growing crowds of visitors. Likewise, as part of a major effort to increase the economic boon of cultural tourism, Venice was undertaking a major renovation of the museum and palace that line St. Mark's Square. Work also began during the year on Florence's renowned Uffizi Gallery to significantly expand the museum. Meanwhile, in Rome, the Borghese Gallery, one of the world's finest art collections, finally reopened in 1997 after 14 years of renovation. The famous Van Gogh Museum in Amsterdam closed for six months for extensive renovations and the construction of a new wing.

The year was also marked by struggle and change in the museums of the former communist nations. The reunification of Berlin's museums began as Old Master paintings that had been divided between museums in East and West Berlin were moved to the new Gemäldegalerie, scheduled to open in 1998. In Moscow the Tretyakov Gallery, which housed the world's finest collection of medieval icons, was heavily in debt owing to cutbacks in government support. Meanwhile, amid attacks from art critics and historians, Moscow funded a new museum dedicated to the art of Aleksandr Shilov, a living artist whose ultrarealistic portraits were considered kitsch by many. Belarus displayed an exhibit of masterpieces by its native son Marc Chagall in Minsk. Because his works previously had been banned by Soviet authorities, not one piece was permanently displayed in Belarus.

The issue of art displaced during World War II remained prominent during the year. In France a government report noted nearly 2,000 works in French museums that had been seized or purchased by the Nazis from Jews in France. These works, distributed among various French museums, were highlighted for exhibits in an attempt to promote claims by rightful owners or their heirs. Some criticized the French for having retained these works without undertaking an active search for their owners. Russia's parliament passed nearly unanimously, overriding Pres. Boris Yeltsin's veto, a law that vested ownership in Russia of nearly 200,000 works taken by the Soviet army from German museums and private collections following the war. Russia argued that the works were rightfully theirs, small payment for their losses during the war.

The problem of thefts from museums continued to be a significant issue. London became the centre of an illegal trade in treasures from Iraq, where economic sanctions resulted in the looting of museums and archaeological sites for economic gain.

(HELEN J. WECHSLER)

Many in the American media called 1997 a golden age for art museums; audiences thronged to learn—and also to shop, dine, and socialize. Not surprisingly, policy makers looked at museums and saw an answer to their every problem. Revitalize downtown? Attract tourists? Celebrate the millennium? Let museums do it. Thus, the question that emerged was how museums could satisfy public expectations for delivering every kind of social benefit while somehow remaining true to their mission of preserving scientific, historical, and artistic artifacts and interpreting them for the public.

One initiative that began to take shape during the year was a data-collection project to address a huge gap in available information. As of the end of 1997, there were no answers to the most basic questions on the number of museums in the U.S. or the size of their collections and audiences.

The most spectacular event of the year was not a blockbuster exhibition but rather the opening of a blockbuster institution—the Getty Center in Los Angeles. The billion-dollar campus, including a museum as well as centres for art history, conservation, and education, was gradually introduced to the public by a series of tours, press accounts, and conferences beginning in January. The official opening occurred in December.

(ANDREW FINCH)

See also Art, Antiques, and Collections.

This article updates the *Macropædia* article MUSEUMS.

Life Sciences

ZOOLOGY

Advances in zoology were made during 1997 in understanding primate behaviour and the evolutionary relationship between wolves and dogs. Two independent long-term field experiments, one with lizards and one with fish, provided evidence suggesting that animals that have been introduced to new environmental situations can evolve rapidly in the wild in response to natural selection.

Linear dominance hierarchies were known to exist among females in the social communities of some primates, such as macaques and baboons, but had not been unequivocally observed in chimpanzees. Because female dominance had been seldom observed in chimpanzee groups, especially within stable groups in the wild, many researchers did not consider the dominance rank of a female to be of particular importance to her reproductive success. To investigate the issue of female dominance in chimpanzees, Anne Pusey and Jennifer Williams of the University of Minnesota and Jane Goodall of the Jane Goodall Institute, Ridgefield, Conn., used data from 35 years of observations of a group of chimpanzees in Gombe National Park, Tanzania. The investigators were able to assess dominance relationships by analyzing "pant-grunt" responses recorded among females in the group from 1970 to 1992. A pant-grunt is accepted as an indicator of submissiveness by one chimpanzee in response to the aggressive behaviour of another. Most of the 10–18 female chimpanzees observed in the group since 1970 were able to be placed in a dominance hierarchy of high, middle, or low. When the investigators eliminated from their analyses one clearly dominant but sterile female that had been part of the group for 28 years, a dominance pattern emerged that correlated with reproductive success. A higher-ranking female was more likely to live longer, produce young more often, have a higher infant-survival rate, and have daughters that matured at an earlier age than females of lower ranking. The investigators attributed the enhanced reproductive success of higher-ranking females to better nutritional status as a consequence of acquiring more suitable areas for foraging.

Carles Vilà and Robert K. Wayne of the University of California, Los Angeles, and colleagues used molecular genetics techniques to conclude that the wolf (*Canis lupus*) is the one and only wild ancestor of the domestic dog (*C. familiaris*). The investigators analyzed specific sequences of mitochondrial DNA that had been sampled from 162 wolves worldwide (27 localities) and from 140 dogs (67 breeds). (Mitochondria are cell organelles that contain their own genetic material, distinct from that of the cell nucleus.) They also examined corresponding sequences taken from all other wild species of the genus *Canis* (coyotes and three species of jackals). Dogs were found to be significantly more similar genetically to wolves than to coyotes or jackals. As observed in comparisons of fossils, wolves were distinct morphologically (*i.e.,* in form and structure) from coyotes about a million years ago. Using molecular clock techniques to time the divergence between the species, the investigators calculated that domesticated dogs were distinct genetically from wolves as far back as 135,000 years ago. Archaeological evidence had previously suggested that dogs originated about 14,000 years ago. One interpretation of the disparity in dates of dog origin is that dogs did not become morphologically distinct from wolves until humans developed agricultural societies 10,000–15,000 years ago, even though they had become genetically distinct earlier. Hence, dog fossils found associated with preagricultural human populations would not have been distinguishable from those of wolves.

To study the speed of evolution in a species, David N. Reznick of the University of California, Riverside, and colleagues carried out experiments on the effects of predation on natural populations of guppies in Trinidad. The investigators initially selected two streams with waterfalls. The stream sections below the waterfalls contained guppies and were determined to be high-predation habitats, whereas those sections above the waterfalls had neither guppies nor many predators because the falls served to exclude both. Guppies were then experimentally introduced to the sections above the waterfalls in both streams. Comparisons of life-history traits of the below-falls, or control, guppy populations and the above-falls, or experimental, populations were made at 4 and 7.5 years for one stream system and at 11 years for the other. After four years, *i.e.,* after only about seven generations, the experimental males above the waterfall were seen to mature sexually at older ages and to have larger body sizes than control males. (The predators in the guppies' original habitats preferred large, sexually mature prey, which thus put selective pressure on the guppies to mature at an early age.) After 11 years both sexes in the experimental population matured later and at larger sizes than in the high-predator sites. The rapid adaptive responses to a changed environment were evaluated in the laboratory and found to have a genetic basis. Moreover, these adaptations and other traits identified in the experimental populations were the same traits found in guppies living in naturally occurring low-predation habitats and were consistent with results derived from mathematical theories of life-history evolution, which had predicted how organisms should evolve in response to external sources of mortality.

©STEPHEN J. KRASEMANN—ALLSTOCK

In 1997 scientists concluded that the wolf (*Canis lupus*) is the one and only wild ancestor of the domestic dog (*C. familiaris*).

An experiment with the lizard *Anolis sagrei* on islands in the Bahamas by Jonathan B. Losos of Washington University, St. Louis, Mo., and colleagues demonstrated rapid changes in morphology in response to changed environmental conditions. In 1977 and 1981 lizards were collected on relatively heavily vegetated Staniel Cay and released onto 14 nearby islands that were much smaller, had few trees, and were covered primarily by vegetation with narrow-diameter stems and branches. Previous studies of the more than 150 *Anolis* species in the Caribbean had revealed a positive relationship between hind-limb length and mean diameter of vegetation perches. Earlier studies also had indicated that long-legged species maximize sprinting ability whereas short-legged species are better able to maintain a grip on narrow surfaces. A comparison in 1991 of hind-limb measurements of adult male lizards on Staniel Cay and from the small islands still supporting the introduced populations demonstrated that lizard morphology had diverged in response to the magnitude of difference between a small island's vegetation and that on Staniel Cay. If the differences observed in the experimental populations of guppies and lizards were inherited genetically and brought about by natural selection, then the studies would support the conclusion that evolution in both life-history and morphological traits can occur rapidly in response to abrupt changes in environmental conditions.

In the area of conservation ecology, investigations of the semiaquatic chicken turtle (*Deirochelys reticularia*) in the southeastern U.S. uncovered information suggesting that humans' traditional patterns of land use can endanger the survival of species whose evolved traits are poorly understood. Kurt Buhlmann of the University of Georgia's Savannah River Ecology Laboratory reported on the ecology of chicken turtles, which differ from most North American turtles by nesting in autumn and winter instead of spring and summer. During a four-year study the investigator documented that chicken turtles hibernate underground on land and thus spend more than half their life in the terrestrial habitat. He also found that when chicken turtle eggs are laid in the fall, as long as 20 months may elapse before the young leave the nest, enter adjacent wetland

(continued on page 242)

SPECIAL REPORT

The Uses and Ethics of Cloning

by Ian Wilmut

The announcement in February 1997 of the birth of Dolly the sheep, the first clone of an adult mammal, attracted international attention because of the new medical and agricultural opportunities and the new ethical concerns raised by the breakthrough. The term *cloning* (derived from the Greek word *klon,* meaning "twig") strictly indicates the taking of a cutting, as in plant breeding, but it has also come to be used to describe the production, by means of a process known as nuclear transfer, of genetically identical animals. Nuclear transfer involves removing the chromosomes from an unfertilized egg and replacing them with a nucleus from a donor cell. As it is the transferred nucleus that determines almost all of the characteristics of the resulting offspring, a clone will resemble its "parent," the animal from which the donor cell was taken.

While the most obvious use of cloning is to produce groups of animals that are genetically identical, nuclear transfer also may be used for the introduction of precise genetic changes in mammals. Although other methods have been employed to add genes to mammals, nuclear transfer makes it possible for the first time to change any function of existing genes. Another application of cloning technology is the production of undifferentiated (embryonic) cells, which could be helpful in treating certain diseases. Before there can be significant use of these applications, however, some practical difficulties must be resolved, as only a small proportion of the embryos thus far produced by nuclear transfer have become live offspring. Ethical choices must also be made. The public response to cloning suggests that countries differ widely in their perceptions of this new technology. Immediately after the announcement of Dolly's birth, for example, Italy banned the cloning of any mammal, whereas a number of groups in the U.S. welcomed the technique.

All of the different tissues of an adult animal or person are derived from the single cell of a fertilized egg. In the early stages of development, the dividing embryonic cells are able to contribute to all of the tissues of the developing embryo before the cells differentiate, progressively, as a result of changes in gene expression. The birth of Dolly by means of an already differentiated adult cell for nuclear transfer showed that the process of differentiation is reversible, at least in some cases. This raises the revolutionary thought that it may be possible to take cells from a human patient and cause them to dedifferentiate to a state in which they are able to contribute to all tissues. If necessary, a genetic change could be made in the cells before they are stimulated to differentiate to the type required for treating a specific disease before return to the patient. Since the cells are identical to the patient, no immune response is expected. This approach has been suggested for the treatment of such varied conditions as AIDS, Duchenne muscular dystrophy, and Parkinson's disease.

At present the only way to induce dedifferentiation is to form an embryo from the donor cell and to culture the embryo to the stage when it has a few hundred cells but has not begun to differentiate. As the nervous system would not have begun to develop at that stage, the embryo would have no means of feeling pain or sensing the environment. At this point the cells would be separated and grown in culture. Some people object strongly to this procedure on religious grounds, holding that the embryo has a soul at the moment

MIKE THEILER—REUTERS

Scottish embryologist Ian Wilmut testifies on cloning before a U.S. Senate subcommittee in March. Although Wilmut had not heard of any morally acceptable reason to clone a human being, he warned against a broadly worded ban that could prohibit related research to treat or prevent human disease.

of conception. As the embryo would have the potential to become a person, they find it deeply disturbing to consider using cells from that embryo for any purpose that would deprive that person of life. An alternative view is that it is justifiable to use the cells since the developing embryo does not become a sentient being until much later in development. Whatever the ethical views, it would be much more practical to develop such cell-based therapies if dedifferentiation could be induced without the production of embryos. Research in 1997 was beginning to assess this possibility.

Although the use of cloning to produce copies of humans has been suggested, many people would judge this to be morally wrong. In addition, the prospect of cloning humans raises false expectations, since human personality is only partly determined by genes. Cloning a sick or dying relative would provide a genetically identical copy of that person, but this new individual would likely develop a quite different personality. Similarly, a copy of an athlete, movie star, entrepreneur, or scientist might well choose another career because of chance events during his or her lifetime. One hypothetical scenario involves an infertile couple who wish to make a copy of one or the other partner rather than having a child by artificial insemination. The social concern is that the parents would not be able to treat naturally a child who was a copy of one of them.

REUTERS

The first clone of an adult mammal, Dolly the sheep stands in her pen at the Roslin Institute, near Edinburgh. Her birth was announced in February.

The impetus behind the research that led to Dolly was not to find a way to clone humans but rather to develop genetically engineered animals that would serve a variety of purposes. As there are great genetic differences in cattle herds and sheep flocks, breeding copies of selected livestock would increase the efficiency of agricultural productivity and help boost the quality of such commercial products as milk, beef, and wool. As in the management of other breeding schemes, it will be important for scientists to maintain the balance between intense selection of livestock and the maintenance of genetic variability. Preservation of frozen cells from a large number of representatives of different breeds would allow nuclei from those donor cells to be used as required. The ethical issues in animal cloning are perhaps less controversial than with humans; nevertheless, some people worry that producing large numbers of animal clones only increases the likelihood that these animals will be mistreated.

Genetic modification of livestock will also provide new opportunities in medicine and research. Today many patients in need of transplants die before organs become available from suitable donors. Cloning pigs has been suggested as a means of rapidly achieving xenotransplantation, the use of animal organs to replace organs in human patients. Organs transplanted between species are in danger of being destroyed within minutes by the acute immune response of the body receiving the transplant; however, strategies are being developed to modify pigs genetically so that rejection by the immune system may be effectively prevented.

Another potential medical application of cloning involves cystic fibrosis research. A common hereditary disease of humans caused by errors in a single gene, cystic fibrosis is characterized by difficulty in breathing due to the accumulation of mucus in the lungs. At present new treatments for cystic fibrosis are assessed by being administered either to human patients or to mice bred with the disease. There is, of course, a limit to the risks that may be taken with human patients, and there are significant differences between the respiratory systems of mice and humans. Cloning sheep bred with cystic fibrosis would provide an inexhaustible supply of animals on which to experiment and would overcome the disadvantages of experimenting on humans and mice.

There have been a variety of responses to these proposals. To some people it is ethically unacceptable to alter a species genetically, but those advancing this view must acknowledge that conventional genetic selection has already brought about profound changes in livestock and pet animals. While many people welcome the availability of organs from animals, others are disturbed at the suggestion of deliberately making animals ill, and some would prohibit such a practice whatever the benefit. Provided that a judgment is made that the advance in medical treatment justifies the distress caused to the animal, most societies accept the benefits from studies involving animal experimentation. In most countries legislation permits such research only under strict supervision.

Experience shows that predictions as to the value and uses of new techniques are often wrong and that society changes its assessment of a new procedure over time. Many religious leaders were initially scandalized by the introduction of methods for the artificial insemination of cattle, a procedure that helped eliminate sexually transmitted diseases and provided the single biggest advance in livestock breeding. Great concern was raised at the time of the birth of Louise Brown, the first baby to be produced after in vitro fertilization. Since then thousands of babies have been born to previously infertile couples, and the technique of artificial insemination is widely accepted. It remains to be seen how methods of cloning will be used and how they will be accepted.

Ian Wilmut, leader of the research team that produced the first clone of an adult mammal, is an embryologist at the Roslin Institute, near Edinburgh.

KURT A. BUHLMANN, SAVANNAH RIVER ECOLOGY LABORATORY, THE UNIVERSITY OF GEORGIA

A chicken turtle tagged with a radio transmitter is returned to its habitat. Telemetry allowed ecologists to find the turtles' nesting and hibernation sites in the southeastern U.S. A study completed in 1997 suggested that terrestrial buffer zones around wetlands were critical to such wetland species' survival.

(continued from page 239)

areas, and begin feeding. The dependency of this unusual species on both the aquatic habitat and the peripheral terrestrial habitat reinforces the conviction of some ecologists that large terrestrial buffer zones around wetlands are critical to the survival of some wetland species and need to be accommodated in land-development projects.

A study of fossils from the late Precambrian in northern Russia by Mikhail A. Fedonkin of the Russian Academy of Sciences, Moscow, and Benjamin M. Waggoner of the University of California, Berkeley, revealed that large triploblastic organisms (those having three primary embryonic layers) existed and began to diversify before the start of the Cambrian Period, which began about 540 million years ago. When first discovered in the 1950s, *Kimberella quadrata* was thought to be a jellyfish. Recent discovery by the investigators of abundant, well-preserved fossils of the species, however, allowed them to reinterpret the earlier findings. *Kimberella* was actually a bilaterally symmetrical, bottom-dwelling multicellular animal that resembled a mollusk. The finding suggested an earlier origin for some higher groups of animals than previously suspected. Meanwhile, David Jablonski of the University of Chicago used fossil mollusks from about 81 million to 66.4 million years ago, near the end of the Cretaceous Period, to test the evolutionary generalization known as Cope's rule, which presupposes that evolutionary lineages will tend toward larger body sizes because of their survival and reproductive advantages. In examining 1,086 species representing 191 identifiable lineages of bivalve and gastropod mollusks, the investigator observed that directional increases in body size within a lineage occurred no more frequently than decreases or expansions in the upper and lower limits of the size; thus, Cope's rule was not supported.

(J. WHITFIELD GIBBONS)

Entomology. The discovery of the chemical substance chitin in fossil beetles in Enspel, Ger., in Oligocene shales deposited 24.7 million years ago greatly extended the known time of its persistence in fossil animals. A horny material that is chemically a polysaccharide (complex sugar), chitin is abundant in the bodies of living arthropods but had not been detected in organisms fossilized more than about 130,000 years ago. B. Artur Stankiewicz and Derek E.G. Briggs of the University of Bristol, Eng., and colleagues used analytic pyrolysis (heating) techniques and scanning electron microscopy to document the presence of chitin in the insect fossils. The findings suggested that preservation of chitin is regulated not by time per se but by the chemical nature of the environment in which fossilization occurs. The authors concluded that the chitin was preserved as the result of biochemical and geochemical factors on the lake bottom that was the source of the shale.

New insight was provided into the previously recognized mutualism between ants and acacia trees, in which ants defend the trees from herbivorous insects and other animals while the trees provide food and shelter for the ants. Because the flowers of *Acacia zanzibarica* and *A. drepanolobium* in Africa are pollinated by insects other than ants, P.G. Willmer of the University of St. Andrews, Scot., and G.N. Stone of the University of Oxford sought to determine how such pollination is achieved when the trees are guarded by ants. The acacia trees that served in the study were pollinated mainly by solitary bees during the midday period. The investigators noted that the ants protected the flowers from insects during early development but avoided young flowers once they had matured to a stage suitable for pollination. Then, as the flowers aged and began producing seeds, the guarding ants returned. The researchers hypothesized that new flowers produce a chemical that acts as an ant deterrent; such a substance would allow the bees to pollinate the flowers without being attacked by guarding ants. To test the hypothesis, they wiped old flowers with new flowers. The ants, normally present around old flowers, avoided those that had been wiped with new flowers—a behaviour that supported the idea of a chemical deterrent.

Sanford D. Porter of the Center for Medical, Agricultural, and Veterinary Entomology, Gainesville, Fla., and colleagues provided support for the position that the success of the imported fire ant (*Solenopsis invicta*) in North America since its introduction in the early 20th century resulted from the absence of many natural enemies found in its native South American habitat. The investigators examined ant mounds and colonies in the spring and fall in 13 regions in South America and 12 in North America. The areas sampled on each continent, primarily roadsides and grazing sites, included different climatic conditions. Sizes of fire ant colonies were found to be larger, mound densities higher, and ant abundances four to seven times greater in North America than in South America. Factors including climate, habitat type, seasonal variability, and ant population structure did not appear to explain the observed differences between the two continents, which bolstered the idea that natural predators, parasites, and competitors control the species in South America. Confirmation that fire ants' success in North America is primarily a consequence of escape from natural enemies was an important objective when biological control of this exotic pest was considered.

(ANNE R. GIBBONS)

This article updates the *Macropædia* article INSECTS.

Ornithology. In a review of major significance published in 1997, Sharmila Choudhury of the Wildfowl and Wetlands Trust, Slimbridge, Eng., compared various hypotheses that had been advanced to explain "divorce" in birds. Most avian mating systems are monogamous; the key to understanding the circumstances under which divorce occurs lies in determining the costs and benefits of both pair fidelity and divorce. Individuals can be expected to divorce when the benefits outweigh the costs. Hypotheses included incompatibility, preference for a better-quality mate, accidental loss of mate, and intrusion of a third party.

As part of a study by G.L. Kooyman and T.G. Kooyman of the Scripps Institution of Oceanography, La Jolla, Calif., adult emperor penguins in Antarctica were fitted with time-and-depth recorders to monitor their ocean dives while foraging. Most dives were found to be to depths of 20–40 m (65–130 ft) for times between four and five minutes. The deepest individual dive was 534 m (1,752 ft), and the longest was 15.8 minutes. The closely related king penguins dive similarly, but the breaths they snatch while briefly resurfacing are not enough to restore their oxygen fully. Yvon Le Maho of the Centre for Ecology and Physiology Energetics, Strasbourg, France, suggested that submerging king penguins cope by deliberately creating hypothermia. In depressing their core temperature, they reduce their oxygen need.

Birds were known to have two complex navigation systems, one that relies on the position of the stars and another that uses the Earth's magnetic field. It had been thought that either system was adequate to guide migrating birds. Nevertheless, according to Wolfgang Wiltschko and co-workers of Johann Wolfgang Goethe University, Frankfurt am Main, Ger., garden warblers, at least, cannot navigate by the stars alone when flying south for the winter; they also need information from the Earth's magnetic field if they are to fly off on exactly the right heading. At the end of each summer, central Europe's garden warblers set off southwest to the Iberian peninsula, then south to Sierra Leone, and finally southeast toward South

Africa. Although born with those instructions, the birds need an external reference system to lay in the correct flight path. The researchers raised two groups of warbler chicks to about six weeks of age. Both groups were exposed to an artificial sky with 16 fake stars rotating once per day to mimic the motion of real stars. While one group experienced the Earth's magnetic field, the other group was exposed to artificial fields, which canceled out the natural field. In August, at the onset of migratory restlessness, the birds' activity was recorded to determine the direction in which they intended to fly. Warblers that had been exposed to the stars and the Earth's magnetic field oriented themselves in the correct southwesterly direction. The other birds, however, prepared to set out wrongly, almost due south.

The spectacled eider, a species of sea duck, was classified as threatened in 1993 after populations in western Alaska had declined more than 90% in 30 years because of unknown causes. The species spends the summer and breeds in the coastal tundra, but its wintering sites had been unknown. To discover where the eiders went in winter, about two dozen individuals were fitted with radio transmitters and tracked until the batteries became too weak to send strong signals. At that time the eiders were dispersed in the Bering Sea south of St. Lawrence Island, where the ocean had not yet frozen solid. Unexpectedly, after six months of inactivity a transmitter emitted a freak signal. U.S. Fish and Wildlife biologists Greg Balough and Bill Larned chartered a plane and flew in search of the source—300 km (190 mi) within the Arctic ice pack. They discovered first hundreds and then thousands of ducks jammed into tiny holes in the Bering Sea ice pack, which the birds kept open to the ocean by their own body warmth and movements. A rough count gave about 150,000 spectacled eiders, estimated to be at least half the total wintering population.

(JEFFERY BOSWALL)

This article updates the *Macropædia* article BIRDS.

MARINE BIOLOGY

Concern over the enlargement of ozone holes—thinned regions of the Earth's protective stratospheric ozone layer—above the polar regions generated interest in the effects on marine organisms of the associated increase in solar ultraviolet (UV) radiation reaching the surface. To study such effects researchers cultured algae known as diatoms under six spectrally different light regimes near Palmer Research Station, Antarctica. Under conditions simulating daily exposure to ambient UV radiation, the diatoms showed a 34% reduction on average in carbon fixation (the organism's essential assimilation of carbon into organic compounds via photosynthesis).

In the tropical seas a challenge was made to the common assumption that damaging UV wavelengths penetrate to considerable depths in oligotrophic (clear) waters, posing a potential threat to coral reefs. A U.K. study that made use of a semisubmersible scanning spectroradiometer at various sites around the central Indian Ocean and Andaman Sea demonstrated that damaging UV radiation attenuated very rapidly with depth, even in very clear waters around the Maldives.

The International Year of the Reef was declared for 1997 to focus attention on the current and increasing plight of coral reefs, particularly the damage being caused by human activity. (*See* ENVIRONMENT: *Special Report*.) The bleaching and consequent death of corals following the disruption of the association with their pigmented symbiotic microorganisms (zooxanthellae) was one major concern, and the causes of bleaching were being actively sought. During the year the phenomenon was reported in the Mediterranean coral *Oculina patagonica* after infection of its zooxanthellae by a species of the bacterium *Vibrio*. Building on the recent discovery that corals can act as host for more than one species of zooxanthellae, another study showed that bleaching might be reversible, since some zooxanthellae are resistant to bacterial infection.

Colonies of species of massive corals (notably *Favites abdita, Montastrea curta,* and *M. annuligera*) on reefs at Heron Island, northeastern Australia, were found to be regularly spaced. Studies revealed that they formed a structural matrix, each colony releasing a chemical that inhibited settlement and growth of neighbouring colonies within a certain distance. A novel method of artificial transplantation of corals was reported by German investigators, who inserted pieces of living coral into a steel mesh that was positioned at the new underwater site and made to function as the cathode in a electrolytic circuit. Passing direct current through seawater between the electrodes induced the accretion of calcium and magnesium minerals at the cathode and thereby generated in situ a new coral substrate having a limestone character. A unique feeding strategy was reported for a soft coral, *Gersemia antarctica*, which grows upright to a height of 1–2 m (3.3–6.6 m). Instead of feeding on suspended plankton, assumed to be the normal feeding mode, observed specimens flexed the upper body downward, which brought polyps into feeding contact with bottom sediment.

Spread of the introduced tropical alga *Caulerpa taxifolia* into the western Mediterranean continued to cause concern along the coasts of France, Spain, and Italy. Reported at new record depths near 100 m, the alga was penetrating far deeper than expected for a photoautotrophic alga (one requiring light and using only inorganic compounds as nutrients), which suggested that it also employs heterotrophic metabolism—*i.e.,* that it can live off organic compounds. A Spanish study reported that close proximity to *Caulerpa* inhibited the growth of native algae such as *Cystoseira* and *Gracilaria*. The inhibitor, called caulerpene, was found to be a secondary metabolite produced by *Caulerpa*, which also made the alga repellent to grazing marine animals and to colonization by epiphytes (plant species that rely on other plants for physical support). A grazing-activated chemical defense was reported for the first time in a single-celled planktonic alga, *Emiliania huxleyi,* when grazed by the protozoan *Oxyrrhis marina*. Feeding resulted in the production of dimethyl sulfide by means of an enzyme-mediated reaction. When experimentally offered algal cell mixtures, the protozoan selected algae showing low activity of the enzyme involved in the reaction.

A Canadian study reported different daily patterns of vertical migration in populations of the veliger larval stage of the sea scallop *Placopecten magellanicus*. Each pattern favoured transport of the veligers by currents back to their particular parental scallop beds.

Historical data on catch localities of the sperm whale (*Physeter macrocephalus*) in the 19th century were compared with contemporary satellite-derived data on the distribution of chlorophyll in the ocean, which can be interpreted as a measure of productivity. On large spatial scales the abundance of chlorophyll, measured by ocean colour, was found to be a good predictor of areas of ocean where sperm whales should be abundant. In a Ukrainian study humpback whales (*Megaptera novaeangliae*) of the Arabian Sea were reported to remain in the same area year-round. Having no northern outlet from the Arabian Sea, they did not migrate to high latitudes in summer for feeding, as did other Northern Hemisphere stocks of humpbacks.

(ERNEST NAYLOR)

This article updates the *Macropædia* articles CRUSTACEANS; FISHES; MOLLUSKS; etc.

BOTANY

In 1997 the genetic engineering of plants continued to make impressive contributions to the development of improved agricultural crops. The gene in baker's yeast that allows the cells to revive after being totally desiccated was introduced into tobacco plants; when the plants' leaves were cut and left to dry, they were still fresh a day later. The advance opened up a new way to protect crops from both severe drought and frost. Plants were also being engineered with greater tolerance of aluminum, the cause of a problem that afflicts 40% of arable land, mainly in the tropics, where acid soils release toxic aluminum ions into the groundwater. Tobacco plants were genetically altered such that their roots released citric acid, an organic acid that tied up aluminum ions in the soil, preventing the aluminum from entering and damaging the roots.

The importance of engineering corn (maize) was highlighted when the U.S. Congress announced plans to analyze the entire genetic makeup, or genome, of the plant, the first crop plant designated to have all its genes mapped and DNA sequenced, in a $40 million project considered to be as significant as the Human Genome Project. The corn genome comprises three billion pairs of bases, the molecular building blocks of DNA, and 30,000 genes, which makes the task comparable in size to unraveling the human genome. By helping to unravel the genetic mysteries of corn, the project could help researchers engineer other major grain crops. The Japanese government pledged to map and sequence the rice genome, six times smaller than the corn genome.

Making productive decisions about the genetic engineering of plants requires a thorough understanding of plant physiology. Biotechnologists had been eager to eliminate a process in plants called photorespiration, a side reaction of photosynthesis that seems to waste a plant's synthesized food by turning it back into carbon dioxide. Akiko Kozaki and Go Takeba of Kyoto (Japan) University, however, discovered that photorespiration actually protects plants from the harmful effects of strong light. Using genetically modified tobacco plants, they reported

APRIL SAUL—KRT

In a laboratory at the University of Pennsylvania, a biologist inspects plants being cultivated as part of a $12 million plant genome project. Genetic engineering of plants continued to play an important role in the development of improved agricultural crops.

that the more a plant photorespires, the better it withstands high-intensity light.

Because plants are rooted to one spot and unable to run from danger, they have evolved an immense array of self-defense systems against pests. Investigators took genes that had been discovered to give both wild beets and snowdrops the ability to repel nematode soil worms and introduced them into grapevines to protect their roots. Commercial spin-offs of the achievement could be considerable; currently, vines infected with nematodes were treated with methyl bromide, a fumigant that was scheduled to be banned in the U.S. in the year 2001.

Since the early 1990s an astonishing airborne communication system between plants had been deciphered. Researchers learned that plants under attack by pests send out messages in the form of volatile compounds to their still-unassaulted neighbours that tell them to prepare their defenses against the insects. Work during the year by Vladimir Shulaev and colleagues of Rutgers University, New Brunswick, N.J., showed that the chemical message system extends to viral attacks. Plants infected with tobacco mosaic virus release methyl salicylate, better known as the fragrant oil of wintergreen, which switches on the defense mechanisms of nearby healthy plants.

Work on plant defenses had also revealed that plants under attack from such insects as caterpillars release airborne insect repellants or broadcast chemical signals to predatory wasps, which attack the pests. Recently, a plant called molasses grass was discovered giving off such signals when unmolested. In field trials in Kenya during the year, molasses grass planted with corn and sorghum cut massive pest devastation to those crops by 95% and thus offered a promising alternative to chemical pesticides.

Knowledge of the ways that plants and animals can cooperate advanced with the discovery, in mangrove trees in Belize, of the first known symbiosis between sponges and trees. Large sponges were found attached to the exposed roots of the trees, with both parties benefiting. Roots with attached sponges were almost four times the size of roots without sponges, and the attached sponges grew faster, perhaps by feeding off nutrients drawn up by the roots.

Some root symbioses had enormous potential for improving crop yields. Legume plants are nourished by root-dwelling *Rhizobium* bacteria that take nitrogen from the air and turn it into nitrate compounds on which the roots feed. For decades a holy grail of crop-plant research had been to find a way to feed other crops in the same manner to boost their growth, and during the year plant scientists found such promise in rice. One group of researchers uncovered a species of *Rhizobium* growing symbiotically in rice plant roots, and a second group discovered previously unknown nitrogen-fixing bacteria of the genus *Azoarcus* that can colonize rice plants. The finds opened up enormous possibilities for reducing the amount of chemical fertilizers currently used in rice farming.

(PAUL SIMONS)

MOLECULAR BIOLOGY

Toward a Therapy for CGD. Chronic granulomatous disease (CGD) is an inherited loss of the ability to ward off infection by bacteria and fungi. Affected persons suffer a series of life-threatening infections to which they finally succumb.

The seat of the problem in CGD is a subset of the white blood cells called phagocytes, which normally engulf and kill invading microorganisms. When they become activated, normal phagocytes dramatically increase their consumption of oxygen in a process called the respiratory burst. The increase is actually accomplished by a chain of chemical reactions, some catalyzed by enzymes (protein molecules that regulate specific reactions), that ultimately yield hypochlorite (OCl^-). Hypochlorite is the active ingredient of laundry bleach and is intensely lethal to the engulfed microorganisms. Phagocytes from people with CGD cannot mount a respiratory burst and are defective in their microbicidal activity.

The first step in the respiratory burst is the activation of a membrane-associated enzyme called NADPH oxidase. The active enzyme requires the interaction of two proteins in the cell fluid, or cytosol, with two proteins in the cell membrane. A defect in any one of those four proteins disarms the respiratory burst. CGD can be caused by a mutation of any one of the four genes that code for the four components of the active NADPH oxidase. In fact, medical researchers have identified cases of CGD that are traceable to defects in each of the four genes.

It should be possible to cure CGD by replacing the defective gene with a normal one. Investigators recently tested the validity of that approach, using cultured lymphocytes taken from a CGD patient. When DNA bearing a normal copy of the defective gene responsible for the CGD was introduced into the lymphocytes, the cells regained the ability to mount a respiratory burst. The next step would be to attempt this gene replacement therapy in the living body. A lasting cure would depend on genetic modification of the body's stem cells. Located in the bone marrow, the stem cells are the long-lived progenitors of the circulating phagocytes. Toward this end, researchers sought to develop an animal model of CGD so that the best therapeutic approach could be worked out prior to attempting it in humans.

One way to create an animal model—for example, a mouse model—of a genetic disease is to eliminate the function of a specific gene. The method involves the introduction of a modified, dysfunctional form of the desired gene into cells that have been derived from an early-stage mouse embryo. Those cells in which the modified gene has successfully replaced the normal gene are injected into early mouse embryos, which are placed into the uterus of a mouse so that development can proceed. Those resultant mouse pups that express the modified gene are used to develop a breeding colony. In this way researchers produced mice that lacked one of the cytosolic components of the NADPH oxidase and whose phagocytes thus could not mount the respiratory burst. The mice exhibited the hallmarks of CGD, being extremely susceptible to infection.

In 1997 the animal-model research was extended to humans when five patients with GCD were treated at the National Institutes of Health, Bethesda, Md., with their own stem cells into which functional genes had been introduced. In each case the outcome was encouraging, with the genetically engineered stem cells producing functionally normal white blood cells for an average of three months.

One Protein, Several Functions. Why are most enzymes in nature so much larger than their substrates—*i.e.,* the molecules that they act upon? The question had long puzzled enzymologists, who thought that smaller catalysts would be more efficient at facilitating the many reactions that go on in cells. One answer is that many enzymes do much more than simply speed up a specific chemical reaction.

An example of the multiple functions that a single protein can serve recently came to light. That protein is glyceraldehyde-3-phosphate dehydrogenase (GDH). It was first isolated in the 1930s as the enzyme that functions in cell metabolism to catalyze the oxidation of glyceraldehyde-3-phosphate (which possesses one phosphate group) in the presence of inorganic phosphate to yield 1,3-diphosphoglycerate (which possesses two phosphates). This reaction is particularly important in that it conserves the energy that is liberated during oxidation of the aldehyde group in the energy-requiring synthesis of a high-energy phosphate bond. An abundant enzyme, GDH plays a crucial role in the process by which the nutrient sugar glucose is converted in the cell to lactic acid, with concomitant production of high-energy phosphate bonds that are used to power cellular processes.

In the 1990s, however, GDH was found to serve other, unrelated roles. One was the repair of defects in DNA that, if left unattended, would result in mutation. DNA normally contains the four nitrogenous bases adenine, thymine, guanine, and cytosine. It should not contain the base uracil, which is a normal component of RNA, but its cytosine base can slowly and spontaneously lose ammonia, or deaminate, and thus be converted to uracil. This instability is compensated by enzymes, collectively called uracil glycosylases, that remove uracil from DNA so that other enzymes can then replace it with cytosine. When the major uracil glycosylase was isolated from human cells and characterized, it proved to be identical to GDH.

Yet another function served by GDH was found to be the transport of transfer RNA (tRNA) out of the cell nucleus. Molecules of tRNA are made in the nucleus but used in the cell cytoplasm (the protoplasm outside the nucleus) during protein synthesis. A carrier protein serves to conduct tRNA from the nucleus into the cytoplasm. When characterized, it too proved to be GDH. Moreover, the versatility of GDH is not exhausted by the foregoing functions. GDH was found to be one component of the complex structure required for the replication of DNA. It also proved to be one of the microtubule-associated proteins that regulate the assembly and function of this ubiquitous element of the cytoskeleton, the network of protein fibres that gives shape and support to the cell.

These multiple functions of GDH should be reflected both in the regulation of GDH and in its location within the cell. The amount and the intracellular location of any protein can be assessed by the use of antibodies that have been prepared to bind specifically to the protein of interest and tagged with a fluorescent substance that stands out distinctly under the microscope. When researchers applied this technique to human cells in culture for visualization of GDH, they observed that nongrowing cells had GDH only in the cytoplasm, in keeping with its role in glucose metabolism and its binding to microtubules. By contrast, growing and dividing cells had GDH in both the nucleus and the cytoplasm, as predicted by its additional roles in tRNA transport, DNA repair, and DNA replication. Such functional versatility may well turn out to be a common feature of proteins. Given the potential for many of the approximately 50,000 different cellular proteins to perform multiple functions, the life of the cell may prove to be even more complicated than previously thought. (IRWIN FRIDOVICH)

A Lamb Named Dolly. In 1997 cloning became a household term, thanks to Ian Wilmut and colleagues of the Roslin Institute, near Edinburgh, who reported in February the first successful cloning of an adult mammal. The centre of attention, a Finn Dorset ewe named Dolly, by her very existence dispelled decades of presumption that adult mammals could not be cloned and ignited a debate concerning the many possible uses and misuses of mammalian cloning technology.

The concept of cloning in mammals, even in humans, was nothing new. Naturally occurring genetic clones, or individuals genetically identical to one another, had long been recognized in the form of monozygotic (identical) twins, triplets, and so on. Unlike Dolly, however, such clones are derived, as their scientific name indicates, from a single zygote, or fertilized egg. Moreover, clones had been generated previously in the laboratory, but only from embryonic cells or from the adult cells of plants and "lower" animals such as frogs. Decades of attempts to clone mammals from existing adults had met with repeated failure, which led to the presumption that something special and irreversible must happen to the DNA of mammalian cells during the animal's development. Indeed, until 1997 it had been generally accepted dogma that adult mammalian cells are no longer genetically totipotent, or capable of giving rise to all of the different cell and tissue types (*e.g.,* liver, brain, and bone) required for making a complete and viable mammal. It was presumed that somatic-cell differentiation, the process by which a single fertilized egg is converted into all of the different cell types found in an adult, involved some irreversible step. That Dolly remained alive and well long after her birth—that she had a functional heart, liver, brain, and other organs, all derived genetically from the nuclear DNA of an adult mammary-gland cell—proved otherwise. At the very minimum, the specific tissue from which Dolly's nuclear DNA was derived must have been totipotent. By extension, it was reasonable to suggest that the nuclear DNA of other adult tissues also remains totipotent. With the success of Dolly, this speculation became a testable hypothesis.

To appreciate more fully the ramifications of Dolly's existence, it is necessary to consider in some detail the circumstances of her creation. Dolly did not spring from the laboratory bench fully formed but developed to term normally in the womb of a Scottish Blackface ewe. Although the DNA in her cell nuclei was derived from a mammary-gland cell taken from an adult Finn Dorset ewe, that DNA had to be fused by electrical pulses with an unfertilized egg cell, the nucleus of which had been removed. The egg cell was taken from a Scottish Blackface ewe, and later another sheep of the same breed served as a surrogate mother. Furthermore, in order for the DNA to be accepted and functional within the context of the egg, the donor mammary-gland cells first had to be induced to abandon the normal cycle of growth and division and enter a quiescent stage. To do this, researchers deliberately withheld nutrients from the cells. The importance of this step had been determined experimentally, and although a number of hypotheses had been raised to explain its necessity, which, if any, of them was correct remained unclear. Nevertheless, a number of fused couplets formed embryos, which were transferred to surrogate ewes. Of 13 recipient ewes, one became pregnant, and 148 days later, which is essentially normal gestation for a sheep, Dolly was born.

Dolly's unusual conception and normal birth raised a host of questions—some scientific, others social, ethical, or even religious. Some of the questions were answerable, and others were not. Of the scientific questions, at least two were thought to be experimentally approachable from studies of Dolly or her offspring.

The first question addressed the issue of X-chromosome inactivation, the process by which normal mammalian females limit the expression of most of the genes located on their X chromosomes. In brief, a normal mammalian male receives an X chromosome from the mother and a Y chromosome from the father and so carries only one X chromosome; a female, on the other hand, receives an X from each parent and so carries two. To avoid the overexpression of genes that would occur with two active X chromosomes, a female effectively shuts down nearly all of the genes on one of her two X chromosomes very early in embryonic development. Which X is inactivated in each individual cell of the female, however, appears to be a matter of chance. Some cells inactivate the maternally derived X; others, the paternally derived X. As the embryo grows and develops and the cells divide and differentiate, the progeny of each cell "remember" the original decision, so that normal adult females end up as mosaics, with some of their cells expressing genes only from their maternally derived X chromosomes and others only from their paternally derived X chromosomes.

The implication for cloning using DNA from adult female cells is that unless the X-chromosome inactivation that exists in the donor cell is somehow reversed and then randomly reestablished in the cells of the developing embryo, the resultant female clones will not be mosaic. All of their cells will express only those genes on the X chromosome that had not been inactivated in the donor cell. If that chromosome carries any abnormal genes, the female clones could fail to express the normal equivalents of those genes present on their other (inactivated) X chromosome and, as a result, be afflicted with any of a range of biological abnormalities early or later in life. That Dolly appeared healthy suggested either that the X-chromosome inactivation was reversed and rerandomized in her cells or that none of her essential X-chromosome genes were abnormal. This was a testable distinction.

A second scientific question raised by Dolly's creation involved the mitochondria, cell organelles that carry their own set of genes distinct from the nuclear genes and that exist outside the nucleus in the cell cytoplasm. Even though the two sets of genes exist independently, they must operate interdependently for the cell to function normally. Since Dolly's mitochondria were derived from a Scottish Blackface donor egg and nuclei from a Finn Dorset mammary-gland cell, an important question was whether there would be any incompatibility. Clearly, Dolly's good health suggested otherwise. An extension of this question remained, nevertheless. Could mammalian

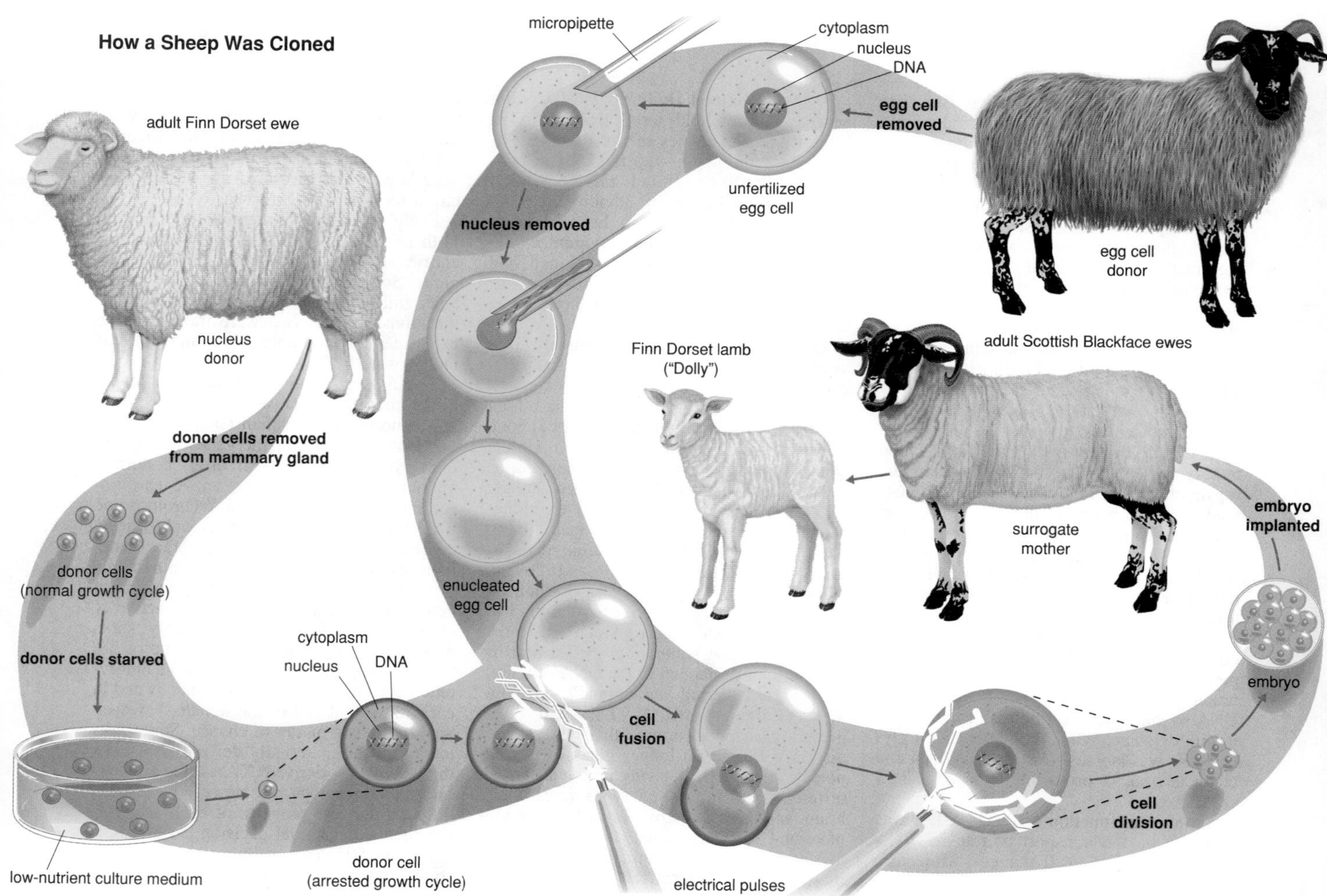

cloning technology be applied to study experimentally the effect of mitochondrial DNA mutations on whole organisms, rather than only on cultured cells, as had been done in the past?

Finally, both scientists and nonscientists were confronting the social and ethical Pandora's box of questions raised by mammalian cloning. On the positive side, cloning of nonhuman animals may greatly simplify the otherwise cumbersome manipulation of domestic livestock currently required for engineering genetic improvements in resistance to disease. It may also facilitate the production of lifesaving pharmaceuticals for human use—*e.g.,* the production of human insulin in nonhuman animal milk. In addition, the application of cloning to the creation of founder individuals in a breeding population of animals could aid in saving endangered species otherwise doomed to extinction.

On the other hand, would racehorse owners attempt to clone champions rather than breed them? If so, how would this approach be regarded by the horse-racing industry? Much more important, what of cloning humans? Does the concept of cloning violate the sanctity of the individual? During the year some observers voiced concerns about misguided zealots attempting to clone political or religious leaders; others envisioned hope for desperate parents of children in need of a perfectly matched donor for a bone-marrow transplant, pointing out that some parents were already opting to pursue pregnancy after pregnancy in an attempt to create such a donor. In 1997 human reproductive technology allowed for in-vitro fertilization, genetic characterization of early embryos prior to implantation, and a multitude of genetic and other forms of both pre- and postnatal presymptomatic testing. One could only wonder to what new accepted practices human cloning might lead. (*See* Special Report.)

(JUDITH L. FRIDOVICH-KEIL)

PALEONTOLOGY

The year 1997 was an active and exciting one for paleontology, as new discoveries and interpretations of fossil vertebrates, invertebrates, and plants advanced scientists' understanding of past ecosystems. In vertebrate paleontology the efforts of the joint expeditions of the American Museum of Natural History and the Mongolian Academy of Sciences to the Gobi Desert of Mongolia continued to produce exceptional vertebrate fossils from the Cretaceous Period (approximately 144 million to 66.4 million years ago). In total the skeletons of more than 150 dinosaurs and 300 lizards and the skulls of 240 mammals were collected. The most famous was a complete skeleton of the small theropod dinosaur *Oviraptor* preserved on top of a nest of eggs. Identification of the embryonic skeletons within the eggs confirmed that the oviraptor was actually sitting on its own nest rather than stealing eggs from the nest of another dinosaur species. This finding was in contrast to interpretations of fossil evidence found in the 1920s, which had incorrectly assumed that the animal was raiding nests for food and hence had led to the genus name *Oviraptor,* meaning "egg thief."

Important new vertebrates were also discovered by an expedition of the State University of New York (SUNY) at Stony Brook to Madagascar. Birds and primitive mammals of the Mesozoic Era (about 245 million to 66.4 million years ago) were among the new fossils under study from this collection. Many of the fossils represented new species within extinct groups of mammals previously known only from South America.

One of the more unusual finds was described in a preliminary report from Chinese paleontologists given at the Jurassic Symposium held at the Museum of Northern Arizona in late 1996. Intriguing pictures showed small theropod dinosaurs that appeared to have feathers preserved along the vertebral column (backbone), although some experts argued that the features in question might be connective-tissue fibres that supported a midline structure down the back of the animal. In another development, researchers at Dinosaur National Monument, Utah, reported that a number of small theropods possessed furculae (wishbones in birds). The two discoveries further strengthened the theory that birds evolved from small carnivorous theropod dinosaurs.

In mid-1997 a paleontologist from the University of Notre Dame, Ind., reported to the media the finding of what might be the largest skeleton of *Tyrannosaurus*. The ownership of the specimen, from Montana, was under dispute, and most of it had yet to be collected; hence, the significance of the find remained unclear. Ownership of the largest and most complete tyrannosaur specimen known to date, which was discovered in

1990 in South Dakota and nicknamed "Sue" had also been a subject of controversy for several years. The courts finally resolved the issue, which cleared the way for the designated owner to auction off the skeleton to the highest bidder. Sue was bought by Chicago's Field Museum of Natural History in October for $8,360,000.

A new skeleton representing one of the very earliest groups of mammals in the fossil record was reported for the first time from the Late Triassic Period (230 million to 208 million years ago) of Greenland by paleontologists from Harvard University. In addition to the fact that fossil vertebrates from Greenland were relatively rare, the new specimen suggested that these early mammals were not closely related to the multituberculates, an extinct primitive group of rodentlike mammals, of the later Mesozoic Era, as had been thought.

Laboratory studies made significant contributions to paleontology during the year. Researchers at Montana State University reported that for the first time organic molecules had been discovered preserved in dinosaur bone. In particular, molecules resembling collagen, a type of protein, were found in nonpetrified samples of *Tyrannosaurus* bones. In a second study, analysis of the rates of genetic change by researchers working on fossil invertebrates at SUNY at Stony Brook suggested that the origin of the major animal phyla may date to 1 billion–1.2 billion years ago. This age is much older than previous estimates, since the first known fossils of metazoans (multicelled animals) date back only to about half that age.

Other invertebrate studies focused on using fossils to document ecological change. For instance, the distribution of corals, which are very sensitive to temperature variations, was being used to track global climate change through portions of the Earth's history (particularly more recent times). The results of this research were stimulating the growth of projects designed to find links between the distribution of climate-sensitive shallow-water marine organisms and environmental change.

Interesting new discoveries of Paleozoic invertebrates reported during the year included a unique group of soft-bodied Silurian fossils from northeastern Iowa and southern Wisconsin. These unusually well-preserved specimens included numerous arthropods, annelid worms, and fish, some of which represented new genera. Like the famous assemblage from the Burgess Shale of the Canadian Rockies, this could turn out to be one of the most significant collections of soft-bodied-animal fossils from North America.

Exopaleontology, the study of ancient organisms from other planets, emerged as a new field of research following a report in 1996 of fossil evidence of primitive life preserved in a Martian meteorite from Antarctica. The report was controversial, and experts continued to debate whether life existed on Mars some 3.6 billion years ago. Nevertheless, it stimulated studies by NASA scientists on ancient underwater vent and seep sites on Earth that produced fossils and represent environments in which organisms derive energy from chemical compounds rather than sunlight. Such sites were of interest to NASA because they may be similar to the type of environment that would allow life to originate on a planet like Mars.

PETER TYSON—AP/WIDE WORLD/EARTHWATCH

In Montana a paleontologist measures the pubic bone of a *Tyrannosaurus*. The bone was part of what was believed to be the largest *Tyrannosaurus* skeleton ever found. The ownership of the specimen was under dispute.

In paleobotany the content of coprolites (fossil dung) was increasingly being employed to determine the nature of early terrestrial plant communities. One such study indicated that the very earliest trees of Middle to Late Devonian age (387 million to 360 million years ago) grew in types of soils very different from those of later ages. The origin and early evolution of the flowering plants was another topic of considerable recent interest to paleobotanists. A paper published in a recent book on the topic identified the oldest angiosperm (flowering plant) known to date, from very Early Cretaceous deposits of Israel.

Permian and Triassic age plants from Antarctica also continued to add to scientists' understanding of plant evolution. Permineralized peat deposits from the Transantarctic Mountains contained some of the best-preserved cell structures of any fossil plants. Reproductive structures from these peats provided vital new information about the early evolution of seed plants.

(WILLIAM R. HAMMER)

See also Anthropology; The Environment.

This article updates the *Macropædia* articles AGRICULTURE; Animal BEHAVIOUR; BIOCHEMICAL COMPONENTS OF ORGANISMS; The BIOLOGICAL SCIENCES; BIOSPHERE; CELLS; CONSERVATION OF NATURAL RESOURCES; DISEASE; The Theory of EVOLUTION; The Principles of GENETICS AND HEREDITY; GEOCHRONOLOGY; MAMMALS; PLANTS; REPRODUCTION AND REPRODUCTIVE SYSTEMS; REPTILES.

Literature

In 1997 the world of publishing was as fickle as ever. The sudden death of Diana, princess of Wales (*see* OBITUARIES), occasioned an outpouring of books that were devoured by the public, even as critics decried the impulse behind them. Although major publishing houses owned by multinational corporations continued their hegemony, an increasing number of highly regarded small presses came to represent a kind of literary samizdat. The virtual bookstore became a reality so overwhelming that many physical bookstores began to feel the effects. In the United States in particular, the best-seller lists were unexpected homes to a good number of dense and imposing literary titles by writers such as Thomas Pynchon (*Mason & Dixon*) and Don DeLillo (*Underworld*), and the winners of major literary fiction prizes (the National Book Award for Fiction in the U.S. and the Booker Prize in Great Britain) were big commercial successes in advance of the awarding of the prizes themselves, which disputed the initial common wisdom that the memoir was supplanting the novel as the literary form du jour. Both prizes, however, were increasingly vexed; the shortlists ignored any number of important titles in both the U.S. and the U.K., and both were won by first-time novelists, which caused many in publishing to shake their heads in disbelief and dismay.

Throughout the world the approaching millennium sent writers fleeing to the past for subject matter. In the U.S. major novels explored the 18th century, the Civil War, the Cold War, and the 1960s. In Britain Jim Crace's *Quarantine* took place in 1st-century Judea, and France's Prix Goncourt was won by *La Bataille,* an account of an 1809 Napoleonic battle told from the combatants' point of view. Germany's cult hit *Starfish Rules* was set in the U.S. during the 1930s, and a major Danish novel explored the religious and political struggles of 14th-century Denmark. Throughout Latin America fiction meditated on recent historical outrages.

The persecution of writers by the state continued in many parts of the world, notably in the Middle East and Africa. The International Parliament of Writers, headed by Nobel Prize winner Wole Soyinka of Nigeria, mailed out an appeal for funds, citing censorship, harassment, imprisonment, and even murder in places like Algeria, Iran, China, Nigeria, and Uzbekistan.

Highly regarded new English translations of Horace's *Odes* and Ovid's *Metamorphoses* appeared. The 75th anniversary of James Joyce's *Ulysses* was marked by the publication in the U.K. of a "reader's edition," which most critics regarded as a travesty. Other highlights of the year included the sudden high visibility of expatriate Indian writers, as well as new works by such internationally known authors as Haruki Murakami, Philip Roth, Peter Handke, Peter Carey, Robert Stone, Cynthia Ozick, John Updike, Saul Bellow, Norman Mailer, Colleen McCullough, Beryl Bainbridge, Peter Findley, Ben Okri, J.M. Coetzee, Athol Fugard, Hélène Cixous, Aharon Appelfeld, Joyce Carol Oates, Mario Vargas Llosa, A.B. Yehoshua, Aleksandr Solzhenitsyn, Kurt Vonnegut, Mario Benedetti, and Lyudmila Petrushevskaya. (STEVEN BAUER)

ENGLISH

United Kingdom. In 1997 literary critics widely agreed that there were no new standout novels. Other literary forms, however, such as the memoir, seemed to many to give better expression to the fin de siècle mood of the country. Stephen Moss, *The Guardian*'s literary editor, complained about what he regarded as a lacklustre 1997 Booker Prize shortlist, writing, "The death of the novel is an endlessly replayed...subject, but any objective observer of the events surrounding this year's Booker would have to conclude that fiction was in a parlous state. Breathing, but only just."

The Booker shortlist drew criticism both for its obscurity on the one hand and for pandering to popularity on the other. Three lesser-known titles shortlisted were Mick Jackson's *The Underground Man,* Madeleine St. John's *The Essence of the Thing,* and Tim Parks's *Europa.* The three more prominent titles, however, were considered more likely to win. Although *Grace Notes* by the well-established short-story writer Bernard MacLaverty from Northern Ireland was expected to gain the award, Booker Prize administrator Martyn Goff said that the panel felt that the book was really three short stories strung together, and its status as a novel was thus weakened. Jim Crace's *Quarantine* was many literary critics' favourite. An ambitious historical novel set in Judea in the 1st century AD, the action took place in the desert during the time when Jesus undertook his 40-day fast. Other characters took up residence there as well, including a dying and wily merchant whom Jesus saves, a woman trying to cure her infertility, and a group of pilgrims intent on settling in the caves. Although *Quarantine* earned praise for its humane intelligence and superb writing, the book nevertheless failed to win. In the voting the judges were divided but eventually arrived at a unanimous decision, announced October 14. The prize of £20,000 was awarded to Arundhati Roy, a first-time author from New Delhi, for *The God of Small Things.* The story, a saga of love, death, and intercaste relations, focused on twins growing up in the southern Indian state of Kerala. In the author's native India, critics charged that the book corrupted public morals. It nevertheless enjoyed strong sales in Britain and North America, and by the day before the winner was announced, the book had emerged as the favourite. Although Gillian Beer, the chairwoman of the judges, praised the book's "extraordinary linguistic inventiveness," Carmen Callil, 1996 chairwoman, in an interview just after the announcement, derided the decision of the judges as "execrable." Moss dismissed comparisons of Roy to V.S. Naipaul and Salman Rushdie as the "fantasies of publicists" and concluded that the year's choice had been "disastrous" for the award and "profoundly depressing."

The Whitbread Award was less controversial but notable in that the overall winner was not a novel. The respective winners in each of four categories—first novel, novel, poetry, and biography or autobiography—were John Lanchester's *The Debt to Pleasure* (1996), Beryl Bainbridge's *Every Man for Himself* (1996), Seamus Heaney's *The Spirit Level* (1996), and Diarmaid MacCulloch's *Thomas Cranmer: A Life* (1996). Although Bainbridge's novel, a tale about the sinking of the *Titanic,* was favoured to take top honours as the Book of the Year, nine judges, chaired by Malcolm Bradbury, settled on Heaney's poetry collection. "It was a tightly fought battle and the decision...was not unanimous," said Bradbury, "but [Heaney] represents some of the most powerful, original, and energetic work in the language." Heaney, the Northern Ireland-born poet and winner of the 1995 Nobel Prize for Literature, had been hailed as Ireland's greatest poet since William Butler Yeats.

The second Orange Prize for Fiction, awarded for the best novel written by a woman, went to Anne Michaels's *Fugitive Pieces.* The book was the Canadian poet's first novel and probed the memories of a Holocaust survivor through his journal. It was a late submission and was considered only after one of the judges of the award called on the publishers, Bloomsbury Publishing PLC, to enter it for the prize. The novel also won *The Guardian* Fiction Award.

Whereas many critics were less than enthusiastic about the year's literary fiction, genre fiction, particularly the crime novel, rose to ever more popular heights. P.D. James published her 12th traditional English crime novel, *A Certain Justice.* A story of a murder in London's Inns of Court, it went straight onto the best-seller lists, along with Ruth Rendell's latest Inspector Wexford novel, *Road Rage.* These established queens of crime were joined by such newcomers as noir stylists Nicholas Blincoe, with *Jello Salad;* Glaswegian writer Christopher Brookmyre, with *Country of the Blind;* and Neil Tidmarsh, whose *Fear of the Dog* was a smooth-paced thriller about amoral dealings in London's 1990s art world. Counterbalancing crime novels set in the gritty modern day was a rush of historical detective fiction. Iain Pears's *An Instance of the Fingerpost* was set in Oxford in the 1660s, and authors Peter Tremayne and Kate Ross, respectively, produced a 7th-century nun and a Regency dandy as sleuths. *The Guardian* praised the best of these offerings for prose styles "at least equivalent to that of, for example, Madeleine St. John, Booker-shortlisted this year." As if envious of the genre's popularity, literary fiction writers Ian McEwan and Martin Amis both produced books obeying elements of the crime novel. McEwan's *Enduring Love* featured a stalker, and Amis's *Night Train* presented a case that might have been murder or suicide.

Other novels that won critical acclaim were Rose Tremain's *The Way I Found Her,* a story of summer love in Paris narrated by a 13-year-old boy, and Edna O'Brien's *Down by the River,* a disturbing story of a 14-year-old girl seeking an abortion after becoming pregnant as a result of an incestuous relationship with her father. A short novel, *The Reader,* a love story set in post-World War II Germany by Bernhard Schlink, was acclaimed by several reviewers for its terse and haunting prose, and *Do White Whales Sing at the Edge of the World?* by Paul Wilson was hailed by *The Independent* as "not a nice novel, but...grim and fantastic."

One of the most controversial books of the year was a new edition of James Joyce's *Ulysses.* Coinciding with the 75th anniversary of the book's publication and appearing on Bloomsday, June 16 (the day on which the action in *Ulysses* takes place), *Ulysses* was edited by Danis Rose, a Joyce scholar in Dublin. Rose claimed to have purged some of Joyce's errors and won praise from, among others, Irish poet and novelist Seamus Deane, who hailed it as "one of the most important editions...in a long time." Many critics were stridently disparaging, however. The *London Review of Books* remarked that Rose's approach "violates every principle and procedure of critical editing," and John Kidd, director of the James Joyce Research Center at Boston University, commented, "No responsible editor has ever undertaken the scale of mutilation that Danis Rose has perpetrated on this text." The Joyce estate, led by Joyce's grandson Stephen James Joyce, threatened to stop the book's publication on copyright grounds.

The memoir threatened to oust the novel as the literature of choice, with *Angela's Ashes* (1996), Frank McCourt's poignant tale of growing up in the slums of Limerick, Ire., winning praise in both the U.K. and the U.S., though sales in the U.S. were greater. *Skating to Antarctica* by Jenny Diski was a memoir of a traumatic childhood, overshadowed by a father who was a con man and a mentally disturbed mother who had aspirations of making her daughter into an ice-skating champion. Along with impoverished and abusive childhoods, illness was another favoured subject for autobiographical comment. *The Diving Bell and the Butterfly,* Jean-Dominique Bauby's account of his suffering as a result of a paralyzing stroke—dictated by blinks of his eye—won high praise when it appeared in the U.K. in a translation by Jeremy Leggatt. *The Independent* declared it a "hugely absorbing narrative" reminiscent of the "icy clarity" of Simone de Beauvoir's description of Jean-Paul Sartre's descent into blindness and confusion. Bauby died in March. (*See* OBITUARIES.) Fiona Shaw's *Out of Me,* an account of a postnatal breakdown, was a passionately written piece about life at the edge of an emotional abyss. More self-reflection came from Elizabeth Kaye, whose book *Mid-Life: Notes from the Halfway Mark* (1995; published in London in 1997) was a wistful but colourful account of coping with aging.

Literary biography continued to thrive as a robust form. The first volume of R.F. Foster's biography of Yeats appeared under the title *The Apprentice Mage, 1865–1914* and was hailed by *The Literary Review* as being as rewarding as it was long awaited; it was especially celebrated for its "brilliantly" handled examination of Yeats's relation to political events in Ireland. Fintan O'Toole's biography of another Anglo-Irish writer, Richard Brinsley Sheridan, was also well received, as was Phyllis Grosskurth's *Byron: The Flawed Angel,* the first substantial account of the life of the poet for more than 30 years and much applauded for its balance and restraint. A stirring account of the life of Daniel Defoe, author of *Moll Flanders* and *Robinson Crusoe,* was produced by Richard West, with a title reminiscent of his subject's writing style: *The Life & Strange Surprising Adventures of Daniel Defoe.* Although little was known about Defoe's life, West coped with this exigency by supplying a lively historical backdrop to his narrative, encompassing such events as the Great Plague of London, the Great Fire of London, and the Popish Plot.

JERRY BAUER

Frank McCourt

Other warmly received biographies included Jennifer S. Uglow's *Hogarth: A Life and a World,* a rich evocation of the artist and his London hometown. A.N. Wilson's *Paul: The Mind of the Apostle* conveyed the subject's enormous intelligence and literary skill amid a backdrop of vexed Mediterranean politics in the 1st century. *Wellington: A Personal History* by Christopher Hibbert provided new insights into the duke's personal life. The author had used newly found archives that had come to light since Elizabeth Longford's major study appeared 25 years earlier.

Other nonfiction works included Hugh Thomas's *The Slave Trade: The Story of the Atlantic Slave Trade, 1440–1870.* Three decades in the writing, it was hailed as one of the most rounded and complete studies of the slave trade to date. David Crystal's *English as a Global Language* examined the rise of the English language, from its murky origins in the Dark Ages to its present-day status as a language to which, Crystal claimed, approximately one-third of the people on the planet were routinely exposed. (*See* Spotlight: *English Language Imperialism*). Equally ambitious in scope were Felipe Fernández-Armesto's *Millennium,* a history of the world over the past 1,000 years, and Roy Porter's authoritative *The Greatest Benefit to Mankind: A Medical History of Humanity.*

Two remarkable compilations were also published. *The Penguin Book of Columnists,* edited by Christopher Silvester, brought together in 640 pages the most vibrant of the U.K.'s newspaper columnists. *The Papacy,* edited by Michael Walsh, was a compact history of the papacy as it approached the 3rd millennium. The book ended with the conclusion that there would be a pope in Rome for as long as there was a human race. One of the most highly sought-after edited collections, however, was a new and comprehensive edition of the letters of the Brontë family. *The Brontës: A Life in Letters,* edited by Juliet Barker, was celebrated for its intimate portrayal of Yorkshire life in the vicarage at Haworth; the book's popularity spoke to the enduring fascination among British readers with this family of geniuses.

(SIOBHAN DOWD)

United States. Fiction is dying—the memoir is the thing. This seemed to be the conventional wisdom in 1997 among the big American publishing houses, where the previous year's mood of desperation born of declining sales of serious fiction and growing returns of unsold books fed a frenzy of hype and aesthetic blindness. Kathryn Harrison's confessional memoir *The Kiss,* her deliberately opaque account of her incestuous affair with her father, became the focus of the hysteria. For a while the controversy over this book—obscene or not? a subtle masterpiece or an empty bit of titillation?—dominated the talk about new books. Ultimately, the year was marked by the publication of some of the biggest books of the decade, which allowed serious readers and critics alike to focus their attention on questions of quality rather than on gossip.

Mason & Dixon, Thomas Pynchon's long-awaited novel set in the pre-Civil War U.S., took centre stage for a time, though the massive 700-page volume, which included cameo appearances by Ben Franklin and George Washington and was peppered with Pynchon's signature wit and song lyrics, received a mixed response from critics. The initial reception of another huge novel, *Underworld,* Don DeLillo's 800-page-plus exploration of American life at the advent of the Atomic Age, was much more positive. Its resonant opening line—"He speaks in your voice, American, and there's a shine in his eye that's halfway hopeful...."—and its masterly opening set-piece (the final game of the 1951 National League play-offs, with Frank Sinatra, Jackie Gleason, and J. Edgar Hoover, among others, in the crowd) immediately swept most readers into the action.

Pynchon and DeLillo were not the only established novelists to produce major new works. Philip Roth's *American Pastoral,* a look back at the 1960s, elicited a favourable critical response. Novelist and naturalist Peter Matthiessen focused once again on pre-World War I Florida in *Lost Man's River,* the second volume in a trilogy with the enigmatic quasi-historical E.J. Watson at the centre of things. John Updike anticipated the next century in his science-fiction knockoff *Toward the End of Time.* Kurt Vonnegut proclaimed *Timequake* his "last" novel even as it began to appear on best-seller lists around the country. The only one of this well-recognized group to strike out was Norman Mailer, with his oddly experimental revision of the Jesus story, *The Gospel According to the Son.*

Among other seasoned novelists, San Francisco-based Herbert Gold published his urbane comedy about an older man in the throes of romance, *She Took My Arm as if She Loved Me,* and Cynthia Ozick revived an old character in new dress in *The Puttermesser Papers.* Joyce Carol Oates produced *Man Crazy,* a novel episodic in design and, like her 1996 work *We Were the Mulvaneys,* set in upstate New York. Frederick Busch used an upstate New York winter as the backdrop for *Girls,* his best novel in years. Ward Just returned to Washington, D.C., for the scene of *Echo House,* one of his most successful works of fiction.

Nicholas Delbanco employed a variation on the legend of the doomed 12th-century lovers Héloïse and Abelard for the motif of his wonderfully engaging contemporary love story *Old Scores.* Edmund White's *The Farewell Symphony* and Allan Gurganus's *Plays Well with Others* were two novels that dealt with the impact of the AIDS epidemic, but neither to very good effect. *Terminal Velocity,* Blanche McCrary Boyd's novel set in the 1970s in a California lesbian commune, was much more successful in its treatment of somewhat similar material. The highly regarded Denis Johnson produced what he called "a California Gothic" titled—aptly, according to most reviewers—*Already Dead.* It had the distinction of being the worst book of the year by a good writer, which, given Mailer's flop, was saying a great deal.

Heading straight to the top of the best-seller lists and staying there was *Cold Mountain,* a debut novel by North Carolina writer Charles Frazier. The story of a wounded Confederate veteran's valiant attempts to put war behind him and return to his mountain home, the book was a wonderful blend of forceful narrative, striking imagery, and engaging characters. The debut of playwright Joseph Skibell as a novelist in *A Blessing on the Moon,* a story of the Holocaust, also won deserved attention. Kathleen Alcalá signed in with *Spirits of the Ordinary,* a charming historical fiction set on the northern border of Mexico in the late 1800s. Jay Parini turned to history again in *Benjamin's Crossing,* a novel based on the last days of the German-Jewish literary critic Walter Benjamin.

Sticking with a contemporary setting with good effect was novelist Kem Nunn in *The Dogs of Winter,* a beautifully composed thriller with a cast of surfers and other California renegades. Craig Nova used a Southern California setting with fine results in *The Universal Donor.* Cristina García, author of the acclaimed *Dreaming in Cuban* (1992), transported readers to Cuba and Miami, Fla., in *The Agüero Sisters,* a novel blessed with wonderful prose rhythms and poignant scenes from Caribbean family life. Darcey Steinke's third novel, *Jesus Saves,* the story of a Virginia minister's daughter and the perils of suburban life, showed off the author's powerful dark lyric style.

MARION ETTLINGER—OUTLINE

Charles Frazier

It was also a good year for novellas and short fiction. Saul Bellow produced a gem of a work in his 100-page story *The Actual.* Two notable novella collections appeared: David Leavitt's *Arkansas* and Francine Prose's *Guided Tours of Hell.* Whether they were considered novellas or simply three long stories, the work in former Pulitzer Prize and PEN/Faulkner winner Richard Ford's *Women with Men* brought him more well-deserved national attention. *Bear and His Daughter* collected all of the gifted novelist Robert Stone's brilliant short fiction from the past several decades. Some important fiction reprints also appeared during the year, namely, *The Complete Stories of Bernard Malamud* and Larry Woiwode's impressive 1975 novel *Beyond the Bedroom Wall.*

American poets produced less controversy than their prose counterparts but nonetheless issued some excellent volumes of verse. Pulitzer Prize winner Mary Oliver came out with *West Wind*—"If there is life after the earth-life, will you come with me?/ Even then? Since we're bound to be something, why not/ together? Imagine Two little stones, two fleas under the/wing of a gull, flying along through the fog...." In *Eating Bread and Honey* Pattiann Rogers also turned, with great effect, to the natural world.

Award-winning poet Frank Bidart—recipient of the 1997 O.B. Hardison Jr. Poetry Prize—published *Desire.* Jane Hirshfield signed in with *The Lives of the Heart* ("There is more and more I tell no one/ Strangers nor loves...."), Stanley Plumly with *The Bride in the Trees,* Charles Wright with *Black Zodiac,* and Hilda Raz with *Divine Honors.* Cynthia MacDonald (*I Can't Remember*), A.R. Ammons (*Glare*), and Jorie Graham (*Errancy*) also brought out new volumes during the year. In *Ceremonies of the Damned,* Adrian C. Louis produced lyrics on Indian reservation life, and Elizabeth Alexander played on black family motifs in *Body of Life.* With the publication of the collection *When People Could Fly,* the prose poem found a marvelous godfather in Morton Marcus ("There was a time when stones flowered. I need to believe that. In forests and fields, layers of black rock cracked open after rain, and slick pink petals swarmed into wet sunlight....").

As to the year's nonfiction prose, certainly some of the memoirs offered the most interesting passages, though Harrison's *The Kiss* was not among the books memorable for their achievement rather than their content. *Burning the Days,* by novelist and screenwriter James Salter, was in this select group, however. "There are certain houses near the river in secluded towns, their wooden fences weathered brown. Near the door in sunlight, stiff-legged, a white cat pulls itself up in an arc. Clothes on a half-hidden line drift in the light. It is here I imagine the wives, their children long grown, at peace with life and now drawn close to the essence of it, the soft rain flattening the water, trees thick with foliage bending to the wind, flowers beneath the kitchen window, quiet days. Men are important no longer, nor can they know such tranquillity, here in perfect exile, if it can be had that way, amid nature, in the world that was bequeathed to us...."—this was Salter in what was perhaps the single most impressive book of prose published all year in any genre.

Memoirs, good and bad, abounded in 1997. In *North Country,* Howard Frank Mosher plumbed the difficulties of approaching middle-age as a "mid-list" novelist. Albert French turned to the Vietnam War for his subject matter in *Patches of Fire.* The difficulties of kinship and siblings were featured in Jay Neugeboren's *Imagining Robert: My Brother, Madness, and Survival.* Another work focusing on family relationships was *My Brother,* Jamaica Kincaid's loosely constructed story of her brother's death from AIDS and her own response to his passing. Phyllis Rose conducted a gracious tour of a recent year in her life, with some excursions into her past, in the felicitously composed *The Year of Reading Proust.* Novelist Paul Auster's autobiography *Hand to Mouth* was a decided failure in the eyes of just about every reviewer of merit. American Indian writer N. Scott Momaday collected his essays in *The Man Made of Words.* Journalist and civil libertarian Nat Hentoff cobbled together a memoir out of essays and newspaper columns under the title *Speaking Freely.*

Literary figures were the subjects of a large portion of the year's best biographies—a category that included Michael Reynolds's *Hemingway: The 1930s, Walker Percy* by Patrick Samway, S.J., *Robert Penn Warren* by Joseph Blotner, *John Ciardi* by Edward M. Cifelli, and *Misfit: The Strange Life of Frederick Exley* by Pulitzer Prize-winning critic Jonathan Yardley—though other creative individuals, painters, photographers, and composers came under scrutiny, notably in *Duchamp* by Calvin Tomkins, *Steichen* by Penelope Niven, and *Johannes Brahms* by Jan Swafford. Sylvia Jukes Morris chose a notable 20th-century woman as her subject in *Rage for Fame: The Ascent of Clare Boothe Luce*. The selected letters of the poet Hart Crane were edited by Langdon Hammer and Brom Weber under the title *O My Land, My Friends.* Literature professor Bonnie Costello edited *The Selected Letters of Marianne Moore.*

Important literary criticism came from elder statesman Alfred Kazin in *God and the American Writer.* Columbia University professor Andrew Delbanco received well-deserved attention for *Required Reading,* his essays on classic American writing. Poet John Hollander put together 23 essays on *The Work of Poetry.* Poet Jane Hirshfield demonstrated an interesting approach in *Nine Gates: Entering the Mind of Poetry,* and Henry Louis Gates's *Thirteen Ways of Looking at a Black Man* demonstrated a critical mind working well in the realm of journalism. Arguably the best work of the year by a younger critic was James Bloom's *The Literary Bent: In Search of High Art in Contemporary American Writing.*

Mark Edmundson's *Nightmare on Main Street* stood as one of the year's best books of cultural criticism. Former *Harper's Magazine* executive editor Michael Pollan, a self-proclaimed "unhandy" man, narrated the story of the construction—by his own hands—of a small building in *A Place of My Own.* Janna Malamud Smith won some notice for her work on privacy in American culture, *Private Matters.* California novelist James Houston focused on American-Asian affinities and differences in his resonant travel memoir *In the Ring of Fire.*

In the realm of historical narrative and public affairs, John Lukacs assessed the extant Hitler biographies in *The Hitler of History.* Maury Klein wrote of the coming of the Civil War in *Days of Defiance.* David K. Shipler took up the subject of race relations in *A Country of Strangers: Blacks and Whites in America.* Novelist Susan Richards Shreve and her writer son, Porter, edited an interesting collection of essays by various hands under the title *Outside the Law: Narratives on Justice in America,* and veteran *New York Times* reporter Serge Schmemann painted an affecting portrait of his ancestral home in Russia in *Echoes of a Native Land: Two Centuries of a Russian Village.*

DOMINIQUE NABOKOV—GAMMA LIAISON

Bharati Mukherjee

Among the year's awards the Pulitzer Prize for Fiction went to Stephen Millhauser for his novel about a visionary entrepreneur, *Martin Dressler.* Short-story writer Gina Berriault received the PEN/Faulkner Award for Fiction for *Women in Their Beds.* Frazier's *Cold Mountain* won the National Book Award for fiction; William Meredith's *Effort at Speech: New and Selected Poems* took the award for poetry; and Joseph Ellis's *American Sphinx: The Character of Thomas Jefferson* won for nonfiction. New Jersey-born Robert Pinsky was named the new poet laureate. (ALAN CHEUSE)

Canada. In 1997 the millennium was too close for comfort yet too distant for reality—an ideal condition for poetry, which feeds on time and death, the beat, and the silence between beats, as evidenced in *Time Capsule: New and Selected Poems,* which eloquently demonstrated why Pat Lowther's 1975 death was a great loss to Canadian literature. Anne Szumigalski soared forth *On Glassy Wings: Poems New & Selected,* a 25-year flight of verbal aerobatics, and *Selected Poems: 1978–1997* was Patrick Lane's latest offering of poems as enigmatic as the volume's title. P.K. Page's collected works required two volumes to reveal the many dimensions of *The Hidden Room: Collected Poems.*

Poets were the original blue-sky pilots, like the voyagers to the *Long Lost Planet: Lesley Choyce and the Surf Poets,* a talking book in which images blazed like meteors across the dark night of the mind; Francis Sparshott in *Home from the Air,* viewing a landscape charged with balloons and sinners, graves and academics; or Dionne Brand's dazzling displays of controlled metaphorics in *Land to Light On.* In contrast was Don McKay's austere, astutely crafted *Apparatus,* instrumental in stopping the eye on the nearly invisible present as it flashes past, swift as childhood. Those moving horizons were circumscribed by Linda Rogers in *Heaven Cake,* a delicious concoction of celestial visions and earthly delights.

Robert Priest, seeking *Resurrection in the Cartoon,* sketched multiple perspectives with the tip of his mordant wit, whereas Al Purdy used a broader brush of humour, loaded with mixed messages, in *The Gods of Nimrud Dag.* Rosemary Aubert's audacious *Picking Wild Raspberries: The Imaginary Love Poems of Gertrude Stein* served as counterpoint to bill bissett's *Loving Without Being Vulnrabul.* Laura Lush, a poetic seismograph, mapped *Fault Lines* in meticulous detail, and George Bowering raced down the tracks of *Blonds on Bikes,* telling tales all the way.

The tellers of real tall tales were found in short-story collections, as in Timothy Findley's *Dust to Dust,* elegiac reconstructions of lives too early lost, or too long extended; Holley Rubinsky's *At First I Hope for Rescue,* lives lived in the narrow valleys of the interior of British Columbia linked into a chain, each binding each; the inspired forgery of John Weier's *Friends Coming Back as Animals,* transformations under the hammer of events; and Maggie Helwig's *Gravity Lets You Down,* a descent into society's underbelly and back again.

In one sense *Larry's Party,* Pulitzer Prize winner Carol Shields' latest novel, lasted for 20 years; in another it was over where it began, at the centre of Larry's labyrinthine heart, where everyone eventually arrives—amazed, bemused, and wonderfully confused. Funnily enough, Mordecai Richler

(continued on page 254)

SPECIAL REPORT

English-Language Children's Literature

by Shannon Maughan

"Jack, be nimble." In 1997 publishers of children's literature appeared to heed this sage advice from Mother Goose as they adapted their book programs to an ever-changing marketplace—one that embraced both a blend of timeless classics and a flurry of new contemporary titles. Overall, fewer new titles were released in 1997, as publishers focused on those considered surefire hits, such as titles from established best-selling authors, tie-ins to movies and television programs, and paperback series for intermediate (ages 8–12) and young adult readers (ages 12 and up) in such popular genres as horror and adventure. Nonetheless, in the U.S. about 5,000 new titles were introduced, some sure to become enduring classics that would fuel the booming $1.5 billion business in children's books.

As a result, one of of the largest publishing mergers of 1996, the new U.S. company Penguin Putnam Inc., began 1997 boasting more than eight different children's imprints in the U.S. and a roster of best-selling authors and illustrators, including Jan Brett (*The Mitten* and *The Hat*), Tomie De Paola (*Strega Nona*), Eric Hill (the Spot books), S.E. Hinton (*The Outsiders*), and such classic properties as *Madeline* by Ludwig Bemelmans, novels by British author Roald Dahl, and Beatrix Potter's beloved Peter Rabbit titles.

Bookstores greeted customers in 1997 with a barrage of books featuring the stars of popular children's television programs and films. In addition, licensed properties gained a stronger foothold in the children's book market, whether it was Blinky Bill or Bananas in Pajamas from Australia, Noddy in the U.K., Rugrats or the Sesame Street gang in the U.S., or any of the globally recognized Disney characters.

It was no surprise that behemoth Disney led the licensing pack in 1997 with tie-ins to *Hercules,* its animated summer release. The animated November release of *Anastasia* from 20th-Century Fox, however, was poised to give Disney a run for its money at the box office and in the bookstores. HarperCollins, the U.S. publishing division and sister company to Fox, released 12 books related to the film, which was set in Russia at the time of the Bolshevik Revolution of 1917. Big-budget action films with PG-13 ratings also muscled their way onto the children's book scene with tie-ins and novelizations of *The Lost World, Men in Black,* and *Batman & Robin.*

Just as TV and film spawned books, the reverse was also true. Classic children's literature inspired a record number of television spin-offs, featuring such enduring characters as Babar the elephant king, Madeline the Parisian schoolgirl, spunky gadabout Pippi Longstocking, and Thomas the Tank Engine (*see* OBITUARIES: *Wilbert Vere Awdry*). "Wishbone," a live-action TV program about an imaginative dog, introduced children to classic adult literature, including such books as Charles Dickens's *A Tale of Two Cities.* In addition, "The Busy World of Richard Scarry," "The Wubbulous World of Dr. Seuss," and the aardvark of the hour, "Arthur," were just a few of the television series based on children's books that continued to gain a phenomenal number of young fans. Although "Arthur" began airing on PBS in late 1996, in 1997 Marc Brown's original Arthur books, many of which were first published nearly 20 years ago, began routinely selling one million copies per month owing to the show's great popularity. The beloved aardvark made his debut in *Arthur's Nose,* published in 1976.

While licensed books represented the up-to-the-minute trends, many classic children's books proved their staying power in 1997 by marking significant anniversaries. Parents continued to share with their own little ones the titles that they had loved as children. In 1997 Rudyard Kipling's adventure story *Captains Courageous* reached the century mark, A.A. Milne's *Now We Are Six* hit 70, and J.R.R.

One of the first books to be targeted specifically to infants and toddlers, *Goodnight Moon* celebrated its 50th anniversary in 1997.

Tolkien's *The Hobbit* turned 60. One of the best-loved bedtime stories of all times, *Goodnight Moon* by Margaret Wise Brown, celebrated its 50th anniversary. The book had sold more than seven million copies and was among the titles most frequently purchased for newborns. Also celebrating a half century of enduring popularity was Esphyr Slobodkina's *Caps for Sale,* a cautionary tale about what can happen when one is napping. *The Cat in the Hat,* starring the irrepressible feline in a striped top hat, one of the creations of verse virtuoso Dr. Seuss, turned 40 in 1997, as did the green galoot who ultimately grows a larger heart in *How the Grinch Stole Christmas.* Also 40 and sharing the spotlight were the groundbreaking "I Can Read" series of books from HarperCollins. Along with the Grinch and the Cat, such I Can Read titles as *Little Bear* by Else Holmelund Minarik and Maurice Sendak, *Frog and Toad Together* by Arnold Lobel, and *Danny and the Dinosaur* by Syd Hoff have been helping children learn to read for decades.

Several books for older readers were feted in 1997 as well. *Misty of Chincoteague,* a tale of wild horses by Marguerite Henry (*see* OBITUARIES), passed a 50-year milestone, and *The Outsiders,* a young-adult coming-of-age novel about teenage boys, turned 30 and reigned as the highest-selling children's trade paperback. British author Brian Jacques's fantasy-adventure Redwall series—first published in 1986—continued to sell briskly. The 11 books about the brave mice who defended Redwall Abbey against cruel rats and other woodland marauders became equally popular with British, American, and other English-language readers.

Top-selling children's titles experienced a good deal of crossover readership in the various English-language territories. The tender tale of Little Nutbrown Hare and his father proved to be a hit with children around the globe as *Guess How Much I Love You* by Sam McBratney, illustrated by Anita Jeram, appeared on best-seller lists in several countries. Authors such as Canadian Robert N. Munsch (*Love You Forever*) and Australian Mem Fox (*Wilfrid Gordon McDonald Partridge, Time for Bed*) joined the list of authors whose works have become increasingly well known outside their homeland. This phenomenon was especially true of books that garnered their respective country's top children's book honours, including two U.S. awards presented by the American Library Association, the Newbery Medal for excellence in fiction or nonfiction and the Caldecott Medal for excellence in illustration, and the U.K. equivalents, the Carnegie Medal for outstanding fiction and the Kate Greenaway Medal for excellence in illustration, the latter two given by Britain's Library Association.

The subject matter in the books nominated for the Carnegie Medal also pointed to a trend in children's literature toward realism and the darker aspects of life. The 1997 shortlist of nominees included Melvin Burgess's *Junk,* a story about drug use; Fine's *The Tulip Touch,* which broached such topics as a suspected murder and arson; and Michael Coleman's *Weirdo's War,* which addressed the kind of incessant bullying that could lead to suicide. In the U.S. author Judy Blume had begun broaching teenage coming-of-age issues some 25 years earlier. She had discussed such subjects as menstruation, puberty, and divorce in the family at a time when those topics were not greeted enthusiastically by librarians. Nonetheless, Blume's *Tales of a Fourth Grade Nothing* (1972), a story about sibling rivalry, ranked as the third highest selling children's trade paperback, behind *The Outsiders* and E.B. White's *Charlotte's Web.* As early as 1963 writer and illustrator Sendak had introduced younger readers to *Where the Wild Things Are,* a vivid depiction of grotesque monsters. He followed with two others in a trilogy—*In the Night Kitchen* (1970) and *Outside Over There* (1981), all of which raised controversy because of their frank and possibly frightening story lines.

When adolescents were seeking mystery and intrigue, they gravitated to series of books by R.L. Stine. These included *Fear Street,* in which teenagers solve mysteries under frightening circumstances, and *Goosebumps,* which were slightly scary suburban mysteries.

All in all, children's book publishers in 1997 managed to get the jump on nimble Jack, not only making it over the candlestick unsinged but also using its light to tally their profits.

Shannon Maughan is a freelance editor-writer for Publishers Weekly *magazine.*

(continued from page 251)
snarled his characters in contradictions and myth in *Barney's Version,* for which he won Canada's $25,000 Giller Prize. For *The Time Being* Mary Meigs arranged the meeting of two women in the wilds of Australia and turned them loose with startling results. In *Evening Light* Harold Horwood saw clear to the core of the outport soul in his rendering of a Newfoundlander's life; Jane Urquhart used the medium of a minimalist artist to limn her meaning in *The Underpainter,* winner of the 1997 Governor-General's Award for English-language fiction; and Marilyn Bowering charted mysterious customs in *Visible Worlds.*

In Austin Clarke's *The Origin of Waves,* immigrants meeting in Toronto after a hiatus of 50 years while away time in a bar during a blizzard; Margaret Gibson, in a storm of memories and pain, re-created the past in *Opium Dreams.* In *Sleeping Weather* Cary Fagan described a waking nightmare of invasion by the irrational and the irresistible. Even scarier was Bharati Mukherjee's protagonist in *Leave It to Me,* a goddess of revenge stalking the parents who abandoned her in infancy. Erika De Vasconcelos celebrated generations of women in *My Darling Dead Ones,* and Nino Ricci completed his trilogy with *Where She Has Gone.*

(ELIZABETH WOODS)

Other Literature in English. Literary works by writers from Australia, New Zealand, and sub-Saharan Africa highlighted 1997. From Australia Madeleine St. John's novel *The Essence of the Thing* was a finalist for Great Britain's increasingly controversial Booker Prize. Peter Carey, winner of the Booker in 1988, released his latest novel, *Jack Maggs;* and poet Les Murray, nominated for the 1998 Neustadt International Prize for Literature, offered a selection of his prose writings in *A Working Forest.* Also in Australia, the best-selling author Colleen McCullough brought out *Caesar: Let the Dice Fly,* her ninth novel and the fifth in an ambitious series on ancient Rome. Other important works included Gail Jones's wide-ranging short-story collection *Fetish Lives* and Robert Dessaix's *Night Letters: A Journey Through Switzerland and Italy* (1996), a marvelously imaginative personal, epistolary, and literary journey set against a changing backdrop of time and place.

New Zealand writers offered a comparable range of literary talent. Heading the list in poetry were Allen Curnow with *Early Days Yet: New and Collected Poems, 1941–1997* and C.K. Stead with *Straw into Gold: Poems New and Selected.* In fiction established authors continuing to draw attention and acclaim were Maurice Shadbolt with *Dove on the Waters* (1996) and Lauris Edmond with *In Position.* In Maurice Gee's latest work, *The Fat Man,* the protagonist threatens to control the lives of an 11-year-old boy and his family as part of his plan for revenge for the mistreatment he suffered as a schoolboy.

Outstanding new literature, both innovative and engaging, emerged from writers in Africa. The Nigerian-born award-winning novelist Ben Okri released *Dangerous Love* (1996), a lyrical novel about a doomed affair between star-crossed lovers; it was hailed as his "most accessible and disarming novel yet." Other standouts included memoirs from two of South Africa's finest writers not noted for such personal revelations—novelist J.M. Coetzee's *Boyhood: Scenes from Provincial Life* and playwright Athol Fugard's *Cousins: A Memoir.* The new works of other South Africans met with both critical and popular success as well, including Lynn Freed's *The Mirror,* Christopher Hope's *Me, the Moon, and Elvis Presley,* Rayda Jacobs's *Eyes of the Sky* (1996), and W.P.B. Botha's *A Duty of Memory.*

The essay collection of Kenyan Ngugi wa Thiong'o, *Penpoints, Gunpoints, and Dreams,* explored the relationship between art and political power. Censorship was the topic in Margreet de Lange's *The Muzzled Muse: Literature and Censorship in South Africa.* Nobelist Wole Soyinka, a victim of censorship and continued threats from Nigeria's government, drew support from such literary luminaries as Kenzaburō Ōe, Nadine Gordimer, and Toni Morrison, who issued a formal statement of protest in his defense.

The year in African letters was also marked by the news of the death of Nigerian author Amos Tutuola, whose grisly tales were inspired by Yoruba folklore. (*See* OBITUARIES.)

(DAVID D. CLARK)

GERMANIC

German. The controversy that had surrounded German-language literature since German reunification in 1990 finally began to abate in 1997. The year saw the 50th anniversary of the first meeting of the legendary Group 47, which had profoundly influenced the creation and reception of postwar German-language literature. The most visible sign of improvement was an agreement at the spring meeting of the two German PEN clubs to work toward the organizational unification of German writers. In previous years the push toward unification of the PEN clubs had been blocked by members of the West German club critical of some of their East German colleagues.

The most disputatious ongoing controversy of 1997 was the German spelling reform decided on by the educational and cultural authorities of the German-speaking nations of Central Europe and scheduled to go into effect in 1998. Many of the most prominent German-speaking authors, including Ilse Aichinger, Ulla Hahn, Sarah Kirsch, Martin Walser, Günter Grass, Hans Magnus Enzensberger, and Siegfried Lenz, protested against the reform during the year, arguing that because of it their literary works would be changed without permission, sometimes to the detriment of intended meaning. Owing to the many legal challenges mounted against the spelling reform in the Federal Republic, it was unclear at the end of the year whether the reform would actually be carried through as planned.

Botho Strauß continued his critical reflections on modern life in his book *Die Fehler des Kopisten,* a blending of aphorism and observation typical for the author. The work centred on the narrator's relationship to his young son, for whom the narrator would like to provide beautiful childhood memories and whom he must soon partially relinquish to the school system. This dilemma furnished the opportunity for critical reflections on contemporary education and child rearing. At the same time, the joyous presence of the son gave the book a more positive tone than Strauß's other recent work.

Peter Handke's novel *In einer dunklen Nacht ging ich aus meinem stillen Haus* was a return to fictional narration after the massive, plotless meandering of *Mein Jahr in der Niemandsbucht* (1994) and the political controversy of Handke's intervention in favour of Serbia in 1996. The hero of the novel is a lonely Salzburg pharmacist who is hit over the head one night and becomes mute. He then sets out on an adventurous trip to Spain, where, after a long pilgrimage, he ultimately regains the power of speech. The novel was full of references both to Handke's earlier works and to Cervantes's *Don Quixote;* Handke sought to re-create the miraculous and the wonderful in an alienated postmodern world.

In his novel *Von allem Anfang an,* Christoph Hein made a valuable contribution to the growing body of literature that seeks to reexamine life in the former German Democratic Republic (GDR) with an honesty difficult to achieve prior to 1989. Set in November 1956, the story revolved around Daniel, the son of a Silesian pastor whose family was forced to move to Saxony at the end of World War II. Combining family memories of war and devastation with Daniel's own coming of age and reflections on the 1956 Hungarian Revolution, this story realistically depicted both the problematic early decades of the GDR and the lack of warmth and friendliness in the West. In his much-less-successful work, *Amerikahaus und der Tanz um die Frauen,* Friedrich Christian Delius also combined a coming-of-age story with a political awakening, this time set in the Berlin of the mid-1960s and focusing on a loser figure with no compelling power.

Perhaps the most important novel by a young author in 1997 was Tobias O. Meißner's cult hit *Starfish Rules,* an unwieldy, apocalyptic fantasy set in a mythical U.S. in the years 1937–39 but including anachronistic characters like Jimi Hendrix and the rap group Public Enemy. The "starfish" of the title was a symbol for the U.S. and its supposed five driving forces: hatred, violence, chaos, sex, and revolution. Heavily influenced by the paranoid brilliance of Thomas Pynchon, Meißner here attempted a postmodern pastiche of pop culture and grand narrative; his novel demonstrated how important American postmodern literature had become for many of the young German authors.

Günter Kunert, who had experienced both the Nazi dictatorship and the socialism of the GDR, published his memoirs, *Erwachsenenspiele,* containing fascinating and humorous reflections on figures such as Bertolt Brecht, Johannes R. Becher, Herbert Marcuse, and Uwe Johnson. Herbert Achternbusch's undisciplined but gripping *Der letzte Schliff* was the semiautobiographical story of a failed love affair. Wilhelm Genazino's *Das Licht brennt ein Loch in den Tag* (1996) contained a lyrical series of observations and memories. The year also saw the publication of Robert Gernhardt's clever and thoughtful poems *Lichte Gedichte,* based partially on Gernhardt's painful experience of a heart bypass operation during the previous year.

Jurek Becker, whose life work bridged the East-West and German-Jewish divides, died on March 14. (STEPHEN BROCKMANN)

Netherlandic. Literary critic and poet Kester Freriks, commenting on the nominees for the VSB prize for poetry for 1997, lamented, "Dutch poetry doesn't sing anymore." In the place of melody we find a degree of cerebral grind that makes many poems inaccessible to many readers. Freriks evaluated the work of the nominees Elisabeth Eybers with her bilingual *Tydverdryf/ Pastime,* Gerrit Kouwenaar, the eventual winner, with *De tijd staat open,* Robert Anker with *In het vertrek,* Judith Herzberg with *Wat zij wilde schilderen,* Flemish poet Leonard Nolens with *En verdwijn met mate,* and Toon Tellegen with *Als wij vlammen waren.* Nolens at 50 was the youngest of the nominees, which led Freriks to say, "I miss the dashing, equivocal capricious debutantes and not only among the debutantes but in the field of poetry in general as well."

Of prose it could well have been said that the place of the storyteller's art had been taken by writers' preoccupation with structure and contemplation of social problems, often of a personal nature. Prominent examples were Arnon Grunberg with *Figuranten* and Joost Zwagerman with *Chaos en rumoer.* Now the end of the 20th century appeared to be witnessing a revival of traditional storytelling. Indications of this could be found in the work of the nominees for the Libris Prize, such as Flemish author Hugo Claus with *De geruchten* (1996), A.F.Th. van der Heijden with *Het hof van barmhartigheid,* Margriet de Moor with *Hertog van Egypte* (1996), and J.J. Voskuil with *Het bureau.* In the works of these authors, one recognized an element that, though still mainly autobiographical, portrayed a situation that reached beyond the exclusively personal.

Internationally well-known writer Harry Mulisch's 70th birthday in July was celebrated with an exhibition dedicated to him in the City Museum of Amsterdam. An equally well-known author of that generation, Marga Minco, cast light on *Nagelaten dagen.*

(MARTINUS A. BAKKER)

Danish. A number of 1996 and 1997 Danish publications captured international attention in 1997. In Anne Marie Ejrnæs's *Thomas Ripenseren* (1996), a young Dane is caught up in 14th-century religious and political struggles in Denmark; Brugge, Belg.; and Paris. Mette Winge's *Når fisken fanger solen* (1996) told the sad fate of Danish astronomer Tycho Brahe's sister Sophia, who followed an alchemist into exile and ended up living in dire poverty. Merete Pryds Helle's *Men Jorden står til evig tid* (1996) mixed scientific meticulousness with musicality and myth, and Kirsten Hammann produced a second fantastic novel, *Bannister.* Ib Michael's *Prins* combined fantasy with realism, starting with the discovery by a 12-year-old boy of a well-preserved body floating off the Danish coast.

In Anders Bodelsen's *Den åbne dør,* a 40-year-old mystery is solved, and Tage Skou-Hansen's *På sidelinjen* (1996) was the latest installment in his series of novels about Holger Mikkelsen. Jens Smærup Sørensen's *Kulturlandsbyen* (1996) was a modern-day judgment on a Danish village that saw its native culture disappear after it was proclaimed a European Union village of culture. Suzanne Brøgger's *Jadekatten* traced the rise, fall, and disintegration of a Jewish immigrant family. Social and ethical disintegration were seen in Jens-Martin Eriksen's *Vinter ved daggry,* which was inspired by ethnic cleansing in Bosnia and Herzegovina; that theme was also the setting for Jan Stage's *De andres krig.*

Three established writers produced volumes of short stories: Klaus Rifbjerg's *Andre Tider* recounted the moments that change lives; Henrik Stangerup's *Lille Håbs rejse* contained three youthful fables that seemed to echo many of the themes in his mature work; and Peter Seeberg's *Halvdelen af natten* was a collection of short stories and essaylike reflections.

Naja Marie Aidt published *Huset overfor: Digte* (1996), more poems in her delicate yet incisive style, and Thomas Boberg reinforced his position as a leading poet of the 1990s with *Under Hundestjernen,* a mixture of verse and prose. Morti Vizki, another '90s poet, found inspiration in Egyptian King Akhenaton for *Sol,* and Jørgen Gustava Brandt's selected poems were published in three volumes. A very different writing style characterized *Sila* (1996), a collection of Greenlandic short stories translated into Danish and edited by Aqqaluk Lynge.

(W. GLYN JONES)

Norwegian. Two Norwegian works of 1997 stood out as examples of publishing at its best: Atle Næss's *Ibsens Italia,* which recaptured both pictorially and lyrically the atmosphere of Italy during two long periods that Henrik Ibsen spent there, and Stein Mehren's *Kjærlighetsdikt,* a book of sensual love poems featured along with 81 reproductions of the poet's abstract paintings.

Among novels, Ketil Bjørnstad's monumental *Veien til Dhaka* brilliantly depicted the moral mess of modern humans, and Finn Carling's *Skumring i Praha* told of a painter who travels to Prague to capture the city at twilight but instead is accused of having murdered his wife and becomes involved in a kafkaesque court case. Anne Holt analyzed in intimate detail a disastrous lesbian relationship between a young woman and a married mother of four in *Mea culpa,* and Sissel Lie's *Svart due* was a surrealistic portrait of a middle-aged woman's attempt to cope with aging. The breakdown of a marriage between a doctor and her husband was recounted in Liv Køltzow's *Verden forsvinner,* winner of the prestigious Brage Prize. Knut Faldbakken's *Eksil* was a psychological thriller set in the seedier districts of Oslo. Gerd Brantenberg's semidocumentary *Augusta og Bjørnstjerne* was largely a retelling of Norwegian cultural and social history in the first half of the 19th century, and Bengt Calmeyer's *Hundreårsromanen. Mennesker* surveyed Norwegian history in the 20th century. Tor Åge Bringsværd's *GOBI. Baghdad* was the fifth in a series of novels about the Mongolian empire.

Short-story collections included Lars Saabye Christensen's *Den misunnelige frisøren,* Kjersti Wold's *Prinsessene lander,* and Toril Brekke's *Blindramme.* Poems by Gunvor Hofmo were collected in *Etterlatte dikt,* which showcased works discovered since her death in 1995.

In the biographical genre, Tor Bomann-Larsen's *Det usynlige blekk: Sigurd Christiansens liv* fascinatingly portrayed the intimate relationship between Christiansen's enigmatic private life and his literary works. Liv Bliksrud's *Sigrid Undset,* and Harald S. Næss's *Knut Hamsuns brev 1915–1924* illuminated interesting aspects of those two Norwegian Nobel Prize winners.

(TORBJØRN STØVERUD)

Swedish. The number of Swedish novels and volumes of poetry and essayistic writings was larger than usual in 1997—1,898 new books were published, and many of the works of well-established authors vied for attention with those produced by a younger generation of writers.

Works of poetry and prose by women figured prominently, with Carina Rydberg's *Den högsta kasten* arousing great debate among the literary cognoscenti; the disappointing tell-all revealed personal information about well-known personalities. Esteemed writer Marianne Fredriksson produced *Enligt Maria Magdalena,* a pale follow-up to her 1996 novels.

Well-regarded works included Anna-Karin Palm's *Målarens döttrar,* a modern rendition of Shakespeare's *The Tempest;* first-time novelist Gabriella Håkansson's pseudoscientific novel *Operation B;* and Inger Edelfeldt's *Betraktandet av hundar,* a story about a lonely schizoid high-school teacher.

Two standout themes—death and dying—characterized many works. The title of Eva Runefelt's book of poetry, *Soft Darkness,* was the metaphor she used for death, and Inger Alfvén's *Berget dit fjärilarna flyger för att dö* told of a slowly dying 38-year-old man. Lennart Sjögren's *Fågeljägarna* was a poetic magnum opus about hunters drowning, and Verner Aspenström's posthumously published *Israpport* overshadowed the literary scene with its haunting beauty.

Another recurring theme was societal outcasts, with the best examples being Björn Ranelid's fictionalized autobiography *Till alla människor pa jorden och i himlen,* the sixth novel in a series; Poet Kjell Espmark's *Glädjen,* about those living in "the other Sweden"; and Anita Goldman's tales from a Jewish family, *Rita Rubinstein åker tunnelbana i den bästa av världar.* Also in this category was *Man måste det man önskar,* Stig Claesson's hilarious love story about two pensioners.

Two novels dealt with the past: Peeter Puide's *Samuil Brachinskys forsvunna vrede,* a contemporary *J'accuse* about the fate of the Estonian Jews during the Nazi era, and Per Holmer's *Svindel,* a story painted on the 1914–43 European canvas about Jewish everyman Herschel Meier; a frightening tale of disintegration of values and ideological battles, it was one of the most discussed and praised books of 1997.

(ROSE-MARIE G. OSTER)

FRENCH

France. Although the emphasis on authors' individuality continued to prevent the precedence of any one literary movement, during 1997 a group of diverse novels had themes whose cohesion compensated for the lack of a unified theory. One predominant theme was that of the drifting social outcast. Jean Echenoz's *Un An* told of a young woman, falsely implicated in her boyfriend's death, who flees across France for a year, slowly sinking into poverty and abasement. The meanderings of an abandoned boy in Emmanuel Darley's *Un Gâchis* were even more somber; he finds love with a lost little girl, only to lose it owing to their inability to communicate and hounding by the police. Finally, in Jean-Christophe Rufin's *L'Abyssin,* a 17th-century French ambassador exiles himself from his own culture when his travels cause him to fear of the imperialistic spread of Christianity and French power.

In contrast to the theme of exile, two successful novels dealt with the inescapable effects of home. The young academic of Jean-Philippe Toussaint's *La Télévision* decides to stop wasting time watching television in order to write, but slowly all of his energy is diverted from his work into the fight against television, and his life is absorbed by the very passivity he had tried to avoid. Home was a source of lasting trauma in Patrick Villemin's *La Morsure,* in which a young man attempts to make sense of his painful childhood, during which he was victimized by his parents, teachers, and classmates.

Three novels were coming-of-age stories. In Jean-Marie Gustave Le Clézio's *Poisson d'or,* an African girl, stolen in infancy and abandoned at age 13, learns to fend for herself in France and the United States as she discovers pride in her heritage. In Tahar Ben Jelloun's *La Nuit de l'erreur,* a Moroccan girl learns to fight for independence as she avenges the cowardly hypocrisy of men by destroying them with her sexuality. The lessons of Morgan Sportès's *Lu* were less laudable; a vacuous woman interested solely in her own beauty learns to use her wiles to marry into money and thus take advantage of a world that had always taken advantage of her.

Two best-selling novels maintained the French tradition of satire. Jean d'Ormesson's *Casimir mène la grande vie* recounted the misadventures of a fallen nobleman, his nostalgic grandfather, a young Trotskyite, and an Arab woman—who agree that the world must be changed but disagree on how to go about it—as they become modern-day Robin Hoods, stealing from the rich to give to the poor. In former thriller writer Tonino Benacquista's *Saga,* four screenwriters, hired without a budget to fill the government's quota of French-produced television series, manage against all odds to come up with a hit. The novel engaged readers in the lives of the struggling writers while poking fun at television and its audience.

In the realm of autobiography, Annie Ernaux's *La Honte* recounted the author's claustrophobic small-town childhood and the shame she suffered over her vindictive neighbours' knowledge of her father's attempt to kill her mother. On a lighter note, in Hélène Cixous's *Or: les lettres de mon père,* the writer discovers the existence of her dead father's love letters to her mother. Before reading them, she imagines what they will say and how they will resurrect the past and bring back to life a man she had thought lost forever.

Two major essays aimed alarmist criticism at France. Pierre Bourdieu's *Sur la télévision* (1996) denounced television's growing control over books in general and of the press in particular, whereas in *La Guerre des rêves,* Marc Augé attacked the steady impoverishment of collective and individual imagination at the hands of what he considers totalitarian and imperialistic image makers, particularly the theme park and mass tourism trades.

Poetry was marked by two divergent foci. The first was the foreignness of everyday objects, as in Nathalie Quintane's *Chaussure,* a collection obsessively preoccupied with shoes, feet, and walking. A second poetic trend, inherited from Surrealism, was the exploration of dreams. In *Anatolie* Marie Etienne attempts to put her dreams on display in the hope that they will gain solidity and reveal the unconscious, a hope sadly unrealized at the end of the collection. Between these two trends, Lionel Ray's *Syllabes de sable* (1996) attempted to discover the inner self by examining a person's reaction to loss—be it the loss of a friend, the loss of youth, or separation from home.

The 1997 Prix Goncourt was awarded to Patrick Rambaud for *La Bataille,* the meticulously researched novelization of an 1809 Napoleonic battle told from the soldiers' point of view. Pascal Bruckner won the Prix Renaudot for *Les Voleurs de beauté,* the philosophical tale of a couple who kidnap and disfigure beautiful women in order to redress the injustice of their own ugliness. The Prix Femina went to Dominique Noguez's *Amour noir,* the story of an all-consuming passion that ends inevitably in death, and Philippe Le Guillou won the Prix Médicis for *Les Sept Noms du peintre,* the tale of a young painter's mystic initiation into sexuality and spirituality.

(VINCENT AURORA)

Canada. In 1997 Quebec writers joined the wave of stage performance in the literary arts. The Quebec Writers Union's literature festival in May was a decidedly youthful affair, mixing disciplines and moving away from the tradition of writers declaiming their works before chair-bound audiences in a hall. More established writers such as Suzanne Jacob and Madeleine Gagnon participated too, in October, with a joint French-English cabaret event that featured writers who represented both language communities.

Leading thinkers such as essayist François Charron questioned the assumptions and uses of Quebec nationalism, long a mainstay of literary life in the province. Influential journalist, essayist, and editor Richard Martineau did the same, using his column in the entertainment weekly *Voir* to give the Quebec writing scene new room for political debate. On the language front, Georges Dor questioned the value of Quebec's celebrating its own patois in the work *Anna braillé ène shot* (1996). François Ricard extended his exploration of one of French Canada's greatest writers with his biography of Gabrielle Roy.

In a surprising move, the Can$10,000 City of Montreal Book Prize was awarded to the little-known *Cristoforo,* a lively and well-researched historical novel about the colonization of New France. The work was penned by a newcomer writing under the pseudonym Willie Thomas. The Governor General's Literary Award for fiction broke no new ground; the Can$10,000 award was given to Aude for her book *Cet imperceptible mouvement,* a short-story collection diaphanous in tone.

An exceptional, almost unclassifiable work by Robert Lalonde was the year's commercial and esthetic success. In *Le Monde sur le flanc de la truite,* which follows in the tradition of Annie Dillard's *Pilgrim at Tinker Creek,* Lalonde meditates on writing and nature and comments on and translates into French a variety of books heretofore unknown in French Quebec.

Hard on the heels of Michel Tremblay's early 1997 best-seller *Quarante-quatre minutes, quarante-quatre secondes,* the perennially popular author weighed in with a second novel in the fall, *Un Objet de beauté.* Tremblay's success proved that in Quebec, like everywhere else, romanticized accounts of a people's history were always eagerly read.

(DAVID HOMEL)

ITALIAN

While academics were disputing in 1997 the authenticity of Eugenio Montale's 1996 *Diario postumo,* actor and playwright Dario Fo was awarded the Nobel Prize for Literature, much to Fo's amazement and the Italian literary establishment's discomfiture. (*See* NOBEL PRIZES.) Also sparking controversy were the "cannibals"—a vociferous band of young pulp-fiction writers, whose works were united in the anthology *Gioventù cannibale.* Susanna Tamaro, author of the exceptionally successful *Va' dove ti porta il cuore* (1994), incensed critics without enthralling many readers with her new novel, *Anima mundi,* which introduced as protagonist a worthless young man who moved from Trieste to Rome, there to be all too suddenly converted. Most intriguing among the other distinguished works by women writers was Marta Morazzoni's *Il caso Courrier,* which painted a picture of provincial life in 1917 in the Auvergne region of France and culminated in the unexpected suicide of its central character. In *Dolce per sé* Dacia Maraini recounted a love affair between a much-traveled middle-aged woman and a violinist 20 years her junior. The woman's resulting self-portrait was unusually structured as a series of letters that she (the narrator) sends to the musician's six-year-old niece. Memories of childhood and adolescence in Naples and Rome during the 1950s and '60s were the subject of Elisabetta Rasy's *Posillipo,* a sober and terse narrative in which beauty and pain are inextricably interwoven. At the other end of the spectrum was Francesca Sanvitale's collection of short stories, *Separazioni,* about loss, old age, and loneliness. A rare example of a present-day narrative was found in Francesca Duranti's *Sogni mancini,* in which an Italian woman, an academic, finds independence, perhaps significantly, not in Italy but in New York City.

Whereas the autobiographical novel was favoured by women writers, the thriller was particularly popular among male authors. Antonio Tabucchi's *La testa perduta di Damasceno Monteiro,* a story about a murder and the collusion between police and drug traffickers in Oporto, Port., had some of the stylistic qualities of his earlier *Sostiene Pereira,* but it lacked the latter's narrative rhythm and structural coherence. More compelling was Daniele Del Giudice's *Mania,* a collection of six short stories that were subtly united by the theme of death. The first, "L'orecchio assoluto," was a remarkable example of a classic plot that went back to Edgar Allan Poe. The consistently high quality of the collection gave further proof of Del Giudice's unusual ability to combine a rich and mobile imagination with a rigorous control of style. Very impressive for its inventiveness and stylistic novelty was *Silenzio in Emilia,* Daniele Benati's first book. In the 11th tale the characters of the previous 10 make up, as in a Federico Fellini movie, a fantastic soccer team. In fact, they are all dead souls of ordinary men haunting their homeland in the Emilia region and still talking, and thinking, in its inimitable language.

Claudio Magris's *Microcosmi,* winner of the Strega Prize, was a fascinating journey of exploration through ever-changing public and private microcosms, including the literary, artistic, historical, and scientific. The narrative—a combination novel, essay, journal, and autobiography—involves animals, woods, mountains, rivers, and seas, as well as dead and living people, and ancient and contemporary settings. At journey's end, however, the points of departure and arrival turn out to be on either side of Trieste's public gardens, which suggests perhaps that the journey of life never took place. Difficult to classify was *Ombre dal Fondo* by Maria Corti. Like Magris, she was a university professor, scholar, and part-time creative writer. Her book chronicles how a collection of manuscripts by contemporary writers was developed at the university of Pavia; each manuscript evokes the shadow of its author, at times in a very moving manner. University life and education were again central to Luigi Meneghello's latest prose collection, *La materia di Reading,* which contained autobiographical essays and reflections on his previous writings and offered further insights into contemporary culture in Italy and Britain.

History from the Middle Ages to the 20th century inspired several novels. The first crusade served as the background for Franco Cardini's *L'avventura de un povero crociato;* Sebastiano Vassalli's *Cuore di pietra* explored national disappointments following major historical events since Italy's unification, such as World War I and the Resistance against Fascism; and Enrico Palandri's *Le colpevoli ambiguità di Herbert Markus* focused on the ideological crisis that followed the fall of the Berlin Wall. Most popular in this category was *La parola ebreo,* a narrative by Rosetta Loy that compellingly told of both the heroism and the indifference of Italian Catholics concerning the persecution of Italian Jews before and during World War II.

Two major projects were completed for the prestigious "Meridiani" collection of Italian classics: Dante's *Commedia* and Petrarch's vernacular works, painstakingly annotated by Anna Maria Chiavacci Leonardi and Marco Santagata, respectively.

(LINO PERTILE)

SPANISH

Spain. Late in 1996 Ana María Matute broke a literary silence of 25 years and astounded critics with *Olvidado Rey Gudú,* a massive allegorical folk-epic that spanned four generations of rulers, gnomes, witches, and other creatures in the make-believe medieval kingdom of Olar. Also published late in 1996 was *Las máscaras del héroe* by Juan Manuel de Prada, a gifted newcomer on the literary scene. His work had been attracting new readers for nearly a year when the author won the coveted Planeta Prize for his second novel, *La tempestad,* set in contemporary Venice; there Giorgione's famously cryptic landscape painting, "The Tempest," supplied the key to a mysterious web that ensnared a Spanish art historian.

TONY SICA—GAMMA LIAISON

Dario Fo

Adding another volume to his prodigious output, Gonzalo Torrente Ballester published *Los años indecisos,* a curious amalgam of semiautobiography, metaliterary narrative technique, and confessional reminiscences in the voice of a failed, self-doubting journalist. *La forja de un ladrón,* by Francisco Umbral, evoked the postwar squalor of Valladolid, whereas in *El pequeño heredero,* Gustavo Martín Garzo offered a compelling story about growing up in rural Castile. The two best-sellers of the year explored deep psychological transformations and engaged weighty moral themes. In Rosa Montero's *La hija del caníbal,* the protagonist's search for her kidnapped husband draws her into uncharted territories of her identity—as a daughter, woman, wife, and citizen of an imperfect world. Antonio Muñoz Molina's tenacious inspector in *Plenilunio,* a taut, grimly realistic analysis of random psychopathic violence, learns that evil wears a disconcertingly ordinary face.

In an introspective novella, *La mirada del alma,* and in the collected vignettes of *Días del desván,* Luis Mateo Díez captured the subtle interplay of remembered images, sensations, and impressions that clarify life's most intimate meanings. Other exceptional fictions included *Placer licuante,* Luis Goytisolo's disturbing novel of triangulated desire and revenge; *No existe tal lugar,* a meditation on utopia by Miguel Sánchez-Ostiz; and Carlos Cañeque's bizarre metanarrative, *Quién,* the Nadal Prize winner. Steeped in the atmosphere of 17th-century Madrid, *El capitán Alatriste* (1996) and *Limpieza de sangre,* by master yarn spinner Arturo Pérez-Reverte, were the first two of six promised volumes devoted to the adventures of the central character, Don Diego Alatriste y Tenorio, in the treacherous court of Philip IV.

In December the Cuban novelist Guillermo Cabrera Infante received the Cervantes Prize, the highest award in Hispanic letters.

(ROGER L. UTT)

Latin America. Life under military rule, particularly the period from the mid-1960s to the mid-1980s, continued to dominate the writing of Latin-American authors. A major issue relating to the history of military tyranny was the treatment of women prisoners, and a guilty secret of this history was the collaboration between women and their male torturers that provided information about other suspects. Liliana Heker's novel, *El fin de la historia,* dealt with this issue through the parallel stories of two women who were childhood friends; an added dimension was provided by the fact that one was a Jew.

Ana María Shua was known for the dry wit with which she wrote about the tensions of daily life in Argentina, often with specific reference to the Jewish community. Her wit was a vehicle for incisive representations of the very real sense of horror over the injustices and conflicts those tensions may create. *La muerte como efecto secundario* was set somewhat in the future and described the despair of attempting to survive in a society undergoing late capitalist collapse. In *El escriba* (1996), a fictitious account of the great Argentine writer Roberto Arlt, Pedro G. Orgambide captured the tumultuous texture of life in Buenos Aires on the eve of the country's first military dictatorship.

Argentine writers also explored a wide range of social issues. Marco Denevi delved into sexual ambiguity in *Nuestra señora de la noche.* Using minimalist prose and other postmodern conventions, Martín Rejtman's series of short stories in *Velcro y yo* (1996) captured the tone of present-day consumer society in Buenos Aires. In *El llamado de la especie,* Sergio Chejfec added to his numerous treatments of Jewish collective memory with a story about lifetime friendship among a group of women. César Aira, perhaps the most accomplished Argentine representative of postmodernist antiliterature, returned to the theme of neoliberalism in modern-day Argentina in *La abeja* (1996).

Elsewhere in Latin America, writers pursued political and social themes with comparable depth and acuity. In Nicaragua Milagros Palma redressed the neglect of women's issues in Nicaraguan literature with her allegorical novel *El pacto* (1996). The book chronicled the diabolical aspects of tyrannical governments in Latin America and the social and historical contradictions that beleaguered political revolutions. Honduran writer Leonel Alvarado presented a series of ingenious rewritings of major works of Latin-American fiction in *Diario del odio.*

A study of a contemporary Latin-American city under the influence of neoliberalist economic policies, Alberto Fuguet's *Tinta roja* (1996) covered the life of a crime reporter who discovered a series of sordid stories in modern Santiago, Chile.

Zoé Valdés's *Te di la vida entera,* considered by many to be one of the most important works to be published by a contemporary Cuban woman writer, presented an ironic allegory of 20th-century Cuban social life as seen through the eyes of a humble provincial woman. In a complex narrative of personal and sociocultural identity, Jesús Díaz, one of Cuba's best-known novelists, portrayed the search for lost Cubans of the post-1959 diaspora in *La piel y la máscara* (1996).

Mexican popular culture continued to earn accolades as one of the most creative in the world. Jordi Soler's *La cantante descalza y otros casos oscursos del rock,* a collection of stories based on popular metropolitan motifs, explored the world of rock music. In *Mal de amores* (1996), best-selling Mexican novelist Angeles Mastretta drew parallels between the relationship of a married couple and Mexican sociocultural history. In a much more experimental novel entitled *Apariciones* (1996), feminist critic Margo Glantz delivered a complex meditation on love and romance that explored female subordination to both divine and secular definitions of love. Using the figure of Iphigenia as the springboard for a meditation on violence and death, Aline Pettersson also explored gender issues in *La noche de las hormigas.*

Puerto Rican writer Edgardo Rodríguez Juliá continued to probe American influences on the island's Hispanic culture. In *Peloteros* he examined the growing charisma of American baseball after World War II, when Puerto Rico increased its social and political involvement with the United States.

A new Spanish-language edition of Rosario Ferré's *The House on the Lagoon* answered critics who charged that the feminist writer deserted her native language by first publishing the 1995 book in English. *La casa de la laguna* presented the story of a woman struggling against enormous violent odds to write her own version of the history of a family whose vicissitudes and treacheries epitomized the sociopolitical history of Puerto Rico.

JERRY BAUER

Nélida Piñon

Although Mario Vargas Llosa's strident repudiations of the Latin-American left had cost him much of his former prestige, he continued to exert considerable influence over Peruvian culture. Rendered with a fine degree of demystifying and ironic humour, *Los cuadernos de don Rigoberto* told the story of a man devoted to sexual hedonism. Mario Benedetti, the dean of Uruguayan letters, chose the format of an autobiographical novel in *Andamios* (1996) to explore the themes of exile and return that typified the work of many fellow authors writing in Latin America's young democracies.

(DAVID WILLIAM FOSTER)

PORTUGUESE

Portugal. The year 1997 was a good one for Portuguese authors and publishers. At the Frankfurt (Ger.) Book Fair, where Portugal was the theme, more titles for translation were sold than ever before, which indicated a steadily growing interest in the country and its literature. Another major coup was the awarding of Mobil's Pegasus Prize for Literature—given annually to the best foreign work of fiction—to Mário de Carvalho, the first Portuguese recipient of the prize, for his novel *A God Strolling in the Cool of the Evening* (1997). The book was first published in Portuguese, as *Um deus passeando pela brisa da tarde,* in 1994. The winner of the 1997 Prize of the International Association of Literary Critics (Portuguese Section) was Augusto Abelaira for his novel *Outrora Agora.* Abelaira probed, with great subtlety, the past and present conflicts arising from the generation gap. The novel, based on a triangular relationship, explored the identities of two female characters belonging to two different generations and exposed some male myths with wit and understanding.

Totally different was a book by José Cardoso Pires. *De Profundis, Valsa Lenta* was a brilliant and pungent account of the stroke from which he recovered admirably. In this narrative Pires became the character of his own fiction. The first symptoms of alienation from the environment, the loss of his own personality, and a sense of the inner movement into the other side of Alice's looking glass were seized with implacable lucidity and courage, which made this work a unique testimony to the resilience of human nature.

An outstanding book of poetry, *O Monhé das Cobras,* was published by Rui Knopfli. His book of memory and memoirs presents fragmentary images of an African childhood, of a lost birthplace that is never to be recovered in his nostalgic peregrination throughout Europe. Loose images—a name, a place, a statue—are deftly woven around the magic of the snake charmer of his youth, gaining the poetic cohesion and the unity of a great work of art.

(L.S. REBELO)

Brazil. The year 1997 was dominated by the deaths of major literary and cultural figures whose works had commented upon and profoundly influenced the direction of Brazilian culture over the past 40 years. Among them was novelist and playwright Antônio Callado, author of *Quarup* (1967), *Reflexos do baile* (1976), *Sempreviva* (1981), and other distinguished works—all of which confronted the social and political injustices in Brazil. Callado had been an outspoken defender of human rights and was imprisoned by the military regime that ruled Brazil from 1964 to 1985. Anthropologist, politician, and novelist Darcy Ribeiro, who had fled into exile when the military took control, used Brazilian Indians' myths to eloquently question their destiny in modern Brazil, notably in the fictional work *Maira* (1976). Political novelist and dramatist Paulo Francis was Brazil's premier international newsman, and Carybé was known for his drawings, which depicted Brazilian street life within an Afro-Brazilian context; he also illustrated novels by Jorge Amado and Gabriel García Márquez, among others. Sociologist Herberto (Betinho) de Souza and illustrious educator Paulo Freire also died. (*See* OBITUARIES.)

Márcio Souza's new novel, *Lealdade,* dealt with his native state of Amazonas during the 19th century. Antônio Olinto's *Alcácer Quibir,* a historical novel about Portugal's fall to Spanish domination in 1580, returned to his favourite themes—the relationship of Portugal, Africa, and Brazil. Sérgio Sant'Anna, Autran Dourado, and Antônio Torres all published new fictional works. Moacyr Scliar's latest collection of short stories was *O amante de Madonna & outras histórias.* A young writer, Antônio Fernando Borges, was awarded the Nestlé Short Fiction Prize for his collection *Que fim levou Brodie?,* which echoed themes characteristic of the works of Argentine writer Jorge Luis Borges. Suzana Vargas published a new volume of poetry, *Caderno de outono e outros poemas. Para sempre,* a new play by Maria Adelaide Amaral, dealt with the intricacies of personal relationships.

In late 1996 Valéria Lamego's *A farpa na lira* offered a new perspective of the poet Cecília Meireles, and *Cecília e Mário,* with an introduction by Alfredo Bosi, was a collection of the correspondence between Meireles and Mário de Andrade. Josué Montello published a new study of Machado de Assis, and, finally, novelist Nélida Piñon was elected president of the Brazilian Academy of Letters, the first woman to hold the position in the academy's 100-year history.

(IRWIN STERN)

RUSSIAN

As had been the case for many years, in 1997 the classics of the "Thaw" generation of the 1950s and 1960s continued to play a significant role in Russian literature. Collected works from Andrey Bitov and Bella Akhmadulina were published to coincide with their 60th birthdays; the death of the popular poet, novelist, and singer of the 1960s Bulat Okudzhava was treated as a national loss. The stream of books and articles on the late Nobel Prize winner Joseph Brodsky continued, and new works appeared from such well-known figures as Vasily Aksyonov, Aleksandr Solzhenitsyn, and Lyudmila Petrushevskaya.

At the same time, the reputation of authors of the succeeding generation, those associated with Russian postmodernism, seemed largely secure. High-quality editions appeared of selected works from two of the leading Moscow Conceptualists, Lev Rubinshteyn and Dmitry Prigov. Also, Viktor Yerofeyev's 50th birthday was marked with the release of his selected works in three volumes, including his new and controversial novel, *Strashnyi sud* ("The Last Judgment").

The attention of both readers and critics was largely centred on other authors, however. In this regard the list of nominees for the 1997 Russian Booker Prize was revealing: Anatoly Azolsky's *Kletka* ("The Cage")—the eventual winner of the prize, worth $12,500; Dmitry Lipskerov's *Sorok let Chanchzhoye* ("Forty Years of Chanchzhoye"); Lyudmila Ulitskaya's *Medya i y dety* ("Medea and her Children") and Anton Utkin's *Khorovod* ("Round Dance"). Surprising perhaps, but the list was nevertheless consistent; there was an absence of playful, postmodernist works and emphasis on intensely emotional and psychological fiction.

Among the prose works receiving substantial critical attention in 1997 were "mythological" novels (Yury Buyda's *Boris i Gleb* ["Boris and Gleb"]), confessional and nonfiction works (Sergey Faybisovich's *Dydya Adik* ["Uncle Adik"] and Aleksandr Melikhov's *Roman s prostatitom* ["Novel with Prostatitis"]), thoroughly traditional realistic novels (O. Pavlov's *Delo Matyushina* ["The Matyushin Affair"]), and even a parody on the fantasy genre (M. Uspensky's *Tam, gde nas net* ["There, Where We Are Not"]).

While some contemporary Russian authors tried to revive the "grand style," others sought artistic discoveries on the level of the page, paragraph, even sentence. For example, Vladimir Gubin published an extremely hermetic but charming and finely wrought novella, entitled *Illarion i karlik* ("Hilarion and the Dwarf"), on which he had worked for several decades. In many ways similar to Gubin, Oleg Yuryev, in his volume of short stories *Frankfurtsky byk* ("The Ox of Frankfurt"), successfully combined a densely metaphysical style with an anti-utopian and grotesque depiction of contemporary Europe. This theme of the "Russian in Europe" was also quite important to Nina Sadur, who published a brief but lively novel, *Nemets* ("The German"). On the other hand, Zinovy Zinik, in *Ostorozhno. Dveri zakryvayutsya* ("Attention. The Subway Doors Are Closing"), explored the experience of an émigré returning to a "different country" after many years' absence.

Several Russian authors, sensing an irrevocable break with the not-so-distant past, tried to sum up this recent chapter in Russian history. Boris Khazanov, a former dissident, depicted the end stages of Soviet society in his novel *Posle nas potop* ("After Us, the Deluge"), and Grigory Kanovich concluded his multivolume treatment of Lithuanian Jewry with his bitter novel *Park zabytikh yevreyev* ("The Park of Forgotten Jews"). Even the literary and philological life of the 1970s and '80s became the subject of belated treatment (Anatoly Nayman's *B.B. i drugiye* ["B.B. and Others"]).

In poetry Yelena Shvarts remained the central figure; her style, combining high lyricism, mysticism, and the grotesque, exerted a noticeable influence on her younger contemporaries. Her latest book of poetry, *Zapadno-vostochny veter* ("The West-East Wind"), was permeated with a spirit of divine madness, the quest for the "fifth cardinal point of the Earth." Poets whose works appeared either in literary journals or in separate books included several impressive debuts (Dmitry Vodennikov from Moscow, Dmitry Kachurov from Murmansk, and Viktor Yefimov from St. Petersburg). Generally speaking, the work of the young generation of poets was characterized by a visionary, fantastic, and mythological bent (in sharp contrast with the total irony and linguistic play dominant only a few years earlier).

In the shakedown among the "thick" journals from the Soviet period, the survivors became clear: *Znamya* ("The Banner") and *Oktyabr* ("October") in Moscow, *Zvezda* ("The Star") in St. Petersburg, and *Volga* in Saratov. Most of the magazines and publishing houses that appeared after perestroika had either ceased to exist or found a particular niche in the nation's literary life, as, for example, *Mitin' zhurnal* ("Mitya's Magazine") and *Postkriptum* ("Postscript") in St. Petersburg and *Lepta* ("The Mite"), *Kommentarii* ("Commentaries"), and *Novy Vavilon* ("New Babylon") in Moscow. Among the new periodicals to appear in 1997, the most significant was the Moscow magazine *Pushkin*. (VALERY SHUBINSKY)

EASTERN EUROPEAN

During 1997 Polish literary circles showed a renewed interest in the poetry of Wisława Szymborska, who had won the Nobel Prize for Literature in 1996. Once again, of all the genres, poetry proved to be the most vital one in Poland. In her volume *Adresat nieznany: Notatnik poetycki 1993–1996* ("Unknown Addressee: A Poetic Notebook 1993–1996"), Agata Tuszyńska exhibited a precision and lyricism that was devoid of sentimentality. Artur Szlosarek, whose earlier poetry was marked by influences of poets Rainer Rilke and Paul Celan, developed a voice of his own in *Popiół i miód* ("Ash and Honey"), which was free of the exaltation and egotism that characterized his earlier work. Paweł Marcinkiewicz received the 1997 Award of the Foundation for Culture for his volume of verse *Świat dla opornych* ("The World for Insubordinates"); Marcinkiewicz, one of the most interesting poets of the younger generation, experimented with poetic conventions in his latest effort. With the publication of Nobel laureate Czesław Miłosz's collections of essays *Piesek przydrożny* ("A Little Side-Road Dog") and *Zycie na wyspach* ("Life on Islands"), he remained visible mainly as a critic of mass culture and the superficial values so prevalent in the late 20th century. Finally, a long-overdue biographical work appeared that was dedicated to the late poet Miron Białoszewski. Carefully edited by Hanna Kirchner, *Miron: Wspomnienia o poecie* ("Miron: Memories of the Poet") offered a wide assortment of personal recollections by friends and critics and thereby gave readers a new dimension to his life. Although residing in Italy, Gustaw Herling-Grudziński marked his presence with the appearance of *Gorący oddech pustyni* ("Heated Breath of a Desert"), a collection of short stories written in 1993–95 and representative of the writer's metaphysical meditations.

Serbian literature, which had been dominated for 50 years by traditional historical fiction, found new expression with postmodern "self-reflective" metafiction; most illustrative of this trend was David Albahari's 1996 novel *Mamac* ("Lure"), which won the prestigious 1997 NIN Award. In the book, Albahari, who had lived in Canada since 1994, sought shelter in the Serbo-Croatian language while exploring the process of dying; in the end, language became the only palpable reality. Another postmodern novel, published in 1997 by Svetislav Basara with the English title *Looney Tunes,* became a best-seller; it offered an absurdist picture of a political establishment. A shorter work not written in the realistic mode was Basara's "Uncle Vanja," considered by *NIN* the best short story of 1997. Historical fiction, the traditional centre of Serbian literature, was best represented by Milica Mićić-Dimovska's *Poslednji zanosi MSS* ("The Final Raptures of MSS"); the novel evokes the life and dynamic personality of Milica Stojadinović Srpkinja, the 19th-century nationalist and woman activist. In the field of poetry, much praise was given to Miroslav Maksimović, an award-winning representative of middle-aged poets. His recent collection of verse, *Nebo* ("The Sky"), deals with the political reality of urban life in a cool, ironic voice. Matija Bećković, a prominent figure in Serbian literary circles and known for his anticommunist and royalist proclivities, published a collection of poems, *Ćeraćemo se još* ("We Will See Each Other in Court Again"); his poems were recited in the streets of Belgrade during the November 1996–February 1997 pro-democracy demonstrations.

Like most other Eastern European literature, the Czech literary market was dominated by translations, mostly from English. Besides the death of internationally known writer Bohumil Hrabal (*see* OBITUARIES), the Czech literary year was distinguished by new editions and reeditions of other Czech masters, such as Milan Kundera's novel *Valčík na rozloučenou* ("The Farewell Party"), which included a forward by the author. The works of Jaroslav Seifert, the first Czech to win a Nobel Prize (1984), were also reedited, notably one of his most memorable collections of verse, *Maminka* ("Dear Mom"). The appearance of Ivan Slavík's juvenile poetry, *Snímání s kříže* ("Descent from the Cross"), was hailed by critics and showed the author's fascination with the poetry of Arthur Rimbaud and Charles Baudelaire. Eda Kriseová's long historical novel *Kočiči životy* ("Cats' Lives") was cited for its lyricism and transported readers from the beginning of the 20th century to the present day in multiethnic Volhynia. Václav Havel, best known for his plays, published *'96,* a volume of his recent speeches and articles.

In Romania the Writers' Union awarded the National Prize to Ştefan Bănulescu, renowned for his prose, and poet Marta Petreu was awarded a prize for her latest volume, *Cartea mâniei* ("The Book of Anger"), and Andrei Pleşu was recognized for his collection of essays *Chipuri şi măsti ale tranziţiei* ("Faces and Masks of the Transition"). Newly elected members to the Romanian Academy were literary critic Nicolae Manolescu, critic and historian Mircea Zaciu, and novelists Nicolae Breban and Dumitru Radu Popescu.

(BOŻENA SHALLCROSS)

JEWISH

Hebrew. The premier event in Hebrew fiction in 1997 was the publication of A.B. Yehoshua's novel *Masa el tom haelef* ("Voyage to the End of the Millennium"), which examined societal and cultural issues in contemporary Israel by means of a plot that takes place near the end of the first millennium. Other works by veteran writers included Aharon Appelfeld's *Mihkre hakerah* ("The Ice Mine"), his first attempt to describe the horrors of a German labour camp, and collections of short stories—Yitzhak Orpaz's *Laila beSanta Paulina* ("A Night in Santa Paulina") and Dalia Rabikovitz's *Kvutzat hakaduregel shel Winnie Mandela* ("Winnie Mandela's Football Team"). The most interesting novels published by the younger generation were Gidi Nevo's *Ad kan* ("So Far"; 1996), an intriguing dialogue with Ya'akov Shabtai's *Past Continuous,* and Tsruya Shalev's *Hayei ahava* ("Love Life"). Other important books were Nurit Zarchi's *Mekhonit kemo orchidea* ("A Car like an Orchid"), Leah Aini's *Hardufim* ("Oleanders"), Rachel Gil's *Isha yoshevet* ("A Woman Sitting"), and Eyal Megged's *Sodot Mongolia* ("Secrets of Mongolia"). Hanna Bat Shahar (the pseudonym of a female writer who used a pen name because of her Orthodox family) published her fourth book, *Sham sirot hadayig* ("Look, the Fishing Boats"). Other books that showed traces of the authors' religious background were Rina Brandle's *K. lo shel Kafka* ("K. Not Kafka's") and Judith Rotem's *Kri'a* ("Mourning"; 1996).

The most significant books of poetry were the second volume of the collected poems of Avot Yeshurun and the first volume (the long poems) of the collected poems of Abba Kovner (1996). Other notable books of poetry were Aharon Shabtai's *Behodesh May hanifla* ("During the Wonderful Month of May"), Mordechai Geldman's *Sefer Sh'al* ("Book of Ask"), Yigal Ben Arieh's *Kav parashat hazman* ("Time Dividing Line"), and Zvia Ben-Yosseph Ginor's *Isha bor* ("Womanswell"; 1996). Such works as Asher Reich's *Musikat horef* ("Winter Music"; 1996) and Itamar Yaoz-Kest's *Dlatot tsrifim od niftahot bi* ("Doors of Bunks Are Still Opened in Me") examined the Holocaust. First books of poetry were offered by Daliah Fallah, *Dodi hashofet hamehozi Dorban* ("My Uncle the Circuit Judge Dorban") and Shimon Adaf, *Hamonologue shel Icarus* ("Icarus's Monologue").

Works of literary scholarship included Dan Laor's *Hayei Agnon* ("The Life of S.Y. Agnon") and Dan Miron's *Hahim bea'po shel hanetzah* ("Posterity Hooked: The Travail and Achievement of U.N. Gnessin"). Hamutal Bar Yosef studied the decadent trends in the writings of Hayyim Bialik, Micah Berdychevski, and Joseph Brenner, and Nitza Ben-Dov wrote about erotic frustrations in Agnon's fiction. Yigal Schwartz examined Appelfeld's world view (1996), and Uzi Shavit discussed enlightenment (Haskala), poetry, and modernism (1996).

(AVRAHAM BALABAN)

Yiddish. Most of the Yiddish writings in 1997 appeared in the accessible form of short stories and sketches. Some, like Avraham Karpinovitsh's exciting tapestry *Geven, geven amol Vilne* ("There Was Once Upon a Time Vilna"), brought a wealth of memory to a retrospective—a reconstruction of the Jerusalem of the North. Yoysef Burg's companion volumes *Tsvey veltn* ("Two Worlds") and *Tseviklte stezshkes* ("Unfolded Paths") propelled characters dramatically through the desperate and unreal circumstances of the Holocaust era. Shire Gorshman's narratives in *On a gal* ("Without Bitterness") traversed a time frame that extended from the medieval era of Rashi to the traumatic experiences of Jews in the Soviet Union. Boris Sandler's intriguing stories in *Toyern* ("Towers") were a mixture—some were allegorical and others realistic—and Moyshe Shkliar's *Moln di amoln* ("Portraying the Past") provided prosaic and poetic reminiscences of school days in Warsaw. Eli Shekhtman produced an ambitious autobiographical volume, *Tristia* (1996), or "Gloom" in Latin, an evocative chronicle of a physical and emotional journey from a childhood in the Soviet Union to the Auschwitz gas chambers and crematoriums in Poland.

Other notable works included Mikhal Feldzenbaum's *Der nakht-malekh* ("The Night Angel"), a modernist drama in an absurdist key, and Heshl Klepfish's *Der kval far doyres* ("The Source for Generations"), essays that covered the panorama of Jewish life in Eastern Europe. Shloyme Vorzoger completed a series of superbly researched and interrelated essays, *Mit zikh un mit andere* ("With Myself and with Others"), capturing in painstaking detail the achievement of Israeli Yiddish writers.

Collections of poetry included Moyshe Bernshteyn's *A toyb in fentster* ("A Dove in the Window"), in which he returned to the theme of a world destroyed. An illustrated album of 80 poems by Mordkhe Gebirtig, *Mayn fayfele* ("My Whistle"), brought to light the renowned Galician folksinger's work, which had spent 40 years in obscurity in Israeli and American archives. *Vu' mit an alef* ("'Where' Spelled with an Aleph") by Boris Karlov (the pen name of Dov Ber Kerler) was his first book of lyrical sonnets and ballads, ranging from the earnest and polemical to the whimsical and satirical. Simkhe Simkhovitsh gathered 50 years of poetic creativity in the anthology *Funken in zshar* ("Sparks in Embers").

Three scholarly volumes also appeared: Chaim M. Weiser's *Frumspeak: The First Dictionary of Yeshivish,* Yitskhak Niborski and Shimen Noyberg's *Verterbukh fun loshn-koydesh-shtamike verter* ("Dictionary of Words Stemming from Hebrew-Aramaic"), and Kazuo Ueda's *Shmuesn Yapanish-English-Yiddish* ("Chats in Japanese-English-and-Yiddish").

In July Yiddish literary authority Chone Shmeruk died in Warsaw.

(THOMAS E. BIRD)

TURKISH

No masterpieces, many fascinating works, and much debate (about human rights and freedom of speech) marked the Turkish literary scene in 1997. Its major event was Frankfurt Book Fair's decision to honour Yashar Kemal, who also won the German Publishers Association's Peace Prize. Turkey's Nobel hopeful published a book of dirges he had collected in southern Anatolia and in late November began to serialize *Fırat suyu kan akıyor baksana* ("Look, the Euphrates Is Flowing Bloody"), the first part of a planned trilogy, in the daily *Milliyet.*

Prominent woman novelist Adalet Ağaoğlu won the $40,000 Aydın Doğan Prize, and Yıldırım Keskin received the 25th annual Orhan Kemal Award. Habib Bektaş, a novelist living in Germany, was awarded the 70th Anniversary Prize of İnkılâp Kitabevi, a major publishing house.

Ahmet Altan's *Tehlikeli masallar* ("Dangerous Tales"), the Turkish translation of

Paulo Coelho's *The Alchemist,* and Ayse Kulin's semifictionalized biography of Aylin Radomişli, a Turkish-American woman psychiatrist in New York and a U.S. Army lieutenant colonel, who died mysteriously, dominated the best-seller lists.

The 51st annual Yunus Nadi Prizes were awarded to Erendiz Atasü for her short stories and Burhan Günel for his latest novel. Ayla Kutlu and Hasan Öztürk shared the screenplay prize; Enver Ercan and Derya Çolpan, the award for poetry. Ercan was also the recipient of the Cemal Süreya poetry prize. The Necatigil Poetry Prize went to Haydar Ergülen. Cahit Külebi, one of Turkey's major poets, passed away at age 80, a few months after he received the Presidential Arts Award.

In the U.S., Kemal Silay edited *An Anthology of Turkish Literature,* featuring selections from the past 1,000 years. *The New Life,* Güneli Gün's translation of Orhan Pamuk's 1994 best-seller, was published in the U.S. to favourable reviews. Pamuk was also featured in a cover story in *The New York Times Magazine*.

(TALAT S. HALMAN)

PERSIAN

In Iran the literary community experienced an escalation in harassment by the government during the first six months of the year. Although the election of a former culture minister to the presidency raised hopes for some relaxation in censorship, official measures to ease it were sporadic. Meanwhile, essayist Faraj Sarkuhi, Iran's most famous jailed dissident, was sentenced to one year in prison. War and civil strife in Afghanistan and Tajikistan left little room for literary activity there.

Although the number of novels, plays, and collections of poetry and short stories published in Iran increased substantially, no noteworthy work appeared in print. *Dar dam-e shah* ("In the Trap of the Shah"), ostensibly the memoirs of a former actress and onetime courtesan of Mohammad Reza Shah Pahlavi, was the most widely read new title. In Sweden veteran novelist Reza Baraheni published his latest novel, *Azadeh khanom va nevisandeh-ash* ("Ms. Azadeh and Her Writer"), an ambitious work in the Postmodern vein. In the United States Shokuh Mirzadegi's *Guldin ark* ("Golden Ark") and Reza Ghasemi's *Hamnava'i-ye shabaneh-ye orkestr-e chubha* ("The Nocturnal Chorus of the Wooden Orchestra") led the list of important additions to expatriate Persian literature.

Perhaps the most significant literary trip of the year was Modernist poet Feraydun Moshiri's visit to the U.S. He read his poems, once considered mediocre at best, to enthusiastic crowds of expatriates in a score of American cities. His selected poems, *Yek aseman parandeh* ("A Skyful of Birds"), thus became the best-selling title of the year in Persian poetry.

The year marked the passing of several notable writers, including Iranian novelist and short-story writer Bozorg Alavi; novelist Taqi Modarressi; Mohammad-Ali Jamalzadeh, who was considered the founder of modern Persian fiction (*see* OBITUARIES); and Tajik writer Satem Ologhzadeh, perhaps the most important fiction writer of Soviet Tajikistan.

(AHMAD KARIMI-HAKKAK)

CHINESE

Chinese literary works received two major awards in 1997. The first, the Third National Book Award, was shared by Tang Haoming and Zhu Shucheng's biographical novel *Kuangdai yicai—Yang Du* ("Outstanding Talent—Yang Du") and Zhou Meisen's *Renjian zhengdao* ("The Way of Living in the World"), published at the end of 1996. *Kuangdai yicai* portrayed Yang Du, a controversial reformer of early republican China, as a complex historical figure, illustrating his experimentation with a broad range of philosophies and his eventual conversion to Buddhism near the end of his life.

The second major award was the Mao Dun Literature Award, given once every three years. Sharing the award were Wang Huo's *Zhanzheng yu ren* ("War and People"), a multivolume portrait of the war against Japan (1937–45) featuring many grand scenes; Cheng Zhongshi's *Bailu yuan* ("White Deer Plain"), which aroused considerable controversy with its weighty implications; and Liu Sifen's *Baimen liu* ("Willow at Baimen"), which depicted famous intellectuals in Chinese history.

The number of fictional works published in 1997 was about the same as in 1996—more than 800. While most lacked depth in spirit or imagination and taste, some were better. *Wo shi taiyang* ("I Am the Sun") by Deng Yiguang portrayed a soldier's inspiring but somehow tragic life with none of the old stereotypical expressions. *Qianjuan yu juejue* ("Close Affection and Breaking Up") by Zhao Changfa was a complicated and fascinating tale of love and hate in a landlord's family and of the relationship between farmers and the land. *Bai lazhu* ("White Candle") by Wang Zhaojun concerned the difficult times of the early 1960s but was unlike other such works in its meek and touching nature. Ge Fei's *Qingshui huanxiang* ("Clear Water Illusions") was a story with a classical flair; it told of a landlord's concubine who, while bathing in a pond, recalls the decline of members of the landlord's family. *Xianggang de zaochen* ("Hong Kong Morning") by Hong Kong writer Liu Wenyong was an autobiographical novel written in strong and colourful language and depicted all types of people in Hong Kong as well as the author's own struggle with himself.

Also attracting interest was the work of Mosuo writer Lamu Gatusa, a three-time winner of China's Minority People Literature Award. Gatusa, who spent two months recording a shaman's recitation of the entire oral history of the Mosuo people in Yunnan province, finished translating the recitation into Chinese in 1997. The work was to be published by the Yunnan Academy of Social Sciences.

Chinese poetry remained at a critical juncture as poets pursued such innovative and bizarre techniques that even critics wondered how the poems should be read. In contrast, Taiwanese poet Yu Guangzhong's touching poems on his travels to the mainland were rich in imagination and flavour.

(QIAN ZHONGWEN)

JAPANESE

Two best-sellers—a novel and a nonfiction work—were the standouts in Japanese literature during 1997. The curious pair comprised Jun'ichi Watanabe's *Shitsuraku-en* ("Paradise Lost") and Haruki Murakami's *Āndāguraundo* ("Underground").

Although there was little similarity between Watanabe's highly erotic story of extramarital love, which ends in double suicides, and John Milton's biblical epic of the same title, the allusive title seemed to add a mysterious flavour to the novel, especially for nonreligious Japanese. A newspaper serialization of the work proved remarkably popular, and the two-volume hardcover edition sold more than one million copies. The novel was then adapted for a motion picture and serialized on television.

Murakami's nonfictional *Underground* was a collection of more than 60 interviews of the victims of the underground disaster on March 20, 1995, in which members of the religious cult Aum Shinrikyo released the deadly nerve gas sarin in a crowded Tokyo subway. Although there had been numerous sensational reports of the event in the mass media, Murakami was the first to use a subdued tone in order to meticulously detail the touching yet vivid account of the victims' panic, confusion, and suffering, which for some lasted long after their initial hospitalization.

Nobuo Kojima's *Uruwashiki hibi* ("Beautiful Days") was another example of a literary triumph marked by quiet appeal. This novel detailed the domestic predicament of an elderly couple whose divorced, middle-aged son turns into an incorrigible alcoholic and becomes hospitalized. Although obviously autobiographical and at times rather monotonous, the story, however, was not gloomy. The title befitted the work, and the pervasive tone was consoling and even humorous—an amazing tour de force on the part of Kojima.

Two remarkable collections of short stories appeared, and, although their settings and subjects were quite different, both were refreshingly vivid and moving. Taku Miki's *Roji* ("Alley"), winner of the Tanizaki Jun'ichirō Prize, evoked the monotony of life in Kamakura, a historic city not far from Tokyo. Each story recounts, vividly and effectively, the petty drama of various types of eccentrics. Aiko Kitahara's *Edo fūkyōden* ("Biographies of Edo Eccentrics"), winner of the Women Writers' Prize, showcased the author's narrative skill and her remarkable ability to portray an assortment of amusing, artistic, and scholarly eccentrics during the feudalistic Edo period.

Takanori Irie's *Taiheiyō bunmei no kōbō* ("The Rise and Fall of the Pacific Civilization") was a brilliant book about cultural history and criticism, both readable and broad in historical perspective. The 1997 Sakutaro Hagiwara Prize in Poetry was awarded to Kōsuke Shibusawa for *Yukueshirezu shō* ("Missing Forever"), a personal and philosophical reflection.

Yu Miri (*see* BIOGRAPHIES) won Japan's top award for young writers, the Akutagawa Prize, for her novel *Kazoku shinema* ("Family Cinema"). A second-generation Korean living in Japan, Yu attracted wide praise for her story about a broken family that reunites to film a semifictional documentary about themselves, but her book also stirred controversy. Japan's conservative press accused Yu of portraying the Japanese as fools, and right-wing terrorists threatened to bomb her Tokyo book signing.

(SHOICHI SAEKI)

Mathematics and Physical Sciences

MATHEMATICS

A major topic occupying mathematicians in 1997 was the nature of randomness. Popular notions often differ from mathematical concepts; reconciling the two in the case of randomness is important because of the use of randomization in many aspects of life, from gambling lotteries to the selection of subjects for scientific experiments.

Although the result of a coin toss, *i.e.,* heads or tails, is determined by physical laws, it can be regarded as random because it is not predictable, provided that the coin rotates many times. Similarly, numbers from a computer random-number generator are accepted as random, even though such numbers are usually produced by a purely mechanistic process of computer arithmetic.

Since the two sides of a coin are quite similar, people agree that heads and tails are equally likely to turn up. Other methods of randomization, however, such as spinning the coin on a tabletop or standing it on edge and striking the table, may favour one outcome over the other if the coin is not absolutely symmetrical. One's perception of the probability of a random event may be based on physical principles such as symmetry (*e.g.,* the six sides of a die are equally likely to come up), but it also may have a less-tangible basis, such as long experience (one rarely wins a big lottery) or subjective belief (some people are lucky).

Statisticians regard a sequence of outcomes as random if each outcome is independent of the previous ones—that is, if its probability is not affected by previous outcomes. Most people agree that tosses of a coin are independent; the coin has no "memory" of previous tosses or cosmic duty to even out heads and tails in the long run. The belief that after a long sequence of heads, tails is more likely on the next toss is known as the "gambler's fallacy."

For heads (H) and tails (T) being equally likely, the three sequences HHHHHHHH, HTHTHTHT, and HTHHTHTT are all random, and the first two are as likely to occur as the third. If one of the first two occurs, however, the result does not appear random. Many people believe that a random sequence should have no "obvious" patterns; that is, later elements of the sequence should not be predictable from early ones. In the 1960s a team of mathematicians suggested measuring randomness by the length of the computer program needed to reproduce the sequence. For a sequence in which tails always follows heads, the program instructions are simple—just write HT repeatedly. A sequence with no discernible pattern requires a longer program, which enumerates each outcome of the sequence. Requiring a long program is equivalent to having the sequence pass certain statistical tests for randomness.

According to this measure, however, the first million decimal digits of pi are not random, since very short computer programs exist that can reproduce them. That conclusion contradicts mathematicians' sense that the digits of pi have no discernible pattern. Nevertheless, the spirit of the approach does correspond to human intuition. Research published in 1997 by Ruma Falk of the Hebrew University of Jerusalem and Clifford Konold of the University of Massachusetts at Amherst concluded that people assess the randomness of a sequence by how hard it is to memorize or copy.

In 1997 freelance mathematician Steve Pincus of Guilford, Conn., Burton Singer of Princeton University, and Rudolf E. Kalman of the Swiss Federal Institute of Technology, Zürich, proposed assessing randomness of a sequence in terms of its "approximate entropy," or disorder. To be random in this sense, a sequence of coin tosses must be as uniform as possible in its distribution of heads and tails, of pairs, of triples, and so forth. In other words, it must contain (as far as possible given its length) equal numbers of heads and tails, equal numbers of each of the possible adjacent pairs (HH, HT, TH, and TT), equal numbers of each of the eight kinds of adjacent triples, and so forth. This must hold for all "short" sequences of adjacent outcomes within the original sequence—ones that are significantly shorter than the original sequence (in technical terms, for all sequences of length less than $\log_2 \log_2 n + 1$, in which n is the length of the original sequence and logarithms are taken to base 2).

When this definition is applied to the 32 possible sequences of H and T having a length of five, the only random ones among them are HHTTH, HTTHH, TTHHT, and THHTT. In this case the short sequences under scrutiny have a length less than $\log_2 \log_2 5 + 1$, or about 2.2. Thus, a random sequence with a length of five must have, as far as possible, equal numbers of heads and tails—hence, two of one and three of the other—and equal numbers of each pair—here, exactly one of each among the four successive adjacent pairs. Furthermore, when this definition is applied to the decimal digits of pi, they do form a random sequence. In the case of a nonrandom sequence, the approximate entropy measures how much the sequence deviates from the "ideal."

Other investigators have used the concept of approximate entropy to investigate the possibility that symptoms anecdotally ascribed to "male menopause" may be sufficiently nonrandom to indicate the existence of such a condition and to assess how randomly the prices of financial stocks fluctuate.

(PAUL J. CAMPBELL)

This article updates the *Macropædia* articles PROBABILITY THEORY; STATISTICS.

CHEMISTRY

Chemical Nomenclature. Decades of controversy over official names for a group of heavy elements ended in 1997 after the International Union of Pure and Applied Chemistry (IUPAC) adopted revised names substantially different from those that it had proposed in 1994. IUPAC is an association of national chemistry organizations formed in 1919 to set uniform standards for chemical names, symbols, constants, and other matters. The action cleared the way for the adoption of official names for elements 101–109 on the periodic table.

The elements were synthesized between the 1950s and the 1980s by researchers in the U.S., Germany, and the Soviet Union, but official names were never adopted because of disagreements over priority of discovery. After an international scientific panel resolved the priority disputes in the early 1990s, IUPAC was free to consider names for the elements proposed by the discoverers. When, however, it rejected some of those proposals and substituted its own names, it received sharp criticism. Discoverers of new elements traditionally have had the right to pick names. IUPAC's rejection of the name seaborgium for element 106 caused special dismay in the U.S., where discoverers of the element had named it for Nobel laureate Glenn T. Seaborg, codiscoverer of plutonium and several other heavy elements.

The dispute led the over-151,000-member American Chemical Society (ACS) to support a largely different group of names and to use them in its many publications. An IUPAC committee subsequently proposed a revised list of names, which were accepted by IUPAC's governing body and the ACS in mid-1997. The official names and symbols of the nine elements were: 101, mendelevium (Md); 102, nobelium (No); 103, lawrencium (Lr); 104, rutherfordium (Rf); 105, dubnium (Db); 106, seaborgium (Sg); 107, bohrium (Bh); 108, hassium (Hs); and 109, meitnerium (Mt). Resolution of the conflict cleared the way for naming the recently discovered elements 110, 111, and 112. The scientists who discovered them had decided not to propose names until the earlier controversy ended.

Inorganic Chemistry. The periodic table of elements graphically depicts the periodic law. This cornerstone of chemistry states that many physical and chemical properties of elements recur in a systematic fashion with increasing atomic number. Confidence in the law as it applies to very heavy elements was shaken, however, when previous studies concluded that rutherfordium and dubnium (elements 104 and 105, respectively) departed from periodicity. For instance, although dubnium is positioned under tantalum in the table, in water solutions it exhibited behaviour different from that of tantalum. During the year a research group headed by Matthias Schädel of the Institute for Heavy Ion Research, Darmstadt, Ger., restored confidence in the law with studies of the chemistry of seaborgium (element 106). Working with just seven atoms of the element, they concluded that seaborgium does behave like its lighter counterparts—including molybdenum and tungsten—in group 6 on the table, as periodic law predicts. Schädel used gas chromatography and liquid chromatography experiments to show that seaborgium forms the same kind of compounds as other group 6 elements.

The first synthesis of mesoporous silica in 1992 led to many predictions that the material would have widespread commercial and industrial applications. Mesoporous silica is silicon dioxide, which occurs in nature as sand and quartz, but it differs from natural forms in that it is riddled with billions of pores, each only a few nanometres (nm), or billionths of a metre, in diameter. (Materials with pores 2–50 nm in diameter are usually called mesoporous; those with pores less than 2 nm in diameter are microporous.) The pores give the silica an amazingly large surface area; a single gram has about 1,500 sq m (16,000 sq ft) of surface. The large surface area seemed to make it ideal for adsorbing materials or perhaps as a catalyst in accelerating chemical reactions. Nevertheless, few such applications materialized.

Jun Liu of the Pacific Northwest National Laboratory, Richland, Wash., and associates reported one of the first potential practical applications for the material. They found that mesoporous silica coated with monolayers (single molecular layers) of tris(methoxy)mercaptopropylsilane had a remarkable ability to bind and remove heavy metals from contaminated water and thus could have important applications in remediating environmental pollution. In laboratory tests on heavily contaminated water, the coated material reduced levels of mercury, silver, and lead to near zero. Liu said the coating could be modified such that the material selectively adsorbed some metals, but not others, to suit different specialized situations. It could be used as a powder packed into treatment columns or fabricated into filtration disks.

Zeolites are microporous materials with many practical uses. They serve as catalysts in refining gasoline, water softeners in laundry detergents, and agents for separating gases. Zeolites work because their internal structure is riddled with highly uniform molecular-sized pores, which allow them to act as molecular sieves, controlling the entry and exit of molecules by size. Natural zeolites are minerals having a three-dimensional aluminosilicate framework, and for several decades scientists have developed synthetic zeolites and zeolite-like materials consisting, initially, of aluminosilicates like the natural minerals and, later, of aluminophosphates, substituted aluminophosphates, zincophosphates, and other combinations of elements. Efforts have also been made to synthesize such materials incorporating cobalt, since inclusion of that element would provide catalytic activity of potential use in many industrial processes. During the year Galen D. Stucky and colleagues of the University of California, Santa Barbara, announced the development of a general method for synthesizing cobalt phosphate zeolite-like materials. Their process yielded materials of new chemical types and structural configurations. The cobalt content could be tailored to fit specific intended applications by adjustment of the electrical charge and structure of amide molecules used in the synthesis.

Organic Chemistry. The buckminsterfullerene molecule (C_{60}) comprises 60 carbon atoms bound together into a spherical cage having a bonding structure that resembles the seams on a soccer ball. In recent years chemists had synthesized a number of dimers of C_{60}—that is, molecules made of two connected C_{60} units. They included such dimers as $C_{121}H_2$ and $C_{120}O_2$, in which two C_{60} molecules are connected with various linkages. The simplest C_{60} dimer, which is C_{120}, had eluded synthesis, however.

During the year Koichi Komatsu and associates at Kyoto (Japan) University and the Rigaku Corp., Tokyo, reported synthesis of the C_{120} dimer. It consists of C_{60} cages linked by a single shared four-carbon ring. The configuration gives the dimer the distinctive shape of a dumbbell, with the shared ring forming a handle that connects the two C_{60} spheres. Komatsu developed a new solid-state mechanical-chemical technique for the synthesis that makes use of a vibrating mill. High-speed vibrations activate the reaction by bringing the reagents into very close contact and providing extra mechanical energy. The mill consisted of a stainless-steel capsule containing a stainless-steel ball and a solid mixture of C_{60} and potassium cyanide (used as a catalyst) under nitrogen gas. Researchers vibrated the mill forcefully for 30 minutes, producing 18% yields of C_{120}. Komatsu reported that the vibrating-mill method could be used in the preparation of dimers of other fullerene molecules—*e.g.,* C_{140} from C_{70}.

The framework of the cubane molecule (C_8H_8) consists of eight carbon atoms linked together in the shape of a cube, a structure that has challenged traditional concepts about chemical bonding. Cubane has properties, including highly strained 90° bonds storing enormous amounts of energy, that make it an ideal candidate for a new generation of powerful explosives, rocket propellants, and fuels. Substitution of nitro groups (–O–N=O) for the eight hydrogen atoms, for instance, would create an explosive expected to be twice as powerful as TNT. Furthermore, the rigid cubic structure appeared useful as the molecular core in the synthesis of antiviral agents and other drugs. Such applications lagged, however, in part because chemists knew little about its basic chemistry and behaviour. Advances in 1997 added to knowledge about cubane, which was first synthesized in 1964.

Scientists at the National Institute of Standards and Technology, Gaithersburg, Md., and the University of Chicago reported determination of cubane's crystal structure at high temperatures. They used X-ray crystallography to show that the basic unit of solid cubane remains a rhombohedron even at temperatures near its melting point. In a second report scientists from the University of Minnesota and the University of Chicago announced determination of several key properties of cubane in the gas phase, including the first experimental values for its bond dissociation energy, heat of hydration, heat of formation, and strain energy.

Applied Chemistry. Researchers in industrial settings were working to develop new ways of synthesizing chemical compounds by means of reactions that do not require toxic ingredients or generate toxic by-products. Such efforts, sometimes termed "green chemistry" or "waste reduction," promised to benefit both the environment and the economy in that they would reduce the use of toxic chemicals and the volume of hazardous waste that would need costly treatment or disposal. Walter V. Cicha and associates of the Du Pont Co., Wilmington, Del., reported a new method for making phosgene that substantially reduced formation of unwanted carbon tetrachloride (CCl_4). Large quantities of phosgene are produced and used annually in the manufacture of polycarbonates and polyurethane plastics, pesticides, and other products. The traditional process for making phosgene involves the reaction of carbon monoxide and chlorine with carbon-based catalysts; it forms substantial amounts of CCl_4, a known carcinogen. Phosgene producers use high-temperature incineration to eliminate the CCl_4, but incineration produces hydrogen chloride, which has to be scrubbed from incinerator exhaust gases before their release into the environment. The Du Pont researchers worked out the mechanism of CCl_4 formation in the phosgene reaction and examined dozens of alternative catalysts. They eventually identified one that produced high yields of phosgene but formed 90% less CCl_4 than the traditional catalyst.

Aldol condensation reactions have been a mainstay in organic chemistry, widely used to synthesize chemicals having important commercial and industrial applications. They involve a transfer of hydrogen between molecules in a reaction to form a new molecule, called an aldol, that is both an aldehyde and an alcohol. The first in a new generation of catalysts for accelerating hundreds of different aldol condensations became commercially available in 1997. It is a catalytic antibody, called 38C2, that was developed by researchers at the Scripps Research Institute, La Jolla, Calif., and the Sloan-Kettering Institute for Cancer Research, New York City, and marketed by the Aldrich Chemical Co., Milwaukee, Wis. Catalytic antibodies, or abzymes (a contraction of "antibody enzymes"), are substances derived from the immune systems of living organisms that selectively accelerate organic chemical reactions by attaching to and stabilizing intermediate structures produced as a reaction progresses. Researchers reported that 38C2 was very efficient in catalyzing an extremely broad range of chemical reactions and that a number of similar catalysts would be commercially available in the near future. (MICHAEL WOODS)

This article updates the *Macropædia* articles CHEMICAL COMPOUNDS; CHEMICAL ELEMENTS; CHEMICAL REACTIONS; Chemical Process INDUSTRIES; The PHYSICAL SCIENCES: *Chemistry*.

In 1997 researchers at the University of California, Santa Barbara, announced the development of a method for synthesizing cobalt phosphate-based zeolite analogs. Their process yielded crystals of new structural configurations.

DR. GALEN STUCKY, DR. XIANHUI BU AND PINGYUN FENG, UNIVERSITY OF CALIFORNIA, SANTA BARBARA

PHYSICS

The physics community worldwide acknowledged 1997 as the centenary of the discovery of the electron—the first identification of a subatomic particle—by the British physicist J.J. Thomson. Subatomic particles, and the particles of which they are constituted, also were at the centre of several interesting experimental results reported during the year, some of which had implications for both physics and cosmology. Evidence continued to underscore the dramatic differences between the reality of quantum physics and normal experience, and researchers reported developing the first atom laser.

Particle Physics. An atom consists of a cloud of electrons surrounding a tiny nucleus. The nucleus in turn is made up of particles called hadrons—specifically, protons and neutrons—which themselves are built up from more fundamental units called quarks. The standard model, the central theory of fundamental particles and their interactions, describes how the quarks are held together in hadrons via the strong force, which is mediated by field particles known as gluons. A proton or neutron comprises three quarks tied together by gluons. Other hadrons called mesons comprise two quarks bound by gluons. Theorists had predicted, however, that "exotic" mesons could also exist. One type could consist of two quarks held together by distinctive, energetically excited gluons; another type could be made of four quarks bound by gluons in a more ordinary way.

In 1997 experimenters at the Brookhaven National Laboratory, Upton, N.Y., claimed to have observed effects due to exotic mesons. The evidence was indirect, since the lifetime of the particles was expected to be about 10^{-23} seconds. The Brookhaven team used a beam of high-energy pions, a type of meson, to bombard protons in a hydrogen target. The characteristics of a small fraction of the debris from the pion-proton collisions suggested that a new particle had formed briefly. The claim was supported by experimenters at CERN (European Laboratory for Particle Physics), near Geneva, who observed similar results by means of a different method involving the annihilation of antiprotons, the antimatter counterpart of protons. If confirmed, the results would be further validation of the standard model.

The standard model considers quarks to be "point particles," with no spatial size, but evidence continued to collect that quarks themselves may have structure. At the DESY (German Electron Synchrotron) laboratory, Hamburg, experiments were being carried out in which positrons, the antimatter counterparts of electrons, were smashed into protons at very high energy and their scattering pattern compared with that from theoretical calculations incorporating the assumption that protons consist of pointlike quarks. For the vast majority of collisions, the results agreed well with theory. For the most violent collisions, however, the dependence of the scattering pattern on energy seemed to be different. This deviation was interpreted as possible evidence for structure within the quark itself or, alternatively, for the transient appearance of a previously unobserved particle.

Of great significance for particle physicists, astrophysicists, and cosmologists is the question of whether another fundamental particle, the neutrino, has a small mass. Neutrinos are very common, but they very rarely interact with other matter and so are difficult to observe. The idea of massless neutrinos is an assumption built into the standard model, but there is no compelling theoretical reason for them to have exactly zero mass. Indeed, the existence of a small mass for neutrinos could help explain both the shortfall of neutrinos, compared with theoretical predictions, detected from the Sun and the fact that the universe behaves as if it has much more mass (so-called missing mass or dark matter) than the total amount of luminous matter currently known to exist.

Evidence from three groups during the year added to previous data suggesting some small mass for the neutrino. Research groups at the Liquid Scintillator Neutrino Detector at Los Alamos (N.M.) National Laboratory (LANL), the Soudan 2 detector in the Soudan iron mine in Minnesota, and the Super-Kamiokande detector in Japan reported results from ongoing experiments that point to a finite mass. At least three other groups around the world were also carrying out experiments intended to give a definite upper boundary for the possible mass of the particle.

Quantum Theory. Several experiments confirmed predictions of quantum theory that had not been experimentally verified previously. Scientists were long familiar with the phenomenon of particle annihilation, in which a collision between a particle and its antiparticle converts both into a burst of electromagnetic radiation. Only during the year, however, did physicists at the Stanford (Calif.) Linear Accelerator Center (SLAC) demonstrate the reverse process. Photons (the particle-like energy packets that constitute light radiation) from a super-powerful short-pulse glass laser, producing a half trillion watts of power in a beam 6 micrometres (0.0002 in) across, were arranged to interact with a pulsed beam of high-energy electrons. Some of the photons collided with the electrons, gaining a huge energy boost, and recoiled back along the line of the laser beam. A number of those energetic photons collided with oncoming laser photons and, in so doing, sufficiently broke down the vacuum to produce pairs of electrons and positrons. The experiment marked the first time that the creation of matter from radiation had been directly observed.

To some the SLAC experiment might seem almost mundane compared with that of Nicolas Gisin's group at the University of Geneva. One of the best-known debates within quantum physics has been that over the Einstein-Podolsky-Rosen paradox. In the 1930s, to express their dissatisfaction with quantum theory, Einstein and two colleagues proposed a thought experiment based on a part of the theory that allows the states of two particles to be quantum mechanically "entangled." For example, two particles with opposite spins could be created together in a combined state having zero spin. A measurement on one particle showing that it is spinning in a certain direction would automatically reveal that the spin of the other particle is in the other direction. According to quantum theory, however, the spin of a particle exists in all possible states simultaneously and is not even defined until a measurement has been made on it. Consequently, if a measurement is made on one of two entangled particles, only then, at that instant, would the state of the other be defined. If the two particles are separated by some distance before the measurement is made, then the definition of the state of the second particle by the measurement on the first would seem to require some faster-than-light "telepathy," as Einstein called it, or "spooky actions at a distance."

For Einstein this conclusion demonstrated that quantum mechanics could not be a complete description of reality. Nevertheless, in 1982 the French physicist Alain Aspect and co-workers showed that such action at a distance indeed exists for photons a short distance apart. In 1997 Gisin and his co-workers extended the experiment for particles separated by large distances. They set up a source of pairs of entangled photons, separated them, and piped them over optical fibres to laboratories in two villages several kilometres apart. Measurements at the two sites showed that each photon "knew" its partner's state in less time than a signal traveling at light speed could have conveyed the information—a vindication of the theory of quantum mechanics but a problem, for some, for theories of causation.

An even stranger experiment confirmed a prediction made in the late 1940s by Dutch physicist Hendrik Casimir. In acoustics the vibration of a violin string may be broken down into a combination of normal modes of oscillation, defined by the distance between the ends of the string. Oscillating electromagnetic fields can also be described in terms of such modes—for example, the different possible standing wave fields in a vacuum inside a metal box. According to classical physics, if there is no field in the box, no energy is present in any normal mode. Quantum theory, however, predicts that even when there is no field in the box, the vacuum still contains normal modes of vibration that each possess a tiny energy, called the zero-point energy. Casimir realized that the number of modes in a closed box with its walls very close together would be restricted by the space between the walls, which would make the number smaller than the number in the space outside. Hence, there would be a lower total zero-point energy in the box than outside. This difference would produce a tiny but finite inward force on the walls of the box. At the University of Washington, Steven Lamoreaux, now at LANL, measured this force for the first time—the bizarre effect produced by the difference between two nonexistent electromagnetic fields in a vacuum. The amount of the force, less than a billionth of a newton, agreed with theory to within 5%.

Atomic Physics. An optical laser emits photons of light all in the same quantum state. As a result, a beam of laser light is of a single pure colour and is coherent; *i.e.,* all the components of the radiation are in step. During the year Wolfgang Ketterle and his co-workers at the Massachusetts Institute of Technology created an analogous quantum state of coherence in a collection of atoms and then released them as a beam, thus producing the first atom laser. The coherent state, created in a gas of sodium atoms, was achieved by means of technique perfected two years earlier for trapping atoms and chilling them to temperatures just billionths of a degree above absolute zero (0 K, −273.15° C, or −459.67° F) to form a new kind of matter called a Bose-Einstein condensate (BEC). In a BEC the constituent atoms exist in the same quantum state and act coherently as a single entity. To make the atom laser, Ketterle's group devised a way to allow a portion of the trapped BEC to emerge as a beam. The beam behaved as a single "matter wave" that could be manipulated like laser light. Although much development was needed, in the future an atom laser might bear the same relation to an optical laser as an electron microscope does to an optical one. Researchers foresaw applications in precision measurement and the precise deposition of atoms on surfaces for the manufacture of submicroscopic structures and devices. (DAVID G.C. JONES)

This article updates the *Macropædia* articles ELECTROMAGNETIC RADIATION; MECHANICS: *Quantum Mechanics;* Principles of PHYSICAL SCIENCE; The PHYSICAL SCIENCES: *Physics;* SUBATOMIC PARTICLES; Principles of THERMODYNAMICS.

ASTRONOMY

Throughout 1997 the universe revealed its secrets to astronomers equipped with a bevy of new telescopes, spacecraft, and novel scientific instruments. Optical astronomy received a major boost in February with an upgrade by space shuttle astronauts to the Earth-orbiting Hubble Space Telescope's (HST's) scientific instruments. Space astronomy missions included a flyby of asteroid Mathilde and the arrival of two spacecraft at Mars, and major astronomical payload launches concluded with the successful, though controversial, liftoff of the Cassini spacecraft, headed for a rendezvous with the giant planet Saturn in the year 2004. (See *Space Exploration,* below.) In early 1997 Comet Hale-Bopp put on a spectacular naked-eye celestial display for people everywhere. Late in the year astronomers using the 5-m (200-in) Hale telescope on Mt. Palomar, California, reported the discovery of two additional moons in orbit around Uranus, raising the number known to 17.

Solar System. The search for the origins of life and for signs of past or present life beyond Earth remained one of the most exciting challenges in science. During the year several space missions shed new light on these issues. On July 4 NASA's Pathfinder spacecraft arrived at Mars, providing the first close-up view of the "red planet" in 21 years. Embodying the new NASA creed of "cheaper, faster, better," Mars Pathfinder made use of a novel landing strategy employing air bags to cushion its final descent to the planetary surface. Two days later Sojourner, a kind of roving robot geologist, wheeled away from Pathfinder, becoming the first moving vehicle ever deployed on another planet. The landing site appeared to be a rock-strewn plain, once swept by water floods. Images from the two craft indicated that some of the rocks may be sedimentary material called conglomerate, which further supports the idea of free-flowing water on the Martian surface in the past. In addition, chemical evidence that the rocks had been repeatedly heated and cooled suggested that Mars had a geologic history somewhat like that of Earth. All told, during their 83 days of operation, Pathfinder and Sojourner collected 16,000 photographs and a vast array of other data on Mars's geology, geochemistry, and atmosphere, which researchers had only begun to analyze in detail by year's end. Overall, scientists already seemed to agree that the data supported the notion that early in its history Mars may have had the necessary conditions to support life.

In September the Mars Global Surveyor orbiting spacecraft reached its destination. It was designed to monitor the Martian climate and to map the planet's surface with a resolution of about 1.4 m (5 ft). To prepare for the start of those activities in March 1999, the spacecraft began readjusting its highly elliptical orbit into a circular, low-altitude orbit by dipping repeatedly into the upper atmosphere, using it as a brake. At the same time, the craft allowed its onboard magnetometer to measure the Martian magnetic field. Early Surveyor results indicated that Mars has a weak global magnetic field, about 1% that of Earth, but later measurements showed the field to exist only as local patches each a few hundred kilometres across, with their magnetic axes pointing in different directions. The local field regions were thought to be remnants of an earlier, stronger global magnetic field, which could have protected the surface of Mars from incoming cosmic rays and enhanced the chances for past life.

DON F. FIGER, UCLA/NASA

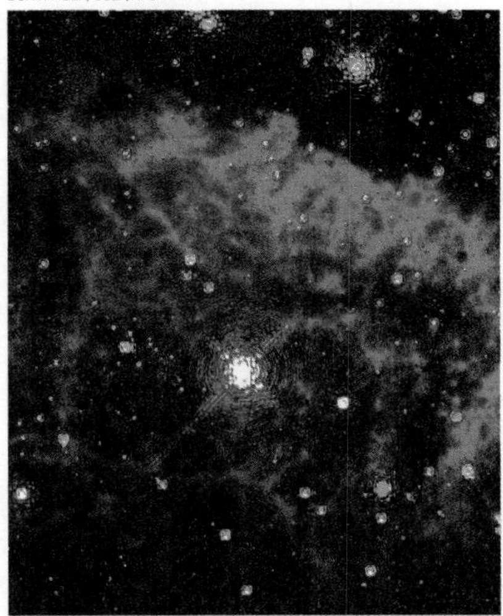

What may be the brightest star in our galaxy was photographed by astronomers in September using NASA's Hubble Space Telescope. The star—25,000 light-years from Earth—has the radiance of 10 million Suns.

Earth Perihelion and Aphelion, 1998

Jan. 4	Perihelion, 147,099,830 km (91,403,420 mi) from the Sun
July 4	Aphelion, 152,095,600 km (94,507,640 mi) from the Sun

Equinoxes and Solstices, 1998

March 20	Vernal equinox, 19:55[1]
June 21	Summer solstice, 14:03[1]
Sept. 23	Autumnal equinox, 05:37[1]
Dec. 22	Winter solstice, 01:56[1]

Eclipses, 1998

Feb. 26	Sun, total (begins 14:50[1]), the beginning visible in the eastern Pacific Ocean about the Equator, the Galápagos Islands, the Panama-Colombia border region; the end visible in the eastern Atlantic Ocean near Morocco.
March 13	Moon, penumbral (begins 02:14[1]), the beginning visible throughout the Americas (excluding northwestern North America), Greenland, and the Arctic, Europe, Africa, western Asia; the end visible in the Americas, eastern Asia, extreme western Africa, extreme western Europe, and part of Antarctica.
Aug. 8	Moon, penumbral (begins 01:32[1]), the beginning visible in the Americas, southern Greenland, Europe, extreme western Asia, Africa, most of Antarctica; the end visible in the Americas (excluding northwestern North America), Africa (excluding the east coastal areas), most of Europe, most of Antarctica.
Aug. 21–22	Sun, annular (begins 23:10[1]), the beginning visible in the Eastern Indian Ocean, northern Sumatra (Indonesia), Malaysia (including Singapore); the end visible in the southwestern Pacific Ocean (northeast of New Zealand).
Sept. 6	Moon, penumbral (begins 09:14[1]), the beginning visible in the Americas (excluding the easternmost regions), eastern Australia, New Zealand, most of Antarctica; the end visible in western North America, Australia, New Zealand, eastern half of Asia, most of Antarctica.

[1]Universal time.
Source: *The Astronomical Almanac for the Year 1998 (1997).*

After arriving at Jupiter in late 1995, the Galileo spacecraft spent the next two years photographing the giant planet and its moons. In February 1997 Galileo came within 586 km (364 mi) of the fractured-ice surface of the Jovian moon Europa. Images taken during that flyby supported earlier speculation that Europa may have a thin icy surface overlying oceans of liquid water or slush that is being warmed by the tidal energy dissipation produced by Jupiter. In addition, some of the images showed surface areas that appeared to be comparatively smooth and crater-free, which stirred debate over whether part or all of Europa had been resurfaced by upwelling water in relatively recent times (within the past few million years) or whether the surface dates back to the early days of the formation of the solar system. If there is liquid water in Europa's interior—and if the moon possesses the kinds of organic compounds that Galileo detected during the year on two other Jovian satellites, Ganymede and Callisto—Europa could be one of the best candidate hosts in the solar system for extraterrestrial life.

For many people 1997 was the year of the great Comet Hale-Bopp, which was witnessed by more individuals than any other comet in history. Surveys showed that by April more than 80% of the U.S. population had seen the comet. Scientifically, other than Halley's Comet, Hale-Bopp was the most photographed and best-studied comet in history. Following just a year after the naked-eye appearance of the bright Comet Hyakutake, Hale-Bopp put on a spectacular show lasting several months; at its brightest it was outshone only by the Moon and a handful of bright planets and stars. Gas and dust shells from the comet were recorded by many instruments, as was its elongated plasma tail. Spectrometers detected more than three dozen organic compounds present in the tail, including ones never before seen in comets. Since many of those molecules had been detected in dense interstellar molecular clouds, this observation strengthened the link between comets and primitive prestellar material. From their orbits above Earth, two astronomical observatory satellites, ROSAT and the Extreme Ultraviolet Explorer, detected X-rays from the comet, as they had from Hyakutake and several other comets. A variety of models for producing the X-rays had been proposed, but at year's end their origin remained unclear.

Stars. The distance to a star is one of the most important pieces of information used to determine its properties. It is also a link in the chain of reasoning employed to establish both the size and the age of the universe. The only direct way to measure stellar distances is to use the phenomenon of parallax. Each year, as the Earth orbits the Sun, nearby stars appear to swing back and forth slightly in their angular position with respect to the very distant stars. By measuring this angular shift and using their knowledge of the diameter of the Earth's orbit, scientists can triangulate the distance to nearby stars. Because Earth's atmosphere limits the precision with which stellar positions can be measured from its surface, the European Space Agency launched the Hipparcos satellite in 1989 to survey the sky and determine accurately the positions of nearby stars. Results of the Hipparcos survey were announced in early 1997. They included determinations of positions for more than 100,000 stars with a precision 100 times better than ever before achieved on Earth and of positions for an additional 1,000,000 stars with somewhat lower precision.

Among the most important results from Hipparcos was a new determination of the distance to, and therefore the luminosity of, the Cepheid variable stars in the Milky Way. These stars, which pulse regularly in brightness, are used to calibrate the distances to remote galaxies. On the basis of Hipparcos's determinations, both Cepheids and galaxies appeared to be about 10% farther away than previously thought. The Hipparcos data also led to a revision of the distance and age determinations of the stars in globular clusters, thought to be the oldest stellar members of the Milky Way Galaxy. They appeared to be 11 billion years old rather than the previously estimated 14 billion–16 billion years. Taken together, the results appeared to resolve the discrepancy between the age of the universe deduced from the ages of the oldest stars and the age found from the observed recession of distant galaxies. They suggested that the universe is about 12 billion years old.

Stars have been observed in a wide variety of sizes and masses, from one-tenth to perhaps 20–50 times the mass of the Sun. Using a newly installed near-infrared camera and multiobject spectrometer on the HST, a team of astronomers headed by Donald F. Figer of the University of California, Los Angeles, announced the discovery of perhaps the brightest and most massive star ever seen. Although hidden from optical view within a region of gas and dust called the Pistol Nebula, it was detectable at infrared wavelengths. The object appeared to radiate 10 million times the luminosity of the Sun. If it is indeed a single star, its present mass is perhaps 60 times that of the Sun, and at birth it may have been as much as 200 solar masses.

Galaxies and Cosmology. Brief bursts of gamma rays coming from the sky were first detected in 1973 by satellites sent aloft to look for the gamma rays that would accompany surreptitious nuclear weapons testing. Since that time these burst events have been detected by a variety of civilian and military satellites and spacecraft. After its launch in 1991, the orbiting Compton Gamma Ray Observatory began detecting about one burst per day, which would bring the total number of events observed to date to more than 2,000. The bursts appeared to arrive at Earth from random directions over the sky. Until 1997 no gamma-ray burst had ever been associated with any star, galaxy, or other known celestial object. The problem in accurately determining their locations was due to the poor angular resolution of current gamma-ray telescopes and the brief duration of the bursts—only seconds on average. In 1996, however, the Italian-Dutch BeppoSAX satellite was launched to search for X-rays from celestial objects, find their precise positions, and study their luminosity variations. It also had the ability to monitor the sky for X-rays that accompany gamma-ray bursts and the capability of being pointed to the region of a burst within hours of the event.

In February 1997 BeppoSAX found an X-ray counterpart for a gamma-ray burst. Subsequent optical observations by the HST revealed two possible optical counterparts, one fuzzy and one starlike, but neither object was bright enough to identify. A gamma-ray burst in May, however, also was followed by the appearance of an X-ray source. Its detection by BeppoSAX quickly led to the discovery of an associated optical object. Pointing one of the twin Keck 10-m (400-in) telescopes in Hawaii to this dim optical counterpart only 56 hours after the initial gamma-ray burst, Mark Metzger and colleagues of the California Institute of Technology measured the spectrum of what turned out to be a distant galaxy. Its red shift of 0.835 placed the source of the burst at a distance of at least 10 billion light-years. The discovery made it clear that gamma-ray bursts arrive at the Earth from cosmological distances, rather than somewhere within or near the Milky Way Galaxy, and that they release more energy in a few seconds than the Sun radiates in its lifetime. The ultimate cause of the bursts remained to be determined, though many astronomers favoured a model involving the coalescence of two neutron stars in a binary system, resulting in a giant explosion and a rapidly expanding fireball.

The brightest objects in the universe are the enigmatic quasars. Since their discovery in 1963, quasars, rather than the far more plentiful but far less luminous galaxies, had held the record for the most distant objects that had been seen in space. In 1997, however, a galaxy was discovered with a red shift of 4.92, displacing the previous record holder, the quasar PC1247+34. The discovery came about when Marijn Franx and collaborators of the Kapteyn Institute, Groningen, Neth., using the Hubble telescope, found a red arc of light near the centre of a relatively nearby cluster of galaxies. A spectrum of the arc taken with one of the Keck telescopes revealed that it was, in fact, a distant and quite young galaxy. It was observable only because the nearer cluster of galaxies acted as a gravitational lens, distorting but magnifying the light from the distant galaxy as it passed through the cluster. (KENNETH BRECHER)

This article updates the *Macropædia* articles The COSMOS; GALAXIES; The PHYSICAL SCIENCES: *Astronomy;* The SOLAR SYSTEM; STARS AND STAR CLUSTERS.

SPACE EXPLORATION

Tracks on the planet Mars and tribulations on Russia's space station *Mir* vied for centre stage in space exploration during 1997. Meanwhile, preparations continued apace for the first launch of parts of the International Space Station (ISS).

Manned Spaceflight. Ten manned space launches were made during the year, most in support of plans to assemble the ISS beginning in 1998. Three U.S. space shuttle missions and two Russian Soyuz missions went to *Mir;* four other shuttle flights carried science missions; and one shuttle flight visited the Hubble Space Telescope (HST) on a servicing mission.

Atlantis made all of the U.S.'s shuttle trips to *Mir.* Although the flights had been meant to give U.S. astronauts experience on a space station, they became part of *Mir*'s lifeline as the aging station (launched in 1986) experienced a series of major mishaps. On February 23, a month after *Atlantis*'s first visit, the space station had a fire, one of the most serious accidents that can happen aboard a spacecraft. Six people were aboard, rather than the usual three, because Soyuz TM-25, which had been carrying a replacement crew, had recently docked. A solid-chemical oxygen canister burned for more than a minute, which forced the crew to don breathing equipment and seriously damaged the station's main electrolysis-based oxygen-generating system. In April an unmanned Progress resupply ferry delivered fresh oxygen canisters and fire extinguishers to *Mir,* and *Atlantis*'s second mission in May included a replacement oxygen generator.

On June 25 *Mir* suffered a near-fatal mishap when a Progress ferry being docked via remote control by Russian cosmonaut Vasily Tsibliyev accidentally rammed into the Spektr science module, putting a hole in the pressure vessel and damaging its solar arrays beyond use. To salvage the station, which consisted of a core, a connecting node, and five science modules, crew members severed electrical and data connections between Spektr and the rest of the station and then sealed off the module. They saved the station but lost about half of their electrical power.

Problems subsequently cascaded as *Mir*'s main computer shut down and had to be jury-rigged to keep working. A planned internal space walk in July to repair the station was postponed when Tsibliyev developed an irregular heartbeat and officials in Moscow decided that the crew was too fatigued to work safely. The toll on the crew became apparent when on July 17 one of them accidentally disconnected a computer cable, which caused the station to drift and its solar panels to point away from the Sun.

With a Progress resupply visit in July, the Soyuz TM-26 crew-replacement mission in August, and the year's third visit by *Atlantis* in September–October, *Mir* had a fresh crew and all needed repair equipment, including a special hatch with electrical connectors to allow Spektr's lines to be reconnected. In activities inside and outside *Mir* between August and November, the crew restored most of the lost power and the main oxygen-generating system (which had experienced renewed problems after the June collision), replaced the onboard computer with a new unit, and installed new solar arrays, although they remained unable to locate the exact point of the hole in Spektr.

Assembly of the ISS was delayed from a late-1997 start to mid-1998 after Russia ran into financial and technical problems with the space station's service module, which was built from what once had been planned as *Mir 2.* The first ISS element, dubbed the FGB, was to be launched in June, with a space shuttle carrying up the first U.S.-built components a month later.

Two shuttle missions, which had to be accomplished with three flights, concentrated on microgravity materials sciences. Soon after launch of the Microgravity Science Laboratory (MSL-1) mission aboard *Columbia* in April, the malfunction of an electricity-generating fuel cell left the shuttle with no reserve and forced its return after only four days in space. Because of the importance of the mission's results to future ISS research, NASA exploited a gap in the shuttle flight schedule to refly the entire mission and crew, a first for the shuttle program. On July 1 MSL-1 was relaunched aboard *Columbia,* and all the experiments were conducted as planned.

In November *Columbia* flew again, carrying the fourth U.S. Microgravity Payload (USMP-4) and Spartan 201, a deployable pair of solar instruments. After *Columbia*'s robot arm put Spartan into space, it was unable to relock onto the craft for retrieval. NASA took advantage of a scheduled space walk by astronauts Winston E. Scott and Takao Doi for testing ISS assembly techniques by having the two catch Spartan by hand and pull it into the shuttle's open payload bay. A second, unscheduled space walk was held just before the end of the mission in order to make up some of the tests that were skipped during the unplanned spartan retrieval.

The year's other science mission for the shuttle was flown in August by *Discovery.* Its major payload was Germany's CRISTA-SPAS-2, a collection of spectrometers and telescopes that the shuttle deployed in space for observations of the Earth's atmosphere.

In February *Discovery* astronauts made the second service call on the orbiting HST since its launch in 1990. In five space walks, they installed more than two tons of equipment, including new spectrographic and imaging instruments, and patched insulation blankets that were found to have eroded under conditions in orbit.

JPL/NASA

After landing on Mars on July 4, NASA's Pathfinder spacecraft and its roving sidekick Sojourner transmitted photographs from a rocky Martian plain. There were signs that water may have once flowed freely at the landing site.

The *Mir* space station's Spektr science module reveals damage to the solar panel at right and a nearby radiator. On June 25 *Mir* suffered a near-fatal mishap when an unmanned ferry being docked via remote control was accidentally rammed into the module.
NASA

Space Probes. Mars, quite simply, was the planet of the year as Mars Pathfinder and its deployed rover beamed back images from the surface and as Mars Global Surveyor started settling into its planned orbit.

Launched the previous December, Pathfinder entered the Martian atmosphere on July 4, 1997. Its descent was braked by a heat shield, a parachute, and rockets and finally by air bags, on which it bounced to rest on the surface. Once down, the tetrahedral craft deployed solar arrays, a colour stereo camera, and instruments for atmospheric and meteorologic studies. Early images revealed the landing area to be a rock-strewn plain showing signs that liquid water once had run through the area. Pathfinder then deployed its six-wheeled rover, Sojourner, which carried colour cameras and a special spectrometer for geologic and geochemical studies of Martian rocks, soil, and dust. After thousands of images were returned from the lander and rover, the mission ended in November. During their operation Pathfinder and Sojourner demonstrated a number of new technologies for future Mars missions. (See *Astronomy,* above.)

Launched a month earlier than Pathfinder, Mars Global Surveyor went into an elliptical orbit around Mars on September 11. It then dipped into the upper Martian atmosphere in a series of aerobraking maneuvers designed to take the satellite into a lower orbit better suited for mapping. A solar array that had not properly deployed after launch began to flex excessively, which prompted NASA to suspend the aerobraking for several weeks while engineers developed gentler maneuvers that would not endanger the craft.

The Near Earth Asteroid Rendezvous (NEAR) spacecraft remained on course to the asteroid Eros, which it was to orbit in 1999 and study for approximately a year. On June 27 NEAR passed within 1,200 km (750 mi) of asteroid Mathilde and took many multispectral images.

The Cassini mission to Saturn lifted off October 15 after a flurry of protests and lawsuits attempted to block the launch. Cassini drew its electric power from the heat generated by the decay of radioactive plutonium. Protesters had claimed that a launch accident could expose Earth's population to plutonium dust, but NASA countered that the casks encasing the plutonium were robust enough to survive any mishap. The ambitious mission was to be the first to orbit Saturn and the first to land on the moon of an outer planet. Cassini was scheduled to reach Saturn in 2004, after which it would send its Huygens probe parachuting into the methane-rich atmosphere of Titan.

The Galileo spacecraft ended its primary mission to Jupiter on December 7, two years after reaching the planet. NASA and the U.S. Congress, however, approved a two-year mission extension during which Galileo would study Jupiter's moons Europa and Io.

Unmanned Satellites. The United States launched the Advanced Composition Explorer (ACE) on August 25 to study the makeup of the solar wind from a "halo orbit" centred on L-1, a gravitational balance point between Earth and the Sun about 1.5 million km (930,000 mi) away from Earth. ACE carried instruments to monitor the magnetic field, solar-wind electrons and ions, and cosmic-ray ions.

Japan's HALCA radio-astronomy satellite was launched on an M-5 rocket from the Kagoshima Space Center on February 12. The 830-kg (1,830-lb) satellite carried an 8-m (26-ft) wire-mesh dish antenna that deployed in orbit. With an apogee of 21,400 km (13,300 mi), the satellite was being used in conjunction with ground-based radio telescopes for very long baseline interferometry to give the effect of a radio antenna more than twice Earth's diameter.

Launched Dec. 24, 1996, the U.S.-Russian-French Bion 11 mission, which had been opposed by animal rights groups, carried two monkeys and a variety of other organisms into orbit to study their physiological responses to weightlessness. After the Bion capsule returned to Earth January 7, one of the monkeys died while under anesthesia for tissue biopsies. Scientists later decided that the whole process was too traumatic and suspended flight experiments with primates for an indefinite time.

India launched its fourth remote-sensing satellite, IRS-1D, on its locally developed PSLV-C1 (Polar Satellite Launch Vehicle) rocket from Sriharikota Island on September 29. The 1,200-kg (2,650-lb) craft had a black-and-white camera with a resolution of 5 m (16.5 ft), a linear imaging colour scanner with a resolution of 23.5 m (78 ft), and a wide-field sensor.

Losses of Japan's Midori (Advanced Earth Observation Satellite) and the U.S.'s Lewis satellites marred the year's activities. Midori, launched in August 1996 to monitor changes in the global environment, ceased operation in June when its solar array failed. Lewis was written off shortly after launch on August 23. The first of two Small Spacecraft Technology Initiative missions planned by NASA, the satellite carried visible and infrared Earth imagers and an ultraviolet cosmic background imager in a small 445-kg (980-lb) package. A few days after launch, its attitude control system failed, which caused it to reenter the atmosphere in late September. Launch of its companion craft, Clark, was delayed to March 1998 to ensure that the problem was not repeated.

Launch Vehicles. The U.S. Air Force surprised the aerospace industry when it decided to choose both finalists in the Evolved Expendable Launch Vehicle (EELV) competition. Selection of a single winner had been expected in June 1998, but the large backlog of planned communications-satellite launches and its own desire to negotiate the best possible launch prices led the Air Force to announce that it would buy services from both Lockheed Martin Corp. and the Boeing Co. Lockheed Martin was to develop a series of EELV launchers based on its Atlas II family; Boeing was to develop its Delta III and IV families.

Europe remained competitive with its Ariane 4 family of launchers and the successful launch in October of its second Ariane 5 vehicle. Investigation of the failed first launch of the Ariane 5 in 1996 revealed that the rocket's guidance system had been adapted from the Ariane 4 design without proper modifications. A management shake-up and a rigorous review of the entire design followed. (DAVE DOOLING)

See also Media and Publishing: *Television.*

This article updates the *Macropædia* articles EXPLORATION: *Space Exploration;* TELESCOPES.

Media and Publishing

TELEVISION

Programming. Television flashed the first news of the automobile accident that took the life of Diana, princess of Wales, on Aug. 31, 1997. (*See* OBITUARIES.) The BBC replaced regular programming with round-the-clock coverage. Six billion viewers in 44 countries watched the funeral in London on September 6 through BBC and Independent Television (ITV) News, the only two networks allowed inside Westminster Abbey. Both were forbidden to shoot close-ups of the royal family.

A week later Roman Catholic nun Mother Teresa, a Nobel Peace Prize winner, was interred in Calcutta amid the pomp of a state funeral that was televised live internationally. (*See* OBITUARIES.) A month to the day after her death, Mother Teresa's life was dramatized on International Family Entertainment (IFE) Inc.'s Family Channel cable network. Completed months before her death, the TV movie *Mother Teresa: In the Name of God's Poor* was written by French journalist and author Dominique Lapierre.

The British handover of Hong Kong to China on June 30/July 1 was widely reported live. The BBC covered everything from the departure from Government House of Gov. Chris Patten to the lowering of the U.K.'s flag and the raising of China's, as well as Patten's departure with Prince Charles aboard the royal yacht *Britannia.*

With six highly competitive broadcasting networks and more than 30 viable national cable networks, the 98 million American homes with TV sets had a wide variety of programming from which to choose—and they were promised even more. Dozens of small cable networks looked for space on cable systems, and, perhaps more important, two aggressive entrepreneurs laid plans for what might become the seventh and eight broadcast networks. Fox Network cofounder and Home Shopping Network chairman Barry Diller bought some of the assets of Universal Television, including its television production operations and two established cable networks—USA and the Sci-Fi Channel. The production operations could help Diller create a TV network that combined some national programming with a heavy dose of local programs. Meanwhile, Paxson Communications Corp. chairman Lowell ("Bud") Paxson revamped his earlier plans for an infomercial-style network and set his sights on launching his own "family values" network, to debut in fall 1998.

The big three broadcasters—ABC, CBS, and NBC—watched their shares of TV viewership in prime time continue to erode from the competition provided by the other broadcast networks and the proliferating cable networks. (A rating is the percentage of the TV households tuned to a show. The share is the percentage of households with sets in use during that time period that were watching it.) For the end of the 1996–97 season, which extended from September through May, the big three's combined share dropped to just 49%. The other three broadcast networks—Fox, UPN, and Time Warner Inc.'s the WB—attracted 21%. That left 30% for the Public Broadcasting Service and cable networks like Nickelodeon, TNT, and ESPN. Unlike the big broadcast networks, which reached nearly all TV homes, cable networks covered only 66% through more than 11,000 local cable systems.

NBC won in the 1996–97 TV season ratings, again on the strength of its powerhouse Thursday night, which was anchored by "Seinfeld" and framed by "Friends" and "ER." Jerry Seinfeld's decision to leave the airwaves at the end of the 1997–98 season, however, left NBC scrambling for replacement programming. CBS narrowly beat out ABC for second place with the Sunday-night help of such strong performers as "Cosby" and "Touched by an Angel," a drama whose religious theme effectively counterprogrammed the more sensationalistic fare elsewhere. In the fall ABC was hoping the return of "The Wonderful World of Disney" and well-received comedies like "Dharma & Greg" would boost it out of third place.

NBC and HBO were the big winners at the Emmy awards ceremonies in September. NBC won 24 statues, despite what proved to be a virtual shutout for its "ER," the year's most nominated show. The acclaimed medical drama received only 3 technical Emmys. HBO was second with 19 trophies, including 5 for its TV movie *Miss Evers' Boys.* Although HBO's "The Larry Sanders Show" had garnered 16 nominations, a record for a sitcom, it failed to claim a single award.

NBC's "Frasier" won for best comedy series for the fourth year in a row, whereas the surprise winner for best drama was the network's "Law & Order," a perennial runner-up to ABC's "NYPD Blue." In the comedy category NBC claimed best actor (John Lithgow, "3rd Rock from the Sun") and best actress (Helen Hunt, "Mad About You"), whereas ABC could claim best actor in a drama (Dennis Franz, "NYPD Blue") and Fox could boast best actress in a drama (Gillian Anderson, "The X-Files").

Arguably the highest-profile cable channel to be launched in 1997 was CBS's Eye on People, which debuted March 31 with 14 original programs and about two million subscribers. In the year's other big cable programming news, News Corp.'s Rupert Murdoch and his partner at Fox Kids Worldwide, Inc., Haim Saban, paid $1.9 billion for the Rev. Pat Robertson's Family Channel. The goal was to fill the channel with kid shows and compete with Nickelodeon, Cartoon Network, and the Disney Channel.

Women figured prominently in some of the high-profile programming stories of 1997. Hollywood's worst-kept secret became official on the evening of April 30 when the character played by comedian Ellen DeGeneres (*see* BIOGRAPHIES) on the ABC sitcom "Ellen" admitted she was gay. The episode earned a 23.4 rating and a 35 share, according to Nielsen Media Research. In September talk show queen Oprah Winfrey made happy men of Roger and Michael King, the brothers whose King World Productions, Inc., distributed her syndicated TV show (a program distributed directly to stations rather than via a network). On September 15 she announced that she had renewed her contract for two more years.

The HBO TV movie *Miss Evers' Boys,* starring Laurence Fishburne and Alfre Woodard, won five Emmy awards in 1997. The movie was inspired by the notorious "Tuskegee experiment," in which black men suffering from syphilis were left untreated for years so the U.S. government could study the disease.

BOB GREENE—HOME BOX OFFICE/REUTERS

News programming began to make its way into prime-time TV in numbers too big to ignore. "Dateline," the NBC news magazine, increased its frequency to four times a week. CBS wooed departing "Today Show" cohost Bryant Gumbel to the network to anchor his own newsmagazine, "Public Eye," and ABC's "20/20" could have been rechristened "40/40" as it added a second weekly airing. The reason for the proliferation was that such shows usually generated strong ratings while costing far less than entertainment offerings.

ABC News started the year on a downbeat in January when a federal jury in North Carolina ordered it to pay $5.5 million to the Food Lion supermarket chain. A month earlier the same jury had found that ABC had committed fraud and trespass in securing its information for an investigative report on meat-handling practices. What troubled many journalists was that the accuracy of the story was not challenged. Although a district court judge eventually reduced the fine to $315,000, the "terrible precedent" remained, as one news producer put it.

Fox Network, which celebrated its 10th anniversary during the year, played host to its first Super Bowl, including what may have been the world's longest pregame show (5 hours 18 minutes). The show gave the network its best-ever ratings, with a 43.3 rating and a 65 share. Each 30-second advertisement in the game cost more than $1.2 million.

Fox may have had the Super Bowl, but it was a Tiger that gave broadcasters one of their biggest sports stories. Generating record ratings for his record-setting win at the Masters golf tournament, Tiger Woods (*see* BIOGRAPHIES) gave a boost to the Professional Golfers' Association tour and to golf on TV. Women also reached a new milepost in television sports. NBC became the first broadcast network to provide weekly coverage of a professional women's sports league when it inaugurated coverage June 21 with a women's professional basketball game between the Los Angeles Sparks and the New York Liberty. In November NBC and Turner Sports (a unit of Time Warner) retained the TV rights to the National Basketball Association for four more years. They had to pay $2.6 billion, however, more than double what they had been paying under their previous contracts.

With a glance at the upper lefthand corner of their TV screens, viewers in the U.S. could quickly gauge whether a program was suitable for their families. Under pressure from the government and children's advocacy groups, most broadcast and cable networks in January began labeling their shows with a ratings system based on the familiar movie-ratings system. For example, instead of an R rating, TV programs with the most explicit sex or violence would carry a TV-MA (mature audience) rating.

Advocates of ratings were still unhappy, however. They kept the heat on, and in October broadcasters and cable programmers modified the ratings to include specific content warnings. Thus, the TV-MA rating might also include one or more of the letters S for sex, V for violence, and L for inappropriate language. Insisting that the ratings violated their First Amendment rights and despite threats from the government, NBC stood alone among major networks in refusing to go along with the content ratings.

In other developments, after five years of self-imposed exile in Europe, Li Nam-ok, the 31-year-old "adopted" daughter of North Korean leader Kim Jong Il, made her first television appearance in London before CNN World Affairs correspondent Ralph Begleiter. Li confirmed that she fled Pyongyang in 1992 when "Papa" cut off the food supply to the household after being angered by the drunken behaviour of son Kim Jong Nam.

A BBC documentary uncovered Swiss national bank documents showing "intent to deceive" over coins stamped with prewar dates to disguise their origins. The coins were reportedly produced from gold stolen from Jews, including gold teeth and possessions of Nazi concentration camp victims.

Sinn Fein, the political wing of the Irish Republican Party, and Ulster Unionists, Northern Ireland's main Protestant British party, held their first live TV debate. They were represented, respectively, by Martin McGuinness, a former commander of the IRA, who rejected a Parliament seat won in May because it required an oath of allegiance to Queen Elizabeth II; and Ken Maginnis, a retired British army major who had sat in Parliament since 1983.

A Brazilian soap opera "Xica da Silva" continued winning viewers for TV Manchete, Brazil's third largest network. Walter Avancini, the director of "Xica," was credited with having raised Manchete's ratings by using sex, violence, and history. "Xica" star Taís Araújo's nudity onscreen three days after her 18th birthday created an uproar because the scenes were apparently taped while she was still a minor, which violated an existing ban. France's most controversial TV anchorman, Patrick Poivre d'Arvor, or PPDA, as he was better known, promoted his book *"Lettre ouverte aux vio-*

One of the most eagerly awaited events on television during the 1996–97 season was the April 30 episode of the ABC sitcom "Ellen," in which the title character, portrayed by comedian Ellen DeGeneres (left), confided to a character played by Laura Dern that she was gay.

HO—ABC-TV/REUTERS

Oprah's Book Club

In 1996 top-rated daytime television talk-show host Oprah Winfrey, the most financially successful female star on TV, expanded her media empire into the realm of publishing with the introduction of Oprah's Book Club. In an effort to restructure "The Oprah Winfrey Show" and because she was a voracious reader herself and wanted to "get the whole country [the U.S.] reading again," Winfrey began endorsing books she felt were of literary merit. The concept quickly took flight, increasing the show's audience to some 20 million viewers, propelling sales of the book-club selections into the stratosphere, and making Winfrey a literary tastemaker with a newfound ability to spark the interest of nonreaders.

Each month Winfrey chose a book, often fiction, and presented it to her audience, allowing sufficient time (two to four weeks) to read the selection thoroughly. The author of the book then appeared on the show to discuss the work with a small group of the readers. The venues for the discussions were often cozy and comfortable, ranging from dinner at Winfrey's home to an all-female slumber party at author Maya Angelou's house. Afterward, the author would often hold a discussion of the book on-line on the Internet as well.

On the basis of daytime television standards, Winfrey's book selections might seem daunting—most were intense, stark dramas. The first selection was the somewhat obscure *The Deep End of the Ocean,* a heart-wrenching story about a Midwestern family coping with the disappearance of a child. Written by first-time novelist Jacquelyn Mitchard, the book had a first-run printing of 100,000 copies. After Winfrey touted the work in her club, however, an additional 640,000 copies were printed. Other recommendations included Wally Lamb's *She's Come Undone,* a hard-hitting story about an overweight rape victim; Ursula Hegi's *Stones from the River,* the story of a dwarf ostracized in a small town in Nazi Germany; and Jane Hamilton's award-winning novel *The Book of Ruth,* a backlist title that sold 750,000 additional copies.

Winfrey's second pick, Toni Morrison's critically acclaimed *Song of Solomon,* was a powerful novel about a Southern black man's search for his identity. Though a backlist title, *Song of Solomon* burst back onto bookstore shelves with renewed vigour once it had been announced as a club selection; an additional 870,000 copies were sold. Winfrey's book-club endorsements ensured instant success; an additional 10 million copies of her first eight selections were sold.

Publishing companies, though pleased by the burgeoning sales, were unprepared for the overwhelming interest in Winfrey's selections. To avoid stock shortages, she began shipping editions to warehouses wrapped in covers that read "Untitled Oprah's Book Club #__." Winfrey then decided to notify publishers ahead of time but asked that in return they donate 10,000 copies of her book-of-the-month selection to libraries.

Winfrey also bought film rights to a number of these books, which promised to make the stories accessible to an even greater portion of the population. She insisted, however, that her financial stake in these films would not influence her club selections.

(JACKIE ORIHILL)

leurs de vie privée," in which he accused colleagues of succumbing to an "Anglo-Saxon disease"—gutter journalism.

Islamic Taliban police in Afghanistan arrested the European Union's Emma Bonino, commissioner for humanitarian affairs, and 18 of her companions, including aid workers, CNN correspondent Christiane Amanpour, and other journalists. The police had been "enraged by the presence of news cameras" in a women's hospital in Kabul. Taliban policy forbids photography of a woman by an unrelated man. Bonino and her delegation were released unharmed after three hours.

BBC's 24-hour news service, "News 24," initially planned for digital TV, was launched November 9 on cable. Because the service was free, News Corp.'s British Sky Broadcasting (BSkyB) Group PLC, Britain's biggest pay-TV company, which ran "Sky News," a similar 24-hour news service, complained to the Department for Culture, Media, and Sport, especially after cable companies made plans to drop "Sky News" for "News 24."

Embattled Pres. Alberto Fujimori of Peru took over Lima TV channel Frecuencia Latina on July 13 after it reported that government security agents were tapping phones. Hours later, station owner Baruch Ivcher, an Israeli-born businessman, was stripped of his Peruvian citizenship. Since foreigners could not own local media, pro-government minority shareholders Samuel and Mendel Winter took over the channel.

Television stations in 60 countries linked up on October 19, World Food Day, for the first TeleFood global telecast based on the theme "Food for All." Organized by the United Nations Food and Agriculture Organization in collaboration with Italian broadcasting company RAI International, the show ran for 8½ hours on RAI and was relayed via the RAI International satellite.

Organization. Central European Media Enterprises Ltd., controlled by former U.S. ambassador to Austria Ronald S. Lauder, claimed that Hungary's National Radio and Television Commission gave broadcast licenses to lower bidders. They included CLT-Ufa, Europe's biggest broadcasting group, and a media consortium consisting of Scandinavian Broadcasting System and MTM Communications, the largest TV production company in Hungary.

Rupert Murdoch's News Corp. agreed to trade satellite assets (including a valuable orbital slot he controlled with MCI) for a nonvoting minority stake in Primestar, a cable-controlled satellite broadcaster in which Time Warner owned 31%. Primestar cable partners MediaOne, Comcast, and Cox approved of the deal because it made News Corp. an ally instead of a competitor.

Compagnie Générale des Eaux SA sold control of its cable TV unit to Canal Plus SA, Europe's biggest pay-TV company. Canal Plus thus raised its stake in Compagnie Générale des Videocommunication to 76% from 20%. Générale des Eaux maintained a 15% interest.

Pierre Lescure, chief executive of Canal Plus, in March bought troubled Amsterdam-based digital pay-TV NetHold for $1.2 billion. His challenge was to turn around NetHold's Telepiu channel in Italy, which lost $190 million in 1996. Canal Plus also faced new competition at home from AB Sat and Television Pay Service.

Britain's most successful and popular association football (soccer) club, Manchester United, on September 30 announced the fall 1998 launch of a channel with BSkyB and Granada. This reinforced BSkyB's broadcast of Britain's major soccer matches.

Flemish socialist MP Louis Vanvelthoven dealt a blow against tobacco advertising and promotions in Belgium. Although tobacco ads on TV had been forbidden there for 20 years, Vanvelthoven's new initiative ended tobacco sponsorship of sports, many of which were telecast.

The European Association of Advertising Agencies urged international channels to create a reliable database similar to those used by many national broadcasters. Pan-European channels did little audience research except for the European Media and Marketing Survey, which showed that apart from Eurosport, international European channels like European Business News, NBC Super Channel, Euronews, and MTV Europe lost some of their audience in 1997.

In November William Kennard took over the Federal Communications Commission (FCC), the first African-American to do so. Kennard, who had been the regulatory agency's top lawyer, was expected to continue the policies of his predecessor, Reed Hundt, pushing for specific public-interest obligations that broadcasters had to meet in exchange for their TV and radio licenses. In this regard, Hundt's legacy was a requirement that TV stations air three hours of educational children's programming each week. The requirement went into effect on September 1.

Technology. The German alliance of Kirch Group, Bertelsmann AG, and Deutsche Telekom AG allowed existing pay-TV channels—analog Premiere and digital DF-1—to broadcast cable digital programming beginning in October. Since digital compression provided for more channels than analog, broadcasters in Britain—among them Cable & Wireless Communications, British Digital Broadcasting, and Flextech, a subsidiary of the U.S.'s Tele-Communications Inc.—were expected to begin using this new technology.

Tokyo Broadcasting System, Inc., bought a 10% stake in PerfecTV Corp., Japan's first digital satellite broadcasting venture, developed by Itochu Corp., Nissho Iwai Corp.,

Mitsui and Co., and Sumitomo Corp. Murdoch persuaded Sony Corp. and Fuji Television Network to invest in Japan Sky Broadcasting (JSkyB) Co. Ltd. Hughes Electronics Corp. hoped to develop an antenna and decoder system that would work with all three digital satellite services to shore up DirecTV, Hughes's consortium with Matsushita Electric and Tokuma Shoten Publishing Co. All three companies had to compete with the semipublic Japan Broadcasting Corp., which operated the world's only high-definition television (HDTV) service, the advanced analog format offering the wide-screen pictures, rich colours, and movielike detail that many once believed would become the worldwide standard.

The FCC in April opened a new era in TV broadcasting in the U.S., tentatively awarding each of the nation's nearly 1,600 TV stations in the country a second channel for digital broadcasting. Most broadcasters planned to use the channel for HDTV, but some, notably the ABC and Fox networks, were also interested in using their extra channels for multicasting—that is, the broadcasting of several channels of standard-definition TV, wide-screen pictures with resolution little better than that of conventional television. By late fall most broadcasters said they would broadcast HDTV during some parts of the day and multicast during others.

In any event, consumers were reminded that there was no need to throw out their conventional analog TV sets or to rush to buy digital TVs, which were expected to cost several thousand dollars when they reached retail stores in 1998. The government ruled that TV stations could keep their analog channels and continue broadcasting their existing services until 85% of homes in their markets had digital receivers. Most industry observers believed that this decision delayed the digital-only date by at least a decade.

Australia's major media group Publishing and Broadcasting Ltd. became an entrant to the Internet. It teamed up with Microsoft Corp. to form Nine MSN to provide on-line news, sports, entertainment, and weather shows, as well as financial and retail services.

Interactive TV, the next generation of television sets, was launched in 1997 by H. Thomas Telesis. It acquired 6.8 million subscribers in the U.S., 10 million in Japan, and 21 million in Western Europe, using direct-to-home television broadcast via satellite. It also reached Malaysia, the Middle East, and Latin America. New markets being targeted included the Philippines, Taiwan, China, South Korea, Indonesia, and India.

RADIO

Just before the handover of Hong Kong from Britain to China, radio shows in Hong Kong gave mainland Chinese a taste of freedom of speech and other democratic ways by giving them a chance to say things they never could on government-run radio at home. From these Chinese callers, people in Hong Kong gained insights into life on the mainland. Radio Television Hong Kong considered itself editorially independent and wanted to remain so under the "high degree of autonomy" China had promised Hong Kong.

Vietnam announced it would step up internal vigilance and increase domestic propaganda to counter broadcast plans by U.S. radio station Radio Free Asia. A commentary in the Communist Party's *Nhan Dan* newspaper described the U.S.-funded station as "an assault tool of the hostile forces."

In June consumer electronics leaders Hitachi Ltd., Panasonic (Matsushita), Sanyo, and JVC announced agreements with WorldSpace, headquartered in Washington, D.C., to develop and mass-produce a new generation of portable radios capable of receiving broadcast programs directly from satellites. WorldSpace was founded in 1990 to provide direct satellite delivery of digital audio communications services to the emerging markets of the world.

In the U.S. it was the year of Thomas Hicks in radio. The Dallas investor went on a radio station shopping spree and by November owned or had agreed to buy 418 stations, more than any other radio operator in the nation. Hicks's binge was part of a rapid consolidation of the radio industry that began in 1996 after the government effectively eliminated most radio ownership limits. At midyear *Broadcasting & Cable* magazine found that 13% of the nation's 10,273 commercial radio stations were in the hands of the 25 largest station groups. The consolidation of the industry did not escape the notice of government regulators concerned not so much with how many stations a company owned nationwide but how many it owned in a single market. In November the Justice Department filed suit in federal court to block a deal that would have given a Hicks-owned company control of four stations serving New York's Long Island, which together accounted for 65% of the advertising revenue in the market.

Driving all the buying and selling was the healthy advertising market, a reflection of the strong overall U.S. economy. According to the Radio Advertising Bureau, August was the 60th straight month of increased advertising sales. Sales for the month were 12% greater than in August 1996.

Although it may have seemed to some that the U.S. marched to a rock beat, radio studies continued to find that country music was the most prevalent and popular radio format. According to Simons Research, some 43 million Americans 18 years or older tuned in to country each week. The runners-up were adult contemporary (36 million weekly listeners) and news/talk (31 million). The average American in 1997 listened to radio each week for 3 hours 24 minutes on weekdays and 5 hours 51 minutes on weekends, according to SRI Radio.

(RAMONA MONETTE S. FLORES; HARRY A. JESSELL; LAWRENCE B. TAISHOFF)

Amateur Radio. Despite the rise of the Internet, more than two million people throughout the world in 1997 continued to communicate over the air as amateur radio operators. Most of these hams—nearly 700,000, by the FCC's count—were in the U.S. The American Radio Relay League (ARRL) reported that it started off the year with 175,000 members, the most in its 83-year history. Hams used their radios mostly for personal communications, but on occasion they were called on to provide emergency communications, as was the case in 1997 with the flooding in the western U.S., and to provide backup communications, as they did for the New York City Marathon. The hams also provided educational opportunities. In the fall NASA scheduled amateur communications between schools and astronaut and ham David Wolf aboard the troubled *Mir* space station.

Despite the number of enthusiasts and their well-documented good work, hams in the U.S. fought a seemingly never-ending battle to preserve the radio frequencies they used. In 1997 the threat came primarily from proposed low-Earth-orbiting satellites. In addition to guarding spectrum in Washington, the ARRL also successfully worked to water down a bill in Congress that would have restricted the use of scanners and affected the manufacture of amateur radio equipment.

(HARRY A. JESSELL; LAWRENCE B TAISHOF)

See also Business and Industry Review: *Advertising; Telecommunications;* Performing Arts: *Motion Pictures; Music.*

This article updates the *Macropædia* article BROADCASTING.

NEWSPAPERS

The death of Diana, princess of Wales *(see* OBITUARIES), in a high-speed car crash in Paris on Aug. 31, 1997, generated more press coverage than any other news event in the 20th century. In the month following the accident, 35% of British news stories were devoted to Diana. In contrast, the biggest events of World War II, including the final defeat of Nazi Germany, earned only 27%.

Photojournalists worldwide were attacked in the backlash of public outrage against the paparazzi who had given chase to the car and were thought to bear responsibility for the accident. Amid talk of legislative curbs, British newspapers called for self-restraint and self-regulation. They also agreed to respect the privacy of the young princes, at least until they reached the age of 18.

The British newspaper industry continued to consolidate, with larger chains buying smaller ones rather than individual newspapers. This trend accelerated, spurred by the need to cut costs in order to offset higher paper expenses and reduced advertising. Mirror Group, publisher of the *Daily Mirror* and the *Sunday Mirror* and owner of other publishing and broadcasting interests, in July acquired Midland Independent Newspapers.

Conrad Black, head of Hollinger International, Inc., had in 1996 taken control of half the daily newspapers in Canada when he bought out the Southam family chain. Across Canada the Southam's 32 papers, which included the *Vancouver* (B.C.) *Sun,* the *Calgary* (Alta.) *Herald,* the *Hamilton* (Ont.) *Spectator,* and the *Montreal Gazette,* shifted content, style, appearance, and editorial point of view. The *Ottawa Citizen,* the flagship paper, which had been owned by the Southam family for 100 years, had offered light and local stories in a traditionally liberal city. The new *Citizen* featured long analytic articles, international news, extensive parliamentary coverage, an expanded editorial section, and a deeply conservative editorial board.

Journalists in Latin America were concerned with staying alive. In the last nine years, more than 170 journalists had been assassinated in the region. In Argentina José Luis Cabézas, a photographer for *Noticias,* was gunned down after taking the first known photograph of a businessman who

Der Spiegel at 50

On Jan. 4, 1997, Germany's leading weekly for news and analysis, *Der Spiegel,* celebrated its 50th anniversary. The magazine had long been something of a fat and mischievous only child in the German journalistic community. In 1947, when Rudolf Augstein received a license from the British zonal authorities to publish a newsmagazine, Germany's situation was sensational and scandalous enough, so the 23-year-old entrepreneur hardly needed to turn to sensationalism and scandal. Because this was the type of magazine that was launched, however, *Der Spiegel* soon found its access to authoritative sources progressively reduced. Comparatively few respectable public figures would lend themselves to a *Spiegel* interview (Chancellor Helmut Kohl consistently refused to be interviewed by *Der Spiegel,* and he was noticeably absent at Augstein's 70th birthday celebration in 1993), so *Der Spiegel* turned to other sources, exposing the underside of the upper classes, particularly the political class. The gleanings were served up in each issue in five or six long narrative articles, garnished with anecdote and innuendo and sauced with almost subliminal derogatory suggestion.

Despite all this—indeed, because of it—*Der Spiegel* was the most important publication in Germany. On the one hand, since it trafficked in suspicion and resentment, it acquired a large constituency of grudge-bearing readers; on the other, it lent itself to all forms of political opposition. Instead of splitting away, dissident factions of political parties went into hiding and emerged in the offices of the magazine. *Der Spiegel* penetrated all political parties, and the range of its political coverage was unmatched in Germany. Above all, the magazine was the standard-bearer of Germany's confused and resentful postwar intellectuals. It also struck fear into the hearts of the elite and so brought comfort to the dispossessed and disaffected little people of Germany. In this way the magazine worked as a palliative to the country's enduring epidemic of envy.

The success of *Der Spiegel* rested on Augstein's diagnosis of the deep psychological wounds of the German body politic. The division of Germany prolonged the confusion of moral values caused by the Third Reich, treason in one part of Germany constituting by definition heroism in the other. Augstein exploited these infirmities in pursuit of his own goal: a neutralist, antimilitaristic West Germany. In short, *Der Spiegel*'s editorial policy was tailored to the Cold War and to a separate West Germany. Augstein called the desire of the West Germans for reunification the *Lebenslüge* ("life-sustaining lie") of the Federal Republic; however, he simply ignored the desire of the East Germans for reunification.

With the end of the Cold War and the disappearance of West and East Germany, *Der Spiegel* lost much of its editorial traction. The launching of the weekly newsmagazine *Focus* in January 1993 broke the monopoly *Der Spiegel* had enjoyed for 46 years. Within four years *Focus* had all but matched the dwindling circulation (roughly one million copies sold) of *Der Spiegel.* If reunification wrapped up the postwar period for Germany, perhaps *Der Spiegel*'s era had also come to an end.

(GEORGE BAILEY)

had been accused of being a mafia chief but also had close ties to Pres. Carlos Menem. Ten months later high-tech telephone traces revealed 100 calls between the businessman and the minister of justice, who was forced to resign. Cabézas's killing was widely seen as an attack on a free press—an attack on journalists trying to expose public corruption. The publisher of *Noticias,* Hector D'Amico, stated, "People stop me in the street constantly with stories they are afraid to bring to police or a judge. We're being asked to do the job of investigators. And it's not a small group of people who are afraid. It's everyone." Mexico was one of the most dangerous nations in 1997; three journalists were killed, four kidnapped, 20 physically attacked, and three threatened with death.

Russian Telegraph, first published in September, became the 14th daily newspaper in Moscow. Owned by Vladimir Potanin's Uneximbank, Russia's most powerful financial group, which already had a large stake in *Komsomolskaya pravda* and *Izvestia*, the new paper aimed to be respectable, be conservative, provide strong business coverage, and, according to its young editor, Leonid Zlotin, offer "no reports of mafia shootouts." Russia's best-selling newspaper remained *Argumentiy i faktiy* ("Arguments and Facts"). The weekly, which had become prominent during the glasnost era, continued its straightforward style with short, factual articles, interviews, and advice columns. Its circulation of 3.1 million was almost three times that of its nearest competitor.

Journalists in Hong Kong reported that whereas there had been no overt crackdown on the press since the British colony reverted to China in July, there had developed self-censorship, a concern that accurate reporting on China would bring forth reprisals. For example, the mass-circulation newspaper *Apple Daily,* which had been critical of China, was denied accreditation to cover news from mainland China. The paper was also not allowed to cover a reception organized by the Chinese Foreign Ministry, which was held in Hong Kong in September. A. Lin Neumann, Asia program coordinator of the Committee to Protect Journalists, reported deep concern about self-censorship in Hong Kong, noting its place as "the principal safe haven for professional, independent Chinese-language reporting about the internal political and economic affairs of the People's Republic."

In the United States 1997 was a good year to own a newspaper. Advertising revenues showed great gains—by October classified ads had gained 12.5% over 1996, retail ads were up 5.7%, and national ads had gained 14.2%. Share prices of newspaper stocks also took part in the "irrational exuberance" of the U.S. stock market climb. The bull market generated a windfall of financial services ads. In 1996 mutual funds and brokerages spent a record $255.4 million to advertise in the country's 50 biggest markets, a record many expected to be broken in 1997. In addition to the booming economy, newspapers themselves added such efficiencies as clustering their markets, developing niche publications, and building networks to make national advertising easier. The cost of newsprint, which had been expected to rise, instead dropped from $700 a ton in 1996 to $500 a ton. Even the anticipated postal increases were delayed until 1998.

Although circulation remained stagnant or dropped off to a small extent, this was often offset by increases in the prices of newspapers. In some instances the papers themselves chose to stop distributing in outlying areas.

Antipornography activist Donna Rice Hughes speaks with reporters on March 19 in Washington, D.C., after the Supreme Court heard arguments challenging the 1996 Communications Decency Act. In June the court struck down the law that regulated what individuals and publishers could put on the Internet.

SUSAN WALSH—ASSOCIATED PRESS

DAMON WINTER—ASSOCIATED PRESS

In the early-morning hours of August 31, *Time* art director Arthur Hochstein redesigns the cover of the magazine after news broke that Diana, princess of Wales, had been killed in a Paris car crash. The princess's death generated more press coverage than any other news event in the 20th century.

Day in and day out, sports stories remained the most popular news events. Among the trends that became more explicit in 1997 was the propensity of media moguls to purchase baseball teams. Rupert Murdoch, chairman of the News Corp., declared that sports, more than anything else, attracted subscribers. In Great Britain sports routinely constituted 23% of news coverage.

The *New York Times* made itself over in 1997. No longer the "Old Gray Lady," the newspaper moved to full-colour production in September. Arthur Ochs Sulzberger, chairman and chief executive of the New York Times Co., retired in October, passing the leadership of the company to his son Arthur Sulzberger, Jr., already the publisher of the paper. The elder Sulzberger stated that his biggest news decision came in 1971 when he decided to publish the Pentagon Papers, the secret government history of the Vietnam War. That resulted in the Supreme Court's ruling that upheld a newspaper's right to publish free of a government's prior restraint.

The Wall Street Journal began publication of a WSJ Special Edition in German. The weekly edition appeared in *Der Tagesspiegel,* a Berlin newspaper. Published in 11 languages, *The Wall Street Journal* by 1997 was being sold in 28 countries.

The *New York Daily News,* then under the leadership of Pete Hamill, created an immigration desk in order to cover the city's various ethnic groups. The industry trend toward immigrant coverage was an attempt to gain new readers for mainstream papers and also to provide papers with access to news stories in different communities.

Still ethnic in any language, the *Forward* marked its 100th anniversary during the year. Begun as a Yiddish daily that could speak to the Jewish immigrants from Eastern Europe in their own language about life in the U.S., the *Forward* by 1997 had become a weekly published in three separate editions in three languages—Yiddish, directed toward its original audience; Russian, for more recent immigrants; and English.

With few independent papers standing alone, the industry trend of larger chains' buying smaller chains continued. Knight-Ridder, Inc., purchased the *Kansas City* (Mo.) *Star,* the *Fort Worth* (Texas) *Star-Telegram,* and two smaller papers from the Disney Co. for $1,650,000,000. Second in size only to the Gannett chain, Knight-Ridder moved against the trend toward diversification into other media. It had sold its broadcast units in 1989 and its share in a cable system in 1996 and planned to sell its on-line information services. The strategy of clustering groups of papers to generate more revenue was exemplified by Conrad Black's expansion in the Chicago area. With the addition of the *Gary* (Ind.) *Post-Tribune,* Black owned the *Chicago Sun-Times*, *Daily Southtown*, Star Newspapers, and the Pioneer Press chain of weeklies for a total of at least 68 papers in the metropolitan area.

While ever-fewer U.S. cities offered more than one daily newspaper, San Juan, P.R., grew to a six-daily city. During the year each of the three existing papers expanded to launch a new morning paper. The *San Juan Star,* the only English-language daily, launched a Spanish version; *El Nuevo Dia* offered *Primera Hora;* and *El Vocero* produced *El Nuevo Mundo.*

In a lawsuit brought by U.S. freelance writers that challenged the practice of newspaper and magazine publishers' reproducing their articles in electronic databases and on CD-ROMs without the writers' permission or additional payment, a U.S. District Court judge ruled against the authors. The judge noted that "copyright law may not have kept pace with today's technology" and that congressional legislation might be necessary. A similar case involving the Canadian Copyright Act was filed by writers in Canada but at the year's end had not been decided.

Construction began in Bloomfield, Mo., of a museum for *Stars and Stripes,* the nation's paper for those in military service. The paper was first published in 1861 by Union troops during the U.S. Civil War. It was revived during World War I, was reborn in World War II, and since then had been published continuously. (ANNE ROBY)

MAGAZINES

The World Trade Organization in January 1997 ruled that Canada could not try to ban American magazines by imposing an 80% tax on split-run editions, those in which U.S. titles are reprinted in Canada with a few pages of Canadian content added in order to attract Canadian advertising. Canadian publishers had argued that the U.S. titles were a form of dumping—selling foreign products at less than their actual cost—since the costs of production had been covered in the American market. An appeal panel in July again turned down the tax and also overturned a postal rate subsidy for Canadian magazines. Almost half the magazines circulated in Canada and some 80% of those on newsstands were American, and the Canadian government's efforts to protect its own industry were viewed by some as protecting the cultural sector from Americanization. And, as the *Globe and Mail* reported, "For Canadians, culture is a nation-building exercise. In the United States, it is simply an enormous industry."

Cultural differences showed up in a different way in Great Britain. Even as the American magazine *Wired* won a National Magazine award for general excellence, the British edition ceased publication. Such British computer magazines as *Loaded, .net, Internet,* and *Stuff* thrived by offering practical, factual consumer information. *Wired*'s revolutionary rhetoric and its brand of pop futurism did not set well with the British, who mostly wanted to know how the new technology worked. The *Guardian* noted that "U.S.-style digital elitism was out of place in a very different British magazine culture."

Founded in 1947, the German magazine *Der Spiegel* marked its 50th year of publication. (*See* Sidebar.) Brazil introduced *Brazil Raca,* the country's first magazine directed toward people of colour. Its first run of 250,000 copies sold out in two days. Articles focused on such topics as mixed marriages and job discrimination along with profiles of successful black Brazilians.

The World Wide Web offered an ever-growing number of newspapers and magazines on-line. While many of the sites were free to all, some charged for information or, in some cases, offered only brief teasers, with most of their content protected by firewalls. The leading U.S. newspapers, with the exception of the *Wall Street Journal,* charged nothing. The *Journal* set two tiers of fees for access, depending on whether one already subscribed to the print edition. Britain's *The Economist* allowed subscribers to access back editions, using codes on its mailing labels. The Medline database, which offered medical articles from around the world, announced that its information would be shared freely with all. How long the idea of free flow of information across the Web would prevail remained a question.

The American magazine industry seemed to offer something for everyone in 1997.

Capitalizing on the interest in sports, three new entries for women were launched. Time-Warner published two trial issues of *Sports Illustrated Women/Sport*, the first in April. Copies were sent to all the women's names on the subscription list of *Sports Illustrated.* The new magazine, like its counterpart for men, was tailored to the young adult who was more likely to be a spectator than a participant in sports. *Jump,* launched by Weider Publications in August, was designed to appeal to teenage girls. *Sports for Women,* introduced by Condé Nast in September, was directed toward the sports participant or sports-minded woman of any age.

Old favourites expanded in foreign editions to new markets. Overseas editions of *Cosmopolitan* appeared for the first time in Italy, Turkey, Russia, Hong Kong, and Japan. With 33 *Cosmopolitan* editions, the Hearst Corp. expected that international profits would account for 50% of the magazine's earnings within a few years, double the current 25%. *Condé Nast Traveler* started a British edition, titled *Traveller,* in October. *Reader's Digest* during the year published 48 overseas editions in 19 languages; they were sold to 27 million readers, nearly double the magazine's 15 million U.S. readers. In one major change the magazine began selling space on its back cover in an effort to increase advertising sales.

Nowhere was change more evident than at the National Geographic Society. Beginning in 1888, *National Geographic* published long, leisurely articles that might take months or even years to develop. By 1997, however, "having the commitment to wait 21 days for a gorilla to take a bath" had given way to more and shorter articles. The society became a for-profit organization and began exploring other media, including full-length feature films, cable and television broadcasting, and CD-ROMs.

Highly specialized niche magazines continued to grow. No matter what one's interest might be, it seemed almost certain that there was a magazine devoted to it, especially in such fields as health and computers. (*See* COMPUTERS AND INFORMATION SYSTEMS: *Sidebar.*) (ANNE ROBY)

BOOK PUBLISHING

The global book market continued its process of consolidation in 1997. A notable deal involved Pearson PLC, which bought Putnam Berkley for $336 million from MCA, the media group controlled by Seagram, and thereby made Pearson's Penguin subsidiary the second largest English-language trade-book publisher in the world. Reed Elsevier was particularly intent upon restructuring with a view to specializing in a limited number of markets. To this end it bought Tolley Publishing from Thomson Corp. at the end of January and promptly followed this up by selling to Random House for approximately $20 million the trade-book division of Reed Books, which included such long-established imprints as William Heinemann, Secker & Warburg, and Methuen. On a somewhat smaller scale, in April the leading Swiss art and architecture publisher Birkhäuser acquired a substantial stake in Princeton Architectural Press of the U.S.; Penguin bought the Victor Gollancz children's list from Cassell; and the German publishers Econ and List and Südwest Verlag GmbH agreed to merge.

The annual output of new titles and reprints in Great Britain exceeded 100,000 for the first time. This was accompanied, predictably, by a sharp increase in returns as well as reports of widespread financial difficulties among publishers.

There were further repercussions from the European Union Directive that in January 1996 had extended the duration of copyrights to the life of the author plus 70 years. Under Britain's Duration of Copyrights and Rights in Performances Regulations, for example, publishers could do anything with copyrighted works as long as they served notice and paid reasonable royalties to the authors. In March Penguin announced that it had agreed to pay substantial royalties to deceased authors' estates, but Oxford University Press and Wordsworth claimed to be exempt from payment of royalties on works for which they had "existing arrangements" before January 1996.

The multimedia scene remained confused, and there were no signs of European collaboration to compete with the U.S. In Britain multimedia CD prices were falling, and many publishers were leaving the business, but those that remained were publishing more titles as booksellers became more receptive. Restructuring was evident elsewhere in Europe. In Germany, Bertelsmann closed down B Electronic Publishing at the end of 1996 after only six months in existence, and in May 1997 the Holtzbrinck group acquired from Burda a majority stake in the loss-making German CD-ROM publisher Navigo Multimedia. The intention was to merge it with Systhema.

Publishers in France encountered difficult trading conditions for the third consecutive year. According to the French Publishers' Association, unit sales had not declined but the average price had fallen, which indicated that the public was willing to wait for cheap editions to appear before buying. In May, Maxi-Livres/Profrance, a publisher, distributor, and bargain bookseller previously thought of as highly successful, collapsed suddenly. In contrast, Hachette Livre prospered after acquiring strategic minority interests in Anne Carriere, Michel Lafon/Ramsay, and Mille et Une Nuits.

Worldwide exports of English-language texts, especially those in the educational field, continued to be buoyant and were likely to remain so because information systems and computers normally use English. (*See* Spotlight: *English-Language Imperialism.*) European publishers were, nevertheless, trying to break into new markets. For the first time in China, Bertelsmann acquired a 49% stake in a publishing joint venture with Shanghai Scientific and Technical Publishers and launched a book club.

A fire at the Calcutta Book Fair in February destroyed hundreds of stands set up by small Bengali publishers who normally did half their annual business there. Few of them were insured. (PETER J. CURWEN)

Janet Dailey, author of 93 romance novels that had sold 200 million copies in 98 countries and 19 languages, shocked her fans in August when she admitted to having plagiarized the work of Nora Roberts, also a best-selling romance writer. In May a reader noticed the similarities between two of the authors' novels and posted her findings electronically on America Online, where Roberts saw them. When confronted, Dailey admitted guilt and added that she had purloined prose from two other Roberts novels as well. Roberts announced her intention to sue Dailey for copyright infringement, adding that any money she won would be donated to Literacy Volunteers of America. She claimed to have discovered plagiarized passages in six of Dailey's novels.

Seymour Hersh, a Pulitzer Prize-winning investigative writer, also had his professional behaviour called into question when it was revealed late in the year that some of the documents he was planning to use in his book *The Dark Side of Camelot,* scheduled to be released shortly thereafter, were fake. The documents contained alleged proof that U.S. Pres. John F. Kennedy had annulled a first marriage, had contact with Mafia mobster Sam Giancana, and agreed to bribe actress Marilyn Monroe to be quiet about their purported affair. ABC-TV's newsmagazine "20/20" revealed that some of the documents were forgeries. Hersh claimed that he knew this and had decided not to use them, a statement some questioned, since he had already been given $2 million for the rights to develop a documentary based on the material. Little, Brown, the publisher, proceeded with the November publication, minus the questionable passages.

HarperCollins came in for its share of criticism when it announced in June that it was canceling 106 books that it had planned to publish, 36 of which were ready for publication and had been featured in the fall catalog. Anthea Disney, HarperCollins president, said the decision was not a financial one but based on her need to "refocus" the company. HarperCollins had a poor financial year, with earnings for fiscal 1997 down 60% as of March. The authors of the canceled books were not required to return their advances and would be paid in full for those that were outstanding. In September HarperCollins' parent organization, News Corp., announced that HarperCollins and the corporation's U.S. magazine and on-line publishing divisions would be combined into the News America Publishing Group.

The year was also notable for the "Oprah effect." Television talk-show host Oprah Winfrey began an on-air Book Club on her successful show. (*See* Sidebar.)

The 1997 Pulitzer Prize for Fiction was awarded to Steven Millhauser for *Martin Dressler: The Tale of an American Dreamer* (Crown), and Richard Kluger won the general nonfiction prize with *Ashes to Ashes: America's Hundred-Year Cigarette War* (Alfred A. Knopf). The National Book Award for fiction went to Charles Frazier for *Cold Mountain* (Atlantic Monthly Press), and the award for nonfiction went to Joseph Ellis for *American Sphinx: The Character of Thomas Jefferson* (Alfred A. Knopf). Fiction best-sellers for 1996, as reported by *Publishers Weekly,* were *The Runaway Jury* by John Grisham (2,775,000 copies), *Executive Orders* by Tom Clancy (2,371,602), and *Desperation* by Stephen King (1,542,077). Nonfiction best-sellers were *Make the Connection* by Oprah Winfrey and Bob Greene (2,302,697), *Men Are from Mars, Women Are from Venus* by John Gray (1,485,089), and *The Dilbert Principle* by Scott Adams (1,319,507). Total book sales in the U.S. increased 4% in 1996 to more than $20 billion. (BETH LEVINE)

See also Literature.

This article updates the *Macropædia* article PUBLISHING.

Military Affairs

In a dramatic illustration of just how much security relationships had changed in Europe over a decade, NATO in July 1997 invited three of its former Warsaw Pact adversaries in Eastern Europe to join the alliance. The NATO-led coalition force in Bosnia and Herzegovina—which included contingents from 20 non-NATO nations—was successful in maintaining a troubled peace in that war-weary country. Peace, however, was hardly a universal condition in 1997. As the year ended, there were some 30 conflicts of varying size and intensity ongoing throughout the world. In the Middle East, Iraq's Pres. Saddam Hussein once again balked at cooperating with UN weapons inspectors and seemed determined to provoke a military confrontation with the United States. Central Africa was a particularly volatile region, with national borders of little use in containing the violence. Civil war continued to ravage Afghanistan and Sri Lanka. The armed forces of Albania and Zaire disintegrated when put to the test, and the death of a princess and the awarding of a prestigious international prize added momentum to a unique international movement to ban antipersonnel land mines.

Arms Control and Disarmament. U.S. and Russian nuclear disarmament was restrained by the continued reluctance of the Russian State Duma (the legislature's lower house) to ratify the 1993 Strategic Arms Reduction Talks II (START-II) treaty. At their March summit meeting in Helsinki, Fin., U.S. Pres. Bill Clinton and Russian Pres. Boris Yeltsin agreed on a framework for the follow-up START-III treaty, which would cut each country's strategic nuclear arsenal to no more than 2,500 warheads. In an effort to make the START-II treaty more palatable to the State Duma, they also agreed to extend the treaty's reduction period by five years. A protocol incorporating this provision was signed by the two countries in September, along with several documents relating to the 1972 antiballistic missile (ABM) treaty. These named Belarus, Russia, Kazakstan, and Ukraine as successors to the Soviet Union for the purposes of the treaty and defined the parameters of the shorter-range missile defense systems that would not be subject to the treaty.

With the UN Conference on Disarmament (CD) dragging its heels on negotiating a ban on antipersonnel land mines, the impetus in this field shifted to the "Ottawa Process"—named after the site of an October 1996 conference sponsored by Canada with the express aim of achieving a global ban at the earliest possible date. In addition to nations, the process included a number of nongovernmental organizations. The most notable of these was the International Campaign to Ban Landmines (ICBL), a coalition of more than 1,000 organizations in over 60 countries. A treaty text was adopted at a follow-up conference in Oslo in September. Diana, princess of Wales—who had been the world's most visible advocate of a land mine ban and was to have addressed the Oslo conference—was killed in an automobile accident on August 31. (*See* OBITUARIES.) The U.S. had preferred the CD as the forum for regulating land mines and rather reluctantly joined the Oslo conference. American efforts to amend the draft treaty to allow several exceptions—such as the continued use of antipersonnel mines in Korea—failed, and President Clinton announced that the U.S. would not sign the treaty. He did, however, launch an initiative to raise $1 billion each year for mine-clearing operations with the goal of eradicating by 2010 all land mines threatening civilian populations. A number of countries with large stockpiles of land mines—such as Russia and China—did not attend the Oslo meeting. When the ICBL and its American coordinator, Jody Williams, were jointly awarded the 1997 Nobel Peace Prize in October, President Yeltsin announced that Russia would support the treaty. (*See* NOBEL PRIZES.) It was opened for signature in Ottawa on December 3 and within a few days was signed by the representatives of 123 countries. Despite Yeltsin's earlier statements, Russia did not immediately sign. Other significant absentees included China and the United States.

The Chemical Weapons Convention entered into force in April, and José Mauricio Bustani of Brazil was elected the first director-general of the Organization for the Prohibition of Chemical Weapons, the treaty's implementing body. The U.S. ratified the convention in April, and Russia followed suit in November. India, China, and South Korea were among the signatories that for the first time acknowledged having chemical-weapons programs.

United States. Once again, Congress appropriated more money for defense than the Clinton administration had requested, passing a $247.7 billion Department of Defense budget for fiscal 1998. President Clinton exercised restraint in using his new line item veto authority, trimming just 13 projects worth $144 million from the bill. These included the money to operate the SR-71 "Blackbird" spy planes—a program that Congress had kept alive since the air force had tried in 1989 to retire the supersonic reconnaissance aircraft. Clinton signed the authorization bill despite reservations about provisions that dealt with the closing of several air force maintenance depots.

In May the Pentagon completed its Quadrennial Defense Review, which concluded that the U.S. must retain the ability to win two regional wars at the same time. The report recommended a modest reduction in total military personnel strength while maintaining 100,000 troops in both Europe and Asia and called for another round of military base closings. In November Secretary of Defense William Cohen announced a Defense

French troops arrive at the Albanian port of Durrës in April as part of a UN-sponsored peacekeeping force sent to oversee relief efforts in the country. Riots had erupted across Albania in January after thousands of people lost investments in failed pyramid schemes. The peacekeeping force included troops from a number of countries, primarily Italy.

ALBERTO PIZZOLI—SYGMA

Reform Initiative, which aimed to streamline the organization and operation of his department and thereby generate savings to help fund the development and procurement of a new generation of information-based weapons systems. Highlights of the plan included the reduction over 18 months of one-third of the personnel in the Office of the Secretary of Defense and the creation of a Threat Reduction & Treaty Compliance Agency by consolidation of the On-Site-Inspection Agency, the Defense Special Weapons Agency, and the Defense Technology Security Administration.

The U.S.'s armed forces suffered more from troubles of their own making during the year than from any foreign foe. Celebrations of the air force's 50th anniversary were clouded by the unprecedented early retirement of the service's chief of staff and several high-visibility cases of alleged sexual misconduct. Gen. Ronald Fogleman resigned in protest over plans to discipline the general in charge of an air force facility in Saudi Arabia struck by a terrorist bomb in June 1996. An earlier air force investigation had cleared the officer of any responsibility for the incident. The air force's first female B-52 pilot, charged with adultery and fraternization, accepted a general discharge rather than face a court-martial, and an air force general who was the leading candidate to replace Gen. John Shalikashvili as chairman of the Joint Chiefs of Staff took his name out of contention after allegations that he had had an adulterous affair more than a decade earlier were made. As a result, Gen. Henry Shelton in October became the third successive army incumbent in the nation's top military post, which had traditionally been rotated among the three services.

The sergeant major of the army—the service's top enlisted man—was first suspended from his duties and then replaced to face a court-martial after he was charged with sexual harassment. In a report released in September, a senior army review panel concluded that sexual harassment and discrimination existed throughout the service. A Defense Department panel in December recommended reducing the integration of men and women in the armed services.

The high operational requirements resulting from the U.S's many overseas commitments took a toll on pilot retention, especially those flying high-performance fighter aircraft. More than 700 experienced pilots left the air force during the year. The Pentagon in July suspended indefinitely military participation in the antidrug patrols along the border with Mexico after a marine shot and killed an 18-year-old Texan. A spate of military aircraft accidents in September prompted the secretary of defense to order all the services to implement a 24-hour "safety stand-down." During the year the air force rolled out its first F-22 "Raptor" air superiority fighter, and the B-2 stealth bomber was declared to be ready for operational use.

NATO. Despite strong Russian objections, leaders of the 16 NATO countries in July offered membership to the Czech Republic, Hungary, and Poland. The accession process was expected to take two years. The heads of state also signed a Founding Act that regulated NATO's special relationship with Russia and a Charter with a similar purpose with Ukraine. To strengthen its links with other nonmembers, NATO bolstered its Partnership for Peace program and established the Euro-Atlantic Partnership Council. The 36,000-strong NATO-led Stabilization Force (SFOR) in Bosnia and Herzegovina maintained a fragile peace between the three ethnic communities, but it became clear that a sizable NATO presence would be required in that country after the SFOR's mandate ended in mid-1998. In December NATO foreign ministers tasked their military authorities to provide early in 1998 options for a follow-on force.

Russian participation in the SFOR remained an example of the close cooperation that could be achieved at the working level. The Russian-NATO Joint Permanent Council established by the Founding Act held several meetings, at both the ministerial and ambassadorial levels. In October Russia appointed a military representative to NATO headquarters in Brussels.

The alliance continued to refine the plans to modernize its command structure. France decided to postpone its return to NATO's integrated military structure after the U.S. refused to give up command of the alliance's Southern Command, but the French indicated they would not block the military reorganization. In March U.S. Army Gen. Wesley Clark was named to replace Gen. George Joulwan as the supreme Allied commander, Europe.

The misdeeds of some NATO soldiers during the 1993 UN intervention in Somalia continued to have repercussions. In Canada a royal commission found that Canadian officers in Somalia and Ottawa had covered up the torture and murder of civilians by Canadian paratroops. Two Italian generals resigned after a newsmagazine alleged that Italian troops had abused and killed unarmed Somalis. The Italian government pledged to conduct a full inquiry.

United Kingdom. In March a contract was signed for the production of three new "Astute"-class nuclear-powered attack submarines, which were scheduled to enter service early in the next century. In May George Robertson was named secretary of state for defense in the new Labour Party government. Despite its strong antinuclear tradition, the Labour Party at its annual conference voted to retain Britain's nuclear deterrent. In October the government confirmed that it would buy seven more American Trident D5 missiles, to be delivered in 1998. They were to be fitted with British-made nuclear warheads. This would increase the British inventory of these submarine-launched ballistic missiles to 58.

France. Alain Richard was named defense minister in the Socialist Party Cabinet that took power in June. The new government announced that it would pare down its troop levels in Africa and would no longer intervene in the domestic affairs of its former colonies there. (*See* Spotlight: *France's New African Policy.*) It also modified a controversial plan of the previous government to call up young people for five days to assess their suitability for the military and to lecture them on patriotism as France made the transition to an all-volunteer force over the next few years. Instead, they would be called up for a single day before their 18th birthday to learn about defense issues. The government also pledged more than F 80 billion for military procurement in 1998, down from the F 90 billion in the previous government's plans.

Germany. German troops involved in an operation in March to rescue foreigners from the anarchy in Albania opened fire on Albanian gunmen in what was described as the first foreign combat by the German military since the end of World War II. The public and government proudly marked the event as another step in overcoming the taboos that had grown from the reactions to Germany's militaristic past. Germans were less pleased with the behaviour of some of their troops at home. Bullying within the ranks was on the increase, and several times during the year soldiers were involved in vicious attacks on foreign workers.

Turkey. The Turkish military, which regarded itself as the defender of Turkey's secular tradition, made no secret of its displeasure with the Islamist government of Prime Minister Necmettin Erbakan and was credited with a major role in his overthrow in June. In little more than a year, the armed forces expelled more than 200 officers charged with having extreme Islamist tendencies. Ismet Sezgin was named defense minister in the new government. He endorsed the previous government's $31 billion 10-year weapons-acquisition program. In midyear and again in September, Turkish troops conducted major incursions into northern Iraq to attack bases of the Kurdistan Workers' Party. Some 8,000 remained in Iraq to police a security buffer zone. The controversial Russian sale of its sophisticated S-300 air defense missile system to the Republic of Cyprus raised tensions between Turkey, Greece, and Russia. Turkey warned that it would not tolerate the missiles' deployment and searched several third-country ships it suspected of carrying the weapons as they passed through the Turkish Straits. Greece, Russia, and the Greek Cypriot government suggested that the missiles would not be deployed if Turkey agreed to the demilitarization of Cyprus.

Commonwealth of Independent States (CIS). In a February decree Russian Pres. Boris Yeltsin ordered a 200,000-man cut in the armed forces, reducing them to an authorized strength of 1.2 million by the end of the year. Dissatisfied with the slow pace of military reform, Yeltsin in May fired both the defense minister and the chief of the general staff. They were replaced by Gen. Igor Sergeyev, the chief of the strategic rocket forces, and Gen. Anatoly Kvashnin. This new team supported Yeltsin's major reform proposals made public in July. The downsizing of the armed forces would continue, reaching a low of 1.2 million authorized military personnel by the end of 1998. Reorganization of Russia's five major services began by combining the strategic rocket forces, the military space troops, and the strategic defense assets of the air defense troops. The air force and the rest of the air defense troops were scheduled to be merged by the end of 1998.

As Russia's conventional military strength deteriorated, increased emphasis was placed on nuclear deterrence, including the possibility of using nuclear weapons to counter a conventional attack. Production of a new intercontinental ballistic missile began, and work started on the first of a new class of strategic missile-carrying submarines. Fulfilling a pledge President Yeltsin had made in May, Russia no longer aimed its nuclear missiles at targets in NATO countries. The bloated defense industry inherited from the

Soviet Union remained in trouble, with frequent strikes. The Defense Ministry lacked the money to pay the enterprises so that they in turn could pay their workers and suppliers. In military procurement the government could afford only to fund prototypes of new conventional weapons in an effort to stay abreast of the latest military technology and to seek foreign sales to sustain the most important enterprises. Such new weapons included the S-37 experimental jet fighter developed by Sukhoi. With wings that were swept forward, the plane was touted as an equal to the American F-22. A new "Black Eagle" main battle tank was also displayed for the first time.

Russia and Ukraine finally settled their long dispute over the division of the former Soviet Black Sea Fleet. Ukraine agreed to lease base facilities in Sevastopol and several other locations on the Crimean Peninsula to Russia for 20 years. The two sides could not agree, however, on the terms for Russia to buy back some 40 strategic bombers inherited by Ukraine when the Soviet Union dissolved. These included the bulk of the supersonic Tu-160 "Blackjacks" that had been in the Soviet inventory.

Despite the presence of a large CIS peacekeeping force in Tajikistan, fighting went on there throughout most of the year between troops loyal to the government and those that had turned against it. In August the government declared victory over the mutineers. Members of illegal armed groups were given until November 17 to turn in their weapons. Uzbekistan, fearing that the conflicts in Tajikistan and Afghanistan might spill over onto its territory, continued to build up its armed forces.

Georgia's Pres. Eduard Shevardnadze again threatened to end the mandate of the Russian peacekeeping force in the Georgian breakaway province of Abkhazia unless the Russians protected returning ethnic Georgians, who had been expelled from the region. At a CIS summit meeting in October, the mandate was extended only until the end of the year. The U.S. bought 21 MiG-29 jet fighters from Moldova after there were reports that Iran was interested in them. Some of the planes were capable of delivering nuclear weapons.

The Rest of Europe. In the civil unrest that broke out in Albania in March, the armed forces proved unwilling or unable to stand up to the rebel groups. Troops deserted; most of the country's arsenals were looted of their weapons; and the defense minister fled the country. A 6,000-strong international force led by Italy moved into the country to distribute food and medicine and to help restore order. The new government fired most of the generals in the army, and several NATO countries offered to help rebuild the Albanian military as a smaller security force. Only 45,000 weapons were turned in during an amnesty period ended on September 30, and government officials estimated that some 600,000 military weapons remained in the hands of the population.

The Muslim and Croat military forces in Bosnia and Herzegovina continued to receive shipments of military equipment—including tanks, heavy artillery, and helicopters—in a controversial program sponsored by the U.S., Kuwait, and Saudi Arabia and designed to give those forces parity with the Bosnian Serbs. In the 18 months that the June 1996 Agreement on Sub-Regional Arms Control had been in effect, the four Balkan parties—Croatia, Yugoslavia, Bosnia and Herzegovina, and the Bosnian Serbs—had destroyed almost 6,600 pieces of heavy military equipment.

Middle East. The UN Security Council refused to lift the economic sanctions it had imposed on Iraq in 1990 because of its concerns that it had not received a full accounting of Iraq's weapons of mass destruction but postponed a decision on an Anglo-American proposal to impose additional sanctions. President Hussein retaliated by briefly expelling the Americans from the UN weapons inspection teams in Iraq and threatening to shoot down American U-2 reconnaissance planes, whereupon the Security Council passed the added sanctions. In October Iranian and Iraqi warplanes violated the no-fly zone established in southern Iraq, which prompted the U.S. to speed up the deployment of an aircraft carrier battle group to the Persian Gulf. The Iranian planes had bombed anti-Iranian rebels located in Iraq. Iran's military strength and its self-sufficiency in arms production continued to grow, as the U.S. had mixed results in its efforts to prevent other countries from providing Iran with advanced weapons technology. China agreed to stop selling Iran cruise missiles, but the Russian government denied that it was supplying Iran with ballistic missile technology despite American and Israeli intelligence reports that individual Russian scientists and enterprises were involved in this activity.

Israel and Turkey continued to cooperate in defense matters. The two countries agreed to produce jointly a long-range air-to-surface missile, a development Egypt warned could trigger a regional arms race. In Lebanon Islamic guerrillas ambushed and killed an elite Israeli naval commando team as it attempted a raid on a guerrilla headquarters near Sidon; this revived the debate within Israel on the value of military operations inside Lebanon.

South and Central Asia. In Afghanistan the Taliban Islamic militia saw its fortunes ebb and flow after its forces pushed northward from the capital, Kabul, in January. In February Taliban fighters seized the strategic Shibar Pass and broke into northern Afghanistan for the first time. For a brief time they held the important city of Mazar-e Sharif after one of the allies in Gen. ʿAbd ar-Rashid Dostam's northern coalition joined forces with the Taliban. Four days later Gen. Abdul Malik changed sides again, and the Taliban were driven from the city. An offensive by another opposition leader, Ahmad Shah Masoud, drove the Taliban back to within 15 km (9.5 mi) of Kabul, and the capital was repeatedly bombed. By early September the Taliban forces were once more at the gates of Mazar-e Sharif, and by the end of the month they had cut the opposition's supply route by capturing the town of Hairatam, on the border with Uzbekistan. In mid-October, however, the opposition again pushed the Taliban back from Mazar-e Sharif.

In Sri Lanka the government seemed no closer to crushing the rebel Liberation Tigers of Tamil Eelam (LTTE) by military means than it had been in the previous 14 years of this bitter conflict. In two major offensives government troops were unable to gain control of the strategic highway leading to the LTTE's stronghold in the north of the island. In August a top Sri Lankan air force officer, Vice-Marshal Elmo Perera, was fired for allegedly having participated in a scheme to buy several armed Mi-24 attack helicopters from Ukraine and then turn them over to the LTTE.

Indian Defense Minister Mulayam Singh Yadav said in July that India was prepared to resume development of the Agni long-range ballistic missile. Work on this nuclear-capable weapon had been suspended in 1994. Both India and Pakistan continued to upgrade their armed forces. India took delivery of a number of Russian-built Su-30 fighters, and Pakistan received the first of 320 Tu-80 main battle tanks it had ordered from Ukraine. In early October Indian and Pakistani forces exchanged artillery fire

AVENTURIER/BUU/HIRES—GAMMA LIAISON

Chinese troops enter Hong Kong upon the return of the British colony to Chinese rule on July 1. Although the U.S. and Britain criticized China's decision to deploy some 4,000 soldiers during the handover, China made assurances that it would respect the freedom of Hong Kong residents.

CHRIS STEELE-PERKINS—MAGNUM

A Senegalese member of the West African peacekeeping force ECOMOG stays on the lookout at a checkpoint in Liberia. In 1997 ECOMOG troops presided over the disarming of various militias in Liberia prior to presidential elections in the country.

across their disputed border in Kashmir. Stung by U.S. criticism of its human rights record, Indonesia in June canceled a contract for nine American-built F-16 fighters, turning instead to Russia for 12 Su-30 jets.

East and Southeast Asia, Oceania. North Korea, lacking enough food to feed its population, remained a major threat to stability in the region. In April the most senior North Korean official ever to have defected warned that North Korea had plans to use both nuclear and chemical weapons against South Korea and Japan should war break out on the peninsula. Concern about the North's nuclear capability was fueled by Hans Blix, head of the International Atomic Energy Agency, who announced in May that North Korea had hidden an unknown amount of plutonium from his inspectors.

Efforts to convene four-power peace talks to end the Korean War officially, involving the two Koreas, China, and the U.S., made little progress. Two preparatory meetings broke down after the North Koreans demanded extensive food aid as a precondition for the talks and insisted that American military withdrawal from South Korea be on the agenda. Additional talks were held in December. In July North and South Korean troops exchanged heavy gunfire across the demilitarized zone. In its annual White Paper, the Japanese Defense Ministry listed North Korea as "a serious source of instability in the region." During the year the U.S. and Japan reviewed and updated the 1978 guidelines that had regulated their bilateral defense cooperation, and spelled out the sort of noncombat support Japan would provide should the U.S. have to become militarily involved in the region.

Soldiers of the British army's Black Watch regiment mounted a last ceremonial guard in Hong Kong before some 4,000 soldiers of the Chinese Peoples' Liberation Army moved into the former British colony when it was returned to Chinese rule on July 1. Turning its attention to Taiwan, China later the same month exercised its East Sea Fleet in what were described as the largest Chinese naval maneuvers in 30 years. The Chinese continued to upgrade the quality of their weaponry. Arms imports from Russia included Su-27 jet fighters, advanced artillery systems, and a diesel-powered submarine. In September Pres. Jiang Zemin announced that China's armed forces—the largest in the world—would be reduced by 500,000 over the next three years.

Civil war flared again in Cambodia after Second Prime Minister Hun Sen (*see* BIOGRAPHIES) ousted his co-premier, Prime Minister Prince Norodom Ranariddh, in a coup. By October royalist troops held only a few pockets along the border with Thailand.

Caribbean and Latin America. Ending its virtual ban on the sale of high-technology weapons to Latin-American countries, the Clinton administration announced in August that requests for such weapons in the future would be considered on a case-by-case basis. Earlier in the year Lockheed Martin had been allowed to offer its F-16 jet fighters to Chile. Many feared that this new policy would trigger an arms race in the region.

Although the military remained the final arbiter of power in Ecuador, it played a restrained role in the political crisis that followed the ouster of Pres. Abdalá Bucaram Ortíz in February. In Colombia the armed forces continued their sometimes uneven struggle against the two left-wing insurgent groups—the Revolutionary Armed Forces of Colombia (FARC) and the National Liberation Army—which were often allied with drug traffickers. The wealth derived from the drug business gave the groups access to advanced technology that matched or surpassed that used by the military. In a peace overture the FARC in June released 70 servicemen it had held for nearly a year. In August the government offered to withdraw its troops from some parts of the country in order to prepare for peace talks.

Widespread complaints of physical and mental abuse to conscripts in the Chilean military led to calls by legislators and human rights groups to end compulsory military service. During a visit to Argentina in October, President Clinton announced that he would ask Congress to approve Argentina as a non-NATO strategic security partner of the U.S.—the first country in the hemisphere to be so designated.

Africa South of the Sahara. An arc of violence stretched from the Red Sea to the South Atlantic Ocean in 1997. Ill-equipped and seldom paid, the demoralized army of Zaire's Pres. Mobutu Sese Seko (*see* OBITUARIES) was powerless to stop the advances of the rebel Alliance of Democratic Forces for the Liberation of Congo-Zaire (ADFL) led by Laurent Kabila. (*See* BIOGRAPHIES.) Aided by troops from Rwanda and Uganda, the ADFL broke out of its eastern stronghold in February. Foreign mercenaries hired by Mobutu—many of them from former Yugoslavia—did little to slow the offensive. As the ADFL approached the capital, the Zairean armed forces melted away. On May

17 the ADFL captured Kinshasa; Kabila named himself president of the country, renaming it the Democratic Republic of the Congo.

Unfortunately, the ouster of Mobutu did not bring peace to Central Africa. Tutsi-Hutu animosities, especially in the eastern Congo (Kinshasa), generated renewed attacks by various rebel groups into neighbouring Rwanda, Uganda, and Burundi. Within Congo itself, anti-Tutsi feelings prompted several groups that had once supported Kabila to turn against his army, portraying it as a foreign invader.

Even more serious fighting rocked the neighbouring Republic of the Congo, where more than 4,000 American, British, Belgian, French, and Portuguese troops had been deployed in case they were needed to evacuate their citizens from Kinshasa. In early June fighting between government forces and the militia loyal to former Congolese ruler Gen. Denis Sassou-Nguesso broke out in the capital, Brazzaville. In August it spread to the interior of the country. Fierce fighting in the capital continued through September and October, with the airport changing hands several times and artillery fire often falling on neighbouring Kinshasa. In October some 1,000 Angolan troops from the enclave of Cabinda entered the conflict, fighting alongside Sassou-Nguesso's Cobra militia in southern Congo. Warning that the expanding conflict was a serious threat to peace in west-central Africa, UN Secretary-General Kofi Annan (*see* BIOGRAPHIES) asked the Security Council to approve a peacekeeping force for the Congo (Brazzaville), but Nguesso claimed victory before the UN could act.

Fighting continued throughout most of the year in southern Sudan as the govern-

Approximate Strengths of Selected Regular Armed Forces of the World

Country	Military personnel in 000s				Warships: Submarines				Combat aircraft[1]				Defense expenditure as % of 1996 GDP
	Total	Army	Navy	Air Force[2]	Nuclear	Diesel	Aircraft Carriers/ Cruisers	Destroyers/ Frigates	Bombers and fighter-ground attack	Fighters	Recon-nais-sance	Tanks[3]	
I. NATO													
Belgium	44.5[4]	28.5	2.7	12.0	—	—	—	3	132		—	326	1.6
Canada	61.6[4]	21.9	9.4	14.6	—	3	—	20	122	—	18	114	1.5
Denmark	32.9	19.0	6.0	7.9	—	5	—	3	64	—	—	353	1.7
France	380.8[4]	219.9	63.3[5]	83.4	10	4	3	39	372	121	71	768	3.1
Germany	347.1[4]	239.9	27.8	76.9	—	16	—	15	296	177	53	3,248	1.7
Greece	162.3	116.0	19.5	26.8	—	8	—	15	209	110	29	1,735	4.8
Italy	325.1[4]	188.3	44.0	63.6	—	8	2	30	235	24	45	1,325	2.2
Netherlands, The	57.2[4]	27.0	13.8	12.0	—	4	—	16	171	—	15	600	2.1
Norway	33.6[4]	15.8	9.0	7.9	—	12	—	4	58	15	6	170	2.4
Portugal	59.3[4]	32.1	14.8	7.7	—	3	—	10	91	—	5	186	2.8
Spain	197.5	128.5	39.0[5]	30.0	—	8	1	17	47	149	21	776	1.5
Turkey	639.0	525.0	51.0[5]	53.0	—	15	—	21	259	165	39	4,205	3.9
United Kingdom	213.8	112.2	44.9[5]	56.7	15	—	3	35	316	107	67	541	3.0
United States	1,447.6	495.0	570.4[5]	382.2	93	—	42	101	3,849	332	236	8,239	3.6
II. NON-NATO EUROPE													
Albania	unk	unk	2.5	6.0	—	1	—	—	47	51	—	721	6.7
Armenia	60.0[4]	58.6	—	—	—	—	—	—	5	1	—	102	6.2
Austria	45.5	45.5	—	—	—	—	—	—	53	—	—	169	0.9
Azerbaijan	66.7	53.3	2.2	11.2	—	—	—	2	15	19	2	270	5.8
Belarus	81.8[4]	50.5	—	22.0	—	—	—	—	129	89	12	1,778	4.2
Bosnia and Herzegovina	56.0	56.0	—	—	—	—	—	—	—	—	—	130	6.3
Bosnian Serbs	30.0	30.0	—	—	—	—	—	—	20	—	—	570	n/a
Bulgaria	101.5[4]	50.4	6.1	19.3	—	2	—	1	112	84	21	1,475	3.3
Croatia	58.0	50.0	3.0	5.0	—	1	—	—	30	—	—	285	6.8
Czech Republic	61.7[4]	27.0	—	17.0	—	—	—	—	57	72	—	952	2.4
Finland	31.0	27.0	2.1	1.9	—	—	—	—	—	98	—	196	2.0
Georgia	33.2[4]	12.6	2.0	3.0	—	—	—	2	7	—	—	79	3.4
Hungary	49.1	31.6	—	17.5	—	—	—	—	—	80	—	797	1.7
Poland	241.7	168.6	17.0	56.1	—	3	—	2	109	231	16	1,729	2.8
Romania	226.9[4]	129.3	17.5[5]	47.6	—	1	—	7	88	203	24	1,255	2.3
Slovakia	41.2[4]	23.8	—	12.0	—	—	—	—	33	76	5	478	2.6
Sweden	53.3	35.1	9.5	8.7	—	10	—	—	162	193	33	539	2.9
Ukraine	387.4[4]	161.5	16.0[5]	124.4	—	3	—	4	450	456	112	4,063	3.0
Yugoslavia	114.2	90.0	7.5[5]	16.7	—	4	—	4	123	80	38	1,270	8.7
III. RUSSIA													
Russia	1,240.0[4]	420.0	220.0[5]	400.0[6]	97	32	23	37	1,321	1,490	344	15,780	6.5
IV. MIDDLE EAST AND NORTH AFRICA; SUB-SAHARAN AFRICA; LATIN AMERICA													
Algeria	124.0	107.0	7.0	10.0	—	2	—	3	55	116	10	890	4.0
Egypt	450.0	320.0	20.0	110.0	—	8	—	9	189	363	20	3,700	4.5
Iran	518.0	450.0	38.0[5]	30.0	—	3	—	4	170	124	14	1,390	5.0
Iraq	387.5	350.0	2.5	35.0	—	—	—	2	136	180	—	2,700	8.3
Israel	175.0	134.0	9.0	32.0	—	3	—	—	426	—	22	4,300	12.1
Jordan	104.0	90.0	0.6	13.4	—	—	—	—	65	32	—	1,141	5.6
Lebanon	55.1	53.3	1.0	0.8	—	—	—	—	—	3	—	315	4.4
Libya	65.0	35.0	8.0	22.0	—	4	—	3	200	209	11	985	5.1
Morocco	196.3	175.0	7.8	13.5	—	—	—	1	70	15	4	524	4.3
Oman	43.5[4]	25.0	4.2	4.1	—	—	—	—	47	—	—	103	15.6
Saudi Arabia	105.5	70.0	13.5[5]	22.0	—	—	—	8	187	139	10	1,055	12.8
Sudan, The	79.7	75.0	1.7	3.0	—	—	—	—	50	6	—	280	4.3
Syria	320.0	215.0	5.0	100.0[2]	—	3	—	4	240	335	14	4,600	4.8
Tunisia	35.0	27.0	4.5	3.5	—	—	—	—	44	—	—	84	2.0
United Arab Emirates	64.5	59.0	1.5	4.0	—	—	—	—	72	28	8	5	5.2
Yemen	66.3	61.0	1.8	3.5	—	—	—	—	29	32	—	1,125	3.7
Angola	110.5	98.0	1.5	11.0	—	—	—	—	14	4	9	300	6.4
Burundi	22.0[4]	18.5	—	—	—	—	—	—	6	—	—	—	4.1

ment's war with the rebel Sudan People's Liberation Army (SPLA) entered its 14th year. Both sides claimed significant gains, but the government had some success in attracting rebel faction leaders to its side. Meanwhile, officials in Kampala charged that Sudanese government troops and planes had crossed into northern Uganda to support Ugandan rebels. In September SPLA leader John Garang agreed to resume peace talks, and they convened in Nairobi, Kenya, the following month. The talks quickly broke down, however, and were recessed until April 1998.

Elsewhere in Africa an army coup in May overthrew the government of Sierra Leone. Some 200 U.S. troops were deployed to Freetown to evacuate American and third-country personnel to a U.S. amphibious assault ship offshore. The Nigerian-led West African peacekeeping force (ECOMOG) in Sierra Leone was humiliated by the new government, which claimed to have captured more than 400 Nigerian troops in heavy fighting in October. The Nigerians bombed and shelled the capital and its harbour in an effort to enforce an economic blockade of the junta. ECOMOG was more successful in neighbouring Liberia, where it presided over the disarming of the various militias prior to the June elections that brought former warlord Charles Taylor (*see* BIOGRAPHIES) to power. In October Taylor announced plans to form a new national army.

New Technology. Australian scientists developed a handheld land mine detector; it combined a ground-probing radar and a conventional metal detector that could detect both metal and plastic mines.

(DOUGLAS L. CLARKE)

This article updates the *Macropædia* article The Technology of WAR.

Approximate Strengths of Selected Regular Armed Forces of the World (continued)

Country	Military personnel in 000s: Total	Army	Navy	Air Force[2]	Warships: Submarines: Nuclear	Diesel	Aircraft Carriers/ Cruisers	Destroyers/ Frigates	Combat aircraft[1]: Bombers and fighter-ground attack	Fighters	Recon-naissance	Tanks[3]	Defense expenditure as % of 1996 GDP
Cameroon	22.1[4]	11.5	1.3	0.3	—	—	—	—	15	—	—	—	2.4
Chad	30.3[4]	25.0	—	0.3	—	—	—	—	4	—	—	60	2.7
Congo, Dem. Rep. of	unk	unk	unk		—	—	—	—	unk	unk	unk	60	2.8
Eritrea	46.0	unk	unk	unk	—	—	—	1	6	—	—	unk	7.5
Ethiopia	120.0[4]	100.0	—	unk	—	—	—	—	85	—	0	350	2.0
Kenya	24.2	20.5	1.2	2.5	—	—	—	—	30	—	—	76	2.2
Nigeria	77.0	62.0	5.5	9.5	—	—	—	1	92	—	—	200	3.5
Rwanda	62.0[4]	55.0	—	—	—	—	—	—	—	—	—	—	6.3
South Africa	79.4[4]	54.3	8.0	11.1	—	3	—	—	114	—	8	224	1.8
Tanzania	34.6	30.0	1.0	3.6	—	—	—	—	—	24	—	65	2.5
Uganda	55.0	55.0	—	—	—	—	—	—	1	—	—	80	2.4
Zambia	21.6	20.0	—	1.6	—	—	—	—	49	14	—	30	1.8
Zimbabwe	39.0	35.0	—	4.0	—	—	—	—	29	12	15	32	3.9
Argentina	73.0	41.0	20.0[5]	12.0	—	3	—	13	227	—	5	326	1.5
Bolivia	33.5	25.0	4.5[5]	4.0	—	—	—	—	15	18	—	—	2.1
Brazil	314.7	200.0	64.7[5]	50.0	—	6	1	21	249	16	4	—	2.1
Chile	94.3	51.0	29.8[5]	13.5	—	4	—	8	73	15	16	130	3.5
Colombia	146.3	121.0	18.0[5]	7.3	—	2	—	4	59	—	13	—	2.6
Cuba	53.0	38.0	5.0[5]	10.0	—	2	—	1	10	120	—	1,500	5.4
Dominican Republic	24.5	15.0	4.0[5]	5.5	—	—	—	—	10	—	—	—	1.1
Ecuador	57.1	50.0	4.1[5]	3.0	—	2	—	2	42	14	—	3	3.4
El Salvador	28.4	25.7	1.1[5]	1.6	—	—	—	—	12	—	8	—	1.5
Guatemala	40.7	38.5	1.5[5]	0.7	—	—	—	—	14	—	—	—	1.4
Mexico	175.0	130.0	37.0[5]	8.0	—	—	—	7	101	10	23	—	0.8
Peru	125.0	85.0	25.0[5]	15.0	—	8	2	5	70	23	7	300	1.9
Uruguay	25.6	17.6	5.0[5]	3.0	—	—	—	3	33	—	1	—	2.3
Venezuela	79.0[4]	34.0	15.0[5]	7.0	—	2	—	6	99	—	19	70	1.2
V. SOUTH AND CENTRAL ASIA; EAST ASIA AND OCEANIA													
Australia	57.4	25.4	14.3	17.7	—	3	—	10	103	—	23	71	2.2
Bangladesh	121.0	101.0	10.5	9.5	—	—	—	4	49	—	—	140	1.7
Cambodia	140.5[4]	84.0	5.0	1.5	—	—	—	—	2	21	—	100	5.7
China	2,840.0	2,090.0	280.0[5]	470.0	6	55	—	54	816	3,161	298	8,500	5.7
India	1,145.0	980.0	55.0[5]	110.0	—	17	1	24	411	380	54	3,314	2.8
Indonesia	461.0[4]	220.0	43.0[5]	21.0	—	2	—	17	68	12	52	—	2.1
Japan	235.6[4]	147.7	42.5	44.1	—	16	—	58	110	228	140	1,110	1.0
Kazakstan	35.1	20.0	0.1	15.0	—	—	—	—	69	32	12	630	2.6
Korea, North	1,055.0	923.0	47.0	85.0	—	26	—	3	607	—	—	3,000	27.2
Korea, South	672.0	560.0	60.0[5]	52.0	—	6	—	40	303	130	51	2,190	3.3
Laos	29.0	25.0	0.5	3.5	—	—	—	—	30	—	—	30	4.1
Malaysia	111.5	85.0	14.0	12.5	—	—	—	4	54	33	7	—	4.2
Myanmar (Burma)	429.0	400.0	20.0[5]	9.0	—	—	—	—	55	36	—	130	7.6
Nepal	46.0	46.0	—	—	—	—	—	—	—	—	—	—	0.9
Pakistan	587.0	520.0	22.0[5]	45.0	—	9	—	11	168	242	26	2,120	5.7
Philippines	110.5	70.0	24.0[5]	16.5	—	—	—	1	12	5	30	—	2.0
Singapore	70.0	55.0	9.0	6.0	—	—	—	—	94	37	8	60	5.5
Sri Lanka	117.0	95.0	12.0	10.0	—	—	—	—	22	—	—	25	6.5
Taiwan	376.0	240.0	68.0[5]	68.0	—	4	—	36	402	—	31	719	4.9
Thailand	266.0	150.0	73.0[5]	43.0	—	—	1	14	161	50	55	277	2.5
Uzbekistan	70.0[4]	45.0	—	4.0	—	—	—	—	49	64	10	370	3.8
Vietnam	492.0	420.0	42.0[5]	30.0	—	—	—	7	71	124	4	1,315	4.0

Note: Data exclude most paramilitary, security, and irregular forces. Naval data exclude vessels of less than 100 tons standard displacement. Figures are for June 1997. Because of substantive changes in national forces and reassessments of evidence, data may not be comparable with previous editions.

[1]Includes combat aircraft from all services, including naval and air defense. Light strike/counterinsurgency aircraft are included in bomb/fighter–ground attack category. Reconnaissance includes maritime reconnaissance and antisubmarine warfare aircraft.

[2]Includes air defense troops.

[3]Main battle tanks (MBT), weighing at least 16.5 metric tons with gun of at least 75-mm calibre.

[4]Some countries have staffs, centrally controlled units, support services, military police, regular armed forces not responsible to Ministry of Defense, and the like, which means total armed forces are greater than the sum of the three armed forces.

[5]Includes marines or naval infantry.

[6]Includes strategic missile forces.

Source: International Institute for Strategic Studies, 23 Tavistock Street, London, *The Military Balance 1997–1998.*

Performing Arts

MUSIC

Classical. Although the general atmosphere in the world of classical concerts and especially opera had been increasingly pessimistic in recent years, the approach of the millennium was bringing a sense of anticipation that could be described only as healthy. Although nothing specific had occurred to bring this about, there seemed to be a growing determination to make the 21st century an artistic success. One of the most encouraging aspects of the current situation was that during recent decades the leading educational faculties in music had found highly motivated and inspirational teachers, who had been able to release the inherent gifts within their students. For several years New York's Juilliard School, the Curtis Institute of Music in Philadelphia, Stanford University, the Indiana University School of Music, London's Royal Academy of Music and Royal College of Music, the Royal Northern College of Music in Manchester, Eng., the Franz Liszt Hochschule für Musik in Weimar, Ger., the Hochschule der Kunste in Berlin, and the Conservatoire International de Musique de Paris had been among the schools producing first-class musicians.

On a more discouraging note, as individual patrons were forced to tighten their purse strings and governments were unable to balance their books, the cash available for many orchestras, opera houses, and even some local festivals was depleted. The greatest survived, and those performers who became household names continued to flourish. Nevertheless, many talented artists were unable to find work.

One country that defied the economic gloom in 1997 was Spain, where there was both government and private money for the arts. From the striking new Guggenheim Museum in Bilbao to the Palace of Music in Valencia and the Festivals in the Canaries and the Jérez de la Frontera, music and opera were thriving at all levels. After having overcome many problems and having spent billions of pesetas, Madrid, as befitted the nation's capital, reopened the rebuilt Teatro Real, filling a void that had blighted the city's music life for more than seven decades. Tenor Plácido Domingo sang in the premiere of Antón García Abril's opera *Divinas Palabras* during the opening week.

In Argentina the world-famous Teatro Colón in Buenos Aires was confronted with budgetary problems. Whereas other theatres were forced to cancel some new productions, the Colón's authorities decided to double the price of the standing-room-only tickets. In Brazil the uneasy economic climate seemed certain to affect the coming seasons at São Paulo's Teatro Municipal, which was suffering from public indifference to its new works. In Chile, by contrast, the Teatro Municipal in Santiago was enjoying both artistic and economic success.

In London during the year, there was great controversy concerning the fate of the city's two opera companies. The Royal Opera closed on July 14 for expensive major redevelopment and planned to reopen with Verdi's *Falstaff* in 1999. In the meantime, the English National Opera, an old Victorian theatre with excellent acoustics, was being forced to make a decision involving the maintenance of the building. The cost of rebuilding and taking the theatre into the 21st century was astronomical, and the administration was considering finding another site on which it could build a new opera house, incorporating many innovations. Many of the opera's patrons, however, did not want to lose the old building.

A much-needed new opera house overshadowed all other cultural subjects in Oslo. One problem that delayed construction was the rivalry between the eastern and western parts of the city, each of which was insisting that the new opera house be built in its area. In the meantime, the growing reputation of the Norwegian Opera was being stifled by having to operate in a small theatre with few facilities. During the year its repertoire included an imaginative production of *My Fair Lady,* and the company took its remarkably effective production of Wagner's complete *Ring* cycle—the first ever to be staged in Norway—to the innovative Theatre Royal in Norwich, Eng. Another great Norwegian institution was the Oslo Philharmonic Orchestra, which was invited to be orchestra in residence at the Musikverein in Vienna during the autumn.

The Theatre Royal became an important operatic and ballet venue during 1997, thanks to the enterprising direction of Peter Wilson, who not only brought to it the *Ring* cycle but also helped produce the first staging of William Alwyn's operatic setting of August Strindberg's *Miss Julie.* The theatre's season was an example of the internationalism of the music world, which had become a constant feature in recent years. No concert season seemed complete without a visiting orchestra and artists, and audiences were often given a taste of new music.

Anniversaries of four composers whose names were always in programs were celebrated in 1997. Brahms died on April 3, 1897; Mendelssohn died on Nov. 4, 1847; Schubert was born on Jan. 31, 1797; and Donizetti was born on Nov. 29, 1797. Needless to say, these anniversaries gave orchestras the opportunity to air those composers' music, including some works that were often neglected.

Another centenary was that of the Czech-born Erich Korngold, who was born in Brno on May 29, 1897. Those who had thought of him only as a Hollywood film music composer had their ears opened during 1997, when a wealth of enthralling and often beautiful work emerged, including a violin concerto, a left-hand piano concerto, and operas, including *Der Ring des Polycrates* and *Violanta.* Korngold was probably the youngest composer to have had his music played at one of the famous Promenade Concerts in London; when Korngold was only 15, Sir Henry Wood conducted one of his works. Argentina celebrated the centenary of the tango by taking the Orquestra Mariano Mores to London's Royal Festival Hall on July 24, delighting an enthusiastic audience.

In the United States the New York Philharmonic opened its season with a concert that celebrated both the centenary of Brahms's death and the 70th birthday of music director Kurt Masur. The New York City Opera opened its season with a successful modern-dress production of Verdi's *Macbeth* and later enjoyed acclaim for its production of Handel's *Xerxes.* The Metropolitan Opera won praise for its production of Wagner's *Das Rheingold.* A highlight at New York's Carnegie Hall was a performance by the Music Festival of India in celebration of the 50th anniversary of Indian independence. In Chicago a $110 million renovation of Orchestra Hall was completed, and the new Symphony Center opened in October, in time for the beginning of the Chicago Symphony Orchestra's new season. A threatened strike by the orchestra's musicians was averted at the last minute when they reached agreement on a new three-year contract. Lyric Opera of Chicago presented the world premiere of Anthony Davis's *Amistad,* about a rebellion aboard a slave ship in the 19th century.

Among the most interesting premieres during 1997 were two works by the German composer Hans Werner Henze. His opera *Venus and Adonis* was staged in Munich, Ger., at the National Theatre in January, and his long-awaited Ninth Symphony was premiered in Berlin in September. There seemed little doubt that both would be performed on the international circuit before the decade ended. Maria Bosse-Sparleder staged another of Henze's operas, *The Bassarids,* in a German version by Dresden's Semperoper on May Day. Helmut Lachenmann was not yet as well known as Henze, but his opera *The Little Match Girl,* which was first presented in Hamburg in January, seemed likely to find its way onto the world's stages. Also much debated was a full-length symphonic poem, *Standing Stone,* by Sir Paul McCartney, which received its premiere by the London Symphony Orchestra on October 14.

The Festival of Perth in Western Australia was the setting for the first performance of Richard Barrett's *Opening of the Mouth,* a song cycle of four poems by Paul Celan. The intention of the 90-minute work was to address the atrocities of the Holocaust, which Celan had survived. It was scored for singers, instrumentalists, and electronics. The premiere was given in a huge abandoned railway workshop, which provided a sense of hell on Earth.

Recent works by the veteran Greek composer Yannis Xenakis concentrated complex ideas into short time periods, and his *Omega* at the Huddersfield Festival in Great Britain was particularly impressive in that regard. Another important Huddersfield premiere was Pascal Dusapin's *Romeo et Juliette.* The Edinburgh Festival introduced James Dillon's *Blitzschlag,* a work for flute and orchestra, which the composer had begun some years earlier. Rossini's rarely seen opera *Eduardo e Cristina* was staged at the Wildbad Festival in Germany, one of several of the composer's works that had been resurrected following his bicentenary in 1992.

Many operas were currently known only through concert performances of their overtures, and it was especially heartwarming to see them properly staged. During the year some German opera houses were delving into this repertoire with highly successful results. One of the most notable was the production on May 3 of Dmitry Kabalevsky's *Colas Breugnon* in the Deutsch-Sorbisches Volkstheater of Bautzen, near Dresden.

Violinist Nigel Kennedy made a welcome return to the concert platform, directing a Bach violin concerto and the Double Concerto, with Katherine Gowers, and also play-

JACK VARTOOGIAN

Jazz master Wynton Marsalis leads the Lincoln Center Jazz Orchestra in his three-hour operatic composition *Blood on the Fields,* a powerful work inspired by the experience of African slaves in America. *Blood on the Fields* was awarded the Pulitzer Prize for music in 1997.

ing the Beethoven violin concerto with the English Chamber Orchestra. Kennedy and Gowers toured in Britain, opening in Birmingham's sumptuous Symphony Hall and also appearing in London's Barbican Hall. These concerts also brought the Japanese conductor Shuntaro Sato to a wide audience, as he had been appointed associate conductor of the English Chamber Orchestra. An exciting young conductor, he had an impact similar to that of the young Simon Rattle.

Among the distinguished musical figures who died during 1997 were the great Russian pianist Sviatoslav Richter, the recorder virtuoso and teacher Carl Dolmetsch, the harpsichordist and Baroque specialist George Malcolm, the British composers Robert Simpson and Wilfred Josephs, and the conductor Georg Solti. (*See* OBITUARIES.)

(DENBY RICHARDS)

Jazz. The Pulitzer Prize music jury in 1965 recommended awarding a special prize for lifetime achievement to Duke Ellington. The Pulitzer advisory board rejected the recommendation. Two of the three music jurists resigned in protest, and a storm of criticism appeared in the American press, whereas the 66-year-old Ellington only said, "Fate is being kind to me. Fate doesn't want me to be too famous too young." The incident was recalled in 1997 because that was the year an extended work by an Ellington enthusiast, Wynton Marsalis, was awarded the Pulitzer Prize for music. Marsalis's award-winning composition was *Blood on the Fields,* a cantata about slavery, first performed in 1994. When the album was released in 1997, *Blood on the Fields* gained praise for the composer's ingenuity of orchestration and criticism for his melodic and libretto-writing weaknesses.

Another composer in the jazz and classical music worlds experienced a replay of coincidence. Anthony Davis's opera *Amistad,* based on an 1839 slave rebellion, premiered at Lyric Opera of Chicago in November just weeks before the release of Steven Spielberg's major film of the same story. Five years earlier the recording of Davis's previous opera, *X, The Life and Times of Malcolm X*, was released in the same year as Spike Lee's popular film on the same subject.

The major composer-improviser Ornette Coleman received a mixed reception for what was billed as a historic four-day concert series titled *? civilization* at New York City's Avery Fisher Hall. Few of his extended-form, large-scale works had been publicly performed, apart from *Skies of America* (1972), which reappeared in this series. As revised by Coleman, *Skies* alternated sections played by the New York Philharmonic, conducted by Kurt Masur, with sections played by Coleman and his jazz-rock band Prime Time. A second ensemble reunited Coleman, on alto saxophone, with two colleagues, Charlie Haden (bass) and Billy Higgins (drums), who had joined him in inventing free jazz in 1958; this was a straightforward jazz concert, joined by trumpeter Wallace Roney and pianist Kenny Barron. Prime Time returned for the final concert, which consisted of Coleman's work *Tone Dialing,* featuring musicians, rappers, dancers, a sword-swallower, acrobats, and singers Lou Reed and Laurie Anderson. Probably Coleman's major work of the year was *Colors* (Harmolodic/Verve), his album of brilliantly lyrical improvised duets with pianist Joachim Kühn.

New York City became a jazz hotbed for two weeks in June when George Wein's venerable JVC Jazz Festival and the first annual Texaco New York Jazz Festival (formerly the What Is Jazz? Festival) were held simultaneously, each at a number of Manhattan venues. The JVC festival, as usual, concentrated on older jazz traditions and young bop-oriented players, including concert tributes to Hoagy Carmichael, Bix Beiderbecke, and Louis Armstrong, and used marginally jazz (an 80th-birthday Lena Horne concert) and nonjazz shows (Aretha Franklin's Gospel Crusade for AIDS) to attract crowds. The Texaco New York festival included longtime bop, pop, and Latin jazz masters but emphasized more modern idioms, especially free jazz, from big bands to solo concerts. The competition apparently was a healthy stimulus to both festivals—Wein claimed his gross was double that of the previous year, and the Knitting Factory nightclub, centre of the Texaco festival, reportedly sold out every night but one. Meanwhile, the Monterey (Calif.) Jazz Festival, one of the first important annual jazz events, was 40 years old in 1997.

The International Association of Jazz Educators was the best-known jazz recipient of a National Endowment for the Arts grant. In 1947 the University of North Texas, then North Texas State University, introduced

(continued on page 286)

SPECIAL REPORT

Listening to the Music of the World

by Chris Heim

"World Music"—What Is It? The dawning of a new musical "global village" or an unfocused, unsuccessful marketing ploy? The revitalization of time-honoured cultural traditions or cynical pop exploitation and New Age natterings? Old field recordings or brave new electronic blends? It may, in fact, be all those things, none of them, and perhaps even something more. In the most general and accepted sense, "world music" expresses the new interest on the part of the West in musical styles and traditions outside its own mainstream and from other countries and cultures. Since its emergence in about 1983, world music has come to embrace everything from field recordings of isolated peoples to new urban styles, traditional revivals to New Age explorations, 1950s "exotica" reissues to 1990s "ethnotechno" recordings.

Among the styles that have attracted attention in recent years under the banner of world music are a variety of African urban dance musics (including Congolese *soukous,* Nigerian *juju,* north African *rai,* and South African *mbaqanga*); contemporary pop flamenco (for example, the Gipsy Kings); a tango revival (aided by the 1996 film *Evita* and reissues of albums by nuevo tango master Astor Piazzolla); the growing boom in Latin-American rock, pop, and salsa (*see* BIOGRAPHIES: *Celia Cruz*); a strong new Celtic scene spurred by the success of theatrical productions such as *Riverdance* and *Lord of the Dance* (*see* BIOGRAPHIES: *Michael Flatley*) and featuring a new generation of traditional and Celtic-rock bands; a host of traditional revivals such as klezmer (music of the Eastern European Jews) and *qawwali* (the songs of the Sufi mystics; *see* OBITUARIES: *Nusrat Fateh Ali Khan*); various Scandinavian folk musics; Cajun and zydeco from Louisiana; Afro-Peruvian; Hawaiian slack-key guitar; and even the banned prewar Berlin cabaret music (*see* BIOGRAPHIES: *Ute Lemper*). Influenced by world music, New Age and smooth jazz artists have introduced world-music instruments and simplified rhythms into their work. In jazz, Afro-Cuban and Brazilian influences have seen a powerful resurgence in recent years. Fueled by the success of the Deep Forest project, which mixed dance music with Pygmy song, a new wave of "ethnotechno" bands have scored hits on the dance music charts with tunes that combine synthesizer and heavy-rhythm tracks with samplings of voices and styles from around the world.

World Music Emerges. Western interest in music from other cultures is not new. Art music (in works by such composers as Edvard Grieg, Claude Debussy, Antonin Dvorak, Bela Bartok, and Louis Moreau Gottschalk) has a long history of incorporating folk influences. Moreover, rock, jazz, blues, and even country music arose from the fusion of African and European forms. The 1950s witnessed the golden age of the mambo, with origins in Cuba, followed by other Latin-American dance crazes. Performers such as Martin Denny, Arthur Lyman, and Esquivel beckoned listeners to ersatz musical holidays with "exotica," a giddy pop that simulated, supposedly, the sounds of faraway, enchanting places. Still later, the folk music boom focused attention on more authentic traditional musics from around the world. Also in the early 1960s, the world was captivated by the melding of jazz and Brazilian music into bossa nova. When the Beatles traveled to India later in the decade, ragas were the rage.

A number of trends began to converge in the 1980s to stimulate the modern world music movement. These included an expanding global communications system, growing interest in diversity and multiculturalism, and improvements in technology that made it easier to make and distribute high-quality audio recordings anywhere in the world. New impetus came from some of rock's more adventurous artists, such as David Byrne, Peter Gabriel, Brian Eno, and Ry Cooder, who helped bring styles, rhythms, and musicians from other parts of the world to Western pop audiences. The most popular and commercially successful such effort was surely Paul Simon's 1986 *Graceland* album. Inspired by and employing South African musicians, including the vocal group Ladysmith Black Mambazo, this award-winning project opened the door to a host of new musics and musicians.

Passing Fad or Underground Phenomenon? Almost as soon as *Graceland* piqued audience interest, some pundits were declaring world music dead. Indeed, few records or performers have attracted a mass audience, racked up platinum record sales, or won broad-based media interest. For every declaration about the death of world music, however, there are other signs that point to its slow rise and steady growth.

JACK VARTOOGIAN

Nicolas Reyes of the Gipsy Kings performs at Radio City Music Hall.

First, world music had little in the way of industry structure to support it a decade ago. Musicians now have a variety of options for live performance: clubs that specialize in world music; package tours such as the WOMAD (World of Music, Arts and Dance) Festival, Africa Fête, and Reggae Sunsplash; and such major international festivals as the New Orleans Jazz and Heritage Festival and similar conclaves in Istanbul; Montreux, Switz.; Montreal; Toronto; and Vancouver, B.C.—to name but a few. Second, all manner of books, magazines, and guides to world music have become available. Radio (usually noncommercial community and public radio in the U.S.) offers local and syndicated world and ethnic music programming. The syndicated radio show *Afropop Worldwide,* for example, was by 1997 heard on 120 stations in the U.S. as well as stations in Europe and Africa.

Third, the music itself has become easier to find and own. A decade ago only a handful of U.S. and European labels offered world titles. Scores of labels with names such as Shanachie, Stern's Africa, Tinder, Rounder, Island, Xenophile, Qbadisc, Hemisphere, Earthworks, Luaka Bop, Nonesuch, World Circuit, Ellipsis Arts..., GlobeStyle, Putumayo, Music of the World, Mesa, and Earthbeat have popped up. New distribution channels include catalog and Internet outlets and such nontraditional retail outlets as bookstores, museum shops, arts and crafts stores, coffeehouses, and gourmet cooking shops. World music seems to be establishing itself as a small but sturdy niche music. By way of comparison, jazz and classical music each account for only about 2–4% of annual record sales in the U.S.; folk music and blues are somewhat smaller slices of the market—but they are not considered failures for lack of mass acceptance.

Brave New World Music. Looking to the future of world music, some fear that this melange of styles is the harbinger of an impending global cultural disaster, a multinational megamedia tsunami that will wipe out all "authentic" musical forms and replace them with one slick, all-encompassing, hideous musical blob. Even while frothy international pop is the lingua franca of music around the world and artists such as Madonna, Michael Jackson, and Mariah Carey regularly top sales charts in many countries, local artists and musics remain a strong force. A number of ethnomusicological studies suggest that every culture deals with new musical influences, encounters, and even invasions in different ways, and the results are different and very distinctive musical syntheses. As has been seen, many of today's most treasured musical expressions are themselves the result of previous cultural interactions. Still, traditional musical revivals all across the globe suggest an enduring resistance to global cultural homogenization.

Chris Heim is Music Director of WBEZ, the National Public Radio station in Chicago.

JACK VARTOOGIAN

The buoyant, energetic style of the popular group Tarika is rooted in the traditional music of Madagascar.

E. CATARINA—RETNA

Bono, lead singer of the Irish band U2, sings during a July concert in Rotterdam, Neth., where the group kicked off its PopMart world tour. U2 later staged a huge show in war-torn Sarajevo, Bosnia and Herzegovina.

(continued from page 283)

dance band as a major field of study for a bachelor's degree. Famed big bands, most notably those of Woody Herman and Stan Kenton, recruited its graduates, and in 1981 the school began offering master's degrees in jazz studies. In its 50th year, the school had nine laboratory bands, a jazz repertory band, and many small ensembles of student musicians. At JazzFest USA, held at Universal Studios, Orlando, Fla., the studios, *Down Beat* magazine, and the Thelonious Monk Institute played host to more than 300 student musicians from middle school to college age and offered more than $600,000 in scholarships.

Rock elements dominated jazz in acid jazz, which continued to attract audiences and record buyers with mixtures of post-James Brown funk and hip-hop rhythms, bop-and-funk melodies, and rappers. The best-known performers included Liquid Soul, featuring tenor-sax soloist Mars Williams, and saxophonist Branford Marsalis's acid-jazz band Buckshot LeFonque, which toured and offered the Columbia compact disc *Music Evolution*.

Jazz reissues began to appear on CD-ROMs with mixed results. N2K Encoded Music issued *Gerry Mulligan Legacy,* with eight tracks (35 minutes) of the arranger-saxophonist's recordings and three video snippets of him playing, two from the famed *The Sound of Jazz* video, and snatches of Mulligan and Patti Austin singing, Art Farmer and Wynton Marsalis talking, and a poem by Mulligan to his mother. The CD-ROM of John Coltrane's *Blue Train* (Blue Note) was considerably more successful, comprising the original 1957 album and alternate takes (59 minutes of music), extensive reminiscences of Coltrane by seven colleagues, a televised Coltrane tenor-saxophone solo, a rare interview with recording engineer Rudy Van Gelder, and a series of photographs of Coltrane sessions by Frank Wolff.

Evan Parker Chicago Solo (OkkaDisk) was the first unaccompanied tenor-saxophone album by British improviser Evan Parker, creator of several previous soprano-sax solo works. Pianist Horace Tapscott offered the sparkling *Thoughts of Dar Es Salaam* (Arabesque), and Australian alto saxophonist Bernie McGann made his U.S. debut at the Chicago Jazz Festival and also led his band in the CD *Playground* (Terra Nova). Tenor saxophonist Fred Anderson led a freely improvising trio in *Fred* (Southport) and then sparred with fellow tenorist Ken Vandermark in *Fred Anderson/DKV Trio* (OkkaDisk). Roscoe Mitchell created unaccompanied solos on woodwinds and percussion in *Sound Songs* (Delmark), and then orchestrated some of those solo works for his nine-piece band at the Texaco New York festival. Guitarists Pat Metheny and Derek Bailey, joined by drummers Gregg Bendian and Paul Wertico, created the three-CD set *The Sign of 4* (Knitting Factory Works), and Metheny and bassist Charlie Haden duetted in *Beyond the Missouri Sky* (Verve).

The year's deaths included big-band blues singer Jimmy Witherspoon, violinist Stéphane Grappelli, trumpeter Doc Cheatham, blues guitarist Jimmy Rogers, drummer Tony Williams (*see* OBITUARIES), drummer Charles Moffett, critic Robert Palmer, British swing trombonist George Chisholm, and arranger George Handy. Two noteworthy biographies, *Louis Armstrong: An Extravagant Life* by Laurence Bergreen and *Space Is the Place: The Lives and Times of Sun Ra* by John Szwed, the latter a remarkable job of research, were published.

(JOHN LITWEILER)

Popular. In Great Britain 1997 would be remembered for the tragic, untimely death of Diana, princess of Wales, and the remarkable scenes of public grief that followed her funeral on September 6. (*See* OBITUARIES.) For many, the most poignant moment of the service at Westminster Abbey was the appearance by her friend Elton John singing a specially rewritten version of his hit "Candle in the Wind." Originally a song dedicated to Marilyn Monroe, it was refashioned and became a tribute to "England's rose," and a single, recorded directly after John's appearance at the funeral, was rush-released to raise money for the Diana, Princess of Wales Memorial Fund. The record became an instant best-seller and the fastest-selling record in British pop history. After 37 days it had sold almost 32 million copies, and it thereby became the best-selling single of all time (succeeding Bing Crosby's "White Christmas," which sold 30 million copies). It was estimated that the single would raise some £25 million for the fund.

Later in September pop musicians were involved in other large-scale, highly publicized events to raise money for charity. A concert at London's Royal Albert Hall to aid victims of the volcanic eruption on the island of Montserrat featured a lineup that included Sir Paul McCartney—the former Beatle who earlier in the year had been knighted for his services to the music industry—along with John (who, in late December, was also knighted), Sting, Mark Knopfler, and Eric Clapton. A few days later the Irish band U2 staged its PopMart show—hailed as the most complicated and expensive live rock show ever assembled—in Sarajevo, the capital of Bosnia and Herzegovina, and promised to give away any profits to charity. Tickets were sold cheaply in recognition of the country's postwar poverty and were made available in both Serbian and Croatian areas of the country so that those opponents in the conflict could come together for the concert.

Such events showed that pop music could still—occasionally—be used for idealistic ends and also that veteran performers could still dominate the headlines and best-seller lists. Further proof that age was no barrier to international success came with the release of the Rolling Stones' new album, *Bridges to Babylon,* to coincide with the start of the band's highly successful North American tour. Mick Jagger, now 54, continued to leap across the stage and sing the hits the band recorded in the 1960s.

The younger end of the British pop market was dominated by two very different groups, the Spice Girls (*see* BIOGRAPHIES) and Oasis, both of which were helped by skillful marketing strategies that ensured enormous coverage in the popular press. The Spice Girls, a pouting, feisty gang who mixed highly commercial dance songs with an even more impressive flair for self-publicity, topped the British charts with songs like "Wannabe" and reached the number one slot in the U.S. Oasis, the guitar band led by the brothers Noel and Liam Gallagher, released a third album, *Be Here Now,* and thus proved that the band had survived the brothers' much-publicized feuding the previous year. A mixture of grand, tuneful rock ballads and aggression, the album was not as original as their earlier work but nonetheless became an instant best-seller. Other bands showed that the "Britpop" movement was still capable of considerable variety. Radiohead mixed guitar rock with inventive, doomy ballads on its album *OK Computer,* and The Verve made clever use of strings on its much-praised *Urban Hymns*. Outside Britain it was a good year for the quirky Icelandic singer Björk, who showed she had moved on from charming, idiosyncratic pop songs to a more sombre, mature style with her new album, *Homogenic*.

In Asia and in Africa, the international music scene was marked by the deaths of two major performers. Nusrat Fateh Ali Khan (*see* OBITUARIES), who died of a heart attack at the age of 49, had became a superstar in his native Pakistan and throughout Asia and much of the West as a result of his rapid-fire treatment of *qawwali*, the Sufi mystical poetry of Islam. His style was steeped in tradition, yet songs like "Mast, Mast" (about intoxication) crossed over to become best-sellers in the pop market.

Fela Anikulapo Kuti, who died of AIDS at the age of 58, was a popular and highly controversial musician in Africa. He had used his music to attack successive military regimes in Nigeria and suffered as a result. In the 1970s his club and home in Lagos were attacked by the army, and in the 1980s, after he was jailed on currency charges, Amnesty International declared him a political prisoner. (*See* OBITUARIES.)

Death rocked the hip-hop world again in 1997. In March, just six months after the death of rapper Tupac Shakur, 24-year-old Brooklyn, N.Y., native Christopher Wallace, better known as Biggie Smalls, or the Notorious B.I.G., was shot to death as he left a party in Los Angeles. (*See* OBITUARIES.) Within weeks of his death, Wallace's double

CD, *Life After Death,* in which he posed on the cover next to a hearse with a license plate bearing his name, was released. A complex collection of love songs, street anthems, and sexual boasts, *Life After Death* rose immediately to number one on the pop album charts. Driven by the chart-topping single "Hypnotize," the album went on to sell more than three million copies.

Sean ("Puffy") Combs, who had produced and marketed Wallace's recordings on his Bad Boy record label, emerged as a commercially successful artist; calling himself Puff Daddy, he was also a producer, songwriter, and remixer for recordings by others. His single "I'll Be Missing You," recorded with Wallace's widow, Faith Evans, paid tribute to Wallace and featured a generous sample from the Police's 1983 pop hit "Every Breath You Take." By the year's end the single had sold more than three million copies; profits went to Wallace's two children. Combs also released a best-selling solo album, *No Way Out*, as "Puff Daddy and the Family."

Not all pop music reflected the shadow of death and the menace of the streets. Hanson—brothers Isaac, Taylor, and Zac, from Tulsa, Okla.—blended peppy harmonies on an infectious bubblegum single, "MMMbop." The trio became teenage heartthrobs and sold three million copies of their first album, *Middle of Nowhere*.

Marilyn Manson—Canton, Ohio, native Brian Warner and his band—created controversy with his updating of Alice Cooper-style shock rock. Manson titled an album *Antichrist Superstar* and proclaimed himself a member of Anton LaVey's Church of Satan. Scheduled concerts in East Rutherford, N.J.; Richmond, Va.; and Somerset, Wis., were threatened with cancellation when organizers became concerned about public reaction. The possibility of lawsuits, however, caused the New Jersey and Virginia authorities to allow Manson to perform, and the Wisconsin concert was moved to Minneapolis, Minn.

Country music singer Garth Brooks drew 250,000 fans to Manhattan's Central Park for a summer concert and live cable TV telecast. Seven weeks later he captured the Country Music Association's top award for Entertainer of the Year. In November, after resolving a disagreement with his record label, Brooks released a new studio album, *Sevens*. The disc sold 897,000 copies in its first week, the most ever by a country artist, and within three weeks had been certified by the Recording Industry Association of America (RIAA) for shipments of five million copies. LeAnn Rimes (*see* BIOGRAPHIES) made history in February when her *Unchained Melody: The Early Years* became the first country album by a woman to debut at number one on Billboard's Top 200 pop chart. The album went on to sell more than two million copies, and a later release, *You Light Up My Life: Inspirational Songs,* also hit the top of the pop chart. At the end of the year, the RIAA declared Rimes the top recording artist of 1997 in recognition of shipments of 12.5 million units (albums and singles).

Fleetwood Mac's lineup for the band's best-selling 1977 album *Rumours* reunited for the first time since 1982, recorded live versions of some of their best-known hits, and mounted a successful tour. Sarah McLachlan and an ever-changing, all-women cast that included Jewel, Fiona Apple, and Sheryl Crow, among others, toured nationally in the Lilith Fair festival.

KARL GEHRING—GAMMA LIAISON

Sarah McLachlan performs at the Lilith Fair summer music festival, which featured only female soloists and "girl bands." Other performers included Jewel, Fiona Apple, and Sheryl Crow.

Singer-songwriter Bob Dylan survived a life-threatening infection around his heart, played for Pope John Paul II in Italy, and released a strong new album, *Time out of Mind*, even as his son, Jakob Dylan, emerged as a star with his own rock band, the Wallflowers. From Dallas, Texas, singer Erykah Badu showed sophistication and style on her debut album, *Baduizm,* drawing comparisons to such artists as Billie Holiday and Bob Marley. Also from Dallas, Kirk Franklin and the members of the vocal group God's Property scored mainstream success when they collaborated on the album *Stomp* and the hit single of the same name.

The Bee Gees, Buffalo Springfield, Joni Mitchell, the Jackson 5, the Rascals, Crosby, Stills & Nash, Bill Monroe, Mahalia Jackson, Syd Nathan, and Parliament-Funkadelic joined the Rock and Roll Hall of Fame. Harlan Howard, Cindy Walker, and Brenda Lee were inducted into the Country Music Hall of Fame.

Elvis Presley's manager, "Colonel" Tom Parker; singer Michael Hutchence of INXS; singer-songwriters John Denver, Townes Van Zandt, Jeff Buckley, and Laura Nyro; and rhythm-and-blues great La Vern Baker were among the major pop music figures who died during 1997. (*See* OBITUARIES.)

(ROBIN DENSELOW; JAY ORR)

This article updates the *Macropædia* article The History of Western MUSIC.

DANCE

North America. No singular force or theme dominated Terpsichore's realm in North America in 1997. American Ballet Theatre (ABT) ambitiously commissioned its first original multiact ballet, *Othello*. Conceived in partnership with San Francisco Ballet, the production was scheduled to enter that repertory in the spring of 1998. Called a "Dance in Three Acts," *Othello* featured choreography by modern-dance practitioner Lar Lubovitch based on Shakespearean source material, but the result was thin ballet fare. The welcome presence of former Alvin Ailey American Dance Theater (AAADT) dancer Desmond Richardson as the first-cast Othello counted for too little, given the choreography's lack of individuality. ABT's new presentations of Ronald Hynd's old-world production of *The Merry Widow* and of Frederic Franklin's old-fashioned *Coppélia* fared mildly better as ballet and as theatre. The company's eight-week season at New York City's Metropolitan Opera House was specifically planned as a "big ballet" season, with mostly multiact ballets making up the repertory. Mixed programs were generally reserved for a second New York season in the fall at City Center. In both instances it was individual dancers who stood out as most newsworthy. Notable among these was the company debut of former New York City Ballet (NYCB) virtuoso Ethan Stiefel, who captured attention with his clean yet impetuous dancing and noticeably thoughtful acting. Other especially remarkable performances came from semi-newcomers Vladimir Malakhov and Angel Corella and from principal dancer Julie Kent.

NYCB's winter season was distinguished by the premiere of Jerome Robbins's *Brandenburg,* a marvelous dance suite of aptly playful and baroque dancing that showed the past master of ballet in top form. The troupe's spring season opened with a run of Peter Martins's staging of *The Sleeping Beauty* and added six new ballets to its repertory with another of its Diamond Project presentations. Although none had the gravity of Robbins's work, efforts by Miriam Mahdaviani, Christopher Wheeldon, and Robert La Fosse made the company dancers look best. Principal dancer Miranda Weese staked further claims to being one of her generation's leading lights, and the very talented Monique Meunier, whose career had had its ups and downs, finally danced with renewed power and ease and was promoted to soloist. In the fall NYCB split into two units and toured South America and the Pacific Rim region. NYCB's winter season opened with a special tribute and farewell performance for Merrill Ashley (*see* BIOGRAPHIES), who celebrated her 30th anniversary with the company.

The Joffrey Ballet of Chicago, still maintaining something of a low profile after its move out of New York City, capped its year with two weeks in Washington, D.C.'s Kennedy Center, performing *The Nutcracker* and a mixed repertory that included artistic director Gerald Arpino's *Kettentanz.* Houston Ballet's (HB's) new multiact *Dracula,* by artistic director Ben Stevenson, captured some national attention, as did the dancing of two of HB's leading dancers, Carlos Acosta and Lauren Anderson. At Boston Ballet (BB) longtime artistic director Bruce Marks relinquished his post to Anna-Marie Holmes, his former assistant. During this transitional year the troupe offered the first complete American staging of the 19th-century *Le Corsaire,* which BB billed as *The Pirate.* The company also presented a new staging of *Cinderella* by classical ballet champion Michael Corder. Dance Theatre of Harlem's (DTH's) year included a labour dispute with its dancers and a major

Martha Butler and Ethan Stiefel (foreground) dance in the American Ballet Theatre production of *Coppélia,* a ballet based on a love story by E.T.A. Hoffmann. Butler became an ABT soloist in 1995; Stiefel joined ABT as a principal dancer in 1996.

Kennedy Center season, which included the premieres of *Sasanka,* an African dance-styled ballet by South Africa's Vincent Mantsoe, and *Crossing Over,* a ballet requiem by company member Robert Garland. When these ballets were given with others in a New York season that used taped music and had scant publicity, their newness had to yield to a more newsworthy event, the local debut of Alicia Graf, an 18-year-old ballerina of wondrous gifts and beautiful presence. Pacific Northwest Ballet launched its silver anniversary year, which included a focus on new ballets.

Miami (Fla.) City Ballet (MCB) performed at home and on tour, bringing to the New York area programs that included Paul Taylor's *Company B* and Jimmy Gamonet De Los Heros's *The Big Band SUPER-MEGATROID* alongside Balanchine's *Western Symphony* and *Scotch Symphony.* In December MCB founder and director Edward Villella was presented with one of the annual Kennedy Center Honors. Victoria Morgan took over direction of the Cincinnati (Ohio) Ballet, and Jonas Kåge assumed the reins at Ballet West in Salt Lake City, Utah. Indianapolis (Ind.) Ballet Theater changed its name to Ballet Internationale and offered the first American performances of *Creation of the World,* a multiact Genesis-inspired ballet by Russian choreographers Natalya Kasatkina and Vladimir Vasilyov. The company, run by former Kirov dancer Eldar Aliyev, figured prominently in a *New York Times* article on the post-Soviet Union influx of Russians into U.S. companies. Colorado Ballet, which presented a new *A Midsummer Night's Dream* by NYCB's Wheeldon, was also included in the story. Russian ballet itself came in the form of a tour by "Stars of the Kirov Ballet" and a stellar one-night program, "Tribute to Sergey Diaghilev," that featured little about the renowned impresario but much new Russian ballet talent, most notably Svetlana Zakharova and Diana Vishneva.

Modern dance's leading lights continued to make their mark. The Paul Taylor Dance Company showed two different and diverting new works in New York City, the elegiac *Eventide* and the vaudevillian *Prime Numbers,* as well as the tango-based *Piazzolla Caldera* at the American Dance Festival in Durham, N.C. Merce Cunningham was feted in the spring for 60 years of dancing and in the fall presented *Scenario,* a dance wherein naked limbs worked marvelously out of artfully lumpen torsos devised by eccentric haute-couturier Rei Kawakubo. The Mark Morris Dance Group honoured composer Lou Harrison with an all-Harrison bill on which the new *Rhymes with Silver* stood out, glowing with physical beauty and lyrical mystery. The Limón Dance Company celebrated a grand golden anniversary with special revivals. These performances helped kick off the 65th anniversary of the Jacob's Pillow Dance Festival in Becket, Mass. Ballet's modern convert Mikhail Baryshnikov toured widely with his White Oak Dance Project and presented in New York City the premiere of *Remote,* a ghostly creation by the intriguing Meg Stuart. In a program simply called "Tharp!," Twyla Tharp showed a happy sampling of her current work and an impressive group of dancers. Notable among her offerings was *Heroes,* an elegantly sinister work devoted to Philip Glass. A select sampler of five British contemporary dance organizations played in New York City; Jonathan Burrows's sharp, imaginative, and engrossing work stood out among these.

Lincoln Center Festival '97 included the welcome presence of Great Britain's Royal Ballet, dominated by glorious appearances of Darcey Bussell, especially in Sir Frederick Ashton's masterful *Cinderella.* The Brooklyn (N.Y.) Academy of Music's Next Wave Festival presented Pina Bausch's funky extravaganza *Der Fensterputzer,* as well as Anne Teresa De Keersmaeker's earthy and sensual *Woud* and Eiko and Koma's indoor re-creation of their outdoor *River.* The Kennedy Center's "America Dancing" kicked off its third year with China's Guangdong Modern Dance Company, a troupe specifically inspired by American modern dance. The newly inaugurated New Jersey Performing Arts Center, in Newark, included in its initial season holiday offerings by ABT of *Cinderella* and Donald Byrd/The Group's *The Harlem Nutcracker.* Byrd also created a new work, *Fin de siècle,* to enrich the AAADT's popular annual New York season.

The National Ballet of Canada's (NBC) Karen Kain spent the year performing her farewell tour, and the company's history was the subject of a prizewinning book, *Power to Rise,* by James Neufeld. In addition to performing its own repertory and offering what it divided into "Grand Classical" and "Grand Contemporary" works, Les Grands Ballets Canadiens celebrated a 40th-anniversary season by being host to appearances by other dance troupes, including NBC, DTH, and the Royal Winnipeg Ballet (RWB). RWB presented the Zürich (Switz.) Ballet in October while it was on a European tour. Montreal's eighth Festival International de Nouvelle Danse focused on the dance of Spain and Portugal, with select representatives of Canadian and U.S. dance as well. After closing the series, Ballet Cristina Hoyos played a successful New York season. In addition to the return of *Riverdance,* Irish step dancing writ large came in the form of Michael Flatley's *Lord of the Dance.* (*See* BIOGRAPHIES.) Charming Australian tappers, in their show called *Tap Dogs,* also made their mark, as did two tango shows, *Forever Tango* and a new edition of *Tango × 2.*

Deaths included dancers Lubov Rostova, Bernard Johnson, Christopher Boatwright, Leon Danielian (*see* OBITUARIES), Carld Jonaissant, Chuck Green, Sylvester Campbell, Anna Scarpova Youskevitch, Leslie ("Bubba") Gaines, Alexandra Danilova (*see* OBITUARIES), and Lotte Goslar; writers Walter Sorell, Anita Finkel, and Martha Duffy; and pedagogues Bessie Schönberg and Stanley Williams.

(ROBERT GRESKOVIC)

Europe. Classical ballet often exists on a precarious footing, and 1997 brought several reminders of this. After an international symposium, "What Future Is There for Classical Dance?," in Lausanne, Switz., aired concerns such as the scarcity of outstanding creative talent, ballet in Great Britain took several hard knocks. Scottish Ballet, the region's only classical ensemble, found itself threatened with closure. The Scottish Arts Council agreed to release funds for the company's 1997–98 season only on condition that a new board of directors be chosen and that the artistic director, Galina Samsova, resign with immediate effect. Because of cuts in their funding, the planned world premiere of Robert Cohan's *The Magic Lamp* had to be replaced by Ashton's *La Fille mal gardée,* using sets and costumes generously lent by Birmingham Royal Ballet. Future funding would probably continue at a reduced level, and cuts in staffing and more changes in repertoire were feared.

The Royal Ballet (along with the Royal Opera) slid into crisis in October, only three months after having vacated the Royal Opera House to allow costly and extensive rebuilding. As a result of mismanagement, the two companies were forced to shuttle between a variety of unsuitable theatres during the two years away from their home. Poor marketing and financial planning led to disastrous ticket sales for the Royal Ballet's first run of performances on the road. Faced with a combined ballet and opera deficit of £4.7 million, the Royal Opera House Board was expected to announce further staff cutbacks and possibly even a suspension of performances. All this came in the wake of highly publicized in-house disputes in which the chief executive, Genista McIntosh, left abruptly only a few months after her appointment.

Other developments, however, counterbalanced this gloomy picture. In Britain the Birmingham Royal Ballet, which had previously operated as the Royal Ballet's smaller touring sister, became completely autonomous on the grounds that this would allow it to move forward more forcefully. The company's director, David Bintley, scored a big hit with his powerfully dramatic three-act *Edward II,* which he originally created for the Stuttgart (Ger.) Ballet in 1995. In Denmark Peter Schaufuss, the former director of the Royal Danish Ballet, launched the Peter Schaufuss Ballet, a touring troupe with funding and premises provided by the city of Holstebro. In France the fears that the Ballet du Rhin and the Nice Opera Ballet would be melted down into compact, less-costly modern dance ensembles proved largely unfounded, although budgets were cut. The new appointees—Bertrand d'At at the Ballet du Rhin and Marc Ribaud at the Nice Opera Ballet—indicated that their repertoires would give more emphasis to contemporary work but would remain in the realm of ballet.

DEE CONWAY

Sabrina Lenzi, in the role of Isabella, and Joseph Cipolla, as Mortimer, star in *Edward II,* choreographer David Bintley's powerful new work for the Birmingham Royal Ballet. *Edward II* proved to be a big hit for Bintley, who based his ballet on Christopher Marlowe's play.

In Russia, despite economic turmoil, not a single state ballet company had closed since the demise of communism in 1991. The number of companies actually increased, although new ones survived on erratic sponsorship and ticket sales and often had trouble paying staff. The wrangles at the Mariinsky (formerly Kirov) Ballet calmed down. Oleg Vinogradov, the target of much suspicion and hostility in his later years, retired as artistic director, and the celebrated conductor Valery Gergiyev, in overall charge of the Mariinsky Theatre's opera and ballet, seemed to keep a firm grasp on the reins of control. He did not, however, name a successor to Vinogradov. The Mariinsky Ballet enjoyed success on its foreign tours, including a long summer season in London, where its most popular evenings were two "Ballets Russes" programs of works by classical choreographer Michel Fokine. Fokine's granddaughter Isabelle was scheduled to stage new productions of *Le Spectre de la rose, Polovtsian Dances from Prince Igor,* and *The Dying Swan,* based on Fokine's notes and photographs. In the end, the Mariinsky Ballet rejected her *Prince Igor* and *Dying Swan* in favour of its own versions, which they considered superior and equally authentic, given that they were inherited from Fokine himself during his early years at the Mariinsky.

At the Bolshoi Theatre in Moscow, the ongoing turmoil was not completely stamped out. Vladimir Vasilyev, the former Bolshoi Ballet star who in 1995 assumed the same overarching post at the Bolshoi Theatre that Gergiyev held at the Mariinsky, received brickbats for his radical reworking of *Swan Lake.* This version dispensed with the evil Odile and featured instead a Black King and his son, the Prince, locked in rivalry for Odette's love. Rivalry also extended to relations inside the Bolshoi Theatre, and this, to general surprise, provoked Vasilyev into declaring on television that he would not renew the contract of the ballet's director, Vyacheslav Gordeyev, when it expired in July. A former dancer, Aleksandr Bogatyrev, was appointed as an interim replacement.

Elsewhere other company directors were on the move. In Germany Valeriy Panov's contract with the Bonn Ballet was not renewed, and Cologne closed down its company, Tanz-Forum; Jochen Ulrich, its head since 1978, consequently lost his job. Once regarded as the most innovative company in

Germany, the Tanz-Forum had entered a long artistic decline, and Ulrich's swan song, *Citizen Kane,* did nothing to suggest a belated reversal. In Italy Mauro Bigonzetti accepted the directorship of Aterballetto, based in Reggio Emilia. He replaced Amedeo Amodio, who resigned after 18 years because of artistic and financial problems and took the vacant directorial post at the Rome Opera Ballet. Elisabetta Terabust also resigned as director of the ballet of La Scala, Milan, after three conflict-ridden years—to be succeeded by no one, since the theatre decided to rely, at least temporarily, on a succession of ballet masters. Carla Fracci, who had retired as Italy's most famous ballerina, was accused of excessive expenditure as director of the Arena di Verona's company and was dismissed. Her replacement was Robert North, an American who had made his name in England and who was opting for a repertoire featuring modern rather than traditional ballets. Dance in Italy, however, was not only about directors coming and going. There were glimmers of hope in government plans to establish choreographic centres and to organize a more equitable division of government subsidies. Consequently, funds would be based on artistic merit rather than merely on the size, popularity, or age of a company, and a fairer share thus would be given to new or smaller ensembles.

Among the highlights of the year were the Paris Opéra Ballet's acquisition of Pina Bausch's much-admired modern dance *The Rite of Spring* (to the Igor Stravinsky score); this was the first time that Bausch had mounted a piece for a company other than her own Tanztheater Wuppertal. The Stuttgart Ballet organized a two-week Cranko Festival, a showcase of the ballets of John Cranko, the company's inspirational founder, who died in 1973. Maurice Béjart, the French choreographer who headed the Béjart Ballet Lausanne, was 70 on January 1. The occasion was marked by a gala in which Béjart himself made an ironic appearance as a hypochondriac in an armchair, confused by doctors and their masks; he then closed the evening by dancing a meditative solo. Roland Petit marked his 25th year at the head of the Ballet National de Marseille with performances in June on a 450-sq m (4,844-sq ft) floating stage in the city's Old Harbour.

Important deaths included those of Danish dancer and choreographer Frank Schaufuss (father of Peter) at 75 and Peter van Dyk (age 67), the first German dancer made a principal at the Paris Opéra Ballet.

(NADINE MEISNER)

THEATRE

Great Britain and Ireland. In 1997 the London stage was aglow with three great double acts. Dame Maggie Smith and Eileen Atkins (*Evening Standard* best actress award) locked horns in Edward Albee's *A Delicate Balance*. Ute Lemper (*see* BIOGRAPHIES) and Ruthie Henshall set the town alight in the concert-form revival of John Kander, Fred Ebb, and Bob Fosse's *Chicago*. Finally, and more unexpectedly, comedy favourite Richard Briers and the ever-glorious Geraldine McEwan scored a triumph as the nonagenarian suicidal married couple in a brilliantly reverberative and well-timed revival of Eugène Ionesco's *The Chairs*.

Chicago proved the sort of galvanic musical hit London had not seen for a few years and became an instant hot ticket. The Walt Disney Co.'s *Beauty and the Beast* proved a popular fixture at the Dominion, a spectacular pantomime that arrived in the spring. Jerry Lewis led another well-liked import, the latest revival of *Damn Yankees*.

The native British musical languished under the not ideally serious influence of Stephen Sondheim. Good new song and dance seemed to be in abeyance. Sir Cameron Mackintosh and Lord Lloyd-Webber offered, respectively, *The Fix* and *Enter the Guardsman* at the Donmar Warehouse. The first was a grim, depressing fable of the American presidency, and the second was a winsome adaptation of a Ferenc Molnar comedy. Neither really hit home, and neither was much fun. Even worse was the musical *Maddie,* which made only a brief appearance after a bizarre and unprecedented campaign by the *Daily Telegraph* critic to raise money for its production among his readers.

Britain's new Labour Party government worked no instant new wonders for the arts. Although celebrities from sports and show business lined up for meetings with Prime Minister Tony Blair, the harsh realities indicated a collapse of morale and ambition among the nation's theatres. A major problem was the waste of lottery funds. To be fair, the arts world had only itself to blame.

Ute Lemper (centre) and other cast members of the hit musical *Chicago* perform at the Adelphi Theatre in London. Featuring hot and jazzy music, *Chicago* tells the story of two showgirls who murder their lovers and manipulate the media in order to secure their freedom and boost their vaudeville careers.

DONALD COOPER—PHOTOSTAGE

When then prime minister John Major's heritage secretary, Virginia Bottomley, asked what the money was needed for, she was told improved facilities. The lottery, consequently, generated £250 million for capital investment, whereas the Treasury offered only £186 million for revenue funding. The result was a building and refurbishment program that was likely to equip the nation with marvelous venues that had nothing to put on their stages.

The prestigious, unsubsidized Chichester Festival Theatre announced big losses. Artistic director Duncan Weldon was forced to resign after a season that included successful revivals of J.M. Barrie's *The Admirable Crichton* and Sandy Wilson's *Divorce Me, Darling!* (his sequel to *The Boy Friend*).

Cuts in local funding in London threatened the futures of the Greenwich Theatre, the King's Head Theatre in Islington, and the remarkable Gate Theatre in Notting Hill—where the actors were unpaid but whose alumni include the departing artistic director of the Royal Court Theatre, Stephen Daldry; the administrator of the Young Vic, Caroline Maude; and the literary manager of the Royal Shakespeare Company, Simon Reade. Daldry, who masterminded the £22 million restoration and rebuilding of the Royal Court, was leaving to pursue a new career in motion pictures, though he was rumoured to be part of Trevor Nunn's plans at the National Theatre. His successor as the Court's artistic director was Ian Rickson, a close colleague of Daldry with a good track record in new plays.

The new Globe Theatre played to enthusiastic audiences during its first full season in the summer, with Mark Rylance as Henry V scoring a particular success. The open-air re-creation of Shakespeare's theatre became an instant tourist attraction, and the cheap ticket prices ensured lively participation from students and foreign spectators.

The Old Vic finally lost its patrons, Ed and David Mirvish of Toronto, after some 15 years of adventurous programming and mounting losses. The resident Peter Hall Company, incumbents for the last year under the Mirvishes, offered an ambitious repertoire of classics and modern plays, and critics and audiences responded enthusiastically. Highlights of the season included Alan Howard and Ben Kingsley in a wonderful revival by Hall of *Waiting for Godot*—some 40 years after he had made his reputation by directing the British premier of the play; Felicity Kendal and Michael Pennington in a new version by Sir Tom Stoppard (*see* BIOGRAPHIES) of Anton Chekhov's *The Seagull;* Alan Howard as a majestic, myopic King Lear; and a bouncy version of Sir John Vanbrugh's *The Provok'd Wife*. The Vic's new plays fared less well, but they built up a good following on Sunday and Monday nights. April de Angelis's *Playhouse Creatures* and Chris Hannan's *Shining Souls* were the best of the lot.

On the other side of the Thames, the Royal National Theatre (RNT) completed a glorious decade of achievement under Sir Richard Eyre. Three of the best plays of the year were presented there, two of them directed by Eyre. Stoppard's *The Invention of Love* (ES best play) was a sumptuously intricate analysis of the parched love life of A.E. Housman, a Victorian poet best known for "A Shropshire Lad." He was played by John Wood, that most scintillating of Stoppard actors, as the older Housman and also by Paul Rhys as the younger man. Alongside this view of the past, Patrick Marber's *Closer* (ES best comedy) was a bristling comedy of manners for the 1990s, a sharp and savage sexual quadrille that contained the theatre's first sex-on-the-Internet scene. Finally, David Hare's *Amy's View* mounted an eloquent defense of the theatre in the portrayal of an actress finding her place there after years in the cultural wilderness. Dame Judi Dench as the actress gave one of her finest performances as she battled for professional survival and the love of her wayward daughter (Samantha Bond).

BILLIE RAFAELLI—PERFORMING ARTS LIBRARY

Actor Ian Holm appears in March in the title role of Shakespeare's *King Lear* at the Royal National Theatre in London. Holm, who passionately conveyed the turbulent inner thoughts of the king in his spiral toward self-destruction, was applauded by critics for his moving performance in a well-known role.

Both *Closer* and *Amy's View* were slated for transfer to the commercial (West End) theatre in 1998. The West End itself had a good year. *Art* continued with its fourth first-class cast within a year of opening. Ben Elton's *Popcorn* was a thrilling having-it-both-ways Shavian debate about the new violence in cinema, with a Quentin Tarantino-type director held hostage by two natural-born killers.

In Hugh Whitemore's cleverly crafted *A Letter of Resignation,* Edward Fox slipped comfortably into the role of former prime minister Harold Macmillan at the time of the security scandal involving Cabinet minister John Profumo. Michael Gambon and Alec McCowen also played real-life politicians—respectively, the disreputable socialist Tom Driberg and the prim Labour Party Prime Minister Clement Attlee—in Stephen Churchett's *Tom & Clem.* Alan Bates was in characteristic self-lacerating form as a husband sitting at his wife's deathbed in Simon Gray's *Life Support*.

The mania for the impersonation of real people onstage continued. In the West End, Sian Phillips was a superlative Marlene Dietrich in a backstage confession plus cabaret performance devised by Pam Gems. And Jean Fergusson appeared in *She Knows You Know!,* her tribute to the popular vaudeville and television star Hylda Baker.

As Nunn took over the RNT reins from Eyre, he directed *Mutabilitie* by the Irish playwright Frank McGuinness, in which William Shakespeare (Anton Lesser) goes to Ireland—which he never did—and meets his fellow poet Edmund Spenser, who is working there—which he really was—as a civil servant in the aftermath of the Munster wars. The play was, however, not one of McGuinness's best, and Nunn made a more auspicious early impact with his revival of Henrik Ibsen's *An Enemy of the People,* newly translated by Christopher Hampton, in which Sir Ian McKellen was a magnificent Doctor Stockmann, the principled doctor who undermines a spa town's prosperity by discovering contamination in the water and corruption in the works.

Even Sir Ian was upstaged by Ian Holm in the title role of *King Lear* (ES best actor) at the National, again directed by Eyre. This was an outstanding Lear year, with four to record. Kathryn Hunter—(if Fiona Shaw can play Richard II, Hunter can certainly play Lear)—opened the account in Lear's home town of Leicester, and the production later moved to the Young Vic. Later, Hunter's former Théâtre de Complicité colleague Tim Barlow, a totally deaf actor, had his moments of minor splendour in the role at the Crucible Theatre in Sheffield. In between, there was Alan Howard's version and, topping everyone else's, Holm's. He played the role with the most ferocious energy in a simple, uncluttered domestic setting oddly susceptible to the elements. Holm stripped down stark naked on the heath, as did Paul Rhys as the disguised Edgar, and their plaintive wailings achieved a crescendo of poignancy rare even in this great play.

The Royal National Theatre's books were balanced by a triumphant return of Eyre's production of Frank Loesser's *Guys and Dolls,* and other notable evenings included the belated London premiere of Kurt Weill's *Lady in the Dark* (ES best musical), starring Maria Friedman; *The Cripple of Inishmaan,* a cracking new comedy by 1996's wunderkind Martin McDonagh; Lindsay Duncan peerless, dangerous, and sexy in Harold Pinter's *The Homecoming;* and Juliet Stevenson leading a spirited *The Caucasian Chalk Circle*.

In contrast, the Royal Shakespeare Company reported poor houses in London and Stratford and an operating deficit of £1.6 million. The company's condition was not helped by a public confusion as to where and exactly when they were playing. Stratford seasons began in November, and the Newcastle tour was moved from February to October and supplemented by another residency in Plymouth. New plays and experimental productions were increasingly confined to small studio spaces, and there was no identifiable stream of work as had been characterized by the regimes of Sir Peter Hall, Nunn, and Terry Hands, or the careers of RSC associates John Barton and David Jones.

Artistic director Adrian Noble's Stratford production of *Twelfth Night* was dismal, though many admired his main-stage *Cymbeline* and his Swan Theatre revival of Ibsen's *Little Eyolf,* both starring his wife, Joanne Pearce. There were sturdy RSC touring productions of *Cyrano de Bergerac* (with Antony Sher) and of *Henry V* (with rising new star Michael Sheen). The RSC's work so rarely seemed intellectually driven or radical that the new *Hamlet,* with Alex Jennings in the lead, directed by Matthew Warchus with great bite and energy, seemed aberrantly exceptional.

The Royal Court's exile in the West End continued to be lively, with Martin McDonagh's *The Leenane Trilogy* a highlight at the Duke of York's Theatre and good new work from Martin Crimp and Conor McPherson, whose *The Weir* (ES most promising new playwright), a haunting quartet of interconnecting monologues, confirmed an exciting new voice from Ireland.

In Ireland itself the Dublin Theatre Festival focused on two disappointing new plays at the Abbey and Gate theatres: Thomas Kilroy's *The Secret Fall of Constance Wilde,* which added little to the folklore about Oscar Wilde and did so in a monotonously arid production by Patrick Mason, and Joseph O'Connor's *The Weeping of Angels,* an enjoyably raucous compendium of Roman Catholic jokes stemming from the fact that the last three religious sisters in Ireland were having their roof fixed by workmen called Michael and Gabriel. Brenda Fricker returned to the Dublin stage in the latter.

(MICHAEL COVENEY)

U.S. and Canada. In the American theatre 1997 was a year of artistic retrenchment and uncertainty. Despite widespread commitment to new works on stages across the country, few important new plays emerged, and a number of well-known playwrights made missteps that failed to please critics and audiences. On Broadway the arrival of two blockbusters—the Walt Disney Co.'s musical stage version of its 1994 animated film *The Lion King* and Livent Inc. of Canada's musicalization of the E.L. Doctorow novel *Ragtime*—generated excitement and intense speculation, in no small part because of the changes in the business and real-estate environment that the shows represented for New York's theatre district.

Artistically, the highlight of the year may have been *Peter and Wendy,* a modest but inventively conceived treatment of Barrie's *Peter Pan,* created by the New York City-based experimental troupe Mabou Mines. Using an eclectic assortment of puppets, an exhilarating musical score by Scottish fiddler Johnny Cunningham, and a single actress—the remarkable Karen Kandel, who acted as the story's narrator and gave voice to all the characters—adapter Liza Lorwin and director Lee Breuer conveyed not only the charm and whimsy of the famous film and theatrical versions but also the darker themes of loss of innocence and nascent sexuality that make Barrie's 1904 work so memorable and unsettling.

Modesty was also a hallmark of one of the season's most provocative dramas, Paula Vogel's *How I Learned to Drive,* a memory play about the complexities and consequences of pedophilia. Vogel's hopscotch-through-time evocation of a young girl's secret sexual relationship with her uncle by marriage is theatrically spare, unexpectedly funny, and, despite its almost clinical examination of taboo subject matter, achingly poetic. *How I Learned to Drive* won a spate of awards after its debut at New York's Vineyard Theatre, and it went on to be staged in several other cities.

The single most widely produced work of the season was *Having Our Say,* Emily Mann's stage adaptation of the autobiography of the Delany sisters, two 100-something-year-old African-American sisters who reminisce about the often harrowing but always hopeful century they've spent living as "Negroes" in the United States. With distinguished actresses Gloria Foster and Mary Alice portraying the Delanys, *Having Our Say* had premiered in 1995 at the McCarter Theatre in Princeton, N.J., where Mann was artistic director, transferred to Broadway for a brief run, and received productions at scores of theatres nationwide.

The country's African-American heritage was also examined in Keith Glover's widely produced *Thunder Knocking on the Door,* a drama with music (the playwright referred to it as a "blusical") about an enigmatic Alabama blues singer. Questions of race received a more experimental treatment in the staging by the Shakespeare Theatre of Washington, D.C., of a race-reversed *Othello,* with Patrick Stewart in the title role surrounded by a black supporting cast; a bravura interpretation by New York's avant-garde Wooster Group of Eugene O'Neill's *The Emperor Jones,* with actress Kate Valk playing the leading role in blackface; and a buoyant, elastic retelling by New York City's Drama Dept. of *Uncle Tom's Cabin,* drawing on various stage adaptations, minstrel shows, and slave narratives as well as Harriet Beecher Stowe's 1852 novel.

Showing up in strong form were David Mamet, whose triptych of short plays *The Old Neighborhood* won accolades for its intense portrait of a man coming to terms with his past; and Alfred Uhry, who, in *The Last Night of Ballyhoo,* his first new play since *Driving Miss Daisy,* used the conventional form of a classic romantic comedy to tell an unconventional story about southern anti-Semitism; it won the 1997 Tony award for best play.

Terry Beaver, Jessica Hecht, Celia Weston, and Dana Ivey perform a scene from Alfred Uhry's *The Last Night of Ballyhoo.* It is the story of a Jewish family in pre-World War II Atlanta, Ga., dealing with Southern anti-Semitism during the social event of the holiday season. It received the 1997 Tony award for best play.

T. CHARLES ERICKSON

The lion's share of the Tonys were captured by two musicals: a slick-as-glass revival of *Chicago* and Peter Stone and Maury Yeston's unlikely spectacle *Titanic.* Riding high on the *Titanic* zeitgeist—fueled by the end-of-year release of the James Cameron film, TV documentaries, and coverage of the real-life exploration of the ship's wreckage—the musical sailed into a potentially profitable long run despite its improbable subject, technical crises during previews, and $10 million price tag. Two charismatic performers, Lillias White and Chuck Cooper, in Cy Coleman's musical about Times Square hookers in the 1980s, *The Life,* earned musical acting Tonys, and Christopher Plummer scored an expected leading-actor nod for his star turn in the one-man play *Barrymore.*

As usual, there was a dearth of serious dramas on Broadway, but that did not slow down escalating box-office revenues. After near-record holiday grosses were recorded, pundits were predicting that 1997 could be one of the commercial theatre's most financially successful years. Ever-climbing ticket prices received part of the credit, as did the sensational advance sales racked up by *The Lion King* and *Ragtime,* shows that their corporate producers made into juggernauts through multimedia "event marketing."

With an advance of some $20 million already pocketed, *The Lion King* opened November 13 at Disney's glitteringly restored New Amsterdam Theatre following a standing-room-only tryout engagement in Minneapolis, Minn. Most critics were breathless in their praise, especially for the eye-popping puppetry and visual effects of director Julie Taymor, who publicly praised the Disney organization for respecting her individual creative approach.

The December 26 preopening preview of *Ragtime* at Livent's new 1,821-seat Ford Center for the Performing Arts (a replacement of the landmark Lyric and Apollo Theatres) marked the culmination of the most extensive advance-marketing campaign ever mounted for a Broadway production. Hundreds of print, television, and radio advertisements had been in circulation for a year prior to the show's arrival, predating the completion of Terrence McNally's script and even the hiring by producer Garth Drabinsky and director Frank Galati of composers and lyricists for the show.

In Canada significant new plays were also in short supply, with the notable exceptions of John Mighton's *Possible Worlds,* a philosophical comedy-thriller remounted in Toronto after it swept the small theatre division of the 1996 Dora Mavor Moore Awards, and Djanet Sears's *Harlem Duet,* a riff on the Othello story devised by Toronto's Nightwood Theatre. Veteran playwright George F. Walker made a triumphant reentry onto the Canadian scene (and revivified Toronto's faltering Factory Theatre) with just half a play—three episodes of his *Suburban Motel,* a mordantly comic play cycle in six parts, the other three of which were due in spring 1998.

Thriving under new leadership, Canada's Shaw Festival found a gem in its namesake's rarely seen drama *In Good King Charles's Golden Days,* a sort of historic dinner party with fascinating and bitchy guests. In Quebec City the French-Canadian auteur Robert Lepage, who was at work on a piece about American architect Frank Lloyd Wright, unveiled La Caserne Dalhousie, the new home of his Ex Machina company, in a cupola-topped fire station renovated over five years at a cost of Can$7.5 million.

Theatre figures who died in 1997 included agent Helen Merrill, who represented some of the U.S.'s most important playwrights; teacher and theorist Michael Kirby, author of *The Art of Time;* character actor Burgess Meredith (*see* Obituaries); and ground-breaking lighting designer Abe Feder. (JIM O'QUINN)

MOTION PICTURES

Diminished surprises and excitement in the programs of the great international film festivals in 1997 seemed to reflect widespread stagnation in the international cinema, no doubt the eventual and inevitable effect of years of domination of world markets by imported Hollywood productions. Many countries with previously rich and inventive small cinemas had little to show during the year. Outside Hollywood, with its well-established commercial patterns, the most vital areas of production were Great Britain, enjoying a sense of renascence, and the Far East, with cinema activity burgeoning economically and artistically in a period of impending political change.

Cinema in English-Speaking Countries. From Hollywood, big-budget box-office winners of the year included Steven Spielberg's *The Lost World: Jurassic Park,* with magical special-effects creations of prehistoric animals but a banal script and two-dimensional human characters; Barry Sonnenfeld's cool and witty science fantasy *Men in Black,* about sombre-suited agents battling extraterrestrials; Wolfgang Petersen's suspense adventure *Air Force One,* which imagined Russian terrorists hijacking the aircraft of the U.S. president, played by Harrison Ford (*see* BIOGRAPHIES); and Paul Verhoeven's *Starship Troopers,* a violent science-fiction fantasy about a teenage military force facing technologically advanced bugs from outer space. Other significant commercial successes were Hong Kong director John Woo's tough crime thriller *Face/Off;* Tom Shadyac's comedy *Liar Liar,* with Jim Carrey (*see* BIOGRAPHIES) as a ruthless lawyer bewitched so that he can speak only the truth for 24 hours; P.J. Hogan's attractive *My Best Friend's Wedding,* starring Julia Roberts as a woman determined to prevent the marriage of the man she wrongly thought she did not want; and *Boogie Nights,* written and directed by Paul Thomas Anderson, about Hollywood's pornographic film industry in the 1970s. Hollywood economic theories were, however, shaken by the surprising success of more modestly budgeted but inventive films like the British comedies *Bean* and *The Full Monty* and "sleepers" like Jay Roach's *Austin Powers: International Man of Mystery,* a parody of James Bond–style spy thrillers.

As is often the case, many of the year's best movies were released in December. They included James Cameron's $200 million blockbuster *Titanic;* Spielberg's *Amistad,* about a rebellion aboard a 19th-century slave ship and the legal aftermath; Gus Van Sant's *Good Will Hunting,* depicting the redemption of a drifting young man; James Brooks's *As Good As It Gets,* a romance with a star turn by Jack Nicholson; Martin Scorsese's *Kundun,* about the Dalai Lama with an all-Tibetan cast; and Barry Levinson's satirical *Wag the Dog.*

Hollywood's traditionally most creative directors were in good form. Woody Allen's *Deconstructing Harry* was a characteristic portrait—comic, painful, and complex in structure—of a writer beset by wives, lovers, psychiatrists, and his own immaturity. Oliver Stone refreshingly set aside sociopolitical pretensions in a fresh and gripping genre thriller, *U-Turn.* Paul Schrader effectively adapted Russell Banks's novel *Affliction,* about a backwoods sheriff (Nick Nolte) battling his own intrinsic failure. Clint Eastwood demonstrated his craft as storyteller with *Absolute Power,* a thriller about a burglar who accidentally witnesses a murder in which the American president himself is an accessory, and followed this with *Midnight in the Garden of Good and Evil,* based on John Berendt's book about a real-life killing in Savannah, Ga. Alan J. Pakula's action drama *The Devil's Own* offered an intriguing moral conflict between an Irish republican terrorist and a New York cop. Robert Zemeckis's *Contact,* based on the novel by Carl Sagan, was a thoughtful and intelligent science-fiction speculation. The actor Robert Duvall wrote, directed, and starred in *The Apostle,* a finely constructed portrait of a preacher who flees the outcome of a crime of passion to seek spiritual redemption, and Francis Ford Coppola effectively adapted John Grisham's *The Rainmaker.*

African-American directors turned to history. Bill Duke attempted a *Godfather*-style treatment of a 1930s black racketeer, Ellsworth Johnson (played by Laurence Fishburne), in *Hoodlum.* In *Rosewood* John Singleton recalled a long-forgotten atrocity of 1923 when a black Florida township was destroyed by whites crazed by racial hatred. Spike Lee's first documentary, *4 Little Girls,* was a sober and powerful investigation of the 1963 bombing of a church in Birmingham, Ala., in which four black children were killed. A view of contemporary African-American life was offered by the winner of the audience prize at the Sundance Film Festival, Theodore Witcher's *love jones,* a romantic melodrama set in a well-to-do community of young blacks in Chicago.

An exceptional number of foreign directors were active in Hollywood. The Polish director Agnieszka Holland made a glossy but indifferent adaptation of Henry James's *Washington Square,* with a serviceable Anglo-American cast. The Taiwanese director Ang Lee shrewdly traced the progress of a failing Watergate-era marriage in *The Ice Storm.* French director Luc Besson directed *The Fifth Element,* a costly, spectacular, and mindless fantasy set in New York City 250 years in the future. Germany's Wim Wenders made the complex suspense thriller *The End of Violence.*

British directors also chalked up Hollywood successes: Mike Newell with *Donnie Brasco,* based on the true story of an undercover FBI agent committed to undoing the Mafia hoodlum who has become his mentor; Ridley Scott with *G.I. Jane,* a crisp morality story about a woman (Demi Moore) fighting for her right to go through the toughest of naval training; and Mike Figgis with *One Night Stand,* a study of human relationships and the long-term effects upon a husband (Wesley Snipes) of a brief casual infidelity. Adrian Lyne undertook a coarse version of Vladimir Nabokov's *Lolita.*

Among more unusual projects was Betty Thomas's *Private Parts,* the professional biography of the purposefully outrageous radio celebrity Howard Stern (*see* BIOGRAPHIES), which was chronicled with intelligence and surprising charm. The most distinguished independent production of the year was Neil LaBute's debut feature *In the Company of Men,* a finely written, ferocious portrait of two young corporate executives who relieve their anxieties by brutally manipulating the affections of a deaf female coworker.

The Grand Jury Prize at the Sundance Film Festival was won by Jonathan Nossiter's *Sunday,* the story of the encounter of two lonely and self-hating middle-aged people in the New York City borough of Queens. Another Sundance prizewinner, Morgan J. Freeman's debut feature *Hurricane,* was an unusually fresh and believable study of a boy confronting the temptations of urban delinquency.

The British cinema was in a state of euphoria that encouraged production to burgeon and even risked overproduction, given the limited exhibition outlets for the ordinary run of British films. The new Labour Party administration granted new tax concessions to the industry, and large injections of lottery money were promised. U.S. companies, notably Miramax Films, developed new British interests. Most significantly, two modestly budgeted comedies rocketed to unprecedented international commercial success. Mel Smith's *Bean* found a worldwide audience for the very visual comedy style of the eccentric British star Rowan Atkinson. The strength of a much richer comedy, Peter Cattaneo's *The Full Monty,* was the firm social reality and truthful characters at the base of its farcical story, about a group of unemployed and unlovely workingmen from the depressed North putting on a Chippendale-style strip act.

British filmmakers continued to favour literary and costume subjects. Iain Softley adapted James's *The Wings of the Dove,* and Phil Agland did Thomas Hardy's *The Woodlanders.* Beeban Kidron made *Swept from the Sea,* an ambitious version of Joseph Conrad's short story "Amy Foster." The Dutch director Marleen Gorris's adaptation of Virginia Woolf's *Mrs. Dalloway* was notable for Vanessa Redgrave's performance in the title role. Best of the adaptations was the Monty Python alumni's clever and charming update of Kenneth Grahame's children's classic *The Wind in the Willows,* directed by Terry Jones.

Notable among biographical studies were Brian Gilbert's *Wilde,* with the gay actor-humorist-author Stephen Fry giving conviction to the role of the tragic author, and John Madden's *Mrs. Brown,* a restrained and touching record of the friendship of Queen Victoria with her loyal but independent-minded Scottish servant John Brown, the two roles splendidly interpreted by Judi Dench and Billy Connolly.

It was an impressive year for British and Irish directorial debuts. The actor Gary Oldman made *Nil by Mouth,* a ferocious and foul-mouthed personal memory of dysfunctional family life in the East End of London. Another actor, Alan Rickman, adapted Sharman MacDonald's stage play *The Winter Guest,* about a group of Scots in a frozen seacoast town. The playwright Jez Butterworth adapted his own stage play *Mojo,* a group portrait of 1950s London lowlife, set in a sleazy club where promising rock singers are bought, sold, and seduced. Two very young first-time directors were Shane Meadows with *TwentyFourSeven,* a funny and serious impression of the life of young people in the depressed Midlands, and, from Ireland, Graham Jones with the low-budget *How to Cheat in the Leaving Certificate,* a comic story that directed serious criticism at outdated educational systems.

The most attractive film from Australia was unquestionably Chris Kennedy's *Doing Time for Patsy Cline,* a whimsical road movie about a teenage aspirant to country-music stardom on the first modest but trouble-prone leg of his journey. Also effective was Bill Bennett's road comedy-thriller *Kiss or Kill.*

From Canada's Atom Egoyan (*see* BIOGRAPHIES), *The Sweet Hereafter* adapted Russell Banks's novel about the feelings and relationships of a small community in the aftermath of a fatal schoolbus accident. Egoyan also completed the medium-length

LOREY SEBASTIAN—MPTV

Steven Spielberg's *Amistad,* about an 1839 slave rebellion, opened in December four days after a federal court in Los Angeles denied a motion to enjoin the film until a trial could determine whether its characters and scenes were illegally copied from author Barbara Chase-Riboud's book *Echo of Lions* (1989).

TOM HILTON—THE KOBAL COLLECTION

Peter Cattaneo's surprising smash comedy *The Full Monty,* about a group of unemployed British workingmen who decide to raise some money by putting on a one-time strip act at a local club, won rave reviews from movie critics and delighted audiences in 1997. The film marked the debut of screenwriter Simon Beaufoy.

Sarabande, about a mixed group of characters variously connected by a Bach concert performed by Yo Yo Ma.

Continental Europe. Some of the best French films of the year concentrated on individual problems and intimate communities. Alain Berliner's *Ma vie en rose* was the wryly comic story of a small boy's gender confusions. Manuel Poirier's *Marion* was a kindly and credible observation of the relationship of modest villagers and a couple of Parisian weekenders. Subsequently, Poirier directed *Western,* a quirky and no-less-attractive road movie about two foreigners journeying through France. Bruno Dumont's debut feature, *La Vie de Jésus* (*The Life of Jesus*) was a deeply felt impression of the boredom of teenagers in a remote provincial town. A Franco-Italian-Swiss co-production, Fabio Carpi's *Homère—portrait de l'artiste dans ses vieux jours* (*Homer—Portrait of the Artist as an Old Man*), with an impressive performance by Claude Rich as an elderly poet embittered by blindness and suspicion, won many festival prizes.

Italian cinema maintained its concern with issues of crime and official abuse. Pasquale Pozzessare's *Testimone a rischio* (*Eyewitness*) told the true story of a salesman who accidentally witnesses a Mafia killing, conscientiously reports it to the police, and subsequently finds his family's life in ruins, thanks to the inadequate provisions for protecting witnesses. Another work about official failure, Franco Bernini's *Le Mani forte* (*The Grey Zone*) looked at the likely involvement of the Italian secret service in many of the terrorist bombings of the 1960s and '70s. Winner of the Grand Jury Prize at the Venice Film Festival, Paolo Virzi's *Ovosodo* (*Hardboiled Egg*) was a seriocomic story of the life from birth to 20-something of a lad from the depressed area of Livorno.

Adaptations of historical novels were in vogue, two examples being Marco Bellocchio's version of Heinrich von Kleist's *Il Principe di Homburg* (*The Prince of Homburg*) and *Marianna Ucrìa,* Roberto Faenza's handsome adaptation of Dacia Maraini's novel *La lunga vita di Marianna Ucria,* the story of an independent-minded deaf aristocratic woman. A new addition to the school of director-clowns and a master of physical comedy, Antonio Albanese directed *Uomo d'acqua dolce* (*Freshwater Man*), the story of a man who returns home after a five-year attack of amnesia, the result of a blow on the head while he was buying mushrooms to satisfy the craving of his pregnant wife.

Although German production failed to make much international impression, it did offer a rare homemade box-office success in Helmut Dietl's *Rossini: oder die mörderische Frage, wer mit wem schlief...* (*Rossini, or the Fatal Question, Who Slept with Whom...*), set entirely in a smart restaurant where the habitués—people of the film world—trade business, careers, and bodies. Austria had some international success with *Funny Games,* Michael Haneke's horrific story of a family terrorized by homicidal psychopaths, and with Reinhard Schwabenitzky's *Hannah,* the story of an assertive young woman who discovers that the management of the family firm where she works is riddled with neo-Nazism.

One of the most attractive films to emerge from Spain was Montxo Armendáriz's fine picture of childhood in the Franco-era 1960s; *Segretos del corazón* (*Secrets of the Heart*) explored secrets of sex, death, and skeletons in family closets through the wondering eyes of a nine-year-old boy. Another elegant, evocative memory of growing up in Franco's Spain, José Luís García Sánchez's *Tranvía a la Malvarrosa* (*Tramway to Malvarrosa*) was based on the memoirs of the writer Manuel Vincent.

Spain's Pedro Almodóvar instilled a Spanish atmosphere and his own brand of irony into an adaptation of Ruth Rendell's *Carne trémula* (*Live Flesh*). Bigas Luna's Franco-Spanish *La femme de chambre du*

Georges du Fresne stars in French director Alain Berliner's 1997 film *Ma vie en rose,* the story of a young boy who decides one day that he wants to be a girl. Although *Ma vie en rose* dealt with a tough topical issue, it ended optimistically, with the boy's family eventually accepting his decision.

JEAN-CLAUDE LOTHER—THE KOBAL COLLECTION

Titanic (*The Chambermaid and the Titanic*) was adapted from Didier Decoin's novel about a man who fantasizes a brief encounter into a public show. Félix Sabroso's *Perdona bonita, pero Lucas me quería a mí* typified the flourishing Spanish school of absurdist, postmodern, pop culture comedy thrillers. Portugal's Manoel de Oliveira, at 89 the world's oldest working director, clearly intended autobiographical reflections in his *Viagem ao princípio do mundo* (*Journey to the Beginning of the World*), with Marcello Mastroianni, in his final role, as an elderly film director looking back on his life.

A year of modestly distinguished pan-Scandinavian co-productions included the Norwegian-Danish-German *Mendel,* written and directed by Alexander Røsler, which described with feeling the psychological effects upon a bright young Jewish boy of emigration from postwar-Germany to a small Norwegian community; and Bille August's *Smilla's Sense of Snow,* a Swedish-Danish-German co-production, with a largely British cast, adapted from Peter Høeg's novel about a part-Inuit woman scientist who becomes an amateur private investigator.

The runaway Danish box-office hit of the year, Stellan Olsson's sharp and touching *En loppe kan også gø* (*Fleas Bark Too, Don't They?*) was based on Jens Peder Larsen's novel about a teenage heroine who has only one leg. The main character was played with charm and spirit by a similarly afflicted actress, Christina Brix Christensen. Also from Denmark came Anders Rønnow-Klarlund's auspicious debut film, *Den Attende*

INTERNATIONAL FILM AWARDS 1997

Golden Globes, awarded in Beverly Hills, Calif., in January 1997	
Best motion picture drama	*The English Patient* (U.S.; director, Anthony Minghella)
Best musical or comedy	*Evita* (U.S.; director, Alan Parker)
Best director	Milos Forman (*The People vs. Larry Flynt,* U.S.)
Best actress, drama	Brenda Blethyn (*Secrets & Lies,* U.K.)
Best actor, drama	Geoffrey Rush (*Shine,* Australia)
Best actress, musical or comedy	Madonna (*Evita,* U.S.)
Best actor, musical or comedy	Tom Cruise (*Jerry Maguire,* U.S.)
Best foreign-language film	*Kolya* (Czech Republic; director, Jan Sverák)
Sundance Film Festival, awarded in Park City, Utah, in January 1997	
Grand Jury Prize, dramatic film	*Sunday* (U.S.; director, Jonathan Nossiter)
Grand Jury Prize, documentary	*Girls like Us* (U.S.; directors, Jane C. Wagner, Tina DiFeliciantonio)
Audience award, dramatic film	*Hurricane* (U.S.; director, Morgan J. Freeman) and *love jones* (U.S.; director, Theodore Witcher)
Audience award, documentary	*Paul Monette: The Brink of Summer's End* (U.S.; director, Monte Bramer)
Berlin International Film Festival, awarded in February 1997	
Golden Berlin Bear	*The People vs. Larry Flynt* (U.S.; director, Milos Forman)
Special Jury Prize	*The River* (Taiwan; director, Tsai Ming-liang)
Best director	Eric Heumann (*Port Djema,* France/Italy/Greece)
Best actress	Juliette Binoche (*The English Patient,* U.S.)
Best actor	Leonardo DiCaprio (*William Shakespeare's Romeo & Juliet,* U.S.)
Césars (France), awarded in February 1997	
Best French film	*Ridicule* (director, Patrice Leconte)
Best director	Patrice Leconte (*Ridicule*) and Bertrand Tavernier (*Capitaine Conan*)
Best actress	Fanny Ardant (*Pédale douce*)
Best actor	Philippe Torreton (*Capitaine Conan*)
Best first film	*Y Aura-t-il de la neige à Noel?* (director, Sandrine Veysset)
Academy of Motion Picture Arts and Sciences (Oscars, U.S.), awarded in Los Angeles in March 1997	
Best film	*The English Patient* (U.S.; director, Anthony Minghella)
Best director	Anthony Minghella (*The English Patient,* U.S.)
Best actress	Frances McDormand (*Fargo,* U.S.)
Best actor	Geoffrey Rush (*Shine,* Australia)
Best supporting actress	Juliette Binoche (*The English Patient,* U.S.)
Best supporting actor	Cuba Gooding, Jr., (*Jerry Maguire,* U.S.)
Best foreign-language film	*Kolya* (Czech Republic; director, Jan Sverák)
British Academy of Film and Television Arts, awarded in London in April 1997	
Best film	*The English Patient* (U.S.; director, Anthony Minghella)
Best director	Joel Coen (*Fargo,* U.S.)
Best actress	Brenda Blethyn (*Secrets & Lies,* U.K.)
Best actor	Geoffrey Rush (*Shine,* Australia)
Best supporting actress	Juliette Binoche (*The English Patient,* U.S.)
Best supporting actor	Paul Scofield (*The Crucible,* U.S.)
Best foreign-language film	*Ridicule* (France; director, Patrice Leconte)
Cannes International Film Festival, France, awarded in May 1997	
Palme d'Or	*The Eel* (Japan; director, Shohei Imamura) and *The Taste of Cherry* (Iran; director, Abbas Kiarostami)
Grand Jury Prize	*The Sweet Hereafter* (Canada; director, Atom Egoyan)
Special Jury Prize	*Western* (France; director, Manuel Poirier)
Best director	Wong Kar-wai (*Happy Together,* Hong Kong)
Best actress	Kathy Burke (*Nil by Mouth,* U.K.)
Best actor	Sean Penn (*She's So Lovely,* U.S.)
Caméra d'Or	*Suzaku* (Japan; director, Naomi Kawase)
International Critics' Prize	*The Sweet Hereafter* (Canada; director, Atom Egoyan)
Locarno International Film Festival, Switzerland, awarded in August 1997	
Golden Leopard	*The Mirror* (Iran; director, Jafar Panahi)
Silver Leopard	*Gadjo Dilo* (France; director, Tony Gatlif) and *Fools* (France/South Africa/Mozambique/Zimbabwe; director, Ramadan Suleman)
Best actress	Rona Hartner (*Gadjo Dilo,* France)
Best actor	Valerio Mastandrea (*We All Fall Down,* Italy)
Montreal World Film Festival, awarded in September 1997	
Best film (Grand Prix of the Americas)	*The Children of Heaven* (Iran; director, Majid Majidi)
Best actress	Frances O'Connor (*Kiss or Kill,* Australia)
Best actor	Sam Rockwell (*Lawn Dogs,* Great Britain)
Best director	Carlos Saura (*Pajarico,* Spain) and Juni Ichikawu (*Tokyo Lullaby,* Japan)
Special Grand Prix of the Jury	*Homer—Portrait of the Artist as an Old Man* (Italy/France/Switzerland; director, Fabio Carpi)
Best screenplay	Fabio Carpi (*Homer—Portrait of the Artist as an Old Man,* Italy/France/Switzerland)
International cinematographic press award	*Homer—Portrait of the Artist as an Old Man* (Italy/France/Switzerland; director, Fabio Carpi)
Venice Film Festival, awarded in September 1997	
Golden Lion	*Hana-bi* (Japan; director, Takeshi Kitano)
Special Jury Prize	*Ovosodo* (Italy; director, Paolo Virzi)
Volpi Cup, best actress	Robin Tunney (*Niagara, Niagara,* U.S.)
Volpi Cup, best actor	Wesley Snipes (*One Night Stand,* U.S.)
International Film Critics' Prize	*Histoire Milosne* (Poland; director, Jerzy Stuhr)
Chicago International Film Festival, awarded in October 1997	
Best feature film	*The Winter Guest* (U.K.; director, Alan Rickman)
Special Jury Prize	*The River* (Taiwan; director, Tsai Ming-liang)
Best actress	Pernilla August (*Private Confessions,* Sweden)
Best actor	Sergey Bodrov (*The Brother,* Russia)
Best director	Michael Haneke (*Funny Games,* Austria)
Best cinematography	Tibor Mathe (*The Witman Boys,* Hungary)
International Film Critics' Prize for debut feature	*La Vie de Jésus* (France; director, Bruno Dumont)
San Sebastián International Film Festival, Spain, awarded in September 1997	
Jury Prize	*I Went Down* (Ireland; director, Paddy Breathnach)
Best director	Claude Chabrol (France, *Rien ne va plus*)
Best actress	Julie Christie (U.S.; *Afterglow*)
Best actor	Federico Luppi (Spain/Argentina; *Martin*)
Special Jury Prize	*Firelight* (U.K.; director, William Nicholson)
Gold Shell	*Rien ne va plus* (France; director, Claude Chabrol)
Tokyo International Film Festival, awarded in November 1997	
Grand Prix	*Beyond Silence* (Germany; director, Caroline Link) and *The Perfect Circle* (Bosnia and Herzegovina; director, Ademir Kenovic)
Special Jury Prize	*Brassed Off* (U.K.; director, Mark Hermon)
Vancouver International Film Festival, British Columbia, awarded in October 1997	
Federal Express Award	*The Hanging Garden* (Canada; director, Thom Fitzgerald)
Air Canada Award	*Beyond Silence* (Germany; director, Caroline Link)
Rogers Award	Thom Fitzgerald (*The Hanging Garden,* Canada)
Best animated film	*Flatworld* (U.K.; director, Daniel Greaves)
Best Western Canadian film	*Kitchen Party* (director, Gary Burns)
Best documentary	*Let Me Go* (Canada; director, Anne Claire Poirier)
Dragons and Tigers Award for Young Cinema	*Green Fish* (South Korea; director, Lee Chang-dong)
European Film Awards, awarded in Berlin in December 1997	
Best European film	*The Full Monty* (U.K.; director, Peter Cattaneo)
Best European actress	Juliette Binoche (*The English Patient,* U.S.)
Best European actor	Bob Hoskins (*TwentyFourSeven,* U.K.)
Outstanding European Achievement in World Cinema	Milos Forman (U.S., *The People vs. Larry Flynt*)

(*The Eighteenth*), an ingenious, progressive intertwining of three disparate groups of characters on the day that Denmark voted to enter the European Union.

Finnish director Paul Anders Simma's *Ministern* (*The Minister of State*) was an attractive, unpretentious myth about a fleeing soldier in World War II who is mistaken for a high-ranking politician, and first-time Norwegian director Erik Skjoldbjærg made an intelligent and polished psychological crime thriller, *Insomnia,* with Stellan Starsgård as a policeman obsessed with the investigation of a young girl's killing. Ingmar Bergman provided the script—a reminiscence of the marital troubles of his own priest-father—for the former actress Liv Ullmann's third film, *Enskilda samtal* (*Private Confessions*).

Among the great indifferent mass of Russian production, the runaway commercial success of the year was Aleksey Balabanov's *Brat* (*The Brother*), a thriller about organized crime wars in St. Petersburg, starring the charismatic young Sergey Bodrov, Jr. Pavel Chukhrai's *Vor* (*The Thief*) was the story of a boy growing up in the 1950s Soviet Union and the trauma he suffers when he discovers that the handsome army officer he has accepted as his father figure is a burglar and pickpocket. International festival favourites of the year were Kira Muratova's sophisticated and entertaining *Tri istorii* (*Three Stories*), which related three black comedies of murder, and Aleksandr Sokurov's painfully slow, if visually beautiful, *Mat i syn* (*Mother and Son*).

The gifted Polish actor Jerzy Stuhr directed and played four roles in the witty and ingenious *Historie milosne* (*Love Stories*), which intertwined the predicaments of four middle-aged men, each confronted by a problematic woman. Filip Bajon's *Poznan '56* was an evocative period piece, an adult's memories of a brave, failed, strike of Polish workers in his childhood, 40 years earlier.

Hungarian cinema showed some signs of recovery. Peter Timar's *Csinibaba* (*Dollybirds*) was an ironic-nostalgic lighthearted musical comedy about the life of a community under communism. Janos Szasz's *Witman Fiúk* (*The Witman Boys*), based on an early-20th-century novel, offered an eerie and richly stylistic tale of a pair of traumatized siblings obsessed by death and sex. Sandor Sara's unsparing *A Vad* (*The Prosecution*) related a terrible tale, based on true events, of the looting and slaughter of a peasant family by the Red Army in the winter of 1944.

Of a number of films inspired by the wars in former Yugoslavia, the finest was certainly a Bosnian-French co-production, Ademir Kenovic's *Savrseni krug* (*The Perfect Circle*), which succeeded in showing the human spirit triumphing over even the most crushing tragedy. The story centres on a feckless poet unwillingly saddled with two war orphans but discovering a sense of responsibility and community that had eluded him in his own previous family life.

Latin America. From Argentina, Eliseo Subiela's *Despabílate amor* (*Wake Up Love*) was a very personal look at the reunion of a group of middle-aged people remembering at once old political traumas and emotional involvements. The prizewinner at Mexico's national festival of Guadalajara, Juan Pablo Viliaseñor's *Por si no te vuelvo a ver* (*If I Never See You Again*) was the seductive tale of a group of old men who escape from the old folks' home to tour with their band. From Brazil, Bruno Barreto's *O que é isso, companheiro?* (*Four Days in September*) scrupulously re-created the real incidents of the 1969 kidnapping of the American ambassador by left-wing revolutionaries.

Asia. Though Iran's most distinguished director, Abbas Kiarostami, incurred official wrath with his film *Ta'm e guilass* (The Taste of Cherry), about a man planning suicide and searching for someone willing to bury him, the film went on to share the Cannes (France) International Film Festival Palme d'Or. Other Iranian directors, either from commercial considerations or because of political caution, stuck to charming and innocuous studies of children. Jafar Panahi used the child actress of his *Badkonake sefid* (*The White Balloon;* 1995) in the less-successful *Ayneh* (*The Mirror*), and Majid Majidi's *Bacheha-ye aseman* (*The Children of Heaven*) featured two ingratiating children and a lost pair of shoes.

Japan triumphed at international festivals. Shohei Imamura's *Unagi* (*The Eel*), about a former convict who prefers his pet eel to other humans, shared the Cannes Film Festival Palme d'Or. International cult director Takeshi Kitano won the Venice Film Festival's Golden Lion with *Hana-bi,* the story of a policeman-turned-bank-robber, marked by the director's characteristic mixture of elegiac melancholy, absurdist humour, chillingly matter-of-fact violence, and pure filmcraft. Masahiro Shinoda's *Setouchi munraito serenade* (*Moonlight Serenade*) observed postwar attitudes through a family traveling to dispose of their soldier-son's ashes.

China's most internationally celebrated director, Zhang Yimou, demonstrated a startling change of mood and style with *You hua hao hao shuo* (*Keep Cool*), a free-wheeling comedy about a bookseller's obsession with a beautiful girl, fascinating for its revelation of the ordinary life of contemporary Beijing. Despite continuing official harassment, including a ban on his employment and withdrawal of his passport, the independent filmmaker Zhang Yuan completed, clandestinely, *Dong gong xi gong* (*East Palace, West Palace*), the first Chinese film to break the taboo on homosexuality. Wang Xiaoshuai, the director of another clandestine Chinese film, *Jidu hanleng* (*Frozen*), about a performance artist who stages his own death, had to conceal his identity under the pseudonym Wu Ming ("No Name").

Hong Kong production entered an energetic phase in the last months before the Chinese takeover. The best film to date of the prolific young Peter Chan, *Tianmimi* (*Comrades: Almost a Love Story*) was an engaging, intelligent romantic study of two mainlanders in Hong Kong during the eventful last decade. Allen Fong returned to the humane charm of his earlier films with *Yi sheng yi tai xi* (*A Little Life-Opera*), the adventures of a small opera troupe in China. Jackie Chan's latest Hong Kong thriller, *Yatgo ho yan* (*Mr. Nice Guy*), directed by Samo Hung, was deliberately aimed, with its largely English dialogue, at the international market.

From Taiwan came *He liu* (*The River*), the third and best film in Tsai Ming-liang's trilogy about a severely dysfunctional family. The son contracts a painful affliction of the neck after being immersed in the polluted Tanshui River; the estranged parents try to help, and the climax is a startling scene of gay incest.

In *Festival,* South Korea's veteran director Im Kwon Taek viewed the ceremonial of a Buddhist funeral through the eyes of the different participants. Hong Sang Soo enjoyed international success with *Daijiga umule pajinnal* (*The Day a Pig Fell into the Well*), a quirky contemporary story of four intersecting lives in present-day Seoul, each character being scripted by a different writer.

From India the most notable new directorial talent was the actress Santwana Bardoloi; her *Adajya* (*The Flight*) was a hard examination of the marginal existence forced on Hindu widows in the 1940s. Shyam Benegal's fascinating *Sardari Begum* reconstructed through flashbacks the imaginary life of a classical thumri singer.

Africa. The leading director of Burkina Faso, Idrissa Ouédraogo, made the most technically ambitious African film to date, *Kini and Adams,* the story of the tried friendship of two poor farmers. Also from Burkina Faso, Gaston Kaboré's *Buud Yam*, top winner at the Ouagadougou film festival, was a mythical tale of a youth who sets out on a quest to find the medicine to restore his mysteriously sick foster sister to health.

From Mali, Abdoulaye Ascofare's *Faraw! Mother of the Dunes* was a powerful portrait of a village woman sustaining her family against the odds of direst poverty. The strange, arid landscapes were finely and evocatively caught by the photography of the Greek master Yorgos Arvanitis. Adama Drabo's *Taafé Fanga* told the humorous story of how the women of a Mali village manipulate their menfolk's superstitious fears to force them to change places and do the hard work of cooking, cleaning, and carrying. A modest film from Guinea, Mohamed Camara's *Dakan* (*Destiny*) was nevertheless historic—and locally reviled—as the first African film to deal openly with the theme of homosexuality.

(DAVID ROBINSON)

Nontheatrical Films. Ken Burns continued in 1997 to earn accolades as he brought history alive. His latest historical documentary, *Lewis and Clark,* again displayed his skill in digging up historical nuggets and then weaving them into a fascinating tale.

Jessica Yu's *Breathing Lessons: The Life and Work of Mark O'Brien* captured prizes throughout the world. This sensitive story of the poet-journalist confined for life in an iron lung won the 1997 Oscar for best documentary short subject and the grand prize at Vila do Conde, Port.

Two educational subjects from the National Geographic Society, *Survivors from the Past: Living Fossils* and *What We Learn About Earth from Space*, garnered several honours, including a silver certificate at Parma, Italy (Prix Leonardo Scientific Film Festival). *Survivors* tells about dinosaurs' succumbing to geologic changes while the nautilus, cockroach, horseshoe crab, and other animals living at that time survived. *What We Learn* revealed the perspective on the Earth gained by looking down on it from space and seeing it as a geologic unit without political boundaries. (THOMAS W. HOPE)

See also Art, Antiques, and Collections: *Photography;* Media and Publishing: *Radio; Television.*

This article updates the *Macropædia* article MOTION PICTURES.

Population Trends

DEMOGRAPHY

At midyear 1997 world population stood at 5,840,000,000, according to estimates prepared by the Population Reference Bureau. The 1997 figure was more than 800 million higher than in 1987, when world population first reached five billion. It was now clear that a six billion total in world population would be reached before 2000, most probably in 1999. The 1997 figure represented an increase of about 86 million over the previous year. The annual rate of increase declined to about 1.47% in 1997 from 1.52% in 1996, a result of birthrate declines in some less-developed countries (LDCs). If the 1997 growth rate were to continue, the world's population would double in 47 years. In 1997, 139 million babies were born, 126 million (over 90%) of them in LDCs. About 53 million people died worldwide. A smaller proportion (77%) of these were in the LDCs, a result of their much younger age structure.

Worldwide, 56% of married couples in 1997 used some method of contraception, and half of all couples were using a "modern" method, such as clinically supplied contraceptives or sterilization. In the LDCs 54% were practicing some form of family planning, and 49% were using a modern one, the latter a slight increase over 1996. The proportion of couples using modern family-planning methods in LDCs excluding China was much lower, only 36%. Regionally, this figure was 58% in Latin America and the Caribbean, 54% in Asia, and only 18% in Africa.

Worldwide, 32% of the population was below the age of 15 in 1997, but that figure was 38% in LDCs excluding China. In more developed countries (MDCs) only 20% were below age 15, as a result of the persistently low birthrate throughout Europe and in Japan. The continued younger age distribution of the LDCs in 1997 would result in a large number of people entering the childbearing ages in the near future, and so there was considerable potential for population growth in those areas. Only 4% of the population in LDCs excluding China was over the age of 65, compared with 14% in the MDCs. Sweden remained the country with the highest percentage of population above age 65 at 18%.

Nearly half, 43%, of the world population in 1997 lived in urban areas. In the LDCs 36% of the population was classified as urban, a slight increase over the previous year, compared with 74% in the MDCs. Among the world's least urbanized countries was Rwanda, with only 5% living in urban centres.

Worldwide, life expectancy at birth was 64 years for males and 68 for females. In the MDCs the same figures were 71 and 78 and in the LDCs 62 and 65, respectively. The 1997 world infant mortality rate stood at 59 infant deaths per 1,000 live births. The lowest infant mortality rates were in Western and Northern Europe, at 5 and 6 infant deaths per 1,000 live births, respectively. Although there were small decreases in some LDCs, the overall rate remained at a high level, 64.

Less-Developed Countries. In 1997 the population of the LDCs grew at 1.81% per year, 2.09% for LDCs excluding China. The total population of the LDCs was 4,666,000,000, 80% of the world total. Of the 86 million people added annually to the world population, 98% were in the LDCs. In LDCs excluding China, women still averaged four children each, unchanged from a year earlier. This remained far from the "two-child family" essential to slowing population growth to zero and stabilizing world population size.

During 1997 Africa remained the region with by far the highest fertility, an average of 5.6 children per woman, 6 in sub-Saharan Africa. New survey data released in 1997 indicated, however, that there was a continued slow decline in fertility in the region. The 1997 Demographic and Health Survey in Senegal indicated that the average number of children per woman declined from about 6 in 1992–93 to 5.7 in 1997. A similar survey in Zambia showed a decline from 6.5 in 1992 to 6.1 in 1996.

Africa's population in 1997 totaled 743 million, an increase of about 20 million since 1996. The continent's annual growth rate was 2.6%, the world's highest by a wide margin and sufficient to double population size in only 26 years. In 1997 life expectancy in Africa, at 52 years for males and 55 for females, was the world's lowest. Infant mortality was the world's highest at 89 infant deaths per 1,000 live births.

In 1997 Latin America's population stood at 490 million, with an annual growth rate of 1.8%, slightly lower than in 1996. The average number of children per woman fell slightly in 1997, to 3, ranging from 5.2 in Honduras to 1.5 in Cuba. Life expectancy remained at 66 years for males and 72 for females. Infant mortality stood at 39.

Asia's population was about 3.6 billion in 1997, by far the largest of the world's regions, up from 3.5 billion in 1996. The region's growth rate remained at about 1.6%, which resulted in a population increase of about 56 million. Life expectancy in Asia in 1997 stood at about 64 for males and 67 for females. Women averaged 2.9 children each, 3.5 excluding China. During 1997 data released for India in 1995 showed

SEBASTIÃO SALGADO—CONTACT PRESS IMAGES

Overpopulation continued to be a major problem in India, where crowded train stations, like this one in Bombay (Mumbai), were common sights. As its number of residents approached one billion in 1997, India moved closer to overtaking China as the most populous nation in the world.

World's 25 Most Populous Urban Areas[1]					
		City proper		Metropolitan area	
Rank	City and country	Population	Year	Population	Year
1	Tokyo, Japan	7,966,195	1995 cen.	27,242,000	1996 est.
2	Mexico City, Mex.	9,815,795	1990 cen.	16,908,000	1996 est.
3	São Paulo, Braz.	9,393,753	1995 est.	16,792,000	1996 est.
4	New York City, U.S.	7,380,906	1996 est.	16,390,000	1996 est.
5	Bombay (Mumbai), India	9,925,891	1991 cen.	15,725,000	1996 est.
6	Shanghai, China	8,930,000	1993 est.	13,659,000	1996 est.
7	Los Angeles, U.S.	3,553,638	1996 est.	12,576,000	1996 est.
8	Calcutta, India	4,399,819	1991 cen.	12,118,000	1996 est.
9	Buenos Aires, Arg.	2,988,006	1995 est.	11,931,000	1996 est.
10	Seoul, S.Kor.	10,776,201	1995 est.	11,768,000	1996 est.
11	Jakarta, Indon.	9,160,500	1995 est.	11,500,000	1995 est.
12	Beijing, China	6,690,000	1993 est.	11,414,000	1996 est.
13	Lagos, Nigeria	1,518,000	1996 est.	10,878,000	1996 est.
14	Tianjin, China	5,000,000	1993 est.	10,687,000	1995 est.
15	Osaka, Japan	2,602,352	1995 cen.	10,618,000	1996 est.
16	Delhi, India	7,206,704	1991 cen.	10,298,000	1996 est.
17	Rio de Janeiro, Braz.	5,473,033	1995 est.	10,264,000	1996 est.
18	Karachi, Pak.	5,208,132	1981 cen.	10,119,000	1996 est.
19	Cairo, Egypt	6,849,000	1994 est.	9,900,000	1996 est.
20	Paris, France	2,156,766	1991 cen.	9,469,000	1995 est.
21	Manila, Phil.	1,654,761	1995 est.	9,280,000	1995 est.
22	Moscow, Russia	8,436,447	1996 est.	9,233,000	1995 est.
23	Dhaka, Bangladesh	3,839,000	1991 cen.	8,500,000	1996 est.
24	Istanbul, Tur.	7,774,169	1995 est.	7,817,000	1995 est.
25	Lima, Peru	5,706,127	1993 est.	7,452,000	1995 est.

[1]Ranked by population of metropolitan area.

that the country's birthrate did not decline as much as expected. Early reports indicated that the number of new users of family planning fell sharply in 1996 as the government dropped specific demographic goals for its population program.

More Developed Countries. The population of the MDCs in 1997 was 1,175,000,000, only 4,000,000 higher than in 1996. The growth rate of these countries was barely over zero, at 0.1% annually. During 1997 Europe continued to report a negative rate of natural increase (birthrate minus death rate) of –0.1%, the first time in history that a major world region had done so. This was due primarily to the sharp drop of the birthrate in the European republics of the former Soviet Union and to continued low fertility in Western Europe. Latvia's record low rate of natural decrease continued at –0.7%. Once again, 13 European countries reported natural decrease rates: Belarus, Bulgaria, Croatia, the Czech Republic, Estonia, Germany, Hungary, Italy, Latvia, Lithuania, Romania, Russia, and Ukraine. Italy and Spain again exhibited the lowest birthrates in the world, with an average number of children per woman of only 1.2; Bulgaria, Czech Republic, and Latvia also registered rates of 1.2.

Life expectancy at birth in Europe (including the European republics of the former Soviet Union) was 69 for males and 77 for females. A major development was the end of the life-expectancy decline in Russia. Life expectancy in Russia was reported to have risen in 1996 to 59.6 for males, up 1.3 years from 1995, and to 72.7 for women, up one year. Japan maintained its leading position on life expectancy, 83 for females and 77 for males. With a rate of 3.9 infant deaths per 1,000 live births, Finland reported the lowest infant mortality in the world, thereby replacing Japan, whose rate of 4 was tied with Singapore for second best.

United States. The resident population of the U.S. was 267,575,000 on July 1, 1997, up from 265,284,000 a year earlier. This represented an increase of 2,291,000, or 0.86%. The National Center for Health Statistics (NCHS) reported that during the 12 months ended in January 1997, natural increase—births minus deaths—amounted to 1,574,000, the net result of 3,882,000 births and 2,308,000 deaths. During that period the birthrate was 14.6 births per 1,000 population, compared with 14.7 in the 12 months ended in January 1996. This represented a much smaller decrease than for the same period in 1995–96. The average number of children per woman stood at about 2 as 1997 began. The U.S. infant mortality rate continued to fall, reaching its lowest level ever at 7.2 for the 12-month period ended in January 1997. Approximately 32% of the births during the 12 months ended June 1996 were reported as having occurred outside of marriage, about the same proportion as in the previous period.

Causes of Death in the United States (January–December)		
	Rate per 100,000 population	
Rank in 1996	1995	1996
1. Diseases of the heart	278.1	275.0
2. Malignant neoplasms	204.1	204.5
3. Cerebrovascular diseases	59.7	59.8
4. Chronic obstructive pulmonary diseases	39.4	39.8
5. Accidents and adverse effects	34.2	34.2
6. Pneumonia and influenza	30.5	30.8
7. Diabetes mellitus	22.2	23.2
8. HIV infection	16.1	11.8
9. Suicide	11.4	11.4
10. Nephritis, nephrotic syndrome, and nephrosis	9.8	10.2
11. Chronic liver disease and cirrhosis	9.5	9.2
12. Septicemia	8.1	8.2
13. Homicide and legal intervention	8.5	7.9
14. Atherosclerosis	6.2	5.9
15. Certain conditions of the perinatal period	5.1	4.9

The age-adjusted death rate for 1996, 492.5 per 100,000 population, declined 2% from 1995. In 1997 the NCHS reported that in 1995 life expectancy at birth rose to a new high, 75.8 years. Female life expectancy was 78.9, a slight decline from the previous year, while male life expectancy rose slightly to 72.5. Life expectancy for white females approached 80 years, at 79.6, while that of white males was 73.4. Black men had the lowest life expectancy of all groups, 65.2 years, while for black females the figure was 73.9.

There were 2,351,000 marriages in the United States in the 12-month period ended in January 1997, a slight increase from 2,324,000 one year earlier. The marriage rate was 8.9 marriages per 1,000 population, virtually the same as in the previous 12-month period. The number of divorces decreased from 1,167,000 to 1,148,000.

(CARL V. HAUB)

See also World Data.

REFUGEES AND INTERNATIONAL MIGRATION

By 1997 the massive humanitarian crises that arose during the first half of the 1990s had largely abated, although longer-term rehabilitation and reconstruction efforts continued on behalf of the people uprooted by those events. Overall, the world's refugee population decreased from 15.5 million in 1996 to 13.2 million in 1997. Similarly, the overall population of concern to the Office of the United Nations High Commissioner for Refugees (UNHCR) fell to some 22.7 million, representing one out of every 255 people on Earth. Of this figure, in addition to the 13.2 million refugees, 3.3 million were returnees, 4.9 million were internally displaced persons (persons in a refugee-like situation but who had not crossed an international border), and 1.4 million were others of humanitarian concern, mainly victims of conflict. UNHCR continued to implement its distinctive international protection mandate in respect to those persons, which involved safeguarding and developing principles of refugee protection, strengthening international commitments, and promoting durable solutions, be they in the form of voluntary repatriation, local integration, or resettlement.

More than two million refugees returned to their countries of origin in the latter half of 1996 and the first half of 1997, which highlighted the fact that repatriation is the preferred solution for many of the world's refugees. Often, however, they returned to fragile or unstable situations.

The Great Lakes region of Africa, where more than two million Rwandans and Burundians fled their countries in 1994, remained a major focus of humanitarian concern. The events in former Zaire (now the Democratic Republic of the Congo; Congo [Kinshasa]) during the first months of 1997 led to the return of Rwandan refugees from that country to their homeland. Locating refugees after they dispersed from camps in eastern Zaire became a predominant objective early in the year. In spite of the harsh conditions and the ongoing conflict, tens of thousands of refugees were found surviving in the surrounding forests, living in dismal conditions. Repatriation operations were mounted, using all means available, and some 180,000 of these refugees were returned to Rwanda. Though more than 860,000 Rwandan refugees were returned to Rwanda in the last half of 1996 and in 1997,

SEBASTIÃO SALGADO—CONTACT PRESS IMAGES

Kurdish refugees in the Atroosh camp in northern Iraq ready themselves to leave as the camp prepared to shut down. Because the Kurdish homeland was divided between Iraq, Turkey, Iran, and Syria, millions of Kurds had been forced to become refugees in recent years.

thousands remained away from their homeland, spread among 10 countries in the region, while up to 190,000 more remained unaccounted for. The forced repatriation of several hundred Rwandan refugees in August and September 1997 from countries in the region raised great concern and caused UNHCR to suspend its operations on behalf of Rwandan refugees in the Congo (Kinshasa). In Rwanda itself the country was struggling with the aftermath of the Hutu-Tutsi conflict while trying to absorb the estimated 2.8 million refugees who had returned since 1994. At the end of 1997, some 74,000 Congolese (former Zairian) refugees remained in Tanzania, although their gradual repatriation was under way. There were also large groups of Burundian refugees in Tanzania and the Congo (Kinshasa). Their return was contingent on the restoration of stability in Burundi.

In southern Africa the violence that not so long ago had permeated the region was replaced by relative peace, stability, and national reconciliation. The implementation of the 1994 peace accord that ended 20 years of civil war in Angola raised hopes that the more than 300,000 refugees currently outside the country could begin returning home in the near future, this being the largest remaining refugee population in the region. Despite setbacks in the peace process, as of mid-1997 a total of some 96,000 refugees had spontaneously returned to Angola.

In western Africa renewed violence in Sierra Leone delayed the planned repatriation of some 375,000 refugees, who, for the most part, had sought asylum in Guinea and Liberia. The coup on May 25 in Freetown resulted in the outflow of an additional 38,000 refugees into those neighbouring countries. In Liberia the peace process made progress. The successful disarmament and demobilization exercise conducted in February and the holding of legislative and presidential elections in July were expected to lead to the return of the more than 500,000 Liberian refugees who were living in Guinea, Côte d'Ivoire, Ghana, and Nigeria and thus bring to an end one of the worst civil wars on the African continent. In Western Sahara renewed efforts to reinvigorate the United Nations Settlement Plan were beginning to reinstill hope that this long-standing dispute could be resolved peace-

In order to support themselves, refugees at the La Miel farm camp in Ibagué, Colom., make *panela,* a hardened candy produced from sugarcane. By 1997 an estimated one million people in Colombia had been displaced by intermittent guerrilla warfare, civil unrest, and drug wars.

PEDRO UGARTE—AGENCE FRANCE-PRESSE

fully and allow for some 165,000 refugees to return to their homeland.

During the first half of 1997 in the Horn of Africa and eastern Africa, a region emerging from years of prolonged conflict, approximately 7,000 Ethiopian refugees returned home from The Sudan and more than 7,000 Somali refugees were repatriated from eastern Ethiopia to northwestern Somalia. The onset of the rainy season, however, postponed further returns until later in the year. The return of more than 320,000 Eritrean refugees from The Sudan, however, was delayed by a stalemate in discussions over the procedures to be followed for their repatriation.

In Bosnia and Herzegovina the guns had fallen silent following the signing of the Dayton Accords in December 1995. More than 250,000 people had by mid-1997 settled or resettled in areas where their ethnic group was in the majority, by far the largest numbers coming from Germany. The return of ethnic minorities to their former homes, however, continued to be difficult. UNHCR, the lead agency for humanitarian operations in former Yugoslavia, was attempting to overcome the persistent obstacles to the return of displaced persons and refugees to these so-called minority areas by launching an "Open Cities" initiative, whereby towns and areas in Bosnia and Herzegovina were invited to declare their readiness to accept the return of former inhabitants, regardless of their origins. A number of towns and areas responded favourably, but significant progress was slow. The return of refugees to Croatia was also negligible, despite commitments established between the government of Croatia, UNHCR, and the United Nations Transitional Administration for Eastern Slavonia, Baranja, and Western Sirmium (UNTAES) to accelerate movements into and out of Krajina and Eastern and Western Slavonia.

Elsewhere in Europe negotiations were under way on the conflict between Georgia and its breakaway regions of Abkhazia and South Ossetia, which had displaced an estimated 38,000 persons from Georgia, forcing them to seek asylum in Russia. In the countries of the Commonwealth of Independent States, legislation to address refugee flows and migratory movements affecting an estimated nine million persons was beginning to be fostered. In Central Europe during the first half of 1997, some 31,000 Albanian refugees fled unrest and uncertainty in the country, seeking temporary asylum in Italy and Greece. Many later returned to Albania following the deployment of a Multinational Protection Force and moves by the authorities in Albania to restore stability to the country. In Western Europe the number of people seeking asylum continued to decline, partly as a result of stricter visa requirements, reinforced border controls, and, in some countries, restricted social benefits. The rate of recognition of those who were applying for refugee status dropped from 42% in 1984 to some 10% by the mid-1990s. New applications for asylum declined nearly 10% in 1996 from a year earlier.

The Soviet invasion of Afghanistan in 1979 and the subsequent 18 years of civil war led to the uprooting of more than six million Afghans, one-third of the nation's population. Afghan refugees constituted the largest refugee caseload of concern to UNHCR, with 1.4 million persons in Iran and 1.2 million in Pakistan. In addition, up to one million persons were displaced inside the country, most of them since 1993. Between Oct. 1, 1996, and May 1, 1997, more than a quarter of a million people were displaced within Afghanistan or became refugees in Pakistan; approximately 80% of them had left Kabul for a variety of reasons, including fear of persecution by the new conservative faction that controlled much of the nation and its prohibition on women's working outside the home and receiving education. Despite the ongoing conflict, several thousand refugees returned to areas of relative safety in Afghanistan, mainly rural regions.

CAROL GUZY—THE WASHINGTON POST

One of the more than four million Sudanese refugees rests in a hut in the Mangalatore camp for the displaced. Civil war in The Sudan had claimed the lives of the 72-year-old farmer's sons, and he had also lost all of his land and cattle.

Afghanistan also had served as host to some 60,000 Tajik refugees who had fled the 1992–93 civil war in Tajikistan. Most of them had returned to their homeland by mid-1997, about 20,000 remaining in northern Afghanistan. The peace talks in Tajikistan, initiated in the first quarter of 1997, were aimed at improving political and security conditions in that nation and served as an encouragement for higher levels of repatriation.

In Southeast Asia the recent power struggle in Cambodia overshadowed the successful operations with respect to refugees in the region. In July and August some 28,000 Cambodians fled renewed fighting in Cambodia, crossing the border into Thailand. More than 3,000 of them later returned voluntarily despite the precarious conditions at the border area. Following the conclusion of the Comprehensive Plan of Action in June 1996, more than 24,000 Vietnamese boat people returned to Vietnam in late 1996 and the first half of 1997. Some 1,700 Vietnamese remained in Hong Kong after the transfer of the territory to Chinese sovereignty on July 1. In Myanmar (Burma) more than 220,000 Muslim refugees from Rakhine state, who had fled their country in late 1991 and 1992, returned to their homes. Some 21,000 remained in camps in Bangladesh, pending discussions between the two nations on possible solutions to their plight. Elsewhere in Asia more than 90,000 Bhutanese of Nepalese origin remained stranded in southeastern Nepal after having been uprooted from their country in 1991 and 1992. Renewed military activities in Sri Lanka caused large-scale internal displacement in the north of the country. More than 500,000 persons were forced to flee by the fighting, and some 8,000 arrived in India, the first outflow of people from Sri Lanka in recent years.

New waves of internal displacement in Colombia, caused by the actions of leftist guerrillas and right-wing paramilitary groups and security forces, caused increased concern in the region. As many as one million persons were estimated to be internally displaced in Colombia. The numbers seeking refuge across international borders were, however, negligible, owing in part to the rugged terrain in that part of the country. Guatemalan refugees, approximately 38,000 of whom remained in camps and settlements in Mexico, continued to return to their country.

In North America recent changes in immigration laws placed new requirements and limitations on asylum seekers. Stricter deadlines for filing applications and tighter control of ports of entry were among new initiatives to discourage illegal immigration. Despite these tendencies toward further restrictions on immigration, the United States and Canada were increasing their efforts to address the issues of requests for asylum by those who had suffered from sexual violence and from discrimination based on gender.

(UNHCR)

This article updates the *Macropædia* article POPULATION.

Religion

Ecumenical and interfaith relations suffered some serious blows during 1997, although the year was also marked by a historic agreement between four Protestant denominations. Some churches dealt with dissidents in their ranks through excommunication. Church-state conflicts intensified in the United States and Europe, and increased attention was drawn to the persecution of Christians throughout the world.

The Georgian Orthodox Church withdrew its membership from the World Council of Churches (WCC) in May, claiming that the international ecumenical body failed to take Orthodox interests into account. It was the first time since the WCC was founded in 1948 that an Orthodox church had left the 330-member organization.

Disagreements between Orthodox churches and their ecumenical partners led Orthodox Ecumenical Patriarch Bartholomew I of Constantinople to boycott the second European Ecumenical Assembly in Graz, Austria, and prompted Russian Orthodox Patriarch Aleksey II to refuse a meeting with Pope John Paul II. In an address in Washington, D.C., in October, Bartholomew stressed the differences between Orthodox and Roman Catholic Christians, saying that "the manner in which we exist has become ontologically different."

A proposed agreement between the 2.5 million-member Episcopal Church and the 5.2 million-member Evangelical Lutheran Church in America was defeated at the ELCA convention in Philadelphia in August. Opposition to the authority of bishops in the Episcopal tradition was a major factor in the defeat of the proposal, but the Lutherans agreed to begin a two-year process of discussion that might lead to a new concordat proposal.

On a more positive note, the ELCA approved a joint declaration with the Roman Catholic Church on the doctrine of justification, saying, "We confess together that all persons depend completely on the saving grace of God for their salvation." Each of the 123 member churches of the Lutheran World Federation was voting independently on the declaration, and the Vatican was continuing to study the document. The ELCA also became the fourth denomination to ratify an agreement to share full communion with three churches in the Reformed tradition—the 3.7 million-member Presbyterian Church (U.S.A.), the 300,000-member Reformed Church in America, and the 1.5 million-member United Church of Christ. A 1995 decision by the 285,000-member Christian Reformed Church to allow its 47 regional bodies the option of ordaining women as ministers, elders, and evangelists led two smaller bodies—the 278,000-member Presbyterian Church in America and the 22,000-member Orthodox Presbyterian Church—to break fellowship with it in 1997.

As a measure calling on officers to live "in fidelity within the covenant of marriage of a man and a woman or chastity in singleness" took effect in the Presbyterian Church (U.S.A.), its General Assembly in Syracuse, N.Y., adopted a new proposal in June calling on church officers to "demonstrate fidelity and integrity in marriage or singleness, and

UPI

Members of the Church of Scientology stage a protest outside the German embassy in Washington, D.C. In June the German government announced that for a year the church would be under nationwide surveillance, possibly the target of tapped telephones and intercepted mail.

in all relationships of life." That measure, which would replace the "fidelity and chastity" amendment, then was submitted to presbyteries for approval.

A proposal to recognize same-sex marriages in the Episcopal Church was narrowly rejected by the denomination's General Convention in Philadelphia in July. The convention also apologized to gays and lesbians for what it called "years of rejection and maltreatment by the church." The Germantown (Pa.) Mennonite Church, the oldest Mennonite church in the U.S., was expelled from its regional conference as of 1998, and its pastor, Richard Lichty, was stripped of his clergy status because the congregation had declared its unconditional acceptance of homosexuals.

Dissent among some fundamentalists and conservative evangelicals led the International Bible Society to drop plans for what it called a "gender-accurate" Bible translation in the United States. A report in *World,* an evangelical magazine published in Asheville, N.C., charging that the translation was motivated by a feminist agenda led to an outcry. Whereas the Bible Society said that the report was inaccurate, its president, Lars Dunberg, said the organization had concluded that to move ahead with the translation "would cause division within the body of Christ."

In March the 600-member Union of Orthodox Rabbis of the United States and Canada proclaimed that the Conservative and Reform movements "are not Judaism at all." The edict took the two rival movements to task for condoning interfaith marriages and homosexuality and asserted that conversions to Judaism within those movements were not valid. The Rabbinical Council of America, an organization of about 1,000 Orthodox rabbis, said that the smaller group's declaration "does not reflect the sentiments of mainstream Orthodox Jewish thought since it implies the disenfranchisement of Jews as Jews."

In the interfaith sphere, the Roman Catholic Church made several gestures toward the Jewish people in 1997, including Pope John Paul II's condemnation of anti-Semitic interpretations of the New Testament and his hailing of the Jews as the people who gave Jesus Christ to all mankind. On the negative side, Southern Baptists and Jews exchanged angry letters prompted by concerns about a 1996 resolution urging Southern Baptists to renew their emphasis on witnessing to Jews.

The Vatican's chief doctrinal overseer, Joseph Cardinal Ratzinger, told a French publication in March that Buddhism is "an erotic spirituality" that poses a challenge to the church. However, the Dalai Lama preached from the pulpit in the Washington National Cathedral in April and declared that "all major religious traditions carry basically the same message—that is, love, compassion and forgiveness." And a Buddhist temple in Cambodia agreed to be host of the tomb of a Catholic bishop who died in 1977 in a Khmer Rouge labour camp.

The Rev. Tissa Balasuriya, a Sri Lankan Oblate priest, was excommunicated by the Vatican in January because of his positions on original sin, papal infallibility, Mary, and Christ's role in salvation. Objections to his book *Mary and Human Liberation* (1990) figured prominently in the action, which Balasuriya described as "the most severe treatment of a Catholic theologian since Vatican II."

Gleb Yakunin, who was defrocked as a Russian Orthodox priest in 1993, was formally excommunicated in February, as was Patriarch Filaret, the leader of the Ukrainian Autocephalous Orthodox Church. Yakunin was expelled for supporting the Ukrainian and Estonian Orthodox churches in their bid to split from the Russian Orthodox Patriarchate. After Russian Pres. Boris Yeltsin vetoed a bill to restrict the influence of non-Orthodox Christians in Russia, the Russian parliament passed a similar bill in September that Yeltsin signed.

The Russian moves to restrict some churches were among situations cited in an 83-page U.S. State Department report on the persecution of Christians around the world. The report highlighted China as one of the leading offenders and described Saudi Arabia as a country where "freedom of religion does not exist."

In a 6–3 ruling in June, the U.S. Supreme Court struck down the four-year-old Religious Freedom Restoration Act, saying that Congress had overstepped its bounds in enacting the measure in response to a 1990 Supreme Court ruling that curtailed protections for religious practice. Two months after the ruling, U.S. Pres. Bill Clinton issued a set of guidelines to "clarify and reinforce the right of religious expression in the federal workplace." On another church-state matter, the high court ruled 5–4 to reverse a 12-year-old decision forbidding publicly financed teachers to tutor children in religious schools. The 1985 ruling, *Aguilar* v. *Felton,* had concluded that allowing public employees to work within religious schools would advance religion, but the 1997 *Agostini* v. *Felton* decision said government programs do not impermissibly advance religion where they create no financial incentives to religious activity.

In January the U.S. Court of Appeals for the 9th Circuit declared that it is unconstitutional for government officials to tape-record a sacramental confession to a priest by a prisoner. In March the House of Representatives declared that displays of the Ten Commandments should be permitted in government offices and courthouses because they are "a declaration of fundamental principles that are the cornerstone of a fair and just society."

Forty U.S. Orthodox, Protestant, and Roman Catholic leaders issued a statement in July declaring that court rulings have denied the concept of moral truths and given people motivated by religion the status of second-class citizens. The statement cited the 1973 Supreme Court ruling that struck down state abortion laws as a prime example.

Legal restrictions in Germany against the Church of Scientology were criticized in the U.S. State Department's annual survey of human rights around the world. Earlier, 34 prominent Americans from the entertainment industry had compared the restrictions to the way Germany treated Jews in the 1930s. In June the German government announced that for a year the church would be under nationwide surveillance, including the possibility of tapped telephones and intercepted mail.

Michael Drosnin's *The Bible Code* became a runaway best-seller in 1997. The book described the discovery of a code in the Bible that allegedly revealed references to major events of the 20th century as well as predictions about the future.

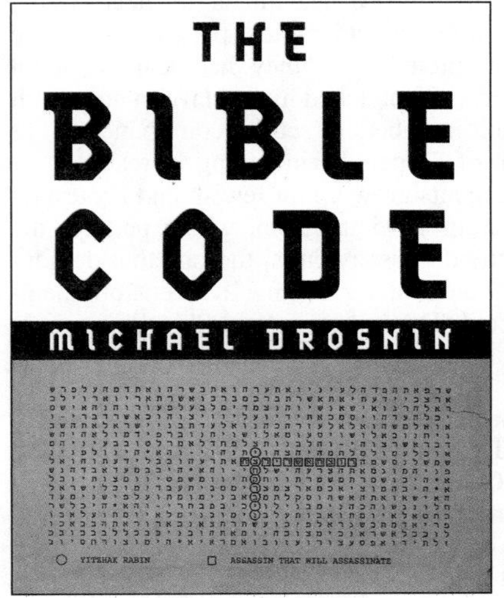

German officials' assertions that Scientology is more of a dangerous cult than a real religion were paralleled by a 600-page report by the Belgian Parliamentary Commission on Cults that applied the label to 189 religious groups. In March the State Secretariat for Cults in Romania barred construction permits for any place of worship not affiliated with one of the 16 religious groups recognized by the state.

Concern about fringe religious movements was heightened in March with the suicide of 39 members of the Heaven's Gate group in a mansion in a suburb of San Diego. Marshall Applewhite, a Presbyterian minister's son who was a cofounder of the group, had constructed a religion that blended elements of Christianity, Gnosticism, theosophy, and a belief in extraterrestrial life. Members of the group believed that they were aliens who had been planted on Earth by a UFO, and that through a mixture of drugs, alcohol, and suffocation, they would be transported to a spacecraft hiding behind the Comet Hale-Bopp. *(See* Special Report.*)*

Several observers of religious movements considered Heaven's Gate to be an example of a preoccupation with apocalyptic prophecies in connection with the coming of a new millennium. Stephen O'Leary of the University of Southern California, cofounder of the Center for Millennial Studies, predicted that "there will be more bizarre incidents and gruesome deaths in anticipation of prophetic fulfillment or in the aftermath of apocalyptic disappointment." In the most publicized religious gathering of the year, hundreds of thousands of men assembled on the Mall in Washington, D.C., in October under the auspices of Promise Keepers, a Christian men's group founded in 1990. The movement stressed reconciliation across denominational and racial boundaries as well as the need for men to practice spiritual, moral, ethical, and sexual purity. Its emphasis on male leadership in family life led the National Organization for Women to call it "the greatest danger to women's rights."

Prophetic fulfillment was the theme of *The Bible Code* (1997), a best-selling book by Michael Drosnin that described the discovery of a code in the text of the Hebrew Bible that contains hidden predictions. The book claimed that the code contains specific references to such events as the assassination of Israeli Prime Minister Yitzhak Rabin, the Oklahoma City, Okla., bombing, and most of the major historical events of the 20th century. Israeli mathematician Eliyahu Rips, whose discovery was the basis of the book, repudiated Drosnin's use of his method to allegedly find predictions of specific events.

A more mainstream religious book that also sold well was *Just as I Am* (1997), the memoirs of evangelist Billy Graham, who turned 79 in November. Another of the century's towering religious figures, Mother Teresa, the Nobel Prize-winning founder of the Order of the Missionaries of Charity, died in September in Calcutta, where for decades she had fed and ministered to the poorest of the city's people. *(See* Obituaries.) Pandurang Shastri Athavale, a Hindu who founded a self-help movement for poor villagers in India, was the 1997 winner of the $1.2 million Templeton Prize for Progress in Religion. Athavale's *swadhyaya,* or "self-study," movement was estimated to have reached 20 million people in 100,000 villages with its teachings that inner divinity can enable people to overcome self-hatred, prejudice, and the misery of poverty.

Another saga that reflected the year's religious ferment was the conversion to Islam of Benjamin F. Chavis, Jr. (now Benjamin Chavis Muhammad), former executive director of the National Association for the Advancement of Colored People. He had been ordained to the ministry of the United Church of Christ (UCC) in 1980 and sought to retain that status after joining the Nation of Islam, declaring that "the God who called me into the Christian church is the same God who is calling me into the Nation of Islam." A regional panel of the UCC disagreed, however, stating that he had joined "another faith" and therefore had to forfeit his UCC clergy status.

(DARRELL J. TURNER)

PROTESTANT CHURCHES

Anglican Communion. Debate over the morality of homosexuality dominated the Anglican Communion in 1997. In February delegates to the Second Anglican Encounter in the South, representing the church's South American, African, and Pacific provinces, adopted the Kuala Lumpur statement on sexual morality. Named after the Malaysian city in which the meeting was held, it declared that "all sexual promiscuity is sin," including "homosexual practices." Soon afterward, the Anglican church in Southeast Asia unanimously adopted the Kuala Lumpur statement and declared itself in communion only "with that part of the Anglican Communion which accepts and endorses the principles." Meanwhile, the bishops of the Southern Africa province issued a statement in March apologizing to homosexual people who had been hurt by years of "unacceptable prejudice" within the church. The General Convention of the Episcopal Church in the U.S., meeting in Philadelphia in July, adopted a similar apology.

The Episcopal convention in the U.S. refused to ratify the Kuala Lumpur statement and referred it to an interim body for further study. The same convention gave dioceses the option to extend employee health insurance to same-sex couples but refused to authorize pension benefits for them. It also narrowly defeated a provision to develop liturgical rites for the blessing of same-sex couples. The Rt. Rev. Frank T. Griswold III, bishop of Chicago, was elected the Episcopal Church's presiding bishop for a nine-year term following his January 1998 installation. He succeeded the Rt. Rev. Edmond Browning, who served from 1985 to 1997. The Philadelphia convention approved the Concordat of Agreement, which would have established full communion with the Evangelical Lutheran Church in America. A month later, however, the Lutheran conven-

(continued on page 306)

SPECIAL REPORT

Doomsday Cults

by Martin E. Marty

Waco, Heaven's Gate, Solar Temple, Aum Shinrikyo ("Supreme Truth"), and People's Temple, or Jonestown, are shorthand terms often used to recall places, movements, and events associated with groups known as doomsday cults. Hearing predictions that there are likely to be more such cults as the year 2000 approaches, many who do not belong to them are trying to make sense of these movements, which they find both strange and threatening.

The first thing people do when they are puzzled by something complex is turn to the experts, in this case the scholars. The first thing most of those who study cults say is do not use the word *cult,* or be careful when you do use it, and perhaps keep it in quotation marks. They hold that while the word *cult* originally was intended to be neutral and innocent, since Jim Jones in 1978 provoked mass suicide among his followers, many have associated cults with killing. That assumption, state the scholars, is unfair to all those who belong to quite peaceful and harmless movements. Yet no one has settled on a satisfactory alternative term, though some speak of NRMs ("new religious movements").

In addition, if people use the word *cult* carefully, they would do well to attach adjectives to it each time. Sometimes the adjective used is *apocalyptic.* Because of the Christian shading of the term *apocalypse* ("involving or portending widespread devastation or ultimate doom"), however, many prefer a word that stretches across the religions and therefore advocate the word *doomsday.*

Doomsday cults have a long history in the United States. Beginning in colonial times, preachers and leaders of many spiritual movements often made the final judgment of a person's life and the subsequent threat of his or her doom central to their proclamations and appeals. Rarely would these leaders proclaim that everyone was doomed. Instead, they would draw on old biblical stories or invent new ones, stories that described how a minority would be saved, while many, maybe most, would be "lost" forever. In order to be saved, followers were instructed that they had to respond to the appeals, change their ways, believe what the leader taught them, and, frequently, form tightly bonded groups so that they could stay at some distance from lures and distractions—including, often, members of their own families. In their closed-in, cultic circles, they would receive the messages of truth, affirm one another, screen out other interpretations of reality, and support each other through ordeals that the group envisioned.

In the 19th century two newly developing religions had elements that led them to be regarded, especially by their many rivals and enemies, as something like today's doomsday cults. Most familiar of these movements was the gathering on a hilltop in New York of followers who had been persuaded by William Miller that they should sell all their possessions, gather, and greet Jesus Christ, who was returning, making a "Second Advent" in 1843 or 1844. When Jesus failed to appear, the disappointed regathered in what is today Seventh-day Adventism. Students and followers of Charles Taze Russell foresaw doom at various times, notably 1914. They survive as Jehovah's Witnesses. In neither case did the followers physically come and stay together in communes or other enclaves, however. Unlike those in many present-day cults, they had and have regular jobs, regular lives.

The charismatic leader has been central in the groups thought of as doomsday cults in the late-20th-century U.S. This is often a person who draws on ancient scriptures and prophecies and then interprets what the Bible calls "the signs of the times." All around, this leader sees evil and corruption and views them, sometimes even including natural disasters, as tokens of divine wrath and signals of judgment, doom, and the end of the world. Immorality, relativism, the competition between religions, the loss of meaning, wars, and rumours of war—all count as such tokens. But there is a way to avoid doom, say such leaders: join the tightly formed group; keep your distance from others; obey what the leader says, especially as new prophecies come forth. Then, be ready to do what you are told to avoid the wrath to come.

Many of these features are present in the cases of the best-known leaders. Jones began his ministry as a conventional mainstream Protestant (Disciples of Christ) pastor. He came to lead the People's Temple movement, eventually from bases in the United States to a remote area in Guyana. While the movement was being observed and exposed by U.S. governmental and other agencies and scholars, Jones evidently talked his hundreds of followers into simultaneous mass suicide.

Similarly, David Koresh had been brought up in orthodox Seventh-day Adventism, a religious movement not considered dangerous by other Christians and the public at large. Koresh's new revelations, however, went beyond the bounds of the Bible and early Adventist leaders and inspired him to lead his Branch Davidians to near Waco, Texas. There federal officials, having lost patience and quite likely having misinterpreted what they had learned about Koresh's followers, in 1993 attacked his enclave in an assault that prompted the cult members to set the compound on fire and led to the death of 74 people, including Koresh.

Not all such movements grow up on Jewish and Protestant soil, as became clear in 1995 in Japan, where perhaps the most dangerous of the doomsday cults, the one that demonstrated the greatest potential for killing innocent nonmembers, formed and acted. This was the Aum Shinrikyo group, led by Shoko Asahara, who was later arrested and accused of murder. Largely on the basis of Japanese religious resources—where talk of an end of history is less frequent—Asahara proclaimed that only he and his followers should control history. In Quebec and Switzerland in 1994, many members of the Order of the Solar Temple, a group that combined elements of feminism and apocalypse, were murdered or committed suicide.

In the U.S. another doomsday cult showed that even on the soil of a nation where 80–90% of the people professed a faith grounded in the Bible, there could develop intense religious movements that had little, if any, biblical prophetic base. This was the movement called, in the end, Heaven's Gate. It had been led by two people who at one time called themselves "Bo" and "Peep." It was leader Marshall Applewhite ("Bo") who talked his followers into being sequestered into a single community. They committed suicide in 1997, as their previously taped testimonies revealed, in order to leave Earth to ride Comet Hale-Bopp to "Heaven's Gate." They stated that they would willingly shrug off and shed their bodies in order to reach the new state and place—while the rest of the human world sped on toward doom.

Are there more groups like these? Will there be more like them? Gnostic sects (groups that claim esoteric knowledge) and eschatological hysteria (anxieties about the end of the world) are as old as religion itself and have occurred in many places and times. In our times there have been Shi'ite Islamic fundamentalist terrorists, Jews who interpret biblical texts and follow new leaders, and various Christian groups and even secular "militias" in the United States that arm themselves and keep others at a distance. Most of them can be studied and classified in the context of old religions newly interpreted, but most of them are also similar to the doomsday cults in their view that they are a specially selected people. They believe that they alone hear the voice of God accurately, that they alone act upon what they hear, and that they and their leader foresee doom for others. The result of their actions can be lethal. They, however, are less divorced from inherited and host religions than are the fully identified doomsday cults.

Why do these cults exist? Human action, especially responses to leaders who invoke the sacred, the divine, is always complex. Cult followers tend to be people who are unsatisfied by the complexities, contradictions, and ambiguities of life—including life as interpreted by the mainstream religions. They seek answers, and the modern world, with its pluralism and its rapid communications, can confuse them and undercut their belief systems and their "orthodox" communities. The cult leader offers a single answer, keeps the rest of the world at bay, and reinforces only one belief system.

The turning of the calendar page to 2000 is inspiring—and will almost certainly inspire all kinds of prophecies and movements. Some may become dangerous. It will be a time that should not be faced complacently.

Martin E. Marty is a professor of religion at the Divinity School of the University of Chicago, a senior editor of Christian Century *magazine, director of the Public Religion Project, and author of many books and articles.*

Doomsday cults almost invariably revolve around a charismatic leader. In Japan cult leader Shoko Asahara (opposite page) ordered his followers to carry out a deadly nerve-gas attack on the Tokyo subway system in 1995. Asahara, who claimed supernatural powers, called himself "Tokyo's Christ." In St. Casimir, Que. (above), investigators leave a house where five members of the Order of the Solar Temple died in a fire in March 1997. Also in March, 39 Heaven's Gate members committed suicide outside San Diego, Calif. Authorities remove bodies (right) from the lavish mansion where they were discovered. Heaven's Gate leader Marshall Applewhite (inset) presided over the mass suicide.

(OPPOSITE) SANKEI SHIMBUN—REUTERS; (ABOVE) JACQUES BOISSINOT—AP/WIDE WORLD/CANAPRESS; (RIGHT) DAVE GATLEY—SIPA PRESS; (INSET) REUTERS

DAVID MAIALETTI—AP/WIDE WORLD

Bishop Frank Griswold III strains to hear a question during a July press conference in Philadelphia. In 1997 Griswold became the Episcopal Church's new presiding bishop when fellow bishops elected him to a nine-year term.

(continued from page 303)
tion failed to ratify it in a vote that fell six votes short of the required two-thirds majority. The Episcopal convention also adopted a canonical change that required mandatory ordination of women in every diocese. The four dioceses that did not now ordain women (Quincy, Ill.; San Joaquin, Calif.; Fort Worth, Texas; and Eau Claire, Wis.) were given three years to implement the new requirements.

An April survey in the Church of England reported that women constituted 10% of its clergy. Since the first ordinations in March 1994, approximately 2,000 women had been ordained in the church's 43 dioceses. About 400 of them were rectors or vicars in charge of parishes.

In December 1996 the Nippon Sei Ko Kai (Anglican Church in Japan) adopted a statement admitting the church's responsibility and sin for supporting Japan's "war of aggression" during World War II. Instead of standing beside "those who are oppressed and suffering," the church made compromises with the "militarism that drove the war effort," the statement acknowledged.

The Rt. Rev. John Elbridge Hines, the Episcopal Church's 22nd presiding bishop, died July 19 in Austin, Texas. He was presiding bishop from 1965 to 1974 and led the church through a stormy period of civil rights activism. (*See* OBITUARIES.)

In late 1996 the Episcopal Church's national office reported errors in statistical reports that gave the impression the church gained 90,000 members between 1991 and 1994. The report acknowledged that the church actually lost 26,000 members during those years. (DAVID E. SUMNER)

Baptist Churches. Frustrated by the lack of results of an earlier protest, the Southern Baptist Convention at its annual meeting called for a boycott of the Walt Disney Co. by all of its 15 million members. On June 18, 1997, 12,000 delegates gathered in Dallas, Texas, urged the boycott to protest Disney's support of homosexuals, exemplified by the provision of health benefits for the partners of the company's homosexual employees. The convention's vote to support the recommended boycott was so overwhelming that a count of the vote was not taken.

At the March meeting of the Baptist World Alliance in McLean, Va., representatives from Baptist bodies throughout the world gathered to report progress and challenges. It was reported that churches in Cuba had been packed, and at one service in the western part of the island, 100 young people responded to a call to the ministry. Samuel Fadeji, president of the All-Africa Baptist Fellowship, reported an increase in new churches to add to the 5,600 churches and more than one million baptized believers in the Nigerian Baptist Convention.

In Azerbaijan Pastor Zaur Balayev and a deacon of the church in Aliabad were arrested. The two men allegedly were put in prison only because of their positions of responsibility with the Baptist Church. The Baptist general secretary, Karl Heinz Walter of the European Baptist Federation, protested to the president of Azerbaijan, stating, "We can assure you that the members of Baptist churches have always been faithful citizens of the countries where they live, but at the same time have insisted on religious freedom for every person."

In the United States the Alliance of Baptists, a moderate group formed in 1987 after disagreeing with the conservative leadership of the Southern Baptist Convention, reported that it had begun discussions with the United Church of Christ about ways in which the two might work together. The Alliance, which included Baptists from a variety of denominations, had changed from a protest group within the Southern Baptist Convention to an independent organization.

Along similar ecumenical lines, Baptists in England, specifically members of the Covenanted Baptist Churches of the Baptist Union of Great Britain, joined in considering a proposal that the world's first ecumenical bishop be appointed. The bishop would be the head of five denominations, including the Baptists.

In August it was revealed that the Rev. Henry Lyons, the president of the National Baptist Convention USA, Inc., had purchased expensive personal items with money that the denomination had earned from business deals. Documents indicated that Lyons and Bernice Edwards, the church's public relations director, had used at least $187,000 in church money toward buying a house, a Mercedes-Benz, and a time-share unit.

(NORMAN R. DE PUY)

Christian Church (Disciples of Christ). More than 8,400 members of the Christian Church (Disciples of Christ) gathered in Denver, Colo., in July 1997, passing resolutions restating the General Assembly's opposition to the U.S. trade embargo on Cuba, demanding increased police accountability, and asking congregations to monitor welfare reform. The decision-making body also lobbied for improved job training and employment opportunities for African-American males, called for removal of the U.S. military from Okinawa, Japan, and emphasized Jerusalem's importance to Christian, Muslim, and Jewish traditions.

The assembly also initiated a test run of a discernment process, designed to help the church listen for God's will on divisive or controversial issues instead of seeking a majority vote. Biblical authority and racism were the issues discussed during the initial round. In other action voters elected the Rev. Michael W. Mooty of Lexington, Ky., moderator of the General Assembly through 1999.

In keeping with the assembly's call for more accountability for law-enforcement officials, the denomination's general minister and president, Richard L. Hamm, issued a pastoral letter in August condemning the beating of a Haitian member of the Disciples by New York City police. "We must

Members of the Southern Baptist Convention cast their votes in support of a resolution to boycott the Walt Disney Co. Southern Baptists opposed Disney's practice of holding "Gay Days" at its theme parks and giving health benefits to partners of the company's homosexual employees.

VICTOR R. CAIVANO—AP/WIDE WORLD

stand for zero tolerance of police abuse and for renewed commitment to public accountability of law enforcement officers and their agencies," said Hamm.

In March approximately 300 volunteers gathered near tiny Chelford, Ark., to help rebuild an African-American church destroyed by arson in 1995. The Burned Churches ministry of the National Council of Churches later honoured the Disciples for the 10-day reconstruction of St. Mark's Missionary Baptist Church. The 35-member congregation held its first formal service in the new structure on Easter morning.

(CLIFFORD L. WILLIS)

Churches of Christ. "Africans Claiming Africa," an evangelistic conference, drew to Harare, Zimb., 1,745 leaders of the Churches of Christ from 17 African countries, speaking 47 languages. Participants reported that there were 9,398 Churches of Christ congregations in Africa, an increase of 34% in five years. They attributed this growth to two factors: the growth of brotherhood schools and the World Bible School correspondence courses. The church celebrated the 100th anniversary of its establishment in Zimbabwe.

Four books written by members of Churches of Christ were on the Evangelical Christian Publishers Association best-seller list during 1997, including two by Max Lucado, *God's Inspirational Promises* and *In the Grip of Grace.* Two scholarly books with great impact were *The Church of Christ: A Biblical Ecclesiology for Today* (1996) by Everett Ferguson and *Reviving the Ancient Faith: The Story of Churches of Christ in America* (1996) by Richard T. Hughes.

"Saving the American Family," a national conference in San Antonio, Texas, highlighted a major emphasis in the Churches of Christ in 1997. This included training in spiritual leadership for men at a rally in Tulsa, Okla., that drew men from 14 states. Abstinence-based sex-education programs for young people were gaining in popularity.

(M. NORVEL YOUNG)

Church of Christ, Scientist. The increased demand for spirituality and healing was the focus of the Church's 102nd annual meeting in Boston. The church president, J. Thomas Black of Michigan, remarked to those present that this reach toward spirituality was changing the ways in which people think about theology, science, and medicine. Black saw this "spiritual hunger that now reaches across ages and races" as a reflection of humanity's "longing to know God's true identity." He said the church was well prepared to meet this longing because of the teachings of the Bible in the light of *Science and Health with Key to the Scriptures* by Mary Baker Eddy, the discoverer of Christian Science. "And the proof is in nearly 125 years of consistent healing based on these books," Black concluded.

Other speakers discussed the beneficial effect of the increased distribution of *Science and Health.* A former registered nurse shared how reading *Science and Health* transformed her life from sickness to health, into the full-time practice of Christian Science healing; others talked about Christian Science lectures that had been held at a major medical school in the United States and at two large hospitals in India.

The growing interest in the beneficial role of prayer for physical healing was demonstrated when a church representative served on the faculty at two major conferences in Boston (December 1996) and Los Angeles (March 1997) entitled "Spirituality and Healing in Medicine," sponsored by Harvard Medical School.

Other significant events during 1997 included a favourable decision for the church when the Massachusetts Supreme Judicial Court endorsed the administrative and fiscal autonomy of churches and other public charities, an award from the Laymen's National Bible Association acknowledging the church's long-standing promotion of the Bible, and establishment of a restoration program to upgrade church facilities.

(VICTOR M. WESTBERG)

Church of Jesus Christ of Latter-day Saints. In 1997 the nearly 10 million-member Church of Jesus Christ of Latter-day Saints conducted a yearlong celebration of the entrance of their Mormon forebears into the Salt Lake Valley 150 years earlier. The festivities included theatrical performances, television documentaries, celebratory literature, special exhibits in the Church Museum of History and Art, and, above all, a reliving of the trek from the Missouri Valley to the Salt Lake Valley by hundreds of horse-drawn wagons and handcarts—a journey that required three months. The wagon trains were made up of volunteer men, women, and children, dressed in pioneer clothing, and included church members from as far away as Siberia, with a considerable number from Great Britain and continental Europe as well as from all parts of the United States and Canada. The finale was their entrance into the Salt Lake Valley on July 23, to participate in the giant sesquicentennial parade of July 24. July 19 was designated Pioneer Heritage Day, and each local congregation throughout the world was asked to contribute a minimum of 150 hours of community service. Perhaps as many as 10,000 local service projects were completed on this and following days. The church's women's organization, the Relief Society, conducted a worldwide campaign to improve literacy. A special event in San Francisco celebrated the 238 men, women, and children who traveled west on the ship *Brooklyn,* which landed in Yerba Buena (San Francisco) in 1846.

Church president Gordon B. Hinckley conducted services in many parts of the world in connection with local history celebrations, the dedication of temples, the opening of visitors centres, and the holding of area conferences. He made special visits to major cities in Europe, Asia, Central and South America, and Australia and New Zealand.

Church authorities began construction of a "great hall" across from Temple Square in downtown Salt Lake City to accommodate 21,000 persons for religious services and other church purposes such as the presentation of sacred pageants and community cultural events. The building, scheduled for completion in April 2000, was expected to cost approximately $240 million.

(LEONARD J. ARRINGTON)

Jehovah's Witnesses. On May 29, 1997, the European Court of Human Rights rendered an important decision in favour of the plaintiffs in the cases of *Tsirlis and Kouloumpas* v. *Greece* and *Georgiadis* v. *Greece.* The plaintiffs were Jehovah's Witnesses ministers, who as Christian clergy were exempted from military service by Greek law but who claimed to have been wrongfully denied that status. The court ruled in favour of the ministers, setting a precedent for future cases concerning conscientious objection.

Earlier that month Jehovah's Witnesses again promoted the importance of adhering strongly to one's principles. On May 15 the videotape *Jehovah's Witnesses Stand Firm Against Nazi Assault* was screened publicly in Moscow and was simultaneously aired on television in St. Petersburg. The documentary recounts the little-known story of the courageous stand of Jehovah's Witnesses during the Hitler era. By late 1997 it had been viewed at more than 160 public showings in Germany and was being used in classrooms in the United States. Regarding the integrity of Jehovah's Witnesses, Swiss Protestant theologian Theophile Bruppacher said, "Not the great churches, but these slandered and scoffed-at people were the ones who stood up first against the rage of the Nazi demon and who dared to make opposition according to their faith."

(MILTON HENSCHEL)

Lutheran Communion. The Lutheran World Federation (LWF) celebrated its 50th anniversary by holding its ninth assembly in Hong Kong on July 8–16, within days after the handover of that city to China. The assembly, the LWF's highest decision-making body, normally meets every six years. Representatives from 122 member churches took part in the event. The assembly reviewed the work of the LWF since the last conference (in Curitiba, Braz., in 1990) and heard addresses on human rights, mission, the church in China, and Christian unity. Edward Cardinal Cassidy of the Vatican delivered an encouraging report on the proposed joint declaration between Lutherans and Roman Catholics on the nonapplicability of the 16th-century condemnations by the Roman Catholic Church of the doctrine of justification by grace through faith. A final decision on the joint declaration by Lutherans and Roman Catholics was expected in 1998. Hong Kong's chief executive Tung Chee Hwa greeted the assembly and gave a commitment to freedom of religion in the Hong Kong special administrative region. After some debate the assembly decided not to make a statement on human rights in China. This decision subsequently became a matter of some controversy, particularly in regard to criticism raised by some in the German media. In a break with tradition, the assembly elected a president from outside the region of the meeting, selecting Christian Krause, a bishop from Brunswick, Ger.

The Evangelical Lutheran Church in Canada reelected Telmor G. Sartison as its bishop and took official action to develop closer ties with the Anglican Church in Canada. The Evangelical Lutheran churches in Germany and the Mennonites agreed to provide occasional eucharistic hospitality to each other's members. The Church of Sweden, the largest Lutheran church in the world, elected Christina Odenberg as its first woman bishop; Bishop K.G. Hammer became the archbishop of Uppsala, Swed. In the U.S. the Lutheran Church Missouri Synod celebrated its 150th anniversary.

The biennial assembly of the Evangelical Lutheran Church in America (ELCA), the second largest Lutheran church in the world, was dominated by ecumenical decisions. With 81.3% of the delegates voting "yes," the ELCA approved a relationship of full communion with three Reformed churches: the Presbyterian Church (USA), the Reformed Church in America, and the United Church of Christ. By a vote of 958–25, the ELCA adopted the joint declaration on justification, stating that a consensus on this doctrine existed between Lutherans and Roman Catholics. This decision was now shared with the LWF as it sought to determine if a consensus existed among its member churches. The ELCA rejected the proposal for full communion with the Episcopal Church by a vote of 684–351, just short of the required two-thirds majority.

(WILLIAM G. RUSCH)

Methodist Churches. Figures published in 1997 showed a 14% increase in the membership of churches belonging to the World Methodist Council (WMC) compared with 1992 (the last census). Total membership was 33,011,100, with the largest increase—89%—being in Asia. There were 14,767,000 Methodists (45% of the total) in the United States.

The European Methodist Council, meeting in Copenhagen in September, discussed a paper suggesting various options for its future, as did the Executive Committee of the WMC meeting in Rome later the same month; there, members were being asked to decide on the role and function of the council appropriate for the new century. Both bodies expressed concern over the restrictions to religious liberty in Russia that would result from the new legislation regarding freedom of conscience and religious association. The new law introduced a two-level system for religious associations, with only those in the first group—religious organizations that had been active in Russia for 50 years and were represented widely geographically—enjoying full rights and therefore able to operate in a normal way. The European Methodist Council sent a letter to Russian Pres. Boris Yeltsin, and the WMC Executive Committee agreed to a letter inviting fellow Christians in Russia "to enter a mutual dialogue so that we may recognize the ties that bind us together and such common ways for the proclamation of the gospel."

The Methodist Church in Hong Kong published a pastoral letter to its members supporting Hong Kong's change to become a special administrative region within China but also emphasizing that the new government has responsibilities for upholding and defending the sovereignty of the nation, serving the people, and defending their dignity and rights. For the first time, the World Methodist Peace Award was given not to an individual but to an organization, the Roman Catholic community of St. Egidio, a volunteer service group organized along the lines of Catholic lay movements of Renaissance Italy.

After 20 years of discussions, the Orthodox and Methodist churches moved from a preparatory to an official stage in order "not only to enjoy sisterly relations, but also to bear joint witness to the Gospel before the world." Ecumenical discussions between Methodists and Roman Catholics continued during the year. Leaders of the World Methodist Council Executive Committee met with Pope John Paul II, who gave "thanks to God for the progress made in the official dialogue between our two communions."

(JOHN C.A. BARRETT)

Pentecostal Churches. Pentecostals and charismatics were heavily involved in the largest religious gathering in the history of the United States on Oct. 4, 1997, when as many as 1.5 million Christian men, who belonged to the organization Promise Keepers, gathered on the Mall in Washington, D.C. Leaders from the charismatic tradition, such as Promise Keepers founder Bill McCartney and pastors Jack Hayford and Joseph Garlington, were prominent on the platform. Other groups also served as host for large gatherings. A week earlier the world conference of the Assemblies of God reported that more than one million persons had attended the conference's final rally in São Paulo, Braz.

In June, after Pat Robertson sold his television company, the Family Channel, he gave $150 million of the proceeds to Regent University, Virginia Beach, Va., which made it the most richly endowed evangelical university in the U.S. Indeed, there was a boom in Pentecostal education during the year. Lee College, Cleveland, Tenn. (Church of God), was upgraded to university status, while Emmanuel College (Pentecostal Holiness), in Franklin Springs, was the fastest-growing college in Georgia for the second year in a row. Also in September the Assemblies of God Theological Seminary dedicated its new $4.5 million building debt free.

Among the Pentecostal denominations several major changes in leadership occurred during the year. In July, John R. Holland resigned under pressure as president of the International Church of the Foursquare Gospel. He was succeeded by Harold E. Helms, the longtime pastor of Angelus Temple in Los Angeles. In August, James D. Leggett was elected to head the International Pentecostal Holiness Church in Kansas City, Mo., while in the same month in Indianapolis, Ind., the Assemblies of God reelected Thomas E. Trask to the office of general superintendent for a four-year term.

The 1997 meeting of the interracial Pentecostal/Charismatic Churches of North America, which met in Washington, D.C., in October, chose to elect co-chairmen for the next two years. Elected were Bishop Gilbert E. Patterson of the Church of God in Christ and Trask.

On the international scene 400 church leaders and theologians gathered in Prague in September under the leadership of Michael Harper and the International Charismatic Consultation on World Evangelism. Designed especially for Eastern Europeans, the organization for the first time attracted significant numbers of Russian Orthodox charismatics as participants.

(VINSON SYNAN)

Reformed, Presbyterian, and Congregational Churches. "Break the Chains of Injustice" was the theme of the 23rd General Council of the World Alliance of Reformed Churches (WARC), which took place in Debrecen, Hung., in August 1997. The General Council meets every seven to eight years to seek a common response to the challenges facing Reformed churches locally and globally. More than 400 delegates from member churches took part in the meeting.

Topping the council's list of "chains" was global economic injustice. World hunger and misery, the yawning gulf between underdeveloped and developed countries, the debt crisis that cripples the poor, and the environmental crisis that threatens everyone had been of concern to Reformed churches for many years. Responding to a strong plea from member churches in the South in particular, however, the council declared that these were not just moral issues but questions close to the heart of the Christian gospel and touching on the integrity of Christian faith. It called member churches to a *processus confessionis,* a "committed process of progressive recognition, education, and confession within all WARC member churches at all levels regarding economic injustice and ecological destruction."

In 1982 the 21st council had suspended the Dutch Reformed Church (DRC) in South Africa from full membership in WARC because of its theological and practical support for apartheid. The 23rd council agreed to lift this suspension, provided the General Synod of the DRC, meeting in 1998, acknowledged unequivocally that "apartheid is wrong and sinful not simply in its effects and operations but also in its fundamental nature." Elected president of WARC was Song Choan-seng, a minister in the Presbyterian Church of Taiwan.

In March WARC held a consultation in Geneva to look afresh at human rights from a theological perspective. Bilateral dialogues were conducted with the Oriental Orthodox on "Holy Scripture: its authority and inspiration" and "the function of theological reflection and the work of theologians" in Kottayam, Kerala, India, in January and with the Pentecostals on "the role and place of the Holy Spirit in the church" in Chicago in May.

Three new member churches were admitted to WARC in 1997: the Evangelical Church in the Dominican Republic, the United Church of Christ Congregational in the Marshall Islands, and the United Church of Christ in the Solomon Islands. In 1997 WARC linked more than 70 million Christians in 211 churches in 103 countries.

(PÁRAIC RÉAMONN)

The Religious Society of Friends. Nearly 300 representatives from more than 70 autonomous groups of Friends (Quakers) from throughout the world gathered for the 19th Triennial meeting of the Friends World Committee for Consultation (FWCC) at Westhill College, Birmingham, Eng., during the last week of July 1997. The theme was "Answering the Love of God: Living our Testimonies." Those gathered were reminded that God loves us with a boundless, unconditional, self-giving love and that we are called to express that love in specific ways to one another, to our families, to our neighbours, to the needy—even to those who act as enemies.

Decisions made at the Triennial included the naming of new leadership for the FWCC. This resulted in a notable shift of responsibility, with Friends from the Southern Hemisphere taking on some of the key posts. David Purnell (Australia) was appointed clerk, Duduzile Mtshazo (South Africa) assistant clerk, and Elizabeth Duke (New Zealand) general secretary. All were scheduled to begin three-year terms in January 1998, as would Patricia Thomas of the U.S., who was named associate secretary.

Issues on which those at the Triennial called for action by all Friends included further support of the work by the Quaker

United Nations Office in Geneva opposing the use of children in armed conflict. The meeting affirmed Friends' long-standing opposition to the use of violence in any conflict. The concern for children was part of this wider commitment.

Some other issues calling for action included sexual discrimination, harassment, and abuse among Friends; truth and integrity in public affairs (challenging Friends to dialogue with their governments); climate change (stemming from a call by the World Council of Churches to address the problem of global warming); and refugees (many of them Quaker) in central Africa.

(THOMAS F. TAYLOR)

Salvation Army. On Dec. 12, 1996, Queen Elizabeth II of the United Kingdom officially opened Edward Alsop Court in London. Developed by the Salvation Army, it offered accommodations, training, and rehabilitation for homeless men.

During 1997 the Salvation Army focused its attention on South Africa. A report submitted to that nation's Truth and Reconciliation Commission maintained that the Army's contribution to South African society had been positive. The Army admitted, however, that its apolitical attitude toward apartheid was not representative of its tradition of promoting universal justice. The presentation concluded by promising to fight racism whenever necessary.

In Cape Town 500 participants aged 18–25, representing the Army's 50 world territories, met for the first time as the International Youth Forum. They were addressed on behalf of South African Pres. Nelson Mandela by Geraldine Fraser-Moleketi, the nation's minister of welfare and population development. She encouraged them to take their responsibilities seriously and to meet the needs of the next millennium.

During the year the Army prayed and petitioned for greater freedoms for Christians in many parts of the world; particular concerns were for those in Pakistan and Russia. World prayer was also invoked for continued religious freedom for the people of Hong Kong following its restoration to Chinese rule. (CHARMAINE FLETCHER)

Seventh-day Adventist Church. In 1997 Brazil surpassed the United States as the country with the largest number of Seventh-day Adventists. Although the church originated in North America, it continued to grow faster in Central and South America, Africa, and Asia. At the end of 1996, North America accounted for only 10% of the world membership, which numbered 9,296,127 in 207 countries.

Plans for the church to achieve worldwide communication via satellite continued to progress. The church developed a satellite network in North, Central, and South America and set in motion a strategy for a worldwide network in 40 languages within the next two years. The Adventist satellite network was intended to provide programs for communicating news and information, spiritual nurture, evangelism, and educational and health care instruction.

The church's humanitarian arm, the Adventist Development and Relief Agency (ADRA), worked in more than 140 countries during 1997. ADRA signed a Memorandum of Understanding with the UN World Food Programme under which the agency would be responsible for the final distribution and monitoring of all food commodities delivered to it by the World Food Programme.

At its highest level the church voted to issue a statement on child sexual abuse that called the Adventists to increase their awareness of the problem, to be actively involved in its prevention, to assist abused and abusive individuals and their families spiritually, and to hold church professionals and church lay leaders accountable for maintaining appropriate personal behaviour. In another important thrust, world president Robert S. Folkenberg called on the church for personal and corporate spiritual accountability among all its clergy, educators, health care workers, and administrators.

Dialogue with the Lutheran World Federation continued in a third round of consultations held at Jongny, Switz. Discussions focused on theological doctrine and authority. The church also engaged in further official dialogue with representatives of the Worldwide Church of God.

(WILLIAM G. JOHNSSON)

Unitarian (Universalist) Churches. By 1997 approximately 50% of all active ministers and a majority of the students studying for Unitarian Universalist–related careers were women. The positions of executive editor of *World,* the official magazine of the denomination, and director of the Beacon Press, its main book-publishing house, were occupied by women.

Attended by some 3,300 delegates, the annual General Assembly of the Unitarian Universalist Association of Churches was held in Phoenix, Ariz., June 19–24. The theme of the meeting was "Building Interfaith Cooperation." Reelected for second four-year terms were the Rev. John A. Buehrens as president and Denise Taft Davidoff as moderator.

The Unitarian Universalist Service Committee during the year established partnerships with appropriate groups and specialists working on women's and children's rights, refugee relief, and health in Mexico, Myanmar (Burma), Kenya, Burundi, Rwanda, and eastern Zaire (now Democratic Republic of the Congo). Services were being supplied through these channels.

The International Council of Unitarians and Universalists in April held its second annual meeting in England and a training session in Klingborg, Ger. Twenty-two countries and regions were represented, including for the first time Finland and Tierra del Fuego.

The buildings of the Prague Unitarian congregation, once the world's largest, were taken over by a dissident group of parishioners, who locked out the mainstream followers. Unitarians throughout the world protested. Local Prague courts declared the action illegal. As of late 1997, however, the Ministry of Culture had not returned the property to the traditional body.

In Romania Arpad Szabo became the new bishop of the consistory of the Unitarian Church. Resolutions were passed by the General Assembly of the British Unitarian movement calling (among others) for an end to the manufacture, trade, and use of antipersonnel land mines; and for year-round shelters for homeless people in Britain.

(JOHN NICHOLLS BOOTH)

The United Church of Canada. National meetings of the General Council highlighted the year for the United Church of Canada in 1997. The meetings were held in Camrose, Alta., August 14–21. The council elected the Rev. William Phipps for a three-year term as moderator of Canada's largest Protestant denomination. Phipps succeeded Marion Best. The 379 delegates agreed to ask district presbyteries to endorse a standard three-year term between council meetings, beginning in the year 2000.

A major decision was to extend the United Church's apology that was offered to native congregations in 1986. The council did so by expressing its deep regret and sorrow to the First Nations people for the injustices of residential schools and for the church's role in them. In 1997 the United Church was named as a defendant in connection with a former school near Port Alberni, B.C. A fund to support healing projects for victims of the native residential schools raised 40% of its $1 million goal.

Among other business, delegates adopted a plan to help congregations discover their mission and to support and develop congregational life. The council also opposed programs forcing the poor to work, voted to review the systems for resource distribution within the church, endorsed the development of a code of ethical behaviour, and reaffirmed its commitment to youth work.

During the last fiscal year, the denomination's nearly two million known members and adherents raised Can$313,360,727 for all purposes. Contributions to the church's national mission fund continued to stagnate as congregations directed more of their support toward local mission projects. The surplus of clergy reported in 1996 continued through 1997.

Sales of the church's new hymnbook, *Voices United,* remained at a high level. To accompany this popular hymnal, the church planned to prepare a new liturgical resource book. Also in 1997, the church's national United Church Women's organization marked the 35th anniversary of its founding.

(DOUGLAS L. FLANDERS)

United Church of Christ. In July 1997, in a historic vote, the 21st General Synod of the United Church of Christ voted to declare full communion with the Evangelical Lutheran Church in America (ELCA). In so doing, the UCC joined its two partners, the Presbyterian Church (USA) and the Reformed Church in America, which had voted full communion with the ELCA in June. In August the ELCA voted affirmatively, and so, pending confirmation by two-thirds of the presbyteries of the Presbyterian Church (USA), these historic affirmations would bring together in full communion these Reformed and Lutheran bodies for the first time since the Reformation, more than 400 years ago.

The 21st General Synod also celebrated the 40th anniversary of the UCC and the 150th anniversary of the American Missionary Association; reaffirmed the church's commitment to be and become a multiracial, multicultural church; supported "a comprehensive global ban" on land mines; expressed concern about the cloning of humans and other mammals and called on UCC national agencies to develop a proposal for action on this issue at the 1999 Synod; condemned the 1996 Welfare Reform Act as "unconscionable"; affirmed that Jerusalem should be an open city that respects the human and political rights of Palestinians and Israelis and the rights of all three religious groups residing there—

Christians, Muslims, and Jews; reaffirmed "fidelity and integrity" as standards for sexual and relational behaviour; recommended new patterns of giving to fund church ministries; and voted to join in a formal partnership with the Council of Churches in Cuba. Paul H. Sherry was reelected president of the UCC.

Throughout the year significant attention was given to church growth and development and stewardship and financial concerns. The need to identify, support, and train new clergy and lay leadership was increasingly acknowledged.

(PAUL H. SHERRY)

ROMAN CATHOLIC CHURCH

After a year in which violence against Roman Catholic clergy was particularly pronounced, 1997 proved somewhat less dangerous. Even so, six priests were murdered in Rwanda, and another was killed by Hutu in Zaire (now Democratic Republic of the Congo). An Irish Franciscan missionary was killed in Kenya for protesting electoral corruption. Twelve churches and more than 800 homes were destroyed by Islamic extremists in Pakistan. China continued to be a difficult place for the Catholic Church. In March the Chinese government took steps aimed at eradicating the underground Catholic Church (which attempted to maintain ties with Rome and was outlawed in favour of the government-controlled Patriotic Catholic Church). On March 4 police officers ransacked the home of underground Bishop Joseph Fan Zhongliang of Shanghai. Police removed Bibles, missals, breviaries, and rosaries. Apparently an attempt was being made to preempt Easter celebrations. The Chinese government promised that religious freedom would prevail after Hong Kong's handover to mainland authorities on July 1.

The church was active in promoting international peace. In the Central African Republic and the Republic of the Congo, local bishops tried to reconcile warring factions. In his January 13 address to the Vatican diplomatic corps, Pope John Paul II called for international nuclear disarmament, a ban on land mines, and the implementation of foreign policies that align with correct moral principles and not mere political advantage. As the Middle East peace process was collapsing in the summer, the pope wrote to Israeli Prime Minister Benjamin Netanyahu and Palestinian leader Yasir Arafat pleading with them to resume peaceful cooperation.

The pope visited Bosnia and Herzegovina and the Czech Republic in April, Lebanon in May (the pope's first visit to that country), Poland in June (the seventh visit to his homeland), and Brazil in October. After Fidel Castro's visit to the Vatican in late 1996, much energy was devoted in 1997 to planning a January 1998 papal visit to Cuba.

Throughout the world the church struggled with only limited success to promote its own social and theological views. In Africa and Latin America, the church vigorously opposed policies to impose contraception and sterilization. Catholic bishops testified before the U.S. Congress and before the Colombian legislature in opposition to physician-assisted suicide. The church staved off efforts to liberalize Portugal's abortion law but could not prevent the legalization of the practice in South Africa. In traditionally Catholic countries such as Argentina, Brazil, Mexico, and Spain, as well as in minority Catholic areas in Africa, the church worked to maintain control over parochial schools and, in some places, to prevent them from closing. The Pontifical Academy for Life spoke eloquently about the dangers of human cloning, calling the practice "a radical manipulation of the constitutive relationality and complementarity which is at the origin of human procreation in both its biological and strictly personal aspects." Earlier in the year the pope himself had spoken on the need for ethics in science, saying that "knowledge must be joined to conscience."

PAUL HANNA—REUTERS

On his first visit to Lebanon, Pope John Paul II blesses worshipers attending Sunday mass in Beirut. In 1997 the pope also visited Bosnia and Herzegovina, the Czech Republic, Poland, and Brazil.

International hunger and malnutrition was a particular theme of papal teaching and Vatican activity in 1997. This effort began with a speech to the International Food Summit in Rome in November 1996. Then, in a long address to the Academy of Social Sciences on April 25, the pope lamented the sheer numbers of the world's poor and hungry and their exploitation by untrammeled market forces. In a speech on May 15 to food-processing executives gathered in Rome, the pope called on them to institute business practices that promoted good nutrition alongside profit. These speeches could be understood in conjunction with two others. One was addressed to the European Convention on the church's social doctrine and challenged leaders to prevent a legitimate quest for privacy from having the effect of putting politics above ethics in such a way as to promote the interests of the individual over the justice of the many. The second was addressed to international advertising executives and called for an ethic in advertising that promoted the "service of man" over the selling of products. Complaints were lodged against spending hundreds of billions of dollars per year on advertising in a world that did not feed its people.

In addition to grappling with the wider world, the church addressed a number of its own internal concerns. The Pontifical Council for the Family initiated a major effort to provide improved pastoral counseling to divorced and remarried Catholics, who constituted a growing number of people separated from the sacraments and alienated from the church. In a series of Wednesday public audience addresses and in a June pronouncement, the pope sought to clarify certain aspects of the church's devotion to Mary. Some ambiguous references in 19th-century papal documents to Mary as *co-redemptorix* had led to confusion in some circles. The pope explained that Jesus Christ alone is to be regarded as redeemer but that Mary, from her agreement at the Annunciation to her vigil at the cross through her exemplary later life, is the *co-operator* in human redemption by showing a perfect model to others.

In ecumenical affairs there were successes and failures. George Leonard Carey, the archbishop of Canterbury and spiritual head of the world's Anglican community, visited Rome in December 1996. Also in December, Pope John Paul and Orthodox leader Karekin I of Armenia brought to a close 1,500 years of separation. During the summer the church and the Evangelical Lutheran Church in America, along with some Lutheran groups in Scandinavia and Germany, signed a formal agreement on the doctrine of "Justification by Faith," a primary source of contention in the 16th-century Reformation. The Orthodox Church in Russia, alleging theological problems and Catholic proselytism, refused to entertain either a papal visit or a meeting with papal officials.

(THOMAS F.X. NOBLE)

See WORLD AFFAIRS: *Vatican City State.*

THE ORTHODOX CHURCH

The year 1997 was one of transitions, crises, and conflicts in the Orthodox churches throughout the world. In Alexandria, Egypt, the metropolitan of Cameroon, Petros Papapetros, was elected the new patriarch on February 21, succeeding Parthenios III, who died in July 1996. The newly established metropolitanate of Hong Kong on January 12 enthroned as its first metropolitan Nikitas Lulias, formerly chancellor of the diocese of Chicago. The new far-flung metropolitanate included Orthodox parishes in several nations on the western Pacific Rim.

The ecumenical patriarchate of Constantinople (Istanbul) became embroiled in controversies with both the government and the Church of Greece over several issues. Among them was the public indication during an August visit to the island of Chios that the ecumenical patriarchate may wish to reclaim authority over the "New Lands" dioceses in Greece that had been placed in the Church of Greece's care in 1928 following the Balkan Wars.

In Russia legislation designed to limit the influence of foreign religious bodies in the nation, supported by Russian Orthodox Patriarch Aleksey, was vetoed by Pres. Boris Yeltsin. A revised version was resubmitted to the parliament by Yeltsin in September for consideration. By a vote of 358–6, the parliament passed a bill that protected the Russian Orthodox Church from competition from other Christian denominations.

Plans for Ecumenical Patriarch Bartholomew I of Constantinople, Patriarch Aleksey of Moscow, and Pope John Paul II to meet privately at the second European Ecumenical Assembly, sponsored by the Conference of European Churches and held June 23–29 in Graz, Austria, were canceled by the Orthodox leaders at the last moment because it was felt that the conditions were not ripe for such a meeting. In Bulgaria on May 1, the canonically recognized head of the Bulgarian Orthodox Church, Patriarch Maxim, filed a complaint with the European Human Rights Commission in protest against a July 1996 ruling of the Bulgarian Supreme Court that supported an alternative government-approved synod, headed by another patriarch, Pimen.

The Holy Synod of the Autocephalous (self-governing) Orthodox Church of Georgia voted on May 20 to withdraw from membership in the World Council of Churches as a result of conservative pressure from four of the church's major monasteries. Tensions, nevertheless, continued to remain high.

In Greece the Orthodox Church was in turmoil because of financial discrepancies in the accounts maintained by the Holy Synod. Archbishop Seraphim, 84 years old and in failing health, in June was challenged to resign by aspirants to his position. Seraphim rejected the suggestion and presided in August over synodic meetings called to address the financial issue. In the United States Archbishop Spyridon of the Greek Orthodox Archdiocese of America dismissed the president and three professors at the Holy Cross Greek Orthodox School of Theology, Brookline, Mass., causing widespread reaction both inside and outside the archdiocese.

An issue of ecumenical importance, the date of the celebration of Pascha (Easter), was addressed by a conference sponsored by the World Council of Churches in which a significant role was played by Orthodox representatives. Held in Aleppo, Syria, March 5–10, the conference, "Towards a Common Date for Easter," led to a proposal—announced on March 24 by Orthodox, Protestant, and Roman Catholic leaders—calling for all Christian churches, beginning in 2001, to set the same date for their Easter observances.

(STANLEY S. HARAKAS)

ORIENTAL ORTHODOX CHURCHES

At the Second European Ecumenical Assembly, held in Graz, Austria, June 23–29, 1997, the first ranking hierarch of the Armenian Church, the Catholikos of Etchmiadzin Karekin I, expressed severe criticism against "some Western European churches" for proselytizing in Orthodox lands. He specifically condemned them for taking advantage of the disorder that occurred after the dissolution of the Soviet Union to enlarge their own churches. He maintained that a policy supportive of the Orthodox would have expressed the ecumenical spirit. In July Ecumenical Patriarch Bartholomew I of Constantinople conducted an official visit to the Armenian Orthodox Church. He was welcomed by Karekin I and members of the Armenian Holy Synod.

Early in February Islamic fundamentalists attacked a Coptic Orthodox Church youth meeting in St. Mary Guirguis Church in Al-Minya province, 255 km (160 mi) south of Cairo, killing 10 and wounding 5. A month later, on March 13, at the predominantly Coptic village of Ezbet Dawoud, masked Islamic terrorists randomly killed 13 villagers. In April Mustafa Mashoor, the leader of Egypt's largest Islamic fundamentalist group, called for a purge of Christians from the Egyptian army and for the reimposition of the "head tax" on Christians and Jews that had been collected in the Ottoman Empire.

In the meantime, the spiritual renewal fostered by Coptic Patriarch Anba Shenouda III, who attracted thousands to his weekly Cairo Bible studies, contributed to the revival of Christian monasticism in Egypt, where it had begun 1,700 years earlier.

(STANLEY S. HARAKAS)

JUDAISM

Late in December 1996 Pres. Ezer Weizman of Israel came under fire from gay and lesbian groups, who alleged that he had attacked homosexuals in answering questions from students at a Haifa high school. Though the furor eased, it highlighted a major rift among Jews. The Orthodox unreservedly condemned homosexual acts, in accordance with biblical law, even if they might show some measure of compassion to homosexual individuals. Reform assemblies remained divided on the issue; an English Reform rabbi, Elizabeth Sarah, resigned her post in March after having come under constant pressure as a result of her proposal, announced months earlier but never implemented, to perform a "commitment" ceremony for two lesbians.

Tensions between religious and secular Jews and between the religious denominations continued to cause concern, particularly in Israel. Especially important was the issue of conversions to Judaism of persons in Israel, on which the Orthodox claimed a monopoly. When the Israeli Knesset (parliament) reopened in November, the (Orthodox) religious parties hoped for the enactment of a law codifying their de facto monopoly. The Israeli government appointed a committee to find a solution to the crisis generated by the proposed bill. In October the committee proposed establishing a "conversion institute" with Reform and Conservative participation and with all conversions performed by the Orthodox; the Orthodox rejected this proposal.

Relationships between Orthodox and non-Orthodox Jews deteriorated still further when non-Orthodox groups praying at the Western Wall in Jerusalem were pelted with stones and excrement by extremists. During the Shavuot and Tisha be-Av observances, on June 11 and August 12, respectively, Reform and Conservative Jews praying at the back of the plaza of the Western Wall were dispersed by the police, whom they charged with the use of excessive force. The Orthodox complained that these prayer groups were provocative because they consisted of men and women and because of the content of some of the prayers; such groups, especially at what the Orthodox regarded as their holiest site, were deeply offensive to them. Among Orthodox leaders deeply critical of extremist tendencies was Yehuda Friedlander, rector of Bar-Ilan University, Tel Aviv. In an outspoken statement

An Israeli policeman pushes a Conservative Jewish woman away from the Western Wall in Jerusalem. In August some 200 Reform and Conservative Jews praying at a special area at the holy site were forcibly evicted by police after Orthodox Jews complained about their presence.

DAVID SILVERMAN—REUTERS

in August, he warned of the danger of civil war in Israel if religious extremism was not curbed.

The conversion bill and the disturbances at the Western Wall raised fears that non-Orthodox rabbis would call for a boycott of the United Jewish Appeal for funds for Israel. The central Jewish fund-raising establishment in the U.S., therefore, agreed in September to help raise money for Reform and Conservative institutions in Israel in exchange for a pledge of solidarity from their leadership; this was an indication of the growth of non-Orthodox forms of Judaism in Israel.

On the interfaith front, major meetings included the Colloquium of the International Council of Christians and Jews, held in Rome in September and addressed by Pope John Paul II. Earlier in the year Vatican officials had announced that the pope had instructed a commission to examine the persecution of Jews in the Inquisition, as part of a program in which the church aimed to seek pardon for past mistakes. Toward the end of September, French bishops offered a formal "repentance" for the Roman Catholic Church's failure to condemn the persecution of Jews during the Vichy regime that governed France during much of World War II.

The centenary of the First Zionist Congress, convened by Theodor Herzl in Basel, Switz., was celebrated in August there. The Basel city council expressed the hope that the centennial events would "have a positive influence on the current discussions of the role of Switzerland in the Second World War." In October the bicentenary of the death of Elijah ben Solomon, the "Vilna Gaon" ("excellency"), was marked with, among other events, an academic conference in Vilnius, Lithuania, devoted to the work of this major scholar and teacher of the Jewish religious world.

Interesting theological issues were raised by the publication and rise to best-seller status of Michael Drosnin's *The Bible Code* (1997), based on the work of mathematicians Eliyahu Rips, credited as the discoverer of the code (who denounced the book), Yoav Rosenberg, and Doron Witztum. Scholars debated as to whether biblical text encodes detailed knowledge of future events and names and, if so, whether that would demonstrate its divine origin. There were others who believed that any such discussion would debase scripture and distract attention from its important teachings.

(NORMAN SOLOMON)

BUDDHISM

In December 1996 Burmese insurgents exploded time bombs at Kaba Aye temple near Yangon (Rangoon), where thousands flocked daily throughout the month to honour a tooth relic of the Buddha on loan from China. The blasts killed or maimed 22 Buddhists, including two government officials. Three Burmese monks were killed and 100 arrested during March 1997 after mobs in Mandalay smashed mosque windows and burned copies of the Qur'an (Koran). The rioting was sparked by reports that a Muslim had molested a Buddhist girl, though the deeper causes remained unclear. Some reports associated the monk-led violence with a recent decision by Myanmar's military government to prevent a rally protesting government mishandling of a temple-restoration project and also with the deaths of 16 monks in government prisons, though other reports that monks in the mob were seen wearing army boots bolstered government claims that conservative forces had incited the riots to discredit Myanmar's bid for membership in the Association of Southeast Asian Nations.

The Dalai Lama assumes a meditative posture during an "enlightenment meeting" in March for Buddhist faithful in Kao-hsiung, Taiwan. Despite criticism from China, Taiwan allowed the Dalai Lama to open an office in Taipei in September.

SIMON KWONG—REUTERS

In January 1997 a number of high-ranking Sri Lankan monks quit the Supreme Advisory Council of the Buddha Sasana Ministry to protest the government's plans for resolving the civil war. In August Sri Lanka's main opposition United National Party called on citizens to tie yellow ribbons at Buddhist temples and churches as an expression of support for free and fair elections. During April and May, Sri Lankans joined Buddhists and Muslims throughout the world to demand preservation of the colossal Buddha image at Bamiyan, Afg., after a leader of the Islamic fundamentalist Taliban group threatened to destroy it.

Taiwan welcomed the Dalai Lama for the first time in March and in September allowed him to establish an office in Taipei, despite harsh criticism from China, which in April also criticized U.S. Pres. Bill Clinton for meeting the Tibetan leader. In May China imprisoned a senior Tibetan monk accused of helping the Dalai Lama to nominate his own candidate for Panchen Lama, a young boy who was not seen after that time. Indian police arrested nine Chinese agents posing as Tibetans at the Dalai Lama's Kalachakra ceremony in Siliguri, India, in December 1996. Followers of an anti-Dalai Lama Tibetan sect were blamed for the February 1997 murder of three of his close associates in Dharmsala, India.

Vietnam continued its crackdown on the opposition United Buddhist Church when security forces raided a central temple in Hue in November 1996 and arrested two church leaders. Vietnamese police also reportedly razed a pagoda near Dalat. In September 1997 the UN reported that forces of Cambodian strongman Hun Sen had used Buddhist temples as crematoriums for scores of political opponents executed since his takeover of the government in July. Cambodian patriarch Maha Ghosananda in August led more than 1,000 Buddhist monks, nuns, and laymen in prayers for peace on the streets of Phnom Penh. Later that month King Norodom Sihanouk returned to hold Buddhist ceremonies for reconciliation at Angkor Wat.

Throughout the year U.S. Vice Pres. Al Gore fended off criticism of fund-raising activities at a tax-exempt Buddhist temple in California. During January scientists voiced concern about the ecological impact of popular Chinese Buddhist practices in New York City, especially releasing domesticated goldfish, birds, and turtles to gain merit. Thai monks combating deforestation celebrated the ordination of their 50 millionth tree in February 1997.

(JONATHAN S. WALTERS)

HINDUISM

As the 50th year of India's independence, 1997 was marked by close scrutiny of the nation's record in meeting the goals of a secular and classless society that were set forth by the framers of its constitution. The unprecedented election in 1997 of a member of the lowest Hindu class as India's president dramatically underscored the momentous strides taken by the nation toward achieving those goals, whereas ongoing communal conflict pointed to the need for further change.

On January 30 the remaining ashes of the venerated Hindu champion of Indian independence Mohandas Gandhi were deposited by his great-grandson, Tushar Gandhi, into the Ganges River at the point of its confluence with the Yamuna at Allahabad, one of the holiest sites in India. Assassinated by a Hindu fanatic on Jan. 30, 1948, Gandhi was cremated and, in accordance with Hindu practice, his remains were distributed to the Indian states for deposit in sacred rivers. Mysteriously, the urn of ashes sent to Orissa remained in a bank vault for nearly 49 years until Tushar Gandhi was able to gain release of the urn by court order. The ritual immersion of the ashes was conducted by Hindu priests and attended by representatives of various religions.

In March a convert from Hinduism was named as a successor to Mother Teresa. Sister Nirmala ("Pure"), whose Hindu parents sent her to a Roman Catholic missionary school in order for her to learn English well, converted to Catholicism at the age of 24 and became one of Mother Teresa's first missionary sisters to work with the sick and poor in Calcutta. The conversion of Hindus, particularly from the lower castes, to Christianity had been denounced repeatedly by Hindu nationalists as a threat to their efforts to achieve a "pure" Hindu nation ("Hindutva").

On July 11 the nation witnessed one of the worst outbreaks of communal violence in recent years. More than 2,200 people were arrested, scores severely injured, and at least 12 killed when members of the lowest caste rioted in Bombay (Mumbai) and throughout Maharashtra state in response to the desecration of a bust of B.R. Ambedkar, the architect of the Indian constitution and a vigorous proponent of a secular state and the welfare of the lowest caste, of which he was himself a member. While Gandhi taught that the lowest members of Hinduism's caste system are "Harijans" ("children of God") and that Hindus must abandon the practice of ritual impurity, or "untouchability," in order to achieve a just society, today's "untouchables," who called themselves "Dalits" ("The Oppressed"), regarded Gandhi as a Brahmin elitist committed to the continuation of the caste structure. Ambedkar, on the other hand, was regarded by Dalits as the champion of a truly casteless society and virtually an incarnation of deity. The draping of a garland of leather shoes around his image in a Bombay slum by an unknown culprit was, therefore, for the Dalits tantamount to sacrilege and provided further evidence of their oppression in modern Indian society.

In sharp contrast to the bloody riots, on July 25 India for the first time inaugurated a Dalit as its president. Vice Pres. K.R. Narayanan, a scholar and one-time ambassador to the United States and to China, was chosen for the largely ceremonial post by an overwhelming majority of federal and state lawmakers. *(See* BIOGRAPHIES.*)* Overcoming every obstacle, he made his way from a primary school in his Kerala village to achieve highest honours at the London School of Economics and then entry into the Indian foreign service. Dalit leaders expressed their hope that President Narayanan would prove to be a new Ambedkar, bringing freedom from oppression to the members of his caste, who constituted one-quarter of India's population.

(H. PATRICK SULLIVAN)

DIMOTIA PICTURE AGENCY/SIPA PRESS

Nearly a half century after the death of venerated Indian leader Mohandas Gandhi, the last of his ashes was deposited in the sacred waters of the Ganges River on January 30. Gandhi's great-grandson, Tushar Gandhi, is shown carrying the casket in which the ashes were sealed.

ISLAM

Two trends noticeable in recent years remained conspicuous during 1997: outbreaks of violence, including attacks by some Muslims against governing authorities in a number of countries, and the continually increasing awareness in Western European nations and in North America of the presence there of Muslim communities and the need for authorities to be sensitive to that presence.

Violence, seemingly unabated, continued in a number of places. In Algeria there were bloody attacks on civilians, as there had been during the previous five years; these attacks, by Muslims against other Muslims, were aimed at bringing down the Algerian government, which had set aside the election results of January 1992, in which the Islamists apparently had been voted into power. Elections in Algeria in June, in which moderates were returned to power, did not stop the violence. In August there was an especially ferocious outbreak during which some 300 persons were killed; by the end of September, more than 600 people had been reported to have been killed in a two-month period. Since 1992 outbreaks of violence in Algeria had killed more than 60,000 people, almost all of them civilians, including women and children.

Violence also erupted sporadically in Egypt, South Asia, and the Xinjiang region of China. Violent incidents, bombings, and confrontations marked the year in and around Jerusalem, the West Bank, Gaza, and adjacent areas in Israel. The civil war continued in Afghanistan, where the ruling Islamist Taliban forces could not bring the northern part of the country under their control, and in the southern Sudan, where a guerrilla force of non-Muslims continued its insurgency against the Islamic-dominated Sudanese government.

In Turkey an Islamist party had formed a parliamentary coalition to govern the nation in June 1996 and began to carry out its program of increasing Islamic influence. The Turkish military, however, continued to purge its ranks of Islamists and increased its pressure on the government during the winter and spring of 1997; in June it forced the prime minister out of office and then oversaw the installation of a secular government. Elections in Iran in May brought a moderate, Mohammad Khatami (*see* BIOGRAPHIES), to the presidency; there were no apparent important changes in religious policies in that country.

The increasing visibility of Muslims in Western European countries and in the United States could be noticed in a number of different ways. Public-school systems in the Washington, D.C., area found it necessary to recognize the needs of Muslim schoolchildren during the fast of Ramadan in January. The Board of Education in New York City in June agreed to the display of Muslim symbols in certain school settings where Jewish and Christian symbols were already present. Also in June, Nike Inc. agreed to withdraw a brand of basketball shoes that bore a logo that could be interpreted as the name of God in Arabic; the company apologized to Muslims for any offense it may have caused. In May the U.S. publisher Simon & Schuster withdrew a children's book that portrayed the prophet Muhammad in a derogatory way. In Hartford, Conn., the Hartford Seminary, long interested in Christian-Muslim interfaith dialogue and study, and the University of Hartford appointed the first incumbent of a newly endowed chair: visiting professor in Abrahamic religions. The visiting appointee was Sulayman Nyang, a Muslim and professor of African Studies at Howard University, Washington, D.C. Such a chair was a rarity and represented a significant intellectual and religious point of view. The three faiths Judaism, Christianity, and Islam were increasingly being seen by many scholars and others as a continuous religious development and thus meriting the term Abrahamic faiths. In Europe, unused church buildings were increasingly being turned into mosques and used by Muslim congregations.

(REUBEN W. SMITH)

This article updates the *Macropædia* articles The Buddha and BUDDHISM; CHRISTIANITY; EASTERN ORTHODOXY; HINDUISM; Muhammad and the Religion of ISLAM; JUDAISM; PROTESTANTISM; The Study and Classification of RELIGIONS; ROMAN CATHOLICISM; and *Micropædia* entries on the various denominations.

Worldwide Adherents of All Religions by Six Continental Areas, Mid-1997

	Africa	Asia	Europe	Latin America	Northern America	Oceania	World	%	Number of countries
Christians	**350,892,000**	**289,784,000**	**552,183,000**	**455,882,000**	**257,129,000**	**24,117,000**	**1,929,987,000**	**33.0**	**244**
Unaffiliated Christians	30,689,000	10,381,000	21,443,000	2,041,000	35,748,000	4,637,000	104,939,000	1.8	201
Affiliated Christians	320,203,000	279,403,000	530,740,000	453,841,000	221,381,000	19,480,000	1,825,048,000	31.2	243
Roman Catholics	117,990,000	111,215,000	286,902,000	442,657,000	73,880,000	7,710,000	1,040,354,000	17.8	240
Protestants	87,190,000	44,654,000	85,924,000	41,829,000	95,063,000	6,253,000	360,913,000	6.2	237
Orthodox	32,880,000	15,403,000	166,908,000	620,000	6,698,000	695,000	223,204,000	3.8	137
Anglicans	20,551,000	641,000	24,338,000	874,000	3,145,000	5,236,000	54,785,000	0.9	167
Other Christians	68,357,000	125,213,000	5,645,000	40,231,000	47,585,000	826,000	287,857,000	4.9	213
Non-Christians	**407,502,000**	**3,248,670,000**	**176,986,000**	**36,047,000**	**44,589,000**	**4,958,000**	**3,918,752,000**	**67.0**	**244**
Atheists	423,000	117,789,000	24,038,000	2,612,000	1,385,000	368,000	146,615,000	2.5	163
Baha'is	2,263,000	3,606,000	104,000	880,000	740,000	73,000	7,666,000	0.1	213
Buddhists	136,000	348,559,000	1,478,000	645,000	2,132,000	191,000	353,141,000	6.0	123
Chinese folk religionists	28,000	362,013,000	216,000	184,000	832,000	61,000	363,334,000	6.2	88
Confucianists	0	6,078,000	10,000	0	0	24,000	6,112,000	0.1	14
Ethnic religionists	90,365,000	138,469,000	1,220,000	1,060,000	331,000	249,000	231,694,000	4.0	141
Hindus	2,378,000	740,633,000	1,520,000	776,000	1,129,000	361,000	746,797,000	12.8	109
Jains	65,000	3,946,000	0	0	5,000	0	4,016,000	0.1	10
Jews	290,000	4,497,000	2,932,000	1,173,000	5,904,000	94,000	14,890,000	0.3	137
Mandeans	0	40,000	0	0	0	0	40,000	0.0	2
Muslims	306,606,000	803,605,000	31,347,000	1,632,000	4,066,000	238,000	1,147,494,000	19.6	204
New-Religionists	27,000	97,263,000	122,000	611,000	649,000	27,000	98,699,000	1.7	57
Nonreligious	4,798,000	597,804,000	113,165,000	15,144,000	26,127,000	3,242,000	760,280,000	13.0	238
Shintoists	0	2,611,000	0	7,000	54,000	0	2,672,000	0.0	8
Sikhs	52,000	21,464,000	497,000	0	491,000	14,000	22,518,000	0.4	32
Spiritists	3,000	2,000	78,000	11,229,000	148,000	7,000	11,467,000	0.2	54
Zoroastrians	1,000	268,000	0	0	3,000	0	272,000	0.0	16
Other religionists	67,000	23,000	259,000	94,000	593,000	9,000	1,045,000	0.0	78
Total population	**758,394,000**	**3,538,454,000**	**729,169,000**	**491,929,000**	**301,718,000**	**29,075,000**	**5,848,739,000**	**100.0**	**244**

Continents. These follow current UN demographic terminology. UN practice began in 1949 by dividing the world into 5 continents, then into 18 regions (1954), then into 8 major continental areas (called macro regions in 1987) and 24 regions (1963), then into 7 major areas and 22 regions (1988), and most recently into the 6 major areas shown above, and 21 regions (1994). *See* United Nations, *World Population Prospects: The 1996 Revision* (New York: UN, 1997), with populations of all continents, regions, and countries covering the period 1950–2025. The table above therefore combines its former columns "East Asia" and "South Asia" into one single continental area, "Asia," which also now includes the former Soviet Central Asian states. Note also that "Europe" now extends eastward to Vladivostok, the Sea of Japan, and the Bering Strait.
Countries. The last column enumerates sovereign and nonsovereign countries in which each religion or religious grouping has a numerically significant following.
Adherents. As defined and enumerated for each of the world's countries in *World Christian Encyclopedia* (1982), projected to mid-1997, adjusted for recent data.
Christians. Followers of Jesus Christ affiliated with churches (church members, including children: 1,782,809,000) plus persons professing in censuses or polls to be Christians though not so affiliated. The four major ecclesiastical blocs are ranked by number of adherents at world level.
Other Christians. This term denotes Catholics (non-Roman), marginal Protestants, crypto-Christians, and adherents of African, Asian, Black, and Latin-American indigenous churches.
Atheists. Persons professing atheism, skepticism, disbelief, or irreligion, including antireligious (opposed to all religion).
Buddhists. 56% Mahayana, 38% Theravada (Hinayana), 6% Tantrayana (Lamaism).
Chinese folk religionists. Followers of the traditional Chinese religion (local deities, ancestor veneration, Confucian ethics, Taoism, universism, divination, some Buddhist elements).
Confucians. Non-Chinese followers of Confucius and Confucianism, mostly Koreans in Korea.
Ethnic religionists. Followers of local, tribal, animistic, or shamanistic religions.
Hindus. 70% Vaishnavites, 25% Shaivites, 2% neo-Hindus and reform Hindus.
Jews. Adherents of Judaism. For detailed data on "core" Jewish population, *see* the annual "World Jewish Populations" article in the American Jewish Committee's *American Jewish Year Book.*
Muslims. 83% Sunnites, 16% Shi'ites, 1% other schools. Up to 1990 the ethnic Muslims in the former U.S.S.R. who had embraced communism were not included as Muslims in this table. After the collapse of communism in 1990–91, these ethnic Muslims are once again enumerated as Muslims if they had returned to Islamic profession and practice.
New-Religionists. Followers of Asian 20th-century New Religions, New Religious movements, radical new crisis religions, and non-Christian syncretistic mass religions, all founded since 1800 and most since 1945.
Nonreligious. Persons professing no religion, nonbelievers, agnostics, freethinkers, dereligionized secularists indifferent to all religion.
Other religionists. Including 70 minor world religions and over 5,000 national or local religions, and a large number of spiritist religions, New Age religions, quasi religions, pseudo religions, parareligions, religious or mystic systems, religious and semireligious brotherhoods of numerous varieties.
Total Population. UN medium variant figures for mid-1997, as given in *World Population Prospects: The 1996 Revision* (New York: UN, 1997).

Religious Adherents in the United States of America, AD 1900–2000

Adherents	Year 1900	%	mid-1970	%	mid-1990	%	Annual Change, 1990–1995 Natural	Conversion	Total	Rate (%)	mid-1995	%	mid-2000	%
Christians	**73,270,000**	**96.4**	**189,321,000**	**90.1**	**217,024,000**	**85.4**	**2,222,100**	**–19,900**	**2,202,200**	**0.99**	**228,035,000**	**85.4**	**236,768,000**	**85.2**
Professing Christians	73,270,000	96.4	189,321,000	90.1	217,024,000	85.4	2,222,100	–19,900	2,202,200	0.99	228,035,000	85.4	236,768,000	85.2
Unaffiliated Christians	18,845,000	24.8	36,120,000	17.2	31,473,000	12.4	322,300	–177,100	145,200	0.46	32,199,000	12.1	31,678,000	11.4
Affiliated Christians	54,425,000	71.6	153,201,000	72.9	185,551,000	73.0	1,899,800	157,200	2,057,000	1.08	195,836,000	73.3	205,090,000	73.8
Roman Catholics	10,775,000	14.2	48,391,000	23.0	56,665,000	22.3	580,200	–23,200	557,000	0.96	59,450,000	22.3	61,800,000	22.2
Protestants	35,000,000	46.1	70,653,000	33.6	82,072,000	32.3	840,300	–154,700	685,600	0.82	85,500,000	32.0	88,800,000	32.0
Evangelicals	26,598,000	35.0	50,689,000	24.1	67,743,000	26.7	693,600	273,800	967,400	1.39	72,580,000	27.2	76,815,000	27.6
Anglicans (Episcopalians)	1,600,000	2.1	3,234,000	1.5	2,480,000	1.0	25,400	–51,400	–26,000	–1.07	2,350,000	0.9	2,203,000	0.8
Orthodox	400,000	0.5	4,387,000	2.1	4,250,000	1.7	43,500	232,700	276,200	5.79	5,631,000	2.1	6,260,000	2.3
Black Christians	5,750,000	7.6	19,679,000	9.4	32,598,000	12.8	333,800	106,600	440,400	1.32	34,800,000	13.0	37,200,000	13.4
Black Evangelicals	5,320,000	7.0	13,551,000	6.4	17,248,000	6.8	176,600	57,800	234,400	1.32	18,420,000	6.9	19,548,000	7.0
Catholics (non-Roman)	100,000	0.1	473,000	0.2	646,000	0.3	6,600	6,200	12,800	1.91	710,000	0.3	800,000	0.3
Other Christians	800,000	1.1	6,384,000	3.0	9,680,000	3.8	99,100	104,900	204,000	2.02	10,700,000	4.0	12,100,000	4.4
Non-Christians	**2,724,800**	**3.6**	**20,789,000**	**9.9**	**37,079,000**	**14.6**	**379,700**	**19,900**	**399,600**	**1.06**	**39,077,000**	**14.6**	**41,054,000**	**14.8**
Atheists	1,000	0.0	200,000	0.1	770,000	0.3	7,900	12,900	20,800	2.57	874,000	0.3	925,000	0.3
Baha'is	2,800	0.0	138,000	0.1	600,000	0.2	6,100	10,500	16,600	2.63	683,000	0.3	750,000	0.3
Buddhists	30,000	0.0	200,000	0.1	1,680,000	0.7	17,200	19,600	36,800	2.10	1,864,000	0.7	2,000,000	0.7
Chinese folk religionists	70,000	0.1	90,000	0.0	76,000	0.0	800	–1,200	–400	–0.53	74,000	0.0	70,000	0.0
Hindus	1,000	0.0	100,000	0.0	650,000	0.3	6,700	22,300	29,000	4.11	795,000	0.3	950,000	0.3
Jews	1,500,000	2.0	6,700,000	3.2	5,535,000	2.2	56,700	–60,100	–3,400	–0.06	5,518,000	2.1	5,500,000	2.0
Muslims	10,000	0.0	800,000	0.4	3,600,000	1.4	36,900	–3,500	33,400	0.91	3,767,000	1.4	3,950,000	1.4
Black Muslims	0	0.0	200,000	0.1	1,250,000	0.5	12,800	17,200	30,000	2.29	1,400,000	0.5	1,650,000	0.6
New-Religionists	0	0.0	110,000	0.1	575,000	0.2	5,900	–300	5,600	0.96	603,000	0.2	675,000	0.2
Nonreligious	1,000,000	1.3	11,730,000	5.6	22,233,000	8.7	227,600	4,600	232,200	1.02	23,394,000	8.8	24,554,000	8.8
Sikhs	0	0.0	1,000	0.0	160,000	0.1	1,600	4,400	6,000	3.50	190,000	0.1	220,000	0.1
Tribal religionists	100,000	0.1	70,000	0.0	280,000	0.1	2,900	2,100	5,000	1.73	305,000	0.1	350,000	0.1
Other religionists	10,000	0.0	650,000	0.3	920,000	0.4	9,400	8,600	18,000	1.88	1,010,000	0.4	1,110,000	0.4
Total population	**75,994,800**	**100.0**	**210,110,000**	**100.0**	**254,103,000**	**100.0**	**2,601,800**	**0**	**2,601,800**	**1.00**	**267,112,000**	**100.0**	**277,822,000**	**100.0**

Methodology. This table extracts a microcosm of the world table above. It depicts the United States, the country with the largest number of adherents to Christianity, the world's largest religion. Statistics for five points in time across the 20th century are presented. Also analyzed is each religion's *Annual change* by: *Natural* increase (births minus deaths, plus immigrants minus emigrants) per year and *Conversion* (new converts minus new defectors per year, which together constitute the *Total* increase per year. *Rate* is then computed as percentage per year.
Structure. Vertically the table lists 27 major religious categories. The 12 major religions (including nonreligion) in the U.S. are listed alphabetically with largest (Christians) first. Indented names of groups in the "Adherents" column are subcategories of the groups above them and are also counted in these unindented totals, so they should not be added twice into the column total. Figures for Christians in 1970 and 1990 are built upon detailed head counts by churches, usually to the last digit. Totals are then rounded to the nearest 1,000. Because of rounding, the corresponding percentage figures may sometimes not total exactly 100%. Figures for AD 2000 are projections based on current long-term trends.
Christians. Professing Christians are all persons who profess publicly to follow Jesus Christ as Lord and Saviour. This category is subdivided into **affiliated Christians** (church members) and **unaffiliated** (nominal) **Christians** (professing Christians not affiliated with any church). The six major ecclesiastical blocs are ranked by number of adherents in AD 2000.
Evangelicals. Churches, agencies, and individuals that call themselves by this term usually emphasize five or more of several fundamental doctrines (salvation by faith, personal acceptance, verbal inspiration of Scripture, depravity of man, Virgin Birth, miracles of Christ, atonement, evangelism, Second Advent).
Black Christians. Members of denominations initiated by Africans, Caribbean islanders, African-Americans.
Other Christians. This term denotes members of denominations and churches that regard themselves as outside mainline Protestant/Catholic/Orthodox Christianity.
Jews. Core Jewish population relating to Judaism, excluding Jewish persons professing a different religion.

(DAVID B. BARRETT; TODD M JOHNSON)

Social Protection

The financial viability of social protection programs continued to cause concern worldwide in 1997. The U.S. government began to revamp such programs as Medicaid, Medicare, and Social Security, while Canada struggled with funding its health care system and delivering services in a timely manner. In Western Europe reforms were implemented in an effort to reduce rising expenditures on health care, old-age, and unemployment benefits, and countries in Central and Eastern Europe experimented with different welfare models, both public and private. In industrialized Asia and the Pacific, measures were taken to improve the delivery of social services and to place greater responsibility on benefit recipients. Nations in Latin America continued to privatize social security pensions, while emerging and less-developed countries in Africa and Asia made efforts to extend benefits and initiate reform.

North America. After introducing landmark welfare reform in 1996, the United States in 1997 moved to overhaul other social protection programs, including Medicaid, Medicare, and Social Security. Although lawmakers sidestepped comprehensive reforms in these areas, significant changes were made, debate was accelerated, and panels were established to study further action.

Meanwhile, the new welfare system, which was not without problems and critics, officially took effect on July 1. Federal guarantees of cash grants to all eligible poor people were eliminated, and states were invested with broad authority and flexibility to move recipients from welfare rolls to jobs. As a result of the new reforms, the welfare caseload fell by more than one million in 1997 to under 11 million, including about 7 million children—a 26% decline since the peak year of 1994 and the lowest level in 25 years.

Two major factors were cited in explaining the sharp reduction—a strong economy that created more jobs and the reform legislation that nudged recipients into those jobs. A White House report in May concluded that the economy played the biggest role in caseload reduction, but critics of reform contended that much of the decline resulted from people being forced off welfare rolls. Whatever the reason, the decline helped produce an unexpected windfall that eased the first-year impact of reform. Since the new block grants issued to states from Washington, D.C., were based on the caseloads each state had had in previous years, states received about $2.6 billion more from the federal government than they would have received on the basis of 1997 caseloads. With greater freedom to experiment and with added federal funds, states turned one-size-fits-all welfare assistance into a variety of programs.

About one-half of the states offered one-time cash payments to help families through financial emergencies and to keep them from entering or returning to welfare. Kentucky and West Virginia extended relocation allowances so that welfare recipients from the jobless areas of Appalachia could work in cities in the region. Illinois earmarked $100 million for improving child care, and New Jersey created a $3.7 million transportation fund. At least 30 states experimented with allowing welfare recipients to keep more of their benefits after they secured jobs. Some experiments, however, ran into problems. A federal district court judge in Philadelphia ruled that Pennsylvania had acted illegally by paying new residents lower welfare benefits than it did to long-time residents. Although the decision applied only to Pennsylvania, it created a concern for at least 12 other states with similar laws.

MORRY GASH—ASSOCIATED PRESS

A welfare mother in Milwaukee, Wis., feeds her 15-month-old son while her 3-year-old daughter looks on. In 1997 Wisconsin ended cash assistance for virtually all of its residents on welfare.

Wisconsin's ambitious program, which was initiated before passage of federal reform, ended cash assistance for virtually everyone on welfare and imposed strict work requirements. The plan, however, offered former welfare recipients substantial help in getting and keeping jobs and provided an average of $15,700 for every family on welfare. In addition, child care and health care were extended to all low-income families, thousands of community service jobs were created, and private industries were encouraged to provide work. The state's welfare rolls plummeted by more than 60% from their peak.

Despite the varied efforts, however, fewer than one-half of the states met the initial October 1 federal deadline for reform standards—having at least one person working in 75% of all two-parent families. States had an easier time with a second rule that required them to have 25% of all welfare families in work activities. More than 30 states also failed to receive federal approval of new computer systems to track child-support cases. States that were unable to meet these standards faced a loss of some federal funds. Both the work rates and penalties were scheduled to rise annually until 2002, when states would have to have 50% of all welfare families and 90% of two-parent families working.

When he signed the reform law on Aug. 22, 1996, Pres. Bill Clinton promised to "fix" those parts of the law that he disliked. Some "fixing" was accomplished in 1997. Clinton received assurances from Congress that all legal immigrants residing in the U.S. at the time the law was signed would be eligible for Supplemental Security Income (SSI), which provided cash to the low-income aged and disabled. He also won a continuance of Medicaid coverage for disabled children who stood to lose their SSI benefits.

The ultimate verdict on welfare reform, however, would not be in for years. In some high-poverty areas, efforts were hampered both by politics and by a lack of jobs and funds for support services. It was uncertain what would happen nationwide when the economy slowed, federal funding shrank, and more states reduced support services.

Early in 1997 it appeared that the push for reform would target Social Security because of concern about the financial stability of the 62-year-old program, which in 1997 provided retirement income and survivor and disability benefits to 44 million people. In 1950, 16 workers paid payroll taxes to support each beneficiary of the program, but that ratio had since dwindled to about 3 to 1 and, with the population aging, by 2030 would shrink to 2 to 1. Experts predicted that the trust fund would be totally depleted by 2029. A 13-member Advisory Council on Social Security, however, issued a report that contradicted the experts, saying that the system did not face a massive crisis and that careful, sensible planning could fund it through the next 75 years. In what would be a basic change, however, panel members agreed that part of the Social Security taxes that had been invested exclusively in government bonds should be shifted into higher-earning private securities. Three different plans were offered for accomplishing this, including one that would give individuals a greater say in how their retirement money was invested, but the panel did not make a recommendation and postponed action pending further study.

The annual cost-of-living increase for Social Security and SSI beneficiaries would be 2.1% in 1998, raising benefits for the average retiree to $765 a month from $749. An average couple who both received benefits would receive $1,288. The payroll tax rate paid by both employees and employers would remain unchanged at 6.2%, but the maximum earnings on which the tax was calculated would increase to $68,400 from $65,400. To finance Medicare, workers and employers would each pay an additional 1.45% of their earnings.

Another ailing area in which broad overhaul was postponed in favour of short-term fixes was health care—Medicaid for the poor and Medicare for the elderly. As part of the balanced budget bill, Congress made several important changes to Medicare, including expansion of health care plan options and the addition of preventive health care coverage. Lawmakers, however, avoided the toughest, most explosive Medicare issue—the program's long-term-funding problems. Instead, a bipartisan commission was created to study structural and financial issues, including raising the eligibility age and making seniors contribute more. The balanced budget package greatly expanded states' roles in administering Medicaid programs but did not convert Medicaid into a block grant. Spurred by welfare changes that left many former recipients without health coverage when they moved to jobs, states embarked on a major expansion of Medicaid that would eventually provide free or low-cost health care to at least one-half of the 10 million uninsured children in the U.S. Despite cuts in federal funding, Medicaid remained the nation's largest health insurer for children and for those needing maternity and nursing-home care.

While social protection programs were changing, the ranks of poor Americans needing assistance did not. The Census Bureau reported that the number (36.5 million) and percentage (13.7%) of people living below the poverty line ($16,036 for a family of four) in 1996 remained virtually unchanged from the previous year.

In Canada the national health care system, popularly referred to as "medicare," came under scrutiny by many who felt that the program was underfunded, that the waiting period for hospital care (averaging about 11 weeks) was unacceptable, and that, as a result, quality care was compromised. About 17,000 more patients were waiting for hospital treatment in 1997 than in 1996, and medical intervention took about 15% longer than what physicians considered to be clinically reasonable. Some proposed the introduction of a two-tier health plan, but newly appointed Health Minister Allan Rock dismissed such a notion. He believed that the current system was adequately funded, even though transfer payments to the provinces were significantly reduced. He acknowledged that the system had some problems, but he believed that the introduction of another plan would only complicate matters. Rock reiterated the government's commitment to expanding the system through national home care and pharmacare programs and its promise, made during the June election, not to institute $700 million of planned cuts to the Canada Health and Social Transfer in 1998–99 and $1.4 billion the following fiscal year.

Western Europe. High unemployment and an aging population continued to generate concern about the financial stability of Western Europe's social security programs. (*See* Spotlight: *Europe's Crumbling Social Network.*) In Spain, where unemployment hovered around 22%, the entire social protection system was overhauled, and business and labour leaders reached agreement on reforms that would foster the hiring of permanent, rather than part-time, employees. Social security benefits would be financed through payroll deductions, whereas other benefits would be paid for through general taxation. In addition, pensions would be calculated on the basis of the last 15 years rather than the last 8 years of a worker's base salary.

Rising costs in health care led to reform in Austria, where the funding system for hospitals was completely redesigned. Payments made by the social insurance scheme for hospital treatment would be subject to an annual cap linked to future contributions. In addition, a new billing system was introduced whereby reimbursement would be based on the diagnosis rather than the type of hospital. A uniform hospital plan was also adopted, which led to the closing of certain hospitals or departments within them.

In Germany the third stage of the health care reform process came into effect in July. Although draft legislation initially had dropped certain items approved for reimbursement in the catalog of covered items, these proposals were withdrawn following heated public protest. In the end, co-payments were raised and elements were introduced that previously had been found only in private health insurance schemes. For example, refunds would be made to those who had contributed to the plan but had not made claims for benefits. Participants in the scheme were also given the opportunity to reduce the amount of their premiums, but in doing so they would increase their own costs for treatment.

In Norway the national insurance benefit regulations were revised. Beginning in January pensioners between the ages of 67 and 70 who had an income from employment in addition to a pension had their pensions reduced, but by less than in previous years. Starting in May, pensioners with employed spouses had their national insurance benefits reduced.

Physicians in France signed "loyalty contracts." Under the program individuals could select a general practitioner who had signed an agreement with the social security health fund stating that fees would be limited to approved charges. In February legislation was passed establishing private retirement savings funds. Following the installation of Socialist Prime Minister Lionel Jospin (*see* BIOGRAPHIES), however, regulations to implement the funds were not enacted as planned. The new government viewed the private funds as undermining the mandatory pay-as-you-go systems and declared that the legislation would be revised.

Political change in the United Kingdom also led to the cancellation of reforms sponsored by the outgoing Conservative government. Prime Minister Tony Blair's (*see* BIOGRAPHIES) new Labour government voided a new formula that would have reduced housing benefits by essentially lowering the housing standards on which benefits were calculated. The new government also introduced a bill that would modernize welfare delivery and launched programs that would help single parents and disabled people find work.

In Switzerland cuts were made in daily unemployment allowances, and the waiting period for unemployment benefits was extended by one day for short-time workers (those compelled to reduce working hours temporarily). Measures were taken to encourage early retirement to help ease unemployment. A mandatory minimum occupational pension provision was also introduced for the unemployed. Similarly, in Denmark pension coverage was made available—under the Danish Labour Market Supplementary Pension Scheme—to people during breaks in their job history in the labour market. The provision would help relieve the large social disparities between pensioners with an extensive working career and those who did not have the opportunity to work most of their lives. Finland experimented with shorter working hours to tackle the unemployment problem and implemented pilot projects in both the private and public sectors. To address the problem of unemployment in Iceland, a national labour market authority was created that would conduct nationwide job placement through a centralized system.

Central and Eastern Europe. A two-tier mandatory pension system, effective for those entering the labour force in 1998, was created in Hungary. While 25% of social security contributions would be paid to pension funds managed by private-sector companies, the remaining 75% would continue to go to the social security agency. Voluntary contributions would form a third tier of the system. In Poland reform legislation that laid the foundation for a similar system was approved by the lower house of the Sejm (parliament).

The Romanian government introduced a draft law intended to establish a single public pension and social security system guaranteed by the state. The health care system also would be reformed. One proposal was that employees and employers would be required to contribute to the cost of medical services and that special funds would be created to administer these contributions.

A new system of mandatory health insurance was implemented in Lithuania. Under the plan a separate health insurance fund was responsible both for compensating patients, which had been done previously by the social insurance fund, and for providing health care services previously financed from state and local budgets.

Industrialized Asia and the Pacific. The federal government in Australia created a new service-delivery agency. The various government departments would focus on policy development and would contract the agency to deliver services such as benefit payments.

Beginning in 1997 customized service was available to all income-support clients in New Zealand. This encompassed personalized, one-to-one contact for beneficiaries and ensured that they saw the same customer-service officer for all income-support issues. The work test (requiring an active search for employment) was extended to single parents, widowed beneficiaries, and spouses of the unemployed, and annual interviews were introduced to encourage beneficiaries to move toward employment. Concern over the costs of maintaining the existing social security system led the government to propose the establishment of a mandatory retirement-savings scheme.

In Japan individuals were made to bear a greater share of expenditures for health care. Contributions to health insurance were augmented and larger co-payments demanded. Major worker unrest in South Korea occurred following a change in the labour law that would have permitted companies to dismiss employees more easily, introduce variations from the standard working hours, and replace striking employees with temporary workers.

Emerging and Less-Developed Countries. In Mexico private pension funds began operations in July, when rules on investments were published. In Argentina and Chile the constant switching of private pension funds between providers was considered a problem because it generated large administrative and marketing costs. Argentina proposed making transfers more complicated, whereas Chile suggested charging lower transfer fees to members who stayed with funds for a specified time. Peru unveiled an overhauled health care system that allowed for the establishment of health plans and programs outside both the social health system and the state health service.

Although many countries in Africa and Asia were plagued by problems of financial imbalances and inadequate coverage, in certain places benefits were increased and some reforms were proposed and implemented. More than seven million people in Egypt benefited from increases in old-age, disability, and survivors pensions, and in Tunisia benefits for private-sector employees were increased in an effort to equalize them with those received by workers in the public sector. India introduced a new medical insurance policy for the poor. It was structured as a social rather than a business venture, with premiums set at a low level. A Pakistani task force on pension funds proposed that the government consider an ambitious three-phase expansion in coverage of the existing scheme. The Philippines started to set up a computerized identification system to facilitate social welfare benefit claims.

(CHRISTIANE KUPTSCH; DAVID M. MAZIE)

HUMAN RIGHTS

During 1997 greater efforts were made both to arrest and convict war criminals in former Yugoslavia and Rwanda and to adopt an international agreement banning the manufacture and use of land mines. In addition, human rights issues emerged when Hong Kong reverted to Chinese control (*see* Spotlight: *Hong Kong's Return to China*) and when Irish Pres. Mary Robinson was appointed UN high commissioner for human rights. Special attention also was given to the activities of "truth commissions" in South Africa and Haiti, Switzerland's alleged financial dealings with the Nazis during the Holocaust (*see* WORLD AFFAIRS: *Switzerland:* Sidebar), continued problems with minority rights and forced migrations of refugees in Turkey, and abuses taking place in the Democratic Republic of the Congo (Congo [Kinshasa]). New concerns were raised about dealing with corporations and other private groups that benefited from or participated in major human rights abuses and the differing perceptions of human rights in less-developed and industrialized countries.

War Crimes and the Punishment of Human Rights Violations. The International Criminal Tribunal for the Former Yugoslavia, located in The Hague, convicted a Bosnian Croat, Drazen Erdemovic, who pleaded guilty and was sentenced to 10 years' imprisonment for his role in the 1995 massacre of unarmed Muslims in northeastern Bosnia and Herzegovina. Bosnian Serb Dusan Tadic was later found guilty on 11 counts of atrocities (5 war crimes and 6 against humanity) and was sentenced to 20 years in jail. In Düsseldorf, Ger., where a court was relieving the overburdened tribunal in The Hague, another Bosnian Serb, Nikola Jorgic, was sentenced to life in prison on 11 counts of genocide and 30 lesser counts of murder. Although NATO-led military forces monitoring implementation of the Dayton peace accords had previously declined to play a role in war-crimes prosecution for fear of jeopardizing the fragile peace agreement in Bosnia, they launched a more aggressive stance and arrested 76 criminals who had been previously indicted for war crimes. In other NATO actions Milan Kovacevic was arrested and Simo Drljaca was shot dead in July while resisting arrest in the Prijedor area; an additional 10 war criminals were later apprehended.

The International Criminal Tribunal for Rwanda moved much more slowly, with 21 persons indicted and arrested and 8 other suspects taken into custody. Three trials were under way, but no convictions were made at the international level, which resulted in major criticism of the effectiveness of the tribunal. The government of Rwanda, operating under its own specially enacted law on genocide, arrested thousands accused of war crimes and put a number of them on trial. The government itself, however, was accused of human rights abuses as a result of the overcrowded and abusive conditions in the prisons, where scores of detainees awaiting trial died.

South Africa and Haiti developed "truth commissions" to deal with human rights violations committed by previous regimes. The primary goal of these bodies was to bring the full facts of past atrocities to light, rather than to punish individual violators. The Truth and Reconciliation Commission in South Africa, however, was criticized for granting amnesty too easily. Massive public demonstrations occurred in August after two men who arranged the 1993 Easter Sunday murder of Chris Hani (a chief lieutenant to Nelson Mandela) applied for amnesty in return for their public confessions.

The dual issues of war crimes and accountability developed over the role played by Swiss banks in laundering gold and other assets confiscated from those arrested and killed by the Nazis during World War II. Special efforts were being made to identify those victims whose assets had been confiscated and transferred to Swiss banks, and the Swiss government helped to establish special funds to reimburse Holocaust survivors, their relatives, and other victims of human rights violations. The first checks for $400 (from a fund unrelated to the dormant bank accounts) were presented to 80 Holocaust survivors in November.

Land Mine Prohibition. In September about 90 nations adopted the text of a proposed treaty banning the manufacture and use of antipersonnel mines by the end of the century. The formal signing of the treaty took place in December, with individual nations ratifying it thereafter. The U.S. government declined to approve the draft, citing concerns about the security of U.S. troops along the demilitarized zone between North and South Korea, although the U.S. pledged to end use of the weapon by 2003 at all sites except in Korea.

Minority Rights and Refugee Issues. Minority rights issues emerged in the Congo (Kinshasa), where Pres. Laurent Kabila (*see* BIOGRAPHIES) refused to allow a UN team to investigate complaints that his rebel forces

A woman wipes away tears while testifying in front of South Africa's Truth and Reconciliation Commission. Her son, an antiapartheid activist, was murdered by white policemen, who later admitted that the black youth had done nothing to provoke the killing.

PETER TURNLEY—DETROIT FREE PRESS/BLACK STAR

STEPHEN GILL—PANOS

This boy prostitute is one of an estimated 28,000 underage sex workers in Sri Lanka. A growing outcry over the child-sex trade, which flourished in Southeast Asia, brought long-needed crackdowns in a number of countries, including Thailand and the Philippines.

had massacred large numbers of Rwandan Hutu refugees during their seven-month campaign to oust dictator Mobutu Sese Seko. (*See* Obituaries.) Some of the executed Hutu had been involved in the slaughter of up to 500,000 Tutsi in 1994.

The Turkish government engaged in a major campaign against rebel Kurds, including a number of military incursions aimed at rebel strongholds inside Iraq and highly repressive measures against political parties and human rights groups representing Kurdish interests. In Myanmar (Burma) forced labour, rape, disappearances, and torture became hallmarks of the ruling State Law and Order Restoration Council's efforts to end independence attempts by Mon, Rohingya, and Karen minorities (among others). In The Sudan the militant Islamic regime used a minority insurrection on the southern frontier as a justification for continuing repression and human rights violations. All-party talks were convened for the first time in Northern Ireland in an effort to resolve that region's long-standing religious conflict, despite renewed acts of terrorism designed to prevent the peace process from taking place.

Major civilian massacres took place in Algiers and other cities in Algeria, resulting in tens of thousands of casualties. Terrorism and the killing of civilians had erupted in 1992 after the military-backed government annulled the second round of parliamentary elections because it seemed likely that the Islamic Salvation Front would gain political control.

The Israeli peace settlement process with the newly installed Palestinian authorities ground to a halt owing to Israel's policy of expanding Jewish settlements in Palestinian territory and the Palestine Liberation Organization's inability to control and prevent violent protests and acts of terrorism. Disputes between the Indian government and Kashmir heated up.

New High Commissioner for Human Rights. Robinson, a long-time human rights advocate, was named high commissioner for human rights by UN Secretary-General Kofi Annan, replacing the largely ineffectual and widely criticized José Ayala Lasso. Robinson was the first head of state to visit Rwanda after the genocide there, the first to visit Somalia during its 1992 famine, and the first to attend the International Criminal Tribunal for the Former Yugoslavia.

Hong Kong's Return to China. One of the most dramatic events with major human rights implications was the July 1 return of Hong Kong to the jurisdiction of China. Major concerns were voiced in the period leading up to the takeover that emerging democratic institutions, including a locally elected legislature and vocal human rights advocates and organizations, would be placed in jeopardy under China's communist government. Although some protests were allowed, China appointed its own legislative body and executive and posted military troops in the territory to establish control.

Other Issues. The role that Swiss banks played in providing economic assistance to the Nazi regime during the Holocaust brought attention to the question of corporate and private responsibility for human rights violations. Traditionally, human rights had focused on the actions (or inactions) of governments and did not attempt to reach the issue of the responsibility of private entities. Criticism, however, was beginning to be directed against corporations, such as large international oil companies like Shell, TOTAL, and UNICAL, which had commercial interests in countries that engaged in gross human rights violations—such as Nigeria, Myanmar, and Iran. Initiatives were taken to allow human rights enforcement efforts to reach private individuals and paramilitary groups, whose connections with government were too far removed to allow them to be covered by traditional human rights laws. In one notable example, a lawsuit was filed in the U.S. seeking to establish financial liability for corporations that gained economic benefit from forced-labour practices in Myanmar.

The so-called North-South debate over human rights focused on the issue of whether the emphasis that Western democracies placed on civil and political rights was appropriate in less-developed countries that preferred to emphasize economic-development concerns. The questions needing resolution were twofold: Were the two approaches compatible, and could a common ground exist that did not give exclusive priority to one over the other.

In late December the Egyptian Supreme Administrative Court upheld that country's 1996 ban on female circumcision, ending months of contention between human-rights groups and Islamic fundamentalists.

(Morton Sklar)

See also Business and Industry Review: *Insurance;* Education; Health and Disease.

This article updates the *Macropædia* article Social Welfare.

Sports and Games

In 1997 Athens, the city where the modern Olympic Games began in 1896, learned that in 2004 it would play host to its first Olympics in more than a century. A bid to play host to the 1996 Games had failed, which led the city's representatives to admit that they had campaigned on the assumption that the Greek capital deserved the Centennial Games on the basis of history alone. For its 2004 bid the Athens committee demonstrated a realistic approach toward solving problems that might stand in the way of such an event's being held there. Attorney Gianna Angelopoulos headed the group that made the bid, and Stratis Stratigis, a lawyer, was appointed to chair the city's Olympic organizing committee.

In November the last of 32 finalists qualified for the 1998 association football (soccer) World Cup. Four countries (South Africa, Jamaica, Croatia, and Japan) reached the finals for the first time, and five others (Tunisia, Iran, Nigeria, Denmark, and Saudi Arabia) made only their second appearance. Defending champion Brazil, led by its 1994 hero, Romário, was considered the early favourite.

In the U.S. two women's professional basketball leagues completed their inaugural seasons during the year. In March the Columbus Quest won the championship of the American Basketball League (ABL); in August the Houston Comets prevailed in the Women's National Basketball Association (WNBA). The ABL, which comprised teams playing in smaller markets, had an average attendance of 3,536, whereas the WNBA averaged 9,669 per game. The level of play in the ABL was generally regarded as superior, but the WNBA had the public-relations muscle of the National Basketball Association behind it. Observers believed that the ABL's only hope of long-term survival was to merge with its more popular rival, but the league began its second season in the fall amid reports of increased attendance.

A change of rules in open-wheel automobile racing signaled a step toward compromise in a dispute that had emerged in recent years. The Indy Racing League (IRL) removed its guarantee of 25 of the 33 starting spots for its own cars in the Indianapolis 500. This increased the chances of the star drivers of the rival Championship Auto Racing Teams (CART) circuit to compete in the event, which had lost some of its allure after the IRL invoked the rule in 1996. Cars in the race were still required to abide by the IRL's unique equipment standards, however, which meant that CART teams would have to maintain IRL-approved cars for only one race per year.

(ANTHONY G. CRAINE)

ARCHERY

In August 1997 the biennial Fédération Internationale de Tir à l'Arc (FITA) world target championships were held in Victoria, B.C., with preliminary rounds shot at 90 m, 70 m, 50 m, and 30 m (1 m = 3.28 ft). One-on-one shooting determined the champions. In the women's Olympic (recurve) division, Kim Du Ri of South Korea defeated Cornelia Pfohl of Germany. The men's Olympic division was won by Kim Kyung Ho of South Korea, with a narrow 108–107 victory over Christophe Peignois of Belgium. Fabiola Palazzini of Italy captured the gold medal in the women's compound bow, and Catherine Pellen of France won silver. Dee Wilde won the men's compound title over fellow American Terry Ragsdale 109–105.

At the U.S. National Field Archery Association (NFAA) indoor championship in March, the top male unlimited professional division ended in a three-way tie at 118 x-rings out of 120. Ken Young, Roger Hoyle, and George Ryals shot two ends of five arrows to determine Young the winner by one x-ring. Pro women's unlimited champion Michelle Ragsdale posted an impressive 117 score on the same difficult 4-cm (1.6-in) centre-ring target. She also swept the same division at the NFAA outdoor championship in July. Russ Weatherbee won the men's outdoor pro unlimited trophy, and Steve Gibbs was the limited men's winner in this five-day, 500-arrow tournament. Waldo Cleland was awarded the Shooter of the Year title for posting the highest total score for all four NFAA championships held during the year.

The U.S. National Archery Association (NAA) indoor champions were Richard Johnson and Janet Dykman in the Olympic bow division, while Mark Penaz and Becky Pearson won in the compound bow division. At the NAA national target championship in August, Richard ("Butch") Johnson won the men's Olympic bow division with a score of 2,631 out of a maximum 2,880. The women's Olympic bow winner was Dykman with 2,606. In the largest compound division ever, the winners were Kevin Eldredge with 2,637 and Diane Hooper with 2,594.

(LARRY WISE)

AUTOMOBILE RACING

Grand Prix Racing. Formula One racing sustained its worldwide interest in 1997 and continued to represent a substantial financial income for the U.K., where many of the components of the highly technical cars were made. The Williams-Renault team remained in the ascendant, strengthened by the excellence of the French Renault engines.

British driver Damon Hill, the defending world champion, moved to the Arrows team but failed to maintain his 1996 form. The fight for the 1997 World Drivers' Championship went to the very last race in Spain, with two-time champion Michael Schumacher of Germany one point ahead of French-Canadian Jacques Villeneuve. Villeneuve won the title, however, after his German rival drove into him during a controversial maneuver.

The season opened at Melbourne, where the Australian Grand Prix was won by Scottish driver David Coulthard in a McLaren-Mercedes with a British-built Ilmor engine. Schumacher took second and Mika Hakkinen of Finland third place for Ferrari and McLaren-Mercedes, respectively. The Brazilian Grand Prix was then won by Villeneuve over Austrian Gerhard Berger's Benetton-Renault. In Argentina the victor was again Villeneuve, with Briton Eddie Irvine's Ferrari second. At Imola, Italy, Heinz-Harald Frentzen of Germany won the San Marino Grand Prix for Williams.

The Monaco Grand Prix, run over the only true road circuit, produced all its usual glitz and glamour, with rain creating an extra hazard. Schumacher displayed his skills, winning on Ferrari's 50th birthday. To three-time drivers' champion Jackie Stewart's gratification, his Stewart-Ford, in its first season of Grand Prix racing, was second, driven by Rubens Barrichello. The field then moved to Barcelona for the Spanish Grand Prix, where Villeneuve won. Another new model, one of Alain Prost's Prost-Mugen-Hondas, driven by Olivier Panis of France, was second. After the long haul to Canada for the race at Montreal, Schumacher finished first for Ferrari, with Jean Alesi second in a Benetton-Renault.

The French Grand Prix at Magny-Cours proved that Ferrari was back on form. Schumacher finished first, with Frentzen's Williams-Renault sandwiched between the winner and the other Ferrari, driven by Irvine. The British Grand Prix was won by Villeneuve, pursued by the two Benetton-Renaults of Alesi and Alexander Wurz. This was followed by the German Grand Prix over the Hockenheim circuit, where Berger put on an impressive performance, keeping Schumacher at bay. At the Hungarian Grand Prix, Hill drove a splendid race until hydraulic problems put him behind Villeneuve on the last lap.

The very fast Spa-Francorchamps circuit then played host to the Belgian Grand Prix. In "impossible" conditions of heavy rain, the race started as a procession behind the pace car. When the field was released, Schumacher showed his superiority in adverse conditions and came home the winner. Italy held its Grand Prix at Monza, but national hopes were dashed when Ferrari could do

(continued on page 322)

FITA Outdoor World Target Archery Championships*

Year	Men's individual: Winner	Points	Men's team: Winner	Points
1989	S. Zabrodsky (U.S.S.R.)	332	U.S.S.R.	985
1991	S. Fairweather (Austl.)	334	South Korea	998
1993	Park Kyung Mo (S.Kor.)	113	France	249
1995	Lee Kyung Chul (S.Kor.)	109	South Korea	255
1997	**Kim Kyung Ho (S.Kor.)**	**108**	**South Korea**	**254**
Year	**Women's individual: Winner**	**Points**	**Women's team: Winner**	**Points**
1989	Kim Soo Nyung (S.Kor.)	338	South Korea	995
1991	Kim Soo Nyung (S.Kor.)	333	South Korea	1,030
1993	Kim Hyo Jung (S.Kor.)	104	South Korea	236
1995	N. Valeyeva (Moldova)	113	South Korea	247
1997	**Kim Du Ri (S.Kor.)**	**105**	**South Korea**	**242**

*Olympic (recurve) division.

SPECIAL REPORT

Alternative Sports

by Brett Forrest

In the 1990s so-called alternative sports made inroads into the imagination and recreation time of people around the world—but especially in the United States. Figures from the National Sporting Goods Association showed a decline in participation by Americans in traditional sports, including football and baseball, in favour of such new sports as in-line skating and snowboarding. Even "extreme" sports, the playground of adrenaline junkies, high-speed addicts, and alterna-athletes, were becoming more mainstream in 1997 than ever before.

Thanks in large part to the annual winter and summer ESPN X Games, which drew 219,900 spectators, such relatively new sports as wakeboarding, aggressive in-line skating, and street luge continued to experience a meteoric rise in participation and exposure that served to further legitimize them. By comparison with these domains of dyed hair, tattoos, and body piercings, sports such as mountain biking and beach volleyball seemed rather establishmentarian; indeed, both had become official Olympic events in 1996. In general, alternative sports could be divided into three groups: those that had already moved from the fringe into the mainstream, those that were fast approaching mainstream status, and those still very much on the fringe.

Mainstream. Paola Pezzo of Italy dominated the women's side of the mountain biking World Cup in 1997, winning 8 of the tour's 10 cross-country events. Missy Giove of the U.S. did likewise in downhill, capturing her second consecutive World Cup title, but she encountered technical problems at the world championships, which allowed Anne-Caroline Chausson of France to take first place. On the men's side, Corrado Herin of Italy won his first downhill World Cup title, and Chausson's teammate Nicolas Vouilloz captured his sixth consecutive downhill world championship.

The Brazilian team of Sandra Pires and Jackie Silva won the women's beach volleyball world championship in September, edging out the American team of Holly McPeak and Lisa Arce, who had won 7 of 12 events on the professional tour. It was a Brazilian show on the men's side as well, with Jose Loiola reaching three major milestones: he became the first non-American player to reach the top ranking on the men's tour; he achieved the $1 million mark in career earnings; and he won the illustrious King of the Beach title.

Canada edged the U.S. for the overall men's freestyle skiing World Cup team title, with Jean-Luc Brassard leading the way. American Olympic moguls champion Donna Weinbrecht had an average season, but aerialist Eric Bergoust provided inspiration for the American team, recovering from a crash that shattered his collarbone in six places to win a silver medal at the world championships in Nagano, Japan. Meanwhile, freestyle's third discipline, acrobatic, continued to struggle for popularity.

Close to Mainstream. In 1997 it was a huge year for snowboarding for two reasons. World-class boarders throughout the world were prepping for the first Olympic competition in 1998, and official figures in midyear proclaimed the sport as the fastest-growing one in the U.S. Top Americans Mike Jacoby and Sondra Van Ert won medals at the world championships, and the sport continued to branch out into four disciplines: downhill, slalom, halfpipe, and boardercross. The Snowboard Retailers Association reported that 1.5 million new snowboarders had emerged since the inaugural X Games.

An enormously popular sport in the early-to-mid-1980s, skateboarding, thanks in large part to television exposure on MTV and ESPN, had a breakout year professionally in 1997. Chriss Finn and Andy MacDonald won the street and halfpipe vert titles, respectively, on the World Cup tour. Tony Hawk, at 29 an elder statesman in the sport, drew crowds wherever he skated, and his gold-medal vert performance at the X Games was widely considered perhaps the best run in competition history. Cara-Beth Burnside took the vert title at the all-women Vans Skate Jam, the first competition of its kind.

From 1990 to 1995 the explosive growth of jet skis—powered personal watercraft—was accompanied by at least a fourfold increase in injuries, according to a report released in 1997. Several high-profile recreational fatalities underlined the report's findings, casting a shadow on the popular sport. Competition, however, continued unfazed, highlighted by Frenchwoman Karine Paturel's women's world title. Jeff Jacobs and Tera Crimson won American championships, and 11 countries participated in the Asia Pacific Jet Racing King's Cup in Bangkok.

One of the U.S.'s fastest-growing sports, in-line hockey, experienced a roller-coaster year. Popularity continued to soar as new rinks sprang up nationwide, with many in warm-weather areas such as Arizona and Nevada, where ice hockey (the sport's progenitor) was anything but a native game. The flagship professional league, Roller Hockey International, fought rumours throughout the year that owing to financial difficulties this, its fifth season, would be its last. The talk did not shake the Anaheim Bullfrogs, who, behind the strong goaltending of David Goverde, won the Murphy Cup, the team's second national title in five years.

Still on the Fringe. Darin Shapiro, the man who practically invented wakeboarding, made a triumphant return after having missed the entire 1996 season because of an ankle injury. He won the professional wakeboard series but was strongly challenged by the duo of Jeremy Kovak and 16-year-old phenomenon Parks Bonifay. Shapiro needed to win the final stop on the tour to win his fifth overall pro series title, and he came through, edging Kovak by just 64 points. Kovak captured titles at the X Games and wakeboard world championships, and Bonifay took the American championships and finished second at the world meet. The sport's total participation swelled to some 1,250,000.

The third year of the Aggressive Skaters Association was the best ever; the professional tour averaged 25,000 spectators over 12 events. The pro tour was augmented by the X Games and MTV's Ultimate Inline Challenge, which gave the sport more publicity than ever before. Taig Khris of France won the men's vert, and Australian Dion Antony took the street title on the overall tour. On the women's side, American Katie Brown won the women's vert title, and Switzerland's Salima Sanga won the street crown.

Organizers for skateboarding-inspired street luge—in which competitors can reach wheel-melting speeds of up to 113 km/h (70 mph), racing down pavement just 5 cm (2 in) above the ground while lying atop 2.4-m (8-ft)-long metal boards—spent the year trying to professionalize the sport and streamline its rules, which thus would make it more attractive to corporate sponsorship. This made-for-TV sport gained increased attention at the X Games, where Michael ("Biker") Sherlock, wearing the standard full leather motorcycle suit and crash helmet, took two gold medals and one silver. Chris Ponseti won the other gold.

Brett Forrest is a reporter for the magazine Men's Journal.

(ABOVE) WILLIAM SALLAZ—DUOMO; (RIGHT) BRIAN BAHR—ALLSPORT; (BELOW) JOAN C. FAHRENTHOLD—ASSOCIATED PRESS

(Above) American Sondra Van Ert speeds downhill in a U.S. Snowboard Grand Prix race in January. Snowboarding was set to make its Olympic debut at the 1998 Winter Games in Nagano, Japan. (Right) Mountain biker Hubert Pallhuber of Italy competes in July in the cross-country World Cup. (Below) Fabiola de Silva of Brazil flies high during the final round of the women's aggressive vertical in-line skating event at the X Games in June.

Formula One Grand Prix Race Results, 1997

Race (distance)	Driver	Winner's time (hr:min:sec)	Fastest lap (km/h)
Australian GP (307.5 km)	D. Coulthard	1:30:28.718	H.-H. Frentzen, 216.618
Brazilian GP (309 km)	J. Villeneuve	1:36:06.990	J. Villeneuve, 205.135
Argentine GP (306.5 km)	J. Villeneuve	1:52:01.215	G. Berger, 172.039
San Marino GP (305.7 km)	H.-H. Frentzen	1:31:00.613	H.-H. Frentzen, 207.541
Monaco GP (208.69 km)	M. Schumacher	2:00:05.654	M. Schumacher, 107.562
Spanish GP (302.469 km)	J. Villeneuve	1:30:35.896	G. Fisichella, 207.003
Canadian GP (237.34 km)	M. Schumacher	1:17:40.646	D. Coulthard, 199.719
French GP (305.814 km)	M. Schumacher	1:38:50.492	M. Schumacher, 196.501
British GP (303.260 km)	J. Villeneuve	1:28:01.665	M. Schumacher, 220.319
German GP (307.035 km)	G. Berger	1:20:59.046	G. Berger, 232.278
Hungarian GP (305.536 km)	J. Villeneuve	1:45:47.149	H.-H. Frentzen, 182.268
Belgian GP (306.577 km)	M. Schumacher	1:33:46.717	J. Villeneuve, 223.892
Italian GP (305.785 km)	D. Coulthard	1:17:04.608	M. Hakkinen, 246.359
Austrian GP (306.933 km)	J. Villeneuve	1:27:35.999	J. Villeneuve, 216.579
Luxembourg GP (189.669 km)	J. Villeneuve	1:31:27.843	H.-H. Frentzen, 208.172
Japanese GP (310.596 km)	M. Schumacher	1:29:48.446	H.-H. Frentzen, 343.371
European GP (305.532 km)	M. Hakkinen	1:38:57.771	H.-H. Frentzen, 191.631

WORLD DRIVERS' CHAMPIONSHIP: Villeneuve 81 points, Schumacher 78 points (later stripped), Frentzen 42 points.
CONSTRUCTORS CHAMPIONSHIP: Williams-Renault 123 points, Ferrari 102 points, Benetton-Renault 67 points.

International Cup for Formula One Manufacturers

Year	Car	Year	Car
1992	Williams/Renault	1995	Benetton/Renault
1993	Williams/Renault	1996	Williams/Renault
1994	Williams/Renault	**1997**	**Williams/Renault**

World Championship of Drivers

Year	Winner	Car
1993	A. Prost (Fr.)	Williams/Renault
1994	M. Schumacher (Ger.)	Benetton/Ford
1995	M. Schumacher (Ger.)	Benetton/Renault
1996	D. Hill (U.K.)	Williams/Renault
1997	**J. Villeneuve (Can.)**	**Williams/Renault**

Le Mans 24-Hour Grand Prix d'Endurance

Year	Car	Drivers
1993	Peugeot	G. Brabham, C. Bouchut, E. Helary
1994	Dauer Porsche	Y. Dalmas, H. Haywood, M. Baldi
1995	McLaren	Y. Dalmas, J.J. Lehto, M. Sekiya
1996	Joest TWR Porsche	M. Reuter, D. Jones, A. Wurz
1997	**Joest Porsche**	**M. Alboreto, S. Johansson, T. Kristensen**

Monte-Carlo Rally

Year	Car	Driver, co-driver
1993	Toyota Celica	Auriol, Occelli
1994	Ford Escort	Delecour, Grataloup
1995	Subaru Impreza	Sainz, Moya
1996	Ford Escort	Bernardini
1997	**Subaru**	**Liatti, Pons**

(continued from page 319)
no better than sixth. The winner was Coulthard for McLaren, with Alesi second.

The Austrian Grand Prix was taken by Villeneuve for Williams, but Coulthard's McLaren outpaced the other Williams car to take second place. By then the World Drivers' Championship was a matter of keen interest because Villeneuve was only one point behind Schumacher. The Luxembourg race over the shortened Nürburgring showed immense drama when Schumacher's brother Ralf took the world champion leader off at the first corner. This left Villeneuve to lead the impressive first four Renault-engined cars home; he was followed by Alesi, Frentzen, and Berger. Excitement was therefore intense at Suzuka for the Japanese Grand Prix. The Ferrari drivers drove a calculated race, with Irvine assisting Schumacher to victory and leaving the German only one point behind Villeneuve.

Thus, the Drivers' Championship was not decided until the final race, which was moved to Jerez de la Frontera, Spain, when work on the Estoril track in Portugal could

(Above) Formula One race-car driver Jacques Villeneuve of Canada celebrates atop the shoulders of two competitors after his third-place finish in the European Grand Prix in October. The performance gave Villeneuve enough points to win the 1997 World Drivers' Championship. (Right) With five hours to go in the Le Mans 24-Hour Grand Prix d'Endurance, Tom Kristensen maneuvers his Porsche around the 13.7-km (8.5-mi) circuit. Michele Alboreto, Stefan Johansson, and Kristensen combined for the victory with 361 laps completed.

PHOTOS, ASSOCIATED PRESS; (ABOVE) RYAN REMIORZ—CANADIAN PRESS; (RIGHT) LAURENT REBOURS not be completed in time. It was a storybook bit of drama as a slowing Schumacher drove into Villeneuve's Williams just as it came up inside him at a corner. The Canadian's car was not badly damaged, and he continued, nursing it home behind the two McLaren-Mercedes of Hakkinen and Coulthard, to take third place and the season title. Schumacher failed to continue and was in some disgrace. Although the Fédération Internationale de l'Automobile, the world governing body of the sport, declined to punish him, Schumacher, as a result of the collision, was later disallowed his championship points. (WILLIAM C. BODDY)

Rallies and Other Races. The historic Monte Carlo Rally returned to the World Rally Championship (WRC) series in January after a one-year downgrade in status. It was won by Subaru's Piero Liatti of Italy in his first-ever WRC victory. At the British RAC rally in November, Colin McRae of Great Britain challenged defending champion Tommi Mäkinen of Finland for the WRC drivers championship. Mäkinen, however, finished sixth in the race and held on to the title by one point. For the second consecutive year, a Joest Porsche won the grueling Le Mans 24-hour endurance event in June. The winning drivers, Michele Alboreto, Stefan Johansson, and Tom Kristensen, combined to cover more than 4,910 km (3,050 mi) at an average speed of 204.2 km/h (126.9 mph).

U.S. Auto Racing. American auto racing enjoyed a year of unprecedented prosperity and popularity in 1997, manifested in the inauguration of multimillion-dollar race tracks in California, Illinois, and Texas and the success of the Indy Racing League (IRL), the single-seater series born of the clash of wills between Indianapolis Motor Speedway management and Championship Auto Racing Teams (CART). Several race series sponsored by the National Association for Stock Car Auto Racing (NASCAR) also continued to grow.

Not only was the Indianapolis 500-mi classic, the world's oldest motor race, held without the CART driving stars, but the IRL also proved its passenger car engine-based race-car formula was viable. The organization began building a new roster of star drivers that attracted crowds at such places as the Pikes Peak (Colorado) International Raceway and the Charlotte (N.C.) Motor Speedway.

The first Indianapolis 500 raced under new rules designed specifically for oval closed courses was won by Dutch-born Arie Luyendyk in an Oldsmobile Aurora-powered G-Force chassis at an average speed of 145.827 mph. He also was the only repeat victor in the 10-race IRL series, winning the inaugural Texas 500. At Indy, which was delayed by rain for two days, Luyendyk bested Treadway Racing teammate Scott Goodyear of Canada by 0.570 sec in a controversial finish when a green flag dropped suddenly while the track's caution lights remained on.

At the new California Speedway's Marlboro 500, the finale of the 17-race CART PPG World Series, Brazilian Mauricio Gugelmin set an American pole record of 240.942 mph in a qualifying lap, but Britisher Mark Blundell won the race for Mercedes. The series championship, the runner-up spot, and third place all went to Reynard Honda as Alex Zanardi of Italy finished first, French-born Gil de Ferran was second, and defending champion Jimmy Vasser was third. Mercedes won the engine manufacturers crown. The series visited Australia, Brazil, and Canada, and CART announced a race in Japan for 1998.

NASCAR continued to be the dominant sanctioning body in the U.S. Its 32-event Winston Cup series enjoyed its closest finish in history. Jeff Gordon (Chevrolet Monte Carlo) reclaimed his driver crown by 14 points over Dale Jarrett (Ford Thunderbird), with another Thunderbird, Mark Martin, 15 points behind Jarrett. Gordon posted 22 top-

Indy Car Champions

Year	Driver
1993	N. Mansell
1994	A. Unser, Jr.
1995	J. Villeneuve
1996	J. Vasser
1997	**A. Zanardi**

Indianapolis 500

Year	Winner	Avg. speed in mph
1993	E. Fittipaldi	157.207
1994	A. Unser, Jr.	160.872
1995	J. Villeneuve	153.616
1996	B. Lazier	147.956
1997	**A. Luyendyk**	**145.827**

National Association for Stock Car Auto Racing (NASCAR) Winston Cup Champions

Year	Winner
1993	D. Earnhardt
1994	D. Earnhardt
1995	J. Gordon
1996	T. Labonte
1997	**J. Gordon**

Stock-car-racing king Jeff Gordon (24) takes the checkered flag to win the Daytona 500 in February, narrowly beating out Chevrolet teammate Terry LaBonte. The 26-year-old Gordon went on to claim the Winston Cup season points championship for the second time in three years.

PIERRE DUCHARME—REUTERS

World Badminton Championships				
Year	Men's singles	Women's singles	Men's doubles	Women's doubles
1989	Yang Yang (China)	Li Lingwei (China)	Li Yongbo, Tian Bingyi (China)	Lin Ying, Guan Weizhen (China)
1991	Zhao Jianhua (China)	Tang Jiuhong (China)	Park Joo Bong, Kim Moon Soo (S.Kor.)	Guan Weizhen, Nong Qunhua (China)
1993	J. Suprianto (Indon.)	S. Susanti (Indon.)	R. Subagja, R. Gunawan (Indon.)	Nong Qunhua, Zhou Lei (China)
1995	H. Arbi (Indon.)	Ye Zhaoying (China)	R. Subagja, R. Mainaky (Indon.)	Gil Young Ah, Jang Hye Ock (S.Kor.)
1997	**P. Rasmussen (Den.)**	**Ye Zhaoying (China)**	**B. Sigit, C. Wijaya (Indon.)**	**Ge Fei, Gu Jun (China)**

All-England Championships—Singles		
Year	Men	Women
1993	H. Arbi (Indon.)	S. Susanti (Indon.)
1994	H. Arbi (Indon.)	S. Susanti (Indon.)
1995	P.-E. Hoyer-Larsen (Den.)	Lim Xiao Qing (Swed.)
1996	P.-E. Hoyer-Larsen (Den.)	Bang Soo Hyun (S.Kor.)
1997	**Dong Jiong (China)**	**Ye Zhaoying (China)**

Uber Cup (women)		
Year	Winner	Runner-up
1987–88	China	S.Korea
1989–90	China	S.Korea
1991–92	China	S.Korea
1993–94	Indonesia	China
1995–96	Indonesia	China

Thomas Cup (men)		
Year	Winner	Runner-up
1987–88	China	Malaysia
1989–90	China	Malaysia
1991–92	Malaysia	Indonesia
1993–94	Indonesia	Malaysia
1995–96	Indonesia	Denmark

five finishes and won 10 races. (*See* BIOGRAPHIES.)

At Daytona Gordon led an unprecedented 1-2-3 sweep for Rick Hendrick Motorsports, with Terry LaBonte finishing second and Ricky Craven third. Six laps from the end, the trio set out after Ford's Bill Elliot, with Gordon elbowing past on a daring dive almost on the infield grass. Ironically, Jarrett, who was to win seven times himself, was involved in the crash that gained the lead for the Hendrick trio.

Chevrolet was also the makers' titlist in NASCAR's other major series. Jack Sprague won the Craftsman Truck series, and in the Busch Grand National, Randy Lajoie defended his championship successfully.

American sports-car racing produced another season of flux. Andy Evans, a Seattle, Wash.-area multimillionaire racer, bought the International Motor Sports Association (IMSA), changed its name to Professional SportsCar Racing (SportsCar), and was in the winning Ferrari 333 SP (with Stefan Johannsen, Fermin Velez, and Yannick Dalmas) at the 12 Hours of Sebring in March. The final race under the generation-old IMSA name was the 24 Hours of Daytona in January. There, two American-engined cars with Riley & Scott (R&S) chassis sandwiched Evans's 333 SP in a contest that was unusually exciting for an endurance race. The winning R&S Ford was owner Rob Dyson's backup car and had seven drivers, including eventual SportsCar national champion Butch Leitzinger. Third was an Oldsmobile-powered R&S with Eduardo Dibos of Peru, Jim Pace, and Barry Waddell. The victor was still in doubt into the final half hour of the race.

At the end of the season, Bill France, Jr., owner of the Daytona Speedway and president of NASCAR, awarded the contract to run the 24 Hours of Daytona race to Sports Car Club of America (SCCA). He also announced a new jointly owned series, U.S. Road Racing Championship. Meanwhile, SCCA's venerable Trans-Am series again crowned Tom Kendall and Ford champions.

(ROBERT J. FENDELL)

Denmark's Peter Rasmussen hits an overhead shot during a volley with China's Sun Jun in the world badminton championships men's final in June. Rasmussen won the grueling two-hour match 16–17, 18–13, 15–10.

PETER KEMP—ASSOCIATED PRESS

BADMINTON

The major international badminton events of 1997 were thoroughly dominated by players from China. At the All-England championships in Birmingham, Eng., in March, Chinese athletes claimed titles in four of the five divisions. Dong Jiong defeated 1996 Olympic gold medalist Poul-Erik Hoyer-Larsen of Denmark in the semifinals of the men's singles event and then beat teammate Sun Jun in the final. In another all-Chinese final, Ye Zhaoying confirmed her world number-one ranking by overpowering Gong Zhichao 11–1, 11–3 for the women's singles crown. Olympic gold medalists Ge Fei and Gu Jun took the women's doubles title, defeating Indonesians Eliza and Resiana Zelin. Ge Fei then teamed with Liu Yong to claim the mixed doubles title with a victory over the top-seeded Indonesian pair of Trikus Heryanto and Minarti Timur. Kang Kyung Jin and Ha Tae Kwon of South Korea prevented a Chinese sweep by winning the men's doubles title over Denmark's Michael Sogaard and Jon Holst-Christensen.

The Sudirman Cup, an international mixed-team competition held every other year, was contested in Glasgow, Scot., in May. South Korea scored a mild upset in the semifinals with a close 3–2 win over Denmark, setting up a final-round confrontation with China. China had earlier advanced to the finals by narrowly defeating Indonesia 3–2. In the championship round China defeated South Korea in all five events to capture its second consecutive title.

The world championships were staged in Glasgow immediately after the Sudirman Cup. Chinese players advanced to four of the five title matches, with two events featuring all-Chinese finals. In a rematch of the one-sided All-England women's singles final, defending world champion Ye Zhaoying again bested compatriot Gong Zhichao. Denmark gained some revenge on China in the men's singles final, with Peter Rasmussen edging Sun Jun in a marathon two-hour match. In the men's doubles competition, the Indonesian team of Budiarto Sigit and Chandra Wijaya overcame the Malaysian duo of Cheah Soon Kit and Yap Kim Hock in an impressive 8–15, 18–17, 15–7 comeback victory.

(DONN GOBBIE)

BASEBALL

Major league baseball, though still scarred by a damaging strike in 1994, enjoyed signs of revival in 1997. Paid attendance for the season exceeded 63 million spectators, an increase of about 3.5 million over the previous year. National League and American League teams also played a limited schedule of interleague games, a historic development that cultivated renewed interest, particularly in regions that had franchises in both leagues, such as New York City, Chicago, Los Angeles–Anaheim, and San Francisco–Oakland.

World Series. The Florida Marlins, who joined the National League in 1993, won the World Series by defeating the Cleveland Indians four games to three in the best-of-seven series. The Marlins thus achieved a championship in their fifth season of existence. The 1969 New York Mets, who won the World Series in their eighth season, had established the previous mark for upward mobility by an expansion team.

The Marlins did not have an easy time of it, however, before vanquishing Cleveland 3–2 in 11 innings for the clinching victory on October 27. The Marlins trailed 2–1 entering the bottom of the ninth before a raucous crowd of 67,204 at their Pro Player Stadium. Craig Counsell hit a sacrifice fly to right field, scoring Moises Alou with the tying run. Then in the bottom of the 11th, Florida shortstop Edgar Renteria lined a two-out, bases-loaded single to centre off Charles Nagy to score Counsell with the winning run.

The Marlins had opened the series at home on October 18 by beating Cleveland 7–4. Alou hit a three-run home run off Orel Hershiser in the fourth inning, and Livan Hernández, the Marlins' rookie right-hander, pitched 5⅔ innings toward the victory. The Indians drew even the next night by defeating the Marlins 6–1 behind Chad Ogea, who pitched 6⅔ innings. Bip Roberts had a two-run single for Cleveland in the fifth, and Sandy Alomar, Jr., belted a two-run homer in the sixth.

On October 21 the series shifted to Cleveland's Jacobs Field, where the weather was frigid and the quality of play mediocre. The Marlins rallied for seven runs in the ninth inning to outlast the Indians 14–11 in a 4-hour 12-minute marathon marred by 17 walks and 6 errors, 3 of which were committed by Cleveland during the ninth inning. It was the second highest scoring game in series history, falling short only of the 29 runs produced in game four of the 1993 series between Philadelphia and Toronto. The Indians led 7–3 after five innings, but their relief pitchers surrendered nine runs in three innings. Gary Sheffield batted in five runs for Florida.

In game four at Cleveland on October 22, the Indians tied the series 2–2 by routing the Marlins 10–3. The game-time temperature was 2° C (35° F), but the blustery conditions did not bother Jaret Wright, the Indians' rookie, who pitched six effective innings. Alomar batted in three runs, Manny Ramírez belted a two-run homer, and Matt Williams hit a home run and two singles.

The Marlins responded in game five on October 23 by beating the Indians 8–7 at Cleveland, where the weather had improved slightly. Before another sellout crowd, the Marlins rallied for four runs in the sixth inning to gain a 6–4 lead. They then survived a three-run Cleveland outburst in the ninth to take a 3–2 lead in the series. Hernández, who worked eight innings, again outpitched Hershiser, the veteran who had enjoyed remarkable success in previous postseason assignments. Alou collected three hits, including a home run, and batted in four runs.

Final Major League Standings, 1997

AMERICAN LEAGUE

East Division				Central Division				West Division			
Club	W.	L.	G.B.	Club	W.	L.	G.B.	Club	W.	L.	G.B.
Baltimore*	98	64	—	Cleveland*	86	75	—	Seattle*	90	72	—
New York*	96	66	2	Chicago	80	81	6	Anaheim	84	78	6
Detroit	79	83	19	Milwaukee	78	83	8	Texas	77	85	13
Boston	78	84	20	Minnesota	68	94	18½	Oakland	65	97	25
Toronto	76	86	22	Kansas City	67	94	19				

NATIONAL LEAGUE

East Division				Central Division				West Division			
Club	W.	L.	G.B.	Club	W.	L.	G.B.	Club	W.	L.	G.B.
Atlanta*	101	61	—	Houston*	84	78	—	San Francisco*	90	72	—
Florida*	92	70	9	Pittsburgh	79	83	5	Los Angeles	88	74	2
New York	88	74	13	Cincinnati	76	86	8	Colorado	83	79	7
Montreal	78	84	23	St. Louis	73	89	11	San Diego	76	86	14
Philadelphia	68	94	33	Chicago	68	94	16				

*Gained play-off berth.

World Series*

Year	Winning team	Losing team	Results
1993	Toronto Blue Jays (AL)	Philadelphia Phillies (NL)	4–2
1994	not held		
1995	Atlanta Braves (NL)	Cleveland Indians (AL)	4–2
1996	New York Yankees (AL)	Atlanta Braves (NL)	4–2
1997	**Florida Marlins (NL)**	**Cleveland Indians (AL)**	**4–3**

*AL—American League; NL—National League.

Rookie shortstop Edgar Renteria gives the Florida Marlins their first World Series crown with a two-out, bases-loaded single to score teammate Craig Counsell in the 11th inning of game 7. The Marlins won the World Series in only their fifth season of existence, having joined the National League in 1993.

MARC SEROTA—REUTERS

On October 25, with an audience of 67,498 poised to celebrate a title back in South Florida, the Indians quieted the mood by defeating the Marlins 4–1. Ogea shocked the crowd by delivering a two-run single in the second inning. He also doubled in the fifth and scored a third run as the Indians beat Kevin Brown, Florida's ace pitcher who also lost game two.

The Marlins completed their unlikely journey to the top one night later, in the first game seven played since the 1991 World Series. Hernández, who had defected from Cuba, was voted the Most Valuable Player (MVP) of the series for his two victories, despite his 5.27 earned run average. The crestfallen Indians, three outs from securing their first World Series crown since 1948, lost baseball's marquee event for the second time in three seasons, having fallen to the Atlanta Braves in six games in 1995.

Play-offs. The success story of the Marlins was even more extraordinary in that they earned a World Series title without finishing in first place in their division. The Marlins were a wild card entry, having achieved the best record of any second-place team in the National League.

The Marlins, from the East Division, first opposed the San Francisco Giants, who won the West. The Marlins swept the best-of-five series, winning 2–1 and 7–6 at home and then 6–2 in San Francisco. Meanwhile, the Braves, champions of the East, swept the Houston Astros, who had finished first in the Central Division.

In the best-of-seven National League Championship Series, the Marlins scored five unearned runs off Greg Maddux, the Braves' most decorated pitcher, to register a 5–3 victory in the opener at Atlanta on October 7. The Braves, behind Tom Glavine's pitching and home runs by Chipper Jones and Ryan Klesko, downed Florida the next day 7–1.

The Marlins went home to win game three 5–2 on October 10, then lost 4–0 the next night on a complete-game four-hitter by Atlanta's Denny Neagle. In game five on October 12, though the Braves loaded the bases in the first inning, Hernández struck out the side. He then completed the game by striking out 15 Braves in a tense 2–1 victory over Maddux, and Florida assumed a 3–2 lead in the series.

Glavine, an estimable postseason performer, started for the Braves in game six at Atlanta on October 14, but he was rocked for four runs in the first inning, and the Marlins won 7–4 behind Brown to clinch the series over the defending league champion Braves. The outcome was considered an upset, although the Marlins had beaten Atlanta in 8 of 12 regular-season games.

The Indians, who were decided underdogs when they began the postseason, squandered a 5–0 first-inning lead before losing the opener of their division series to the Yankees 8–6 at New York on September 30. On October 2 the Indians won 7–5, but they were routed 6–1 in Cleveland on October 4. The Indians won the next two games 3–2 and 4–3 on October 5 and 6, respectively to eliminate the defending world champion Yankees. Wright was the winning pitcher in games two and five of the series.

The Indians thus advanced to the American League Championship Series (ALCS) against the Baltimore Orioles, who eliminated the Seattle Mariners three games to one in the other division play-offs. In game one of the ALCS at Baltimore on October 8, the Orioles beat Cleveland 3–0. The Indians then won three in a row—by 5–4 at Baltimore and 2–1 and 8–7 at home. The Orioles then won 4–2 in Cleveland but lost to the Indians 1–0 in 11 innings at Baltimore on October 15. Tony Fernández hit the game-winning home run to earn the Indians an American League pennant.

Regular Season. The Braves, led by their excellent starting pitchers, won 101 of 162 games and finished nine games ahead of the Marlins, who were 92–70. San Francisco, which received scant mention from the experts as a contender, was the surprise winner of the National League West, two games better than the Los Angeles Dodgers. Houston was the only team to play above .500 in the Central Division as the Astros outdistanced the Pittsburgh Pirates by five games.

The Orioles crafted the best record in the American League with 98 victories, two more than the Yankees, who finished second in the East and gained a wild-card play-off berth. The Indians struggled for much of the summer but still posted an 86–75 record to win the Central Division by six games over the Chicago White Sox. Seattle wound up with a 90–72 record and won the West by six games over the Anaheim Angels.

Individual Accomplishments. Home runs were an ongoing theme all season. Mark McGwire, who was traded from the Oakland A's to the St. Louis Cardinals, hit a total of 58 home runs, and Ken Griffey, Jr., the American League's MVP, hit 56 for the Mariners. Both fell short of the major

Jackie Robinson: A 50th Anniversary Remembrance

Nearly 54,000 people—among them U.S. Pres. Bill Clinton—jammed New York City's Shea Stadium on April 15, 1997. Although the Los Angeles Dodgers and New York Mets baseball teams played that evening, the impressive turnout had more to do with a ball game played exactly 50 years earlier at Ebbets Field in nearby Brooklyn. That game marked the debut of a rookie named Jack Roosevelt Robinson, an African-American whose presence in the Dodgers lineup marked the first time in the 20th century that a member of his race had played in a major league ball game. The Shea Stadium crowd gathered to honour the memory of the man who had withstood taunts, death threats, and other forms of abuse from players and fans alike as he broke baseball's colour barrier and helped to spark the civil rights movement. "If Jackie Robinson were here today," Clinton told the crowd during a 15-minute ceremony, "he would say we have done a lot of good in the last 50 years, but we could do a lot better."

Major league baseball spent the summer commemorating Robinson's achievement. The theme was "breaking barriers," and Robinson's impact on the sport and race relations in the U.S. was celebrated. The integration of baseball had opened the athletic arena to minorities, and eventually Hispanics and Asians followed Robinson's lead. By 1959, every major league baseball team had at least one African-American on its roster; some 17% of baseball's players were black, and blacks had also been accepted in professional football and basketball. By 1997, 80% of the players in the National Basketball Association were black, as were 67% of the players in the National Football League (NFL). In baseball, however, that number had dropped to 15% by 1997. Curiously, the Dodgers opened the season with the same number of African-Americans on their roster as they had had in 1947: one. Hispanics, however, accounted for 20% of major league players.

As Clinton suggested in his address, minorities were now welcome on the playing fields, but stereotypes and other barriers lingered. Leadership positions both on the field (catcher in baseball and quarterback in football) and off were rarely filled by blacks. Not until 1975—three years after Robinson's death—did a major league baseball team hire an African-American to be a field manager, and in 1997 only four teams had black managers. In the NFL only four blacks had ever served as head coaches, and, although 11 of the 30 head-coaching positions changed hands during the 1996 season, none went to blacks. No major sports franchise in the U.S. had ever had an African-American as a majority owner.

As Robinson's Hall of Fame career and his place in history were recognized in big league ballparks throughout the season, a baseball team known as the Colorado Silver Bullets—the only all-women's professional team in the country—spent the summer barnstorming from town to town to play exhibition games, just as teams of blacks and players from the Negro Leagues had done during the first half of the century. The Silver Bullets served as a reminder of the fact that until at least one more barrier was broken, a full one-half of the population remained effectively banned from playing major league baseball.

(ANTHONY G. CRAINE)

Nothing excited a crowd quite like the sight of Jackie Robinson stealing home plate. During a game in 1948, Robinson slides safely home as Boston catcher Bill Salkeld bobbles a throw.

ASSOCIATED PRESS

league record established by Roger Maris, who hit 61 homers for the Yankees in 1961. Only Babe Ruth and Maris had hit more home runs than had McGwire in one season.

Frank Thomas of the White Sox won the American League batting title with a .347 average, while Tony Gwynn (*see* BIOGRAPHIES) batted .372 for the San Diego Padres to earn his eighth National League title. Colorado Rockies slugger Larry Walker was close behind Gwynn, with a .366 average, and became the first native Canadian player to be named MVP. Roger Clemens, acquired from the Boston Red Sox as a free agent, won the American League Cy Young Award with 21 victories for the Toronto Blue Jays. Seattle's Randy Johnson won 20. Neagle, of the star-studded Atlanta staff, was the only National League pitcher to win 20 games, but he lost in the Cy Young voting to Pedro Martínez of the Montreal Expos, who fanned 305 batters and posted the best earned run average, 1.90 per nine innings. Randy Myers of the Orioles led both leagues in saves by relief pitchers with 45, and Curt Schilling of the Philadelphia Phillies led in strikeouts with 319. The Phillies' Scott Rolen and Nomar Garciaparra of the Red Sox were both voted unanimously Rookie of the Year in the National League and American League, respectively. Dusty Baker of the Giants was selected National League Manager of the Year. Davey Johnson unexpectedly resigned from the Orioles just hours before being named American League Manager of the Year.

Other Developments. On June 12 the Giants beat the Texas Rangers 4–3 at Arlington, Texas, in the first regular-season interleague game in major league history. The American League beat the National League 3–1 at Cleveland in the 69th All-Star Game on July 8. Paul Beeston, former president and chief executive officer of the Blue Jays, was named president and chief operating officer for major league baseball. Bud Selig remained interim commissioner.

KYODO NEWS

Members of the Yakult Swallows toss Katsuya Nomura, their manager, high into the air after defeating the Seibu Lions four games to one to win the 1997 Japan Series in October.

After the World Series the long-awaited phase one of league realignment was announced, but the changes were less severe than had been feared. In order to better accommodate the new expansion teams, the Arizona Diamondbacks in the National League West and the Tampa Bay Devil Rays in the American League East, only the Detroit Tigers and the Milwaukee Brewers were transferred. The Tigers remained in the American League, switching from the East Division to the Central, and, in a surprisingly well-received decision, the Brewers moved from the American League Central to the National League Central.

(ROBERT WILLIAM VERDI)

Latin America. The 1997 Caribbean Series was held in Hermosillo, Mex., February 4–9. After losing its first two games, the Northern Eagles (Águilas del Cibao), representing the Dominican Republic, rebounded to win the championship with a 4–2 record. Mexico's Culiacán Tomato Growers (the 1996 winners) and the Magallanes Navigators of Venezuela tied for second place with 3–3 records. Puerto Rico's champions, the Mayagüez Indians, finished last at 2–4.

Cuba lost the gold medal game to Japan 11–2 in the Intercontinental Cup Tournament held in Barcelona, Spain, in August. The loss ended Cuba's 10-year unbeaten streak in international baseball competition.

The Mexico City Tigers defeated the Mexico City Red Devils four games to one in the championship series of the Mexican League. It was the Red Devils' third consecutive appearance (and third loss) in the finals; the Monterrey Sultans defeated them in 1995 and 1996.

In major league baseball Francisco Córdova and Ricardo Rincón, both from the Mexican state of Veracruz, combined to pitch a no-hit game on July 12 as the Pittsburgh Pirates defeated the Houston Astros 3–0 in 10 innings. It was the first combined extra-inning no-hit game in U.S. baseball history. Córdova pitched nine innings and was relieved by Rincón, who worked the 10th inning and officially won the game.

A team from Guadalupe, Mex., a suburb of Monterrey, captured the Little League World Series in Williamsport, Pa., in August with a come-from-behind 5–4 win over a team from Mission Viejo, Calif. The victory came 40 years to the day after Mexico won its first Little League crown.

(MILTON JAMAIL)

Japan. The Yakult Swallows of the Central League, which had won two Japan Series in the previous four seasons, defeated the Seibu Lions of the Pacific League four games to one in the 1997 postseason championship series. After a one-game-to-one tie in the two games played at the Lions' stadium in Tokorozawa, the Swallows swept the three-game series at Tokyo's Jingu Stadium, their home ballpark. Swallows skipper Katsuya Nomura had won the league championship four times in the last six years and the Japan Series three times in his eight years as Yakult manager.

A key element in the 1997 season was baserunning. Both champions had the most stolen bases in their respective leagues. The Lions, which as a team had stolen 200 bases, including 62 by league leader Kazuo Matsui, had 83 more stolen bases than the runner-up Chiba Lotte Marines. The Swallows, with 123 stolen bases, were followed by the runner-up Hiroshima Toyo Carp with 117. The Swallows and the Lions also led their respective leagues in most other offense categories, including base hits, doubles, triples, and runs batted in, but not in home runs. Makoto Kosaka, rookie shortstop for the Marines, had 56 stolen bases, the best record for a rookie player, and was voted Rookie of the Year in the Pacific League.

Yutaka Ohno, a left-handed starter for the Carp, won the best earned-run-average title in the Central League with an ERA of 2.85. At age 42, he was the oldest player ever to have won a title in Japanese baseball. Ichiro Suzuki of the defending champion Orix BlueWave, with 185 hits and a batting average of .345, was the leading hitter in the Pacific League for the fourth straight year.

(TOSHIHIKO SUZUKI)

Caribbean Series

Year	Winning team	Country
1993	Santurce Crab Pickers	Puerto Rico
1994	Licey Tigers	Dominican Republic
1995	San Juan Senators	Puerto Rico
1996	Culiacán Tomato Growers	Mexico
1997	**Northern Eagles**	**Dominican Republic**

Japan Series*

Year	Winning team	Losing team	Results
1993	Yakult Swallows (CL)	Seibu Lions (PL)	4–3
1994	Yomiuri Giants (CL)	Seibu Lions (PL)	4–2
1995	Yakult Swallows (CL)	Orix BlueWave (PL)	4–1
1996	Orix BlueWave (PL)	Yomiuri Giants (CL)	4–1
1997	**Yakult Swallows (CL)**	**Seibu Lions (PL)**	**4–1**

*CL—Central League; PL—Pacific League.

BASKETBALL

United States. *Professional.* In 1997 it took the advent of two new women's leagues, the Women's National Basketball Association (WNBA) and the American Basketball League (ABL), finally to divert some attention from Michael Jordan of the Chicago Bulls. Dominating the competition as usual, Jordan drove the Bulls to their fifth National Basketball Association (NBA) championship in seven years with his matchless mixture of superb skill and indomitable will.

The Bulls' "Drive for Five" was not easy, despite Chicago's 69 regular-season victories, because the Utah Jazz put up a terrific fight before falling four games to two in the best-of-seven NBA finals. Once again, forward Dennis Rodman provided the sideshow with his multicoloured hair and penchant for the outrageous. He was heavily fined and suspended for kicking a photographer during a regular-season game. He returned in time for the play-offs, during which he was fined again for making derogatory remarks about Utah's Mormon community. The Bulls, sparked by the incomparable Jordan, who also won his fifth play-off Most Valuable Player (MVP) award, rose to every challenge, including the twin threat of Utah's Karl ("The Mailman") Malone (the regular-season MVP) and John Stockton in the finals.

Bulls' fans were more concerned about whether the whole dynasty would unravel after the playoffs. Jordan vowed to retire immediately if the Bulls traded forward Scottie Pippen or failed to sign Coach Phil Jackson for another year. Without "Air" Jordan's commanding presence, the NBA in general and the Chicago franchise in particular would see a golden era end abruptly, but to the fans' immense relief, the Jordan saga continued. The superstar, reacting favourably to Jackson's rehiring, agreed to a one-year, $36 million contract.

Meanwhile the NBA's coaching merry-go-round picked up speed. Rick Pitino led the charge by switching from the University of Kentucky to become coach and general manager of the Boston Celtics, and the Orlando Magic lured 68-year-old Chuck Daly out of retirement. Larry Brown jumped from the Indiana Pacers to the Philadelphia 76ers, and Celtics' icon Larry Bird, an Indiana native, signed to coach the Pacers.

In the midst of all this activity, the women's leagues opened their inaugural seasons with high hopes and considerable fanfare. With the global image and marketing skills of the NBA helping with promotion, the WNBA gained the larger share of media and fan attention as well as the majority of stars from colleges, the 1996 U.S. Olympic team, and other countries. The WNBA consisted of two four-team conferences: the Eastern Conference, comprising the Charlotte Sting, Cleveland Rockers, Houston Comets, and New York Liberty;

(LEFT) JOHN MCDONOUGH—SPORTS ILLUSTRATED; (RIGHT) MATTHEW STOCKMAN—ALLSPORT

(Left) Steve Kerr of the Chicago Bulls makes the game-winning shot to beat the Utah Jazz in Game 6 of the NBA championship finals. The win clinched the best-of-seven series for the Bulls. (Right) Michael Jordan (23) and Scottie Pippen celebrate the Bulls' fifth NBA title in seven years.

National Basketball Association (NBA) Championship

Season	Winner	Runner-up	Results
1992–93	Chicago Bulls	Phoenix Suns	4–2
1993–94	Houston Rockets	New York Knicks	4–3
1994–95	Houston Rockets	Orlando Magic	4–0
1995–96	Chicago Bulls	Seattle SuperSonics	4–2
1996–97	**Chicago Bulls**	**Utah Jazz**	**4–2**

NBA Final Standings, 1996–97

EASTERN CONFERENCE

Team	Won	Lost
Atlantic Division		
*Miami	61	21
*New York	57	25
*Orlando	45	37
*Washington	44	38
New Jersey	26	56
Philadelphia	22	60
Boston	15	67
Central Division		
*Chicago	69	13
*Atlanta	56	26
*Detroit	54	28
*Charlotte	54	28
Cleveland	42	40
Indiana	39	43
Milwaukee	33	49
Toronto	30	52

WESTERN CONFERENCE

Team	Won	Lost
Midwest Division		
*Utah	64	18
*Houston	57	25
*Minnesota	40	42
Dallas	24	58
Denver	21	61
San Antonio	20	62
Vancouver	14	68
Pacific Division		
*Seattle	57	25
*L.A. Lakers	56	26
*Portland	49	33
*Phoenix	40	42
*L.A. Clippers	36	46
Sacramento	34	48
Golden State	30	52

*Gained play-off berth.

and the Western Conference, consisting of the Los Angeles Sparks, Phoenix Mercury, Sacramento Monarchs, and Utah Starzz. The Comets, guided by league MVP Cynthia Cooper, defeated the Liberty, led by Rebecca Lobo, 65–51 in a one-game final play-off on August 30 to capture the first WNBA championship.

The ABL, which began playing in October 1996, also enjoyed a competitive debut season. It consisted of eight charter members: the Atlanta Glory, Columbus Quest, New England Blizzard, and Richmond Rage in the Eastern Conference; and the Colorado Xplosion, Portland Power, San Jose Lasers, and Seattle Reign in the Western Conference. The Quest and the Rage clashed in the best-of-five final play-offs in March 1997, with Columbus prevailing three games to two. Valerie Still, named the top play-off performer, sparked the Quest to a 31–9 regular-season record. After the regular season the ABL announced the addition of the expansion Long Beach StingRays in the Western Conference and the move of the Rage from Richmond to Philadelphia.

College. Arizona's stunning 84–79 overtime upset over Kentucky in the championship game of the men's National Collegiate Athletic Association (NCAA) tournament championship provided a fitting climax to an exciting season. As interest in women's basketball was reaching new heights, on both collegiate and professional levels, Tennessee's 68–59 conquest of Old Dominion in the NCAA final gave the Lady Volunteers their second straight national title.

The meteoric rise in interest, media coverage, and quality of play throughout women's college basketball continued in 1996–97. Although attendance at women's games lagged well behind the overall NCAA figure of 30 million for men's competition during the season, it rose to an unprecedented total of 6.4 million. Tennessee's triumphal sweep through the tournament was accompanied by record attendance and television ratings. In a dramatic Midwest Regional showdown, Tennessee eliminated previously unbeaten Connecticut 91–81 to end the 33–1 Lady Huskies' dream of a second undefeated season in three years.

JOHN BIEVER—SPORTS ILLUSTRATED

Miles Simon of Arizona heads upcourt during the NCAA championship game against Kentucky. He was named the Final Four's Most Outstanding Player after Arizona captured the title in overtime.

Competition in the men's ranks was equally ferocious. The Arizona Wildcats put it all together at the right time, upsetting a trio of teams seeded number one in their regionals—Kansas, North Carolina, and Kentucky. Arizona stunned Kansas, almost everybody's pretournament choice, and then moved into the Final Four by surviving a nerve-shattering overtime battle with Providence.

It was the shot at vindication needed by Arizona Coach Lute Olson. His team had finished fifth in the Pacific-10 race and went into the tournament seeded fourth in the Southeast Regional, expected to continue its frustrating habit of early NCAA exits. Not this time. Arizona proved it belonged by ousting favoured North Carolina 66–58 to put an Olson-coached team in the title clash for the first time.

Arizona then made the most of its opportunity, silencing a mostly hostile crowd of 47,028 in the Indianapolis (Ind.) RCA Dome. Skeptics thought Kentucky's blend of experience and Pitino coaching legerdemain would be too much to overcome. The Southeast Conference powerhouse had survived a bruising semifinal struggle with Big Ten champion Minnesota 78–69, but its hopes for back-to-back NCAA titles got run down. Despite a roster with no seniors, Olson's Wildcats outfought the defending champions, using blazing speed and defensive pressure to shut down Kentucky's shooters. Arizona's three-guard lineup, featuring Miles Simon and Michael Dickerson, along with 1.85-m (6-ft 1-in) freshman playmaker Mike Bibby, created havoc. A match-up zone defense limited Kentucky's all-American Ron Mercer to three first-half points, and Simon earned his tournament Most Outstanding Player laurels with a game-high 30 points. Kentucky rallied late to tie the game at 74–74 and force overtime but had too little left to sustain its momentum. Arizona scored all 10 of its overtime points at the free-throw line.

Still, the outstanding achievement of the year belonged to North Carolina's legendary coach, Dean Smith. (*See* BIOGRAPHIES.) The Tar Heels' second-round NCAA tournament decision over Colorado was the 877th victory of Smith's career, breaking the all-time record set by Kentucky's Adolph Rupp. Smith added two more victories in the East Regional before bowing to Arizona in the NCAA semifinals.

Tennessee's Chamique Holdsclaw drives to the basket past Amber Eller-Paul of Old Dominion in the NCAA women's tournament's final game. Tennessee won 68–59 for its second straight title. Holdsclaw, twice All-American, scored 24 points and was named the Final Four's Most Valuable Player.

HEINZ KLUETMEIER—SPORTS ILLUSTRATED

Division I National Collegiate Athletic Association (NCAA) Championship—Men

Year	Winner	Runner-up	Score
1993	North Carolina	Michigan	77–71
1994	Arkansas	Duke	76–72
1995	UCLA	Arkansas	89–78
1996	Kentucky	Syracuse	76–67
1997	**Arizona**	**Kentucky**	**84–79**

Division I National Collegiate Athletic Association (NCAA) Championship—Women

Year	Winner	Runner-up	Score
1993	Texas Tech	Ohio State	84–82
1994	North Carolina	Louisiana Tech	60–59
1995	Connecticut	Tennessee	70–64
1996	Tennessee	Georgia	83–65
1997	**Tennessee**	**Old Dominion**	**68–59**

National Invitation Tournament (NIT) Championship

Year	Winner	Runner-up	Score
1993	Minnesota	Georgetown	62–61
1994	Villanova	Vanderbilt	80–73
1995	Virginia Tech	Marquette	65–64
1996	Nebraska	St. Joseph's	60–56
1997	**Michigan**	**Florida State**	**82–73**

World Amateur Basketball Championship—Men		
Year	**Winner**	**Runner-up**
1988	U.S.S.R.	Yugoslavia
1990	Yugoslavia	U.S.S.R.
1992	United States	Croatia
1994	United States	Russia
1996	United States	Yugoslavia

World Amateur Basketball Championship—Women		
Year	**Winner**	**Runner-up**
1988	United States	Yugoslavia
1990	United States	Yugoslavia
1992	Unified Team	China
1994	Brazil	China
1996	United States	Brazil

In other developments, the Big Ten Conference decided to join the crowd by staging a postseason tournament, to begin in 1998. That left the Pacific-10 Conference and the Ivy League as the only major holdouts for a postseason tourney. In Chicago, De Paul University fired Coach Joey Meyer, ending a 55-year family reign over the Blue Demons, 43 of them under Joey's father, the legendary Ray Meyer. (ROBERT G. LOGAN)

International. The Fédération Internationale de Basketball, the world governing body of the sport, boasted a membership of 202 national federations in 1997. In addition, there were some 250 million basketball players worldwide and nearly 2,000 international referees.

The final rounds of the European championships for men and women were the major basketball events of 1997 in Europe. Yugoslavia, favoured to win the men's gold medal, succeeded in defeating Italy 61–49 in the final, which was played in Barcelona, Spain. Russia took bronze with a 97–77 win over Greece. In the women's competition in Budapest, Lithuania won the gold medal, beating Slovakia 72–62 in the final. Germany defeated Hungary 86–61 to capture the bronze.

The second world championship for men 22 and under was played in Melbourne, Australia, and was won by the host nation, which defeated Puerto Rico 88–73 in the final. The fourth world championship for junior (18 and under) women took place in Natal, Braz., and was won by the United States, which defeated Australia 78–74 in the final. The European winners at the cadet (under 16) level were Yugoslavia in the men's championship and Russia in the women's tournament. Runners-up were Russia and the Czech Republic, respectively.

The major club competition during the 1996–97 European season, the European Championship for Men's Clubs, was won by Olympiakos (Greece), which defeated Barcelona (Spain), runner-up the previous season as well, 73–58 in Rome. In the other European competitions, Real Madrid (Spain) won the European Cup by beating Verona (Italy); Aris Salonica (Greece) defeated the Turkish team Bursa to take the European Korac Cup; Bourges (France) gained the Women's European Champions Cup with a victory over the reigning champions, Wuppertal (Germany); and the Ronchetti Cup went to Moscow with C.S.K.A. defeating Parma (Italy). These championships marked the 40th anniversary of international club competitions in Europe. During the 1996–97 season 236 teams participated in the European competitions, watched by a record 2.6 million spectators.

A new event, Euro Stars, was contested for the first time in December 1996. The cream of players from the East and West played out a thrilling contest (the East winning 117–114) in front of 14,000 spectators in the Abdi Ipecki Arena in Istanbul.

During the year the sport recorded the deaths of five important basketball personalities: Federico Slinger (Uruguay), Abdel Azim Ashry (Egypt), Raimundo Saporta (Spain), Luis Andres Martin (Argentina), and Michel Rouiller (Switzerland).

(MARK HANNEN)

BILLIARD GAMES

Carom Billiards. The Billiards World Cup Association (BWA) three-cushion billiard world championship was won in 1996 for an unprecedented third consecutive year by Torbjörn Blomdahl of Sweden. It was his sixth career world title, as he had previously won the BWA world's event in 1988, 1991, 1992, 1994, and 1995.

The BWA championship is determined by a four-stop annual international tour with a round-robin format. Points are awarded in accordance with each player's final position in each event and accumulate throughout the tour. Therefore, it is possible to win the world title without actually winning any of the qualifiers. Indeed, Blomdahl captured his 1994 championship in that exact manner, but that was far from the case in 1996. Blomdahl claimed his latest crown by finishing third at the Dutch Open, fourth at the Korean Open, and then first at both the Belgian Open and the tour finale, the Efes Pilsen Open in Istanbul. The tour runner-up was Dick Jaspers of The Netherlands, with Marco Zanetti of Italy in third overall. Eight-time U.S. national champion Sang Lee finished a close fourth.

Lee was perhaps even more impressive in an invitational tournament in Queens, N.Y., in late 1996. A field of 32 of North America's finest carom players was reduced to 8 over two days of preliminary rounds. As national champion, Lee was seeded into the nine-player round-robin finals, but he accepted a very unusual handicap: he would play his games to 57 points, whereas all of his opponents would need only 40 points to win. Despite this onerous burden, Lee tied with two other players with 6–2 records and then prevailed in a play-off to capture a very hard-earned and prestigious championship. Lee's points-per-inning (PPI) average was a stunning 1.594. Next-best was the 1.061 mark of tournament runner-up Pedro Piedrabuena, a stylish young player from Ecuador. No other contestant reached the 1.000 PPI threshold.

World Three-Cushion Championship	
Year	**Winner**
1992	T. Blomdahl (Swed.)
1993	Sang Lee (U.S.)
1994	T. Blomdahl (Swed.)
1995	T. Blomdahl (Swed.)
1996	T. Blomdahl (Swed.)

WPA World Nine-Ball Championships	
Year	**Men's champion**
1993	Chao Feng-pang (Taiwan)
1994	T. Okumura (Japan)
1995	O. Ortmann (Ger.)
1996	R. Souquet (Ger.)
1997	**J. Archer (U.S.)**
Year	**Women's champion**
1993	L.J. Jones (U.S.)
1994	E. Mataya-Laurance (U.S.)
1995	G. Hofstatter (Austria)
1996	A. Fisher (U.K.)
1997	**A. Fisher (U.K.)**

Pocket Billiards. The Professional Billiards Tour (PBT), the principal organization representing the men's pocket billiard professionals for the past decade, suffered what many industry observers believed could be fatal blows during 1997. RJ Reynolds' Camel brand cigarettes, the PBT tour's major sponsor in 1996, canceled their affiliation completely, citing "a lot of politics out there... holding the game/sport up from getting a lot of corporate involvement." At the same time, Camel expanded its sponsorship of the American Poolplayers Association (a national amateur league pool organization) and announced plans to conduct a seven-stop "Camel Pro Billiard Series" with well over $500,000 in prize money. The series would be totally independent of any players' group, with neither the PBT nor its newer rival, the Professional Cuesports Association (PCA), having any input or involvement in the venture, but all players would be eligible to participate.

Controversial PBT Commissioner Don Mackey, promising that bad prize-money checks from some 1996 PBT tour events would be made good, was also threatening litigation over the loss of Camel sponsorship. The PBT tour became essentially nonexistent, with a nine-month void on its 1997 tournament schedule. The PBT finally "released" its member players to participate in any tournament or event they wished. The PCA did only slightly better in generating tournaments, and both groups were, at best, leery about the new Camel series events.

The Women's Professional Billiard Association (WPBA) concluded the tour year at the WPBA Nationals in Crystal City, Calif., where former English snooker star Allison Fisher was victorious. Given her stunning dominance on the tour, she easily won the 1996 women's Player of the Year honours. She continued on the winning track in 1997, taking her second consecutive World Pool-Billiard Association world nine-ball title in October.

In the men's ranks the conflicting sanctioning groups led *Pool & Billiard Magazine* to name both C.J. Wiley (PCA) and Johnny Archer (PBT) as 1996 Players of the Year. Both led their respective organization's annual point standings; Wiley won the PCA inaugural Dallas (Texas) Million $ Challenge, and Archer took the 1996 PBT Pro Tour Championship in Providence, R.I.

A national nine-ball Senior Tour for players aged 50 and older was established by the Mizerak Group (headed by hall-of-famer

World Professional Snooker Championship			
Year	**Winner**	**Year**	**Winner**
1992	S. Hendry	1995	S. Hendry
1993	S. Hendry	1996	S. Hendry
1994	S. Hendry	**1997**	**K. Doherty**

Steve Mizerak). Player and fan response was enthusiastic, and the first eight tournaments produced eight different winners.

Dagenham, Eng., was the site for the third Mosconi Cup competition in December 1996, pitting seven-man squads from the U.S. and Europe in team competition. Although trailing 9–12 on the final day, the Americans pulled out a stunning comeback victory 15–13.

The Billiard Congress of America inducted Arthur ("Babe") Cranfield and Ruth McGinnis into the BCA Hall of Fame in ceremonies in Las Vegas, Nev. Cranfield was the only person to win the U.S national junior, national amateur, and world professional pocket billiard titles. McGinnis, who died in 1974, was acclaimed as women's world champion 1932–40, had had a high run of 128 balls, and had toured the U.S. extensively, giving exhibitions.

(BRUCE H. VENZKE)

Snooker. Snooker, too, was plagued with sponsorship problems in 1997. The world professional championship, held annually at Sheffield, Eng., stood to lose its lifeblood after 1997 when the British government proposed a ban on tobacco advertising, including the sponsorship of sporting events. Existing sponsorship contracts were later allowed to run their full course, which thereby granted the world championship and the Masters tournament at Wembley, London, a new lease on life, but alternative sponsorship had to be found within five years. The Grand Prix event at Bournemouth, Eng., in October was again unsponsored, but the annual U.K. championship at Preston in November was boosted by a £4 million sponsorship package for four years.

Four of the top 10 world-ranking events in 1997 were held outside the U.K.: two tournaments in Bangkok, the German Open in Bingen am Rhein, and the European Open in Malta. An invitational tournament was also played in Beijing. In October Stephen Hendry of Scotland received the Player of the Year award for the seventh time in eight years despite having lost the world title 18–12 to former world amateur champion Ken Doherty of Ireland in May.

(SYDNEY E. FRISKIN)

Professional Bowlers Association (PBA) Tournament of Champions

Year	Champion	Year	Champion
1992	M. McDowell	1995	M. Aulby
1993	G. Branham	1996	D. D'Entremont
1994	N. Duke	**1997**	**J. Gant**

BOWLING

World Tenpins. The 1996–97 international bowling season started early when the world youth championships were held in August 1996 in Hong Kong. Owing to the travel cost and the full calendar of European tournaments, many top European countries could not participate. The winners of the 10 events came from Colombia, Japan, Taiwan, Venezuela, and South Korea.

In October Colombia and Venezuela dominated the lanes at the South American championships in Brasília, Braz. Colombian bowlers took 7 of the 12 events, while Venezuelans captured 4, leaving the Uruguayan winners of the men's doubles as the only exceptions.

The European Individual Cup for the national champions of each country closed the year in November in Nottingham, Eng. Jaana Strömberg of Finland, two-time world youth champion, prevailed over top-seeded Isabelle Saldjian of France 402–387 to capture the title. In the men's division the host nation's Wayne Greenall defeated Sweden's Göran Carlsson 427–373 to gain England its first men's victory.

Calendar year 1997 opened with the East Asian Games in Pusan, S.Kor., where China pulled a stunning upset by sweeping the men's and women's titles. Jun Zhao defeated heavily favoured Tagata Kengo of Japan 415–380 to win the men's gold medal. Liying Liang completed China's remarkable triumph, winning 427–420 over South Korea's Yeau Jin Kim in the final women's competition.

At the end of June, Europe's top bowlers were again in Nottingham, this time for the European championships. Susanne Erlandsson of Sweden won the singles, and bowlers from The Netherlands swept the other gold medals in the women's events. Patrik Johansson of Sweden won the men's singles, with Sweden winning two other men's events and one gold each going to Germany, Belgium, and Norway.

In global qualification tournaments 24 countries qualified to send their best female and best male bowler to Lahti, Fin., for the fifth world games in August 1997. The mixed doubles title was unexpectedly captured by Malaysia, which, in a tension-filled final, defeated Australia 838–816. In singles competition top-seeded Patricia Schwarz of Germany had no problem defeating Saldjian 395–345 to take home the gold medal. In the men's final Gery Verbruggen of Belgium upset Vernon Peterson of the U.S. 463–430.

(YRJÖ SARAHETE)

JEFF BEIERMAN—THE NEW YORK TIMES

University of Nebraska sophomore Jeremy Sonnenfeld made history in 1997 when he became the first U.S. bowler on record to roll three perfect games in a row.

U.S. Tenpins. Bowling suffered a much-publicized setback in 1997 when the ABC television network announced that it would no longer carry the championship round of Professional Bowlers Association (PBA) tournaments, a Saturday afternoon feature on ABC for 36 years. The cancellation of the live telecasts was the latest in a series of reverses for the tenpin game. Many bowling centres had closed, and membership in the American Bowling Congress and the Women's International Bowling Congress (WIBC) continued to decline. To compensate for the loss of ABC, the PBA reached an agreement with the CBS network, which would broadcast the final round of nine tournaments beginning in April 1998. The PBA contracted with the ESPN cable network, which had carried some of the professional tournaments for many years, to telecast 23 meets in 1998.

In a final match delayed by computer glitches and other technical problems, John Gant of Winston-Salem, N.C., defeated former champion Mike Aulby 208–187 at the PBA's 1997 Brunswick World Tournament of Champions, held at the National Bowling Stadium in Reno, Nev., in January. At the WIBC championship tournament at the same venue in July, Kendra Cameron of Gambrills, Md., won the all-events title with

ABC Bowling Championships—Regular Divisions

Year	Singles	Score	All-events	Score
1993	D. Bock	798	J. Nimke	2,254
1994	J. Weltzien	810	T. Holt	2,190
1995	M. Surina	826	J. Kwiatkowski	2,191
1996	D. Scudder, Jr.	823	S. Kurtz	2,224
1997	**J. Socha**	**847**	**J. Richgels**	**2,241**

WIBC Bowling Championships—Open Division

Year	Singles	Score	All-events	Score
1993	K. Collura, K. Murph (tie)	747	A.M. Duggan	1,990
1994	V. Fifield	716	W. Macpherson-Papanos	1,940
1995	B. Owen	749	B. Owen	1,983
1996	C. Berlanga	723	L. Nichols	1,985
1997	**J. Schmidt**	**765**	**K. Cameron**	**2,039**

FIQ World Bowling Championships—Men

Year	Singles	Pairs	Triples	Team (fives)
1983	T. Cariello (U.S.)	Australia	Sweden	Finland
1987	P. Rolland (Fr.)	Sweden	United States	Sweden
1991	Ying Chieh Ma (Taiwan)	United States	United States	Taiwan
1995	M. Doi (Can.)	Sweden	Netherlands	Netherlands

FIQ World Bowling Championships—Women

Year	Singles	Pairs	Triples	Team (fives)
1983	L. Sulkanen (Swed.)	Denmark	West Germany	Sweden
1987	E. Piccini (Mex.)	United States	United States	United States
1991	M. Beckel (Ger.)	Japan	Canada	South Korea
1995	D. Ship (Can.)	Thailand	Australia	Finland

a record nine-game total of 2,039. Jeff Richgels, of Oregon, Wis., captured the all-events title (2,241 points) at the men's American Bowling Congress tournament in July in Huntsville, Ala., while John Socha of New Berlin, Wis., racked up a record 847 series to win the singles.

A highlight of the 1997 bowling season was the first 900 series in American Bowling Congress-sanctioned competition. Jeremy Sonnenfeld, a 20-year-old sophomore at the University of Nebraska, rolled three successive perfect games in a tournament at Sun Valley Lanes in Lincoln, Neb., on February 2. Sonnenfeld's feat was even more remarkable because the right-hander shot each game on a different pair of lanes. Meanwhile, Walter Ray Williams, Jr., a PBA Hall of Famer and three-time Player of the Year, was favoured to win the title again in 1997. (*See* BIOGRAPHIES.)

(JOHN J. ARCHIBALD)

BOXING

The reputation of boxing's heavyweight division sank to an all-time low in 1997 with the disqualification of former undisputed world champion Mike Tyson for biting the ears of Evander Holyfield (*see* BIOGRAPHIES) during a World Boxing Association (WBA) heavyweight title bout in Las Vegas, Nev., on June 28. Tyson received a warning from referee Mills Lane after biting a chunk out of Holyfield's right ear in the third round. When the fight resumed, Tyson sank his teeth into Holyfield's other ear, and Lane was forced to disqualify him.

Declaring Tyson a "discredit to boxing," the Nevada State Athletic Commission suspended him for at least one year and fined him 10% of his $30 million purse, the maximum penalty permitted under existing rules. Subsequently, however, the commission gave itself the power to confiscate the entire purse of a boxer who commits a serious offense.

World Heavyweight Champions No Weight Limit
WBA
Evander Holyfield (U.S.; 11/6/93)
Michael Moorer (U.S.; 4/22/94)
George Foreman (U.S.; 11/5/94) stripped of title in 1995
Bruce Seldon (U.S.; 4/8/95)
Mike Tyson (U.S.; 9/7/96)
Evander Holyfield (U.S.; 11/9/96)
WBC
Oliver McCall (U.S.; 9/24/94)
Frank Bruno (U.K.; 9/2/95)
Mike Tyson (U.S.; 3/16/96) gave up title in 1996
Lennox Lewis (U.K.; 2/7/97)
IBF
Evander Holyfield (U.S.; 11/6/93)
Michael Moorer (U.S.; 4/22/94)
George Foreman (U.S.; 11/5/94) gave up title in 1995
Frans Botha (S.Af.; 12/9/95) stripped of title in 1996
Michael Moorer (U.S.; 6/22/96)
Evander Holyfield (U.S.; 11/8/97)

World Cruiserweight Champions Top Weight 195 Pounds
WBA
Bobby Czyz (U.S.; 3/8/91) vacant
Orlin Norris (U.S.; 11/6/93)
Nate Miller (U.S.; 7/22/95)
Fabrice Tiozzo (Fr.; 11/8/97)
WBC
Carlos de Léon (P.R.; 5/17/89)
Massimiliano Duran (Italy; 7/27/90)
Anaclet Wamba (Fr.; 7/20/91)
Marcelo Dominguez (Arg.; 4/19/96)
IBF
Alfred Cole (U.S.; 7/30/92) gave up title in 1996
Adolpho Washington (U.S.; 8/31/96)
Uriah Grant (U.S.; 6/21/97)
Imamu Mayfield (U.S.; 11/8/97)

Apart from the Tyson horror show, several contests for other versions of the heavyweight crown only tarnished the division further. A fight for the vacant World Boxing Council (WBC) title ended in a farce as Lennox Lewis avenged a knockout loss to Oliver McCall (U.S.). McCall, who had been in and out of drug rehabilitation programs in the months prior to the rematch, showed a complete reluctance to throw punches and sometimes turned his back on his opponent. After five frustrating rounds the referee stopped the bout, disqualifying McCall for refusing to defend himself.

In another dreary exhibition early in the year, Henry Akinwande (Eng.) retained the World Boxing Organization (WBO) crown by defeating reluctant challenger Scott Welch (Eng.). In July Akinwande relinquished the WBO title to challenge Lewis for what was considered the more prestigious WBC championship. During the bout, which was held in South Lake Tahoe, Nev., and also refereed by Lane, Akinwande did little more than force clinches with Lewis. In the fifth round Lane disqualified Akinwande for "blatant and persistent holding."

World Boxing Association heavyweight champion Evander Holyfield grimaces in pain after Mike Tyson bit off part of his ear during their rematch bout in Las Vegas, Nev., on June 28. Tyson, who was disqualified in the third round by referee Mills Lane (left), was later suspended from boxing for one year.

JED JACOBSOHN—ALLSPORT

An International Boxing Federation (IBF) title match between champion Michael Moorer and challenger Vaughan Bean (U.S.) provided no great boost to the unhappy heavyweight situation as Moorer outpointed Bean over 12 lacklustre rounds.

Fortunately, some excitement came late in the year in two separate fights involving Lewis and Holyfield. In a bout held in Atlantic City, N.J., in October, Lewis raised his standing in the eyes of many boxing enthusiasts by destroying Polish-born challenger Andrew Golota (U.S.) in only 95 seconds to retain the WBC crown. Golota, whose penchant for throwing low blows had cost him two disqualification losses to former champion Riddick Bowe (U.S.), suffered a seizure in his dressing room after the fight, and at year's end his future in boxing seemed uncertain.

In November Holyfield restored some pride to the heavyweight division in an impressive performance against Moorer, knocking Moorer to the canvas five times before the referee, on advice from the ringside physician, stopped the fight in the eighth round. Holyfield was declared the winner by technical knockout and added Moorer's IBF championship belt to the WBA belt he already held. Named Fighter of the Year by the Boxing Writers Association of America, Holyfield hoped to face Lewis in a unification match in 1998.

The 48-year-old former heavyweight champion George Foreman made news in November as well, in part because of the respectable performance he put in against Shannon Briggs, who was nearly half his age, and in part because of his announcement—for the second time—of his retirement from the ring. Foreman lost the controversial majority-decision fight to Briggs in Atlantic City, N.J.; the crowd was clearly convinced that Foreman, at 118 kg (260 lb), should have won, but two of the judges scored the match for Briggs and the ring referee called it even.

Among the champions in the lower weight divisions, Oscar de la Hoya proved outstanding again, remaining undefeated after 27 bouts. After retaining the WBC light-

World Light Heavyweight Champions Top Weight 175 Pounds
WBA
Virgil Hill (U.S.; 9/92)
Dariusz Michalczewski (Ger.; 6/13/97) stripped of title in 1997
Lou Del Valle (U.S.; 9/20/97)
WBC
Mike McCallum (Jam.; 7/23/94)
Fabrice Tiozzo (Fr.; 6/16/95)
Roy Jones, Jr. (U.S.; 11/23/96)
Montell Griffin (U.S.; 3/21/97)
Roy Jones, Jr. (U.S.; 8/7/97) vacant
IBF
Virgil Hill (U.S.; 11/23/96)
Dariusz Michalczewski (Ger.; 6/13/97) gave up title in 1997
William Guthrie (U.S.; 7/19/97)

World Middleweight Champions Top Weight 160 Pounds
WBA
John David Jackson (U.S.; 10/2/93) stripped of title in 1994
Jorge Castro (Arg.; 8/12/94)
Shinji Takehara (Japan; 12/19/95)
William Joppy (U.S.; 6/24/96)
Julio César Green (Dom.Rep.; 8/23/97)
WBC
Gerald McClellan (U.S.; 5/8/93) vacant
Julian Jackson (U.S.; 3/17/95)
Quincy Taylor (U.S.; 8/19/95)
Keith Holmes (U.S.; 3/16/96)
IBF
James Toney (U.S.; 5/10/91) gave up title in 1993
Roy Jones (U.S.; 5/22/93) gave up title in 1994
Bernard Hopkins (U.S.; 4/29/95)

World Welterweight Champions Top Weight 147 Pounds
WBA
Aaron Davis (U.S.; 7/8/90)
Meldrick Taylor (U.S.; 1/19/91)
Crisanto España (Venez.; 10/31/92)
Ike Quartey (Ghana; 6/4/94)
WBC
Simon Brown (Jam.; 3/18/91)
James McGirt (U.S.; 11/29/91)
Pernell Whitaker (U.S.; 3/6/93)
Oscar de la Hoya (U.S.; 4/12/97)
IBF
Simon Brown (Jam.; 4/23/88) gave up title in 1991
Maurice Blocker (U.S.; 10/4/91)
Felix Trinidad (P.R.; 6/19/93)

World Super Middleweight Champions Top Weight 168 Pounds
WBA
Christophe Tiozzo (Fr.; 3/30/90)
Victor Cordoba (Pan.; 4/5/91)
Michael Nunn (U.S.; 9/12/92)
Steve Little (U.S.; 2/26/94)
Frank Liles (U.S.; 8/12/94)
WBC
Nigel Benn (U.K.; 10/3/92)
Thulane Malinga (S.Af.; 3/2/96)
Vincenzo Nardiello (Italy; 7/6/96)
Robin Reid (U.K.; 10/12/96)
Thulane Malinga (S.Af.; 12/19/97)
IBF
Iran Barkley (U.S.; 1/10/92)
James Toney (U.S.; 2/13/93)
Roy Jones (U.S.; 11/18/94) **gave up title in 1997**
Charles Brewer (U.S.; 6/21/97)

World Junior Middleweight Champions Top Weight 154 Pounds (also called super welterweight)
WBA
Pernell Whitaker (U.S.; 3/4/95) gave up title in 1995
Carl Daniels (U.S.; 6/16/95)
Julio César Vásquez (Arg.; 12/16/95)
Laurent Boudouani (Fr.; 8/21/96)
WBC
Simon Brown (U.S.; 12/18/93)
Terry Norris (U.S.; 5/7/94)
Luis Santana (Dom.Rep.; 11/12/94)
Terry Norris (U.S.; 8/19/95)
Keith Mullings (U.S.; 12/6/97)
IBF
Vincent Pettway (U.S.; 9/17/94)
Paul Vaden (U.S.; 8/12/95)
Terry Norris (U.S.; 12/16/95) **gave up title in 1997**
Raul Marquez (U.S.; 4/12/97)
Yory Boy Campas (Mex.; 12/6/97)

World Junior Welterweight Champions Top Weight 140 Pounds (also called super lightweight)
WBA
Juan Martin Coggi (Arg.; 1/12/93)
Frankie Randall (U.S.; 9/17/94)
Juan Martin Coggi (Arg.; 1/13/96)
Frankie Randall (U.S.; 8/16/96)
Khalid Rahilou (Fr.; 1/11/97)
WBC
Julio César Chávez (Mex.; 5/13/89)
Frankie Randall (U.S.; 1/29/94)
Julio César Chávez (Mex.; 5/7/94)
Oscar de la Hoya (U.S.; 6/7/96) **gave up title in 1997**
IBF
Charles Murray (U.S.; 5/15/93)
Jake Rodriguez (P.R.; 2/13/94)
Kostya Tszyu (Austl.; 1/28/95)
Vince Phillips (U.S.; 5/31/97)

weight crown against Miguel González (Mex.), de la Hoya moved up and captured the WBC welterweight crown from highly rated Pernell Whitaker, albeit on a controversial decision. De la Hoya later silenced loudmouth Hector ("Macho") Camacho (U.S.) in a 12-round decision before administering a sound beating to Wilfredo Rivera (P.R.), which the referee stopped in the eighth round. De la Hoya's purse total for 1997 was $33 million, an amount seldom seen outside the heavyweight ranks.

Another extraordinarily talented champion, Roy Jones, Jr., carelessly gave away the WBC light heavyweight title in a fight with Montell Griffin (U.S.) in March. After flooring Griffin in the ninth round, Jones threw two quick punches while his opponent was down. The referee had no choice but to disqualify him. A rematch between the two in August was aptly billed under the slogan "Unfinished Business," and it did not take long for Jones to settle matters; he knocked out Griffin in the first round for the title.

Ricardo López made his 19th defense of the WBC strawweight crown by beating Mongkol Charoen (Thai.). A victory over Alex Sanchez later in the year boosted López's record to 46–0. IBF welterweight king Felix Trinidad moved up a division and flattened Troy Waters (Austr.) in the first round. WBC super welterweight champion Terry Norris blew his chance for a future meeting with de la Hoya when he was

British boxer Prince Naseem Hamed (right) connects with a left hook to the head of José Badillo of Puerto Rico during their featherweight championship bout in October. Hamed retained his World Boxing Organization title and preserved his undefeated record by stopping Badillo in the seventh round.

DAN CHUNG—REUTERS

World Lightweight Champions Top Weight 135 Pounds
WBA
Joey Gamache (U.S.; 6/13/92)
Tony Lopez (U.S.; 10/24/92)
Dingaan Thobela (S.Af.; 6/26/93)
Olzubek Nazarov (Russia; 10/30/93)
WBC
Miguel González (Mex.; 8/24/92) gave up title in 1996
Jean-Baptiste Mendy (Fr.; 4/20/96)
Steve Johnston (U.S.; 3/1/97)
IBF
Fred Pendleton (U.S.; 1/10/93)
Rafael Ruelas (U.S.; 2/19/94)
Oscar de la Hoya (U.S.; 5/6/95) gave up title in 1995
Philip Holiday (S.Af.; 8/19/95)
Shane Mosley (U.S.; 8/2/97)

World Junior Lightweight Champions Top Weight 130 Pounds (also called super featherweight)
WBA
Joey Gamache (U.S.; 6/28/91) gave up title in 1991
Genaro Hernandez (U.S.; 11/22/91) gave up title in 1995
Choi Yong Soo (S.Kor.; 10/21/95)
WBC
Azumah Nelson (Ghana; 2/29/88)
Jesse James Leija (U.S.; 5/7/94)
Gabriel Ruelas (U.S.; 9/17/94)
Azumah Nelson (Ghana; 12/1/95)
Genaro Hernandez (U.S.; 3/22/97)
IBF
Juan Molina (P.R.; 2/22/92) vacant
Eddie Hopson (U.S.; 4/22/95)
Tracy Patterson (U.S.; 7/9/95)
Arturo Gatti (U.S.; 12/15/95)

World Featherweight Champions Top Weight 126 Pounds
WBA
Park Yung Kyun (S.Kor.; 3/30/91)
Eloy Rojas (Venez.; 12/4/93)
Wilfredo Vasquez (P.R.; 5/18/96)
WBC
Gregorio Vargas (Mex.; 4/28/93)
Kevin Kelley (U.S.; 12/4/93)
Alejandro González (Mex.; 1/7/95)
Manuel Medina (Mex.; 9/23/95)
Luisito Espinosa (Phil.; 12/11/95)
IBF
Troy Dorsey (U.S.; 6/3/91)
Manuel Medina (Mex.; 8/12/91)
Tom Johnson (U.S.; 2/26/93)
Naseem Hamed (U.K.; 2/8/97) gave up title in 1997
Hector Lizarraga (U.S.; 12/13/97)

World Junior Featherweight Champions Top Weight 122 Pounds (also called super bantamweight)
WBA
Raul Pérez (Mex.; 10/7/91)
Wilfredo Vásquez (P.R.; 3/27/92)
Antonio Cermeno (Venez.; 5/13/95) vacant
WBC
Thierry Jacob (Fr.; 3/20/92)
Tracy Patterson (U.S.; 6/23/92)
Hector Acero-Sánchez (U.S.; 8/26/94)
Daniel Zaragoza (Mex.; 11/6/95)
Erik Morales (Mex.; 9/6/97)
IBF
José Sanabria (Venez.; 5/21/88)
Fabrice Benichou (Fr.; 3/10/89)
Welcome Ncita (S.Af.; 3/10/90)
Kennedy McKinney (U.S.; 12/2/92)
Vuyani Bungu (S.Af.; 8/20/94)

World Bantamweight Champions Top Weight 118 Pounds
WBA
John Michael Johnson (U.S.; 4/22/94)
Daorung Chuvatana (Thai.; 7/16/94)
Veeraphol Sahaprom (Thai.; 9/17/95)
Nana Konadu (Ghana; 1/28/96)
Daorung Chuvatana Siriwat (Thai.; 10/26/96)
Nana Konadu (Ghana; 6/21/97)
WBC
Byun Jong-Il (S.Kor.; 3/28/93)
Yasuei Yakushiji (Japan; 12/22/93)
Wayne McCullough (N.Ire.; 7/30/95)
Sirimongkol Singmanassuk (Thai.; 8/10/96)
Joichiro Tatsuyoshi (Japan; 11/22/97)
IBF
Orlando Canizales (U.S.; 7/9/88) gave up title in 1994
Harold Mestre (Colom.; 1/21/95)
Mbulelo Botile (S.Af.; 4/29/95)
Tim Austin (U.S.; 7/19/97)

World Junior Bantamweight Champions Top Weight 115 Pounds (also called super flyweight)
WBA
Katsuya Onizuka (Japan; 4/10/92)
Lee Hyung Chul (S.Kor.; 9/18/94)
Alima Goitia (Venez.; 7/22/95)
Yokthai Sithoar (Thai.; 8/24/96)
Satoshi Iida (Japan; 12/23/97)
WBC
Nana Konadu (Ghana; 11/7/89)
Moon Sung Kil (S.Kor.; 1/20/90)
José Luis Bueno (Mex.; 11/13/93)
Hiroshi Kawashima (Japan; 5/4/94)
Gerry Peñalosa (Phil.; 2/20/97)
IBF
Harold Grey (Colom.; 8/29/94)
Carlos Salazar (Arg.; 10/7/95)
Harold Grey (Colom.; 4/27/96)
Danny Romero (U.S.; 8/24/96)
Johnny Tapia (U.S.; 7/18/97)

World Flyweight Champions Top Weight 112 Pounds
WBA
Kim Yong Kang (S.Kor.; 6/1/91)
Aquiles Guzmán (Venez.; 9/26/92)
David Griman (Venez.; 12/92)
San Sow Ploenchit (Thai.; 2/13/94)
José Bonilla (Venez.; 11/14/96)
WBC
Sot Chitalada (Thai.; 6/3/89)
Muangchai Kittlkasem (Thai.; 2/15/91)
Yury Arbachakov (Russia; 6/23/92)
Chatchai Dutchboygym (Sasakul) (Thai; 5/9/97)
IBF
Phichit Sithbangprachan (Thai.; 11/29/92) vacant
Francisco Tejedor (Colom.; 2/95)
Danny Romero (U.S.; 4/22/95) gave up title in 1996
Mark Johnson (U.S.; 5/4/96)

World Junior Flyweight Champions Top Weight 108 Pounds
WBA
Yuh Myung Woo (S.Kor.; 11/18/92) gave up title in 1993
Leo Gamez (Venez.; 10/21/93)
Choi Hi Yong (S.Kor.; 2/4/95)
Carlos Murillo (Pan.; 1/13/96)
Keiji Yamaguchi (Japan; 5/21/96)
Pichitnoi Siriwat (Thai.; 12/3/96)
WBC
Michael Carbajal (U.S.; 3/13/93)
Chiquita Gonzalez (Mex.; 2/19/94)
Saman Sorjaturong (Thai.; 7/15/95)
IBF
Michael Carbajal (U.S.; 7/29/90)
Chiquita Gonzalez (Mex.; 2/19/94)
Saman Sorjaturong (Thai.; 7/15/95) vacant
Michael Carbajal (U.S.; 3/16/96)
Mauricio Pastrana (Colom.; 1/18/97) vacant
Mauricio Pastrana (Colom.; 12/13/97)

World Mini-flyweight Champions Top Weight 105 Pounds (also called strawweight)
WBA
Kim Bong Jun (S.Kor.; 4/16/89)
Choi Hi Yong (S.Kor.; 2/2/91)
Ohashi Hideyuki (Japan; 10/14/92)
Chana Porpaoin (Thai.; 2/10/93)
Rosendo Alvarez (Nic.; 12/2/95)
WBC
Napa Kiatwanchai (Thai.; 11/13/88)
Choi Jum Hwan (S.Kor.; 11/12/89)
Ohashi Hideyuki (Japan; 2/7/90)
Ricardo López (Mex.; 10/25/90)
IBF
Falan Lookmingkwan (Thai.; 2/21/90)
Manny Melchor (Phil.; 9/6/92)
Ratanapol Vorapin (Thai.; 12/10/92) stripped of title in 1996
Ratanapol Vorapin (Thai.; 5/16/96)
Zolani Lepetelo (S.Af.; 12/27/97)

stopped in the ninth round by 7–1 underdog Keith Mullings in December.

WBO featherweight champion Naseem Hamed won the IBF title by stopping Tom Johnson (U.S.) in eight rounds. Hamed later defeated Billy Hardy (Eng.) in one round, Juan Cabrera (Arg.) in two, and José Badillo (P.R.) in seven. Before his fight with Badillo, Hamed gave up the IBF crown rather than agree to a mandatory defense against Hector Lizarraga. The 23-year-old Hamed made a highly publicized U.S. debut on December 19 at Madison Square Garden in New York City against Kevin Kelley (U.S.). In a wild match that saw each fighter hit the canvas three times, Hamed eventually prevailed, knocking out Kelley in the fourth round. With the win, Hamed, who was born in Great Britain to Yemeni parents, boosted his record to 29–0.

In 1997 boxing suffered a double blow from the deaths of two former world champions, Willie Pastrano (U.S.) and Edwin Rosario (P.R.). (*See* OBITUARIES.) Pastrano won the light heavyweight title in June 1963, defended the title twice before losing it to José Torres (U.S.) in 1965, and retired with

KATHY WILLENS—ASSOCIATED PRESS

It took more than five hours for 34-year-old world chess champion Garry Kasparov and IBM's Deep Blue computer program to play to a draw in the fourth game of their six-game match in New York City in May. Kasparov eventually lost the match, dropping the final game in only 19 moves.

a record of 63–13–8. Rosario, a three-time world lightweight champion active in the 1980s and '90s, had a career record of 43–6. His death was believed to be related to drug abuse, a problem he battled for most of his career. Zambian Felix Bwalya fell into a coma and died on December 23 after a two-day drinking spree to celebrate winning the Commonwealth light welterweight title.

(FRANK BUTLER)

CHESS

The year 1997 was dominated by the blow to Garry Kasparov's prestige when he lost a six-game challenge rematch in New York City to the Deep Blue computer program developed by IBM. The match, played May 3–11, was a follow-up to the dramatic contest won by the Russian champion in 1996. The prize money was much greater in 1997, with $700,000 to the winner and $400,000 to the loser. Yet much more than this was at stake, for the immense interest generated by the contest and the machine's success led to a rise in IBM stock prices and to the assumption by the general public that a computer program had finally proved superior to the best of humankind.

Interestingly, this latter conclusion was not the view of chess experts, who would have required a more rigorous proof under tournament conditions against a variety of human opponents over at least 11 rounds. Kasparov, too, assumed that he would get the chance of a replay, so IBM's low-key announcement in September that the program was being devoted to things other than chess was a grave disappointment to him. He even drew a comparison between IBM and the old Central Committee of the Communist Party of the Soviet Union, with which he had had difficult dealings.

The course of the match proved dramatic. Kasparov won the first game in 45 moves but then made the error of resigning in the second game after 45 moves, in a position that was shown subsequently to be a forced draw had Black played for perpetual check. This proved a grave psychological blow to Kasparov, who reacted badly by giving vent to the suspicion that some outside human intervention had helped the program in making certain positional decisions earlier in the game.

Having thus lost his equanimity and, some would say, objectivity, the champion drew the next three games and then went down ignominiously in only 19 moves in the final game. (*See* TABLE.) This was his worst defeat ever and showed a lack of his usual preparation, for the gambit variation essayed by Deep Blue had already been tried in a game the previous October between a Fritz program (of Dutch origin) and Gennady Timoshchenko (a former second to Kasparov). It was assumed that Kasparov must not have known of this game; otherwise, he would surely not have played the loosening pawn move at his 11th turn.

Kasparov was scheduled to defend his world title against Russian archrival Anatoly Karpov in October. Lawyers for both sides had reached agreement on the terms, but the principals were unable to bring the match to fruition, largely owing to lack of sponsorship. This in turn was the result of several recent inferior performances by Karpov, notably his joint third place at Dos Hermanas, Spain, in April, behind Vladimir Kramnik of Russia and Viswanathan Anand of India, and his shared sixth place at Dortmund,

Caro-Kann Defense

White: Deep Blue		Black: Garry Kasparov	
White	Black	White	Black
1 e4	c6	11 Bf4	b5
2 d4	d5	12 a4	Bb7
3 Nc3	dxe4	13 Re1	Nd5
4 Nxe4	Nd7	14 Bg3	Kc8
5 Ng5	Ngf6	15 axb5	cxb5
6 Bd3	e6	16 Qd3	Bc6
7 N1f3	h6	17 Bf5	exf5
8 Nxe6	Qe7	18 Rxe7	Bxe7
9 0-0	fxe6	19 c4	resigns
10 Bg6+	kd8		

Olympiad—Men

Year	Winner	Runner-up
1989	U.S.S.R.	Yugoslavia
1992	Russia	Uzbekistan
1994	Russia	Bosnia
1996	Russia	Ukraine

Olympiad—Women

Year	Winner	Runner-up
1988	Hungary	U.S.S.R.
1992	Georgia	Ukraine
1986	U.S.S.R.	Hungary
1994	Georgia	Hungary
1996	Georgia	China

World Chess Championship—Men

Year	Winner	Runner-up
1987	G. Kasparov (U.S.S.R.)	A. Karpov (U.S.S.R.)
1990	G. Kasparov (U.S.S.R.)	A. Karpov (U.S.S.R.)
1993	A. Karpov (Russia)	J. Timman (Neth.)
1996	A. Karpov (Russia)	G. Kamsky (U.S.)

World Chess Championship—Women

Year	Winner	Runner-up
1988	M. Chiburdanidze (U.S.S.R.)	N. Ioseliani (U.S.S.R.)
1991	Xie Jun (China)	M. Chiburdanidze (U.S.S.R.)
1993	Xie Jun (China)	N. Ioseliani (Georgia)
1996	Z. Polgar (Hung.)	Xie Jun (China)

Ger., in July, when Kramnik led Anand by a point to finish first. In fact, the results in 1997 indicated that Kramnik, still only 22 years old, was the logical successor to Kasparov, once financing could be raised for such a match.

The Fédération Internationale des Échecs (FIDE), the world ruling body, endeavoured to regularize the anomaly of two world champions, Kasparov and Karpov, when it arranged a knockout contest for the 100 likeliest contenders, which would start in early December and conclude in January 1998. This event was marked by meticulous planning, including the issuing of exacting contracts to the players in which the old question of the copyright of games was raised. Kasparov, however, refused to take part, indicating that the short matches of the envisaged knockout format was a break with 111 years of chess history. Precedent demanded that the title change hands only after a long match of, say, a minimum of 18 games.

Kasparov failed to prove his superiority when he could only tie for first place at the Tilburg, Neth., tournament in early October. After a start of 5.5/6, he lost in the seventh round to 21-year-old Peter Svidler of St. Petersburg, who for four years had shown excellent form in the Russian championships. The outcome was a tie on 8 points out of 11 for Kasparov, Svidler, and Kramnik. In the other strong tournament of the year, at Linares, Spain, in February, the top scores were Kasparov 8.5/11, Kramnik 7.5, Michael Adams of England and Veselin Topalov of Bulgaria both 6.5, Judit Polgar of Hungary 6, and Anand 5.5.

In team contests England won the European championship at Pula, Croatia, in mid-May after a tie on points with Russia, 22.5 points out of 36; Armenia finished third with 22 points. Russia recovered at the world team championship in October by beating the Georgian women 4–0 in the last round. This single whitewash of the whole event led to some dark mutterings among the American team, which had led throughout the tournament until then. The final scores at the top were Russia 23.5 out of 36, the U.S. 23, Armenia 21, and England 20.5.

In individual contests the West had a rare success in the world junior (under-20) championships at Zagan, Pol., in July. In the boys section Tal Shaked of the U.S. made 9.5/13 to head the massed ranks of former Soviet and other Eastern European players who normally dominated such events. An even greater break with tradition came when Harriet Hunt of Oxford, Eng., took the girls title with a late burst of six wins and a draw in her last seven games.

(BERNARD CAFFERTY)

CONTRACT BRIDGE

The two most important world championships in contract bridge, the Bermuda Bowl and the Venice Cup, which is restricted to women, took place in Hammamet, Tun., Oct. 19–Nov. 1, 1997. The Bermuda Bowl was won by France, which defeated the United States 328–301 in the final. Norway finished third. The winning team comprised Alain Lévy, Christian Mari, Hervé Mouiel, Frank Multon, Paul Chemla, and Michel Perron, with Jean-Louis Stoppa as the nonplaying captain. (The first four players were part of the French team that won the 1996 World Team Olympiad.) The silver medalists were the defending champions, Nick Nickell, Dick Freeman, Bob Hamman, Bobby Wolff, Jeff Meckstroth, and Eric Rodwell, with Walt Walvick as the nonplaying captain.

The Venice Cup was won by the U.S., which defeated China 249–184 in the final. Third was the other U.S. team. The winners were Mildred Breed, Tobi Sokolow, Marinesa Letizia, Lisa Berkowitz, Jill Meyers, and Randi Montin, with Sue Picus as the nonplaying captain. The Chinese team consisted of Sun Ming, Lu Yan, Gu Ling, Zhang Yalan, Wang Wenfei, and Zhang Yu, with Hu Ji Hong as the nonplaying captain.

Two more world championships took place in 1997, each one for players under 25 years of age. In Forlì, Italy, in July, Stefan Solbrand and Olle Wademark from Sweden won the world junior pairs title. Second were Mette Drøgemuller from Denmark and Sebastian Reim from Germany, and finishing third were Boye Brogeland and Trond Hantveit of Norway.

In Hamilton, Ont., in August, Denmark won the world junior teams trophy. The players were the brothers Lars and Morten Lund Madsen, Freddi Brøndum, Jacob Røn, Mik Kristensen, and Mikkel Nøhr, with Kirsten Steen Møller as the nonplaying captain. In the final they beat Norway 248–178. Norway was represented by Boye Brogeland, Øyvind Saur, Espen Erichsen, Thomas Charlsen, Bjørn Morten Mathisen, and Christer Kristoffersen, with Sten Bjertnes as the nonplaying captain. The Russian team placed third.

The first Transnational Open Teams tournament, also held in the autumn at Hammamet, was won convincingly by a combined Italian-Polish team consisting of Leandro Burgay, Dano DeFalco, Carlo Mariani, Marcin Lesniewski, and Krzysztof Martens. In the final they defeated the Polish team of Krzysztof Jassem, Piotr Tuszynski, Ireneusz Kowalczyk, and Marek Witek 132–40.

The 12th worldwide pairs tournament, held on June 6 and 7 at sites throughout the world, was once again the biggest contest of the year in terms of the number of competitors; more than 80,000 took part. The highest score, 1,906, was achieved by Zhang Jie and Zhao Jinlong of China, playing in the Great Hall of China in Beijing.

(PHILLIP ALDER)

World Contract Bridge Pair Championship

Year	Open winners	Women's winners	Mixed winners
1990	Marcelo Branco, Gabriel Chagas (Braz.)	Kerri Shuman, Karen McCallum (U.S.)	Peter Weichsel, Juanita Chambers (U.S.)
1994	Marcin Lesniewski, Marek Szymanowski (Pol.)	Carla Arnolds, Bep Vriend (Neth.)	Danuta Hocheker, Apolinare Kowalski (Pol.)

World Team Olympiad

Year	Open winner	Open runner-up	Women's winner	Women's runner-up
1988	United States	Austria	Denmark	United Kingdom
1992	France	United States	Austria	United Kingdom
1996	France	Indonesia	United States	China

The best-played deal of the year, in the opinion of the International Bridge Press Association, was declared by the Norwegian Geir Helgemo. The deal occurred while Helgemo and his teammates, Bart Bramley, Brian Glubok, Edgar Kaplan, Norman Kay, and Walter Schafer, were winning the Open Swiss Teams national title at the American Spring Nationals in Dallas, Texas, in March.

NORTH
♠ 9 7 3
♥ 9 7 6 2
♦ K 10 8 6
♣ 9 2

WEST
♠ 8 4
♥ K Q J 8 4
♦ 5
♣ K 10 7 5 3

EAST
♠ Q J 10 5
♥ A 10 5 3
♦ 3
♣ Q J 6 4

SOUTH
♠ A K 6 2
♥ —
♦ A Q J 9 7 4 2
♣ A 8

Dealer: West
Vulnerable: Both

WEST	NORTH Kaplan	EAST	SOUTH Helgemo
2♥	Pass	4♥	6♦
Pass	Pass	Pass	

Opening lead: ♥ K.

West opened with a modern weak two-bid. Then, over East's jump to game, Helgemo took a reasonable shot at six diamonds. A club lead would have been lethal, but not surprisingly West selected the king of hearts. Helgemo ruffed and drew the missing trumps. Helgemo was sure to lose one spade trick. To avoid losing a club as well, he had to win three spade tricks. The obvious possibility was to find the missing spades splitting 3–3. Then, on his 13th spade, declarer could discard a club from the dummy. Rather than put all his eggs in that one omelet by playing spades from the top, however, Helgemo started with a low spade from hand, putting in dummy's seven when West played the four. East won with a deceptive jack and returned the five of spades. Helgemo paused to assess the situation.

Being vulnerable, East probably had four trumps to jump to four hearts. If West had opened with a five-card suit, Helgemo judged he was more likely to have begun with 2–5–1–5 distribution than with 3–5–1–4. If West had begun with a doubleton spade, there would be only one hope. Therefore, Helgemo played the six of spades from his hand, winning the trick with dummy's nine! Helgemo cashed the ace-king of spades, discarding a club from the dummy, took the ace of clubs, and ruffed his club loser in the dummy.

Bermuda Bowl

Year	Winner	Runner-up
1991	Iceland	Poland
1993	Netherlands	Norway
1995	United States	Canada
1997	**France**	**United States**

CRICKET

Driven ever harder by the demands of television, sponsors, and players, international cricket experienced another hectic season in 1996–97. Whether the quality of the cricket matched the quantity was open to question, but barely a week passed without a Test or one-day international being contested somewhere in the world. There were 45 Tests from Oct. 1, 1996, to Oct. 1, 1997, and more than 100 one-day internationals. By the end, Australia had confirmed its position as the strongest of the nine Test-playing nations, winning 8 of its 15 Tests, including series against the West Indies and South Africa and a record fifth successive victory in the Ashes series against England. The 3–2 score flattered the English, who won the first and last Tests but were comprehensively outplayed in between.

In G.D. McGrath and S.K. Warne, Australia had bowlers of contrasting styles but similar effectiveness. McGrath, tall, slender, and fast, took 77 wickets in 15 Tests, including 36 (average 19.47) against England, while Warne continued his surge toward the list of all-time greats by becoming the most prolific leg-spinner in Test history. With his ninth wicket of the Ashes series, Warne surpassed R. Benaud's 248 Test wickets, and by the end of the series, he had taken 264 wickets in 58 Tests at an average of just under 24 each. Aggressively led by M.A. Taylor, Australia scored its runs fast and took its wickets quickly—win or lose. Of 15 Tests in the 1996–97 season, only one—in England at Lord's when the first two days were all but lost to rain—was drawn.

The statistical highlight of the year was recorded in Colombo, Sri Lanka, where the home side's 962 for 6 beat, by 49 runs, the previous highest Test innings, 903 for 7 by England against Australia in 1938. With S.T. Jayasuriya within sight of breaking the individual Test record on the final morning of the first match, a crowd of 32,000 gathered in Colombo to witness history. Sadly, the Sri

Test Series Results, October 1996–September 1997

Test	Host country	Ground	Date	Scores	Result
1st	India	Delhi	Oct. 10–13	Australia 182 and 234; India 361 and 58 for 3	India won by 7 wickets
1st	Pakistan	Sheikhupura	Oct. 17–21	Zimbabwe 375 and 241 for 7; Pakistan 553	Match drawn
2nd	Pakistan	Faisalabad	Oct. 24–26	Zimbabwe 133 and 200; Pakistan 267 and 69 for 0	Pakistan won by 10 wickets
1st	India	Ahmedabad	Nov. 20–23	India 223 and 190; South Africa 244 and 105	India won by 64 runs
2nd	India	Calcutta	Nov. 27–Dec. 1	South Africa 428 and 367 for 3 dec; India 329 and 137	South Africa won by 329 runs
3rd	India	Kanpur	Dec. 8–12	India 237 and 400 for 7 dec; South Africa 177 and 180	India won by 280 runs
1st	Pakistan	Lahore	Nov. 21–24	New Zealand 155 and 311; Pakistan 191 and 231	New Zealand won by 44 runs
2nd	Pakistan	Rawalpindi	Nov. 28–Dec. 1	New Zealand 249 and 168; Pakistan 430	Pakistan won by an innings and 13 runs
1st	Australia	Brisbane	Nov. 22–26	Australia 479 and 217 for 6 dec; West Indies 277 and 296	Australia won by 123 runs
2nd	Australia	Sydney	Nov. 29–Dec. 3	Australia 331 and 312 for 4 dec; West Indies 304 and 215	Australia won by 124 runs
3rd	Australia	Melbourne	Dec. 26–28	Australia 219 and 122; West Indies 255 and 87 for 4	West Indies won by 6 wickets
4th	Australia	Adelaide	Jan. 25–28	West Indies 130 and 204; Australia 517	Australia won by an innings and 183 runs
5th	Australia	Perth	Feb. 1–3	Australia 243 and 194; West Indies 384 and 57 for 0	West Indies won by 10 wickets
1st	Zimbabwe	Bulawayo	Dec. 18–22	Zimbabwe 376 and 234; England 406 and 204 for 6	Match drawn
2nd	Zimbabwe	Harare	Dec. 26–30	England 156 and 195 for 3; Zimbabwe 215	Match drawn
1st	South Africa	Durban	Dec. 26–28	South Africa 235 and 259; India 100 and 66	South Africa won by 328 runs
2nd	South Africa	Cape Town	Jan. 2–6	South Africa 529 for 7 dec and 256 for 6 dec; India 359 and 144	South Africa won by 282 runs
3rd	South Africa	Johannesburg	Jan. 16–20	India 410 and 266 for 8 dec; South Africa 321 and 228 for 8	Match drawn
1st	New Zealand	Auckland	Jan. 24–28	New Zealand 390 and 248 for 9 dec; England 521	Match drawn
2nd	New Zealand	Wellington	Feb. 6–10	New Zealand 124 and 191; England 383	England won by an innings and 68 runs
3rd	New Zealand	Christchurch	Feb. 14–18	New Zealand 346 and 186; England 228 and 307 for 6	England won by 4 wickets
1st	South Africa	Johannesburg	Feb. 28–March 4	South Africa 302 and 130; Australia 628 for 8 dec	Australia won by an innings and 196 runs
2nd	South Africa	Port Elizabeth	March 14–17	South Africa 209 and 168; Australia 108 and 271 for 8	Australia won by 2 wickets
3rd	South Africa	Centurion Park	March 21–24	Australia 227 and 185; South Africa 384 and 32 for 2	South Africa won by 8 wickets
1st	West Indies	Kingston	March 6–10	West Indies 427 and 241 for 4 dec; India 346 and 99 for 2	Match drawn
2nd	West Indies	Port of Spain	March 14–18	West Indies 296 and 299 for 6; India 436	Match drawn
3rd	West Indies	Bridgetown	March 27–31	West Indies 298 and 140; India 319 and 81	West Indies won by 38 runs
4th	West Indies	St. John's	April 4–8	West Indies 333; India 212 for 2	Match drawn (rain)
5th	West Indies	Georgetown	April 17–21	India 355; West Indies 145 for 3	Match drawn (rain)
1st	New Zealand	Dunedin	March 7–10	New Zealand 586 for 7 dec; Sri Lanka 222 and 328	New Zealand won by an innings and 36 runs
2nd	New Zealand	Hamilton	March 14–17	New Zealand 222 and 273; Sri Lanka 170 and 205	New Zealand won by 120 runs
1st	Sri Lanka	Colombo	April 19–23	Sri Lanka 330 and 423 for 8 dec; Pakistan 378	Match drawn
2nd	Sri Lanka	Colombo	April 26–30	Sri Lanka 331 and 386 for 4 dec; Pakistan 292 and 285 for 5	Match drawn
1st	England	Birmingham	June 5–8	Australia 118 and 477; England 478 for 9 dec and 119 for 1	England won by 9 wickets
2nd	England	London (Lord's)	June 19–23	England 77 and 266 for 4 dec; Australia 213 for 7 dec	Match drawn
3rd	England	Manchester	July 3–7	Australia 235 and 395 for 8 dec; England 162 and 200	Australia won by 268 runs
4th	England	Leeds	July 24–28	England 172 and 268; Australia 501 for 9 dec	Australia won by an innings and 61 runs
5th	England	Nottingham	Aug. 7–10	Australia 427 and 336; England 313 and 186	Australia won by 264 runs
6th	England	London (Oval)	Aug. 21–23	England 180 and 163; Australia 220 and 104	England won by 19 runs
1st	West Indies	St. John's	June 13–15	Sri Lanka 223 and 152; West Indies 189 and 189 for 4	West Indies won by 6 wickets
2nd	West Indies	Kingstown	June 20–24	West Indies 147 and 343; Sri Lanka 222 and 233 for 8	Match drawn
1st	Sri Lanka	Colombo	Aug. 2–6	India 537 for 8 dec; Sri Lanka 952 for 6 dec	Match drawn
2nd	Sri Lanka	Colombo	Aug. 9–13	Sri Lanka 332 and 415 for 7 dec; India 375 and 281 for 5	Match drawn
1st	Zimbabwe	Harare	Sept. 18–22	Zimbabwe 298 and 311 for 9 dec; New Zealand 207 and 304 for 8	Match drawn
2nd	Zimbabwe	Bulawayo	Sept. 25–29	Zimbabwe 461 and 227 for 8 dec; New Zealand 403 and 275 for 8	March drawn

Lankan opener succumbed to nerves and was out 35 runs short of the world record of 375, having faced 578 balls in an innings lasting 13½ hours. The second wicket partnership of 576 with R.S. Mahanama was comfortably the highest for any wicket in Test cricket and was just one run short of being the highest in first-class cricket.

While Colombo produced a wicket almost perfect for batsmen, the pitches in England for the Ashes series favoured the bowlers, mostly the Australians. England scored a handsome victory in the opening Test when Australia lost eight wickets before lunch on the first day and, with N. Hussain scoring a career-best 207 for the home team, never recovered. In the second Test the rain at Lord's helped England gain a draw when McGrath took 8 for 38. The critical Test was the third at Old Trafford. England had the best of the conditions but had no one to match the wiles of Warne or the determination of S.R. Waugh, who enhanced his reputation as the best batsman in the world by becoming only the third Australian to score a hundred in each innings of an Ashes Test. After that victory Australia did not look back, winning the next two Tests and the Ashes. J.N. Gillespie, a promising young fast bowler, took 7 for 37 at Leeds, while Warne took a total of nine wickets at Nottingham. Only in the final Test at the Oval, on another questionable pitch, did England strike back, bowling Australia out for 104 on the third day, P.C.R. Tufnell taking 11 for 93 in his first Test of the series. For M.A. Atherton, the England captain, it was too little too late. M.T.G. Elliott of Australia was the leading run-scorer, with 556 at 55.60. For England, G.P. Thorpe scored 453 runs at 50.33, and A.R. Caddick fulfilled his potential with 24 wickets at 26.42.

In the unofficial world championship, Australia beat South Africa 2–1. G.S. Blewett and S.R. Waugh set up an innings win in the first Test with a partnership of 385, and twin brother M.E. Waugh—known as "Junior" because he was born four minutes after Steve—guided Australia to a two-wicket victory in the second Test with an innings of 116 on a bouncy pitch. (*See* BIOGRAPHIES: *Waugh, Mark and Steve.*)

West Indies was still undergoing a rebuilding program when it was beaten decisively by Australia, though S. Chanderpaul confirmed his reputation as a determined middle-order batsman and, on occasion, C. Ambrose recovered his old fire. In B.K.V. Prasad, A. Kumble, and J. Srinath, India found a trio of world-class bowlers to add to the batting prowess of its young captain, S.R. Tendulkar, and two promising newcomers, R.S. Dravid and S.C. Ganguly.

CLIVE MASON—ALLSPORT

S.K. Warne of Australia bowls against England during the pivotal third Test of the Ashes series at Old Trafford in Manchester, Eng. Australia won the Test to even the series 1–1 and then went on to win the next two Tests and the Ashes. By the end of the series, Warne had taken 264 wickets in 58 Tests.

In England concern over declining standards and interest, especially among young people, prompted a complete overhaul of the structure of the domestic game, both recreational and first-class. A move to change the format of the county championship was defeated, however, which caused some of the more powerful counties to threaten a breakaway. Glamorgan, led by M. Maynard, captured its first county championship title in 28 years. Essex won the NatWest Trophy, Surrey the Benson and Hedges Cup, and Warwickshire the Sunday league. In Australia Queensland secured the Sheffield Shield; Bombay (Mumbai) won India's Ranji Trophy; Barbados captured the Red Stripe Cup in the West Indies; and Canterbury took New Zealand's Shell Trophy. Natal dominated South African cricket, winning both the four-day Super Sport title and the Standard Bank one-day cup. Bangladesh, Kenya, and Scotland qualified for the 1999 World Cup. In April D.C.S. Compton, one of England's most gifted batsmen, died at age 78. (*See* OBITUARIES.) (ANDREW LONGMORE)

Cricket World Cup

Year	Result			
1979	West Indies	286–9	England	194
1983	India	183	West Indies	140
1987	Australia	253–5	England	246–8
1992	Pakistan	249–6	England	227
1996	Sri Lanka	245–3	Australia	241

All-Time First-Class Test Cricket Standings (as of Sept. 30, 1997)

	England			Australia			South Africa			West Indies			New Zealand		
	Wins	Draws	Losses	W	D	L	W	D	L	W	D	L	W	D	L
England v.	—	—	—	92	85	114	47	43	20	27	40	48	36	38	4
Australia v.	114	85	92	—	—	—	33	15	14	35	22*	29	13	11	7
South Africa v.	20	43	47	14	15	33	—	—	—	0	0	1	12	6	3
West Indies v.	48	40	27	29	22*	35	1	0	0	—	—	—	10	14	4
New Zealand v.	4	38	36	7	11	13	3	6	12	4	14	10	—	—	—
India v.	14	38	32	9	18*	24	2	4	4	7	35	28	13	16	6
Pakistan v.	9	32	14	11	15	14	0	0	1	7	12	12	18	16	5
Sri Lanka v.	1	1	3	0	3	7	0	2	1	0	2	1	2	7	6
Zimbabwe v.	0	2	0	†			0	0	1	†			0	5	1

	India			Pakistan			Sri Lanka			Zimbabwe		
	W	D	L	W	D	L	W	D	L	W	D	L
England v.	32	36	14	14	32	9	3	1	1	0	2	0
Australia v.	24	18*	9	14	15	11	7	3	0	†		
South Africa v.	4	4	2	1	0	0	1	2	0	1	0	0
West Indies v.	28	35	7	12	12	7	1	2	0	†		
New Zealand v.	6	16	13	5	16	18	6	7	2	1	5	0
India v.	—	—	—	4	33	7	7	8	1	1	1	0
Pakistan v.	7	33	4	—	—	—	9	7	3	5	2	1
Sri Lanka v.	1	8	7	3	7	9	—	—	—	2	3	0
Zimbabwe v.	0	1	1	1	2	5	0	3	2	—	—	—

*Including one tie. †No matches.

CURLING

Sweden won its first men's world curling crown in 20 years at the 1997 world championships held in Bern, Switz., in April, injecting some fresh blood into the sport's reigning hierarchy in preparation for the 1998 Winter Olympics in Nagano, Japan. Represented by Ostersund and skipped by Peter Lindholm, Sweden defeated Germany, represented by Füssen and skipped by Andy Kapp, 6–3 in the final. Scotland had earned the silver medal in four of the previous five world championships but slipped to third place, beating Canada in the men's bronze medal final. Canadian men, who had claimed the world title for the last four years in a row, were shut out of the medals for the first time since 1984. Rounding out the top 10, in order, were Denmark, the United States, Australia, Norway, Switzerland, and Finland.

In the women's competition Canada maintained form when Regina, skipped by Sandra Schmirler, defeated Norway, repre-

World Curling Championship—Men		
Year	Winner	Runner-up
1993	Canada	Scotland
1994	Canada	Sweden
1995	Canada	Scotland
1996	Canada	Scotland
1997	**Sweden**	**Germany**

World Curling Championship—Women		
Year	Winner	Runner-up
1993	Canada	Germany
1994	Canada	Scotland
1995	Sweden	Canada
1996	Canada	United States
1997	**Canada**	**Norway**

sented by Snaroen and skipped by Dordi Nordby, 8–4 in the final. Schmirler, who had claimed the title in 1993 and 1994 under her maiden name, Sandra Peterson, became the first woman to win three world championships. Nordby also had won twice previously. For Canada it was the second women's world crown in a row and the fourth in five years. The remaining top 10 finishers in order were Denmark, Japan, Sweden, Germany, the United States, Finland, Scotland, and Switzerland.

Curling, which was first introduced as a demonstration sport at the 1988 Winter Olympics in Calgary, Alta., was set to be a full medal sport for the first time at the Games in Nagano. The eight men's countries that qualified were, in order of ranking, Canada, Scotland (which was representing the U.K.), Sweden, Germany, the U.S., Norway, Switzerland, and Japan. The eight qualifying countries on the women's side were, in order of ranking, Canada, Norway, Sweden, the U.S., Germany, Denmark, Japan, and Scotland. (BRUCE CHEADLE)

CYCLING

In 1997 cycling's world governing body, the Union Cycliste Internationale (UCI), introduced random blood testing in an attempt to curtail the use of erythropoietin (EPO), the hormone that stimulates the production of oxygen-rich red blood cells. A safe level of hematocrit (the amount of red cells in the blood) was set at 50% (55% for riders from high-altitude countries), and any rider found to exceed the limit was eliminated from the event. Riders who tested above the agreed-upon level were not allowed to compete again until a further test had determined that the level had dropped to within the accepted parameters.

The UCI also continued to study limitations on bicycle design and confirmed a restriction on handlebar extension to eliminate finally the extended-arm position that had helped cyclists establish a number of world records in track racing in 1996. The UCI indicated that further limitations on frame design and wheel dimensions would be phased in over the next two years.

The Tour de France, held in July, was won by the German rider Jan Ullrich, who, at 23 years 7 months, was the youngest champion since Laurent Fignon triumphed in 1983 at age 22. Ullrich, who had finished second in 1996, took the lead after the 10th of the 21 stages and held on to win by 9 min 9 sec

Tour de France		
Year	Winner	Kilometres
1993	M. Indurain (Spain)	3,700
1994	M. Indurain (Spain)	3,978
1995	M. Indurain (Spain)	3,635
1996	B. Riis (Den.)	3,764
1997	**J. Ullrich (Ger.)**	**3,944**

Cycling World Track Championships—Women		
Year	Sprint	3-km pursuit
1993	T. Dubnicoff (Can.)	R. Twigg (U.S.)
1994	G. Yenyukhina (Russia)	M. Clignet (Fr.)
1995	F. Ballanger (Fr.)	R. Twigg (U.S.)
1996	F. Ballanger (Fr.)	M. Clignet (Fr.)
1997	**F. Ballanger (Fr.)**	**J. Arndt (Ger.)**

Cycling World Track Championships—Men*			
Year	Sprint (amateur)	Pursuit (amateur)	Motor-paced (amateur)
1994	M. Nothstein (U.S.)	C. Boardman (U.K.)	C. Podlesch (Ger.)
1995	D. Hill (Austl.)	G. Obree (U.K.)	not held
1996	F. Rousseau (Fr.)	C. Boardman (U.K.)	not held
1997	**F. Rousseau (Fr.)**	**P. Ermenault (Fr.)**	**not held**

*From 1993 professionals and amateurs competed in the same event.

Cycling World Road-Racing Championships			
Year	Men (amateur)	Men (professional)	Women (amateur)
1993	J. Ullrich (Ger.)	L. Armstrong (U.S.)	L. van Moorsel (Neth.)
1994	A. Pedersen (Den.)	L. Leblanc (Fr.)	M. Valvik (Nor.)
1995	D. Nelissen (Neth.)	A. Olano (Spain)	J. Longo (Fr.)
1996*		J. Museeuw (Belg.)	B. Heeb (Switz.)
1997		**L. Brochard (Fr.)**	**A. Cappellotto (Italy)**

*From 1996 professionals and amateurs competed in the same event.

Cycling Champions, 1997		
Event	Winner	Country
WORLD CHAMPIONS—TRACK		
Men		
Sprint	F. Rousseau	France
Individual pursuit	P. Ermenault	France
Kilometre time trial	S. Kelly	Australia
40-km points	S. Martinello	Italy
Team pursuit	M. Benetton, A. Capelli, C. Citton, A. Collinelli	Italy
Keirin	F. Magne	France
Olympic sprint	V. Le Quellec, F. Rousseau, A. Tournant	France
50-km Madison	M. Alzamora, J. Llaneras	Spain
Women		
Sprint	F. Ballanger	France
Individual pursuit	J. Arndt	Germany
500-m time trial	F. Ballanger	France
25-km points	N. Karimova	Russia
WORLD CHAMPIONS—ROAD		
Men		
Individual road race	L. Brochard	France
Individual time trial	L. Jalabert	France
Women		
Individual road race	A. Cappellotto	Italy
Individual time trial	J. Longo-Ciprelli	France
WORLD CHAMPION—CYCLO-CROSS		
	D. Pontoni	Italy
WORLD CHAMPIONS—MOUNTAIN BIKES		
Men		
Individual cross-country	H. Pallhuber	Italy
Individual downhill	N. Vouilloz	France
Women		
Individual cross-country	P. Pezzo	Italy
Individual downhill	A.-C. Chausson	France
MAJOR PROFESSIONAL ROAD-RACE WINNERS		
Tour de France	J. Ullrich	Germany
Tour of Italy	I. Gotti	Italy
Tour of Spain	A. Zülle	Switzerland
Milan–San Remo	E. Zabel	Germany
Tour of Flanders	R. Sorensen	Denmark
Paris–Roubaix	F. Guesdon	France
Liège–Bastogne–Liège	M. Bartoli	Italy
Amstel Gold	B. Riis	Denmark
San Sebastian Classic	D. Rebellin	Italy
Rochester Classic	A. Tafi	Italy
Grand Prix Suisse	D. Rebellin	Italy
Paris–Tours	A. Tchmil	Ukraine
Paris–Nice	L. Jalabert	France
Ghent–Wevelgem	P. Gaumont	France
Flèche Wallonne	L. Jalabert	France
Tour of Romandie	P. Tonkov	Russia
Dauphiné Libéré	U. Bölts	Germany
Midi-Libre	A. Elli	Italy
Dunkirk 4-Day	J. Museeuw	Belgium
Grand Prix of Frankfurt	M. Bartoli	Italy

RICHARD MARTIN—VANDYSTADT/ALLSPORT

German cyclist Jan Ullrich (foreground) speeds through a crowd of enthusiastic spectators on his way to winning the Tour de France, which covered 3,944 km (2,450 mi). At 23 years 7 months, Ullrich was the youngest cyclist to win the event since 22-year-old Laurent Fignon triumphed in 1983.

over Richard Virenque of France (who for the fourth year won the competition for the best mountain climber). It was the greatest winning margin since 1984.

Djamolidin Abdoujaparov of Uzbekistan was disqualified from the Tour after testing positive for the stimulant bromantan and the anabolic steroid clenbuterol following the second stage of the three-week race. Abdoujaparov had won nine stages of the Tour over the years and had won the points competition on three occasions.

The world track championships were held in Perth, Australia, in August. France dominated the competition, winning six gold medals and setting a world record of 44.926 sec in the three-man Olympic sprint over 750 m (2,460 ft). Felicia Ballanger won both the women's sprint and the 500-m time trial for the third successive year. Jean-Pierre Van Zyl became the first South African cyclist to win a world championship medal since his country's return to international competition when he finished second in the keirin.

The world road championships took place in San Sebastián, Spain, in October. Laurent Brochard was an unexpected winner of the men's road race for France, which also won the individual time trial with Laurent Jalabert, the top-ranked road racer in the world on rating points gained for performances throughout the year. (JOHN R. WILKINSON)

EQUESTRIAN SPORTS

Thoroughbred Racing. *United States.* Numerous thoroughbred luminaries were revealed during 1997, but at season's end no one star shone brightest. This left Horse of the Year honours a toss-up among five standouts: the undefeated two-year-old colt Favorite Trick, Kentucky Derby and Preakness Stakes winner Silver Charm, and handicap division rivals Skip Away, Gentlemen, and Formal Gold.

Favorite Trick ended a brilliant freshman campaign on Breeders' Cup Day (November 8) at Hollywood Park in California by scoring a 5½-length victory in the Juvenile, his eighth straight win of an unblemished season. He was ridden by Pat Day, whose nine Breeders' Cup wins and $14,692,600 in purse earnings ranked first among all jockeys in the 14-year history of the event.

Silver Charm held off Captain Bodgit by a head to win the 123rd Kentucky Derby on May 3 at Churchill Downs in Louisville, Ky. The winner was trained by Bob Baffert, who had lost the 1996 "Run for the Roses" when his Cavonnier was beaten by a nose by Grindstone. It was the third Kentucky Derby win in nine years for jockey Gary Stevens, who was elected to thoroughbred racing's Hall of Fame three days before the race.

In the tightest finish in the last 65 runnings of the Preakness Stakes, Silver Charm bested Free House by a head, with Captain Bodgit another head back in third, in the 122nd running of that race, at Pimlico Race Course in Baltimore, Md. A stretch battle for the ages culminated in a pulsating three-horse photo finish. Three weeks later at Belmont Park on Long Island, N.Y., Silver Charm was the first horse in eight years to enter the Belmont Stakes with the opportunity to become the U.S.'s 12th Triple Crown winner. He was thwarted in his bid, however, and finished second by three-quarters of a length to Touch Gold with Chris McCarron aboard. Free House was third. The victory was especially rewarding for Touch Gold, which had finished fourth in the Preakness in spite of going to his knees and nose at the start of the race. Silver Charm was later diagnosed with a blood disorder and missed part of the season.

Skip Away, the 1996 Eclipse Award–winning three-year-old colt, returned in 1997 and wrapped up the year ranked as North America's second leading money-winning thoroughbred of all time, with career earnings of $6,876,360 (Cigar was first with $9,999,813). Skip Away won only four races in 1997 but was never worse than third in his 11 starts. Gentlemen won four of his six starts in 1997, including Grade-I stake triumphs in the Hollywood Gold Cup, Pacific Classic, and Pimlico Special, a race in which he defeated Skip Away. Gentlemen would have been the heavy favourite in the Breeders' Cup Classic but was sidelined with a virus. Formal Gold, which defeated Skip Away in the Woodward Stakes (Grade-I), also was seeking to enhance his record in the Breeders' Cup Classic but was withdrawn nine days before the race with a fracture in his right hind leg.

It was announced in September that Arlington International Racecourse, near Chicago, was withdrawing its request for racing dates in 1998. Arlington owner Richard Duchossois said increased competition from riverboat casinos, regulatory commission restraints, and lack of Illinois state legislative support had created an economic climate too harsh for world-class racing in Chicago to survive. Duchossois had rebuilt the track at a reported cost of $200 million and reopened it in 1989 after a 1985 fire destroyed the original structure.

Silver Charm (centre), ridden by jockey Gary Stevens, edges Captain Bodgit (left) and Free House (right) to win the 122nd Preakness Stakes at Pimlico Race Course in Baltimore, Md., on May 17. Silver Charm was the first horse in eight years to win both the Preakness and the Kentucky Derby.

SUSAN WALSH—ASSOCIATED PRESS

Major Thoroughbred Race Winners, 1997

Race	Won by	Jockey
United States		
Acorn	Sharp Cat	G. Stevens
Apple Blossom	Halo America	C. Borel
Arlington Million	Marlin	G. Stevens
Beldame	Hidden Lake	R. Migliore
Belmont	Touch Gold	C. McCarron
Beverly D.	Memories of Silver	J. Bailey
Breeders' Cup Juvenile	Favorite Trick	P. Day
Breeders' Cup Juvenile Fillies	Countess Diana	S. Sellers
Breeders' Cup Sprint	Elmhurst	C. Nakatani
Breeders' Cup Mile	Spinning World	C. Asmussen
Breeders' Cup Distaff	Ajina	M. Smith
Breeders' Cup Turf	Chief Bearhart	J. Santos
Breeders' Cup Classic	Skip Away	M. Smith
Champagne	Grand Slam	G. Stevens
Charles H. Strub Stakes	Victory Speech	J. Bailey
Cigar Mile Handicap	Devious Course	J.F. Chavez
Coaching Club American Oaks	Ajina	M. Smith
Donn Handicap	Formal Gold	J. Bravo
Eddie Read	Expelled	J.A. Garcia
Florida Derby	Captain Bodgit	A. Solis
Futurity	Grand Slam	G. Stevens
Gulfstream Park Handicap	Mt. Sassafras	J. Bailey
Haskell Invitational	Touch Gold	C. McCarron
Hollywood Derby	Subordination	J. Bailey
Hollywood Futurity	Real Quest	K. Desormeaux
Hollywood Gold Cup	Gentlemen	G. Stevens
Hollywood Turf Cup	River Bay	A. Solis
Hollywood Turf Handicap	Rainbow Dancer	A. Solis
International	Influent	J.-L. Samyn
Jockey Club Gold Cup	Skip Away	J. Bailey
Kentucky Derby	Silver Charm	G. Stevens
Kentucky Oaks	Blushing K.D.	L.J. Meche
Man o' War	Influent	J. Bailey
Matriarch Stakes	Ryafan	A. Solis
Matron	Beautiful Pleasure	J. Bailey
Metropolitan	Langfuhr	J.F. Chavez
Mother Goose	Ajina	M. Smith
Oaklawn Handicap	Atticus	S. Sellers
Oak Tree Turf Championship	Rainbow Dancer	A. Solis
Pacific Classic	Gentlemen	G. Stevens
Pimlico Special	Gentlemen	G. Stevens
Preakness	Silver Charm	G. Stevens
Santa Anita Derby	Free House	K. Desormeaux
Santa Anita Handicap	Siphon	D. Flores
Secretariat	Honor Glide	G. Gomez
Spinster	Clear Mandate	P. Day
Super Derby	Deputy Commander	C. McCarron
Travers	Deputy Commander	C. McCarron
Turf Classic	Val's Prince	M. Smith
Whitney	Will's Way	J. Bailey
Woodward	Formal Gold	K. Desormeaux
England		
One Thousand Guineas	Sleepytime	K. Fallon
Two Thousand Guineas	Entrepreneur	M. Kinane
Derby	Benny The Dip	W. Ryan
Oaks	Reams of Verse	K. Fallon
St. Leger	Silver Patriarch	P. Eddery
Coronation Cup	Singspiel	F. Dettori
Ascot Gold Cup	Celeric	P. Eddery
Eclipse Stakes	Pilsudski	M. Kinane
King George VI and Queen Elizabeth Diamond Stakes	Swain	J. Reid
Sussex Stakes	Ali-Royal	K. Fallon
International Stakes	Singspiel	F. Dettori
Dubayy Champion Stakes	Pilsudski	M. Kinane
France		
Poule d'Essai des Poulains	Daylami	G. Mosse
Poule d'Essai des Pouliches	Always Loyal	F. Head
Prix du Jockey-Club	Peintre Celebre	O. Peslier
Prix de Diane	Vereva	G. Mosse
Prix Royal-Oak	Ebadiyla	G. Mosse
Prix Ganay	Helissio	O. Peslier
Prix Lupin	Cloudings	O. Peslier
Grand Prix de Paris	Peintre Celebre	O. Peslier
Grand Prix de Saint-Cloud	Helissio	C. Asmussen
Prix Vermeille	Queen Maud	O. Peslier
Prix de l'Arc de Triomphe	Peintre Celebre	O. Peslier
Grand Critérium	Second Empire	M. Kinane
Ireland		
Irish Two Thousand Guineas	Desert King	C. Roche
Irish One Thousand Guineas	Classic Park	S. Craine
Irish Derby	Desert King	C. Roche
Irish Oaks	Ebadiyla	J. Murtagh
Irish St. Leger	Oscar Schindler	S. Craine
Irish Champion Stakes	Pilsudski	M. Kinane
Italy		
Derby Italiano	Single Empire	D. Harrison
Gran Premio del Jockey-Club	Caitano	A. Starke
Germany		
Deutsches Derby	Borgia	O. Peslier
Grosser Preis von Baden	Borgia	K. Fallon
Deutschland Preis	Luso	L. Dettori
Europa Preis	Taipan	S. Guillot
United Arab Emirates		
Dubayy World Cup	Singspiel	J. Bailey
Australia		
Caulfield Cup	Might and Power	J. Cassidy
Melbourne Cup	Might and Power	J. Cassidy
Japan		
Japan Cup	Pilsudski	M. Kinane

The Kentucky Derby

Year	Horse	Jockey
1993	Sea Hero	J. Bailey
1994	Go For Gin	C. McCarron
1995	Thunder Gulch	G. Stevens
1996	Grindstone	J. Bailey
1997	**Silver Charm**	**G. Stevens**

The Belmont Stakes

Year	Horse	Jockey
1993	Colonial Affair	J. Krone
1994	Tabasco Cat	P. Day
1995	Thunder Gulch	G. Stevens
1996	Editor's Note	R. Douglas
1997	**Touch Gold**	**C. McCarron**

The Preakness Stakes

Year	Horse	Jockey
1993	Prairie Bayou	M. Smith
1994	Tabasco Cat	P. Day
1995	Timber Country	P. Day
1996	Louis Quatorze	P. Day
1997	**Silver Charm**	**G. Stevens**

Triple Crown Champions—U.S.

Year	Horse
1946	Assault
1948	Citation
1973	Secretariat
1977	Seattle Slew
1978	Affirmed

In March it was revealed that Cigar had proved to be infertile. The two-time Horse of the Year (1995 and 1996) was retired at the end of the 1996 racing season and had been booked to be bred to 71 mares in 1997, his first seaon at stud. Forego, age 27, one of the greatest thoroughbreds of all time and three-time Horse of the Year (1974, 1975, and 1976), had to be put to death after he broke a hind leg in a paddock accident.

Jerry Bailey, winner of the Eclipse Award as the U.S.'s outstanding jockey in 1995 and 1996, had another incredible year in 1997, with more than $17 million in purse earnings. Meanwhile, on August 25 Day became the fifth jockey in racing history to reach the 7,000 plateau in career victories. In November Eddie Arcaro, a legend in the turf world who was regarded by many as the greatest jockey of all time, succumbed to liver cancer at the age of 81. (*See* OBITUARIES.)

(JOHN G. BROKOPP)

International. Singspiel, which ended 1996 with a victory in the world's richest race on turf, the Japan Cup, started 1997 with a triumph in the race offering the richest first prize on dirt, the Dubayy World Cup. He added two important races at home in Great Britain during the summer but suffered a career-ending fracture on November 5, two days before he should have run in the Breeders' Cup Turf. Pilsudski, which had ended 1996 with a 1¼-length defeat of Sing-

2,000 Guineas

Year	Horse	Jockey
1993	Zafonic	P. Eddery
1994	Mister Baileys	J. Weaver
1995	Pennekamp	T. Jarnet
1996	Mark of Esteem	F. Dettori
1997	**Entrepreneur**	**M. Kinane**

The Derby

Year	Horse	Jockey
1993	Commander in chief	M. Kinane
1994	Erhaab	W. Carson
1995	Lammtarra	W.R. Swinburn
1996	Shaamit	M. Hills
1997	**Benny The Dip**	**W. Ryan**

The St. Leger

Year	Horse	Jockey
1993	Bob's Return	P. Robinson
1994	Moonax	P. Eddery
1995	Classic Cliche	L. Dettori
1996	Shantou	F. Dettori
1997	**Silver Patriarch**	**P. Eddery**

Triple Crown Champions—British

Year	Winner
1915	Pommern
1917	Gay Crusader
1918	Gainsborough
1935	Bahram
1970	Nijinsky

Melbourne Cup

Year	Horse	Jockey
1993	Vintage Crop	M. Kinane
1994	Jeune	W. Harris
1995	Doriemus	D. Oliver
1996	Saintly	D. Beadman
1997	**Might and Power**	**J. Cassidy**

The Hambletonian Trot

Year	Horse	Driver
1993	American Winner	R. Pierce
1994	Victory Dream	M. Lachance
1995	Tagliabue	J. Campbell
1996	Continentalvictory	M. Lachance
1997	**Malabar Man**	**M. Burroughs**

spiel in the Breeders' Cup Turf, finished 1997 with a triumph by a neck over Air Groove in the Japan Cup, his fourth success in a Group 1 contest during the year. Singspiel was retired to stud at Newmarket, Eng., while Pilsudski, which had already been sold, was retired to a farm on Hokkaido in Japan.

Both these five-year-olds were trained by Michael Stoute at Newmarket and, after having been slow to reach peak form, showed tremendous consistency over their final two seasons. Peintre Celebre, however, was a more instant champion. He won the Prix du Jockey-Club (French Derby) and Grand Prix de Paris in his fourth and fifth races, respectively. Although Peintre Celebre was beaten—under controversial circumstances—in the Prix Niel after a 12-week absence, he defeated Pilsudski by five lengths in the Prix de l'Arc de Triomphe on October 5; in the process he cut 1.7 sec off the course record and gave his sire, Nureyev, his 100th win in a European Pattern race.

Spinning World, another son of Nureyev, established himself as the best miler in Europe with wins in the Prix Jacques le Marois and Prix du Moulin. He was sparingly raced, however, as his owners, the Niarchos family, had just one aim—to improve on his second-place finish in the 1996 Breeders' Cup Mile, which he did with a two-length victory in the 1997 race.

Helissio started as favourite for the King George VI and Queen Elizabeth Diamond Stakes, but he was not allowed an easy lead, and soft ground further compromised his chance. Swain, third in the 1996 Breeders' Cup Turf behind Pilsudski and Singspiel, scored a surprising victory. He finished one length in front of Pilsudski, followed by Helissio and Singspiel.

Olivier Peslier had ridden Helissio to win the 1996 Arc but was claimed to ride Peintre Celebre in all the colt's races in 1997. Peslier, who went on to be champion jockey in France for the second time, rode Helissio to an impressive victory in the Prix Ganay in April, but he was replaced by Cash Asmussen when the colt won the Grand Prix de Saint-Cloud.

Pat Eddery, an 11-time champion in Britain, became only the third jockey to have ridden 4,000 winners there, reaching that milestone on Silver Patriarch in the St. Leger. The pair had been beaten in the Derby in a photo finish by the America colt Benny The Dip with Willie Ryan aboard.

Aiden O'Brien, champion trainer over jumps each season since he was first licensed in 1993, became the first Irish trainer to send out over 200 winners in a year. His victories included the Irish 1,000 and 2,000 Guineas and the Irish Derby in a season in which Irish horses won all five home classics for the first time since 1964. O'Brien also gained Group 1 victories in England, France, and Ireland with the two-year-olds Saratoga Springs, Second Empire, and King of Kings. Second Empire won the Grand Criterium on a day when, after many horses had been prevented from traveling to the course by a stable workers' demonstration, only two of the scheduled eight races could be run. Heinz Jentzsch, the dominant trainer in Germany for almost 40 years, retired after saddling his 4,024th winner on November 8. Peter Schiergen, who rode a European-record 270 victories in 1995, was on Jentzsch's final winner and then retired to take over his stable.

JULIAN HERBERT—ALLSPORT

In one of the most exciting finishes in the history of Epsom Derby, Benny The Dip (right) holds off Silver Patriarch to win the race on June 7. Ridden by journeyman jockey J.W. Ryan, Kentucky-bred Benny The Dip completed the 2⅖-km (1½-mi) course in a time of 2 min 35.77 sec.

DANIEL HULSHIZER—ASSOCIATED PRESS

Malvern Burroughs celebrates after crossing the finish line with three-year-old Malabar Man to win the Hambletonian, North America's premier harness race, at the Meadowlands in East Rutherford, N.J., on August 9. The 56-year-old Burroughs was the first amateur to win the race since 1948.

In Australia, Might and Power, a four-year-old gelding trained by Jack Denham and ridden by Jim Cassidy, led all the way in both the Caulfield and Melbourne cups. Doriemus, second by seven lengths in the Caulfield Cup and beaten only by a nose, or a "short half head," in the Melbourne Cup, had won both races in 1995.

South African horses were allowed to run abroad for the first time since the 1970s, when a ban had been imposed because of African horse sickness. The first to try elsewhere was London News, successful in the Queen Elizabeth II Cup in Hong Kong in April. Hong Kong racing itself continued with little change after the Chinese takeover in July.

(ROBERT W. CARTER)

Harness Racing. For Malvern Burroughs the dream of winning the big race came true in 1997. In driving his three-year-old trotter Malabar Man to victory in the 1997 Hambletonian, harness racing's greatest classic in North America, the 56-year-old Burroughs achieved special recognition because he was not a professional driver. Instead, he was a businessman who drove his own horses as a hobby and gave his driving fees to charity. In the mid-1970s Burroughs had been a young New Jersey contractor whose firm had won the bid to build a new racetrack called the Meadowlands. He became interested in harness racing and obtained a license to drive in races. In 1981 the Hambletonian was moved to the Meadowlands. After Malabar Man's win, one official said, "Mal, you built this track. Now you own it!"

Malabar Man had taken championship honours as a two-year-old in 1996 and swept through 13 wins in 16 starts in 1997, ending his career with two impressive wins in Italy in early November. His earnings for the season totaled more than $1.4 million. His accomplishments overshadowed the fact that North America had its first Triple Crown winner in 14 years as the three-year-old Western Dreamer swept the Cane Pace, Little Brown Jug, and Messenger Stakes to become the eighth pacing Triple Crown champion. Immediately after his Triple Crown triumph, Western Dreamer was upset in the Breeders Crown in Canada. On that same night, the three-year-old filly Stienam's Place easily won her Breeders Crown race and vaulted into competition as top pacer of 1997.

In Europe the year began with a popular triumph in the Prix d'Amerique, the grueling endurance test contested over 2,700 m (1⅝ mi) near Paris in January. The nine-year-old Abo Volo swept to victory for driver Jos Verbeeck. It was a poignant triumph for the Viel family, owners of Abo Volo, because the family patriarch, Albert Viel, was gravely ill at the time of the race and died a few weeks later.

The fastest trotters in the world gathered at the Solvalla racecourse in Sweden in May to determine which was the best over the 1,600-m (1-mi) distance. The race was touted as a match between the Swedish hero Zoogin and the Norwegian Gentle Star. The traditional rivalry between the two Nordic nations was in full bloom on Elitlopp Day as partisans waved flags and shouted their support. Disaster struck, however, when Zoogin lost a shoe early in his elimination heat, broke stride twice, and was disqualified. Then the crowd groaned in dismay as Gentle Star broke stride at the start of his elimination and failed to qualify for the final. The Elitlopp final was won by Gum Ball, an American-bred horse owned in Sweden, as master horseman Stig Johansson controlled the race from the start.

The Inter-Dominion championships, pitting the best "down under" harness horses, were held at Globe Derby Park in Adelaide, S.Aus., in March, and they furnished Aussie racing fans with unforgettable finishes. The winner of the pacing final was Our Sir Vancelot, driven by Brian Hancock, who held off a fast-closing Rainbow Knight. In the trotting championship the well-traveled New Zealand mare Pride of Petite staged one of the most dramatic stretch drives ever to win in the last possible stride for driver Tony Herlihy. (DEAN A. HOFFMAN)

Steeplechasing. The Irish Republican Army forced the postponement of the 150th Grand National on April 5 by telephoning two coded bomb warnings. It was run two days later, as the only race of the afternoon before a crowd of 20,000. The New Zealand-bred Lord Gyllene led virtually throughout for a 25-length win. Martell increased the prize money and confirmed its continued sponsorship until 2004.

Mr. Mulligan was a surprise winner of the Cheltenham Gold Cup, his first race since falling in the 1996 King George VI Chase, won by One Man, 11 weeks earlier. Al Capone II, the best jumper in France, won his first Grand Steeplechase de Paris in June. In November he won the Prix de la Haye Jousselin for the fifth consecutive year.

Show Jumping and Dressage. Germany, the reigning Olympic and world champions, won the team event at the 1997 European show jumping championships at Mannheim, Ger., the first time it had done so since 1981. Ludger Beerbaum won the individual championship, beating Hugo Simon of Austria on ET. Simon and ET had won all three legs of the Volvo World Cup at Göteborg, Swed., in May. He was the first rider to win this event three times and only the third to win all three legs.

Anky van Grunsven of The Netherlands won the Volvo World Dressage Cup on Bonfire in April but was narrowly, and controversially, beaten by Isabell Werth of Germany and Gigolo in the European dressage championships at Verden, Ger., in August. American rider David O'Connor won the Badminton Horse Trials Three Day Event on Custom Made in May, and New Zealander Mark Todd won the Burghley Trials in September.

(ROBERT W. CARTER)

Polo. In April 1997 Memo Gracida, the new leader of Isla Carroll, won his sixth consecutive and a record 15th career U.S. Open by defeating White Birch in the final at the Palm Beach (Fla.) Polo Club. Isla Carroll also gained the World Cup and the Gold Cup of the Americas, and White Birch won its eighth USPA Gold Cup. Grant's Farm Manor and Peapacton obtained the Sterling and Challenge cups, respectively.

In England, Black Bears won the Warwickshire Cup in Cirencester, and Isla Carroll obtained the Queen's Cup in Windsor. Hubert Perrodo's Labegorce, lining up Gracida's brother Carlos and Javier Novillo Astrada of Argentina, outclassed Isla Carroll in the Gold Cup at Cowdray Park. Labegorce beat Black Bears for the Prince Philip Trophy and returned the Westchester Cup to Great Britain after 83 years as it defeated the U.S. 12–9. In Deauville, France, Ellerston White bested defending champion Labegorce to obtain the Gold Cup.

Segurbier won the Gold Cup in Sotogrande, Spain, beating Scapa in the final, and the local Santa Maria and Belgium's Scapa triumphed in the Silver and Bronze cups, respectively. Jerudong Park, led by the sultan of Brunei's son, lined up cousins Bautista and Eduardo Heguy from Argentina and took the Zobel Cup.

In Argentina, La Baronesa (comprising brothers Sebastian and Pite Merlos, Matias

World Fencing Championships—Men

Year	Individual			Team		
	Foil	Épée	Sabre	Foil	Épée	Sabre
1991	I. Weissenborn (Ger.)	A. Shuvalov (U.S.S.R.)	G. Kirienko (U.S.S.R.)	Cuba	U.S.S.R.	Hungary
1992	P. Omnès (Fr.)	E. Srecki (Fr.)	B. Szabo (Hung.)	Germany	Germany	Unified Team
1993	A. Koch (Ger.)	P. Kolobkov (Russia)	G. Kirienko (Russia)	Germany	Italy	Hungary
1994	R. Tucker (Cuba)	P. Kolobkov (Russia)	F. Becker (Ger.)	Germany	France	Russia
1995	D. Chevtchenko (Russia)	E. Srecki (Fr.)	G. Kirienko (Russia)	Cuba	Germany	Italy
1996	A. Puccini (Italy)	A. Beketov (Russia)	S. Pozdnyakov (Russia)	Russia	Italy	Russia
1997	**S. Golubitsky (Ukr.)**	**E. Srecki (Fr.)**	**S. Pozdnyakov (Russia)**	**France**	**Cuba**	**France**

World Fencing Championships—Women

Year	Individual foil	Team foil	Individual épée	Team épée
1992	G. Trillini (Italy)	Italy	M. Horvath (Hung.)	Hungary
1993	F. Bortolozzi (Italy)	Germany	O. Jermakova (Est.)	Hungary
1994	B. Szabo (Rom.)	Romania	L. Chiesa (Italy)	Spain
1995	L. Badea (Rom.)	Italy	J. Jakimiuk (Pol.)	Hungary
1996	L. Badea (Rom.)	Italy	L. Flessel (Fr.)	France
1997	**G. Trillini (Italy)**	**Italy**	**M. Garcia-Soto (Cuba)**	**Hungary**

Eric Srecki of France (left) parries an attack by Russia's Pavel Kolobkov en route to winning the men's individual épée final at the world fencing championships in Cape Town. Srecki's triumph added to French victories in the team foil and team sabre competitions.

MacDonough, and Tommy Fernández Llorente), won the Los Indios Tortugas Open. Ellerstina (Adolfo Cambiaso, Mariano Aguerre, Gonzalo Pieres, and Lolo Castagnola) captured the most important tournament in the world, the Argentine Open, for the second time. Both quartets had to define the Hurlingham Open, but the match, after many suspensions, was finally canceled because of rain.

(JORGE ADRIÁN ANDRADES)

FENCING

During the 1997 world championships in July in Cape Town, René Roch, president of the Fédération Internationale d'Escrime (FIE—the international governing body of fencing) announced changes designed to simplify the sport and make it more interesting for television viewers and nonexperts while retaining the essence of the game. The most important changes involved the establishment of World Cup circuit team events, the introduction of the transparent mask, and the use of wireless scoring. Additionally, women's sabre became an official event.

The transparent mask had been undergoing development for several years in various countries. An acceptable design emerged from the U.S. manufacturer Zivkovic Modern Fencing Equipment, Inc., and it was authorized for use on the World Cup circuit as of Jan. 1, 1998. A decision on wireless scoring was expected late in 1997. Wireless scoring employed a device that eliminated the need for trailing wires and should result in fewer equipment failures.

The World Cup team circuit was considered necessary for fencing to become more popular throughout the world. The proposed circuit would include all the best teams in the world but would also ensure representation from all continents.

In the world championships France was the most successful, gaining victories in the individual men's épée, team sabre, and team men's foil and earning four bronze medals for a total of seven. Italy and Cuba followed with two championships apiece; Italy triumphed in the individual and team women's foil, and Cuba finished first in the women's individual épée and men's team épée.

(GRAHAM MORRISON)

FIELD HOCKEY

A new annual event, the World Hockey Series, that was to have been launched for men in November 1997 was postponed indefinitely in September for the want of sponsorship and television support. International competition on a continental basis was planned initially at four venues, the winners gaining eligibility to play, along with several automatic qualifiers, in the second round at three other sites. The three survivors from this round were scheduled to appear, along with the host nation, in a final four-nation competition at a new venue. Unfortunately, only 34 of the 119 countries affiliated with the Fédération Internationale de Hockey (FIH) expressed interest in participating, and the refusal by some leading nations, notably The Netherlands, to play in the inaugural event hastened a period of reappraisal.

Despite the FIH's efforts to make field hockey more attractive by changing its laws, the world's television networks remained unconvinced. The experimental no-offside rule that came into force in August 1996 was extended for another year, although at the international level the expected harvest of goals did not materialize. Another change in the rules aimed at inducing both men and women to score more goals was introduced on Sept. 1, 1997. A penalty corner awarded at the end of each period of play had to be completed even if time ran out.

For the 2000 Olympic Games at Sydney, Australia, England was given the right to stage the qualifying tournament for women. The number of participating teams was increased from 8 to 10. The men's qualifying tournament was assigned to Osaka, Japan, where eight teams would be in contention.

Australia, the World Cup holder and defending Olympic champion, continued to dominate the women's game by winning the Champions Trophy at Berlin—in a 2–1 victory over Germany—for the fourth successive time in June 1997. The tables were turned in October when Germany beat Australia 3–2 in the men's Champions Trophy final held in Australia. (SYDNEY E. FRISKIN)

World Cup Field Hockey Championship—Men

Year	Winner	Runner-up
1986	Australia	England
1990	The Netherlands	Pakistan
1994	Pakistan	The Netherlands

World Cup Field Hockey Championship—Women

Year	Winner	Runner-up
1986	The Netherlands	West Germany
1990	The Netherlands	Australia
1994	Australia	Argentina

FOOTBALL

Association Football (Soccer). *Europe.* While qualification for the finals of the 1998 World Cup in France occupied the attention of the majority of the 197 member nations of the Fédération Internationale de Football Association (FIFA), the escalation of transfer fees continued despite the so-called Bosman ruling in 1995, which allowed players not under contract to change teams freely. The move of Brazilian striker Ronaldo Luiz Nazario de Lima, known as Ronaldo (*see* BIOGRAPHIES), from Barcelona (Spain) to Internazionale of Italy created protracted and complicated issues. Although it seemed that the original deal would cost a world-record £17 million, investigations by FIFA revealed that the player, or those acting for him, had bought out his employment contract with the Spanish club. Under FIFA rules, however, this did not constitute a formal transfer fee, and Ronaldo was allowed to join Internazionale while the two clubs involved discussed the financial arrangements, which increased the final cost to £18.2 million.

FIFA World Cup				
Year	**Result**			
1986	Argentina	3	West Germany	2
1990	West Germany	1	Argentina	0
1994	Brazil*	0	Italy	0

*Won on penalty kicks.

In a bid to replace Ronaldo, Barcelona spent £29 million on two other Brazilians, Vito Barbosa Ferreira Rivaldo, a midfielder from Deportivo La Coruna (£16 million), and Sonny Anderson da Silva, a striker from the French club Monaco (£13 million). Real Betis of Seville, Spain, agreed to pay £21.4 million for the services of Denilson de Oliveira, a 20-year-old midfielder from São Paulo, Braz., even though he would not be able to play for the Spanish club until after the 1998 World Cup finals.

In the three major European cup competitions, German clubs won the European Cup of Champion Clubs and the Union des Associations Européenes de Football (UEFA) Cup, while Barcelona took the Cup-Winners' Cup. At Munich on May 28, in the Champions League Cup final, the culmination of the European Cup, Borussia Dortmund, in its first appearance in the final, gained a surprising 3–1 victory over much-favoured Juventus of Italy. Ironically, four members of the German team had played previously for Juventus. The Italians dominated the opening exchanges as had been predicted, initially revealing superior skill. Dortmund withstood the onslaught, however, and took the lead in the 29th minute when Juventus goalkeeper Angelo Peruzzi was unable to clear Andy Moller's left-wing corner properly. Paul Lambert returned the ball to the far post, where Karlheinz Riedle, arguably standing offside, chested it down and drove hard into the net. Five minutes later it was 2–0, and the game appeared to be drifting away from the Italians. Following another corner from Moller, Riedle headed in from the near post, having told colleagues the day before the match that he had had a dream of scoring twice. Back came Juventus, but it was denied a goal when Christian Vieri's score was disallowed because he handled the ball. Tactical substitutions brought the Italians back into contention in the second half. Alen Boksic turned the Dortmund defense on the left, and substitute Alessandro Del Peiro scored from close range in the 64th minute. Coach Marcello Lippi might have put Juventus back in with a chance of saving the match, but his opposite number, Ottmar Hitzfeld, topped it with a double replacement that produced instant results. Lars Ricken had been on the field just 16 seconds when he lobbed Peruzzi from 27.4 m (30 yd) to restore Dortmund's two-goal advantage in the 71st minute.

In the Cup-Winners' Cup final at Rotterdam, Neth., on May 14, Barcelona, making a record 14th appearance in a European final, won the competition for the fourth time by beating the defending champion, Paris St.-Germain, 1–0. While the French hoped they could unsettle their opponents' undoubted rhythm, it proved a vain gesture. When Barcelona's Fernando Couto had a 26th-minute goal disallowed for an infringement, it seemed just a matter of time before his team would take the lead legitimately.

European Cup-Winners' Cup				
Season	**Result**			
1992–93	Parma (Italy)	3	Royal Antwerp	1
1993–94	Arsenal (Eng.)	1	Parma (Italy)	0
1994–95	Real Zaragosa (Spain)	2	Arsenal (Eng.)	1
1995–96	Paris-St. Germain	1	Rapid Vienna	0
1996–97	**Barcelona**	**1**	**Paris-St. Germain**	**0**

European Cup of Champion Clubs				
Season	**Result**			
1992–93	Olympique Marseille	1	AC Milan	0
1993–94	AC Milan	4	Barcelona	0
1994–95	Ajax Amsterdam	1	AC Milan	0
1995–96	Juventus (Italy)*	1	Ajax Amsterdam	1
1996–97	**Borussia Dortmund (Ger.)**	**3**	**Juventus (Italy)**	**1**

*Won on penalty kicks.

Association Football National Champions		
Nation	**League winners**	**Cup winners**
Albania		Partizani
Andorra	Principat	Principat
Argentina	Velez Sarsfield	
Armenia	Pyunik	Ararat Erevan
Austria	Salzburg	Sturm Graz
Azerbaijan	Neftchi Baku	Kopaz
Belarus	MPKC Mozyr	Belshina
Belgium	Lierse	Ekeren
Bolivia	Bolivar	
Brazil	Gremio	Cruzeiro
Bulgaria	CSKA Sofia	CSKA Sofia
Chile	Colo Colo	
Colombia	Deportivo Cali	
Croatia	Croatia Zagreb	Croatia Zagreb
Cyprus	Anorthosis	Apoel
Czech Republic	Sparta Prague	Slavia Prague
Denmark	Brondby	FC Copenhagen
Ecuador	Emelec	
England	Manchester United	Chelsea
Estonia	Lantana	Sadam
Faroe Islands	GI Gotu	GI Gotu
Finland	Jazz Pori	HJK Helsinki
France	Monaco	Nice
Georgia	Dynamo Tbilisi	Dynamo Tbilisi
Germany	Bayern Munich	Stuttgart
Greece	Olympiakos	AEK Athens
Hungary	MTK Budapest	MTK Budapest
Iceland	IA Akranes	IA Akranes
Ireland	Derry City	Shelbourne
Israel	Beitar Jerusalem	Hapoel Beersheva
Italy	Juventus	Vicenza
Latvia	Skonto Riga	RAF Yelgava
Liechtenstein	—	Balzers
Lithuania	Kareda	Zalgiris
Luxembourg	Jeunesse Esch	Jeunesse Esch
Macedonia	Sileks	Sileks
Malta	Valletta	Valletta
Moldova	Constructorul	Zimbru Chisinau
Netherlands, The	PSV Eindhoven	Roda Kerkrade
Northern Ireland	Crusaders	Glenavon
Norway	Rosenborg	Tromso
Paraguay	Cerro Porteno	
Peru	Sporting Cristal	
Poland	Widzew Lodz	Legia Warsaw
Portugal	Porto	Boavista
Romania	Steaua	Steaua
Russia	Alania	Lokomotiv Moscow
San Marino	Folgore	Murata
Scotland	Rangers	Kilmarnock
Slovakia	Kosice	Slovan Bratislava
Slovenia	Branik Maribor	Branik Maribor
Spain	Real Madrid	Barcelona
Sweden	IFK Göteborg	AIK Stockholm
Switzerland	Sion	Sion
Turkey	Galatasaray	Kocaelispor
Ukraine	Dynamo Kiev	Donetsk
Uruguay	Penarol	
Venezuela	Minerven	
Wales	Barry Town	Barry Town
Yugoslavia	Partizan Belgrade	Red Star Belgrade

BEN RADFORD—ALLSPORT

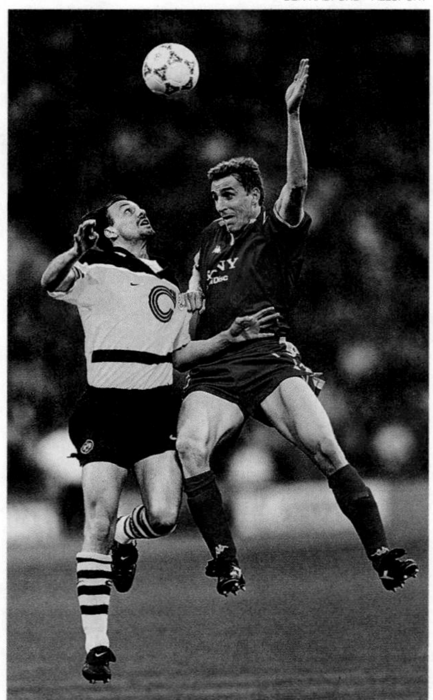

Alen Boksic (right) of Juventus (Italy) outjumps Jürgen Kohler of Borussia Dortmund (Germany) during the Champions League Cup final in May. Dortmund gained a 3–1 victory.

Nine minutes later Barcelona did score. Ivan de la Pena combined with Luis Enrique to send Ronaldo into the penalty area, where the striker was unfairly tackled by Bruno Ngotty. Ronaldo then scored on the resulting penalty kick.

Schalke 04 completed the German double triumph against Italian opposition by beating Internazionale in the UEFA Cup to gain its first trophy in Europe. In the first leg at Gelsenkirchen, Ger., on May 7, a 69th-minute strike by Belgian forward Marc Wilmots from fully 18.3 m (20 yd) gave the Germans a slender lead for the return leg at Milan on May 21. In that contest Internazionale was unable to score until six minutes from the end of regulation time, when Chilean striker Ivan Zamorano connected. With no further addition to the score during the overtime period, a penalty shoot-out decided the outcome. Zamorano was one of two failures for Internazionale from the penalty spot as Schalke won 4–1. Germany completed a remarkable season by winning the European championship for women, beating Italy 2–0 at Oslo on July 12.

For the 1997–98 season a record 188 clubs, representing 48 of UEFA's 51 member associations (only Albania, Bosnia and Herzegovina, and San Marino did not compete), embarked on an expected 439 matches in the three major tournaments. Among the changes made during the year were that the runners-up in the top eight ranking European domestic championships would also compete in the Champion Clubs' Cup and the decision that the final of the UEFA Cup would fall in line with the other two tournaments and stage its final in one match at a neutral venue.

In Bulgaria, CSKA Sofia won both the League and Cup competitions, a feat equaled by Principat (Andorra), Croatia Zagreb (Croatia), GI Gotu (Faroe Islands), MTK Budapest (Hungary), IA Akranes (Iceland), Jeunesse Esch (Luxembourg), Sileks (Macedonia), Valletta (Malta), Steaua (Romania), Branik Maribor (Slovenia), Sion (Switzerland), and Barry Town (Wales). In Georgia, Dynamo Tbilisi achieved its sixth consecutive double triumph. Jeunesse Esch remained unbeaten in its 22 league games, while in Andorra, Spordany Juvenil lost all 22.

In Scotland the Rangers achieved their 47th league championship and their 9th in succession, equaling Celtic's run from 1966 to 1974. The top goal scorer in Europe was Tony Bird of Barry Town with 42 league goals. In contrast to the trading of superstars, Bird was transferred to Swansea City (Wales) for a modest £40,000.

Among several alterations to the Laws of the Game, it was agreed that a goal could be scored directly from the kickoff without another player's having touched the ball and that goalkeepers could not handle a throw-in from one of their own players or hold on to the ball for more than six seconds but could legitimately move their feet when facing a penalty kick.

Qualification matches for the 32 places available in the 1998 World Cup finals included a record score for the competition when Iran beat the Maldives 17–0 on June 2 at Damascus, Syria. Karim Bagheri, with seven goals, also tied the individual record. After the end of hostilities in former Yugoslavia, Bosnia and Herzogovina was allowed to stage matches in Sarajevo, but Albania was forced to play home games in Spain and Switzerland because of civil unrest.

(JACK ROLLIN)

The Americas. The countdown to the World Cup overshadowed Latin-American soccer for the second straight year in 1997. The longest-ever South American qualifying tournament of 16 games per team ended with Argentina, Colombia, Paraguay, and Chile—which would make its first final appearance in 16 years—as qualifiers. In the Central/North American zone, the lengthy qualifying process ended with Mexico, the U.S., and Jamaica—the first-ever finalist from the English-speaking Caribbean—headed for France in 1998.

At the South American Championship (Copa America), played in Bolivia with Central America's Mexico and Costa Rica as guests, many major stars were missing because they were playing in Europe and the clubs were obliged to release them for international duty only a maximum seven times a year. Only Bolivia, Paraguay, and defending World Cup champion Brazil fielded full-strength sides. Brazil, led by World Player of the Year Ronaldo (*see* BIOGRAPHIES), was the winner, as expected, beating Bolivia 3–1 in the final—a final helped by Brazil's playing all its preliminary games in low-lying Santa Cruz and Bolivia's playing all its games in the high altitude of La Paz. Brazil continued to look like the best team in the region in a series of friendly internationals played at home and abroad in 1997.

Libertadores de América Cup

Year	Winner (country)	Runner-up (country)	Scores
1993	São Paulo (Braz.)	Universidad Catolica (Chile)	5–1, 0–2
1994	Vélez Sarsfield (Arg.)	São Paulo (Braz.)	1–0, 0–1, 5–3*
1995	Grêmio (Braz.)	Atletico Nacional (Colom.)	3–1, 1–1
1996	River Plate (Arg.)	América (Colom.)	0–1, 2–0
1997	**Cruzeiro (Braz.)**	**Sporting Cristal (Peru)**	**0–0, 1–0**

*Winner determined in penalty shootout after tiebreaking game.

Brazil's Cruzeiro (Belo Horizonte) beat Sporting Cristal of Peru 1–0 on aggregate home and away in the Libertadores de América Cup final for South America's top club teams, but Cruzeiro was beaten by the European champion, Juventus, in the Intercontinental Cup. The Super Cup for past Libertadores Cup winners was won by Argentina's River Plate, the strongest club side in South America. It won its country's 1996–97 season-closing championship and then made it three domestic titles in a row with the 1997–98 opening championship. Brazil's Atletico Mineiro won the minor CONMEBOL Cup after serious fighting between players and spectators at the end of the first leg against Lanus (Argentina).

In the U.S., D.C. United captured its second consecutive major league soccer championship on October 26. United, which finished the regular season with a league-topping 20–11 record, defeated the Colorado Rapids (14–18) 2–1 at Washington's Robert F. Kennedy Stadium before a sellout crowd of 57,431.

(ERIC WEIL)

U.S. Football. *College.* The Universities of Michigan and Nebraska shared the national championship of college football in 1997–98 when voters in the two major polls selected different number one teams for the third time in eight years. As the only two undefeated teams in Division I-A of the National Collegiate Athletic Association (NCAA), Big Ten Conference champion Michigan (12–0) won the writers' poll, and Big 12 champion Nebraska (13–0) narrowly won the coaches' poll.

Michigan finished its season on Jan. 1, 1998, by winning the Rose Bowl 21–16 over Pacific-10 champion Washington State, which made its first trip to the Pasadena, Calif., game in 67 years. Nebraska earned its third championship in four years by defeating Southeastern Conference champion Tennessee (11–2) by a score of 42–17 in the Orange Bowl at Miami, Fla., the next day. The polls agreed on Atlantic Coast Conference champion Florida State (11–1) at number three after the Seminoles led Division I-A in rushing defense with a yield of 51.9 yd per game and bested the Big Ten's Ohio State (10–3) 31–14 in the Sugar Bowl at New Orleans, La. It was the Seminoles' 11th consecutive season in the top four college teams.

The 1997 season was the third in four years that the Rose Bowl's commitment from the Big Ten and Pac-10 champions

U.S. College Football National Champions

Season	Champion
1992–93	Alabama
1993–94	Florida St.
1994–95	Nebraska
1995–96	Nebraska
1996–97	Florida
1997–98	**Michigan*/Nebraska***

*Tied.

MARK J. TERRILL—ASSOCIATED PRESS

Michigan cornerback and Heisman Trophy winner Charles Woodson (2) leaps high in the end zone to intercept a pass from Washington State quarterback Ryan Leaf during the Rose Bowl on Jan. 1, 1998. Michigan defeated Washington State 21–16 to secure its first national championship in 49 years.

prevented a national championship game between the only two major college teams undefeated in the regular season. Beginning with the 1998 season, the Rose Bowl would cooperate with the Orange, Sugar, and Fiesta bowls to ensure a championship game between the two highest-ranked teams in the regular season.

While Michigan won its first national championship since 1948, Wolverine junior cornerback Charles Woodson became the first primarily defensive player ever to win the Heisman Trophy, which was awarded every year to honour the best college football player in the nation. Woodson, who also won the similar but less-prestigious Walter Camp Award, ranked second nationally with seven interceptions, scored two touchdowns with 11 catches as a part-time wide receiver, and scored once as a punt returner. He also won the Chuck Bednarik and Jim Thorpe awards for best defensive player and best defensive back, respectively, as Michigan's defense led the country by allowing only an

Rose Bowl

Season	Result			
1992–93	Michigan	38	Washington	31
1993–94	Wisconsin	21	UCLA	16
1994–95	Penn State	38	Oregon	20
1995–96	Southern California	41	Northwestern	32
1996–97	Ohio State	20	Arizona State	17
1997–98	**Michigan**	**21**	**Washington State**	**16**

Orange Bowl

Season	Result			
1992–93	Florida St.	27	Nebraska	14
1993–94	Florida St.	18	Nebraska	16
1994–95	Nebraska	24	Miami	17
1995–96	Florida St.	31	Notre Dame	26
1996–97	Nebraska	41	Virginia Tech	21
1997–98	**Nebraska**	**42**	**Tennessee**	**17**

Sugar Bowl

Season	Result			
1992–93	Alabama	34	Miami (Fla.)	13
1993–94	Florida	41	West Virginia	7
1994–95	Florida State	23	Florida	17
1995–96	Virginia Tech	28	Texas	10
1996–97	Florida	52	Florida State	20
1997–98	**Florida State**	**31**	**Ohio State**	**14**

Cotton Bowl

Season	Result			
1992–93	Notre Dame	28	Texas A&M	3
1993–94	Notre Dame	24	Texas A&M	21
1994–95	Southern California	55	Texas Tech	14
1995–96	Colorado	38	Oregon	6
1996–97	Brigham Young	19	Kansas State	15
1997–98	**UCLA**	**29**	**Texas A&M**	**23**

RAY STUBBLEBINE—REUTERS

With less than two minutes remaining in Super Bowl XXXII, Denver Broncos running back Terrell Davis (30) darts through a gaping hole in the Green Bay Packers' defensive line to score the game-winning touchdown. Davis was named Most Valuable Player in the Broncos' 31–24 upset of the Packers.

average 8.9 points, 206.9 total yards, and 115.9 passing yards per regular-season game.

Nebraska coach Tom Osborne retired after 25 seasons and a 255–49–3 record, including 60–3–0 in his last five years. The Cornhuskers' offense led the country with per-game averages of 47.1 points, 392.6 rushing yards, and 513.7 total yards. Nebraska was the first team since 1980 with players who won both of the top awards for linemen; the Vince Lombardi/Rotary Award went to defensive end Grant Wistrom, and the Outland Trophy for interior linemen was awarded to guard Aaron Taylor.

Tennessee star quarterback Peyton Manning, the Heisman runner-up who had been considered the favourite to win the award, won the Maxwell Award as player of the year, as well as the Scholar-Athlete Award and the Davy O'Brien National Quarterback Award. Rose Bowl coaches Mike Price of Washington State and Lloyd Carr of Michigan won different Coach of the Year awards, and Grambling State coach Eddie Robinson retired after 57 seasons with a record of 408–165–15, the most victories in college football history.

Other conference winners in Division I-A were Syracuse (9–4) in the Big East, Southern Mississippi (9–3) in Conference USA, Colorado State (11–2) in the Western Athletic, Utah State (6–6) and Nevada (5–6) in the Big West, and Marshall (10–3) in the Mid-American. In Division I-AA, Southwestern Athletic Conference champion Southern University (11–1) won the Heritage Bowl for predominantly black colleges on Dec. 27, 1997, in Atlanta, Ga., 34–28 over South Carolina State (9–3). Other Division I-AA conference champions were Harvard (9–1) in the Ivy League, Villanova (12–1) in the Atlantic 10, Eastern Washington (12–2) in the Big Sky, Western Illinois (11–2) in the Gateway, and Hampton (10–2) in the Mid-Eastern Athletic.

In Division III, 14–0 Mount Union (Ohio) defeated 12–1 Lycoming (Pa.) 61–12. Mount Union earned its second consecutive championship with the country's longest winning streak, 28 games, behind quarterback Bill Borchert, who won the Gagliardi Trophy as the top player in Division III and set all-division career records with 141 regular-season touchdown passes and a 194.08 efficiency rating. The outstanding players in the other divisions were Villanova wide receiver Brian Finneran, who won the Walter Payton Player of the Year Award in Division I-AA, and Bloomsburg University running back Irv Sigler, who was awarded the Harlon Hill Trophy in Division II.

Professional. After four previous Super Bowl losses (three with veteran quarterback John Elway at the helm), the underdog Denver Broncos finally captured the National Football League (NFL) championship, defying the odds and outplaying the defending champion Green Bay Packers, led by quarterback Brett Favre (*see* BIOGRAPHIES), by a score of 31–24 in Super Bowl XXXII on Jan. 25, 1998, in San Diego, Calif. Denver was the first American Football Conference (AFC) champion to win the Super Bowl since the Raiders (then in Los Angeles) in 1984 and only the second wild-card team ever to win it (the Raiders won as a wild card in 1981).

Elway, at age 37 the oldest quarterback ever to win the Super Bowl, passed for only 123 yd, compared with Favre's 256 passing yards, but Denver took advantage of three Green Bay turnovers and a tired Packer defense to put the game away. Broncos running back Terrell Davis, who was named the game's Most Valuable Player (MVP), carried the ball 30 times for 157 yd and three touchdowns (a Super Bowl record), despite being forced to sit out much of the second quarter after a blow to the head left him suffering from a migraine headache.

The Broncos, the first wild-card team even to reach the Super Bowl since the Buffalo Bills in 1992, trounced the Jacksonville Jaguars 42–17 in the wild-card round and slipped past the Kansas City Chiefs 14–10 in the division play-offs. In the AFC championship, Elway passed for two touchdowns with less than two minutes remaining in the first half, and with the help of four forced turnovers in the second half, Denver held on for a 24–21

Super Bowl

	Season	Result			
XXVII	1992–93	Dallas Cowboys (NFC)	52	Buffalo Bills (AFC)	17
XXVIII	1993–94	Dallas Cowboys (NFC)	30	Buffalo Bills (AFC)	13
XXIX	1994–95	San Francisco 49ers (NFC)	49	San Diego Chargers (AFC)	26
XXX	1995–96	Dallas Cowboys (NFC)	27	Pittsburgh Steelers (AFC)	17
XXXI	1996–97	Green Bay Packers (NFC)	35	New England Patriots (AFC)	21
XXXII	**1997–98**	Denver Broncos (AFC)	31	Green Bay Packers (NFC)	24

NFL Final Standings, 1997

AMERICAN CONFERENCE

Eastern Division	W	L	T	Central Division	W	L	T	Western Division	W	L	T
*New England	10	6	0	*Pittsburgh	11	5	0	*Kansas City	13	3	0
*Miami	9	7	0	*Jacksonville	11	5	0	*Denver	12	4	0
New York Jets	9	7	0	Tennessee	8	8	0	Seattle	8	8	0
Buffalo	6	10	0	Cincinnati	7	9	0	Oakland	4	12	0
Indianapolis	3	13	0	Baltimore	6	9	1	San Diego	4	12	0

NATIONAL CONFERENCE

Eastern Division	W	L	T	Central Division	W	L	T	Western Division	W	L	T
*New York Giants	10	5	1	*Green Bay	13	3	0	*San Francisco	13	3	0
Washington	8	7	1	*Tampa Bay	10	6	0	Carolina	7	9	0
Philadelphia	6	9	1	*Detroit	9	7	0	Atlanta	7	9	0
Dallas	6	10	0	*Minnesota	9	7	0	New Orleans	6	10	0
Arizona	4	12	0	Chicago	4	12	0	St. Louis	5	11	0

*Qualified for play-offs.

victory over the Pittsburgh Steelers. The Packers, with their third consecutive National Football Conference (NFC) Central Division title, earned a bye in the wild-card play-offs. They beat the Tampa Bay Buccaneers 21–7 in the division play-offs and won the NFC championship 23–10 over the San Francisco 49ers as Favre passed for 222 yd and one touchdown.

The Packers were one of three teams to repeat as division winners. The Steelers won their fourth consecutive title in the AFC Central, and the New England Patriots took their second in a row in the AFC East. The New York Giants won the NFC East for the first time since 1990, and the Buccaneers ended a 15-year absence from the play-offs by earning one of the wild-card berths for the top three division runners-up in each conference. None of the other 10 play-off teams had missed postseason play for more than one year.

The New York Jets' eight-game improvement to 9–7 tied the biggest in NFL history, whereas the Indianapolis Colts had the worst decline, six games to 3–13. The Giants improved by 4½ games and played in one of the league's two tie games, its first since 1989. The Dallas Cowboys' six-year streak of play-off appearances ended, and the Steelers and 49ers were left with league-high streaks of six apiece. The Bills missed the play-offs for only the second time in 10 seasons.

The 1997–98 season was characterized by resurgent rushing attacks, with the most yards on the ground since 1988. Players rushed seven times for at least 200 yd in a game, the most in NFL history, and 121 times for at least 100 yd, the most since the NFL's 1970 merger with the American Football League. Corey Dillon of the Cincinnati Bengals ran for 246 yd in a December 4 game against the Tennessee Oilers, breaking the rookies' record that Jim Brown had set 40 years earlier. Detroit Lions running back Barry Sanders, who shared the regular-season MVP award with Favre, became the third player to run for at least 2,000 yd in a season when he led the league with 2,053. Sanders also reached a career total of 13,319 yd and became the second leading rusher in NFL history, behind Walter Payton.

The NFL's leading offensive teams were the Broncos, with 29.5 points and 367 total yards per game; Pittsburgh, with 154.9 rushing yards; and the Seattle Seahawks, with 247.4 passing yards behind 41-year-old quarterback Warren Moon. Detroit led the NFC in rushing and total yards, and Green Bay led the conference in passing yards. Pittsburgh also had the best defense against the run, allowing only 82.4 yd per game. Defensive tackle Dana Stubblefield won the Defensive Player of the Year award for San Francisco, which led the NFC in rushing defense, and Denver and Indianapolis led the AFC in total defense and pass defense, respectively. John Randle was the first defensive tackle ever to lead the NFL in sacks, with 15.5 for the Minnesota Vikings, and Ryan McNeil led the league with 9 interceptions for the St. Louis Rams.

The Lions' Herman Moore caught more than 100 passes for a record third consecutive season and tied Oakland Raider Tim Brown for the NFL lead, with 104 receptions. Other receiving leaders were Rob Moore, with 1,584 yd for the Arizona Cardinals; Cris Carter, with 13 touchdowns for the Vikings; and Pittsburgh's Yancey Thigpen, with 17.7 yd per catch. Tennessee's Ronnie Harmon became the first back to gain more than 6,000 yd receiving in his career.

Steve Young of San Francisco led NFL passers for the sixth time in seven seasons with a 104.7 passer rating and also led with 8.5 yd per pass attempt. Oakland's Jeff George passed for a league-best 3,917 yd, and Indianapolis's Jim Harbaugh's four interceptions for the Colts gave him a 1.3 interception percentage, the NFL's lowest. Denver's Super Bowl hero, Davis, also led the AFC for the season with 1,750 yd rushing, and his 15 touchdown runs tied for the NFL lead with the Miami Dolphins' Karim Abdul-Jabbar, who led the league with 16 total touchdowns. Kicker Mike Hollis of Jacksonville led NFL scorers with 134 points.

(KEVIN M. LAMB)

Canadian Football. The Toronto Argonauts became the first Canadian Football League (CFL) team since 1982 to win two consecutive championships when they defeated the Saskatchewan Roughriders 47–23 in the Grey Cup at Edmonton, Alta., on Nov. 16, 1997. Toronto quarterback Doug Flutie, the game's Most Valuable Player (MVP), was superb, completing 30 of 38 passes attempted for 352 yd and scoring three touchdowns passing and one running. He also won the regular season's MVP award for the sixth time in seven years. Flutie led CFL passers with 47 touchdowns, 5,505 total yards, and a 97.8 efficiency rating.

Toronto, which won the Eastern Division with a 15–3 record, featured league leaders Robert Drummond, with 18 touchdowns; Mike Clemons, with 122 catches; and Mike Vanderjagt, with 190 points scored. Saskatchewan was only 8–10 in the regular season, tied for third behind the Western Division winners, the Edmonton Eskimos (12–6).

Edmonton linebacker Willie Pless was the league's top defensive player for the fourth consecutive season. Other Toronto award winners were centre Mike Kiselak, the top offensive lineman, and slotback Derrell Mitchell, the top rookie and a league leader with 17 touchdown catches. British Columbia Lions running back Sean Millington was voted the top Canadian player, and Calgary Stampeders kicker Mark McLoughlin won the Tom Pate Award for sportsmanship. Milt Stegall of the Winnipeg Blue Bombers led the league with 1,616 yd receiving; the Montreal Alouettes' Mike Pringle had a league-topping 1,775 yd rushing; and Montreal's Elfrid Payton had 14 sacks.

(KEVIN M. LAMB)

Australian Football. Adelaide FC won its first premiership in the Australian Football League (AFL) in 1997—in its seventh season in the competition. A crowd of 99,645 packed into the Melbourne Cricket Ground and saw Adelaide come from behind to defeat St. Kilda. Adelaide, in its first grand final, won the match 19.11 (125) to 13.16 (94) to become only the second club from outside Victoria to have won the title (West Coast won in 1992 and 1994). St. Kilda, the crowd favourite, was in its first grand final since 1971 and was seeking its first premiership since 1966. The victory was a triumph for Malcolm Blight, in his first season as Adelaide's coach, who had tasted bitter grand final defeat three times as coach of Geelong (1989, 1992, and 1994).

It was a record-breaking 101st season for the AFL, with attendances, club membership, and television ratings all reaching new marks. A total of 5,842,591 watched the 176 first-round games and a further 560,406 the eight finals, for a grand total of 6,402,997. This bettered the 5,694,960 of the 1996 season. Port Adelaide played its first season in the AFL and fared brilliantly, narrowly missing the finals. It replaced Fitzroy, which merged with Brisbane. Footscray had a name change and became known as the Western Bulldogs.

The major award winners for the year were: Brownlow Medal (awarded to the best and fairest player in the competition), Robert Harvey of St. Kilda; Norm Smith Medal (for best player in the grand final), Andrew McLeod of Adelaide; Coleman Medal (given to the leading goalkicker in home and away rounds), Tony Modra of Adelaide, with 81. Several of the game's greats retired after the 1997 season, including Stephen Kernahan and Greg Williams (both of Carlton), Gary Ablett (Geelong), and Chris Langford and John Platten (both Hawthorn).

(GREG HOBBS)

Rugby Football. In 1997 Rugby Union was all about one side—the New Zealand All Blacks—as they became possibly the best-ever Union team. Two years after losing the Rugby Union World Cup in 1995, the All Blacks had become the undisputed "unofficial" champions, a title they gained without Jonah Lomu, perhaps the world's best player. Lomu was out for most of the 1997 season with a rare kidney disease, but even without him the All Blacks defeated the world's second and third best sides, South Africa and Australia, home and away, to win their second successive Tri-Nations championship. Defeat for South Africa and Australia in the Tri-Nations caused both nations to part company with their national coaches, Greg Smith and Carel du Plessis, respectively.

AFL Final Standings, 1997
(League ladder after round 22)

Team*	W	L	D	Points
St. Kilda	15	7	0	60
Geelong	15	7	0	60
Western Bulldogs	14	8	0	56
Adelaide	13	9	0	52
West Coast	13	9	0	52
Sydney	12	10	0	48
North Melbourne	12	10	0	48
Brisbane	10	11	1	42

*Teams that qualified for play-offs.

Grey Cup

Year	Result			
1993	Edmonton Eskimos (WFC)	33	Winnipeg Blue Bombers (EFC)	23
1994	British Columbia Lions (WFC)	26	Baltimore Stallions (EFC)	23
1995	Baltimore Stallions (SD)	37	Calgary Stampeders (ND)	20
1996	Toronto Argonauts (ED)	43	Edmonton Eskimos (WD)	37
1997	**Toronto Argonauts (ED)**	**47**	**Saskatchewan Roughriders (WD)**	**23**

SIMON BAKER—REUTERS

During a Tri-Nations rugby match held in Dunedin, N.Z., on August 16, Taine Randell (with ball) of the New Zealand All Blacks scores despite an attempt by Australia's James Holbeck to tackle him. The All Blacks won by a score of 36–24 to secure their second consecutive Tri-Nations championship.

Not content with domination in Test matches, New Zealand also had the world's best club team in 1997. The Auckland Blues won the Super 12 championship for the second successive year.

Great Britain thought it had produced world beaters when the Lions, which had lost 2–1 to the All Blacks in 1993, beat South Africa in South Africa 2–1 in a historic series. The series was won in dramatic fashion in Durban with a drop goal (three points) from English centre Jeremy Guscott in the dying minutes. The Lions—a team made up of the best from England, Scotland, Wales, and Ireland—had never played in the World Cup, but with the gulf between the Southern and Northern Hemisphere sides growing every season, many commentators felt that it was the only Northern team that could compete with New Zealand, South Africa, and Australia. England lost to Australia in the summer, the match before England coach Jack Rowell resigned and was replaced by former international competitor Clive Woodward.

In the Five Nations championship, France took the title and the Grand Slam with a perfect record in its four matches, scoring 14 tries. Later it was announced that Italy would be welcomed into rugby's oldest tournament in 2000.

Money was a factor with English clubs in 1997. Even though the clubs were losing money, Va'aiga Tuigamala of Western Samoa became the first £1 million player when he moved from Wigan (a Rugby League team) to the Newcastle Falcons. England's Will Carling retired from international competition after the Five Nations to concentrate on his club, the Harlequins, and a career in the media. In December, however, Carling broke his hand, which put him on the sidelines and led to some speculation that his playing days might soon be over.

Australian teams dominated Rugby League during the year. The Brisbane Broncos captured both the Super League Telstra Cup with a 26–8 win over the Cronulla Sharks in September and the World Club Challenge, defeating the Hunter Mariners 36–12 in October. Meanwhile, the Australian national side beat Great Britain in two out of three Test matches and split with New Zealand, winning the Anzac Day Test 34–22 and then losing the second Test 30–12. France drew with Ireland 30–30 but edged past Scotland 22–20. (PAUL MORGAN)

Five Nations Championship

Year	Result
1993	France
1994	Wales
1995	England*
1996	England
1997	**France***

Rugby Union World Cup

Year	Result			
1987	New Zealand	29	France	9
1991	Australia	12	England	6
1995	South Africa	15	New Zealand	12

Rugby League World Cup

Year	Result			
1975*	Australia†			
1977*	Australia	13	Great Britain	12
1988	Australia	25	New Zealand	12
1992	Australia	10	Great Britain	6
1995	Australia	16	England	8

*Called International Championship from 1975 to 1977.
†Championships played without a grand final match; England was the runner-up.

Record of International Test Matches 1871 to Aug. 31, 1997

	England Wins	England Draws	England Losses	Scotland Wins	Scotland Draws	Scotland Losses	Ireland Wins	Ireland Draws	Ireland Losses	Wales Wins	Wales Draws	Wales Losses	British Isles* Wins	British Isles* Draws	British Isles* Losses
England v.	—	—	—	58	17	39	64	8	38	43	12	48	—	—	—
Scotland v.	39	17	58	—	—	—	58	1	45	44	2	55	—	—	—
Ireland v.	38	8	64	45	1	58	—	—	—	37	6	58	—	—	—
Wales v.	48	12	43	55	2	44	58	6	37	—	—	—	—	—	—
British Isles* v.	—	—	—	—	—	—	—	—	—	—	—	—	—	—	—
South Africa v.	8	1	4	6	0	3	8	1	1	9	1	0	19	4	10
New Zealand v.	14	0	4	18	2	0	12	1	0	13	0	3	23	2	6
Australia v.	13	0	7	8	0	7	11	0	6	11	0	8	2	0	8
France v.	27	7	40	34	3	32	41	5	25	30	3	38	—	—	—

	South Africa Wins	South Africa Draws	South Africa Losses	New Zealand Wins	New Zealand Draws	New Zealand Losses	Australia Wins	Australia Draws	Australia Losses	France Wins	France Draws	France Losses
England v.	4	1	8	4	0	14	7	0	13	40	7	27
Scotland v.	3	0	6	0	2	18	7	0	8	32	3	34
Ireland v.	1	1	8	0	1	12	6	0	11	25	5	41
Wales v.	0	1	9	3	0	13	8	0	11	38	3	30
British Isles* v.	10	4	19	6	2	23	8	0	2	—	—	—
South Africa v.	—	—	—	22	3	22	24	0	11	16	5	5
New Zealand v.	22	3	22	—	—	—	70	5	27	24	0	8
Australia v.	11	0	24	27	5	70	—	—	—	10	2	13
France v.	5	5	16	8	0	24	13	2	10	—	—	—

*The British Isles ("British Lions") is a combined team from the four "Home Unions" (England, Ireland, Scotland, and Wales).

GOLF

A new word entered the golfing lexicon in 1997: *Tigermania.* No player in the long history of the game had attracted publicity to the extent that Eldrick ("Tiger") Woods (*see* BIOGRAPHIES) did in his first full year as a professional. And the sport smiled all the way to the bank.

The arrival on the scene of the young Californian helped to produce an explosion of interest. According to figures released by the Associated Press, ticket sales at the tournaments he played were up 25%, souvenir sales were up 20%, and American television audiences for the final day of the four major championships (the Masters, U.S. Open, British Open, and U.S. Professional Golfers' Association of America [PGA] championship) increased by nearly 60%. Golf apparel and footwear sales for his main sponsor, Nike, improved 100% to $120 million in the fiscal year ended May 31, which made the five-year, $40 million contract the company signed with Woods when he left the amateur ranks in August 1996 appear a bargain.

The PGA TOUR organization in the United States, meanwhile, concluded talks with the major television networks with deals that would produce a doubling of income for the organization to $650 million over four years. "We believe golf is at the beginning of an unprecedented growth cycle," stated the tour's commissioner, Tim Finchem. "The substantial investment our television partners have made in the future of the game will enable us to assist the World Golf Foundation in building facilities that will serve as entry points for kids to be introduced to the game. Right now only 2% of kids between the ages of 12 and 17 are involved in the game. We need to change that."

STEVE MUNDAY—ALLSPORT

Eldrick ("Tiger") Woods celebrates after sinking a putt on the 18th hole of the Augusta (Ga.) National golf course to clinch victory in the Masters Tournament. Woods earned the coveted green champion's jacket after producing rounds of 70, 66, 65, and 69 for a total of 270—the lowest in Masters history.

To act as the catalyst for all this, Woods had to recapture as a professional the success he had enjoyed as an amateur (three successive U.S. Junior Amateur titles followed by three successive U.S. Amateur titles). After winning two of his first eight professional events in 1996, he began 1997 with another victory in the Mercedes championship at La Costa Resort and Spa, in Carlsbad, Calif., and then produced the single most outstanding performance of the entire season in the Masters at the Augusta (Ga.) National Golf Club. In what was his first major championship as a professional, Woods produced rounds of 70, 66, 65, and 69 for an 18-under-par total of 270—the lowest aggregate in Masters history. His 12-stroke winning margin over fellow American Tom Kite was also a record, and he was the youngest champion of one of the four major tournaments in 66 years.

Easily the longest hitter in the event (John Daly was not competing), Woods was so dominant that inevitably talk turned to whether he could become the first player ever to win all four majors in one season, especially when he won his next tournament as well, the GTE Byron Nelson Classic in Irving, Texas. It did not happen; in fact, Woods never even came close in the other three. He did, however, become the first player to win more than $2 million in one season on the PGA tour, and he also enjoyed

British Open Tournament (men)

Year	Winner
1993	G. Norman (Austl.)
1994	N. Price (Zimb.)
1995	J. Daly (U.S.)
1996	T. Lehman (U.S.)
1997	**J. Leonard (U.S.)**

United States Open Championship (men)

Year	Winner
1993	L. Janzen (U.S.)
1994	E. Els (S.Af.)
1995	C. Pavin (U.S.)
1996	S. Jones (U.S.)
1997	**E. Els (S.Af.)**

Masters Tournament

Year	Winner
1993	B. Langer (Ger.)
1994	J. Olazábal (Spain)
1995	B. Crenshaw (U.S.)
1996	N. Faldo (U.K.)
1997	**T. Woods (U.S.)**

U.S. Professional Golfers' Association (PGA) Championship

Year	Winner
1993	P. Azinger (U.S.)
1994	N. Price (Zimb.)
1995	S. Elkington (Austl.)
1996	M. Brooks (U.S.)
1997	**D. Love III (U.S.)**

British Amateur Championship (men)

Year	Winner
1993	I. Pyman (U.K.)
1994	L. James (U.K.)
1995	G. Sherry (U.K.)
1996	W. Bladon (U.K.)
1997	**C. Watson (U.K.)**

United States Amateur Championship (men)

Year	Winner
1993	J. Harris (U.S.)
1994	T. Woods (U.S.)
1995	T. Woods (U.S.)
1996	T. Woods (U.S.)
1997	**M. Kuchar (U.S.)**

Women's British Open Championship

Year	Winner
1993	K. Lunn (Austl.)
1994	L. Neumann (Swed.)
1995	K. Webb (Austl.)
1996	E. Klein (U.S.)
1997	**K. Webb (Austl.)**

Ladies' British Amateur Championship

Year	Winner
1993	C. Lambert (U.K.)
1994	E. Duggleby (U.K.)
1995	J. Hall (U.K.)
1996	K. Kuehne (U.S.)
1997	**A. Rose (U.K.)**

United States Women's Open Championship

Year	Winner
1993	L. Merten (U.S.)
1994	P. Sheehan (U.S.)
1995	A. Sorenstam (Swed.)
1996	A. Sorenstam (Swed.)
1997	**A. Nicholas (U.K.)**

United States Women's Amateur Championship

Year	Winner
1993	J. McGill (U.S.)
1994	W. Ward (U.S.)
1995	K. Kuehne (U.S.)
1996	K. Kuehne (U.S.)
1997	**S. Cavalleri (Italy)**

Ladies' Professional Golf Association (LPGA) Championship

Year	Winner
1993	P. Sheehan (U.S.)
1994	L. Davies (U.K.)
1995	K. Robbins (U.S.)
1996	L. Davies (U.K.)
1997	**C. Johnson (U.S.)**

a short spell at the top of the official world golf ranking. During the year Tom Lehman of the U.S. and Ernie Els of South Africa also reached that pinnacle, but for most of the season, Greg Norman led the rankings. The Australian did not win a major, but he took the $1 million first prize at the Andersen Consulting world championship and two PGA tour titles.

Els won the U.S. Open at the Congressional Country Club in Bethesda, Md. It was his second victory in the championship in four years, and, as in 1994, Scotland's Colin Montgomerie finished second. Tied with two holes to play, Montgomerie scored a bogey five on the 17th and lost by a single shot to Els's four-under-par total of 276.

The British Open was staged at the Royal Troon Golf Club in Troon, Scot. With a round to go, Sweden's Jesper Parnevik led Northern Ireland's Darren Clarke by two shots and Americans Fred Couples and Justin Leonard by five. With six holes remaining, Parnevik was still two ahead, but now of Leonard, and at the end he could not hold off the 25-year-old Texan, a former U.S. Amateur champion. Leonard scored a closing 65 to Parnevik's 73 and won by three with a 12-under-par aggregate of 272.

The PGA championship at Winged Foot Golf Club in Mamaronek, N.Y., also resulted in an American's winning his first major. Leonard was prominent again, and after three rounds he and Davis Love III were tied for the lead, seven strokes ahead of the rest of the field. This time, however, Love conquered all. His last round, 66 for an 11-under-par total of 269, was five better than Leonard could manage.

With major winners Woods, Leonard, and Love on the team, the United States was favoured to regain the Ryder Cup, held on continental Europe for the first time, at Valderrama Golf Club in southern Spain. For the second successive year, however, Europe won by the narrowest possible margin, 14½–13½. After Europe took a five-point lead into the 12 concluding singles, the Americans staged a comeback, but they had too much ground to cover. Germany's Bernhard Langer made sure that Europe gained a tie in the tournament and therefore retained the trophy by beating Brad Faxon, and on the final green of the final game, Montgomerie secured Europe's victory in the match by halving with Scott Hoch. Montgomerie was the top points scorer, with 3½ out of a possible 5, while Love lost all his four games. Leonard halved two and lost two, and Woods finished with one win, one half, and three defeats.

Montgomerie and Langer were the most consistent performers on the PGA European tour. The German won four times to Montgomerie's two, but the Scot nevertheless won a record fifth successive Order of Merit title. He earned £798,947 to Langer's £692,398. Special mention should also be made of ninth-placed José-María Olazábal, who returned in February after nearly 18 months out with an injury. The former U.S. Masters champion had been diagnosed as suffering from rheumatoid arthritis in his feet, but a German physician believed a herniated disc in his lower back was the cause of his problems and gave Olazábal an exercise program. Five months later he was playing tournament golf again, winning a tournament and regaining his Ryder Cup place.

Woods finished the PGA tour with $2,066,833, just under $200,000 more than David Duval, who after seven second-place finishes in his career suddenly had three successive victories at the end of the season, climaxing in the tour championship at the Champions Golf Club near Houston, Texas. The men who achieved the most wins and earned the most official money during 1997, however, were Hale Irwin and Gil Morgan on the PGA Senior tour. Irwin tied the tour record for most titles with nine and won $2,343,364, whereas Morgan won six and finished with $2,160,562. Tommy Horton retained his position as leading money winner on the European Seniors tour, although Gary Player of South Africa won the Senior British Open at Royal Portrush Golf Club, Portrush, N.Ire.

Walker Cup (men; amateur)	
Year	**Result**
1989	Britain and Ireland 12½, United States 11½
1991	United States 14, Britain and Ireland 10
1993	United States 19, Britain and Ireland 5
1995	Britain and Ireland 14, United States 10
1997	**United States 18, Britain and Ireland 6**

World Cup (men; professional)	
Year	**Winner**
1993	United States (F. Couples and D. Love III)
1994	United States (F. Couples and D. Love III)
1995	United States (F. Couples and D. Love III)
1996	South Africa (E. Els and W. Westner)
1997	**Ireland (P. Harrington and P. McGinley)**

Curtis Cup (women; amateur)	
Year	**Result**
1988	Britain and Ireland 11, United States 7
1990	United States 14, Britain and Ireland 4
1992	Britain and Ireland 10, United States 8
1994	Britain and Ireland 9, United States 9
1996	Britain and Ireland 11½, United States 6½

Ryder Cup (men; professional)	
Year	**Result**
1989	Europe 14, United States 14
1991	United States 14½, Europe 13½
1993	United States 15, Europe 13
1995	Europe 14½, United States 13½
1997	**Europe 14½, United States 13½**

Justin Leonard follows through on a swing during the final round at the British Open. The 25-year-old Texan scored a closing 65 and won by three strokes with a 12-under-par total of 272.

England's Alison Nicholas lines up a putt during the U.S. Women's Open championship. Nicholas defeated Nancy Lopez (U.S.) by a single shot with a 10-under-par aggregate of 274.

Els narrowly failed in his bid to win the Toyota World Match Play championship for a fourth successive time, losing on the final green of the final round to Fiji's Vijay Singh at the Wentworth (Surrey, Eng.) Club. A week later, however, he linked up with Retief Goosen and David Frost to give South Africa its first victory in the Alfred Dunhill Cup at the Royal and Ancient Golf Club of St. Andrews in Fife, Scot. They beat Sweden 2–1 in the final.

Sweden's Annika Sorenstam scored six victories and earned $1,236,789 in becoming the leading player on the Ladies' Professional Golf Association (LPGA) tour for the second time, but she could not make it three U.S. Women's Open championships in a row. That trophy went to England's Alison Nicholas, who defeated Hall of Famer Nancy Lopez of the U.S. by one shot with a 10-under-par total of 274 at Pumpkin Ridge Golf Club in Cornelius, Ore. Nicholas also finished at the top of the European Women's Tour Order of Merit with £94,589. Karrie Webb of Australia won her second Weetabix Women's British Open at Sunningdale, Berkshire, Eng., by eight strokes over American Rosie Jones with a record-low 19-under total of 269. Webb also came in second among the LPGA money leaders, taking home $987,606.

The U.S. Women's Amateur was won by Silvia Cavalleri of Italy at the Brae Burn Country Club in West Newton, Mass., and the U.S. men's amateur team regained the Walker Cup, beating Great Britain and Ireland 18–6 at Quaker Ridge Golf Club in Scarsdale, N.Y. Matthew Kuchar succeeded Woods as the men's U.S. Amateur champion.

The year saw the death at the age of 84 of Ben Hogan (*see* OBITUARIES), one of golf's greatest-ever exponents. Hogan won the U.S. Open four times, the Masters and the PGA twice each, and the British Open once.

(MARK GARROD)

World Gymnastics Championships—Men				
Year	All-around Team	All-around Individual	Horizontal bar	Parallel bars
1994	China	I. Ivankov (Bela.)	V. Sherbo (Bela.)	Liping Huang (China)
1995	China	Li Xiaoshuang (China)	A. Wecker (Ger.)	V. Sherbo (Bela.)
1996	not held	not held	J. Carballo (Spain)	R. Charipov (Ukr.)
1997	**China**	**I. Ivankov (Bela.)**	**J. Tanskanen (Fin.)**	**Zhang Jinjing (China)**
Year	**Pommel horse**	**Rings**	**Vault**	**Floor exercise**
1994	M. Urzica (Rom.)	Y. Chechi (Italy)	V. Sherbo (Bela.)	V. Sherbo (Bela.)
1995	Li Donghua (Switz.)	Y. Chechi (Italy)	A. Nemov (Russia)* G. Misutin (Ukr.)*	V. Sherbo (Bela.)
1996	Pae Gil Su (N.Kor.)	Y. Chechi (Italy)	A. Nemov (Russia)	V. Sherbo (Bela.)
1997	**V. Belenki (Ger.)**	**Y. Chechi (Italy)**	**S. Fedorchenko (Kazak.)**	**A. Nemov (Russia)**

*Tied.

World Gymnastics Championships—Women			
Year	All-around Team	All-around Individual	Balance beam
1994	Romania	S. Miller (U.S.)	S. Miller (U.S.)
1995	Romania	L. Podkopayeva (Ukr.)	Mo Huilan (China)
1996	not held	not held	D. Kochetkova (Russia)
1997	**Romania**	**S. Khorkina (Russia)**	**G. Gogean (Rom.)**
Year	**Uneven parallel bars**	**Vault**	**Floor exercise**
1994	Li Luo (China)	G. Gogean (Rom.)	D. Kochetkova (Russia)
1995	S. Khorkina (Russia)	S. Amanar (Rom.)* L. Podkopayeva (Ukr.)*	G. Gogean (Rom.)
1996	S. Khorkina (Russia)* Ye. Piskun (Bela.)*	G. Gogean (Rom.)	G. Gogean (Rom.)* Kui Yuanyuan (China)*
1997	**S. Khorkina (Russia)**	**S. Amanar (Rom.)**	**G. Gogean (Rom.)**

*Tied.

PATRICK KOVARIK—AFP

Li Xiaopeng of China performs on the parallel bars during the men's team final at the world gymnastics championships in September. China captured the men's title.

GYMNASTICS

The Fédération Internationale de Gymnastique (FIG), which governs the sport of gymnastics, announced that beginning in 1997 there would no longer be compulsory competition in world championships and the Olympic Games. Only the optional competition, in which each gymnast is allowed to create a unique routine, would be held. The FIG also raised the minimum age for women from 15 to 16 in the year of the competition and elected a new president, Italy's Bruno Grandi. This brought to an end Yury Titov's 20-year reign as president.

The artistic world championship events were held in Lausanne, Switz., on September 1–7. The women's competition was won by Romania, followed by Russia, China, Ukraine, France, and the United States. On the men's side China won the title, followed by Belarus, Russia, Japan, the U.S., and Germany.

At the rhythmic world gymnastics championships in October, Ukraine's Yelena Vitrichenko claimed the all-around title, winning the clubs and ribbon competitions with perfect 10 scores. Russia won the team title, followed by Belarus, Ukraine, Germany, Bulgaria, and Italy.

FABRIZIO BENSCH—REUTERS

Svetlana Khorkina of Russia staged a last-minute comeback on the uneven bars to jump from fourth to first in the all-around competition. Romania's Simona Amanar was second, and Russia's Yelena Produnova took third. Belarus's Ivan Ivankov won his second men's all-around title. Aleksey Bondarenko of Russia took the silver, and Japan's Naoya Tsukahara earned the bronze.

In the men's events Aleksey Nemov of Russia won the floor exercise, Kazakstan's Sergey Fedorchenko took the vault, and China's Zhang Jinjing won the parallel bars. Yuri Chechi of Italy captured his fifth straight world title on the still rings, and Finland's Jani Tanskanen won the horizontal bar, gaining his country's first gold medal in 47 years. On the pommel horse three gymnasts finished with an identical score of 9.700. In a new rule intended to avoid ties, the gold medal was awarded to Valeri Belenki of Germany on the basis of his qualifying score. Eric Poujade of France received the silver, and the 1996 winner, North Korea's Pae Gil Su, was granted the bronze.

The four women's events were won by three gymnasts representing two countries, Romania and Russia. Amanar won the vault, Khorkina took the uneven bars, and Romania's Gina Gogean won the balance beam and floor exercise.

The rhythmic world championships were held in Berlin on October 23–26. Russia earned the team title, followed by Belarus, Ukraine, Germany, Bulgaria, and Italy. Ukraine's Yelena Vitrichenko took the all-around title, followed by Russia's Nataliya Likovskaya and Yana Batyrchina. Russia and Ukraine swept the individual events, with Batyrchina winning the rope, Likovskaya taking hoop with a perfect 10, and Vitrichenko earning the clubs and ribbon titles with scores of a perfect 10 on each.

(LUAN PESZEK)

ICE HOCKEY

North America. The National Hockey League (NHL) season for 1996–97 saw the Detroit Red Wings win the Stanley Cup for the first time in 42 years. But the long-awaited fan celebration ended three days after the Wings' victory parade when a limousine crash left defenseman Vladimir Konstantinov hospitalized and fighting for his life with a critical head injury. The crash similarly injured Sergey Mnatsakanov, the Red Wings' masseur, and hurt defenseman Vyacheslav Fetisov.

A key event in the Red Wings' championship season occurred on Oct. 9, 1996, when the franchise made a bold trade and acquired left wing Brendan Shanahan and defenseman Brian Glynn from the Hartford Whalers for Paul Coffey, centre Keith Primeau, and a number one draft choice. Shanahan's impact on the Red Wings was immediate. He was named an alternate captain, helped the team to a 2–0 victory over Edmonton in his Detroit debut, and went on to lead the club in scoring with 88 points on 47 goals and 41 assists. Shanahan also recorded consecutive hat tricks (three-goal games) against Pittsburgh and San Jose. Among other milestones, Wings coach Scotty Bowman (see BIOGRAPHIES) reached his 1,000th NHL victory on Feb. 8, 1997, when Detroit outlasted Pittsburgh 6–5 in overtime, and Sergey Federov, one of five Russians on the roster, scored five goals in an overtime win against Washington.

In the 82-game season contested by the NHL's 26 teams before the play-offs began, the division winners were defending champion Colorado, which compiled the league's highest total for victories (49) and points (107), Dallas (104), New Jersey (104), and Buffalo (92). They led the 16-team field into the play-offs.

Like the Red Wings, the Philadelphia Flyers made amends for a lengthy streak of disappointing seasons by reaching the Stanley Cup final series for the first time since 1974–75. The Flyers moved through the play-offs to the Eastern Conference championship by defeating the Pittsburgh Penguins, Buffalo Sabres, and New York Rangers, in that order, all by four games to one. Detroit had a more competitive struggle on its way to the Western Conference title. The Red Wings ousted the St. Louis Blues four games to two and defeated the Anaheim Mighty Ducks 4–0, three of the games being decided in overtime. A remarkable defensive effort enabled the Wings to outshoot the Ducks 232–131 in a series that was a prelude to a redemptive four-games-to-two victory over the Colorado Avalanche—the team that had knocked Detroit out of the play-offs one year earlier.

Detroit's combination of speed, power, and stifling defense proved an insoluble problem for Philadelphia as the final series evolved into a startling mismatch. It produced the 19th series sweep in Stanley Cup history and the Flyers' first four-game losing streak since 1994. The Red Wings never trailed after any period in the series, thanks to the play of goalie Mike Vernon, who limited the opposition to two or fewer goals in 17 of 20 play-off games. The Red Wings won the first two games in Philadelphia by identical 4–2 scores and routed the Flyers 6–1 when the series moved to Detroit for game three. On June 7 in Detroit, before a crowd of 19,983 at Joe Louis Arena, the Red Wings took the decisive fourth game 2–1 as Vernon stopped 26 of 27 shots. The series proved a major embarrassment to centre Eric Lindros, the Flyers' team captain, who scored only one goal during the Wings' sweep, and to his coach, Terry Murray, who was fired six days after it ended.

Trent Klatt (20) of the Philadelphia Flyers tries to sneak a shot by goalie Mike Vernon (29) of the Detroit Red Wings during game 4 of the Stanley Cup finals. The Red Wings won the game 2–1 to complete a four-game sweep against the Flyers and earn the Stanley Cup for the first time in 42 years.

AL BELLO—ALLSPORT

Vernon won the Conn Smythe Trophy as the most valuable player in the Stanley Cup, and Dominik Hasek of Buffalo took the Vezina Trophy for goaltending during the regular season. Hasek also won the Hart Trophy as the regular season's most valuable player and added a dubious entry to his résumé by drawing a three-game suspension and $10,000 fine—the year's most severe punishment—for assaulting a reporter. Mario Lemieux of Pittsburgh, in his final NHL season, won the Ross Trophy as the league's highest scorer (122 points).

Brian Leetch of the Rangers won the Norris Trophy as the outstanding defenseman, and Mike Peca of Buffalo won the Selke Trophy as the best defensive forward. The Lady Byng Trophy for good sportsmanship went to Paul Kariya of Anaheim for the second straight season, and defenseman Bryan Berard of the New York Islanders took the Calder Trophy as the season's top rookie. The Jack Adams Award for the outstanding coach went to Ted Nolan of Buffalo, who nevertheless was fired.

Off the ice, the NHL announced plans to become a 30-team league with the addition of expansion franchises in Nashville, Tenn. (starting in 1998–99), Atlanta, Ga. (1999–2000), and Columbus, Ohio, and Minneapolis-St. Paul, Minn. (2000–2001).

(RON REID)

International. In the 61st world ice hockey championship, contested by 36 nations, Dean Evason and Owen Nolan of Canada scored the vital goals against Sweden to capture their nation's 21st title at the Pool A tournament in Helsinki, Fin., in May. It was Canada's second victory in four years and the third time in five years that the Swedes had had to settle for the silver medal. The first final to be decided in a best-of-three series, it reached a climax in a tension-filled third game.

The two finalists had played one another in one of the two initial groups. At that time Sweden cruised to a 7–2 victory and then went on to win the six-team group without defeat, with Canada second and the United States third. The three qualified for the medal round along with the top three in the other group, the Czech Republic, Finland, and Russia. Sweden again beat Canada in the medal round, but the Canadians, with teamwork steadily improving, proved a clear second best, ahead of the Russians and Czechs.

Sweden won the first game of the best-of-three final 3–2 but lost 3–1 in the second game, setting the stage for a nail-biting finale. Evason, the Canadian captain and the only member of the team without a National Hockey League contract, put the puck home from the edge of the crease to open the scoring in the 19th minute. Two minutes into the second period, a pass from Travis Green found Nolan perfectly placed to slide in what proved to be the winning goal. From then on, Canada's confidence was brimming over. Sweden could make little impression until, with a little over a minute left, Michael Nylander scored a goal in a feverish late onslaught, but Canada held on for a hard-earned 2–1 victory. It came as no surprise when Canada's Sean Burke and Sweden's Tommy Salo were voted the top two goalies in the tournament.

The Czechs beat the Russians 4–3 for the bronze medal, with Finland fifth and the U.S. sixth, followed by Latvia, Italy, Slovakia, France, Germany, and Norway, the latter failing to win a single game. Attendance exceeded 13,000 for each of the 13 major matches at Helsinki's new Hartwell Arena. The top 11 teams qualified automatically for the 1998 Pool A tournament in Switzerland, but because this had been expanded from 12 to 16 teams, they were to be joined by Belarus (1997 Pool B winners), Switzerland (the host nation), Japan (as best Far East team), and the two leaders of a qualifying tournament to be held between Norway, Kazakstan, Austria, and Poland.

Belarus won all of its seven games in the Pool B tournament in Poland; Ukraine topped Slovenia at the head of Pool C in Estonia; and Croatia triumphed over South Korea in Pool D in Andorra. Vacancies left by the expansion of Pool A enabled the promotion of Ukraine, Slovenia, and Estonia from Pool C to B and of Croatia, South Korea, Spain, and Yugoslavia from Pool D to C.

The 20th European Cup, open to national club champions, was won by Lada Togliatti of Russia, which defeated Modo Domsjö of Sweden 4–3 in the final at Oberhausen, Ger. Düsseldorfer from Germany took the bronze medal. A new interclub European League consisting of 20 teams from 12 nations was won by TPS Turku of Finland. A projected revamped format for 1998 would allow the league to replace the European Cup as the sport's major competition in Europe. It had taken more than 20 years to develop the league, and subsequent further enlargement was envisioned, with the possible addition of North American participation.

Canada defeated the U.S. 4–3 in the final of the fourth women's world ice hockey championship at Kitchener, Ont. Finland finished third. Six nations qualified for the first women's Olympic Games tournament at Nagano, Japan, in 1998. (HOWARD BASS)

ICE SKATING

Figure Skating. In 1997 figure-skating competition at the top level continued to be highly remunerative for the most successful performers, in marked contrast to what had been a virtually amateur sport only two years previously. For the second season in a row, lucrative prize money provided added incentives for top skaters to continue skating in competitive events. A total of nearly $1 million was again awarded to 144 skaters at the world championships in Lausanne, Switz., from $50,000 for the men's and women's winners and $75,000 for the leading pair and dance couples down to $2,500 for the 24th singles skaters and $3,750 for the 24th partnerships.

Whereas women skaters once tended to reach peak form in their early 20s, the dominance of teenagers became progressively apparent at the world championships. With the degree of athleticism rapidly advancing, growing concerns about the physical and mental demands led to new minimum age limits, precluding skaters under 15 from senior championships but, significantly, exempting any below that age who had already competed before this change of rule. The chief beneficiary of the exemption was Tara Lipinski, who made history with a technically brilliant performance to become the youngest women's champion ever. The American mighty mite took gold at the age of 14 years, 9 months, and 12 days—32 days younger than the 1927 champion, Sonja Henie of Norway. Weighing only 34 kg (75 lb) and standing only 1.42 m (4 ft 8 in) tall, Lipinski landed seven triple jumps in her free program, including her unique combination of two triple toe loop jumps. Lipinski's title-defending compatriot, 16-year-old Michelle Kwan, finished a close runner-up.

Setting new jumping standards, Canada's Elvis Stojko (*see* BIOGRAPHIES) became the first skater in a world championship to land a combination of quadruple and triple toe loops. He also included six other triples and

NHL Final Standings, 1997

EASTERN CONFERENCE	Won	Lost	Tied	Points
Atlantic Division				
*New Jersey	45	23	14	104
*Philadelphia	45	24	13	103
*Florida	35	28	19	89
*New York Rangers	38	34	10	86
Washington	33	40	9	75
Tampa Bay	32	40	10	74
New York Islanders	29	41	12	70
Northeast Division				
*Buffalo	40	30	12	92
*Pittsburgh	38	36	8	84
*Ottawa	31	36	15	77
*Montreal	31	36	15	77
Hartford	32	39	11	75
Boston	26	47	9	61

WESTERN CONFERENCE	Won	Lost	Tied	Points
Central Division				
*Dallas	48	26	8	104
*Detroit	38	26	18	94
*Phoenix	38	37	7	83
*St. Louis	36	35	11	83
*Chicago	34	35	13	81
Toronto	30	44	8	68
Pacific Division				
*Colorado	49	24	9	107
*Anaheim	36	33	13	85
*Edmonton	36	37	9	81
Vancouver	35	40	7	77
Calgary	32	41	9	73
Los Angeles	28	43	11	67
San Jose	27	47	8	62

*Qualified for play-offs.

The Stanley Cup

Season	Winner	Runner-up	Games
1992–93	Montreal Canadiens	Los Angeles Kings	4–1
1993–94	New York Rangers	Vancouver Canucks	4–3
1994–95	New Jersey Devils	Detroit Red Wings	4–0
1995–96	Colorado Avalanche	Florida Panthers	4–0
1996–97	**Detroit Red Wings**	**Philadelphia Flyers**	**4–0**

World Hockey Championship

Year	Winner
1993	Russia
1994	Canada
1995	Finland
1996	Czech Republic
1997	**Canada**

finished with a sequence of seven Arabian cartwheels to regain the men's title from the American runner-up and defending champion, Todd Eldredge. Stojko vaulted from fourth place after the short program to claim his third triumph in four years.

In a very close pairs contest, Germany's Mandy Wötzel and Ingo Steuer took their first pairs title after having twice finished second, toppling the defending Russians, Marina Yeltsova and Andrey Bushkov, in a tight split judges' decision. Russians Oksana Grishuk and Yevgeny Platov swept comfortably to their fourth consecutive ice-dance success, again outpointing their compatriots Anjelike Krylova and Oleg Ovsyannikov.

The meeting was clouded by the death of Carlo Fassi (*see* OBITUARIES), the Italian-born coach of several famous past champions, after he suffered a severe heart attack. His latest pupil, American Nicole Bobek, was clearly affected while bravely completing the women's event.

JEAN LOUP GAUTREAU—AFP

At the world figure-skating championships, American Tara Lipinski landed seven triple jumps in her free program. The 14-year-old Lipinski became the youngest women's champion ever.

The second Champions Series was again based on results at six venues and awarded prize money of more than $2 million. Ending two weeks before the world championships, the series provided a foretaste of what was to follow. Stojko, runner-up the previous year, finished ahead of Eldredge in the men's competition, and Lipinski defeated Kwan. Wötzel and Steuer won the pairs, but the ice dance differed from the world championships as the Canadians Shae-Lynn Bourne and Victor Kraatz scored an upset to defeat Krylova and Ovsyannikov.

The International Skating Union (ISU) ordered a review of the complex placing system for the judging of figure skating. "We have made huge steps forward in recent years," said the ISU president, Ottavio Cinquanta, "but it is crucial that the public can more easily understand how our extremely technical sport is judged and we must develop a fair and comprehensible method." In support, this change was resolutely urged by the influential International Olympic Committee president, Juan Antonio Samaranch.

Speed Skating. The season's prize money budget of $5 million spread among major ISU events included, for the second year, both large-circuit and short-track speed skating. At the world championships, held at the new arena constructed for the 1998 Winter Olympic Games in Nagano, Japan, Ids Postma of The Netherlands became the new men's champion, and Germany's Gunda Niemann gained her third successive women's crown and her fifth overall title in six years.

Both champions were among those competitors wearing a popular new-style "clap" skate that features a quick release at the heel and thereby provides a stronger push for the skater. When the foot is lifted from the ice, the blade snaps back into position. First seen in a more basic form on the Dutch canals in the late 19th century, the updated 1997 version proved to be faster than traditional blades. Coaches agreed that this development improved times appreciably, particularly over the longer distances, and a general changeover appeared imminent.

At the world sprint championships, in Hamar, Nor., Russia's Sergey Klevchenya retained the men's title, and Germany's Franziska Schenk became the new women's

World Figure Skating Champions—Men

Year	Winner
1993	K. Browning (Can.)
1994	E. Stojko (Can.)
1995	E. Stojko (Can.)
1996	T. Eldredge (U.S.)
1997	**E. Stojko (Can.)**

World Figure Skating Champions—Women

Year	Winner
1993	O. Baiul (Ukr.)
1994	Y. Sato (Japan)
1995	Chen Lu (China)
1996	M. Kwan (U.S.)
1997	**T. Lipinski (U.S.)**

World Figure Skating Champions—Pairs

Year	Winners
1993	I. Brasseur, L. Eisler (Can.)
1994	Ye. Shishkova, V. Naumov (Russia)
1995	R. Kovarikova, R. Novotny (Cz.Rep.)
1996	M. Yeltsova, A. Bushkov (Russia)
1997	**M. Wötzel, I. Steur (Ger.)**

World Ice Dancing Champions

Year	Winners
1993	M. Usova, A. Zhulin (Russia)
1994	O. Grichuk, Ye. Platov (Russia)
1995	O. Grichuk, Ye. Platov (Russia)
1996	O. Grichuk, Ye. Platov (Russia)
1997	**O. Grichuk, Ye. Platov (Russia)**

World Ice Speed-Skating Records Set in 1997 on Major Tracks

Event	Name	Country	Time
	MEN		
1,500 m	Neal Marshall	Canada	1 min 50.05 sec

World All-Around Speed-Skating Champions—Men

Year	Winner
1993	F. Zandstra (Neth.)
1994	J.O. Koss (Nor.)
1995	R. Ritsma (Neth.)
1996	R. Ritsma (Neth.)
1997	**I. Postma (Neth.)**

World All-Around Speed-Skating Champions—Women

Year	Winner
1993	G. Niemann (Ger.)
1994	E. Hunyady (Austria)
1995	G. Niemann (Ger.)
1996	G. Niemann (Ger.)
1997	**G. Niemann (Ger.)**

World Ice Speed-Skating Records Set in 1997 on Short Tracks

Event	Name	Country	Time
	MEN		
1,000 m	Marc Gagnon	Canada	1 min 28.230 sec
5,000-m relay	Kim Sun Tae	S. Korea	7 min 0.042 sec
	Lee Jun Hwan		
	Kim Don Sung		
	Lee Ho Eung		
	WOMEN		
500 m	Isabelle Charest	Canada	44.867 sec
1,000 m	Chun Lee Kyung	S. Korea	1 min 32.340 sec
3,000-m relay	Chun Lee Kyung	S. Korea	4 min 17.630 sec
	Won Hye Kyung		
	Kim Sun Mi		
	An Sang Mi		

World Speed-Skating Sprint Championships

Year	Men	Women
1993	I. Zhelezovsky (Bela.)	Ye Qiaobo (China)
1994	D. Jansen (U.S.)	B. Blair (U.S.)
1995	Kim Yoon Man (S.Kor.)	B. Blair (U.S.)
1996	S. Klevchenya (Russia)	C. Witty (U.S.)
1997	**S. Klevchenya (Russia)**	**F. Schenk (Ger.)**

World Short-Track Speed-Skating Championships—Overall Winners

Year	Men	Women
1993	M. Gagnon (Can.)	N. Lambert (Can.)
1994	M. Gagnon (Can.)	N. Lambert (Can.)
1995	Chae Ji Hoon (S.Kor.)	Chun Lee Kyung (S.Kor.)
1996	M. Gagnon (Can.)	Chun Lee Kyung (S.Kor.)
1997	**Kim Dong Sung (S.Kor.)**	**Chun Lee Kyung (S.Kor.), Yang Yang (China)**

DEB THORNE-LATTA—CALGARY HERALD/ASSOCIATED PRESS

Canada's Neal Marshall crosses the finish line in first place in the men's 1,500-m speedskating race at the single-distance championships in Canada in March. Marshall set a new world record in the event with a time of 1 min 50.05 sec.

champion. The second world single-distance championships, in Warsaw, underlined Niemann's dominance during the season as she won three of the five women's events. Rintje Ritsma of The Netherlands was the only man to win two events. The 12th World Cup series was contested over 10 meetings in 10 countries, and only Ritsma finished best in two of the four men's distances. Niemann, with a first and a second, emerged the most successful among the women.

At the world short-track championships in Nagano, Kim Dong Sung of South Korea captured the men's title, relegating the Canadian defender and three-time former champion Marc Gagnon to second place. Chun Lee Kyung, also of South Korea, gained her third successive women's title but had to share the gold medal with China's first champion, Yang Yang.

(HOWARD BASS)

World Judo Championships—Men

Year	Open weights	60 kg	65 kg	71 kg
1989	N. Ogawa (Japan)	A. Totikashvili (U.S.S.R.)	D. Becanovic (Yugos.)	T. Koga (Japan)
1991	N. Ogawa (Japan)	T. Koshino (Japan)	G. Quellmalz (Ger.)	T. Koga (Japan)
1993	R. Kubacki (Pol.)	R. Sonada (Japan)	Y. Nakamura (Japan)	Yung Chung Hoon (S.Kor.)
1995	D. Douillet (Fr.)	N. Ojeguine (Russia)	U. Quellmalz (Ger.)	D. Hideshima (Japan)
1997	**R. Kubacki (Pol.)**	**T. Nomura (Japan)**	**Kim Hyuk (S.Kor.)**	**K. Nakamura (Japan)**
Year	**78 kg**	**86 kg**	**95 kg**	**+95 kg**
1989	Kim Bying Ju (S.Kor.)	F. Canu (Fr.)	K. Kurtanidze (U.S.S.R.)	N. Ogawa (Japan)
1991	D. Lascau (Ger.)	H. Okada (Japan)	S. Traineau (Fr.)	S. Kosorotov (U.S.S.R.)
1993	Chun Ki Young (S.Kor.)	Y. Nakamura (Japan)	A. Kovacs (Hung.)	D. Douillet (Fr.)
1995	T. Koga (Japan)	Chun Ki Young (S.Kor.)	P. Nastula (Pol.)	D. Douillet (Fr.)
1997	**Cho In Chul (S.Kor.)**	**Jeon Ki Young (S.Kor.)**	**P. Nastula (Pol.)**	**D. Douillet (Fr.)**

World Judo Championships—Women

Year	Open weights	48 kg	52 kg	56 kg
1989	E. Rodríguez (Cuba)	K. Briggs (U.K.)	S. Rendle (U.K.)	C. Arnaud (Fr.)
1991	Zhuang Xiaoyan (China)	C. Nowak (Fr.)	A. Giungi (Italy)	M. Blasco (Spain)
1993	B. Maksymow (Poland)	R. Tamura (Japan)	R. Verdecia (Cuba)	N. Fairbrother (U.K.)
1995	M. van der Lee (Neth.)	R. Tamura (Japan)	M.-C. Restoux (Fr.)	D. González (Cuba)
1997	**D. Beltran (Cuba)**	**R. Tamura (Japan)**	**M.-C. Restoux (Fr.)**	**I. Fernández (Spain)**
Year	**61 kg**	**66 kg**	**72 kg**	**+72 kg**
1989	C. Fleury (Fr.)	E. Pierantozzi (Italy)	I. Berghmans (Belg.)	Fengliang Gao (China)
1991	F. Eickoff (Ger.)	E. Pierantozzi (Italy)	Kim Mi Jong (S.Kor.)	Moon Ji Yoon (S.Kor.)
1993	G. van de Cavaye (Belg.)	Cho Min Sun (S.Kor.)	Leng Chin Hui (China)	J. Hagn (Ger.)
1995	Jung Sung Sook (S.Kor.)	Cho Min Sun (S.Kor.)	C. Luna (Cuba)	A. Seriese (Neth.)
1997	**S. Vandenhende (Fr.)**	**K. Howey (U.K.)**	**N. Anno (Japan)**	**C. Cicot (Fr.)**

JUDO

International judo competition in 1997 began with the first women's judo world cup team tournament in Osaka, Japan, in January. The Cuban team defeated South Korea 5–2, and Japan and France shared third place. Competition shifted into high gear in February, with both the French and German international judo tournaments serving as a warm-up and preview of the world championships in October. Japanese *judoka,* appearing for the first time in a European competition in all-blue *judogi* (uniforms), won 7 of the 14 titles at stake in the French tournament.

At the world championships in Paris on October 9–12, with 90 countries competing, Japan edged out France as top country—10 medals to 9—by a single bronze medal. The South Korean men emerged with three gold medals, followed by Poland with two. The French women, with three, took the most gold medals. Olympic champion Jeon Ki Young of South Korea won his third straight world title in the men's 86-kg event; Rafal Kubacki of Poland captured his second open crown; and David Douillet of France took his third straight over-95-kg gold. In the women's events Isabel Fernández of Spain took the 56-kg title, and Ryoko Tamura of

World Lawn Bowls Championships

Year	Singles	Pairs	
1988	D. Bryant (Eng.)	New Zealand	
1992	T. Allcock (Eng.)	Scotland	
1996	T. Allcock (Eng.)	Ireland	
	Triples	**Fours**	**Team**
1988	New Zealand	Ireland	England
1992	Israel	Scotland	Scotland
1996	Scotland	England	Scotland

Japan won her third consecutive title in the women's 48-kg class. (ANDY ADAMS)

LAWN BOWLS

In the 1980s and '90s, the traditional game of lawn bowls was boosted in the British Isles by a switch in the winter months to carpeted indoor stadiums (by 1997 there were some 400 of them), which attracted large memberships. Television had embraced this indoor game by the creation of a single purpose-built rink (flanked by tiered seating), on which the annual world indoor championship was played. An adaptation of the outdoor game on similar lanes seemed likely with the formation in 1997 of the World Bowls Tour by the Professional Bowls Association, which attracted a worldwide membership.

In 1997 Scotland's Hugh Duff won his second world indoor singles title (he had won in 1988). Six-time pairs winner (and 1996 outdoor singles champion) Tony Allcock of England returned to the winner's circle after four years, this time with a new partner, Mervyn King, while their teammate Norma Shaw captured her first singles title.

At the women's third biennial Atlantic Rim tournament in August, the host nation, Wales, won the team championship as well as the triples event. England finished second with victories in the singles and pairs, and South Africa's win in the fours put it in third place overall. The World Bowls Board, the ruling body of international lawn bowls, reported a decline in membership in the 35 registered countries. In 1997 the board's total affiliated membership figure was 560,000, with Australia (230,000) at the top, followed by England (130,000) and Scotland (83,000). (DONALD J. NEWBY)

RODEO

Records fell at the 1997 National Finals Rodeo (NFR), the $3.4 million championship-deciding competition of the world's largest rodeo organization, the Professional Rodeo Cowboys Association (PRCA). Held at the Thomas & Mack Center at the University of Nevada at Las Vegas, the 39th NFR took place December 5–14. Saddle bronc riding ace Dan Mortensen of Manhattan, Mont., claimed rodeo's most prestigious award, the world champion all-around cowboy title, by earning $184,559. (PRCA world championships in the all-around and individual rodeo events are based upon regular-season earnings as well as money earned at the season-ending NFR.) Joe Beaver of Huntsville, Texas, came in second without winning an individual world title.

Mortensen, however, claimed his fourth individual world title in saddle bronc riding with $182,636 in earnings. Bareback rider Eric Mouton of Weatherford, Okla., set a new NFR record for the highest score on 10 horses (796 points) en route to his first PRCA world title. Mouton rose from eighth place in the world standings to first place on the strength of $77,091 in NFR earnings. He finished the season with $133,196.

Calf ropers received standing ovations on December 13 as the NFR arena record of 7.1 sec (set only the day before by Ronnie Hyde of Bloomington, Ind.) was broken three times. Blair Burk of Durant, Okla., roped a calf in 7 sec. Minutes later Fred Whitfield of Hockley, Texas, wrapped up a 6.9-sec run; that record held for less than one minute before Jeff Chapman of Athens, Texas, scored in 6.8 sec. Cody Ohl of Orchard, Texas, earned $154,950 for the year and the 1997 world title.Team roping partners Speed Williams of Jacksonville, Fla., and Rich Skelton of Llano, Texas, took top honours in their specialty event with $114,700 and $112,242, respectively. Williams, a three-time champion in the rival International Professional Rodeo Cowboys Association, won championships in both associations.

In steer wrestling the oldest of 15 contestants, 52-year-old Butch Myers of Athens, Texas, toppled 10 steers in 43.3 sec to shave a full second off the record he set in 1986. Myers, the 1980 PRCA world champ, finished second in the 1997 title chase to Brad Gleason of Ennis, Mont. Gleason banked $120,890 en route to his first world title.

Kristie Peterson of Elbert, Colo., defended her 1996 barrel racing championship with $165,238 in earnings. Peterson made

Men's World All-Around Rodeo Championship

Year	Winner	Year	Winner
1992	T. Murray	1995	J. Beaver
1993	T. Murray	1996	J. Beaver
1994	T. Murray	**1997**	**D. Mortensen**

The Diamond Challenge Sculls

Year	Winner	Min:s
1993	T. Lange (Ger.)	7:39
1994	X. Müller (Grasshopper, Switz.)	7:35
1995	J. Jaanson (Parnu, Est.)	7:24
1996	M.L.O. Vervoorn (Delft, Neth.)	7:42
1997	**G.M.P. Searle (Molesey B.C.)**	**7:38**

Grand Challenge Cup

Year	Winner	Min:s
1993	Dortmund, Ger.	6:11
1994	Charles River and San Diego	6:13
1995	San Diego Training Center	5:59
1996	Imperial College and Queens Tower	6:11
1997	**Institutes of Sport, Australia**	**6:03**

World Rowing Championships—Men

Year	Single sculls	Min:s	Double sculls	Min:s	Coxed pairs	Min:s		
1993	D. Porter (Can.)	6:59.03	Y. Lamarque, S. Barathay (Fr.)	6:24.69	J. Searle, G. Searle (U.K.)	7:01.50		
1994	A. Willims (Ger.)	6:46.33	R. Thorsen, L. Bjoenness (Nor.)	6:08.33	T. Frankovic, I. Boraska (Croatia)	6:42.16		
1995	I. Cop (Slov.)	6:52.93	L. Christensen, M. Haldbo-Hansen (Den.)	6:17.01	L. Sartori, G. DeStabile (Italy)	7:35.11		
1996	X. Müller (Switz.)	6:44.85	D. Tizzano, A. Abbagnale (Italy)	6:16.90	Y. Schulte, L. Prevot (Fr.)	7:18.26		
1997	**J. Koven (U.S.)**	**6:44.86**	**S. Volkert, A. Hajek (Ger.)**	**6:13.35**	**S. Fentress, J. Irving (U.S.)**	**6:56.30**		
Year	**Coxless pairs**	**Min:s**	**Coxed fours**	**Min:s**	**Coxless fours**	**Min:s**	**Eights**	**Min:s**
1993	S. Redgrave, M. Pinsent (U.K.)	6:37.11	Romania	6:14.64	France	6:04.54	Germany	5:37.08
1994	S. Redgrave, M. Pinsent (U.K.)	6:18.65	Romania	6:06.69	Italy	5:48.44	United States	5:24.50
1995	S. Redgrave, M. Pinsent (U.K.)	6:28.11	United States	6:37.50	Italy	5:58.28	Germany	5:53.40
1996	S. Redgrave, M. Pinsent (U.K.)	6:20.09	Romania	6:25.74	Australia	6:06.37	Netherlands	5:42.74
1997	**M. Andrieux, J.-C. Rolland (Fr.)**	**6:27.69**	**France**	**6:04.17**	**United Kingdom**	**5:52.40**	**United States**	**5:27.20**

World Rowing Championships—Women

Year	Single sculls	Min:s	Double sculls	Min:s	Quadruple sculls	Min:s
1993	J. Thieme (Ger.)	7:26.00	P. Baker, B. Lawson (N.Z.)	7:03.42	China	6:21.07
1994	T. Hansen (Den.)	7:23.96	P. Baker, B. Lawson (N.Z.)	6:45.30	Germany	6:11.73
1995	M. Brandin (Swe.)	7:26.00	M. McBean, K. Heddle (Can.)	6:55.76	Germany	6:40.80
1996	Ye. Khodotovich (Bel.)	7:32.21	M. McBean, K. Heddle (Can.)	6:56.84	Germany	6:27.44
1997	**Ye. Khodotovich (Bel.)**	**7:29.30**	**E. Meike, K. Boron (Ger.)**	**6:51.07**	**Germany**	**6:16.15**
Year	**Coxless pairs**	**Min:s**	**Coxless fours**	**Min:s**	**Eights**	**Min:s**
1993	C. Gosse, H. Cortin (Fr.)	7:24.74	China	6:42.06	Romania	6:18.88
1994	C. Gosse, H. Cortin (Fr.)	7:01.77	Netherlands	6:30.76	Germany	6:07.42
1995	M. Still, K. Slatter (Austl.)	7:12.70	United States	7:03.53	United States	6:50.73
1996	M. Still, K. Slatter (Austl.)	7:01.39	United States	6:49.48	Romania	6:19.73
1997	**E. Robinson, A. Korn (Can.)**	**7:08.09**	**United Kingdom**	**6:40.30**	**Romania**	**6:02.40**

10 penalty-free runs at Las Vegas to sew up the rodeo's cumulative "average" award in the time of 143.28 sec. Peterson, who had won the average competition for four consecutive years, gained her third barrel racing world championship.

For the first time in NFR history, an entire round of bull riding went by without a qualified eight-second ride. The 1997 field featured nine NFR rookies, and the inexperience showed. Veteran Scott Mendes of Weatherford, Texas, captured his first world championship with $120,364 in earnings and won the bull riding average contest with a score of 557 points on seven bulls ridden.

(GAVIN FORBES EHRINGER)

ROWING

World rowing made significant progress in 1997 by establishing a new pattern to meet the changing needs of the sport. This was illustrated in the world championships on Lake Aiguebelette, France, where two dozen restructured rowing and sculling events attracted 981 competitors from 52 nations. The 14 events for men and 10 for women included 14 heavyweight and 10 lightweight classes. In all, 20 nations finished in the medal table. The leading nations overall were Germany, the U.S., Denmark, Italy, France, the U.K., and Australia. The U.S. headed the men's events with three titles, and whereas Germany captured four women's championships, it owed its overall supremacy to its depth in men's events. Germany and Italy won all their gold medals for sculling, and Australia, Denmark, and the U.S. were the only nations to triumph in both disciplines. The leaders in the heavyweight events were France, the U.K., Germany, and the U.S.; the best lightweights were Australia, Denmark, and Germany.

Eight of the titles were decided by less than a second. Australia gained the closest victory in men's lightweight eights, winning by 0.03 sec over the British team, with Canada 0.88 sec farther behind. The U.S. defeated Australia by little more in men's coxed pairs—0.06 sec. Germany took the women's lightweight quadruple sculls by 0.53 sec from Canada, and the U.S. triumphed narrowly over Romania by 0.56 sec in men's eights. Denmark defeated France by the same margin in men's lightweight coxless fours, and Switzerland denied Ireland the men's lightweight coxless pairs title by 0.70 sec. The two other narrow victories were Britain's first women's heavyweight gold medal in coxless fours with 0.83 sec to spare against Romania and Germany's 0.84-sec defeat of Denmark in women's lightweight double sculls. In men's heavyweight coxless fours the British team, which outraced France by a full 3.94 sec, was anchored by Steven Redgrave and Matthew Pinsent, who had previously won the coxless pairs six times (Redgrave had also won coxless pairs twice with another partner). The duo had made the switch to coxless fours after the 1996 Olympic Games.

The International Olympic Committee decision that rowing had to reduce its competitors in the 2000 Games in Sydney to 550 from the 606 allowed in Atlanta, Ga., in 1996 overshadowed the 1997 season. Another controversial issue was the possibility of further changes to the Olympic program, either by reduction of the number of boats or elimination of the eights altogether.

MIKE HEWITT—ALLSPORT

Australia's Justine Joyce (left) and Eliza Blair pose with their gold medals after winning the lightweight coxless pairs at the world rowing championships in Savoie, France, in September.

A new international event introduced early in the regatta season was the World Cup series held in Munich, Ger.; Paris; and Lucerne, Switz. The final scores were Germany 209 points, Britain 101, Romania 88, Denmark 73, and France 70. In the world junior championships held at Hazewinkel, Belg., the outstanding countries were Germany, with five titles, and Romania, with four.

At the Henley Royal Regatta in England, there were only four overseas winners. Australian crews won the Grand (eights) and Double Sculls challenge cups; the Augusta (Ga.) Sculling Center took the Queen Mother Challenge Cup (quadruple sculls); and Maria Brandin of Sweden became the first winner of the new Princess Royal Challenge Cup for women's sculls. The first all-British final of the Diamond Challenge Sculls since 1983 was won by the 1992 Olympic gold medal oarsman Greg Searle in his first season in single sculls. In the 143rd University Boat Race, Cambridge won the best contest in many years by two lengths, increasing its lead over Oxford to 74–68 in the series.

(K.L. OSBORNE)

SAILING (YACHTING)

The year 1997 began with an unfolding drama in the South Atlantic, where water-ballasted monohulls of increasingly radical design met extreme weather conditions in the single-handed, nonstop circumnavigation race called the Vendee Globe. Only 6 of the 16 entries finished the race, during which four boats and one skipper were lost at sea. The Australian rescue services responded superbly, but many questioned the extraordinary expense involved in the rescues, which also risked the lives of the rescue personnel. The winner of the race was Christophe Auguin, who established a new record of 105 days 20 hr 31 min.

In December 1996 a new Sydney–Hobart Race record was established by Hasso Plattner's *Morning Glory*, which finished in 2 days 14 hr 7 min. The Newport (R.I.)–Bermuda passage record was also broken in late 1996 as *CCP/Cray Valley*, a 15.2-m (1 m=3.28 ft) Jean-Marie Finot design skippered by Jean-Pierre Mouligne, completed the 1,078-km (670-mi) course in 2 days 5 hr 56 min. The 1905 transatlantic record, held by the schooner *Atlantic*, was broken in April 1997 by the 24.4-m water-ballasted sloop *Nicorette*, with an elapsed time of 11 days 13 hr 22 min. Some 1,098 km (682 mi) were covered in the first 48 hours of the voyage. In May the fully crewed nonstop circumnavigation time was cut by 3½ days

In July the USS *Constitution* celebrated the 200th anniversary of her original launch on Oct. 21, 1797, by taking to the seas off Marblehead, Mass., the first time the ship had sailed under her own power in 116 years. The *Constitution* was the oldest commissioned warship in the world.

JOHN E. GAY—REUTERS

America's Cup

Year	Winning yacht	Owner	Skipper	Losing Yacht	Owner
1983	*Australia II* (Australia)	A. Bond and syndicate	J. Bertrand	*Liberty* (U.S.)	Maritime College at Fort Schuyler Foundation, Inc.
1987	*Stars & Stripes* (U.S.)	Sail America syndicate	D. Conner	*Kookaburra III* (Australia)	K. Parry and syndicate
1988	*Stars & Stripes* (U.S.)	Sail America syndicate	D. Conner	*New Zealand* (New Zealand)	M. Fay
1992	*America³* (U.S.)	America³ Foundation	B. Koch	*Il Moro di Venezia* (Italy)	Compagnia della Vela di Venezia
1995	*Black Magic* (N.Z.)	P. Blake and Team New Zealand	R. Coutts	*Young America*	Pact 95 syndicate

Bermuda Race

Year	Winning yacht	Owner
1988	*Congere*	B. Koeppel
1990	*Denali*	L. Huntington
1992	*Constellation*	U.S. Naval Academy
1994	*Gaylark*	K. Smith
1996	*Boomerang*	G. Coumantaros

Transpacific Race

Year	Winning yacht	Owner
1989	*Silver Bullet*	J. DeLaura
1991	*Chance*	R. McNulty
1993	*Silver Bullet*	J. DeLaura
1995	*Merlin*	D. Sinclair
1997	***Ralphie***	**J. Montgomery**

Admiral's Cup

Year	Winning team
1989	United Kingdom
1991	France
1993	Germany
1995	Italy
1997	**United States**

World Class Boat Champions, 1997

Class	Winner	Country
Etchells 22	P.R. Hoj-Jensen	Denmark
Europe	Margriet Matthysse	Netherlands
Finn	Fredrik Loof	Sweden
470 (men)	Petri Leskinen	Finland
470 (women)	Ruslana Taran	Ukraine
505	Mark Upton Brown	U.K.
Hobie 16 (women)	Gwenael Roth	France
J/24	Vince Brun	U.S.
Laser	Robert Scheidt	Brazil
Optimist	Luca Bursic	Italy
Snipe	Mauricio Santa-Cruz	Brazil
Star	Alexander Hagen	Germany
Tornado	Roland Gaebler	Germany

when Olivier de Kersauson of France finished in 71 days 14 hr 22 min with a six-man crew in a 26.2-m trimaran. In July Roy Disney's 21.3-m turbo-sled *Pyewacket* sliced almost a full day off the Transpacific (Los Angeles–Honolulu) Race record held by *Merlin* since 1977. Bruno Peyron's 26.2-m catamaran set a new multihull record for the same race, with an elapsed time of 5 days 9 hr 18 min.

After its spring 1997 meeting the International Sailing Federation (ISAF, formerly the International Yacht Racing Union) asked the International Olympic Committee (IOC) to add an 11th medal to the 2000 Olympic Regatta in order to restore the Star class boat to the roster of events. This reflected the highly charged political atmosphere in the ISAF since the annual meeting in November 1996, at which the Star was bounced to make way for the high-performance double-trapeze dinghy, the 49er, which was felt to be well suited to Sydney Harbour. Most observers had expected either the 470 or the Finn to be omitted, but well-prepared defenses by the 470 and Finn classes deflected the knife.

The appeal to the IOC was not successful, and the lineup for the Sydney Olympic Regatta remained: 49er, Laser, Europe (women), Finn (men), 470 (separate categories for men and women), Mistral boards (separate categories for men and women), Tornado catamarans, and Solings.

In an exciting final Fastnet Race against defending champion Italy, the United States won the Champagne Mumm Admiral's Cup in August after 28 years out of the winner's circle. The U.S. team consisted of *Flash Gordon 3, MK Café,* and *Jameson.* The 1997–98 Whitbread Round-the-World Race started in late September from Southhampton, Eng.

In March the America's Cup trophy was damaged severely in a sledgehammer attack by a Maori nationalist. Garrands of London, which had crafted it originally, restored the Cup and returned it to Auckland, N.Z. A record 18 clubs filed Cup challenges, including nine syndicates from Europe.

(JOHN B. BONDS)

SKIING

Alpine Skiing. The 1997 world championships enjoyed favourable snow conditions in Sestriere, Italy, particularly welcome after the difficulties experienced during recent years. Deborah Compagnoni virtually deposed Alberto Tomba as Italy's skiing superstar by winning both the women's slalom and giant slalom, the only racer at the meeting to gain more than one title. Hers was a commendable comeback in a career fraught with injuries.

Another Italian, Isolde Kostner, added to the home crowd's delight by successfully defending the supergiant slalom (super G) title; her championship a year earlier was the first by an Italian woman since 1932. In her 11th season Hilary Lindh of the United States atoned for the absence of her injured titleholding compatriot, Picabo Street, by winning the downhill. The combined title went to Renate Götschl of Austria, who unexpectedly outpointed the favourite, Katja Seizinger of Germany.

Three of the five men's events were won by Norwegians, Atle Skaardal retaining the super G, Tom Stiansen claiming the slalom despite a late surge from Tomba, and Kjetil Andre Aamodt emphasizing his versatility by taking the combined. Bruno Kernen gave Switzerland its first gold medal in four years by upsetting the favoured racers in the downhill, and another Swiss, Michael von Grünigen, was a less-surprising giant slalom victor.

Appreciated more than the world championship meeting because it reflected a season's consistency of form, the 31st Alpine World Cup series suffered minimally from snow problems, thanks to an early start in

Alpine World Cup

Year	Men	Women
1993	M. Girardelli (Lux.)	A. Wachter (Austria)
1994	K.A. Aamodt (Nor.)	V. Schneider (Switz.)
1995	A. Tomba (Italy)	V. Schneider (Switz.)
1996	L. Kjus (Nor.)	K. Seizinger (Ger.)
1997	**L. Alphand (Fr.)**	**P. Wiberg (Swed.)**

World Alpine Skiing Championships—Slalom

Year	Men's slalom	Men's giant slalom	Men's supergiant	Women's slalom	Women's giant slalom	Women's supergiant
1993	K.A. Aamodt (Nor.)	K.A. Aamodt (Nor.)	not held	K. Buder (Austria)	C. Merle (Fr.)	K. Seizinger (Ger.)
1994	T. Stangassinger (Austria)	M. Wasmeier (Ger.)	M. Wasmeier (Ger.)	V. Schneider (Switz.)	D. Compagnoni (Italy)	D. Roffe-Steinrotter (U.S.)
1995	not held					
1996	A. Tomba (Italy)	A. Tomba (Italy)	A. Skaardal (Nor.)	P. Wiberg (Swed.)	D. Compagnoni (Italy)	I. Kostner (Italy)
1997	**T. Stiansen (Nor.)**	**M. von Grünigen (Switz.)**	**A. Skaardal (Nor.)**	**D. Compagnoni (Italy)**	**D. Compagnoni (Italy)**	**I. Kostner (Italy)**

World Alpine Skiing Championships—Downhill

Year	Men	Women
1993	U. Lehmann (Switz.)	K. Pace (Can.)
1994	T. Moe (U.S.)	K. Seizinger (Ger.)
1995	not held	
1996	P. Ortlieb (Austria)	P. Street (U.S.)
1997	**B. Kernen (Switz.)**	**H. Lindh (U.S.)**

World Alpine Skiing Championships—Combined

Year	Men	Women
1993	L. Kjus (Nor.)	M. Vogt (Ger.)
1994	L. Kjus (Nor.)	P. Wiberg (Swed.)
1995	not held	
1996	M. Girardelli (Lux.)	P. Wiberg (Swed.)
1997	**K. A. Aamodt (Nor.)**	**R. Götschl (Austria)**

DIETHER ENDLICHER—ASSOCIATED PRESS

Deborah Compagnoni of Italy speeds past spectators and course officials on her way to winning the women's giant slalom at the world Alpine skiing championships in February. A victor in the women's slalom as well, Compagnoni was the only racer at the competition to gain more than one title.

reliable conditions in North America. Luc Alphand, ranking first in the downhill and super G, won the overall men's trophy at the last tournament when runner-up Aamodt failed to finish high enough to overtake him in the slalom at Vail, Colo. The first French champion since Jean-Claude Killy in 1968, Alphand also became the first downhill specialist to win the cup since Karl Schranz of Austria in 1970.

Norwegians and Swedes, once prominent only in Nordic skiing, were becoming more numerous in Alpine events. Emphasizing this development, Sweden's Pernilla Wiberg became the first Scandinavian to win the women's crown, comfortably ahead of Seizinger, her predecessor and closest rival. Finishing first in the slalom, Wiberg demonstrated her ability in contrasting disciplines by placing fourth in the downhill. The concurrently decided Nations Cup was won by the Austrian men and German women.

Because of recurring knee injuries, Marc Girardelli, an Austrian-born skier representing Luxembourg, reluctantly announced his retirement at 33 after a distinguished 17-year career. He was the overall World Cup champion five times and won 46 cup races plus four gold, four silver, and three bronze medals in six world championships. Tomba, another veteran expected to quit, pledged to compete at one more Winter Olympics in 1998. A bizarre moment occurred during the season when the International Ski Federation belatedly awarded France's Marielle Goitschel a gold medal for the 1966 world championship downhill. The woman who had beaten her, Erika Schinegger of Austria, subsequently became Erik after surgery.

Nordic Skiing. At the world championships in Trondheim, Nor., Bjørn Daehlie, on

Nordic World Cup

Year	Men	Women
1993	B. Daehlie (Nor.)	L. Yegorova (Russia)
1994	V. Smirnov (Kazak.)	M. Di Centa (Italy)
1995	B. Daehlie (Nor.)	Ye. Vyalbe (Russia)
1996	B. Daehlie (Nor.)	M. Di Centa (Italy)
1997	**B. Daehlie (Nor.)**	**Ye. Vyalbe (Russia)**

World Nordic Skiing Championships—Men

Year	10-km	15-km	30-km	50-km	Relay
1993	S. Sivertsen (Nor.)	B. Daehlie (Nor.)	B. Daehlie (Nor.)	T. Mogren (Swed.)	Norway
1994	B. Daehlie (Nor.)	B. Daehlie (Nor.)	T. Alsgaard (Nor.)	V. Smirnov (Kazak.)	Italy
1995	V. Smirnov (Kazak.)	V. Smirnov (Kazak.)	V. Smirnov (Kazak.)	S. Fauner (Italy)	Norway
1996	not held				
1997	**B. Daehlie (Nor.)**	**B. Daehlie (Nor.)**	**A. Prokurorov (Russia)**	**M. Myllyla (Fin.)**	**Norway**

World Nordic Skiing Championships—Women

Year	5-km	10-km	15-km	30-km	Relay
1993	L. Lazhutina (Russia)	S. Belmondo (Italy)	Ye. Vyalbe (Russia)	S. Belmondo (Italy)	Russia
1994	L. Yegorova (Russia)	L. Yegorova (Russia)	M. Di Centa (Italy)	M. Di Centa (Italy)	Russia
1995	L. Lazhutina (Russia)	L. Lazhutina (Russia)	L. Lazhutina (Russia)	Ye. Vyalbe (Russia)	Russia
1996	not held				
1997	**Ye. Vyalbe (Russia)**	**Ye. Vyalbe (Russia)**	**Ye. Vyalbe (Russia)**	**Ye. Vyalbe (Russia)**	**Russia**

World Nordic Skiing Championships—Ski Jump

Year	90-m hill	120-m hill	Team jump	Combined	Team combined
1993	M. Harada (Japan)	E. Bredeson (Nor.)	Norway	K. Ogiwara (Japan)	Japan
1994	E. Bredesen (Nor.)	J. Weissflog (Ger.)	Germany	F.-B. Lundberg (Nor.)	Japan
1995	T. Okabe (Japan)	T. Ingebrigtsen (Nor.)	Finland	F.-B. Lundberg (Nor.)	Japan
1996	not held				
1997	**J. Ahonen (Fin.)**	**M. Harada (Japan)**	**Finland**	**K. Ogiwara (Japan)**	**Norway**

ARMANDO TROVATI—ASSOCIATED PRESS

Sweden's Pernilla Wiberg (left) and France's Luc Alphand show off their trophies after earning the overall titles in the 31st Alpine World Cup series. Wiberg was the first Scandinavian to win the women's crown, and Alphand was the first French men's champion since Jean-Claude Killy in 1968.

World Open Championship—Men

Year	Winner
1993	Jan. Khan (Pak.)
1994	Jan. Khan (Pak.)
1995	Jan. Khan (Pak.)
1996	Jan. Khan (Pak.)
1997	**R. Eyles (Austl.)**

World Open Championship—Women

Year	Winner
1993	M. Martin (Austl.)
1994	M. Martin (Austl.)
1995	M. Martin (Austl.)
1996	S. Fitz-Gerald (Austl.)
1997	**S. Fitz-Gerald (Austl.)**

British Open Championship—Men

Year	Winner
1992–93	Jan. Khan (Pak.)
1993–94	Jan. Khan (Pak.)
1994–95	Jan. Khan (Pak.)
1995–96	Jan. Khan (Pak.)
1996–97	**Jan. Khan (Pak.)**

British Open Championship—Women

Year	Winner
1992–93	M. Martin (Austl.)
1993–94	M. Martin (Austl.)
1994–95	M. Martin (Austl.)
1995–96	M. Martin (Austl.)
1996–97	**M. Martin (Austl.)**

home terrain, and Yelena Vyalbe (*see* BIOGRAPHIES) of Russia were dominant in the cross-country men's and women's events, respectively. It was Dæhlie's fifth overall title in six years, and Vyalbe won all five gold medals, the first person ever to accomplish this.

In the 18th Nordic World Cup series, Dæhlie and Vyalbe also proved the most successful during the 15 tournaments. Primoz Peterka of Slovenia ranked ahead of Germany's Dieter Thoma in the Jumping World Cup, and the separate Combined World Cup title was comfortably won by Samppa Lajunen of Finland.

Several major venues, notably Planica, Slovenia; Kulm, Austria; Garmisch-Partenkirchen, Ger.; Sapporo, Japan; and Lahti, Fin., offered improved jumping facilities during the year. The spectacular visual appeal of this sport resulted in increased international television coverage.

Freestyle Skiing. An appreciably higher degree of skill and greater media support accompanied the 18th Freestyle World Cup series, with 11 sites serving as host of 74 men's and women's events, culminating in a final at Hundfjället, Swed. Darcy Downs of Canada and Stacey Blumer of the U.S. won, respectively, the men's and women's overall championships. Canada gained the Nations Cup, ahead of the U.S. and France.

The biennial world championships successfully tested the new Olympic facilities in Nagano, Japan. The men's titles went to Fabrice Becker of France (acro) and Canadians Jean-Luc Brassard (moguls) and Nicolas Fontaine (aerials). The women's winners were Oksana Kushenko of Russia (acro), Candice Gilg of France (moguls), and Kirstie Marshall of Australia (aerials).

(HOWARD BASS)

SQUASH

While the squash world looked forward to first-time participation in the 1998 Commonwealth and Asian games, there was little tangible progress in 1997 on the road to inclusion in the Olympics. Though last-ditch efforts to gain a place at the Sydney (Australia) Games in 2000 were being made, the door seemed closed.

Meanwhile, the World Squash Federation was continuing its twin thrusts of promoting doubles squash and enforcing the mandatory use of eye protection for juniors competing in world championships. Goggles were also mandated by regional federations for juniors competing in their events.

On court, for the first time a world squash championship was contested in South America, as Rio de Janeiro played host to the junior women's event. The team championship was won by England, which beat surprising finalist New Zealand on the last day. The individual title also went to England when top seed Tania Bailey beat Isabelle Stoehr of France in the final.

The women's World Open in Sydney in October featured an all-Australian final. Sarah Fitz-Gerald held on to the title that she had won for the first time 12 months earlier, defeating former champion Michelle Martin 9–5, 5–9, 6–9, 9–2, 9–3 in the final. The match was a reversal of their contest in April, when Martin defeated Fitz-Gerald to take her fifth consecutive British Open title.

Meanwhile, Jansher Khan (*see* BIOGRAPHIES), who won his sixth British Open in a grueling 126-minute marathon over Peter Nicol of Scotland, decided for personal reasons against trying to add to his tally of eight World Open titles. The championship was won by Rodney Eyles of Australia, who beat Nicol 15–11, 15–12, 15–12 in the final. First-time finalist Canada was beaten by defending champion England in the team final, which followed the individual event.

(ANDREW SHELLEY)

SWIMMING

It was a turbulent year in the world of swimming in 1997, with record-setting performances in the water and conflict on the pool deck. Drugs were the subject of most of the on-deck strife; doping charges continued to be leveled at Ireland's Michelle Smith-de Bruin, a surprising triple gold medalist at the 1996 Olympic Games. Smith-de Bruin vigorously denied the accusations. The drug controversy flared up again when China's women reemerged at the Chinese national games in Shanghai in October to dominate women's swimming after two years in the doldrums. In December three top Russians and a Brazilian tested positive for steroids and were suspended from competition. Meanwhile, Germany saw the first of more than 100 trials of former East German coaches, trainers, and physicians charged with having systematically administered steroids to their athletes.

China's performances in women's swimming drew the ire of experts throughout the world as Chinese women set two world records, posted the world's top times in 8 of the 13 individual women's events, and had at least 5 of the world's top 10 times in 7 of those events. Four of the Chinese champions had not previously been ranked among the world's top 150 swimmers in their events. The pattern of Chinese performances had been seen only twice before: in East Germany during the 1970s and '80s and in China in the early '90s. In both cases, drugs were later proved to have been involved. From 1991 to 1996, 23 Chinese swimmers tested positive for anabolic steroids, compared with 3 from the rest of the world.

Controversy also swirled around two rule changes proposed for enactment in 1998: a 15-m limit in the distance a swimmer could use the underwater dolphin kick at the start and at turns in the butterfly and a reduction in the penalty for testing positive for banned drugs from a four-year suspension to two years.

In the water, with the world championships in January 1998 looming, the competition was fast and furious. Competing at the short-course (25-m pool) world championships in Göteborg, Swed., in April, Costa Rica's Claudia Poll set world records for the 200-m (1 min 54.17 sec) and 400-m (4 min 0.03 sec) freestyle. She kept up her unbeaten streak by repeating her triumphs at the year's premier long-course (50-m pool) meet, the Pan Pacific championships, held in Fukuoka, Japan, in August. At year's end Poll, a 1996 Olympic champion, was named the female World Swimmer of the Year by *Swimming World* magazine. It marked the first time a Central or South American swimmer had been granted the coveted award.

Seven short-course men's records fell during the year. Russia's Denis Pankratov, a double Olympic champion in 1996, lowered all three butterfly marks: 23.35 sec for 50 m, 51.78 sec for 100 m, and 1 min 52.64 sec for 200 m. Surprisingly, he swam poorly at Göteborg and at the European championships in Seville, Spain, failing to win a

CRAIG PRENTIS—ALLSPORT

Claudia Poll of Costa Rica raises her arms in triumph after setting a world record in the 400-m freestyle (4 min 0.03 sec). Poll was named the 1997 female World Swimmer of the Year.

World Swimming Records Set in 1997 in 50-m Pools

Event	Name	Country	Time
MEN			
100-m butterfly	Michael Klim	Australia	52.15 sec
WOMEN			
200-m individual medley	Wu Yanyan	China	2 min 09.72 sec
400-m individual medley	Chen Yan	China	4 min 34.79 sec

World Swimming Records Set in 1997 in 25-m Pools

Event	Name	Country	Time
MEN			
50-m backstroke	Chris Renaud	Canada	24.25 sec
50-m breaststroke	Mark Warnecke	Germany	26.97 sec
50-m butterfly	Denis Pankratov	Russia	23.35 sec
100-m butterfly	Denis Pankratov	Russia	51.78 sec
200-m butterfly	Denis Pankratov	Russia	1 min 52.64 sec
400-m individual medley	Marcel Wouda	Netherlands	4 min 05.41 sec
4 x 100-m medley relay	Australia national team	Australia	3 min 30.66 sec
4 x 200-m freestyle relay	Australia national team	Australia	7 min 02.74 sec
WOMEN			
200-m freestyle	Claudia Poll	Costa Rica	1 min 54.17 sec
400-m freestyle	Claudia Poll	Costa Rica	4 min 00.03 sec
50-m breaststroke	Han Xue	China	30.77 sec
50-m butterfly	Jenny Thompson	U.S.	26.48 sec
100-m butterfly	Jenny Thompson	U.S.	57.79 sec
4 x 100-m freestyle relay	China national team	China	3 min 34.55 sec
4 x 200-m freestyle relay	China national team	China	7 min 51.92 sec

World Swimming and Diving Championships—Men

	Freestyle				
Year	50 m	100 m	200 m	400 m	1,500 m
1982		J. Woithe (E.Ger.)	M. Gross (W.Ger.)	V. Salnikov (U.S.S.R.)	V. Salnikov (U.S.S.R.)
1986	T. Jager (U.S.)	M. Biondi (U.S.)	M. Gross (W.Ger.)	R. Henkel (W.Ger.)	R. Henkel (W.Ger.)
1991	T. Jager (U.S.)	M. Biondi (U.S.)	G. Lamberti (Italy)	J. Hoffmann (Ger.)	J. Hoffmann (Ger.)
1994	A. Popov (Russia)	A. Popov (Russia)	A. Kasvio (Fin.)	K. Perkins (Austl.)	K. Perkins (Austl.)

	Backstroke		Breaststroke		Butterfly	
	100 m	200 m	100 m	200 m	100 m	200 m
1982	D. Richter (E.Ger.)	R. Carey (U.S.)	S. Lundquist (U.S.)	V. Davis (Can.)	M. Gribble (U.S.)	M. Gross (W.Ger.)
1986	I. Polyansky (U.S.S.R.)	I. Polyansky (U.S.S.R.)	V. Davis (Can.)	J. Szabo (Hung.)	P. Morales (U.S.)	M. Gross (W.Ger.)
1991	J. Rouse (U.S.)	M. López Zubero (Spain)	N. Rozsa (Hung.)	M. Barrowman (U.S.)	A. Nesty (Suriname)	M. Stewart (U.S.)
1994	M. López Zubero (Spain)	V. Selkov (Russia)	N. Rozsa (Hung.)	N. Rozsa (Hung.)	R. Szukala (Pol.)	D. Pankratov (Russia)

	Individual medley		Team relays		
	200 m	400 m	4 x 100-m freestyle	4 x 200-m freestyle	4 x 100-m medley
1982	A. Sidorenko (U.S.S.R.)	R. Prado (Braz.)	United States	United States	United States
1986	T. Darnyi (Hung.)	T. Darnyi (Hung.)	United States	East Germany	United States
1991	T. Darnyi (Hung.)	T. Darnyi (Hung.)	United States	Germany	United States
1994	J. Sievinen (Fin.)	T. Dolan (U.S.)	United States	Sweden	United States

	Diving		
	1-m springboard	3-m springboard	Platform
1982		G. Louganis (U.S.)	G. Louganis (U.S.)
1986		G. Louganis (U.S.)	G. Louganis (U.S.)
1991	E. Jongejans (Neth.)	K. Ferguson (U.S.)	Sun Shuwei (China)
1994	E. Stewart (Zimb.)	Yu Zhuocheng (China)	D. Saoutine (Russia)

medal. Only one men's world record was set during the year in long-course competition. In October Australia's Michael Klim lowered the world mark for the 100-m butterfly to 52.15 sec. Klim, who also ranked first in the world in the 200-m freestyle, was named the male World Swimmer of the Year by *Swimming World.*

China's Chen Yan and Wu Yanyan were the focus of an international uproar when they obliterated long-course world records. Chen stroked the women's 400-m individual medley in 4 min 34.79 sec, breaking the last of the East German drug-enhanced marks. Wu swam the 200-m individual medley in 2 min 9.72 sec, carving an astonishing two seconds off the record set by Lin Li at the 1992 Olympic Games in Barcelona, Spain. Neither woman had ranked in the top 50 in the world before their swims, and critics charged that they (and other Chinese) were using drugs. No swimmer outside the world top 50 had ever before set a world record, and swimmers outside the top 50 were not subject to unannounced drug tests. Misty Hyman and Brooke Bennett were the only American women to rank first in the world in 1997, Hyman in the 100-m butterfly (58.72 sec) and Bennett in the 800-m (8 min 26.36 sec) and 1,500-m (16 min 10.24 sec) freestyle.

At the European championships in Seville, Spain, in August, Aleksandr Popov of Russia demonstrated that he had recovered fully from a near-fatal stabbing in Moscow after the 1996 Olympics by winning his third-straight European titles in both the 50-m (22.30 sec) and 100-m (49.02 sec) freestyle sprints. Hungary's 16-year-old Agnes Kovacs set a European record of 2 min 24.9 sec in the 200-m breaststroke, the third fastest time in history. Smith-de Bruin kept the fires of controversy surrounding her Olympic performance stoked by winning the 200-m freestyle and 400-m individual medley.

Diving. The biggest diving event of the year was the 10th Fédération Internationale de Natation Amateur Diving World Cup, held in Mexico City, September 10–14.

Russian diver Dmitry Sautin shows perfect form en route to winning the gold medal in the 10-m event at the 10th Fédération Internationale de Natation Amateur Diving World Cup.

ANDREW WINNING—REUTERS

Once again, Russia's 1996 Olympic champion Dmitry Sautin confirmed his place as the world's best male diver. Sautin won double gold, taking the 3-m springboard by less than a point over Zhou Yilin of China and the 10-m platform ahead of Mexico's Fernando Platas. China's Liu Ben won the 1-m springboard title, besting 17-year-old American Troy Dumais. In synchronized diving China's Gong Ming and Xu Hao took the 3-m title, and teammates Li Chengwei and Huang Quiang won the gold medal in the 10-m event.

Canadians Eryn Bulmer and Myriam Boileau were surprising winners. Bulmer edged Yulia Pakhalina of Russia by only 0.12 of a point on the 3-m springboard, and Boileau was five points better than China's Wang Rui on the 10-m platform. In the 1-m event Zhang Jing and Tan Shuping of China finished first and second. It was a Chinese sweep for the gold in the synchronized diving events, with Zhang Jing and Shi Lei taking the 3-m competition and Chi Bin and Wang Rui winning the 10-m. China also won the men's, women's, and overall team titles.

In August Dumais won his fifth and sixth U.S. national titles, taking both the 1-m and 3-m springboard competitions. Justin Dumais, his 19-year-old brother, finished second in the 3-m event, and the Dumaises became the first brother combination in U.S. diving history to finish first and second in the same event at a national championship.

Synchronized Swimming. The stately world of synchronized swimming experienced many changes in 1997. For years the U.S. had dominated the sport, but with the retirement of the entire 1996 Olympic gold medal-winning American team, the door was left open for other countries to excel. That was exactly what happened at the World Cup, held in July in Guangzhou (Canton), China, where Russia's Olga Sedakova took the solo crown. The Russians made it a clean sweep by also winning the duet and team titles, followed in both events by Japan and Canada.

In the U.S. Anna Kozlova notched a "grand slam," taking solo, duet, team, and figures titles at the national championships. The Russian-born Kozlova was due to become a U.S. citizen in 1999. Bill May finished third at nationals, becoming the first male member of a U.S. national team. He would be allowed to compete at the Goodwill Games in 1998. (PHILLIP WHITTEN)

World Swimming and Diving Championships—Women

	Freestyle					
Year	50 m	100 m	200 m	400 m	800 m	
1982		B. Meineke (E.Ger.)	A. Verstappen (Neth.)	C. Schmidt (E.Ger.)	K. Linehan (U.S.)	
1986	T. Costache (Rom.)	K. Otto (E.Ger.)	H. Friedrich (E.Ger.)	H. Friedrich (E.Ger.)	A. Strauss (E.Ger.)	
1991	Zhuang Yong (China)	N. Haislett (U.S.)	H. Lewis (Austl.)	J. Evans (U.S.)	J. Evans (U.S.)	
1994	Le Jingyi (China)	Le Jingyi (China)	F. van Almsick (Ger.)	Yang Aihua (China)	J. Evans (U.S.)	
	Backstroke		**Breaststroke**		**Butterfly**	
	100 m	200 m	100 m	200 m	100 m	200 m
1982	K. Otto (E.Ger.)	C. Sirch (E.Ger.)	U. Geweniger (E.Ger.)	S. Varganova (U.S.S.R.)	M.T. Meagher (U.S.)	I. Geissler (E.Ger.)
1986	B. Mitchell (U.S.)	C. Sirch (E.Ger.)	S. Gerasch (E.Ger.)	S. Hörner (E.Ger.)	K. Gressler (E.Ger.)	M. Meagher (U.S.)
1991	K. Egerszegi (Hung.)	K. Egerszegi (Hung.)	L. Frame (Austl.)	E. Volkova (U.S.S.R.)	Qian Hong (China)	S. Sanders (U.S.)
1994	He Cihong (China)	He Cihong (China)	S. Riley (Austl.)	S. Riley (Austl.)	Liu Limin (China)	Liu Limin (China)
	Individual medley		**Team relays**			
	200 m	400 m	4×100-m freestyle	4×200-m freestyle	4×100-m medley	
1982	P. Schneider (E.Ger.)	P. Schneider (E.Ger.)	East Germany		East Germany	
1986	K. Otto (E.Ger.)	K. Nord (E.Ger.)	East Germany	East Germany	East Germany	
1991	Lin Li (China)	Lin Li (China)	United States	Germany	United States	
1994	Lu Bin (China)	Dai Guohong (China)	China	China	China	
	Diving					
	1-m springboard	3-m springboard	Platform			
1982		M. Neyer (U.S.)	W. Wyland (U.S.)			
1986		Gao Min (China)	Chen Lin (China)			
1991	Gao Min (China)	Gao Min (China)	Fu Mingxia (China)			
1994	Chen Lixia (China)	Tan Shuping (China)	Fu Mingxia (China)			

TABLE TENNIS

At the 1997 world table tennis championships in Manchester, Eng., China again dominated play, winning six of the seven titles. The men's team from China defeated France (the first time since 1948 France had reached the final), while the women's team downed North Korea. Deng Yaping, the 24-year-old 1992 and 1996 Olympic champion, won her third world singles championship, then announced her retirement. In men's doubles 1995 world singles champion Kong Linghui and 1996 Olympic champion Liu Guoliang took gold, just as they had in Atlanta, Ga., in 1996. Only Sweden's 1989 world and 1992 Olympic champion Jan-Ove Waldner broke the pattern, beating Belarus's Vladimir Samsonov in the men's singles. Deng and Kong were also the 1996 singles winners in the grand final of the International Table Tennis Federation's (ITTF) newly inaugurated Pro Tour.

The historic "Ping-Pong Diplomacy" breakthrough exchange visits of the U.S. team to China in 1971 and the Chinese team to the U.S. in 1972 were commemorated in 25th anniversary reunions in both the U.S. and China.

The ITTF considered staging one-table centre-court matches in a boxing ring or theatre-like setting that would bring the action closer to the spectators. Given the increased firepower of the glued-on sponge-rubber rackets that encourage very aggressive, even risky, serve and serve-return follow-up play, the ITTF also sought to continue experiments with a larger ball.

(TIM BOGGAN)

ALEX LIVESEY—ALLSPORT

Members of the men's table tennis team celebrate their victory at the 1997 world championships in Manchester, Eng. China once again proved its supremacy by defeating France, which had reached the final for the first time since 1948.

TENNIS

Becoming only the second man in the modern era of "open tennis" to finish five consecutive years as the world's top-ranked player, Pete Sampras garnered two more Grand Slam titles in a stellar 1997 campaign. Sampras dominated the men's Association of Tennis Professionals (ATP), winning his second consecutive and fourth career ATP Tour world championship. He also finished the year as the ATP's top money winner, with $6,498,311, more than twice that of the runner-up, Yevgeny Kafelnikov. Switzerland's Martina Hingis (*see* BIOGRAPHIES) established herself as the best in the women's game, sweeping three of the four major championships before turning 17 and ending the season as the top women's money winner, with $3,400,196. Capturing men's Grand Slam crowns for the first time were Australia's Patrick Rafter and Brazil's Gustavo Kuerten. Meanwhile, Iva Majoli of Croatia won her first major title.

Three of Germany's great players came to different crossroads, as did the enigmatic American Andre Agassi. Steffi Graf—world champion for 8 of the previous 10 years—had knee surgery in June and was forced off the courts for the rest of 1997. Michael Stich, 1991 Wimbledon champion, retired at age 28, and Boris Becker moved into semiretirement as he approached the age of 30. Agassi married actress Brooke Shields in April and wandered indifferently through most of the year, sinking to number 122 on the end-of-season computer ranking list.

Australian Open. When Hingis moved relentlessly through the field at Melbourne to stake her claim as the youngest Grand Slam singles titlist of the century, she did not concede a set in the entire event and obliterated Mary Pierce 6–2, 6–2 in the final. Graf was ousted 6–2, 7–5 in the fourth round by the surging South African Amanda Coetzer, who concluded the season as the number four player in the world.

Sampras started his season in high style, recording a second championship run in Melbourne. The resolute American handled the oppressive weather conditions admirably, surviving two five-set contests and then halting Spain's surprising Carlos Moya 6–2, 6–3, 6–3 in a meticulous final-round display. Moya toppled defending champion Becker in a five-set opening-round skirmish and upended second-seeded Michael Chang 7–5, 6–2, 6–4 in the semifinal round. Austria's indefatigable Thomas Muster achieved a major breakthrough on the hard courts, reaching the semifinals with unexpected wins over two-time former titlist Jim Courier and the explosive Goran Ivanisevic. Muster then lost in straight sets to Sampras.

French Open. Ranked 66th in the world coming into the world's preeminent clay court event, Kuerten proceeded to defeat three former champions on his way to a startling success at Roland Garros. The 20-year-old knocked out 1995 winner Muster in a five-set third-round showdown, came through again in five arduous sets against

Table Tennis World Cup

Year	Men
1993	Z. Primorac (Croatia)
1994	J.-P. Gatien (Fr.)
1995	Kong Linghui (China)
1996	Liu Guoliang (China)
1997	**Z. Primorac (Croatia)**
Year	**Women**
1996	Deng Yaping (China)
1997	**Wang Nan (China)**

1997 Table Tennis World Rankings

Men	Women
1. Jan-Ove Waldner (Sweden)	1. Deng Yaping (China)
2. Kong Linghui (China)	2. Li Ju (China)
3. Vladimir Samsonov (Belarus)	3. Wang Nan (China)
4. Liu Guoliang (China)	4. Chen Jing (Taiwan)
5. Wang Tao (China)	5. Wang Chen (China)

World Table Tennis Championships—Men

Year	St. Bride's Vase (singles)	Iran Cup (doubles)	Swaythling Cup (team)
1991	J. Persson (Swed.)	P. Karlsson, T. Von Scheele (Swed.)	Sweden
1993	J.-P. Gatien (Fr.)	Wang Tao, Lu Lin (China)	Sweden
1995	Kong Linghui (China)	Wang Tao, Lu Lin (China)	China
1997	**J.-O. Waldner (Swed.)**	**Kong Linghui, Liu Guoliang (China)**	**China**

World Table Tennis Championships—Mixed

Year	Heydusek Prize
1989	Yoo Nam Kyu, Hyung Jung Hwa (S.Kor.)
1991	Wang Tao, Liu Wei (China)
1993	Wang Tao, Liu Wei (China)
1995	Wang Tao, Liu Wei (China)
1997	**Liu Guoliang, Wu Na (China)**

World Table Tennis Championships—Women

Year	G. Geist Prize (singles)	W.J. Pope Trophy (doubles)	Corbillon Cup (team)
1991	Deng Yaping (China)	Gao Jun, Chen Zihe (China)	Korea
1993	Hyun Jung Hwa (S.Kor.)	Liu Wei, Qiao Yunping (China)	China
1995	Deng Yaping (China)	Deng Yaping, Qiao Hong (China)	China
1997	**Deng Yaping (China)**	**Deng Yaping, Yang Ying (China)**	**China**

GARY M. PRIOR—ALLSPORT

Gustavo Kuerten, ranked 66th in the world going into the French Open, was the lowest-ranked player to win the event and the first man from Brazil to capture a Grand Slam championship.

defending champion Yevgeny Kafelnikov, and then was thoroughly uninhibited in a straight-set conquest of 1993–94 victor Sergi Bruguera. Kuerten was the first man from Brazil to win the French tournament. The top-seeded Sampras, slowed by a stomach virus, lost in the third round to Sweden's Magnus Norman.

Hingis had been away from tennis for seven weeks prior to the French Open, but even so she seemed certain to finish on top. After having won six consecutive tournaments and 37 matches in a row during the year, she was soundly taken apart 6–4, 6–2 by an authoritative Majoli. Searching for a third-straight title and a sixth overall, Graf contested her last match of the year and injured herself seriously with 64 unforced errors in a 6–1, 6–4 quarterfinal loss to Coetzer. The South African was narrowly eliminated by Majoli in a hard-fought three-set semifinal confrontation. Hingis defeated 1990–92 champion Monica Seles in another suspenseful three-set semifinal. No match was more compelling than Majoli's 5–7, 6–4, 6–2 fourth-round escape against Lindsay Davenport of the U.S. Davenport won the first set 7–5 and was leading in the second 4–0, 40–15, but she collapsed thereafter. Majoli retaliated audaciously and never looked back.

Wimbledon. Taking the most coveted title in tennis for the fourth time in five years, Sampras was first-rate. He lost his serve only twice in seven matches, winning an astonishing 116 of 118 service games. In the final he routed Cédric Pioline of France 6–4, 6–2, 6–4, repeating the straight-set victory he had achieved against the same opponent four years earlier in the U.S. Open final. Sealing his 10th Grand Slam singles title at the All-England Club, Sampras placed himself within striking distance of Roy Emerson, who collected a record 12 major championships in the 1960s.

Until Sampras restored order in the end, it was a tournament of upsets as rain disrupted the first week of play. The second week was so crowded with extra matches that Sampras was on court all but one afternoon. The favourite, however, was surrounded by three unseeded players in the semifinal round. Pioline subdued Stich in a spirited five-set struggle that ended minutes before darkness. Earlier, Sampras was a confident straight-set victor over Australia's Todd Woodbridge. After beating Becker in a four-set quarterfinal, Sampras listened incredulously at the net as the German told him, "This was my last match at Wimbledon, and I just want you to know that it has been a pleasure playing against you."

Also bowing out in the quarterfinals were Tim Henman and Greg Rusedski, the two top British competitors. Not since 1936, when Fred Perry collected his third title in a row, had a British man been triumphant in the singles at Wimbledon, but both Henman and Rusedski had seemed capable of claiming the crown this time around. Much to the chagrin of many seasoned British observers, Rusedski suffered a four-set quarterfinal loss to Pioline on the same day that Henman faltered in a straight-set loss to Stich.

Hingis was eager to make amends for her Paris disappointment, and she did precisely that. In the final the top seed confronted third-seeded Jana Novotna, whose all-court virtuosity was at first too much for the teenager, but Hingis's agile mind and superior strategic acumen ultimately enabled her to recover for a 2–6, 6–3, 6–3 triumph in her first Wimbledon final. Hingis was the youngest player to capture the All-England

Australian Open Tennis Championships—Singles

Year	Men	Women
1993	J. Courier (U.S.)	M. Seles (Yugos.)
1994	P. Sampras (U.S.)	S. Graf (Ger.)
1995	A. Agassi (U.S.)	M. Pierce (Fr.)
1996	B. Becker (Ger.)	M. Seles (U.S.)
1997	**P. Sampras (U.S.)**	**M. Hingis (Switz.)**

French Open Tennis Championships—Singles

Year	Men	Women
1993	S. Bruguera (Spain)	S. Graf (Ger.)
1994	S. Bruguera (Spain)	A. Sánchez Vicario (Spain)
1995	T. Muster (Austria)	S. Graf (Ger.)
1996	Ye. Kafelnikov (Russia)	S. Graf (Ger.)
1997	**G. Kuerten (Braz.)**	**I. Majoli (Cro.)**

All-England (Wimbledon) Tennis Championships—Singles

Year	Men	Women
1993	P. Sampras (U.S.)	S. Graf (Ger.)
1994	P. Sampras (U.S.)	C. Martínez (Spain)
1995	P. Sampras (U.S.)	S. Graf (Ger.)
1996	R. Krajicek (Neth.)	S. Graf (Ger.)
1997	**P. Sampras (U.S.)**	**M. Hingis (Switz.)**

United States Open Tennis Championships—Singles

Year	Men	Women
1993	P. Sampras (U.S.)	S. Graf (Ger.)
1994	A. Agassi (U.S.)	A. Sánchez Vicario (Spain)
1995	P. Sampras (U.S.)	S. Graf (Ger.)
1996	P. Sampras (U.S.)	S. Graf (Ger.)
1997	**P. Rafter (Austl.)**	**M. Hingis (Switz.)**

Australian Open Tennis Championships—Doubles

Year	Men	Women
1993	D. Visser, L. Warder	G. Fernandez, N. Zvereva
1994	P. Haarhuis, J. Eltingh	G. Fernandez, N. Zvereva
1995	J. Palmer, R. Reneberg	A. Sánchez Vicario, J. Novotna
1996	S. Edberg, P. Korda	A. Sánchez Vicario, C. Rubin
1997	**T. Woodbridge, M. Woodforde**	**M. Hingis, N. Zvereva**

French Open Tennis Championships—Doubles

Year	Men	Women
1993	L. Jensen, M. Jensen	G. Fernandez, N. Zvereva
1994	B. Black, J. Stark	G. Fernandez, N. Zvereva
1995	P. Haarhuis, J. Eltingh	G. Fernandez, N. Zvereva
1996	Ye. Kafelnikov, D. Vacek	L. Davenport, M.J. Fernandez
1997	**Ye. Kafelnikov, D. Vacek**	**G. Fernandez, N. Zvereva**

All-England (Wimbledon) Tennis Championships—Doubles

Year	Men	Women
1993	T. Woodbridge, M. Woodforde	G. Fernandez, N. Zvereva
1994	T. Woodbridge, M. Woodforde	G. Fernandez, N. Zvereva
1995	T. Woodbridge, M. Woodforde	A. Sánchez Vicario, J. Novotna
1996	T. Woodbridge, M. Woodforde	H. Sukova, M. Hingis
1997	**T. Woodbridge, M. Woodforde**	**G. Fernandez, N. Zvereva**

United States Open Tennis Championships—Doubles

Year	Men	Women
1993	K. Flach, R. Leach	A. Sánchez Vicario, H. Sukova
1994	P. Haarhuis, J. Eltingh	A. Sánchez Vicario, J. Novotna
1995	T. Woodbridge, M. Woodforde	G. Fernandez, N. Zvereva
1996	T. Woodbridge, M. Woodforde	G. Fernandez, N. Zvereva
1997	**Ye. Kafelnikov, D. Vacek**	**L. Davenport, J. Novotna**

Davis Cup (men)			
Year	Winner	Runner-up	Results
1993	Germany	Australia	4–1
1994	Sweden	Russia	4–1
1995	United States	Russia	3–2
1996	France	Sweden	3–2
1997	**Sweden**	**United States**	**5–0**

Fed Cup (women)			
Year	Winner	Runner-up	Results
1993	Spain	Australia	3–0
1994	Spain	United States	3–0
1995	Spain	United States	3–2
1996	United States	Spain	5–0
1997	**France**	**Netherlands**	**4–1**

championship since Lottie Dodd in 1887. In the semifinals Hingis was a straight-set winner over the glamorous Russian 16-year-old Anna Kournikova, and Novotna easily dismissed 1995–96 finalist Arantxa Sánchez Vicario. Second-seeded Seles could not convert a match point against Sandrine Testud of France and lost tamely in the third round.

U.S. Open. With his movie star appearance and muscular physique, Rafter was an immensely popular figure in Flushing Meadows, N.Y., as the players assembled for the last Grand Slam event of the season. At 24 the Australian demonstrated irrefutably that he had come of age. He had lost five finals without winning a tournament leading up to the U.S. contest, but he raised the level of his game markedly and performed more powerfully than ever before. In the final he eliminated Rusedski 6–3, 6–2, 4–6, 7–5. Not since Pat Cash triumphed at Wimbledon 10 years earlier had an Australian won a major championship.

Rafter toppled two highly regarded Americans en route to his groundbreaking triumph. In the fourth round he was dazzling under the lights in a four-set victory over 1994 champion Agassi, and in the semifinals he played what was perhaps the match

Martina Hingis beams after having defeated Venus Williams (left) in the women's U.S. Open final. She became only the sixth woman to win at least three Grand Slam titles in a year.

PAUL J. SUTTON—DUOMO

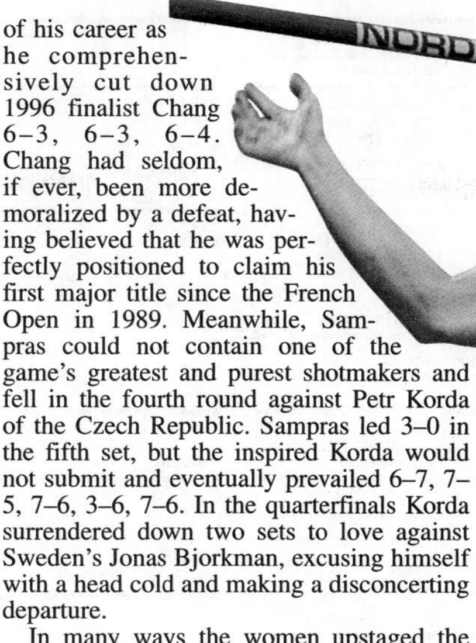

of his career as he comprehensively cut down 1996 finalist Chang 6–3, 6–3, 6–4. Chang had seldom, if ever, been more demoralized by a defeat, having believed that he was perfectly positioned to claim his first major title since the French Open in 1989. Meanwhile, Sampras could not contain one of the game's greatest and purest shotmakers and fell in the fourth round against Petr Korda of the Czech Republic. Sampras led 3–0 in the fifth set, but the inspired Korda would not submit and eventually prevailed 6–7, 7–5, 7–6, 3–6, 7–6. In the quarterfinals Korda surrendered down two sets to love against Sweden's Jonas Bjorkman, excusing himself with a head cold and making a disconcerting departure.

In many ways the women upstaged the men at tournament. Venus Williams became the first African-American female to appear in the final since Althea Gibson won the crown in 1958. Unseeded and largely an unrealized talent until her remarkable performance, Williams advertised her astonishing athleticism and her strong will to win throughout the competition. In the final she was simply beaten by a decidedly better match player, her weaknesses thoroughly exposed by Hingis in a 6–0, 6–4 loss. Hingis consequently became only the sixth woman ever to capture at least three Grand Slam titles in a single year. It was apparent, however, that Williams stirred more emotions than any other player in the field. She upended 8th-seeded Anke Huber in the third round and toppled number 11 Irina Spirlea in an excruciatingly tight semifinal meeting, saving two match points to win 7–6, 4–6, 7–6.

That match was marred by an incident at a changeover in which the two competitors seemed to deliberately bump into each other. Richard Williams—the father of Venus—accused the Romanian player of racism after the match but later apologized to Spirlea and retracted his accusation.

Other Events. After an agonizing loss in the 1996 Davis Cup final, in which they were three times within a point of defeating France, Sweden came back unwaveringly in 1997 to become the champion nation for the sixth time. The Swedish men beat the United States 5–0 in the late November final at Göteborg, Swed. Sampras, who suffered a muscle tear in his calf, was forced to retire after having split sets with Magnus Larsson. Bjorkman—who ascended from number 69 to number 4 in 1997—was the chief architect of the triumph. In the Fed Cup final for the women, France was triumphant for the first time, overcoming The Netherlands 4–1 at Den Bosch, Neth. Pierce and Testud ably joined forces to lead France to the triumph.

(STEVE FLINK)

TRACK AND FIELD SPORTS (ATHLETICS)

A year in which African distance runners produced a flurry of new world records, 1997 also featured indoor and outdoor world championship competition and a pair of highly publicized million-dollar match races.

GARY M. PRIOR—ALLSPORT

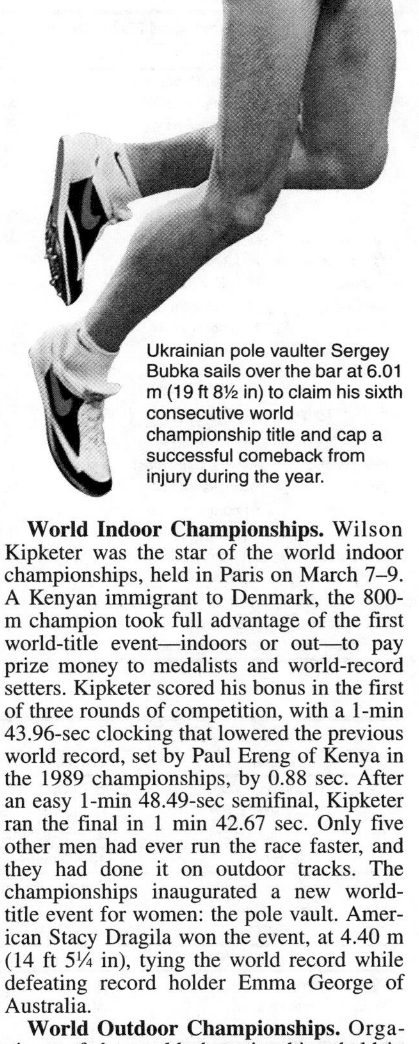

Ukrainian pole vaulter Sergey Bubka sails over the bar at 6.01 m (19 ft 8½ in) to claim his sixth consecutive world championship title and cap a successful comeback from injury during the year.

World Indoor Championships. Wilson Kipketer was the star of the world indoor championships, held in Paris on March 7–9. A Kenyan immigrant to Denmark, the 800-m champion took full advantage of the first world-title event—indoors or out—to pay prize money to medalists and world-record setters. Kipketer scored his bonus in the first of three rounds of competition, with a 1-min 43.96-sec clocking that lowered the previous world record, set by Paul Ereng of Kenya in the 1989 championships, by 0.88 sec. After an easy 1-min 48.49-sec semifinal, Kipketer ran the final in 1 min 42.67 sec. Only five other men had ever run the race faster, and they had done it on outdoor tracks. The championships inaugurated a new world-title event for women: the pole vault. American Stacy Dragila won the event, at 4.40 m (14 ft 5¼ in), tying the world record while defeating record holder Emma George of Australia.

World Outdoor Championships. Organizers of the world championships, held in Athens on August 1–10, put on a memorable event that boosted their city's ultimately successful bid to serve as host of the 2004 Olympic Games. The sixth edition of the championships—the first to award prize money—yielded a number of new champions but no world records, despite the enticement of $100,000 world-record bonuses.

1997 World Outdoor Records—Men

Event	Competitor and country	Performance
800 m	Wilson Kipketer (Den.)	1 min 41.73 sec*
	Wilson Kipketer (Den.)	1 min 41.24 sec
	Wilson Kipketer (Den.)	1 min 41.1 sec
3,000-m steeplechase	Wilson Boit Kipketer (Kenya)	2 min 59.08 sec
	Bernard Barmasai (Kenya)	2 min 55.72 sec
2 mi†	Haile Gebrselassie (Eth.)	8 min 1.08 sec
	Daniel Komen (Kenya)	7 min 58.61 sec
5,000 m	Haile Gebrselassie (Eth.)	12 min 41.86 sec
	Daniel Komen (Kenya)	12 min 39.74 sec
10,000 m	Haile Gebrselassie (Eth.)	26 min 31.32 sec
	Paul Tergat (Kenya)	26 min 27.85 sec

*Equals world record. †Not an officially ratified event; best performance on record.

1997 World Outdoor Records–Women

Event	Competitor and country	Performance
5,000 m	Dong Yanmei (China)	14 min 31.27 sec
	Jiang Bo (China)	14 min 28.09 sec
Pole vault	Emma George (Austl.)	4.55 m (14 ft 11 in)
Hammer throw	Olga Kuzenkova (Russia)	71.22 m (233 ft 8 in)
	Olga Kuzenkova (Russia)	73.10 m (239 ft 10 in)

1997 World Indoor Records—Men

Event	Competitor and country	Performance
800 m	Wilson Kipketer (Den.)	1 min 43.96 sec
	Wilson Kipketer (Den.)	1 min 42.67 sec
1,500 m	Hicham El Guerrouj (Morocco)	3 min 31.18 sec
Mile	Hicham El Guerrouj (Morocco)	3 min 48.45 sec
5,000 m	Haile Gebrselassie (Eth.)	12 min 59.04 sec
Triple jump	Aliecer Urrutia (Cuba)	17.83 m (58 ft 6 in)

1997 World Indoor Records—Women

Event	Competitor and country	Performance
4x400-m relay	Russia (Tatyana Chebykina, Svetlana Goncharenko, Olga Kotlyarova, Tatyana Alekseyeva)	3 min 26.84 sec
5,000 m	Jiang Bo (China)	14 min 28.09 sec
Pole vault	Stacy Dragila (U.S.)	4.40 m (14 ft 5¼ in)*

World Track and Field Championships—Men

Event	1995	1997
100 m	D. Bailey (Can.)	M. Greene (U.S.)
200 m	M. Johnson (U.S.)	A. Boldon (Trin.)
400 m	M. Johnson (U.S.)	M. Johnson (U.S.)
800 m	W. Kipketer (Den.)	W. Kipketer (Den.)
1,500 m	N. Morceli (Alg.)	H. El Guerrouj (Mor.)
5,000 m	I. Kirui (Kenya)	D. Komen (Kenya)
10,000 m	H. Gebrselassie (Eth.)	H. Gebrselassie (Eth.)
steeplechase	M. Kiptanui (Kenya)	W.B. Kipketer (Kenya)
110-m hurdles	A. Johnson (U.S.)	A. Johnson (U.S.)
400-m hurdles	D. Adkins (U.S.)	S. Diagana (Fr.)
marathon	M. Fiz (Spain)	A. Anton (Spain)
20-km walk	M. Didoni (Italy)	D. García (Mex.)
50-km walk	V. Kononen (Fin.)	R. Korzeniowski (Pol.)
4×100-m relay	Canada (R. Esmie, G. Gilbert, B. Surin, D. Bailey)	Canada (R. Esmie, G. Gilbert, B. Surin, D. Bailey)
4×400-m relay	United States (M. Ramsey, D. Mills, B. Reynolds, M. Johnson)	United States (J. Young, A. Pettigrew, C. Jones, T. Washington)
high jump	T. Kemp (Bahamas)	J. Sotomayor (Cuba)
pole vault	S. Bubka (Ukr.)	S. Bubka (Ukr.)
long jump	I. Pedroso (Cuba)	I. Pedroso (Cuba)
triple jump	J. Edwards (U.K.)	Y. Quesada (Cuba)
shot put	J. Godina (U.S.)	J. Godina (U.S.)
discus throw	L. Riedel (Ger.)	L. Riedel (Ger.)
hammer throw	A. Abduvaliyev (Tajik.)	H. Weis (Ger.)
javelin throw	J. Zelezny (Cz.Rep.)	M. Corbett (S.Af.)
decathlon	D. O'Brien (U.S.)	T. Dvorak (Cz.Rep.)

World Track and Field Championships—Women

Event	1995	1997
100 m	G. Torrence (U.S.)	M. Jones (U.S.)
200 m	M. Ottey (Jam.)	Z. Pintusevich (Ukr.)
400 m	M.-J. Pérec (Fr.)	C. Freeman (Austl.)
800 m	A. Quirot (Cuba)	A. Quirot (Cuba)
1,500 m	H. Boulmerka (Alg.)	C. Sacramento (Port.)
5,000 m	S. O'Sullivan (Ire.)	G. Szabo (Rom.)
10,000 m	F. Ribeiro (Port.)	S. Barsosio (Kenya)
100-m hurdles	G. Devers (U.S.)	L. Engquist (Swed.)
400-m hurdles	K. Batten (U.S.)	N. Bidouane (Mor.)
marathon	M. Machado (Port.)	H. Suzuki (Japan)
10-km walk	I. Stankina (Rus.)	A. Sidoti (Italy)
4x100-m relay	United States (C. Mondie-Milner, C. Guidry, C. Gaines, G. Torrence)	United States (C. Gaines, M. Jones, I. Miller, G. Devers)
4x400-m relay	United States (K. Graham, R. Stevens, C. Jones, J. Miles)	Germany (A. Feller, U. Rohlander, A. Rucker, G. Breuer)
high jump	S. Kostadinova (Bul.)	H. Haugland (Nor.)
long jump	F. May (Italy)	L. Galkina (Russia)
triple jump	I. Kravets (Ukr.)	S. Kasparkova (Cz.Rep.)
shot put	A. Kumbernuss (Ger.)	A. Kumbernuss (Ger.)
discus throw	E. Zvereva (Bel.)	B. Faumuina (N.Z.)
javelin throw	N. Shikolenko (Bel.)	T. Hattestad (Nor.)
heptathlon	G. Shouaa (Syria)	S. Braun (Ger.)

IAAF World Cup—Men

	100 metre	200 metre	400 metre	800 metre	1,500 metre
1989	L. Christie (Gr.Brit.)	R. Caetano da Silva (Amer.)	R. Hernandez (Amer.)	T. McKean (Gr.Brit.)	A. Bile (Africa)
1992	L. Christie (Gr.Brit.)	R. Caetano da Silva (Amer.)	S. Bada (Africa)	D. Sharpe (U.K.)	M. Suleiman (Asia)
1994	L. Christie (Gr.Brit.)	J. Regis (Gr.Brit.)	A. Pettigrew (U.S.)	M. Everett (U.S.)	N. Morceli (Africa)
	5,000 metre	**10,000 metre**	**Steeplechase**	**110-m hurdles**	**400-m hurdles**
1989	S. Aouita (Africa)	S. Antibo (Europe)	J. Kariuki (Africa)	R. Kingdom (U.S.)	D. Patrick (U.S.)
1992	F. Bayesa (Africa)	A. Abebe (Africa)	P. Barkutwo (Africa)	C. Jackson (U.K.)	S. Matete (Africa)
1994	B. Lahlafi (Africa)	K. Skah (Africa)	M. Kiptanui (Africa)	T. Jarrett (Gr.Brit.)	S. Matete (Africa)
	4×100-m relays	**4×400-m relays**	**Triple jump**	**High jump**	**Pole vault**
1989	United States	Americas	M. Conley (U.S.)	P. Sjoberg (Europe)	P. Collet (Europe)
1992	United States	Africa	J. Edwards (U.K.)	Y. Sergeyenko (UT)	I. Potapovich (UT)
1994	Great Britain	Great Britain	Y. Quesada (Amer.)	J. Sotomayor (Amer.)	O. Brits (Africa)
	Long jump	**Shot put**	**Discus throw**	**Hammer throw**	**Javelin throw**
1989	L. Myricks (U.S.)	U. Timmermann (E.Ger.)	J. Schult (E.Ger.)	H. Weis (Europe)	S. Backley (Gr.Brit.)
1992	I. Pedroso (Amer.)	M. Stulce (U.S.)	T. Washington (U.S.)	T. Gécsek (Europe)	J. Zelezny (Europe)
1994	F. Salle (Gr.Brit.)	C.J. Hunter (U.S.)	V. Dubrovshchik (Europe)	A. Abduvaliyev (Asia)	S. Backley (Gr.Brit.)
	Team				
1989	United States				
1992	Africa				
1994	Africa				

Ukrainian pole vaulter Sergey Bubka, who because of injury had competed just four times in 1997 before the championships, won his sixth consecutive world title with panache. When the bar reached 5.96 m (19 ft 6½ in) and only three vaulters remained in the competition, he could have taken the lead with a first-attempt clearance. Instead, he boldly elected to pass and raise the bar to 6.01 m (19 ft 8½ in), a height he had not cleared since May 1996. This time Bubka cleared with room to spare, and no competitor could match him.

Wilson Kipketer runs to a new world record of 1 min 42.67 sec in the 800 m.

MICHEL LIPCHITZ—ASSOCIATED PRESS

Merlene Ottey, the 37-year-old women's sprint star from Jamaica, placed third in the 200 m to collect a record 14th world outdoor championship medal. The athlete with the next largest collection, American Carl Lewis (10 medals), did not compete in Athens and closed out his illustrious career at the conclusion of the 1997 season.

Repeat champions, however, were few and far between, as just 13 winners from the 1995 meet and 10 of 44 champions from the 1996 Olympics prevailed. To boost participation, the International Amateur Athletic Federation (IAAF) issued "wild card" invitations to defending world champions. The move was precipitated largely by the fact that two defending world and Olympic champions, Michael Johnson (200 m and 400 m) and Dan O'Brien (decathlon), missed the U.S. championships, citing injuries, and did not qualify for their country's team. Several defending champions accepted the invitations, and for the first time at a major world-level championship since the 1928 Olympics, a nation was allowed to field more than three athletes in an individual event. A quartet of runners from the U.S. made the 400-m final, and Johnson rebounded from his thigh injury to win the world title for a third consecutive time.

Men's International Competition. Perhaps the biggest news in 1997 was that Olympic 100-m champion Donovan Bailey of Canada would race Johnson over 150 m in the Toronto Skydome. The made-for-television spectacle would ostensibly settle the question of which man was the "world's fastest human." It would also pay the two sprinters a guaranteed $500,000 each to appear, with the winner taking an additional $1 million. In the event, however, the June 1 meet treated approximately 25,000 attendees and millions more television viewers to an anticlimactic race. Bailey strode to an early lead on the specially constructed track. Shortly after entering the straight, Johnson grimaced and then clutched his left thigh before stopping. Bailey finished alone in 14.99 sec and in the race's aftermath accused Johnson of feigning injury and of cowardice. Bailey later apologized.

A day before the Bailey-Johnson showdown, in Hengelo, Neth., promoters underwritten by shoe manufacturer adidas put up a $1 million purse for a two-mile race between two other Olympic champions, Haile Gebrselassie of Ethiopia and Noureddine

TATIA PAULE— ASSOCIATED PRESS

Daniel Komen of Kenya is lifted by teammates after he broke a 10-day-old world record in the 5,000 m. Komen's time of 12 min 39.74 sec eclipsed Haile Gebrselassie's mark by 2.12 sec.

Morceli of Algeria. The payout, however, was contingent on the winner's covering the two miles in less than eight minutes. Morceli, the 1,500-m and one-mile world-record holder, proved far from up to the task, and Gebrselassie, the 5,000-m world-record holder, ran the last three laps alone. Gebrselassie's time of 8 min 1.08 sec lowered the old world best (two miles was not an officially recognized world-record distance) by 2.46 sec but did not earn the $1 million.

For Gebrselassie, who had run a two-mile world best in 1995 only to see it surpassed by Daniel Komen of Kenya in 1996, the race began a back-and-forth flurry of record breaking that continued through the summer. On July 4 in Oslo the Ethiopian cut almost seven seconds from the 10,000-m world record with a 26-min 31.32-sec clocking. Komen promptly took back the two-mile standard on July 19 in Hechtel, Belg., lowering it to 7 min 58.61 sec.

At the world championships Gebrselassie won his third consecutive title at 10,000 m, and Komen won the 5,000 m. Three nights after Komen's gold-medal race, in a 5,000-m event at the Weltklasse Invitational in Zürich, Switz., Gebrselassie sprinted away from Komen and Paul Tergat of Kenya in the final 200 m to win in a world-record 12

IAAF World Cup—Women

	100 metre	200 metre	400 metre	800 metre	1,500 metre
1989	S. Echols (U.S.)	S. Moller (E.Ger.)	A. Quirot (Amer.)	A. Quirot (Amer.)	P. Ivan (Europe)
1992	N. Voronova (UT)	M.-J. Pérec (Europe)	J. Miles (U.S.)	M. Mutola (Africa)	Y. Podkopayeva (UT)
1994	I. Privalova (Europe)	M. Ottey (Amer.)	I. Privalova (Europe)	M. Mutola (Africa)	H. Boulmerka (Africa)
	3,000 metre	**10,000 metre**	**100-m hurdles**	**400-m hurdles**	**4×100-m relays**
1989	Y. Murray (Europe)	K. Ullrich (E.Ger.)	C. Oschkenat (E.Ger.)	S. Farmer-Patrick (U.S.)	East Germany
1992	D. Tulu (Africa)	D. Tulu (Africa)	A. López (Amer.)	S. Farmer-Patrick (U.S.)	Asia
1994	Y. Murray (Gr.Brit.)	E. Meyer (Africa)	A. López (Amer.)	S. Gunnell (Gr.Brit.)	Africa
	4×400-m relays	**Triple Jump**	**High jump**	**Long jump**	**Shot put**
1989	Americas		S. Costa (Amer.)	G. Chistyakova (U.S.S.R.)	Zhihong Huang (Asia)
1992	Americas		I. Quintero (Amer.)	H. Drechsler (Ger.)	B. Laza (Amer.)
1994	Great Britain	A. Biryukova (Europe)	B. Bilac (Europe)	I. Kravets (Europe)	Zhihong Huang (Asia)
	Discus throw	**Javelin throw**	**Team**		
1989	I. Wyludda (E.Ger.)	P. Felke (E.Ger.)	East Germany		
1992	M. Marten (Amer.)	T. Sanderson (U.K.)	Unified Team		
1994	I. Wyludda (Europe)	T. Hattestad (Europe)	Europe		

min 41.86 sec. In Brussels nine days later, Gebrselassie watched from the stands as first Komen in the 5,000 m (12 min 39.74 sec) and then Tergat in the 10,000 m (26 min 27.85 sec) erased his world records.

The event most thoroughly dominated by one man was the 800 m, which Kipketer never lost in 1997. He equaled British runner Sebastian Coe's 16-year-old outdoor mark of 1 min 41.73 sec, the oldest world record on the books, in Stockholm on July 7 and subsequently broke it on August 13 in Zürich. Kipketer won the indoor and outdoor world titles with ease and then displayed astonishing tactical versatility in subsequent meets. His 1-min 42.98-sec victory at the Grand Prix final in Fukuoka, Japan, raised his 1997 total of races faster than 1 min 43 sec to eight, one more than the record of seven he had established in 1996.

Women's International Competition. The most startling development early in the summer season was the emergence of sprinter Marion Jones of the U.S., a former high-school track star, who at age 16 had missed qualifying for the 1992 Olympics in the 200 m by a single place (and just 0.07 sec). Although Jones had excelled as a basketball player through three seasons at the University of North Carolina, her progress in track had stalled until she reeled off a 10.92-sec 100-m race in the semifinals of the 1997 U.S. championships and followed it up by winning the final in 10.97 sec. She then handed Jackie Joyner-Kersee her first long-jump defeat at the U.S. championships or U.S. Olympic trials since Joyner-Kersee's first such title in 1987, but Jones failed to qualify for the world championships final in that event.

She went on to win 11 of her 14 major 100-m and 200-m races in Europe and Japan, defeating two-time Olympic 100-m champion Gail Devers in two of three meetings and Ottey in six of eight races. Jones also won the world 100-m title and produced the year's fastest times in the 100 m (10.76 sec) and 200 m (21.76 sec).

The $250,000 IAAF Grand Prix circuit points leadership for 1997 went to shot-putter Astrid Kumbernuss. The 27-year-old German lost the world indoor championship to rival Vita Pavlysh of Ukraine, snapping a streak of 53 consecutive wins for the Olympic champion since February 1995. After losing to Pavlysh once more in early May, Kumbernuss was perfect—winning 27 times in succession, including nine Grand Prix circuit meets and the outdoor world title. Cathy Freeman, the 1996 Olympic runner-up and Australia's first Aboriginal track star, was undefeated at 400 m in nine meets, including the world championships, which she won in 49.77 sec. (*See* BIOGRAPHIES.)

China's national games in October shocked the track and field world, much as that sports festival's 1993 edition had, with world records and stunningly high-level performances, often by athletes previously unknown outside China. The 1,500-m heats and final yielded the 13 fastest times of the year, although no Chinese athlete had even entered that event at the world championships. In the heats alone, four teenage girls surpassed the previous world junior record of 3 min 58.91 sec (set by Wang Yuan at the 1993 national games), and each ran yet faster in the final. Winner Jiang Bo's 3-min 50.98-sec clocking missed the world record by 0.52 sec. The 5,000-m world record fell twice during the meet, with Jiang lowering it the farthest with her 14-min 28.09-sec win in the final. Ma Junren, coach to many of the barrier-smashing distance runners, denied widespread speculation that he had given his athletes banned drugs and instead credited secret nutritional supplements and hard training.

Cross Country and Marathon Running. At the world cross country championships, in Turin, Italy, in March, Tergat won the men's individual title for the third year in a row. Derartu Tulu of Ethiopia claimed the women's crown, and her nation won the women's team title. Kenya won three of the four team championships (junior and senior men and junior women), bringing its tally to 28 of 32 titles awarded in the 1990s.

At the world championships in Athens, Spain's Abel Antón outkicked his countryman, defending champion Martin Fiz, to win the men's marathon in 2 hr 13 min 16 sec. The women's gold medal went to Hiromi Suzuki of Japan in 2 hr 29 min 48 sec.

The men's and women's winners of other

CHRISTOPH RUCKSTUHL—AFP

U.S. sprinter Marion Jones (right) narrowly defeats Ukraine's Zhanna Pintussevich (foreground) in the women's 100-m final at the world track and field championships in Athens on August 3. Sevatheda Fynes (rear) of The Bahamas finished third.

World Cross Country Championships—Men (12,000 m)

Year	Individual	Team
1993	W. Sigei (Kenya)	Kenya
1994	W. Sigei (Kenya)	Kenya
1995	P. Tergat (Kenya)	Kenya
1996	P. Tergat (Kenya)	Kenya
1997	**P. Tergat (Kenya)**	**Kenya**

World Cross Country Championships—Women (5,000 m)

Year	Individual	Team
1993	A. Dias (Port.)	Kenya
1994	H. Chepngeno (Kenya)	Portugal
1995	D. Tulu (Eth.)	Kenya
1996	G. Wami (Eth.)	Kenya
1997	**D. Tulu (Eth.)**	**Ethiopia**

World Marathon Cup*

Year	Men	Women
1989	K. Metaferia (Eth.)	S. Marchiano (U.S.)
1991	Y. Tolstikov (U.S.S.R.)	R. Mota (Port.)
1993	R. Nerurkar (U.K.)	Wang Junxia (China)
1995	D. Wakiihuri (Kenya)	A. Catuna (Rom.)
1997	**Spain**	**Japan**

*Team event from 1997.

Boston Marathon

Year	Men	h:min:s
1993	C. N'Deti (Kenya)	2:09:33
1994	C. N'Deti (Kenya)	2:07:15
1995	C. N'Deti (Kenya)	2:09:22
1996	M. Tanui (Kenya)	2:09:16
1997	**L. Aguta (Kenya)**	**2:10:34**
Year	**Women**	**h:min:s**
1993	O. Markova (Russia)	2:25:27
1994	U. Pippig (Ger.)	2:21:45
1995	U. Pippig (Ger.)	2:25:11
1996	U. Pippig (Ger.)	2:27:12
1997	**F. Roba (Eth.)**	**2:26:23**

New York City Marathon

Year	Men	h:min:s
1993	A. Espinosa (Mex.)	2:10:04
1994	G. Silva (Mex.)	2:11:21
1995	G. Silva (Mex.)	2:11:00
1996	G. Leone (Italy)	2:09:54
1997	**J. Kagwe (Kenya)**	**2:08:12**
Year	**Women**	**h:min:s**
1993	U. Pippig (Ger.)	2:26:24
1994	T. Loroupe (Kenya)	2:27:37
1995	T. Loroupe (Kenya)	2:28:06
1996	A. Catuna (Rom.)	2:28:18
1997	**F. Rochat-Moser (Switz.)**	**2:28:43**

major marathons were: Osaka, Japan, women's, Katrin Dörre-Heinig (Germany) 2 hr 25 min 57 sec; Tokyo, Koji Shimizu (Japan) 2 hr 10 min 9 sec and Makiko Ito (Japan) 2 hr 27 min 45 sec; Fukuoka, men's, Josiah Thugwane (South Africa) 2 hr 7 min 28 sec; Nagoya, Japan, women's, Madina Biktagirova (Belarus) 2 hr 29 min 30 sec; Paris, John Kemboi (Kenya) 2 hr 10 min 14 sec and Helena Rozdrogina (Russia) 2 hr 29 min 11 sec; London, Antonio Pinto (Portugal) 2 hr 7 min 55 sec and Joyce Chepchumba (Kenya) 2 hr 26 min 51 sec; Rotterdam, Neth., Domingos Castro (Portugal) 2 hr 7 min 51 sec and Tegla Loroupe (Kenya) 2 hr 22 min 7 sec; Boston, Lameck Aguta (Kenya) 2 hr 10 min 34 sec and Fatuma Roba (Ethiopia) 2 hr 26 min 23 sec; Berlin, Elijah Lagat (Kenya) 2 hr 7 min 41 sec and Catherina McKiernan (Ireland) 2 hr 23 min 44 sec; Chicago, Khalid Khannouchi (Morocco) 2 hr 7 min 10 sec and Marian Sutton (U.K.) 2 hr 29 min 3 sec; New York City, John Kagwe (Kenya) 2 hr 8 min 12 sec and Franziska Rochat-Moser (Switzerland) 2 hr 28 min 43 sec.

(SIEG LINDSTROM)

VOLLEYBALL

In 1997 volleyball ranked among the fastest-growing sports in the world. More than 200 nations were members of the Fédération Internationale de Volley Ball (FIVB), the world governing body for the sport, and more than 130 million people played volleyball annually, according to the FIVB. In an attempt to adapt the sport and to reduce the length of matches, which often exceeded three hours, the FIVB was exploring several options. The increased use of rally scoring (point-per-serve scoring) was one of the major components of these plans, as was the potential introduction of a halftime. In addition, some playing tactics were being revised. The utilization of jump serves and overhand serve receptions was on the increase, and back-row hitters were becoming a more integral part of the offensive attack.

The inaugural World Grand Champions Cup, the major international tournament of the year, took place in Japan in November. Russia captured the women's title, and Brazil claimed the men's crown. In the men's World League, established in 1990, Italy won its sixth title. Russia captured the women's World Grand Prix. On the U.S. scene, Stanford won both the men's and women's National Collegiate Athletic Association volleyball titles.

At the FIVB World Championships of Beach Volleyball, held in Los Angeles in September, U.S. men's and women's four-person teams both captured gold. The men defeated Brazil two games to none in just over an hour, with scores of 12–4 and 12–6, while the U.S. women needed only 40 minutes to beat Australia 2–0 (12–2, 12–5). Brazil beat the American teams to win the gold medal in both the men's and women's pairs. Owing to the increasing popularity of beach volleyball, the number of professional and amateur tournaments throughout the world, as well as prize moneys for the pro tours, was increased for 1998.

(RICHARD S. WANNINGER)

World Volleyball Championships

Year	Men	Women
1988	United States	U.S.S.R.
1990	Italy	U.S.S.R.
1992	Brazil	Cuba
1994	Italy	Cuba
1996	Netherlands	Cuba

WEIGHT LIFTING

At the 1997 world championships, held in December in Chiang Mai, Thai., China dominated both the men's and the women's competition, as it had at the 1995 championships, held in Guangzhou (Canton), China. (*See* TABLE, page 372.)

In the men's events China won three overall gold medals, three silver, and one bronze and scored 637 points to win the team competition. Bulgaria won three gold medals, and Moldova, Poland, Russia, and Slovakia won one gold each. In the final tally, Bulgaria was second to China, with a total of five overall medals. Poland won four, Turkey three, and Russia two.

Superheavyweight Andrey Chemerkin of Russia, the Olympic champion in 1996, won the clean and jerk and the overall title with a new world record of 462.5 kg (1,019.6 lb). American Wes Barnett won a bronze overall in the 108-kg division, the first U.S. overall medal at the world championships since 1976. Four world records were broken in the men's competition.

In the women's events China won six overall gold medals and one silver and scored 657 points to win the team competition. Indonesia won two overall gold medals, and Turkey captured one. China's seven overall medals topped the final tally, followed by Indonesia, Turkey, and Taiwan, with three each. Fifteen world records were broken in the women's competition, 12 by China and 3 by Turkey.From 1998 the men's competition would include only eight bodyweight classes; women weight lifters, who would finally be included in the Olympics at the 2000 Summer Games in Sydney, Australia, would compete in seven classes.

(DRAGOMIR CIOROSLAN)

WRESTLING

Freestyle and Greco-Roman. On Jan. 1, 1997, eight new men's weight classes (down from 10), which had been approved by the Fédération Internationale des Luttes Associées (FILA) in August 1996, became effective. This was the biggest rule change since 1969 and applied to all FILA-sanctioned events.

At the freestyle world championships, held in Krasnoyarsk, Russia, on August 28–

Three-time Olympic champion Aleksandr Karelin of Russia (right) manhandles Deak Mihaly of Hungary en route to winning the 130-kg-class gold medal at the Greco-Roman wrestling world championships in Wroclaw, Pol., in September. The Russians won two other gold medals to take the team title.

CZAREK SOKOLOWSKI—ASSOCIATED PRESS

31, 44 teams competed. The host Russian team captured two gold medals and claimed the team title with 61 points, followed by Ukraine with 45 points and Iran with 40. The U.S. took only two medals, one gold as Les Gutches took the title at 85 kg and one silver from Cary Kolat at 63 kg. Both were competing in their first world championship. The U.S. team finished sixth with 29 points, one point behind Cuba and Turkey.

The Russian team duplicated its freestyle win in the Greco-Roman world championships, held in Wroclaw, Pol., on September 10–13. Russian wrestlers took three gold medals en route to the team title with 60 points, followed by Turkey with 38 points and Germany with 31 points. Russian superheavyweight Aleksandr Karelin, winner of a record three Olympic gold medals in wrestling, won the title at 130 kg.

At the 67th U.S. collegiate championships, held in Cedar Falls, Iowa, on March 20–22, defending champion University of Iowa won its 17th title with a record 170 points and five champions over runner-up Oklahoma State. A record 17,436 fans—the largest amateur wrestling crowd in U.S. history—witnessed the finals. (JOHN HOKE)

Sumo. In 1997, for the fourth consecutive year, *yokozuna* (grand champion) Takanohana emerged as the leading figure in Japanese sumo wrestling, winning 78 of the 90 annual bouts and three of the six *basho* (tournaments). Wakanohana opened the year with a victory in January. His hopes of gaining promotion to *yokozuna* in March were sidetracked by an injury, and Takanohana captured the Emperor's Cup after a four-way play-off. Hawaiian-born Akebono came on strong at the end of the May *basho,* beating Takanohana in their final bout and again in a play-off to take the *yusho* (victory) for his ninth championship. Takanohana bounced back in July, decisively defeating Akebono on the final day to clinch the Nagoya *basho* title. Takanohana made it two in a row by winning the Aki *basho* in September after a play-off with Musashimaru to boost his *yusho* total to 18. In the year's final tournament, Takanonami surprised his stablemate Takanohana in a play-off to claim the title—his second.

Another highlight of the year was the retirement of Hawaiian-born former *ozeki* (champion) Konishiki after an outstanding 15-year career. The heaviest-ever in sumo history at more than 278 kg (612 lb), Konishiki won three titles and in 1992 narrowly missed promotion to *yokozuna*.

(ANDY ADAMS)

World Weight Lifting Champions, 1997

Weight	Winner and country	Performance
MEN		
54 kg (119 lb)	Lan Shizang (China)	287.5 kg (633.8 lb)
59 kg (130 lb)	Stefan Georgiev (Bulgaria)	295 kg (650.4 lb)
64 kg (141 lb)	Xiao Jiangang (China)	317.5 kg (700 lb)
70 kg (154.5 lb)	Zlatan Vanev (Bulgaria)	355 kg (782.6 lb)
76 kg (167.5 lb)	Yoto Yotov (Bulgaria)	367.5 kg (810.2 lb)
83 kg (183 lb)	Andrzej Cofalik (Poland)	380 kg (837.8 lb)
91 kg (200.5 lb)	Vadim Vacarciuc (Moldova)	387.5 kg (854.3 lb)
99 kg (218 lb)	Martin Tesovic (Slovakia)	400 kg (881.8 lb)
108 kg (238 lb)	Cui Wenhua (China)	415 kg (914.9 lb)
+108 kg (+238 lb)	Andrey Chemerkin (Russia)	462.5 kg (1,019.6 lb)
WOMEN		
46 kg (101 lb)	Liu Ling (China)	175 kg (385.8 lb)
50 kg (110 lb)	Winarni (Indonesia)	185 kg (407.9 lb)
54 kg (119 lb)	Meng Xianjuan (China)	205 kg (451.9 lb)
59 kg (130 lb)	Patmawati (Indonesia)	212.5 kg (468.5 lb)
64 kg (141 lb)	Chen Yanqing (China)	230 kg (507 lb)
70 kg (154 lb)	Xiang Fenglan (China)	235 kg (518.1 lb)
76 kg (167.5 lb)	Hua Ju (China)	247.5 kg (545.6 lb)
83 kg (183 lb)	Derya Acikgoz (Turkey)	262.5 kg (578.7 lb)
+83 kg (+183 lb)	Ma Runmei (China)	252.5 kg (556.7 lb)

1997 Sumo Tournament Champions

Tournament	Location	Winner	Winner's record
Hatsu *basho* (New Year's tournament)	Tokyo	Wakanohana	14–1
Haru *basho* (spring tournament)	Osaka	Takanohana	13–2
Natsu *basho* (summer tournament)	Tokyo	Akebono	13–2
Nagoya *basho* (Nagoya tournament)	Nagoya	Takanohana	13–2
Aki *basho* (autumn tournament)	Tokyo	Takanohana	13–2
Kyushu *basho* (Kyushu tournament)	Fukuoka	Takanonami	13–2

World Wrestling Championships—Freestyle*

Year	48 kg	52 kg (54 kg)	57 kg (58 kg)	62 kg (63 kg)	68 kg (69 kg)
1992	Park II (N.Kor.)	Li Hak (N.Kor.)	A. Puerto (Cuba)	J. Smith (U.S.)	A. Fadzaev (UT)
1993	A. Vila (Cuba)	V. Jordanov (Bulg.)	Terry Brands (U.S.)	Tom Brands (U.S.)	A.A. Fallah (Iran)
1994	A. Vila (Cuba)	V. Jordanov (Bulg.)	A. Puerto (Cuba)	M. Azizov (Russia)	A. Leipold (Ger.)
1995	V. Orudzhev (Russia)	V. Jordanov (Bulg.)	Terry Brands (U.S.)	E. Tedeev (Ukr.)	A. Gevorkian (Arm.)
1996	Kim II (N.Kor.)	V. Jordanov (Bulg.)	K. Cross (U.S.)	Tom Brands (U.S.)	V. Bogiyev (Russia)
1997		**W. Garcia (Cuba)**	**M. Talaee (Iran)**	**A. Kenari (Iran)**	**A. Gevorkian (Arm.)**
Year	**74 kg (76 kg)**	**82 kg (85 kg)**	**90 kg**	**100 kg (97 kg)**	**130 kg (130 kg)**
1992	Park Jang (S.Kor.)	K. Jackson (U.S.)	M. Khadartsev (UT)	L. Khabelov (UT)	B. Baumgartner (U.S.)
1993	Park Jang (S.Kor.)	S. Ozturk (Tur.)	A. Jadidi (Iran)	L. Khabelov (Russia)	B. Baumgartner (U.S.)
1994	T. Ceylan (Tur.)	L. Jabrailov (Moldova)	R. Khadem (Iran)	A. Sabejey (Ger.)	M. Demir (Tur.)
1995	B. Saytyev (Russia)	K. Jackson (U.S.)	R. Khadem (Iran)	K. Angle (U.S.)	B. Baumgartner (U.S.)
1996	B. Saytyev (Russia)	Kh. Magomedov (Russia)	R. Khadem (Iran)	K. Angle (U.S.)	M. Demir (Tur.)
1997	**B. Saytyev (Russia)**	**L. Gutches (U.S.)**		**K. Kuramagomedov (Russia)**	**Z. Guclu (Tur.)**

*Figures in parentheses represent new weight classes established in 1997.

World Wrestling Championships—Greco-Roman Style*

Year	48 kg	52 kg (54 kg)	57 kg (58 kg)	62 kg (63 kg)	68 kg (69 kg)
1992	O. Kucherenko (UT)	J. Ronningen (Nor.)	An Han Bong (S.Kor.)	A. Pirim (Tur.)	A. Repka (Hung.)
1993	W. Sánchez (Cuba)	R. Martínez (Cuba)	A. Manukjan (Arm.)	S. Martynov (Russia)	I. Duguchiyev (Russia)
1994	W. Sánchez (Cuba)	A. Mkrtchyan (Ger.)	J. Melnichenko (Kazak.)	S. Martynov (Russia)	I. Duguchiyev (Russia)
1995	Sim Kwon Ho (S.Kor.)	S. Danielane (Russia)	D. Hall (U.S.)	S. Martynov (Russia)	R. Adzhy (Ukr.)
1996	Sim Kwon Ho (S.Kor.)	A. Nazaryan (Arm.)	Y. Melnichenko (Kazak.)	W. Zawadzki (Pol.)	R. Wolny (Pol.)
1997		**E. Yildiz (Tur.)**	**Y. Melnichenko (Kazak.)**	**S. Eroglu (Tur.)**	**Son Sang Pil (S.Kor.)**
Year	**74 kg (76 kg)**	**82 kg (85 kg)**	**90 kg**	**100 kg (97 kg)**	**130 kg (130 kg)**
1992	M. Iskandarian (UT)	P. Farcas (Hung.)	M. Bullmann (Ger.)	H. Milian (Cuba)	A. Karelin (UT)
1993	N. Alamanza (Cuba)	M. Yerlikaya (Tur.)	G. Koguchavili (Russia)	M. Ljungberg (Swed.)	A. Karelin (Russia)
1994	M. Iskandarian (Russia)	T. Zander (Ger.)	G. Koguchavili (Russia)	A. Wronski (Pol.)	A. Karelin (Russia)
1995	Y. Riemer (Fr.)	H. Yerlikaya (Tur.)	H. Baser (Tur.)	M. Ljungberg (Swed.)	A. Karelin (Russia)
1996	F. Ascuy (Cuba)	H. Yerlikaya (Tur.)	V. Oleynyk (Ukr.)	A. Wronski (Pol.)	A. Karelin (Russia)
1997	**M. Yli-Hannuksela (Fin.)**	**S. Tsuir (Russia)**		**G. Koguashvili (Russia)**	**A. Karelin (Russia)**

*Figures in parentheses represent new weight classes established in 1997.

Transportation

Two significant transportation policy shifts were discernible in 1997. The first was that simple outright privatization was not necessarily the only solution for reviving rail systems and that "concessioning"—the purchase of operating rights—had as much to offer. Financial restructuring and further advances in technology were moving the railway industry into a new era of sustained and sustainable growth. The second was that governments were recognizing not only that the integration of services was the most economical organizational structure but also that it provided the proper framework for the development of public transportation and intermodal freight services. These policy directions, with ever-increasing emphasis on environmentally friendly systems and vehicles and service improvements ranging from new safety measures to quicker point-to-point journeys, were expected to contribute significantly to reducing congestion in urban areas and reducing atmospheric pollution.

(JOHN H. EARP)

AVIATION

Although the world airline industry in 1996 experienced both its highest-ever load factor (the proportion of seats offered that were sold) and a decline in net interest charges on purchase or lease of aircraft, the record profitability of 1995 was not sustained. According to the International Air Transport Association (IATA), profitability in 1996 on international scheduled services was $3 billion, compared with $5.2 billion the previous year. This drop reflected increasing cost pressures, notably from higher aviation fuel prices and the higher value of the U.S. dollar in relation to other world currencies. Pierre Jeanniot, IATA director general, commented, "The airlines will need to do much better than that during 1997 in order to complete their recovery from the losses of 1990–93. In theory, the prospects for this are good. Traffic growth remains buoyant, driven by fundamentally favourable economic conditions. Record load factors are being achieved. Indications are that unit costs continue to fall." The IATA projected that future profitability depended on moderation in adding capacity and on success in controlling unit costs.

IATA airlines carried some 1,185,000,000 passengers in 1996 on their scheduled services, 8.4% over 1995 on international flights and 4.4% higher in the domestic sector. Overall freight tonnage grew by 4.6% to almost 24 million.

At the end of 1996, 11,711 Western-built jet aircraft and 5,221 turbo-prop aircraft were in commercial service. The jets, operated by 650 airlines, during the year flew 30 million hours. By mid-1997 rapidly rising orders for new aircraft were placing an immense strain on the production capacity of the two remaining major Western aerospace companies, Boeing-McDonnell Douglas (now officially known as the Boeing Co.) and the European consortium Airbus Industrie, with Boeing struggling to meet what it termed "the steepest production increases since the dawn of the jet age." The Seattle, Wash.-based manufacturer increased its staff by 14,000 over 1996–97 in its attempt to increase deliveries by mid-1998 to 43 airliners a month, compared with about 18 a month in 1996.

Air safety continued to be a prime concern. A total of 19 jet aircraft losses occurred during 1996, a loss rate of 0.63 per million hours. This compared with 1995 figures of 17 losses and a rate of 0.65 per million hours. Although the number of aircraft losses was similar, 1996 was a worse year for fatalities, with 1,189 passenger and 97 crew deaths, compared with 383 passengers and 39 crew members in 1995. Also, 21 acts of unlawful interference, including hijackings, were committed against civil aviation during 1996, four more than in 1995 but considerably down from 1994 and 1993, when the figures were 42 and 49, respectively.

Overall, airlines continued to enjoy bullish conditions. Most forecasters saw an annual increase in number of passengers of about 6% per year during the 1997–2001 period, with highest average passenger growth rates in Asia (7.4%), the South Pacific (7.3%), Latin America and Africa (6.6%), Europe (6.2%), North America (6.1%), and the Middle East (5.1%).

Any euphoria was, however, tempered by a number of worries. The U.S. air traffic control system suffered a series of freak

The new passenger terminal at the National Airport in Washington, D.C., opened on July 27. Part of a decade-long, $1 billion renovation project at the airport, the terminal featured a ceiling with 54 domes and windows overlooking the Potomac River. The terminal was designed by noted architect Cesar Pelli.

ROBERT REEDER—THE WASHINGTON POST

WOJTEK LASKI—GAMMA LIAISON

In March it was announced that the historic shipyard in Gdansk, Pol., where the Solidarity labour movement was born, would close and that all 3,700 of the shipyard's employees would be laid off. The shipyard was $150 million in debt.

accidents at several facilities in the fall, including "impossible" power failures at National Airport in Washington, D.C., and the air traffic control centre in Kansas. As skies became increasingly crowded, the industry accelerated progress to implement fully FANS (Future Air Navigation System), a global network of satellites aimed at making use of airspace capacity more efficient by improving communication systems and achieving greater accuracy in navigation and air traffic surveillance.

In 1996 airport landing and related charges, at $6.5 billion, and air navigation charges, at $5.2 billion, were each $300 million higher than in 1995. Together they amounted to 8.9% of the industry's worldwide international operating costs—but for some airlines they were as much as 25%. In addition, the industry, the IATA warned, faced "new threats of environmental and value-added taxes, both of which are often discriminatory and can distort competition."

Airlines continued to forge marketing mergers with one another in an effort to stem the rise in costs, although activity in this sector became less frenetic than in previous years. In an effort to maximize profits, many carriers improved their business- and first-class sections, and the IATA established a multidisciplinary task force to study the possible future effects of European monetary union on airline costs and revenues.

(ARTHUR REED)

SHIPPING AND PORTS

According to figures released by Lloyd's Register of Shipping, the world fleet at the end of 1996 stood at a new high of 507.9 million gt (gross tons), an increase of 17.2 million gt over the previous year. This confirmed the steady growth of the world fleet during the past 30 years. The oil tanker component of the fleet grew by 2.1 million gt to 146.4 million gt, and the bulk carrier fleet increased by 5 million gt to a total of 151 million gt.

A significant increase was in the containership fleet, which, boosted by deliveries of large vessels, increased by 11% to 43.1 million gt. Because there was little scrapping of containerships, the fleet was growing at a rate some considered alarming. Unless traffic volumes became greater than expected, as some industry observers had predicted, the market appeared to be in danger of chronic overcapacity.

Concern about the ability of a substantial part of the world fleet to meet the July 1998 International Safety Management Code deadline was voiced by William O'Neil of the International Maritime Organization and seconded by ship classification societies. O'Neil warned the industry that the deadline would not be altered, even though only a small percentage of the 19,000 ships required to be certified had achieved that status. Failure to comply would place owners in breach of the International Convention for Safety of Life at Sea and cause ships to be detained by a number of important maritime countries, with serious consequences for international trade.

Because the world's ports mirrored shipping industry trends, there was an increasing need for the large container ports to become hubs that would be able to serve the newly formed liner consortia. In the Asia-Pacific region, Hong Kong and Singapore were the main exponents of this role, but the same was also true of such European ports as Hamburg, Ger., Rotterdam, Neth., Antwerp, Belg., and Felixstowe, Eng., and, in the U.S., New York City.

The level of scrapping decreased by about 1.7 million gt to 7.8 million gt. India, Bangladesh, and Pakistan remained the most active areas for ship demolition.

(EDWARD CROWLEY)

FREIGHT AND PIPELINES

The inland collection and distribution of containerized freight was dominated in 1997 by road transportation, although there were signs in Europe that rail and barge traffic was making inroads as a result of environmental considerations. Worldwide, freight moved most often from Asian ports, which accounted for two-thirds of the movement in the top 20 ports. Hong Kong and Singapore continued to lead the world, each handling nearly 14 million TEU (20-ft equivalent units). Within the area Japan's eight leading containerports handled nearly 10 million TEU, and in Vietnam, Ho Chi Minh City opened a new container-handling facility and announced a $1.4 billion master plan for its ports. In Europe, Italian ports benefited from the privatization of terminal operations, and the strong growth of U.S. Pacific ports led to a new $2 billion project in the Alameda corridor serving Los Angeles.

Growth in pipeline construction was modest, up 8% from 28,165 km (1 km=0.62 mi) in 1996 to an expected 30,250 km in 1997. Continued concern with economic risks, together with increased competition and regulatory changes, accounted for some caution in an otherwise positive outlook. In Europe the focus remained on the North Sea, particularly the NorFra (Norway–France) 830-km pipeline project with its terminal at Dunkirk, France.

Farther east a trans-Eurasian pipeline network was planned to link Turkmenistan to China and Japan. Myanmar (Burma) joined Malaysia and Thailand with major pipeline proposals to meet internal needs. Australia began a 1,500-km gas line project to link into fields in Western Australia. In China construction began on a $1,750,000,000 crude oil line from Korla to Luoyang and a $724 million products line linking Guangdong province to Hainan Island.

In August a 465-km-long, 61-cm (24-in)-diameter pipeline linking Argentina to Chile was completed. A 3,020-km gas line to link Bolivia to Brazil was projected. There were plans for a $200 million fuel pipeline to link the Texas Gulf Coast to Oklahoma, Kansas, and Colorado, extending an existing 1,450-km line by more than 640 km.

ROADS AND TRAFFIC

The remorseless growth of traffic was in 1997 yielding ever-greater congestion in urban areas and ever-growing concern for air quality and the environment. Vehicle emissions were estimated to contribute nearly half of the carbon dioxide that was considered to be the primary cause of global warming. In deciding whether they should encourage the expansion of urbanization, governments were torn between quality-of-life issues, such as increased pollution and congestion, and wealth creation, which is linked to improved distribution networks. Paris experimented with banning cars with odd/even registration numbers on alternate days, a practice already common in Athens. In London an expressway section to the airport was designated for bus/coaches only, and San Diego, Calif., experimented with an automated traffic-management system on its freeways. Traffic control measures seemed likely to have a greater future than new expressways in major cities, although some limited construction of underground routes and major bridge links continued.

The opening in March–April of the 1.6-km (1-mi) dual three-lane Cheung Ching tunnel and the Tsing Ma bridge, the longest dual-deck bridge in the world, provided key links in the access to the new Chek Lap Kok airport on Lantau Island in Hong Kong. The project was part of the strategic network of transport development in China that also included the $200 million Jiangyin Bridge across the Chang Jiang (Yangtze River). South Korea reopened the Songsu Bridge in Seoul, which had collapsed in 1994. In Portugal the second crossing of the Tagus River, the 18-km Vasco da Gama Bridge, was the biggest private-sector infrastructure project under construction in Europe. It was taking place a short distance upstream from the Tagus bridge, which was undergoing a complex strengthening exercise. The Melbourne (Australia) Citylink, including twin 1.6-km tunnels, was a 34-year project devised under a build-own-operate-transfer arrangement; it reflected the twin ambitions of private-sector involvement and environmental concern. The worldwide squeeze on funding for new roads was typified by the slow progress on the main highway on Vancouver Island, British Columbia.

INTERCITY RAIL

The revival of intercity rail service continued in 1997, although achieving financial viability remained a difficult goal. World expenditure on track and rolling stock during the year totaled more than $20 billion. Much railway development was being financed by privatization, but no single approach prevailed. Both Swiss and German railways chose to restructure their companies so as to retain state control. Less-wealthy countries, including Peru, Pakistan, Mozambique, and the Czech Republic, opted for direct privatization.

Japan introduced 300-km/h service on its 554-km line from Shin Osaka to Hakata and thereby regained the world's fastest timetabled service (1 km=0.62 mi). Japan also began testing a 550-km/h prototype train and planned to develop a 320-km/h service that would produce less noise and require less maintenance than its other lines. Belgian National Railways completed its high-speed Thalys line from Antoing to Brussels. Italy and Germany continued to plan extensions to their networks, the latter allocating funds for a 280-km magnetically levitated line linking Hamburg and Berlin. China planned to introduce 180-km/h intercity services on four routes from Beijing, which would enable journeys up to 1,500 km to be undertaken without overnight travel.

By 1997 tilting trains were no longer a novelty. Almost 1,400 were in service, and an additional 1,200 were on order. Other advances in services included special facilities for disabled persons on Spanish trains and electronic way-finding facilities for blind passengers in London.

Switzerland planned to increase the rolling motorway services of its Lötschberg Tunnel in order to meet its constitutional commitment for rail rather than road to carry freight across the nation by 2004. Increasing rapprochement between Argentina and Chile led to a feasibility study of a 25-km railway tunnel through the Andes Mountains. The United Arab Emirates were examining the possibility of a rail link from Dubayy to Abu Dhabi for reasons of pollution reduction. Russia was seeking to encourage the development of a 3,100-km section from Baikal to Amur, to parallel the Trans-Siberian railway. It also completed a new 100-km link between Zarubino, Russia, and Hunchun, China.

URBAN MASS TRANSIT

As a counter to continued public unease arising from growth in car ownership, urban congestion, and air pollution, urban mass transit systems continued to proliferate and expand in 1997. An estimated $6.5 billion was being invested in mass transit systems in major cities throughout the world.

New light-rail lines (lines usually powered by electricity) were opened or extended in Amsterdam; La Coruña, Spain; Dallas, Texas; Jena, Ger.; Rouen, France; Sydney, Australia; and Toronto. New openings did not, however, reflect the significant numbers of systems under construction. In the Pacific Rim, Kuala Lumpur, Malaysia, planned to have three integrated lines open by 2000, and Inchon, S.Kor., was on track to have a fully automated system by 1999. Manila, Hong Kong, and Singapore were also working on extensions of their systems. In Europe lines were under construction in Bratislava, Slovakia; Croydon and Docklands (London); Cagliari, Italy; Dublin; Izmir, Tur.; Montpellier, France; Turin, Italy; Utrecht, Neth.; and Valencia, Spain. Many more light-rail systems were in the planning stage, including those in Cali, Colom.; Bordeaux, France; and Denver, Colo. In Vancouver, B.C., the skytrain system was being extended.

Many cities, including Stockholm, Toronto, and New York, were refurbishing stations and/or rolling stock. New or extended lines opened in Bilbao, Spain; Belo Horizonte, Braz.; Madrid; Shanghai; Taipei, Taiwan; and Tokyo. New lines were planned for Budapest; Puerto Rico; Istanbul; Ho Chi Minh City, Vietnam; Lima, Peru; and Alexandria, Egypt. New light-rail service was established for airports in Oslo; Hong Kong; Salt Lake City, Utah; and Kyoto, Japan. As with intercity rail, the private sector was funding many of these developments.

Buses remained the backbone of urban services. The year saw significant progress in the development of buses with low floors for handicapped riders and in the use of commercial hydrogen fuel cells.

(JOHN H. EARP)

See also Architecture and Civil Engineering; Business and Industry Review: *Aerospace; Automobiles; Energy;* The Environment.

This article updates the *Macropædia* article TRANSPORTATION.

Beneath the concrete support beams of an elevated railway under construction in Bangkok, a Buddhist monk crosses the tracks of the State Railway of Thailand. World expenditure on track and rolling stock during the year totaled more than $20 billion.

CHARLES DHARAPAK—ASSOCIATED PRESS

World Affairs

The future of NATO and the European Community continued to preoccupy the diplomats during 1997. Poland, the Czech Republic, and Hungary were invited to join the 16 NATO member states following the signing of the Founding Act on Mutual Relations, Cooperation and Security, which had been concluded earlier in the year between Russia and NATO. This resulted in the addition of 350,000 soldiers to the North Atlantic alliance, but it also involved considerable expense because of the need to modernize the armed forces of the new member nations. In some circles in the United States and, to a lesser extent in Europe, there were doubts or even opposition to enlarging NATO, partly because of isolationist trends in those countries and partly because it was suspected that broadening the alliance would mean making it less effective. Russia had accepted this step most reluctantly and had expressed violent opposition to any further expansion of NATO toward the east (including Ukraine, Estonia, Latvia, and Lithuania) even though NATO had undertaken not to deploy nuclear weapons on the territory of the new members. Several pacts were signed in September concerning the implementation of the Strategic Arms Reduction Talks II (START-II) treaty, which provided for the dismantling of nuclear weapons systems. Also during the year Russia became a full, permanent member of the Group of Seven (G-7, now G-8) of the major economic powers.

The movement to make a dramatic advance on the road to achieving closer European unity, including the introduction of a common European currency, made little headway. Whereas the French and Italian governments declared their support and the Germans, who had been its most steadfast advocates, continued to declare that the provisions of the Maastricht Treaty would be met fully and in time, there was growing public lethargy and even dissent. The introduction of the far-reaching reforms was predicated on certain levels of economic performance (such as a low budget deficit), which, given the poor performance of many European economies, seemed unattainable; either the stipulations of the treaty had to be watered down, which would make it less ambitious, or there had to be postponements in the timetable.

Some observers had believed they had detected a worldwide trend away from a system of planned (or mixed) economy and from socialism, but those surmises were not confirmed by events in 1997. In Great Britain and France governments of the left won the general elections, and the "tiger" economies of East and Southeast Asia as well as Japan were doing poorly compared with their past performances. True, the socialism of the Labour Party in Britain and the Socialist Party in France had been subject to considerable erosion, but it was still a far cry from the enthusiasm for an unfettered market economy shown, for instance, by Margaret Thatcher when she was Britain's prime minister. China tried to combine strict political control with relative economic freedom; the results were mixed, marked by considerable economic advances for many Chinese on one hand and stresses and strains in the cities and the countryside on the other. Deng Xiaoping, who had been the power behind the throne even after he officially retired in 1989, died in February. (*See* OBITUARIES.) If there was a subsequent struggle for power in Beijing, it did not percolate to the outside world. The transfer of power in Hong Kong on June 30/July 1 after 156 years of British rule proceeded in an orderly fashion and held no surprises. (*See* Spotlight: *Hong Kong's Return to China.*)

As India was moving toward becoming the most populous country in the world, overtaking China in the process, it was showing a mixed balance sheet. The predictions about economic disaster, mass starvation, and increased tension with Pakistan had not come true. On the contrary, India had become one of the world's leading rice exporters, and steps were taken toward a normalization of relations with Pakistan. On the other hand, the Congress Party, which had provided leadership to India ever since the country attained independence, was further weakened; the strongly nationalist Hindu parties became increasingly powerful, and the internal tensions based on ethnic and linguistic differences persisted.

Among the main causes of ferment in many countries in 1997 were the activities of the radical elements in the Muslim world. In Iran a relative moderate, Mohammad Khatami (*see* BIOGRAPHIES), was elected president with a considerable majority against a more orthodox candidate, and in Turkey Necmettin Erbakan, a leader of the conservative Muslim forces, was compelled to resign under pressure from the military. There was no major change in Iranian foreign policy, however, and radical Islamic elements continued their military attacks in Algeria as well as in Egypt and Lebanon and against Israel. The peace process between Israel and the Palestinians came to a virtual standstill under the impact of terrorist attacks and the lack of cooperation of the Israeli government. In the Afghan civil war, the Taliban forces, fanatically Islamic in inspiration, suffered some setbacks but still ruled the capital, Kabul, and large parts of the country.

Though the situation in former Yugoslavia remained relatively stable as a result of the presence of international military forces, fissures and regroupings were already beginning to form in anticipation of their eventual departure. In central Africa the bloodshed continued in Rwanda. Pres. Mobutu Sese Seko (*see* OBITUARIES) was forced to step down in Zaire following the defeat of his army by opposition military forces; Laurent Kabila (*see* BIOGRAPHIES) subsequently declared himself head of state, but the conditions in the country, renamed the Democratic Republic of the Congo, remained unsettled, and the killing continued, though on a smaller scale. Generally speaking, Africa remained a focus of much international concern, directed especially toward a possible governmental breakdown in Nigeria, civil wars in northern Uganda and southern Sudan, and riots in Kenya and in various West African countries. Following the negative experience of the Western attempt to restore order in Somalia, however, there was little enthusiasm by those countries to engage in similar experiments elsewhere in Africa.

Russia in 1996 had experienced a bad year, full of forebodings concerning an imminent national breakdown. Fortunately, the worst predictions with regard to political instability and economic crisis did not come true. Violent internal dissent continued, with neocommunists and extreme nationalists often making common cause in attacking the government. The administration, nonetheless, showed greater resilience than many had expected, and there was modest progress at least in some regions of the country. The outlook was grimmer in other parts of the former Soviet Union with the exception of the Baltic countries and the oil-rich republics; economically and politically they were, at best, marking time.

Globalization continued to be one of the main slogans in international politics, but it manifested itself mainly in economic matters, and its impact in political developments was hardly visible to the naked eye. There was only limited collaboration between nations even with regard to confronting dangers menacing all of them, such as ecological disaster, organized crime, and the international drug trade. Terrorist operations continued in many parts of the world. A peaceful settlement was found for Chechnya, and in Ireland negotiations were under way, not for the first time, between the Irish Republican Army and the Protestant loyalists of Northern Ireland. Europe, with the exception of Spain, was relatively free of terrorism, but elsewhere, especially in North Africa and the Middle East, there was a new upsurge. Attacks elsewhere, from Peru and Colombia to Sri Lanka and Kashmir, revealed that this was not a specific Muslim problem but that ethnic and religious antagonisms were likely to express themselves in guerrilla warfare and terrorism rather than in full-scale military operations, which had become too costly and too risky even for large and powerful nations.

(WALTER LAQUEUR)

This article updates the *Macropædia* article 20th-Century INTERNATIONAL RELATIONS.

UNITED NATIONS

Kofi Annan of Ghana (*see* BIOGRAPHIES) took office on Jan. 1, 1997, as the new secretary-general of the United Nations, and change was in the air throughout the year. Annan's reforms were controversial, but the General Assembly approved most of them. In other major developments, the UN's authority was seriously challenged by Iraq and the Democratic Republic of the Congo (Congo [Kinshasa]; formerly Zaire), and it faced declining enthusiasm for its development and refugee programs.

Organization and Budget. The UN was owed more than $2 billion by its member nations; the U.S. alone owed $1.3 billion. On January 9 Annan declared that the UN "cannot be expected to move forward if it is dragged down by unpaid dues." He also described some criticisms of the organization as "misinformation and disinformation." In a meeting with Annan on January 23, U.S. Pres. Bill Clinton promised to urge the U.S. Congress to pay its back dues. He acknowledged that the U.S. could not expect "to lead through the United Nations unless we are prepared to pay our own way." He also urged Annan to eliminate waste, streamline the UN staff, and wipe out "overlap and abuse."

On March 17 Annan outlined plans for

streamlining the UN. He proposed reducing the UN budget of $2,480,000,000 for 1998 and 1999 by $123,000,000, shifting some $200,000,000 million from administrative expenses to development aid, leaving 1,000 empty staff posts unfilled, merging three separate departments dealing with economic and social issues into one, coordinating field operations more tightly, consolidating the separate administrative, personnel, and procurement services that aid agencies maintained in New York City, overhauling the information department, reducing paper output by 25%, and drawing up a staff code of conduct. Referring to the U.S. Congress's commitment to pay if the UN reformed, he said, "We are giving them reform. I hope they will deliver on their part of the bargain." On November 13, however, Congress made what a White House spokesman called the "boneheaded" decision not to erase the U.S. debt.

On July 17, at a special General Assembly session, Annan proposed a further "quiet revolution." He suggested creating executive committees for four central areas of the organization's work: peace and security, economic and social affairs, development operations, and humanitarian affairs. A Senior Management Group would act as a Cabinet. His plan reduced the number of top-level administrators from about 25 to fewer than a dozen. His proposal to appoint a deputy secretary-general to take charge when he himself was away from New York City was accepted by the General Assembly. He also proposed funding a $1 billion revolving fund to carry the UN through its financial problems; disbanding staff offices serving the Trusteeship Council, which had completed the tasks set for it in the Charter; and appointing a commission to study possible changes in the Charter and in the role of the specialized agencies. Annan asked the world not to judge the UN by proposed cuts or changed structures but "by the relief and refuge that we provide to the poor, to the hungry, the sick and threatened: the peoples of the world whom the United Nations exists to serve." Before the Assembly adjourned, it approved Annan's proposals.

On February 1 Annan urged the World Economic Forum, a meeting of hundreds of business and government leaders, to invest in the poorest countries, 100 of which were worse off currently than 15 years earlier. A good example was set by Ted Turner, founder of the Cable News Network, who pledged on September 18 to contribute as much as $1 billion of Time Warner Inc. stock over 10 years to support UN programs and called on other wealthy people to follow his example. Annan called the donation "a wonderful gesture."

UN Forces. UN members evinced a cautious mood about peacekeeping and tended to favour placing the responsibility for new operations on coalitions of interested countries that would use their own forces with Security Council approval. Italy adopted this approach to meet Albania's request for assistance in quelling civil unrest stemming from the collapse of fraudulent "pyramid" savings schemes. On March 28, by a vote of 14–0 with one abstention (China, which called the matter "internal"), the Council dispatched 6,000 troops to Albania to oversee international relief efforts, help restore order, and put an end to civil strife.

Angola. On October 29 the Council voted unanimously to impose travel sanctions against the National Union for the Total Independence of Angola (UNITA) to punish the organization for flouting peace accords signed in 1994 that required UNITA to disarm its fighters and integrate them into a national army. The sanctions were designed to prevent UNITA from buying arms abroad and flying them into parts of the country that it controlled. UN members were ordered to ban all flights departing from or landing at unauthorized Angolan airfields, where about 40 weekly flights previously operated illegally, garnering $500,000 a year in illicit diamond exports.

Iraq. On April 9 an Iraqi plane flew more than 100 religious pilgrims to Saudi Arabia, violating the air embargo imposed after the Persian Gulf War in 1991. Despite U.S. pressure, the Security Council failed to condemn the flight. On June 4 the Security Council agreed to permit Iraq to sell $2 billion in oil to pay for food, medicine, and other essential civilian items for a second six-month period. The U.S. approved but criticized the UN Department of Humanitarian Affairs for failing to have enough monitors in place and for delaying the distribution of supplies.

Iraq refused throughout the year to allow UN inspectors full access to its arms installations. On October 23 the Security Council's hard line against Iraq seemed to weaken when China, Egypt, France, Kenya, and Russia declined to support a resolution expressing the Council's "firm intention" to ban the travel of Iraqi officials who obstructed inspections. On October 29 Iraq moved to expel all Americans working for the UN Special Commission (UNSCOM), which was in charge of destroying weapons in Iraq, accusing them of spying. It then barred two American weapons inspectors and one American representative of the International Atomic Energy Agency from entering the country and refused to allow UN inspection teams with American members to carry on their work. This order led the Security Council unanimously on the same day to warn Iraq of "serious consequences" if it did not reverse its decision, and the UN teams refused as of November 3 to operate without their American colleagues. Thus, Iraqi orders aimed at the Americans effectively restored the unity of the Council.

Richard Butler, an Australian diplomat and arms control expert who succeeded Rolf Ekeus as executive chairman of UNSCOM in July, condemned the Iraqi move and said that he would not allow his teams to work "on the basis that Iraq can say...which person from which country is or isn't acceptable." Ekeus and Butler both affirmed that in the previous 6½ years the Iraqi government had lied, told half-truths, hidden or destroyed evidence and documents, delayed UNSCOM's work, barred inspectors from talking with officials or employees in factories who could supply them with information, and shuffled weapons and materials around the country.

JOHN MOORE—ASSOCIATED PRESS

On the flight deck of the USS *Nimitz* aircraft carrier in the Persian Gulf, a maintenance worker gestures to a colleague from the wing of a fighter plane. U.S. forces were deployed to the area in November after Iraq obstructed the work of UN inspection teams in charge of destroying weapons in the country.

During November Iraqi officials threatened several times to shoot down any U-2 surveillance planes flying over Iraqi territory, which prompted the U.S. to warn that any such attack would be an "act of war." The flights were temporarily suspended while Annan dispatched diplomats to Iraq to attempt to defuse the crisis, but the diplomats returned to New York City empty-handed. The surveillance flights resumed on November 10 without incident. Meanwhile, UNSCOM charged Iraq with moving equipment out of camera range, disabling surveillance equipment by covering camera lenses, and turning off lights trained on suspected weapons sites. On November 12 the Council banned Iraqi officials who did not cooperate with UNSCOM from traveling abroad and warned of "further action" if Iraq continued to defy the UN. It also condemned Iraq's threats against the U-2 planes and its attempts to hide equipment, calling these acts threats to international peace and security. On November 13 Butler ordered all members of all the teams to withdraw from Iraq. On November 21 UN inspectors returned to Baghdad in accordance with an agreement brokered by Russian Foreign Minister Yevgeny Primakov. They resumed work on November 22, although Iraq barred them from inspecting "palaces" belonging to Saddam Hussein and other "sensitive" sites, some with ideal space for producing or storing weapons.

Libya. The Arab League on September 21 voted to defy UN sanctions by permitting planes carrying Col. Muammar al-Qaddafi, the Libyan leader, to land on the territory of member nations and to permit flights to Libya for humanitarian and religious purposes. The sanctions were imposed on Libya in 1992 over its refusal to surrender suspects wanted in the U.S. and Britain in connection with the 1988 bombing of a Pan American plane over Lockerbie, Scot., which killed 270 people. Pres. Nelson Mandela of South Africa visited Libya in late October, crossing the frontier by road in order to comply with the embargo, and while in Libya called for the lifting of sanctions and suggested that the Lockerbie case go before an international tribunal.

Environment. The UN Framework Convention on Climate Change of 1992, ratified by 165 countries, was in 1997 the subject of intense negotiations in Germany and Japan over government commitments to reduce greenhouse gas emissions to 1990 levels by the year 2000. Scientists had been warning for years that if the heat-trapping carbon dioxide in the atmosphere doubled over the preindustrial levels in the 19th century, the worldwide consequences would be very serious. On June 23 representatives of 131 nations gathered in New York City to assess their progress and concluded that it would be difficult, if not impossible, to avoid the carbon dioxide increase because the world's economic and political systems could not change their practices rapidly enough. The final negotiations at Kyoto, Japan, in December produced an agreement to reduce emissions between the years 2008 and 2012 by 8% in European Union countries, by 7% in the U.S., and by 6% in Japan. Less-developed nations such as China and India committed themselves only to reducing emissions voluntarily.

Human Rights. For the seventh straight year, the Human Rights Commission failed to condemn China's human rights record. The vote on April 15 was 27–17, the widest margin ever. Calling the vote "a victory of cooperation over confrontation," China's delegate, Wu Jianmin, criticized the draft resolution as "an outrageous distortion of China's reality" reflecting Western attempts to "dominate China's fate."

Another group composed of individual experts, the UN Committee on Human Rights, condemned Israel on May 9 for sanctioning torture in questioning suspected terrorists. The committee acknowledged "the terrible dilemma that Israel confronts in dealing with terrorist threats" but argued that the 1987 Convention Against Torture and Other Cruel, Inhuman or Degrading Treatment or Punishment prohibited torture even during wartime or when a threat of war existed.

A special investigator, Carl-Johan Groth of Sweden, reported to the Commission on Human Rights in March that Cuba's destruction of two civil airplanes on Feb. 24, 1996, violated the pilots' right to life. Groth pointed out that Cuba had other means available, including radio communication, for warning off the planes but instead deliberately proceeded to destroy them. Groth added that Cuba was continuing a campaign of repression against dissident groups in the country.

On March 10 the UN International Criminal Tribunal for the Former Yugoslavia at The Hague opened a trial of three Muslims and a Croat accused of having raped, tortured, and killed Serbs during the war in Bosnia and Herzegovina. The tribunal on June 24 began the trial of Gen. Tihomir Blaskic, Bosnian Croat commander of a strategic region in central Bosnia, who was charged with the bombarding, plundering, and pillaging of four towns in the Lasva Valley, where more than 100 Muslim civilians were murdered, tortured, or driven from their homes. On July 14 the tribunal sentenced Dusan Tadic, a Bosnian Serb, to 97 years in prison for 11 counts of killing and torturing his Muslim and Croat neighbours during the Bosnian civil war. The longest sentence imposed for any single crime was 20 years, the other sentences to run concurrently. On October 6, 10 Bosnian Croats, including one of the most wanted war crimes suspects in Bosnia, Dario Kordic, accused of having engineered an "ethnic cleansing" campaign, turned themselves in to the tribunal, which then had 20 suspects in custody.

On February 28 Annan called for the UN to send a military force to help deliver relief and extricate tens of thousands of refugees caught in the spreading warfare in eastern Zaire, but the Security Council declined to do so, a decision that Annan considered mistaken. Laurent Kabila (*see* BIOGRAPHIES), president of Congo (Kinshasa), who toppled Pres. Mobutu Sese Seko (*see* OBITUARIES) on May 17, soon began a "cat and mouse" game with the UN. He repeatedly rebuffed efforts to search for evidence that Rwandans supporting his rebellion had helped kill more than 500,000 people, most of them Tutsi, and that other massacres had taken place well after his forces dominated the fighting. The secretary-general in May and October had to recall forensic investigators from the Congo because Kabila's government prevented them from carrying out their mission. Investigators resumed their work on December 8 but were forced to stop again on December 15 after mobs, purportedly government-inspired, demonstrated outside their camp.

Arms. The Chemical Weapons Convention prepared by the Disarmament Conference and signed by 167 nations, 102 of which ratified it, went into effect on April 29. The treaty prohibited nations from developing, producing, stockpiling, or using chemical arms and called on them to destroy existing stocks within 10 years. The U.S. Senate consented to its ratification on April 24, and the Russian lower house approved it on October 31. Iraq, Libya, and Syria, which had chemical weapons, did not ratify the treaty.

(RICHARD N. SWIFT)

COMMONWEALTH OF NATIONS

In 1997 the Commonwealth received increasing international attention. Following the return of Pakistan (1991) and South Africa (1994) and the admittance of Cameroon and Mozambique (both 1995), two more countries, Rwanda and Yemen, applied to join the organization. The Palestine National Authority also inquired about membership. The increasing number of members had prompted Commonwealth leaders in 1995 to form a high-level committee to regularize previously ad hoc arrangements by setting firm criteria for admittance. It proposed that a country should have had a constitutional association with an existing member; comply with the principles of the 1991 Harare Declaration, in which members pledged to work for just and honest government, fundamental human rights, equality of women, universal access to education, and sound economic management; accept English as the medium of inter-Commonwealth relations; and acknowledge the role of the British monarch as head of the Commonwealth.

At Edinburgh neither Yemen nor Rwanda was admitted. Their applications were to be "kept under review." Palestine could not be considered until it became sovereign. The new rules made entry more difficult, but the return of Ireland and Myanmar (Burma), both of which left in the 1940s, was seen as an eventual possibility. The Edinburgh summit, the first in the U.K. for 20 years, attracted a record number of 51 countries—43 represented by heads of government. Nigeria, suspended since 1995, was excluded.

The meeting, addressed by Queen Elizabeth II for the first time in Commonwealth history, was the first international summit to be chaired by new British Prime Minister Tony Blair. (*See* BIOGRAPHIES.) His Labour Party had made an election promise to raise the U.K.'s Commonwealth profile.

Fiji, whose Commonwealth membership had lapsed in 1987 following a coup led by Col. Sitiveni Rabuka, was readmitted on October 1. Its return had been blocked because its constitution discriminated against Fijians of Indian origin. The new constitution was regarded as fairer, and Rabuka, as prime minister, attended the Commonwealth Heads of Government Meeting (CHOGM) in Edinburgh (October 24–27).

The emphasis at CHOGM was on trade and investment. The meeting dealt specifically with means of fostering cooperation between the public and private sectors, and with problems of globalization, particularly those confronting small and weak nations. A new Trade and Investment Access Facility was established to help less-developed countries. Training centres would enhance export management; a business council would increase private-sector involvement in trade and investment promotion; and a Commonwealth code of good practice for national policies would attract private capital flows.

West Africa remained the Commonwealth focus in regard to issues of democracy and good governance. Despite several meetings and a visit to Nigeria, the Commonwealth Ministerial Action Group (CMAG) of eight foreign ministers made little firm progress toward achieving the release of political prisoners or a quick return to civilian rule. A serious setback was the military over-

PATRICK ZACHMANN—MAGNUM

In Strasbourg, France, demonstrators protest the March convention of the National Front, the French fascist party led by Jean-Marie Le Pen. A strong showing by the National Front in the French parliamentary elections was a major factor in the Socialist Party's triumph over the ruling centre-right coalition.

throw in May of the recently elected civilian government in Sierra Leone. The Commonwealth supported Nigerian-led efforts to restore Pres. Tejan Kabbah. He was invited to Edinburgh—the first deposed leader to attend a Commonwealth summit.

A Commonwealth group observed Pakistan's elections in February. Constitutional changes effected later were attributed to its recommendations. The Cameroon parliamentary elections were also observed, and the team was highly critical of their conduct. In his increasing "good offices" role, the Commonwealth's secretary-general, Chief Emeka Anyaoku, visited Papua New Guinea in March and helped defuse the tense situation that followed the hiring of mercenaries to fight in Bougainville. Papua New Guinea's prime minister, Sir Julius Chan, stepped down, and the Commonwealth observed subsequent elections.

(DEREK INGRAM)

EUROPEAN UNION

Agreement on the final stages of preparation for European economic and monetary union, an accord on a new treaty on closer political union, and the first tentative steps toward a major future expansion in its membership dominated developments within the European Union (EU) in 1997. A year that began amid serious doubts about the likelihood of achieving a successful transition to a single European currency by the target date of January 1999 ended with considerably greater confidence about the inevitability of monetary union.

In spite of these promising developments, the EU in 1997 was again confronted with a much slower than expected recovery from recession in the major Western European economies. Persistent mass unemployment remained a cause of growing social and political concern, which led to an emergency EU heads of government summit in Luxembourg in November dedicated exclusively to the struggle to reduce the numbers of the jobless.

In political terms the two most influential events in 1997 were the British and the French general elections. A clear leftward tilt was given to the political balance within the European Union as a result of the landslide victory of Tony Blair's Labour Party in the British general election in May. This was followed a month later by the unexpected decision by Pres. Jacques Chirac to call early elections to the French National Assembly and the even more unexpected subsequent defeat by the left of the centre-right government.

The triumph of the French Socialists under Lionel Jospin (*see* BIOGRAPHIES) meant that for the first time in its history, the European Union's Council of Ministers had a numerical majority of social democratic and/or labour-led governments. Taken together, the two elections seemed to signal a growing discontent among European voters with the economic policies of economic deregulation and government budget austerity that were followed in the 15 EU countries in the late 1980s and early 1990s.

By the time the EU celebrated the 40th anniversary of the original European Community in March, it was increasingly clear that a majority of member states would probably fulfill the strict economic qualification tests for monetary union that had been laid down in the Maastricht Treaty in 1991. During the first six months of 1997, the Dutch government, which held the rotating post of EU presidency, succeeded in achieving agreement on the final details of the arrangements for the single currency (the Euro) and for a framework of economic disciplines that would be binding on countries taking part in the monetary union. It was agreed that the final decision as to which countries would be invited to join the Euro group would be made at a special EU heads of government summit to be held in May 1998. The deadline for starting the final stage of monetary union was set at January 1999, to be followed by a transition period leading to the complete replacement of national currencies by the Euro ending in the middle of 2002.

By the end of 1997, it seemed probable that the successful candidate countries in the "first wave" group to join the single currency would be Belgium, The Netherlands, Luxembourg, France, Germany, Austria, Finland, Portugal, and Ireland. There was also a growing view that Italy would succeed in qualifying as well. This followed a period of political upheaval in the early autumn during which the efforts of the centre-left Italian government, led by Romano Prodi, to push through the financial reforms that were necessary for the nation to achieve monetary union appeared doomed to failure.

Three additional countries—Great Britain, Denmark, and Sweden—were expected to meet the economic qualifications for monetary union but to delay their formal accession to the single currency until some years after the 1999 launch. In November, however, the new British Labour government—in a sharp break with the strongly "Euroskeptical" policy pursued by previous Conservative regimes—announced that it was now committed in principle to joining the single currency.

As the adoption of the single European currency drew nearer, there was increasing debate about the wider economic implications of the move to the Euro, both for the European economies and for the world financial system. During the year EU finance ministers debated the need for closer coordination of economic policy, including sensitive areas touching on such traditional national sovereignty concerns as employment and taxation.

EU governments were divided between supporters and critics of the "Anglo-Saxon" model of sharply deregulated labour markets. There was universal concern, however, about the persistence of high unemployment—notably in France and Germany—and the need to accelerate economic reforms designed to create jobs and reduce Europe's numbers of workless to more acceptable levels. This led to the adoption, at a special employment summit in Luxembourg in November, of a series of broad targets to improve labour market flexibility and boost job-creation initiatives in a range of sectors, including small and medium-sized business and the social services.

During 1997 there was also increased international awareness of the implications of the emergence of the Euro as a major world currency for the future roles of the United States dollar and gold in the global financial system. This was a major subject of debate at the annual meetings of the International Monetary Fund and the World Bank in Hong Kong during October.

The return to power of the British Labour Party government defused a range of tensions between the United Kingdom and its EU partners that had emerged during the years of Margaret Thatcher's prime ministership. The change of British strategy was emphasized when Prime Minister Blair announced in June that Britain would become a full participant in the social policy chapter of the 1991 European Union Maastricht Treaty. The decision by the government in London to adopt a more constructive role in EU affairs was widely welcomed in other European capitals.

The clear progress made by the EU during 1997 toward the goal of a single currency was in marked contrast to the difficulties in negotiating a new treaty on closer political union, difficulties that came to a climax at the EU heads of government summit in Amsterdam in June. The original idea had been to reform the EU decision-making institutions and processes agreed upon in the 1991 Maastricht Treaty while at the same time giving the EU a more "human face."

The importance of the latter was emphasized by continuing evidence of a growing gulf between the EU's political elites and their electorates about the pace and direction of closer European integration. In an effort to meet these concerns, EU governments agreed to write into the new treaty a series of commitments covering areas such as human rights, equality, defense of the environment, and social protection as well as greater powers for the European Parliament and measures to make EU decision making more transparent. The Amsterdam summit also agreed to transfer responsibility for key areas on internal security—including the fight against transnational crime—from member states to the European Union itself.

In spite of intense diplomatic efforts to achieve an accord, EU governments failed to agree on hoped-for reforms of the way in which the Council of Ministers makes decisions. The new treaty provided for a modest extension of the system of majority voting to a limited number of new policy areas, but it deferred agreement on making majority-vote decisions the norm instead of the exception. This inconclusive outcome of what had been hailed as a major milestone on the road to a politically more united Europe was seen by some EU governments as a threat to the goal of EU enlargement. They argued that without further far-reaching institutional reform, it would be impossible for the EU to integrate all those countries in Central and Eastern Europe that either had already sought or were shortly expected to seek EU membership.

In July the European Commission published a major study of the political, economic, and other implications of EU enlargement—"Agenda 2000." In its report the commission recommended that 6 of the 12 applicant nations be selected for initial enlargement negotiations. They included Poland, Hungary, the Czech Republic, Slovenia, Estonia, and Cyprus. A second EU heads of government summit in Luxembourg in December confirmed this decision, and formal accession negotiations were scheduled to begin in early 1998. Romania, Bulgaria, Slovakia, Lithuania, and Latvia were to prepare for accession later.

In selecting the countries with which to begin negotiations, the EU used both political and economic criteria. Only those nations that met a series of democratic and human rights tests would be accepted. The great majority of the applicant countries were seen as meeting these requirements—with the exception of Slovakia, whose drift toward antidemocratic rule had been a cause of concern in the EU for more than two years.

Aware of the political problems that might be created by a decision to open accession talks with some but not all applicant countries, EU governments discussed arrangements that would encourage closer cooperation with all of them. Late in 1997 EU member states debated the setting up of a standing European Conference. This would comprise the 15 existing EU countries, the 6 "first wave" applicants, and Bulgaria, Romania, Latvia, Slovakia, and Lithuania.

This conference would include a wide range of issues for cooperation, ranging from transportation and the fight against crime to foreign policy and the environment. While all the Central and Eastern European countries were expected to become full EU members at some future time, however, Turkey was still not considered even a potential future member in view of its poor record on democracy and human rights.

The accelerating momentum behind EU enlargement was given further impetus by the decision by NATO at its conference in Madrid in July to accept Poland, Hungary, and the Czech Republic as members as of mid-1999. But this development added a further complicating factor to the already complex web of relations linking both Western and Eastern European countries and to the debate about the extent to which the EU itself should take responsibility for European security and defense.

This debate was given a new focus by the continuing NATO peacekeeping operation in Bosnia and Herzegovina and speculation about whether the U.S. would withdraw its troops from that area in 1998. The year also ended without a clear-cut agreement between NATO and the Western European Union—the security organization run by a majority of the EU states—under which the WEU would be able to use NATO military resources in peacekeeping operations supported by the EU. (JOHN PALMER)

COMMONWEALTH OF INDEPENDENT STATES

The borders of the Western alliance drew closer to the former Soviet Union in 1997 as Poland, Hungary, and the Czech Republic, all formerly included in the Warsaw Pact, were formally invited to join NATO, with a target date of April 1999. This historic development raised questions about how Russia would protect its geostrategic interests in the CIS and beyond. For 1997, at least, Moscow answered the challenge by trying to put its diplomatic house in order.

In May, Russian Pres. Boris Yeltsin signed a charter establishing a NATO-Russia council with representation in Brussels. Also concluded was a peace accord with Pres. Aslan Maskhadov of the breakaway Russian republic of Chechnya, almost three years after the start of hostilities that left the Caucasian republic in ruins. The accord helped clear the way for the conclusion in July of a crucial agreement on the export of oil from Azerbaijan's Caspian Sea fields through Chechnya to Russia. After five years of stalling, Yeltsin traveled to Kiev in May to sign a far-reaching treaty recognizing Ukrainian territorial integrity and sovereignty over Crimea. With Moscow's agreement to the terms of the lease on the key naval base at Sevastopol, a settlement was also reached on the disposition of the Black Sea Fleet. Upon the conclusion in June of a bilateral treaty with Romania, Ukraine achieved what it had sought since the CIS was formed: recognition of its borders by all neighbouring countries. At the same time, Ukraine rejected a Russian offer of security guarantees. Rather, at the NATO summit in Madrid, it accepted an invitation to form a NATO-Ukraine consultative council similar in intent and purpose to the NATO-Russia council.

In a case of déjà vu, Russia and its closest ally, Belarus, agreed in April to integrate their states into a "union" open to the participation of other CIS countries. There were no takers, and pan-CIS initiatives were limited by and large to continued peacekeeping in Georgia's secessionist Abkhazia republic. Disquiet was evident in the Russian-Belarusian alliance itself when Moscow protested the mistreatment of Russian journalists in Belarus. The deteriorating civil rights situation in that country raised alarm in Western capitals.

In Central Asia attention was focused on the radical Taliban's advance into northern Afghanistan and the dual spectre of destabilization and refugees in that region. The Afghanistan situation was partly responsible for prompting the warring sides in Tajikistan's civil conflict—the Russian-backed government and the Afghan-based United Tajik Opposition—to sit down at the peace table in June in order to sign a power-sharing agreement.

The CIS as a whole achieved positive economic growth (a projected 0.4%) in 1997, although figures varied greatly by country. The highest growth rates (over 4%) were posted in Georgia, Armenia, Azerbaijan, and Kyrgyzstan; the lowest was posted in Turkmenistan, where gross domestic product declined by 14.5%. Ukraine's performance was stagnant owing to the slow pace of reforms. A survey by the European Bank for Reconstruction and Development found that the CIS ranked highest in the world for corruption.

(KATHLEEN MIHALISKO)

MULTINATIONAL AND REGIONAL ORGANIZATIONS

On May 31, 1997, the foreign ministers of the member states of the Association of Southeast Asian Nations (ASEAN) met in Kuala Lumpur, Malaysia, and announced that they would embrace Myanmar (Burma), Laos, and Cambodia as full members at the group's 30th anniversary meeting in July. The announcement was controversial because, in the words of Nobel Peace Prize winner Daw Aung San Suu Kyi, ASEAN's endorsement of her native Myanmar would make its military leaders "even more obdurate and oppressive." Indonesia and Malaysia argued, however, that including Myanmar was a step toward "constructive engagement" that emphasized economic relationships over political and human rights issues. Both the U.S. and the European Union protested, but Myanmar and Laos were admitted as full members of ASEAN on July 23. Earlier in the month ASEAN had announced that although it had decided to delay Cambodia's admission to the organization indefinitely, it would help that nation conduct elections in 1998 to keep it from resuming the civil war that pitted its two prime ministers, Prince Norodom Ranariddh and Hun Sen (*see* BIOGRAPHIES), against each other. On July 19 Hun Sen said that he would not allow three ASEAN foreign ministers to broker a settlement of the conflict. Under pressure from the ASEAN Regional Forum, however, he changed his mind. ASEAN then admitted Hun Sen's foreign minister as an observer of the annual meeting of ASEAN foreign ministers on July 24–25.

Just before the 21-member ASEAN Regional Forum convened in Malaysia on July 27, U.S. Secretary of State Madeleine Albright (*see* BIOGRAPHIES) criticized a call by Malaysian Prime Minister Dato Seri Mahathir bin Mohamad for member states to review the Universal Declaration of Human Rights. Mahathir said that the 1948 declaration was "formulated by the superpowers which did not understand the needs of poor countries." Insisting that less-developed nations conform to its ideals, he added, was a form of oppression. Albright responded by saying that she did not think that any nations, religions, and cultural or ethical systems wanted to tolerate torture or abrogate human rights and that the U.S. would oppose any attempts to change the Universal Declaration.

As Asia's economic crisis worsened, U.S. Pres. Bill Clinton and Asian leaders tentatively agreed in late November on a $68 billion bailout for the region. The plan, worked out by representatives of the Asia-Pacific Economic Cooperation group, called for the International Monetary Fund to provide the money in the form of loans to Asian countries in order to help them overcome recent bankruptcies and currency devaluations. Some economists, however, worried that $68 billion might not be enough to bail out all of the troubled countries.

On May 14–16 trade ministers of 34 countries in the Americas met in Belo Horizonte, Braz., for the Americas Business Forum, where they discussed the future of the Free Trade Area of the Americas (FTAA), a hemispheric free-trade organization first proposed at the Summit of the Americas in 1994. The member states of the Southern Cone Common Market (Mercosur) clashed with the U.S. representatives over the pace of future negotiations to remove hemispheric trade barriers. Both sides wanted the FTAA in place by the year 2005, but the U.S. preferred to begin comprehensive talks after the second Summit of the Americas (March 1998), while the Latin-American states wanted to deal with one issue at a time. Mercosur representatives, led by Brazilian Foreign Minister Luiz Felipe Lampreia, proposed discussing customs procedures first, then quotas and surtaxes, and finally tariffs and market access in 2003. A compromise reached on May 16 provided for negotiations to begin after the March 1998 summit, though the trade ministers would not decide upon the "objective, approaches, structure, and venue" of the talks until they met in Costa Rica in February 1998.

At the World Economic Forum in São Paulo, Braz., in September, speakers praised Mercosur's advances in promoting regional trade. They also noted that the U.S. had done little to advance President Clinton's 1994 pledge at the Summit of the Americas to establish the FTAA "from Alaska to Tierra del Fuego" by 2005. Lampreia asserted that trade between the four Mercosur members (Argentina, Brazil, Paraguay, Uruguay) was soaring and that the alliance was signing accords with the European Union and the Andean Pact, a trade group in western South America. At a summit meeting in Uruguay in December, the presidents of the four Mercosur countries agreed to facilitate the exchange of services between their countries and to protect their industries from illegal competition from abroad.

Pres. Robert Mugabe of Zimbabwe addressed the UN General Assembly on September 25 on behalf of the Organization of African Unity (OAU). Mugabe called for restricting or abolishing the power of veto among members of the Security Council. He specified, however, that if the power of veto was retained, any new permanent members added to the Security Council should also have it. During 1997 the OAU was also involved in brokering talks between the government of the Comoros, a three-island republic in the Indian Ocean, and the inhabitants of Anjouan, who sought to secede from the Comoros and rejoin France.

(RICHARD N. SWIFT)

DEPENDENT STATES

Europe and the Atlantic. In late 1997 the ongoing dispute between Spain and Great Britain over the status of Gibraltar threatened to derail reforms that would integrate Spain more fully into NATO's military structure. In December Britain backed off on a threat to veto the creation of a NATO command in Madrid, and Spain agreed to lift restrictions on the use of Gibraltar in NATO operations—but only on a case-by-case basis. The question of the territory's status was at a stalemate, however, as Spain proposed shared sovereignty leading to eventual return of the British colony to Spanish control, whereas Gibraltarian Chief Minister Peter Caruana offered a counterproposal that would end Gibraltar's colonial status while allowing it to remain under British sovereignty.

On St. Helena, 1,950 km (1,200 mi) west of Africa, there were reports of antigovernment riots and arson in April after two members of the five-member Executive Council resigned in protest against budget cuts and Gov. David Smallman's "dictatorial" rule. The island's 6,800 residents, who had been deprived of British citizenship by the U.K.'s Nationality Act of 1981, faced unemployment of up to 18%, inadequate job training, and high costs accrued in the continuing fight to regain citizenship. Smallman called new elections for July 9. The 300 residents of Tristan da Cunha raised the same question of British citizenship during Smallman's annual visit in January. A 10-year contract to operate Tristan's lucrative lobster-fishing concession, which was awarded in 1996 to a South African firm, went into effect on January 1.

On November 11 an agreement was signed establishing a maritime boundary between the islands of Jan Mayen, Greenland, and Iceland. The 1,934-sq km (747-sq mi) area of Arctic Ocean had remained a source of contention since 1993, when the International Court of Justice settled the rival claims between Norway and Denmark covering most of the region.

Caribbean and Bermuda. Gov. Pedro Rosselló was sworn in for a second term in Puerto Rico in January. In a message to mark the occasion, U.S. Pres. Bill Clinton promised to support legislation in Congress to allow the holding of a referendum on Puerto Rico's future political status. Puerto Ricans had last voted on various constitutional options in November 1993, when the continuation of commonwealth status was confirmed by a narrow margin.

The Soufrière Hills volcano worsened during the year in Montserrat, with the capital, Plymouth, destroyed and the southern and central parts of the British colony having to be evacuated. Only about 4,000 people were left in the northern "safe zone" after thousands had moved to nearby Antigua, Britain, or other parts of the Caribbean. A new chief minister, David Brandt, took over in August from Bertrand Osborne, who resigned when residents protested against inadequate conditions in evacuation centres. A new British governor was appointed in September, and, in keeping with its responsibilities to the islanders, the U.K. announced a £41 million assistance package that consisted of emergency aid for housing and other amenities, budgetary support, and capital grants. Nineteen people were killed in June in the worst of the many eruptions of hot rocks and gas that had been taking place at intervals since the volcano roared back to life in July 1995.

Dependent States[1]

Australia	**Portugal**
Christmas Island	Macau
Cocos (Keeling) Islands	**United Kingdom**
Norfolk Island	Anguilla
Denmark	Bermuda
Faroe Islands	British Virgin Islands
Greenland	Cayman Islands
France	Falkland Islands
French Guiana	Gibraltar
French Polynesia	Guernsey
Guadeloupe	Hong Kong
Martinique	Isle of Man
Mayotte	Jersey
New Caledonia	Montserrat
Réunion	Pitcairn Island
Saint Pierre and Miquelon	Saint Helena and Dependencies
Wallis and Futuna	
Netherlands, The	Turks and Caicos Islands
Aruba	**United States**
Netherlands Antilles	American Samoa
New Zealand	Guam
Cook Islands	Northern Mariana Islands
Niue	Puerto Rico
Tokelau	Virgin Islands (of the U.S.)
Norway	
Jan Mayen	
Svalbard	

[1]Excludes territories (1) to which Antarctic Treaty is applicable in whole or in part, (2) without permanent civilian population, (3) without internationally recognized civilian government (Western Sahara, Gaza Strip), or (4) representing unadjudicated unilateral or multilateral territorial claims.

On June 25 a major eruption of the Soufrière Hills volcano on the island of Montserrat devastated the southern two-thirds of the island and killed at least 19 persons. Some 8,000 of Montserrat's 12,000 residents were evacuated, and the island's only airport was forced to close.

KEVIN WEST—GAMMA LIAISON

Strong opposition from the business community and the general public in March forced the Cayman Islands to withdraw tax and duty increases imposed in the 1997 budget. Following consultations on alternative revenue-raising measures, the government agreed to increase the ceiling on its authorized borrowing instead. In Anguilla in June it was announced that a new airport, with almost double the present runway length, would be built. The $25 million cost would be borne by private investors. In July the British Virgin Islands government approved a three-year development plan, which included the expansion of the existing cruise-ship pier at a cost of $2 million and construction of a terminal building and a tourism information centre.

The Aruba legislature was dissolved in September following a dispute between the two main parties in the governing coalition led by Prime Minister Henny Eman. The argument centred on allegedly insulting remarks made by a member of the Aruba People's Party, the senior coalition partner, against the Aruban Liberal Organization, the junior partner. The balance of power in the legislature was unchanged after the December 12 election, with the coalition retaining a 12–9 majority over the opposition People's Electoral Movement.

Environment Minister Pamela Gordon was named leader of the ruling United Bermuda Party and, therefore, prime minister of Bermuda in March. She succeeded David Saul, who said that he was resigning because he wanted to devote more time to his own business activities.

Pacific. The Cook Islands were the focus of regional attention in 1997, especially on November 1, when Cyclone Martin, arguably the Pacific's most severe storm of the century, caused heavy damage, especially on the northern islands, which were mostly low-lying atolls. Virtually all buildings were destroyed on Manihiki, where 9 people died and 10 were missing. In December Cyclone Pam caused damage (but no loss of life), mostly on Rarotonga. Earlier in the year Rarotonga was host to the South Pacific Forum, which had been the scene of strong debate between small island states and their metropolitan neighbours, Australia and New Zealand, over global climate change and the control of greenhouse-gas emissions. A drop of 16% in the Cook Islands' gross domestic product was predicted for 1997, even before the hurricane damage, and under a public-sector reform initiative with assistance of the Asian Development Bank, about 50% of those employed in the public service had been laid off. The projected sale of rights to manage the national airport and other utilities prompted debate and widespread opposition. Tokelau, one of the world's smallest dependencies, linked its islands to one another and to the outside world through the installation of a modern telephone system.

French Polynesia was also hit by Cyclone Martin, causing the loss of nine lives and widespread damage. In the French elections, Ai'a Api Party candidates secured both territorial seats in the French Assembly, but the party's decreased support was indicative of dissatisfaction with the local government over the brief resumption of nuclear tests at Mururoa atoll in 1995. Economically, the territory continued to benefit from the $200 million a year payable until 2003 to compensate for the economic adjustment that was required following the cessation of testing. In New Caledonia the Kanak Socialist National Liberation Front continued to confront the government in its attempts to secure nickel-mining rights in that part of the northern province over which it had political control. A proposed joint venture with a Canadian partner would generate substantial economic development but would threaten other nickel interests.

American Samoa protested in July when the neighbouring nation of Western Samoa adopted "Samoa" as its official name, arguing that this implied an assumption of paramountcy over all of the Samoan group of islands. In April American Samoa mourned the death of Peter Tali Coleman, who formerly had served as governor for 11 years in three terms, despite his administration's being charged with overspending and mismanagement.

After an inconclusive first round of gubernatorial elections in November 1996, former lieutenant governor Tauese Sunia was successful in the second round. In the Commonwealth of the Northern Marianas, the reelection of Pedro Pangelinan Tenorio as governor was challenged on constitutional grounds because he had served two terms in the 1980s. In Guam the legislature switched from Democratic to Republican in the 1996 elections.

East Asia. The history-making handover of Hong Kong from British to Chinese sovereignty at midnight on June 30/July 1 divided 1997 neatly in half. Other than a plethora of Chinese and new Hong Kong flags around the city immediately after the big event, the transformation was not obvious. Just beneath the surface, however, were a multitude of significant changes that could be expected to shape Hong Kong in the years to come.

Tung Chee Hwa (*see* BIOGRAPHIES) became the first chief executive of the Hong Kong special administrative region and, therefore, the first ethnic Chinese to rule this city of some 6.3 million people, 95% of them Chinese. A 60-person legislature, about half of whom were popularly elected in 1995, was disbanded as of July 1 to make way for a temporary body selected by a Beijing-endorsed group of Hong Kong politicians and businesspeople. Balloting was scheduled for May 1998 to elect a new legislative body.

In the months following the handover, as protesters criticized the new Hong Kong government and China with rare police intervention, the signs were good that civil liberties would survive in Hong Kong under Chinese stewardship. The style of government in Hong Kong did, however, change slightly. The U.K. had not introduced territorywide democracy until the waning years of its reign, but the last British governor, Chris Patten, had frequently emphasized his support of democracy and civil liberties. After he was replaced by Tung, however, the emphasis shifted onto such bread-and-butter issues as the rising price of housing in Hong Kong, the quality (and deficiency) of education, and the lack of a mandatory retirement plan for local workers.

Throughout the hottest months, which produced the wettest year for the territory in more than a century, the local stock market thrived. Tourism was disappointing, but the economy in general was strong. Although the Hang Seng stock index fell in the autumn, Hong Kong generally avoided the currency turmoil that swept much of the region and remained a relatively safe haven for business. (*See* Spotlight: *Hong Kong's Return to China*.)

The political atmosphere in nearby Macau, a Portuguese colony that was scheduled to be returned to China on Dec. 20, 1999, was decidedly calmer than in Hong Kong. Gang violence, often revolving around gambling, plagued the city, however, and early in the year drive-by shootings and gangland-style executions seemed an almost weekly occurrence. By the fourth quarter, prominent business figures in the territory such as Stanley Ho, one of the richest men in Asia and the one who controlled gambling in Hong Kong, had apparently put a stop to the violence.

(TIM HEALY; BARRIE MACDONALD; DAVID RENWICK; MELINDA C. SHEPHERD)

This article updates the *Macropædia* articles HONG KONG; PACIFIC ISLANDS; The WEST INDIES.

ANTARCTICA

Ice averaging 2,160 m (7,087 ft) in thickness covers 98% of the continent of Antarctica, which has an area of 14 million sq km (5.4 million sq mi). There is no indigenous human population. Human activity consists mainly of scientific research at approximately 40 year-round stations and additional summer-only camps; the population is about 4,100 in summer and 1,000 in winter. In addition, several thousand tourists (most of them ship-based) visit Antarctica annually in summer. The 42-nation Antarctic Treaty, which is the managerial mechanism for the region south of latitude 60° S, reserves the area for peaceful purposes, encourages scientific cooperation, prescribes environmental protection measures, allows inspections to verify adherence, and defers the issue of territorial sovereignty.

The debate over how quickly the Antarctic ice sheet could melt reached beyond the science community in 1997 when a *Popular Science* cover story in February examined findings by glacial "dynamicists" (researchers who think Antarctica's ice sheet may have receded as recently as 3 million years ago) and "stablists" (those who believe the ice sheet has been stable for the last 10 million to 15 million years). The scientific debate was important because agreement on a clear picture of the past could help to cast a more accurate vision of Earth's future. The debate was also significant because 90% of the world's ice is on Antarctica, and if all this ice were to melt, the worldwide sea level would rise some 60 m (200 ft). The dynamicists, led by Peter Webb of Ohio State University and David Harwood of the University of Nebraska, reported that they had found sediments in the Transantarctic Mountains containing marine microfossils only three million years old, which suggested that the climate at that time may have been warm enough to melt the eastern part of Antarctica's ice sheet and enable ocean water to flood Antarctica's subglacial basins. If the eastern ice sheet shrank significantly then, another big thaw would be possible if Antarctica's temperature rose a similar amount. The stablists collected rock and ash samples from the same sedimentary layer studied by the dynamicists and found no sign of wetting or erosion, which suggested that the layers were not disturbed by a receding ice sheet as recently as three million years ago. The stablists theorized that the fossils might have blown in. It was believed that further research, including a large, six-nation drilling project at Cape Roberts that began in October 1997, might shed light on the answer to one of Antarctica's most perplexing questions.

Meanwhile, the West Antarctic Ice Sheet, which would raise sea level 6 m (20 ft) if it were to collapse, was the subject of scrutiny. The ice in West Antarctica is unstable because it is situated on land below sea level; when glaciologists went to Antarctica, they found ice streams in the process of collapse. Climatologist Peter deMenocal told *Time* magazine in April, "When I began my Ph.D. in 1986, the conventional wisdom was that it took 1,000 years to end an ice age; in '91 that figure was lowered to 100 years, and then just two years later Richard Alley at Penn State published a paper about climate changing in two to five years." Robert Bindschadler of NASA said he suspected that West Antarctic ice had been collapsing for thousands of years and final collapse might not occur for a couple of thousand more, but there was no guarantee the collapse would be orderly and predictable. In late 1997 a large research camp at Siple Dome in West Antarctica was continuing investigations of the ice sheet's behaviour.

At sea, ships and oceanographers of seven nations measured the potentially enormous climatic role of carbon and other biogenic elements within the Southern Ocean and between the ocean, the atmosphere, and the seafloor. The region had been deemed a source of carbon dioxide (a gas thought to contribute to the greenhouse effect), which would mean that the Southern Ocean contributed to global warming. The new cruises showed instead that the Southern Ocean seemed to be absorbing about 200 million to 400 million tons of carbon per year. It appeared likely that this represented a change in the behaviour of the ocean and not just a better data set. The oceanographers found that movement of carbon between the Southern Ocean and the atmosphere was highly susceptible to perturbation and was less well understood than fluxes in less-remote areas. The international program, called the Southern Ocean Joint Global Ocean Flux Study, was expected to continue most of the decade.

More evidence was found that Antarctic plants and animals, always thought of as hardy survivors because of the harsh climate, are susceptible to human-caused change. Biologists found the first direct evidence that abnormally high levels of ultraviolet rays, which penetrate the protective ozone layer during the period of Antarctica's infamous ozone hole, cause damage to the DNA of higher animals. Kirk Malloy and William Detrich, both of Northeastern University, Boston, found extensive DNA lesions in the eggs and larvae of icefish—Antarctic fish that lack hemoglobin. Meanwhile, up to two-thirds of emperor and Adélie penguins in rookeries near Australia's Mawson research station were found to have a poultry virus, probably caused by human disposal of poultry products. Penguins at a remote site were free of the virus. The virus also could have been spread by movement of people carrying it on footwear, clothing, equipment, and vehicles.

An estimated 7,322 shipborne tourists visited Antarctica in the 1996–97 summer, down from the 9,212 of the previous year. The International Association of Antarctica Tour Operators, however, projected that the annual number would exceed 10,000 in 1997–98 and future years. Perhaps 100 tourists landed by airplane, and additional sightseers were aboard commercial flights that did not land in the Antarctic. Forty-eight percent of the shipborne tourists were from the United States. Germany, Great Britain, Japan, and Australia also contributed significant numbers. The Antarctic Peninsula was the most popular destination, with Cuverville Island the most visited spot.

It was reported that a vast iceberg that could supply a fifth of the world's drinking water for a year had broken off East Antarctica and begun a 10-year drift to the north. Neal Young, an Australian glaciologist, said the berg covered more than 3,000 sq km (1,160 sq mi) when it calved from the West Ice Shelf in May 1996. It broke into five or six bergs, the biggest of which was an estimated 300 m (985 ft) deep and was grounded off the coast north of Australia's Davis Station. The total amount of ice involved was equivalent to about a third of all the ice Antarctica dumps into the sea each year.

(GUY G. GUTHRIDGE)

This article updates the *Macropædia* article ANTARCTICA.

ARCTIC REGIONS

During 1997 U.S. and Canadian oil and gas companies made renewed efforts to proceed with exploration and development in environmentally sensitive areas of arctic Alaska and the northern part of Canada's Yukon. In January BP Exploration Alaska Inc. announced plans to increase capital spending in Alaska by $1 billion to $3.5 billion over the next five years and reverse the fall in oil production from Alaska's North Slope. The company expected to increase its share of oil production to nearly 600,000 bbl a day by 2002, a reversal from the decline once considered inevitable. The firm also hoped to add five billion barrels in recoverable oil reserves over the following decade, in addition to possible development in the National Petroleum Reserve-Alaska, a federally owned reserve west of Prudhoe Bay, or in the Arctic National Wildlife Refuge (ANWR). Reports that BP Exploration and

JOANNA PINNEO—AURORA

An Inuit woman dances after a seal feast. In 1999 the Inuit were to take over what was to become Canada's third official territory, Nunavut ("our land"). Stretching well above the Arctic Circle, the new territory of Nunavut would comprise an area larger than Alaska and California combined.

Chevron USA were proceeding to develop the 100 million-bbl Sourdough Prospect oil field as early as 1998 raised concern among environmental groups. The Alaska Wilderness League feared that the project, which bordered the ANWR and the 600,000-ha (1.5 million-ac) coastal plain, could result in a network of pipelines, roads, and drilling pads that might affect the wildlife in the 7.7 million-ha (19 million-ac) refuge, which was also the birthing grounds of the 150,000 porcupine caribou herd that migrated into the Yukon and Northwest Territories (NWT). In February a wilderness bill was introduced in the U.S. Congress to give permanent wilderness protection to the coastal plain.

A dispute between Alaska and the U.S. government over ownership of the tidelands, offshore lagoons, and estuaries along the approximately 200-km (125-mi) Arctic Refuge coastline could also affect development. Alaska planned to lease these lands to oil and gas companies, whereas the U.S. wanted to protect them as part of the ANWR. In May a Yukon company, Northern Cross Ltd., applied for permits to reopen 25-year-old wellheads for testing purposes near Eagle Plains—an area that was part of the porcupine caribou herd's winter feeding range. By June the Canadian government had approved the company's plans to begin redeveloping its natural gas property. Environmental groups were concerned that the project would give pro-development lobbyists ammunition to encourage development in the herd's North Slope calving grounds.

The 13 regional for-profit corporations created under the Alaska Native Claims Settlement Act celebrated their 26th anniversary in 1997. The largest of the corporations reported a net worth of $265 million in 1997 and paid out over $13 million to its aboriginal shareholders. In southeastern Alaska native corporations provided an estimated one in 10 jobs. The Trans-Alaska pipeline marked its 20th anniversary.

According to a report issued in October by the Northwest Territories, the cost estimated for carving a new territory, Nunavut, out of the NWT in 1999 would be almost double (about $286 million) the amount that the federal government originally had budgeted ($150 million). The additional funds would be needed to establish a government and infrastructure for Nunavut. The NWT would decentralize its main government departments in communities across the Arctic in an effort to spread employment opportunities among the widely dispersed communities, where average unemployment hovered around 30%.

Two mines planned for the Northwest Territories could make Canada one of the world's top diamond-producing nations. Joint ventures by British, Canadian, and Australian companies—led by Broken Hill Pty. Co. (BHP) and Rio Tinto PLC—could produce 10% of global diamond output. The NWT's 43 diamond projects outnumbered gold and other mining ventures. The BHP and Rio Tinto projects, costing an estimated $900 million and $750 million, respectively, were expected to yield 11 million carats of high-quality diamonds as early as 1998.

In September, faced with an extensive environmental-impact assessment process and demands by the Innu and Inuit aboriginal groups for impact and benefits agreements, Inco Ltd., the world's largest nickel producer announced a one-year delay, until late 2000 at the earliest, in the proposed start-up of its Voisey Bay nickel project in northern Labrador. Inco had already paid $4.3 billion to acquire the project—billed as the largest nickel find ever—and had planned to invest another $1.4 billion–$2 billion in a mine, mill, and smelter.

Also in September, after four years of negotiations, it was reported that a $28 billion U.S.-Russian oil venture to develop the Priobskoye oil field in Siberia had broken down because of financial disagreements between the Russian oil giant Yukos and Amoco, its American partner. After spending more than $100 million, and with proven reserves of some 600 million tons of oil, Amoco expected to boost its own reserves significantly. The Amoco deal was the second major U.S.-Russian venture to unravel in the same period. Citing "legal" difficulties, the Russian government in August annulled the results of a bid won by the Exxon Corp. to develop huge oil fields in Russia's far north.

In January former Canadian prime minister John Turner, acting on behalf of the World Wildlife Fund, dropped a lawsuit after reaching an agreement with the federal government that a system of protected places—free from mining and other resource development—would be established in the NWT by the year 2000. The federal and NWT governments agreed to set aside 12% of the NWT as ecologically protected areas and acknowledged that project proponents and environmental-impact assessors would take into account the notion of "potentially protected natural areas" in the course of evaluating the impacts of future resource developments.

After four years of research, the biggest conservation project in North America moved closer to reality. The creation of the "Y2Y," a 3,000-km (1,800-mi) expanse of parks and wilderness preserves stretching through the northern Rocky Mountains from Yellowstone National Park in Wyoming to the Yukon and NWT, was announced in October. The purpose of Y2Y was to create a development-free corridor of prime habitat so that wildlife could move freely between Canada and the U.S. The wildlife population there included 27,000 moose, 15,000 elk, 9,000 sheep, 5,000 mountain goats, 3,500 woodland caribou, 1,000 wolves, and 1,000 grizzly and black bears.

In June a study by the Arctic Monitoring and Assessment Program reported that ozone depletion, ultraviolet (UV) radiation, climate change, and pollutants generated by humans were a more serious threat to the Arctic environment than had previously been believed. The occurrence of ozone "holes" in the Arctic atmosphere in the spring was particularly damaging because humans and ecosystems were more vulnerable to UV radiation at that time. The report also concluded that the impact of the warming climate in the Arctic, already under way, could influence the rest of the Earth both by increasing the sea level through glacial melt and by altering oceanic circulation, which was responsible for transporting colder water from the Arctic to lower latitudes.

(KENNETH DE LA BARRE)

This article updates the *Macropædia* article The ARCTIC.

WORLD LEGISLATIVE ELECTION RESULTS

The following table is a guide to the principal political parties and coalitions of the world. All countries that were independent on Dec. 31, 1997, are included, except the Vatican City State. In most instances parties are included only if represented in elected parliaments (in the lower house in bicameral legislatures). (Party names may be condensed or omitted for reasons of space or to more clearly indicate party groupings.) The first column under "Parliamentary representation" indicates the number of seats obtained in the most recent general election and excludes nonelective seats and seats still undecided. If only a portion of the seats were at stake, the figure given indicates the total number of seats held by each party after the election. The column in parentheses represents the number of seats won in the penultimate election. Single-party penultimate election results may be combined if a coalition was formed at the most recent election. The date of the most recent election follows the name of the country.

The capital letters in the column "Affiliation" show the relative positions of the parties within the political spectrum of each country. The key chosen is as follows: ER-extreme right; R-right; CR-centre right; C-centre; CL-centre left; SD-social democratic; S-strictly defined socialist; L-broadly defined left (may or may not be Marxist); K-strictly defined communist; and EL-extreme left. In addition, within some countries there are political organizations that exist chiefly to advance a special interest as distinct from a political orientation. These are represented by lowercase letters as follows: x-parties that have repudiated former communist affiliation; e-parties based on distinct regional, ethnic, or linguistic identity; r-parties based on religion, often fundamentalist; g-environmental, or Green; and p-parties based largely on personalities.

The number in the column "Voting strength" indicate proportions of the valid votes cast for the respective parties. (STEPHEN NEHER; MELINDA C. SHEPHERD)

World Legislative Election Results

Country / Name of party	Affiliation	Voting strength (%)	Parliamentary representation	
Afghanistan				
Multifactional warfare from January 1993	—	—	—	
Albania (June–July 1997)				
Democratic Party	CR	25.7	29	(122)
Social Democratic Party	S	2.5	8	—
Socialist Party of Albania	x	52.8	101	(10)
Greek minority party	e	2.8	4	(3)
Others	—	16.2	13	(5)
Algeria (June 1997)				
Islamic Salvation Front	ERr		*	
Islamic Renaissance Movement (Nahda)	r	9.9	34	
Movement of the Islamic Society (Hamas)	Cr	16.8	69	
National Democratic Rally	C	38.3	156	
National Liberation Front	S	16.1	62	
Pro-Berber parties	e	9.9	39	
Other parties	—	3.8	9	
Independents	—	5.2	11	
Andorra (February 1997)				
Liberal Union	CR	...	18	(5)
National Democratic Grouping	CR	...	6	(8)
New Democracy	CL	...	2	(5)
Others and independents	—	...	2	(10)
Angola (September 1992)				
Popular Liberation Movement of Angola–Labour Party (MPLA–PT)	x	53.7	129	(203)
National Union for the Total Independence of Angola (UNITA)	—	34.1	70	—
Others	—	12.2	21	—
Antigua and Barbuda (March 1994)				
Antigua Labour Party	C	54.4	11	(15)
United Progressive Party	C	43.7	5	(1)
Barbuda People's Movement	e	1.4	1	(1)
Argentina (October 1997)				
Justicialist National Movement (Peronist)	CR–CL	36.1	119	(136)
Radical Civic Union }	CL	45.7	106	(69)
Front for a Country in Solidarity (Frepaso coalition) }				(26)
Others	—	18.2	32	(26)
Armenia (July 1995)				
Republic Bloc (coalition)	—	42.7	119	
National Democratic Union	—	7.5	5	
Shamiram Women's Movement	—	16.9	8	
Armenian Communist Party	K	12.1	7	
Others and independents	—	20.8	51	
Australia (March 1996)				
National Party of Australia	R	8.2	18	(16)
Liberal Party of Australia	C	38.7	76	(49)
Australian Labor Party	L	38.7	49	(80)
Others and independents	—	14.4	5	(2)
Austria (December 1995)				
Freedom Movement	R	21.9	40	(42)
Liberal Forum	—	5.5	10	(11)
Austrian People's Party	C	28.3	53	(52)
Austrian Social Democratic Party	SD	38.1	71	(65)
The Green Alternative	Lg	4.8	9	(13)
Azerbaijan (November 1995–February 1996)				
New Azerbaijan Party and allies	p	...	115	
Others	—	...	9	
Bahamas, The (March 1997)				
Free National Movement	CR	57.0	34	(34)
Progressive Liberal Party	C	42.0	6	(15)
Bahrain				
Consultative Council (advisory body)	—	—	—	
Bangladesh (June–September 1996)				
Bangladesh Nationalist Party	CR	...	113	(212)
National Party	CR	...	33	†
Awami League	SD	...	176	†
Bangladesh Islamic Assembly	r	...	3	†
Others	—	...	5	(2)
Barbados (September 1994)				
Democratic Labour Party	C	38.8	8	(18)
National Democratic Party	—	12.1	1	(0)
Barbados Labour Party	SD	48.8	19	(10)
Belarus				
House of Representatives	—	—	110	
Belgium (May 1995)				
National Front (French)	ERe	2.3	2	(1)
Vlaams Blok (Flemish)	ERe	7.8	11	(12)
Volksunie (Flemish)	Re	4.7	5	(10)
Liberals { Flemish	CR	13.1	21	(26)
Liberals { French	CR	10.3	18	(20)
Social Christians { Flemish	C	17.2	29	(39)
Social Christians { French	C	7.7	12	(18)
Socialist { Flemish	SD	12.6	20	(28)
Socialist { French	SD	11.9	21	(35)
Greens { Flemish	g	4.4	5	(7)
Greens { French	g	4.0	6	(10)
Others	—	4.0	0	(6)
Belize (June 1993)				
United Democratic Party	R	48.8	16	(13)
People's United Party	C	51.2	13	(15)
Benin (March–May 1995)				
Government party and allies	—	...	32	
Opposition parties	—	...	50	
Bhutan				
National Assembly, nonparty	—	—	105	
Bolivia (June 1997)				
Civic Solidarity Union	R	15.9	21	(20)
Nationalist Revolutionary Movement	CR	17.7	26	(52)
Nationalist Democratic Action	p	22.3	33 }	(35)
Movement of the Revolutionary Left	SD	16.7	25 }	
Conscience of the Fatherland	CL	15.8	17	(13)
Free Bolivia Movement	L	2.5	4	(7)
United Left (coalition)	L–K	3.7	4	(0)
Others	—	5.4	0	(3)
Bosnia and Herzegovina (September 1996)				
Muslim-nationalist party	er	37.8	19	
Serb-nationalist party	er	24.0	9	
Croat-nationalist party	er	14.0	8	
Pro-multiethnic parties	—	11.3	4	
Others	—	12.9	2	
Botswana (October 1994)				
Botswana Democratic Party	C	54.4	27	(31)
Botswana National Front	CL	37.1	13	(3)
Brazil (October 1994)				
Progressive Renewal Party	CR	...	52	(22)
Social Democrats and allies	C	...	192	(177)
Brazilian Democratic Movement	CL	...	107	(109)
Workers' Party and ally	L	...	66	(46)
Democratic Labour Party	L	...	34	(46)
Others	—	...	62	(103)
Brunei				
Legislative Council (nonelected)	—	—	—	
Bulgaria (April 1997)				
Bulgarian Business Bloc	R	4.9	12	(13)
United Democratic Forces (coalition)	CR	52.3	137	(87)
Euro-Left (coalition)	SD	5.5	14	—
Democratic Left (coalition)	L	22.1	58	(125)
Movement for Rights and Freedoms (Turkish)	e	7.6	19	(15)
Burkina Faso (May–June 1997)				
Government party and allies	...	76.0	103	(84)
Opposition parties	...	16.6	8	(23)
Burundi (June 1993)				
Burundi Democratic Front	—	72.6	65	
Unity for National Progress	—	21.9	16	
Cambodia (May 1993)				
Funcinpec	CR	45.5	58	
Buddhist Liberal Democrats	L	3.8	10	
Cambodian People's Party	x	38.2	51	
Others	—	12.5	1	
Cameroon (May 1997)				
Government party	R	...	116	(88)
Allied party	e	...	1	(6)
Cameroon People's Union	—	...	1	(18)
National Union for Democracy and Progress (Islamist)	Cr	...	13	(68)
Social Democratic Front	SD	...	43	†
Others	—	...	6	(0)
Canada (June 1997)				
Reform Party of Canada	R	19.4	60	(52)
Progressive Conservative Party	CR	18.9	20	(2)
Liberal Party of Canada	C	38.4	155	(177)
New Democratic Party	SD	11.0	21	(9)
Bloc Québécois	e	10.7	44	(54)
Others and independents	—	1.6	1	(1)
Cape Verde (December 1995)				
Movement for Democracy	—	61.3	50	(56)
African Party for the Independence of Cape Verde	—	29.8	21	(23)
Democratic Convergence Party	—	6.7	1	—
Central African Republic (August–September 1993)				
Central African People's Liberation Movement	—	...	34	
Others	—	...	51	
Chad (January–February 1997)				
Patriotic Salvation Movement	p	...	63	
Allied party	—	...	15	
Union for Renewal and Democracy	p	...	29	
Others	—	...	16	
Chile (December 1997)				
Union for the Progress of Chile	ER–R	36.3	47	(50)
Coalition of Parties for Democracy	C–L	50.6	70	(70)
Leftist alliance	L–EL	7.6	0	(0)
Others	—	5.7	3	(0)
China (September 1992–March 1993)				
National People's Congress	K	...	2,978	
Colombia (March 1994)				
Social Conservative Party	R	...	56	(15)
Other rightist parties	R	...	2	(24)
Liberal Party	C	...	89	(86)
Democratic Alliance–April 19 Movement	L	...	2	(15)
Others	—	...	14	(21)
Comoros				
Transitional government from September 1997				
Congo, Democratic Republic of the				
Military government from May 1997				
Congo, Republic of the				
Military-backed transitional government from November 1997				
Costa Rica (February 1994)				
Social Christian Unity Party	CR	40.4	25	(29)
National Liberation Party	CL	44.6	28	(25)
Others	—	15.0	4	(3)
Côte d'Ivoire (November 1995–December 1996)				
Democratic Party of Côte d'Ivoire	—	...	149	(147)
Rally of Republicans	C	...	13	(14)
Ivorian Popular Front	SD	...	13	(10)
Croatia (October 1995)				
Croatian Party of Rights	ERe	5.0	4	(5)
Croatian Democratic Union	Re	45.2	75	(85)
Moderate opposition coalition	R–C	18.3	20	(6)
Croatian Social-Liberal Party	CL	11.6	11	(14)
Social Democratic Party	x	8.9	9	(11)
Others and independents	—	11.0	8	(17)
Cuba (February 1993)				
Government (single) party	K	...	589	(499)
Cyprus				
Greek Zone (May 1996)				
Democratic Rally/Liberals	R	34.5	20	(20)
Democratic Party	CR	16.4	10	(11)
EDEK–SK (Socialists)	CL	8.1	5	(7)
Free Democrats Movement	CL	3.7	2	—
Progressive Party of the Working People	L	33.0	19	(18)
Turkish Zone (December 1993)				
National Unity Party	CR	29.9	17	
Democrat Party	—	29.2	15	
Communal Liberation Party	CL	13.3	5	
Republican Turkish Party	S	24.2	13	
Czech Republic (May–June 1996)				
Association for the Republic–Czech Republican Party	ER	8.0	18	(14)
Governing coalition	R–CR	44.1	99	(105)

World Legislative Election Results

Country / Name of party	Affiliation	Voting strength (%)	Parliamentary representation	
Czech Social Democratic Party	SD	26.4	61	(16)
Liberal Social Union (coalition)	Lg	—	—	(16)
Communist (reformed) party	x	10.3	22	(35)
Left Bloc	K	1.8	0	
Others	—	9.4	0	(14)
Denmark (September 1994)				
Progress	ER	6.4	11	(12)
Liberal	R	23.3	42	(29)
Conservative People's	R	15.0	27	(30)
Christian People's	CR	1.8	0	(4)
Centre Democrats	C	2.8	5	(9)
Radical Liberal	C	4.6	8	(7)
Social Democrats	CL	34.6	62	(69)
Socialist People's	L	7.3	13	(15)
Red-Green Unity List	Lg	3.1	6	(0)
Faroe Islands and Greenland	—	—	4	(4)
Independents	—	1.0	1	(0)
Djibouti (December 1997)				
Popular Rally for Progress and allies	—	78.6	65	(65)
Dominica (June 1995)				
Dominica Freedom Party	CR	35.8	5	(11)
Dominica United Workers' Party	CL	34.4	11	(6)
Labour Party	L	29.6	5	(4)
Independents/others	—	0.2	0	(1)
Dominican Republic (May 1994)				
Social Christian Reformist Party	CR	39.7	50	(40)
Dominican Revolutionary Party and allies	L	42.7	57	(36)
Dominican Liberation Party	L	16.1	13	(44)
Ecuador (May 1996)				
Social Christian Party	CR	30.7	27	(26)
Popular Democracy	C	10.4	12	(4)
Ecuadorian Roldosist Party	C	19.9	19	(11)
Democratic Left	SD	6.3	4	(8)
Alfarist Radical Front	L	6.8	3	(2)
Democratic Popular Movement	EL	4.4	2	(8)
New Country–Pachakutik Movement (indigenous interests)	e	10.9	8	—
Others	—	10.6	7	(18)
Egypt (November–December 1995)				
Muslim Brotherhood	r	—	*	*
New Wafd Party	R	...	6	†
National Democratic Party	CR	...	317	(348)
National Progressive Unionist	L	...	5	(6)
Other parties	—	...	3	—
Independents	—	...	113	(83)
El Salvador (March 1997)				
National Conciliation Party	R	8.6	11	(4)
Nationalist Republican Alliance (Arena)	R	34.9	28	(39)
Liberal Democratic Party	p	3.1	2	—
Christian Democratic Party and ally	C	11.7	10	(18)
Other centrist parties	CR–CL	9.2	6	(2)
Farabundo Martí National Liberation Front	L	32.5	27	(21)
Equatorial Guinea (November 1993)				
Democratic Party	—	...	68	(41)
Principal opposition parties	—	—	†	—
Others	—	...	12	—
Eritrea				
Transitional government from May 1993	—	—	—	
Estonia (March 1995)				
Republican and Conservative People's Party	R	5.0	5	—
Pro Patria ("Fatherland") Coalition	CR	7.9	8	(29)
Estonian Reform Party	CR	16.2	19	—
Estonian Centre Party	CL	14.2	16	—
Coalition and Rural People's Union	CL/x	32.2	41	(17)
Moderates	SD	6.0	6	(12)
Our Home Is Estonia (pro-Russian alliance)	e	5.9	6	—
Others	—	12.6	0	(43)
Ethiopia (May–June 1995)				
Ethiopian People's Revolutionary Democratic Front	—	...	493	
Major opposition parties	—	—	†	
Others and independents	—	...	54	
Fiji (February 1994)				
Ethnic Fijian seats	e	...	37	(37)
Ethnic Indian seats	e	...	27	(27)
Chinese/European seats	e	...	4	(4)
Multiracial seat	e	...	1	(1)
Rotuma Island	e	...	1	(1)
Finland (March 1995)				
Finnish Christian Union	R	3.0	7	(8)
National Coalition	CR	17.9	39	(40)
Swedish People's Party	e	5.1	12	(12)
Finnish Centre	C	19.9	44	(55)
Social Democratic Party	S	28.3	63	(48)
Left-Wing Alliance	L–K	11.2	22	(19)
Green Union	g	6.5	9	(10)
Others	—	8.1	4	(8)
France (May–June; 1st round %s)				
National Front	ER	14.9	1	(0)
Rally for the Republic	R	15.7	139	(247)
Other right-wing parties	R	6.6	8	(24)
Union for French Democracy	CR	14.2	109	(213)
Socialist Party	S	23.5	246	(54)
Other left-wing parties	L	4.2	29	(16)
French Communist Party	K	9.9	37	(23)
The Greens	g	6.8	8	(0)
Gabon (December 1996–January 1997)				
Gabonese Democratic Party	p	...	82	(66)
National Rally of Woodcutters	C	...	12	(17)
Gabonese Progress Party	—	...	8	(19)
Others and independents	—	...	18	(18)
Gambia, The (January 1997)				
Alliance for Patriotic Reorientation and Construction	p	52.1	33	
Opposition parties	—	44.1	10	
Independents	—	3.8	2	
Georgia (November–December 1995)				
All-Georgian Union of Revival (Adzharian Muslim)	er	6.8	32	—
National Democratic Party	CR	8.0	34	(12)
Citizens' Union of Georgia	C	23.7	106	—
Others and independents	—	61.5	63	(228)
Germany (October 1994)				
Christian Social Union	R	7.3	50	(51)
Christian Democratic Union	CR	34.2	244	(268)
Free Democratic Party	C	6.9	47	(79)
Social Democratic Party	SD	36.4	252	(239)
Party of Democratic Socialism	x	4.4	30	(17)
Greens/Alliance '90	g	7.3	49	(8)
Others	—	3.5	0	(0)
Ghana (December 1996)				
National Democratic Congress	p	...	134	(189)
New Patriotic Party	CR	...	60	(0)
Others	—	...	6	(11)
Greece (September 1996)				
Political Spring	CR	2.9	0	(10)
New Democracy	CR	38.1	108	(111)
Panhellenic Socialist Movement (Pasok)	S	41.5	162	(170)
Democratic Social Movement	L	4.4	9	
Progressive Left Coalition	L–K	5.1	10	(0)
Communist Party	K–EL	5.6	11	(9)
Grenada (June 1995)				
Grenada United Labour Party	R	26.8	2	(4)
National Democratic Congress	C	31.1	5	(7)
New National Party	C	32.7	8	(2)
Others	—	9.4	0	(2)
Guatemala (November 1995)				
National Advancement Party	Rp	34.7	43	(24)
Guatemalan Republican Front	Rp	19.5	21	(32)
Other rightist parties	R	8.7	3	(3)
National Alliance (coalition)	C	13.0	7	(21)
New Guatemala Democratic Front	CL	8.5	6	—
Guinea (June 1995)				
Presidential party and allies	—	...	76	
Opposition parties	—	...	38	
Guinea-Bissau (July 1994)				
African Party for the Independence of Guinea and Cape Verde	L	46.0	62	(150)
Guinea-Bissau Resistance	—	19.2	19	—
Other opposition parties	—	34.8	19	—
Guyana (December 1997)				
People's National Congress (black interests)	Le	40.6	22	(31)
People's Progressive Party (East Indian interests)	Le	55.3	29	(32)
Others	—	2.7	2	(2)
Haiti (June–September 1995)				
Lavalas movement	C–L	...	68	
Others and independents	—	...	15	
Honduras (November 1997)				
National Party	R	41.5	55	(55)
Liberal Party	CR	49.6	67	(71)
Christian Democratic Party	C	2.6	2	(0)
National Innovation and Unity Party–Social Democratic	SD	4.1	3	(2)
Democratic Unification Party	L–EL	2.1	1	—
Hungary (May 1994)				
Independent Smallholders'	R	8.8	26	(43)
Hungarian Democratic Forum	CR	11.7	37	(165)
Christian Democratic People's Party	CR	7.1	22	(21)
Alliance of Free Democrats	CL	19.8	70	(92)
Federation of Young Democrats	L	7.0	20	(21)
Hungarian Socialist Party	x	33.0	209	(33)
Others and independents	—	12.6	2	(11)
Iceland (April 1995)				
Independence Party	R	37.1	25	(26)
Progressive Party	C	23.3	15	(13)
Women's Alliance	CL	4.9	3	(5)
People's Movement	CL	7.2	4	(10)
Social Democratic Party	SD	11.4	7	
People's Alliance	L	14.3	9	(9)
India (April–May 1996)				
Bharatiya Janata Party	Rr	20.3	161	(119)
Allied parties	Rr	...	34	(4)
Congress (I)	C	28.8	136	(226)
Allied parties	C	...	5	(17)
Janata Dal and leftist allies	CL–K	...	112	(115)
Allied regional parties	e	...	58	(16)
Others (includes vacant seats)	—	...	37	(46)
Indonesia (May 1997)				
Governing coalition of groups	—	74.3	325	(282)
United Development Party (Muslim interests)	r	22.6	89	(62)
Party representing Christian and nationalist interests	—	3.1	11	(56)
Iran (March 1996–February 1997)				
Association of Combatant Clergy "group"	ERr	...	113	(155‡)
Servants of Construction "group"	Rr	...	86	(115‡)
Others	—	...	62	
Iraq (March 1996)				
Ba.th Party	—	...	160	(250)
Allied independents	—	...	60	
Ireland (June 1997)				
Progressive Democrats	R	4.7	4	(10)
Fianna Fail (Republican)	C	39.3	77	(68)
Fine Gael (United Ireland)	C	27.9	54	(45)
Labour Party	SD	10.4	17	(33)
Democratic Left	S	2.5	4	(4)
Sinn Fein ("Ourselves Alone")	EL	2.6	1	(0)
Green Alliance	g	2.8	2	(1)
Others and independents	—	9.8	7	(5)
Israel (May 1996)				
Moledet	ER	2.3	2	(3)
United Torah Judaism (orthodox)	r	3.2	4	(4)
Shas (orthodox)	r	8.5	10	(6)
National Religious Party	r	7.8	9	(6)
Likud and allies	R	25.1	32	(40)
Israel for Immigration (Russian)	Ce	5.7	7	—
The Third Way	C	3.1	4	—
Israel Labor Party	SD	26.8	34	(44)
Meretz	CL	7.4	9	(12)
United Arab List	e	2.9	4	(2)
Hadash	L	4.2	5	(3)
Italy (April 1996)				
Northern League	Re	10.1	59	(366)
Right-wing alliance	R	44.0	246	
National Alliance	R	15.7	107	(109)
Forza Italia	R	20.6	110	(112)
United Christian Democrats	CR	5.8	29	—
Centrist parties	C	43.4	319	(46)
Left-wing pact/alliance	L			(213)
Democratic Party of the Left	SD	21.1	163	(114)
Green Federation	g	2.5	...	(11)
Communist Refoundation Party	K	8.6	35	(41)
Others	—	2.5	6	(5)
Jamaica (December 1997)				
Jamaica Labour Party	CL	39	11	(8)
People's National Party	L	56	49	(52)
Japan (October 1996)				
Liberal-Democratic Party	R	38.6	239	(223)
Democratic Party	—	10.1	52	—
New Frontier Party (Shinshinto)	R–SD	28.0	156	(160)
Social Democratic Party	SD	2.2	15	(70)
Japan Communist Party	L	12.5	26	(15)
Others and independents	—	8.6	12	(43)
Jordan (November 1997)				
Islamic Action Front	r	—	†	(16)
Tribal/traditional candidates	C	...	62	(49)
Independent Islamists	C	...	8	(10)
Leftists and Nationalists	L	...	10	
Kazakstan (December 1995–February 1996)				
Pro-presidential parties	—	...	53	
Opposition	—	...	14	
Kenya (December 1997)				
Kenya African National Union	—	...	109	(100)
Forum for Restoration of Democracy	—	...	21	(62)
Democratic Party	—	...	39	(23)
National Development Party	—	...	21	(0)
Others	—	...	19	(3)
Kiribati (July 1994)				
Christian Democratic Party	p	...	13	
Gilbertese National Progressive Party	p	...	7	
Independents	—	...	19	
Korea, North (April 1990)				
Korean Workers' Party	K	99.8	687	
Korea, South (April 1996)				
United Liberal Democrats	R	16.2	50	—
New Korea Party	R	34.5	139	(149)
National Congress for New Politics	C	25.3	79	—
Democratic Party	CL	11.2	15	(97)
Others and independents	—	12.8	16	(53)
Kuwait (October 1996)				
Islamic moderates and fundamentalists	r	...	14	(19)
Government supporters	—	...	19	(15)
Tribal candidates and independents	—	...	11	
Liberal opposition	—	...	4	(6)
Kyrgyzstan (February–April 1995)				
Pro-government independents	—	...	90	
Others	—	...	15	

World Legislative Election Results

Country Name of party	Affili- ation	Voting strength (%)	Parlia- mentary represen- tation	
Laos (December 1997)				
Government (single) party	K	...	98	(85)
Nonparty	—	...	1	(0)
Latvia (September–October 1995)				
Popular Movement for Latvia	ERp	14.9	16	—
Fatherland and Freedom	ERe	11.9	14	(6)
National Conservative Party	Re	6.3	8	(15)
Farmer's Union and allies	CR	6.3	8	(18)
Latvian Way Union	C	14.6	17	(36)
Master Democratic Party	CL	15.2	18	(5)
National Harmony Party (pro-Russian)	—	5.6	6	(13)
Latvian Socialist Party (pro-Russian)	—	5.6	5	(7)
Latvian Unity Party	K	7.1	8	—
Lebanon (August–September 1996)				
Christian	—	—	64	
Maronite	—	—	34	
Greek Orthodox	—	—	14	
Greek Catholic	—	—	8	
Armenian Orthodox	—	—	5	
Others	—	—	3	
Muslim/Druze	—	—	64	
Sunnite	—	—	27	
Shi.ite	—	—	27	
Druze	—	—	8	
.Alawite	—	—	2	
Lesotho (March 1993)				
Basotho Congress Party	—	74.8	65	
Basotho National Party	—	22.7	0	
Liberia (July 1997)				
National Patriotic Front of Liberia	p	...	49	
Others	—	...	15	
Libya				
General People's Congress	—	—	760	
Liechtenstein (January–February 1997)				
Progressive Citizens' Party	CR	39.2	10	(11)
Fatherland Union	C	49.2	13	(13)
Free List	g	11.6	2	(1)
Lithuania (October 1996–March 1997				
Christian Democrats	CR	12.2	16	(13)
Homeland Union	CR	29.8	70	—
Reform Movement (Sajudis)	CR	—	—	(29)
Centre Union	C	8.2	13	(2)
Social Democratic Party	SD	6.6	12	(8)
Democratic Labour Party	x	9.5	12	(74)
Others and independents	—	33.7	15	(15)
Luxembourg (June 1994)				
Christian Social People's Party	CR	29.3	21	(22)
Democratic Party	C	11.6	12	(11)
Socialist Workers' Party	S	33.5	17	(18)
Communist Party	K	2.8	0	(1)
Action Committee for Democracy and Justice	—	7.1	5	(4)
Green Alternative	g	10.2	5	(4)
Macedonia (October–November 1994)				
Alliance of Macedonia	x	...	95	
Pro-government Albanian party	e	...	10	
Antigovernment Albanian party	e	...	4	
Other opposition	—	...	11	
Madagascar (June 1993)				
Living Forces coalition	—	...	75	
Others	—	...	59	
Malawi (May 1994)				
United Democratic Front	—	46.4	84	—
Malawi Congress Party	—	33.6	55	(136)
Alliance for Democracy	—	18.9	36	—
Malaysia (April 1995)				
Islamic parties	CR	17.4	13	(15)
National Front coalition	e	64.0	162	(127)
Democratic Action Party	SD	12.1	9	(20)
Others and independents	—	6.5	8	(18)
Maldives (December 1994)				
People's Council, nonparty	—	...	40	
Mali (July–August 1997)				
Alliance for Democracy in Mali	p	...	128	(74)
Principal opposition parties	—	—	†	—
Others	—	...	19	(42)
Malta (October 1996)				
Nationalist Party	R	47.8	34	(34)
Malta Labour Party	SD	50.7	35	(31)
Marshall Islands (November 1995)				
House of Representatives, nonparty	—	—	33	
Mauritania (October 1996)				
Government party	R	...	70	(67)
Principal opposition parties	...	...	1	(†)
Others and independents	—	...	8	(12)
Mauritius (December 1995)				
Mauritian Socialist Movement and allied parties	—	19.7	0 }	(59)
Mauritian Militant Movement } Mauritian Labour Party and allied parties }	—	65.2	60	(3)
Others	—	15.1	2	—
Mexico (July 1997)				
National Action Party (PAN)	CR	26.9	122	(119)
Institutional Revolutionary Party (PRI)	C–CL	38.5	239	(300)
Democratic Revolutionary Party	SD	25.8	125	(71)
Labour Party	L	2.6	6	(10)
Mexican Green Ecologist Party	g	4.0	8	(0)
Micronesia, Federated States of (March–April 1997)				
Congress, nonparty	—	...	14	(14)
Moldova (February 1994)				
Popular Front alliance	Re	7.5	9	
Peasants/Intellectuals bloc	Ce	9.2	11	
Agrarian Democratic Party	C–x	43.2	56	
Socialist/Unity bloc (Russian)	xe	22.0	28	
Others	—	18.1	0	
Monaco (January 1993)				
Campora list	p	...	15	
Others	p	...	3	
Mongolia (June 1996)				
United Heritage Party	R	1.6	1	—
Democratic Alliance coalition	C–SD	47.0	50	(5)
People's Revolutionary Party	—	40.5	25	(71)
Morocco (November–December 1997)				
Justice and Welfare (Islamist)	r	—	*	*
National Entente (coalition)	CR	24.7	100	(129)
Centre (coalition)	CR	27.3	97	(66)
Democratic Bloc (coalition)	CL–L	34.3	102	(114)
Others	—	13.7	26	(24)
Mozambique (October 1994)				
Mozambique Liberation Front (Frelimo)	x	44.3	129	(250)
Mozambique National Resistance (Renamo)	—	37.8	112	
Democratic Union	—	5.2	9	
Myanmar				
Military government since September 1988	—	—	—	
Namibia (December 1994)				
Democratic Turnhalle Alliance	C	20.8	15	(21)
South West Africa People's Organization (SWAPO)	L	73.9	53	(41)
Others	—	5.3	4	(10)
Nauru (February 1997)				
Parliament, nonparty	p	—	18	(18)
Nepal (November 1994)				
National Democratic Party	R	17.9	20	(4)
Nepali Congress Party	C	33.4	83	(110)
Communist parties	K	30.9	88	(82)
Others and independents	—	17.8	14	(9)
Netherlands, The (May 1994)				
Christian Democratic Appeal	CR	22.2	34	(54)
People's Party for Freedom and Democracy	CR	19.9	31	(22)
Democrats 66	CL	15.5	24	(12)
Labour Party	SD	24.0	37	(49)
Green Left	Lg	3.5	5	(6)
General Union of the Elderly	—	4.5	6	—
Others	—	10.4	13	(7)
New Zealand (October 1996)				
New Zealand First	CR	13.1	17	(2)
National Party	CR	34.1	44	(50)
United New Zealand	C	0.9	1	—
ACT New Zealand (libertarian)	—	6.2	8	—
Labour Party	CL	28.3	37	(45)
The Alliance (coalition)	L	10.1	13	(2)
Nicaragua (October 1996)				
National Opposition Union	—	—	—	(51)
Right-wing parties	R	7.6	9	(1)
Liberal Alliance coalition	R–C	46.0	42	—
Sandinist National Liberation Front	CL–EL	36.5	36	(39)
Others	—	9.9	6	(1)
Niger (November 1996–January 1997)				
Government party	—	...	59	—
Major opposition parties	—	—	† }	(83)
Others and independents	—	...	24 }	
Nigeria				
Military government since 1993	—	—	—	
Norway (September 1997)				
Progress Party (nationalist)	R	15.3	25	(10)
Conservative Party	R	14.3	23	(28)
Christian People's Party	CR	13.7	25	(13)
Centre Party	CR	7.9	11	(32)
Liberal Party	C	4.5	6	(1)
Labour Party	SD	35.0	65	(67)
Socialist Left	S	6.0	9	(13)
Others	—	3.3	1	(1)
Oman				
Consultative Council (advisory body)	—	—	—	
Pakistan (February 1997)				
Pakistan Muslim League (Nawaz)	—	...	134	(73)
Pakistan Muslim League (Junejo)	—	...	0	(6)
Pakistan People's Party	CL	...	18	(86)
Awami National Party	CL	...	9	(3)
Muhajir National Movement	e	...	12	(†)
Others and independents	—	...	31	(39)
Palau (November 1996)				
House of Delegates, nonparty	—	—	16	
Panama (May 1994)				
Democratic Revolutionary Party and allies	—	...	31	(12)
Others	—	...	41	(55)
Papua New Guinea (June 1997)				
People's Progress Party	Rp	...	16	(10)
People's Democratic Movement	Rp	...	10	(15)
United Party (Pangu Pati)	Cp	...	13	(22)
Others	p	...	30	(31)
Independents	—	...	40	(31)
Paraguay (May 1993)				
Colorado Party	R	43.0	38	(48)
Authentic Radical Liberal Party	CL	35.1	33	(19)
National Encounter coalition	—	17.1	9	—
Others	—	4.8	0	(5)
Peru (April 1995)				
Popular Christian Party	R	3.1	3	(8)
Popular Action	CR	3.3	4	—
Change 90-New Majority (coalition of independents)	p	52.1	67	(44)
Union for Peru	p	14.0	17	—
Independent Moralizing Front	p	4.9	6	(7)
American Popular Revolutionary Alliance	CL	6.5	8	—
Others	—	16.1	15	(21)
Philippines (May 1995)				
National People's Coalition	R	...	28	(48)
Centrist parties	C	...	13	(15)
People Power–National Union of Christian Democrats	p	...	126	(51)
Democratic Filipino Struggle	—	...	28	(87)
Others and independents	—	...	9	(0)
Poland (September 1997)				
Movement for the Reconstruction of Poland	R	5.6	6	—
Solidarity Electoral Alliance	R–CR	33.8	2.1	—
Other rightist parties/groups	R–CR	...	0	(38)
Freedom Union	C	13.4	60	(74)
Labour Union	L	4.4	0	(41)
Democratic Left Alliance	—	27.1	164	(171)
Polish Peasant Party	—	7.3	27	(132)
German minority	e	...	2	(4)
Portugal (October 1995)				
Popular Party	R	9.1	15	(5)
Social Democratic Party	CR	34.0	88	(135)
Portuguese Socialist Party	CL	43.9	112	(72)
Unified Democratic Coalition	L–K	8.6	15	(17)
Others	—	4.4	0	(1)
Qatar				
Consultative Council (advisory body)	—	—	—	
Romania (November 1996)				
Romanian National Unity Party	ERe	4.4	18	(30)
Greater Romania Party	ERe	4.5	19	(16)
Democratic Convention of Romania	CR	30.2	122	(82)
Social Democratic Union	SD	12.9	53	(43)
Social Democracy Party	x	21.5	91	(117)
Hungarian Democratic Union	e	6.6	25	(27)
Others	—	19.9	0	(13)
Russia (December 1995)				
Liberal Democratic Party	ERe	11.2	51	(64)
Power to the People (right–left nationalist)	e	1.8	9	—
Our Home Is Russia	CR	10.1	55	—
Russia's Democratic Choice	CR	3.9	9	(76)
Congress of Russian Communities	Ce	4.3	5	—
Forward Russia!	C	1.9	3	—
Yabloko (Bloc of Three)	CL	6.9	45	(28)
Women of Russia	CL	4.6	3	(24)
Communist Party	L	22.3	157	(45)
Agrarian Party	L	3.8	20	(55)
Workers' Russia	EL	4.5	1	(0)
Other parties	—	...	15	(137)
Independents	—	...	77	(21)
Rwanda				
Transitional government from July 1994	—	—	—	
Saint Kitts and Nevis (July 1995)				
People's Action Movement	CL	...	1	(4)
St. Kitts-Nevis Labour Party	L	...	7	(4)
Concerned Citizens' Movement	e	...	2	(2)
Nevis Reformation Party (pro-secessionist)	e	...	1	(1)
Saint Lucia (May 1997)				
United Workers' Party	C	36.6	1	(11)
St. Lucia Labour Party	CL	61.3	16	(6)
Saint Vincent and the Grenadines (February 1994)				
New Democratic Party	C	54.9	12	(15)
St. Vincent Labour Party	SD	26.5	2	(0)
Movement for National Unity	L	17.4	1	(0)
Samoa (April 1996)				
Human Rights Protection Party	—	43.5	24	(30)
National Development Party	—	26.1	11	(14)
Independents and other	—	30.4	14	(3)

World Legislative Election Results

Country Name of party	Affiliation	Voting strength (%)	Parliamentary representation	
San Marino (May 1993)				
Popular Democratic Alliance	C	7.7	4	—
Christian Democrats	CR	41.4	26	(27)
Socialist Party	S	23.7	14	(7)
Progressive Democratic Party	x	18.6	11	(18)
Other parties	—	8.6	5	(8)
São Tomé and Príncipe (October 1994)				
Party of Democratic Convergence	C	17	14	(33)
Movement for the Liberation of São Tomé and Príncipe	L	43	27	(21)
Independent Democratic Action	—	26	14	—
Others	—	4	0	(1)
Saudi Arabia				
Consultative Council (advisory body)	—	—	—	
Senegal (May 1993)				
Socialist Party	SD	56.6	84	(103)
Senegalese Democratic Party	—	30.2	27	(17)
Let Us Unite Senegal	EL	4.9	3	—
Other parties	—	8.3	6	—
Seychelles (July 1993)				
People's Progressive Front	L	57.5	28	(23)
Others	—	42.5	5	—
Sierra Leone				
Military regime from May 1997				
Singapore (January 1997)				
People's Action Party	p	65.0	81	(77)
Singapore People's Party	C	2.3	1	—
Singapore Democratic Party	CL	10.6	0	(3)
Workers' Party	L	14.2	1	(1)
Slovakia (September–October 1994)				
Slovak National Party	Re	5.4	9	(15)
Movement for a Democratic Slovakia	CR	35.0	61	(74)
Democratic Union	C	8.6	15	—
Christian Democratic Movement	CL	10.1	17	(18)
Common Choice coalition	CL–x	10.4	18	(29)
Hungarian minority coalition	e	10.2	17	(14)
Others	—	20.3	13	(0)
Slovenia (November 1996)				
Slovenian National Party	ER	3.2	4	(12)
Slovenian People's Party	R	19.4	19	(10)
Slovenian Christian Democrats	CR	9.6	10	(15)
Social Democratic Party	C–SD	16.1	16	(4)
Liberal Democracy of Slovenia	CL	27.0	25	—
Centre-left parties	CL	—	—	(33)
United List of Social Democrats	x	9.0	9 }	(14)
Pensioner's party	—	4.3	5 }	
Hungarian/Italian minorities	e	—	2	(2)
Solomon Islands (August 1997)				
Mamaloni supporters	p	...	24	(21)
Alliance for Change (coalition)	—	...	26	(17)
Others and independents	—	...	0	(9)
Somalia				
No government since 1991	—	—	—	
South Africa (April 1994)				
Freedom Front	ER	2.2	9	
National Party	CR	20.4	82	
Inkatha Freedom Party	e	10.5	43	
Democratic Party	C	1.7	7	
African National Congress	CL	62.7	252	
Pan-Africanist Congress	EL	1.2	5	
Others	—	1.3	2	
Spain (March 1996)				
Popular Party	CR	38.7	156	(141)
Basque Nationalist Party	Ce	1.3	5	(5)
Canarian Coalition	Ce	0.9	4	(4)
Convergence and Union (Catalan)	CLe	4.6	16	(17)
Spanish Socialist Workers' Party	SD	37.6	141	(159)
United Left	L–K	10.5	21	(18)
Galician Nationalist Bloc	Le	0.9	2	(0)
Herri Batasuna (Basque radicals)	ELe	0.7	2	(2)
Other regional parties	e	1.6	3	(4)
Sri Lanka (August 1994)				
United National Party	CR	44.0	94	(125)
People's Alliance	CL	48.9	105 }	(86)
Others and independents	—	3.6	14 }	
Sri Lanka Muslim Congress	r	1.8	7	(4)
Tamil United Liberation Front	e	1.7	5	(10)
Sudan, The (March 1996)				
Government supporters	—	...	264	
Principal opposition forces	—	—	†	
Suriname (May 1996)				
National Democratic Party	p	25.6	16	(12)
Democratic Alternative '91	SD	12.4	4 }	(9)
Pendawa Lima (Javan party)	e	10.0	4 }	
New Front coalition	CLe	41.4	24	(30)
Alliance	—	9.3	3	—
Swaziland (September–October 1993)				
House of Assembly, nonparty	—	—	55	
Sweden (September 1994)				
New Democracy	R	1.2	0	(24)
Christian Democrats	R	4.1	15	(27)
Moderate Coalition Party	CR	22.4	80	(80)
Centre Party	CR	7.7	27	(31)
Liberal People's Party	C	7.2	26	(33)
Social Democrats	S	45.3	161	(138)
Left Party	x	6.2	22	(16)
Greens	g	5.0	18	(0)
Switzerland (October 1995)				
Freedom Party	R	4.0	7	(8)
Swiss People's Party	R	14.9	29	(25)
Christian Democrats	CR	17.0	34	(36)
Liberal Party	CR	2.7	7	(10)
Radical Democrats	C	20.2	45	(44)
Social Democrats	SD	21.8	54	(42)
Green Party	g	5.0	9	(14)
Others	—	14.4	15	(21)
Syria (August 1994)				
Ba.th Party and allies	—	...	167	(166)
Independents	—	...	83	(84)
Taiwan (December 1995)				
New Party (pro-unification)	R	12.9	21	—
Nationalist (Kuomintang)	—	46.1	85	(96)
Democratic Progressive Party (pro-independence)	—	33.2	54	(50)
Others and independents	—	7.8	4	(15)
Tajikistan (February–March 1995)				
Communist Party	K	...	60	
Others and independents	—	...	119	
Western/Islamic parties			*	
Tanzania (October–November 1995)				
NCCR–Maguezi	C	...	16	—
Government party	S	...	186	(216)
Civic United Front (pro-Zanzibar autonomy)	e	...	24	—
Others	—	...	6	—
Thailand (November 1996)				
Thai Nation	R	...	39	(92)
Thai Citizens	Rp	...	18	(18)
National Development Party	Rp	...	52	(53)
Social Action Party	CR	...	20	(22)
New Aspiration Party	p	...	125	(57)
Democrat Party	C	...	123	(86)
Others	—	...	16	(63)
Togo (February 1994–August 1996)				
Rally of the Togolese People	p	...	40	
Allied party and independents	—	...	3	
Action Committee for Renewal	—	...	33	
Union for Democracy	—	...	5	
Tonga (January 1996)				
Noble representatives	—	—	9	(9)
People's Party (pro-democracy commoners)	—	...	6	(6)
Other commoners	—	...	3	(3)
Trinidad and Tobago (November 1995)				
People's National Movement	C	48.8	17	(21)
National Alliance for Reconstruction	C	4.8	2	(2)
United National Congress	SD	45.7	17	(13)
Tunisia (March 1994)				
Government party	CL	97.7	144	(141)
Opposition parties	—	2.3	19	(0)
Turkey (December 1995)				
Nationalist Action Party	ER	8.2	0 }	(62)
Welfare (Refah) Party	Rr	21.3	158 }	
True Path Party	CR	19.2	135	(178)
Motherland Party	CR	19.7	132	(115)
Democratic Left Party	CL	14.7	76	(7)
Republican People's Party	CL	10.7	49	—
Other leftist	CL–L	...	0	(88)
Turkmenistan (December 1994)				
Government (single) party	x	...	50	
Tuvalu (November 1993)				
Parliament, nonparty	—	—	12	
Uganda (June 1996)				
National Assembly, nonparty	—	—	276	
Ukraine (March 1994–February 1996)				
Extreme nationalist parties	ERe	...	5	
Less-extreme nationalist parties	CRe	...	15	
Ukrainian Popular Movement (Rukh)	Ce	...	21	
Centrist parties	C	...	17	
Communist Party and allies	K–EL	...	132	
Independents	—	...	230	
United Arab Emirates				
Federal National Council (advisory body)	—	—	—	
United Kingdom (May 1997)				
U.K. Unionist Party	ERe	0.04	1	(1)
Democratic Unionist Party	ERe	0.3	2	(3)
Ulster Unionist Party	Re	0.8	10	(9)
Conservative Party	R–CR	30.7	165	(336)
Liberal Democrats	C–CL	16.8	46	(20)
Social Democratic and Labour Party (Northern Ireland)	CLe	0.6	3	(4)
Labour Party	CL–L	43.2	418	(271)
Sinn Fein (Northern Ireland)	ELe	0.4	2	(0)
Scottish National Party	e	2.0	6	(3)
Plaid Cymru (Welsh nationalists)	e	0.5	4	(4)
Other	—	4.6	2	(0)
United States (November 1996)				
Republican	R–CR	...	227	(230)
Democratic	C–L	...	207	(204)
Other	L	...	1	(1)
Uruguay (November 1994)				
National (Blanco) Party	C	31.4	31	(39)
Colorado Party	C	32.5	32	(30)
New Space	CL	5.1	5	(9)
Progressive Encounter	L	30.8	31	—
Broad Front	L	—	—	(21)
Uzbekistan (December 1994–January 1995)				
People's Democratic Party and allies	x	100.0	250	
Opposition parties			*	
Vanuatu (November 1995)				
Union of Moderate Parties (Francophone)	—	...	17	(19)
National United Party	p	...	9	(10)
Unity Front coalition (Anglophone)	—	...	20	(16)
Others and independents	—	...	4	(1)
Venezuela (December 1993)				
COPEI (Social Christians)	CR–CL	22.8	54	(67)
Democratic Action	SD	23.9	55	(97)
National Convergence }	L	24.4	50	—
Movement to Socialism }				(18)
The Radical Cause	EL	21.1	40	(3)
Others	—	7.8	0	(16)
Vietnam (July 1997)				
Vietnamese Communist Party	K	...	384 }	(395)
Allies	—	...	63 }	
Independents	—	...	3	—
Yemen (April 1997)				
Yemeni Alliance for Reform	Rr	18.5	54	(62)
General People's Congress	p	57.4	187	(123)
Yemeni Socialist Party	L	—	†	(56)
Others and independents	—	24.1	60	(60)
Yugoslavia (November 1996)				
Serbian Radical Party	ERe	18.5	16	(34)
Zajedno (Together) (four-party coalition) }	CR–CLe	23.9	22	
Serbian Democratic Movement }	Ce			(20)
Democratic Party }	C			(5)
Socialist Party of Serbia and allies	xe	48.1	64	(47)
Democratic Party of Socialists of Montenegro	xe	...	20	(17)
People's Party (Montenegrin pro-Serbian)	e	...	8	(4)
Others	—	...	8	(11)
Zambia (November 1996)				
Movement for Multiparty Democracy	50	60.1	131	(125)
United National Independence Party	p	—	†	(25)
Others and independents	—	39.9	19	(0)
Zimbabwe (April 1995)				
Zimbabwe African National Union-Patriotic Front	—	82.3	118	(117)
Others and independents	—	17.7	2	(3)

*Banned. †Boycotted. ‡Approximate.

AFGHANISTAN

Area: 652,225 sq km (251,825 sq mi)
Population (1997 est.): 23,738,000 (including Afghan refugees estimated to number more than 1,500,000 in Pakistan and about 1,400,000 in Iran)
Capital: Kabul
Chief of state: President Burhanuddin Rabbani; de facto Taliban leader, Mohammad Rabbani
Head of government: until July, Prime Minister Gulbuddin Hekmatyar

Afghanistan in 1997 had two de facto governments. A Taliban government, recognized by Pakistan, Saudi Arabia, and the United Arab Emirates, ruled about two thirds of the country, mainly in the south, including the capital, Kabul. The Taliban acknowledged as its leader Mohammad Omar Akhund ("Akhund" indicates "mullah"), who was honoured with an ancient Islamic title, "commander of the faithful." Their government, however, had been put together in Kandahar under the direction of an interim council, headed by Mullah Mohammad Rabbani, who could thus be considered the head of the Taliban government.

An "opposition" government under Burhanuddin Rabbani continued to control large areas of the traditionally non-Pushtun north of the country. Rabbani's representative was allowed to occupy Afghanistan's UN seat, while the Organization of the Islamic Conference declared Afghanistan's seat vacant.

In May a dispute within the opposition Jumbish-i-Milli party forced Gen. 'Abd ar-Rashid Dostam out of his stronghold in Mazar-e Sharif in the north. Dostam, who had used his Uzbek militia to bring down the communist government in 1992, was himself overthrown when one of his own generals, 'Abd al-Malik Pahlawan, turned against him. Dostam was forced to flee to Turkey, and Pahlawan opened Mazar-e Sharif to Taliban forces. It seemed that the last major centre of resistance to Taliban rule had been taken, and Pakistan became the first country to recognize the legitimacy of the Taliban government. Within a few days, however, Pahlawan again changed sides, and the Taliban were driven out of Mazar-e Sharif in a bloody battle in which several thousand of them were taken captive.

In July, following an initiative by the UN special representative in Afghanistan, Norbert Holl, to build a broad-based government, a new anti-Taliban government with its capital in Mazar-e Sharif was announced. Gulbuddin Hekmatyar, who had been prime minister of the government driven from Kabul by the Taliban in September 1996, was not included. Burhanuddin Rabbani was retained in the office of president, and a Cabinet of technocrats was to be led by 'Abd ar-Rahim Ghafuzai (who died in a plane crash in September). More significantly, Ahmad Shah Masoud was renamed defense minister, and Pahlawan was to be foreign minister. In fact, this government was little more than a cover for the northern alliance's military effort to retake Kabul.

LUC DELAHAYE—MAGNUM

Troops under the command of Ahmad Shah Masoud combat Taliban forces near Kabul, Afg. Despite fierce fighting in Afghanistan throughout 1997, the political division of the country at year's end remained largely the same as it had been in 1996.

The reinvigorated northern alliance of Pahlawan's and Masoud's forces plus Hazara Shi'ite militias pushed the Taliban back to within a few kilometres of Kabul. When a second Taliban attack on Mazar-e Sharif in September was repulsed, Dostam returned and Pahlawan was forced to flee.

The situation at the end of the year was much as it had been in the beginning. Afghanistan was divided along ethnic lines—the Pashtun south and east unified under the Taliban and the Tajik, Uzbek, Turkmen, and Hazara areas in the north.

The Taliban (Persian for "students") had first appeared in Afghanistan in late 1994 as youthful fighters from religious schools in Pakistan. They pledged to replace with Islamic law the destructive factionalism that had marked Afghan political life since the fall of the communist regime in 1992. Popular support and military success followed their progress, especially in Pashtun areas of Afghanistan. Within two years Kabul had fallen to them with little armed resistance.

To the discomfort of the international aid agencies seeking to provide assistance, the severe Taliban interpretation of Islamic law called for public floggings and stoning to enforce rigid social restrictions, including a ban on many activities by women—*e.g.,* attending school, working, or appearing in public unaccompanied by a male relative.

Among Afghanistan's neighbours, Pakistan was sympathetic with the Taliban, if not indeed a supplier of material support and direction. Iran, at ideological odds with the Sunni Taliban, continued to align itself with the Shi'ite Hazara and Persian-speaking Tajiks of the opposition. The Muslim states of Central Asia were openly alarmed when the Taliban twice temporarily occupied Mazar-e Sharif. The local authorities in Dushanbe worried that refugees from Afghanistan might endanger Tajikistan's fragile political balance. (STEPHEN SEGO)

ALBANIA

Area: 28,748 sq km (11,100 sq mi)
Population (1997 est.): 3,293,000
Capital: Tiranë
Chief of state: Presidents Sali Berisha until July 23 and, from July 24, Rexhep Mejdani
Head of government: Prime Ministers Aleksander Meksi until March 2, Bashkim Fino from March 11, and, from July 24, Fatos Nano

The year 1997 would go into the books as one of the most tragic in Albanian history. In February the country suddenly plunged into chaos, and by March public order had broken down entirely. The drama was triggered by the collapse of pyramid investment schemes, which overnight rendered one out of three Albanians penniless. With astonishing speed the entire military establishment melted away, the security service dissolved, and the people broke into military depots and armed themselves with every type of weapon, including Kalashnikovs and even tanks—an estimated 650,000 weapons were seized. Most of the southern half of the country fell into the hands of ragtag rebels and criminal gangs. More than 10,000 persons fled to Italy, which in turn caused a governmental crisis in Rome. Calls came from all sides demanding the resignation of Pres. Sali Berisha. Albania became virtually without state rule, and several high government officials, including Defense Minister Safet Zhulali, fled abroad.

On March 2 the People's Assembly pro-

(continued on page 394)

Pyramid Schemes in Eastern Europe

For many citizens of postcommunist Eastern Europe in the 1990s, enhanced intellectual and political freedom paled in comparison with the opportunity to accumulate wealth. Exposure to Western European and North American consumer culture opened up a new world of possibilities to those who had languished under inefficient state-run economies. In their haste to embrace the benefits of the free market, however, some of the fledgling capitalists of Eastern Europe found themselves vulnerable to one of the oldest con games in the book: the pyramid scheme.

While the structure of individual pyramid schemes varies, the basic premise is that a person gives those managing the scheme a set sum of money and is promised a huge financial return on the "investment." The managers never actually invest the money. Instead, the person is repaid from the money received from the next people to get involved in the scheme, and they in turn are repaid from the funds invested by those who follow them. For such a plan to work, there must be a continuous flow of capital from new investors, for once the cash flow has stopped, no more money can be paid out.

The promise of incredible returns on a relatively small amount of money can prove to be a strong lure for unsophisticated investors. Nowhere was this more evident in 1997 than in Albania, which had emerged from

communism as the poorest nation in Europe. Foreign aid and economic-reform programs had seemingly started the country on the road to a market economy, but Albania's lack of strong financial institutions provided an ideal environment for pyramid schemes to flourish. By 1996 individual investors—often the people least able to afford it—had invested more than $1 billion in such plans.

By 1997 the inflow of money had decreased, the pyramid schemes were collapsing, and Albanians who had invested their life savings found themselves destitute. In desperation they turned their anger on the government, blaming the administration of Pres. Sali Berisha for failing to impose regulatory controls. The nation faced anarchy as armed mobs took to the streets, and there was fear that the violence in Albania could spread beyond its borders. Berisha froze the assets of the schemes and ordered the resignation of Prime Minister Aleksander Meksi. The damage had been done, however, as the government could not order financial compensation without spurring hyperinflation. The deployment of an Italian-led peacekeeping force in April stabilized the political situation to a degree but could do little to repair the economic devastation.

These photographs capture scenes in the Albanian seaport of Durrës. They were taken by James Nachtwey, whose work has appeared in many international publications.

PHOTOGRAPHS, JAMES NACHTWEY—MAGNUM

Following the collapse of pyramid schemes that cost many their entire life savings, Albanians storm the gates of the port at Durrës in a mad scramble to board ships bound for Italy.

A masked gunman, recruited by the government to help quell disorder, mans an improvised checkpoint.

Panic sets in for one of the countless families in Albania devastated by the crisis.

Hoping to board a ship and flee the country, a man and child face an uncertain future.

With only survival as their goal, desperate residents look for any means of escaping Albania's chaotic conditions.

(continued from page 389)
claimed a state of emergency. Prime Minister Aleksander Meksi and his Democratic Party of Albania (PDS) Cabinet resigned and were replaced by a national reconciliation government headed by Bashkim Fino. New national elections were set for June 29. In late March the UN Security Council approved dispatching a multinational military force to Albania to oversee the distribution of international humanitarian aid and maintain order. Some 7,000 troops from eight European countries under Italian leadership participated in "Operation Alba."

The Socialist Party of Albania (PSS; the former Communist Party) and its allies won a landslide victory in the relatively peaceful June elections. Berisha resigned, and former physics professor Rexhep Mejdani, secretary of the PSS, was elected president in July. A new 20-member multiparty Cabinet (excluding the PDS) was formed, with Fatos Nano, a PSS leader, as prime minister.

The Albanian economy also suffered grievously. Unemployment soared over the 25% mark, and inflation had risen 28% by July. Gross domestic product, which had registered 8–11% increases in the previous few years, dropped by 7%. The currency was devalued from 108 to more than 150 leks to the dollar. (LOUIS ZANGA)

This article updates the *Macropædia* article BALKAN STATES: *Albania.*

ALGERIA

Area: 2,381,741 sq km (919,595 sq mi)
Population (1997 est.): 29,476,000
Capital: Algiers
Chief of state: President Liamine Zeroual
Head of government: Prime Minister Ahmed Ouyahia

The situation in Algeria throughout 1997 was highly complex. On the one hand, the government moved ahead with its constitutional reform process, holding legislative elections in June and municipal elections at the end of the year. On the other hand, violence reached new levels of horror, with repeated massacres occurring in the hinterland of Algiers that the security services appeared to be unable to control. At the same time, the economy improved, with an enlarged trade surplus and the promise of significant foreign investment in the non-oil sector for the first time since 1990.

The year opened (and closed) with intensified outrages during the fast month of Ramadan, giving the lie to Prime Minister Ahmed Ouyahia's claim that only "residual terrorism" remained to threaten the nation. Early in the year, preparations for the legislative elections began, with the formation in March of a new political party closely aligned with Pres. Liamine Zeroual, the National Democratic Rally (RND), and with other parties adjusting to the new electoral law that banned religion and ethnicity from their platforms. In January the expected leader of the RND, 'Abd al-Haq Benhamouda, was assassinated, apparently by an opposition faction in the regime.

The elections, on June 5, resulted in the expected victory for the RND, which gained 37% of the vote and 41% of the seats (156) and thus, together with the pro-government National Liberation Front's (FLN's) 62 seats, enjoyed a majority in the 380-member lower house of the legislature (the upper house, which controls the legislative process, is indirectly elected). Two Islamist parties, Society for Peace (MSP, formerly Hamas) and an-Nahda, won 96 seats, and the veteran Socialist Forces Front, largely because of electoral manipulation, obtained only 20 seats.The new government, appointed in July, reflected the electoral results, with the RND taking 20 of the 28 ministerial posts and the remainder being split between the FLN (4), MSP (3), and an-Nahda (1). In essence, the government team did not change. Charging widespread fraud, the opposition vehemently protested the conduct of the local elections in October.

Despite claims by the government that it had mastered the security situation, the tempo of horrifying massacres in central Algeria increased throughout the year, culminating in hours-long incidents on the outskirts of the capital and with a reprise in the last days of 1997. The perpetrators—ostensibly the Armed Islamic Group—appeared to reflect the increasingly complex political situation, with the security forces, paramilitary units, and even government representatives also being accused of involvement. The massacres seemed to result from an intensifying struggle within the regime between the presidency and the army leadership over the ultimate control of Algeria's fate. Further disagreements were caused by a decision in July to release from prison two Islamic Salvation Front leaders, Abbasi Madani and 'Abd al-Kader Hachani, and a truce negotiated between the government and the Army of Islamic Salvation—the other major Islamist armed group—for October.

Despite the turbulent political situation, economic circumstances appeared to improve, with the half-year trade surplus rising to $3,140,000,000, compared with $1,640,000,000 a year earlier, a result of rising oil and gas prices. Gas exports were expected to increase to 60 billion cu m per year by 2000 as a result of the new trans-Maghreb pipeline, which began operations in November 1996. (GEORGE JOFFÉ)

This article updates the *Macropædia* article NORTH AFRICA: *Algeria.*

ANDORRA

Area: 468 sq km (181 sq mi)
Population (1997 est.): 64,600
Capital: Andorra la Vella
Chiefs of state: Co-princes of Andorra, the president of France and the bishop of Urgell, Spain
Head of government: Prime Minister Marc Forné Molné

Led by Prime Minister Marc Forné Molné, the ruling Liberal Union (UL) party swept the parliamentary elections held Feb. 16, 1997. The UL, calling for greater deregulation of the economy and willingness to allow foreign investment, won 18 of the 28 seats in the General Council of the Valleys and would for the first time rule outright without the necessity of forming coalitions with smaller parties. The liberal National Democratic Grouping captured six seats, while the New Democracy and the National Democratic Initiative parties each won two seats.

Officials expressed concern over the economy, as the number of visitors has dropped in recent years. Some shops closed, and import tax revenue fell. Import tariffs provided three-fourths of the country's revenues, which made possible its lack of income and corporation taxes. There were still some bargains to be found in Andorra—for example, alcohol, tobacco, perfume, and gasoline, all of which were heavily taxed in neighbouring France and Spain. Visitors looking for duty-free luxury goods could find bargains, as shopkeepers were able to maintain low profit margins because of their large sales volume. (ANNE ROBY)

This article updates the *Micropædia* article ANDORRA.

ANGOLA

Area: 1,246,700 sq km (481,354 sq mi)
Population (1997 est.): 10,624,000
Capital: Luanda
Chief of State: President José Eduardo dos Santos
Head of government: Prime Minister Fernando José França van-Dúnem

In spite of their nation's being the largest producer of oil in southern Africa, with the prospect of an ever-larger output, and in spite also of the enthusiastic involvement of international mining companies in the country's lucrative diamond-mining industry, the vast majority of the people of Angola had little to rejoice about in 1997. Continuing fears of a breakdown in the peace process restrained recovery from some 20 years of civil war, while the presence of an estimated 10 million–15 million concealed land mines, a relic of that same struggle and a topic much discussed worldwide during the year, not only caused thousands of casualties but also discouraged farmers from producing the food the country so badly needed.

Faced with the continuing mistrust between the government and the opposition National Union for the Total Independence of Angola (UNITA), the UN repeatedly felt constrained to revise its plan for the withdrawal of its peacekeeping force. In January the planned inauguration of a government of national unity was abandoned because Jonas Savimbi, the UNITA leader, refused to leave his headquarters at Bailundo in the central highlands, believing his life would be in danger if he visited Luanda. Moreover, after having been encouraged in his campaign against the government and supplied with arms for years by the U.S. and South Africa, he was reluctant to modify his own political aspirations to bring them into line with the less-sympathetic policies of a new South

JOHN VINK—MAGNUM

Schoolchildren attend a class in a bombed-out building in Kuito, Angola. Though a UN peacekeeping force maintained stability in Angola in 1997, many feared that the country's fragile peace process might be headed for a crisis as government officials and opposition leaders traded threats and accusations.

African government and of the U.S. More specifically, he balked at surrendering control of the roughly 80% of Angola's diamond trade that remained in UNITA's hands, arguing that since the government controlled the entire oil industry, it was unrealistic to expect him to be satisfied with the reduced proportion of the diamond trade that the government was offering to UNITA.

In March the UN Security Council threatened economic sanctions against UNITA if the movement refused to join a government of national unity immediately. This seemed to spur Savimbi into action, and he said his followers would cooperate. When representatives of the ruling Popular Liberation Movement of Angola and UNITA met in Luanda on April 11 for the swearing-in ceremony, however, Savimbi himself did not attend. Likewise, UNITA had not implemented a number of clauses in the Lusaka peace accord of 1994. Nevertheless, UNITA representatives were appointed to a number of ministries, while Savimbi himself was granted a special role as leader of the opposition, with a generous salary and the right to question Pres. José Eduardo dos Santos on political issues.

In a vain attempt to bolster its military position, UNITA sent reinforcements to Zaire (now Democratic Republic of the Congo) to assist the movement's one remaining significant foreign ally, Pres. Mobutu Sese Seko, in his efforts to turn back the advancing rebel forces led by Laurent Kabila. The government, however, sent troops to support Kabila, and the joint intervention in the Zairean war on opposing sides posed a serious threat to the peace process.

The overthrow of Mobutu weakened UNITA's bargaining power, and in May the government felt confident enough to press harder for a settlement of its diamond-mining allocation offer by launching a military offensive against UNITA-held diamond-rich territory in the northeastern province of Lunda Norte. After initial setbacks UNITA forces reacted vigorously, which caused UN officials to express serious doubts about the credibility of reports that UNITA was disbanding troops to meet the terms of the Lusaka peace accord. Eventually, the UN Security Council gave the go-ahead for air and travel sanctions to be imposed on UNITA from October 30 in response to the rebels' failure to promote the peace process.

Also in October, Angolan troops played a vital role in the restoration of Gen. Denis Sassou-Nguesso as president of the Republic of the Congo while at the same time destroying UNITA bases in the republic.

(KENNETH INGHAM)

This article updates the *Macropædia* article SOUTHERN AFRICA: *Angola.*

ANTIGUA AND BARBUDA

Area: 442 sq km (171 sq mi)
Population (1997 est.): 64,500 (excluding evacuees from Montserrat)
Capital: Saint John's
Chief of state: Queen Elizabeth II, represented by Governor-General James Carlisle
Head of government: Prime Minister Lester Bird

The offshore banking sector created major problems for Antigua and Barbuda in 1997, the government having to announce in February that it intended to close four out of five such banks owned by Russians and Ukrainians on the grounds of "irregularities" in their operations. There was some uncertainty, however, over whether existing law permitted such action.

In August the so-called European Union Bank, which claimed to be the first offshore Internet bank, went into receivership following the disappearance of its two Russian founders. A "fraud alert" was issued for the two. U.S. officials had in 1996 identified

Russian criminal elements as being active in money laundering through Caribbean offshore banking locations. Antigua and Barbuda had almost 60 registered offshore banks, but the government decided in 1997 not to issue any new licenses for the time being.

Control of local government in Barbuda passed to the Barbuda People's Movement in March when the party captured all five seats under the country's partial election system, which takes place at two-year intervals. The party already controlled the other four seats on the Barbuda Council.

(DAVID RENWICK)

This article updates the *Macropædia* article The WEST INDIES: *Antigua and Barbuda.*

ARGENTINA

Area: 2,780,092 sq km (1,073,400 sq mi)
Population (1997 est): 35,409,000
Capital: Buenos Aires
Head of state and government: President Carlos Saúl Menem, assisted by Ministerial Coordinator Jorge Rodríguez

Pres. Carlos Menem experienced a year of mixed fortunes in 1997. His popularity, which had reached a low point in late 1996 following a series of corruption allegations against members of his government launched by former economy minister Domingo Cavallo, underwent a modest revival after a successful visit to the U.S. in December 1996. Menem's discussions with U.S. Pres. Bill Clinton partly secured special status for Argentina as a non-NATO ally. This was confirmed by U.S. Secretary of State Madeleine Albright in August 1997. Early in the year it became apparent that the economic recovery was strengthening significantly after a strong final quarter of 1996, and this increased the prospect that the economy would grow more than the 5% officially projected for the year.

Local political developments were less encouraging. Talks between the opposition Radical Civic Union and the Frepaso grouping over possible joint electoral tactics for the midterm congressional polls (to elect half the Chamber of Deputies) began in late 1996 and continued into 1997. At the beginning of August, the two parties announced that they would form an electoral alliance (the so-called Alliance for Work, Justice, and Education) for both the congressional polls in October 1997 and the presidential elections in 1999.

Menem also encountered difficulties with the judiciary following court rulings early in the year that his efforts to push through further labour reforms by decree were unconstitutional. A pact in May between the government and the nation's major labour federation also failed to advance the reforms.

Differences between Menem and his likely successor for the Justicialist National Movement (Peronist) presidential nomination in 1999, Buenos Aires Gov. Eduardo Duhalde, intensified in the wake of the murder of journalist José Luis Cabezas in January and flared up over other issues on repeated occasions during the year. In mid-February another bone of contention was the introduction of a bill by a close associate of Menem concerning the use of national referenda to decide on constitutional reforms; this was viewed as a possible attempt to embark on making changes that would allow Menem to run for a third term as president in 1999.

After months of speculation about possible Cabinet dismissals in the wake of repeated allegations that several members had had illicit dealings with business magnate (and alleged planner of organized crime activities within the government) Alfredo Yabrán, Justice Minister Elías Jassán resigned on June 26. He was replaced by Raúl Granillo Ocampo, who had been serving as ambassador to the U.S. In late September there were signs that Menem was considering replacing the Chief of Cabinet Jorge Rodríguez, whose efforts to fulfill that role apparently had failed to meet the president's expectations, but Rodríguez was still in office at year's end.

In the October 26 elections the opposition Alliance (Alianza), took 46% of the vote while the ruling Peronists (PJ) won only 36%. It lost its slim majority and took 52 of the 127 seats up for renewal; the Alliance received 61 seats, with the remainder divided among smaller parties. In the state of Buenos Aires, the victory of the Alliance's Graciela Fernández Meijide over Hilda Duhalde (wife of the PJ provincial governor, Eduardo Duhalde) by a wide margin (54% to 38%) reduced the likelihood that the governor would secure his party's nomination to run for the presidency in 1999.

Concerning the economy, the publication of first-quarter gross domestic product (GDP) figures in June showed that expansion was strong, with an increase of 8.1% compared with the same period of 1996, when there was a decline of 3.2%. The performance continued during the second quarter, with GDP growth provisionally put at 7.8%, giving an average of 8% for the first half of the year; Economy Minister Roque Fernández predicted growth of at least 7% for the whole year.

Despite robust growth and continuing low inflation (0.8% for the year to the end of August), unemployment continued at a high level and in May stood at 16.1% (down from 17.3% in October 1996). Menem pledged to reduce this to 6–8% by the end of his term in 1999, but the creation of new jobs did not appear to be rapid enough by the final quarter of 1997 to help the Peronists avert a significant defeat by the opposition alliance in the October elections.

During the first three quarters of 1997, the country's trade account registered a sharp deficit of some $2,980,000,000, compared with a surplus of $491,000,000 in the same period of 1996. For the year as a whole, the Economy Ministry was predicting a deficit of $4.1 billion (revised up from $2 billion at the start of the year), increasing the current-account deficit to more than $8 billion.

At the annual meetings of the International Monetary Fund and the World Bank in late September, it was indicated that Argentina (which had met its first-half fiscal deficit target agreed upon with the IMF) would sign an agreement for a $1 billion loan from the Fund by the end of the year.

(SUSAN M. CUNNINGHAM)

ARMENIA

Area: 29,743 sq km (11,484 sq mi). The disputed Nagorno-Karabakh region, with an area of 4,400 sq km (1,700 sq mi), and has been part of Azerbaijan since 1923.
Population (1997 est.): officially 3,773,000; actually about 3,000,000 (plus 150,000 in Nagorno-Karabakh)
Capital: Yerevan
Chief of state: President Levon Ter-Petrosyan
Head of government: Prime Ministers Armen Sarkisyan and, from March 20, Robert Kocharyan

The unresolved Karabakh conflict continued to have an impact on both domestic politics and foreign policy in Armenia in 1997. In March Pres. Levon Ter-Petrosyan appointed as prime minister Robert Kocharyan, president of the unrecognized Nagorno-Karabakh republic, who embarked on a crackdown on corruption and tax evasion. Powerful Yerevan Mayor Vano Siradegyan was elected chairman of the ruling Pan-Armenian National Movement in July. Although Kocharyan and other senior officials met with representatives of the banned main opposition Dashnak (Armenian Revolutionary Federation) party in April to discuss conditions for its reinstatement, the trial of 31 Dashnak members on charges of terrorism continued. Ter-Petrosyan's announcement in September that Armenia had accepted a peace plan for Nagorno-Karabakh that required major unnamed compromises from Armenia provoked calls by the opposition for his resignation and new parliamentary elections.

In May several tiny left-wing political groups began lobbying for Armenia's accession to the Russia-Belarus union, collecting over a million signatures in favour. Ter-Petrosyan and Russian Pres. Boris Yeltsin signed a major treaty on friendship, cooperation, and mutual assistance in August. A second agreement on supplying Russian gas to Armenia and its export via Armenia to Turkey was also signed.

(ELIZABETH FULLER)

This article updates the *Macropædia* article TRANSCAUCASIA: *Armenia.*

AUSTRALIA

Area: 7,682,300 sq km (2,966,200 sq mi)
Population (1997 est.): 18,508,000
Capital: Canberra
Chief of state: Queen Elizabeth II, represented by Governor-General Sir William Deane
Head of government: Prime Minister John Howard

Domestic Affairs. Despite a reputation for weak leadership, Prime Minister John

(continued on page 398)

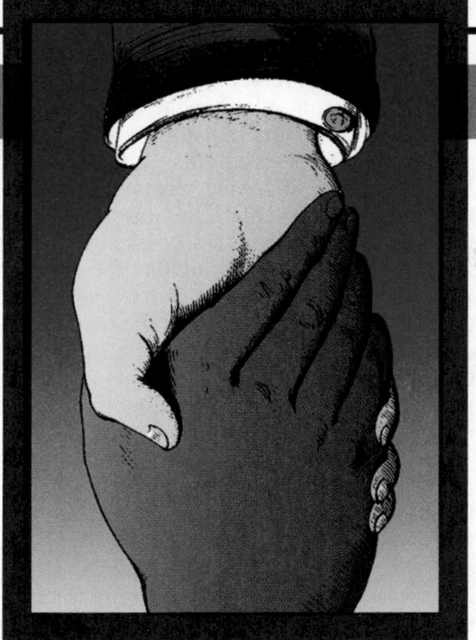

SPOTLIGHT

RACIAL INTEGRATION IN AUSTRALIA AND NEW ZEALAND

by A.R.G. Griffiths

Illustration by Cathy Hull

By 1997 public opinion in Australia and New Zealand was demanding that a solution be found to the great gap in the standards of living between the indigenous people of each nation and those who arrived later. The governments of Australia and New Zealand and the Aboriginal and Maori people all agreed that as the new millennium approached, reconciliation was vital. For two centuries a variety of programs had been tried, including assimilation, benevolent neglect, integration, and a small amount of self-determination, but they all failed. Driving the reconciliation process were decisions by the High Court in Australia to allow Aboriginals to claim the titles of their traditional lands.

Until 1992 Australia had been regarded by an 18th-century legal concept as an empty continent where the indigenous inhabitants had no rights to ownership. But a High Court ruling overturned two centuries of legal practice by deciding that Eddie Mabo and other residents of the Murray Islands in the Torres Strait, who brought a case against the commonwealth, owned customary title to their land. This sensational and unexpected judgment, known as the Mabo decision, established that Aboriginals had the right to claim title to traditional lands. When Prime Minister Paul Keating's Australian Labor Party passed the act of Parliament in 1993 and turned the High Court ruling into law, however, the government excluded pastoral leases (very large tracts of land leased to farmers and ranchers) from native claims. The legislation led to a crisis of confidence in the mining and resource industries. Uncertain about the ownership of land, investors were inhibited in their prospecting and exploitation of minerals, oil, and gas. The Queensland premier, Rob Borbidge, called for an emergency premiers' conference; the National Farmers Federation asked for action to overrule the decision; and many Australians believed that every backyard in Australia was under threat from an Aboriginal land claim.

Keating's Labor government fell in 1996, and the new conservative administration under Prime Minister John Howard set out to rewrite the statute book as far as Aboriginal land rights were concerned. Howard moved quickly as soon as the High Court had ruled on a second watershed case brought by the Wik people. The High Court ruled on Dec. 23, 1996, that pastoral leases and native title could coexist. Howard was aghast to find that potentially 78% of Australia's land was claimable by Aboriginals under the Wik judgment. The National Party (the junior partner in the government) led the chorus of outrage against the High Court judgment. Howard made several visits to outback Australia, where pastoralists held title to properties as large as small European nations, and after a divisive and abusive period of negotiation devised a 10-point plan. The Howard government eliminated many of the Keating reforms. Claims dealing with water and offshore resources were to be wiped out, as were claims in which government infrastructure was involved. Aboriginals would be able to enter land to hold ceremonies, visit sacred sites, obtain water, and gather food, but they would not be permitted to interfere with crops, livestock, pastures, or fences.

The complex new legislation, 400 pages long, contained, according to the jubilant deputy prime minister, Tim Fischer, "bucket loads of extinguishment." Native title was to be abolished on pastoral leases when it would interfere with the rights of the pastoralist. The Aboriginals in return ominously promised payback in the form of "bucket loads of litigation," which, they threatened, would ultimately cost taxpayers millions of dollars.

Whereas the debate in Australia centred on the Mabo and Wik cases, in New Zealand the largest and oldest land claim in the nation's history neared settlement. The New Zealand government and the Ngai Tahu, a South Island Maori tribe, agreed to bury the hatchet in a dispute that had begun with the Treaty of Waitangi in 1840. Although it might have appeared to them that they were slightly better off under the Treaty of Waitangi than under the legal concept by which the Australian Aboriginals were dispossessed, the Maori still considered that they had been forced to sell 14 million ha (34.5 million ac) for the pitiful sum of £14,750. In September 1997 the New Zealand Parliament agreed with their long-standing complaints and made a compensation settlement of $NZ 170 million. This paled into insignificance compared with the Maori claim that their economic losses from the government land purchases were over $NZ 20 billion. The New Zealand government expressed profound regret and apologized unreservedly for the past suffering and grave injustices that had significantly impaired the Ngai Tahu economic, social, and cultural development.

Some influential Australians tried to learn from Maori experiences the best ways to achieve reconciliation, and at a community level the clouds over New Zealand and Australia contained fewer thunderstorms than had been predicted by such controversial political figures as Winston Peters and Pauline Hanson. (*See* BIOGRAPHIES.) For every Peters and Hanson, however, there were many in each country who were striving to achieve close racial harmony.

Nevertheless, whereas New Zealand took every opportunity to apologize, Australia flew in the face of public opinion. At a special staged reconciliation meeting with Aboriginals in Melbourne, Howard said only that he was sorry for the hurt and trauma many continued to experience as a consequence of past practices and that he himself felt a deep sorrow for those of his fellow Australians who suffered injustice under the practices of past generations toward indigenous people. Howard insisted, however, that "in facing the realities of the past we must not join those who would portray Australia's history since 1788 as little more than a disgraceful record of imperialism, exploitation, and racism."

A.R.G. Griffiths is Associate Professor in History at Flinders University of South Australia and author of Contemporary Australia.

(continued from page 396)
Howard, the leader of the centre-right Liberal Party, made great and potentially lasting changes to the fabric of Australian society in 1997. In his first term in office, the prime minister introduced legislation to modify the High Court's ruling on Aboriginal land rights, changed the direction of the tariff-versus-protection debate, undertook a massive overhaul of the taxation system, and set up a constitutional convention as a first step toward creating an Australian republic. He was, however, unable to resolve a difficult challenge to his authority from a new force on the scene, Queensland member of Parliament Pauline Hanson. (*See* BIOGRAPHIES.) Within months of her first election in 1996 to the House of Representatives for the Queensland seat of Oxley, Hanson founded a new political party, the One Nation Party. Its policies included an end to immigration, an end to measures that favoured Aborigines, and tariff protection for Australian industry.

Hanson's party quickly took centre stage with the Australian media, and her comments were widely reported overseas. After public opinion polls in April predicted that the One Nation Party would win Senate seats in Queensland and New South Wales in the event that both houses of Parliament were dissolved, the Queensland premier, Bob Borbidge, urged Howard to heed the alarm bells. Borbidge pointed out that Hanson's impact could not be swept under the carpet and that defections to the One Nation Party had come from those conservatives who had elected Howard to stand up for them against the Australian Labor Party's pro-Aboriginal and pro-multicultural policies. At that point Howard moved quickly. The government decided to set an immigration quota of 68,000 for 1997–98, a reduction of 20% over a two-year period.

The Economy. During the year the nation's treasurer, Peter Costello, was frequently at odds with the prime minister on the major economic difficulties facing the government: unemployment, taxation reform, and tariff reduction. Costello focused on reducing the nation's deficit, while Howard concentrated on trying to reduce the effect of unemployment on families. On May 13 Costello declared that eliminating the deficit was central to his economic program. "Our country has been on a losing strategy, a path of deficit and debt," said the treasurer, and his response was to slash spending by $A 1.7 billion.

The main feature of the 1997 budget was a program of savings incentives. A 15% tax rebate of up to $A 450 on personal super-contributions or net income from savings and investments was offered. Cash payments were to be given to workers who delayed their retirement by five years. A "Federation Fund" of $A 1 billion was set up to initiate national infrastructure projects to mark in 2001 the centenary of the establishment of the Commonwealth of Australia. Chief among these was the proposal to complete the Adelaide-to-Darwin railway, with the Commonwealth providing $A 100 million toward the line and the South Australian and Northern Territory governments adding $A 100 million each.

The differences of emphasis between Howard and Costello continued through the year. Despite five cuts in interest rates in 12 months, consumer confidence remained low. Unemployment remained Australia's most significant economic headache throughout 1997. By June the Australian Bureau of Statistics had assessed the jobless rate at 8.8%, with 809,800 Australians out of work. Howard declared that solving unemployment was "my strongest commitment and my top priority." Admitting that the decision was "significantly influenced by jobs," the Howard government rejected the recommendation of the productivity commission that car tariffs be slashed to 5% by 2004. Instead, the Cabinet bowed to public opinion and decided to freeze tariff cuts.

In a decision welcomed by the nation's automobile industry, the state premiers, and the labour unions, Howard announced that tariffs would be cut from 22.5% to 15% by the year 2000 and kept at that level until 2005, when legislation would reduce tariffs to 10%. Mitsubishi, Ford, and Holden-General Motors all applauded the decision. Following the success of their fellow workers in the automobile industry, members of the textile, clothing, and footwear (TCF) unions harried local MPs about potential job losses in their factories. The TCF unions predicted a loss of 50,000 jobs, mainly those of migrant women, if their campaign to stop tariff reduction failed.

In September the Howard Cabinet again bowed to public opinion. In the face of opposition from farmers, miners, and the productivity commission itself, the prime minister posed for television cameras in Bond's clothing factory as he announced his decision to maintain tariff protection. Howard declared a five-year freeze on tariff reduction, protecting Australia's TCF industries until the year 2000. Recognizing the political importance of saving jobs, Howard said that he had made a "very good decision for the battlers of Australia."

Primary producers were the group most unimpressed, with sugar growers leading the complaints. Their chairman, Harry Bonnano, said that sugar growers had no tariff protection. He warned the coalition that it faced an electoral backlash if it continued to treat the agricultural sector with contempt. Queensland Premier Borbidge also attacked Howard for inconsistency, saying that what was good for the goose was good for the gander: "You can't have one rule for Victoria and another rule for Queensland."

On August 5 a judgment by the High Court ruled invalid about $A 5 billion in tobacco, alcohol, and gasoline taxes collected by the states and territories. The court ruled that only the federal government had the power to levy such taxes. In the wake of the mass confusion caused by the ruling, the federal government agreed to collect tobacco, alcohol, and gasoline taxes on behalf of the states.

Then, in his boldest and most risky act as prime minister, saying that he had been spurred on by the High Court ruling on state taxes, Howard decided to open up the whole question of the inefficiency of the Australian taxation system itself. While sticking to his core promise not to increase taxes in his first term as prime minister, Howard announced that he was prepared to take the dangerous path and make taxation reform an issue in the next election. He maintained that anybody who had the national economic interest at heart knew that Australia could not go into the 21st century with the existing tax system. Howard pledged to consider the introduction of a broad-based indirect tax, including the introduction of a goods and services tax, to replace some existing indirect taxes.

Foreign Affairs. Australia moved a step closer toward becoming a republic in 1997 when the government appointed the first delegates to attend a convention on Feb. 2–13, 1998, to decide whether Australia was to remain a constitutional monarchy. From a list drawn up from nominations submitted by republicans, monarchists, the federal Australian Labor Party, the Democrats, the state governments, and federal ministers, Howard, who supported the status quo, chose 76 government appointees, largely in the constitutional monarchist camp. Of the 76 appointed delegates, 40 were MPs—20 from the commonwealth and 20 from the states. The other convention delegates were to be elected by popular vote. Republicans and monarchists had less than four weeks to select candidates before nominations closed on October 8.

On December 23 it was announced that 45 Republicans, 27 monarchists, and 4 independent or undecided nominees had been elected. The constitutional convention's mandate was to determine whether the constitution should be amended to create a republic, which model would be best, and what the timetable for change would be.

In an unexpected turn of events, support for the monarchy dropped to below 50% in the wake of the death of Diana, princess of Wales, an event that left the nation in mourning. The Australian Broadcasting Commission calculated that six million Australians watched the funeral of Diana on television. A later poll conducted by the *Australian* revealed that 34% of Australians supported a republic; this marked the first significant shift in opinion in three years.

While relations with Britain were altered by the new phase in the republican debate, Foreign Minister Alexander Downer released a White Paper on foreign policy in August. This gave a completely new assessment of the government's foreign-policy objectives. Downer moved Australia's foreign relations toward a closer relationship with Asia, with a top priority being given to trade and Australia's economic development. Called *In the National Interest,* the 84-page document reaffirmed Australia's commitment to the Asian Pacific region. The White Paper identified the four most important bilateral relationships as those with the United States, Indonesia, Japan, and China. The central point Downer stressed was that the national interest was at the heart of the matter (so far as foreign policy was concerned) and that such international issues as global warming and human rights had to be made subordinate to trade questions.

In an editorial, the *Advertiser* observed that to say an Australian government must put Australia first was not a lot more substantial than remarking that sin was bad, but that, nevertheless, almost for the first time Australian foreign-policy conclusions would be read with approval "by decision makers in the capitals of greatest importance to us." The White Paper followed Australia's decision to put its money where its mouth was by helping to bail out the Thai economy with a $A 1.3 billion loan as part of an International Monetary Fund operation. Australia's practical assistance to help achieve regional stability by helping Thailand was recognized in Southeast Asia as being more important than any other event in establishing closer relations between Australia and their countries.

Although Australia's foreign-policy makers made great strides forward in the country's relationship with China and Southeast Asia, Australia's foreign relations with its closest and smaller neighbours in the South Pacific were damaged when a confidential and often inaccurate report on the personal characteristics of many leaders of the South Pacific nations was carelessly left on a table in a hotel in Cairns, Queen. The Australian government declined to make a formal apology, saying that the document did not represent official government policy. At the meeting of the South Pacific Forum, however, the offending Cairns papers were added to the list of attacks on Australian policy on global warming, the sea transport of nuclear waste, and the protection of local industry. (A.R.G. GRIFFITHS)

See also *Dependent States.*

AUSTRIA

Area: 83,859 sq km (32,378 sq mi)
Population (1997 est.): 8,087,000
Capital: Vienna
Chief of state: President Thomas Klestil
Head of government: Chancellors Franz Vranitzky and, from January 28, Viktor Klima

The beginning of 1997 was marked in Austria by a change in government leadership. Chancellor Franz Vranitzky, who had taken office in June 1986, resigned on January 19, saying that 10 years were "a sufficient spell" for the job and that he wanted to make way for a younger generation.

Vranitzky designated as his successor Finance Minister Viktor Klima, who was sworn in as chancellor on January 28. Klima, who was well known for having successfully brokered a difficult 1996–97 budget, quickly appointed a new Cabinet and in his formal declaration of government policy called maintaining a high level of employment in Austria "the central question for the future."

Despite the smooth transition of power, Vranitzky's resignation came at an uncertain time for the country's ruling two-party coalition, made up of the Social-Democratic Party of Austria (SPÖ) and the right-of-centre Austrian People's Party (ÖVP). Local elections showed declining support for the ÖVP and the growing popularity of the extreme nationalist party, the Freedom Party of Austria (FPÖ), led by the outspoken Jörg Haider. The FPÖ was renowned for its controversial anti-immigrant stance and its severe criticism of the European Union (EU). Increasingly, however, it became clear that the party's appeal lay partly in its opposition to the long-standing privileges enjoyed by the two coalition members and to the exclusion of other parties from established political processes.

The long-delayed privatization of the state-owned Creditanstalt Bankverein, a bank heavily influenced by the ÖVP, seemed only to confirm the political establishment's resistance to change and fear of outside influence. A non-Austrian consortium had been interested in purchasing Creditanstalt since 1994, but the government's desire to sell the bank to an Austrian investor was not a secret. In January Creditanstalt was finally sold to the country's leading bank, Bank Austria AG, which had ties to the SPÖ.

Fear of change no doubt stemmed from the fact that the Austrian economy had been sluggish ever since the country joined the EU in 1995. By 1997 economic growth was slowly accelerating, thanks to exports and business investment in machinery and equipment, but growth in gross domestic product was only an estimated 1.6%, still below the EU average. The government's attempts at pension reform proved unpopular, and Austrians endured their second year of harsh government budget cuts designed to ensure Austria's qualification to take part in a single European currency, which was due to take place in 1999.

Despite accusations that the government was too slow to change, the new chancellorship did seem to herald a shift in emphasis for the policies of the dominant SPÖ. Under the leadership of Vranitzky, the SPÖ had moved closer to the centre ground of politics, and Klima moved the party even farther in this direction, tightening up on immigration laws and pushing ahead with privatization, both traditional policies of the right. Unlike his predecessor, however, Klima was willing to communicate with Haider, although by the end of the year, the political threat posed by the FPÖ had become less significant.

The economy finally seemed on the path to recovery, and unemployment had begun to fall. In October the ÖVP defied opinion polls by gaining seats in the local parliamentary elections in Upper Austria. Moreover, the budget was well on course to meet the requirements for joining the EU's economic and monetary union.

Having endured some difficulties in its first two years as a member of the European Union, Austria looked forward to being in a strong position when it took over the six-month rotating presidency of the EU at the beginning of July 1998. (FIONA MULLEN)

AZERBAIJAN

Area: 86,600 sq km (33,400 sq mi), including the 5,500-sq km (2,100-sq mi) exclave of Nakhichevan
Population (1997 est.): 7,617,000 (including 326,000 in Nakhichevan)
Capital: Baku
Head of state and government: President Heydar Aliyev, assisted by Prime Minister Artur Rasizade

Despite domestic political setbacks in the early spring, 1997 was in many respects a year of triumph for Azerbaijan and for Pres. Heydar Aliyev personally. In January National Security Minister Namik Abbasov announced the arrest of some 40 people who

CHARLES CROWELL—BLACK STAR

Workers confer at a yard that builds offshore oil platforms in Baku, Azerbaijan. During the 1990s exploitation of the vast oil fields under the Caspian Sea was complicated by political instability in Azerbaijan, Russian claims on the Caspian fields, and disputes over the location of new pipelines.

had allegedly planned a coup at the beginning of the year, and in February historian Ziya Bunyadov, a prominent member of the ruling New Azerbaijan Party and a close associate of Aliyev, was assassinated. During the summer, however, Aliyev was lionized in Washington for his "distinguished career of public service," and he presided over the signing of oil contracts worth $8 billion with three U.S.-led consortia to exploit separate Caspian Sea oil fields.

A preliminary agreement concluded in July with two major Russian oil companies to develop the Serdar Caspian oil field was suspended after Turkmenistan protested that Serdar lay in its sector of the Caspian and threatened to contest ownership of Serdar and one other Caspian deposit in an international court. In December, however, Aliyev and Pres. Saparmurad Niyazov of Turkmenistan agreed to set up a working group to designate the division between their national sectors.

In November the first oil to be extracted by one of the eight international consortia to begin operations in Azerbaijan began flowing northward from Baku to the Russian port of Novorossiysk. U.S. and Turkish government officials expressed their support for construction of an export pipeline from Baku to the Turkish port of Ceyhan that would minimize Azerbaijan's dependence on Moscow in shipping its oil to international markets. The Azerbaijanis also conducted intensive talks with Georgia, Ukraine, Bulgaria, and Romania about possible alternative oil-export routes.

Mindful of his country's increased international profile, Aliyev issued a decree in September that abolished military censorship of the media; it was, however, not implemented. Leading members of the opposition Azerbaijan Popular Front were prevented several times during the summer from visiting former president Abulfaz Elchibey, who had fled to his native village in the exclave of Nakhichevan during a bloodless coup in July 1993. In early November, though, Elchibey was permitted to return to Baku.

Harassment of less-prominent opposition political figures continued, as did the trials of former police officials charged with complicity in earlier failed coup attempts. Three opposition women politicians were accused of spying for Western intelligence services.

Beginning in May the cochairmen of the Organization for Security and Cooperation in Europe's Minsk Group, charged with mediating a political settlement of the deadlocked Nagorno-Karabakh conflict between Armenia and Azerbaijan, undertook several missions to the region in an attempt to persuade the two nations to agree to a peace plan that provided for the withdrawal of Armenian forces from occupied Azerbaijani territory and bestowed on the disputed enclave broad autonomy within Azerbaijan. Azerbaijan agreed to the proposals unconditionally, and Armenia accepted them as a basis for further talks.

Arkady Gukasyan, the former Karabakh foreign minister who was elected president of the enclave in August, continued, however, to insist on a "package" solution to the conflict that would resolve all contentious issues within one framework document.

(ELIZABETH FULLER)

This article updates the *Macropædia* article TRANSCAUCASIA: *Azerbaijan.*

BAHAMAS, THE

Area: 13,939 sq km (5,382 sq mi)
Population (1997 est.): 287,000
Capital: Nassau
Chief of state: Queen Elizabeth II, represented by Governor-General Orville Turnquest
Head of government: Prime Minister Hubert Ingraham

Former Bahamas prime minister Sir Lynden Pindling was criticized by the commission of inquiry that had been established to probe the management of state enterprises under the administration of his Progressive Liberal Party (PLP) government. When the commission presented its report on the Hotel Corp. in February, Sir Lynden was found to have acted improperly when he accepted loans of $750,000 from two businessmen who held contracts with the corporation, of which he was chairman. The committee, however, did not recommend any action against him.

In March the Free National Movement, led by Prime Minister Hubert Ingraham, solidified its hold on office by winning the general election with an increased majority of 34 seats, 6 being retained by the PLP. The number of seats in the House of Assembly had been reduced from 49 to 40 for the election to create more evenly balanced constituencies. Sir Lynden held on to his own seat but promptly resigned as PLP leader, giving way to Perry Christie, a former minister of agriculture and trade.

After a 25-year career, during which he took The Bahamas to independence from Great Britain, Sir Lynden in July announced his withdrawal from active politics. He admitted to "failures and disappointments" in his farewell address to the parliament and offered "regrets" for his political shortcomings.

(DAVID RENWICK)

This article updates the *Macropædia* article The WEST INDIES: *The Bahamas.*

BAHRAIN

Area: 694 sq km (268 sq mi)
Population (1997 est.): 620,000
Capital: Manama
Chief of state: Emir Isa ibn Sulman al-Khalifah
Head of government: Prime Minister Khalifah ibn Sulman al-Khalifah

Since the end of 1994, Bahrain had witnessed bouts of political unrest and violence perpetrated mainly by the Muslim Shi'ite opposition in an attempt to persuade the government to restore the parliament, which was abolished in 1975. International human rights organizations, such as Amnesty International and Human Rights Watch, recorded cases of human rights abuses by the Bahraini authorities against those arrested or imprisoned for their political activities. In addition to their political demands, the Shi'ites were asking for economic reforms and jobs for the unemployed. In 1997 foreign workers constituted 63% of Bahrain's labour force. In late November it was reported that eight exiled opposition leaders had been sentenced in absentia to 5–15 years in prison.

On June 12, 1996, in an attempt to bring the situation under control, Emir Isa ibn Sulman al-Khalifah published a decree dividing the country into four provinces, each with a governor responsible for the preservation of law and order in his province. Governors were also responsible for overseeing economic and educational development in their provinces.

A decree issued by the emir in January announced the establishment of a National Guard, which was to become a military force independent of the army and a backup for it. The goal of the National Guard was to reach a force of 1,000, mostly drawn from non-Bahraini recruits; it was to be headed by the emir's son, Sheikh Muhammad ibn Isa al-Khalifah.

(LOUAY BAHRY)

This article updates the *Macropædia* article ARABIA: *Bahrain.*

BANGLADESH

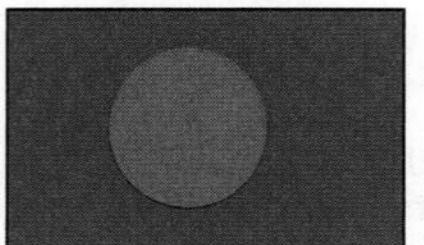

Area: 147,570 sq km (56,977 sq mi)
Population (1997 est.): 125,340,000
Capital: Dhaka
Chief of state: President Shahabuddin Ahmed
Head of government: Prime Minister Sheikh Hasina Wazed

Although the political situation in Bangladesh in 1997 was relatively stable compared with the previous year, the Awami League (AL) government of Prime Minister Sheikh Hasina Wazed was, nevertheless, confronted with strong opposition from the Bangladesh Nationalist Party (BNP), headed by former prime minister Khaleda Zia, and from the main Islamic fundamentalist party, the Islami Oikyo Jote. The BNP, the Islami Oikyo Jote, and a breakaway faction of the National Party, which supported the government, led a nationwide general strike on August 24 in protest against fuel price hikes of as much as 63%. At least 150 people were injured in clashes between protesters and police during the strike. The BNP attempted to increase the political pressure on the government when all its members stormed out of Parliament on August 30 in protest against the prime minister's economic policies.

The political climate had been inflamed in January when the High Court ruled that the government had acted lawfully in repealing a long-standing indemnity ordinance that had protected those accused of being involved in the 1975 coup in which Pres. Sheikh Mujibur Rahman, father of Sheikh Hasina, was assassinated along with nine members of his family. The trial of six of the accused began in May. This issue took

Overcrowded streets like this one are common sights in Dhaka, the capital of Bangladesh. One of the poorest countries in the world, Bangladesh experienced turmoil in 1997 when opposition parties led a nationwide general strike in protest against fuel price hikes by the government.

FRANK FOURNIER—CONTACT PRESS IMAGES

on personal overtones for Zia, whose husband was accused by the secretary-general of the AL of involvement in the 1975 coup.

The government and the Parbattaya Chattagram Jana Sanghati Samity (PCJSS), the political wing of the Shanti Bahini, a guerrilla group that had been fighting a 24-year insurgency for greater regional autonomy for the indigenous population of the Chittagong Hill Tracts in southeastern Bangladesh, achieved a major breakthrough in bilateral talks in May, and on December 5 the PCJSS and the government signed a peace agreement. A new administrative system would substantially address desires for autonomy, and a general amnesty for all members of Shanti Bahini was proposed.

On May 19 more than 1.5 million people in Bangladesh were rendered homeless and at least 100 persons were killed when a cyclone struck the southeastern region of the country. The effects of the storm were compounded by the tidal waves that accompanied it, with more than 50 islands and districts affected by the flooding that followed. On July 13 floods again swept the same area of Bangladesh, killing at least 57 people and leaving a quarter of a million homeless. On September 27 another cyclone ravaged the southeastern part of the country. Although more than 600,000 people had been evacuated before the storm hit the coastal areas, at least 60 people were killed, hundreds were injured, and thousands were once again left homeless.

Following up on their landmark treaty for sharing water from the Ganges River, which came into effect on January 1, Bangladesh and India agreed to share the flow of a second common river, the Teesta. The government's decision to grant Indian vehicles transit rights through Bangladesh was, however, rejected by the opposition parties in Parliament. This led to a daylong strike that resulted in one death and more than 100 injuries in clashes with the police.

(CLAUDE RAKISITS)

BARBADOS

Area: 430 sq km (166 sq mi)
Population (1997 est.): 265,000
Capital: Bridgetown
Chief of state: Queen Elizabeth II, represented by Governor-General Sir Clifford Husbands
Head of government: Prime Minister Owen Arthur

The Barbados government in March appointed a British consulting firm, Maxwell Stamp, to study the regulation of the nation's offshore financial sector. Offshore banking was expected to grow in Barbados from the relatively modest base in 1997 of about 37 banks with Bar$13.6 billion in assets.

Although Barbados's main industry, tourism, continued to do well during the year, not all hotels shared in its success, especially the smaller ones. This prompted the government in April to launch a U.S. $15 million investment fund to help hotels that faced financial difficulties. About 4,500 of the 6,500 hotel rooms in Barbados were in hotels classified as "small."

The third party in the Barbados House of Assembly, the National Democratic Party (NDP), lost further ground in July when two of its leaders defected back to the official opposition Democratic Labour Party. The NDP had captured one seat in the 1994 election, but its ambition to be a credible "third force" in Barbados politics now seemed to be wishful thinking.

(DAVID RENWICK)

BELARUS

Area: 207,595 sq km (80,153 sq mi)
Population (1997 est.): 10,360,000
Capital: Minsk
Head of state and government: President Alyaksandr Lukashenka, assisted by Prime Minister Syarhey Ling (acting in that position until his confirmation on February 19)

Political turbulence again characterized the year in Belarus. Pres. Alyaksandr Lukashenka continued to consolidate his authority through a series of dubious constitutional changes begun in November 1996, after he won a heavily manipulated referendum.

The chief political event of 1997 was the union with Russia, declared on April 2 and ratified by both countries on June 11. Apparently, Russia had some reservations from the start, however, and the original 18-page document drawn up by the Belarusian side was reduced to 3 pages by the Russian delegation. Moscow seemed especially wary about a merger of the two currencies and assumption of Belarusian debts. Lukashenka, too, later distanced himself somewhat from the union, and by September he was saying that Belarus would always retain its sovereign status.

Acts of political repression and breaches of human rights in Belarus continued to elicit international concern. Virtually every major political figure in opposition was subjected to harassment; in one particularly egregious example, Tamara Vinnikava, head of the National Bank of Belarus, was arrested in January and held in solitary detention, isolated and ill, without having been brought to trial. She was finally released in early November. On March 16 the head of the Belarusian Soros Foundation was deported, and that same month the Belarusian state security organization began to audit all nongovernmental organizations.

On March 23 the first secretary of the U.S. embassy was declared persona non grata for having taken part in an "illegal" demonstration on that day; the U.S. retaliated by expelling a Belarusian diplomat and recalling Ambassador Kenneth Yalowitz. At least six journalists were attacked and beaten by militia on April 2 during a demonstration against union with Russia; about 100 people were detained. Russia was outraged by and formally protested the Belarusian government's detention in July of Russian television journalists; one journalist had previously been expelled. As a measure of the seriousness with which Russia took these incidents, a planned visit there by President Lukashenka had to be called off when his airplane was refused permission to enter Russian air space. Yeltsin later made it clear that the visit was contingent on the release of Russian journalist Pavel Sheremet (who was released on October 7 on condition that he remain in Belarus).

A fact-finding delegation from the Organization for Security and Cooperation in Europe was sent to Minsk in April following two months of bitter street confrontations between Lukashenka and his opponents. The Soros Foundation and Citihope International later closed their offices in Minsk.

Zyanon Paznyak, a resident of the United States, was reelected leader of the Belarusian Popular Front, the main opposition force, at the party's fifth congress in June. President Lukashenka sought to counter its growing popularity among young people, however, by establishing a Belarusian Patriotic Union of Youth (comparable to the former Komsomol), led by Usevalad Yancheuski, a 22-year-old student of Belarusian State University.

Government figures indicating economic recovery, a growth rate of 2.6% in 1996, and spectacular growth in 1997 were illusory and based on the inclusion of unsold stocks accumulating in warehouses. Still, foreign investments continued, and a new Ford automotive plant opened near Minsk during the year. Belarus remained in debt to Russia for oil and gas supplies, while it continued to operate a budget deficit of almost 5% of gross domestic product.

The exchange rate for the Belarusian rubel had fallen to 28,000 to the U.S. dollar by September, compared with 11,500 in 1996. Prices rose by 141% in the first quarter of 1997, the highest rate in the former Soviet Union. (DAVID R. MARPLES)

BELGIUM

Area: 30,528 sq km (11,787 sq mi)
Population (1997 est.): 10,189,000
Capital: Brussels
Chief of state: King Albert II
Head of government: Prime Minister Jean-Luc Dehaene

The pedophile scandal that rocked Belgium in 1996 continued to be a significant force in the country throughout 1997, fueling pressure for reform of the political, judicial, and police systems. The suspect at the centre of the scandal, Marc Dutroux, was charged with having kidnapped and murdered four girls, aged 8 to 19; with having kidnapped, imprisoned, and raped two others, aged 12 and 14; with having murdered an accomplice, Bernard Weinstein; and with criminal conspiracy. He and at least four other defendants were unlikely to be brought to trial before autumn 1998.

An inquiry—unanimously approved by Parliament in April—identified 30 individuals whose actions had contributed to the tragedies and singled out one politician—former justice minister Melchior Wathelet, who had approved Dutroux's release in 1992 before completion of a 13-year prison sentence for rape. Acting on the inquiry's recommendations, the government in mid-September introduced new procedures for handling incidents involving missing people and required each police force to appoint a magistrate specifically for such cases. To end the counterproductive rivalry the case revealed between the gendarmerie (responsible to the Interior Ministry) and the judicial police (accountable to the courts), the government proposed merging both forces into a federal unit. Approval was given for the creation in Belgium of the European Centre for Missing Children—inspired by the U.S. National Center for Missing and Exploited Children—as had been promised by the government after the October 1996 White March, when 300,000 people demonstrated in Brussels against the authorities' handling of the Dutroux case. Public anger against the police and judicial systems was heightened by the discovery in March of the body of Loubna Benaïssa in a garage a few hundred metres from her Brussels home five years after the girl was reported missing.

If the Dutroux case were not enough, in October Andras Pandy, a Protestant pastor, was arresed in Brussels on suspicion of having murdered and dismembered his two wives and four of his children beginning a decade earlier.

One political spin-off of the Dutroux case was the nationwide popularity of Flemish Liberal legislator Marc Verwilghen, who had chaired the parliamentary inquiry into the case. His success was matched by the strong showing of his party and of its French-speaking Liberal counterpart. With Belgium's next general election scheduled to be held by May 1999 at the latest, the Liberals moved to the front in the race to form the next government.

Industrial news during the year was dominated by the controversial closing in the summer of the Renault plant in Vilvoorde, on the outskirts of Brussels, with the loss of 2,700 jobs and the transfer of production to France and Spain. The French company's announcement in February provoked unsuccessful protests from the Belgian government, trade unions, and employees and was implemented despite being judged illegal by Belgian and French courts because of the absence of prior consultation with the unions.

Further gloom was caused by the demise of Wallonia's iron and steel industry. The end came when production at the ailing steelmaker Forges de Clabecq was brought to a halt in January after the company had been declared bankrupt. In its heyday in the late 1970s, it employed 6,000 people, but by the beginning of 1997, the numbers had dwindled to 1,800. Despite the industrial setbacks, the country appeared on course to meet the economic entry criteria for the European single currency, the euro. Belgium's National Bank predicted that the 1997 budget deficit would be 2.8% of gross domestic product and thus under the 3% ceiling required for economic and monetary union membership. (RORY WATSON)

BELIZE

Area: 22,965 sq km (8,867 sq mi)
Population (1997 est.): 228,000
Capital: Belmopan
Chief of state: Queen Elizabeth II, represented by Governor-General Colville Young
Head of government: Prime Minister Manuel Esquivel

In municipal elections held on March 11, 1997, the opposition People's United Party (PUP) won all seven town boards for the first time in Belize's history. Johnny Briceño, the deputy PUP leader, received the most votes, 3,173, in Orange Walk, while Pinita Espejo topped the list for the United Democratic Party with 2,133 votes. General elections were scheduled for mid-1998 after a full reregistration of the electorate.

Prime Minister Manuel Esquivel made several Cabinet changes in April: Salvador Fernández was transferred from his post as minister of trade and industry to that of health and sports; Elito Urbina replaced Alfredo Martínez (appointed minister of trade and industry) as ambassador to Mexico; Hubert Elrington was named minister of home affairs and labour; and Ruben Campos, former minister of health and sports, was appointed minister of national coordination and mobilization.

The approved 1997–98 budget comprised expenditures of Bz$402.7 million and revenues of $297.1 million. The prime minister projected the yield from the value-added tax at Bz$76.7 million. Esquivel said that in 1996 the official reserves had reached their highest level in six years. During the year sugar, banana, and citrus exports increased. (INES PARKER)

This article updates the *Macropædia* article CENTRAL AMERICA: *Belize.*

BENIN

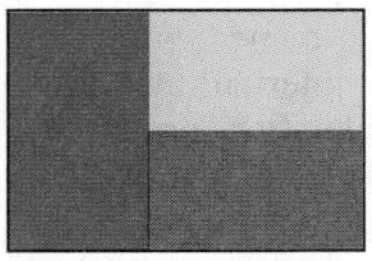

Area: 112,680 sq km (43,500 sq mi)
Population (1997 est.): 5,902,000
Capital: Porto-Novo (executive and ministerial offices remain in Cotonou)
Head of state and government: President Mathieu Kérékou, assisted by Prime Minister Adrien Houngbedji

Benin's chronically weak economy produced mixed results in 1997 as labour unions stepped up their resistance to the government's efforts at liberalization. Protesting the government's plans to transfer control of loading and unloading to four private firms, dockers staged a 24-hour walkout on February 14 that effectively shut down the country's main port at Cotonou, a major channel of foreign-exchange earnings. Two months later office workers went on strike in protest against Pres. Mathieu Kérékou's decision to replace the port authority's management team, labeling it another attempt to politicize the harbour. SONICOG, the state-owned edible oils, butter, and soap producer, was finally privatized in June, after buyers had agreed to the government's condition that all 870 workers be retained. The sale marked the eighth privatization in Benin since 1990, generating about $35 million to the government.

The National Assembly agreed to issue private broadcast licenses for radio and television stations but incorporated into them harsh penalties for libel and defamation. Japan granted Benin $14 million for the construction of 65 new schools. Long a source of cheap, illegal child labour for neighbouring countries, Benin was preparing to stiffen penalties against exploiting minors. This followed the arrest in July of five traffickers preparing to ship 90 minors, some only eight years old, to Gabon.

In March the army held joint military exercises with Burkina Faso and Togo. The Economic Community of West African States held its summit in Cotonou during the last week of August.

(NANCY ELLEN LAWLER)

This article updates the *Macropædia* article WESTERN AFRICA: *Benin.*

BHUTAN

Area: 47,000 sq km (18,150 sq mi)
Population (1997 est.): 860,000 (excluding Bhutanese of Nepalese origin declared stateless by the Bhutanese government in late 1990, nearly 100,000 of whom are now refugees in Nepal)
Capital: Thimphu
Head of state and government: Druk Gyalpo (King) Jigme Singye Wangchuk

In August 1997 the foreign secretary of Nepal, Kumar Gyawali, met with Bhutan's king, Jigme Singye Wangchuk, in Bhutan's capital, Thimphu. The main topic of discussion was the repatriation to Bhutan of the nearly 100,000 Bhutanese of Nepalese origin who had taken shelter in eight UN-monitored refugee camps in eastern Nepal since 1990, when Bhutan launched a national policy that everyone adhere to Bhutanese Buddhist traditions. Although the outcome of the meeting was not disclosed, the fact that the king had met with Gyawali led to speculation that this issue was close to being resolved. During previous discussions Bhutan had always insisted that only the refugees who had been forcefully evicted would be allowed back in Bhutan. Nepal, however, maintained that most refugees had been forced to sign statements of voluntary migration, thus forfeiting, according to Bhutanese law, their right to return.

In August Bhutan entered into discussion with Bangladesh to export to that country 125 MW of electricity. It was expected that an agreement between the two nations would soon be signed after further talks.

(CLAUDE RAKISITS)

BOLIVIA

Area: 1,098,581 sq km (424,164 sq mi)
Population (1997 est.): 7,767,000
Capitals: La Paz (administrative) and Sucre (judicial)
Head of state and government: Presidents Gonzalo Sánchez de Lozada Bustamente and, from August 6, Hugo Bánzer Suárez

DILIP MEHTA—CONTACT PRESS IMAGES

Prayer flags flutter on a hillside in Thimphu, Bhutan. During the 1990s Bhutan enforced a national policy that required everyone to adhere to Buddhism. In 1997 there were indications that at least some of the nearly 100,000 Bhutanese who had fled to Nepal to escape the policy would be repatriated.

In the June 1997 election, a former dictator of Bolivia, Hugo Bánzer Suárez, and his party, Nationalist Democratic Action, emerged as winners. They secured 22% of the vote and became the dominant party in a new government coalition with the Movement of the Revolutionary Left (MIR), Civic Solidarity Union, and Conscience of the Fatherland. This coalition gave Bánzer a broad basis from which to govern, with a large majority of seats in the legislature.

The election campaign was marked by a bitter rivalry between the MIR leader, Jaime Paz Zamora, and the outgoing president, Gonzalo Sánchez de Lozada Bustamente, whose party finished second. Sánchez de Lozada focused on the allegations that the MIR had received money from drug traffickers during the 1989 campaign. It was for this alleged reason that Paz Zamora's U.S. visa was revoked, and the U.S. ambassador reiterated that his country would have no relations with anyone implicated in the drug trade. Bánzer, however, managed to persuade the MIR to accept exclusion from ministerial positions in order to appease the U.S. government.

The coalition program, entitled Alliance for Democracy, set out its general aims but made no mention of Bánzer's election promises to review the privatization and capitalization contracts awarded by the previous administration. Bánzer had been an opponent of the sale of national assets, particularly the state-owned oil company. In reality, however, the new coalition had little choice but to continue the process of economic reform begun by the government of Sánchez de Lozada. The policies of trade liberalization, privatization, encouragement of foreign investment, and strict monetary control seemed certain to continue.

In other developments the Organization of American States (OAS) Inter-American Commission on Human Rights began an investigation of the "Christmas massacre" of December 1996. This incident occurred when the occupation of two gold mines in the Potosí department, to prevent the exploitation of gold reserves on sacred ancestral lands, ended with violent clashes between miners and the government troops, leaving 11 dead and about 50 wounded. The chief of the national police, accused of having ordered troops to open fire on the occupants, was dismissed. The dark spectre of military rule was also raised in January when the president of the Inter-American Commission on Human Rights was abducted and beaten by members of a police intelligence unit.

(ALAN MURPHY)

BOSNIA AND HERZEGOVINA

Area: 51,129 sq km (19,741 sq mi)
Population (1997 est.): 3,124,000, excluding about 1,000,000 refugees in adjacent countries and Western Europe
Capital: Sarajevo
Heads of state: Tripartite presidency headed by Alija Izetbegovic
Heads of government: Two cochairmen of the Council of Ministers

The Republic of Bosnia and Herzegovina concluded a second year of relative peace following three and a half years of bloodshed. The Dayton Peace Agreement, signed on Dec. 14, 1995, was intended to end the vicious fighting, lay the foundation for a new constitutional order, and provide the framework for a multiethnic state with pluralistic and democratic institutions. On all points some progress was reported, but serious problems remained.

The fundamental issue was the very definition of the state, which was sharply divided after the Dayton accords along ethnic and geographic lines. The Federation of Bosnia and Herzegovina (Federation) included the areas populated predominantly by Croats and Muslims, while Republika Srpska (Serb Republic), a crescent-shaped area north and east of the Federation, was home to most ethnic Bosnian Serbs. Ethnic Serbs and Croats in Bosnia continued to identify with—and show loyalty to—the adjacent states of Serbia or Croatia, rather than the central Bosnian government in Sarajevo. Worse, the Croat areas of Bosnia and Herzegovina, nominally part of the Federation, were de facto a part of Croatia—and this was almost true as well in the case of Republika Srpska and Serbia. Consequently, the notion of "Bosnia and Herzegovina" often seemed like a historical relic, and many wondered if it could become a unified state commanding even minimal loyalty from the majority of its inhabitants. The two ministates in Bosnia and Herzegovina had so far failed to create even the minimum conditions for establishing a democratic country with free elections: a politically neutral environment was absent; indicted war criminals, for the most part Bosnian Serbs, continued to exert powerful influence behind the scenes; freedom of movement and expression remained restricted; many disenfranchised refugees were still unable to return home; and nationalists on all three sides remained committed to setting up their separate, "ethnically pure" states.

Under these handicaps municipal elections, postponed from 1996, were held on September 13–14. Councils were elected in 135 municipalities—74 in the Federation and 61 in Republika Srpska. As expected, the three nationalist ruling parties (the predominantly Muslim Party of Democratic Action, the Serbian Democratic Party, and the Croatian Democratic Union) won a clear majority of the council seats. Nonnational parties—those that did not exclusively represent one ethnic group—won only 6% of council seats throughout the country, and independent candidates also fared poorly.

A significant power struggle between Bosnian Serb leaders reemerged in June, hampering reform efforts in Republika Srpska. In July the republic's president, Biljana Plavsic, accused war crimes suspect Radovan Karadzic and several of his allies of corruption. In November a parliamentary election was held in the republic. Plavsic and her coalition Serbian National Alliance failed to win a majority, but the Serbian Democratic Party and its ally, the Radical Party, fell three seats short of an overall majority. The situation remained tense, and deep rifts continued to impede progress.

Not surprisingly, Bosnia and Herzegovina began 1997 in near economic paralysis, and little improvement was seen in the months that followed. More than 50% of the workers in the Federation and nearly 70% in Republika Srpska were unemployed. Most companies were still state-owned; few were operating. Under heavy international pressure, in October the Federation parliament approved part of a package of privatization laws in an effort to jump-start the economy. Bosnia and Herzegovina had to import almost everything it consumed, and black-marketing in tobacco and alcohol was widespread, especially in Republika Srpska. Billions of dollars in foreign aid were arriving to help rebuild housing, bridges, and airports, and a number of small and medium-sized companies were able to take advantage of lending programs from international agencies and the United States. Still, Bosnian enterprises were severely hampered by heavy taxes, bureaucratic red tape, and sometimes corrupt police officials.

Key questions still hovered over Bosnia and Herzegovina: was there a way to partition the country in a fair and stable way along ethnic lines, and if the NATO-led UN forces withdrew on schedule in June 1998, would war resume? At the end of the year, the U.S. government concluded that it would be necessary to keep some American troops in Bosnia and Herzegovina after their current mission ended and that a continued Western military presence was a prerequisite for even minimal stability.

(MILAN ANDREJEVICH)

This article updates the *Macropædia* article BALKAN STATES: *Bosnia and Herzegovina.*

BOTSWANA

Area: 581,730 sq km (224,607 sq mi)
Population (1997 est.): 1,501,000
Capital: Gaborone
Head of state and government: President Sir Ketumile Masire

As Botswana celebrated the 30th anniversary of its independence on Sept. 30, 1996, it appeared to be on the brink of another surge in economic growth. The 1997–98 budget was presented on Feb. 10, 1997, by Vice Pres. and Minister of Finance Festus Mogae; he forecast a surplus and substantial growth in the mining sector. Revenues and grants were expected to total 7.8 billion pula, exceeding expenditures by 763 million pula. There was to be a 5% cut in income tax at a cost of 50 million pula. The main allocations were 25% to education, 20% for land and housing development, and 13% to defense, police, and the office of the president. The biggest problem the country faced was that of finding new jobs for the rapidly growing labour force and reducing unemployment, which in late 1997 stood at 21%. Botswana's growth during recent years was one of the highest in Africa, with gross domestic product increasing by 7% in 1995–96 and by 6.8% during 1996–97. Growth by sector for 1996–97 was mining 9.9%, trade 7.3%, and manufacturing 6.5%.

(GUY ARNOLD)

This article updates the *Macropædia* article SOUTHERN AFRICA: *Botswana.*

CARLOS HUMBERTO—CONTACT PRESS IMAGES

Demonstrators in Brazil protest the government's decision to privatize Companhia Vale do Rio Doce, the world's largest iron-ore mining company. By the final quarter of 1997, preparations were also well advanced for the sale of state assets in the telecommunications and electrical power industries.

BRAZIL

Area: 8,547,404 sq km (3,300,171 sq mi)
Population (1997 est.): 159,691,000
Capital: Brasília
Head of state and government: President Fernando Henrique Cardoso

Domestic Affairs. The year 1997 began with the federal legislature called into a special session by Pres. Fernando Cardoso, who was attempting to ensure that progress would be made on a number of legislative matters, including the constitutional amendment concerning the reelection of the president of the nation and also of state governors and mayors. The reelection amendment was approved in two rounds of voting by the Chamber of Deputies in late January and late February, each by the required three-fifths majority. It took almost three more months before the Senate approved the bill, also in two rounds. Passage of the amendment effectively cleared the way for Cardoso to run for another four-year term of office in the elections scheduled for 1998.

Legislative maneuverings concerning the reelection were influenced early in the year by elections in both chambers of the federal legislature. Former Bahia state governor Antônio Carlos Magalhães of the Liberal Front Party (PFL) was elected to head the Senate, replacing José Sarney of the Party of the Brazilian Democratic Movement (PMDB), who was president of Brazil from 1985 to 1990. The Chamber of Deputies elected Michel Temer of the PMDB to replace Luis Eduardo Magalhães (son of Antônio and also from the PFL). These outcomes were favoured by Cardoso as part of the effort to gain votes from the loose alliance of parties backing his minority Brazilian Social Democratic Party.

At the end of March, an inquiry into the allegedly illegal authorization of several billion dollars of bond payments by some state and municipal governments contributed to delays on the reelection bill. Further problems arose in May when a leading São Paulo newspaper broke a story alleging that bribes had been offered to federal legislators in exchange for votes in favour of the reelection amendment.

Deliberations on other pending constitutional amendments moved slowly, although in early April first-round approval was given by the Chamber of Deputies to the administrative reform bill that would set salary limits and remove job guarantees for public employees. Second-round approval was granted in November. The social security reform bill, which was being reworked by the Senate after the bill was diluted in the lower house in 1996, was approved by early October but had to return to the Chamber of Deputies for two rounds of votes.

Two changes were made in the Cabinet in the second half of May, to replace Justice Minister Nelson Jobim, who was elevated to head the Supreme Court, and Transport Minister Odacir Klein, who had resigned in late 1996. The Justice post was filled by Sen. Iris Resende, and Eliseu Padilha moved from the Chamber of Deputies to Transport. Both were from the PMDB (as were their predecessors), and the balance of parties in the Cabinet was thereby maintained. In late July, Gustavo Loyola resigned as head of the central bank and was replaced by Gustavo Franco, who had previously been the bank's director of international affairs. The transition was a smooth one, with Franco's appointment heralding policy continuity.

The Economy. Gross domestic product (GDP) figures for the first half of 1997 revealed an increase of 4.3% from the same period of 1996. This growth, which was underpinned by a sound industrial performance, was expected to slow slightly in the second half of the year, particularly since interest rates were unlikely to come down further, and consumer credit would thus be kept relatively tight. By October it appeared likely that GDP would increase by about 4% for the year. The annual rate of inflation was expected to be about 5% for 1997.

Brazil's main difficulties concerned the deficits on the public sector and current accounts. In 1996 there was an operational deficit (balance of public-sector accounts including interest payments) of 3.9% of GDP with a primary surplus (the balance excluding interest payments) of 0.4% of GDP. For 1997 the government hoped to improve on that position, although in September, Planning Minister Antônio Kandir acknowledged that the target of achieving a primary surplus of 1.5% of GDP was unlikely to be met, with 0.6% viewed as more viable. This was the case despite the government's moving ahead with the sale of state assets, including a major stake in the state mining concern, Companhia Vale do Rio Doce, in May. By the final quarter of the year, preparations were well advanced for the disposal of government-owned assets in the telecommunications and electrical power industries.

(SUSAN M. CUNNINGHAM)

BRUNEI

Area: 5,765 sq km (2,226 sq mi)
Population (1997 est.): 308,000
Capital: Bandar Seri Begawan
Head of state and government: Sultan and Prime Minister Haji Hassanal Bolkiah Mu'izzaddin Waddaulah

In 1997 Brunei's leaders continued to discuss the need to open their tiny, oil-rich country to outsiders. Tourism was seen as a particularly lucrative way to diversify an economy heavily dependent on nonrenewable natural resources like oil. At the same time, however, the nation struggled with the realities of opening up a relatively closed, quiet religious society.

One reality hit home in March when Sultan Haji Hassanal Bolkiah and his brother, Prince Haji Jefri Bolkiah, were sued by a former Miss U.S.A., Shannon Marketic, who claimed she had been kept as a virtual prisoner and had been expected to engage in sexual activities while a guest of the sultan. The sultan denied Marketic's allegations, and in September a U.S. federal court judge in Los Angeles ruled that the suit could not go forward because the sultan and his brother enjoyed diplomatic immunity. Nevertheless, Brunei received a public relations black eye.

Brunei continued to entice tourists, however. Although the ultraconservative Islamic sultanate had traditionally frowned on alcohol and unveiled women in public, this seemed to be changing. By 1997 many restaurants served beer out of teapots, unveiled women were a common sight (as was sexy window advertising at chic boutiques), and a wide range of entertainment was available via satellites, video rental stores, and new movie theatres. (TIM HEALY)

This article updates the *Macropædia* article SOUTHEAST ASIA: *Brunei.*

BULGARIA

Area: 110,994 sq km (42,855 sq mi)
Population (1997 est.): 8,329,000
Capital: Sofia
Chief of state: Presidents Zhelyu Zhelev and, from January 19, Petar Stoyanov
Head of government: Prime Ministers Georgi Parvanov until February 12, Stefan Sofiyanski until April 24 and, from April 24, Ivan Kostov

At the end of 1996, Bulgaria was in deep crisis. The currency was in free fall, and the International Monetary Fund (IMF) had refused any further help until a currency board was introduced to control the exchange rate and limit government spending. The response of the incumbent Bulgarian Socialist Party (BSP) was to change its leadership, with Georgi Parvanov replacing Zhan Videnov. The public view was that this was more of the same. On Jan. 3, 1997, crowds began to demonstrate in favour of early elections. On the same day, the opposition Union of Democratic Forces (UDF) made elections a condition of their agreeing to the establishment of a currency board. On January 10 the UDF walked out of the parliament, and that evening serious clashes between demonstrators and police took place outside the parliament building. On January 19 the new president, Petar Stoyanov, took office and was required by the constitution to ask Nikolay Dobrev of the BSP to form an administration. The prospect of continued BSP rule intensified the protests; by the end of the month, a general strike was threatened.

On February 4 Dobrev conceded. He would not form a government, and elections would be held in April. Stoyanov admitted that civil war might well have been the alternative. An interim administration under the UDF mayor of Sofia, Stefan Sofiyanski, took office on February 12. On February 24 it resumed negotiations with the IMF, suspended in November, the assumption being that a currency board would be introduced; in March the IMF agreed in principle to a financial support package of $167 million.

The elections of April 19 gave a resounding victory to the UDF, which won 137 of the 240 seats in the parliament. The Democratic Left, the main element of which was the BSP, won 58 seats. On April 24 a new government was formed under the UDF leader, Ivan Kostov, and on July 1 the currency board came into operation. Kostov also committed his administration to speeding up economic change and privatization, especially of land; to the more rigorous combating of crime and corruption; and to seeking membership in NATO and the European Union.

On July 7 the new government introduced a bill, which became effective in September, opening the files of the former state security police. A government commission in October named 23 high-ranking public officials as former collaborators with the security police.

(RICHARD J. CRAMPTON)

This article updates the *Macropædia* article BALKAN STATES: *Bulgaria.*

BURKINA FASO

Area: 274,400 sq km (105,946 sq mi)
Population (1997 est.): 10,891,000
Capital: Ouagadougou
Chief of state: President Blaise Compaoré
Head of government: Prime Minister Kadré Désiré Ouédraogo

Pres. Blaise Compaoré's ruling Congress for Democracy and Progress (CDP) increased its majority in the country's second multiparty parliamentary elections, held on May 11, 1997. Although 569 persons representing 13 parties campaigned for seats in the Assembly of People's Deputies, only the CDP fielded candidates in all 111 districts. The results of the first round of voting gave it 97 seats outright. The voter turnout was 44%, a 9% improvement over the 1992 elections, which had been boycotted by the opposition. On June 11 Compaoré shuffled the composition of his 30-person Cabinet, all of whom were CDP members.

Several student leaders were arrested in early January after antigovernment demonstrations protesting living and working conditions erupted in Ouagadougou and Bobo Dioulasso. Another four were detained on February 2, which triggered a week of strikes and disorder. After considerable public pressure the government freed them a week later, and the students agreed to suspend their strike while talks began. Nevertheless, a second 72-hour strike started on February 13.

Burkina Faso agreed to send troops to Liberia and the Central African Republic to aid African peacekeeping efforts. The 15th Pan-African Film and Television Festival of Ouagadougou, attended by competitors from 25 countries, was held in February.

(NANCY ELLEN LAWLER)

This article updates the *Macropædia* article WESTERN AFRICA: *Burkina Faso.*

BURUNDI

Area: 27,816 sq km (10,740 sq mi)
Population (1997 est.): 6,053,000
Capital: Bujumbura
Head of state and government: President Pierre Buyoya, assisted by Prime Minister Pascal-Firmin Ndimira

A number of violent clashes between Burundi's Tutsi-dominated army and Hutu rebels were reported in the first few months of 1997. On January 5, it was alleged, Tutsi civilians led by army troops slaughtered some 400 people in Muramvya province. Five days later, at a detention centre in Muyinga province, troops shot dead 126 Hutu refugees who had been expelled from Tanzania, an incident the army acknowledged. Hutu rebels retaliated in March in a succession of attacks across the country, and by early April the army was reportedly using aircraft to bombard rebel positions. On April 3 the UN Department of Humanitarian Affairs described "dangerously unsanitary conditions" in refugee camps used to hold some 500,000 Burundians whom the army had forcibly removed from their homes in order to undermine Hutu support in the countryside.

On April 16, at a regional summit in Arusha, Tanz., Pres. Pierre Buyoya met with the heads of state of Ethiopia, Kenya, Rwanda, Tanzania, Uganda, and Zambia to discuss the situation in Burundi. The leaders of those nations agreed that they would ease some sanctions imposed against Burundi following the military coup in July 1996 that put Buyoya in office. The Hutu-led National Council for the Defense of Democracy denounced the summit and criticized regional leaders for treating Buyoya as a legitimate head of government. One week prior to the summit, Jean Minami, the exiled leader of the opposition Front for Democracy in Burundi, alleged that the Buyoya regime had been responsible for killing 50,000 people since it came to power.

In June former president Sylvestre Ntibantunganya, who had been ousted in the 1996 coup, left the sanctuary of the U.S. embassy in Bujumbura, where he had spent nearly a year; although it was unclear what political role, if any, Ntibantunganya would play in the future, he immediately called for negotiations between the government and Hutu rebels. At a meeting with foreign diplomats in Bujumbura on June 26, Buyoya appealed to the international community for help in bringing peace to Burundi. In late August, however, the government pulled out of peace talks with rebels that took place in Tanzania, claiming that Hutu were receiving military training and weapons in refugee camps in Tanzania in preparation for renewed attacks. Reports of attacks by rebels against civilians continued throughout the year.

(GUY ARNOLD)

This article updates the *Macropædia* article CENTRAL AFRICA: *Burundi.*

CAMBODIA

Area: 181,916 sq km (70,238 sq mi)
Population (1997 est.): 10,385,000
Capital: Phnom Penh
Chief of state: King Norodom Sihanouk
Head of government: First Prime Minister Norodom Ranariddh, assisted by Second Prime Minister Hun Sen

When two men became prime ministers of Cambodia after the United Nations-organized 1993 elections, many people assumed the worst. The two, Hun Sen (*see* BIOGRAPHIES) and Prince Norodom Ranariddh, were unlikely partners. First Prime Minister Ranariddh, son of King Norodom Sihanouk and the elected victor, was an ineffectual leader with little authority. Second Prime Minister Hun Sen bullied his way into power when his party lost but was by far the stronger leader.

PHILIP JONES GRIFFITHS—MAGNUM

Monks walk past a defaced statue at one of the Angkor temples near Siem Reap, Cambodia. The most impressive religious site in Cambodia, Angkor repeatedly was the scene of fighting between the troops of Hun Sen and those of Prince Norodom Ranariddh.

For three years the coleaders kept their mutual antipathy in check, but by 1997 relations between them were increasingly tense. The stage was set for a showdown that would pitch Cambodia toward civil war and put in doubt the future of democracy there. Early in the year there were reports that soldiers loyal to each man were stockpiling arms. In March a grenade attack on a political rally organized by the opposition killed 19 people. Hun Sen denied having ordered the attack.

The conflict was then intensified by the efforts of both Hun Sen and Ranariddh to enlist the Khmer Rouge guerrillas as allies. While the Khmer Rouge were still vilified for their genocidal 1975–79 rule, they continued to wield power in gem-mining regions of Cambodia. By wooing the guerrillas, each man hoped to boost his fighting strength and his chances in the elections scheduled for 1998. Moreover, whoever engineered the collapse of the guerrilla group would surely win national and international applause.

When Ranariddh began negotiating with Khmer Rouge factions in the spring of 1997, Hun Sen accused his co-prime minister of illegally and unilaterally making a devil's pact with the enemy. In June Ranariddh announced that the Khmer Rouge was in its death throes and that its notorious leader, Pol Pot, was on the run from a breakaway Khmer Rouge faction. (Few believed this until August, when Pol Pot was sentenced to life in prison at a jungle trial held by his erstwhile followers.) In October Pol Pot was interviewed in prison and expressed no remorse for his role in the Khmer Rouge rule; he also stated that the genocide figures had been exaggerated.

In June soldiers loyal to Hun Sen and those loyal to Ranariddh traded fire in downtown Phnom Penh; four of Ranariddh's men died in the exchange. The next month Hun Sen issued a warning that Khmer Rouge were massing in the capital. There was no proof of this, though Ranariddh's chief of security had deployed former guerrillas to guard his boss's residence. Hun Sen, however, used this as the pretext for making his move. All-out fighting erupted on July 5 near the international airport. By the time the shooting stopped 48 hours later, Ranariddh and many of his supporters had fled the country. Others were rounded up and allegedly tortured, and at least one was executed. Ranariddh's forces retreated to western Cambodia and dug in for a battle with Hun Sen's soldiers. Hun Sen appointed as first prime minister Ung Huot, a pliable member of Ranariddh's party, a move grudgingly endorsed by Ranariddh's father, King Sihanouk, who left Cambodia in October, saying he might never return. Hun Sen ordered Ranariddh's arrest on charges of conspiracy with the Khmer Rouge and arms smuggling.

Hun Sen's coup was awkward for the Association of Southeast Asian Nations, which had agreed in principle to expand its membership to include Laos, Myanmar (Burma), and Cambodia. But with the latter verging on civil war, the seven existing members (Thailand, Singapore, Indonesia, Malaysia, Brunei, Vietnam, and the Philippines) decided to postpone Cambodia's entry. Hun Sen's power grab was also problematic for the UN, which had spent $2 billion to bring peace and democracy to the country. In September, Hun Sen and Ranariddh appeared at the General Assembly to demand official recognition. The UN chose to leave Cambodia's seat vacant for the year.

(ROBIN PAUL AJELLO)

This article updates the *Macropædia* article SOUTHEAST ASIA: *Cambodia.*

CAMEROON

Area: 475,442 sq km (183,569 sq mi)
Population (1997 est.): 14,678,000
Capital: Yaoundé
Chief of state: President Paul Biya
Head of government: Prime Minister Peter Mafany Musonge

Cameroon's second multiparty legislative elections, postponed from early March 1997, were held on May 17, two months after the National Assembly was dissolved. The announcement followed weeks of unrest in the English-speaking northwest of the country during which 10 people died. Forty-five parties fielded 1,800 candidates in the elections. Pres. Paul Biya's ruling People's Democratic Movement added to its absolute majority, taking 116 of the 180 seats. The main opposition party, the Social Democratic Front, led by John Fru Ndi, won 43 seats, while Bello Bouba Maigari's National Union for Democracy and Progress took 13. Eight seats went to four other parties. Despite opposition calls for the results to be annulled amid charges of election rigging, Ndi announced that his party would not boycott the new session of the National Assembly. International observers concluded that the polls were generally conducted fairly. In July the government rejected opposition demands that it relinquish its state monopoly of television and radio. The presidential election took place in October, and Biya won with 92% of the vote.

In May a deal was signed giving China the right to mine bauxite in Cameroon. After announcing that the economy grew by an estimated 5% in 1996, Biya presented the 1997–98 budget to the Assembly in July. Although a 13% increase in spending over the previous year was projected, he claimed it would achieve a fiscal balance. The opposition denounced the budget as no more than a propaganda device that was designed to impress international donors, but the National Assembly overwhelmingly passed it on July 15.

Relations with Nigeria remained tense. In May the government denied that its troops had attacked Nigerian forces on the oil-rich Bakassi peninsula. The Cameroonian army was put on full alert on its southern borders in August, responding to reports that Nigeria had reinforced its base near the Equatorial Guinea border. (NANCY ELLEN LAWLER)

This article updates the *Macropædia* article WESTERN AFRICA: *Cameroon*.

CANADA

Area: 9,970,610 sq km (3,849,674 sq mi)
Population (1997 est.): 30,287,000
Capital: Ottawa
Chief of state: Queen Elizabeth II, represented by Governor-General Roméo LeBlanc
Head of government: Prime Minister Jean Chrétien

Domestic Affairs. Still concerned with the nagging problem of the possible secession of Quebec, Canadians went to the polls on June 2, 1997, in a general election. The results were indecisive. The governing Liberal Party under Prime Minister Jean Chrétien saw its House of Commons majority reduced, while the opposition was reconstituted as four regional blocs. A fractious Parliament appeared to be a sure prospect for the future.

The Chrétien government, in power since November 1993, decided to hold the election five months before the end of the four-year term customary for Canadian governments. The government campaigned on its record, especially its success in cutting the federal deficit from $45.7 billion when it came into office to an estimated $17 billion for fiscal year 1997–98. Its other policies were based on those of the previous Progressive Conservative Party administration of Brian Mulroney: enhanced free trade with the United States, a goods and services tax, and the improvement of Canada's international competitiveness. The Liberals' cuts in health and social programs, carried out to reduce spending, aroused voter dissatisfaction, especially in the poorer regions of Canada. Its cautious stance on Quebec separatism also disappointed voters, especially in the western provinces. Thus, the Chrétien government took a risk in going to the public before the end of its mandate.

The election result showed that Canadians were, on the whole, pleased with Chrétien's approach to the problems of the country. The Liberal majority of 174 of the 295 seats in the House of Commons was, however, cut to 155 in an expanded 301-seat House. This majority depended heavily on Ontario, where the Liberals captured 101 of the province's 103 seats. The Liberals suffered a severe setback in that part of Canada on the Atlantic Ocean, a traditional base of support. The cuts they had made in unemployment insurance benefits hurt them in that region, where the jobless rate was above the average. Two Cabinet ministers from the region were defeated. In Quebec, an area critical to the future of the country, the Liberals made gains, winning 26 of 75 seats. (They had taken 19 seats in the previous election.) Another federalist party, the Progressive Conservatives, also took votes away from the separatist Bloc Québécois, whose sole function in federal politics was to advocate the breakup of the country. In the Prairie Provinces (Alberta, Saskatchewan, and Manitoba) and in British Columbia, the Liberals won only 15 seats, a decline from their previous standing. Chrétien held his own seat in Quebec but by a margin much closer than in the 1993 election.

The Bloc Québécois, which had been the official opposition in the previous Parliament, lost that position. Its share of the popular vote dropped in Quebec, the only province in which it fielded candidates. In 1993 it had won 50 of 75 seats in Quebec; in 1997 it took only 44. A new leader who did not inspire confidence, Gilles Duceppe, was one explanation for the decline; another was the unpopularity of its provincial counterpart, the Parti Québécois, struggling as a government to put Quebec's financial house in order.

The 1997 election catapulted a party only 10 years old, the Reform Party, into the official opposition. Led by a populist figure from Alberta, Preston Manning (*see* BIOGRAPHIES), the Reform Party appealed to western Canada's belief that its interests in the federation were continually being subordinated to those of Ontario and Quebec. Manning made a strenuous effort to win seats in Ontario and thus elevate Reform into national party status, but it was shut out in the large central province. It captured 35 seats in the three Prairie Provinces and 25 in British Columbia, however, which gave it 60 seats in the new Parliament. For the first time, a regional protest party had become Canada's official opposition party.

The Progressive Conservatives, who had won only two seats in 1993 after nine years in power under Mulroney, made respectable gains in 1997. Under Jean Charest, an attractive young leader who was a strong federalist, the party took 5 seats in Quebec, 13 in the Atlantic Provinces (New Brunswick, Newfoundland, Nova Scotia, and Prince Edward Island), and one each in Ontario and Manitoba.

The New Democratic Party, starting from a base of nine members of Parliament, also improved its standing. For the first time in its history, the party achieved a breakthrough in the Maritime Provinces (New Brunswick, Nova Scotia, and Prince Edward Island), long dominated by the old-line parties. In Nova Scotia, led by a lively new leader from Halifax, Alexa McDonough, the party took 6 of the province's 11 seats. In New Brunswick it won 2 seats, and the remaining 12 seats were won in the Prairie Provinces, British Columbia, and Yukon, which gave the New Democrats a representation of 21 seats in the Commons. It seemed likely that the party's strengthened presence in the federal government would bring a social-progressive voice to parliamentary deliberations.

The voter turnout in the 1997 election was about 67%, slightly lower than that of 1993. Of the total vote, the Liberals took 38%, Reform and the Progressive Conservatives tied at 19%, and the New Democratic Party and the Bloc Québécois each captured 11%. The four opposition parties appeared to be too diverse to combine forces against the government, and so the Liberals seemed to be in no danger of being defeated in Parliament. The election did, however, bring regional differences into the open and thus possibly make it more difficult to reach consensus on national questions. In addition, each of the opposition parties achieved official party status, which allowed them additional funds for research and a guaranteed allocation of time at the parliamentary question period. With the parties promising searching criticism of the Liberal government's policies, politics in Canada seemed certain to be more turbulent than in the last session of Parliament.

Chrétien adopted two strategies in 1997 to improve federal-provincial relations. One was the familiar process of devolution, which he had always favoured as an effective response to Quebec's restlessness in the federation. He therefore turned over partial control of immigration to those provinces that had requested the transfer. By an agreement of April 21, he surrendered job-training programs to Quebec, a power that the province had long demanded. Other provinces were also given responsibility for educating unemployed workers who wished to reenter the labour force.

Chrétien's other strategy, and this marked a departure for his government, was to go on the offensive against some of the assumptions and claims of the Quebec separatists. In this contest his spokesman was Stéphane Dion, a young law professor from Montreal who had been appointed minister for intergovernmental affairs in 1996. In two strongly worded open letters released on August 11 and 26, Dion wrote to the Quebec government to point out that Quebec could not leave the union unilaterally without the possibility of dangerous consequences. He rejected three assertions made by the Parti Québécois government: that international law permitted secession, that a majority of 50% plus one was a sufficient threshold for secession, and that international law ruled out any changes to a seceding state's boundaries. Dion's letters, which were intended to convince moderate opinion in Quebec that independence could not be achieved by the painless process advanced by the separatists, struck a popular chord in the rest of Canada. They showed a more determined stance against the secessionists than at any other time since the Chrétien government came to power. At the same time, the federal government went ahead with its challenge to the legality of separation, which was to be argued before the Supreme Court of Canada in February 1998.

The premiers of all the provinces except Quebec also made their contribution to the debate over unity. At their annual conference, held in St. Andrews, N.B., August 6–8, they decided to hold a special meeting to prepare a pro-union statement for Quebec. This meeting was held in Calgary, Alta., on September 14. A seven-point statement was drafted recognizing Quebec's "unique character" within the federation while insisting that all provinces and all citizens enjoyed "equality of status."

There was only one provincial election in 1997. In Alberta, Ralph Klein, noted for his rigorous control over governmental expenditures, led the Progressive Conservative Party to a decisive victory on March 11. Klein's party captured 63 of the 83 seats in the legislature.

The Economy. The Canadian economy moved ahead strongly in 1997, with growth in gross domestic product (GDP) expected to be almost 4%. A consumer spending spree demonstrated that Canadians were more confident about the future. With low interest rates and marginal levels of inflation (the consumer price index ranged between 1.5% and 2% for the year), the conditions for economic growth were favourable. The only cloud in the sky was the continuing high rate of unemployment. During the four years of the Liberal government, it had fallen from 11% to 9% but had not declined further. Unemployment among young people 15–24 years of age was a particular problem.

Among the proudest achievements of the Chrétien government was Finance Minister Paul Martin's success in bringing the national deficit under control. In a budget submitted on February 18, he announced a deficit target of $17 billion for the 1997–98 fiscal year. A second financial statement on October 15 revealed that the actual deficit for the year 1996–97 had been only $8.9 billion, the lowest in 20 years. There seemed little doubt that the target for 1997–98 would be easily met and that a balanced budget would soon follow.

Foreign Affairs. Commercial salmon fishing off the northwestern coast of North America became a subject of contention between Canada and the United States in 1997. At issue were the conservation and equitable sharing of fish stocks that move through the coastal waters of one country to find spawning rivers in the other. Off the panhandle of Alaska, for instance, fishermen from that state intercept chinook and sockeye salmon as they make their way in from the Pacific to the streams in British Columbia where they hatched. At the south end of Vancouver Island, Canadian fishermen catch coho salmon, a threatened species, as they swim toward rivers in Washington. The harvest of migrating salmon, worth about $500 million a year, was supposed to be regulated by the Pacific Salmon Treaty, negotiated in 1985. The treaty had, however, been ineffective for several years. One weakness lay in the fact that ocean fishing fell under different jurisdictions in the two countries. In Canada the regulation of fisheries was a federal responsibility, while in the U.S. it was a function of the states. Private fishing interests and aboriginal groups also had to be consulted in each country. In the U.S. their weight was strong enough to dictate

CARLO ALLEGRI—AFP

Near Winnipeg, Man., a member of the Canadian military motors a boat past a sign for the Red River during a patrol for residents needing assistance. A massive flood that began in April forced some 25,000 persons from their homes and inundated more than 800 farms.

the American position in negotiations with Canada. Commercial fish farming was another complicating factor. An increasingly important form of harvest, it had caused salmon prices to drop in recent years. This had led to the danger of overfishing as fishermen tried to maintain their incomes.

Talks between the two countries to implement the salmon treaty broke down before the opening of the fishing season. Premier Glen Clark of British Columbia, hoping to put pressure on the U.S., threatened to cancel an agreement allowing U.S. naval vessels to use a submarine-testing facility north of Nanaimo on the inside coast of Vancouver Island. On July 19 a ferry traveling between Washington and Alaska was blockaded for three days at the British Columbia port of Prince Rupert by almost 200 boats belonging to Canadian fishermen angry at what they perceived as overfishing by their Alaskan neighbours. The issue had been taken up with U.S. Pres. Bill Clinton by Prime Minister Chrétien when they met on June 20. Chrétien pressed for the complicated dispute to go to binding arbitration, but Clinton disagreed. In August the two countries sent the dispute to two "eminent persons," who were charged with finding a way to reestablish negotiated quotas through consultation with the fishing interests on both sides of the border. They were William Ruckelshaus, a former director of the U.S. Environmental Protection Agency, and David Strangway, retiring president of the University of British Columbia.

A three-man commission of inquiry, appointed in 1995 to look into the torture and death of a civilian by Canadian peacekeepers during a UN mission to Somalia in 1993, issued its report on June 30. It found "organizational and leadership failures" in the Canadian high command, who had overlooked known disciplinary problems in the airborne regiment sent to Somalia and had later tried to manipulate information to cover up misbehaviour there. The commission's five-volume report, *Dishonoured Legacy,* singled out 11 senior officers for censure. A key recommendation in the report, that the military police and justice system be placed under an independent authority, was rejected by the Chrétien government. The government did announce, however, that it would implement many of the more than 160 recommendations in the report.

(D.M.L. FARR)

CAPE VERDE

Area: 4,033 sq km (1,557 sq mi)
Population (1997 est.): 394,000
Capital: Praia
Chief of state: President Antonio Mascarenhas Monteiro
Head of government: Prime Minister Carlos Veiga

Cape Verde's economy remained stable during 1997, though unemployment continued to affect approximately 25% of the population. In mid-June Prime Minister Carlos Veiga announced the signing of an agreement with Italy aimed at increasing Italian investments in Cape Verde, particularly in the tourism industry. On June 26 the African Development Bank (ADB) awarded a loan worth $4.9 million to Cape Verde to finance road-rehabilitation projects on four of its islands, a loan the ADB said Cape Verde would have 50 years to repay. Gualberto do Rosario, the minister for economic cooperation, stated in late July that Cape Verde would aim at having no state deficit in 1998.

On August 29 Cape Verde and Angola signed accords proclaiming their intention to work together in the fields of health and social welfare. In September Prime Minister Veiga visited Angola in a further effort to strengthen bilateral ties with that southern African country, where nearly 100,000 of the 600,000 Cape Verdeans living abroad resided. In late October, accompanied by a political and economic delegation, Veiga paid his first official visit to China. By 1997 China had provided loans to Cape Verde estimated at $19.8 million. (GUY ARNOLD)

This article updates the *Macropædia* article WESTERN AFRICA: *Cape Verde.*

CENTRAL AFRICAN REPUBLIC

Area: 622,436 sq km (240,324 sq mi)
Population (1997 est.): 3,342,000
Capital: Bangui
Chief of state: President Ange-Félix Patassé
Head of government: Prime Ministers Jean-Paul Ngoupande and, from January 30, Michel Gbezera-Bria

As a result of the army mutiny that began in November 1996, the third in less than a year, Bangui was brought virtually to a standstill. On Jan. 4, 1997, despite the extension of a temporary truce between the mutineers and the government, two French army officers serving with an international mediation team were killed. In reprisal, French troops stationed in Bangui attacked the mutineers' bases in the city on January 5, killing at least 10. To prevent further escalation of the fighting, Pres. Ange-Félix Patassé and rebel leader Capt. Anicet Saulet signed a pact in late January, agreeing that African peacekeepers should replace those of France. On February 12, small units from Chad, Burkina Faso, Gabon, Mali, Senegal, and Togo took over from French troops.

All those detained following the November 1996 mutiny were freed on March 17 as disarmament talks between the opposing sides continued. In February an effort at national reconciliation brought eight opposition deputies into the government. Most of the mutineers agreed in April to return to their barracks. Further disturbances, however, erupted when three rebels were killed by security forces on May 2. Blaming Patassé for the deaths, opposition parties pulled out of the government and called for a general strike. On June 24, after four days of violent clashes, the African peacekeeping force shelled Bangui. At least 100 died, thousands fled the city, and many foreign embassies were closed. Negotiations reopened, and by the end of July, most of the army dissidents had returned to their units.

(NANCY ELLEN LAWLER)

This article updates the *Macropædia* article CENTRAL AFRICA: *Central African Republic.*

CHAD

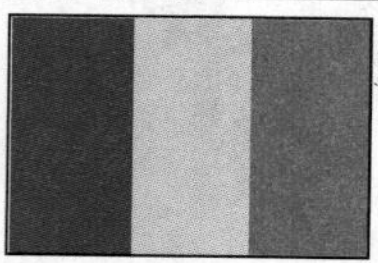

Area: 1,284,000 sq km (495,755 sq mi)
Population (1997 est.): 7,166,000
Capital: N'Djamena
Chief of state: President Lieut. Gen. Idriss Déby
Head of government: Prime Ministers Djimasta Koibla and, from May 16, Nassour Ouaidou Guelendouksia

Legislative elections for the 125-member National Assembly, which had originally been scheduled for November 1996, were postponed until early 1997; the polling took place in two rounds—on January 5 and February 23. The elections, part of a transition to democracy in Chad that had begun in January 1993, were pronounced "free and fair" by international observers in spite of allegations of minor irregularities. Pres. Idriss Déby's Patriotic Salvation Movement gained 55 seats, the Union for Renewal and Democracy 31, the National Union for Development and Renewal 15, and other parties 24.

In January the International Federation of Human Rights Leagues (FIDH) reported an increase in human rights abuses in Chad. The FIDH stated that scores of people had been summarily executed by the nation's security forces in recent months and produced a copy of a government order, allegedly issued to the forces in November 1996, that told officers that "robbers must not be the object of normal procedures [of arrest]. If one is caught in the act, you must proceed with his physical elimination." The FIDH report echoed findings published earlier by Amnesty International.

On April 18 the government signed a peace agreement with the rebel Armed Forces for a Federal Republic (FARF) that granted general amnesty to FARF members and provided for the transformation of FARF into a political party. In May President Déby replaced Prime Minister Koibla with Nassour Ouaidou Guelendouksia, who announced a new Cabinet on May 21.

The leaders of 21 opposition parties in August denounced the presence of French troops in Chad. They claimed that the troops represented an outmoded colonialism and that they were there to bolster the personal rule of Déby.

(GUY ARNOLD)

This article updates the *Macropædia* article WESTERN AFRICA: *Chad.*

CHILE

Area: 756,626 sq km (292,135 sq mi)
Population (1997 est.): 14,583,000
Capitals: Santiago (national) and Valparaíso (legislative)
Head of state and government: President Eduardo Frei Ruiz-Tagle

Two events dominated politics in Chile in 1997: the midterm elections in December and the impending retirement of Gen. Augusto Pinochet Ugarte as army commander in chief, scheduled for March 1998. Observers believed that the elections, for all 120 seats in the Chamber of Deputies and half of the elected senators, might decide the choice of the governing coalition's presidential candidate in 1999. Within the coalition the Socialists and the Party for Democracy favoured Ricardo Lagos, a Socialist whom polls rated the country's most popular politician, but one faction of the Christian Democrats (PDC) was hostile to nominating a Socialist candidate.

In the election the governing coalition won 50.5% of the vote, a drop of almost 5% from the 1993 vote. It retained its overall majority in the legislature but by a reduced margin. Almost 18% of the electorate cast either blank or spoiled ballots. Within the coalition the Socialists fared best, strengthening the candidacy of Lagos.

Though Pinochet, president of the military government of 1973–90, publicly insisted that the choice of his successor was in the hands of Pres. Eduardo Frei, he was reported to have told friends that he had submitted a list of seven candidates. Frei ultimately chose Gen. Ricardo Izurieta, the army chief of staff.

The importance of Pinochet's departure was emphasized by the failure of a government bill to amend the constitution and end the system under which nine senators were nominated, several of them indirectly by the armed forces. As in 1996, the government made a deal with the right-wing National Renovation (RN) party, but the bill was blocked when several RN senators sided with the extreme right-wing Independent Democratic Union. Frei announced that the government would try again in March 1998, by which time Pinochet and three of the nominated senators would have retired. Though Pinochet, as a former president, would become a senator, Frei would appoint three new senators, probably enough to give his administration a majority in the Senate and thereby amend the constitution.

In January plans to privatize the 13 water companies were dropped after running into opposition from the right in the Senate, which wanted more flexible regulation, and from the PDC, which opposed privatization. In April 150 years of coal mining at Lota ended, and 1,100 people were left unemployed, after attempts by Enacar, the state company, to modernize the mine and reduce the workforce had broken down in 1996. By contrast, prospects for Chile's main export, copper, remained buoyant; a report predicted increased output of 9.7% in 1997 to 3.4 million tons and projected output in 2000 of 4.8 million tons.

Though the U.S. made new efforts to gain the authority to quickly negotiate Chilean entry to the North American Free Trade Agreement, opposition from the Democrats in the U.S. Congress remained an obstacle. The U.S. decision to remove the ban on high-technology arms sales to South America led to speculation that Chile would buy F-16 fighter jets and raised fears of a regional arms race as Peru, Chile's arch rival, bought MiG fighters from Belarus.

Export earnings were projected to grow more slowly than imports, which would result in a widening of the trade deficit from

$1,147,000,000 in 1996 to $1,900,000,000. Gross domestic product was expected to grow by 5.8%, down from 7.2% in 1996. Consumer prices were projected to rise by 5.5%, down from 6.6%. Unemployment was estimated at 5.4% at the end of the year. The exchange rate held steady at about U.S. $1 = 425 Chilean pesos. (CHARLIE NURSE)

CHINA

Area: 9,572,900 sq km (3,696,100 sq mi), including Tibet and excluding Taiwan (See *Taiwan,* below.)
Population (1997 est., excluding Taiwan): 1,227,740,000
Capital: Beijing
Chief of state: President Jiang Zemin
Head of government: Premier Li Peng

China formally entered a new era in 1997. On February 19 paramount leader Deng Xiaoping, one of China's key statesmen in the 20th century, died at the age of 92. (*See* OBITUARIES.) At the 15th Congress of the Communist Party of China (CPC) in September, Deng's designated successor, Jiang Zemin, further consolidated his authority and initiated an effort to solve the nagging problem of China's deficit-ridden state-owned enterprises. The Chinese economy continued to hum along at a better than 9% growth rate, with work continuing on the huge Three Gorges Dam. (*See* ARCHITECTURE AND CIVIL ENGINEERING: *Sidebar.*) China's difficult relations with the U.S. improved modestly as Jiang paid his first state visit to Washington, D.C., in late October.

Politics and the Economy. After years of declining health, Deng, who had joined the Chinese communist movement in the early 1920s, finally succumbed to Parkinson's and lung disease. In economic and social terms, the China he left behind had changed more rapidly during his 18-year reign than during any other period in modern history. There was no mistaking Deng's impact on his country. While maintaining a tight grip on power and ruthlessly suppressing any real or perceived challenges to the authority of the CPC, Deng liberated China from the fetters of Mao Zedong's economic policies and feudal social restrictions. Facilitating market-opening reforms in China, Deng also allowed a considerable measure of personal autonomy to Chinese citizens as long as they refrained from trespassing into the forbidden zone of politics. Deng was a tough-minded pragmatist who had little patience for the niceties of Marxist-Leninist theory. He was perhaps best known for his anti-ideological aphorism that it does not matter whether the cat is black or white as long as it catches mice. Deng's last political initiative had come in early 1992 when he restarted the sputtering engine of economic reform by extolling the policies of opening to the world and promoting market socialism that his conservative critics had faulted. Among Deng's other major accomplishments were the normalization of relations with the U.S. and the Soviet Union, the Sino-British agreement regarding the handover of Hong Kong, and the transfer of power to a successor generation. Deng's responsibility for the June 4, 1989, massacre in Beijing's Tiananmen Square and his absolute intolerance for dissent were consistent with his reputation as a CPC hatchet man during the earlier stages of his revolutionary career.

Among Deng's conservative critics had been Peng Zhen (*see* OBITUARIES), another tough-minded first-generation revolutionary who survived the Cultural Revolution (1966–76) to become a leading hard-liner in the 1980s. As head of the National People's Congress (NPC), Peng was a modern incarnation of the ancient Chinese Legalist tradition, in which the law was viewed as an instrument of authoritarian rule. In January, Sun Yaoting, the last of the once-powerful fraternity of eunuchs who served the Chinese imperial court, died at the age of 93. One after the other, the mooring lines that had secured China to its imperial and revolutionary pasts were fraying and breaking.

(continued on page 414)

A Buddhist monk meditates on the roof of the Jonkhong temple in Tibet. In 1997 Chinese authorities remained unwilling to engage the Dalai Lama in a genuine dialogue or to countenance Tibetan autonomy. China's continued suppression of political and religious freedoms in Tibet led to mounting criticism in the West and numerous protests by human rights organizations.

JEFFREY AARONSON—NETWORK/ASPEN

SPOTLIGHT

HONG KONG'S RETURN TO CHINA

by Steven I. Levine

Illustration by Cathy Hull

At midnight on June 30/July 1, 1997, the crown colony of Hong Kong officially reverted to Chinese sovereignty, ending 156 years of British rule. After a formal handover ceremony on July 1, the colony became the Hong Kong special administrative region (HKSAR) of the People's Republic of China. The ceremony culminated a 13-year transition that had been initiated by the Sino-British Joint Declaration on the Question of Hong Kong, signed by the heads of the two governments in December 1984. The agreement stipulated that under Chinese rule the HKSAR would enjoy a high degree of autonomy, except in matters of foreign relations and defense, and that the social and economic systems as well as the lifestyle in Hong Kong would remain unchanged for 50 years after 1997. Many observers, however, expressed considerable skepticism about China's pledge to abide by the "one country, two systems" plan outlined in the agreement. They feared that China would drastically curtail the rights and freedoms of Hong Kong residents.

Great Britain had acquired Hong Kong Island from China in 1842, when the Treaty of Nanking was signed at the end of the first Opium War (1839–42). Unsatisfied with incomplete control of the harbour, the British forced China to cede Kowloon Peninsula south of what is now Boundary Street and Stonecutters Island less than 20 years later, after the second Opium War (1856–60). By the Convention of 1898, the New Territories together with 235 islands were leased to Britain for 99 years from July 1, 1898. After the communists took power in China in 1949, Hong Kong became a sanctuary for hundreds of thousands of refugees fleeing communist rule. In the following decades the Chinese government insisted that the treaties giving Britain sovereignty over Hong Kong were invalid.

Although in 1984 Britain and China agreed on the terms of the handover of Hong Kong, Sino-British cooperation during the transition period deteriorated after the appointment in 1992 of Chris Patten as Hong Kong's last colonial governor. Sharply breaking with past practice, Patten initiated a series of political reforms designed to give the people of Hong Kong a greater voice in government via democratic elections to the Legislative Council (LegCo). China's crackdown on the student-led democracy movement in 1989 fed anxiety in Hong Kong regarding the handover and led to the political awakening of a previously quiescent population. Beijing made efforts to stonewall Patten's reforms, which it condemned as a betrayal of London's earlier promises to manage the transition as an exercise in which Hong Kong had no voice of its own. When Hong Kong's Democratic Party, led by barrister Martin Lee, routed pro-Beijing politicians in the 1995 LegCo elections, Beijing denounced Patten and began a series of strong measures aimed at reestablishing its influence. On March 24, 1996, China's 150-member Preparatory Committee, which had been created to oversee the handover, voted to dissolve LegCo and install a provisional legislature after Hong Kong returned to Chinese sovereignty. In December 1996 a China-backed special election committee selected the 60 members of the provisional body, just days after it had overwhelmingly elected 59-year-old shipping magnate Tung Chee-hwa (*see* BIOGRAPHIES) the first chief executive of the HKSAR. Tung, whose tottering corporate empire had been salvaged by a large infusion of government-supplied capital in the 1980s, soon signaled his intention to roll back Patten's reforms, announcing in April 1997 proposals to restrict political groups and public protests after the handover. In essence, what Lee called the "Singaporization" of Hong Kong—*i.e.,* the imposition of authoritarian control—had begun even before the Union Jack was lowered in the colony for the last time.

Pomp and pageantry marked the formal handover ceremony. In attendance were numerous dignitaries from around the world, including Pres. Jiang Zemin and Premier Li Peng of China, British Prime Minister Tony Blair, Prince Charles, and U.S. Secretary of State Madeleine Albright (*see* BIOGRAPHIES). Prince Charles, who gave a short speech in which he congratulated the colony on its political, economic, and social successes, told the people of Hong Kong, "We shall not forget you, and we shall watch with the closest interest as you embark on this new era of your remarkable history." President Jiang, the first mainland Chinese head of state to visit Hong Kong since 1842, reassured residents that China would carry out the "one country, two systems" plan of local autonomy, which had been contrived principally by Chinese paramount leader Deng Xiaoping. Deng had passed away on February 19, just four and a half months before the handover he had hoped to witness. (*See* OBITUARIES.) On the morning of the handover, several thousand specially trained troops of the Chinese People's Liberation Army were deployed in Hong Kong as garrison forces symbolizing the reassertion of China's sovereignty. Chinese authorities did not attempt to suppress several rallies outside the LegCo building on June 30–July 1, even when Lee addressed thousands of demonstrators from a balcony after LegCo had officially been dissolved. The protests proceeded peacefully.

Tung, in his first speech as chief executive, skirted the issues of political rights and democracy, choosing to espouse "traditional Chinese values." He also dwelled on mundane but important issues such as housing and education, vowing to increase the rate of home ownership in Hong Kong to 70% in the next 10 years and to provide better training for teachers. Tung counted on enhanced social programs, including government payments to the elderly poor, and continuing prosperity to marginalize political opposition to his new administration. Most citizens of Hong Kong, of whom 95% were ethnic Chinese, appeared ready to give him the benefit of the doubt, at least for the time being. Tung and the provisional legislature prepared for the first posthandover legislative elections in mid-1998 by reworking the rules of the political game. On July 8 it was announced that only 20 of the 60 legislative seats would be filled via a system of proportional representation. The remaining 40 seats would be chosen by electoral colleges and an election committee, as they were in the period prior to the implementation of Patten's reforms. This change virtually ensured the dominance of Hong Kong's business and professional elite, most of whose members valued stability—which they identified with their own power—over democratic representation. In the first months after the handover, Hong Kong was indeed stable. The outlook for the free exercise of political and civil rights in Hong Kong was clouded, however. Members of the Democratic Party protested that the new electoral system was created to minimize their influence, and Lee predicted that the Democrats would win no more than 10 of the 20 directly elected seats.

CHRISTOPHER MORRIS—BLACK STAR

Two children who took part in a Buddhist ceremony were among the thousands of celebrants in Hong Kong as the British colony reverted to Chinese rule.

President Jiang hailed the "return of Hong Kong to the motherland" as a great historical event that presaged Taiwan's eventual reunification with mainland China. Both Taiwan's ruling Kuomintang and its main opposition, the Democratic Progressive Party, vigorously rejected Jiang's assertion and vowed to resist Beijing's attempts to exert pressure on the island nation. In late June Taiwan conducted live-fire military exercises, which were intended as a signal to China that Taiwan would resist any attempts at reunification. On June 28 approximately 70,000 people in Taiwan attended a "Say No to China" antireunification rally. Although the Taiwanese government encouraged China to protect freedom in Hong Kong, it made it clear that Taiwan would not be absorbed in a similar manner.

The United States, rather than Great Britain, was the principal Western power interested in holding China to its pledge of respecting Hong Kong's political and economic autonomy. Both U.S. Pres. Bill Clinton and Secretary of State Albright informed Beijing that its behaviour with respect to Hong Kong would be considered a touchstone in Sino-American relations, and U.S. congressional leaders reinforced this message. Chinese leaders, meanwhile, severely restricted the access of their own citizens to Hong Kong, whose per capita gross domestic product of more than $24,000 was roughly 40 times that of China and whose habits of free expression and political participation were not ones that Beijing wished its own citizens to emulate.

Steven I. Levine is a Senior Research Associate at Boulder Run Research and the author of Anvil of Victory: The Communist Revolution in Manchuria.

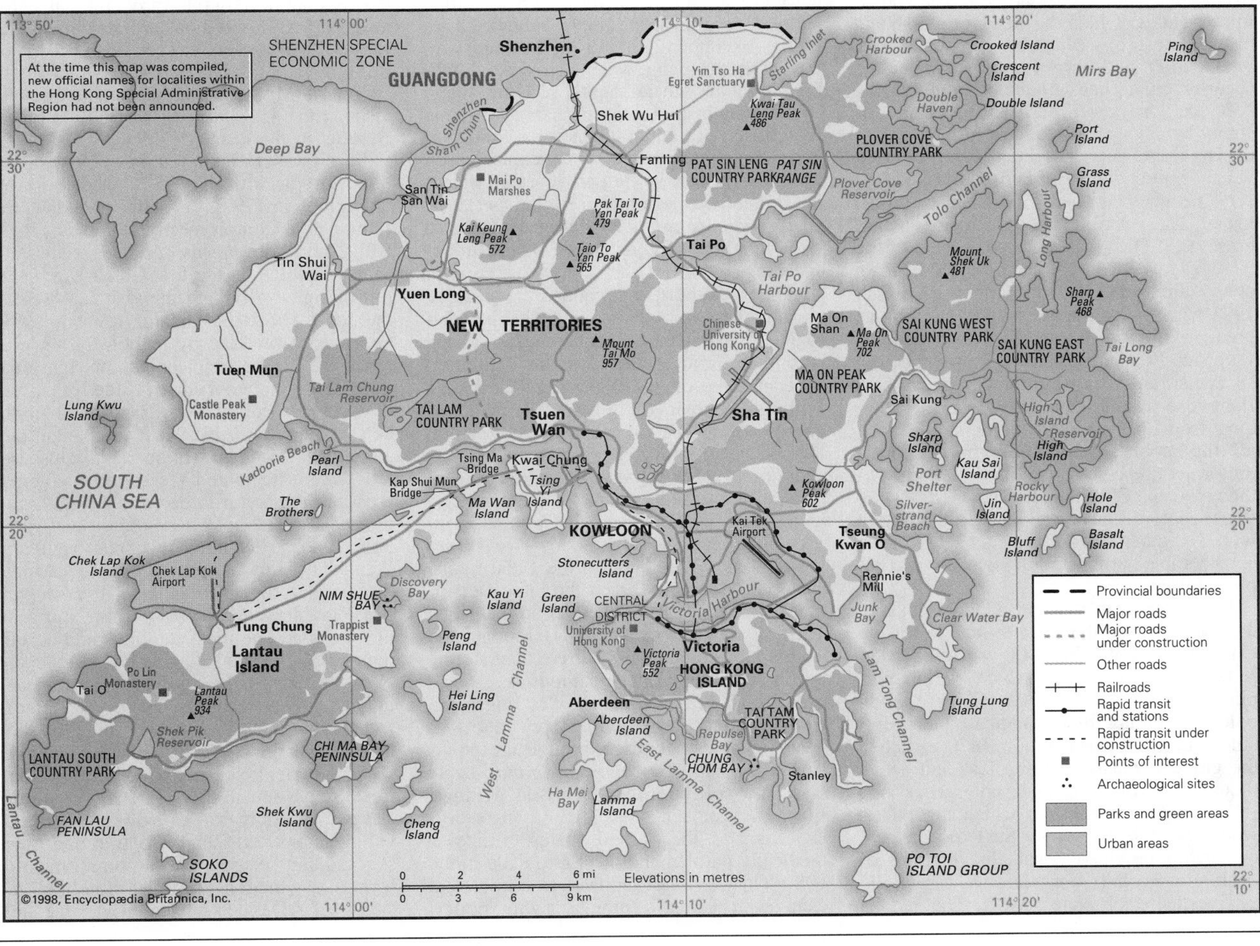

(continued from page 411)

The prolonged deathwatch over Deng, who had gradually yielded his authority to Jiang over a number of years, provided time for his successor to consolidate his power. Considered a bantamweight when he vaulted from the leadership of Shanghai to that of the CPC in 1989, Jiang had proved the skeptics wrong by demonstrating considerable skills as a political infighter as well as a statesman. In 1997 Jiang successfully passed four tests of leadership, beginning with Deng's death and concluding with his state visit to the U.S. that left him at year's end in a significantly stronger political position. First, like the hapless Hua Guofeng who briefly succeeded Mao in 1976, Jiang wrapped himself in the mantle of his departed predecessor. At Deng's public memorial, Jiang pledged to continue the policies of reform that Deng had initiated in 1978. Unlike Hua at the time of his patron's demise, however, Jiang had already enjoyed nearly eight years at the helm of the CPC by the time Deng died. Second, Jiang was centre stage at the ceremony in Hong Kong that marked the handover of the British colony to China, an important milestone in the historical process of national reintegration. (*See* Spotlight: *Hong Kong's Return to China.*)

The third, and the most important of Jiang's tests, came at the Congress of the CPC. There he succeeded both in ousting one of his chief rivals, Qiao Shi, from the seven-person Standing Committee of the Political Bureau, the inner sanctum of political power, and in seeding the 22-member Political Bureau as well as the CPC Central Committee with his supporters. The forced retirement of Qiao, the head of the NPC, caught most observers by surprise. Qiao, who earlier had served as China's public security chief, had gradually built up the NPC as his power base in the name of strengthening the rule of law in China. Under his leadership the NPC became a forum where limited debate and circumscribed dissent from government policies were allowed. This role might soon come to an end, however, if Qiao was replaced as head of the NPC by Li Peng, who, according to China's constitution, had to step down in March 1998 when he completed his second term as premier. Waiting in the wings to replace Li was Vice-Premier Zhu Rongji, an economic specialist ranked third in the CPC hierarchy. Jiang also ousted the elderly Gen. Liu Huaqing from the Standing Committee, which left the People's Liberation Army without a uniformed representative in that body, although Gen. Chi Haotian and Gen. Zhang Wannian joined the Political Bureau along with six other new members. This was a considerable turnover although not a complete sweep.

In his report to the 15th Congress, Jiang finally addressed the issue of how to reform China's roughly 300,000 deficit-ridden state-owned enterprises, which were a running financial sore on the Chinese body politic. Avoiding the ideologically unacceptable concept of privatization, Jiang sketched the gradual transformation of all but a few thousand of the core state enterprises into joint stock companies in which the public would be able to invest. Such prospective ownership provided a socialist fig leaf of "public ownership" for what was essentially a divestment of state assets. The details remained to be worked out. The CPC would somehow have to cushion the potentially explosive problem of widespread urban unemployment if money-losing factories were shut down as well as try to block avaricious Communist Party officials from transforming state firms into their own private assets. The CPC had made little headway in stemming the rising tide of corruption, although it finally decided to prosecute Chen Xitong on charges of corruption more than two years after the former Beijing CPC boss was removed from power. The lurid story of Chen's depravity formed the basis for an underground Chinese best-seller, *Wrath of Heaven* (1997), published under a pseudonym by an unknown author and packed with scenes of money scheming, blackmail, and illicit sex.

Although Jiang appeared to have things well in hand in Beijing, CPC control in the farther reaches of China was another matter. Growing worker and farmer protests over economic issues and continuing ethnic unrest in Tibet and Xinjiang underlay the CPC's preoccupation with stability and its resort to repression. One of the larger protests, involving tens of thousands of unemployed workers, took place in July in the city of Mianyang in Sichuan province, where the police arrested scores of demonstrators. In early February Turkic-speaking Uygur nationalists, protesting what they said was China's execution of 30 fellow Muslim activists, rioted in Yining in the northwestern province of Xinjiang, which led to further crackdowns and arrests as China's Islamic neighbours in Central Asia watched uneasily from across their borders. An internal CPC document in May 1996 identified national separatism and illegal religious activities as integral threats to Beijing's authority in Xinjiang, where terrorist bombings in the provincial capital of Urumqi and assassinations of local officials by Islamic separatists prompted Chinese officials to make thousands of arrests. An explosion on a municipal bus in Beijing in early March that killed two persons raised the spectre of ethnic violence in the capital itself, home to large numbers of Uygurs and other Turkic-speaking minorities.

Chinese authorities remained unwilling to engage the Dalai Lama in a genuine dialogue or to countenance meaningful Tibetan autonomy. Among other acts, they sentenced Tibetan musicologist Ngawang Choepel, a Fulbright scholar, to 18 years in prison on charges of spying for the U.S. and Chatral Rinpoche, a senior Tibetan lama, to six years on charges of maintaining illegal contacts with the Dalai Lama. Foreign interest in the fate of Tibet, which China had invaded in 1950, was fueled by two Hollywood films sympathetic to the Dalai Lama. The U.S. Congress forced the State Department to appoint a special coordinator on Tibet, a move denounced by Beijing, and chapters of Students for a Free Tibet sprung up on American college campuses.

Meanwhile, the voice of Wei Jingsheng, China's best-known political prisoner, was heard in other countries through the publication of *The Courage to Stand Alone* (1997), a collection of his prison writings. In mid-November, soon after Jiang's official visit to the United States, Wei was medically paroled and went into exile in the U.S. This did not appear to indicate a change in China"s human rights policy, however, as many other lesser-known opponents of the regime remained in prison.

Ever since Deng's reforms hollowed out Chinese Marxism, the legitimacy of the CPC had rested on economic performance. In 1997 China's gross domestic product grew at an annual rate of 9.6%, the highest of any less-developed country. Industrial production was up 11%, whereas consumer prices increased only a modest 2%. China's foreign currency reserves of $128 billion (July) were second only to Japan's. Although the Hong Kong stock market rode a roller coaster in the last quarter of the year, Chinese stock markets, which climbed sharply in the first half of the year, were scarcely affected by global vicissitudes. An estimated 25 million–30 million Chinese invested in the stock market in 1997, a number that could increase sharply if Jiang's plan to sell off the majority of state-owned enterprises was implemented. In May Zhou Daojiong, the chairman of the Securities Regulatory Commission, was replaced in an effort to strengthen state control over the stock market.

China's prosperity drew strength from its export-oriented industries, in which average monthly wages were only a small fraction of those in Taiwan and South Korea, to say nothing of developed countries like Japan and the U.S. This was the main reason foreign investment continued to flow into China in 1997. In 1996, the last year for which figures were available, China attracted more than a third of total global foreign investment in manufacturing, or $42 billion, far ahead of the $6.4 billion invested in second-place Mexico. Beijing used its new economic clout toward political ends, awarding a $1.5 billion aircraft contract to Europe's Airbus Industrie on the occasion of French Pres. Jacques Chirac's visit to Beijing in May and sweetening Jiang's state visit to the U.S. with a multibillion-dollar contract to the Boeing Co.

Foreign Relations. China's burgeoning trade surplus with the U.S., expected to top $40 billion in 1997, was on the agenda when Jiang held a summit meeting with U.S. Pres. Bill Clinton during his eight-day state visit to the U.S. It was the first China-U.S. summit in eight years, and the visit represented the fourth of Jiang's major tests in 1997. Greeted everywhere by demonstrators protesting China's policies on human rights and Tibet, Jiang hobnobbed with top executives of American corporations, rang the opening bell at the New York Stock Exchange, and paid visits to Pearl Harbor, Williamsburg, Va. (where he toured the restored colonial area and donned a three-cornered hat), and the Liberty Bell in Philadelphia. He allowed himself to be lectured on human rights by President Clinton and U.S. congressional leaders but defended China's record with considerable skill, asserting China's priority of "social and political stability" and declaring that China had responded correctly to what he termed the "political disturbance" in Tiananmen Square in 1989. On the subject of Tibet, Jiang likened China's policy toward the region to the emancipation of slaves in the U.S., saying that China had freed some one million Tibetan "serfs and slaves." In return for a pledge to stop providing nuclear assistance to Iran and other states, Jiang secured a U.S. commitment to lifting the sanctions that had prohibited the export of American nuclear power technology to China, to the delight of the floundering American nuclear power industry. A midyear report by the CIA identified China as a major supplier of missile technology and chemical warfare equipment to Iran and Pakistan, and it remained to be seen whether Beijing would honour its new pledge. Notwithstanding China's ambivalence toward the U.S., which it viewed as a hegemonic power attempting to obstruct China's rise, Jiang and the leaders of the CPC saw the summit meeting with the U.S. president as an important indicator of international recognition that China was now a world power that no country, not even the U.S., could afford to ignore. In that sense, Jiang's state visit to Washington was, from China's perspective, a notable success.

Playing the world statesman, Jiang visited Moscow in April, solidifying a rhetorical alignment with Russia that was based on mutual suspicion of the U.S. as well as Chinese purchases of advanced Russian military technology, particularly jet aircraft. In November, Russian Pres. Boris Yeltsin met with Jiang in Beijing, and the two leaders agreed on the final demarcation of the eastern sector of their border.

Renewing its warnings about the supposed dangers of Japanese militarism, China objected to the new guidelines announced by Tokyo and Washington governing U.S.-Japanese security cooperation. Beijing's economic diplomacy, in which the lure of the China market was the trump card of visiting Chinese leaders, had muted most European criticism of Chinese human rights abuses and thereby enabled China once again to defeat U.S. efforts in the UN Commission on Human Rights to subject China's record to international scrutiny.

China eased its pressure on Taiwan in 1997 after its sabre rattling of the previous two years, but it continued to oppose any efforts by Taiwan to gain official recognition by foreign countries or international organizations. The next test of China's policy toward Taiwan would come if Taiwan's ruling Kuomintang lost its parliamentary majority and was forced into a coalition with overtly or covertly pro-independence oppositionists. Once the Portugese-ruled enclave of Macau returned to China's sovereignty in 1999, political pressures in Beijing should force CPC leaders to step up their campaign "to return Taiwan to the embrace of the motherland."

Mao's death in 1976 had been heralded by the devastating Tangshan earthquake, which killed at least 200,000 people—a small fraction, to be sure, of the some 30 million lives claimed by the famine of 1959–61. In 1977 the Great Helmsman's embalmed body was laid in the mausoleum where it still resided. Within weeks of Mao's death, however, his successors began to dismantle his legacy. Deng's death scarcely created a ripple among the Chinese people, for whom politics was no longer in command as in Mao's day. The difference in the modes of exit of these two men was instructive. The increasingly smaller shadows cast by China's top leaders in the succession from Mao to Deng to Jiang boded well for the Chinese people, who in 1997 focused on the task that Deng had legitimized, namely, working to improve their daily lives in a society where the political struggles of the past were a fading memory.

(STEVEN I. LEVINE)

COLOMBIA

Area: 1,141,568 sq km (440,762 sq mi)
Population (1997 est.): 36,200,000
Capital: Santafé de Bogotá, D.C.
Head of state and government: President Ernesto Samper Pizano

The political situation in Colombia did not improve in 1997. The actions taken by Pres. Ernesto Samper to better his own and his government's position seemed only to increase his vulnerability. In 1996 the U.S. had removed Colombia from the list of countries believed to be making progress against illegal drug traffickers. In dealing with the thorny problem of extradition of criminals from Colombia for trials elsewhere, the Colombian legislature in November approved a constitutional amendment that allowed for nonretroactive extradition. This was not strong enough for the U.S., and so Colombia remained "decertified." This virtually eliminated the possibility of any U.S. government aid and also posed the threat of commercial sanctions. Particularly galling for Colombia was that Bolivia and Mexico, in similar drug-related difficulties, were "certified."

In January President Samper decreed an "economic state of emergency," which allowed for increases in taxes, principally stamp duties and taxes on foreign borrowings, to combat the growing national deficit and inflation pressures. In March the Constitutional Court ruled the "emergency" unjustified and annulled the fiscal changes. Subsequently, several of Samper's closest allies left his government, including Alfonso Valdivieso, the prosecutor general, and Horacio Serpa, the interior minister, both to prepare bids for the presidential elections of May 1998. Also, Carlos Medellín, who as justice minister was strongly in favour of changing the law on extradition, resigned in April. Later in the year the economy strengthened.

The most dramatic event of 1997 was the release by the largest guerrilla group, the Colombia Revolutionary Armed Forces (FARC), of 60 soldiers kidnapped in Putumayo in August 1996 and of 10 marines captured in Chocó in January 1997. After much negotiation the army evacuated 13,000 sq km (5,000 sq mi) of territory in the jungles of Caquetá, where the hostages were released. Although claimed as a satisfactory end to the hostage crisis, the fact that FARC was in overt control of an area of Colombian territory for more than four weeks was not lost on the public. A poll showed that 64% of Colombians thought that the government was losing the war against the guerrillas.

Indeed, the threat to democracy in Colombia in 1997 significantly increased. Attacks on economic targets by FARC and the other main left-wing terrorist group, the National Liberation Army (ELN), intensified. Oil installations were, as usual, a main objective, with damage achieved in more than 50 of the attacks. Several of these caused spillage of crude oil into rivers that flow into Venezuela, which created another problem for Colombia. A specific tactic emerged to disrupt the municipal elections of October 26. Widespread intimidation of declared candidates, apparently by agents of FARC and ELN working together, caused many to withdraw. From the other end of the political spectrum, right-wing militias, formed by landowners to protect their own interests, made similar threats to left-leaning candidates, forcing further withdrawals.

In the midst of this serious challenge, Samper appointed a Commission of National Conciliation in July to explore the possibility of a peace accord with FARC and ELN. This was not well received by the military and did not impress the guerrilla groups, which felt they had gained the initiative. An initial meeting in Cúcuta was called off, and a month later Sen. Jorge Cristo was assassinated in Cúcuta when Pres. Rafael Caldera of Venezuela was due to meet Samper there to discuss the strained relations between the two countries.

In the elections at the end of October, Samper's Liberal Party again was victorious. Voter turnout was low, however, and there were reports of cancellation of ballots due to intimidation.

(PETER POLLARD)

COMOROS

Area: 1,862 sq km (719 sq mi), excluding the 373-sq km (144-sq mi) island of Mayotte, a de facto dependency of France since 1976
Population (1997 est.): 514,000 (excluding 128,000 on Mayotte)
Capital: Moroni
Chief of state: President Mohamed Taki Abdoulkarim
Head of government: Prime Ministers Ahmed Abdou and, from December 7, Nourdine Bourhane

During August 1997 two of Comoros's islands—Anjouan and Moheli—announced their secession from the nation despite promises by Pres. Mohamed Taki of greater island autonomy. They wanted to reestablish their connection with France. The French government reaffirmed its support for the territorial integrity of Comoros, and the Organization of African Unity (OAU) appealed for calm and said the separation of Anjouan was "totally unacceptable." OAU-sponsored peace talks followed. Early in September, however, government troops from Moroni set out by boat to recapture Anjouan despite appeals from the OAU and France to negotiate instead. The 300 troops met fierce resistance, and though the government at first claimed it had regained control of the island, it later admitted defeat. The government expressed "profound regret" that France had refused to offer support and also complained to the UN Security Council that foreign mercenaries had taken part in the conflict on the side of Anjouan. President Taki on December 7 appointed Nourdine Bourhane, a native of Anjouan, prime minister.

(GUY ARNOLD)

This article updates the *Micropædia* article COMOROS.

CONGO, DEMOCRATIC REPUBLIC OF THE (ZAIRE)

Area: 2,344,858 sq km (905,354 sq mi)
Population (1997 est.): 46,674,000
Capital: Kinshasa
Chief of state: Presidents Mobutu Sese Seko until May 16 and, from May 29, Head of State and Government Laurent Kabila
Head of government: First State Commissioners (Prime Ministers) Léon Kengo wa Dondo until March 18, Étienne Tshisekedi from April 2 to April 9, and Likulia Bolongo from April 9 to May 16

By the beginning of 1997, the rebellion that had begun in the eastern province of Kivu in October 1996 had made significant progress. In January the government launched a counteroffensive under new military leadership and supported by some 300 European mercenaries. The Zairean troops, even though they were backed by air strikes, were no match for the rebels, however, and retreated before the rebels' advance, looting the villages they were meant to protect as they did so. The ailing president, Mobutu Sese Seko, tried, unsuccessfully, to enlist the aid of other African countries, but even so, the claim of the rebel leader, Laurent Kabila (*see* BIOGRAPHIES), in February that unless Mobutu surrendered power within two weeks he would be overthrown by military force seemed wildly optimistic.

After talks with U.S. officials and a number of African leaders—among them Pres. Robert Mugabe of Zimbabwe, who supplied arms and equipment to Kabila, and Pres. Yoweri Museveni of Uganda (*see* BIOGRAPHIES), who sympathized with the rebel cause—Pres. Nelson Mandela of South Africa announced in late February that an attempt would be made to initiate discussions between Kabila and representatives of President Mobutu. This was the first of a series of efforts by Mandela and U.S. officials to bring the leaders together, all of which failed because of Kabila's unwillingness to call a halt to his victorious advance until Mobutu agreed to resign and the president's refusal to do so. In the meantime, disillusioned Zairean leaders became convinced that Western powers, and the U.S. in particular, were eager to abandon their longtime ally, having no further need of Mobutu's government as a bastion against communism in sub-Saharan Africa.

Zairean hopes that popular support for the rebels might be undermined by the parliament's dismissal on March 18 of Prime Minister Léon Kengo wa Dondo—an act later endorsed by Mobutu—and his replacement on April 2 by a longtime leader of the opposition to Mobutu, Étienne Tshisekedi, were short-lived. Faced with a new rebel offensive in April, hundreds of Zairean troops defected to the enemy.

Mobutu's decision to dismiss Tshisekedi on April 9 caused further splits among Zaire's leaders. At that time international mining companies, forseeing Kabila's rise to power, hurriedly began making deals with the rebel leader to protect or extend their interests in Zaire. Advancing westward through Zaire at an astonishing speed, Kabila's forces, spearheaded by Tutsi warriors trained in Uganda and Rwanda, entered Kinshasa without serious opposition on May 17. Mobutu fled to Morocco, where he died on September 7 in Rabat. (*See* OBITUARIES.) An attempt by Tshisekedi to lay claim to the office of prime minister was not successful. Kabila became president and signed a 15-point constitutional decree giving himself full legislative, executive, and military powers, pending the adoption of a new constitution by a constituent assembly. Zaire was renamed the Democratic Republic of the Congo.

To outside observers Kabila was an unknown factor, but backed by the goodwill of a number of foreign powers, including the U.S. and most members of the European Union though not France, he was able within a few months to bring some order into the chaotic economy he had inherited from Mobutu, and civil servants were paid regularly for the first time in many years. The delay before he finally agreed in late November to permit foreign observers to investigate allegations of atrocities committed by his troops during their advance across the country may have signaled an unwillingness to be dictated to by outsiders, but it also threatened to discourage external donors.

(KENNETH INGHAM)

This article updates the *Macropædia* article CENTRAL AFRICA: *Zaire*.

CONGO, REPUBLIC OF THE

Area: 342,000 sq km (132,047 sq mi)
Population (1997 est.): 2,583,000
Capital: Brazzaville
Chief of state: Presidents Pascal Lissouba and, from October 25, Denis Sassou-Nguesso
Head of government: Prime Ministers David Charles Ganao and, from September 8, Bernard Kolelas

ROGER LEMOYNE—GAMMA LIAISON

Rwandan children are evacuated back to their homeland from a transit centre in Kisangani, Zaire. More than 100,000 Rwandan refugees in eastern Zaire were forced to flee their camps as rebel forces clashed with government troops. The rebels, led by Laurent Kabila, overthrew the government in May.

In the first half of 1997, outbreaks of fighting between militias loyal to Pres. Pascal Lissouba and those allied with former head of state Denis Sassou-Nguesso escalated into full-scale civil war. On February 1 former Sassou-Nguesso militiamen in the process of integration into the national army mutinied at their training base in Loudima, some 250 km (150 mi) west of Brazzaville. Although the army restored order within days, tensions remained high, erupting into armed confrontations again in June, with widespread looting in the capital. At least 2,000 people died. French troops evacuated an estimated 5,000 foreign nationals and then withdrew from the country. On June 14 a fierce artillery attack was launched on the airport. Brazzaville was effectively split between the two factions, with neither side willing to negotiate despite calls from the UN Security Council and neighbouring states. Finally, on July 5, Lissouba and Sassou-Nguesso accepted terms of a truce brokered by Gabonese Pres. Omar Bongo. Sporadic shooting continued, however, for the next two months. On September 14 the presidents of eight African countries and other representatives met in Libreville, Gabon, to find a more permanent solution to the troubles, even as government helicopter gunships attacked opponents' positions in Brazzaville. Hopes of a peaceful resolution were dashed when, in October, Sassou-Nguesso's forces, aided by 3,500 soldiers from neighbouring Angola, seized control of Brazzaville and Pointe Noire. On October 19 Lissouba fled to Burkina Faso, while members of his government sought asylum in the Democratic Republic of the Congo, and on October 25 Sassou-Nguesso assumed the presidency.

The economy of the oil-rich nation was badly hit by the fighting, and the educational system was in turmoil. In March security forces used tear gas to break up a student demonstration called to protest the 16-month delay in payments of their grants. There were fears that a second invalid school year would have to be declared.

(NANCY ELLEN LAWLER)

This article updates the *Macropædia* article CENTRAL AFRICA: *Congo*.

COSTA RICA

Area: 51,100 sq km (19,730 sq mi)
Population (1997 est.): 3,468,000
Capital: San José
Head of state and government: President José María Figueres Olsen

In the months preceding the general elections to be held in early 1998, the candidate of the opposition Social Christian Unity Party, Miguel Angel Rodríguez, held the lead in opinion polls over José Miguel Corrales of the ruling National Liberation Party (PLN). Corrales's nomination as PLN candidate was tainted by charges of ballot rigging. This did not help the party's image, already at a low ebb as Pres. José María Figueres was judged the least popular president of recent history, owing to corruption scandals and mishandling of the economy. In 1996, with the growth of gross domestic product under 1%, inflation almost 15%, and a fiscal deficit of 5.5% of GDP, Costa Rica's performance was among the least successful in Latin America. Targets set in a central bank economic recovery plan at the beginning of 1997 had to be revised by the third quarter; projected GDP growth was lowered from 3% to 2.5%, and the public-sector deficit, forecast at 3.5% of GDP, was exceeding 4%.

Further discredit to the country's institutions resulted from allegations that legislators and judicial officials were among many involved in the narcotics trade between South America and the U.S. With only a lightly armed police force and no army, Costa Rica was hard-pressed to combat either the drug traffickers or money launderers. In this light, when Rodríguez sought investment from Carlos Hank González of Mexico's Institutional Revolutionary Party, who was under investigation in the U.S. for money laundering, his presidential candidacy was damaged. (BEN BOX)

This article updates the *Macropædia* article CENTRAL AMERICA: *Costa Rica.*

CÔTE D'IVOIRE

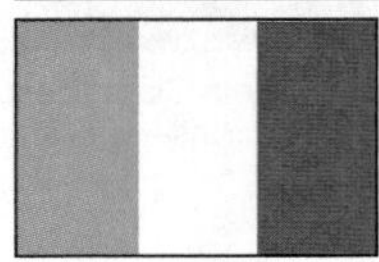

Area: 322,463 sq km (124,504 sq mi)
Population (1997 est.): 14,986,000
Seats of government: predominantly Abidjan; some ministries have relocated to Yamoussoukro
Chief of state: President Henri Konan Bédié
Head of government: Prime Minister Daniel Kablan Duncan

By-elections were held on Dec. 29, 1996, in six constituencies where outbreaks of violence had closed polls during the 1995 legislative elections. The ruling Democratic Party of Côte d'Ivoire (PDCI) added three seats to its overwhelming majority in the National Assembly. In August the government announced a constitutional reform bill that would, among other things, establish a Senate whose president would automatically become interim successor to the chief of state in case of death or incapacitation.

Once again, student unrest fractured the academic year. One student was killed after police broke up a demonstration outside the Ministry of Security in January. Students rioted at the Abidjan campus and closed the National University. In April the University of Bouaké was closed after protesters burned down the Welfare Services Centre. The banned Federation of Students and Pupils announced a new boycott of classes, beginning April 22, because of the government's failure to improve working and living conditions. In mid-June new talks began to deal with the students' grievances.

Further economic liberalization took place as import restrictions on used vehicles were eased. Efforts to determine the ownership of rural land were undertaken in hopes of creating a more viable property market and allowing greater access to credit. Coffee production was expected to increase in anticipation of the government's freeing of prices. The government, however, remained reluctant to allow a similar liberalization for cocoa despite considerable pressure from the World Bank. (NANCY ELLEN LAWLER)

This article updates the *Macropædia* article WESTERN AFRICA: *Côte d'Ivoire*.

CROATIA

Area: 56,610 sq km (21,857 sq mi)
Population (1997 est.): 4,774,000
Capital: Zagreb
Chief of state: President Franjo Tudjman
Head of government: Prime Minister Zlatko Matesa

In 1997 Croatia continued to struggle out of the morass left by the Balkan conflicts and toward national reconstruction. The reintegration of Croatia's eastern Slavonia region, which had been occupied by Serb forces, claimed a great deal of attention during the year. In April a mixed Croat-Serb Transitional Police Force was formed. On May 1 a state commission was established to reintroduce all Croatian state bodies gradually into the region, and in August the Croatian educational system, with special facilities for Serbs, was reestablished. Communications, postal, and transport services were restored; public enterprises returned; and pensions were paid to about 20,000 Serb residents. Under United Nations supervision but with many irregularities reported, the region participated in the national elections on April 13. The ruling Croatian Democratic Union (HDZ) and the Independent Democratic Serb Party won a majority of votes cast, and the two ethnic-based parties formed coalition administrations in the main Slavonian towns of Vukovar and Beli Manastir. Serb representatives took their seats in Osijek for the first time since war broke out six years earlier.

Administrative progress was not matched by smooth repopulation of eastern Slavonia and other areas of Croatia by the hundreds of thousands of Serbs who had fled or had been forced out during hostilities. (Neither were the large numbers of Croats who had been displaced from their homes in Serb-held territories eager to return, however.) The slow pace of repatriation in Croatia and the frequent reports of anti-Serb incidents led to the UN Security Council's decision to extend the UN mandate in the region beyond July 15 and to criticize Croatia formally on September 18.

In July the World Bank and the International Monetary Fund postponed action on large loans intended to assist Croatia's economic-stabilization program. The action—or inaction—was taken in reaction to what the U.S. State Department called Croatia's "insufficient compliance" with the provisions of the Dayton peace accords, including resistance to the repatriation of Serb refugees and lack of cooperation in bringing persons accused of war crimes to trial at the international tribunal in The Hague.

In the local elections on April 13 and

presidential elections on June 15, the opposition tried to trade on public frustration with perceived widespread government corruption and concerns regarding Pres. Franjo Tudjman's authoritarian style. The Organization for Security and Cooperation in Europe criticized the HDZ for misusing government prerogatives, including its control over the state media. Even so, the incumbent HDZ scored impressive victories and regained control of the capital, Zagreb. President Tudjman himself won about 60% of votes cast and earned a second five-year term. Voter turnout was quite low, however, which indicated that opposition parties had failed to offer a meaningful alternative, and their leaders bickered openly instead of focusing their criticism on the HDZ.

Responding to public pressure, the government initiated a campaign against official corruption. On September 13 the assistant minister of economy and his top aide were jailed for accepting bribes. Five days later in Split, the local commander of the military police and 10 others were arrested for their alleged involvement in a narcotics and stolen vehicles trafficking ring.

The economy continued its general recovery in 1997, led by a tourism industry that in many places returned to prewar levels. Upgrading the country's transportation system, especially airports and highways, became a key national objective. With much fanfare the Karlovac–Rijeka highway, connecting the country's interior to the Istrian coast, was partially opened in March. On September 20 Karl Habsburg, heir to the Habsburg throne, baptized his son Ferdinand Zvonimir in Zagreb in deference to the last Croatian king, Zvonimir, who ruled during the 11th century.

(MAX PRIMORAC)

This article updates the *Macropædia* article BALKAN STATES: *Croatia.*

JOHN MCCONNICO—ASSOCIATED PRESS

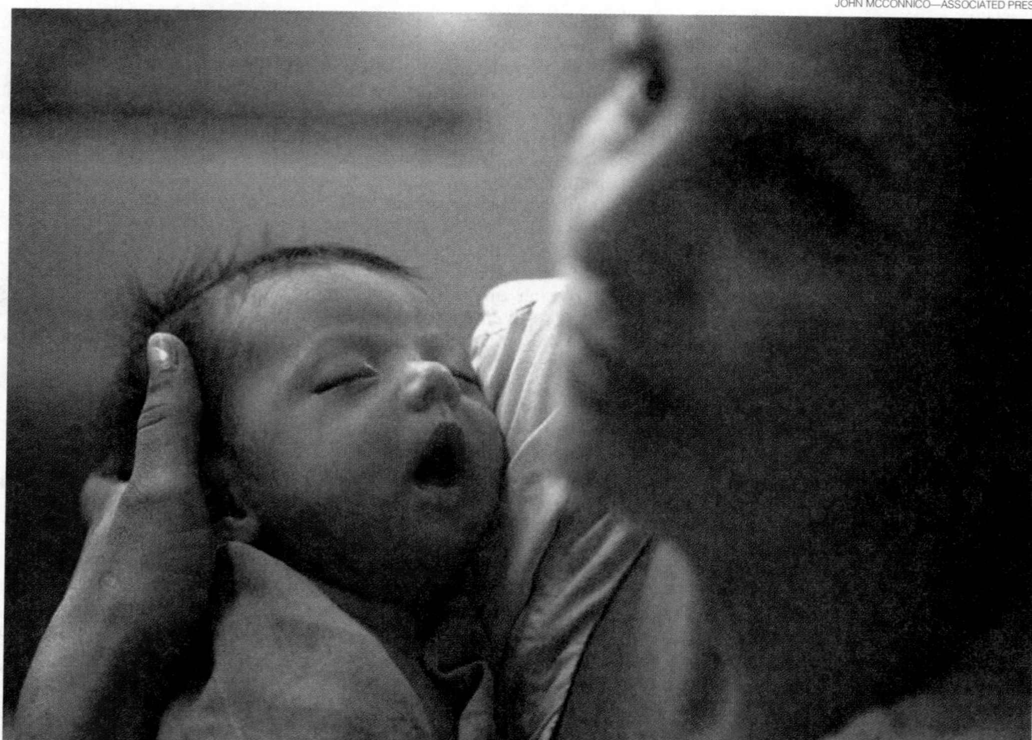

A mother holds her month-old daughter at a hospital in Santa Clara. Despite a long U.S.-led economic embargo on Cuba, the country's infant mortality rate—9 deaths per 1,000 live births—was among the world's lowest, and medical progress was still being made even with access to medicine limited.

CUBA

Area: 110,861 sq km (42,804 sq mi)
Population (1997 est.): 11,190,000
Capital: Havana
Head of state and government: President of the Council of State and President of the Council of Ministers Fidel Castro Ruz

The year 1997 began on a positive note, with the economy showing significant gains, real gross domestic product growing 7.8% in 1996 despite the damage caused by Hurricane Lili in October 1996. Nickel production increased more than 30%, and the number of tourist arrivals passed the one million mark for the first time, an increase of 35% over 1995. The shortage of foreign exchange remained critical, however, and the 1996 trade deficit of $1,729,000,000 made the country increasingly vulnerable to pressure from the U.S. trade embargo. The 1997 sugar harvest was insufficiently financed because of the reticence of lenders to provide funds for any sugar produced from cane fields that had formerly been U.S.-owned, and output was expected to be less than the 4,450,000 metric tons harvested in 1996.

Despite worldwide condemnation of the Helms-Burton legislation enacted in 1996, which extended sanctions to non-U.S. companies that did business in Cuba and allowed U.S. citizens to sue foreign companies for conducting business in confiscated American property in Cuba, a complaint brought by the European Union against the U.S. at the World Trade Organization was suspended. U.S. Pres. Bill Clinton was expected to ask the U.S. Congress to amend Title IV of the legislation (concerning the denial of U.S. entry visas to employees and shareholders of "trafficking" companies), and he was expected to continue to waive Title III (authorizing court cases against those "trafficking" in expropriated assets). Supporters of the law, however, introduced their own amendments to the U.S. Congress that would have the effect of tightening the legislation. The Cuban government mounted a diplomatic campaign against the new legislation, with senior officials visiting every country in Latin America as well as promoting relations with the island's Caribbean neighbours. The heads of state of Jamaica, Barbados, and Saint Vincent and the Grenadines paid official visits to Cuba, and ambassadors of Caribbean nations in the U.S. issued a rejection of U.S. legislative proposals that would impose sanctions on their countries for doing business with Cuba.

In May Cuba accused the U.S. of using a crop-spraying aircraft to cause an infestation of thrips in the province of Matanzas. The UN Food and Agriculture Organization provided assistance in controlling the plague. Cuba requested a hearing under the UN convention on biological warfare to consider the case, and a consultative meeting in Geneva in late August ended inconclusively.

The tourist industry was rocked by several bombings, first in April at the Meliá Cohiba hotel and later in July at the Capri and Nacional hotels, all in Havana. Another bomb went off in the Meliá Cohiba in August. The bombings were the first since the 1960s, and the government blamed Cuban refugee extremists in Miami, Fla. Also in July the U.S. Coast Guard prevented a refugee flotilla from entering Cuban waters, and the national baseball team of Cuba pulled out of a series in the U.S. because of threats from Miami exiles. The first bombing fatality occurred at the beginning of September, when an Italian was killed by an explosion in one of three hotels on Havana's seafront that were bombed on the same day along with a popular tourist restaurant. About a week later the Interior Ministry announced that it was holding a former paratrooper from El Salvador, Raúl Ernesto Cruz León, who had confessed to working as a mercenary and planting six bombs. Although he did not reveal for whom he was working, Cuba accused the Miami-based Cuban American National Foundation (CANF) of being behind the bombings, an allegation it denied. Influential CANF Chairman Jorge Mas Canosa died in Miami in November. (*See* OBITUARIES.)

On July 12 there was a ceremonial homecoming for the remains of revolutionary leader Ernesto ("Che") Guevara and six Cuban guerrillas who were killed in Bolivia on Oct. 9, 1967. Their bodies were exhumed from a secret grave and returned to Cuba to lay in state. More than 12,500 delegates attended the 14th World Festival of Youth and Students, held in Havana at the end of July, although only 5,000 had been expected. Despite warnings by U.S. authorities that their attendance contravened the Trading with the Enemy Act, 849 Americans attended, and the U.S. delegation was the largest of any country.

In October the Cuban Communist Party held its first Congress since 1991. No new policy initiatives or changes in leadership were announced. For the first time since the revolution, Christmas was declared an official holiday in Cuba.

(SARAH CAMERON)

This article updates the *Macropædia* article THE WEST INDIES: *Cuba*.

CYPRUS

Area: 9,251 sq km (3,572 sq mi) for the entire island; the area of the Turkish Republic of Northern Cyprus (TRNC), proclaimed unilaterally (1983) in the occupied northern third of the island, 3,355 sq km (1,295 sq mi)
Population (1997 est.): island 860,000; TRNC only, 198,000 (including recent Turkish settlers and Turkish military)
Capital: Lefkosia/Lefkosa (also known as Nicosia)
Head(s) of state and government: President Glafcos Clerides; of the TRNC, President Rauf Denktash

Cyprus in 1997 remained dominated by the conflicts between the Greek and Turkish segments of the population, which had resulted in the island's geographic partition. Incidents along the dividing line between the Greek and Turkish sectors continued, although the border was quieter than in 1996. Residents of each sector were allowed to cross the border to visit sites of religious and historical importance, a measure that helped improve relations. The presidents of each sector, Glafcos Clerides and Rauf Denktash, met for one-on-one talks, first in New York City and then in Switzerland. Although the talks produced no specific results, the dialogue was expected to continue. Despite the partition, negotiations for membership in the European Union continued, with formal accession talks scheduled to begin in early 1998.

The UN force in Cyprus continued its peacekeeping mission. The British Sovereign Base Areas, which were maintained under British rule when Cyprus achieved independence in 1960, were the targets of criticism and demonstrations, both from environmentalists and from Cypriots resenting the bases' separate administration.

Another source of tension came in the form of a Greek Cypriot proposal to buy a Russian air defense missile system costing $600 million. The missiles, which were scheduled to be delivered in mid-1998, would dramatically change the strategic balance between the two Cypriot regimes. The missile deal was representative of the increased economic links between Greek Cyprus and Eastern Europe.

The economy, always stronger on the Greek side, experienced a slowdown in 1997 but recovered, and gross domestic product rose 3% over the previous fiscal year. Offshore investment continued, with Greek Cyprus ranking fifth in the world in merchant shipping (down from fourth in 1996). Work began on a desalinization plant to overcome the island's chronic water shortage.

(GEORGE H. KELLING)

CZECH REPUBLIC

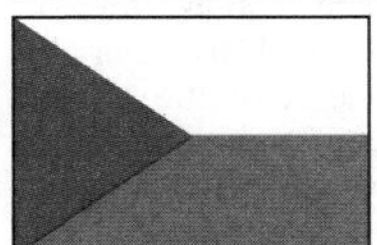

Area: 78,866 sq km (30,450 sq mi)
Population (1997 est.): 10,307,000
Capital: Prague
Chief of state: President Vaclav Havel
Head of government: Prime Ministers Vaclav Klaus until November 30 and, from December 16, Josef Tosovsky

For the Czech Republic, 1997 was a year of foreign policy success and economic disappointment. It was the year the country "returned to Europe," being offered membership in NATO on July 8 and being invited on July 16 to start membership talks with the European Union (EU). These long-awaited developments, however, were overshadowed by the economic and political crisis that emerged in the spring. Although Prime Minister Vaclav Klaus had claimed as early as January 1994 that the Czech economic transition was over, in the first months of 1997 it became apparent that much work remained. Many problems were caused by the government's failure to ensure adequate firm restructuring and to create transparent financial market regulations. The Cabinet's delay in dealing with health care, energy, transportation, education, and housing reform was also criticized.

Another problem was the government's inability to communicate effectively with the opposition or with the country's population in general. The public's frustration was already apparent a year earlier, in the May–June 1996 elections, when the three parties supporting Klaus won just 99 of 200 parliamentary seats. By late March 1997, however, Klaus's minority government had gained a parliamentary majority, thanks to support from two deputies who had been expelled from the opposition Czech Social Democratic Party (CSSD).

On April 16 the government announced a package of austerity measures to address the rising trade and budget deficits and growing public-sector wages. Most controversial was the introduction of a 20% import deposit, which was canceled in August following criticism from the EU. With opinion polls showing a steady fall in the public's confidence in the government, Pres. Vaclav Havel began calls for the Cabinet's resignation.

The economic crisis reached a climax in the last two weeks of May when the Czech National Bank drove up interest rates and spent approximately $3 billion to defend the koruna, which was under continuing pressure from speculators. On May 26 the bank abolished the 15% trading band in which the exchange rate was allowed to fluctuate. The next day the koruna lost 10% of its value against the dollar, and seven years of currency stability ended.

The chairmen of the three ruling coalition parties announced radical measures aimed at resolving the economic crisis, and Klaus was forced to admit to economic policy errors. The government was also reshuffled, with Industry and Trade Minister Vladimir Dlouhy and Finance Minister Ivan Kocarnik resigning on May 23 and May 24, respectively. Other Cabinet changes included the replacement of Deputy Prime Minister Jan Kalvoda and Minister of Local Development Jaromir Schneider. Kalvoda's exit from politics brought in the more popular Michael Zantovsky to replace him in March as Civic Democratic Alliance chairman.

On June 10 the government barely survived a parliamentary vote of confidence, called for by Klaus and used for the first time in Czech history. The two former CSSD deputies helped bring the government a 101–99 victory. The two junior coalition parties finally abandoned Klaus, however, as the Christian Democratic Union caused controversies over his economic and defense policies. Klaus resigned on November 30. Two weeks later Havel appointed a nonparty figure, National Bank Director Josef Tosovsky, to form a caretaker government.

The economic crisis had a strong impact on the economy, bringing annual gross domestic product growth down to just 1.2% in the second quarter. The economy was also adversely affected by a five-day railroad workers strike in February and by severe flooding in July. The floods, the worst of the century, caused at least 47 deaths and an estimated 50 billion koruny in damage. The strike cost the country an estimated 1 billion koruny and was the most serious case of labour unrest since November 1989. Meanwhile, the koruna's collapse contributed to the failure of at least 10 travel agencies during the summer, and troubles in the banking sector continued to surface.

In foreign affairs a long-awaited Czech-German declaration aimed at improving bilateral ties was ratified by the two countries' parliaments by early March. Relations with Slovakia reached a low point, and Slovakia temporarily recalled its ambassador to the Czech Republic on April 9. On the other hand, the issue of the common state border was definitively settled on July 25 with the swap of two villages and other borderland. Czech-Canadian ties were complicated after an August 7 TV report that depicted Czech Roma (Gypsies) living well in Canada led some 1,000 Roma to request refugee status in that country by late September.

(SHARON FISHER)

This article updates the *Macropædia* article CZECH AND SLOVAK REPUBLICS: *Czech Republic*.

DENMARK

Area: 43,094 sq km (16,639 sq mi)
Population (1997 est.): 5,284,000
Capital: Copenhagen
Chief of state: Queen Margrethe II
Head of government: Prime Minister Poul Nyrup Rasmussen

Political concern in Denmark throughout 1997 focused primarily on the country's relationship with the European Union (EU). At a summit in Amsterdam in June, Prime Minister Poul Nyrup Rasmussen and the other heads of government of EU member states agreed on the Amsterdam Treaty, amendments to the Maastricht Treaty, which included making job creation a formal EU goal and increasing cooperation in matters of security and foreign affairs. In a speech to the Folketing (national legislature) in October, Rasmussen announced that a national referendum would be held on the Amsterdam Treaty in May 1998, after a Supreme Court ruling on the constitutional legality of existing EU treaties. An opinion poll showed 46% of Danes in favour of ratifying the treaty, 31% opposed, and the remainder undecided.

A premature general election was averted in the fall when the opposition Liberal and Conservative parties reached an agreement with Denmark's Social Democrat-led government on a compulsory pension savings scheme that was part of an austerity package to cool the overheated economy. The package, designed to curb galloping private consumption, also included increased stamp duties on housing loans and extra public expenditure cuts in the state budget for 1998.

In local elections that took place throughout the nation in November, the Social Democratic Party retained its position as Denmark's strongest party. Its level of support, however, fell from 34.1% in the 1993 local polls to 33.1%. Contesting its first election, the far-right Danish People's Party won 6.8% of the vote.

The year brought hope of peace in the four-year-old feud between rival motorcycle gangs in Scandinavia. In September leather-clad leaders of the Hell's Angels and Bandidos gangs appeared on television to announce a truce and pledged to work on a pact to end their conflict, which had killed 10 people and wounded over 70 in Denmark, Sweden, Finland, and Norway since the summer of 1993. Danish authorities were unimpressed by the truce, however. Tight legislation curbing biker activity remained in force, and police surveillance of the gangs continued amid fears that the end of the feud might mean an escalation of gang involvement in drug trafficking, arms trading, and prostitution. Police efforts had also attracted attention earlier in the year when seven suspected neo-Nazis were arrested in Copenhagen on January 18 for allegedly planning to send letter bombs to British left-wing activists and to sports personalities in racially mixed marriages.

In June Queen Margrethe II inaugurated the $5 billion, 18-km (11-mi) Great Belt (Storebælt) rail tunnel and bridge connecting the eastern island of Zealand, on which Copenhagen stands, and the central island of Funen. The completion of the construction project ended 114 years of ferry service across the Store Strait and cut the crossing time from more than one hour to just seven minutes. In addition, a suspension bridge spanning the strait was due to open in 1998, and work was well under way on building a road and railroad bridge-tunnel link over The Sound (Øresund) between Copenhagen and southern Sweden, which was scheduled to open in 2000.

During 1997 Denmark held the chairmanship of the Organization for Security and Cooperation in Europe, steering a program of peace promotion in countries of the former Soviet Union. On July 12 U.S. Pres. Bill Clinton visited Copenhagen to thank Denmark for its stalwart championing of the independence of the Baltic states (Estonia, Latvia, and Lithuania) after the breakup of the Soviet Union and for its participation in multinational peacekeeping operations in former Yugoslavia. Clinton's visit drew a tumultuous response from Danes, tens of thousands of whom flocked to hear his open-air address in the heart of the capital. It was the first time that a U.S. president had visited Denmark while in office.

(CHRISTOPHER FOLLETT)

This article updates the *Macropædia* article DENMARK.

DJIBOUTI

Area: 23,200 sq km (8,950 sq mi)
Population (1997 est.): 622,000
Capital: Djibouti
Chief of state: President Hassan Gouled Aptidon
Head of government: Prime Minister Barkat Gourad Hamadou

On Sept. 2, 1997, 11 Djibouti soldiers were killed and 16 were injured in an attack in the northern part of the nation. Though no group claimed responsibility for the action, most government officials blamed it on Afar rebels who belonged to the Front for the Restoration of Unity and Democracy. Two days later Pres. Hassan Gouled Aptidon met with French Pres. Jacques Chirac to discuss the situation. In August France had announced that its 3,100 garrison troops in Djibouti might be reduced. This could be a serious economic setback for Djibouti, since the troops had created an estimated one-third of the country's gross domestic product.

Four former leaders of the ruling party, the Popular Rally for Progress, were released from prison on January 10. They had been jailed in August 1996 for insulting President Aptidon. In addition, they were to be deprived of their civil rights for the next five years, a penalty they sought to have nullified when they were released from prison.

(GUY ARNOLD)

This article updates the *Macropædia* article EASTERN AFRICA: *Djibouti*.

DOMINICA

Area: 750 sq km (290 sq mi)
Population (1997 est.): 74,400
Capital: Roseau
Chief of state: President Crispin Anselm Sorhaindo
Head of government: Prime Minister Edison James

Opposition parties in January 1997 strongly objected to the sale of the Dominica Electricity Services Co. (Domlec) to Great Britain's Commonwealth Development Corporation (CDC), arguing that the purpose of the transaction could not be easily understood, a view with which the Dominica Association of Industry and Commerce seemed to agree. After the sale CDC owned 73% of Domlec and said it would invest up to $19 million to increase generation capacity and improve transmission and distribution.

In April the British government agreed to provide $1 million to fund badly needed work to protect the coastline from erosion. This was in addition to the $5 million from Britain that had already been allotted for development aid.

Dominica in 1997 became the first Caribbean country to participate in the work of Green Globe, the environmental division of the World Travel and Tourism Council, when it accepted an offer of technical assistance for an environmental management program. The government's aim was to make Dominica a model eco-tourism destination.

In his 1997–98 budget speech in July, Finance Minister Julius Timothy announced that Dominica's offshore financial sector was to be expanded by the addition of an international ship registry and by incentives to trust and insurance companies to incorporate locally. The fee for registering an international business company was reduced to $90 plus an annual license charge of $150.

(DAVID RENWICK)

This article updates the *Macropædia* article The WEST INDIES: *Dominica*.

DOMINICAN REPUBLIC

Area: 48,671 sq km (18,792 sq mi)
Population (1997 est.): 7,802,000
Capital: Santo Domingo
Head of state and government: President Leonel Fernández Reyna

Pres. Leonel Fernández and the legislature began 1997 at loggerheads over the budget. The president introduced two measures that did not require legislative approval: unification of the exchange rate and an increase in fuel prices, both of which in the future would fluctuate in line with the world market. The controversial budget package included increases in indirect taxation, cuts in direct taxation, higher wages for government workers, and lower import duties. A modified version of his budget, approved by both houses, was vetoed by the president, who increased wages for government workers by decree. He submitted a revised budget at the end of April. Price increases, rising unemployment, and electricity shortages resulted in protest strikes and violent demonstrations. These took place despite growth of 6.9% in gross domestic product during the first half of the year, inflation of 4.4% in the same period, and substantial state spending on infrastructure and construction works. In June a law was passed allowing private capital to be invested in several state corporations, including sugar and electricity, to help reduce their deficits.

At the beginning of the year, the state sugar company, Consejo Estatal de Azúcar, announced plans to employ 16,000 Haitian cane cutters for the 1997 harvest. The news led to a sharp increase in Haitian immigration, which coincided with a rising number of Haitian beggars in Santo Domingo. The result was a wave of anti-Haitian feeling, and more than 15,000 Haitians were deported. The presidents of the two countries reached an agreement in February to halt large-scale repatriations and respect human rights.

The government began investigations into corruption in the previous administration. It was alleged that military officers and senior government officials had bought and sold government-protected land, some of which was later sold for tourist development. A senior member of the Social Christian Reformist Party was arrested, accused of selling public land in the area around Puerto Plata to other officials at low prices. In September, however, the president dismissed the Santo Domingo public prosecutor, Guillermo Moreno, who had become a symbol of the fight against human rights abuses and corruption.

(SARAH CAMERON)

This article updates the *Macropædia* article The WEST INDIES: *Dominican Republic.*

ECUADOR

Area: 272,045 sq km (105,037 sq mi), including the 8,010-sq km (3,093-sq mi) Galápagos Islands
Population (1997 est.): 11,937,000 (Galápagos Islands, nearly 15,000)
Capital: Quito
Chief of state and head of government: Presidents Abdalá Bucaram Ortíz until February 6, Rosalía Arteaga Serrano from February 9 to 11, and, from February 11, Fabián Alarcón Rivera

By the end of 1996, Ecuador's new president, Abdalá Bucaram Ortíz, had managed to alienate almost all sectors of society. His government's unpopularity deepened early in 1997 with the announcement of large increases in utility prices that most adversely affected those sectors of society that had voted for Bucaram. Further proposals were, however, blocked by an unprecedented degree of unity among opposition parties.

The situation worsened when the president proposed additional price increases. A series of antigovernment demonstrations culminated in a general strike on February 5. The next day Bucaram was voted out of office by Congress on the grounds of mental incapacity, only six months after his election. Following the vote Bucaram barricaded himself in the presidential palace and refused to move. Faced with potentially violent protests, the military withdrew its support for the president, leaving him no option but to flee the country. Congress leader Fabián Alarcón was elected interim president, despite protests by Vice Pres. Rosalía Arteaga that constitutionally the presidency should pass to her.

Owing to the fact that his mandate came from Congress and not from the electorate, Alarcón was in a weak position to deal with the country's political and economic woes. His position was strengthened, however, by the results of a referendum held on May 25, asking the people to ratify Congress's removal of the previous incumbent and its appointment of Alarcón as interim president until the 1998 elections. He was given an overwhelming majority in both cases.

Ecuador endured another crisis in early July when Congress voted to dismiss the entire Supreme Court, arguing that it had become too politicized. In April the president of the court, Carlos Solórzano, had issued arrest warrants for various officials and members of Congress suspected of corruption during the Bucaram administration. The centre-right Social Christian Party was the winner in elections in November for a temporary National Assembly to reform the constitution.

(ALAN MURPHY)

EGYPT

Area: 997,739 sq km (385,229 sq mi)
Population (1997 est.): 62,110,000
Capital: Cairo
Chief of state: President Hosni Mubarak
Head of government: Prime Minister Kamal al-Janzuri

Continued support of the Middle East peace process was a major concern for Egyptian Pres. Hosni Mubarak in 1997. Early in the year Mubarak held talks with both Palestine Liberation Organization leader Yasir ʿArafat and King Hussein of Jordan, and during the World Economic Forum in Davos, Switz., in February, he met with Israeli Prime Minister Benjamin Netanyahu. In March Netanyahu

A visitor enters one of four new tunnels constructed to take fresh water from the Nile River to the Sinai Desert in northeastern Egypt. The tunnels were part of an $810 million irrigation project inaugurated in January by Egyptian Pres. Hosni Mubarak.

JASPER MORTIMER—ASSOCIATED PRESS

visited Cairo to discuss the peace process as well as espionage charges against an Israeli Arab, ʿAzzam ʿAzzam, whom Egypt's state security court sentenced in August to 15 years of hard labour for spying for Israel. Another meeting between the two leaders was held in May in Sharm ash-Shaykh, Egypt. Also in May, Mubarak tried to revive Israeli-Syrian negotiations, meeting with Syrian Pres. Hafez al-Assad in Sharm ash-Shaykh for that purpose. By the end of 1997, the Middle East peace process was in such doldrums—despite Mubarak's efforts—that Egypt decided not to attend the Middle East and North Africa Economic Summit in Qatar on November 16–18.

During the year Egypt attempted to mend fences with both Iran and Iraq. On May 6 Iranian Foreign Minister ʿAli Akbar Velayati visited Egypt to discuss bilateral relations with his Egyptian counterpart, ʿAmr Musa. Egyptian-Iraqi relations improved, and Egypt opposed the use of force after U.S. members of the UN Special Commission overseeing the elimination of Iraqi weapons of mass destruction were asked to leave Iraq. Consequently, Iraqi Deputy Prime Minister Tariq ʿAziz visited Egypt on November 20.

In June Mubarak met Libyan leader Muammar al-Qaddafi in Tobruk, Libya. The tangible result of the meeting between the two leaders was the decision to establish a joint free-trade zone and to construct a joint airport. The close relationship between Egypt and Libya became particularly controversial when U.S. officials claimed in September that the kidnapping of a prominent Libyan opposition leader, Mansur al-Kikhya, by Libyan agents in Egypt in December 1993 had been done in complicity with Egyptian security officers. Mubarak categorically denied the charges.

Sectarian tensions came to the forefront of public attention when Mustafa Mashhur, the leader of the Muslim Brotherhood, one of the two major political opposition organizations in Egypt, said in an interview in April that Copts (Egyptian Christians) should not serve in the Egyptian army and should pay a religious tax, which implied that Copts could not be trusted. The uproar that followed led to a claim by Mashhur that he was misquoted but left the impression that anti-Coptic feeling was strong even among the mainstream Islamic fundamentalists. Copts were again the target of terrorist attacks by Islamic militants in Upper Egypt. On February 12 militants of the al-Jamaʿa al-Islamiya (Islamic Group) attacked a Coptic church in Abu Qurqas, killing 10 worshipers and wounding at least 4. On March 13 militants suspected of belonging to the Islamic Group killed 13 people in the mostly Coptic village of Najʿ Dawud.

The Egyptian government's struggle against the militants of the Islamic Group and the al-Jihad organization continued unabated but was marred by major setbacks in 1997. On September 18 a tour bus in Cairo was attacked, and the Egyptian driver and nine German tourists were killed. On November 17 militants of the Islamic Group attacked tourists in the Temple of Queen Hatshepsut at Luxor in Upper Egypt, killing some 60 foreign tourists, more than the total number of foreigners previously killed by Islamic militants in Egypt since their violent campaign began in 1992. It was regarded as the bloodiest incident by Islamic militants since the assassination of Anwar as-Sadat on Oct. 6, 1981. The militants had a number of demands, among them the release of their spiritual leader, Sheik Omar Abdel-Rahman, who was serving a life sentence in the U.S. for plotting to blow up the World Trade Center in 1993. The booming Egyptian tourist industry, which brought in $3 billion per year and had an estimated record number of 4.2 million visitors in 1997, suffered a major blow. Mubarak reacted by increasing the security measures in tourist areas.

Unless Mubarak opened up the political system by allowing free elections (the last free elections in Egypt were held in January 1950) and poured massive aid to the underdeveloped regions of Upper Egypt, the recruitment of militants among unemployed and impoverished Egyptian youth was likely to continue. On February 23 the People's Assembly approved a presidential decree extending martial law for three more years. Martial law allowed detention without trial and extended the jurisdiction of military courts to civilians. One of the basic demands of all political opposition parties in Egypt was the abrogation of martial law.

(MARIUS K. DEEB)

EL SALVADOR

Area: 21,041 sq km (8,124 sq mi)
Population (1997 est.): 5,662,000
Capital: San Salvador
Head of state and government: President Armando Calderón Sol

Elections were held on March 16, 1997, for the 84 members of the national legislature and for 262 mayors. With more than half the electorate staying away from the polls, the vote was a resounding success for the former guerrilla force, the Farabundo Martí National Liberation Front (FMLN), now a social democratic rather than a Marxist party. As well as winning the powerful post of mayor of San Salvador, the FMLN won 39% of the vote and gained 27 seats in the legislature. The ruling Nationalist Republican Alliance (ARENA) gained 35% of the vote and managed to win 28 seats in the legislature. The next largest party, the right-wing National Conciliation Party, won 11 seats.

Pres. Armando Calderón said that economic policy would not change despite the strong gains by the FMLN, but the election result immediately cast doubt on the government's privatization program. This concern was borne out when all opposition parties in the legislature united in May to vote in favour of repealing the telecommunications privatization law. The law would have allowed 51% of the company, ANTEL, to be held by one strategic investor, and 10% by employees, while the remainder was to be sold to private investors through the local stock market. The opposition parties favoured keeping 51% in the hands of the government. The president refused to veto the repeal, saying he would seek other ways of finding fresh capital for ANTEL, but this led to the resignation of Alfredo Mena Lagos, the state modernization commissioner and architect of the privatization program. On July 24 the legislature passed a law that divided ANTEL into two companies, one to control the physical plant and terrestrial network and one to manage the sale of frequencies. The government was a minority shareholder; a foreign investor could acquire 51% and employees retain 10%.

The financial markets were rocked by the discovery of a large-scale fraud. Roberto Mathies Hill, a prominent business sup-

An El Salvadoran fisherman who lost his leg in a land-mine explosion in 1985 is carried from his boat on his wife's back. The effects of a civil war that claimed 75,000 lives and injured thousands more in the 1980s and early '90s were still being felt in 1997.

TOMASZ TOMASZEWSKI—VISUM

porter of ARENA, was arrested for having diverted funds from two finance companies, Finsepro and Insepro, to prop up other companies that he owned and that were on the verge of bankruptcy. Some 1,400 depositors were affected, and losses were calculated at $113 million. The nation's superintendent of financial operations was sacked for not having spotted the fraud earlier, and the FBI was called in to investigate possible money laundering.

(SARAH CAMERON)

This article updates the *Macropædia* article CENTRAL AMERICA: *El Salvador.*

EQUATORIAL GUINEA

Area: 28,051 sq km (10,831 sq mi)
Population (1997 est.): 443,000
Capital: Malabo
Chief of state: President Brig. Gen. Teodoro Obiang Nguema Mbasogo
Head of government: Prime Minister Angel Serafin Seriche Dougan

In May 1997 Spain's prime minister, José María Aznar, sent a message to Pres. Teodoro Obiang Nguema that urged him to make progress in the transition to democracy. Aznar called upon the president to implement the Document of Assessment of the National Pact and Legislative Agreement 1997, which had been signed in April by the government and 13 opposition parties. In June Spain agreed to investigate whether an Equatorial Guinean opposition leader, Severo Moto, then living in Spain, had been involved in a 1996 coup attempt in his country; if so, he would lose his status as a political refugee.

When Spain decided to maintain Moto's status, Equatorial Guinea responded by placing a freeze on diplomatic relations with Spain. President Obiang banned the main opposition Progress Party, which had been led by Moto. This followed the interception by Angolan authorities in May of a Russian ship carrying arms apparently bound for Equatorial Guinea.

In July President Obiang said it was possible he would share power with "an opposition government" following legislative elections scheduled for 1998. He had been urged to do so by both Spain and the U.S. At the beginning of September, the Ministry of Defense closed the country's mainland air and sea borders "until further notice" in order "to ensure" that the anniversary of independence on October 12 proceeded normally.

In September the government announced that French would join Spanish as an official language of the country. Spain's foreign minister, Abel Matutes Juan, responded to the decision by stating that he respected Equatorial Guinea's right to introduce a second official language "in a region of Africa where French has a great presence." He said that Spain would continue to provide aid to the nation.

(GUY ARNOLD)

This article updates the *Macropædia* article WESTERN AFRICA: *Equatorial Guinea.*

ERITREA

Area: 121,144 sq km (46,774 sq mi)
Population (1997 est.): 3,590,000 (including about 350,000 refugees in The Sudan)
Capital: Asmara
Head of state and government: President Isaias Afwerki

In 1997 the government of Eritrea continued its measured and resolute steps to reconstruct society and to create a unique brand of democracy. While the establishment of opposition parties was contemplated, the official rhetoric of the sole functioning political party, the People's Front for Democracy and Justice (PFDJ), seemed to discourage their formation. Nevertheless, strides were made toward the implementation of a democratic constitution. The constitution was ratified on May 23, 1997, but at the year's end had yet to be implemented. The commitment to democracy could be seen, however, in the political structures that had been established, particularly at the regional level in the form of popularly elected local and district governments.

Though economic progress continued to be slow, Eritrea was able to rely upon strong political and economic support from the West, particularly the U.S. and Italy. Early in the year it was estimated that more than $300 million had been either invested or committed to business in Eritrea, and the PFDJ regime enthusiastically welcomed foreign direct investment. Most notably, new foreign investments in mining and petroleum exploration were made. Late in the year, however, the government began restricting foreign grants for health and education and informed a number of private agencies, including OXFAM-Canada, that it no longer required their aid.

Perhaps the most significant economic development was the unveiling of the new national currency, the nakfa, which was pegged to the Ethiopian birr. Steady progress was also made in the development of infrastructure such as roads and port facilities.

Relations with Ethiopia continued to be warm and supportive. In addition, Eritrea demonstrated its strong leadership in the region by sending military support to a joint international force in Africa's Great Lakes region. Eritrea was also instrumental in providing leadership in the establishment of the Intergovernmental Authority on Development as an effective instrument of regional economic cooperation.

Relations with The Sudan continued to be strained, with each country accusing the other of conspiracies to overthrow their respective governments. The Sudanese National Democratic Alliance, a united front comprising groups from northern and southern Sudan, bent on overthrowing the Sudanese government, set up headquarters in Asmara. In contrast to the troubles with The Sudan, Eritrea's relations with Yemen improved significantly in 1997.

(EDMUND J. KELLER)

This article updates the *Micropædia* article ERITREA.

ESTONIA

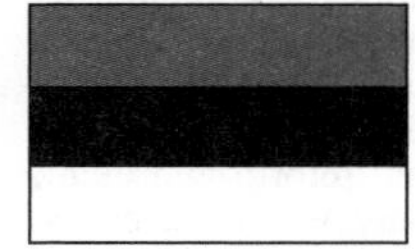

Area: 45,227 sq km (17,462 sq mi)
Population (1997 est.): 1,463,000
Capital: Tallinn
Chief of state: President Lennart Meri
Head of government: Prime Ministers Tiit Vähi and, from March 17, Mart Siimann

Estonian politics were turbulent in 1997. Prime Minister Tiit Vähi resigned on February 25 in a scandal involving the privatization of real estate in Tallinn. The governing coalition nonetheless survived, with Mart Siimann of the Estonian Coalition Party becoming the new prime minister. A new clash erupted in September, this time between the president and the Cabinet on one side and the Ministry of Defense and the military on the other following the drowning of 14 soldiers during training in the strait between the island of Suur Pakri and the port of Kurkse.

Still another scandal, which broke in late October, involved illegal surveillance by a security firm belonging to Koit Pikaro, who had been forced to resign in 1996 from a high police office. Pikaro worked as a consultant to Tallinn's City Council chairman and Estonian Centre Party functionary Edgar Savisaar, who himself had been forced out of Vähi's Cabinet in late 1995 as minister of the interior under allegations that he had spied on his political rivals.

Fueled by foreign investments, economic advances continued unabated in 1997. The European Commission (EC) recommended that Estonia begin accession talks for membership in the European Union, which somewhat soured relations with Latvia and Lithuania, which were not extended the EC's recommendation. At the end of 1997, Estonia opened a free-trade zone at Muuga harbour, northeast of Tallinn, to facilitate transit trade with Russia.

A major achievement was the inauguration of visa-free travel with Estonia's Nordic neighbours. Relations with Russia improved a bit, even though Moscow postponed the signing of a border treaty. In 1997 the Council of Europe ended its monitoring of Estonia's treatment of its ethnic Russian minority, and the U.S. State Department's annual human rights report of January 1997 gave Estonia a comparatively clean bill of health.

(TÕNU PARMING)

This article updates the *Macropædia* article BALTIC STATES: *Estonia.*

ETHIOPIA

Area: 1,133,882 sq km (437,794 sq mi)
Population (1997 est.): 58,733,000
Capital: Addis Ababa
Chief of state: President Negasso Gidada
Head of government: Prime Minister Meles Zenawi

In 1997 Ethiopia continued to receive high marks from the international community for its progress toward achieving good government. Among Ethiopians, however, there existed widespread disaffection with such government policies as land reform and ethnic federalism. The economy was on a course to grow at an annual rate approaching 7%, the most dynamic sector being agriculture, with a growth rate of nearly 15%. Drought returned to Tigre and the Ogaden regions, however, and this could negatively affect the country's economic progress.

Donor nations seemed most impressed with Ethiopia's attacks on official corruption. Early in the year the former prime minister and minister of defense, Tamirat Layne, remained under house arrest. Along with some business associates, he had been arrested late in 1996 on allegations of corruption. Later in 1997, 261 members of the executive committee of the city government were sacked on allegations and charges of incompetence and corruption. Many observers believed, however, that corruption continued to be rampant and that government rhetoric and periodic action had done little to address it adequately. Nevertheless, the International Monetary Fund and the World Bank vigorously supported Ethiopia's efforts at economic reform, expressing concern only over the pace of the action. For example, foreign private investment in the economy remained weak, and the move toward privatization continued to be slow.

Rights to both rural and urban property were an ongoing source of tension between the government and some segments of the population. Early in the year farmers in the Amhara regional state protested against the state's agrarian reforms. They claimed discrimination based upon whether families had owned property under the imperial regime or whether individuals had been granted a certain amount of property for their support of the deposed regime of Mengistu Haile Mariam. People falling into either of those categories could claim only one hectare (2.47 ac) of rural land, while those who supported the ruling Ethiopian People's Revolutionary Democratic Front (EPRDF) were allowed to own up to three hectares. Farmers were particularly incensed by the fact that EPRDF soldiers had been used to confiscate some rural property.

In the cities confusion persisted over compensation for nationalized property. The government announced that it intended to sell 18,000 properties that had been nationalized under the previous regime. It was not clear, however, what formula would be used to compensate the previous owners.

Armed opposition to the regime continued, particularly in areas where the Oromo Liberation Front and the Somali-based al-Ittihad movement were active, but attacks on government troops were sporadic. There were also occasional bomb and grenade attacks aimed at destabilizing the government, mostly in Addis Ababa. Nonmilitarized opposition tended to be ineffective, as the EPRDF had all but co-opted or suppressed civilian opposition parties.

On the diplomatic front Ethiopia attempted to play the role of statesman. It moderated its rhetoric against The Sudan and attempted to broker talks aimed at reuniting Somalia. At the same time, it continued to quietly support the activities of the National Democratic Alliance, a united front of northern and southern Sudanese engaged in political and military efforts to depose the Islamic fundamentalist regime in that country.

(EDMOND J. KELLER)

This article updates the *Macropædia* article EASTERN AFRICA: *Ethiopia.*

FIJI

Area: 18,272 sq km (7,055 sq mi)
Population (1997 est.): 778,000
Capital: Suva
Chief of state: President Rautu Sir Kamisese Mara
Head of government: Prime Minister Sitiveni Rabuka

In July 1997 the House of Representatives and Senate unanimously approved a new constitution for Fiji. Acceptance of proposals based on recommendations of a constitutional commission represented a triumph for Prime Minister Sitiveni Rabuka, who had worked with opposition leader Jai Ram Reddy to overcome the distrust engendered by the coups of 1987. The new constitution, scheduled to take effect in July 1998, provided for a multiracial Cabinet and raised the prospect of a coalition government. Following the approval of the new constitution, Fiji was readmitted to the Commonwealth of Nations. In May Fiji played host to the Melanesian Spearhead Group, an organization that emphasized opportunities for cooperative development and trade.

The 1997 budget provided for expenditures of just over $1 billion. Inflation stood at 3.5% for the fiscal year. The year's sugar harvest was disrupted by strike action by mill workers. The Malaysian government joined in a venture to encourage entrepreneurial activity among ethnic Fijians, who in 1996 constituted approximately 51% of Fiji's population; 43% was Indian.

In early March Cyclone Gavin wreaked havoc in Fiji, causing damage estimated at $25 million–$30 million. The cyclone also claimed at least 26 lives, 10 of them in the loss at sea of a fishing vessel.

(BARRIE MACDONALD)

This article updates the *Macropædia* article PACIFIC ISLANDS: *Fiji.*

FINLAND

Area: 338,145 sq km (130,559 sq mi)
Population (1997 est.): 5,145,000
Capital: Helsinki
Chief of state: President Martti Ahtisaari
Head of government: Prime Minister Paavo Lipponen

In 1997 Mauno Koivisto, president of Finland from 1982 to 1994, complained that his presidential office had been swept clear of important records by the time that he took over from his ailing predecessor, Urho Kekkonen, who was known to have formed close links with Soviet leaders during his 25 years of office. Koivisto wrote in memoirs published in September that notes of face-to-face talks with foreign leaders had evidently been removed to the archives of a private foundation. In 1997 he was still being allowed only restricted access to the records. Kekkonen, forced to retire in 1981 with diagnosed symptoms of dementia, led Finland through a period during which the country was accused in the West of undue acquiescence to the wishes of Moscow.

Unlike its Nordic neighbours, Finland in 1997 refused to endorse a global movement to ban antipersonnel land mines. Finland also differed from Denmark and Sweden in vowing that it would be in the first wave of countries to join the third stage of the European Union's (EU's) economic and monetary union, EMU. This was scheduled to become operational at the beginning of 1999 and would eventually introduce a common EU currency. A poll showed that despite resistance from the agrarian-based opposition Finnish Centre Party and from some members of the ruling coalition parties, Parliament was likely to endorse accession in a vote early in 1998.

Finland continued to be plagued by high unemployment, running at above 12% according to the figures used for EU comparison but at a much higher rate according to the number of persons the Labour Ministry reported as receiving unemployment benefits. The nation taxed incomes at a rate above 48%, exceeded in the EU only by Denmark and Sweden and up by almost 10% from 1996, compared with a rise of 4.5% in gross domestic product.

The government called for more flexibility in the labour market, in which a rising proportion of the workforce was absorbed by the service sector. But it also urged the renewal of the national collective agreement between employers and unions that regulated the nonunionized workforce. The unions urged tighter statutory rules for sectors not under union control.

(EDWARD M. SUMMERHILL)

FRANCE

Area: 543,965 sq km (210,026 sq mi)
Population (1997 est.): 58,616,000
Capital: Paris
Chief of state: President Jacques Chirac
Head of government: Prime Ministers Alain Juppé and, from June 3, Lionel Jospin

The year 1997 was dominated by the upset victory of the left, bringing to power in midyear the Socialist-led coalition of Prime Minister Lionel Jospin (*see* BIOGRAPHIES), who then governed France in "cohabitation" with the right-wing president, Jacques Chirac. The new government included three Communist Party ministers (two in the Cabinet), the leader of the Green Party (which entered Parliament for the first time) as its

JEAN GAUMY—MAGNUM

Jean-Marie Le Pen, the controversial founder of the far-right National Front (FN), acknowledges supporters at the party's convention in March. Playing on fears of rising unemployment and a loss of national identity, the FN helped oust the ruling centre-right majority in France's parliamentary elections.

environment minister, and five women holding Cabinet positions.

In policy terms the defeat of the centre-right coalition did not spell the end of France's quest to qualify for the single European currency, as some of Jospin's Communist allies might have hoped. Thanks to an upturn in the economy, the new Socialist prime minister was able to reduce the public-sector deficit without imposing the austerity measures against which he had campaigned. The victory of the left, however, led to a dashing of any remaining hope that France in 1997 might be reintegrated into NATO and also to a reappraisal of the links that right-wing French Gaullists had long entertained with military dictators in former French colonies in Africa. (*See* Spotlight: *France's New African Policy.*)

At home—to combat the country's stubbornly high unemployment rate of more than 12% of the workforce—the new government launched an ambitious jobs program. It set about creating or subsidizing 350,000 new government jobs and challenged private employers to match that figure. It relaxed the previous government's squeeze on health spending and increased its expenditure on education while raising taxes on companies and canceling planned reductions in the income tax.

Domestic Affairs. By the spring of 1997, the Gaullist Alain Juppé had lost almost all of the radical reforming zeal that he had shown when he became prime minister in 1995. A rare exception was parliamentary approval in late January of a restructuring of French railways, freeing French National Railways from carrying debt that would in the future be attached to a state-backed rail company.

The government also had to cope with a variety of ancient and modern scandals. Allegations that it had hushed up corruption in the Gaullist administration of the city of Paris led President Chirac in January to appoint a judicial commission to prevent political interference with the course of justice and to better protect the rights of the accused. In July this commission produced some modest proposals, including a limitation on the rights of investigating magistrates to hold suspects in preventive detention; these proposals had, however, already been eclipsed by the Jospin government's earlier announcement that it would no longer try to influence prosecutors in individual cases. On a more serious level and as part of a general European move to try to rectify wartime wrongs to Jews, the Juppé government—following revelations that French museums were still holding some 2,000 works that had once had Jewish owners—also announced in January that a commission was being formed to trace property seized from Jews in 1940–44. Meanwhile, on October 8 Maurice Papon went on trial in Bordeaux for complicity in the deportation of more than 1,500 Jews to death camps during World War II. The 87-year-old Papon was secretary-general of the Gironde prefecture in 1942–44. He was the highest-ranking French official of the Vichy regime to go on trial and, given the time span, probably the last to do so.

Residual sensitivities about the Vichy period also lay behind the furor that erupted in February over one method proposed by the Juppé government to carry out its promise to crack down on illegal immigration. This concerned a plan for French hosts to report to their local town hall the departure of any visa-bearing foreign visitors they had housed. Protesting against this return of the "informer," French intellectuals and entertainers led demonstrations that, at their peak on February 22, put tens of thousands of people on the streets of Paris. The government backed down, acknowledging the strength of a movement that took everyone, including the Socialist Party, by surprise.

Also fueling this controversy was rising fear of the far-right National Front (FN). On February 9 Catherine Mégret, wife of Bruno Mégret, who ranked second in the FN hierarchy, was elected mayor of Vitrolles, a residential suburb of Marseille. For the FN, whose few previous victories had depended on a divided opposition, it was the first time it had ever won an absolute electoral majority in a two-way contest. The FN's founder, Jean-Marie Le Pen, was reelected its president, though the most popular leader among the FN rank and file appeared to be Bruno Mégret. The impression of division within the FN ranks, coupled with the calculation (correct, as it turned out) that Le Pen was simply too controversial to be able to contest a parliamentary seat himself, was one of the many factors that led President Chirac to make his fateful decision to call on April 21 for an early "snap" election.

Chirac's main motive in calling the election was damage control. After the pendulum moved so far to the right in 1993, when right-wing candidates won 465 of the 577 National Assembly seats, it seemed inevitable—quite apart from high unemployment and the low personal popularity of Juppé—that it would swing back a bit. The right was therefore bound to lose some seats in the parliamentary election, which, if the National Assembly had served its full five-year term, would have been held in March 1998. Chirac concluded that these losses would be all the more certain because the 1998 budget would require extra austerity measures for France to qualify for the European economic and monetary union (EMU). The president reckoned he could minimize these losses by calling a snap election, giving his opponents on the left and far right less time to mobilize and thereby retaining a working parliamentary majority for the rest of his term, until 2002.

Early in the campaign the left drew even with the government coalition in the opinion polls. Jospin, Chirac's runoff opponent in the 1995 presidential election, once again showed himself to be an effective cam-

(continued on page 428)

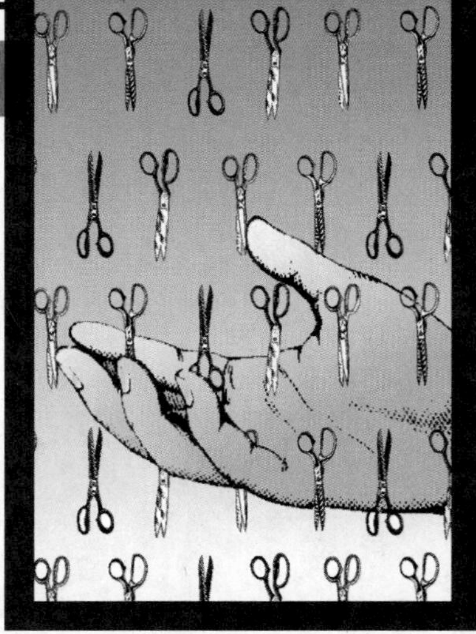

SPOTLIGHT

EUROPE'S CRUMBLING SOCIAL NETWORK

by Birna Helgadottir

Illustration by Cathy Hull

The European welfare state suffered a year of crisis in 1997. In the years after World War II, generations of Europeans had grown accustomed to levels of social protection that were generous and comprehensive compared with, for example, the United States or Asia. In recent years, however, various factors had sent welfare budgets shooting upward to unsustainable heights. For example, the increasing globalization of the world economy was causing Europe to face intense competition from cheaper job markets. Unemployment reached record levels—almost 21 million in 1994 in the European countries of the Organisation for Economic Co-operation and Development; consequently, more people in those countries were relying on state handouts than were working for wages. People were living longer, and so governments had to pay out more pensions, and an aging population put an increasing strain on government health services.

In Eastern Europe, meanwhile, people continued to struggle with the harsh realities of postcommunism. From the primitive rural society of Albania to the relatively evolved economies of the Baltic nations (Estonia, Latvia, and Lithuania), the former regimes had been oppressive, but most had provided basic welfare safety nets. As those countries transformed their economies according to free-market principles, they also suffered a sharp fall in social security benefits and health standards, a widening wealth gap, and a rise in organized crime. In Romania, for example, living standards were found to be 20% lower in 1997 than they were in 1990.

Perhaps nowhere were the contrasts between current privations and former security so marked as in Sweden—the country that is often called the cradle of the welfare state. The Swedish crisis began in the recession of the early 1990s, which forced the government to embark on a series of severe cuts in public spending. In 1997 the economy was at last showing signs of recovery, but years of austerity had taken their toll. A survey early in the year by the consumer office at the nation's second largest city, Göteborg, showed that half its households were living on or below the poverty line and 6% could not afford to visit a physician. The Swedish welfare system is two-tiered: the national government provides social insurance and benefits, whereas regional authorities hand out allowances that are meant to ensure that everyone has enough to live decently. These allowances were originally intended as emergency payments, but by 1997 they had become a long-term source of income for many households. Consequently, municipalities became so financially stretched that they imposed rigorous checks on claimants, and only the most determined received payments. A national board of health and welfare report estimated that 150,000 households entitled to benefits received nothing. Religious charities such as the Salvation Army were left to pick up the pieces; in Stockholm, a city of just over 1.5 million, the City Mission charity dealt with 2,500 families during the year, while the Salvation Army day centre received 11,250 visitors and handed out 4,500 parcels of food and clothing.

Single-income earners, single parents, and pensioners were particularly hard hit by the cuts. In the summer of 1997, Stockholm had its bid to serve as host of the 2004 Olympic Games effectively sabotaged by a bombing campaign carried out by an unlikely terrorist group called We Who Built Sweden. The group was believed to be made up of disaffected pensioners whose bitterness over welfare cuts expressed itself in an agenda of racism and violence. Elsewhere in Europe, countries that had lined up to join the first wave of the single European currency, scheduled for introduction in 1999, found themselves having to slash public spending in order to become members of the currency group. The rules for joining the economic and monetary union (EMU), known as the convergence criteria, were tough; they included a budget deficit of no more than 3% of gross domestic product and low rates of inflation. Most prospective members—including France, Germany, and, particularly, Italy—were struggling to meet these requirements. Some economists and social scientists voiced their doubts over the wisdom of the economic policies being imposed in order to meet the convergence criteria. They argued that tight fiscal restraint, which curbed economic growth, was not what was needed at a time when there were 20 million people unemployed in the European Union and an estimated 50 million living in poverty. Christopher Allsopp, editor of the *Oxford Review of Economic Policy* and a member of the Court of the Bank of England, wrote in the October edition of *New College News:* "Viewed dispassionately, the process looks like a large scale system failure...public perceptions naturally associate fiscal cuts with unemployment and blame the Maastricht process and moves towards currency union for the mess that Europe is in."

In May thousands of trade union members from across the continent marched in Brussels, headquarters of the European Union, on the European Day for Employment to support increased rights for workers. The unions accused the EU of concentrating too much on benefits to the business sector rather than on the private citizen. In France the centre-right government, led by Prime Minister Alain Juppé, became increasingly unpopular as it attempted to introduce harsh cuts needed to tackle a $10 billion deficit in the state social security fund. In the weeks before the general election in May and June, there were persistent strikes and public protests. State employees, from teachers to air traffic controllers, walked out of their jobs and onto the streets. Even the medical profession took part, with doctors refusing to answer emergency calls during the strikes. France's new Socialist government led by Lionel Jospin (*see* BIOGRAPHIES) put increased emphasis on job creation and protection of workers rights, but Jospin's government was also forced to make cuts to the welfare budget. Within a month of the election, the protesters were back on the streets as family groups gathered outside the National Assembly in Paris to show their outrage over the government's plans to scrap universal child benefits.

European Social Security and Welfare Spending

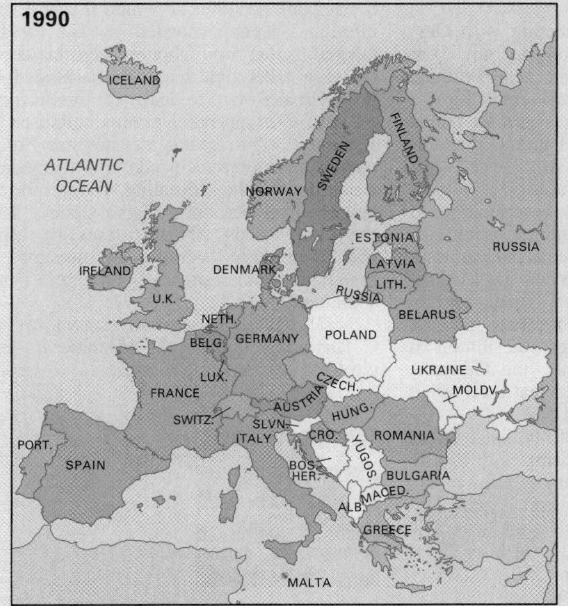

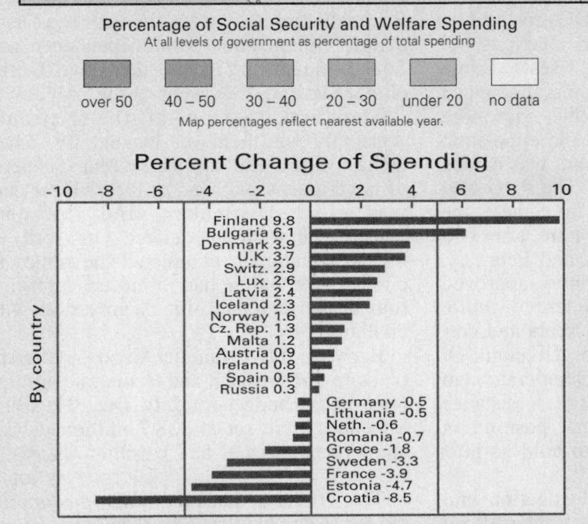

In October the Italian centre-left government fell when the Communist Refoundation Party, which held the balance of power in the Chamber of Deputies, refused to support proposed budget cuts. In order to meet EMU requirements, Prime Minister Romano Prodi needed to overhaul the welfare system, and, in what he called "a budget for Europe," he announced $3 billion of public spending cuts. Those who were to bear the brunt of the cuts were the so-called baby pensioners; under the previous system workers had been entitled to state pensions after a certain number of years of employment, so those who had started work at the old school-leaving age of 14 could retire as young as 50. In November, after four months of negotiations, Italy's trade unions accepted a government plan to raise the minimum retirement age to 55 in 1999 and 57 in 2002.

Germany was a country whose industrial power had in the past been supported by excellent labour relations. The welfare crisis ended that. The government and employers insisted that mass unemployment needed to be addressed by cutting labour costs, but unions and employees fought to maintain benefits. Many industries, such as the automobile, chemical, and engineering sectors, were hit by mass strikes, which cost companies such as Daimler-Benz and Ford hundreds of millions of dollars. Late in November thousands of students marched through Bonn in a demonstration protesting the underfinancing of Germany's colleges and universities that had resulted in overcrowding and cuts in teaching staffs. Thousands more boycotted classes throughout the country.

Although the problem was perhaps most acute in those countries planning early entry into the EMU, nearly every European government faced some kind of public-spending dilemma. In Britain the outgoing Conservative government had spent many years chipping away at the welfare system. Whereas living standards as a whole had increased, there was increased inequality of wealth; in 1997, 13.7 million people were estimated to be living below the poverty line, compared with 5 million in 1979. The criteria for receiving money from the government were made much more rigorous, and the number of people who were being rejected for benefits had risen from 113,000 to 317,000 a year in the past three years.

Even with these cuts, however, Britain's welfare system was continuing to cost the country approximately $144 billion a year. The centre-left Labour Party, elected with a large majority in May after 18 years in opposition, may have presented a more compassionate face to the voters, but it soon showed itself equally intent on slimming down the welfare budget. The new government said it would adhere to plans devised by the previous regime to make $800 million worth of welfare cuts and also announced various "welfare-to-work" schemes, such as one that would move single parents back into the job market as soon as their children had reached school age.

No government, however, had found a real solution to the welfare crisis. In a report to the Council of Europe in June, Ann Cathrine Haglund, special adviser to the UN secretary-general, wrote, "Western European countries have reacted to [recession and unemployment] by notably adapting their social protection to make it more restrictive. The welfare state has had increasing difficulty in combating poverty and exclusion. Employment policies have had little success. Most countries are looking for new ideas and seem to have objective difficulties in tackling the situation and finding solutions at the national level."

Birna Helgadottir is an editor on the staff of The European, *London.*

(continued from page 425)
paigner and managed to forge an electoral pact with the Greens and minor left-wing parties and a looser arrangement with the more powerful Communists that papered over policy differences. The Gaullists of the Rally for the Republic and the Union for French Democracy centre-right had the advantage of presenting a common platform and joint candidates, but their weakness lay in the unpopularity of their leader, Juppé. As the campaign continued, Juppé increasingly hinted that he would resign, and, indeed, on May 26, the day after the first round of voting, in which the forces of the left outpolled those of the right, he announced he would.

In the runoff election on June 1, the Socialist Party and small splinter groups won 274 seats, and their Communist and Green allies took 38 and 7 seats, respectively, against 257 for the centre-right. For the first time in a decade, the FN won a seat in Parliament. Its sole victory, in the southern port city of Toulon, greatly understated the importance of its role elsewhere in splitting the right-wing vote.

Jospin waited for an audit of the nation's public finances on July 21 to announce his first budgetary decisions. The audit estimated that the 1997 deficit would be 3.5–3.7% of gross domestic product (GDP), well adrift of the EMU-qualifying target of 3%. To help plug the gap, spending was cut F 10 billion and corporate taxes raised by F 22 billion. By the time the government unveiled on September 24 its draft budget for 1998, which planned to raise an extra F 14 billion in taxes while keeping public spending just below the inflation rate, the finance minister was confident that economic growth would reduce the 1997 deficit to 3.1% of GDP, which was within negotiating range of the EMU target.

Despite the election defeat, President Chirac signaled during his Bastille Day press conference on July 14 that he did not intend to be just a figurehead. While calling for a "constructive cohabitation" with Jospin, the president also criticized the Socialist government's various early moves to restrict family allowances for the middle class, to allow amnesty for illegal immigrants, to restrain employers from laying off workers, and to shut down the Superphénix nuclear reactor. As the autumn wore on, however, the president ventured increasingly less into domestic policy and focused more on foreign affairs, where the constitution gave him more power.

Foreign Relations. Aside from a reappraisal of France's Africa policy in response to the overthrow of Pres. Mobutu Sese Seko in Zaire (now Democratic Republic of the Congo), the main focus of French foreign policy in 1997 was in Europe. France sought to recalibrate both the EMU project and NATO more to French tastes but in both areas met with limited success.

The background to the EMU issue lay in French frustration at having to accept Germany's terms for the single currency. This came to the fore during the French election campaign, in which the Socialists campaigned for a looser interpretation of the deficit criterion to qualify for EMU; for the early inclusion in EMU of countries with similar languages and cultures, such as Italy and Spain; for some political counterweight to the European central bank planned on the German model; and for a higher European priority on job creation. Once in power, however, the Socialists had to moderate their demands.

After a difficult first meeting with German Chancellor Helmut Kohl on June 13 at the Franco-German summit near Poitiers, France, Jospin—with President Chirac's support—went on to press his demands about jobs at the European Union (EU) summit at Amsterdam the following week. The upshot was a summit declaration about the importance of tighter EU coordination to promote jobs and growth and the promise to hold in Luxembourg a special EU autumn summit on employment. When the Luxembourg summit convened on November 21, little was accomplished, however. By the time of the next Franco-German summit in Weimar, Ger., in September, the Germans were substantially reassured that the French would not rock the EMU boat.

President Chirac successfully insisted that NATO forge a new relationship with Russia to balance the enlargement of its membership by the inclusion of several Eastern European countries. His efforts were acknowledged in the signing in Paris on May 27 of the Founding Act on Mutual Relations, Cooperation and Security, which set up a permanent consultative mechanism between Russia and NATO. This did not change Russia's opposition in principle to the NATO enlargement, but it finally removed the vestiges of the Cold War, as Russian Pres. Boris Yeltsin made clear at the Paris ceremony, where he announced that Russian nuclear weapons would no longer be targeted at any NATO country. (DAVID BUCHAN)

See also *Dependent States*.

GABON

Area: 267,667 sq km (103,347 sq mi)
Population (1997 est.): 1,190,000
Capital: Libreville
Chief of state: President Omar Bongo
Head of government: Prime Minister Paulin Obame-Nguéma

Following the smashing victory of the Gabonese Democratic Party (PDG) in the December 1996 parliamentary elections, in which it won 100 of the 120 seats, Prime Minister Paulin Obame-Nguéma announced his new Cabinet on Jan. 29, 1997. Alexandre Sambat, the only member of the opposition coalition to be given a portfolio, was named minister of youth and sports. The PDG also won an absolute majority in the Senate, the new upper house of the legislature, after two rounds of polling in January and February. In March the National Assembly approved a draft law that lengthened the term of future presidents from five to seven years and created the post of vice president. Divungui-Di N'Dingue of the opposition Democratic and Republican Alliance and High Resistance Council was appointed to that position in May. Gabon was scheduled to hold its next presidential election in 1998.

The continuing French investigation into the misuse of corporate funds by the Elf oil firm's Gabon subsidiary reportedly increased tensions between France and Gabon. Judicial interest in the case centred on Swiss bank accounts in which illegal "commissions" were deposited by Elf for the alleged use of top Gabonese politicians.

Peace talks that had been arranged by Pres. Omar Bongo to deal with the disarmament of Chadian rebel groups collapsed on January 9. Throughout the summer Bongo played a major role in attempts to mediate a solution to the escalating troubles in the neighbouring Republic of the Congo. With the cooperation of presidents of other French-speaking countries in the area, he organized a committee to negotiate a peace settlement.

(NANCY ELLEN LAWLER)

This artcle updates the *Macropædia* article CENTRAL AFRICA: *Gabon*.

GAMBIA, THE

Area: 10,689 sq km (4,127 sq mi)
Population (1997 est.): 1,248,000
Capital: Banjul
Head of state and government: President Capt. Yahya Jammeh

On Nov. 8, 1996, a group of unknown assailants attacked a military barracks at Farafenni near the Senegal border, leaving a number of soldiers dead and wounded. The government then announced a postponement of the legislative elections, which were to be held on December 11; they were rescheduled for Jan. 2, 1997. The government also banned all political rallies indefinitely; it had been angered by weekly rallies called by the opposition leader, Ousainou Darboe, the principal presidential rival to Pres. Yahya Jammeh in the elections of the previous September.

The postponed elections were held in January 1997 and resulted in victory for Jammeh's Alliance for Patriotic Reorientation and Construction, which won 33 of 45 seats and so obtained the more than two-thirds majority required for it to be allowed to alter the constitution. Darboe's United Democratic Party won seven seats, the National Reconciliation Party two, the People's Democratic Organization for Independence and Socialism one, and independents two. Of the eligible voters, 73% went to the polls.

The first session of the National Assembly was held on January 16. Mustapha Wadda, the former secretary-general of government and head of the civil service, was elected speaker, and the new constitution went into effect. On April 17 President Jammeh completed the return to civilian rule that he had promised, replacing four of the regional military governors with civilians.

Early in July Dominic Mendy, secretary of state for finance and economic affairs, presented a budget for July–Dec. 31, 1997. Revenues were set at 338.7 million dalasis and expenditures at 558.1 million dalasis.

(GUY ARNOLD)

This article updates the *Macropædia* article WESTERN AFRICA: *The Gambia*.

GEORGIA

Area: 69,492 sq km (26,831 sq mi)
Population (1997 est.): 5,377,000
Capital: Tbilisi
Head of state and government: President Eduard A. Shevardnadze, assisted by Minister of State Nikoloz Lekishvili

Georgia's strained relationship with Russia was the major factor determining the country's domestic as well as foreign policy in 1997. Both the leadership and the opposition accused Moscow of seeking to use the conflict over the breakaway Black Sea province of Abkhazia to undermine Georgia's sovereignty; in December a leading Georgian parliamentarian charged that Russia was plotting to assassinate Pres. Eduard Shevardnadze and return the Communist Party to power.

Early in the year Shevardnadze proclaimed a new campaign against corruption, and in July Security Minister Shota Kviraya was forced to resign following accusations by opposition National Democratic Party leader Irina Sarishvili-Chanturia that he was engaged in black-market trading in cigarettes and gasoline. Two former influential political figures who had helped engineer Shevardnadze's return to power in Georgia in 1992 were brought to trial. In September former prime minister Tengiz Sigua was ordered to repay $5.8 million compensation for losses allegedly incurred by his decision in early 1992 to continue using former Soviet foreign exchange rates. Sigua accused Shevardnadze of fabricating the charges against him. The trial of Djaba Ioseliani, former leader of the Mkhedrioni paramilitary formation, and 14 of his associates opened in early December. They were charged with terrorism and involvement in the failed assassination attempt against Shevardnadze in August 1995, but proceedings were immediately suspended because of the illness of one of the defense lawyers.

The Commonwealth of Independent States summit in Moscow in late March agreed to Shevardnadze's demand that the CIS peacekeeping force deployed since July 1994 along the internal border between Georgia and Abkhazia be given broader powers to protect ethnic Georgians who had fled their homes in Abkhazia during the 1992–93 war and wished to return. The Abkhaz leadership, however, protested this decision, which Moscow then failed to implement. Instead, the Russian foreign ministry mediated several rounds of talks between Abkhaz and Georgian leaders in Moscow in June and July, but he failed to persuade both sides to sign a draft protocol intended to serve as a basis for a political settlement of the conflict. Abkhaz leader Vladislav Ardzinba flew to Tbilisi in August for a face-to-face meeting with Shevardnadze; at that meeting the two men renounced the use of force in bilateral relations. Meeting in Geneva in late November under UN auspices, Georgian and Abkhaz delegations agreed to create working groups to expedite the resumption of economic ties and the repatriation of Georgian displaced persons.

From early summer onward, Russian border guards systematically refused to permit vehicles transporting alcohol to enter Russian territory from Georgia. Georgians perceived this ban as intended to undermine the country's potential role as a transport artery and thus to deprive it of lucrative customs tariffs. Also in early summer, Russian border guards arbitrarily moved a frontier post 1,300 m (1,420 yd) into Georgian territory, which elicited protests from the Georgian government. Anti-Russian feeling was further fueled by the disclosure in October that several Georgian soldiers had contracted radiation sickness from radioactive substances abandoned at a former Soviet military base.

Shevardnadze alternated in his official statements between reproaching Moscow for its alleged anti-Georgian bias and declaring Russia a strategic ally. During a visit to the U.S. in August, he sought American support for his country's potential role as one of the export routes for Azerbaijan's Caspian Sea oil. In November Shevardnadze announced a moratorium on implementing death sentences handed down by Georgian courts—one of the preconditions set for full membership in the Council of Europe, in which Georgia in 1997 had "special guest" status. In October, however, the presidents of Georgia, Ukraine, Azerbaijan, and Moldova announced an alternative alignment reflecting their shared security concerns and the desire to profit jointly from the transport of Caspian oil through their territories.

(ELIZABETH FULLER)

This article updates the *Macropædia* article TRANSCAUCASIA: *Georgia.*

GERMANY

Area: 357,022 sq km (137,847 sq mi)
Population (1997 est.): 82,143,000
Capital: Bonn; capital designate: Berlin
Chief of state: President Roman Herzog
Head of government: Chancellor Helmut Kohl

The all-important task facing the Federal Republic of Germany in 1997 was the implementation of decisions taken the year before in light of the discovery that Germany, by dint of its advanced social welfare policies and labour legislation, had all but priced itself out of international competition. Indeed, in terms of attractiveness as an industrial location, Germany had disqualified itself as an effective competitor even within the bounds of the European Union (EU).

Politics and the Economy. The reasons for this predicament were clear enough. Germany had been caught squarely within a complex of developments converging on Europe from all sides: the disappearance of customs barriers within the Common Market, programmed but unprepared for; the sudden collapse of the entire communist bloc on its eastern border, unexpected and uncomprehended; and the precipitous self-annexation of East Germany (the German Democratic Republic; GDR) to the Federal Republic, unforeseen and confounding in its consequences. The end result of this series of upheavals was an astronomical drain on the financial stability of the federation (over DM 700 billion in seven years), not least because the West German government in its euphoria had been rash enough to exchange East Germany's entire cash holdings in East Marks for West Marks at the rate of one to one (a rate of four to one would have been generous). This was before it was discovered that East Germany's total debt was more than DM 400 billion (West).

The main challenge was to render Germany competitively attractive as an industrial location by radically reducing taxes so as to attract investment capital, foreign and domestic, within the EU and thus lower the rate of unemployment, which had reached a high of 11.2% (as against 10.6% for the previous year). While Chancellor Helmut Kohl may have announced the "tax reform of the century" in the spring of 1996, the big economic story in Germany in 1997 was the legislative flop of the century: the tax reform coming to nothing in a series of tortuous negotiations, blocked at every turn by the Social Democratic Party (SPD), which enjoyed a majority in the Bundesrat (Federal Council), Germany's second legislative chamber. The same fate befell the second most important measure in abeyance, the reform of the pension fund, which faced actuarial occlusion—*i.e.,* the reversal of the ratio of wage earners to pensioners, from 78% versus 22% to 45% versus 55%—in less than four decades.

It became obvious by midyear that the whole process of reform had been foreclosed by the federal elections looming in the fall of 1998. The SPD meant to make an electoral issue of the failure (which they could guarantee) of the governing coalition to pass a tax law before the election. This standoff forced the coalition to abandon the effort to enact revisionary tax legislation altogether rather than accept a compromise with an intransigent opposition. There remained, then, the fallback position of enacting only those measures whose passage was exempted from approval by the Bundesrat. Under this heading the so-called solidarity surcharge, a decrease of 2% from 7.5%, was passed on September 30 to the exasperation of the helpless opposition. Providing relief of approximately DM 30 a month for the average family, it was little enough, but it was a step in the right direction, a demonstration of the government's earnest intention to lower taxes—if election results permitted. It was also evidence that the coalition was not at odds with itself, as the SPD insisted.

The disadvantage of the solidarity surcharge was its title, which led to the false impression that only the western Germans were being taxed in obligatory solidarity with their eastern cousins. On the other hand, the reduction by only 2% was interpreted as a slap on the wrist of eastern Germany for its failure to put the gift of the surcharge to good use.

The chronic increase in unemployment was due preeminently to changes in the economic and social structure in Germany, particularly in the eastern region. The throwing open of the EU to unrestricted economic competition ruled out the immobility characteristic of mass organizations and collectives. The emphasis had shifted from mass to mobility, to swift and imaginative adaptation to changes in customs and clientele. In an address on September 30, Gerhard Schröder, one of the tandem of SPD candidates for chancellor, made it clear "that we cannot load anything more on our social system." For the Socialists it was a matter of defending what they had achieved, but even this required rapid innovation on the part of enterprises, more flexibility of organization for wage work, reform of training and retraining, and a more production-effective state. Here, however, Schröder's reliance on the state as the prime regulatory factor stuck out like a sore thumb. The new spirit of small, flexible enterprises was turned against big business as well as big government. What characterized the large multinational corporations was their subjection to the economy of scale, where spectacular increases in per capita productive capacity dictated spectacular decreases in the number of places of work. Another sign of the times was the privatization during the year of two large concerns, Deutsche Telekom, the telephone company, and Lufthansa, the German airline, as well as the breakup of the postal monopoly formerly enjoyed by Deutsche Bundespost.

Like most enterprises in 1997, German trade unions continued to lose membership. The Textile and Clothing Union (GTB) had lost more than 70% of its membership (from 700,000 to 200,000) in less than seven years. On October 28, in its 103rd year, the GTB announced its dissolution and the transfer of its remaining membership to IG Metall, which, despite dwindling numbers, remained the largest (2,752,226 members) of the unions. In mid-October the chemical union, IG Chemie-Papier-Keramik (694,897), the miners union, IG Bergbau und Energie (364,331), and the small leather-workers union, Gewerkschaft Leder (21,904), announced their merger into the IG Bergbau, Chemie und Energie conglomerate, a million strong—for the moment. Across the board Germany's unions lost an average 5% of their membership during the year. The single exception was the Police Union, with an increase of 0.3% (to 199,421).

Pains of Reunification. The great complicating factor in Germany was that the Federal Republic was founded twice—as a "part-state" in 1949 and then again as the reunited whole nation in 1990. The circumstances of the two travails were entirely different. In the first there was the exhilaration of deliverance from the worst war humanity had ever known coupled with a new departure in German history amply financed by the world's richest nation. The Germans responded by creating the "economic miracle." In the second there was the financial and administrative responsibility for reclaiming an East Germany devastated by almost half a century of communist economic mismanagement.

In 1997—seven years after embarking on this mission, complicated as it was by the process of uniting the whole of Western Europe (with 30% of the EU's contributions to Brussels coming from Germany)—the Germans produced a miraculous muddle. This fiasco was particularly dismaying to the eastern Germans, who had entered the period with vaulting hopes of economic opportunity, social justice, and a high standard of living. Instead, after seven years of massive subsidies, tax breaks, and venture capital investment, the new states fashioned from the former East produced hardly 3% of Germany's exports. The financial misery of eastern German hospitals had become legendary—a total deficit of more than a billion Marks. The eastern states were bedeviled by an unemployment rate of 18%. More ominously, they proved to be a millstone around the neck of the republic as a whole, making for a record unemployment rate throughout Germany and the highest national debt in the history of the federation.

Matching the two foundings of the state, Germany had the legacies of two tyrannies to deal with, adjudicate, and otherwise dispose of—that which ended in 1945 and that which ended in 1990. The process of retroactive judgment and punishment for crimes committed under the misrule of the GDR was broadly gauged and costly. In August, Egon Krenz, Erich Honecker's successor as GDR leader, was sentenced to 6½ years' imprisonment on charges of manslaughter in three cases that occurred under his brief (seven-week) authority as head of state. At the same time, on like charges concerning the notorious order to open fire on citizens emboldened to "flee the republic," two top GDR communist leaders, Günter Schabowski and Günther Kleiber, were sentenced to three years' imprisonment each. This was part of the ongoing process of bringing to justice those responsible for the deaths of at least 753 people at the Berlin Wall and the intra-German border over a 28-year period. By mid-1997 six GDR generals had likewise been sentenced to terms of imprisonment ranging from 6½ years to 22 months (suspended in this one case). A number of officers of lesser rank, noncommissioned officers, and soldiers were brought to trial, all in connection with the deaths of refugees at the border. By autumn the number of these trials had risen to 65, at which some 80 persons were sentenced to various terms in prison. In most cases, however, sentences were suspended. On September 30 the District Court of Frankfurt am Main, in a trial that had lasted a full two years, exonerated seven former GDR judges of complicity in sentencing the philosopher Robert Havemann to 2½ years of house arrest in 1979 on trumped-up charges. The prosecution immediately appealed the court's decision.

All this was wearisome and expensive enough, but it was also true that with the ending of the Cold War, subsidies and emergency investments came to an abrupt halt. The Meteor Theatre in East Berlin entered receivership in midyear, following the Schiller Theatre, one of West Berlin's largest and most prestigious theatres, two years earlier.

Also accountable for the financial straits of the nation was the Klondike atmosphere throughout eastern Germany and particularly in the former East Berlin. Indeed, Berlin as a whole had become the world's largest construction site, much of it the result of breakneck investment. A good example was the multibillion-dollar complex at the Berlin Wall's Checkpoint Charlie undertaken by the Central European Development Corp., an American enterprise headed by Ronald S. Lauder of the cosmetics concern. On September 29 Lauder announced his departure from the firm, and the project was curtailed drastically, with construction halted on two of the five blocks, with 116,000 sq m (1,250,000 sq ft) of space. A Lauder partner avowed that it made no sense to continue construction under prevailing circumstances. Buildings already completed in the area had failed to attract tenants in any numbers if at all. The investors concerned had calculated, wrongly, that the political *renommé* of Checkpoint Charlie would constitute an attraction, and they had jumped the gun in anticipating the transfer of the federal government from Bonn in 1999. The number of bankruptcies in Germany in 1997 increased by 14% over 1996; the average was more than twice as high in the eastern states as it was in former West Germany.

Still, the government had succeeded in lowering the costs incidental to employment by reducing the amount payable on sick leave to 80% of the employee's regular income, saving employers DM 10 billion–DM 12 billion a year. The cancellation of the notorious tax on capital investment on January 1 saved another DM 4 billion–DM 8 billion. The repeal of the property tax brought still another DM 9 billion worth of relief. These measures had, it was argued, removed much of the objection to exorbitant employment costs.

The major political parties, the Christian Democratic Union/Christian Social Union (CDU/CSU), the SPD, and the Greens, were all split, for and against an unhampered market economy and the downsizing of government at every level. Traditional party lines in each case were lopped off at the middle. The increasingly evident slogan was "nothing sacred." Chancellor Kohl became as likely a target within his own party as Oskar Lafontaine of the SPD and Joschka Fischer of the Greens within theirs. The introduction of the Euro, the coin of the common currency-to-be, was another divisive issue. While Kohl staked his political future on the fulfillment of the Maastricht

PHOTO NEWS/GAMMA LIAISON

German workers protest the loss of mining jobs. During 1997 the unemployment rate in Germany reached a high of 11.2%. Many employed workers were asked to give up some of their benefits to satisfy criteria for the country's entry into the European economic and monetary union.

Treaty to the letter, other CDU/CSU political leaders, such as Saxony's president, Kurt Biedenkopf, and Bavaria's president, Edmund Stoiber, called for postponement.

Foreign Affairs. The intractable refugee problem continued to cause concern, and in midyear statisticians linked the rising crime rate in the cities to the increase in the number of foreigners entering Germany. (There was one respect in which government intervention was welcome: the protection of the citizen against the rising crime rate.) The SPD's Schröder, in a statement that alienated many of his followers, said that any refugee convicted of a crime should be forthwith deported. As if in answer, a 10.6% decrease in the number of applicants for asylum in Germany was registered in 1997.

George Bush belatedly reaped his reward for having been the only ally of Germany who unreservedly welcomed German reunification. The former U.S. president was invited to attend the official celebration of the Day of Unity on September 30 as guest speaker. Mikhail Gorbachev was not. Said Erwin Teufel, president of Baden-Württemberg, "We don't owe the United States of America much—we owe them everything!" "Though much has changed in the past few years," said Helmut Kohl, who followed Teufel as speaker, "the axis of our foreign policy has not shifted." The chancellor added that Germany was regarded in all the capitals of Europe and in the U.S. as an "element of stability" in the international political scene. This could not be said of the prospective SPD-Green coalition, the Greens presenting in mid-October a position paper calling for the reduction of the Bundeswehr (armed forces) by more than half, an increase in the price of gasoline from DM 1.66 to DM 4 per litre (about $9.55 per gallon), and the dissolution of NATO. The SPD lost no time in denouncing the program as a "rejection of reality."

(GEORGE BAILEY)

GHANA

Area: 238,533 sq km (92,098 sq mi)
Population (1997 est.): 18,101,000
Capital: Accra
Head of state and government: Chairman of the Provisional National Defense Council and President Jerry John Rawlings

The elections of December 1996 resulted in a resounding victory for Pres. Jerry Rawlings, who received 57.2% of the vote, as opposed to 39.8% for his principal rival, John Kufuor. Similarly, in the legislative elections the ruling National Democratic Congress (NDC) won 133 of 200 seats, while 60 went to the New Patriotic Party. Nonetheless, these results provided the first real opposition to Rawlings and the NDC in 15 years. The turnout of voters was a highly respectable 76.8%. President Rawlings was sworn in for his new term on Jan. 7, 1997.

In his 1997–98 budget, presented at the end of February, Finance Minister Kwame Peprah said the government would introduce a bill with the aim of reintroducing the value-added tax (VAT), an incremental excise that is levied at each stage of the development of a product and has the effect of a sales tax on the ultimate consumer. Following widespread protests the tax had been dropped after its introduction in 1995. Concern about the new VAT continued to surface throughout the year. In September it was proposed that the tax be introduced during the July–September 1998 harvest season. The minister of communications, Ekow Spio-Garbrah, said, however, that the tax would not be introduced until the people were fully prepared for it.

In May a partnership between Leo Shield Exploration NL and the Canadian exploration company Golden Knight Resources Inc. announced the discovery of gold reserves totaling almost 14,175 kg (31,250 lb) on the Oda River in southwestern Ghana. Several new gold-mining projects were begun during the year. In Accra Coca-Cola Co. opened a new $9 million bottling plant.

(GUY ARNOLD)

This article updates the *Macropædia* article WESTERN AFRICA: *Ghana*.

GREECE

Area: 131,957 sq km (50,949 sq mi)
Population (1997 est.): 10,541,000
Capital: Athens
Chief of state: President Konstantinos Stephanopoulos
Head of government: Prime Minister Konstantinos Simitis

The political situation in Greece in 1997 was characterized by increasing dissatisfaction with the social cost of the government's economic policies. On January 28 farmers resumed protests they had interrupted in December 1996. Their demonstrations continued until February 8 and included road blocks in Thessaly that effectively halted traffic between central and northern Greece. On January 20 secondary-school teachers went on a strike that lasted until March 16, causing major problems in the educational sector and almost forcing Education Minister Gerasimos Arsenis to extend the school year. The health sector was affected by a three-week strike in June and July. Workers and employees in several other sectors, including waste removal and pharmacy, also staged shorter strikes throughout the year. Despite their overall conciliatory tone, Prime Minister Konstantinos ("Kostas") Simitis and Finance and Economics Minister Ioannis Papantoniou made it clear that they would stick to their tight fiscal policies.

In the spring the government tried to initiate a "social dialogue" aimed at reaching a consensus on the future course of Greece's social and economic policies. On May 14 Simitis officially launched the dialogue. The tripartite coordinating committee, comprising government, trade union, and employers' representatives, first met on May 27; the parliament debated the issue on June 10, and several commissions were established. Although the social dialogue began with cautious optimism on most sides, little came of it during the year. Discussions on a revision of the constitution proved equally fruitless. The central issue involved a proposed change to the article stipulating that early parliamentary elections must be held if the parliament fails to elect a new state president by a three-fifths majority in the third round of voting. Most opposition parties rejected a proposal by the ruling Panhellenic Socialist Movement (Pasok) to lower the requirement to a simple majority and to separate the presidential election from early parliamentary votes. On June 12 a 50-member parliamentary commission was set up to deal with the constitutional revision.

In late March the main opposition party, New Democracy, held its fourth congress. The meeting was intended to put an end to seven months of uncertainty after the party's loss in the parliamentary elections of September 1996 and to bridge the gap between conservative and liberal forces within the party. On March 21 Konstantinos ("Kostas") Karamanlis of the conservative wing, a nephew of the former longtime Greek prime minister and president of the same name, was elected new party leader with 70% of the delegates' vote.

The government experienced two changes in 1997. Deputy Foreign Minister Christos Rozakis resigned on January 2 because of bad health and was replaced on February 4 by Ioannis Kranidiotis. Transport Minister Charalambos Kastanidis resigned on September 1 after statements by Simitis that were critical of the Transport Ministry's work were leaked to the media. He was replaced by Simitis confidant Anastasios Mantelis.

In foreign policy 1997 was dominated by relations with Turkey and events in Albania. Greek-Turkish relations remained tense because of long-standing disputes regarding the Aegean Sea and because of Cyprus. One major issue was the purchase of Russian S-300 surface-to-air missiles by Cyprus in January and Turkey's negative reaction to the planned deployment of those arms on the divided island. On September 4 Defense Minister Apostolos Tsochatzopoulos said that Greece would consider a Turkish strike against the missiles cause for war between the two nations. A meeting between Simitis and Pres. Suleyman Demirel of Turkey during the Madrid NATO summit on July 8 resulted in a joint communiqué stating both sides' commitment to peace, security, and good neighbourly relations; respect for each other's sovereignty, international law, and international agreements; respect "for each other's legitimate, vital interests and concerns in the Aegean"; and the peaceful settlement of disputes without the threat of force. The meeting and the communiqué did not, however, address major disputed issues such as the territorial waters in the Aegean, and the communiqué was criticized by large parts of the political opposition in Athens. In November Simitis and Demirel formally agreed to carry out the provisions in the communiqué.

Events in Albania were relevant for Greece because of the Greek minority living in southern Albania and because of the possibility of a mass exodus of refugees from Albania to Greece. Along with Italy, Greece was one of the main contributors to the multinational force deployed in Albania. Greek troops were stationed in Albania from mid-April to early August. On September 25 Greece and Albania signed three defense-cooperation agreements.

Relations with Macedonia remained unchanged, with no breakthrough on the dispute over that country's name. Greek-Bulgarian relations remained calm, with no apparent shift in policy on either side following the Bulgarian elections in April.

The Greek economy continued its upward course in 1997. Gross domestic product was expected to grow by 3.5% (up from 2.6% in 1996). Inflation fell to a 25-year low of 5.6% in August, compared with 7.5% at the end of 1996. Greece continued, however, to be plagued by a large trade deficit of $18.8 billion (April 1997), and unemployment rose to 10.4%. Simitis pledged to continue his economic policies but predicted that 1998 would be "another hard year."

In August Athens served as host of the sixth track and field world championships, and on September 5 the Greek capital was awarded the 2004 Olympic Games.

(STEFAN KRAUSE)

GRENADA

Area: 344 sq km (133 sq mi)
Population (1997 est.): 98,400
Capital: Saint George's
Chief of state: Queen Elizabeth II, represented by Governor-General Daniel Williams
Head of government: Prime Minister Keith Mitchell

In March 1997 the Grenadan government's Mercy Committee, a government-appointed body that adjudicates requests for leniency for those convicted of murder, rejected a request from the Conference of Churches of Grenada that Phyllis Coard and Colville (Kamau) McBarnette—2 of the 14 people serving life sentences for the October 1983 murder of Prime Minister Maurice Bishop—be released from prison on humanitarian grounds. The Jamaica-born Coard—wife of Bishop's deputy Bernard Coard, who led the rebellion against Bishop and who was also serving a life sentence—was said to be experiencing severe psychiatric disorder, and McBarnette was described as suffering from persistent abdominal pains. Most Grenadans strongly opposed any leniency for Bishop's killers.

Grenada's relations with Cuba, which had been broken following the ouster by U.S. troops in 1983 of the extreme left-wing group that had seized power from Bishop, were fully restored in April when Prime Minister Keith Mitchell paid an official visit to Cuban Pres. Fidel Castro, during which an economic cooperation agreement was signed. Cuba had extended substantial assistance to Grenada during the Bishop regime, the outstanding example being the multimillion-dollar international airport.

Grenada's veteran politician and former prime minister Sir Eric Gairy died in August. (*See* OBITUARIES.) He founded the Grenada United Labour Party and a labour union, and the working class became his main support base.

(DAVID RENWICK)

This article updates the *Macropædia* article The WEST INDIES: *Grenada*.

GUATEMALA

Area: 108,889 sq km (42,042 sq mi)
Population (1997 est.): 11,242,000
Capital: Guatemala City
Head of state and government: President Alvaro Arzú Irigoyen

Following the peace treaty between the government and the guerrillas of the Guatemalan National Revolutionary Unity (URNG) on Dec. 29, 1996, a 155-member UN military observer mission went to Guatemala in February to oversee the demobilization of the rebel forces. By March 3, six camps totaling 3,614 armed URNG guerrillas had been set up for a 60-day disarmament process. In July the first major groups of refugees arrived from Mexico to occupy land bought for them by the government. About 10,000 of the estimated 30,000 refugees in Mexico were expected to return by the end of 1997. Several mass graves of Indians presumed killed by the army in 1981–82 were uncovered in Quiché province. It was claimed that there were at least 100 mass graves in the country, possibly containing some of the 45,000 people who disappeared during the civil war.

The cost of implementing the peace accords was estimated at $2.6 billion over five years, of which more than half would come from other countries. The International Monetary Fund criticized the government's tax policy and urged reforms that would increase the government's income. In 1996 tax revenues were only 8.4% of gross domestic product, the second lowest in the region, with only Haiti lower at 7%. Peace brought economic rewards; tourism boomed, with an expected 10% increase to 500,000 visitors in 1997, while in January–June tourism income rose 11% to $153 million.

The government pushed ahead with its plan to privatize state-owned companies. Empresa Guatemalteca de Telecomunicaciones (Guatel) was the biggest firm offered for sale in 1997, although there was opposition to that sale. A privatization bill was passed by Congress in March allowing state assets to be converted into shares, 5% of which would be sold to employees of the privatized companies. Appeals were made against the legislation, but in September the constitutional court upheld the law, clearing the way for the privatization of Guatel by the end of the year. Two power-generating stations were also sold as a first step toward privatizing the state electricity company, and others on the list included the railway company, airports, ports, the post and telegraph company, banks, and the tourism institute.

(SARAH CAMERON)

GUINEA

Area: 245,857 sq km (94,926 sq mi)
Population (1997 est.): 7,405,000 (including nearly 700,000 refugees from Liberia and Sierra Leone)
Capital: Conakry
Head of state and government: President Gen. Lansana Conté, assisted by Prime Minister Sidya Touré

During 1997 the government of Prime Minister Sidya Touré sought to broaden its role in inter-African affairs. In January Foreign Minister Lamine Camara met with top UN officials and expressed Guinea's willingness to mediate in the ongoing conflict between Cameroon and Nigeria over the oil-rich Bakassi peninsula. Both countries immediately accepted the offer. Following the May

Former Guatemalan National Revolutionary Unity (URNG) guerrilla members receive training for civilian life as part of a UN-brokered peace agreement between the URNG and the Guatemalan government. Some 3,600 guerrillas were placed in temporary camps around the country.

THOMAS HOEPKER—MAGNUM

25 military coup in Sierra Leone that overthrew the elected government of Pres. Ahmad Tejan Kabbah, Guinea's Pres. Lansana Conté announced that 1,500 soldiers would be sent to join the Nigerian-led West African ECOMOG force seeking to restore civilian rule. In August Sierra Leonean and Liberian citizens living in Guinea claimed that the presence of the exiled Kabbah in Conakry had caused the government to arrest large numbers of them for supposedly backing the rebel government in Sierra Leone.

Repercussions from Guinea's 1996 army mutiny continued to be felt. Seventy-five Liberians who had been imprisoned for months on charges of helping Guinean rebels were freed in April, but many mutineers remained in jail awaiting trial. On June 23 a special State Security Court was created to deal with them. Opposition parties attacked the court as being unconstitutional. In August the manager and the editor in chief of *L'Oeil,* a weekly newspaper in opposition to the government, were arrested and charged with libel and the publication of false information.

Despite a plunge in world gold prices, the Ghanaian-based Ashanti Goldfields Co. Ltd. continued its preparations for opening a new mine at Siguiri, in northeastern Guinea. The mine was expected to produce 4,252 kg (9,375 lb) annually when it reached full production.

(NANCY ELLEN LAWLER)

This article updates the *Macropædia* article WESTERN AFRICA: *Guinea.*

GUINEA-BISSAU

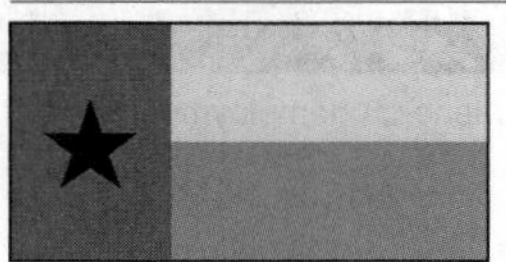

Area: 36,125 sq km (13,948 sq mi)
Population (1997 est.): 1,179,000
Capital: Bissau
Chief of state: President João Bernardo Vieira
Head of government: Prime Ministers Manuel Saturnino da Costa until May 27 and, from June 5, Carlos Correia

On June 5, 1997, Pres. João Vieira replaced Prime Minister Manuel Saturnino da Costa, whom he had dismissed on May 27 because of a serious political crisis, with a former prime minister, Carlos Correia. The crisis that led to da Costa's dismissal and required the deployment of troops in the capital and other towns to quell rioting arose out of protests by government employees against nonpayment of wages and poor working conditions. The new prime minister carried out a series of Cabinet changes between June 6 and 14.

A labour dispute broke out in August following Guinea-Bissau's entry into the Communauté Financière Africaine (CFA) franc zone, in which the nation gave up the peso for the CFA franc in order to improve its regional trade position. After talks with the government had failed, the nation's main trade union staged a three-day strike of government workers. The union wanted salaries to be aligned with those in the CFA franc zone in order to compensate for the sharp rise in food prices and the reduced purchasing power of workers that had resulted from the country's entry into the zone.

(GUY ARNOLD)

This article updates the *Macropædia* article WESTERN AFRICA: *Guinea-Bissau.*

GUYANA

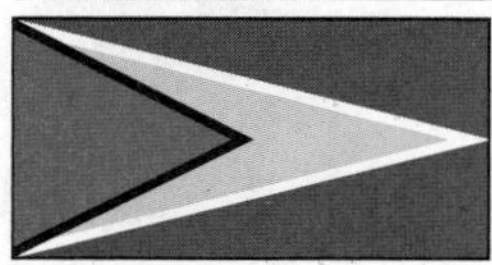

Area: 215,083 sq km (83,044 sq mi)
Population (1997 est.): 773,000
Capital: Georgetown
Chief of state: Presidents Cheddi Jagan and, from March 6, Sam Hinds
Head of government: Prime Ministers Sam Hinds and, from March 17, Janet Jagan

Guyana's outstanding political figure of the century, Pres. Cheddi Jagan, died March 6, 1997. (*See* OBITUARIES.) Jagan, who founded the People's Progressive Party (PPP) in 1950 as a socialist party, became in 1953 the first popularly elected premier in what was then British Guiana. Prime Minister Sam Hinds succeeded Jagan as president, as required by the constitution, and appointed the former president's widow, the American-born Janet Jagan, prime minister. In September Janet Jagan was nominated as PPP/Civic candidate for president in the general election scheduled for late 1997. In the election, on December 15, Jagan defeated former president Desmond Hoyte of the People's National Congress party. Hoyte vowed to contest the election, which he claimed had been rigged.

On June 29 Guyana and Cuba signed the final document of the 19th Mixed Intergovernmental Commission. The two countries agreed to strengthen their ties with one another and cooperate in such fields as public health, agriculture, fishing, and education.

(DAVID RENWICK)

This article updates the *Macropædia* article GUYANA.

HAITI

Area: 27,700 sq km (10,695 sq mi)
Population (1997 est.): 6,611,000
Capital: Port-au-Prince
Chief of state: President René Préval
Head of government: Prime Minister Rosny Smarth

Plagued by the desperately low living standards of many of its people, Haiti was a troubled nation at the beginning of 1997. During January there were violent demonstrations in Port-au-Prince and street protests throughout the country, together with a general strike on January 16 that included calls for the resignation of Prime Minister Rosny Smarth. Gang warfare broke out in the slum area of Cité Soleil near Port-au-Prince, and about 20 people were killed. There were more clashes in February, marked by widespread criticism of the new police force and calls for the UN police trainers to remain in Haiti until the end of the year. A second wave of violence in February resulted in 50 deaths. Another general strike on March 20 caused an outbreak of violence in Cap-Haïtien, and UN observers there had to be evacuated.

Many people blamed the disturbances on a conspiracy to destabilize the government, plotted by factions within the ruling Lavalas coalition. Supporters of former president Jean-Bertrand Aristide formed a breakaway movement, the Fanmi Lavalas (Lavalas Family), which registered as a political party in order to contest the April 6 Senate and municipal elections. The main opposition parties boycotted the elections, held for 9 of the 27 Senate seats, 2 deputies, members of 564 local assemblies, and 133 municipal representatives; less than 10% of the electorate voted. The Lavalas Family campaigned to replace Prime Minister Smarth with Aristide but failed to oust him in a vote of no confidence in the Chamber of Deputies on March 27.

The electoral board, the Conseil Electoral Provisoire (CEP), agreed on May 22 to postpone the second round of the Senate elections from May 25 to June 15 because of accusations of fraud in the first round and additional street violence and strikes. On June 9 Prime Minister Smarth resigned after having held office for 15 months. He criticized the CEP for failing to annul the results of the April elections and accused a group within Lavalas of stirring up political unrest. The CEP then announced the indefinite postponement of the elections, claiming that its preparations for the event were incomplete. This followed a warning from the U.S. that if the first round was not rerun in several areas, it would not recognize the election and might cut aid to Haiti. Pres. René Préval resisted calls to dismiss the CEP, which was widely seen as dominated by supporters of Aristide. He also delayed appointing a new prime minister, and Smarth remained temporarily in office pending a decision. Préval claimed that the electoral crisis should be resolved before a new prime minister was appointed and that the national legislature was the only body constitutionally able to take action concerning the CEP. The UN civilian mission suspended its technical aid for the CEP on August 19 after the latter had confirmed the controversial results of the first round of senatorial elections, which gave two seats to the Lavalas Family. The UN declared that the suspension would last until "honesty and credibility" had been reestablished.

President Préval nominated an official of the Inter-American Development Bank, Ericq Pierre, to be prime minister, but the Chamber of Deputies rejected his appointment on August 26 on the grounds that it had not been consulted in advance and that a politician rather than a professional bureaucrat was needed for the post. Late in the year the president had still not nominated another candidate, and on October 20 Smarth announced that he would stop running the government and called on his ministers to do the same. In mid-October a series of local elections was finally completed, and a permanent electoral council was formed. Aristide supporters dominated the elections.

More than 172 people were believed

Rotting garbage litters an urban area in Haiti, where living standards were desperately low. During the year the economy worsened, unemployment and crime levels rose, electricity blackouts were frequent, and the quality of other public services declined.

JEAN-LÉO DUGAST—PANOS

drowned in September when an overloaded ferry capsized as it tried to dock at Montrouis, on the west coast. It was transporting passengers from the Ile de la Gonâve, and when they all crowded to one side, the boat tipped over and sank in 35 m (115 ft) of water, some 50 m (165 ft) from shore. About 60 survivors swam to shore. (*See* DISASTERS.)

(SARAH CAMERON)

This article updates the *Macropædia* article The WEST INDIES: *Haiti.*

HONDURAS

Area: 112,492 sq km (43,433 sq mi)
Population (1997 est.): 5,823,000
Capital: Tegucigalpa
Head of state and government: President Carlos Roberto Reina Idiaquez

Two parties dominated the campaigning for the general elections on Nov. 30, 1997, the ruling Liberal Party (candidate Carlos Flores Facussé) and the National Party (candidate Nora Gunera de Melgar). Also contesting the elections were the National Innovation and Unity Party, the Christian Democrats, and the newly formed left-wing Democratic Unity. As well as concentrating on improving living standards, both leading candidates focused on public security in the light of rising crime. Flores was the winner in the election, gaining about 53% of the vote.

In March the government, private business, and labour unions signed a Social Pact designed to resolve a crisis stemming largely from a sharp rise in living costs in 1996. During the following month, however, the government accepted new economic adjustment conditions required by the International Monetary Fund (IMF), several of which contravened accords in the Social Pact. In 1996, for the third consecutive year, Honduras failed to meet IMF targets on inflation, the elimination of subsidies, privatization, and reduction of the fiscal deficit.

Following the murder of two Chortí Indian leaders in April, 2,000 indigenous people marched to Tegucigalpa to confront Pres. Carlos Roberto Reina. Subsequently, other ethnic minority leaders were killed; in all cases land disputes were the cause. Lack of progress in the handover of land promised to the Chortí led to a hunger strike by their leaders. This ended in August after the government pledged immediate action.

Honduras was involved in border negotiations in 1997 with both El Salvador and Nicaragua. The former revolved around the demarcation of logging areas, while at the end of May, Nicaraguan and Honduran gunboats exchanged fire in the disputed waters of the Gulf of Fonseca. Efforts to improve Honduran-Nicaraguan relations were made in order to promote a commercial corridor from Corinto, Nic., to Puerto Cortés, Honduras, as an alternative to the Panama Canal.

(BEN BOX)

This article updates the *Macropædia* article CENTRAL AMERICA: *Honduras.*

HUNGARY

Area: 93,030 sq km (35,919 sq mi)
Population (1997 est.): 10,157,000
Capital: Budapest
Chief of state: President Arpad Goncz
Head of government: Prime Minister Gyula Horn

The year 1997 in Hungary was marked by continued growth of the economy, significant changes in the electorate's party preferences, and increasing public debate over joining NATO. Financial problems in traditional state-sponsored sectors such as health care and education resulted in considerable public discontent and led to trade-union protests. The crisis-ridden agricultural sector also had a rough year; in the spring, farmers blocked roads across the country, protesting government plans to raise their taxes and contributions to the social security system.

Annual inflation dropped to 18% from 24% in 1996, and annual growth in gross domestic product (GDP) increased to 3% from 0.5%. Hungary continued to attract the largest amount of direct foreign investment in East-Central Europe, and the Budapest stock market strengthened its position as the region's strongest exchange. Even so, official growth figures stayed behind those of the fastest-growing economies in the region, partly because the government was unable to curtail the operations of the underground economy, which produced an estimated 30% of GDP. During the year the government launched a major campaign to update the pension system, and the National Assembly passed a pension-reform plan in July.

In April, Ivan Peto stepped down as chairman and caucus leader of the junior coalition party, the Alliance of Free Democrats. With his resignation, which came in the wake of growing public distrust in the governing parties after a privatization scandal in 1996, Peto wanted to give his party renewed dynamism before the 1998 general elections. By the end of the year, the senior coalition member, the Hungarian Socialist Party, had regained most of the supporters it had lost since 1996, despite a strengthening of opposition parties. Early in the year it appeared that the popularity of the moderate, centre-right Federation of Young Democrats-Hungarian Civic Party and the populist, radical right-wing Independent Smallholders' Party had reached that of the Socialists. That occurred partly as a result of general discontent with the economic austerity program launched in 1995 and partly because of high-level corruption scandals throughout 1996.

The rest of the opposition fell apart. In July 1997 the Christian Democratic People's Party split in two, and in the autumn parties formerly associated with the defunct Hungarian Democratic Forum and the Christian Democrats forged electoral alliances with the major opposition parties. The Young Democrats joined with the remains of the Democratic Forum and the moderate group of the Christian Democrats, while the Smallholders struck an alliance with the Christian Democrats' radical splinter group; thus, the political scene was divided into three major power blocs. In the meantime, extraparliamentary parties on the extreme left and extreme right also became significantly stronger; both extremes were fiercely opposed to Hungary's bid to become a member of NATO.

The long-anticipated offer came in July; Hungary, along with the Czech Republic and Poland, was invited to join NATO. Hungary was subsequently extended a special consultative status. Meanwhile, in its country reports on East-Central European associate countries, the European Union (EU) had given Hungary the best rating regarding its commitment to democracy, its economic competitiveness, and its advancement in adjusting its laws to EU standards.

In a November referendum, Hungarians overwhelmingly supported the country's NATO membership. Prior to that, however, the issue sparked a loud political and public debate. A suggestion put forward by the Young Democrats in September to hold a fully binding referendum on NATO membership prompted the Cabinet to call one itself. But the referendum plan was bogged down in a political scandal owing to the government's decision to link it with a referendum on a controversial passage of the land-reform bill, on which the opposition had initiated another referendum.

Opposition parties exploited public protests against government plans to allow foreign capital to enter the country's strategic agricultural sector and pushed for a total ban on planned foreign ownership. Their effort to put their own questions on referendum were turned down by the coalition parties, which held more than two-thirds of the seats in the National Assembly. The Constitutional Court finally ruled that in the opposition-supported land referendum, the original questions rather than those of the government should be asked, which prompted the National Assembly to postpone the issue until the next year.

Relations with the Roman Catholic Church were normalized in June when Prime Minister Gyula Horn signed an agreement with the Vatican; Hungary agreed that the state would return buildings and property seized from the church under communism or else pay compensation. In September the International Court of Justice in The Hague ruled that both Hungary and Slovakia were at fault in their bitter dispute over the Gabcikovo-Nagymaros hydroelectric project; Hungary had broken international law when it canceled construction work in 1989 and when it unilaterally withdrew from the 1977 bilateral agreement, while Slovakia did not have the right to divert the waters of the Danube to its own territory.

(ZSOFIA SZILAGYI)

ICELAND

Area: 102,819 sq km (39,699 sq mi)
Population (1997 est.): 271,000
Capital: Reykjavík
Chief of state: President Ólafur Ragnar Grímsson
Head of government: Prime Minister Davíd Oddsson

The economy of Iceland continued to grow in 1997. Gross domestic product was estimated to have increased by 3.5%, following a growth of 5.7% in 1996. The growth in 1997 was led primarily by domestic demand; private consumption rose 5% and gross fixed investment 20%. Exports, on the other hand, increased only 3%.

Most of the rise in investment was in the expansion of aluminum production capacity. The enlargement of the aluminum plant owned by the Alusuisse-Lonza Group was completed in 1997, and construction on a new aluminum plant owned by Columbia Ventures Corp., a U.S. company, began in 1997 and was scheduled to be completed in 1998. Another source of the surge in investment was enlargement by the National Power Company (Landsvirkjun) of its hydroelectric production capacity to meet the demand for power from the two plants. Furthermore, Norsk Hydro, a Norwegian company, was considering building in Reydarfjordur in the northeast of the country an aluminum plant that would initially produce 200,000 tons a year and eventually 500,000 tons.

Iceland's dispute with Norway and Russia over fishing by Icelandic vessels in a small pocket outside the 200-mi economic zones of each country continued in 1997, although with less intensity than in the two previous years owing to the fact that fish catches were down and fewer Icelandic vessels entered the area. The Norwegian and Icelandic coast guards maintained their vigilance toward each other's vessels and made one arrest each of fishing boats, arrests that were considered controversial. The boats were brought to harbour and fined for allegedly not reporting their catch and whereabouts in accordance with fishing regulations.

In October the vice president of Taiwan, Lien Chan, paid an unofficial visit to Iceland with a large delegation of Taiwanese officials and businessmen. His being greeted by Prime Minister Davíd Oddsson prompted a strong protest from the government of China, which demanded that Lien be turned away; the Icelandic authorities refused. A spokesman for China hinted that by allowing the visit, Iceland would have to take the consequences of its actions. Subsequently, China canceled several impending contracts with Icelandic businesses in order to emphasize its displeasure. (BJÖRN MATTHÍASSON)

INDIA

Area: 3,165,596 sq km (1,222,243 sq mi)
Population (1997 est.): 967,613,000
Capital: New Delhi
Chief of state: Presidents Shankar Dayal Sharma and, from July 25, Kocheril Raman Narayanan
Head of government: Prime Ministers H.D. Deve Gowda and, from April 21 to November 28, Inder Kumar Gujral

India commemorated 50 years of independence in 1997, but the celebrations were muted owing to concern about widespread corruption and crime in public life. Persistent political friction between the ruling 13-party United Front and the Congress (I) party resulted in the dissolution of the Lok Sabha (House of the People) on December 4. As the year ended, the country was facing a new general election after only 18 months.

Domestic Affairs. In April the Congress (I) party withdrew its support of Prime Minister H.D. Deve Gowda. The reason given was that although his minority United Front government was dependent upon the Congress, he did not consult the party about policies. On April 11 Deve Gowda lost a motion of no confidence in the Lok Sabha by 292 votes to 158. In his place the United Front elected the minister for external affairs, Inder Kumar Gujral, as leader. With the Congress backing him, Gujral was sworn in as prime minister on April 21 and gained the endorsement of Parliament the next day. He retained most of the members of the outgoing Council of Ministers and

STEVE MCCURRY—MAGNUM

Construction on the Sardar Sarovar Dam, one of a series of controversial dams planned for the Narmada River basin in India, continued in 1997. The long-delayed dam was expected to become one of the country's largest producers of hydroelectric power and to supply water for extensive irrigation.

later added four female ministers of state to increase women's representation.

In November a commission of inquiry issued a report stating that the Dravida Munnetra Kazhagam (DMK) party shared responsibility for the assassination of former prime minister Rajiv Gandhi in 1991. The Congress party then demanded that the United Front drop the DMK from its government. When the Front refused to do so, Congress withdrew its support from the government on November 28. Having lost his majority, Prime Minister Gujral resigned the same day. With no party or group in a position to form a viable government, the president dissolved the Lok Sabha on December 4 and called for new elections early in 1998.

In July, Kocheril Raman Narayanan (*see* BIOGRAPHIES) was elected president of India, defeating T.N. Seshan, to succeed Shankar Dayal Sharma. He was sworn in on July 25. The governor of Andhra Pradesh, Krishna Kant, was elected vice president to replace Narayanan. He defeated Surjit Singh Barnala.

Elections were held for the State Assembly of Punjab in February, and the ruling Congress (I) party was routed. The Bharatiya Janata Party (BJP) and the Shiromani Akali Dal (Badal), which campaigned as a coalition, won 93 of the 117 seats and formed a government with Prakash Singh Badal as chief minister. In Uttar Pradesh the BJP formed an alliance with the Bahujan Samaj Party (BSP); as a result, the president's rule was revoked, and on March 21 a government was installed with Mayawati of the BSP as chief minister. Under the terms of the deal, she stepped down after six months, and on September 21 Kalyan Singh of the BJP became chief minister. One of the first things he did was announce that a temple for Lord Rama would be built in Ayodhya. Earlier in September a special judge of Lucknow had ordered BJP leaders Kalyan Singh, L.K. Advani, and Murali Manohar Joshi, the Shiv Sena leader Bal Thackeray, and 45 others to stand trial for their role in the events that had culminated in the demolition of the Babri Mosque in Ayodhya in December 1992.

The chief minister of Bihar, Laloo Prasad Yadav, resigned on July 25 after the governor of the state sanctioned his prosecution along with that of another former chief minister, Jagannath Mishra, and others for misuse of public funds in the state veterinary department totaling Rs 9.5 billion. Yadav's wife, Rabri Devi, was elected leader of his party and took over as chief minister. In December the state was jolted when 61 persons belonging to landless labourers' families were massacred by a private army of landowners in the Jehanabad district.

Former prime minister P.V. Narasimha Rao was directed by the Delhi court to stand trial on charges of having bribed members of the Jharkhand Mukti Morcha political party in order to win a no-confidence motion in Parliament in 1993. The conviction of a former central minister, Kalpnath Rai, under the Terrorist and Disruptive Activities (Prevention) Act for having harboured a terrorist was struck down by the Supreme Court in November.

Parliament proclaimed primary education to be a fundamental right. A bill to set aside one-third of the seats in legislatures for women was stalled owing to lack of agreement among the parties. The Prasar Bharati Act, by which the government-owned radio and television stations were to be handed over to an autonomous organization, came into force in September.

The Supreme Court had, in December 1996, ordered the closing of 292 factories in order to curb pollution around the Taj Mahal in Agra. In 1997 the court directed that the felling of trees in forests be stopped. The court also asked government and industries to frame rules for the prevention of sexual harassment of women in workplaces.

On September 29 a 294-metric ton polar satellite launch vehicle was sent up from the space range at Sriharikota, Andhra Pradesh; the vehicle, in turn, launched a remote sensing satellite, IRS-1D. It was discovered, however, that the satellite's orbit required correction. Another Indian satellite, Insat-2D, which had been launched in June by a French rocket, developed trouble and was abandoned on October 5, disrupting the country's telecommunications and stock exchange operations.

The death on September 5 in Calcutta of Mother Teresa, the Albanian nun who had made India her home and had devoted her life to caring for the poor, was widely mourned. She was given a state funeral that was attended by dignitaries from several countries. (*See* OBITUARIES.)

The Economy. The financial crisis in East Asia affected the Indian economy, causing turmoil in the nation's stock market. The rupee plunged in value after August, reaching a low of Rs 39.82=$1 on December 2. Action by the Reserve Bank enabled the rupee to reach Rs 38.92=$1 by December 4.

In June the World Bank announced that it would provide India with $6.7 billion for carrying out economic reforms. The government monopoly in coal and lignite mining was ended. Proposals for disinvestment in several public-sector undertakings, including the Indian Oil Corporation, were also announced.

Despite a slowdown in exports, a growth rate of above 6% was forecast for the year. The growth rate in 1996–97 was placed at 6.8%, and the rate of savings at 25.6% of gross domestic product.

In his budget for 1997–98, presented on February 28, the finance minister, Palaniappan Chidambaram, announced further reductions in income and corporate taxes. Customs duties were also cut. The allocation for development plans was Rs 628,520,000,000, an increase of Rs 79,580,000,000, and for defense Rs 356,200,000,000, an increase of Rs 61,220,000,000. A voluntary tax disclosure scheme was announced to increase the number of income tax payers above the current 12 million.

During the year the government assumed a further burden of Rs 150 billion by accepting the recommendation of a pay commission to increase the salaries of four million government employees. To reduce the fiscal deficit, a surcharge of 3% on imports was levied. Prices of petroleum products were increased in August to curtail the deficit incurred by oil imports.

Foreign Relations. Elevation to the prime ministership enabled Inder Kumar Gujral to pursue with greater vigour the "Gujral Doctrine" of seeking better relations with India's immediate neighbours without demanding reciprocity. For example, a 30-year agreement with Bangladesh to share the waters of the Ganges River went into effect on January 1. A similar agreement was negotiated during the year to share the waters of the Teesta River. Transit facilities were extended to Nepal so that it would be able to use Bangladesh ports.

At a meeting of the South Asian Association for Regional Cooperation held in Male, Maldives, in May, it was decided to convert the South Asian Preferential Trading Arrangement into a South Asian Free Trade Area. The prime ministers of India and Pakistan met in Male and again in New York City in September to discuss bilateral matters. In September and October, however, an exchange of fire across the line of control in the disputed territory of Jammu and Kashmir by the armies of the two countries created a new complication.

Prime Minister Gujral met U.S. Pres. Bill Clinton in New York City in September. In an address to the UN General Assembly, Gujral advanced India's claim to a permanent seat in the enlarged Security Council. India also reiterated its opposition to the Comprehensive Test Ban Treaty. Earlier it had been announced that international inspection of two of the nation's nuclear reactors would be allowed. Over U.S. objections, Russia reaffirmed its decision to supply two nuclear reactors to India. During the year Russian Sukhoi SU-30 fighter aircraft were introduced into the Indian air force.

(H.Y. SHARADA PRASAD)

INDONESIA

Area: 1,919,317 sq km (741,052 sq mi)
Population (1997 est.): 199,544,000
Capital: Jakarta
Head of state and government: President Suharto

In 1997 it was hard to be an optimist in Indonesia. National elections in May provided little hope to those calling for a more open political system. During the campaign season the rumblings of discontent were the loudest, and most violent, in 25 years. Prior to the elections more than 200 people were killed as demonstrations by opposition parties turned into riots. The election commission banned Megawati Sukarnoputri, onetime leader of the Indonesian Democratic Party and daughter of the country's popular first president, from contesting a seat. She may have been one of the few able to upset the country's tightly controlled government. The results of the parliamentary polls on May 29 were not surprising. Leaders of Golkar—the longtime ruling party backed by President Suharto, the military, and big business—had confidently predicted that the party would take just over 70% of the vote. Golkar won a record 74.4%.

A day after the elections, the two legal opposition parties attributed Golkar's overwhelming victory to widespread balloting fraud; for the first time ever, the government acknowledged some election breaches and held new polls in nearly 90 locations. The new results did not significantly affect the national outcome. Golkar won 325 of the 425 seats being contested in the House of Representatives.

Golkar's win virtually ensured that the new legislature would reelect Suharto to another five-year presidential term in 1998, but those who believed Suharto's style of government was out of touch with society remained disaffected. The middle class became increasingly critical of the country's closed political system. Many in the business community felt cheated by the blatant abuse of power by the relatives of senior officials, and the poor were frustrated by a growing income gap. Nevertheless, the government saw its victory as support for its policies.

During the year there was even more speculation than usual about Suharto's successor. The 76-year-old president was typically silent on the subject, but many others had drawn up lists of vice presidential candidates. Among those often mentioned was the eldest of Suharto's children, Siti Hardyanti Rukmana (known as Tutut). She was Indonesia's foremost businesswoman—her diversified conglomerate PT Citra Lamtoro Gung Persada was worth an estimated $1 billion—and a top official in Golkar. Though Tutut hardly needed additional exposure, the campaign season heralded her real coming out as she traveled throughout Java, Indonesia's most populous island, to woo voters. Despite Tutut's popularity, she would not necessarily be a welcome choice for vice president, however. Such obvious nepotism would anger many Indonesians and frustrate hopes for more open political and economic systems.

Indonesia's economic prospects did not look bright, particularly during the second half of the year. Currency turmoil in Southeast Asia roiled Indonesia as well. The rupiah depreciated nearly 30% against the dollar, and confidence in the Indonesian economy plummeted. The government announced it would defer $35 billion worth of projects, but that was not enough to calm

(continued on page 440)

A mother and child cross a footbridge in a riverside slum in Indonesia, where political, economic, and environmental problems persisted throughout the year. Whereas the ruling Golkar party prospered, many Indonesians complained of social injustice and blamed the government for rising unemployment.

GREG GIRARD—CONTACT PRESS IMAGES

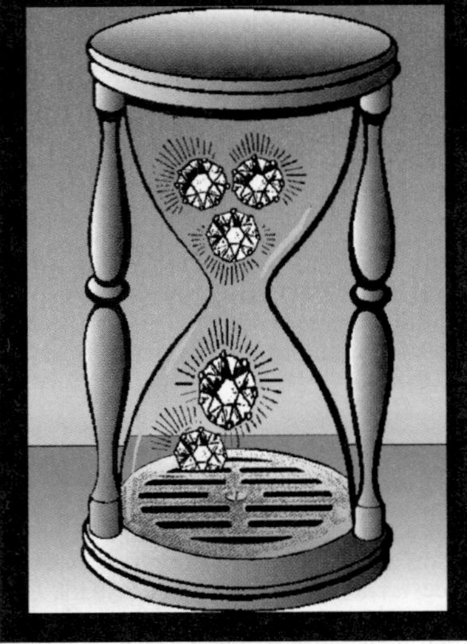

SPOTLIGHT

POVERTY IN SOUTH ASIA

by H.Y. Sharada Prasad

Illustration by Cathy Hull

The South Asian region, which comprises India, Pakistan, Bangladesh, Nepal, Sri Lanka, Bhutan, and Maldives, in 1997 accounted for one-fifth of the world's population, two-thirds of its absolute poor, and one-half of its illiterate adults. According to a well-researched study by Mahbub ul-Haq published in 1997, "South Asia is fast emerging as the poorest, most-illiterate, the most malnourished, the least gender-sensitive—indeed, the most deprived region in the world." Of the region's 1,191,000,000 inhabitants (mid-1993 estimate), 527 million earned less than $1 per day, 337 million had no access to safe drinking water, and half of the children were underweight. South Asia's annual per capita income of $309 was less than even that of sub-Saharan Africa, which stood at $551.

The region was not always so abysmally poor. Until 200 years ago, India (which also included the present Pakistan and Bangladesh) was a byword for wealth, the home of much-sought-after goods like cotton textiles, spices, sugar, and precious stones. Its affluence, however, paved the way for its poverty by attracting adventurers and invaders from the rest of Asia and from Europe. When European powers overran and colonized the region, they systematically drained its resources, a feature of colonialism. The rulers did introduce new technology and enlarge the area that was under irrigation, but their overall economic policies were not conducive to capital formation and access to the industrial know-how essential for industrialization and the modernization of agriculture. When Great Britain withdrew from the Indian subcontinent in 1947, the percentage of people deriving their livelihoods from industry was lower than it had been in the second half of the 18th century. Even during the centuries of affluence, however, Indian society was marred by extreme disparities, with the low-caste "untouchables" condemned to dire poverty.

The South Asian countries cannot blame colonialism for all their misfortunes. By 1997 they had been free for 50 years, and the policies they adopted are no less responsible for their plight. Several countries in the neighbouring region of East and Southeast Asia had also been colonized. Per capita incomes in both regions were roughly similar in 1968, but in the 30 years since that time, many of the East and Southeast Asian countries have made spectacular economic progress. According to Mahbub, "East Asia (excluding China) now enjoys 27 times the per capita income of South Asia."

The main reasons for East Asia's success include a move toward adoption of export-led growth, improvement of human capital through adult literacy and technical education, increased provision of health facilities, and land reforms. Another factor is the comparative stability of its governments, although many are authoritarian.

In contrast, the South Asian countries pursued government-led growth with extensive bureaucratic controls. India, for example, adopted centralized planning in 1952, which in the following three decades resulted in what was dubbed the "Hindu rate of growth" of 2–3% per year. While India is proud of its democracy, the system has led to a multiplicity of subsidies. Pakistan, which alternated between civilian and military rule, nevertheless achieved an annual growth rate of 6% for nearly four decades but with little impact on income disparities among its population. It has lagged behind its neighbours in literacy, health care, and population control. Sri Lanka has a creditable record of literacy and health services—the levels being comparable to those in many advanced countries—but has remained unable to accelerate its growth rate because of ethnic strife that has necessitated a defense outlay of 4.7% of gross domestic product (GDP). India and Pakistan also spend a high proportion of GDP on defense (3.6% in India and 7% in Pakistan).

Whatever else does or does not grow in South Asia, population does. During the last

CAROL GUZY—THE WASHINGTON POST

Calcutta, India

(Above) Thimphu, Bhutan; (right) Dhaka, Bangladesh

PHOTOS, CONTACT PRESS IMAGES; (TOP) DILIP MEHTA; (BOTTOM) FRANK FOURNIER

50 years, its population has almost tripled; it grew from 563 million in 1960 to the present 1,191,000,000. Because of modern drugs and national campaigns against epidemics, the mortality rate was easier to control than the birthrate. To be effective, birth control requires education, particularly of women, and well-organized public health services. Even though the percentage of people living below the poverty line in India was falling, there were more poor in India in 1997 than at the time of independence. In 1993 the number of poor people was estimated at 416 million, compared with a total population of only 361 million in the 1951 census. The region's average annual population growth rates between 1990 and 1995 were: India 1.8%, Pakistan 2.9%, Bangladesh 1.6%, Nepal 2.5%, and Sri Lanka 1.2%.

It is not as though there are no success stories in the region. India has achieved self-sufficiency in food production and has an array of technologically advanced industries. Pakistan has maintained a high economic growth rate. Bangladesh has brought down its population growth rate from 2.4% in 1980–90 to 1.6% in 1990–95 and has vibrant nongovernmental organizations working to develop the nation's economy. Sri Lanka has effective health services.

Mohandas Gandhi once described the essence of freedom as "wiping every tear from every eye." After 50 years of freedom, the percentage of those suffering hardship in South Asia is higher than in any other region of the world. The countries of the region have in recent months relaxed their rigid economic controls and begun giving the private sector a greater role in growth. By maintaining economic liberalization; allocating greater resources to literacy, technical education, and health services; and pursuing population-control measures with greater vigour, South Asia can within a generation cease to be the sick region of the world.

H.Y. Sharada Prasad is the former information adviser to the prime minister of India.

(continued from page 437)
investors. In October the government stated that it would work with the International Monetary Fund and the World Bank to reform the economy. Suharto ordered Widjojo Nitisastro, a respected economist and an old friend, to take charge of the overhaul. In early November the IMF agreed to a $23 billion assistance package for Indonesia. In return, Indonesia agreed, among other things, to close down 16 ailing banks and reform its financial industry. Japan and Singapore also announced that they would each extend $5 billion in stand-by credit to Indonesia.

Many in Indonesia hoped that the government's well-regarded technocrats, led by Widjojo, would press Suharto to eliminate monopolies and other privileged business arrangements, in particular the "national car," a controversial automaking venture that was headed by Suharto's youngest son and exempt from the luxury tax and tariffs. The growth of the economy was expected to slow during the coming year. In 1997 the economic growth rate was an estimated 6.8%, down from 7.5% in 1996. In 1998 that figure could drop to as low as 4.8%.

Another major problem casting a pall over Indonesia in 1997 was a months-long toxic haze. Forest fires, set by plantation owners and small farmers to clear land, burned out of control as the nation suffered from a drought exacerbated by El Niño. In August the smoke spread from the islands of Indonesia throughout Southeast Asia. Cities throughout the region declared their air quality hazardous. Thousands of people were sickened, schools and offices closed, and airline flights were canceled because of poor visibility. On September 26, in what was described as Indonesia's worst aviation disaster, a Garuda Indonesia plane encountered heavy smoke and crashed near Medan, killing all 234 people on board. (*See* DISASTERS.) It was impossible to calculate the long-term health and economic costs of the fires. Finally, in November, Indonesia experienced its first tropical downpours in six months.

(SUSAN BERFIELD)

IRAN

Area: 1,645,258 sq km (635,238 sq mi)
Population (1997 est.): 62,305,000 (excluding about 1.4 million Afghan refugees and 600,000 Iraqi refugees)
Capital: Tehran
Supreme political and religious authority: *Rahbar* (Spiritual Leader) Ayatollah Sayyed Ali Khamenei
Head of state and government: Presidents Hojatolislam Ali Akbar Hashemi Rafsanjani and, from August 4, Mohammad Khatami

Iran's Islamic regime celebrated its 18th year in power in 1997 by taking a major step toward more constitutional legitimacy and liberal conduct of state affairs. On May 23 the comparatively moderate Mohammad Khatami (*see* BIOGRAPHIES) was elected president in an unexpected landslide against the apparently strong conservative factions. No fewer than 91% of the electorate cast their votes, 69% in favour of Khatami. The popular mood for political change was in part a rejection of conservative hard-line policies, such as the Islamic dress code and constraints on economic growth, that caused a large number of women and young people to vote for Khatami. Others looked to Khatami to implement reforms that might lead to greater prosperity. The clear mandate given to the new president also offered him a genuine opportunity to achieve such political goals as the formation of political parties and greater civil rights.

The pace of reform after the elections was slowed by the continuing strength of the conservatives. Ali Akbar Nategh-Nouri, Khatami's main rival in the presidential election, remained speaker of the *Majlis* (parliament), and Ayatollah Sayyed Ali Khamenei remained the country's spiritual leader. The election of Khatami also did not affect the key councils of state, such as the Council of Guardians or the Expediency Council, which regulated constitutional affairs. Nonetheless, following the swearing in of Khatami on August 4, the new Cabinet appointments showed that reformist policies were most to be expected in cultural and domestic arenas, with cautious moves for modernization elsewhere. The 22 Cabinet appointees were all male, with Hassan Habibi retaining the post of first vice president and Abdullah Nouri becoming the minister of the interior. Important posts in the hands of supporters of Khatami's liberal policies were Kamal Kharrazi as minister of foreign affairs, Bijan Namdar-Zanganeh as oil minister, Ataollah Mohajerani as minister of Islamic culture and guidance, and Hossein Nemazi as minister of economic affairs and finance. The conservatives retained the Ministry of Intelligence under Dorri Najafabadi and the Ministry of Justice under Esmail Shushtari but were heavily outnumbered in this youthful Cabinet, confirmed by the *Majlis* on August 20. As a strong gesture in recognition of an improved role for females in the new administration, Massoumeh Ebtekar was appointed vice president for environmental affairs, and several deputy ministerial posts were also allocated to women. During the vote in the *Majlis,* the conservatives never won more than 96 of the 270 seats available, which showed that the balance of power in the *Majlis* appeared for the first time since the revolution to favour the progressive wing of the regime.

The retiring president, Hashemi Rafsanjani, made it clear in February that he would retain an influential and watchful position within the Islamic regime even after resigning office. He became chairman of the Expediency Council in February with a term of five years as arbiter of policy making.

A warning of political change was issued in June when Khamenei endorsed a campaign against corruption in public life. During the year several senior officials, including a former commander of the Revolutionary Guards, were imprisoned for embezzlement of public funds and for having taken bribes.

The new Iranian president made it clear in a speech on June 1 that he was not, in principle, against a renewal of ties with the United States, and in December he said that he hoped to reestablish a discussion with the American people. In late September there were fears voiced in Israel that Iran had acquired advanced missile and nuclear technology from Russian sources, which suggested that, contrary to U.S. wishes, Iran was still pursuing development of weapons of mass destruction. Iran's support for Islamic movements dedicated to halting the Arab-Israeli peace process and its alleged involvement in international terrorism—as, for example, in a 1992 bombing of a Berlin café—created added tensions to relations with the U.S. U.S. sanctions on Iran remained in place but were challenged in September when a $2 billion gas-development project in Iran was sponsored by companies from France and Russia.

The economy made moderately good progress because of buoyant oil revenues,

Women, wearing dark-coloured, loose-fitting garments and face coverings in public as required by Islamic code, board a bus in Mashhad. Along with the young and middle class, women played a large role in the landslide victory of the moderate Mohammad Khatami in Iran's presidential election in May.

IAN BERRY—MAGNUM

estimated at $16 billion in 1997, with growth in national income rising to more than 5% and foreign debt reduced to $19 billion. The annual rate of inflation fell to 25%, but unemployment remained at some two million. (KEITH S. MCLACHLAN)

IRAQ

Area: 435,052 sq km (167,975 sq mi)
Population (1997 est): 22,219,000
Capital: Baghdad
Head of state and government: President and Prime Minister Saddam Hussein

During 1997 UN Security Council Resolution 986 permitted Iraq to export $2 billion of oil each six months for a maximum of $4 billion in order to meet the country's humanitarian needs. The proceeds were to be used for food, medicine, and other necessities of life; as reparations to victims of the war against Kuwait; and as payment for the costs of UN operations in Iraq. Still under a general sanctions regime, Iraq had no direct control over oil revenues; the oil income went into an escrow account, and contracts for purchases had to be approved by a UN sanctions committee. After many previous rejections of the plan, Iraq announced its acceptance of the "oil for food" resolution, and oil began flowing on Dec. 10, 1996.

The second six-month period of oil exports was delayed by the Iraqi government and the UN until a new distribution plan could be worked out. An agreement was finally reached, and on Aug. 19, 1997, Iraq once again began exporting oil. According to the agreement, Iraq was responsible for the distribution of food and medicine in central and southern Iraq, but in doing so it was closely monitored by UN inspection teams. In the northern, Kurdish-controlled areas of Iraq, the UN Department of Humanitarian Affairs was responsible for the distribution.

Goods purchased by Iraq under the terms of the agreement started to arrive in Iraq in March. The government, however, complained that the UN was too slow in approving contracts that Iraq had signed with foreign companies.

In the summer of 1997, Ambassador Rolf Ekeus stepped down as head of the UN Special Commission (UNSCOM) on Iraq and was replaced by Richard Butler, the Australian ambassador to the UN and an expert on arms control. Butler assumed his new position on July 1, 1997, and visited Baghdad later that month. Previously, on June 21, after several incidents designed to prevent UNSCOM officials from inspecting locations in search of documents and weapons, the UN Security Council threatened Iraq with additional sanctions if it continued to hinder the work of the UNSCOM search teams.

In October, after further challenges, the UN Security Council, led by the U.S., debated adding new sanctions on Iraq but was unable to produce a unanimous resolution; instead, it decided to postpone applying new sanctions. Iraq, on its part, announced on October 29 that it would expel the American members of the UNSCOM team. This act generated a new crisis with the UN. The Security Council condemned Iraq and insisted that inspectors of all nationalities remain on the UNSCOM team. On November 4 Iraq agreed to postpone the date when the Americans would be expelled. On November 13 Iraq expelled six American weapons inspectors. The U.S. then threatened military action against Iraq, and on November 20 Iraq allowed the U.S. inspectors to return. A conflict then arose over sites, particularly the many palaces of Saddam Hussein, that remained closed to the inspectors, and at the year's end it had not been resolved.

After bloody fighting in 1996, the two rival Kurdish parties, the Kurdish Democratic Party (KDP), led by Mas'ud al-Barzani, and the Patriotic Union of Kurdistan, led by Jalal at-Talabani, signed a cease-fire agreement on Oct. 23, 1996. After intermittent skirmishing, the cease-fire broke down on Oct. 12, 1997, with serious military clashes between the two parties. In May and again in October 1997, Turkey undertook major military incursions into northern Iraq in pursuit of guerrillas of the Kurdish Workers' Party (PKK), a separatist group of Turkish Kurds that was using northern Iraq as a base for raids into Turkey. The incursion inflicted heavy losses on the PKK fighters. The Turks allied themselves with Barzani and the KDP, whose forces helped the Turks in their offensives and to whom they relinquished some territory.

Relations between Iraq and its Arab neighbours, particularly Syria and Jordan, improved in 1997. Relations between Syria and Iraq, both ruled by competing factions of the Arab Socialist Ba'th Party, had deteriorated in 1980 when Syria sided with Iran during the Iran-Iraq War. Syria took the initiative in easing relations by sending a commercial delegation to Baghdad in May 1997. In August the two countries opened an official border crossing point and exchanged several trade delegations. Iraqi-Jordanian relations also improved when King Hussein of Jordan appointed 'Abd as-Salam al-Majali prime minister.

(LOUAY BAHRY)

IRELAND

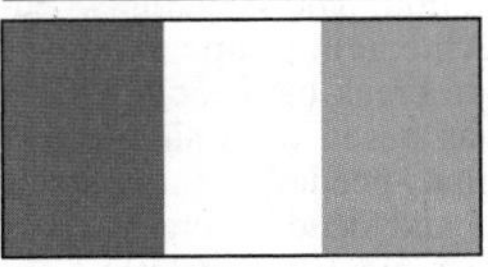

Area: 70,285 sq km (27,137 sq mi)
Population (1997 est.): 3,644,000
Capital: Dublin
Chief of state: Presidents Mary Robinson and, from November 11, Mary McAleese
Head of government: Prime Ministers John Bruton and, from June 26, Bertie Ahern

Political issues past, present, and future merged in 1997, an eventful year dominated by an inconclusive general election. Power changed hands but without any clear shift in voting patterns, and a new government emerged that had to depend not only on the involvement of a partner but also on the uncertain support of independent deputies. Radical change took place in Northern Ireland, with the close involvement of the Dublin government, but there again no clear resolution emerged.

Prime Minister John Bruton called the election for June 6 and declared the main plank in his program to be that of his own leadership and the coherent and united performance of what had become known as the "rainbow coalition," a centre-left partnership of his own Fine Gael Party and the Labour and Democratic Left parties. Their performance had undoubtedly been effective, and they were riding on a tide of economic success that was the envy of many larger European countries. This resurgence in growth and economic development justified electoral promises from all candidates, among them reduction in taxation, and led to a keenly fought campaign. It was inconclusive, however, the main loser being the Labour Party, whose fall in public support meant that the Bruton-led administration did not return to power. It was replaced by a centre-right coalition led by Fianna Fail and supported by the Progressive Democrats and independents that included Sinn Fein, the political wing of the Irish Republican Army. On June 26 Parliament voted to replace Bruton as prime minister with Bertie Ahern, leader of Fianna Fail.

A major judicial inquiry into corruption focusing on a leading Irish businessman's cash gifts to politicians was suspended during the election campaign. On its resumption sensational revelations emerged about the former prime minister, Charles Haughey, who had financed his lavish personal life with gifts and possibly with bribes from wealthy Irish businessmen. The country was rocked by unprecedented revelations involving offshore bank accounts in which unnamed Irish people of wealth held funds, apparently in defiance of revenue and taxation laws.

The inquiry, under Judge Brian McCracken, not only leveled adverse judgments against Haughey but also raised many additional queries about possible corruption. These were directed at those men and women appointed to the new Ahern administration who had previously been part of governments led by Haughey. Two additional inquiries were established, one of them investigating the newly appointed foreign affairs minister, Ray Burke; under constant siege by opposition parties and the press, he was forced to resign both his appointment and his seat in the legislature. The inquiries destabilized the government, despite protestations to the contrary from the participating parties, and also damaged the standing of Ireland with many Northern Ireland politicians, who felt that the delicate peace talks were not helped by their being conducted by a minister under accusation of wrongdoing.

The McCracken tribunal also raised questions about other ministers in the government, and the wrangling about possible corruption continued into the autumn, with few people optimistic about the full-term survival of the Ahern administration. In September Jim Kemmy, a senior member of the Labour Party, died, and the government was confronted with a second by-election.

Pres. Mary Robinson announced in March that she would not run for a second term when her seven-year term drew to a close in November. The effect of this news was to throw every political party into confusion. They sought agreement to appoint

John Hume, leader of the Northern Ireland Social and Democratic Labour Party, to the office. This would make an election unnecessary. There was, however, considerable controversy over Hume because of his involvement in the Northern Ireland peace process, and he consequently withdrew his name from consideration. As the election neared, there were five candidates for the presidency, four of them women. The leading contender was the Fianna Fail candidate, Mary McAleese, a Catholic nationalist from the North of Ireland and pro-vice chancellor of Queen's University, Belfast. Attempts by the opposition parties to link her name with Sinn Fein following her endorsement by Gerry Adams, leader of that party, served only to increase her popularity, and in October she was elected president by a large majority.

The nation's economy prospered throughout the year. It demonstrated its effectiveness by producing generous budgetary surpluses and, at 1%, the lowest annual inflation rate in the European Union. This provided the minister for finance, Charlie McCreevy, with great leeway over tax and development programs for his December budget. It was welcome news for a government otherwise beset with difficulties.

(MAVIS ARNOLD)

See also *United Kingdom.*

ISRAEL

Area: 20,320 sq km (7,846 sq mi), not including territory occupied in the June 1967 war
Population (1997 est.): 5,652,000
Capital: Jerusalem is the proclaimed capital of Israel (since Jan. 23, 1950) and the actual seat of government, but recognition has generally been withheld by the international community.
Chief of state: President Ezer Weizman
Head of government: Prime Minister Benjamin Netanyahu

The year 1997 began with a major agreement between Israel and the Palestinians. After months of procrastination, Israeli Prime Minister Benjamin Netanyahu finally agreed on January 15 to withdraw Israeli troops from most of the West Bank town of Hebron. The pullback marked the completion of a key phase in the Oslo peace process—the handover by Israel of seven major West Bank towns to Palestinian rule.

The move was hailed as a historic watershed. Netanyahu, who in opposition had led a vehement campaign against the Oslo accords, now seemed to recognize their necessity. He agreed to additional Israeli pullbacks from the West Bank, and there were hopes that he would have the authority to reconcile most of the disaffected right-wing Israelis to the peacemaking process with the Palestinians.

Within weeks, however. Netanyahu, under right-wing pressure from within his government coalition, announced his intention to build a new Jewish settlement in the East Jerusalem site Har Homa (known as Jabal Abu Ghneim to Palestinians) on land claimed by the Palestinians. The decision sparked Palestinian protests and accusations of bad faith. Palestinian mistrust of Israeli motives was compounded on March 7 when the Israeli government announced that in the first phase of further withdrawal from the West Bank, Israel would hand over only 2% of "area C," land controlled exclusively by Israel, and 7% of "area B," land controlled jointly, to the Palestinian Authority (PA). The Palestinians, who had expected some 30%, spurned the Israeli offer, and the peace process faltered. It broke down completely when a terrorist bomb ripped through the Apropos Cafe in Tel Aviv on March 21, killing three young women. Although the suicide bomber was a member of the Hamas fundamentalists, who were opposed to accommodation with Israel, Netanyahu accused Palestine Liberation Organization Chairman Yasir 'Arafat of giving a "green light" to terrorism. Mutual recrimination and growing mistrust led to a breakdown in security cooperation.

To revive the peace process, Netanyahu postponed deadlocked interim negotiations and proposed moving directly to "final status" talks on the key issues of borders, Jewish settlements, Palestinian refugees, and Jerusalem. His final status proposals, however, fell far short of minimal Palestinian aspirations. Although never precisely articulated, his plan offered the Palestinians about 50% of the West Bank, in five separate areas cut off from each other by "strategic roads" that would remain under Israeli control.

On July 30 two more suicide bombers blew themselves up in the Mahane Yehuda fruit and vegetable market in Jerusalem, killing 16 people. Netanyahu declared that there would be no further land transfers to the Palestinians until the terrorism stopped, a statement seen by some as signaling the end of the Oslo process. The situation deteriorated further when at least four more Israelis were killed in a triple suicide bombing in Jerusalem at the Ben Yehuda pedestrian mall on September 4.

Netanyahu responded to the terror by closing off Palestinian areas and holding back some $40 million in Palestinian tax payments, measures that exacerbated economic hardship and drew widespread international condemnation. The Egyptians, Europeans, and Americans spearheaded mediation efforts to break the deadlock. The American plan was based on a simple formula: the Palestinians needed to show determination in word and deed to crack down on terror, and the Israelis had to refrain from further unilateral actions like the construction at Har Homa.

In September, U.S. Secretary of State Madeleine Albright (*see* BIOGRAPHIES) visited Israel and urged Netanyahu to accept a "time-out" on settlement activity for the duration of peace negotiations. The Israelis insisted that both the scope and the duration of the time-out be more closely defined. In early November, Israeli Foreign Minister David Levi met Palestinian deputy leader Mahmoud Abbas (Abu Mazen) in Washington, D.C., but failed to establish a basis for final status talks. Meanwhile, in December Netanyahu said that the West Bank up to the Jordan River would always belong to Israel.

As the peace process with the Palestinians floundered, relations between Israel and other Arab countries suffered, including those with its closest peace partner, Jordan. After the decision to build at Har Homa, Jordan's King Hussein wrote an angry letter to Netanyahu accusing him of endangering regional stability. A few days later, on March 13, a Jordanian soldier opened fire on a group of Israeli schoolgirls visiting a border tourist site, killing seven. Hussein, showing both compassion and courage, visited the bereaved families in Israel, a gesture that did much to restore confidence in the resilience of the Israel-Jordan peace.

The close strategic relations between the two countries frayed in late September, however, after Israeli Mossad intelligence agents tried to kill a fundamentalist Hamas leader on Jordanian soil. Hussein, who only weeks before had been host to Mossad Chief Dani Yatom, felt betrayed. It was, he said, as if a guest he had invited into his home had raped his daughter. To assuage the king's wrath, Netanyahu was forced to release the jailed Hamas spiritual leader, Sheikh Ahmad Yassin, whom Hussein had hoped to use as a lever to boost his influence on the West Bank. The key questions, though, were whether the ailing 61-year-old Yassin, after eight years in Israeli imprisonment, retained his influence over the militant wing of Hamas and, if he did, whether he would use it to curb or promote terror.

Relations between Israel and Egypt, the other Arab country with which Israel had a formal peace treaty, also soured in the wake of the Israeli-Palestinian deadlock and sank to their lowest ebb in years when an Israeli businessman, 'Azzam 'Azzam, was sentenced in Cairo on August 31 to 15 years on charges of spying for Israel. Israeli government and opposition leaders assured the Egyptians of 'Azzam's innocence, but Egyptian Pres. Hosni Mubarak refused to intervene on 'Azzam's behalf, arguing that Netanyahu had made this impossible by criticizing the Egyptian legal system.

The most volatile of Israel's borders remained that with Lebanon. Fighting between Israel and the Iranian- and Syrian-backed Hezbollah troops in southern Lebanon took a heavy toll. In a helicopter crash in February, 73 Israeli military personnel were killed on their way to Israel's self-declared security zone. In September, 12 more Israeli soldiers died in an abortive naval commando raid near Sidon, and calls for a unilateral Israeli pullback from Lebanon mounted. On November 9 former deputy foreign minister Yossi Beilin, of the Labor Party, placed himself at the head of a popular movement for withdrawal. In response, Maj. Gen. Antoine Lahad, commander of the Israeli-backed South Lebanese Army (SLA), warned that if Israel abandoned him and his men, they might join the Hezbollah. Israeli spokesmen insisted that a unilateral pullback would put Israeli towns and villages at risk. They argued that a withdrawal was possible only in the context of a wider peace deal with Syria, the one power in the area that could control the Hezbollah. Peace talks between Israel and Syria remained frozen, however, as Netanyahu refused to continue the negotiations begun by the previous Labor government.

As he seemed to stumble from one controversy to the next, Netanyahu's standing as prime minister was seriously compromised. His appointment in January of Roni Bar-On, a Likud Party functionary, as attor-

CHRISTOPHER MORRIS—BLACK STAR

Palestinians demonstrate against the construction of houses by Israelis in East Jerusalem. The start of the housing projects in March provoked renewed fighting between the two sides that disrupted the delicate peace process.

ney general sparked a police inquiry. After an investigation that lasted nearly three months, during which the prime minister was interrogated, Elyakim Rubinstein, the new attorney general, decided not to press charges against him.

At one time during the year, it seemed as if his government might fall over the question of religious conversions to Judaism, after Conservative and Reform Jews petitioned the Supreme Court, challenging the monopoly of the Orthodox Jews on this practice. The Orthodox parties demanded that Netanyahu push through legislation that would enshrine their position on this issue and threatened to bring his government down if he did not do so. Netanyahu's secular coalition partners threatened to bring the government down if he did.

American Jews, most of them Conservative or Reform, warned of a schism if the proposed legislation was enacted and threatened to reduce their fund-raising for Israel in that event. Netanyahu set up a committee to work out a compromise, and when its proposals were rejected by the Orthodox in October, all sides agreed to allow an additional three months for devising a solution.

On June 3 the Labor Party elected former army chief of staff Ehud Barak to become its new leader. In a bid to break the mold of Israeli politics, he apologized to the Jews who had moved to Israel in large waves during the late 1940s and early '50s from Arab countries, many of whom supported the Likud Party, for any slights they may have received at the hands of the Labor movement.

The year was not a good one for the Israeli economy. Growth was down to 2.1% after a 4% rise in 1996. Another concern was the rise in unemployment, up from 6.7% to about 8%. There were some positive signs, however. Inflation declined from 10% to about 8%, and foreign currency reserves rose to a staggering $19 billion as abnormally high interest rates and an intensive privatization campaign attracted foreign investors.

(LESLIE D. SUSSER)

ITALY

Area: 301,323 sq km (116,341 sq mi)
Population (1997 est.): 57,511,000
Capital: Rome
Chief of state: President Oscar Luigi Scalfaro
Head of government: Prime Minister Romano Prodi

The first centre-left coalition to govern Italy since the proclamation of the Italian Republic in 1946 continued to do so throughout 1997 despite a crisis that tested the unity of the Italian left and threatened to bring down the government. The year was also marked by an exceptional succession of devastating earthquakes that left thousands of people homeless.

The crisis involved the so-called Olive Tree coalition (L'Ulivo) led by the centrist Prime Minister Romano Prodi but with, as its "trunk," Italy's largest party, the Democratic Party of the Left (PDS), once the Communist Party. The coalition emerged from elections held in April 1996, and it collided with trouble in October, following 17 months in office largely devoted to brisk economic housecleaning aimed at enabling Italy to qualify to be among the first to adhere to the European economic and monetary union (EMU), a goal seen by all parties as vital for the country's future competitiveness. The process consisted partly of attempts, judged by outsiders as praiseworthy, both to narrow the percentage gap between deficit and productivity and to cut spending. To further help balance its books, the government levied a special, one-time-only, "Euro tax" on its citizens. Although many did so grudgingly, the Italians paid the tax and thus signified, the government concluded, public awareness of the importance of the EMU. Prime Minister Prodi commented that his overall purpose was to turn Italy into a "normal country"—that is, to rid it of notoriously inefficient public services and political seesawing.

Another key aim of the Prodi government was constitutional reform, again seen by both left and right as essential for stabilizing Italy's chronic political instability. To that end a 70-member Parliamentary Commission was established in February, chaired by the leader of the PDS, Massimo D'Alema, and including the right-of-centre opposition Forza Italia movement, headed by media magnate and former prime minister Silvio Berlusconi (who was later convicted of financial misdeeds). In June the commission voted unexpectedly to favour a "semipresidential" constitution for Italy, one similar to that of France. Berlusconi and the leader of the extreme right-wing National Alliance, Gianfranco Fini, supported this decision. The commission also urged adoption of a far-reaching new federal structure, marked by a wholesale devolution to the country's 20 regions of powers previously held by the national government. In September it set about drafting final recommendations, which, to be adopted, needed a two-thirds majority in both houses of the legislature.

In northern Italy, Umberto Bossi, the leader of the Northern League, which accused the national government of squandering northern wealth, dropped his campaign for federalism in favour of outright secession for an ill-defined land in the north he called "Padania." Paramilitary squads called "Green Guards" appeared at Bossi's rallies, and they clashed with police during a visit to Verona by Pres. Oscar Scalfaro in September. Though Bossi announced his desire to form a "Padanian parliament," his candidates were defeated in local elections in April in Milan, Turin, and Trieste. The most vivid demonstration of secessionist feeling took place in May when an eight-man commando group scaled the tall bell tower overlooking St. Mark's Square in Venice and from it unfurled the flag of the old (independent) Venetian Republic, claiming to be champions of its resuscitation. In the square was a homemade armoured car that they had transported across the lagoon from the mainland aboard a hijacked ferry. The men envisaged, it later transpired, a republic with its own coinage and its own Olympic Games. Four of them were later given jail terms of six years; the others, four years and nine months.

The year's major disturbance took place in October when the Communist Refoundation Party, led by Fausto Bertinotti and belonging to neither the Olive Tree nor the Cabinet, suddenly withdrew its parliamentary support from the government. Left without a majority in the legislature, Prime Minister Prodi tendered his resignation to President Scalfaro amid dismay over sabotage of the left by the left. Ostensibly, Bertinotti's purpose was to obstruct a stringent, Europe-oriented budget that curbed social services and pensions. But most Italian commentators saw it instead as a call for attention from old-style, loyally orthodox militant communists afraid of being overtaken in a changing Italy moving toward social democracy.

Within a week the revolt ended. Bertinotti reconsidered and finally signed a one-year extendable nonbelligerence pact with the government so as not to hinder Italy's entry into the EMU and reform at home. In return he won a pledge for a law establishing a 35-hour workweek by 2001. He then agreed to the budget and backed a confidence motion that the government won by 319 votes to 285.

In September violent earth tremors struck the regions of Umbria and Marche in central Italy and, unusually, continued to do so with unabated force and on two broad fronts for a period of weeks. The repeated quakes, at times numbering more than 100 a day, inflicted severe damage. They wreaked havoc on 48 townships, wiping some off the map, destroying art treasures and (Parliament was told) 1,150 historic buildings in the process. In the third week of the tremors, the government counted 38,000 homeless. They were forced, as winter approached, into tents, trailers, and prefabricated structures. Eleven people were killed and some 100 injured. Four of the dead, two of them members of a Roman Catholic religious order, perished under vaults that crashed down from the roof of the Upper Church of the famed 13th-century Basilica of St. Francis in the Umbrian hill town of Assisi. Two large ceiling frescoes lost in the church were a masterpiece (showing St. Mark) by Cimabue (*c.* 1250–1302) and a St. Jerome attributed to his pupil, Giotto (1266?–1337). Giotto's famous fresco cycle illustrating the life of St. Francis was relatively unharmed. Prodi promised that Assisi would be fully restored by 2000.

In its endless contest with the Mafia crime organization, the government scored a success with the capture in June of Pietro Aglieri, regarded as the second in command in the hierarchy of the Mafia, behind the jailed "boss of bosses" Salvatore ("Toto") Riina. On the wanted list for eight years, Aglieri simply put his hands up and surrendered when 50 police, with 250 others behind them, used stun grenades to burst into his hideout, a high-walled farmhouse near Palermo, Sicily. A well-educated and cool gunman already facing a life sentence for murder, Aglieri was also wanted for his alleged part in the killings in 1992 of Judge Giovanni Falcone, Italy's top investigator of the Mafia, and two months later his colleague Paolo Borsellino.

Also during the year the Camorra, as the Mafia in and around Naples was called, plunged into an especially vicious bout of bloodletting between rival clans following a lengthy truce between them; in July, after dozens of killings, the government sent some 500 troops into Naples. Some 200 other police were rushed to the nearby province of Caserta, where eight clans had gone to war with one another.

Italian troops were also dispatched to Albania in April as part of an eight-nation, 6,000-strong protection force, proposed and led by Italy under the auspices of the UN, the aim of which was, over three months, to ensure the safe passage of humanitarian aid to a civilian population suffering from the effects of antigovernment insurrection and anarchy in Albania in the wake of mass pauperization after a major financial scandal. During the crisis an estimated 10,000 Albanians were perilously ferried (by Albanian delinquents, claimed Italy) across the then often stormy Adriatic to the Italian coast, swelling to a calculated 63,000 the number of Albanians in Italy, which made them the second largest foreign community, after that of Morocco (119,000). One rusting former Albanian minesweeper making for Italy with would-be refugees was sunk after it collided with the Italian naval corvette *Sibilla.* It was later salvaged from a depth of 800 m (2,624 ft), after which the Italians established the number of drowned in the incident at 59.

In July a military court in Rome at a retrial sentenced Erich Priebke, an 83-year-old former Nazi officer who had been extradited from Argentina, to 15 years in jail for responsibility in the massacre in 1944 of 335 Italians. The Nazis had ordered the executions in reprisal for a Rome street ambush of a German patrol by Italian partisans. The court sentenced Karl Haas, a former Nazi major who told the court he had killed two of the victims himself, to 10 years. Each man was, however, "excused" 10 years of his punishment. Judge Luigi Maria Flamini later explained that both men had deserved life sentences but had been spared them because of their advanced ages. Flamini said he had found Priebke guilty of a key role in the arrest and torture of the Italians.

In April fire ravaged a chapel in the Turin cathedral that for four centuries had housed the Holy Shroud, revered by many as the winding cloth used to wrap the body of Christ after the Crucifixion, though found by experts in 1988 to be a medieval forgery. To the applause of a weeping crowd, firemen rescued the glass-and-zinc-encased shroud, which was later pronounced undamaged. In May two electricians were jailed for having started the blaze that gutted the famous La Fenice ("The Phoenix") opera house in Venice in 1996. The alleged arsonists were said to have so acted to escape a contractual penalty of 15 million lire (about $10,000) for being two months behind schedule in their work.

(DEREK WILSON)

Flames rise from the roof of a chapel in the cathedral in Turin that for four centuries had housed the Holy Shroud, revered by many as the cloth used to wrap the body of Christ after the Crucifixion, though in 1988 it was found by experts to be a forgery. The shroud was not damaged by the fire.

BALBONTIN-NERI/SYGMA

JAMAICA

Area: 10,991 sq km (4,244 sq mi)
Population (1997 est.): 2,536,000
Capital: Kingston
Chief of state: Queen Elizabeth II, represented by Governor-General Sir Howard Cooke
Head of government: Prime Minister Percival J. Patterson

The government of Jamaica moved to salvage the nation's beleaguered garment industry, one of the country's largest employers, when it allocated J$200 million in January 1997 to subsidize 5% of the operating costs of 180 factories. This was meant to help maintain the industry's competitive edge in the U.S. market, where exporters had been losing ground to Mexican garments, which had faced no import restrictions since Mexico's accession to the North American Free Trade Agreement in 1992. Later in the year, in August, another J$160 million was added to the rescue package.

In May the Jamaican parliament ratified the "Shiprider Agreement" with the U.S. after amendments were made that satisfied Jamaica's desire to preserve sovereignty over its territorial waters. The agreement committed both nations to cooperating closely in the war against drug trafficking in the Caribbean.

In June two of the country's leading bauxite and alumina firms, Alpart and Jamalco, announced they would merge in January 1998 in a move designed to strengthen the industry. Alpart, partly owned by Kaiser Aluminum and Chemical Corp. of the U.S., was Jamaica's largest alumina refiner.

In March Michael Manley, prime minister of Jamaica in 1972–80 and 1989–92, died. (*See* OBITUARIES.) In parliamentary elections in December, the ruling People's National Party was returned to power.

(DAVID RENWICK)

This article updates the the *Macropædia* article The WEST INDIES: *Jamaica.*

JAPAN

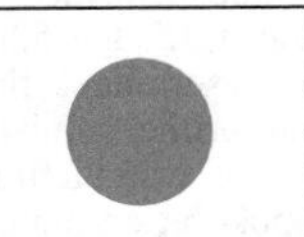

Area: 377,819 sq km (145,877 sq mi)
Population (1997 est.): 126,110,000
Capital: Tokyo
Chief of state: Emperor Akihito
Head of government: Prime Minister Ryutaro Hashimoto

On Jan. 20, 1997, Prime Minister Ryutaro Hashimoto opened the 140th ordinary session of the Diet (parliament) by pledging reforms in six sectors: administration, finance, social security, the economy, the monetary system, and education. They were designed to make Japan's markets "free, fair, and global" by 2001. The media named the plan the "Big Bang" after a deregulation program undertaken in London in 1986. Reform dominated domestic politics in 1997 and offered some promise of cutting costs to internationally competitive levels by the 21st century.

Domestic Affairs. In October 1996 Hashimoto's Liberal-Democratic Party (LDP), which had dominated politics from 1955 to 1993, won a plurality but not a majority in the election for the House of Representatives. The new Cabinet was made up entirely of LDP members. Passage of bills, however, depended on ad hoc coalitions, since the LDP also did not control the House of Councillors. Informal alliances were made with the Social Democratic Party (SDP) and the New Harbinger Party (Sakigake). The opposition was spearheaded by the New Frontier Party (Shinshinto). The Democratic Party of Japan (DPJ) was the second largest opposing group but, like the Shinshinto, cooperated with the LDP-led government on a case-by-case basis and seemed to hold a balance of power.

The distribution of seats in the 1997 Diet was as follows: (House of Representatives) LDP 244, Shinshinto 141, DPJ 52, Japanese Communist Party (JCP) 26, SDP 15, Sakigake 2, independents, minor parties 20 (total 500); (House of Councillors) LDP 112, SDP 22, DPJ 22, JCP 14, Sakigake 3, independents, minor parties 79 (total 252).

All of these parties were subject to the turmoil of factions, splinters, and shifting alliances. In February, after a threatened members' revolt, the Shinshinto united under the leadership of Ichiro Ozawa, a former rival of Hashimoto within the LDP. In March a DPJ convention decided to remain in opposition, to support the government on some issues, and to resolve a leadership problem. In December Shinshinto officially disbanded because of internal disputes.

On April 17 a controversial bill designed to revise leases of land occupied by U.S. forces on Okinawa passed the Diet. Surprisingly, opposition forces in Shinshinto and in the DPJ supported the legislation. The SDP, which remained in the informal coalition with the LDP, and the communists opposed it. On April 19 the SDP chairwoman, Takako Doi, appealed to members in the SDP's annual convention to rebuild the party, "which represents ordinary and weak citizens."

On June 18 the Diet ended its regular session. In 150 days the LDP-led alliance had passed 100 laws and approved 16 treaties. Legislation included a revision of the 1952 Okinawa bases law, creation of a body to supervise financial institutions, and deregulation of the Nippon Telegraph & Telephone Corp. The Okinawa legislation allowed the U.S. forces stationed there to remain as legal occupants of their bases after May 14, when the U.S. leases expired.

An election of the 127-member Tokyo Metropolitan Assembly on July 6 proved to be a political indicator in several ways. First, the turnout (40.8%, the lowest on record) revealed public apathy. Second, the LDP did well, winning 54 seats, but the JCP made a spectacular gain by doubling its seats to 26. Allies of the LDP and other opposition parties did poorly.

On September 11 Prime Minister Hashimoto was named president of the LDP, an office for which he was unopposed. His selection coincided with the LDP's achieving a majority (251 seats) in the House of Representatives, its first in four years, after recruiting seven independents.

Hashimoto then reshuffled his Cabinet, carefully selecting party members who represented factions of the LDP. Thus, Hiroshi Mitsuzuka was retained as finance minister and Fumio Kyuma as defense minister. An old ally, Keizo Obuchi, became foreign minister. At the request of the 62-man faction led by a former prime minister, Yasuhiro Nakasone, Hashimoto selected Koko Sato to lead the effort to reform domestic politics as minister of management and coordination. Immediately, the Cabinet's reputation suffered. In the 1970s in the Lockheed procurement scandal, Sato had been convicted of having accepted a bribe. A *Kyodo News* opinion survey conducted September 14–15 showed that 59% of those polled did not support the new Cabinet. On September 22 Sato resigned from the Cabinet to save the prime minister further embarrassment. One week later Hashimoto apologized to the Diet for the appointment.

On August 29 the Supreme Court reached a decision on a prolonged case. It ruled in favour of an 83-year-old historian, Saburo Ienaga. The professor had referred in a textbook to experiments on live captives by the Japanese army in China during World War II. The Education Ministry had ordered the passage deleted, but the court ordered the government to pay the author $3,500 in damages and to reinstate the passage. The court did not, however, hold that such screening violated the constitution.

During the year Japan suffered more than its share of man-made disasters. On January 2 the Russian tanker *Nakhodka* broke up off the Oki Islands in the Sea of Japan, spilling at least 3.7 million litres (one million gallons) of fuel oil onto the shores of Shimane prefecture. A few days later the prime minister admitted that the government had "misjudged" the scope of the environmental impact. Six months later a Japanese-owned tanker struck a shoal in Tokyo Bay, 6 km (3.7 mi) southeast of the port of Yokohama. In this case maritime safety forces moved promptly to confine the 1.5 million-litre (390,000-gal) spill.

The public was understandably sensitive to delayed reports of a nuclear accident, the worst ever in peacetime Japan. On March 11 leaks of radioactive substances—including plutonium—increased eightfold after an explosion at a plant operated by the state-owned Power Reactor and Nuclear Fuel Development Corp. in Tokai, north of Tokyo. Although the accident occurred at about 8 PM, people in Tokai did not find out about it until the next morning. Officials claimed that there was no threat to the environment.

The Economy. Demographic trends affected Japan's economy during the year. The Management and Coordination Agency announced that at the end of 1996, the number of children (through the age of 14) totaled 19.5 million, the lowest figure since the first census (1920). Meanwhile, the number of those aged 65 and over passed the 19 million mark, and this group was expected to make up 20% of the total population by 2006. The number of children plus those over 65 was equal to 44.4% of those in the productive ages (15–64), and this percentage was expected to rise. To help serve the aging population, the Diet on March 28 passed a $640 billion budget for fiscal year 1997, a $75 billion increase over the previous year.

The year had begun with projections of a 2.3% growth in gross domestic product (GDP) for 1997. In the second quarter, however, the economy suffered its biggest drop in 23 years. According to the Economic Planning Agency, GDP shrank at an annualized rate of 11.2%, which was largely attributed to an increase in the consumption tax. In May the unemployment rate matched the record-high rate of 3.5% (2,440,000 jobless). Fortunately, inflation remained low. In 1996 the consumer price index rose only 0.1%, and by June 1997 it had shown no further increase.

On May 15 the government unveiled the "Big Bang," more formally the Action Plan for Economic Structural Reform and Creation. The next day the Diet abolished the monopoly held by Japanese banks in transactions involving foreign exchange. By June 13 three plans for reform had been released by the Securities and Exchange, the Financial System Research, and the Insurance councils. The plans called for the introduction of comprehensive securities accounts in brokerage houses and a review of the tax system by 2000, including abolition of the securities transaction tax. Eventually banks would be allowed to sell insurance.

Reforms could not come too soon. Throughout the year Japan was buffeted by a storm of investigations, indictments, arrests, and resignations, many of which involved the nation's most prestigious financial houses. The trouble began on March 14 when Hideo Sakamaki stepped down as head of the biggest firm, Nomura Securities Co., Ltd. He also resigned as chairman of the Securities Dealers Association, admitting illicit dealing with a corporate racketeer (*sokaiya*). On May 20 prosecutors raided headquarters of the Dai-Ichi Kangyo Bank Ltd. and some 10 local offices of Nomura. That same week the bank's president, Katsuhiko Kondo, and chairman, Tadashi Okuda, resigned after having assumed "moral responsibility" for ties with *sokaiya*. The prime minister commented, however, that "resignations were not enough," and on July 30 Finance Minister Mitsuzuka imposed harsh penalties. Many of the two firms' major credit transactions were suspended, some until December. On November 3 Sanyo Securities filed for bankruptcy protection, and on November 24 Yamaichi Securities decided to close down business after 100 years of operation. (*See* ECONOMIC AFFAIRS: *Banking*.)

Foreign Affairs. Despite the turmoil in Tokyo and a nagging recession, Japan for the sixth consecutive year retained its status as the world's leading nation in net external assets. Public and private holdings abroad minus liabilities totaled $850 billion.

Measured by high-level exchanges of visitors, relations with the U.S. continued to be Japan's most important international contact. In February, Secretary of State Madeleine Albright went to Tokyo, where she agreed with Prime Minister Hashimoto that the two nations would strengthen their security alliance. In March, Vice Pres. Al Gore, in Tokyo during an Asian trip, was more specific: the U.S. wanted to maintain its Marine garrison on Okinawa. In an April 25 speech in Washington, D.C., after a meeting with Pres. Bill Clinton, Hashimoto urged Americans to be "sensitive" to the issue of Okinawa, where most of the U.S. troops in Japan were on an island that was only 0.6% of the nation's area; in a referendum later in the year, Okinawans voted against the establishment of a new military base on the island. In August Tokyo welcomed Clinton's nomination of Thomas Foley, former speaker of the House of Representatives, to be ambassador to Japan. Ambassador Foley was scheduled to arrive in Tokyo the week of November 17.

The Japanese public was particularly concerned with a joint draft security plan unveiled by Tokyo and Washington on June 8. Projecting the highest Japanese military profile in the Asia-Pacific region since World War II, it provided for peacetime coordination of defense planning, a joint response to any aggression against Japan, and Japan's cooperation in conflicts occurring in undefined "areas around Japan." Critics denounced the scheme as violating Japan's no-war constitution.

Late in the year, talks between Japan and the U.S. returned to trade issues, which had perennially dominated relations between the two countries. At a conference in Denver, Colo., in June, Hashimoto noted Clinton's concern over the U.S. trade deficit with Japan, which reached a total of $35.9 billion in 1996. Earlier in Washington, D.C., a small independent agency had taken a policy step that echoed the problem and reverberated through the shipping sectors of each nation. The Federal Maritime Commission announced that it planned to levy fines on Japanese vessels in retaliation for restrictions imposed on American ships by the politically powerful Japan Harbor Transportation Association. Indeed, on September 4 sanctions of $100,000 per ship were applied to three Japanese firms, the first such trade penalty in a decade. In October diplomats from both nations arranged a temporary suspension of sanctions, but the imposed fines remained intact.

Looking toward its neighbours, Japan continued in somewhat tentative fashion to atone for its past. On August 15, the 52nd anniversary of the nation's surrender that ended World War II, the prime minister expressed "deep remorse" for war victims, particularly in Asia. He spoke at an annual Tokyo ceremony designed to mourn Japanese casualties and attended by the emperor.

On February 20 at the Chinese embassy in Tokyo, Hashimoto offered Japan's respects on the death of China's longtime leader, Deng Xiaoping. On March 30 Foreign Minister Yukihiko Ikeda became the highest-ranking official to visit Beijing after Deng's death. Ikeda announced the resumption of a $14 million loan program, which had been suspended in 1996 to protest Chinese nuclear tests.

Islands located between the two nations continued to be sources of debate. On May 6 a conservative member of Shinshinto, accompanied by a reporter, landed on one of the Senkaku Islands and planted a Japanese

The Peopling of Japan

Perhaps the most universal of heirlooms passed down from parent to child are stories of family—stories that address the questions, Who are we? Where did we come from? Like others, the peoples of Japan had been asking these questions for generations. Archaeological, linguistic, and other anthropological data all supported the idea that at least two major migrations brought human populations from the Asian continent to the Japanese archipelago: the Jomon people, who were principally hunters, fishers, and foragers, were thought to have entered Japan some 10,000–12,000 years ago via a land bridge, and the Yayoi people, who farmed rice, were thought to have traveled by boat to Japan starting about 2,300 years ago. At least three different hypotheses had been raised, however, to explain the relative contributions of each wave of immigrants to the modern Japanese. Recent genetic studies finally helped to resolve at least some of the uncertainty.

Michael Hammer of the United States and Satoshi Horai of Japan, together with their colleagues, applied studies of genetic polymorphisms (variations in the sequence of nucleotides in the DNA molecule) in both the mitochondrial DNAs and Y chromosomal DNAs of a variety of East Asian populations and found differences in the relative frequencies of these polymorphisms that enabled clear distinctions to be made between the different groups. Polymorphisms in both mitochondrial and some Y chromosomal DNAs can be particularly useful for identifying and tracking human populations because both are passed from parent to child without recombination (a process by which the majority of genes in the nucleus of a cell may "mix and match," which thereby uncouples them from their neighbours). Mitochondrial DNA is passed only from mothers to their children, and Y chromosomal DNA is passed only from fathers to their sons. By comparing the relative frequencies of specific sets of polymorphisms, called haplotypes, in the peoples of Japan and other Asian nations, the researchers were able to distinguish populations exhibiting similar haplotypes from those exhibiting clearly different haplotypes.

The results of Hammer and Horai's work indicated that the modern mainland Japanese resulted from genetic contributions of both the ancient Jomon people and the Yayoi immigrants. They thereby supported the "hybridization" model and refuted the "replacement" and "transformation" models. Indeed, about 65% of the gene pool of the mainland Japanese was now suspected of reflecting gene flow from the continent of Asia after the Yayoi migration. Only the Ainu inhabitants of the northern island of Hokkaido and the Ryukyuans living on the island of Okinawa appeared to represent the true modern descendants of the Jomon people. Furthermore, whereas the Yayoi were believed to have come from the Korean peninsula or from mainland China, the geographic origins of the Jomon remained unclear. The family history was not yet complete.

(JUDITH L. FRIDOVICH-KEIL)

JEFFREY AARONSON—NETWORK/ASPEN

An 80-year-old rice farmer from the village of Hosokawa, in the urban prefecture of Kyoto, is one of more than 19 million Japanese citizens aged 65 and over. To help serve Japan's aging population, the Diet passed a $640 billion budget for fiscal year 1997, a $75 billion increase over the previous year.

flag. Located between Okinawa and Taiwan, these rocky, uninhabited islets had been under Japanese control for a century but were claimed by China and Taiwan. Authorities in Tokyo insisted that quiet diplomacy should resolve the issue.

On January 25 the prime minister found it necessary to apologize for a loose remark by Chief Cabinet Secretary Seiroku Kajiyama. Serving as host to Pres. Kim Young Sam of South Korea, Hashimoto received a vigorous denunciation from Kim of Kajiyama's statement that the Japanese army's use of "comfort women" (a euphemism for involuntary prostitutes) in Korea during World War II emerged from a "social background." Even Japan had licensed prostitution, Kajiyama added. President Kim represented Koreans and many other Asians by noting that Japan had not in all ways come to grips with its past.

The two leaders had met to improve bilateral relations as well as to nudge along, with the aid of the U.S. and China, peaceful reunification of the Korean peninsula. Japan had recognized South Korea but also maintained informal relations with North Korea. On August 22 at the Japanese embassy in Beijing, Japanese and North Korean negotiators agreed to reopen normalization talks at high diplomatic levels. On September 5 Tokyo announced a loan to North Korea, through UN channels, of $20 million for the purchase of Japanese rice.

Prime Minister Hashimoto had visited Moscow in 1996, hoping to move talks along toward a peace treaty with Russia. Tokyo had normalized relations with Moscow in 1956, but a formal pact ending World War II continued to stall over a minor territorial dispute. It involved four small islands in the southern Kurils, historically Japanese but occupied by the Russians since 1945. On May 17 Igor Rodionov, the first Russian defense minister to visit Japan, informed Japan's Defense Minister Kyuma that Russian garrisons on the disputed Kurils were soon to be reduced. Later the Russians indicated that they would no longer deploy missiles aimed at Japan. On June 20 at the conference in Denver, Hashimoto and Russian Pres. Boris Yeltsin agreed to plan reciprocal visits to resolve disputes and to improve bilateral relations. Yeltsin also expressed support of Japan's effort to obtain a permanent seat on the United Nations Security Council.

Outsiders were often surprised to learn that the Japanese had long had ties with Latin America. In late 1996 its considerable trade and investment interests were dramatically revealed by a hostage crisis at Japan's embassy in Lima, Peru. Túpac Amaru Revolutionary Movement guerrillas seized some 600 guests, who were celebrating the emperor's birthday. Through a four-month hostage crisis, Japan urged patience, but on April 22 it welcomed a forceful rescue of victims. Ambassador Morihisa Aoki and 23 other Japanese citizens had been among the hostages. On May 10 Hashimoto traveled to Lima to convey Japan's gratitude to Pres. Alberto Fujimori, a Peruvian of Japanese ancestry.

(ARDATH W. BURKS)

JORDAN

Area: 89,326 sq km (34,489 sq mi)
Population (1997 est.): 4,522,000 (including about 1.3 million Palestinian refugees)
Capital: Amman
Head of state and government: King Hussein, assisted by Prime Ministers ʿAbd al-Karim Kabariti and, from March 19, ʿAbd as-Salam al-Majali

Jordan found it increasingly difficult to halt the deterioration in its relations with Israel and to make further progress toward democratization in 1997; relations with its Arab Gulf neighbours and with the United States continued to improve, however, and privatization measures were enacted. A new Cabinet was formed on March 19 under ʿAbd as-Salam al-Majali after the king lost confidence in ʿAbd al-Karim Kabariti's year-old government owing to differences on how to handle relations with Israel and the inability of the government to carry out reforms in the civil service and army. The new regime did, however, continue the moves initiated by the former government to improve relations with Arab Gulf states and to liberalize investment laws. Trade with Kuwait resumed after a six-year break, and an exchange of ambassadors was expected; relations with Saudi Arabia improved; and trade agreements were concluded with Egypt, Bahrain, and Qatar. Progress was also being made in regard to economic and military cooperation with the U.S., and joint military exercises were held.

Relations with Israel started well with Israel's decision to withdraw from most of the West Bank town of Hebron in February, an agreement that Jordan helped facilitate. It was all downhill from there, however, as Israeli Prime Minister Benjamin Netanyahu refused to compromise on allowing Israelis to expand their settlements in the West Bank and laid the blame for Palestinian suicide bombings at the door of the Palestinian Authority. Attempts by Jordan and Egypt to mediate the conflict produced no significant results. The crowning blow came in late September when Israel's Mossad intelligence agency tried to assassinate a Hamas leader in Jordan. Two Mossad agents were captured, and in order to secure their release, Israel had to release Sheikh Ahmad Yassin, the spiritual leader of Hamas, from prison in an apparent deal with Jordan. King Hussein expressed his exasperation with Netanyahu, but he made a point of signaling his determination to adhere to the new relationship with Israel by pointedly receiving the credentials of the new Israeli ambassador on October 5. Trade with Israel remained insignificant, although a scheme for sharing water from Lake Tiberias went into effect.

King Hussein dissolved the National Assembly (which had been in recess since March 19) on September 1, and elections for the House of Deputies were held on November 4. A new pro-government party, the National Constitutional Party (NCP), was formed through the merger of nine parties. The NCP's platform advocated measures to revitalize the economy, combat unemployment, and introduce a value-added tax. The Islamic Action Front, which protested the one-man, one-vote system, which had weakened its electoral fortunes, declared that it would boycott the elections, along with smaller leftist and pan-Arab parties. In the election, which the opposition parties boycotted, the pro-government independents won 62 of the 80 seats. A voter turnout of 54.6% was reported, the lowest total since the democratization process was launched by King Hussein in 1989.

Jordan began negotiating with the United States about membership in the World Trade Organization. The government was determined to attract foreign investment; the 50% ceiling it had established on foreign ownership of banking and insurance firms was eliminated but was kept in force for mining and construction companies.

(JENAB TUTUNJI)

SPOTLIGHT

WATER CRISIS IN THE MIDDLE EAST AND NORTH AFRICA

by Peter Rogers

Illustration by Cathy Hull

Water availability has for millennia shaped the culture of the people in the part of the world now commonly referred to as the Middle East and North Africa. This huge region extends from the Maghreb, comprising Morocco, Algeria, Tunisia, Libya, and sometimes Mauritania, into the Mashriq, comprising Egypt, The Sudan, Lebanon, Israel, Jordan, Iraq, Syria, Saudi Arabia, Kuwait, Bahrain, Qatar, the United Arab Emirates, Oman, Yemen, and parts of Turkey. The World Bank (1994) also included Iran with this region.

The annual renewable water resources of the region were given by the World Bank (1994) to be about 350 billion cu m (1 cu m=35.3 cu ft), with almost 50% of this water crossing national boundaries. This amounts to about 1,400 cu m per person per year, which is much less than 20% of the global average. The accompanying table shows the water availability in the Middle Eastern and North African countries. Of the 17 nations listed, only 6 had per capita availability of more than 1,000 cu m per person per year in 1990, and 6 had less than 500 cu m per capita per year. The figures of 1,000 and 500 cu m are often assumed to be the lower limits on water availability, below which countries experience severe water stress. Estimates of the 1990 withdrawals of water from the rivers and aquifers reveal that fully 87% was withdrawn for agriculture, mostly for irrigation.

One seeming anomaly is that five of the countries—Libya, Qatar, Saudi Arabia, the United Arab Emirates, and Yemen—used more than 100% of their total available water. They achieved this by drawing on groundwater on a very large scale. In addition to those nations that exceeded their available water, Egypt, Israel, and Jordan were essentially at their limit.

This very tight resource situation was further complicated by the fact that both the rainfall and the streamflows in the region are highly variable, both within a year and between the years, which makes water resources difficult and expensive to manage. For example, in addition to the severely water-stressed countries, Algeria, Iran, Morocco, and Tunisia suffer serious deficits. The table also points to a major problem brewing for the future; by 2025 the water availability per capita will have dropped to less than one-half its present unsatisfactory level, and only two countries, Iran and Iraq, will be above 1,000 cu m per capita per year.

Potential for Conflict. Despite much talk about water's being the cause of the next war in the Middle East, there is little evidence that water has been a major cause of war in modern history, although disputes over it may have been one of many contributing causes. Not "causing" wars does not imply, however, that water disputes are not major sources of international friction. There are 23 international rivers in the region. At one time or another, there have been disputes between countries over most of them, but the most contentious remain the Nile, Euphrates, Tigris, Yarmuk, and Jordan. Conflicts also have arisen from the use of groundwater aquifers that cross national boundaries, notably between Israel and the Palestinians, and between Jordan and Saudi Arabia. There could also be strife between Egypt and Libya over the latter's extensive $30 billion development of the Nubian Aquifer to supply its coastal cities by means of its "Great Man-Made River."

Some of the water available to countries in the region comes from other nations. Obviously, the higher the percentage of the total received in that way, the greater the potential for conflict. Egypt, for example, in recent years received 97% of its water from outside its boundaries, Iraq 66%, and Israel 20%. Syria was in the ambiguous situation of receiving large amounts from upstream Turkey but passing even more on to downstream Iraq.

Since 1993 further complications have been added to the transboundary disputes with the incorporation of the Palestinian region into the water balance between Israel and Jordan. Also, the relations between Turkey and its downstream neighbours, Syria and Iraq, can only worsen as Turkey pushes forward with its giant water-development program in the Tigris and Euphrates basins. The Nile basin is also becoming more contentious, with the Ethiopians challenging the Egyptian and Sudanese claims to 80% of the flow of the Nile. Conflict over the use of the aquifers in the West Bank and Gaza will remain a major stumbling block to a final peace settlement in that region unless the issue can be addressed creatively.

The conflicts about water use are not restricted to international problems but can also occur within countries. The major conflict in such circumstances is between agricultural and urban uses. Irrigation is by far the largest use for water in each country in the region and is predicted to continue increasing far beyond the water availability for the region as a whole. Nonagricultural demands are also increasing, even more rapidly than those for irrigation.

Another major conflict is between human use of water and the needs of the environment. In many areas rivers and aquifers are becoming polluted, and wetlands are drying up. Ten of the countries in the region suffer from severe water-quality problems; the only ones rated as having moderate problems are those very arid countries where water use currently exceeds 100% of available supplies but that have few or no perennial streams. They include Bahrain, Israel, Kuwait, Libya, Oman, Qatar, Saudi Arabia, the United Arab Emirates, and Yemen.

Possible Solutions. Despite the gloomy prognoses, there are several promising approaches to water management in the region that suggest there will be enough water for all reasonable demands well into the middle of the next century. The most effective of them are expected to be integrated management of water resources and rational water pricing. During the next decade, the water managers in the various countries will have to face up to rationalizing water uses in such a way that the water goes to the users who will derive the greatest value from it while still maintaining the quality of the surrounding environment. Fortunately, the water used in agriculture dwarfs any of the other uses, and its economic value is typically less than one-tenth of that of water for

Water Availability				
	Net annual renewable water resources	Renewable resources per capita		
		1960	1990	2025
Country	BCM[1]	Cubic metres per year[2]		
Algeria	18.40	1,704	737	354
Bahrain[3]	—	—	—	—
Egypt	58.30	2,251	1,112	645
Iran	117.50	5,788	2,152	1,032
Iraq	100.00	14,706	5,285	2,000
Israel	2.15	1,024	467	311
Jordan	0.86	529	224	91
Lebanon	3.94	2,000	1,407	809
Libya	0.70	538	154	55
Morocco	29.70	2,560	1,185	651
Oman	2.00	4,000	1,333	421
Qatar[3]	0.00	—	—	—
Saudi Arabia	2.20	537	156	49
Syria	5.50	1,196	439	161
Tunisia	4.35	1,036	532	319
United Arab Emirates	0.30	3,000	189	113
Yemen	2.50	481	214	72

[1]Billion cubic metres.
[2]1 cu m=35.3 cu ft.
[3]Figures not available.
Sources: World Resources Institute (1991–92 and 1992–93); World Bank (1995).

urban or industrial consumers. Consequently, a small percentage of water diverted from agriculture would yield abundant quantities for all other uses at little cost. Removing 200 ha (500 ac) from irrigation would provide 50 litres (13.2 gal) of water per person per day for almost 200,000 urban dwellers.

There is, however, great resistance to the reallocation of agricultural water in most government agencies, particularly those concerned with food production and "food self-sufficiency." There are two reasons that indicate that this concern is misplaced: first, in most countries a 10% improvement in irrigation efficiency is generally very inexpensive to attain; and second, the concept of food self-sufficiency should be replaced by the concept of food security. In this case the water reallocated from agriculture can be replaced by importing food that would have required considerable irrigation if grown locally.

Even for the rapidly growing urban demands, more than 50% is typically used for toilet flushing and other sanitary activities. Moving away from water-based sanitation to dry toilets will save considerable amounts of water in the future. Water losses in municipal systems continue to be very large and could be greatly reduced by better maintenance and management of the systems. Conservation of water in households and industry can also be useful. Finally, pricing of water remains a powerful tool that can be used to help implement the reallocations between water users and to stimulate improved efficiency of water use. Establishment of tradable water rights and markets for water along with privatization of the water-supply utilities would also go a long way toward achieving a less-water-constricted future.

The solutions described above are typically characterized as "demand-side" options. Unfortunately, most of the current proposals are still linked to what are called "supply-side" options. For example, the large-scale Libyan diversions from the Nubian Aquifer are designed to increase the supply to the coastal cities at huge expense without requiring Libyans to face up to the real environmental costs of supplying the water. Apart from additional investment in desalination for urban or industrial users, the era of supply-side development has all but come to an end in the region, and it is unrealistic to expect that any such megaprojects will be economically and environmentally sustainable.

Peter Rogers is a professor of applied science at Harvard University.

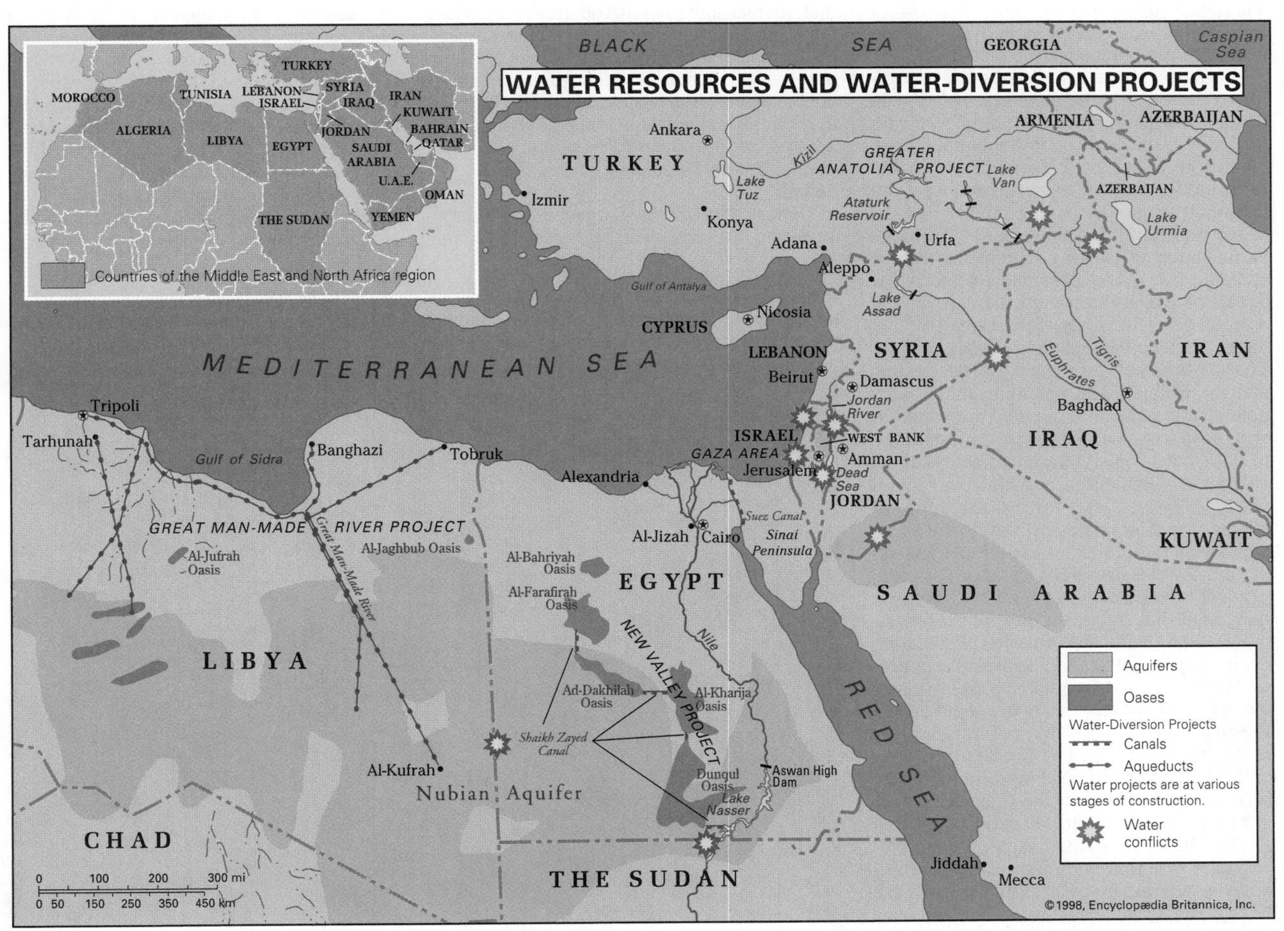

KAZAKSTAN

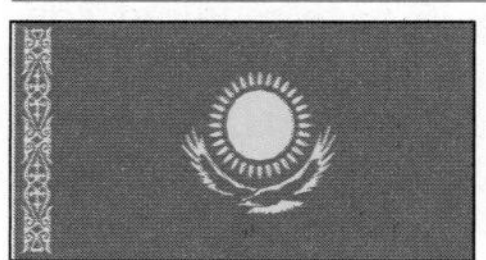

Area: 2,724,900 sq km (1,052,090 sq mi)
Population (1997 est.): 16,554,000
Capital: Almaty until December 10; thereafter Aqmola
Head of state and government: President Nursultan Nazarbayev, assisted by Prime Ministers Akezhan Kazhegeldin and, from October 10, Nurlan Balgimbayev

The economy was the main focus of attention for the government and population of Kazakstan in 1997. Modest upturns in some industrial production figures indicated that government efforts to reverse the post-Soviet economic decline were paying off, but little improvement was visible in the living standard of the population. At the end of March, a coalition of political opposition groups held an unauthorized demonstration in Almaty to protest the continuing decline in living conditions; two weeks later the same groups demanded that the government resign for having caused the economic and social crisis in the country. Dissatisfaction with government economic policies continued to build throughout the year, and on October 10 Prime Minister Akezhan Kazhegeldin resigned following a massive demonstration by unemployed miners. He was replaced by Nurlan Balgimbayev, a former oil and gas industry minister, whose ministry had been folded into a new Ministry of Energy that was created as part of an effort to reduce the bureaucracy.

Kazakstan's leaders discovered that efforts to overcome the economic crisis with the aid of foreign investment did not always have the desired effect; in September, Pres. Nursultan Nazarbayev complained that firms under foreign management were attempting to evade paying taxes, and he called for limits on the extent of foreign participation in existing enterprises. At the end of May, 2,000 pensioners took to the streets of Almaty to protest increases in the cost of gas, electricity, and water that put these services beyond their ability to pay. The government responded by demanding that the Belgian firm operating the Almaty power system install individual usage meters at its own expense; the firm then threatened to back out of its contract in Kazakstan.

Human rights activists maintained that a newly instituted fee for broadcasting licenses was a government ploy to force independent radio and television stations off the air. By the beginning of May, 27 independent broadcasters had shut down because they could not afford the license fees.

Relations with the Russian Federation cooled somewhat in 1997 as Kazakstan protested the use of Cossack troops to patrol the border between the two countries and President Nazarbayev rejected Russian demands that Russian oil firms be given preference in obtaining development rights to offshore oil deposits in the Caspian Sea. A group of parliamentary deputies criticized the leasing of weapons testing sites in Kazakstan to the Russian military. In June Nazarbayev warned that Kazakstan might have to fight for its independence if Russia tried to force the country into a union similar to that between Russia and Belarus. In a move widely interpreted as an effort to dilute Russian-majority regions in the northern part of Kazakstan, two Russian-majority oblasts were fused with neighbouring oblasts having Kazak majorities.

Plans went ahead to move Kazakstan's capital to Aqmola, despite the expense involved in the move. The inauguration of the new capital took place on December 10.

(BESS BROWN)

This article updates the *Macropædia* article Central Asia: *Kazakstan.*

KENYA

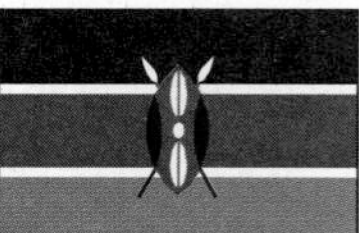

Area: 582,646 sq km (224,961 sq mi)
Population (1997 est.): 28,803,000
Capital: Nairobi
Head of state and government: President Daniel arap Moi

The attention of both Kenyan and foreign observers was mainly focused upon two issues throughout 1997, both arising from Pres. Daniel arap Moi's mostly uncompromising attitude toward his critics. First, the president's fierce opposition to demands for reform of the constitution before the next elections—scheduled to be held before the end of the year—caused recurrent protests that increasingly led to outbreaks of violence. Second, the president's failure to take effective action to combat high-level corruption caused donor agencies to have grave doubts about Kenya's future, even though they readily acknowledged the government's success in introducing economic reforms that had cut inflation and reduced the budget deficit.

Donor concern was sharpened on January 15 when the president reappointed to his Cabinet the former energy and industry minister, Nicholas Biwott. Biwott had been deeply involved in allegations of corruption in connection with the award of contracts for building the Turkwell Gorge dam in northern Kenya in 1986. In March two additional controversial contracts, awarded by the state-owned Kenya Power and Lighting Company in 1996, led both the International Monetary Fund (IMF) and the World Bank to demand clarification regarding the process of bidding for contracts.

In late May Moi rejected demands from church leaders and opposition parties for constitutional reforms aimed at increasing civil liberties and eliminating the ruling party's unfair advantage in elections. Criminal gangs not directly involved in politics then took advantage of an unlicensed opposition rally in Nairobi to indulge in violence and looting. On July 7, amid clashes between security forces and protesters taking part in pro-reform rallies across the nation, police took violent action against worshippers in Nairobi's All Saints Anglican Cathedral; this incident led to further confrontation between security forces and protesters demanding constitutional reform. It also encouraged donor nations to urge the president to agree to repeal laws that appeared to weigh the polls in his favour.

When a court case in which leading government officials were accused of involvement in serious fraud was dismissed in June on a technicality, the IMF threatened to suspend its loan agreement, and donor countries canceled a meeting scheduled for late July. Faced with such pressure, the president appeared to give way, offering to help pass legislation through the current legislature to enact reform. His proposal contributed to the existing divisions among his opponents. Some were prepared to take the offer of reform legislation at its face value, but the majority insisted on continuing their protest. These divisions had been reinforced in June by the decision of Kenneth Matiba, chairman of the opposition Forum for Restoration of Democracy-Asili party, to resign from the legislature and to boycott any elections, a

At the International School of Kenya in Nairobi, a young man peers through a microscope in a biology laboratory as his teacher talks with another student. Political problems in Kenya in 1997 overshadowed many recent advances in the country, particularly in the areas of education and economic reform.

CAROL GUZY—THE WASHINGTON POST

course of action that other opponents of the government declined to follow.

Late in July, to the consternation of donor agencies, Moi dismissed his most senior customs officer, Samuel Chebii, who had been playing a vital role in campaigning against corruption. A few days later the finance minister, Musalia Madavadi, wrote an official letter to the managing director of the IMF agreeing to reinstate Chebii and suggesting other measures that the government might take to check corruption and improve the economy. On July 31, however, the letter was withdrawn on the order of Moi himself, and at that point the IMF suspended its loan program. The immediate result was a sharp drop in the value of the Kenyan shilling, which caused grave concern in Kenyan financial circles. The IMF relented on August 23, offering to recommend payment of the second part of the loan if the government took steps to secure the independence of the Revenue and Anti-Corruption Authorities, to improve the management of its energy sector, and to ensure accountability for past financial infractions.

On September 11 the legislature agreed to measures repealing laws allowing detention without trial and the regulation of political gatherings. Moi gave his own assent on November 7, and on November 12 it was announced that presidential and legislative elections would take place on December 29. Because of logistic problems, the election was extended to December 30. On the last day of the year, amid charges of fraud from all sides, it appeared that President Moi would be reelected. (KENNETH INGHAM)

This article updates the *Macropædia* article EASTERN AFRICA: *Kenya*.

T. HASKELL—SYGMA

As the famine in North Korea continued to worsen, many residents resorted to planting crops, using whatever tools were available. During the year UNICEF estimated that 80,000 children in the country were in immediate danger of dying and another 800,000 were suffering from malnutrition.

KIRIBATI

Area: 811 sq km (313 sq mi)
Population (1997 est.): 82,400
Capital: Bairiki, on Tarawa
Head of state and government: President Teburoro Tito

With the government of Pres. Teburoro Tito remaining in firm control of domestic politics in Kiribati in 1997, the president himself adopted a high international profile. Following a visit to China in late 1996, where he signed a treaty promoting mutual respect and trade, Tito visited Rabi Island in Fiji to attend ceremonies marking the 50th anniversary of the resettlement of the Banaban people to Rabi following World War II. In December 1996 Tito also spoke at the opening of the seventh Nuclear Free and Independent Pacific Conference in Fiji, voicing his support for Fiji's call for a permanent and complete ban of nuclear testing worldwide.

In August 1997 Kiribati and another Pacific nation, Tuvalu, signed a Treaty of Friendship, the purpose of which was to strengthen and improve relations.

Kiribati continued to court controversy in 1997 over its 1995 act of moving the international date line far to the east, so that it went around Kiribati's Line Islands group. The move, which fulfilled one of Tito's campaign promises, was intended to enable Kiribati to become the first country to reach midnight on Dec. 31, 1999; consequently, elaborate plans to hold the world's first New Year's celebration on Jan. 1, 2000, were under way. Tonga, New Zealand, and Fiji, each arguing that "the party of the millennium" should be theirs, protested against Kiribati's tampering with the date line, but the Royal Greenwich Observatory in England, which created the international system of timekeeping, stated that Kiribati was within its rights when it made the change. (BARRIE MACDONALD)

This article updates the *Macropædia* article PACIFIC ISLANDS: *Kiribati*.

KOREA, DEMOCRATIC PEOPLE'S REPUBLIC OF

Area: 122,762 sq km (47,399 sq mi)
Population (1997 est.): 24,317,000
Capital: Pyongyang
Chief of state: President Kim Jong Il (designated)
Head of government: Chairmen of the Council of Ministers (Premier) Kang Song San and, from February 21 (acting Premier), Hong Sang Nam.

On March 5, 1997, representatives from North Korea attended a meeting in New York City with U.S. and South Korean diplomats to discuss proposed peace negotiations aimed at formally ending the state of war on the Korean peninsula. The meeting marked the first official contact between North and South Korea in three years and paved the way for joint talks with South Korea, the U.S., and China in Geneva in December. Although no solid agreements were reached, the meetings represented a significant step forward in the process of determining a security arrangement to replace the armistice that had put an unofficial end to the 1950–53 Korean War. The negotiations were, however, expected to be lengthy and difficult.

Some observers viewed North Korea's increased willingness to participate in peace talks as a sign of its desire to enhance its diplomatic standing and to receive food aid to help feed a population devastated by famine. According to the UN World Food Programme, most North Koreans had come to depend on government rations, which were cut to 100–150 g (3.5–5.3 oz) per person per day in 1997. UNICEF estimated that 80,000 children were in immediate danger of dying and another 800,000 were suffering from malnutrition. On May 26 South Korea agreed to send 50,000 tons of food to the North by August. The U.S. also provided North Korea with about $50 million in surplus grain during the year.

In August North Korea and Japan reopened bilateral negotiations that had been suspended for five years. A central issue was that of allowing Japanese women who had married North Korean men in the late 1950s to visit their families in Japan; more than 1,800 Japanese women went to North Korea during those years and were never heard from again. Tokyo had refused to send food aid to the beleaguered North in anger over this and over reports that North Korean agents had kidnapped Japanese citizens in the 1970s.

Ground was broken in August on a barren section of North Korea's eastern seaboard for the construction of two nuclear power plants to be used for nonmilitary purposes. The power plants were part of a deal negotiated with the U.S. in October 1994, in which the North was provided two 1,000-MW light-water reactors and fuel oil in exchange for freezing its own nuclear development, which many suspected was aimed at obtaining material for nuclear weapons.

Two prominent North Korean officials defected in 1997. In February Hwang Jang Yop, the architect of North Korea's official ideology of *juche,* or self-reliance, entered the South Korean consulate in Beijing and asked for asylum in South Korea. Hwang was sent first to the Philippines and then to Seoul, where he periodically issued warnings of Pyongyang's intentions to attack the South and perhaps Japan with missiles and nuclear weapons. In August North Korea's ambassador to Egypt, Chang Sung Gil, along with his brother and both of the men's families, defected at the U.S. embassy in Cairo. Chang had reportedly been an important figure in North Korean missile sales to the Middle East, and he was considered by U.S. intelligence to be a valuable source of information.

The third anniversary of the death of longtime dictator Kim Il Sung on July 8, 1994, passed without his son and successor Kim Jong Il formally taking the office of president. On October 8, however, Kim Jong Il officially assumed the leadership of the Korean Workers' (Communist) Party.

(GEORGE T. CROWELL)

This article updates the *Macropædia* article KOREA: *North Korea.*

KOREA, REPUBLIC OF

Area: 99,268 sq km (38,328 sq mi)
Population (1997 est.): 45,628,000
Capital: Seoul
Head of state and government: President Kim Young Sam, assisted by Prime Minister Lee Soo Sung and, from March 4, Koh Kun

In January 1997 the Hanbo Group, one of South Korea's largest steel and construction conglomerates, collapsed with debts of about $6 billion. After carrying out an investigation into the collapse, the Supreme Public Prosecutor's Office (SPPO) indicted at least four members of Pres. Kim Young Sam's ruling New Korea Party (NKP), accusing them of taking millions from Hanbo in exchange for helping to arrange bank loans for the ailing firm. After being questioned by the SPPO on February 12, Interior Minister Kim Woo Suk resigned from his post. In a live television broadcast on February 25, President Kim issued a public apology for the Hanbo scandal. On March 4 Kim appointed Koh Kun, president of Myongji University, Yongin, and a former mayor of Seoul, to replace Lee Soo Sung as prime minister. The following day Kim reshuffled his Cabinet, replacing eight ministers, including Finance Minister Han Seung Soo. Succeeding Han was Kang Kyong Shik, who had served as finance minister in 1982–83.

Another scandal erupted in May when Kim Hyun Chul, the son of President Kim, was arrested on charges of bribery and tax evasion. The president's son, who had helped manage his father's presidential campaign in 1992, was accused of having accepted $3.6 million in bribes from two businessmen seeking lucrative government contracts and licenses. He was also charged with having accepted $3.8 million from four other businessmen and having then laundered the money to avoid paying taxes. Kim's son was formally indicted on June 5, four days after thousands of students had congregated on the streets and campuses of Seoul to demand Kim's resignation.

The Hanbo scandal and the arrest of Kim's son helped to turn South Korea's presidential race into a wide-open contest between three serious candidates. Kim, restricted by the constitution from succeeding himself, was too weakened politically to dictate his successor. Lee Hoi Chang, a onetime Supreme Court judge with a reputation for incorruptibility, emerged as the ruling party's nominee at the NKP national convention in July. The runner-up at the convention, Rhee In Je, governor of South Korea's central Kyonggi province, refused to abandon his campaign for the presidency, however, and two months later quit the NKP to run as an independent in the December 18 election. Making the race even more unpredictable was the entry of the popular mayor of Seoul, Cho Soon, who later withdrew to support Lee.

J.M. TURPIN—GAMMA LIAISON

Striking workers protest new labour laws in South Korea. Some 145,000 workers affiliated with the Korean Federation of Trade Unions walked out of factories in January. Production losses due to the strikes amounted to about $2.6 billion.

In August, Lee's campaign ran into trouble when it was disclosed that his two sons had been exempted from compulsory military service for being underweight. Many Koreans suspected that Lee's sons, who each dropped 10 kg (22 lb) after an initial physical examination, had deliberately dieted in order to get below the minimum weight requirement of 50 kg (110 lb). Although no laws were broken, the scandal still managed to tarnish Lee's image as a man of integrity, and his poll ratings plummeted. Lee was dealt a further political blow when President Kim rejected Lee's proposal of an early release for former presidents Chun Doo Hwan and Roh Tae Woo, who had been found guilty in 1996 of having plotted the coup that followed the assassination of longtime strongman Park Chung Hee in 1979.

Late in the race venerable campaigner Kim Dae Jung (*see* BIOGRAPHIES), who had unsuccessfully contested each South Korean presidential election since 1971, found himself in the unfamiliar role of front-runner. With the ruling party in disarray as a result of splits and scandals, Kim Dae Jung, sensing victory, toned down his rhetoric and moderated his leftist positions, recruited several retired generals to his side, and made an effort to court business groups. He was, however, embarrassed when his adviser Oh Ik Je defected to North Korea. The defection rekindled suspicions that Kim was too sympathetic to the North.

In the election Kim Dae Jung won with more than 40.4% of the vote; Lee Hoi Chang finished second with 38.6%. Kim was the first president who was not a member of the NKP. One of his first moves, in December, was to grant immediate pardons to Chun and Roh, who had been his bitter enemies.

In foreign affairs the most significant event of 1997 for South Korea was a meeting with North Korea and the U.S. in New York City on March 5. Representatives of the three countries met to discuss a 1996 proposal by President Kim and U.S. Pres. Bill Clinton for peace talks aimed at formally ending the state of war on the Korean peninsula; the proposed talks would also include China. Seoul agreed to attend the meeting after Pyongyang expressed "regret" over sending a submarine loaded with commandos into South Korean waters in 1996. Although no breakthroughs were reported, the meeting marked the first official contact between North and South Korea in three years and was seen by international observers as an important step forward in North-South relations. After his election Kim Dae Jung announced his intention to seek a summit meeting with North Korean leaders.

Statistics indicate more economic troubles on the horizon for South Korea. The Samsung Economic Research Institute forecast that growth of gross domestic product would amount to about 5% at best in 1997, far below the 9% average of previous years. In January factory production sank to 77% of capacity, a four-year low. The trade deficit expanded. Speaking on the 78th anniversary of the March 1 Independence Declaration, President Kim urged the country to reform key institutions and to take measures to strengthen South Korea's international competitiveness.

In July the Kia Group, the country's third largest maker of automobiles, sought protection from bankruptcy after it was unable to repay about $314 million in outstanding loans. In December the the Halla Group, the nation's 12th largest conglomerate, collapsed after failing to repay some $200 million in debt.

The general weakness in the economy was felt by the financial sector. Probably worst hit was Korea First Bank, the fourth largest bank in the country. Korea First had large outstanding loans with both Hanbo and Kia as well as some other risky ventures and posted a $400 million loss for the first half of 1997, with the expectation that the number would exceed $1 billion before the end of the year. With the currency falling, Seoul finally sought a bailout from the International Monetary Fund. On December 3 South Korea agreed to an international rescue package amounting to $57 billion, the largest such rescue ever. The money was to be used to help increase the nation's depleted foreign currency reserves, which in turn was expected to slow the devaluation of the won and help the nation pay off foreign debt. Late in December commercial lenders gave South Korean borrowers a one-month extension on $15 billion of loans due at the end of the year.

(GEORGE T. CROWELL)

This article updates the *Macropædia* article KOREA: *South Korea.*

KUWAIT

Area: 17,818 sq km (6,880 sq mi)
Population (1997 est.): 1,809,000
Capital: Kuwait City
Head of state and government: Emir Sheikh Jabir al-Ahmad al-Jabir as-Sabah, assisted by Prime Minister Crown Prince Sheikh Saad al-Abdullah as-Salim as-Sabah

Domestic politics absorbed the attention of Kuwaitis in 1997, highlighted by exposures of corruption in government and an assassination attempt against a prominent critic of the regime. The new government got off to a shaky start. Election of the speaker of the 1996 National Assembly resulted in a 30–29 vote for the incumbent, Ahmad ʿAbd al-ʿAziz as-Saʿdoun. His opponent in the race, a former finance minister, Jassim al-Kharafi, challenged the election in court on the grounds that the speaker had not received an absolute majority of the votes of all 60 members, and it was not until early 1997 that Saʿdoun's entitlement to his office was judicially confirmed.

Some critics concluded that the new Cabinet, appointed shortly after the October election, was among the least distinguished since the adoption of the 1962 constitution. Kuwaitis' disappointment at some ministerial choices was reinforced by allegations of ministerial malfeasance and nonfeasance that surfaced shortly after the new Cabinet took office. One of the most troubling and complex of these came to light at a December 1996 press conference called by the managing director of the Kuwait Oil Tanker Co., a subsidiary of Kuwait's national oil company from which millions of dollars had been embezzled during the Iraqi occupation. A former oil and finance minister and also a member of the ruling family, Sheikh ʿAli al-Khalifah as-Sabah, was among those charged with the crime.

In 1997 political parties were illegal in Kuwait, but voluntary associations with political goals were not. A new organization of this type, founded late in the spring of 1997, was formed by a group of middle-class Kuwaitis, many of them professors at Kuwait University, including a female former dean, Moudhi al-Hamoud. Dissatisfied with the already existing political groups yet concerned that independent candidacies were retarding the progress of democratization in Kuwait, the group had begun meeting informally after the 1996 election. The new organization, the Nahdha Party/National Democratic Rally, aspired to be the political home of what one founding member, Shamlan al-ʿEisa, called "the silent majority"—that is, Kuwaitis interested in liberalization of the economy and government but who were neither Arab Nationalists, Socialists, nor religious ideologues.

The hopefulness engendered by the appearance of a centrist political grouping was rapidly dissipated on June 6 when an assassination attempt was made on the life of parliamentarian ʿAbdullah an-Naibari. Naibari had been a strong critic of fiscal malfeasance in Kuwait for many years and the nemesis of Sheikh ʿAli al-Khalifah as-Sabah throughout most of the latter's government service. A report by a member of a prominent merchant family, Jassim as-Saqr, that he had received a death threat by telephone the day after the assassination attempt evoked fears that the attempt on Naibari's life was part of a larger plot. The prompt arrest of those responsible, however, one of whom was a cousin of the finance minister, Nasser ʿAbdullah ar-Roudhan, both quieted fears of subsequent attempts on the lives of other dissidents and stirred concern that the minister himself might be involved.

(MARY ANN TÉTREAULT)

This article updates the *Macropædia* article ARABIA: *Kuwait.*

KYRGYSTAN

Area: 199,900 sq km (77,200 sq mi)
Population (1997 est.): 4,595,000
Capital: Bishkek
Head of state and government: President Askar Akayev, assisted by Prime Minister Apas Jumagulov

Kyrgyzstan experienced further setbacks in the democratization process in 1997 as a result of prosecutions of government opponents and independent journalists. In January, Topchubek Turganaliyev, head of the opposition Democratic Party of Free Kyrgyzstan, was given a 10-year sentence on a previously dismissed embezzlement charge; many attributed the move to the government's desire to silence an influential critic. The prosecution in May of the chief editor of one of the main independent newspapers resulted in an international outcry; the journalist was later freed by the Supreme Court.

The output of a new gold-refining mill, a Canadian-Kyrgyz joint venture, gave Kyrgyzstan the highest percentage increase in industrial production in the Commonwealth of Independent States for the first half of 1997, but other enterprises continued to languish, and living conditions for most of the country's population failed to improve. In July the Communist Party and several Slavic interest groups appealed to the Kyrgyz leadership to form a union with the Russian Federation, on the model of the union between Russia and Belarus, as a way out of the economic crisis. The government of Kyrgyzstan ignored the appeal, which was repeated in the following months.

Authorities in Kyrgyzstan were increasingly concerned during 1997 about the growth of the illegal narcotics trade in the country. Not only was Kyrgyzstan being used as a conduit for drugs in transit from Afghanistan and Tajikistan to Western Europe, but illegal drug-processing laboratories were discovered within Kyrgyzstan itself. The government appealed for international help.

(BESS BROWN)

This article updates the *Macropædia* article CENTRAL ASIA: *Kyrgyzstan.*

LAOS

Area: 236,800 sq km (91,429 sq mi)
Population (1997 est.): 5,117,000
Capital: Vientiane (Viangchan)
Chief of state: President Nouhak Phoumsavan
Head of government: Prime Minister Gen. Khamtai Siphandon

On July 23, 1997, Laos realized a longtime goal when it became a member of the Association of Southeast Asian Nations (ASEAN). Laos also joined the ASEAN Free Trade Area and undertook to integrate intraregional and external trade tariffs by 2007. While other ASEAN members pledged to lend the country technical and administrative support, Laos in turn agreed to permit citizens of ASEAN states to travel visa-free within its borders. In early September the Laotian legislature was accepted into the ASEAN Inter-Parliamentary Organization. A flurry of high-level state visits to Vientiane commemorated the country's new status: President Suharto of Indonesia traveled to Laos in February, Singapore Prime Minister Goh Chok Tong in March, Cambodia Co-Prime Minister Hun Sen in April, Thailand Prime Minister Chavalit Yongchaiyudh in June, Vietnam Prime Minister Vo Van Kiet in August, and Philippines Pres. Fidel Ramos in October. Laotian Prime Minister Khamtai Siphandon paid visits during the year to Myanmar (Burma), Cuba, and India.

In February a concession was granted to a Thai company to build and operate Laos's first railway, a 1,500-km (930-mi) network linking Vientiane to neighbouring countries. A 20-km (12-mi) stretch between the capital and Nong Khai, Thai., via the existing Mekong River Bridge was to be completed by late 1998. An accord to build a second Mekong bridge, financed by Japan and joining the southern Laotian province of Suvannakhet with the Thai border town Mukdahan, was signed on May 1. In July Vientiane was host of a World Bank meeting on building the long-delayed $1.2 billion Nam Theun-2 Dam along a tributary of the Mekong. The dam's proposed 615-MW hydroelectric power station was fiercely resisted by environmentalists and human rights activists from other countries who opposed the relocation of hill-tribe people. Consequently, the World Bank asked the government to do additional environmental impact studies before the project could go forward.

The economy was inevitably hurt by the monetary crises that beset Southeast Asia in 1997. The devaluation of the Thai baht after July 2 resulted in a black market in currency dealings in Vientiane as the government tried in vain to prevent the kip from plunging with the closely tied Thai unit.

In elections during December for members of the National Assembly, candidates of the Lao People's Revolutionary Party won 98 of the 99 seats. The party, which tolerated no organized opposition, allowed four independents to contest the vote.

(ROBERT WOODROW)

This article updates the *Macropædia* article SOUTHEAST ASIA: *Laos.*

LATVIA

Area: 64,610 sq km (24,946 sq mi)
Population (1997 est.): 2,472,000
Capital: Riga
Chief of state: President Guntis Ulmanis
Head of government: Prime Ministers Andris Skele and, from July 28, Guntars Krasts

Latvia's coalition government experienced difficulties in 1997. Andris Skele, who resigned as prime minister in January when Pres. Guntis Ulmanis criticized his choice for finance minister, was quickly voted back into office. On February 13 Parliament confirmed Skele's new five-party coalition by 70 votes to 17. Skele, an entrepreneur with no political affiliation, was widely credited with having turned Latvia's economy around during his first year in office. He had delivered the country's first balanced budget and instituted other economic reforms, especially in banking, which improved Latvia's relationship with the International Monetary Fund and gained a BBB investment grade rating from Standard and Poor's. The country's gross domestic product was expected to grow 4% in 1997. In July, however, Skele resigned as prime minister following the collapse of his coalition; several high-ranking government officials faced charges of corruption. Guntars Krasts, a former minister of the economy and supporter of free-market reforms, replaced Skele as prime minister.

Latvia's bid to join the European Union was not accepted in talks that began in September. In addition to improving its administrative systems, Latvia was told that it had to speed up naturalization of minorities, in particular its large number of Russians.

Latvia received support from a number of Western countries in its quest to become a member of NATO, but all three Baltic states were turned down. Russia remained fiercely opposed to their joining the Western alliance and offered its own security guarantees. Though these were rejected, Prime Minister Krasts declared that more economic cooperation with Russia would be welcome.

Efforts to privatize the economy continued. For sale were the Latvian Shipping Company and the big utility companies, Latvenergo and Latvia Gas. Russian gas supplier RAO Gazprom and two German companies bought a one-third share in the gas company, the largest privatization to date.

(ANNE ROBY)

This article updates the *Macropædia* article BALTIC STATES: *Latvia.*

LEBANON

Area: 10,400 sq km (4,016 sq mi)
Population (1997 est.): 3,112,000 (excluding Palestinian refugees estimated to number about 350,000)
Capital: Beirut
Chief of state: President Elias Hrawi
Head of government: Prime Minister Rafiq al-Hariri

Fighting in southern Lebanon resumed on Jan. 8, 1997, when a Katyusha rocket was fired from southern Lebanon into northern Israel. The ensuing clashes between Israeli soldiers and Lebanon's Hezbollah forces ended the cease-fire that had been in effect since April 1996. Fighting between the two continued throughout the year. In June the United Nations General Assembly endorsed a nonbinding resolution assessing Israel $1.7 million in damages for the shelling of the UN headquarters in Qana. The resolution was opposed by Israel and the United States. In September discussions began between Israel and Lebanon over reducing casualties in southern Lebanon. The Lebanese government reiterated its position on southern Lebanon, basing it on UN Security Council Resolution 425, which stipulates Israeli withdrawal from Lebanon without any preconditions.

The resumption of the conflict in southern Lebanon was also a reflection of Hezbollah's increasing legitimization. With its acceptance of the accords that ended Lebanon's civil war and its participation in the 1996 elections, sending a noncleric, Muhammad Funaysh, to the National Assembly, it became more than a guerrilla organization. Hezbollah developed a political infrastructure, educational and health care services, and media organs. Its avowed goal in 1997 was to drive Israel from southern Lebanon but not necessarily into the sea. This mellowing of doctrine led to splits in the party and the reemergence of Sheikh Subhi at-Tufayli.

Forced to step down as secretary-general of Hezbollah in 1990 for being too extremist, Tufayli resurfaced in 1997 as a protest figure. The hunger strike he advocated in late spring materialized on July 4 when, despite government deployment of troops in the region as a show of force, some 10,000 Lebanese converged on Baalbek to protest the government's economic policies. This "revolution of the hungry" was an expression of discontent in northern Al-Biqaʿ (Bekaa Valley) over the government's policy of forcing farmers to stop cultivating illegal drugs in return for compensation—which never materialized. Tufayli advocated nonpayment of taxes and electricity and water bills and threatened to march on Beirut. The demonstration was also an expression of discontent over economic corruption, debt, and overspending on roads, airports, and a new stadium in Beirut.

The Ta'if accord of 1989 retained the tradition in Lebanon of a Maronite Christian president, a Sunni Muslim prime minister, and a Shiʿite Muslim speaker of the National Assembly and allowed increased power for the prime minister and speaker. Competition between the leaders in 1997 led to accusations by the speaker, Nabih Berri, that Prime Minister Rafiq al-Hariri was wielding more power than he was entitled to and had unilaterally pushed bills through the legislature, while Hariri accused Berri of obstructing the reconstruction program by stalling bills in the Assembly. At times, mediation by Syria to resolve the disputes was necessary.

Pope John Paul II visited Beirut on May 10–11. The trip, which had been scheduled for 1994 but was postponed owing to a bomb attack on a Maronite church, was the first visit by a pope to the Middle East since 1964 and the first-ever official papal visit to Lebanon. In a mass celebrated by the pope in downtown Beirut and attended by some 300,000 people, the pontiff called on all religious factions to work together.

(REEVA S. SIMON)

LESOTHO

Area: 30,355 sq km (11,720 sq mi)
Population (1997 est.): 2,008,000
Capital: Maseru
Chief of state: King Letsie III
Head of government: Prime Minister Ntsu Mokhehle

Lesotho experienced a troubled year in 1997, one that included a police mutiny and an attempt to dismiss Prime Minister Ntsu Mokhehle from the leadership of the Basotho Congress Party (BCP). On February 7 about 100 Royal Lesotho Mounted Police seized police headquarters in Maseru in order to force the withdrawal of murder charges against eight of the officers; the charges had been brought against them in 1985, when three police officers were killed. By mid-February some 2,000 of the approximately 3,000 police were on strike, and the government had to deploy troops to recapture police headquarters. Ten police were subsequently charged with having subverted state authority.

At the beginning of March, the BCP discharged Mokhehle as party leader because he had not performed "effectively and effi-

CHRIS STEELE-PERKINS—MAGNUM

Two men urge support for Charles Taylor prior to Liberia's national elections in July. Taylor, who had launched the Liberian civil war more than seven years earlier, won a landslide victory and was inaugurated on August 2. He said his first task was to heal the wounds of the civil war.

ciently." Most BCP members of the National Assembly, however, supported the prime minister, and on April 18 the High Court ruled that the BCP decision was invalid. In June, however, BCP dissidents again challenged Mokhehle's position, claiming that at age 78 he was incapable of maintaining a "meaningful and coherent" leadership. On June 6 a violent confrontation took place at Qachas Nek between Mokhehle's supporters and opponents, and two deaths resulted. Mokhehle then announced that he was forming a new party, the Lesotho Congress for Democracy, and a number of BCP members resigned to join it. Mokhehle was able to continue as prime minister because he had the support of a majority in the Assembly, although opposition parties called his action a coup and demanded new general elections.

(GUY ARNOLD)

This article updates the *Macropædia* article SOUTHERN AFRICA: *Lesotho.*

LIBERIA

Area: 97,754 sq km (37,743 sq mi)
Population (1997 est.): 2,602,000 (excluding Liberian refugees temporarily residing in surrounding countries estimated to number about 650,000)
Capital: Monrovia
Head of state and government: Chairman of the Council of State Ruth Perry and, from August 2, President Charles Taylor

On July 19, 1997, presidential and legislative elections were held throughout Liberia, and Charles Taylor, who had launched the Liberian civil war more than seven years earlier, won a sweeping victory. With 75% of the votes, his National Patriotic Front of Liberia Party won 21 of 26 seats in the Senate and 49 of 64 seats in the House of Representatives. Taylor's closest rival for the presidency, Ellen Johnson-Sirleaf of the Unity Party, won 10% of the votes; her party gained three seats in the Senate and seven seats in the House of Representatives.

Taylor was inaugurated as Liberia's 21st president on August 2. He said that his first task was to heal the wounds of the civil war. Leaders of the neighbouring countries that had played a part in a peacekeeping mission for Liberia attended the inauguration ceremony, and Taylor thanked them for their efforts. President Taylor then established a nine-man National Security Council. The new government faced a bankrupt economy with no money in the state coffers and $2 billion of international debt.

During the early part of the year, it had been touch and go as to whether the August 1996 peace agreement forged in Nigeria (the 14th such agreement) would work. Despite setbacks, however, the process of disbanding and disarming the armed forces of the different factions was carried out successfully.

(GUY ARNOLD)

This article updates the *Macropædia* article WESTERN AFRICA: *Liberia.*

LIBYA

Area: 1,757,000 sq km (678,400 sq mi)
Population (1997 est.): 5,648,000
Capital: Tripoli (policy-making body meets in Surt)
Chief of state: (de facto) Col. Muammar al-Qaddafi; (nominal) Secretary of the General People's Congress Zanati Muhammad az-Zanati
Head of government: Secretary of the General People's Committee (Premier) ʿAbd al-Majid al-Qaʿud

Libya's international relations in 1997 were again dominated by the decade-long consequences of the December 1988 bombing of a U.S. airliner over Lockerbie, Scot. Libya's leader, Col. Muammar al-Qaddafi, refused to allow the two Libyan nationals accused

Tuareg tribespeople in Libya journey through the desert toward the Ghadamis oasis. Since 1990 Tuareg uprisings and government massacres in Niger and Mali had sent thousands of refugees to Libya, Burkina Faso, Algeria, and Mauritania.

YVES GELLIE

of the crime by Scottish investigators to be tried in a Scottish court. The U.S. government remained adamant that there could be no compromise on the issue and continued to insist that the damaging U.S.-led and UN-endorsed air-traffic and selective trade embargo should remain in place against Libya.

Colonel Qaddafi indicated his personal frustration with the flight embargo by flying in his own jet to Niger and Nigeria for diplomatic meetings in the spring. He knew that most Middle Easterners and Africans did not agree with Western governments on many aspects of the Lockerbie case. Egypt, for example, counseled compromise and urged that the case be tried in a neutral court in a neutral country, and Pres. Nelson Mandela of South Africa, who met with Qaddafi in Tripoli in October, expressed his belief that the accused Libyans would not receive a fair trial in Great Britain. Jim Swire, the most prominent of the bereaved family campaigners in the impasse, stated that the bereaved also wanted a trial in a neutral venue.

At home the year started with the execution on January 2 of eight Libyans—six army officers and two civilians—after they had been found guilty of spying with equipment supplied by the CIA. The accused came from the Warfalla, one of the three tribes on which Qaddafi had depended for support since the revolution in September 1969. Attempts by Qaddafi to persuade the Warfalla to deal with the problem failed. The decision to execute the men was seen as an attempt by Qaddafi to signal to the Warfalla that his leadership of the country remained strong.

The economy was steady in 1997. Libyan oil remained in demand by European importers. Though the inconvenience of the trade embargo remained, the period of austerity in its most unpleasant form was consigned to the past.

A significant economic initiative was the change in the official attitude toward tourism. The government gave the green light to a sector that had been regarded throughout the 1970s and '80s as an unimportant and undignified activity. International travel consultants and local entrepreneurs were active throughout the year. An emphasis was being placed on "desert tourism." (J.A. ALLAN)

This article updates the *Macropædia* article NORTH AFRICA: *Libya*.

LIECHTENSTEIN

Area: 160 sq km (62 sq mi)
Population (1997 est.): 31,300
Capital: Vaduz
Chief of state: Prince Hans Adam II
Head of government: Mario Frick

The longest-serving ruling coalition in Europe dissolved after almost 60 years when the Progressive Citizens' Party (FBP) quit in March 1997 to form an opposition group in the parliament. The coalition of the FBP and the Fatherland Union (VU) party had been formed in 1938 during fears of invasion by Nazi Germany. The VU formed a new government in April. In elections on February 2, the FBP lost a seat to the Free List (FL) party, which left it 10 seats (instead of 11) in the 25-member parliament. The VU held on to its 13 seats, while the FL moved up from 1 to 2 seats.

Prince Hans Adam II, meanwhile, urged the adoption of constitutional reforms that would reduce the role of the parliament and rely more on direct democracy, in which the people vote directly on specific issues. Opposition politicians charged that his call for change was only a ploy to gain more power for himself.

Liechtenstein's royal family, unlike most in Europe, paid for its own upkeep—its castle and royal household—and was probably the country's largest taxpayer. Though a remark by the prince about selling Liechtenstein to Bill Gates and renaming it Microsoft was not meant seriously, in July, when faced by politicians opposing his effort to gain the power to appoint judges, he ended discussions by saying he would pack his bags and move Princess Maria, the children, and himself to Vienna. (ANNE ROBY)

This article updates the *Micropædia* article LIECHTENSTEIN.

LITHUANIA

Area: 65,301 sq km (25,213 sq mi)
Population (1997 est.): 3,706,000
Capital: Vilnius
Chief of state: President Algirdas Brazauskas
Head of government: Prime Minister Gediminas Vagnorius

In 1997 the coalition of the Homeland Union (Conservatives of Lithuania; TS-LK) and the Christian Democrats, victorious in parliamentary elections in fall 1996, successfully implemented structural and legislative reforms in Lithuania that attracted greater foreign direct investments. Investments were expected to grow further with continuing cash privatization of strategic state enterprises. Even with an increased trade deficit, the annual rate of inflation was brought down to 9%.

Lithuania's difficulties in overcoming the legacy of one-party communist rule and establishing a pluralist, democratic system was shown by the victory of nonparty candidates, lawyer Arturas Paulauskas and émigré environmentalist Valdas Adamkus, over TS-LK chairman Vytautas Landsbergis in the first round of the presidential elections on December 21. Runoff elections were to take place in early January 1998.

The decision by the European Commission (EC) in July to exclude Lithuania from the Eastern European states recommended to begin formal negotiations in 1998 for European Union (EU) membership prompted Prime Minister Gediminas Vagnorius to wage an active campaign to alter this position. At its summit meeting in December, the EU ignored Vagnorius's plea but gave the EC the task of reviewing the country's situation and deciding when Lithuania had made sufficient reforms to begin membership discussions. A border treaty was signed by the Russian and Lithuanian presidents on October 24.

(SAULIUS A. GIRNIUS)

This article updates the *Macropædia* article BALTIC STATES: *Lithuania*.

LUXEMBOURG

Area: 2,586 sq km (999 sq mi)
Population (1997 est.): 420,000
Capital: Luxembourg
Chief of state: Grand Duke Jean
Head of government: Prime Minister Jean-Claude Juncker

On July 1, 1997, Luxembourg assumed the rotating presidency of the European Union (EU) from The Netherlands for a six-month term. Jean-Claude Juncker, Luxembourg's prime minister since 1995, became president just two weeks after a failed EU summit in Amsterdam. His priorities were to resolve the unanswered questions left by the Dutch and to keep on track the drive toward the establishment of a single currency by January 1999, even as such larger countries as France and Germany struggled to meet the requirements for monetary union. (See *European Union*, above.)

The domestic economy continued to grow, especially financial and banking services. The industrial sector was becoming more diversified, with increased movement into high-tech firms. On January 14 the Luxembourg-based television company Cie. Luxembourgeoise de Telediffusion (CLT) and the German media group Bertelsmann AG merged their broadcasting operations. The consolidated firm controlled 19 television stations and 23 radio stations in 10 European countries. (ANNE ROBY)

MACEDONIA

Area: 25,713 sq km (9,928 sq mi)
Population (1997 est.): 1,984,000
Capital: Skopje
Chief of state: President Kiro Gligorov
Head of government: Prime Minister Branko Crvenkovski

Ethnic tensions were on the rise in Macedonia in 1997. Early in the year ethnic Albanian and ethnic Macedonian students demonstrated over the pros and cons of Albanian-language teaching at Skopje University's pedagogical faculty; in early May the Constitutional Court ruled in favour of Albanian-language instruction. That same month the government indicted officials of the predominantly Albanian towns of Gostivar and Tetovo for flying the Albanian national flag from public buildings illegally. The Assembly passed a law on July 8 enabling ethnic minorities to use their national symbols under certain circumstances but

PASCAL MAITRE—MATRIX

A shaman stands on crumbling steps outside a house in the village of Amberode, Madagascar. Shamans played an important role in Madagascar, where health care was poor and some 75% of the population lived in poverty.

barring them from flying their flags from public buildings.

On the following day three ethnic Albanians were killed and dozens more were wounded in clashes with the police in Gostivar. Mayor Rufi Osmani was sentenced to 13 years 8 months in jail on September 17, convicted of "fanning national, racial, and ethnic intolerance, inciting rebellion, and disregarding the Constitutional Court" for allowing Albanian and Turkish flags to fly from the Gostivar town hall. Even while acknowledging the problems faced by the Albanian minority, in late September, Elisabeth Rehn, special envoy to the UN Commission on Human Rights, recommended that Macedonia be excluded from her mandate because of its improved human rights record.

Amid growing public dissatisfaction with the government, a major reshuffle took place on May 27. Among those replaced were Deputy Prime Minister Jane Miljovski and Foreign Minister Ljubomir Frckovski, both prominent reformers. Frckovski was replaced by Defense Minister Blagoj Handziski, who was succeeded by Lazar Kitanovski.

Only minor economic changes were registered in 1997. The economy continued to grow, and inflation and the budget deficit remained acceptably low. Other indexes, such as Macedonia's trade deficit and unemployment, remained uncomfortably high, however.

In early March the national bank suspended operations of Macedonia's largest savings house, and as a result, about 30,000 clients lost an estimated total of $28 million–$80 million. The government promised compensation of $12 million, and trials of top financial officials began in October. In June the national bank depreciated the denar 16% against the German mark.

Tensions over the status of Macedonia's Albanian minority continued to prejudice relations with Albania. Macedonia's relationship with Greece was stable, and, even though the disputed issue of Macedonia's name remained unresolved, the year saw the first exchange of ministerial visits between the Balkan neighbours. In December the UN Security Council voted to extend the mandate for its peacekeeping force, UNPREDEP, to August 1998.

(STEFAN KRAUSE)

This article updates the *Macropædia* article BALKAN STATES: *Macedonia*.

MADAGASCAR

Area: 587,041 sq km (226,658 sq mi)
Population (1997 est.): 14,062,000
Capital: Antananarivo
Chief of state: Presidents Norbert Ratsirahonana (acting) and, from January 31, Didier Ratsiraka
Head of government: Prime Ministers Norbert Ratsirahonana and, from February 21, Pascal Rakotomavo

During the first round of Madagascar's presidential elections, which were held on Nov. 3, 1996, Didier Ratsiraka took the lead with 36.61% of the vote, followed by former president Albert Zafy with 23.39%. The second round was held on December 29. Voter turnout was low in this round, but Ratsiraka secured the necessary majority to win, tallying 50.71% to Zafy's 49.29%, and was formally declared president on Jan. 31, 1997.

Ratsiraka, a former military leader, had ruled Madagascar for 16 years before his overthrow in 1991. On February 21 Ratsiraka made the surprising appointment of Pascal Rakotomavo, the chief executive of a finance firm, as prime minister. Most observers had expected Norbert Ratsirahonana to remain in that office. In April Rakotomavo named his Cabinet, which included a number of ministers who had served in the outgoing government.

Legislative elections, which were originally scheduled to be held in August, were pushed back for at least 10 months in order to allow time for the distribution of identity cards to Madagascar's four million eligible voters. In early May the government passed a law that required citizens to possess the cards in order to register to vote and participate in elections.

The delay, which allowed 138 members of the National Assembly to continue in office well past the expiration of their mandate, angered opposition leaders. Zafy accused the government of acting in "flagrant violation of the constitution" and called in vain for Ratsiraka to step down.

Swarms of locusts caused major damage in Madagascar in 1997. Crops, including rice plantations, were destroyed after locusts overran several districts on the island. Bush fires used to ward off the locusts were also responsible for destroying vegetation. The Agriculture Ministry assured residents that it would eradicate all of the swarms by October.

(GUY ARNOLD)

MALAWI

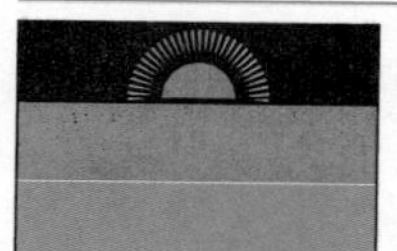

Area: 118,484 sq km (45,747 sq mi)
Population (1997 est.): 9,609,000
Capital: A capital is not designated in the 1994 constitution. Current government operations are divided between Lilongwe (ministerial and financial), Blantyre (executive and judicial), and Zomba (legislative)
Head of state and government: President Bakili Muluzi

The campaign to reduce Malawi's dependence on external aid and to increase foreign investment remained among the government's top priorities. At the same time, the marked improvement in the management of the economy since the change of government in 1994 resulted in a sharp decline in inflation and interest rates, and this encouraged foreign donors to offer aid totaling $319 million for 1997. Pres. Bakili Muluzi, nevertheless, remained conscious of the fact that 64% of the population lived in poverty.

In an attempt to reduce the impact of heavy transportation costs caused by landlocked Malawi's remoteness from the sea, the government tried to encourage the processing of more products near their point of origin. Meanwhile, the privatization of tobacco production, Malawi's biggest export earner, continued to be a priority.

On April 3 the leading opposition party, the Malawi Congress Party (MCP), announced that it would end its 10-month boycott of the national legislature. The boycott had been imposed after the MCP accused the ruling United Democratic Front of trying to persuade MCP legislators to shift their party allegiance in order to protect its majority, but President Muluzi agreed to introduce a constitutional amendment that would prevent such political chicanery. In November former president Hastings Kamuzu Banda died. (*See* OBITUARIES.)

(KENNETH INGHAM)

This article updates the *Macropædia* article SOUTHERN AFRICA: *Malawi.*

MALAYSIA

Area: 329,733 sq km (127,311 sq mi)
Population (1997 est.): 21,767,000
Capital: Kuala Lumpur
Chief of state: *Yang di-Pertuan Agong* (Paramount Ruler) Tuanku Ja'afar ibni al-Marhum Tuanku Abdul Rahman
Head of government: Prime Minister Dato Seri Mahathir bin Mohamad

Malaysia's sometimes prickly relationship with Singapore entered a difficult period in March 1997 because of comments in an affidavit filed by Singapore Senior Minister Lee Kuan Yew. His description of Johor, the Malaysian state across the causeway from Singapore, as being notoriously crime-ridden sparked outrage. Lee apologized, and the row died down, but the remarks rankled.

Raging scrub and forest fires in Indonesia produced a noxious pall that enveloped Kuala Lumpur and other parts of Malaysia for months. Sarawak, on the island of Borneo, the worst-hit state, declared a 10-day state of emergency in September because of the smog.

Differences over the practice of Islam, which was controlled by religious authorities in individual states, seemed likely to become a growing source of friction in the mainly Muslim country. The federal government and Muslim clerics clashed over several religious rulings, including bans for the faithful on beauty and body-building contests. Prime Minister Dato Seri Mahathir bin Mohamad warned that rigid devotion to Islamic ritual could hurt economic development. His call for Muslims to reform their attitudes toward their religion angered Islamic conservatives.

There was continuing speculation about Deputy Prime Minister Anwar Ibrahim's chances of inheriting the presidency of the United Malays National Organization (UMNO) from Mahathir. UMNO was the dominant party in the ruling National Front coalition, and, consequently, its president heads the government. In part, the succession rumours were fueled by apparent differences between Mahathir and Anwar in handling issues affecting the economy.

Mahathir's unprecedented decision in May to delegate sweeping powers to Anwar while he was away on a long vacation seemed to dispel notions that he was less than fully supportive of his deputy. The country's economic woes, however, drew attention to their contrasting approaches. Conventional wisdom initially held that Malaysia would not be badly affected by the regional currency turmoil that spilled over from Thailand when that nation devalued its currency in July. Sales of the ringgit by offshore funds combined with investor jitters, however, sent the Malaysian currency and stock market on a downward spin. The prime minister blamed foreigners bent on sabotaging the economy. He then intervened to shore up the market, apparently sidelining Anwar, who was also serving as finance minister.

Measures that were taken included a directive to state-managed funds to buy shares in Malaysian companies and a short-lived ban on the short selling of some stocks, which was lifted when it prompted a massive sell-off by fund managers. Between January and September about $110 billion—more than four times the country's foreign currency reserves—were wiped from the market capitalization of the Kuala Lumpur stock exchange.

In October the government presented an "austerity" budget to bring about a medium-term recovery. The program included export incentives and tighter fiscal policy. Import taxes were raised to reduce the current-account deficit, estimated at 13.1 billion ringgit on October 17. Several large-scale projects were deferred, including the Bakun dam in Sarawak; the Linear City, a shopping mall to be built over a river in Kuala Lumpur; a highway linking hill resorts; and a series of bridges linking Malaysia and Indonesia. The corporate income tax was cut from 30% to 28%.

Many believed that the measures did not go far enough to trim the fat from Malaysia's decade-long boom. In December Anwar announced tougher plans to cope with the deepening woes. These included an 18% cut in 1998 government spending, curbs on big imports such as airplanes, and a freeze on new stock listings. Growth of gross domestic product was officially revised downward to 7% for 1997 and 4–5% in 1998, but private-sector economists believed the rate was likely to be lower.

Mahathir's bitter attacks on "rogue speculators," hints of a "Jewish plot," and threat to ban currency trading drew international criticism. Domestically, however, his National Front partners rallied behind him. Especially in rural areas of Malaysia, the prime minister was seen as a hero who dared to stand up to developed nations.

(CHOONG TET SIEU)

This article updates the *Macropædia* article SOUTHEAST ASIA: *Malaysia.*

MALDIVES

Area: 298 sq km (115 sq mi)
Population (1997 est.): 267,000
Capital: Male
Head of state and government: President Maumoon Abdul Gayoom

The ninth summit of the South Asian Association for Regional Co-operation (SAARC) was held in Male on May 12–14, 1997. Pres. Maumoon Abdul Gayoom and other heads of state of the SAARC nations resolved to improve political and economic cooperation and reiterated their commitment to eradicating poverty in the region. They also agreed upon several initiatives related to the protection of the environment, including the implemention of recommendations of two regional studies that had focused on the greenhouse effect and the causes and consequences of natural disasters. In a speech to UN delegates at the Earth Summit Plus 5 in July, Gayoom said that global warming threatened his nation's existence and called for international help in combating the problem. Researchers had recently detected a slight rise in the Indian Ocean around Maldives. In October Gayoom made a similar plea when he spoke at an executive session of the Commonwealth heads of government.

For his efforts to give Maldives a stronger voice in the Commonwealth and the international community, Queen Elizabeth II awarded Gayoom the Grand Cross of St. Michael and St. George (GCMG), the highest order accorded to foreign dignitaries by the British monarchy. Gayoom was the only Maldivian citizen ever to have received the GCMG order.

Maldives made slow but steady economic and social progress in 1997. With an average per capita income of $990, Maldives had risen above the lowest-income countries. Its social indicators were modestly encouraging, with average life expectancy at 63 years and adult literacy at 93%. Just over 31% of the population was urban-based. The country spent 9.2% of its budget on education and 5% on health. (GUY ARNOLD)

This article updates the *Micropædia* article MALDIVES.

MALI

Area: 1,248,574 sq km (482,077 sq mi)
Population (1997 est.): 9,945,000
Capital: Bamako
Chief of state: President Alpha Oumar Konaré
Head of government: Prime Minister Ibrahima Boubacar Keita

Preparatory to Mali's second multiparty national elections, a new electoral code was adopted in January 1997, and the 34-person Independent National Electoral Commission was created. Logistic problems forced the postponement of the legislative elections from March to April. Some 1,500 candidates from 21 parties campaigned for the 147 seats in the country's new National Assembly.

The voter turnout was heavy, but lack of ballots, incomplete and incorrect voting lists, and other irregularities created delays, and charges of election fraud were brought by the opposition. The ruling Alliance for Democracy in Mali (ADEMA) took an early lead in the first round of voting on April 13. Opposition protests escalated, however, and on April 26 the Constitutional Court nullified the results of the voting and suspended the next day's scheduled second round.

To prevent further chaos, Pres. Alpha Oumar Konaré also pushed back the presidential election from May 4 to May 11. The opposition responded with a boycott of the presidential election that was largely successful, with only 27% of the electorate going to the polls. Konaré, who was running virtually unopposed, took 84% of the vote and was inaugurated on June 8. New legislative elections, which had been rescheduled for July 20 and August 3, were also boycotted by most opposition parties. As a result, ADEMA won 130 of the 147 seats. (NANCY ELLEN LAWLER)

This article updates the *Macropædia* article WESTERN AFRICA: *Mali.*

MALTA

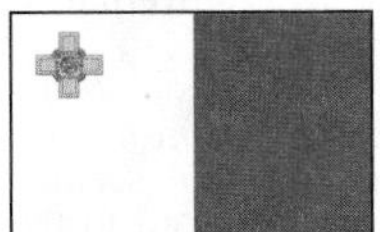

Area: 316 sq km (122 sq mi)
Population (1997): 375,000
Capital: Valletta
Chief of state: President Ugo Mifsud Bonnici
Head of government: Prime Minister Alfred Sant

Immediately after the election of October 1996, the new Labour Party government withdrew Malta from the NATO Partnership for Peace program. Prime Minister Alfred Sant declared that Malta would use its constitutional neutrality as a basis for its efforts to promote stability and security in the Mediterranean region. The new government also froze Malta's application to join the European Union (EU) but said it would seek the gradual introduction of an industrial free-trade zone between Malta and the EU and would also work for cooperation in the commercial, technical, financial, cultural and educational sectors.

The value-added tax (VAT), introduced in 1995 by the Nationalist Party government to supplant customs duties, was replaced on July 1, 1997, by a new taxation system, a combination of customs and excise duties. In March Minister of Finance Lino Spiteri, citing the country's weak economy, resigned and questioned publicly the wisdom of the decision to replace the VAT; previously, he had also criticized the freezing of Malta's EU application.

The budget for 1997 estimated that a deficit of 101.2 million Maltese lira between revenue and expenditure would be reduced to 82.6 million lira by means of foreign grants and loans. In September, however, it was predicted that the actual deficit would be between 120 million lira and 130 million lira. Faced with this financial gap and increased unemployment, the government was planning an austerity budget for 1998. (ALBERT GANADO)

MARSHALL ISLANDS

Area: 181 sq km (70 sq mi)
Population (1997 est.): 60,300
Capital: Majuro
Head of state and government: President Imata Kabua

In January 1997 the national legislature elected Imata Kabua president of the Marshall Islands. He succeeded his cousin, Amata Kabua, who died in December 1996.

The budget for 1997 was $84.8 million, down from $91.7 million in 1996. The Compact of Free Association with the U.S., which was expected to bring approximately $1 billion to the economy over 15 years (75% of all government expenditure), was scheduled to expire in 2001. Consequently, the government began a reform of the public service that was designed to reduce the number of jobs by 25%. South Korean investors announced plans for a major resort development that would cause the relocation of affected populations on Mili, Majuro, and Arno atolls.

Consultant scientists reported in late 1996 that by the removal of some soil and saturation of agricultural areas with potassium fertilizers, Bikini atoll, which had been the site of 23 nuclear tests during the 1940s and 1950s, could be resettled. In July President Kabua deferred plans for a feasibility study of a controversial proposal to develop Bikini as a commercial nuclear-waste dump for radioactive material produced by Asian power plants. (BARRIE MACDONALD)

MAURITANIA

Area: 1,030,700 sq km (398,000 sq mi)
Population (1997 est.): 2,411,000
Capital: Nouakchott
Chief of state: President Col. Maaouya Ould Sidi Ahmad Taya
Head of government: Prime Minister Cheikh Afia Ould Mohamed Khouna

Relations between the government and opposition groups deteriorated in 1997. On January 25 leaders of the six main opposition parties, along with many of their supporters, were arrested on charges of conspiracy and detained for several weeks. In March a new opposition coalition, formed to coordinate strategy for the presidential elections in December, called for a new electoral code, access to the state-owned media, and the formation of an independent electoral commission. The government refused to consider these demands. In April, despite a ban on demonstrations, several opposition parties marched to protest sharp rises in the cost of living. In July the opposition coalition announced that it would boycott the presidential election and thus virtually ensured the reelection of Pres. Maaouya Ould Sidi Ahmad Taya in December.

After mediation by Tunisia, Mauritania and Libya agreed in March to restore full diplomatic relations, which had been broken off in 1995 when Mauritania established ties with Israel. Talks with Senegal were held in June, with both nations seeking to improve cooperation on matters of common concern, including trade and security.

On July 14 the International Monetary Fund approved a $20 million loan for Mauritania's structural-reform program, praising the country's efforts over the past five years to liberalize the economy. The economy was expected to grow by 5% in 1997, though prices were also projected to rise by 5%, owing in part to a severe drought that affected much of the nation. (NANCY ELLEN LAWLER)

This article updates the *Macropædia* article WESTERN AFRICA: *Mauritania.*

MAURITIUS

Area: 2,040 sq km (788 sq mi)
Population (1997 est.): 1,143,000
Capital: Port Louis
Chief of state: President Cassam Uteem
Head of government: Prime Minister Navin Ramgoolam

Although the coalition of the Mauritian Labour Party of Navin Ramgoolam and the Mauritian Militant Movement (MMM) of Paul Berenger governed Mauritius for 18 months after the elections of December 1995, the alliance was an uneasy one. On June 21, 1997, after months of conflict the coalition was brought to an end when Prime Minister Ramgoolam dismissed Berenger, who had been the deputy prime minister and the minister of foreign affairs and regional cooperation. Berenger's dismissal was followed by the resignation of seven of the nine MMM members of the Cabinet.

(GUY ARNOLD)

This article updates the *Micropædia* article MAURITIUS.

MEXICO

Area: 1,958,201 sq km (756,066 sq mi)
Population (1997 est.): 94,275,000
Capital: Mexico City
Head of state and government: President Ernesto Zedillo Ponce de León

Having enjoyed a firm economic recovery in 1996, when gross domestic product (GDP) grew by 5.1%, Mexico began 1997 on a positive note for the administration of Pres. Ernesto Zedillo. Authorities and members of the ruling Institutional Revolutionary Party (PRI) realized from the outset, however, that there could be setbacks following the midterm congressional elections, the first-ever poll for mayor of Mexico City, and some local and provincial elections, when the population would register at the ballot box its response to the handling of the economy in the wake of the financial crisis in late 1994 and early 1995. In addition, the ruling party itself appeared to be increasingly subject to rifts and defections, and from December 1996 onward, Zedillo redoubled efforts to restore party unity but was unable to prevent a wave of senior figures from defecting to other parties.

In large measure the first half of 1997 was dominated by campaigning for the midterm elections, held on July 6. From the beginning the focus was on the Mexico City mayoral race, which the National Action Party (PAN) initially appeared likely to win. When, however, it selected Carlos Castillo Peraza as its candidate on March 2 (with former presidential candidate Diego Fernández de Cevallos choosing not to run) and the other main opposition grouping, the Democratic Revolutionary Party (PRD), decided to field its cofounder, Cuauhtémoc Cárdenas Solórzano (*see* BIOGRAPHIES), it soon became evident that Cárdenas was the front-runner. The PRI's choice was Alfredo del Mazo, who had served as governor of Mexico state from 1981 to 1986.

A further omen of the impending defeat for the ruling PRI in the congressional polls was the result of the municipal and legislative elections in the state of Morelos, held on March 16. The number of municipalities controlled by the PRI was reduced from 32 (of 33) to 17, with the PRD taking 13 and PAN 2. In the state legislature the opposition parties together won a majority of seats (11 for PRD and 5 for PAN) as against 13 for the PRI.

All 500 seats in the national Chamber of Deputies were up for renewal on July 6, with 300 of them directly elected and 200 allocated proportionally. In the election the PRI won 38.5% of the vote, which was below the minimum of just over 42% needed to qualify for a simple majority of seats. In the final tally the PRI won 165 seats by direct vote and 74 indirectly, which left the party a dozen short of a majority. The PRD and PAN received similar shares of the vote (25.8% and 26.9%, respectively), although the PRD won several more seats (125 versus 121) owing to the method of allocation. In the elections for the Senate, the PRI took 13 of the 32 vacant seats, which left it with 77 of 128 seats overall; PAN took 9 and PRD 8 for totals of 33 and 16, respectively. The small opposition groupings—the Mexican Green Ecologist Party (PVEM) and the Labour Party (PT)—which took 4% and 2.5% of the vote, won 8 and 7 deputies' seats, respectively, and one each in the Senate.

A Mexican policeman in the state of Jalisco carries a large bundle of marijuana toward a bonfire for incineration in August. Despite continued efforts by Washington to pressure Mexico to eradicate its marijuana and poppy fields, drug activity in the country continued to increase.

DANIEL AGUILAR—REUTERS

The damaging effect of the election for the PRI was the opposition's accord to operate together in a loose alliance in the legislature with a view to gaining greater bargaining power with the government on policy issues. They were particularly interested in budgetary matters and the reduction of sales taxes, which had been sharply increased (from 10% to 15%) in the wake of the 1994–95 economic crisis.

Though the PRI strongly contested the opposition alliance's bid for control of many of the key congressional committees (including the budget committee), it did not prevail. Porfirio Muñoz Ledo of PRD also became the first non-PRI leader of the Chamber of Deputies.

As was expected, PRD's Cárdenas won the Mexico City mayoralty by a wide margin (he took 48% of the vote), with 25.5% for del Mazo (PRI) and 16% for Castillo Peraza (PAN). Cárdenas began his three-year term in December. He met with Zedillo in September and October on financial and security matters (the federal government controls funding for the capital).

Cárdenas appeared to have won assurances that he would be involved in the appointment of the police chief but seemed unlikely to have much say in regard to the city's budget.

Other election results in July 1997 included wins for the PRI in the states of San Luis Potosí, Colima, Campeche, and Sonora, while PAN won in Nuevo León and Querétaro. The PRI's loss of its majority in the Chamber of Deputies led to the departure on September 9 of the party's president, Humberto Roque Villanueva; he was succeeded by Mariano Palacios Alcocer, who had previously served as governor of Querétaro state.

Fidel Velázquez, the veteran leader of the Confederation of Mexican Workers (CTM), linked to the PRI, died in June. (*See* OBITUARIES.) He was succeeded by Leonardo Rodríguez Alcaine. The CTM's umbrella organization, the Congress of Labour, showed signs during the year of increasing disunity as several groups defected to the rival Forum for New Trade Unionism. These developments prevented the negotiation of the annual tripartite pact between government, business, and unions, which was usually concluded before the following year's budget launch.

Late in December in a tiny village in southern Mexico, 45 people, many of them women and children, were killed. Sixteen men, possibly members of a paramilitary group, were charged with the murders.

On the economic front the recovery evident during 1996 continued in the first half of 1997, with an expansion of some 7% (based on 6% growth in the first quarter and 7.4% in the second). This was underpinned by the strong performance of manufacturing (up 9.1%) and construction (up 10.2%) as well as fair growth in services (6.3%) and agriculture (5.8%).

By early November, when the 1998 budget proposals were submitted, the government estimated that GDP would increase 6.5% in 1997, up from the 6% foreseen in September and the 4–4.5% at the start of the year. Throughout the year unemployment appeared to be declining gradually, with the rate for the end of the year projected at 4.5%, compared with 5.5% at the end of 1996. It was also expected, however, that inflation would rise to 15.5–16%.

The external accounts remained relatively strong, although the trade surplus, which was over $6 billion in 1996, was reduced as imports rose. By the end of September, the accumulated surplus stood at $1,840,000,000. The reduced trade deficit and other payment obligations were officially expected to push the current account deficit up to $6,700,000,000 by the end of the year, from $1,760,000,000 a year earlier.

The authorities remained committed to the floating-exchange-rate regime established in early 1995 in the wake of the economic crisis, with the rate against the U.S. dollar holding up well during the first nine months of the year, when it traded mostly in the range 7.7–7.9 pesos per $1.

(SUSAN M. CUNNINGHAM)

MICRONESIA, FEDERATED STATES OF

Area: 701 sq km (271 sq mi)
Population (1997 est.): 107,000
Capital: Palikir, on Pohnpei
Head of state and government: President Jacob Nena

In elections that took place during March 1997, the 10 incumbent senators were all returned to office without opposition. In November 1996 Pres. Bailey Olter, who had suffered a stroke in July, was replaced by Vice Pres. Jacob Nena, who became acting president. In May 1997 Nena was sworn in as president.

Economic difficulties continued as the government tried to plan for the ending in 2001 of the Compact of Free Association with the United States. Over the 15-year life of the current agreement, Micronesia was to receive approximately $1,355,000,000. No indication was given as to future levels of funding. In response to the possible reduction in support, the government in March offered an early-retirement package that sought to reduce the public service employment by 20%. In April the Asian Development Bank announced a loan of $18 million for public-service reform and development of the private sector.

At the end of December 1996, Typhoon Fern caused damage to private houses, public utilities, and crops. In March U.S. Pres. Bill Clinton declared Yap a disaster area, which thus allowed the U.S. to provide assistance to the hard-hit areas.

(BARRIE MACDONALD)

This article updates the *Macropædia* article PACIFIC ISLANDS: *Micronesia.*

MOLDOVA

Area: 33,700 sq km (13,000 sq mi)
Population (1997 est.): 4,363,000
Capital: Chisinau
Chief of state: Presidents Mircea Snegur and, from January 15, Petru Lucinschi
Head of government: Prime Ministers Andrei Sangheli and, from January 16, Ion Ciubuc

Petru Lucinschi was sworn in as Moldova's new president on Jan. 15, 1997. The following day he called upon economist Ion Ciubuc to form a new Cabinet. Lucinschi, who had won the December 1996 runoff election against Mircea Snegur, soon found himself confronting the legislature much as his predecessor had done in 1995–96. Growing opposition from the Socialist Unity faction, the Communists' Party, and segments of the Agrarian Democratic Party hindered the adoption of badly needed reform legislation. Eyeing the March 1998 parliamentary elections, on February 8 Lucinschi's supporters set up the Movement for a Democratic and Prosperous Moldova. In June Snegur's Party of Revival and Accord of Moldova and the pro-Romanian Christian Democratic Popular Front joined forces as the Democratic Convention of Moldova.

In an attempt to resolve the conflict with the breakaway Dniester region, on May 8 Lucinschi and Dniester leader Igor Smirnov signed a memorandum in Moscow on normalizing mutual relations, with Russia, Ukraine, and the Organization for Security and Cooperation in Europe as guarantors.

The state of the economy remained desolate. In early November the International Monetary Fund and the World Bank, pointing to a budgetary deficit that was expected to reach 7% of gross domestic product in 1997, decided that they would withhold further loan installments.

(DAN IONESCU)

MONACO

Area: 1.95 sq km (0.75 sq mi)
Population (1997 est.): 31,900
Chief of state: Prince Rainier III
Head of government: Ministers of State Paul Dijoud and, from February 3, Michel Leveque

Beginning with a mass in the cathedral and continuing with a multimedia waterfront extravaganza that depicted scenes from the principality's long history, yearlong festivities opened in Monaco on Jan. 8, 1997, to mark the 700th year of rule by the Grimaldi family. Prince Rainier III unveiled a statue of the dynasty's founder, François Grimaldi, who on Jan. 8, 1297, disguised himself as a monk to get inside the gates of Monaco and then opened them to his forces and seized control.

Amid speculation about the succession, Rainier, who had stated that he would hand over rule of the principality to Prince Albert when he thought his son was ready, was expected to continue ruling Monaco at least until May 9, 1999, the 50th anniversary of his reign.

Once the mainstay of the economy, revenue from the state-controlled Société des Bains de Mer, which operated the casinos, had been declining for a few years. These losses were offset, however, by a relatively diverse underlying economy comprising more than 100 industries along with tourism and banking and financial services. A telecommunications industry was being developed, and construction was strong as Monaco continued to expand in the only directions it could—underground and out into the sea.

(ANNE ROBY)

This article updates the *Micropædia* article MONACO.

MONGOLIA

Area: 1,566,500 sq km (604,800 sq mi)
Population (1997 est.): 2,373,000
Capital: Ulaanbaatar
Chief of state: Presidents Punsalmaagiyn Ochirbat and, from June 20, Natsagiyn Bagabandi
Head of government: Prime Minister Mendsaikhan Enkhsaikhan

The result of the May 1997 presidential elections clearly suggested growing voter disenchantment with the coalition government formed by the Democratic Alliance (DA). It had achieved modest success in its first year of attempting to accelerate economic reform but at the cost of increasing poverty and unemployment. The DA nominated the incumbent president, Punsalmaagiyn Ochirbat, for reelection. The opposition Mongolian People's Revolutionary

Party (MPRP) selected its chairman, Natsagiyn Bagabandi, as its presidential candidate. The third parliamentary party, the United Heritage (conservative) Party, nominated Jambyn Gombojav, a member of the Great Hural (parliament) who had recently resigned from the MPRP. Bagabandi won the election with 60.8% of the vote, compared with Ochirbat's 29.8% and Gombojav's 6.6%.

The election of the opposition candidate to the presidency, with its right of veto, threatened to produce legislative logjams in the Great Hural. Because the DA was one seat short of a two-thirds majority, MPRP members had already hindered legislation. Moreover, the autumn 1997 session opened amid rumours of a split between the coalition partners over social policy. Between October 1996 and April 1997, the proportion of poor households (monthly income less than $20) rose from 17% to 20%. Registered unemployment rose slightly to 60,800, but with the addition of those leaving school and demobilized soldiers, the true figure reached 227,200.

Mongolia was not short of foreign grants and loans for infrastructure development and balance of payments support, although Japan, the biggest bilateral donor, and the Asian Development Bank were critical of the nation's slow implementation of aid programs. The first 15,000 bbl of oil extracted from Mongolia by U.S. companies were dispatched to China in 1996. By mid-1997 currency reserves were rising, the tugrik had stabilized, and inflation was falling.

Mongolia's relations with China and Russia were marred by cross-border smuggling and poaching. Low-key military cooperation with the U.S. signaled its growth as Mongolia's "third neighbour."

(ALAN J.K. SANDERS)

MOROCCO

Area: 458,730 sq km (177,117 sq mi) (Area and population figures refer to Morocco as constituted prior to the purported division of Western Sahara between Morocco and Mauritania and the subsequent Moroccan occupation of the Mauritanian zone in 1979.)
Population (1997 est.): 27,225,000
Capital: Rabat
Chief of state: King Hassan II
Head of government: Prime Minister ʿAbd al-Latif Filali

For Morocco 1997 was a year of constitutional restructuring, alongside the ongoing restructuring of the economy. The constitutional changes approved by referendum in 1996 came into effect, with municipal elections in June and legislative elections for the new bicameral parliament in November. The municipal elections returned a 56% vote for the centre and right-wing parties, to the surprise of most observers, who had expected the left-of-centre Democratic Bloc (Koutla) to do better than its rivals. The Democratic Bloc won only 32% of the vote in a 75.13% turnout of eligible voters. The municipal elections were important for the legislative elections later in the year because the municipalities would choose 60% of the members of the new upper chamber, all of whom were to be indirectly elected, with the professional associations electing the remaining 40%.

As the legislative elections neared, the Democratic Bloc alliance broke up in late September. Consequently, a National Entente victory was anticipated, with the pro-government Constitutional Union and National Assembly of Independents playing key roles in the government that would emerge. This development also fed anxieties that unless the parties could demonstrate political maturity as they governed, popular support for the new constitutional arrangements—a critical part of the king's vision for transition to a constitutional monarchy—would be fatally undermined. The elections, which were held on November 14 for the 325-seat House of Representatives, produced 102 seats for the Koutla, 100 for the right-wing National Entente (Wifaq) alliance, 97 for the centre parties, 9 for the Islamists, and 17 for the others. The voter turnout was 58.3%.

Morocco's major diplomatic problem, the Western Sahara dispute, apparently moved closer to solution when the UN secretary-general, Kofi Annan, appointed a former U.S. secretary of state, James Baker, as his special envoy. After four meetings in which Morocco and the opposition Polisario Front met face-to-face, Baker announced in October that terms had been reached that would enable the long-delayed referendum for self-determination to be held in 1998. Morocco abandoned some of its demands for voter registration, and the Polisario Front made similar concessions over voting procedures.

In economic terms Morocco experienced modest growth after the outstanding recovery in 1996 as a result of the record grain harvest of 10 million metric tons. Growth was expected to be between 1% and 2.5%, compared with 11.8% in 1996; the harvest was estimated to total 3,350,000 metric tons. As a result, grain imports were expected to reach 2.5 million metric tons in 1997–98.

(GEORGE JOFFÉ)

This article updates the *Macropædia* article NORTH AFRICA: *Morocco*.

MOZAMBIQUE

Area: 812,379 sq km (313,661 sq mi)
Population (1997 est.): 18,165,000
Capital: Maputo
Head of state and government: President Joaquim Chissano, assisted by Prime Minister Pascoal Mocumbi

Heavy rains early in 1997 caused tens of thousands of Mozambicans to seek refuge in Malawi to avoid floods in their own districts. Supplying the refugees with food presented the government with a severe problem, and a call for aid was made to the international community. The rains also further delayed the inevitably slow minesweeping operations in several provinces. The rains did provide some benefits, however; they helped to maintain the increased production of cereal grains, which was gradually reducing the country's dependence on emergency food assistance. The lack of roads and other transport links between producer and consumer continued to discourage farmers from growing more crops than they needed for their own use, and by the middle of the year 177,000 people still required immediate food aid and would continue to do so for at least four months.

Nevertheless, donor agencies were pleased with Mozambique's progress. The vast road-building project was progressing, with the restoration of the link between Maputo and Witbank, S.Af., high among the priorities, as too was the construction of major roads that would provide access to the Nacala and Beira regions. The privatization program, launched in 1989, was also advancing steadily, with more than 700 companies privatized by mid-1997 and the probable addition of 300–400 by the year's end.

In July the International Finance Corp. approved an investment package to establish an aluminum smelter plant near Maputo. The construction of the plant would create 5,000 temporary jobs, and after its completion there would be permanent employment for 900 workers. Eventually the plant would triple the country's output of aluminum, earning annually approximately $430 million in foreign exchange.

The full development of democracy in Mozambique, strongly urged by the donor countries, continued to be hampered by the difficulty encountered by the main opposition party, Mozambique National Resistance (Renamo), in formulating policies that differed in any essential respects from those of the government. Renamo, with a few exceptions, lacked leaders of proven ability, so many of the donor countries that were stressing the importance of democracy were not anxious to see it in power.

In July, Prime Minister Pascoal Mocumbi denied reports that arms were being smuggled through Mozambican ports to the opposition National Union for the Total Independence of Angola party. The government, he said, was not involved in any such transactions, nor, to the best of his knowledge, was any private citizen in Mozambique.

(KENNETH INGHAM)

This article updates the *Macropædia* article SOUTHERN AFRICA: *Mozambique*.

MYANMAR (BURMA)

Area: 676,577 sq km (261,228 sq mi)
Population (1997 est.): 46,822,000
Capital: Yangon (Rangoon)
Head of state and government: Chairman of the State Law and Order Restoration Council (from November 15, State Peace and Development Council) Gen. Than Shwe

In 1997, as in the previous year, Myanmar's military junta, the State Law and Order Restoration Council (SLORC), arrested more than 250 supporters of the opposition National League for Democracy (NLD). Eager to show signs of flexibility, however, the head of the SLORC's military intelligence, Lieut. Gen. Khin Nyunt, met with the NLD chairman, Aung Shwe, prior to the July 25 summit meeting of the Association of Southeast Asian Nations (ASEAN), at which Myanmar was officially admitted as a new ASEAN member.

In an attempt to placate growing U.S. and European Union (EU) criticism of its human rights record, the SLORC allowed the NLD to hold its party congress for the first time in seven years. Although the SLORC had authorized only 300 delegates to attend the congress, which was held on September 27–28 at the Yangon residence of NLD leader Daw Aung San Suu Kyi, about 600 party members were eventually allowed to participate. Suu Kyi, fearing that the SLORC might attempt to divide the party leadership, later rejected an invitation to a meeting between the SLORC and the NLD's Aung Shwe. Suu Kyi declared that all future meetings between the SLORC and the NLD would have to include her. In an attempt to infuse new blood into the government and accelerate the rate of economic development, the SLORC was dissolved on November 15 and replaced by an all-military, 19-member State Peace and Development Council (SPDC). Only the four senior members of SLORC were included in the SPDC.

While Myanmar's relations with the U.S. and the EU continued to deteriorate over the SLORC's human rights abuses and its alleged profiteering from the drug trade, relations with countries in Southeast Asia steadily improved. In January Myanmar and China signed an agreement to exchange military intelligence information. Former strongman U Ne Win met with Indonesia's President Suharto in Yangon in February and again in Jakarta in September. Philippine Pres. Fidel Ramos met with the SLORC leadership on an official visit to Myanmar in October.

Over 20,000 refugees from Myanmar fled to Thailand in January and February as a result of the SLORC's military offensive against the Karen National Union, the last remaining ethnic guerrilla group refusing to negotiate with the government.

(CLAUDE RAKISITS)

This article updates the *Macropædia* article SOUTHEAST ASIA: *Myanmar.*

NAMIBIA

Area: 825,118 sq km (318,580 sq mi)
Population (1997 est.): 1,727,000
Capital: Windhoek
Chief of state: President Sam Nujoma
Head of government: Prime Minister Hage Geingob

At the 1997 congress of the ruling South West Africa People's Organization (SWAPO), held on May 28–June 1 in Windhoek, Pres. Sam Nujoma, running unopposed, won a third term as party president and was recommended for a third term as president of Namibia. The deliberations of the congress were held behind closed doors, and critics of SWAPO continued to accuse the party of authoritarian practices. Hifikepunye Pohamba, the minister of fisheries and marine resources, was elected secretary-general of SWAPO to replace Netumbo Ndaitwah.

The government refused to become involved in the South African Truth and Reconciliation Commission process and its continuing failure to hold an inquiry in Namibia into human rights violations committed during the decades-long guerrilla war that preceded Namibian independence in 1990. Namibia's refusal to grant the request remained a source of tension between the two countries. The government was also accused by health organizations of not doing enough to halt the spread of AIDS. By 1997 the number of Namibians infected with HIV had reached 150,000.

A key event of 1997 was the breaking of a devastating drought; the best rains in many decades fell in Namibia in February. The fishing industry continued in the doldrums as the catch remained small. Some mines scaled down operations, though production at the giant Rossing uranium mine slowly increased. Many former members of the SWAPO army remained jobless, and some participated in a series of protests against unemployment, which the government largely ignored, just as it ignored protests against its plan to build a giant hydroelectric plant at Epupa on the Kunene River in the north of the country. The seminomadic Himba people who lived in the vicinity of the proposed dam would have to be relocated.

(CHRISTOPHER SAUNDERS)

A Buddhist monk looks over the Irrawady River in Myanmar. In recent years ethnic conflict, authoritarian rule, and economic stagnation in the country had contributed to political instability, which had a disruptive effect on the local Buddhist communities.

LE BRACQUER—PRADO/GAMMA LIAISON

This article updates the *Macropædia* article SOUTHERN AFRICA: *Namibia.*

NAURU

Area: 21.2 sq km (8.2 sq mi)
Population (1997 est.): 10,400
Capital: Government offices in Yaren district
Head of state and government: Presidents Reuben Kun (interim) and, from February 13, Kinza Clodumar

Declining phosphate prices, the high cost of maintaining an international airline, and investments that did not perform well combined to make governing difficult for Pres. Kinza Clodumar in 1997. Clodumar, who had previously served as finance minister, was elected president on February 13, becoming Nauru's fifth president in four months. Nauru's political upheavals began in the closing months of 1996. One of the world's smallest parliaments, with only 18 members, elected Kennan Adeang on November 26, replacing Bernard Dowiyogo, who had himself been elected on November 7 as a substitute for Lagumot Harris. Adeang was subsequently defeated in a no-confidence vote, and Reuben Kun acted as interim president until Clodumar was chosen. Clodumar made positive steps to consolidate Nauru's offshore investments, buying a major central business district building from the Victoria state government in Australia. Assuring his audience that Nauru was "very much on the move again," Clodumar said that Nauru would be sensitive to local feelings with its development proposals for the Southern Cross site at the corner of Burke and Exhibition streets in Melbourne.

(A.R.G. GRIFFITHS)

This article updates the *Macropædia* article PACIFIC ISLANDS: *Nauru.*

NEPAL

Area: 147,181 sq km (56,827 sq mi)
Population (1997 est.): 21,424,000
Capital: Kathmandu
Chief of state: King Birendra Bir Bikram Shah Dev
Head of government: Prime Ministers Sher Bahadur Deuba until March 6, Lokendra Bahadur Chand from March 12 until October 4, and, from October 7, Surya Bahadur Thapa

In 1997 politics in Nepal proved once again to be volatile and unstable. In an attempt to shore up support, Prime Minister Sher Bahadur Deuba expanded and reshuffled his Cabinet on January 8 to include members of the legislature who had recently participated in a no-confidence motion against him. The move, however, did not save the prime minister's three-party coalition government from another no-confidence motion on March 6. After the second motion was made, King Birendra asked Lokendra Bahadur Chand, leader of a splinter faction of the centre-right Rashtriya Prajatantra Party (RPP), to form a new government.

Chand's new ruling coalition—Nepal's fifth in seven years—was an uneasy alliance made up of his faction of the RPP, the promonarchist Nepal Sadbhavana Party (NSP), and the United Communist Party of Nepal. Even though it pursued economic liberalization and privatization, the new government was itself unable to avoid a no-confidence motion, registered by the National Congress Party (NCP) on October 4. As a result, King Birendra asked former prime minister Surya Bahadur Thapa, an RPP leader, to form yet another three-party coalition government. Although Thapa's new coalition included the RPP, NCP, and NSP, it was decided that the NCP would head the government after one year. During Indian Prime Minister Inder Kumar Gujral's visit to Nepal in June, Kathmandu and New Delhi signed trade and civil aviation agreements and a pact ensuring Nepalese transit rights through India to Bangladesh.

(CLAUDE RAKISITS)

NETHERLANDS, THE

Area: 41,526 sq km (16,033 sq mi)
Population (1997 est.): 15,619,000
Capital: Amsterdam; seat of government, The Hague
Chief of state: Queen Beatrix
Head of government: Prime Minister Wim Kok

A major conference of the European Union (EU) was held June 16–18, 1997, in Amsterdam. The European leaders were hoping to reach an agreement on establishing the European economic and monetary union (EMU) in 1999, which would result in the Euro (a common European currency). The leaders also discussed the possible future inclusion of other—particularly Eastern European—countries in the EU and the institutional mechanisms needed to accomplish this. (See *European Union,* above.)

Queen Beatrix delivered her traditional speech to open the new parliamentary year. In it she expressed optimism for the country, based on the steady growth of the economy and good economic prospects for the near future. On July 1 Wim Duisenberg, president of the central bank of The Netherlands, was appointed the new president of the European Monetary Institute, the most powerful monetary institution in Europe. Duisenberg had served as minister of finance in the left-wing Cabinet of Joop den Uyl from 1973 to 1977.

On March 19 a public referendum was held in Amsterdam to discuss the expansion of the city into the waters of the IJmeer, a lake on the east side of the city. Ecologists were strongly opposed to the plan because of the damage it would cause to the environment. A majority of the population (62%) voted against the expansion, but in spite of the vote, the City Council decided to go ahead with the project. They justified their decision on the fact that only 40% of the electorate voted.

On April 15 a visit of a Dutch trade mission to China, led by the minister of economic affairs, was canceled by the Chinese government. The minister had supported a resolution by the EU condemning the human rights situation in China. The cancellation of the visit resulted in a significant deterioration in relations between The Netherlands and China.

U.S. Pres. Bill Clinton visited The Netherlands in May to meet Prime Minister Wim Kok, who was also serving as chairman of the EU. Together with 50 European leaders and Queen Beatrix, they commemorated the 50th anniversary of the Marshall Plan. Kok urged the establishment of a new Marshall Plan for the rebuilding of Eastern European economies.

On Jan. 4, 1997, after an interruption of 10 years, a severe winter once again allowed ice skaters to compete in the Elfstedentocht, a 200-km (125-mi) race that passes through 11 cities in Friesland province. Traditionally, this event causes a feeling of excitement throughout The Netherlands, partly because the Dutch climate seldom allows the race to be held. More than 16,000 people participated in the event, which was won by a farmer, Henk Angenent.

(KLAAS J. HOEKSEMA)

See also *Dependent States,* above.

NEW ZEALAND

Area: 270,534 sq km (104,454 sq mi)
Population (1997 est.): 3,653,000
Capital: Wellington
Chief of state: Queen Elizabeth II, represented by Governor-General Sir Michael Hardie-Boys
Head of government: Prime Ministers Jim Bolger and, from December 8, Jennifer Shipley

In 1997 the first full year of mixed-member proportional government, in which a party's representation in the legislature is a mixture of those elected by the public and those appointed by political parties according to the aggregate percentage of votes for those parties, was traumatic for New Zealand's politicians. Following the October 1996 general elections, neither the governing National Party (NP), with 44 seats, nor its rival for 60 years, the Labour Party (LP), with 37 seats, had the majority to form a government without calling on each other or on a newcomer party to form a coalition. The NP, led by Prime Minister Jim Bolger, was the more daring in negotiating an agonizingly detailed basis for a coalition with the New Zealand First Party (NZFP), which held the balance of power with 17 seats and included in its representation all Maori districts. While the LP remained aloof from new liaisons, Bolger was considered too accommodating by many observers in regard to the number of Cabinet positions he offered to so inexperienced a partner. The chief beneficiary was the NZFP's charismatic leader, Winston Peters, who took over as deputy prime minister and treasurer in the new coalition government.

During 1997 the electorate became so frustrated by a lack of clear direction for government policy, particularly in regard to privatization of health care, that by the year's end the NP's popularity was down from 34% at the elections to 28% and the NZFP was down from 13.1% to an insignificant 1%.

An outstanding reversal for the NZFP and for Peters personally was the size of the defeat of a referendum seeking approval of a national compulsory superannuation (retirement savings) scheme. More than 80% of the electorate voted, and of those, 91.8% said "no." As treasurer, Peters in the June budget attempted to balance social policy spending promises against the need for a tight grip on the purse strings. An expected budget surplus had been halved, the question of superannuation was still unresolved, and beneficiaries would be required to follow a code of social responsibility. For the unemployed this referred to seeking work; for parents it was looking after their children.

In early October, with calls for his resignation increasing, Bolger signaled a return to some of the NP's old privatization policies and assured party critics that the agreement with the NZFP would not work as a "strait-jacket." However, in November a majority of NP members of Parliament lobbied to replace Bolger with Minister of Transport Jennifer Shipley. Bolger resigned; the NP Caucus duly elected Shipley New Zealand's first woman prime minister; and the NZFP continued in the coalition.

In a positive step for race relations, the government finally addressed a long-held Maori grievance concerning land rights. (*See* Spotlight: *Racial Integration in Australia and New Zealand.*) One agreement, which had been worked on by the NP for some years, was a settlement with the leading Maori tribe of South Island in reparation for the colonial administration's laying aside, in the 1850s, of insufficient areas for native reserves. In September the government returned a 1,150-ha (2,842-ac) tract of forest to a Maori tribe on North Island.

(JOHN A. KELLEHER)

See also *Dependent States*, above.

NICARAGUA

Area: 131,812 sq km (50,893 sq mi)
Population (1997 est.): 4,632,000
Capital: Managua
Head of state and government: Presidents Violeta Barrios de Chamorro and, from January 10, Arnoldo Alemán

On Jan. 10, 1997, Arnoldo Alemán, the candidate of a coalition of right-wing parties, was sworn in as president of Nicaragua, having won the election held on Oct. 20, 1996. The leftist Sandinista National Liberation Front boycotted the inauguration in protest against a Supreme Court ruling that 80 laws passed by the outgoing Sandinista-dominated National Assembly after Nov. 22, 1996, were illegal.

The new president promised to create 500,000 jobs during his five-year term. Savings and investment were to be promoted, accompanied by government honesty and discipline. Tourism was identified for expansion, targeted to be the biggest foreign exchange earner by 2002. Nine new hotels were authorized to be built, and a target of $80 million was set for tourism revenues in 1997, up from $58 million in 1996. On March 31 the government-owned telecommunications company, Empresa Nicaragüense de Telecomunicaciones, was auctioned; 80% of the money raised was to be used to compensate people whose property had been confiscated by the Sandinistas, and 20% would be spent on housing and infrastructure.

A relief plan for the rural debt problem, estimated at $150 million, was announced in February. Debtors would be allowed to clear their debts immediately and escape interest and penalties or have their debt cut by half and repay it over 10 years with interest.

Talks between the government and the Sandinistas were held intermittently during the year. The government convened a "national dialogue," made up of 45 organizations, including political parties and groups from the private sector. The dialogue was undermined, however, when it was revealed that the government and the Sandinistas had reached a secret agreement on compensation for properties expropriated under the Sandinista government. There were 1,293 foreign claims unresolved for restitution or compensation. The U.S. granted Nicaragua another year to sort out property rights involving U.S. citizens and thereby postponed a threatened suspension of U.S. aid.

(SARAH CAMERON)

This article updates the *Macropædia* article CENTRAL AMERICA: *Nicaragua.*

NIGER

Area: 1,267,000 sq km (489,000 sq mi)
Population (1997 est.): 9,389,000
Capital: Niamey
Head of state and government: President Gen. Ibrahim Baré Maïnassara, assisted by Prime Ministers Amadou Boubacar Cissé and, from November 27, Ibrahim Assane Mayaki

Prime Minister Amadou Boubacar Cissé chose a new 27-member Cabinet in December 1996. Among his selections was Senoussi Jackou, deputy head of the opposition party Democratic and Social Convention (CDS); Jackou was immediately suspended by the CDS for accepting the post. On Jan. 11, 1997, demonstrators demanding restoration of full democracy to Niger clashed with police in Niamey. Three opposition leaders, one of them former president Mahamane Ousmane, were arrested within a few days. After two weeks of violent demonstrations in Niamey and Zinder, Pres. Ibrahim Baré Maïnassara released the three detainees. In March police broke up an opposition rally near the National Assembly, and a ban on all demonstrations was declared. In April the government accused Canada, Germany, and the U.S. of supporting opposition groups it claimed were trying to destabilize the country. Dozens of opposition supporters were arrested by security forces after clashes in Maradi, Zinder, and Tahoua.

On June 2, following an attack by Tuareg rebels on a military supply vehicle in Agadez, army soldiers staged a rebellion, taking hostage the region's three most senior government officials, all of whom were Tuaregs. Defense Minister Issoufou Ousmane Oubandawaki led negotiations with the mutinous soldiers, and the hostages were released the following day. In August Oubandawaki announced that the Democratic Renewal Front, the only Tuareg rebel group that had not signed the peace accord of April 1995, had finally agreed to do so.

In a radio broadcast to the nation on November 24, President Mainassara announced that he was discharging the administration of Prime Minister Cissé on the grounds that it had not effectively dealt with such problems as the threat of famine and government security. He appointed a former foreign minister, Ibrahim Assane Mayaki, as prime minister.

(NANCY ELLEN LAWLER)

This article updates the *Macropædia* article WESTERN AFRICA: *Niger.*

NIGERIA

Area: 923,768 sq km (356,669 sq mi)
Population (1997 est.): 103,460,000
Capital: Abuja; judiciary and some ministries remain in Lagos, the former capital
Head of state and government: Chairman of the Provisional Ruling Council Gen. Sani Abacha

The first national conventions of the five political parties that had been granted legal status were held in November 1996. The parties elected their leaders as follows: Committee for National Consensus, Abel Ubeku; Democratic Party of Nigeria, Ali Ahmed; Grassroot Democratic Movement, Gambo Lawan; National Centre Party of Nigeria, Mugaji Abdulahi; and United Nigeria Congress Party, Isa Mohamed Argungu. In February 1997 Gen. Sani Abacha indicated that he might run for president in the 1998 elections; he claimed success in his efforts to restore civilian rule and economic stability. He also commented that other nations had been unfair in criticizing his government's attempts to comply with human rights reform.

The first step in the return to civilian rule began in February with the registration of voters at more than 100,000 centres. Then on March 15 (three months behind schedule), local government elections were held, and in some areas the participation rate was an incredible 90%. These were the first elec-

(continued on page 468)

SPOTLIGHT

FRANCE'S NEW AFRICAN POLICY

by David Buchan

Illustration by Cathy Hull

During 1997 a gradual sea change in France's policy toward Africa reached its culmination. Gone or going was France's paternalism toward French-speaking Africa, its tendency to want to keep others out of its African *pré carré* (backyard), and its ingrained habit of playing the feudal potentate in former colonies or of propping up local dictators. Instead came a new emphasis on democracy and human rights as a help rather than a hindrance to prosperity, a better appreciation of the role of international institutions in promoting economic development and resolving conflicts in Africa, and a wider focus on the rest of Africa so as to increase France's commercial and political influence in English- and Portuguese-speaking parts of the continent.

Thus, speaking to the annual gathering of French ambassadors in Paris, French Pres. Jacques Chirac enunciated on Aug. 27, 1997, two new "rules of conduct." First, he said, France must "refrain from any interference whatsoever, be it of political, military, or of any other nature," adding that "France would not accept it at home; it must not resort to it in other countries." Second, France must "encourage our African partners to strengthen, in the manner and at the pace of their choosing, the rule of law and good governance," because this was essential for foreign investors to feel confident enough to do business in Africa.

These new rules of conduct were all the more striking for coming from a traditional Gaullist like Chirac, steeped in the personal and financial links that have bound French African rulers to Paris ever since their countries achieved independence in 1960. In June 1997, however, the Socialists won the general election and returned to government in Paris under a new prime minster, Lionel Jospin. (*See* BIOGRAPHIES.) Jospin's administration promised an African policy that was different not only from its immediate predecessor, the right-wing government of Gaullist Prime Minister Alain Juppé, but also from that conducted by Chirac's predecessor, Socialist Pres. François Mitterrand, between 1981 and 1995.

Mitterrand had paid lip service to democracy and human rights, but he operated an old-fashioned policy toward Africa that was partly overseen by his own son, Jean-Christophe, at the president's Élysée Palace. During the Mitterrand presidency French troops intervened 10 times in sub-Saharan Africa to evacuate French citizens or to protect friendly leaders from rebellions. On taking office in 1995, Chirac largely continued the same policy, though with different men—he brought back as an adviser Jacques Foccart, who had steered African policy under former presidents Charles de Gaulle and Georges Pompidou.

The last years under Mitterrand and the first two years of Chirac's presidency produced, however, a disastrous sequence of setbacks to French influence, which came to a head in 1997 with the ousting of French-backed Pres. Mobutu Sese Seko of Zaire (renamed the Democratic Republic of the Congo [Congo (Kinshasa)]). Ironically, the setbacks came in Zaire, Rwanda, and Burundi, all of which had been Belgian rather than French colonies. The chain of events started in 1994 when Rwandan Pres. Juvénal Habyarimana, a Hutu who had enjoyed French support, died in an airplane crash that ignited simmering tensions and set off mass executions by Hutu of Tutsi. This in turn brought about an invasion of Rwanda by Tutsi rebel forces from Uganda. France intervened in 1994 to stabilize the situation but was accused by the newly installed Tutsi-dominated Rwandan government of merely helping Hutu killers find refuge in Zaire. This also helped destabilize Zaire, where the long-standing rebellion of Laurent Kabila (*see* BIOGRAPHIES) drew support from Rwanda and other neighbouring countries to mount a successful anti-Mobutu offensive that was also increasingly anti-French in tone. After he gained power, Kabila boycotted the summit of French-speaking countries in Hanoi in November.

Long after the U.S. had reversed its Cold War-era support for Mobutu and called for the dictator to go, and long after it was clear that Kabila would prevail, the right-wing Juppé government continued to give Mobutu qualified backing and appealed for some negotiated solution to the civil war. The reason was less one of economic self-interest—French trade and investment in Mobutu's Zaire had shrunk sharply by 1997 and was far less than that of Belgium or the U.S.—and more from an inability to imagine Zaire's staying intact without Mobutu's iron hold over it. In particular, Paris was worried that a breakup of Zaire would destabilize the already shaky French-speaking Republic of the Congo (Congo [Brazzaville]) and the Central African Republic (CAR) to the north.

In the event, Congo (Kinshasa) did not break up, perhaps partly because Kabila threatened to be as autocratic as his predecessor. After occupying Kinshasa and taking power in May 1997, he repeatedly refused to let United Nations investigators make on-the-spot inquiries into allegations of massacres committed by his own troops. The possibility that Kabila may prove almost as bad as Mobutu, however, did not alter the fact that the change of power in Kinshasa was a serious setback for French influence.

Even before the almost simultaneous changing of the guard in Paris and Kinshasa, France was beginning to alter its military and economic relationships with French-speaking Africa. In late 1997 it based 7,900 French troops in Djibouti, the CAR, Chad, Gabon, Côte d'Ivoire, and Senegal under agreements that dated from 1960. Under plans already approved by its Gaullist predecessors, the Jospin government intended to make a gradual 40% cut in the number of those troops in Africa as it created a smaller, fully professional army at home. The latter would, if necessary, be able to send reinforcements to Africa, using transport and communications not available in 1960. French troops planned to completely quit the CAR, where they found themselves increasingly caught up in local mutinies, contrary to the 1960 agreements, which, ostensibly, provided for French intervention only in cases of external aggression.

Such mutinies have in fact become a general hazard in Africa, aggravated by International Monetary Fund (IMF)

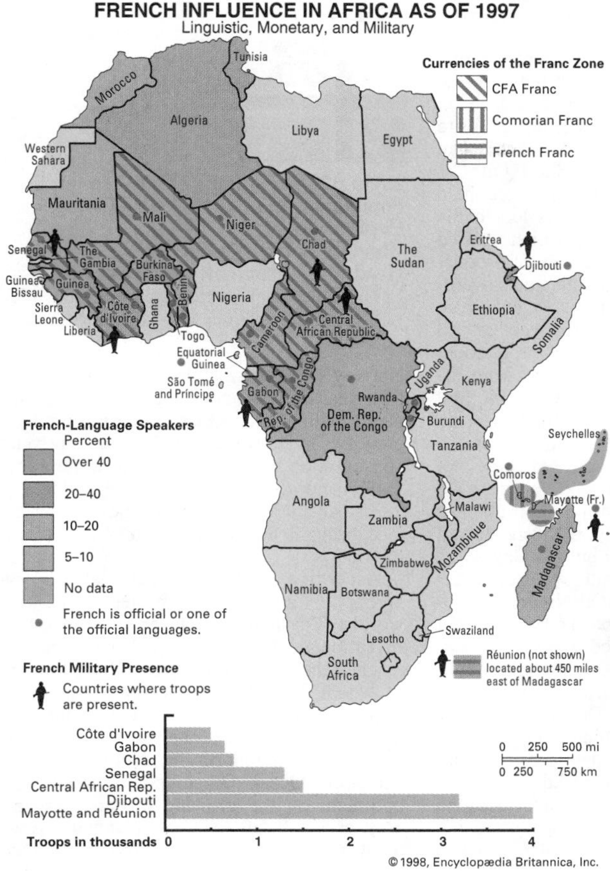

and World Bank programs that seek to restrain or cut government payrolls, including those of the military. Paris has therefore sought to convince those institutions of the need to act carefully and flexibly. In Chad, which has had a relatively big army, France has cofinanced with the World Bank a program to demobilize and retrain some 27,000 soldiers. France has also joined Great Britain and the U.S. in a concerted effort to train African forces to take over more of the peacekeeping in Africa.

Once at odds with the IMF and the World Bank over Africa, France by 1997 was working hand in glove with them. An early success of this cooperation was their joint push for the January 1994 devaluation of the CFA (for Communauté Financière Africaine) franc, which at that time was being used by 14 West and Central African states. Though resisted by many leaders in Africa and some in France (including Chirac, before he became president), this long overdue adjustment of the CFA franc from a rate of two French centimes set in 1948 to one centime boosted exports and growth in Africa without setting off any prolonged inflation spiral.

By 1997 almost all the CFA member countries had programs with the International Monetary Fund and the World Bank. A standard feature of these is the requirement of privatizing state companies by competitive bids. Despite rivalry from U.S. companies in telecommunications and oil exploration and from Asian groups in forestry, French companies have won many of these bids. This may be because of French companies' greater knowledge of the local market and its risks. Realizing that they can no longer regard French-speaking Africa as their protected patch, French companies have launched a major drive to win other markets, notably South Africa.

Behind their setbacks, many French have seen the hand of the United States, accusing it of spearheading a drive to anglicize French-speaking Africa. But Franco-American competition to provide aid could work to Africa's benefit. Charles Josselin, French minister for cooperation in charge of African policy, has affirmed, "The U.S. is not driving France out of Africa; France is not fading away at its approach." It would be a pity if France did fade out, for Paris is the second biggest provider—behind Japan—of official development aid and a persistent preacher on behalf of Africa.

David Buchan is Paris Correspondent for the Financial Times.

ADIL BRADLOW—ASSOCIATED PRESS

A French soldier disembarks from a military transport in Brazzaville, Republic of the Congo. French troops evacuated thousands of civilians from the war-torn city in June.

(continued from page 465)
tions in the process that was scheduled to culminate on Oct. 1, 1998, with the transfer of power to a civilian president. Some violence occurred, and at Onitsha police used tear gas to disperse 2,000 demonstrators. Periodically throughout the year, bomb explosions upset government hopes for a peaceful political transition. An explosion in Lagos on January 7 killed 2 soldiers and wounded 27 others, as well as 2 civilians; the bomb was detonated as an army bus passed a bus stop. Another bomb in Lagos during February injured five soldiers and three civilians. In May there were similar incidents in Lagos, Ibadan, and Onitsha. The government accused the opposition National Democratic Coalition, led by exiled author Wole Soyinka, of having staged the attacks. In March the government charged Soyinka and 14 others with treason, accusing them of responsibility for the bomb explosions and of waging war on General Abacha.

The finance minister, Anthony Ani, presented the 1997 budget in mid-January. He doubled expenditure on the rural sector of the economy for the year. Of a total expenditure of 146 trillion naira, 32.4% was allotted to infrastructure, agriculture, water resources, and rural development, while education and health were also given increases. Defense spending, at 17.5 billion naira, rose in 1997 to 12% of the budget from 10.9% in 1996. The increases were made possible by a rise of $1 on a barrel of oil to $17 per barrel, which increased foreign exchange resources from $1,440,000,000 to $4,090,000,000. Oil production for 1997 was projected at 2,040,000 bbl per day, which was expected to provide revenue of more than $11 billion, up 13.5% over 1996.

In April there were outbreaks of fighting in the Delta region near Warri between the Ijo and Itsekiri ethnic groups over a decision to remove municipal offices from an Ijo to an Itsekiri location. The unrest, which began in March, involved nearby Shell Oil Co. workers, nearly 100 of whom were held hostage by the combatants; this led to the shutdown of 11 oil wells, which caused Shell to lose 210,000 bbl per day of production. By the end of the month, the government had sent troops to the area to restore order; altogether the disturbances caused Shell to lose 1.5 million bbl of production. Lagos and the surrounding areas were affected by gasoline shortages during the first three weeks of April, and troops were sent to several gas stations to maintain order. Shell claimed that the shortages were not due to the regional disturbances but were the result of technical and distribution problems, and for a few weeks exports were halved from the normal 900,000 bbl per day.

When the Commonwealth Ministerial Action Group (CMAG) visited Nigeria in November 1996, it met Abacha but was not given access to imprisoned opposition leaders such as Moshood Abiola. Nigeria insisted that its suspension from the Commonwealth was unjustified. On November 17 Abacha dissolved his Cabinet and promised to release some political detainees. On December 21 the army announced that it had foiled an attempted coup against Abacha and had arrested his second in command, Lieut. Gen. Oladipo Diya. (GUY ARNOLD)

This article updates the *Macropædia* article WESTERN AFRICA: *Nigeria.*

Chaos reigns in the streets of Lagos, Nigeria's largest city and one of the largest in sub-Saharan Africa. In 1997 Lagos was a city with no mayor, little government or street planning, and few signs of law and order. Bomb explosions erupted in the city in January and February.

DANIEL LAINE—MATRIX

NORWAY

Area: 323,758 sq km (125,004 sq mi)
Population (1997 est.): 4,405,000
Capital: Oslo
Chief of state: King Harald V
Head of government: Prime Ministers Thorbjørn Jagland and, from October 17, Kjell Magne Bondevik

Norway's economy in 1997 experienced its fifth year of continuous solid growth. Compared with 1996, gross domestic product grew by 3.9%, wages by about 4%, private consumption by 3%, public consumption by 2.4%, and the consumer price index by 2.5%. An increase of 3% in the number of jobs brought the unemployment rate down to about 4%.

According to the International Energy Agency, Norway was expected to be the world's fifth largest producer of oil in 1997. Investments in the oil and gas sectors reached the record sum of 66 billion kroner, of which 36 billion kroner were spent on developing existing fields on the continental shelf and 10 billion kroner on searching for new fields in the North Sea, Norwegian Sea, and Arctic Ocean. Oil companies based their optimism on the growing demand for energy, especially in Asia, and planned investments on the same scale in 1998. A contract signed in 1997 for 25 years of annual delivery of 6 billion cu m (212 cu ft) of natural gas to Italy revealed the growing importance of the rich gas fields on the continental shelf and indicated the necessity of continuing to build pipelines to southern Europe and of constructing facilities in Norway to produce and store liquefied natural gas. The oil and gas sectors contributed 23% of Norway's total income of some 480 billion kroner.

On September 15, 75% of the nation's eligible voters went to the polls to elect the 165 members of the Storting, the single-chamber national legislature. Before the elections Prime Minister Thorbjørn Jagland declared that his Labour Party government would resign should the result be weaker than in 1993 (36.9% of the votes, 67 seats). The outcome was 35% and 65 seats. A coalition of the three parties in the political centre (Christian People's Party, Centre Party, and Liberal Party) obtained 42 seats, the Socialist Left Party 9, and the Conservative Party 23; unexpectedly, the populist right-wing Progress Party won 25 seats to become the new Storting's second largest party. The Labour government had time to present its draft budget for 1998 to the Storting before it resigned in mid-October in favour of the new centre coalition government, headed by theologian Kjell Magne Bondevik of the Christian People's Party. During the budget debates late in the year, the new government found that constant compromise was required in order for it to remain in power. All the political parties agreed at the end of November that, as in 1997, the surplus of the 1998 state budget should be transferred to the Government Petroleum Fund for investments abroad.

(GUDMUND SANDVIK)

See also *Dependent States,* above.

OMAN

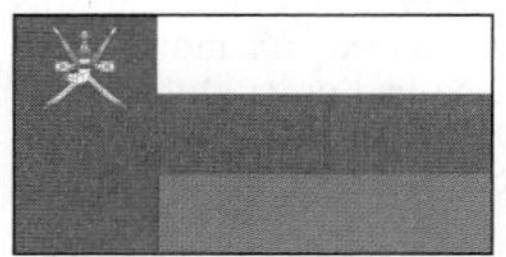

Area: 309,5000 sq km (119,500 sq mi)
Population (1997 est.): 2,265,000
Capital: Muscat
Head of state and government: Sultan and Prime Minister Qabus ibn Sa'id

Foreign affairs were a major focus of activity for Oman during 1997. The nation had taken the lead among Arab countries in establishing diplomatic and commercial relations with Israel following the signing of the Hebron accord in January, but in March Oman reversed this course after the Arab League's decision to halt normalization with Israel owing to the construction of new Israeli settlements in East Jerusalem. Oman canceled its agreement to allow Israeli firms to participate in trade shows in Oman scheduled for March and April and rejected Israeli participation in Muscat's fourth international fair in October.

Also in March, Oman signed an agreement with 13 other countries to form the Indian Ocean Rim Association for Regional Cooperation. In May Oman and Yemen signed maps defining the border between the two countries. Numerous high-level exchanges occurred in 1997 between Omani and Iranian officials, and the two sides reached agreements to cooperate on the development of shared natural gas deposits and to establish closer commercial ties.

Oman witnessed several significant developments in its petroleum and natural gas industries during 1997. In April Oman participated in talks with Indonesian officials on establishing an organization for gas-exporting countries modeled on OPEC. In May the Caspian Pipeline Consortium, of which Oman held a 7% share, signed a final agreement on financing the 1,500-km (930-mi) pipeline from Kazakstan to the Russian Black Sea port of Novorossiysk.

(DAVID COLVIN)

This article updates the *Macropædia* article ARABIA: *Oman*.

PAKISTAN

Area: 796,095 sq km (307,374 sq mi), excluding the 83,716-sq km Pakistani-administered portion of Jammu and Kashmir
Population (1997 est.): 136,183,000, excluding 3.9 million residents of Pakistani-administered Jammu and Kashmir and 1.2 million Afghan refugees
Capital: Islamabad
Chief of state: Presidents Farooq Ahmed Leghari and, from December 3, Wasim Sajjad (acting)
Head of government: Prime Ministers Malik Meraj Khalid (acting) and, from February 17, Mohammed Nawaz Sharif

On Feb. 3, 1997, Pakistanis went to the polls for the fourth time in eight years to elect a new government. For the second time in five years, the country voted in the Pakistan Muslim League (PML) with a thumping majority, ousting the government of Benazir Bhutto's Pakistan People's Party (PPP). PML leader Nawaz Sharif (*see* BIOGRAPHIES) returned to the office of prime minister after a nearly four-year hiatus. For the third time since 1988, Bhutto was back in the role of opposition leader.

The PML won 134 seats in the 217-seat National Assembly. Bhutto's PPP managed to win just 17 seats—the party's worst-ever showing. A third party, Movement for Justice, led by popular former cricketer Imran Khan, failed to win a single seat in the election despite polling nearly 5% of votes nationwide.

The elections had been forced when Pres. Farooq Ahmed Leghari, a longtime PPP loyalist, ousted Bhutto in November 1996, accusing her of corruption and ineptitude. Bhutto had been dismissed before on similar charges in 1990, and Sharif himself had been ousted for corruption in 1993. Bhutto had appealed Leghari's action, but Pakistan's Supreme Court ruled just days before the polls that the sacking was legal and ordered the polls to proceed as scheduled.

Sharif's landslide put him on a collision course with President Leghari. In April the new government used its majority in the parliament to amend the constitution, abolishing, among other executive powers, the president's power to dismiss an elected government. Sharif's administration also abolished the Council for Defence and National Security, which formalized the military's role in Pakistani politics. The military remained a formidable political force in the country, however.

Despite his huge mandate, Sharif continued to face strong opposition, not only from Bhutto but from other centres of power in the country. He battled with the judiciary over the appointment of new judges, and in September Chief Justice Sajjad Ali Shah took his case to the president and indirectly to Army Chief of Staff Gen. Jehangir Karamat. Stripped of his executive powers, President Leghari could only comment on Sharif's "unconstitutional" interference with the judiciary. The chief justice was eventually suspended in early December. Rather than appoint a replacement for the chief justice, President Leghari unexpectedly resigned. Mohammad Rafiq Tarar, a former senator and Supreme Court judge and close confidant of Sharif, was elected president on December 31.

In August Sharif and associates charged Bhutto with illegally amassing wealth in Swiss bank accounts. Bhutto denied the charge but admitted that she and her family had long held Swiss accounts. The government said some, if not most, of the money had been collected either as bribes or as proceeds from drug trafficking involving Bhutto's husband, Asif Ali Zardari, who was in jail facing corruption charges.

At the end of 1997, Pakistan's economic picture remained dismal. Though agricultural production was likely to boost economic growth to 5.5% from just 3.1% in 1996, Pakistan still had a large current-account deficit (6.5% of gross domestic product), budget deficit (6.3% of GDP), and low savings rate (just 13% of GDP). Inflation remained high at above 12%. Foreign debt climbed to nearly $50 billion. In July, under pressure from the International Monetary Fund, Pakistan expedited its privatization program, putting more government-controlled banks, industrial units, and utilities up for sale. In October the government devalued the rupee by 8.7%—the second devaluation in 11 months.

(ASSIF A. SHAMEEN)

The children below are among the thousands of untouchable Hindus, known as haris, born into bonded slavery in Pakistan. Owing largely to the recent efforts of activists, some 1,500 haris have been freed. One of the world's most populous and poorest nations, Pakistan faced dire economic problems in 1997.

PER A. PETTERSSON—BLACK STAR

PALAU

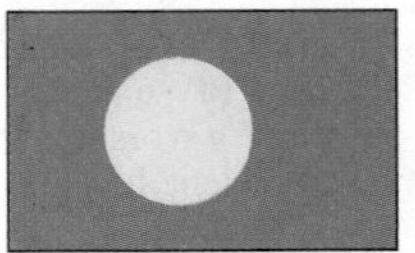

Area: 488 sq km (188 sq mi)
Population (1997 est.): 17,200
Provisional capital: Koror; a site on Babelthuap was designated to be the permanent capital
Head of state and government: President Kuniwo Nakamura

In 1997 Pres. Kuniwo Nakamura made good use of opportunities to develop trade relationships and forge vital links with Palau's neighbours. He made his first visit to China accompanied by the president of the Palau Senate, Isidoro Rudimch, and the speaker of the House of Delegates, Ignacio Anastacio. This was the most senior delegation the country had sent abroad since independence in 1994. The importance of the trip was underlined by the meeting of Palau's leaders with Qiao Shi, chairman of the Standing Committee of the Chinese National People's Congress.

During the year Palau formally agreed to establish diplomatic exchanges with the Philippines. Relations between the two nations had been strained by the detention of Filipino fishermen arrested for unlawful entry and fish poaching in Palauan waters. Palauan Minister of State Andres Uherbelau assured Philippine Pres. Fidel Ramos that the 5,000 overseas Filipino workers in Palau would be accorded fair, just, and reasonable working conditions.

On April 3 President Nakamura was on hand when a draft agreement on Taiwanese aviation exchanges was initialed by Palau's commerce and trade minister, George Ngirarsaol. Further links were made with Taipei when Taiwan's Wallant International Development Holding Co. agreed to cooperate with Palau's Pacific Development Corp. on the establishment of Palau's first university. The projected university, which was expected to attract Taiwanese students, would include lakeside villas, a golf course, and a commercial centre. On August 3 a pontoon-type bridge, designed and built by the Japanese, opened between Koror and Babelthuap islands as a temporary replacement for the 241-m (790-ft) bridge that collapsed in 1996.

(A.R.G. GRIFFITHS)

This article updates the *Macropædia* article PACIFIC ISLANDS: *Palau.*

PANAMA

Area: 75,517 sq km (29,157 sq mi)
Population (1997 est.): 2,719,000
Capital: Panama City
Head of state and government: President Ernesto Pérez Balladares

The imminent U.S. handover in 1999 of the Panama Canal to Panama raised a number of issues during 1997. Among them was the approval by the Panamanian legislature of a new, autonomous and financially independent Panama Canal Authority. The body would assume responsibility for the waterway after Dec. 31, 1999, and would succeed the Panama Canal Commission, which would oversee the transition. In September attendees at a Universal Congress of the Panama Canal discussed concerns about international shipping and tariff policy, efficiency, and the need to improve the canal's infrastructure in order to accommodate larger vessels.

On December 24 agreement was reached that U.S. troops could remain in Panama after the handover of the canal. The Panamanian government proposed the establishment of a multinational antidrug centre at Howard Air Force Base. Although some potential members of such a centre worried that U.S. involvement would take on a military rather than a civilian role, their concerns could not be addressed until the matter was put before the Panamanian electorate in a referendum.

Another contentious issue was the proposal by the ruling Revolutionary Democratic Party to amend the constitution so that Pres. Ernesto Pérez Balladares could run for reelection in 1999 to ensure continuity for the canal handover and the economy. Any constitutional change, however, would have to be submitted to a referendum.

After gaining entry into the World Trade Organization in September, Panama was involved in international trade agreements with Pacific, Latin-American, and European partners. The banking centre shed its image as a money launderer and was host to a conference on techniques to eradicate this crime. Although economic performance improved as a result of an influx of foreign investment from privatizations, growth in the Colón Free Zone, and a boom in construction, serious problems persisted, including a 14% unemployment rate.

(BEN BOX)

This article updates the *Macropædia* article CENTRAL AMERICA: *Panama.*

PAPUA NEW GUINEA

Area: 462,840 sq km (178,704 sq mi)
Population (1997 est): 4,496,000
Capital: Port Moresby
Chief of state: Queen Elizabeth II, represented by Governor-General Wiwa Korowi and, from November 13, Silas Atopare
Head of government: Prime Ministers Sir Julius Chan, John Giheno (acting) from March 27, Sir Julius Chan from June 2, and, from July 22, Bill Skate

In 1997 Papua New Guinea faced "mercenary mayhem" after the government hired Sandline International mercenary soldiers to fight on the island of Bougainville in order to end the long-running secessionist crisis. Disgruntled Papua New Guinean soldiers, who had been fighting in Bougainville for nine years and who were fed up with low pay and poor conditions, triggered civil unrest. Brig. Gen. Jerry Singirok, who was later dismissed, announced on national radio on March 17 that he had ordered the Sandline contract to be suspended and called on Prime Minister Sir Julius Chan to resign. After politicians were blockaded inside Parliament House by soldiers and protesters, Chan acted. Although he survived a vote asking him to stand aside, Chan voluntarily stepped down, called elections, and set up an official commission of inquiry. The commission cleared Chan of corrupt practices and illegal actions, and he resumed office.

In the ensuing elections, however, Bill Skate replaced Chan as prime minister. Skate had the difficult task of dealing with the aftermath of the mutiny and trying to restore consensus in the country while at the same time being pressed by the serious food shortages faced by up to 700,000 people following a severe drought and harsh frosts in the highlands.

In July representatives from Bougainville, after meeting for two weeks at the Burnham army camp in New Zealand, issued the "Burnham Declaration," in which they called for a cease-fire, demilitarization of the island, an end to the military blockade, and installation of a UN peacekeeping force. In August, during his first visit to Bougainville, Skate endorsed the declaration and vowed to seek a peaceful settlement. Australia promised $A 600,000 for drought relief and reconstruction and rehabilitation on Bougainville.

(A.R.G. GRIFFITHS)

This article updates the *Macropædia* article PACIFIC ISLANDS: *Papua New Guinea.*

PARAGUAY

Area: 406,752 sq km (157,048 sq mi)
Population (1997 est.): 5,089,000
Capital: Asunción
Head of state and government: President Juan Carlos Wasmosy

The year 1997 was dominated by the Colorado Party's primary elections to choose a candidate for the 1998 presidential elections and by the banking crisis that struck Paraguay in June. The primaries led to intensified rivalry between Pres. Carlos Wasmosy and Luis María Argaña, defeated by Wasmosy for the nomination in 1992 and now party president. The primaries, held in September, were won by Lino Oviedo, a retired general, who polled 36.8%, against 35% for Argaña and 22.5% for Wasmosy's candidate, former finance minister Carlos Facetti.

This result left Wasmosy as a lame-duck president, opposed by most of his party and, since 1993, without a majority in the legislature. The vote was seen as a victory for those who favoured a return to more authoritarian government and opposed the tentative market reforms of the past decade. Meanwhile, Oviedo, defiant of Wasmosy, found his candidacy for the presidency under challenge in court, and in October he went into hiding from the government, which charged him with sedition.

RON GILING—PANOS

Peru was home to an increasing number of sprawling slums. During 1997 it was estimated that half the population in the Andean nation lived below the poverty level, up from 38% in 1985. The country's economic plight contributed to Pres. Alberto Fujimori's declining popularity.

Early in the year extensive withdrawals by depositors at three banks caused a liquidity crisis and forced the central bank to close the three institutions. After the closing the central bank announced that nine more financial institutions were "under observation." Unofficial estimates put the cost to the Treasury of honouring deposits at the failed banks at $350 million, but legislation introduced in August increased the guaranteed payment to each depositor from $2,300 to $11,500. This would, according to the central bank, require a $1 billion contingency fund, or about 60% of the annual budget.

The crisis affected the economy severely. Asunción supermarkets reported a 10–13% drop in sales, and Paraguay's annual economic growth was expected to decline from the 4% predicted to 2.5%, the same rate as in 1996. Consumer price inflation was predicted to fall from 8.1% in 1996 to 6%, and the trade deficit was expected to rise from $1.4 billion to $1.7 billion.

(CHARLIE NURSE)

PERU

Area: 1,285,216 sq km (496,225 sq mi)
Population (1997 est.): 24,371,000
Capital: Lima
Head of state and government: President Alberto Fujimori

Early in 1997 Peru was dominated by the Lima hostage crisis, which thrust the country onto the international stage. The crisis had begun on Dec. 17, 1996, when 14 Túpac Amaru (MRTA) rebels gained entry to the Japanese ambassador's residence during a reception and took more than 600 hostages, including many foreign diplomats. The rebels demanded the release of some of their imprisoned comrades and improvements in prison conditions for others in exchange for the release of the hostages. Pres. Alberto Fujimori refused to accept the former demand, but he was under pressure from the international community—in particular Japan—to resolve the crisis peacefully. The rebels had released most of the hostages, and talks seemed to be making progress when Cuba and the Dominican Republic offered asylum to the rebels, but they were stalled when the rebel commander, Nestor Cerpa, accused the government of digging a tunnel under the residence.

On April 22 the siege was ended in a dramatic attack by elite Peruvian commandos. The remaining 72 hostages were rescued, though one died later from heart failure. All 14 rebels and 2 soldiers were killed in the fighting.

Though Fujimori's gamble had paid off, his tough, uncompromising style came under attack. The Japanese government, in particular, criticized his decision not to inform it of his plans for ending the siege. Despite the nation's initial relief at the ending of the 126-day ordeal, the president's approval rating sank to an all-time low in mid-July. One of the main reasons was the controversial dismissal of three judges of the Constitutional Tribunal, which decides on the constitutionality of laws. Public outrage prompted demonstrations in Lima and other major cities, as well as condemnation from the U.S. government.

Fujimori's standing was further shaken when the armed forces accused Baruch Ivcher, the owner of the TV station Frecuencia Latina, of carrying out a campaign to discredit them. Ivcher, a naturalized Peruvian, was also accused of selling arms to Ecuador and of having obtained Peruvian citizenship illegally. Following the station's broadcast of a program alleging more violations by security forces, Ivcher's citizenship was revoked and control of Frecuencia Latina wrested from him. A storm of criticism ensued, but Fujimori did not intervene, which led to a further collapse of support for the president. The day after the Ivcher incident, the foreign minister, Francisco Tudela, resigned for "reasons of conscience." Soon afterward it was announced that the defense minister, Tomas Castillo, would be replaced by Gen. César Saucedo, who was considered closely allied with Fujimori's discredited intelligence adviser, Vladimiro Montesinos. This was seen as evidence of the growing power of the army in relation to that of Fujimori.

Opposition parties began campaigning for a referendum on whether Fujimori should be allowed to run for a third term of office in 2000, but opposition remained fragmented. The most popular alternative candidate, Lima Mayor Alberto Andrade, had already signaled his desire to campaign for mayor again in 1998.

In autumn the weather also conspired against Fujimori's hopes for reelection to a third term. The catastrophic climatic effects of possibly the worst El Niño of the century caused the failure of the fish harvest and a severe drought. This made a reversal of the downturn in economic growth of the last two years very unlikely.

(ALAN MURPHY)

PHILIPPINES

Area: 300,076 sq km (115,860 sq mi)
Population (1997 est.): 71,539,000
Capital: Quezon City (designated national government centre and the location of the lower house of the legislature and some ministries); many government offices are in Manila or suburbs
Head of state and government: President Fidel V. Ramos

Economic problems hurt the Philippines in 1997. Its economic growth rate slipped from 7.5% in the first half of 1996 to 5.9% in the first half of 1997 and declined further in the second half of the year. One reason for the decline was the drought that affected half of the country's rice-growing areas. Another was the financial turmoil in Southeast Asia that triggered a fall in the international value of the Philippines's currency, the peso, by 36% from July through December. Consequently, more pesos were needed to repay foreign loans, most of which were in U.S. dollars. Although exports increased, the stock market fell, interest rates soared, and some banks were stuck with domestic loans that could not be repaid.

The problems interrupted the steady economic growth enjoyed by the Philippines since Fidel Ramos became president in 1992. Ramos was credited with having pulled the Philippines out of earlier economic problems but blamed for hesitancy in dealing with the recent trouble at a time when his attention seemed fixed on politics. Ramos repeatedly denied that he wanted the constitution changed so that he could seek another six-year presidential term in elections scheduled for May 1998. Despite this, opposition politicians and the media accused him of scheming to run again. His supporters collected signatures for a referendum on amending the constitution, but on March 18 the Supreme Court ruled that the referendum law did not apply to this situation. Supporters in Congress, a third of whose members would also be barred from new terms, began efforts to abolish term limits.

Talk of another term, or extending Ramos's original term, was opposed by former president Corazon Aquino and Jaime Cardinal Sin, archbishop of Manila and an influential voice in the predominately Roman Catholic country. Sin said Ramos's administration had lost the people's trust and respect and his continuation as president would mean a return to "political dynasties, warlordism, corruption, sham democracy, and debilitating poverty."

Support for keeping Ramos in office came from many businessmen. They appreciated his economic improvements and feared that he might be succeeded by Joseph Estrada. Estrada, a former star of B movies, had been elected vice president on a separate ticket from Ramos's in 1992. Lacking administrative or economic experience, he campaigned for the 1998 elections on the basis of simple populist slogans. He accused Ramos on August 21 of mishandling economic problems. Estrada's main rival in presidential opinion polls was Gloria Macapagal-Arroyo, who supported economic reform. On December 8 Ramos endorsed José de Venecia, speaker of the lower house of Congress, for president.

The government's 1996 treaty with the Moro National Liberation Front failed to bring peace to the southern islands. The Moro Islamic Liberation Front (MILF), a hard-line faction that rejected the treaty, continued the struggle. It claimed 120,000 fighters, but the government estimated only 8,000. Its chairman, Hashim Salamat, called his headquarters at Camp Abubakre on Mindanao the capital of an "Islamic republic." Rejecting government efforts to negotiate, the MILF carried out guerrilla attacks and terrorist bombings. The government accused it of operating kidnapping syndicates to raise money.

Tension continued between the Philippines and China over reefs in the South China Sea that were part of the Spratly Islands and claimed by both nations. After China occupied Mischief Reef in 1995, the Philippines began patrolling the area. A Chinese structure was discovered on another reef in April 1997, but after Filipino complaints China abandoned the reef on May 1 and four armed Chinese vessels withdrew from the area. (HENRY S. BRADSHER)

POLAND

Area: 312,685 sq km (120,728 sq mi)
Population (1997 est.): 38,802,000
Capital: Warsaw
Chief of state: President Aleksander Kwasniewski
Head of government: Prime Minister Wlodzimierz Cimoszewicz and, from October 31, Jerzy Buzek

Parliamentary elections in September 1997 brought a dramatic reversal in Polish politics. The Solidarity Electoral Action (AWS), a loose coalition of some 30 right-wing groups dominated by the Solidarity trade union, handily defeated the formerly communist Democratic Left Alliance (SLD), which had governed since 1993. The AWS won 33.8% of the popular vote in elections to the Sejm (lower house of parliament); the SLD finished second with 27.1%. The centrist Freedom Union (UW), the party of Poland's leading reformers, was third with 13.4%. The election was fought over issues of "history" rather than economics; the divide between the heirs to Solidarity and the successors to the communist party remained the most important fault line in politics.

The balloting defied opinion polls, which for months before the elections had forecast a tie between the AWS and the SLD. Many voters opted at the last minute to shift their support to the AWS from smaller right-of-centre groupings as the best means of defeating the former communists. The elections thus spurred further consolidation in Polish politics. Only two other parties won seats in the Sejm as voters chose moderate pro-market parties over an assortment of radicals and reactionaries. The Polish Peasant Party, which had governed in coalition with the SLD since 1993, dropped from 15.4% of the popular vote to 7.3%. The populist Movement for the Reconstruction of Poland won just six seats—and promptly disintegrated.

The AWS sought quickly to ally with the UW to form a new "Solidarity" government. Jerzy Buzek, a mild-mannered chemical engineering professor from Silesia who had drafted the AWS economic program, was named prime minister. Leszek Balcerowicz, the UW chairman and architect of Poland's initial "shock therapy" in 1990, returned to government as finance minister and deputy prime minister. The power broker of the new arrangement was AWS leader and Solidarity chairman Marian Krzaklewski. Although the AWS included both populists and free-market liberals, the coalition with the UW seemed likely to guarantee progress on crucial reform issues, such as privatization and deregulation.

The coalition set a conservative social agenda. One of the new majority's first acts was to ratify the concordat with the Vatican that had languished in the Sejm since 1993. Another priority was to enact a final settling of accounts (if belated and largely symbolic) with communism. Persons associated with past communist abuses were removed from the state security apparatus, the civil service, and public broadcasting.

Poland's economy chalked up its sixth straight year of growth in 1997. Gross domestic product (GDP) rose by 7%, and inflation sank to a new year-on-year low of 13% in December. The country's current-account deficit also expanded sharply, however, from under 1% of GDP in 1996 to nearly 5% in 1997. Optimists stressed that the deficit was driven by imports of vital investment goods. Pessimists noted that consumer spending, fueled by a dramatic expansion in household loans, was outpacing growth in productivity. Some economists worried that Poland risked a currency collapse like the one that hit the Czech Republic in early 1997. The new government undertook the unpalatable task of tightening budget plans for 1998 to dampen overstimulated consumer spending.

Economic growth seemed unaffected by the catastrophic flooding that shut down western Poland in July. More than 50 people died, 140,000 were evacuated, 40,000 were left homeless, and the cities of Raciborz, Opole, and Wroclaw were heavily damaged as two flood waves swept north along the Odra (Oder) River, Poland's border with Germany. The floods exposed the frail condition of Poland's infrastructure. Phones stopped working as soon as the water hit, and 160 bridges and 1,500 km (900 mi) of roads were washed away. Overcentralization hampered official rescue efforts.

Poland adopted a new constitution in May 1997, after eight years of debate, but public support was lukewarm. The sticking point, reflected in heated debate over the preamble, was a question of world view: should the constitution invoke secular or Christian values? The final wording was a clumsy compromise that papered over deep differences between Poles on religion: "We, the Polish Nation, citizens of the Republic, both those believing in God as the source of truth, justice, good, and beauty, and those who do not share this belief but derive these universal values from other sources."

(LOUISA VINTON)

PORTUGAL

Area: 92,135 sq km (35,574 sq mi)
Population (1997 est.): 9,943,000
Capital: Lisbon
Chief of state: President Jorge Sampaio
Head of government: Prime Minister António Guterres

Portugal's Socialist government continued to take advantage of rosy economic conditions in 1997 as it appeared increasingly likely that the country would become a founding member of the European economic and monetary union (EMU) at the scheduled Jan. 1, 1999, start date. Thanks to strong economic growth—3.5% in 1997—lower interest rates, and a continuing crackdown on tax evasion, the government was able to increase spending on social programs like health care and education without threatening the budget-deficit target of 2.9% of gross domestic product. In October the government of Prime Minister António Guterres unveiled another EMU-friendly budget that again proposed increased social spending while further reducing the deficit. Characterizing the budget as "rigorous, but with a social conscience," Finance Minister António Sousa Franco stressed that it would guide Portugal through the transition to monetary union.

Throughout the country the effects of economic good health were visible. Construction—much of it centred on the site of Lisbon's World Exposition, scheduled to open in May 1998—continued apace. The capital continued its facelift for EXPO '98: work progressed on the new Vasco da Gama automobile bridge across the Tagus River; the subway system was being renovated; and new roads, office complexes, and apartment buildings were under construction. The Iberian peninsula's largest shopping mall opened in Lisbon, and the government began intensive study of plans for a new airport for the capital on the southern bank of the Tagus by early in the next century.

The stock market enjoyed a banner year, rising almost 70% during the first nine months as interest rates fell further and the privatization program gained momentum. The U.S. investment bank Morgan Stanley lauded the country's progress and upgraded its rating of the Lisbon exchange to a developed market from an emerging one. Dow Jones Global Indexes also announced it was adding the Lisbon exchange to its portfolio. The government, meanwhile, said it would take in more than 800 billion escudos from the sale of shares in Portugal Telecom, the electric utility Electricidade de Portugal, and the highway operator Brisa, among others. Tax benefits and aggressive marketing encouraged hundreds of thousands of first-time investors to enter the market. Unemployment, running at a modest 6.7% at the end of the third quarter, seemed on track to decline further.

On the political front, parliamentary deputies narrowly rejected a law that would have allowed unrestricted abortions during the first 12 weeks of pregnancy. The new law, which would have replaced one of Europe's most restrictive statutes, spurred heated legislative debate and led to confrontations between pro-choice and antiabortion supporters. The controversy brought to light deep divisions in the culture of this predominantly Roman Catholic country, where an estimated 16,000 illegal abortions were performed each year. Another issue that promised to animate the 1998 political agenda was the government proposal for "regionalization," or the devolution of some governmental power to regional authorities. The Socialists, for whom regionalization was a key platform plank in the 1995 general election, claimed it would make government more sensitive to local needs, whereas the opposition expressed fears that it would burden the budget and create national divisions. Regionalization faced a national referendum in 1998.

Portugal during the year celebrated the 500th anniversary of explorer Vasco da Gama's historic departure for India, which opened a new era of trade and helped elevate the country to world superpower status in 1497. The country's only museum of international modern art opened in a gloriously refurbished 19th-century casino in Sintra.

(ERIK BURNS)

See also *Dependent States,* above.

QATAR

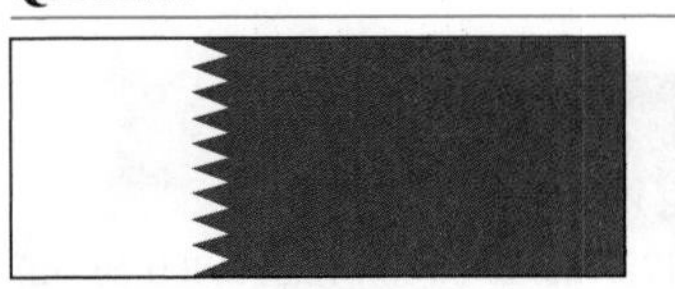

Area (including Hawar Islands, also claimed by Bahrain): 11,437 sq km (4,416 sq mi)
Population (1997 est.): 561,000
Capital: Doha
Head of state and government: Emir Sheikh Hamad ibn Khalifah ath-Thani, assisted by Prime Minister Sheikh Adbullah ibn Khalifah ath-Thani

Major events in Qatar during 1997 focused on the emirate's foreign relations and oil and natural gas industries. The dispute between Qatar and Bahrain over control of a number of islands in the Persian Gulf cooled off in March after both sides agreed to let the International Court of Justice decide the issue. The two countries also agreed to establish an embassy in each other's capital for the first time since they achieved independence in 1971. Qatar froze its relations with Israel following the Arab League's decision in March to reactivate the Arab boycott of Israel but, as part of the peace process, agreed to be host of a regional economic summit in November in Doha.

Significant progress was made in 1997 to develop oil and natural gas resources. As part of the North Field Development Project, Qatar Liquefied Gas, the world's largest liquefied gas export facility, was inaugurated in February at Ras Laffan. The Ras Laffan project was a joint venture of the Qatar General Petroleum Corp. (70%) and Mobil Corp. (30%). An agreement was signed in March with an international consortium to build a $340 million oil refinery in Qatar.

(DAVID COLVIN)

This article updates the *Macropædia* article ARABIA: *Qatar.*

ROMANIA

Area: 237,500 sq km (91,699 sq mi)
Population (1997 est.): 22,572,000
Capital: Bucharest
Chief of state: President Emil Constantinescu
Head of government: Prime Minister Victor Ciorbea

The year 1997 in Romania began with great expectations following the victory of the democrats in the November 1996 parliamentary and presidential elections. In January the new president, Emil Constantinescu, vowed to do something about rampant corruption and organized crime, and in February the coalition government led by Prime Minister Victor Ciorbea kicked off its "shock therapy" economic program.

Despite the will for change and an initially high level of public confidence in the new leadership, a thoroughgoing reform of the economy and society proved difficult. Restructuring of mammoth state industries was fitful, and privatization proceeded much more slowly than envisaged. The government sought to place the blame for this dysfunction on the old bureaucratic structures and initiated a drive to streamline various departments from the top down—changes that were promptly denounced as "political purges" by the leftist and nationalist opposition.

The main reason that needed reform could not be properly implemented was that homogeneity and consensus in the government itself were lacking. The ruling coalition consisted of three political alliances: the centre-right Democratic Convention of Romania (CDR), the Social Democratic Union (USD), and the Hungarian Democratic Union of Romania (UDMR). Widespread disagreement and tension surfaced within each of the three groupings, as well as between them, and nearly every political formation was plagued by infighting and rifts. In October, for example, Sen. Constantin Ticu Dumitrescu of the National Peasant Party–Christian Democratic, the main component of the CDR, was suspended from the party after he criticized its leadership for delaying the passage of a law that would allow access to the secret files of the communist political police.

Perpetual friction within the coalition often delayed the adoption of laws by the parliament. The Cabinet had to resort to "urgent ordinances" to speed up decision making, a practice that many felt circumvented normal democratic procedures. Coalition solidarity was more in evidence, however, when the government rejected the flurry of no-confidence and nonbinding opposition motions directed at the government, such as the one introduced in mid-December that would have held the government responsible for the plummeting living standards.

In August the Cabinet admitted that economic reform had stalled and announced the closing of 17 of the biggest loss-making enterprises (the number was later cut to 14). A government reshuffle, primarily aimed at

DAVID TURNLEY—THE DETROIT FREE PRESS

In Botiza, Rom., a miner smokes a cigarette before beginning an all-night shift at a salt mine, where he earns only $150 a month. Having embarked on a rigorous program of economic reform since the 1996 elections, Romania continued to search for ways to combat its deepening poverty.

consolidating the economic ministries, was announced in late October but could be completed only on December 2. One-third of the ministerial posts, including finance, reform, and industry and commerce, were affected. A privatization ministry was created to replace several institutions with overlapping responsibilities. Only days later, however, the Cabinet was again plunged into crisis when the two UDMR ministers boycotted meetings to protest the coalition's failure to permit education of the country's large Magyar minority in the Hungarian language in all subjects. In yet another scandal, Foreign Minister Adrian Severin of the Democratic Party (PD, the leading force in the USD) resigned on December 23 after he claimed that some party leaders and media directors were working for foreign secret services. Another PD minister, Traian Basescu (Transport), had to quit on December 29 for criticizing the Cabinet.

Growing dissatisfaction with government policies led to a wave of protests by workers, students, and others that peaked in October. The left-wing opposition parties proved unable to harness this popular discontent, however, chiefly because they too were divided. Former president Ion Iliescu's Party of Social Democracy in Romania split in June, and in December the new Alliance for Romania proclaimed itself "a third force" in the political arena.

Early in the year Romania launched a diplomatic offensive to improve its image abroad. President Constantinescu received senior foreign officials, including French Pres. Jacques Chirac (February) and U.S. Pres. Bill Clinton (July). Joining NATO and the European Union were proclaimed Romania's top foreign policy priorities. With these objectives in mind, Romania sought to improve relations with its neighbours and signed a basic treaty with Ukraine in June. The country was nonetheless passed over in the first wave of expansion by both NATO and the EU. (DAN IONESCU)

This article updates the *Macropædia* article BALKAN STATES: *Romania*.

RUSSIA

Area: 17,075,400 sq km (6,592,800 sq mi)
Population (1997 est.): 147,231,000
Capital: Moscow
Chief of state: President Boris Yeltsin
Head of government: Prime Minister Viktor Chernomyrdin

Domestic Affairs. Pres. Boris Yeltsin bounded back into the political fray in March 1997 after eight months' absence caused by sickness. His first action was to reshuffle the Cabinet to include new ministers with strong reform credentials. Anatoly Chubais, Russia's most determined reformer, was appointed first deputy prime minister and finance minister. Boris Nemtsov, one of Russia's youngest and most popular regional leaders, was appointed first deputy prime minister alongside Chubais. Together, the "young reformers" announced plans to overhaul taxation, housing, and welfare; restore central control over headstrong regional leaders; and curb the power of Russia's monopolies (natural gas, electricity, and railways). Stock markets and foreign investors were jubilant, confident that Russia was beginning a new round of economic liberalization. By year's end, however, many of the brave intentions of the new team were still confined to paper, stalled by opposition from Russia's communist-dominated Duma (the lower house of the Russian parliament) and vested interests in finance, industry, and the increasingly autonomous regions.

The new government's avowed determination to move Russia from the "crony capitalism" of the early Yeltsin years to a more liberal, transparent model brought it into conflict with the group of financiers who had bankrolled Yeltsin's 1996 reelection campaign. In return for services rendered, the bankers had been allowed to take their pick of influential government posts and companies being privatized. Chubais and Nemtsov argued that this relationship between government and big business was distorting the operation of Russia's fledgling market, degrading the government in the eyes of the population, and deterring foreign investment.

In July the government sold a 25% stake in Svyazinvest, the national telecommunications holding company. The auction was the first in which the winning bid was significantly higher than the reserve price, so the government realized an appreciable cash profit rather than simply privatizing a previously state-owned enterprise. Won by Unexim Bank, Russia's largest private bank, it was judged by many to be the most straightforward and fair of Russia's privatization transactions to date, but it earned Chubais the bitter enmity of the losing consortium, which unleashed a media war accusing him of being as corrupt as anyone else.

Matters came to a head in November when it was revealed that Chubais and several of his associates had accepted improbably high advance royalties on a book from a company owned by Unexim Bank. Yeltsin stripped Chubais of his post as finance minister but kept him on as first deputy prime minister in an apparent effort to reassure the international financial community that economic reform remained on track.

Debate over military reform continued throughout the year. Defense Minister Igor Rodionov was replaced in May by Gen. Igor Sergeyev, but expectations that Sergeyev's appointment would accelerate reforms were unfulfilled. At the end of the year, Yeltsin approved a "National Security Concept" designed to orient Russian policy makers in the post–Cold War period. There were hopes that the new document, which concluded that Russia faced no immediate danger of large-scale external aggression, would allow resources to be directed away from defense.

A major shift in the balance of power between the federal government and the provinces followed the election of regional leaders in Russia's 89 increasingly autonomous republics and regions. The republic of Chechnya continued to assert that it was a sovereign state, whereas the federal government insisted it was part of the Russian Federation. In January former guerrilla leader Aslan Maskhadov was elected president of Chechnya, but the territory remained divided among local warlords, and it was questionable how much control Maskhadov exercised outside the capital. Yeltsin and Maskhadov signed a provisional peace treaty in May but left the question of Chechnya's eventual status undetermined.

The Economy. The recovery of output, predicted by the Russian government for each of the past three years, failed once more to materialize. Gross domestic product (GDP), however, as officially recorded, did stop falling in 1997. Indeed, some analysts reckoned that the official statistics were failing to capture a recovery that had in fact begun; if so, this would be the first time the economy had grown since 1989.

One important factor contributing to the growth of optimism was the government's continued success in curbing inflation. Consumer-price inflation was 11.3% in 1997, down from 21.8% in 1996.

At the start of the year, the situation had looked a great deal more fragile. The country was riddled with payment arrears—large tax debts to the state budget, large state payments behind schedule both to state employees and to government suppliers, and chains of overdue payments between firms and between firms and their employees. As a result, the use of barter and of a variety of money surrogates was growing.

The situation changed dramatically in March when the government reshuffle brought in what enthusiasts called a "dream team" of reformers. They promptly set about putting macroeconomic stabilization on a sounder, more durable footing. The first step was to make federal government taxing and spending plans more realistic. Federal spending plans were cut in a "sequestration" of the 1997 budget designed to bring spending closer to the level of revenue raising that was achievable in practice. This entailed large cuts in subsidies to producers; though these were resisted by the Duma, the government pressed ahead.

The "young reformers" followed up by increasing pressure on some of the largest tax debtors, including the giant natural gas monopoly, Gazprom. This allowed the government to make good some of its own arrears, such as state pension payments. These were emergency measures, however. The need remained to put federal government finances on a sustainable basis over the following year and beyond. The government embarked on two more battles with the Duma—over the 1998 budget and a new tax code.

The draft budget for 1998 was a logical successor to the "sequestrated" version of the 1997 budget and was correspondingly unpopular with the communist-dominated Duma. The new tax code aimed to simplify the existing tax structure by cutting the number of taxes from 200 to 28. Western investors, especially, saw the introduction of the new tax code as a major step forward in reducing the turbulence and unpredictability of the existing Russian tax system. Many were therefore disheartened when, in October, President Yeltsin, fighting to stave off a Duma vote of no confidence in the government, conceded a delay in the attempt to push the new code through. Most Russian analysts, however, were less impressed by the new code. They considered that it had been drafted in a hurry and would cause problems if implemented without revision.

The new government team also launched a long-term program to cut state spending on housing maintenance and housing utilities (gas, water, heating, and electricity supplies to domestic dwellings). Many, probably most, Russian city budgets were dominated by housing subsidies, distributed indiscriminately to all households regardless of their income levels. Privatization of more than half the urban housing stock had not disposed of the problem. Charges for maintenance and utilities had continued to be subsidized for all—whether municipal tenants or new owners. The housing-reform program, led by Nemtsov, aimed to raise these charges in steps until they covered costs by the year 2003. At the same time, part of the public spending released would be targeted at direct support for low-income households. This policy was highly sensitive politically; Yeltsin appeared in the fall to be hinting at concessions on that front, too.

Thus, after initial successes the initiatives of the new reform team had begun to run into difficulties by the fall. The rate of tax collection, after some major tax arrears had been captured, remained low; federal tax revenue in the first eight months of the year was down to only 8.1% of GDP. As a result, the government's ability to reduce the state deficit and the rate of government borrowing (with total government debt, external plus internal, around 50% of GDP and rising) remained in doubt. The government was, therefore, still borrowing at levels that tended to "crowd out" borrowing for private-sector investment. Indeed, investment continued to fall in 1997—not a good augury for the recovery expected (once more) by the government "next year" (1998).

Finance from abroad, however, increased. Having gained an international sovereign credit rating in late 1996, the government had begun to issue Eurobonds on Western markets. This access to Western financial markets was also gained by several Russian cities and provinces, including Moscow, St. Petersburg, and Nizhny Novgorod.

The increased inflow of foreign private capital, though undoubtedly welcome in many respects, carried some dangers. In the first half of the year, the total inflow was $6.7 billion, accounting for more than a third of the cumulative stock of foreign investment at midyear. Much of this new surge, however, was portfolio rather than direct investment, and a further large slice was private-sector borrowing rather than equity investment. That meant that the flows in could easily be reversed and become flows out. Meanwhile, a good deal of smart Russian money continued to be placed offshore, so on balance there probably remained a net outflow of capital. Qualms about the prospects for a sustained recovery seemed to be borne out at year's end when, in an indication of the extent to which the Russian economy had been integrated into the global economy, the Russian government found itself forced to raise interest rates to protect the ruble against the turmoil afflicting emerging markets worldwide.

Foreign Affairs. Tensions persisted throughout the year over NATO's potential enlargement to include former Soviet allies in Central and Eastern Europe. In the event, Russia did not carry out its early threat to abandon some of its arms control commitments if NATO went ahead with eastward expansion. Instead, in May Yeltsin signed the Russia-NATO Founding Act—a political agreement that established a consultative council and promised Russia "a voice but no veto" in the affairs of the alliance.

Russia worked hard throughout the year to cultivate relations with China, India, and Japan. Moscow's declared aim was to construct a "multipolar" system of international relations in contrast to the "unipolar," U.S.-dominated system seen as having replaced the bipolar world of the Cold War era. In addition, Moscow declared its intention to follow through on a nuclear construction project in Iran that aroused strong U.S. opposition. Russia also announced a series of new oil deals with its old ally, Iraq.

In April Russia and Belarus agreed to ratify a treaty of union calling for union of the two nations, common citizenship, coordinated security and economic policies, and a single currency. The reform wing of the Russian government expressed strong reservations, as did liberal opinion in Belarus, and the terms of the treaty were confined to paper only.

In May Russia and Ukraine finally resolved their five-year dispute over the division of the Black Sea Fleet and signed a long-awaited friendship treaty under which Russia formally acknowledged its neighbour's independence and territorial integrity.

(ELIZABETH TEAGUE)

Snow accumulates on the decks of boats docked along the Pregolya River in the Russian seaport city of Kaliningrad. Wedged between Lithuania and Poland, Kaliningrad *oblast* (province) was an often forgotten part of Russia, though its ice-free port and tariff-free status were significant assets.

DENNIS CHAMBERLAIN—BLACK STAR

RWANDA

Area: 26,338 sq km (10,169 sq mi)
Population (1997 est.): 7,738,000
Capital: Kigali
Head of state and government: President Pasteur Bizimungu in conjunction with Vice President Paul Kagame and Prime Minister Pierre Celestin Rwigema

Another deeply troubled year for Rwanda was dominated by refugee problems, additional massacres, and a slow process of trials for genocidal acts. In August 1996 an agreement had been signed by Prime Minister Pierre Celestin Rwigyema and his Zairean counterpart, Léon Kengo wa Dondo, for the return to Rwanda of 1.3 million refugees from more than 30 camps in eastern Zaire. The next month, however, tensions developed between the two countries following a number of border incidents. At the same time, 400,000 refugees were reported by the UN High Commissioner for Refugees to have returned voluntarily to Rwanda.

MARC SCHLOSSMAN—PANOS

Rwandan refugees wait at the airport in Kigali after having been airlifted back to their homeland from eastern Zaire (Democratic Republic of the Congo). Officials estimated that 400,000 refugees returned home voluntarily. Some 1.3 million Hutu had fled in 1994 to escape an advancing Tutsi army.

At the beginning of December 1996, the Tanzanian government ordered all Rwandan refugees to return home, and by the end of the month, some 700,000 were reported to have left Tanzania. Many thousands were thought to have abandoned the camps and headed into the countryside, however. On Jan. 3, 1997, a court in Kibungo sentenced two Hutu to death on charges of genocide and crimes against humanity during 1994. Three others, also Hutu, were sentenced to death later in the month, and 90,000 people awaited trial in Rwandan prisons.

Hutu extremists were reported to have been responsible for 60 deaths, including 3 Spanish aid workers, near Ruhengeri in January. Additional murders included some UN personnel in February, an estimated 424 Tutsi along the border with Zaire in March, and some 270 more Tutsi in December.

In August the government appealed for emergency food aid to cope with the results of a poor harvest and the return of huge numbers of refugees. It estimated that 175,000 metric tons would be needed for the following six months. (GUY ARNOLD)

This article updates the *Macropædia* article CENTRAL AFRICA: *Rwanda.*

SAINT KITTS AND NEVIS

Area: 269 sq km (104 sq mi)
Population (1997 est.): 41,800
Capital: Basseterre
Chief of state: Queen Elizabeth II, represented by Governor-General Cuthbert Sebastian
Head of government: Prime Minister Denzil Douglas

The Concerned Citizens Movement (CCM), headed by Vance Amory, premier of Nevis, was returned to power in the Nevis Assembly election in February 1997, retaining the three seats it had held in the previous house. The Nevis Reformation Party (NRP) kept its two seats.

After threatening to secede from the Federation of St. Kitts and Nevis for some time, the CCM finally took the plunge in October, when it presented a motion to the Nevis Assembly calling for separation from St. Kitts. The motion received the support of the NRP. A referendum to confirm the resolution was to be held in Nevis within six months. A bill to establish a St. Kitts and Nevis defense force was accepted by the National Assembly in July. Prime Minister Denzil Douglas said the force would be used particularly in counternarcotics operations. (DAVID RENWICK)

This article updates the *Macropædia* article The WEST INDIES: *Saint Kitts and Nevis.*

SAINT LUCIA

Area: 617 sq km (238 sq mi)
Population (1997 est.): 148,000
Capital: Castries
Chief of state: Queen Elizabeth II, represented by Governor-General George Mallet
Head of government: Prime Ministers Vaughan Lewis and, from May 24, Kenny Anthony

During its final months in office in 1997, the United Workers' Party (UWP) government of Prime Minister Vaughan Lewis introduced legislation requiring government ministers, MPs, and senior civil servants to declare their assets publicly. St. Lucia thus became the fifth Caribbean nation to adopt a form of integrity legislation.

The UWP, which had been in power for all but 3 of the last 33 years, was severely trounced in the May general election, retaining only one seat in the 17-seat parliament. The St. Lucia Labour Party (SLP), with 61.3% of the vote, won the other 16. Even UWP leader Lewis lost his seat. On May 24 Kenny Anthony, a lawyer, was sworn in as prime minister of the SLP government. Among the new government's first acts was to establish a commission of inquiry into alleged corruption under the UWP administration. A controversial decision of the new government was the establishment of diplomatic relations with China, replacing those with Taiwan. (DAVID RENWICK)

This article updates the *Macropædia* article The WEST INDIES: *Saint Lucia.*

SAINT VINCENT AND THE GRENADINES

Area: 389 sq km (150 sq mi)
Population (1997 est.): 112,000
Capital: Kingstown
Chief of state: Queen Elizabeth II, represented by Governor-General Sir David Jack
Head of government: Prime Minister Sir James Fitz-Allen Mitchell

In August 1997 a U.S. couple, James and Penella Fletcher, were freed on a charge of having murdered a St. Vincent boat-taxi operator when a judge ruled there was insufficient evidence for a conviction. The incident attracted intense attention from the U.S. media, which aroused the ire of the prime minister, Sir James Mitchell, when aspersions were cast on the efficiency of the country's legal system and the integrity of the government. Among the allegations made was that government officials had tried to extort money from the Fletchers.

The House of Assembly in August passed legislation that provided for both a fine and a term of imprisonment for those found guilty of money laundering, which often was linked to drug trafficking in the Caribbean. The legislation also required banks to divulge information about suspect accounts to the police. (DAVID RENWICK)

This article updates the *Macropædia* article The WEST INDIES: *Saint Vincent and the Grenadines*.

SAMOA

Area: 2,831 sq km (1,093 sq mi)
Population (1997 est.): 169,000
Capital: Apia
Chief of state: O le Ao o le Malo (Head of State) Malietoa Tanumafili II
Head of government: Prime Minister Tofilau Eti Alesana

In July 1997 the Legislative Assembly of Western Samoa voted 41–1 to change the country's name to Samoa. Issues of open government achieved prominence when legislation was passed to restrict the term of office of the auditor general to three years, applied retroactively. The change allowed the government to dismiss the incumbent, who had been suspended since 1994 for having accused ministers and senior public servants of financial mismanagement. In another defensive measure, the government weakened the voice of its critics by restricting its advertising to the government-owned newspaper. In November opposition leaders organized a large public demonstration and called on the government to resign.

Economic growth for 1997 was predicted at 6–7%, after 3–4% in 1996 and 9.6% in 1995. Returns from exports rose 25% in 1996, and tourism increased 16%. The stronger performance also reflected recovery from the hurricane damage of 1994 and a reduced impact from the disease that had destroyed export crops in recent years. (BARRIE MACDONALD)

This article updates the *Macropædia* article PACIFIC ISLANDS: *Western Samoa*.

SAN MARINO

Area: 61.1 sq km (23.6 sq mi)
Population (1997 est.): 25,600
Capital: San Marino
Heads of state and government: The republic is governed by two *capitani reggenti*, or coregents, appointed every six months by a popularly elected Great and General Council.

During 1997 tiny San Marino continued to exercise a vigorous role in the conduct of both domestic affairs and international relations. The country boasted numerous visits from distinguished foreign representatives and itself launched an energetic diplomatic campaign to protect its role as a force to be reckoned with. The diplomatic high point was the official visit of the republic's longtime state secretary for foreign and political affairs, Gabriele Gatti, to Cuba, where he met with Fidel Castro and discussed investment opportunities for San Marino businesses. San Marino received a visit from Italy's foreign minister, who discussed opportunities for future collaboration with his nation within the context of a united Europe.

San Marino inaugurated its Museum of the Emigrant, bearing witness to a trend that had recently been reversed as increasing numbers of immigrants sought citizenship there. Concern regarding the integrity of the people was echoed in the effort to preserve the republic's ancient democratic spirit through only slight modifications of the electoral system.

The Great Council, however, also voted to throw out laws on the books that prohibited "libidinous acts with persons of the same sex," which had been punishable by prison terms, and approved the construction of skateboarding and in-line skating facilities, both actions sure indications that San Marino was fully part of the modern era. (GREGORY O. SMITH)

This article updates the *Micropædia* article SAN MARINO.

SÃO TOMÉ AND PRÍNCIPE

Area: 1,001 sq km (386 sq mi)
Population (1997 est.): 137,000
Capital: São Tomé
Chief of state: President Miguel Trovoada
Head of government: Prime Minister Raul Bragança Neto

The economy of São Tomé and Príncipe in 1997 remained heavily dependent upon international assistance, with just over 60% of the budget derived from grants; most of this came from the European Union. A major development program under way during the year included job creation and new health centres and medical equipment. Financed by the European Development Fund, the program was also providing technical assistance as well as new drainage, sanitation, and environmental protection facilities.

In May the government and the South African group Wadco signed an agreement to establish a customs-free zone on the west coast of Príncipe. Covering between 400 and 600 ha (1,000 and 1,500 ac), it was located near the island's airport and could become the site of a deep-water port and provide services for oil operators in the Gulf of Guinea. In September there were indications that the country was considering joining the Central African Economic and Monetary Zone. (GUY ARNOLD)

This article updates the *Macropædia* article CENTRAL AFRICA: *São Tomé and Príncipe*.

SAUDI ARABIA

Area: 2,248,000 sq km (868,000 sq mi)
Population (1997 est.): 19,072,000
Capital: Riyadh
Head of state and government: King Fahd

Since the bomb attack against the U.S. military housing complex at Al-Khubar in 1996, United States investigators had expressed frustration at the poor cooperation between American and Saudi investigators. The Saudis proposed and later dropped plans to extradite from Canada a Shi'ite suspect, Hani as-Sayegh. After learning about Sayegh, the United States flew him to Washington in June. In exchange for being provided information about the attack against the American military personnel housed in the apartment bloc, the U.S. agreed to reduced charges and guaranteed that Sayegh would not be extradited to Saudi Arabia. In September the U.S. dropped all terrorist-related charges against Sayegh for lack of evidence but set in motion plans to deport him.

Two British nurses, Deborah Parry and Lucille McLauchlan, were arrested in December 1996 and charged with the murder of an Australian nurse, Yvonne Gilford. Both women were found guilty. Parry was sentenced to beheading and McLauchlan to an eight-year prison term and 500 lashes. According to Saudi law, the victim's family could, in exchange for monetary compensation, waive the death penalty, and Gilford's brother accepted an offer of $1,250,000.

Strong oil prices, accounting for 80% of Saudi revenues, were responsible for a government surplus of 700 million rials at the end of 1996, the first officially recorded annual surplus since 1983. The 1997 budget projected a deficit of 17 billion rials in a budget of 164 billion rials. Infrastructure, education, and health and social services were allocated more funding. Anticipated joint ventures in the energy sector were discussed at a conference in October, but the government made it clear that Saudi Arabia would maintain ownership and control of any expansion efforts in oil and gas.

Talks continued with Yemen over border issues, and Iran resumed direct flights to Saudi Arabia during the annual Muslim hajj for the first time since the Iranian Islamic revolution in 1979. An Iraqi plane flew more than 100 passengers to Saudi Arabia in April for the hajj, and helicopters crossed the no-fly zone, landing at the Saudi border to pick up pilgrims returning to Iraq. Although the United States considered the flights violations of the UN-imposed flight ban, the United Nations did not condemn the flights.

During the annual pilgrimage to Mecca, a fire killed more than 300 people. It was believed that a gas cylinder had exploded, and flames spread through the more than 70,000 tents that housed the pilgrims near Mecca. More than half of the victims were from India and Pakistan. (REEVA S. SIMON)

This article updates the *Macropædia* article ARABIA: *Saudi Arabia*.

SENEGAL

Area: 196,712 sq km (75,951 sq mi)
Population (1997 est.): 9,404,000
Capital: Dakar
Chief of state: President Abdou Diouf
Head of government: Prime Minister Habib Thiam

After several months of relative calm in the troubled Casamance region, clashes between separatists belonging to the Movement of Democratic Forces of Casamance and the Senegalese army erupted in March 1997. Two soldiers were killed on March 23, and 25 were slain in a rebel ambush on August 19. In September 20 civilians were killed in two separate attacks, 11 of them in the village of Diogue, near the resort area of Cap Skirring. In response, 2,500 troops swept thought the region, destroying two rebel bases and killing 22 rebels. Thousands of villagers fled across the border to Guinea-Bissau to escape the violence. The government, fearing a drop in income from tourism, the country's second largest foreign-currency earner, dispatched additional troops to protect the resorts.

Secondary-school teachers went on strike on March 27, demanding better living conditions. As the prospect of a lost school year loomed, students rioted in Dakar. A settlement was reached in July when the teachers were granted higher housing allowances.

In March Senegal agreed to extend its fishing protocol with the European Union for an additional four years. Senegal would receive annual compensation of $10.4 million from the EU, an increase of 33% over the previous arrangement. The sale of a one-third interest in the state-owned telephone company to French Telecom was accomplished in the summer. Relations with Taiwan grew closer in 1997, with the Asian nation pledging financial and technical assistance to Senegal's program of achieving self-sufficiency in food production. Taiwan announced in October that Senegal would replace South Africa as its home port in Africa.

(NANCY ELLEN LAWLER)

This article updates the *Macropædia* article WESTERN AFRICA: *Senegal*.

SEYCHELLES

Area: 455 sq km (176 sq mi)
Population (1997 est.): 77,300
Capital: Victoria
Head of state and government: President France-Albert René

On Feb. 2, 1997, a fire in Victoria partially destroyed the international conference centre that was contained within the headquarters of the ruling Seychelles People's Progressive Front. Damage was estimated at $1 million. The police said the fire could have been the result of arson and linked it to an arson attack on the presidential palace in October 1996.

With an average per capita income of $6,210, Seychelles was no longer dependent upon aid, though it continued to require various forms of technical assistance. Only about 1.1% of the budget was derived from grants. Seychelles qualified for assistance from the European Development Fund, which provided financing for the rehabilitation of the Victoria Market, for the Anse Royale landfill, and for the Nial water-treatment-plant extension. (GUY ARNOLD)

This article updates the *Micropædia* article SEYCHELLES.

SIERRA LEONE

Area: 71,740 sq km (27,699 sq mi)
Population (1997 est.): 4,424,000
Capital: Freetown
Head of state and government: President Ahmad Tejan Kabbah until May 25 and, from June 17, Maj. Johnny Paul Koroma

On May 25, 1997, junior army officers and enlisted men staged a coup and overthrew Pres. Ahmad Tejan Kabbah, who fled the country. The coup began with the storming of the capital's top security prison and release of 600 captives, many of them dissident soldiers. Maj. Johnny Paul Koroma declared himself head of state and announced the abolition of the constitution and a ban on political parties.

There was immediate international condemnation of the coup, and Nigeria said it would lead a regional military force to restore Kabbah. Nigeria then dispatched troops to Freetown while naval vessels stood

CAROL GUZY—THE WASHINGTON POST

Senegalese fishermen cast nets from two boats into the glistening waters of the Atlantic Ocean. In March Senegal agreed to extend its fishing protocol with the European Union for an additional four years.

CORRINE DUFKA—REUTERS

Women attending a June peace rally in Freetown, Sierra Leone, look past a heavily armed Sierra Leonean soldier. Some 4,600 Nigerian-led ECOMOG troops were sent to Freetown, and by year's end it seemed they had succeeded in restoring deposed Pres. Ahmad Tejan Kabbah to power.

offshore; an additional 1,500 troops from neighbouring Guinea joined the Nigerians. In June there was widespread lawlessness throughout Sierra Leone; this was made worse by the failure of Nigeria to overthrow the coup. As many as 300,000 people had left Sierra Leone by mid-June.

Meanwhile, on June 1, Koroma announced the formation of a 20-member Armed Forces Revolutionary Council (AFRC), including Foday Sankoh (the former leader of the Revolutionary United Front, which had been opposed to the government) as deputy chairman. The AFRC rejected British, Ghanaian, and Nigerian efforts at mediation. The Nigerians—acting for ECOMOG, the peacekeeping forces of the Economic Community of West African States (ECOWAS)—occupied the Freetown international airport and seaport, and early in June Nigerian naval vessels bombarded Freetown; by June 4 there were some 4,600 ECOMOG troops in Freetown, but they failed to restore the ousted president, and a stalemate ensued. On June 17 Koroma was sworn in as Sierra Leone's president.

While lawlessness and clashes between Koroma and Kabbah supporters continued through June and July, the Commonwealth of Nations demanded the unconditional reinstatement of Kabbah. Talks to end the crisis were held in Abidjan, Côte d'Ivoire, during August, but these collapsed when Koroma demanded that he stay in power for four years. ECOWAS applied sanctions to Sierra Leone to force it to return to democratic legitimacy, and most aid agencies pulled out of the country.

Fighting continued into the autumn. Finally, in Conakry, Guinea, in late October, the foreign ministers of Côte d'Ivoire, Ghana, Guinea, Liberia, and Nigeria prevailed upon the military government of Sierra Leone to agree to restore Kabbah to the presidency in April 1998. Koroma would receive immunity from prosecution for his role in the May coup.

(GUY ARNOLD)

This article updates the *Macropædia* article WESTERN AFRICA: *Sierra Leone.*

SINGAPORE

Area: 646 sq km (249 sq mi)
Population (1997 est.): 3,104,000
Chief of state: President Ong Teng Cheong
Head of government: Prime Minister Goh Chok Tong

On Jan. 2, 1997, the ruling People's Action Party (PAP) overwhelmingly won Singapore's parliamentary elections. In a major personal victory for Prime Minister Goh Chok Tong, the PAP garnered 65% of the vote and reclaimed two of the four seats held by the opposition. It was a hard-fought campaign that provoked some international criticism over PAP tactics, which included threatening to delay property-upgrading programs in districts that voted for the opposition. Such tactics were particularly effective in a country where 86% of the populace lived in government-built housing.

The government also caused a stir by launching an all-out legal offensive against one of its defeated opponents, the previously little-known lawyer Tang Liang Hong, whom the PAP accused of being a "Chinese chauvinist." In eight separate suits brought by Goh, Senior Minister Lee Kuan Yew, and other officials, the PAP charged Tang with defamation when he accused the government of lying during the campaign. Tang fled the country and was later charged with tax evasion. The court initially awarded the PAP more than $5 million in damages, but that was later reduced by more than half. In a separate defamation case against Tang's running mate, Joshua Benjamin Jeyaretnam, Goh also prevailed but won only a fraction of the damages he had sought.

On the economic front the Asian currency crisis had serious effects on Singapore. Once thought of as a safe haven amid its less-stable neighbours, Singapore watched in horror as speculators turned on its dollar after ravaging the Thai baht, Malaysian ringgit, Indonesian rupiah, and Philippine peso. Between the end of June and the end of December, the Singapore dollar depreciated by 9%. The benchmark Straits Times Industrials Index had dropped 31% since the beginning of the year.

Local companies that had expanded aggressively throughout the region in recent years were also hit hard by the currency crisis, since trade with Malaysia, Thailand, Indonesia, and the Philippines accounted for 27% of Singapore's total trade. The economic picture was not expected to improve soon. Analysts downgraded regional growth predictions from 8–10% to 4–6% for the year.

Looking for positive signs amid the regional gloom, Singapore's defenders pointed to its economic strengths. Unlike its neighbours, Singapore had no foreign debt, had consistently run current-account and budget surpluses, and had low inflation (roughly 2%). In addition, its commercial banks were strong, with the highest credit rating in Asia and, luckily, less than 5% of their loans in troubled Thailand. (ANDREA HAMILTON)

This article updates the *Macropædia* article SOUTHEAST ASIA: *Singapore.*

SLOVAKIA

Area: 49,036 sq km (18,933 sq mi)
Population (1997 est.): 5,404,000
Capital: Bratislava
Chief of state: President Michal Kovac
Head of government: Prime Minister Vladimir Meciar

In Slovakia 1997 would be remembered as the year the country fell from the group of fast-track states for entry into NATO and the European Union (EU). Over 90% of eligible voters boycotted a May referendum on NATO membership after Interior Minister Gustav Krajci removed from the ballot a question on direct presidential elections that had been added by the opposition. Another controversy centred on the parliament's refusal in September to reinstate the mandate of Frantisek Gaulieder, who was stripped of his seat in December 1996 after he quit the ruling Movement for a Democratic Slovakia (HZDS). The feud between Pres. Michal Kovac and Prime Minister Vladimir Meciar continued, and several politically related cases remained unresolved, including the 1995 kidnapping of Kovac's son. The ruling coalition squabbled over bank and television privatization and the 1998 state budget. Five opposition parties formed the Slovak Democratic Coalition (SDK), which immediately surpassed the HZDS in opinion polls. The SDK signed a cooperation agreement with the opposition Hungarian coalition, while the postcommunist Party of the Democratic Left preferred to remain an "independent opposition party."

In June the EU-Slovak parliamentary committee recommended that Slovakia improve government-opposition relations, alter the composition of parliamentary committees to achieve a fair coalition-opposition ratio, and pass a minority language law in order to move toward EU membership. Kovac and Meciar issued a rare joint statement in October promising to cooperate in achieving these goals. After three years of anticipation, on November 19 the parliament voted to expand the parliamentary committees overseeing the secret service and military intelligence to include three SDK deputies.

Annual growth in Slovakia's gross domestic product was expected to fall to 4% by December, and year-end inflation was predicted to rise to 8%. Problem areas included the mounting state budget and trade deficits. Although the import surcharge was lifted on January 1, the worsening trade deficit led Slovakia to introduce 7% import tariffs in July.

A dispute with the Czech Republic over disposition of remaining common property led Slovakia to withdraw its ambassador for three weeks in April; however, talks between Meciar and his Czech counterpart, Vaclav Klaus, in October helped to resolve some problems. Ties were strained with another neighbour as well, Hungary, when it complained that Slovakia was not fulfilling the bilateral state treaty and when suggestions about a possible population exchange became public.

(SHARON FISHER)

This article updates the *Macropædia* article CZECH AND SLOVAK REPUBLICS: *Slovakia.*

SLOVENIA

Area: 20,256 sq km (7,821 sq mi)
Population (1997 est.): 1,955,000
Capital: Ljubljana
Chief of state: President Milan Kucan
Head of government: Prime Minister Janez Drnovsek

On Feb. 27, 1997, Slovenia's legislature finally broke a deadlock and approved a new coalition government, again led by Janez Drnovsek, prime minister since 1992. Legislative elections in November 1996 had given Drnovsek's centre-left Liberal Democracy of Slovenia 25 of 90 seats, which made it the largest party. After prolonged negotiations the right-wing Slovenian People's Party (19 seats) agreed to enter the government, and its leader, Marjan Podobnik, became deputy prime minister. The centre-left DeSUS Party (5 seats), primarily representing retirees, also joined the coalition. Government policies remained unchanged.

Milan Kucan, president since 1990, was elected in November to a second five-year term. The former head of Slovenia's Communist Party, Kucan ran as a nonparty candidate and received 56% of the vote. His nearest competitor in the eight-candidate field won 18%.

Slovenia's economic growth rate remained moderate at 3.5%. The rate of inflation was 9.5%, and unemployment stood at 14%. At the end of October, the country had $4,185,000,000 of foreign exchange reserves and a foreign debt of $4,060,000,000.

On March 5 Msgr. Franc Rode was appointed archbishop and titular head of the Roman Catholic Church in Slovenia, replacing Archbishop Alojzij Sustar, who retired. He proved more forceful than his predecessor in defending the church's interests, particularly in the still-delayed return of forest land and other property confiscated by the communist government after World War II.

Although disappointed by the decision of NATO members in July to exclude Slovenia in the first round of expansion, Slovenia's government pledged to work toward the country's inclusion in the projected second round and in the meantime to continue participation in the NATO-sponsored Partnership for Peace. A small Slovene military unit joined the SFOR peacekeeping force in Bosnia and Herzegovina in November. On July 16 the European Union formally invited Slovenia to join in negotiations aimed at eventual membership. In October the UN General Assembly elected Slovenia to serve a two-year term (1998–99) as a nonpermanent member of the Security Council, replacing Poland. (RUDOLPH M. SUSEL)

This article updates the *Macropaedia* article BALKAN STATES: *Slovenia.*

SOLOMON ISLANDS

Area: 28,370 sq km (10,954 sq mi)
Population (1997 est.): 411,000
Capital: Honiara
Chief of state: Queen Elizabeth II, represented by Governor-General Moses Pitakaka
Head of government: Prime Ministers Solomon Mamaloni and, from August 27, Bartholomew Ulufa'alu

After general elections in August 1997, Bartholomew ("Bart") Ulufa'alu was chosen prime minister by the legislature. From Malaita, Ulufa'alu was the leader of the Liberal Party and headed the Alliance for Change coalition. An economics graduate from the University of Papua New Guinea, he served as leader of the opposition from 1976 to 1980 and minister of finance from 1981 to 1984.

In May the minister of finance acknowledged earlier mismanagement and said that the country could not pay its debts but also argued that the economy was fundamentally sound. At that time the government carried internal debt of $117 million, external debt of $116 million, and debt-servicing arrears of some $25 million. Forestry remained the major source of overseas earnings, though controversy continued over government management of the sector. The new Gold Ridge gold-mining venture on Guadalcanal promised significant economic growth.

Despite progress in talks on border management and defense cooperation, the border with Papua New Guinea (PNG) remained a source of tension. Incursions into Solomon Islands territory by PNG forces countering secessionist action in Bougainville gave rise to formal protests in March and April. (BARRIE MACDONALD)

This article updates the *Macropædia* article PACIFIC ISLANDS: *Solomon Islands.*

SOMALIA

Area: 637,000 sq km (246,000 sq mi; including the 176,000-sq km [68,000-sq mi] area of the unilaterally declared [in 1991] and unrecognized Republic of Somaliland)
Population (1997 est.): 6,870,000 (including 4,200,000 residents of Somaliland; excluding 450,000 refugees in neighbouring countries)
Capital: Mogadishu; Hargeysa is the capital of Somaliland
Head of state and government: Somalia had no functioning government in 1997.

Disastrous floods ravaged southern Somalia in 1997; meanwhile, up to the end of the year, there was little success in the attempts to bring peace and rebuild central government in a country still divided between rival clan-based factions. In the northwest the self-declared Republic of Somaliland continued to function in spite of its failure to gain international recognition. In the rest of the country, however, the factions were grouped into two loose alliances: the Somali Salvation Alliance (SSA), headed by Ali Mahdi Muhammad, and the Somali National Alliance, first formed by Gen. Muhammad Farah Aydid, who died in 1996, and in 1997 led by his son Hussein Aydid. Both claimed to head governments and used the title "president." A third force was that of Osman Hassan Ali ("Ato"), formerly the elder Aydid's financier and right-hand man but now allied with Ali Mahdi.

There were two concurrent peace processes. In January at the resort town of Sodere, Eth., leaders of 26 factions affiliated with the SSA created a National Salvation Council with a mandate to organize a transitional government. This was followed by a meeting in Addis Ababa, Eth., in July. This peace process, though backed by the Organization of African Unity, was boycotted by both Hussein and the president of Somaliland, Muhammad Ibrahim Egal.

The other initiative, backed by Pres. Daniel arap Moi of Kenya, involved Hussein, Ali Mahdi, and Ato. In May Ato and Hussein signed a peace declaration in Yemen, and later that month Hussein and Ali Mahdi attended a meeting in Cairo chaired by Pres. Hosni Mubarak of Egypt. In November talks were finally held in Cairo between the Hussein and Ali Mahdi factions, and a National Reconciliation Conference was scheduled for 1998.

Fighting nevertheless continued in several areas: in Mogadishu in January there were clashes between the militias of Hussein, Ato, and Ali Mahdi; in the south Somali plain, the local Rahanweyn clans contested Hussein's control; and in the southeast, conflict continued in spite of a peace conference for the region held at Afmadow in December 1996. A significant role was played by Islamist militia groups, particularly the

Sudan-backed al-Ittihad. The latter were driven from their bases in the southwest in June after repeated cross-border attacks by Ethiopian troops, who were retaliating for bomb attacks in Ethiopia.

In November and December freak rains led to severe flooding of the rivers Jubba and Shabelle in the south of the country. More than a thousand lives were lost, communities were made homeless, and food stores were destroyed. An international relief effort was belatedly mounted.

In Somaliland the National Communities Conference in February reelected President Egal by a landslide and announced that a new constitution would be operative for an interim period of three years, after which a public referendum would be held to ratify it. In spite of occasional clashes, Somaliland remained generally peaceful, and the economy, especially the important livestock trade, was strong. (VIRGINIA R. LULING)

This article updates the *Macropædia* article EASTERN AFRICA: *Somalia.*

SOUTH AFRICA

Area: 1,219,090 sq km (470,693 sq mi)
Population (1997 est.): 42,446,000
Capitals (de facto): Pretoria (executive); Bloemfontein (judicial); Cape Town (legislative)
Head of state and government: President Nelson Mandela

South Africa in 1997 experienced shuffling and upheavals in its political parties, a sign of the approach of parliamentary elections in 1999. Crime continued as a major concern throughout the year. Police figures indicated an average of 52 murders each day, a rape every 30 minutes, a car stolen every 9 minutes, and an armed robbery every 11 minutes.

Domestic Affairs. Opening Parliament on February 7, Pres. Nelson Mandela spoke of the fostering of a "new patriotism" and emphasized the government's commitment to its economic strategy, which involved cutting the budget deficit, restructuring state assets, and increasing exports. He pointed to the achievements of the African National Congress (ANC) government in the fields of nutrition, health care, education, housing, and provision of water and electricity. By November 1996 nearly two million hectares (five million acres) of land had been redistributed under the government's reform program. By mid-1997 more than one million households had been given access to clean piped water since 1994, and 900,000 electricity connections had been made in the preceding two years; by September 322,000 houses had been built since 1994 or were under construction. The minister of health generated controversy by introducing bills aimed at reducing the price of medicines and improving access to health care.

In March Lieut. Gen. Siphiwe Nyanda, former leader of Umkhonto we Sizwe, the armed wing of the ANC, was appointed deputy chief of the National Defence Force and was slated to succeed Gen. George Meiring as chief when the latter's contract expired at the end of 1998. A national Council of Traditional Leaders, with limited powers, was inaugurated.

The Truth and Reconciliation Commission, chaired by Archbishop Desmond Tutu, continued its hearings into gross violations of human rights between 1960 and 1993. Testimony from victims continued to be heard. In addition, a committee considered applications for amnesty from perpetrators. There were also a number of special hearings. F.W. de Klerk, testifying for the National Party (NP), denied that the party had presided over systematic criminal activity or that assassination had formed a part of its policy in the 1980s. This prompted Tutu to state at a press conference that he found this hard to understand, which, in turn, caused the NP to suspend participation in the commission and take it to court, demanding an apology from Tutu and the resignation of the commission's vice-chairman. By late in the year, police had admitted to the use of torture and hired killers during the NP regime in the 1980s, and it was also confirmed that newspapers had been infiltrated by security police spies during that time. As the hearings continued, a conflict developed between police personnel, who asserted they had been ordered to "eliminate," *i.e.,* kill, black political opponents of the government, and politicians and senior police and military officials, who insisted that the police had misunderstood them and that words such as *eliminate* meant merely to "politically neutralize." Former president P.W. Botha had been subpoenaed to appear before the commission, but this was postponed for health reasons. The ANC admitted to a number of human rights violations, including a plan to assassinate Chief Mangosuthu Gatsha Buthelezi, leader of the Inkatha Freedom Party (IFP), which was countermanded by ANC headquarters.

ADIL BRADLOW—ASSOCIATED PRESS

Demonstrators stage a rally outside city hall in Benoni, S.Af., where the Truth and Reconciliation Commission held an amnesty hearing for the convicted killers of South African Communist Party leader Chris Hani, who was slain in 1993.

Former president F.W. de Klerk resigned as leader of the NP at the end of August on the grounds that he was a burden to the party because his opponents viewed him as a "symbol of the past." He was succeeded by Marthinus van Schalkwyk, who took over a party that, apart from its base in the Western Cape, was described as "in tatters" by commentators.

In February Roelf Meyer stepped down as secretary-general of the NP to head a task force that was to examine ways of reforming the party, including dissolving it to form a new political movement. In May he was relieved of this job, and shortly afterward he resigned from the NP. He formed the New Movement Process to canvass for a new party, which attracted numbers of local leaders of the NP. Soon he linked up with Bantu Holomisa, who had been expelled from the ANC in 1996 and had then formed the National Consultative Forum. Holomisa obtained support from Lucas Mangope, former president of Bophuthatswana, and from Sifiso Nkabinde, ANC leader from Richmond in Natal, who had been expelled from the ANC in April as a police spy. Mangope was indicted on 208 charges of fraud, theft, and attempted theft during the year, involving more than R 16 million. Nkabinde, with 17 others, was arrested in September on 18 charges of murder dating back to 1993, including the killing of five men—two ANC councillors among them—in July. Holomisa and Meyer launched the United Democratic Movement in September, excluding Mangope and Nkabinde on the grounds that both were subject to criminal charges.

In December the ANC held a conference at which Nelson Mandela was replaced as president by Thabo Mbeki, establishing the latter as the presumptive successor to Mandela as president of the country.

Buthelezi, president of the IFP and minister of home affairs, was appointed acting president several times during the year during the absences abroad of President Mandela and Deputy President Mbeki. This symbolized a growing rapprochement between the ANC and the IFP and a substantial diminution of violence between them. Walter Felgate, an IFP stalwart and leading adviser to Buthelezi for 20 years, surprised observers by resigning from the IFP to join the ANC.

The Congress of South African Trade Unions (COSATU), with a membership of approximately 1.8 million (up from 1.3 million in 1994), on June 2 called a 24-hour general strike against the Basic Conditions of Employment Bill; it claimed a participation of more than two million. It held a one-hour stoppage on August 4 with a similar turnout, successful regional general strikes during August 19–23, and a two-day general strike on October 27–28. The employment bill reduced the workweek from 46 hours to 45 and granted four months of unpaid maternity leave, but COSATU wanted a 40-hour workweek and six months of maternity leave, of which four were to be paid. COSATU also opposed the government's economic strategy, arguing that its focus on reduction of the budget deficit would not promote job creation.

In April Eugene Terreblanche, leader of the extreme-right-wing Afrikaanse Weerstandsbeweging, was convicted of the attempted murder of a black worker and serious assault on another. Clarence Makwetu was replaced as leader of the Pan-Africanist Congress (PAC) in December 1996 by Stanley Mogoba. His supporters refused to accept the change, and eventually Makwetu was expelled from the PAC for three years. In one of a series of advances for black business, Mzi Khumalo's Capital Alliance-led African Mining Group took over the mining house JCI.

The Economy. Economic growth slowed during the year. In 1996 gross domestic product had grown by 3.1%, boosted by agriculture in the first part of the year. In the first quarter of 1997, GDP fell by 1%, but in the second quarter it grew by 2.1%, and growth of 2–2.5% was estimated for the year.

As in the past, economic growth was not matched by growth in employment. Registered unemployment in December 1996 was 4.2 million (29.3% of the economically active population). The government estimated that 71,000 jobs were lost in the nonagricultural sector in 1996 and 42,000 in the first quarter of 1997, against the government's target of creating 126,000 jobs in 1996. Since 1990, 422,000 workers, 7% of the workforce, had lost their jobs.

The rate of inflation in 1996 was 7.4%, the lowest since 1972, but it was projected to increase to 9% in 1997. The bank rate, which had been raised from 16% to 17% in November 1996, was cut to 16% in October 1997. The budget in March estimated 1997–98 spending at R 186,747,000,000 (an increase of 6.1% over the previous year). Education and interest payments on the national debt were the largest items, consuming 21% each. The budget deficit was projected to be 4% of GDP. As of July 1, some exchange controls were relaxed, with residents allowed to invest R 200,000 abroad.

Foreign Affairs. Beginning in February, as Laurent Kabila's (*see* BIOGRAPHIES) Alliance of Democratic Forces for the Liberation of Congo started the military capture of cities in Zaire, President Mandela and Deputy President Mbeki moved to the centre of the African diplomatic stage. They took the lead in mediating between Kabila and Pres. Mobutu Sese Seko of Zaire for a peaceful and democratic transition of power; this included the first face-to-face meeting between Mobutu and Kabila.

Binational commissions similar to that established with the United States were established with Germany and Great Britain. Arms sales continued to provoke controversy. In January the U.S. criticized the government for proposing to sell arms to Syria. A South African newspaper was almost taken to court for having revealed a proposed arms deal with Saudi Arabia. The National Conventional Arms Control Committee, established to oversee arms sales, blocked sales to Turkey. President Mandela made two official state visits to Asian countries, which signifed a "south to south" emphasis in foreign policy.

(MARTIN LEGASSICK)

This article updates the *Macropædia* article SOUTHERN AFRICA: *South Africa.*

SPAIN

Area: 505,990 sq km (195,364 sq mi)
Population (1997 est.): 39,323,000
Capital: Madrid
Chief of state: King Juan Carlos I
Head of government: Prime Minister José María Aznar López

The Popular Party (PP) in 1997 demonstrated that it was adept at leading the coalition it had formed with the various nationalist parties. It was successful despite comments made by the parties during the March election campaign that reinforced the belief that poor relations between the centre-right parties and the centre-left Convergence and Union (Catalan) coalition would preclude any form of cooperation. The fact that the PP plurality in the 1996 election was small gave hope to the Spanish Socialist Workers' Party (PSOE) that it would not be out of power for long.

The PSOE continued to be adversely affected by its connection to the Antiterrorist Liberation Groups (GAL) investigation. GAL, a shadowy organization that carried out a number of extrajudicial killings in the 1980s, was perhaps the turning point in the PSOE electoral defeat. A judicial investigation into the Cesid (state intelligence agency) papers on the case dominated the PSOE's retreat from government. Felipe González Márquez's party leadership was brought into such question over the affair that he was weakened and the PSOE appeared directionless and in disrepute with the judiciary.

Despite GAL's being very useful to the PP in its campaigning against the PSOE, there was pressure on the new government to release sensitive information regarding the case. This fueled further speculation about the role of the civil leadership in Spain. Whereas the scandal suited the PP in opposition, by the end of the year it was turning into an issue that both parties would prefer settled.

In November the benefits of Javier Solana's 1995 appointment to the position of secretary-general of the NATO alliance appeared to reap dividends. These were realized by the promise of considerable progress in the incorporation of Spain into the Integrated Military Command of NATO. The national legislature overwhelmingly supported the PP's position favouring incorporation, which thus seemed to resolve a problem that had dogged Spain's defense planners since the 1980s. The final resolution of the issue, however, hinged upon the status of Gibraltar within NATO and, more significantly for the PP, the status of the Canary Islands. The latter existed within the Portuguese mandate of the Eastern Atlantic and were of concern to the Canarian coalition, a partner in the governing bloc.

Relations with Cuba suffered some deterioration in 1997 when the government inflamed Cuban and Spanish commercial interests by warning Spanish tourists away from the island. This appeared to be retaliation for the poor legal treatment of a Spanish tourist by the Cuban judiciary. An attempt to distance itself from the previous government's position on Cuba raised a number of problems for the PP. Cuba represented one of Spain's most lucrative opportunities for investment, and commercial interests were obviously wary of any interruption to the trade that appeared set to expand.

DUS KO DESPOTOVIC—SYGMA

In Ermua, Spain, a large crowd of mourners look on as pallbearers carry the coffin of Miguel Ángel Blanco, the popular young politician whose death at the hands of Basque separatists in July set off a wave of demonstrations across the country.

Latin America also emerged as a judicial question. After many unsuccessful years in the Chilean courts, Gen. Augusto Pinochet Ugarte, head of state of Chile from 1973 to 1990, was indicted in Spain on charges of genocide and crimes against humanity in connection with the deaths of Spanish nationals following the military coup of September 1973. The issue then shifted to Argentina and the behaviour of military officers there during the "dirty war" of the late 1970s, when thousands of citizens were killed, were imprisoned, or disappeared.

The Basque separatists group Euskadi Ta Askatasuna (ETA) continued to strain the political process, and popular revulsion grew throughout the year against ETA and its political wing, Herri Batasuna. By March a large increase in murders by the organization had heightened tension within the Basque provinces and pressured the Basque Nationalist Party (PNV) to support the government's position of nonnegotiation. Following the July kidnapping and fatal wounding by Basque separatists of a young PP politician, Miguel Ángel Blanco, millions demonstrated in the streets as the parties united to condemn the fatal attack. Finally, on December 1, 23 members of the top leadership of Herri Batasuna were found guilty of aiding ETA and were each sentenced to seven years in prison.

After the PP's first year in office, the goodwill between it and the major nationalist parties in the legislature, the Catalan and the PNV, appeared to have lost strength. Both parties had enjoyed leverage over the previous PSOE government, and the PNV in particular stepped back from colluding too closely with the government.

Perhaps the most significant domestic event of the year was the replacement of González as secretary-general of the PSOE. At the 34th congress of the party, he resigned after 23 years in the post. His replacement, Joaquín Almunia, represented continuity, however, as he was the favoured candidate of González.

The United Left group, led by Julio Anguita, finally succumbed to factionalism. The leadership of Anguita was called into question by the defection of the New Left and of groupings in Galicia and Catalonia. The third largest party in Spain and the inheritors of the communist tradition, the United Left suffered an identity crisis that was intensified by a weak electoral performance in 1996. Some observers considered it possible that the new leadership of the PSOE could move toward increased cooperation with the United Left.

(BENNY POLLACK)

SRI LANKA

Area: 65,610 sq km (25,332 sq mi)
Population (1997 est.): 18,663,000
Capitals: Sri Jayawardenepura Kotte (legislative and judicial); Colombo (executive)
Head of state and government: President Chandrika Kumaratunga, assisted by Prime Minister Sirimavo Bandaranaike

The 14-year-old civil war in Sri Lanka continued unabated in 1997. The Liberation Tigers of Tamil Eelam (LTTE), the guerrilla group that had been fighting the central government since 1983 in its quest for an independent homeland for Sri Lanka's two million Tamils, began the new year with an attack against the army's northern garrison at Paranthan. On January 9 about 3,000 LTTE fighters attacked the camp and captured its main weapons. More than 500 LTTE fighters and more than 200 government personnel died in the assault. Two months later the LTTE conducted simultaneous attacks on the army camp at Vavunatheevu, 217 km (135 mi) east of Colombo, and on the China Bay air force base, 80 km (50 mi) to the north. The LTTE's losses were great; of the 800 guerrillas who fought in the two battles, more than 200 were killed, and about 65 army personnel lost their lives.

Determined to end these attacks, on May 13 the government launched the biggest military offensive yet in the civil war. Operation Sure Victory, which involved more than 20,000 troops, had the objective of recapturing a strategic 72.5-km (45-mi)-long road that linked Jaffna Peninsula with the rest of the island. Within five days government forces had captured Omanthai and Nedunkeni, two strategically located towns on the Vavuniya–Kilinochchi highway. The capture of these two towns cost the lives of more than 250 guerrillas and 53 government soldiers.

On June 10 and June 25, the LTTE launched counterattacks on the army camp at Thandikulam, about five kilometres (three miles) from Vavuniya, the gateway to the Northern province. More than 600 LTTE guerrillas infiltrated government lines and destroyed the ammunition depot at the camp. The LTTE claimed that more than 376 government soldiers had been killed, and the government claimed that over 200 guerrillas had died in battle. More devastating to civilian morale was a powerful bomb that exploded on October 15 in a parking lot in the centre of Colombo, killing 18 and injuring more than 100.

As a result of the bomb attack, the government offered to stop the military offensive if the LTTE was willing to discuss proposals that involved granting increased autonomy to the regional councils administered by Tamils and Muslims. The government, however, also maintained its basic position on talks with the LTTE—the guerrilla group would need to lay down its arms first and agree to arrive at a settlement within a stipulated time frame. This was unacceptable to the LTTE. On April 3 the government and the main opposition, the United National Party, with the help of the British government, agreed to present a common front in negotiations with the LTTE.

(CLAUDE RAKISITS)

SUDAN, THE

Area: 2,503,890 sq km (966,757 sq mi)
Population (1997 est.): 32,594,000
Capitals: Khartoum (executive and ministerial) and Omdurman (legislative)
Head of state and government: President and Prime Minister Lieut. Gen. Omar Hassan Ahmad al-Bashir

In December 1996 former prime minister Sadiq al-Mahdi fled to Eritrea, where he joined forces with the rebel Sudan National Democratic Alliance (NDA). Early in January rebels from the NDA and John Garang's Sudan People's Liberation Army (SPLA) captured Kurmuk and Qeissan, two towns near the Ethiopian border. The Ethiopian authorities strongly denied Sudanese claims that Ethiopian troops had been involved in the attack. Sudanese Pres. Omar al-Bashir nevertheless appealed to the UN Security Council to stop Ethiopian violations of Sudanese territory and also declared a jihad (holy war) against the rebels.

Relations with Uganda also remained strained. In January Ugandan Pres. Yoweri Museveni urged the Organization of African Unity to designate as a colonial war the continuing conflict in southern Sudan, where the SPLA was claiming new successes in his war against the government. Soon afterward the Sudanese minister of defense accused Uganda of having invaded his country at the instigation of the U.S.

Significant changes in government policy were suggested in April by the terms of an agreement between the government and six

Having lost all of their cattle in the ongoing civil war in The Sudan, members of the Dinka tribe attempt to cultivate the land. In 1997 the UN made an urgent call for financial assistance to meet the emergency humanitarian needs of an estimated 4.2 million displaced and war-affected people in the country.

CAROL GUZY—THE WASHINGTON POST

small southern rebel groups that had split from the SPLA in 1991. Under the agreement the government accepted that there should be a referendum on southern self-determination, to be held in 2001, and that legislation imposing the Islamic religious law on the predominantly non-Muslim south would be suspended. This posed a problem for the rebel movement because the northern branch of the NDA insisted upon the unity of The Sudan whereas the SPLA wanted independence for the south. Behind this struggle for supremacy were the emergency humanitarian needs of an estimated 4.2 million displaced and war-affected people in the country.

Persistent attempts to restore peace by Pres. Nelson Mandela of South Africa and Pres. Daniel arap Moi of Kenya seemed to be bearing fruit when Museveni and Bashir agreed to start "a new chapter of cooperation" after a meeting under Moi's chairmanship in Eldoret, Kenya, in May. This was followed by a meeting in Pretoria, S.Af., in August, with Mandela as host, at which progress was made toward easing the tension between The Sudan and Uganda. In September representatives of the government and the SPLA agreed to meet for talks in Nairobi, Kenya, on October 28. The rebel movement was given a boost in December, however, when the U.S. secretary of state met with Garang and NDA leaders in Uganda.

(KENNETH INGHAM)

SURINAME

Area: 163,820 sq km (63,251 sq mi)
Population (1997 est.): 424,000
Capital: Paramaribo
Head of state and government: President Jules Wijdenbosch

On April 28, 1997, The Netherlands declared that it would prosecute the former military dictator of Suriname, Dési Bouterse. At the time, Bouterse was the president of the main government party, the National Democratic Party, to which Pres. Jules Wijdenbosch also belonged, and was considered by most to be the power behind the throne in Suriname. Bouterse was suspected of being one of the leaders of the so-called Suriname Drug Cartel and was to be charged for trafficking in cocaine on a large scale. Interpol issued a request for his arrest. Probably as a reaction to this accusation against Bouterse, President Wijdenbosch created for him the position of adviser of the state, which gave him a diplomatic passport. On August 25 President Wijdenbosch discharged his minister of finance, Motilal (Atta) Mungra, for refusing to adhere to the policy of increasing government spending and inflationary financing. In response, the Hindustan Party of Mungra withdrew from the government coalition, which then held only 22 seats of the 51 in the National Assembly. Many feared that this crisis could be a prelude to the formal return to power of Bouterse as the so-called rescuer of the country.

On October 26 Wijdenbosch announced that the police and the army had foiled an attempted coup. Arrested were 5 civilians and 12 low-ranking soldiers disgruntled with economic, not political, conditions.

(KLAAS J. HOEKSEMA)

SWAZILAND

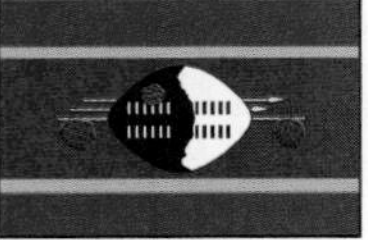

Area: 17,364 sq km (6,704 sq mi)
Population (1997 est.): 1,032,000
Capitals: Mbabane (administrative and judicial), Lozitha and Ludzidzini (royal), and Lobamba (legislative)
Chief of state: King Mswati III
Head of government: Prime Minister Sibusiso Barnabas Dlamini

During 1997 King Mswati III appeared to be playing a cat-and-mouse game with the forces demanding democracy in his country. On July 26, 1996, he had appointed Sibusiso Barnabas Dlamini his new prime minister and announced the creation of a 30-member constitutional review committee. The king called for nationwide submissions of proposed constitutional changes to the committee. These changes had followed an emergency meeting of regional leaders on July 24 in Maputo, Mozambique, to discuss Swaziland's political circumstances.

The slow progress toward change provoked unrest in February 1997 when the Swaziland Federation of Trade Unions coordinated opposition groups that called for amendments to the constitution to end the absolute monarchy and create a multiparty political system. A three-week nationwide strike that began in February halted the country's transportation system and disrupted the important sugar and timber businesses.

The government reacted angrily, and the police used live ammunition to break up crowds of demonstrators. Four labour union leaders were arrested and charged with intimidation, and the strike ended in early March. Talks scheduled for March 5 to address the union demands failed when the government representatives did not appear.

(GUY ARNOLD)

This article updates the *Macropædia* article SOUTHERN AFRICA: *Swaziland.*

SWEDEN

Area: 449,964 sq km (173,732 sq mi)
Population (1997 est.): 8,863,000
Capital: Stockholm
Chief of state: King Carl XVI Gustaf
Head of government: Prime Minister Göran Persson

When they looked back on 1997, Sweden's government ministers would be able to reflect on one major achievement. After an arduous process begun in 1991, they could finally claim victory in their battle to stabilize the government's finances. The national budget, burdened throughout the 1990s by economic weakness and overspending on welfare, would be balanced in 1998, the government announced in its April budget.

This represented a notable achievement, considering that Sweden's annual budget deficit had recently been 12.3% of gross domestic product. It came, though, at the price of popularity for the ruling Social Democratic Labour Party (SAP). Public discontent with high unemployment and continued cuts in welfare spending triggered a downward swing in the SAP's opinion-poll standings. Midyear polls showed the SAP, long unchallenged as Sweden's largest political grouping, trailing the main opposition conservative Moderate Coalition Party for the first time in many years. As 1997 ended, however, the SAP—facing a general election in 1998—had regained a narrow lead.

As the year wore on, Prime Minister Göran Persson's administration could take solace in a decline in the unemployment rate. The official unemployment figure—which excluded the tens of thousands on government-funded work and training projects—had hovered persistently at 8% since the government took power in 1994. In November, however, the figure fell suddenly to 272,000, or 6.5%, the lowest level in five years. Economists attributed the improvement to a healthier economy and the impact of a large-scale government training program announced earlier in the year.

Indeed, such was the newfound health of the economy that Sweden found itself among the group of European Union countries qualified to form the planned European single currency in 1999. The nation was, however, deeply skeptical about many of the plans of the EU, and it came as no surprise in June when the government announced the country's nonparticipation in the monetary union, declaring the project to be "very uncertain."

Outside the political and economic domain, 1997 was punctuated by a string of revelations that discomfited the establishment. The year got off to a sour start in January with newspaper revelations that Sweden may have used as much as seven metric tons of gold bought from Nazi Germany, despite suspicions that the gold may have been stolen from victims of persecution. The disclosures, based upon documents in the Riksbank (central bank) archives, set the scene for the launch of a government inquiry in February into neutral Sweden's role during World War II.

In August the country was rocked by allegations that some 60,000 people, mostly women, were forcibly sterilized as part of a government-sponsored eugenics program between 1935 and 1976. The Health and Social Affairs Ministry ordered an independent inquiry into the role played by politicians and medical officials in regard to the sterilization of the mentally retarded and of Swedes from non-Nordic ethnic backgrounds, under laws that were not repealed until 1976.

Barely a month later a fresh political row erupted. This time the claims were that Säpo, Sweden's security service, had breached a parliamentary edict that in the 1960s banned the keeping of dossiers on citizens because of their political views. It emerged that well into the 1970s Säpo had monitored and compiled files on people with left-wing leanings. The formerly communist Left Party and four other parties demanded an independent commission to examine Säpo's actions. The government conceded the establishment of a parliamentary inquiry but rejected the setting up of a commission, saying it was confident that the compilation of dossiers for political reasons had not been prevalent.

Perhaps the most significant decision made during the year was to begin the controversial shutdown of Sweden's nuclear power industry. Defying a hail of criticism from industry, trade unions, and opposition parties, the SAP announced that the first of the country's 12 reactors would close in 1998, in line with a referendum decision in 1980. As of 1997, nuclear power supplied half of Sweden's electricity needs, but the government insisted that the country could meet the deficit by saving energy and increasing the use of alternative energy sources.

(GREG MCIVOR)

SWITZERLAND

Area: 41,285 sq km (15,940 sq mi)
Population (1997 est.): 7,116,000
Capitals: Bern (administrative) and Lausanne (judicial)
Head of state and government: President Arnold Koller

Many Swiss were considerably startled in 1997 at finding themselves being buffeted by an onslaught of criticism, some of it from within Switzerland itself, concerning their country's actions during and after World War II. (*See* Sidebar.) At the same time, they were confronted throughout the year by announcements of widespread layoffs, attributed largely to the restructuring and takeovers of companies. These, in conjunction with the slow emergence from economic depression and near-zero growth, contributed to rising long-term unemployment. Average overall unemployment, however, decreased to about 5% by late in the year, and despite a depressing number of commercial bankruptcies, economic forecasts became cautiously optimistic. While salaries declined marginally in real terms, as they had since 1990, the cost of health insurance continued to rise inexorably, and many families had to struggle to balance their monthly budgets.

If such were among common everyday concerns for most Swiss, they were overshadowed in the media by periodic blow-by-blow accounts of the federal government's efforts to achieve an agreement with the European Union (EU) on a provisional association of Switzerland with the European Economic Area (EEA)—seen as a move toward full membership in the EU. The staunchly pro-EU government had been rebuffed in a 1992 referendum by rejection of its advocacy, solidly supported by industry and banks, of entry into the EEA. After more than two years of negotiations, its hopes were again dashed in early November when the EU found unacceptable what Switzerland described as its "final" proposals on taxes for 40-ton trucks and on employment and residence in Switzerland of EU nationals. Within a week or so of this setback, however, both sides were reaffirming their confidence that the impasse would be overcome and that, given time, an accord was within reach.

Faced by a national debt approaching $5,750,000,000, the government applied a range of economies—including graduated salary cuts, of 1% to 3% according to grade, for public officials. This example strengthened the resolve of indebted cantonal governments, Geneva and Vaud in particular, to do likewise.

In the cities there was a trend to the political left. To reduce unemployment, unions were supporting a 36-hour week (instead of 40) without wage reductions. Apart from occasional sit-ins and demonstrations, reaction to the layoffs took the form of sometimes heated public discussions regarding the "social and moral responsibility" of large companies that had abruptly laid off workers who then became a financial burden to the government. In the same context, multinational firms were criticized for moving manufacturing plants and other facilities to wherever labour was cheaper. The government, meanwhile, proceeded with plans for clearing the national debt and ensuring a balanced federal budget within five years. Various means, including higher taxes, were being considered for increasing government revenue.

The public was startled again, if momentarily, on September 1 by a mid-morning holdup at a Zürich post office in which five men, armed but not masked, got away with Sw F 55 million. They left several million more behind, there being no more room in their small stolen van disguised as a postal vehicle and fitted with newly stolen official plates. The money, stored in steel boxes, was awaiting transport by an armoured security vehicle to the nearby Swiss National Bank. It was said to have been by far the largest sum thus stolen in the country's history. A Sw F 1 million reward was offered. By mid-October, 17 persons had been arrested in Spain, Italy, and Germany, and some Sw F 25 million had been recovered.

(ALAN MCGREGOR)

Swiss Banks in Disarray

In 1997 the reputation for integrity of the Swiss banking industry, long established as a pillar of Switzerland's economy, was already in question by the time the banks finally announced what they called a "definitive" total in dormant accounts, many opened by German Jews prior to World War II. For years the banks had been slow in coming forward with the totals: $142,857 in 1947, $428,571 in 1949, and $589,286 in 1956. In 1962, after a new law called for identification of all accounts believed to have been opened by persons put to death by the Nazis, the figure was close to $6,790,000. Following 1995 Swiss press reports of still more funds lying in such accounts—plus reaction by the World Jewish Congress (WJC) in conjunction with information from U.S. archives on Swiss banks' and other companies' wartime business with the Third Reich—the total was stated in February 1996 to be just over $27 million. By October 1997 the figure was $42 million, and by year's end, according to a prominent Swiss banker in a televised discussion, it was about $57 million, of which $8.6 million was in accounts under Swiss names.

As 1996 drew to a close, the Swiss government, alarmed that the country's overall image was being harmed, ordered banks not to destroy whatever remained in their archives relating to the period involved. In January 1997, however, security guard Christoph Meili, on his nightly round at the Union Bank of Switzerland (UBS) in Zürich, noticed a bin of documents for shredding, including papers relating to prewar property transactions in Berlin, some of which had apparently Jewish names. He smuggled a few folders out of the bank and told the media what he had done, thereby coming to the attention of the WJC. Meili was sacked and accused of violating banking security, but the case against him was dropped, the judicial authorities realizing how invidious it appeared to the world at large. Invited to the U.S. by the WJC, he went on to visit Israel, where he was acclaimed a virtual hero.

For the banks it was the worst possible scenario. Several U.S. states favoured boycotting the "big three" Swiss banks (UBS, Swiss Bank Corp., and Crédit Suisse). In response, the banks, insurance companies, and business interests, together with the Swiss National Bank (the central bank), set up a special fund for Holocaust survivors (totaling $191 million by the end of 1997). The federal government announced plans for the creation of a Solidarity Foundation—to aid the needy in general—with a capital of $4,640,000,000 to be financed by sales of Switzerland's gold reserves after they were revalued. In the public mind the situation seemed to be linked with Switzerland's wartime dealings with Germany and with the Basel-based Bank for International Settlements, as well as with Nazi thefts of bullion from occupied Europe and of gold, including dental fillings, from extermination camp victims.

Provisional estimates of the cost for these and other conciliatory measures were $286 million for 1997 alone, with much of it being spent on organizing commissions, teams of lawyers, and U.S. public relations firms. By the year's end the banks had issued three lists of dormant accounts, one in July, with 1,872 names of non-Swiss, and the other two in October, with the names of 3,687 non-Swiss and 10,875 Swiss individuals.

(ALAN MCGREGOR)

SYRIA

Area: 185,180 sq km (71,498 sq mi)
Population (1997 est.): 15,009,000
Capital: Damascus
Head of state and government: President Gen. Hafez al-Assad, assisted by Prime Minister Mahmoud Zuabi

Syria assumed a more active role in Middle Eastern affairs in 1997 than it had played in recent years. Confronted with a steadily strengthening strategic partnership between Israel and Turkey, Syria took steps to construct a countervailing alliance by improving relations with Iraq, strengthening ties with Iran, and collaborating more closely with Saudi Arabia.

Reconciling with Iraq served as the linchpin of Syria's new regional diplomacy. In mid-May a trade delegation led by the head of the country's chambers of commerce traveled to Baghdad to discuss ways in which Syria might supply Iraq with food, soap, and medicine in exchange for oil. The border between the two nations, which had been closed for more than 15 years, was formally reopened at the beginning of June. Vice Pres. ʿAbd al-Halim ibn Said Khaddam subsequently welcomed a delegation representing Iraq's chambers of commerce to Damascus, noting that Syria's overtures to Iraq had been undertaken as a response to persistent Turkish efforts to seize control of Kurdish areas in northern Iraq. Syrian officials enlarged and upgraded harbour facilities in Latakia and Tartus in anticipation of heightened activity at those two ports once trade with Iraq revived. Meanwhile, Minister of Foreign Affairs Farouk ash-Shara toured capitals of Persian Gulf nations to assure the leaders of the Gulf Cooperation Council states that his government's budding rapprochement with Iraq would conform to the principles laid down in the 1991 Damascus Declaration, which had called for the establishment of an Arab force as part of a security and economic plan for the region in the aftermath of the Gulf War.

At the same time, Syria moved to solidify its ties to Iran, even as it took steps to mediate between Iran and Saudi Arabia. Iranian Minister of Foreign Affairs Ali Akbar Velayati visited Syria in early July to discuss the future of Persian Gulf security, and Syrian diplomats in Tehran arranged for a Saudi minister of state to confer with Iran's Pres. Hojatolislam Ali Akbar Hashemi Rafsanjani. At the end of July, Syria's Pres. Hafez al-Assad undertook a rare official visit to Tehran to bid farewell to Rafsanjani and offer congratulations to his successor, President-elect Mohammed Khatami. Several of Syria's senior military commanders accompanied President Assad on the trip, ostensibly to discuss ways to improve "strategic regional cooperation and coordination" with their Iranian counterparts.

At the end of June, Syrian officials invited the eight signatories of the Damascus Declaration to Latakia for talks concerning the creation of an Arab common market. The stimulus for the conference was the growing likelihood that Israeli goods and investment capital would penetrate the regional economy as Israel normalized its relations with Jordan, Morocco, Qatar, and Oman. In the wake of the meeting, Syrian leaders took the lead in publicly criticizing the U.S.-sponsored Middle Eastern economic summit that was planned to convene in Qatar at the end of November. Damascus argued that taking part in a multilateral conference attended by Israeli leaders would convince the government of Benjamin Netanyahu that it could enjoy the economic rewards of peace without resolving the major issues that continued to divide Israel from Syria and Lebanon. The potential for Syrian-Israeli conflict escalated in late August when Israel announced that it planned to build a dam across the Yarmuk River at a point on the Syrian side of the pre-1967 boundary. Damascus immediately charged that the proposal "proves that Netanyahu does not want peace and wants only to escalate tensions in the region."

At home, Syrian authorities launched a highly publicized campaign to eradicate corruption in public-sector enterprises. Credit for directing the campaign was given to the president's son, Bashar.

(FRED H. LAWSON)

TAIWAN

Area: 36,179 sq km (13,969 sq mi)
Population (1997 est.): 21,616,000
Capital: Taipei
Chief of state: President Lee Teng-hui
Head of government: Presidents of the Executive Yuan (Premiers) Lien Chan until August 21 and, from September 1, Vincent Siew

At Taiwan's National Development Conference in December 1996, the ruling Kuomintang (KMT, or Nationalist Party) and the opposition Democratic Progressive Party (DPP) agreed on several proposals to revamp the political system. The most important of these gave the president authority to nominate the premier without the consent of the legislature. In return, the legislature was given the power to force the resignation of the Cabinet through a no-confidence vote passed by a simple majority and to impeach and remove the president and vice president by a two-thirds vote on charges of sedition or treason. Another change agreed upon was a drastic reduction in the power and scope of the Taiwan Provincial Government, which was responsible for handling general administrative affairs. In protest against this change, the Taiwan provincial governor, James Soong Chu-yu, a KMT stalwart, submitted his resignation to Pres. Lee Teng-hui, who, however, refused to accept it.

A widespread perception that social order was deteriorating in Taiwan was reinforced in 1997 by the kidnapping and brutal murder of Pai Hsiao-yen, the teenage daughter of popular television entertainer Pai Ping-ping. The slaying, the third in a series of high-profile killings on the island, triggered mass demonstrations in Taipei in May. Protesters criticized the government for not doing enough to enforce law and order and demanded the resignation of the Cabinet. President Lee tried unsuccessfully to mollify public opinion by engineering a limited Cabinet shakeup. Premier Lien Chan announced that he would step down once the National Assembly had adopted the constitutional changes that the KMT and DPP had agreed upon at the National Development Conference. Meeting in extended session, the National Assembly accomplished this task by midsummer, and Lien kept his promise to resign. In his place President Lee appointed KMT legislator Vincent Siew, who had previously held a series of top

A woman is among those praying at Long Shan Buddhist temple in Taiwan. The Dalai Lama, the Buddhist spiritual leader of Tibet, made his first trip to Taiwan in March. The visit, which was opposed by Beijing, underscored the tension between China and Taiwan over the question of sovereignty.

PETER TURNLEY—NEWSWEEK/BLACK STAR

diplomatic and economic management posts. Siew promised to focus on improving social order, raising the quality of life, undertaking a program of spiritual revitalization, and pursuing economic development while enhancing national security and improving ties with China.

Throughout the year President Lee reaffirmed Taiwan's commitment to playing a larger role in world affairs. In March the Dalai Lama paid his first visit to Taiwan. This was followed by a visit in April from U.S. Speaker of the House Newt Gingrich, who departed from official U.S. policy by unequivocally pledging support to Taiwan if China threatened Taiwan's security by military force. Taiwan unveiled its first fleet of 70 domestically built fighter planes named after the late Pres. Chiang Ching-kuo and in April began accepting delivery of 150 U.S.-built F-16s. The U.S. also agreed to sell Taiwan Super Cobra attack helicopters to bolster its defense capabilities.

The greatest cause of uneasiness for Taiwan remained its troubled relationship with China. In late June, one week before China reestablished its sovereignty over Hong Kong (*see* Spotlight: *Hong Kong's Return to China*), Taiwan conducted live-fire military exercises, which international observers interpreted as a signal to China that Taiwan would resist any attempts at reunification. On June 28 an estimated 70,000 people attended a "Say No to China" antireunification rally in Taipei. The government later urged China to protect freedom in Hong Kong but made it clear that Taiwan would not be absorbed in a similar manner. Taiwan had repeatedly rejected Beijing's view that Hong Kong's return to Chinese control under a "one country, two systems" pledge of local autonomy was a model for Taiwan's own eventual return to China. In the November municipal elections, the "shocking" victories of the DPP, which favoured independence for Taiwan, emphasized the problem.

On September 7–10 President Lee led a Taiwanese delegation to the Universal Congress of the Panama Canal, which was intended as a forum for international leaders to discuss the future of the canal once it reverted to Panamanian control after Dec. 31, 1999. In terms of tonnage shipped through the canal, both Taiwan and China were among the top 10 users of the waterway. Taiwan's support of the conference, however, caused China to lead a boycott by a number of heads of state who had planned to attend.

In 1997 Taiwan's economy expanded at a rate in excess of 6%. Inflation remained under control, and exports increased.

(STEVEN I. LEVINE)

TAJIKISTAN

Area: 143,100 sq km (55,300 sq mi)
Population (1997 est.): 6,054,000
Capital: Dushanbe
Chief of state: President Imomali Rakhmonov
Head of government: Prime Minister Yahyo Azimov

Tajikistan's civil war ended officially on June 27, 1997, with the signing in Moscow of peace accords between the government of Pres. Imomali Rakhmonov and the United Tajik Opposition (UTO), a coalition of largely Islamic groups that had been fighting government forces since the end of 1992. Leaders of the two sides agreed in December 1996 to begin a final round of peace negotiations, and during the first half of 1997, hard bargaining over the terms of the accords preceded the signing. The final version of the accords set up a National Reconciliation Commission, to be headed by UTO chief Sayed Abdullo Nuri, with Parliament Speaker Abdulmajid Dostiyev as vice-chairman, and gave the UTO one-third of all government and judicial positions at all levels and in all regions of the country, including areas where there had never been an opposition presence.

Negotiators for the UTO repeatedly expressed concern that the National Revival Bloc of former prime minister Abdumalik Abdullojonov, which represented the interests of northern Tajikistan, was excluded from the peace process at the insistence of the government. In April President Rakhmonov was wounded in an assassination attempt in Khujand, the major city of northern Tajikistan. Opposition and outside observers attributed the attack to anger in the region over the failure to include northern representatives in the final peace negotiations, but the government in Dushanbe used the assault as an excuse for large-scale arrests of northern political activists, including Abdullojonov's brother, who was dying of cancer.

Many small bands of fighters who were outside the control of either the government or the opposition were excluded from the peace process as well. These groups made their presence felt throughout the year, with attacks on both government and opposition forces and the taking of hostages. In February one armed band seized several military observers from the UN Mission in Tajikistan, some staff members of the International Committee of the Red Cross, four Russian journalists, and the minister of security, who had been sent from Dushanbe to negotiate the release of the international hostages. In August Col. Makhmud Khudoiberdiyev, formerly a government supporter, attacked government troops in the vicinity of Dushanbe. After heavy fighting against the regular army, Khudoiberdiyev and his supporters were driven out of their headquarters in the southern part of the country and disappeared. Rumours that Khudoiberdiyev had found refuge in Uzbekistan were hotly denied by Uzbek authorities. The deputy head of the UTO, Akbar Turajonzoda, commented that the only solution to violence by groups left out of the peace process was to bring them into it.

Opposition chief Nuri arrived in Dushanbe on September 11 to take up his duties as chairman of the National Reconciliation Commission, somewhat later than expected owing to several bombings in the city, including one in the Dushanbe hotel where opposition leaders were to live. Despite continuing violence in the capital, the commission began its work of implementing the peace accords.

In mid-October a group of some 70 gunmen attacked the barracks of the Presidential Guard in Dushanbe, killing 14 guardsmen and demonstrating the fragility of the peace in Tajikistan. Opposition spokesman Davlat Usmon stated that the attackers were probably from a group that was formerly part of the UTO but had rejected the peace accords.

(BESS BROWN)

This article updates the *Macropædia* article CENTRAL ASIA: *Tajikistan*.

TANZANIA

Area: 945,090 sq km (364,901 sq mi)
Population (1997 est.): 29,461,000
De facto capital: Dar es Salaam; the legislature meets in Dodoma, the capital designate
Chief of state: President Benjamin William Mkapa
Head of government: Prime Minister Frederick Tulway Sumaye

Pres. Benjamin Mkapa's campaign to root out corruption in high places was bolstered in 1997 by the resignation in late 1996 of two ministers named in a comprehensive report submitted by the nine-man Anti-Corruption Commission appointed by the president. The resignation of Simon Mbilinyi, minister of finance, in November was followed by that of Juma Alifa Ngasongwa in December. Both men said that they had resigned in order to clear the way for a thorough government investigation. A third man, Kilonzo Mporogonyi, deputy minister of finance, was dismissed by President Mkapa in February 1997.

On January 21 it was announced that the largest state-owned bank, the National Bank of Commerce, which had incurred heavy losses over a long period, was to be split into three smaller banks. This was part of the effort to bring greater efficiency into banking and into the economy generally. Faced with having to set aside 40% of its revenue for the year to service the foreign debt, and with a further 40% earmarked for the salaries of state employees, the government, however, had little income left to finance the development programs the country needed.

Fortunately, foreign donors remained willing to help. Following aid of $211 million provided by the European Union late in 1996, the Paris Club of creditors agreed in January to cancel $1 billion of the country's debt and to reschedule an additional $700 million. Ireland, too, offered to make aid to Tanzania a priority, with a promise of £19 million over a three-year period. After Tanzania and Uganda had reaffirmed their interest in cross-border transport links in April, President Mkapa met with the presidents of Kenya and Uganda on April 29 to discuss further measures aimed at creating an East Africa Common Market.

All efforts to improve the country's economic performance and the welfare of its people were, however, hampered by the worst drought in 40 years. The production of coffee and cotton, Tanzania's two biggest foreign-currency earners, had been in decline for several years and dropped again sharply in 1997, and other projects were hard hit by the severe water shortage. Appealing to the international community for aid in September, President Mkapa said that 13 of the country's 20 mainland regions would be unable to produce sufficient food to meet their needs. He forecast that the total food deficit would amount to 916,000 metric tons, of which the bulk would be bought on the open market, but asked foreign donors to provide 92,000 metric tons.

In January Tanzania's exemplary record in dealing with refugees was threatened when Amnesty International sent a delegation to Dar es Salaam to urge the government to stop the forcible repatriation of refugees from the camps in the northwest of the country that had begun in December 1996. In February a new dimension was added to the refugee problem when supporters of Pres. Mobutu Sese Seko of Zaire sought sanctuary in the western region of Kigoma from the attacks of rebels attempting to overthrow his government.

(KENNETH INGHAM)

This article updates the *Macropædia* article EASTERN AFRICA: *Tanzania.*

THAILAND

Area: 513,115 sq km (198,115 sq mi)
Population (1997 est.): 60,602,000
Capital: Bangkok
Chief of state: King Bhumibol Adulyadej
Head of government: Prime Ministers Chavalit Yongchaiyudh until November 6 and, from November 9, Chuan Leekpai

Within weeks of its election in November 1996, the six-party coalition government of Prime Minister Chavalit Yongchaiyudh was encountering considerable social unrest as workers, farmers, students, and businessmen noisily aired their grievances. By early 1997 a growing financial crisis, exacerbated by scandals in banking and property development, had rapidly plunged the nation into its worst recession in decades. The army had to be persuaded to accept huge cuts in military expenditure. On September 8, when opposition parties submitted a no-confidence motion in the National Assembly, the government survived only after Chavalit gave way on constitutional reform. But demands for his ouster intensified, and on November 6 he resigned. Two former prime ministers, Chatichai Choonhavan and Chuan Leekpai, vied to succeed him. Chuan gathered sufficient numbers in the 393-member House of Representatives to form an eight-party coalition with a slim majority, and on November 9 King Bhumibol Adulyadej appointed him prime minister.

A 99-member assembly charged with writing the new constitution began its deliberations in January. The key Drafting Committee was chaired by former prime minister Anand Panyarachun. Despite early criticism that members were being pressured by patronage-dispensing politicians, the document, finalized in August, was much admired for measures to curb vote buying, limit corruption, inject transparency into administration, codify rights of citizens, and eliminate military influence in the Senate. Alarmed at the erosion of their powers, government politicians at first planned to reject the charter, but when the army declared itself in favour and the king intimated support, opposition evaporated, and the new constitution passed a joint sitting of the National Assembly on September 27 by 578 votes to 16. Promulgated October 11, it set a 240-day limit for the government to pass laws establishing a new legislative framework before elections.

Lagging exports, declining labour productivity, excess liquidity, and massive overinvestment in real estate triggered attacks on the baht by international currency speculators in May and June. Though at first these attacks were beaten back by the central bank, pressure continued, which led to the resignation on June 19 of Finance Minister Amnuay Viravan, an implacable foe of devaluation. Thanong Bidaya, a banker, replaced him and immediately announced help for overstretched banks and relaxed limits on foreign shareholding. But the Bank of Thailand was soon forced to suspend operations at 16 finance companies. On July 2, just two days after Prime Minister Chavalit had assured the nation that there would be no devaluation, the central bank, having lost billions of dollars defending the currency, abandoned the peg to a dollar-dominated basket of hard currencies. Within hours the baht had been effectively devalued by almost 20%. On July 29 the bank's governor, Rerngchai Marakanond, was replaced by Chaiyawat Wibulswasdi. As negotiations with the International Monetary Fund (IMF) began, another 42 finance firms were suspended; fully half the nation's banks and quasi banks had been put out of business. On August 11 the IMF detailed a rescue package, soon reaching $17.2 billion, that included contributions from Japan and other neighbouring countries, the Asian Development Bank, and the IMF itself. At the behest of the IMF, $2 billion was cut from the budget, fuel prices were increased, and the value-added tax was hiked from 7% to 10%. The baht, however, continued its slide. Inflation mounted and interest rates soared, even as the stock market plunged to record lows and growth of gross domestic product declined toward zero. On October 19, as a result of Chavalit's decision to reverse the fuel-price increase, Finance Minister Thanong resigned. As the new prime minister, Chuan, began putting together a Cabinet in November, the baht had lost 37% of its value and the situation remained volatile.

(ROBERT WOODROW)

This article updates the *Macropædia* article SOUTHEAST ASIA: *Thailand.*

An investor in Bangkok reads a local newspaper reporting the planned resignation of Thai Prime Minister Chavalit Yongchaiyudh in November. The Thai stock exchange, which had plunged after the devaluation of the nation's currency in July, rose 6.9% on the news of Chavalit's imminent departure.

THAKSINA KHAIKAEW—ASSOCIATED PRESS

TOGO

Area: 56,785 sq km (21,925 sq mi)
Population (1997 est.): 4,736,000
Capital: Lomé
Chief of state: President Gen. Gnassingbé Eyadéma
Head of government: Prime Minister Klutse Kwassi

Togo played an active role in inter-African relations during 1997. In February Pres. Gnassingbé Eyadéma called for an emergency Organization of African Unity summit to deal with the crisis in Zaire. This followed the government's denial in January that Togolese mercenaries were serving with the forces of Zairean Pres. Mobutu Sese Seko. In March the army participated in military exercises with Benin and Burkina Faso. The West African Economic and Monetary Union, consisting of seven French-speaking West African countries, met in Lomé on June 23. In a joint statement, they condemned the May 25 military coup in Sierra Leone and demanded a return to constitutional rule in that nation.

Political activity centred on preparations for the April 1998 presidential elections. In July leaders of the three main opposition parties—the Action Committee for Renewal, the Union of Forces of Change, and the Party for Democracy and Renewal—agreed to unite and choose a single candidate to run against Eyadéma. In October about 500 opposition party members marched through Lomé and accused the government of planning to fix the election.

Togo's cocoa and coffee exports increased by 200% for the 1996–97 season. The European Union agreed to provide $30 million in aid to assist government projects in the areas of health care, education, culture, and the construction of rural roads.

(NANCY ELLEN LAWLER)

This article updates the *Macropædia* article WESTERN AFRICA: *Togo*.

TONGA

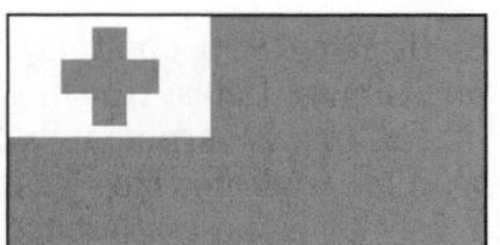

Area: 750 sq km (290 sq mi)
Population (1997 est.): 97,600
Capital: Nuku'alofa
Head of state and government: King Taufa'ahau Tupou IV, assisted by Prime Minister of Privy Council Baron Vaea

Political dissension that began in late 1996 continued into 1997. Three journalists, one also a legislator, associated with the prodemocracy movement had been imprisoned by the Legislative Assembly for contempt in September 1996 because they had published a motion of impeachment against a government minister before the case was officially opened. They had subsequently been released by the chief justice because due process had not been followed. When the speaker of the Legislative Assembly criticized the chief justice's decision, he was found guilty of contempt by the Supreme Court and fined T$1,000.

In March Cyclone Hina caused damage to crops and buildings, mostly on Tongatapu; one person was reported killed. Australia provided aid funds for the development of an environmental management strategy, and the Asian Development Bank provided assistance for agriculture. Prospects for exporting squash to Japan improved following a dismal 1996, when exports were less than half of 1994 levels. In addition, increased spending power was anticipated because of a 6–7% increase in funds remitted by Tongans working overseas.

(BARRIE MACDONALD)

This article updates the *Macropædia* article PACIFIC ISLANDS: *Tonga*.

TRINIDAD AND TOBAGO

Area: 5,128 sq km (1,980 sq mi)
Population (1997 est.): 1,276,000
Capital: Port of Spain
Chief of state: Presidents Noor Mohammed Hassanali and, from March 19, Arthur Napoleon Raymond Robinson
Head of government: Prime Minister Basdeo Panday

The official opposition party, the People's National Movement (PNM), lost two of its members in the House of Representatives in February when both Vincent Lasse and Rupert Griffith crossed the floor to join forces with the coalition government in the capacity of "independents." Both men were given ministerial posts, though they were not invited to join the Cabinet. Their defection reduced the PNM's strength in the House to 15 seats while boosting the United National Congress-led coalition government's support to 21.

Arthur Napoleon Raymond Robinson, prime minister of Trinidad and Tobago when the National Alliance for Reconstruction (NAR) party was in power during 1986–91, was elected president by an electoral college on February 14 and was sworn in on March 19. He replaced Noor Mohammed Hassanali, who retired after having served two five-year terms. In July the NAR, whose sole member in the House was part of the coalition, elected a new leader, Nizam Mohammed. Mohammed was given a mandate to "reestablish the party as an independent political organization."

(DAVID RENWICK)

This article updates the *Macropædia* article The WEST INDIES: *Trinidad and Tobago*.

TUNISIA

Area: 164,150 sq km (63,378 sq mi)
Population (1997 est.): 9,245,000
Capital: Tunis
Chief of state: President Gen. Zine al-Abidine Ben Ali
Head of government: Prime Minister Hamed Karoui

At the start of 1997, Pres. Zine al-Abidine Ben Ali strengthened his control over the government by reshuffling his Cabinet, moving his confidant, Abdallah Kallel, to the justice portfolio. The most important diplomatic event for Tunisia was President Ben Ali's visit to France in October. It had proved difficult to arrange because of a series of contentious issues between the two nations, ranging from the mysterious implication of the president's brother in a drug-smuggling ring in 1995 to the ongoing anxieties in Europe about Tunisia's human rights record. During the visit the Tunisian leader was frequently reminded of French concerns—both official and unofficial—in regard to human rights. Despite these issues, however, the visit was successful in reinforcing economic relations between the two countries and capped a series of ministerial exchanges that had begun with the French defense minister's visit to Tunis in March.

European anxieties over Tunisia's human rights behaviour had led to the release of the veteran politician Mohamed Mouada from house arrest in September. Mouada, a former leader of the opposition party Mouvement des Démocrates Socialistes, had originally been sentenced in early 1996 to 11 years in prison for contacts with a foreign power (Libya) but had been released into house arrest in December 1996. Despite this hopeful development, however, reports of arrests and imprisonment for political reasons continued to emerge throughout the year, causing considerable tensions in Tunisia's diplomatic relationships. Other measures included controls on academic freedom and threats of treason charges against any Tunisian deemed to have misrepresented Tunisia abroad.

At the same time, Tunisia's regional role increased in stature. In March the Tunisian government was able to persuade Libya and Mauritania to reactivate their memberships in the Union Maghreb Arabe—the regional organization that also included Algeria and Morocco but that had been virtually moribund since the start of the 1990s. Relations with Libya also continued to improve and proposals were made to link the two countries' electricity grids by the year 2000 at a cost of $130 million and the ratification of the Gulf of Gabes offshore joint-venture agreement, which would involve a $30 million investment over the next five years and would contribute to the recovery of Tunisia's position as a net oil exporter. Foreign investors, such as British Gas, also reported encouraging exploration results in the oil and gas sector during the year.

In June the International Monetary Fund called for economic reform to be accelerated, with particular reference to the privatization of government-owned assets, a new round of which—designed to raise $1.4 billion—had begun in March. The IMF also pointed to the unemployment level of 15% as too high.

(GEORGE JOFFÉ)

TURKEY

Area: 779,452 sq km (300,948 sq mi)
Population (1997 est.): 63,528,000
Capital: Ankara
Chief of state: President Suleyman Demirel
Head of government: Prime Ministers Necmettin Erbakan and, from June 30, Mesut Yilmaz

The year 1997 in Turkey was dominated by the struggle between Islamists and secularists. Tension between the coalition government formed in June 1996 by Necmettin Erbakan, leader of the Islamist Welfare Party (RP), and the secularist opposition, supported by the armed forces, came to a head at the beginning of the year. On February 1 the secularists were outraged by speeches at a meeting organized by the RP mayor of the Ankara suburb of Sincan to commemorate Ayatollah Ruhollah Khomeini's call for the "liberation" of Jerusalem. The Iranian ambassador, Mohammad Reza Bagheri, who spoke at the meeting and denounced the U.S. and Israel, was forced to leave the country; the Turkish ambassador in Tehran was expelled in retaliation; and the mayor of Sincan was arrested.

On February 4 the armed forces showed their hand by sending a column of armoured vehicles through the streets of Sincan. On February 28, at a meeting of the National

Security Council, the commanders of the armed forces declared that religious reaction had become a greater danger than Kurdish separatism and demanded that the government legislate eight-year compulsory secular education. This demand would entail the closing of religious "middle schools" (for 12–16-year olds) and the limitation of enrollment in religious high schools to the staffing needs of mosques. Erbakan agreed in principle, but he delayed action, and the secularist opposition put pressure on the RP's junior partner, Tansu Ciller's True Path Party (DYP), to quit the coalition.

Pressure on the coalition increased on May 21 when the chief prosecutor asked the Constitutional Court to order the dissolution of the RP for activities against the secular character of the republic. On the same day, labour and employers organizations issued a joint declaration demanding the government's resignation.

As defections from the DYP threatened to deprive the coalition of its slender majority, Erbakan agreed to cede the premiership to Ciller and call early elections. A small right-wing group, the Great Unity Party, promised to support Ciller, who was therefore confident of securing the nomination. Pres. Suleyman Demirel decided, however, to entrust the formation of the new government to Mesut Yilmaz, leader of the centre-right Motherland Party, the second largest party in the national legislature. On June 30 Yilmaz succeeded in forming a minority coalition with the centre-left Democratic Left Party of Bulent Ecevit and with DYP dissidents inside and outside the Democratic Turkey Party. The new secularist government secured legislative endorsement on July 12, by 281 votes to 256, thanks to the support of a second centre-left party, the Republican People's Party, led by Deniz Baykal.

On August 16 the legislature passed the education law demanded by the military. In November the budget bill introduced a three-year stabilization program designed to cure chronic inflation. At the end of the year, the government sought the backing of the International Monetary Fund and the World Bank for the program, which aimed at halving annual economic growth to 3% and reducing inflation to 50% by the end of 1998.

Erbakan's efforts to give an Islamic slant to Turkish foreign policy culminated in the formation of "D8," the grouping of Islamic less-developed countries, at a summit meeting in Istanbul on June 14–15, just as his government was about to fall. Little was heard of this new organization after the change of government.

The new prime minister, Yilmaz, and his foreign minister, Ismail Cem, turned their attention to relations with the West. Their efforts to have Turkey included in the list of countries considered for eventual full membership in the European Union suffered a setback on December 13, when the EU heads of government meeting in Luxembourg decided to invite Turkey to a standing European conference, but refused to commit themselves further. They also stressed that Turkey had to resolve its problems with Greece, assist a Cyprus settlement, and improve its human rights record before it could be considered for membership. Yilmaz turned down the invitation. His principled position earned him popular support at home but perplexed the foreign ministries of the EU nations, which felt the Luxembourg decision was eminently fair. Turkey also went its own way at the December Islamic summit meeting in Iran; President Demirel departed early, apparently to snub protests from Islamic nations over the growing importance of his country's ties with Israel.

Attempts at dialogue with Greece culminated in a meeting between Yilmaz and Greek Prime Minister Konstantinos Simitis in Crete in November, but they succeeded only in preventing clashes and did not advance a solution. There was no letup either in the insurgency led by the radical Kurdish Workers' Party (PKK) in southeastern Turkey. Turkish troops crossed repeatedly into the Kurdish areas of northern Iraq to destroy PKK bases. They secured the cooperation of Mas'ud al-Barzani's Kurdish Democratic Party and supported it against its rival, Jalal at-Talabani's Patriotic Union of Kurdistan.

(ANDREW MANGO)

TURKMENISTAN

Area: 488,100 sq km (188,500 sq mi)
Population (1997 est.): 4,695,000
Capital: Ashgabat
Head of state and government: President Saparmurad Niyazov

The government's decision at the beginning of January 1997 to end subsidized allocations of flour for all citizens was an indication that Turkmenistan's economy was suffering from the failure of its customers within the Commonwealth of Independent States (CIS) to pay for deliveries of Turkmen gas. During a state visit to Moscow in August, Pres. Saparmurad Niyazov charged that Russia was hampering the export of Turkmen gas to customers outside the CIS who would pay in hard currency because Russia wanted to monopolize the export market. The U.S. decision in July not to oppose a pipeline project to transport Turkmen gas across Iran represented a major boost for Turkmenistan's gas industry by freeing the country from its dependence on Russia for access to foreign markets.

During most of 1997 Turkmenistan was embroiled in quarrels with Azerbaijan over the ownership of offshore oil deposits in the Caspian Sea. The disputes were the result of the failure of the Caspian littoral states to agree on national delimitations of the sea. An argument over the Serdar field in the first half of 1997 was resolved when Azerbaijan accepted the Turkmen claim. In July Turkmen Foreign Minister Boris Shikhmuradov proposed the creation of a joint Turkmen-Azerbaijani commission to establish the sea boundaries of the two countries. The proposal was not acted upon, however, and at the end of September, Turkmenistan demanded that Azerbaijan and an international petroleum consortium pay compensation for the development of two offshore oil fields that Turkmenistan considered to be at least partially its property. (BESS BROWN)

This article updates the *Macropædia* article CENTRAL ASIA: *Turkmenistan.*

TUVALU

Area: 25.6 sq km (9.9 sq mi)
Population (1997 est.): 10,300
Capital: Government offices in Vaiaku, Fongafale islet, of Funafuti atoll
Chief of state: Queen Elizabeth II, represented by Governor-General Tulaga Manuella
Head of government: Prime Minister Bikenibeu Paeniu

The political crisis of late 1996 continued with Prime Minister Kamuta Latasi refusing to test the support for his government by calling Parliament into session. He was, however, defeated 7–5 on a no-confidence motion when Parliament met in December and was replaced a week later by former prime minister Bikenibeu Paeniu. Paeniu restored the Union Jack to the national flag of the former British colony and throughout 1997 adopted a strong stance on the need to control emissions of greenhouse gases in order to ensure the survival of low-lying island nations.

The economy remained heavily dependent on aid and income from citizens living abroad. The Tuvalu Trust Fund performed well, providing some $A 3.9 million for distribution and allowing the reinvestment of $3 million, bringing the total in the fund to $A 35.3 million. The government continued its efforts to find opportunities for overseas employment, as the jobs of about 1,000 of its citizens currently working in Nauru were jeopardized by the projected exhaustion of that country's phosphate deposits within a decade.

(BARRIE MACDONALD)

This article updates the *Macropædia* article PACIFIC ISLANDS: *Tuvalu.*

UGANDA

Area: 241,038 sq km (93,065 sq mi)
Population (1997 est.): 20,605,000
Capital: Kampala
Head of state and government: President Yoweri Museveni, assisted by Prime Minister Kintu Musoke

Uganda's record of economic reform, backed by generous assistance from donor countries, resulted in the nation's becoming the first to qualify for help under a World Bank project to ease the burden of debt of the 20 most heavily indebted countries. The terms appeared generous, but satisfaction turned to dismay when it was learned that aid would not be received until April 1998. Consequently, plans to provide universal primary education with the help of the money saved by the debt-relief measures had to be postponed.

Drought in the eastern part of the country early in the year was followed by famine. In

FRED HOOGERVORST—PANOS

A boy carries a load of bricks in Bigodi, Uganda. Pres. Yoweri Museveni, through the National Poverty Eradication Plan, launched an initiative to enhance rural development, improve health care, and provide universal primary education for Uganda, where about half the population was under age 15.

March, as the first consignment of relief food was distributed in Kumi district, the most severely affected region, the district agricultural officer said that people were starving in 8 of the district's 16 counties. The Ministry of Labour and Social Services estimated that $24 million would be needed to combat the famine, which by June was affecting half of Uganda's population. This was a particularly serious setback for a country where food was normally plentiful.

Throughout the year attempts at mediation by Iran, by Pres. Daniel arap Moi of Kenya, and by Pres. Nelson Mandela of South Africa testified to the obstinate nature of the long-running dispute between Uganda and its neighbour, The Sudan, with each side offering assistance to rebel movements challenging the authority of their respective governments. The bitterness of the campaign was highlighted in a report, published in June, by an Amnesty International team that spent two weeks in northern Uganda. The team claimed to have been shocked by the systematic nature of the gross abuses perpetrated by the rebels but added that the Ugandan army, though not nearly so culpable, was not wholly innocent of human rights abuses.

Sporadic fighting also disturbed the western borderland. Insurgents of the Allied Democratic Forces, having enlisted additional recruits from armed groups in eastern Zaire, posed an increasing threat both to the villagers living on the slopes of the Ruwenzori Mountains and to plans to extract valuable cobalt from the waste dumps from the Kilembe mines. Uganda's favourable standing in the eyes of donor countries was illustrated by the fact that funds for the cobalt-processing plant were being provided by a French-Australian mining company, La-Source, and grants and loans were made by the European Union and North Korea to set up a hydroelectric power station, a foundry to supply spare parts for the whole western region, and a limestone quarry.

Because of the role played by Pres. Yoweri Museveni in the campaigns against The Sudan and against Pres. Mobutu Sese Seko of Zaire, the U.S. was particularly well-disposed toward Uganda, supplying arms and military training. A less-beneficial result of the government's military activities, however, was revealed in the annual budget, in which 20% of the nation's revenue was revealed to have been allocated to defense spending. Further concern was aroused by the news that the growth rate, which had peaked at 10% in 1995, was expected to fall to 5% in 1997. (KENNETH INGHAM)

This article updates the *Macropædia* article EASTERN AFRICA: *Uganda.*

UKRAINE

Area: 603,700 sq km (233,100 sq mi)
Population (1997 est.): 50,668,000
Capital: Kiev
Chief of state: President Leonid Kuchma
Head of government: Prime Ministers Pavlo Lazarenko until July 2 and, from July 16, Valery Pustovoytenko

The year 1997 proved a complex one for Ukraine, with continuing tensions between president and parliament and between president and prime minister. In July, shortly after leading a trade delegation on a much-publicized visit to Canada, Prime Minister Pavlo Lazarenko formally resigned and was replaced two weeks later by Valery Pustovoytenko, formerly the mayor of Dnipropetrovsk. Lazarenko had been criticized publicly by Pres. Leonid Kuchma for his failure to deal with corruption—and even possibly being a part of it himself. Pustovoytenko inherited the Clean Hands program, initiated by Kuchma in mid-February to root out government corruption. These efforts were denounced by Serhy Holovaty, the reform-minded minister of justice, who also lost his position in August.

The political arena remained volatile, notably because the parliament was chaired by Socialist Party chief Oleksandr Moroz, who was often at odds with President Kuchma. The 1997 budget, for example, was not passed until June. Kuchma was clearly unhappy with the most significant legislation of the year, a new law on parliamentary elections that divided the 450-seat legislature into two 225-seat parts for the elections scheduled for March 29, 1998; half the deputies were to be elected in single-mandate territorial districts, the other half from slates of parties or blocs. It took 13 tries to get the bill through the parliament before it was accepted on September 24 by a bare majority and reluctantly signed by the president on October 22. The election law and the process it went through were hailed by some as evidence that Ukraine maintained—by post-Soviet standards—a relatively strong legislature.

The rifts among political leadership focused attention on the parliamentary elections in 1998 and the presidential elections in 1999. Four candidates had already announced their intention to seek the presidency: Kuchma; Lazarenko, now the government leader of Dnipropetrovsk region; former prime minister and police chief Yevhen Marchuk; and Holovaty.

Despite optimistic official statements and generous aid from the International Monetary Fund (IMF), Ukraine continued to struggle economically. During the first nine months of the year, gross domestic product fell by 5% compared with the same period in 1996, which indicated that the economic decline had not yet "bottomed out." By November failure to pay debts had resulted in the impounding of Ukrainian ships at some foreign ports.

Kuchma convoked the Supreme Economic Council on September 12 to hammer out a socioeconomic policy to the year 2000. It was anticipated that some of the $2.4 billion backlog of wages owed to government workers and $3.7 billion due to the pension fund would be met by the year's end. Unemployment continued to rise and reached 516,358 by April.

Foreign investment, on the other hand, led by companies in the U.S. and Germany, rose by a healthy 46.1% in the first half of the year (over the 1996 figure). The IMF and President Kuchma alike stressed the importance for the future of establishing small and medium-sized private businesses, which had yet to receive adequate incentives from the parliament.

In July, Minister of Health Andriy Serdyuk announced that over the past six years, life expectancy among males had fallen from 64.7 to 61.2 years and that the population overall had fallen by 1,150,000 to 50,900,000 by Jan. 1, 1997. For the past few years, the mortality rate had exceeded the birthrate, apparently linked to the continuing drop in living standards. Crime rates remained high; Borys Derevyanko, the editor in chief of the main independent newspaper in Odessa, was assassinated on August 11.

In the international sphere an accord was reached with Russia on May 28 on the long-disputed question of the disposition of the Black Sea Fleet. Russia was given about 80% of the fleet and use of two of the main Black Sea ports, Sevastopol and South Bay. Ukraine received the more distant Striletskaya Bay and $526 million in compensation for the loss of ships. Russia agreed to lease facilities at Sevastopol for $100 million a year for 20 years, with the payments marked off against Ukraine's existing $3 billion debt to Russia. This accord cleared the way for the 10-year political treaty signed three days later by which, among other provisions, Russia recognized the political and territorial integrity of Ukraine, including the Crimean Peninsula. Though partly symbolic, the treaty stabilized relations with Russia for the first time since Ukraine declared independence in August 1991. Another round of bilateral talks in Kiev and Moscow in November led to the resolution of a trade dispute between the two countries, and both agreed to abolish the 20% value-added tax that they had been imposing on imports from the other country.

In mid-July the Kiev-based Social Monitoring Centre announced the results of a poll, based on more than 2,000 respondents from all regions, that indicated that 44% of Ukrainians supported the idea of joining the Russia-Belarus union (announced on April 2, 1997), 32% were opposed, and 24% were undecided.

Relations with the West, and particularly the U.S., remained cordial. Foreign Affairs Minister Hennady Udovenko visited Washington, D.C., in March and had discussions on NATO expansion with Secretary of State Madeleine Albright. (*See* BIOGRAPHIES.) On July 9 Kuchma and the leaders of the 16 NATO countries signed a charter on a "Distinctive Partnership Between NATO and Ukraine," which provided for regular consultations and cooperation on a number of issues but did not go as far as the Ukrainians wished—namely, to provide a NATO guarantee of the security of Ukraine and military status within NATO. A similar document was signed by Russia and the NATO states at the same time.

In September, by acclamation, Udovenko was elected president of the 52nd session of the United Nations General Assembly.

(DAVID R. MARPLES)

UNITED ARAB EMIRATES

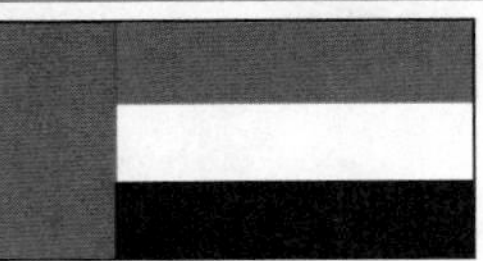

Area: 83,600 sq km (32,280 sq mi)
Population (1997 est.): 2,580,000
Capital: Abu Dhabi
Chief of state: President Sheikh Zaid ibn Sultan an-Nahayan
Head of government: Prime Minister Sheikh Maktum ibn Rashid al-Maktum

The economy of the United Arab Emirates (UAE) continued its robust expansion in 1997. Gross domestic product (GDP) grew about 10% in 1996, the highest rate in the Middle East, and in 1997 it rose a substantial 4.4%. Significantly, two-thirds of the growth was from sources other than oil. The UAE's per capita income was highest in the region at $21,322. The country was a significant foreign donor, giving nearly 4% of its GDP to 13 international development organizations, including the International Monetary Fund and the World Bank.

Despite the government's effort to reduce the number of resident foreigners, the country remained heavily dependent on foreign labour, which constituted more than 80% of the workforce. At the same time, the government invested substantially in education for its citizens, with enrollment at the university and the colleges of technology growing to 15,000; in addition, several thousand were studying abroad.

Iran was the Emirates' primary foreign policy concern in 1997 even after the election to the Iranian presidency in May of Mohammad Khatami (*see* BIOGRAPHIES), who called for improved relations with Iran's neighbours. UAE officials protested Iranian military activities in the Persian Gulf, especially in regard to the ownership of three Gulf islands, which had been the subjects of disputes for many years. Most Arab governments supported the UAE in this confrontation.

(WILLIAM A. RUGH)

UNITED KINGDOM

Area: 244,100 sq km (94,251 sq mi)
Population (1997 est.): 58,919,000
Capital: London
Chief of State: Queen Elizabeth II
Head of Government: Prime Ministers John Major and, from May 2, Tony Blair

Domestic Affairs. Three separate events—one widely predicted, one long-hoped-for, and one a sudden shock—made 1997 an important year for the United Kingdom. The widely predicted event was the election on May 1 of a Labour government after 18 years in opposition (*see* Sidebar) and the resultant arrival of a new prime minister, Tony Blair. (*See* BIOGRAPHIES.) The long-hoped-for event was the renewal of the Irish Republican Army's (IRA's) cease-fire on July 20. (See *Northern Ireland,* below.) The sudden shock was the death of Diana, princess of Wales, in Paris on August 31. (*See* OBITUARIES.)

Following Labour's election victory, Blair said, "We ran for office as New Labour and we will govern as New Labour." By this, the new prime minister indicated that his government would keep to the centrist political strategy he had developed in opposition and not revert to the party's former left-wing policies. On May 7 Blair addressed a meeting of Labour MPs and warned them not to step out of line: "You are here because of the Labour Party under which you fought. You are the ambassadors for New Labour and ambassadors for the Government." Only a tiny minority of MPs, describing themselves as "old Labour," were reluctant to accept this discipline. The great majority acquiesced, either because they were enthusiastically pro-Blair or because they acknowledged that the size of Labour's victory owed much to the way Blair had transformed the party since his election as leader in July 1994.

Blair appointed Labour's deputy leader, John Prescott, deputy prime minister and secretary of state for the environment, transport, and the regions; his long-standing political ally Gordon Brown chancellor of the Exchequer; one of Labour's sharpest brains and best debaters, Robin Cook, foreign secretary; the man who had run Blair's party leadership campaign in 1994, Jack Straw, home secretary; the U.K.'s first blind Cabinet minister, David Blunkett, education secretary; and Lord Simon, former chairman of British Petroleum, the minister for trade and competitiveness in Europe. (*See* BIOGRAPHIES.)

On May 14 the Queen's Speech (a ritual event at the beginning of each parliamentary session) set out the new government's priorities. These included measures to reduce class sizes and raise education targets in state-run schools, a "welfare-to-work" plan, and legislation to introduce a national minimum wage. The Queen's Speech also contained a package of constitutional measures, including an exploration of the need for a Freedom of Information Act and the incorporation into British law of the European

Convention on Human Rights. Two of the most significant proposals concerned referenda on devolution in Scotland and Wales.

Scotland's referendum was held on September 11. This comprised two separate questions. First, did the Scots want to set up their own parliament in Edinburgh, with wide law-making powers and control over services such as health and education? Second, did the Scots want this new parliament to have the power to vary the standard rate (which would still be levied on a U.K.-wide basis from London) of income tax and set a rate that would differ from the rest of the country by up to 3%? On a 60% turnout, both questions produced an emphatic "yes" majority, with 74% voting "yes" on question one and 63% on question two.

Wales's referendum, held on September 18, had one question on the ballot: Did the Welsh want their own assembly, with the power to administer public services in Wales? (Since the assembly would not have its own powers to levy taxes or pass laws, it was not to be called a parliament.) The Welsh proved less enthusiastic than the Scots. On a 50% turnout, voters divided 50.3% "yes" and 49.7% "no." Despite the narrowness of the victory, Blair claimed a mandate to proceed with the legislation to set up both a parliament for Scotland and an assembly for Wales.

In spite of Labour's large majority, Blair established a special Cabinet committee on constitutional issues and invited the Liberal Democrats to join it. The committee's purpose was to establish as broad a cross-party consensus as possible on steps toward incorporating the European Convention on Human Rights into British law, reform of the House of Lords, and the implementation of a preelection agreement between the two parties to hold a referendum, due in 1999, on whether to change the voting system for the House of Commons.

The Conservatives, meanwhile, had to come to terms with their massive defeat. On May 2 John Major, having lost his post as prime minister, announced his intention to resign as party leader. In both of the first two ballots, on June 10 and June 17, the pro-European former chancellor of the Exchequer Kenneth Clarke held a narrow lead, but he failed to secure an outright majority. In the third ballot William Hague (*see* BIOGRAPHIES) defeated Clarke by 92 votes to 70.

Hague immediately announced a radical overhaul of the party: changes in its constitution to give ordinary members a greater say in its affairs, a ban on foreign donations to party funds (an issue that had embarrassed the Conservatives before the election), and the publication of the sources and details of all large donations. His biggest organizational task was to revive the party's membership, which had fallen by 80% in 20 years from 1,500,000 to 300,000.

Hague's early months as Tory leader were plagued by continuing divisions within the party over its policy toward Europe. In October Hague announced that he would oppose British membership in Europe's single

Labour's Return to Power

On May 1, 1997, the voters of the U.K. dispatched the Conservative Party into opposition after 18 years in power and replaced it with the Labour Party and a new prime minister, Tony Blair. (*See* BIOGRAPHIES.) The election set a number of records:

- It gave Labour more seats (418) and a bigger majority (179) than the party had ever achieved before.
- The number of women elected to the House of Commons, 120, easily beat the previous record of 60.
- The Conservatives suffered their lowest share of the popular vote (30.7%) since 1832 and won their fewest number of seats (165) since 1906.
- For the first time ever, the Conservatives emerged from the election with no MPs from Scotland or Wales.
- Seven outgoing Cabinet ministers were defeated in their own local constituencies—the largest number at any election in the 20th century.
- The Liberal Democrats won more seats (46) than at any election since 1929.

Conservative Prime Minister John Major's outgoing government had never recovered completely from "Black Wednesday"—Sept. 16, 1992—the day the U.K. was forced to leave the European exchange-rate mechanism and devalue the pound. During the next two years, a series of tax increases were implemented in order to restore equilibrium to the U.K.'s public finances.

Labour, meanwhile, had made itself more appealing to the electorate, choosing the charismatic Blair as leader in July 1994 and ridding itself of its traditional commitment to state socialism in April 1995. The party rebranded itself as New Labour in an effort to show voters that it had changed. In particular it promised not to increase the standard (23%) or higher (40%) rates of income tax.

During the six-week election campaign, two other factors harmed the Conservatives: they remained divided over Britain's relations with the rest of the European Union (EU), and they failed to rid themselves of their reputation for individual malpractice, or "sleaze." The former trade and industry minister, Neil Hamilton, refused to stand down as Tory candidate for the normally strongly Conservative constituency of Tatton in the north of England despite having been accused of taking bribes from Egyptian-born businessman Mohammed Al Fayed. (*See* BIOGRAPHIES). By contract, Labour and the Liberal Democrats withdrew their candidates in favour of an independent candidate, Martin Bell, a well-known former war correspondent for BBC television. This widely publicized local contest embarrassed the Conservatives nationally and culminated in a clear victory for Bell, who became the first independent MP since 1950.

The election saw the intervention of a new party, the Referendum Party, founded by the financier Sir James Goldsmith (*see* OBITUARIES) to campaign for a referendum on Britain's relationship to the EU. He spent £20 million—as much as Labour or the Conservatives—on a campaign to support candidates in 547 of the U.K.'s 659 constituencies, but his party won only 2.6% of the vote, and none of its candidates was elected.

(PETER KELLNER)

British Prime Minister Tony Blair acknowledges a cheering crowd as he begins to promote his program to eliminate welfare dependency. Blair had become prime minister after leading the Labour Party to its largest parliamentary majority ever in the general election on May 1.

ROY LETKEY—FSP/GAMMA

currency union throughout the current Parliament and the following one—that is, for up to 10 years.

Apart from politics, the event that overshadowed the year was the death of Diana almost exactly one year after her divorce from Prince Charles. (*See* BIOGRAPHIES.) In a spontaneous outpouring of public grief, crowds of people laid millions of bouquets of flowers worth an estimated £25 million outside the princess's London residence, Kensington Palace, and outside Buckingham Palace. In addution, many thousands stood in line for hours at Buckingham Palace and elsewhere to sign books of condolence. At her funeral, in Westminster Abbey on September 6, the singer Elton John performed a new version of his song "Candle in the Wind," the CD of which quickly set sales records worldwide.

The reaction of Great Britain's royal family to Diana's death came under criticism from sections of the media, which questioned Queen Elizabeth's reluctance to allow the union flag to fly at half-staff over Buckingham Palace. Tradition dictated that the only flag to adorn the large pole was the royal standard, and then only when the queen was in residence. At the time of Diana's death, the queen was on holiday at Balmoral Castle in Scotland, and the pole was empty. Eventually, the queen relented; the union flag flew at half-staff over Buckingham Palace on the day of Diana's funeral. This incident sparked a wider debate about the future role of the monarchy in British life. By year's end feelings about the royal family had improved somewhat. Prince Charles had worked to improve his public image; the queen and Prince Philip celebrated their 50th wedding anniversary; and several popular reforms were announced, including plans to convert Kensington Palace to a museum.

Diana's brother, Charles, Earl Spencer, among others, blamed the press for her death. In response to widespread public revulsion at the aggressive photographers known as paparazzi and the use of their photographs by some British newspapers, the leading editors announced that they would henceforth not buy pictures obtained under circumstances that invaded the privacy of public figures, except when justified by compelling public interest. In particular, the editors agreed to abide by a request from Prince Charles that his and Diana's two sons, Princes William and Henry, be allowed to grow up without being harassed by reporters or photographers.

Economic Affairs. The first major decision of the incoming Labour government was to grant the Bank of England the right to determine interest rates independently of the chancellor of the Exchequer. The bank was instructed to operate within a general framework of keeping inflation down but also of maintaining steady economic growth. This decision, announced on May 6, was widely welcomed by London's financial community as a sign of the government's intention to maintain inflation within its new target range of 1.5–3.5%.

The bank used its powers to increase its base interest rates in a series of quarter-point steps, from 6% at the time of the election to 7% by August. Clarke, the outgoing Conservative chancellor, rejected criticism that he had kept the base rate artificially low before the election. The bank acted in order to prevent Britain's economy from overheating. In July the government forecast that output would grow by 3.5% in 1997 and 2.5% in 1998. Unemployment continued to fall throughout 1997, from 1.9 million in December 1996 to 1.4 million a year later, the lowest figure since 1980.

The new government decided to confirm the overall levels of public spending that had been set for 1997–98 and 1998–99 by the previous Conservative administration—with one exception. On July 2, in his first budget speech, Brown announced a windfall tax totaling £5.2 billion on the profits of utility companies—such as gas, water, and electricity—that had been privatized during the 1980s and early '90s. Most of the money was to be spent on a new welfare-to-work program aimed at providing training, job subsidies, child care, and other support services to help people join, or rejoin, the labour market. Brown also announced extra funds for health and education in 1998–99, but this money was to come from the contingency reserve (general, unallocated funds) and not increase the overall total of public spending.

Brown reported modest increases in taxation in order to reduce government borrowing, which he forecast would fall from £13,250,000,000 in 1997–98 to £5.5 billion, or well under 1% of gross domestic product, in 1998–99. Although Brown redeemed Labour's election promise not to increase income tax rates, he revealed plans for tax relief on mortgage interest payments and changes in company taxation that would reduce the value of the tax shelter enjoyed by people building up a company or private pension.

On October 27 Brown ruled out British participation in the European Union's (EU's) single currency until after the next general election (due by June 2002), "barring fundamental unforeseen change in economic circumstances." Brown also announced that preparations would begin to enable Britain to join the single currency shortly after the next election if conditions were right.

Foreign Affairs. On May 12 Foreign Secretary Cook launched a mission statement outlining the foreign policy aims and objectives of the incoming Labour government. Its overall purpose was uncontroversial—"to promote the national interests of the United Kingdom and to contribute to a strong world economy." What received the most attention, however, was a specific pledge "to spread the values of human rights, civil liberties and democracy which we demand for ourselves."

On May 21 the government announced a complete ban on the manufacture, transfer, export, and import of antipersonnel land mines. At midnight on June 30/July 1 the U.K. handed Hong Kong over to China in a short ceremony attended by Blair and Prince Charles. (*See* Spotlight: *Hong Kong's Return to China.*) Hong Kong had been the last significant colony ruled by Britain; the few remaining dependent territories all had tiny populations. On July 1 the U.K. rejoined UNESCO.

On July 28 the government announced that in line with its ethical principles, "we will not issue an export license if there is a clearly identifiable risk that the proposed export might be used for internal repression." Despite this declaration, the government allowed the delivery to Indonesia of Hawk jets and Alvis armoured vehicles, even though the former Conservative government had admitted that previous British-supplied armoured vehicles had been used to suppress protests against the Indonesian government. Cook defended the sale on the grounds that export licenses had been used before Britain's general election and could not be revoked.

The new Labour government pursued a policy on Europe which differed from that of its Conservative predecessors. As well as signifying a wish in principle to join the EU's single currency, though not in the first wave (see *Economic Affairs*, above), the new government signed the social chapter of the 1992 Maastricht Treaty. Britain also agreed to sign the "Amsterdam Treaty" following the summit of EU heads of government in Amsterdam in June; this reversed the policy of the previous Conservative government.

Northern Ireland. The IRA continued its campaign of sporadic violence during the early months of 1997, although at a more subdued level than before the 1995–96 cease-fire.

On June 25 Blair announced that a new round of talks on the future of Northern Ireland would start in September, whether or not the IRA had called a new cease-fire. The prime minister told the House of Commons that the British government had written to Sinn Fein (the political arm of the IRA) that it could participate in the new talks six weeks after the IRA had called a new cease-fire. The British and Irish governments published joint proposals on an agreement that there would have to be "some decommissioning" of weapons during negotiations on a long-term political settlement but that Sinn Fein would be able to take part in those negotiations before the IRA started to hand over any of its weapons.

On July 19 the IRA announced that a new cease-fire would come into effect at noon the following day, and on August 6 Marjorie Mowlam, the Northern Ireland secretary for Great Britain, met Gerry Adams, the president of Sinn Fein, for talks in Belfast. Mowlam announced on August 29 that Sinn Fein would be admitted to the peace talks, which were scheduled to start on September 15. A small IRA splinter group, calling itself the Continuity IRA, rejected the cease-fire, but its attempts to maintain a campaign of violence against British rule proved to be more of a minor irritant during the latter months of 1997 than a serious threat to the peace process.

Initially both of the main Unionist parties refused to join the talks. On September 17, however, David Trimble, the leader of the larger of the two parties, the Ulster Unionist Party, announced that his party would join the talks in order to "expose their [Sinn Fein's] fascist character." Trimble initially refused to conduct face-to-face negotiations with Sinn Fein, but tense talks began on September 23.

On December 11 the IRA received a further bonus from its cease-fire when Blair welcomed two leading members of Sinn Fein to the prime minister's residence in Downing Street, the first time since 1921 that leading figures associated with the IRA had been received there.

(PETER KELLNER)

See also *Commonwealth of Nations; Dependent States.*

UNITED STATES

Area: 9,363,364 sq km (3,615,215 sq mi), including 204,446 sq km of inland water but excluding the 155,534 sq km of the Great Lakes that lie within U.S. boundaries
Population (1997 est.): 267,839,000
Capital: Washington, D.C.
Head of state and government: President Bill Clinton

In 1997 the United States experienced a truly vintage year: a time of peace, prosperity, relative harmony, and rising prospects—favourable indicators that had not been seen for at least 25 years. On the world stage the U.S. stood unchallenged as the globe's sole superpower, and at home a business expansion already some seven years old continued. The U.S. was also at the centre of a global reorganization of production—the so-called new economy of computers and the Internet. As financial storms battered other parts of the world, U.S. stock markets were at an all-time high, and unemployment was at a 25-year low and shrinking. Inflation, the bane of fiscal conservatives during any economic surge, was virtually nonexistent, even though wages, for years stagnant as the economy endured painful restructuring, were finally on the rise. Unlike 25 years earlier, no great social or political conflicts shook the nation. Crime, the blight of the urban U.S., was on a sustained decline, and welfare rolls were shrinking dramatically.

Domestic Affairs. In Washington, D.C., Pres. Bill Clinton showed himself to be less of a master bridge builder than a shrewd fence straddler. In the wake of his resounding 1996 election victory, Clinton, the first Democrat to have won reelection since Franklin D. Roosevelt, continued to follow his "triangulation" strategy—placing himself to the right of most Democrats and to the left of most Republicans. His popularity ratings stayed consistently above 50% through much of the year, despite a variety of alleged and interminable scandals and investigations that had become a hallmark of his presidency. Even with a Republican-dominated Congress, Clinton achieved a goal that had eluded presidents since 1969—an extraordinary bipartisan agreement to balance the federal budget by the year 2002. In the process he presided over the largest U.S. tax cut since 1981, including reductions in capital gains (the maximum rate would drop from 28% to 20%) and estate taxes (the basic $600,000 exemption would double over time). In all, the tax reductions were estimated to be worth $96 billion over five years and $282 billion over a decade. In addition, Clinton doled out billions in additional subsidies for middle-class college education and health insurance for children.

The main parts of the deal included a $58 billion reduction in nonmilitary spending, about $12 billion more than Clinton had originally proposed. More than $115 billion was also anticipated in savings from Medicare programs. Despite the austerity, the agreement provided $34 billion for important presidential priorities, including health insurance for up to 10 million children not covered by private or public plans. It also allowed for restoration of welfare benefits to legal immigrants who had been dropped during the budgetary wars of 1996, expansion of student loan programs, and new funding for early childhood assistance through Head Start programs. The $135 billion tax cuts were offset somewhat by the $50 billion saved by raising tax revenues on airline tickets and by closing alleged tax loopholes. Both the spending and the tax portions of the budget passed the two houses of Congress by wide margins.

The sudden breakthrough in fiscal probity was attributed to economic growth, which changed government projections for social outlays and tax inflows and reduced the estimated budget deficit in 1997 to a comparatively paltry $22.6 billion. The agreement on such a sweeping deal between Clinton and Congress was a tribute to the president's political skills as well as a sign that the nation had retreated from a confrontational mood and expected politicians to do the same.

The tangible decentralization of power showed itself in a multitude of ways, but one of the most obvious was welfare reform. Since 1996, when Congress passed the welfare-reform law, state and local governments had used their power to change dramatically their systems of social protection. Revised work and eligibility rules for welfare had cut rolls in Wisconsin by 55% since the start of the decade. Oregon, Indiana, West Virginia, Rhode Island, and Connecticut all experienced decreases of 40% or more. Throughout the Midwest and most of the old South, welfare rolls fell anywhere from 20% to 40%. Only California registered an increase.

Americans endorsed mayors who followed federal and state trends toward spinning off government services to private contractors, balancing budgets, and reshaping old-fashioned labour-management relations while dealing briskly with crime. As a result, such urban areas as Philadelphia and Cleveland, Ohio, cities that had been fiscal sinkholes in the 1980s, were reporting substantial surpluses, better services for residents, and renewed optimism.

In Los Angeles low-key Republican Richard Riordan soundly defeated Democratic Sen. Tom Hayden to win reelection to a second term as mayor in a city where Democrats outnumbered Republicans by two to one. In New York City Republican Rudolph Giuliani coasted to a similar victory in an even more stalwart Democratic stronghold.

The Economy. The reinvigoration, however, would not have been possible without the phenomenal performance of the economy, which entered the year growing at nearly a 4% rate, with unemployment hovering around 5.3%, and the Dow Jones industrial average heading toward 7000. Debate grew over whether the pace could be sustained without a revival in inflation, which had hit a meagre 2.4% in 1996. As growth surged at 5.9% in the first quarter of the year, Federal Reserve Board Chairman Alan Greenspan fired a warning shot by raising the federal funds' interest rate by 25 basis points, to 5.5%, the first interest-rate rise in two years. During the first half of the year, the economy continued to boom at a 4.1% rate—roughly double the pace at which economists generally feared a reignition of inflation. Yet Greenspan took no further action.

LISA QUINONES—BLACK STAR

In October African-American women from around the U.S. gathered in Philadelphia for the Million Woman March. The march was intended to help create positive changes in black communities.

The most striking economic phenomenon of 1997 was an enormous surge in jobs that did not bring about a corresponding rise in prices, even as real U.S. wages began to climb. By November the unemployment rate had fallen to 4.7%, the lowest since 1973. Meanwhile, over the 12-month period ended in November, Americans' incomes rose 4.1%, a real gain of 2% when adjusted for inflation—the highest rate recorded since the mid-1970s.

(continued on page 498)

SPOTLIGHT

ENGLISH LANGUAGE IMPERIALISM

by Gerald Knowles

Illustration by Cathy Hull

Seen in its simplest terms, language imperialism involves the transfer of a dominant language to other peoples. The transfer is essentially a demonstration of power—traditionally military power but also in the modern world economic power—and aspects of the dominant culture are usually transferred along with the language. In view of the prestige of the dominant power and its culture, the transfer may not be imposed but actually be demanded by the peoples who adopt the dominant language. It is likely to be regarded as an intrinsically superior language and accorded alleged virtues—*e.g.,* that it is more logical, more beautiful, or easier to learn than the dominated languages. Among the most successful imperial languages are Latin, Arabic, and English.

The dominant language can survive the collapse of the imperial power itself. At this stage the original native speakers lose control of the language, which eventually passes to a new evolving power structure. For example, Latin survived for 1,000 years as the language of the Roman Catholic Church, and it spread to areas such as Scandinavia that had never been part of the Roman Empire. During its period of dominance, the position of a language may appear to be unassailable, but it can be destroyed by successful challenges to the power structure on which it depends. Latin declined after the rise of the nation state and the Protestant Reformation, both of which led to the rise of national languages, including English.

By the time the English language began to spread overseas in the wake of British military and mercantile expansion, the written language was already on the way to standardization. Leaving aside some differences in vocabulary—and some minor variations in spelling, such as British *colour* and American *color*—essentially the same written form has been adopted worldwide. In the absence of a true standard of pronunciation, correct spoken English was assumed to be the preserve of polite London society, a view that was eventually formalized in the British Received Pronunciation of the early 20th century.

In America, and later Australia and New Zealand and South Africa, new varieties of English were developed by native speakers coming from the British Isles. Early colonists would not in general have moved in fashionable circles in London, and consequently colonial speech was generally regarded by Londoners as an inferior form of English. The first Americanism to be condemned was the use of *bluff* as "headland," first recorded in 1735. Even among quite advanced ancient Asian civilizations, 19th-century colonial administrators sought to impose the English language and culture. In 1813 the official education policy in India was to impart "to the Native population knowledge of English literature and science through the medium of the English language." English came to be used as an official language not only in southern Asia but also in Singapore and Hong Kong, Malaya and the East Indies, and later in East Africa.

A very different situation developed in West Africa. There special trade languages, or pidgins, had long been in use for communication with Portuguese traders, and they used elements from Portuguese and African languages. When the British arrived, they began to incorporate elements from English. Mixed groups of Africans transported to the Caribbean by slave traders would not have a language in common, and pidgins would form the most effective means of communication. Eventually they would be adopted as a native language, called a creole.

The total number of English speakers was small before 1800, but since then the number has grown rapidly. Great Britain was indisputably the dominant English-speaking power in the 19th century, but it was already being overtaken by the United States both in population and as an economic power. International English in the 20th century has consequently been dominated by American rather than British English. The use of English has spread far beyond the old British Empire. It has even begun to replace French in Francophone Africa—*e.g.,* Algeria and the former Zaire. English has some special status as official or second language in more than 70 countries. (*See* MAP.) By the 1990s immigration and natural growth in the former colonies had created a population of some 350 million people who spoke English as their mother tongue, most of them in the United States. A further 250 million to 350 million people use English in some way as a second language. The number of people using English as a foreign language is impossible to assess, since it is arbitrary at what point someone with a limited knowledge counts as an English speaker. Something like a quarter of the world's population has some competence in English, and the vast majority are not native speakers of the language.

The demand for English from nonnative speakers has created a huge international English-language-teaching industry. Although American English has been the dominant partner, the British Council was set up after 1945 to promote the English language and British culture. By the 1990s the council had some 120,000 students learning English through its offices abroad and some 400,000 candidates for its English exams.

Up to the late 19th century, developments in mass communications—printing, newspapers, and the telegraph—had involved the written language. For the next century, beginning with the telephone and the phonograph, developments were to involve the spoken language. The film industry grew rapidly in importance after the addition of sound to moving picture, and since the main centre was in Hollywood rather than London, it was American English that was spread with the new medium. At about the same time, the broadcasting industry—initially radio and later television—developed first in Great Britain but was soon dwarfed by its American counterpart. People's lives began to be controlled, in English-speaking countries and elsewhere, by the American-dominated advertising industry. Popular music found its way onto the airwaves, but following the introduction of rock and roll in the 1950s, broadcasters began to determine what kind of music was popular. The dominant language in this medium has always been American English.

The existence of modern mass communications has made it possible to set up international bodies and organize events on a global scale. The United Nations, the World Bank, and the European Union all have several official languages, as do international conferences and learned journals. Practical realities nearly always dictate that English be one of the official languages and also the one most used. The use of several official languages means that documents have to be translated from the original language into other official languages, but this is often viewed as a waste of time and money. There is thus a tension between the demands of equity, leading to the recognition of the importance of several languages, and the convenience of using only one.

Computer-based technology has led to a massive extension in the use of English, both in computer software and on the Internet. Computer languages are based on English, and English is the language normally used to communicate with the user. Software can, of course, use other languages, but it will doubtless make use of English-based commands. Texts in other languages can be found on the Internet, including Arabic and Japanese, but these few exceptions only underline the basic fact that the vast majority (about 85%, according to one recent French study) are in English. Anybody can in principle contact anybody else anywhere in the world, but in practice they can do this only if they are sufficiently proficient in English.

English is now used by so many people on an international scale and in so many areas of everyday life that its role as the language of the world might seem assured and permanent. Already within the last 50 years, however, there have been signs of a reaction against English and in favour of a local language, particularly where English was introduced as an imperial language. One day people everywhere might want to use their own languages. Erasmus wrote in Latin and modern Dutch intellectuals write in English, but in the future Dutch scholars might want to write in Dutch.

Moreover, the control exercised by the mass media is highly likely to provoke a reaction. The media increasingly determine the details of people's lives: the way they speak to each other, how they wear a baseball cap, and even how they blow their noses. There could come a time when people object to having their culture and their social identities constructed by the mass media. As the means through which that power of the media is exercised, such a reaction would in all probability lead to a rejection of English, much as the reaction against church control once led to the rejection of Latin.

Finally, there is an obvious threat from computer technology to the status of English as an international lingua franca. Machine translation, if it can be fully automated, will make it possible for users of any language to access information. Translation linked to the technology that enables computers to recognize and produce speech will lead to automatic interpretation. Some automatic teller machines already give the user a choice of language, and Web sites are beginning to appear on the Internet with a choice of languages. In this way, although computer technology has in the short term given a massive boost to the use of English, it is likely in the longer term to make language use a matter of choice. Of course, nobody can see into the future, but sooner or later the dominant position of the English language is going to be successfully challenged.

Gerald Knowles is a professor in the department of linguistics at the University of Lancaster, Eng., and author of A Cultural History of the English Language.

(continued from page 495)

The combined effect on the U.S. stock market of high growth, low unemployment, rising wages, and low inflation was galvanic. The Dow Jones industrial average broke through 8000 in July, and economists predicted that it might reach 10000 or even 12000 without a significant retrenchment. As a major financial crash in Southeast Asia cast clouds on the horizon, American optimism continued undiminished—until a minicrash came on October 27 that knocked 554 points off the Dow Jones in a single day. Yet 24 hours later the bull market regained momentum as the market climbed 337 points in a single session, the biggest rise in a decade.

Organized labour, however, showed its resentment at Clinton's perceived bias in favour of conservative economic policies and corporate globalism. During his first term Clinton had strongly supported passage of the North American Free Trade Agreement between the U.S., Canada, and Mexico. During the deal making, he had traded away renewal of the administration's "fast-track" authority to negotiate trade agreements that could be approved or denied by Congress only without amendment. Without such authority the president was weakened in his position to reach agreements on trade issues with other nations. In November, however, the White House was forced to announce that it would not seek renewal of the fast-track authorization, chiefly because of opposition from Democrats, heavily supported by organized labour, who opposed free trade because they believed it resulted in job losses for Americans. Clinton vowed to seek the authorization again in early 1998, but the setback was a blow to his international prestige.

ANDY BLANKISH—KRT

Air Force Lieut. Kelly J. Flinn stands before a B-52 bomber at an air force base in Minot, N.D. Flinn, who had an affair with a man married to an enlisted woman, avoided being court-martialed in May by accepting the lighter punishment of a general discharge. Her case attracted wide publicity in 1997.

Ethics in Government. The president and his administration continued to be troubled by a number of scandals. The most personal accusation was the charge of sexual harassment made by Paula Corbin Jones, who had been an Arkansas state employee when Clinton was governor. The White House argued before the Supreme Court that a president in office should be allowed to postpone until the end of his term civil suits derived from past actions. The court, however, did not agree, and by the end of the year, the country was facing the prospect of the president's being forced to give testimony in court.

Flowers for Gianni Versace sit outside his boutique on Rodeo Drive in Beverly Hills, Calif. In July the celebrated designer was gunned down in front of his Miami Beach, Fla., home by Andrew Cunanan, a suspect in four other slayings.

MINGASSON—GAMMA LIAISON

First lady Hillary Rodham Clinton also sought, and failed, to create a Supreme Court precedent in the Whitewater affair. Her attorneys argued, and lost, an assertion that notes taken by White House lawyers during conversations with her were privileged under lawyer-client confidentiality and could be withheld from Kenneth Starr, the special prosecutor investigating the case. The court gave Starr access to the documents, but they did not lead to any startling changes in the three-year, $30 million probe of various real-estate deals conducted while Clinton was in Arkansas.

All paled, however, before the outcry that arose, both in Republican circles and in the press, over the financing of the 1996 election campaign. At no time in U.S. history had more money been spent on electoral politics—$2.2 billion at all levels. A substantial amount of Democratic campaign funds, it appeared, had come from questionable sources, especially from businessmen with Asian backgrounds and often, it seemed, with interests in China. Revelations about Democratic Party fund-raising, which had trickled out even during the campaign, caused the Democratic National Committee (DNC) eventually to return $2.8 million in donations. The accusations became even more serious as various members of the U.S. national security establishment questioned the appropriateness of visits by some of the donors to the White House.

Much was made of the activities of Charles Yah Lin Trie, a Taiwanese-born entrepreneur who ran a Little Rock, Ark., restaurant and who eventually became a top Democratic fund-raiser; he had visited the White House 23 times. Clinton admitted that it was "clearly inappropriate" for Trie, who had helped raise a substantial amount of money for the Democrats and for the Clintons' legal defense, to have escorted a known Chinese weapons dealer through the White House.

Another figure in the fund-raising effort was California businessman Johnny Chung, who had donated a total of $366,000 to the DNC, all of which was later returned because the source of the money could not be verified. Among other indiscretions, Chung had managed to pass on a $50,000 check to the DNC through Hillary Clinton's then chief of staff, Margaret Williams. Two days later he escorted a number of Chinese business associates to a taping of Clinton's weekly radio address. The donation raised the issue of possible impropriety on the part of Williams for having accepted a campaign contribution on government property.

The Republican-led furor over these and other revelations took on a shriller tone after it was discovered that Clinton and Vice Pres. Al Gore had made a number of fund-raising calls from their executive offices. The actions raised the spectre of a possible violation of the Pendleton Act, which forbids federal employees to solicit contributions on federal property. Although both denied wrongdoing, Gore said that he made calls on only "a few occasions," and the president claimed little recollection.

Eventually, the campaign fund-raising issue came before a Senate investigating committee, chaired by Fred Thompson of Tennessee, who charged that the alleged scandal involved a plot on the part of China's gov-

CURT WILCOTT—GAMMA LIAISON

Texas Department of Public Safety spokesman Mike Cox (left) announces the peaceful surrender of an armed separatist group, known as the Republic of Texas, to state police after a weeklong standoff. Terence O'Rourke (right), attorney for Republic of Texas leader Richard McLaren, stands beside Cox.

ernment to influence U.S. politics. His committee issued 52 subpoenas, and fund-raiser Trie, for one, fled to China rather than testify. The hearings aired secret communications intercepts that indicated that Chinese officials in Beijing and Washington at least discussed how to increase their government's influence with U.S. local, state, and federal officials. In addition, the committee heard testimony that the Republican National Committee (RNC) had also received questionable support from abroad, dating back to 1994. The major donor was Hong Kong businessman Ambrous Tung Young, who had introduced Haley Barbour, then chairman of the RNC, to top Chinese officials. The RNC ultimately returned a $100,000 Young donation.

Serious strains developed between Attorney General Janet Reno and FBI Director Louis Freeh over the fund-raising controversy. The dispute involved different interpretations of the 1978 Independent Counsel Act. Freeh believed that the act could be read broadly to ensure an impartial investigation; he urged Reno to turn the entire fund-raising matter over to an independent prosecutor because she, as a Cabinet official, faced a conflict of interest in investigating her own boss. Reno, however, took a narrower view of the legal grounds for appointing a special prosecutor. She insisted, with the backing of departmental attorneys, that only clear evidence of wrongdoing could trigger an independent investigation. Reno was shaken, however, when soon after she had made one of her clearest assertions of the lack of need for outside investigation, the White House began releasing videotapes of Clinton's meetings with various campaign donors, including controversial figures. Although none revealed anything illicit, Reno had not been informed of the existence of the tapes. In the end she remained firm—an independent counsel would not be appointed.

The entire fund-raising issue clearly established that U.S. campaign-financing laws were in a quagmire, with bewildering distinctions between "hard" and "soft" campaign donations. As Clinton declared, reform of some kind was highly desirable, and several proposals were aired in Congress.

Foreign Affairs. Relations with China marked the point of greatest difficulty in making the distinction between foreign and domestic affairs in a globalized economy as greater numbers of Asians immigrated to the U.S. and more business was done with China. Greater commercial dealing with Asia's authoritarian regimes also raised larger questions of how to impress upon them the need for increased observance of human rights. All of these issues came to a head in late October and early November when Chinese Pres. Jiang Zemin made his first trip to the U.S., the first by a Chinese head of state in 12 years. His visit, coming only months after the return of Hong Kong to Chinese sovereignty, raised the issue of democracy and trade to a special level of sensitivity. In more than two hours of conversations with Clinton at the White House, and again in public, Clinton took unusual pains to stress that on the issue of democracy China's leadership was "on the wrong side of history." Jiang seemed unfazed by the admonition. On a more practical level, China pledged to cut off nuclear aid to Iran in exchange for future sales of American nuclear reactors to China.

Late in the year the Clinton administration orchestrated a series of multibillion-dollar bailouts to shore up the short-circuited economies of Thailand, Malaysia, Indonesia, and South Korea, among others, which were caught up in a dominoes-style financial collapse. The International Monetary Fund was called in to provide what could prove to be upwards of $100 billion in interim financing, and the U.S. was embarrassed as a recalcitrant Congress refused to approve $3.5 billion in IMF contributions.

In Europe U.S. foreign policy was on surer ground. In July the U.S.-led NATO alliance welcomed three new members to the security alliance—Poland, Hungary, and the Czech Republic—all of which would become members in 1999. The enlargement of NATO had been preceded by a lively debate within the administration over its advisability and had encountered vociferous Russian opposition. Nonetheless, the move proceeded as planned, with the alliance promising that it would deploy no combat troops or nuclear weapons in its new regions.

Although most of the world's nations gathered in Ottawa in December to sign a treaty banning the use of antipersonnel land mines, the United States was not among the signatories. Clinton explained that treaty negotiators would not allow an interim exemption for the U.S., which had requested the continued use of antipersonnel mines to protect antitank defenses of vital importance in the Korean peninsula, where 40,000 U.S. troops and their South Korean allies were vastly outnumbered by the forces of North Korea.

Clinton's most difficult foreign-policy challenge involved an old nemesis—Iraqi dictator Saddam Hussein, who had repeatedly shown an uncanny ability to win political advantage while still enduring the military and economic straitjacket imposed by a U.S.-led alliance after the Persian Gulf War. When teams of UN weapons inspectors apparently closed in on secret stocks of biological and chemical weapons, Hussein declared that American inspectors would no longer be allowed on the UN team hunting for Iraqi weapons of mass destruction. He eventually forced UN personnel to leave the country. Although the UN Security Council unanimously condemned Iraq but initially refused to follow an American lead of further sanctions against Baghdad, it later imposed additional sanctions because of Hussein's continued unwillingness to cooperate and his threats to U.S. reconnaissance aircraft. When Hussein threatened to shoot down American U-2 spy planes overflying sensitive Iraqi areas, Clinton ordered three carrier groups to operate within striking range and massed aircraft in Saudi Arabia and Turkey. Hussein shrewdly backed down and invited UN inspectors back into the country but refused to grant them entree to some 47 rebuilt presidential compounds. Although the U.S. sought to balance threats of continued economic embargo against incentives for further Iraqi cooperation, the consensus was that U.S. dependence on coalition building had perhaps resulted in a shift of political momentum toward its most dangerous regional adversary.

(GEORGE RUSSELL)

See also *Dependent States.*

DEVELOPMENTS IN THE STATES, 1997

State governments enjoyed a prosperous yet contentious year at the centre of national public policy debates. Strong economic conditions in most states produced record revenues and allowed a third consecutive year of multibillion-dollar state tax cuts. The black ink was augmented by the success of state-inspired welfare reform, which had cut nearly two million recipients from public assistance rolls during recent months.

The state financial outlook was brightened further by a historic accord with the U.S. tobacco industry. Two states negotiated major settlements, and the industry agreed to pay other states a settlement worth billions of dollars.

The first effects of challenges to a decades-long affirmative action trend were felt in states during the year. States continued to struggle with the federal government over a variety of issues ranging from environmental rules to the distribution of the tobacco-settlement funds. Growing use of the Internet, too, led states to wrestle with a host of new taxation, privacy, and legal concerns. All 50 states held regular legislative sessions during 1997, and 11 staged special sessions.

Party Strengths. No significant change was demanded by voters in limited off-year elections for governors and state legislatures during 1997. In New Jersey and Virginia gubernatorial races, Republicans retained seats won four years earlier. The partisan governors' lineup for 1998 thus remained at 32 Republicans, 17 Democrats, and one independent (in Maine).

Only a few seats changed hands in 226 legislative races nationwide. The only significant move occurred in Virginia, where the Republicans gained control of the equally represented state Senate by capturing the governor's office. After November balloting, the partisan lineup was unchanged at 50 chambers controlled by Democrats, 46 by Republicans, and two tied. (Nebraska has a unicameral, nonpartisan legislature.) Going into 1998, Republicans had two-chamber control of 18 legislatures, Democrats dominated both houses in 20 states, and 11 state legislatures were split or tied.

Government Structures and Powers. By a margin of nearly two to one, New York voters rejected a proposed 1999 state constitutional convention to address issues such as term limits for public officials, caps on state indebtedness, and ballot initiatives. Opponents portrayed the proposal as a "playground for politicians."

In a law targeted at gangsta rap, Texas became the first state to prohibit state agency pension funds from investing in companies producing sexually explicit or violent music lyrics. Michigan became the 14th state to reform its juvenile justice system, lowering the permissible age for charging offenders as adults from 15 to 14 and expanding applicable crimes from 9 to 20. Oklahoma revamped its state corrections system, approving a truth-in-sentencing law that would virtually abolish parole.

Charging overreaching by activists, the European Union filed a World Trade Organization (WTO) complaint against Massachusetts for its politically inspired boycott of products made in Myanmar (Burma). Under WTO rules, only economic considerations could be considered in such decisions.

New York became the first state victim of new line-item-veto authority granted to the president in 1996. Pres. Bill Clinton disallowed New York permission to impose a health-provider tax to match federal Medicaid dollars. The veto cost the state an estimated $200 million.

Government Relations. Federalism, the relationship between state and federal governments, continued to generate controversy during the year. Although the Republican-controlled Congress voiced support for devolving duties to states, actual progress was slight, and arguments broke out on numerous fronts. States argued with the federal government over air-quality standards, mandates in federal programs, welfare regulations, tobacco industry settlements, and highway funding.

States rights received a boost from a 5–4 U.S. Supreme Court decision invalidating part of the Brady Handgun Violence Protection Act. The court ruled that local law-enforcement officials could not be forced to conduct the background check required by the federal law. The high court also strengthened state autonomy in regard to reapportionment, election rules, and operation of federal programs.

Several states also contested a Clinton administration plan to use statistical sampling procedures in the upcoming 2000 national census. At year's end Congress elected to test the procedures but did not commit to using them. Following yet another federalism-oriented debate, both houses of the Oregon legislature asked that states be allowed to undertake Social Security reform by enacting their own retirement plans.

Finances. A booming national economy during 1997 helped produce the biggest state treasury surpluses in two decades. The good news prompted states to reduce taxes

At the new Franklin D. Roosevelt Memorial in Washington, D.C., a reporter uses a flashlight to look for the wheelchair under Roosevelt's cape. That the wheelchair was not more prominent in the sculpture enraged disability activists, who staged a protest at the memorial when it was unveiled in May.

DAYNA SMITH—THE WASHINGTON POST

for the third consecutive year, this time by a net $1.7 billion.

Even so, the surpluses produced arguments. Legislators in Colorado, Missouri, and Oregon rejected spending ideas and required that excess revenues be returned to taxpayers. Some observers suggested that capital gains taxes from stock market profits contributed to black ink in state treasuries. Others credited the work requirement in welfare reform, which helped prompt a dramatic drop in welfare expenditures and a resultant increase in taxpaying jobholders.

Twenty-one states reduced taxes specifically to offset higher-than-expected revenues, and 18 used a portion of higher revenues to shore up their "rainy day" funds. Another 18 targeted programs for one-time or extraordinary funding increases. Six reduced state debt.

Nineteen states reduced personal income taxes, with significant reductions occurring in Arizona, Connecticut, Iowa, Massachusetts, and Minnesota. Other major tax reductions included cuts in sales taxes on food in Georgia, Louisiana, and Missouri and property tax reductions in Kansas and Montana.

Tax increases were few in number. Michigan, Pennsylvania, and Utah raised motor-fuel taxes. Colorado voters rejected a gas tax hike to finance highway and infrastructure repairs. Alaska, Maine, New Jersey, Oregon, Rhode Island, and Utah boosted levies on cigarettes and tobacco. Alaska's boost in cigarette taxes to $1 per pack resulted in a price of about $3 per pack in that state. A Maine law providing for taxation of charities that benefit nonresidents was invalidated by the U.S. Supreme Court.

Education. Ohio and Vermont joined a majority of states under court order to equalize school funding between rich and poor districts by reducing state reliance on local property tax revenues. New York voters turned down a school bond referendum.

Health and Welfare. Tobacco dominated state health and fiscal news during 1997. As individuals began to win judgments alleging their health problems were affected by tobacco-related complications, the attorneys general of Mississippi and Florida were able to negotiate multibillion-dollar settlements with tobacco companies in order to repay the states for their tobacco-caused health expenditures. Mississippi Attorney General Michael Moore announced the first state settlement, a $3,366,000,000 payout over 25 years. Florida Attorney General Bob Butterworth later revealed a similar pact, this one for $11.3 billion. At one time during the year, 40 states were pursuing tobacco lawsuits, citing similar grounds.

After extensive negotiations with two dozen state attorneys general and plaintiffs' lawyers, the tobacco firms finally agreed to a historic $368.5 billion settlement. The agreement said the funds would compensate states and class-action individual plaintiffs for costs of smoking-related illness, fund antismoking programs, and provide health care for uninsured children. The proposed pact provided for states to share in an $8.5 billion payout by tobacco companies for 5 years, followed by $15 billion in payments for 20 additional years.

The pact, however, required congressional and U.S. executive branch approval. The federal government was spending about 60% of government health care dollars through the Medicare program, and at year's end many congressmen were objecting to terms of the settlement. They demanded that the U.S. government share in settlement proceeds and that up to $25 billion in payments to plaintiffs' trial lawyers be markedly reduced.

States also continued to grapple with the consequences of the historic 1996 federal welfare-reform law, which required able-bodied welfare recipients to find a job within two years or face a cutoff of benefits. Seventeen states passed new laws accommodating the federal mandate, often setting up stringent welfare-to-work programs.

Aided by a booming national economy, welfare-reform statistics were startling; a federal study at the end of the year indicated that 1.9 million recipients had been removed from state welfare rolls over the previous two years, with every jurisdiction except Hawaii and the District of Columbia showing a marked decline. Reform advocates hailed the development, saying the shift from welfare to work reduced despair among recipients and dramatically enriched state treasuries.

Washington state voters turned down two health-related ballot initiatives. One would have legalized the medicinal use of marijuana, LSD, and heroin. The other would have allowed workers to retain their individual physicians if they changed their health care coverage.

Oregon voters again endorsed the state's unique Death with Dignity Act, this time by a 60% favourable vote. The measure legalized physician-assisted suicide. In 1994 a similar measure had been approved by a 51–49% margin, but legal challenges delayed its implementation and led to the second vote.

When a federal ban was vetoed by President Clinton, 14 states outlawed "partial-birth" abortion, a late-term procedure attacked by pro-life advocates. New Jersey's legislature enacted a ban on that procedure over Gov. Christine Todd Whitman's veto. The California Supreme Court overturned the state's 10-year-old law requiring notification of parents before teenagers could receive an abortion. The court based its decision on privacy rights it found in the state constitution and thus avoided federal court review.

A nationwide drive to toughen drunk-driving laws made progress during 1997. Fifteen states followed National Highway Traffic Safety Administration recommendations and lowered the blood-alcohol-content standard from 0.10% to 0.08%. Other states moved to confiscate automobiles, impound license plates, or confiscate registration papers for drunk-driving felonies or repeat offenders.

Law and Justice. According to statistics released during the year, serious crime dropped by 3% nationwide, the fifth consecutive annual decline. Paced by an overall drop in the murder rate of 9%, incidents of violent crime fell by 6%, and more numerous property crimes were down by 2%. The national juvenile arrest rate also fell. Authorities attributed the trend to tougher sentencing, a crackdown on minor offenses, and the aging national population. Gun-control advocates suffered a setback in November when Washington voters rejected 71–29% a proposal to require trigger guards on weapons sold in the state.

States executed 74 men during 1997, the highest total since capital punishment was reintroduced in 1976. Half of the national total, 37 men, were put to death in Texas, and 9 more were executed in Virginia. The surge of executions in Texas was facilitated by court approval of a 1995 state law designed to shorten death-row stays by allowing state and federal appeals to run concurrently.

The upward trend in executions continued even in the face of adverse publicity. On March 25 fire erupted from the leather face mask of an inmate being put to death in the 74-year-old electric chair at the Florida State Prison in Starke. After a medical report indicated that the convict had died instantly, Florida Gov. Lawton Chiles announced there would be no change in the procedure.

At year's end, of 38 states with a death penalty statute, only Florida, Alabama, Georgia, Kentucky, Nebraska, and Tennessee relied solely on the electric chair for executions. The remaining states all offered lethal injection as an option.

In a controversial decision, the U.S. Supreme Court upheld a 1994 Kansas law allowing the state to confine violent sexual offenders even after their prison terms had been served. Five other states had similar laws.

Louisiana became the first state explicitly allowing motorists who feared for their life to shoot and kill carjackers. Reversing a decades-long trend toward easy divorce, Louisiana also became the first state to toughen its marriage laws and narrow the grounds for divorce. Couples seeking a Louisiana marriage license would now choose between marriage vows with strict divorce requirements or the standard license, which allowed no-fault divorce.

In a novel case arising from an Internet discussion on sport hunting, an El Paso, Texas, student was arrested for suggesting that a pro-hunting California state senator be "hunted down and skinned and mounted for our viewing pleasure." The accused became the first to be charged with making an on-line threat to a public official, a felony in California.

Kentucky became the first among 15 states with victim-notification laws to automate its system fully. Individuals who registered with the state received a computer-generated call within 10 minutes when an inmate was released or transferred to a new facility.

Ethics. Arizona Gov. J. Fife Symington III was convicted on September 3 on seven felony counts of defrauding lenders to his troubled real-estate empire. Symington resigned two days later and was replaced by Arizona's secretary of state, Jane Dee Hull, another Republican. Symington was the 11th state governor to be forced from office during this century because of scandal and the third during the 1990s.

Massachusetts State Sen. Dianne Wilkerson pleaded guilty to four counts of failure to file income tax returns and was sentenced to six months of home detention. The senator said she failed to pay because death threats she received as a lawyer for the National Association for the Advancement of Colored People (NAACP) forced her to spend her money on security.

Prisons. The growth rates of both prison construction and inmate populations slowed during 1997. Penal construction expenditures rose 4.8% during the year, well under the average increase for the 1990s.

SAM DEANER—ASSOCIATED PRESS

Student demonstrators opposed to Proposition 209, an anti-affirmative-action measure passed in California in 1996, hold a rally outside the administration building of the University of California, Berkeley. Black and Hispanic admissions at the university's law school dropped sharply in 1997.

Statistics released at midyear showed that the number of prisoners housed in state and federal prisons increased by 5% to 1,182,169, also well under the 7.3% average population growth of the 1990s. Another 518,000 adults were held in local jails on a typical day in 1997.

Gambling. For the third consecutive year, opponents of legalized gaming were encouraged by a slowdown in gambling's expansion. Countering a national trend, voters in the Navajo Reservation, the country's largest, rejected casino gambling on their land in Arizona, Utah, and New Mexico. Oregon voters, however, approved a statewide lottery to finance construction and computer equipment purchases for public schools.

Environment. Conflicts in Washington, D.C., continued to dominate environmental news during the year. Despite objections from some states, the federal government imposed tough new ozone standards, which led to predictions of job losses and economic hardship in some areas.

The U.S. Department of the Interior reneged on a 1993 decision to sell federal Mojave Desert land to California to be used as a low-level nuclear-waste facility. Both state and federal tests had pronounced the area safe for the site, but owing to environmental concerns, the Clinton administration reversed the decision, which had been made during the presidency of George Bush. California filed suit to enforce the agreement.

Equal Rights. A three-decade trend of growth for affirmative-action programs was slowed and sometimes even reversed during the year. The U.S. Supreme Court refused to hear a challenge to California's 1996 Proposition 209, which barred race- or gender-based preferences in school admissions, public hiring, and public contracting.

The court decision, along with a similar outcome in a 1996 Texas case, led to the abolition of affirmative-action admissions programs at Texas and California universities and a resultant drop in admissions of African-American and Hispanic law-school applicants. Proponents of 209 said the court action would clear the way for similar anti-affirmative-action proposals that were pending in 26 states.

Advocates of additional legal protection for homosexuals enjoyed mixed success. In Washington voters rejected a proposal barring discrimination on the basis of sexual orientation. Responding to the nation's first court decisions legalizing the action, the Hawaii legislature amended the state constitution to bar same-sex marriages. New Jersey, however, became the first state to allow homosexual partners to adopt jointly, treating them the same as married couples.

Rejecting a claim that mere advantage on the civil service test was sufficient, the Illinois Supreme Court ruled that the state must give "absolute preference" to veterans applying for state jobs. Maine voters rejected a proposal to extend voting rights to the mentally ill under guardianship; other individuals with guardians, including the mentally retarded, had such rights in the state.

Consumer Protection. The growing popularity of computers and the Internet led to numerous state policy and funding debates during 1997. Many states grappled with novel problems arising from Internet use, including privacy of medical records, gambling availability, and other issues.

All states moved to address the serious computer network problem that would result from the change from 1999 to 2000. To save money and space, most programming in the past few decades had used only the final two digits in the date; consequently, computers in 2000 would assume the date was 1900, which would throw state payments, receipts, and other functions into disarray. One consulting firm estimated that fixing the problem could cost upwards of $600 billion during the next few years. Nevada became the first state to address year 2000 liability concerns. A new Nevada law provided immunity to state and local governments "from any civil action...caused by a computer that produced, calculated or generated an incorrect date."

When several states objected, a congressional effort to bar states from imposing extra taxes on Internet commercial transactions was stalled in the federal government during the year. States also moved to protect tax revenue from Internet expansion by cracking down on interstate wine and liquor sales. By the year's end, 21 states prohibited direct shipping of wine, with Georgia, Kentucky, and Florida classifying direct shipment as a felony. At the end of 1997, nine state attorneys general announced they were initiating an antitrust investigation against the Microsoft Corp. for monopolizing the market for operating-systems software.

(DAVID C. BECKWITH)

URUGUAY

Area: 176,215 sq km (68,037 sq mi)
Population (1997 est.): 3,185,000
Capital: Montevideo
Head of state and government: President Julio María Sanguinetti

The Broad Front (FA) alliance, in opposition to the coalition of the Blanco and Colorado parties, lost its second leader within 12 months in 1997 when Tabaré Vázquez, elected leader in December 1996, resigned in September. He had been expected to be the FA's presidential candidate in the 1999 elections. In subsequent elections for the FA leadership, the alliance experimented with a free vote for all the electorate, plus those aged between 14 and 18 (voting age is officially 18), but few people turned out, and a large proportion of their votes had to be scrutinized for fraud. Radicals within the FA objected to the broad scope of the election, claiming that it would marginalize the left.

The internal disputes within the FA were forecast to assist the ruling coalition in the months before the elections. Similarly beneficial were the continued improvements in many productive and service sectors, which led to growth in gross domestic product close to 1996's 4.9%. Inflation for 1997 was forecast to be between 15% and 20%, maintaining a downward trend. Unemployment, at about 11%, was also falling, although trade unions argued that in parts of the country there remained pockets of unacceptably high joblessness.

The tourist sector started the year well, with arrivals in January–March up by 17% from January–March 1996 and earnings, at $423.6 million, up 25.5%. A major oil spill from a Panamanian tanker in February at Punta del Este and a rise in violent crime in Montevideo threatened to reduce the year's overall figures, however. Both travel and real-estate agents were concerned that Uruguay's heavily armed bandit gangs would undermine the country's safe image.

(BEN BOX)

UZBEKISTAN

Area: 447,400 sq km (172,700 sq mi)
Population (1997 est.): 23,664,000
Capital: Tashkent
Chief of state: President Islam Karimov
Head of government: Prime Minister Otkir Sultonov

In 1997 Uzbekistan maintained its reputation for political stability but made little progress in the development of a civil society. Concealed censorship of the information media remained, although there was some improvement in the reporting of international events. Although its economy was widely considered to be the strongest in Central Asia, Uzbekistan's successes were offset by high inflation and severe restrictions on imports, which adversely affected the living standard of the population. International lending agencies were disillusioned by Uzbekistan's failure to honour its commitment to making its currency fully convertible. On the other hand, the automobile plant in Andijon, an Uzbek–South Korean joint venture, could not keep up with demand for its cars, and the start-up of an oil refinery in Bukhara in August made a major contribution toward ensuring energy self-sufficiency for the nation. Meanwhile, economic ties between Russia and Uzbekistan declined as political relations between the two countries cooled.

Uzbekistan's main foreign policy concerns in 1997 were its eastern and southern neighbours. The Uzbek leadership sought international support to help end the fighting in Afghanistan, proposing the establishment of a contact group under the auspices of the UN and the Organization of the Islamic Conference to seek a peaceful settlement between the warring Afghan factions. The contact group envisaged in the Uzbek proposal would consist of the countries bordering Afghanistan, as well as the U.S. and Russia. Uzbekistan refused to sign the peace accords in June that formally ended the civil war in Tajikistan, arguing that the accords would lead only to political instability because too many Tajik groups had been excluded from the peace process. Subsequent events in Tajikistan seemed to bear out the validity of the Uzbek doubts, but by autumn Uzbekistan had signed the Tajik accords.

(BESS BROWN)

This article updates the *Macropædia* article CENTRAL ASIA: *Uzbekistan.*

VANUATU

Area: 12,190 sq km (4,707 sq mi)
Population (1997 est.): 176,000
Capital: Vila
Chief of state: President Jean-Marie Leye
Head of government: Prime Minister Serge Vohor

The aftermath of earlier financial mismanagement issues continued to influence political developments in Vanuatu in 1997. In October 1996, after a no-confidence vote against the government of Maxime Carlot Korman, Serge Vohor emerged as prime minister heading a coalition of his own Union of Moderate Parties, the Melanesian Progressive Party of Deputy Prime Minister Barak Sope, and the National United Party led by former prime minister Walter Lini. Shortly afterward, Vohor sacked Sope after damaging revelations were made by the national ombudsman, who recommended that Sope be banned from all public office because of his alleged role in a financial scandal. Vohor then brought Donald Kalpokas of the Vanua'aku Party into the government as deputy prime minister, only to replace him with Sope in May. In late 1997 the legislature voted to greatly reduce the powers of the ombudsman, charging that its investigations concentrated only on politicians. Pres. Jean-Marie Leye refused to sign the bill into law, however, until its constitutionality had been tested in court.

Opposition to Vohor continued to mount, and late in the year members of the legislature sought to oust him on a motion of no confidence. In late November Leye, frustrated with the political wrangling, dissolved the legislature and called for new elections in January 1998. On December 4 a Supreme Court judge overturned Leye's order, nullifying the dissolution of the legislature and triggering a frenzied day of activity. Vohor's opponents called for a legislative debate of the no-confidence motion, while the administration filed a last-minute appeal. By early the next day, Vohor and his opponents had agreed to a parliamentary truce until a hearing by the Court of Appeal could be convened.

(BARRIE MACDONALD)

This article updates the *Macropædia* article PACIFIC ISLANDS: *Vanuatu.*

VATICAN CITY STATE

Area: 44 ha (109 ac)
Population (1997 est.): 850
Chief of state: (sovereign pontiff) Pope John Paul II
Head of administration: Secretary of State Angelo Cardinal Sodano, who heads a pontifical commission of five cardinals

Pope John Paul II spent 1997 on a tireless campaign to promote his ecumenical vision of the Vatican in the new millennium. On the Italian front, the pope personally distributed copies of St. Mark's Gospel, which 12,000 volunteer missionaries planned to continue to distribute to the Roman Catholic faithful until the church's millennial Jubilee in 2000.

During the year the pope made apostolic visits to Bosnia and Herzegovina, the Czech Republic, Lebanon, Poland, and Brazil. His visit to Lebanon was his first and culminated in the concelebration of the Eucharist with a crowd of nearly half a million people, including a strong gathering of Muslims. The tour of his native Poland on May 31–June 10 was the longest of the pope's sojourns. A papal visit to Cuba in January 1998 was also announced.

The most serious diplomatic setback for the Vatican in 1997 was the last-minute decision by Russian Patriarch Aleksey II to cancel a planned meeting with the pope in Austria. This decision was clarified in a strongly worded statement that decried the Vatican's alleged excesses in evangelizing among the Orthodox faithful in countries of the former Soviet Union.

(GREGORY O. SMITH)

See also RELIGION: *Roman Catholic Church.*

This article updates the *Micropædia* article VATICAN CITY.

VENEZUELA

Area: 912,050 sq km (352,144 sq mi)
Population (1997 est.): 22,777,000
Capital: Caracas
Head of state and government: President Rafael Caldera

In February and March large-scale strikes by physicians, university professors, and government employees, combined with rumours of a military coup and worries about the health of Pres. Rafael Caldera, created an atmosphere of uncertainty. The government managed to diffuse labour unrest but only by acceding to demands for large pay increases for government workers. Caldera's annual state of the union address ended talk of his imminent demise.

Divisions between and within the political parties effectively brought the legislature to a halt during the first quarter of the year, leaving little time to discuss the government's reform program Agenda Venezuela. Among the proposed reforms were privatization of the aluminum, steel, and electricity industries; reform of the judicial system; and the reorganization of public finances. Legislative support for such politically sensitive issues grew less and less likely as the year wore on and as the competing parties began their campaigns for the next election, to be held in December 1998. The main political party, Democratic Action (AD), put up resistance to the proposed reforms. AD and the Social Christian Party (COPEI), the other main party, rejected the government's proposal to hold a special session in July to discuss the contract for privatization of the government-owned steel company, Sidor.

Because all government reforms required approval by the legislature, and Caldera's party, National Convergence, controlled fewer than 10% of the seats, the president needed support from elsewhere. However, his party's most consistent supporter, the Movement to Socialism (MAS), split into two factions, and the support of COPEI could not be guaranteed. The only remaining alternative, AD, seemed certain to demand major concessions to the government's liberal economic policies in exchange for its support. In addition to

(continued on page 505)

SPOTLIGHT

LATIN AMERICA'S NEW INVESTORS

by Carmelo Mesa-Lago

Illustration by Cathy Hull

Individual retirement accounts for workers were not significant in Latin America before the 1990s. They were limited to a tiny number of people who were employed in large enterprises where such accounts were established through collective bargaining and funded by payroll contributions from both the employers and the workers. In some cases the enterprise managed the pension fund itself, whereas in others it was done by outside administrators. The fund was generally invested in many types of financial instruments, including stocks.

In 1980, however, Chile reformed its traditional pension funds (more than 50, each with its own administration, financing, and benefits) and created a new system. The old funds were financed by premiums paid by the workers and employers (in some by the government also). Most of them applied the pay-as-you-go method, in which the present generation of workers finances current pensions and future generations finance the pensions of the current workers. The new pension system, which began to function in Chile in 1981, used a financing method—fully funded individual (FFI)—that was based only on the worker's premiums, which were fixed indefinitely. The system is "individual" because premiums are deposited in individual accounts owned by the workers, the pension fund is invested, and the capital returns or yields from the investments are added to the individual accounts. There is a strict relationship between premiums and benefits; consequently, the worker's pension is based on the fund accumulated in his or her individual account at the time of retirement.

The FFI system is administered by private for-profit corporations that can perform only that function; banks, insurance companies, and other financial intermediaries are not allowed to manage FFI schemes directly. Such corporations compete among themselves for clients (who can select freely among them) and charge commissions for their services; the workers neither participate in the administration of such corporations nor have representation in their public supervisory agencies. The Chilean government subsidizes the new system (which means it pays the deficit of the old system, the transfer of contributions to those who move from the public to the private system, and a minimum pension in the latter for those who have not accumulated enough funds in their individual accounts) and provides a series of guarantees to new members.

In the 1980s the Chilean FFI was the only scheme in operation in the region, but during 1993–97 seven other Latin-American countries introduced their own pension reforms: Peru in 1993, Argentina and Colombia in 1994, Uruguay in 1996, and Bolivia, El Salvador, and Mexico in 1997. These schemes differ among themselves and from the pioneering Chilean system. For instance, the administration of the pension fund is not exclusively private but is also public or mixed in half of the countries; the employer contribution was not eliminated in five of the countries; and state guarantees in the system vary significantly. In Bolivia, El Salvador, and Mexico the FFI replaced the old social insurance system (as in Chile); in Argentina and Uruguay it was combined with a reformed previous social insurance pension fund; and in Colombia and Peru a worker can choose between the FFI and a reformed previous social insurance pension fund. At the end of 1997, 26,000,000 workers had become investors in FFI plans in Latin America: 11,000,000 in Mexico, 5,400,000–5,500,000 in Chile and Argentina, 2,000,000 in Colombia, 1,300,000 in Peru, and 250,000–350,000 in Bolivia, El Salvador, and Uruguay.

The FFI funds in 1997 were invested in many kinds of financial instruments, and one or more agencies (public, private, or both) classified the instruments according to their risks. The distribution of the portfolio varied greatly among the eight FFIs: from 8% to 100% in government securities, 1% to 18% in mortgage bonds, 4% to 29% in bank deposits, 0.2% to 25% in corporate stocks, 5% to 20% in corporate bonds, 2.5% to 33% in other bonds and real estate, 2% to 13% in other lending institutions and mutual funds, and 0% to 0.5% in foreign instruments. Excluding Colombia and Peru, which had 10% and 8% of their FFIs invested in government securities, respectively, the range of that instrument was from 42% to 100%. In Bolivia and Mexico all of the fund had to be in this instrument in the first year at least.

In 1997 only three countries had a substantial part of their FFI funds invested in stocks: 25% in Chile, 23% in Peru, and 18% in Argentina; Colombia had only 0.2%, and the other countries had none (no data were available for Uruguay). The reason for this was that the capital markets were not well developed in the majority of countries of the region; consequently, few stocks were traded in such markets. Until capital markets evolve and become more secure and attractive, this instrument will not be important in the investment of FFI funds in most countries. Legal prohibition (El Salvador, Mexico, Uruguay), as well as fears of capital flight and disinvestment, was a significant barrier to investment in foreign instruments.

Finally, FFI schemes seem to work best in countries with the following four characteristics: (1) a large majority of the labour force that is urban and salaried; (2) universal or near-universal coverage of the labour force by the scheme; (3) a substantially large number of workers in the system (at least one million) in order to provide an ample base for the operation of several administrators and competition; and (4) the existence of a capital market regulated by the government. In countries with a majority of the labour force informal, self-employed, and/or rural, extension of coverage is extremely difficult. Also, the nonexistence of a regulated capital market or the lack of potential for it in small poor countries makes portfolio diversification almost impossible, which causes investment to be concentrated heavily in government securities.

Carmelo Mesa-Lago is Distinguished Service Professor of Economics and Latin American Studies at the University of Pittsburgh, Pa.

(continued from page 503)
MAS, the other main left-wing party, the Radical Cause, also split in two. This left both parties as secondary players in the legislature and ended their pact with COPEI as the "Triple Alliance."

At the end of May, the mayor of Chacao, Irene Sáez, applied to register her party—Integration, Representation, New Hope (IRENE)—on a national level. Despite attacks from rivals, she remained the main presidential contender, with 33% of the voters' support, according to a midyear poll. As an independent, Sáez avoided contact with the traditional political parties but drew support from within all of them. COPEI remained divided over whether to back Sáez.

In June a new labour law was passed to reform the complex and outmoded severance pay system. This was designed to stimulate employment and productivity by reducing the cost to employers of hiring and firing workers. The trade union confederation was criticized for making too many concessions in the labour law negotiations but regained credibility with its members by calling a one-day general strike in July to protest the 27% increase in gasoline (petrol) prices and the private sector's failure to increase salaries, which they claimed were part of the deal that had included government-worker pay increases. This strike followed hard on the heels of a walkout by 3,000 Caracas subway workers.

Prospects for the country's ailing economy looked brighter in 1997, with growth for the year at 5.1%—a faster-than-expected recovery. The oil sector was responsible for much of the expansion, gaining 8.8%. Economic recovery was also helped by the huge government-worker pay increases of about 70%, which boosted private consumption. Growth in bank lending also helped, as did a real appreciation of the bolívar, which fueled rapid import growth. On the downside the large pay increases to government workers caused the government's 1997 inflation target of 25% to rise, and by July the inflation rate was 40.5%.

(ALAN MURPHY)

Rescue workers sift through the rubble after an earthquake jolted the coastal region east of Caracas, Venez., on July 9. The quake, which had a magnitude of 6.9, killed at least 79 people.

ROBERTO SCHMIDT—AFP

VIETNAM

Area: 331,041 sq km (127,816 sq mi)
Population (1997 est.): 75,124,000
Capital: Hanoi
Chief of state: Presidents Le Duc Anh and, from September 17, Tran Duc Luong
Head of government: Prime Ministers Vo Van Kiet and, from September 25, Phan Van Khai

As expected, Vietnam's ruling Communist Party replaced the national leadership in 1997. The government used the closely controlled National Assembly elections on July 20 to bring new blood into the legislature, which over the years had become more vocal in challenging official policy. Although it was no surprise that the Communist Party remained dominant, taking 381 of the 450 seats, three independent candidates—including a former soldier in the South Vietnamese army—were unexpected victors. All but 108 of the legislators were elected for the first time. Women won 117 seats, and ethnic minority groups took 78.

The political highlight of 1997 was, however, the long-awaited appointment of a new president and prime minister. When the National Assembly convened in September, among its first acts was to appoint Phan Van Khai prime minister to replace Vo Van Kiet. Khai, a Russian-trained technocrat and a dominant force behind Hanoi's economic reforms, had long been expected to succeed Kiet. In a surprising move, the National Assembly also chose Tran Duc Luong to take over from ailing Pres. Le Duc Anh. A Russian-trained geologist from central Vietnam, Luong was ranked only 12th in the 18-member Politburo. At a special plenum in late December, the Communist Party's Central Committee named military political commissar Le Kha Phieu, a conservative northerner who ranked fifth in the Politburo, to succeed Do Muoi as the ruling party's general secretary. Phieu thereby became Vietnam's most powerful politician.

While the drama on the political stage unfolded, the Vietnamese government faced daunting economic challenges. Despite official forecasts of another strong year and for annual growth to continue at between 9% and 10% through 2000, independent analysts indicated that growth was slowing and could fall to between 7% and 8% in 1997 and to 5% in 1998. Inflation for the first six months of the year stood at just 1.1%. Exports maintained solid growth, though the electronics sector slowed sharply. Because it was not freely convertible, the local currency was largely shielded from the Asian currency crisis. During the year, however, central bank authorities at least twice effectively devalued the dong. Serious worries about the banking system emerged after several banks, including the largest state-owned commercial bank, Vietcombank, defaulted on letters of credit. As a mark of its concern, the National Assembly in September rejected the nomination of Cao Si Kiem to remain as governor of the central bank. Disenchantment continued to grow among foreign investors, dismayed by Vietnam's bureaucratic red tape, corruption, flagging zeal for reform, and the lack of an adequate legal infrastructure. Unprofitable government-owned firms remained a major drain on the economy.

On the diplomatic front, Vietnam experienced substantial progress. Adm. Joseph Prueher, commander in chief of the U.S. Pacific Command, visited Hanoi in March, followed three months later by U.S. Secretary of State Madeleine Albright. (*See* BIOGRAPHIES.) Do Muoi traveled to China in July. The next month China and Vietnam held talks on their simmering maritime and border disputes, including conflicting claims on the Spratly Islands. In November French Pres. Jacques Chirac paid a state visit to Vietnam, which preceded a summit of French-speaking nations and territories in Hanoi. Russian Prime Minister Viktor Chernomyrdin also visited the nation in November. At the Asia-Pacific Economic Cooperation (APEC) forum, held in Vancouver, B.C., November 21–25, Vietnam, Russia, and Peru were admitted as APEC members from 1998.

An era came to a close on July 31 when the last reigning emperor of Vietnam, Bao Dai (*see* OBITUARIES), died in exile in Paris at the age of 83.

(ALEJANDRO REYES)

This article updates the *Macropædia* article SOUTHEAST ASIA: *Vietnam.*

YEMEN

Area: 555,000 sq km (214,300 sq mi)
Population (1997 est.): 16,496,000
Capital: San'a'
Chief of state: President Maj. Gen. Ali Abdallah Salih
Head of government: Prime Ministers 'Abd al-Aziz 'Abd al-Ghani and, from May 15, Faraj Said ibn Ghanem

Yemen held the second parliamentary election in its history on April 27, 1997. The General People's Congress (GPC) party of Pres. Ali Abdallah Salih won 187 of the 301 seats, and the Islah Party finished second with 53. After the election some successful independent candidates joined those two parties, increasing their seats to 226 and 59, respectively. The Yemeni Socialist Party had won 56 seats in the 1993 election, but in 1997 it boycotted the vote, charging election fraud. Yet international election observers, including the National Democratic Institute, found the voting by and large fair. On May 15 a new prime minister, Faraj Said ibn Ghanem, formed a new 28-member Cabinet, including 24 from the GPC.

Yemen made progress in 1997 toward resolving its territorial dispute with Eritrea over Greater Hanish Island, submitting the problem to arbitration in The Hague. Yemeni-Saudi relations also improved somewhat with intensified negotiations over the nondemarcated portion of their common border.

The government implemented a structural adjustment program to revive the economy, which was suffering the effects of the recent

At-Tawilah, Yemen, was among the areas struggling with absorbing unemployed repatriated workers and other problems after the 1990–91 Persian Gulf War. The Yemeni government won worldwide support in 1997 for planned economic reforms and improved international relations.

J.H. MORRIS—PANOS

civil war and the loss of subsidies from many Arab and Western nations. Comprehensive reforms, including privatization, won endorsement and funding support from the World Bank and the International Monetary Fund. (WILLIAM RUGH)

YUGOSLAVIA

Area: 102,173 sq km (39,449 sq mi)
Population (1997 est.): 10,632,000
Capital: Belgrade
Chief of state: Presidents Zoran Lilic until June 25, Srdja Bozovic (acting) until July 23, and, from July 23, Slobodan Milosevic.
Head of government: Prime Minister Radoje Kontic

Yugoslavia's economic and social situation continued to deteriorate in 1997. The easing of its international isolation after the signing of the Dayton peace accords in December 1995 had little tangible effect on living standards, although the country's straitened circumstances did appear to have eroded the authority of strongman Slobodan Milosevic.

After almost three months of protests against his regime's decision to annul opposition victories in 32 municipal elections held on Nov. 17, 1996, Milosevic decided to recognize his Socialist Party of Serbia's (SPS's) defeat. The Socialists, in alliance with two other leftist parties (one led by Milosevic's wife), still dominated Serbia's parliament and retained control of the media, security forces, and municipal budgets. Constitutionally barred from another term as president of Serbia, Milosevic became president of the Federal Republic of Yugoslavia (comprising Serbia and Montenegro) in July.

Many voters in Serbia's parliamentary and presidential elections in September and October turned to the right, and candidates of the nationalist Serbian Radical Party (SRS) finished second behind Milosevic's much-weakened SPS. The SRS leader and mayor of Zemun, Vojislav Seselj, received more votes than SPS candidate Zoran Lilic in the second round of presidential balloting, but the post remained vacant because of an unacceptably low voter turnout. Lilic was replaced by Yugoslav Foreign Minister Milan Milutinovic as the Socialists' candidate for the December 7 runoff elections, but the results again were inconclusive, and a new election was held on December 21. Milutinovic was the winner and was sworn in as president on December 29.

Another indication of Milosevic's waning influence came in Montenegro, where his protégé, Pres. Momir Bulatovic, was defeated by Prime Minister Milo Djukanovic in presidential balloting in October. The two men had cofounded the ruling Democratic Party of Socialists of Montenegro, but they and the party split over relations with Serbia and economic and political reforms. Djukanovic was slated to take over the presidency in January 1998, but Bulatovic main-

A homeless woman in Yugoslavia finds refuge in a privately owned hotel. The difficult economic situation in Yugoslavia, brought about by government mismanagement and the high cost of the war in Bosnia and Herzegovina, left many formerly middle-class people bankrupt and homeless.

ABBAS—MAGNUM

tained that the election was fraudulent. The parliament drafted a new electoral law and scheduled extraordinary parliamentary elections for May 1998 but could not break the impasse.

The situation in Serbia's predominately ethnic Albanian province of Kosovo remained tense. Less than a year after Milosevic and Ibrahim Rugova, head of the shadow government of the "Republic of Kosovo," signed an agreement calling for the reintegration of Kosovo schools and the return of some 300,000 Albanian-speaking children to classes, clashes between Serbian security forces and Albanians intensified. The agreement, which had been pushed by Western countries and was hailed as the first major breakthrough in normalizing relations between Serbs and Albanians, was never implemented. Rugova appealed for Western mediation, but Milosevic was unenthusiastic. Several European countries and the U.S. advocated a special status for Kosovo to guarantee local autonomy but emphasized that secession was not an option.

The federal Yugoslav economy, devastated by international trade sanctions, years of mismanagement, failure to push privatization, half-hearted reforms, and lack of interest by foreign investors, showed little signs of improvement. Belgrade economists predicted that the overall economic picture throughout Yugoslavia would remain bleak for at least five more years. On the last day of 1996, Milosevic had promised that 1997 would be a year of reforms, and the Serbian government reiterated that pledge for reforms in October. Deputy Prime Minister Danko Djunic, a nonparty economist who was well-connected internationally, was entrusted with the task of guiding reforms and improving Yugoslavia's image abroad.

In July Serbia's parliament passed a voluntary privatization scheme to take effect on October 31. The valuation procedures were lengthy and cumbersome, however, and seemed likely to remain unattractive to foreign investors. International financial and aid institutions were also demanding greater compliance with the Dayton peace agreement. Nevertheless, a number of foreign companies toured Serbia and Montenegro looking for firms to buy. One success was the purchase of 49% of Serbia's postal and telephone company by Italian and Greek companies for something under $1 billion.

(MILAN ANDREJEVICH)

ZAMBIA

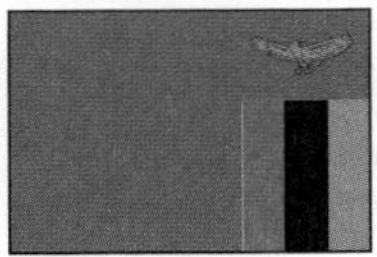

Area: 752,614 sq km (290,586 sq mi)
Population (1997 est.): 9,350,000
Capital: Lusaka
Head of state and government: President Frederick Chiluba

Zambia's success in 1997 in implementing the program of structural adjustment established by the International Monetary Fund and the World Bank continued to guarantee the loyalty of multilateral donors. The World Bank itself promised to provide $123 million in balance of payments support, and in March the European Union granted the nation $200 million. But to the people of Zambia, structural adjustment appeared less rewarding. The stringent controls imposed upon the economy contributed to the growing poverty of the rural population, and the privatization of overstaffed public companies led to the loss of 150,000 jobs, mainly in the towns. Impending cuts in the inflated civil service inherited from Pres. Kenneth Kaunda's days in office also caused disquiet, and members of the civil service threatened strike action if their demands for pay increases were not met.

To add to his troubles, Pres. Frederick Chiluba faced hostility from bilateral donors, who remained critical of the manner in which he had prevented former president Kaunda from competing in the presidential elections in 1996. The action of those donors who had either suspended aid or threatened to do so forced Minister of Finance Ronald Penza to introduce measures into his February budget to encourage self-reliance, though he still hoped for foreign aid to ensure that his cautious optimism about the economy was justified. In April, however, accusations of autocratic behaviour leveled against President Chiluba for proposing legislation to regulate the press resulted in the postponement of the bill.

The privatization of Zambia Consolidated Copper Mines, which was to have been completed by the end of the year, made little progress. The government argued that the fate of an industry that was responsible for 90% of the country's foreign exchange earnings could not be determined without careful consideration of the various options.

Heavy-handed intervention by police, who fired on an opposition rally on August 23, wounding Kaunda and another antigovernment campaigner, created serious tensions in Lusaka, but an attempted military coup on October 28 was easily thwarted. Nevertheless, the professed objective of the coup—to stop the country from going to ruin—provided evidence of the failure of the government's policies to gain the confidence of the general public. At the same time, the stern measures adopted by the government in the wake of the failed coup confirmed critics in their view that democracy no longer prevailed in Zambia. On December 25 Kaunda was arrested on charges of inciting the attempted coup. Six days later he was released but placed under house arrest.

(KENNETH INGHAM)

This article updates the *Macropædia* article SOUTHERN AFRICA: *Zambia.*

ZIMBABWE

Area: 390,757 sq km (150,872 sq mi)
Population (1997 est.): 11,423,000
Capital: Harare
Head of state and government: President Robert Mugabe

Pres. Robert Mugabe's consistent refusal in 1997 to respond to external pressures to change policies that he professed to be in the interests of the black population of his country made potential foreign donors cautious and caused would-be foreign investors to hesitate. At the same time, Mugabe's frequently reiterated threat to acquire mainly white-owned land without compensating the owners, except where improvements had clearly been made, aroused disquiet among the nation's white farmers. On November 28 the government published a list of 1,503 mostly white-owned commercial farms that would be forcibly purchased. The owners had until December 28 to appeal the ruling.

Typical of the president's stance was his announcement in February of a new tariff structure that gave increased protection to local industry. This was in clear conflict with the World Bank policy on trade liberalization. Then, in March, a bill was published legalizing affirmative action to permit discrimination that would benefit "persons disadvantaged by previous discrimination." Later in the month Mugabe stated that recent reforms had left the country "ripe for investment" and that the government would continue to play an important role in the choice of foreign partners and would ensure that the privatization program was used to encourage black entrepreneurs so as to redress the legacy of minority rule.

These moves failed to harmonize with allegations that senior party officials, including the president's brother-in-law, had lied in order to receive substantial benefits in compensation for nonexistent wounds said to have been received in fighting for black majority rule. In April evidence in court revealed that Mugabe's wife and others had illegally borrowed millions of dollars from a finance fund set up by the U.S. to help house the urban poor of Zimbabwe.

An outbreak of strikes induced the government to offer pay increases of more than 30% to public-service employees in July. This forced other employers, who had hoped to keep wage increases to the level of inflation, to concede similar pay awards. The strain that the increases imposed on the finance minister's attempts to balance the budget was considerable, yet the World Bank claimed in August to have seen sufficient improvement in Zimbabwe's fiscal situation to justify the renewal of financial support suspended in 1995.

Mugabe soon caused the bank to reverse its decision. The revelation in March of bogus compensation claims for war wounds had led to the suspension of compensation payments. This was followed by increasingly noisy protests from genuine guerrilla veterans that culminated in the disruption of a ceremony marking Heroes' Day in August. In the face of protests from the minister of finance, Mugabe offered a generous package of payments and other benefits to all veterans of the freedom struggle.

The World Bank's subsequent decision in October to delay disbursement of its aid was a severe setback, but the ever-resilient Mugabe seized the opportunity provided by his visit to the U.K. to attend the Commonwealth Heads of Government Meeting later in the month to ask the British government to provide compensation to the white farmers whose land he proposed to acquire for redistribution among the black population. Britain, however, refused to pay, stating that the farmers were now Zimbabwean citizens.

(KENNETH INGHAM)

This article updates the *Macropædia* article SOUTHERN AFRICA: *Zimbabwe.*

CONTRIBUTORS

Adams, Andy. Editor and Publisher, *Sumo World.* Author of *Sumo; Sumo World Record Book.* •SPORTS AND GAMES: *Judo; Wrestling:* Sumo

Ajello, Robin Paul. Associate Editor, *Asiaweek* magazine. •WORLD AFFAIRS: *Cambodia*

Alder, Phillip. Syndicated Bridge Columnist. Author of *Get Smarter at Bridge.* •SPORTS AND GAMES: *Contract Bridge*

Alexander, Steve. Freelance. •COMPUTERS AND INFORMATION SYSTEMS

Allaby, Michael. Writer and Lecturer. Author of *Basic Environmental Science; Facing the Future.* •THE ENVIRONMENT: *Environmental Issues; International Environmental Activities*

Allan, J.A. Professor of Geography, School of Oriental and African Studies, University of London. Author of *Water and Peace in the Middle East.* •WORLD AFFAIRS: *Libya*

Andrades, Jorge Adrián. •SPORTS AND GAMES: *Equestrian Sports:* Polo

Andrejevich, Milan. U.S.-based Writer and Consultant •WORLD AFFAIRS: *Bosnia and Herzegovina; Yugoslavia*

Archibald, John J. Retired Feature Writer, St. Louis (Mo.) *Post-Dispatch;* Adjunct Professor, Washington University, St. Louis. Member of the American Bowling Congress Hall of Fame. •SPORTS AND GAMES: *Bowling:* U.S. Tenpins

Arnold, Guy. Freelance Writer. Author of *South Africa: Crossing the Rubicon; Modern Nigeria;* and others. •WORLD AFFAIRS: *Botswana; Burundi; Cape Verde; Chad; Comoros; Djibouti; Equatorial Guinea; Gambia, The; Ghana; Guinea-Bissau; Lesotho; Liberia; Madagascar; Maldives; Mauritius; Nigeria; Rwanda; São Tomé and Príncipe; Seychelles; Sierra Leone; Swaziland*

Arnold, Mavis. Freelance Journalist, Dublin. •WORLD AFFAIRS: *Ireland*

Arrington, Leonard J. Formerly Church Historian, Church of Jesus Christ of Latter-day Saints. Coauthor of *The Mormon Experience* and others. •RELIGION: *Church of Jesus Christ of Latter-day Saints*

Aurora, Vincent. Preceptor of French Literature, Columbia University, New York City. •LITERATURE: *French:* France

Baber, Bonnie. Senior Editor, *Footwear News* magazine. •BUSINESS AND INDUSTRY REVIEW: *Apparel:* Footwear

Backe, Everett E. Senior Scientist and Professor, Institute of Textile Technology. Author of *Cotton Ginners Handbook.* •BUSINESS AND INDUSTRY REVIEW: *Textiles:* Cotton; Wool

Bahry, Louay. Adjunct Professor of Political Science, Washington, D.C. Author of *The Baghdad Bahn.* •WORLD AFFAIRS: *Bahrain; Iraq*

Bailey, George. Author of *Galileo's Children; Germans.* •MEDIA AND PUBLISHING: *Magazines:* Sidebar; WORLD AFFAIRS: *Germany*

Bakker, Martinus A. Professor of Germanic Languages, Calvin College, Grand Rapids, Mich. Editor of *Studies in Netherlandic Culture and Literature.* •LITERATURE: *Netherlandic*

Balaban, Avraham. Professor of Modern Hebrew Literature, University of Florida. Author of *A Different Wave of Hebrew Fiction: Postmodernist Israel.* •LITERATURE: *Jewish:* Hebrew

Balmforth, Dennis. Visiting Professor Emeritus, Institute of Textile Technology. •BUSINESS AND INDUSTRY REVIEW: *Textiles:* Introduction; Manmade Fibres

Barrett, David B. Research Professor of Missiometrics, Regent University, Virginia Beach, Va. Author of *World Christian Encyclopedia; Schism and Renewal in Africa.* •RELIGION: *Tables* (in part)

Barrett, John C.A. Headmaster, the Leys School; Secretary, British Committee, World Methodist Council. Author of *Family Worship in Theory and Practice.* •RELIGION: *Methodist Churches*

Bass, Howard. Journalist and Author; formerly Editor, *Winter Sports;* Ice Hockey Correspondent, *Daily Telegraph;* Skiing and Skating Correspondent, *Daily Mail.* Author of 19 books on winter sports. •SPORTS AND GAMES: *Ice Hockey:* International; *Ice Skating; Skiing*

Bauer, Steven. Professor of English, Miami University, Oxford, Ohio. Author of *Daylight Savings,* winner of the Peregrine Smith Poetry Prize. •LITERATURE: *Introduction*

Beckwith, David C. Director of Government Relations, Electronic Data Systems, Inc., Washington, D.C. •WORLD AFFAIRS: *United States:* State and Local Affairs

Belaski, Ann M. Multimedia Content Editor, McDougal Littel. •BIOGRAPHIES *(in part)*

Bell, Tom. Classifier, Encyclopædia Britannica •OBITUARIES *(in part)*

Berfield, Susan. Senior Writer, *Asiaweek* magazine. •WORLD AFFAIRS: *Indonesia*

Bickelhaupt, David L. Professor Emeritus, Fisher College of Business, Ohio State University. •BUSINESS AND INDUSTRY REVIEW: *Insurance*

Binczewski, George J. Principal Technical Adviser, S.C. Systems, Moraga, Calif. •BUSINESS AND INDUSTRY REVIEW: *Materials and Metals:* Light Metals

Bird, Thomas E. Co-director of the Jewish Studies Program and the Center for Jewish Studies, Queens College, City University of New York. •LITERATURE: *Jewish:* Yiddish

Blackmore, Heather. Editorial Assistant, Encyclopædia Britannica •BIOGRAPHIES *(in part)*

Boddy, William C. Founder and Editor, *Motor Sport,* London. Author of *Aero-Engined Racing Cars, etc.,* and MBE. •SPORTS AND GAMES: *Automobile Racing:* Grand Prix Racing

Bodeker, Gerard C. Member, Health Services Research Unit, University of Oxford, Oxford, Eng. •HEALTH AND DISEASE: *Special Report:* Alternative Medicine *(in part)*

Boden, Edward. Publications Adviser, British Veterinary Association. •HEALTH AND DISEASE: *Veterinary Medicine*

Boggan, Tim. Historian, U.S.A. Table Tennis Association (USATT). Author of *Winning Table Tennis.* •SPORTS AND GAMES: *Table Tennis*

Bonds, John B. Adjunct Professor, The Citadel. •SPORTS AND GAMES: *Sailing*

Booth, John Nicholls. Lecturer and Writer. Author of *The Quest for Preaching Power; Psychic Paradoxes;* and others. •RELIGION: *Unitarian (Universalist) Churches*

Boswall, Jeffery. Freelance Lecturer on Wildlife Television. •LIFE SCIENCES: *Ornithology*

Box, Ben. Editor, Footprint Handbooks. •WORLD AFFAIRS: *Costa Rica; Honduras; Panama; Uruguay*

Boye, Roger. Formerly Coin Columnist, *Chicago Tribune.* •ART, ANTIQUES, AND COLLECTIONS: *Numismatics*

Bradsher, Henry S. Foreign Affairs Writer. •WORLD AFFAIRS: *Philippines*

Brazee, Rutlage J. Geophysical Consultant. •EARTH SCIENCES: *Geophysics*

Brecher, Kenneth. Professor of Astronomy and Physics, Boston University. •MATHEMATICS AND EARTH SCIENCES: *Astronomy*

Brockmann, Stephen. Assistant Professor of German Studies, Carnegie Mellon University •LITERATURE: *German*

Brokopp, John G. Specialist in publicity, public relations, and writing about equestrian racing. •SPORTS AND GAMES: *Equestrian Sports:* Thoroughbred Racing: *United States*

Brown, Bess. Human Dimensions Specialist, OSCE Liaison Office for Central Asia. Author of *Authoritarianism in the New States of Central Asia.* •WORLD AFFAIRS: *Kazakstan; Kyrgyzstan; Tajikistan; Turkmenistan; Uzbekistan*

Brundtland, Gro Harlem. Physician and Former Prime Minister of Norway. •COMMENTARY: *Shifting Attitudes in a Changing World*

Buchan, David. Correspondent, *Financial Times,* Paris. •WORLD AFFAIRS: *France;* SPOTLIGHT: *France's New African Policy*

Burks, Ardath W. Professor Emeritus of Asian Studies, Rutgers University, New Brunswick, N.J. Author of *Japan: A Postindustrial Power.* •WORLD AFFAIRS: *Japan*

Burns, Erik. Bureau Chief, AP-Dow Jones News Services, Lisbon. •WORLD AFFAIRS: *Portugal*

Butler, Frank. Formerly Sports Editor, *News of the World.* Author of *The Good, the Bad and the Ugly: A Story of Boxing.* •SPORTS AND GAMES: *Boxing*

Cafferty, Bernard. Associate Editor, *British Chess Magazine.* •SPORTS AND GAMES: *Chess*

Cameron, Sarah. Freelance Writer and Editor, Footprint Handbooks. •WORLD AFFAIRS: *Cuba; Dominican Republic; El Salvador; Guatemala; Haiti; Nicaragua*

Campbell, Paul J. Professor of Mathematics and Computer Science, Beloit College, Beloit, Wis. •MATHEMATICS AND PHYSICAL SCIENCES: *Mathematics*

Campbell, Robert. Architect and Architecture Critic. Author of *Cityscapes of Boston;* Coauthor of *American Architecture of the 1980s.* •ARCHITECTURE AND CIVIL ENGINEERING: *Architecture*

Carter, Robert W. Journalist, London. •SPORTS AND GAMES: *Equestrian Sports:* Show Jumping and Dressage; Steeplechasing; Thoroughbred Racing: *International*

Chappell, Duncan. Deputy President, Federal Administrative Appeals Tribunal, Sydney, Australia. •LAW, CRIME, AND LAW ENFORCEMENT: *Crime; Law Enforcement*

Chapple, Abby. Writer and Consultant, Consumer Communications, Largent, W.Va. •BUSINESS AND INDUSTRY REVIEW: *Home Furnishings:* Furniture

Cheadle, Bruce. Reporter, The Canadian Press. •SPORTS AND GAMES: *Curling*

Cheuse, Alan. Writing Faculty, English Department, George Mason University, Fairfax, Va.; Book Commentator, National Public Radio. Author of *The Light Possessed* and others. •LITERATURE: *English:* United States

Choong Tet Sieu. Associate Editor, *Asiaweek* magazine. •WORLD AFFAIRS: *Malaysia*

Cioroslan, Dragomir. National Coach for U.S.A. Weightlifting, Inc. •SPORTS AND GAMES: *Weight Lifting*

Clark, David D. Managing Editor, *World Literature Today.* •LITERATURE: *English:* Other Literature in English

Clarke, Douglas L. Captain, U.S. Navy (ret.); Military Analyst. Author of *The Missing Man: Politics and the MIA.* •MILITARY AFFAIRS

Clarke, R.O. Lecturer and Consultant on Industrial Relations, London. •ECONOMIC AFFAIRS: *Labour-Management Relations*

Cogle, T.C.J. Consultant, *Electrical Review.* •BUSINESS AND INDUSTRY REVIEW: *Electrical*

Colvin, David. Managing Editor, *The Middle East Journal.* •WORLD AFFAIRS: *Oman; Qatar*

Corzine, Robert. Energy Correspondent, *Financial Times.* •BUSINESS AND INDUSTRY REVIEW: *Energy:* Alternative Energy; Natural Gas; Petroleum

Cosgrave, Bronwyn. Health and Beauty Editor, U.K. *Cosmopolitan.* •BIOGRAPHIES *(in part);* FASHIONS; OBITUARIES *(in part)*

Coveney, Michael. Theatre Critic, *The Daily Mail.* Author of *The World According to Mike Leigh* and others. •PERFORMING ARTS: *Theatre:* Great Britain and Ireland

Craine, Anthony G. Associate Editor, *Inside Sports* magazine. •BIOGRAPHIES *(in part);* SPORTS AND GAMES: *Baseball:* Sidebar; *Introduction*

Crampton, Richard J. Professor of East European History and Fellow of St. Edmund Hall, University of Oxford, Oxford, Eng. Author of *Eastern Europe in the Twentieth Century and others.* •WORLD AFFAIRS: *Bulgaria*

Crowell, George T. Senior Writer, *Asiaweek* magazine. •WORLD AFFAIRS: *Korea, Democratic People's Republic of; Korea, Republic of*

Crowley, Edward. Editor, Baltic Magazine Supplements; Director, Technical Writing Services.

•BUSINESS AND INDUSTRY REVIEW: *Shipbuilding;* TRANSPORTATION: *Shipping and Ports*

Cunningham, Susan M. Economic and Political Analyst; Freelance Writer. Author of *Latin America Since 1945.* •WORLD AFFAIRS: *Argentina; Brazil; Mexico*

Curwen, Peter J. Professor of Business, Sheffield (Eng.) Business School. Author of *The U.K. Publishing Industry* and others. •MEDIA AND PUBLISHING: *Book Publishing* (international)

Deam, John B. Retired Technical Director, AMT—The Association for Manufacturing Technology, McLean, Va. •BUSINESS AND INDUSTRY REVIEW: *Machinery and Machine Tools*

Deanin, Rudolph D. Professor, Department of Plastics Engineering, University of Massachusetts at Lowell. Author of *Plastics Additives.* •BUSINESS AND INDUSTRY REVIEW: *Materials and Metals:* Plastics

Deeb, Marius K. Professor, SAIS, Johns Hopkins University, Washington, D.C. Author of *Political Parties and Democracy in Egypt.* •WORLD AFFAIRS: *Egypt*

de la Barre, Kenneth. Director, the Bridge Group. •WORLD AFFAIRS: *Arctic Regions*

Denselow, Robin. Rock Music Critic, *The Guardian;* Current Affairs Reporter, BBC Television. Author of *When the Music's Over: The Politics of Pop.* •PERFORMING ARTS: *Music:* Popular (international)

de Puy, Norman R. Minister, American Baptist Churches; Editor and Publisher, *Cabbages and Kings* newsletter. •RELIGION: *Baptist Churches*

Dicks, Geoffrey R. U.K. Economist, NatWest Markets. Author of *Sources of World Financial and Banking Information.* •BUSINESS AND INDUSTRY REVIEW: *Introduction*

Dixon, Bernard. Science Writer; Consultant; Editor, *Medical Science Research.* Author of *Power Unseen: How Microbes Rule the World* and others. •HEALTH AND DISEASE: *Medicine* (international); *Mental Health*

Doll, Susan. Freelance Writer, Instructor of Film History, School of the Art Institute of Chicago and Oakton Community College. Author of *Best of Elvis and others.* •BIOGRAPHIES *(in part);* BUSINESS AND INDUSTRY REVIEW: *Home Furnishings:* Housewares; OBITUARIES *(in part)*

Dooling, Dave. Freelance Aerospace Writer, D^2 Associates. •MATHEMATICS AND PHYSICAL SCIENCES: *Space Exploration*

Dowd, Siobhan. Columnist, *Literary Review* (London); *Glimmer Train* (U.S.). Author of *This Prison Where I Live.* •LITERATURE: *English:* United Kingdom

Eadington, William R. Professor of Economics, Director, Institute for Study of Gambling and Commercial Gaming, University of Nevada, Reno. •BUSINESS AND INDUSTRY REVIEW: *Special Report:* Gambling

Earp, John H. Director, Halcrow Fox and Associates. •TRANSPORTATION: *Introduction; Freight and Pipelines; Intercity Rail; Roads and Traffic; Urban Mass Transit*

Edmondson, Lesley. Freelance Writer. •BIOGRAPHIES *(in part)*

Ehringer, Gavin Forbes. Rodeo Columnist, *Western Horseman.* •SPORTS AND GAMES: *Rodeo*

Ellis, Roger. Editor, *Mining Journal,* London. •BUSINESS AND INDUSTRY REVIEW: *Mining*: Sidebar

Eron, Carol L. Director, Editorial Concepts. •BUSINESS AND INDUSTRY REVIEW: *Materials and Metals:* Ceramics *(in part)*

Fagan, Brian. Professor of Anthropology, University of California, Santa Barbara. Author of *Time Detectives.* •ANTHROPOLOGY AND ARCHAEOLOGY: *Archaeology:* Western Hemisphere

Farr, D.M.L. Professor Emeritus of History, Carleton University, Ottawa. •WORLD AFFAIRS: *Canada*

Fendell, Robert J. Board Member, Amelia Island Concours d'Elegance. Columnist, *Sport Scene Florida.* Author of *Encyclopedia of Motor Racing Greats* and others. •SPORTS AND GAMES: *Automobile Racing:* U.S. Auto Racing

Finch, Andrew. Assistant Director, Government and Public Affairs, American Association of Museums. •LIBRARIES AND MUSEUMS: *Museums* (United States)

Fischer, Adelheid. Associate Editor, *Yearbook of Science and the Future,* Encyclopædia Britannica. •BIOGRAPHIES *(in part);* OBITUARIES *(in part)*

Fisher, Sharon. Central European Specialist, London. •WORLD AFFAIRS: *Czech Republic; Slovakia*

Flagg, Gordon. Managing Editor, *American Libraries.* •LIBRARIES AND MUSEUMS: *Libraries* (United States)

Flanders, Douglas L. Development Officer, *The United Church Observer.* •RELIGION: *The United Church of Canada*

Fletcher, Charmaine. Media and Press Officer, the Salvation Army. •RELIGION: *Salvation Army*

Flink, Steve. Senior Correspondent, *Tennis Week* magazine; formerly Editor, *World Tennis* magazine. •SPORTS AND GAMES: *Tennis*

Flores, Ramona Monette S. Professor, University of the Philippines; Editorial Consultant, *Masks and Voices;* Editor-in-Chief, *Pahinungód Annual Journal.* •MEDIA AND PUBLISHING: *Radio* (international); *Television* (international)

Fogle, Douglas. Curatorial Assistant, Walker Art Center, Minneapolis, Minn. •ART, ANTIQUES, AND COLLECTIONS: *Paintings and Sculpture*

Follett, Christopher. Denmark Correspondent, *The Times;* Danish Correspondent, Radio Sweden; Newscaster, Radio Denmark, affiliated to Reuters News Agency, Copenhagen. Author of *Fodspor paa Cypern.* •WORLD AFFAIRS: *Denmark*

Forrest, Brett. Reporter, *Men's Journal* •SPORTS AND GAMES: *Special Report:* Alternative Sports

Foster, David William. Chair, Regents' Professor of Spanish, Humanities, and Women's Studies, Arizona State University. Author of *Violence in Argentine Literature* and others. •LITERATURE: *Spanish:* Latin America

Frank, Stephen E. Staff Reporter, *The Wall Street Journal.* •ECONOMIC AFFAIRS: *Banking: United States*

Freeman, Laurie. Freelance Writer and Editor. •BUSINESS AND INDUSTRY REVIEW: *Advertising*

Fridovich, Irwin. James B. Duke Professor of Biochemistry, Duke University Medical Center, Durham, N.C. •LIFE SCIENCES: *Molecular Biology (in part)*

Fridovich-Keil, Judith L. Assistant Professor, Department of Genetics, Emory University School of Medicine, Atlanta, Ga. •LIFE SCIENCES: *Molecular Biology (in part);* WORLD AFFAIRS: *Japan:* Sidebar

Friedrich, Mary Jane. Life Sciences Editor, Encyclopædia Britannica. •BIOGRAPHIES *(in part)*; OBITUARIES *(in part)*

Friskin, Sydney E. Hockey Correspondent, *The Times.* •SPORTS AND GAMES: *Billiard Games:* Snooker; *Field Hockey*

Fuller, Elizabeth. Editor, *Newsline,* Radio Free Europe, Radio Liberty, Prague. •WORLD AFFAIRS: *Armenia; Azerbaijan; Georgia*

Gaddum, Anthony H. Chairman, H.T. Gaddum and Co.; Vice President, International Silk Association. •BUSINESS AND INDUSTRY REVIEW: *Textiles:* Silk

Ganado, Albert. Lawyer. Coauthor of *A Study in Depth of 143 Maps Representing the Great Siege of Malta of 1565* and others. •WORLD AFFAIRS: *Malta*

Garrod, Mark. Golf Correspondent, PA Sport, U.K. Contributor to *Golf World* and *Amateur Golf* magazines. Secretary of the Association of Golf Writers. •SPORTS AND GAMES: *Golf*

Gaughan, Thomas. Associate Director of Libraries, Illinois Institute of Technology, Chicago. •LIBRARIES AND MUSEUMS: *Libraries* (international)

Gibbons, Anne R. Freelance Writer. •LIFE SCIENCES: *Entomology*

Gibbons, J. Whitfield. Professor of Ecology, Savannah River Ecology Laboratory, University of Georgia. Author of *Keeping All the Pieces* and others. •LIFE SCIENCES: *Zoology*

Gill, Martin J. Information and Computer Expert, F.A.O. EASTFISH. •AGRICULTURE AND FOOD SUPPLIES: *Fisheries*

Girnius, Saulius A. State Consultant, Republic of Lithuania Government •WORLD AFFAIRS: *Lithuania*

Gobbie, Donn. Director of Publicity and Media Relations, U.S. Badminton Association. •SPORTS AND GAMES: *Badminton*

Goldsmith, Arthur. Freelance Writer. Author of *The Camera and Its Images.* •ART, ANTIQUES, AND COLLECTIONS: *Photography;* BUSINESS AND INDUSTRY REVIEW: *Photography*

Gottlieb, Jean S. Freelance Editor; Bibliographer. Author of *A Checklist of the Newberry Library's Printed Books in Science, Medicine, Technology, and the Pseudosciences, ca. 1460–1750.* •BIBLIOGRAPHY

Greeman, Adrian Lee. Editor, *Civil Engineer International.* •ARCHITECTURE AND CIVIL ENGINEERING: *Bridges*

Green, Anthony L. Copy Supervisor, Encyclopædia Britannica. •BIOGRAPHIES *(in part)*

Green, Theresa. Information Officer. •BUSINESS AND INDUSTRY REVIEW: *Materials and Metals:* Glass

Greskovic, Robert. Dance Reviewer, *A&E Entertainment Almanac;* Freelance Writer. •PERFORMING ARTS: *Dance:* North America

Griffiths, A.R.G. Associate Professor in History, Flinders University of South Australia. Author of *Contemporary Australia; Beautiful Lies.* •WORLD AFFAIRS: *Australia; Nauru; Palau; Papua New Guinea; Spotlight:* Racial Integration in Australia and New Zealand

Grumet, Robert S. Anthropologist, New Hope, Pa. Author of *Historic Contact* and others. •ANTHROPOLOGY AND ARCHAEOLOGY: *Anthropology:* Cultural

Gutek, Gerald Lee. Professor, Educational Leadership and Policy Studies, Loyola University, Chicago. Author of *A History of the Western Educational Experience* and others. •EDUCATION (U.S.); EDUCATION: *Sidebar*

Guthridge, Guy G. Manager, Polar Information Program, U.S. National Science Foundation. •WORLD AFFAIRS: *Antarctica*

Halman, Talat S. Distinguished Visiting Professor, Bilkent University, Ankara. Author of *Poetry of Ancient Anatolia and Near East.* •LITERATURE: *Turkish*

Hamilton, Andrea. Staff Correspondent, *Asiaweek* magazine. •WORLD AFFAIRS: *Singapore*

Hammer, William R. Professor and Chair, Department of Geology, Augustana College, Rock Island, Ill. Author of contributions to Dinofest II International Proceedings, National Academy of Sciences, Philadelphia; *Antarctic Paleobiology.* •LIFE SCIENCES: *Paleontology*

Hannen, Mark. Competitions Officer, English Basket Ball Association. •SPORTS AND GAMES: *Basketball:* International

Harakas, Stanley S. Emeritus Archbishop Iakovos Professor of Orthodox Theology, Holy Cross Greek Orthodox School of Theology. Author of *Health and Medicine in the Eastern Orthodox Tradition* and others. •RELIGION: *Oriental Orthodox Church; The Orthodox Church*

Haub, Carl V. Demographer, Population Reference Bureau. Author of *Population Change in the Former Soviet Union* and others. •POPULATION TRENDS: *Demography*

Hawkland, William D. Chancellor Emeritus of Law and Boyd Professor, Louisiana State University. •LAW, CRIME, AND LAW ENFORCEMENT: *Court Decisions*

Healy, Tim. General Editor, *Asiaweek* magazine. •WORLD AFFAIRS: *Brunei; Dependent States:* East Asia

Heim, Chris. Music Director and Freelance Writer, WBEZ Radio, Chicago. •PERFORMING ARTS: *Music:* Special Report: *Listening to the Music of the World*

Heinzl, John. Business Reporter, *Toronto Globe and Mail.* •BUSINESS AND INDUSTRY REVIEW: *Retailing*

Helgadottir, Birna. Senior Reporter, *The European.* •WORLD AFFAIRS: *Spotlight:* Europe's Crumbling Social Network

Hendershott, Myrl C. Professor of Oceanography, Scripps Institution of Oceanography, La Jolla, Calif. •EARTH SCIENCES: *Oceanography*

Hennelly, James. Assistant Editor, Encyclopædia Britannica. •BIOGRAPHIES *(in part);* ECONOMIC

AFFAIRS: *Labour-Management Relations:* Sidebar; OBITUARIES *(in part)*

Henschel, Milton. President, Watchtower Bible and Tract Society. •RELIGION: *Jehovah's Witnesses*

Hering, Howard. Administrative Manager, Frederick Wildman and Sons. •BUSINESS AND INDUSTRY REVIEW: *Beverages:* Wine

Higgs, Kimball. Assistant Vice President, Sotheby's Book Department. •ART, ANTIQUES, AND COLLECTIONS: *Antiquarian Books*

Hobbs, Greg. Chief Writer, Australian Football League. Author of books on Australian Football. •SPORTS AND GAMES: *Football:* Australian

Hoeksema, Klaas J. Staff Member, Institute for Polytechnics, Amsterdam. •WORLD AFFAIRS: *Netherlands, The; Suriname*

Hoffman, Dean A. Executive Editor, *Hoof Beats* magazine. •SPORTS AND GAMES: *Equestrian Sports:* Harness Racing

Hoke, John. Publisher, *Amateur Wrestling News.* •SPORTS AND GAMES: *Wrestling*

Hollar, Sherman. Assistant Editor, Encyclopædia Britannica. •BIOGRAPHIES *(in part)*; DISASTERS

Homel, David. Author of *Rat Palms* and others. •LITERATURE: *French:* Canada

Hope, Thomas W. Chairman/CEO, Hope Reports, Inc. Author of *America's Top 100 Contract Producers.* •PERFORMING ARTS: *Motion Pictures:* Nontheatrical Films

Hunnings, Neville March. Editor, *Encyclopedia of European Union Law—Constitutional Texts.* •LAW, CRIME, AND LAW ENFORCEMENT (international)

IEIS. International Economic Information Services. •ECONOMIC AFFAIRS: *World Economy; Stock Exchanges* (international)

Ingham, Kenneth. Emeritus Professor of History, University of Bristol, Eng. Author of *Politics in Modern Africa: The Uneven Tribal Dimension* and others. •WORLD AFFAIRS: *Angola; Congo, Democratic Republic of the (Zaire); Kenya; Malawi; Mozambique; Sudan, The; Tanzania; Uganda; Zambia; Zimbabwe*

Ingram, Derek. Consultant Editor, Gemini News Service. Author of *Commonwealth for a Colour-Blind World; The Imperfect Commonwealth.* •WORLD AFFAIRS: *Commonwealth of Nations*

Ionescu, Dan. Journalist, Radio Free Europe, Romanian/Moldovan Desk. Former Senior Research Analyst with Open Media Research Institute, Prague. •WORLD AFFAIRS: *Moldova; Romania*

Jackson, Peter S. Wyse. Secretary-General, Botanic Gardens Conservation International, U.K. •THE ENVIRONMENT: *Botanical Gardens*

Jamail, Milton. Lecturer, Department of Government, University of Texas at Austin. •SPORTS AND GAMES: *Baseball:* Latin America

Jessell, Harry A. Executive Editor, *Broadcasting & Cable.* •MEDIA AND PUBLISHING: *Radio:* (U.S., *in part*); *Radio:* Amateur Radio *(in part)*; *Television* (U.S., *in part*)

Joffé, George. Journalist and Writer on North African and Middle Eastern Affairs. Deputy Director, RIIA, London. •WORLD AFFAIRS: *Algeria; Morocco; Tunisia*

Johnson, Todd M. Senior Researcher, World Evangelization Research Center. Coauthor of *World Christian Encyclopedia.* •RELIGION: *Tables* (in part)

Johnsson, William G. Editor, *Adventist Review.* Author of *Behold His Glory* and others. •RELIGION: *Seventh-day Adventist Church*

Jones, David G.C. Honorary Lecturer in Physics, University of Sussex, Brighton, Eng. Author of *Atomic Physics.* •MATHEMATICS AND PHYSICAL SCIENCES: *Physics*

Jones, W. Glyn. Professor Emeritus of Scandinavian Studies, University of East Anglia, Norwich, Eng. Author of *Colloquial Danish* and others. •LITERATURE: *Danish*

Jotischky, Helma. Head of Business Intelligence, Paint Research Association. Author of *The Americas* and others. •BUSINESS AND INDUSTRY REVIEW: *Paints and Varnishes*

Kang, Taehi. Associate Professor of Art Theory, The Korean National University of Arts, Seoul. •BIOGRAPHIES *(in part)*

Karimi-Hakkak, Ahmad. Associate Professor of Persian Languages and Literature, University of Washington. •LITERATURE: *Persian*

Kelleher, John A. Journalist, New Zealand. Formerly Editor, *Dominion* and *Dominion Sunday Times* (Wellington). •WORLD AFFAIRS: *New Zealand*

Keller, Edmond J. Professor, Political Science, University of California, Los Angeles. •WORLD AFFAIRS: *Eritrea; Ethiopia*

Kelling, George H. Historian, Wilford Hall Air Force Medical Center. Author of *Countdown to Rebellion: British Policy in Cyprus 1939–1955.* •WORLD AFFAIRS: *Cyprus*

Kellner, Peter. Political Commentator, BBC Television; Columnist, *The Observer,* London. Author of *The Civil Servants: An Inquiry into Britain's Ruling Class* and others. •BIOGRAPHIES *(in part)*; WORLD AFFAIRS: *United Kingdom;* Sidebar

Knapp, Rebecca. Managing Editor, *Art & Antiques.* •ART, ANTIQUES, AND COLLECTIONS: *Introduction*

Knowles, Gerald. Professor, Department of Linguistics, University of Lancaster, Lancaster, Eng. Author of *A Cultural History of the English Language.* •WORLD AFFAIRS: *Spotlight:* English Language Imperialism

Knox, Richard A. Specialist Energy Writer, Technical Press Services. •BUSINESS AND INDUSTRY REVIEW: *Energy:* Nuclear

Koberstein, Wayne. Editor, *Pharmaceutical Executive* magazine. •BUSINESS AND INDUSTRY REVIEW: *Pharmaceuticals*

Koelsch, James R. Freelance Journalist, Discrete Parts Manufacturing Industry. •BUSINESS AND INDUSTRY REVIEW: *Materials and Metals:* Metalworking

Kovel, Ralph and Terry. Authors; Publishers. Authors of *Kovels' Antiques & Collectibles Price List 1996.* •ART, ANTIQUES, AND COLLECTIONS: *Collectibles*

Kowalski, Lawrence. Copy Supervisor, Encyclopædia Britannica. •OBITUARIES *(in part)*

Krause, Stefan. Historian and Balkan Specialist, London. •WORLD AFFAIRS: *Greece; Macedonia*

Kroll, Thomas E. Lecturer, Roosevelt University and Northwestern University, Chicago; President, Thomas Kroll Associates. Author of *Introduction to Data Processing; C Language Programming.* •BUSINESS AND INDUSTRY REVIEW: *Microelectronics; Telecommunications*

Kuiper, Kathleen. Associate Editor, Encyclopædia Britannica. Editor, *Merriam-Webster's Encyclopedia of Literature.* •BIOGRAPHIES *(in part);* OBITUARIES *(in part)*

Kuptsch, Christiane. Research Officer, ISSA. •SOCIAL PROTECTION (international)

Lamb, Kevin M. Special Projects Writer, *Dayton* (Ohio) *Daily News.* Author of *Quarterbacks, Nickelbacks & Other Loose Change.* •SPORTS AND GAMES: *Football:* Canadian, U.S.

Lamb, Robert E. Executive Director, American Philatelic Society. •ART, ANTIQUES, AND COLLECTIONS: *Philately*

Langeneckert, Sandra. Copy Editor, Encyclopædia Britannica. •BIOGRAPHIES *(in part)*; OBITUARIES *(in part)*

Laqueur, Walter. Chairman, International Research Council, Center for Strategic and International Studies, Washington, D.C. Author of *Europe in Our Time* and others. •WORLD AFFAIRS: *Introduction*

Latham, Arthur. Freelance Writer. •BIOGRAPHIES *(in part)*; OBITUARIES *(in part)*

Lavallée, H.-Claude. Director of Graduate Studies, Pulp and Paper Research Centre, University of Quebec at Trois-Rivières. •BUSINESS AND INDUSTRY REVIEW: *Wood Products:* Paper and Pulp

Lawler, Nancy Ellen. Professor Emeritus, Oakton Community College, Des Plaines, Ill. Author of *Soldiers of Misfortune* and others. •WORLD AFFAIRS: *Benin; Burkina Faso; Cameroon; Central African Republic; Congo; Côte d'Ivoire; Gabon; Guinea; Mali; Mauritania; Niger; Senegal; Togo*

Lawson, Fred H. James Irvine Professor of Government, Mills College, Oakland, Calif. •WORLD AFFAIRS: *Syria*

Lawson, Richard L. General, USAF (retired). President and Chief Executive Officer, National Mining Association. •BUSINESS AND INDUSTRY REVIEW: *Energy:* Coal

Lee, Jungbock. Professor, Department of Political Science, Seoul National University. •BIOGRAPHIES *(in part)*

Legassick, Martin. Professor, History Department, University of Western Cape, Bellville, S.Af. •WORLD AFFAIRS: *South Africa*

Lehman, Richard L. Professor, College of Engineering, Rutgers University, New Brunswick, N.J. Author of *Handbook on Continuous Fiber Reinforced Ceramic Composites.* •BUSINESS AND INDUSTRY REVIEW: *Materials and Metals:* Ceramics *(in part)*

Levine, Beth. Freelance Writer. Author of *Divorce: Young People Caught in the Middle* and others. •MEDIA AND PUBLISHING: *Book Publishing* (United States)

Levine, Steven I. Senior Research Associate, Boulder Run Research. •WORLD AFFAIRS: China; *Spotlight:* Hong Kong's Return to China; Taiwan

Lindstrom, Sieg. Managing Editor, *Track & Field News.* •SPORTS AND GAMES: *Track and Field Sports*

Litweiler, John. Jazz Critic; Contributor to *Down Beat, Chicago Tribune,* and others. Author of *Ornette Coleman: A Harmolodic Life.* •OBITUARIES *(in part)*; PERFORMING ARTS: *Music:* Jazz

Logan, Robert G. Sportswriter, *Daily Herald* (Arlington Heights, Ill.). Author of *Cubs Win* and others. •SPORTS AND GAMES: *Basketball:* United States

Longmore, Andrew. Chief Sports Feature Writer, *The Independent;* formerly Assistant Editor, *The Cricketer.* •BIOGRAPHIES *(in part)*; SPORTS AND GAMES: *Cricket*

Luling, Virginia R. Social Anthropologist. •WORLD AFFAIRS: *Somalia*

Macdonald, Barrie. Professor of History, Massey University, Palmerston, N.Z. •WORLD AFFAIRS: *Dependent States:* Pacific; *Fiji; Kiribati; Marshall Islands; Micronesia, Federated States of; Samoa; Solomon Islands; Tonga; Tuvalu; Vanuatu*

McElroy, John. Editorial Director, *Automotive Industries.* •BUSINESS AND INDUSTRY REVIEW: *Automobiles*

McGregor, Alan. Freelance Contributor, *The Times; The Lancet;* Swiss Radio International; CBS Radio. •WORLD AFFAIRS: *Switzerland; Switzerland:* Sidebar

McIvor, Greg. Stockholm Correspondent, *Financial Times.* •WORLD AFFAIRS: *Sweden*

McLachlan, Keith S. Professor Emeritus, School of Oriental and African Studies, University of London. Author of *Boundaries of Modern Iran.* •WORLD AFFAIRS: *Iran*

Mango, Andrew. Foreign Affairs Analyst. Author of *Turkey: The Challenge of a New Role.* •WORLD AFFAIRS: *Turkey*

Mantzavrakos, Afrodite. Copy Editor, Encyclopædia Britannica. •BIOGRAPHIES *(in part)*; OBITUARIES *(in part)*

Marples, David R. Professor of History, University of Alberta. Author of *Belarus: From Soviet Rule to Nuclear Catastrophe* and others. •WORLD AFFAIRS: *Belarus; Ukraine*

Marty, Martin E. Professor, University of Chicago. Director, Public Religion Project. Author of *The One and the Many; Under God, Indivisible;* and others. •RELIGION: *Special Report:* Doomsday Cults

Mathews, John H. Copy Editor, Encyclopædia Britannica. •BIOGRAPHIES *(in part);* OBITUARIES *(in part)*

Matthíasson, Björn. Economist, Ministry of Finance, Iceland. •WORLD AFFAIRS: *Iceland*

Maughan, Shannon. Freelance Writer and Editor, *Publishers Weekly; Crayola Kids.* •LITERATURE: *Special Report:* English-Language Children's Literature

Mazie, David M. Staff Writer, *Reader's Digest;* Freelance Writer. •SOCIAL PROTECTION (U.S.)

Meisner, Nadine. Freelance Dance Critic. •PERFORMING ARTS: *Dance:* European

Mermel, T.W. Consulting Engineer; formerly Chairman, Committee on World Register of

Dams, International Commission on Large Dams. •ARCHITECTURE AND CIVIL ENGINEERING: *Dams*

Mesa-Lago, Carmelo. Distinguished Service Professor of Economics and Latin American Studies, University of Pittsburgh. •WORLD AFFAIRS: *Spotlight:* Latin America's New Investors

Michael, Tom. Assistant Editor, Encyclopædia Britannica. •BIOGRAPHIES *(in part);* NOBEL PRIZES *(in part);* OBITUARIES *(in part)*

Mihalisko, Kathleen. Network Administrator for Calibre Systems, Inc. •WORLD AFFAIRS: *Commonwealth of Independent States*

Millikin, Sandra. Freelance Art Historian. •ART, ANTIQUES, AND COLLECTIONS: *Art Exhibitions*

Monti, Steven. Senior Information Manager, Encyclopædia Britannica. •COMPUTERS AND INFORMATION SYSTEMS: *Sidebar*

Morgan, Paul. Deputy Editor, *Rugby World.* •SPORTS AND GAMES: *Football:* Rugby Football

Morris, Jacqui M. Editor, *Oryx.* •THE ENVIRONMENT: *Wildlife Conservation*

Morrison, Graham. Press Officer, British Fencing Federation; Correspondent, *Daily Telegraph; Country Life; Déléqué de Presse, Fédération Internationale D'Escrime.* •SPORTS AND GAMES: *Fencing*

Mullen, Fiona. Editor, The Economist Intelligence Unit, London. •WORLD AFFAIRS: *Austria*

Munns, Thomas E. Senior Program Officer, National Materials Advisory Board, National Research Council. •BUSINESS AND INDUSTRY REVIEW: *Materials and Metals:* Advanced Composites *(in part)*

Murphy, Alan. Associate Editor, Footprint Handbooks. •WORLD AFFAIRS: *Bolivia; Ecuador; Peru; Venezuela*

Naylor, Ernest. Professor Emeritus, University of Wales, Bangor. •LIFE SCIENCES: *Marine Biology*

Neher, Stephen. Assistant Editor, Encyclopædia Britannica. •WORLD AFFAIRS: *World Legislative Election Results (in part)*

Newby, Donald J. Formerly Bowls Correspondent, *Daily Telegraph;* formerly Editor, *World Bowls.* Author of various bowls publications. •SPORTS AND GAMES: *Lawn Bowls*

Noble, Thomas F.X. Professor of History, University of Virginia. Author of *Soldiers of Christ: Saints and Saints' Lives.* •RELIGION: *Roman Catholic Church*

Nurse, Charlie. Lecturer, Politics Department, Anglia Polytechnic University, England. •WORLD AFFAIRS: *Chile; Paraguay*

O'Donoghue, Michael. Lecturer in Gemology, London Guildhall University. •BUSINESS AND INDUSTRY REVIEW: *Gemstones*

Ogden, Shepherd. President, The Cook's Garden. Author of *Step by Step Organic Flower Gardening* and others. •THE ENVIRONMENT: *Gardening; Gardening:* Sidebar

O'Quinn, Jim. Editor in Chief, *American Theatre* magazine. •PERFORMING ARTS: *Theatre:* U.S. and Canada

Orihill, Jackie. Index Editor and Freelance Writer, Encyclopædia Britannica. •BIOGRAPHIES *(in part)*; MEDIA AND PUBLISHING: *Television and Radio:* Sidebar

Orr, Jay. Music Writer, *Nashville* (Tenn.) *Banner.* •PERFORMING ARTS: *Music:* Popular (U.S.)

Osborne, K.L. Editor, *British Rowing Almanack.* Author of *Boat Racing in Britain, 1715–1975* and *One Man Went to Row.* •SPORTS AND GAMES: *Rowing*

Oster, Rose-Marie G. Professor, Department of Germanic Studies, University of Maryland. •LITERATURE: *Swedish*

Palmer, John. European Editor, *The Guardian.* Author of *Europe Without America: The Crisis in Atlantic Relations.* •WORLD AFFAIRS: *European Union*

Parker, Ines. Freelance Writer. •WORLD AFFAIRS: *Belize*

Parker, Sandy. Publisher, fur industry newsletter; Co-publisher, *Fur World.* •BUSINESS AND INDUSTRY REVIEW: *Apparel:* Furs

Parming, Tõnu. President, Estonian Publishing Co. •WORLD AFFAIRS: *Estonia*

Pertile, Lino. Professor of Romance Languages and Literature, Harvard University. Author of *Cambridge History of Italian Literature.* •LITERATURE: *Italian*

Peszek, Luan. Publications Director, U.S.A. Gymnastics; Editor, *U.S.A. Gymnastics* magazine; *Technique* magazine. •SPORTS AND GAMES: *Gymnastics*

Pfeffer, Irving. Attorney. Author of *The Financing of Small Business.* •ECONOMIC AFFAIRS: *Stock Exchanges* (North America)

Pollack, Benny. Professor of Iberian and Latin American Politics, University of Liverpool. •WORLD AFFAIRS: *Spain*

Pollard, Peter. Associate Editor, Footprint Handbooks. •WORLD AFFAIRS: *Colombia*

Prasad, H.Y. Sharada. Formerly Information Adviser to the Prime Minister of India. •WORLD AFFAIRS: *India;* Spotlight: *Poverty in South Asia*

Primorac, Max. President, Center for Civil Society in Southeastern Europe, Washington, D.C. •WORLD AFFAIRS: *Croatia*

Prince, Greg W. Executive Editor, *Beverage World.* •BUSINESS AND INDUSTRY REVIEW: *Beverages:* Beer; Soft Drinks; Spirits

Qian Zhongwen. Senior Research Fellow, Literature Institute, Chinese Academy of Social Sciences. •LITERATURE: *Chinese*

Rakisits, Claude. International Affairs Consultant. •WORLD AFFAIRS: *Bangladesh; Bhutan; Myanmar (Burma); Nepal; Sri Lanka*

Rauch, Robert. Freelance Editor and Writer. •BIOGRAPHIES *(in part)*

Réamonn, Páraic. Communications Director, World Alliance of Reformed Churches. •RELIGION: *Reformed, Presbyterian, and Congregational Churches*

Rebelo, L.S. Reader Emeritus; Visiting Professor, Department of Portuguese Studies, King's College, University of London. •LITERATURE: *Portuguese:* Portugal

Reed, Arthur. Senior Editor, Europe, *Air Transport World.* Author of *Britain's Aircraft Industry;* Coauthor of *RAE Farnborough.* •TRANSPORTATION: *Aviation*

Reid, Ron. Staff Sportswriter, *Philadelphia Inquirer.* •SPORTS AND GAMES: *Ice Hockey:* North America

Rengers, Maria Ottolino. Copy Editor, Encyclopædia Britannica. •BIOGRAPHIES *(in part)*

Renwick, David. Freelance Journalist. •WORLD AFFAIRS: *Antigua and Barbuda; Bahamas, The; Barbados; Dependent States*: Caribbean and Bermuda; *Dominica; Grenada; Guyana; Jamaica; Saint Kitts and Nevis; Saint Lucia; Saint Vincent and the Grenadines; Trinidad and Tobago*

Reyes, Alejandro. Senior Correspondent, *Asiaweek* magazine. •WORLD AFFAIRS: *Vietnam*

Richards, Denby. Editor, *Musical Opinion.* •PERFORMING ARTS: *Music:* Classical

Ridgway, Laurence. Consultant, Contributor, and Producer of Symposia, *World Tobacco* magazine. •BUSINESS AND INDUSTRY REVIEW: *Tobacco*

Robinson, David. Film Critic and Historian. Author of *A History of World Cinema; Chaplin: His Life and Art.* •PERFORMING ARTS: *Motion Pictures*

Roby, Anne. Freelance Writer and Editor. •MEDIA AND PUBLISHING: *Magazines; Newspapers;* WORLD AFFAIRS: *Andorra; Latvia; Liechtenstein; Luxembourg; Monaco*

Rogers, Peter. Gordon McKay Professor of Environmental Engineering and Professor of City Planning, Harvard University. •WORLD AFFAIRS: *Spotlight:* The Water Crisis in the Middle East and North Africa

Rollin, Jack. Executive Editor, *Rothmans Football Yearbook.* Compiler of Playfair Football *Who's Who.* Author of *World Cup 1930–1990* and others. •BIOGRAPHIES *(in part)*; SPORTS AND GAMES: *Football:* Association Football (Soccer): *Europe*

Romano, Frank J. Professor of Graphic Arts, School of Printing Management and Sciences, Rochester (N.Y.) Institute of Technology. •BUSINESS AND INDUSTRY REVIEW: *Printing*

Rugh, William A. President, AMIDEAST. •WORLD AFFAIRS: *United Arab Emirates; Yemen*

Rundall, Rebecca. Copy Editor, Encyclopædia Britannica. •BIOGRAPHIES *(in part)*; OBITUARIES *(in part)*

Rusch, William G. Director, Commission on Faith and Order, National Council of Churches of Christ. •RELIGION: *Lutheran Communion*

Russell, Cristine. Freelance Science Writer and Special Health Correspondent, *Washington Post.* •HEALTH AND DISEASE: *Medicine* (U.S.)

Russell, George. International Editor, *Time* magazine. Author of *Eyewitness: A History of Photojournalism.* •WORLD AFFAIRS: *United States*

Russell, James S. Managing Senior Editor, *Architectural Record* magazine. •ARCHITECTURE AND CIVIL ENGINEERING: *Buildings*

Rutherford, Andrew. Professor, University of Southampton, Eng. Author of *Transforming Criminal Policy* and others. •LAW, CRIME, AND LAW ENFORCEMENT: *Prisons and Penology*

Saeki, Shoichi. Professor Emeritus, Tokyo University. Author of *Japanese Autobiographies.* •LITERATURE: *Japanese*

Sanders, Alan J.K. Lecturer in Mongolian Studies, School of Oriental and African Studies, University of London. Author of *The Historical Dictionary of Mongolia* and others. •WORLD AFFAIRS: *Mongolia*

Sandvik, Gudmund. Professor Emeritus of Legal History, Faculty of Law, University of Oslo. •WORLD AFFAIRS: *Norway*

Sarahete, Yrjö. General Secretary, Fédération Internationale des Quilleurs. •SPORTS AND GAMES: *Bowling:* World Tenpins

Saunders, Christopher. Associate Professor, History Department, University of Cape Town, S.Af. Author of *The Making of the South African Past.* •WORLD AFFAIRS: *Namibia*

Schafrik, Robert E. Director, Division of Materials, Mechanics, and Manufacturing, National Research Council. •BUSINESS AND INDUSTRY REVIEW: *Materials and Metals:* Advanced Composites *(in part)*

Schalet, Benjamin. Classifier, Information Management & Retrieval, Encyclopædia Britannica. •BIOGRAPHIES *(in part)*; OBITUARIES *(in part)*

Sego, Stephen. Freelance Journalist; formerly Director, Radio Free Afghanistan. •WORLD AFFAIRS: *Afghanistan*

Shackleford, Peter. Chief of Environment, Planning, and Finance, World Tourism Organization. •BUSINESS AND INDUSTRY REVIEW: *Tourism*

Shallcross, Bożena. Assistant Professor, Indiana University, Bloomington. Author of *Homes of the Romantic Artists* and others. •LITERATURE: *Eastern European*

Shameen, Assif A. Regional Correspondent for *Asiaweek* magazine. •WORLD AFFAIRS: *Pakistan*

Sharma, Hari. Professor Emeritus and Former Director, Cancer Prevention and Natural Products Research, Department of Pathology, College of Medicine, The Ohio State University, Columbus. Fellow, National Academy of Ayurveda, Ministry of Health and Family Welfare, Government of India. Author of *Freedom from Disease; Contemporary Ayurveda: Medicine and Research in Maharishi Ayur-Veda.* •HEALTH AND DISEASE: *Special Report:* Alternative Medicine *(in part)*

Sharples, Jerry A. Private Consultant. Coauthor of *Imperfect Competition and Political Economy.* •AGRICULTURE AND FOOD SUPPLIES: *International Issues; Agricultural Commodities*

Shelley, Andrew. Chairman, JSM, London. •BIOGRAPHIES *(in part)*; SPORTS AND GAMES: *Squash Rackets*

Shepherd, Melinda C. Associate Editor, Encyclopædia Britannica. •ECONOMIC AFFAIRS: *Banking;* International; OBITUARIES *(in part);* WORLD AFFAIRS: *Dependent States*: Europe and the Atlantic; *World Legislative Election Results (in part)*

Sherry, Paul H. President, United Church of Christ. •RELIGION: *United Church of Christ*

Shimizu, Teiji. Freelance Reporter. •BIOGRAPHIES *(in part)*

Shoemaker, Alan H. Collection Manager, Riverbanks Zoological Park. •THE ENVIRONMENT: *Zoos*

Shubinsky, Valery. Literary Columnist, *Vechernyi Peterburg.* •LITERATURE: *Russian*

Simon, Reeva S. Assistant Director, Middle East Institute, Columbia University, New York City. •WORLD AFFAIRS: *Lebanon; Saudi Arabia*

Simons, Paul. Writer; Television Producer. Author of *Weird Weather.* •LIFE SCIENCES: *Botany*

Sklar, Morton. Director, World Organization Against Torture; Judge, Administrative Tribunal for OAS. Editor, *The Status of Human Rights in the United States* and *Torture in the U.S.* Author of *The Right to Travel* and others. •SOCIAL PROTECTION: *Human Rights*

Slayman, Andrew. Associate Editor, *Archaeology* magazine. •ANTHROPOLOGY AND ARCHAEOLOGY: *Archaeology:* Eastern Hemisphere

Smith, Donald. Editor, *Rubber World.* •BUSINESS AND INDUSTRY REVIEW: *Materials and Metals:* Rubber

Smith, Gregory O. Dean of Academic Affairs, Rome International University. •WORLD AFFAIRS: *San Marino; Vatican City State*

Smith, Reuben W. Emeritus Professor of History, University of the Pacific, Stockton, Calif. •RELIGION: *Islam*

Solomon, Norman. Fellow, Oxford Centre for Hebrew and Jewish Studies, Oxford, Eng. Author of *The Analytic Movement.* •RELIGION: *Judaism*

Sparks, Karen J. Managing Editor, Encyclopædia Britannica. •OBITUARIES *(in part)*

Spence, Jonathan. Sterling Professor of History, Yale University. •ARCHITECTURE AND CIVIL ENGINEERING: *Dams:* Sidebar

Spencer, Peter L. Editor, *Consumers' Research* magazine. •ECONOMIC AFFAIRS: *Consumer Affairs* (U.S.)

Stern, Irwin. Former Senior Lecturer in Portuguese, Columbia University, New York City. •LITERATURE: *Portuguese:* Brazil

Støverud, Torbjørn. Honorary Research Fellow, University College, London. •LITERATURE: *Norwegian*

Sullivan, H. Patrick. Dean and Professor Emeritus of Religion, Vassar College, Poughkeepsie, N.Y. •RELIGION: *Hinduism*

Summerhill, Edward M. Part-Time Staff Member, Reuters; Freelance Writer, Finnish News Agency. •WORLD AFFAIRS: *Finland*

Sumner, David E. Journalism Professor; Contributor to Episcopal Church periodicals. Author of *The Episcopal Church's History: 1945–1985* and others. •RELIGION: *Anglican Communion*

Susel, Rudolph M. Editor, *American Home; Our Voice.* •WORLD AFFAIRS: *Slovenia*

Susser, Leslie D. Diplomatic Correspondent, *The Jerusalem Report.* Coauthor of *Shalom Friend: The Life and Legacy of Yitzhak Rabin.* •WORLD AFFAIRS: *Israel*

Suzuki, Toshihiko. Communication Officer, the Delegation of the European Commission, Japan. •SPORTS AND GAMES: *Baseball:* Japan

Swan, Russ. Editor-in-Chief, *World Highways.* •ARCHITECTURE AND CIVIL ENGINEERING: *Roads*

Swift, Richard N. Professor Emeritus of Politics, New York University. •WORLD AFFAIRS: *Multinational and Regional Organizations; United Nations*

Synan, Vinson. Dean, School of Divinity, Regent University, Virginia Beach, Va. Author of *Holiness-Pentecostal Tradition; Pentecostal Churches.* •RELIGION: *Pentecostal Churches*

Szilagyi, Zsofia. Freelance Writer, UNHCR, Budapest Office. •WORLD AFFAIRS: *Hungary*

Taishoff, Lawrence B. Chairman Emeritus, *Broadcasting & Cable.* •MEDIA AND PUBLISHING: *Radio* (U.S., *in part*); *Radio:* Amateur Radio *(in part); Television* (U.S., *in part*)

Tanner, Wendy. Copy Editor, Encyclopædia Britannica. •BIOGRAPHIES *(in part)*

Taylor, Thomas F. General Secretary, Friends World Committee for Consultation. •RELIGION: *Religious Society of Friends*

Teague, Elizabeth. Senior Analyst, Jamestown, United Kingdom. •WORLD AFFAIRS: *Russia*

Tesoro, José Manuel. Staff Writer, *Asiaweek* magazine. •WORLD AFFAIRS: *Cambodia*

Tétreault, Mary Ann. Professor of Political Science, Iowa State University. Author of *The Kuwait Petroleum Corporation and the Economics of the New World Order* and others. •WORLD AFFAIRS: *Kuwait*

Thomas, Robert Murray. Professor Emeritus of Education and Head, Program in International Education, University of California, Santa Barbara. •EDUCATION (international)

Tikkanen, Amy. Assistant Editor, Encyclopædia Britannica. •BIOGRAPHIES *(in part)*; OBITUARIES *(in part)*

Todd, Amy. Manager, Sotheby's; Freelance Journalist. •ART, ANTIQUES, AND COLLECTIONS: *Art Auctions and Sales*

Trickett, Anthony. General Manager, Economic Affairs, International Iron and Steel Institute. •BUSINESS AND INDUSTRY REVIEW: *Materials and Metals:* Iron and Steel

Tugend, Alina. Press and Publications Officer, Consumers International. •ECONOMIC AFFAIRS: *Consumer Affairs* (international)

Turner, Darrell J. Religion Writer, *Journal Gazette* (Fort Wayne, Ind.). •RELIGION: *Introduction*

Tutunji, Jenab. Assistant Professorial Lecturer, Political Science, George Washington University, Washington, D.C. •WORLD AFFAIRS: *Jordan*

Ulak, James T. Curator of Japanese Art, Freer Gallery of Art and Arthur M. Sakler Gallery, Smithsonian Institution, Washington, D.C. Coauthor of *Asian Art in the Art Institute of Chicago* and *Reflections of Reality in Japanese Art.* •MACROPÆDIA: *East Asian Arts*

UNHCR. The Office of the United Nations High Commissioner for Refugees. •POPULATION TRENDS: *Refugees and International Migration*

Utt, Roger L. Editor, *Puerta del Sol;* formerly Assistant Professor of Spanish, Department of Romance Languages and Literatures, University of Chicago. •LITERATURE: *Spanish:* Spain

Venzke, Bruce H. Associate Editor, *Pool & Billiard Magazine;* Past President, Billiard Congress of Wisconsin. •SPORTS AND GAMES: *Billiard Games:* Carom Billiards; Pocket Billiards

Verdi, Robert William. Sports Columnist, *Chicago Tribune.* Coauthor of *Once a Bum, Always a Dodger; Holy Cow!;* and others. •SPORTS AND GAMES: *Baseball* (U.S.)

Vinton, Louisa. Editor-in-Chief, Economist Intelligence Unit, Vienna. •WORLD AFFAIRS: *Poland*

Wallenfeldt, Jeff. Assistant Editor, Encyclopædia Britannica. •BIOGRAPHIES *(in part)*

Wallis, Shani. Independent Technical Journalist. •ARCHITECTURE AND CIVIL ENGINEERING: *Tunnels*

Walters, Jonathan S. Assistant Professor of Religion and Asian Studies, Whitman College, Walla Walla, Wash. Author of *History of Kelaniya.* •RELIGION: *Buddhism*

Wandycz, Piotr S. Bradford Durfee Professor of History, Yale University. Author of *The Lands of Partitioned Poland, 1795–1918* and others. •MACROPÆDIA: *Poland*

Wanninger, Richard S. •SPORTS AND GAMES: *Volleyball*

Warren, J. Robert. Editor, Asia-Pacific Report, *Chemical Market Reporter.* •BUSINESS AND INDUSTRY REVIEW: *Chemicals*

Watson, Rory. Deputy Editor, *European Voice.* Coauthor of *American Express Guide to Brussels.* •WORLD AFFAIRS: *Belgium*

Way, Diane Lois. Lawyer; Historical Researcher. •BIOGRAPHIES *(in part)*

Wechsler, Helen J. Senior Manager, International Programs, American Association of Museums. •LIBRARIES AND MUSEUMS: *Museums* (international)

Weil, Eric. Sports Editor, Buenos Aires Herald; South American Correspondent for *World Soccer* magazine. •SPORTS AND GAMES: *Football:* Association Football (Soccer): *Latin America*

Westberg, M. Victor. Manager of Committees on Publication, the First Church of Christ, Scientist, Boston. •RELIGION: *Church of Christ, Scientist*

Whitney, Barbara. Copy Supervisor, Encyclopædia Britannica. •BIOGRAPHIES *(in part)*; BUSINESS AND INDUSTRY REVIEW: *Games and Toys; Games and Toys:* Sidebar; OBITUARIES *(in part)*

Whitten, Phillip. Editor-in-Chief, *Swimming World* magazine. •SPORTS AND GAMES: *Swimming*

Wilkinson, Clive R. Coordinator, Global Coral Reef Monitoring Network. Author of *Global Climate Change and Coral Reefs.* •THE ENVIRONMENT: *Special Report:* Coral Reefs: The Forgotten Rain Forests of the Sea

Wilkinson, John R. Sportswriter, Coventry Newspapers. •SPORTS AND GAMES: *Cycling*

Willis, Clifford L. Director of News and Information, Office of Communication, Christian Church (Disciples of Christ). •RELIGION: *Christian Church (Disciples of Christ)*

Wilmut, Ian. Doctor, Principal Investigator, Roslin Institute. •LIFE SCIENCES: *Zoology:* Special Report: *The Uses and Ethics of Cloning*

Wilson, Derek. Correspondent, BBC, Rome. Author of *Rome, Umbria and Tuscany.* •WORLD AFFAIRS: *Italy*

Wilson, Michael. Freelance Aviation Writer and Consultant. •BUSINESS AND INDUSTRY REVIEW: *Aerospace*

Winokur, Robert S. Acting Assistant Administrator for Weather Services, National Oceanic and Atmospheric Administration. •EARTH SCIENCES: *Meteorology and Climate*

Wise, Larry. Golden Eagle Archery Staff. Author of *Tuning Your Compound Bow* and others. •SPORTS AND GAMES: *Archery*

Wolf, Allison Wheeler. Freelance Writer. Formerly Director of Communications, American Apparel Manufacturers Association. •BUSINESS AND INDUSTRY REVIEW: *Apparel:* Clothing

Woodrow, Robert. Formerly Assistant Managing Editor, *Asiaweek* magazine. •WORLD AFFAIRS: *Laos; Thailand*

Woods, Elizabeth. Writer. Author of *If Only Things Were Different (I): A Model for a Sustainable Society; Bird Salad;* and others. •LITERATURE: *English:* Canada

Woods, Michael. Science Editor, Block News Alliance. Author of *Science on Ice: Research in Antarctica.* •MATHEMATICS AND PHYSICAL SCIENCES: *Chemistry;* NOBEL PRIZES *(in part)*

Woollen, Anthony. Former Editor, *Food Manufacture.* Former Editor, *Food Industries Manual.* •AGRICULTURE AND FOOD SUPPLIES: *Food Processing*

World Forest Institute. Information Specialists. •BUSINESS AND INDUSTRY REVIEW: *Wood Products:* Wood

Wright, Andrew G. Associate Editor, *Engineering News-Record.* •BUSINESS AND INDUSTRY REVIEW: *Building and Construction*

Wyllie, Peter John. Professor, Division of Geological and Planetary Sciences, California Institute of Technology. Author of *The Dynamic Earth; The Way the Earth Works.* •EARTH SCIENCES: *Geology and Geochemistry*

Young, M. Norvel. Chancellor Emeritus, Pepperdine University, Malibu, Calif. Author of *Preachers of Today.* •RELIGION: *Churches of Christ*

Zanga, Louis. Freelance Journalist. •WORLD AFFAIRS: *Albania*

Zegura, Stephen L. Professor of Anthropology, University of Arizona. •ANTHROPOLOGY AND ARCHAEOLOGY: *Anthropology:* Physical

Bibliography: Recent Books

The following list encompasses more than 130 recent books in English that have been judged significant contributions to learning in their respective fields. Each citation includes a few lines of commentary to indicate the tenor of the work. The citations are organized by broad subject area, using the 10 parts of the *Propædia* as an outline.

Matter and Energy

Richard Morris, *Achilles in the Quantum Universe* (1997), a historical study of the concept of infinity and the philosophers and mathematicians who have explored its meaning.

Michael Springford (ed.), *Electron: A Centenary Volume* (1997), essays by 11 physicists on the form and function of the electron, whose discovery by J.J. Thomson in 1897 has influenced scientific research from molecular biology to astrophysics.

Alexander Yu. Grosberg and Alexei R. Khokhlov, *Giant Molecules Here, There, and Everywhere* (1997), a description of the class of giant molecules of which natural substances such as DNA and synthetic polymers are composed.

Nickolas Solomey, *The Elusive Neutrino: A Subatomic Detective Story* (1997), a discussion of the neutrino, whose detection has given astronomers and physicists stunning insights into the beginnings of the universe.

Helga Nowotny and Ulrike Felt, *After the Breakthrough: The Emergence of High-Temperature Superconductivity as a Research Field* (1997), a study of the influence of the revolutionary breakthrough in superconductivity on social and economic behaviour.

Alfred K. Mann, *Shadow of a Star: The Neutrino Story of Supernova 1987A* (1997), a scientist's eyewitness account of a stellar explosion (the first one seen since 1604), explaining the event and its aftermath and what was learned about the composition of the star.

David Park, *The Fire Within the Eye: A Historical Essay on the Nature and Meaning of Light* (1997), an essay on the spiritual, natural, and scientific preeminence of light.

Timothy Ferris, *The Whole Shebang: A State-of-the-Universe(s) Report* (1997), an overview of recent scientific depictions of the universe, detailing current research that may point to the existence of multiple universes, each governed by its own physical laws.

Alan H. Guth, *The Inflationary Universe: The Quest for a New Theory of Cosmic Origins* (1997), a theory of the universe that attempts to explain the origin, nature, and indestructibility of matter.

Martin Rees, *Before the Beginning: Our Universe and Others* (1997), a discussion of black holes, dark matter, nucleosynthesis of the elements, and related astrophysical phenomena.

Lee Smolin, *The Life of the Cosmos* (1997), a reflection on the possibility of constructing a single unified theory that would successfully merge Einstein's theory of relativity with quantum theory.

Piers Bizony, *The Rivers of Mars: Searching for the Cosmic Origins of Life* (1997), a work that examines the question of whether the chemical essentials for life on Earth were sown from space and whether they also exist on other heavenly bodies, particularly Mars.

The Earth

Ernest Zebrowski, Jr., *Perils of a Restless Planet: Scientific Perspectives on Natural Disasters* (1997), case studies of catastrophic natural events, employing scientific methodology for developing theories, technologies, and public policy to minimize damage and possibly predict occurrences.

Joanna Burger, *Oil Spills* (1997), a historical survey of oil spills, their effect on the biosphere, and efforts to contain or prevent them.

William J. Broad, *The Universe Below: Discovering the Secrets of the Deep Sea* (1997), a firsthand account of deep-sea exploration and how the release of previously secret technologies has accelerated the pace and scope of biological discoveries and recovery of sunken treasure.

Walter A. Lyons, *The Handy Weather Answer Book* (1997), an explanation of weather and related phenomena in a question-and-answer format.

Richard V. Fisher, Grant Heiken, and Jeffrey B. Hulen, *Volcanoes: Crucibles of Change* (1997), a study of volcanoes, enumerating their types and causes as well as events that foreshadow volcanic activity, with firsthand accounts of eruptions and a worldwide guide to sites of active volcanoes.

Thomas Fairchild Sherman, *A Place on the Glacial Till: Time, Land, and Nature Within an American Town* (1997), a geologic, archaeological, and paleontological overview of an area near Oberlin, Ohio, describing both living and extinct flora and fauna.

Life on Earth

Walter Alvarez, *T. Rex and the Crater of Doom* (1997), a theory about the mass extinction of dinosaurs that occurred 65 million years ago, pointing to geologic evidence for a comet or asteroid impact off the Yucatan Peninsula.

Lionel R. Milgrom, *The Colours of Life: An Introduction to the Chemistry of Porphyrins and Related Compounds* (1997), a biochemical discussion of colours, explaining why grass is green and blood is red and exploring pigments at the molecular level.

Jared Diamond, *Why Is Sex Fun? The Evolution of Human Sexuality* (1997), a speculation on whether the development of such exclusively human sexual behaviours as preference for sex in private may have given humans an evolutionary advantage over other mammals.

Boyce Rensberger, *Life Itself: Exploring the Realm of the Living Cell* (1997), an introduction to the fundamentals of cellular biology and the study of genes.

Frans de Waal and Frans Lanting, *Bonobo: The Forgotten Ape* (1997), a study of the bonobo, contrasting its social behaviour with that of the chimpanzee.

Michael Sims, *Darwin's Orchestra: An Almanac of Nature in History and the Arts* (1997), brief essays, in one-a-day format, on aspects of natural history, ranging from a battle-halting eclipse in 585 BC to a method for studying the hearing of earthworms.

Susan Allport, *A Natural History of Parenting: From Emperor Penguins to Reluctant Ewes, a Naturalist Looks at How Parenting Differs in the Animal World and Ours* (1997), an overview of parenting behaviours throughout the animal kingdom.

Mark Kurlansky, *Cod: A Biography of the Fish That Changed the World* (1997), an account of the decimation of the cod, one of the world's major food resources.

Christopher McGowan, *The Raptor and the Lamb: Predators and Prey in the Living World* (1997), a study of the symbiotic relationship between predator and prey that shows how an ingenious offense and a resourceful defense promote traits that contribute to the survival of both species.

Martha A. Strawn, *Alligators: Prehistoric Presence in the American Landscape* (1997), a pictorial as well as verbal plea for protection of an ancient species, with photographs and essays depicting the habitat, life, and often violent death at human hands of the American alligator.

Stephen H. Schneider, *Laboratory Earth: The Planetary Gamble We Can't Afford to Lose* (1997), a state-of-the-Earth report.

Human Life

Roger Lewin, *Patterns in Evolution: The New Molecular View* (1997), an account of the effect of molecular science on evolutionary studies.

Milford Wolpoff and Rachel Caspari, *Races and Human Evolution: A Fatal Attraction* (1997), a discussion of the "Eve" theory of human evolution (one common ancestor) as contrasted with multiregionalism, the hypothesis that posits diverse origins—possibly different species—for the variety of modern human races.

Noel T. Boaz, *Eco Homo: How the Human Being Emerged from the Cataclysmic History of the Earth* (1997), a work relating early humans to their ecological setting and asserting that the evolutionary success of hominids arose in large part from their rapid response to extreme fluctuations in the prehistoric African climate.

Stephen S. Hall, *A Commotion in the Blood: Life, Death, and the Immune System* (1997), the story of immunology and immunotherapy in the treatment of various cancers as seen in the work and lives of some of the principal researchers in the field.

Richard Rhodes, *Deadly Feasts: Tracking the Secrets of a Terrifying New Plague* (1997), a work that predicts the spread of several virulent fatal contagious diseases that have already surfaced around the globe and urges prevention research and international public health measures.

Jon Arrizabalaga, John Henderson, and Roger French, *The Great Pox: The French Disease in Renaissance Europe* (1997), a history of what was thought to be a new disease and another plague, with a description of changes in medical practice and hospital care that affected its treatment.

Bernard J. Baars, *In the Theater of Consciousness: The Workspace of the Mind* (1997), an examination of the way humans experience themselves and their world, with discussions on the phenomena of dreaming and sleeping.

Deborah Blum, *Sex on the Brain: The Biological Differences Between Men and Women* (1997), an evolutionary approach to sexual differences that speculates on the influence of gender on aggressiveness, risk taking, and endurance.

Lacy Baldwin Smith, *Fools, Martyrs, Traitors: The Story of Martyrdom in the Western World* (1997), an exploration into the psyches, personalities, and politics of martyrs of all persuasions, from Socrates to Gandhi.

Corinne Smith and Lisa Strick, *Learning Disabilities: A to Z* (1997), a guide to learning disabilities and suggestions for evaluation and treatment.

Human Society

Art Wolfe with Deirdre Skillman, *Tribes* (1997), essays and photographs depicting traditional clothing and body ornamentation worn by indigenous tribes from every continent except Antarctica.

Kwame Anthony Appiah and Henry Louis Gates, Jr. (eds.), *The Dictionary of Global Culture: The Global Citizen's Guide to Culture, Emphasizing the Achievement of the Non-Western World—What Every American Needs to Know as We Enter the Next Century* (1997), a comprehensive survey of global culture, including references to non-Western personalities in literature and the arts.

Rosina Lippi-Green, *English with an Accent: Language, Ideology, and Discrimination in the U.S.* (1997), a study of language as a marker of class.

Robin Blackburn, *The Making of New World Slavery: From the Baroque to the Modern* (1997), a history of European doctrines of slavery from the Middle Ages to the early modern period, relating the rise of plantation slavery to burgeoning consumer markets.

Regina M. Schwartz, *The Curse of Cain: The Violent Legacy of Monotheism* (1997), an argument that ethnic discrimination and other exclusionary human behaviours originated with God's rejection of Cain.

Thomas Lynch, *The Undertaking: Life Studies from the Dismal Trade* (1997), reflections of a poet-mortician on life and death and on the role of the undertaker in society.

Randall Kennedy, *Race, Crime, and the Law* (1997), a provocative examination of the crossroads at which race relations in the U.S. intersect with the criminal justice system.

Martha C. Nussbaum, *Cultivating Humanity: A Classical Defense of Reform in Liberal Education* (1997), an argument for continued support of liberal education in colleges and universities, suggesting curricular reform and attitudinal changes among faculty and students.

James Youniss and Miranda Yates, *Community Services and Social Responsibility in Youth* (1997), an account of a high-school program that encourages students to become involved in community service.

Michele M. Hoyman, *Power Steering: Global Automakers & the Transformation of Rural Communities* (1997), a study of the long- and short-term effects on a small rural community when it is selected as the site of a major auto-manufacturing plant.

David M. Blitzer, *What's the Economy Trying to Tell You? Everyone's Guide to Understanding and Profiting from the Economy* (1997), a primer on economics and the market, defining economics, explaining markets and business cycles, and describing the roles of policy makers, government, and consumers.

William Greider, *One World, Ready or Not: The Manic Logic of Global Capitalism* (1997), an analysis of the effect of global capitalism on human society, emphasizing the need to correct the worldwide maldistribution of wealth.

William Wolman and Anne Colamosca, *The Judas Economy: The Triumph of Capital and the Betrayal of Work* (1997), an argument that global economics in the post-Cold War era has undercut organized labour in the U.S.

Kiren Aziz Chaudhry, *The Price of Wealth: Economies and Institutions in the Middle East* (1997), a study of the domestic political economies of Saudi Arabia and Yemen before, during, and after the oil boom.

Robert Kuttner, *Everything for Sale: The Virtues and Limits of Markets* (1997), a history of markets that makes the case for a mixed economy in which government acts as a stabilizer and expresses societal desires for progress and improved technology.

Arlie Russell Hochschild, *The Time Bind: When Work Becomes Home and Home Becomes Work* (1997), observations on the problems faced by working parents in their attempt to meet both family and work responsibilities.

Jonathan Williams (ed.), *Money: A History* (1997), a historical and geographic overview of mediums of exchange from the ancient world to the present day.

Rebecca M. Blank, *It Takes a Nation: A New Agenda for Fighting Poverty* (1997), a study of the nature of poverty in the U.S. that defends the need for continuing broad-based government participation in efforts to improve opportunities for the poor.

Ronald I. McKinnon and Kenichi Ohno, *Dollar and Yen: Resolving Economic Conflict* (1997), a discussion of exchange-rate economics and the need to stabilize currencies.

Vaclav Havel (trans. Paul Wilson *et al.*), *The Art of the Impossible: Politics as Morality in Practice* (1997), a group of essays tracing the development of Havel's thinking during his confinement in prison under a totalitarian communist regime and later when he was leader of the fledgling Czech democracy.

Nicholas Mercuro and Steven G. Medema, *Economics and the Law: From Posner to Post-Modernism* (1997), an overview of current schools of thought in the fields of law and economics.

William Ayers, *A Kind and Just Parent: The Children of Juvenile Court* (1997), an argument by a teacher in Chicago's Juvenile Detention Center school urging deeper understanding of both young criminals and their victims.

James M. Banner, Jr., and Harold C. Cannon, *The Elements of Teaching* (1997), a deceptively simple but persuasive description of the art of teaching, its ideals, and its difficulties, with an analysis of what constitutes a good teacher.

Phillip C. Schlechty, *Inventing Better Schools: An Action Plan for Educational Reform* (1997), an evaluation of strategies for improving public education.

Laurel N. Tanner, *Dewey's Laboratory School: Lessons for Today* (1997), a history of the first hundred years of the University of

Chicago Laboratory School, emphasizing how its policies and practices can be adapted for today's curriculum.

Art

Theodor W. Adorno (trans. Robert Hullot-Kentor), *Aesthetic Theory* (1997), a new translation of Adorno's major work, a defense of modernism that expresses his belief that "art is the sedimented history of human misery."

Philip Kotler and Joanne Scheff, *Standing Room Only: Strategies for Marketing the Performing Arts* (1997), suggestions for ways to attract contemporary audiences to theatre, symphony, dance, and opera without compromising artistic integrity.

Edward R. Tufte, *Visual Explanations: Images and Quantities, Evidence and Narrative* (1997), design strategies for presenting visual information.

Helen C. Evans and William D. Wixom (eds.), *The Story of Byzantium: Art and Culture of the Middle Byzantine Era, A.D. 843–1261* (1997), a look at the secular, political, and religious culture of the Byzantine Empire.

E.P. Thompson, *The Romantics: England in a Revolutionary Age* (1997), a posthumously published group of lectures on English writers of the 1790s, tracing the intellectual influences of that period on the work of Samuel Taylor Coleridge, Mary Wollstonecraft, and others.

David Wiles, *Tragedy in Athens: Performance Space and Theatrical Meaning* (1997), a study of Athenian performance and stagecraft, based on the archaeological evidence of vase paintings and the remains of altars, theatres, and other structures.

Peter Bogdanovich, *Who the Devil Made It?* (1997), conversations with 16 pioneering motion picture directors, including Howard Hawks and Alfred Hitchcock, illustrating the importance of the director's influence on the filmmaking process.

Garry Wills, *John Wayne's America: The Politics of Celebrity* (1997), a study of the relationship between politics and popular culture in the United States as exemplified by the career of the legendary actor who personified American patriotism and self-reliance.

Jessie Ann Owens, *Composers at Work: The Craft of Musical Composition, 1450–1600* (1997), an attempt, based on extant manuscripts, treatises, and textbooks, to reconstruct how early composers worked.

Timothy D. Taylor, *Global Pop: World Music, World Markets* (1997), a study of the influence of popular music on musical theory, composition, and performance around the world.

Steven L. Cantor, *Innovative Design Solutions in Landscape Architecture* (1997), a description of 50 architectural projects by firms of various sizes.

James E. Packer, *The Forum of Trajan in Rome: A Study of the Monuments* (1997), a three-volume history of Trajan's Forum, detailing its construction, its significance in Rome in the 2nd century, and its later descent into obscurity.

David Stevens, *Roof Gardens, Balconies, and Terraces* (1997), a commentary on the innovative use of small garden areas in such varied environments as Italy, Africa, and North and South America.

Marcia Pointon, *Strategies for Showing: Women, Possession, and Representation in English Visual Culture, 1665–1800* (1997), a study of the lives of English women in the 17th and 18th centuries.

Technology

Janet H. Murray, *Hamlet on the Holodeck: The Future of Narrative in Cyberspace* (1997), a discussion of the way computer technology is reshaping traditional narrative as new digital systems interact with conventional literature.

Bettyann Holtzmann Kevles, *Naked to the Bone: Medical Imaging in the 20th Century* (1997), a consideration of X-ray technology and its influence on society.

Keith Wailoo, *Drawing Blood: Technology and Disease Identity in Twentieth-Century America* (1997), an assertion that medical technology has changed the way diseases are diagnosed.

John D. Graham and Jennifer Kassalow Hartwell (eds.), *The Greening of Industry: A Risk Management Approach* (1997), case studies of six industries showing the effect of risk management practices on controlling and preventing pollution.

Paul Bianchina, *Builder's Guide to New Materials and Techniques* (1997), an introduction to new technologies that are profoundly influencing building design and construction.

Derek Phillips, *Lighting Historic Buildings* (1997), an analysis of lighting and its relationship to changing concepts of interiors and exteriors of buildings, with remarks on the importance of minimizing anachronistic lighting in historic structures.

Bert S. Hall, *Weapons & Warfare in Renaissance Europe: Gunpowder, Technology, and Tactics* (1997), a history of military technology, describing the changes in weaponry and battle tactics associated with the development and refinement of gunpowder.

Ken Alder, *Engineering the Revolution: Arms and the Enlightenment in France, 1763–1815* (1997), an examination of French politics and economics in light of the technology introduced by French military engineers who crafted the first interchangeable parts for gun and cannon manufacture.

Religion

Michael Drosnin, *The Bible Code* (1997), an examination of the claim that a code concealed in the text of the Bible has predicted a number of world events, such as the collapse of communism and the assassinations of John Kennedy and Yitzhak Rabin.

A.N. Wilson, *Paul: The Mind of the Apostle* (1997), a critical discussion of the origins of Christianity and the man responsible for the transformation of the religion into a potent force during the 1st century AD.

Claudine Fabre-Vassas (trans. Carol Volk), *The Singular Beast: Jews, Christians, & the Pig* (1997; first published in France in 1994), a historical examination of the ritual and symbolic role of the pig in Christian and Jewish traditions.

Jeffrey Burton Russell, *A History of Heaven: The Singing Silence* (1997), an examination of the concept of heaven and its various depictions by artists, writers, and philosophers.

Gerald Messadié (trans. Marc Romano), *A History of the Devil* (1997), a biographical history of Satan, naming Iran as his birthplace in the 6th century BC and positing a connection between the devil and harsh landscapes and climates.

Marcus Borg (ed.), *Jesus and Buddha: The Parallel Sayings* (1997), a study pointing out the numerous correspondences in teachings on the conduct of life by two of humanity's revered spiritual leaders.

Lama Surya Das, *Awakening the Buddha Within: 8 Steps to Enlightenment, Tibetan Wisdom for the Western World* (1997), a description of the Buddhist way of life, emphasizing its applicability to the Western lifestyle through its pragmatic, nonsectarian training in self-realization.

Steven B. Smith, *Spinoza, Liberalism, and the Question of Jewish Identity* (1997), a literary biography of Spinoza, focusing on his writings in defense of autonomy, religious toleration, and intellectual freedom.

Peter Brown, *The Rise of Western Christendom: Triumph and Diversity, AD 200–1200* (1997), a survey of the spread of Christianity, with accounts of Christian enclaves in Asia, among Islamic populations, and in northern and western Europe.

Jan Assmann, *Moses the Egyptian: The Memory of Egypt in Western Monotheism* (1997), an account of the ways historical and fictional characters in religious life have changed over time, taking Moses and the long history of Mosaic studies as an example.

Don Cupitt, *After God: The Future of Religion* (1997), a chronological account of the evolution of religious belief, contemplating the many varieties of faith in the modern world.

The History of Mankind

Daniel C. Snell, *Life in the Ancient Near East* (1997), a description—drawn principally from cuneiform writings, the Bible, and Egyptian inscriptions—of everyday life in early Turkey, Syria, Persia, Israel, Egypt, and other ancient Middle Eastern countries.

Pat Southern, *Domitian: Tragic Tyrant* (1997), a psychological study of Vespasian's second son that questions whether the emperor has been maligned by history.

John Julius Norwich, *A Short History of Byzantium* (1997), the life story of Constantinople from its days as the Greek port of Byzantium to its defeat by the Turks in 1453.

Mauro Ambrosoli (trans. Mary McCann Salvatorelli), *The Wild and the Sown: Botany and Agriculture in Western Europe, 1350–1850* (1997), a history of the French, Italian, and English farmers, botanists, and landowners who together promoted new farming methods based on crop rotation and livestock raising.

David Cressy, *Birth, Marriage, and Death: Ritual, Religion, and the Life-Cycle in Tudor and Stuart England* (1997), a historic account of the interaction between clergy and laity, men and women, public officials and the public at life's milestones.

Erik Hildinger, *Warriors of the Steppe: A Military History of Central Asia, 500 B.C. to 1700 A.D.* (1997), a history of the nomadic Central Asian armies, describing their tactics, their commanders, and their abiding influence on cavalry warfare.

Reinhold C. Mueller, *The Venetian Money Market: Banks, Panics, and the Public Debt, 1200–1500* (1997), an account of money and banking in Venice from the standpoint of bankruptcies, liquidations, and panics, with an evaluation of the relationship between public debt and private wealth.

Pamela Kyle Crossley, *The Manchus* (1997), a history of the Manchurian peoples from their beginnings as early fishing and hunting communities of eastern Asia to their consolidation into the Manchu state, which conquered and ruled China from 1644 to 1912.

Daniel R. Brower and Edward J. Lazzerini (eds.), *Russia's Orient: Imperial Borderlands and Peoples, 1700–1917* (1997), a series of essays describing the disparate ethnic groups in Russia's distant borderlands, their history, and the effect of their distinctive identities on post-Soviet Russia.

Elizabeth Isichei, *A History of African Societies to 1870* (1997), an exploration of the African past from remotest prehistory, with historiographical observations on ways to avoid the confinement of the Western academic perspective.

Nancy G. Siraisi, *The Clock and the Mirror: Girolamo Cardano and Renaissance Medicine* (1997), a study of the writings of Renaissance physician Cardano and what they reveal about his era.

Tim Judah, *The Serbs: History, Myth, and the Destruction of Yugoslavia* (1997), a history of the Serbs from the 14th century to the present that aims to deliver a dispassionate and balanced account rather than a justification or indictment.

Christiane Harzig, Maria Anna Knothe, Margareta Matovic, Deirdre Mageean, and Monika Blaschke, *Peasant Maids—City Women: From the European Countryside to Urban America* (1997), an account of the lives of German, Irish, Polish, and Swedish women immigrants in Chicago in the late 19th and early 20th centuries.

Pauline Maier, *American Scripture: Making the Declaration of Independence* (1997), an exploration into the collective process that resulted in the Declaration of Independence, dismissing the traditional view that Jefferson was its sole author.

Matthew Restall, *The Maya World: Yucatec Culture and Society, 1550–1850* (1997), a description of the lives of the Maya under Spanish rule, based on legal and other documents written in the Mayan language.

Donald Denoon, with Stewart Firth, Jocelyn Linnekin, Malama Meleisea, and Karen Nero, *The Cambridge History of the Pacific Islanders* (1997), a comprehensive and authoritative history of the people of the Pacific Islands.

Osumaka Likaka, *Rural Society and Cotton in Colonial Zaire* (1997), an examination of the effects of colonialism on traditional rural African culture.

Roy Richard Grinker and Christopher B. Steiner (eds.), *Perspectives on Africa: A Reader in Culture, History, & Representation* (1997), a study showing how ethnic, cultural, and linguistic diversity in Africa and the arrival and ongoing presence of Europeans have been represented and interpreted over time.

Boutros Boutros-Ghali, *Egypt's Road to Jerusalem: A Diplomat's Story of the Struggle for Peace in the Middle East* (1997), recollections of the period when, as Anwar as-Sadat's minister of state for foreign affairs, Boutros-Ghali participated in the Egypt-Israeli negotiations that culminated in the Camp David Accords.

Jeffrey M. Paige, *Coffee and Power: Revolution and the Rise of Democracy in Central America* (1997), an account of the connection between coffee growing and political power in Central America.

Willem van Kemenade, *China, Hong Kong, Taiwan, Inc.: The Dynamics of a New Empire* (1997), an analysis of the social, economic, political, and moral challenges that China faces as its growth threatens the autonomy of other nations in East Asia and as it attempts to come to terms with a changing global role.

Bruce Cumings, *Korea's Place in the Sun: A Modern History* (1997), a portrait of a nation whose people struggle to pursue modernization and industrial development against a backdrop of political turmoil, poverty, and war.

Kwame Gyekye, *Tradition and Modernity: Philosophical Reflections on the African Experience* (1997), a meditation on postcolonial life, examining the diversity of multifaceted African cultures alongside Western moral and political philosophy and proposing social and political models of modernity congenial to African traditions.

Matthew H. Edney, *Mapping an Empire: The Geographical Construction of British India* (1997), an account of mapmaking as a political and scientific undertaking in British India.

Redmond O'Hanlon, *No Mercy: A Journey to the Heart of the Congo* (1997), an account of travels into an exotic and often dangerous region.

Brian Ladd, *The Ghosts of Berlin: Confronting German History in the Urban Landscape* (1997), a meditation on the relationship of architecture, urban design, and history in Berlin.

William J. Murtagh, *Keeping Time: The History and Theory of Preservation in America* (rev. ed., 1997), an account of historic preservation of objects, archaeological sites, and buildings, with guidelines and discussions of social, legal, ethical, and economic issues.

The Branches of Knowledge

J. François Gabriel (ed.), *Beyond the Cube: The Architecture of Space Frames and Polyhedra* (1997), a description of a type of construction consisting of hollow geometric forms, enumerating its properties, virtues, relationship to crystal formation, and future applications.

Jan Gullberg, *Mathematics from the Birth of Numbers* (1997), a history of numbers and their symbols, with discussions ranging from the four rules of arithmetic to calculus and differential equations.

Maurizio Forte and Alberto Siliotti (eds. and comps.), *Virtual Archaeology: Recreating Ancient Worlds* (1997), a collection of three-dimensional high-definition computer reconstructions, along with hundreds of full-colour maps, diagrams, and photographs, providing readers with a sense of how significant archaeological sites around the world once looked, including Pompeii, Giza, Troy, and Abu Simbel.

Sara Schechner Genuth, *Comets, Popular Culture, and the Birth of Modern Cosmology* (1997), an account of the interrelated effects of comet lore and popular culture on early modern science.

Ernst Mayr, *This Is Biology: The Science of the Living World* (1997), a study of the history, philosophy, and methodology of the life sciences, emphasizing the ways in which biologists are developing increasingly precise information about the living world.

Terrence W. Deacon, *The Symbolic Species: The Co-evolution of Language and the Brain* (1997), an investigation of the ability of humans to create and manipulate language symbols.

Roald Hoffmann and Shira Leibowitz Schmidt, *Old Wine, New Flasks: Reflections on Science and Jewish Tradition* (1997), a meditation on science and religion that explores the philosophical issues concerning humanity's domination of nature.

Michael D. Resnik, *Mathematics as a Science of Patterns* (1997), a look at the philosophical underpinnings of mathematics as a science of patterns and at the relationship of mathematics to realism and empiricism.

D.N. Rodowick, *Gilles Deleuze's Time Machine* (1997), a study of the reciprocal relationship between cinema and philosophy as expressed in the writings of French philosopher Gilles Deleuze.

(JEAN S. GOTTLIEB)

Major New Revisions from *Encyclopædia Britannica*

This section of the *Britannica Book of the Year* consists of articles or parts of articles that have recently been revised or rewritten for publication in the 1998 edition of *Encyclopædia Britannica* and have also been incorporated in *Britannica Online*™, an electronic version of the encyclopædia. The articles appearing here have been chosen by the yearbook editors for their general interest or their timeliness.

The selection from the article EAST ASIAN ARTS has been revised to include a new assessment of the visual arts in Japan. The recent history of Poland has been revised and selected from the article POLAND.

Subscribers desiring update sheets to put in their encyclopaedia to indicate that an article has been revised or added and owners of older sets wishing information about the exact articles being replaced by the reprints should address their requests to EB Direct, Inc., P.O. Box 22393, Denver CO 80222-9422. There is no charge for the article update sheets.

East Asian Arts

Japanese visual arts

GENERAL CHARACTERISTICS

Most Japanese art bears the mark of extensive interaction with or reaction to outside forces. Buddhism, which originated in India and developed throughout Asia, was the most persistent vehicle of influence. It provided Japan with an already well-established iconography and also offered perspectives on the relationship between the visual arts and spiritual development. Notable influxes of Buddhism from Korea occurred in the 6th and 7th centuries. The Chinese T'ang international style was the focal point of Japanese artistic development in the 8th century, while the iconographies of Chinese Esoteric Buddhism were highly influential from the 9th century. Major immigrations of Chinese Ch'an (Japanese: Zen) Buddhist monks in the 13th and 14th centuries and, to a lesser degree, in the 17th century placed indelible marks on Japanese visual culture. These periods of impact and assimilation brought not only religious iconography but also vast and largely undigested features of Chinese culture. Whole structures of cultural expression, ranging from a writing system to political structures, were presented to the Japanese.

Various theories have thus been posited which describe the development of Japanese culture and, in particular, visual culture as a cyclical pattern of assimilation, adaptation, and reaction. The reactive feature is sometimes used to describe periods in which Japanese art's most obviously unique and indigenous characteristics flourish. The notion of cyclical assimilation and then assertion of independence requires extensive nuancing, however. It should be recognized that, while there were periods in which either continental or indigenous art forms were dominant, usually the two forms coexisted.

Importance of nature

Another pervasive characteristic of Japanese art is an understanding of the natural world as a source of spiritual insight and an instructive mirror of human emotion. An indigenous religious sensibility that long preceded Buddhism perceived that a spiritual realm was manifest in nature. Rock outcroppings, waterfalls, and gnarled old trees were viewed as the abodes of spirits and were understood as their personification. This belief system endowed much of nature with numinous qualities. It nurtured, in turn, a sense of proximity to and intimacy with the world of spirit as well as a trust in nature's general benevolence. The cycle of the seasons was deeply instructive and revealed, for example, that immutability and transcendent perfection were not natural norms. Everything was understood as subject to a cycle of birth, fruition, death, and decay. (Imported Buddhist notions of transience were thus merged with the indigenous tendency to seek instruction from nature.)

Attentive proximity to nature developed and reinforced an aesthetic that generally avoided artifice. In the production of works of art, the natural qualities of constitutive materials were given special prominence and understood as integral to whatever total meaning a work professed. When, for example, Japanese Buddhist sculpture of the 9th century moved from the stucco or bronze T'ang models and turned for a time to natural, unpolychromed woods, already ancient iconographic forms were melded with a preexisting and multileveled respect for wood.

Union with the natural was also an element of Japanese architecture. Architecture seemed to conform to nature. The symmetry of Chinese-style temple plans gave way to asymmetrical layouts that followed the specific contours of hilly and mountainous topography. The borders existing between structures and the natural world were deliberately obscure. Elements such as long verandas and multiple sliding panels offered constant vistas on nature—although the nature was often carefully arranged and fabricated rather than wild and real.

Preference for imperfections

The perfectly formed work of art or architecture, unweathered and pristine, was ultimately considered distant, cold, and even grotesque. This sensibility was also apparent in tendencies of Japanese religious iconography. The ordered hierarchical sacred cosmology of the Buddhist world generally inherited from China bore the features of China's earthly imperial court system. While some of those features were retained in Japanese adaptation, there was also a concurrent and irrepressible trend toward creating easily approachable deities. This usually meant the elevation of ancillary deities such as Jizo Bosatsu or Kannon Bosatsu to levels of increased cult devotion. The inherent compassion of supreme deities was expressed through these figures and their iconography.

The interaction of the spiritual and natural world was

also delightfully expressed in the many narrative scroll paintings produced in the medieval period. Stories of temple foundings and biographies of sainted founders were replete with episodes describing both heavenly and demonic forces roaming the earth and interacting with the populace on a human scale. There was a marked tendency toward the comfortable domestication of the supernatural. The sharp distinction between good and evil was gently reduced, and other worldly beings took on characteristics of human ambiguity that granted them a level of approachability, prosaically flawing the perfect of either extreme.

Even more obviously decorative works such as the brightly polychromed overglaze enamels popular from the 17th century selected the preponderance of their surface imagery from the natural world. The repeated patterns found on surfaces of textiles, ceramics, and lacquerware are usually carefully worked abstractions of natural forms such as waves or pine needles. In many cases pattern, as a kind of hint or suggestion of molecular substructure, is preferred to carefully rendered realism.

The everyday world of human endeavour has been carefully observed by Japanese artists. For example, the human figure in a multiplicity of mundane poses was memorably recorded by the print artist Hokusai (1760–1849). The quirky and humorous seldom eluded the view of the many anonymous creators of medieval hand scrolls or 17th-century genre screen paintings. Blood and gore, whether in battle or criminal mayhem, were vigorously recorded as undeniable aspects of the human. Similarly, the sensual and erotic were rendered in delightful and uncensorious ways. The reverence and curiosity about the natural extended from botany to every dimension of human activity.

In summary, the range of Japanese visual art is extensive, and some elements seem truly antithetical. An illuminated sutra manuscript of the 12th century and a macabre scene of ritual disembowelment rendered by the 19th-century print artist Tsukioka Yoshitoshi can be forced into a common aesthetic only in the most artificial way. The viewer is thus advised to expect a startling range of diversity. Yet within that diverse body of expression certain characteristic elements seem to be recurrent: art that is aggressively assimilative; a profound respect for nature as a model; a decided preference for delight over dogmatic assertion in the description of phenomena; a tendency to give compassion and human scale to religious iconography; and an affection for materials as important vehicles of meaning.

STYLISTIC AND HISTORICAL DEVELOPMENT

Formative period. The terminology and chronology used in describing pre- and protohistoric Japan is generally agreed to be that of a Paleolithic, or Pre-Ceramic, stage dating from approximately 30,000 BC (although some posit an initial date as early as 200,000 BC); the Jōmon period (*c.* 10,500 BC–3rd century BC), variously subdivided; the Yayoi period (3rd century BC–3rd century AD); and the Tumulus, or Kofun, period (3rd century AD–AD 710).

Paleolithic stage. Until about 18,000 years ago, what is now known as the Japanese archipelago was connected to the East Asian landmass at several points. Similarly, the now divided islands were also joined at some points. These land passages account for the discovery of the remains of both prehistoric animals and microlithic cultures (but no pottery) of types usually associated with the continent. Continued warming trends, beginning about 20,000 years ago, eventually raised sea levels, thus cutting off all but the northern passage from Siberia.

The earliest human populations on the archipelago had subsisted on hunting and foraging, but with the warming trends the bounty of large, easy-to-fell animals began to die out while the variety and density of plant life rose dramatically. The increase in the number of sites discovered dating from 15,000 to 18,000 years ago suggests that once-roaming bands of hunter-gatherers were becoming gradually more sedentary and less dependent on foraging. As further evidence, the remains of charred cooking stones, indicating prolonged periods of use, have been discovered, and manufactured projectile points, including worked obsidian, dating from this period provide evidence of the people's adaptive skill in bringing down smaller, swifter game.

Mesolithic stage

Approximately 12,000 to 10,000 years ago, the definitive conditions for what is termed a Mesolithic stage became apparent: a hunting culture employed microliths and, in addition, manufactured pottery. Just as the use of microlith weapons increased as a result of a decline in the numbers of big game, the manufacture of pottery was probably necessitated by a food supply crisis that required a means of storage and, perhaps, a method for boiling or otherwise cooking plants.

Jōmon period. Beginning in 1960, excavations of stratified layers in the Fukui Cave, Nagasaki prefecture in northwestern Kyushu, yielded shards of dirt-brown pottery with applied and incised or impressed decorative elements in linear relief and parallel ridges. The pottery was low-fired, and reassembled pieces are generally minimally decorated and have a small round-bottomed shape. Radiocarbon dating places the Fukui find to approximately 10,500 BC, and the Fukui shards are generally thought to mark the beginning of the Jōmon period. This early transitional period seems to lack convincing evidence of plant cultivation which would, along with microlith and pottery production, allow it to meet the criteria for a Neolithic culture.

The name Jōmon is a translation for "cord marks," the term the American zoologist Edward Sylvester Morse used in his book *Shell Mounds of Ōmori* (1879) to describe the distinctive decoration on the prehistoric pottery shards he found at Ōmori in southwestern Tokyo. Other names, such as "Ainu school pottery" and "shell mound pottery," were also applied to pottery from this period, but, after some decades, although cord marks are not the defining decorative scheme of the type, the term *jōmon* was generally accepted. The earliest stage of the period, to which the Fukui shards belong, has been given various names, including Incipient Jōmon and Subearliest Jōmon. Some scholars even call it Pre-Jōmon and argue that life during this stage showed only a slight advance from that of the Paleolithic. In 1937 Yamanouchi Sugao suggested the subdivisions Earliest, Early, Middle, Late, and Latest Jōmon for the remainder of the period. With refinements in chronology and the addition of some subsets, this terminology remains in use.

Earliest Jōmon

The period called Earliest, or Initial, Jōmon (*c.* 7500–5000 BC) produced bullet-shaped pots used for cooking or boiling food. The tapered bases of the pots were designed to stabilize the vessels in soft soil and ash at the centre of a fire pit. Decorative schemes included markings made by pressing shells and cords or by rolling a carved stick into the clay before it hardened. The shapes and worked surface textures of these early vessels suggest their probable precursors—leather, bark, or woven reed containers reinforced with clay. The Hanawadai site in Ibaraki prefecture constitutes the first recognized Earliest Jōmon community.

Early Jōmon (5000–3500 BC) sites suggest a pattern of increased stabilization of communities, the formation of small settlements, and the astute use of abundant natural resources. A general climatic warming trend encouraged habitation in the mountain areas of central Honshu as well as coastal areas. Remains of pit houses have been found arranged in horseshoe formations at various Early Jōmon sites. Each house consisted of a shallow pit with a tamped earthen floor and a grass roof designed so that rainwater runoff could be collected in storage jars.

Early Jōmon vessels generally continued the fundamental profile of a cone shape, narrow at the foot and gradually widening to the rim or mouth, but most had flat bottoms, a feature found only occasionally in the Earliest Jōmon period. The characteristic markings were impressed on damp clay with a twisted cord or cord-wrapped stick to produce a multiplicity of patterns. Other techniques, including shell impressions, were also used. In addition to the flared-mouth jars, shallow bowls and narrow-necked bottles were also introduced. The discovery of

Earliest Jōmon vessel, clay, *c.* 5000 BC. In the Hakodate Municipal Museum, Japan. Height 16.6 cm.
Hakodate Municipal Museum, Japan

increasing varieties of flat-bottomed vessels appropriate for cooking, serving, and providing storage on flat earthen floors correlates with the evidence of the gradual formation of pit-house villages.

While pottery was the main form of visual expression in the Early Jōmon period, wood carving and lacquering are among the other significant forms of expression, suggesting the development of a more complex culture. Ropes, reed baskets, and wooden objects have been found at the Torihama mound site in Fukui prefecture. The oldest known examples of Japanese lacquerware—bowls and a comb—are also from this site.

The Middle Jōmon period (3500–2500 BC) witnessed a dramatic increase both in population and in the number of settlements. Signs of incipient agriculture can be detected in this period, but this may have involved settling near wild plants and storing them effectively. Vessels began to take on heavy decorative schemes employing applied clay. The use of vessels for purposes beyond cooking and storage is also noted. Clay lamps, drum shells, and figurines strongly suggest an expanding use of the medium for religious symbolic expression. Fertility images of clay female figurines with exaggerated breasts and hips and of stone phalli have been located on stone platforms placed on the northwest side of dwellings. These platforms may represent early household altars. During this period jars were used for burial and were characteristically damaged so as to prohibit any other type of use.

Three distinct vessel styles were produced during the Middle Jōmon. The Katsusaka type, produced by mountain dwellers, has a burnt-reddish surface and is noted especially for extensive and flamboyant applied decorative schemes, some of which may have been related to a snake cult. The Otamadai type, produced by lowland peoples, was coloured dirt-brown with a mica additive and is somewhat more restrained in design. The Kasori E type has a salmon-orange surface. During this period a red ocher paint was introduced on some vessel surfaces, as was burnishing, perhaps in an attempt to reduce the porosity of the vessels.

In the Late Jōmon (2500–1000 BC) colder temperatures and increased rainfall forced migration from the central mountains to the eastern coastal areas of Honshu. There is evidence of even greater interest in ritual, probably because of the extensive decrease in population. From this time are found numerous ritual sites consisting of long stones laid out radially to form concentric circles. These stone circles, located at a distance from habitations, may have been related to burial or other ceremonies. Previously disparate tribes began to exhibit a greater cultural uniformity. Artifacts discovered in diverse coastal areas show a uniform vocabulary of expression and a consistent decorative system, suggesting more sophisticated methods of manufacturing, such as controlled firing of pottery, and increased specialization. The technique of erased cord marking, in which areas around applied cord marks were smoothed out, was increasingly used. This relates to a more general practice or interest in polished pottery surfaces. A unique black polished pottery type called Goryo has been found in central Kyushu. Some scholars suggest that this may in some way be imitative of Chinese black Lung-shan pottery (*c.* 2200–1700 BC).

Evidence from the Latest, or Final, Jōmon (*c.* 1000–3rd century BC) suggests that inhospitable forces, whether contagious disease or climate, were at work. There was a considerable decrease in population and a regional fragmentation of cultural expression. Particularly noteworthy was the formation of quite distinct cultures in the north and south. The discovery of numerous small ritual implements, including pottery, suggests that the cultures developing in the north were rigidly structured and evinced considerable interest in ritual.

More than 50 percent of the Latest Jōmon sites are in northern Honshu, where significant quantities of polished or burnished pottery and lacquerware have been found. In fact, it is from this time that lacquer working—used for both decorative and waterproofing purposes—begins to emerge as a distinct craft. In general, the northern distinction between utilitarian and ritual ware became more pronounced, and the ritual ware became more elaborately conceived. The latter phenomenon is clearly illustrated by the unusual clay figurines with enormous goggle eyes that are characteristic of the Latest Jōmon.

In the south mobility and informality were the emerging characteristics of social organization and artistic expression. In distinction to the northern culture, the south seemed more affected by outside influences. Indeed, the incursions of continental culture would, in a few centuries, be based in the Kyushu area.

Yayoi period. In 1884 a shell mound site in the Yayoi district of Tokyo yielded pottery finds that were initially thought to be variants of Jōmon types but were later linked to similar discoveries in Kyushu and Honshu. Scholars gradually concluded that the pottery exhibited some continental influences but was the product of a distinct culture, which has been given the name Yayoi.

Both archaeological and written evidence point to increasing interaction between the mainland and the various polities on the Japanese archipelago at this time. Indeed, the chronology of the Yayoi period (3rd century

Clay figurine dating from Latest Jōmon period, excavated at Ebisuda, Miyagi prefecture. In the collection of Tōhoku University, Sendai, Japan. Height 35.6 cm.
By courtesy of the Archaeological Seminar, Tohoku University, Sendai, Japan

BC–3rd century AD) roughly corresponds with the florescence of the aggressively internationalized Chinese Han dynasty (206 BC–AD 220).

The Yayoi culture thus marked a period of rapid differentiation from the preceding Jōmon culture. Jōmon, a hunting-and-gathering culture with possibly nascent forms of agriculture, experienced changes and transitions primarily in reaction to climatic and other natural stimulants. Yayoi, however, was greatly influenced by knowledge and techniques imported from China and Korea. The impact of continental cultures is decidedly clear in western Japan from about 400 BC, when primitive wet-rice cultivation techniques were introduced. Attendant to the emerging culture based on sedentary agriculture was the introduction of a significant architectural form, the raised thatched-roof granary. Bronze and iron implements and processes of metallurgy were also introduced and quickly assimilated, as the Yayoi people both copied and adapted types and styles already produced in China and Korea. Thus, while the decorative instincts of the Jōmon culture were limited primarily to the manipulation of clay, a variety of malleable materials, including bronze, iron, and glass, were increasingly available to artisans of the Yayoi period. The introduction of these various technologies, the development of a stable agricultural society, and the growth of a complex social hierarchy that characterized the period became the springboards for various forms of creative expression and provided increasing opportunities for the development of artistic forms.

The Yayoi period is most often defined artistically by its dramatic shift in pottery style. The new type of pottery, reflecting continental styles, was made first in western Japan. It then moved eastward and became assimilated with existing Jōmon styles. Jōmon pottery was earthenware formed from readily available sedimentary clay and was generally stiff. Yayoi pottery was formed from a fine-grained clay of considerable plasticity found in the delta areas associated with rice cultivation. It was smooth, reddish orange in colour, thinly potted, symmetrical, and minimally decorated. The simpler, more reserved styles and forms emulated Chinese earthenware. It was also at this time that pottery began to be produced in sets, including pieces made for the storing, cooking, and serving of food.

Dōtaku bells

In addition to the characteristic pottery that gave its site name to the period, the production of metal objects, particularly the *dōtaku* bells, represents a significant artistic manifestation of the Yayoi period. The *dōtaku* were cast in bronze and imitative of a Chinese musical instrument.

Earthenware jar excavated from Kugahara, Tokyo, Yayoi period. In the Tokyo National Museum. Height 36.3 cm.
By courtesy of the Tokyo National Museum

Dōtaku (bell-shaped bronze) with design of whirlpools, excavated from Uzumora, Hyōgo prefecture, Yayoi period. In the Tokyo National Museum.
By courtesy of the International Society for Educational Information, Tokyo

More than 400 indigenously produced *dōtaku* have been discovered in Japan. These bells range from 4 to 50 inches in height. Their quality suggests a rather advanced state of technical acumen. Figural and decorative relief bands on these bells offer some, albeit highly interpretive, insights into Yayoi culture and suggest that shamanism was the dominant religious modality. The *dōtaku* appear not to have been used as musical instruments in Japan. Instead, like the bronze mirrors and other distinguished and precious implements transferred and adapted from Chinese and Korean forms, the *dōtaku* took on talismanic significance, and their possession implied social and religious power.

Tumulus, or Kofun, period. About AD 300 there appeared new and distinctive funerary customs whose most characteristic feature was chambered mound tombs. These tumuli, or kofun ("old mounds"), witnessed significant variations over the following 400 years but consistently dominated the period to which they gave their name. Some authorities have suggested that the development of these tombs was a natural evolution from a Yayoi-period custom of burial on high ground overlooking crop-producing fields. While partially convincing, this theory alone does not account for the sudden florescence of mound tombs, nor does it address the fact that some aspects of the tombs are clearly adaptations of a form preexisting on the Korean peninsula. Indeed, implements and artifacts discovered within these tombs suggest a strong link to peninsular culture.

Changes in tomb structure, as well as the quantity, quality, and type of grave goods discovered, offer considerable insight into the evolution of Japan's sociopolitical development from a group of interdependent agricultural communities to the unified state of the early 8th century. Of course, the material culture of the Kofun period extended far beyond the production of funerary art. For example, it is in this time that an essential form of Japanese expression, the Chinese writing system, made its appearance on the archipelago—a fact known from such evidence as inscribed metal implements. This system had a profound and comparatively quick influence not only on written language but also on the development of painting in Japan. Nevertheless, tombs are the repositories of the period's greatest visual achievements and are excellent indicators of more general cultural patterns at work. And, in that wider context, three distinct shifts in tomb style can be discerned that define the chronology of the period: Early Kofun of the 4th century, Middle Kofun covering the 5th and early 6th centuries, and Late Kofun, which lasted until the beginning of the 8th century and during which tomb burials were gradually replaced by Buddhist cremation ceremonies. The Late Kofun roughly coincides with the periods known to art historians as the Asuka (mid-6th century–645) and the Hakuhō (645–710).

Tombs of the Early Kofun period made use of and customized existing and compatible topography. When viewed from above, the tomb silhouette was either a rough circle or, more characteristically, an upper circle combined with a lower triangular form, suggesting the shape of an old-fashioned keyhole. The tombs contained a space for a wooden coffin and grave goods. This area was accessed through a vertical shaft near the top of the mound and was sealed off after burial was completed. The deceased were buried with materials that were either actual or symbolic indicators of social status. The grave goods were intended, as well, to sustain the spirit in its journey in the afterlife. They included bronze mirrors, items of jewelry made from jade and jasper, ceramic vessels, and iron weapons. Adorning the summit of the mound and at points on the circumference midway, at the base, and at the entrance to the tomb were variously articulated clay cylinder forms known as *haniwa* ("clay circle").

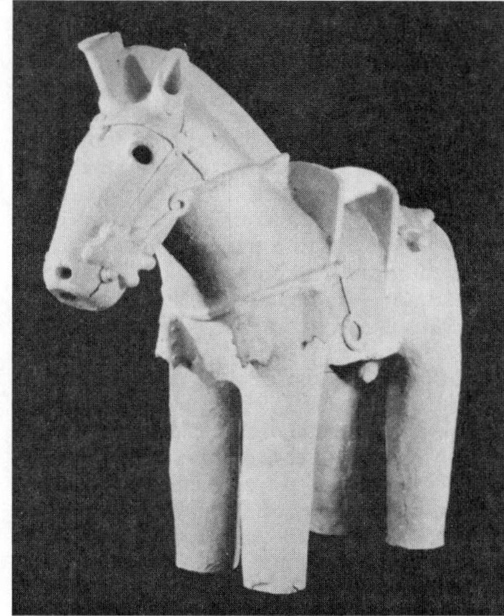

Haniwa horse, clay, 5th–6th century. In the Tokyo National Museum. Height 83.8 cm.

By courtesy of the International Society for Educational Information, Tokyo

Haniwa sculpture

Haniwa were an unglazed, low-fired, reddish, porous earthenware made of the same material as a type of daily-use pottery called *haji* ware. These clay creations were shaped from coils or slabs and took the form of human figures, animals, and houses. The latter shape was usually set at the peak of the burial hillock. Many attempts have been made to interpret the function of *haniwa*. They seem to have served both as protective figures and as some type of support for the deceased in the afterlife. There is some suggestion that, similar to tomb figurines found in other cultures, they symbolized a retinue of living servants who might otherwise have been sacrificed upon the demise of their master. They are regionally distinctive and show a stylistic development from the decidedly schematic to realistic.

Another type of ceramic prominent in the Kofun period was *sue* ware. Distinct from *haji* ware, it was high-fired and in its finished form had a gray cast. Occasionally, accidental ash glazing is found on the surface. Until the 7th century, *sue* ware was a product reserved for the elite, who used it both for daily ware and on ceremonial occasions. *Sue* ware was more closely identified with Korean ceramic technology and was the precursor for a variety of medieval Japanese ceramic types. Interestingly, both *haji* and *sue* ware found roles in funerary art.

After the 4th century, tomb builders abandoned naturally sympathetic topography and located mounds in clusters on flat land. There are differences in mound size, even within the clusters, suggesting levels of social status. The scale of these tombs, together with construction techniques, changed considerably. The tomb generally assumed to be that of the late 4th-century emperor Nintoku, located near the present-day city of Ōsaka, measures nearly 1,600 feet in length and covers 80 acres (32 hectares). It is alternately surrounded by three moats and two greenbelts. Approximately 20,000 *haniwa* were thought to have been placed on the surface of this huge burial mound.

In the later part of the 5th century, the vertical shaft used to access the early pit tomb was replaced by the Korean-style horizontal corridor leading to a tomb chamber. This made multiple use of the tomb easier, and the notion of a family tomb came into existence. Also notable from the 5th century is the archaeological evidence of

Mausoleum of Nintoku, at Sakai, largest of the "keyhole" type tombs of the Tumulus, or Kofun, period. Circumference 2,718 m, height 21 m.

By courtesy of the International Society for Educational Information, Tokyo horse trappings and military hardware in tombs. *Haniwa* representing warriors and stylized military shields are also prominent. Records of diplomatic and military forays combine with the grave goods of the period to suggest a strong military cast to 5th- and 6th-century culture. However, in time these accoutrements of war and symbols of physical power are found in ancillary tombs rather than in the grave sites of known leaders. This suggests a gradual consolidation of power and the formation of a specialized military service within the kingdoms.

Japan's close relationship with Korean and Chinese cultures during the Kofun period effected an influx of peninsular craftsmen. This is reflected in the production of *sue* ware mentioned above and in the high quality of metalwork achieved. Mirrors are a particularly fine example of the development of metal craft. The typical East Asian mirror of the time is a metal disk brought to a high reflective finish on one side and elaborately decorated on the reverse. Such mirrors did not originate in Japan but seem to have been made and used there for religious and political purposes. The dominant Japanese creation myth describes the Sun Goddess, Amaterasu Omikami, being coaxed from hiding by seeing her reflection in a mirror. This may well have imparted a magico-religious quality to mirrors and caused them to be understood as authority symbols. Of particular note is the so-called *chokkomon* decorative scheme found on some of these mirrors and on other Early Kofun metalwork. *Chokkomon* means "patterns of straight line and arcs," and the motif has also been found chiseled on a wall in a Late Kofun tomb at the Idera tomb in Kyushu. It has been suggested that the abstract interweaving pattern may symbolize rope binding the dead to the tomb, an aspect of Chinese cosmology of the Han dynasty.

Metalwork

Late Kofun tombs are characterized by schemes of wall decoration within the burial chambers. Two especially important tombs have been excavated in the area just to the south of present-day Nara. The Takamatsu tomb (1972) and the Fujinoki tomb (1985) suggest high levels of artistic achievement and a sophisticated assimilation of continental culture. The Takamatsu tomb is noted for its wall paintings containing a design scheme representing a total Chinese cosmology. Included are especially fine female figure paintings. At Fujinoki exquisite and elaborate metalwork, including openwork gold crowns, a gilt bronze saddle bow, and gilt bronze shoes, was discovered. Design motifs show evidence of Chinese, Central Asian, and Indian sources.

Asuka period. The Asuka period was a time of transformation for Japanese society. It is named for the Asuka area at the southern end of the Nara (Yamato) Basin (a few miles to the south of the present-day city of Nara), which was the political and cultural centre of the country at the time. From there, the imperial court ruled over a loose confederation of rival clans, the most powerful of which were the Soga, Mononobe, and Nakatomi.

Japan's interest in and contacts with continental cultures continued to increase in the Asuka. A wide range of political and cultural relations with the Korean kingdoms of Koguryŏ, Silla, and, in particular, Paekche provided an opportunity for comparatively systematic assimilation of vast amounts of Korean culture, Chinese culture read through a Korean prism, and the religious beliefs of Buddhism. It was within that period of intensive relations with Paekche that critical foundations were constructed for a radical shift in the direction of Japanese visual arts.

Introduction of Buddhism

The most significant change, of course, was the introduction of Buddhism. Historians debate the actual date of the arrival of Buddhist texts, implements of worship, and iconography in Japan, but according to tradition a Paekche delegation to the emperor Kimmei in 538 or 552 made the presentation of certain religious articles. Given the extent of contact with Korea, however, various "unofficial" introductions of Buddhism had probably already occurred. The religion soon found favour in Japan and flourished under the powerful regent Prince Shōtoku (574–622), who established it as the state religion.

Buddhism was already a thousand years old when it arrived in Japan. It had transformed and been transformed by the iconography and artistic styles of the various cultures along its path of expansion from India. The central message of Gautama Buddha (6th–5th centuries BC) had also experienced multiple interpretations, as evidenced by the numerous sectarian divisions in Buddhism. The artistic forms necessary to provide the proper environment for the practice of the religion were well defined, however—calligraphy, painting, sculpture, liturgical implements, and temple architecture—and these were the means by which nearly all continental modes of Buddhism were absorbed and adapted by the Japanese culture.

During this period of intensive peninsular contact, Korean artisans skilled in metalwork, sculpture, painting, ceramics, and other fields necessary to the production of Buddhist iconography immigrated to or were brought to Japan in large numbers. While the practice of most of the above-mentioned forms was the purview of professionals, the calligraphic rendering of the written word was a skill available to the educated elite of the period. Thus, in the Asuka period the foundations of both individualized and public forms of visual expression were secured.

Architecture. Buddhism was established in Japan as a site-oriented faith. Temples with designs initially based on continental models became centres of worship. In contrast to the importance of funerary art in the Kofun period, the artistic expression of the Asuka period was developed within the matrix of public and privately commissioned temples. By the close of the Asuka period in the mid-7th century, nearly all vestiges of tomb burial customs were actually outlawed as the new faith made extensive inroads.

The most important temple complexes of the period are the Shitennō Temple at Ōsaka, the Wakakusa Temple near Nara (both constructed by Prince Shōtoku), and the Asuka Temple at Asuka. All three are known only through archaeological remains, although Wakakusa, Shōtoku's private temple, which was destroyed by fire in

Shaka Triad by Tori, comprising the Buddha Śākyamuni and a pair of bodhisattvas, bronze, 623, Asuka period. In the *kondō* of the Hōryū Temple, Nara. Heights of figures: (left) 92 cm, (centre) 86.4 cm, (right) 93.9 cm.
Asuka-En

Asuka temple layout

670, was reincarnated as the Hōryū Temple (see below). These temple complexes replicated forms popular in Paekche and Koguryŏ. They were walled compounds in which stood a second rectangular compound bordered by a continuous roofed corridor. This second enclosure was entered through a central gate on its south side and contained a variety of internal structures, such as a pagoda (a form derived from the Indian stupa that served the dual functions of cosmological diagram and reliquary of important personages) and a Golden Hall (*kondō*), both used for worship. Support buildings, such as lecture halls, a belfry, and living quarters, lay outside and to the north of the inner cloister. True to the continental style, the buildings and gates were sited along a south-north axis and were symmetrical in layout. It was within the various buildings, particularly the *kondō*, that sculptures representing various figures in the Buddhist pantheon were placed.

Roof tiles, stone, and cryptomeria wood were the essential building materials, all indigenous or locally produced. Structures relied on the placement of vertical wood pillars secured on finished stone bases. Horizontal elements were added in varying degrees of complexity, and structural balance was based on the essential pillar concept.

Sculpture. While the structures of these temples did not survive, certain important sculptures did, and these images are generally associated with the name of Kuratsukuri Tori (also known as Tori Busshi). Tori was descended from a family of saddlemakers. Excellence in this trade required mastery of the component media of lacquer, leather, wood, and metal, each of which was, in various ways, also used in the production of sculpture.

A large, seated, gilt-bronze image of Shaka (the Japanese name for Śākyamuni Buddha, the historical Buddha) survives from the Asuka Temple and is dated to 606. Also extant is the gilt-bronze Shaka Triad of Hōryū Temple, which is dated by inscription to 623. The Asuka Buddha, heavily restored, is attributed to Tori based on the stylistic similarity of its undisturbed head to the renderings found in the Shaka Triad, which is confidently assigned to the master sculptor's hand. A more controversial work is a gilt bronze Yakushi (the healing Buddha), which carries an inscription of 607. It is very close to the style of Tori, but many date the work to the latter part of the century. The Triad and the Yakushi are now housed in Hōryū Temple. An inscribed dedication found on the halo of the central figure of the Triad suggests that the ensemble was dedicated to the recently deceased Shōtoku and his consort. A stylistically related work is the wooden statue of the bodhisattva Kuze Kannon in the Yumedono ("Hall of Dreams") of the Hōryū Temple. The Tori style seen in these works reveals an interpretive dependence on Chinese Buddhist sculpture of the Northern Wei dynasty (386–534/535), such as that found in the cave sites at Lung-men. Symmetry, a highly stylized linear treatment of draped garments, and a reserved and gentle facial expression with a characteristic archaic smile are the prominent distinguishing features of this sculpture. The Japanese interpretations in bronze and wood advance the frontally focused Chinese relief sculptures by beginning to suggest more fully rounded figures.

Tori style

Painting. Buddhist temples were decorated not only with sculpture but also with religious paintings, tapestries, and other objects. Most such works from the Asuka period have not survived. An exception is the Tamamushi Shrine, which consists of a miniature *kondō* affixed to a rectangular pedestal or base. This assemblage of wood, metal, and lacquer provides an excellent view of what a *kondō* of the period may have looked like and, perhaps more important, is decorated with the only known painting from the Asuka period. The painting program on the miniature *kondō* seems to depict, through images on various panels and doors, the deities normally found in sculptural form within the hall. Paintings on the panels of the base show aspects of Buddhist cosmology and scenes from jataka tales, those narratives that tell of exemplary incidents in the previous incarnations of the Buddha. Perhaps best known is the jataka of the Hungry Tigress, in which the Buddha prior to enlightenment chances upon a tigress and her cubs starving in a desolate ravine and offers his own body to them. The painting depicts a sequential narrative in one panel, showing the saint removing his robe, leaping from a cliff, and being eaten by the tigers. The painting style suggests an Indian prototype vastly influenced by the fluid linearity of Chinese Wei styles. (JAMES T. ULAK)

Poland

POLAND IN THE 20TH CENTURY

The rebirth of Poland. The outbreak of World War I was accompanied by two major political trends among the Poles. Piłsudski, distancing himself from socialist politics, became a military leader and commander of a brigade that fought on the Austrian side. His cooperation with the Central Powers was tactical, part of his pursuit of the goal of complete independence. Expecting a collapse of the three partitioners, he prepared for a Polish fait accompli. In 1915 the Germans and the Austrians drove out the Russians from Congress Poland, and on Nov. 5, 1916, they issued the Two Emperors' Manifesto proclaiming the creation of the Polish kingdom. Its status and borders remained undefined, but the document internationalized the Polish question. Piłsudski, who refused to raise Polish troops without binding political commitments from the Central Powers, came into conflict with them and in 1917 was imprisoned in Germany.

Dmowski's alternate policy of linking the Polish cause with the Franco-Russian alliance appeared promising when the first formal offer of Polish autonomy and unification came from the Russian commander in chief, Grand Duke Nicholas, on Aug. 14, 1914. Subsequent moves by the Russian government, however, revealed the hollowness of such promises. Russian concessions to the Poles, culminating in the tsar's Christmas Day 1916 order, were made only in reaction to the Central Powers' initiatives and victories. The chances of Polish independence increased radically in 1917 when the United States entered the war and two revolutions shook Russia. U.S. President Woodrow Wilson, to whom the great Polish patriot and pianist Ignacy Paderewski had gained access, already spoke of a united and autonomous Poland in a January 1917 address. The Russian Provisional Government, somewhat ambiguously, and the Petrograd (St. Petersburg) Soviet of Workers' and Soldiers' Deputies more explicitly, declared their recognition of Poland's right to independence in March 1917. At the Brest-Litovsk conference (Dec. 22, 1917–March 3, 1918) the Bolsheviks denounced the Central Powers' handling of the Polish question. On Jan. 8, 1918, Wilson's Fourteen Points appeared. Point 13 declared that an independent Polish state should be composed of indisputably Polish inhabitants, with a secure access to the sea. The Inter-Allied conference (June 1918) endorsed Polish independence, thus crowning the efforts of Dmowski, who had promoted the Polish cause in the West since 1915. In August 1917 he had set up a Polish National Committee in Paris, which the French viewed as a quasi-government. Under its aegis a Polish army composed mainly of volunteers from the United States was placed under the command of General Józef Haller.

Russian concessions

With the end of the war on Nov. 11, 1918, Piłsudski, released by the German revolutionaries, returned to

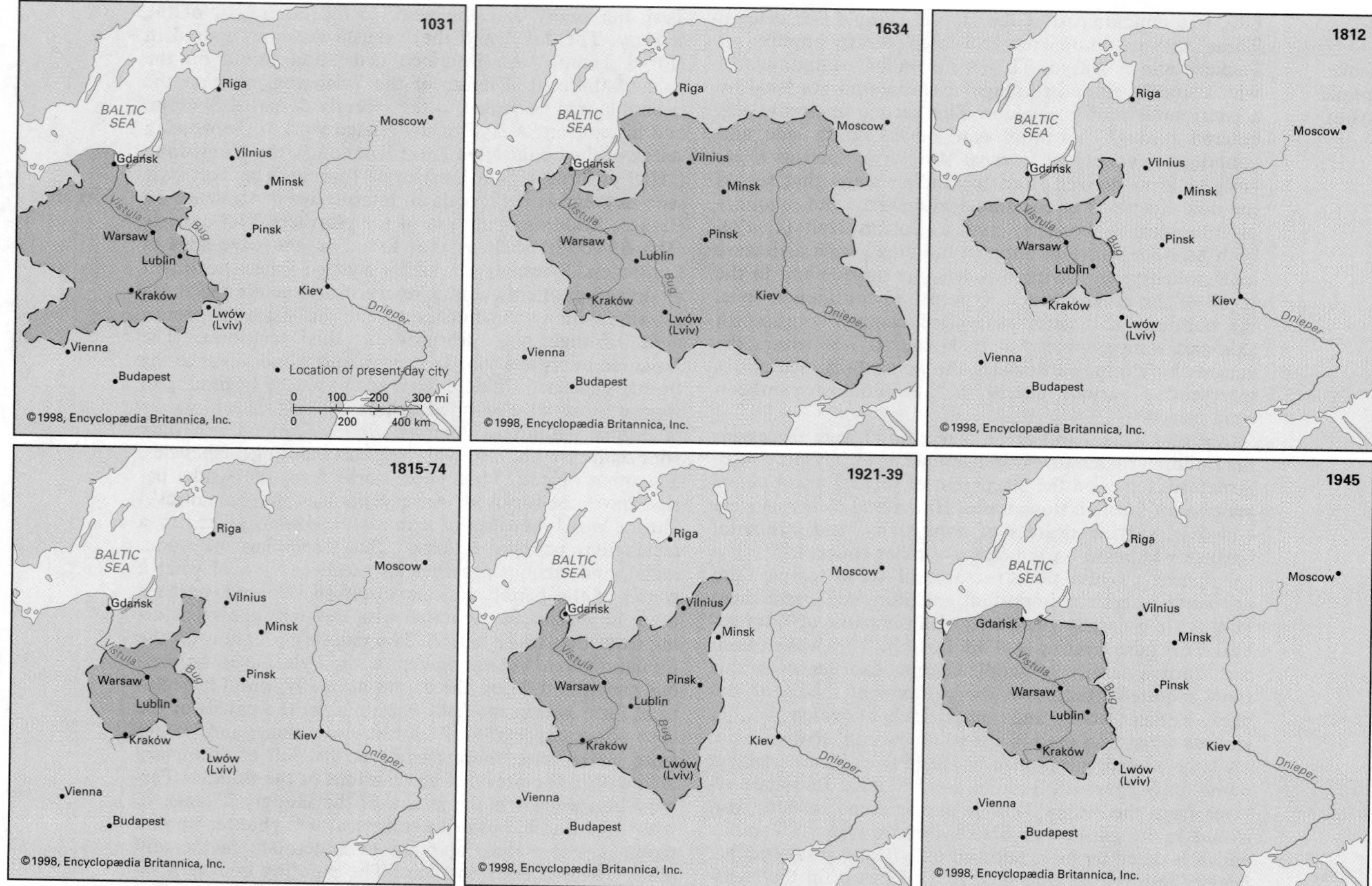

Changes in Poland's territory from 1031 to 1945.

Warsaw. The German-appointed Regency Council handed over its powers to him, and Piłsudski successfully negotiated a German evacuation of the kingdom. A leftist government in Lublin headed by Daszyński resigned in his favour, but not Dmowski's Polish National Committee, representing the Polish political right. The danger of two rival governments was avoided through the mediation of Paderewski. Under a compromise implemented in January 1919, Piłsudski remained chief of state and commander in chief; Paderewski, who became premier and foreign minister, and Dmowski represented Poland at the Paris Peace Conference.

At that stage the Polish government controlled only Congress Poland and western Galicia. In the east the Ukrainians, having proclaimed their own republic, battled the Poles. Farther east the Poles clashed with the Bolsheviks who were advancing into Belarusian and Lithuanian lands. A Polish uprising in Poznania led to a partial seizure of the province, but the fate of Prussian Poland lay in the hands of the peacemakers.

The struggle between Piłsudski and Dmowski

From the Treaty of Versailles to the Treaty of Riga. The Polish program at the Paris Peace Conference was affected by the Piłsudski-Dmowski dualism. Piłsudski's approach was "federalist," Dmowski's "incorporationist." The former strove to establish a bloc of states corresponding to pre-partition Poland. The latter postulated a centralized Polish state, with its eastern border determined by the Second Partition but also including Upper Silesia and parts of East Prussia transferred from Germany. France favoured strengthening Poland at Germany's expense, but Britain opposed that approach. Wilson occupied a middle position. The borders drawn under the Treaty of Versailles (June 1919) roughly corresponded to Polish-German frontiers before the partitions, except that Gdańsk became the Free City of Danzig, and plebiscites were held in parts of East Prussia and Upper Silesia to determine which nation these regions wished to join. The East Prussian plebiscite of July 1920 (at the height of the Russo-Polish War) was won by Germany. In the Silesian plebiscite of March 1921—preceded and followed by three Polish uprisings—682 communes voted for Poland and 792 for Germany. The region was formally divided in October 1921.

The drawing of the southern border under the Treaty of Saint-Germain (September 1919) was preceded by an armed Czech-Polish clash in January 1919 in the Duchy of Cieszyn. In July 1920 the area was divided, leaving a sizable Polish minority in Czechoslovakia. As for the embattled eastern Galicia, the Allies authorized a Polish administration and military occupation in 1919. Final recognition of Polish sovereignty came only in 1923, the delay being due to the Russian situation.

An armed struggle between the Bolsheviks and Poland resulted from Russian attempts to carry the revolution westward and from Piłsudski's federalist policy. The Great Powers failed to pursue either an all-out intervention against the Bolsheviks or a policy of peace. An Allied proposal for a temporary border between Bolshevik Russia and Poland (called the Curzon Line) was unacceptable to either side. Except for an alliance with the Ukrainian leader Symon Petlyura (April 1920), whose troops accompanied the Poles as they captured Kiev in May, Poland fought in isolation. An offensive by the Red Army drove the Poles back to the outskirts of Warsaw, but the country was saved from catastrophe by Piłsudski's counterattack on August 16 (the "Miracle of the Vistula"). In the compromise Peace of Riga (March 1921), the Bolsheviks abandoned their plans to communize Poland, but the Poles had to abandon their federalist concepts. The new border, which corresponded roughly to the 1793 frontier, cut across mixed Ukrainian and Belarusian territories. In the north it included Wilno, captured by General Lucjan Żeligowski, a move that dug a chasm between Lithuania and Poland.

The Second Republic. Interwar Poland with an area of about 150,000 square miles and more than 27 million inhabitants (more than 35 million by 1939) was the sixth largest country in Europe. Devastated by the years of hostilities, the state had to be reconstructed of three parts with different political, economic, and judicial systems and traditions. More than three-fifths of the population was dependent on agriculture that was badly in need of structural change: agrarian reform and redistribution of land that would relieve the demographic pressure (*e.g.*, hidden unemployment) and modernization of production that could alleviate the disparity between agrarian and industrial prices ("the price scissors"). Industrialization was essential, but local capital was insufficient, and foreign investors did not always operate in Poland's interests. Nonetheless, the Polish economy made important strides in the mid-1920s through the reforms of Władysław Grabski. After being severely hit by the Great Depression of the 1930s, it began to recover under the guidance of Eugeniusz Kwiatkowski, whose earlier achievements included the building of a new port and town of Gdynia.

Dependence on agriculture

Economic difficulties were interwoven with and augmented by political problems, among which the minority issues ranked high. Ukrainians (some 16 percent of the total population, according to recent estimates), Jews (about 10 percent), Belarusians (about 6 percent), and Germans (about 3 percent) lived in a state that, although multiethnic, was based on single-nation ideology. The Ukrainians never fully accepted Polish rule, and Ukrainian extremists engaged in terrorism to which the Poles responded with brutal "pacifications." In the case of the large and unassimilated Jewish population, concentrated in certain areas and professions, anti-Semitism was rampant, especially in the 1930s, though Poland never introduced anti-Jewish legislation.

Interwar politics centred to a large extent on the search for a constitutional model that would reconcile traditional Polish strivings for liberty with the need for a strong government. Piłsudski gave up his provisional powers to a Sejm elected in January 1919 but continued as the head of state under a provisional "Little Constitution." The Sejm quickly became an arena of interparty strife, with the right grouped around the National Democrats, the left around the PPS and radical Populists, and the centre represented mainly by the Polish Peasant Party-Piast. The illegal Communist Party, formed in 1918, was of marginal importance. The constitution of 1921 made the parliament supreme vis-à-vis the executive. The proportional system of universal suffrage (which included women) necessitated coalition cabinets, and the left and the right almost never cooperated. The assassination of the first president of the republic, Gabriel Narutowicz, in 1922 by a nationalist fanatic showed the extent of blind partisanship.

In May 1926 Piłsudski (who had held the title of marshal since 1920) came out of his three-year retirement. Demanding moral and political cleansing (*sanacja*), he staged an armed demonstration intended to force President Stanisław Wojciechowski to dismiss the government. Fighting in Warsaw ensued and ended in victory for Piłsudski. His candidate, Ignacy Mościcki, became president and remained in office until World War II. Piłsudski rejected fascism and totalitarianism but promoted an authoritarian regime in which his former legionnaires played a key role. Worshiped by his supporters and hated by his opponents, he became a father figure for large segments of the population. The pro-Piłsudski Non-Party Bloc of Cooperation with the Government (BBWR) became his political instrument, used at first against the opposition rightist National Democrats. In 1930 Piłsudski responded to the challenge of the centre-left opposition (Centrolew) by ordering the arrest and trial of its leaders, including three-time premier Witos. The brutal Brześć affair (named for the fortress in which the politicians involved were imprisoned) was seen as a blot on the Piłsudski regime, even though the sentences were light and some of the accused emigrated.

The Brześć affair

Following the 1930 elections BBWR had a majority in the Sejm. In April 1935 it was able to push through a new constitution, which placed the president above all other branches of government. An electoral law undercut the political parties that boycotted the 1935 parliamentary elections. In May Piłsudski died, leaving the country as a dictatorship without a dictator. His legend could not be bequeathed. A decomposition of the *sanacja* regime (sometimes called that of the colonels) ensued. Attempts to pass on Piłsudski's mantle to the new commander in chief, Marshal Edward Śmigły-Rydz, were unsuccessful, as was the artificial creation of a governmental party—the Camp of National Unity. The peasant parties (now united); the increasingly chauvinist National Party (as the National Democrats were by then known), with its fascist splinter party, the National Radical Camp; and the socialists all opposed the regime and showed success in municipal elections. Socioeconomic tension was translated into peasant strikes in the countryside and riots in towns.

Political and socioeconomic difficulties contrasted with the richness of intellectual, artistic, and scholarly life of the period. Twenty years of independence had given the Poles a new confidence that proved essential in the trials of World War II. Poland's international position between an inimical and revisionist Germany (which constantly denounced the "corridor" separating it from East Prussia) and the Soviet Union was dangerous from the start. The tasks of Polish diplomacy in the interwar period were exceedingly difficult. The only option was to remain neutral in regard to its two giant neighbours while concluding alliances (in 1921) with France and Romania. An alliance with Czechoslovakia foundered on basic differences of approach to international relations, particularly when Colonel Józef Beck became Piłsudski's foreign minister in 1932.

In 1932 Poland succeeded in signing a nonaggression pact with Soviet Russia and in 1934 a declaration of nonaggression with Nazi Germany. The enmity of the Nazis for the Soviets seemed to preclude a rapprochement (such as the Russo-German agreement at Rapallo, Italy, in 1922). The French alliance was maintained, though its value to Poland was diminished by the treaties of Locarno (1925) and subsequent Franco-German cooperation. Warsaw vainly sought to encourage Paris to adopt a strong line against Nazi Germany. But the French did not react forcibly even to the German remilitarization of the Rhineland (1936). Poland continued its policy of balance, but, in profiting from the German action against Czechoslovakia by gaining the disputed part of Cieszyn (October 1938), it gave the impression of being in collusion with Adolf Hitler. However, when confronted with German demands for an extraterritorial road through the "corridor" and the annexation of Danzig, as well as with an invitation to join the Anti-Comintern Pact, Beck knew that his country's independence was at stake. Accepting British Prime Minister Neville Chamberlain's guarantee of March 1939 and turning it into a full-fledged alliance with Britain, Warsaw rejected German demands. On Sept. 1, 1939, Hitler, having secured Soviet cooperation through the German-Soviet (Molotov-Ribbentrop) Nonaggression Pact a week earlier, launched an all-out attack against Poland.

The German-Soviet pact

World War II. The Poles, fighting alone against the Wehrmacht's overwhelming might, particularly in air power and armour, were doomed. On September 17 the Red Army invaded Poland, and on September 28 Hitler and Stalin agreed on a final partition, the Soviets taking eastern Galicia and lands east of the Bug River (*i.e.*, more than half of the country, where the Poles constituted about two-fifths of the population). After farcical plebiscites these territories were incorporated into Soviet Ukraine and Belorussia. Between 1940 and 1941 about 1.5 million people were deported to the U.S.S.R. Wilno was handed over to Lithuania, which by 1940 had become one of the Soviet republics. While the Soviets singled out class enemies, the Germans—who split the area they occupied into a central region called the General Government and territories annexed to the Reich—emphasized race. The Holocaust claimed the lives of some three million Polish Jews, herded into ghettoes and killed in extermination camps, of which Auschwitz (Oświęcim) was but one. Thousands of Jews died fighting, as in the Warsaw Ghetto Uprising in 1943. The Nazis also engaged in mass terror, deporting and executing Poles in an attempt to destroy the intelligentsia and reduce Polish culture to the lowest level.

A large Polish underground resisted the Nazis from 1939 through a veritable secret state and a Home Army (AK) loyal to the Polish government in exile. The latter was a legal successor of the government that on Sept. 17, 1939, had crossed into Romania and was interned there. Set up in Paris and moved after the collapse of France to London, it was led by the premier and commander in chief General Władysław Sikorski. Under his command Polish troops, organized in the west, fought in Europe and North Africa. Polish pilots played a disproportionately large role in the Battle of Britain (1940–41), and the small Polish navy distinguished itself. A major Polish contribution to the war effort lay in discovering and passing on to the Allies the secret of the German ciphering machine Enigma.

The German attack on the Soviet Union in June 1941 changed drastically Poland's position, for one of its foes now became a member of the Grand Alliance. Under British pressure the Polish government in exile reestablished relations with the Soviet Union through the Sikorski-Maysky accord, accepting the annulment of the Ribbentrop-Molotov treaty without an explicit Soviet renunciation of annexed Polish territory. The Soviets promised to release the deported Poles and agreed to the creation of a Polish army—more than 230,000 Poles had been prisoners of war since 1939—under the command of General Władysław Anders. Difficulties appeared almost from the start, however. The Soviets sought British and U.S. approval for their territorial gains. Friction developed regarding the Polish army in Russia, which in 1942 was evacuated to the Middle East. Meanwhile, the Soviets were promoting Polish communist activity both in the U.S.S.R. and in occupied Poland, where a Polish Workers' Party (PPR) emerged in 1942 with its own small People's Guard.

The emergence of the Polish Workers' Party

British Prime Minister Winston Churchill, not appreciating fully Stalin's hegemonic designs, believed that timely territorial concessions to the U.S.S.R. would preserve the internal independence of postwar Poland. During three visits to Washington, D.C. (1941–42), Sikorski outlined his ideas about postwar security in east-central Europe, including a Czechoslovak-Polish confederation; however, U.S. President Franklin D. Roosevelt regarded Polish issues as secondary. For him, as for Churchill, the importance of the Soviet Union as an ally was crucial, and neither leader was prepared to see relations with Stalin founder on the Polish rock. This became apparent when they were undeterred by the German announcement on April 13, 1943, of the discovery in the Katyn Forest of mass graves of more than 4,000 Polish officers who had been captured by the Red Army. Only in 1992 did post-communist Moscow publicly acknowledge its guilt in this matter.

Sikorski's death in a mysterious plane crash in Gibraltar (July 1943) was a great blow to the Poles at a time when Soviet offensives after the victories of Stalingrad and Kursk brought the Red Army closer to the prewar Polish borders. The new prime minister and Peasant Party leader, Stanisław Mikołajczyk, could not rival Sikorski's standing and was at odds with the new commander in chief, General Kazimierz Sosnkowski. The Soviets demanded as the price for reestablishing relations with the Polish government not only territorial concessions but also the dismissal of several of its members. Their backing of Polish communists—the Union of Polish Patriots in Moscow and the National Committee of the Homeland, headed by Bolesław Bierut and set up in Poland in December 1943—was evident. At the Tehrān Conference late in 1943, Churchill's proposal that the Soviet-Polish border coincide with the Curzon Line (roughly similar to the Ribbentrop-Molotov line) and that Poland be compensated at Germany's cost was accepted by Roosevelt and Stalin. The Mikołajczyk government, which was opposed to such a territorial deal, was not informed.

Roosevelt suggested to Mikołajczyk that the AK show its goodwill by cooperating with the Red Army. Such cooperation, however, when attempted in areas that had been part of prewar eastern Poland, was followed by arrests and deportation or conscription into the Soviet-sponsored Polish Kościuszko Division commanded by General Zygmunt Berling. On Aug. 1, 1944, just as Mikołajczyk, prompted by the British, came to Moscow, the AK, under the supreme command of General Tadeusz Bór-Komorowski, rose in Warsaw against the retreating Germans. The Warsaw Uprising constitutes one of the most tragic and controversial events of the war. The AK planned to capture the capital and act on behalf of Mikołajczyk's government as host to the entering Red Army. It was assumed that the Soviets would not dare to disregard this demonstration of the Polish right to self-determination. In the absence of Soviet military assistance, the rising was doomed, yet had the AK not risen it would have been accused of inactivity by the communists. The insurgents fought alone for 63 days, because the Soviets not only halted their own offensive but also refused to allow Allied planes to help resupply the AK. When Warsaw capitulated, the city had been almost totally destroyed, and 200,000 civilians and more than 10,000 combatants had perished.

The Warsaw Uprising

Stalin had no interest in assisting the Polish underground and did not hesitate to defy world public opinion when, in March 1945, he had 16 leaders of the underground arrested and tried in Moscow. Their elimination was linked to the process of building a communist-dominated Polish state. In July 1944 a Polish Committee of National Liberation was set up in Moscow, issued its Lublin Manifesto (July 22), and signed a secret territorial accord with the U.S.S.R. Mikołajczyk, caught between British pressure and the resistance of his government, resigned in November 1944. Ignoring the socialist Tomasz Arciszewski, who succeeded Mikołajczyk as premier, Roosevelt and Churchill agreed with Stalin at the Yalta Conference (February 1945) to create a Provisional Polish Government of National Unity. Its core was the Lublin Polish Committee of National Liberation (already recognized by Stalin as the government), to which some politicians from Poland and abroad were added. Britain and the United States recognized that government on July 5, 1945, simultaneously withdrawing recognition from the government in London. A large Polish political emigration emerged as a voice of a free Poland and remained active during the next 40 years.

Communist Poland. The postwar Polish republic, renamed in 1952 the Polish People's Republic, occupied an area some 20 percent smaller than prewar Poland, and its population of almost 30 million rose to nearly 39 million in the following four decades. After the Holocaust, the expulsion of several million Germans, and population transfers with the U.S.S.R., Poland was virtually ethnically homogenous. The expulsion of the Germans was approved by the Potsdam Conference, but the final decision regarding the new German-Polish border along the Oder-Neisse Line was left to a future peace conference. The U.S.S.R. cleverly capitalized on its status as the sole guarantor of this border, which gave Poland a long seacoast, with such harbours as Szczecin and Gdańsk, and such natural resources as coal and zinc in Silesia. But, if Poland became potentially wealthier, it nevertheless was devastated (cities like Warsaw, Wrocław, and Gdańsk lay in ruins), and social conditions bordered on chaos. Huge migrations, mainly to the ex-German "western territories," added to the instability. Fighting against the remnants of the Ukrainian Liberation Army was followed by the mass relocation of the Ukrainians (Operation Vistula) in 1947. Persecutions of the AK and political opponents (the National Party was outlawed) by the communists led to armed clashes that continued for several years. It was under these conditions that a Jewish pogrom occurred in Kielce in June 1946, claiming more than 40 lives.

Operation Vistula

Bierut, who was formally nonpartisan but in fact was an old communist, became president. In a cabinet headed by a socialist and dominated by communists and fellow travelers, Mikołajczyk became deputy prime minister. He successfully re-created a genuine Polish Peasant Party (PSL), which was larger than the PPR and its socialist and democratic satellite parties (the PPS and SD, respectively). Supported by all enemies of communism, Mikołajczyk sought to challenge the PPR in the "free and unfettered" elections stipulated by the Yalta accords. His opponents included the ruthless secretary-general of the PPR, Władysław Gomułka, a "home communist," and the men in charge of security (Jakub Berman) and of the economy (Hilary Minc), who had returned from Russia.

The Sovietization of Poland, accompanied by terror, included the nationalization of industry and the expropriation of privately owned land parcels larger than 125 acres (50 hectares). Yet in some areas (namely, matters concerning the church and foreign policy) the communists trod lightly during this transition period. The test of strength between Mikołajczyk and the PPR first occurred during the referendum of 1946—the results of which, favourable to Mikołajczyk, were falsified—and then in the general elections of 1947, which were hardly "free and unfettered." Mikołajczyk, fearing for his life, fled the country. The victorious communists completed their monopoly of power in 1948 by absorbing the increasingly dependent PPS to become the Polish United Workers' Party (PUWP).

Over the next few years the Bierut regime closely followed the Stalinist model in politics (adopting the Soviet-style 1952 constitution), economics (emphasizing heavy industry and collectivization of agriculture), military affairs (appointing the Soviet Marshal Konstantin Rokossovsky as commander of Polish forces and adhering to the Warsaw Pact of 1955), foreign policy (joining the Communist Information Bureau, the agency of international communism), culture, and the rule of the secret police. Political terror in Poland, however, did not include, as elsewhere, show trials of fallen party leaders-Gomułka, denounced as a "Titoist" and imprisoned in 1951, was spared such a trial. Moreover, the primate of Poland, Stefan Wyszyński, could still negotiate a modus vivendi in 1950, though he was arrested in September 1953.

The Gomułka regime

The death of Stalin in March 1953 opened a period of struggle for succession and change in the U.S.S.R. that had repercussions throughout the Soviet bloc. The interlude of liberalization that followed culminated in the Soviet leader Nikita Khrushchev's denunciation of Stalinism at the 20th Party Congress in February 1956. With the sudden death of Bierut, anti-Stalinists in Poland raised their heads; a violently suppressed workers' strike in Poznań in June 1956 shook the whole country. Gomułka, who believed in a "Polish road to socialism," became a candidate for the leadership of the party. What appeared as his confrontation with Khrushchev, who came to Warsaw in October and threatened intervention, made Gomułka popular throughout Poland. In reality the Polish leader convinced Khrushchev of his devotion to communism and of the need for a reformist approach to strengthen its doctrine. Important changes followed, among them Polish-Soviet accords on trade and military cooperation (Rokossovsky and most Soviet officers left the country), a significant reduction of political terror, an end to forced collectivization, the release of Cardinal Wyszyński (followed by some concessions in the religious field), and contacts with the West, including freer travel. Gomułka's objective, however, was to bridge the gap between the people and the party, thereby legitimizing the latter. Hence, the period of reform known as "Polish October" did not prove to be the beginning of an evolution of communism as revisionists at home and politically motivated emigres had hoped.

Within a decade economic reform slowed down, the activity of the church was circumscribed, and intellectuals were subjected to pressures. Demonstrations by students in favour of intellectual freedom led to reprisals in March 1968 that brought to an end the so-called "little stabilization" that Gomułka succeeded in achieving. Ever more autocratic, Gomułka became involved in an "anti-Zionist" campaign that resulted in purges within the party, administration, and army. Thousands of people of Jewish origin emigrated. Also in 1968 Polish troops joined the Soviet-led intervention in Czechoslovakia. In 1970 Gomułka registered a foreign policy success by signing a treaty with West Germany that involved a recognition of the Oder-Neisse border. In December 1970, however, major strikes in the shipyards at Gdańsk, Gdynia, and Szczecin, provoked by price increases, led to bloody clashes with police and troops in which many were killed. Gomułka was replaced as first secretary by the more pragmatic Edward Gierek.

The Gierek decade (1970–80) began with ambitious attempts to modernize the economy and raise living standards. Exploiting the East-West détente, he attracted large foreign loans and investments. But initial successes turned sour as the world oil crisis and mismanagement of the economy produced huge budget deficits, which Gierek tried to cover through increased borrowing. The policy of consumerism failed to strengthen the system, and new price increases in 1976 led to workers' riots in Ursus and Radom, which once again were brutally suppressed.

A Workers' Defense Committee (KOR) arose and sought to unite the intelligentsia, which had been isolated in 1968, and the workers, who had received no support in 1970. Dissidents such as Jacek Kuroń and Adam Michnik became internationally known. Other committees appeared that claimed the legality of their activity and protested reprisals as contrary to the 1975 Helsinki Accords. The PUWP responded with measures of selective intimidation. In 1978 the election of Karol Cardinal Wojtyła, the archbishop of Kraków, as Pope John Paul II gave the Poles a father figure and a new inspiration. The coalition of workers and intellectuals, operating largely under the protective umbrella of the church, was in fact building a civil society. The pope's visit to Poland in 1979 endowed that society with national, patriotic, and ethical dimensions. The barrier of fear was broken as another strike was staged at the Gdańsk shipyard that forced an accord with the government on Aug. 31, 1980. Out of the strike led by a charismatic electrician, Lech Wałęsa, there emerged the almost 10-million-strong Independent Self-Governing Trade Union Solidarity (Solidarność), which the government was forced to recognize. Here was an unprecedented working-class revolution directed against a "socialist" state, an example to other peoples of the Soviet bloc.

The pope's visit

A huge movement that sought not to govern but rather to ensure freedom through a "self-limiting revolution," Solidarity could not have been homogenous. The opponents of communism ranged from those who opposed the system as contrary to liberty and democracy, to those who saw it as inimical to national and Christian values, to those who felt that it had not lived up to its socioeconomic promises. These three attitudes all resurfaced after the fall of communism and explain a good deal about the developments in the 1989–96 period.

Gierek did not survive politically the birth of Solidarity, and he was replaced by Stanisław Kania, who was followed by General Wojciech Jaruzelski. By the autumn of 1981 Jaruzelski had become premier, first secretary of the party, and commander in chief. His decision to break Solidarity through the introduction of martial law in December 1981 may well have stemmed from a conviction that the constant tug of war between Solidarity and the government was leading the country toward anarchy that had to be ended by Polish or by Soviet hands. It is likely that he could not conceive of any Poland except a communist one. Martial law effectively broke Solidarity by paralyzing the country and imprisoning virtually all of the movement's leadership, Wałęsa included. It did not, however, destroy it. After the lifting of martial law in 1983, the government could not establish its legitimacy. A political deadlock was worsened by a catastrophic economic situation. In 1984 a popular priest, Jerzy Popieluszko, was murdered by the secret police, but for the first time in such a case state agents were arrested and charged with the crime.

The advent of Mikhail Gorbachev as the leader of the Soviet Union in 1985 and his policies of reform (glasnost and perestroika) started a process that led to the collapse of communism in eastern Europe and the disintegration of the U.S.S.R. The Jaruzelski regime realized that broad reforms were unavoidable and that a revived Solidarity had to be part of them. The roundtable negotiations under the auspices of the church—Józef Cardinal Glemp succeeded Wyszyński as primate—resulted in a "negotiated revolution." Solidarity was restored and participated in partly free elections in June 1989 that brought it victory.

Poland since 1989. Detaching the satellite (populist and democratic) parties from the PUWP, Wałęsa negotiated a compromise by virtue of which Jaruzelski was elected president, while Wałęsa's adviser, the noted Catholic politician Tadeusz Mazowiecki, became premier. This was the first government led by a noncommunist since World War II. The tasks it faced were immense. A "shock therapy" (the Balcerowicz Plan) was adopted in the throes of the financial and structural crisis to rapidly convert the communist economic model into a free-market system and to reintegrate the Polish economy into the global economy. It proved a success, but the social cost was high. The difficulties of redirecting trade previously linked to the Soviet bloc were great. The new government achieved, however, two major successes: a formal recognition of the Oder-Neisse border by the reunited Germany and the powers and, after the dissolution of the Warsaw Pact in 1991, the evacuation of Soviet troops from the country (1992).

"Shock therapy"

Poland's reentry into western Europe, from which it had been forcibly separated since the end of World War II, was a slow process. Nonetheless, by 1996 the country had become a member of the Council of Europe, had established economic ties with the European Union, and was admitted to the Organisation for Economic Co-operation and Development. Successive Polish governments also sought membership in the North Atlantic Treaty Organization despite Russian opposition. Russia's unsettled political situation in the 1990s cast a shadow on Polish foreign policy and complicated its options. Accords were signed with Ukraine and Lithuania, and limited regional cooperation was established by the formation of the Visegrad Group (Poland, the Czech Republic, Slovakia, and Hungary).

By the mid-1990s the Polish economy—more than half privatized—was making important strides, including significant reductions in the annual inflation rate and the budget deficit. Moreover, the annual growth rate of Poland's gross national product became the highest in Europe. But progress was uneven geographically, and economic sectors such as the coal-mining and the building industries experienced slumps. The gap between the rich and the poor grew, adding to the bitterness and frustration reflected in a political life that was far less stable than expected.

The disintegration of Solidarity, accelerated by political and personality clashes, became apparent in the 1990 election, in which Wałęsa defeated Mazowiecki for the presidency. Voters' dissatisfaction was reflected in the surprising support for the dark-horse candidate Stanisław Tyminski, a Polish émigré businessman from Canada. Several cabinets succeeded one another in the early 1990s, of which that headed by Jan Olszewski fell as a result of a clumsy attempt to produce a list of former high-ranking communist collaborators, while that of the first woman prime minister, Hanna Suchocka, was unexpectedly defeated by a somewhat frivolous no-confidence vote. The centrist Freedom Union, which bore the brunt of the transition to democracy, remained largely a party of the intelligentsia. The rightists, split into several groups, accused Wałęsa and the roundtable negotiators of selling out to communists who were able to profit financially from the collapse of the economy and to reorganize as the party Social Democracy of the Republic of Poland. Indeed, the latter exploited the increased frustration over the inequalities of a capitalist economy and the political infighting of the Solidarity camp. Well-organized and disciplined, they won the legislative election in alliance with the PSL in 1993 and the presidency in November 1995. Wałęsa's defeat by the young, dynamic postcommunist Aleksander Kwasniewski—whose campaign asked voters to look to the future rather than the past—may have been symptomatic of a generational change that was visible also in the attitude toward the church. The high prestige of the church suffered as its efforts to influence politics and to be a national rallying point in the increasingly secularized postcommunist society occasionally backfired.

The election of Kwasniewski

Whether the postcommunists' victory will lead ultimately to the emergence of a real and responsible left, centre, and right and whether a new constitution will provide a mechanism for a smoothly functioning democracy depend in no small degree on the growing sophistication and experience of the electorate. Many of the problems faced by Poland—increased crime, drug use, and corruption, as well as the lowering of ethical standards—are common to all of Europe. (PIOTR S. WANDYCZ)

For later developments in the history of Poland, see the BRITANNICA BOOK OF THE YEAR.

1998 Britannica World Data

Encyclopædia Britannica, Inc.
Chicago
Auckland/London/Manila/Paris/Rome
Seoul/Sydney/Tokyo

CONTENTS

INTRODUCTION

Britannica World Data provides a statistical portrait of some 217 countries and dependencies of the world, at a level appropriate to the significance of each. It contains 194 country statements (the "Nations of the World" section), ranging in length from one to four pages, and permits, in the 24 major thematic tables (the "Comparative National Statistics" [CNS] section), comparisons among these larger countries and 23 smaller states.

Updated annually, *Britannica World Data* is particularly intended as direct, structured support for many of Britannica's other reference works—encyclopaedias, yearbooks, atlases—at a level of detail that their editorial style or design do not permit.

Like the textual, graphic, or cartographic modes of expression of these other products, statistics possess their own inherent editorial virtues and weaknesses. Two principal goals in the creation of *Britannica World Data* were up-to-dateness and comparability, each possible to maximize separately, but not always possible to combine. If, for example, research on some subject is completed during a particular year (x), figures may be available for 100 countries for the preceding year ($x - 1$), for 140 countries for the year before that ($x - 2$), and for 180 countries for the year before that ($x - 3$).

Which year should be the basis of a thematic compilation for 217 countries so as to give the best combination of up-to-dateness and comparability? And, should $x - 1$ be adopted for the thematic table, ought up-to-dateness in the country table (for which year x is already available) be sacrificed for agreement with the thematic table? In general, the editors have opted for maximum up-to-dateness in the country statistical boxes and maximum comparability in the thematic tables.

Comparability, however, also resides in the meaning of the numbers compiled, which may differ greatly from country to country. The headnotes to the thematic tables explain many of these methodological problems; the Glossary serves the same purpose for the country statistical pages. Published data do not always provide the researcher or editor with a neat, unambiguous choice between a datum compiled on two different bases (say, railroad track length, or route length), one of which is wanted and the other not. More often a choice must be made among a variety of official, private, and external intergovernmental (UN, FAO, IMF) sources, each reporting its best data but each representing a set of problems: (1) of methodological variance from (or among) international conventions; (2) of analytical completeness (data for a single year may, successively, be projected [based on 10 months' data], preliminary [for 12 months], final, revised or adjusted, etc.); (3) of time frame, or accounting interval (data may represent a full Gregorian calendar year [preferred], a fiscal year, an Islamic or other national or religious year, a multiyear period or average [when a one-year statement would contain unrepresentative results]); (4) of continuity with previous data; and the like. Finally, published data on a particular subject may be complete and final but impossible to summarize in a simple manner. The education system of a single country may include, for example, public and private sectors; local, state, or national systems; varying grades, tracks, or forms within a single system; or opportunities for double-counting or fractional counting of a student, teacher, or institution. When no recent official data exist, or they exist, but may be suspect, the tables may show unofficial estimates, a range (of published opinion), analogous data, or no data at all.

The published basis of the information compiled is the statistical collections of Encyclopædia Britannica, Inc., some of the principal elements of which are enumerated in the Bibliography. Holdings for a given country may include any of the following: the national statistical abstract; the constitution; the most recent censuses of population; periodic or occasional reports on vital statistics, social indicators, agriculture, mining, labour, manufacturing, domestic and foreign trade, finance and banking, transportation, and communications. Further information is received in a variety of formats—telephone, letter, fax, microfilm and microfiche, and most recently, in electronic formats such as computer disks, CD-ROMs, and the Internet. So substantial had the resources of the Internet become by the current research year that it was thought possible, for the first time, to add uniform resource locators (URLs) to the great majority of country pages and a number of the CNS tables (summary world sites with data on all countries still being somewhat of a rarity) so as to apprise the reader of the possibility and means to access current information on these subjects year-round.

The recommendations offered are usually to official sites (national statistical offices, general national governments, central banks, embassies, intergovernmental organizations [especially the UN Development Programme], and the like). Though often dissimilar in content, they will usually be updated year-round, expanded as opportunity permits, and lead on to related sites, such as parliamentary offices, information offices, diplomatic and consular sites, news agencies and newspapers, and, beyond, to the myriad academic, commercial, and private sites now accessible from the personal computer. While these URLs were correct and current at the time of writing, they may be subject to change.

The great majority of the social, economic, and financial data contained in this work should not be interpreted in isolation. Interpretive text of long perspective, such as that of the *Encyclopædia Britannica* itself; political, geographic, and topical maps, such as those in the *Britannica Atlas;* and recent analysis of political events and economic trends, such as that contained in the articles of the *Book of the Year,* will all help to supply analytic focus that numbers alone cannot. By the same token, study of those sources will be made more concrete by use of *Britannica World Data* to supply up-to-date geographic, demographic, and economic detail.

GLOSSARY

A number of terms that are used to classify and report data in the "Nations of the World" section require some explanation.

Those italicized terms that are used regularly in the country compilations to introduce specific categories of information (*e.g., birth rate, budget*) appear in this glossary in italic boldface type, followed by a description of the precise kind of information being offered and how it has been edited and presented.

All other terms are printed here in roman boldface type. Many terms have quite specific meanings in statistical reporting, and they are so defined here. Other terms have less specific application as they are used by different countries or organizations. Data in the country compilations based on definitions markedly different from those below will usually be footnoted.

Terms that appear in small capitals in certain definitions are themselves defined at their respective alphabetical locations.

Terms whose definitions are marked by an asterisk (*) refer to data supplied only in the larger two- to four-page country compilations.

access to services, a group of measures indicating a population's level of access to public services, including electrical power, treated public drinking water, sewage removal, and fire protection.*

activity rate, *see* participation/activity rates.

age breakdown, the distribution of a given population by age, usually reported here as percentages of total population in 15-year age brackets. When substantial numbers of persons do not know, or state, their exact age, distributions may not total 100.0%.

area, the total surface area of a country or its administrative subdivisions, including both land and inland (nontidal) water area. Land area is usually calculated from "mean low water" on a "plane table," or flat, basis.

area and population, a tabulation usually including the first-order administrative subdivisions of the country (such as the states of the United States), with capital (headquarters, or administrative seat), area, and population. When these subdivisions are especially numerous or, occasionally, nonexistent, a planning, electoral, census, or other nonadministrative scheme of regional subdivisions has been substituted.

associated state, *see* state.

atheist, in statements of religious affiliation, one who professes active opposition to religion; "nonreligious" refers to those professing only no religion, nonbelief, or doubt.

balance of payments, a financial statement for a country for a given period showing the balance among: (1) transactions in goods, services, and income between that country and the rest of the world, (2) changes in ownership or valuation of that country's monetary gold, SPECIAL DRAWING RIGHTS, and claims on and liabilities to the rest of the world, and (3) unrequited transfers and counterpart entries needed (in an accounting sense) to balance transactions and changes among any of the foregoing types of exchange that are not mutually offsetting. Detail of national law as to what constitutes a transaction, the basis of its valuation, and the size of a transaction visible to fiscal authorities all result in differences in the meaning of a particular national statement.*

balance of trade, the net value of all international goods trade of a country, usually excluding reexports (goods received only for transshipment), and the percentage that this net represents of total trade.

Balance of trade refers only to the "visible" international trade of goods as recorded by customs authorities and is thus a segment of a country's BALANCE OF PAYMENTS, which takes all visible and invisible trade with other countries into account. (Invisible trade refers to imports and exports of money, financial instruments, and services such as transport, tourism, and insurance.) A country has a favourable, or positive (+), balance of trade when the value of exports exceeds that of imports and negative (−) when imports exceed exports.

barrel (bbl), a unit of liquid measure. The barrel conventionally used for reporting crude petroleum and petroleum products is equal to 42 U.S. gallons, or 159 litres. The number of barrels of crude petroleum per metric ton, ranging typically from 6.20 to 8.13, depends upon the specific gravity of the petroleum. The world average is roughly 7.33 barrels per ton.

birth rate, the number of live births annually per 1,000 of midyear population. Birth rates for individual countries may be compared with the estimated world annual average of 25.0 births per 1,000 population between 1990 and 1995.

budget, the annual receipts and expenditures—of a central government for its activities only;

Abbreviations

Measurements

cu m	cubic metre(s)
kg	kilogram(s)
km	kilometre(s)
kW	kilowatt(s)
kW-hr	kilowatt-hour(s)
metric ton-km	metric ton-kilometre(s)
mi	mile(s)
passenger-km	passenger-kilometre(s)
passenger-mi	passenger-mile(s)
short ton-mi	short ton-mile(s)
sq km	square kilometre(s)
sq m	square metre(s)
sq mi	square mile(s)
troy oz	troy ounce(s)
yr	year(s)

Political Units and International Organizations

CACM	Central American Common Market
Caricom	Caribbean Community and Common Market
CFA	Communauté Financière Africaine
CFP	Comptoirs Françaises du Pacifique
CIS	Commonwealth of Independent States
CUSA	Customs Union of Southern Africa
E.Ger.	East Germany
EC	European Communities
EU	European Union
FAO	United Nations Food and Agriculture Organization
IMF	International Monetary Fund
OECD	Organization for Economic Cooperation and Development
OECS	Organization of Eastern Caribbean States
U.A.E.	United Arab Emirates
U.K.	United Kingdom
UNDP	United Nations Development Programme
U.S.	United States
U.S.S.R.	Union of Soviet Socialist Republics
W.Ger.	West Germany

Months

Jan.	January	Oct.	October
Feb.	February	Nov.	November
Aug.	August	Dec.	December
Sept.	September		

Miscellaneous

AIDS	Acquired Immune Deficiency Syndrome
avg.	average
c.i.f.	cost, insurance, and freight
commun.	communications
CPI	consumer price index
est.	estimate(d)
excl.	excluding
f.o.b.	free on board
GDP	gross domestic product
GNP	gross national product
govt.	government
incl.	including
mo.	month(s)
n.a.	not available (in text)
n.e.s.	not elsewhere specified
no.	number
pl.	plural
pos.	position
pub. admin.	public administration
PVC	Polyvinyl Chloride
SDR	Special Drawing Right
SITC	Standard International Trade Classification
svcs.	services
teacher tr.	teacher training
transp.	transportation
voc.	vocational
$	dollar (of any currency area)
£	pound (of any currency area)
...	not available (in tables)
—	none, less than half the smallest unit shown, or not applicable (in tables)

does not include state, provincial, or local governments or semipublic (parastatal, quasi-nongovernmental) corporations unless otherwise specified. Figures for budgets are limited to ordinary (recurrent) receipts and expenditures, wherever possible, and exclude capital expenditures—*i.e.,* funds for development and other special projects originating as foreign-aid grants or loans.

When both a recurrent and a capital budget exist for a single country, the former is the budget funded entirely from national resources (taxes, duties, excises, etc.) that would recur (be generated by economic activity) every year. It funds the most basic governmental services, those least able to suffer interruption. The capital budget is usually funded by external aid and may change its size considerably from year to year.

capital, usually, the actual seat of government and administration of a state. When more than one capital exists, each is identified by kind; when interim arrangements exist during the creation or movement of a national capital, the de facto situation is described.

Anomalous cases are annotated, such as those in which (1) the de jure designation under the country's laws differs from actual local practice (*e.g.,* Benin's designation of one capital in constitutional law, but another in actual practice), (2) international recognition does not validate a country's claim (as with the proclamation by Israel of a capital on territory not internationally recognized as part of Israel), or (3) both a state and a capital have been proclaimed on territory recognized as part of another state (as with the Turkish Republic of Northern Cyprus).

capital budget, *see* budget.

causes of death, as defined by the World Health Organization (WHO), "the disease or injury which initiated the train of morbid events leading directly to death, or the circumstances of accident or violence which produced the fatal injury." This principle, the "underlying cause of death," is the basis of the medical judgment as to cause; the statistical classification system according to which these causes are grouped and named is the *International List of Causes of Death,* the latest revision of which is the Tenth. Reporting is usually in terms of events per 100,000 population. When data on actual causes of death are unavailable, information on morbidity, or illness rate, usually given as reported cases per 100,000 of infectious diseases (notifiable to WHO as a matter of international agreement), may be substituted.

chief of state/head of government, paramount national governmental officer(s) exercising the highest executive and/or ceremonial roles of a country's government. In general usage, the chief of state is the formal head of a national state. The primary responsibilities of the chief of state may range from the purely ceremonial—convening legislatures and greeting foreign officials—to the exercise of complete national executive authority. The head of government, when this function exists separately, is the officer nominally charged (by the constitution) with the majority of actual executive powers, though they may not in practice be exercised, especially in military or single-party regimes in which effective power may reside entirely outside the executive governmental machinery provided by the constitution. A prime minister, for example, usually the actual head of government, may in practice exercise only Cabinet-level authority.

In communist countries an official identified as the chief of state may be the chairman of the policy-making organ, and the official given as the head of government the chairman of the nominal administrative/executive organ.

c.i.f. (trade valuation): *see* imports.

colony, an area annexed to, or controlled by, an independent state but not an integral part of it; a non-self-governing territory. A colony has a charter and may have a degree of self-government. A crown colony is a colony originally chartered by the British government.

commonwealth (U.K. and U.S.), a self-governing political entity that has regard to the common weal, or good; usually associated with the United Kingdom or United States. Examples include the Commonwealth of Nations (composed of independent states [from 1931 onward]), Puerto Rico since 1952, and the Northern Marianas since 1979.

communications, collectively, the means available for the public transmission of information within a country. Data are tabulated for: daily newspapers and their total circulation; radio and television as total numbers of receivers; telephone data as "main lines," or the number of subscriber lines (not receivers) having access to the public switched network; cellular telephones as number of subscribers; and facsimile machines and personal computers as number of units. For each, a rate per 1,000 persons is given.

constant prices, an adjustment to the members of a financial time series to eliminate the effect of inflation year by year. It consists of referring all data in the series to a single year so that "real" change may be seen.

constitutional monarchy, *see* monarchy.

consumer price index (CPI), also known as the retail price index, or the cost-of-living index, a series of index numbers assigned to the price of a selected "basket," or assortment, of basic consumer goods and services in a country, region, city, or type of household in order to measure changes over time in prices paid by a typical household for those goods and services. Items included in the CPI are ordinarily determined by governmental surveys of typical household expenditures and are assigned weights relative to their proportion of those expenditures. Index values are period averages unless otherwise noted.

coprincipality, *see* monarchy.

current prices, the valuation of a financial aggregate as of the year reported.

daily per capita caloric intake (supply), the calories equivalent to the known average daily supply of foodstuffs for human consumption in a given country divided by the population of the country (and the proportion of that supply provided, respectively, by vegetable and animal sources). The daily per capita caloric intake of a country may be compared with the corresponding recommended minimum daily requirement. The latter is calculated by the Food and Agriculture Organization of the United Nations from the age and sex distributions, average body weights, and environmental temperatures in a given region to determine the calories needed to sustain a person there at normal levels of activity and health. The daily per capita caloric requirement ranges from 2,200 to 2,500.

de facto population, for a given area, the population composed of those actually present at a particular time, including temporary residents and visitors (such as immigrants not yet granted permanent status, "guest" or expatriate workers, refugees, or tourists), but excluding legal residents temporarily absent.

de jure population, for a given area, the population composed only of those legally resident at a particular time, excluding temporary residents and visitors (such as "guest" or expatriate workers, refugees, or tourists), but including legal residents temporarily absent.

deadweight tonnage, the maximum weight of cargo, fuel, fresh water, stores, and persons that may safely be carried by a ship. It is customarily measured in long tons of 2,240 pounds each, equivalent to 1.016 metric tons. Deadweight tonnage is the difference between the tonnage of a fully loaded ship and the fully unloaded tonnage of that ship.

See also gross ton.

death rate, the number of deaths annually per 1,000 of midyear population. Death rates for individual countries may be compared with the estimated world annual average of 9.3 deaths per 1,000 population between 1990 and 1995.

density (of population), usually, the DE FACTO POPULATION of a country divided by its total area. Special adjustment is made for large areas of inland water, desert, or other uninhabitable areas—*e.g.,* excluding the ice cap of Greenland.

dependent state, constitutionally or statutorily organized political entity outside of and under the jurisdiction of an independent state (or a federal element of such a state) but not formally annexed to it (*see* Table).

Dependent states[1]

Australia
Christmas Island
Cocos (Keeling) Islands
Norfolk Island
China
Hong Kong
Denmark
Faroe Islands
Greenland
France
French Guiana
French Polynesia
Guadeloupe
Martinique
Mayotte
New Caledonia
Réunion
Saint Pierre and Miquelon
Wallis and Futuna
Netherlands, The
Aruba
Netherlands Antilles
New Zealand
Cook Islands
Niue
Tokelau
Norway
Jan Mayen
Svalbard
Portugal
Macau
United Kingdom
Anguilla
Bermuda
British Virgin Islands
Cayman Islands
Falkland Islands
Gibraltar
Guernsey
Isle of Man
Jersey
Montserrat
Pitcairn Island
Saint Helena and Dependencies
Turks and Caicos Islands
United States
American Samoa
Guam
Northern Mariana Islands
Puerto Rico
Virgin Islands (of the U.S.)

[1]Excludes territories (1) to which Antarctic Treaty is applicable in whole or in part, (2) without permanent civilian population, (3) without internationally recognized civilian government (Western Sahara, Gaza Strip), or (4) representing unadjudicated unilateral or multilateral territorial claims.

direct taxes, taxes levied directly on firms and individuals, such as taxes on income, profits, and capital gains. The *immediate* incidence, or burden, of direct taxes is on the firms and individuals thus taxed; direct taxes on firms may, however, be passed on to consumers and other economic units in the form of higher prices for goods and services, blurring the distinction between direct and indirect taxation.

distribution of income/wealth, the portion of personal income or wealth accruing to households or individuals constituting each respective decile (tenth) or quintile (fifth) of a country's households or individuals.*

divorce rate, the number of legal, civilly recognized divorces annually per 1,000 population.

doubling time, the number of complete years required for a country to double its population at its current rate of natural increase.

earnings index, a series of index numbers comparing average wages in a collective industrial sample for a country or region with the same industries at a previous period to measure changes over time in those wages. It is most commonly reported for wages paid on a daily, weekly, or monthly basis; annual figures may represent total income or averages of these shorter periods. The scope of the earnings index varies from country to country; the index is often limited to earnings in manufacturing industries. The index for each country applies to all wage earners in a designated group and ordinarily takes into account basic wages (overtime is normally distinguished), bonuses, cost-of-living allowances, and contributions toward social security. Some countries include payments in kind. Contributions toward social security by employers are usually excluded, as are social security benefits received by wage earners.

economically active population, *see* population economically active.

education, tabulation of the principal elements of a country's educational establishment, classified as far as possible according to the country's own system of primary, secondary, and higher levels (the usual age limits for these levels being identified in parentheses), with total number of schools (physical facilities) and of teachers and students (whether full- or part-time). The student-teacher ratio is calculated whenever available data permit.

educational attainment, the distribution of the population age 25 and over with completed educations by the highest level of formal education attained or completed; it must sometimes be reported, however, for age groups still in school or for the economically active only.

emirate, *see* monarchy.

enterprise, a legal entity formed to conduct a business, which it may do from more than one establishment (place of business or service point).

ethnic/linguistic composition, ethnic, racial, or linguistic composition of a national population, reported here according to the most reliable breakdown available, whether published in official sources (such as a census) or in external analysis (when the subject is not addressed in national sources).

exchange rate, the value of one currency compared with another, or with a standardized unit of account such as the SPECIAL DRAWING RIGHT, or as mandated by local statute when one currency is "tied" by a par value to another. Rates given usually refer to free market values when the currency has no, or very limited, restrictions on its convertibility into other currencies.

exports, material goods legally leaving a country (or customs area) and subject to customs regulations. The total value and distribution by percentage of the major items (in preference to groups of goods) exported are given, together with the distribution of trade among major trading partners (usually single countries or trading blocs). Valuation of goods exported is free on board (f.o.b.) unless otherwise specified. The value of goods exported and imported f.o.b. is calculated from the cost of production and excludes the cost of transport.

external debt, public and publicly guaranteed debt with a maturity of more than one year owed to nonnationals of a country and repayable in foreign currency, goods, or services. The debt may be an obligation of a national or subnational governmental body (or an agency of either), of an autonomous public body, or of a private debtor that is guaranteed by a public entity. The debt is usually either outstanding (contracted) or disbursed (drawn).

external territory (Australia), *see* territory.

federal, consisting of first-order political subdivisions that are prior to and independent of the central government in certain functions.

federal republic, *see* republic.

federation, union of coequal, preexisting political entities that retain some degree of autonomy and (usually) right of secession within the union.

fertility rate, *see* total fertility rate.

financial aggregates, tabulation of seven-year time series, providing principal measures of the financial condition of a country, including: (1) the exchange rate of the national currency against the U.S. dollar, the pound sterling, and the International Monetary Fund's SPECIAL DRAWING RIGHT (SDR), (2) the amount and kind of international reserves (holdings of SDRs, gold, and foreign currencies) and reserve position of the country in the IMF, and (3) principal economic rates and prices (central bank discount rate, government bond yields, and industrial stock [share] prices). For BALANCE OF PAYMENTS, the origin in terms of component balance of trade items and balance of invisibles (net) is given.*

fish catch, the live-weight equivalent of the aquatic animals (including fish, crustaceans, mollusks, etc., but excluding whales, seals, and other aquatic mammals) caught in freshwater or marine areas by national fleets and landed in domestic or foreign harbours for commercial, industrial, or subsistence purposes.

f.o.b. (trade valuation): *see* exports.

food, *see* daily per capita caloric intake.

form of government/political status, the type of administration provided for by a country's constitution—whether or not suspended by extralegal military or civil action, although such de facto administrations are identified—together with the number of members (elected, appointed, and ex officio) for each legislative house, named according to its English rendering. Dependent states (*see* Table) are classified according to the status of their political association with the administering country.

gross domestic product (GDP), the total value of the final goods and services produced by residents and nonresidents within a given country during a given accounting period, usually a year. Unless otherwise noted, the value is given in current prices of the year indicated. The *System of National Accounts* (SNA, published under the joint auspices of the UN, IMF, OECD, EC, and World Bank) provides a framework for international comparability in classifying domestic accounting aggregates and international transactions comprising "net factor income from abroad," the measure that distinguishes GDP and GNP.

gross national product (GNP), the total value of final goods and services produced both from within a given country *and* from external (foreign) transactions in a given accounting period, usually a year. Unless otherwise noted, the value is given in current prices of the year indicated. GNP is equal to GROSS DOMESTIC PRODUCT (*q.v.*) adjusted by net factor income from abroad, which is the income residents receive from abroad for factor services (labour, investment, and interest) less similar payments made to nonresidents who contribute to the domestic economy.

gross ton, volumetric unit of measure (equaling 100 cubic feet [2.83 cu m]) of the permanently enclosed volume of a ship, above and below decks available for cargo, stores, or passenger accommodation. Net, or register, tonnage exempts certain nonrevenue spaces—such as those devoted to machinery, bunkers, crew accommodations, and ballast—from the gross tonnage. *See also* deadweight tonnage.

head of government, *see* chief of state/head of government.

health, a group of measures including number of accredited physicians currently practicing or employed and their ratio to the total population; total hospital beds and their ratio; and INFANT MORTALITY RATE.

household, economically autonomous individual or group of individuals living in a single dwelling unit. A family household is one composed principally of individuals related by blood or marriage.

household income and expenditure, data for average size of a HOUSEHOLD (by number of individuals) and median household income. Sources of income and expenditures for major items of consumption are given as percentages.

In general, household income is the amount of funds, usually measured in monetary units, received by the members (generally those 14 years old and over) of a household in a given time period. The income can be derived from (1) wages or salaries, (2) nonfarm or farm SELF-EMPLOYMENT, (3) transfer payments, such as pensions, public assistance, unemployment benefits, etc., and (4) other income, including interest and dividends, rent, royalties, etc. The income of a household is expressed as a gross amount before deductions for taxes. Data on expenditure refer to consumption of personal or household goods and services; they normally exclude savings, taxes, and insurance; practice with regard to inclusion of credit purchases differs markedly.

immigration, usually, the number and origin of those immigrants admitted to a nation in a legal status that would eventually permit the granting of the right to settle permanently or to acquire citizenship.*

imports, material goods legally entering a country (or customs area) and subject to customs regulations; excludes financial movements. The total value and distribution by percentage of the major items (in preference to groups of goods) imported are given, together with the direction of trade among major trading partners (usually single countries), trading blocs (such as the European Union), or customs areas (such as Belgium-Luxembourg). The value of goods imported is given free on board (f.o.b.) unless otherwise specified; f.o.b. is defined above under EXPORTS.

The principal alternate basis for valuation of goods in international trade is that of cost, insurance, and freight (c.i.f.); its use is restricted to imports, as it comprises the principal charges needed to bring the goods to the customs house in the country of destination. Because it inflates the value of imports relative to exports, more countries have, latterly, been estimating imports on an f.o.b. basis as well.

incorporated territory (U.S.), *see* territory.

independent, of a state, autonomous and controlling both its internal and external affairs. Its date usually refers to the date from which the country was in effective control of these affairs within its present boundaries, rather than the date independence was proclaimed or the date recognized as a de jure act by the former administering power.

indirect taxes, taxes levied on sales or transfers of selected intermediate goods and services, including excises, value-added taxes, and tariffs, that are ordinarily passed on to the ultimate consumers of the goods and services. Figures given for individual countries are limited to indirect taxes levied by their respective central governments unless otherwise specified.

infant mortality rate, the number of children per 1,000 live births who die before their first birthday. Total infant mortality includes neonatal mortality, which is deaths of children within one month of birth.

invisibles (invisible trade), *see* balance of trade.

kingdom, *see* monarchy.

labour force, portion of the POPULATION ECONOMICALLY ACTIVE (PEA) comprising those most fully employed or attached to the labour market (the unemployed are considered to be "attached" in that they usually represent persons previously employed seeking to be reemployed), particularly as viewed from a short-term perspective. It normally includes those who are self-employed, employed by others (whether full-time, part-time, seasonally, or on some other less than full-time basis), and, as noted above, the unemployed (both those previously employed and those seeking work for the first time). In the "gross domestic product and labour force" table, the majority of the labour data provided refer to population economically active, since PEA represents the longer-term view of working population and, thus, subsumes more of the marginal workers who are often missed by shorter-term surveys.

land use, distribution by classes of vegetational cover or economic use of the land area only (excluding inland water, for example, but not marshland), reported as percentages. The principal categories utilized include: (1) forest, which includes natural and planted tracts, (2) meadows and pastures, which includes land in temporary or permanent use whose principal purpose is the growing of animal fodder, (3) agricultural and under permanent cultivation, which includes temporary and permanent cropland, as well as land left fallow less than five years, but capable of being returned to production without special preparation, and (4) other, which includes built-up, wasteland, watercourses, and the like.

leisure, the principal monetary expenditures, uses, or reported preferences in the use of the individual's free time for recreation, rest, or self-improvement.*

life expectancy, the number of years a person born within a particular population group (age cohort) would be expected to live, based on actuarial calculations.

literacy, the ability to read and write a language with some degree of competence; the precise degree constituting the basis of a particular national statement is usually defined by the national census and is often tested by the census enumerator. Elsewhere, particularly where much adult literacy may be the result of literacy campaigns rather than passage through a formal educational system, definition and testing of literacy may be better standardized.

major cities, usually the five largest cities proper (national capitals are always given, regardless of size); fewer cities may be listed if there are fewer urban localities in the country. For multipage tables, 10 or more may be listed.* Populations for cities will usually refer to the city proper—*i.e.,* the legally bounded corporate entity, or the most compact, contiguous, demographically urban portion of the entity defined by the local authorities. Occasionally figures for METROPOLITAN AREAS are cited when the relevant civil entity at the core of a major agglomeration had an unrepresentatively small population.

manufacturing, mining, and construction enterprises/retail sales and service enterprises, a detailed tabulation of the principal industries in these sectors, showing for each industry the number of enterprises and employees, wages in that industry as a percentage of the general average wage, and the value of that industry's output in terms of value added or turnover.*

marriage rate, the number of legal, civilly recognized marriages annually per 1,000 population.

material well-being, a group of measures indicating the percentage of households or dwellings possessing certain goods or appliances, including automobiles, telephones, television receivers, refrigerators, air conditioners, and washing machines.*

merchant marine, the privately or publicly owned ships registered with the maritime authority of a nation (limited to those in Lloyd's of London statistical reporting of 100 or more GROSS TONS) that are employed in commerce, whether or not owned or operated by nationals of the country.

metropolitan area, a city and the region of dense, predominantly urban, settlement around the city; the population of the whole usually has strong economic and cultural affinities with the central city.

military expenditure, the apparent value of all identifiable military expenditure by the central government on hardware, personnel, pensions, research and development, etc., reported here both as a percentage of the GNP, with a comparison to the world average, and as a per capita value in U.S. dollars.

military personnel, *see* total active duty personnel.

mobility, the rate at which individuals or households change dwellings, usually measured between censuses and including international as well as domestic migration.*

monarchy, a government in which the CHIEF OF STATE holds office, usually hereditarily and for life, but sometimes electively for a term. The state may be a coprincipality, emirate, kingdom, principality, sheikhdom, or sultanate. The powers of the monarch may range from absolute (*i.e.,* the monarch both reigns and rules) through various degrees of limitation of authority to nominal, as in a constitutional monarchy, in which the titular monarch reigns but others, as elected officials, effectively rule.

monetary unit, currency of issue, or that in official use in a given country; name, spelling, and abbreviation in English according to International Monetary Fund recommendations or local practice; name of the lesser, usually decimal, monetary unit constituting the main currency; and valuation in U.S. dollars and U.K. pounds sterling, usually according to free-market or commercial rates.

See also exchange rate.

natural increase, also called natural growth, or the balance of births and deaths, the excess of births over deaths in a population; the rate of natural increase is the difference between the BIRTH RATE and the DEATH RATE of a given population. The estimated world average during 1990–95 was 15.7 per 1,000 population, or 1.57% annually. Natural increase is added to the balance of migration to calculate the total growth of that population.

net material product, *see* material product.

nonreligious, *see* atheist.

official language(s), that (or those) prescribed by the national constitution for day-to-day conduct and publication of a country's official business or, when no explicit constitutional provision exists, that of the constitution itself, the national gazette (record of legislative activity), or like official documents. Other languages may have local protection, may be permitted in parliamentary debate or legal action (such as a trial), or may be "national languages," for the protection of which special provisions have been made, but these are not deemed official. The United States, for example, does not yet formally identify English as "official," though it uses it for virtually all official purposes.

official name, the local official form(s), short or long, of a country's legal name(s) taken from the country's constitution or from other official documents. The English-language form is usually the protocol form in use by the country, the U.S. Department of State, and the United Nations.

official religion, generally, any religion prescribed or given special status or protection by the constitution or legal system of a country. Identification as such is not confined to constitutional documents utilizing the term explicitly.

organized territory (U.S.), *see* territory.

overseas department (France), *see* department.

overseas territory (France), *see* territory.

parliamentary state, *see* state.

part of a realm, a dependent Dutch political entity with some degree of self-government and having a special status above that of a colony (*e.g.,* the prerogative of rejecting for local application any law enacted by The Netherlands).

participation/activity rates, measures defining differential rates of economic activity within a population. Participation rate refers to the percentage of those employed or economically active who possess a particular characteristic (sex, age, etc.); activity rate refers to the fraction of the total population who *are* economically active.

passenger-miles, or **passenger-kilometres,** aggregate measure of passenger carriage by a specified means of transportation, equal to the number of passengers carried multiplied by the number of miles (or kilometres) each is transported. Figures given for countries are often calculated from ticket sales and ordinarily exclude passengers carried free of charge.

people's republic, *see* republic.

place of birth/national origin, if the former, numbers of native- and foreign-born population of a country by actual place of birth; if the latter, any of several classifications, including those based on origin of passport at original admission to country, on cultural heritage of family name, on self-designated (often multiple) origin of (some) ancestors, and on other systems for assigning national origin.*

political status, *see* form of government/political status.

population, the number of persons present within a country, city, or other civil entity at the date of a census of population, survey, cumulation of a civil register, or other enumeration. Unless otherwise specified, populations given are DE FACTO, referring to those actually present, rather than DE JURE, those legally resident but not necessarily present on the referent date. If a time series, noncensus year, or per capita ratio referring to a country's total population is cited, it will usually refer to midyear of the calendar year indicated.

population economically active, the total number of persons (above a set age for economic labour, usually 10–15 years) in all employment statuses—self-employed, wage- or salary-earning, part-time, seasonal, unemployed, etc. The International Labour Organisation defines the economically active as "all persons of either sex who furnish the supply of labour for the production of economic goods and services." National practices vary as regards the treatment of such groups as armed forces, inmates of institutions, persons seeking their first job, unpaid family workers, seasonal workers and persons engaged in part-time economic activities. In some countries, all or part of these groups may be included among the economically active, while in other countries the same groups may be treated as inactive. In general, however, the data on economically active population do not include students, persons occupied solely in family or household work, retired persons,

persons living entirely on their own means, and persons wholly dependent upon others.

See also labour force.

population projection, the expected population in the years 2000 and 2010, embodying the country's own projections wherever possible. Estimates of the future size of a population are usually based on assumed levels of fertility, mortality, and migration. Projections in the tables, unless otherwise specified, are medium (*i.e.,* most likely) variants, whether based on external estimates by the United Nations, World Bank, or U.S. Department of Commerce or on those of the country itself.

price and earnings indexes, tabulation comparing the change in the CONSUMER PRICE INDEX over a period of seven years with the change in the general labour force's EARNINGS INDEX for the same period.

principality, *see* monarchy.

production, the physical quantity or monetary value of the output of an industry, usually tabulated here as the most important items or groups of items (depending on the available detail) of primary (extractive) and secondary (manufactured) production, including construction. When a single consistent measure of value, such as VALUE ADDED, can be obtained, this is given, ranked by value; otherwise, and more usually, quantity of production is given.

public debt, the current outstanding debt of all periods of maturity for which the central government and its organs are obligated. Publicly guaranteed private debt is excluded. For countries that report debt under the World Bank Debtor Reporting System (DRS), figures for outstanding, long-term EXTERNAL DEBT are given.

quality of working life, a group of measures including weekly hours of work (including overtime); rates per 100,000 for job-connected injury, illness, and mortality; coverage of labour force by insurance for injury, permanent disability, and death; workdays lost to labour strikes and stoppages; and commuting patterns (length of journey to work in minutes and usual method of transportation).*

railroads, mode of transportation by self-driven or locomotive-drawn cars over fixed rails. Length-of-track figures include all mainline and spurline running track but exclude switching sidings and yard track. Route length, when given, does not compound multiple running tracks laid on the same trackbed.

recurrent budget, *see* budget.

religious affiliation, distribution of nominal religionists, whether practicing or not, as a percentage of total population. This usually assigns to children the religion of their parents.

republic, a state with elected leaders and a centralized presidential form of government, local subdivisions being subordinate to the national government. A *federal republic* (as distinguished from a unitary republic) is a republic in which power is divided between the central government and the constituent subnational administrative divisions (*e.g.,* states, provinces, or cantons) in whom the central government itself is held to originate, the division of power being defined in a written constitution and jurisdictional disputes usually being settled in a court; sovereignty usually rests with the authority that has the power to amend the constitution. A *unitary republic* (as distinguished from a federal republic) is a republic in which power originates in a central authority and is not derived from constituent subdivisions. A *people's republic,* in the dialectics of Communism, is the first stage of development toward a communist state, the second stage being a *socialist republic.* An *Islamic republic* is structured around social, ethical, legal, and religious precepts central to the Islamic faith.

retail price index, *see* consumer price index.

retail sales and service enterprises, *see* manufacturing, mining, and construction enterprises/retail sales and service enterprises.

roundwood, wood obtained from removals from forests, felled or harvested (with or without bark), in all forms.

rural, *see* urban-rural.

self-employment, work in which income derives from direct employment in one's own business, trade, or profession, as opposed to work in which salary or wages are earned from an employer.

self-governing, of a state, in control of its internal affairs in degrees ranging from control of most internal affairs (though perhaps not of public order or of internal security) to complete control of all internal affairs (*i.e.,* the state is autonomous) but having no control of external affairs or defense. In this work the term self-governing refers to the final stage in the successive stages of increasing self-government that generally precede independence.

service/trade enterprises, *see* manufacturing, mining, and construction enterprises/retail sales and service enterprises.

sex distribution, ratios, calculated as percentages, of male and female population to total population.

sheikhdom, *see* monarchy.

social deviance, a group of measures, usually reported as rates per 100,000, for principal categories of socially deviant behaviour, including specified crimes, alcoholism, drug abuse, and suicide.*

social participation, a group of measures indicative of the degree of social engagement displayed by a particular population, including rates of participation in such activities as elections, voluntary work or memberships, trade unions, and religion.*

social security, public programs designed to protect individuals and families from loss of income owing to unemployment, old age, sickness or disability, or death and to provide other services such as medical care, health and welfare programs, or income maintenance.

socialist republic, *see* republic.

sources of income, *see* household income and expenditure.

Special Drawing Right (SDR), a unit of account utilized by the International Monetary Fund (IMF) to denominate monetary reserves available under a quota system to IMF members to maintain the value of their national currency unit in international transactions.*

state, in international law, a political entity possessing the attributes of: territory, permanent civilian population, government, and the capacity to conduct relations with other states. Though the term is sometimes limited in meaning to fully independent and internationally recognized states, the more general sense of an entity possessing a *preponderance* of these characteristics is intended here. It is, thus, also a first-order civil administrative subdivision, especially of a federated union. An *associated state* is an autonomous state in free association with another that conducts its external affairs and defense; the association may be terminated in full independence at the instance of the autonomous state in consultation with the administering power. A *parliamentary state* is an independent state of the Commonwealth that is governed by a parliament and that may recognize the British monarch as its titular head.

structure of gross domestic product and labour force, tabulation of the principal elements of the national economy, according to standard industrial categories, together with the corresponding distribution of the labour force (when possible POPULATION ECONOMICALLY ACTIVE) that generates the GROSS DOMESTIC PRODUCT.

sultanate, *see* monarchy.

territory, a noncategorized political dependency; a first-order administrative subdivision; a dependent political entity with some degree of self-government, but with fewer rights and less autonomy than a colony because there is no charter. An *external territory* (Australia) is a territory situated outside the area of the country. An *organized territory* (U.S.) is a territory for which a system of laws and a settled government have been provided by an act of the United States Congress. An *overseas territory* (France) is an overseas subdivision of the French Republic with elected representation in the French Parliament, having individual statutes, laws, and internal organization adapted to local conditions.

ton-miles, or **ton-kilometres,** aggregate measure of freight hauled by a specified means of transportation, equal to tons of freight multiplied by the miles (or kilometres) each ton is transported. Figures are compiled from waybills (nationally) and ordinarily exclude mail, specie, passengers' baggage, the fuel and stores of the conveyance, and goods carried free.

total active duty personnel, full-time active duty military personnel (excluding militias and part-time, informal, or other paramilitary elements), with their distribution by percentages among the major services.

total fertility rate, the sum of the current age-specific birth rates for each of the child-bearing years (usually 15–49). It is the probable number of births, given present fertility data, that would occur during the lifetime of each woman should she live to the end of her child-bearing years.

tourism, service industry comprising activities connected with domestic and international travel for pleasure or recreation; confined here to international travel and reported as expenditures in U.S. dollars by tourists of all nationalities visiting a particular country and, conversely, the estimated expenditures of that country's nationals in all countries of destination.

transfer payments, *see* household income and expenditure.

transport, all mechanical methods of moving persons or goods. Data reported for national establishments include: for railroads, length of track and volume of traffic for passengers and cargo (but excluding mail, etc.); for roads, length of network and numbers of passenger cars and of commercial vehicles (*i.e.,* trucks and buses); for merchant marine, the number of vessels of more than 100 gross tons and their total deadweight tonnage; for air transport, traffic data for passengers and cargo and the number of airports with scheduled flights.

unincorporated territory (U.S.), *see* territory.

unitary republic, *see* republic.

urban-rural, social characteristic of local or national populations, defined by predominant economic activities, "urban" referring to a group of largely nonagricultural pursuits, "rural" to agriculturally oriented employment patterns. The distinction is usually based on the country's own definition of urban, which may depend only upon the size (population) of a place or upon factors like employment, administrative status, density of housing, etc.

value added, also called value added by manufacture, the gross output value of a firm or industry minus the cost of inputs—raw materials, supplies, and payments to other firms—required to produce it. Value added is the portion of the sales value or gross output value that is actually created by the firm or industry. Value added generally includes labour costs, administrative costs, and operating profits.

The Nations of the World

Afghanistan

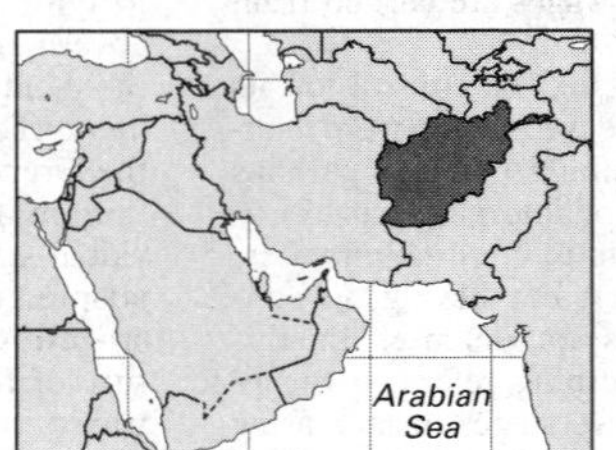

Official name[1]: Islamic Emirate of Afghanistan (Persian and Pashtu long-form names, n.a.).
Form of government: Islamic emirate.
Chief of state: President.[2]
Head of government: Prime Minister[3].
Capital: Kabul.
Official languages: Pashto; Dari (Persian).
Official religion: Islam.
Monetary unit: 1 afghani (Af) = 100 puls (puli); valuation (Oct. 3, 1997) 1 U.S.$ = Af 4,750; 1 £ = Af 7,657.

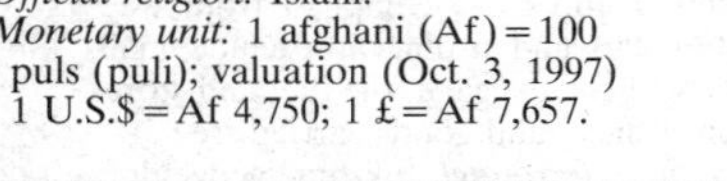

Area and population[4]	area		population
			1993
Regions	sq mi	sq km	estimate
Central	11,657	30,192	3,481,400
East	9,802	25,386	1,567,500
East-central	21,739	56,304	685,600
North	29,520	76,457	2,421,900
North-east	30,233	78,304	2,518,300
South	19,525	50,569	1,659,600
South-west	77,000	199,430	2,188,700
West	46,187	119,624	1,497,500
TOTAL	251,825[5]	652,225[5]	16,020,500

Demography

Population (1997): 23,738,000[6].
Density (1997): persons per sq mi 94.3, persons per sq km 36.4.
Urban-rural (1995): urban 20.0%; rural 80.0%.
Sex distribution (1997): male 51.50%; female 48.50%.
Age breakdown (1997): under 15, 43.0%; 15–29, 27.4%; 30–44, 16.2%; 45–59, 8.9%; 60–74, 3.8%; 75 and over, 0.7%.
Population projection: (2000) 26,668,000; (2010) 34,098,000.
Doubling time: 24 years.
Ethnic composition (early 1990[6]): Pashtun 38%; Tajik 25%; Ḥazāra 19%; Uzbek 6%; Chahar Aimak, Turkmen, Balochi, and other 12%.
Religious affiliation (1990): Sunnī Muslim 84%; Shīʿī Muslim 15%; other 1%.
Major cities (1988): Kabul 700,000[7]; Kandahār (Qandahār) 225,500; Herāt 177,300; Mazār-e Sharīf 130,600.

Vital statistics

Birth rate per 1,000 population (1997): 43.0 (world avg. 25.0).
Death rate per 1,000 population (1997): 18.0 (world avg. 9.3).
Natural increase rate per 1,000 population (1997): 25.0 (world avg. 15.7).
Total fertility rate (avg. births per childbearing woman; 1997): 6.1.
Life expectancy at birth (1996): male 46.4 years; female 45.2 years.

National economy

Budget (1987–88). Revenue: Af 79,800,000,000. Expend.: Af 105,800,000,000.
Gross domestic product (1995): U.S.$13,598,000,000 (U.S.$600 per capita).

Structure of gross domestic product and labour force	1992–93			
	in value Af '000,000[8]	% of total value	labour force	% of labour force
Agriculture	61,400	48.5	4,276,100	67.2
Manufacturing / Mining and public utilities	32,800	25.9	298,900	4.7
Construction	12,400	9.8	81,400	1.3
Transp. and commun.	5,300	4.2	139,900	2.2
Trade	12,400	9.8	420,600	6.6
Pub. admin., services	2,400 (with Other)	1.9 (with Other)	929,300	14.6
Other			214,300	3.4
TOTAL	126,700	100.0[9]	6,360,500	100.0

Public debt (external, outstanding; 1993): U.S.$5,381,000,000.
Production (metric tons except as noted). Agriculture, forestry, fishing (1997): wheat 1,700,000, corn (maize) 360,000, grapes 330,000, rice 300,000, potatoes 235,000, barley 180,000, almonds 9,000, opium poppy 600–3,000; livestock (number of live animals) 14,300,000 sheep, 2,200,000 goats, 1,500,000 cattle, 300,000 horses, 265,000 camels; roundwood (1995) 7,680,000 cu m; fish catch (1994) 1,300. Mining and quarrying (1995): salt 13,000; copper 5,000; gypsum 3,000; barite 2,000. Manufacturing (by production value in Af '000,000; 1988–89): food products 4,019; leather and fur products 2,678; textiles 1,760; printing and publishing 1,070; industrial chemicals (including fertilizers) 1,053; footwear 999. Construction (Af '000,000; 1985): 1,094. Energy production (consumption): electricity (kW-hr; 1994) 687,000,000 (815,000,000); coal (metric tons; 1994) 6,000 (6,000); petroleum products (metric tons; 1994) none (280,000); natural gas (cu m; 1994) 175,032,000 (175,032,000).
Population economically active (1994)[10]: total 5,557,000; activity rate of total population 29.4% (participation rates: female 9.0%; unemployed 3.4%).

Consumer price index (1990 = 100)	1988	1989	1990	1991	1992	1993	1994
Consumer price index	64.3	83.1	100.0	266.0	420.8	563.9	676.7

Tourism: receipts (1993) U.S.$1,000,000; expenditures (1987) U.S.$1,000,000.
Land use (1994): forested 2.9%; meadows and pastures 46.0%; agricultural and under permanent cultivation 12.4%; other 38.7%.

Foreign trade[11]

Balance of trade (current prices)	1989	1990	1991	1992	1993	1994
U.S.$'000,000	−249	−351	−265	−236	+234	−306
% of total	29.1%	38.7%	27.4%	24.7%	15.5%	34.1%

Imports (1994): U.S.$602,000,000 (1989–90; machinery 37.7%, basic manufactures 18.3%, minerals and fuels 10.9%). *Major import sources* (1994): Japan 14.4%; Singapore 7.1%; China 5.2%; India 5.0%; Pakistan 4.6%.
Exports (1994): U.S.$296,000,000 (1992; dried fruits and nuts 51.3%, carpets and rugs 13.1%, karakul wool and hides 4.9%, cotton 1.4%). *Major export destinations* (1994): Belgium-Luxembourg 3.8%; Pakistan 3.7%.

Transport and communications

Transport. Railroads (1995): length 25 km. Roads (1995): total length 21,000 km (paved 13%). Vehicles (1995): passenger cars 34,000; trucks and buses 31,000. Merchant marine: none. Air transport (1993): passenger-km 197,000,000; metric ton-km cargo 11,000,000[12]; airports (1996) 3.

Communications Medium	date	unit	number	units per 1,000 persons
Daily newspapers	1994	circulation	216,000	11.0
Radio	1996	receivers	1,670,000	73.7
Television	1995	receivers	180,000	10.0
Telephones	1995	main lines	29,000	1.4

Education and health

Educational attainment (1980). Population age 25 and over having: no formal schooling 88.5%; some primary education 6.8%; complete primary 0.3%; some secondary 1.2%; postsecondary 3.2%. *Literacy* (1995): Total population age 15 and over literate 31.5%; males 47.2%; females 15.0%.

Education (1994–95)	schools	teachers	students	student/ teacher ratio
Primary	1,753[13]	20,055[14]	1,312,197	...
Secondary	819[13]	17,548[14] (with Voc., teacher tr.)	512,851 (with Voc., teacher tr.)	...
Voc., teacher tr.	33[13]			
Higher[15]	5[16]	444[17]	9,367[17]	21.1

Health (1988–93): physicians 2,347 (1 per 6,690 persons); hospital beds 5,331 (1 per 2,945 persons); infant mortality rate (1997) 147.0.
Food (1992): daily per capita caloric intake 1,523 (vegetable products 89%, animal products 11%); 62% of FAO recommended minimum requirement.

Military

Total active duty personnel (1996): no identifiable military units appear to represent the central government. *Military expenditure as percentage of GNP* (1990): 15.0% (world 4.4%); per capita expenditure U.S.$29.

[1]In 1997 the Taleban army changed the name of the country to Islamic Emirate of Afghanistan from Islamic State of Afghanistan. [2]The Taleban army, made up of former students, ousted the president, captured the capital city, Kabul, and gained a stronghold in the country on Sept. 27, 1996. In November 1996 other factional groups were negotiating a national coalition government. [3]Ousted by the Taleban army. [4]In 1993 an administrative reorganization created 32 provinces (*wilayah*), but detailed breakdown of area and population is unavailable. [5]Detailed breakdown does not account for 6,162 sq mi (15,960 sq km), which is included in the total. [6]Including Afghan refugees estimated to number about 1.2 million in Pakistan and about 1.4 million in Iran. [7]1993 estimate. [8]Detail does not add to total given because of rounding. [9]Based on settled population only; unemployed data is 1990. [10]At prices of 1978–79. [11]Exports are f.o.b. and imports are c.i.f. [12]1992. [13]1992–93. [14]1993–94. [15]Includes universities only. [16]1988–89. [17]1989–90.

Internet resources for further information:
- **Afghanistan Today http://frankenstein.worldweb.net/afghan**
- **Arthur Paul Afghanistan Collection http://www.unomaha.edu/Qworld/cas/collection.html**

Albania

Official name: Republika e Shqipërisë (Republic of Albania).
Form of government: unitary multiparty republic with one legislative house (People's Assembly [155])[1].
Chief of state: President.
Head of government: Prime Minister.
Capital: Tiranë.
Official language: Albanian.
Official religion: none.
Monetary unit: 1 lek = 100 qindars; valuation (Oct. 3, 1997) 1 U.S.$ = 148.25 leks; 1 £ = 238.98 leks.

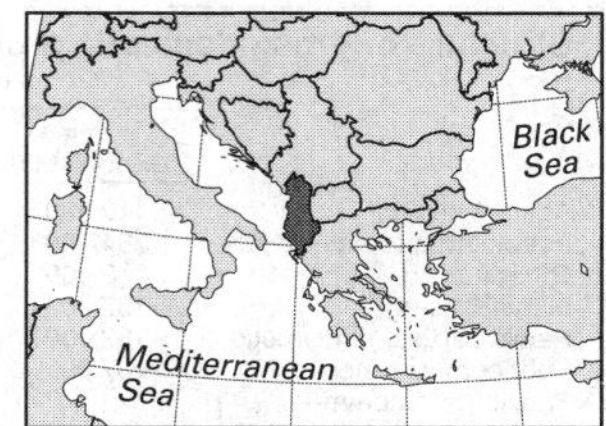

Area and population		area		population
				1990
Provinces	Capitals	sq mi	sq km	estimate
Berat	Berat	396	1,027	180,489
Dibër	Peshkopi	605	1,568	153,775
Durrës	Durrës	327	848	251,029
Elbasan	Elbasan	572	1,481	248,676
Fier	Fier	454	1,175	251,115
Gjirokastër	Gjirokastër	439	1,137	67,392
Gramsh	Gramsh	268	695	44,791
Kolonjë	Ersekë	311	805	25,291
Korçë	Korçë	842	2,181	218,219
Krujë	Krujë	234	607	109,876
Kukës	Kukës	514	1,330	104,731
Lezhë	Lezhë	185	479	63,505
Librazhd	Librazhd	391	1,013	73,871
Lushnjë	Lushnjë	275	712	137,830
Mat	Burrel	397	1,028	78,754
Mirditë	Rrëshen	335	867	51,701
Përmet	Përmet	359	929	40,419
Pogradec	Pogradec	280	725	73,333
Pukë	Pukë	399	1,034	50,286
Sarandë	Sarandë	424	1,097	89,459
Shkodër	Shkodër	976	2,528	241,549
Skrapar	Çorovoda	299	775	47,605
Tepelenë	Tepelenë	315	817	51,022
Tiranë	Tiranë	478	1,238	374,483
Tropojë	Bajram	403	1,043	45,965
Vlorë	Vlorë	621	1,609	180,725
TOTAL		11,100[2]	28,748	3,255,891

Demography

Population (1997): 3,293,000.
Density (1997): persons per sq mi 296.6, persons per sq km 115.0.
Urban-rural (1995): urban 42.4%; rural 57.6%.
Sex distribution (1995): male 49.50%; female 50.50%.
Age breakdown (1996): under 15, 34.1%; 15–29, 24.2%; 30–44, 20.1%; 45–59, 12.4%; 60–74, 7.5%; 75 and over, 1.7%.
Population projection: (2000) 3,427,000; (2010) 3,860,000.
Doubling time: 47 years.
Ethnic composition (1989): Albanian 98.0%; Greek 1.8%; Macedonian 0.1%.
Religious affiliation (1996): a significant portion of the population are nonreligious; believers identify themselves as Muslim 70%, Orthodox 6%, Roman Catholic 3%, other 21%.
Major cities (1990): Tiranë 243,000; Durrës 85,400; Elbasan 83,300.

Vital statistics

Birth rate per 1,000 population (1996): 22.6 (world avg. 25.0).
Death rate per 1,000 population (1996): 7.7 (world avg. 9.3).
Natural increase rate per 1,000 population (1996): 14.9 (world avg. 15.7).
Total fertility rate (avg. births per childbearing woman; 1996): 2.7.
Marriage rate per 1,000 population (1990): 8.9.
Divorce rate per 1,000 population (1990): 0.8.
Life expectancy at birth (1995): male 68.5 years; female 74.3 years.
Major causes of death per 100,000 population: n.a.; however, principal health problems in the mid-1990s included malnutrition (especially of children).

National economy

Budget (1995). Revenue: 54,024,000,000 leks (taxes 73.6%, of which excise taxes 19.3%, social security contributions 17.1%, import duties and export taxes 11.5%, value-added tax 10.3%; nontax revenue 26.4%). Expenditures: 77,134,000,000 leks (current expenditure 76.1%, of which personnel costs 23.9%, social security 18.2%, government operations and maintenance 15.9%, service of public debt 6.5%; capital expenditure 23.9%).
Public debt (1995): U.S.$556,700,000.
Production (metric tons except as noted). Agriculture, forestry, fishing (1996): cereals 537,600; vegetables and melons 459,500 (mainly beans, peas, onions, tomatoes, cabbage, eggplants, and carrots), potatoes 137,000; livestock (number of live animals) 2,500,000 sheep, 1,900,000 goats, 850,000 cattle, 4,300,000 poultry; roundwood (1994) 409,000 cu m; fish catch (1995) 3,488. Mining and quarrying (1995): copper ore 258,000; chromite 243,000. Manufacturing (value of production in '000 leks; 1993)[3]: food products 824,000; textiles 263,000; clothing 139,000. Construction (1990): 12,428 units. Energy production (consumption): electricity (kW-hr; 1994) 3,903,000,000 (3,903,000,000); coal (metric tons; 1994) 179,000 (179,000); crude petroleum (barrels; 1994) 3,527,800 (2,703,500); petroleum products (metric tons; 1994) 261,000 (261,000); natural gas (cu m; 1994) 77,000,000 (77,000,000).
Gross national product (1995): U.S.$2,199,000,000 (U.S.$670 per capita).

Structure of gross domestic product and labour force	1994		1995	
	value '000,000 leks	% of total value	labour force	% of labour force
Agriculture	92,254	55.5	778,000	58.7
Manufacturing, mining, public utilities	20,966	12.6	95,000	7.2
Construction	15,732	9.5	21,000	1.6
Transp. and commun.	5,546	3.3	30,000	2.3
Trade			62,000	4.7
Pub. admin., defense	31,799	19.1	...	...
Services			79,000	6.0
Other	—	—	260,000[4]	19.6
TOTAL	166,297	100.0	1,325,000	100.0[2]

Population economically active (1995): total 1,325,000; activity rate of total population 63.0% (1993; participation rates: ages 15–64, 90.2%; female 49.0%; unemployed 12.9%).

Price and earnings indexes (1991 = 100)	1991	1992	1993	1994	1995	1996
Consumer price index	100.0	325.2	602.0	737.8	794.7	896.0
Earnings index	...	...	...	...	...	...

Household income and expenditure. Average household size (1989) 4.7; annual income per rural household 80,835 leks (U.S.$ value, n.a.); sources of income: wages 53.0%, transfers from relatives abroad 21.5%, social insurance 11.4%; expenditure: n.a.

Foreign trade

Balance of trade (current prices)	1990	1991	1992	1993	1994	1995
'000,000 leks	−150	−308	−454	−490	−460	−474
% of total	24.5%	60.3%	76.4%	68.6%	62.0%	53.6%

Imports (1995): U.S.$679,000,000 (food, beverages, live animals, and tobacco 22.3%; manufactured goods 21.2%; machinery and transport equipment 20.3%; mineral fuels 9.7%; chemicals 6.8%). *Major import sources:* Italy 37.9%; Greece 26.8%; Bulgaria 8.0%; Germany 4.6%; Turkey 4.1%.
Exports (1995): U.S.$205,000,000 (miscellaneous manufactured articles 45.6%; crude materials 24.7%; manufactured goods 14.1%). *Major export destinations:* Italy 51.5%; Greece 9.9%; Turkey 6.2%; Belgium-Luxembourg 5.4%.

Transport and communications

Transport. Railroads: length (1996) 670 km; passenger-km 197,000,000; metric ton-km cargo 428,000. Roads (1995): total length 15,500 km (paved 30%). Vehicles (1995): passenger cars 58,682; trucks and buses 34,441. Merchant marine (1992): vessels (100 gross tons and over) 24; total deadweight tonnage 80,954. Air transport (1995): passenger-km 3,519,000; short ton-mi 223,000, metric ton-km 325,000; airports (1997) with scheduled flights 1.

Communications				units
Medium	date	unit	number	per 1,000 persons
Daily newspapers	1995	circulation	185,000	54
Radio	1996	receivers	550,000	157
Television	1995	receivers	300,000	89
Telephones	1995	main lines	42,000	12
Facsimile machines	1995	units	600	0.2

Education and health

Educational attainment (1989). Population age 10 and over having: primary education 65.3%; secondary 29.1%; higher 5.6%. *Literacy* (1989): total population age 10 and over literate 91.8%; males 95.5%; females 88.0%.

Education (1993)	schools	teachers	students	student/ teacher ratio
Primary (age 6–13)	1,777	32,098	535,713	16.7
Secondary (age 14–17)	47[5]	4,149	73,259	17.7
Voc., teacher tr.[5]	466	7,390	138,000	18.7
Higher	8[5]	1,774	30,185	17.0

Health (1994): physicians 6,154 (1 per 552 persons); hospital beds 10,200 (1 per 333 persons); infant mortality rate per 1,000 live births (1996) 49.2.
Food (1995): daily per capita caloric intake 2,324 (vegetable products 64%, animal products 36%); 96% of FAO recommended minimum requirement.

Military

Total active duty personnel (1996): 54,000 (army 83.3%, navy 4.6%, air force 12.1%). *Military expenditure as percentage of GNP* (1995): 1.1% (world 2.8%); per capita expenditure U.S.$14.

[1]A transitional constitution was adopted on April 29, 1991. The proposed text of a permanent constitution was rejected in a referendum on Nov. 6, 1994. [2]Detail does not add to total given because of rounding. [3]Value of production in constant prices of 1990. [4]Includes 171,000 undistributed unemployed. [5]1990.

Internet resources for further information:
- **UNDP Human Development Report—Albania 1996**
http://www.undp.tirana.al/hdr96/hdrindex.html
- **Albanian Ministry of Foreign Affairs**
http://www.tirana.al/minjash/

Algeria

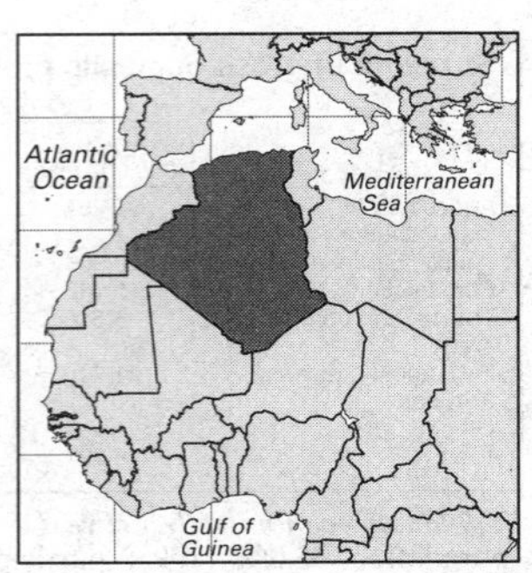

Official name: Al-Jumhūrīyah al-Jazā'irīyah ad-Dīmuqrāṭīyah ash-Sha'bīyah (Arabic) (Democratic and Popular Republic of Algeria).
Form of government: multiparty republic with two legislative bodies (Council of Nation [144][1]; National People's Assembly [380]).
Chief of state: President.
Head of government: Prime Minister.
Capital: Algiers.
Official language: Arabic.
Official religion: Islam.
Monetary unit: 1 Algerian dinar (DA) = 100 centimes; valuation (Oct. 3, 1997) 1 U.S.$ = DA 58.72; 1 £ = DA 94.66.

Population (1987 census)

Provinces	population	Provinces	population	Provinces	population
Adrar	217,678	Djelfa	494,494	Oum el-Bouaghi	403,936
Aïn Defla	537,256	Ghardaïa	216,140	Relizane	544,877
Aïn Temouchent	274,990	Guelma	353,309	Saïda	235,494
Alger	1,690,191	Illizi	18,930	Sétif	1,000,694
Annaba	455,888	Jijel	472,312	Sidi bel-Abbès	446,277
Batna	752,617	Khenchela	246,541	Skikda	622,510
El-Bayadh	153,254	Laghouat	212,388	Souk Ahras	296,077
Béchar	185,346	Mascara	566,901	Tamanrasset	95,822
Bejaïa	700,952	Médéa	652,863	Et-Tarf	275,315
Biskra	430,202	Mila	511,605	Tébessa	410,233
Blida	702,188	Mostaganem	505,932	Tiaret	575,794
Bordj Bou Arreridj	424,828	M'Sila	604,693	Tindouf	16,428
Bouira	526,900	Naâma	113,700	Tipaza	620,151
Boumerdes	650,975	Oran	932,473	Tissemsilt	228,120
Ech-Chleff	684,192	Ouargla	284,454	Tizi Ouzou	936,948
Constantine	664,303	El-Oued	376,909	Tlemcen	714,862
				TOTAL	23,038,942[2]

Demography

Area: 919,595 sq mi, 2,381,741 sq km.
Population (1997): 29,476,000.
Density (1997): persons per sq mi 32.1, persons per sq km 12.4.
Urban-rural (1995): urban 55.8%; rural 44.2%.
Sex distribution (1995): male 50.60%; female 49.40%.
Age breakdown (1995): under 15, 39.0%; 15–29, 29.6%; 30–44, 17.3%; 45–59, 8.2%; 60–74, 4.6%; 75 and over, 1.3%.
Population projection: (2000) 31,410,000; (2010) 38,479,000.
Doubling time: 31 years.
Ethnic composition (1992): Arab *c.* 80%; Berber *c.* 20%, of which Kabyle *c.* 13%, Shawia *c.* 6%.
Religious affiliation (1990): Muslim 99.9%, of which Sunnī 99.5%, Ibāḍīyah 0.4%; Roman Catholic 0.1%.
Major cities (1987): Algiers (1995) 2,168,000 (metro area; 3,702,000); Oran 609,823; Constantine 440,842; Annaba 222,518; Batna 181,601.

Vital statistics

Birth rate per 1,000 population (1996): 28.5 (world avg. 25.0).
Death rate per 1,000 population (1996): 5.9 (world avg. 9.3).
Natural increase rate per 1,000 population (1996): 22.6 (world avg. 15.7).
Total fertility rate (avg. births per childbearing woman; 1996): 3.6.
Marriage rate per 1,000 population (1993): 5.7.
Life expectancy at birth (1996): male 67.2 years; female 69.5 years.
Notified cases of infectious diseases per 100,000 population (1990): hepatitis 15.1; typhoid fever 11.3; measles 7.2; cholera 5.2; tuberculosis 4.8.

National economy

Budget (1995). Revenue: DA 600,900,000,000 (export taxes on hydrocarbons 50.8%; value-added taxes 16.1%). Expenditures: DA 627,700,000,000 (current expenditure 70.8%, development expenditure 23.1%; other 6.1%).
Land use (1994): forested 1.6%; meadows and pastures 13.3%; agricultural and under permanent cultivation 3.4%; other (mostly desert) 81.7%.
Production (metric tons except as noted). Agriculture, forestry, fishing (1996): wheat 2,800,000, barley 1,690,000, potatoes 1,150,000, tomatoes 718,000, dates 360,600, olives 313,300, onions 312,900, oranges 236,700, grapes 132,300; livestock (number of live animals) 17,565,000 sheep, 2,895,000 goats; roundwood (1995) 2,517,000 cu m; fish catch (1995) 106,246. Mining and quarrying (1996): iron ore (gross weight) 2,245,000; phosphate rock (gross weight) 1,051,000; mercury 10,669 flasks. Manufacturing (value added in U.S.$'000,000; 1994): food products 686; iron and steel 594; fabricated metal products 489; cement, bricks, and tiles 358; transport equipment 333; electrical machinery 227. Construction (dwellings completed; 1995): 166,900. Energy production (consumption): electricity (kW-hr; 1994) 19,888,000,000 (18,764,000,000); coal (metric tons; 1994) 20,000 (1,280,000); crude petroleum (barrels; 1995) 278,860,000 ([1994] 160,307,000); petroleum products (metric tons; 1994) 39,543,000 (10,862,000); natural gas (cu m; 1995) 60,600,000,000 ([1994] 19,209,000,000).
Household income and expenditure. Average household size (1992) 6.9; income per household: n.a.; sources of income (1995): wages and salaries 43.1%, self-employment 38.3%, transfers 18.6%; expenditure (1988): food and beverages 52.3%, transportation and communications 12.0%, clothing and footwear 8.6%, housing and energy 6.7%, other 20.4%.
Gross national product (1995): U.S.$44,609,000,000 (U.S.$1,600 per capita).

Structure of gross domestic product and labour force

	1994		1990	
	in value DA '000,000	% of total value	labour force	% of labour force
Agriculture	140,500	9.5	907,490	15.9
Petroleum and natural gas	334,200[3]	22.7[3]	55,000	1.0
Other mining	2,200	0.2	...	...
Manufacturing	137,000[3]	9.3[3]	646,390	11.3
Public utilities, construction	182,100	12.4	651,370	11.4
Pub. admin., defense	187,000	12.7	1,318,370	23.1
Transp. and commun. }			252,230	4.4
Trade }	488,400[4]	33.2[4]	444,970	7.8
Other }			1,435,180[5]	25.1[5]
TOTAL	1,471,400	100.0	5,711,000	100.0

Population economically active (1994): total 6,814,000; activity rate of population 24.8% (participation rates [1987] ages 15–64, 44.3%; female 9.2%; unemployed [1995] more than 28%).

Price and earnings indexes (1990 = 100)

	1990	1991	1992	1993	1994	1995	1996
Consumer price index	100.0	125.9	165.8	199.8	257.8	340.8	420.1[6]
Earnings index[7]	100.0	131.1	170.2	199.1	203.8	224.2	246.6

Public debt (external, outstanding; 1995): U.S.$30,442,000,000.
Tourism: (1995) receipts from visitors U.S.$27,000,000; expenditures by nationals abroad U.S.$135,000,000.

Foreign trade[8]

Balance of trade (current prices)

	1990	1991	1992	1993	1994	1995
U.S.$'000,000	+3,215	+4,107	+2,489	+1,312	−1,005	+429
% of total	14.2%	21.1%	12.6%	7.0%	5.5%	2.0%

Imports (1994): U.S.$9,599,000,000 (food 29.4%, of which cereals and preparations 13.8%; nonelectrical machinery 14.7%, iron and steel 9.5%). *Major import sources* (1995): France 29.6%; Spain 10.5%; Italy 8.2%; U.S. 8.0%; Germany 5.6%.
Exports (1994): U.S.$8,594,000,000 (crude petroleum 45.7%, natural gas 31.2%, refined petroleum 18.8%). *Major export destinations* (1995): Italy 18.8%; U.S. 14.8%; France 11.8%; Spain 8.0%; Germany 7.9%.

Transport and communications

Transport. Railroads (1995): route length 2,965 mi, 4,772 km; (1994) passenger-km 2,524,000,000; metric ton-km cargo 2,400,000,000. Roads (1995): total length 102,424 km (paved 69%). Vehicles (1995): passenger cars 871,000; trucks and buses 566,000. Air transport (1996)[9]: passenger-km 2,644,000,000; metric ton-km cargo 14,826,000; airports (1996) 28.

Communications

Medium	date	unit	number	units per 1,000 persons
Daily newspapers	1994	circulation	1,440,000	52
Radio	1996	receivers	3,500,000	122
Television	1995	receivers	2,000,000	71
Telephones	1995	main lines	1,176,300	42
Cellular telephones	1995	subscribers	4,700	0.2
Facsimile machines	1995	units	5,200	0.2
Personal computers	1995	units	85,000	3.0

Education and health

Educational attainment (1989). Percentage of economically active population age 16 and over having: no formal schooling 38.2%; Qur'ānic education 0.9%; primary 20.8%; secondary 11.1%; vocational 19.7%; higher 9.3%. *Literacy* (1995): total population age 15 and over literate 10,531,000 (61.6%); males literate 6,368,000 (73.9%); females literate 4,163,000 (49.0%).

Education (1995–96)

	schools	teachers	students	student/ teacher ratio
Primary (age 6–11)	17,186	169,010	4,617,000	27.3
Secondary (age 12–17)	3,954	150,397	2,544,864	16.9
Higher[10]	...	14,475	233,019	16.1

Health (1994): physicians 25,796 (1 per 1,066 persons); hospital beds 53,612 (1 per 513 persons); infant mortality rate per 1,000 live births (1996) 48.7.
Food (1995): daily per capita caloric intake 3,042 (vegetable products 90%, animal products 10%); 127% of FAO recommended minimum requirement.

Military

Total active duty personnel (1996): 123,700 (army 86.5%, navy 5.4%, air force 8.1%). *Military expenditure as percentage of GNP* (1995): 3.2% (world 2.8%); per capita expenditure U.S.$43.

[1]Seats of the Council of Nation are to be filled in late 1997, 48 of which will be appointed by the president. [2]De facto population. [3]Petroleum and natural gas includes (and Manufacturing excludes) refined petroleum and manufacture of hydrocarbons. [4]Includes import duties of DA 119,100,000,000. [5]Includes 1,141,278 unemployed. [6]Average of 2nd quarter. [7]Public workers only; all data based on January averages of gross income. [8]Imports c.i.f.; exports f.o.b. [9]Air Algérie. [10]1994–95.

Internet resources for further information:

- **Office National de Statistiques (French) http://ist.cerist.dz/sie/ons/ons.htm**
- **Permanent Mission of Algeria to the UN http://www.undp.org/missions/algeria/**

Andorra

Official name: Principat d'Andorra; (Principality of Andorra).
Form of government: parliamentary coprincipality with one legislative house (General Council [28]).
Chiefs of state: President of France; Bishop of Urgell, Spain.
Head of government: Head of Government.
Capital: Andorra la Vella.
Official language: Catalan.
Official religion: none[1].
Monetary unit: There is no local currency of issue; the French franc and Spanish peseta are both in circulation. 1 franc (F) = 100 centimes; 1 peseta (Pta) = 100 céntimos.
Valuation (Oct. 3, 1997)
1 U.S.$ = F 5.92, 1 £ = F 9.55;
1 U.S.$ = Ptas 148.85,
1 £ = Ptas 239.94.

Area and population		area		population
				1997[2]
Parishes	**Capitals**	sq mi	sq km	estimate
Andorra la Vella	Andorra la Vella	49[3]	127[3]	21,721
Canillo	Canillo	74	191	2,518
Encamp	Encamp			9,800
La Massana	La Massana	25	65	5,785
Les Escaldes-Engordany	—	[3]	[3]	15,182
Ordino	Ordino	33	85	1,931
Sant Julià de Lòria	Sant Julià de Lòria	[3]	[3]	7,542
TOTAL		181	468	64,479

Demography

Population (1997): 64,600.
Density (1997): persons per sq mi 356.9, persons per sq km 138.0.
Urban-rural (1995): urban 62.5%; rural 37.5%.
Sex distribution (1996): male 52.71%; female 47.29%.
Age breakdown (1993): under 15, 16.3%; 15–29, 27.7%; 30–44, 27.2%; 45–59, 15.1%; 60–74, 9.9%; 75 and over, 3.8%.
Population projection: (2000) 66,000; (2010) 71,000.
Doubling time: 92 years.
Ethnic composition (by nationality; 1997): Spanish 44.4%; Andorran 20.2%; Portuguese 10.7%; French 6.8%; other nationality 6.6%; undeclared nationality 11.3%.
Religious affiliation (1992): Roman Catholic 92.0%; Protestant 0.5%; Jewish 0.4%; other 7.1%.
Major cities (1997): Andorra la Vella 21,984[4]; Les Escaldes 15,182; Encamp 9,800.

Vital statistics

Birth rate per 1,000 population (1996): 10.9[5] (world avg. 25.0).
Death rate per 1,000 population (1996): 3.1[5] (world avg. 9.3).
Natural increase rate per 1,000 population (1996): 7.8[5] (world avg. 15.7).
Total fertility rate (avg. births per childbearing woman; 1996): 1.1.
Marriage rate per 1,000 population (1995): 2.2.
Life expectancy at birth (1995): male 75.6 years; female 81.7 years.
Major causes of death per 100,000 population: n.a.; however, health problems are those of a developed country—cardiovascular disease, hypertension, malignant neoplasms (cancers).

National economy

Budget (1996). Revenue: Ptas 25,449,000,000 (indirect taxes on commodities 76.6%, property income 11.4%). Expenditures: Ptas 25,795,000,000 (administrative costs 26.2%, capital expenditures 24.0%, education and recreation 15.9%, general public services 8.7%, social welfare 5.1%, health 3.3%).
Public debt (1994): about U.S.$125,000,000.
Production. Agriculture (1996): tobacco 1,023 metric tons; other traditional crops include hay, potatoes, and grapes; livestock (number of live animals; 1996) 1,965 sheep[6], 1,141 cattle, 682 horses. Quarrying: small amounts of marble are quarried. Manufacturing (value of recorded exports in Ptas '000; 1996): motor vehicles and parts 1,190,000; electrical machinery and apparatus 779,000; clothing 778,000; newspapers and periodicals 613,000; furniture 276,000; other products include cigars and cigarettes and liqueurs. Construction (approved new building construction; 1996): 175,000 sq m. Energy production (consumption): electricity (kW-hr; 1996) 109,000,000 (335,000,000); coal, none (n.a.); crude petroleum, none (n.a.); petroleum products, none (n.a.); natural gas, none (n.a.).
Tourism (1997): about 6,000,000 visitors; number of hotels (1996) 222.
Population economically active (1996)[7]: total 28,071; activity rate of total population 43.5% (participation rates: ages 15–64, 59.4%; female, n.a.; unemployed, unofficially, none[8]).

Price and earnings indexes (1991 = 100)	1991	1992	1993	1994	1995	1996	1997[9]
Consumer price index[10]	100.0	105.9	110.8	116.1	121.4	125.8	127.7
Annual earnings index[11]	100.0	107.6	114.4	117.1	121.2	127.3	...

Gross domestic product (1996): U.S.$1,123,000,000 (U.S.$17,420 per capita)[12].

Structure of labour force[7]	1996	
	labour force	% of labour force
Agriculture Mining	192	0.7
Manufacturing	1,233	4.4
Construction	4,598	16.4
Public utilities	...	...
Transp. and commun.	...	...
Trade	5,438	19.4
Restaurants, hotels	5,367	19.1
Finance, real estate, insurance	1,254	4.5
Pub. admin., defense	3,452	12.3
Services	5,005	17.8
Other	1,532	5.4
TOTAL	28,071	100.0

Land use (1994): forested 22.0%; meadows and pastures 56.0%; agricultural and under permanent cultivation 2.0%; other 20.0%.
Household income and expenditure. n.a.

Foreign trade

Balance of trade (current prices)	1991	1992	1993	1994	1995	1996
Ptas '000,000	...	−112,177	...	−117,846	−125,510	−129,575
% of total	...	93.0%	...	89.7%	91.1%	91.7%

Imports (1996): Ptas 135,460,000,000 (food, beverages, and tobacco 29.0%; machinery and apparatus 14.1%; chemicals and chemical products 9.1%; transport equipment 7.6%; textiles and wearing apparel 7.6%; photographic and optical goods and watches and clocks 4.6%). *Major import sources:* Spain 40.9%; France 30.8%; Germany 4.3%; U.S. 4.0%; U.K. 3.9%.
Exports (1996): Ptas 5,881,000,000 (motor vehicles and parts 20.2%; electrical machinery and apparatus 13.2%; clothing 13.2%; newspapers and periodicals 10.4%; food and beverages 5.9%). *Major export destinations:* Spain 49.9%; France 39.4%; Germany 1.3%; Switzerland 1.3%.

Transport and communications

Transport. Railroads: none; however, both French and Spanish railways stop near the border. Roads (1994): total length 167 mi, 269 km (paved 74%). Vehicles (1996): passenger cars 35,358; trucks and buses 4,238. Merchant marine: vessels (100 gross tons and over) none. Airports (1997) with scheduled flights: none.

Communications **Medium**	date	unit	number	units per 1,000 persons
Daily newspapers	1994	circulation	4,000	62
Radio	1996	receivers	10,000	156
Television	1993	receivers	20,000	315
Telephones	1996	main lines	30,964	480
Cellular telephones	1996	subscribers	5,343	83
Facsimile machines	1995	units	1,300	20

Education and health

Educational attainment (mid-1980s). Percentage of population age 15 and over having: no formal schooling 5.5%; primary education 47.3%; secondary education 21.6%; postsecondary education 24.9%; unknown 0.7%. *Literacy:* resident population is virtually 100% literate.

Education (1996–97)	schools	teachers	students	student/ teacher ratio
Primary/Lower secondary (age 7–15)	12	...	5,424	...
Upper secondary	6	...	2,655	...
Higher	—	—	—	—

Health: physicians (1994) 132 (1 per 491 persons); hospital beds (1993) 114 (1 per 556 persons); infant mortality rate per 1,000 live births (1995) 7.7.
Food (1995)[13]: daily per capita caloric intake 3,463 (vegetable products 67%, animal products 33%); 139% of FAO recommended minimum requirement.

Military

Total active duty personnel (1996): none. France and Spain are responsible for Andorra's external security; a 32-person police force is assisted in alternate years by either French gendarmerie or Barcelona police.

[1]Roman Catholicism enjoys special recognition in accordance with Andorran tradition. [2]January 1. [3]Andorra la Vella includes Les Escaldes-Engordany and Sant Julià de Lòria. [4]1995. [5]Official government figures. [6]Large herds of sheep and goats from Spain and France feed in Andorra in the summer. [7]Labour force receiving wages only; total population economically active equals 31,775. [8]The restricted size of the indigenous labour force necessitated high levels of immigration in the late 1980s and early 1990s to serve the tourist trade; emigration exceeded immigration in 1994 and 1995 because of a labour force surplus. [9]June. [10]Consumer price index of Spain. [11]Per Andorran Office of Social Security. [12]Tourism (including winter-season sports, fairs, festivals, and income earned from low-duty imported manufactured items) and the banking system (of some importance as a tax haven for foreign financial investment and transactions) are the primary sources of GDP. [13]Composite values derived from Spanish and French food data.

Internet resources for further information:

- **Andorra National Information Centre**
  http://www.andorra.ad/cniauk.html
- **The Principality of Andorra**
  http://www.xmission.com/Qdderhak/andorra.htm

Angola

Official name: República de Angola (Republic of Angola).
Form of government: unitary multiparty republic[1] with one legislative house (National Assembly [220]).
Head of state and government: President[2].
Capital: Luanda.
Official language: Portuguese.
Official religion: none.
Monetary unit: 1 readjusted Kwanza[3] = 100 lwei; valuation (Oct. 3, 1997) 1 U.S.$ = readjusted Kwanza 257,128; 1 £ = readjusted Kwanza 414,491.

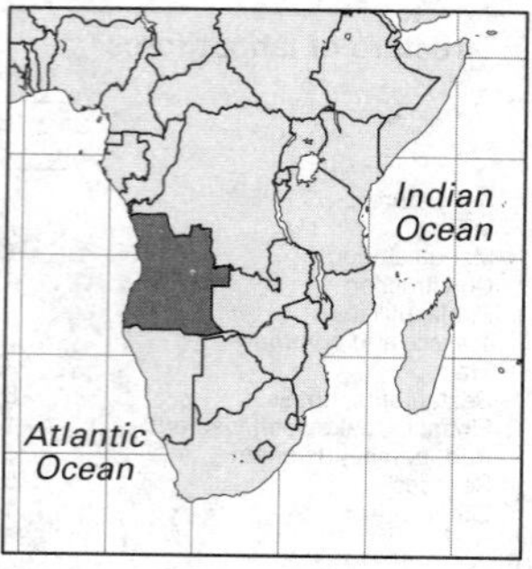

Area and population

Provinces	Capitals	area sq mi	area sq km	population 1997 estimate[4]
Bengo	Caxito	12,112	31,371	...
Benguela	Benguela	12,273	31,788	...
Bié	Kuito	27,148	70,314	...
Cabinda	Cabinda	2,807	7,270	...
Cunene	N'Giva	34,495	89,342	...
Huambo	Huambo	13,233	34,274	...
Huíla	Lubango	28,958	75,002	...
Kuando Kubango	Menongue	76,853	199,049	...
Kuanza Norte	N'Dalatando	9,340	24,190	...
Kuanza Sul	Sumbe	21,490	55,660	...
Luanda	Luanda	934	2,418	...
Lunda Norte	Lucapa	39,685	102,783	...
Lunda Sul	Saurimo	17,625	45,649	...
Malanje	Malanje	37,684	97,602	...
Moxico	Lwena	86,110	223,023	...
Namibe	Namibe	22,447	58,137	...
Uíge	Uíge	22,663	58,698	...
Zaire	M'Banza Kongo	15,494	40,130	...
TOTAL		481,354[5]	1,246,700	10,624,000

Demography

Population (1997): 10,624,000.
Density (1997): persons per sq mi 22.1, persons per sq km 8.5.
Urban-rural (1996): urban 31.6%; rural 68.4%.
Sex distribution (1997): male 50.41%; female 49.59%.
Age breakdown (1997): under 15, 44.7%; 15–29, 25.8%; 30–44, 15.8%; 45–59, 8.9%; 60 and over, 4.8%.
Population projection: (2000) 13,400,000; (2010) 18,082,000.
Doubling time: 26 years.
Ethnic composition (1983): Ovimbundu 37.2%; Mbundu 21.6%; Kongo 13.2%; Luimbe-Nganguela 5.4%; Nyaneka-Humbe 5.4%; Chokwe 4.2%; Luvale (Luena) 3.4%; Luchazi 2.4%; Ambo (Ovambo) 2.4%; Lunda 1.2%; Mbunda 1.2%; Portuguese 0.5%; mestizo 0.5%; other 0.4%.
Religious affiliation (1995): Christian 70.1%, of which Roman Catholic 50.7%, Protestant 14.6%; traditional beliefs 29.9%.
Major cities (1995): Luanda 2,081,000; Huambo 203,000[6]; Benguela 155,000[6]; Lobito 150,000[6]; Lubango 105,000[7].

Vital statistics

Birth rate per 1,000 population (1996): 44.6 (world avg. 25.0).
Death rate per 1,000 population (1996): 17.7 (world avg. 9.3).
Natural increase rate per 1,000 population (1996): 26.9 (world avg. 15.7).
Total fertility rate (avg. births per childbearing woman; 1996): 6.3.
Marriage rate per 1,000 population (1972): 4.5.
Life expectancy at birth (1996): male 44.7 years; female 49.1 years.
Major causes of death (percentage of total deaths; 1990): diarrheal diseases 25.8%; malaria 19.4%; cholera 7.3%; acute respiratory infections 6.8%; measles 6.2%.

National economy

Budget (1997). Revenue: NKz 694,600,000,000[3] (1994; tax revenue 98.4%, of which income taxes 71.8%, petroleum taxes 19.0%, import duties 4.3%; nontax revenue 1.6%). Expenditures: NKz 521,300,000,000[3] (1994; defense and internal security 56.5%; administration 29.0%; health 3.4%; education 2.6%; other 8.5%).
Public debt (external, outstanding; 1995): U.S.$9,533,000,000.
Tourism: receipts from visitors (1994) U.S.$13,000,000; expenditures by nationals abroad (1993) U.S.$66,000,000.
Production (metric tons except as noted). Agriculture, forestry, fishing (1996): cassava 2,500,000, corn (maize) 398,000, sugarcane 330,000, bananas 295,000, sweet potatoes 190,000, dry beans 175,000, millet 102,000, palm oil 52,000, peanuts (groundnuts) 23,000, coffee 5,000; livestock (number of live animals) 3,309,000 cattle, 1,470,000 goats, 810,000 pigs, 245,000 sheep, 6,500,000 chickens; roundwood (1995) 7,005,000 cu m; fish catch (1995) 93,847. Mining and quarrying (1994): diamonds 1,350,000 carats. Manufacturing (1994): bread 15,082; wheat flour 4,496; sugar 3,190[8]; pasta 3,190[8]; corn flour 2,513; laundry soap 530; leather shoes 132,000 pairs[8]; beer 123,300 hectolitres; soft drinks 69,050 hectolitres[7]; fabric 3,038,000 sq m; matches 6,357,000 boxes[7]. Construction (value in NKz '000,000[3]; 1986); residential 608; nonresidential 1,977. Energy production (consumption): electricity (kW-hr; 1992) 1,855,000,000 (1,855,000,000); coal, none (none); crude petroleum (barrels; 1992) 192,634,000 (10,373,000); petroleum products (metric tons; 1992) 1,317,000 (346,000); natural gas (cu m; 1992) 166,576,000 (166,576,000).
Gross national product (1995): U.S.$4,422,000,000 (U.S. $410 per capita).

Structure of gross domestic product and labour force

	1994 in value NKz '000,000,000[3]	1994 % of total value	1991 labour force	1991 % of labour force
Agriculture	85,567	11.9	2,892,000	69.4
Mining	367,436	51.1	}	}
Manufacturing	24,448	3.4	}	}
Construction	11,505	1.6	}	}
Finance	3,595	0.5	438,000	10.5
Trade	72,624	10.1	}	}
Public utilities	—	—	}	}
Transp. and commun.	15,100	2.1	}	}
Pub. admin., defense } Services	138,778	19.3	}	}
Other	...	...	836,000	20.1
TOTAL	719,053	100.0	4,166,000	100.0

Population economically active (1991): total 4,166,000; activity rate of total population 40.3% (participation rates over age 10, 60.1%; female 38.4%).

Price and earnings indexes (1991 = 100)

	1991	1992	1993	1994
Consumer price index	100.0	595.0	11,534.0	123,639.0
Monthly earnings index	100.0	150.0	1,000.0	8,800.0

Household income and expenditure. Average household size (1980) 4.8; annual income per household: n.a.; sources of income: n.a.; expenditure: n.a.
Land use (1995): forested 18.5%; meadows and pastures 43.3%; agricultural and under permanent cultivation 2.8%; other 35.4%.

Foreign trade

Balance of trade (current prices)

	1990	1991	1992	1993	1994	1995
U.S.$'000,000	+1,276	+2,080	+1,160	+1,551	+1,565	+2,180
% of total	25.1%	43.6%	19.0%	35.2%	37.6%	39.1%

Imports (1995): U.S.$1,700,000,000 (1991; current consumption goods 50.2%, capital goods 20.2%, intermediate consumption goods 18.9%, transport equipment 6.8%). *Major import sources* (1991): Portugal 29.8%; U.S. 10.5%; France 9.7%; Japan 7.8%; Brazil 7.3%.
Exports (1995): U.S.$3,880,000,000 (mineral fuels 74.6%, diamonds 2.5%). *Major export destinations* (1991): U.S. 56.6%; Germany 5.6%; Brazil 4.9%; The Netherlands 4.2%; U.K. 3.4%; Belgium 3.3%.

Transport and communications

Transport. Railroads (1988): route length 1,739 mi, 2,798 km; passenger-mi 203,000,000, passenger-km 326,000,000; short ton-mi cargo 1,178,000,000, metric ton-km cargo 1,720,000,000. Roads (1995): total length 45,128 mi, 72,626 km (paved 25%). Vehicles (1995): passenger cars 197,000; trucks and buses 26,000. Merchant marine (1992): vessels (100 gross tons and over) 113; total deadweight tonnage 123,479. Air transport (1993)[9]: passenger-mi 589,000,000, passenger-km 948,000,000; short ton-mi cargo 77,000,000, metric ton-km cargo 113,000,000; airports (1997) with scheduled flights 17.

Communications

Medium	date	unit	number	units per 1,000 persons
Daily newspapers	1995	circulation	121,500[10]	11[10]
Radio	1995	receivers	450,000	39
Television	1995	receivers	550,000	48
Telephones	1995	main lines	60,000	5.2
Cellular telephones	1995	subscribers	2,000	0.2

Education and health

Educational attainment: n.a. *Literacy* (1990): percentage of population age 15 and over literate 41.7%; males literate 55.6%; females literate 28.5%.

Education (1990–91)

	schools	teachers	students	student/ teacher ratio
Primary (age 7–10)	6,308[11]	31,062	990,155	31.9
Secondary (age 11–16)	5,276[11]	5,138[12]	166,812	...
Voc., teacher tr.	...	566[12]	19,687	...
Higher	1[11]	439	6,534	14.9

Health (1990): physicians 662 (1 per 15,136 persons); hospital beds 11,857 (1 per 845 persons); infant mortality rate per 1,000 live births (1995) 142.1.
Food (1995): daily per capita caloric intake 1,927 (vegetable products 93%, animal products 7%); 82% of FAO recommended minimum requirement.

Military

Total active duty personnel (1997): 98,000 (army 89.5%, navy 1.4%, air force 9.1%). *Military expenditure as percentage of GNP* (1995): 3.1% (world 2.8%); per capita expenditure U.S.$22.

[1]National unity government sworn in April 11, 1997, lacked effective control in much of eastern and southern Angola in November 1997. [2]President assisted by Prime Minister. [3]In July 1995 a readjusted Kwanza, equivalent to 1,000 New Kwanza (NKz) was introduced; previously in September 1990 the Kwanza (Kz) was replaced at par, by the New Kwanza (NKz). [4]Unified national estimates and projections based on sample surveys, partial censuses, and analysis of provincial vital statistics. [5]Detail does not add to total given because of rounding. [6]1983. [7]1984. [8]1989. [9]TAAG Airline only. [10]Circulation for four newspapers only. [11]1985–86. [12]1989–90.

Internet resources for further information:
- **Official Home Page of the Republic of Angola http://www.angola.org/**

Antigua and Barbuda

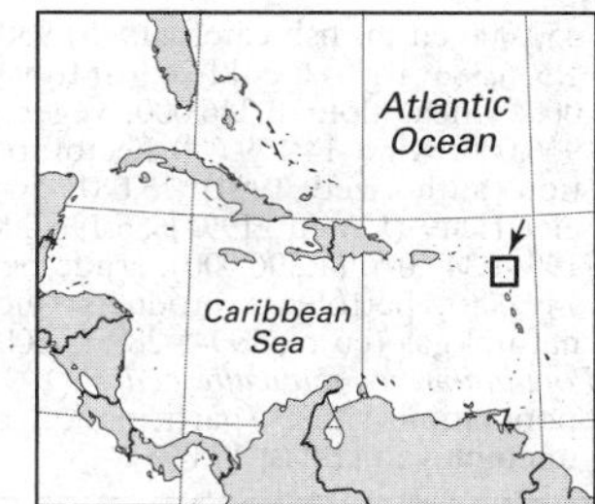

Official name: Antigua and Barbuda.
Form of government: constitutional monarchy with two legislative houses (Senate [17]; House of Representatives [17[1]]).
Chief of state: British Monarch represented by Governor-General.
Head of government: Prime Minister.
Capital: Saint John's.
Official language: English.
Official religion: none.
Monetary unit: 1 Eastern Caribbean dollar (EC$) = 100 cents; valuation (Oct. 3, 1997) 1 U.S.$ = EC$2.70; 1 £ = EC$4.35.

Area and population

	area		population
	sq mi	sq km	1991 census
Parishes[2]			
Saint George	9.3	24.1	4,473
Saint John's	28.5	73.8	35,635
Saint Mary	22.0	57.0	5,303
Saint Paul	18.5	47.9	6,117
Saint Peter	12.7	32.9	3,622
Saint Phillip	17.0	44.0	2,964
Islands[2]			
Barbuda	62.0	160.6	1,241
Redonda	0.5	1.3	[3]
TOTAL	170.5	441.6	59,355[4]

Demography

Population (1997): 64,500[5].
Density (1997): persons per sq mi 378.3, persons per sq km 146.1.
Urban-rural (1995): urban 36.5%; rural 63.5%.
Sex distribution (1991): male 48.20%; female 51.80%.
Age breakdown (1991): under 15, 30.4%; 15–29, 27.8%; 30–44, 20.5%; 45–59, 10.2%; 60–74, 7.7%; 75 and over, 3.4%.
Population projection: (2000) 65,000; (2010) 66,000.
Doubling time: 50 years.
Ethnic composition (1994): black 91.3%; mixed 3.7%; white 2.4%; Syrian/Lebanese 0.6%; Indo-Pakistani 0.4%; Amerindian 0.3%; other 1.3%.
Religious affiliation (1991): Protestant 73.7%, of which Anglican 32.1%, Moravian 12.0%, Methodist 9.1%, Seventh-day Adventist 8.8%; Roman Catholic 10.8%; Jehovah's Witness 1.2%; Rastafarian 0.8%; other religion/no religion/not stated 13.5%.
Major cities (1991): Saint John's 22,342.[6]

Vital statistics

Birth rate per 1,000 population (1995): 20.9 (world avg. 25.0); (1988) legitimate 23.4%; illegitimate 76.6%.
Death rate per 1,000 population (1995): 6.7 (world avg. 9.3).
Natural increase rate per 1,000 population (1995): 14.2 (world avg. 15.7).
Total fertility rate (avg. births per childbearing woman; 1996): 1.7.
Marriage rate per 1,000 population (1988): 4.9.
Divorce rate per 1,000 population (1988): 0.2.
Life expectancy at birth (1996): male 71.5 years; female 75.8 years.
Major causes of death per 100,000 population (1988): diseases of the circulatory system 237.5; malignant neoplasms (cancers) 44.5; diseases of the respiratory system 44.5; endocrine and metabolic disorders 25.4; ill-defined conditions 68.6.

National economy

Budget (1995). Revenue: EC$289,600,000 (taxes on international transactions 35.2%, of which import duties 15.8%; consumption taxes 26.6%; nontax revenue 13.4%; income taxes 9.8%). Expenditures: EC$355,400,000 (current expenditures 86.1%; development expenditures 13.9%).
Public debt (external, outstanding; end of 1995): U.S.$235,500,000.
Production (metric tons except as noted). Agriculture, forestry, fishing (1996): tropical fruit (including papayas, guavas, soursops, and oranges) 5,500, mangoes 1,300, eggplants 250, lemons and limes 220, carrots 210, "Antiguan Black" pineapples 150; livestock (number of live animals) 15,700 cattle, 12,200 sheep; roundwood, n.a.; fish catch (1995) 470. Mining and quarrying: crushed stone for local use. Manufacturing (1994): beer and malt 166,000 cases; T-shirts 179,000 units; other manufactures include cement, handicrafts, small appliances, and electronic components. Construction (1995): gross value of building applications EC$154,000,000. Energy production (consumption): electricity (kW-hr; 1994) 117,500,000 (105,700,000); coal, none (none); crude petroleum, none (none); petroleum products (metric tons; 1994) negligible (101,000); natural gas, none (none).
Population economically active (1991): total 26,753; activity rate of total population 45.1% (participation rates: ages 15–64, 69.7%; female 45.6%; unemployed [1994] 6.7%).

Price and earnings indexes (1990 = 100)

	1990	1991	1992	1993	1994	1995
Consumer price index	100.0	105.7	108.9	112.2	116.2	119.5
Weekly earnings index[7]	100.0	100.0	112.7	...	...	...

Household income and expenditure. Average household size (1991) 3.2; income per household: n.a.; sources of income: n.a.; expenditure (1974)[8]: food and nonalcoholic beverages 42.9%, housing 23.3%, transportation 10.0%, clothing and footwear 7.5%, energy 5.5%, alcoholic beverages and tobacco 3.6%, other 7.2%.
Gross national product (at current market prices; 1994): U.S.$453,000,000 (U.S.$6,970 per capita).

Structure of gross domestic product and labour force

	1995		1991	
	in value EC$'000,000	% of total value	labour force	% of labour force
Agriculture, fishing	43.5	3.2	1,040	3.9
Quarrying	20.6	1.5	64	0.2
Manufacturing	22.7	1.7	1,444	5.4
Construction	119.3	8.8	3,109	11.6
Public utilities	52.9	3.9	435	1.6
Transp. and commun.	215.8	15.9	2,395	9.0
Trade, restaurants, and hotels	255.8	18.9	8,524	31.9
Finance, real estate	171.5	12.6	1,454	5.4
Pub. admin., defense	217.9	16.1	2,572	9.6
Services	81.2	6.0	5,207	19.5
Other	154.0[9]	11.4[9]	509	1.9
TOTAL	1,355.2	100.0	26,753	100.0

Land use (1994): forested 11.0%; meadows and pastures 9.0%; agricultural and under permanent cultivation 18.0%; other 62.0%.
Tourism: receipts from visitors (1995) U.S.$328,500,000; expenditures by nationals abroad (1994) U.S.$25,000,000.

Foreign trade[10]

Balance of trade (current prices)

	1989	1990	1991	1992	1993	1994
U.S.$'000,000	−316	−325	−326	−347	−375	−403
% of total	83.4%	83.0%	76.7%	71.4%	78.6%	83.1%

Imports (1992): U.S.$417,000,000 ([11]agricultural products 9.0%, other [including petroleum products for reexport] 91.0%). *Major import sources* (1989)[11]: United States 27.0%; United Kingdom 16.0%; Canada 4.0%; OECS 3.0%; Italy 3.0%.
Exports (1992): U.S.$70,000,000 ([11]reexports [significantly, petroleum products reexported to neighbouring islands] 78.0%, domestic exports 22.0%). *Major export destinations* (1989)[11]: United States 41.0%; United Kingdom 19.0%; Germany 19.0%.

Transport and communications

Transport. Railroads[12]. Roads (1995): total length 152 mi, 245 km (paved 56%). Vehicles (1995): passenger cars 13,588; trucks and buses 1,342. Merchant marine (1992): vessels (100 gross tons and over) 292; total deadweight tonnage 997,381. Air transport (1993): passenger-mi 140,000,000, passenger-km 225,000,000; (1991) short ton-mi cargo 137,000, metric ton-km cargo 200,000; airports (1996) with scheduled flights 2.

Communications

Medium	date	unit	number	units per 1,000 persons
Daily newspapers	1994	circulation	—	—
Radio	1996	receivers	50,000	776
Television	1995	receivers	28,000	435
Telephones	1995	main lines	20,000	311

Education and health

Educational attainment (1991). Percentage of population age 25 and over having: no formal schooling 1.1%; primary education 50.5%; secondary 33.4%; higher (not university) 5.4%; university 6.2%; other/unknown 3.4%.
Literacy (1990): total population age 15 and over literate 40,000 (90.0%).

Education (1994–95)

	schools	teachers	students	student/teacher ratio
Primary (age 5–11)	43[13]	439	11,506	26.2
Secondary (age 12–16)	12[13]	277	4,294	15.5
Higher	1	16	46	2.9

Health (1992): physicians 59 (1 per 1,083 persons); hospital beds 369 (1 per 173 persons); infant mortality rate per 1,000 live births (1996) 17.2.
Food (1995): daily per capita caloric intake 2,406 (vegetable products 65%, animal products 35%); 102% of FAO recommended minimum requirement.

Military

Total active duty personnel (1995): a 100-member defense force is part of the Eastern Caribbean regional security system.

[1]Directly elected seats only; attorney general and speaker may serve ex officio if they are not elected to House of Representatives. [2]Community councils on Antigua and the local government council on Barbuda are the organs of local government. [3]Uninhabited. [4]Unadjusted de jure population excluding institutionalized population; de jure population adjusted for undercount (including institutionalized population) is 63,896. [5]Excludes evacuees from Montserrat. [6]Large settlements include (1991): All Saints 2,230; Liberta 1,473; Codrington 814. [7]Construction sector. [8]Weights of consumer price index components. [9]Net indirect taxes less imputed bank service charges. [10]Exports f.o.b.; imports c.i.f. [11]Estimated percentages. [12]Privately owned tracks are mostly nonoperative. [13]1991–92.

Internet resources for further information:
- **Antigua and Barbuda High Commission (London) http://antigua-barbuda.com/**

Argentina

Official name: República Argentina (Argentine Republic).
Form of government: federal republic with two legislative houses (Senate [72]; Chamber of Deputies [257]).
Head of state and government: President[1].
Capital: Buenos Aires.
Official language: Spanish.
Official religion: Roman Catholicism.
Monetary unit: 1 peso (pl. pesos)[2] (Arg$) = 100 centavos; valuation (Oct. 3, 1997) 1 U.S.$ = Arg$1.00; 1 £ = Arg$1.61.

Area and population

		area		population
				1995
Provinces	Capitals	sq mi	sq km	estimate
Buenos Aires	La Plata	118,754	307,571	13,333,670
Catamarca	Catamarca	39,615	102,602	287,567
Chaco	Resistencia	38,469	99,633	890,548
Chubut	Rawson	86,752	224,686	396,800
Córdoba	Córdoba	63,831	165,321	2,914,972
Corrientes	Corrientes	34,054	88,199	852,685
Entre Ríos	Paraná	30,418	78,781	1,063,416
Formosa	Formosa	27,825	72,066	444,367
Jujuy	San Salvador de Jujuy	20,548	53,219	551,804
La Pampa	Santa Rosa	55,382	143,440	280,876
La Rioja	La Rioja	34,626	89,680	246,158
Mendoza	Mendoza	57,462	148,827	1,500,818
Misiones	Posadas	11,506	29,801	877,904
Neuquén	Neuquén	36,324	94,078	460,395
Río Negro	Viedma	78,384	203,013	556,674
Salta	Salta	60,034	155,488	952,174
San Juan	San Juan	34,614	89,651	550,641
San Luis	San Luis	29,633	76,748	320,109
Santa Cruz	Río Gallegos	94,187	243,943	180,115
Santa Fe	Santa Fe	51,354	133,007	2,934,220
Santiago del Estero	Santiago del Estero	52,645	136,351	696,092
Tierra del Fuego[3]	Ushuaia	8,210	21,263	96,917
Tucumán	San Miguel de Tucumán	8,697	22,524	1,209,716
Other federal entity				
Distrito Federal	Buenos Aires	77	200	2,988,006
TOTAL		1,073,399[4]	2,780,092	34,586,635[4]

Demography

Population (1997): 35,409,000[5].
Density (1997): persons per sq mi 33.0, persons per sq km 12.7.
Urban-rural (1991): urban 86.9%; rural 13.1%.
Sex distribution (1995): male 49.06%; female 50.94%.
Age breakdown (1995): under 15, 28.9%; 15–29, 24.8%; 30–44, 19.0%; 45–59, 14.1%; 60–74, 9.8%; 75 and over, 3.4%.
Population projection: (2000) 36,648,000; (2010) 40,755,000.
Ethnic composition (1986): European 85%; mestizo and Amerindian 15%.
Religious affiliation (1995): Roman Catholic 90.9%; other 9.1%.
Major cities (1991)[6]: Buenos Aires (1995) 2,988,006 (Greater Buenos Aires 11,295,555); Greater Córdoba 1,208,713; Greater Rosario 1,118,984.

Vital statistics

Birth rate per 1,000 population (1995–2000): 19.9 (world avg. 25.0).
Death rate per 1,000 population (1995–2000): 7.9 (world avg. 9.3).
Natural increase rate per 1,000 population (1995–2000): 12.0 (world avg. 15.7).
Total fertility rate (avg. births per childbearing woman; 1995–2000): 2.6.
Life expectancy at birth (1995–2000): male 69.6 years; female 76.8 years.
Major causes of death per 100,000 population (1993): heart disease 247.1; neoplasms (cancers) 143.5; diseases of the brain 75.8; accidents 32.8.

National economy

Budget (1995). Revenue: U.S.$55,650,600,000 (current revenue 96.9%, of which tax revenue 90.0%, nontax revenue 6.5%, other 0.4%; capital revenue 3.1%). Expenditure: U.S.$55,560,600,000 (1989; social security 35.3%; economic services 16.0%; education 9.9%; defense 9.9%; debt service 7.4%).
Public debt (external, outstanding; 1995): U.S.$62,181,000,000.
Gross national product (1995): U.S.$278,431,000,000 (U.S.$8,030 per capita).

Structure of gross domestic product and labour force

	1994		1980	
	in value Arg$'000,000[2]	% of total value	labour force	% of labour force
Agriculture	13,665.7	4.8	1,200,992	12.0
Mining	4,672.7	1.7	47,171	0.5
Manufacturing	56,443.3	20.0	1,985,995	19.9
Construction	18,858.5	6.7	1,003,175	10.1
Public utilities	4,735.5	1.7	103,256	1.0
Transp. and commun.	15,234.5	5.4	460,476	4.6
Trade	41,132.0	14.6	1,702,080	17.0
Finance	50,267.0	17.8	395,704	4.0
Pub. admin., defense; Services	71,970.8	25.6	2,399,039	24.0
Other	4,665.0[7]	1.7[7]	691,302	6.9
TOTAL	281,645.0[4]	100.0	9,989,190	100.0

Production (metric tons except as noted). Agriculture, forestry, fishing (1996): sugarcane 17,600,000, wheat 15,200,000, soybeans 12,654,000, corn (maize) 10,466,000, sunflower seeds 5,300,000, grapes 2,728,000; livestock (number of live animals) 54,000,000 cattle, 17,000,000 sheep; roundwood (1995) 11,450,000 cu m; fish catch (1995) 930,592. Mining and quarrying (1995): silver 1,536,386 troy oz; gold 26,910 troy oz. Manufacturing (1994): cement 6,306,000; wheat flour 3,346,000; vegetable oil 3,027,000; sugar 1,110,000; paper 966,000; wine 14,179,000 hectolitres; beer 11,293,000 hectolitres. Construction (authorized; 1994): 15,081,456 sq m. Energy production (consumption): electricity (kW-hr; 1994) 66,196,000,000 (67,162,000,000); coal (metric tons; 1994) 348,000 (1,596,000); crude petroleum (barrels; 1994) 245,053,000 (173,749,000); petroleum products (metric tons; 1994) 21,499,000 (19,743,000); natural gas (cu m; 1994) 28,675,000,000 (31,293,000,000).
Population economically active (1995): total 14,345,171; activity rate of total population 41.5% (participation rates: ages 15–64, 64.5%; female 36.9%; unemployed [1996] 17.0%).

Price and earnings indexes (1990 = 100)[2]

	1991	1992	1993	1994	1995	1996
Consumer price index	272.0	339.0	375.0	391.0	404.0	405.0
Monthly earnings index[8]	249.0	324.0	365.0	390.0	384.0	386.0

Household size and expenditure. Average household size (1991) 3.8; expenditure (1985–86): food 38.2%, transportation 11.6%, housing 9.3%, energy 9.0%, clothing 8.0%, health 7.9%, recreation 7.5%, other 8.5%.
Tourism (1995): receipts U.S.$4,306,000,000; expenditures U.S.$2,067,000,000.
Land use (1994): forest 18.6%; pasture 51.9%; agriculture 9.9%; other 19.6%.

Foreign trade[9]

Balance of trade (current prices)

	1991	1992	1993	1994	1995	1996
U.S.$'000,000	+4,572	−1,388	−1,576	−4,002	+2,985	+1,621
% of total	23.6%	5.4%	5.7%	11.3%	7.7%	3.5%

Imports (1994): U.S.$21,590,000,000 (machinery and transport equipment 52.0%, chemical products 14.0%, manufactured products 12.9%, food products and live animals 4.6%). *Major import sources:* U.S. 22.8%; Brazil 19.9%; Italy 6.6%; Germany 6.4%; France 5.0%; Chile 3.9%; Uruguay 3.7%.
Exports (1994): U.S.$15,839,000,000 (food products and live animals 35.2%, manufactured products 12.5%, machinery and transport equipment 11.2%, petroleum and petroleum products 10.4%, vegetable and animal oils 9.6%, chemical products 5.9%). *Major export destinations:* Brazil 23.1%; U.S. 11.0%; The Netherlands 7.5%; Chile 6.3%; Italy 4.1%; Uruguay 4.1%.

Transport and communications

Transport. Railroads (1995): route length 33,821 km; passenger-km (1994) 6,460,159,000; metric ton-km cargo 7,613,000,000. Roads (1995): total length 134,278 mi, 216,100 km (paved 29%). Vehicles (1995): passenger cars 4,665,329; commercial vehicles and buses 1,181,569. Air transport (1995): passenger-km 11,785,000,000; metric ton-km cargo 1,330,000,000; airports (1997) with scheduled flights 39.

Communications

Medium	date	unit	number	units per 1,000 persons
Daily newspapers	1992	circulation	4,780,000	137
Radio	1996	receivers	21,500,000	614
Television	1995	receivers	12,000,000	347
Telephones	1995	main lines	5,531,700	160
Cellular telephones	1995	subscribers	340,700	9.9
Facsimile machines	1995	units	50,000	1.4
Personal computers	1995	units	850,000	25

Education and health

Educational attainment (1991). Percentage of population age 25 and over having: no formal schooling 5.7%; less than primary education 22.3%; primary 34.6%; incomplete secondary 12.5%; complete secondary 12.8%; higher 12.0%. *Literacy* (1995): percentage of total population age 15 and over literate 96.2%; males literate 96.2%; females literate 96.2%.

Education (1994–95)

	schools	teachers	students	student/ teacher ratio
Primary (age 6–12)	25,448	286,885	5,126,307	17.9
Secondary (age 13–17)[10]	7,239	233,564	2,238,091	9.6
Higher	1,705	118,695	926,793	7.8

Health (1992): physicians 88,800 (1 per 376 persons); hospital beds 147,000 (1 per 227 persons); infant mortality rate (1995–2000) 22.0.
Food (1995): daily per capita caloric intake 3,110 (vegetable products 70%, animal products 30%); 131% of FAO recommended minimum requirement.

Military

Total active duty personnel (1997): 73,000 (army 56.2%, navy 27.4%, air force 16.4%). *Military expenditure as percentage of GNP* (1995): 1.7% (world 2.8%); per capita expenditure U.S.$137.

[1]Assisted by a ministerial coordinator who exercises general administration of the country. [2]On Jan. 1, 1992, the austral was replaced by the peso at a ratio of 10,000 to 1. [3]Area of Tierra del Fuego (province since 1991) excludes claims to British-held islands in the South Atlantic Ocean. [4]Detail does not add to total given because of rounding. [5]Includes 2 million illegal immigrants from Bolivia and Paraguay. [6]*Municipios.* [7]Import duties. [8]Manufacturing sector only. [9]Import figures are f.o.b. in balance of trade and c.i.f. in commodities and trading partners. [10]Secondary includes vocational and teacher training.

Internet resources for further information:
- **National Institute of Statistics and Censuses (Spanish only) http://www.indec.mecon.ar/default.htm**

Armenia

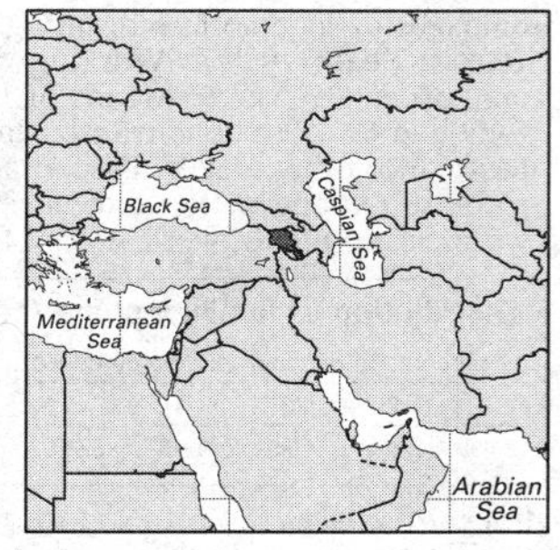

Official name: Hayastani Hanrapetut'yun (Republic of Armenia).
Form of government: unitary multiparty republic with a single legislative body (National Assembly [190]).
Head of state: President.
Head of government: Prime Minister.
Capital: Yerevan.
Official language: Armenian.
Official religion: none[1].
Monetary unit[2]: 1 dram = 100 lumas; valuation (Oct. 3, 1997) official, 1 U.S.$ = 501.10 drams; 1 £ = 807.77 drams.

Area and population	area		population
			1995
Regions	sq mi	sq km	estimate
Aragatsotn	1,064	2,755	161,700
Ararat	812	2,104	302,100
Armavir	479	1,241	314,000
Gegharkunik	1,573	4,073	255,800
Lori	1,464	3,791	391,700
Kotayk	811	2,100	327,100
Shirak	1,034	2,679	357,600
Syunik	1,739	4,505	161,400
Vayots-Dzor	891	2,308	69,700
Tavush	1,043	2,702	170,000
Cities			
Yerevan	81	210	1,248,700
Other	493[3]	1,278[3]	
TOTAL	11,484[4]	29,743[4, 5]	3,759,800[5]

Demography

Population (1997): 3,773,000 (de jure); *c.* 3,000,000 (de facto)[6].
Density (1997): persons per sq mi 327.3, persons per sq km 126.4.
Urban-rural (1995): urban 67.6%; rural 32.4%.
Sex distribution (1994): male 48.42%; female 51.58%.
Age breakdown (1993): under 15, 30.1%; 15–29, 24.4%; 30–44, 22.4%; 45–59, 12.3%; 60–74, 8.6%; 75 and over, 2.2%.
Population projection: (2000) 3,787,000; (2010) 3,892,000.
Doubling time: n.a.; doubling time exceeds 100 years.
Ethnic composition (1989): Armenian 93.3%; Azerbaijani 2.6%; other 4.1%.
Religious affiliation: believers are predominantly Armenian Apostolic.
Major cities (1991): Yerevan 1,283,000; Gyumri 163,000[7]; Kirovakan 76,000[7].

Vital statistics

Birth rate per 1,000 population (1995): 13.3 (world avg. 25.0); (1993) legitimate 86.0%; illegitimate 14.0%.
Death rate per 1,000 population (1995): 6.5 (world avg. 9.3).
Natural increase rate per 1,000 population (1995): 6.8 (world avg. 15.7).
Total fertility rate (avg. births per childbearing woman; 1994): 2.0.
Marriage rate per 1,000 population (1995): 4.2.
Divorce rate per 1,000 population (1995): 0.8.
Life expectancy at birth (1994): male 67.0 years; female 73.7 years.
Major causes of death per 100,000 population (1993): circulatory diseases 395.6; cancers 78.6; respiratory diseases 38.3; accidents and violence 24.2.

National economy

Budget (1995). Revenue: 103,834,000,000 drams (tax revenue 64.0%, of which enterprise profits tax 23.0%, value-added tax 16.4%, payroll tax 10.3%, income tax 6.6%, other taxes 7.7%; grants 18.3%; nontax 17.7%). Expenditures: 155,492,000,000 drams (current expenditures 75.6%, of which pensions and social welfare 16.0%, interest 10.4%, wages 8.7%, health and education 8.3%, other 32.3%[8]; capital expenditure and net lending 24.4%).
Land use (1994): forest 13.4%; pasture 23.1%; agriculture 20.1%; other 43.4%.
Gross national product (1995)[9]: U.S.$2,752,000,000 (U.S.$730 per capita).

Structure of net material product and labour force	1995			
	in value '000,000 drams	% of total value	labour force	% of labour force
Agriculture	167,475	32.7	492,000	31.5
Manufacturing, mining Public utilities	164,834	31.6	352,000	22.5
Construction	48,368	9.3	96,000	6.2
Transp. and commun.	17,687	3.4	27,000	1.7
Trade	42,927	8.2	63,000	4.0
Pub. admin., defense	—	—	29,000	1.9
Services	—	—	341,000	21.8
Other	80,994	14.8	162,000[10]	10.4[10]
TOTAL	522,285	100.0	1,562,000	100.0

Production (metric tons except as noted). Agriculture, forestry, fishing (1996): potatoes 423,163, tomatoes 180,361, wheat 168,000, grapes 158,200, apples 118,000, barley 105,000; livestock (number of live animals) 561,000 sheep and goats, 496,500 cattle, 79,000 pigs, 2,700,000 poultry; roundwood (1991) 44,100 cu m; fish catch (1995) 4,500. Mining and quarrying (1995): copper 10,000,000; perlite 200,000; molybdenum 5,000. Manufacturing (value in '000,000 drams; 1994): machine-building and metalworking equipment 18,436; food products 13,842; chemicals 5,330; metals 5,259; construction materials 3,154; textiles 2,500; leather products 2,335. Construction (1995): 284,000 sq m.

Energy production (consumption): electricity (kW-hr; 1995) 5,560,000,000 (5,674,000,000); coal (metric tons; 1994) none (36,000); crude petroleum (barrels; 1994) none (1,195,000); petroleum products (metric tons; 1994) none (356,000); natural gas (cu m; 1994) none (883,773,000).
Population economically active (1995): total 1,562,000; activity rate of total population 41.5% (1994; participation rates: ages 16–59 [male], 16–54 [female] 75.4%; female [1994] 45.0%; unemployed 4.3%).

Price and earnings indexes (1992 = 100)	1992	1993	1994	1995	1996
Consumer price index	100	1,075	86,355	237,947	282,384
Earnings index	...	...	...	...	...

Household income and expenditure. Average household size (1989) 4.7; income per household (1994) 47,352 drams (U.S.$153); sources of income (1994): wages and salaries 52.3%, agricultural income 7.7%, other 40.0%; expenditure (1994): goods and services 78.0%, taxes and payments to government 22.0%.

Foreign trade

Balance of trade (current prices)	1993	1994	1995	1996
'000,000 drams	−20.0	−128.3	−354.5	−468.1
% of total	5.1%	22.9%	39.6%	44.6%

Imports (1995): U.S.$672,900,000 (food products 33.4%, mineral products 33.1%, jewelry 4.3%, other 29.2%). *Major import sources:* former Soviet Union (FSU) 49.6%, of which Russia 19.9%, Turkmenistan 19.2%, other FSU 10.6%; non-FSU 50.4%, of which U.S., Iran, France, and Belgium are the biggest sources.
Exports (1995): U.S.$270,900,000 (jewelry 33.1%, machinery and equipment 14.7%, mineral products 10.6%). *Major export destinations:* FSU 61.7%, of which Russia 32.6%, Turkmenistan 25.3%, other FSU 3.8%; non-FSU 38.3%, of which Iran 13.0%, Belgium 11.3%, Germany 3.7%.

Transport and communications

Transport. Railroads (1996): length 515 mi, 829 km; (1995) passenger-mi 196,000,000, passenger-km 316,000,000; short ton-mi cargo 3,345,000,000, metric ton-km cargo 4,884,000,000. Roads (1996): length 4,600 mi, 7,500 km (paved 98%). Vehicles (1991): passenger cars 2,782, trucks and buses 12,034. Air transport (1990): passenger-mi 3,453,000,000, passenger-km 5,556,900,000; short ton-mi cargo 34,000,000, metric ton-km cargo 49,000,000; airports (1997) 1.

Communications Medium	date	unit	number	units per 1,000 persons
Daily newspapers	1995	circulation	80,000	23
Television	1995	receivers	900,000	241
Telephones	1995	main lines	583,000	155
Facsimile machines	1995	units	300	0.1

Education and health

Educational attainment (1989). Percentage of population age 25 and over having: primary education or no formal schooling 7.4%; some secondary 18.6%; completed secondary and some postsecondary 57.7%; higher 13.8%.
Literacy (1989): total population age 15 and over literate 98.8%; males literate 99.4%; females literate 98.1%.

Education (1994–95)	schools	teachers	students	student/ teacher ratio
Primary (age 6–13) Secondary (age 14–17)	1,400	54,000[8]	574,500	11.0[8]
Voc., teacher tr.	69[8]	...	25,200[8]	...
Higher	14	...	36,500	...

Health (1994): physicians 13,000 (1 per 288 persons); hospital beds 30,000 (1 per 125 persons); infant mortality rate 14.7.

Military

Total active duty personnel (1997): *c.* 58,600 (army 100%). *Military expenditure as percentage of GNP* (1995): 0.9% (world 2.8%); per capita expenditure: U.S.$23.

[1]The constitution provides for the right to practice the religion of one's choice. In practice, the law imposes restrictions on religious freedom. The 1991 Law on Religious Organizations establishes the separation of church and state, but recognizes the Armenian Apostolic Church (the Armenian Orthodox Church) as having special status. The law requires all nonapostolic religious denominations to register with the Ministry of Justice and prohibits proselytizing. [2]The Armenian dram was introduced on Nov. 22, 1993, to replace the Russian ruble, at a rate of 200 Russian rubles to 1 dram. [3]Area of Lake Sevan. [4]Armenia claims the nearby Naxçivan (Nagorno-Karabakh) region (area 4,400 sq km; pop. [1997 est.] 150,000), which has been part of Azerbaijan since 1923. [5]Detail does not add to total given because of rounding. [6]About ⅕ of Armenia's population has left the country since 1993 because of an energy crisis. [7]1989; reduced in population by evacuation following Dec. 7, 1988, earthquake. [8]1993–94. [9]Ruble-area national accounts and GNP data are very speculative. [10]Includes 106,000 unemployed and 56,000 undistributed employed.

Internet resources for further information:
- **Armenia Human Development Report 1996 http://www.undp.org/undp/rbec/nhdr/1996/armenia/**
- **Trade Point Armenia Home Page http://tpa-gw1.amilink.net/**

Australia

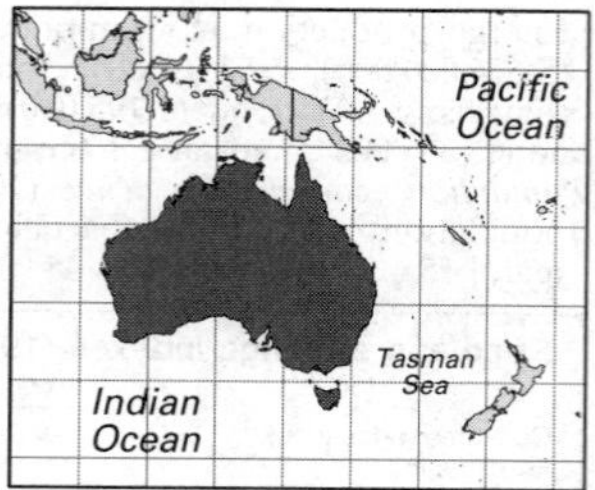

Official name: Commonwealth of Australia.
Form of government: federal parliamentary state (formally a constitutional monarchy) with two legislative houses (Senate [76]; House of Representatives [148]).
Chief of state: British Monarch represented by Governor-General.
Head of government: Prime Minister.
Capital: Canberra.
Official language: English.
Official religion: none.
Monetary unit: 1 Australian dollar ($A) = 100 cents; valuation (Oct. 3, 1997) 1 U.S.$ = $A 1.37; 1 £ = $A 2.21.

Area and population

		area		population
States	**Capitals**	sq mi	sq km	1996 census
New South Wales	Sydney	309,500	801,600	6,038,696
Queensland	Brisbane	666,900	1,727,200	3,368,850
South Australia	Adelaide	379,900	984,000	1,427,936
Tasmania	Hobart	26,200	67,800	459,659
Victoria	Melbourne	87,900	227,600	4,373,520
Western Australia	Perth	975,100	2,525,500	1,726,095
Territories				
Australian Capital Territory	Canberra	900	2,400	299,243
Northern Territory	Darwin	519,800	1,346,200	195,101
TOTAL		2,966,200	7,682,300	17,892,423[1]

Demography

Population (1997): 18,508,000.
Density (1997): persons per sq mi 6.2, persons per sq km 2.4.
Urban-rural (1996): urban 85.0%; rural 15.0%.
Sex distribution (1996): male 49.46%; female 50.54%.
Age breakdown (1996): under 15, 21.6%; 15–24, 14.5%; 25–44, 30.8%; 45–64, 21.0%; 65 and over, 12.1%.
Population projection: (2000) 19,058,000; (2010) 20,830,000.
Doubling time: 99 years.
Ethnic composition (1996): white 95.2%; aboriginal 2.0%; Asian 1.3%; other 1.5%.
Religious affiliation (1991): Christian 74.0%, of which Roman Catholic 27.3%, Anglican Church of Australia 23.8%, other Protestant 20.1% (Uniting Church and Methodist 8.2%, Presbyterian 4.3%), Orthodox 2.8%; Muslim 0.9%; Buddhist 0.8%; Jewish 0.4%; no religion 12.9%; other 11.0%.
Major cities (1995): Sydney 3,772,700; Melbourne 3,218,100; Brisbane 1,489,-100; Perth 1,262,600; Adelaide 1,081,000; Newcastle 466,000; Canberra-Queanbeyan 331,800; Gold Coast–Tweed 326,900; Wollongong 253,600; Hobart 194,700.
Place of birth (1996): 73.9% native-born; 26.1% foreign-born, of which Europe 12.4% (United Kingdom 6.3%[2], Italy 1.3%, Greece 0.7%, Germany 0.6%, The Netherlands 0.5%, other Europe 3.0%), Asia and Middle East 5.6%, New Zealand 1.6%, Africa, the Americas, and other 6.5%.
Mobility (1995–96). Population age 15 and over living in the same residence as in 1994: 81.6%; different residence between states, regions, and neighbourhoods 18.4%.
Households (1993–94). Total number of households 6,616,800. Average household size 2.6; 1 person 21.8%, couples only 25.8%, couples with dependent children only 23.7%, nonfamily members 12.4%, single parent with children 6.6%, other 9.7%.
Immigration (1996): permanent immigrants admitted 96,970, from United Kingdom and Ireland 12.8%, New Zealand 11.8%, China 7.6%, Vietnam 4.8%, Hong Kong 4.6%, India 4.4%, Philippines 3.9%, South Africa 3.2%, Bosnia and Herzegovina 3.2%, Yugoslavia 3.1%, Sri Lanka 2.2%. Refugee arrivals (1994–95): 13,600.

Vital statistics

Birth rate per 1,000 population (1996): 14.1 (world avg. 25.0); (1993) legitimate 75.0%; illegitimate 25.0%.
Death rate per 1,000 population (1996): 6.9 (world avg. 9.3).
Natural increase rate per 1,000 population (1996): 7.2 (world avg. 15.7).
Total fertility rate (avg. births per childbearing woman; 1996): 1.82.
Marriage rate per 1,000 population (1996): 6.0.
Divorce rate per 1,000 population (1996): 2.7.
Life expectancy at birth (1996): male 75.4 years; female 81.1 years.
Major causes of death per 100,000 population (1995): diseases of the circulatory system 296.0; cancers 190.0; respiratory diseases 52.0; accidents, poisoning, and violence 41.0; endocrine, nutritional, and metabolic diseases 23.0; digestive system diseases 21.0; nervous system diseases 17.0.

Social indicators

Educational attainment (1995). Percentage of population age 15 to 64 having: no formal schooling 0.3%; incomplete secondary education 36.3%; completed secondary 17.8%[3, 4]; postsecondary, technical, or other certificate/diploma 33.7%; university 11.9%.
Quality of working life (1995–96). Average workweek: 40.5 hours (16.8%[4] overtime). Annual rate per 100,000 workers for: accidental injury and industrial disease, 3,200[5]; death, n.a. Proportion of employed persons insured for damages or income loss resulting from: injury 100%[5]; permanent disability 100%[5]; death 100%[5]. Working days lost to industrial disputes per 1,000 employees (1995): 79. Means of transportation to work (1986): private automobile 69.4%; public transportation 10.1%; motorcycle and bicycle 3.2%; foot 6.6%; other 10.7%. Discouraged job seekers (considered by employers to be too young or too old, having language or training limitations, or no vacancies in line of work; 1995): 1.3% of labour force.

Distribution of family income (1990[6])

percentage of family income by decile

1	2	3	4	5	6	7	8	9	10 (highest)
1.4%	3.1%	4.2%	5.5%	6.9%	8.6%	10.6%	13.3%	17.2%	29.2%

Access to services (1976). Proportion of dwellings having access to: electricity 99.5%; bathroom 96.0%; flush toilet 92.2%; kitchen 97.9%; public sewer 73.4%.
Social participation. Eligible voters participating in last national election (1996): 95.8%; voting is compulsory. Population age 16 and over participating in voluntary work: n.a. Trade union membership in total workforce (1996): 31%.
Social deviance (1996). Offense rate per 100,000 population for: murder 3.8; sexual assault 78.7; assault 620.8; auto theft 672.2; unarmed robbery, burglary, and housebreaking 4,608.2; armed robbery 34.0. Incidence per 100,000 in general population of: alcoholism, n.a.; prisoners with drug offenses (1994) 8.8; suicide (1995) 13.1.
Material well-being (1995). Households possessing: automobile 85%; telephone 95%; refrigerator 99.7%; air conditioner 32.3%[7]; personal computers 23.0%[4]; washing machine 90.0%; central heating 3.9%[7]; swimming pool 10.1%[7].

National economy

Gross national product (1995): U.S.$337,909,000,000 (U.S.$18,720 per capita).

Structure of gross domestic product and labour force

	1994–95[8]		1995–96	
	in value $A '000,000	% of total value	labour force	% of labour force
Agriculture	13,592	3.3	421,900	4.7
Mining	17,983	4.4	85,300	0.9
Manufacturing	64,623	15.7	1,111,400	12.3
Construction	27,031	6.5	600,300	6.6
Public utilities	13,449	3.3	80,800	0.9
Transp. and commun.	36,978	9.0	546,700	6.0
Trade[9]	78,442	19.0	2,106,500	23.2
Finance, real estate	91,176	22.1	1,111,400	12.3
Pub. admin., defense	15,226	3.7	378,700	4.2
Services	56,324	13.6	1,844,200	20.3
Other	−2,231[10]	−0.6[10]	779,200[11]	8.6[11]
TOTAL	412,593	100.0	9,066,400	100.0

Budget (1996–97). Revenue: $A 130,160,000,000 (income tax 71.2%, of which individual 50.7%, corporate 15.1%; excise duties and sales tax 21.0%). Expenditures: $A 129,686,000,000 (social security and welfare 37.7%; health 15.0%; economic and public services 12.7%; transfers to state governments 12.9%; interest on public debt 7.5%).
Public debt (1996): $A 97,659,000,000.
Tourism (1996): receipts from visitors U.S.$8,127,500,000; expenditures by nationals abroad U.S.$5,038,800,000.

Manufacturing, mining, and construction enterprises (1994–95)[12]

	no. of establishments[13]	no. of employees	Turnover per person employed ($A '000)[13]	annual turnover ($A '000,000)
Manufacturing				
Food, beverages, and tobacco	3,514	163,100	243.4	41,010
Metal products	7,522	147,400	229.6	34,691
Machinery and equipment	8,988	202,800	178.0	38,189
Chemical, petroleum, and coal products	3,009	91,100	330.0	30,462
Printing and publishing	5,265	94,200	139.0	13,621
Miscellaneous manufacturing	5,973	54,000	102.1	5,754
Wood and paper products	3,973	63,800	174.1	11,360
Nonmetallic mineral products	1,909	39,000	225.4	8,951
Textile, clothing, footwear, and leather	4,456	76,600	124.6	9,786
Mining				
Coal, oil, and gas	254	29,600	...	17,023
Metallic minerals	261	25,700	...	11,913
Nonmetallic minerals[14]	699	8,799	...	2,240
Construction[15]	98,100	518,200	...	34,407

Production (gross value in $A '000 except as noted). Agriculture, forestry, fishing (1995–96): livestock slaughtered 6,066,400 (cattle 3,474,300, sheep and lambs 1,005,000, poultry 964,600, pigs 589,200); wheat 4,602,000, wool 2,686,-800, barley 1,347,000, sugarcane 1,319,700, cotton 851,000[16], grapes 680,600, potatoes 378,000[16], oats 311,000[16], apples 269,800[16], bananas 254,700[16], sorghum 242,000[16], oranges 214,800[16], rice 216,000[16], tomatoes 166,000[16], carrots 133,000[16], pears 73,400[16], onions 54,100, peaches 50,000[16], pineapples 43,300[16], corn (maize) 41,000, tobacco 40,000[16], cauliflower 33,700[5]; livestock (number of live animals; 1997) 121,900,000 sheep, 26,250,000 cattle, 2,410,000 pigs, 73,509,000 poultry; roundwood (1995) 22,458,000 cu m; fish catch (1995) 219,499 metric tons. Mining and quarrying (metric tons [tons of contained metal]; 1995–96): iron ore 142,936,000; bauxite 42,655,000; zinc 930,000; lead 455,000; copper 437,000; tin 8,175; gold 253,504 kg; diamonds 40,693,000 carats. Manufacturing (value added in U.S.$'000,000 except as noted; 1994): food products 10,043; transport equipment 5,860; metal products 5,234; printing and publishing 4,946; non-ferrous metals 4,624; woven woolen cloth 8,624,000 sq m[16]. Construction (buildings completed, by value in $A '000; 1995–96): new dwellings 12,105,700; alterations and additions to dwellings 2,283,500; nonresidential 10,728,400.

Retail and service enterprises (1991–92)

	no. of establishments	no. of employees	total wages and salaries ($A '000,000)	annual turnover ($A '000,000)
Retail				
Motor vehicle dealers, gasoline and tire dealers	37,305	220,661	2,572[17]	44,954
Food stores	53,166	406,299	2,461[17]	43,963[16]
Department and general stores	459	87,148	1,175[17]	11,209[16]
Clothing, fabrics, and furniture stores	21,688	91,138	965[17]	7,957[16]
Household appliances and hardware stores	14,268	75,355	629	12,588[16]
Recreational goods	...	...	...	6,299[16]
Services[5]				
Real estate agents	7,265	51,922	...	2,798.7
Architectural services	4,409	16,204	...	945.2
Surveying services	1,175	6,964	...	481.2
Consulting engineering services	5,454	28,208	...	2,325.2
Legal services	8,850	63,108	...	5,105.2
Accounting services	8,699	60,000	...	4,051.2
Computing services	4,894	30,062	...	3,928.8
Advertising services	858	9,083	...	842.1
Market research services	174	8,064	...	251.7
Business management services	686	4,933	...	506.6

Energy production (consumption): electricity (kW-hr; 1994) 167,151,000,000 (167,151,000,000); coal (metric tons; 1994) 176,078,000 (52,678,000); crude petroleum (barrels; 1994) 159,160,000 (202,490,000); petroleum products (metric tons; 1994) 33,086,000 (33,707,000); natural gas (cu m; 1994) 25,185,000,000 (17,438,000,000).

Population economically active (1995–96): total 9,066,400; activity rate of total population 49.9% (participation rates: over age 15, 63.7%; female 42.9%; unemployed 8.5%).

Price and earnings indexes (1990 = 100)

	1991	1992	1993	1994	1995	1996	1997[18]
Consumer price index	103.2	104.2	106.1	108.1	113.2	116.1	116.5
Weekly earnings index	105.1	109.3	111.3	115.0	120.8	125.7	129.9

Household income and expenditure (1993–94). Average household size 2.6; average annual income per household $A 37,700 (U.S.$27,585); sources of income: wages and salaries 72.7%, transfer payments 13.0%, self-employment 7.5%, other 6.8%; expenditure: food and beverages 18.7%, transportation and communications 15.3%, housing 13.9%, recreation 13.3%, household durable goods 6.6%, clothing and footwear 5.7%, health 4.6%, energy 2.8%, other 19.1%.

Financial aggregates

	1991	1992	1993	1994	1995	1996	1997[19]
Exchange rate, $A 1.00 per:							
U.S. dollar	0.78	0.74	0.68	0.73	0.74	0.80	0.73
£	0.44	0.42	0.45	0.48	0.47	0.51	0.46
SDR	0.53	0.50	0.49	0.53	0.50	0.55	0.54
International reserves (U.S.$)							
Total (excl. gold; '000,000)	16,535	11,208	11,102	11,285	11,896	14,534	16,189
SDRs ('000,000)	290	96	82	73	55	37	23
Reserve pos. In IMF ('000,000)	351	577	550	506	502	482	491
Foreign exchange ('000,000)	15,894	10,536	10,470	10,706	11,340	14,016	15,676
Gold ('000,000 fine troy oz)	7.93	7.93	7.90	7.90	7.9	7.9	3.16[20]
% world reserves	0.8	0.8	0.9	0.9	0.9	0.9	...
Interest and prices							
Central bank discount (%)	10.99	6.96	5.83	5.75	5.75	5.75[18]	...
Govt. bond yield (short-term; %)	9.94	7.25	5.63	7.65	7.60[20]	7.53	5.58[21]
Industrial share prices (1990 = 100)	96.4	100.3	104.7	112.9	114.2	152.0	180.3[21]
Balance of payments (U.S.$'000,000)							
Balance of visible trade	+3,529	+1,640	−29	−3,280	−4,166	−891	...
Imports, f.o.b.	38,833	41,173	42,666	50,611	57,311	60,955	15,562[18]
Exports, f.o.b.	42,362	42,813	42,637	47,331	53,145	60,064	17,599[18]
Balance of invisibles	−11,036	−10,971	−9,666	−16,364	−19,040	−15,977	−2,010[18]
Balance of payments, current account	−11,131	−11,076	−9,876	−16,717	−19,107	−15,870	−2,043[18]

Land use (1995): agricultural and under permanent cultivation 6.3%; other 93.7% (of which, meadows and pastures [1994] 54.2%).

Foreign trade

Balance of trade (current prices)

	1992	1993	1994	1995	1996	1997[21]
$A '000,000	2,850	427	−3,188	−5,803	−1,197	−312
% of total	2.5%	0.3%	2.4%	3.9%	0.8%	0.2%

Imports (1995–96): $A 77,819,000,000 (machinery 33.4%, of which office machines and automatic data-processing equipment 7.7%; basic manufactures 14.2%, of which textile yarn and fabrics 3.0%, paper and paper products 2.5%, iron and steel 1.8%; transport equipment 13.5%, of which road motor vehicles 10.2%; chemicals and related products 11.4%; mineral fuels and lubricants 5.5%; food and live animals 3.7%; crude materials [inedible] excluding fuels 2.0%; beverages and tobacco 0.6%). *Major import sources:* U.S. 22.6%; Japan 13.9%; U.K. 6.3%; Germany 6.2%; China 5.1%.

Exports (1995–96): $A 75,999,000,000 (food and live animals 20.1%, of which cereals and cereal preparations 6.5%, meat and meat preparations 4.3%, sugar, sugar preparations, and honey 2.3%, dairy products 2.2%; crude materials excluding fuels 19.4%, of which metalliferous ores and metal scrap 11.4%, textile fibres and their waste 5.3%; mineral fuels and lubricants 16.6%, of which coal, coke, and briquettes 10.3%, petroleum, petroleum products, and natural gas 4.2%; basic manufactures 12.9%). *Major export destinations:* Japan 21.6%; South Korea 8.7%; New Zealand 7.4%; U.S. 6.0%; China 5.0%; Singapore 4.7%; Taiwan 4.5%; Hong Kong 4.0%.

Trade by commodity group (1995–96)

		imports		exports	
SITC Group		U.S.$'000,000	%	U.S.$'000,000	%
00	Food and live animals	2,159	3.8	9,671	18.3
01	Beverages and tobacco	374	0.6	431	0.8
02	Crude materials, excluding fuels	1,297	2.3	10,127	19.1
03	Mineral fuels, lubricants, and related materials	2,916	5.1	8,882	16.8
04	Animal and vegetable oils, fat, and waxes	193	0.3	190	0.4
05	Chemicals and related products, n.e.s.	6,112	10.6	2,090	3.9
06	Basic manufactures	8,495	14.8	7,647	14.4
07	Machinery and transport equipment	26,939	46.9	6,764	12.8
08	Miscellaneous manufactured articles	8,096	14.1	1,877	3.5
09	Goods not classified by kind	842	1.5	5,295	10.0
TOTAL		57,423	100.0	52,974	100.0

Direction of trade (1995–96)

	imports		exports	
	U.S.$'000,000	%	U.S.$'000,000	%
Africa	361	0.6	763	1.6
Asia	21,463	37.7	28,651	58.4
Japan	8,869	15.6	11,369	23.2
South America	641	1.1	553	1.1
North and Central America	13,720	24.1	4,351	8.9
United States	12,577	22.1	3,423	7.0
Europe	15,414	27.1	6,152	12.5
EEC	14,405	25.3	5,795	11.8
Russia	27	0.05	108	0.2
Other Europe	982	1.7	249	0.5
Oceania	3,262	5.7	5,364	10.9
New Zealand	2,491	4.4	3,921	8.0
Other	2,020	3.6	3,239	6.6
TOTAL	56,881	100.0[22]	49,073	100.0

Transport and communications

Transport. Railroads[23]: route length (1995) 22,385 mi, 36,026 km; passenger journeys 407,170,000[4]; short ton-mi cargo 67,716,000,000[24, 25], metric ton-km cargo 98,864,000,000[24, 25]. Roads (1995): total length 556,145 mi, 895,030 km (paved 38.6%). Vehicles (1995): passenger cars 8,370,000; trucks and buses 2,640,300. Merchant marine (1994): vessels (150 gross tons and over) 90; total deadweight tonnage 3,499,527. Air transport (1996)[26]: passenger-mi 44,687,000,000, passenger-km 71,917,000,000; short ton-mi cargo 1,257,000,000, metric ton-km cargo 1,836,000,000; airports (1996) with scheduled flights 400.

Communications

Medium	date	unit	number	units per 1,000 persons
Daily newspapers	1994	circulation	4,600,000	258
Radio	1996	receivers	21,000,000	1,148
Television	1995	receivers	11,565,000	641
Telephones	1996	main lines	9,500,000	519
Cellular telephones	1996	subscribers	3,815,000	209
Facsimile machines	1995	units	475,000	26
Personal computers	1996	units	5,700,000	312

Education and health

Literacy (1996): total population literate, virtually 100%[27].

Education (1995)

	schools	teachers	students	student/teacher ratio
Primary (age 6–12) } Secondary (age 13–17) }	9,865	202,401	1,833,681 1,275,656	... ...
Vocational[28]	234[29]	19,210[30]	917,801	47.8
Higher	95[31]	25,916[31]	604,177	...

Health: physicians (1995–96) 45,800 (1 per 400 persons); hospital beds (1994–95) 77,494 (1 per 226 persons); infant mortality rate (1996) 5.7.

Food (1995): daily per capita caloric intake 3,068 (vegetable products 66%, animal products 34%); 115% of FAO recommended minimum requirement.

Military

Total active duty personnel (1997): 57,400 (army 44.3%, navy 24.9%, air force 30.8%). *Military expenditure as percentage of GNP* (1995): 2.5% (world 2.8%); per capita expenditure U.S.$465.

[1]Total includes 3,323 persons in nondelimited areas. [2]Includes both Northern Ireland and Republic of Ireland. [3]Completed highest level of secondary school available. [4]1994. [5]1992–93. [6]December. [7]1983. [8]At 1989–90 prices. [9]Trade includes hotels and restaurants. [10]Less imputed bank service charges. [11]Mostly unemployed. [12]Excludes operations of single-establishment enterprises employing fewer than four persons. [13]1993–94. [14]1990–91. [15]1991–92. [16]1994–95. [17]1985–86. [18]Second quarter. [19]August. [20]Fourth quarter. [21]July. [22]Detail does not add to total given because of rounding. [23]Government railways only. [24]1995–96. [25]Includes government and private freight. [26]Includes Qantas and Ansett Australia. [27]A national survey conducted in 1996 put the number of persons who had very poor literacy and numeracy skills at about 17% of the total population (age 15 to 64). [28]Includes special education. [29]1986. [30]Full-time staff. [31]1989.

Internet resources for further information:
- **Australian Bureau of Statistics http://www.abs.gov.au**

Austria

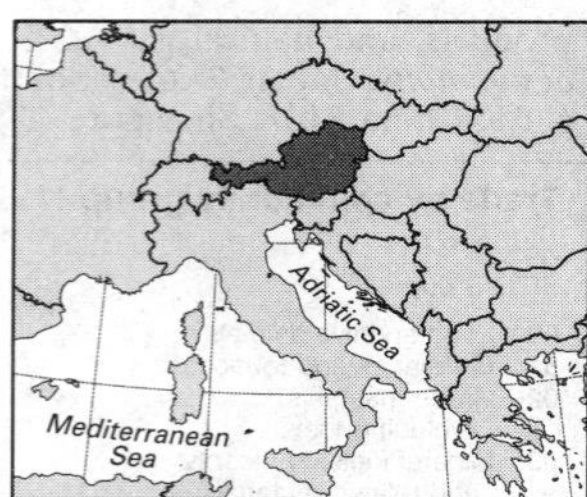

Official name: Republik Österreich (Republic of Austria).
Form of government: federal multiparty republic with two legislative houses (Federal Council [64]; National Council [183]).
Chief of state: President.
Head of government: Chancellor.
Capital: Vienna.
Official language: German.
Official religion: none.
Monetary unit: 1 Austrian Schilling (S) = 100 Groschen; valuation (Oct. 3, 1997) 1 U.S.$ = S 12.40; 1 £ = S 19.99.

Area and population

		area		population
States	Capitals	sq mi	sq km	1995 estimate
Burgenland	Eisenstadt	1,531	3,966	274,000
Kärnten	Klagenfurt	3,681	9,533	561,000
Niederösterreich	Sankt Pölten	7,403	19,174	1,518,000
Oberösterreich	Linz	4,625	11,979	1,386,000
Salzburg	Salzburg	2,763	7,155	507,000
Steiermark	Graz	6,327	16,388	1,206,000
Tirol	Innsbruck	4,883	12,648	658,000
Vorarlberg	Bregenz	1,004	2,601	343,000
Wien (Vienna)	—	160	415	1,593,000
TOTAL		32,378[1]	83,859	8,047,000[1]

Demography

Population (1997): 8,087,000.
Density (1997): persons per sq mi 249.8, persons per sq km 96.4.
Urban-rural (1991): urban 64.5%; rural 35.5%.
Sex distribution (1995): male 48.50%; female 51.50%.
Age breakdown (1995): under 15, 17.5%; 15–29, 21.4%; 30–44, 23.2%; 45–59, 18.1%; 60–74, 13.6%; 75 and over, 6.2%.
Population projection: (2000) 8,149,000; (2010) 8,283,000.
Doubling time: not applicable; population is stable.
Ethnic composition (national origin; 1991): Austrian 93.4%; citizens of former Yugoslavia 2.5%; Turkish 1.5%; German 0.7%; other 1.9%.
Religious affiliation (1991): Roman Catholic 78.0%; nonreligious and atheist 8.6%; Lutheran 4.8%; Muslim 2.0%; Jewish 0.2%; other (mostly Christian) 2.7%; unknown 3.7%.
Major cities (1991): Vienna 1,539,848; Graz 237,810; Linz 203,044; Salzburg 143,978; Innsbruck 118,112.

Vital statistics

Birth rate per 1,000 population (1996): 10.8 (world avg. 25.0); (1995) legitimate 72.6%; illegitimate 27.4%.
Death rate per 1,000 population (1996): 9.9 (world avg. 9.3).
Natural increase rate per 1,000 population (1996): 0.9 (world avg. 15.7).
Total fertility rate (avg. births per childbearing woman; 1996): 1.5.
Marriage rate per 1,000 population (1995): 5.3.
Divorce rate per 1,000 population (1995): 2.3.
Life expectancy at birth (1995): male 73.5 years; female 80.1 years.
Major causes of death per 100,000 population (1995): diseases of the circulatory system 539.9; malignant neoplasms (cancers) 243.5.

National economy

Budget (1994). Revenue: S 819,990,000,000 (tax revenue 90.8%, of which social security contributions 38.8%, individual income taxes 17.2%, value-added taxes 14.9%). Expenditures: S 915,900,000,000 (social security and welfare 46.4%; health 13.5%; education 9.6%; defense 2.2%).
National debt (end of year 1996): U.S.$127,440,000,000.
Production (metric tons except as noted). Agriculture, forestry, fishing (1995): sugar beets 2,886,000, corn (maize) 1,474,000, barley 1,065,000, wheat 1,301,000, potatoes 724,000, apples 324,000, rye 314,000, grapes 290,000, rapeseed 263,000, pears 124,000; livestock (number of live animals) 3,706,000 pigs, 2,326,000 cattle, 13,157,000 chickens; roundwood (1995) 14,405,000 cu m; fish catch (1995) 4,458. Mining and quarrying (1995): iron ore 2,107,000; magnesite 783,000; high-grade graphite 12,000. Manufacturing (value added in S '000,000,000; 1994): electrical machinery and apparatus 47.1; nonelectrical machinery and apparatus 37.3; beverages and tobacco products 31.0; chemicals and chemical products 26.8; fabricated metals 24.9; transport equipment 23.9. Construction (completed in S '000,000,000; 1994): residential 31.1; nonresidential 28.9. Energy production (consumption): electricity (kW-hr; 1995) 56,587,000,000 (54,077,000,000); coal (metric tons; 1994) 1,391,000 ([1995] 4,651,000); crude petroleum (barrels; 1995) 7,309,000 ([1994] 65,465,000); petroleum products (metric tons; 1994) 8,460,000 (10,330,000); natural gas (cu m; 1995) 1,482,000,000 (7,193,000,000).
Tourism (U.S.$'000,000; 1996): receipts U.S.$13,821; expenditures U.S.$12,105.
Population economically active (1995): total 3,808,000; activity rate of total population 47.3% (participation rates: ages 15–64 [1993] 69.3%; female 41.8%; unemployed [1996] 7.0%).

Price and earnings indexes (1990 = 100)

	1990	1991	1992	1993	1994	1995	1996
Consumer price index	100.0	103.3	107.5	111.4	114.7	117.3	119.4
Monthly earnings index	100.0	105.2	110.3	116.1	120.7	126.0	...

Gross national product (at current market prices; 1995): U.S.$216,547,000,000 (U.S.$26,890 per capita).

Structure of gross domestic product and labour force

	1995			
	in value S '000,000	% of total value	labour force	% of labour force
Agriculture	35,500	1.6	243,800	6.4
Mining	8,250	0.4	11,000	0.3
Manufacturing	466,800	20.5	806,900	21.2
Construction	169,130	7.4	330,800	8.7
Public utilities	64,450	2.8	37,000	1.0
Transp. and commun.	141,820	6.2	233,900	6.1
Trade, restaurants	375,560	16.5	756,500	19.9
Finance, real estate	464,800	20.5	338,400	8.9
Pub. admin., defense	360,030	15.8	861,400	22.6
Services	105,750	4.7		
Other	80,180[2]	3.5[2]	188,300[3]	4.9[3]
TOTAL	2,272,280[1]	100.0[1]	3,808,000	100.0

Household income and expenditure. Average household size (1995) 2.5; net median income per household (1993) S 291,930 (U.S.$25,110); expenditure (1993): food and beverages 17.4%, transportation 16.3%, housing 14.5%, cafe and hotel expenditures 10.7%.
Land use (1994): forested 39.2%; meadows and pastures 24.3%; agricultural and under permanent cultivation 18.3%; other 18.2%.

Foreign trade[4]

Balance of trade (current prices)

	1990	1991	1992	1993	1994	1995
S '000,000,000	–90.2	–112.9	–106.4	–97.7	–116.4	–88.0
% of total	8.8%	10.5%	9.8%	9.5%	10.2%	7.1%

Imports (1995): S 668,000,000,000 (machinery and transport equipment 36.9%, of which road vehicles 11.4%, electrical machinery and apparatus 6.6%; chemicals and related products 10.7%; food products 5.3%; clothing 4.7%). *Major import sources:* Germany 43.6%; Italy 8.8%; France 4.9%; United States 4.2%; Switzerland 3.8%; The Netherlands 3.4%.
Exports (1995): S 580,000,000,000 (machinery and transport equipment 39.0%, of which electrical machinery and apparatus 7.5%, road vehicles 7.3%; chemical products 9.2%; paper and paper products 6.3%; iron and steel 5.7%). *Major export destination:* Germany 38.4%; Italy 8.8%; Switzerland 5.4%; France 4.4%; Hungary 3.6%; United Kingdom 3.3%.

Transport and communications

Transport. Railroads (1995)[5]: length 5,672 km; passenger-km 10,476,000,000; (1996) metric ton-km cargo 13,908,000,000. Roads (1995): total length 130,023 km (paved 100%). Vehicles (1995): passenger cars 3,593,588; trucks and buses 300,042. Air transport[6] (1995): passenger-km 7,566,000,000; metric ton-km cargo 175,595,000; airports (1996) with scheduled flights 6.

Communications

Medium	date	unit	number	units per 1,000 persons
Daily newspapers	1994	circulation	3,736,000	465
Radio	1996	receivers	4,710,000	584
Television	1995	receivers	2,706,000	336
Telephones	1995	main lines	3,749,000	466
Cellular telephones	1995	subscribers	383,500	48
Facsimile machines	1995	units	284,700	35
Personal computers	1995	units	124,200	15

Education and health

Educational attainment (1993). Percentage of population age 25 and over having: lower-secondary education 37.5%; vocational education ending at secondary level 44.6%; completed upper secondary 6.1%; higher vocational 5.5%; higher 6.3%. *Literacy:* virtually 100%.

Education (1995–96)

	schools	teachers	students	student/teacher ratio
Primary/lower secondary (age 6–13)	4,557	65,977	649,994	9.9
Upper secondary/voc. (age 14–17)	693	39,553	295,473	7.5
Higher	44[7]	14,322[7]	222,095	15.9[7]

Health (1996): physicians 27,869[8] (1 per 289 persons); hospital beds 68,641 (1 per 117 persons); infant mortality rate per 1,000 live births 5.0.
Food (1995): daily per capita caloric intake 3,417 (vegetable products 65%, animal products 35%); 130% of FAO recommended minimum requirement.

Military

Total active duty personnel (1996): 55,800 (army 92.3%; navy, none; air force 7.7%). *Military expenditure as percentage of GNP* (1994): 1.0% (world 3.0%); per capita expenditure U.S.$232.

[1]Detail does not add to total given because of rounding. [2]Value-added tax plus import duties (S 196,990,000,000) less imputed bank service charges (S 116,810,000,000). [3]Includes 173,000 unemployed. [4]Imports c.i.f., exports f.o.b. [5]Federal railways only. [6]Austrian Airlines, Lauda Air, and Tyrolean Airways. [7]1994–95. [8]Includes 6,506 doctors in training.

Internet resources for further information:
- **Austrian Central Office of Statistics http://www.oestat.gv.at**
- **Austrian Press and Information Service (Washington, D.C.) http://www.austria.org/index.html**

Azerbaijan

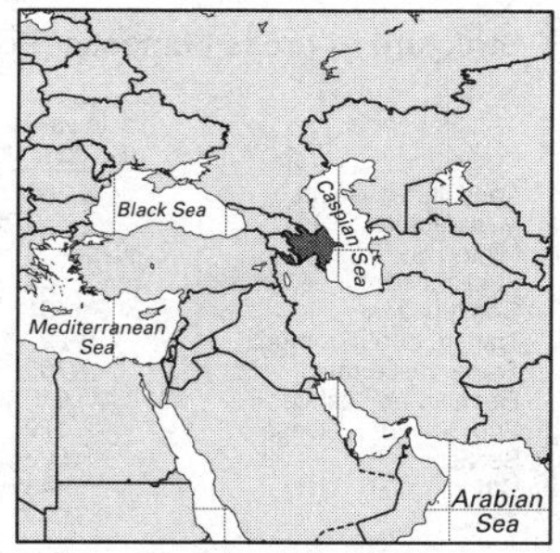

Official name: Azärbayjan Respublikasi (Azerbaijani Republic).
Form of government: federal multiparty republic with a single legislative body (National Assembly [124[1]]).
Head of state and government: President assisted by prime minister.
Capital: Baku (Azerbaijani: Bakı).
Official language: Azerbaijani.
Official religion: none.
Monetary unit: 1 manat (A.M.)[2] = 100 gopik; valuation (Oct. 3, 1997) free rate, 1 U.S.$ = A.M. 3,950; 1 £ = A.M. 6,367.

Area and population

Republics	Capitals	area sq mi	area sq km	population 1991 estimate
Naxçıvan (Nakhichevan)	Naxçıvan (Nakhichevan)	2,100	5,500	305,700
Qarabağ[3] (Nagorno Karabakh)	Xankändi (Stepanakert)	1,700	4,400	193,300
Regions under republican jurisdiction	—	29,600	76,700	4,924,300
Cities				
Baku (Bakı)	—	...	...	1,713,300
TOTAL		33,400	86,600	7,136,600

Demography

Population (1997): 7,617,000.
Density (1997): persons per sq mi 228.1, persons per sq km 88.0.
Urban-rural (1995): urban 53.0%; rural 47.0%.
Sex distribution (1995): male 49.20%; female 50.80%.
Age breakdown (1995): under 15, 33.2%; 15–29, 26.1%; 30–44, 18.1%; 45–59, 10.1%; 60–69, 5.8%; 70 and over, 6.7%.
Population projection: (2000) 7,783,800; (2010) 8,284,600.
Doubling time: 50 years.
Ethnic composition (1989): Azerbaijani 82.7%; Russian 5.6%; Armenian 5.6%; Lezgin 2.4%; Avar 0.6%; Ukrainian 0.5%; Tatar 0.4%; other 2.2%.
Religious affiliation (1997): Muslim (mostly Shīʿī) 93.3%; Russian Orthodox 1.1%; Armenian Apostolic (Orthodox) 1.1%; other 4.5%.
Major cities (1995): Baku (metro area) 2,500,000; Gäncä (formerly Kirovabad) 291,000; Sumqayıt (Sumgait) 268,000; Mingacevir (Mingechaur) 96,000.

Vital statistics

Birth rate per 1,000 population (1996): 16.9 (world avg. 25.0); (1994) legitimate 94.8%; (1994) illegitimate 5.2%.
Death rate per 1,000 population (1996): 6.5 (world avg. 9.3).
Natural increase rate per 1,000 population (1996): 10.4 (world avg. 15.7).
Total fertility rate (avg. births per childbearing woman; 1993): 2.8.
Marriage rate per 1,000 population (1994): 6.3.
Divorce rate per 1,000 population (1994): 0.8.
Life expectancy at birth (1994): male 65.2 years; female 73.9 years.
Major causes of death per 100,000 population (1994): diseases of the circulatory system 336.3; accidents, poisoning, and violence 99.1; diseases of the respiratory system 98.6; malignant neoplasms (cancers) 67.6; diseases of the digestive system 31.7; infectious and parasitic diseases 29.0; endocrine and metabolic disorders 14.2; diseases of the nervous system 12.1.

National economy

Budget (1995). Revenue: A.M. 1,872,500,000,000 (tax revenue 52.2%, of which enterprise profits tax 21.8%, value-added tax 9.4%, individual income tax 6.2%, excise tax 4.7%, other 10.1%; nontax revenue 34.0%, of which foreign exchange revenue 16.9%, customs 3.7%; other 13.8%). Expenditures: A.M. 2,395,300,000,000 (goods and services 30.5%; social protection 22.3%; wages and salaries 16.3%; subsidies 9.7%; capital expenditure 3.3%; other 17.9%).
Public debt (external, outstanding; 1995): U.S.$206,000,000.
Production (metric tons except as noted). Agriculture, forestry, fishing (1996): cereals 1,032,000, fruit 957,000, vegetables (except potatoes) 377,000, cotton 274,000, potatoes 209,000, tobacco 68,000, tea 4,000; livestock (number of live animals) 4,574,000 sheep and goats, 1,658,000 cattle, 32,000 horses, 31,000 pigs, 16,000,000 poultry; roundwood (1993) 17,000 cu m; fish catch (1995) 38,000. Mining and quarrying (1995): iron ore 1,000,000; alunite 600,000. Manufacturing (value of production in A.M. '000,000; 1994): textiles 110,265; processed foods 107,943; machine-building and metalworking equipment 82,939; chemical products 60,977; construction materials 34,164; ferrous and nonferrous metals 23,184; meat and dairy products 22,540; clothing 11,847. Construction (1994): completed residential 779,000 sq m. Energy production (consumption): electricity (kW-hr; 1994) 17,600,000,000 (17,800,000,000); coal (metric tons; 1994) none (8,000); crude petroleum (barrels; 1994) 70,393,000 (76,672,000); petroleum products (metric tons; 1994) 6,259,000 (6,208,000); natural gas (cu m; 1994) 5,549,000,000 (7,706,000,000).
Household income and expenditure. Average household size (1989) 4.8; income per household (1994): A.M. 71,443 (U.S.$, n.a.[4]); sources of income (1993): wages and salaries 50.9%, agricultural income 24.0%, social benefits 10.2%; expenditure: food 61.2%, clothing 11.1%, services 3.0%.
Gross national product (at current market prices; 1995): U.S.$3,601,000,000 (1994; U.S.$480 per capita)[4].

Structure of gross domestic product and labour force

	1993 in value A.M. '000,000	1993 % of total value	1994 labour force	1994 % of labour force
Agriculture	42,653	26.8	899,000	34.4
Mining, Manufacturing, Public utilities	39,035	24.5	374,000	14.3
Construction	11,438	7.2	192,000	7.4
Transp. and commun.	12,532	7.9	176,000	6.7
Trade	8,452	5.3	141,000	5.4
Finance	11,278	7.1	13,000	0.5
Pub. admin., defense	9,415	5.9	49,000	1.9
Services	24,016	15.1	698,000	26.7
Other	626	0.4	72,000[5]	2.8
TOTAL	159,445[6]	100.0[6]	2,614,000	100.0[6]

Population economically active (1994): total 2,614,000, activity rate of total population 35.1% (participation rates: ages 16–59 [male], 16–54 [female] 71.5%; female 45.0%; unemployed [1995] 1.0%).

Price and earnings indexes (1993 = 100)

	1993	1994	1995
Consumer price index	100.0	728.9	2,884
Monthly earnings index	100.0	1,887	3,483

Tourism (1995): receipts from visitors U.S.$2,000,000; expenditures by nationals abroad U.S.$4,000,000.
Land use (1994): forest 11.0%; pasture 25.4%; agriculture 48.5%; other 15.1%.

Foreign trade

Balance of trade (current prices)

	1993	1994	1995
U.S.$'000,000	−160	−121	−121
% of total	10.6%	4.0%	10.0%

Imports (1995): U.S.$668,000,000 (food products 41.5%, machinery and equipment 18.4%, chemical products 10.9%, metals 6.3%). *Major import sources:* Turkey 21.1%; Russia 13.2%; Iran 12.0%; Turkmenistan 7.6%; Ukraine 5.1%; Kazakstan 2.7%.
Exports (1995): U.S.$547,000,000 (petroleum products 57.8%, cotton 21.4%, machinery and equipment 8.4%, food products 7.1%, metals 3.3%). *Major export destinations:* Iran 29.8%; Russia 18.1%; United Kingdom 9.0%.

Transport and communications

Transport. Railroads (1994): length 2,120 km; passenger-km 1,081,000,000; metric ton-km cargo 4,416,000,000. Roads (1995): total length 57,770 km (paved 93.8%). Vehicles (1995): passenger cars 289,000; trucks and buses 88,800. Merchant marine: vessels (100 gross tons and over) n.a.; total deadweight tonnage, n.a. Air transport (1994): passenger-km 2,026,000,000; metric ton-km cargo 49,000,000; airports (1997) with scheduled flights 3.

Communications

Medium	date	unit	number	units per 1,000 persons
Daily newspapers	1995	circulation	210,000	28
Television	1995	receivers	1,600,000	212
Telephones	1995	main lines	640,000	86
Cellular telephones	1995	subscribers	6,000	0.8
Facsimile machines	1995	units	2,500	0.1

Education and health

Educational attainment (1995). Percentage of population age 15 and over having: primary education or no formal schooling 12.1%; some secondary 9.1%; completed secondary and some postsecondary 27.5%; higher 7.6%.
Literacy (1989): percentage of total population 15 and over literate 97.3%; males literate 98.9%; females 95.9%.

Education (1994–95)

	schools	teachers	students	student/ teacher ratio
Primary (age 6–13), Secondary (age 14–17)	4,502	156,000	1,486,000	9.5
Voc., teacher tr.	78	...	73,000	...
Higher	23	...	89,100	...

Health (1994): physicians 29,000 (1 per 256 persons); hospital beds 74,000 (1 per 100 persons); (1996) infant mortality rate per 1,000 live births 20.3.

Military

Total active duty personnel (1997): 66,700 (army 80.0%, navy[7] 3.3%, air force 16.7%). *Military expenditure as percentage of GNP* (1995): *c.* 2.8% (world 2.8%); per capita expenditure (1995) U.S.$40.

[1]Excludes one vacant seat reserved for Nagorno-Karabakh representative. [2]The manat was introduced on Aug. 15, 1992, at a 10-to-1 ratio with the Russian ruble and circulated parallel with it; on June 20, 1993, the manat became the sole legal tender. [3]In November 1991 the Azerbaijan Supreme Soviet abolished Nagorno Karabakh's autonomous status. [4]Ruble-area GNP and exchange-rate data are very speculative. [5]Includes 24,000 undistributed unemployed and 48,000 undistributed employed. [6]Detail does not add to total given because of rounding. [7]Azerbaijan shares a portion of the Caspian flotilla.

Internet resources for further information:
- **Azerbaijan http://ourworld.compuserve.com/homepages/Azerbaijan/**
- **Azerbaijan Republic http://www.president.az/azerbaijan/azerbaijan.htm**

Bahamas, The

Official name: The Commonwealth of The Bahamas.
Form of government: constitutional monarchy with two legislative houses (Senate [16]; House of Assembly [40]).
Chief of state: British Monarch represented by Governor-General.
Head of government: Prime Minister.
Capital: Nassau.
Official language: English.
Official religion: none.
Monetary unit: 1 Bahamian dollar (B$) = 100 cents; valuation (Oct. 3, 1997) 1 U.S.$ = B$1.00; 1 £ = B$1.61.

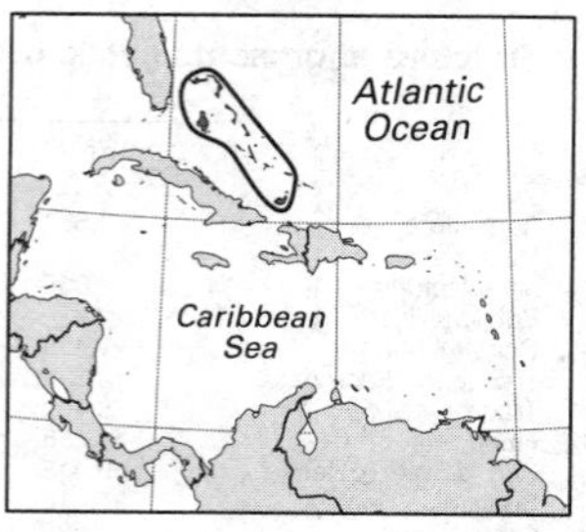

Area and population

	area[1]		population
Islands and Island Groups[2]	sq mi	sq km	1990 census
Abaco, Great and Little	649	1,681	10,034
Acklins	192	497	405
Andros	2,300	5,957	8,187
Berry Islands	12	31	628
Bimini Islands	9	23	1,639
Cat Island	150	388	1,698
Crooked and Long Cay	93	241	412
Eleuthera	187	484	7,993
Exuma, Great, and Exuma Cays	112	290	3,556
Grand Bahama	530	1,373	40,898
Harbour Island	3	8	1,219
Inagua, Great and Little	599	1,551	985
Long Island	230	596	2,954
Mayaguana	110	285	312
New Providence	80	207	172,196
Ragged Island	14	36	89
Rum Cay	30	78	53
San Salvador	63	163	465
Spanish Wells	10	26	1,372
Other uninhabited cays and rocks	9	23	—
TOTAL	5,382	13,939[3]	255,095

Demography

Population (1997): 287,000.
Density (1997)[4]: persons per sq mi 73.8, persons per sq km 28.5.
Urban-rural (1995): urban 86.0%; rural 14.0%.
Sex distribution (1995): male 48.91%; female 51.09%.
Age breakdown (1995): under 15, 29.3%; 15–29, 28.6%; 30–44, 23.2%; 45–59, 11.6%; 60–74, 5.1%; 75 and over, 2.2%.
Population projection: (2000) 295,000; (2010) 321,000.
Doubling time: 42 years.
Ethnic composition (1993): black 85.0%; white 12.0%; Asian or Hispanic 3.0%.
Religious affiliation (1990): non-Anglican Protestant 46.4%[5], of which Baptist 31.1%; Anglican 16.0%; Roman Catholic 16.0%; other 21.6%.
Major cities (1990): Nassau 172,196[6]; Freeport/Lucaya 26,574; Marsh Harbour 3,611; Bailey Town 1,490; Dunmore Town (Harbour Island) 1,219.

Vital statistics

Birth rate per 1,000 population (1995): 22.5 (world avg. 25.0); (1994) legitimate 44.7%; illegitimate 55.3%.
Death rate per 1,000 population (1995): 5.9 (world avg. 9.3).
Natural increase rate per 1,000 population (1995): 16.6 (world avg. 15.7).
Total fertility rate (avg. births per childbearing woman; 1996): 2.0.
Marriage rate per 1,000 population (1994): 9.2.
Divorce rate per 1,000 population (1994): 1.7.
Life expectancy at birth (1996): male 68.0 years; female 77.2 years.
Major causes of death per 100,000 population (1994): circulatory diseases 137.8; infectious diseases 99.1, of which AIDS 88.1; cancers 86.6.

National economy

Budget (1996–97). Revenue: B$714,900,000 (import taxes 47.2%, stamp taxes 17.8%, departure taxes 8.3%, fines and forfeits 6.3%, business and professional licenses 5.1%). Expenditures: B$765,800,000 (education 17.4%, health 13.8%, general administration 13.8%, public works and water supply 12.4%, interest on public debt 11.7%, public order 10.4%, defense 2.8%).
National debt (March 1997): U.S.$1,556,000,000.
Production (value of export production in B$'000 except as noted). Agriculture, forestry, fishing (1996): crayfish 54,000, poultry products 26,300, citrus (particularly grapefruits and limes) 12,000, sponges 1,100, other marine products 2,500; roundwood (1995) 117,000 cu m. Mining and quarrying (value of export production; 1996): salt 18,100; aragonite 4,900. Manufacturing (value of export production; 1996): pharmaceuticals and other chemical products (1995) 74,200; rum 5,200. Construction (value of construction completed in B$'000,000; 1996): residential 92; nonresidential 65. Energy production (consumption): electricity (kW-hr; 1995) 1,254,000,000 (1,085,000,000); coal, none (none); crude petroleum, none (none); petroleum products (metric tons; 1994) negligible (555,000); natural gas, none (none).
Tourism (1996): receipts U.S.$1,458,000,000; expenditures U.S.$240,000,000.
Household income and expenditure. Average household size (1994) 3.9; income per household (1994) B$27,000 (U.S.$27,000); sources of income: n.a.; expenditure (1995)[7]: housing 32.8%, transportation and communications 14.8%, food and beverages 13.8%, household furnishings 8.9%.
Gross national product (1995): U.S.$3,297,000,000 (U.S.$11,940 per capita).

Structure of gross domestic product and labour force

	1992		1994	
	in value B$'000,000	% of total value	labour force[8]	% of labour force
Agriculture, fishing	89	2.9	6,614	4.7
Manufacturing } Mining }	105	3.4	5,060	3.6
Public utilities	88	2.9 } (Mining, Public utilities)	2,010	1.4
Construction	91	3.0	8,651	6.1
Transp. and commun.	227	7.4	10,821	7.7
Trade, restaurants	705	23.0	36,507	25.9
Finance, real estate	610	19.9	11,940	8.5
Pub. admin., defense	179	5.8 }	40,063	28.4
Services	523	17.1 }		
Other	443[9]	14.5[9]	19,348[10]	13.7[10]
TOTAL	3,059[3]	100.0[3]	141,014	100.0

Population economically active (1994)[11]: total 138,700; activity rate of total population 50.7% (participation rates: ages 15–64, 77.8%; female 46.8%; unemployed [1996] 13%).

Price and earnings indexes (1991 = 100)

	1991	1992	1993	1994	1995	1996	1997
Consumer price index	100.0	105.8	108.6	110.2	112.4	114.0	114.6[12]
Annual earnings index[13]	100.0	112.8	116.8[12]	...	...	...	...

Land use (1994): forest 32.4%; pasture 0.2%; agriculture 1.0%; other 66.4%.

Foreign trade[14, 15]

Balance of trade (current prices)

	1990	1991	1992	1993	1994	1995
B$'000,000	−874	−866	−845	−792	−904	−1,067
% of total	64.7%	65.8%	68.7%	70.9%	73.0%	75.2%

Imports (1995): B$1,243,000,000 (machinery and transport equipment 24.8%; food products 16.8%; petroleum for domestic use 12.6%; chemicals and chemical products 8.1%). *Major import sources*[16]: U.S. 92.8%; EC 2.8%.
Exports (1995): B$176,000,000 (domestic exports 52.6%, of which crayfish 31.9%, salt 7.7%; reexports 47.4%, of which machinery and transport equipment 26.1%). *Major export destinations:* U.S. 81.1%; EC 9.2%; Canada 1.9%.

Transport and communications

Transport. Railroads: none. Roads (1995): total length 1,522 mi, 2,450 km (paved 57%). Vehicles (1994): passenger cars 46,089; trucks and buses 11,858. Merchant marine (1992): vessels (100 gross tons and over) 1,061; total deadweight tonnage 33,081,652. Air transport (1994): passenger-mi 119,000,000, passenger-km 191,000,000; short ton-mi cargo 12,300, metric ton-km cargo 18,000; airports (1997) with scheduled flights 22.

Communications

Medium	date	unit	number	units per 1,000 persons
Daily newspapers	1994	circulation	35,000	126
Radio	1996	receivers	80,000	282
Television	1995	receivers	50,000	179
Telephones	1995	main lines	77,000	277
Cellular telephones	1995	subscribers	2,400	8.6
Facsimile machines	1995	units	500	1.8

Education and health

Educational attainment (1990). Percentage of population age 25 and over having: no formal schooling 3.5%; incomplete primary education 25.4%; complete primary/incomplete secondary 57.6%; complete secondary/higher 13.5%. *Literacy* (1995): total percentage age 15 and over literate 98.2%.

Education (1993–94)

	schools	teachers	students	student/ teacher ratio
Primary (age 5–10)	115	1,581	33,343	21.1
Secondary (age 11–16)	...	1,775	28,363	16.0
Higher[17]	1	300	3,201	10.7

Health: physicians (1992) 373 (1 per 709 persons); hospital beds (1993) 1,081 (1 per 249 persons); infant mortality rate per 1,000 live births (1995) 19.0.
Food (1995): daily per capita caloric intake 2,498 (vegetable products 68%, animal products 32%); 103% of FAO recommended minimum requirement.

Military

Total active duty personnel (1996): 860 (coast guard 100%). *Military expenditure as percentage of GNP* (1996)[18]: 0.6% (world, n.a.); per capita expenditure U.S.$74.

[1]Includes areas of lakes and ponds, as well as lagoons and sounds almost entirely surrounded by land; area of land only is about 3,890 sq mi (10,070 sq km). [2]Family (Out) Islands (all islands other than New Providence) are administered by commissioners assigned by the central government. [3]Detail does not add to total given because of rounding. [4]Land area only. [5]Four largest Protestant bodies only. [6]Population cited is for New Providence Island. [7]Weights of retail price index components. [8]Survey date of official figures is unknown. [9]Includes net indirect taxes (B$430,000,000) and statistical discrepancy (B$13,000,000). [10]Includes 594 not adequately defined and 18,754 unemployed. [11]As of May 1. [12]May. [13]Annual mean household income. [14]Imports c.i.f.; exports f.o.b. [15]Official Bahamian statistics exclude trade data for crude petroleum imported for storage by foreign companies, hormones, and inorganic and organic chemicals. [16]Excludes all petroleum imports. [17]College of The Bahamas only. [18]Includes police.

Internet resources for further information:
- **The Government of The Bahamas http://www.bahamas.net.bs/government**

Bahrain

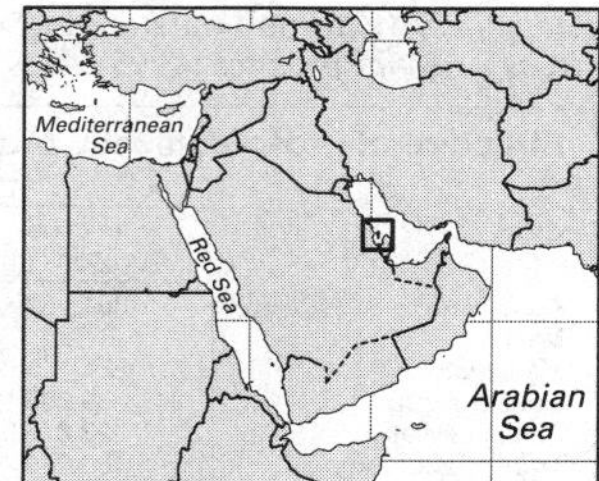

Official name: Dawlat al-Baḥrayn (State of Bahrain).
Form of government: monarchy (emirate)[1].
Chief of state: Emir.
Head of government: Prime Minister.
Capital: Manama.
Official language: Arabic.
Official religion: Islam.
Monetary unit: 1 Bahrain dinar (BD) = 1,000 fils; valuation (Oct. 3, 1997) 1 BD = U.S.$2.65 = £1.65.

Area and population

Regions[2]	area sq mi	area sq km	population 1991 census
Al-Gharbīyah (Western)	60.3	156.1	22,034
Al-Ḥadd	2.3	6.0	8,610
Jidd (Judd) Ḥafṣ	8.3	21.6	44,769
Al-Manāmah (Manama)	10.0	25.8	136,999
Al-Muḥarraq	6.2	16.0	74,245
Ar-Rifāʿ	112.6	291.6	49,752
Ash-Shamālīyah (Northern)	14.2	36.8	33,763
Ash-Sharqīyah (Eastern)	...	...	3,242[3]
Sitrah	11.1	28.8	36,755
Al-Wusṭā (Central)	13.6	35.2	34,304
Towns with special status			
Ḥammād	5.1	13.1	29,055
Madīnat ʿĪsā	4.8	12.4	34,509
Islands			
Ḥawār[4] and other	19.5	50.6	[2]
TOTAL	268.0	694.2[5]	508,037

Demography

Population (1997): 620,000.
Density (1997): persons per sq mi 2,313.4, persons per sq km 893.1.
Urban-rural (1995): urban 90.3%; rural 9.7%.
Sex distribution (1994): male 57.78%; female 42.22%.
Age breakdown (1994): under 15, 31.5%; 15–29, 25.5%; 30–44, 30.8%; 45–59, 8.5%; 60–74, 3.0%; 75 and over, 0.6%.
Population projection: (2000) 660,000; (2010) 780,000.
Doubling time: 32 years.
Ethnic composition (1991): Bahraini Arab 63.6%; Persian, Indian, Pakistani, and other Asians 30.3%; other Arab 3.5%; European 1.2%; other 1.4%.
Religious affiliation (1995): Muslim 81.8%, of which Shīʿī 57.3%, Sunnī 24.5%; Christian 8.5%; other 9.7%.
Major cities (1991): Manama (1992) 140,401; Ar-Rifāʿ 45,956; Al-Muḥarraq 45,337; Madīnat ʿĪsā 34,509.

Vital statistics

Birth rate per 1,000 population (1994): 27.4 (world avg. 25.0); legitimate 100%.
Death rate per 1,000 population (1994): 5.4 (world avg. 9.3).
Natural increase rate per 1,000 population (1994): 22.0 (world avg. 15.7).
Total fertility rate (avg. births per childbearing woman; 1994): 3.6.
Marriage rate per 1,000 population (1993): 6.4.
Divorce rate per 1,000 population (1993): 1.3.
Life expectancy at birth (1994): male 69.0 years; female 72.4 years.
Major causes of death per 100,000 population (1991): diseases of the circulatory system 100.4; malignant neoplasms (cancers) 34.1; diseases of the respiratory system 29.7; accidents and violence 28.5; endocrine, nutritional, and metabolic diseases 17.4; congenital anomalies 13.8.

National economy

Budget (1996). Revenue: BD 633,300,000 ([1995] entrepreneurial and property income 57.7%, import duties 8.4%, foreign grants 6.7%). Expenditures: BD 627,300,000 ([1995] general administration and public order 28.5%, defense 17.3%, education 13.4%, fuel and energy 9.6%, health 9.3%, transportation and communications 9.0%).
Public debt (external, outstanding; 1991): U.S.$1,810,000,000[6].
Population economically active (1991): total 226,448; activity rate of total population 44.6% (participation rates: ages 15–64, 66.1%; female 17.5%; unemployed [1997] *c.* 30%).

Price and earnings indexes (1990 = 100)

	1990	1991	1992	1993	1994	1995	1996
Consumer price index	100.0	100.8	100.6	103.1	104.0	106.8	106.6
Earnings index	...	...	...	...	...	...	...

Production (metric tons except as noted). Agriculture, forestry, fishing (1997): fruit (excluding melons) 25,095, cow's milk 20,000, dates 20,000, tomatoes 5,000, hen's eggs 3,050; livestock (number of live animals) 29,400 sheep, 18,000 goats, 16,500 cattle; fish catch (1994) 9,031. Manufacturing (barrels; 1994): gas oil 28,900,000; fuel oil 20,900,000; kerosene 10,400,000; gasoline 7,700,000; jet fuel 7,100,000; naphtha 1,860,000; propane 1,500,000; butane 1,190,000; aluminum (1996) 461,200 metric tons. Construction (permits issued; 1991): residential 5,931; nonresidential 718. Energy production (consumption): electricity (kW-hr; 1994) 4,550,000,000 (4,550,000,000); crude petroleum (barrels; 1996) 14,124,000 ([1994] 89,516,000); petroleum products (metric tons; 1996) 13,100,000 (538,000); natural gas (cu m; 1996) 10,210,000,000 (10,210,000,000).

Gross national product (1995): U.S.$4,525,000,000 (U.S.$7,840 per capita).

Structure of gross domestic product and labour force

	1996 value in BD '000,000[7]	1996 % of total value	1991 labour force	1991 % of labour force
Agriculture	22.0	1.1	5,108	2.3
Mining	396.0	19.7	3,638	1.6
Manufacturing	393.5	19.5	26,618	11.8
Construction	98.8	4.9	26,738	11.6
Public utilities	35.6	1.8	2,898	1.3
Transp. and commun.	184.5	9.2	13,789	6.1
Trade	207.4	10.3	29,961	13.2
Finance	371.7	18.4	17,256	7.6
Pub. admin., defense	373.7	18.5	83,944	37.1
Services	105.1	5.2		
Other	−172.6	−8.6	16,498	7.3
TOTAL	2,015.7	100.0	226,448	100.0[5]

Household income and expenditure. Average household size (1991) 5.8; income per household: n.a.; sources of income: n.a.; expenditure (1984): food and tobacco 33.3%, housing 21.2%, household durable goods 9.8%, transportation and communications 8.5%, recreation 6.4%, clothing and footwear 5.9%, education 2.7%, health 2.3%, energy and water 2.2%.
Land use (1994): meadows and pastures 5.8%; agricultural and under permanent cultivation 2.9%; built-on and wasteland 91.3%.
Tourism (1995): receipts from visitors U.S.$288,000,000; expenditures by nationals abroad U.S.$163,000,000.

Foreign trade

Balance of trade (current prices)

	1991	1992	1993	1994	1995	1996
BD '000,000	−227.3	−300.3	−50.6	−49.3	+149.3	+191.7
% of total	7.9%	10.3%	1.8%	1.8%	5.1%	5.9%

Imports (1995): BD 1,397,100,000 (crude petroleum products 35.8%, transport equipment and machines 16.0%, food and live animals 9.3%; chemicals 8.9%). *Major import sources:* United States 8.3%; United Kingdom 5.9%; Saudi Arabia 4.9%; Australia 4.8%; Japan 4.1%; Germany 4.0%.
Exports (1995): BD 1,546,400,000 (petroleum products 59.7%, basic manufactured goods 27.3%). *Major export destinations:* Saudi Arabia 6.1%; South Korea 3.8%; Japan 3.5%; United States 3.2%; India 2.5%.

Transport and communications

Transport. Railroads: none. Roads (1995): total length 2,835 km (paved 74.6%). Vehicles (1995): passenger cars 141,901; trucks and buses 29,584. Merchant marine (1992): vessels (100 gross tons and over) 87; total deadweight tonnage 192,487. Air transport (1996)[8]: passenger-km 2,758,800,000; metric ton-km cargo 105,754,000; airports (1997) with scheduled flights 1.

Communications

Medium	date	unit	number	units per 1,000 persons
Daily newspapers	1994	circulation	70,000	128
Radio	1995	receivers	320,000	555
Television	1995	receivers	255,000	442
Telephones	1995	main lines	140,900	244
Cellular telephones	1995	subscribers	27,600	48
Facsimile machines	1995	units	5,700	9.9
Personal computers	1995	units	29,000	50

Education and health

Educational attainment (1991). Percentage of population age 25 and over having: no formal education 38.4%; primary education 26.2%; secondary 25.1%; higher 10.3%. *Literacy* (1995): percentage of population age 15 and over literate 85.2%; males literate 89.1%; females literate 79.4%.

Education (1994–95)

	schools	teachers	students	student/teacher ratio[9]
Primary (age 6–11)	124	3,536[10]	72,329	20.8
Secondary (age 12–17)	35[11]	2,305[10]	48,944	20.2
Voc., teacher tr.	9[11]	820[10]	7,113	8.2
Higher	4[11]	655[12]	7,676[12]	11.7

Health (1993): physicians 482 (1 per 1,115 persons); hospital beds 1,529 (1 per 352 persons); infant mortality rate per 1,000 live births (1994) 23.8.

Military

Total active duty personnel (1997): 11,000 (army 77.3%, navy 9.1%, air force 13.6%). *Military expenditure as percentage of GNP* (1995): 5.4% (world 2.8%); per capita expenditure U.S.$473.

[1]Appointed 40-member Consultative Council is an advisory body only. [2]The creation of four administrative units began in 1997, but the regions have no administrative function; the six major cities of Bahrain were administered by a single municipal council. [3]Ash-Sharqīyah includes population of Ḥawār and other islands. [4]Also claimed by Qatar. [5]Detail does not add to total given because of rounding. [6]Includes long-term private debt not guaranteed by the government. [7]In purchasers' value at current prices. [8]One-fourth apportionment of international flights of Gulf Air (jointly administered by the governments of Bahrain, Oman, Qatar, and the United Arab Emirates). [9]1993–94. [10]Teachers in public education only. [11]1987–88. [12]1993–94.

Internet resources for further information:
- **University of Bahrain http://www.uob.bh/**
- **Bahrain Telephone Company http://www.batelco.com.bh/dbahrain/intro.htm**

Bangladesh

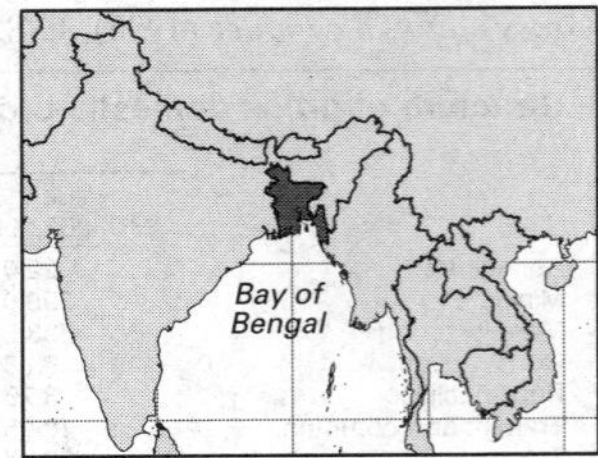

Official name: Gana Prajātantrī Bangladesh (People's Republic of Bangladesh).
Form of government: unitary multiparty republic with one legislative house (Parliament [330[1]]).
Chief of state: President.
Head of government: Prime Minister.
Capital: Dhākā.
Official language: Bengali.
Official religion: Islam.
Monetary unit: 1 Bangladesh taka (Tk) = 100 paisa; valuation (Oct. 3, 1997) 1 U.S.$ = Tk 44.55; 1 £ = Tk 71.81.

Area and population

Divisions[2]	Administrative centres	area sq mi	area sq km	population 1991 census[3]
Barisal	Barisal	5,134	13,297	7,757,334
Chittagong	Chittagong	13,039	33,771	21,865,850
Dhākā	Dhākā	12,015	31,119	33,939,848
Khulna	Khulna	8,600	22,274	13,243,054
Rājshāhi	Rājshāhi	13,326	34,513	27,499,727
Sylhet	Sylhet	4,863	12,596	7,149,372
TOTAL		56,977	147,570	111,455,185

Demography

Population (1997): 125,340,000.
Density (1997): persons per sq mi 2,200, persons per sq km 849.4.
Urban-rural (1997): urban 20.0%; rural 80.0%.
Sex distribution (1996): male 51.72%; female 48.28%.
Age breakdown (1996): under 15, 42.0%; 15–29, 26.4%; 30–44, 17.8%; 45–59, 8.9%; 60–74, 3.8%; 75 and over, 1.1%.
Population projection: (2000) 132,081,000; (2010) 153,195,000.
Doubling time: 48 years.
Ethnic composition (1991): Bengali 98.8%; tribal 1.1%, of which Chakmā 0.2%, Saontāl 0.2%, Marma 0.1%; other 0.1%.
Religious affiliation (1991): Muslim 88.3%; Hindu 10.5%; Buddhist 0.6%; Christian 0.3%; other 0.3%.
Major cities (1991)[4]: Dhākā 6,105,160; Chittagong 2,040,663; Khulna 877,388; Rājshāhi 517,136; Mymensingh 185,517[5].

Vital statistics

Birth rate per 1,000 population (1997): 26.8 (world avg. 25.0).
Death rate per 1,000 population (1997): 12.2 (world avg. 9.3).
Natural increase rate per 1,000 population (1997): 14.6 (world avg. 15.7).
Total fertility rate (avg. births per childbearing woman; 1997): 3.2.
Marriage rate per 1,000 population (1995): 10.2.
Divorce rate per 1,000 population (1981): 3.6.
Life expectancy at birth (1997): male 58.0 years; female 58.0 years.
Major causes of death (1990; percentage of recorded deaths): typhoid fever 19.8%; old age 14.8%; tetanus 10.1%; tuberculosis and other respiratory diseases 8.7%; diarrhea 6.4%; suicide, accidents, and poisoning 5.1%; high blood pressure and heart diseases 5.0%.

National economy

Budget (1994–95). Revenue: Tk 216,940,000,000 (revenue receipts 62.9%, of which sales tax 20.2%, customs duties 14.8%, income taxes 9.7%, dividends and profits from public enterprises 7.2%; development receipts 37.1%). Expenditures: Tk 196,084,000,000 (development expenditure 49.0%; employee compensation 22.0%; goods and services 13.8%; transfer payments 12.9%).
Production (metric tons except as noted). Agriculture, forestry, fishing (1996): paddy rice 27,000,000, sugarcane 7,446,000, wheat 1,320,000, jute 770,000, bananas 630,000, pulses 545,000, oilseeds 520,000, mangoes 189,000, pineapples 150,000, tea 51,000; livestock (number of live animals) 30,330,000 goats, 24,340,000 cattle, 1,155,000 sheep, 882,000 buffalo, 123,000,000 chickens, 16,200,000 ducks; roundwood (1995) 32,044,000 cu m; fish catch (1995) 1,170,365. Mining and quarrying (1995): marine salt 350,000; industrial limestone 23,500. Manufacturing (value added in U.S.$'000,000; 1994): textiles 617; chemicals 473; food products 359; wearing apparel 225; tobacco products 225; electrical machinery 88; paper and paper products 86. Construction: n.a. Energy production (consumption): electricity (kW-hr; 1994) 10,010,000,000 (10,010,000,000); coal (metric tons; 1994) none (198,000); crude petroleum (barrels; 1994) 134,000 (8,966,000); petroleum products (metric tons; 1994) 1,104,000 (2,006,000); natural gas (cu m; 1994) 6,635,000,000 (6,635,000,000).
Household income. Average household size (1991) 5.6; average annual income per household (1991–92) Tk 40,092 (U.S.$1,061); sources of income (1991–92): self-employment 51.6%, wages and salaries 23.1%, transfer payments 10.3%, other 15.0%; expenditure (1991–92): food and drink 66.6%, housing and rent 10.4%, energy 5.6%, clothing and footwear 4.7%, other 12.7%.
Population economically active (1990): total 51,200,000; activity rate of total population 46.9% (participation rates: over age 10, 69.7%; female 39.3%; unemployed 1.0%[6]).

Price and earnings indexes (1990 = 100)

	1990	1991	1992	1993	1994	1995	1996
Consumer price index	100.0	107.2	111.8	111.8	115.8	122.5	125.8
Earnings index[7]	100.0	104.9	109.3	114.8	121.7	...	...

Public debt (external, outstanding; 1995): U.S.$15,543,000,000.
Gross national product (1995): U.S.$28,599,000,000 (U.S.$240 per capita).

Structure of gross domestic product and labour force

	1994–95 in value Tk '000,000	1994–95 % of total value	1990 labour force	1990 % of labour force
Agriculture	361,367	30.9	33,303,000	65.0
Mining	112,948	9.7	15,000	—
Manufacturing			5,925,000	11.6
Construction	69,209	5.9	525,000	1.0
Public utilities	23,646	2.0	40,000	0.1
Transp. and commun.	139,049	11.9	1,611,000	3.1
Trade	100,548	8.6	4,285,000	8.4
Finance	23,127	2.0	296,000	0.6
Public admin., defense	62,308	5.3	5,200,000	10.2
Services and other	278,059	23.8		
TOTAL	1,170,261	100.0[8]	51,200,000	100.0

Land use (1994): forest 14.6%; pasture 4.6%; agriculture 74.5%; other 6.3%.
Tourism (1995): receipts U.S.$23,000,000; expenditures U.S.$229,000,000.

Foreign trade

Balance of trade (current prices)

	1991	1992	1993	1994	1995	1996
Tk '000,000	−48,564	−55,276	−52,113	−59,665	−107,719	−110,988
% of total	28.2%	25.3%	22.5%	21.9%	29.7%	28.7%

Imports (1994–95): Tk 234,530,000,000 (textile yarn, fabrics, and made-up articles 22.6%; machinery and transport equipment 12.4%; petroleum and products 6.1%; chemicals 5.9%; cereals and preparations 4.2%; iron and steel 3.5%). *Major import sources* (1993): Japan 12.5%; India 9.5%; Hong Kong 8.0%; South Korea 6.9%; China 5.1%; Singapore 4.6%; U.S. 4.3%.
Exports (1994–95): Tk 131,310,000,000 (ready-made garments 56.6%; jute manufactures 10.4%; fish and prawns 10.1%; hides, skins, and leather 6.7%; fertilizers 2.4%; raw jute 2.0%; tea 1.0%). *Major export destinations* (1993): Western Europe 40.2%; U.S. 33.6%; Association of Southeast Asian Nations (ASEAN) 4.0%; Hong Kong 2.7%; Japan 2.5%.

Transport and communications

Transport. Railroads (1994–95): route length 1,681 mi, 2,706 km; passenger-mi 2,508,000,000, passenger-km 4,037,000,000; short ton-mi cargo 521,000,000, metric ton-km cargo 760,000,000. Roads (1995): total length 104,709 mi, 168,513 km (paved 9%). Vehicles (1994): passenger cars 82,198; trucks and buses 104,860. Merchant marine (1992): vessels (100 gross tons and over) 301; total deadweight tonnage 566,775. Air transport (1993–94)[9]: passenger-mi 1,763,000,000, passenger-km 2,838,000,000; short ton-mi cargo 82,000,000, metric ton-km cargo 121,000,000; airports with scheduled flights (1997) 8.

Communications

Medium	date	unit	number	units per 1,000 persons
Daily newspapers	1994	circulation	51,000	0.4
Radio	1996	receivers	8,000,000	65
Television	1995	receivers	600,000	5.0
Telephones	1995	main lines	286,600	2.4
Cellular telephones	1995	subscribers	2,500	—
Facsimile machines	1995	units	4,000	—

Education and health

Educational attainment (1991). Percentage of population age 25 and over having: no formal schooling 65.4%; primary education 17.1%; secondary 13.8%; postsecondary 3.7%. *Literacy* (1991): total population age 15 and over literate 34.8%; males literate 45.2%; females literate 23.7%.

Education (1993–94)

	schools	teachers	students	student/ teacher ratio
Primary (age 6–10)	66,168	242,252	15,185,000	62.7
Secondary (age 11–17)	11,019	135,217	4,884,000	36.1
Voc., teacher tr.	152	1,857	29,923	16.1
Higher	1,268	36,000	1,032,635	28.7

Health (1994): physicians 24,911 (1 per 4,759 persons); hospital beds 35,800 (1 per 3,312 persons); infant mortality rate (1997) 79.
Food (1995): daily per capita caloric intake 2,017 (vegetable products 97%, animal products 3%); 87% of FAO recommended minimum requirement.

Military

Total active duty personnel (1997): 121,000 (army 83.5%, navy 8.7%, air force 7.8%). *Military expenditure as percentage of GNP* (1995): 1.7% (world 2.8%); per capita expenditure U.S.$4.

[1]Includes 30 seats reserved for women. [2]Geographic reorganization at the district level took place in 1993; each division is now divided into the following number of new districts: Barisal 6, Chittagong 11, Dhākā 17, Khulna 10, Rājshāhi 16, and Sylhet 4. [3]Adjusted for underenumeration. [4]Metropolitan population. [5]Municipal population. [6]Excluding underemployment. [7]Wage earnings in manufacturing. [8]Detail does not add to total given because of rounding. [9]Bangladesh Biman only.

Internet resources for further information:
- **Permanent Mission to the United Nations http://www.undp.org:81/missions/bangladesh/**
- **Asian Development Bank: Statistics of DMCs: Bangladesh http://internotes.asiandevbank.org/notes/ban1/BANNACT.htm**

Barbados

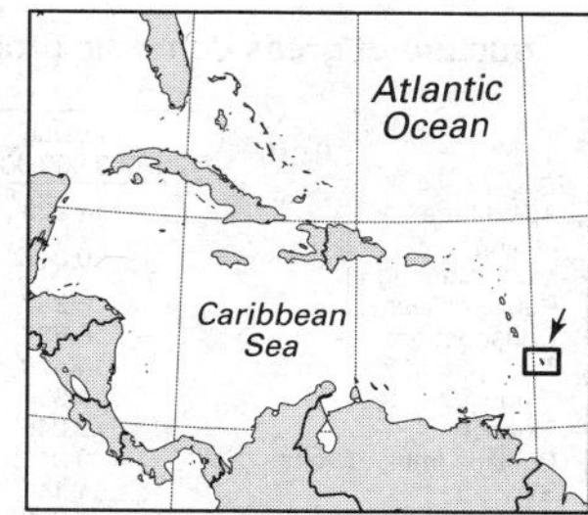

Official name: Barbados.
Form of government: constitutional monarchy with two legislative houses (Senate [21]; House of Assembly [28]).
Chief of state: British Monarch represented by Governor-General.
Head of government: Prime Minister.
Capital: Bridgetown.
Official language: English.
Official religion: none.
Monetary unit: 1 Barbados dollar (BDS$) = 100 cents; valuation (Oct. 3, 1997) 1 U.S.$ = BDS$2.01; 1 £ = BDS$3.24.

Area and population	area		population
Parishes[1]	sq mi	sq km	1990 census
Christ Church	22	57	47,050
St. Andrew	14	36	6,346
St. George	17	44	17,905
St. James	12	31	21,001
St. John	13	34	10,206
St. Joseph	10	26	7,619
St. Lucy	14	36	9,455
St. Michael[2]	15	39	97,516
St. Peter	13	34	11,263
St. Philip	23	60	20,540
St. Thomas	13	34	11,590
TOTAL	166	430[3]	260,491

Demography

Population (1997): 265,000.
Density (1997): persons per sq mi 1,596, persons per sq km 616.
Urban-rural (1990): urban 37.9%; rural 62.1%.
Sex distribution (1996): male 47.86%; female 52.14%.
Age breakdown (1996): under 15, 23.8%; 15–29, 25.8%; 30–44, 24.8%; 45–59, 12.8%; 60–74, 7.9%; 75 and over, 4.9%.
Population projection: (2000) 266,000; (2010) 270,000.
Doubling time: n.a.; doubling time exceeds 100 years.
Ethnic composition (1990): black 92.5%; white 3.2%; mixed 2.8%; other 1.5%.
Religious affiliation (1990): Anglican 33.0%; other Protestant 29.8%, of which Pentecostal 12.7%, Methodist 5.9%; nonreligious 20.2%; Roman Catholic 4.4%; not stated 2.7%; other 9.9%.
Major cities (1990): Bridgetown 6,070 (urban area 85,000); Speightstown, *c.* 3,500.

Vital statistics

Birth rate per 1,000 population (1996): 13.3 (world avg. 25.0); (1979) legitimate 26.9%; illegitimate 73.1%.
Death rate per 1,000 population (1996): 9.1 (world avg. 9.3).
Natural increase rate per 1,000 population (1996): 4.2 (world avg. 15.7).
Total fertility rate (avg. births per childbearing woman; 1996): 1.8.
Marriage rate per 1,000 population (1993): 8.5.
Divorce rate per 1,000 population (1993): 16.7.
Life expectancy at birth (1996): male 71.6 years; female 77.2 years.
Major causes of death per 100,000 population (1992): diseases of the circulatory system 366.8; malignant neoplasms (cancers) 178.5; endocrine and metabolic disorders 120.2; accidents, poisonings, and violence 40.3; diseases of the respiratory system 40.0; diseases of the digestive system 28.9; infectious and parasitic diseases 19.0; diseases of the nervous system 17.1.

National economy

Budget (1996–97). Revenue: BDS$1,231,064,000[4] (tax revenue 91.9%, of which goods and services taxes 39.1%, personal income and company taxes 32.3%, import duties 7.4%; nontax revenue 8.1%). Expenditures: BDS$1,359,104,000 (current expenditure 83.5%, of which education 18.1%, health 11.8%, economic services 10.4%, social security and welfare 8.2%).
Production (metric tons except as noted). Agriculture, forestry, fishing (1995): raw sugar 38,500, sweet potatoes 5,202, yams 2,570, lettuce 1,909, cabbage 1,823, onions 1,804, cucumbers 1,428, carrots 1,305, tomatoes 1,153, pumpkins 1,080, cassava 818; livestock (number of live animals; 1993) 66,000 sheep, 45,000 pigs, 38,000 goats, 33,000 cattle; roundwood, n.a.; fish catch 3,286. Manufacturing (value added in BDS$'000; 1995): food, beverages, and tobacco (mostly sugar, molasses, rum, beer, and cigarettes) 108,000; paper products, printing, and publishing 33,400; metal products and assembly-type goods (mostly electronic components) 28,000; textiles and wearing apparel 11,700. Construction (value added in BDS$; 1996): 151,400,000. Energy production (consumption): electricity (kW-hr; 1994) 571,000,000 (571,000,000); coal, none (none); crude petroleum (barrels; 1994) 452,000 (1,909,000); petroleum products (metric tons; 1996) 255,000 (314,000); natural gas (cu m; 1994) 22,065,000 (22,065,000).
Household income and expenditure. Average household size (1990) 3.5; income per household (1988) BDS$13,455 (U.S.$6,690); sources of income: n.a.; expenditure (1994): food 39.4%, housing 16.8%, transportation 10.5%, household operations 8.1%, alcohol and tobacco 6.4%, fuel and light 5.2%, clothing and footwear 5.0%, other 8.6%.
Population economically active (1996): total 135,800; activity rate of total population 51.5% (participation rates: ages 15 and over, 67.6%; female 61.9%; unemployed 15.8%).

Price and earnings indexes (1990 = 100)	1990	1991	1992	1993	1994	1995	1996
Consumer price index	100.0	106.3	112.7	114.0	114.1	116.2	119.0
Hourly earnings index	100.0	...	...	...	...	...	...

Gross national product (1995): U.S.$1,745,000,000 (U.S.$6,560 per capita).

Structure of gross domestic product and labour force	1996			
	in value BDS$'000,000	% of total value	labour force	% of labour force
Agriculture, fishing	205.6	5.2	6,000	4.4
Mining	18.7[5]	0.5[5]	...	...
Manufacturing	206.7	5.2	9,700	7.1
Construction	151.4	3.8	9,900	7.3
Public utilities	115.8[5]	2.9[5]	1,800	1.3
Transp. and commun.	315.5	7.9	4,400	3.2
Trade, restaurants	1,054.7	26.5	28,200	20.8
Finance, real estate	563.6	14.1	8,300	6.1
Pub. admin., defense	598.9	15.0	46,100	34.0
Services	146.1	3.6		
Other	610.8[6]	15.3[6]	21,400[7]	15.8[7]
TOTAL	3,987.8	100.0	135,800	100.0

Public debt (external, outstanding; 1995): U.S.$369,600,000.
Tourism: receipts from visitors (1995) U.S.$680,000,000; expenditures by nationals abroad (1993) U.S.$52,000,000.

Foreign trade[8]

Balance of trade (current prices)	1991	1992	1993	1994	1995	1996
BDS$'000,000	−984.6	−568.8	−689.3	−753.8	−917.0	−1,106
% of total	53.6%	42.6%	48.9%	50.9%	49.3%	49.6%

Imports (1996): BDS$1,667,287,000 (retained imports 92.0%, of which machinery 17.8%, food and beverages 15.6%, construction materials 6.8%, chemicals 6.4%, fuels 5.4%; reexported imports 8.0%). *Major import sources* (1996): U.S. 40.5%; Trinidad and Tobago 10.8%; U.K. 8.4%; Canada 5.1%; Jamaica 1.6%.
Exports (1996): BDS$556,690,000 (domestic exports 76.3%, of which sugar 12.8%, chemicals 9.8%, electrical components 9.7%, rum 2.1%, margarine and lard 2.1%, clothing 1.4%; reexports 23.7%). *Major export destinations* (1996): U.K. 16.8%; U.S. 13.5%; Jamaica 7.5%; Trinidad and Tobago 6.3%; Canada 4.4%; St. Lucia 3.8%; Guyana 2.9%.

Transport and communications

Transport. Railroads: none. Roads (1995): total length 1,000 mi, 1,610 km (paved 95%). Vehicles (1995): passenger cars 43,711; trucks and buses 10,583[9]. Merchant marine (1992): vessels (100 gross tons and over) 37; total deadweight tonnage 84,000. Air transport (1995): passenger arrivals 699,000, passenger departures 707,400; cargo unloaded 8,382 metric tons, cargo loaded 4,717 metric tons; airports (1997) with scheduled flights 1.

Communications Medium	date	unit	number	units per 1,000 persons
Daily newspapers	1994	circulation	41,405	157
Radio	1996	receivers	300,000	1,134
Television	1995	receivers	75,000	287
Telephones	1995	main lines	90,100	345
Cellular telephones	1995	subscribers	4,600	17.7
Facsimile machines	1995	units	1,800	6.8
Personal computers	1995	units	15,000	57.5

Education and health

Educational attainment (1990). Percentage of population age 25 and over having: no formal schooling 0.4%; primary education 23.7%; secondary 60.3%[10]; higher 11.2%; other 4.4%. *Literacy* (1995): total population age 15 and over literate 97.4%; males literate 98.0%; females literate 96.8%.

Education (1989–90)	schools	teachers	students	student/ teacher ratio
Primary (age 3–11)[11]	106	1,553	26,662	17.2
Secondary (age 12–16)	33	1,406	21,259	15.1
Vocational[12]	8	79	996	12.6
Higher[13]	1	153	1,314	8.6

Health (1992): physicians 312 (1 per 842 persons); hospital beds 1,966 (1 per 134 persons); infant mortality rate per 1,000 live births (1996) 14.2.
Food (1995): daily per capita caloric intake 3,207 (vegetable products 74%, animal products 26%); 133% of FAO recommended minimum requirement.

Military

Total active duty personnel (1997): 610 (army 82.0%, navy 18.0%). *Military expenditure as percentage of GNP* (1995): 0.8% (world 2.8%); per capita expenditure U.S.$50.

[1]Parishes and city of Bridgetown have no local administrative function. [2]Includes city of Bridgetown. [3]Detail does not add to total given because of rounding. [4]Current revenue only. [5]Mining excludes natural gas; Public utilities includes natural gas. [6]Net indirect taxes. [7]Unemployed. [8]Import figures are f.o.b. in balance of trade and c.i.f. in commodities and trading partners. [9]Includes taxis. [10]Includes composite senior. [11]1991–92. [12]1987–88. [13]University of the West Indies, Cave Hill campus.

Internet resources for further information:
- **Central Bank of Barbados http://www.bajan.com/cenbnet/welcome.html**

Belarus

Official name: Respublika Belarus (Republic of Belarus).
Form of government[1]: unitary multiparty republic with two legislative bodies (Council of the Republic [64]; House of Representatives [110]).
Head of state and government: President.
Capital: Minsk.
Official languages: Belarusian; Russian.
Official religion: none.
Monetary unit[2]: rubel (Rbl; plural rubli) valuation (Oct. 3, 1997) free rate, 1 U.S.$ = Rbl 43,337; 1 £ = Rbl 69,859.

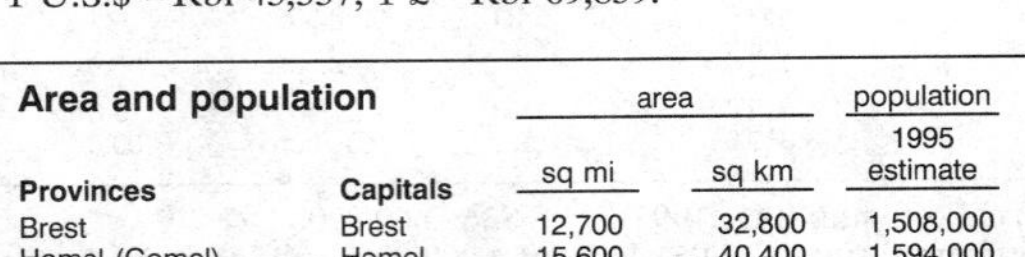
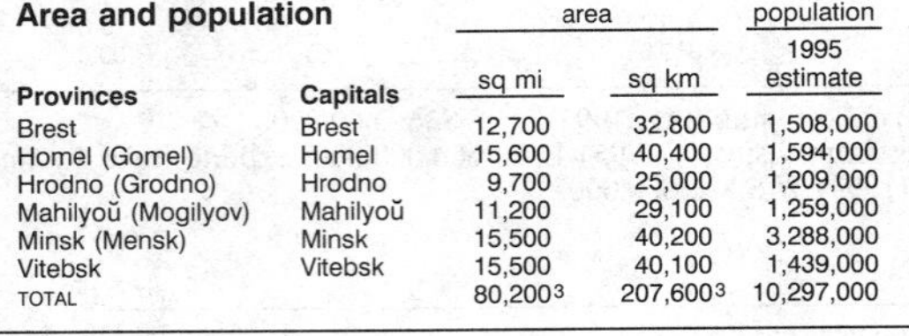

Area and population

Provinces	Capitals	area sq mi	area sq km	population 1995 estimate
Brest	Brest	12,700	32,800	1,508,000
Homel (Gomel)	Homel	15,600	40,400	1,594,000
Hrodno (Grodno)	Hrodno	9,700	25,000	1,209,000
Mahilyoŭ (Mogilyov)	Mahilyoŭ	11,200	29,100	1,259,000
Minsk (Mensk)	Minsk	15,500	40,200	3,288,000
Vitebsk	Vitebsk	15,500	40,100	1,439,000
TOTAL		80,200[3]	207,600[3]	10,297,000

Demography

Population (1997): 10,360,000.
Density (1997): persons per sq mi 129.2, persons per sq km 49.9.
Urban-rural (1996): urban 68.9%; rural 31.1%.
Sex distribution (1995): male 47.00%; female 53.00%.
Age breakdown (1995): under 15, 22.0%; 15–29, 20.8%; 30–44, 23.6%; 45–59, 16.1%; 60–69, 10.4%; 70 and over, 7.1%.
Population projection: (2000) 10,456,000; (2010) 10,831,000.
Doubling time: not applicable; population is declining.
Ethnic composition (1991): Belarusian 77.9%; Russian 13.5%; Ukrainian 3.0%; Jewish 0.7%; other 4.9%.
Religious affiliation (1997): Belarusian Orthodox 31.6%; Roman Catholic 17.8%; other 50.6%.
Major cities (1995): Minsk 1,695,000; Homel 514,000; Mahilyoŭ 366,000.

Vital Statistics

Birth rate per 1,000 population (1996): 9.3 (world avg. 25.0); (1994) legitimate 87.9%; illegitimate 12.1%.
Death rate per 1,000 population (1996): 13.0 (world avg. 9.3).
Natural increase rate per 1,000 population (1996): −3.7 (world avg. 15.7).
Total fertility rate (avg. births per childbearing woman; 1993): 1.9.
Marriage rate per 1,000 population (1994): 7.3
Divorce rate per 1,000 population (1994): 4.3.
Life expectancy at birth (1994): male 63.5 years; female 74.3 years.
Major causes of death per 100,000 population (1994): diseases of the circulatory system 621.4; malignant neoplasms (cancers) 181.4; accidents and violence 138.5; diseases of the respiratory system 65.2.

National economy

Budget (1995). Revenue: Rbl 35,018,000,000,000[2] (value-added tax 28.4%, taxes on profits 23.8%, taxes on income 9.4%, excise taxes 8.0%, Chernobyl surcharges 7.9%, taxes on international trade 5.7%, other 16.8%). Expenditures: Rbl 37,888,000,000,000[2] (education 17.5%, health 15.2%, subsidies 10.8%, transfers 9.4%, Chernobyl expenditures 7.9%, lending minus repayments 5.1%, capital expenditure 4.1%, other 30.0%[4]).
Public debt (external, outstanding; 1995): U.S.$1,255,000,000.
Household income and expenditure. Average household size (1989) 3.2; income per household (1995) Rbl 2,400,000[2]; sources of income (1994): wages and salaries 47.1%, transfers 45.6%, agricultural income 7.3%; expenditure (1994): retail goods 70.6%, taxes 4.6%, health services 3.8%.
Production (metric tons except as noted). Agriculture, forestry, fishing (1996): potatoes 10,881,000, cereal 5,318,000, other vegetables 1,176,000, sugar beets 1,011,000, fruit 377,000; livestock (number of live animals) 5,054,000 cattle, 3,895,000 pigs, 262,000 sheep and goats, 229,000 horses, 39,000,000 poultry; roundwood (1996) 10,015,000 cu m; fish catch (1995) 15,000. Mining and quarrying (1995): peat 4,000,000; potash 3,200,000. Manufacturing (value of production in Rbl '000,000[2]; 1994): machine-building equipment 1,086,650; chemical products 659,438; food products 562,438; construction materials 142,555. Construction (1991): 5,395,000 sq m. Energy production (consumption): electricity (kW-hr; 1995) 24,918,000,000 (32,113,000,000); coal (1994) none (1,199,000); crude petroleum (barrels; 1995) 14,162,000 (94,463,000); petroleum products (1994) 10,735,000 (10,002,000); natural gas (cu m; 1995) 266,000,000 (13,840,000,000).
Population economically active (1995): 4,636,000; activity rate of total population 45.2% (participation rate: ages 16–59 [male], 16–54 [female] 83.5%; female [1991] 53.3%; unemployed 2.4%).

Price and earnings indexes (1990 = 100)

	1990	1991	1992	1993	1994	1995
Consumer price index	100.0	183.5	1,962	25,265	c. 586,000	c. 1,430,000
Monthly earnings index	100.0	300.0	3,150	40,950	c. 696,150	...

Gross national product (1995)[5]: U.S.$21,356,000,000 (U.S.$2,070 per capita).

Structure of gross domestic product and labour force

	1995 in value Rbl '000,000,000[2, 6]	% of total value	labour force	% of labour force
Agriculture	14,223	12.0	804,000	17.3
Mining, Manufacturing	30,342	25.6	1,161,000	25.0
Public utilities	6,282	5.3	...	...
Construction	6,637	5.6	279,000	6.0
Transp. and commun.	14,578	12.3	279,000	6.0
Trade	14,934	12.6	222,000	4.8
Finance	9,245	7.8	44,000	0.9
Public admin., defense	3,911	3.3	63,000	1.4
Services	11,141	9.4	827,000	17.8
Other	7,230[7]	6.1	957,000[8]	20.6
TOTAL	118,523	100.0	4,636,000	100.0[9]

Tourism: receipts from visitors, n.a.; expenditures by nationals abroad, n.a.
Land use (1994)[10]: forested 33.7%; meadows and pastures 14.1%; agricultural and under permanent cultivation 30.5%; other 21.7%.

Foreign trade

Balance of trade (current prices)

	1993	1994	1995	1996
U.S.$'000,000	−1,051	−710	−528	−1,655
% of total	15.7%	11.8%	5.4%	15.7%

Imports (1996): U.S.$6,919,000,000 (1995; Commonwealth of Independent States [CIS] 93.8%, mainly petroleum, natural gas, rolled metal, coal; non-CIS 6.2%, mainly intermediate inputs [rubber, paint, rolled metal] and consumer goods [cars, shoes, cotton textiles]). *Major import sources:* Russia 46.2%; Ukraine 14.3%; Germany 9.3%; Lithuania 4.3%; Poland 3.9%.
Exports (1996): U.S.$5,264,000,000 (1995; CIS 88.9%, mainly trucks, diesel fuel, synthetic fibres, refrigerators, tires, potassium fertilizer, milk and milk products, tractors; non-CIS commodities 11.1%, potassium and nitric fertilizers, trucks, refrigerators, tires, tractors, consumer durables). *Major export destinations:* Russia 47.0%; Ukraine 16.7%; Poland 4.8%; Germany 4.5%.

Transport and communications

Transport. Railroads (1995): length 5,488 km; passenger-km 16,000,000,000; (1994) metric ton-km cargo 27,963,000,000. Roads (1995): total length 51,547 km (paved 98.6%). Vehicles (1995): passenger cars 955,256; trucks and buses 9,289. Merchant marine (1992): vessels (100 gross tons and over) n.a.; total deadweight tonnage 18,373,000,000. Air transport (1994): passenger-km 1,390,000,000; metric ton-km cargo 10,000,000; airports (1997) 1.

Communications

Medium	date	unit	number	units per 1,000 persons
Daily newspapers	1995	circulation	1,899,000	187
Radio	1996	receivers	3,200,000	311
Television	1995	receivers	2,700,000	265
Telephones	1995	main lines	1,968,000	190
Cellular telephones	1995	subscribers	5,900	600
Facsimile machines	1995	units	8,900	900

Education and health

Educational attainment (1989). Percentage of population age 25 and over having: no formal schooling or primary education only 23.0%; some secondary 16.8%; completed secondary and some postsecondary 49.4%; higher 10.8%.

Education (1995–96)

	schools	teachers	students	student/ teacher ratio
Primary (age 6–13), Secondary (age 14–17)	4,900	127,000	1,561,000	12.3
Voc., teacher tr.	149	...	122,400	...
Higher	59	16,900[11]	197,400	10.5[11]

Literacy (1989): total population age 15 and over literate 7,690,000 (97.9%); males literate 3,661,000 (99.4%); females literate 4,029,000 (96.6%).
Health (1995): physicians 46,000 (1 per 224 persons); hospital beds 127,000 (1 per 81 persons); infant mortality rate per 1,000 live births 12.6.

Military

Total active duty personnel (1997): 81,800 (army 61.7%, air force and air defense 26.9%, other 11.4%). *Military expenditure as percentage of GNP* (1995): 0.8% (world 2.8%); per capita expenditure U.S.$32.

[1]Legal status of new constitution approved by referendum on Nov. 27, 1996, and legislative bodies established per this constitution are controversial. [2]On Aug. 20, 1994, the rubel became the unit of account replacing the Belarusian ruble, which was formally recognized as the sole legal tender on May 18, 1994. The conversion took place at the rate of 10 Belarusian rubles per 1 rubel. [3]Rounded area figures; exact area figures are 80,153 sq mi (207,595 sq km). [4]Includes expenditure arrears and statistical discrepancy. [5]Ruble-area GNP and exchange rate data very speculative. [6]Provisional estimates. [7]Includes Rbl 1,256,000,000,000 and Rbl 5,884,000,000,000 of imputed payments to financial intermediaries. [8]Includes 131,000 unemployed and 692,000 undistributed employed. [9]Detail does not add to total given because of rounding. [10]25% of Belarusian territory severely affected by radioactive fallout from Chernobyl. [11]1993–94.

Internet resources for further information:

- **The Native Byelorussian WWW-server for Businessmen http://www.belarus.net/**
- **United Nations Office in Belarus http://www.un.minsk.by**

Belgium

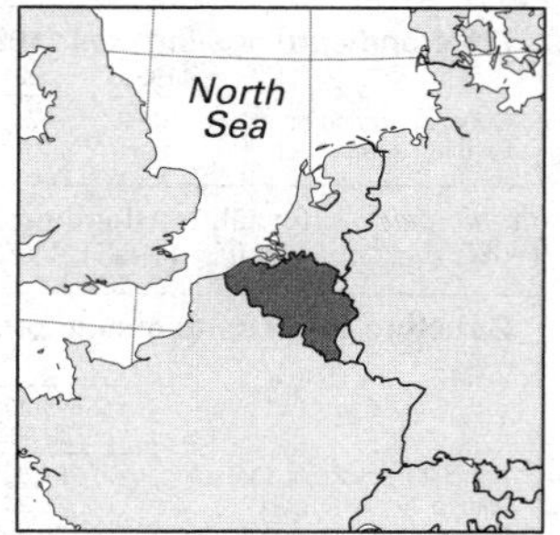

Official name: Koninkrijk België (Dutch); Royaume de Belgique (French) (Kingdom of Belgium).
Form of government: federal constitutional monarchy with a Parliament composed of two legislative chambers (Senate [71[1]]; House of Representatives [150]).
Chief of state: Monarch.
Head of government: Prime Minister.
Capital: Brussels.
Official languages: Dutch; French; German.
Official religion: none.
Monetary unit: 1 Belgian franc (BF) = 100 centimes; valuation (Oct. 3, 1997) 1 U.S.$ = BF 36.38; 1 £ = BF 58.64.

Area and population

Regions[3] Provinces	Capitals	area sq mi	area sq km	population 1996[2] estimate
Brussels-Capital	—	62	161	948,122
Flanders	—	5,221[4]	13,522	5,880,357
Antwerp	Antwerp	1,107	2,867	1,631,243
East Flanders	Ghent	1,151	2,982	1,351,777
Flemish Brabant[5]	Leuven	813	2,106	999,186
Limburg	Hasselt	935	2,422	775,302
West Flanders	Brugge	1,214	3,145	1,122,849
Wallonia	—	6,504[4]	16,844	3,314,568
Hainaut	Mons	1,462	3,786	1,284,761
Liège	Liège	1,491	3,862	1,013,729
Luxembourg	Arlon	1,714	4,440	241,339
Namur	Namur	1,415	3,666	435,677
Walloon Brabant[5]	Wavre	421	1,091	339,062
TOTAL		11,787	30,528[4]	10,143,047

Demography

Population (1997): 10,189,000.
Density (1997): persons per sq mi 864.4, persons per sq km 333.8.
Urban-rural (1996[6]): urban 96.8%; rural 3.2%.
Sex distribution (1996[6]): male 49.02%; female 50.98%.
Age breakdown (1994[2]): under 15, 18.1%; 15–29, 20.7%; 30–44, 22.7%; 45–59, 17.3%; 60–74, 15.1%; 75 and over, 6.1%.
Population projection: (2000) 10,353,000; (2010) 10,189,000.
Doubling time: not applicable; doubling time exceeds 100 years.
Nationality (1992): Belgian 91.0%; Italian 2.4%; Moroccan 1.4%; French 0.9%; Turkish 0.8%; Dutch 0.6%; other 2.9%.
Religious affiliation (1980): Roman Catholic 90.0%; Muslim 1.1%; Protestant 0.4%; nonreligious and atheist 7.5%; other 1.0%.
Major cities (1996[2]): Brussels 136,424[7] (948,122[8]); Antwerp 455,852; Ghent 226,464; Charleroi 205,591; Liège 190,525.

Vital statistics

Birth rate per 1,000 population (1996): 11.4 (world avg. 25.0); (1989) legitimate 88.7%; illegitimate 11.3%.
Death rate per 1,000 population (1996): 10.4 (world avg. 9.3).
Natural increase rate per 1,000 population (1996): 1.0 (world avg. 15.7).
Total fertility rate (avg. births per childbearing woman; 1990–95): 1.6.
Marriage rate per 1,000 population (1994): 5.1.
Divorce rate per 1,000 population (1994): 2.2.
Life expectancy at birth (1991–93): male 73.0 years; female 79.8 years.
Major causes of death per 100,000 population (1989): diseases of the circulatory system 412.8; malignant neoplasms (cancers) 274.6; accidents and violence 64.6; diseases of the respiratory system 50.1.

National economy

Budget (1994). Revenue: BF 2,292,500,000,000 (direct taxes 52.3%, indirect taxes 40.8%). Expenditures: BF 2,668,700,000,000 (government departments 27.9%, debt service 27.7%, domestic transfers 16.3%).
Public debt (1996[2]): U.S.$314,300,000,000.
Production (metric tons except as noted). Agriculture, forestry, fishing (1997[6]): sugar beets 5,245,000, potatoes 2,490,000, wheat 1,910,000, barley 435,500, apples 302,400, tomatoes 300,000; livestock (number of live animals) 7,050,000 pigs, 3,000,000 cattle, 161,000 sheep, 24,000 horses; roundwood (1995[6]) 4,185,000 cu m; fish catch (1995) 36,445. Mining and quarrying (1994): quartz 500,000; barite 30,000; granite (Belgium bluestone) 2,105,000 cu m; marble 330 cu m. Manufacturing (value added in U.S.$'000,000; 1994): chemicals 4,771; transport equipment 3,632; textiles 2,056; plastics 2,045; printing 1,968; furniture 1,632. Construction (1993): residential 33,063,000 cu m; nonresidential 42,864,000 cu m. Energy production (consumption): electricity (kW-hr; 1994) 72,236,000,000 (76,219,000,000); coal (metric tons; 1994) 753,000 (13,050,000); crude petroleum (barrels; 1994) none (206,706,000); petroleum products (metric tons; 1994) 25,373,000 (17,036,000); natural gas (cu m; 1994) 1,351,000 (11,531,000,000).
Tourism (1995[6]): receipts U.S.$5,593,700,000; expenditures U.S.$9,038,100,000.
Household income and expenditure. Avg. household size (1991) 2.7; sources of income (1992): wages 49.6%, transfer payments 20.7%, property income 18.8%, self-employment 10.9%; expenditure (1992): food 18.0%, housing 17.0%, transp. 13.3%, health 11.8%, durable goods 10.7%, clothing 7.7%.
Gross national product (1995): U.S.$250,710,000,000 (U.S.$24,710 per capita).

Structure of gross domestic product and labour force

	1996 in value BF '000,000	1996 % of total value	1996 labour force	1996 % of labour force
Agriculture	101,900	1.2	104,100	2.5
Mining	20,600	0.2	10,000	0.2
Manufacturing	1,761,900	21.2	754,400	18.0
Construction	391,700	4.7	254,100	6.1
Public utilities	204,300	2.5	29,400	0.7
Transp. and commun.	634,500	7.6	286,200	6.8
Trade } Finance }	2,213,000	26.6	682,500	16.3
			401,400	9.6
Pub. admin., defense } Services }	2,612,600	31.5	1,244,700	29.7
Other	364,300[9]	4.4[9]	429,300[10]	10.2[10]
TOTAL	8,305,000[4]	100.0[4]	4,196,000[4]	100.0[4]

Population economically active (1996): total 4,196,000; activity rate 41.3% (participation rates: ages 14–64, 61.1%; female 41.6%; unemployed 9.6%).

Price and earnings indexes (1990 = 100)

	1990	1991	1992	1993	1994	1995	1996
Consumer price index	100.0	103.2	105.7	108.6	111.2	112.8	115.2
Hourly earnings index	100.0	105.1	110.1	112.4	114.7	...	...

Land use (1994[6]): forest 21.3%; pasture 21.0%; agriculture 24.2%; other 33.5%.

Foreign trade[6]

Balance of trade (current prices)

	1991	1992	1993	1994	1995	1996
BF '000,000	+30,900	+67,500	+370,500	+513,000	+427,700	+402,000
% of total	0.4%	0.9%	4.7%	5.9%	4.4%	4.5%

Imports (1994): BF 4,206,413,900,000 (machinery 25.6%; chemicals 13.0%; food 8.9%; diamonds 7.2%; mineral fuels 6.9%; petroleum products 4.8%). *Major import sources:* Germany 20.2%; The Netherlands 17.7%; France 16.1%; U.K. 9.4%.
Exports (1994): BF 4,588,184,500,000 (machinery 28.1%; chemicals 16.7%, of which plastics 5.1%; food 9.1%; diamonds 6.8%; iron and steel 6.0%; textiles 5.0%; petroleum products 2.8%). *Major export destinations:* Germany 21.0%; France 19.0%; The Netherlands 13.2%; U.K. 8.5%.

Transport and communications

Transport. Railroads (1995): route length 3,368 km; passenger-km 6,757,000,000; metric ton-km cargo 7,787,000,000. Roads (1995): total length 142,555 km (paved 97%). Vehicles (1996): passenger cars 4,339,231; trucks and buses 431,376. Merchant marine (1992): vessels (100 gross tons and over) 232; total deadweight tonnage 218,506. Air transport (1994): passenger-km 7,496,412,000; metric ton-km cargo 422,249,000; airports (1997) 2.

Communications

Medium	date	unit	number	units per 1,000 persons
Daily newspapers	1995	circulation	3,089,000	304
Radio	1994	receivers	7,690,000	757
Television	1995	receivers	4,700,000	464
Telephones	1995	main lines	4,632,100	457
Cellular telephones	1995	subscribers	235,000	23.2
Facsimile machines	1995	units	165,000	16.3
Personal computers	1995	units	1,400,000	138

Education and health

Educational attainment (1981). Percentage of population age 15 and over having: less than secondary education 44.4%; lower secondary 26.5%; upper secondary 17.0%; vocational 2.9%; teacher's college 0.6%; university 3.5%.
Literacy (1995): virtually 99% literate.

Education (1993–94)

	schools	teachers	students	student/ teacher ratio
Primary (age 6–12)	4,453	72,589[11, 12]	731,527	...
Secondary (age 12–18)	1,950	110,599[13]	796,914	...
Voc., teacher tr.[13]	304	14,548[14]	155,192	...
Higher[13]	21	10,517[14]	123,320	...

Health: physicians (1996[2]) 38,363 (1 per 264 persons); hospital beds (1994) 77,181 (1 per 131 persons); infant mortality rate (1996) 5.6.
Food (1995): daily per capita caloric intake 3,530 (vegetable products 68%, animal products 32%); 134% of FAO recommended minimum requirement.

Military

Total active duty personnel (1997): 44,450 (army 64.1%, navy 6.1%, air force 27.0%, medical service 2.8%). *Military expenditure as percentage of GNP* (1996): 1.7% (world 2.8%); per capita expenditure U.S.$439.

[1]Excludes certain members of the royal family serving ex officio. [2]January 1. [3]Corresponding to three language-based federal community councils: Dutch (Flanders), French (Wallonia), and bilingual (Brussels-Capital) having authority in cultural affairs; a fourth (German) community council lacks expression as an administrative region. [4]Detail does not add to total given because of rounding. [5]Former Brabant province divided on Jan. 1, 1995. [6]Includes Luxembourg. [7]1991. [8]Région Bruxelloise. [9]Represents a statistical correction. [10]Includes 404,200 unemployed. [11]Includes preschool teachers. [12]1992–93. [13]1991–92. [14]1987–88.

Internet resources for further information:
- **Belgian Federal Government On Line http://belgium.fgov.be/**

Belize

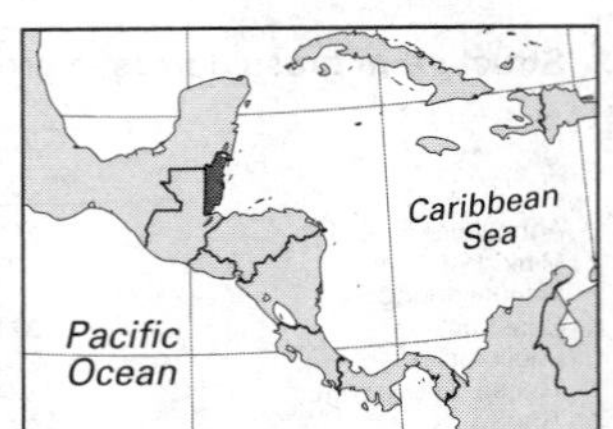

Official name: Belize.
Form of government: constitutional monarchy with two legislative houses (Senate [8[1]]; House of Representatives [29[2]]).
Chief of state: British Monarch represented by Governor-General.
Head of government: Prime Minister.
Capital: Belmopan.
Official language: English.
Official religion: none.
Monetary unit: 1 Belize dollar (BZ$) = 100 cents; valuation (Oct. 3, 1997) 1 U.S.$ = BZ$2.00[3]; 1 £ = BZ$3.22.

Area and population

		area		population
Districts	Capitals	sq mi	sq km	1994 estimate
Belize	Belize City	1,663	4,307	62,939
Cayo	San Ignacio	2,006	5,196	41,594
Corozal	Corozal	718	1,860	31,412
Orange Walk	Orange Walk	1,790	4,636	33,855
Stann Creek	Dangriga	986	2,554	19,957
Toledo	Punta Gorda	1,704	4,413	19,243
TOTAL		8,867[4]	22,965[4, 5]	209,000

Demography

Population (1997): 228,000.
Density (1997): persons per sq mi 25.7, persons per sq km 9.9.
Urban-rural (1994): urban 47.5%; rural 52.5%.
Sex distribution (1996): male 50.02%; female 49.98%.
Age breakdown (1996): under 15, 41.6%; 15–29, 26.4%; 30–44, 16.3%; 45–59, 8.6%; 60 and over, 7.1%.
Population projection: (2000) 248,000; (2010) 307,000.
Doubling time: 26 years.
Ethnic composition (1991): mestizo (Spanish-Indian) 43.6%; Creole (predominantly black) 29.8%; Mayan Indian 11.0%; Garifuna (black-Carib Indian) 6.7%; white 3.9%; East Indian 3.5%; other or not stated 1.5%.
Religious affiliation (1991): Roman Catholic 57.7%; Protestant 34.3%, of which Anglican 7.0%, Pentecostal 6.3%, Methodist 4.2%, Seventh-day Adventist 4.1%, Mennonite 4.0%; other Christian 1.7%; other 0.3%; none or not stated 6.0%.
Major cities (1996): Belize City 52,670; Orange Walk 14,960; San Ignacio/Santa Elena 11,315; Corozal 8,020; Belmopan 6,490.

Vital statistics

Birth rate per 1,000 population (1996): 32.8 (world avg. 25.0); (1992) legitimate 41.6%; illegitimate 58.4%.
Death rate per 1,000 population (1996): 5.7 (world avg. 9.3).
Natural increase rate per 1,000 population (1996): 27.1 (world avg. 15.7).
Total fertility rate (avg. births per childbearing woman; 1996): 4.1.
Marriage rate per 1,000 population (1994): 6.3.
Divorce rate per 1,000 population (1993): 0.6.
Life expectancy at birth (1996): male 66.6 years; female 70.6 years.
Major causes of death per 100,000 population (1990): accidents 92.6; heart diseases 84.7; diseases of the respiratory system 57.1; malignant neoplasms (cancers) 52.4; cerebrovascular disease 47.6; diabetes mellitus 37.0.

National economy

Budget (1996–97). Revenue: BZ$302,800,000 (current revenue 88.3%; development revenue 11.7%). Expenditures: BZ$375,000,000 (current expenditures 71.2%; development expenditures 28.8%, of which foreign grants and loans 27.0%).
Tourism (1995): receipts from visitors U.S.$78,000,000; expenditures by nationals abroad U.S.$21,000,000.
Production (metric tons except as noted). Agriculture, forestry, fishing (1996): sugarcane 1,091,000, oranges 127,900, bananas 67,000, grapefruits 44,000, corn (maize) 28,200, rice 9,600, coconuts 3,200, red kidney beans 3,100, cacao 182, honey (1994) 72; livestock (number of live animals) 60,000 cattle, 22,000 pigs, 1,300,000 chickens; roundwood (1994) 187,600 cu m; fish catch (1995) 1,366, of which shrimp 635, lobsters 392, conchs 184, freshwater and marine fish 155. Mining and quarrying (1995): sand and gravel 320,000; limestone 310,000. Manufacturing (1995): sugar (1996) 110,500; molasses 46,500; fertilizer 26,600; flour 11,500; orange concentrate (1996) 113,000 hectolitres; beer 41,100 hectolitres; grapefruit concentrate (1996) 34,000 hectolitres; cigarettes 94,000,000 units; garments (1996) 2,100,000 units. Construction (publicly financed buildings under construction; 1991): residential 180 units; nonresidential, n.a. Energy production (consumption): electricity (kW-hr; 1994) 110,000,000 (110,000,000); coal, none (none); crude petroleum, none (none); petroleum products (metric tons; 1994) none (81,000); natural gas, none (none).
Household income and expenditure. Average household size (1991) 4.9; average annual income of employed head of household (1993) BZ$6,450[6] (U.S.$3,225[6]); sources of income: n.a.; expenditure (1990): food, beverages, and tobacco 34.0%, transportation 13.7%, energy and water 9.1%, housing 9.0%, clothing and footwear 8.8%, household furnishings 8.0%.
Population economically active (1996): total 75,450; activity rate of total population, 34.1% (participation rates: ages 14–64, 58.5%; female 30.8%; unemployed 13.8%).

Price and earnings indexes (1990 = 100)

	1990	1991	1992	1993	1994	1995	1996
Consumer price index	100.0	102.3	104.7	106.2	109.0	112.1	115.6
Earnings index	...	...	...	...	...	...	...

Public debt (external, outstanding; 1995): U.S.$220,300,000.
Gross national product (1995): U.S.$568,000,000 (U.S.$2,630 per capita).

Structure of gross domestic product and labour force

	1995		1996	
	in value BZ$'000[7]	% of total value	labour force	% of labour force
Agriculture, fishing, forestry	205,800	20.9	18,650	24.7
Mining	6,200	0.6	85	0.1
Manufacturing	135,600	13.7	6,770	9.0
Construction	65,400	6.6	3,250	4.3
Public utilities	36,400	3.7	925	1.2
Transp. and commun.	100,700	10.2	3,845	5.1
Trade, restaurants	170,400	17.3	13,815	18.3
Finance, real estate, insurance	121,300	12.3	1,760	2.3
Pub. admin., defense	123,900	12.6	15,015	19.9
Services	59,800	6.1		
Other	−39,500[8]	−4.0[8]	11,335[9]	15.0[9]
TOTAL	986,000	100.0	75,450	100.0[5]

Land use (1994): forested 92.1%; meadows and pastures 2.2%; agricultural and under permanent cultivation 3.6%; other 2.1%.

Foreign trade[10]

Balance of trade (current prices)

	1991	1992	1993	1994	1995	1996
BZ$'000,000	−222.5	−217.2	−237.8	−170.6	−144.4	−129.4
% of total	31.4%	27.9%	30.3%	22.0%	18.3%	16.2%

Imports (1995): BZ$517,000,000 (machinery and transport equipment 25.8%; food and beverages 18.3%; mineral fuels and lubricants 11.5%; chemicals and chemical products 10.7%). *Major import sources:* U.S. 54.0%; Mexico 11.0%; U.K. 6.3%; Netherlands Antilles 5.0%; Canada 3.0%.
Exports (1995): BZ$323,400,000 (domestic exports 88.4%, of which raw sugar 29.5%, orange concentrate 13.9%, bananas 13.6%, marine products 9.6%, garments 9.0%; reexports 11.6%). *Major export destinations:* U.K. 42.0%; U.S. 36.0%; Germany 5.0%; Canada 4.0%.

Transport and communications

Transport. Railroads: none. Roads (1995): total length 1,721 mi, 2,770 km (paved 19%). Vehicles (1993): passenger cars 10,667; trucks and buses 6,108. Merchant marine (1992): vessels (100 gross tons and over) 32; total deadweight tonnage 45,706. Air transport (1995)[11]: passenger arrivals 174,824, passenger departures 191,409; cargo loaded 299 metric tons, cargo unloaded 1,176 metric tons. Airports (1997) with scheduled flights 9.

Communications

Medium	date	unit	number	units per 1,000 persons
Radio	1996	receivers	29,620	133
Television	1995	receivers	23,547	109
Telephones	1995	main lines	28,900	134
Cellular telephones	1995	subscribers	1,200	5.6
Facsimile machines	1995	units	500	2.3
Personal computers	1995	units	6,000	28

Education and health

Educational attainment (1991). Percentage of population age 25 and over having: no formal schooling 13.0%; primary education 64.3%; secondary 14.9%; higher 6.6%; other 1.2%. *Literacy* (1991): total population age 14 and over literate 75,500 (70.3%).

Education (1996–97)

	schools	teachers	students	student/ teacher ratio
Primary (age 5–12)	245	1,976[12]	52,994	25.9[12]
Secondary (age 13–16)	30	740[12]	10,648	13.7[12]
Higher	11	...	2,469	...

Health: physicians (1995) 139 (1 per 1,546 persons); hospital beds (1993) 585 (1 per 350 persons); infant mortality rate per 1,000 live births (1996) 33.9.
Food (1992): daily per capita caloric intake 2,662 (vegetable products 75%, animal products 25%); 118% of FAO recommended minimum requirement.

Military

Total active duty personnel (1996): 1,050 (army 95.2%, maritime wing 4.8%). *Military expenditure as percentage of GNP* (1995): 1.6% (world 2.8%); per capita expenditure U.S.$41.

[1]Excludes president of the Senate, who may be elected by the Senate from outside its appointed membership. [2]Excludes speaker of the House of Representatives, who may be elected by the House from outside its elected membership. [3]The Belize dollar is officially pegged to the U.S. dollar. [4]Includes offshore cays totaling 266 sq mi (689 sq km). [5]Detail does not add to total given because of rounding. [6]Estimated figure for about 33,000 employed heads of household. [7]At factor cost. [8]Less imputed bank service charges. [9]Includes 910 not adequately defined and 10,425 unemployed. [10]Import figures are f.o.b. in balance of trade and c.i.f. in commodities and trading partners. [11]Belize international airport only. [12]1994–95.

Internet resources for further information:
- **Belize Information Service Home Page http://www.belize.gov.bz/bis.htm**

Benin

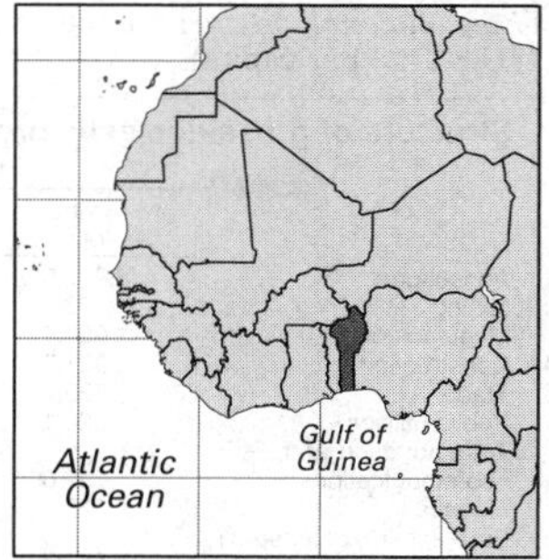

Official name: République du Bénin (Republic of Benin).
Form of government: multiparty republic with one legislative house (National Assembly [83[1]]).
Head of state and government: President, assisted by Prime Minister.
Capital[2]: Porto-Novo.
Official language: French.
Official religion: none.
Monetary unit: 1 CFA franc (CFAF) = 100 centimes; valuation (Oct. 3, 1997) 1 U.S.$ = CFAF 592.29; 1 £ = CFAF 954.76.

Area and population		area		population
				1992
Provinces[3]	**Capitals**	sq mi	sq km	census
Atacora	Natitingou	12,050	31,200	648,330
Atlantique	Cotonou	1,250	3,200	1,060,310
Borgou	Parakou	19,700	51,000	816,278
Mono	Lokossa	1,500	3,880	646,954
Ouémé	Porto-Novo	1,800	4,700	869,492
Zou	Abomey	7,200	18,700	813,985
TOTAL		43,500	112,680	4,855,349

Demography

Population (1997): 5,902,000.
Density (1997): persons per sq mi 135.7, persons per sq km 52.4.
Urban-rural (1994): urban 41.0%; rural 59.0%.
Sex distribution (1997): male 48.83%; female 51.17%.
Age breakdown (1997): under 15, 48.0%; 15–29, 27.5%; 30–44, 13.5%; 45–59, 7.2%; 60–74, 3.1%; 75 and over, 0.7%.
Population projection: (2000) 6,517,000; (2010) 8,955,000.
Doubling time: 21 years.
Ethnic composition (1992): Fon 39.7%; Yoruba (Nago) 12.1%; Adjara 11.1%; Bariba 8.6%; Aizo 8.6%; Somba (Otomary) 6.6%; Fulani 5.6%; other 7.7%.
Religious affiliation (1991): traditional beliefs, including voodoo 62.0%; Christian 23.3%, of which Roman Catholic 21.0%, Protestant 2.3%; Muslim 12.0%; other 2.7%.
Major cities (1992): Cotonou 533,212; Porto-Novo 177,660; Djougou 132,192; Abomey-Calavi 125,565; Parakou 106,708.

Vital statistics

Birth rate per 1,000 population (1997): 46.0 (world avg. 25.0).
Death rate per 1,000 population (1997): 13.0 (world avg. 9.3).
Natural increase rate per 1,000 population (1997): 33.0 (world avg. 15.7).
Total fertility rate (avg. births per childbearing woman; 1997): 6.6.
Marriage rate per 1,000 population (1980–85): 12.8.
Divorce rate per 1,000 population (1980–85): 0.8.
Life expectancy at birth (1996): male 50.7 years; female 54.7 years.
Major causes of death per 100,000 population (1995): n.a.; however, of the 13,680 reported cases of selected infectious diseases (notifiable to the World Health Organization), measles 77%, tuberculosis 18%, leprosy 4%, acquired immune deficiency syndrome (AIDS) 2%, neonatal tetanus 0.2%.

National economy

Budget (1997). Revenue: CFAF 183,984,000,000 (1996; current receipts 68.2%, of which nonpetroleum fiscal receipts and customs duties 56.3%, other nonfiscal receipts 11.9%). Expenditures: CFAF 295,547,000,000 (1996; current expenditures 63.9%, of which salaries 24.9%, debt service 12.2%).
Production (metric tons except as noted). Agriculture, forestry, fishing (1997): cassava 1,451,628, yams 1,346,040, corn (maize) 503,818, seed cotton 444,124, sorghum 111,843, tomatoes 71,714, peanuts (groundnuts) 84,206, dry beans 58,966, sweet potatoes 67,732, millet 28,758, coconuts 20,000, sugarcane 29,594, karité nuts (shea nuts) 15,000, paddy rice 21,788, palm kernels 13,300[4], bananas 13,000, mangoes 12,000, oranges 12,000, pineapples 3,000, tobacco 325; livestock (number of live animals; 1997) 1,350,000 cattle, 1,012,960 goats, 601,183 sheep, 584,000 pigs, 25,000,000 chickens; roundwood (1995) 5,899,000 cu m; fish catch (1995) 37,000. Mining and quarrying (1993): limestone 500,000, marine salt 100. Manufacturing (1994): cement 380,000[5]; cotton fibre 103,000; meat 68,000; wheat flour 11,515; palm oil 9,432. Construction: n.a. Energy production (consumption): electricity (kW-hr; 1994) 6,000,000 (248,000,000); coal, none (none); crude petroleum (barrels; 1994) 2,130,000 (41,000); petroleum products (metric tons; 1994) none (144,000); natural gas, none (none).
Land use (1995): agricultural and under permanent cultivation 17.0%; other 83.0% (of which [1994] forested 30.7%, meadows and pastures 4.0%).
Tourism (1995): receipts from visitors U.S.$27,000,000; expenditures by nationals abroad U.S.$19,000,000[6].
Population economically active (1992): total 2,085,400; activity rate of total population 43.0% (participation rates: ages 15–64, 73.4%; female 42.6%; unemployed, n.a.).

Price and earnings indexes (1991 = 100)	1991	1992	1993	1994	1995	1996	1997[7]
Consumer price index	100.0	104.0	104.5	144.7	165.7	173.7	181.1
Hourly earnings index[8]	100.0	100.0	100.0	144.1	...	...	...

Gross national product (1995): U.S.$2,034,000,000 (U.S.$370 per capita).

Structure of gross domestic product and labour force	1995		1992	
	in value CFAF '000,000,000	% of total value	labour force	% of labour force[9]
Agriculture	351.5	33.9	1,147,746	55.0
Mining	7.2	0.7	661	0.0
Manufacturing	83.7	8.1	160,406	7.7
Public utilities	6.8	0.7	1,176	0.1
Construction	49.6	4.8	51,655	2.5
Transportation and communications	78.0	7.5	52,837	2.5
Trade }	215.6	20.8	432,501	20.7
Finance }			3,106	0.1
Pub. admin., defense	79.8	7.7 }	164,544	7.9
Services	103.6	10.0 }		
Other	60.0	5.8	70,814	3.4
TOTAL	1,035.8	100.0	2,085,446	100.0[10]

Public debt (external, outstanding; 1995): U.S.$1,514,000,000.
Household income and expenditure. Average household size (1992) 5.9; income per household (1983) U.S.$240; sources of income: self-employment 73.7%, wages and salaries 26.3%; expenditure: n.a.

Foreign trade

Balance of trade (current prices)	1991	1992	1993	1994	1995	1996
CFAF '000,000,000	−41.1	−50.1	−50.3	−33.5	−104.2	−64.0
% of total	17.8%	20.3%	18.8%	7.2%	20.1%	12.9%

Imports (1996): CFAF 280,200,000,000 (1990; manufactured goods 28.8%, of which cotton yarn and fabric 10.7%; food products 24.7%, of which cereals 17.6%; machinery and transport equipment 10.9%; chemical products 10.0%; refined petroleum products 8.5%; beverages and tobacco 7.3%). *Major import sources* (1995): France 27.1%; United Kingdom 9.6%; China 9.3%; Thailand 9.1%; Hong Kong 8.8%; The Netherlands 5.6%; United States 4.8%; Germany 4.3%.
Exports (1996): CFAF 216,200,000,000 (cotton yarn 49.6%, crude petroleum 2.9%, seed cotton 2.3%). *Major export destinations* (1995): Brazil 18.2%; Portugal 13.5%; Morocco 10.3%; Libya 7.5%; India 6.5%; Italy 4.5%; United States 4.5%.

Transport and communications

Transport. Railroads (1994): length 359 mi, 578 km; passenger-mi 66,500,000, passenger-km 107,000,000; short ton-mi cargo 173,000,000, metric ton-km cargo 253,000,000. Roads (1995): total length 5,257 mi, 8,460 km (paved 31.4%). Vehicles (1995): passenger cars 22,200; trucks and buses 12,400. Merchant marine (1992): vessels (100 gross tons and over) 12; total deadweight tonnage 210. Air transport (1996)[11]: passenger-mi 139,644,000, passenger-km 224,736,000; short ton-mi cargo 11,247,000, metric ton-km cargo 16,420,000; airports (1997) with scheduled flights 1.

Communications				units
Medium	date	unit	number	per 1,000 persons
Daily newspapers	1994	circulation	12,000	2
Radio	1995	receivers	400,000	73
Television	1995	receivers	20,000	4
Telephones	1995	main lines	27,500	5
Cellular telephones	1995	subscribers	1,100	0.2
Facsimile machines	1995	units	500	0.1

Education and health

Educational attainment (1992). Percentage of population age 25 and over having: no formal schooling 78.5%; primary education 10.8%; some secondary 8.2%; secondary 1.2%; postsecondary 1.3%. *Literacy* (1995): total percentage of population age 15 and over literate 37.0%; males literate 48.7%; females literate 25.8%.

Education (1993–94)	schools	teachers	students	student/ teacher ratio
Primary	2,889	12,343	602,069	48.8
Secondary	145	2,384	97,480	40.9
Voc., teacher tr.	14	283	4,873	17.2
Higher	16	602	9,964	16.5

Health: physicians (1993) 363 (1 per 14,216 persons); hospital beds (1993) 1,235 (1 per 4,182 persons); infant mortality rate per 1,000 live births (1997) 103.0.
Food (1995): daily per capita caloric intake 2,405 (vegetable products 96%, animal products 4%); 105% of FAO recommended minimum requirement.

Military

Total active duty personnel (1997): 4,800 (army 93.8%, navy 3.1%, air force 3.1%). *Military expenditure as percentage of GNP* (1995): 1.2% (world 2.8%); per capita expenditure U.S.$4.

[1]Includes one seat that was to remain vacant per the electoral code. [2]Porto-Novo, the official capital established under the constitution, is the seat of the legislature, but the president and most government ministers reside in Cotonou. [3]In 1997 an administrative reorganization created 12 *départements*, but detailed breakdown of area and population is unavailable. [4]1996. [5]1993. [6]1994. [7]May. [8]Minimum hourly industrial wage; January 1. [9]Age 10 years and over. [10]Detail does not add to total given because of rounding. [11]Represents 1/11 of the traffic of Air Afrique, which is operated by 11 West African states.

Bhutan

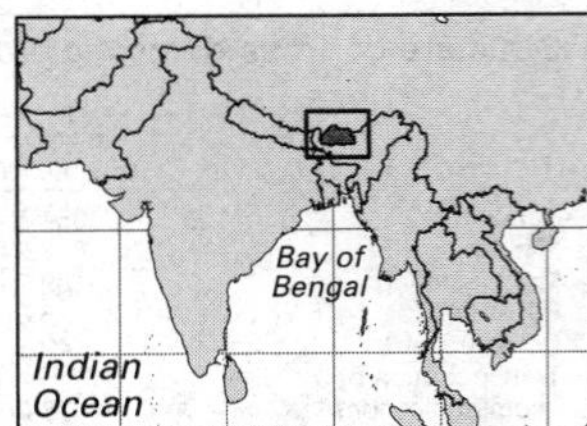

Official name: Druk-Yul (Kingdom of Bhutan).
Form of government: constitutional[1] monarchy with one legislative house (National Assembly [152[2]]).
Head of state and government: Monarch (*druk gyalpo*).
Capital: Thimphu.
Official language: Dzongkha (a Tibetan dialect).
Official religion: Mahāyāna Buddhism.
Monetary unit: 1 ngultrum[3] (Nu) = 100 chetrum; valuation (Oct. 3, 1997) 1 U.S.$ = Nu 36.17; 1 £ = Nu 58.31.

Area and population

Districts	Capitals	area sq mi	area sq km	population 1997 estimate
Bumthang	Jakar	1,150	2,990	...
Chhukha	Chhukha	...	...	...
Chirang	Damphu	310	800	...
Dagana	Dagana	540	1,400	...
Gaylegphug	Gaylegphug	1,020	2,640	...
Ha	Ha	830	2,140	...
Lhuntshi	Lhuntshi	1,120	2,910	...
Mongar	Mongar	710	1,830	...
Paro	Paro	580	1,500	...
Pema Gatsel	Pema Gatsel	150	380	...
Punakha	Punakha	2,330	6,040	...
Samchi	Samchi	830	2,140	...
Samdrup Jongkhar	Samdrup Jongkhar	900	2,340	...
Shemgang	Shemgang	980	2,540	...
Tashigang	Tashigang	1,640	4,260	...
Thimphu	Thimphu	630	1,620	...
Tongsa	Tongsa	570	1,470	...
Wangdi Phodrang	Wangdi Phodrang	1,160	3,000	...
TOTAL		18,150[4, 5]	47,000[4, 5]	860,000[6]

Demography

Population (1997): 860,000[6].
Density (1997): persons per sq mi 47.4, persons per sq km 18.3.
Urban-rural (1997): urban 7.0%; rural 93.0%.
Sex distribution (1988): male 50.97%; female 49.03%.
Age breakdown (1988): under 15, 40.3%; 15–29, 26.4%; 30–44, 16.5%; 45–59, 10.5%; 60–74, 5.2%; 75 and over, 1.1%.
Population projection: (2000) 916,000; (2010) 1,129,000.
Doubling time: 26 years.
Ethnic composition (1993): Bhutiā (Ngalops) 50.0%; Nepalese (Gurung) 35.0%; Sharchops 15.0%.
Religious affiliation (1980): Buddhist 69.6%; Hindu 24.6%; Muslim 5.0%; other 0.8%.
Major cities (1993): Thimphu 30,340; Phuntsholing 10,000[7].

Vital statistics

Birth rate per 1,000 population (1997): 41.3 (world avg. 25.0); legitimate, n.a.; illegitimate, n.a.
Death rate per 1,000 population (1997): 13.9 (world avg. 9.3).
Natural increase rate per 1,000 population (1997): 27.4 (world avg. 15.7).
Total fertility rate (avg. births per childbearing woman; 1997): 5.9.
Marital status of population 15 years and over (1985): married 71.2%; single 19.7%; widowed 7.5%; divorced 1.6%.
Divorce rate per 1,000 population: n.a.
Life expectancy at birth (1997): male 51.0 years; female 53.0 years.
Major causes of death (percentage distribution; 1989): respiratory tract infections 19.5%; diarrhea/dysentery 15.2%; skin infections 12.2%; parasitic worm infestations 10.0%; malaria 9.4%.

National economy

Budget (1996–97). Revenue: Nu 5,107,000,000 (internal revenue 38.8%, grants from UN and other international agencies 33.5%, grants from government of India 27.7%). Expenditures: Nu 5,663,000,000 (capital expenditures 61.2%, current expenditures 38.8%).
Public debt (external, outstanding; 1995): U.S.$86,600,000.
Production (metric tons except as noted). Agriculture, forestry, fishing (1996): oranges 58,000, rice 50,000, corn (maize) 39,000, potatoes 34,000, sugarcane 13,000, green peppers and chilies 8,500, millet 7,000, apples 5,500, wheat 5,000, barley 4,000, pulses 1,600; livestock (number of live animals) 435,000 cattle, 75,000 pigs, 59,000 sheep, 42,000 goats, 30,000 horses; roundwood (1995) 1,399,000 cu m; fish catch (1995) 340. Mining and quarrying (1995): limestone 267,000; dolomite 249,000; gypsum 52,000. Manufacturing (value in Nu '000,000; 1994): chemical products 419.0; cement 255.1; wood board products 230.6; distillery products 178.3; processed fruits 103.0. Construction (number of buildings completed; 1977–78): residential 10; nonresidential (guest house) 1. Energy production (consumption): electricity (kW-hr; 1994) 1,682,000,000 (230,000,000); coal (metric tons; 1994) 2,000 (20,000); crude petroleum, none (n.a.); petroleum products (metric tons; 1994) none (31,000); natural gas, none (n.a.).
Household income and expenditure. Average household size (1980) 5.4[6]; income per household: n.a.; sources of income: n.a.; expenditure (1979): food 72.3%, clothing 21.2%, energy 3.7%, household durable goods 0.7%, personal effects and other 2.1%.

Gross national product (at current market prices; 1995): U.S.$295,000,000 (U.S.$420 per capita).

Structure of gross domestic product and labour force

	1995 in value Nu '000,000	1995 % of total value	1984 labour force	1984 % of labour force
Agriculture	3,912.8	41.6	303,000[8]	87.2
Mining	193.1	2.0	3,000[8]	0.9
Manufacturing	1,088.8	11.6		
Construction	921.9	9.8		
Trade	730.7	7.8		
Public utilities	826.1	8.8		
Transportation and communications	687.6	7.3		
Finance	525.2	5.6		
Pub. admin., defense	751.4	8.0	12,000[8]	3.4
Services			30,000[8]	8.5[9]
Other	−231.0[10]	−2.5[10]	...	...
TOTAL	9,406.6	100.0	348,000	100.0

Population economically active (1984)[6]: total 348,000; activity rate of total population 53.4% (participation rates: ages 15–64, 94.8%; female 55.0%; unemployed 6.5%).

Price and earnings indexes (1990 = 100)

	1989	1990	1991	1992	1993	1994	1995
Consumer price index	90.9	100.0	112.3	130.2	144.8	155.0	168.3
Earnings index	...	...	...	...	...	...	...

Land use (1994): forested 66.0%; meadows and pastures 5.8%; agricultural and under permanent cultivation 2.8%; other 25.4%.
Tourism (1995): receipts from visitors U.S.$5,830,000; expenditures by nationals abroad, n.a.

Foreign trade[11]

Balance of trade (current prices)

	1989–90	1990–91	1991–92	1992–93	1993–94	1994–95
Nu '000,000	−481.6	−583.5	−687.9	−1,633.6	−966.2	−1,337.4
% of total	17.5%	18.3%	17.4%	30.8%	18.7%	23.1%

Imports (1994–95): Nu 3,562,400,000 ([12]petroleum products 7.4%, rice 6.9%, motor vehicles and parts 5.1%, iron and steel products 2.0%, fabrics 1.2%, machinery parts 0.4%). *Major import source:* India 77.2%.
Exports (1994–95): Nu 2,225,000,000 ([12]electricity 24.9%, cement 12.8%, timber and wood manufactures 11.5%, fruit and vegetables 9.5%). *Major export destination:* India 93.8%.

Transport and communications

Transport. Railroads: none. Roads (1995): total length 1,998 mi, 3,216 km (paved [1991] 79%). Vehicles (1988): passenger cars 2,590; trucks and buses 1,367. Merchant marine: none. Air transport (1996): passenger-mi 29,000,000, passenger-km 46,000,000; metric ton-km cargo, n.a.; airports (1997) with scheduled flights 1.

Communications

Medium	date	unit	number	units per 1,000 persons
Radio	1996	receivers	23,000	27
Television	...	receivers	...	...
Telephones	1995	main lines	5,200	6.3
Facsimile machines	1995	units	300	0.4

Education and health

Educational attainment: n.a. *Literacy* (1995 est.): total population age 15 and over literate 42.2%; males literate 56.2%; females literate 28.1%.

Education (1990)

	schools	teachers	students	student/teacher ratio
Primary (age 7–11)[13]	235	1,859	56,773	30.5
Secondary (age 12–16)	31	662	15,984	24.1
Voc., teacher tr.	8	149	1,822	12.2
Higher	2	57	519	9.1

Health: physicians (1994) 100 (1 per 8,000 persons); hospital beds 970 (1 per 825 persons); infant mortality rate per 1,000 live births (1997) 105.
Food (1975–77): daily per capita caloric intake 2,058 (vegetable products 98%, animal products 2%); 89% of FAO recommended minimum requirement.

Military

Total active duty personnel (1993): about 7,000 (army 100%).

[1]There is no formal constitution, but a form of constitutional monarchy is in place. [2]Includes 47 nonelective seats occupied by representatives of the King and religious groups. [3]Indian currency is also accepted legal tender; the ngultrum is at par with the Indian rupee. [4]2,700 sq mi (7,000 sq km) are not included in the district area totals. [5]Includes Chhukha area. [6]The figure stated is an estimate based on recent reported figures resulting from the repudiation of the 1980 census by the King and from the existence of a large number of Nepalese refugees; as such the actual population could range from 700,000 to 1,800,000. [7]1982. [8]Derived value. [9]Includes 6.5% with no occupation. [10]Imputed bank service charges. [11]Import figures are c.i.f. in balance of trade, commodities, and trading partners. [12]Trade data with India only. [13]1993.

Bolivia

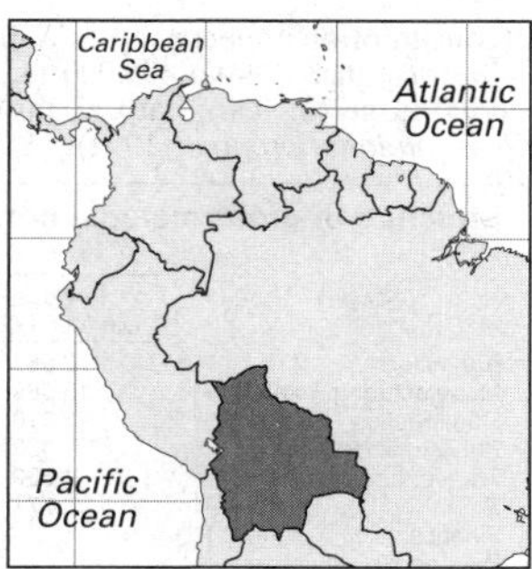

Official name: República de Bolivia (Republic of Bolivia).
Form of government: unitary multiparty republic with two legislative houses (Chamber of Senators [27]; Chamber of Deputies [130]).
Head of state and government: President.
Capitals: La Paz (administrative); Sucre (judicial).
Official languages: Spanish, Aymara, Quechua.
Official religion: Roman Catholicism.
Monetary unit: 1 boliviano (Bs) = 100 centavos; valuation (Oct. 3, 1997) 1 U.S.$ = Bs 5.30; 1 £ = Bs 8.54.

Area and population

Departments	Capitals	area sq mi	area sq km	population 1997 estimate
Beni	Trinidad	82,458	213,564	336,633
Chuquisaca	Sucre	19,893	51,524	549,835
Cochabamba	Cochabamba	21,479	55,631	1,408,071
La Paz	La Paz	51,732	133,985	2,268,824
Oruro	Oruro	20,690	53,588	383,498
Pando	Cobija	24,644	63,827	53,124
Potosí	Potosí	45,644	118,218	746,618
Santa Cruz	Santa Cruz	143,098	370,621	1,651,950
Tarija	Tarija	14,526	37,623	368,506
TOTAL		424,164	1,098,581	7,767,059

Demography

Population (1997): 7,767,000.
Density (1997): persons per sq mi 18.3, persons per sq km 7.1.
Urban-rural (1997): urban 61.2%; rural 38.8%.
Sex distribution (1997): male 49.68%; female 50.32%.
Age breakdown (1995): under 15, 40.6%; 15–29, 27.5%; 30–44, 16.3%; 45–59, 9.6%; 60–74, 5.0%; 75 and over, 1.0%.
Population projection: (2000) 8,329,000; (2010) 10,229,000.
Doubling time: 29 years.
Ethnic composition (1996): Indian 55.0%; mestizo 30.0%; white 15.0%.
Religious affiliation (1995): Roman Catholic 88.5%; Protestant 10.4%.
Major cities (1993): La Paz 784,976; Santa Cruz 767,260; Cochabamba 448,756; El Alto 446,189; Oruro 201,831; Sucre 144,994.

Vital statistics

Birth rate per 1,000 population (1997): 33.5 (world avg. 25.0).
Death rate per 1,000 population (1997): 9.2 (world avg. 9.3).
Natural increase rate per 1,000 population (1997): 24.3 (world avg. 15.7).
Total fertility rate (avg. births per childbearing woman; 1997): 4.4.
Marriage rate per 1,000 population (1980): 4.8.
Life expectancy at birth (1997): male 59.6 years; female 62.9 years.
Major causes of death (percentage of total registered deaths; 1980–81): infectious and parasitic diseases 23.9%; diseases of the circulatory system 19.5%; diseases of the respiratory system 14.0%; accidents, homicides, and violence 9.8%; diseases of the digestive system 8.6%.

National economy

Budget (1995). Revenue: Bs 5,256,100,000 (taxes on goods and services 39.5%, income of government enterprises 24.6%, property taxes 10.2%, taxes on international trade 6.7%, social security contributions 6.5%, income taxes 2.5%). Expenditures: Bs 6,801,600,000 (education 19.3%, social security 16.0%, public services 14.0%, transportation and communications 12.3%, defense 8.4%, public order and safety 8.1%, health 6.2%).
Production (metric tons except as noted). Agriculture, forestry, fishing (1996): sugarcane 4,120,000, soybeans 862,000, potatoes 715,000, corn (maize) 613,000, bananas and plantains 495,000, rice 344,000, cassava 311,000, wheat 99,000, coffee 22,000; livestock (number of live animals) 8,039,000 sheep, 6,118,000 cattle, 2,482,000 pigs, 1,496,000 goats, 631,000 asses, 322,000 horses; roundwood (1995) 2,208,000 cu m; fish catch (1995) 6,308. Mining and quarrying (metric tons of pure metal; 1996): zinc 144,764; lead 16,538; tin 14,778; silver 384; gold 14.9. Manufacturing (value added in U.S.$'000; 1994): petroleum products 375; food products 169; beverages 99; nonmetal mineral products 36; textiles 23; printing and publishing 19; nonferrous metals 18. Construction (1985)[1]: residential dwellings 226. Energy production (consumption): electricity (kW-hr; 1994) 2,876,000,000 (2,892,000,000); coal, none (none); crude petroleum (barrels; 1994) 8,937,000 (9,268,000); petroleum products (metric tons; 1994) 1,183,000 (1,257,000); natural gas (cu m; 1994) 3,425,000,000 (1,159,000,000).
Population economically active (1992): total 2,530,409; activity rate of total population 33.6% (participation rates: ages 15–64, 63.6%; female 39.0%; unemployed 2.5%).

Price and earnings indexes (1990 = 100)

	1990	1991	1992	1993	1994	1995	1996
Consumer price index	100.0	121.4	136.1	147.7	159.3	175.6	197.4
Monthly earnings index[2]	100.0	113.8	131.8	152.6	177.1	195.9	...

Public debt (external, outstanding; 1995): U.S.$4,452,000,000.
Gross national product (at current market prices; 1995): U.S.$5,905,000,000 (U.S.$800 per capita).

Structure of gross domestic product and labour force

	1996 in value Bs '000[3]	1996 % of total value[3]	1992 labour force[4]	1992 % of labour force[4]
Agriculture	2,906,264	14.9	984,407	38.9
Mining	1,923,665	9.9	52,623	2.1
Manufacturing	3,264,962	16.8	222,485	8.8
Construction	705,764	3.6	129,409	5.1
Public utilities	418,125	2.2	6,086	0.2
Transp. and commun.	1,944,309	10.0	116,800	4.6
Trade	2,359,237	12.1	232,429	9.2
Finance	2,221,079	11.4	54,711	2.2
Pub. admin., defense	1,796,796	9.3	406,928	16.1
Services	839,871	4.3		
Other	1,066,142[5]	5.5[5]	324,531	12.8
TOTAL	19,446,214	100.0	2,530,409	100.0

Household income and expenditure. Average household size (1992): 3.8; average annual income per household: n.a.; sources of income: n.a.; expenditure (1988): food 35.5%, transportation and communications 17.7%, housing 14.8%, household durable goods 7.3%, clothing and footwear 5.1%, beverages and tobacco 4.5%, recreation 2.7%, health 2.1%, education 0.3%.
Tourism (1995): receipts from visitors U.S.$146,000,000; expenditures by nationals abroad U.S.$148,000,000.
Land use (1994): forested 53.5%; meadows and pastures 24.4%; agricultural and under permanent cultivation 2.2%; other 19.9%.

Foreign trade[6]

Balance of trade (current prices)

	1991	1992	1993	1994	1995	1996
U.S.$'000,000	+59.0	−294.4	−384.1	−89.3	−162.5	−313.4
% of total	3.6%	17.2%	20.9%	4.1%	6.9%	12.1%

Imports (1996): U.S.$1,635,023,000 (capital goods 39.1%, of which capital goods for industry 22.0%, transport equipment 15.9%; raw materials 36.8%, of which raw materials for industry 26.5%; consumer goods 21.2%, of which durable consumer goods 10.7%, nondurable consumer goods 10.5%). *Major import sources* (1995): United States 18.2%; Brazil 14.5%; Japan 13.8%; Argentina 10.4%; Chile 7.5%; Peru 5.0%; Germany 4.7%.
Exports (1996): U.S.$1,295,308,000 (soybeans 15.5%; zinc 11.7%; petroleum 10.9%; gold 9.7%; natural gas 7.3%; tin 6.4%; timber 6.4%; silver 4.9%). *Major export destinations* (1995): U.S. 23.3%; U.K. 15.1%; Peru 14.2%; Argentina 12.0%; Germany 5.4%; The Netherlands 4.3%; France 3.6%.

Transport and communications

Transport. Railroads (1993): route length 2,295 mi, 3,694 km; passenger-mi 216,800,000, passenger-km 348,900,000; short ton-mi cargo 521,900,000, metric ton-km cargo 761,900,000. Roads (1995): total length 34,478 mi, 55,487 km (paved 5%). Vehicles (1995): passenger cars 213,666; trucks and buses 133,984. Merchant marine (1992): vessels (100 gross tons and over) 1; total deadweight tonnage 15,765. Air transport (1996): passenger-mi 912,000,000, passenger-km 1,468,000,000; short ton-mi cargo 31,655,000, metric ton-km cargo 46,216,000; airports (1997) with scheduled flights 14.

Communications

Medium	date	unit	number	units per 1,000 persons
Daily newspapers	1994	circulation	500,000	69
Radio	1996	receivers	4,250,000	560
Television	1995	receivers	1,500,000	202
Telephones	1995	main lines	347,800	47
Cellular telephones	1995	subscribers	7,200	1.0

Education and health

Educational attainment (1992). Percentage of population age 25 and over having: no formal schooling 23.3%; some primary 20.3%; primary education 21.7%; some secondary 9.0%; secondary 6.5%; some higher 5.0%; higher 4.8%; not specified 9.4%. *Literacy* (1992): total population age 15 and over literate 79.5%; males literate 87.7%; females literate 71.8%.

Education (1990–91)

	schools[7]	teachers	students	student/teacher ratio
Primary (age 6–13)	9,758	51,763	1,278,775	24.7
Secondary (age 14–17)	724	12,434	219,232	17.6
Voc., teacher tr.	47			
Higher[8]	10	4,261	109,503	25.7

Health (1994): physicians 1,976 (1 per 3,663 persons); hospital beds 7,203 (1 per 1,005 persons); infant mortality rate per 1,000 live births (1997) 67.
Food (1995): daily per capita caloric intake 2,192 (vegetable products 83%, animal products 17%); 92% of FAO recommended minimum requirement.

Military

Total active duty personnel (1997): 33,500 (army 74.6%, navy 13.4%, air force 12.0%). *Military expenditure as percentage of GNP* (1995): 2.3% (world 2.8%); per capita expenditure U.S.$18.

[1]National government sponsored only. [2]Private-sector earnings in La Paz. [3]In 1990 prices. [4]Population 7 years of age and over. [5]Net import duties. [6]Import figures are f.o.b. in balance of trade and c.i.f. for commodities and trading partners. [7]1986–87. [8]1991–92.

Internet resources for further information:
- **Instituto Nacional de Estadística http://www.ine.gov.bo/**
- **UNDP Bolivia http://guf.pnud.bo/bolbrief.htm**

Bosnia and Herzegovina[1]

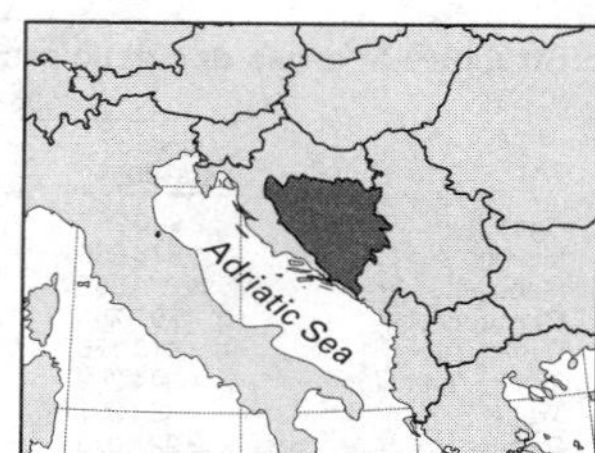

Official name: Bosna i Hercegovina (Bosnia and Herzegovina).
Form of government: federal multiparty republic with bicameral legislature (Senate [15[2]]; House of Representatives [42]).
Chief of state: Chairman of the tripartite presidency.
Heads of government: Two cochairmen of the Council of Ministers.
Capital: Sarajevo.
Official language: Serbo-Croatian.
Official religion: none.
Monetary unit: 1 Bosnian dinar[3] (BD) = 100 para; valuation (Oct. 3, 1997) 1 U.S.$ = BD 176.25; 1 £ = BD 284.11.

Area and population (1991 census)[4]

Districts	population	Districts	population	Districts	population
Banja Luka	195,139	Grude	15,976	Pucarevo	30,624
Banovići	26,507	Han Pijesak	6,346	Rogatica	21,812
Bihać	70,896	Jablanica	12,664	Rudo	11,572
Bijeljina	96,796	Jajce	44,903	Sanski Most	60,119
Bileća	13,269	Kakanj	55,857	Sarajevo	525,980
Bosanska Dubica	31,577	Kalesija	41,795	Šekovići	9,639
Bosanska Gradiška	60,062	Kalinovik	4,657	Šipovo	15,553
Bosanska Krupa	58,212	Kiseljak	24,081	Skender Vakuf	19,416
Bosanski Brod	33,962	Kladanj	16,028	Sokolac	14,833
Bosanski Novi	41,541	Ključ	37,233	Srbac	21,660
Bosanski Petrovac	15,552	Konjic	43,636	Srebrenica	37,211
Bosanski Šamac	32,835	Kotor Varoš	36,670	Srebrenik	40,769
Bosansko Grahovo	8,303	Kreševo	6,699	Stolac	18,845
Bratunac	33,575	Kupres	10,728	Tešanj	48,390
Brčko	87,332	Laktaši	29,910	Teslič	59,632
Breza	17,266	Lištica	26,437	Titov Drvar	17,079
Bugojno	46,843	Livno	39,526	Tomislavgrad	29,261
Busovača	18,883	Ljubinje	4,162	Travnik	70,402
Čajniće	8,919	Ljubuški	27,182	Trebinje	30,879
Capljina	27,852	Lopare	32,400	Tuzla	131,861
Cazin	63,406	Lukavac	56,830	Ugljevik	25,641
Celinac	18,666	Maglaj	43,294	Vareš	22,114
Citluk	14,709	Modriča	35,413	Velika Kladuša	52,921
Derventa	56,328	Mostar	126,067	Višegrad	21,202
Doboj	102,546	Mrkonjič Grad	27,379	Visoko	46,130
Donji Vakuf	24,232	Neum	4,268	Vitez	27,728
Foča	40,513	Nevesinje	14,421	Vlasenica	33,817
Fojnica	16,227	Odžak	30,651	Zavidovići	57,153
Gacko	10,844	Olovo	16,901	Zenica	145,577
Glamoč	12,421	Orašje	28,201	Žepče	22,840
Goražde	37,505	Posušje	16,659	Živinice	54,653
Gornji Vakuf	25,130	Prijedor	112,470	Zvornik	81,111
Gracanica	59,050	Prnjavor	46,894	TOTAL	4,365,639
Gradačac	56,378	Prozor	19,601		

Demography

Area: 19,741 sq mi, 51,129 sq km.
Population (1997)[5]: 3,124,000.
Density (1997)[5]: persons per sq mi 158.2, persons per sq km 61.1.
Urban-rural (1981): urban 36.2%; rural 63.8%.
Sex distribution (1991): male 49.79%; female 50.21%.
Age breakdown (1991): under 15, 23.4%; 15–29, 26.5%; 30–44, 22.8%; 45–64, 16.0%; 65 and over, 11.3%.
Population projection: (2000) 3,012,000; (2010) 3,328,000.
Ethnic composition (1991): Muslim 49.2%; Serb 31.3%; Croat 17.3%.
Religious affiliation (1992): Muslim 40%; Serbian Orthodox 31%; Roman Catholic 15%; Protestant 4%; other 10%.
Major cities (1991): Sarajevo (1997) 360,000; Banja Luka 143,079; Zenica 96,027; Tuzla 83,770; Mostar 75,865.

Vital statistics

Birth rate per 1,000 population (1996): 7.9 (world avg. 25.0); (1993) legitimate 92.6%; illegitimate 7.4%.
Death rate per 1,000 population (1996): 15.4 (world avg. 9.3).
Natural increase rate per 1,000 population (1996): −8.5 (world avg. 15.7).
Total fertility rate (avg. births per childbearing woman; 1996): 1.0.
Marriage rate per 1,000 population (1991): 6.0.
Divorce rate per 1,000 population (1991): 0.3.
Life expectancy at birth (1996): male 51.2 years; female 61.4 years.
Major causes of death per 100,000 population (1989): circulatory diseases 344.1; malignant neoplasms (cancers) 122.6; accidents, violence, and poisoning 47.1; digestive system diseases 29.2; respiratory diseases 29.0.

National economy

Budget (1997). Revenue: DM 618,000,000 (primarily customs duties). Expenditures: DM 598,500,000 (defense 41.0%, disability benefits 29.3%).
Production (metric tons except as noted). Agriculture, forestry, fishing (1996): corn (maize) 589,000, potatoes 347,000, wheat 166,000, barley 47,000; livestock (head) 314,000 cattle, 276,000 sheep, 165,000 pigs; roundwood (1995) 40,000 cu m; fish catch (1995) 2,500. Mining (1995): iron ore (gross weight) 150,000; bauxite 75,000; barite (concentrate) 2,000. Manufacturing (1995): cement 150,000; crude steel 115,000; pig iron 100,000; coke 100,000. Construction (residential units constructed; 1990): 26,568. Energy production (consumption): electricity (kW-hr; 1994) 1,921,000,000 (2,081,000,000); coal (metric tons; 1994) 1,400,000 (1,400,000); petroleum products (metric tons; 1994) none (35,000); natural gas (cu m; 1994) none (378,000,000).
Gross national product (1994)[6]: U.S.$2,470,000,000 (U.S.$700 per capita).

Structure of gross material product and labour force

	1989		1990	
	in value Din '000,000[7]	% of total value	labour force[8]	% of labour force[8]
Agriculture	2,963	10.9	39,053	3.8
Manufacturing, mining	15,589	57.6	496,190	48.3
Construction	1,918	7.1	74,861	7.3
Public utilities	403	1.5	22,345	2.2
Transp. and commun.	1,600	5.9	68,798	6.7
Trade	3,777	13.9	130,914	12.8
Finance }	834 }	3.1 }	38,686	3.8
Pub. admin., defense }			155,411 }	15.1 }
Services }				
Other }				
TOTAL	27,084	100.0	1,026,258	100.0

Population economically active (1991): total 992,000; activity rate of total population 22.7% (participation rates: ages 15–64, 35.6%; female [1990] 37.7%; unemployed [1996] 75.0%).

Price and earnings indexes (1985 = 100)

	1984	1985	1986	1987	1988	1989	1990
Consumer price index	58	100	188	400	1,188	16,169	109,000
Monthly earnings index	...	...	...	...	...	...	...

Household income and expenditure. Average household size (1991) 3.4; income per household (1990) Din 72,850[6] (U.S.$6,437); sources of income (1990): wages 53.2%, transfers 18.2%, self-employment 12.0%, other 16.6%; expenditure (1988): food 41.3%, clothing 8.3%, fuel and lighting 7.8%, housing 7.8%, transportation 6.0%, beverages and tobacco 5.7%.

Foreign trade[6]

Balance of trade (current prices)

	1991	1992	1993	1994	1995	1996
U.S.$'000,000	...	...	−339	−614	−891	−1,708
% of total	...	...	66.6%	89.5%	89.7%	83.3%

Imports (1996)[6]: U.S.$1,879,000,000. *Major import sources:* Croatia 32%; Slovenia 15%; Germany 13%; Italy 13%; Hungary 6%.
Exports (1996)[6]: U.S.$171,000,000. *Major export destinations:* Croatia 34%; Italy 26%; Germany 16%; Slovenia 8%; United States 5%.

Transport and communications

Transport. Railroads (1991): route length 1,021 km; passenger-km 554,000,000; metric ton-km cargo 1,946,000,000. Roads (1991): total length 21,168 km (paved 54%). Vehicles (1990): passenger cars 438,080; trucks and buses 50,578. Airports (1997) with scheduled flights 1[9].

Communications

Medium	date	unit	number	units per 1,000 persons
Daily newspapers	1995	circulation	520,000	150
Television	1995	receivers	325,000	94
Telephones	1995	main lines	237,800	69

Education and health

Educational attainment (1981). Percentage of population age 15 and over having: less than full primary education 49.5%; primary 24.2%; secondary 21.7%; postsecondary and higher 4.3%. *Literacy* (1981): total population age 10 and over literate 2,962,400 (85.5%); males 96.5%; females 76.6%.

Education (1990–91)

	schools	teachers	students	student/ teacher ratio
Primary (age 7–14)	2,205	23,369	539,875	23.1
Secondary (age 15–18)	238	9,030	172,063	19.1
Higher	44	2,802	37,541	13.4

Health: physicians (1996) 4,500[6] (1 per 703 persons); hospital beds (1990) 19,858 (1 per 217 persons); infant mortality rate (1996) 43.2.

Military

Total active duty personnel (1997): 40,000 (army 100%).

[1]Government structure provided for by Dayton accords and constitutions of 1993 and 1994 is being implemented in stages since formal signing of peace accord on Dec. 14, 1995. [2]All seats are nonelective. [3]The Bosnian dinar is pegged to the Deutsche Mark (DM) at a 100 to 1 ratio; a new Bosnian currency, the convertible Mark (pegged to the DM at a 1 to 1 ratio) is to be introduced in early 1998. [4]First-order subdivisions as of late 1996 comprised two autonomous regions: the *c.* 26,100 sq km Federation of Bosnia and Herzegovina (which is further divided into 10 cantons) and the *c.* 25,000 sq km Republika Srpska. [5]Excludes about 1,000,000 refugees in adjacent countries and Western Europe. [6]Estimated figures. [7]Yugoslav new dinar (Din). [8]Excludes 28,000 workers in the private sector. [9]Sarajevo Airport reopened in August 1996.

Internet resources for further information:

- **Embassy of Bosnia and Herzegovina (Washington, D.C.)**
  http://www.bosnianembassy.org/
- **Office of the High Representative in Bosnia and Herzegovina**
  http://www.ohr.int/

Botswana

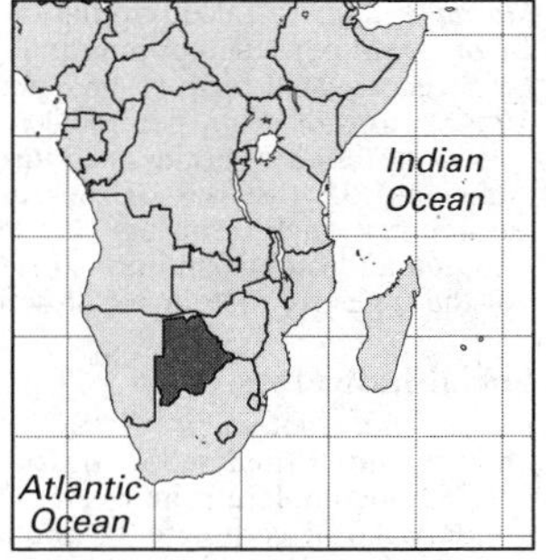

Official name: Republic of Botswana.
Form of government: multiparty republic with one legislative body[1] (National Assembly [46[2]]).
Head of state and government: President.
Capital: Gaborone.
Official language: English[3].
Official religion: none.
Monetary unit: 1 pula (P) = 100 thebe; valuation (Oct. 3, 1997) 1 U.S.$ = P 3.68; 1 £ = P 5.94.

Area and population

Districts	Capitals	area sq mi	area sq km	population 1991 census
Barolong	...	773	2,003	18,400
Central	Serowe	57,039	147,730	412,970
Ghanzi	Ghanzi	45,525	117,910	24,719
Kgalagadi	Tsabong	41,290	106,940	31,134
Kgatleng	Mochudi	3,073	7,960	57,770
Kweneng	Molepolole	13,857	35,890	170,437
Ngwaketse	Kanye	10,219	26,467	128,989
North East	Masunga	1,977	5,120	43,354
North West				
Chobe	Kasane	8,031	20,800	14,126
Ngamiland	Maun	33,359	86,400	57,811
Okavango	Orapa	8,776	22,730	36,723
South East	Ramotswa	687	1,780	43,584
Towns[4]				
Francistown	—	31	79	65,244
Gaborone	—	65	169	133,468
Jwaneng	—	39	100	11,188
Lobatse	—	16	42	26,052
Orapa	—	7	17	8,827
Selebi-Pikwe	—	19	50	39,772
Sowa	—	61	159	2,228
TOTAL		224,607[5]	581,730	1,326,796

Demography

Population (1997): 1,501,000.
Density (1997): persons per sq mi 6.7, persons per sq km 2.6.
Urban-rural (1996): urban 29.2%; rural 70.8%.
Sex distribution (1996): male 49.02%; female 50.98%.
Age breakdown (1995): under 15, 43.2%; 15–29, 28.5%; 30–44, 16.5%; 45–59, 7.9%; 60–74, 3.2%; 75 and over, 0.7%.
Population projection: (2000) 1,557,000; (2010) 1,598,000.
Doubling time: 23 years.
Ethnic composition (1983): Tswana 75.5%; Shona 12.4%; San (Bushman) 3.4%; Khoikhoin (Hottentot) 2.5%; Ndebele 1.3%; other 4.9%.
Religious affiliation (1980): traditional beliefs 49.2%; Protestant 29.0%; African Christian 11.8%; Roman Catholic 9.4%; other 0.6%.
Major cities (1993): Gaborone 156,803; Francistown 75,678; Selebi-Pikwe 42,350; Molepolole 41,730; Kanye 34,233.

Vital statistics

Birth rate per 1,000 population (1991–95): 37.1 (world avg. 25.0); (1986) legitimate 28.8%[6]; illegitimate 71.2%[6].
Death rate per 1,000 population (1991–95): 6.6 (world avg. 9.3).
Natural increase rate per 1,000 population (1991–95): 30.5 (world avg. 15.7).
Total fertility rate (avg. births per childbearing woman; 1996): 4.3.
Marriage rate per 1,000 population (1987): 1.6.
Life expectancy at birth (1993): male 59.5 years; female 65.6 years.
Major causes of death (as percentage of total of inpatient deaths[7]; 1992): respiratory diseases 14.3%; pneumonia 10.0%; digestive diseases 8.9%; cerebrovascular disease 4.2%; AIDS 3.9%; kidney disease 3.0%.

National economy

Budget (1996–97). Revenue: P 5,421,300,000 (mineral royalties 47.4%, customs and excise taxes 20.1%, property income 17.8%, interest income 4.6%). Expenditures: P 6,057,000,000 (1995–96; economic services 40.4%, education 20.8%, public order and safety 3.5%, social welfare 3.0%, health 2.5%).
Population economically active (1991): total 441,203; activity rate of total population 33.2% (participation rates: ages 15–64, 59.6%; female 38.4%; unemployed 13.9%).

Price and earnings indexes (1990 = 100)

	1990	1991	1992	1993	1994	1995	1996
Consumer price index	100.0	111.8	129.8	148.4	164.1	181.3	199.6
Monthly earnings index	100.0	113.6	133.5	162.0	169.8	181.6	...

Public debt (external, outstanding; 1995): U.S.$682,100,000.
Tourism (1995): receipts U.S.$162,000,000; expenditures U.S.$145,000,000.
Production (metric tons except as noted). Agriculture, forestry, fishing (1996): cereals 82,900 (of which sorghum 55,100, corn [maize] 23,000, millet 4,000), vegetables and melons 16,000, pulses 14,000, fruits 10,500, tubers 9,000; livestock (number of live animals) 1,950,000 cattle, 1,900,000 goats, 250,000 sheep, 237,500 mules and asses, 31,500 horses; roundwood (1995) 1,584,000 cu m; fish catch (1993) 2,000. Mining and quarrying (1996): copper 20,979; nickel 17,461; cobalt 405; diamonds 17,707,062 carats. Manufacturing (value added in P '000,000; 1994): food products 164.3; wearing apparel 78.9; paper and paper products 28.0; industrial chemicals 18.7; wood products 17.5. Construction (value added in P '000,000; 1995–96): 877,900. Energy production (consumption): electricity (kW-hr; 1993) 970,000,000 (970,000,000); coal (metric tons; 1992) 901,452 (n.a.); crude petroleum, none (n.a.).
Gross national product (1994): U.S.$4,037,000,000 (U.S.$2,800 per capita).

Structure of gross domestic product and labour force

	1995–96 in value P '000,000	1995–96 % of total value	1991 labour force	1991 % of labour force
Agriculture	546,200	3.7	97,626	22.1
Mining	5,084,800	34.2	13,264	3.0
Manufacturing	686,200	4.6	26,470	6.0
Construction	877,900	5.9	57,510	13.0
Public utilities	312,500	2.1	6,388	1.4
Transp. and commun.	507,200	3.4	11,398	2.6
Trade	2,474,000	16.6	35,194	8.0
Finance	1,231,300	8.3	13,286	3.0
Pub. admin., defense	2,517,700	16.9	34,002	7.7
Services	638,800	4.3	72,064	16.3
Other	...	...	74,001[8]	16.8[8]
TOTAL	14,876,600	100.0	441,203	100.0[5]

Household income and expenditure (1991). Average household size 4.8; average annual income per household (1985–86) P 3,910 (U.S.$2,080); sources of income (1987): wages and salaries 73.3%, self-employment 15.9%, transfers 10.8%; expenditure: food 39.4%, household durable goods 14.0%, rent and services 13.3%, transportation 13.1%, clothing 5.6%, health 2.3%.
Land use (1994): forest 46.8%; pasture 45.2%; agriculture 0.7%; other 7.3%.

Foreign trade[9]

Balance of trade (current prices)

	1990	1991	1992	1993	1994	1995
P '000,000	241.3	398.1	299.1	668.4	1,216.3	1,623.6
% of total	3.8%	5.6%	4.2%	8.4%	14.0%	15.6%

Imports (1995): P 5,304,800,000 (1994; machinery and transport equipment 29.6%, of which transport equipment 12.0%; food, beverages, and tobacco 17.6%; chemical and rubber products 9.7%; metal and metal products 9.4%; textiles and footwear 8.9%; wood and paper 5.8%; mineral fuels 5.7%). *Major import sources:* Customs Union of Southern Africa (CUSA) 73.9%; South Korea 7.1%; Zimbabwe 5.5%; U.K. 2.5%; U.S. 2.0%.
Exports (1995): P 5,931,600,000 (1994; diamonds 79.9%; copper-nickel matte 5.6%; textiles 3.8%; meat products 3.7%). *Major export destinations:* U.K. 37.5%; CUSA 21.5%; Zimbabwe 3.0%; U.S. 0.9%.

Transport and communications

Transport. Railroads (1995): length 603 mi, 971 km; passenger-km 86,000,000; metric ton-km cargo 1,710,000[10]. Roads (1995): total length 11,388 mi, 18,327 km (paved 25%). Vehicles (1994): passenger cars 27,058; trucks and buses 42,696. Merchant marine: none. Air transport (1994)[11]: passenger-km 58,370,000; metric ton-km cargo 540,000; airports (1997) 4.

Communications

Medium	date	unit	number	units per 1,000 persons
Daily newspapers	1995	circulation	42,100	29.0
Radio	1995	receivers	1,190,000	821
Television	1995	receivers	35,000	24.0
Telephones	1995	main lines	59,700	41.1
Facsimile machines	1995	units	3,100	2.1

Education and health

Educational attainment (1991). Percentage of population age 25 and over having: no formal schooling 42.9%; primary education 17.3%; some secondary 32.3%; complete secondary 3.9%; postsecondary 3.7%. *Literacy* (1995): total population over age 15 literate 591,700 (69.8%); males literate 324,900 (80.5%); females literate 266,800 (59.9%).

Education (1994)

	schools	teachers	students	student/teacher ratio
Primary (age 6–13)	669	11,726	310,050	26.4
Secondary (age 14–18)	188	4,712	86,684	18.4
Voc., teacher tr.	45	966	6,373	6.6
Higher	1	507	5,062	10.0

Health (1994): physicians 339 (1 per 4,395 persons); hospital beds (1993) 3,299 (1 per 434 persons); infant mortality rate 39.0.
Food (1995): daily per capita caloric intake 2,153 (vegetable products 83%, animal products 17%); 93% of FAO recommended minimum requirement.

Military

Total active duty personnel (1997): 7,500 (army 93.3%, navy, none [landlocked], air force 6.7%). *Military expenditure as percentage of GNP* (1995): 5.3% (world 2.8%); per capita expenditure U.S.$155.

[1]In addition, the House of Chiefs, a 15-member body consisting of chiefs, subchiefs, and associated members, serves in an advisory capacity to the government. [2]Including four specially elected members and two nonelective seats. [3]Tswana is the national language. [4]Areas are included with respective district totals; population figures are not included with district totals. [5]Detail does not add to total given because of rounding. [6]Registered births only. [7]Represents nearly 30% of all deaths. [8]Includes 61,265 unemployed. [9]Import figures are f.o.b. in balance of trade and c.i.f. in commodities and trading partners. [10]1994. [11]Air Botswana only.

Brazil

Official name: República Federativa do Brasil (Federative Republic of Brazil).
Form of government: multiparty federal republic with 2 legislative houses (Senate [81]; Chamber of Deputies [513]).
Chief of state and government: President.
Capital: Brasília.
Official language: Portuguese.
Official religion: none.
Monetary unit: 1 real[1] = 100 centavos; valuation (Oct. 3, 1997) 1 U.S.$ = 1.10 reais; 1 £ = 1.77 reais.

Area and population

		area		population
States	**Capitals**	sq mi	sq km	1995 estimate[2]
Acre	Rio Branco	59,132	153,150	455,200
Alagoas	Maceió	10,785	27,933	2,685,400
Amapá	Macapá	55,388	143,454	326,200
Amazonas	Manaus	609,200	1,577,820	2,320,200
Bahia	Salvador	219,034	567,295	12,646,000
Ceará	Fortaleza	56,505	146,348	6,714,200
Espírito Santo	Vitória	17,836	46,194	2,786,700
Goiás	Goiânia	131,772	341,289	4,308,400
Maranhão	São Luís	128,713	333,366	5,231,300
Mato Grosso	Cuiabá	350,120	906,807	2,313,600
Mato Grosso do Sul	Campo Grande	138,286	358,159	1,912,800
Minas Gerais	Belo Horizonte	227,176	588,384	16,505,300
Pará	Belém	483,850	1,253,165	5,448,600
Paraíba	João Pessoa	21,848	56,585	3,340,000
Paraná	Curitiba	77,108	199,709	8,712,800
Pernambuco	Recife	38,200	98,938	7,445,200
Piauí	Teresina	97,444	252,379	2,725,000
Rio de Janeiro	Rio de Janeiro	16,954	43,910	13,296,400
Rio Grande do Norte	Natal	20,582	53,307	2,582,300
Rio Grande do Sul	Pôrto Alegre	108,905	282,062	9,578,600
Rondônia	Pôrto Velho	92,090	238,513	1,339,500
Roraima	Boa Vista	86,918	225,116	262,200
Santa Catarina	Florianópolis	36,851	95,443	4,836,600
São Paulo	São Paulo	96,066	248,809	33,699,600
Sergipe	Aracaju	8,514	22,050	1,605,300
Tocantins	Palmas	107,499	278,421	1,007,000
Federal District				
Distrito Federal	Brasília	2,248	5,822	1,737,800
Disputed areas[3]		1,149	2,977	—
TOTAL		3,300,171[4, 5]	8,547,404[4, 5]	155,822,400[4]

Demography

Population (1997): 159,691,000.
Density (1997): persons per sq mi 48.4, persons per sq km 18.7.
Urban-rural (1995)[6]: urban 79.0%; rural 21.0%.
Sex distribution (1995)[6]: male 48.99%; female 51.01%.
Age breakdown (1995)[6]: under 15, 32.2%; 15–29, 26.9%; 30–44, 20.6%; 45–59, 11.9%; 60 and over, 8.4%.
Population projection: (2000) 164,163,000; (2010) 179,995,000.
Doubling time: 60 years.
Racial composition (1995)[6]: white 54.4%; mulatto and mestizo 40.1%; black and black/Amerindian 4.9%; Asian 0.5%; Amerindian 0.1%.
Religious affiliation (1995): Catholic 74.3%[7], of which Roman Catholic 72.3%[7]; Protestant 22.5%, of which Pentecostal 19.1%; other Christian 0.9%; other 2.3%.
Major cities (1991)[8] *and metropolitan areas/urban agglomerations* (1995): São Paulo 9,393,753 (16,417,000[9]); Rio de Janeiro 5,473,909 (9,888,000[9]); Salvador 2,070,296 (2,819,000[9]); Belo Horizonte 1,529,566 (3,899,000[9]); Brasília 1,492,542 (1,778,000[10]); Recife 1,296,995 (3,168,000[9]); Pôrto Alegre 1,237,223 (3,349,000[9]); Manaus 1,005,634 (1,189,000[10]); Goiânia 912,136 (1,033,000[10]); Curitiba 841,882 (2,270,000[9]); Belém 765,476 (1,574,000[9]); Campinas 748,076 (1,607,000[10]); Fortaleza 743,335 (2,660,000[9]).

Other principal cities (1991)[8]

	population		population		population
Aracaju	401,676	Natal	459,827	São Bernardo do Campo	550,030[12]
Campo Grande	516,403	Niterói	400,586[11]	São Jose dos Campos	385,879
Guarulhos	544,698[12]	Nova Iguaçu	562,062[11]	Sorocaba	348,952
João Pessoa	497,306	Osasco	566,949[12]	Teresina	556,073
Juiz de Fora	377,538	Ribeirão Preto	416,186	Uberlândia	354,710
Londrina	355,062	Santo André	518,272[12]		
Maceió	554,727	Santos	415,554[13]		

Place of birth/national origin (1991): native-born Brazilians 99.47%; naturalized citizens 0.11%; foreigners 0.42%.
Families (1990)[6]. Average family size 3.9; 1–2 persons 26.2%, 3 persons 21.3%, 4 persons 21.5%, 5–6 persons 22.3%, 7 or more persons 8.7%.
Emigration: Emigration for economic opportunity accelerated in the 1980s. By 1995 it was officially estimated that 1–2.5 million Brazilians lived outside of Brazil. Emigrants' most popular destinations in order of preference are the United States, Japan, and the United Kingdom.

Vital statistics

Birth rate per 1,000 population (1996): 20.8 (world avg. 25.0).
Death rate per 1,000 population (1996): 9.2 (world avg. 9.3).
Natural increase rate per 1,000 population (1996): 11.6 (world avg. 15.7).
Total fertility rate (avg. births per childbearing woman; 1996): 2.3.
Marriage rate per 1,000 population (1994): 5.0.
Divorce rate per 1,000 population (1994): 0.6.
Life expectancy at birth (1996): male 56.7 years; female 66.8 years.
Major causes of death per 100,000 population (1994)[14]: diseases of the circulatory system 238; accidents, murder, and violence 104; malignant neoplasms (cancers) 94; diseases of the respiratory system 79; endocrine, metabolic, and nutritional disorders 45; infectious and parasitic diseases 41; birth trauma and other conditions originating in the perinatal period 37; diseases of the digestive system 36; ill-defined conditions 147.

Social indicators

Educational attainment (1995)[6]. Percentage of population age 10 and over having: no formal schooling or less than one year of primary education 16.2%; incomplete primary 55.9%; complete primary 7.6%; incomplete secondary 4.6%; complete secondary 9.1%; incomplete undergraduate 2.4%; complete undergraduate 3.9%; unknown 0.3%.

Distribution of income (1988)[6, 15]

percentage of national income by decile

1	2	3	4	5	6	7	8	9	10 (highest)
0.7	1.7	2.2	3.4	3.9	5.0	6.8	9.9	15.9	50.5

Quality of working life. Annual estimated rate per 100,000 insured workers (1990) for: on-the-job injury 2,032; industrial illness 17; death 4. Proportion of labour force participating in national social insurance system (1990): 50.1%. Proportion of formally employed population receiving minimum wage (1993): 25.0%.
Access to services (1995)[6]. Proportion of households having access to: electricity 91.7%, of which urban households having access 98.6%, rural households having access 62.9%; safe public (piped) water supply 71.3%, of which urban households having access 85.4%, rural households having access 11.6%; public (piped) sewage system 39.5%, of which urban households having access 48.2%, rural households having access 3.2%; no sewage disposal 11.4%, of which urban households having no disposal 3.5%, rural households having no disposal 40.9%.
Social participation. Voting is mandatory for national elections; in the October 1994 elections blank or otherwise invalid ballots accounted for as many as 15% of all votes cast. Trade union membership in total workforce (1991): 16,748,155. Practicing Roman Catholic population in total affiliated Roman Catholic population (1990): 25%.
Social deviance (1990). The incidence of crime is not accurately reported. Crimes resulting in imprisonment: 159,071, of which murder 7.3%, assault 11.0%, theft, burglary, and housebreaking 26.6%, robbery and extortion 12.2%, narcotics trafficking 6.3%, narcotics usage 4.5%. Suicide: 5,142.
Leisure. Favourite leisure activities include: playing soccer, dancing, rehearsing all year in neighbourhood samba groups for celebrations of Carnival, and competing in water sports, volleyball, and basketball.
Material well-being (1995)[6]. Households possessing: telephone 22.3%, of which urban 26.7%, rural 3.5%; colour television receiver 60.9%, of which urban 69.8%, rural 23.3%; refrigerator 74.8%, of which urban 83.4%, rural 38.7%; washing machine 26.6%, of which urban 31.2%, rural 7.3%.

National economy

Gross national product (1995): U.S.$579,787,000,000 (U.S.$3,640 per capita).

Structure of gross domestic product and labour force

	1995		1993	
	in value R$'000,000[1, 16]	% of total value	labour force[6]	% of labour force
Agriculture	68,290	12.2	18,253,856	25.7
Mining	5,867	1.0	...	...
Public utilities	14,198	2.5	...	...
Manufacturing	123,821	22.0	9,486,435	13.4
Construction	45,124	8.0	4,289,159	6.0
Transportation and communications	30,702	5.5	2,283,978	3.2
Trade	38,037	6.8	8,474,935	11.9
Finance, real estate	42,824	7.6	1,929,077	2.7
Pub. admin., defense	70,154	12.5	3,044,332	4.3
Services	162,097	28.9	17,418,896	24.5
Other	−39,333[17]	−7.0[17]	5,784,710[18]	8.2[18]
TOTAL	561,781	100.0	70,965,378	100.0[4]

Budget. Revenue (1995): R$320,178,000,000 (development receipts 62.6%, of which credits 58.4%; current receipts 37.4%, of which social contributions 19.3% [including social security 9.2%], taxes 13.3%). Expenditures: R$320,178,000,000 (administration and planning 59.5%; social welfare 13.9%; regional development 6.0%; health and sanitation 4.9%; agriculture 3.1%; education 2.7%; defense and public order 2.6%).
Public debt (external, outstanding; 1995): U.S.$96,609,000,000.
Production ('000 metric tons except as noted). Agriculture, forestry, fishing (1996): sugarcane 324,414, corn (maize) 32,011, cassava 24,569, soybeans 23,171, oranges 21,848, rice 10,039, bananas 5,738, wheat 3,277, dry beans 2,776, potatoes 2,656, tomatoes 2,650, papayas 2,200, coffee 1,264, cashew apples 1,250, pineapples 1,052, seed cotton 1,032, coconuts 984, onions 944, tangerines 760[19], grapes 731, sweet potatoes 655, apples 653, cottonseed 650, lemons and limes 495, tobacco 476, mangoes 435, cotton lint 360, sorghum 310, cacao beans 313, cashews 187, peanuts (groundnuts) 154, maté 150, sisal 133, palm oil 76, garlic 57, castor beans 48, natural rubber 30, brazil nuts 25; livestock (number of live animals) 165,000,000 cattle, 36,600,000 pigs, 18,000,000 sheep, 6,300,000 horses; roundwood (1995) 220,263,000 cu m, of which fuelwood 114,052,000 cu m, sawlogs and veneer logs 47,779,000 cu m, pulpwood 30,701,000 cu m; fish catch (1995) 800, of which freshwater fishes 202. Mining and quarrying (value of export production in U.S.$'000,000; 1996): iron ore 2,668; semifinished copper 165; ferroniobium 153; bauxite

115; granite 97; semifinished tin 68; kaolin (clay) 65; manganese 55; asbestos 35; gemstones (1994) 27; gold production for both domestic use and export 1,833,000 troy oz; Brazil is also a world-leading producer of high-quality grade quartz and tantalum. Manufacturing (value added in U.S.$'000,000; 1994): food products 19,450; transport equipment 16,050; paints, soaps, drugs, and medicines 15,600; electrical machinery 12,350; nonelectrical machinery 11,600; industrial chemicals 11,000; iron and steel 8,800; textiles 7,100; fabricated metals 6,000; cement, bricks, and tiles 5,700; paper and paper products 5,250. Construction (authorized[20]; 1987): residential 20,090,000 sq m; nonresidential 8,180,000 sq m.
Land use (1994): forested 57.7%; meadows and pastures 21.9%; agricultural and under permanent cultivation 6.0%; other 14.4%.

Manufacturing enterprises (1992)

	no. of enter-prises	number of labourers	wages of labourers as a % of avg. of all mfg. wages	value added in producer's prices (in CR$'000,000,000[1])[21]
Chemical products (incl. pharmaceuticals)	2,795	360,800	170.4	1,351
Food products	5,241	548,400	63.8	1,040
Nonelectrical machinery	2,086	297,000	120.7	994
Fabricated metals, iron and steel, and nonferrous metals	2,325	377,200	123.9	923
Transport equipment	830	282,000	162.1	784
Electrical machinery	1,366	215,900	135.5	591
Textiles	1,439	242,600	64.4	379
Nonmetallic mineral products	1,638	145,200	91.5	369
Paper and paper products	824	116,900	103.6	296
Clothing and footwear	2,480	459,200	37.6	272
Publishing and printing	920	103,000	121.7	226
Plastics	828	106,500	83.5	193
Beverages	508	84,900	93.0	178
Rubber products	439	54,500	97.9	91
Wood and wood products (excl. furniture)	860	79,500	45.4	91
Furniture	845	72,100	48.9	86

Population economically active (1993)[6]: total 70,965,378; activity rate of total population 47.9% (participation rates: ages 15–59, 72.7%; female 39.6%; unemployed [May 1996] 5.9%[22, 23]).

Price and earnings indexes (1993 = 100)

	1992	1993	1994	1995	1996	1977[24]
Consumer price index	5.9	100.0	2,769.4	5,106.1	6,036.8	6,466.7
Monthly earnings index[25]	4.3	100.0	...	...	...	...

Tourism (1995): receipts U.S.$2,171,000,000; expenditures U.S.$4,245,000,000.

Retail trade enterprises (1993)

	no. of enterprises	total no. of employees	annual wage as a % of all trade wages	annual values of sales in Cr$'000,000,000
Vehicles, new and used; parts	5,239	241,299	133.8	1,939
General merchandise stores (including food products)	3,260	328,303	93.0	1,432
Gas stations	11,302	139,348	94.5	942
Clothing, footwear, and apparel	4,654	189,980	90.2	479
Electronics, furniture, kitchenware, and antiques	2,476	101,439	100.1	446
Metal products, lumber, glass, and construction materials	6,192	126,136	85.7	395
Food, beverages, and tobacco	3,423	64,432	73.2	246
Pharmaceutical and cosmetic products	1,816	55,069	94.4	241
Agricultural and industrial equipment and machinery	1,980	43,171	115.3	189

Family income and expenditure (1993). Average family size 3.7[6]; annual income per family Cr$608,364 (U.S.$2,178[6, 26]); sources of income (1987–88)[27]: wages and salaries 62.4%, self-employed 14.7%, transfers 10.9%, other 12.0%; expenditure (1987–88)[27]: food and beverages 25.3%, housing, energy, and household furnishings 21.3%, transportation and communications 15.0%, clothing and footwear 12.9%, health care 9.1%.

Financial aggregates[28]

	1992	1993	1994	1995	1996	1997[29]
Exchange rate, reais[1] per:						
U.S. dollar	.002	.049	.846	.973	1.039	1.064
£	.003	.073	1.322	1.508	1.506	1.734
SDR	.006	.163	1.235	1.446	1.495	1.453
International reserves (U.S.$)						
Total (excl. gold; '000,000)	22,521	30,604	37,070	49,708	58,323	54,117
SDRs ('000,000)	1	2	—	1	1	—
Reserve pos. in IMF ('000,000)	—	—	—	—	—	—
Foreign exchange ('000,000)	22,520	30,602	37,069	49,707	58,322	54,117
Gold ('000,000 fine troy oz)	2.23	2.93	3.71	4.58	3.69	4.75
% world reserves	0.24	0.32	0.37	0.50	0.41	0.53
Interest and prices						
Central bank discount (%)	1,489	5,757	56	39	24	22
Govt. bond yield (%)	...	...	...	...	...	...
Industrial share prices	...	...	...	...	...	...
Balance of payments (U.S.$'000,000)						
Balance of visible trade	+15,239	+14,329	+10,861	−3,157	...	...
Imports, f.o.b.	20,554	25,711	33,241	49,663	...	...
Exports, f.o.b.	35,793	39,630	44,102	46,506	...	...
Balance of invisibles	−9,150	−14,309	−12,014	−14,979	...	...
Balance of payments, current account	+6,089	+20	−1,153	−18,136	...	...

Energy production (consumption): electricity (kW-hr; 1996) 273,827,000,000 ([1995] 243,836,000,000); coal (metric tons; 1996) 5,400,000 ([1994] 16,434,000); crude petroleum (barrels; 1996) 293,997,000 ([1994] 469,227,000); petroleum products (metric tons; 1994) 55,111,000 (57,042,000); natural gas (cu m; 1996) 9,181,000,000[30] ([1994] 4,103,000,000); carburant alcohol (cu m; 1995) 9,946,000 (9,946,000).

Foreign trade

Balance of trade (current prices)

	1991	1992	1993	1994	1995	1996
U.S.$'000,000	+10,578	+15,239	+13,299	+10,466	−3,115	−5,539
% of total	20.1%	27.4%	20.8%	13.7%	3.3%	5.5%

Imports (1995): U.S.$49,621,000,000 (nonelectrical and electrical machinery and apparatus 27.7%, chemicals and chemical products 12.7%, mineral fuels 12.5%, transport equipment 11.9%). *Major import sources:* United States 23.9%; Argentina 11.0%; Germany 10.4%; Italy 5.5%; Japan 5.1%; France 2.7%; South Korea 2.4%; Saudi Arabia 2.3%; Canada 2.2%; Chile 2.2%.
Exports (1995): U.S.$46,506,000,000 (iron and steel 8.7%, nonelectrical machinery and apparatus 8.5%, mineral ores 5.9%, motor vehicles 5.9%, wood pulp, paper, and paper products 5.9%, coffee 4.4%, refined sugar and confectionery 4.3%, aluminum and related products 3.3%, electrical machinery and apparatus 3.2%, footwear and other leather products 3.2%). *Major export destinations:* United States 18.7%; Argentina 8.7%; Japan 6.7%; The Netherlands 6.3%; Germany 4.6%; Italy 3.7%; Belgium 3.4%; United Kingdom 2.9%; Paraguay 2.8%; Chile 2.6%.

Transport and communications

Transport. Railroads: route length (1995) 18,578 mi, 29,899 km; passenger-mi 9,009,000,000, passenger-km 14,498,000,000; short ton-mi cargo 93,455,000,000, metric ton-km cargo 136,442,000,000. Roads (1995): total length 1,205,000 mi, 1,939,000 km (paved 9%). Vehicles (1995): passenger cars 12,000,000; trucks and buses 3,160,689. Air transport (1996)[31]: passenger-mi 22,471,000,000, passenger-km 36,164,000,000; short ton-mi cargo 1,118,000,000, metric ton-km cargo 1,632,000,000; airports (1995) with scheduled flights 139.

Communications

Medium	date	unit	number	units per 1,000 persons
Daily newspapers	1994	circulation	7,200,000	47
Radio	1996	receivers	55,000,000	348
Television	1995	receivers	30,000,000	193
Telephones	1995	main lines	12,082,600	78
Cellular telephones	1995	subscribers	1,285,500	8.2
Facsimile machines	1995	units	200,000	1.3
Personal computers	1995	units	2,000,000	13

Education and health

Literacy (1995)[32]: total population age 15 and over literate 91,100,000 (83.3%); males literate 45,200,000 (83.3%); females literate 45,900,000 (83.2%).

Education (1994)

	schools	teachers	students	student/ teacher ratio
Primary (age 7–14)	195,545	1,335,270	31,101,662	23.3
Secondary (age 15–17)	13,449	295,542	4,510,199	15.3
Higher	851	155,776	1,661,034	10.7

Health: physicians (1993) 222,658 (1 per 681 persons); hospital beds (1993) 509,270 (1 per 298 persons); infant mortality rate per 1,000 live births (1996) 55.3.
Food (1995): daily per capita caloric intake 2,834 (vegetable products 81%, animal products 19%); 119% of FAO recommended minimum requirement.

Military

Total active duty personnel (1996): 295,000 (army 66.0%, navy 17.0%, air force 17.0%). *Military expenditure as percentage of GNP* (1995): 1.7% (world 2.8%); per capita expenditure U.S.$68.

[1]The real (R$) replaced the cruzeiro real (CR$) on July 1, 1994, at a rate of 2,750 cruzeiros reais to 1 real (a rate par to the U.S.$ on that date). Previously, the cruzeiro real replaced the cruzeiro (Cr$) at a rate of 1,000 cruzeiros to 1 cruzeiro real on Aug. 2, 1993; the cruzeiro replaced the new cruzado (NCz$) at a rate of 1 to 1 on March 16, 1990; and the new cruzado replaced the (old) cruzado (Cz$) at a rate of 1,000 (old) to 1 new on Jan. 15, 1989. [2]Projection based on 1991 census. [3]Area in dispute between Ceará and Piauí. [4]Detail does not add to total given because of rounding. [5]Land area excluding inland water is 3,265,076 sq mi (8,456,508 sq km). [6]Excludes rural population of Acre, Amapá, Amazonas, Pará, Rondônia, and Roraima. [7]Includes syncretic Afro-Catholic cults having Spiritist beliefs and rituals. [8]Revised preliminary census. [9]Officially defined metropolitan area. [10]Officially defined urban agglomeration. [11]Within Rio de Janeiro metropolitan area. [12]Within São Paulo metropolitan area. [13]1995 population estimate of urban agglomeration is 1,173,000. [14]Projected rates based on about 67% of total deaths. [15]As of 1992, 33,000,000 Brazilians lived in extreme poverty (more than half of whom lived in the nine states of the northeast). [16]At factor cost. [17]Less imputed bank service charges. [18]Includes 1,389,089 not adequately defined and 4,395,621 unemployed. [19]Includes mandarin oranges, satsuma oranges, and clementines. [20]Urban construction only for 74 cities. [21]1993. [22]Six largest metropolitan regions only. [23]Excludes workers in the extremely large informal sector. [24]May. [25]Minimum wages. [26]Based on end-of-year exchange rate. [27]Based on 10,408,833 families in Brazil's nine largest metropolitan regions. [28]End-of-period figures. [29]April. [30]Includes wasted gas. [31]TAM, Transbrasil, VARIG, and VASP airlines only. [32]By official estimate; functional literacy, however, may be as low as 42% of total population over age 15.

Internet resources for further information:

- **IBGE: Instituto Brasileiro de Geografia e Estatística (Portuguese version) http://www.ibge.gov.br/**
- **IBGE: Instituto Brasileiro de Geografia e Estatística (English version) http://www.ibge.gov.br/english/e-home.htm**

Brunei

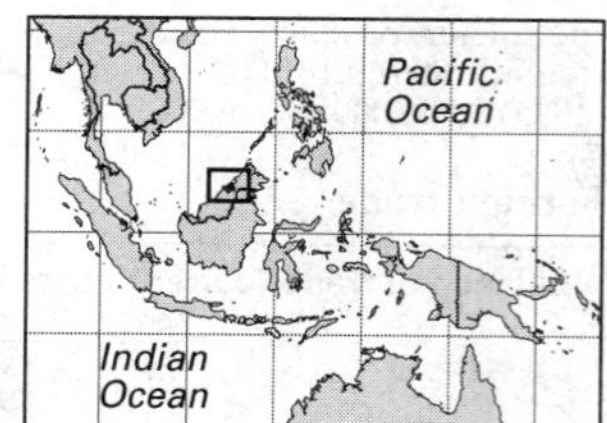

Official name: Negara Brunei Darussalam (State of Brunei, Abode of Peace).
Form of government: monarchy (sultanate)[1].
Head of state and government: Sultan.
Capital: Bandar Seri Begawan.
Official language: Malay[2].
Official religion: Islam.
Monetary unit: 1 Brunei dollar (B$) = 100 cents; valuation (Oct. 3, 1997) 1 U.S.$ = B$1.54; 1 £ = B$2.49.

Area and population

Districts	Capitals	area sq mi	area sq km	population 1995 estimate
Belait	Kuala Belait	1,052	2,724	60,000
Brunei and Muara	Bandar Seri Begawan	220	571	195,000
Temburong	Bangar	504	1,304	8,500
Tutong	Tutong	450	1,166	32,500
TOTAL		2,226	5,765	296,000

Demography

Population (1997): 308,000.
Density (1997): persons per sq mi 138.4, persons per sq km 53.4.
Urban-rural (1997): urban 58.0%; rural 42.0%.
Sex distribution (1995): male 52.91%; female 47.09%.
Age breakdown (1993): under 15, 34.0%; 15–29, 28.0%; 30–44, 24.9%; 45–59, 8.7%; 60 and over, 4.4%.
Population projection: (2000) 331,000; (2010) 410,000.
Doubling time: 35 years.
Ethnic composition (1992): Malay 67.1%; Chinese 15.4%; other indigenous 6.0%; Indian and other 11.5%.
Religious affiliation (1991): Muslim 67.2%; Buddhist 12.8%; Christian 10.0%; other religions and nonreligious 10.0%.
Major cities (1991): Bandar Seri Begawan 45,867[3]; Kuala Belait 21,163; Seria 21,082; Tutong 13,049.

Vital statistics

Birth rate per 1,000 population (1997): 23.3 (world avg. 25.0); (1982) legitimate 99.6%; illegitimate 0.4%.
Death rate per 1,000 population (1997): 3.0 (world avg. 9.3).
Natural increase rate per 1,000 population (1997): 20.3 (world avg. 15.7).
Total fertility rate (avg. births per childbearing woman; 1997): 2.9.
Marriage rate per 1,000 population (1993): 7.1.
Divorce rate per 1,000 population (1992): 1.1.
Life expectancy at birth (1997): male 73.0 years; female 78.0 years.
Major causes of death per 100,000 population (1992): cardiovascular disease 55.3; malignant neoplasms (cancers) 37.3; accidents, poisoning, and violence 30.6; cerebrovascular diseases 19.0; pneumonia 12.3; hypertensive diseases 9.7; congenital anomalies 9.7.

National economy

Budget (1995). Revenue: B$3,538,000,000 (nontax revenue 68.4%, of which property income 19.4%, commercial receipts 7.7%; tax revenue 31.6%, of which corporate income tax 22.8%, import duty 2.8%). Expenditures: B$3,649,000,000 (current expenditure 62.1%; development expenditure 19.8%; charged expenditure 12.6%).
Public debt (external, outstanding): none.
Tourism (1990): receipts from visitors U.S.$35,000,000; expenditures by nationals abroad, n.a.
Production (metric tons except as noted). Agriculture, forestry, fishing (1996): vegetables and melons 8,500, fruits (excluding melons) 4,890, cassava 1,500, rice 1,000, pineapples 650; livestock (number of live animals) 5,000 goats, 4,000 pigs, 3,500 buffalo, 1,800 cattle, 2,500,000 chickens; roundwood (1995) 295,000 cu m; fish catch (1995) 4,812. Mining and quarrying (1992): other than petroleum and natural gas, none except sand and gravel for construction. Manufacturing (1994): gasoline 172,000; diesel oils 122,000; jet fuels 59,000; fuel oil 55,000; kerosene 4,000. Construction (value in B$'000,000; 1989): residential 26.2; nonresidential 5.1. Energy production (consumption): electricity (kW-hr; 1994) 1,315,000,000 (1,315,000,000); coal, none (none); crude petroleum (barrels; 1994) 59,087,000 (1,930,000); petroleum products (metric tons; 1994) 856,000 (852,000); natural gas (cu m; 1994) 8,794,000,000 (1,938,000,000).
Population economically active (1991): total 111,955; activity rate of total population 43.0% (participation rates: ages 15–64, 67.6%; female 32.9%; unemployed 4.7%).

Price and earnings indexes (1990 = 100)

	1989	1990	1991	1992	1993	1994	1995
Consumer price index	98.0	100.0	101.6	102.9	107.3	109.9	116.5
Monthly earnings index[4]	...	...	76.9	87.5	...	...	...

Household income and expenditure. Average household size (1991) 5.8; income per household: n.a.; sources of income: n.a.; expenditure (1990): food 38.7%, transportation and communications 19.9%, housing 18.6%, clothing 6.4%, other 16.4%.

Gross national product (at current market prices; 1994): U.S.$3,975,000,000 (U.S.$14,240 per capita).

Structure of gross domestic product and labour force

	1995 in value B$'000,000	1995 % of total value	1991 labour force	1991 % of labour force
Agriculture	188	2.7	2,162	1.9
Mining / Manufacturing	2,756	39.0	9,397	8.4
Construction	405	5.7	14,145	12.6
Public utilities	74	1.1	2,223	2.0
Transportation and communications	299	4.2	5,392	4.8
Trade	596	8.4	15,404	13.8
Finance	549	7.8	5,807	5.2
Services	2,390	33.8	52,121	46.6
Other	−188	−2.7	5,304[5]	4.7[5]
TOTAL	7,069	100.0	111,955	100.0

Land use (1994): forested 85.4%; meadows and pastures 1.1%; agricultural and under permanent cultivation 1.3%; other 12.2%.

Foreign trade

Balance of trade (current prices)

	1989	1990	1991	1992	1993	1994
B$'000,000	+1,998	+2,197	+2,417	+1,946	+1,672	+866
% of total	37.4%	37.7%	39.2%	33.7%	29.3%	14.7%

Imports (1994): B$2,517,000,000 (machinery and transport equipment 40.0%, manufactured goods 21.5%, miscellaneous manufactured articles 17.2%, food and live animals 11.2%, chemicals 4.9%, crude materials 2.3%, beverages and tobacco 2.1%). *Major import sources:* ASEAN 47.0%, of which Singapore 28.9%, Malaysia 11.9%; EEC 17.3%; United States 11.3%; Japan 9.2%.
Exports (1994): B$3,383,200,000 (crude petroleum 45.8%, natural gas 41.8%, petroleum products 3.1%). *Major export destinations:* Japan 54.6%; ASEAN 26.1%, of which Thailand 11.0%, Singapore 10.6%; South Korea 13.7%; Taiwan 2.7%.

Transport and communications

Transport. Railroads (1993)[6]: length 12 mi, 19 km. Roads (1994): total length 1,527 mi, 2,457 km (paved 59%). Vehicles (1995): passenger cars 141,371; trucks and buses 16,557. Merchant marine (1992): vessels (100 gross tons and over) 51; total deadweight tonnage 349,718. Marine transport (1992): cargo loaded 20,411,000 metric tons, cargo unloaded 1,377,000 metric tons. Air transport (1996): passenger-mi 1,685,000,000, passenger-km 2,712,000,000; short ton-mi cargo 74,028,000, metric ton-km cargo 108,079,000; airports (1996) with scheduled flights 1.

Communications

Medium	date	unit	number	units per 1,000 persons
Daily newspapers	1994	circulation	20,000	70
Radio	1996	receivers	125,000	417
Television	1995	receivers	90,000	308
Telephones	1995	main lines	68,100	233
Cellular telephones	1995	subscribers	35,900	123
Facsimile machines	1995	units	2,000	6.8
Personal computers	1995	units	8,000	27

Education and health

Educational attainment (1991). Percentage of population age 25 and over having: no formal schooling 17.0%; primary education 43.3%; secondary 26.3%; postsecondary and higher 12.9%; not stated 0.5%. *Literacy* (1991): total population age 15 and over literate 149,901 (87.8%); males literate 84,425 (92.5%); females literate 65,476 (82.5%).

Education (1995)

	schools	teachers	students	student/ teacher ratio
Primary (age 5–11)[7]	170	3,380	55,241	15.5
Secondary (age 12–20)	37	2,157	27,801	13.4
Voc., teacher tr.	6	370	1,966	5.2
Higher	4	325	1,606	4.7

Health (1993): physicians 197 (1 per 1,398 persons); hospital beds 967 (1 per 285 persons); infant mortality rate per 1,000 live births (1997) 9.0.
Food (1995): daily per capita caloric intake 2,849 (vegetable products 78%, animal products 22%); 127% of FAO recommended minimum requirement.

Military

Total active duty personnel (1996): 5,000[8] (army 78.0%, navy 14.0%, air force 8.0%). *Military expenditure as percentage of GNP* (1995): 6.0% (world 2.8%); per capita expenditure U.S.$920.

[1]A nonelective 21-member body advises the sultan on legislative matters. [2]All official documents that must be published by law in Malay are, however, also required to be issued in an official English version as well. [3]1988 metropolitan area population estimate. [4]Nonagricultural sectors only; 1985 = 100. [5]Mostly unemployed. [6]Privately owned. [7]Includes preprimary. [8]All services form part of the army.

Internet resources for further information:
- **Brunei Darussalam http://brunet.bn/**

Bulgaria

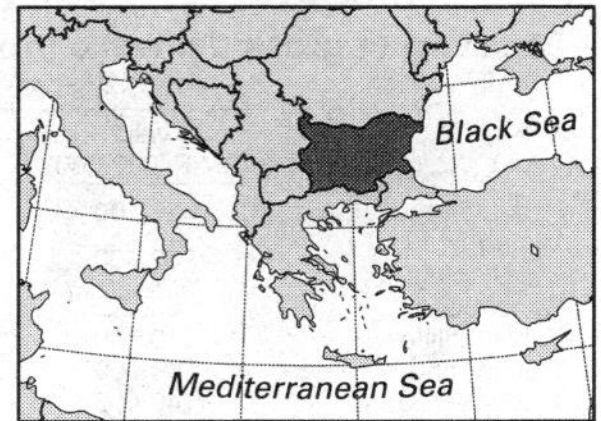

Official name: Republika Bŭlgaria (Republic of Bulgaria).
Form of government: unitary multiparty republic with one legislative body (National Assembly [240]).
Chief of state: President.
Head of government: Prime Minister.
Capital: Sofia.
Official language: Bulgarian.
Official religion: none[1].
Monetary unit: 1 lev (leva) = 100 stotinki; valuation (Oct. 3, 1997) 1 U.S.$ = 1,754 leva; 1 £ = 2,827 leva.

Area and population		area		population
		sq mi	sq km	1996 estimate
Regions	**Capitals**			
Burgas	Burgas	5,685	14,724	846,524
Khaskovo	Khaskovo	5,338	13,824	897,863
Lovech	Lovech	5,849	15,150	990,307
Montana	Mikhaylovgrad	4,095	10,607	615,629
Plovdiv	Plovdiv	5,245	13,585	1,213,966
Ruse	Ruse	4,187	10,843	760,029
Sofiya	Sofia (Sofiya)	7,344	19,021	966,502
Varna	Varna	4,606	11,929	901,160
City Commune				
Sofiya	Sofia (Sofiya)	506	1,311	1,192,735
TOTAL		42,855	110,994	8,384,715

Demography

Population (1997): 8,329,000.
Density (1997): persons per sq mi 194.4, persons per sq km 75.0.
Urban-rural (1996): urban 52.6%; rural 47.4%.
Sex distribution (1996): male 47.80%; female 52.20%.
Age breakdown (1995): under 15, 16.9%; 15–29, 20.5%; 30–44, 20.0%; 45–59, 19.4%; 60–74, 17.6%; 75 and over, 5.6%.
Population projection: (2000) 8,218,000; (2010) 7,898,000.
Doubling time: not applicable; population is declining.
Ethnic composition (1992): Bulgarian 85.7%; Turkish 9.4%; Gypsy 3.6%; other 1.3%.
Religious affiliation (1992)[2]: Bulgarian Orthodox 85.7%; Sunnī Muslim 12.1%; Shīʿī Muslim 1.0%; other 1.2%.
Major cities (1996): Sofia 1,116,823; Plovdiv 344,326; Varna 301,421; Burgas 199,470; Ruse 168,051.

Vital statistics

Birth rate per 1,000 population (1996): 8.6 (world avg. 25.0); (1995) legitimate 74.3%; illegitimate 25.7%.
Death rate per 1,000 population (1996): 14.0 (world avg. 9.3).
Natural increase rate per 1,000 population (1996): −5.4 (world avg. 15.7).
Total fertility rate (avg. births per childbearing woman; 1995): 1.2.
Marriage rate per 1,000 population (1996): 4.3.
Divorce rate per 1,000 population (1995): 1.3.
Life expectancy at birth (1995): male 67.1 years; female 74.9 years.
Major causes of death per 100,000 population (1995): diseases of the circulatory system 869.8; malignant neoplasms (cancers) 192.4; accidents, poisoning, and violence 66.0; diseases of the respiratory system 63.0; diseases of the digestive system 42.8; endocrine and metabolic disorders 27.3.

National economy

Budget (1995). Revenue: 328,328,900,000 leva (tax revenue 79.8%, of which social insurance 22.4%, value-added tax 18.1%, income tax 11.1%, profit tax 10.1%, excises 7.1%, customs and duties 6.5%, other 4.5%; nontax revenue 15.2%; other 5.0%). Expenditures: 377,923,300,000 leva (debt service 32.9%, social insurance 24.6%, defense 9.4%, education 9.4%, economic services 4.7%).
Tourism (1995): receipts from visitors U.S.$473,000,000; expenditures by nationals abroad U.S.$195,000,000.
Production (metric tons except as noted). Agriculture, forestry, fishing (1996): wheat 1,788,000, corn (maize) 1,198,000, sunflower seeds 530,000, barley 459,000, grapes 350,000, tomatoes 330,000, potatoes 302,000; livestock (number of live animals) 3,383,000 sheep, 2,140,000 pigs, 757,000 goats, 632,000 cattle; roundwood (1995) 1,970,000 cu m; fish catch (1995) 23,400. Mining and quarrying (1995): zinc 75,000. Manufacturing (value of production in '000,000 leva; 1995): chemical and oil processing 186,592; food, beverages, and tobacco 162,596; metallurgy and ore mining 96,394; machine and metalworking 81,156; electronic and electrical equipment 37,871; other goods 220,947. Construction (1995): residential 429,972 sq m; nonresidential 156,890. Energy production: electricity (kW-hr; 1994) 39,306,000,000; coal (metric tons; 1994) 30,833,000; crude petroleum (barrels; 1995) 343,100; petroleum products (metric tons; 1993) 4,010; natural gas (cu m; 1995) 60,094,000.
Household income and expenditure. Average household size (1995) 3.0; income per household (1995) 189,523 leva (U.S.$2,824); sources of income (1995): wages and salaries 37.5%, self-employment in agriculture 25.2%, transfer payments 15.7%; expenditure (1995): food 42.8%, housing and energy 7.5%, clothing 7.2%, transportation 6.6%, household durable goods 4.0%, health care 3.5%, education and culture 2.9%.
Land use (1995): forested 30.2%; meadows and pastures 16.2%; agricultural and under permanent cultivation 38.0%; other 15.6%.
Gross national product (1995): U.S.$11,225,000,000 (U.S.$1,334 per capita).

Structure of gross domestic product and labour force	1995			
	in value '000,000 leva	% of total value	labour force	% of labour force
Agriculture	239,451	12.9	783,000	21.1
Manufacturing, mining	767,083	41.2	956,000	25.8
Construction	99,454	5.3	188,000	5.1
Transp. and commun.	136,480	7.3	251,000	6.8
Trade	196,845	10.6	357,000	9.6
Public utilities, housing	142,059	7.6	81,000	2.2
Finance	73,883	4.0	51,000	1.4
Pub. admin., defense	67,530	3.6	76,000	2.1
Services	135,804	7.3	532,000	14.4
Other	2,414	0.1	430,000[3]	11.6[3]
TOTAL	1,861,003	100.0[4]	3,705,000	100.0[4]

Population economically active (1995): total 3,705,000; activity rate of total population 44.2% (1992; participation rates: ages 16–59 [male], 16–54 [female] 70.2%; female 48.4%; unemployed 11.4%).

Price and earnings indexes (1990 = 100)	1990	1991	1992	1993	1994	1995	1996
Consumer price index	100.0	438.5	786.6	1,228	2,296	3,722	8,300
Monthly earnings index	100.0	267.3	622.1	965.0	1,485	2,170	3,793

Public debt (external, outstanding; 1995): U.S.$9,574,000,000.

Foreign trade

Balance of trade (current prices)	1991	1992	1993	1994	1995	1996
'000,000 leva	+12,235.0	−12,748.3	−28,645.7	−10,815.9	−20,348.5	−87,297.9
% of total	11.9%	6.5%	12.2%	2.4%	2.8%	5.0%

Imports (1996): 905,613,000,000 leva (1995; machine-building and metalworking equipment 13.8%; electrical and electronic equipment 7.6%; food, beverages, and tobacco 7.1%; textiles and knitwear 4.5%). *Major import sources:* C.I.S. 40.5%; Germany 10.9%; Italy 5.9%; Greece 3.4%; France 3.0%.
Exports (1996): 818,315,000,000 leva (1995; chemicals and plastics 25.9%; food, beverages, and tobacco 16.9%; machine-building and metalworking equipment 16.9%; textiles and knitwear 3.3%). *Major export destinations:* C.I.S. 19.4%; Italy 9.7%; Germany 9.1%; Turkey 8.2%.

Transport and communications

Transport[5]. Railroads (1995): track length 6,507 km; (1996) passenger-km 5,065,000,000; metric ton-km cargo 7,549,000,000. Roads (1995): length 37,320 km (paved 92%). Vehicles (1995): cars 1,647,571; trucks and buses 20,495. Merchant marine (1995): vessels (100 gross tons and over) 61; deadweight tonnage 391,000. Air transport (1995): passenger-mi 1,765,000,000, passenger-km 2,840,000,000; short ton-mi cargo 24,100,000, metric ton-km cargo 35,200,000; airports (1996) with scheduled flights 3.

Communications				units
Medium	date	unit	number	per 1,000 persons
Daily newspapers	1995	circulation	1,179,000	141
Television	1995	receivers	3,011,000	359
Telephones	1995	main lines	2,563,000	306
Cellular telephones	1995	subscribers	20,900	2.5
Facsimile machines	1995	units	15,000	1.8
Personal computers	1995	units	180,000	21.5

Education and health

Educational attainment (1992). Percentage of population age 25 and over having: no formal schooling 4.7%; incomplete primary education 12.5%; primary 31.9%; secondary 35.7%; higher 15.0%. *Literacy* (1992): total population age 15 and over literate 97.9%; males literate 98.7%; females literate 97.1%.

Education (1995–96)	schools	teachers	students	student/ teacher ratio
Primary (age 6–14) Secondary (age 15–17)	3,325	70,763	963,582	13.6
Voc., teacher tr.	535	19,141	213,337	11.1
Higher	88	25,339	248,571	9.8

Health (1995): physicians 29,069 (1 per 288 persons); hospital beds 89,190 (1 per 94 persons); (1996) infant mortality rate per 1,000 live births 15.6.
Food (1995): daily per capita caloric intake 2,907 (vegetable products 78%, animal products 22%); 116% of FAO recommended minimum requirement.

Military

Total active duty personnel (1995): 101,900 (army 75.9%, navy 2.9%, air force 21.2%). *Military expenditure as percentage of GNP* (1995): 2.8% (world 2.8%); per capita expenditure U.S.$125.

[1]Bulgaria has no official religion; the 1991 constitution, however, refers to Eastern Orthodoxy as the "traditional" religion. [2]Census data reflect the traditional religious identity of Bulgaria but apparently disregard the nonreligious, who may exceed half the adult population. [3]Includes 6,455 undistributable employed and 423,773 unemployed. [4]Detail does not add to total given because of rounding. [5]Public sector.

Internet resources for further information:
- **National Statistical Institute of the Republic of Bulgaria http://www.acad.bg/BulRTD/nsi/index.htm**

Burkina Faso

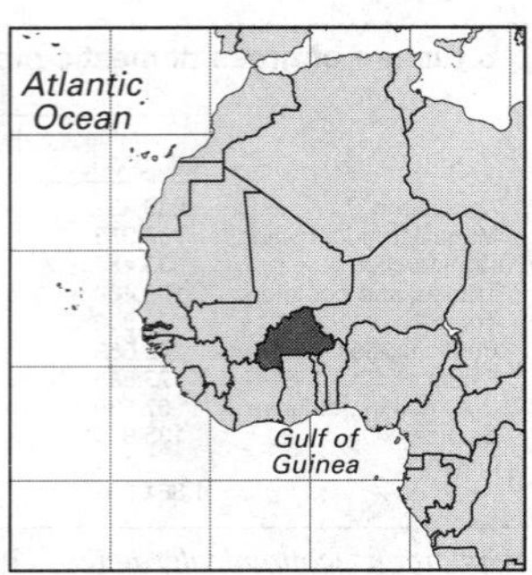

Official name: Burkina Faso (Burkina Faso).
Form of government: multiparty republic with one advisory body (House of Representatives [178]) and one legislative body (Assembly of People's Deputies [111]).
Chief of state: President.
Head of government: Prime Minister.
Capital: Ouagadougou.
Official language: French.
Monetary unit: 1 CFA franc (CFAF) = 100 centimes; valuation (Oct. 3, 1997) 1 U.S.$ = CFAF 592.29; 1 £ = CFAF 954.76.

Area and population

Provinces	Capitals	area sq mi	area sq km	population 1991 estimate
Bam	Kongoussi	1,551	4,017	173,516
Bazéga	Kombissiri	2,051	5,313	352,104
Bougouriba	Diébougou	2,736	7,087	242,986
Boulgou	Tenkodogo	3,488	9,033	465,845
Boulkiemde	Koudougou	1,598	4,138	393,900
Comoé	Banfora	7,102	18,393	296,083
Ganzourgou	Zorgho	1,578	4,087	223,555
Gnagna	Bogandé	3,320	8,600	272,203
Gourma	Fada N'Gourma	10,275	26,613	350,336
Houé	Bobo-Dioulasso	6,438	16,672	724,803
Kadiogo	Ouagadougou	451	1,169	652,377
Kénédougou	Orodara	3,207	8,307	162,010
Kossi	Nouna	5,088	13,177	389,360
Kouritenga	Koupéla	628	1,627	227,060
Mouhoun	Dédougou	4,032	10,442	329,115
Nahouri	Pô	1,484	3,843	119,144
Namentenga	Boulsa	2,994	7,755	214,564
Oubritenga	Ziniaré	1,812	4,693	328,682
Oudalan	Gorom Gorom	3,879	10,046	123,495
Passoré	Yako	1,575	4,078	232,278
Poni	Gaoua	4,000	10,361	258,647
Sanguie	Réo	1,994	5,165	234,079
Sanmatenga	Kaya	3,557	9,213	404,563
Sèno	Dori	5,202	13,473	269,892
Sissili	Léo	5,303	13,736	297,598
Soum	Djibo	5,154	13,350	217,972
Sourou	Tougan	3,663	9,487	313,355
Tapoa	Diapaga	5,707	14,780	187,785
Yatenga	Ouahigouya	4,746	12,292	558,318
Zoundwéogo	Manga	1,333	3,453	175,166
TOTAL		105,946	274,400	9,190,791

Demography

Population (1997): 10,891,000.
Density (1997): persons per sq mi 102.8, persons per sq km 39.7.
Urban-rural (1991): urban 14.0%; rural 86.0%.
Sex distribution (1997): male 48.65%; female 51.35%.
Age breakdown (1997): under 15, 48.1%; 15–29, 27.0%; 30–44, 12.6%; 45–59, 7.5%; 60–74, 3.9%; 75 and over, 0.9%.
Population projection: (2000) 11,684,000; (2010) 14,150,000.
Ethnic composition (1983): Mossi 47.9%; Mande 8.8%; Fulani 8.3%; Lobi 6.9%; Bobo 6.8%; Senufo 5.3%; Grosi 5.1%; Gurma 4.8%; Tuareg 3.3%.
Religious affiliation (1980): traditional beliefs 44.8%; Muslim 43.0%; Christian 12.2%, of which Roman Catholic 9.8%, Protestant 2.4%.
Major cities (1993): Ouagadougou 690,000; Bobo-Dioulasso 300,000; Koudougou 105,000; Ouahigouya 38,902[1]; Banfora 35,319[1].

Vital statistics

Birth rate per 1,000 population (1996): 47.0 (world avg. 25.0).
Death rate per 1,000 population (1996): 20.0 (world avg. 9.3).
Natural increase rate per 1,000 population (1996): 27.0 (world avg. 15.7).
Total fertility rate (avg. births per childbearing woman; 1996): 6.8.
Life expectancy at birth (1996): male 43.5 years; female 42.9 years.
Major causes of death (ages 15 and under; 1991): malaria, respiratory diseases, intestinal infectious diseases, meningitis.

National economy

Budget (1995). Revenue: CFAF 224,800,000,000 (1993; import duties 23.4%, personal income taxes 18.8%, sales taxes 14.7%). Expenditures: CFAF 244,800,000,000 (wages and salaries 25.2%, debt service 6.2%).
Public debt (external, outstanding; 1995): U.S.$1,136,000,000.
Tourism: receipts (1995) U.S.$22,000,000; expenditures (1994) U.S.$23,000,000.
Production (metric tons except as noted). Agriculture, forestry, fishing (1996): sorghum 1,314,000, millet 785,000, sugarcane 400,000, corn (maize) 222,000, peanuts (groundnuts) 213,300, seed cotton 170,000, rice 124,000, pulses 22,000, sweet potatoes 20,000, sesame 6,000, cassava 2,000; livestock (number of live animals) 7,300,000 goats, 5,800,000 sheep, 4,350,000 cattle, 19,000,000 chickens; roundwood (1995) 10,033,000 cu m; fish catch (1995) 8,000. Mining and quarrying (1995): gold 672 kg[2]; silver 100 kg[3]. Manufacturing (1995): sugar 47,107; flour 31,046; soap 5,787; edible oils 4,286; soft drinks and beer 287,000 hectolitres; printed fabric 5,297,000 sq m; bicycles 11,150 units; mopeds 8,673 units; cigarettes 47,000,000 packets. Construction (value added in CFAF; 1995): 62,400,000,000. Energy production (consumption): electricity (kW-hr; 1994) 216,000,000 (216,000,000); crude petroleum, none (n.a.); petroleum products (metric tons; 1994) none (309,000).
Gross national product (1995): U.S.$2,417,000,000 (U.S.$230 per capita).

Structure of gross domestic product and labour force

	1995 in value CFAF '000,000	1995 % of total value	1991 labour force	1991 % of labour force
Agriculture	367,100	31.6	4,293,784	91.8
Mining }	232,300	20.0	2,590	0.1
Manufacturing }			51,694	1.1
Construction	62,400	5.4	11,016	0.2
Public utilities	10,600	0.9	3,844	0.1
Transp. and commun.	44,700	3.8	15,041	0.3
Trade	140,400	12.1	120,314	2.6
Finance	...	...	2,075	—
Pub. admin., defense }	248,200	21.3	111,556	2.4
Services }				
Other	57,200[4]	4.9[4]	67,279[5]	1.4[5]
TOTAL	1,163,000[6]	100.0	4,679,193	100.0

Population economically active (1991): total 4,679,193; activity rate 50.9% (participation rates: over age [1988] 10, 78.1%; female 48.7%; unemployed 1.1%).

Price and earnings indexes (1990 = 100)

	1990	1991	1992	1993	1994	1995	1996
Consumer price index	100.0	102.5	100.5	101.1	126.5	135.8	144.2
Hourly earnings index[7]	100.0	100.0	100.0	...	...	...	...

Household income and expenditure. Average household size (1985) 6.2; average annual income per household CFAF 303,000 (U.S.$640); sources of income: n.a.; expenditure (1985)[8]: food 38.7%, transportation 18.6%, electricity and fuel 13.7%, beverages 9.0%, health 5.2%, housing 5.1%.
Land use (1994): forested 50.5%; meadows and pastures 21.9%; agricultural and under permanent cultivation 13.0%; other 14.6%.

Foreign trade[9]

Balance of trade (current prices)

	1991	1992	1993	1994	1995	1996
CFAF '000,000	+99.80	+93.10	+69.30	−22.90	+1.96	−122.85
% of total	22.8%	24.4%	18.1%	5.6%	0.3%	28.3%

Imports (1995): CFAF 242,100,000,000 (capital equipment 31.1%, food products 14.4%, petroleum products 10.6%, raw materials 8.7%). *Major import sources* (1993): France 24.5%; Côte d'Ivoire 17.9%; Nigeria 6.6%; Japan 6.4%; China 5.6%; United States 4.3%; The Netherlands 4.3%.
Exports (1995): CFAF 164,400,000,000 (raw cotton 42.2%, live animals 18.9%, gold 12.1%, hides and skins 8.9%). *Major export destinations* (1993): Côte d'Ivoire 34.9%; France 21.1%; Mali 5.4%; Taiwan 3.5%; Japan 3.5%.

Transport and communications

Transport. Railroads (1995)[10]: route length 386 mi, 622 km; passenger-km 202,000,000; metric ton-km cargo 45,000,000. Roads (1995): total length 7,771 mi, 12,506 km (paved 16%). Vehicles (1995): passenger cars 16,800; trucks and buses 17,222. Merchant marine: none. Air transport (1993): passenger-km 217,154,000; metric ton-km cargo 34,204,000; airports (1997) 2.

Communications

Medium	date	unit	number	units per 1,000 persons
Daily newspapers	1995	circulation	17,000[11]	1.6[11]
Radio	1996	receivers	512,500	48.3
Television	1995	receivers	45,500	4.4
Telephones	1995	main lines	30,000	2.9

Education and health

Educational attainment (1985). Percentage of population age 10 and over having: no formal schooling 86.1%; some primary 7.3%; general secondary 2.2%; specialized secondary and postsecondary 3.8%; other 0.6%. *Literacy* (1995): percentage of total population age 15 and over literate 18.2%; males literate 29.5%; females literate 9.2%.

Education (1993–94)

	schools	teachers	students	student/ teacher ratio
Primary	2,971	10,300	600,032	58.2
Secondary	173[12]	3,346	116,033	34.7
Vocational	22[12]	639	8,808	13.8
Higher	9[12]	571	8,815	15.4

Health (1991): physicians 341 (1 per 27,158 persons); hospital beds 5,041 (1 per 1,837 persons); infant mortality rate (1996) 117.8.
Food (1995): daily per capita caloric intake 2,155 (vegetable products 96%, animal products 4%); 91% of FAO recommended minimum requirement.

Military

Total active duty personnel (1997): 5,800 (army 96.6%, air force 3.4%). *Military expenditure as percentage of GNP* (1995): 2.9% (world 2.8%); per capita expenditure U.S.$7.

[1]1985. [2]Officially marketed gold only; does not include substantial illegal production. [3]1992. [4]Includes indirect taxes less imputed bank service charges and subsidies. [5]Includes 49,819 unemployed. [6]Detail does not add to total given because of rounding. [7]January 1; index refers to the *S.M.I.G.* (*salaire minimum interprofessionnel guaranti*), a form of minimum professional wage. [8]Weights of consumer price index components; Ouagadougou only. [9]Imports figures are c.i.f. in balance of trade and f.o.b. in commodities and trading partners. [10]Passenger-km and metric ton-km cargo figures are based on traffic between Abidjan, Côte d'Ivoire, and Ouagadougou. [11]Circulation for 3 newspapers only. [12]1991–92.

Burundi

Official name: Republika y'u Burundi (Rundi); République du Burundi (French) (Republic of Burundi).
Form of government: military regime with one legislative house (National Assembly [81])[1].
Head of state and government: President, assisted by Prime Minister.
Capital: Bujumbura.
Official languages: Rundi; French.
Official religion: none.
Monetary unit: 1 Burundi franc (FBu) = 100 centimes; valuation (Oct. 3, 1997) 1 U.S.$ = FBu 349.04; 1 £ = FBu 562.66.

Area and population

		area		population
				1990
Provinces	**Capitals**	sq mi	sq km	census
Bubanza	Bubanza	420	1,089	222,953
Bujumbura	Bujumbura	509	1,319	608,931
Bururi	Bururi	952	2,465	385,490
Cankuzo	Cankuzo	759	1,965	142,707
Cibitoke	Cibitoke	631	1,636	279,843
Gitega	Gitega	764	1,979	565,174
Karuzi	Karuzi	563	1,457	287,905
Kayanza	Kayanza	476	1,233	443,116
Kirundo	Kirundo	658	1,703	401,103
Makamba	Makamba	757	1,960	223,799
Muramvya	Muramvya	593	1,535	441,653
Muyinga	Muyinga	709	1,836	373,382
Ngozi	Ngozi	569	1,474	482,246
Rutana	Rutana	756	1,959	195,834
Ruyigi	Ruyigi	903	2,339	238,567
TOTAL LAND AREA		10,019	25,949	
INLAND WATER		721	1,867	
TOTAL		10,740	27,816	5,292,793[2]

Demography

Population (1997): 6,053,000[3].
Density (1997)[4]: persons per sq mi 604.1, persons per sq km 233.3.
Urban-rural (1990): urban 6.3%; rural 93.7%.
Sex distribution (1995): male 48.94%; female 51.06%.
Age breakdown (1995): under 15, 46.2%; 15–29, 25.9%; 30–44, 16.4%; 45–59, 7.0%; 60–74, 3.5%; 75 and over, 1.0%.
Population projection: (2000) 6,493,000; (2010) 8,229,000.
Doubling time: 28 years.
Ethnic composition (1983): Rundi 97.4%, of which Hutu 82.9%, Tutsi 13.6%; Twa Pygmy 1.0%; other 2.6%.
Religious affiliation (1990): Roman Catholic 65.1%; Protestant 13.8%; Muslim 1.6%; nonreligious 18.6%; traditional beliefs 0.3%; other 0.6%.
Major cities (1990): Bujumbura (1994) 300,000; Gitega 101,827; Bururi 15,816; Ngozi 14,511; Cibitoke 8,280.

Vital statistics

Birth rate per 1,000 population (1996): 42.7 (world avg. 25.0).
Death rate per 1,000 population (1996): 17.8 (world avg. 9.3).
Natural increase rate per 1,000 population (1996): 24.9 (world avg. 15.7).
Total fertility rate (avg. births per childbearing woman; 1996): 6.5.
Marriage rate per 1,000 population: n.a.
Divorce rate per 1,000 population: n.a.
Life expectancy at birth (1996): male 44.3 years; female 47.3 years.
Major causes of death: n.a.; however, major health problems include malaria, influenza, diarrheal diseases, measles, and AIDS.

National economy

Budget (1995). Revenue: FBu 59,600,000,000 (customs duties 37.1%, excise duties 22.6%, income tax 19.2%, taxes on goods and services 14.6%, administrative receipts 2.4%). Expenditures: FBu 69,100,000,000 (wages and salaries 27.5%, goods and services 18.4%, subsidies and transfers 9.8%, public debt 6.3%).
Tourism (1995): receipts from visitors U.S.$1,000,000; expenditures by nationals abroad U.S.$25,000,000.
Production (metric tons except as noted). Agriculture, forestry, fishing (1996): bananas 1,544,000, sweet potatoes 670,000, cassavas 549,000, dry beans 288,000, sugarcane 148,000, corn (maize) 144,000, yams and taros 103,000, sorghum 66,000, potatoes 42,000, rice 42,000, coffee 25,000, millet 11,000, peanuts (groundnuts) 10,000, wheat 9,000; livestock (number of live animals) 900,000 goats, 390,000 cattle, 320,000 sheep, 4,000,000 chickens; roundwood (1995) 4,969,000 cu m; fish catch (1995) 21,100. Mining and quarrying (1991): peat 10,026; kaolin clay 6,682; lime 86; gold 804 troy oz. Manufacturing (1994): beer 1,382,670 hectolitres; carbonated beverages 201,400 hectolitres; cigarettes 584,580,000 units; blankets 248,438 units; footwear 74,890 pairs. Construction: n.a. Energy production (consumption): electricity (kW-hr; 1994) 147,000,000 (192,000,000); coal, none (n.a.); crude petroleum, none (n.a.); petroleum products (metric tons; 1994) none (71,000); natural gas, none (n.a.); peat (metric tons; 1994) 12,000 (12,000).
Land use (1994): forested 12.7%; meadows and pastures 38.6%; agricultural and under permanent cultivation 45.9%; other 2.8%.
Gross national product (at current market prices; 1995): U.S.$984,000,000 (U.S.$160 per capita).

Structure of gross domestic product and labour force

	1995		1990	
	in value FBu '000,000	% of total value	labour force	% of labour force
Agriculture	126,664	47.8	2,574,443	93.1
Mining }	1,296	0.5	1,419	—
Public utilities }			1,672	0.1
Manufacturing	27,855	10.5	33,867	1.2
Construction	11,436	4.3	19,737	0.7
Transportation and communications	8,892	3.4	8,504	0.3
Trade	8,709	3.3	25,822	0.9
Finance	...	...	2,005	0.1
Pub. admin., defense	37,866	14.3 }	85,191	3.1
Services	4,648	1.7 }		
Other	37,623[5]	14.2[5]	13,270	0.5
TOTAL	264,990[2]	100.0	2,765,945[2]	100.0

Public debt (external, outstanding; 1995): U.S.$1,095,000,000.
Population economically active (1991): total 2,779,777; activity rate of total population 52.9% (participation rates: ages 15–64, 91.4%; female 52.6%; unemployed, n.a.).

Price and earnings indexes (1990 = 100)

	1990	1991	1992	1993	1994	1995	1996
Consumer price index	100.0	109.0	111.0	121.7	139.8	166.7	210.8
Earnings index	...	...	...	...	...	...	...

Household income and expenditure. Average household size (1990) 4.6; income per household: n.a.; sources of income: n.a.; expenditure[6]: food 59.6%, clothing and footwear 11.1%, furniture and household goods 6.0%, energy and water 5.8%, housing 4.4%, other 13.1%.

Foreign trade

Balance of trade (current prices)

	1991	1992	1993	1994	1995	1996
FBu '000,000	−28,144	−30,751	−26,417	−22,603	−24,018	−26,039
% of total	45.8%	50.0%	44.0%	29.9%	31.1%	53.5%

Imports (1995): FBu 52,082,000,000 (1994; machinery and transport equipment 21.3%, food and food products 17.9%, petroleum products 8.2%, pharmaceutical products 6.4%). *Major import sources:* Belgium-Luxembourg 14.8%; France 9.2%; Germany 8.8%; Japan 6.1%; United States 5.7%; The Netherlands 4.5%; Kenya 4.3%.
Exports (1995): FBu 28,872,000,000 (coffee 80.7%, tea 7.8%, cotton 1.6%, animal hides and skins 1.2%). *Major export destinations:* Germany 21.6%; Belgium-Luxembourg 17.6%; France 10.9%; United States 6.7%; Rwanda 3.6%; United Kingdom 3.6%; The Netherlands 2.3%; Zaire 1.6%.

Transport and communications

Transport. Railroads: none. Roads (1995): total length 8,997 mi, 14,480 km (paved 7%). Vehicles (1995): passenger cars 16,800; trucks and other vehicles 15,000. Merchant marine (1979): vessels (100 gross tons and over) 1; total gross tonnage 385. Air transport (1994)[7]: passenger arrivals 28,762, departures 33,750; cargo loaded 1,760 short tons (1,597 metric tons), unloaded 14,841 short tons (13,463 metric tons); airports (1997) with scheduled flights 1.

Communications

Medium	date	unit	number	units per 1,000 persons
Daily newspapers	1996	circulation	20,000	3.4
Radio	1996	receivers	300,000	50
Television	1995	receivers	40,000	7.0
Telephones	1995	main lines	17,200	2.7
Cellular telephones	1995	subscribers	300	0.1
Facsimile machines	1995	units	100	—

Education and health

Educational attainment: n.a. *Literacy* (1995): percentage of total population age 15 and over literate 35.3%; males literate 49.7%; females literate 22.5%.

Education (1992–93)

	schools	teachers	students	student/ teacher ratio
Primary (age 6–11)	1,418	10,400	651,086	62.6
Secondary (age 12–18)	113[8]	2,562	55,713	21.7
Higher	8	556	4,256	7.6

Health (1990): physicians 168 (1 per 31,777 persons); hospital beds 10,370 (1 per 515 persons); infant mortality rate per 1,000 live births (1996) 104.8.
Food (1995): daily per capita caloric intake 1,749 (vegetable products 97%, animal products 3%); 75% of FAO recommended minimum requirement.

Military

Total active duty personnel (1996): 18,500 (army 100%). *Military expenditure as percentage of GNP* (1995): 4.4% (world 2.8%); per capita expenditure U.S.$6.

[1]The new military government from July 1996 reinstated the National Assembly in September 1996; transitional government announced in September 1996 to be in place until September 1999. [2]Detail does not add to total given because of rounding. [3]Population is not adjusted for casualties or refugees of the recent civil war. [4]Based on land area. [5]Indirect taxes less subsidies. [6]Weights of consumer price index components. [7]Figures for Bujumbura airport only. [8]1990–91.

Cambodia

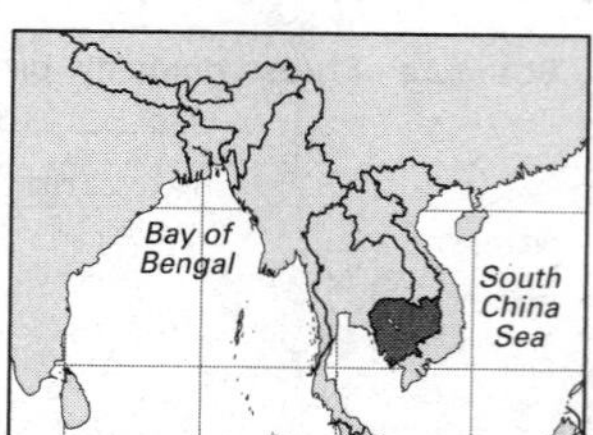

Official name: Preah Reach Ana Pak Kampuchea (Kingdom of Cambodia)[1].
Form of government: constitutional monarchy with one legislative house (National Assembly [120]).
Chief of state: King.
Heads of government: Co-premiers[2].
Capital: Phnom Penh.
Official language: Khmer.
Official religion: Buddhism.
Monetary unit: 1 riel = 100 sen; valuation (Oct. 3, 1997) 1 U.S.$ = 3,192 riels; 1 £ = 5,145 riels.

Area and population

Provinces	Capitals	area sq mi	area sq km	population 1987 estimate
Bântéay Méan Cheăy	...	[3]	[3]	[3]
Bătdâmbâng	Bătdâmbâng	7,353[3]	19,044[3]	837,000[3]
Kâmpóng Cham	Kâmpóng Cham	4,053	10,498	1,244,000
Kâmpóng Chhnăng	Kâmpóng Chhnăng	2,131	5,520	257,000
Kâmpóng Spœ	Kâmpóng Spœ	2,709	7,016	396,000
Kâmpóng Thum	Kâmpóng Thum	4,730	12,251	441,000
Kâmpôt	Kâmpôt	3,808	9,862	412,000
Kândal	...	1,472	3,813	838,000
Kaôh Kŏng	Krŏng Kaôh Kŏng	4,301	11,140	30,000
Krâchéh	Krâchéh	4,283	11,094	182,000
Môndôl Kiri	Senmonorom	5,517	14,288	18,000
Ŏtdâr Méan Cheăy[4]	...	...	...	...
Poŭthĭsăt	Poŭthĭsăt	4,900	12,692	204,000
Preăh Vihéar	Phnum Tbéng Méan Cheăy	5,541	14,350	80,000
Prey Vêng	Prey Vêng	1,885	4,883	782,000
Rôtânăh Kiri	Lumphăt	4,163	10,782	52,000
Siĕmréab[4]	Siĕmréab	4,207	10,897	555,000
Stœ̆ng Trêng	Stœ̆ng Trêng	4,328	11,209	46,000
Svay Riĕng	Svay Riĕng	1,145	2,966	340,000
Takêv	Takêv	1,474	3,818	618,000
Municipalities				
TOTAL LAND AREA		68,045	176,238	
Phnom Penh		18	46	564,000
Preăh Seihânŭ		27	69	61,000
Kêb		...	...	...
INLAND WATER		2,192	5,678	
TOTAL		70,238[5]	181,916	7,957,000

Demography

Population (1997): 10,385,000.
Density (1997)[6]: persons per sq mi 147.9, persons per sq km 57.1.
Urban-rural (1995): urban 21%; rural 79%.
Sex distribution (1997): male 48.24%; female 51.76%.
Age breakdown (1997): under 15, 45.4%; 15–29, 25.3%; 30–44, 17.1%; 45–59, 7.6%; 60–74, 3.8%; 75 and over, 0.8%.
Population projection: (2000) 11,267,000; (2010) 14,602,000.
Ethnic composition (1994): Khmer 88.6%; Vietnamese 5.5%; Chinese 3.1%; Cham 2.3%; other (Thai, Lao, and Kola) 0.5%.
Religious affiliation (1994): Buddhist 95%; Muslim 2%; other 3%.
Major cities (1987): Phnom Penh 920,000[7]; Bătdâmbâng 45,000; Kâmpóng Cham 33,000; Pursat 16,000; Kâmpóng Chhnăng 15,000.

Vital statistics

Birth rate per 1,000 population (1997): 43.0 (world avg. 25.0).
Death rate per 1,000 population (1997): 15.0 (world avg. 9.3).
Natural increase rate per 1,000 population (1997): 28.0 (world avg. 15.7).
Total fertility rate (avg. births per childbearing woman; 1997): 5.8.
Life expectancy at birth (1997): male 52 years; female 55 years.
Major causes of death per 100,000 population: n.a.; however, major health problems include tuberculosis, malaria, and pneumonia. Violence, acts of war, and military ordnance (especially unexploded mines) remain hazards.

National economy

Budget (1996). Revenue: 797,500,000,000 riels (taxes on international trade 46.9%; indirect taxes 22.3%, of which consumption taxes 8.3%; nontax revenue 27.6%). Expenditures: 1,395,100,000,000 riels (current expenditure 61.2%, of which economic and financial affairs 26.8%, defense 21.4%, education 12.3%, public health 8.7%; development expenditure 38.8%).
Public debt (external, outstanding; 1995): U.S.$1,942,000,000.
Tourism (1995): receipts U.S.$100,000,000; expenditures U.S.$8,000,000.
Production (metric tons except as noted). Agriculture, forestry, fishing (1996): rice 3,500,000, sugarcane 205,000, bananas 140,000, roots and tubers 138,000 (of which cassava 90,000, sweet potatoes 30,000), corn (maize) 60,000, oranges 60,000, rubber 40,000, mangoes 30,000, soybeans 18,000, tobacco leaves 10,000; livestock (number of live animals; 1997) 2,800,000 cattle, 2,050,000 pigs, 770,000 buffalo, 14,300,000 chickens and ducks; roundwood (1995) 7,765,000 cu m; fish catch (1995) 112,510. Mining and quarrying (1995): legal mining is confined to fertilizers, salt, and construction materials. Manufacturing (value of production in '000,000 riels; 1988): cigarettes 1,064.5; food 116.9; chemical products (including rubber) 83.5; light industries (including textiles) 63.2; mechanical equipment and parts 46.8; building materials 4.5. Construction: n.a. Energy production (consumption): electricity (kW-hr; 1994) 187,000,000 (187,000,000); petroleum products (metric tons; 1994) none (159,000).
Household income and expenditure. Average household size (1980) 5.6.

Gross domestic product (1995): U.S.$2,718,000,000 (U.S.$270 per capita).

Structure of gross domestic product and labour force

	1995 in value '000,000,000 riels	1995 % of total value	1996 labour force	1996 % of labour force
Agriculture	3,826	53.1	3,732,000	72.6
Mining	20	0.3	1,406,000	27.4
Manufacturing	367	5.1		
Construction	561	7.8		
Public utilities	50	0.7		
Transp. and commun.	248	3.4		
Trade	983	13.7		
Public admin., defense	283	3.9		
Services / Other	862	12.0		
TOTAL	7,200	100.0	5,138,000	100.0

Population economically active (1993): total 4,010,000; activity rate of total population 43.1% (participation rates: ages 15–64, 86.2%; female 55.8%).

Price and earnings indexes (1994 = 100)

	1991	1992	1993	1994	1995	1996	1997
Consumer price index	31.8	64.7	119.7	100.0	105.3	115.9	129.5[8]
Earnings index	...	...	...	...	...	...	...

Land use (1994): forested 69.1%; meadows and pastures 8.5%; agricultural and under permanent cultivation 21.7%; other 0.7%.

Foreign trade[9]

Balance of trade (current prices)

	1991	1992	1993	1994	1995	1996
U.S.$'000,000	−33.0	−86.0	−203.0	−275.0	−382.0	−395.0
% of total	7.1%	14.0%	31.7%	22.9%	19.1%	24.3%

Imports (1996): U.S.$1,010,000,000 (1995; gold 32.8%; cigarettes 20.7%; gasoline and diesel oil 11.7%; motorcycles 3.9%; motor vehicles 2.4%). *Major import sources* (1995): Singapore 35.7%; Thailand 23.8%; Vietnam 6.8%.
Exports (1996): U.S.$615,000,000 (1995; reexports 50.4%; domestic exports 49.6%, of which sawn timber 16.5%, logs 11.8%, rubber 5.6%). *Major export destinations* (1995): Thailand 42.7%; Singapore 11.1%; India 7.6%

Transport and communications

Transport. Railroads (1995): length 380 mi, 612 km; passengers transported (1994) 500,000; cargo transported (1994) 100,000 metric tons. Roads (1995): total length 7,643 mi, 12,300 km (paved 34%). Vehicles (1996): passenger cars 42,210; trucks and buses 9,005. Merchant marine (1992): vessels (100 gross tons and over) 3; total deadweight tonnage 3,839. Air transport (1977): passenger-mi 26,098,800, passenger-km 42,000,000; short ton-mi cargo 274,000, metric ton-km cargo 400,000; airports (1997) with scheduled flights 8.

Communications

Medium	date	unit	number	units per 1,000 persons
Radio	1995	receivers	1,192,000	124.0
Television	1995	receivers	76,900	8.0
Telephones	1996	main lines	10,100	1.0
Cellular telephones	1995	subscribers	14,400	1.5
Facsimile machines	1995	units	960	0.1

Education and health

Educational attainment: n.a. *Literacy* (1993): total population age 15 and over literate 3,895,000 (65.3%); males literate 79.7%; females literate 53.4%.

Education (1994–95)

	schools	teachers	students	student/ teacher ratio
Primary (age 6–10)	4,539[10]	37,827	1,703,316	45.0
Secondary (age 11–16)	440[10]	16,349	297,555	18.2
Voc., teacher tr.	65[10]	2,618[10]	16,350	...
Higher	9[10]	784	11,652	14.9

Health: physicians (1994) 1,200 (1 per 7,900 persons); hospital beds (1994) 12,098[11] (1 per 791 persons); infant mortality rate (1997) 106.
Food (1995): daily per capita caloric intake 2,012 (vegetable products 94%, animal products 6%); 91% of FAO recommended minimum requirement.

Military

Total active duty personnel (1997)[12]: 140,500 (army 59.8%, navy 3.6%, air force 1.0%, provincial 35.6%). *Military expenditure as percentage of GNP* (1995): 3.1% (world 2.8%); per capita expenditure U.S.$9.

[1]The United Nations Transitional Authority in Cambodia (UNTAC) assumed administrative responsibility for Cambodia in March 1992. Cambodian sovereignty, however, was retained by a Supreme National Council (SNC) until UN-supervised elections were held May 23–29, 1993. The Kingdom of Cambodia was proclaimed from Sept. 24, 1993. [2]The first premier is serving extraconstitutionally from July 1997. [3]Bântéay Méan Cheăy included in Bătdâmbâng. [4]The area and population of Ŏtdâr Méan Cheăy is included with Siĕmréab. [5]Detail does not add to total given because of rounding. [6]Based on land area. [7]1994 estimate. [8]August. [9]Trade statistics do not indicate whether imports are c.i.f. or f.o.b.; illegal or undeclared trade is not accounted for in the foreign-trade figures shown here. [10]1992–93. [11]Public hospitals only. [12]Figures include provincial and exclude paramilitary forces.

Internet resources for further information:
- **Cambodian Information Center http://www.cambodia.org**

Cameroon

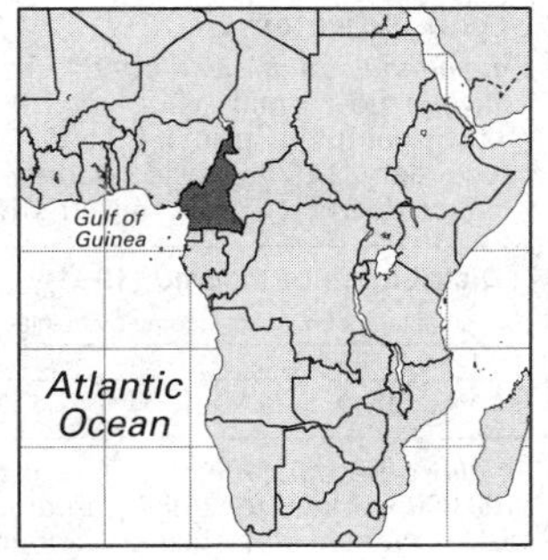

Official name: République du Cameroun (French); Republic of Cameroon (English).
Form of government: unitary multiparty republic with one legislative house (National Assembly [180]).
Chief of state: President.
Head of government: Prime Minister.
Capital: Yaoundé.
Official languages: French; English.
Official religion: none.
Monetary unit: 1 CFA franc (CFAF) = 100 centimes; valuation (Oct. 3, 1997) 1 U.S.$ = CFAF 592.29; 1 £ = CFAF 954.76.

Area and population

Provinces	Capitals	area sq mi	area sq km	population 1987 census
Adamoua	Ngaoundéré	24,591	63,691	495,200
Centre	Yaoundé	26,613	68,926	1,651,600
Est	Bertoua	42,089	109,011	517,200
Extrême-Nord	Maroua	13,223	34,246	1,855,700
Littoral	Douala	7,814	20,239	1,354,800
Nord	Garoua	25,319	65,576	832,200
Nord-Ouest	Bamenda	6,877	17,810	1,237,400
Ouest	Bafoussam	5,356	13,872	1,339,800
Sud	Ebolowa	18,189	47,110	373,800
Sud-Ouest	Buea	9,448	24,471	838,000
LAND AREA		179,519	464,952	
INLAND WATER		4,051	10,492	
TOTAL		183,569[1]	475,442[1]	10,495,700

Demography

Population (1997): 14,678,000.
Density (1997)[2]: persons per sq mi 81.8, persons per sq km 31.6.
Urban-rural (1991): urban 41.2%; rural 58.8%.
Sex distribution (1991): male 49.88%; female 50.12%.
Age breakdown (1991): under 15, 46.4%; 15–29, 24.4%; 30–44, 15.1%; 45–59, 8.6%; 60 and over, 5.5%.
Population projection: (2000) 15,966,000; (2010) 20,630,000.
Doubling time: 25 years.
Ethnic composition (1983): Fang 19.6%; Bamileke and Bamum 18.5%; Duala, Luanda, and Basa 14.7%; Fulani 9.6%; Tikar 7.4%; Mandara 5.7%; Maka 4.9%; Chamba 2.4%; Mbum 1.3%; Hausa 1.2%; French 0.2%; other 14.5%.
Religious affiliation (1990): Roman Catholic 34.7%; animist 26.0%; Muslim 21.8%; Protestant 17.5%.
Major cities (1991): Douala 1,200,000; Yaoundé 1,000,000; Bafoussam 200,000; Garoua 120,000; Maroua 80,000.

Vital statistics

Birth rate per 1,000 population (1995–2000): 39.3 (world avg. 25.0).
Death rate per 1,000 population (1995–2000): 11.9 (world avg. 9.3).
Natural increase rate per 1,000 population (1995–2000): 27.4 (world avg. 15.7).
Total fertility rate (avg. births per childbearing woman; 1995–2000): 5.3.
Life expectancy at birth (1995–2000): male 54.5 years; female 57.2 years.
Major causes of death per 100,000 population: n.a.; however, major health problems include measles, malaria, tuberculosis of respiratory system, anemias, meningitis, and intestinal obstruction and hernia.

National economy

Budget (1995–96). Revenue: CFAF 654,900,000,000 (petroleum royalties 21.8%; taxes on goods and services 19.7%; customs duties 18.0%). Expenditures: CFAF 775,200,000,000 (current expenditure 94.4%, of which debt services 45.1%, wages and salaries 24.3%, goods and services 15.1%).
Public debt (external, outstanding; 1995): U.S.$8,061,000,000.
Gross national product (1995): U.S.$8,615,000,000 (U.S.$650 per capita).

Structure of gross domestic product and labour force

	1995–96 in value CFAF '000,000,000	1995–96 % of total value	1985 labour force	1985 % of labour force
Agriculture	1,836	40.2	2,900,871	74.0
Mining	334	7.3	1,793	0.1
Manufacturing	453	9.9	174,498	4.5
Construction }	220	4.8	66,684	1.7
Public utilities }			3,522	0.1
Transp. and commun. }			51,688	1.3
Trade }	1,230	26.9	154,014	3.9
Finance }			8,009	0.2
Services }		8.1 }	292,922	7.5
Public admin., defense	370			
Other	128	2.8	263,634	6.7
TOTAL	4,571	100.0	3,917,635	100.0

Household income and expenditure. Average household size (1980) 5.2; average annual income per household (1983)[3] U.S.$420; sources of income: n.a.; expenditure (1993)[3]: food 49.1%, housing 18.0%, transportation and communications 13.0%, health 8.6%, clothing 7.6%, recreation 2.4%.
Tourism (1993): receipts U.S.$47,000,000; expenditures U.S.$225,000,000.
Population economically active (1991): total 4,740,000; activity rate of total population 40.0% (participation rates [1985]: ages 15–69, 66.3%; female 38.5%; unemployed, n.a.).

Price and earnings indexes (1992 = 100)

	1991	1992	1993	1994	1995	1996
Consumer price index	100.1	100.0	96.8	130.8	149.0	156.0
Earnings index	...	...	...	...	...	...

Production (metric tons except as noted). Agriculture, forestry, fishing (1996): sugarcane 1,350,000, cassava 1,300,000, bananas 980,000, plantains 970,000, corn (maize) 654,000, vegetables and melons 385,000, sweet potatoes 180,000, palm oil 130,000, cacao 120,000, yams 110,000, peanuts (groundnuts) 100,000, millet 100,000, rice 80,000, palm kernels 56,000; livestock (number of live animals) 4,900,000 cattle, 3,800,000 sheep, 3,800,000 goats, 1,410,000 pigs; roundwood (1994) 13,948,000 cu m; fish catch (1995) 63,947. Mining and quarrying (1994): marble 200,000; pozzolana 130,000; aluminum 85,000; limestone 57,000; tin ore and concentrate 4. Manufacturing (value added in CFAF '000,000; 1994): beverages 49,314; wood and wood products 42,756; rubber and plastic products 38,928; food products 30,030; iron and steel products 29,424; textiles 20,113; refined petroleum products 17,888; industrial chemicals 8,559; pottery, china, and earthenware 6,773; paper products 3,652. Construction (1983): residential 230,400 sq m; nonresidential 51,100 sq m. Energy production (consumption): electricity (kW-hr; 1994) 2,740,000,000 (2,740,000,000); coal (metric tons; 1994) 1,000 (1,000); crude petroleum (barrels; 1993) 39,462,000 (7,889,000); petroleum products (metric tons; 1994) 1,023,000 (1,014,000); natural gas, none (n.a.).
Land use (1994): forested 77.1%; meadows and pastures 4.3%; agricultural and under permanent cultivation 15.1%; other 3.5%.

Foreign trade[4]

Balance of trade (current prices)

	1989	1990	1991	1992	1993	1994
CFAF '000,000,000	+40.3	+141.5	+198.6	+197.6	+249.7	+387.4
% of total	5.2%	14.8%	22.3%	25.9%	30.6%	34.5%

Imports (1994–95): CFAF 464,700,000,000 (semifinished goods 18.8%; food, beverages, and tobacco 14.2%; industrial equipment 12.4%; transport equipment 11.0%). *Major import sources* (1995): France 39.2%; United States 9.7%; Germany 9.1%; Japan 6.9%; Belgium-Luxembourg 6.8%; Italy 4.5%; The Netherlands 4.3%; United Kingdom 3.9%.
Exports (1994–95): CFAF 811,000,000,000 (crude petroleum 38.1%; lumber 11.0%; cocoa 8.4%; coffee 7.3%; aluminum 6.7%; cotton 3.7%). *Major export destinations* (1995): France 29.7%; Italy 16.6%; Spain 14.3%; The Netherlands 13.0%; South Korea 2.8%; Germany 2.3%.

Transport and communications

Transport. Railroads (1995): route length 625 mi, 1,006 km; passenger-mi 197,000,000, passenger-km 317,000,000; short ton-mi cargo 556,000,000, metric ton-km cargo 812,000,000. Roads (1991): total length 30,074 mi, 48,400 km (paved 8%). Vehicles (1995): passenger cars 92,200; trucks and buses 60,000. Merchant marine (1992): vessels (100 gross tons and over) 47; total deadweight tonnage 39,797. Air transport (1992): passenger-mi 196,000,000, passenger-km 315,000,000; short ton-mi cargo 26,712,000, metric ton-km cargo 39,000,000; airports (1997) with scheduled flights 5.

Communications

Medium	date	unit	number	units per 1,000 persons
Daily newspapers	1995	circulation	66,000	5.0
Radio	1995	receivers	4,100,000	325
Television	1995	receivers	960,000	72.1
Telephones	1995	main lines	59,700	4.5
Cellular telephones	1995	subscribers	2,800	0.2

Education and health

Educational attainment (1976). Percentage of population age 15 and over having: no schooling 51.1%; primary education 41.7%; some postprimary 0.2%; secondary 5.7%; some postsecondary 0.3%; higher 0.2%; other 0.8%.
Literacy (1995): percentage of total population age 15 and over literate 63.4%; males literate 75.0%; females literate 52.1%.

Education (1994–95)

	schools	teachers	students	student/ teacher ratio
Primary (age 6–14)	6,801	40,970	1,896,722	46.3
Secondary (age 15–24)	388[5]	14,917	459,068	30.8
Vocational	220[5]	5,885	91,779	15.6
Higher[6]	5[5]	1,086	33,177	30.5

Health: physicians (1989) 945 (1 per 11,848 persons); hospital beds (1988) 29,285 (1 per 371 persons); infant mortality rate (1995–2000) 58.0.
Food (1995): daily per capita caloric intake 2,214 (vegetable products 94%, animal products 6%); 95% of FAO recommended minimum requirement.

Military

Total active duty personnel (1997): 13,100 (army 87.8%, navy 9.9%, air force 2.3%). *Military expenditure as percentage of GNP* (1994): 1.9% (world 3.0%); per capita expenditure U.S.$8.

[1]Detail does not add to total given because of rounding. [2]Based on land area. [3]Weights of consumer price index components. [4]Import figures are f.o.b. in balance of trade and c.i.f. for commodities and trading partners. [5]1986–87. [6]1990–91.

Internet resources for further information:
- **Presidency of the Republic of Cameroon**
http://www.camnet.cm/celcom/anglais/homepr.htm

Canada

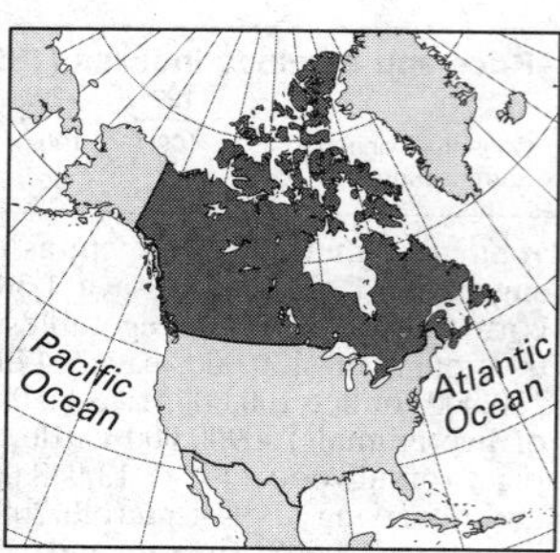

Official name: Canada.
Form of government: federal multiparty parliamentary state with two legislative houses (Senate [104]; House of Commons [301]).
Chief of state: Queen of Canada (British Monarch).
Representative of chief of state: Governor-General.
Head of government: Prime Minister.
Capital: Ottawa.
Official languages: English; French.
Official religion: none.
Monetary unit: 1 Canadian dollar (Can$) = 100 cents; valuation (Oct. 3, 1997) 1 U.S.$ = Can$1.37; 1 £ = Can$2.21.

Area and population

		area		population
Provinces	**Capitals**	sq mi	sq km	1996 census
Alberta	Edmonton	255,287	661,190	2,847,000
British Columbia	Victoria	365,948	947,800	3,933,300
Manitoba	Winnipeg	250,947	649,950	1,145,200
New Brunswick	Fredericton	28,355	73,440	762,000
Newfoundland	St. John's	156,649	405,720	563,600
Nova Scotia	Halifax	21,425	55,490	947,900
Ontario	Toronto	412,581	1,068,580	11,407,700
Prince Edward Island	Charlottetown	2,185	5,660	137,200
Quebec	Quebec	594,860	1,540,680	7,419,900
Saskatchewan	Regina	251,866	652,330	1,023,500
Territories				
Northwest Territories[1]	Yellowknife	1,322,910	3,426,320	67,500
Yukon Territory	Whitehorse	186,661	483,450	31,600
TOTAL		3,849,674	9,970,610	30,286,600[2]

Demography

Population (1997): 30,287,000.
Density (1997)[3]: persons per sq mi 8.5, persons per sq km 3.3.
Urban-rural (1996): urban 77.9%; rural 22.1%.
Sex distribution (1997): male 49.53%; female 50.47%.
Age breakdown (1997): under 15, 19.8%; 15–29, 20.7%; 30–44, 25.5%; 45–59, 17.7%; 60–74, 11.0%; 75 and over, 5.3%.
Population projection: (2000) 31,472,000; (2010) 35,065,000.
Doubling time: not applicable; doubling time exceeds 100 years.
Ethnic origin (1991): French 22.8%; British 20.8%; German 3.4%; Italian 2.8%; Chinese 2.2%; Amerindian and Inuktitut (Eskimo) 1.7%; Ukrainian 1.5%; Dutch 1.3%; multiple origin and other 43.5%[4].
Religious affiliation (1991): Roman Catholic 45.2%; Protestant 36.4%; Eastern Orthodox 1.9%; Jewish 1.2%; Muslim 0.9%; Buddhist 0.6%; Hindu 0.6%; nonreligious 12.5%; other 0.7%.
Major metropolitan areas (1996): Toronto 4,263,757; Montreal 3,326,510; Vancouver 1,831,665; Ottawa-Hull 1,010,498; Edmonton 862,597; Calgary 821,628; Quebec 671,889; Winnipeg 667,209; Hamilton 624,360; London 398,616.

Other metropolitan areas (1996)

	population		population		population
Chicoutimi-Jonquière	160,454	Regina	193,652	Sherbrooke	147,384
Halifax	332,518	St. Catharines–Niagara	372,406	Sudbury	160,488
Kitchener	382,940	St. John's	174,051	Trois Rivières	139,956
Oshawa	268,773	Saskatoon	219,056	Victoria	304,287
				Windsor	278,685

Place of birth (1991): 84.6% native-born; 15.4% foreign-born, of which United Kingdom 2.6%, other European 5.9%, Asian countries 3.8%, United States 0.9%, other 2.2%.
Mobility (1991). Population living in the same residence as in 1986: 53.3%; different residence, same municipality 23.2%; same province, different municipality 15.9%; different province 3.9%; different country 3.7%.
Households (1995). Total number of households 11,243,000. Average household size 2.6; 1 person 24.9%, 2 persons 32.9%, 3 persons 16.5%, 4 persons 16.8%, 5 or more persons 8.9%. Family households (1995): 7,879,700 (70.1%), nonfamily 3,363,300 (29.1%, of which 1 person 83.3%).
Immigration (1994): permanent immigrants admitted 223,875, from Hong Kong 19.7%, Philippines 8.5%, India 7.7%, China 5.6%, Taiwan 3.3%, Sri Lanka 3.0%, United States 2.8%, Vietnam 2.8%, United Kingdom 2.7%; refugee arrivals 19,089.

Vital statistics

Birth rate per 1,000 population (1996): 12.5 (world avg. 25.0); (1985) legitimate 83.8%; illegitimate 16.2%.
Death rate per 1,000 population (1996): 7.2 (world avg. 9.3).
Natural increase rate per 1,000 population (1996): 5.3 (world avg. 15.7).
Total fertility rate (avg. births per childbearing woman; 1993): 1.9.
Marriage rate per 1,000 population (1995): 5.4.
Divorce rate per 1,000 population (1995): 2.7.
Life expectancy at birth (1996): male 74.9 years; female 81.2 years.
Major causes of death per 100,000 population (1994): diseases of the circulatory system 247.1; malignant neoplasms (cancers) 196.0; diseases of the respiratory system 55.4; accidents and violence 42.5 (including suicide 12.8).

Social indicators

Educational attainment (1991). Percentage of population age 25 and over having: no formal schooling 1.0%; less than complete primary education 4.0%; complete primary 11.7%; lower-level secondary 34.3%; upper-level secondary 27.7%; postsecondary 21.4%; graduates by level (1987): 4-year higher degree 101,960, master's 15,790, doctorate 2,385.

Distribution of income (1991)

percentage of national income by quintile

1	2	3	4	5 (highest)
5.3%	13.6%	19.7%	25.9%	35.5%

Quality of working life (1995). Average workweek: 38.4 hours. Annual rate per 100,000 workers for (1990): injury, accident, or industrial illness 3,320; death 5.1[5]. Average days lost to labour stoppages per 1,000 employee-workdays (1995): 0.5. Average duration of journey to work (1983): 23 minutes[6] (automobile 72.8%, public transportation 17.3%, other 9.9%). Rate per 1,000 workers of discouraged (unemployed no longer seeking work; 1983): 10.5.
Access to services (1990). Proportion of households having access to: electricity 100.0%; public water supply 99.8%; public sewage collection 99.3%.
Social participation. Eligible voters participating in last national election (June 1997): *c.* 70%. Population over 18 years of age participating in voluntary work (1987): 27.0%. Union membership in total workforce (1992): 29.7%. Practicing religious population in total affiliated population (1991): 87.6%.
Social deviance (1994). Offense rate per 100,000 population for: violent crime 1,037, of which assault 8.8[7], sexual assault 111.0[7], homicide 1.8; property crime 5,212, of which auto theft 546, burglary 1,326. Incidence per 100,000 in general population of: alcoholism 2,285; drug abuse 258.
Leisure (1992). Favourite leisure activities (hours weekly): television 15.3; social time 12.7; reading 3.5; sports and entertainment 0.9.
Material well-being (1995). Households possessing: automobile 74.5%, of which two or more 21.7%; telephone 98.5%; radio 98.9%; colour television 98.5%; refrigerator 99.7%; central air conditioner 24.6%[8]; cable television 73.4%; video recorder 82.1%; microwave oven 83.4%.

National economy

Gross national product (1995): U.S.$573,695,000,000 (U.S.$19,380 per capita).

Structure of gross domestic product and labour force

	1995		1996	
	in value Can$'000,000[9]	% of total value	labour force	% of labour force
Agriculture	15,421	2.8	453,300	3.0
Mining	23,678	4.4	279,900	1.8
Manufacturing	102,384	18.9	2,082,500	13.8
Construction	27,221	5.0	718,600	4.7
Public utilities	17,632	3.2	147,000	1.0
Transp. and commun.	48,605	9.0	872,600	5.8
Trade	65,494	12.1	2,361,200	15.6
Finance	86,772	16.0	799,900	5.3
Pub. admin., defense	32,690	6.0	820,100	5.4
Services	122,110	22.5	5,141,200	33.9
Other	—	—	1,469,200[10]	9.7[10]
TOTAL	542,007[11]	100.0[2]	15,145,400[2]	100.0

Budget (1995–96). Revenue: Can$145,453,000,000 (individual income taxes 45.1%, value-added tax 15.2%, corporate income tax 9.9%, import duties 2.6%). Expenditures: Can$177,703,000,000 (1995–96; social services 32.5%, public debt interest 26.9%, defense 8.2%, health 4.7%, education 2.9%).
National debt (1996): Can$569,691,000,000.
Tourism (1996): receipts U.S.$8,811,500,000; expenditures U.S.$11,168,000,000.

Manufacturing, mining, and construction enterprises (1993)

	no. of estab-lishments	no. of employees	weekly wages as a % of avg. of all mfg. wages	annual value added (Can$'000,000)
Manufacturing				
Food and beverages	3,202	216,000	100.7	20,110
Transport equipment	1,224	187,000	144.3	19,430
Chemicals and related products	1,396	97,000	142.0	12,860
Machinery	4,000	129,000	125.0	9,130
Electrical and electronic products	1,176	104,000	133.6	8,520
Printing, publishing, and related products	4,655	125,000	111.1	8,500
Paper and related products	651	101,000	152.1	7,890
Wood	2,201	100,000	109.3	7,880
Primary metals	417	85,000	155.2	7,790
Metal fabricating	3,287	106,000	113.6	6,290
Rubber and plastic	1,394	85,000	112.3	5,900
Textiles	1,057	60,000	88.4	3,600
Nonmetallic mineral products	1,519	44,000	125.4	3,440
Wearing apparel	1,923	85,000	67.4	3,220
Petroleum and coal products	170	16,000	189.5	2,560
Furniture and fixtures	1,965	50,000	91.5	2,310
Tobacco products industries	17	5,000	184.5	1,220
Mining[12]	1,232	113,000	...	29,650
Construction[13]	...	800,000	121.7	28,182

Production (metric tons except as noted). Agriculture, forestry, fishing (1996): wheat 23,024,000, barley 13,590,000, corn (maize) 7,000,000, rapeseed 6,089,000, potatoes 3,800,000, oats 3,475,000, soybeans 2,820,000, vegetables 2,098,883 (of which tomatoes 500,590, carrots 330,920, onions 174,051, cabbage 143,000), dry peas 1,690,000, linseed 1,115,000, sugar beets 1,030,000, apples 560,000; livestock (number of live animals) 12,767,300 cattle, 12,223,700 pigs, 622,300 sheep, 350,000 horses; roundwood (1996) 188,432,000 cu m; fish catch (1995) 1,010,582. Mining and quarrying (1996): iron ore 36,030,000; zinc 1,187,829; copper 655,891; lead 246,083; nickel 184,548; uranium 11,448; molybdenum 8,845; silver 1,228 kg; gold 164.1 kg. Manufacturing (value-added in Can$'000,000[9]; 1996): transportation equipment 16,181.7; electrical products 12,570.7; food 10,556.6; chemical products 8,159.1; paper products 7,755.9; metal products 6,467.8; wood products 5,371.4; printing and publishing 4,288.8; rubber and plastic products 3,890.4; machinery 3,797.0; wearing apparel 2,079.0; textiles 2,008.3; furniture 1,774.7. Construction (value-added in Can$'000,000[9]; 1996): residential 6,683.8; nonresidential 20,001.7.

Service enterprises (1988)

	no. of enter-prises	no. of employees[14]	weekly wages as a % of all wages	annual sales (Can$'000,000)
Retail trade				
Motor vehicle dealers	...	79,800	...	35,917
Food stores	...	213,400	...	35,187
Service stations	...	63,700	...	14,612
Department stores	...	[15]	...	13,271
Clothing stores	...	50,200	...	7,486
Pharmacies	...	52,400	...	7,459
Furniture and appliance stores	...	62,100	...	4,447
Automotive stores	...	31,500	...	3,767
General merchandise	...	231,700[15]	...	3,109
Sporting goods	...	...	...	2,669
General stores	...	[15]	...	2,415
Hardware stores	...	17,300	...	1,824
Shoe stores	...	18,400	...	1,599
Jewelry stores	...	14,000	...	1,215
Variety stores	...	45,100	...	1,057

Energy production (consumption): electricity (kW-hr; 1994) 554,186,000,000 (510,272,000,000); coal (metric tons; 1994) 72,824,000 (52,229,000); crude petroleum (barrels; 1994) 638,633,000 (507,557,000); petroleum products (metric tons; 1994) 87,161,000 (77,264,000); natural gas (cu m; 1994) 148,129,000,000 (78,223,000,000).

Population economically active (1996): total 15,145,400; activity rate of total population 50.5% (participation rates: ages 15–64, 64.8%; female 45.2%[16]; unemployed 9.7%).

Price and earnings indexes (1990 = 100)

	1990	1991	1992	1993	1994	1995	1996
Consumer price index	100.0	105.6	107.2	109.2	109.4	111.8	113.5
Hourly earnings index[17]	100.0	105.5	108.2	110.5	111.5	113.1	116.7

Household income and expenditure (1995). Average household size 2.6; average annual income per family (1994) Can$54,153 (U.S.$39,655); sources of income (1995): wages and salaries 57.0%, transfer payments 20.7%, property and entrepreneurial income 13.7%, profits 8.6%; expenditure (1992): housing 24.7%[18], food 15.5%, transp. and commun. 15.3%, household durable goods 9.1%, recreation 8.4%, clothing 5.1%, health 4.3%, education 3.0%.

Financial aggregates

	1992	1993	1994	1995	1996	1997[19]
Exchange rate, Can$ per:						
U.S. dollar	1.21	1.29	1.36	1.37	1.36	1.39
£	2.14	1.94	2.09	2.17	2.13	2.26
SDR	1.75	1.82	2.05	2.03	1.97	1.95
International reserves (U.S.$)						
Total (excl. gold; '000,000)	11,431	12,481	12,286	15,049	20,422	21,818
SDRs ('000,000)	1,039	1,062	1,148	1,177	1,168	1,146
Reserve pos. in IMF ('000,000)	1,011	948	919	1,243	1,226	1,135
Foreign exchange ('000,000)	9,382	10,471	10,219	12,629	18,028	19,536
Gold ('000,000 fine troy oz)	9.94	6.05	3.89	3.41	3.09	3.09
% world reserves	1.07	0.65	0.43	0.38	0.34	0.35
Interest and prices						
Central bank discount (%)	7.36	4.11	7.43	5.79	3.25	3.50[20]
Govt. bond yield (%)	8.77	7.85	8.63	8.28	7.50	5.99[20]
Industrial share prices (1990 = 100)	99.5	114.1	125.2	129.6	154.0	205.8[20]
Balance of payments (U.S.$'000,000)						
Balance of visible trade,	5,981	7,612	12,202	22,341	30,062	...
of which:						
Imports, f.o.b.	–126,370	–136,418	–151,290	–167,513	–175,737	...
Exports, f.o.b.	132,351	144,030	163,492	189,854	205,799	...
Balance of invisibles	–27,951	–31,481	–29,590	–31,034	–27,254	...
Balance of payments, current account	–22,060	–23,869	–17,388	–8,693	–2,808	...

Land use (1994): forested 53.6%; meadows and pastures 3.0%; agricultural and under permanent cultivation 4.9%; built-on, wasteland, and other 38.5%.

Foreign trade

Balance of trade (current prices)

	1991	1992	1993	1994	1995	1996
Can$'000,000,000	5.2	8.2	12.1	19.3	38.7	36.4
% of total	2.1%	3.2%	3.4%	4.5%	7.9%	7.1%

Imports (1996): Can$239,576,900,000 (machinery and transport equipment 53.4%, of which motor vehicles 21.4%; food, feed, beverages, and tobacco 11.8%; petroleum and energy products 4.0%; forestry products 0.8%). *Major import sources:* U.S. 67.4%; Japan 4.5%; Mexico 2.5%; U.K. 2.5%; Germany 2.1%; China 2.1%; France 1.5%; Italy 1.2%; South Korea 1.2%.

Exports (1996): Can$280,566,300,000 (machinery and transport equipment 44.8%, of which motor vehicles 22.6%; mineral fuels 9.1%, of which crude petroleum 3.5%; food 8.7%, of which wheat 2.0%; lumber 5.6%; newsprint and paper products 4.4%; wood pulp 2.2%). *Major export destinations:* U.S. 82.3%; Japan 3.7%; U.K. 1.4%; Germany 1.2%; China 1.0%; South Korea 1.0%; France 0.6%; The Netherlands 0.6%.

Trade by commodities (1995)

SITC Group	imports U.S.$'000,000	imports %	exports U.S.$'000,000	exports %
00 Food and live animals	8,228.8	5.0	11,472.2	6.0
01 Beverages and tobacco	750.6	0.5	869.7	0.4
02 Crude materials, excluding fuels	5,856.7	3.6	23,684.2	12.3
03 Mineral fuels, lubricants, and related materials	6,004.4	3.6	16,108.8	8.4
04 Animal and vegetable oils, fats, and waxes	...	...	...	...
05 Chemicals and related products, n.e.s.	12,858.5	7.8	10,900.3	5.7
06 Basic manufactures	21,761.6	13.2	32,268.3	16.8
07 Machinery and transport equipment	84,554.2	51.4	75,069.9	39.1
08 Miscellaneous manufactured articles	19,051.6	11.6	9,613.2	5.0
09 Goods not classified by kind	5,034.9	3.1	10,495.1	5.5
TOTAL	164,333.6[21]	100.0[21]	192,132.1[21]	100.0[21]

Direction of trade (1996)

	imports U.S.$'000,000	imports %	exports U.S.$'000,000	exports %
Africa	1,516	0.9	907	0.4
Asia	21,683	12.8[2]	17,081	8.5
China	3,610	2.1	2,067	1.0
Japan	7,664	4.5	7,471	3.7
Taiwan	2,099	1.2	1,020	0.5
Other	8,310	4.9	6,523	3.3
Americas	122,129	71.8	168,437	84.2[2]
United States	114,626	67.4	164,761	82.3
Mexico	4,281	2.5	855	0.4
Other Americas	3,222	1.9	2,821	1.4
Europe	20,412	12.0	12,661	6.3
EU	16,704	9.8	10,783	5.4
Other Europe	3,708	2.2	1,878	0.9
Oceania	1,189	0.7	859	0.4
TOTAL	170,038[21, 22]	100.0[21, 22]	200,146[21]	100.0[21]

Transport and communications

Transport. Railroads (1995): length 71,592 km; passenger-km 1,430,000,000; metric ton-km cargo 271,032,000,000. Roads (1995): total length 1,021,000 km (paved 35%). Vehicles (1995): passenger cars 14,280,000; trucks and buses 3,895,600. Merchant marine (1993): vessels (100 gross tons and over) 1,049; total deadweight tonnage 1,910,000. Air transport (1996): passenger-km 56,016,000,000; metric ton-km cargo 1,780,980,000; airports (1997) with scheduled flights 269.

Communications

Medium	date	unit	number	units per 1,000 persons
Daily newspapers	1995	circulation	6,330,000	215
Radio	1994	receivers	26,878,000	919
Television	1995	receivers	18,917,000	647
Telephones	1995	main lines	17,457,300	590
Cellular telephones	1995	subscribers	2,589,800	87.5
Facsimile machines	1995	units	525,000	18.1
Personal computers	1995	units	5,700,000	192

Education and health

Literacy (1986): total population age 15 and over literate 18,745,000 (96.6%); males literate (1975) 8,003,000 (95.6%); females literate (1975) 8,182,000 (95.7%).

Education (1994–95)

	schools	teachers	students	student/ teacher ratio
Primary (age 6–14)	12,700	148,724	2,413,126	17.8
Secondary (age 14–18)	3,324	133,358	2,469,552	...
Postsecondary and higher[23]	265	64,100[24]	1,209,386[25]	14.4[24]

Health: physicians (1994) 54,786 (1 per 534 persons); hospital beds (1993) 163,399 (1 per 177 persons); infant mortality rate (1995) 6.1.

Food (1995): daily per capita caloric intake 3,093 (vegetable products 71%, animal products 29%); 116% of FAO recommended minimum requirement.

Military

Total active duty personnel (1997): 61,600 (army 35.6%, navy 15.3%, air force 23.7%, not identified by service 25.4%). *Military expenditure as percentage of GNP* (1995): 1.7% (world 2.8%); per capita expenditure U.S.$318.

[1]On May 25, 1993, the Prime Minister and Inuit representatives signed an agreement (following a number of territory-wide referendums), officially establishing Nunavut as a territory in 1999. It would comprise 2,201,400 sq km (844,960 sq mi) of the eastern part of Northwest Territories, with a population of 22,000 (17,500 Inuit). [2]Detail does not add to total given because of rounding. [3]Based on land area of 3,558,096 sq mi (9,215,430 sq km). [4]Includes 4.0% who are of both French and British origin. [5]1992. [6]Urban areas. [7]1991. [8]1989. [9]At prices of 1986. [10]Unemployed. [11]GDP at current values in 1995 is Can$776,299,000,000. [12]1990. [13]1988. [14]1984. [15]Department and General stores included with General merchandise. [16]1995. [17]Manufacturing only. [18]Includes energy and utilities. [19]October. [20]September. [21]Detail does not add to total because of discrepancies in estimates. [22]Total for imports includes U.S.$3,220,000,000 (1.9% of total imports; mostly special transactions) not distributable by region. [23]1996–97. [24]1993–94. [25]Includes 248,231 part-time university students.

Internet resources for further information:

- **Statistics Canada http://www.statcan.ca**

Cape Verde

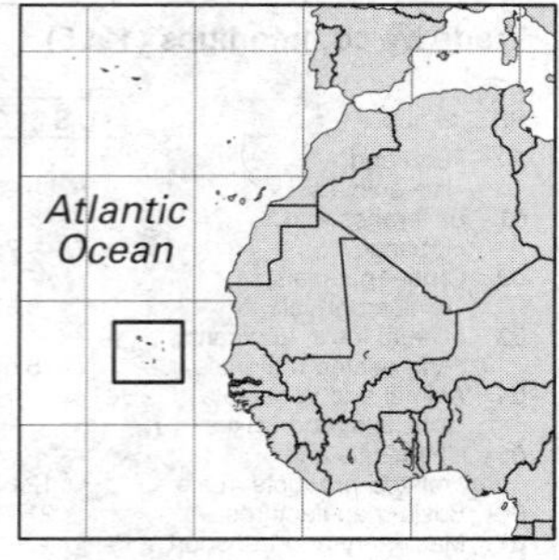

Official name: República de Cabo Verde (Republic of Cape Verde).
Form of government: multiparty[1] republic with one legislative house (National People's Assembly [72]).
Chief of state: President.
Head of government: Prime Minister.
Capital: Praia.
Official language: Portuguese.
Official religion: none.
Monetary unit: 1 escudo (C.V.Esc.) = 100 centavos; valuation (Oct. 3, 1997) 1 U.S.$ = C.V.Esc. 94.75; 1 £ = C.V.Esc. 152.74.

Area and population

Island Groups / Islands/Counties[2] / Counties	Capitals	area sq mi	area sq km	population 1990 census
Leeward Islands		696[3]	1,803	221,537
Brava	Nova Sintra	26	67	6,975
Fogo				
Mosteiros[4]	...	184	476	33,902
São Filipe	São Filipe			
Maio	Porto Inglês	104	269	4,969
Santiago		383	991	175,691
Praia	Praia	153	396	82,802
Santa Catarina	Assomada	94	243	41,584
Santa Cruz	Pedra Badejo	58	149	25,892
São Domingos[4]		...	...	...
Tarrafal	Tarrafal	78	203	25,413
Windward Islands		861[3]	2,230	119,954
Boa Vista	Sal Rei	239	620	3,452
Sal	Santa Maria	83	216	7,715
Santo Antão		300	779	43,845
Paúl	Pombas	21	54	8,121
Porto Novo	Porto Novo	215	558	14,873
Ribeira Grande	Ponta do Sol	64	167	20,851
São Nicolau	Ribeira Brava	150	388	13,665
São Vicente[5]	Mindelo	88	227	51,277
TOTAL		1,557	4,033	341,491

Demography

Population (1997): 394,000.
Density (1997): persons per sq mi 253.1, persons per sq km 97.8.
Urban-rural (1990): urban 29.7%; rural 70.3%.
Sex distribution (1990): male 47.29%; female 52.71%.
Age breakdown (1990): under 15, 45.1%; 15–29, 27.2%; 30–44, 11.4%; 45–59, 7.9%; 60 and over, 8.4%.
Population projection: (2000) 411,000; (2010) 464,000.
Doubling time: 25 years.
Ethnic composition (1986): mixed 71.0%; black 28.0%; white 1.0%.
Religious affiliation (1995): Roman Catholic 95.9%; Protestant and other 4.1%.
Major cities (1990): Praia 61,644; Mindelo 47,109; São Filipe 5,616.

Vital statistics

Birth rate per 1,000 population (1997): 35.5 (world avg. 25.0); (1989) legitimate 28.9%; illegitimate 71.1%.
Death rate per 1,000 population (1997): 7.8 (world avg. 9.3).
Natural increase rate per 1,000 population (1997): 27.7 (world avg. 15.7).
Total fertility rate (avg. births per childbearing woman; 1997): 5.2.
Marriage rate per 1,000 population (1990): 4.5.
Divorce rate per 1,000 population: n.a.
Life expectancy at birth (1997): male 66.8 years; female 73.4 years.
Major causes of death per 100,000 population (1987): enteritis and other diarrheal diseases 97.4; heart disease 77.9; malignant neoplasms (cancers) 47.9; pneumonia 46.4; accidents, poisoning, and violence 44.0.

National economy

Budget (1995). Revenue: C.V.Esc. 8,404,000,000 (import duties 44.7%; income taxes 25.4%; property income taxes 5.8%; transfers 5.1%; municipal taxes 1.2%). Expenditures: C.V.Esc. 19,128,000,000 (capital expenditure 51.5%; current expenditure 48.5%, of which wages and salaries 20.6%, transfers 8.7%, public debt 6.3%, goods and services 1.5%).
Public debt (external, outstanding; 1995): U.S.$191,400,000.
Tourism (1995): receipts from visitors U.S.$10,000,000; expenditures by nationals abroad U.S.$12,000,000.
Land use (1994): forest 0.2%; pasture 6.2%; agriculture 11.2%; other 82.4%.
Production (metric tons except as noted). Agriculture, forestry, fishing (1996): sugarcane 12,500, bananas 6,000, coconuts 5,000, vegetables (including melons) 4,200, fruits (except melons) 4,000, cassava 3,000, potatoes 2,090, sweet potatoes 1,150; livestock (number of live animals) 460,000 pigs, 109,000 goats, 21,000 cattle; roundwood, n.a.; fish catch (1995) 7,081. Mining and quarrying (1992): salt 4,000. Manufacturing (1994): bread 3,926[6]; paint 492; canned tuna 273; cigarettes 94; beer 4,162,033 litres; soft drinks 932,154 litres; other items also manufactured are rum and flour. Construction (1982): residential C.V.Esc. 365,800,000; nonresidential C.V.Esc. 1,700,000. Energy production (consumption): electricity (kW-hr; 1994) 59,527,000 (46,570,000); coal, none (none); crude petroleum, none (none); petroleum products (metric tons; 1995) none (70,329); natural gas, none (none).
Gross national product (1995): U.S.$366,000,000 (U.S.$960 per capita).

Structure of gross domestic product and labour force

	1993 in value C.V.Esc. '000,000	1993 % of total value	1990 labour force	1990 % of labour force
Agriculture	4,878	20.7	29,876	24.7
Manufacturing	1,515	6.4	5,520	4.6
Public utilities	698	3.0	883	0.7
Mining	67	0.2	410	0.3
Construction	4,814	20.4	22,722	18.9
Transp. and commun.	2,898	12.3	6,138	5.1
Trade	5,634	23.9	12,747	10.6
Finance	939	4.0	821	0.7
Pub. admin., defense	1,936	8.2	17,358	14.4
Services	221	0.9		
Other	...	...	24,090	20.0
TOTAL	23,600[3]	100.0[3]	120,565	100.0

Population economically active (1990): total 120,565; activity rate of total population 35.3% (participation rates: ages 15–64, 64.3%; female 38.0%; unemployed, 25.8%).

Price and earnings indexes (1990 = 100)

	1990	1991	1992	1993	1994	1995
Consumer price index	100.0	110.0	113.0	120.0	128.0	138.0
Monthly earnings index	100.0	117.0	140.0	121.0	124.0	141.0

Household income and expenditure. Average household size (1990) 5.1; income per household: n.a.; sources of income: n.a.; expenditure (1988): food 51.1%, housing, fuel, and power 13.5%, beverages and tobacco 11.8%, transportation and communications 8.8%, household durable goods 6.9%, other 7.9%.

Foreign trade[7]

Balance of trade (current prices)

	1989	1990	1991	1992	1993	1994
C.V.Esc. '000,000	−8,179	−9,097	−10,031	−11,907	−12,075	−13,678
% of total	88.6%	92.0%	92.0%	94.8%	95.1%	95.1%

Imports (1994): C.V.Esc. 14,012,000,000 (1993; food 34.6%, transport equipment 13.3%, machinery and apparatus 11.4%, nonmetallic mineral products 10.3%, metal products 7.3%). *Major import sources* (1993): Portugal 33.6%; The Netherlands 8.5%; Germany 4.9%; France 4.4%; U.S. 3.5%.
Exports (1994): C.V.Esc. 333,300,000 (1993; fish and fish preparations 62.6%, bananas 11.7%). *Major export destinations* (1993): Portugal 48.8%; Angola 16.0%; The Netherlands 3.4%.

Transport and communications

Transport. Railroads: none. Roads (1995): total length 680 mi, 1,095 km (paved 78%). Vehicles (1993): passenger cars 6,479; trucks and buses 2,099. Merchant marine (1992): vessels (100 gross tons and over) 42; total deadweight tonnage 30,921. Air transport (1994)[8]: passenger-mi 106,000,000, passenger-km 171,000,000; short ton-mi cargo 13,156,000, metric ton-km cargo 19,207,000; airports (1997) with scheduled flights 9.

Communications

Medium	date	unit	number	units per 1,000 persons
Radio	1995	receivers	57,000	146
Television	1995	receivers	1,000	2.6
Telephones	1995	main lines	21,500	55
Facsimile machines	1995	units	1,000	2.6

Education and health

Educational attainment (1990). Percentage of population age 25 and over having: no formal schooling 47.9%; primary 40.9%; incomplete secondary 3.9%; complete secondary 1.4%; higher 1.5%; unknown 4.4%. *Literacy* (1995): total population age 15 and over literate 71.6%; males literate 81.4%; females literate 63.8%.

Education (1993–94)

	schools	teachers	students	student/ teacher ratio
Primary (age 7–12)	370[6]	2,657	78,173	29.4
Secondary (age 13–17)	16[9]	438	11,808	27.0
Voc., teacher tr.	3[9]	94[10]	2,289	...
Higher	...	...	...	...

Health (1987): physicians 77 (1 per 4,208 persons); hospital beds 625 (1 per 550 persons); infant mortality rate per 1,000 live births (1995) 55.9.
Food (1994): daily per capita caloric intake 3,031 (vegetable products 83%, animal products 17%); 129% of FAO recommended minimum requirement.

Military

Total active duty personnel (1997): 1,100 (army 90.9%, air force 9.1%). *Military expenditure as percentage of GNP* (1995): 1.0% (world 3.0%); per capita expenditure U.S.$10.

[1]Constitution revised Sept. 28, 1990, to adopt a multiparty system; first multiparty elections took place on Jan. 13, 1991. [2]Island/county areas are coterminous except Fogo, Santiago, and Santo Antão islands. [3]Detail does not add to total given because of rounding. [4]Created after the 1990 census; adjusted areas and populations not available. [5]Includes Santa Luzia Island, which is uninhabited. [6]1991. [7]Imports are c.i.f. [8]TACV airline only. [9]1986–87. [10]Vocational teachers only.

Internet resources for further information:
- **Embassy of Cape Verde (Washington, D.C.) http://www.capeverdeusembassy.org/**

Central African Republic

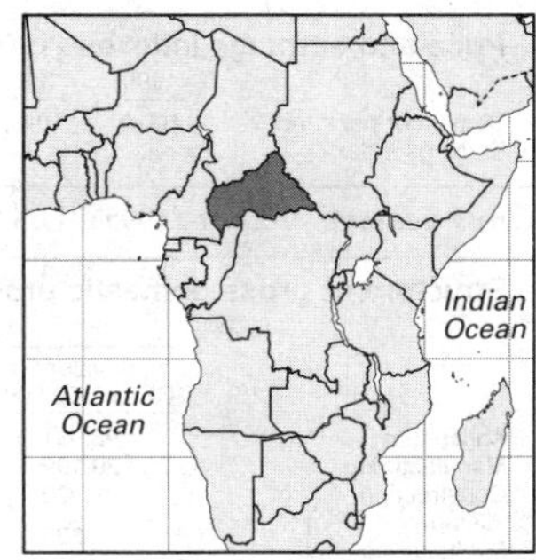

Official name: République Centrafricaine (Central African Republic).
Form of government: multiparty republic with one legislative body (National Assembly [85])[1].
Chief of state: President.
Head of government: Prime Minister.
Capital: Bangui.
Official languages: French; Sango.
Official religion: none.
Monetary unit: 1 CFA franc (CFAF) = 100 centimes; valuation (Oct. 3, 1997) 1 U.S.$ = CFAF 592.29; 1 £ = CFAF 954.76.

Area and population

		area		population
				1988
Prefectures	**Capitals**	sq mi	sq km	census
Bamingui-Bangoran	Ndélé	22,471	58,200	28,643
Basse-Kotto	Mobaye	6,797	17,604	194,750
Haut-Mbomou	Obo	21,440	55,530	27,113
Haute-Kotto	Bria	33,456	86,650	58,838
Kemo	Sibut	6,642	17,204	82,884
Lobaye	Mbaïki	7,427	19,235	169,554
Mambéré-Kadéï	Berbérati	11,661	30,203	230,364
Mbomou	Bangassou	23,610	61,150	119,252
Nana-Gribizi	Kaga-Bandoro	7,721	19,996	95,497
Nana-Mambéré	Bouar	10,270	26,600	191,970
Ombella-M'poko	Boali	12,292	31,835	180,857
Ouaka	Bambari	19,266	49,900	208,332
Ouham	Bossangoa	19,402	50,250	262,950
Ouham-Pendé	Bozoum	12,394	32,100	287,653
Sangha-Mbaéré	Nola	7,495	19,412	65,961
Vakaga	Birao	17,954	46,500	32,118
Autonomous commune				
Bangui	Bangui	26	67	451,690
TOTAL		240,324	622,436	2,688,426

Demography

Population (1997): 3,342,000.
Density (1997): persons per sq mi 13.9, persons per sq km 5.4.
Urban-rural (1996): urban 39.0%; rural 61.0%.
Sex distribution (1997): male 49.30%; female 50.70%.
Age breakdown (1997): under 15, 44.1%; 15–29, 27.3%; 30–44, 15.1%; 45–59, 8.2%; 60–74, 4.2%; 75 and over, 1.1%.
Population projection: (2000) 3,539,000; (2010) 4,177,000.
Doubling time: 30 years.
Ethnolinguistic composition (1988): Baya (Gbaya) 23.7%; Banda 23.4%; Mandjia 14.7%; Ngbaka 7.6%; Sara 6.5%; Mbum 6.3%; Kare 2.4%; French 0.1%; other 15.3%.
Religious affiliation (1995): Protestant 25.0%; Roman Catholic 25.0%; traditional 24.0%; Muslim 15.0%; other (Christian majority) 11.0%.
Major cities (1994): Bangui 524,000; Berbérati 47,000; Bouar 43,000; Bambari 41,000; Carnot 41,000; Bossangoa 33,000.

Vital statistics

Birth rate per 1,000 population (1997): 39.0 (world avg. 25.0); legitimate, n.a.; illegitimate, n.a.
Death rate per 1,000 population (1997): 17.0 (world avg. 9.3).
Natural increase rate per 1,000 population (1997): 22.0 (world avg. 15.7).
Total fertility rate (avg. births per childbearing woman; 1997): 5.2.
Marriage rate per 1,000 population: n.a.
Divorce rate per 1,000 population: n.a.
Life expectancy at birth (1996): male 47.0 years; female 52.0 years.
Mortality: n.a.; however, principal causes of death in the mid-1990s included respiratory infections (especially tuberculosis and pneumonia), diseases of the digestive system, meningitis, diarrheal diseases, malnutrition, cardiovascular diseases, malaria, viral hepatitis, and AIDS.

National economy

Budget (1996). Revenue: CFAF 45,800,000,000 (taxes 96.1%, nontax receipts 3.9%). Expenditures: CFAF 114,400,000,000 (capital expenditure 50.5%, current expenditure 49.5%).
Public debt (external, outstanding; 1995): U.S.$852,000,000.
Production (metric tons except as noted). Agriculture, forestry, fishing (1997): cassava 578,700, yams 320,000, bananas 100,000, peanuts (groundnuts) 97,800, plantains 78,000, corn (maize) 65,000, seed cotton 50,000, sesame seeds 32,000, pulses 26,000, sorghum 25,000, oranges 20,000, coffee 18,000, cottonseed 10,000[2], paddy rice 9,000, cotton lint 7,000[2]; livestock (number of live animals) 2,926,000 cattle, 1,350,000 goats, 596,000 pigs, 3,600,000 chickens; roundwood (1995) 3,864,000 cu m; fish catch (1995) 13,300. Mining and quarrying (1996): gold 98 kg[3], diamonds 487,300 carats[4]. Manufacturing (value added in U.S.$'000; 1994): food, beverages, and tobacco 19,000; chemical products 3,000; wood products 2,000; textiles, wearing apparel, and leather products 1,000; transport equipment 1,000. Construction (1992)[5]: residential 10,052 sq m; nonresidential 82,411 sq m. Energy production (consumption): electricity (kW-hr; 1994) 101,000,000 (101,000,000); coal, none (none); crude petroleum, none (none); petroleum products (metric tons; 1994) none (79,000); natural gas, none (none).
Gross national product (1995): U.S.$1,123,000,000 (U.S.$340 per capita).

Structure of gross domestic product and labour force

	1995		1988	
	in value CFAF '000,000[6]	% of total value	labour force	% of labour force
Agriculture	282,800	53.4	1,113,900	80.4
Mining	32,700	6.2	15,400	1.1
Manufacturing	46,600	8.8	22,400	1.6
Construction	25,000	4.7	7,000	0.5
Public utilities	4,300	0.8	1,500	0.1
Transp. and commun.	15,600	2.9	1,500	0.1
Trade	56,600	10.7	118,000	8.5
Other services	25,200	4.8	15,600	1.1
Pub. admin., defense	41,000	7.7	91,700	6.6
TOTAL	529,800	100.0	1,387,000	100.0

Land use (1994): forest 75.0%; meadows 4.8%; agriculture 3.2%; other 17.0%.
Tourism (1993): receipts U.S.$3,000,000; expenditures U.S.$43,000,000[2].
Population economically active (1988): total 1,186,972; activity rate of total population 48.2% (participation rates: ages 15–64, 78.3%; female 46.8%; unemployed 7.5%).

Price and earnings indexes (1990 = 100)

	1990	1991	1992	1993	1994	1995	1996
Consumer price index[5]	100.0	97.8	96.5	93.6	116.6	139.0	143.7
Earnings index	...	...	...	...	...	...	...

Household income and expenditure. Average household size (1988) 4.7; average annual income per household CFAF 91,985 (U.S.$435); sources of income: n.a.; expenditure (1991)[7]: food 70.5%, clothing 8.5%, other manufactured products 7.6%, energy 7.3%, services (including transportation and communications, recreation, and health) 6.1%.

Foreign trade

Balance of trade (current prices)

	1990	1991	1992	1993	1994	1995
CFAF '000,000,000	−9.3	−13.0	−10.1	−4.5	+4.3	−0.7
% of total	12.4%	32.9%	15.2%	6.7%	2.7%	0.4%

Imports (1995): CFAF 94,203,000,000 (1992; food products 22.2%, transportation equipment 16.6%, chemical products 13.7%, energy products 11.0%). *Major import sources:* France 37.0%; Japan 24.3%; Cameroon 6.3%; Germany 3.7%; Belgium-Luxembourg 3.2%; United States 2.6%.
Exports (1995): CFAF 93,524,000,000 (diamonds 49.7%, coffee 15.7%, wood products 15.0%, cotton 12.1%). *Major export destinations:* Belgium-Luxembourg 40.1%; France 16.0%; Democratic Republic of the Congo 2.1%; Republic of the Congo 1.1%; United Kingdom 1.1%.

Transport and communications

Transport. Railroads: none. Roads (1996): total length 14,900 mi, 24,000 km (paved 2%). Vehicles (1995): passenger cars 9,500; trucks and buses 7,000. Merchant marine: vessels (100 gross tons and over) none. Air transport (1996)[8]: passenger-mi 139,644,000, passenger-km 224,736,000; short ton-mi cargo 11,247,000, metric ton-km cargo 16,420,000; airports[9] (1997) 1.

Communications

Medium	date	unit	number	units per 1,000 persons
Daily newspapers	1995	circulation	2,000	1.0
Radio	1995	receivers	245,000	75.0
Television	1995	receivers	16,000	5.0
Telephones	1995	main lines	7,800	2.4
Cellular telephones	1995	subscribers	100	0.03
Facsimile machines	1995	units	200	0.06

Education and health

Educational attainment (1988). Percentage of population age 10 and over having: no formal schooling 59.3%; primary education 29.6%; lower secondary 7.5%; upper secondary 2.3%; higher 1.3%. *Literacy* (1995): total population age 15 and over literate 60.0%; males literate 68.5%; females literate 52.4%.

Education (1991–92)

	schools	teachers	students	student/ teacher ratio
Primary (age 6–11)	930[10]	4,004[10]	277,961	...
Secondary (age 12–18)	46[10]	845[10]	42,263	...
Vocational	[11]	[11]	1,477	...
Higher[12]	1	139	2,923	21.0

Health (1992): physicians 157 (1 per 18,660 persons); hospital beds (1991) 4,258 (1 per 672 persons); infant mortality rate (1997) 108.0.
Food (1995): daily per capita caloric intake 1,885 (vegetable products 91%, animal products 9%); 83% of FAO recommended minimum requirement.

Military

Total active duty personnel (1997): 2,650[13] (army 94.3%; navy, none; air force 5.7%). *Military expenditure as percentage of GNP* (1994): 3.2% (world 3.0%); per capita expenditure U.S.$10.

[1]New constitution promulgated on Jan. 14, 1995. [2]1994. [3]1995. [4]An unknown but substantial amount is believed to be smuggled out of the country annually. [5]Bangui only. [6]At factor cost. [7]Weights of consumer price index components. [8]Represents 1/11 of the traffic of Air Afrique, which is operated by 11 West African states. [9]International air service only. [10]1990–91. [11]Included with secondary. [12]University of Bangui only. [13]Excludes 2,300 gendarmerie, who are part of the armed forces.

Internet resources for further information:
- **Central African Republic http://www.africa.co.uk/country/cenafrep.htm**

Chad

Official name: Jumhūrīyah Tshad (Arabic); République du Tchad (French) (Republic of Chad).
Form of government: unitary republic with one legislative body (National Assembly [125]).
Chief of state: President.
Head of government: Prime Minister.
Capital: N'Djamena.
Official languages: Arabic; French.
Official religion: none.
Monetary unit: 1 CFA franc (CFAF) = 100 centimes; valuation (Oct. 3, 1997) 1 U.S.$ = CFAF 592.29; 1 £ = CFAF 954.76.

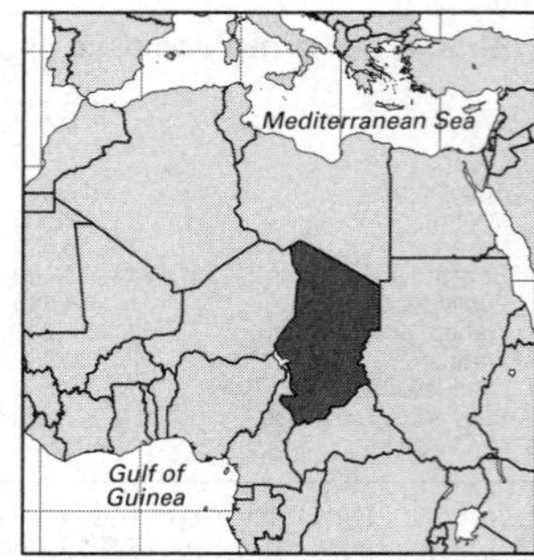

Area and population

Préfectures	Capitals	area sq mi	area sq km	population 1993 census
Batha	Ati	34,285	88,800	288,458
Biltine	Biltine	18,090	46,850	184,807
Borkou-Ennedi-Tibesti	Faya Largeau	231,795	600,350	73,185
Chari-Baguirmi	N'Djamena	32,010	82,910	1,251,906
Guéra	Mongo	22,760	58,950	306,253
Kanem	Mao	44,215	114,520	279,927
Lac	Bol	8,620	22,320	252,932
Logone Occidental	Moundou	3,357	8,695	455,489
Logone Oriental	Doba	10,825	28,035	441,064
Mayo-Kebbi	Bongor	11,625	30,105	825,158
Moyen-Chari	Sarh	17,445	45,180	738,595
Ouaddaï	Abéché	29,436	76,240	543,900
Salamat	Am Timan	24,325	63,000	184,403
Tandjilé	Laï	6,965	18,045	453,854
TOTAL		495,755[1]	1,284,000	6,279,931

Demography

Population (1997): 7,166,000.
Density (1997): persons per sq mi 14.5, persons per sq km 5.6.
Urban-rural (1995): urban 21.4%; rural 78.6%.
Sex distribution (1993): male 48.46%; female 51.54%.
Age breakdown (1993): under 15, 47.9%; 15–29, 24.5%; 30–44, 14.6%; 45–59, 7.1%; 60–74, 4.2%; 75 and over, 1.3%.
Population projection: (2000) 7,760,000; (2010) 10,055,000.
Doubling time: 27 years.
Ethnolinguistic composition (1993): Sara 27.7%; Sudanic Arab 12.3%; Mayo-Kebbi peoples 11.5%; Kanem-Bornu peoples 9.0%; Ouaddaï peoples 8.7%; Hadjeray (Hadjaraï) 6.7%; Tangale (Tandjilé) peoples 6.5%; Gorane peoples 6.3%; Fitri-Batha peoples 4.7%; Fulani (Peul) 2.4%; other 4.2%.
Religious affiliation (1993): Muslim 53.9%; Christian 34.7%, of which Roman Catholic 20.3%, Protestant 14.4%; traditional beliefs 7.4%; other 4.0%.
Major cities (1993): N'Djamena 530,965; Moundou 282,103; Bongor 196,713; Sarh 193,753; Abéché 187,936; Doba 185,461.

Vital statistics

Birth rate per 1,000 population (1995): 44.6 (world avg. 25.0).
Death rate per 1,000 population (1995): 17.7 (world avg. 9.3).
Natural increase rate per 1,000 population (1995): 26.9 (world avg. 15.7).
Total fertility rate (avg. births per childbearing woman; 1995): 5.9.
Life expectancy at birth (1995): male 44.9 years; female 49.6 years.

National economy

Budget (1996). Revenue: CFAF 110,170,000,000 (taxes 89.1%, of which taxes on income and profits 36.1%, taxes on international trade 31.2%, taxes on goods and services 18.6%; nontax revenue 10.9%). Expenditures: CFAF 151,794,000,000 (current expenditure 50.9%, of which government salaries 20.3%, government matériel 11.2%, defense 8.4%, debt service 5.5%, transfer payments 2.5%; capital expenditure 49.1%).
Tourism: receipts from visitors (1994) U.S.$36,000,000; expenditures by nationals abroad U.S.$26,000,000.
Production (metric tons except as noted). Agriculture, forestry, fishing (1996): sorghum 444,146[2], sugarcane 330,000[2], millet 257,631[2], yams 240,000, seed cotton 213,000[2], cassava 195,000, rice 97,728[2], corn (maize) 74,631[2], peanuts (groundnuts) 64,400, sweet potatoes 58,000, pulses 34,000, mangoes 32,000, dates 18,000, onions 14,000, sesame seeds 13,088, potatoes 8,000; livestock (number of live animals) 4,959,000 cattle, 3,271,000 goats, 2,219,000 sheep, 656,946 camels, 4,400,000 chickens; roundwood (1995) 4,512,000 cu m; fish catch (1995) 60,000. Mining and quarrying (1996): aggregate (gravel) 170,000; limited commercial production of natron (10,000) and salt; artisanal gold production. Manufacturing (1996): cotton fibre 61,700; refined sugar 27,455; soap 2,958; woven cotton fabrics 881,000 metres; edible oil 125,491 hectolitres; beer 117,100 hectolitres; cigarettes 35,000,000 packs; bicycles 3,444 units. Construction: n.a. Energy production (consumption): electricity (kW-hr; 1996) 92,066,000 (68,638,000); petroleum products (metric tons; 1994) none (31,000).
Household income and expenditure (1993). Average household size 5.0; average annual income per household CFAF 96,806 (U.S.$458); sources of income (1995–96; urban) "informal"[3]-sector employment and entrepreneurship 36.7%, transfers 24.8%, wages 23.6%, ownership of real estate 8.6%; expenditure (1983)[4]: food 45.3%, health 11.9%, energy 5.8%, clothing 3.3%.
Population economically active (1993): total 2,719,497; activity rate of total population 43.9% (participation rates: over age 15, 72.0%; female 47.9%; unemployed 0.6%).

Price and earnings indexes (1990 = 100)

	1990	1991	1992	1993	1994	1995	1996
Consumer price index	100.0	104.2	100.9	93.8	131.7	143.6	161.4
Earnings index	...	...	...	...	...	...	...

Gross national product (1995): U.S.$1,144,000,000 (U.S.$180 per capita).

Structure of gross domestic product and labour force

	1996 in value CFAF '000,000	1996 % of total value	1993 labour force	1993 % of labour force
Agriculture	98,931	43.2	1,903,492	83.0
Manufacturing	29,109	12.7	33,670	1.5
Construction	1,909	0.8	10,885	0.5
Mining }	1,833	0.8	756	—
Public utilities }			2,026	0.1
Transp. and commun. }	63,176	27.6	13,252	0.6
Trade and finance }			179,169	7.8
Pub. admin., defense }	22,257	9.7	61,875	2.7
Services }			79,167	3.4
Other	11,843	5.2	9,311	0.4
TOTAL	229,058	100.0	2,293,603	100.0

Public debt (external, outstanding; 1995): U.S.$839,600,000.
Land use (1994): forested 25.7%; meadows and pastures 35.7%; agricultural and under permanent cultivation 2.6%; other 36.0%.

Foreign trade

Balance of trade (current prices)

	1992	1993	1994	1995	1996
CFAF '000,000,000	−16.6	−15.1	−42.6	−13.9	−21.2
% of total	14.8%	14.9%	22.1%	5.3%	7.4%

Imports (1996): CFAF 153,900,000,000 (1983; petroleum products 16.8%; cereal products 16.8%; pharmaceutical products and chemicals 11.5%; machinery and transport equipment 8.5%, of which transport equipment 7.3%; electrical equipment 5.7%; textiles 2.9%; raw and refined sugar 2.3%). *Major import sources* (1996[5]): France 34.7%; Cameroon 24.1%; Belgium-Luxembourg 7.4%; Nigeria 6.5%; Portugal 5.6%.
Exports (1996[5]): CFAF 132,700,000,000 (1995; cotton lint 59.4%; live cattle 10.9%; live sheep and goats 4.9%). *Major export destinations* (1996): Portugal 34.7%; Germany 11.3%; Costa Rica 6.5%; United States 5.6%; France 5.6%.

Transport and communications

Transport. Railroads: none. Roads (1995): total length 32,700 km (paved 1%). Vehicles (1995): passenger cars 9,630; trucks and buses 14,360. Air transport (1996)[6]: passenger-km 224,736,000; metric ton-km cargo 16,420,000; airports (1997) with scheduled flights 1.

Communications

Medium	date	unit	number	units per 1,000 persons
Daily newspapers	1995	circulation	1,500	0.2
Radio	1995	receivers	1,310,000	205.9
Television	1995	receivers	50,000	7.9
Telephones	1995	main lines	5,300	0.8
Facsimile machines	1995	units	200	0.03

Education and health

Educational attainment (1993). Percentage of economically active population age 15 and over having: no formal schooling 81.1%; Qur'ānic education 4.2%; primary education 11.2%; secondary education 2.7%; higher education 0.3%; professional education 0.5%. *Literacy* (1995): percentage of total population age 15 and over literate 48.1%; males literate 62.1%; females literate 34.7%.

Education (1994–95)

	schools	teachers	students	student/ teacher ratio
Primary (age 6–12)	2,447	9,404[7]	591,784[7]	62.9[7]
Secondary (age 13–19)	66[8]	2,046	82,559	40.4
Voc., teacher tr.	25[9]	157	3,277	20.9
Higher[10]	4	311	3,049	9.8

Health (1993): physicians 217 (1 per 27,765 persons); hospital beds 3,962 (1 per 1,521 persons); infant mortality rate per 1,000 live births (1995) 122.
Food (1995): daily per capita caloric intake 1,913 (vegetable products 94%, animal products 6%); 80% of FAO recommended minimum requirement.

Military

Total active duty personnel (1997): 30,350 (army 82.4%, navy, none, air force 1.2%, paramilitary 16.4%). *Military expenditure as percentage of GNP* (1995): 3.1% (world 2.8%); per capita expenditure U.S.$5.

[1]Detail does not add to total given because of rounding. [2]1996–97. [3]Not reported to fiscal authorities. [4]Capital city only. [5]Based on direction of trade data (analysis of reports of trading partners, rather than country's own customs data). [6]One-eleventh portion of total traffic of Air Afrique, which is operated by 11 West African states. [7]1995–96. [8]1988–89. [9]1987. [10]Universities and equivalent institutions only.

Internet resources for further information:

- **CIA World Factbook—Chad**
  http://www.odci.gov/cia/publications/nsolo/factbook/cd.htm
- **Chad—A Country Study**
  http://lcweb2.loc.gov/frd/cs/tdtoc.html

Chile

Official name: República de Chile (Republic of Chile).
Form of government: multiparty republic with two legislative houses (Senate [47[1]]; Chamber of Deputies [120]).
Head of state and government: President.
Capital: Santiago[2].
Official language: Spanish.
Official religion: none.
Monetary unit: 1 peso (Ch$) = 100 centavos; valuation (Oct. 3, 1997) 1 U.S.$ = Ch$414.35; 1 £ = Ch$667.93.

Area and population[3]

Regions	Capitals	area sq mi	area sq km	population 1995 estimate
Aisén del General Carlos Ibáñez del Campo	Coihaique	42,095	109,025	88,782
Antofagasta	Antofagasta	48,820	126,444	415,487
Araucanía	Temuco	12,300	31,858	853,187
Atacama	Copiapó	29,179	75,573	202,810
Bío-Bío	Concepción	14,258	36,929	1,753,662
Coquimbo	La Serena	15,697	40,656	525,432
Libertador General Bernardo O'Higgins	Rancagua	6,319	16,365	684,179
Los Lagos	Puerto Montt	25,868	66,997	957,212
Magallanes y la Antártica Chilena	Punta Arenas	50,979	132,034	181,551
Maule	Talca	11,700	30,302	902,646
Santiago, Región Metropolitana de	Santiago	5,926	15,349	5,783,703
Tarapacá	Iquique	22,663	58,698	410,343
Valparaíso	Valparaíso	6,331	16,396	1,478,281
TOTAL		292,135[4]	756,626[4]	14,237,275[5]

Demography

Population (1997): 14,583,000.
Density (1997): persons per sq mi 49.9, persons per sq km 19.3.
Urban-rural (1995): urban 85.8%; rural 14.2%.
Sex distribution (1995): male 49.40%; female 50.60%.
Age breakdown (1994): under 15, 30.5%; 15–29, 25.5%; 30–44, 22.1%; 45–59, 12.7%; 60–74, 6.9%; 75 and over, 2.3%.
Population projection: (2000) 15,086,000; (2010) 16,480,000.
Doubling time: 50 years.
Ethnic composition (1992): European and mestizo 89.7%; Araucanian (Mapuche) 9.6%; Aymara 0.5%; Rapa Nui Polynesian 0.2%.
Religious affiliation (1992): Roman Catholic 76.7%; Protestant 13.2%; atheist and nonreligious 5.8%; other 4.3%.
Major cities (1995): Greater Santiago 5,076,808; Concepción 350,268; Viña del Mar 322,220; Valparaíso 282,168; Talcahuano 260,915; Temuco 239,340.

Vital statistics

Birth rate per 1,000 population (1995): 19.7 (world avg. 25.0).
Death rate per 1,000 population (1995): 5.5 (world avg. 9.3).
Natural increase rate per 1,000 population (1994): 14.2 (world avg. 15.7).
Total fertility rate (avg. births per childbearing woman; 1994): 2.3.
Life expectancy at birth (1995): male 71.8 years; female 77.8 years.
Major causes of death per 100,000 population (1993): diseases of the circulatory system 157.4; malignant neoplasms (cancers) 111.5; accidents and adverse effects 66.1; diseases of the respiratory system 64.9.

National economy

Budget (1994). Revenue: Ch$4,843,100,000,000 (income from taxes 84.3%, nontax revenue 15.7%). Expenditures: Ch$4,481,980,000,000 (social security and welfare 33.3%, economic affairs and services 15.4%, education 13.9%.
Public debt (external, outstanding; 1995): U.S.$7,178,000.
Population economically active (1995): total 5,274,200; activity rate of total population 37.8% (participation rates: ages 15–64, 58.6%; female 32.4%; unemployed 4.7%).

Price and earnings indexes (1990 = 100)

	1990	1991	1992	1993	1994	1995	1996
Consumer price index	100.0	122.0	141.0	158.0	177.0	191.0	205.0
Monthly earnings index	100.0	121.2	146.2	...	...	...	...

Production (metric tons except as noted). Agriculture, forestry, fishing (1996): sugar beets 2,804,000, grapes 1,527,000, tomatoes 1,370,000, wheat 1,227,000, corn (maize) 932,000, apples 910,000, potatoes 828,000, onions (dry) 390,000, oats 200,000, rice 154,000, barley 64,000; livestock (number of live animals) 4,516,000 sheep, 3,858,000 cattle, 1,486,000 pigs; roundwood (1995) 31,365,000 cu m; fish catch (1995) 7,590,900. Mining (1995): iron 8,174,000; copper 2,488,000; zinc 30,000; molybdenum 17,889; silver 1,032,000 kg; gold 39,180 kg. Manufacturing (value added in U.S.$'000; 1994): food products 2,725,000; metal and metal products 2,123,000; petroleum and petroleum products 1,042,000; paper and paper products 782,000; beverages 671,000; nonmetallic mineral products 535,000. Construction (1994)[6]: residential 7,049,369 sq m; nonresidential 2,875,935 sq m. Energy production (consumption): electricity (kW-hr; 1994) 25,250,000,000 (25,250,000,000); coal (metric tons; 1994) 1,182,000 (3,145,000); crude petroleum (barrels; 1994) 4,459,000 (54,141,000); petroleum products (metric tons; 1994) 7,136,000 (8,399,000); natural gas (cu m; 1994) 1,954,000,000 (1,865,000,000).
Gross national product (1995): U.S.$59,151,000,000 (U.S.$4,160 per capita).

Structure of gross domestic product and labour force

	1994 in value Ch$'000,000[7]	1994 % of total value	1995 labour force	1995 % of labour force
Agriculture	486,595	8.3	809,700	15.4
Mining	470,974	8.0	93,200	1.8
Manufacturing	1,003,765	17.1	861,500	16.3
Construction	322,992	5.5	410,700	7.8
Public utilities	160,600	2.8	28,100	0.5
Transp. and commun.	454,329	7.8	400,500	7.6
Trade	993,408	17.0	974,100	18.5
Finance	972,559	16.6	340,100	6.4
Pub. admin., defense	159,952	2.7	1,322,800	25.1
Services	397,881	6.8		
Other	431,956[8]	7.4[8]	33,500[9]	0.6[9]
TOTAL	5,855,011	100.0	5,274,200	100.0

Household income and expenditure. Average household size (1994) 3.8; average annual income per household (1994) Ch$5,981,706 at November prices (U.S.$12,552); sources of income (1990): wages and salaries 75.1%, transfer payments 12.0%, other 12.9%; expenditure (1989): food 27.9%, clothing 22.5%, housing 15.2%, transportation 6.4%.
Tourism (1995): receipts U.S.$900,000,000; expenditures U.S.$774,000,000.

Foreign trade[10]

Balance of trade (current prices)

	1991	1992	1993	1994	1995	1996
U.S.$'000,000	+1,575	+749	−979	+660	+1,384	−1,147
% of total	9.7%	3.9%	5.1%	2.9%	4.5%	3.6%

Imports (1994): U.S.$11,359,400,000 (intermediate goods 51.8%; capital goods 28.7%; consumer goods 17.5%). *Major import sources:* U.S. 23.2%; Japan 8.9%; Brazil 8.8%; Argentina 8.4%; Germany 4.9%; France 3.2%.
Exports (1994): U.S.$11,645,100,000 (industrial products 44.9%, of which foodstuffs 18.6%, paper and paper products 7.9%, chemical and petroleum products 6.3%; mining 43.8%). *Major export destinations:* U.S. 17.3%; Japan 17.0%; Argentina 5.5%; Brazil 5.2%; Germany 5.0%; Taiwan 4.6%.

Transport and communications

Transport. Railroads (1995): length 4,084 mi, 6,572 km; passenger-km 689,000,000; metric ton-km cargo 2,329,246,000[11]. Roads (1995): total length 49,550 mi, 79,750 km (paved 14%). Vehicles (1995): passenger cars 888,645; trucks and buses 469,142. Air transport (1995): passenger-km 6,332,843,000; metric ton-km cargo 1,348,083,000; airports (1997) with scheduled flights 23.

Communications

Medium	date	unit	number	units per 1,000 persons
Daily newspapers	1994	circulation	1,411,000	101
Radio	1996	receivers	4,400,000	305
Television	1995	receivers	4,000,000	280
Telephones	1995	main lines	1,884,800	132
Cellular telephones	1995	subscribers	197,300	13.8
Facsimile machines	1995	units	15,000	1.0
Personal computers	1995	units	540,000	37.8

Education and health

Educational attainment (1992). Percentage of population age 25 and over having: no formal schooling 5.7%; primary education 44.2%; secondary 42.2%; higher 7.9%. *Literacy* (1995): total population age 15 and over literate 95.2%; males 95.4%; females 95.0%.

Education (1994)

	schools	teachers	students	student/ teacher ratio
Primary (age 6–13)	8,323	78,813	2,119,737	26.9
Secondary (age 14–17)[12]	2,956[13]	50,187	664,498	13.2
Higher	201[13]	18,084[14]	315,653[15]	...

Health (1994): physicians 16,000 (1 per 875 persons); hospital beds 43,076 (1 per 326 persons); infant mortality rate per 1,000 live births (1995) 11.1.
Food (1995): daily per capita caloric intake 2,769 (vegetable products 78%, animal products 22%); 113% of FAO recommended minimum requirement.

Military

Total active duty personnel (1997): 94,300 (army 54.1%, navy 31.6%, air force 14.3%). *Military expenditure as percentage of GNP* (1995): 3.8% (world 2.8%); per capita expenditure U.S.$158.

[1]Includes 8 nonelective seats. [2]Legislative bodies meet in Valparaíso. [3]Excludes the 480,000-sq mi (1,250,000-sq km) section of Antarctica claimed by Chile (and administered as part of Magallanes y la Antártica Chilena region) and "inland" (actually tidal) water areas. The 1992 census population of Chilean-claimed Antarctica was 126. [4]Includes 205 sq mi (530 sq km) of waters, known as Laguna del Desierto, lost in a border dispute with Argentina, resolved on Oct. 21, 1994. [5]Population projection based on 1992 census. [6]Construction approved and already begun only. [7]In constant prices of 1986. [8]Less imputed bank service charges. [9]Includes unemployed not previously employed. [10]Import figures are f.o.b. in balance of trade and c.i.f. for commodities and trading partners. [11]1994. [12]Includes vocational. [13]1988. [14]Universities only. [15]1993.

Internet resources for further information:

- **Ministry General Secretariat of the Government; International Press Department http://www.segegob.cl/seg-ingl/index2i.html**

China

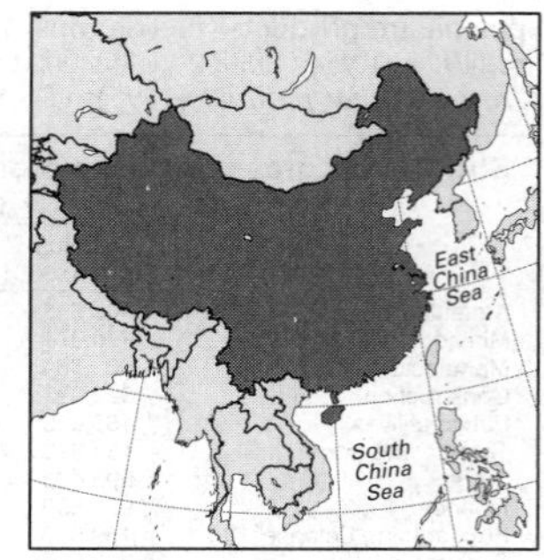

Official name: Chung-hua Jen-min Kung-ho-kuo (People's Republic of China).
Form of government: single-party people's republic with one legislative house (National People's Congress [2,978]).
Chief of state: President.
Head of government: Premier.
Capital: Peking (Beijing).
Official language: Mandarin Chinese.
Official religion: none.
Monetary unit: 1 Renminbi (yuan) (Y) = 10 jiao = 100 fen; valuation (Oct. 3, 1997) 1 U.S.$ = Y 8.28; 1 £ = Y 13.36.

Area and population[1, 2]

Provinces	Capitals	area sq mi	area sq km	population 1996[3] estimate
Anhwei (Anhui)	Ho-fei (Hefei)	54,000	139,900	60,130,000
Chekiang (Zhejiang)	Hang-chou (Hangzhou)	39,300	101,800	43,190,000
Fukien (Fujian)	Fu-chou (Fuzhou)	47,500	123,100	32,370,000
Hainan (Hainan)	Hai-k'ou (Haikou)	13,200	34,300	7,240,000
Heilungkiang (Heilongjiang)	Harbin	179,000	463,600	37,010,000
Honan (Henan)	Cheng-chou (Zhengzhou)	64,500	167,000	91,000,000
Hopeh (Hebei)	Shih-chia-chuang (Shijiazhuang)	78,200	202,700	64,370,000
Hunan (Hunan)	Ch'ang-sha (Changsha)	81,300	210,500	63,920,000
Hupeh (Hubei)	Wu-han (Wuhan)	72,400	187,500	57,720,000
Kansu (Gansu)	Lan-chou (Lanzhou)	141,500	366,500	24,380,000
Kiangsi (Jiangxi)	Nan-ch'ang (Nanchang)	63,600	164,800	40,630,000
Kiangsu (Jiangsu)	Nanking (Nanjing)	39,600	102,600	70,660,000
Kirin (Jilin)	Ch'ang-ch'un (Changchun)	72,200	187,000	25,920,000
Kwangtung (Guangdong)	Canton (Guangzhou)	76,100	197,100	68,680,000
Kweichow (Guizhou)	Kuei-yang (Guiyang)	67,200	174,000	35,080,000
Liaoning (Liaoning)	Shen-yang (Shenyang)	58,300	151,000	40,920,000
Shansi (Shanxi)	T'ai-yüan (Taiyuan)	60,700	157,100	30,770,000
Shantung (Shandong)	Chi-nan (Jinan)	59,200	153,300	87,050,000
Shensi (Shaanxi)	Sian (Xi'an)	75,600	195,800	35,140,000
Szechwan (Sichuan)	Ch'eng-tu (Chengdu)	210,800	546,000	98,650,000
Tsinghai (Qinghai)	Hsi-ning (Xining)	278,400	721,000	4,810,000
Yunnan (Yunnan)	K'un-ming (Kunming)	168,400	436,200	39,900,000
Autonomous regions				
Inner Mongolia (Nei Monggol)	Hu-ho-hao-t'e (Hohhot)	454,600	1,177,500	22,840,000
Kwangsi Chuang (Guangxi Zhuang)	Nan-ning (Nanning)	85,100	220,400	45,430,000
Ningsia Hui (Ningxia Hui)	Yin-ch'uan (Yinchuan)	25,600	66,400	5,130,000
Sinkiang Uighur (Xinjiang Uygur)	Wu-lu-mu-c'hi (Urumqi)	635,900	1,646,900	16,610,000
Tibet (Xizang)	Lhasa	471,700	1,221,600	2,400,000
Municipalities				
Chungking (Chongqing)	—	8,900	23,000	14,600,000
Peking (Beijing)	—	6,500	16,800	12,510,000
Shanghai (Shanghai)	—	2,400	6,200	14,150,000
Tientsin (Tianjin)	—	4,400	11,300	9,420,000
TOTAL		3,696,100[4]	9,572,900[4]	1,211,210,000[5]

Demography

Population (1997): 1,227,740,000.
Density (1997): persons per sq mi 332.2, persons per sq km 128.3.
Urban-rural (1997): urban 32.0%; rural 68.0%.
Sex distribution (1995): male 51.03%; female 48.97%.
Age breakdown (1990): under 15, 27.7%; 15–29, 31.0%; 30–44, 20.7%; 45–59, 12.0%; 60–74, 6.9%; 75 and over, 1.7%.
Population projection: (2000) 1,261,480,000; (2010) 1,348,957,000.
Doubling time: 77 years.
Ethnic composition (1990): Han (Chinese) 91.96%; Chuang 1.37%; Manchu 0.87%; Hui 0.76%; Miao 0.65%; Uighur 0.64%; Yi 0.58%; Tuchia 0.50%; Mongolian 0.42%; Tibetan 0.41%; Puyi 0.23%; Tung 0.22%; Yao 0.18%; Korean 0.17%; Pai 0.14%; Hani 0.11%; Kazak 0.10%; Tai 0.09%; Li 0.09%; other 0.51%.
Religious affiliation (1980): nonreligious 51.9%; Chinese folk-religionist 20.1%; atheist 12.0%; Buddhist 8.5%; Muslim 1.4%; Christian 0.1%; other 6.0%.
Major cities (1990): Shanghai 7,496,509; Peking 5,769,607; Tientsin 4,574,689; Shen-yang 3,603,712; Wu-han 3,284,229; Canton 2,914,281; Harbin 2,443,398; Chungking (Chongqing) 2,266,772; Nanking 2,090,204; Sian 1,959,044; Ta-lien (Dalian) 1,723,302; Ch'eng-tu 1,713,255; Ch'ang-ch'un 1,679,270; T'ai-yüan 1,533,884; Tsinan 1,480,915; Ch'ing-tao (Qingdao) 1,459,195; An-shan (Anshan) 1,203,986; Fu-shun 1,202,388; Lan-chou 1,194,640; Cheng-chou 1,159,679; Tzu-po (Zibo) 1,138,074; K'un-ming 1,127,411.
Households (1995). Average rural household size 4.5; urban household size 3.2. Family households (1990): 277,390,000 (99.4%); collective 1,671,000 (0.6%).

Vital statistics

Birth rate per 1,000 population (1997): 16.4 (world avg. 25.0).
Death rate per 1,000 population (1997): 7.1 (world avg. 9.3).
Natural increase rate per 1,000 population (1997): 9.3 (world avg. 15.7).
Total fertility rate (avg. births per childbearing woman; 1997): 1.8.
Marriage rate per 1,000 population (1995): 7.7.
Divorce rate per 1,000 population (1995): 0.9.
Life expectancy at birth (1997): male 68.0 years; female 72.0 years.
Major causes of death per 100,000 population (percentage distribution; 1995)[6]: diseases of the circulatory system 22.2%; malignant neoplasms (cancers) 21.9%; diseases of the respiratory system 15.7%; diseases of the heart 15.3%; injuries and poisoning 6.9%; digestive diseases 3.3%.

Social indicators

Educational attainment (1990). Percentage of population age 25 and over having: no schooling 29.3%; incomplete primary 34.3%; completed primary 34.4%; postsecondary 2.0%.

Distribution of urban household income (1995)

avg. per capita income by quintile (avg. Y 4,288)

first quintile	second quintile	third quintile	fourth quintile	fifth quintile
Y 2,478	Y 3,364	Y 4,074	Y 4,958	Y 7,134

Quality of working life (1991). Average workweek: 48 hours. Annual rate per 100,000 workers for: injury or accident, n.a.; industrial illness, n.a.; death, n.a. Funds for pensions and social welfare relief (1995): Y 154,180,000,000. Average days lost to labour stoppages per 1,000 workdays: n.a. Average duration of journey to work: n.a. Method of transport: n.a. Rate per 1,000 workers of discouraged (unemployed no longer seeking work): n.a.
Access to services. Proportion of communes having access to electricity (1979) 87.1%. Percentage of urban population with: safe public water supply (1995) 93.0%; public sewage collection, n.a.; public fire protection, n.a.
Social participation. Eligible voters participating in last national election: n.a. Population participating in voluntary work: n.a. Trade union membership in total labour force (1991): 17.9%. Practicing religious population in total affiliated population: n.a.
Social deviance. Annual reported arrest rate per 100,000 population (1986) for: property violation 20.7; infringing personal rights 7.2; disruption of social administration 3.3; endangering public security 1.0[7].
Leisure. Favourite leisure activities: n.a.
Material well-being (1995). Urban families possessing (number per family): bicycles 1.9; televisions 1.2; washing machines 0.9; refrigerators 0.7; sewing machines 0.6; cameras 0.3. Rural families possessing (number per family): bicycles 1.5; televisions 0.8; sewing machines 0.7; washing machines 0.2.

National economy

Gross national product (at current market prices; 1995): U.S.$744,890,000,000 (U.S.$620 per capita).

Structure of gross national product and labour force

	1995 in value Y '000,000,000	% of total value	labour force ('000)[8]	% of labour force[8]
Agriculture	1,199.30	20.6	330,180	52.9
Mining }	2,435.37	41.8	10,670	1.7
Manufacturing }			98,030	15.7
Construction	381.96	6.6	33,220	5.3
Public utilities	...	...	2,580	0.4
Transp. and commun.	323.65	5.6	19,420	3.1
Trade	509.44	8.7	42,920	6.9
Finance	...	...	3,560	0.6
Pub. admin.	...	...	10,420	1.7
Services	976.33	16.7	28,050	4.5
Other	...	...	44,830	7.2
TOTAL	5,826.05	100.0	623,880	100.0

Budget (1996). Revenue: Y 736,661,000,000 (taxes 93.7%; funds collected for energy and transport projects and others 6.3%). Expenditures: Y 791,438,000,000 (culture, education, and public health 21.5%; capital construction 11.2%; government administration 8.1%; enterprise development 6.7%; agricultural development 6.6%; defense 4.7%; urban public works 3.7%).
Public debt (external, outstanding; 1995): U.S.$94,675,000,000.
Tourism: receipts from visitors (1995) U.S.$8,733,000,000; expenditures by nationals abroad U.S.$3,688,000,000.

Retail and service enterprises (1992)

	no. of enter-prises	no. of employees	annual wage as a % of all wages	annual gross output value (Y '000,000)
Retail trade	10,063,000	24,345,000	...	...
Grocery stores	171,000	1,213,000	...	...
Department stores	174,000	2,120,000	...	...
Other food shops	120,000	824,000	...	...
Agricultural supplies stores	100,000	508,000	...	...
Electrical appliances stores	96,000	930,000	...	...
Household supplies stores	71,000	377,000	...	...
Grain and oil shops	81,000	783,000	...	...
Textile stores	40,000	288,000	...	...
Drugstores	32,000	251,000	...	...
Bookstores	28,000	151,000	...	...
Coal stores	16,000	200,000	...	...
Service trade	1,842,000	4,522,000	...	...
Repair shops	742,000	1,110,000	...	...
Barbershops	508,000	779,000	...	...
Hotels	189,000	1,427,000	...	...
Photo studios	98,000	225,000	...	...

Production (metric tons except as noted). Agriculture, forestry, fishing (1996): grains—rice 197,200,000, corn (maize) 127,810,000, wheat 110,315,000, sorghum 4,098,000, barley 3,500,000, millet 2,701,000; oilseeds—soybeans 13,010,000, peanuts (groundnuts) 10,230,000, rapeseed 9,166,000, sunflower seeds 1,290,000; fruits and nuts—watermelons 21,708,000, apples 17,058,000, oranges 8,050,000, cantaloupes 5,962,000, pears 5,921,000; other—sweet potatoes 100,196,000, sugarcane 70,840,000, potatoes

36,769,000, sugar beets 16,726,000, cabbage 16,214,000, tomatoes 15,532,-000, cucumbers 13,351,000, seed cotton 12,609,000, eggplants 9,325,000, onions 9,630,000, garlic 8,574,000, tobacco leaves 3,210,000, tea 614,000; livestock (number of live animals) 452,199,000 pigs, 149,908,000 goats, 127,261,000 sheep, 108,910,000 cattle, 23,315,000 water buffalo, 10,745,-000 asses, 10,071,000 horses, 2,902,000,000 chickens, 483,000,000 ducks; roundwood (1995) 297,653,000 cu m; fish catch (1995) 24,433,321. Mining and quarrying (1996): metal concentrates—zinc 1,119,000, copper 906,000, lead 530,000, antimony 99,000, tin 56,000, tungsten 24,000; metal ores—iron ore 250,000,000, bauxite 5,500,000, manganese ore 5,000,-000[9], silver 250[9], gold 140[9]; nonmetals—salt 28,990,000, gypsum 7,500,000, phosphates 7,000,000[9], talc 2,500,000, fluorspar 2,000,000, barite 1,500,000, graphite 350,000[9], asbestos 250,000. Manufacturing (1996): cement 490,-000,000; rolled steel 86,110,000; chemical fertilizer 26,600,000; paper and paperboard 24,000,000[9]; sulfuric acid 18,890,000; sugar 6,500,000; cotton yarn 4,900,000; cotton fabrics 22,120,000,000 m; cigarettes 34,420,000 cases; colour television sets 21,090,000 units; household washing machines 9,448,-000 units[9]; household refrigerators 9,280,000 units; motor vehicles 1,490,000 units. Construction (1995): residential 1,074,330,000 sq m; nonresidential 381,670,000 sq m. Distribution of industrial production (percentage of total value of output by sector; 1978 [1995]): state-operated enterprises 80.6% (34.0%); collectives 19.2% (36.6%); privately operated enterprises 0.2% (29.4%). Retail sales (percentage of total sales by sector; 1978 [1995]): state-operated enterprises 90.5% (29.8%); collectives 7.4% (19.3%); privately operated enterprises 2.1% (50.9%).

Manufacturing and mining enterprises (1995)

	no. of enter-prises	no. of employees[10]	annual wages as a % of avg. of all wages[11]	annual gross output value (Y '000,000)
Manufacturing				
Machinery, transport equipment, and metal manufactures,	131,810	17,740,000	96.7	1,462,671
of which,				
Metal products	30,728	1,930,000	...	165,072
Industrial equipment	29,631	4,050,000	...	236,569
Transport equipment	19,445	3,700,000	...	330,328
Electronic goods	7,997	1,720,000	...	253,048
Measuring equipment	5,637	860,000	...	42,570
Textiles	25,686	6,730,000	95.5	460,400
Garments	20,007	1,750,000	...	147,015
Foodstuffs,	61,983	4,760,000	87.5	620,008
of which,				
Food processing	30,711	1,980,000	...	304,510
Beverages	14,719	1,210,000	...	115,568
Tobacco manufactures	423	330,000	...	100,423
Chemicals,	59,010	7,470,000	92.1	733,852
of which,				
Pharmaceuticals	5,388	1,020,000	...	96,126
Plastics	19,255	1,090,000	...	112,765
Secondary forest products (including paper and stationery)	38,130	2,410,000	96.1	164,602
Primary forest products	1,237	1,160,000	114.3	16,493
Mining				
Nonferrous and ferrous metals	5,915	840,000	107.6	43,410
Crude petroleum	134	1,280,000	...	142,846
Coal	11,953	5,210,000	119.8	115,516

Energy production (consumption): electricity (kW-hr; 1994) 928,083,000,000 (926,037,000,000); coal (metric tons; 1994) 1,239,902,000 (1,231,928,000); crude petroleum (barrels; 1994) 1,069,320,000 (1,024,375,000); petroleum products (metric tons; 1994) 106,629,000 (114,972,000); natural gas (cu m; 1994) 17,540,000,000 (17,540,000,000).

Financial aggregates[12]

	1990	1991	1992	1993	1994	1995	1996
Exchange rate, Y per:							
U.S. dollar	5.22	5.43	5.75	5.80	8.45	8.32	8.31
£	10.06	10.16	8.70	8.59	13.18	12.90	12.96
SDR	7.43	7.77	7.91	7.97	12.33	12.36	11.93
International reserves (U.S.$)							
Total (excl. gold; '000,000)	29,586	43,674	20,620	22,387	52,914	75,377	107,039
SDRs ('000,000)	562	577	419	484	539	582	614
Reserve pos. in IMF ('000,000)	430	433	758	704	755	1,216	1,396
Foreign exchange	28,594	42,664	19,443	21,199	51,620	73,579	105,029
Gold ('000,000 fine troy oz)	12.7	12.7	12.7	12.7	12.7	12.7	12.7
% world reserves	1.4	1.4	1.4	1.4	1.4	1.4	1.4
Interest and prices							
Central bank discount (%)	...	...	...	...	...	...	...
Govt. bond yield (%)	...	...	...	...	...	...	...
Industrial share prices	...	...	...	...	...	...	...
Balance of payments (U.S.$'000,000)							
Balance of visible trade,	+9,165	+8,743	+5,183	−10,654	+7,290	+18,050	+19,535
of which:							
Imports, f.o.b.	−42,354	−50,176	−64,385	−86,313	−95,271	−110,060	−131,542
Exports, f.o.b.	51,519	58,919	69,568	75,659	102,561	128,110	151,077
Balance of invisibles	+2,833	+5,022	+1,218	−955	−758	−11,774	−12,437
Balance of payments, current account	+11,998	+13,765	+6,401	−11,609	+6,532	+6,276	+7,098

Household income and expenditure. Average household size (1995) 3.7; rural household 4.5, urban household 3.2. Average annual income per household Y 11,555; rural household Y 10,474, urban household Y 13,851. Sources of income: rural household (1995)—income from household businesses 80.3%, wages 15.2%, other 4.5%; urban household (1995)—wages 80.6%, business income 5.7%, other 13.7%. Expenditure (1995): rural household—food 58.6%, housing 13.9%, cultural activities 7.8%, clothing 6.9%, household materials 5.2%, health 3.2%, transportation 2.6%; urban household—food 49.9%, clothing 13.5%, cultural activities 8.8%, household materials 8.4%, housing 7.1%, transportation 4.8%, health 3.1%.

Population economically active (1995): total 696,600,000; activity rate of total population 57.8% (participation rates: over age 15, 76.8%[13]; female 49.7%[13]; unemployed 10.4%). Urban workforce by sector 1978 (1995): state enterprises 74,500,000 (109,550,000); collectives 20,000,000 (30,760,000); self-employment or privately run enterprises 150,000 (8,770,000).

Price and earnings indexes (1990 = 100)

	1990	1991	1992	1993	1994	1995	1996
Consumer price index	100.0	105.1	114.1	133.5	165.9	193.9	210.0
Annual earnings index[14]	100.0	109.3	126.7	157.5	212.1	257.0	...

Land use (1994): forested 14.0%; meadows and pastures 42.9%; agricultural and under permanent cultivation 10.3%; other 32.8%.

Foreign trade[15]

Balance of trade (current prices)

	1991	1992	1993	1994	1995	1996
U.S.$'000,000	+8,743	+5,183	−10,654	+7,290	+18,050	+19,535
% of total	8.0%	3.9%	6.6%	3.7%	7.6%	6.9%

Imports (1995): U.S.$132,078,000,000 (machinery and transport equipment 39.9%; products of textile industries, rubber and metal products 21.8%; chemical and related products 13.1%; inedible raw materials 7.7%; food and live animals 4.6%; mineral fuels and lubricants 3.9%). *Major import sources:* Japan 22.0%; United States 12.2%; Taiwan 11.2%; South Korea 7.8%; Hong Kong 6.5%; Germany 6.1%; Russia 2.9%; Singapore 2.6%; Italy 2.4%; France 2.0%; Australia 2.0%.

Exports (1995): U.S.$148,770,000,000 (products of textile industries, rubber and metal products 21.7%; machinery and transport equipment 21.1%; food and live animals 6.7%; chemicals and allied products 6.1%; mineral fuels and lubricants 3.6%; inedible raw materials 2.9%). *Major export destinations:* Hong Kong 24.2%; Japan 19.1%; United States 16.6%; South Korea 4.5%; Germany 3.8%; Singapore 2.4%; The Netherlands 2.2%; Taiwan 2.1%.

Transport and communications

Transport. Railroads (1995): length 45,319 mi, 72,934 km; passenger-mi 220,319,000,000, passenger-km 354,570,000,000; short ton-mi cargo 881,539,-000,000, metric ton-km cargo 1,287,000,000,000. Roads (1995): total length 718,931 mi, 1,157,009 km (paved 90%). Vehicles (1995): passenger cars 4,179,000; trucks and buses 5,213,270. Merchant marine (1992): vessels (100 gross tons and over) 2,390; total deadweight tonnage 20,657,996. Air transport (1995): passenger-mi 42,334,000,000, passenger-km 68,130,000,000; short ton-mi cargo 1,527,000,000, metric ton-km cargo 2,230,000,000; airports (1996) with scheduled flights 113.

Communications

Medium	date	unit	number	units per 1,000 persons
Daily newspapers	1994	circulation	27,790,000	23
Radio	1996	receivers	215,950,000	177
Television	1995	receivers	227,880,000	189
Telephones	1995	main lines	40,706,000	34
Cellular telephones	1995	subscribers	3,629,000	3.0
Facsimile machines	1995	units	270,000	0.2
Personal computers	1995	units	2,600,000	2.2

Education and health

Literacy (1990): total population age 15 and over literate 636,112,000 (77.7%); males literate 364,687,000 (87.0%); females literate 271,425,000 (68.0%).

Education (1995)

	schools	teachers	students	student/ teacher ratio
Primary (age 7–13)	849,123	6,539,000	159,064,000	24.3
Secondary (age 13–17)	81,020	3,334,000	53,710,000	16.1
Secondary specialized	14,196	549,000	8,205,000	14.9
Higher	1,054	401,000	2,906,000	7.2

Health (1995): physicians 1,918,000 (1 per 628 persons); hospital beds 3,141,-000 (1 per 384 persons); infant mortality rate per 1,000 live births (1997) 39.

Food (1995): daily per capita caloric intake 2,741 (vegetable products 82%, animal products 18%); 116% of FAO recommended minimum requirement.

Military

Total active duty personnel (1997): 2,840,000 (army 73.6%, navy 9.9%, air force 16.5%). *Military expenditure as percentage of GNP* (1995): 2.3% (world 2.8%); per capita expenditure U.S.$53.

[1]Names of the provinces, autonomous regions, and municipalities are stated in conventional form, followed by Pinyin transliteration; names of capitals are stated in conventional form or Wade-Giles transliteration, followed by Pinyin transliteration. [2]Data for Taiwan, Quemoy and Matsu (parts of Fukien province occupied by Taiwan), and Hong Kong (which reverted to China from British administration July 1, 1997) are excluded. [3]January 1. [4]Includes 4,600 sq mi (11,900 sq km) not shown separately. [5]Total includes servicemen not assigned to any political division and discrepancies between provincial and national estimates. [6]Based on urban sample population. [7]Excludes arrests for anti-Communist activities. [8]Employed only. [9]1995. [10]In state-owned and collective-owned industries only. [11]1979. [12]Exchange rates and international reserves are end-of-year figures. [13]1987. [14]Average annual wage in industrial establishments in urban areas. [15]Imports and exports f.o.b.

Internet resources for further information:

- **Embassy of The People's Republic of China http://www.china-embassy.org/**

Colombia

Official name: República de Colombia (Republic of Colombia).
Form of government: unitary, multiparty republic with two legislative houses (Senate [102]; House of Representatives [165]).
Head of state and government: President.
Capital: Santafé de Bogotá, D.C.
Official language: Spanish.
Official religion: none.
Monetary unit: 1 peso (Col$) = 100 centavos; valuation (Oct. 3, 1997) 1 U.S.$ = Col$1,245; 1 £ = Col$2,006.

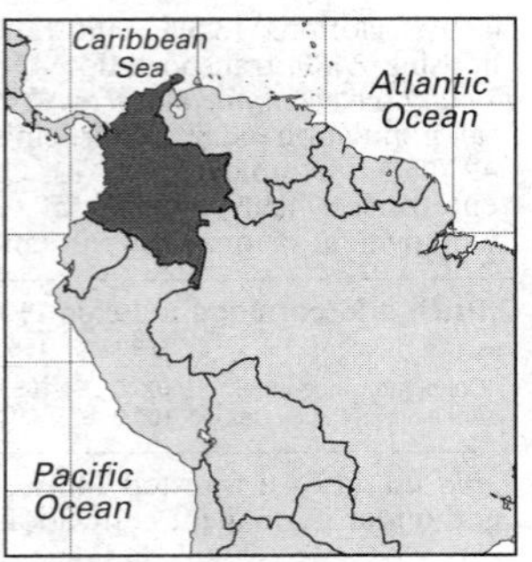

Area and population

Departments	Capitals	area sq mi	area sq km	population 1993 census[1]
Antioquia	Medellín	24,445	63,312	4,919,619
Atlántico	Barranquilla	1,308	3,388	1,837,468
Bolívar	Cartagena	10,030	25,978	1,702,188
Boyacá	Tunja	8,953	23,189	1,315,579
Caldas	Manizales	3,046	7,888	1,030,062
Caquetá	Florencia	34,349	88,965	367,898
Cauca	Popayán	11,316	29,308	1,127,678
Cesar	Valledupar	8,844	22,905	827,219
Chocó	Quibdó	17,965	46,530	406,199
Córdoba	Montería	9,660	25,020	1,275,623
Cundinamarca	Santafé de Bogotá, D.C.	8,735	22,623	1,875,337
Huila	Neiva	7,680	19,890	843,798
La Guajira	Riohacha	8,049	20,848	433,361
Magdalena	Santa Marta	8,953	23,188	1,127,691
Meta	Villavicencio	33,064	85,635	618,427
Nariño	Pasto	12,845	33,268	1,443,671
Norte de Santander	Cúcuta	8,362	21,658	1,162,474
Orinoquía-Amazonía	...	186,519	483,083	688,805
Quindío	Armenia	712	1,845	495,212
Risaralda	Pereira	1,598	4,140	844,184
San Andrés y Providencia	San Andrés	17	44	61,040
Santander	Bucaramanga	11,790	30,537	1,811,741
Sucre	Sincelejo	4,215	10,917	701,105
Tolima	Ibagué	9,097	23,562	1,286,078
Valle	Cali	8,548	22,140	3,736,090
Capital District				
Santafé de Bogotá, D.C.		613[2]	1,587[2]	5,484,244
TOTAL		440,762[2]	1,141,568[2]	37,422,791

Demography

Population (1997): 36,200,000.
Density (1997): persons per sq mi 82.1, persons per sq km 31.7.
Urban-rural (1990): urban 70.3%; rural 29.7%.
Sex distribution (1996): male 49.24%; female 50.76%.
Age breakdown (1996): under 15, 33.5%; 15–29, 28.1%; 30–44, 21.5%; 45–59, 10.4%; 60–74, 5.3%; 75 and over, 1.2%.
Population projection: (2000) 37,822,000; (2010) 42,959,000.
Doubling time: 35 years.
Ethnic composition (1985): mestizo 58.0%; white 20.0%; mulatto 14.0%; black 4.0%; mixed black-Indian 3.0%; Amerindian 1.0%.
Religious affiliation (1995): Roman Catholic 95.2%; other 4.8%.
Major cities (1993): Santafé de Bogotá, D.C., 5,484,244; Cali 1,847,176; Medellín 1,834,881; Barranquilla 1,090,916.

Vital statistics

Birth rate per 1,000 population (1996): 25.9 (world avg. 25.0).
Death rate per 1,000 population (1996): 5.9 (world avg. 9.3).
Natural increase rate per 1,000 population (1996): 20.0 (world avg. 15.7).
Total fertility rate (avg. births per childbearing woman; 1996): 2.9.
Life expectancy at birth (1996): male 65.4 years; female 73.3 years.
Major causes of death per 100,000 population (1990)[3]: homicide with firearms 101.0; malignant neoplasms (cancers) 82.6; ischemic heart disease 70.4; accidents 49.0; infectious and parasitic diseases 25.5.

National economy

Budget (1995). Revenue: Col$13,405,350,000,000 (indirect taxes 36.9%, direct taxes 26.8%, credit resources 22.3%). Expenditures: Col$9,510,848,000,000 (education 20.2%, finance and public credit 16.9%, defense 12.4%).
Public debt (external, outstanding; 1995): U.S.$12,983,000,000.
Tourism (1995): receipts U.S.$851,000,000; expenditures U.S.$822,000,000.
Production (metric tons except as noted). Agriculture, forestry, fishing (1996): sugarcane 32,500,000, plantains 3,212,000, potatoes 2,594,000, bananas 2,100,000, rice 1,787,000, corn 1,058,000, coffee 821,800; livestock (no. of live animals) 26,088,000 cattle, 3,708,000 vicuña[4], 2,540,000 sheep, 2,431,000 pigs; roundwood (1995) 20,491,000 cu m; fish catch (1995) 167,080. Mining and quarrying (1996): iron ore 605,716; salt 560,252; gold 710,013 troy oz[5]; silver 169,252 troy oz[5]; emeralds 6,305,903 carats[5]. Manufacturing (value added in Col$'000,000; 1992): processed food 1,160,600; beverages 953,400; textiles and clothing 631,700; machinery and electrical apparatus 351,200; paper products 266,500. Construction (no. of permits; 1996)[6]: residential 6,118; nonresidential 3,138. Energy production (consumption): electricity (kW-hr; 1994) 43,474,000,000 (43,617,000,000); coal (metric tons; 1994) 22,527,000 (6,476,000); petroleum (barrels; 1994) 168,202,000 (97,085,000); petroleum products (metric tons; 1994) 12,510,000 (11,682,000); natural gas (cu m; 1994) 5,111,119,000 (5,111,119,000).
Gross national product (1995): U.S.$70,263,000,000 (U.S.$1,910 per capita).

Structure of gross domestic product and labour force

	1995 in value Col$'000,000	1995 % of total value	1980 labour force	1980 % of labour force
Agriculture	9,513,515	13.1	2,412,413	28.5
Mining	3,973,366	5.5	49,740	0.6
Manufacturing	13,573,048	18.8	1,136,735	13.4
Construction	4,628,555	6.4	242,191	2.9
Public utilities	2,344,821	3.2	44,233	0.5
Transp. and commun.	6,897,403	9.5	352,623	4.2
Trade	7,184,183	9.9	1,261,633	14.9
Finance			278,210	3.2
Pub. admin., defense / Services / Other	24,292,123	33.6	1,998,460	23.6
Other			690,762[7]	8.2[7]
TOTAL	72,407,014	100.0	8,467,000	100.0

Population economically active (1985): total 9,558,000; activity rate 34.3% (participation rates: over age 12, 49.4%; female 32.8%; unemployed 4.3%).

Price and earnings indexes (1990 = 100)

	1990	1991	1992	1993	1994	1995	1996
Consumer price index	100.0	130.4	165.6	203.1	251.5	304.2	365.8
Monthly earnings index[8]	100.0	126.1	158.9	198.7	...	...	...

Household income and expenditure. Average household size (1985) 4.7; sources of income (1992): wages 45.1%, self-employment 35.4%, transfer payments 14.2%; expenditure (1992): food 34.2%, transportation 18.5%, housing 7.8%, health care 6.4%, household durable goods 5.7%, clothing 4.5%.
Land use (1994): forest 22.0%; pasture 18.2%; agriculture 5.7%; other 54.1%.

Foreign trade[9]

Balance of trade (current prices)

	1991	1992	1993	1994	1995	1996
U.S.$'000,000	+2,720.1	+920.1	−1,970.0	−2,640.7	−3,157.6	−2,206.7
% of total	23.2%	7.1%	12.2%	13.6%	13.9%	9.4%

Imports (1996): U.S.$13,676,000,000 (machinery and transport equipment 45.3%, chemicals 24.7%, vegetable products 7.5%, metals 6.6%, food and tobacco 6.1%, paper and paper products 3.5%). *Major import sources* (1995): U.S. 39.1%; Venezuela 9.8%; Japan 7.6%; Germany 5.8%.
Exports (1996): U.S.$10,574,000,000 (petroleum products 27.4%, coffee 14.9%, chemicals 10.2%, forestry and fisheries 10.0%, textiles and apparel 8.1%, coal 8.0%, food 7.1%). *Major export destinations* (1995): U.S. 34.9%; Germany 7.3%; Peru 6.1%; Venezuela 5.5%; Ecuador 4.1%; Japan 3.6%.

Transport and communications

Transport. Railroads (1992): route length (1994) 3,230 km; passenger-km 15,524,000; metric ton-km cargo 242,917,000. Roads (1995): total length 106,600 km (paved 12%). Vehicles (1995): cars 1,150,000; trucks 550,000. Merchant marine (1992): vessels (100 gross tons and over) 101; deadweight tonnage 403,047. Air transport (1995): passenger-km 4,565,477,000; metric ton-km cargo 965,828,000; airports (1997) 43.

Communications

Medium	date	unit	number	units per 1,000 persons
Daily newspapers	1994	circulation	1,910,020[10]	55[10]
Radio	1996	receivers	5,400,000	151
Television	1995	receivers	7,314,000	188
Telephones	1995	main lines	3,872,800	100
Cellular telephones	1995	subscribers	274,600	7.1
Personal computers	1995	units	630,000	16

Education and health

Educational attainment (1985). Percentage of population age 25 and over having: no schooling 15.3%; primary education 50.1%; secondary 25.4%; higher 6.8%; not stated 2.4%. *Literacy* (1995): population age 15 and over literate 91.3%; males literate 91.2%; females literate 91.4%.

Education (1994)

	schools	teachers	students	student/teacher ratio
Primary (6–10)	46,707	170,526	4,327,507	25.4
Secondary (11–16)	8,161	141,484	2,879,681	20.3
Higher[11]	235[12]	54,164	510,649	9.4

Health: physicians (1992) 33,498 (1 per 1,078 persons); hospital beds (1989) 45,888 (1 per 693 persons); infant mortality rate (1995) 26.9.
Food (1995): daily per capita caloric intake 2,758 (vegetable products 84%, animal products 16%); 119% of FAO recommended minimum requirement.

Military

Total active duty personnel (1997): 146,300 (army 82.7%, navy 12.3%, air force 5.0%). *Military expenditure as percentage of GNP* (1995): 2.6% (world 2.8%); per capita expenditure U.S.$55.

[1]Adjusted figures. [2]Detail does not add to total given because of rounding. [3]Estimates based on about 75% of total deaths. [4]1991. [5]1995. [6]Construction permits for 7 metropolitan areas and 10 cities. [7]Includes unemployed. [8]Minimum legal wages revised annually January 2. [9]Import figures are f.o.b. in balance of trade and c.i.f. in commodities and trading partners. [10]Circulation for 26 newspapers only. [11]1992. [12]1987.

Internet resources for further information:
- **National Administration Department of Statistics http://www.sin.com.co/Clientes/DANE/home.html**

Comoros[1]

Official name: Jumhurīyat al-Qumur al-Ittihādīyah al-Islāmīyah (Arabic); République Fédérale Islamique des Comores (French) (Federal Islamic Republic of the Comoros).
Form of government: transitional regime[2].
Head of state and government[2]: President.
Capital: Moroni.
Official languages: Comorian; Arabic; French.
Official religion: Islam.
Monetary unit: 1 Comorian franc (CF) = 100 centimes; valuation (Oct. 3, 1997) 1 U.S.$ = CF 447.95; 1 £ = CF 722.10.

Area and population

Islands[3]	Capitals	area sq mi	area sq km	population 1995 estimate
Mwali (Mohéli)[4]	Fomboni	112	290	27,600
Nzwani (Anjouan)[4, 5]	Mutsamudu	164	424	211,900
Ngazidja (Grande-Comore)	Moroni	443	1,148	250,500
TOTAL		719	1,862	490,000

Demography

Population (1997): 514,000.
Density (1997): persons per sq mi 714.9, persons per sq km 276.0.
Urban-rural (1995)[6]: urban 30.8%; rural 69.2%.
Sex distribution (1991): male 49.49%; female 50.51%.
Age breakdown (1995)[6]: under 15, 48.5%; 15–29, 26.4%; 30–44, 13.8%; 45–59, 7.3%; 60–74, 3.4%; 75 and over, 0.6%.
Population projection: (2000) 549,000; (2010) 689,000.
Doubling time: 20 years.
Ethnic composition (1995): nearly all Comorian (a mixture of Bantu, Arab, Malay, and Malagasy peoples).
Religious affiliation (1994): Sunnī Muslim 98.9%; Roman Catholic 1.1%.
Major cities (1991): Moroni 30,000; Mutsamudu 20,000; Domoni (1990) 8,000; Fomboni (1990) 5,600.

Vital statistics

Birth rate per 1,000 population (1996): 45.8 (world avg. 25.0).
Death rate per 1,000 population (1996): 10.3 (world avg. 9.3).
Natural increase rate per 1,000 population (1996): 35.5 (world avg. 15.7).
Total fertility rate (avg. births per childbearing woman; 1996): 6.7.
Marriage rate per 1,000 population: n.a.[7]
Divorce rate per 1,000 population: n.a.
Life expectancy at birth (1996): male 56.4 years; female 61.0 years.
Major causes of death per 100,000 population: n.a.; however, major diseases include malaria (afflicts 80–90% of the adult population), tuberculosis, leprosy, and kwashiorkor (a nutritional deficiency disease).

National economy

Budget (1996). Revenue: CF 22,873,000,000 (tax revenue 43.5%, grants 36.0%, loans 14.6%, nontax revenue 5.9%). Expenditures: CF 29,513,000,000 (current expenditures 61.8%, development expenditures 38.2%).
Production (metric tons except as noted). Agriculture, forestry, fishing (1996): coconuts 60,000[6], bananas 57,000, cassava 49,700, pulses 8,760, taro 8,300, corn (maize) 3,700, cloves 2,000, vanilla 150, ylang-ylang essence 40, other export crops grown in small quantities include coffee, cinnamon, and tuberoses; livestock (number of live animals[6]) 128,000 goats, 50,000 cattle, 14,500 sheep; roundwood, n.a.; fish catch (1995) 13,200. Mining and quarrying: sand, gravel, and crushed stone from coral mining for local construction. Manufacturing: products of small-scale industries include processed vanilla and ylang-ylang, cement, handicrafts, soaps, soft drinks, woodwork, and clothing. Construction: n.a. Energy production (consumption): electricity (kW-hr; 1996) 30,900,000 ([1994] 17,742,000); coal, none (none); crude petroleum, none (none); petroleum products (metric tons; 1994) none (22,000); natural gas, none (none).
Population economically active (1991): total 215,000; activity rate of total population 44.4% (participation rates: ages 10 years and over, 57.8%; female 40.0%; unemployed 20%).

Price and earnings indexes (1993 = 100)

	1992	1993	1994	1995	1996
Consumer price index	98.2	100.0	125.0	133.9	138.7
Monthly earnings index	...	100.0	121.0	137.0	...

Tourism (1996): receipts from visitors U.S.$20,300,000; expenditures by nationals abroad U.S.$5,100,000.
Public debt (external, outstanding; 1995): U.S.$186,700,000.
Household income and expenditure. Average household size (1985) 5.6; income per household: n.a.; sources of income: n.a.; expenditure (1993)[10]: food and beverages 67.3%, clothing and footwear 11.6%, tobacco and cigarettes 4.1%, energy 3.8%, health care 3.2%, household furnishings 3.0%, other 7.0%.
Gross national product (at current market prices; 1995): U.S.$237,000,000 (U.S.$470 per capita).

Structure of gross domestic product and labour force

	1996 in value CF '000,000	1996 % of total value	1980 labour force[11]	1980 % of labour force
Agriculture, fishing	31,636	38.6	53,063	53.3
Mining	...	...	62	0.1
Manufacturing	4,361	5.3	3,946	4.0
Construction	5,054	6.2	3,267	3.3
Public utilities	1,068	1.3	129	0.1
Transportation and communications	3,093	3.8	2,118	2.1
Trade, restaurants, hotels	22,832	27.9	1,873	1.9
Finance, insurance	3,115	3.8	237	0.2
Public admin., defense	12,114	14.8	2,435	2.5
Services	401	0.5	4,646	4.7
Other	−1,827[12]	−2.2	27,687[12]	27.8[12]
TOTAL	81,847	100.0	99,463	100.0

Land use (1994)[6]: forested 17.9%; meadows and pastures 6.7%; agricultural and under permanent cultivation 44.9%; other 30.5%.

Foreign trade[13]

Balance of trade (current prices)

	1993	1994	1995	1996
CF '000,000,000	−7.9	−14.2	−15.8	−17.1
% of total	39.3%	61.2%	65.1%	77.1%

Imports (1996): CF 24,659,000,000 (rice 13.5%, petroleum products 13.5%, vehicles 7.6%, meat and fish 6.0%, iron and steel 3.7%, other 40.4%). *Major import sources:* France 39.4%; Pakistan 7.7%; South Africa 6.6%; United Arab Emirates 6.3%.
Exports (1996): CF 2,436,000,000 (vanilla 42.5%, ylang-ylang 26.5%, cloves 8.6%). *Major export destinations:* France 48.9%; Germany 13.6%; United States 11.8%; Réunion and Madagascar 11.8%.

Transport and communications

Transport. Railroads: none. Roads (1995): total length 544 mi, 875 km (paved 76%). Vehicles (1995): passenger cars 7,080; trucks and buses 4,870. Merchant marine (1992): vessels (100 gross tons and over) 6; total deadweight tonnage 3,579. Air transport (1994): passenger-mi 1,900,000, passenger-km 3,000,000; short ton-mi cargo, n.a., metric ton-mi cargo, n.a.; airports (1997) with scheduled flights 2.

Communications

Medium	date	unit	number	units per 1,000 persons
Radio	1996	receivers	61,000	122
Television	1993	receivers	200	0.4
Telephones	1996	main lines	4,980	9.9
Facsimile machines	1995	units	100	0.2

Education and health

Educational attainment (1980). Percentage of population age 25 and over having: no formal schooling 56.7%; Qur'anic school education 8.3%; primary 3.6%; secondary 2.0%; higher 0.2%; not specified 29.2%. *Literacy* (1995)[6]: total population age 15 and over literate 192,000 (57.0%); males literate 108,000 (64.0%); females literate 84,000 (50.0%).

Education (1993–94)

	schools	teachers	students	student/ teacher ratio
Primary (age 7–12)	275	1,737[14]	77,837	43.0[14]
Secondary (age 13–19)	...	613[15]	17,474	25.5[15]
Teacher training	...	...	163	...
Higher	...	...	400	...

Health: physicians (1993) 77[16] (1 per 6,600[16] persons); hospital beds (1990) 649 (1 per 715 persons); infant mortality rate per 1,000 live births (1996) 75.3.
Food (1995): daily per capita caloric intake 1,850 (vegetable products 94%, animal products 6%); 79% of FAO recommended minimum requirement.

Military

Total active duty personnel (1995): 800[17]. *Military expenditure as percentage of GNP:* n.a.

[1]Excludes Mayotte, a *collectivité territoriale* ("territorial collectivity") of France, unless otherwise indicated. [2]From Sept. 13, 1997. [3]Island names in Comorian (French), respectively. [4]Unilateral independence declared in early August 1997. [5]Formal secession as of approved referendum of Oct. 26, 1997, was not internationally recognized. [6]Includes Mayotte. [7]In the early 1990s, 20% of adult men had more than one wife. [8]Moroni only. [9]July average for government employees only. [10]Weights of consumer price index components for Moroni. [11]The wage labour force was very small in 1995; total of less than 7,000 including government employees, and less than 2,000 excluding them. [12]Not adequately defined. [13]Imports are f.o.b. in balance of trade and c.i.f. in commodities and trading partners. [14]Public education only. [15]1991–92. [16]Estimated figure. [17]Permanent presence of French military personnel in the Comoros to be expected per agreement ratified in December 1996.

Internet resources for further information:
- **Welcome to the World Wide Web site of the Comoro Islands (unofficial) http://www.ksu.edu/sasw/comoros/comoros.html**

Congo, Democratic Republic of the

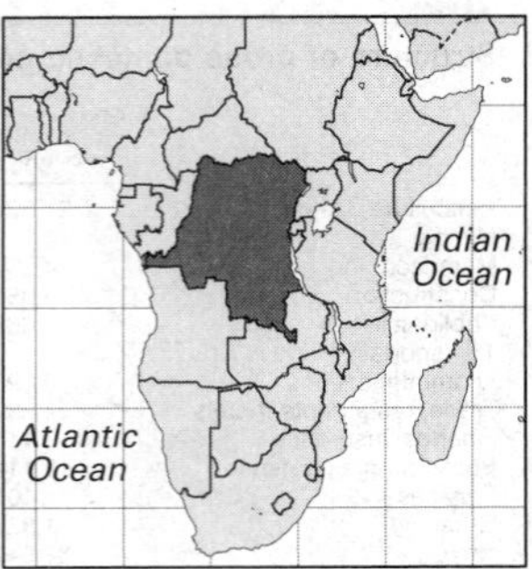

Official name: République Democratique du Congo (Democratic Republic of the Congo).
Form of government: revolutionary military regime[1].
Chief of state: President[1].
Capital: Kinshasa.
Official language: French.
Official religion: none.
Monetary unit: new zaïre (NZ)[2]; valuation (Oct. 3, 1997) 1 U.S.$ = NZ 137,500; 1 £ = NZ 221,650.

Area and population

Provinces	Capitals	area sq mi	area sq km	population 1994 estimate
Bandundu	Bandundu	114,154	295,658	4,907,000
Bas-Zaïre	Matadi	20,819	53,920	2,578,000
Equateur	Mbandaka	155,712	403,292	4,789,000
Haute-Zaïre	Kisangani	194,302	503,239	5,432,000
Kasai-Occidental	Kananga	59,746	154,742	3,117,000
Kasai-Oriental	Mbuji-Mayi	65,754	170,302	3,778,000
Kinshasa	—	3,848	9,965	4,655,000
Maniema	Kindu	51,062	132,250	1,048,000[3]
Nord-Kivu	Goma	22,967	59,483	3,546,000[3]
Shaba	Lubumbashi	191,845	496,877	5,602,000
Sud-Kivu	Bukavu	25,147	65,130	3,093,000[3]
TOTAL		905,354[4]	2,344,858	42,545,000[3]

Demography

Population (1997): 46,674,000.
Density (1997): persons per sq mi 51.6, persons per sq km 19.9.
Urban-rural (1995): urban 29.1%; rural 70.9%.
Sex distribution (1995): male 49.41%; female 50.59%.
Age breakdown (1995): under 15, 47.3%; 15–29, 25.9%; 30–44, 14.1%; 45–59, 8.1%; 60–74, 3.8%; 75 and over, 0.8%.
Population projection: (2000) 51,136,000; (2010) 68,876,000.
Ethnic composition (1983): Luba 18.0%; Kongo 16.1%; Mongo 13.5%; Rwanda 10.3%; Azande 6.1%; Bangi and Ngale 5.8%; Rundi 3.8%; Teke 2.7%; Boa 2.3%; Chokwe 1.8%; Lugbara 1.6%; Banda 1.4%; other 16.6%.
Religious affiliation (1995): Roman Catholic 41.0%; Protestant 32.0%; indigenous Christian 13.4%, of which Kimbanguist 13.0%; other Christian 0.8%; Muslim 1.2%; traditional beliefs and other 11.6%.
Major cities (1994): Kinshasa 4,655,313; Lubumbashi 851,381; Mbuji-Mayi 806,475; Kisangani 417,517; Kananga 393,030.

Vital statistics

Birth rate per 1,000 population (1990–95): 47.5 (world avg. 25.0).
Death rate per 1,000 population (1990–95): 14.5 (world avg. 9.3).
Natural increase rate per 1,000 population (1990–95): 33.0 (world avg. 15.7).
Total fertility rate (avg. births per childbearing woman; 1990–95): 6.7.
Life expectancy at birth (1990–95): male 50.4 years; female 53.7 years.
Major causes of death per 100,000 population: n.a.; however, major causes in the early 1990s included malaria, measles, diarrhea, acute respiratory infections, and AIDS.

National economy

Budget (1996). Revenue: U.S.$374,000,000 (customs duties and taxes on international trade 33.4%; taxes on mining production 11.2%; other revenues 55.3%). Expenditures: U.S.$1,163,000,000 (debt service 71.5%, of which external 62.7%, domestic 8.8%; wages and salaries 6.4%; foreign-financed capital expenditure 5.2%).
Public debt (external, outstanding; 1995): U.S.$9,621,000,000.
Land use (1994): forested 76.7%; meadows and pastures 6.6%; agricultural and under permanent cultivation 3.5%; other 13.2%.
Production (metric tons except as noted). Agriculture, forestry, fishing (1996): cassava 18,000,000, plantains 2,270,000, sugarcane 1,300,000, corn (maize) 1,100,000, peanuts (groundnuts) 580,000, rice 430,000, bananas 412,000, sweet potatoes 410,000, yams 315,000, mangoes 212,000, papayas 210,000, palm oil 181,000, oranges 156,000, pineapples 145,000, dry beans 125,000, seed cotton 77,000, palm kernels 72,000, coffee 60,000, natural rubber 11,000[5]; livestock (number of live animals) 4,172,000 goats, 1,480,000 cattle, 1,157,000 pigs, 1,043,000 sheep, 34,000,000 chickens; roundwood (1995) 48,747,000 cu m; fish catch (1995) 158,627. Mining and quarrying (1996): copper (metal content) 39,647; cobalt (metal content) 4,041; zinc (metal content) 3,162; gold 1,252 kg; diamonds 22,240,000 carats. Manufacturing (1995): iron and steel 965,000; cement 194,000; sugar 82,461; soap 46,773; tires 50,000 units; printed fabrics 15,728,000 sq m; matches 3,305,000 packs; shoes 1,600,000 pairs; beer 1,781,000 hectolitres; soft drinks 807,000 hectolitres. Energy production (consumption): electricity (kW-hr; 1994) 5,545,000,000 (4,523,-000,000); coal (metric tons; 1995) 14,400 ([1994] 136,000); crude petroleum (barrels; 1995) 10,087,000 ([1994] 2,782,000); petroleum products (metric tons; 1994) 350,000 (1,024,000); natural gas, none (none).
Household income and expenditure. Average household size (1982) 6.0; average annual income per household Z 1,200[2] (U.S.$209); sources of income: n.a.; expenditure (1985): food 61.7%, housing and energy 11.5%, clothing and footwear 9.7%, transportation 5.9%, furniture and utensils 4.9%.
Gross national product (1995): U.S.$5,313,000,000 (U.S.$120 per capita).

Structure of gross domestic product and labour force

	1995 in value Z '000,000[2]	1995 % of total value	1991 labour force	1991 % of labour force
Agriculture	21,248,000	58.0	9,021,000	65.1
Mining	1,591,000	4.3		
Manufacturing	2,365,000	6.5		
Construction	845,000	2.3	2,200,000	15.9
Public utilities	604,000	1.6		
Transp. and commun.	1,023,000	2.8		
Trade	6,114,000	16.7		
Pub. admin., defense	483,000	1.3	2,627,000	19.0
Finance and services	2,038,000	5.6		
Other	313,000	0.9		
TOTAL	36,622,000[4]	100.0	13,848,000	100.0

Population economically active (1991): total 13,848,000; activity rate 35.9% (participation rates [1987]: over age 10, 57.4%; female 40.8%).

Price and earnings indexes (1992 = 10)

	1992	1993	1994	1995	1996
Consumer price index	10	199	47,501	304,915	2,313,781
Earnings index	...	...	...	...	...

Tourism (1993): receipts U.S.$6,000,000; expenditures U.S.$16,000,000.

Foreign trade[6]

Balance of trade (current prices)

	1991	1992	1993	1994	1995	1996
U.S.$'000,000	+108	+403	+477	+643	+581	+708
% of total	3.4%	18.5%	26.3%	33.8%	25.0%	27.8%

Imports (1995): U.S.$870,200,000 (non-oil 94.0%; oil 6.0%). *Major import sources*[7, 8] (1995): Belgium-Luxembourg 15.0%; U.S. 6.7%; Germany 6.0%; France 4.2%; The Netherlands 4.0%; China 3.6%; Italy 3.3%.
Exports (1995): U.S.$1,451,500,000 (diamonds 17.2%, crude petroleum 11.4%, coffee 8.8%, copper 7.9%). *Major export destinations*[7] (1995): Belgium-Luxembourg 36.3%; U.S. 16.9%; Italy 9.7%; Japan 5.0%.

Transport and communications

Transport. Railroads (1994)[9]: length (1996) 5,138 km; passenger-km 29,000,-000; metric ton-km cargo 176,000,000. Roads (1995): total length 154,027 km (paved 2%). Vehicles (1995): passenger cars 762,000; trucks and buses 55,000. Air transport (1991)[10]: passenger-km 144,242,000; metric ton-km cargo 21,046,000; airports (1997) with scheduled flights 22.

Communications

Medium	date	unit	number	units per 1,000 persons
Daily newspapers	1995	circulation	120,000	2.7
Radio	1995	receivers	3,480,000	79.3
Television	1995	receivers	22,000	0.5
Telephones	1995	main lines	36,000	0.8
Cellular telephones	1995	subscribers	10,000	0.2
Facsimile machines	1995	units	5,000	0.1

Education and health

Educational attainment: n.a. *Literacy* (1995): percentage of total population age 15 and over literate 77.3%; males literate 86.6%; females literate 67.7%.

Education (1994–95)

	schools	teachers	students	student/teacher ratio
Primary (age 6–11)	14,885	121,054	5,417,506	44.8
Secondary (age 12–17)	4,276[11]	59,325[11]	640,298[12]	22.6[11]
Voc., teacher tr.	[11]	[11]	701,148[12]	[11]
Higher	...	3,873[13]	93,266	15.9[13]

Health: physicians (1990) 2,469 (1 per 15,584 persons); hospital beds (1986) 68,508 (1 per 487 persons); infant mortality rate (1990–95) 93.
Food (1995): daily per capita caloric intake 1,879 (vegetable products 97%, animal products 3%); 85% of FAO recommended minimum requirement.

Military

Total active duty personnel (1997): Former Zairean armed forces disbanded 1997; some 20,000–40,000 personnel of the Congo Liberation Army subsequently constituted the national armed forces. *Military expenditure as percentage of GNP* (1995): 0.3% (world 2.8%); per capita expenditure U.S.$0.

[1]The government of the Democratic Republic of the Congo was formed by proclamation on May 23, 1997, replacing the former Republic of Zaire. Head of state assumed title of president, but named no prime minister, as provided by 1994 constitutional law. [2]The new zaïre (NZ) replaced the (old) zaïre (Z) at a rate of 3,000,000 (old) zaïres to 1 NZ on Oct. 22, 1993. [3]Estimated to account for division of former Kivu province. [4]Detail does not add to total given because of rounding. [5]1995. [6]Imports c.i.f.; exports f.o.b. [7]DOT (Direction of Trade) valuation; the valuation as the sum of all known trading partners, by external analysis, rather than as the reported sum of the country's own trade data. [8]The DOT valuation is approximately 45% higher than values shown. [9]Traffic statistics are for services operated by the Zaire National Railways (SNCZ), which controls more than 90% of the country's total rail facility. [10]Air Zaire only; declared bankrupt 1995. [11]Secondary includes Voc., teacher tr. [12]1993–94. [13]1989.

Internet resources for further information:
- **Zaire—A Country Study**
http://lcweb2.loc.gov/frd/cs/zrtoc.html

Congo, Republic of the

Official name: République du Congo (Republic of the Congo).
Form of government: transitional[1] republic with a Parliament consisting (until October 1997) of two legislative chambers (Senate [60]; National Assembly [125]).
Chief of state: President[1].
Capital: Brazzaville.
Official language: French[2].
Official religion: none.
Monetary unit: 1 CFA franc (CFAF) = 100 centimes; valuation (Oct. 3, 1997) 1 U.S.$ = CFAF 592.29; 1 £ = CFAF 954.76.

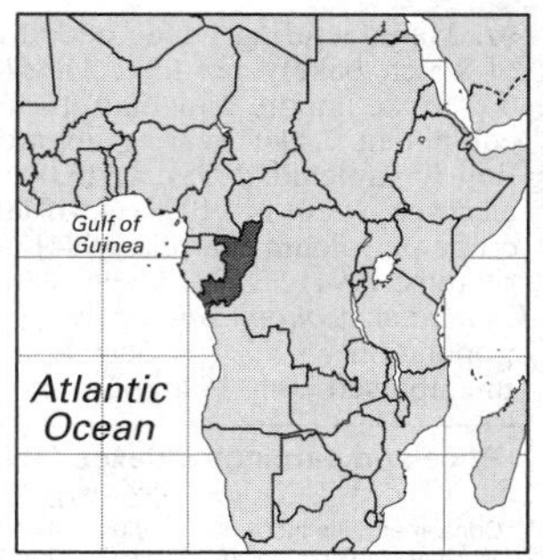

Area and population

Regions	Capitals	area sq mi	area sq km	population 1992 estimate
Bouenza	Madingou	4,733	12,258	177,357
Cuvette Est	Owando	28,900	74,850	151,839
Cuvette Ouest	Ewo			
Kouilou	Pointe-Noire	5,270	13,650	89,296
Lékoumou	Sibiti	8,089	20,950	74,420
Likouala	Impfondo	25,500	66,044	70,675
Niari	Loubomo	10,007	25,918	120,077
Plateaux	Djambala	14,826	38,400	119,722
Pool	Kinkala	13,110	33,955	182,671
Sangha	Ouesso	21,542	55,795	35,961
Communes				
Brazzaville	—	39	100	937,579
Loubomo	—	7	18	83,605
Mossendjo	—	2	5	16,405
Nkayi	—	3	8	42,465
Ouesso	—	2	5	16,171
Pointe-Noire	—	17	44	576,206
TOTAL		132,047	342,000	2,694,449

Demography

Population (1997): 2,583,000.
Density (1997): persons per sq mi 19.6, persons per sq km 7.6.
Urban-rural (1991): urban 41.1%; rural 58.9%.
Sex distribution (1995): male 48.92%; female 51.08%.
Age breakdown (1995): under 15, 45.6%; 15–29, 26.4%; 30–44, 14.6%; 45–59, 8.1%; 60–74, 4.2%; 75 and over, 1.0%.
Population projection: (2000) 2,750,000; (2010) 3,298,000.
Doubling time: 23 years.
Ethnic composition (1983): Kongo 51.5%; Teke 17.3%; Mboshi 11.5%; Mbete 4.8%; Punu 3.0%; Sango 2.7%; Maka 1.8%; Pygmy 1.5%; other 5.9%.
Religious affiliation (1997): Roman Catholic 40.9%; traditional beliefs 32.9%; Protestant 24.2%; Muslim 2.0%.
Major cities (1992): Brazzaville 937,579; Pointe-Noire 576,206; Loubomo 83,605; Nkayi 42,465; Mossendjo 16,405.

Vital statistics

Birth rate per 1,000 population (1990–95): 44.7 (world avg. 25.0).
Death rate per 1,000 population (1990–95): 14.9 (world avg. 9.3).
Natural increase rate per 1,000 population (1990–95): 29.8 (world avg. 15.7).
Total fertility rate (avg. births per childbearing woman; 1990–95): 6.3.
Life expectancy at birth (1990–95): male 48.9 years; female 53.8 years.
Major causes of morbidity and mortality in the early 1990s included malaria, acute respiratory infections, diarrhea, trauma, helminthiasis[3], and sexually transmitted diseases.

National economy

Budget (1996). Revenue: CFAF 353,750,000,000 (petroleum revenue 59.6%; nonpetroleum receipts 40.4%, of which [1995] customs duties 19.2%, income tax 12.6%). Expenditures: CFAF 380,500,000,000 (debt service 39.6%; salaries 27.9%; transfers and subsidies 8.7%, goods and services 7.1%).
Public debt (external, outstanding; 1995): U.S.$4,955,000,000.
Production (metric tons except as noted). Agriculture, forestry, fishing (1996): cassava 720,000, sugarcane 460,000, plantains 99,000, bananas 46,000, peanuts (groundnuts) 28,000, corn (maize) 26,000, avocados 26,000, yams 17,000, palm oil 17,000, pineapples 13,000, cacao beans 2,000, coffee 1,000; livestock (number of live animals) 312,000 goats, 114,000 sheep, 70,000 cattle; roundwood (1995) 3,834,000 cu m; fish catch (1995) 35,024. Mining and quarrying (1997): artisanal extraction of gold only. Manufacturing (1994): residual fuel oil 288,000; cement 87,400; distillate fuel oils 95,000; aviation gas 58,000; gasoline 58,000; kerosene 52,000; refined sugar 27,000; wheat flour 15,131[4]; dried, cured, or salted fish 4,000[5]; cigarettes 655,000,000 cartons; mechanical cultivators 294,404 units[5]; beer 507,000 hectolitres; soft drinks 220,000 hectolitres; cotton textiles 1,800,000 m[4]; veneer sheets 35,000 cu m[4]; footwear 300,000 pairs[6]. Energy production (consumption): electricity (kW-hr; 1994) 435,000,000 (547,000,000); crude petroleum (barrels; 1996) 80,300,000 ([1994] 8,040,000); petroleum products (metric tons; 1994) 570,000 (540,000); natural gas (cu m; 1994) 5,125,000 (5,125,000).
Household income and expenditure. Average household size (1984) 5.2; income per household: n.a.; sources of income: n.a.; expenditure (1977)[7, 8]: food, beverages, and tobacco 62.0%, housing 10.1%, transportation and recreation 8.6%, clothing and footwear 6.9%, fuel, energy, and water 5.7%, health and medical care 3.8%.
Gross national product (1995): U.S.$1,784,000,000 (U.S.$680 per capita).

Structure of gross domestic product and labour force

	1996 in value CFAF '000,000[9]	1996 % of total value	1991 labour force	1991 % of labour force
Agriculture, forestry, fishing	119,600	9.7	471,000	59.1
Petroleum	500,700	40.6		
Manufacturing, mining	94,300	7.6	101,000	12.7
Construction	18,000	1.5		
Public utilities	15,800	1.3		
Trade	137,700	11.2		
Transp. and commun.	90,800	7.4	225,000	28.2
Pub. admin., defense	124,000	10.0		
Services	80,200	6.5		
Other	53,600	4.3	—	—
TOTAL	1,234,700	100.0[10]	797,000	100.0

Population economically active (1992): total 886,000; activity rate of total population 37.4% (participation rates [1984]: ages 15–64, 54.0%; female 45.6%; unemployed[11] 2.3%).

Price and earnings indexes (1990 = 100)

	1990	1991	1992	1993	1994	1995
Consumer price index[7]	100.0	109.2	111.3	113.6	170.1	206.5
Earnings index	...	...	...	...	...	...

Land use (1994): forested 58.3%; meadows and pastures 29.3%; agricultural and under permanent cultivation 0.5%; other 11.9%.
Tourism (1995): receipts U.S.$4,000,000; expenditures U.S.$39,000,000.

Foreign trade

Balance of trade (current prices)

	1991	1992	1993	1994	1995	1996
CFAF '000,000,000	+169.6	+195.9	+175.3	+192.1	+261.8	+32.2
% of total	37.2%	45.8%	38.2%	22.0%	28.7%	2.2%

Imports (1995): CFAF 333,900,000,000 (1991[12]; machinery and transport equipment 38.0%, basic manufactures 27.4%, food and live animals 11.2%, chemicals and chemical products 8.4%, mineral fuels 3.2%, beverages and tobacco 2.3%). *Major import sources:* France 32.0%; U.S. 9.6%; The Netherlands 6.6%; Italy 4.4%; Belgium-Luxembourg 3.8%; Germany 3.3%.
Exports (1995): CFAF 624,100,000,000 (petroleum and petroleum products 84.6%, wood and wood products 8.4%, other 7.0%). *Major export destinations:* U.S. 22.6%; Italy 15.4%; The Netherlands 12.5%; France 9.2%.

Transport and communications

Transport. Railroads: (1995) length 795 km; passenger-km 302,000,000; metric ton-km cargo 267,000,000. Roads (1995): total length 12,760 km (paved 10%). Vehicles (1995): passenger cars 36,100; trucks and buses 15,600. Air transport (1996)[13]: passenger-km 224,736,000; metric ton-km cargo 16,420,000; airports (1997) with scheduled flights 10.

Communications

Medium	date	unit	number	units per 1,000 persons
Daily newspapers	1992	circulation	19,000	8.0
Radio	1995	receivers	808,000	312
Television	1995	receivers	44,000	17.0
Telephones	1995	main lines	21,400	8.1
Facsimile machines	1995	units	100	0.4

Education and health

Educational attainment (1984). Percentage of population age 25 and over having: no formal schooling 58.7%; primary education 21.4%; secondary education 16.9%; postsecondary 3.0%. *Literacy* (1995): total population age 15 and over literate 74.9%; males literate 83.1%; females literate 67.2%.

Education (1995–96)

	schools	teachers	students	student/ teacher ratio
Primary (age 6–13)	1,612	7,060	497,305	70.4
Secondary (age 14–18)	238[14]	5,710	189,381	33.2
Voc., teacher tr.	60[14]	1,463	25,269	17.3
Higher	12[14]	656[15]	13,806[15]	21.0[15]

Health: physicians (1990) 613 (1 per 3,595 persons); hospital beds (1989) 4,817 (1 per 446 persons); infant mortality rate per 1,000 live births (1990–95) 84.
Food (1995): daily per capita caloric intake 2,141 (vegetable products 93%, animal products 7%); 96% of FAO recommended minimum requirement.

Military

Total active duty personnel (1997): 10,000 (army 80.0%, navy 8.0%, air force 12.0%). *Military expenditure as percentage of GNP* (1995): 2.5% (world 2.8%); per capita expenditure U.S.$19.

[1]Transitional constitution proclaimed Nov. 3, 1997, vesting executive power in president and legislative power in a national transitional council. [2]"Functional" national languages are Lingala and Monokutuba. [3]Parasitic infestation by helminthic worms. [4]1993. [5]1992. [6]1990. [7]African households only; Brazzaville. [8]Cost-of-living components. [9]At current factor cost. [10]Detail does not add to total given because of rounding. [11]Previously employed only. [12]Based on c.i.f. valuation. [13]Represents 1/11 of the traffic of Air Afrique, which is operated by 11 African states. [14]1989. [15]1992.

Internet resources for further information:

- **Congo: Official Web of the Presidence of Congo http://www.amb-congo.fr/congo/_index.htm**

Costa Rica

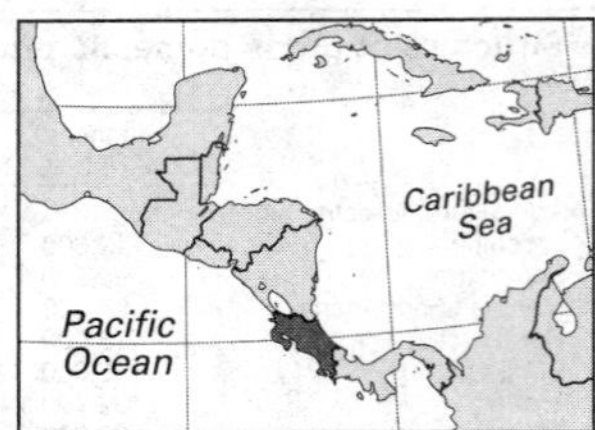

Official name: República de Costa Rica (Republic of Costa Rica).
Form of government: unitary multiparty republic with one legislative house (Legislative Assembly [57]).
Head of state and government: President.
Capital: San José.
Official language: Spanish.
Official religion: Roman Catholicism.
Monetary unit: 1 Costa Rican colón (₡) = 100 céntimos; valuation (Oct. 3, 1997) 1 U.S.$ = ₡238.30; 1 £ = ₡384.14.

Area and population		area		population
				1996[1] estimate
Provinces	**Capitals**	sq mi	sq km	
Alajuela	Alajuela	3,766	9,753	601,674
Cartago	Cartago	1,207	3,125	378,188
Guanacaste	Liberia	3,915	10,141	266,198
Heredia	Heredia	1,026	2,657	270,096
Limón	Limón	3,548	9,188	255,248
Puntarenas	Puntarenas	4,354	11,277	375,639
San José	San José	1,915	4,959	1,220,412
TOTAL		19,730[2]	51,100	3,367,455

Demography

Population (1997): 3,468,000.
Density (1997): persons per sq mi 175.8, persons per sq km 67.9.
Urban-rural (1995): urban 44.0%; rural 56.0%.
Sex distribution (1996): male 50.50%; female 49.50%.
Age breakdown (1996): under 15, 34.5%; 15–29, 27.0%; 30–44, 21.2%; 45–59, 10.4%; 60–74, 5.4%; 75 and over, 1.5%.
Population projection: (2000) 3,687,000; (2010) 4,401,000.
Doubling time: 36 years.
Ethnic composition (1993): white 87.0%; mestizo 7.0%; black/mulatto 3.0%; East Asian (mostly Chinese) 2.0%; Amerindian 1.0%.
Religious affiliation (1992): Roman Catholic 80.0%; Evangelical Protestant 15.0%; other 5.0%.
Major cities (1996): San José 324,011[3] (metropolitan area 968,367); Limón 57,216; Alajuela 49,568; San Isidro de El General 41,912; Desamparados 39,221[4].

Vital statistics

Birth rate per 1,000 population (1995): 23.8 (world avg. 25.0); legitimate 53.4%; illegitimate 46.6%.
Death rate per 1,000 population (1995): 4.2 (world avg. 9.3).
Natural increase rate per 1,000 population (1995): 19.6 (world avg. 15.7).
Total fertility rate (avg. births per childbearing woman; 1995): 2.8.
Marriage rate per 1,000 population (1995): 7.1.
Divorce rate per 1,000 population (1992): 1.1.
Life expectancy at birth (1990–95): male 71.9 years; female 77.5 years.
Major causes of death per 100,000 population (1994): diseases of the circulatory system 126.6, of which ischemic heart disease 59.8, cerebrovascular disease 29.6; malignant neoplasms (cancers) 80.0; diseases of the respiratory system 40.6; accidents 36.1; diseases of the digestive system 24.6.

National economy

Budget (1995). Revenue: ₡427,400,000,000 (tax revenue 85.5%, of which social security contributions 25.9%, sales tax 20.2%, import duties 11.5%, income taxes 11.0%; nontax revenue 14.1%). Expenditures: ₡472,200,000,000 (health 20.7%, social security and welfare 19.9%, interest payments 19.3%, education 16.8%, general public services 6.7%, public order 6.2%).
Public debt (external, outstanding; 1995): U.S.$3,132,000,000.
Gross national product (1995): U.S.$8,884,000,000 (U.S.$2,610 per capita).

Structure of gross domestic product and labour force	1995			
	in value ₡'000,000	% of total value	labour force	% of labour force
Agriculture, forestry, fishing	289	17.4	252,500	20.5
Mining }	308	18.6	2,500	0.2
Manufacturing }			192,100	15.6
Construction	38	2.3	73,900	6.0
Public utilities	56	3.4	12,300	1.0
Transp. and commun.	88	5.3	61,600	5.0
Trade, restaurants	335	20.2	225,400	18.3
Finance, real estate	202	12.2	50,500	4.1
Public administration	232	14.0 }	287,000	23.3
Services	109	6.6 }		
Other	—	—	73,900[5]	6.0
TOTAL	1,659[2]	100.0	1,231,600[2]	100.0

Production (metric tons except as noted). Agriculture, forestry, fishing (1996): sugarcane 3,620,000, bananas 2,100,000, pineapples 260,000, rice 186,400, oranges 165,000, coffee 142,600, cassava 125,000, plantains 105,000, palm oil 96,800, potatoes 63,900, other products include other tropical fruits, cut flowers, and ornamental plants grown for export; livestock (number of live animals) 1,585,000 cattle, 300,000 pigs, 16,500,000 chickens; roundwood (1995) 4,806,000 cu m; fish catch (1994) 20,849, of which shrimp 5,468. Mining and quarrying (1995): limestone (1994) 1,700,000; gold 16,000 troy oz. Manufacturing (value added in ₡'000,000; 1993): food products 51,902, of which bakery products 11,651; soft drinks and carbonated waters 11,044; malt liquors and malt 10,561; radio, television, and communications equipment 7,494; wearing apparel 6,943; plastic products 6,800. Construction (completed; 1995): 1,515,000 sq m. Energy production (consumption): electricity (kW-hr; 1995) 4,843,000,000 (4,342,000,000); coal, none (none); crude petroleum (barrels; 1994) none (4,757,000); petroleum products (metric tons; 1994) 538,000 (1,396,000); natural gas, none (none).
Population economically active (1994): total 1,187,005; activity rate of total population 38.7% (participation rates: ages 15–69, 59.7%; female 30.1%; unemployed [July 1996] 6.2%).

Price and earnings indexes (1990 = 100)	1990	1991	1992	1993	1994	1995	1996
Consumer price index	100.0	128.7	156.8	172.1	195.4	240.7	282.9
Monthly earnings index[6]	100.0	120.3	144.5	176.2	207.6	250.0	...

Tourism (1995): receipts U.S.$661,000,000; expenditures U.S.$332,000,000.
Household income and expenditure. Average household size (1996) 4.1[7]; average annual household income (1996) ₡1,247,867 (U.S.$5,980)[7]; sources of income (1987–88): wages and salaries 61.0%, self-employment 22.6%, transfers 9.6%, other 6.8%; expenditure (1987–88): food and beverages 39.1%, housing and energy 12.1%, transportation 11.6%, household furnishings 10.9%, other 26.3%.
Land use (1994): forested 30.8%; meadows and pastures 45.8%; agricultural and under permanent cultivation 10.4%; other 13.0%.

Foreign trade[8]

Balance of trade (current prices)	1991	1992	1993	1994	1995	1996
U.S.$'000,000	–97.5	–364.0	–611.6	–490.2	–236.8	–322.3
% of total	3.0%	9.0%	13.3%	9.9%	4.2%	5.5%

Imports (1995): U.S.$3,024,800,000 (raw materials for industry 37.2%; nondurable consumer goods 18.7%; capital goods for industry 14.4%; durable consumer goods 10.9%). *Major import sources:* U.S. 44.2%; Japan 5.5%; Venezuela 5.5%; Mexico 4.5%; other Central American countries 7.6%.
Exports (1995): U.S.$2,624,100,000 (bananas 23.7%; coffee 15.5%; textiles, clothing, and footwear 5.7%[9]; fish and shrimp 4.6%[10]; ornamental plants, leaves, and flowers 4.3%). *Major export destinations*[11]: U.S. 50%; Germany 8%; Nicaragua 3%; Canada 3%; United Kingdom 3%.

Transport and communications

Transport. Railroads (1995): route length 590 mi, 950 km[12]. Roads (1995): total length 22,121 mi, 35,600 km (paved 17%). Vehicles (1995): passenger cars 259,000; trucks and buses 132,940. Merchant marine (1992): vessels (100 gross tons and over) 24; total deadweight tonnage 8,368. Air transport (1995)[13]: passenger-mi 1,135,000,000, passenger-km 1,827,000,000; short-ton mi cargo 29,982,000, metric ton-km cargo 43,773,000; airports (1996) 14.

Communications				units
Medium	date	unit	number	per 1,000 persons
Daily newspapers	1994	circulation	333,000	102
Radio	1996	receivers	760,000	224
Television	1995	receivers	340,000	102
Telephones	1995	main lines	557,200	167
Cellular telephones	1995	subscribers	18,700	5.6
Facsimile machines	1995	units	2,200	0.1

Education and health

Educational attainment (1996)[7]. Percentage of population age 5 and over having: no formal schooling 11.7%; incomplete primary education 28.5%; complete primary 25.8%; incomplete secondary 16.0%; complete secondary 9.0%; higher 8.5%; other/unknown 0.5%. *Literacy* (1995): total population age 15 and over literate 2,118,000 (94.8%); males literate 1,054,000 (94.7%); females literate 1,064,000 (95.0%).

Education (1995)	schools	teachers	students	student/ teacher ratio
Primary (age 7–12)	3,544	15,806[14]	508,923	31.4[14]
Secondary (age 13–17)	285	...	207,231	...
Higher	29	...	79,959	...

Health (1996): physicians 4,422 (1 per 763 persons); hospital beds 5,961 (1 per 566 persons); infant mortality rate per 1,000 live births (1995) 13.3.
Food (1992): daily per capita caloric intake 2,883 (vegetable products 83%, animal products 17%); 129% of FAO recommended minimum requirement.

Military

Paramilitary expenditure as percentage of GNP (1995): 0.3% (world, n.a.); per capita expenditure U.S.$8. The army was officially abolished in 1948. Paramilitary (police) forces had 7,000 members in 1996.

[1]January 1. [2]Detail does not add to total given because of rounding. [3]Population of San José canton. [4]Within San José metropolitan area. [5]Includes 63,500 unemployed. [6]Data for July average of each year. [7]Based on a July 1996 survey. [8]Import figures are f.o.b. in balance of trade and c.i.f. for commodities and trading partners. [9]Based on 1993 data. [10]Based on 1994 data. [11]Estimated figures. [12]Rail service suspended in June 1995 because of a lack of funds. [13]Lacsa (Costa Rican Airlines) only. [14]1994.

Internet resources for further information:

- **Bienvenido a las paginas del Gobierno de Costa Rica http://www.casapres.go.cr/**

Côte d'Ivoire

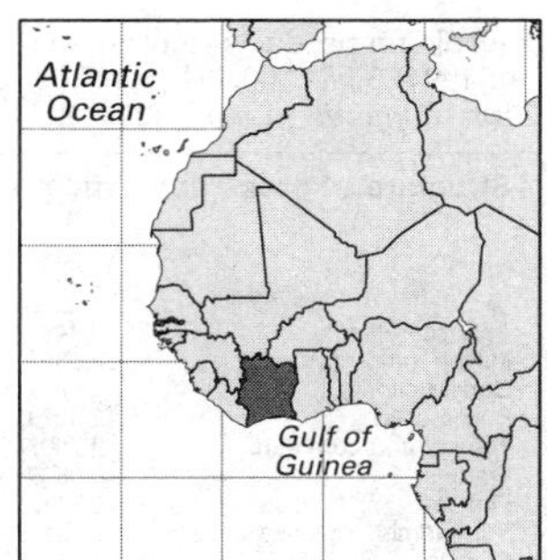

Official name: République de Côte d'Ivoire (Republic of Côte d'Ivoire [Ivory Coast][1]).
Form of government: multiparty republic with one legislative house (National Assembly [175]).
Chief of state: President.
Head of government: Prime Minister.
Capital: Abidjan (de facto; legislative).
Capital designate: Yamoussoukro (de jure; administrative).
Official language: French.
Official religion: none.
Monetary unit: 1 CFA franc (CFAF) = 100 centimes; valuation (Oct. 3, 1997) 1 U.S.$ = CFAF 592.29; 1 £ = CFAF 954.76.

Area and population (1988 census)

Department	area sq km	population	Department	area sq km	population
Abengourou	5,200	216,058	Guiglo	11,220	170,321
Abidjan	8,550	2,485,847	Issia	3,590	195,663
Aboisso	6,250	225,895	Katiola	9,420	130,635
Adzopé	5,230	237,870	Korhogo	12,500	390,229
Agboville	3,850	203,493	Lakota	2,730	116,771
Agnibilékrou	1,700	84,349	Man	4,990	294,724
Bangolo	2,060	79,979	Mankono	10,660	123,362
Béoumi	2,820	90,327	M'bahiakro	5,460	102,531
Biankouma	4,950	98,236	Odiénné	20,600	169,764
Bondoukou	10,040	174,251	Oumé	2,400	141,268
Bongouanou	5,570	224,958	Sakassou	1,880	59,362
Bouaflé	3,980	165,822	San-Pédro	6,900	170,669
Bouaké	4,700	450,594	Sassandra	5,190	108,090
Bouna	21,470	135,813	Séguéla	11,240	121,235
Boundiali	7,895	127,847	Sinfra	1,690	121,903
Dabakala	9,670	81,820	Soubré	8,270	310,790
Daloa	5,450	359,753	Tabou	5,440	58,147
Danané	4,600	222,839	Tanda	6,490	204,070
Daoukro	3,610	86,494	Tengréla	2,200	54,847
Dimbokro	4,920	141,968	Tiassalé	3,370	133,708
Divo	7,920	387,106	Touba	8,720	107,886
Duékoué	2,930	102,168	Toumodi	2,780	80,802
Ferkessedougou	17,728	172,893	Vavoua	6,160	168,292
Gagnoa	4,500	276,217	Yamoussoukro	6,160	281,442
Grand-Lahou	2,280	52,559	Zuénoula	2,830	114,027
			TOTAL	320,763[2]	10,815,694

Demography

Population (1997): 14,986,000.
Density (1997): persons per sq mi 121.0, persons per sq km 46.7.
Urban-rural (1995): urban 43.6%; rural 56.4%.
Sex distribution (1993): male 50.77%; female 49.23%.
Age breakdown (1993): under 15, 48.8%; 15–29, 24.7%; 30–44, 14.1%; 45–59, 8.1%; 60–64, 1.7%; 65 and over, 2.6%.
Ethnolinguistic composition (1988)[3]: Akan 41.8%; Voltaic 16.3%; Malinke 15.9%; Kru 14.6%; Southern Mande 10.7%; other 0.7%.
Religious affiliation (1988): Muslim 38.7%; Catholic 20.8%; animist 17.0%; atheist 13.4%; Protestant 5.3%, excluding Harrism (1.4%); other 3.4%.
Major cities (1988): Abidjan (1990) 2,168,000; Bouaké 329,850; Daloa 121,842.

Vital statistics

Birth rate per 1,000 population (1990–95): 49.9 (world avg. 25.0).
Death rate per 1,000 population (1990–95): 15.1 (world avg. 9.3).
Natural increase rate per 1,000 population (1990–95): 34.8 (world avg. 15.7).
Total fertility rate (avg. births per childbearing woman; 1990–95): 7.4.
Life expectancy at birth (1990–95): male 49.7 years; female 52.4 years.
Major causes of death per 100,000 population: n.a.; however, AIDS was a major cause of both morbidity and mortality among adults in the mid-1990s.

National economy

Budget (1996). Revenue: CFAF 1,272,400,000,000 (current revenues 81.8%, principally (1995) import taxes and duties 22.8%, taxes on income, goods, and services 18.3%, export taxes 16.1%). Expenditures: CFAF 1,062,900,000,000 (wages and salaries 36.7%, debt service 30.1%; other 28.6%).
Production (metric tons except as noted). Agriculture, forestry, fishing (1996): yams 2,824,000[4], cassava 1,564,000[4], plantains 1,300,000[4], sugarcane 1,236,000[4], paddy rice 1,223,000[4], cacao beans 1,254,480, corn (maize) 552,000, palm oil 265,693, bananas 258,026, cotton seed 217,216; coconuts 213,000, coffee 195,981, rubber 79,299; livestock (number of live animals) 1,314,000 sheep, 1,277,000 cattle, 1,027,000 goats; roundwood (1995) 14,290,000 cu m; fish catch (1995) 70,526. Mining and quarrying (1994): gold 1,500 kg; diamonds 15,000 carats. Manufacturing (value added in CFAF '000,000,000; 1993): meat products 717, chemicals 357, cocoa and chocolate 275, leather products 275, fabricated metal products 191, photographic and optical goods 129. Energy production (consumption): electricity (kW-hr; 1995) 2,915,000,000 (2,140,000,000); crude petroleum (barrels; 1994) 2,441,000 (24,623,000); petroleum products (metric tons; 1994) 2,320,000 (2,306,000).
Household income and expenditure. Average household size (1988) 5.4; average annual income per household (1980) CFAF 500,000 (U.S.$2,200); sources of income: self-employment 49.9%, wages 44.9%, transfers 5.2%; expenditure (1992–93)[5]: food 48.0%, transportation 12.2%, clothing 10.1%, energy and water 8.5%, housing 7.8%, household equipment 3.4%.
Gross national product (1995): U.S.$9,248,000,000 (U.S.$660 per capita).

Structure of gross domestic product and labour force

	1995 in value CFAF '000,000,000	1995 % of total value	1994 labour force	1994 % of labour force
Agriculture	1,572.9	31.3	2,886,000	51.1
Manufacturing and mining	876.8	17.4	650,000	11.5
Construction and public utilities	99.1	2.0		
Transp. and commun.	362.9	7.2	2,112,000	37.4
Trade	1,024.6	20.4		
Public admin., defense	442.2	8.8		
Services	395.9	7.9		
Other (customs receipts)	257.0	5.1		
TOTAL	5,031.4	100.0[6]	5,648,000	100.0

Public debt (external, outstanding; 1995): U.S.$11,899,000,000.
Population economically active (1994): total 5,648,000; activity rate of total population 41.1% (participation rates: over age 10, 64.3%; female 33.8%).

Price and earnings indexes (1990 = 100)

	1990	1991	1992	1993	1994	1995	1996
Consumer price index	100.0	101.7	106.0	108.3	136.5	156.0	159.9
Hourly earnings index[7]	100.0	100.0	100.0	100.0	100.0	110.0	110.0

Tourism (1995): receipts U.S.$72,000,000; expenditures U.S.$159,000,000.

Foreign trade

Balance of trade (current prices)

	1990	1991	1992	1993	1994	1995
U.S.$'000,000	+1,297.6	+880.1	+961.6	+734.5	+1,260.9	+1,450.3
% of total	27.6%	19.4%	19.5%	17.1%	28.2%	23.1%

Imports (1995): CFAF 1,379,200,000,000 (food and food products 18.9%, crude and refined petroleum 17.0%, transport equipment 9.0%, plastics 4.7%, paper and paper products 4.7%, pharmaceuticals 4.5%, electrical equipment 4.1%). *Major import sources:* France 32.0%; Nigeria 19.6%; U.S. 5.9%; Ghana 4.0%; Germany 3.9%; Italy 3.8%.
Exports (1995): CFAF 1,931,800,000,000 (cocoa beans and products 33.5%, coffee and coffee products 11.0%, wood and wood products 9.3%, petroleum products 9.2%, fish products 6.5%, cotton and cotton cloth 4.4%). *Major export destinations:* France 18.1%; The Netherlands 8.3%; Germany 7.8%; Italy 7.6%; Mali 5.9%; Burkina Faso 5.0%.

Transport and communications

Transport. Railroads (1995): route length 639 km; passenger-km 129,000,000; metric ton-km cargo 58,000,000. Roads (1995): total length 50,160 km (paved 9.6%). Vehicles (1995): passenger cars 271,000; trucks and buses 150,000. Air transport (1996)[8]: passenger-km 224,736,000; metric ton-km cargo 16,420,000; airports (1997) 5.

Communications

Medium	date	unit	number	units per 1,000 persons
Daily newspapers	1995	circulation	198,000	13.9
Radio	1995	receivers	1,600,000	112
Television	1995	receivers	810,000	56.8
Telephones	1995	main lines	115,800	8.1

Education and health

Educational attainment (1988). Percentage of population age 6 and over having: no formal schooling 60.0%; Koranic school 3.6%; primary education 24.8%; secondary 10.7%; higher 0.9%. *Literacy* (1995): percentage of population age 15 and over literate 40.1%; males 49.9%; females 30.0%.

Education (1994–95)

	schools	teachers	students	student/ teacher ratio
Primary (age 7–12)	7,185	36,058	1,609,929	44.6
Secondary (age 13–19)[9]	147	9,505	463,810	48.8
Vocational	...	1,424	11,037	7.8
Higher[10]	...	...	51,215	...

Health: physicians (1990) 1,020 (1 per 11,745 persons); hospital beds (1993) 7,928 (1 per 1,698 persons); infant mortality rate (1990–95) 92.0.
Food (1995): daily per capita caloric intake 2,517 (vegetable products 96%, animal products 4%); 109% of FAO recommended minimum requirement.

Military

Total active duty personnel (1997): 8,400 (army 81.0%, navy 10.7%, air force 8.3%). *Military expenditure as percentage of GNP* (1995): 1.1% (world avg. 2.8%); per capita expenditure U.S.$7.

[1]Since 1986, Côte d'Ivoire has requested that the French form of the country's name be used as the official protocol version in all languages. [2]Total area per more recent survey is 322,463 sq km; breakdown of that area by department is not available. [3]"Ivoirian" nationals only, representing about 65% of the de facto population. [4]1996. [5]Weights of consumer price index components for a worker's family living in the capital city. [6]Detail does not add to total given because of rounding. [7]January 1; index refers to the S.M.I.G. (*salaire minimum interprofessionel garanti*), a form of minimum professional wage. [8]Represents 1/11 share of traffic of Air Afrique, which is operated by 11 West African states. [9]Data exclude 208 private schools, with (1992) 107,096 students. [10]1993–94.

Internet resources for further information:

- **Côte d'Ivoire—A Country Study**
http://lcweb2.loc.gov/frd/cs/citoc.html

Croatia

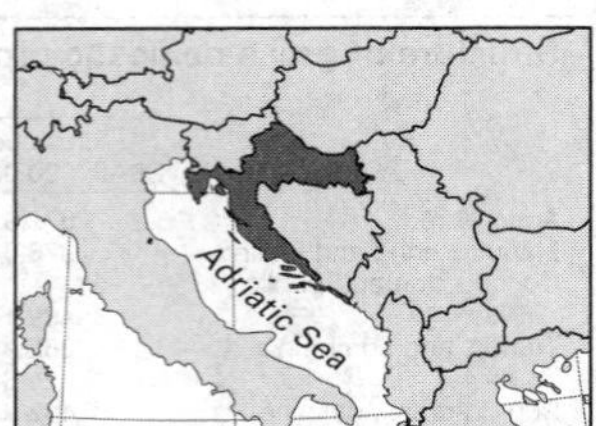

Official name: Republika Hrvatska (Republic of Croatia).
Form of government: multiparty republic with a two-chambered legislature (House of Zupanije[1] [68[2]]; House of Representatives [127[3]]).
Head of state: President.
Head of government: Prime Minister.
Capital: Zagreb.
Official language: Croatian.
Official religion: none.
Monetary unit: 1 kuna (plural kune)[4] = 100 lipa; valuation (Oct. 3, 1997) 1 U.S.$ = 6.21 kune; 1 £ = 10.01 kune.

Area and population (1991 census)

City	Capitals	area sq mi	area sq km	population 1991 census
Zagreb	—	497	1,288	867,717
County				
Bjelovar-Bilogora	Bjelovar	1,019	2,640	144,042
Dubrovnik-Neretva	Dubrovnikvn	689	1,784	126,329
Istria	Pazin	1,087	2,815	204,346
Karlovac	Karlovac	1,278	3,311	174,105
Koprivnica-Križevci	Koprimica	688	1,783	129,907
Krapina-Zagorje	Krapina	477	1,235	149,534
Lika-Senj	Gospić	1,447	3,748	71,215
Međimurje	Čakovec	282	730	119,866
Osijek-Baranja	Osijek	1,397	3,619	331,979
Požega-Slavonija	Požega	917	2,374	134,548
Primorje-Gorski Kotar	Rijeka	1,381	3,578	323,130
Šibenik	Šibenik	722	1,871	109,171
Sisak-Moslavina	Sisak	1,976	5,117	287,002
Slavonski Brod-Posavina	Slavonski Brod	782	2,026	174,998
Split-Dalmatia	Split	1,745	4,520	474,019
Varaždin	Varaždin	478	1,238	187,343
Virovitica-Podravina	Virovitica	798	2,068	104,625
Vukovar-Srijem	Vukovar	943	2,442	231,241
Zadar-Knin	Zadar	2,453	6,352	272,003
Zagreb	Zagreb	800	2,071	167,145
TOTAL		21,359	55,322	4,784,265

Demography

Population (1997): 4,774,000.
Density (1997): persons per sq mi 223.5, persons per sq km 86.3.
Urban-rural (1991): urban 54.2%; rural 45.8%.
Sex distribution (1991): male 48.50%; female 51.50%.
Age breakdown (1991): under 15, 19.4%; 15–29, 20.7%; 30–44, 22.7%; 45–59, 18.3%; 60–74, 12.9%; 75 and over, 4.5%; not stated 1.5%.
Population projection: (2000) 4,771,000; (2010) 4,761,000.
Doubling time: not applicable; population is declining.
Ethnic composition (1991): Croat 78.1%; Serb 12.1%; Muslims 0.9%; Hungarians 0.5%; Slovene 0.5%; other 7.9%.
Religious affiliation (1997): Roman Catholic 72.1%; Eastern Orthodox 14.1%; Muslim 1.3%; other 12.5%.
Major cities (1991): Zagreb 867,717; Split 200,459; Rijeka 167,964.

Vital statistics

Birth rate per 1,000 population (1995): 10.5 (world avg. 25.0); (1994) legitimate 92.4%; illegitimate 7.6%.
Death rate per 1,000 population (1995): 10.6 (world avg. 9.3).
Natural increase rate per 1,000 population (1995): −0.1 (world avg. 15.7).
Total fertility rate (avg. births per childbearing woman; 1993): 1.5.
Marriage rate per 1,000 population (1994): 5.3.
Divorce rate per 1,000 population (1994): 1.0.
Life expectancy at birth (1991): male 68.6 years; female 76.0 years.
Major causes of death per 100,000 population (1993): diseases of the circulatory system 533.2; cancers 218.0; accidents, violence, and poisoning 95.0; diseases of the digestive system 49.7; diseases of the respiratory system 45.3.

National economy

Budget (1996). Revenue: 31,085,318,000 kune[4] (sales tax 63.2%, customs and import fees 15.6%, income tax 14.2%). Expenditures: 31,621,691,000 kune[4] (defense 36.6%, social insurance 13.8%, education 11.7%).
Land use (1994): forest 37.1%; pasture 19.3%; agriculture 21.6%; other 22.0%.
Population economically active (1991): total 2,040,000; activity rate 42.6% (participation rates: ages 15–64, 57.2%; female 42.8%; unemployed 11.2%).

Price and earnings indexes (1990 = 100)

	1991	1992	1993	1994	1995	1996
Consumer price index	100.0	735.3	11,663	24,162	25,148	25,879
Annual earnings index	100.0	414.9	6,659	15,529	22,623	25,276

Production (metric tons except as noted). Agriculture, forestry, fishing (1996): corn (maize) 1,883,000, sugar beets 906,000, wheat 741,000, potatoes 665,000, grapes 373,000, barley 88,000, plums 38,215; livestock (number of live animals) 1,196,000 pigs, 462,000 cattle, 427,000 sheep; roundwood 2,912,000 cu m; fish catch (1995) 31,533. Mining and quarrying (1995): lime 150,000; gypsum 50,000. Manufacturing (value added in U.S.$'000,000; 1996): food products 895; transport equipment 425; electrical machinery 362; textiles 285; wearing apparel 260. Construction (value in kune; 1994): residential 1,966,315; nonresidential 4,590,289. Energy production (consumption): electricity (kW-hr; 1994) 8,275,000,000 (11,840,000,000); coal (metric tons; 1994) 96,000 (460,000); crude petroleum (barrels; 1994) 11,559,000 (37,280,000); petroleum products (metric tons; 1994) 4,462,000 (3,148,000); natural gas (cu m; 1994) 3,054,000,000 (1,427,000,000).
Gross domestic product (1995): U.S.$15,508,000,000 (U.S.$3,250 per capita).

Structure of gross domestic product and labour force

	1994 in value '000,000 kune[4]	1994 % of total value	1991 labour force	1991 % of labour force
Agriculture	9,248.8	11.0	265,000	13.0
Mining, manufacturing	23,538.1	28.0	613,000	30.0
Construction	1,792.0	2.1	98,000	4.8
Public utilities	12,927.0	15.4	32,700	1.6
Transp. and commun.	3,750.9	4.5	120,000	5.9
Trade	10,057.3	12.0	163,000	8.0
Finance	6,741.0	8.0	60,400	3.0
Pub. admin., defense	12,541.6	15.0	315,000	15.4
Services	3,327.8	4.0	80,700	4.0
Other			292,200[5]	14.3[5]
TOTAL	83,924.5	100.0	2,040,000	100.0

Household income and expenditure. Average household size (1991) 3.1; income per household (1990) Din 165,813[4] (U.S.$14,650); sources (1990): self-employment 40.8%, wages 40.2%, transfers 12.1%, other 6.9%; expenditure (1988): food 34.2%, transportation 9.3%, clothing 8.6%, housing 8.3%, energy 7.6%, drink and tobacco 5.1%, durable goods 4.5%, health care 4.3%.

Foreign trade[6]

Balance of trade (current prices)[7]

	1990	1991	1992	1993	1994	1995
'000,000 kune[4]	−11,333	−7,160	−3,877	−1,636	−3,604	−5,962
% of total	13.7%	7.8%	2.2%	5.5%	10.0%	18.7%

Imports (1996): U.S.$7,787,000,000 (1994; machinery and transport equipment 25.9%; products classified by constituent material 15.2%; miscellaneous ready-made products 14.6%; mineral fuels, lubricants, and similar products 11.8%; chemical products 10.4%; food and live animals 9.5%; raw materials except fuel 2.9%; beverages and tobacco 1.2%). *Major import sources:* Germany 20.6%; Italy 18.3%; Slovenia 9.9%; Austria 7.7%.
Exports (1996): U.S.$4,512,000,000 (1994; miscellaneous ready-made products 29.0%; machinery and transport equipment 17.5%; products classified according to constituent material 15.2%; chemical products 12.9%; mineral fuels, lubricants, and similar products 9.3%; food and live animals 9.3%; raw materials except fuel 5.0%; beverages and tobacco 1.6%). *Major export destinations:* Italy 21.0%; Germany 18.6%; Slovenia 13.5%; Bosnia 12.2%.

Transport and communications

Transport. Railroads (1994): length 2,699 km; passenger-km 962,000,000; metric ton-km cargo 1,563,000,000. Roads (1995): total length 26,929 km (paved 82%). Vehicles (1994): passenger cars 698,391; trucks and buses 53,860. Merchant marine (1994): cargo ships 155. Air transport (1997): passenger-km 563,000,000; metric ton-km cargo 2,268,000; airports (1997) 4.

Communications

Medium	date	unit	number	units per 1,000 persons
Daily newspapers	1995	circulation	2,600,000	575
Radio	1996	receivers	1,100,000	230
Television	1995	receivers	1,100,000	230
Telephones	1995	main lines	1,287,000	269
Cellular telephones	1995	subscribers	34,000	7.1
Facsimile machines	1995	units	38,000	8.0
Personal computers	1995	units	100,000	21

Education and health

Educational attainment (1991). Percentage of population age 15 and over having: no schooling or unknown 10.1%; less than full primary education 21.2%; primary 23.4%; secondary 36.0%; postsecondary and higher 9.3%.
Literacy (1991): total population age 15 and over literate 96.7%; males 98.8%; females 94.8%.

Education (1994–95)

	schools	teachers	students	student/ teacher ratio
Primary (age 7–14)	1,928	24,194	431,795	17.8
Secondary (age 15–18)	482	15,269	196,740	12.9
Voc., teacher tr.	3	79	2,660	33.7
Higher	61	5,814	77,525	13.3

Health (1994): physicians 9,138 (1 per 524 persons); hospital beds 28,230 (1 per 169 persons); (1995) infant mortality rate per 1,000 live births 8.9.

Military

Total active duty personnel (1997): 58,000 (army 86.2%, navy 5.2%, air force and air defense 8.6%). *Military expenditure as percentage of GNP* (1995): 5.0% (world 2.8%).

[1]Translated as communes or municipalities. [2]Includes 5 nonelective seats. [3]Includes 12 seats reserved for Croatians abroad. [4]On Jan. 1, 1990, the Yugoslav new dinar (Din), equal to 10,000 Yugoslav old dinars (Din), was introduced. On Dec. 23, 1991, the Croatian dinar (HrD) was introduced at parity with the Yugoslav new dinar, which it replaced as Croatia's official currency. On May 30, 1994, the kuna, equal to 1,000 Croatian dinars, was introduced. [5]Includes unemployed and private sector. [6]Import figures are f.o.b. in balance of trade and c.i.f. for commodities and trading partners. [7]Balance of trade recalculated to reflect currency changes.

Internet resources for further information:
- **Central Bureau of Statistics http://www.dzs.hr/index-eng.html**

Cuba

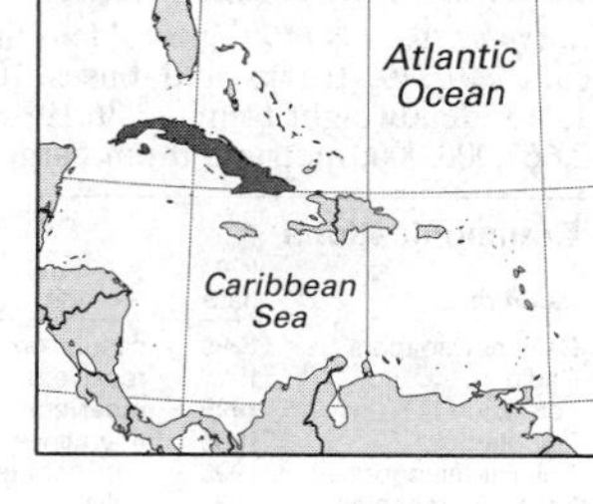

Official name: República de Cuba (Republic of Cuba).
Form of government: unitary socialist republic with one legislative house (National Assembly of the People's Power [589]).
Head of state and government: President.
Capital: Havana.
Official language: Spanish.
Official religion: none.
Monetary unit: 1 Cuban peso (CUP) = 100 centavos; valuation (Oct. 3, 1997) 1 U.S.$ = 1.00 CUP[1]; 1 £ = 1.61 CUP.

Area and population

		area		population
Provinces	**Capitals**	sq mi	sq km	1990[2] estimate
Camagüey	Camagüey	6,174	15,990	744,744
Ciego de Avila	Ciego de Avila	2,668	6,910	367,489
Cienfuegos	Cienfuegos	1,613	4,178	366,531
Ciudad de la Habana[3]	—	281	727	2,107,557
Granma	Bayamo	3,232	8,372	793,868
Guantánamo	Guantánamo	2,388	6,186	499,182
Holguín	Holguín	3,591	9,301	997,735
La Habana[4]	Havana	2,213	5,731	647,280
Las Tunas	Las Tunas	2,544	6,589	495,133
Matanzas	Matanzas	4,625	11,978	612,268
Pinar del Río	Pinar del Río	4,218	10,925	694,306
Sancti Spíritus	Sancti Spíritus	2,604	6,744	430,662
Santiago de Cuba	Santiago de Cuba	2,382	6,170	995,370
Villa Clara	Santa Clara	3,345	8,662	810,249
Special municipality				
Isla de la Juventud	Nueva Gerona	926	2,398	73,319
TOTAL		42,804	110,861	10,635,693[5]

Demography

Population (1997): 11,190,000.
Density (1997): persons per sq mi 261.4, persons per sq km 100.9.
Urban-rural (1995): urban 76.0%; rural 24.0%.
Sex distribution (1994): male 50.20%; female 49.80%.
Age breakdown (1994): under 15, 22.8%; 15–29, 28.0%; 30–44, 21.8%; 45–59, 15.2%; 60–74, 8.4%; 75 and over, 3.8%.
Population projection: (2000) 11,385,000; (2010) 11,911,000.
Ethnic composition (1994): mixed 51.0%; white 37.0%; black 11.0%; other 1.0%.
Religious affiliation (1997): nonreligious 57.9%; Roman Catholic 39.5%; Protestant 2.4%; other 0.2%.
Major cities (1993): Havana 2,175,995; Santiago de Cuba 440,084; Camagüey 293,961; Holguín 242,085; Guantánamo 207,796.

Vital statistics

Birth rate per 1,000 population (1997): 13.2 (world avg. 25.0).
Death rate per 1,000 population (1997): 7.4 (world avg. 9.3).
Natural increase rate per 1,000 population (1997): 5.8 (world avg. 15.7).
Total fertility rate (avg. births per childbearing woman; 1997): 1.5.
Marriage rate per 1,000 population (1992): 17.7.
Divorce rate per 1,000 population (1993): 6.0.
Life expectancy at birth (1997): male 72.8 years; female 77.7 years.
Major causes of death per 100,000 population (1992): heart disease 173.4; malignant neoplasms (cancers) 115.5; cerebrovascular disease 60.9; accidents 45.8; diseases of the blood vessels 23.5; influenza and pneumonia 22.7.

National economy

Budget (1990). Revenue: CUP 12,463,200,000. Expenditures: CUP 14,448,400,000 (capital investment 37.7%; education and public health 20.4%; social, cultural, and scientific activities 17.3%; defense, internal security 9.5%).
Production (metric tons except as noted). Agriculture, forestry, fishing (1996): sugarcane 40,000,000, potatoes 364,000, oranges and tangerines 291,000, grapefruit 261,000, bananas and plantains 260,000, cassava 250,000, rice 223,000; livestock (number of live animals) 4,650,000 cattle, 1,500,000 pigs, 19,000,000 chickens; roundwood (1995) 3,152,000 cu m; fish catch (1995) 93,435. Mining and quarrying (1996): nickel 50,000; chromite 30,000. Manufacturing (value added in U.S.$'000,000; 1990): tobacco products 2,629; food products 1,033; beverages 358; chemical products 354; transport equipment 225; nonelectrical machinery 176. Construction (gross value of construction in CUP '000,000; 1989): residential 227; nonresidential 872. Energy production (consumption): electricity (kW-hr; 1996) 8,654,000,000 (8,654,000,000); coal (metric tons; 1994) none (153,000); crude petroleum (barrels; 1994) 6,552,000 (38,326,000); petroleum products (metric tons; 1994) 4,456,000 (7,905,000); natural gas (cu m; 1994) 39,004,000 (39,004,000).
Public debt (external, outstanding; 1996): U.S.$12,000,000,000.
Household income and expenditure. Average household size (1990) 3.7; average annual income per household (1982) CUP 3,680 (U.S.$4,330); sources of income (1982): wages and salaries 57.3%, bonuses and other payments 42.7%; personal consumption (1989): food 26.7%, other retail purchases 60.5%, transportation services 5.4%, energy 2.7%, value of self-produced and consumed food 1.5%, household repairs 1.3%, other 1.9%.
Population economically active (1988): total 4,570,236; activity rate of total population 43.7% (participation rates: over age 15, 56.9%; female 36.1%; unemployed 6.0%).

Price and earnings indexes (1985 = 100)

	1983	1984	1985	1986	1987	1988	1989
Implicit consumer price deflator index	94.9	98.0	100.0	101.4	102.8	103.1	...
Monthly earnings index[6]	95.9	99.0	100.0	100.1	98.1	99.6	100.0

Tourism: receipts from visitors (1995) U.S.$1,100,000,000; expenditures by nationals abroad (1990) U.S.$48,000,000.
Gross national product (1991): U.S.$17,000,000,000 (U.S.$1,580 per capita).

Structure of gross domestic product and labour force

	1994		1989	
	in value[7] CUP '000,000	% of total value	labour force[6]	% of labour force
Agriculture	879.4	6.8	721,100	20.4
Mining	97.5	0.8	767,500	21.8
Manufacturing	3,340.6	26.0		
Public utilities	350.0	2.7		
Construction	383.9	3.0	344,300	9.8
Transp. and commun.	708.7	5.5	235,900	6.7
Finance, insurance	492.4	3.8	21,700	0.6
Trade	2,935.2	22.8	395,300	11.2
Public administration	—	—	151,700	4.3
Services	3,680.6	28.6	835,700	23.7
Other	—	—	53,400	1.5
TOTAL	12,868.3[8]	100.0	3,526,600	100.0

Land use (1994): forested 23.7%; meadows and pastures 27.0%; agricultural and under permanent cultivation 30.7%; other 18.6%.

Foreign trade[9]

Balance of trade (current prices)

	1991	1992	1993	1994	1995	1996
U.S.$'000,000	−1,332	−412	−551	−797	−1,166	−1,179
% of total	38.4%	15.1%	19.2%	24.4%	28.3%	24.4%

Imports (1996): U.S.$3,010,000,000 (1992; mineral fuels and lubricants 39.4%, food and live animals 25.4%, machinery and transport equipment 15.8%, chemicals 6.9%, basic manufactures 6.6%, inedible crude materials 3.2%). *Major import sources:* Spain 17.0%; Russia 16.9%; Mexico 11.6%; France 7.2%; Canada 6.2%; Argentina 4.5%.
Exports (1996): U.S.$1,831,000,000 (1992; sugar 63.4%, minerals and concentrates 10.6%, fish products 5.9%, raw tobacco and tobacco products 4.6%, citrus and other agricultural products 3.4%). *Major export destinations:* Russia 20.2%; Canada 16.1%; The Netherlands 11.1%; China 6.8%.

Transport and communications

Transport. Railroads (1994): length 2,987 mi, 4,807 km; passenger-km 2,347,000,000; metric ton-km cargo 645,000,000. Roads (1986): total length 28,928 mi, 46,555 km (paved 27%). Vehicles (1988): passenger cars 241,300; trucks and buses 208,400. Air transport (1996): passenger-km 3,450,000,000; metric ton-km cargo 56,300,000; airports with scheduled flights (1997) 14.

Communications

Medium	date	unit	number	units per 1,000 persons
Daily newspapers	1995	circulation	1,315,000	122
Radio	1995	receivers	3,608,000	327
Television	1995	receivers	2,200,000	200
Telephones	1995	main lines	353,200	32
Cellular telephones	1995	subscribers	1,900	0.2
Facsimile machines	1995	units	400	0.1

Education and health

Educational attainment (1981). Percentage of population age 25 and over having: no formal schooling or some primary education 39.6%; completed primary 26.6%; secondary 29.6%; higher 4.2%. *Literacy* (1995 est.): total population age 15 and over literate 95.7%; males literate 96.2%; females literate 95.3%.

Education (1995–96)

	schools	teachers	students	student/ teacher ratio
Primary (age 6–11)	9,862	90,565	1,074,153	11.9
Secondary (age 12–17)	2,175[10]	46,772	460,348	9.8
Voc., teacher tr.	618[10]	27,267	244,253	9.0
Higher	35[10]	22,967	122,346	5.3

Health (1992): physicians 46,860 (1 per 231 persons); hospital beds 80,684 (1 per 134 persons); infant mortality rate per 1,000 live births (1997) 7.3.
Food (1995): daily per capita caloric intake 2,291 (vegetable products 84%, animal products 16%); 99% of FAO recommended minimum requirement.

Military

Total active duty personnel (1997): 60,000 (army 75.0%, navy 8.3%, air force 16.7%). *Military expenditure as percentage of GDP* (1995): 1.6% (world 2.8%); per capita expenditure: U.S.$32.

[1]Official rate; the black-market rate is about 23 pesos (CUP) to 1 U.S.$ at year–end 1997. [2]January 1. [3]Province coextensive with the city of Havana. [4]Province bordering the city of Havana on the east, south, and west. [5]The 1993 census total was 10,900,000; detail, n.a. [6]State sector only; excludes military and unemployed. [7]At constant 1981 prices. [8]At factor cost. [9]Imports c.i.f.; exports f.o.b. [10]1989–90.

Internet resources for further information:
- **CubaNet http://www.cubanet.org/**

Cyprus

Island of Cyprus

Area: 3,572 sq mi, 9,251 sq km.
Population (1997): 860,000[1].

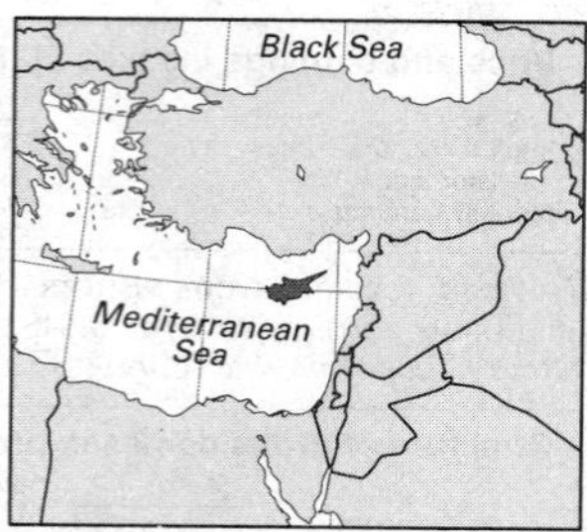

Two de facto states currently exist on the island of Cyprus: the Republic of Cyprus (ROC), predominantly Greek in character, occupying the southern two-thirds of the island, which is the original and still the internationally recognized de jure government of the whole island; and the Turkish Republic of Northern Cyprus (TRNC), proclaimed unilaterally Nov. 15, 1983, on territory originally secured for the Turkish Cypriot population by the July 20, 1974, intervention of Turkey. Only Turkey recognizes the TRNC, and the two ethnic communities have failed to reestablish a single state. Provision of separate data below does not imply recognition of either state's claims but is necessitated by the continuing lack of unified data.

Republic of Cyprus

Official name: Kipriakí Dimokratía (Greek); Kıbrıs Cumhuriyeti (Turkish) (Republic of Cyprus).
Form of government: unitary multiparty republic with a unicameral legislature (House of Representatives [80[2]]).
Head of state and government: President.
Capital: Lefkosia (Nicosia).
Official languages: Greek; Turkish.
Monetary unit: 1 Cyprus pound (£C) = 100 cents; valuation (Oct. 3, 1997) 1 £C = U.S.$1.92 = £1.19.

Demography

Population (1997): 662,000.
Urban-rural (1996[4]): urban 68.5%; rural 31.5%.
Age breakdown (1994[4]): under 15, 25.3%; 15–29, 21.8%; 30–44, 22.4%; 45–59, 15.6%; 60–74, 10.2%; 75 and over, 4.7%.
Ethnic composition (1992): Greek Cypriot 95.1%; British 0.8%; other 4.1%.
Religious affiliation (1995): Cypriot Orthodox 92.0%; Maronite 1.3%; other 6.7%.
Urban areas (1994[4]): Lefkosia 186,400[6]; Limassol 143,400; Larnaca 64,000.

Vital statistics

Birth rate per 1,000 population (1995): 15.4 (world avg. 25.0).
Death rate per 1,000 population (1995): 7.7 (world avg. 9.3).
Natural increase rate per 1,000 population (1995): 7.7 (world avg. 15.7).
Life expectancy at birth (1994–95): male 75.3 years; female 79.8 years.

National economy

Budget (1995). Revenue: £C 1,270,800,000 (indirect taxes 39.2%, direct taxes 25.4%, social security contributions 20.1%). Expenditures: £C 1,310,700,000 (current expenditures 87.9%, development expenditures 11.7%).
Tourism (1996): receipts U.S.$1,679,000,000; expenditures U.S.$340,000,000.
Household expenditure (1992): food and beverages 22.7%, transportation and communications 15.6%, expenditures in cafes and hotels 13.6%.
Gross national product (1995): U.S.$8,607,000,000 (U.S.$13,410 per capita).

Structure of gross domestic product and labour force

	1996			
	in value £C '000,000	% of total value	labour force	% of labour force
Agriculture	179.5	4.4	30,000	9.8
Mining	12.4	0.3	800	0.3
Manufacturing	464.0	11.3	43,300	14.1
Construction	354.0	8.6	25,200	8.2
Public utilities	89.8	2.2	1,500	0.5
Transp. and commun.	337.0	8.2	19,200	6.2
Trade	781.6	19.1	76,900	25.0
Finance, insurance	702.9	17.1	23,300	7.6
Pub. admin., defense	537.3	13.1 }	64,400	21.0
Services	341.6	8.3 }		
Other	301.2	7.4	22,400[7]	7.3[7]
TOTAL	4,101.3	100.0	307,000	100.0

Production. Agriculture (value of production in £C '000,000; 1993): milk 27.9, potatoes 24.1, poultry 24.1, barley 21.8, pork 20.0, grapes 15.6. Manufacturing (value added in £C '000,000; 1994): food 66.8; wearing apparel 44.4; cement, bricks, and tiles 41.7; beverages 41.3; cigarettes and cigars 30.8. Energy production: electricity (kW-hr; 1995) 2,473,000,000.

Foreign trade[8]

Imports (1996): £C 1,857,500,000 (consumer goods 33.1%; transport equipment 10.2%; capital goods 9.2%; mineral fuels 8.4%). *Major import sources:* U.S. 16.8%; U.K. 11.2%; Italy 9.2%; Greece 7.2%; Germany 7.1%.
Exports (1996): £C 648,900,000 (reexports 57.9%[9]; domestic exports 34.1%, of which clothing 5.8%, potatoes 4.3%; ships' stores 8.0%). *Major export destinations:* Russia 17.5%; Bulgaria 15.1%; U.K. 10.4%; Greece 5.8%.

Transport and communications

Transport. Roads (1995): total length 10,150 km (paved 57%). Vehicles (1995): cars 219,749; trucks and buses 103,852. Merchant marine (1992): vessels 1,416; deadweight tonnage 36,198,083. Air transport (1995)[10]: passenger-km 2,667,000,000; metric ton-km cargo 36,187,000; airports (1996) 2.

Communications

Medium	date	unit	number	units per 1,000 persons
Daily newspapers	1995	circulation	86,700	135
Radio	1995	receivers	184,000	287
Television	1995	receivers	102,500	160
Telephones	1995	main lines	347,300	541
Cellular telephones	1995	subscribers	44,500	69
Facsimile machines	1995	units	7,000	11

Education and health

Educational attainment (1992). Percentage of population age 25 and over having: no formal schooling 5.1%; higher education 17.0%. *Literacy* (1992): population age 15 and over literate 95.2%; male 97.8%; female 92.8%.

Education (1994–95)

	schools	teachers	students	student/teacher ratio
Primary (age 6–11)	383	3,498	64,884	18.5
Secondary (age 12–17)	107	3,832	53,738	14.0
Vocational	11	509	4,066	8.0
Higher	32	648	7,765	12.0

Health (1993): physicians 1,455 (1 per 433 persons); hospital beds 3,297 (1 per 191 persons); infant mortality rate per 1,000 live births (1995) 9.0.

Internet resources for further information:
- **The Cyprus Government http://www.pio.gov.cy/**
- **Central Bank of Cyprus http://www.centralbank.gov.cy/cyprus/index.html**

Turkish Republic of Northern Cyprus

Official name: Kuzey Kıbrıs Türk Cumhuriyeti (Turkish) (Turkish Republic of Northern Cyprus).
Capital: Lefkoşa (Nicosia).
Official language: Turkish.
Monetary unit: 1 Turkish lira (LT) = 100 kurush; valuation (Oct. 3, 1997) 1 U.S.$ = LT 175,715; 1 £ = LT 283,253.
Population (1997): 198,000[1] (Lefkoşa 39,973[11, 12]; Gazimağusa 27,742[11, 12]).
Ethnic composition (1993): Turkish 98.6%; other 1.4%.

Structure of gross domestic product and labour force

	1995		1994	
	in value LT '000,000,000	% of total value	labour force	% of labour force
Agriculture and fishing	3,530	10.2	17,738	23.2
Mining and manufacturing	3,168	9.1	8,207	10.7
Construction	1,291	3.7 }	9,584	12.5
Public utilities	1,353	3.9 }		
Transp. and commun.	3,006	8.7	6,228	8.1
Trade, restaurants	6,455	18.6	8,004	10.5
Pub. admin.	7,156	20.6	16,589	21.7
Finance, real estate } Services }	6,398	18.4	9,460	12.4
Other	2,361[13]	6.8[13]	704[14]	0.9[14]
TOTAL	34,718	100.0	76,514	100.0

Budget (1995). Revenue: U.S.$293,300,000 (domestic sources 62.0%, loans 28.5%, aid from Turkey 9.5%). Expenditures: U.S.$293,300,000 (current expenditures 88.3%).
Imports (1995): U.S.$366,100,000 (machinery and transport equipment 16.5%, food 10.9%). *Major import sources:* Turkey 53.2%; U.K. 13.5%.
Exports (1995): U.S.$67,300,000 (ready-made garments 35.4%, citrus fruits 32.8%). *Major export destinations:* U.K. 35.4%; Turkey 30.0%.

Education (1995–96)

	schools	teachers	students	student/teacher ratio
Primary (age 7–11)	92	1,055	15,524	14.7
Secondary (age 12–17)	41	816	11,511	14.1
Vocational	10	342	1,969	5.8
Higher	7	...	17,375	...

Health (1995): physicians 272 (1 per 667 persons); hospital beds 902 (1 per 201 persons); infant mortality rate per 1,000 live births 4.9.

Internet resources for further information:
- **Turkish Republic of Northern Cyprus http://www.cypnet.com/.ncyprus/root.html**

[1]Includes 50,000 "settlers" from Turkey and 35,000 Turkish military in the TRNC; excludes 3,900 British military in the Sovereign Base Areas (SBA) in the ROC and 1,100 UN peacekeeping forces. [2]Twenty-four seats reserved for Turkish Cypriots are not occupied. [3]Excludes British and UN military forces. [4]January 1. [5]Area includes 99 sq mi (256 sq km) of British military SBA and *c.* 107 sq mi (*c.* 278 sq km) of the UN Buffer Zone. [6]ROC only. [7]Includes 9,400 unemployed. [8]Imports c.i.f.; exports f.o.b. [9]Mainly cigarettes and consumer electronics. [10]Cyprus Airways. [11]Preliminary figures. [12]1996. [13]Customs duties. [14]Unemployed.

Czech Republic

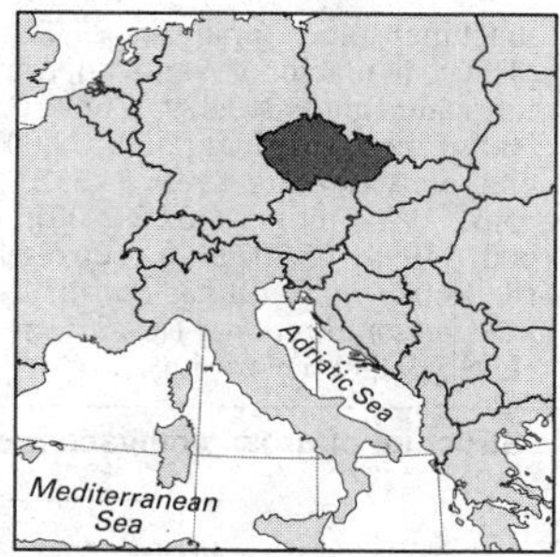

Official name: Česká Republika.
Form of government: unitary multiparty republic with two legislative houses (Senate [81[1]]; Chamber of Deputies [200]).
Chief of state: President.
Head of government: Prime Minister.
Capital: Prague.
Official language: Czech.
Official religion: none.
Monetary unit[2]: 1 koruna (Kč) = 100 halura; valuation (Oct. 3, 1997) 1 U.S.$ = 32.85 Kč; 1 £ = 52.95 Kč.

Area and population

Regions	Capitals	area sq mi	area sq km	population 1996[3] estimate
Jižní Čechy	České Budějovice	4,381	11,346	700,831
Jižní Morava	Brno	5,802	15,028	2,057,239
Severní Čechy	Ustí nad Labem	3,011	7,799	1,178,208
Severní Morava	Ostrava	4,273	11,068	1,972,336
Střední Čechy	Prague	4,253	11,014	1,106,738
Východní Čechy	Hradec Králové	4,340	11,240	1,235,641
Zapadní Čechy	Plzeň	4,199	10,875	860,496
Capital city				
Prague	—	192	496	1,209,855
TOTAL		30,450[4]	78,866	10,321,344

Demography

Population (1997): 10,307,000.
Density (1997): persons per sq mi 338.5, persons per sq km 130.7.
Urban-rural: n.a.
Sex distribution (1995): male 48.60%; female 51.40%.
Age breakdown (1995): under 15, 18.3%; 15–29, 23.3%; 30–44, 21.1%; 45–59, 19.3%; 60–74, 13.4%; 75 and over, 4.6%.
Population projection: (2000) 10,290,000; (2010) 10,377,000.
Doubling time: not applicable; population is declining.
Ethnic composition (1991): Czech 81.2%; Moravian 13.2%; Slovak 3.1%; Polish 0.6%; German 0.5%; Silesian 0.4%; Gypsy 0.3%; Hungarian 0.2%; Ukrainian 0.1%; other 0.4%.
Religious affiliation (1991): Roman Catholic 39.0%; Protestant 4.3%, of which Czechoslovak Brethren Reformed 2.0%, Czechoslovak Hussite 1.7%, Silesian Evangelical 0.3%; Eastern Orthodox 0.2%; Greek Catholic 0.1%; other Christian 0.3%; undenominational 39.9%; other 16.2%.
Major cities (1996): Prague 1,210,000; Brno 388,900; Ostrava 324,800; Plzeň 171,200; Olomouc 104,800.

Vital statistics

Birth rate per 1,000 population (1996): 8.8 (world avg. 25.0); (1995) legitimate 84.4%; illegitimate 15.6%.
Death rate per 1,000 population (1996): 10.9 (world avg. 9.3).
Natural increase rate per 1,000 population (1996): −2.1 (world avg. 15.7).
Total fertility rate (avg. births per childbearing woman; 1995): 1.4.
Marriage rate per 1,000 population (1996): 5.2.
Divorce rate per 1,000 population (1996): 3.2.
Life expectancy at birth (1995): male 70.0 years; female 76.9 years.
Major causes of death per 100,000 population (1995): diseases of the circulatory system 638.4; malignant neoplasms (cancers) 277.1; accidents, poisoning, and violence 82.3; diseases of the respiratory system 49.1; diseases of the digestive system 41.9; diseases of the genitourinary system 15.3.

National economy

Budget (1996). Revenue: Kč 482,800,000,000[2] (taxes 55.6%, of which value-added tax 22.6%, consumer tax 12.7%, income tax 10.1%, external trade tax 4.1%, other taxes 6.1%; social security 36.1%; other revenue 8.3%). Expenditures: Kč 484,400,000,000[2] (current expenditures 83.2%, of which social security 31.2%, subsidies to organizations 26.1%, defense 9.7%, enterprise subsidies 5.6%, health care 3.6%, education 3.5%, transfers to local budgets 3.5%; capital expenditures 11.8%; other 5.0%).
Public debt (external, outstanding; 1995): U.S.$9,610,000,000.
Production (metric tons except as noted). Agriculture, forestry, fishing (1996): cereals 6,683,000 (of which wheat 3,732,000, barley 2,305,000, rye 220,000, corn [maize] 143,000), sugar beets 4,317,000, potatoes 1,758,000; livestock (number of live animals) 4,016,000 pigs, 1,989,000 cattle, 26,600,000 poultry; roundwood (1995) 12,060,000 cu m; fish catch (1995) 22,579. Mining and quarrying (1996): limestone 13,100; kaolin 3,320. Manufacturing (value of production in Kč '000,000[2]; 1995): machinery and transport equipment 71,885; metal products 49,076; food products 36,568; chemical products 17,786; textiles 16,262. Construction (value in Kč '000,000[2]; 1994): residential 6,889; nonresidential 26,416. Energy production (consumption): electricity (kW-hr; 1994) 58,705,000,000 (58,260,000,000); coal (metric tons; 1994) 10,886,000 (6,907,000); crude petroleum (barrels; 1994) 938,000 (48,312,000); petroleum products (metric tons; 1994) 4,384,000 (5,514,000); natural gas (cu m; 1994) 242,000,000 (7,339,000,000).
Household income and expenditure. Average household size (1996) 2.9; income per household (1996) Kč 243,043[2] (U.S.$8,942); sources of income (1996[3]): wages and salaries 66.7%, transfer payments 27.6%, other 5.7%; expenditure (1996): food and beverages 25.6%, housing and utilities 11.3%, household durable goods 7.3%, clothing and footwear 7.2%, other 48.6%.

Population economically active (1997): total 5,469,500; activity rate of total population 53.0% (participation rates: [1996] ages 15–59 [male], 15–54 [female] 96.6%; female 44.0%; [1996] unemployed 3.1%).

Price and earnings indexes (1990 = 100)

	1990	1991	1992	1993	1994	1995	1996
Consumer price index	100.0	170.0	174.0	210.3	231.6	252.6	274.9
Annual earnings index	100.0	116.6	127.3	177.7	209.9	248.7	295.0

Gross national product (1995): U.S.$39,990,000,000 (U.S.$3,870 per capita).

Structure of gross domestic product and labour force

	1995		1997	
	in value Kč '000,000[2]	% of total value	labour force	% of labour force
Agriculture	60,500	5.0	284,000	5.2
Mining and manufacturing	340,000	28.1	1,471,900	26.9
Construction	71,600	5.9	470,600	8.6
Public utilities	63,700	5.3	94,900	1.7
Transportation and communications	72,600	6.0	384,700	7.0
Trade	133,700	11.0	822,500	15.0
Finance	116,100	9.6	345,500	6.3
Pub. admin., defense	118,100	9.7	317,500	5.8
Services	183,900	15.2	743,200	13.6
Other	51,800	4.3	534,700[4]	9.8[4]
TOTAL	1,212,000	100.0[5]	5,469,500	100.0[5]

Land use (1994): forested 33.3%; meadows and pastures 11.3%; agricultural and under permanent cultivation 43.0%; other 12.4%.

Foreign trade

Balance of trade (current prices)

	1991	1992	1993	1994	1995	1996
Kč '000,000[2]	+41,680	−45,300	+10,100	−20,600	−93,892	−157,715
% of total	5.9%	8.4%	1.3%	2.4%	7.6%	11.7%

Imports (1996): Kč 755,278,000,000[2] (machinery and transport equipment 38.2%, manufactured goods 19.3%, chemicals 11.8%, fuels and lubricants 8.7%). *Major import sources:* Germany 29.8%; Slovakia 9.6%; Russia 7.4%; Italy 5.9%; Austria 5.8%.
Exports (1996): Kč 594,952,000,000[2] (manufactured goods 28.8%, machinery and transport equipment 32.7%, miscellaneous manufactured articles 14.8%, chemicals 9.1%, inedible crude materials, except fuel 4.7%, mineral fuels and lubricants 4.7%). *Major export destinations:* Germany 36.0%; Slovakia 14.2%; Austria 6.4%; Italy 3.3%; Russia 3.2%.

Transport and communications

Transport. Railroads (1995): length 9,430 km; passenger-km 8,023,000,000; metric ton-km cargo 25,468,000,000. Roads (1995): total length 124,770 km (paved 13%). Vehicles (1995): passenger cars 3,113,476; trucks and buses 204,238. Merchant marine (1993): vessels (oceangoing) 18; total deadweight tonnage 514,126. Air transport (1995): passenger-km 2,555,062,000; metric ton-km 33,473,000; airports (1996) with scheduled flights 2.

Communications

Medium	date	unit	number	units per 1,000 persons
Daily newspapers	1994	circulation	2,259,000	219
Television	1995	receivers	4,200,000	407
Telephones	1995	main lines	2,444,200	237
Cellular telephones	1995	subscribers	48,900	4.7
Facsimile machines	1995	units	73,600	7.1
Personal computers	1995	units	550,000	53.2

Education and health

Educational attainment (1991). Percentage of adult population having: no schooling and incomplete primary 31.7%; complete secondary 58.6%; higher 8.5%. *Literacy* (1990): total population age 15 and over literate 8,170,442 (100%); males literate 3,914,080 (100%); females literate 4,256,362 (100%).

Education (1995–96)

	schools	teachers	students	student/teacher ratio
Primary (age 6–14)	4,212	63,019	1,004,565	15.9
Secondary (age 15–18)	361	10,903	133,093	12.2
Voc., teacher tr.	832	18,458	229,909	12.5
Higher	23	12,892	139,774	9.4

Health (1995): physicians 38,462 (1 per 268 persons); hospital beds 74,510 (1 per 138 persons); (1996) infant mortality rate per 1,000 live births 6.0.
Food (1995): daily per capita caloric intake 3,175 (vegetable products 71%, animal products 29%); 128% of FAO recommended minimum requirement.

Military

Total active duty personnel (1996): 44,000 (army 63.6%, air force 36.4%). *Military expenditure as percentage of GNP* (1995): 2.3% (world 2.8%); per capita expenditure (1995): U.S.$229.

[1]First Czech Senate elected November 1996. [2]The koruna (Kč) was introduced Feb. 8, 1993, at par with the former Czechoslovak koruna (Kčs), which it replaced. [3]January 1. [4]Includes 204,000 employed with second job, 188,300 people with disabilities, and 16,400 nondistributable. [5]Detail does not add to total given because of rounding.

Internet resources for further information:
- **Czech Statistical Office http://infox.eunet.cz/csu/csu_e.html**

Denmark

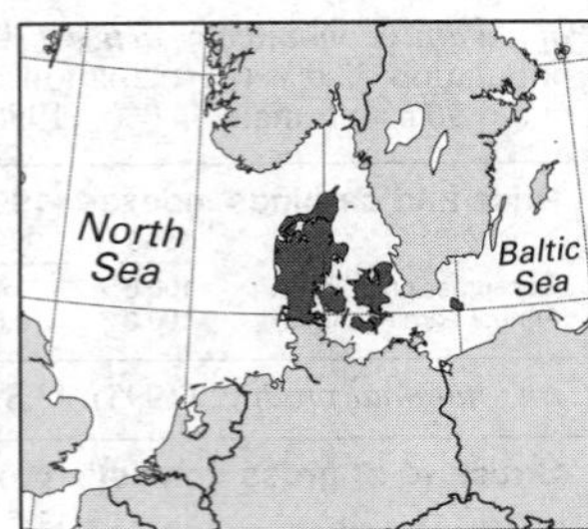

Official name: Kongeriget Danmark (Kingdom of Denmark).
Form of government: parliamentary state and constitutional monarchy with one legislative house (Folketing [179]).
Chief of state: Danish Monarch.
Head of government: Prime Minister.
Capital: Copenhagen.
Official language: Danish.
Official religion: Evangelical Lutheran.
Monetary unit: 1 Danish krone (Dkr; plural kroner) = 100 øre; valuation (Oct. 3, 1997) 1 U.S.$ = Dkr 6.71; 1 £ = Dkr 10.82.

Area and population[1]

Counties	Capitals	area sq mi	area sq km	population 1996[2] estimate
Århus	Århus	1,761	4,561	625,224
Bornholm	Rønne	227	588	45,186
Frederiksborg	Hillerød	520	1,347	353,674
Fyn	Odense	1,346	3,486	470,528
København	—	203	526	607,344
Nordjylland	Ålborg	2,383	6,173	490,836
Ribe	Ribe	1,209	3,132	223,097
Ringkøbing	Ringkøbing	1,874	4,853	271,730
Roskilde	Roskilde	344	891	225,520
Sønderjylland	Åbenrå	1,520	3,938	252,929
Storstrøm	Nykøbing Falster	1,312	3,398	257,495
Vejle	Vejle	1,157	2,997	339,818
Vestsjælland	Sorø	1,152	2,984	289,852
Viborg	Viborg	1,592	4,122	232,254
Municipalities				
Copenhagen (København)	—	34	88	476,751
Frederiksberg	—	3	9	88,789
TOTAL		16,639[3]	43,094[3]	5,251,027

Demography

Population (1997): 5,284,000.
Density (1997): persons per sq mi 317.6, persons per sq km 122.6.
Urban-rural (1995): urban 85.2%; rural 14.8%.
Sex distribution (1996[2]): male 49.37%; female 50.63%.
Age breakdown (1996[2]): under 15, 17.5%; 15–29, 20.8%; 30–44, 22.1%; 45–59, 19.9%; 60–74, 12.7%; 75 and over, 7.0%.
Population projection: (2000) 5,348,000; (2010) 5,504,000.
Doubling time: not applicable; population is stable.
Ethnic composition (1996[2])[4]: Danish 95.8%; Asian 1.6%, of which Turkish 0.7%; residents of former Yugoslavia 0.5%; other Scandinavian 0.4%; African 0.3%; other 1.4%.
Religious affiliation (1995): Evangelical Lutheran 87.0%; other Christian 1.7%; Muslim 1.5%; other/nonreligious 9.8%.
Major urban areas (1994): Greater Copenhagen 1,346,289; Århus 209,404; Odense 143,029; Ålborg 116,567; Frederiksberg 88,789[5, 6].

Vital statistics

Birth rate per 1,000 population (1996): 12.9 (world avg. 25.0); (1995) legitimate 53.5%; illegitimate 46.5%.
Death rate per 1,000 population (1996): 11.6 (world avg. 9.3).
Natural increase rate per 1,000 population (1996): 1.3 (world avg. 15.7).
Total fertility rate (avg. births per childbearing woman; 1995): 1.8.
Marriage rate per 1,000 population (1995): 6.7.
Divorce rate per 1,000 population (1995): 2.5.
Life expectancy at birth (1994–95): male 72.6 years; female 77.8 years.
Major causes of death per 100,000 population (1995): malignant neoplasms (cancers) 296.6; ischemic heart disease 242.3; cerebrovascular disease 105.9.

National economy

Budget (1995)[7]. Revenue: Dkr 589,933,000,000 (direct taxes 52.3%, indirect taxes 29.7%). Expenditures: Dkr 604,806,000,000 (social security assistance 32.6%, education 11.7%, welfare services 9.8%, health 8.4%, defense 2.9%).
National debt (end of year; 1995): Dkr 663,653,000,000.
Tourism (1996): receipts U.S.$3,425,000; expenditures U.S.$4,142,000,000.
Population economically active (1996): total 2,796,501; activity rate of total population 52.7% (participation rates: ages 15–64, 79.1%; female 45.3%; unemployed [April 1996–March 1997] 8.4%).

Price and earnings indexes (1990 = 100)

	1991	1992	1993	1994	1995	1996	1997
Consumer price index	102.4	104.5	105.9	108.0	110.2	112.6	115.0[8]
Hourly earnings index	103.1	106.2	108.6	113.3	117.2	...	...

Household income and expenditure. Average household size (1996) 2.2; income per household (1988) Dkr 199,354 (U.S.$29,613); expenditure (1993): housing 22.9%, food and beverages 17.9%, transportation and communications 15.5%, recreation 8.3%, household furnishings 6.1%, energy 6.1%.
Production (in Dkr '000,000 except as noted). Agriculture, forestry, fishing (value added; 1995): pork 16,005, milk 11,152, beef 3,554, wheat 3,411, barley 2,731, flowers and plants 2,541, mink furs 1,991; roundwood (1995) 2,288,000 cu m; fish catch (1995) 2,041,133 metric tons. Mining and quarrying (1994): sand and gravel 24,829,000 cu m; chalk 3,522,000 cu m. Manufacturing (value added; 1994): food products 38,325, of which meat 11,170; nonelectrical machinery and apparatus 23,331; chemicals and chemical products 18,504; electrical machinery and apparatus 14,428; printing and publishing 9,649; fabricated metals 9,479. Construction (completed; 1995): residential 1,375,000 sq m; nonresidential 3,573,000 sq m. Energy production (consumption): electricity (kW-hr; 1995) 34,332,000,000 ([1994] 36,252,000,000); coal (metric tons; 1994) none (13,087,000); crude petroleum (barrels; 1996) 75,920,000 ([1994] 65,802,000); petroleum products (metric tons; 1994) 8,691,000 (8,069,000); natural gas (cu m; 1994) 4,902,000,000 (2,992,000,000).
Gross national product (at current market prices; 1995): U.S.$156,027,000,000 (U.S.$29,890 per capita).

Structure of gross domestic product and labour force

	1995 in value Dkr '000,000[9]	% of total value	labour force	% of labour force
Agriculture, fishing	34,999	4.2	115,000	4.1
Mining	7,225	0.9	4,000	0.1
Manufacturing	167,943	20.2	521,200	18.6
Construction	47,015	5.7	164,100	5.9
Public utilities	16,172	1.9	16,500	0.6
Transp. and commun.	79,261	9.5	188,800	6.7
Trade, restaurants	108,604	13.1	435,500	15.5
Finance, real estate	158,299	19.0	261,500	9.3
Pub. admin., defense	183,466	22.1	156,800	5.6
Services	52,935	6.4	739,300	26.4
Other	−24,185[10]	−2.9[10]	199,500[11]	7.1[11]
TOTAL	831,733[3]	100.0[3]	2,802,400[3]	100.0[3]

Land use (1994): forested 10.5%; meadows and pastures 7.5%; agricultural and under permanent cultivation 55.9%; other 26.1%.

Foreign trade[12]

Balance of trade (current prices)

	1991	1992	1993	1994	1995	1996
Dkr '000,000	+22,965	+35,166	+43,077	+41,596	+29,500	+31,206
% of total	5.3%	7.7%	9.1%	8.6%	5.9%	5.8%

Imports (1995): Dkr 236,587,000,000 (goods for household consumption 25.8%, transport equipment and parts 11.1%, machinery and apparatus 8.7%). *Major import sources:* Germany 22.8%; Sweden 12.2%; The Netherlands 7.3%; United Kingdom 7.0%; France 5.4%; Norway 5.0%.
Exports (1995): Dkr 266,087,000,000 (nonelectrical and electrical machinery 25.1%, fresh or frozen swine meat 6.0%, pharmaceuticals 4.7%, furniture 4.6%, textiles and clothing 4.5%). *Major export destinations:* Germany 23.2%; Sweden 10.0%; United Kingdom 8.1%; Norway 6.1%; France 5.5%.

Transport and communications

Transport. Railroads (1995): route length 2,865 km; passenger-km 4,834,000,000; metric ton-km cargo 1,985,000,000. Roads (1995): total length 71,420 km (paved 100%). Vehicles (1995): passenger cars 1,729,405; trucks and buses 288,464. Air transport (1996)[13]: passenger-km 5,376,000,000; metric ton-km cargo 170,768,000; airports (1996) with scheduled flights 13.

Communications

Medium	date	unit	number	units per 1,000 persons
Daily newspapers	1995	circulation	1,610,000	308
Radio	1996	receivers	5,200,000	988
Television	1995	receivers	2,700,200	516
Telephones	1995	main lines	3,202,500	612
Cellular telephones	1995	subscribers	822,300	157
Facsimile machines	1995	units	250,000	48
Personal computers	1995	units	1,416,000	270

Education and health

Educational attainment (1995). Percentage of population age 25–69 having: completed lower secondary or not stated 40.0%; completed upper secondary or vocational 40.3%; advanced vocational 6.0%; undergraduate 8.9%; graduate 4.8%. *Literacy:* virtually 100%.

Education (1994–95)

	schools	teachers	students	student/ teacher ratio
Primary/lower secondary (age 7–15)	2,536	58,500[14]	605,798	10.4[14]
Upper secondary (age 16–18)	153	11,000[14]	75,793	6.8[14]
Vocational	237	12,000[14]	168,417	13.6[14]
Higher	158	8,000[14]	155,661	19.5[14]

Health (1994): physicians 14,497 (1 per 358 persons); hospital beds 26,170 (1 per 199 persons); infant mortality rate per 1,000 live births (1996) 5.7.
Food (1995): daily per capita caloric intake 3,704 (vegetable products 54%, animal products 46%); 138% of FAO recommended minimum requirement.

Military

Total active duty personnel (1996): 32,900 (army 57.8%, navy 18.2%, air force 24.0%). *Military expenditure as percentage of GNP* (1994): 1.9% (world 3.0%); per capita expenditure U.S.$522.

[1]Excludes the Faroe Islands and Greenland. [2]January 1. [3]Detail does not add to total given because of rounding. [4]Based on nationality. [5]Within Greater Copenhagen. [6]1996. [7]Includes both central and local governments. [8]May. [9]At factor cost. [10]Imputed bank service charges. [11]Includes 4,000 not adequately defined and 195,500 with previous employment. [12]Imports c.i.f., exports f.o.b. [13]Danish share of Scandinavian Airlines System (scheduled air service only) and Maersk Air. [14]1993–94.

Internet resources for further information:
- **Statistics Denmark http://www.dst.dk/internet/startuk.htm**

Djibouti

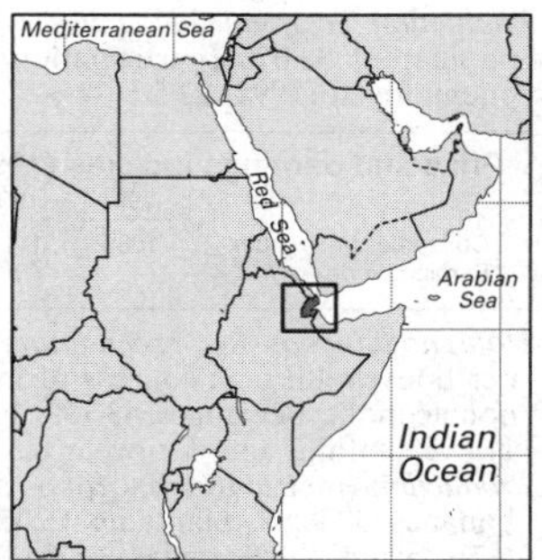

Official name: Jumhūrīyah Jībūtī (Arabic); République de Djibouti (French) (Republic of Djibouti).
Form of government: multiparty republic with one legislative house (National Assembly [65]).
Head of state and government: President.
Capital: Djibouti.
Official languages: Arabic; French.
Official religion: none.
Monetary unit: 1 Djibouti franc (DF) = 100 centimes; valuation (Oct. 3, 1997) 1 U.S.$ = DF 177.72; 1 £ = DF 286.48.

Area and population

		area[1]		population
Districts	Capitals	sq mi	sq km	1982 estimate
'Alī Sabīḥ (Ali-Sabieh)	'Alī Sabīḥ	925	2,400	15,000
Dikhil	Dikhil	2,775	7,200	30,000
Djibouti	Djibouti	225	600	200,000
Obock	Obock	2,200	5,700	15,000
Tadjoura (Tadjourah)	Tadjoura	2,825	7,300	30,000
TOTAL		8,950	23,200	335,000[2]

Demography

Population (1997): 622,000[3].
Density (1997): persons per sq mi 69.5, persons per sq km 26.8.
Urban-rural (1995): urban 82.8%; rural 17.2%.
Sex distribution (1997): male 51.62%; female 48.38%.
Age breakdown (1997): under 15, 42.7%; 15–29, 25.9%; 30–44, 15.1%; 45–59, 11.7%; 60–74, 4.0%; 75 and over, 0.6%.
Population projection: (2000) 680,000; (2010) 916,000.
Doubling time: 32 years.
Ethnic composition (1983): Somali 61.7%, of which Issa 33.4%, Gadaboursi 15.0%, Issaq 13.3%; Afar 20.0%; Arab (mostly Yemeni) 6.0%; European 4.0%; other (refugees) 8.3%.
Religious affiliation (1995): Sunnī Muslim 97.2%; Christian 2.8%, of which Roman Catholic 2.2%, Orthodox 0.5%, Protestant 0.1%.
Major city and towns (1989): Djibouti 383,000[4]; ʿAlī Sabīḥ 4,000; Tadjoura 3,500; Dikhil 3,000.

Vital statistics

Birth rate per 1,000 population (1997): 42.0 (world avg. 25.0).
Death rate per 1,000 population (1997): 15.0 (world avg. 9.3).
Natural increase rate per 1,000 population (1997): 27.0 (world avg. 15.7).
Total fertility rate (avg. births per childbearing woman; 1997): 6.0.
Marriage rate per 1,000 population (1982): 6.7.
Divorce rate per 1,000 population (1982): 1.9.
Life expectancy at birth (1997): male 48.6 years; female 52.6 years.
Major causes of death (percentage of total deaths [infants and children to age 10, district of Djibouti only]; 1984): diarrhea and acute dehydration 16.0%; malnutrition 16.0%; poisoning 11.0%; tuberculosis 6.0%; acute respiratory disease 6.0%; malaria 6.0%; anemia 6.0%; heart disease 2.0%; kidney disease 1.0%; other ailments 19.0%; no diagnosis 11.0%.

National economy

Budget (1996)[5]. Revenue: DF 25,395,000,000 (tax revenue 92.5%, of which domestic taxes [construction, gambling, market fees, licenses] 33.5%, wages and salary tax 14.5%, surcharge on khat 8.8%, income and profit tax 6.4%; nontax revenue 7.5%). Expenditures: DF 30,430,000,000 (current expenditures 88.7%, of which defense and mobilization 23.2%, education 9.8%, health 4.9%; capital expenditures 11.3%).
Tourism (1993): receipts from visitors U.S.$13,000,000; expenditures by nationals abroad U.S.$15,000,000.
Production (metric tons except as noted). Agriculture, forestry, fishing (1997): vegetables and melons 22,390, of which tomatoes 1,000, eggplant 45; livestock (number of live animals) 507,000 goats, 470,000 sheep, 190,000 cattle, 62,000 camels, 8,200 asses; roundwood, n.a.; fish catch (1995) 350. Mining and quarrying: mineral production limited to locally used construction materials and evaporated salt. Manufacturing (1991): structural detail, n.a.; main products include furniture, nonalcoholic beverages, meat and hides, light electromechanical goods, and mineral water. Construction (1989): 53,900 sq m. Energy production (consumption): electricity (kW-hr; 1994) 185,000,000 (185,000,000); firewood and charcoal, n.a. (n.a.)[6]; coal, none (n.a.); crude petroleum, none (n.a.); petroleum products (metric tons; 1994) none (127,000); natural gas, none (n.a.); geothermal, wind, and solar resources are substantial but largely undeveloped.
Population economically active (1991): total 282,000; activity rate of total population 61.5% (participation rates: over age 10, 70.4%; female 40.8%; unemployed [1987] *c.* 40–50%).

Price and earnings indexes (1990 = 100)

	1990	1991	1992	1993	1994	1995	1996
Consumer price index[7]	100.0	106.8	110.4	115.3	122.8	128.8	134.2
Earnings index	...	...	...	...	...	...	...

Household income and expenditure. Average household size (1985)[8] 7.2; income per household: n.a.; sources of income (1976): wages and salaries 51.6%, self-employment 36.0%, transfer payments 10.5%, other 1.9%; expenditure (expatriate households; 1984): food 50.3%, energy 13.1%, recreation 10.4%, housing 6.4%, clothing 1.7%, personal effects 1.4%, health care 1.0%, household goods 0.3%, other 15.4%.
Public debt (external, outstanding; 1995): U.S.$218,000,000.
Gross national product (1994): U.S.$474,000,000 (U.S.$835 per capita).

Structure of gross domestic product and labour force

	1996		1991	
	in value DF '000,000	% of total value	labour force	% of labour force
Agriculture	2,623	3.0	212,000	75.2
Mining	—	— }		
Manufacturing	4,331	5.0 }	31,000	11.0
Construction	4,708	5.5 }		
Public utilities	6,300	7.3 }		
Transp. and commun.	13,231	15.3 }		
Trade	13,378	15.5 }		
Finance	8,261	9.6 }	39,000	13.8
Pub. admin., defense	18,368	21.3 }		
Services	4,023	4.7 }		
Other	10,992	12.7	...	...
TOTAL	86,215	100.0[9]	282,000	100.0

Land use (1994): forested 0.9%; meadows and pastures 56.1%; agricultural and under permanent cultivation[10]; built-on, wasteland, and other 43.0%.

Foreign trade

Balance of trade (current prices)

	1992	1993	1994	1995	1996
U.S.$'000,000	−205.9	−183.9	−180.7	−167.4	−160.9
% of total	65.9%	56.4%	61.6%	69.0%	67.0%

Imports (1996): U.S.$200,500,000 (food, beverages, khat, and tobacco 41.3%; machinery and electric appliances 19.0%; petroleum products 8.0%; clothing and footwear 7.6%; chemical products 4.8%; base metals and base metal products 4.8%; transport equipment 3.4%). *Major import sources:* France 15.0%; Ethiopia 10.9%; Italy 7.8%; Saudi Arabia 7.5%; U.K. 6.0%.
Exports (1996): U.S.$39,600,000 (1991: unspecified special transactions 71.7%; live animals [including camels] 15.5%; food and food products 12.8%). *Major export destinations:* Ethiopia 44.8%; Somalia 38.2%; Yemen 8.2%; Saudi Arabia 3.3%.

Transport and communications

Transport. Railroads (1995): length (1989) 66 mi, 106 km; passenger-mi 173,000,000, passenger-km 279,000,000; short ton-mile cargo 187,000,000[11], metric ton-km cargo 273,000,000[11]. Roads (1995): total length 1,796 mi, 2,890 km (paved 13%). Vehicles (1994): passenger cars 13,500; trucks and buses 3,000. Merchant marine (1992): vessels (100 gross tons and over) 10; total deadweight tonnage 4,090. Air transport (1995)[12]: passengers handled 120,145; metric tons of freight handled 12,291; airports (1997) with scheduled flights 1.

Communications

Medium	date	unit	number	units per 1,000 persons
Daily newspapers	1990	circulation	4,000	7.6
Radio	1995	receivers	48,000	80.0
Television	1995	receivers	26,000	43.0
Telephones	1996	main lines[13]	8,169	13.5
Facsimile machines	1996	units[13]	142	0.2

Education and health

Educational attainment: n.a. *Literacy* (1995): percentage of population age 15 and over literate 46.2%; males literate 60.3%; females literate 32.7%.

Education (1996–97)

	schools	teachers	students	student/ teacher ratio
Primary (age 6–11)	81[14]	1,005[14]	33,960	...
Secondary (age 12–18) } Voc., teacher tr. }	26[15]	628[14]	11,628	...
Higher	1[15]	13[15]	130[16]	...

Health (1989): physicians 97 (1 per 5,258 persons); hospital beds[17] 1,383 (1 per 369 persons); infant mortality rate per 1,000 live births (1997) 105.
Food (1995): daily per capita caloric intake 1,831 (vegetable products 88%, animal products 12%); 79% of FAO recommended minimum requirement.

Military

Total active duty personnel (1997): 9,600[18] (army 83.3%, navy 2.1%, air force 2.1%, paramilitary 12.5%). *Military expenditure as percentage of GNP* (1995): 4.5% (world 2.8%); per capita expenditure U.S.$52.

[1]Original figures are those given in sq km; sq mi equivalent is rounded to appropriate level of generality. [2]Includes 45,000 persons not distributed by district. [3]Excludes about 20,000 Somali and 5,000 Ethiopian refugees. [4]1995 estimate. [5]Preliminary. [6]Represents about 15% of total energy consumption. [7]Based on expatriates' expenditures. [8]City of Djibouti only. [9]Detail does not add to total given because of rounding. [10]In 1988–89 only 1,005 acres (407 hectares) of land were cultivated. [11]Based on total weight of Ethiopian exports and imports transported to and from the port of Djibouti. [12]Djibouti International Airport only. [13]Number of users. [14]1994–95. [15]1991. [16]1995–96. [17]Public health facilities only. [18]Excludes 3,900 French troops.

Internet resources for further information:
- **Bienvenue à Djibouti http://www.intnet.dj/djibouti.html**

Dominica

Official name: Commonwealth of Dominica.
Form of government: multiparty republic with one legislative house (House of Assembly [32[1]]).
Chief of state: President.
Head of government: Prime Minister.
Capital: Roseau.
Official language: English.
Official religion: none.
Monetary unit: 1 East Caribbean dollar (EC$) = 100 cents; valuation (Oct. 3, 1997) 1 U.S.$ = EC$2.70; 1 £ = EC$4.35.

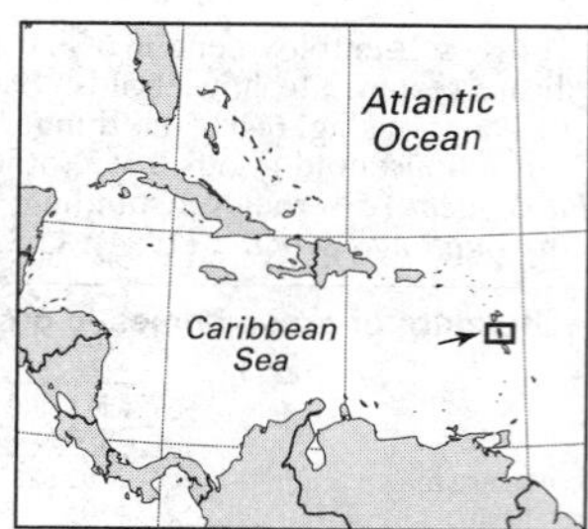

Area and population

Parishes	area sq mi	area sq km	population 1991 census
St. Andrew	69.3	179.6	11,106
St. David	49.0	126.8	6,977
St. George	20.7	53.5	20,365
St. John	22.5	58.5	4,990
St. Joseph	46.4	120.1	6,183
St. Luke	4.3	11.1	1,552
St. Mark	3.8	9.9	1,943
St. Patrick	32.6	84.4	8,929
St. Paul	26.0	67.4	7,495
St. Peter	10.7	27.7	1,643
TOTAL	285.3[2]	739.0[2]	71,183[3]

Demography

Population (1997): 74,400.
Density (1997): persons per sq mi 256.6; persons per sq km 99.2.
Urban-rural: n.a.
Sex distribution (1991): male 49.78%; female 50.22%.
Age breakdown (1991): under 15, 33.3%; 15–29, 28.3%; 30–44, 16.3%; 45–59, 9.7%; 60 and over, 11.8%; unknown, 0.6%.
Population projection: (2000) 75,000; (2010) 76,000.
Doubling time: 54 years.
Ethnic composition (1991): black 89.1%; mixed race 7.2%; Amerindian/Carib 2.4%; white 0.4%; other 0.7%; not stated 0.2%.
Religious affiliation (1991): Roman Catholic 70.1%; six largest Protestant groups 17.2%, of which Seventh-day Adventist 4.6%, Pentecostal 4.3%, Methodist 4.2%; other 8.9%; nonreligious 2.9%; unknown 0.9%.
Major towns (1991): Roseau 15,853; Portsmouth 3,621; Marigot 2,919; Atkinson 2,518; Mahaut 2,372.

Vital statistics

Birth rate per 1,000 population (1996): 18.4 (world avg. 25.0); (1991) legitimate 24.1%; illegitimate 75.9%.
Death rate per 1,000 population (1996): 5.3 (world avg. 9.3).
Natural increase rate per 1,000 population (1996): 13.1 (world avg. 15.7).
Total fertility rate (avg. births per childbearing woman; 1996): 1.9.
Marriage rate per 1,000 population (1990): 3.3.
Divorce rate per 1,000 population (1990): 0.4.
Life expectancy at birth (1996): male 74.5 years; female 80.4 years.
Major causes of death per 100,000 population (1990): diseases of the circulatory system 273.5, of which ischemic heart diseases 120.8, hypertensive disease 88.8; malignant neoplasms (cancers) 116.6; endocrine, metabolic, and nutritional disorders 51.4; diseases of the respiratory system 43.0; infectious and parasitic diseases 37.5.

National economy

Budget (1995–96). Revenue: EC$194,100,000 (tax revenue 67.9%, of which consumption taxes 25.1%, taxes on income and profits 18.3%; grants 15.7%; nontax revenue 14.1%; other 2.3%). Expenditures: EC$219,100,000 (current expenditures 70.4%; development expenditures 29.6%).
Public debt (external, outstanding; 1995): U.S.$102,300,000.
Land use (1994): forested 66.0%; meadows and pastures 3.0%; agricultural and under permanent cultivation 23.0%; other 8.0%.
Tourism (1995): receipts from visitors U.S.$35,700,000; expenditures by nationals abroad U.S.$4,300,000.
Gross national product (at current market prices; 1995): U.S.$218,000,000 (U.S.$2,990 per capita).

Structure of gross domestic product and labour force

	1995 in value EC$'000,000	1995 % of total value	1991 labour force[4]	1991 % of labour force[4]
Agriculture	100.9	19.8	7,344	30.8
Mining	4.4	0.9	65	0.3
Manufacturing	35.8	7.0	1,947	8.2
Construction	44.4	8.7	2,819	11.8
Public utilities	21.0	4.1	304	1.3
Transportation and communications	88.4	17.3	1,202	5.0
Trade, hotels, restaurants	76.7	15.0	3,658	15.4
Finance, real estate } Services }	82.7	16.2	810	3.4
			3,446	14.5
Pub. admin., defense	92.9	18.2	1,520	6.4
Other	−36.8[5]	−7.2[5]	699	2.9
TOTAL	510.3[6]	100.0	23,814	100.0

Population economically active (1991): total 26,364; activity rate of total population 38.0% (participation rates: ages 15–64, 62.4%; female 34.5%; unemployed [1994] 23%).

Price and earnings indexes (1990 = 100)

	1991	1992	1993	1994	1995	1996	1997[7]
Consumer price index	106.2	111.4	113.1	113.1	114.6	116.5	118.6
Earnings index	...	...	...	...	...	...	...

Household income and expenditure. Average household size (1991) 3.6; income per household: n.a.; sources of income: n.a.; expenditure (1984)[8]: food and nonalcoholic beverages 43.1%, housing and utilities 16.1%, transportation 11.6%, clothing and footwear 6.5%, household furnishings 6.0%.
Production (metric tons except as noted). Agriculture, forestry, fishing (1995): bananas 39,928[9], plantains 15,358, root crops 14,818 (of which dasheens 6,710, yams 4,479, tanias 3,326), grapefruit 10,682, coconuts 8,853, oranges 4,340, limes 3,314, mangoes 1,633, pepper 144, bay oil 16; livestock (number of live animals; 1996) 13,400 cattle, 9,700 goats, 7,600 sheep; roundwood, n.a.; fish catch 842 metric tons. Mining and quarrying: pumice, limestone, and sand and gravel are quarried primarily for local consumption. Manufacturing (value of production in EC$'000; 1996): toilet soap 19,633; laundry soap 17,240; crude coconut oil 1,615; bottled spring water 323,000 cases[10]; other products include fruit juices, beer, garments, furniture, paint, and cardboard boxes. Construction (value of starts; 1993): U.S.$12,100,000. Energy production (consumption): electricity (kW-hr; 1994) 52,400,000 (43,500,000); coal, none (none); crude petroleum, none (none); petroleum products (metric tons; 1994) none (23,000); natural gas, none (none).

Foreign trade[11]

Balance of trade (current prices)

	1990	1991	1992	1993	1994	1995
EC$'000,000	−129.3	−110.5	−140.3	−123.6	−137.3	−189.4
% of total	29.9%	26.9%	32.7%	32.3%	35.8%	44.0%

Imports (1995): EC$314,300,000 ([12]machinery and transport equipment 28.5%; basic manufactures 25.1%; food 18.4%; chemicals and chemical products 12.8%). *Major import sources:* Caricom countries 25.8%; U.S. (including Puerto Rico) 23.4%; U.K. 13.7%; France 8.2%; Japan 7.6%.
Exports (1995): EC$115,000,000 (manufactured exports 49.3%, of which coconut-based laundry and toilet soaps 32.9%; agricultural exports 47.7%, of which bananas 38.5%; reexports 3.0%). *Major export destinations*[13]: U.K. 53.5%; Caricom countries 24.2%; U.S. (including Puerto Rico) 15.7%.

Transport and communications

Transport. Railroads: none. Roads (1995): total length 475 mi, 765 km (paved 50%). Vehicles (1995): passenger cars 2,770; trucks and buses 2,839. Merchant marine (1992): vessels (100 gross tons and over) 7; total deadweight tonnage 3,153. Air transport (1991): passenger arrivals 43,312, passenger departures, n.a.; cargo unloaded 259 metric tons, cargo loaded 415 metric tons; airports (1996) with scheduled flights 2.

Communications

Medium	date	unit	number	units per 1,000 persons
Radio	1996	receivers	65,000	875
Television	1995	receivers	5,200	70
Telephones	1995	main lines	17,800	240
Facsimile machines	1995	units	300	4.0

Education and health

Educational attainment (1991). Percentage of population age 25 and over having: no formal schooling 4.2%; primary education 78.4%; secondary 11.0%; higher vocational 2.3%; university 2.8%; other/unknown 1.3%. *Literacy* (1990): total population age 15 and over literate, *c.* 42,000 (90.0%).

Education (1994–95)

	schools	teachers	students	student/teacher ratio
Primary	64 }	641	12,627 }	29.8
Secondary	13[14] }		6,493 }	
Higher[14]	2	34	484	14.2

Health: physicians (1993) 24 (1 per 2,952 persons); hospital beds (1992) 241 (1 per 298 persons); infant mortality rate per 1,000 live births (1996) 9.6.
Food (1995): daily per capita caloric intake 3,032 (vegetable products 79%, animal products 21%); 125% of FAO recommended minimum requirement.

Military

Total active duty personnel (1996): none[15].

[1]Includes 22 seats that are elective (including speaker if elected from outside of the House of Assembly) and 10 seats that are nonelective (including 9 appointees of the president and the attorney general serving ex officio). [2]Area breakdown by parish is based on 1961 survey. Total area of Dominica per more recent survey is 290 sq mi (750 sq km). [3]Includes institutionalized population of 1,717. [4]Employed persons only. [5]Net of indirect taxes less imputed banking service charge. [6]Detail does not add to total given because of rounding. [7]April. [8]Weights of consumer price index components. [9]1996. [10]1990. [11]Imports f.o.b. in balance of trade and c.i.f. in commodities and trading partners. [12]Breakdown based on 1992 imports valued at EC$299,200,000. [13]Excludes reexports. [14]1992–93. [15]300-member police force includes a coast guard unit.

Internet resources for further information:
- **Dominica Online: Statistics http://delphis.netgate.net/stats.htm**
- **Dominica Business Online: The Economy http://delphis.netgate.net/dbeco.htm#STATS**

Dominican Republic

Official name: República Dominicana (Dominican Republic).
Form of government: multiparty republic with two legislative houses (Senate [30]; Chamber of Deputies [120]).
Head of state and government: President.
Capital: Santo Domingo.
Official language: Spanish.
Official religion: none[1].
Monetary unit: 1 Dominican peso (RD$) = 100 centavos; valuation (Oct. 3, 1997) 1 U.S.$ = RD$14.33; 1 £ = RD$23.09.

Area and population

Provinces	area sq km	population 1993 preliminary census	Provinces	area sq km	population 1993 preliminary census
Azua	2,532	194,209	Monte Cristi	1,925	94,429
Baoruco	1,283	101,742	Monte Plata	2,633	162,630
Barahona	1,739	157,772	Pedernales	2,077	16,975
Dajabón	1,021	63,995	Peravia	1,648	199,661
Duarte	1,605	272,277	Puerto Plata	1,857	255,061
El Seíbo	1,786	94,244	Salcedo	440	99,965
Espaillat	838	197,617	Samaná	854	73,094
Hato Mayor	1,329	76,761	San Cristóbal	1,265	409,381
Independencia	2,008	38,185	San Juan	3,571	247,029
La Altagracia	3,010	112,396	San Pedro de Macorís	1,255	212,886
Elías Piña	1,424	59,321	Sánchez Ramírez	1,196	158,218
La Romana	654	158,132	Santiago	2,836	690,548
La Vega	2,286	335,140	Santiago Rodríguez	1,112	60,015
María Trinidad Sánchez	1,271	122,165	Santo Domingo[2]	1,401	2,134,779
Monseñor Nouel	992	144,327	Valverde	823	146,087
			TOTAL	48,671	7,089,041[3]

Demography

Population (1997): 7,802,000.
Density (1997): persons per sq mi 415.2, persons per sq km 160.3.
Urban-rural (1993): urban 55.5%; rural 44.5%.
Sex distribution (1993): male 49.90%; female 50.10%.
Age breakdown (1995): under 15, 35.1%; 15–29, 29.0%; 30–44, 19.8%; 45–59, 9.9%; 60–74, 4.9%; 75 and over, 1.3%.
Population projection: (2000) 8,187,000; (2010) 9,414,000.
Doubling time: 38 years.
Ethnic composition (1993): mixed 73%; white 16%; black 11%.
Religious affiliation (1995): Roman Catholic 91.3%; other 8.7%.
Major urban centres (1993): Santo Domingo 1,555,656[4]; Santiago 364,859; La Romana 132,834; San Francisco de Macorís 129,943; San Pedro de Macorís 123,987.

Vital statistics

Birth rate per 1,000 population (1996): 23.5 (world avg. 25.0).
Death rate per 1,000 population (1996): 5.7 (world avg. 9.3).
Natural increase rate per 1,000 population (1996): 17.8 (world avg. 15.7).
Total fertility rate (avg. births per childbearing woman; 1996): 2.7.
Marriage rate per 1,000 population (1992): 3.6.
Life expectancy at birth (1996): male 66.9 years; female 71.3 years.
Major causes of death per 100,000 population (1985)[5]: diseases of the circulatory system 165; infectious and parasitic diseases 85; malignant neoplasms (cancers) 45; diseases of the respiratory system 41.

National economy

Budget (1995–96). Revenue: RD$26,494,000,000 (tax revenue 87.8%, of which taxes on goods and services 45.5%, import duties 24.7%, income taxes 16.7%; nontax revenue 6.3%; grants and loans 5.9%). Expenditures: RD$26,846,000,000 (development expenditure 53.9%; current expenditure 46.1%).
Public debt (external, outstanding; 1995): U.S.$3,550,000,000.
Gross national product (1995): U.S.$11,390,000,000 (U.S.$1,460 per capita).

Structure of gross domestic product and labour force

	1995 in value RD$'000,000	% of total value	labour force	% of labour force[6]
Agriculture	20,322	12.7	...	12.9
Mining	4,390	2.8	...	0.4
Manufacturing	28,152	17.5	...	17.5
Construction	15,282	9.5	...	4.6
Public utilities	3,051	1.9	...	0.6
Transp. and commun.	16,429	10.2	...	6.5
Trade, restaurants	29,697	18.5	...	21.2
Finance, real estate	16,194	10.1	...	3.4
Pub. admin., defense	13,626	8.5 }	...	24.6
Services	13,314	8.3 }		
Other	—	—	...	8.3[7]
TOTAL	160,456[8]	100.0	...	100.0

Production (metric tons except as noted). Agriculture, forestry, fishing (value of production in RD$'000,000; 1995): coffee 2,067, rice 1,781, chicken meat 1,692, sugarcane 1,586, milk 1,524, plantains 1,238, beef 1,077, beans 1,043, cacao beans 535, eggs 507, bananas 495, fish 110; roundwood (1995) 982,300 cu m. Mining (1996): nickel 30,400; gold 122,501 troy oz. Manufacturing (1995–96)[9]: cement 1,551,000; refined sugar 109,900; beer 2,010,000 hectolitres; rum 395,600 hectolitres; cigarettes 201,800,000 20-unit packs. Construction (value of authorized private construction in RD$'000,000; 1992): 2,519. Energy production (consumption): electricity (kW-hr; 1995) 6,044,000,000 (3,292,000,000); coal (metric tons; 1994) none (104,000); crude petroleum (barrels; 1994) none (14,594,000); petroleum products (metric tons; 1994) 1,782,000 (3,199,000); natural gas, none (none).
Tourism (1995): receipts U.S.$1,604,000,000; expenditures U.S.$85,000,000.
Population economically active (1991)[10]: total 2,758,000; activity rate of total population 37.6% (participation rates: age 10 and over, 50.3%; female 29.0%; unemployed [1994] 28.0%).

Price and earnings indexes (1990 = 100)

	1990	1991	1992	1993	1994	1995	1996
Consumer price index	100.0	153.9	160.9	169.4	183.4	206.4	217.0[11]
Annual earnings index[12]	100.0	130.0	130.0	150.0	150.0	180.0	...

Household income and expenditure. Average household size (1993) 3.9; average income: n.a.; sources of income: n.a.; expenditure (1980–85): food and beverages 46.0%, housing 10.0%, household goods 8.0%.
Land use (1994): forested 12.4%; meadows and pastures 43.4%; agricultural and under permanent cultivation 30.6%; other 13.6%.

Foreign trade[13]

Balance of trade (current prices)

	1991	1992	1993	1994	1995	1996
U.S.$'000,000	−1,071	−1,613	−1,607	−1,919	−2,020	−2,390
% of total	44.8%	58.9%	61.1%	59.8%	56.9%	59.5%

Imports (1995): U.S.$2,786,000,000 (crude petroleum and petroleum products 21.7%; agricultural products 17.2%, of which cereals 5.3%). *Major import sources*[10]: U.S. 44%; Venezuela 11%; Mexico 6%; Japan 5%; Netherlands Antilles 4%.
Exports (1995): U.S.$766,000,000[14] (ferronickel 31.6%; raw sugar 13.3%; raw coffee 10.6%; cacao 7.1%; gold 5.4%). *Major export destinations:* U.S. 47.6%; The Netherlands 14.1%; Puerto Rico 6.5%; South Korea 4.6%; Canada 4.4%.

Transport and communications

Transport. Railroads (1995)[15]: route length 1,083 mi, 1,743 km. Roads (1995): total length 7,643 mi, 12,300 km (paved 49%). Vehicles (1995): passenger cars 209,000; trucks and buses 141,400. Air transport (1994)[16]: passenger-mi 145,396,000, passenger-km 233,992,000; short ton-mi cargo 1,738,000, metric ton-km cargo 2,537,000; airports (1997) 7.

Communications

Medium	date	unit	number	units per 1,000 persons
Daily newspapers	1994	circulation	264,000	35
Radio	1996	receivers	1,180,000	154
Television	1995	receivers	728,000	97
Telephones	1995	main lines	569,000	76
Cellular telephones	1995	subscribers	33,000	4.4
Facsimile machines	1995	units	2,500	0.3

Education and health

Educational attainment (1981). Percentage of population age 25 and over having: no formal schooling 48.0%; incomplete primary education 31.7%; complete primary 4.0%; secondary 14.0%; higher 2.3%. *Literacy* (1995): total population age 15 and over literate, *c.* 4,164,000 (82.1%); males literate, *c.* 2,118,000 (82.0%); females literate, *c.* 2,046,000 (82.2%).

Education (1994–95)

	schools	teachers	students	student/teacher ratio
Primary (age 6–13)	4,001	42,135	1,462,722	34.7
Secondary (age 14–17)	...	10,757	240,441	22.4
Voc. teacher tr.	...	1,297	22,795	17.6
Higher[17]	7	5,091	73,461	14.4

Health (1994): physicians[18] 6,869 (1 per 1,076 persons); hospital beds[18] 8,621 (1 per 858 persons); infant mortality rate per 1,000 live births (1996) 47.7.
Food (1995): daily per capita caloric intake 2,323 (vegetable products 84%, animal products 16%); 103% of FAO recommended minimum.

Military

Total active duty personnel (1996): 24,500 (army 61.2%, navy 16.3%, air force 22.5%). *Military expenditure as percentage of GNP* (1994): 1.1% (world 3.0%); per capita expenditure U.S.$16.

[1]Roman Catholicism is the state religion per concordat with Vatican City. [2]National district. [3]Final census figure is 7,293,390. [4]Urban population of national district. [5]Projected rates based on about 60% of total deaths. [6]Official central bank estimates. [7]Not adequately defined. [8]Detail does not add to total given because of rounding. [9]Excludes free-zone sector for reexport (mostly ready-made garments) employing (1995) 184,000. [10]Estimated figures. [11]Average of 2nd and 3rd quarters. [12]Minimum wage in private sector. [13]Excludes free zones. [14]Excludes 1995 reexports of free zones equaling U.S.$1,764,000,000. [15]Most track is privately owned and serves the sugar industry only. [16]Dominicana and Dominair airlines. [17]Universities only. [18]Public sector only.

Internet resources for further information:
- **Consulate General of the Dominican Republic http://www.consudom-ny.do/**

Ecuador

Official name: República del Ecuador (Republic of Ecuador).
Form of government: unitary multiparty republic with one legislative house (National Congress [82]).
Head of state and government: President.
Capital: Quito.
Official language: Spanish.
Official religion: none.
Monetary unit: 1 Sucre (S/.) = 100 centavos; valuation (Oct. 3, 1997) 1 U.S.$ = S/. 4,151; 1 £ = S/. 6,690.

Area and population

Regions / Provinces	Capitals	area sq mi	area sq km	population 1997 estimate
Amazonica				
Morona-Santiago	Macas	13,100	33,930	131,845
Napo	Tena	9,918	25,690	146,319
Pastaza	Puyo	11,496	29,774	57,339
Sucumbíos	Nueva Loja	7,076	18,327	128,512
Zamora-Chinchipe	Zamora	8,923	23,111	94,339
Costa				
El Oro	Machala	2,259	5,850	524,466
Esmeraldas	Esmeraldas	5,884	15,239	389,967
Guayas	Guayaquil	7,916	20,503	3,201,672
Los Ríos	Babahoyo	2,770	7,175	630,303
Manabí	Portoviejo	7,289	18,879	1,211,064
Insular				
Galápagos	Puerto Baquerizo Moreno	3,093	8,010	14,713
Sierra				
Azuay	Cuenca	3,137	8,125	597,798
Bolívar	Guaranda	1,521	3,940	178,706
Cañar	Azogues	1,205	3,122	210,340
Carchi	Tulcán	1,392	3,605	160,983
Chimborazo	Riobamba	2,536	6,569	412,836
Cotopaxi	Latacunga	2,344	6,072	299,443
Imbabura	Ibarra	1,760	4,559	316,793
Loja	Loja	4,257	11,026	418,292
Pichincha	Quito	4,987	12,915	2,295,739
Tungurahua	Ambato	1,288	3,335	428,116
TOTAL		105,037[1, 2]	272,045[2]	11,936,858[3]

Demography

Population (1997): 11,937,000.
Density (1997): persons per sq mi 113.6, persons per sq km 43.9.
Urban-rural (1997): urban 62.0%; rural 38.0%.
Sex distribution (1997): male 50.23%; female 49.77%.
Age breakdown (1997): under 15, 35.4%; 15–29, 29.1%; 30–59, 28.9%; 60 and over, 6.6%.
Population projection: (2000) 12,646,000; (2010) 14,899,000.
Doubling time: 61 years.
Ethnic composition (1989): Amerindian 40.0%; mestizo 40.0%; white 15.0%; black 5.0%.
Religious affiliation (1995): Roman Catholic 93.4%; other 6.6%.
Major cities (1997): Guayaquil 1,973,880; Quito 1,487,513; Cuenca 255,028.

Vital statistics

Birth rate per 1,000 population (1995): 15.8[4] (world avg. 25.0); (1982) legitimate 67.9%; illegitimate 32.1%.
Death rate per 1,000 population (1995): 4.4[4] (world avg. 9.3).
Natural increase rate per 1,000 population (1995): 11.4[4] (world avg. 15.7).
Total fertility rate (avg. births per childbearing woman; 1994): 3.1.
Marriage rate per 1,000 population (1992): 6.4[4, 5].
Divorce rate per 1,000 population (1992): 0.6[4, 5].
Life expectancy at birth (1994): male 67.5 years; female 72.6 years.
Major causes of death per 100,000 population (1995): circulatory diseases 55.1; accidents, poisoning, and violence 29.2; pneumonia 27.2; diabetes mellitus 15.4; neoplasms (cancers) 12.7; parasitic diseases 12.2.

National economy

Budget (1995). Revenue: S/. 4,972,654,000,000 (income from petroleum 42.8%, indirect taxes 40.1%, direct taxes 17.1%). Expenditures: S/. 4,972,654,000,000 (general administration 48.7%, debt service 16.2%, subsidies 14.5%).
Production (metric tons except as noted). Agriculture, forestry, fishing (1996): sugarcane 6,750,000, bananas 5,309,000, rice 1,346,000, corn (maize) 855,000; livestock (live animals) 5,105,000 cattle, 2,621,000 pigs, 1,709,000 sheep, 63,105,000 chickens; roundwood (1995) 10,361,000 cu m; fish catch (1994) 339,915. Mining and quarrying (1994): limestone 1,900,000; gold 7,000 kg. Manufacturing (value added in S/. '000,000; 1994): chemical products 2,115,314; food products 803,936; nonmetallic mineral products 256,750; textiles 226,901. Construction (in S/.; 1992)[6]: residential 93,166,704,000; nonresidential 58,102,274,000. Energy production (consumption): electricity (kW-hr; 1994) 8,163,000,000 (8,163,000,000); crude petroleum (barrels; 1994) 123,998,000 (35,436,000); petroleum products (metric tons; 1994) 6,499,000 (5,135,000); natural gas (cu m; 1994) 204,000,000 (204,000,000).
Household income and expenditure. Average household size (1990) 4.1; average annual income per household (1995) S/. 9,825,610 (U.S.$3,830); sources of income (1995): self-employment 70.9%, wages 16.0%, transfer payments 6.7%, other 6.4%; expenditure (1995): food and tobacco 37.9%, transportation and communications 15.0%, clothing 9.2%, household furnishings 6.5%, housing and utilities 5.3%, health care 4.6%.

Population economically active (1990): total 3,359,767; activity rate of total population 34.8% (participation rates: ages 8 and over, 44.0%; female 26.4%; unemployed [1994] 7.1%).

Price and earnings indexes (1990 = 100)

	1990	1991	1992	1993	1994	1995	1996
Consumer price index	100.0	148.7	229.9	333.3	424.3	521.6	648.3
Hourly earnings index[7]	100.0	125.0	187.5	206.3	218.8	...	...

Public debt (external, outstanding; 1995): U.S.$12,032,000,000.
Gross national product (1995): U.S.$15,997,000,000 (U.S.$1,390 per capita).

Structure of gross domestic product and labour force

	1995 in value S/. '000,000[8]	1995 % of total value	1990 labour force	1990 % of labour force
Agriculture	37,033	17.2	1,035,712	30.8
Mining	31,348	14.6	20,870	0.6
Manufacturing	32,794	15.3	370,338	11.0
Construction	5,225	2.4	196,716	5.9
Public utilities	2,956	1.4	12,660	0.4
Transp. and commun.	19,313	9.0	131,084	3.9
Trade	31,679	14.7	476,730	14.2
Finance	25,467	11.8	81,357	2.4
Pub. admin., defense	15,579	7.2	838,129 (with Services)	24.9 (with Services)
Services	12,683	5.9		
Other	997[9]	0.5[9]	196,171[10]	5.8[10]
TOTAL	215,074	100.0	3,359,767	100.0[1]

Tourism (1995): receipts U.S.$255,000,000; expenditures U.S.$235,000,000.

Foreign trade[11]

Balance of trade (current prices)

	1991	1992	1993	1994	1995	1996
U.S.$'000,000	+736.0	+1,031.9	+680.7	+508.0	+532.4	+1,510.5
% of total	14.1%	20.7%	13.3%	7.3%	6.6%	18.3%

Imports (1995): U.S.$4,195,159,000 (machines and transport equipment 40.0%, basic manufactures 18.8%, chemicals 17.4%, food and live animals 6.3%, mineral fuels 5.9%). *Major import sources:* U.S. 31.2%; Colombia 9.6%; Japan 7.9%; Venezuela 6.1%; Germany 4.7%; Brazil 4.5%.
Exports (1995): U.S.$4,321,900,000 (food and live animals 47.6%, mineral fuels 30.2%, basic manufactures 2.7%, crude materials 2.3%). *Major export destinations:* U.S. 42.7%; Colombia 5.7%; Chile 4.5%; Italy 4.0%.

Transport and communications

Transport. Railroads (1994): route length 966 km; passenger-km 27,000,000; metric ton-km cargo 9,000,000. Roads (1995): total length 43,106 km (paved 18%). Vehicles (1995): passenger cars 395,000; trucks and buses 58,650. Air transport (1994): passenger-km 1,410,000,000; metric ton-km cargo 162,000,000; airports (1996) 14.

Communications

Medium	date	unit	number	units per 1,000 persons
Daily newspapers	1994	circulation	808,000	72
Radio	1996	receivers	3,240,000	277
Television	1995	receivers	900,000	79
Telephones	1995	main lines	748,200	65
Cellular telephones	1995	subscribers	49,800	4.3
Facsimile machines	1995	units	30,000	2.6
Personal computers	1995	units	45,000	3.9

Education and health

Educational attainment (1990). Percentage of population age 25 and over having: no formal schooling 2.2%; incomplete primary 54.3%; primary 28.0%; postsecondary 15.5%. *Literacy* (1990): total population age 15 and over literate 5,217,543 (88.3%); males 2,616,192 (90.5%); females 2,601,351 (86.2%).

Education (1992–93)

	schools[12]	teachers	students	student/teacher ratio
Primary (age 4–12)	16,146	63,347	1,986,753	31.4
Secondary (age 12–18) / Vocational	2,207	62,630	813,557	13.0
Higher	21	12,856[13]	206,541[13]	16.1[13]

Health: physicians (1993) 12,149 (1 per 904 persons); hospital beds (1992) 17,253 (1 per 623 persons); infant mortality rate (1995) 30.5.
Food (1992): daily per capita caloric intake 2,583 (vegetable products 86%, animal products 14%); 113% of FAO minimum requirement.

Military

Total active duty personnel (1996): 57,100 (army 87.6%, navy 7.2%, air force 5.2%). *Military expenditure as percentage of GNP* (1994): 3.5% (world 3.0%); per capita expenditure U.S.$49.

[1]Detail does not add to total given because of rounding. [2]Includes 884 sq mi (2,289 sq km) in nondelimited areas. [3]Total includes 87,273 persons in nondelimited areas. [4]Excluding nomadic Indian tribes. [5]Based on incomplete registration. [6]Authorized construction in Cuenca, Guayaquil, and Quito only. [7]General minimum wage. [8]At constant 1975 prices. [9]Minus imputed bank services plus gross import duties. [10]Includes unemployed persons not previously employed. [11]Import figures are f.o.b. in balance of trade and c.i.f. for commodities and trading partners. [12]1986–87. [13]1989–90.

Internet resources for further information:
- **Instituto Nacional de Estadistica y Censos (in Spanish) http://www4.inec.gov.ec/**

Egypt

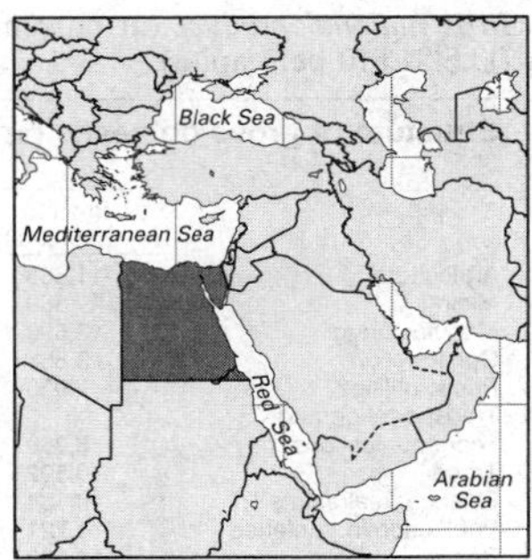

Official name: Jumhūrīyah Miṣr al-'Arabīyah (Arab Republic of Egypt).
Form of government: republic with one legislative house (People's Assembly [454[1]]).
Chief of state: President.
Head of government: Prime Minister.
Capital: Cairo.
Official language: Arabic.
Official religion: Islam.
Monetary unit: 1 Egyptian pound (£E) = 100 piastres; valuation (Oct. 3, 1997) 1 U.S.$ = £E 3.40; 1 £ = £E 5.48.

Area and population

Regions / Governorates	Capitals	area sq mi	area sq km	population 1995 estimate
Frontier				
Al-Baḥr al-Aḥmar	Al-Ghurdaqah	78,643	203,685	115,000
Janūb Sīnā'	Aṭ-Ṭūr	12,796	33,140	35,000
Maṭrūḥ	Marsā Maṭrūḥ	81,897	212,112	186,000
Shamāl Sīnā'	Al-'Arish	10,646	27,574	219,000
Al-Wādī al-Jadīd	Al-Kharijah	145,369	376,505	136,000
Lower Egypt				
Al-Buḥayrah	Damanhūr	3,911	10,130	3,973,000
Ad-Daqahlīyah	Al-Manṣūrah	1,340	3,471	4,226,000
Dumyāṭ	Dumyāṭ	227	589	898,000
Al-Gharbīyah	Ṭanṭā	750	1,942	3,437,000
Al-Ismā'īlīyah (Ismailia)	—	557	1,442	681,000
Kafr ash-Shaykh	Kafr ash-Shaykh	1,327	3,437	2,266,000
Al-Minūfīyah	Shibīn al-Kawm	592	1,532	2,672,000
Al-Qalyūbīyah	Banhā	387	1,001	3,045,000
Ash-Sharqīyah	Az-Zaqāzīq	1,614	4,180	4,220,000
Upper Egypt				
Aswān	Aswān	262	679	1,042,000
Asyūṭ	Asyūṭ	600	1,553	2,843,000
Banī Suwayf	Banī Suwayf	510	1,322	1,836,000
Al-Fayyūm	Al-Fayyūm	705	1,827	1,995,000
Al-Jīzah	Al-Jīzah	32,878	85,153	4,525,000
Al-Minyā	Al-Minyā	873	2,262	3,372,000
Qinā	Qinā	715[2]	1,851[2]	2,607,000
Sawhāj	Sawhāj	597	1,547	3,067,000
Urban				
Būr Sa'īd (Port Said)	—	28	72	467,000
Al-Iskandarīyah (Alexandria)	—	1,034	2,679	3,431,000
Al-Qāhirah (Cairo)	—	83	214	6,955,000
Al-Uqṣur (Luxor)	—	...[2]	...[2]	159,000
As-Suways (Suez)	—	6,888	17,840	411,000
TOTAL		385,229	997,739	58,819,000

Demography

Population (1997): 62,110,000.
Density (1997): persons per sq mi 161.2, persons per sq km 62.3.
Urban-rural (1996): urban 43.0%; rural 57.0%.
Sex distribution (1997): male 50.52%; female 49.48%.
Age breakdown (1997): under 15, 36.5%; 15–29, 28.4%; 30–44, 18.5%; 45–59, 10.8%; 60–74, 4.9%; 75 and over, 0.9%.
Population projection: (2000) 65,604,000; (2010) 77,349,000.
Ethnic composition (1986): Egyptian 99.9%; other 0.1%.
Religious affiliation (1990): Sunnī Muslim *c.* 90%; Christian *c.* 10%[3].
Major cities ('000; 1996): Cairo 9,900[4]; Alexandria 3,700[4]; Al-Jīzah 2,144[5].

Vital statistics

Birth rate per 1,000 population (1997): 28.0 (world avg. 25.0).
Death rate per 1,000 population (1997): 9.0 (world avg. 9.3).
Natural increase rate per 1,000 population (1997): 19.0 (world avg. 15.7).
Total fertility rate (avg. births per childbearing woman; 1997): 3.5.
Life expectancy at birth (1994): male 65.4 years; female 69.5 years.

National economy

Budget (1995–96). Revenue: £E 60,893,000,000 (general taxes 62.8%, of which income tax 22.5%, sales taxes 17.2%, customs duties 13.0%; oil revenue 7.7%; Suez Canal fees 4.9%). Expenditures: £E 63,889,000,000 (current expenditure 81.3%, of which debt servicing 25.1%, wages and salaries 22.0%).
Public debt (external, outstanding; 1995): U.S.$31,325,000,000.
Population economically active (1995–96): total 16,925,000; activity rate 28.1% (participation rates: ages 15–64, 49.0%; unemployed 9.4%).

Price and earnings indexes (1990 = 100)

	1991	1992	1993	1994	1995	1996	1997[6]
Consumer price index	119.7	136.1	152.5	165.0	190.9	204.7	214.7
Annual earnings index[7]	119.9	133.9	155.4	...	...	...	...

Production ('000; metric tons except as noted). Agriculture, forestry, fishing (1997): sugarcane 14,105, wheat 5,600, corn (maize) 5,180, tomatoes 5,038, rice 4,900, oranges 1,608, cotton 890, sorghum 650; livestock ('000; number of live animals) 3,491 sheep, 3,250 goats, 2,800 buffalo, 2,700 cattle, 42,000 chickens, 10,380 pigeons[8]; roundwood (1995) 2,698,000 cu m; fish catch (1995) 310. Mining and quarrying (1995): kaolin 293,381; iron ore 2,430; salt 1,900. Manufacturing (1995–96): cement 17,200; nitrate fertilizers 7,354; sugar 1,131; cotton yarn 275; refrigerators 373,000 units[9]; automobiles 6,800 units[9]. Construction (1992–93): urban residential units 123,098. Energy production (consumption): electricity ('000,000 kW-hr; 1994) 47,920 (47,920); coal ('000 metric tons; 1994) n.a. (1,852); crude petroleum ('000 barrels; 1994) 323,676 (192,342); petroleum products ('000 metric tons; 1994) 26,424 (16,630); natural gas ('000,000 cu m; 1994) 10,544 (10,544).
Gross national product (1995): U.S.$45,507,000,000 (U.S.$790 per capita).

Structure of gross domestic product and labour force

	1995–96[10] in value £E '000,000	1995–96[10] % of total value	1992 labour force	1992 % of labour force
Agriculture	24,470	16.0	5,535,000	35.0
Mining (petroleum)	41,335	26.9	44,900	0.3
Manufacturing			2,014,600	12.7
Construction	7,898	5.1	884,200	5.6
Public utilities	3,190	2.1	147,300	0.9
Transp. and commun.	16,116[11]	10.5[11]	777,700	4.9
Trade	28,545[12]	18.6[12]	1,332,100	8.4
Finance	8,832	5.8	237,100	1.5
Pub. admin., defense, services	11,150	7.3	3,420,200	21.6
Other	11,833	7.7	1,416,000[13]	8.9[13]
TOTAL	153,369	100.0	15,814,800[14]	100.0[14, 15]

Household income and expenditure. Average household size (1986) 4.9; expenditure (1986–87)[16]: food 55.7%, clothing 10.9%, housing 10.5%.
Tourism (1995): receipts U.S.$2,800,000,000; expenditures U.S.$1,278,000,000.

Foreign trade[17]

Balance of trade (current prices)

	1991	1992	1993	1994	1995	1996
U.S.$'000,000	−5,667	−5,231	−6,378	−5,953	−7,597	−8,390
% of total	40.5%	41.6%	47.4%	42.4%	44.8%	46.7%

Imports (1995–96): U.S.$13,826,400,000 (machinery and transport equipment 29.7%; foodstuffs 20.9%; iron and steel products 9.5%; chemical products 3.9%). *Major import sources:* U.S. 18.9%; Germany 9.6%; Italy 7.6%.
Exports (1995–96): U.S.$4,592,800,000 (petroleum and petroleum products 48.5%; cotton yarn, textiles, and clothing 12.5%; basic metals and manufactures 5.4%). *Major export destinations:* Italy 18.6%; U.S. 11.1%.

Transport and communications

Transport. Railroads (1995): length 4,810 km; passenger-km 47,992,000,000[18]; metric ton-km cargo 2,336,000,000[18]. Roads (1995): length 58,000 km (paved 78%). Vehicles (1995): passenger cars 1,280,000; trucks and buses 423,300. Inland water (1996–97): Suez Canal, number of transits 14,704; metric ton cargo 354,591,000. Air transport (1996)[19]: passenger-km 8,742,200,000; metric ton-km cargo 197,974,000; airports (1997) 11.

Communications

Medium	date	unit	number	units per 1,000 persons
Daily newspapers	1995	circulation	2,600,000	43.0
Radio	1995	receivers	19,400,000	312.0
Television	1995	receivers	6,850,000	110.0
Telephones	1995	main lines	2,716,200	46.3
Cellular telephones	1995	subscribers	7,400	0.1
Facsimile machines	1995	units	21,600	0.4
Personal computers	1995	units	235	0.004

Education and health

Literacy (1995): total population age 15 and over literate 51.4%; males 63.6%; females 38.8%.

Education (1995–96)

	schools	teachers	students	student/ teacher ratio
Primary (age 6–11)[20]	16,188	302,916	7,470,437	24.7
Secondary (age 12–17)[20]	7,307[18]	235,313	4,242,245	18.0
Vocational	1,351[18]	133,794	1,900,406	14.2
Teacher training	56[18]	650[7]	2,664[7]	4.1
Higher	12[21]	38,828[18, 22]	696,988[23]	...

Health: physicians (1996) 129,000 (1 per 472 persons); hospital beds (1994) 113,020 (1 per 515 persons); infant mortality rate (1997) 71.0.
Food (1995): daily per capita caloric intake 3,327 (vegetable products 94%, animal products 6%); 132% of FAO recommended minimum requirement.

Military

Total active duty personnel (1997): 450,000 (army 71.1%, navy 4.4%, air force [including air defense] 24.5%). *Military expenditure as percentage of GNP* (1995): 5.7% (world 2.8%); per capita expenditure U.S.$43.

[1]Includes 10 nonelective seats. [2]The area of Al-Uqṣur (Luxor) is included with Qinā governorate. [3]According to the 1986 census, the Christian population of Egypt was 5.9% of the total; this figure is considered by some external authorities to understate the Christian population by as much as 60%. [4]Population of urban agglomeration. [5]1992. [6]July. [7]Average nominal wages for each fiscal year (*e.g.,* 1990–91). [8]1991. [9]1992–93. [10]At 1991–92 constant prices. [11]Transportation includes earnings from traffic on the Suez Canal. [12]Trade includes restaurants and hotels. [13]Unemployed and those seeking work for the first time. [14]Total includes 5,700 persons not classifiable by sector. [15]Detail does not add to total given because of rounding. [16]Weight of consumer price components; urban households only. [17]Import figures are f.o.b. except for commodities and trading partners. [18]1993–94. [19]Egypt Air only. [20]Data exclude 1,770 primary and 1,449 secondary schools in the Al-Azhar education system. [21]Universities only. [22]Excludes Al-Azhar University. [23]1994–95.

Internet resources for further information:
- **Egypt State Information Service http://www.sis.gov.eg/**
- **Egypt's Information Highway http://www.idsc.gov.eg/**
- **Arab Net http://www.arab.net**

El Salvador

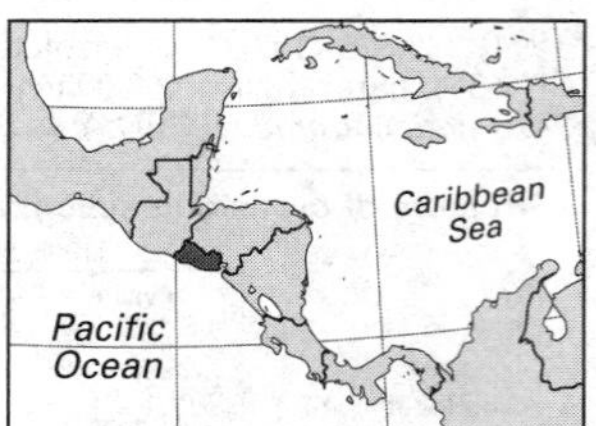

Official name: República de El Salvador (Republic of El Salvador).
Form of government: republic with one legislative house (Legislative Assembly [84]).
Chief of state and government: President.
Capital: San Salvador.
Official language: Spanish.
Official religion: none[1].
Monetary unit: 1 colón (₡) = 100 centavos; valuation (Oct. 3, 1997) 1 U.S.$ = ₡8.76; 1 £ = ₡14.11.

Area and population

		area		population
Departments	Capitals	sq mi	sq km	1992 census
Ahuachapán	Ahuachapán	479	1,240	261,188
Cabañas	Sensuntepeque	426	1,104	138,426
Chalatenango	Chalatenango	779	2,017	177,320
Cuscatlán	Cojutepeque	292	756	178,502
La Libertad	Nueva San Salvador	638	1,653	513,866
La Paz	Zacatecoluca	473	1,224	245,915
La Unión	La Unión	801	2,074	255,565
Morazán	San Francisco	559	1,447	160,146
San Miguel	San Miguel	802	2,077	403,411
San Salvador	San Salvador	342	886	1,512,125
San Vicente	San Vicente	457	1,184	143,003
Santa Ana	Santa Ana	781	2,023	458,587
Sonsonate	Sonsonate	473	1,225	360,183
Usulután	Usulután	822	2,130	310,362
TOTAL		8,124	21,041[2]	5,118,599

Demography

Population (1997): 5,662,000.
Density (1997): persons per sq mi 696.9, persons per sq km 269.1.
Urban-rural (1994): urban 54.8%; rural 45.2%.
Sex distribution (1993): male 47.53%; female 52.47%.
Age breakdown (1993): under 15, 39.9%; 15–29, 27.1%; 30–44, 15.4%; 45–59, 9.7%; 60 and over, 7.9%.
Population projection: (2000) 5,931,000; (2010) 6,850,000.
Doubling time: 33 years.
Ethnic composition (1993): mestizo (white and Indian) 89.0%; Amerindian 10.0%; white 1.0%.
Religious affiliation (1995): Roman Catholic 78.2%; Protestant 17.1%, of which Pentecostal 13.3%; other Christian 1.9%; other 2.8%.
Major cities (1992)[3]: San Salvador 422,570 (metro area 1,522,126); Soyapango 251,811[4]; Santa Ana 202,337; San Miguel 182,817; Mejicanos 145,000[4].

Vital statistics

Birth rate per 1,000 population (1996): 27.7 (world avg. 25.0).
Death rate per 1,000 population (1996): 6.6 (world avg. 9.3).
Natural increase rate per 1,000 population (1996): 21.1 (world avg. 15.7).
Total fertility rate (avg. births per childbearing woman; 1996): 3.2.
Marriage rate per 1,000 population (1992): 4.3.
Divorce rate per 1,000 population (1992): 0.5.
Life expectancy at birth (1996): male 65.5 years; female 72.4 years.
Major causes of death per 100,000 population (1991)[5]: diseases of the circulatory system 109; violence 66; accidents 62; malignant neoplasms (cancers) 44; infectious and parasitic diseases 39; ill-defined conditions 74.

National economy

Budget. Revenue (1995): ₡10,535,000,000 (sales taxes 43.5%, income taxes 26.6%, import duties 16.9%, nontax revenue 5.5%). Expenditures (1994): ₡10,264,300,000 (general public services 13.2%, education 13.2%, police 9.8%, fuel and energy 9.1%, health 8.3%, defense 8.1%).
Production (metric tons except as noted). Agriculture, forestry, fishing (1996): sugarcane 3,900,000, corn (maize) 639,600, sorghum 198,600, coffee 126,000, bananas 62,700, rice 50,500, dry beans 50,500, oranges 41,500, tobacco 1,240; livestock (number of live animals) 1,286,000 cattle, 400,000 pigs, roundwood (1994) 6,504,000 cu m; fish catch (1995) 15,812, of which crustaceans (1994) 4,844. Mining and quarrying (1993): limestone 2,600,000 metric tons. Manufacturing (value added in ₡'000,000[6]; 1995): food products 2,807; chemical products 854; beverages 837; textiles 738; petroleum products 668; nonmetallic mineral products 493; metallic products 471. Construction (buildings completed; 1993): residential 650,000 sq m; nonresidential 296,000 sq m. Energy production (consumption): electricity (kW-hr; 1994) 3,324,000,000 (3,415,000,000); coal, none (none); crude petroleum (barrels; 1994) none (7,469,000); petroleum products (metric tons; 1994) 985,000 (1,343,000).
Household income and expenditure. Average household size (1992–93): 4.8; average income per household (1992–93): ₡22,930 (U.S.$2,562); expenditure (1990–91)[7]: food and beverages 37.0%, housing 12.1%, transportation and communications 10.2%, clothing and footwear 6.7%.
Population economically active (1995): total 2,136,400; activity rate of total population 39.1% (participation rates: ages 15–64, 62.9%; female 37.1%; unemployed 7.6%).

Price and earnings indexes (1991 = 100)

	1991	1992	1993	1994	1995	1996	1997[8]
Consumer price index	100.0	111.2	131.8	145.8	160.4	176.0	184.5
Monthly earnings index[9]	100.0	110.1	127.5	143.4	...	...	...

Gross national product (at current market prices; 1995): U.S.$9,057,000,000 (U.S.$1,610 per capita).

Structure of gross domestic product and labour force

	1995			
	in value ₡'000,000	% of total value	labour force	% of labour force
Agriculture	11,683	13.8	584,900	27.4
Mining	389	0.5	1,100	0.1
Manufacturing	18,598	21.9	402,900	18.9
Construction	3,851	4.5	146,900	6.9
Public utilities	920	1.1	8,300	0.4
Transportation and communications	6,258	7.4	86,400	4.0
Trade	16,592	19.5	413,800	19.4
Finance, real estate	9,384	11.0	27,800	1.3
Public admin., defense	4,721	5.6	432,600	20.2
Services	12,568	14.8		
Other	—	—	31,600	1.5
TOTAL	84,962[2]	100.0[2]	2,136,400[2]	100.0[2]

Public debt (external, outstanding; 1995): U.S.$2,055,000,000.
Tourism (1995): receipts U.S.$75,000,000; expenditures U.S.$72,000,000.
Land use (1994): forested 5.0%; meadows and pastures 29.5%; agricultural and under permanent cultivation 35.2%; other 30.3%.

Foreign trade[10]

Balance of trade (current prices)

	1991	1992	1993	1994	1995	1996
U.S.$'000,000	−518.2	−982.3	−1,141.9	−1,448.9	−1,855.3	−1,646.5
% of total	41.4%	46.9%	44.4%	47.1%	48.2%	44.6%

Imports (1994): U.S.$2,261,600,000 (chemicals and chemical products 16.5%, transport equipment 12.4%, food and beverages 11.7%, nonelectrical machinery and equipment 11.6%). *Major import sources:* U.S. 41.5%; Guatemala 10.7%; Japan 6.3%; Venezuela 6.1%; Mexico 4.7%.
Exports (1994): U.S.$812,700,000 (coffee 32.5%, paper and paper products 7.0%, clothing 4.6%, pharmaceuticals 4.2%, raw sugar 4.2%). *Major export destinations:* U.S. 22.6%; Guatemala 21.9%; Germany 14.9%; Costa Rica 8.9%.

Transport and communications

Transport. Railroads (1995): route length 562 km; (1994) passenger-km 5,540,000; (1994) metric ton-km cargo 29,640,000. Roads (1995): total length 12,320 km (paved 14%). Vehicles (1995): passenger cars 102,000; trucks and buses 159,700. Air transport (1994)[11]: passenger-km 1,978,000,000; metric ton-km cargo 14,333,000; airports (1997) with scheduled flights 1.

Communications

Medium	date	unit	number	units per 1,000 persons
Daily newspapers	1994	circulation	284,000	53
Radio	1996	receivers	2,080,000	373
Television	1995	receivers	500,700	91
Telephones	1995	main lines	284,800	52
Cellular telephones	1995	subscribers	13,500	2.5
Facsimile machines	1990	units	3,500	0.7

Education and health

Educational attainment (1992): Percentage of population over age 25 having: no formal schooling 34.7%; incomplete primary education 37.6%; complete primary[12] 10.8%; secondary 9.4%; higher technical 2.4%; incomplete undergraduate 1.1%; complete undergraduate 2.9%; other/unknown 1.1%.
Literacy (1992): total population age 15 and over literate, 2,326,800 (74.1%); males literate, 1,141,007 (77.4%); females literate, 1,185,793 (71.3%).

Education (1993)

	schools	teachers	students	student/teacher ratio
Primary (age 7–15)	3,961	26,259[13]	1,042,256	39.7[13]
Secondary (age 16–18)	...	...	29,527	...
Voc. teacher tr.	...	...	88,588	...
Higher[14]	...	4,643	77,359	16.7

Health (1993): physicians 4,525 (1 per 1,219 persons); hospital beds 9,379 (1 per 588 persons); infant mortality rate per 1,000 live births (1996) 31.5.
Food (1995): daily per capita caloric intake 2,577 (vegetable products 89%, animal products 11%); 113% of FAO recommended minimum requirement.

Military

Total active duty personnel (1996): 28,400 (army 90.5%, navy 3.9%, air force 5.6%). *Military expenditure as percentage of GNP* (1995): 1.1% (world 2.8%); per capita expenditure U.S.$18.

[1]Roman Catholicism, although not official, enjoys special recognition in the constitution. [2]Detail does not add to total given because of rounding. [3]Population of *municipios* (second-order administrative units). [4]Within San Salvador metropolitan area. [5]Projected rates based on about 80% of total deaths. [6]At constant prices of 1990. [7]536,628 urban households only. [8]June. [9]Private sector only. [10]Imports c.i.f., exports f.o.b. [11]Taca airlines only. [12]Education completed through ninth grade. [13]Public schools only. [14]Universities and equivalent institutions only.

Internet resources for further information:

- **Inter-American Development Bank: Basic Socio-Economic Data http://database.iadb.org/int/basicrep/baslv.htm**
- **Consulado de El Salvador (Miami) http://www.queondas.com/consalvamia/**

Equatorial Guinea

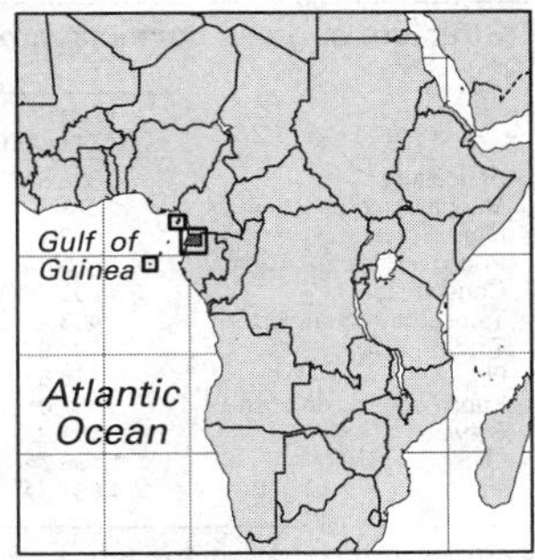

Official name: República de Guinea Ecuatorial (Republic of Equatorial Guinea).
Form of government: republic with one legislative house (Chamber of People's Representatives [80[1]]).
Chief of state: President.
Head of government: Prime Minister.
Capital: Malabo.
Official languages: Spanish; French.
Official religion: none.
Monetary unit[2]: 1 CFA franc (CFAF) = 100 centimes; valuation (Oct. 3, 1997) 1 U.S.$ = CFAF 592.29; 1 £ = CFAF 954.76.

Area and population

Regions / Provinces	Capitals	area sq mi	area sq km	population 1987 estimate
Insular		785[3]	2,034	70,280
Annobón	Palé	7	17	2,360
Bioko Norte	Malabo	300	776	56,600
Bioko Sur	Luba	479	1,241	11,320
Continental		10,045[3]	26,017	259,950
Centro-Sur	Evinayong	3,834	9,931	55,970
Kie-Ntem	Ebebiyin	1,522	3,943	74,050
Litoral[4]	Bata	2,573	6,665	75,640
Wele-Nzas	Mongomo	2,115	5,478	54,290
TOTAL		10,831[3]	28,051	330,230

Demography

Population (1997): 443,000.
Density (1997): persons per sq mi 40.9, persons per sq km 15.8.
Urban-rural (1992): urban 29.4%; rural 70.6%.
Sex distribution (1995): male 49.25%; female 50.75%.
Age breakdown (1995): under 15, 43.2%; 15–29, 25.5%; 30–44, 15.6%; 45–59, 9.3%; 60–74, 5.3%; 75 and over, 1.1%.
Population projection: (2000) 478,000; (2010) 615,000.
Doubling time: 27 years.
Ethnic composition (1983): Fang 82.9%; Bubi 9.6%; Ndowe 3.8%; Annobonés 1.5%; Bujeba 1.4%; other 0.8%.
Religious affiliation (1980): Christian (mostly Roman Catholic) 88.8%; traditional beliefs 4.6%; atheist 1.4%; Muslim 0.5%; other 0.2%; none 4.5%.
Major cities (1983): Malabo 30,418; Bata 24,308; Ela-Nguema 6,179; Campo Yaunde 5,199; Los Angeles 4,079.

Vital statistics

Birth rate per 1,000 population (1994): 40.7 (world avg. 25.0); legitimate, n.a.; illegitimate, n.a.
Death rate per 1,000 population (1994): 14.7 (world avg. 9.3).
Natural increase rate per 1,000 population (1994): 26.0 (world avg. 15.7).
Total fertility rate (avg. births per childbearing woman; 1994): 5.3.
Marriage rate per 1,000 population: n.a.
Divorce rate per 1,000 population: n.a.
Life expectancy at birth (1994): male 50.0 years; female 54.3 years.
Major causes of death per 100,000 population: n.a.; however, major diseases include malaria (about 24% of total mortality), respiratory infections (12% of mortality), cholera, leprosy, trypanosomiasis (sleeping sickness), and waterborne (especially gastrointestinal) diseases.

National economy

Budget (1995). Revenue: CFAF 27,468,000,000 (domestic revenue 49.3%, of which tax revenue 32.1%, nontax revenue 9.9%, oil revenue 7.3%; foreign grants 50.7%). Expenditures: CFAF 29,452,000,000 (capital expenditure 64.2%; current expenditure 34.7%, of which interest 12.0%, salaries 9.0%).
Public debt (external, outstanding; 1995): U.S.$229,600,000.
Gross national product (at current market prices; 1995): U.S.$152,000,000 (U.S.$380 per capita).

Structure of gross domestic product and labour force

	1995 in value CFAF '000,000	1995 % of total value	1983 labour force	1983 % of labour force
Agriculture, forestry	41,479	46.2	59,390	57.9
Manufacturing, mining	23,494	26.2	1,616	1.6
Construction	3,724	4.1	1,929	1.9
Public utilities	2,680	3.0	224	0.2
Transportation and communications	1,606	1.8	1,752	1.7
Trade	7,404	8.2	3,059	3.0
Finance	1,669	1.9	409	0.4
Pub. admin., defense	4,080	4.5	8,377	8.2
Services	2,270	2.5		
Other	1,409	1.6	25,809	25.2
TOTAL	89,815	100.0	102,565	100.0[3]

Production (metric tons except as noted). Agriculture, forestry, fishing (1996): roots and tubers 86,000 (of which cassava 49,000, sweet potatoes 37,000), bananas 17,000, coconuts 8,000, coffee 7,000, palm oil 5,000, cacao beans 4,500, palm kernels 3,000; livestock (number of live animals) 36,000 sheep, 8,100 goats, 5,300 pigs, 4,800 cattle; roundwood (1995) 714,000 cu m; fish catch (1995) 3,800. Mining and quarrying: details, n.a.; however, in addition to quarrying for construction materials, unexploited deposits of iron ore, lead, zinc, manganese, and molybdenum are present; the offshore Alba gas-condensate field, opened in 1992, achieved commercial production of 7,000 barrels of condensate per day in 1994 (11 months). Manufacturing (1995): veneer sheets 9,300. Construction: n.a. Energy production (consumption): electricity (kW-hr; 1994) 20,000,000 (20,000,000); coal, none (n.a.); crude petroleum[5], none (n.a.); petroleum products (metric tons; 1994) none (41,000); natural gas, none (n.a.).
Population economically active (1991): total 148,000; activity rate of total population 41.0% (participation rates [1983]: ages 15–64, 66.7%; female 35.7%; unemployed 24.2%).

Price and earnings indexes (1990 = 100)

	1987	1988	1989	1990	1991	1992	1993
Consumer price index	92.3	93.4	98.9	100.0	96.8	89.9	93.5
Earnings index	...	...	...	...	...	...	...

Household income and expenditure. Average household size (1980) 4.5; income per household: n.a.; sources of income (1988): wages and salaries 57.0%, business income 42.0%, other 1.0%; expenditure (1988): food and beverages 62.0%, clothing and footwear 10.0%, medical care 6.0%.
Tourism: tourism is a government priority but remains undeveloped.
Land use (1994): forested 65.2%; meadows and pastures 3.7%; agricultural and under permanent cultivation 8.2%; built-on, wasteland, and other 22.9%.

Foreign trade

Balance of trade (current prices)

	1990	1991	1992	1993	1994	1995
CFAF '000,000	−8,522	−6,017	−10,932	+2,537	+16,104	+20,454
% of total	29.7%	11.4%	33.5%	7.7%	30.5%	31.5%

Imports (1995): CFAF 37,900,000,000 (capital equipment 52.7%; petroleum products 4.5%; other 42.8%). *Major import sources:* Cameroon 40.6%; Spain 18.2%; France 14.3%; United States 7.8%; Belgium 6.5%; The Netherlands 5.2%; Italy 3.9%.
Exports (1995): CFAF 43,100,000,000 (petroleum products 44.6%; wood 41.6%; food products 5.9%, of which cocoa 5.8%). *Major export destinations:* United States 34.0%; Japan 17.4%; China 12.7%; Spain 12.7%; Portugal 4.6%; The Netherlands 4.6%; France 4.6%; Nigeria 3.5%.

Transport and communications

Transport. Railroads: none. Roads (1993): total length 1,667 mi, 2,682 km (paved 19%). Vehicles (1994): passenger cars 6,500; trucks and buses 4,000. Merchant marine (1992): vessels (100 gross tons and over) 3; total deadweight tonnage 6,699. Air transport (1990): passenger-mi 4,000,000, passenger-km 7,000,000; short ton-mi cargo (1985) 700,000, metric ton-km cargo (1985) 1,000,000; airports (1997) with scheduled flights 1.

Communications

Medium	date	unit	number	units per 1,000 persons
Daily newspapers	1994	circulation	1,000	2.4
Radio	1996	receivers	200,000	464
Television	1995	receivers	37,000	88
Telephones	1995	main lines	2,500	5.9
Facsimile machines	1995	units	100	0.2

Education and health

Educational attainment (1983). Percentage of population age 15 and over having: no schooling 35.4%; some primary education 46.6%; primary 13.0%; secondary 2.3%; postsecondary 1.1%; not specified 1.6%. *Literacy* (1983): percentage of total population age 15 and over literate 62.2%; males literate 77.8%; females literate 48.6%.

Education (1993–94)

	schools	teachers	students	student/ teacher ratio
Primary (age 6–11)	781	1,381	75,751	54.9
Secondary (age 12–17)	9[6]	466	14,511	31.1
Voc., teacher tr.[7]	1[6]	122	2,105	17.3
Higher	4[6]	58	578	10.0

Health: physicians (1990) 99 (1 per 3,532 persons); hospital beds (1990) 992 (1 per 350 persons); infant mortality rate per 1,000 live births (1994) 102.6.
Food (latest): daily per capita caloric intake 2,230; 68% of FAO recommended minimum requirement.

Military

Total active duty personnel (1997): 1,320 (army 83.3%, navy 9.1%, air force 7.6%). *Military expenditure as percentage of GNP* (1995): 1.6% (world 2.8%); per capita expenditure U.S.$5.

[1]Conduct of November 1993 legislative elections was unacceptable to international observers. [2]As of Jan. 1, 1985, Equatorial Guinea became a member of the franc zone, substituting the CFA franc for the previous monetary unit, the ekwele; the CFA franc has a par value of 100 CFA francs to the French franc. [3]Detail does not add to total given because of rounding. [4]Includes three islets in Corisco Bay. [5]Equatorial Guinea announced an oil strike off Bioko in 1995 having an estimated production capacity of 10,000 barrels per day. [6]1987–88. [7]Efforts are being undertaken to provide the training necessary to qualify nondegree teachers for service. Also, teacher-training schools are to be expanded in order to increase the number of primary-school teachers.

Eritrea

Official name: State of Eritrea.
Form of government: transitional regime with one interim legislative body (Constituent Assembly [150][1]).
Head of state and government: President.
Capital: Asmara.
Official language: none.
Official religion: none.
Monetary unit: Ethiopian birr[2] (Br) = 100 cents; valuation (Oct. 3, 1997) 1 U.S.$ = Br 6.69; 1 £ = Br 10.78.

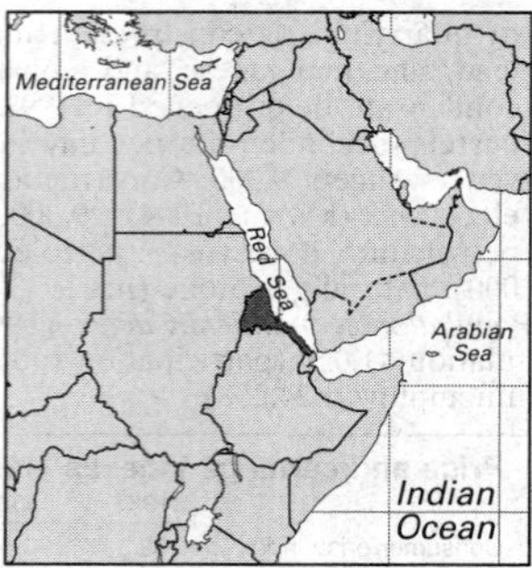

Area and population

		area[3]		population
				1997
Regions[4]	Capitals	sq mi	sq km	estimate
Region 1	Asseb (Aseb)	10,660	27,600	...
Region 2	Massawa (Mitsiwa)	10,730	27,800	...
Region 3	Keren	8,960	23,200	...
Region 4	Barentu	12,820	33,200	...
Region 5	Mendefera	3,090	8,000	...
Region 6	Asmara (Asmera)	500	1,300	...
TOTAL		46,770[5]	121,100	3,590,000

Demography

Population (1997): 3,590,000.
Density (1997): persons per sq mi 76.8, persons per sq km 29.7.
Urban-rural (1992): urban 16.3%; rural 83.7%.
Sex distribution (1997): male 50.00%; female 50.00%.
Age breakdown (1997): under 15, 42.8%; 15–29, 29.3%; 30–44, 13.6%; 45–59, 9.1%; 60–74, 4.2%; 75 and over, 1.0%.
Population projection: (2000) 4,461,000; (2010) 5,956,000.
Doubling time: 28 years.
Linguistic composition (1976): Tigrinya 49.0%; Tigré 31.7%; Afar 4.3%; Hedareb 3.9%; Bilen 3.1%; Saho 3.0%; Kunama 2.7%; Nara 2.1%; Rashaida 0.3%.
Religious affiliation (1993): believers are *c.* 50% Christian and *c.* 50% Muslim; there are also a few animists.
Major cities (1992): Asmara 400,000; Asseb 50,000; Keren 40,000; Massawa 40,000; Mendefera 14,833[6].

Vital statistics

Birth rate per 1,000 population (1995–2000): 39.8 (world avg. 25.0).
Death rate per 1,000 population (1995–2000): 14.7 (world avg. 9.3).
Natural increase rate per 1,000 population (1995–2000): 25.1 (world avg. 15.7).
Total fertility rate (avg. births per childbearing woman; 1995–2000): 5.3.
Marriage rate per 1,000 population (1992): 6.8.
Divorce rate per 1,000 population: n.a.
Life expectancy at birth (1995–2000): male 49.1 years; female 52.1 years.
Major causes of death per 100,000 population: n.a.; morbidity (principal causes of illness) arises mainly in malaria and other infectious diseases, parasitic infections, malnutrition, diarrheal diseases, and dysenteries.

National economy

Budget (1995). Revenue: Br 1,345,200,000 (taxes 53.2%, of which direct taxes 25.3%, import duties 16.7%, indirect taxes 11.2%; nontax revenue 46.8%). Expenditures: Br 2,657,100,000 (current expenditure 80.2%, of which materials 32.0%, wages and salaries 24.3%; capital 19.8%).
Public debt: n.a.
Production (metric tons except as noted). Agriculture, forestry, fishing (1996): cereals 124,000, roots and tubers 110,000, sorghum 80,000, millet 35,000, barley 35,000, pulses 33,000, vegetables and melons 30,000, wheat 12,000, corn (maize) 10,000, sesame seeds 7,000, dry beans 4,000, chickpeas 4,000; livestock (number of live animals) 1,530,000 sheep, 1,400,000 goats, 1,320,000 cattle, 69,000 camels; fish catch (1995) 3,773, of which artisanal fisheries 746. Mining and quarrying (1995): salt 305,120; marble and granite are quarried, as are sand and aggregate (gravel) for construction; deposits of copper, zinc, mica, gold, iron, manganese, nickel, and lead exist but remain unexploited. Manufacturing (gross value in Br '000; 1995): beverages 163,400; food products 122,000; chemical products 101,900; leather products and shoes 57,900; textile products 54,300; metal products 47,000; nonmetallic products 31,300; paper and printing products 19,100; tobacco and matches 13,400. Construction: reconstruction, after some 30 years of civil war, is a principal concern of the government. Energy production: energy resources include hydroelectricity, fossil fuels, geothermal power, coal, biogas, solar power, and wind; commercial electricity production for 1986–87 was 148,664,000 kW-hr.
Household income and expenditure. Average household size (1984) 4.5; average annual income per household: n.a.; sources of income: n.a.; expenditure: n.a.
Persons economically active: n.a.

Price and earnings indexes (December 1992 = 100)

	1991	1992	1993	1994	1995
Consumer price index[7]	91.9	100.0	119.2	127.4	141.3
Earnings index	...	...	...	...	...

Gross national product (at current market prices; 1993): *c.* U.S.$393,415,000 (U.S.$115 per capita).

Structure of gross domestic product and labour force

	1995		1992	
	in value Br '000,000	% of total value	labour force	% of labour force
Agriculture	390.8	8.4	647	2.6
Manufacturing	571.3	12.2	11,894	48.3
Mining	2.1	0.1	292	1.2
Public utilities	59.8	1.3	2,284	9.3
Construction	235.6	5.0	298	1.2
Transp. and commun.	453.4	9.7	3,126	12.7
Trade	921.9	19.7	597	2.4
Finance	136.8	2.9	382	1.6
Public admin., defense	558.0	11.9		
Services	156.2	3.3	5,001	20.3
Other	1,195.7[8]	25.5[8]		
TOTAL	4,681.5[5]	100.0	24,621[5]	100.0[5]

Tourism (1993): 12 major hotels.
Land use (1994): forested 7.3%; agricultural and under permanent cultivation 5.1%; meadows and pastures 69.0%; other (predominantly barren land) 18.6%.

Foreign trade

Balance of trade (current prices)

	1992	1993	1994	1995
U.S.$'000,000	−263.0	−239.0	−331.0	−323.0
% of total	89.8%	76.8%	71.9%	66.6%

Imports (1995): Br 2,608,500,000 (machinery and transport equipment 45.2%, manufactured goods 19.1%, food products 17.1%, chemical products 6.0%, raw materials 2.5%, petroleum and petroleum products 1.9%, animal and vegetable oils 1.2%). *Major import sources:* Saudi Arabia 19.6%[9]; Italy 17.5%; United Arab Emirates 9.2%; Germany 5.9%; United States 5.9%; Ethiopia 5.5%; United Kingdom 3.8%; The Sudan 3.0%.
Exports (1995): Br 529,500,000 (raw materials 29.8%, food products 26.2%, manufactured goods 19.3%, beverages and tobacco 3.8%, machinery and transport equipment 3.8%, chemical products 2.5%). *Major export destinations:* Ethiopia 63.3%; The Sudan 16.4%; Yemen 4.9%; Saudi Arabia 3.7%; Italy 2.2%; Germany 0.5%.

Transport and communications

Transport. Railroads (1997): a 190-mi (306-km) rail line that formerly connected Massawa and Agordat is currently under reconstruction. A 24-mi (38-km) section between Amatere and Demas townships was reopened on Jan. 4, 1997. Roads (1995): total length 2,442 mi, 3,930 km (paved 21%). Vehicles (1995): automobiles 5,350, trucks and buses, n.a. Merchant marine: vessels (100 gross tons and over) n.a. Air transport (1993)[10]: passenger arrivals 47,645[11], passenger departures 42,548[11]; short ton cargo handled 25,907[12], metric ton cargo handled 28,557[12]; airports (1997) with scheduled flights 2.

Communications

Medium	date	unit	number	units per 1,000 persons
Television	1995	receivers	22,000	6.0
Telephones	1995	main lines	17,200	4.8
Facsimile machines	1995	units	800	0.2

Education and health

Literacy (1993): total population literate *c.* 20%.

Education (1995–96)

	schools	teachers	students	student/ teacher ratio
Primary (age 7–12)	537	5,828	241,725	41.5
Secondary (age 13–18)	86[13]	2,031	78,902	38.8
Voc., teacher tr.[14]	4[13]	133	1,246	9.4
Higher[15]	1	144	2,032	14.1

Health (1993): physicians 69 (1 per 36,000 persons); hospital beds (1986–87): 2,449 (1 per 1,100 persons); infant mortality rate per 1,000 live births (1995–2000) 98.0.
Food (1993): daily per capita caloric intake 1,750 (vegetable and animal products, n.a.); 93% of FAO recommended minimum requirement.

Military

Total active duty personnel (1997): estimated strength of Eritrean armed forces (predominantly former guerrillas) is some 45,000 to be reduced to 35,000.

[1]Indirectly elected by regional administrative bodies between January and March 1997; Constituent Assembly will write a constitution and is expected to be replaced by a permanent legislature in about 5 years. [2]The Nakfa was introduced in July 1997 as the new national currency; the Ethiopian birr will eventually be phased out. [3]Approximate figures. The published total area is 46,774 sq mi (121,144 sq km); water area is 7,776 sq mi (20,140 sq km). [4]On May 20, 1995, a resolution was approved dividing the country into six administrative regions, which would then be divided into region, subregion, and village categories. [5]Detail does not add to total given because of rounding. [6]1989. [7]Asmara only; year-end. [8]Including indirect taxes less subsidies. [9]Saudi Arabia is a transshipment point; not all goods included here are of Saudi Arabian origin. [10]Asmara airport only. [11]January to June only. [12]1987–88. [13]1992–93. [14]1994–95. [15]1993–94; full-time students only.

Internet resources for further information:
- **Government of Eritrea http://www.NetAfrica.org/eritrea/**

Estonia

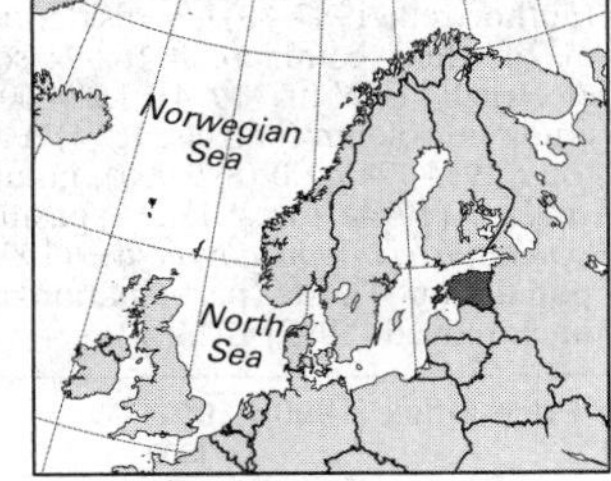

Official name: Eesti Vabariik (Republic of Estonia).
Form of government: unitary multiparty republic with a single legislative body (Riigikogu[1] [101]).
Chief of state: President.
Head of government: Prime Minister.
Capital: Tallinn.
Official language: Estonian.
Official religion: none.
Monetary unit: 1 kroon (EEK) = 100 sents; valuation (Oct. 3, 1997) 1 U.S.$ = EEK 14.10; 1 £ = EEK 22.73.

Area and population

Counties	Capitals	area sq mi	area sq km	population 1995[2] estimate
Harju	Tallinn	1,673	4,333	559,106
Hiiu	Kärdla	395	1,023	11,953
Ida-Viru	Jõhvi	1,299	3,364	206,418
Järva	Paide	1,013	2,623	43,639
Jõgeva	Jõgeva	1,005	2,604	42,146
Lääne	Haapsalu	920	2,383	32,586
Lääne-Viru	Rakvere	1,337	3,464	75,533
Pärnu	Pärnu	1,856	4,806	99,563
Põlva	Põlva	836	2,165	36,315
Rapla	Rapla	1,151	2,980	40,058
Saare	Kuressaare	1,128	2,922	40,759
Tartu	Tartu	1,193	3,090	154,483
Valga	Valga	790	2,047	40,014
Viljandi	Viljandi	1,386	3,589	64,377
Võru	Võru	890	2,305	44,633
TOTAL		17,462[3, 4]	45,227[3, 4]	1,491,583

Demography

Population (1997): 1,463,000.
Density (1997)[5]: persons per sq mi 83.8, persons per sq km 32.3.
Urban-rural (1996): urban 69.4%; rural 30.6%.
Sex distribution (1996): male 47.23%; female 52.77%.
Age breakdown (1995): under 15, 20.7%; 15–29, 21.0%; 30–44, 21.7%; 45–59, 18.1%; 60–74, 13.8%; 75 and over, 4.7%.
Population projection: (2000) 1,430,000; (2010) 1,401,000.
Ethnic composition (1994): Estonian 63.9%; Russian 29.0%; Ukrainian 2.7%; Belarusian 1.6%; Finnish 1.0%; other 1.8%.
Religious affiliation (1997): Estonian Orthodox 19.9%; Evangelical Lutheran 13.7%; other 66.4%.
Major cities (1996): Tallinn 434,763; Tartu 101,901; Narva 75,211; Kohtla-Järve 68,533; Pärnu 51,807.

Vital statistics

Birth rate per 1,000 population (1996): 9.0 (world avg. 25.0); (1994) legitimate 59.1%; illegitimate 40.9%.
Death rate per 1,000 population (1996): 12.9 (world avg. 9.3).
Natural increase rate per 1,000 population (1996): −3.9 (world avg. 15.7).
Total fertility rate (avg. births per childbearing woman; 1995): 1.3.
Marriage rate per 1,000 population (1994): 4.9.
Divorce rate per 1,000 population (1994): 3.7.
Life expectancy at birth (1993): male 62.4 years; female 73.8 years.
Major causes of death per 100,000 population (1993): diseases of the circulatory system 792.9, of which ischemic heart diseases 485.6, cerebrovascular disease 255.6; malignant neoplasms (cancers) 225.3; accidents 110.5.

National economy

Budget (1995). Revenue: EEK 15,952,000,000 (payments for social security and welfare 31.7%, value-added taxes 27.0%, personal income taxes 24.5%, corporate taxes 7.3%). Expenditures: EEK 15,498,000,000 (current expenditure 94.8%, capital expenditure 5.2%).
Public debt (external, outstanding; 1995): U.S.$181,700,000.
Production (metric tons except as noted). Agriculture, forestry, fishing (1996): potatoes 500,000, barley 273,000, oats 100,000, wheat 100,000, rye 70,000, apples 17,000; livestock (number of live animals) 449,000 pigs, 370,400 cattle; roundwood (1996) 3,901,000 cu m; (1995) fish catch 212,000. Mining and quarrying (value of production in EEK '000,000; 1994): oil shale 781; peat 121. Manufacturing (value of production in EEK '000,000; 1994): meat and meat products 1,502; chemicals and chemical products 1,502; dairy products 1,368; fish and fish products 1,156; beverages 1,091; cement, bricks, and tiles 923; wood and wood products (excluding furniture) 922; textiles 908. Construction (value of construction in EEK '000,000; 1994): residential 295; nonresidential 1,836. Energy production (consumption): electricity (kW-hr; 1994) 9,152,000,000 (5,288,000,000); oil shale (metric tons; 1994) 16,000,000[6] (16,299,000); coal and coke (metric tons; 1994) none (97,000); crude petroleum, none (n.a.); natural gas (cu m; 1994) none (645,000,000).
Population economically active (1995): total 726,700; activity rate of total population 48.7% (participation rates [1989]: ages 15–64, 68.5%; female 52.5%; unemployed [1995] 3.6%).

Price and earnings indexes (1994 = 100)[7]

	1994	1995	1996	1997
Consumer price index	100.0	127.0	156.3	172.3
Monthly earnings index	100.0	137.1	173.0	212.4

Household income and expenditure. Average household size (1994) 3.1[8]; average net income per household (1994) EEK 46,303 (U.S.$3,681)[8]; sources of income (1994)[9]: wages and salaries 53.0%, transfers 12.8%, self-employment 5.7%, other 28.5%; expenditure (1994)[9]: food and beverages 41.0%, housing 9.6%, transportation 9.2%, clothing and footwear 8.4%.
Gross national product (1995): U.S.$4,252,000,000 (U.S.$2,860 per capita).

Structure of gross domestic product and labour force

	1994 in value EEK '000,000	1994 % of total value	1995 labour force	1995 % of labour force
Agriculture, fishing	2,787	9.2	85,900	11.8
Mining	540	1.8	10,300	1.4
Manufacturing	5,059	16.7	137,400	18.9
Public utilities	883	2.9	19,600	2.7
Construction	1,666	5.5	47,900	6.6
Trade, restaurants	5,615	18.6	109,300	15.0
Transp. and commun.	2,734	9.1	55,400	7.6
Finance, real estate	2,452	8.1	36,800	5.1
Pub. admin., defense	1,216	4.0	36,500	5.0
Services	2,418	8.0	123,900	17.0
Other	4,858[10]	16.1	63,700	8.8
TOTAL	30,228	100.0	726,700	100.0[11]

Tourism (1995): receipts U.S.$353,000,000; expenditures U.S.$90,000,000.
Land use (1994): forest 44.7%; pasture 7.2%; agriculture 32.2%; other 15.9%.

Foreign trade[12]

Balance of trade (current prices)

	1992	1993	1994	1995	1996
EEK '000,000	+79	−1,309	−4,594	−8,287	−8,061
% of total	0.8%	5.8%	12.0%	16.4%	16.1%

Imports (1996): U.S.$3,209,000,000 (1995; machinery 21.4%, food 14.1%, textiles and clothing 12.8%, chemical products 12.4%, mineral fuels 11.4%). *Major import sources:* Finland 29.1%; Russia 13.4%; Germany 9.9%.
Exports (1996): U.S.$2,077,000,000 (1995; food 16.4%, textiles and clothing 16.1%, wood and paper products 13.4%, machinery 13.1%, chemicals 10.2%). *Major export destinations:* Finland 18.3%; Russia 16.4%; Sweden 11.6%; Latvia 8.2%; Germany 7.1%.

Transport and communications

Transport. Railroads (1996): route length 1,018 km; (1995) passenger-km 421,000,000; metric ton-km cargo 3,612,000,000. Roads (1995): total length 14,992 km (paved 54%). Vehicles (1995): passenger cars 383,000; trucks and buses 96,700. Merchant marine (1992): vessels (100 gross tons and over) 234; (1994) total deadweight tonnage 695,000. Air transport (1996)[13]: passenger-km 120,000,000; metric ton-km cargo 762,000; airports (1997) 1.

Communications

Medium	date	unit	number	units per 1,000 persons
Daily newspapers	1995	circulation	373,000	242
Television	1995	receivers	610,000	411
Telephones	1995	main lines	412,000	277
Cellular telephones	1995	subscribers	31,000	21
Facsimile machines	1995	units	13,000	8.7
Personal computers	1995	units	10,000	6.7

Education and health

Educational attainment (1989). Percentage of persons age 25 and over having: no formal schooling 2.2%; primary education 39.0%; secondary 45.1%; higher 13.7%. *Literacy* (1989): percentage of population age 15 and over literate 99.7%; males literate 99.9%; females literate 99.6%.

Education (1994–95)

	schools	teachers	students	student/ teacher ratio
Primary } Secondary }	741	15,453	218,600	14.1
Vocational	84	1,585	27,806	17.5
Higher	22	...	23,169	...

Health (1994): physicians 4,680 (1 per 319 persons); hospital beds 12,521 (1 per 119 persons); (1996) infant mortality rate per 1,000 live births 12.1.
Food (1995): daily per capita caloric intake 2,836 (vegetable products 65%, animal products 35%); 111% of FAO recommended minimum requirement.

Military

Total active duty personnel (1997): 3,510 (army 95.4%, navy 4.6%). *Military expenditure as a percentage of GNP* (1995): 1.1% (world 2.8%); per capita expenditure U.S.$80.

[1]Official legislation bans translation of parliament's name. [2]January 1. [3]Total includes 1,092 sq mi (2,827 sq km) of inland water, of which the Estonian portion of Lake Peipus (590 sq mi [1,529 sq km]) is not distributed by county. [4]Total includes 1,596 sq mi (4,133 sq km) of Baltic Sea islands. [5]Based on land area only. [6]Estimated figure. [7]Third quarter. [8]Monthly average for December. [9]Annual average. [10]Includes taxes (EEK 4,076,000,000) less subsidies (EEK 675,000,000). [11]Detail does not add to total given because of rounding. [12]Exports f.o.b.; imports c.i.f. [13]Estonian Air.

Internet resources for further information:
- **Estonian Human Development Report http://www.undp.org/undp/rbec/nhdr/1996/estonia/**
- **Estonian Human Development Report http://www.ciesin.ee/undp/nhdr97/eng/index.html**
- **Estonia http://www.vm.ee/etoday/1997/11brief.htm**

Ethiopia

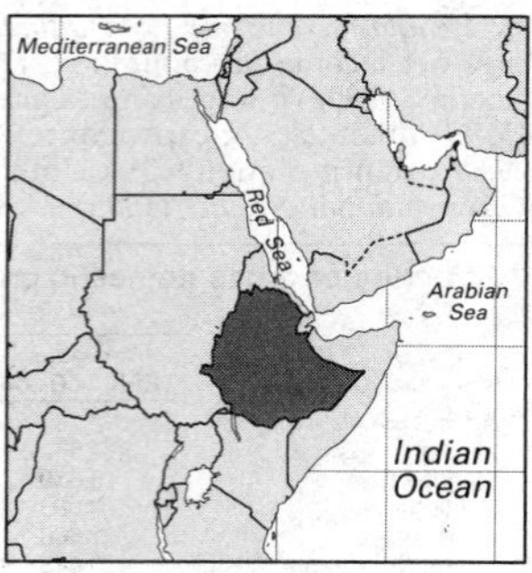

Official name: Federal Democratic Republic of Ethiopia.
Form of government: federal republic[1] with two legislative houses (Federal Council [117]; Council of People's Representatives [548]).
Chief of state: President.
Head of government: Prime Minister.
Capital: Addis Ababa.
Official language: none[2].
Official religion: none.
Monetary unit: 1 birr (Br) = 100 cents; valuation (Oct. 3, 1997) 1 U.S.$ = Br 6.69; 1 £ = Br 10.78.

Area and population

Regions[3]	Capital	area sq mi	area sq km	population 1994 census
Addis Ababa	...	...	...	2,112,737
Affar	...	...	...	1,106,383
Amhara	...	...	...	13,834,297
Benishangul-Gumuz	...	...	...	460,459
Dire Dawa	...	...	...	251,864
Gambela	...	...	...	181,862
Hariai	...	...	...	131,139
Oromiya	...	...	...	18,732,525
Southern Nations, Nationalities and Peoples	...	...	...	10,377,028
Tigray	...	...	...	3,136,267
TOTAL		437,794	1,133,882	...

Demography

Population (1997): 58,733,000.
Density (1997): persons per sq mi 134.2, persons per sq km 51.8.
Urban-rural (1995): urban 11.5%; rural 88.5%.
Sex distribution (1996): male 50.07%; female 49.93%.
Age breakdown (1996): under 15, 45.9%; 15–29, 26.6%; 30–44, 14.8%; 45–59, 8.2%; 60–74, 3.7%; 75 and over, 0.8%.
Population projection: (2000) 63,513,593; (2010) 81,169,000.
Ethnolinguistic composition (1983)[4]: Amhara 37.7%; Galla (Oromo) 35.3%; Tigrinya 8.6%; Gurage 3.3%; Ometo (Omotic) 2.7%; Sidamo 2.4%.
Religious affiliation (1980)[4]: Ethiopian Orthodox 52.5%; Muslim 31.4%; traditional beliefs 11.4%; other Christian 4.5%; other 0.2%.
Major cities (1994): Addis Ababa 2,112,737; Dire Dawa 164,851; Harar 131,139; Nazret 127,842; Gonder 112,249.

Vital statistics

Birth rate per 1,000 population (1995–2000): 48.2 (world avg. 25.0).
Death rate per 1,000 population (1995–2000): 16.2 (world avg. 9.3).
Natural increase rate per 1,000 population (1995–2000): 32.0 (world avg. 15.7).
Total fertility rate (avg. births per childbearing woman; 1995–2000): 7.0.
Life expectancy at birth (1995–2000): male 48.4 years; female 51.6 years.
Major causes of death (1987–88)[4, 5]: infectious and parasitic diseases 33.1%; respiratory diseases 15.7%; digestive system diseases 10.7%.

National economy

Budget (1995–96). Revenue: Br 6,817,300,000 (taxes 69.3%, of which import duties 25.3%, income and profit tax 23.9%, sales tax 14.0%, export duties 1.7%; nontax revenue 30.7%). Expenditures: Br 8,573,200,000 (general services 20.4%; social services 15.9%, of which education 10.6%, public health 3.6%; debt payment 9.8%).
Public debt (external, outstanding; 1995): U.S.$4,958,000,000.
Tourism (1995): receipts U.S.$36,000,000; expenditures U.S.$25,000,000.
Gross national product (1995): U.S.$5,722,000,000 (U.S.$100 per capita).

Structure of gross domestic product and labour force[4]

	1993–94 in value Br '000,000	1993–94 % of total value	1995[6] labour force	1995[6] % of labour force
Agriculture	13,754.1	54.4	21,605,317	88.6
Manufacturing, mining	1,932.3	7.6	401,535	1.6
Construction	736.0	2.9	61,232	0.3
Public utilities	254.8	1.0	17,066	0.1
Transp. and commun.	1,163.5	4.6	103,154	0.4
Trade	2,551.3	10.1	935,937	3.8
Finance	2,035.2	8.0	19,451	0.1
Pub. admin., defense	1,792.7	7.1	} 1,252,224	} 5.1
Services	1,008.2	4.0		
Other	66.6[7]	0.37		
TOTAL	25,294.7	100.0	24,395,916	100.0

Production (metric tons except as noted). Agriculture, forestry, fishing (1996): corn (maize) 3,250,000, sorghum 1,980,000, wheat 1,970,000, sugarcane 1,600,000, barley 1,570,000, millet 360,000, potatoes 350,000, yams 263,000, coffee 230,000, seed cotton 45,500; livestock (number of live animals) 29,900,000 cattle, 21,700,000 sheep, 16,700,000 goats, 8,580,000 horses, mules, and asses, 1,000,000 camels; roundwood (1995) 48,454,000 cu m; fish catch (1995) 6,400. Mining and quarrying (1994)[4]: cement 400,000; limestone 200,000; salt 165,000; gold 128,603 troy oz; platinum 48 troy oz. Manufacturing (gross value in Br '000[8]; 1991–92)[4]: food and beverages 555,800; textiles 251,400; leather and shoes 162,300; cigarettes 106,000; chemicals 53,400. Construction (authorized; 1987–88)[4, 9]: residential 260,251 sq m; nonresidential 63,346 sq m, of which commercial 16,994 sq m. Energy production (consumption)[4]: electricity (kW-hr; 1994) 1,284,000,000 (1,284,000,000); coal, none (n.a.); crude petroleum (barrels; 1994) n.a. (5,637,000); petroleum products (metric tons; 1994) 746,000 (899,000); natural gas, n.a. (n.a.).
Land use (1994): forest 13.3%; pasture 20.0%; agriculture 11.0%; other 55.7%.
Population economically active (1995): total 24,606,100; activity rate of total population 43.4% (participation rates: ages 15–64, 72.2%; female 41.5%; unemployed [1993][4] 62.9%).

Price index (1990 = 100)[4]

	1990	1991	1992	1993	1994	1995	1996
Consumer price index	100.0	135.7	150.0	155.3	167.1	183.9	174.6

Household income and expenditure. Average household size (1984)[4] 4.5; income per household (1981–82)[4] Br 1,728 (U.S.$835); sources of income (1981–82): self-employment 79.5%, wages and salaries 0.2%, other 20.3%; expenditure (1988)[4]: food 66.7%, fuel and power 15.9%, clothing and footwear 6.8%, health care 3.1%, education 2.5%, household goods 2.1%.

Foreign trade

Balance of trade (current prices)[4]

	1989	1990	1991	1992	1993	1994
Br '000,000	−747.6	−1,271.6	−433.1	−1,360.5	−2,325.1	−2,708.3
% of total	29.1%	50.8%	55.5%	60.3%	53.9%	39.6%

Imports (1994–95): Br 6,546,274,000 (motor vehicles 15.5%, petroleum products 15.2%, food and live animals 13.9%, machinery [including aircraft] 10.9%, metal wares 8.6%, fertilizers 5.3%, textiles 3.5%, pharmaceuticals 3.0%, chemicals 2.7%). *Major import sources:* Saudi Arabia 15.1%; U.S. 13.0%; Italy 11.1%; Germany 9.6%; Japan 6.1%; U.K. 4.9%.
Exports (1994–95): Br 2,834,844,000 (coffee 63.5%, hides 13.2%, pulses 3.6%, petroleum products 3.4%). *Major export destinations:* Germany 30.8%; Japan 13.0%; Italy 7.6%; Djibouti 6.8%; U.S. 6.0%; France 5.8%.

Transport and communications

Transport. Railroads (1994–95)[10]: length 782 km; passenger-km 151,000,000; metric ton-km cargo 93,000,000. Roads (1995): total length 19,400 km (paved 15%). Vehicles (1995): passenger cars 45,559; trucks and buses 20,462. Air transport (1996)[11]: passenger-km 1,889,029,000; metric ton-km cargo 118,093,000; airports (1997) 31.

Communications

Medium	date	unit	number	units per 1,000 persons
Daily newspapers	1996	circulation	77,000	1.3
Radio	1996	receivers	9,000,000	153
Television	1995	receivers	230,000	4.0
Telephones	1995	main lines	142,500	2.5
Facsimile machines	1995	units	1,400	—

Education and health

Educational attainment: n.a. *Literacy* (1995): total population age 15 and over literate 35.5%; males 45.5%; females 25.3%.

Education (1994–95)

	schools	teachers	students	student/teacher ratio
Primary (age 7–12)	9,276	83,113	2,722,192	32.8
Secondary (age 13–18)	1,209[12]	22,779	747,142	32.8
Voc., teacher tr.	...	826	9,103	11.0
Higher	11[13]	1,937	32,671	16.9

Health: physicians (1988)[4] 1,466 (1 per 30,195 persons); hospital beds (1986–87)[4] 11,745 (1 per 3,873 persons); infant mortality rate (1995–2000) 107.0.
Food (1992)[4]: daily per capita caloric intake 1,610 (vegetable products 93%, animal products 7%); 69% of FAO recommended minimum.

Military

Total active duty personnel (1997): the estimated strength of Ethiopian armed forces was some 120,000. *Military expenditure as percentage of GNP* (1995): 2.2% (world 2.8%); per capita expenditure U.S.$2.

[1]New republic formally established on Aug. 22, 1995. [2]Amharic is the "working" language of the Federal Democratic Republic of Ethiopia. [3]Ethiopia now has 10 administrative regions as of the 1995 reorganization; area and capital detail were unavailable in late 1997. [4]Includes Eritrea. [5]Percentage of illnesses in a sample population of hospital outpatients. [6]For ages 10 and up. [7]Less imputed bank service charges. [8]At constant prices of 1978–79. [9]Addis Ababa only. [10]Includes 62 mi (100 km) of the Chemin de Fer Djibouti-Ethiopiën (CDE) in Djibouti; excludes 190 mi (306 km) of Northern Ethiopia Railway, not in use since 1978. [11]Ethiopian Airlines only. [12]1985–86. [13]1983–84.

Fiji

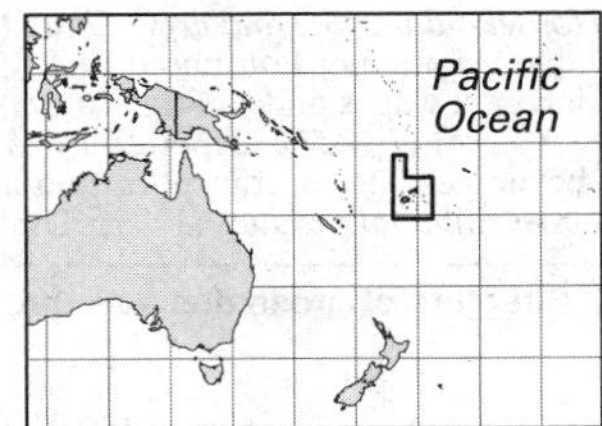

Official name: Sovereign Democratic Republic of Fiji.
Form of government[1]: republic with two legislative houses (Senate [34[2]]; House of Representatives [70]).
Chief of state: President.
Head of government: Prime Minister.
Capital: Suva.
Official language: English.
Official religion: none.
Monetary unit: 1 Fiji dollar (F$) = 100 cents; valuation (Oct. 3, 1997) 1 U.S.$ = F$1.46; 1 £ = F$2.35.

Area and population

Divisions / Provinces	Capitals	area sq mi	area sq km	population 1996 census[3]
Central	Suva			
Naitasiri	—	643	1,666	126,441
Namosi	—	220	570	5,893
Rewa	—	105	272	101,193
Serua	—	320	830	15,495
Tailevu	—	369	955	48,233
Eastern	Levuka			
Kadavu	—	185	478	9,539
Lau	—	188	487	12,203
Lomaiviti	—	159	411	16,203
Rotuma	—	18	46	2,810
Northern	Labasa			
Bua	—	532	1,379	14,977
Cakaudrove	—	1,087	2,816	43,626
Macuata	—	774	2,004	80,151
Western	Lautoka			
Ba	—	1,017	2,634	211,080
Nadroga-Navosa	—	921	2,385	54,049
Ra	—	518	1,341	30,762
TOTAL	—	7,055[4]	18,272[4]	772,655

Demography

Population (1997): 778,000.
Density (1997): persons per sq mi 110.2, persons per sq km 42.6.
Urban-rural (1996): urban 46.4%; rural 53.6%.
Sex distribution (1990): male 50.65%; female 49.35%.
Age breakdown (1990): under 15, 37.3%; 15–29, 28.5%; 30–44, 18.7%; 45–59, 10.0%; 60–74, 4.1%; 75 and over, 1.4%.
Population projection: (2000) 796,000; (2010) 860,000.
Doubling time: 38 years.
Ethnic composition (1996): Fijian 51.1%; Indian 43.6%[5]; other 5.3%.
Religious affiliation (1986): Christian 52.9%; Hindu 38.1%; Muslim 7.8%; Sikh 0.7%; other 0.5%.
Major cities (1996; "urban centres"): Suva 167,421; Lautoka 42,917; Nadi 30,791; Labasa 24,187; Nausori 21,645.

Vital statistics

Birth rate per 1,000 population (1997): 22.7 (world avg. 25.0); (1978) legitimate 82.7%; illegitimate 17.3%.
Death rate per 1,000 population (1997): 4.6 (world avg. 9.3).
Natural increase rate per 1,000 population (1997): 18.1 (world avg. 15.7).
Total fertility rate (avg. births per childbearing woman; 1997): 2.8.
Marriage rate per 1,000 population (1988): 9.6.
Life expectancy at birth (1997): male 70.0 years; female 75.0 years.
Major causes of death per 100,000 population (1987): diseases of the circulatory system 153.4; malignant neoplasms (cancers) 35.5; accidents, poisoning, and violence 32.2; diseases of the respiratory system 31.7; diabetes mellitus 27.3; infectious and parasitic diseases 18.2; birth trauma 16.5.

National economy

Budget (1995). Revenue: F$702,429,000 (income taxes, estate taxes, and gift duties 56.0%; customs duties and port dues 29.6%; fees, royalties, and sales 6.4%). Expenditures: F$681,048,000 (departmental expenditure 72.0%; public-debt charges 23.7%; pensions and gratuities 4.3%).
Public debt (external, outstanding; 1995): U.S.$169,900,000.
Production (metric tons except as noted). Agriculture, forestry, fishing (1996): sugarcane 4,110,000, coconuts 210,000, cassava 25,600, taro 21,900, paddy rice 18,500, bananas 6,300, sweet potatoes 4,000, tomatoes 3,000, yams 2,700, pineapples 2,500; livestock (number of live animals) 354,000 cattle, 211,000 goats, 121,000 pigs; roundwood (1995) 598,200 cu m; fish catch (1995) 34,577. Mining and quarrying (1995): gold 3,477 kg; silver 1,572 kg. Manufacturing (U.S.$'000,000; 1994): food products 84; wearing apparel 28; wood and wood products 16; beverages 15; chemical products 13. Construction (1995): residential 97,000 sq m; nonresidential 64,000 sq m. Energy production (consumption): electricity (kW-hr; 1994) 520,000,000 (520,000,000); coal (metric tons; 1994) none (20,000); crude petroleum, none (n.a.); petroleum products (metric tons; 1994) none (201,000); natural gas, none (n.a.).
Population economically active (1986): total 241,160; activity rate of total population 33.7% (participation rates: ages 15–64, 56.0%; female 21.2%; unemployed [1990] 6.4%).

Price and earnings indexes (1990 = 100)

	1990	1991	1992	1993	1994	1995	1996
Consumer price index	100.0	106.5	111.7	117.5	118.2	120.8	124.5
Earnings index	...	...	...	...	...	...	...

Gross national product (1995): U.S.$1,895,000,000 (U.S.$2,440 per capita).

Structure of gross domestic product and labour force

	1995 in value F$'000[6]	1995 % of total value	1986 labour force	1986 % of labour force
Agriculture	198,235	20.5	106,305	44.1
Mining	1,544	0.2	1,345	0.5
Manufacturing	116,148	12.0	18,106	7.5
Construction	45,782	4.7	11,786	4.9
Public utilities	13,924	1.4	2,154	0.9
Transp. and commun.	156,688	16.2	13,151	5.4
Trade	211,696	21.8	26,010	10.8
Finance	119,595	12.3	6,016	2.5
Pub. admin., defense; Services	138,699	14.3	36,619	15.2
Other	−33,540[7]	−3.4[7]	19,668[8]	8.2[8]
TOTAL	968,771	100.0	241,160	100.0

Household income and expenditure. Average household size (1986) 5.7; income per household (1980) F$2,837 (U.S.$3,546); sources of income (1973): wages and salaries 81.5%, self-employment 9.1%, other 9.4%; expenditure (1991[9]): food, beverages, and tobacco 41.5%, housing and energy 21.4%, transportation and communications 12.9%, household durable goods 6.5%.
Tourism (1995): receipts from visitors U.S.$312,000,000; expenditures by nationals abroad U.S.$55,000,000.
Land use (1994): forested 64.9%; agricultural and under permanent cultivation 14.2%; meadows and pastures 9.5%; other 11.4%.

Foreign trade

Balance of trade (current prices)

	1991	1992	1993	1994	1995	1996
F$'000,000	−279.57	−275.53	−521.42	−409.36	−454.45	−225.26
% of total	20.1%	20.9%	30.7%	20.4%	22.9%	10.9%

Imports (1996): F$1,380,071,000 (durable manufactures 25.9%; machinery and transport equipment 23.8%; food, beverages, and tobacco 15.1%; mineral fuels 13.4%; miscellaneous manufactured consumer articles 11.6%; chemicals 7.4%). *Major import sources:* Australia 44.4%; New Zealand 14.8%; United States 9.3%; Japan 5.2%; Singapore 5.0%; Taiwan 2.6%; China 2.5%; Thailand 1.8%; United Kingdom 1.8%; Hong Kong 1.7%.
Exports (1996)[10]: F$790,960,000 (sugar 34.5%; clothing 23.7%; gold 10.3%; fish 7.6%; timber 5.8%; molasses 2.8%; coconut oil 0.7%). *Major export destinations*[11]: Australia 33.4%; United Kingdom 18.1%; United States 10.0%; Japan 8.6%; New Zealand 4.5%; Portugal 4.4%; Malaysia 3.8%.

Transport and communications

Transport. Railroads (1995)[12]: length 370 mi, 595 km. Roads (1995): total length 3,200 mi, 5,100 km (paved 20%). Vehicles (1995): passenger cars 49,712; trucks and buses 33,928. Merchant marine (1992): vessels (100 gross tons and over) 64; total deadweight tonnage 60,444. Air transport (1996)[13]: passenger-km 1,194,652,000; metric ton-km cargo 75,367,000; airports (1997) with scheduled flights 13.

Communications

Medium	date	unit	number	units per 1,000 persons
Daily newspapers	1995	circulation	54,000	68
Radio	1996	receivers	450,000	561
Television	1995	receivers	70,000	89
Telephones	1995	main lines	64,800	83
Cellular telephones	1995	subscribers	2,200	2.8
Facsimile machines	1995	units	3,000	3.8

Education and health

Educational attainment (1986). Percentage of population age 25 and over having: no formal schooling 28.3%; primary only 19.1%; some secondary 44.1%; secondary 4.1%; postsecondary 3.3%; other 1.1%. *Literacy* (1986): total population age 15 and over literate 87.0%; males literate 90.0%; females literate 84.0%.

Education (1992)

	schools	teachers	students	student/teacher ratio
Primary (age 5–15)	693	4,644	145,630	31.4
Secondary (age 16–19)	142	3,045	60,237	19.8
Voc., teacher tr.	45	625	7,283	11.6
Higher[14]	5[15]	277	7,908	28.5

Health: (1994) physicians 295 (1 per 2,576 persons); hospital beds (1993) 1,747 (1 per 438 persons); infant mortality rate per 1,000 live births (1997) 20.0.
Food (1995): daily per capita caloric intake 3,078 (vegetable products 81%, animal products 19%); 135% of FAO recommended minimum requirement.

Military

Total active duty personnel (1997): 3,600 (army 91.7%, navy 8.3%, air force, none). *Military expenditure as percentage of GNP* (1995): 1.7% (world 2.8%); per capita expenditure U.S.$42.

[1]A new constitution was signed into law on July 25, 1977, and becomes effective in July 1998. [2]All seats are appointed. [3]Preliminary. [4]Detail does not add to total given because of rounding. [5]The emigration of Indian population after the coup in 1987 has resulted in the reemergence of a Fijian majority. [6]Constant 1977 prices. [7]Less imputed bank service charges. [8]Not stated and unemployed. [9]Weights of consumer price index components based on 3,000 urban households. [10]Excludes reexports valued at F$226,438,000. [11]Based on exports of local products only. [12]Owned by the Fiji Sugar Corporation. [13]Air Pacific only. [14]1991. [15]1983.

Finland

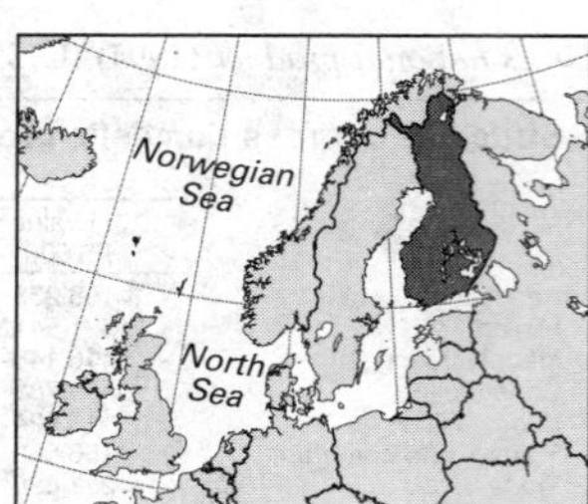

Official name: Suomen Tasavalta (Finnish); Republiken Finland (Swedish) (Republic of Finland).
Form of government: multiparty republic with one legislative house (Parliament [200]).
Chief of state: President.
Head of government: Prime Minister.
Capital: Helsinki.
Official languages: Finnish; Swedish.
Official religion: none[1].
Monetary unit: 1 markka (Fmk) = 100 penniä; valuation (Oct. 3, 1997) 1 U.S.$ = Fmk 5.29; 1 £ = Fmk 8.52.

Area and population[2]

Provinces	Capitals	area sq mi	area sq km	population 1997 estimate
Häme	Hämeenlinna	8,590	22,248	730,500
Keski-Suomi	Jyväskylä	7,486	19,388	258,100
Kuopio	Kuopio	7,704	19,954	258,300
Kymi	Kouvola	4,951	12,824	331,900
Lappi	Rovaniemi	38,200	98,937	201,400
Mikkeli	Mikkeli	8,353	21,633	205,600
Oulu	Oulu	23,777	61,582	451,800
Pohjois-Karjala	Joensuu	8,334	21,585	177,300
Turku ja Pori	Turku	8,000	20,719	702,200
Uusimaa	Helsinki	4,017	10,404	1,326,600
Vaasa	Vaasa	10,548	27,319	447,900
Autonomous Province				
Åland (Ahvenanmaa)	Mariehamn (Maarianhamina)	599	1,552	25,200
TOTAL		130,559[3]	338,145[3]	5,116,800

Demography

Population (1997): 5,145,000.
Density (1997)[4]: persons per sq mi 43.7, persons per sq km 16.9.
Urban-rural (1997): urban 65.1%; rural 34.9%.
Sex distribution (1997): male 48.72%; female 51.28%.
Age breakdown (1997): under 15, 18.9%; 15–29, 18.9%; 30–44, 22.6%; 45–59, 20.4%; 60–74, 13.2%; 75 and over, 6.0%.
Population projection: (2000) 5,209,000; (2010) 5,270,000.
Doubling time: not applicable; population is stable.
Linguistic composition (1997): Finnish 92.9%; Swedish 5.7%; other 1.4%.
Religious affiliation (1997): Evangelical Lutheran 85.7%; Finnish (Greek) Orthodox 1.1%; nonreligious 12.2%; other 1.0%.
Major cities (1997): Helsinki 532,053 (metro area [1995] 874,953); Espoo 196,260[5]; Tampere 186,026; Vantaa 168,778[5]; Turku 166,929; Oulu 111,556.

Vital statistics

Birth rate per 1,000 population (1996): 11.8 (world avg. 25.0); (1995) legitimate 66.9%; illegitimate 33.1%.
Death rate per 1,000 population (1996): 9.6 (world avg. 9.3).
Natural increase rate per 1,000 population (1996): 2.2 (world avg. 15.7).
Total fertility rate (avg. births per childbearing woman; 1996): 1.7.
Marriage rate per 1,000 population (1995): 4.6.
Divorce rate per 1,000 population (1995): 2.7.
Life expectancy at birth (1995): male 72.8 years; female 80.2 years.
Major causes of death per 100,000 population (1994): ischemic heart diseases 262.5; malignant neoplasms (cancers) 192.3; cerebrovascular disease 112.4; diseases of the respiratory system 71.8; accidents 50.8.

National economy

Budget (1996). Revenue: Fmk 192,989,000,000 (value-added taxes 23.6%, loans 20.4%, income and property taxes 20.1%, excise duties 12.7%). Expenditures: Fmk 192,985,000,000 (social security and health 25.0%; state debt 15.2%; education 12.2%; agriculture 5.9%; defense 4.6%).
National debt (September 1996) U.S.$88,873,000,000.
Tourism (in U.S.$'000,000; 1996): receipts 1,674; expenditures 2,366.
Production (metric tons except as noted). Agriculture, forestry, fishing (1995): silage 5,633,000, barley 1,763,000, sugar beets 1,110,000, oats 1,097,000, potatoes 798,000, turnips 125,000; livestock (number of live animals) 1,295,000 pigs, 1,185,000 cattle, 208,000 reindeer; roundwood 50,217,000 cu m; fish catch 184,829. Mining and quarrying (1995): chromite (gross weight) 598,000. Manufacturing (value added in Fmk '000,000; 1994): wood pulp, paper, and paperboard 19,818; nonelectrical machinery 12,091; electrical machinery 9,390; food products 9,193; printing and publishing 7,129; iron and steel 4,806; industrial and basic chemicals 4,611. Construction (completed; 1995): residential 8,700,000 cu m; nonresidential 14,830,000 cu m. Energy production (consumption): electricity (kW-hr; 1996) 66,756,000,000 ([1994] 65,420,000,000); coal (metric tons; 1994) none (7,501,000); crude petroleum (barrels; 1994) none (66,747,000); petroleum products (metric tons; 1994) 10,898,000 (9,734,000); natural gas (cu m; 1994) none (3,390,000,000).
Population economically active (1995): total 2,521,000; activity rate of total population 49.4% (participation rates: ages 15–64, 73.5%; female 47.0%; unemployed [May 1996–April 1997] 15.5%).

Price and earnings indexes (1990 = 100)

	1991	1992	1993	1994	1995	1996	1997[8]
Consumer price index	104.1	107.4	109.7	110.9	112.0	112.6	112.9
Annual earnings index	106.4	108.4	109.2	111.4	116.6	121.1	123.5

Household income and expenditure (1994). Average household size 2.2; disposable income per household Fmk 129,000 (U.S.$24,700); sources of disposable income: wages and salaries 70.1%, transfer payments 8.7%, self-employment 8.7%, other 12.5%; expenditure (1994): housing and energy 28.7%, food and beverages 22.9%, transportation and communications 20.0%.
Gross national product (1995): U.S.$105,174,000,000 (U.S.$20,580 per capita).

Structure of gross domestic product and labour force

	1995 in value Fmk '000,000	% of total value	labour force	% of labour force
Agriculture, fishing	8,713	1.8 }	176,000	7.0
Forestry	12,933	2.7 }		
Mining	1,852	0.4	5,000	0.2
Manufacturing	128,186	26.8	486,000	19.3
Public utilities	13,261	2.8	26,000	1.0
Construction	27,812	5.8	174,000	6.9
Transp. and commun.	41,813	8.8	177,000	7.0
Trade, restaurants	52,590	11.0	353,000	14.0
Finance, real estate	90,157	18.9	198,000	7.8
Pub. admin., defense	91,437	19.1 }	832,000	33.0
Services	13,187	2.8 }		
Other	−4,429	−0.9	96,000[6]	3.9[6]
TOTAL	477,512	100.0	2,521,000[7]	100.0[7]

Land use (1994): forested 76.1%; meadows and pastures 0.4%; agricultural and under permanent cultivation 8.5%; other 15.0%.

Foreign trade[9]

Balance of trade (current prices)

	1991	1992	1993	1994	1995	1996
Fmk '000,000	+5,098	+12,516	+30,849	+33,552	+47,465	+44,802
% of total	2.8%	6.2%	13.0%	12.2%	15.6%	13.7%

Imports (1996): Fmk 140,996,000,000 (raw materials 50.2%; consumer goods 21.2%; mineral fuels 8.9%). *Major import sources:* Germany 15.1%; Sweden 11.9%; U.K. 8.8%; U.S. 7.4%; Russia 7.3%; Japan 5.2%; France 4.5%.
Exports (1996): Fmk 185,798,000,000 (metal products and machinery 40.3%; paper, paper products, and publishing 23.4%; chemicals and chemical products 9.7%). *Major export destinations:* Germany 12.1%; Sweden 10.7%; U.K. 10.2%; U.S. 7.9%; Russia 6.1%; France 4.2%; The Netherlands 4.0%.

Transport and communications

Transport. Railroads: route length (1995) 5,859 km; passenger-km 2,616,000,000; metric ton-km cargo 9,564,000,000. Roads (1996): total length[10] 77,722 km (paved 63%). Vehicles (1996): passenger cars 1,900,855; trucks and buses 260,115. Air transport (1996)[11]: passenger-km 10,709,000,000; metric ton-km cargo 241,302,000; airports (1996) 24.

Communications

Medium	date	unit	number	units per 1,000 persons
Daily newspapers	1995	circulation	2,368,000	464
Radio	1996	receivers	4,950,000	966
Television	1995	receivers	1,900,000	372
Telephones	1995	main lines	2,796,000	547
Cellular telephones	1995	subscribers	1,017,600	199
Facsimile machines	1995	units	132,000	26
Personal computers	1995	units	930,000	182

Education and health

Educational attainment (1995). Percentage of population age 25 and over having: incomplete upper-secondary education 45.1%; complete upper secondary or vocational 41.5%; higher 13.4%. *Literacy:* virtually 100%.

Education (1995–96)

	schools	teachers	students	student/teacher ratio
Primary/Lower Secondary (age 7–15)	4,474	...	588,162	...
Upper Secondary (age 16–18)	477	...	134,851	...
Voc. (incl. higher)	520	21,245[12]	199,200	9.5[12]
Higher	21	7,790[12]	133,359	16.4[12]

Health (1995): physicians 13,771[13] (1 per 371 persons); hospital beds (1994) 49,877[14] (1 per 102 persons); infant mortality rate per 1,000 live births (1996) 3.9.
Food (1995): daily per capita caloric intake 3,022 (vegetable products 59%, animal products 41%); 112% of FAO recommended minimum requirement.

Military

Total active duty personnel (1996): 32,500 (army 80.0%, navy 7.7%, air force 12.3%). *Military expenditure as percentage of GNP* (1994): 2.1% (world 3.0%); per capita expenditure U.S.$386.

[1]The Evangelical Lutheran and Finnish (Greek) Orthodox churches have special recognition. [2]Six provinces only in new 1997 local administrative breakdown; data are unavailable. [3]Total includes land area of 117,604 sq mi (304,593 sq km) and inland water area of 12,955 sq mi (33,552 sq km). [4]Based on land area only. [5]Within Helsinki urban area. [6]Includes 85,000 unemployed persons not previously employed and 11,000 not adequately defined. [7]Detail does not add to total given because of rounding. [8]First quarter average. [9]Imports c.i.f., exports f.o.b. [10]Excludes Åland Islands. [11]Finnair only. [12]1994–95. [13]Registered professionals of working age. [14]Excludes beds in hospitals operated by specialized institutions.

Internet resources for further information:

- **Embassy of Finland (Washington, D.C.) http://www.finland.org/facts.html**
- **Statistics Finland http://www.stat.fi/sf/tilsivue.html**

France

Official name: République Française (French Republic).
Form of government: republic with two legislative houses (Parliament; Senate [321], National Assembly [577]).
Chief of state: President.
Head of government: Prime Minister.
Capital: Paris.
Official language: French.
Official religion: none.
Monetary unit: 1 franc (F) = 100 centimes; valuation (Oct. 3, 1997) 1 U.S.$ = F 5.92; 1 £ = F 9.55.

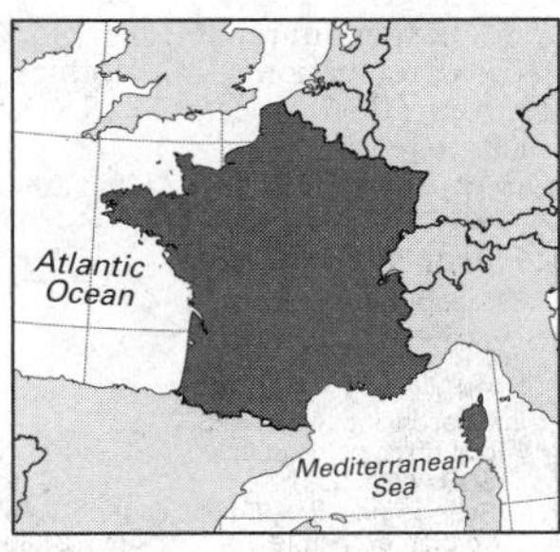

Area and population

Regions / Departments	Capitals	area sq mi	area sq km	population 1995[1] estimate
Alsace				
Bas-Rhin	Strasbourg	1,836	4,755	994,100
Haut-Rhin	Colmar	1,361	3,525	695,700
Aquitaine				
Dordogne	Périgueux	3,498	9,060	388,700
Gironde	Bordeaux	3,861	10,000	1,263,500
Landes	Mont-de-Marsan	3,569	9,243	318,300
Lot-et-Garonne	Agen	2,070	5,361	303,600
Pyrénées-Atlantiques	Pau	2,952	7,645	592,200
Auvergne				
Allier	Moulins	2,834	7,340	352,500
Cantal	Aurillac	2,211	5,726	155,200
Haute-Loire	Le Puy	1,922	4,977	206,600
Puy-de-Dôme	Clermont-Ferrand	3,077	7,970	601,100
Basse-Normandie				
Calvados	Caen	2,142	5,548	633,800
Manche	Saint-Lô	2,293	5,938	484,100
Orne	Alençon	2,356	6,103	294,700
Bourgogne				
Côte-d'Or	Dijon	3,383	8,763	507,300
Nièvre	Nevers	2,632	6,817	230,400
Saône-et-Loire	Mâcon	3,311	8,575	554,800
Yonne	Auxerre	2,868	7,427	331,400
Bretagne				
Côtes-d'Armor	Saint-Brieuc	2,656	6,878	536,600
Finistère	Quimper	2,600	6,733	840,600
Ille-et-Vilaine	Rennes	2,616	6,775	836,700
Morbihan	Vannes	2,634	6,823	633,000
Centre				
Cher	Bourges	2,793	7,235	321,100
Eure-et-Loir	Chartres	2,270	5,880	410,100
Indre	Châteauroux	2,622	6,791	234,400
Indre-et-Loire	Tours	2,366	6,127	545,800
Loir-et-Cher	Blois	2,449	6,343	312,500
Loiret	Orléans	2,616	6,775	609,300
Champagne-Ardenne				
Ardennes	Charleville-Mézières	2,019	5,229	292,000
Aube	Troyes	2,318	6,004	293,100
Haute-Marne	Chaumont	2,398	6,211	200,100
Marne	Châlons-sur-Marne	3,151	8,162	567,300
Corse[2]				
Corse-du-Sud	Ajaccio	1,550	4,014	124,400
Haute-Corse	Bastia	1,802	4,666	135,300
Franche-Comté				
Doubs	Besançon	2,021	5,234	494,100
Haute-Saône	Vesoul	2,070	5,360	229,900
Jura	Lons-le-Saunier	1,930	4,999	252,100
Territoire de Belfort	Belfort	235	609	137,100
Haute-Normandie				
Eure	Évreux	2,332	6,040	535,400
Seine-Maritime	Rouen	2,424	6,278	1,241,500
Île-de-France				
Essonne	Évry	696	1,804	1,145,900
Hauts-de-Seine	Nanterre	68	176	1,405,300
Paris	Paris	40	105	2,130,900
Seine-et-Marne	Melun	2,284	5,915	1,179,300
Seine-Saint-Denis	Bobigny	91	236	1,405,500
Val-de-Marne	Créteil	95	245	1,234,700
Val-d'Oise	Pontoise	481	1,246	1,108,400
Yvelines	Versailles	882	2,284	1,367,700
Languedoc-Roussillon				
Aude	Carcassonne	2,370	6,139	305,300
Gard	Nîmes	2,260	5,853	607,100
Hérault	Montpellier	2,356	6,101	859,900
Lozère	Mende	1,995	5,167	72,800
Pyrénées-Orientales	Perpignan	1,589	4,116	376,200
Limousin				
Corrèze	Tulle	2,261	5,857	236,300
Creuse	Guéret	2,149	5,565	127,100
Haute-Vienne	Limoges	2,131	5,520	355,500
Lorraine				
Meurthe-et-Moselle	Nancy	2,024	5,241	716,200
Meuse	Bar-le-Duc	2,400	6,216	194,000
Moselle	Metz	2,400	6,216	1,015,900
Vosges	Épinal	2,268	5,874	385,400
Midi-Pyrénées				
Ariège	Foix	1,888	4,890	136,600
Aveyron	Rodez	3,373	8,736	266,700
Gers	Auch	2,416	6,257	172,300
Haute-Garonne	Toulouse	2,436	6,309	990,700
Haute-Pyrénées	Tarbes	1,724	4,464	224,000
Lot	Cahors	2,014	5,217	157,000
Tarn	Albi	2,223	5,758	341,700
Tarn-et-Garonne	Montauban	1,435	3,718	205,200
Nord-Pas-de-Calais				
Nord	Lille	2,217	5,742	2,556,800
Pas-de-Calais	Arras	2,576	6,671	1,438,000

Area and population (continued)

Regions / Departments	Capitals	area sq mi	area sq km	population 1995 estimate
Pays de la Loire				
Loire-Atlantique	Nantes	2,631	6,815	1,089,400
Maine-et Loire	Angers	2,767	7,166	721,200
Mayenne	Laval	1,998	5,175	281,900
Sarthe	Le Mans	2,396	6,206	521,600
Vendée	La Roche-sur-Yon	2,595	6,720	525,700
Picardie				
Aisne	Laon	2,845	7,369	539,500
Oise	Beauvais	2,263	5,860	762,700
Somme	Amiens	2,382	6,170	553,100
Poitou-Charentes				
Charente	Angoulême	2,300	5,956	341,200
Charente-Maritime	La Rochelle	2,650	6,864	540,700
Deux-Sèvres	Niort	2,316	5,999	346,800
Vienne	Poitiers	2,699	6,990	390,400
Provence–Alpes–Côte d'Azur				
Alpes-de-Haute-Provence	Digne	2,674	6,925	138,800
Alpes-Maritimes	Nice	1,660	4,299	1,011,100
Bouches-du-Rhône	Marseille	1,964	5,087	1,797,000
Hautes-Alpes	Gap	2,142	5,549	118,800
Var	Toulon	2,306	5,973	872,900
Vaucluse	Avignon	1,377	3,567	489,600
Rhône-Alpes				
Ain	Bourg-en-Bresse	2,225	5,762	500,400
Ardèche	Privas	2,135	5,529	282,900
Drôme	Valence	2,521	6,530	426,800
Haute-Savoie	Annecy	1,694	4,388	617,300
Isère	Grenoble	2,869	7,431	1,064,600
Loire	Saint-Étienne	1,846	4,781	748,500
Rhône	Lyon	1,254	3,249	1,561,900
Savoie	Chambéry	2,327	6,028	366,800
TOTAL		210,026	543,965	58,010,100[3]

Demography

Population (1997): 58,616,000.
Density (1997): persons per sq mi 279.1, persons per sq km 107.8.
Urban-rural (1996): urban 72.9%; rural 27.1%.
Sex distribution (1996): male 48.71%; female 51.29%.
Age breakdown (1995): under 15, 19.7%; 15–29, 21.4%; 30–44, 22.2%; 45–59, 16.9%; 60–74, 13.6%; 75 and over, 6.2%.
Population projection: (2000) 59,351,000; (2010) 61,870,000.
Doubling time: not applicable; doubling time exceeds 100 years.
Ethnolinguistic composition (1990): French (mother tongue) 93.6%, of which fully or substantially bilingual in Occitan 2.7%, German (mostly Alsatian) 2.3%, Breton 1.0%, Catalan 0.4%; Arabic 2.5%; other 3.9%.
Religious affiliation (1992): Roman Catholic 76.3%; Muslim 6.3%; Protestants 2.9%; other 14.5%.
Major cities (1990): Paris 2,152,423 (metropolitan area 9,060,257); Marseille 800,550 (1,231,082); Lyon 415,487 (1,262,223); Toulouse 358,688 (608,430); Nice 342,439 (475,507); Strasbourg 252,338 (338,483); Nantes 244,995 (492,-255); Bordeaux 210,336 (685,456); Montpellier 207,996 (236,788).
National origin (1990): French 93.6%, of which Martiniquais 0.2%, Guadeloupian 0.2%, Réunionese 0.2%; Portuguese 1.1%; Algerian 1.1%; Moroccan 1.0%; Italian 0.4%; Spanish 0.4%; Turkish 0.3%; other 2.1%.
Mobility (1990). Population living in same residence as in 1982: 51.4%; same region 89.0%; different region 8.8%; different country 2.2%.
Households (1993). Average household size 2.6; 1 person 27.7%, 2 persons 32.0%, 3 persons 17.4%, 4 persons 14.7%, 5 persons or more 8.2%. Family households (1990): 14,118,940 (72.1%); nonfamily 5,471,460 (27.9%, of which 1-person 24.6%).
Immigration (1994): immigrants admitted 64,102 (Algeria 13.6%, Morocco 12.3%, Turkey 7.3%, Tunisia 3.4%, Sri Lanka 2.7%, Lebanon 1.3%).

Vital statistics

Birth rate per 1,000 population (1996): 12.6 (world avg. 25.0); (1994) legitimate 63.9%; illegitimate 36.1%.
Death rate per 1,000 population (1996): 9.2 (world avg. 9.3).
Natural increase rate per 1,000 population (1996): 3.4 (world avg. 15.7).
Total fertility rate (avg. births per childbearing woman; 1995): 1.7.
Marriage rate per 1,000 population (1996): 4.8.
Divorce rate per 1,000 population (1993): 1.9.
Life expectancy at birth (1994): male 73.7 years; female 81.8 years.
Major causes of death per 100,000 population (1994): heart disease and other circulatory diseases 286.7; malignant neoplasms (cancers) 247.6; accidents and violence 76.9; respiratory diseases 63.7; digestive tract diseases 43.7.

Social indicators

Educational attainment (1990). Percentage of population age 25 and over having: primary 22.1%; lower secondary 7.8%; higher secondary and vocational 29.4%; postsecondary 11.6%; undeclared attainment 29.1%.

Distribution of income (1984)

percentage of household income by quintile

1	2	3	4	5 (highest)
7.1%	12.3%	17.1%	23.2%	40.3%

Quality of working life. Average workweek (1994): 38.9 hours. Annual rate per 100,000 workers for: injury or accident 5,322 (deaths 0.8); accidents in transit to work 708 (deaths 68.3); industrial illness 16.6[4]; death 4.8[4]. Average days lost to labour stoppages per 1,000 workers (1993): 23.0. Average length of journey to work (1990): 8.7 mi (14 km).
Access to services (1992). Proportion of dwellings having: central heating 86.0%; piped water 97.0%; indoor plumbing 95.8%.
Social participation. Eligible voters participating in last (May and June 1997) national election: *c.* 78%. Population over 15 years of age participating in voluntary associations: 28.0%.

Social deviance. Offense rate per 100,000 population (1994) for: murder 0.8; rape 11.3; other assault 290.8; theft (including burglary and housebreaking) 5,204.2. Incidence per 100,000 in general population of: alcoholism, n.a. (deaths related to alcoholism; 1991) 5.0; suicide (1993) 21.1.
Leisure (1987–88). Participation rate for favourite leisure activities: watching television 82%; reading magazines 79%; listening to radio 75%; entertaining relatives 64%; visiting relatives 61%; attending fairs/expositions 56%.
Material well-being (1994). Households possessing: automobile 79.5%; colour television 92.4%; VCR 52.8%; refrigerator 99.0%; washing machine 89.4%.

National economy

Gross national product (1995): U.S.$1,451,051,000,000 (U.S.$24,990 per capita).

Structure of gross domestic product and labour force

	1995			
	in value F '000,000	% of total value	labour force	% of labour force
Agriculture	183,444	2.6	1,026,000	4.1
Mining	57,507	0.8	118,900	0.5
Manufacturing	1,542,442	21.8	3,992,700	15.8
Construction	342,836	4.8	1,466,600	5.8
Public utilities	178,069	2.5	162,900	0.6
Transp. and commun.	433,518	6.1	1,272,800	5.0
Trade[5]	1,012,441	14.3	3,482,000	13.8
Finance	320,501	4.5	601,900	2.4
Pub. admin., defense	1,323,570	18.7	6,248,100	24.7
Services	1,290,922	18.2	3,953,800	15.7
Other	403,238[6]	5.7[6]	2,934,600[7]	11.6[7]
TOTAL	7,088,488	100.0	25,260,300	100.0

Budget (1996). Revenue: F 1,552,100,000,000 (value-added taxes 49.1%; direct taxes 38.2%; customs taxes 10.2%). Expenditure: F 1,541,300,000,000 (education 22.5%, defense 15.6%, debt service 14.7%, social welfare 10.8%).

Manufacturing enterprises (1995)

	no. of enterprises[8]	no. of employees	annual salaries as a % of avg. of all salaries[8]	annual value added (F '000,000)
Food products	55,197	545,900	87	208,065
Transport equipment	4,293	508,700	108	167,357
Electrical machinery	15,620	433,600	118	156,221
Iron and steel	27,847	403,800	96	131,376
Mechanical equipment	32,134	390,300	104	127,637
Petroleum refineries	180	46,200	174	117,041
Printing, publishing	30,359	231,900	125	83,083
Textiles and wearing apparel	29,701	281,500	78	63,633
Rubber products	5,875	204,200	94	57,758
Chemical products	1,442	102,100	128	51,146
Paper and paper products	1,916	101,500	102	38,585
Metal products	442	43,700	103	28,115
Glass products	1,536	52,400	104	16,638
Footwear	4,236	55,400	75	12,970

Production (metric tons except as noted). Agriculture, forestry, fishing (1997): wheat 34,070,000, sugar beets 32,171,000, corn (maize) 15,110,000, barley 10,161,000, grapes 7,000,000, potatoes 6,500,000, rapeseed 3,512,000, dry peas 3,087,000, sunflower seeds 2,193,000, apples 2,192,000, tomatoes 785,000, carrots 644,000, green peas 575,000, oats 563,000, cauliflower 530,000, lettuce 528,000, peaches 474,000, sorghum 426,000, string beans 325,000, onions 324,000; livestock (number of live animals) 20,300,000 cattle, 14,968,000 pigs, 10,126,000 sheep, 1,114,000 goats; roundwood (1995) 46,345,000 cu m; fish catch (1995) 793,413. Mining and quarrying (1995): iron ore 1,500,000; potash salts 800,000; bauxite 130,800; uranium 840; gold 151,124 troy oz; silver 48,231 troy oz. Manufacturing (1995): cement 19,896,000; crude steel 18,132,000; pig iron 12,876,000; paper products 8,700,000; rubber products 619,400, of which tires 59,268,000 units; aluminum 586,000; automobiles 3,200,000 units. Construction (dwelling units completed; 1993) 299,000.

Retail trade enterprises (1995[1])

	no. of enterprises	no. of employees	weekly wages as a % of all wages	annual turnover (F '000,000)
Large food stores	4,373	385,402	...	617,222
Clothing stores	51,873	195,535	...	126,504
Pharmacies	22,301	126,508	...	121,980
Small food stores	64,565	163,474	...	110,928
butcher shops	21,548	59,962	...	36,732
Furniture stores	7,179	53,080	...	54,390
Electrical and electronics stores	10,990	55,560	...	43,995
Department stores	736	35,074	...	27,741
Publishing and paper	15,083	40,375	...	24,591
Gas, coal, and other energy products	6,042	25,375	...	19,204

Energy production (consumption)[9]: electricity (kW-hr; 1994) 475,622,000,000 (412,454,000,000); coal (metric tons; 1994) 8,039,000 (21,809,000); crude petroleum (barrels; 1994) 20,297,000 (562,907,000); petroleum products (metric tons; 1994) 69,078,000 (66,994,000); natural gas (cu m; 1994) 2,517,200,000 (33,449,900,000).
Population economically active (1995): total 25,260,300; activity rate of total population 43.4% (participation rates: ages 15–64, 67.6%[10]; female 45.0%; unemployed 11.7%).

Price and earnings indexes (1990 = 100)

	1990	1991	1992	1993	1994	1995	1996
Consumer price index	100.0	103.2	105.7	107.9	109.7	111.6	113.9
Earnings index	100.0	104.4	108.4	111.7	115.0	116.0	118.0

Household income and expenditure (1995). Average household size 2.6; average annual income per household F 302,560 (U.S.$60,610); sources of income: wages and salaries 70.0%, self-employment 24.4%, social security 5.6%; expenditure: housing 18.2%, food 16.8%, transportation 14.5%, health 10.4%, recreation 6.9%, clothing 5.4%.
Tourism (1996): receipts U.S.$28,181,700,000; expenditures U.S.$17,505,400,000.
Public debt (1994): F 3,272,800,000,000 (U.S.$624,940,000,000).

Financial aggregates

	1992	1993	1994	1995	1996	1997[10]
Exchange rate, F per:						
U.S. dollar	5.51	5.90	5.35	4.90	5.24	6.05
£	9.37	8.73	8.35	7.60	8.90	9.81
SDR	7.57	8.10	7.80	7.28	7.53	8.25
International reserves (U.S.$)						
Total (excl. gold; '000,000)	27,028	22,649	26,257	26,853	26,796	29,011
SDRs ('000,000)	163	331	362	955	981	968
Reserve pos. in IMF ('000,000)	2,482	2,310	2,375	2,756	2,695	2,400
Foreign exchange	24,384	20,008	23,520	23,142	23,120	25,643
Gold ('000,000 fine troy oz)	81.85	81.85	81.85	81.85	81.85	81.85
% world reserves	8.7	8.7	8.7	9.1	9.0	9.2
Interest and prices						
Central bank discount (%)	9.50	9.50	9.50	...	...	...
Govt. bond yield (%)	8.60	6.91	8.52	7.59	6.39	5.58
Industrial share prices (1990 = 100)	102.3	112.6	112.5	102.5	115.9	152.4
Balance of payments (U.S.$'000,000)						
Balance of visible trade	1,661	8,418	7,868	11,175	15,099	...
Imports, f.o.b.	223,561	187,873	215,593	259,225	258,963	...
Exports, f.o.b.	225,222	196,291	223,461	270,400	274,062	...
Balance of invisibles	1,819	3,503	263	5,268	5,412	...
Balance of payments, current account	3,480	11,921	8,128	16,443	20,511	...

Land use (1994): forest 27.3%; pasture 19.3%; agriculture 35.4%; other 18.0%.

Foreign trade

Balance of trade (current prices)

	1991	1992	1993	1994	1995	1996
F '000,000,000	−29.6	+31.0	+101.7	+87.8	+107.0	+91.6
% of total	1.2%	1.3%	4.5%	3.5%	3.9%	3.2%

Imports (1995): F 1,380,400,000 (machinery and transport equipment 38.5%, of which transport equipment 14.6%; agricultural products 11.9%; chemicals 8.4%; fuels 6.9%). *Major import sources:* Germany 18.3%; Italy 9.9%; U.K. 9.5%; Belgium-Luxembourg 8.8%; Spain 6.1%; U.S. 6.1%.
Exports (1995): F 1,428,800,000 (machinery and transport equipment 42.6%, of which transport equipment 19.5%; agricultural products 15.1%; chemical products 8.4%; plastics 3.2%). *Major export destinations:* Germany 17.7%; Italy 9.5%; Belgium-Luxembourg 8.6%; U.K. 7.6%; U.S. 7.4%.

Transport and communications

Transport. Railroads (1995): route length 31,940 km; passenger-km 55,470,000,000; metric ton-km cargo 47,400,000,000. Roads (1995): total length 812,700 km (paved [1985] 92%). Vehicles (1995): passenger cars 25,100,000; trucks and buses 5,005,000. Merchant marine (1992): vessels (100 gross tons and over) 729; total deadweight tonnage 4,981,027. Air transport (1994): passenger-km 67,500,000,000; metric ton-km cargo 11,300,000,000; airports (1996) with scheduled flights 61.

Communications

Medium	date	unit	number	units per 1,000 persons
Daily newspapers	1994	circulation	13,685,000	235
Radio	1995	receivers	50,000,000	860
Television	1995	receivers	33,600,000	579
Telephones	1995	main lines	32,400,000	558
Cellular telephones	1995	subscribers	1,379,000	23.8
Facsimile machines	1995	units	96,200	1.6
Personal computers	1995	units	7,800,000	134

Education and health

Literacy (1980): total population literate 41,112,000 (98.8%); males literate 19,933,000 (98.9%); females literate 21,179,000 (98.7%).

Education (1994–95)

	schools	teachers	students	student/teacher ratio
Primary (age 6–10)	41,244	301,699[11]	4,012,600	...
Secondary (age 11–18) } Voc., teacher tr.	11,212	454,000[12]	4,486,063 } 1,251,295	12.6[12]
Higher	1,062[13]	52,663[12]	2,107,600	...

Health: physicians (1994) 160,235 (1 per 361 persons); hospital beds (1995) 679,731 (1 per 86 persons); infant mortality rate (1996) 4.9.
Food (1995): daily per capita caloric intake 3,588 (vegetable products 62%, animal products 38%); 142% of FAO recommended minimum requirement.

Military

Total active duty personnel (1996): 398,900 (army 59.3%, navy 15.9%, air force 22.2%, other 2.6%). *Military expenditure as percentage of GNP* (1995): 3.1% (world 2.8%); per capita expenditure U.S.$826.

[1]January 1. [2]In May 1992, Corse was granted local autonomy (with its own directly elected assembly), changing its regional status to "territorial collective." [3]Detail does not add to total given because of rounding. [4]1989. [5]Includes hotels. [6]Imputed rents and imputed bank service charges. [7]Unemployed. [8]1991. [9]All energy statistics include Monaco. [10]August. [11]Includes preprimary teachers. [12]1993–94. [13]1988–89.

Internet resources for further information:
- **Economie et Statistique**
http://www.insee.fr/vf/produits/pub/ecostat/index.htm

Gabon

Official name: République Gabonaise (Gabonese Republic).
Form of government: unitary multiparty republic with a Parliament comprising two legislative houses (Senate [91]; National Assembly [120]).
Chief of state: President.
Head of government: Prime Minister.
Capital: Libreville.
Official language: French.
Official religion: none.
Monetary unit: 1 CFA franc (CFAF) = 100 centimes; valuation (Oct. 3, 1997) 1 U.S.$ = CFAF 592.29; 1 £ = CFAF 954.76.

Area and population

		area		population
Provinces	Capitals	sq mi	sq km	1993 census[1]
Estuaire	Libreville	8,008	20,740	463,187
Haut-Ogooué	Franceville	14,111	36,547	104,301
Moyen-Ogooué	Lambaréné	7,156	18,535	42,316
Ngounié	Mouila	14,575	37,750	77,781
Nyanga	Tchibanga	8,218	21,285	39,430
Ogooué-Ivindo	Makokou	17,790	46,075	48,862
Ogooué-Lolo	Koulamoutou	9,799	25,380	43,915
Ogooué-Maritime	Port-Gentil	8,838	22,890	97,913
Woleu-Ntem	Oyem	14,851	38,465	97,271
TOTAL		103,347[2]	267,667	1,014,976

Demography

Population (1997): 1,190,000.
Density (1997): persons per sq mi 11.5, persons per sq km 4.4.
Urban-rural (1993): urban 73.1%; rural 26.9%.
Sex distribution (1995): male 49.32%; female 50.68%.
Age breakdown (1995): under 15, 39.1%; 15–29, 22.3%; 30–44, 17.2%; 45–59, 12.4%; 60–74, 7.2%; 75 and over, 1.7%.
Population projection: (2000) 1,244,000; (2010) 1,445,000.
Doubling time: 32 years.
Ethnic composition (1983): Fang 35.5%; Mpongwe 15.1%; Mbete 14.2%; Punu 11.5%; other 23.7%.
Religious affiliation (1995): Christian 79.9%, of which Roman Catholic 50.1%, Protestant 18.0%, traditional religion 19.3%; Muslim 0.8%.
Major cities (1993): Libreville 362,386; Port-Gentil 80,841; Franceville 30,246; Oyem 22,669; Moanda 21,921.

Vital statistics

Birth rate per 1,000 population (1990–95): 37.2 (world avg. 25.0).
Death rate per 1,000 population (1990–95): 15.5 (world avg. 9.3).
Natural increase rate per 1,000 population (1990–95): 21.8 (world avg. 15.7).
Total fertility rate (avg. births per childbearing woman; 1990–95): 5.3.
Life expectancy at birth (1990–95): male 51.9 years; female 55.2 years.
Major causes of death per 100,000 population: n.a.; however, in the early 1990s major causes of morbidity and mortality included malaria, shigellosis (infection with dysentery), tetanus, cardiovascular diseases, trypanosomiasis, and tuberculosis.

National economy

Budget (1996). Revenue: CFAF 755,100,000,000 (oil revenues 59.5%; customs duties 16.6%; other current revenues 23.9%). Expenditures: CFAF 676,500,000,000 (current expenditure 75.7%, of which wages and salaries 27.3%, service on public debt 25.6%; capital expenditure 22.8%).
Public debt (external, outstanding; 1995): U.S.$4,099,000,000.
Tourism (1995): receipts from visitors U.S.$4,000,000; expenditures by nationals abroad U.S.$112,000,000.
Production (metric tons except as noted). Agriculture, forestry, fishing (1996): roots and tubers 408,000 (of which cassava 220,000, yams 120,000, taro 65,000), plantains 250,000, sugarcane 220,000, corn (maize) 27,000, peanuts (groundnuts) 15,000, bananas 9,000, palm oil 3,000, cacao beans 1,000; livestock (number of live animals) 172,000 sheep, 165,000 pigs, 84,000 goats, 39,000 cattle, 3,000,000 chickens; roundwood (1995) 4,347,000 cu m; fish catch (1995) 27,978. Mining and quarrying (1996): manganese ore 1,983,000; uranium ore 623,000. Manufacturing (1994): fuel oil 289,000; diesel and gas oil 240,000; cement 147,789; kerosene 100,000; wheat flour 31,000[3]; refined sugar 13,687; beer 816,419[4] hectolitres; soft drinks 415,613[4] hectolitres; cigarettes 399,000,000 units[3]; plywood 47,100,000 cu m; textiles are also significant. Energy production (consumption): electricity (kW-hr; 1995) 1,024,000,000 (794,000,000); crude petroleum (barrels; 1995) 132,500,000 ([1994] 11,600,000); petroleum products (metric tons; 1994) 776,000 (633,000); natural gas (cu m; 1994) 129,000,000 (129,000,000); fuelwood (cu m; 1994) 2,812,000 (2,812,000).
Population economically active (1993): total 375,944; activity rate of total population 37.0% (participation rates [1985]: ages 15–64, 68.2%; female 38.4%; unemployed [1996] 20%).
Household income and expenditure. Average household size (1993) 5.2; income per household: n.a.; sources of income (1983): private sector 73.4%, public sector 26.6%; expenditure (1969)[5]: food and tobacco 54.7%, clothing and footwear 17.5%, housing 13.0%, recreation 6.6%, transportation and communications 6.3%, health care 1.9%.

Price and earnings indexes (1990 = 100)

	1990	1991	1992	1993	1994	1995	1996
Consumer price index	100.0	105.4	100.2	91.3	124.3	136.7	141.8
Earnings index	...	...	...	...	...	...	...

Land use (1994): forested 77.2%; meadows and pastures 18.2%; agricultural and under permanent cultivation 1.8%; other 2.8%.
Gross national product (1995): U.S.$3,759,000,000 (U.S.$3,490 per capita).

Structure of gross domestic product and labour force

	1996		1993	
	in value CFAF '000,000	% of total value	labour force	% of labour force
Agriculture, forestry, fishing	198,700	7.1	156,000[6]	41.6
Mining	1,190,500	42.6	43,000[6]	11.5
Manufacturing	166,300	6.0		
Construction	98,900	3.5		
Public utilities	40,300	1.4		
Transportation and communications	147,600	5.3	115,000[6]	30.7
Trade	424,300	15.2		
Finance	14,900	0.5		
Services	265,900	9.5		
Pub. admin., defense	245,300	8.8	61,000[6]	16.2
TOTAL	2,792,800[2]	100.0[2]	376,000[2]	100.0

Foreign trade

Balance of trade (current prices)

	1991	1992	1993	1994	1995	1996
CFAF '000,000	+386,100	+362,800	+419,400	+882,000	+870,800	+1,095,800
% of total	44.3%	43.6%	46.7%	50.6%	49.3%	52.5%

Imports (1995): CFAF 495,900,000,000 ([1994] machinery and mechanical equipment 32.1%, food and agricultural products 17.5%, transport equipment 15.1%, construction materials 14.0%, chemical products 13.1%). *Major import sources* (1995): France 35.2%; Africa 28.0%; other EEC 20.9%; United States 4.8%; Japan 3.9%.
Exports (1995): CFAF 1,591,700,000 (crude petroleum and petroleum products 81.4%, wood 12.3%, manganese ore and concentrate 4.9%, uranium ore and concentrate 0.8%). *Major export destinations* (1995): United States 50.0%; France 16.3%; other EU 11.9%; Japan 8.3%; Africa 2.3%.

Transport and communications

Transport. Railroads (1995): length 424 mi, 683 km; passenger-km 77,000,000; metric ton-km cargo carried 503,000,000. Roads (1995): total length 4,850 mi, 7,800 km (paved 10%). Vehicles (1992): passenger cars 23,000; trucks and buses 17,000. Merchant marine (1992): vessels (100 gross tons and over) 29; total deadweight tonnage 30,186. Air transport (1996)[7]: passenger-mi 452,000,000, passenger-km 728,000,000; short ton-mi cargo 23,700,000, metric ton-km cargo 34,600,000; airports (1997) with scheduled flights 17.

Communications

Medium	date	unit	number	units per 1,000 persons
Daily newspapers	1996	circulation	40,000	34.1
Radio	1995	receivers	200,000	173
Television	1995	receivers	40,000	34.6
Telephones	1995	main lines	32,000	27.7
Cellular telephones	1995	subscribers	4,000	3.5
Facsimile machines	1995	units	400	0.3
Personal computers	1995	units	6,000	5.2

Education and health

Educational attainment of economically active population (1993): none, or incomplete primary 37.7%; complete primary 32.1%; complete secondary 16.4%; postsecondary certificate or degree 13.8%. *Literacy* (1995): total population age 15 and over literate 63.2%; males literate 73.7%; females literate 53.3%.

Education (1994–95)

	schools	teachers	students	student/ teacher ratio
Primary	1,105	4,709	247,018	52.5
Secondary	51[8]	1,897	56,457	29.8
Voc., teacher tr.	29[8]	485	9,261	19.1
Higher[9, 10]	2	299	3,000	10.0

Health: physicians (1989) 448 (1 per 2,377 persons); hospital beds (1985) 5,156 (1 per 197 persons); infant mortality rate per 1,000 live births (1990–95) 94.
Food (1995): daily per capita caloric intake 2,511 (vegetable products 86%, animal products 14%); 107% of FAO recommended minimum requirement.

Military

Total active duty personnel (1997): 4,700 (army 68.1%, navy 10.6%, air force 21.3%), excluding 600 French troops. *Military expenditure as percentage of GNP* (1995): 2.6% (world 2.8%); per capita expenditure U.S.$90.

[1]De jure; excludes nonnationals numbering 100,000 to 150,000 (mainly West African) prior to their large-scale expulsion in February 1995. [2]Detail does not add to total given because of rounding. [3]1992. [4]1995. [5]Libreville only. [6]Derived values. [7]Air Gabon only. [8]1984–85. [9]Universities only. [10]1991–92.

Internet resources for further information:
- **Welcome to Gabon (official site: Presidency of Gabon)**
http://presidence-gabon.alderan.com/index-a.html

Gambia, The

Official name: The Republic of The Gambia.
Form of government: republic with one legislative body (National Assembly [49])[1].
Head of state and government: President[2].
Capital: Banjul.
Official language: English.
Official religion: none.
Monetary unit: 1 dalasi (D) = 100 butut; valuation (Oct. 3, 1997) 1 U.S.$ = D 10.05; 1 £ = D 16.20.

Area and population

		area		population
				1993
Divisions	**Capitals**	sq mi	sq km	census[3]
Kombo St. Mary[4, 5]	Kanifing	29	76	228,214
Lower River	Mansakonko	625	1,618	65,146
MacCarthy Island	Kuntaur/Georgetown	1,117	2,894	156,021
North Bank	Kerewan	871	2,256	156,462
Upper River	Basse	799	2,069	155,059
Western	Brikama	681	1,764	234,917
City				
Banjul[5]	—	5	12	42,326
TOTAL		4,127[6]	10,689[6]	1,038,145

Demography

Population (1997): 1,248,000.
Density (1997)[7]: persons per sq mi 375.3, persons per sq km 144.9.
Urban-rural (1993): urban 36.7%; rural 63.3%.
Sex distribution (1993): male 50.08%; female 49.92%.
Age breakdown (1993): under 15, 43.8%; 15–29, 27.7%; 30–44, 15.1%; 45–59, 6.8%; 60–74, 3.5%; 75 and over, 1.4%; not stated 1.7%.
Population projection: (2000) 1,381,000; (2010) 1,864,000.
Doubling time: 23 years.
Ethnic composition (1993): Malinke 34.1%; Fulani 16.2%; Wolof 12.6%; Dyola 9.2%; Soninke 7.7%; other 20.2%.
Religious affiliation (1993): Muslim 95.0%; Christian 4.0%; traditional beliefs and other 1.0%.
Major cities/urban areas (1986): Serekunda 102,600[4]; Banjul 42,326 (Greater Banjul 270,540[5, 8]); Brikama 24,300; Bakau 23,600[4]; Farafenni 10,168[9].

Vital statistics

Birth rate per 1,000 population (1997): 43.9 (world avg. 25.0); legitimate, n.a.; illegitimate, n.a.
Death rate per 1,000 population (1997): 13.3 (world avg. 9.3).
Natural increase rate per 1,000 population (1997): 30.6 (world avg. 15.7).
Total fertility rate (avg. births per childbearing woman; 1997): 5.8.
Marriage rate per 1,000 population: n.a.
Divorce rate per 1,000 population: n.a.
Life expectancy at birth (1997): male 51.2 years; female 55.8 years.
Major causes of death per 100,000 population: n.a.; however, major infectious diseases include malaria, gastroenteritis and dysentery, pneumonia and bronchitis, measles, schistosomiasis, and whooping cough.

National economy

Budget (1995–96). Revenue: D 861,700,000 (tax revenue 79.9%, of which import duties and excises 31.8%, income taxes 15.8%, sales tax 7.6%; nontax revenue and grants 20.1%). Expenditures: D 877,700,000 (administrative expenses 24.9%; goods and services 17.4%; interest payments 15.8%; agriculture 11.2%; education and culture 9.2%; transportation and communications 6.9%; public services 2.2%).
Production (metric tons except as noted). Agriculture, forestry, fishing (1996): millet 61,500, peanuts (groundnuts) 46,000, paddy rice 19,600, corn (maize) 10,000, cassava 6,000, seed cotton 4,500, pulses (mostly beans) 4,000, palm oil 2,500, palm kernels 2,000; livestock (number of live animals) 323,000 cattle, 224,000 goats, 159,000 sheep; roundwood (1995) 1,220,700 cu m; fish catch (1993) 20,479, of which Atlantic Ocean 18,079, inland water 2,400. Mining and quarrying: sand and gravel are excavated for local use. Manufacturing (value of production in D '000; 1982): processed food, including peanut and palm-kernel oil 62,878; beverages 10,546; textiles 3,253; chemicals and related products 1,031; nonmetals 922; printing and publishing 358; leather 150. Construction: n.a. Energy production (consumption): electricity (kW-hr; 1994) 75,000,000 (75,000,000); coal, none (none); crude petroleum, none (none); petroleum products (metric tons; 1994) none (75,000); natural gas, none (none).
Public debt (external, outstanding; 1995): U.S.$383,700,000.
Population economically active (1992): total 412,000; activity rate of total population 47.2% (participation rates: [1983] ages 15–64, 78.2%; female 46.3%; unemployed, n.a.).

Price and earnings indexes (1990 = 100)

	1990	1991	1992	1993	1994	1995	1996
Consumer price index	100.0	108.6	118.9	126.6	128.7	137.7	139.3
Earnings index	...	...	...	...	...	...	...

Tourism (1995): receipts from visitors U.S.$23,000,000; expenditures by nationals abroad U.S.$16,000,000.

Household income and expenditure. Average household size (1983) 8.3; income per household: n.a.; sources of income: n.a.; expenditure (1991)[10]: food and beverages 58.0%, clothing and footwear 17.5%, energy and water 5.4%, housing 5.1%, education, health, transportation and communications, recreation, and other 14.0%.
Gross national product (at current market prices; 1995): U.S.$354,000,000 (U.S.$320 per capita).

Structure of gross domestic product and labour force

	1995–96		1983	
	in value D'000,000[11]	% of total value	labour force	% of labour force
Agriculture } Mining }	120.9	21.3	239,940 / 66	73.7 / 0.0
Manufacturing	32.9	5.7	8,144	2.5
Construction	28.2	5.0	4,373	1.3
Public utilities	3.2	0.6	1,233	0.4
Transportation and communications	112.1	19.8	8,014	2.5
Trade	91.2	16.1	16,551	5.1
Finance	36.3	6.4	4,577	1.4
Public administration	60.7	10.6	8,295	2.5
Services	22.3	4.0	9,381	2.9
Other	59.7[12]	10.5[12]	25,049[13]	7.7[13]
TOTAL	567.5	100.0	325,623	100.0

Land use (1994): forested 10.0%; meadows and pastures 19.0%; agricultural and under permanent cultivation 17.2%; built-on area, wasteland, and other 53.8%.

Foreign trade

Balance of trade (current prices)

	1992	1993	1994	1995	1996
D '000,000	−433.8	−516.7	−660.0	−368.5	−744.0
% of total	14.1%	15.7%	21.8%	13.6%	27.4%

Imports (1995–96): D 2,062,900,000 (1993–94; basic manufactures 25.4%; food 24.7%; machinery and transport equipment 23.5%; mineral fuels and lubricants 6.0%; chemicals and related products 5.1%). *Major import sources:* China 24.7%; Belgium-Luxembourg 10.1%; United Kingdom 8.5%; Hong Kong 7.7%; Senegal 5.4%; Thailand 4.9%.
Exports (1995–96): D 1,318,900,000 (1993–94; domestic exports 15.7%, of which groundnuts 8.5%; reexports 84.3%[14]). *Major export destinations:* Belgium-Luxembourg 50.4%; Japan 21.5%; Guinea 6.2%; Hong Kong 4.3%; United Kingdom 3.6%; France 2.6%; Spain 2.2%.

Transport and communications

Transport. Railroads: none. Roads (1995): total length 1,483 mi, 2,640 km (paved 35%). Vehicles (1995): passenger cars 7,950; trucks and buses 8,240. Merchant marine (1992): vessels (100 gross tons and over) 11; total deadweight tonnage 2,029. Air transport (1992): passenger arrivals and departures 275,000; cargo 3,000 metric tons; airports (1997) with scheduled flights 1.

Communications

Medium	date	unit	number	units per 1,000 persons
Daily newspapers	1994	circulation	2,000	2.0
Radio	1995	receivers	140,000	126
Television	1995	receivers	6,000	6.1
Telephones	1995	main lines	19,200	17
Cellular telephones	1995	subscribers	1,400	1.3
Facsimile machines	1995	units	1,000	0.9

Education and health

Educational attainment (1973). Percentage of population age 20 and over having: no formal schooling 90.8%; primary education 6.2%; secondary 2.6%; higher 0.4%. *Literacy* (1995): total population age 15 and over literate 38.6%; males literate 52.8%; females literate 24.1%.

Education (1994)

	schools	teachers	students	student/ teacher ratio
Primary (age 8–14)	250	3,158	105,471	33.4
Secondary (age 15–21)[15]	32	1,126	27,120	24.1
Postsecondary	9[16]	155	1,591	10.3

Health (1990–91): physicians 61 (1 per 14,536 persons); hospital beds 601 (1 per 1,475 persons); infant mortality rate per 1,000 live births (1997) 79.
Food (1994): daily per capita caloric intake 2,157 (vegetable products 95%, animal products 5%); 91% of FAO recommended minimum requirement.

Military

Total active duty personnel (1997): 875. *Military expenditure as percentage of GNP* (1995): 4.8% (world 2.8%); per capita expenditure U.S.$13.

[1]Established by new constitution effective Jan. 16, 1997. [2]Presidential elections of September 1996 did not meet international standards. [3]Preliminary. [4]Kombo St. Mary includes the urban areas of Serekunda and Bakau. [5]Kombo St. Mary and Banjul city make up Greater Banjul. [6]Includes inland water area of 2,077 sq km (802 sq mi). [7]Based on land area only. [8]1993. [9]1983. [10]Low-income population in Banjul and Kombo St. Mary only; weights of consumer price index components. [11]At constant prices of 1976–77. [12]Indirect taxes. [13]Not adequately defined. [14]Mostly unofficial trade with Senegal. [15]Includes teacher training and vocational. [16]1984–85.

Internet resources for further information:
- **Official WWW Site of The Republic of The Gambia http://www.Gambia.com/**

Georgia

Official name: Sakartvelos Respublika (Republic of Georgia).
Form of government: unitary multiparty republic with a single legislative body (Parliament [235]).
Head of state and government: President.
Capital: T'bilisi.
Official language: Georgian.
Official religion: none.
Monetary unit: 1 Georgian lari[1] = 100 tetri; valuation (Oct. 7, 1997), 1 U.S.$ = 1.30 lari; 1 £ = 2.11 lari.

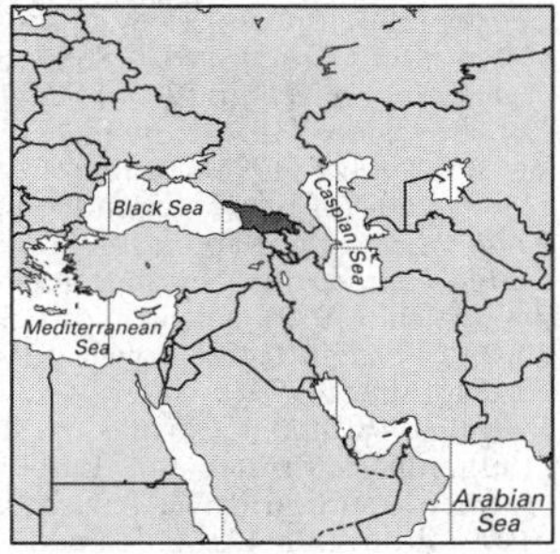

Area and population

Autonomous republics	Capitals	area sq mi	area sq km	population 1993[2] estimate
Abkhazia[3]	Sokhumi (Sukhumi)	3,343	8,660	516,600
Ajaria	Bat'umi	1,120	2,900	386,700
Regions under republican jurisdiction				
Guria	...	785	2,033	160,800
Imereti	...	2,452	6,349	788,900
Kakheti	...	4,717	12,217	464,000
Kvemo Kartli	...	2,615	6,772	601,500
Racha-Lechkumi	...	1,245	3,224	45,400
Samegrelo	...	1,697	4,395	418,100
Samtskhe-Javakheti	...	2,017	5,224	198,800
Shida Kartli	...	3,043	7,882	485,900
Svaneti	...	1,694	4,389	23,200
Tianeti	...	1,569	4,063	43,800
Region under urban council jurisdiction				
T'bilisi	...	534	1,384	1,271,800
TOTAL		26,831	69,493[4]	5,405,400[4]

Demography

Population (1997): 5,377,000.
Density (1997): persons per sq mi 200.4, persons per sq km 77.4.
Urban-rural (1995): urban 55.6%; rural 44.4%.
Sex distribution (1994): male 47.60%; female 52.40%.
Age breakdown (1989): under 15, 24.8%; 15–29, 24.1%; 30–44, 19.2%; 45–59, 17.5%; 60–74, 10.8%; 75 and over, 3.6%.
Population projection: (2000) 5,309,000; (2010) 5,367,000.
Doubling time: n.a.
Ethnic composition (1989): Georgian 70.1%; Armenian 8.1%; Russian 6.3%; Azerbaijani 5.7%; Ossetian 3.0%; Greek 1.9%; Abkhazian 1.8%; other 3.1%.
Religious affiliation (1997): Christian 46.1%, of which Georgian Orthodox 36.6%, Armenian Apostolic 5.6%, Russian Orthodox 2.7%, other Christian 1.2%; Sunnī Muslim 11.0%; other (mostly nonreligious) 42.9%.
Major cities (1997): T'bilisi 1,253,100; K'ut'aisi 240,000; Rust'avi 158,000.

Vital statistics

Birth rate per 1,000 population (1995): 10.9 (world avg. 25.0); (1989) legitimate 82.3%; illegitimate 17.7%.
Death rate per 1,000 population (1995): 8.1 (world avg. 9.3).
Natural increase rate per 1,000 population (1995): 2.8 (world avg. 15.7).
Total fertility rate (avg. births per childbearing woman; 1995): 2.1.
Marriage rate per 1,000 population (1995): 4.0.
Divorce rate per 1,000 population (1995): 0.5.
Life expectancy at birth (1994): male 69.0 years; female 76.0 years.
Major causes of death per 100,000 population (1995): diseases of the circulatory system 569.6; malignant neoplasms (cancers) 63.4; accidents, poisoning, and violence 44.7; diseases of the digestive system 30.3.

National economy

Budget (1997). Revenue: 639,900,000 lari[1] (tax revenue 65.5%, of which value-added tax 41.3%, excise tax 8.1%, customs duties 6.7%, individual income tax 5.4%, company profit tax 3.8%, other taxes 0.2%; grants 9.3%; other revenue 25.2%). Expenditures: 839,900,000 lari[1] (social protection 24.2%; defense and public order 20.9%; housing and services 11.9%; education 6.1%; health care 5.7%; other expenditures 31.2%).
Population economically active (1995): total 1,730,000; activity rate of total population 32.2% (participation rates [1992]: ages 16–59 [male], 16–54 [female] 72.9%; female [1989] 45.9%; unemployed [1996] 6.0%).

Price and earnings indexes (1992 = 1)

	1992	1993	1994	1995
Consumer price index	1.0	15.0	2,362.0	6,207.0
Monthly earnings index	1.0	14.0	3,100.0	7,850.0

Production (metric tons except as noted). Agriculture, forestry, fishing (1996): watermelons 750,000, corn (maize) 395,000, potatoes 360,000, grapes 350,000, tomatoes 220,000, apples 140,000, cabbages 90,000, oranges 66,000; livestock (number of live animals) 980,000 cattle, 725,000 sheep and goats, 353,000 pigs, 12,000,000 poultry; roundwood, n.a.; fish catch (1995) 46,000. Mining and quarrying (1996): manganese ore 97,000. Manufacturing (1995): metallurgy 239; chemical and timber 109; machinery 58. Construction (1994): 12,100 sq m. Energy production (consumption): electricity (kW-hr; 1994) 6,803,000,000 (7,603,000,000); coal (metric tons; 1994) 34,000 (274,000); crude petroleum (barrels; 1994) 542,000 (2,008,000); petroleum products (metric tons; 1994) none (n.a.); natural gas (cu m; 1994) 8,969,000 (2,797,000,000).
Gross national product (1995): U.S.$2,358,000,000 (U.S.$440 per capita)[5].

Structure of net material product and labour force

	1995 in value '000,000 lari[1]	% of total value	labour force[6]	% of labour force
Agriculture	432	31.5	90,000	8.6
Mining				
Manufacturing	401	13.5		
Public utilities			251,700	24.0
Construction	67	4.9		
Transp. and commun.	78	5.7	78,100	7.4
Trade	325	23.7	41,100	3.9
Finance	...	...		
Public administration, defense	...	...	44,100	4.2
Services	...	...	211,100	20.1
Other	284	20.7	334,700[7]	31.9
TOTAL	1,587	100.0	1,050,800	100.0[4]

Public debt (external; 1995): U.S.$988,000,000.
Household income and expenditure. Average household size (1989) 4.1; income per household: n.a.; sources of income (1993): wages and salaries 34.5%, benefits 21.9%, agricultural income 21.6%, other 22.0%; expenditure (1993): taxes 42.5%, retail goods 32.3%, savings 16.4%, transportation 4.2%.

Foreign trade

Balance of trade (current prices)

	1992	1993	1994	1995
U.S.$'000,000	−378	−448	−365	−339
% of total	41.5%	32.9%	32.4%	32.8%

Imports (1994): (1995) U.S.$686,100,000 (oil and gas 47.0%; textiles, clothing, shoes 28.5%; food products 16.1%; electricity 3.0%; petroleum products 2.9%). *Major import sources:* Turkmenistan 71.1%; Turkey 12.6%; Russia 4.2%; Azerbaijan 3.4%; Ukraine 1.2%.
Exports (1994): (1995) U.S.$347,200,000 (food products 30.0%; ferrous metals 29.7%; textiles 7.0%; chemicals 5.0%). *Major export destinations:* Russia 46.0%; Turkey 17.6%; Turkmenistan 8.8%; Kazakstan 6.5%.

Transport and communications

Transport. Railroads (1996): 1,583 km; (1989) passenger-km 17,000,000; cargo traffic, n.a. Roads (1995): 21,000 km (paved 93.5%). Vehicles (1995): passenger cars 441,828; trucks and buses 50,220. Merchant marine: vessels (1,000 gross tons and over) 54; total deadweight tonnage 1,108,068. Air transport (1989): passenger-km 5,295,600,000; metric ton-km cargo, n.a.; airports (1997) with scheduled flights 1.

Communications

Medium	date	unit	number	units per 1,000 persons
Television	1995	receivers	1,200,000	220
Telephones	1995	main lines	554,000	103
Cellular telephones	1995	subscribers	200	0.04
Facsimile machines	1995	units	500	0.1

Education and health

Educational attainment (1989). Percentage of population age 25 and over having: primary education or no formal schooling 12.3%; some secondary 15.2%; completed secondary and some postsecondary 57.4%; higher 15.1%.

Education (1993–94)

	schools	teachers	students	student/teacher ratio
Primary (age 6–13) / Secondary (age 14–17)	3,788	...	815,000	...
Voc., teacher tr.	...	...	29,300	...
Higher	19	...	93,000	...

Health (1993): physicians 29,900 (1 per 182 persons); hospital beds 57,100 (1 per 95 persons); infant mortality rate per 1,000 live births (1995) 17.8.

Military

Total active duty personnel (1997): 17,600 (army 71.6%, air force 17.0%, navy[8] 11.4%). About 8,500 Russian troops remained in Georgia in late 1997. *Military expenditure as percentage of GNP* (1995): 2.4% (world 2.8%); per capita expenditure U.S.$37.

[1]The Georgian lari, introduced Sept. 25, 1995, replaced the Georgian coupon, at a rate of 1,000,000 coupons to 1 lari; on the same date, the Georgian lari became the sole legal tender, floating against all currencies. The Georgian coupon was introduced April 5, 1993, at par with the Russian ruble and circulated parallel with it; on Aug. 20, 1993, the coupon became the sole legal tender, floating against all currencies. [2]January 1. [3]Abkhazia adopted a constitution declaring it an independent state on Nov. 26, 1994; on Feb. 9, 1995, it was granted wider autonomy within Georgia; attainment of full national autonomy remains in dispute. [4]Detail does not add to total given because of rounding. [5]Ruble-area GNP and exchange-rate data are very speculative. [6]State sector only. [7]Includes 65,450 unemployed and 269,250 undistributed employed. [8]A portion of the former U.S.S.R. Black Sea Fleet has been allocated to Georgia.

Internet resources for further information:

- **UNDP Human Development Report Georgia 1996 http://www.undp.org/undp/rbec/nhdr/1996/georgia/**
- **Embassy of Georgia in the United States of America http://www.steele.com/embgeorgia/embassy.htm**
- **Parliament of Georgia http://www.parliament.ge**

Germany

Official name: Bundesrepublik Deutschland (Federal Republic of Germany).
Form of government: federal multiparty republic with two legislative houses (Federal Council [68]; Federal Diet [672]).
Chief of state: President.
Head of government: Chancellor.
Seat of government: Bonn (Berlin is capital designate).
Official language: German.
Official religion: none.
Monetary unit: 1 Deutsche Mark (DM) = 100 Pfennige; valuation (Oct. 3, 1997) 1 U.S.$ = DM 1.76; 1 £ = DM 2.84.

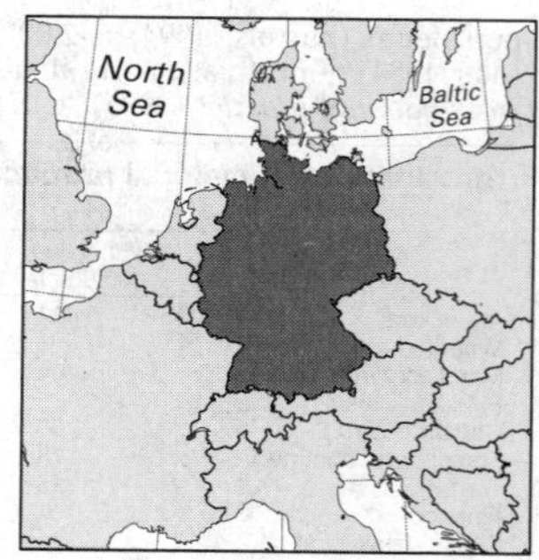

Area and population

States Administrative districts	Capitals	area sq mi	area sq km	population 1996[1] estimate
Baden-Württemberg	Stuttgart	13,804[2]	35,752	10,319,400[2]
Freiburg	Freiburg	3,613	9,357	2,087,000
Karlsruhe	Karlsruhe	2,671	6,919	2,644,400
Stuttgart	Stuttgart	4,076	10,558	3,862,300
Tübingen	Tübingen	3,443	8,918	1,725,600
Bayern	Munich	27,240	70,551[2]	11,993,500[2]
Mittelfranken	Ansbach	2,798	7,246	1,667,300
Niederbayern	Landshut	3,988	10,330	1,143,400
Oberbayern	Munich	6,768	17,530	3,978,100
Oberfranken	Bayreuth	2,792	7,230	1,110,500
Oberpfalz	Regensburg	3,741	9,690	1,054,500
Schwaben	Augsburg	3,859	9,994	1,722,100
Unterfranken	Würzburg	3,294	8,532	1,317,700
Berlin	—	344	891	3,471,400
Brandenburg	Potsdam	11,382	29,479	2,542,000
Bremen	Bremen	156	404	679,800
Hamburg	Hamburg	292	755	1,707,900
Hessen	Wiesbaden	8,152	21,114[2]	6,009,900
Darmstadt	Darmstadt	2,874	7,445	3,684,600
Giessen	Giessen	2,078	5,381	1,055,900
Kassel	Kassel	3,200	8,289	1,269,400
Mecklenburg-Vorpommern	Schwerin	8,946	23,170	1,823,100
Niedersachsen	Hannover	18,382	47,610	7,780,400
Braunschweig	Braunschweig	3,126	8,097	1,679,600
Hannover	Hannover	3,493	9,046	2,139,000
Lüneburg	Lüneburg	5,986	15,504	1,602,100
Weser-Ems	Oldenburg	5,777	14,963	2,359,700
Nordrhein-Westfalen	Düsseldorf	13,158	34,078[2]	17,893,000[2]
Arnsberg	Arnsberg	3,090	8,002	3,827,500
Detmold	Detmold	2,517	6,518	2,012,900
Düsseldorf	Düsseldorf	2,042	5,289	5,290,600
Köln	Köln	2,844	7,365	4,188,600
Münster	Münster	2,665	6,903	2,573,500
Rheinland-Pfalz	Mainz	7,662[2]	19,846[2]	3,977,900
Koblenz	Koblenz	3,117	8,072	1,489,900
Rheinhessen-Pfalz	Mainz	2,646	6,852	1,982,600
Trier	Trier	1,901	4,923	505,400
Saarland	Saarbrücken	992	2,570	1,084,400
Sachsen	Dresden	7,109	18,413	4,566,600
Sachsen-Anhalt	Magdeburg	7,894	20,446	2,738,900
Dessau	Dessau	1,652	4,280	573,100
Halle	Halle/Saale	1,710	4,428	909,400
Magdeburg	Magdeburg	4,532	11,738	1,256,400
Schleswig-Holstein	Kiel	6,089	15,770	2,725,500
Thüringen	Erfurt	6,244	16,171	2,503,800
TOTAL		137,847[2]	357,022[2]	81,817,500

Demography

Population (1997): 82,143,000.
Major cities (1995): Berlin 3,470,200; Hamburg 1,706,800; Munich 1,240,600; Cologne 964,200; Frankfurt am Main 651,200; Essen 616,400; Dortmund 600,000; Stuttgart 587,000; Düsseldorf 571,900; Bremen 549,000; Duisburg 535,200; Hannover 524,600; Nürnberg 494,100.

Other principal cities (1995)

	population		population		population
Aachen	247,400	Heilbronn	121,700	Neuss	148,600
Augsburg	261,000	Herne	179,900	Oberhausen	224,900
Bergisch Gladbach	105,200	Hildesheim	106,000	Offenbach am Main	116,600
Bielefeld	324,000	Ingolstadt	111,900	Oldenburg	150,500
Bochum	400,500	Jena	101,800	Osnabrück	167,900
Bonn	291,700	Kaiserslautern	102,000	Paderborn	132,100
Bottrop	119,900	Karlsruhe	276,600	Pforzheim	118,400
Braunschweig	253,600	Kassel	201,400	Potsdam	137,600
Bremerhaven	130,800	Kiel	247,300	Recklinghausen	127,200
Chemnitz	271,400	Koblenz	109,300	Regensburg	126,000
Cottbus	124,600	Krefeld	249,900	Remscheid	122,700
Darmstadt	139,100	Leipzig	478,200	Reutlingen	108,400
Dresden	472,900	Leverkusen	161,900	Rostock	231,300
Erfurt	212,600	Lübeck	216,900	Saarbrücken	187,800
Erlangen	101,500	Ludwigshafen am Rhein	168,000	Salzgitter	117,700
Freiburg im Breisgau	198,300	Magdeburg	263,000	Schwerin	117,200
Fürth	108,100	Mainz	184,500	Siegen	111,300
Gelsenkirchen	291,800	Mannheim	315,100	Solingen	165,700
Gera	125,000	Moers	107,000	Ulm	115,400
Göttingen	127,200	Mönchengladbach	266,000	Wiesbaden	266,400
Hagen	212,700	Mülheim an der Ruhr	176,700	Witten	105,000
Halle an der Saale	287,400	Münster	264,500	Wolfsburg	126,800
Hamm	183,700			Wuppertal	382,400
Heidelberg	138,400			Würzburg	127,700
				Zwickau	103,900

Density (1997): persons per sq mi 596.0, persons per sq km 230.1.
Urban-rural (1996[1]): urban 86.1%; rural 13.9%.
Population projection: (2000) 82,931,000; (2010) 85,613,000.
Sex distribution (1996[1]): male 48.68%; female 51.32%.
Age breakdown (1996[1]): under 15, 16.2%; 15–29, 19.4%; 30–44, 23.8%; 45–59, 19.6%; 60–74, 14.6%; 75 and over, 6.4%.
Doubling time: not applicable; doubling time exceeds 100 years.
Ethnic composition (by nationality; 1997[1]): German 91.2%; Turkish 2.5%, of which (1990) Kurdish *c.* 0.5%; Yugoslav 1.0%; Italian 0.7%; Greek 0.4%; Bosnian 0.4%; Polish 0.3%; Austrian 0.2%; Croatian 0.2%; Spanish 0.2%; other 2.9%.
Religious affiliation: (former West Germany; 1987) Roman Catholic 42.9%, Lutheran-Reformed and Lutheran traditions 41.6%, Muslim 2.7%, Reformed tradition 0.6%, Jewish 0.1%, other 12.1%; (former East Germany; 1990) Protestant 47.0%, Roman Catholic 7.0%, unaffiliated and other 46.0%.
Households (1996). Number of households 37,281,000; average household size 2.2; 1 person 35.4%, 2 persons 32.3%, 3 persons 15.5%, 4 persons 12.2%, 5 or more persons 4.6%.

Vital statistics

Birth rate per 1,000 population (1995): 9.4 (world avg. 25.0); legitimate 83.9%; illegitimate 16.1%.
Death rate per 1,000 population (1995): 10.8 (world avg. 9.3).
Natural increase rate per 1,000 population (1995): −1.4 (world avg. 15.7).
Total fertility rate (avg. births per childbearing woman; 1994): 1.5.
Marriage rate per 1,000 population (1995): 5.3.
Divorce rate per 1,000 population (1994): 2.0.
Life expectancy at birth (1995): male 73.0 years; female 79.5 years.
Major causes of death per 100,000 population (1995): diseases of the circulatory system 525.8; malignant neoplasms (cancers) 260.7, of which bronchial, lung, and tracheal 45.5; diseases of the respiratory system 66.0, of which pneumonia 21.6, chronic bronchitis 14.2; suicide 15.8.

Social indicators

Educational attainment (1995). Percentage of population age 25 and over having: primary and lower secondary 57.1%; intermediate secondary 18.4%; vocational secondary 7.3%; post-secondary and higher (all levels) 17.2%.
Quality of working life. Average workweek (1995): 39.6 hours. Annual rate per 100,000 workers (1993) for: injuries or accidents at work 4,808; deaths, including commuting accidents, 6.7. Proportion of labour force insured for damages or income loss resulting from: injury, virtually 100%; permanent disability, virtually 100%; death, virtually 100%. Average days lost to labour stoppages per 1,000 workers (1996): 4.1.

Distribution of income (1993)[3]

percentage of household income by quintile

1	2	3	4	5 (highest)
6.5	11.8	17.3	27.2	37.2

Access to services. Proportion of dwellings (1996) having: electricity, virtually 100%; piped water supply, virtually 100%; flush sewage disposal (1993) 98.4%; public fire protection, virtually 100%.
Social participation. Eligible voters participating in last (October 1994) national election 79.1%. Trade union membership in total workforce (1994): *c.* 27%. Practicing religious population (1994): 5% of Protestants and 25% of Roman Catholics "regularly" attend religious services.
Social deviance (1995). Offense rate per 100,000 population for: murder and manslaughter 4.8; sexual abuse 58, of which child molestation 20, rape and forcible sexual assault 14; robbery 78; assault and battery 117; theft 4,712. Incidence per 100,000 in general population (late 1970s) of: alcoholism 2,500–3,000; drug and substance abuse 650; suicide (1995) 15.8.
Material well-being (1996; median income)[3]. Households possessing: automobile 96.1%; telephone 99.5%; colour television receiver 95.9%; refrigerator 79.3%; washing machine 97.7%; home freezer 72.1%; personal computer 48.8%; video recorder 80.1%.

Recreational and leisure activities[3]

(Monthly household expenditures, 1996; median income)

Activity	DM	percentage
Vacations	201	25.0
Expenditures for motor vehicles	115	14.3
Sporting and camping equipment and sporting events	115	14.3
Televisions, radios, and their fees	79	9.8
Books, newspapers, and magazines	66	8.2
Gardening and pets	50	6.2
Games and toys	40	5.0
Visits to theatre and cinema	22	2.7
Photographic and moviemaking equipment and film	18	2.2
Tools	6	0.7
Other activities	92	11.5
TOTAL	803[2]	100.0[2]

National economy

Budget (1996). Revenue: DM 1,753,518,000,000 (taxes 83.9%). Expenditures: DM 1,864,196,000,000 (pensions and other social security payments 33.8%, purchase of current goods and services 22.3%, personnel costs 20.9%).
Total national debt (1995): DM 1,285,900,000,000.
Production (value of production in DM except as noted; 1995–96). Agriculture, forestry, fishing: cereal grains 5,713,000,000, fruits 3,031,000,000, flowers and ornamental plants 2,655,000,000, sugar beets 2,453,000,000, grapes for wine 2,336,000,000, vegetables 2,055,000,000, potatoes 1,862,000,000, tree nurseries 1,710,000,000, oilseed crops 1,018,000,000; livestock (number of live

animals; 1995) 24,377,900 pigs, 15,760,600 cattle, 87,695,200 poultry; roundwood (1996) 38,970,000 cu m; fish catch (metric tons; 1995) 298,017. Mining and quarrying (metric tons; 1996): potash 34,600,000. Manufacturing (value added at factor cost in DM '000,000; 1994): capital equipment 250,212, of which machinery 88,631, transport equipment 70,647; electrical equipment 64,067; chemicals (including pharmaceuticals) 62,401, food and beverages 39,578; plastics and other synthetic products 28,108; glass and ceramic products 24,094; furniture and other wood products 17,024; paper products 12,608; textiles 8,743; clothing 5,847. Construction (newly completed buildings, sq m; 1995): residential 47,263,000; nonresidential 47,229,000.

Manufacturing, mining, and construction enterprises (1995)

	no. of enterprises[6]	no. of employees	wages as a % of avg. of all wages[3, 7]	annual gross production value (DM '000,000)
Manufacturing	39,316	6,644,000	100.0	2,059,072
of which				
Road and motor vehicles	827	694,000	112.6	260,587
Machinery (nonelectric)	5,803	1,039,000	99.6	248,037
Machinery and appliances (electric)	2,427	795,000	106.9	226,297
Chemical	1,292	551,000	102.7	224,693
Food and beverages	4,421	546,000	90.0	218,037
Petroleum and natural gas	54	25,000	124.1	113,716
Rubber and plastic products	2,560	358,000	...	88,127
Glass and ceramics	2,398	282,000	...	74,286
Wood and wood products	2,039	127,000	83.8	31,726
Textiles	1,296	149,000	81.8	31,641
Mining and quarrying	782	188,000	105.3	40,084
Construction	24,738	1,486,000	100.0	259,416

Energy production (consumption): electricity (kW-hr; 1994) 528,221,000,-000 (530,558,000,000); hard coal (metric tons; 1994) 57,623,000 (66,255,-000); lignite (metric tons; 1994) 207,077,000 (209,308,000); crude petroleum (barrels; 1994) 21,535,000 (793,500,000); petroleum products (metric tons; 1994) 99,578,000 (113,839,000); natural gas (cu m; 1994) 20,904,000,000 (92,770,000,000).

Gross national product (at current market prices; 1995): U.S.$2,252,343,000,-000 (U.S.$27,510 per capita).

Structure of gross domestic product and labour force

	1996			
	in value DM '000,000	% of total value	labour force	% of labour force
Agriculture	37,150	1.0	942,000	2.4
Public utilities, mining	82,420	2.3	454,000	1.1
Manufacturing	843,810	23.8	8,356,000	20.9
Construction	217,270	6.1	2,881,000	7.2
Transportation and communications	176,680	5.0	1,923,000	4.8
Trade	294,820	8.3	4,696,000	11.7
Finance, real estate	497,570	14.0	1,182,000	3.0
Services	809,670	22.9	9,728,000	24.3
Pub. admin., defense	387,040	10.9	3,320,000	8.3
Other	194,570	5.5	6,503,000[8]	16.3[8]
TOTAL	3,541,000	100.0[2]	39,985,000	100.0

Population economically active (1996): total 39,985,000; activity rate of total population 48.8% (participation rates: ages 15–64, 71.0%; female 42.9%; unemployed 10.0%).

Price and earnings indexes (1991 = 100)

	1992	1993	1994	1995	1996	1997[9]
Consumer price index	105.1	109.7	112.7	114.8	116.5	119.0
Hourly earnings index	107.1	113.5	115.3	...	...	...

Household income and expenditure. Average annual income per household (1996[3]) DM 82,488 (U.S.$54,816); sources of take-home income: wages 78.8%, self-employment 11.6%, transfer payments 9.6%; expenditure: rent 23.9%, food and beverages 21.2%, transportation 18.0%, entertainment, education, and leisure 11.4%, household operations, durables, and maintenance 7.2%, clothing and footwear 6.4%.

Tourism (1996): receipts U.S.$15,787,500,000; expenditures U.S.$49,557,600,-000.

Financial aggregates[10]

	1991	1992	1993	1994	1995	1996	1997[9]
Exchange rate, DM per:							
U.S. dollar	1.5160	1.6140	1.7263	1.5488	1.4335	1.5548	1.7655
£	2.8360	2.4404	2.1988	2.4207	2.2219	2.6285	2.8481
SDR	2.1685	2.2193	2.3712	2.2610	2.1309	2.2357	2.4103
International reserves (U.S.$)							
Total (excl. gold; '000,000)	63,001	90,967	77,640	77,363	85,005	83,178	77,195
SDRs ('000,000)	1,917	841	962	1,114	2,001	1,907	1,831
Reserve pos. in IMF ('000,000)	3,567	4,239	3,951	4,030	5,210	5,468	5,008
Foreign exchange	57,517	85,877	72,727	72,219	77,794	75,083	70,356
Gold ('000,000 fine troy oz)	95.18	95.18	95.18	95.18	95.18	95.18	95.18
% world reserves	10.13	10.24	10.43	10.46	10.48	10.52	10.67
Interest and prices							
Central bank discount (%)	8.0	8.3	4.8	4.5	3.0	2.5	2.5
Govt. bond yield (%)	8.6	8.0	6.3	6.7	6.5	5.6	5.1
Industrial share prices (1990 = 100)[11]	91.5	87.3	93.6	106.1	103.3	117.9	176.9
Balance of payments (U.S.$'000,000,000)							
Balance of visible trade	19.92	28.72	41.75	51.68	66.12	71.21	...
Imports, f.o.b.	383.48	401.51	340.73	378.59	457.10	488.22	...
Exports, f.o.b.	403.37	430.23	382.49	430.27	523.22	519.44	...
Balance of invisibles	−37.80	−48.11	−55.15	−71.99	−87.10	−84.28	...
Balance of payments, current account	−17.88	−19.39	−13.40	−20.31	−20.98	−13.07	...

Service enterprises (1991)

	no. of enterprises	no. of employees	weekly wage as a % of all wages	annual turnover (DM '000,000)
Gas	151	37,000	...	42,228
Water	183	40,000	...	3,443
Electrical power	462	296,000	...	147,076
Transport				
air	133	57,390	...	20,270
buses	6,054	192,869	...	12,586
rail	1	416,199	...	14,697
shipping	1,449	9,076	...	...
Communications				
press	2,452	240,075	...	31,096
film[4]	615	3,000	...	836
Postal services	17,616[5]	652,573	...	68,346
Hotels and restaurants	135,141	652,251	...	60,257
Wholesale trade	36,605[5]	1,214,000	...	1,015,984
Retail trade	152,629	2,241,000	...	605,755

Land use (1994): forest 30.6%; pasture 15.1%; agriculture 19.9%; other 34.4%.

Foreign trade

Balance of trade (current prices)

	1992	1993	1994	1995	1996
DM '000,000,000	+45.91	+75.81	+88.73	+103.40	+117.27
% of total	3.6%	6.4%	6.8%	7.4%	8.1%

Imports (1996): DM 669,060,500,000 (machinery and transport equipment 33.4%, of which road transport equipment 9.9%, electrical machinery other than office equipment 6.7%, office equipment and computers 4.4%; chemicals and chemical products 8.6%, of which organic chemical products 2.0%, unfabricated plastics 1.6%; food and beverages 7.8%, of which fruits and vegetables 2.7%, meat and meat products 1.2%, coffee, tea, and cocoa 0.9%; mineral fuels 7.7%, of which crude petroleum and petroleum products 5.3%, natural gas 1.9%; clothing 6.4%; iron and steel 2.6%; furniture 1.5%). *Major import sources:* France 10.3%; The Netherlands 8.3%; Italy 8.0%; U.S. 7.1%; U.K. 6.6%; Belgium 6.1%; Japan 4.9%; Switzerland 3.8%; Austria 3.7%.

Exports (1996): DM 771,913,400,000 (machinery and transport equipment 49.6%, of which road transport equipment 16.4%, electrical machinery other than office equipment 7.9%, office equipment 2.4%; chemicals and chemical products 13.1%, of which organic chemical products 2.6%, unfabricated plastics 2.3%). *Major export destinations:* France 10.9%; U.K. 8.0%; U.S. 7.8%; The Netherlands 7.4%; Italy 7.4%; Belgium-Luxembourg 6.2%; Austria 5.6%; Switzerland 4.9%; Spain 3.6%; Japan 2.7%; Sweden 2.4%.

Transport and communications

Transport. Railroads (1995): length 49,094 mi, 80,297 km; passengers carried 1,656,000,000; passenger-mi 39,507,000,000, passenger-km 63,581,000,-000; short ton-mi cargo 48,537,000,000, metric ton-km cargo 70,863,000,000. Roads (1996): total length 142,207 mi, 228,860 km (paved 99%). Vehicles (1997[1]): passenger cars 41,045,200; trucks and buses 2,381,500. Merchant marine (1995): vessels (100 gross tons and over) 1,476; total deadweight tonnage 5,721,000. Air transport (1995): passengers carried 34,584,000; passenger-mi 39,883,016,000, passenger-km 64,185,615,000; short ton-mi cargo 3,997,192,000, metric ton-km cargo 5,835,802,000; airports (1997) 35.

Communications

Medium	date	unit	number	units per 1,000 persons
Daily newspapers	1994	circulation	30,641,000	375
Radio	1995	receivers	150,000,000	1,836
Television	1995	receivers	45,000,000	551
Telephones	1995	main lines	40,400,000	495
Cellular telephones	1995	subscribers	3,750,000	45.9
Facsimile machines	1995	units	1,446,600	17.7
Personal computers	1995	units	13,500,000	165

Education and health

Health (1996): physicians 279,335 (1 per 293 persons); dentists 61,404 (1 per 1,334 persons); hospital beds (1995) 628,658 (1 per 130 persons); infant mortality rate per 1,000 live births 5.3.

Education (1995–96)

	schools	teachers	students	student/ teacher ratio
Primary (age 6–10)	17,910	199,623	3,634,342	18.2
Secondary (age 10–19)	17,711	402,472	5,822,242	14.5
Voc., teacher tr.	9,245	107,548	2,435,753	22.6
Higher	335	152,401	1,838,456	12.1

Food (1995): daily per capita caloric intake 3,265 (vegetable products 68%, animal products 32%); 123% of FAO recommended minimum requirement.

Military

Total active duty personnel (1997): 347,100 (army 69.6%, navy 8.1%, air force 22.3%). *Military expenditure as percentage of GNP* (1995): 1.9% (world 2.8%); per capita expenditure U.S.$496.

[1]January 1. [2]Detail does not add to total given because of rounding. [3]Former West Germany only. [4]1984. [5]1990. [6]Establishments with 20 or more workers only. [7]1994. [8]Includes 4,003,000 unemployed. [9]September. [10]End-of-period figures unless footnoted otherwise. [11]Period averages.

Internet resources for further information:

- **Federal Statistical Office of Germany**
http://www.statistik-bund.de/basis/be_ueber.htm

Ghana

Official name: Republic of Ghana.
Form of government: unitary multiparty republic with one legislative house (House of Parliament [200]).
Head of state and government: President.
Capital: Accra.
Official language: English.
Official religion: none.
Monetary unit: 1 cedi (₵) = 100 pesewas; valuation (Oct. 3, 1997) 1 U.S.$ = ₵2,228; 1 £ = ₵3,591.

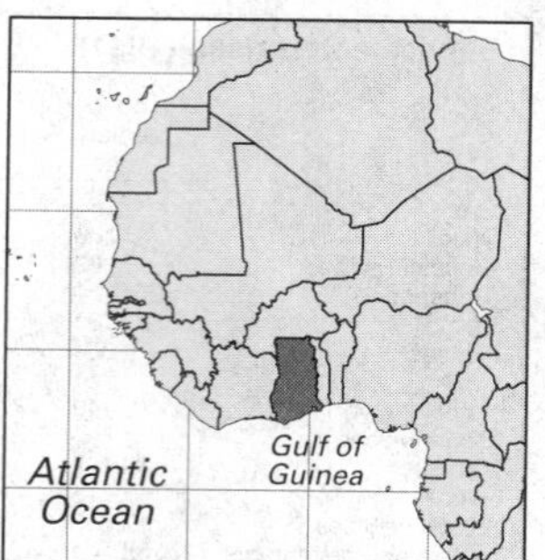

Area and population

Regions[2]	Capitals	area sq mi	area sq km	population 1991[1] estimate
Ashanti	Kumasi	9,417	24,389	2,485,766
Brong-Ahafo	Sunyani	15,273	39,557	1,432,971
Central	Cape Coast	3,794	9,826	1,359,861
Eastern	Koforidua	7,461	19,323	2,003,235
Greater Accra	Accra	1,253	3,245	1,696,170
Northern	Tamale	27,175	70,384	1,389,105
Upper East	Bolgatanga	3,414	8,842	921,196
Upper West	Wa	7,134	18,476	526,398
Volta	Ho	7,942	20,570	1,432,971
Western	Sekondi-Takoradi	9,236	23,921	1,374,483
TOTAL		92,098[3]	238,533	14,622,156

Demography

Population (1997): 18,101,000.
Density (1997): persons per sq mi 196.5, persons per sq km 75.9.
Urban-rural (1996): urban 36.8%; rural 63.2%.
Sex distribution (1996): male 49.66%; female 50.34%.
Age breakdown (1990): under 15, 46.8%; 15–29, 26.2%; 30–44, 14.4%; 45–59, 8.0%; 60–74, 3.8%; 75 and over, 0.8%.
Population projection: (2000) 19,272,000; (2010) 22,929,000.
Doubling time: 23 years.
Ethnolinguistic composition (1983): Akan 52.4%; Mossi 15.8%; Ewe 11.9%; Ga-Adangme 7.8%; Gurma 3.3%; Yoruba 1.3%; other 7.5%.
Religious affiliation (1995): traditional beliefs 38.0%; Muslim 30.0%; Christian 24.0%, of which Roman Catholic 12.1%, Protestant 4.9%, African Christian 4.9%, Anglican 2.1%; other 8.0%.
Major cities (1988[1]): Accra 949,100; Kumasi 385,200; Tamale 151,100; Tema 110,000; Sekondi-Takoradi 103,600.

Vital statistics

Birth rate per 1,000 population (1990–95): 41.7 (world avg. 25.0); legitimate, n.a.; illegitimate, n.a.
Death rate per 1,000 population (1990–95): 11.7 (world avg. 9.3).
Natural increase rate per 1,000 population (1990–95): 30.0 (world avg. 15.7).
Total fertility rate (avg. births per childbearing woman; 1993): 5.9.
Life expectancy at birth (1993): male 53.3 years; female 57.2 years.
Major causes of death per 100,000 population: n.a.; however, principal infectious diseases as a percentage of outpatients (1989): malaria 43.8%, respiratory infections (including tuberculosis) 8.0%, diarrheal diseases 6.7%, intestinal worms 3.1%.

National economy

Budget (1995). Revenue: ₵1,690,791,000,000 (import-export duties 29.6%, of which cocoa export duty 11.5%[4]; excise and value-added taxes 21.5%, of which petroleum tax 13.2%; income taxes 16.3%; divestiture of government assets 6.6%). Expenditures: ₵1,697,893,000,000 (1994; education 22.3%; debt service 20.1%; health 6.9%; transportation and communications 5.3%; social security and welfare 3.6%; defense 2.9%).
Public debt (external, outstanding; 1995): U.S.$4,568,000,000.
Production (metric tons except as noted). Agriculture, forestry, fishing (1997): roots and tubers 10,500,000 (of which cassava 6,800,000, yams 2,250,000, taro 1,450,000), cereals 1,770,000 (of which corn [maize] 1,000,000, sorghum 350,000, rice 220,000, millet 200,000), bananas and plantains 1,804,000, cacao 350,000, coconuts 240,000, tomatoes 160,000, peanuts (groundnuts) 135,000, sugarcane 110,000, oranges 50,000, palm kernels 34,000, lemons and limes 30,000, pulses 20,000; livestock (number of live animals) 2,200,000 goats, 2,100,000 sheep, 1,150,000 cattle, 395,000 pigs, 13,300,000 chickens; roundwood (1996) 26,473,000 cu m; fish catch (1995) 344,460 (of which anchovies 65,497). Mining and quarrying (1996): bauxite 383,370; manganese ore 266,420; gold 50,079 kg; diamonds 773,126 carats. Manufacturing (value added in ₵; 1993): tobacco 71,474,700,000; footwear 60,350,600,000; chemical products 40,347,600,000; beverages 36,167,000,000; metal products 35,121,700,000; petroleum products 32,143,500,000; textiles 18,278,600,000; machinery and transport equipment 9,525,700,000. Construction (value added in ₵; 1994): 171,129,000,000. Energy production (consumption): electricity (kW-hr; 1994) 6,167,000,000 (5,857,000,000); coal (metric tons; 1994) none (3,000); crude petroleum (barrels; 1994) none (7,498,000); petroleum products (metric tons; 1994) 921,000 (1,100,000); natural gas, none (n.a.).
Tourism (1994): receipts U.S.$228,000,000; expenditures U.S.$20,000,000.
Household income and expenditure. Average household size (1984) 4.9; average annual income per household (1978) ₵9,600 (U.S.$[5]); sources of income: n.a.; expenditure (1978): food 57.4%, clothing 14.3%, housing 11.5%, transportation and communications 3.3%, health care 1.3%.
Gross national product (1995): U.S.$6,719,000,000 (U.S.$390 per capita).

Structure of gross domestic product and labour force

	1995 in value ₵'000,000	1995 % of total value	1984 labour force	1984 % of labour force
Agriculture	3,325,912	44.0	3,310,967	59.4
Mining	131,809	1.7	26,828	0.5
Manufacturing	712,467	9.4	588,418	10.5
Construction	255,422	3.4	64,686	1.2
Public utilities	146,288	1.9	15,437	0.3
Transp. and commun.	474,803	6.3	122,806	2.2
Trade	1,152,750	15.2	792,147	14.2
Finance	292,073	3.9	27,475	0.5
Pub. admin., defense }	705,312	9.3	97,548	1.7
Services }			376,168	6.7
Other	360,331[6]	4.8[6]	157,624[7]	2.8[7]
TOTAL	7,557,167	100.0[3]	5,580,104	100.0

Population economically active (1984): total 5,580,104; activity rate of total population 45.4% (participation rates: over age 15, 82.5%; female 51.2%; unemployed 2.8%).

Price and earnings indexes (1990 = 100)

	1990	1991	1992	1993	1994	1995	1996
Consumer price index	100.0	118.0	129.9	162.3	202.7	323.2	473.7
Monthly earnings index	100.0	117.2	...	...	...	...	...

Land use (1994): forest 42.2%; pasture 36.9%; agriculture 19.0%; other 1.9%.

Foreign trade

Balance of trade (current prices)

	1991	1992	1993	1994	1995	1996
U.S.$'000,000	−320.7	−470.2	−664.3	−353.1	−256.6	−366.0
% of total	13.8%	19.2%	23.8%	12.6%	4.6%	10.4%

Imports (1994): U.S.$1,579,900,000 (1987; machinery 28.1%; mineral fuels 14.0%; chemicals 12.0%; food 5.2%). *Major import sources:* Germany 13.7%; U.K. 12.1%; U.S. 11.7%; France 5.4%; Italy 4.8%.
Exports (1994): U.S.$1,226,800,000 (gold 44.7%; food 26.3%, of which cocoa 26.1%; logs and sawn timber 13.5%; electricity 4.6%; diamonds 1.7%). *Major export destinations:* U.K. 15.5%; Italy 7.9%; Japan 6.7%; U.S. 6.6%; Germany 5.5%; France 4.0%.

Transport and communications

Transport. Railroads (1993): route length 592 mi, 953 km; passenger-mi 731,400,000, passenger-km 1,177,000,000; short ton-mi cargo 93,906,000, metric ton-km cargo 137,100,000. Roads (1994): total length 24,000 mi, 38,700 km (paved 40%). Vehicles (1994): passenger cars 86,200; trucks and buses 130,000. Merchant marine (1992): vessels (100 gross tons and over) 155; total deadweight tonnage 130,977. Air transport (1996)[8]: passenger-mi 407,073,000, passenger-km 655,122,000; short ton-mi cargo 20,239,000, metric ton-km cargo 29,549,000; airports (1996) with scheduled flights 1.

Communications

Medium	date	unit	number	units per 1,000 persons
Daily newspapers	1993	circulation	1,060,000	64.4
Radio	1995	receivers	4,300,000	249
Television	1995	receivers	265,000	15.3
Telephones	1995	main lines	60,000	3.5
Cellular telephones	1995	subscribers	6,200	0.4
Facsimile machines	1995	units	4,500	0.3
Personal computers	1995	units	20,000	1.2

Education and health

Educational attainment (1984). Percentage of population age 25 and over having: no formal schooling 60.4%; primary education 7.1%; middle school 25.4%; secondary 3.5%; vocational and other postsecondary 2.9%; higher 0.6%. *Literacy* (1995): total population age 15 and over literate 6,160,000 (64.5%); males literate 3,570,000 (75.9%); females literate 1,850,000 (53.5%).

Education (1991–92)

	schools	teachers	students	student/teacher ratio
Primary (6–12)	11,056	66,068	1,796,490	27.2
Secondary (13–20)	5,540	43,367	816,578	18.8
Voc., teacher tr.[9]	57	422	13,232	31.4
Higher[9]	16	700	9,274	13.2

Health: physicians (1994) 735 (1 per 22,970 persons); hospital beds (1994) 26,455 (1 per 638 persons); infant mortality rate per 1,000 live births (1994) 83.
Food (1996): daily per capita caloric intake 2,622 (vegetable products 96%, animal products 4%); 114% of FAO minimum recommended requirement.

Military

Total active duty personnel (1997): 7,000 (army 71.4%, navy 14.3%, air force 14.3%). *Military expenditure as percentage of GNP* (1995): 1.4% (world 2.8%); per capita expenditure U.S.$5.

[1]January 1. [2]Government administration has been decentralized to the local level of 103 district assemblies, 4 municipal assemblies, and 3 metropolitan assemblies. [3]Detail does not add to total given because of rounding. [4]1994. [5]Unofficial 1978 exchange rate (7.5 to 9.9 times the official rate) does not permit meaningful conversion into other currencies. [6]Import duties and statistical adjustments less imputed bank service charges. [7]Unemployed only. [8]Ghana Airways only. [9]1989–90.

Internet resources for further information:
- **Ghana Fact Sheet http://www.macroint.com/dhs/press/gh-fac.html**

Greece

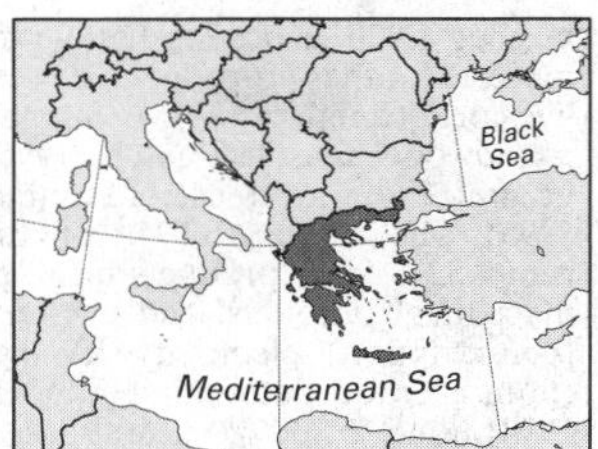

Official name: Ellinikí Dhimokratía (Hellenic Republic).
Form of government: unitary multiparty republic with one legislative house (Greek Chamber of Deputies [300]).
Chief of state: President.
Head of government: Prime Minister.
Capital: Athens.
Official language: Greek.
Official religion: Eastern Orthodox.
Monetary unit: 1 drachma (Dr) = 100 lepta; valuation (Oct. 3, 1997) 1 U.S.$ = Dr 278.32; 1 £ = Dr 448.66.

Area and population

Regions		area sq mi	area sq km	population 1991 census
Anatolikí Makedhonía kaí Thráki	(Eastern Macedonia and Thrace)	5,466	14,157	570,496
Attikí	(Attica)	1,470	3,808	3,523,407
Dhytikí Ellás	(Western Greece)	4,382	11,350	707,687
Dhytikí Makedhonía	(Western Macedonia)	3,649	9,451	293,015
Iónioi Nísoi	(Ionian Islands)	891	2,307	193,734
Ípiros	(Epirus)	3,553	9,203	339,728
Kedrikí Makedhonía[1]	(Central Macedonia)	7,393	19,147	1,710,513
Kríti	(Crete)	3,218	8,336	540,054
Nótion Aiyaíon	(Southern Aegean)	2,041	5,286	257,481
Pelopónnisos	(Peloponnesos)	5,981	15,490	607,428
Stereá Ellás	(Central Greece)	6,004	15,549	582,280
Thessalía	(Thessaly)	5,420	14,037	734,846
Vóreion Aiyaíon	(Northern Aegean)	1,481	3,836	199,231
TOTAL		50,949	131,957	10,259,900

Demography

Population (1997): 10,541,000.
Density (1997): persons per sq mi 206.9, persons per sq km 79.9.
Urban-rural (1996): urban 65.7%; rural 34.3%.
Sex distribution (1996): male 49.23%; female 50.77%.
Age breakdown (1995): under 15, 17.1%; 15–29, 22.6%; 30–44, 20.8%; 45–59, 18.1%; 60–74, 15.4%; 75 and over, 6.0%.
Population projection: (2000) 10,674,000; (2010) 11,132,000.
Doubling time: not applicable; doubling time exceeds 100 years.
Ethnic composition (1983): Greek 95.5%; Macedonian 1.5%; Turkish 0.9%; Albanian 0.6%; other 1.5%.
Religious affiliation (1980): Christian 98.1%, of which Eastern Orthodox 97.6%, Roman Catholic 0.4%, Protestant 0.1%; Muslim 1.5%; other 0.4%.
Major cities (1991): Athens 772,072; Thessaloníki 383,967; Piraeus (Piraiévs) 182,671; Pátrai 152,570; Peristérion 137,288.

Vital statistics

Birth rate per 1,000 population (1996): 9.7 (world avg. 25.0); (1995) legitimate 97.0%; illegitimate 3.0%.
Death rate per 1,000 population (1996): 9.6 (world avg. 9.3).
Natural increase rate per 1,000 population (1996): 0.1 (world avg. 15.7).
Total fertility rate (avg. births per childbearing woman; 1993): 1.4.
Marriage rate per 1,000 population (1995): 6.1.
Divorce rate per 1,000 population (1994): 0.7.
Life expectancy at birth (1990): male 74.6 years; female 79.4 years.
Major causes of death per 100,000 population (1995): diseases of the circulatory system 491.3, of which cerebrovascular disease 181.9, ischemic heart disease 121.3; malignant neoplasms (cancers) 210.6; respiratory disease 55.1.

National economy

Budget (1996). Revenue: Dr 14,578,000,000,000[2] (indirect and excise taxes 30.2%, direct taxes 16.6%, European Community 5.3%). Expenditures: Dr 14,590,553,000,000 (1994; health and social insurance 5.5%, defense 4.0%, education and culture 3.4%, police and justice systems 1.5%).
Public debt (1995): U.S.$25,421,000,000.
Tourism (1996): receipts U.S.$3,684,100,000; expenditures U.S.$1,176,800,000.
Production (metric tons except as noted). Agriculture, forestry, fishing (1997): sugar beets 3,500,000, corn (maize) 2,045,000, wheat 2,016,000, tomatoes 1,903,500, olives 1,600,000, grapes 1,226,800, potatoes 1,050,000, oranges 950,000, peaches and nectarines 530,000, barley 357,000, apples 280,000, cabbages 280,000, rice 230,000, cucumbers 170,000; livestock (number of live animals) 9,606,000 sheep, 5,847,000 goats, 951,000 pigs, 600,000 cattle, 28,500,000 chickens; roundwood (1996) 2,006,000 cu m; fish catch (1995) 198,217. Mining and quarrying (1996): bauxite 1,881,000; zinc 13,000[3]; lead 11,000[3]; chromium ore 5,650[3, 4]. Manufacturing (value added in Dr '000,000; 1995): food, beverages, and tobacco 694,431; chemicals 402,133; textiles 257,555; paper and printing 208,696; transport equipment 148,767; clothing and footwear 137,524. Construction (value of completed buildings in Dr; 1994): residential 801,300,000; nonresidential 31,004,400,000. Energy production (consumption): electricity (kW-hr; 1994) 40,623,000,000 (41,005,000,000); coal (metric tons; 1994) 56,741,000 (59,569,000); crude petroleum (barrels; 1994) 3,589,000 (102,721,000); petroleum products (metric tons; 1994) 15,078,000 (14,311,000); natural gas (cu m; 1994) 55,047,000 (55,047,000).
Household income and expenditure. Average household size (1993–94) 2.9; income per household Dr 3,900,000 (U.S.$15,660); sources of income (1994): property and entrepreneurial income 54.5%, wages and salaries 27.9%, transfer payments 17.6%; expenditure: food 35.7%, transportation 14.7%, clothing and footwear 13.0%, housing 8.6%, education 6.5%, other 21.5%.
Gross national product (1995): U.S.$85,885,000,000 (U.S.$8,210 per capita).

Structure of gross domestic product and labour force

	1995 in value Dr '000,000	% of total value	labour force	% of labour force
Agriculture	2,538,766	14.2	781,900	18.4
Mining	213,615	1.2	15,600	0.4
Manufacturing	2,483,098	13.9	577,700	13.6
Construction	1,102,673	6.2	252,300	5.9
Public utilities	433,992	2.4	41,500	1.0
Transp. and commun.	1,309,314	7.4	248,000	5.8
Trade	2,455,455	13.8	848,700	20.0
Finance	568,044	3.2	241,000	5.7
Pub. admin., defense	3,347,139	18.8	817,200	19.2
Services	1,932,091	10.8		
Other	1,432,478[5]	8.0[5]	424,700[6]	10.0[6]
TOTAL	17,816,664[7]	100.0[7]	4,248,500[7]	100.0

Population economically active (1995): total 4,248,500; activity rate of total population 40.6% (participation rates: ages 15–64, 60.7%; female 38.1%; unemployed 10.0%).

Price and earnings indexes (1990 = 100)

	1990	1991	1992	1993	1994	1995	1996
Consumer price index	100.0	119.5	138.4	158.4	175.7	192.0	207.1
Hourly earnings index	100.0	116.7	132.8	146.7	165.9	187.9	...

Land use (1994): forest 20.3%; pasture 40.7%; agriculture 27.2%; other 11.8%.

Foreign trade

Balance of trade (current prices)

	1990	1991	1992	1993	1994	1995
Dr '000,000,000	−1,613.3	−1,886.1	−2,113.5	−2,536.2	−2,331.9	−3,367.5
% of total	44.3%	37.3%	36.8%	39.6%	33.9%	39.8%

Imports (1995): Dr 5,908,368,000,000 (machinery and transport equipment 32.5%; food 14.0%, of which meat products 4.0%, dairy products 2.2%; chemical products 8.9%; crude petroleum 5.1%). *Major import sources:* Germany 17.9%; Italy 15.7%; U.S. 9.0%; France 8.2%; U.K. 6.9%; The Netherlands 6.6%; Belgium-Luxembourg 3.4%; Spain 2.9%.
Exports (1995): Dr 2,540,891,000,000 (textiles 25.8%; food 25.6%; petroleum products 8.5%; minerals 3.7%; cotton 3.7%). *Major export destinations:* Germany 27.7%; U.S. 17.7%; Italy 8.4%; U.K. 6.6%; France 6.6%.

Transport and communications

Transport. Railroads (1994): route length 1,537 mi, 2,474 km; passenger-mi 869,300,000, passenger-km 1,399,000,000; short ton-mi cargo 210,000,000, metric ton-km cargo 307,000,000. Roads (1995): total length 72,350 mi, 116,440 km (paved 92%). Vehicles (1995): passenger cars 2,204,761; trucks and buses 908,423. Merchant marine (1995): vessels (100 gross tons and over) 2,128; total deadweight tonnage 29,863,000. Air transport (1995): passenger-mi 4,936,800,000, passenger-km 7,945,008,000; short ton-mi cargo 80,370,000, metric ton-km cargo 117,338,000; airports (1997) with scheduled flights 36.

Communications

Medium	date	unit	number	units per 1,000 persons
Daily newspapers	1992	circulation	1,400,000	135
Radio	1995	receivers	4,200,000	402
Television	1995	receivers	4,630,000	442
Telephones	1995	main lines	5,162,800	493
Cellular telephones	1995	subscribers	273,000	26.1
Facsimile machines	1995	units	15,300	1.5
Personal computers	1995	units	350,000	3.3

Education and health

Educational attainment (1991). Percentage of population age 25 and over having: no formal schooling (illiterate) 6.8%; some primary education 10.6%; completed primary 39.7%; lower secondary 10.8%; higher secondary 20.6%; some postsecondary 4.9%; a degree from institution of higher education 6.6%. *Literacy* (1991): total population age 15 and over literate 7,870,000 (95.2%); males literate 3,900,000 (97.7%); females literate 3,970,000 (93.0%).

Education (1992–93)

	schools	teachers	students	student/ teacher ratio
Primary (age 6–12)	7,634	37,549	745,666	19.9
Secondary (age 12–18)	2,988	45,794	700,488	15.3
Voc., teacher tr.	695	14,319	190,443	13.3
Higher[8]	17	9,124	115,464	12.6

Health: physicians (1994) 40,487 (1 per 258 persons); hospital beds (1993) 52,144 (1 per 199 persons); infant mortality rate per 1,000 live births (1996) 8.1.
Food (1995): daily per capita caloric intake 3,815 (vegetable products 78%, animal products 22%); 142% of FAO recommended minimum requirement.

Military

Total active duty personnel (1997): 162,300 (army 71.5%, navy 12.0%, air force 16.5%). *Military expenditure as percentage of GNP* (1995): 5.5% (world 2.8%); per capita expenditure U.S.$482.

[1]Includes Mount Athos (Áyion Óros), an autonomous, self-governing monastic region; 1991 population 1,557. [2]Includes Dr 5,633,000,000,000 of domestic borrowing. [3]Metal content of ore. [4]1994. [5]Income from ownership of buildings. [6]Unemployed. [7]Detail does not add to total given because of rounding. [8]1991–92.

Internet resources for further information:
- **Greek Indexer http://www.hiway.gr/gi/**

Grenada

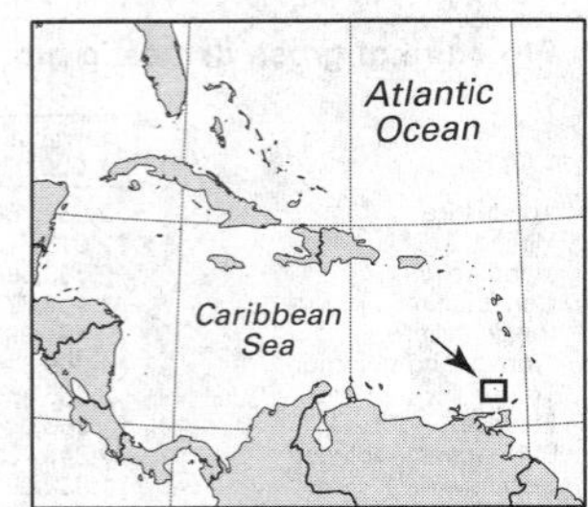

Official name: Grenada.
Form of government: constitutional monarchy with two legislative houses (Senate [13]; House of Representatives [15[1]]).
Chief of state: British Monarch represented by Governor-General.
Head of government: Prime Minister.
Capital: St. George's.
Official language: English.
Official religion: none.
Monetary unit: 1 East Caribbean dollar (EC$) = 100 cents; valuation (Oct. 3, 1997) 1 U.S.$ = EC$2.70; 1 £ = EC$4.35.

Area and population

Local Councils	Principal towns	area sq mi	area sq km	population 1991 census
Carriacou	Hillsborough	10	26	5,726
Petite Martinique	...	3	8	
St. Andrew	Grenville	38	99	24,135
St. David	...	17	44	11,011
St. George	...	25[2]	65[2]	27,373
St. John	Gouyave	14	35	8,752
St. Mark	Victoria	10	25	3,861
St. Patrick	Sauteurs	16	42	10,118
Town				
St. George's	—	[2]	[2]	4,621
TOTAL		133	344	95,597

Demography

Population (1997): 98,400.
Density (1997): persons per sq mi 739.8, persons per sq km 286.0.
Urban-rural (1991)[3]: urban 33.5%; rural 66.5%.
Sex distribution (1991): male 49.20%; female 50.80%.
Age breakdown (1991): under 15, 38.4%; 15–29, 25.8%; 30–44, 16.1%; 45–59, 8.9%; 60–74, 7.6%; 75 and over, 3.2%.
Population projection: (2000) 100,000; (2010) 104,000.
Doubling time: 52 years.
Ethnic composition (1991): black 84.9%; mixed 11.0%; Indo-Pakistani 3.0%; white 0.7%; other 0.4%.
Religious affiliation (1995): Roman Catholic 57.8%; Protestant 37.6%, of which Anglican 14.4%, Pentecostal 8.3%, Seventh-day Adventist 7.0%; other 4.6%, of which Rastafarian *c.* 3.0%.
Major localities (1991): St. George's 4,621; Gouyave 3,000[4]; Grenville 2,000[4].

Vital statistics

Birth rate per 1,000 population (1996): 21.3[5] (world avg. 25.0); (1987) legitimate 18.1%; illegitimate 81.9%.
Death rate per 1,000 population (1996): 7.9[5] (world avg. 9.3).
Natural increase rate per 1,000 population (1996): 13.4[5] (world avg. 15.7).
Total fertility rate (avg. births per childbearing woman; 1996): 3.8.
Marriage rate per 1,000 population (1991): 4.3.
Divorce rate per 1,000 population (1991): 0.8.
Life expectancy at birth (1996): male 68.4 years; female 73.4 years.
Major causes of death per 100,000 population (1987): diseases of the circulatory system 264.3; malignant neoplasms (cancers) 82.8; endocrine and metabolic diseases 57.3; diseases of the respiratory system 45.6; diseases of the digestive system 38.2; ill-defined conditions 209.1.

National economy

Budget (1995). Revenue: EC$226,480,000 (general sales taxes 31.7%, income taxes 19.0%, import duties 15.2%, grants from abroad 9.5%). Expenditures: EC$209,690,000 (education 16.8%, transportation and communications 14.1%, general administration 12.3%, health 10.4%).
Public debt (external, outstanding; 1995): U.S.$98,400,000.
Tourism (1995): receipts from visitors U.S.$58,000,000; expenditures by nationals abroad U.S.$4,000,000.
Gross national product (at current market prices; 1995): U.S.$271,000,000 (U.S.$2,980 per capita).

Structure of gross domestic product and labour force

	1995		1991	
	in value EC$'000,000[6]	% of total value	labour force[7]	% of labour force
Agriculture	61.7	11.9	4,223	17.1
Quarrying	2.6	0.5	126	0.5
Manufacturing	30.7	5.9	1,881	7.6
Construction	36.5	7.0	3,168	12.9
Public utilities	22.4	4.3	350	1.4
Transportation and communications	117.4	22.6	1,614	6.5
Trade, restaurants	109.5	21.1	5,149	20.9
Finance, real estate	67.6	13.0	866	3.5
Pub. admin., defense	89.1	17.1	1,738	7.1
Services	15.1	2.9	3,372	13.7
Other	–32.7[8]	–6.3[8]	2,163	8.8
TOTAL	519.9[9]	100.0	24,650	100.0

Production (metric tons except as noted). Agriculture, forestry, fishing (1996): bananas 8,600, coconuts 6,800, sugarcane 6,500, roots and tubers 3,000, nutmeg 1,920, avocados 1,900, grapefruit 1,900, mangoes 1,700, cacao 1,567, mace 124, other crops include cotton, limes, cinnamon, cloves, and pimiento; livestock (number of live animals) 13,052 sheep, 7,000 goats, 5,300 pigs; roundwood, n.a.; fish catch (1995) 1,486. Mining and quarrying: excavation of gravel for local use. Manufacturing (value of production in EC$'000; 1995): wheat flour 10,174; soft drinks 8,558; beer 7,172; animal feed 4,698; rum 4,520; other products include clothing, edible coconut oil, paints, pharmaceutical products, and cigarettes. Construction: n.a. Energy production (consumption): electricity (kW-hr; 1994) 70,000,000 (70,000,000); coal, none (none); crude petroleum, none (none); petroleum products (metric tons; 1994) none (52,000); natural gas, none (none).
Household income and expenditure. Average household size (1991) 3.7; income per household (1988) EC$7,097 (U.S.$2,629); sources of income: n.a.; expenditure (1987): food, beverages, and tobacco 40.7%, household furnishings and operations 13.7%, housing 11.9%, transportation 9.1%, personal effects and medical care 8.6%.
Population economically active (1988): total 38,920; activity rate of total population 39.9% (participation rates: ages 15–65, 72.7%; female 48.6%; unemployed [1996] 17.5%).

Price and earnings indexes (1990 = 100)

	1990	1991	1992	1993	1994	1995	1996
Consumer price index	100.0	102.6	106.5	109.5	112.4	115.8	118.0
Annual earnings index[10]	100.0	108.0	118.8	124.1	131.5	138.3	...

Land use (1994): forested 9.0%; meadows and pastures 3.0%; agricultural and under permanent cultivation 35.0%; other 53.0%.

Foreign trade[11]

Balance of trade (current prices)

	1990	1991	1992	1993	1994	1995
U.S.$'000,000	–82.6	–102.6	–94.5	–111.7	–123.1	–112.7
% of total	61.2%	67.3%	68.7%	72.2%	71.4%	72.3%

Imports (1995): U.S.$134,300,000 (food 23.8%; machinery and transport equipment 19.7%; basic manufactures 17.3%; chemicals and chemical products 7.9%). *Major import sources*[12]: United States 32%; United Kingdom 14%; Barbados 5%; Japan 4%; St. Vincent and the Grenadines 4%.
Exports (1995): U.S.$21,600,000 (domestic exports 89.4%, of which fish 15.7%, cocoa beans 15.3%, nutmeg 14.4%, bananas 8.8%, clothing 6.0%; reexports 10.6%). *Major export destinations*[12]: United States 18%; Germany 18%; United Kingdom 18%; St. Lucia 7%; Barbados 7%.

Transport and communications

Transport. Railroads: none. Roads (1995): total length 700 mi, 1,127 km (paved 51%). Vehicles (1991)[13]: passenger cars 4,739; trucks and buses 3,068. Merchant marine (1992): vessels (100 gross tons and over) 3; total deadweight tonnage 484. Air transport (1995)[14]: passenger arrivals 158,646, departures 161,232; cargo loaded 1,680 metric tons, cargo unloaded 555 metric tons; airports (1997) with scheduled flights 2.

Communications

Medium	date	unit	number	units per 1,000 persons
Radio	1996	receivers	45,000	460
Television	1995	receivers	15,000	154
Telephones	1995	main lines	23,200	238
Cellular telephones	1995	subscribers	400	4.1
Facsimile machines	1995	units	300	3.1

Education and health

Educational attainment (1991). Percentage of population age 25 and over having: no formal schooling 1.8%; primary education 74.9%; secondary 15.5%; higher 4.7%, of which university 2.8%; other/unknown 3.1%. *Literacy* (1992): total population age 15 and over literate 50,000 (85.0%).

Education (1994–95)

	schools	teachers	students	student/ teacher ratio
Primary (age 5–11)[15]	57	849	23,256	27.4
Secondary (age 12–16)[15]	19	381	7,260	19.1
Vocational	...	...	...	...
Higher[16]	1	66	651	9.9

Health (1996): physicians (1992) 47 (1 per 2,045 persons); hospital beds 439 (1 per 223 persons); infant mortality rate per 1,000 live births 14.3.
Food (1995): daily per capita caloric intake 2,713 (vegetable products 77%, animal products 23%); 112% of FAO recommended minimum requirement.

Military

Total active duty personnel (1993): [17]. *Military expenditure as percentage of GNP:* n.a.; per capita expenditure, n.a.

[1]Excludes the speaker, who may be elected from outside its elected membership. [2]St. George local council includes St. George's town. [3]Urban defined as St. George's town and St. George local council. [4]1987. [5]Based on year of registration. [6]At factor cost in 1990 prices. [7]Employed persons only. [8]Less imputed bank service charges. [9]Detail does not add to total given because of rounding. [10]Private sector only. [11]Imports c.i.f.; exports f.o.b. [12]Estimated figure(s). [13]Registered vehicles only. [14]Point Salines airport. [15]Excludes private schools. [16]1993–94; excludes Grenada Teachers' College. [17]The 750-member police force includes a paramilitary unit and a coast guard unit.

Guadeloupe

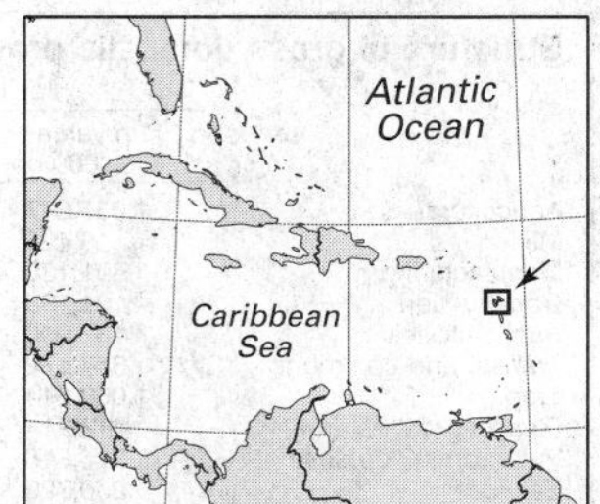

Official name: Département de la Guadeloupe (Department of Guadeloupe).
Political status: overseas department (France[1]) with two legislative houses (General Council [43]; Regional Council [41]).
Chief of state: President of France.
Heads of government: Commissioner of the Republic (for France); President of the General Council (for Guadeloupe); President of the Regional Council (for Guadeloupe).
Capital: Basse-Terre.
Official language: French.
Official religion: none.
Monetary unit: 1 French franc (F) = 100 centimes; valuation (Oct. 3, 1997) 1 U.S.$ = F 5.92; 1 £ = F 9.55.

Area and population

		area		population
Arrondissements	Capitals	sq mi	sq km	1990 census
Basse-Terre[2]	Basse-Terre	332	861	151,979
Pointe-à-Pitre[3]	Pointe-à-Pitre	297	769	192,643
Saint-Martin–Saint-Barthélemy[4]	Marigot	29	75	33,556
TOTAL		687[5]	1,780[5]	378,178[6]

Demography

Population (1997): 433,000.
Density (1997): persons per sq mi 630.3, persons per sq km 243.3.
Urban-rural (1995)[7]: urban 99.4%; rural 0.6%.
Sex distribution (1995): male 48.83%; female 51.17%.
Age breakdown (1995): under 15, 26.1%; 15–29, 27.5%; 30–44, 22.3%; 45–59, 13.1%; 60–74, 7.7%; 75 and over, 3.3%.
Population projection: (2000) 454,000; (2010) 530,000.
Doubling time: 58 years.
Ethnic composition (1991): Creole (mulatto) 77.0%; black 10.0%; Guadeloupe mestizo (French–East Asian) 10.0%; white 2.0%; other 1.0%.
Religious affiliation (1995): Roman Catholic 81.1%; Jehovah's Witness 4.8%; Protestant 4.7%; other 9.4%.
Major communes (1990): Les Abymes 62,605; Saint-Martin 28,518; Pointe-à-Pitre 26,029 (141,000[8, 9]); Le Gosier 20,688; Basse-Terre 14,003 (53,000[8]).

Vital statistics

Birth rate per 1,000 population (1995): 16.3 (world avg. 25.0); (1994) legitimate 38.7%; illegitimate 61.3%.
Death rate per 1,000 population (1995): 5.7 (world avg. 9.3).
Natural increase rate per 1,000 population (1994): 10.6 (world avg. 15.7).
Total fertility rate (avg. births per childbearing woman; 1990–95): 2.2.
Marriage rate per 1,000 population (1995): 4.3.
Divorce rate per 1,000 population (1995): 1.3.
Life expectancy at birth (1990–95): male 71.1 years; female 78.0 years.
Major causes of death per 100,000 population (1992): diseases of the circulatory system 189.0; malignant neoplasms (cancers) 110.3; accidents, violence, and poisoning 66.3; diseases of the digestive system 33.3; infectious and parasitic diseases 29.3; endocrine and metabolic diseases 27.5.

National economy

Budget (1994). Revenue: F 2,971,000,000 (tax revenues 64.8%, of which direct taxes 33.7%; advances, loans, and transfers 29.8%; nontax revenues 4.6%). Expenditures: F 6,199,000,000 (current expenditures 65.6%; capital [development] expenditures 17.2%; advances and loans 17.1%).
Public debt (external, outstanding; 1990[10]): U.S.$58,000,000.
Tourism (1995): receipts from visitors U.S.$458,000,000; expenditures by nationals abroad, n.a.
Production (metric tons except as noted). Agriculture, forestry, fishing (1996): sugarcane 376,000, bananas 116,000, yams 7,000, plantains 6,000, sweet potatoes 5,000, pineapples 4,000, cucumbers and gherkins 4,000, tomatoes 3,000, melons 3,000, and flowers are also produced for export; livestock (number of live animals) 63,000 goats, 60,000 cattle, 14,000 pigs; roundwood (1995) 15,300 cu m; fish catch (1995) 9,530. Mining and quarrying (1993): pumice 210,000. Manufacturing (1996): cement 282,571; raw sugar 48,896; rum 66,483 hectolitres; other products include clothing, wooden furniture and posts, and metalware. Construction (buildings authorized; 1992): residential 358,474 sq m; nonresidential 160,084 sq m. Energy production (consumption): electricity (kW-hr; 1996) 1,098,000,000 (987,600,000); coal, none (none); crude petroleum, none (none); petroleum products (metric tons; 1994) none (446,000); natural gas, none (none).
Population economically active (1993): total 175,500; activity rate of total population 42.0% (participation rates: ages 15–64, 73.2%; [1990] female 45.5%; unemployed [1996] 27.8%).

Price and earnings indexes (1990 = 100)[11]

	1990	1991	1992	1993	1994	1995	1996[12]
Consumer price index	100.0	102.0	104.5	106.7	110.8	114.3	113.5
Monthly earnings index[13]	100.0	102.0	104.7	105.0	106.5	108.7[14]	109.6

Household income and expenditure. Average household size (1990) 3.4; income per household (1988) F 105,400 (U.S.$17,700); sources of income (1988): wages and salaries 78.9%, self-employment 12.7%, transfer payments 8.4%; expenditure (1990): food and beverages 30.9%, transportation and communications 20.5%, housing and lighting 11.3%, household durables 9.3%, clothing and footwear 9.3%, energy and fuel 7.7%.
Gross national product (1990): U.S.$1,160,000,000 (U.S.$2,970 per capita).

Structure of gross domestic product and labour force

	1989		1993	
	in value F '000,000	% of total value	labour force	% of labour force
Agriculture	1,177.4	9.2	9,079	5.2
Mining, manufacturing	758.4	5.9	10,376	5.9
Construction	949.3	7.4	15,564	8.9
Public utilities	38.7	0.3	...	...
Transp. and commun.	773.3	6.1		
Trade	2,499.6	19.6	54,474	31.0
Finance, real estate	848.8	6.6		
Pub. admin., defense	4,242.4	33.2	40,207	22.9
Services	2,056.6	16.1		
Other	−563.3[15]	−4.4[15]	45,800[16]	26.1[16]
TOTAL	12,781.2	100.0	175,500	100.0

Land use (1994): forest 39.1%; pasture 14.2%; agriculture 16.0%; other 30.7%.

Foreign trade

Balance of trade (current prices)

	1990	1991	1992	1993	1994	1995
F '000,000	−8,439	−8,209	−7,505	−7,309	−7,693	−8,655
% of total	86.3%	79.8%	83.8%	83.2%	82.0%	84.3%

Imports (1995): F 9,459,415,000 (consumer goods 26.5%, food and agriculture products 17.3%, machinery and equipment 15.7%, transport vehicles and parts 11.2%). *Major import sources* (1995): France 63.8%; other EEC 13.5%; United States 3.3%; Martinique 2.4%; Japan 2.2%.
Exports (1995): F 804,096,000 (bananas 25.4%, sugar 11.4%, rum 4.4%, melons 2.9%). *Major export destinations* (1995): France 65.8%; Martinique 10.5%; other EEC 10.3%; French Guiana 2.1%.

Transport and communications

Transport. Railroads: none. Roads (1996): total length 1,988 mi, 3,200 km (paved [1986] 80%). Vehicles (1993): passenger cars 101,600; trucks and buses 37,500. Merchant marine (1992): vessels (100 gross tons and over) 20; deadweight tonnage 4,430. Air transport (1996): passenger arrivals and departures 1,854,971; cargo handled 13,473 metric tons, cargo unloaded 4,823 metric tons; airports (1997) with scheduled flights 7.

Communications

Medium	date	unit	number	units per 1,000 persons
Daily newspapers	1995	circulation	35,000	81
Radio	1995	receivers	98,000	226
Television	1995	receivers	114,000	263
Telephones	1995	main lines	158,800	366
Facsimile machines	1995	units	3,400	7.8

Education and health

Educational attainment (1990). Percentage of population age 25 and over having: incomplete primary, or no declaration 59.8%; primary education 14.5%; secondary 19.0%; higher 6.7%. *Literacy* (1982): total population age 15 and over literate 225,400 (90.1%); males literate 108,700 (89.7%); females literate 116,700 (90.5%).

Education (1993–94)

	schools	teachers	students	student/teacher ratio
Primary (age 6–10)	344	3,167	38,092	12.0
Secondary (age 11–17) / Vocational	84	3,834	51,366	13.4
Higher[17]	1	121	4,673	38.6

Health (1991): physicians 590 (1 per 680 persons); hospital beds 3,230 (1 per 122 persons); infant mortality rate per 1,000 live births (1994) 7.9.
Food (1995): daily per capita caloric intake 2,732 (vegetable products 75%, animal products 25%); 129% of FAO recommended minimum requirement.

Military

Total active duty personnel (1994): 535 French troops.

[1]Guadeloupe elects 4 deputies and 2 senators to French parliament. [2]Comprises Basse-Terre 327 sq mi (848 sq km), pop. 149,943, and Îles des Saintes 5 sq mi (13 sq km), pop. 2,036. [3]Comprises Grande-Terre 228 sq mi (590 sq km), pop. 177,570; Marie-Galante 61 sq mi (158 sq km), pop. 13,463; La Désirade 8 sq mi (20 sq km), pop. 1,610; and the uninhabited Îles de la Petite-Terre. [4]Comprises the French part of Saint-Martin 20 sq mi (52 sq km), pop. 28,518; Saint-Barthélemy 8 sq mi (21 sq km), pop. 5,038; and the small, uninhabited island of Tintamarre. [5]Total area includes 29 sq mi (75 sq km) not allocated by arrondissement. [6]Preliminary; final 1990 census total was 386,987. [7]Urban defined as locality with 2,000 or more inhabitants. [8]Urban agglomeration. [9]Includes Les Abymes. [10]Includes external long-term private debt not guaranteed by the government. [11]Base and indexes are end of year unless footnoted. [12]March. [13]Based on minimum-level wage of public employees. [14]June. [15]Less imputed bank service charges. [16]Unemployed. [17]University of Antilles–French Guiana, Guadeloupe campus.

Internet resources for further information:

- **Guadeloupe: Présentation générale (in French) http://www.outre-mer.gouv.fr/domtom/gua.htm**

Guatemala

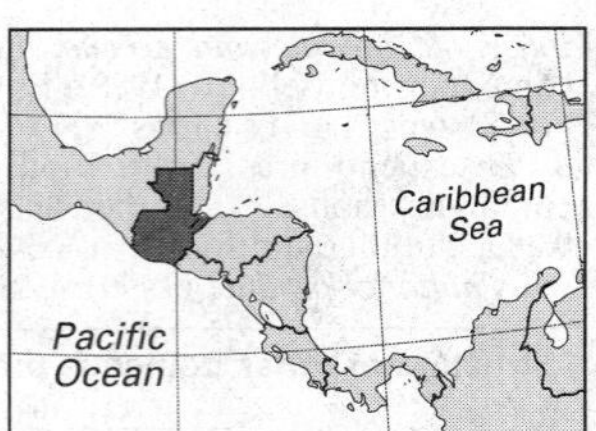

Official name: República de Guatemala (Republic of Guatemala).
Form of government: republic with one legislative house (Congress of the Republic [80]).
Head of state and government: President.
Capital: Guatemala City.
Official language: Spanish.
Official religion: none.
Monetary unit: 1 quetzal (Q) = 100 centavos; valuation (Oct. 3, 1997) 1 U.S.$ = Q 6.12; 1 £ = Q 9.86.

Area and population

Departments	Capitals	area sq mi	area sq km	population 1995 estimate[1]
Alta Verapaz	Cobán	3,354	8,686	670,815
Baja Verapaz	Salamá	1,206	3,124	205,481
Chimaltenango	Chimaltenango	764	1,979	385,856
Chiquimula	Chiquimula	917	2,376	274,091
El Progreso	Guastatoya (Progreso)	742	1,922	117,943
Escuintla	Escuintla	1,693	4,384	610,322
Guatemala	Guatemala City	821	2,126	2,246,170
Huehuetenango	Huehuetenango	2,857	7,400	816,376
Izabal	Puerto Barrios	3,490	9,038	370,538
Jalapa	Jalapa	797	2,063	211,830
Jutiapa	Jutiapa	1,243	3,219	387,177
Petén	Flores	13,843	35,854	310,008
Quetzaltenango	Quetzaltenango	753	1,951	623,571
Quiché	Santa Cruz del Quiché	3,235	8,378	652,022
Retalhuleu	Retalhuleu	717	1,856	268,996
Sacatepéquez	Antigua Guatemala	180	465	202,243
San Marcos	San Marcos	1,464	3,791	790,118
Santa Rosa	Cuilapa	1,141	2,955	291,611
Sololá	Sololá	410	1,061	274,356
Suchitepéquez	Mazatenango	969	2,510	403,618
Totonicapán	Totonicapán	410	1,061	333,634
Zacapa	Zacapa	1,039	2,690	174,450
TOTAL		42,042[2]	108,889	10,621,226

Demography

Population (1997): 11,242,000[3].
Density (1997): persons per sq mi 267.4, persons per sq km 103.2.
Urban-rural (1995): urban 38.7%; rural 61.3%.
Sex distribution (1995): male 50.49%; female 49.51%.
Age breakdown (1994): under 15, 44.0%; 15–29, 26.1%; 30–44, 15.8%; 45–59, 8.3%; 60 and over, 5.8%.
Population projection: (2000) 12,222,000; (2010) 15,827,000.
Doubling time: 24 years.
Ethnic composition (1994): Amerindian 42.8%; non-Amerindian 57.2%.
Religious affiliation (1986): Roman Catholic *c.* 75%, of which Catholic/traditional syncretist *c.* 25%; Protestant (mostly fundamentalist) *c.* 25%.
Major cities (1995): Guatemala City 1,167,495; Mixco 436,668; Villa Nueva 165,567; Chinautla 61,335; Amatitlan 40,229.

Vital statistics

Birth rate per 1,000 population (1994): 35.4 (world avg. 25.0).
Death rate per 1,000 population (1994): 7.5 (world avg. 9.3).
Natural increase rate per 1,000 population (1994): 27.9 (world avg. 15.7).
Total fertility rate (avg. births per childbearing woman; 1994): 4.8.
Marriage rate per 1,000 population (1993): 4.7.
Life expectancy at birth (1994): male 61.9 years; female 67.1 years.
Major causes of death per 100,000 population (1988): infectious and parasitic diseases 121.6; diseases of the respiratory system 110.8; perinatal causes 58.7; malnutrition 50.2; dehydration 18.5.

National economy

Budget (1996). Revenue: Q 8,605,100,000 (tax revenue 94.5%, of which taxes on goods and services 50.9%, income taxes 23.3%, customs duties 18.0%, nontax revenue 5.5%). Expenditures: Q 8,378,500,000 (current expenditures 73.6%, of which disbursements for goods and services 38.7%, transfer payments 23.3%; capital expenditures 26.4%).
Tourism (1995): receipts U.S.$277,000,000; expenditures U.S.$174,000,000.
Land use (1994): forested 53.6%; meadows and pastures 24.0%; agricultural and under permanent cultivation 17.6%; other 4.8%.
Production (metric tons except as noted). Agriculture, forestry, fishing (1996): sugarcane 14,380,000, corn (maize) 1,135,896, bananas 676,692, coffee 207,000, tomatoes 129,168, oil palm fruit 126,000; livestock (number of live animals) 2,291,440 cattle, 950,408 pigs, 21,000,000 chickens; roundwood (1995) 14,123,400 cu m; fish catch (1995) 11,927. Mining and quarrying (1994): gypsum (1993) 60,000; iron ore 3,498; antimony ore 494. Manufacturing (value added in Q '000,000; 1995[4]): food and beverage products 273; clothing and textiles 111; machinery and metal products 51. Construction (value of buildings authorized in Q '000,000; 1991)[5]: residential 170.2; nonresidential 127.5. Energy production (consumption): electricity (kW-hr; 1994) 3,161,000,000 (3,161,000,000); crude petroleum (barrels; 1994) 2,632,000 (6,958,000); petroleum products (metric tons; 1994) 750,000 (1,805,000).
Household income and expenditure. Average household size (1994) 5.2; income per household (1989) Q 4,306 (U.S.$1,529); sources of income: n.a.; expenditure (1981): food 64.4%, housing and energy 16.0%, transportation and communications 7.0%, household furnishings 5.0%, clothing 3.1%.
Gross national product (1995): U.S.$14,255,000,000 (U.S.$1,340 per capita).

Structure of gross domestic product and labour force

	1996 in value Q '000[4]	1996 % of total value	1995 labour force	1995 % of labour force
Agriculture	1,035,227	24.0	1,798,227	58.1
Mining	19,429	0.4	3,095	0.1
Manufacturing	601,138	14.0	420,928	13.6
Construction	91,198	2.1	126,898	4.1
Public utilities	137,008	3.2	9,285	0.3
Transp. and commun.	377,172	8.8	77,377	2.5
Trade	1,060,614	24.6	225,940	7.3
Finance, real estate	418,214	9.7		
Pub. admin., defense	316,818	7.4	371,407	12.0
Services	250,729	5.8		
Other	—	—	61,901[6]	2.0[6]
TOTAL	4,307,547	100.0	3,095,058	100.0

Population economically active (1996): total 3,183,173; activity rate of total population 29.1% (participation rates [1994] ages 15–64, 51.0%; female 19.5%; unemployed 0.5%[7]).

Price and earnings indexes (1990 = 100)

	1990	1991	1992	1993	1994	1995	1996
Consumer price index	100.0	133.2	146.5	163.9	181.7	196.9	218.7
Annual earnings index[8]	100.0	126.6	162.3	203.8	232.7	291.1	349.9

Public debt (external, outstanding; 1995): U.S.$2,493,000,000.

Foreign trade[9]

Balance of trade (current prices)

	1991	1992	1993	1994	1995	1996
U.S.$'000,000	−197.3	−1,190.8	−1,096.2	−755.3	−692.0	−849.7
% of total	7.5%	35.7%	29.0%	19.9%	13.8%	17.3%

Imports (1996): U.S.$3,146,223,700 (machinery 17.1%, mineral products 15.6%, chemical products 14.1%, transport equipment 12.3%, food products 7.7%, metal products 7.4%, plastic products 5.8%). *Major import sources:* United States 43.9%; Mexico 10.3%; Venezuela 5.3%; El Salvador 4.1%.
Exports (1995): U.S.$1,935,516,600 (coffee 23.3%, sugar 9.9%, bananas 7.6%, vegetable seeds 3.6%, legumes 3.3%). *Major export destinations:* United States 36.6%; El Salvador 12.7%; Honduras 6.9%; Germany 5.1%.

Transport and communications

Transport. Railroads (1996): route length 884 km; passenger-km (1991) 12,531,000; metric ton-km cargo 47,233,000. Roads (1995): total length 12,795 km (paved 28%). Vehicles (1994): passenger cars 102,000; trucks and buses 96,800. Air transport (1993)[10]: passenger-km 384,000,000; metric ton-km cargo 21,000,000; airports (1996) 2.

Communications

Medium	date	unit	number	units per 1,000 persons
Daily newspapers	1994	circulation	240,000	29
Radio	1996	receivers	570,000	52
Television	1995	receivers	475,000	45
Telephones	1995	main lines	289,500	27
Cellular telephones	1995	subscribers	30,000	2.8
Facsimile machines	1995	units	10,000	0.9
Personal computers	1995	units	30,000	2.8

Education and health

Educational attainment (1994). Percentage of population age 25 and over having: no formal schooling 45.2%; incomplete primary education 20.8%; complete primary 18.0%; some secondary 4.8%; secondary 7.2%; higher 4.0%. *Literacy* (1994): total population age 15 and over literate 2,809,000 (64.2%); males literate 1,544,000 (71.7%); females literate 1,265,000 (57.3%).

Education (1993)

	schools	teachers	students	student/teacher ratio
Primary (age 7–12)	10,770	44,220	1,393,921	31.5
Secondary (age 13–18)	1,274[11]	20,942	334,883	16.0
Voc., teacher tr.	626[11]			
Higher[12]	5	4,346	69,532	16.0

Health (1988): physicians 2,171 (1 per 3,999 persons); hospital beds (1987) 13,667 (1 per 602 persons); infant mortality rate (1994) 53.9.
Food (1995): daily per capita caloric intake 2,300 (vegetable products 92%, animal products 8%); 105% of FAO recommended minimum requirement.

Military

Total active duty personnel (1996): 44,200 (army 95.0%, navy 3.4%, air force 1.6%). *Military expenditure as percentage of GNP* (1995): 1.3% (world 2.8%); per capita expenditure U.S.$18.

[1]Adjusted for underenumeration in 1994 census. [2]Detail does not add to total given because of rounding. [3]Population of departments and cities taken from official projections based on 1973–81 intercensal growth rates and subsequent vital (birth and death) rates. [4]At prices of 1958. [5]Private construction in Guatemala City metropolitan area only. [6]Persons in activities not adequately defined. [7]Officially unemployed; majority of economically active population is estimated to be underemployed. [8]Based on employees entitled to social security. [9]Import figures are f.o.b. in balance of trade and c.i.f. for commodities and trading partners. [10]Aviateca Airlines only. [11]1991. [12]1989.

Internet resources for further information:
- **Instituto Nacional de Estadística (Spanish only) http://www.gua.gbm.net/ine**

Guinea

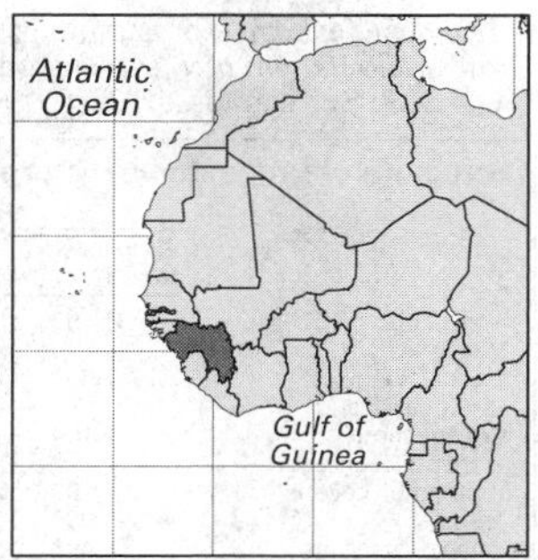

Official name: République de Guinée (Republic of Guinea).
Form of government: unitary multiparty republic with one legislative house (National Assembly [114 seats]).
Head of state and government: President assisted by Prime Minister[1].
Capital: Conakry.
Official language: French.
Official religion: none.
Monetary unit: 1 Guinean franc (GF) = 100 cauris; valuation (Oct. 3, 1997) 1 U.S.$ = GF 1,130; 1 £ = GF 1,822.

Area and population

		area		population
Regions	Capitals	sq mi	sq km	1983 census
Beyla	Beyla	6,738	17,452	161,347
Boffa	Boffa	1,932	5,003	141,719
Boké	Boké	3,881	10,053	225,207
Conakry	Conakry	119	308	705,280
Coyah (Dubréka)	Coyah	2,153	5,576	134,190
Dabola	Dabola	2,317	6,000	97,986
Dalaba	Dalaba	1,313	3,400	132,802
Dinguiraye	Dinguiraye	4,247	11,000	133,502
Faranah	Faranah	4,788	12,400	142,923
Forécariah	Forécariah	1,647	4,265	116,464
Fria	Fria	840	2,175	70,413
Gaoual	Gaoual	4,440	11,500	135,657
Guéckédou	Guéckédou	1,605	4,157	204,757
Kankan	Kankan	7,104	18,400	229,861
Kérouané	Kérouané	3,070	7,950	106,872
Kindia	Kindia	3,409	8,828	216,052
Kissidougou	Kissidougou	3,425	8,872	183,236
Koubia	Koubia	571	1,480	98,053
Koundara	Koundara	2,124	5,500	94,216
Kouroussa	Kouroussa	4,647	12,035	136,926
Labé	Labé	973	2,520	253,214
Lélouma	Lélouma	830	2,150	138,467
Lola	Lola	1,629	4,219	106,654
Macenta	Macenta	3,363	8,710	193,109
Mali	Mali	3,398	8,800	210,889
Mamou	Mamou	2,378	6,160	190,525
Mandiana	Mandiana	5,000	12,950	136,317
Nzérékoré	Nzérékoré	1,460	3,781	216,355
Pita	Pita	1,544	4,000	227,912
Siguiri	Siguiri	7,626	19,750	209,164
Télimélé	Télimélé	3,119	8,080	243,256
Tougué	Tougué	2,394	6,200	113,272
Yomou	Yomou	843	2,183	74,417
TOTAL		94,926[2]	245,857	5,781,014

Demography

Population (1997): 7,405,000.
Density (1997): persons per sq mi 78.0, persons per sq km 30.1.
Urban-rural (1990): urban 25.6%; rural 74.4%.
Sex distribution (1996): male 48.80%; female 51.20%.
Age breakdown (1995): under 15, 47.1%; 15–29, 25.9%; 30–44, 15.0%; 45–59, 7.8%; 60–74, 3.6%; 75 and over, 0.6%.
Population projection: (2000) 7,611,000; (2010) 9,440,000.
Doubling time: 29 years.
Ethnic composition (1990): Fulani 40.3%; Malinke 25.8%; Susu 11.0%; Kissi 6.5%; Kpelle 4.8%; other 11.6%.
Religious affiliation (1983): Muslim 86.9%; traditional beliefs 4.6%; other 8.5%.
Major cities (1983): Conakry (1993) 1,090,610; Kankan 55,010; Nzérékoré 44,598; Kindia 39,121; Kissidougou 30,724.

Vital statistics

Birth rate per 1,000 population (1996): 42.6 (world avg. 25.0).
Death rate per 1,000 population (1996): 18.7 (world avg. 9.3).
Total fertility rate (avg. births per childbearing woman; 1996): 5.7.
Life expectancy at birth (1996): male 42.7 years; female 47.5 years.
Major causes of death per 100,000 population: n.a.; however, in the mid-1990s, the major causes of illness were (in order): malaria, acute respiratory infections, intestinal parasitic diseases, gastroenteritis, and malnutrition.

National economy

Budget (1997). Revenue: GF 628,600,000,000 (current revenues 78.6%, of which mining sector 18.8%, other 59.8%; foreign aid 21.4%). Expenditures: GF 754,700,000,000 (current expenditure 50.8%, of which wages and salaries 23.6%, other goods and services 7.9%; capital spending 49.2%).
Public debt (external, outstanding; 1995): U.S.$2,975,000,000.
Tourism (1995): receipts U.S.$1,000,000; expenditures U.S.$21,000,000.
Production (metric tons except as noted). Agriculture, forestry, fishing (1996): fruits 990,000 (of which plantains 429,000, bananas 150,000, pineapples 67,000), roots and tubers 691,000 (of which cassava 440,000, sweet potatoes 130,000, yams 95,000), paddy rice 668,000, vegetables and melons 420,000, sugarcane 220,000, peanuts (groundnuts) 139,000, corn (maize) 90,000; livestock (number of live animals) 2,212,000 cattle, 760,000 goats, 618,000 sheep, 45,000 pigs, 7,000,000 chickens; roundwood (1995) 5,223,000 cu m; fish catch (1995) 68,766. Mining and quarrying (1996): bauxite 15,888,600; alumina 564,237; gold 7,863 kg[3]. Manufacturing (value of production in GF '000; 1985): corrugated and sheet iron 571,081; plastics 462,242; tobacco products 375,154; cement 326,138; printed matter 216,511. Energy production (consumption): electricity (kW-hr; 1995) 700,000,000 (700,000,000); petroleum products (metric tons; 1994) none (355,000).
Gross national product (1995): U.S.$3,593,000,000 (U.S.$550 per capita).

Structure of gross domestic product and labour force

	1994		1983	
	in value GF '000,000,000	% of total value	labour force	% of labour force
Agriculture, forestry, fishing	415.7	24.1	1,423,615	78.2
Mining	328.6	19.1	12,241	0.7
Manufacturing	79.6	4.6	11,215	0.6
Construction	119.5	6.9	9,115	0.5
Public utilities	3.7	0.2	3,205	0.2
Transp. and commun.	88.4	5.1	29,496	1.6
Trade, finance	448.7	26.0	40,865	2.0
Pub. admin., defense	91.3	5.3	137,600	7.5
Services	102.6	6.0		
Other	45.7	2.7	155,679	8.5
TOTAL	1,723.6[2]	100.0	1,823,031	100.0

Population economically active (1992): total 2,590,000; activity rate of total population 42.3% (participation rates [1983]: ages 15–64, 63.5%; female 39.4%; unemployed, n.a.).

Price and earnings indexes (1990 = 100)

	1989	1990	1991	1992	1993	1994	1995[4]
Consumer price index	83.8	100.0	119.7	139.5	149.5	155.6	163.2
Annual salary index[5]	...	100.0	200.0	262.4	272.6	275.2	...

Household income and expenditure. Average household size (1983) 6.7; average annual income per capita (1984) GS 7,660 (U.S.$305); expenditure (1985): food 61.5%, health 11.2%, clothing 7.9%, housing 7.3%.
Land use (1994): forest 27.3%; pasture 43.5%; agriculture 3.3%; other 25.9%.

Foreign trade[6]

Balance of trade (current prices)

	1990	1991	1992	1993	1994	1995
U.S.$'000,000	+85.5	−7.8	−91.2	−21.6	−169.7	−39.0
% of total	6.8%	0.6%	8.1%	1.9%	14.1%	3.2%

Imports (1994): U.S.$687,000,000 (goods for mining companies 22.2%; goods for public sector 20.1%; other private sector 57.7%). *Major import sources:* France 19.5%; Côte d'Ivoire 16.0%; U.S. 7.1%; Belgium 6.9%.
Exports (1994): U.S.$625,900,000 (bauxite 43.4%; alumina 16.5%; gold 13.3%; coffee 9.1%; diamonds 6.4%; fish 3.1%). *Major export destinations:* Belgium 26.7%; U.S. 15.1%; Ireland 10.0%; Spain 9.6%; France 4.6%.

Transport and communications

Transport. Railroads (1997): route length 662 km; (latest) passenger-km 41,500,000; metric ton-km cargo 7,300,000. Roads (1997): total length 19,215 km (paved 10%). Vehicles (1992): passenger cars 23,155; trucks and buses 13,000. Air transport (1994): passenger-km 32,842,000; metric ton-km cargo 1,241,000; airports (1997) 1.

Communications

Medium	date	unit	number	units per 1,000 persons
Daily newspapers	1988	circulation	13,000	2.0
Radio	1995	receivers	230,000	34.3
Television	1995	receivers	65,000	9.7
Telephones	1995	main lines	10,900	1.6
Cellular telephones	1995	subscribers	1,000	0.15
Facsimile machines	1995	units	200	0.03
Personal computers	1995	units	1,000	0.15

Education and health

Educational attainment of those age six and over having attended school (1983): primary 55.2%; secondary 32.7%; vocational 3.4%; higher 8.7%. *Literacy* (1995): percentage of total population age 15 and over literate 35.9%; males 49.9%; females 21.9%.

Education (1995–96)

	schools	teachers	students	student/ teacher ratio
Primary (age 7–12)	3,237	11,875	584,161	49.2
Secondary (age 13–18)	225[7]	4,690	127,517	27.2
Voc., teacher tr.[8]	35[7]	1,302	9,278	7.1
Higher	10[7]	805[9]	6,245[9]	7.8[9]

Health: physicians (1990) 773 (1 per 7,680 persons); hospital beds (1988) 3,382 (1 per 1,652 persons); infant mortality rate (1996) 134.
Food (1995): daily per capita caloric intake 2,161 (vegetable products 97%, animal products 3%); 94% of FAO recommended minimum requirement.

Military

Total active duty personnel (1997): 9,700 (army 87.6%, navy 4.1%, air force 8.2%). *Military expenditure as percentage of GNP* (1995): 1.5% (world 2.8%).

[1]President created extraconstitutional post of Prime Minister July 1996. [2]Detail does not add to total given because of rounding. [3]1995 reported figure to government of artisanal production; excludes artisanal production smuggled out of country. [4]Through third quarter. [5]Nonmilitary civil service employees. [6]Imports c.i.f.; exports f.o.b. in commodities and direction of trade. [7]1987–88. [8]1992–93. [9]Universities only.

Internet resources for further information:
- **Welcome to Guinea http://www.guinee.net**

Guinea-Bissau

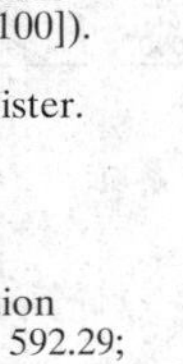

Official name: Républica da Guiné-Bissau (Republic of Guinea-Bissau).
Form of government: multiparty republic with one legislative house (National People's Assembly [100]).
Chief of state: President.
Head of government: Prime Minister.
Capital: Bissau.
Official language: Portuguese.
Official religion: none.
Monetary unit[1]: 1 CFA franc (CFAF) = 100 centimes; valuation (Oct. 3, 1997) 1 U.S.$ = CFAF 592.29; 1 £ = CFAF 954.76.

Area and population

Regions	Capitals	area sq mi	area sq km	population 1991 census[2]
Bafatá	Bafatá	2,309	5,981	143,377
Biombo[3]	Bissau	324	840	60,420
Bolama	Bolama	1,013	2,624	26,691
Cacheu	Cacheu	1,998	5,175	146,980
Gabú	Gabú	3,533	9,150	134,971
Oio	Farim	2,086	5,403	156,084
Quinara	Fulacunda	1,212	3,138	44,793
Tombali	Catió	1,443	3,736	72,441
Autonomous Sector				
Bissau[3]	—	30	78	197,610
TOTAL		13,948[4]	36,125[4]	983,367

Demography

Population (1997): 1,179,000.
Density (1996)[5]: persons per sq mi 108.6, persons per sq km 41.9.
Urban-rural (1996): urban 22.0%; rural 78.0%.
Sex distribution (1997): male 48.52%; female 51.48%.
Age breakdown (1997): under 15, 42.7%; 15–29, 28.1%; 30–44, 15.4%; 45–59, 9.2%; 60–74, 3.8%; 75 and over, 0.8%.
Population projection: (2000) 1,263,000; (2010) 1,579,000.
Doubling time: 33 years.
Ethnic composition (1979): Balante 27.2%; Fulani 22.9%; Malinke 12.2%; Mandyako 10.6%; Pepel 10.0%; other 17.1%.
Religious affiliation (1992): traditional beliefs 54%; Muslim 38%; Christian 8%.
Major cities (1979): Bissau 233,000[6]; Bafatá 13,429; Gabú 7,803; Mansôa 5,390; Catió 5,179.

Vital statistics

Birth rate per 1,000 population (1997): 39.0 (world avg. 25.0); legitimate, n.a.; illegitimate, n.a.
Death rate per 1,000 population (1997): 16.0 (world avg. 9.3).
Natural increase rate per 1,000 population (1997): 23.0 (world avg. 15.7).
Total fertility rate (avg. births per childbearing woman; 1997): 5.3.
Marriage rate per 1,000 population (1981): 0.1.
Divorce rate per 1,000 population: n.a.
Life expectancy at birth (1997): male 47.1 years; female 50.4 years.
Major causes of death per 100,000 population: n.a.; however, major diseases include tuberculosis of the respiratory system, whooping cough, typhoid fever, cholera, bacillary dysentery and amebiasis, malaria, pneumonia, and meningococcal infections; malnutrition is widespread.

National economy

Budget (1996). Revenue: PG 899,500,000,000 (1995; tax revenue 54.7%, of which customs 27.4%, tax on consumption 16.9%; nontax revenue 45.3%, of which fishing licenses 37.7%). Expenditures: PG 2,188,200,000,000 (1995; current expenditures 50.3%, of which goods and services 7.4%, wages and salaries 9.2%; capital expenditures 49.7%).
Production (metric tons except as noted). Agriculture, forestry, fishing (1997): rice 135,000, fruits 65,400[7], roots and tubers (sweet potatoes and cassava) 60,000, cashews 35,000, plantains 29,000, millet 25,000, coconuts 25,000, vegetables 20,000, sorghum 19,000, peanuts (groundnuts) 18,000, corn (maize) 14,000, palm kernels 8,000[7], sugarcane 5,500, bananas 4,000, palm oil 4,500[7], seed cotton 3,400; livestock (number of live animals) 475,000 cattle, 310,000 pigs, 270,000 goats, 255,000 sheep, 850,000 chickens; roundwood (1995) 579,000 cu m; fish catch (1995) 5,595. Mining and quarrying: extraction of construction materials only. Manufacturing (1997): fresh pork 9,720; palm oil 5,000[8]; copra 5,000[7]; fresh beef 3,850; soap 2,900[6]; dried and smoked fish 1,900[6]; animal hides 1,277[8], of which cattle 875[8], goat 194[8], sheep 158[8]; sawlogs 40,000 cu m[8]; distilled liquor 13,000 hectolitres[6]. Construction: n.a. Energy production (consumption): electricity (kW-hr; 1994) 45,000,000 (45,000,000); coal, none (none); crude petroleum, none (none); petroleum products (metric tons; 1994) none (75,000); natural gas, none (none).
Population economically active (1992): total 471,000; activity rate of total population 46.9% (participation rates (1991): over age 10, 67.1%; female 40.5%; unemployed, n.a.).

Price and earnings indexes (1990 = 100)

	1992	1993	1994	1995	1996	1997[9]
Consumer price index	267.3	395.8	455.9	662.7	998.9	1,323.0
Earnings index	...	...	...	...	...	...

Public debt (external, outstanding; 1995): U.S.$848,600,000.
Gross national product (at current market prices; 1995): U.S.$265,000,000 (U.S.$250 per capita).

Structure of gross domestic product and labour force

	1996 in value PG '000,000[10]	1996 % of total value	1994 labour force	1994 % of labour force
Agriculture	35,100	53.0	365,000	77.2
Mining } Manufacturing } Public utilities }	7,500	11.3	21,000 (incl. construction)	4.5
Construction	2,100	3.2		
Transportation and communications	1,600	2.4	87,000 (transportation through pub. admin.)	18.3
Trade	14,900	22.5		
Finance, services	400	0.6		
Pub. admin., defense	4,600	6.9		
TOTAL	66,300[11]	100.0[11]	473,000	100.0

Tourism: n.a.
Land use (1994): forested 38.1%; meadows and pastures 38.4%; agricultural and under permanent cultivation 12.1%; other 11.4%.
Household income and expenditure. Average household size (1981) 4.1; income per household: n.a.; sources of income: n.a.; expenditure: n.a.

Foreign trade[12]

Balance of trade (current prices)

	1991	1992	1993	1994	1995	1996
CFAF '000,000	−3,122	−9,491	−7,062	−2,940	−13,010	−17,216
% of total	57.6%	87.3%	58.8%	29.8%	50.0%	50.5%

Imports (1996): U.S.$63,000,000 (1995; foodstuffs 35.6%, transport equipment 11.7%, fuel and lubricants 11.5%, machinery 10.7%, building materials 10.2%). *Major import sources* (1995): Portugal 36.9%; The Netherlands 13.6%; China 8.3%; Japan 8.0%; Spain 4.3%; U.K. 3.8%; France 3.4%; U.S. 3.2%.
Exports (1996): U.S.$25,800,000 (1995; cashews 85.8%, lumber 6.3%, cotton 5.4%). *Major export destinations* (1995): India 87.8%; Portugal 10.2%; France 1.0%; Spain 0.8%.

Transport and communications

Transport. Railroads: none. Roads (1995): total length 2,703 mi, 4,350 km (paved 10%). Vehicles (1995): passenger cars 6,300; trucks and buses 4,900. Merchant marine (1992): vessels (100 gross tons and over) 19; total deadweight tonnage 1,846. Air transport (1994): passenger-mi 3,700,000, passenger-km 6,000,000; short ton-mi cargo 700,000, metric ton-km cargo 1,000,000; airports (1997) with scheduled flights 2.

Communications

Medium	date	unit	number	units per 1,000 persons
Daily newspapers	1995	circulation	6,000	6.0
Radio	1995	receivers	47,200	42.0
Television	1995	receivers	...	...
Telephones	1995	main lines	9,900	8.8
Facsimile machines	1995	units	563	0.5

Education and health

Educational attainment (1979). Percentage of population age 7 and over having: no formal schooling or knowledge of reading and writing 90.4%; primary education 7.9%; secondary 1.0%; technical 0.5%; higher 0.2%. *Literacy* (1995): total population age 15 and over literate 54.9%; males literate 68.0%; females literate 42.5%.

Education (1988)

	schools	teachers	students	student/ teacher ratio
Primary (age 7–13)	632[13]	3,065[13]	100,369[14]	...
Secondary (age 13–18)	12[15]	824[15]	5,505	...
Voc., teacher tr.	4[13]	107	825	7.7

Health: physicians (1986) 274 (1 per 3,245 persons); hospital beds (1993) 1,300 (1 per 797 persons); infant mortality rate per 1,000 live births (1997) 114.
Food (1995): daily per capita caloric intake 2,433 (vegetable products 93%, animal products 7%); 105% of FAO recommended minimum requirement.

Military

Total active duty personnel (1997): 7,250[16] (army 93.8%, navy 4.8%, air force 1.4%). *Military expenditure as percentage of GNP* (1995): 2.8% (world 2.8%); per capita expenditure U.S.$6.

[1]Since Guinea-Bissau became a member of the French Franc Zone, the Guinea-Bissau peso (PG) was replaced by the CFA franc in May 1997. [2]Preliminary. [3]Biombo region excludes Bissau city. [4]Includes water area of about 3,089 sq mi (8,000 sq km). [5]Based on land area of 10,859 sq mi (28,125 sq km). [6]1995. [7]1996. [8]1993. [9]March. [10]Factor cost at constant 1986 prices. [11]Detail does not add to total given because of rounding. [12]Import figures are c.i.f. in balance of trade and f.o.b. in commodities and trading partners. [13]1987. [14]1994–95. [15]1986. [16]Excludes 2,000 gendarmes, who are part of the armed forces.

Internet resources for further information:
- **Guinea-Bissau http://www.hmnet.com/africa/guineabis/guineabis.html**
- **Guiné-Bissau http://www.portugalnet.pt/encontro/guine/guine.html**

Guyana

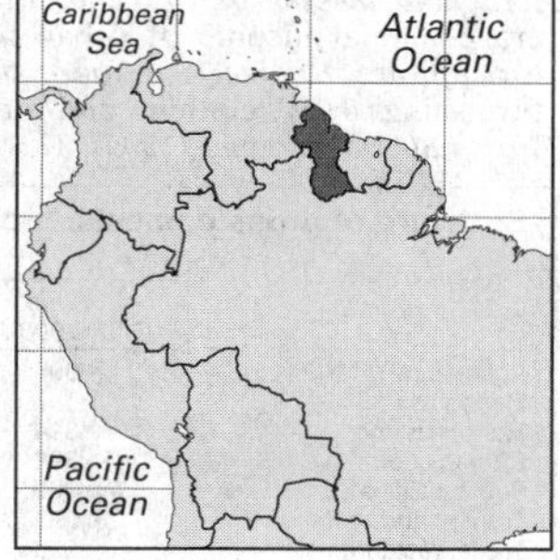

Official name: Co-operative Republic of Guyana.
Form of government: unitary multiparty republic with one legislative house (National Assembly [65[1]]).
Head of state and government: President.
Capital: Georgetown.
Official language: English.
Official religion: none.
Monetary unit: 1 Guyana dollar (G$) = 100 cents; valuation (Oct. 3, 1997) 1 U.S.$ = G$142.50; 1 £ = G$229.71.

Area and population

Administrative Regions	Capitals	area sq mi	area sq km	population 1986 estimate
Region 1 (Barima–Waini)	Mabaruma	7,853	20,339	18,516
Region 2 (Pomeroon–Supenaam)	Anna Regina	2,392	6,195	41,966
Region 3 (Essequibo Islands–West Demerara)	Vreed en Hoop	1,450	3,755	102,760
Region 4 (Demerara–Mahaica)	Paradise	862	2,233	310,758
Region 5 (Mahaica–Berbice)	Fort Wellington	1,610	4,170	55,556
Region 6 (East Berbice–Corentyne)	New Amsterdam	13,998	36,255	148,967
Region 7 (Cuyuni–Mazaruni)	Bartica	18,229	47,213	17,941
Region 8 (Potaro–Siparuni)	Mahdia	7,742	20,052	5,672
Region 9 (Upper Takutu–Upper Essequibo)	Lethem	22,313	57,790	15,338
Region 10 (Upper Demerara–Berbice)	Linden	6,595	17,081	38,598
TOTAL		83,044[2]	215,083[2]	756,072

Demography

Population (1997): 773,000.
Density (1997)[3]: persons per sq mi 10.2, persons per sq km 3.9.
Urban-rural (1995): urban 36.2%; rural 63.8%.
Sex distribution (1995): male 49.46%; female 50.54%.
Age breakdown (1995): under 15, 32.2%; 15–29, 30.1%; 30–44, 22.2%; 45–59, 9.5%; 60–74, 4.8%; 75 and over, 1.2%.
Population projection: (2000) 780,000; (2010) 807,000.
Doubling time: 73 years.
Ethnic composition (1992–93): East Indian 49.4%; black (African Negro and Bush Negro) 35.6%; mixed 7.1%; Amerindian 6.8%; Portuguese 0.7%; Chinese 0.4%.
Religious affiliation (1990): Christian 52.0%, of which Protestant 34.0% (including Anglican 17.0%), Roman Catholic 18.0%; Hindu 34.0%; Muslim 9.0%; other 5.0%.
Major cities (1992): Georgetown 248,500; Linden 27,200; New Amsterdam 17,700.

Vital statistics

Birth rate per 1,000 population (1996): 19.0 (world avg. 25.0).
Death rate per 1,000 population (1996): 9.5 (world avg. 9.3).
Natural increase rate per 1,000 population (1996): 9.5 (world avg. 15.7).
Total fertility rate (avg. births per childbearing woman; 1996): 2.2.
Marriage rate per 1,000 population: n.a.
Divorce rate per 1,000 population: n.a.
Life expectancy at birth (1996): male 57.5 years; female 62.8 years.
Major causes of death per 100,000 population (1990)[4]: diseases of the circulatory system 244.6, of which cerebrovascular disease 103.7, ischemic heart disease 56.8, diseases of pulmonary circulation and other forms of heart disease 49.3; diseases of the digestive system 39.0; endocrine and metabolic disorders 37.3; diseases of the respiratory system 37.3.

National economy

Budget (1996–97). Revenue: G$36,293,000,000 (current revenue 94.3%, of which consumption taxes 29.5%, income taxes on companies 20.9%, personal income taxes 12.7%, import duties 10.2%; development revenue 5.7%, of which external grants 5.3%). Expenditures: G$42,305,000,000 (current expenditure 61.3%, of which debt charges 18.9%, personal emoluments 17.4%; development expenditure 38.7%).
Production (metric tons except as noted). Agriculture, forestry, fishing (1996): rice 334,515, raw sugar 280,066, coconuts 72,800, cassava (manioc) 35,100, plantains 21,000, bananas 17,000, pineapples 10,400; livestock (number of live animals) 190,000 cattle, 130,000 sheep[5], 7,500,000 chickens; roundwood 526,725 cu m; fish catch 58,446, of which shrimps and prawns 17,792. Mining and quarrying (1996): bauxite 2,470,567; gold 386,031 troy oz; diamonds 46,730 carats. Manufacturing (1996): flour 36,600; rum 237,200 hectolitres; cigarettes 400,000,000 units; soft drinks 4,253,000 cases; pharmaceuticals 20,300,000 tablets; other products include cotton cloth and dyed and printed fabrics. Construction: n.a. Energy production (consumption): electricity (kW-hr; 1996) 348,200,000 ([1995] 217,200,000); coal, none (none); crude petroleum, none (none); petroleum products (metric tons; 1994) none (343,000); natural gas, none (none).
Tourism: receipts from visitors (1995) U.S.$32,600,000; expenditures by nationals abroad U.S.$21,100,000.
Land use (1994): forested 83.8%; meadows and pastures 6.3%; agricultural and under permanent cultivation 2.5%; other 7.4%.
Household income and expenditure. Average household size (1980) 5.1; income per household, n.a.; sources of income, n.a.; expenditure, n.a.
Gross national product (1995): U.S.$536,000,000 (U.S.$750 per capita).

Structure of gross domestic product and labour force

	1996 in value G$'000,000[6]	1996 % of total value	1980 labour force	1980 % of labour force
Sugar	16,277[7]	19.4[7]	50,316	20.4
Other agriculture	15,530[8]	18.5[8]		
Fishing, forestry	7,429	8.8		
Mining	15,567	18.5	9,669	3.9
Manufacturing	3,078[9, 10]	3.7[9, 10]	28,980	11.8
Construction	3,747	4.4	7,024	2.8
Public utilities	[10]	[10]	2,850	1.2
Transp. and commun.	4,486	5.3	9,412	3.8
Trade	3,534	4.2	15,231	6.2
Finance, real estate	5,854	7.0	2,944	1.2
Pub. admin., defense	7,393	8.8	29,948	12.1
Services	1,193	1.4	29,295	11.9
Other	—	—	61,002[11]	24.7[11]
TOTAL	84,088	100.0	246,671	100.0

Population economically active (1987): total 270,074; activity rate of total population 35.7% (participation rates: ages 15–64, 60.4%; female 29.9%; unemployed, n.a.

Price and earnings indexes (1990 = 100)

	1990	1991	1992	1993	1994	1995	1996
Consumer price index[12]	100.0	183.1	208.4	224.4	260.5	281.5	294.2
Earnings index	...	...	...	...	...	...	...

Public debt (external, outstanding; 1995): U.S.$1,782,000,000.

Foreign trade[13]

Balance of trade (current prices)

	1991	1992	1993	1994	1995	1996
U.S.$'000,000	−40.7	−61.0	−68.3	−40.6	−40.8	−14.2
% of total	7.1%	7.4%	7.6%	4.2%	4.0%	1.3%

Imports (1995): U.S.$536,800,000 (capital goods 35.0%; consumer goods 21.2%; fuels and lubricants 16.7%). *Major import sources*[14]: U.S. 29%; Italy 18%; Netherlands Antilles 17%; U.K. 11%; Japan 4%.
Exports (1996): U.S.$574,800,000 (domestic exports 96.2%, of which sugar 26.2%, gold 18.1%, rice 16.3%, bauxite 15.0%, timber 8.9%; reexports 3.8%). *Major export destinations* (1995)[14]: Canada 26%; U.S. 25%; U.K. 22%.

Transport and communications

Transport. Railroads: [15]. Roads (1995): total length 4,859 mi, 7,820 km (paved 7%). Vehicles (1995): passenger cars 24,000; trucks and buses 9,000. Merchant marine (1992): vessels (100 gross tons and over) 82; total deadweight tonnage 13,509. Air transport (1994): passenger-mi 139,000,000, passenger-km 224,000,000; short ton-mi cargo 16,000,000, metric ton-km cargo 23,000,000; airports (1996) with scheduled flights 1[16].

Communications

Medium	date	unit	number	units per 1,000 persons
Daily newspapers	1995	circulation	44,500	585
Radio	1996	receivers	350,000	454
Television	1995	receivers	15,000	197
Telephones	1995	main lines	44,600	587
Cellular telephones	1995	subscribers	1,200	1.6

Education and health

Educational attainment (1980). Percentage of population age 25 and over having: no formal schooling 8.1%; primary education 72.8%; secondary 17.3%; higher 1.8%. *Literacy* (1995): total population age 15 and over literate, *c.* 511,000 (98.1%); males literate, *c.* 254,000 (98.6%); females literate, *c.* 257,000 (97.5%).

Education (1994–95)

	schools	teachers	students	student/teacher ratio
Primary (age 6–11)	423[17]	3,453	100,806	29.2
Secondary (age 12–17)	93[17]	1,828	67,039	36.7
Voc., teacher tr.[17]	8	176	5,388	30.6
Higher[18]	...	492	8,257	16.8

Health: physicians (1993) 244 (1 per 3,148 persons); hospital beds (1989) 2,488 (1 per 305 persons); infant mortality rate per 1,000 live births (1996) 51.4.
Food (1995): daily per capita caloric intake 2,460 (vegetable products 88%, animal products 12%); 108% of FAO recommended minimum requirement.

Military

Total active duty personnel (1996): 1,717 (army 93.2%, navy 1.0%, air force 5.8%). *Military expenditure as percentage of GNP* (1994): 1.5% (world 3.0%); per capita expenditure U.S.$9.

[1]Includes 12 indirectly elected seats. [2]Includes inland water area equaling *c.* 7,000 sq mi (*c.* 18,000 sq km). [3]Based on land area only. [4]Based on incomplete data. [5]1995. [6]At factor cost. [7]Includes sugar manufacturing. [8]Includes rice manufacturing. [9]Excludes sugar and rice manufacturing. [10]Manufacturing includes Public utilities. [11]Represents "not stated." [12]Weights of consumer price index components for Georgetown, Linden, and New Amsterdam only. [13]Imports c.i.f.; exports f.o.b. [14]Estimated figure. [15]No public railways. [16]International only; domestic air service is provided on a charter basis. [17]1989–90. [18]1993–94.

Internet resources for further information:

- **Inter-American Development Bank: Guyana: Basic Socio-Economic Data http://database.iadb.org/int/basicrep/baguy.htm**

Haiti

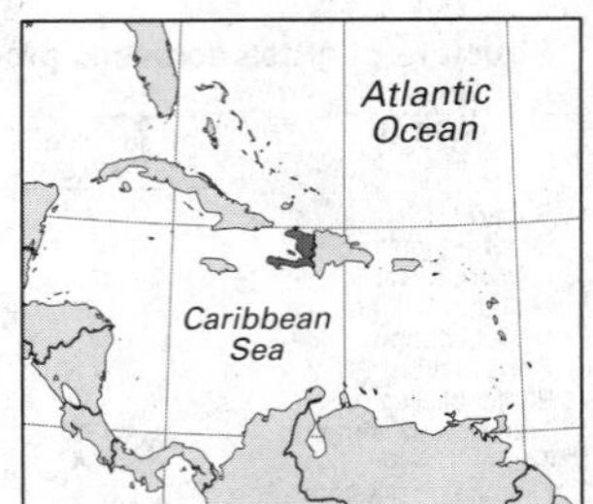

Official name: Repiblik Dayti (Haitian Creole); République d'Haïti (French) (Republic of Haiti).
Form of government: multiparty republic with two legislative houses (Senate [27]; Chamber of Deputies [83]).
Chief of state: President.
Head of government: Prime Minister.
Capital: Port-au-Prince.
Official languages: Haitian Creole; French.
Official religion: none[1].
Monetary unit: 1 gourde (G) = 100 centimes; valuation (Oct. 3, 1997) 1 U.S.$ = G 16.63; 1 £ = G 26.81.

Area and population

		area[2]		population
Departements	**Capitals**	sq mi	sq km	1995 estimate
Artibonite	Gonaïves	1,924	4,984	1,013,779
Centre	Hinche	1,419	3,675	490,790
Grand'Anse	Jérémie	1,278	3,310	641,399
Nord	Cap-Haïtien	813	2,106	759,318
Nord-Est	Fort-Liberté	697	1,805	248,764
Nord-Ouest	Port-de-Paix	840	2,176	420,971
Ouest	Port-au-Prince	1,864	4,827	2,494,862
Sud	Les Cayes	1,079	2,794	653,398
Sud-Est	Jacmel	781	2,023	457,013
TOTAL		10,695	27,700	7,180,294[3]

Demography

Population (1997): 6,611,000.
Density (1997): persons per sq mi 618.1, persons per sq km 238.7.
Urban-rural (1995): urban 32.6%; rural 67.4%.
Sex distribution (1995): male 49.09%; female 50.91%.
Age breakdown (1995): under 15, 40.2%; 15–29, 27.3%; 30–44, 17.0%; 45–59, 9.5%; 60–74, 4.8%; 75 and over, 1.2%.
Population projection: (2000) 6,901,000; (2010) 8,093,000.
Doubling time: 39 years.
Ethnic composition (1993): black 95.0%; mulatto/other 5.0%.
Religious affiliation (1995): Roman Catholic 68.5%[4]; Protestant 24.1%, of which Baptist 5.9%, Pentecostal 5.3%, Seventh-day Adventist 4.6%; other 7.4%.
Major cities (1995): Port-au-Prince 846,247 (metropolitan area 1,425,594); Carrefour 277,662[5]; Delmas 232,142[5]; Cap-Haïtien 100,638; Pétionville 69,543[5].

Vital statistics

Birth rate per 1,000 population (1996): 33.5 (world avg. 25.0).
Death rate per 1,000 population (1996): 15.5 (world avg. 9.3).
Natural increase rate per 1,000 population (1996): 18.0 (world avg. 15.7).
Total fertility rate (avg. births per childbearing woman; 1996): 4.8.
Life expectancy at birth (1996): male 47.3 years; female 51.3 years.
Major causes of death per 100,000 population (1982)[6]: infectious and parasitic diseases 46.0; diseases of the circulatory system 11.9; diseases associated with malnutrition 8.5; ill-defined conditions 115.2.

National economy

Budget (1996)[7]. Revenue: G 3,790,000,000 (customs duties 13.2%, grants 9.3%, other taxes 71.0%). Expenditures: G 4,120,000,000 (current expenditure 83.6%, subsidies 7.2%, interest on public debt 5.8%, development expenditure 3.4%).
Public debt (external, outstanding; 1995): U.S.$751,800,000.
Production (metric tons except as noted). Agriculture, forestry, fishing (1996): sugarcane 1,200,000, cassava (manioc) 350,000, plantains 270,000, bananas 239,200, mangoes 210,000, corn (maize) 204,100, yams 190,000, sweet potatoes 183,300, rice 95,900, sorghum 88,100, dry beans 49,200, avocados 45,000, coffee 27,000, sisal 5,600, cacao 4,200; livestock (number of live animals) 1,657,000 goats, 1,246,000 cattle, 500,000 pigs, 490,000 horses; roundwood (1995) 6,417,000 cu m; fish catch (1995) 5,500. Mining and quarrying: small amounts of limestone, calcareous clay, salt, and marble. Manufacturing (1995–96): cement 84,000[8]; essential oils (mostly amyris, neroli, and vetiver) 227[8]; cigarettes 837,900,000 units; malt liquor 13,800,000 bottles; beer 4,200,000 bottles; articles assembled for reexport (gross export value in U.S.$'000,000) 104.3, of which garments 95.0, sports equipment and toys 5.9, electronic components 2.7. Construction: n.a. Energy production (consumption): electricity (kW-hr; 1995–96) 575,000,000 (257,300,000); coal (metric tons; 1994) none (n.a.); crude petroleum, none (none); petroleum products (metric tons; 1994) none (166,000); natural gas, none (none).
Land use (1994): forested 5.1%; meadows and pastures 18.0%; agricultural and under permanent cultivation 33.0%; other 43.9%.
Population economically active (1990): total 2,679,140; activity rate of total population 41.1% (participation rates: ages 15–64, 64.8%; female 40.0%; unemployed [1996] unofficially more than 50.0%).

Price and earnings indexes (1990 = 100)

	1990	1991	1992	1993	1994	1995	1996
Consumer price index	100.0	115.4	137.8	168.8	240.7	302.0	353.7
Annual earnings index[9, 10]	100.0	100.0	100.0	100.0	100.0	240.0	...

Household income and expenditure. Average household size (1982) 4.4; average annual income of urban wage earners (1984): G 1,545 (U.S.$309); expenditure (1986–87)[11]: food, beverages, and tobacco 51.1%, household furnishings 9.2%, clothing and footwear 8.7%, transportation 7.6%.
Gross national product (1995): U.S.$1,777,000,000 (U.S.$250 per capita).

Structure of gross domestic product and labour force

	1995		1990	
	in value G '000,000[12]	% of total value	labour force	% of labour force
Agriculture	1,395	32.2	1,535,444	57.3
Mining	7	0.2	24,012	0.9
Manufacturing	314	7.3	151,387	5.6
Construction	398	9.2	28,001	1.0
Public utilities	39	0.9	2,577	0.1
Transp. and commun.	93	2.1	20,691	0.8
Trade, restaurants	598	13.8	352,970	13.2
Finance, real estate			5,057	0.2
Services / Pub. admin., defense	1,360	31.4	155,347	5.8
Other	127[13]	2.9[13]	403,654[14]	15.1[14]
TOTAL	4,331	100.0	2,679,140	100.0

Tourism (in U.S.$'000,000; 1995): receipts 81; expenditures 35.

Foreign trade[15, 16]

Balance of trade (current prices)

	1990–91	1991–92	1992–93	1993–94	1994–95	1995–96
U.S.$'000,000	−156.1	−221.1	−233.5	−204.4	−378.7	−548.1
% of total	35.9%	43.9%	46.0%	55.8%	70.4%	73.7%

Imports (1995–96)[17]: U.S.$663,100,000 (food and live animals 33.1%, petroleum and derivatives 10.7%, animal and vegetable oils 9.2%, chemicals and chemical products 8.1%). *Major import sources* (1995)[18]: United States 65%; Japan 5%; France 4%; Germany 3%.
Exports (1995–96)[17]: U.S.$85,900,000 (domestic value added of reexport assembly plants [mostly clothing] 47.6%, handicrafts [includes wood carvings, paintings, and woven sisal products] 15.4%, coffee 7.9%, essential oils 6.6%). *Major export destinations* (1995)[18]: United States 76%; France 7%; Germany 5%; Italy 5%.

Transport and communications

Transport. Railroad (1995):[19]. Roads (1995): total length 2,535 mi, 4,080 km (paved 24%). Vehicles (1995): passenger cars 32,000; trucks and buses 21,000. Air transport (1994)[20]: passenger arrivals 167,882, passenger departures 177,072; cargo unloaded 11,967 metric tons, cargo loaded 10,087 metric tons; airports (1997) with scheduled flights 2.

Communications

Medium	date	unit	number	units per 1,000 persons
Daily newspapers	1994	circulation	45,000	7.1
Radio	1996	receivers	270,000	41
Television	1995	receivers	25,000	3.9
Telephones	1995	main lines	55,302	8.6

Education and health

Educational attainment (1986–87). Percentage of population age 25 and over having: no formal schooling 59.5%; primary education 30.5%; secondary 8.6%; vocational and teacher training 0.7%; higher 0.7%. *Literacy* (1995): total population age 15 and over literate 1,930,000 (45.0%); males literate 992,000 (48.0%); females literate 938,000 (42.2%).

Education (1992–93)

	schools	teachers	students	student/ teacher ratio
Primary (age 6–12)	6,111[21]	27,607	787,553	28.5
Secondary (age 13–18) / Voc., teacher tr.	630[21]	10,174	193,624	19.0
Higher[22, 23]	2	777	11,546	14.9

Health (1993–94): physicians 641[24] (1 per 9,846 persons); hospital beds 6,473 (1 per 975 persons); infant mortality rate per 1,000 live births (1996) 103.8.
Food (1992): daily per capita caloric intake 1,706 (vegetable products 95%, animal products 5%); 75% of FAO recommended minimum requirement.

Military

Total active duty personnel:[25].

[1]Roman Catholicism has special recognition. [2]Estimated. [3]Official population projection based on 1982 census. [4]About 80% of all Roman Catholics also practice voodoo. [5]Within Port-au-Prince metropolitan area. [6]Public health facilities only. [7]Excludes G 6,900,000,000 in foreign aid. [8]1992–93. [9]Standard minimum wage. [10]The majority of Haitians work in subsistence agriculture, a sector where minimum wage legislation does not apply. [11]Based on nationwide sample survey of 3,120 households. [12]At prices of 1975–76. [13]Import duties. [14]Includes 63,975 not adequately defined and 339,679 officially unemployed. [15]Includes domestic value added only of reexport assembly plants. [16]Import figures c.i.f., export figures f.o.b. for fiscal year ending March 31. [17]For fiscal year ending September 30. [18]Estimated figures for calendar year. [19]A 50-mi (80-km) railway is privately owned. [20]Port-au-Prince Airport only. [21]1991–92. [22]Port-au-Prince universities only. [23]1995–96. [24]Public health services only. [25]The Haitian army was disbanded in 1995. A UN force provided security between April 1995 and December 1997 and supervised the creation of a national police force.

Internet resources for further information:
- **Embassy of Haiti (Washington, D.C.) (mostly French language) http://www.haiti.org/embassy/**

Honduras

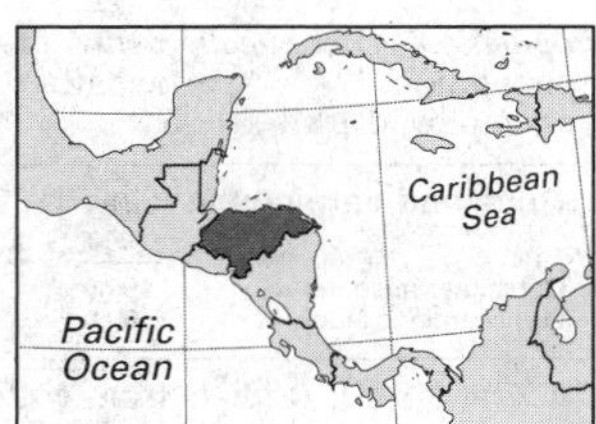

Official name: República de Honduras (Republic of Honduras).
Form of government: multiparty republic with one legislative house (National Assembly [128]).
Head of state and government: President.
Capital: Tegucigalpa[1].
Official language: Spanish.
Official religion: none.
Monetary unit: 1 Honduran lempira (L) = 100 centavos; valuation (Oct. 3, 1997) 1 U.S.$ = L 13.39; 1 £ = L 21.58.

Area and population

		area		population
Departments	Administrative centres	sq mi	sq km	1991 estimate
Atlántida	La Ceiba	1,641	4,251	255,000
Choluteca	Choluteca	1,626	4,211	309,000
Colón	Trujillo	3,427	8,875	164,000
Comayagua	Comayagua	2,006	5,196	257,000
Copán	Santa Rosa de Copán	1,237	3,203	226,000
Cortés	San Pedro Sula	1,527	3,954	706,000
El Paraíso	Yuscarán	2,787	7,218	277,000
Francisco Morazán	Tegucigalpa	3,068	7,946	878,000
Gracias a Dios	Puerto Lempira	6,421	16,630	37,000
Intibucá	La Esperanza	1,186	3,072	130,000
Islas de la Bahía	Roatán	100	261	24,000
La Paz	La Paz	900	2,331	112,000
Lempira	Gracias	1,656	4,290	180,000
Ocotepeque	Nueva Ocotepeque	649	1,680	77,000
Olancho	Juticalpa	9,402	24,351	309,000
Santa Bárbara	Santa Bárbara	1,975	5,115	291,000
Valle	Nacaome	604	1,565	121,000
Yoro	Yoro	3,065	7,939	355,000
TOTAL		43,277[2]	112,088[2]	4,708,000

Demography

Population (1997): 5,666,000.
Density (1997)[3]: persons per sq mi 130.5, persons per sq km 50.4.
Urban-rural (1994): urban 42.9%; rural 57.1%.
Sex distribution (1990): male 50.07%; female 49.93%.
Age breakdown (1990): under 15, 44.6%; 15–29, 28.3%; 30–44, 14.4%; 45–59, 7.8%; 60–74, 3.9%; 75 and over, 1.0%.
Population projection: (2000) 6,323,000; (2010) 7,998,000.
Doubling time: 24 years.
Ethnic composition (1987): mestizo 89.9%; Amerindian 6.7%; black (including Black Carib) 2.1%; white 1.3%.
Religious affiliation (1994): Roman Catholic 91.7%; Protestant (mostly fundamentalist, Moravian, and Methodist) and other 8.3%.
Major cities (1995): Tegucigalpa 813,900[4]; San Pedro Sula 383,900; La Ceiba 89,200; El Progreso 85,400; Choluteca 76,400.

Vital statistics

Birth rate per 1,000 population (1993): 35.8 (world avg. 25.0); legitimate, n.a.; illegitimate, n.a.
Death rate per 1,000 population (1993): 6.4 (world avg. 9.3).
Natural increase rate per 1,000 population (1993): 29.4 (world avg. 15.7).
Total fertility rate (avg. births per childbearing woman; 1993): 4.9.
Marriage rate per 1,000 population (1983): 4.9.
Divorce rate per 1,000 population (1983): 0.4.
Life expectancy at birth (1993): male 64.8 years; female 69.2 years.
Major causes of death per 100,000 population (1983): diseases of the circulatory system 48.4; infectious and parasitic diseases 46.6; accidents and violence 42.2; diseases of the respiratory system 26.3.

National economy

Budget (1995). Revenue: L 9,900,900,000 (current revenue 68.8%, of which excise and sales taxes 23.3%, income taxes 19.6%, import duties 14.4%; capital revenue 31.2%). Expenditures: L 10,502,800,000 (current expenditure 53.6%; capital expenditure 17.9%; public-debt service 16.2%).
Public debt (external, outstanding; 1995): U.S.$3,979,000,000.
Production (metric tons except as noted). Agriculture, forestry, fishing (1996): sugarcane 3,237,000, bananas 927,000, corn (maize) 580,000, pineapples 269,000, plantains 190,000, coffee 131,000, palm oil 76,600, sorghum 68,000, dry beans 55,000, rice 41,000; livestock (number of live animals) 2,182,000 cattle, 600,000 pigs, 14,000,000 chickens; roundwood (1995) 6,362,000 cu m; fish catch (1995) 24,333. Mining and quarrying (1995): gypsum 26,000; salt 25,000; zinc 14,500; lead 2,000; copper 390. Manufacturing (1995): cement 995,100; raw sugar 406,000; wheat flour 216,000; beer 7,989,000 hectolitres; milk 672,260 hectolitres; cigarettes 2,388,500,000 units. Construction (value of private construction in L '000,000; 1995)[5]: residential 340.6; nonresidential 533.5. Energy production (consumption): electricity (kW-hr; 1994) 2,655,000,000 (2,672,000,000); coal, none (none); crude petroleum (barrels; 1992) none (3,064,000); petroleum products (metric tons; 1994) none (950,000).
Household income and expenditure. Average household size (1988) 5.4; income per household: n.a.; sources of income (1985): wages and salaries 58.8%, transfer payments 1.8%, other 39.4%; expenditure (1986): food 44.4%, utilities and housing 22.4%, clothing and footwear 9.0%, household furnishings 8.3%, health care 7.0%, transportation 3.0%, other 5.9%.
Tourism (1995): receipts U.S.$80,000,000; expenditures U.S.$57,000,000.
Gross national product (1995): U.S.$3,566,000,000 (U.S.$600 per capita).

Structure of gross domestic product and labour force

	1995			
	in value L '000,000[6]	% of total value	labour force	% of labour force
Agriculture	7,973	24.5	766,000	42.7
Mining	655	2.0	4,200	0.2
Manufacturing	5,440	16.7	211,500	11.8
Construction	1,853	5.7	118,500	6.6
Public utilities	1,481	4.6	14,400	0.8
Transp. and commun.	1,715	5.3	50,100	2.8
Trade	3,453	10.6	194,000	10.8
Finance, real estate	4,759	14.6	36,700	2.0
Public admin., defense	1,793	5.5	400,800	22.3
Services	3,423	10.5		
TOTAL	32,545	100.0	1,796,200	100.0

Population economically active (1995): total 1,796,200; activity rate of total population 32.6% (participation rates: over age 15 [1992] 58.3%; female 31.7%; unemployed [1990] 40.0%).

Price and earnings indexes (1990 = 100)

	1990	1991	1992	1993	1994	1995	1996
Consumer price index	100.0	134.0	145.7	161.4	196.4	254.3	314.9
Weekly earnings index[7]	100.0	132.9	151.1	170.3	180.3	232.0	...

Land use (1994): forested 53.6%; meadows and pastures 13.8%; agricultural and under permanent cultivation 18.1%; other 14.5%.

Foreign trade[8]

Balance of trade (current prices)

	1991	1992	1993	1994	1995	1996
L '000,000	+11.9	−129.3	−208.6	−113.1	−42.1	−348.5
% of total	0.7%	7.5%	11.4%	6.3%	1.9%	11.7%

Imports (1995): U.S.$1,587,600,000 (machinery and electrical equipment 17.1%, industrial chemicals 14.8%, mineral fuels 14.0%, metal products 8.7%, transport equipment 8.4%, plastics and resins 7.3%). *Major import sources:* United States 42.8%; Japan 4.7%; Germany 3.6%; Mexico 3.0%; Brazil 1.8%; Spain 1.8%; The Netherlands 1.5%.
Exports (1995): U.S.$1,092,900,000 (coffee 32.0%, bananas 19.6%, shrimp and lobsters 14.5%, zinc 2.5%, frozen meats 1.2%). *Major export destinations:* United States 54.2%; Germany 6.9%; Belgium 4.8%; Japan 3.6%; Spain 3.6%; The Netherlands 2.1%; Italy 1.9%.

Transport and communications

Transport. Railroads (1989): length (1993) 614 mi, 988 km; passenger-km 7,700,000; metric ton-km cargo 30,200,000. Roads (1995): total length 9,383 mi, 15,100 km (paved 20%). Vehicles (1995): passenger cars 81,439; trucks and buses 170,006. Merchant marine (1992): vessels (100 gross tons and over) 966; total deadweight tonnage 1,437,321. Air transport (1994): passenger-mi 180,000,000, passenger-km 289,000,000; short ton-mi cargo 26,000,000, metric ton-km cargo 38,000,000; airports (1996) with scheduled flights 8.

Communications

Medium	date	unit	number	units per 1,000 persons
Daily newspapers	1995	circulation	240,000	45
Radio	1996	receivers	1,910,000	337
Television	1995	receivers	160,000	29
Telephones	1995	main lines	160,800	29

Education and health

Educational attainment (1988). Percentage of population age 10 and over having: no formal schooling 33.4%; primary education 50.1%; secondary education 13.4%; higher 3.1%. *Literacy* (1990): total population age 15 and over literate 2,082,000 (73.1%); males literate 1,078,000 (75.5%); females literate 1,004,000 (70.6%).

Education (1995)

	schools	teachers	students	student/ teacher ratio
Primary (age 7–13)	8,168	28,978	1,008,092	34.8
Secondary (age 14–19) Voc., teacher tr.	661	12,480	184,589	14.8
Higher	8	3,676	54,293	14.8

Health: physicians (1990) 2,900 (1 per 1,586 persons); hospital beds (1994) 4,737 (1 per 1,126 persons); infant mortality rate (1993) 47.2.
Food (1995): daily per capita caloric intake 2,359 (vegetable products 88%, animal products 12%); 104% of FAO recommended minimum.

Military

Total active duty personnel (1996): 18,800 (army 85.1%, navy 5.3%, air force 9.6%). *Military expenditure as percentage of GNP* (1995): 1.4% (world 2.8%); per capita expenditure U.S.$8.

[1]Tegucigalpa and adjacent city of Comayagüela jointly form the capital according to the constitution. [2]The 1993 area is 43,433 sq mi (112,492 sq km); breakdown by department is not available. [3]Based on the revised area. [4]Population cited is for Central District (Tegucigalpa and Comayagüela). [5]Tegucigalpa, San Pedro Sula, and 10 other urban centres. [6]At factor cost. [7]Official minimum wages in all sectors. Minimum wages were fixed from June 1981 to Jan. 1, 1990, when new minimum wages were introduced. [8]Import figures are f.o.b. in balance of trade and c.i.f. for commodities and trading partners. [9]1989.

Hong Kong

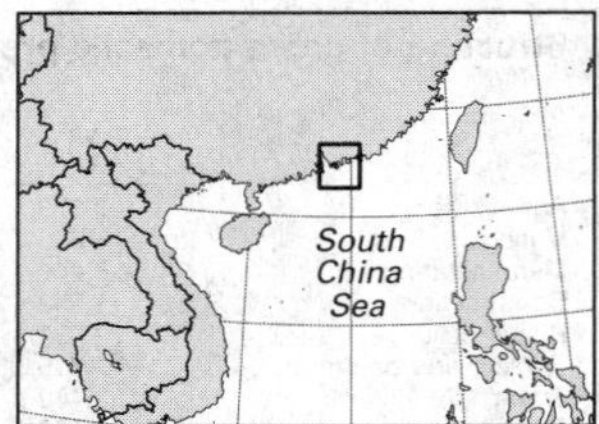

Official name: Hsiang Kang (Chinese); Hong Kong (English)[1].
Political status: Special Administrative Region[2] (People's Republic of China) with one legislative house (Legislative Council [60[3]]).
Head of state and government: Chief Executive.
Capital: none[4].
Official languages: Chinese; English[1].
Official religion: none.
Monetary unit: 1 Hong Kong dollar (HK$) = 100 cents; valuation (Oct. 3, 1997) 1 U.S.$ = HK$7.74; 1 £ = HK$12.47.

Area and population

	area		population
			1996
Area	sq mi	sq km	census
Hong Kong Island	30.9	80.1	1,312,637
Kowloon and New Kowloon	18.0	46.5	1,987,996
New Territories	372.7	965.3	2,906,733
Marine	—	—	10,190
TOTAL	421.6	1,091.9	6,217,556

Demography

Population (1997): 6,491,000.
Density (1997): persons per sq mi 15,396.9, persons per sq km 5,945.0.
Urban-rural (1997): urban 100.0%.
Sex distribution (1996): male 50.06%; female 49.94%.
Age breakdown (1996)[5]: under 15, 18.9%; 15–29, 22.4%; 30–44, 29.4%; 45–59, 15.1%; 60–74, 10.5%; 75 and over, 3.7%.
Population projection: (2000) 6,928,000; (2010) 8,606,000.
Doubling time: not applicable; doubling time exceeds 100 years.
Linguistic composition (1991)[6]: Chinese 96.8%, of which Cantonese 88.7%; English 2.2%; other 1.0%.
Religious affiliation (1997): predominantly Buddhist and Taoist; however, there are about 260,000 Protestants (1994), 254,100 Roman Catholics, 50,000 Muslims, and 12,000 Hindus.

Vital statistics

Birth rate per 1,000 population (1996): 10.0 (world avg. 25.0); (1985) legitimate 94.5%; illegitimate 5.5%.
Death rate per 1,000 population (1996): 4.9 (world avg. 9.3).
Natural increase rate per 1,000 population (1996): 5.1 (world avg. 15.7).
Total fertility rate (avg. births per childbearing woman; 1995): 1.1.
Marriage rate per 1,000 population (1996): 5.9.
Life expectancy at birth (1996): male 75.9 years; female 81.5 years.
Major causes of death per 100,000 population (1996): malignant neoplasms (cancers) 156.1; diseases of the circulatory system 131.3; diseases of the respiratory system 96.6; accidents and poisoning 26.2; diseases of the digestive system 21.6; diseases of the genitourinary system 18.6.

National economy

Budget (1996–97). Revenue: HK$202,276,000,000 (earnings and profit taxes 40.6%; indirect taxes 24.8%, of which entertainment and stamp duties 15.1%, duties 4.1%; capital revenue 18.4%). Expenditures: HK$217,194,000,000 (education 18.0%; housing 11.9%; health 11.5%; transportation and public works 11.1%; law and order 9.2%; social welfare 8.3%; culture and recreation 5.1%).
Gross domestic product (1995): U.S.$142,332,000,000 (U.S.$22,990 per capita).

Structure of gross domestic product and labour force

	1995			
	in value HK$'000,000	% of total value	labour force	% of labour force
Agriculture	1,453	0.1		
Mining	268	—	534,600	17.8
Manufacturing	89,719	8.4		
Construction	49,753	4.6	229,300	7.7
Public utilities	23,562	2.2	7	7
Transp. and commun.	100,129	9.4	327,700	10.9
Trade	278,581	26.0	824,900	27.5
Finance, insurance, and real estate	253,492	23.7	341,700	11.4
Pub. admin., defense, and services	174,448	16.3	609,800	20.3
Other	99,969[8]	9.3[8]	132,700[7, 9]	4.4[7, 9]
TOTAL	1,071,374	100.0	3,000,700	100.0

Production (metric tons except as noted). Agriculture, forestry, fishing (1996): vegetables 76,000, fruits and nuts 5,230, field crops 660, milk 439, eggs 30,600,000 units; livestock (number of live animals) 288,000 pigs[10], 270 cattle, 3,290,000 chickens; roundwood (1995) 200,000 cu m; fish catch 175,130. Manufacturing (value added in HK$; 1994): wearing apparel 13,515,000,000; electrical and electronic products 12,621,000,000; textiles 11,595,000,000; publishing and printed material 9,949,000,000; basic metals and fabricated metal products 5,547,000,000; plastic products 2,495,000,000. Construction (1996): residential 819,000 sq m; nonresidential 1,067,000 sq m. Energy production (consumption): electricity (kW-hr; 1994) 26,741,000,000 (33,236,000,000); coal (metric tons; 1994) none (8,450,000); petroleum products (metric tons; 1994) none (4,472,000).

Population economically active (1996): total 3,093,800; activity rate of total population 49.0% (participation rates: over age 15, 61.8%; female 47.8%; unemployed 2.8%).

Price and earnings indexes (1990 = 100)

	1990	1991	1992	1993	1994	1995	1996
Consumer price index	100.0	111.6	122.0	132.5	143.2	155.7	164.9
Daily earnings index[11]	100.0	110.4	121.4	133.2	143.6	160.4	167.6

Tourism (1995): receipts from visitors U.S.$9,314,000,000.
Household income and expenditure. Average household size (1996) 3.2; monthly income per household (1996) HK$17,500 (U.S.$2,300); sources of income: n.a.; expenditure (1994–95): food 29.5%, housing 28.8%, transportation and vehicles 7.8%, clothing and footwear 6.7%, durable goods 5.5%.
Land use (1995): forested 20.1%; agricultural and under permanent cultivation 5.8%; fishponds 1.5%; built-on, scrublands, and other 72.6%.

Foreign trade

Balance of trade (current prices)

	1991	1992	1993	1994	1995	1996
HK$'000,000	−13,096	−30,342	−26,347	−80,695	−146,994	−137,664
% of total	0.1%	1.6%	1.2%	3.3%	5.2%	4.7%

Imports (1996): HK$1,537,013,000,000 (machinery and transport equipment 37.0%, of which electrical machinery 12.7%, telecommunications equipment 9.2%; textile yarn and fabrics 8.3%; chemicals and other related products 6.9%; apparel and accessories 6.9%). *Major import sources:* China 37.1%; Japan 13.6%; Taiwan 8.0%; U.S. 7.9%; Singapore 5.3%; South Korea 4.8%.
Exports (1996): HK$212,160,000,000[12] (clothing accessories and apparel 32.7%; electrical machinery 14.3%; watches and clocks 7.1%; textile fabrics 6.5%; office and automatic data-processing machines 6.2%; telecommunications equipment 4.0%; articles of artificial resins and plastics 2.7%; metal products 2.7%; paper and paper products 1.4%). *Major export destinations:* China 29.0%; U.S. 25.4%; Germany 5.4%; Japan 5.3%; U.K. 5.0%.

Transport and communications

Transport. Railroads (1995): route length 21 mi, 34 km; passenger-mi 2,231,000,000, passenger-km 3,591,000,000; short ton-mi cargo 68,000,000[13], metric ton-km cargo 99,000,000[13]. Roads (1996): total length 1,083 mi, 1,743 km (paved 100%). Vehicles (1996): passenger cars 325,131; trucks and buses 142,446. Air transport (1996): passenger arrivals 11,692,404, passenger departures 11,785,771; airports (1997) with scheduled flights 1.

Communications

Medium	date	unit	number	units per 1,000 persons
Daily newspapers	1995	circulation	2,951,000[14]	479[14]
Radio	1996	receivers	3,700,000	586
Television	1995	receivers	2,092,000	340
Telephones	1996	main lines	3,508,000	556
Cellular telephones	1995	subscribers	798,400	129
Facsimile machines	1995	units	284,900	46
Personal computers	1995	units	720,000	116

Education and health

Educational attainment (1996). Percentage of population age 15 and over having: no formal schooling 9.5%; primary education 22.6%; secondary 46.6%; matriculation 6.1%; nondegree higher 4.8%; higher degree 10.4%.
Literacy (1985): total population age 15 and over literate 3,668,000 (88.1%); males literate 2,040,000 (94.7%); females literate 1,628,000 (80.9%).

Education (1996–97)

	schools	teachers	students	student/ teacher ratio
Primary (age 6–11)	856	19,710[15]	466,507	23.7[15]
Secondary (age 12–18)	498	22,777[15]	477,708	21.2[15]
Vocational	9	2,488[16]	48,837	18.5[16]
Higher	17	1,422[16]	87,411	32.4[16]

Health (1996): physicians 9,196[17] (1 per 686 persons); hospital beds 29,956 (1 per 211 persons); infant mortality rate per 1,000 live births 4.1.
Food (1995): daily per capita caloric intake 3,285 (vegetable products 68%, animal products 32%); 143% of FAO recommended minimum requirement.

Military

Total active duty personnel (1996): 850[18] (army 53.0%, navy 23.5%, air force 23.5%).

[1]English may also be used as an official language by executive authorities, legislature, and judiciary of Hong Kong. [2]On July 1, 1997, Hong Kong reverted to China as a Special Administrative Region in which the existing socioeconomic system would remain unchanged for a period of 50 years. [3]Includes 27 nonelective seats. The 60-seat provisional legislative body will be replaced with a permanent legislature by June 30, 1998. [4]Victoria, for some time, had been regarded as the capital because it had been the seat of the British administration of the Crown Colony. [5]Excludes transients and Vietnamese refugees. [6]Excludes about 59,900 Vietnamese refugees, about 1% of the population. [7]Other includes Public utilities. [8]Indirect taxes less subsidies. [9]Includes 95,600 unemployed. [10]Excludes local pigs not slaughtered in abattoirs. [11]September. [12]Excludes reexports valued at HK$1,185,758,000,000. [13]1994. [14]Thirty-two newspapers only. [15]1995–96. [16]1987–88. [17]Registered personnel; all may not be present and working in the country. [18]British forces with a few locally enlisted personnel.

Internet resources for further information:
- **Census and Statistics Department http://www.info.gov/censtatd**
- ***Hong Kong 1997* (a reference annual) http://www.info.gov.hk/isd/hk97/e1997/append-e/eapp097r.htm**

Hungary

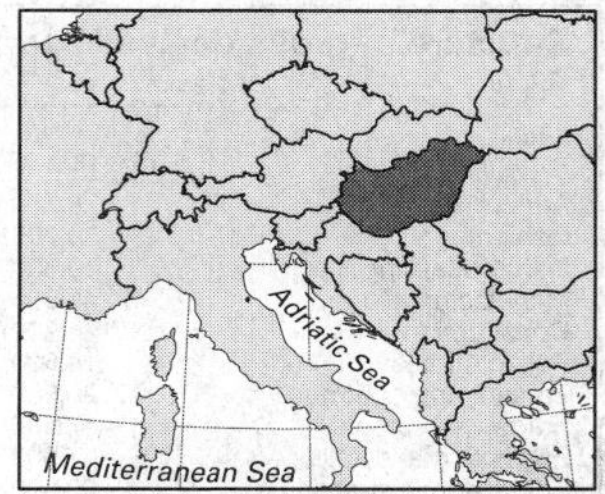

Official name: Magyar Köztársaság (Republic of Hungary).
Form of government: unitary multiparty republic with one legislative house (National Assembly [386[1]]).
Chief of state: President.
Head of government: Prime Minister.
Capital: Budapest.
Official language: Hungarian.
Official religion: none.
Monetary unit: 1 forint (Ft) = 100 filler; valuation (Oct. 3, 1997) 1 U.S.$ = Ft 195.14; 1 £ = Ft 314.56.

Area and population

		area		population
				1997[2]
Counties	**Capitals**	sq mi	sq km	estimate
Bács-Kiskun	Kecskemét	3,251	8,420	538,000
Baranya	Pécs	1,710	4,430	407,000
Békés	Békéscsaba	2,174	5,631	400,000
Borsod-Abaúj-Zemplén	Miskolc	2,798	7,247	742,000
Csongrád	Szeged	1,646	4,263	425,000
Fejér	Székesfehérvár	1,688	4,373	425,000
Győr-Moson-Sopron	Győr	1,568	4,062	425,000
Hajdú-Bihar	Debrecen	2,398	6,211	549,000
Heves	Eger	1,404	3,637	327,000
Jász-Nagykun-Szolnok	Szolnok	2,165	5,607	419,000
Komárom-Esztergom	Tatabánya	869	2,251	311,000
Nógrád	Salgótarján	982	2,544	221,000
Pest	Budapest[3]	2,468	6,393	996,000
Somogy	Kaposvár	2,331	6,036	336,000
Szabolcs-Szatmár-Bereg	Nyíregyháza	2,292	5,937	572,000
Tolna	Szekszárd	1,430	3,704	248,000
Vas	Szombathely	1,288	3,337	271,000
Veszprém	Veszprém	1,791	4,639	378,000
Zala	Zalaegerszeg	1,461	3,784	299,000
Capital City				
Budapest[3]		203	525	1,885,000
TOTAL		35,919[4]	93,030[4]	10,174,000

Demography

Population (1997): 10,157,000.
Density (1997): persons per sq mi 282.8, persons per sq km 109.2.
Urban-rural (1996): urban 62.6%; rural 37.4%.
Sex distribution (1997): male 47.79%; female 52.21%.
Age breakdown (1997): under 15, 17.7%; 15–29, 22.8%; 30–44, 20.9%; 45–59, 19.1%; 60–74, 14.3%; 75 and over, 5.2%.
Population projection: (2000) 10,056,000; (2010) 9,727,000. The population has declined at an average annual rate of 0.3% since 1980.
Ethnic composition (1993): Magyar 92%; Gypsy 3%; German 1%; Slovak 1%; Jewish 1%; Southern Slav 1%; other 1%.
Religious affiliation (1997): Christian 88.6%, of which Roman Catholic 63.1%, Protestant 25.5%; other (mostly nonreligious and atheist) 11.4%.
Major cities (1997[2]): Budapest 1,885,000; Debrecen 210,000; Miskolc 178,000.

Vital statistics

Birth rate per 1,000 population (1996): 10.4 (world avg. 25.0); legitimate 77.6%; illegitimate 22.4%.
Death rate per 1,000 population (1996): 14.1 (world avg. 9.3).
Natural increase rate per 1,000 population (1996): −3.7 (world avg. 15.7).
Total fertility rate (avg. births per childbearing woman; 1996): 1.5.
Marriage rate per 1,000 population (1996): 4.9.
Divorce rate per 1,000 population (1996): 2.2.
Life expectancy at birth (1995): male 65.3 years; female 74.5 years.
Major causes of death per 100,000 population (1996): diseases of the circulatory system 680.4; malignant neoplasms (cancers) 320.0.

National economy

Budget (1997). Revenue: Ft 2,251,896,000,000 (value-added tax 27.8%, income tax 17.8%, payments by enterprises 16.5%, excise duties 11.8%). Expenditures: Ft 2,561,608,000,000 (debt service 32.3%, health 15.9%[5], education 15.7%[5], defense 11.3%[6], social security 8.1%).
Production (metric tons except as noted). Agriculture, forestry, fishing (1996): corn (maize) 5,917,000, sugar beets 4,687,000, wheat 3,924,000, potatoes 1,093,000, barley 930,000; livestock (number of live animals) 5,032,000 pigs, 977,000 sheep; roundwood (1996) 4,415,000 cu m; fish catch (1995) 27,406. Mining and quarrying (1996): bauxite 1,044,000; glass sand 325,000. Manufacturing (value of production in Ft '000,000; 1996): food, beverage, and tobacco products 986,000; machinery and equipment 981,000; chemicals and chemical products 821,000; basic metals and fabricated metal products 419,000. Construction (value of production in Ft '000,000; 1995): residential 23,689[7]; office buildings 21,213. Energy production (consumption): electricity (kW-hr; 1994) 33,486,000,000 (35,520,000,000); coal (metric tons; 1994) 14,111,000 (15,369,000); crude petroleum (barrels; 1994) 10,537,000 (47,138,000); petroleum products (metric tons; 1994) 6,356,000 (7,044,000); natural gas (cu m; 1994) 4,334,000,000 (9,350,000,000).
Land use (1994): forested 19.1%; meadows and pastures 12.4%; agricultural and under permanent cultivation 53.9%; other 14.6%.
Public debt (external, outstanding; 1995): U.S.$23,572,000,000.
Population economically active (1997[8]): total 4,284,200; activity rate of total population 42.2% (participation rates: ages 15–74, 54.9%; female [1996] 49.8%; unemployed 8.6%).

Price and earnings indexes (1990 = 100)

	1990	1991	1992	1993	1994	1995	1996
Consumer price index	100.0	135.0	166.1	203.4	241.6	309.7	382.8
Monthly earnings index	100.0	133.4	165.8	202.1	252.4	289.3	348.3

Gross national product (1995): U.S.$42,129,000,000 (U.S.$4,120 per capita).

Structure of gross domestic product and labour force

	1995		1996	
	in value Ft '000,000[9]	% of total value	labour force	% of labour force
Agriculture	351,100	6.4	326,500	7.3
Mining and manufacturing	1,125,500	20.5	943,400	21.1
Construction	238,700	4.3	218,300	4.9
Public utilities	166,900	3.0	100,200	2.2
Transp. and commun.	480,700	8.8	334,000	7.5
Trade	522,900	9.5	559,400	12.5
Finance, real estate	904,700	16.5	279,300	6.3
Public administration, defense	340,200	6.2	277,600	6.2
Services	731,100	13.3	767,600	17.2
Other	632,000[10]	11.5[10]	663,900[11]	14.9[11]
TOTAL	5,493,800	100.0	4,470,200	100.0[4]

Household income and expenditure. Average household size (1991) 2.8; income per household (1990) Ft 376,195 (U.S.$5,900); sources of income (1995): wages 59.4%, social security benefits (cash) 15.0%, real estate 6.0%; expenditure (1995): food and beverages 40.3%; transportation, communications, and automobile maintenance 19.9%; housing 16.3%; household durable goods 7.1%; culture and recreation 6.2%; clothing 6.1%.

Foreign trade

Balance of trade (current prices)

	1991	1992	1993	1994	1995	1996
Ft '000,000,000	−76.2	−19.5	−317.7	−362.8	−284.8	−466.4
% of total	4.7%	1.1%	16.2%	13.8%	8.3%	10.4%

Imports (1996): Ft 2,468,100,000,000 (manufactured goods 46.9%, machinery and transport equipment 30.5%, fuels and electrical energy 13.6%, food and live animals 5.0%). *Major import sources:* Germany 23.6%; Russia 12.5%; Austria 9.5%; Italy 8.1%; France 4.2%; U.S. 3.5%; U.K. 3.3%.
Exports (1996): Ft 2,001,700,000,000 (manufactured goods 46.8%, machinery and transport equipment 25.5%, food and live animals 18.4%, fuels and electrical energy 4.1%). *Major export destinations:* Germany 29.0%; Austria 10.6%; Italy 8.0%; Russia 6.0%; France 3.7%; U.S. 3.5%.

Transport and communications

Transport. Railroads (1995): 13,181 km; (1996) passenger-km 9,358,000,000; metric ton-km cargo 7,600,000,000. Roads (1996): total length 29,999 km (paved 93%). Vehicles (1996): passenger cars 2,264,165; trucks and buses 322,000. Merchant marine (1992): vessels (100 gross tons and over) 15; total deadweight tonnage 93,204. Air transport (1996)[12]: passenger-km 2,762,000,000; metric ton-km cargo 32,950,000; airports (1997) with scheduled flights 1.

Communications

Medium	date	unit	number	units per 1,000 persons
Daily newspapers	1995	circulation	2,321,000	228
Radio	1996	receivers	6,250,000	590
Television	1995	receivers	4,530,000	444
Telephones	1995	main lines	1,893,000	185
Cellular telephones	1995	subscribers	265,000	26
Facsimile machines	1995	units	45,000	4.4
Personal computers	1995	units	400,000	39

Education and health

Educational attainment (1990). Population age 25 and over having: no formal schooling 1.3%; primary education 57.9%; secondary 30.7%; higher 10.1%. *Literacy* (1984): population age 15 and over literate 8,269,850 (98.9%); males literate 3,934,250 (99.2%); females literate 4,335,600 (98.6%).

Education (1996–97)

	schools	teachers	students	student/ teacher ratio
Primary (age 6–13)	3,765	83,658	966,000	11.5
Secondary (age 14–17)	980	29,462	361,400	12.3
Vocational	363	5,292	143,800	27.2
Higher	89	19,426	141,900	7.3

Health (1995): physicians 42,489 (1 per 240 persons); hospital beds 92,603 (1 per 110 persons); infant mortality rate per 1,000 live births (1996) 10.9.

Military

Total active duty personnel (1997): 49,100 (army 64.4%, air force 35.6%). *Military expenditure as percentage of GNP* (1995): 1.5% (world 2.8%); per capita expenditure U.S.$95.

[1]Includes 8 seats reserved for ethnic minorities. [2]January 1. [3]Budapest has separate county status. The area and population of the city are excluded from the larger county (Pest), which it administers. [4]Detail does not add to total given because of rounding. [5]1993. [6]1994. [7]Includes hotel construction. [8]Second quarter. [9]At purchaser's prices. [10]Taxes on products. [11]Includes 168,000 undistributed employed and 495,900 unemployed. [12]Malév airlines only.

Internet resources for further information:

- **Embassy of the Republic of Hungary http://www.hungaryemb.org/**
- **Hungarian Central Statistical Office http://www.ksh.hu/eng/homeng.html**
- **Hungarian Home Page http://www.fsz.bme.hu/hungary/**

Iceland

Official name: Lýdhveldidh Ísland (Republic of Iceland).
Form of government: unitary multiparty republic with one legislative house (Althing [63]).
Chief of state: President.
Head of government: Prime Minister.
Capital: Reykjavík.
Official language: Icelandic.
Official religion: Evangelical Lutheran.
Monetary unit: 1 króna (ISK) = 100 aurar; valuation (Oct. 3, 1997) 1 U.S.$ = ISK 71.34; 1 £ = ISK 115.00.

Area and population

Constituencies[2]	Principal centres	area sq mi	area sq km	population 1996[1] estimate
Austurland	Egilsstadhir	8,491	21,991	12,684
Nordhurland eystra	Akureyri	8,636	22,368	26,652
Nordhurland vestra	Saudhárkrókur	5,055	13,093	9,989
Reykjanes	...	765[3]	1,982[3]	71,446
Reykjavík	Reykjavík	3	3	105,487
Sudhurland	Şelfoss	9,735	25,214	20,626
Vestfirdhir	Ísafjördhur	3,657	9,470	8,856
Vesturland	Borgarnes	3,360	8,701	13,995
TOTAL		39,699	102,819	269,735

Demography

Population (1997): 271,000.
Density (1997)[4]: persons per sq mi 29.5, persons per sq km 11.4.
Urban-rural (1996): urban 91.9%; rural 8.1%.
Sex distribution (1997): male 50.11%; female 49.89%.
Age breakdown (1997): under 15, 24.0%; 15–29, 22.9%; 30–44, 22.8%; 45–59, 15.2%; 60–74, 10.2%; 75 and over, 4.9%.
Population projection: (2000) 277,000; (2010) 298,000.
Doubling time: 79 years.
Ethnic composition (1995)[5]: Icelandic 95.9%; Danish 0.8%; Swedish 0.5%; persons born in the United States 0.5%; German 0.3%; other 2.0%.
Religious affiliation (1996): Protestant 95.0%, of which Evangelical Lutheran 90.5%, other Lutheran 3.5%; Roman Catholic 1.0%; nonreligious 1.9%; other 2.1%.
Major cities (1996): Reykjavík 105,487 (urban area 160,629); Kópavogur 18,553[6]; Hafnarfjördhur 17,938[6]; Akureyri 15,009; Gardhabær 7,830[6].

Vital statistics

Birth rate per 1,000 population (1995): 16.0 (world avg. 25.0); legitimate 39.1%; illegitimate 60.9%.
Death rate per 1,000 population (1995): 7.2 (world avg. 9.3).
Natural increase rate per 1,000 population (1995): 8.8 (world avg. 15.7).
Total fertility rate (avg. births per childbearing woman; 1995): 2.1.
Marriage rate per 1,000 population (1995): 4.6.
Divorce rate per 1,000 population (1995): 1.8.
Life expectancy at birth (1994–95): male 76.5 years; female 80.6 years.
Major causes of death per 100,000 population (1994): diseases of the circulatory system 300.4, of which ischemic heart diseases 175.6, cerebrovascular disease 69.2; malignant neoplasms (cancers) 166.5; diseases of the respiratory system 80.1.

National economy

Budget (1995). Revenue: ISK 162,757,000,000 (indirect taxes 50.6%, of which value-added taxes 26.4%; direct taxes 41.8%; nontax revenue 7.6%). Expenditures: ISK 178,997,000,000 (health and welfare 40.2%, education 12.3%, communications 7.6%, general administration 4.9%, agriculture 4.1%).
Production (metric tons except as noted). Agriculture, forestry, fishing (1996): potatoes 11,200, silage 1,554,000 cu m, hay 1,338,000 cu m; livestock (number of live animals) 463,900 sheep, 80,500 horses, 74,800 cattle; fish catch (value in ISK '000,000; 1995) cod 14,390, shrimp 10,489, redfish 6,494, Greenland halibut 4,976, haddock 4,412. Mining and quarrying (1995): diatomite 28,100. Manufacturing (value added in ISK '000,000; 1993): preserved and processed fish 17,534; printing and publishing 5,020; fabricated metal products 3,996; meat 2,569; wood furniture 2,275. Construction (completed): residential (1995) 600,000 cu m; nonresidential (1994) 944,000 cu m. Energy production (consumption): electricity (kW-hr; 1996) 5,118,000,000 ([1995] 4,653,000,000); coal (metric tons; 1994) none (71,000); crude petroleum, none (none); petroleum products (metric tons; 1994) none (558,000); natural gas, none (none).
Land use (1994): forested 1.2%; meadows and pastures 22.7%; agricultural and under permanent cultivation 0.1%; other 76.0%.
Population economically active (April 1997): total 145,200; activity rate of total population 53.7% (participation rates: ages 16–74, 77.2%; female 46.3%; unemployed 3.9%).

Price and earnings indexes (1990 = 100)

	1991	1992	1993	1994	1995	1996	1997[7]
Consumer price index	106.8	111.0	115.6	117.4	119.3	122.0	123.8
Annual earnings index	108.3	111.5	113.1	114.5	119.6	127.3	136.0

Tourism (1996): receipts from visitors U.S.$153,700,000; expenditures by nationals abroad U.S.$309,700,000.
Gross national product (1995): U.S.$6,686,000,000 (U.S.$24,950 per capita).

Structure of gross domestic product and labour force

	1995 in value ISK '000,000[8]	1995 % of total value[8]	1997 labour force[9]	1997 % of labour force[9]
Agriculture	8,700	1.9	6,000	4.1
Fishing	33,700	7.4	6,600	3.4
Fish processing	19,600	4.3	7,700	5.3
Manufacturing	41,900	9.2	16,300	11.2
Construction	26,900	5.9	9,500	6.5
Public utilities	14,600	3.2	1,000	0.7
Transp. and commun.	26,900	5.9	9,900	6.8
Trade, restaurants	47,400	10.4	23,600	16.3
Finance, real estate	67,900	14.9	12,700	8.8
Public administration	62,500	13.7	5,900	4.1
Health, education, other services	21,900	4.8	40,200	27.7
Other	83,900[10]	18.4[10]	5,700[11]	3.9[11]
TOTAL	455,900	100.0	145,200[12]	100.0[12]

Public debt (external, outstanding; December 1995): U.S.$3,274,000,000.
Household income and expenditure. Average household size (1990)[13] 3.6; annual income per household (1990)[13] ISK 2,605,563 (U.S.$44,712); sources of income (1995): wages and salaries 74.1%, pension 10.5%, self-employment 2.7%, other 12.7%; expenditure (1993): food and beverages 23.9%, housing 16.0%, transportation and communications 14.5%, recreation 9.6%, household furnishings 7.6%, clothing and footwear 7.5%, expenditures in restaurants and hotels 7.4%.

Foreign trade[14]

Balance of trade (current prices)

	1991	1992	1993	1994	1995	1996
ISK '000,000	−3,253	−392	+12,188	+20,098	+13,068	+1,467
% of total	1.7%	0.2%	6.9%	9.7%	5.9%	0.6%

Imports (1996): ISK 135,995,000,000 (nonelectrical machinery and apparatus 14.4%; electrical machinery and apparatus 8.7%; food products 8.7%; road vehicles 7.7%; crude petroleum and petroleum products 7.4%). *Major import sources:* Norway 13.5%; Germany 10.9%; United Kingdom 10.2%; United States 9.4%; Denmark 8.4%; Sweden 6.7%; The Netherlands 6.0%.
Exports (1996): ISK 126,304,000,000 (marine products 73.3%, of which frozen fish 28.7%, frozen shrimp 12.6%, salted fish 12.4%, fish meal 7.0%; aluminum 9.6%). *Major export destinations:* United Kingdom 19.0%; Germany 12.8%; United States 12.1%; Japan 9.8%; Denmark 7.2%; France 6.7%.

Transport and communications

Transport. Railroads: none. Roads (1996): total length 7,691 mi, 12,378 km (paved 25%). Vehicles (1996): passenger cars 124,909; trucks and buses 16,623. Merchant marine (1992): vessels (100 gross tons and over) 394; total deadweight tonnage 114,851. Air transport (1996)[15]: passenger-mi 1,850,000,000, passenger-km 2,977,000,000; short ton-mi cargo 36,268,000, metric ton-km cargo 52,950,000; airports (1996) with scheduled flights 24.

Communications

Medium	date	unit	number	units per 1,000 persons
Daily newspapers	1994	circulation	137,000	515
Radio	1996	receivers	197,000	733
Television	1995	receivers	76,250	285
Telephones	1995	main lines	148,675	556
Cellular telephones	1995	subscribers	30,900	116
Facsimile machines	1995	units	4,100	15
Personal computers	1995	units	55,000	206

Education and health

Educational attainment: n.a. *Literacy:* virtually 100%.

Education (1996–97)

	schools	teachers	students	student/teacher ratio
Primary/lower secondary (age 7–15)	205	3,549	42,212	11.9
Upper Secondary (age 16–19)	35	1,454	17,970	12.4
Higher	14	508	7,972	15.7

Health: physicians (1995) 797 (1 per 335 persons); hospital beds (1993) 2,798[16] (1 per 95 persons); infant mortality rate (1993–95 avg.) 4.6.
Food (1995): daily per capita caloric intake 3,159 (vegetable products 60%, animal products 40%); 119% of FAO recommended minimum requirement.

Military

Total active duty personnel (1996): 120 coast guard personnel; NATO-sponsored U.S.-manned Iceland Defense Force (1996): 2,200. *Military expenditure as percentage of GNP* (1995): none (world average 2.8%).

[1]December 1. [2]Constituencies are electoral districts. Actual local administration is based on towns or rural districts. [3]Reykjanes includes Reykjavík. [4]Population density calculated with reference to 9,191 sq mi (23,805 sq km) area free of glaciers, lava fields, and lakes. [5]By country of birth. [6]Within Reykjavík urban area. [7]July. [8]Breakdown by sector is estimated. [9]April. [10]Indirect taxes, statistical discrepancy, and production of private nonprofit institution less imputed bank service charges and subsidies. [11]Unemployed. [12]Detail does not add to total given because of rounding. [13]Based on sample survey. [14]Imports f.o.b. in balance of trade and c.i.f. for commodities and trading partners. [15]Icelandair only. [16]Excludes nursing wards in old-age homes.

Internet resources for further information:
- **The Icelandic Government (some Icelandic only) http://www.stjr.is/en/stjren01.htm**
- **Embassy of Iceland (Washington, D.C.) http://www.iceland.org/**

India

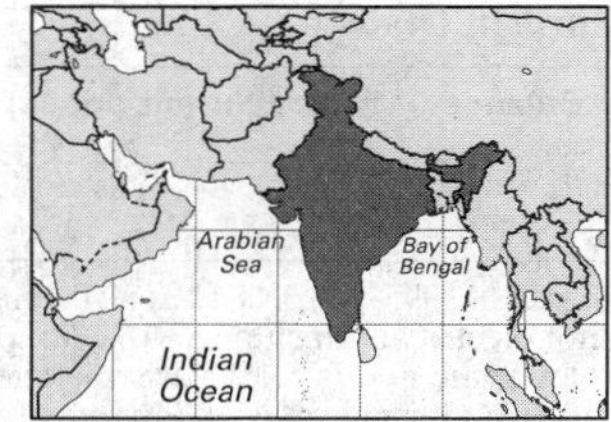

Official name: Bhārat (Hindī); Republic of India (English).
Form of government: multiparty federal republic with two legislative houses (Council of States [245[1]], House of the People [545[2]]).
Chief of state: President.
Head of government: Prime Minister.
Capital: New Delhi.
Official languages: Hindī; English.
Official religion: none.
Monetary unit: 1 Indian rupee (Re, plural Rs) = 100 paise; valuation (Oct. 3, 1997) 1 U.S.$ = Rs 36.17; 1 £ = Rs 58.31.

Area and population

States	Capitals	area sq mi	area sq km	population 1994 estimate
Andhra Pradesh	Hyderābād	106,195	275,045	71,800,000
Arunāchal Pradesh	Itānagar	32,333	83,743	965,000
Assam	Dispur	30,285	78,438	24,200,000
Bihār	Patna	67,134	173,877	93,080,000
Goa	Panaji	1,429	3,702	1,235,000
Gujarāt	Gāndhīnagar	75,685	196,024	44,235,000
Haryāna	Chandīgarh	17,070	44,212	17,925,000
Himāchal Pradesh	Shimla	21,495	55,673	5,530,000
Jammu and Kashmir	Srīnagar	38,830	100,569	8,435,000
Karnātaka	Bangalore	74,051	191,791	48,150,000
Kerala	Trivandrum	15,005	38,863	30,555,000
Madhya Pradesh	Bhopāl	171,215	443,446	71,950,000
Mahārāshtra	Mumbai (Bombay)	118,809	307,713	85,565,000
Manipur	Imphāl	8,621	22,327	2,010,000
Meghālaya	Shillong	8,660	22,429	1,960,000
Mizoram	Āīzawl	8,140	21,081	775,000
Nāgāland	Kohīma	6,401	16,579	1,410,000
Orissa	Bhubaneshwar	60,119	155,707	33,795,000
Punjab	Chandīgarh	19,445	50,362	21,695,000
Rājasthān	Jaipur	132,140	342,239	48,040,000
Sikkim	Gangtok	2,740	7,096	444,000
Tamil Nādu	Chennai (Madras)	50,216	130,058	58,840,000
Tripura	Agartala	4,049	10,486	3,065,000
Uttar Pradesh[3]	Lucknow	113,673	294,411	150,695,000
West Bengal	Calcutta	34,267	88,752	73,600,000
Union Territories				
Andaman and Nicobar Islands	Port Blair	3,185	8,249	322,000
Chandīgarh	Chandīgarh	44	114	725,000
Dādra and Nagar Haveli	Silvassa	190	491	153,000
Damān and Diu	Damān	43	112	111,000
Lakshadweep	Kavaratti	12	32	56,000
Pondicherry	Pondicherry	190	492	894,000
National Capital Territory[4]				
Delhi	Delhi	572	1,483	10,865,000
TOTAL		1,222,243[5]	3,165,596[5]	913,070,000[6]

Demography

Population (1997): 967,613,000.
Density (1997)[5]: persons per sq mi 791.7, persons per sq km 305.7.
Urban-rural (1995): urban 26.8%; rural 73.2%.
Sex distribution (1995): male 51.64%; female 48.36%.
Age breakdown (1995): under 15, 35.2%; 15–29, 27.2%; 30–44, 19.1%; 45–59, 11.2%; 60–74, 5.9%; 75 and over, 1.4%.
Population projection: (2000) 1,012,909,000; (2010) 1,155,830,000.
Doubling time: 43 years.
Linguistic composition (1981)[7]: Hindī (including associated languages and dialects) 38.77%; Telugu 7.96%; Bengalī 7.56%; Marāṭhī 7.28%; Tamil 6.56%; Urdū 5.18%; Gujarātī 4.87%; Kannaḍa 3.95%; Malayālam 3.81%; Oṛiyā 3.36%; Punjābī 2.73%; Assamese 1.18%[8]; Bhīlī/Bhilodī 0.65%; Santhālī 0.62%; Kashmirī 0.47%; Goṇḍī 0.29%; Sindhī 0.29%; Konkaṇī 0.23%; Dogrī 0.22%; Tulu 0.20%; Kurukh 0.19%; Nepālī 0.18%; Khandeshī 0.17%; Manipurī 0.13%; other 3.15%. Hindī (45.00%) and English (2.50%) are also spoken as lingua francas (second languages).
Major cities (1991): (*urban agglomerations;* 1995) Greater Mumbai (Greater Bombay) 9,925,891 (15,093,000); Delhi 7,206,704 (9,882,000); Calcutta 4,399,819 (11,673,000); Chennai (Madras) 3,841,396 (5,906,000); Bangalore 3,302,296 (4,749,000); Hyderābād 3,145,939 (5,343,000); Ahmadābād 2,954,526 (3,688,000); Kānpur 1,879,420 (2,356,000); Nāgpur 1,624,752 (1,847,000); Lucknow 1,619,115 (2,029,000); Pune 1,566,651 (2,940,000); New Delhi[9] 301,297.

Other principal cities (1991)

	population		population		population
Āgra	891,790	Indore	1,091,674	Rājkot	612,458
Allahābād	806,486	Jabalpur	764,586	Rānchi	599,306
Amritsar	708,835	Jaipur	1,458,183	Sholāpur (Solāpur)	
Aurangābād	573,272	Jalandhar (Jullundur)	509,510		604,215
Bareilly	590,661	Jodhpur	666,279	Srīnagar	850,000[13]
Bhopāl	1,062,771	Kalyān[11]	1,014,557	Sūrat	1,505,872
Chandīgarh	510,565	Kota	537,371	Thāne (Thāna)[11]	803,389
Cochin (Kochi)	582,588	Ludhiāna	1,042,740	Trivandrum	699,872
Coimbatore	816,321	Madurai	940,989	Vadodara (Baroda)	
Farīdābād	617,717	Meerut	753,778		1,061,598
Guwāhāti	584,342	Mysore	606,755	Vārānasi (Benares)	
Gwalior	690,765	Nāshik (Nāsik)	656,925		932,399
Howrah (Hāora)[10]	950,435	Patna	917,243	Vijayawāda	701,827
Hubli-Dhārwād	648,298	Pimpri-Chinchwad[12]	517,083	Vishākhapatnam	752,037

Religious affiliation (1991): Hindu 80.3%; Muslim 11.0%, of which Sunnī 8.2%, Shīʿī 2.8%; Christian 3.8%, of which Protestant 1.9%, Roman Catholic 1.7%, Orthodox 0.2%; Sikh 2.0%; Buddhist 0.7%; Jain 0.5%; Zoroastrian 0.01%; other 1.7%.
Households (1991)[14]. Total households 151,032,898. Average household size 5.6; 1–2 persons 12.1%, 3–5 persons 44.4%, 6–8 persons 30.5%, 9 or more persons 13.0%. Average number of rooms per household 2.2; 1 room 40.5%, 2 rooms 30.6%, 3 rooms 13.8%, 4 rooms 7.1%, 5 rooms 3.2%, 6 or more rooms 3.9%, unspecified number of rooms 0.9%. Average number of persons per room 2.6. Shelterless (homeless) population estimated (1987) at more than 100,000,000.

Vital statistics

Birth rate per 1,000 population (1996): 25.9 (world avg. 25.0).
Death rate per 1,000 population (1996): 9.6 (world avg. 9.3).
Natural increase rate per 1,000 population (1996): 16.3 (world avg. 15.7).
Total fertility rate (avg. births per childbearing woman; 1996): 3.2.
Marital status of male (female) population age 6 and over (1992–93): single 48.3% (37.1%); married 47.5% (55.2%); widowed 3.6% (7.2%); divorced or separated 0.6% (0.5%).
Life expectancy at birth (1996): male 59.1 years; female 60.3 years.
Major causes of death per 100,000 population (1987)[15]: diseases of the circulatory system 227; infectious and parasitic diseases 215; diseases of the respiratory system 108; certain conditions originating in the perinatal period 108; accidents, homicide, and other violence 102; diseases of the digestive system 48; diseases of the nervous system 43; malignant neoplasms (cancers) 41; endocrine, metabolic, and nutritional disorders 30; diseases of the blood and blood-forming organs 25; ill-defined conditions 129.

Social indicators

Educational attainment (1981)[16]. Percentage of population age 25 and over having: no formal schooling (illiterate) 64.8%; no formal schooling (literate) 1.0%; some primary education 7.1%; completed primary 10.9%; some secondary 6.2%; completed secondary 7.1%; higher vocational 0.4%; completed undergraduate degree 2.5%.

Distribution of expenditure (1992)

percentage of household expenditure by quintile				
1	2	3	4	5 (highest)
8.5%	12.1%	15.8%	21.1%	42.5%

Quality of working life. Average workweek (1989): 42 hours[17]. Rate of fatal (nonfatal) injuries per 100,000 industrial workers (1989) 17 (3,625)[17]. Employees covered under Employee's State Insurance Scheme (1991) 6,070,000; number of beneficiaries 26,749,000[17]. Agricultural workers in servitude to creditors (early 1990s) 10–20%.
Access to services (1991). Percentage of total (urban, rural) households having access to: electricity for lighting purposes 42.4% (75.8%, 30.5%); attached toilet or nearby latrine 23.7% (63.9%, 9.5%). Source of drinking water: piped water 32.3%, well 32.2%, hand pump or tube well 30.0%, river or canal 2.0%, public tank 1.3%, other 2.2%.
Social participation. Eligible voters participating in last (April/May 1996) national election: 57.9%. Trade union membership (early 1990s): *c.* 9,000,000.
Social deviance (1990)[18]. Offense rate per 100,000 population for: murder 4.1; dacoity (gang robbery) 1.3; theft and housebreaking 56.6; riots 12.0. Rate of suicide per 100,000 population (1991): 9.0.
Material well-being (1994). Households possessing: black and white television receivers 18.8%, colour television receivers 6.3%, videocassette recorders 1.3%, refrigerators 6.9%, washing machines 2.3%.

National economy

Gross national product (1995): U.S.$319,660,000,000 (U.S.$340 per capita).

Structure of gross domestic product and labour force

	1995–96 in value Rs '000,000,000[19]	1995–96 % of total value	1991 labour force[20]	1991 % of labour force[20]
Agriculture, forestry	2,748	27.9	191,340,829	60.9
Mining	197	2.0	1,751,275	0.6
Manufacturing	1,560	15.8	28,671,479	9.1
Construction	566	5.7	5,543,205	1.8
Public utilities	263	2.7	...	...
Transp. and commun.	764	7.8	8,017,746	2.5
Trade, restaurants	1,405	14.3	21,296,337	6.8
Finance, real estate	861	8.7	...	...
Pub. admin., defense	524	5.3	29,311,622	9.3
Services	594	6.0		
Other	376	3.8	28,198,877[21]	9.0[21]
TOTAL	9,858	100.0	314,131,370	100.0

Budget (1996–97). Revenue: Rs 1,982,500,000,000 (tax revenue 59.9%, of which excise taxes 23.5%, customs duties 22.4%, corporation taxes 9.9%; nontax revenue 40.1%, of which economic services 23.5%, interest receipts 10.8%). Expenditures: Rs 2,297,300,000,000 (interest payments and debt servicing 26.1%; transportation 11.5%; grants to state governments 10.1%; defense 8.6%; communications 6.1%; agriculture 4.9%; social services 4.3%).
Public debt (external, outstanding; 1995): U.S.$79,725,000,000.
Production (in '000 metric tons except as noted). Agriculture, forestry, fishing (1996): sugarcane 255,000, cereals 214,082 (of which rice 120,012, wheat 62,620, sorghum 10,500, corn [maize] 8,660, pearl millet 7,000[22], finger millet 2,850[22]; fruits 40,197 (of which mangoes 10,000, bananas 9,935, oranges 2,000, lemons and limes 1,700, apples 1,200), oilseeds 27,361 (of which peanuts [groundnuts] 8,000, rapeseed 6,000, cottonseed 5,101, soybeans 4,200, sunflower seeds 1,450, castor beans 1,000); pulses 15,414 (of which chickpeas

6,000, pigeon peas 3,000), coconuts 8,700, seed cotton 7,651, cotton lint 2,550, jute 1,500, tea 715, tobacco 512, natural rubber 435, betel 248, ginger 210, pepper 46; livestock (number of live animals; 1996) 196,003,000 cattle, 120,270,000 goats, 80,102,000 water buffalo, 45,390,000 sheep; roundwood (1995) 299,163,000 cu m; fish catch (metric tons; 1995) 4,903,659, of which freshwater fish (1994) 2,197,000. Mining and quarrying (1995–96): limestone 94,032; iron ore 66,576; bauxite 5,448; manganese 720[23]; chromium 500[23]; zinc 171[23]; copper 57[23]; lead 42[23]; gold 65,600 troy oz; diamonds 29,900 carats. Manufacturing (in '000 metric tons except as noted; 1995–96): cement 69,032; finished steel 14,533; steel ingots 14,700[24]; refined sugar 14,788; nitrogenous fertilizers 7,950[24]; paper and paperboard 3,100[24]; soda ash 1,465; jute textiles 1,364[24]; aluminum 527; nylon and polyester yarns 357[24]; bicycles 9,426,000 units; motorcycles and scooters 2,035,000 units; power-driven pumps 513,000 units[24]; passenger cars and jeeps 414,200 units; passenger buses and trucks 259,100 units; cotton cloth 17,033,000,000 metres[24]; other important manufactured products include drugs and pharmaceuticals, computer software, gold jewelry, and silk goods. Construction (value of new construction in Rs; 1989–90): 563,670,000,000.

Manufacturing enterprises (1992–93)[25]

	no. of factories	no. of persons engaged	avg. wages as a % of avg. of all wages	annual value added (Rs '000,000)
Chemicals and chemical products,	7,886	640,400	155.6	107,519
of which fertilizers/pesticides	633	100,300	204.6	25,712
drugs and medicine	2,112	167,300	150.5	22,066
synthetic fibres	268	54,400	232.9	19,070
paints, soaps, and cosmetics	1,878	99,600	128.8	16,114
Textiles	14,789	1,397,300	86.7	59,140
Transport equipment,	5,552	718,300	137.9	50,284
of which motor vehicles	3,379	340,700	149.4	29,028
Nonelectrical machinery/apparatus	8,554	505,000	135.2	50,040
Electrical machinery/apparatus,	5,120	402,600	145.6	49,161
of which industrial machinery	1,924	162,600	173.7	21,066
communications equipment/TVs	1,194	124,100	131.3	16,050
Food products,	21,397	1,240,200	60.3	48,462
of which sugar	1,306	351,500	93.4	15,398
Iron and steel	3,388	490,200	147.0	48,123
Refined petroleum	79	24,400	247.1	27,972
Nonferrous basic metals	2,859	176,500	109.1	16,219
Fabricated metal products	7,038	239,900	96.1	13,468
Bricks, cement, plaster products	687	94,300	125.5	12,568
Rubber products	2,172	121,900	105.2	12,541
Tobacco products	7,786	493,700	28.4	12,513

Energy production (consumption): electricity (kW-hr; 1995–96) 380,100,000,000 ([1994] 385,902,000,000); coal (metric tons; 1995) 287,676,000 ([1994] 284,497,000); crude petroleum (barrels; 1995–96) 264,845,000 ([1994] 434,149,000); petroleum products (metric tons; 1994) 43,575,000 (56,722,000); natural gas (cu m; 1995) 17,022,000,000 ([1995–96] 20,388,000,000).

Financial aggregates[26]

	1991	1992	1993	1994	1995	1996	1997[27]
Exchange rate, Rs per:							
U.S. dollar	25.83	26.20	31.38	31.38	35.18	35.93	35.91
£	48.33	39.61	46.48	49.03	54.53	61.01	58.51
SDR	36.95	36.02	43.10	45.81	52.30	51.67	49.80
International reserves (U.S.$)							
Total (excl. gold; '000,000)	3,627	5,757	10,199	19,698	17,922	20,170	22,664
SDRs ('000,000)	46	4	100	2	139	122	2
Reserve pos. in IMF ('000,000)	—	292	292	310	316	306	295
Foreign exchange ('000,000)	3,580	5,461	9,807	19,386	17,467	19,742	22,367
Gold ('000,000 fine troy oz)	11.282	11.348	11.457	11.800	12.780	12.781	12.781
% world reserves	1.2	1.2	1.3	1.3	1.4	1.4	1.4
Interest and prices							
Central bank discount (%)	12.0	12.0	12.0	12.0	12.0	12.0	12.0
Advance (prime) rate (%)	17.9	18.9	16.3	...	...	...	...
Industrial share prices (1990 = 100)[28]	134.8	247.3	202.9	322.1	270.0	246.6	...
Balance of payments (U.S.$'000,000)							
Balance of visible trade	−2,992	−2,107	−522	...	...	...	...
Imports, f.o.b.	21,087	22,126	22,538	...	...	...	...
Exports, f.o.b.	18,095	20,019	22,016	...	...	...	...
Balance of invisibles	−1,300	−2,378	−1,354	...	...	...	...
Balance of payments, current account	−4,292	−4,495	−1,876	...	...	...	...

Land use (1994): forested 23.0%; meadows and pastures 3.8%; agricultural and under permanent cultivation 57.1%; other 16.1%.

Population economically active (1991): total 314,131,370; activity rate of total population 37.5% (participation rates: over age 15 [1981] 60.7%; female 28.6%; unemployed[29]).

Price and earnings indexes (1990 = 100)

	1991	1992	1993	1994	1995	1996	1997[30]
Consumer price index	113.9	127.3	135.4	149.2	164.5	179.2	187.9
Earnings index	...	...	...	...	...	...	...

Household income and expenditure. Average household size (1991)[14] 5.6; income per household: n.a.; sources of income (1984–85): salaries and wages 42.2%, self-employed 39.7%, interest 8.6%, profits and dividends 6.0%, rent 3.5%; expenditure (1993–94): food and beverages 50.9%, transportation and communications 13.0%, clothing and footwear 9.8%, housing 5.7%, energy 4.2%, household furnishings 4.2%.

Service enterprises (net value added at factor cost in Rs '000,000; 1992–93): wholesale and retail trade 766,500; transport and storage 420,610; community and social services 368,850; construction 358,330; finance 242,380; real estate and business services 215,840; electricity, gas, and steam 137,080.

Tourism: receipts from visitors (1995) U.S.$2,754,000,000; expenditures by nationals abroad (1994) U.S.$408,000,000.

Foreign trade[31, 32]

Balance of trade (current prices)

	1990–91	1991–92	1992–93	1993–94	1994–95	1995–96
Rs '000,000	−106,450	−38,100	−96,870	−33,500	−72,970	−151,820
% of total	14.1%	4.1%	8.3%	2.3%	4.2%	6.7%

Imports (1995–96): Rs 1,216,470,000,000 (mineral fuels and lubricants 20.7%; nonelectrical machinery 18.1%; precious and semiprecious stones 5.7%; electronic goods 5.1%; organic chemicals 4.7%). *Major import sources:* U.S. 10.5%; Germany 8.6%; Japan 6.6%; Saudi Arabia 5.5%; Kuwait 5.4%; U.K. 5.3%; Belgium 4.7%; United Arab Emirates 4.4%; Russia 3.3%.

Exports (1995–96): Rs 1,064,650,000,000 (agricultural and allied products 19.1%; cut and polished diamonds and jewelry 16.6%; ready-made garments 11.6%; machinery, transport equipment, metal products, iron and steel, and electronic components 11.4%; cotton yarn, fabrics, and thread 8.1%; chemicals and chemical products 7.4%; leather and leather manufactures 5.4%). *Major export destinations:* U.S. 17.4%; Japan 7.0%; U.K. 6.3%; Germany 6.2%; Hong Kong 5.7%; United Arab Emirates 4.5%; Belgium 3.5%; Russia 3.3%; Bangladesh 3.3%; Italy 3.2%.

Transport and communications

Transport. Railroads (1994–95): route length 38,935 mi, 62,660 km; passenger-mi 198,500,000,000, passenger-km 319,400,000,000; short ton-mi cargo 173,268,000,000, metric ton-km cargo 252,967,000,000. Roads (1995): total length 1,248,700 mi, 2,009,600 km (paved 50%). Vehicles (1995): passenger cars 2,720,000; trucks and buses 2,207,000. Air transport (1995)[33]: passenger-mi 12,563,000,000, passenger-km 20,219,000,000; short ton-mi cargo 437,871,000, metric ton-km cargo 639,280,000; airports (1996) with scheduled flights 66.

Communications

Medium	date	unit	number	units per 1,000 persons
Daily newspapers	1993	circulation	18,800,000	21
Radio	1996	receivers	111,000,000	117
Television	1995	receivers	20,000,000	21
Telephones	1995	main lines	10,600,000	11
Cellular telephones	1995	subscribers	135,600	0.14
Facsimile machines	1995	units	50,000	0.05
Personal computers	1995	units	1,200,000	1.3

Education and health

Literacy (1995): total population age 15 and over literate 315,600,000 (52.0%); males literate 205,100,000 (65.5%); females literate 110,500,000 (37.7%).

Education (1995–96)

	schools	teachers	students	student/ teacher ratio
Primary (age 6–10)	590,421	1,740,736	109,734,292	63.0
Secondary (age 11–17)	265,869	2,657,985	63,521,637	23.9
Higher[34]	8,407	286,000	5,007,000	17.5

Health (1992): physicians 410,875 (1 per 2,173 persons); hospital beds 642,103 (1 per 1,357 persons); infant mortality rate (1996) 71.1.

Food (1995): daily per capita caloric intake 2,388 (vegetable products 93%, animal products 7%); 108% of FAO recommended minimum requirement.

Military

Total active duty personnel (1996): 1,145,000 (army 85.6%, navy 4.8%, air force 9.6%); personnel in paramilitary forces for border security 282,000. *Military expenditure as percentage of GNP* (1995): 2.4% (world 2.8%); per capita expenditure U.S.$8.

[1]Council of States can have a maximum of 250 members; a maximum of 12 of these members may be nominated by the president. [2]Includes 2 nonelective seats. [3]Future creation of the new state of Uttarakhand from part of Uttar Pradesh was announced in August 1996. [4]Effective government of new national capital territory in place from December 1993. [5]Excludes 46,976 sq mi (121,667 sq km) of territory claimed by India as part of Jammu and Kashmir but occupied by Pakistan or China; inland water constitutes 9.0% of total area of India (including all of Indian-claimed Jammu and Kashmir). [6]Detail does not add to total given because of rounding. [7]Mother tongue unless otherwise noted. [8]Estimated figure. [9]Within Delhi urban agglomeration. [10]Within Calcutta urban agglomeration. [11]Within Greater Mumbai urban agglomeration. [12]Within Pune urban agglomeration. [13]1990 estimate. [14]Excludes Jammu and Kashmir. [15]Projected rates based on about 3.5% of total deaths (317,392 registered deaths out of an estimated total of nearly 9,000,000 deaths). [16]Excludes Assam. [17]Data apply to the workers employed in the "organized sector" only (28 million in 1994, of which 20 million are employed in the public sector and 8 million are employed in the private sector); few legal protections exist for the other 348 million workers in the "unorganized sector." [18]Crimes reported to National Crime Records Bureau by police authorities of state governments. [19]At factor cost. [20]All persons aged 5 years or older designated "workers" per 1991 census. [21]Not adequately defined. [22]1995–96. [23]Approximate metal content of ore. [24]1994–95. [25]Establishments with 10 or more workers using electrical power and all establishments employing 20 or more workers. [26]End-of-period unless otherwise noted. [27]March. [28]Annual average. [29]Average number of registered unemployed during the first quarter of 1996 was 36,882,000. [30]February. [31]Imports c.i.f.; exports f.o.b. [32]Fiscal year beginning April 1. [33]Air-India, Indian Airlines, and Jet Airways only. [34]1993–94.

Internet resources for further information:

- **National Informatics Centre: Union Government**
  http://www.nic.in/htm/ug.htm
- **Ministry of External Affairs**
  http://www.meadev.gov.in/
- **Ministry of Finance: Budget and Economic Survey**
  http://www.nic.in/indiabudget/
- **Press Information Bureau (Government of India)**
  http://www.nic.in/India-Image/PIB/

Indonesia

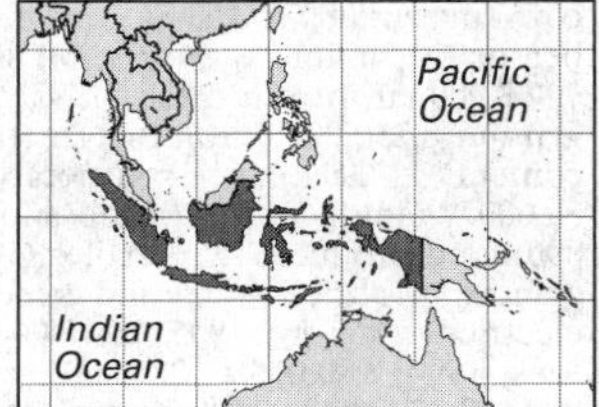

Official name: Republik Indonesia (Republic of Indonesia).
Form of government: unitary multiparty republic with two legislative houses (House of People's Representatives [500[1]]; People's Consultative Assembly [1,000[2]]).
Head of state and government: President.
Capital: Jakarta.
Official language: Bahasa Indonesia.
Official religion: monotheism.
Monetary unit: 1 Indonesian rupiah (Rp) = 100 sen; valuation (Oct. 3, 1997) 1 U.S.$ = Rp 3,640; 1 £ = Rp 5,868.

Area and population

		area		population
Metropolitan district	**Capitals**	sq mi	sq km	1995 estimate
Jakarta Raya	Jakarta	228	590	9,160,500
Provinces				
Bali	Denpasar	2,147	5,561	2,902,200
Bengkulu	Bengkulu	8,173	21,168	1,415,000
Irian Jaya	Jayapura	162,928	421,981	1,956,300
Jambi	Jambi	17,297	44,800	2,383,400
Jawa Barat	Bandung	17,877	46,300	39,336,500
Jawa Tengah	Semarang	13,207	34,206	29,688,100
Jawa Timur	Surabaya	18,502	47,921	33,885,900
Kalimantan Barat	Pontianak	56,664	146,760	3,651,800
Kalimantan Selatan	Banjarmasin	14,541	37,660	2,900,400
Kalimantan Tengah	Palangkaraya	58,919	152,600	1,637,300
Kalimantan Timur	Samarinda	78,162	202,440	2,331,000
Lampung	Tanjung Karang	12,860	33,307	6,680,300
Maluku	Ambon	28,767	74,505	2,094,700
Nusa Tenggara Barat	Mataram	7,790	20,177	3,654,800
Nusa Tenggara Timur	Kupang	18,485	47,876	3,582,800
Riau	Pakanbaru	36,510	94,561	3,924,600
Sulawesi Selatan	Ujung Pandang	28,101	72,781	7,577,800
Sulawesi Tengah	Palu	26,921	69,726	1,947,500
Sulawesi Tenggara	Kendari	10,690	27,686	1,594,000
Sulawesi Utara	Menado	7,345	19,023	2,652,300
Sumatera Barat	Padang	19,219	49,778	4,328,200
Sumatera Selatan	Palembang	40,034	103,688	7,232,700
Sumatera Utara	Medan	27,331	70,787	11,145,300
Timor Timur[3]	Dili	5,743	14,874	843,100
Special autonomous districts				
Aceh	Banda Aceh	21,387	55,392	3,860,000
Yogyakarta	Yogyakarta	1,224	3,169	2,916,700
TOTAL		741,052	1,919,317	195,283,200

Demography

Population (1997): 199,544,000.
Density (1997): persons per sq mi 269.3, persons per sq km 104.0.
Urban-rural (1997): urban 37.0%; rural 63.0%.
Sex distribution (1990): male 49.88%; female 50.12%.
Age breakdown (1990): under 15, 36.5%; 15–29, 28.3%; 30–44, 18.1%; 45–59, 10.7%; 60–74, 5.3%; 75 and over, 1.1%.
Population projection: (2000) 208,706,000; (2010) 237,653,000.
Ethnolinguistic composition (1990): Javanese 39.4%; Sundanese 15.8%; Indonesian (Malay) 12.1%; Madurese 4.3%; Minang 2.4%; other 26.0%.
Religious affiliation (1990): Muslim 87.2%; Christian 9.6%, of which Roman Catholic 3.6%; Hindu 1.8%; Buddhist 1.0%; other 0.4%.
Major cities (1990): Jakarta 8,259,266; Surabaya 2,421,016; Bandung 2,026,893.

Vital statistics

Birth rate per 1,000 population (1997): 22.4 (world avg. 25.0).
Death rate per 1,000 population (1997): 7.9 (world avg. 9.3).
Natural increase rate per 1,000 population (1997): 14.5 (world avg. 15.7).
Total fertility rate (avg. births per childbearing woman; 1997): 2.6.
Marriage rate per 1,000 population (1993–94): 7.8[4].
Life expectancy at birth (1997): male 63.0 years; female 66.0 years.
Major causes of death (percent distribution, 1986): infectious and parasitic diseases 43.5%; diseases of the respiratory system 21.9%; cardiovascular diseases 9.7%; diseases of the nervous system 6.0%.

National economy

Budget (1997–98). Revenue: Rp 88,061,000,000,000 (income tax 33.1%, value-added tax 27.9%, oil and gas revenues 16.9%, nontax revenue 9.6%, excise taxes 5.0%). Expenditures: Rp 89,391,000,000,000 (general public services 33.7%, transfers and subsidies 13.1%, debt repayment 8.4%).
Public debt (external, outstanding; 1995): U.S.$65,347,000,000.
Tourism (1995): receipts U.S.$5,228,000,000; expenditures U.S.$2,172,000,000.
Production (metric tons except as noted). Agriculture, forestry, fishing (1996): rice 51,165,000, sugarcane 32,053,000, cassava 16,000,000, maize 8,925,000, palm oil 4,998,000, natural rubber 1,578,000; livestock (number of live animals) 14,323,000 goats, 11,930,000 cattle, 7,684,000 sheep, 3,140,000 buffalo; roundwood (1995) 185,895,000 cu m; fish catch (1995) 4,118,000. Mining and quarrying (1996): nickel ore 3,400,000; copper concentrate 1,760,000; bauxite 820,000; gold 83,660 kg. Manufacturing (value added in Rp '000,000,000; 1994)[5]: textiles 8,055.4; transport equipment 6,796.7; tobacco products 6,194.6; food products 5,293.3; wood products 5,240.0; machinery 3,185.5. Energy production (consumption): electricity (kW-hr; 1994) 61,370,000,000 (61,370,000,000); coal (metric tons; 1994) 28,549,000 (3,461,000); crude petroleum (barrels; 1994) 561,265,000 (308,820,000); petroleum products (metric tons; 1994) 44,888,000 (36,428,000); natural gas (cu m; 1994) 59,532,000,000 (23,191,000,000).
Gross national product (1995): U.S.$190,105,000,000 (U.S.$980 per capita).

Structure of gross domestic product and labour force

	1996		1995	
	in value Rp '000,000,000	% of total value	labour force[6]	% of labour force[6]
Agriculture	86,212.1	16.3	35,233,270	44.0
Mining	43,893.2	8.3	643,332	0.8
Manufacturing	133,088.5	25.2	10,127,047	12.7
Construction	42,279.2	8.0	3,768,080	4.7
Public utilities	6,561.0	1.2	216,128	0.3
Transp. and commun.	35,553.7	6.7	3,458,155	4.3
Trade	88,451.2	16.7	13,883,682	17.3
Finance, real estate	46,839.6	8.9	658,497	0.8
Pub. admin., defense	29,531.4	5.6	12,121,869	15.1
Services	16,546.5	3.1		
Other	...	...	...	...
TOTAL	528,956.4	100.0	80,110,060	100.0

Population economically active: total (1995) 86,361,300; activity rate 44.3% (participation rates: over age 10, 56.6%; unemployed 7.2%).

Price and earnings indexes (1990 = 100)

	1990	1991	1992	1993	1994	1995	1996
Consumer price index	100.0	109.4	117.7	129.0	140.0	153.2	165.5
Earnings index[7]	100.0	114.6	127.1	150.0	195.8	233.3	...

Household income and expenditure. Average household size (1995) 4.3; income per household: n.a.; sources of income: n.a.

Foreign trade

Balance of trade (current prices)

	1991	1992	1993	1994	1995	1996
U.S.$'000,000	+6,075	+4,937	+8,872	+11,496	+8,883	+5,285
% of total	11.6%	9.2%	13.4%	16.8%	10.8%	5.6%

Imports (1996): U.S.$42,929,000,000 (machinery and transport equipment 40.8%, basic manufactures 15.4%, chemicals 14.0%, mineral fuels 8.5%, crude materials 8.1%). *Major import sources:* Japan 19.8%; U.S. 11.8%; Germany 7.0%; Singapore 6.7%.
Exports (1996): U.S.$49,814,000,000 (crude petroleum 11.5%, natural gas 9.0%, plywood 7.2%, garments 7.2%, processed rubber 4.5%). *Major export destinations:* Japan 25.9%; U.S. 13.6%; Singapore 9.2%; The Netherlands 3.3%.

Transport and communications

Transport. Railroads (1994): route length 6,583 km; passenger-km (1996) 15,924,000,000; metric ton-km cargo (1996) 3,912,000,000. Roads (1995): length 372,414 km (paved 47%). Vehicles (1995): passenger cars 2,107,299; trucks and buses 2,024,702. Air transport (1995): passenger-km 14,330,000,000; metric ton-km cargo 606,848,000; airports (1996) 81.

Communications

Medium	date	unit	number	units per 1,000 persons
Daily newspapers	1994	circulation	3,800,000	20
Radio	1996	receivers	26,000,000	132
Television	1995	receivers	28,000,000	145
Telephones	1995	main lines	3,290,900	17
Cellular telephones	1995	subscribers	218,600	1.1
Facsimile machines	1995	units	85,000	0.4
Personal computers	1995	units	730,000	3.8

Education and health

Educational attainment (1990). Percentage of population age 25 and over having: no schooling 34.6%; less than complete primary 28.2%; primary 23.3%; secondary 12.5%; higher 1.4%. *Literacy* (1995 est.): total population age 15 and over literate 83.8%; males literate 89.6%; females literate 78.0%.

Education (1994–95)

	schools	teachers	students	student/ teacher ratio
Primary (age 7–12)	149,464	1,172,640	26,200,023	22.3
Secondary (age 13–18)	27,177	595,962	8,864,001	14.9
Voc., teacher tr.[8]	3,502	102,114	1,405,220	13.8
Higher	1,236	150,607	2,229,796	14.8

Health (1994): physicians 28,989 (1 per 6,570 persons); hospital beds 116,847 (1 per 1,630 persons); infant mortality rate (1997) 51.
Food (1995): daily per capita caloric intake 2,732 (vegetable products 95%, animal products 5%); 126% of FAO recommended minimum.

Military

Total active duty personnel (1997): 284,000 (army 77.5%, navy 15.1%, air force 7.4%). *Military expenditure as percentage of GNP* (1995): 1.8% (world 2.8%); per capita expenditure U.S.$18.

[1]Includes 75 nonelective seats reserved for the military. [2]Includes the 500 members of the House of People's Representatives plus 500 other delegates. [3]The legality of Indonesian administration of this province is disputed by the United Nations. [4]Muslim population only. [5]Medium and large manufacturing establishments only. [6]Employed people only. [7]Based on minimum monthly wages. [8]1993–94.

Internet resources for further information:
- **Central Bureau of Statistics http://www.bps.go.id/**

Iran

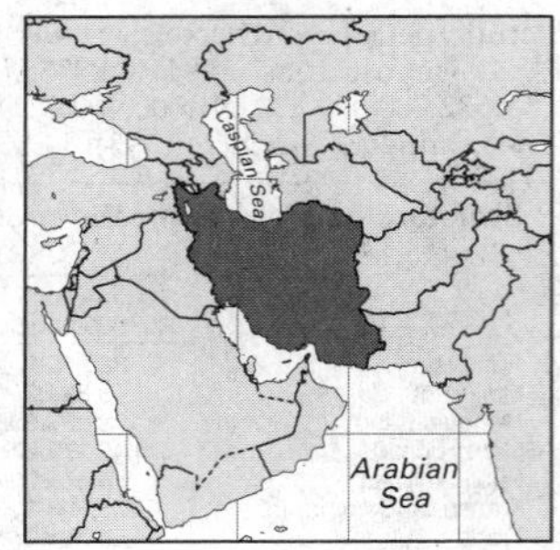

Official name: Jomhūrī-ye Eslāmī-ye Irān (Islamic Republic of Iran).
Form of government: unitary Islamic republic with one legislative house (Islamic Consultative Assembly [270]).
Supreme political/religious authority: Leader[1].
Head of state and government: President.
Capital: Tehrān.
Official language: Farsī (Persian).
Official religion: Islam.
Monetary unit: 1 rial (Rls); valuation (Oct. 3, 1997) 1 U.S.$ = Rls 3,000[2]; 1 £ = Rls 4,836[2].

Area and population

Provinces	area sq km	1991 census population	Provinces	area sq km	population
Ardabīl	17,814	1,141,625	Kohkīlūyeh va		
Āzārbāyjān-e Gharbī	37,588	2,284,208	Būyer Aḥmadī	14,261	496,739
Āzārbāyjān-e Sharqī	49,287	3,278,718	Kordestān	27,855	1,233,480
Būshehr	25,357	694,252	Lorestān	28,803	1,501,778
Chahār Maḥāll va			Markazi	29,530	1,182,611
Bakhtīārī	14,820	747,297	Māzandarān	46,456	3,793,149
Eşfahān	104,650	3,682,444	Qazvīn	[3]	[3]
Fārs	126,489	3,543,828	Qom	10,930	757,147
Gilan	14,811	2,204,047	Semnān	91,538	458,125
Hamadān	19,445	1,651,320	Sīstān va		
Hormozgān	68,476	924,433	Balūchestān	181,471	1,455,102
Ilām	19,086	440,693	Tehrān	53,693[3]	11,001,295[3]
Kermān	186,422	1,862,542	Yazd	72,342	691,119
Kermānshāhān	23,667	1,622,159	Zanjān	[3]	[3]
Khorāsān	313,335	6,013,200	TOTAL	1,645,258	55,837,163
Khūzestān	67,132	3,175,852			

Demography

Population (1997): 62,304,000[4].
Density (1997): persons per sq mi 98.1, persons per sq km 37.9.
Urban-rural (1995–96): urban 58.3%; rural 41.7%.
Sex distribution (1991): male 51.52%; female 48.48%.
Age breakdown (1991): under 15, 44.3%; 15–29, 26.6%; 30–44, 15.1%; 45–59, 8.2%; 60–74, 4.8%; 75 and over 1.0%.
Population projection: (2000) 65,730,000; (2010) 78,567,000.
Doubling time: 26 years.
Ethnic composition (1995): Persian 51%; Azerbaijani 24%; Gīlaki/Mazāndarānī 8%; Kurd 7%; Arab 3%; Lurī 2%; Balochi 2%; other 3%.
Religious affiliation (1994): Muslim 99.1% (Shīʿī 93.4%, Sunnī 5.7%); Bahāʾī 0.6%; Christian 0.1%; Zoroastrian 0.1%; Jewish 0.1%.
Major cities (1994): Tehrān 6,750,043; Mashhad 1,964,489; Eşfahān 1,220,595; Tabriz 1,166,203; Shīrāz 1,042,801; Ahvāz 828,380; Qom 780,453.

Vital statistics

Birth rate per 1,000 population (1996): 33.7 (world avg. 25.0).
Death rate per 1,000 population (1996): 6.6 (world avg. 9.3).
Total fertility rate (avg. births per childbearing woman; 1996): 4.7.
Marriage rate per 1,000 population (1993): 7.9.
Divorce rate per 1,000 population (1993): 0.5.
Life expectancy at birth (1996): male 66.1 years; female 68.7 years.
Major causes of death per 100,000 population (1990)[5]: diseases of the circulatory system 304; accidents and violence 108; malignant neoplasms (cancers) 61; diseases of the respiratory system 48; infectious diseases 34.

National economy

Budget (1996–97). Revenue: Rls 54,369,000,000,000 (oil revenue 51.5%, taxes 19.6%, other 28.9%). Expenditures: Rls 54,619,000,000,000 (current expenditure 58.5%, development expenditure 41.5%).
Public debt (external, outstanding; 1995): U.S.$17,078,000,000.
Tourism (1995–96): receipts U.S.$67,000,000; expenditures U.S.$241,000,000.
Gross national product (1995–96): U.S.$60,792,000,000 (U.S.$1,000 per capita).

Structure of gross domestic product and labour force

	1995–96		1991	
	in value Rls '000,000,000[6]	% of total value[6]	labour force	% of labour force
Agriculture	46,892	25.2	3,205,430	21.7
Petroleum, natural gas	29,069	15.6	100,545	0.7
Other mining	884	0.5		
Manufacturing	25,877	13.9	2,013,724	13.7
Construction	6,346	3.4	1,372,437	9.3
Public utilities	1,854	1.0	129,000	0.9
Transp. and commun.	11,435	6.2	762,178	5.2
Trade, restaurants	27,981	15.0	1,238,305	8.4
Finance, real estate	16,331	8.8	194,686	1.3
Pub. admin., defense	16,832	9.0	3,517,897	23.9
Services	3,283	1.8		
Other	−659[7]	−0.4[7]	2,202,502[8]	14.9[8]
TOTAL	186,125	100.0	14,736,704	100.0

Production (metric tons except as noted). Agriculture, forestry, fishing (1996): wheat 11,200,000, sugar beets 4,000,000, barley 3,000,000, rice 2,300,000, tomatoes 2,150,000, apples 2,000,000, grapes 1,900,000, sugarcane 1,900,000, oranges 1,600,000, onions 1,200,000, dates 795,000, lemons and limes 655,000, corn (maize) 600,000, seed cotton 512,000, pistachios 282,000; livestock (number of live animals) 51,499,000 sheep, 8,492,000 cattle; roundwood (1995) 7,463,000 cu m; fish catch (1995) 368,300. Mining and quarrying (1994–95): gypsum 8,230,000[9]; iron ore (metal content) 4,300,000[10]; copper ore (metal content) 117,900; zinc ore (metal content) 72,900; chromite (metal content) 39,000. Manufacturing (value added in U.S.$'000,000; 1994): iron and steel 890; food products 755; textiles 635; transport equipment 473; electrical machinery 461; bricks, tiles, and cement 451. Energy production (consumption): electricity (kW-hr; 1995–96) 84,969,000,000 (79,128,000,000[10]); coal (metric tons; 1994) 980,000 (1,280,000); crude petroleum (barrels; 1995–96) 1,318,000,000 (343,300,000[10]); petroleum products (metric tons; 1994) 45,500,000 (47,180,000); natural gas (cu m; 1995–96) 39,100,000,000 (39,000,000,000).
Population economically active (1991): total 14,736,704; activity rate 26.4% (participation rates: ages 15–64, 46.8%; female 11.1%; unemployed [1994] 30%).

Price and earnings indexes (1990–91 = 100)

	1990–91	1991–92	1992–93	1993–94	1994–95	1995–96
Consumer price index	100.0	120.7	150.2	184.5	249.3	372.5
Daily earnings index[11]	100.0	113.6	136.9	161.4	200.4	278.2

Household income and expenditure. Average household size (1991): 5.1; income per urban household (1988) Rls 1,339,970 (U.S.$19,536); sources of urban income (1988): wages 37.4%, self-employment 30.5%, other 32.1%; expenditure (1990–91): food, beverages, and tobacco 42.6%[12], housing and energy 24.9%, clothing 11.8%.
Land use (1994): forest 7.0%; pasture 26.9%; agriculture 11.1%; other 55.0%.

Foreign trade

Balance of trade (current prices)

	1990–91	1991–92	1992–93	1993–94	1994–95	1995–96
U.S.$'000,000	+975	−11,016	−10,002	−1,957	+7,633	+6,160
% of total	2.6%	22.8%	20.1%	5.1%	24.4%	20.1%

Imports (1994–95): U.S.$11,795,000,000 (nonelectrical machinery 34.4%, electrical machinery 7.1%, iron and steel 5.9%, grains 5.8%, transportation equipment 5.4%). *Major import sources:* Germany 18.7%; Italy 8.5%; Japan 7.6%; Belgium 5.5%; U.A.E. 5.5%.
Exports (1994–95): U.S.$19,428,000,000 (petroleum and natural gas 75.2%, carpets 11.0%, pistachios 2.0%, iron and steel 1.8%). *Major export destinations:* Japan 15.1%; U.S. 13.9%; U.K. 9.2%; Germany 6.2%; S. Korea 4.8%.

Transport and communications

Transport. Railroads (1995): route length 4,527 mi, 7,286 km; (1993) passenger-km 6,422,000,000; metric ton-km cargo 9,124,000,000. Roads (1995): length 98,200 mi, 158,000 km (paved 59%). Vehicles (1994): passenger cars 1,630,000; trucks and buses 609,000. Merchant marine (1992): vessels (100 gross tons and over) 403; total deadweight tonnage 8,345,269. Air transport (1996)[13]: passenger-km 6,128,000,000; metric ton-km cargo 109,600,000; airports (1996) with scheduled flights 19.

Communications

Medium	date	unit	number	units per 1,000 persons
Daily newspapers	1994	circulation	1,200,000	20
Radio	1996	receivers	13,000,000	213
Television	1995	receivers	7,000,000	117
Telephones	1995	main lines	5,090,400	85
Cellular telephones	1995	subscribers	9,200	0.2
Facsimile machines	1995	units	30,000	0.5

Education and health

Educational attainment (1986). Percentage of population age 25 and over having: no formal schooling 12.8%; secondary education 38.0%; higher 7.8%.
Literacy (1994): total population age 15 and over literate 25,300,000 (72.1%); males literate 14,200,000 (78.4%); females literate 11,100,000 (65.8%).

Education (1994–95)

	schools	teachers	students	student/ teacher ratio
Primary (age 7–11)	61,889	311,531[14]	9,745,600	31.7[14]
Secondary (age 12–18)	30,389[14]	228,869	7,284,611	31.8
Voc., teacher tr.		20,418	368,218	18.0
Higher		36,366	478,455	13.2

Health (1995): physicians (1994) 37,000 (1 per 1,600 persons); hospital beds 93,000 (1 per 650 persons); infant mortality rate (1996) 52.7.
Food (1995): daily per capita caloric intake 2,955 (vegetable products 91%, animal products 9%); 123% of FAO recommended minimum requirement.

Military

Total active duty personnel (1996): 513,000 (revolutionary guard corps 23.4%, army 67.3%, navy 3.5%, air force 5.8%). *Military expenditure as percentage of GNP* (1995): 2.6% (world 2.8%); per capita expenditure U.S.$65.

[1]Not required to be a supreme theological authority. [2]Fixed rate. [3]Tehrān province includes Qazvīn and Zanjān provinces. Qazvīn province was created in January 1997 from part of Zanjān province. [4]De jure estimate excluding refugees. [5]Projected rates based on about 20% of total deaths. [6]At factor cost. [7]Less imputed bank service charge. [8]Includes 1,640,092 unemployed. [9]1995. [10]1994. [11]Construction sector only. [12]Includes café and hotel expenditures. [13]Iran Air. [14]1993–94.

Internet resources for further information:
- **Islamic Republic News Agency http://www.irna.co.uk/**

Iraq

Official name: Al-Jumhūrīyah al-ʿIrāqīyah (Republic of Iraq).
Form of government: unitary multiparty[1] republic with one legislative house (National Assembly [220[2]]).
Head of state and government: President.
Capital: Baghdad.
Official language: Arabic[3].
Official religion: Islam.
Monetary unit: 1 Iraqi dinar (ID) = 20 dirhams = 1,000 fils; valuation (Oct. 3, 1997) 1 U.S.$ = 1,200 ID[4]; 1 £ = 1,934 ID[4].

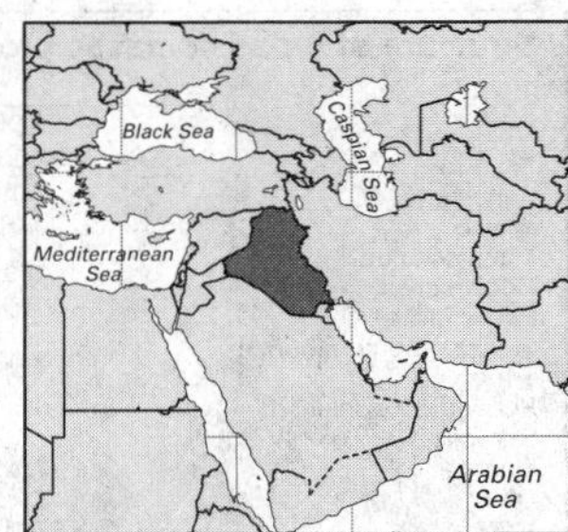

Area and population		area[5]		population
				1991
Governorates	Capitals	sq mi	sq km	estimate
Al-Anbār	Ar-Ramādī	53,208	137,808	865,500
Bābil	Al-Ḥillah	2,163	5,603	1,221,100
Baghdād	Baghdad	1,572	4,071	3,910,900
Al-Baṣrah[5]	Basra	7,363	19,070	1,168,800
Dhī Qār	An-Nāṣirīyah	4,981	12,900	1,030,900
Diyālā	Baʿqūbah	6,828	17,685	1,037,600
Karbalāʾ	Karbalāʾ	1,944	5,034	567,600
Maysān	Al-ʿAmārah	6,205	16,072	524,200
Al-Muthannā	As-Samāwah	19,977	51,740	350,000
An-Najaf	An-Najaf	11,129	28,824	666,400
Nīnawā	Mosul	14,410	37,323	1,618,700
Al-Qādisiyah	Ad-Dīwānīyah	3,148	8,153	595,600
Ṣalāḥ ad-Dīn	Tikrīt	9,407	24,363	772,200
At-Taʾmīm	Karkūk (Kirkūk)	3,737	9,679	605,900
Wāsiṭ	Al-Kūt	6,623	17,153	605,700
Kurdish Autonomous Region[6]				
Dahūk	Dahūk	2,530	6,553	309,300
Irbīl	Irbīl	5,820	15,074	928,400
As-Sulaymānīyah	As-Sulaymānīyah	6,573	17,023	1,124,200
LAND AREA		167,618	434,128	
OTHER[7]		357	924	
TOTAL		167,975	435,052	17,903,000

Demography

Population (1997): 22,219,000[8].
Density (1997): persons per sq mi 132.3, persons per sq km 51.1.
Urban-rural (1997): urban 68.1%; rural 31.9%.
Sex distribution (1996): male 51.23%; female 48.77%.
Age breakdown (1994): under 15, 41.1%; 15–29, 30.5%; 30–44, 16.0%; 45–59, 7.6%; 60–74, 3.7%; 75 and over, 1.1%.
Population projection: (2000) 24,731,000; (2010) 34,545,000.
Doubling time: 29 years.
Ethnic composition (1983): Arab 77.1%; Kurd 19.0%; Azerbaijani 1.7%; Assyrian 0.8%; other 1.4%.
Religious affiliation (1994): Shīʿī Muslim 62.5%; Sunnī Muslim 34.5%; Christian (primarily Chaldean rite and Syrian rite Roman Catholic and Nestorian) 2.7%; other (primarily Yazīdī syncretist) 0.3%.
Major cities (1987): Baghdad (1995; urban agglomeration) 4,478,000; Mosul 664,221; Irbīl 485,968; Karkūk (Kirkūk) 418,624; Al-Baṣrah 406,296.

Vital statistics

Birth rate per 1,000 population (1994): 34.1 (world avg. 26.0).
Death rate per 1,000 population (1994): 9.8 (world avg. 9.2).
Natural increase rate per 1,000 population (1994): 24.3 (world avg. 16.8).
Total fertility rate (avg. births per childbearing woman; 1996): 4.9.
Marriage rate per 1,000 population (1992): 7.8.
Life expectancy at birth (1994): male 57.3 years; female 60.4 years.
Major causes of death. Prior to the Gulf War (1990) the leading causes (in descending order) were: circulatory diseases, injury and poisoning, cancer, and congenital anomalies; since 1990, additional mortality has been attributed to deprivation of medical care and malnutrition consequent upon the imposition of UN sanctions, especially among children and other vulnerable populations.

National economy

Budget (1992). Revenue: ID 13,935,000,000. Expenditures: ID 13,935,000,000. Details of more recent budgets are not available.
Public debt (external, outstanding; 1994): U.S.$20,000,000,000.
Production (metric tons except as noted). Agriculture, forestry, fishing (1996): wheat 1,000,000, clover 820,000, tomatoes 800,000, dates 550,000, barley 500,000, potatoes 380,000, oranges 310,000, grapes 300,000, rice 270,000; livestock (number of live animals) 5,000,000 sheep, 1,000,000 cattle; roundwood (1995) 161,000 cu m; fish catch (1995) 22,550. Mining and quarrying (1995): sulfur 475,000; phosphate rock 440,000. Manufacturing (value added in U.S.$'000,000; 1994): refined petroleum 127; bricks, tiles, and cement 100; industrial chemicals 79; food products 59; metal products 28. Construction (authorized; 1991): residential 4,558,000 sq m; nonresidential 410,000 sq m. Energy production (consumption): electricity (kW-hr; 1994) 27,060,000,000 (27,060,000,000); coal, none (none); crude petroleum (barrels; 1996) 255,500,000 ([1994] 207,200,000); petroleum products (metric tons; 1994) 22,180,000 (21,215,000); natural gas (cu m; 1994) 3,170,000,000 (3,170,000,000).
Household income and expenditure (1988). Average household size 8.9; sources of income: self-employment 33.9%, wages and salaries 23.9%, transfers 23.0%, rent 18.6%; expenditure: food and beverages 50.2%, housing and energy 19.9%, clothing and footwear 10.6%.
Gross domestic product (1996): U.S.$11,500,000,000 (U.S.$540 per capita).

Structure of gross domestic product and labour force	1992		1988	
	in value ID '000,000[9]	% of total value	labour force	% of labour force
Agriculture	20,844	35.1	477,264	11.6
Mining	230	0.4	60,701	1.5
Manufacturing	5,620	9.5	337,293	8.2
Construction	2,259	3.8	460,788	11.2
Public utilities	181	0.3	41,200	1.0
Transp. and commun.	5,947	10.0	266,233	6.4
Trade	15,190	25.6	281,877	6.8
Finance, real estate	4,692	7.9	41,532	1.0
Pub. admin., defense, and services	7,209	12.2	2,160,406	52.3
Other	−2,824	−4.8		
TOTAL	59,348	100.0	4,127,294	100.0

Population economically active (1988): total 4,127,294; activity rate of total population 24.7% (participation rates: ages 15–64, 45.3%; female 12.0%).

Price index (1990 = 100)	1990	1991	1992	1993	1994	1995	1996
Consumer price index	100.0	287	860[10]	2,600[10]	10,000[10]	50,000[10]	275,000[10]

Tourism (1994): receipts U.S.$12,000,000; expenditures, n.a.
Land use (1994): forest 0.4%; pasture 9.1%; agriculture 13.1%; other 77.4%.

Foreign trade[11, 12]

Balance of trade (current prices)	1990[10]	1991[10]	1992[10]	1993[10]	1994[10]	1995[10]
U.S.$'000,000	+5,587	−1,633	−2,199	−1,956	−1,518	−2,081
% of total	36.6%	66.3%	73.3%	68.8%	66.5%	71.3%

Imports (1995): U.S.$2,500,000,000[10] (agricultural products 42.7%, of which cereals 9.9%; unspecified 57.3%). *Major import sources*[13]: Jordan 49.0%; Turkey 17.0%; Hungary 15.0%; Switzerland 8.0%.
Exports (1995): U.S.$419,000,000[10] (mostly crude petroleum and petroleum products). *Major export destinations:* Jordan 98.0%.

Transport and communications

Transport. Railroads (1995): route length 2,032 km; (1993) passenger-km 1,566,000,000; (1993) metric ton-km cargo 1,649,000,000. Roads (1995): total length 46,500 km (paved 86%). Vehicles (1995): passenger cars 672,000; trucks and buses 368,000. Air transport: [14].

Communications				units
Medium	date	unit	number	per 1,000 persons
Daily newspapers	1994	circulation	532,000	27
Radio	1996	receivers	3,700,000	167
Television	1995	receivers	1,000,000	48
Telephones	1995	main lines	675,000	33

Education and health

Educational attainment (1987). Percentage of population age 10 and over having: no formal schooling 52.8%; primary education 21.5%; secondary 11.6%; higher 4.1%; unknown 10.0%. *Literacy* (1995): total population age 15 and over literate 58.0%; males 70.7%; females 45.0%.

Education (1994–95)	schools	teachers	students	student/ teacher ratio
Primary (age 6–11)	8,035	132,030	2,977,800	22.6
Secondary (age 12–17)	2,635	48,961	1,062,204	21.7
Voc., teacher tr.	310	9,903	135,711	13.7
Higher	12	11,847	201,984	17.0

Health (1993): physicians 8,787 (1 per 2,181 persons); hospital beds 27,202 (1 per 704 persons); infant mortality rate per 1,000 live births (1994) 91.9.
Food (1995): daily per capita caloric intake 2,268 (vegetable products 96%, animal products 4%); 94% of FAO recommended minimum requirement.

Military

Total active duty personnel (1997): 387,500 (army 90.3%, navy 0.7%, air force 9.0%). *Military expenditure as percentage of GDP* (1994): 18.0%[10] (world, n.a.); per capita expenditure U.S.$136.

[1]Multipartyism is officially authorized, but political power is in fact concentrated in a single-party apparatus. [2]Elective seats as of March 1996 elections; 30 additional seats allotted to the Kurdish Autonomous Region were filled by presidential appointment. [3]Kurdish is official in the Kurdish Autonomous Region only. [4]Exchange bureau (semi-official) rate. [5]Includes territory ceded to Kuwait as of Jan. 15, 1993. [6]De facto self-government between 1992 and 1996. Iraqi sovereignty over some of the area was reasserted in late 1996. [7]Territorial water at the mouth of the Shaṭṭ al-ʿArab. [8]Census population of Oct. 16, 1997, as cited on Oct. 17, 1997, equaled 22,017,983. [9]At factor cost. [10]Estimated figure(s). [11]Imports c.i.f.; exports f.o.b. [12]UN-imposed trade sanctions in place from August 1990 through October 1997. [13]Based on estimated imports equaling U.S.$608,000,000. [14]No scheduled air service since June 1992.

Internet resources for further information:
- **Permanent Mission of Iraq to the United Nations (official site) http://www.undp.org/missions/iraq**
- **Iraq Foundation (unofficial) http://www.iraqfoundation.org/**

Ireland

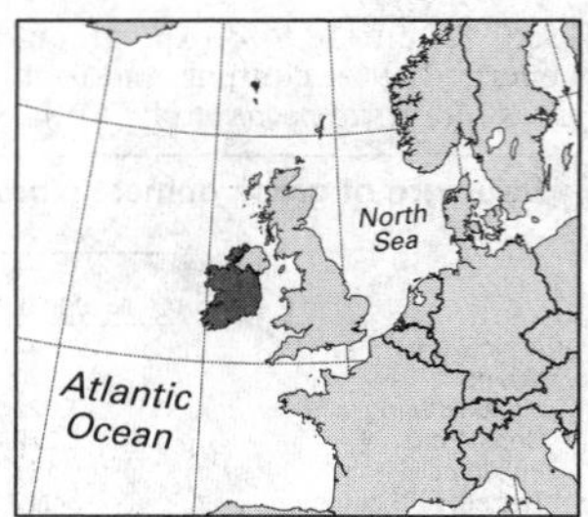

Official name: Éire (Irish); Ireland[1] (English).
Form of government: unitary multi-party republic with two legislative houses (Senate [60[2]]; House of Representatives [166]).
Chief of state: President.
Head of government: Prime Minister.
Capital: Dublin.
Official languages: Irish; English.
Official religion: none.
Monetary unit: 1 Irish pound (£Ir) = 100 new pence; valuation (Oct. 3, 1997) 1 £Ir = U.S.$1.44 = £1.11.

Area and population

Provinces / Counties	area sq mi	area sq km	population 1996 census
Connacht	6,611	17,122	433,000
Galway[3]	2,293	5,940	189,000
Leitrim	581	1,525	25,000
Mayo	2,084	5,398	111,000
Roscommon	951	2,463	52,000
Sligo	693	1,796	56,000
Leinster	7,580	19,633	1,922,000[4]
Carlow	346	896	42,000
Dublin[5]	356	922	1,057,000
Kildare	654	1,694	135,000
Kilkenny	796	2,062	75,000
Laoighis	664	1,719	53,000
Longford	403	1,044	30,000
Louth	318	823	92,000
Meath	902	2,336	109,000
Offaly	771	1,998	59,000
Westmeath	681	1,763	63,000
Wexford	908	2,351	104,000
Wicklow	782	2,025	102,000
Munster	9,315	24,127	1,033,000
Clare	1,231	3,188	94,000
Cork[3]	2,880	7,460	420,000
Kerry	1,815	4,701	126,000
Limerick[3]	1,037	2,686	165,000
Tipperary North Riding	771	1,996	58,000
Tipperary South Riding	872	2,258	75,000
Waterford[3]	710	1,838	95,000
Ulster (part of)	3,093	8,012	234,000[4]
Cavan	730	1,891	53,000
Donegal	1,865	4,830	129,000
Monaghan	498	1,291	51,000
TOTAL LAND AREA	26,600	68,895[4]	
INLAND WATER	537	1,390	
TOTAL	27,137	70,285	3,622,000

Demography

Population (1997): 3,644,000.
Density (1997): persons per sq mi 134.3, persons per sq km 51.8.
Urban-rural (1996): urban 58.0%; rural 42.0%.
Sex distribution (1996): male 49.64%; female 50.36%.
Age breakdown (1996): under 15, 23.7%; 15–24, 17.5%; 25–44, 28.0%; 45–59, 15.6%; 60–74, 12.3%; 75 and over, 2.9%.
Population projection: (2000) 3,702,000; (2010) 3,904,000.
Religious affiliation (1991): Roman Catholic 91.6%; Church of Ireland (Anglican) 2.3%; Presbyterian 0.4%; other 5.7%.
Major cities (1996)[6]: Dublin 480,996; Cork 127,092; Galway 57,095.

Vital statistics

Birth rate per 1,000 population (1996): 13.9 (world avg. 26.0).
Death rate per 1,000 population (1996): 8.7 (world avg. 9.2).
Natural increase rate per 1,000 population (1996): 5.2 (world avg. 16.8).
Total fertility rate (avg. births per childbearing woman; 1994): 1.8.
Life expectancy at birth (1990–92): male 72.3 years; female 77.9 years.
Major causes of death per 100,000 population (1996): heart and circulatory diseases 385.2, of which ischemic heart disease 210.0; malignant neoplasms (cancers) 201.8; respiratory disease 131.6, of which pneumonia 62.7.

National economy

Budget (1997). Revenue: £Ir 13,584,100,000 (income taxes 36.3%, value-added tax 25.5%, excise taxes 18.2%). Expenditures: £Ir 14,996,000,000 (social welfare 30.6%, health 16.5%, debt service 15.2%, education 14.7%).
Public debt (1995): U.S.$48,449,000,000.
Tourism (1995): receipts U.S.$2,688,000,000; expenditures U.S.$2,030,000,000.
Production (metric tons except as noted). Agriculture, forestry, fishing (1996): sugar beets 1,485,000, barley 1,225,000, wheat 771,000, potatoes 733,000, oats 146,000, milk 51,900,000[7] hectolitres; livestock (number of live animals)[8] 7,934,000 sheep, 7,423,000 cattle, 1,620,000 pigs; roundwood (1995) 2,204,000 cu m; fish catch (1995) 412,722. Mining and quarrying (1994): gypsum 367,300; zinc ore 194,000[9]; lead ore 53,700[9]. Manufacturing (value added in £Ir; 1990): metals and engineering goods 3,237,500,000; food products 1,828,300,000; chemical products 1,492,600,000. Construction (1996): residential 4,167,000 sq m; nonresidential 3,531,000 sq m. Energy production (consumption): electricity (kW-hr; 1994) 17,105,000,000 (17,105,000,000); coal (metric tons; 1994) 1,000 (2,695,000); crude petroleum (barrels; 1994) none (16,764,000); petroleum products (metric tons; 1994) 2,213,000 (4,879,000); natural gas (cu m; 1994) 2,565,000,000 (2,565,000,000).
Gross national product (1995): U.S.$52,765,000,000 (U.S.$14,710 per capita).

Structure of gross domestic product and labour force

	1996			
	in value £Ir '000,000[10]	% of total value	labour force	% of labour force
Agriculture	2,858	7.5	136,000	9.2
Mining			5,000	0.3
Manufacturing	14,480	38.4	246,000	16.7
Construction			86,000	5.8
Public utilities			14,000	0.9
Transp. and commun.	6,749	17.9	80,000	5.4
Trade			273,000[11]	18.5[11]
Pub. admin., defense	1,931	5.1	76,000	5.2
Services			369,000	25.0
Finance	11,729	31.1	[11]	[11]
Other			191,000[12]	13.0[12]
TOTAL	37,747	100.0	1,475,000	100.0

Population economically active (1996): total 1,475,000; activity rate 40.7% (participation rates: ages 15–64, 59.2%[13]; unemployed 11.9%[14]).

Price and earnings indexes (1990 = 100)

	1990	1991	1992	1993	1994	1995	1996
Consumer price index	100.0	103.2	106.4	107.9	110.4	113.2	115.1
Weekly earnings index	100.0	104.4	108.6	114.4	117.8	120.5	123.1[15]

Household income and expenditure. Average household size (1996) 3.3; income per household (1994–95): £Ir 16,224 (U.S.$25,100); expenditure (1996)[16]: food 22.8%, transportation 13.9%, rent and household goods 11.6%.

Foreign trade[17]

Balance of trade (current prices)

	1991	1992	1993	1994	1995	1996
£Ir '000,000	2,168	3,549	4,945	5,470	7,206	7,750
% of total	7.7%	11.8%	14.2%	13.7%	14.9%	14.8%

Imports (1995): £Ir 20,347,300,000 (machinery and transport equipment 42.4%, chemicals 12.9%, manufactured goods 11.5%, food 7.2%, petroleum and petroleum products 3.3%, crude materials [inedible] 2.0%, beverages and tobacco 1.0%). *Major import sources:* U.K. 35.5%; U.S. 17.5%; Germany 7.1%; Japan 5.2%; Singapore 4.0%; France 3.8%; The Netherlands 2.7%.
Exports (1995): £Ir 27,680,900,000 (machinery and transport equipment 34.6%, chemical products 18.8%, food 17.5%, manufactured goods 4.8%). *Major export destinations:* U.K. 25.7%; Germany 14.4%; France 9.4%; U.S. 8.2%.

Transport and communications

Transport. Railroads (1995): route length 1,947 km; passenger-km 1,331,900,000; metric ton-km cargo 573,000,000. Roads (1995): length 92,340 km (paved 94%). Vehicles (1995): passenger cars 990,384; trucks and buses 155,153. Air transport (1996)[18]: passenger-km 5,126,177,000; metric ton-km cargo 102,055,000; airports (1996) 9.

Communications

Medium	date	unit	number	units per 1,000 persons
Daily newspapers	1996	circulation	542,000	151
Radio	1996	receivers	2,150,000	597
Television	1995	receivers	1,000,000	279
Telephones	1996	main lines	1,341,719	373
Cellular telephones	1995	subscribers	158,000	44
Facsimile machines	1995	units	80,000	22
Personal computers	1995	units	520,000	145

Education and health

Educational attainment (1991). Percentage of population age 15 and over having: primary education or no schooling 33.7%; secondary 42.7%; some postsecondary 12.6%; university or like institution 11.0%.

Education (1994–95)

	schools	teachers	students	student/ teacher ratio
Primary (age 6–11)[19]	3,319	20,901	491,256	23.5
Secondary (age 12–18)	452	12,635	225,490	17.8
Voc., teacher tr.	327	8,019	146,050	18.2
Higher	29	4,889	88,925	18.2

Health: physicians (1984) 5,180 (1 per 681 persons); hospital beds (1994) 11,853[20] (1 per 301 persons); infant mortality rate (1994) 5.9.
Food (1995): daily per capita caloric intake 3,638 (vegetable products 69%, animal products 39%); 145% of FAO recommended minimum requirement.

Military

Total active duty personnel (1995): 12,900 (army 84.5%, navy 7.7%, air force 7.8%). *Military expenditure as percentage of GNP* (1995): 1.3% (world 2.8%); per capita expenditure U.S.$193.

[1]As provided by the constitution; the 1948 Republic of Ireland Act provides precedent for this longer formulation of the official name but, per official sources, "has not changed the usage *Ireland* as the name of the state in the English language." [2]Includes 11 nonelective seats. [3]Includes county borough(s). [4]Detail does not add to total given because of rounding. [5]Includes the three county councils of Dun Laoghaire–Rathdown, Fingal, and South Dublin. Established Jan. 1, 1994. [6]County boroughs. [7]1995. [8]June. [9]Metal content of ores. [10]At factor cost. [11]Trade includes Finance. [12]Unemployed. [13]1988. [14]April. [15]2nd quarter. [16]November. [17]Import figures are c.i.f. in balance of trade. [18]Aer Lingus only. [19]National schools only. [20]Acute-care public hospitals only.

Internet resources for further information:

- **Central Statistics Office (Ireland) http://www.cso.ie/index.html**

Israel

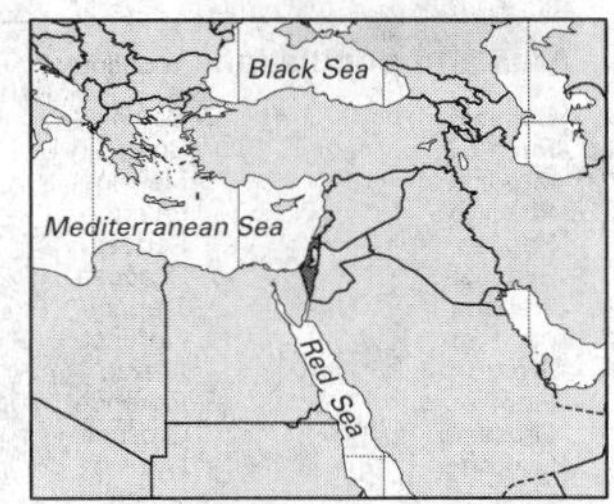

Official name: Medinat Yisra'el (Hebrew); Isrā'īl (Arabic) (State of Israel).
Form of government: multiparty republic with one legislative house (Knesset [120]).
Chief of state: President.
Head of government: Prime Minister.
Capital: Jerusalem is the proclaimed capital of Israel and the actual seat of government, but recognition of its status as capital by the international community has largely been withheld pending final settlement of territorial and other issues through peace talks between Israel and the Arab parties concerned.
Official languages: Hebrew; Arabic.
Official religion: none.
Monetary unit: 1 New (Israeli) sheqel (NIS) = 100 agorot; valuation (Oct. 3, 1997) 1 U.S.$ = NIS 3.50; 1 £ = NIS 5.64.

Area and population

Districts	Capitals	area[1] sq mi	area[1] sq km	population 1996[2] estimate
Central (Ha Merkaz)	Ramla	479	1,242	1,213,200
Haifa (Hefa)	Haifa	330	854	740,300
Jerusalem (Yerushalayim)	Jerusalem	240	622	662,700
Northern (Ha Zafon)	Tiberias	1,284	3,325	952,100
Southern (Ha Darom)	Beersheba	5,447	14,107	770,200
Tel Aviv	Tel Aviv–Yafo	66	170	1,141,900
TOTAL		7,846	20,320	5,480,400[3, 4]

Demography

Population (1997): 5,652,000[3, 4].
Density (1997)[3, 4]: persons per sq mi 720.4, persons per sq km 278.1.
Urban-rural (1996)[2]: urban 91.0%; rural 9.0%.
Sex distribution (1997): male 49.68%; female 50.32%.
Age breakdown (1997): under 15, 28.4%; 15–29, 25.2%; 30–44, 19.7%; 45–59, 13.7%; 60–74, 8.8%; 75 and over, 4.2%.
Population projection: (2000) 5,717,000; (2010) 6,403,000.
Ethnic composition (1997): Jewish 80.5%; Arab and other 19.5%.
Religious affiliation (1997): Jewish 80.5%; Muslim (mostly Sunnī) 14.6%; Christian 3.2%; Druze 1.7%.
Major cities (1997): Jerusalem 602,100; Tel Aviv–Yafo 353,100; Haifa 255,300; Rishon LeZiyyon 171,100; Holon 163,900; Petah Tiqwa 154,500.

Vital statistics

Birth rate per 1,000 population (1997): 20.0 (world avg. 25.0); (1994)[5] legitimate 98.2%; illegitimate 1.8%.
Death rate per 1,000 population (1997): 6.0 (world avg. 9.3).
Natural increase rate per 1,000 population (1997): 14.0 (world avg. 15.7).
Total fertility rate (avg. births per childbearing woman; 1997): 2.7.
Marriage rate per 1,000 population (1996): 6.7.
Divorce rate per 1,000 population (1996): 1.7.
Life expectancy at birth (1997): male 76.3 years; female 80.2 years.
Major causes of death per 100,000 population (1994): heart diseases 211.3; cancers 140.5; cerebrovascular diseases 59.5; accidents 25.5.

National economy

Budget (1998). Revenue: NIS 156,800,000,000 (1996; income tax, property tax, and land improvement tax 39.0%, value-added tax 28.0%, sales tax and fuel tax 9.5%, royalties and interest 2.7%). Expenditures: NIS 164,400,000,000 (1996; defense 22.3%, labour and social welfare 16.8%, education and culture 16.2%, interest on loans 16.2%).
Public debt (1994): U.S.$71,069,000,000.
Gross national product (1995): U.S.$87,875,000,000 (U.S.$15,920 per capita).

Structure of gross domestic product and labour force

	1993		1996	
	in value NIS '000,000	% of total value	labour force	% of labour force
Agriculture	3,197	2.4	51,000	2.4
Manufacturing, mining	29,007	21.5	405,100	18.8
Construction	9,678	7.2	150,000	6.9
Public utilities	2,263	1.7	18,500	0.9
Transp. and commun.	10,238	7.6	124,300	5.8
Trade	15,581	11.6	331,200	15.3
Finance	34,906	25.9	261,200[6]	12.1[6]
Public and community services	5,683	4.2	625,800[7]	29.0[7]
Services	30,482	22.6	33,800[8]	1.6[8]
Other	−6,368[9]	−4.7[9]	156,100[10]	7.2[10]
TOTAL	134,667	100.0	2,157,000	100.0

Production (metric tons except as noted). Agriculture, forestry, fishing (1997): watermelons 450,000, tomatoes 440,000, grapefruit 390,000, potatoes 260,000, wheat 140,000, seed cotton 131,000; livestock (number of live animals) 410,000 cattle, 340,000 sheep, 94,000 goats, 23,000,000 chickens; roundwood (1995) 113,000 cu m; fish catch (1995) 20,564. Mining and quarrying (1996): phosphate rock 2,450,000, potash 2,500,000. Manufacturing (1996): cement 6,723,000; polyethylene 144,147[11]; sulfuric acid 130,000[11]; cardboard 113,278; paper 114,403; chlorine 34,630; wine 12,733,000 litres[11]. Construction (1996): residential 7,010,000 sq m; nonresidential 2,380,000 sq m. Energy production (consumption): electricity (kW-hr; 1994) 28,315,000 (27,985,000); coal (metric tons; 1994) none (6,026,000); crude petroleum (barrels; 1994) 29,000 (88,682,000); petroleum products (metric tons; 1994) 10,589,000 (8,122,000); natural gas (cu m; 1994) 22,025,000 (22,025,000).
Population economically active (1996)[12]: total 2,157,000; activity rate 38.9% (participation rates: over age 15, 53.7%; female 43.5%; unemployed 6.7%).

Price and earnings indexes (1990 = 100)

	1991	1992	1993	1994	1995	1996	1997[13]
Consumer price index	119.0	133.2	147.8	166.0	182.7	203.3	222.0
Daily earnings index	112.8	125.9	140.6	155.6	178.5	203.3	229.8

Household income and expenditure (1996). Average household size 3.6; monthly income per household[14, 15] NIS 6,125 (U.S.$2,034); sources of income (1993)[14]: salaries and wages 63.4%, allowances and assistance 18.9%, self-employment 14.6%, other 3.1%; expenditure (1996): housing 22.6%, food, beverages, and tobacco 21.8%, household durable goods 7.3%, clothing, footwear, and personal goods 5.9%, transportation 4.1%, energy 4.0%.
Tourism (1995): receipts U.S.$2,784,000,000; expenditures U.S.$3,148,000,000.

Foreign trade[16]

Balance of trade (current prices)

	1991	1992	1993	1994	1995	1996
U.S.$'000,000	−5,000.7	−5,654.8	−5,656.4	−6,695.4	−9,239.7	−9,438.8
% of total	17.4%	17.7%	16.0%	16.4%	19.5%	18.7%

Imports (1996): U.S.$29,949,000,000 (investment goods 17.7%; diamonds 14.1%; consumer goods 13.2%; fuel and lubricants 7.1%). *Major import sources:* U.S. 20.0%; Belgium 12.1%; Germany 9.4%; U.K. 8.8%; Italy 7.6%.
Exports (1996): U.S.$20,510,200,000 (machinery and transport equipment 29.5%; diamonds 25.6%; chemicals 11.8%; apparel 4.9%; food, beverages, and tobacco 3.9%; rubber and plastic 3.9%). *Major export destinations:* U.S. 30.6%; U.K. 6.7%; Japan 5.9%; Belgium 5.4%; Hong Kong 5.2%.

Transport and communications

Transport. Railroads (1996): route length 610 km; passenger-km 267,000,000[13]; metric ton-km cargo 1,176,000,000[13]. Roads (1995): total length 14,700 km (paved 100%). Vehicles (1997): passenger cars 1,174,000; trucks and buses 272,000. Merchant marine (1992): vessels (100 gross tons and over) 58; total deadweight tonnage 723,418. Air transport (1996)[17]: passenger-km 11,511,000,000; metric ton-km cargo 1,113,000,000; airports (1997) with scheduled flights 7.

Communications

Medium	date	unit	number	units per 1,000 persons
Daily newspapers	1995	circulation	1,500,000	271.0
Radio	1995	receivers	2,700,000	489.0
Television	1995	receivers	1,600,000	290.0
Telephones	1995	main lines	2,342,600	417.7
Cellular telephones	1995	subscribers	300,000	53.5
Facsimile machines	1995	units	140,000	25.0
Personal computers	1995	units	560,000	99.8

Education and health

Educational attainment (1991). Percentage of population age 25 and over having: no formal schooling 6.7%; primary 22.5%; secondary 39.6%; post-secondary, vocational, and higher 31.2%. *Literacy* (1995): total population age 15 and over literate 95.6%; males literate 97.7%; females literate 93.6%.

Education (1996–97)

	schools[18]	teachers	students	student/ teacher ratio
Primary (age 6–13)	1,937	57,618[18]	691,800	...
Secondary (age 14–17)[19]	797	39,093[20]	478,900	...
Vocational, teacher tr.	435	17,141[20]	142,900	...
Higher	7	7,829[21]	101,700[22]	...

Health (1997): physicians (1996) 27,000 (1 per 206 persons); hospital beds 34,200 (1 per 165 persons); infant mortality rate per 1,000 live births 8.0.
Food (1995): daily per capita caloric intake 3,271 (vegetable products 81%, animal products 19%); 127% of FAO recommended minimum.

Military

Total active duty personnel (1997): 175,000 (army 76.6%, navy 5.1%, air force 18.3%). *Military expenditure as percentage of GNP* (1995): 9.6% (world 2.8%); per capita expenditure U.S.$1,646.

[1]Excluding West Bank (2,270 sq mi [5,879 sq km]), Gaza Strip (146 sq mi [378 sq km]), Golan Heights (454 sq mi [1,176 sq km]), and East Jerusalem (27 sq mi [70 sq km]). [2]January 1. [3]Includes population of Golan Heights (31,500) and East Jerusalem. [4]Excludes Israelis in Jewish localities (pop. 138,600) in the West Bank and Gaza Strip. [5]Jewish population only. [6]Finance includes other business activities. [7]Public and community services includes education, health, social, and personal services. [8]Services includes private households with domestic personnel. [9]Includes statistical discrepancies less imputed bank service charges. [10]Includes 144,200 unemployed. [11]1993. [12]Excludes armed forces; includes Israelis in occupied territories. [13]June. [14]Urban population only. [15]1995. [16]Figures are gross for net imports and exports. [17]El Al only. [18]1995–96. [19]Includes intermediate schools. [20]1992–93. [21]1994–95. [22]1995–96.

Internet resources for further information:
- **Central Bureau of Statistics (Israel) http://www.cbs.gov.il**
- **Facts about Israel http://www.israel-mfa.gov.il/facts/index.html**

Italy

Official name: Repubblica Italiana (Italian Republic).
Form of government: republic with two legislative houses (Senate [325[1]]; Chamber of Deputies [630]).
Chief of state: President.
Head of government: Prime Minister.
Capital: Rome.
Official language: Italian.
Official religion: none.
Monetary unit: 1 lira (Lit, plural lire) = 100 centesimi; valuation (Oct. 3, 1997) 1 U.S.$ = Lit 1,726; 1 £ = Lit 2,783.

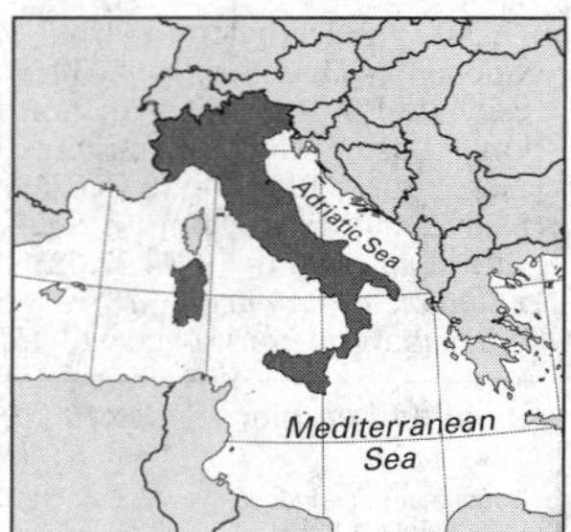

Area and population

Regions / Provinces[3]	Capitals	area sq mi	area sq km	population 1996[2] estimate[4]
Abruzzi	L'Aquila	4,168	10,794	1,270,591
Chieti	Chieti	999	2,587	388,276
L'Aquila	L'Aquila	1,944	5,034	303,879
Pescara	Pescara	473	1,225	292,202
Teramo	Teramo	752	1,948	286,234
Basilicata	Potenza	3,858	9,992	609,238
Matera	Matera	1,331	3,447	208,154
Potenza	Potenza	2,527	6,545	401,084
Calabria	Catanzaro	5,823	15,080	2,075,842
Catanzaro	Catanzaro	924	2,392	384,496
Cosenza	Cosenza	2,568	6,650	753,815
Crotone	Crotone	662	1,716	179,336
Reggio di Calabria	Reggio di Calabria	1,229	3,183	579,009
Vibo Valentia	Vibo Valentia	440	1,139	179,186
Campania	Naples	5,249	13,595	5,762,518
Avellino	Avellino	1,078	2,792	441,675
Benevento	Benevento	800	2,071	295,803
Caserta	Caserta	1,019	2,639	840,737
Napoli	Naples	452	1,171	3,098,397
Salerno	Salerno	1,900	4,922	1,085,906
Emilia-Romagna	Bologna	8,542	22,123	3,924,456
Bologna	Bologna	1,429	3,702	905,838
Ferrara	Ferrara	1,016	2,632	355,341
Forlì-Cesena	Forlì	969	2,510	350,158
Modena	Modena	1,039	2,690	609,723
Parma	Parma	1,332	3,449	392,018
Piacenza	Piacenza	1,000	2,589	266,363
Ravenna	Ravenna	718	1,859	349,992
Reggio nell'Emilia	Reggio nell'Emilia	885	2,292	429,865
Rimini	Rimini	154	400	265,158
Friuli-Venezia Giulia	Trieste	3,029	7,845	1,188,897
Gorizia	Gorizia	180	467	138,041
Pordenone	Pordenone	878	2,273	276,010
Trieste	Trieste	82	212	254,746
Udine	Udine	1,889	4,893	520,100
Lazio	Rome	6,642	17,203	5,202,098
Frosinone	Frosinone	1,251	3,239	489,923
Latina	Latina	869	2,251	497,632
Rieti	Rieti	1,061	2,749	150,305
Roma	Rome	2,066	5,352	3,774,987
Viterbo	Viterbo	1,395	3,612	289,251
Liguria	Genoa	2,092	5,418	1,658,513
Genova	Genoa	709	1,836	933,127
Imperia	Imperia	446	1,155	216,996
La Spezia	La Spezia	341	882	225,285
Savona	Savona	596	1,545	283,105
Lombardia	Milan	9,211	23,857	8,924,870
Bergamo	Bergamo	1,051	2,722	936,667
Brescia	Brescia	1,846	4,782	1,065,172
Como	Como	497	1,288	531,160
Cremona	Cremona	684	1,771	330,946
Lecco	Lecco	315	816	302,575
Lodi	Lodi	302	783	190,196
Mantova	Mantova	903	2,339	368,725
Milano	Milan	765	1,980	3,720,534
Pavia	Pavia	1,145	2,965	494,640
Sondrio	Sondrio	1,240	3,212	177,079
Varese	Varese	463	1,199	807,176
Marche	Ancona	3,743	9,693	1,443,172
Ancona	Ancona	749	1,940	440,239
Ascoli Piceno	Ascoli Piceno	806	2,087	365,826
Macerata	Macerata	1,071	2,774	298,295
Pesaro e Urbino	Pesaro	1,117	2,892	338,812
Molise	Campobasso	1,713	4,438	331,446
Campobasso	Campobasso	1,123	2,909	239,227
Isernia	Isernia	590	1,529	92,219
Piemonte	Turin	9,807[5]	25,399	4,288,866
Alessandria	Alessandria	1,375	3,560	433,300
Asti	Asti	583	1,511	209,798
Biella	Biella	352	913	190,728
Cuneo	Cuneo	2,665	6,903	551,373
Novara	Novara	530	1,373	339,375
Torino	Turin	2,637	6,830	2,220,724
Verbano-Cusio-Ossola	Verbania	858	2,221	161,248
Vercelli	Vercelli	806	2,088	182,320
Puglia	Bari	7,470	19,348	4,082,953
Bari	Bari	1,980	5,129	1,560,347
Brindisi	Brindisi	710	1,838	413,334
Foggia	Foggia	2,774	7,185	699,214
Lecce	Lecce	1,065	2,759	817,524
Taranto	Taranto	941	2,437	592,534
Sardegna	Cagliari	9,301	24,090	1,660,701
Cagliari	Cagliari	2,662	6,895	769,993
Nuoro	Nuoro	2,720	7,044	272,985
Oristano	Oristano	1,016	2,631	158,131
Sassari	Sassari	2,903	7,520	459,592
Sicilia (Sicily)	Palermo	9,926	25,709	5,094,735
Agrigento	Agrigento	1,175	3,042	475,669
Caltanissetta	Caltanissetta	822	2,128	282,999

Area and population (continued)

Catania	Catania	1,371	3,552	1,088,323
Enna	Enna	989	2,562	186,145
Messina	Messina	1,254	3,248	683,315
Palermo	Palermo	1,927	4,992	1,240,252
Ragusa	Ragusa	623	1,614	297,378
Siracusa	Siracusa	814	2,109	406,566
Trapani	Trapani	951	2,462	434,088
Toscana	Florence	8,877	22,992[5]	3,523,238
Arezzo	Arezzo	1,248	3,232	316,735
Firenze	Florence	1,365	3,536	952,908
Grosseto	Grosseto	1,739	4,504	216,713
Livorno	Livorno	468	1,213	336,759
Lucca	Lucca	684	1,773	375,591
Massa-Carrara	Massa-Carrara	447	1,157	201,242
Pisa	Pisa	945	2,448	384,550
Pistoia	Pistoia	373	965	265,995
Prato	Prato	133	344	221,528
Siena	Siena	1,475	3,821	251,217
Trentino-Alto Adige	Bolzano	5,258	13,618	913,169
Bolzano-Bozen	Bolzano	2,857	7,400	451,563
Trento	Trento	2,401	6,218	461,606
Umbria	Perugia	3,265	8,456	825,910
Perugia	Perugia	2,446	6,334	602,276
Terni	Terni	819	2,122	223,634
Valle d'Aosta	Aosta	1,259	3,262	118,723
Veneto	Venice	7,090	18,364	4,433,060
Belluno	Belluno	1,420	3,678	211,996
Padova	Padova	827	2,142	835,029
Rovigo	Rovigo	691	1,789	245,314
Treviso	Treviso	956	2,477	757,864
Venezia	Venice	950	2,460	817,597
Verona	Verona	1,195	3,096	801,363
Vicenza	Vicenza	1,051	2,722	763,897
TOTAL		116,324[6]	301,277[6]	57,332,996

Demography

Population (1997): 57,510,000.
Density (1997): persons per sq mi 494.4, persons per sq km 191.9.
Urban-rural (1996[2]): urban 67.0%; rural 33.0%.
Sex distribution (1996): male 48.62%; female 51.38%.
Age breakdown (1996[2]): under 15, 14.9%; 15–29, 21.9%; 30–44, 21.7%; 45–59, 19.0%; 60–74, 15.8%; 75 and over, 6.7%.
Population projection: (2000) 57,765,000; (2010) 57,614,000.
Doubling time: not applicable; population stable.
Ethnolinguistic composition (1983): Italian 94.1%; Sardinian 2.7%; Rhaetian 1.3%; other 1.9%.
Religious affiliation (1980): Roman Catholic 83.2%; nonreligious 13.6%; atheist 2.6%; other 0.6%.
Major cities (1996[2, 4]): Rome 2,654,187; Milan 1,306,494; Naples 1,050,234; Turin 923,106; Palermo 689,301; Genoa 659,116; Bologna 386,491; Florence 383,594; Catania 341,623; Bari 336,560; Venice 298,915.
National origin (1991): Italian 99.3%; foreign-born 0.7%, of which European 0.3%, African 0.2%, Asian 0.1%, other 0.1%.
Mobility (1991). Population living in the same commune as in 1986: 93.3%; another commune, same province 3.4%; different province 2.5%; abroad 0.8%.
Households. Average household size (1991) 2.7; composition of households: 1 person 19.5%, 2 persons 21.9%, 3 persons 25.2%, 4 persons 21.4%, 5 or more persons 12.0%. Family households (1991): 15,538,335 (73.8%); nonfamily 5,527,105 (26.2%), of which one-person 19.5%.
Immigration (1993): immigrants 100,401, from Europe 54.2%, of which EC countries 17.6%; Asia 16.4%; Africa 15.3%; Western Hemisphere 13.4%.

Vital statistics

Birth rate per 1,000 population (1996): 9.2 (world avg. 25.0); (1994) legitimate 90.2%; illegitimate 9.8%.
Death rate per 1,000 population (1996): 9.5 (world avg. 9.3).
Natural increase rate per 1,000 population (1996): −0.3 (world avg. 15.7).
Total fertility rate (avg. births per childbearing woman; 1996): 1.2.
Marriage rate per 1,000 population (1996): 4.7.
Divorce rate per 1,000 population (1994): 0.5.
Life expectancy at birth (1993): male 74.1 years; female 80.5 years.
Major causes of death per 100,000 population (1993): diseases of the circulatory system 423.7; malignant neoplasms (cancers) 270.5; diseases of the respiratory system 56.2; accidents and violence 49.8; diseases of the digestive system 49.8.

Social indicators

Educational attainment (1995). Percentage of labour force age 15 and over having: basic literacy or primary education 40.4%; secondary 30.5%; postsecondary technical training 5.1%; some college 19.2%; college degree 4.3%.
Quality of working life. Average workweek (1995): 37.0 hours. Annual rate per 100,000 workers (1988) for: injury or accident 3,697; death 5.7. Percentage of labour force insured for damages or income loss (1992) resulting from: injury 100%; permanent disability 100%; death 100%. Number of working days lost to labour stoppages per 1,000 workers (1995): 35. Average duration of journey to work: n.a. Rate per 1,000 workers of discouraged (unemployed no longer seeking work; 1990): 1.1.
Material well-being. Rate per 1,000 of population possessing (1995): telephone 434; automobile 550; television 436.
Social participation. Eligible voters participating in last national election (April 21, 1996): 91.0%. Trade union membership in total workforce (1990): *c.* 28%.
Social deviance (1995). Offense rate per 100,000 population for: murder 2.5; rape 3.2; assault 210.4; theft, including burglary and housebreaking 3,274.
Access to services (1991). Nearly 100% of dwellings have access to electricity, a safe water supply, and toilet facilities.

Leisure (1992). Favourite leisure activities (as percentage of household spending on culture): sporting events 17.8%; cinema 16.3%; theatre 14.0%.

National economy

Gross national product (1995): U.S.$1,088,085,000,000 (U.S.$19,020 per capita).

Structure of gross domestic product and labour force

	1996		1995	
	in value (Lit '000,000,000)	% of total value	labour force	% of labour force
Agriculture	53,302	2.9	1,490,000	6.6
Mining	80,154	4.3	4,622,000	20.3
Manufacturing	302,074	16.4		
Construction	92,943	5.0	1,615,000	7.1
Public utilities	107,653	5.8	257,000	1.1
Transp. and commun.	118,754	6.4	1,061,000	4.7
Trade	345,357	18.7	4,221,000	18.6
Finance	90,051	4.9	733,000	3.2
Pub. admin., defense	411,507[7]	22.3[7]	4,138,000	18.2
Services	244,895	13.3	1,873,000	8.2
Other	[7]	[7]	2,724,000[8]	12.0[8]
TOTAL	1,846,690	100.0	22,734,000	100.0

Budget (1995). Revenue: Lit 472,066,000,000,000 (income taxes 41.0%, of which individual 35.1%, corporate 5.9%; value-added and excise taxes 30.6%). Expenditures: Lit 696,860,000,000,000 (debt service 27.5%; social security 18.4%; education 9.1%; transportation 4.7%; defense 2.8%).
Public debt (1996[9]): U.S.$1,427,300,000,000.
Tourism (1996): receipts U.S.$28,245,200,000; expenditures U.S.$12,681,500,-000.

Manufacturing, mining, and construction enterprises (1993)

	no. of enterprises	no. of employees[10]	hourly wages as a % of avg. of all wages	annual value added (Lit '000,000,000)
Manufacturing				
Machinery (nonelectrical)	4,560	367,990	...	28,774
Electrical machinery	3,089	316,727	...	23,639
Food products	2,734	219,970	...	22,116
Industrial chemicals	1,215	199,279	...	21,444
Transport equipment	1,180	301,859	...	16,007
Textiles	3,514	215,387	...	14,335
Pottery, ceramics, and glass	2,312	159,138	...	13,322
Rubber and plastic products	1,677	112,839	...	9,271
Wearing apparel	4,063	185,072	...	8,592
Printing, publishing	1,383	90,998	...	8,588
Metal products	993	114,301	...	8,548
Paper and paper products	793	63,347	...	5,494
Petroleum and gas	23	9,478	...	3,898
Mining and quarrying	384	24,952	...	4,998
Construction	7,659	1,642,000	...	86,824

Production (metric tons except as noted). Agriculture, forestry, fishing (1997): sugar beets 13,000,000, grapes 9,459,000, corn (maize) 8,500,000, wheat 7,610,000, tomatoes 4,000,000, olives 2,452,000, potatoes 2,120,000, apples 2,071,000, oranges 1,973,000, peaches and nectarines 1,742,000, rice 1,424,000, barley 1,170,000; livestock (number of live animals) 10,531,000 sheep, 7,964,-000 pigs, 7,018,000 cattle, 130,000,000 chickens; roundwood (1995) 9,802,000 cu m; fish catch (1995) 609,768. Mining and quarrying (1995): rock salt 3,430,374; feldspar 2,199,315; potash 1,438,850[11]; barite 85,661; zinc 43,669; lead 22,658. Manufacturing (1995): cement 33,714,914; crude steel 27,635,287; pig iron 11,677,789; glass 3,981,104; sulfuric acid 2,161,796; textiles 1,172,916; wine 62,618,000 hectolitres[11]; beer 10,616,173 hectolitres; olive oil 6,290,000 hectolitres[11]; 6,995,818 washing machines; 5,908,224 refrigerators; 2,913,468 motorized road vehicles, of which 1,372,034 automobiles, 824,597 motorcycles 245,527 trucks and buses; 2,779,827 colour televisions. Construction (1995): residential 77,162,182 cu m; commercial 64,729,419 cu m.

Service enterprises (1995)

	no. of enterprises[12]	no. of employees	hourly wage as a % of all wages	annual value added (Lit '000,000,000)
Public utilities	379	257,000	...	102,495
Transportation, Communications	2,508	1,061,000	...	115,512
Finance	...	733,000	...	88,363
Wholesale and retail trade	9,173	4,221,000	...	327,636
Pub. admin., services	...	4,138,000	...	208,888

Energy production (consumption): electricity (kW-hr; 1994) 231,783,000,-000 (269,382,000,000); coal (metric tons; 1994) 267,000 (16,672,000); crude petroleum (barrels; 1994) 33,422,000 (582,644,000); petroleum products (metric tons; 1994) 83,049,000 (89,500,000); natural gas (cu m; 1994) 20,209,-000,000 (48,326,000,000).
Population economically active (1995): total 22,734,000; activity rate of total population 39.7% (participation rates: ages 15–64, 57.3%; female 37.3%; unemployed 11.3%).

Price and earnings indexes (1990 = 100)

	1990	1991	1992	1993	1994	1995	1996
Consumer price index	100.0	106.3	111.8	116.8	121.5	127.8	132.8
Earnings index	100.0	109.8	115.4	119.8	124.0	127.8	131.9

Household income and expenditure (1995). Average household size 2.7; average annual income per household (1984) Lit 19,692,000 (U.S.$11,208); sources of income (1991): salaries and wages 41.7%, property income and self-employment 38.0%, transfer payments 20.3%; expenditure (1994): food and beverages 21.7%, housing 19.5%, transportation and communications 16.8%, recreation and education 6.4%.

Financial aggregates

	1992	1993	1994	1995	1996	1997[13]
Exchange rate, Lit per:						
U.S. dollar	1,232.4	1,573.7	1,612.4	1,628.9	1,530.6	1,759.5
£	2,175.8	2,363.7	2,469.6	2,571.2	2,690.8	2,864.5
SDR	2,022.4	2,340.5	2,379.2	2,355.7	2,200.9	2,399.2
International reserves (U.S.$)						
Total (excl. gold; '000,000)	27,643	27,545	32,265	34,905	45,948	51,096
SDRs ('000,000)	238	241	125	53[14]	29	55
Reserve pos. in IMF ('000,000)	2,439	2,164	2,033	1,963	1,855	1,728
Foreign exchange ('000,000)	24,966	25,140	30,107	32,942	44,064	49,318
Gold ('000,000 fine troy oz)	66.67	66.67	66.67	66.67	66.67	66.67
% world reserves	7.1	7.3	7.3	7.3	7.3	7.5
Interest and prices						
Central bank discount (%)	12.00	8.00	7.50	9.00	7.50	6.25[15]
Govt. bond yield (%)	13.67	11.21	10.57	11.98	8.93	6.19[15]
Industrial share prices (1990 = 100)	70.5	83.5	104.1	95.4	96.0	138.3[15]
Balance of payments (U.S.$'000,000)						
Balance of visible trade	3,088	32,825	35,497	44,082	60,822	...
Imports, f.o.b.	−175,067	−136,328	−154,308	−187,254	−190,021	...
Exports, f.o.b.	178,155	169,153	189,805	231,336	250,843	...
Balance of invisibles	−31,082	−21,763	−19,875	−18,378	−19,782	...
Balance of payments, current account	−27,994	11,062	15,622	25,704	−41,040	...

Land use (1994): forest 23.0%; pasture 15.4%; agriculture 37.9%; other 23.7%.

Foreign trade

Balance of trade (current prices)

	1991	1992	1993	1994	1995	1996
Lit '000,000,000	−1,913	2,229	50,789	50,957	65,841	67,775
% of total	0.4%	0.5%	10.6%	9.1%	9.6%	9.6%

Imports (1994): Lit 332,409,083,000,000 (machinery and transport equipment 30.7%, of which transport equipment 11.3%, precision machinery 5.7%; chemicals 16.2%; metal 9.9%; food 6.4%; petroleum 4.5%; textiles 4.0%). *Major import sources:* Germany 19.2%; France 13.9%; U.K. 6.1%; The Netherlands 5.5%; Belgium-Luxembourg 4.8%; U.S. 4.8%.
Exports (1995): Lit 376,785,707,000,000 (machinery and transport equipment 42.0%, of which transport equipment 11.2%, electrical machinery 5.2%, precision machinery 3.7%; chemicals 10.3%; textiles 7.8%; wearing apparel 7.3%, of which shoes 2.6%; metal and processed metal 6.7%). *Major export destinations:* Germany 18.9%; France 13.1%; U.S. 7.2%; U.K. 6.2%.

Transport and communications

Transport. Railroads (1995): length 9,944 mi, 16,003 km; passenger-mi 30,-882,000,000, passenger-km 49,700,000,000; short ton-mi cargo 28,499,000,000, metric ton-km cargo 41,608,000,000. Roads (1995): total length 195,334 mi, 314,360 km (paved 100%). Vehicles (1995): passenger cars 31,700,000; trucks and buses 5,127,000. Merchant marine (1994): vessels (100 gross tons and over) 1,966; total deadweight tonnage 7,149,453. Air transport (1993): passenger-mi 18,429,000,000, passenger-km 29,658,600,000; short ton-mi cargo 914,300,000, metric ton-km cargo 1,334,900,000; airports (1997) 34.

Communications

Medium	date	unit	number	units per 1,000 persons
Daily newspapers	1995	circulation	7,237,000	126
Radio	1994	receivers	45,350,000	790
Television	1995	receivers	25,000,000	436
Telephones	1995	main lines	24,854,000	434
Cellular telephones	1995	subscribers	3,864,000	67.4
Facsimile machines	1995	units	202,000	3.5
Personal computers	1995	units	4,800,000	83.4

Education and health

Literacy (1991): total population age 14 and over literate 47,376,663 (97.7%); males literate 22,897,907 (98.8%); females literate 24,478,756 (97.1%).

Education (1995–96)

	schools	teachers	students	student/teacher ratio
Primary (age 6–10)	20,442	289,055	2,825,838	9.8
Secondary (age 11–18)	9,278	214,861	1,907,024	8.9
Voc., teacher tr.	7,888	313,001	2,661,760	8.5
Higher[16, 17]	48	58,874	1,601,873	27.2

Health (1993): physicians 207,319 (1 per 193 persons); hospital beds 380,423 (1 per 147 persons); infant mortality rate per 1,000 live births (1996) 6.0.
Food (1995): daily per capita caloric intake 3,458 (vegetable products 74%, animal products 26%); 137% of FAO recommended minimum requirement.

Military

Total active duty personnel (1997): 325,150 (army 57.9%, navy 13.5%, air force 19.6%, central staff 9.0%). *Military expenditure as percentage of GNP* (1995): 1.8% (world 2.8%); per capita expenditure U.S.$338.

[1]Includes 10 nonelective seats. [2]January 1. [3]Six provinces were created in 1992. [4]Resident population only. [5]Detail does not add to total given because of rounding. [6]The total area for Italy, per the latest survey, is 301,323 sq km (116,341 sq mi). [7]Pub. admin., defense includes other. [8]Unemployed. [9]October 1. [10]Total number of persons engaged. [11]1993. [12]Enterprises with 20 or more persons engaged. [13]August. [14]November. [15]July. [16]Universities only. [17]1994–05.

Internet resources for further information:
- **Tavole statistiche http://www.istat.it**

Jamaica

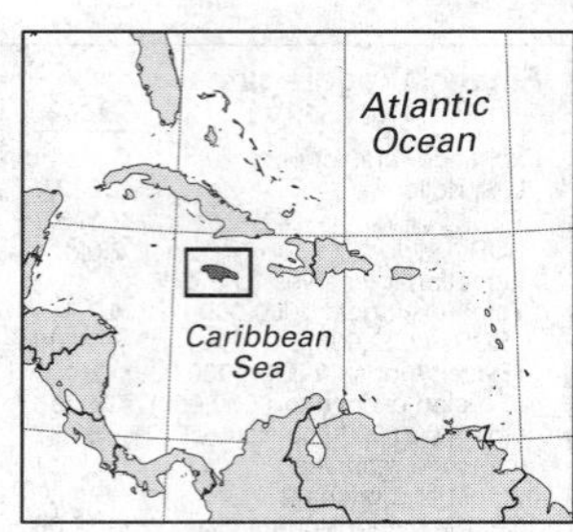

Official name: Jamaica.
Form of government: constitutional monarchy with two legislative houses (Senate [21]; House of Representatives [60]).
Chief of state: British Monarch represented by Governor-General.
Head of government: Prime Minister.
Capital: Kingston.
Official language: English.
Monetary unit: 1 Jamaica dollar (J$) = 100 cents; valuation (Oct. 3, 1997) 1 U.S.$ = J$34.40; 1 £ = J$55.45.

Area and population

Parishes	Capitals	area sq mi	area sq km	population 1994[1] estimate
Clarendon	May Pen	462	1,196	222,500
Hanover	Lucea	174	450	66,600
Kingston	[2]	8	22	[3]
Manchester	Mandeville	321	830	173,100
Portland	Port Antonio	314	814	78,500
Saint Andrew	[2]	166	431	697,000
Saint Ann	Saint Ann's Bay	468	1,213	154,500
Saint Catherine	Spanish Town	460	1,192	370,600
Saint Elizabeth	Black River	468	1,212	146,600
Saint James	Montego Bay	230	595	166,000
Saint Mary	Port Maria	236	611	113,700
Saint Thomas	Morant Bay	287	743	88,900
Trelawny	Falmouth	338	875	74,100
Westmoreland	Savanna-la-Mar	312	807	130,500
TOTAL		4,244	10,991	2,482,600

Demography

Population (1997): 2,536,000.
Density (1997): persons per sq mi 597.5, persons per sq km 230.7.
Urban-rural (1991): urban 50.2%; rural 49.8%.
Sex distribution (1995): male 49.74%; female 50.26%.
Age breakdown (1995): under 15, 32.3%; 15–29, 28.7%; 30–44, 19.7%; 45–59, 9.8%; 60 and over, 9.5%.
Population projection: (2000) 2,589,000; (2010) 2,814,000.
Doubling time: 39 years.
Ethnic composition (1982): black 74.7%; mixed black 12.8%; East Indian 1.3%; other 11.2%, of which not stated 9.5%.
Religious affiliation (1995): Protestant 42.7%, of which Pentecostal 10.5%, Seventh-day Adventist 6.1%, Baptist 5.3%, Anglican 3.7%; Roman Catholic 10.4%; other (including nonreligious) 46.9%[4].
Major cities (1991): Kingston 103,771[5] (metropolitan area 587,798); Spanish Town 92,383; Portmore 90,138; Montego Bay 83,446; May Pen 46,785.

Vital statistics

Birth rate per 1,000 population (1995): 23.2 (world avg. 25.0).
Death rate per 1,000 population (1995): 5.0 (world avg. 9.3).
Natural increase rate per 1,000 population (1995): 18.2 (world avg. 15.7).
Total fertility rate (avg. births per childbearing woman; 1995): 3.0.
Marriage rate per 1,000 population (1994): 6.1.
Life expectancy at birth (1990–95): male 71.4 years; female 75.8 years.
Major causes of death per 100,000 population (1991): diseases of the circulatory system 189.4; malignant neoplasms (cancers) 84.1; endocrine and metabolic disorders 51.3; diseases of the respiratory system 30.1.

National economy

Budget (1995–96). Revenue J$39,642,300,000 (tax revenue 85.6%, of which consumption taxes 32.3%, income taxes 30.6%, stamp duties 3.9%; nontax revenue 14.4%). Expenditures: J$48,334,200,000 (current expenditure 62.8%, of which debt interest 22.4%).
Public debt (external, outstanding; 1995): U.S.$3,409,000,000.
Production (metric tons except as noted). Agriculture, forestry, fishing (1996): sugarcane 2,624,000, yams 240,371, vegetables 218,200, citrus fruits 130,000, bananas 130,000, coconuts 115,000, pumpkins, squash, and gourds 42,000, plantains 34,769, sweet potatoes 33,000, cabbages 33,000, carrots 26,000, tomatoes 24,000; livestock (number of live animals) 440,000 goats, 420,000 cattle, 180,000 pigs; roundwood (1995) 354,700 cu m; fish catch (1995) 13,617. Mining and quarrying (1996): crude bauxite 3,924,800; alumina 3,199,500; (1995) gypsum 208,000. Manufacturing (value added in constant 1991–95 prices, J$'000,000; 1995): machinery and equipment 593.6; food processing 580.3; petroleum products 351.3; rubber and plastic products 324.1; textiles and clothing 257.0; tobacco and tobacco products 255.2; metal and nonmetallic products 223.6. Construction (1995): residential units completed 7,067[6]; factory space completed 6,989 sq m[7]. Energy production (consumption): electricity (kW-hr; 1994) 3,927,000,000 (3,927,000,000); coal, none (none); crude petroleum (barrels; 1994) none (5,893,000); petroleum products (metric tons; 1994) 825,000 (2,748,000); natural gas, none (none).
Population economically active (1995): total 1,150,000; activity rate of total population 46.0% (participation rates: ages 14 and over 58.7%; female 46.3%; unemployed 16.2%).

Price and earnings indexes (1990 = 100)

	1990	1991	1992	1993	1994	1995	1996
Consumer price index	100.0	151.1	267.8	327.0	441.6	529.5	669.3
Earnings index	...	...	...	...	...	...	...

Gross national product (1995): U.S.$3,803,000,000 (U.S.$1,510 per capita).

Structure of gross domestic product and labour force

	1995 in value J$'000,000	% of total value	labour force	% of labour force
Agriculture	15,323.1	9.4	223,200	19.4
Mining	11,711.7	7.2	7,000	0.6
Manufacturing	28,774.6	17.7	104,700	9.1
Construction	20,880.6	12.8	76,000	6.6
Public utilities	3,633.7	2.2	6,800	0.6
Transp. and commun.	13,918.9	8.6	44,500	3.9
Trade	38,505.0	23.7	201,400	17.5
Pub. admin., defense	13,960.2	8.6		
Finance, real estate	21,501.3	13.2	298,700	26.0
Services	6,454.5	4.0		
Other	−12,094.8[8]	−7.4[8]	187,800[9]	16.3[9]
TOTAL	162,568.8	100.0	1,150,000[10]	100.0

Household income and expenditure. Average household size (1991) 4.2; average annual income per household (1988) J$8,356 (U.S.$1,525); sources of income (1989): wages and salaries 66.1%, self-employment 19.3%, transfers 14.6%; expenditure (1988)[11]: food and beverages 55.6%, housing 7.9%, fuel and other household supplies 7.4%, health care 7.0%, transportation 6.4%.
Tourism (1995): receipts U.S.$1,069,000,000; expenditures U.S.$148,000,000.

Foreign trade[12]

Balance of trade (current prices)

	1991	1992	1993	1994	1995	1996
U.S.$'000,000	−654	−636	−1,121	−957.7	−1,342.6	−1,527.3
% of total	22.2%	23.2%	34.9%	28.7%	31.9%	35.6%

Imports (1996): U.S.$2,906,679,000 (raw materials 55.7%, of which fuels 15.4%; consumer goods 25.7%, of which food 7.6%; capital goods 18.6%, of which machinery and apparatus 9.5%). *Major import sources:* U.S. 60.2%; U.K. 4.3%; Japan 4.1%; Venezuela 3.2%; Mexico 3.1%; France 2.8%.
Exports (1996): U.S.$1,379,421,000 (crude materials 49.7%; food 20.2%; beverages and tobacco 3.5%; chemicals 3.3%; machinery and transport equipment 2.3%; manufactured goods 1.4%). *Major export destinations:* U.S. 42.4%; U.K. 11.1%; Canada 9.2%; Norway 5.9%; France 4.6%; Germany 4.2%.

Transport and communications

Transport. Railroads (1991): route length 129 mi, 208 km; passenger-mi 12,127,000[7], passenger-km 19,516,000[7]; short ton-mi cargo 1,700,000, metric ton-km cargo 2,482,000. Roads (1995): total length 11,600 mi, 18,600 km (paved 71%). Vehicles (1994–95): passenger cars 86,791; trucks and buses 41,312. Air transport (1996)[13]: passenger-mi 1,204,001,000, passenger-km 1,937,655,000; short ton-mi cargo 136,014,000, metric ton-km cargo 198,577,000; airports (1997) with scheduled flights 4.

Communications

Medium	date	unit	number	units per 1,000 persons
Daily newspapers	1995	circulation	160,000	65
Radio	1996	receivers	1,859,000	739
Television	1995	receivers	773,000	306
Telephones	1995	main lines	291,800	116
Cellular telephones	1995	subscribers	45,200	18
Facsimile machines	1995	units	1,600	0.6

Education and health

Educational attainment (1982). Percentage of population age 25 and over having: no formal schooling 3.2%; some primary education 79.8%; some secondary 15.0%; complete secondary and higher 2.0%. *Literacy* (1995): total population age 15 and over literate 85%; males literate 80.8%; females literate 89.1%.

Education (1994–95)

	schools	teachers	students	student/ teacher ratio
Primary (age 6–11)[14]	788[15]	11,283	319,298	28.3
Secondary (age 12–16)	126	8,377	207,035	24.7
Voc., teacher tr.	18	950	15,898	16.7
Higher	15[16]	1,047[17]	24,200	17.9[17]

Health (1995): physicians 417[18] (1 per 6,043 persons); hospital beds (1993) 5,023 (1 per 492 persons); infant mortality rate per 1,000 live births 28.6.
Food (1995): daily per capita caloric intake 2,647 (vegetable products 84%, animal products 16%); 118% of FAO recommended minimum requirement.

Military

Total active duty personnel (1997): 3,320 (army 90.4%; coast guard 4.5%; air force 5.1%). *Military expenditure as percentage of GNP* (1995): 0.8% (world 2.8%); per capita expenditure U.S.$11.

[1]January 1. [2]The parishes of Kingston and Saint Andrew are jointly administered from the Half Way Tree section of Saint Andrew. [3]Kingston included with Saint Andrew. [4]Includes *c.* 3.0% Rastafarian. [5]City of Kingston is coextensive with Kingston parish. [6]51% public sector. [7]1990. [8]Less imputed service charges. [9]Includes 186,700 unemployed. [10]Detail does not add to total given because of rounding. [11]Weights of consumer price index components. [12]Import figures are c.i.f. [13]Air Jamaica only. [14]Includes lower-secondary students at all-age schools. [15]1991–92. [16]1988–89. [17]1987–88. [18]Public health only.

Internet resources for further information:
- **Embassy of Jamaica**
  http://www.caribbean-online.com/jamaica/embassy/washdc/

Japan

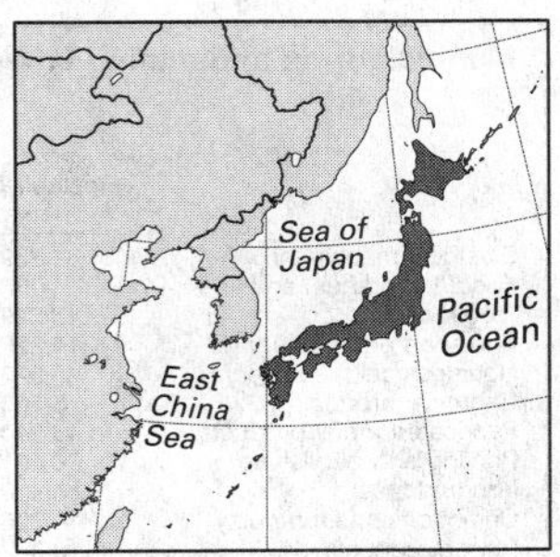

Official name: Nihon (Japan).
Form of government: constitutional monarchy with a National Diet consisting of two legislative houses (House of Councillors [252]; House of Representatives [500]).
Chief of state: Emperor.
Head of government: Prime Minister.
Capital: Tokyo.
Official language: Japanese.
Official religion: none.
Monetary unit: 1 yen (¥) = 100 sen; valuation (Oct. 3, 1997) 1 U.S.$ = ¥122.26; 1 £ = ¥197.08.

Area and population

Regions / Prefectures	Capitals	area sq mi	area sq km	population 1996 estimate
Chūbu				
Aichi	Nagoya	1,984	5,139	6,897,481
Fukui	Fukui	1,619	4,192	828,971
Gifu	Gifu	4,091	10,596	2,106,718
Ishikawa	Kanazawa	1,621	4,198	1,182,300
Nagano	Nagano	5,245	13,585	2,206,290
Niigata	Niigata	4,857	12,579	2,492,352
Shizuoka	Shizuoka	3,001	7,773	3,749,247
Toyama	Toyama	1,642	4,252	1,125,618
Yamanashi	Kōfu	1,723	4,463	886,010
Chūgoku				
Hiroshima	Hiroshima	3,269	8,467	2,882,074
Okayama	Okayama	2,738	7,092	1,952,610
Shimane	Matsue	2,559[1]	6,629[1]	769,941
Tottori	Tottori	1,349[1]	3,494[1]	614,469
Yamaguchi	Yamaguchi	2,358	6,107	1,550,982
Hokkaidō				
Hokkaidō (Territory)	Sapporo	32,247	83,520	5,698,946
Kantō				
Chiba	Chiba	1,989	5,151	5,823,934
Gumma	Maebashi	2,454	6,356	2,011,046
Ibaraki	Mito	2,353	6,094	2,971,524
Kanagawa	Yokohama	928	2,403	8,281,848
Saitama	Urawa	1,467	3,799	6,809,303
Tochigi	Utsunomiya	2,476	6,414	1,992,807
Kinki				
Hyōgo	Kōbe	3,236	8,381	5,410,170
Mie	Tsu	2,231	5,778	1,848,617
Nara	Nara	1,425	3,692	1,438,618
Shiga	Ōtsu	1,551	4,016	1,298,444
Wakayama	Wakayama	1,824	4,725	1,079,579
Kyūshū				
Fukuoka	Fukuoka	1,916	4,963	4,951,909
Kagoshima	Kagoshima	3,539	9,167	1,793,350
Kumamoto	Kumamoto	2,860	7,408	1,861,916
Miyazaki	Miyazaki	2,986	7,735	1,177,436
Nagasaki	Nagasaki	1,588	4,113	1,541,327
Ōita	Ōita	2,447	6,338	1,230,268
Saga	Saga	942	2,440	885,566
Ryukyu				
Okinawa	Naha	871	2,255	1,282,705
Shikoku				
Ehime	Matsuyama	2,190	5,672	1,505,129
Kagawa	Takamatsu	727	1,883	1,027,839
Kōchi	Kōchi	2,744	7,107	815,003
Tokushima	Tokushima	1,601	4,146	831,922
Tohoku				
Akita	Akita	4,484[2]	11,613[2]	1,209,970
Aomori	Aomori	3,714[2]	9,619[2]	1,482,657
Fukushima	Fukushima	5,322	13,784	2,136,181
Iwate	Morioka	5,898	15,277	1,419,595
Miyagi	Sendai	2,815	7,292	2,338,370
Yamagata	Yamagata	3,601	9,327	1,255,863
Metropolis				
Tōkyō[3]	Tokyo	836	2,166	11,771,951
Urban prefectures				
Kyōto[4]	Kyōto	1,781	4,613	2,631,374
Ōsaka[4]	Ōsaka	722	1,869	8,803,792
TOTAL		145,883[5, 6]	377,835[5, 6]	125,864,022

Demography

Population (1997): 126,110,000.
Density (1997): persons per sq mi 864.5, persons per sq km 333.8.
Urban-rural (1995): urban 77.6%; rural 22.4%.
Sex distribution (1996[7]): male 49.03%; female 50.97%.
Age breakdown (1996[7]): under 15, 15.8%; 15–29, 21.8%; 30–44, 19.6%; 45–59, 21.9%; 60–74, 15.0%; 75 and over, 5.9%.
Population projection: (2000) 127,286,000; (2010) 130,344,000.
Doubling time: not applicable; doubling time exceeds 100 years.
Composition by nationality (1995[8]): Japanese 98.9%; Korean 0.5%; Chinese 0.2%; Brazilian 0.1%; other 0.3%.
Place of birth (1995): 99.3% native-born; 0.7% foreign-born (mainly Korean).
Immigration (1995[8]): permanent immigrants/registered aliens admitted 1,354,011, from North and South Korea 50.0%, Taiwan, Hong Kong, and China 16.1%, Brazil 11.8%, Philippines 6.3%, United States 3.2%, Peru 2.6%, Thailand 1.0%, United Kingdom 0.9%, Vietnam 0.6%, Iran 0.6%, Canada 0.5%, Indonesia 0.5%, other 5.9%.
Major cities (1995): Tokyo 11,771,819; Yokohama 3,307,408; Ōsaka 2,602,352; Nagoya 2,152,258; Sapporo 1,756,968; Kyōto 1,463,601; Kōbe 1,423,830; Fukuoka 1,284,741; Kawasaki 1,202,811; Hiroshima 1,108,868; Kita-Kyūshū 1,019,522.

Other principal cities (1995)

	population		population		population
Akashi	287,613	Kakogawa	260,558	Okayama	616,056
Akita	312,035	Kanazawa	453,977	Okazaki	322,615
Amagasaki	488,574	Kashiwa	317,752	Ōmiya	433,768
Aomori	294,165	Kasugai	277,579	Ōtsu	276,331
Asahikawa	360,569	Kawagoe	323,345	Sagamihara	570,594
Chiba	856,882	Kawaguchi	448,801	Sakai	802,965
Fujisawa	368,636	Kōchi	322,077	Sendai	971,263
Fukui	255,601	Koriyama	324,831	Shimonoseki	259,791
Fukushima	285,745	Koshigaya	298,285	Shizuoka	474,089
Fukuyama	374,510	Kumamoto	650,322	Suita	342,794
Funabashi	540,814	Kurashiki	422,824	Takamatsu	330,997
Gifu	407,145	Machida	360,418	Takatsuki	362,259
Hachiōji	503,320	Maebashi	284,780	Tokorozawa	320,448
Hakodate	298,868	Matsudo	461,489	Tokushima	268,712
Hamamatsu	561,568	Matsuyama	460,870	Toyama	325,303
Higashi-Ōsaka	517,228	Miyazaki	300,054	Toyohashi	352,913
Himeji	470,986	Morioka	286,478	Toyonaka	398,912
Hirakata	400,130	Nagano	358,512	Toyota	341,038
Hiratsuka	253,818	Nagasaki	438,724	Urawa	453,300
Ibaraki	258,237	Naha	301,928	Utsunomiya	435,446
Ichihara	277,080	Nara	359,234	Wakayama	393,951
Ichikawa	440,527	Neyagawa	258,440	Yamagata	254,485
Ichinomiya	267,359	Niigata	494,785	Yao	276,658
Iwaki	360,497	Nishinomiya	390,388	Yokkaichi	285,777
Kagoshima	546,294	Ōita	426,981	Yokosuka	432,202

Religious affiliation (1992): Shintō and related religions 51.3%; Buddhism 38.3%; Christian 1.2%; other 9.2%.
Households (1995). Total households 43,447,100; average household size 2.9; composition of households 1 person 24.7%, 2 persons 23.1%, 3 persons 18.6%, 4 persons 19.0%, 5 persons 8.2%, 6 or more persons 6.4%. Family households 32,545,700 (74.9%); nonfamily 10,901,400 (25.1%), of which 1 person 10,768,000 (24.7%).

Type of household (1993)

Total number of occupied dwelling units: 40,835,000

	number of dwellings	percentage of total
by kind of dwelling		
exclusively for living	38,518,000	94.3
mixed use	169,000	0.4
combined with nondwelling	2,148,000	5.3
detached house	24,183,000	59.2
apartment building	14,253,000	34.9
tenement (substandard or overcrowded building)	2,205,000	5.4
other	194,000	0.5
by legal tenure of householder		
owned	24,410,000	59.8
rented	15,721,000	38.5
other	704,000	1.7
by kind of amenities		
flush toilet	30,524,000	74.7
bathroom	38,196,000	93.5
by year of construction		
prior to 1945	2,146,000	5.4
1945–70	9,700,000	24.3
1971–80	12,548,000	31.5
1981–87	9,258,000	23.2
1988–93	6,224,000	15.6

Mobility (October 1990). Population living in same residence as in October 1985, 74.7%; different residence, same town 9.5%; same prefecture 7.9%; different prefecture 7.6%; different country 0.3%.

Vital statistics

Birth rate per 1,000 population (1995): 9.5 (world avg. 25.0); (1985) legitimate 99.0%; illegitimate 1.0%.
Death rate per 1,000 population (1995): 7.4 (world avg. 9.3).
Natural increase rate per 1,000 population (1995): 2.1 (world avg. 15.7).
Total fertility rate (avg. births per childbearing woman; 1995): 1.4.
Marriage rate per 1,000 population (1995): 6.4; median age at first marriage men 28.5 years, women 26.2 years.
Divorce rate per 1,000 population (1995): 1.6.
Life expectancy at birth (1995): male 76.4 years; female 82.8 years.
Major causes of death per 100,000 population (1994): circulatory diseases 239.1, of which cerebrovascular disease 96.9; malignant neoplasms (cancers) 196.4; pneumonia and bronchitis 68.4; accidents and adverse effects 29.1, of which suicide 16.9; nephritis, nephrotic syndrome, and nephrosis 15.1; cirrhosis of the liver 13.3; diabetes mellitus 8.8.

Social indicators

Educational attainment (1990). Percentage of population age 25 years and over having: primary education 34.3%; secondary 44.5%; postsecondary 21.2%.

Distribution of income (1995)

percentage of average household income by quintile

1	2	3	4	5 (highest)
11.5	15.5	19.1	22.7	31.2

Quality of working life. Average workweek (1995): 38.2 hours. Annual rate of industrial deaths per 100,000 workers (1994): 2.6. Proportion of labour force insured for damages or income loss resulting from injury, permanent disability, and death (1991): 50.1%. Average man-days lost to labour stoppages per 1,000,000 workdays (1995): 1.2. Average duration of journey to work (1988)[9]: 26.8 minutes (1983; 26.7% private automobile, 67.4% public transportation, 5.5% taxi, 0.4% other). Rate per 1,000 workers of discouraged (unemployed no longer seeking work; 1993): 87.8.

Access to services (1989). Proportion of households having access to: gas supply 64.6%; safe public water supply 94.0%; public sewage collection 89.4%.

Social participation. Eligible voters participating in last national election (October 1996): 59.6%. Population 15 years and over participating in social-service activities on a voluntary basis (1991): 26.3%. Trade union membership in total workforce (1995): 18.9%.

Social deviance (1994). Offense rate per 100,000 population for: homicide 1.0; rape 1.3; robbery 2.2; larceny and theft 1,246.6. Incidence in general population of: alcoholism, n.a.; drug and substance abuse, n.a. Rate of suicide per 100,000 population: 16.7.

Leisure/use of personal time

Discretionary daily activities (1991)
(Population age 15 years and over)

	weekly average hrs./min.
Total discretionary daily time	5:56[7]
of which	
Hobbies and amusements	0:36
Sports	0:11
Learning (except schoolwork)	0:12
Social activities	0:05
Associations	0:29
Radio, television, newspapers, and magazines	2:23
Rest and relaxation	1:21
Other activities	0:21

Major leisure activities (1991)
(Population age 15 years and over)

	percentage of participation		
	male	female	total
Hobbies and amusements	93.0	90.8	91.9
Sports	84.2	72.1	78.0
Light exercises	30.8	34.1	32.0
Swimming	27.1	20.8	23.8
Bowling	33.0	23.1	27.9
Learning (except schoolwork)	36.3	37.0	36.7
Travel			
Domestic	72.7	68.3	70.4
Foreign	10.4	7.6	9.0

Material well-being (1994). Households possessing: automobile 79.7%; telephone, virtually 100%; colour television receiver 99.3%; refrigerator 98.9%; air conditioner 72.3%; washing machine 99.4%; vacuum cleaner 98.7%; videocassette recorder 82.8%; camera 86.8%; microwave oven 84.3%; compact disc player 53.8%.

National economy

Gross national product (at current market prices; 1995): U.S.$4,810,000,000,000 (U.S.$38,420 per capita).

Structure of gross domestic product and labour force

	1995		1996	
	in value ¥'000,000,000	% of total value	labour force	% of labour force
Agriculture, fishing	9,325.0	1.9	3,560,000	5.3
Mining	1,019.9	0.2	60,000	0.1
Manufacturing	119,294.3	24.7	14,450,000	21.5
Construction	49,692.9	10.3	6,700,000	10.0
Public utilities	13,649.7	2.8	370,000	0.6
Transportation and communications	31,468.9	6.5	4,110,000	6.1
Trade	61,199.6	12.7	14,630,000	21.8
Finance	85,712.0	17.7		
Pub. admin., defense	38,967.6	8.1	20,680,000	30.8
Services	92,977.9	19.2		
Other	−20,377.8[10]	−4.2[10]	2,540,000[11]	3.8[11]
TOTAL	482,930.0	100.0[6]	67,110,000[6]	100.0

Budget (1996). Revenue: ¥54,076,000,000,000 (1995; income tax 34.9%; corporation tax 22.7%; value-added tax 10.3%; liquor and tobacco tax 5.7%; fuel taxes 4.4%; stamp duties 3.1%; customs duties 1.6%; carried-over surplus 1.1%). Expenditures: ¥75,104,924,000,000 (social security 19.0%; debt service 21.8%; public works 12.8%; culture, education, and science 8.3%; national defense 6.4%; pensions 2.2%).

Public debt (1995): U.S.$2,556,900,000,000.

Population economically active (1996): total 67,110,000; activity rate of total population 53.3% (participation rates: age 15 and over, 63.4%[12]; female 40.5%; unemployed 3.4%).

Price and earnings indexes (1990 = 100)

	1991	1992	1993	1994	1995	1996	1997[13]
Consumer price index	103.3	105.1	106.4	107.1	107.0	107.2	109.6
Monthly earnings index	103.4	105.6	107.7	110.2	112.5	114.6	116.1

Household income and expenditure (1995). Average household size 2.8; average annual income per household ¥6,849,800 (U.S.$72,824); sources of income (1992): wages and salaries 59.3%, transfer payments 19.5%, self-employment 10.1%, other 11.1%; expenditure: food 22.6%, transportation and communications 11.0%, recreation 9.5%, housing 6.7%, clothing and footwear 6.0%, fuel, light, and water charges 5.6%, education 5.3%, furniture and household utensils 3.7%, medical care 2.7%.

Tourism (1996): receipts from visitors U.S.$4,281,000,000; expenditures by nationals abroad U.S.$37,977,400,000.

Land use (1994): forested 66.4%; meadows and pastures 1.8%; agricultural and under permanent cultivation 11.7%; other 20.1%.

Manufacturing and mining enterprises (1994)

	no. of establishments	avg. no. of persons engaged	annual wages as a % of avg. of all mfg. wages	annual value added (¥'000,000,000)
Electrical machinery	31,389	1,773,000	100.1	18,382
Food, beverages, and tobacco	46,549	1,237,000	72.9	11,995
Transport equipment	14,226	937,000	122.5	11,626
Nonelectrical machinery	40,320	1,074,000	116.6	11,090
Chemical products	5,160	398,000	136.4	11,379
Fabricated metal products	46,214	813,000	100.6	7,748
Printing and publishing	26,461	536,000	121.2	6,467
Iron and steel	5,830	308,000	141.6	4,647
Ceramic, stone, and clay	19,326	433,000	100.5	5,031
Plastic products	18,862	443,000	92.8	4,134
Paper and paper products	10,410	271,000	100.1	3,062
Textiles	16,745	283,000	81.7	1,883
Apparel products	34,230	634,000	51.9	2,538
Nonferrous metal products	3,709	161,000	120.1	1,756
Precision instruments	5,928	206,000	100.8	1,657
Lumber and wood products	16,532	217,000	78.9	1,550
Furniture and fixtures	15,435	209,000	83.6	1,553
Rubber products	4,334	148,000	104.0	1,472
Petroleum and coal products	1,093	34,000	163.5	1,697
Leather products	4,810	64,000	69.0	378
Mining and quarrying	611	12,000	112.7	100

Energy production (consumption): electricity (kW-hr; 1994) 964,328,000,000 (964,382,000,000); coal (metric tons; 1994) 6,949,000 (123,099,000); crude petroleum (barrels; 1994) 3,958,000 (1,647,000,000); petroleum products (metric tons; 1994) 185,612,000, of which (by volume) diesel 32.8%, heavy fuel oil 25.5%, gasoline 19.8%, kerosene and jet fuel 15.0% (193,545,000); natural gas (cu m; 1994) 2,276,600,000 (61,101,700,000). Composition of energy supply by source (1994): crude oil and petroleum products 55.8%, coal 17.2%, natural gas 11.3%, nuclear power 11.9%, hydroelectric power 3.0%, other 0.8%. Domestic energy demand by end use (1994): mining and manufacturing 42.6%, residential and commercial 25.9%, transportation 24.1%, other 7.4%.

Financial aggregates

	1991	1992	1993	1994	1995	1996	1997[14]
Exchange rate[15], ¥ per:							
U.S. dollar	125.20	124.75	111.85	99.74	102.30	108.78	114.20
£	234.21	188.62	172.27	157.59	158.56	169.88	178.35
SDR	179.09	171.53	153.63	145.61	152.86	166.80	158.80
International reserves (U.S.$)							
Total (excl. gold; '000,000)	72,059	71,623	98,524	125,860	183,250	216,648	221,128
SDRs ('000,000)	2,579	1,094	1,543	2,083	2,707	2,648	2,510
Reserve pos. in IMF ('000,000)	7,722	8,641	8,261	8,100	8,100	6,671	6,051
Foreign exchange ('000,000)	61,758	61,888	88,720	115,146	172,443	207,335	212,566
Gold ('000,000 fine troy oz)	24.23	24.23	24.23	24.23	24.23	24.23	24.23
% world reserves	2.6	2.6	2.6	2.6	2.7	2.7	2.7
Interest and prices							
Central bank discount (%)[15]	4.50	3.25	1.75	1.75	0.50	0.50	0.50
Govt. bond yield (%)	6.53	4.94	3.69	3.71	2.27	2.23	2.03[13]
Industrial share prices (1990 = 100)	84.5	62.6	76.5	73.3	63.3	73.4[16]	...
Balance of payments (U.S.$'000,000,000)							
Balance of visible trade	103.1	132.4	141.6	145.9	132.1	83.56	...
Imports, f.o.b.	203.5	198.5	209.7	238.2	297.2	316.72	...
Exports, f.o.b.	306.6	330.9	351.3	384.2	429.3	400.28	...
Balance of invisibles	−17.7	−14.8	−10.1	−16.7	−20.9	−17.68	...
Balance of payments, current account	35.9	72.9	131.5	129.2	111.2	65.88	...

Retail and wholesale trade and services (1994)

	no. of establishments	avg. no. of employees	annual sales (¥'000,000,000)
Retail trade	1,499,948	7,384,143	143,325
Food and beverages	569,403	2,740,000	43,021
Grocery	65,174	715,000	16,986
Liquors	92,436	278,000	5,966
General merchandise	4,839	494,000	20,391
Department stores	2,267	478,000	19,976
Motor vehicles and bicycles	89,345	569,000	17,539
Apparel and accessories	225,714	789,000	14,269
Gasoline service stations	72,177	441,000	11,818
Furniture and home furnishings	144,368	563,000	11,557
Books and stationery	72,007	679,000	5,158
Wholesale trade	429,302	4,581,000	514,317
Machinery and equipment	97,691	1,165,000	110,808
General machinery except electrical	41,618	425,000	30,991
Motor vehicles and parts	17,942	225,000	29,308
General merchandise	1,159	61,000	91,717
Farm, livestock, and fishery products	42,537	445,000	56,954
Food and beverages	53,687	573,000	47,381
Minerals and metals	19,809	242,000	47,281
Building materials	50,152	406,000	32,641
Textiles, apparel, and accessories	40,970	407,000	30,461
Chemicals	17,011	172,000	21,486
Drugs and toilet goods	19,710	288,000	21,048

Production (metric tons except as noted). Agriculture, forestry, fishing (1997): rice 13,000,000, sugar beets 3,800,000, potatoes 3,365,000, cabbages 2,702,000, sugarcane 1,610,000, onions 1,278,000, sweet potatoes 1,181,000, apples 963,000, cucumbers 826,400, tomatoes 752,900, carrots 724,000, watermelons 616,500, wheat 550,000, lettuce 536,400, eggplants 478,400, pears 426,000, cantaloupes 400,000, grapes 255,000, pumpkins 242,000, barley 220,000, strawberries 201,500, peaches 156,000, oranges 136,000, soybeans 120,000, tea 90,000, green beans 75,000, tobacco 69,700, green peas 44,700; livestock (number of live animals) 9,809,000 pigs,

4,749,000 cattle, 31,000 goats, 30,000 horses, 25,000 sheep, 309,000,000 chickens; roundwood (1994) 18,887,000 cu m; fish catch (1995) 6,757,570, of which mackerel 794,580, sardines 661,390, Alaska pollack 338,507, squid 358,574, oysters 227,319, crabs 57,179, river eels 30,030, carp 19,217. Mining and quarrying (1996): limestone 202,897,000; silica stone 19,015,000; dolomite 3,905,000; pyrophyllite 618,000; zinc 79,700; lead 7,753; copper 1,145; tungsten 578[17]; silver 85,000 kg; gold 8,627 kg. Manufacturing (1994): semifinished steel 102,727,000[18]; crude steel 98,295,000; cement 91,624,000; hot-rolled steel products 87,982,000[18]; pig iron 73,776,000; sulfuric acid 6,594,000; fertilizers 6,047,000; plastic products 5,055,000; newsprint 2,971,800; spun yarn 656,000; synthetic fabrics 2,048,000,000 sq m; cotton fabrics 1,180,000,000 sq m; finished products (in number of units) 442,352,000 watches and clocks, 25,550,000 air conditioners, 20,171,000 electronic desk calculators, 19,202,000 videocassette recorders, 11,842,000 cameras, 9,445,000 colour television receivers, 7,997,000 video cameras, 7,801,000 passenger cars, 6,702,000 bicycles, 5,288,000 facsimile machines, 5,042,000 automatic washing machines, 4,952,000 electric refrigerators, 3,960,000 computers, 3,167,000 microwave ovens, 2,725,000 motorcycles, 2,144,000 photocopy machines. Construction (value in ¥'000,000; 1994): residential 26,870,000; nonresidential 54,559,000.

Foreign trade[19]

Balance of trade (current prices)

	1991	1992	1993	1994	1995	1996
¥'000,000,000	+10,459	+13,484	+13,376	+12,419	+9,998	+6,737
% of total	14.1%	18.6%	20.0%	18.1%	13.7%	8.1%

Imports (1995): ¥31,534,000,000,000 (machinery and transport equipment 25.3%, food products 15.2%, petroleum and petroleum products 8.9%, textiles 7.3%, chemicals and chemical products 7.3%). *Major import sources:* United States 22.4%; China 10.7%; South Korea 5.1%; Australia 4.3%; Taiwan 4.3%; Indonesia 4.2%; Germany 4.1%; Canada 3.2%; Malaysia 3.1%; Thailand 3.0%.

Exports (1995): ¥41,532,000,000,000 (electrical machinery 25.6%, motor vehicles 12.0%, chemicals 6.8%, scientific and optical equipment 4.7%, iron and steel products 4.0%, textiles and allied products 2.0%). *Major export destinations:* United States 27.3%; South Korea 7.1%; Taiwan 6.5%; Hong Kong 6.3%; Singapore 5.2%; China 5.0%; Germany 4.6%; Thailand 4.5%; Malaysia 3.8%; United Kingdom 3.2%.

Trade by commodity group (1995)

	imports		exports	
SITC group	U.S.$'000,000	%	U.S.$'000,000	%
00 Food and live animals; 01 Beverages and tobacco	45,748	13.6	1,612	0.4
02 Crude materials, excluding fuels	34,268[20]	10.2[20]	3,086[20]	0.7[20]
03 Mineral fuels, lubricants, and related materials	53,976	16.1	2,736	0.6
04 Animal and vegetable oils, fats, and waxes	[20]	[20]	[20]	[20]
05 Chemicals and related products, n.e.s.	23,862	7.1	29,254	6.6
06 Basic manufactures	39,847	11.8	49,848	11.2
07 Machinery and transport equipment	75,722	22.5	310,708	70.1
08 Miscellaneous manufactured articles	49,365	14.7	35,661	8.0
09 Goods not classified by kind	13,306	3.9	10,032	2.3
TOTAL	336,094	100.0[6]	442,937	100.0[6]

Direction of trade (1994)

	imports		exports	
	U.S.$'000,000	%	U.S.$'000,000	%
Africa	4,015	1.5	6,652	1.7
Asia	124,955	45.6	167,986	42.5
South America	7,055	2.6	5,598	1.4
North America and Central America	74,053	27.0	136,597	34.5
United States	63,067	23.0	118,693	30.0
other North and Central Am.	10,986	4.0	17,904	4.5
Europe	48,469	17.7	68,256	17.3
EU	36,168	13.2	60,056	15.2
Russia	3,481	1.3	1,167	0.3
other Europe	8,820	3.2	7,033	1.8
Oceania	16,771	6.1	10,676	2.7
TOTAL	274,123[6]	100.0[6]	395,201[6]	100.0[6]

Transport and communications

Transport. Railroads (1995): length 12,511 mi, 20,134 km; rolling stock—locomotives 1,787, passenger cars 25,973, freight cars 12,688; passengers carried 22,598,000,000[21]; passenger-mi 248,584,000,000, passenger-km 400,058,000,000; short ton-mi cargo 17,193,000,000, metric ton-km cargo 25,101,000,000. Roads (1994): total length 706,091 mi, 1,136,346 km (paved 73%). Vehicles (1995): passenger cars 44,680,000; trucks 21,934,000; buses 243,000. Merchant marine (1994): vessels (100 gross tons and over) 7,165; total deadweight tonnage 22,000,000. Air transport (1995): passengers carried 90,780,000; passenger-mi 80,959,200,000, passenger-km 130,291,500,000; short ton-mi cargo 4,486,800,000, metric ton-km cargo 6,550,600,000; airports (1996) with scheduled flights 73.

Distribution of traffic (1994)

	cargo carried ('000,000 tons)	% of national total	passengers carried ('000,000)	% of national total
Road	5,810.0	90.1	59,935.0	72.4
Rail (intercity)	79.0	1.2	22,598.0	27.3
Urban transport	—	—	17,445.0[17]	...
road	—	—	8,445.0[17]	...
rail	—	—	9,000.0[17]	...
Inland water	556.0	8.6	151.0	0.2
Air	0.9	0.0	74.0	0.1
TOTAL	6,445.9	100.0[6]	82,758.0[21]	100.0[21]

Communications

Medium	date	unit	number	units per 1,000 persons
Daily newspapers	1995	circulation	72,518,000	578
Radio	1995	receivers	100,000,000	799
Television	1995	receivers	77,500,000	619
Telephones	1995	main lines	61,106,000	488
Cellular telephones	1995	subscribers	10,204,000	82
Facsimile machines	1995	units	8,000,000	64
Personal computers	1995	units	19,100,000	152

Radio and television broadcasting (1994): total radio stations 1,340, of which commercial 481; total television stations 14,625, of which commercial 7,736. Commercial broadcasting hours (by percentage of programs; 1994): reports—radio 13.0%, television 21.0%; education—radio 3.4%, television 12.0%; culture—radio 14.9%, television 24.7%; entertainment—radio 67.6%, television 40.0%. Advertisements (daily average; 1994): radio 148, television 295.

Other communications media (1995)

	titles		traffic ('000)
Print		**Electronic**[22]	
Books (new)	58,310	Telegram	43,288
of which		Domestic	43,288
Social sciences	12,578	International	270
Fiction	11,427	Fax service	678[23]
Arts	7,540		
Natural sciences	4,460		
Engineering	4,774		
History	3,917	**Post**[22]	
Philosophy	2,731	Mail	23,887,000
Magazines/journals[24]	4,178	Domestic	23,534,000
Weekly	112	International	353,000
Monthly	2,848	Parcels	384,000
		Domestic	378,000
Cinema		International	6,000
Feature films	610		
Domestic	289		
Foreign	321		

Education and health

Literacy: total population age 15 and over literate, virtually 100%.

Education (1995)

	schools	teachers	students	student/teacher ratio
Primary (age 6–11)	24,548	431,000	8,371,000	19.4
Secondary (age 12–17)	16,775	552,000	9,296,000	16.8
Higher	1,223	162,000	3,101,000	19.1

Health (1994): physicians 228,643 (1 per 546 persons); dentists 79,896 (1 per 1,564 persons); nurses 862,013 (1 per 145 persons); pharmacists 157,719 (1 per 792 persons); midwives 22,690[17] (1 per 5,476 persons); hospital beds (1992) 1,686,696 (1 per 74 persons), of which general 75.0%, mental 21.5%, tuberculosis 2.3%, other 1.2%; infant mortality rate per 1,000 live births 4.2.

Food (1995): daily per capita caloric intake 2,887 (vegetable products 79%, animal products 21%); 123% of FAO recommended minimum.

Military

Total active duty personnel (1996): 235,500 (army 62.9%, navy 18.2%, air force 18.9%). *Military expenditure as percentage of GNP* (1994): 1.0% (world 3.0%); per capita expenditure U.S.$366.

[1]Excludes Lake Naka (38 sq mi [98 sq km]), which is part of both Shimane and Tottori prefectures. [2]Excludes Lake Towada (23 sq mi [60 sq km]), which is part of both Akita and Aomori prefectures. [3]Part of Kantō geographic region. [4]Part of Kinki geographic region. [5]1987 survey (includes Lake Naka and Lake Towada); total area per 1994 survey equals 145,877 sq mi (377,819 sq km). [6]Detail does not add to total given because of rounding. [7]April 1. [8]January 1. [9]Applies to passengers carried within metropolitan areas only. [10]Import duties and statistical discrepancy less imputed bank service charge. [11]Includes 2,250,000 unemployed. [12]1995. [13]May. [14]June. [15]End of period. [16]September. [17]1992. [18]1991. [19]Import figures are f.o.b. in balance of trade and c.i.f. in commodities and trading partners. [20]Crude materials includes Animal and vegetable oils, fats, and waxes. [21]Totals do not include Urban transport. [22]1994. [23]Number of subscribers. [24]1996.

Internet resources for further information:

- **Bank of Japan: http://www.boj.or.jp/en/index.htm**
- **Economic Planning Agency of Japan: http://www.epa.go.jp/e-e/menu.html**
- **Statistics Bureau and Statistics Center (Japan): http://www.stat.go.jp/1.htm**

Jordan

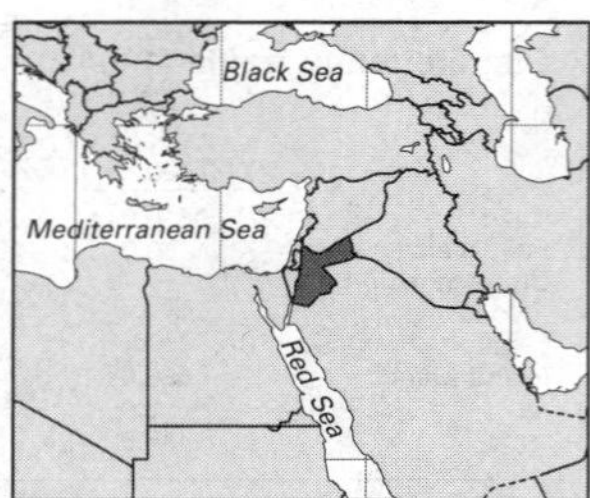

Official name: Al-Mamlakah al-Urdunnīyah al-Hāshimīyah (Al-Urdun) (Hashemite Kingdom of Jordan).
Form of government: constitutional monarchy[1] with a National Assembly comprising two legislative houses (Senate [40 appointed by king]; House of Deputies [80]).
Head of state and government: King assisted by Prime Minister.
Capital: Amman.
Official language: Arabic.
Official religion: Islam.
Monetary unit: 1 Jordan dinar (JD) = 1,000 fils; valuation (Oct. 3, 1997) JD 1.00 = U.S.$1.41 = £0.87.

Area and population

Governorates	Capitals	area sq mi	area sq km	population 1994 census[2]
ʿAjlūn	ʿAjlun	...[3]	...[3]	94,205
ʿAmman	Amman	4,097[4]	10,612[4]	1,567,908
Al-ʿAqabah	Al-ʿAqabah	...[5]	...[5]	79,745
Al-Balqāʾ	Aṣ-Ṣalt	425	1,100	273,489
Irbid	Irbid	985[3]	2,551[3]	745,774
Jarash	Jarash	...[3]	...[3]	123,195
Al-Karak	Al-Karak	1,548	4,010	169,552
Maʿān	Maʿān	13,954[5]	36,141[5]	79,401
Mādabā	Mādabā	...[4]	...[4]	106,308
Al-Mafraq	Al-Mafraq	10,475	27,129	170,903
Aṭ-Ṭafīlah	Aṭ-Ṭafīlah	850	2,202	61,156
Az-Zarqāʾ	Az-Zarqāʾ	2,008	5,201	623,943
TOTAL		34,342[6]	88,946[6]	4,095,579

Demography

Population (1997): 4,522,000.
Density (1997): persons per sq mi 131.7, persons per sq km 50.8.
Urban-rural (1994): urban 78.6%; rural 21.4%.
Sex distribution (1994): male 52.15%; female 47.85%.
Age breakdown (1994): under 15, 41.4%; 15–29, 31.6%; 30–44, 14.8%; 45–59, 8.0%; 60–74, 3.5%; 75 and over, 0.7%.
Population projection: (2000) 5,039,000; (2010) 6,734,000.
Doubling time: 23 years.
Ethnic composition (1995): Arab 98%, of which Palestinian *c.* 50%; Circassian 1%; Armenian 1%.
Religious affiliation (1995): Sunnī Muslim 92.0%; Christian 8.0%.
Major cities (1994): Amman 963,490; Az-Zarqāʾ 344,524; Irbid 208,201; Aṣ-Ṣalt 187,014; Ar-Ruṣayfah 131,130; Al-Mafraq 109,841.

Vital statistics

Birth rate per 1,000 population (1994): 34.3 (world avg. 25.0).
Death rate per 1,000 population (1994): 3.0 (world avg. 9.3).
Natural increase rate per 1,000 population (1994): 31.3 (world avg. 15.7).
Total fertility rate (avg. births per childbearing woman; 1995): 5.9.
Life expectancy at birth (1995): male 64.4 years; female 69.9 years.
Major causes of death per 100,000 population: n.a.

National economy

Budget (1996 est.). Revenue: JD 1,777,600,000 (taxes 49.3%, of which sales tax 22.2%, custom duties 12.7%, income and profits taxes 9.8%; nontax 37.7%, of which licenses and fees 13.4%, postal, telegraph, and telephone 10.5%; external aid 12.9%). Expenditures: JD 1,801,100,000 (current 80.5%, of which defense 23.2%, wages and salaries 19.4%; capital construction 19.5%).
Public debt (external, outstanding; 1995): U.S.$6,904,000,000.
Production (metric tons except as noted). Agriculture, forestry, fishing (1997): tomatoes 474,000, grapes 84,267, olives 82,117, oranges and tangerines 81,204, eggplants 73,500, cucumbers 68,000, cauliflower and cabbage 54,388, wheat 51,000, barley 44,730, lemons and limes 44,259, bananas 38,889; livestock (number of live animals) 2,100,000 sheep, 555,000 goats, 43,000 cattle, 18,000 camels, 78,000 chickens; roundwood (1995) 11,000 cu m; fish catch (1993) 62. Mining and quarrying (1996): phosphate ore 5,360,000; potash 1,800,000. Manufacturing (value added in JD '000; 1994): nonmetallic mineral products, pottery, and china 118,035; chemicals 94,295; food products 78,075; fabricated metal products, except machinery 31,755; refined petroleum 30,458; plastic products 27,181. Construction (1996): 5,471,000 sq m. Energy production (consumption): electricity (kW-hr; 1994) 5,075,000,000 (5,075,000,000); crude petroleum (barrels; 1994) 14,400 (22,056,000); petroleum products (metric tons; 1994) 2,856,000 (3,641,000).
Land use (1994): forest 0.8%; pasture 8.9%; agriculture 4.6%; other 85.7%.
Tourism (1995): receipts U.S.$696,000,000; expenditures U.S.$420,000,000.
Population economically active (1993): total 859,300; activity rate of total population 22.2% (participation rates: over age 15, 43.6%; female 14.0%; unemployed [1996] 13.0%).

Price and earnings indexes (1990 = 100)

	1990	1991	1992	1993	1994	1995	1996
Consumer price index	100.0	108.2	112.5	116.2	120.3	123.1	131.1
Daily earnings index	100.0	100.0	...	...	...	...	...

Gross national product (1995): U.S.$6,354,000,000 (U.S.$1,510 per capita).

Structure of gross domestic product and labour force

	1996 in value JD '000,000[7]	1996 % of total value	1993 labour force	1993 % of labour force
Agriculture	232.9	5.5	54,995	6.4
Mining	153.6	3.6	91,086	10.6
Manufacturing	688.6	16.2		
Construction	341.1	8.0	60,151	7.0
Public utilities	98.2	2.3	6,015	0.7
Transp. and commun.	591.8	13.9	57,573	6.7
Trade	480.1	11.3	129,754	15.1
Finance	766.8	18.0	24,920	2.9
Pub. admin., defense	792.7	18.6	434,806	50.6
Services[8]	201.9	4.7		
Other	−87.3[9]	−2.1[9]		
TOTAL	4,260.4	100.0	859,300	100.0

Household income and expenditure. Average household size (1995) 6.1; income per household (1995) JD 4,010 (U.S.$5,725); sources of income (1995): wages and salaries 51.4%, rent and property income 23.8%, transfer payments 13.7%, self-employment 11.1%; expenditure (1992): food and beverages 40.6%, housing and energy 26.9%, transportation 11.2%, clothing and footwear 8.2%, education 3.5%, health care 2.2%.

Foreign trade[10]

Balance of trade (current prices)

	1991	1992	1993	1994	1995	1996
JD '000,000	−939.7	−1,384.7	−1,588.9	−1,367.4	−1,349.3	−1,851.0
% of total	37.9%	45.5%	47.9%	40.7%	35.2%	41.8%

Imports (1996): JD 3,043,556,000 (machinery and transport equipment 26.0%; food and live animals 22.5%; mineral fuels 12.2%; chemicals and chemical products 10.8%; iron and steel 5.2%). *Major import sources:* Iraq 11.8%; United States 9.7%; Germany 8.0%; Italy 5.9%; France 4.9%.
Exports (1996): JD 1,288,171,000 (domestic goods 80.7%, of which chemicals and chemical products 25.7%, phosphate fertilizers 9.9%, potash 9.8%, fruits, vegetables, and nuts 6.4%, machinery and transport equipment 1.9%; reexports 19.3%). *Major export destinations*[11]: Saudi Arabia 12.5%; Iraq 9.2%; India 7.9%; United Arab Emirates 5.7%; Syria 3.9%.

Transport and communications

Transport. Railroads (1995): route length 677 km; passenger traffic was negligible; metric ton-km cargo 1,336,000,000[12]. Roads (1995): total length 6,750 km (paved 100%). Vehicles (1995): passenger cars 167,828; trucks and buses 82,516. Merchant marine (1995): vessels (1,000 gross tons and over) 1; total deadweight tonnage 15,794. Air transport (1995)[13]: passenger-km 4,394,518,000; metric ton-km cargo 265,226,000; airports (1997) 2.

Communications

Medium	date	unit	number	units per 1,000 persons
Daily newspapers	1994	circulation	250,000	62
Radio	1996	receivers	980,000	224
Television	1995	receivers	740,000	176
Telephones	1995	main lines	317,400	75
Cellular telephones	1995	subscribers	11,500	2.7
Facsimile machines	1995	units	32,000	7.6
Personal computers	1995	units	35,000	8.3

Education and health

Educational attainment (1995). Percentage of population age 25 and over having: no formal schooling 31.8%; primary education 34.5%; secondary 13.9%; postsecondary and vocational 8.4%; higher 11.4%. *Literacy* (1995): percentage of population age 15 and over literate 85.8%; males literate 91.4%; females literate 79.7%.

Education (1993–94)

	schools	teachers	students	student/ teacher ratio
Primary (age 6–14)	2,482	48,158	1,036,079	21.5
Secondary (age 15–17)	741	4,597	93,773	20.4
Voc., teacher tr.	54	2,553	30,052	11.8
Higher	55[14]	4,280[15]	85,934[15]	20.1

Health (1995): physicians 6,839 (1 per 616 persons); hospital beds 7,440 (1 per 567 persons); (1994) infant mortality rate per 1,000 live births 34.0.
Food (1995): daily per capita caloric intake 2,734 (vegetable products 89%, animal products 11%); 111% of FAO recommended minimum requirement.

Military

Total active duty personnel (1997): 104,050 (army 86.5%, navy 0.6%, air force 12.9%). *Military expenditure as percentage of GDP* (1995): 7.7% (world 2.8%); per capita expenditure U.S.$117.

[1]Political parties legalized July 1992; November 1993 legislative elections were multiparty. [2]Preliminary. [3]Irbid includes area of ʿAjlūn and Jarash governorates. [4]ʿAmman includes area of Mādabā governorate. [5]Maʿān includes area of Al-ʿAqabah governorate. [6]Excludes 116 sq mi (300 sq km) of territory per Israel-Jordan treaty of October 1994. [7]At factor cost. [8]Includes domestic help employed in households. [9]Less imputed bank service charges. [10]Imports f.o.b. in balance of trade and c.i.f. in commodities and trading partners. [11]Domestic exports only. [12]For Aqaba Railway Corporation only. [13]Royal Jordanian airlines only. [14]1988–89. [15]Includes community colleges.

Internet resources for further information:

- **The Hashemite Kingdom of Jordan http://www.iconnect.com/jordan/**
- **Jordan National Information System http://www.nic.gov.jo/**

Kazakstan

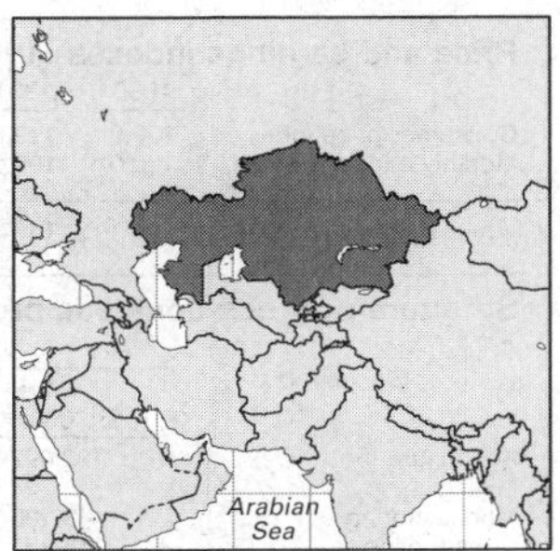

Official name: Qazaqstan Respublikasï (Republic of Kazakstan).
Form of government[1]: unitary republic with a Parliament consisting of two chambers (Senate [47[2]] and Assembly [67]).
Head of state and government[1]: President assisted by Prime Minister.
Capital: Aqmola[3].
Official language: Kazak.
Official religion: none.
Monetary unit[4]: 1 tenge (T) = 100 tiyn; valuation (Oct. 3, 1997) free rate, 1 U.S.$ = 75.81 tenge; 1 £ = 122.21 tenge.

Area and population

		area		population
				1995
Provinces	Capitals	sq mi	sq km	estimate
Almaty (Alma-Ata)	Almaty (Alma-Ata)	86,500[5]	224,200[5]	1,684,600
Aqmola[6]	Aqmola	35,500	92,000	845,700
Aqtöbe	Aqtöbe	116,050	300,600	752,800
Atyraū	Atyraū	45,800	118,600	459,600
Batys Qazaqstan	Oral	58,400	151,300	669,800
Mangghystaū	Aqtaū	63,950	165,600	324,400
Ongtüstik Qazaqstan	Shymkent	45,300	117,300	1,987,800
Pavlodar	Pavlodar	48,200	124,800	943,600
Qaraghandy	Qaraghandy	165,250	428,000	1,754,500
Qostanay[6]	Qostanay	44,000	113,900	1,055,300
Qyzylorda	Qyzylorda	87,250[7]	226,000[7]	606,100
Shyghys Qazaqstan	Shyghys Qazaqstan	109,400	283,300	1,750,500
Soltüstik Qazaqstan	Petropavl	47,500	123,200	1,257,900
Torghay[6]	*Arqalyq*	*43,150*	*111,800*	*305,900*
Zhambyl	Zhambyl (Aullye-Ata)	55,700	144,300	1,039,600
Cities				
Almaty (Alma-Ata)	—	5	5	1,172,400
Baykonur (Leninsk)	—	7	7	68,600
TOTAL		1,052,100[8]	2,724,900	16,679,100

Demography

Population (1997): 16,554,000.
Density (1997): persons per sq mi 15.7, persons per sq km 6.1.
Urban-rural (1996): urban 56.0%; rural 44.0%.
Sex distribution (1994): male 49.00%; female 51.00%.
Age breakdown (1991): under 15, 31.4%; 15–29, 25.1%; 30–44, 21.3%; 45–59, 12.2%; 60–69, 6.1%; 70 and over, 3.9%.
Population projection: (2000) 16,573,000; (2010) 17,181,000.
Ethnic composition (1995): Kazak 46.0%; Russian 34.8%; Ukrainian 4.9%; German 3.1%; Uzbek 2.3%; Tatar 1.9%; other 7.0%.
Religious affiliation: Muslim (mostly Sunnī) 47.0%; Russian Orthodox 8.2%; Protestant 2.1%; other (mostly nonreligious) 42.7%.
Major cities (1995): Almaty (Alma-Ata) 1,172,400; Qaraghandy (Karaganda) 573,700; Shymkent (Chimkent) 397,600; Pavlodar 340,700.

Vital statistics

Birth rate per 1,000 population (1995): 16.7 (world avg. 25.0); (1994) legitimate 86.6%; illegitimate 13.4%.
Death rate per 1,000 population (1995): 10.2 (world avg. 9.2).
Natural increase rate per 1,000 population (1995): 6.5 (world avg. 15.7).
Total fertility rate (avg. births per childbearing woman; 1994): 3.1.
Marriage rate per 1,000 population (1994): 7.3.
Divorce rate per 1,000 population (1994): 2.5.
Life expectancy at birth (1994): male 64.0 years; female 73.0 years.
Major causes of death per 100,000 population (1994): diseases of the circulatory system 459.0; malignant neoplasms (cancers) 134.3; accidents, poisoning, and violence 125.6; diseases of the respiratory system 87.9.

National economy

Budget (1997). Revenue: 270,492,000,000 tenge (taxes on goods and services 32.6%, income, profits and capital gains taxes 31.7%, taxes on international trade 3.1%, nontax revenue 19.4%). Expenditures: 325,469,000,000 tenge (education 18.3%, health 14.5%, defense 5.9%, social security 5.4%).
Public debt (external, outstanding; 1995): U.S.$2,899,000,000.
Population economically active (1995): total 6,976,000; activity rate of total population 41.8% (participation rates: ages 16–59 [male], 16–54 [female] 80.1%; female [1994] 48.0%; unemployed 2.3%).

Price and earnings indexes (1994 = 100)

	1994	1995	1996
Consumer price index	100.0	286.6	389.5
Monthly earnings index	100.0	276.2	384.4

Production (metric tons except as noted). Agriculture, forestry, fishing (1996): wheat 7,678,000, barley 2,696,000, potatoes 1,656,000, oats 359,000, sugar beets 341,000; livestock (number of live animals) 19,953,000 sheep and goats, 6,860,000 cattle, 1,700,000 horses, 1,622,700 pigs; roundwood (1991) 1,974,000 cu m; fish catch (1995) 69,716. Mining and quarrying (1995): iron ore 15,000,000; chrome 2,400,000; lead 190,000; zinc 40,000. Manufacturing (value of production in '000,000 tenge; 1996): food products 107,397; nonferrous metallurgy 89,052; ferrous metallurgy 81,026; machinery 52,168; chemical products 28,974; construction materials 23,239. Construction (1994): residential 2,300,000 sq m. Energy production (consumption): electricity (kW-hr; 1996) 58,657,000,000 (1994; 78,277,000,000); coal (metric tons; 1996) 76,597,000 (1994; 76,357,000); crude petroleum (barrels; 1996) 166,800,000 (1994; 87,004,000); petroleum products (metric tons; 1994) 13,372,000 (14,306,000); natural gas (cu m; 1996) 6,397,000,000 (1994; 9,588,000,000).
Gross national product (1995): U.S.$22,143,000,000 (U.S.$1,330 per capita).

Structure of gross domestic product and labour force

	1995			
	in value '000,000 tenge	% of total value	labour force	% of labour force
Agriculture	123,830	12.1	1,442,000	20.7
Manufacturing, mining, public utilities	238,733	23.4	1,372,000	19.7
Construction	62,459	6.1	364,000	5.2
Transp. and commun.	108,203	10.6	507,000	7.3
Trade	164,481	16.1	1,035,000	14.8
Finance	322,016	31.6	334,000	4.8
Pub. admin., defense; Services			1,664,000	23.9
Other	...	...	258,000[9]	3.7[9]
TOTAL	1,019,122	100.0[8]	6,976,000	100.0[8]

Household income and expenditure. Average household size (1989) 4.0; income per household (1991) 5,290 Russian rubles[4]: U.S.$ equivalent: n.a.[10]; sources of income (1994): salaries and wages 67.7%, social benefits 16.9%, agricultural income 5.8%, other 9.6%; expenditure (1994): retail goods 60.6%, taxes 16.8%, services 11.7%, other 10.9%.

Foreign trade

Balance of trade (current prices)

	1992	1993	1994	1995	1996
U.S.$'000,000	−1,121	−414	−920	−222	−400
% of total	13.6%	4.2%	12.3%	2.1%	3.4%

Imports (1996): U.S.$6,017,000,000 (equipment and mechanical tools 8.7%, chemical industry products 8.3%, foodstuffs 7.4%, vehicles 6.0%, oil and gas condensate 5.2%, electrical equipment 4.9%, oil refining products 1.4%). *Major import sources* (1995): Russia 64.7%; Germany 7.0%; Ukraine 5.3%; Kyrgyzstan 2.7%; Lithuania 2.1%; China 1.8%.
Exports (1996): U.S.$5,617,000,000 (oil and gas condensate 23.9%, rolled ferrous metal 9.6%, refined copper 9.5%, grain 8.0%, coal 5.1%, ferroalloys 3.3%, alumina 2.8%, unrefined zinc 2.4%, cotton fiber 1.7%, iron ores and concentrates 1.4%, oil refining products 1.4%). *Major export destinations* (1995): Russia 64.1%; China 7.4%; Ukraine 6.8%; Italy 3.1%; U.S. 2.8%.

Transport and communications

Transport. Railroads (1994): length 21,600 km; (1995) passenger-km 13,200,000,000; metric ton-km cargo 124,500,000,000. Roads (1995): total length 158,655 km (paved 68.4%). Vehicles (1995): passenger cars 1,030,000; trucks and buses 516,000. Air transport (1994): passenger-km 4,600,000,000; metric ton-km cargo 100,000,000; airports (1997) with scheduled flights 20.

Communications

Medium	date	unit	number	units per 1,000 persons
Television	1995	receivers	4,578,000	275
Telephones	1995	main lines	1,963,000	118
Cellular telephones	1995	subscribers	4,600	0.3
Facsimile machines	1995	units	2,900	0.2

Education and health

Educational attainment (1989). Population age 25 and over having: primary education or no formal schooling 16.2%; some secondary 19.8%; completed secondary and some postsecondary 54.1%; higher 9.9%. *Literacy* (1989): population age 15 and over literate 97.5%; males 99.1%; females 96.1%.

Education (1995–96)

	schools	teachers	students	student/ teacher ratio
Primary (age 7–13); Secondary (age 14–17)	8,700	262,000	3,060,000	11.7
Voc., teacher tr.	3,504[11]	...	984,300[11]	...
Higher	69[11]	...	267,000[11]	...

Health (1995): physicians 62,000 (1 per 267 persons); hospital beds 193,000 (1 per 86 persons); infant mortality rate per 1,000 live births 27.9.

Military

Total active duty personnel (1997): 35,100 (army 57.0%, air force 43.0%). *Military expenditure as percentage of GNP* (1995): 0.9% (world avg. 2.8%); per capita expenditure U.S.$25.

[1]According to a presidential edict of Oct. 16, 1995, implementing the new constitution approved by referendum Aug. 30, 1995. [2]Includes 7 nonelective seats. [3]Almaty until Dec. 10, 1997, thereafter Aqmola. [4]The Kazak tenge was introduced Nov. 18, 1993, to replace the Russian ruble, at a rate of 500 Russian rubles to 1 tenge; on Nov. 25, 1993, the Kazak tenge became the sole legal tender. [5]Area of Almaty city included with Almaty province. [6]Torghay province abolished April 23, 1997; its area and population were divided between Aqmola and Qostanay provinces, but adjusted figures are not yet available. [7]Area of Baykonur city included with Qyzylorda province. [8]Detail does not add to total given because of rounding. [9]Includes 139,600 undistributed unemployed and 118,400 undistributed employed. [10]Ruble-area exchange rates for this period very speculative. [11]1994–95.

Internet resources for further information:
- **Kazakstan Human Development Report 1995 http://www.undp.org/undp/rbec/nhdr/kazakstan/**

Kenya

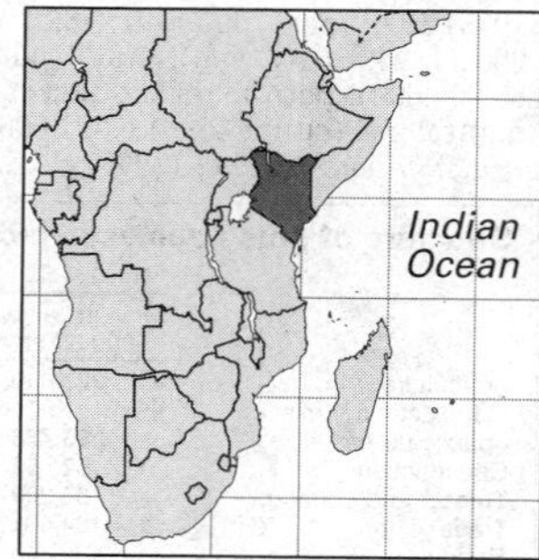

Official name: Jamhuri ya Kenya (Swahili); Republic of Kenya (English).
Form of government: unitary multiparty republic with one legislative house (National Assembly [202[1]]).
Head of state and government: President.
Capital: Nairobi.
Official languages: Swahili; English.
Official religion: none.
Monetary unit: 1 Kenya shilling[2] (K Sh) = 100 cents; valuation (Oct. 3, 1997) 1 U.S.$ = K Sh 61.93; 1 £ = K Sh 99.82.

Area and population

Provinces	Provincial headquarters	area sq mi	area sq km	population 1993 estimate
Central	Nyeri	5,087	13,176	3,626,000
Coast	Mombasa	32,279	83,603	2,155,000
Eastern	Embu	61,734	159,891	4,334,000
North Eastern	Garissa	48,997	126,902	408,000
Nyanza	Kisumu	6,240	16,162	4,041,000
Rift Valley	Nakuru	67,131	173,868	5,690,000
Western	Kakamega	3,228	8,360	3,035,000
Special area				
Nairobi	—	264	684	1,678,000
TOTAL		224,961[3]	582,646	24,967,000

Demography

Population (1997): 28,803,000.
Density (1997): persons per sq mi 128.0, persons per sq km 49.4.
Urban-rural (1995): urban 20.4%; rural 79.6%.
Sex distribution (1997): male 49.99%; female 50.01%.
Age breakdown (1997): under 15, 51.3%; 15–29, 26.5%; 30–44, 12.7%; 45–59, 6.3%; 60–74, 2.7%; 75 and over, 0.5%.
Population projection: (2000) 30,490,000; (2010) 33,920,000.
Doubling time: 33 years.
Ethnic composition (1989): Kikuyu 17.7%; Luhya 12.4%; Luo 10.6%; Kalenjin 9.8%; Kamba 9.8%; other 39.7%.
Religious affiliation (1987): Christian 73.0%, of which Roman Catholic 27.0%, Protestant 19.0%, other Christian (mostly African Indigenous, Anglican, Eastern Orthodox) 27.0%; traditional 19.0%; Muslim 6.0%; other 2.0%.
Major cities (1989): Nairobi 1,504,900[4]; Mombasa 465,000; Kisumu 185,100; Nakuru 162,800; Machakos 92,300[5].

Vital statistics

Birth rate per 1,000 population (1996): 32.4 (world avg. 25.0).
Death rate per 1,000 population (1996): 10.8 (world avg. 9.3).
Natural increase rate per 1,000 population (1996): 21.6 (world avg. 15.7).
Total fertility rate (avg. births per childbearing woman; 1996): 4.3.
Life expectancy at birth (1996): male 54.2 years; female 54.6 years.
Major causes of death per 100,000 population: n.a.; however, major infectious diseases include AIDS, malaria, gastroenteritis, venereal diseases, diarrhea and dysentery, trachoma, amebiasis, and schistosomiasis.

National economy

Budget (1995–96). Revenue: K Sh 151,316,000,000 (goods and services 34.5%, income tax 31.7%, custom and excise duties 14.0%). Expenditures: K Sh 152,555,000,000 (recurrent expenditure 79.6%, development expenditure 20.4%).
Production (metric tons except as noted). Agriculture, forestry, fishing (1996): sugarcane 4,810,000, corn (maize) 2,223,000, cassava 860,000, sweet potatoes 635,000, plantains 370,000, wheat 350,000, pineapples 270,000, pulses 270,000, tea 255,000, bananas 220,000, potatoes 205,000, sorghum 140,000, coffee 98,000, barley 65,000, millet 59,000, coconuts 43,000, sisal 34,000, tomatoes 32,000, cashew nuts 15,000, sunflower seeds 15,000, seed cotton 12,000, tobacco 10,000, cotton seeds 8,000; livestock (number of live animals) 13,800,000 cattle, 7,400,000 goats, 5,600,000 sheep; roundwood (1995) 41,696,000 cu m; fish catch (1995) 241,064, of which freshwater fish 95.3%. Mining and quarrying (1995): soda ash 218,450; fluorite 80,230; salt 71,400. Manufacturing (value added in K£'000[2]; 1994): food products 639,000; machinery and transport equipment 233,000; beverages and tobacco 190,000; chemical products 168,000; metal products 125,000; paper and paper products 87,000; plastic products 65,000; clothing and footwear 55,000. Construction (1990): residential 411,000 sq m; nonresidential 182,000 sq m. Energy production (consumption): electricity (kW-hr; 1994) 3,538,000,000 (3,802,000,000); coal (metric tons; 1994) none (109,000); crude petroleum (barrels; 1994) none (15,928,000); petroleum products (metric tons; 1994) 1,949,000 (1,680,000).
Public debt (external, outstanding; 1995): U.S.$5,927,000,000.
Household income and expenditure. Average household size (1980) 6.2; average annual income per household: n.a.; sources of income: n.a.; expenditure (1980): food 46.5%, housing 10.0%, furniture and utensils 9.4%, transportation 8.4%, clothing and footwear 7.7%, energy 2.6%, health 2.2%.
Tourism (1995): receipts from visitors U.S.$454,000,000; expenditures by nationals abroad U.S.$135,000,000.
Population economically active (1992): total 10,633,000; activity rate of total population 41.1% (participation rates [1985]: ages 15–64, 76.2%; female 40.9%; unemployed, n.a.).

Price and earnings indexes (1990 = 100)

	1990	1991	1992	1993	1994	1995	1996
Consumer price index	100.0	119.8	155.2	226.3	292.0	294.3	320.2
Monthly earnings index	100.0	109.3	...	...	...	...	...

Gross national product (1995): U.S.$7,583,000,000 (U.S.$280 per capita).

Structure of gross domestic product and labour force

	1995 in value K Sh '000,000	% of total value	labour force[6]	% of labour force[6]
Agriculture	122,697	31.0	294,000	18.9
Mining	724	0.2	5,000	0.3
Manufacturing	43,185	10.9	205,000	13.1
Construction	18,353	4.6	76,000	4.9
Public utilities	5,441	1.4	23,000	1.5
Transp. and commun.	30,407	7.8	79,000	5.1
Trade	60,501	15.3	135,000	8.7
Finance	72,335	18.2	78,000	5.0
Pub. admin., defense; Services	42,514	10.7	663,000	42.6
Other	—	—	—	—
TOTAL	396,157	100.0[3]	1,558,000	100.0

Land use (1994): forest 29.5%; pasture 37.4%; agriculture 8.0%; other 25.1%.

Foreign trade[7]

Balance of trade (current prices)

	1991	1992	1993	1994	1995	1996
K Sh '000,000	−11,890	−5,923	−5,938	−16,738	−36,082	−44,762
% of total	16.4%	6.2%	3.7%	8.8%	15.6%	15.9%

Imports (1995): U.S.$3,065,000,000 (machinery and transport equipment 35.4%, chemical products 17.6%, petroleum and petroleum products 13.4%, food and beverages 4.4%). *Major import sources:* United Kingdom 12.4%; United Arab Emirates 8.9%; Japan 8.6%; India 7.5%; South Africa 7.4%; Germany 6.0%; Italy 5.2%; United States 3.6%; Saudi Arabia 2.0%.
Exports (1995): U.S.$1,873,100,000 (tea 17.6%, coffee [not roasted] 15.1%, fruits and vegetables 5.0%, petroleum products 5.0%, cement 1.8%, hides and skins 1.1%, soda ash 1.1%). *Major export destinations:* United Kingdom 11.9%; Germany 9.3%; Uganda 8.7%; Tanzania 7.1%; Pakistan 5.7%; The Netherlands 5.2%; United States 5.1%.

Transport and communications

Transport. Railroads (1993): route length 1,885 mi, 3,034 km; passenger-mi 288,000,000, passenger-km 464,000,000; short ton-mi cargo 898,600,000, metric ton-km cargo 1,312,000,000. Roads (1995): total length 39,558 mi, 63,663 km (paved 14%). Vehicles (1995): passenger cars 271,000; trucks and buses 75,900. Merchant marine (1992): vessels (100 gross tons and over) 29; total deadweight tonnage 11,649. Air transport (1996)[8]: passenger-mi 1,141,800,000, passenger-km 1,837,553,000; short ton-mi cargo 32,746,000, metric ton-km cargo 47,809,000; airports (1997) with scheduled flights 11.

Communications

Medium	date	unit	number	units per 1,000 persons
Daily newspapers	1995	circulation	402,000[9]	14[9]
Radio	1996	receivers	3,000,000	103
Television	1995	receivers	462,000	18
Telephones	1995	main lines	239,600	9.0
Cellular telephones	1995	subscribers	2,300	0.1
Facsimile machines	1995	units	3,800	0.1
Personal computers	1995	units	18,000	0.7

Education and health

Educational attainment (1979). Percentage of population over age 25 having: no formal schooling 58.6%; primary education 32.2%; some secondary 7.9%; complete secondary and higher 1.3%. *Literacy* (1995): total population over age 15 literate 78.1%; males literate 86.3%; females literate 70.0%.

Education (1993)

	schools	teachers	students	student/ teacher ratio
Primary (age 5–11)	15,804	173,002	5,428,600	31.4
Secondary (age 12–17)	2,639	31,657	517,577	16.3
Voc., teacher tr.	63	1,332[10]	29,593	13.4[10]
Higher	14	4,392[11]	88,180	8.1[11]

Health (1994): physicians 4,558 (1 per 5,999 persons); hospital beds 37,271 (1 per 734 persons); infant mortality rate per 1,000 live births (1996): 55.2.
Food (1995): daily per capita caloric intake 1,991 (vegetable products 88%, animal products 12%); 86% of FAO recommended minimum requirement.

Military

Total active duty personnel (1996): 24,200 (army 84.7%, navy 5.0%, air force 10.3%). *Military expenditure as percentage of GNP* (1995) 2.3% (world 2.8%); per capita expenditure U.S.$6.

[1]Includes 14 nonelective seats. [2]Kenya pound (K£) as a unit of account equals 20 K Sh. [3]Detail does not add to total given because of rounding. [4]1990. [5]1983. [6]Employed persons only. [7]Import figures are f.o.b. in balance of trade and c.i.f. in commodities and trading partners. [8]Kenya Airways only. [9]Circulation for four newspapers only. [10]1987–88; teacher training only. [11]1990–91; universities only.

Internet resources for further information:
- **Embassy of the Republic of Kenya http://www.embassyofkenya.com/**

Kiribati

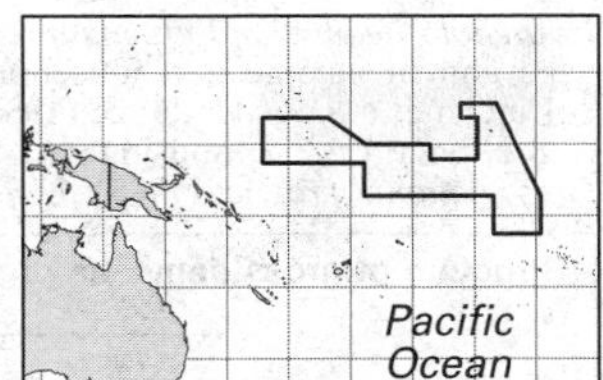

Official name: Republic of Kiribati.
Form of government: unitary republic with a unicameral legislature (House of Assembly [41[1]]).
Head of state and government: President.
Capital: Bairiki, on Tarawa Atoll.
Official language: English.
Official religion: none.
Monetary unit: 1 Australian Dollar ($A) = 100 cents; valuation (Oct. 3, 1997) 1 U.S.$ = $A 1.37; 1 £ = $A 2.21.

Area and population

Island Groups / Islands	Capitals	area[2] sq mi	area[2] sq km	population 1990 census
Gilberts Group	Bairiki Islet	110	286[3]	67,508
Abaiang	Tuarabu	7	18	5,233
Abemama	Kariatebike	11	27	3,218
Aranuka	Takaeang	5	12	1,002
Arorae	Roreti	3	9	1,440
Banaba	Anteeren	2	6	284
Beru	Taubukinberu	7	18	2,909
Butaritari	Butaritari	5	13	3,774
Kuria	Tabontebike	6	16	990
Maiana	Tebangetua	6	17	2,180
Makin	Makin	3	8	1,762
Marakei	Rawannawi	5	14	2,863
Nikunau	Rungata	7	19	1,994
Nonouti	Teuabu	8	20	2,814
Onotoa	Buariki	6	16	2,100
Tabiteuea North	Utiroa	10	26	3,201
Tabiteuea South	Buariki	5	12	1,331
Tamana	Bakaka	2	5	1,385
Tarawa North	Abaokoro	6	15	3,648
Tarawa South	Bairiki	6	16	25,380
Line Group	Kiritimati	192	496	4,782
Northern		167	432	—
Kiritimati (Christmas)	London	150	388	2,537
Tabuaeran (Fanning)	Paelau	13	34	1,309
Teraina (Washington)	Washington	4	10	936
Southern (Millennium, Flint, Malden, Starbuck, Vostok)		25	64	—
Phoenix Group (Birnie, Enderbury, Kanton [Canton], McKean, Manra [Sydney], Nikumaroro [Gardner], Orona [Hull], Rawaki [Phoenix])	Kanton	11	29	45
TOTAL		313	811	72,335

Demography

Population (1997): 82,400.
Density (1996)[4]: persons per sq mi 294.3, persons per sq km 113.5.
Urban-rural (1997): urban 36.0%; rural 64.0%.
Sex distribution (1990): male 49.45%; female 50.55%.
Age breakdown (1990): under 15, 40.3%; 15–29, 27.5%; 30–44, 17.3%; 45–59, 9.2%; 60–74, 4.8%; 75 and over, 0.9%.
Population projection: (2000) 87,000; (2010) 94,700.
Doubling time: 35 years.
Ethnic composition (1990): I-Kiribati 97.4%; mixed (part I-Kiribati and other) 1.5%; Tuvaluan 0.5%; European 0.2%; other 0.4%.
Religious affiliation (1990): Roman Catholic 53.4%; Kiribati Protestant (Congregational) 39.2%; Bahā'ī 2.4%; Seventh-day Adventist 1.9%; Mormon 1.6%; other 1.5%.
Major cities (1990): urban Tarawa 25,154.

Vital statistics

Birth rate per 1,000 population (1994): 31.0 (world avg. 25.0); legitimate, n.a.; illegitimate, n.a.
Death rate per 1,000 population (1994): 11.0 (world avg. 9.3).
Natural increase rate per 1,000 population (1994): 20.0 (world avg. 15.7).
Total fertility rate (avg. births per childbearing woman; 1997): 3.3.
Marriage rate per 1,000 population (1988): 5.2.
Life expectancy at birth (1997): male 62.0 years; female 67.0 years.
Major causes of death per 100,000 population (1993): senility without mention of psychosis 61.2; stroke 39.1; diarrhea 37.8; hepatitis 32.5; diabetes mellitus 28.6; malnutrition 23.4; meningitis 18.2.

National economy

Budget (1995). Revenue: $A 42,200,000 (nontax revenue 71.1%, tax revenue 28.9%). Expenditures: $A 70,600,000 (current expenditure 68.1%, capital expenditure 31.9%).
Public debt (external, outstanding; 1993): U.S.$18,000,000.
Production (metric tons except as noted). Agriculture, forestry, fishing (1996): coconuts 68,000, roots and tubers 8,100 (of which taro 1,600), copra (1994) 8,000, vegetables and melons 5,000, bananas 4,500, seaweed (1994) 1,200; livestock (number of live animals) 9,500 pigs, 300,000 chickens; fish catch (1995) 24,685. Mining and quarrying: none. Manufacturing (1991): processed copra 8,661; other important products are processed fish, baked goods, clothing, and handicrafts. Energy production (consumption): electricity (kW-hr; 1993) 7,000,000 (7,000,000); coal, none (n.a.); crude petroleum, none (n.a.); petroleum products (metric tons; 1993) none (7,000); natural gas, none (n.a.).
Gross national product (1995): U.S.$73,000,000 (U.S.$920 per capita).

Structure of gross domestic product and labour force

	1994 in value $A '000	1994 % of total value	1990 labour force	1990 % of labour force
Agriculture, fishing	11,460	22.5	23,137[5]	71.0[5]
Mining	—	—	—	—
Manufacturing	379	0.7	622	1.9
Construction	1,100	2.2	339	1.0
Public utilities	860	1.7	301	0.9
Transp. and commun.	5,917	11.6	921	2.8
Trade	8,195	16.1	1,341	4.1
Finance	2,040	4.0	441	1.4
Pub. admin., defense	14,775	29.0	2,123	6.5
Services			2,286	7.0
Other	6,200	12.2	1,099[6]	3.4[6]
TOTAL	50,926	100.0	32,610	100.0

Population economically active (1990): total 32,610; activity rate of total population 45.1% (participation rates: over age 15, 75.6%; female 46.4%; unemployed 2.8%).

Price and earnings indexes (1985 = 100)

	1989	1990	1991	1992	1993	1994	1995
Consumer price index	120.8	126.9	131.7	138.3	146.7	154.2	164.2
Earnings index	...	...	...	...	...	...	...

Household income and expenditure. Average household size (1990) 6.6; income per household: n.a.; sources of income (1978): wages 69.7%, self-employment 21.4%, transfer payments 6.0%, other 2.9%; expenditure (1982): food 50.0%, tobacco and alcohol 14.0%, clothing 8.0%, transportation 8.0%, housing, energy, and household operation 7.5%.
Tourism (1995): receipts from visitors U.S.$1,000,000; expenditures by nationals abroad (1994) U.S.$3,000,000.
Land use (1994): forested 2.7%; agricultural and under permanent cultivation 50.7%; other 46.6%.

Foreign trade

Balance of trade (current prices)

	1989	1990	1991	1992	1993	1994
$A '000	–22,161	–30,765	–29,529	–44,017	–35,804	–29,005
% of total	63.3%	80.7%	80.0%	77.2%	77.9%	67.1%

Imports (1994): $A 36,115,000 (food and live animals 31.6%; machinery and transport equipment 17.4%; basic manufactures 13.4%; mineral fuels 9.3%; beverages and tobacco 8.7%; chemicals 6.4%; crude materials 2.1%). *Major import sources:* France 27.6%; United States 26.2%; Australia 16.3%; Fiji 8.3%; Japan 7.5%; New Zealand 2.5%.
Exports (1994): $A 7,110,000 (domestic exports 73.4%, of which copra 63.0%, fish and fish preparations 6.2%, seaweed 4.2%; reexports 26.6%). *Major export destinations:* Japan 32.9%; United States 17.1%; Hong Kong 12.9%; Bangladesh 8.6%; Germany 8.6%; Malaysia 7.1%.

Transport and communications

Transport. Roads (1995): total length 407 mi, 655 km (paved [1991] 5%). Vehicles (1982): passenger cars 307; trucks and buses 130. Merchant marine (1992): vessels (100 gross tons and over) 7; total deadweight tonnage 2,685. Air transport (1993): passenger-mi 6,000,000, passenger-km 10,000,000; short ton-mi cargo 514,000[7], metric ton-km cargo 750,000[7]; airports (1996) with scheduled flights 17.

Communications

Medium	date	unit	number	units per 1,000 persons
Radio	1996	receivers	6,050	75
Television	1995	receivers	685	8.6
Telephones	1995	main lines	2,000	25
Facsimile machines	1995	units	200	2.5

Education and health

Educational attainment (1990)[8]. Percentage of population age 15 and over having: no schooling 6.9%; primary 67.8%; secondary 24.5%; higher 0.6%; not stated 0.2%. *Literacy* (1985): total population age 15 and over literate 90%.

Education (1993)

	schools	teachers	students	student/teacher ratio
Primary (age 6–13)	92	537	16,316	30.4
Secondary (age 14–18)	9[7]	179	3,152	17.6
Voc., teacher tr.	6[7]	40	297	7.4
Higher[9]	—	—	—	—

Health: physicians (1993) 10 (1 per 7,687 persons); hospital beds (1990) 283 (1 per 253 persons); infant mortality rate per 1,000 live births (1996) 54.
Food (1995): daily per capita caloric intake 2,772 (vegetable products 88%, animal products 12%); 122% of FAO recommended minimum requirement.

[1]Includes two nonelective members. [2]Includes uninhabited islands. [3]Detail does not add to total given because of rounding. [4]Based on inhabited island areas (280 sq mi, [726 sq km]) only. [5]Includes 20,568 persons engaged in "village work" (subsistence agriculture or fishing). [6]Includes 900 unemployed. [7]1990. [8]For indigenous population. [9]54 students overseas.

Korea, North

Official name: Chosŏn Minjujuŭi In'min Konghwaguk (Democratic People's Republic of Korea).
Form of government: unitary single-party republic with one legislative house (Supreme People's Assembly [687]).
Chief of state:[1].
Head of government: Premier.
Capital: P'yŏngyang.
Official language: Korean.
Official religion: none.
Monetary unit: 1 won = 100 chŏn; valuation (Oct. 3, 1997) 1 U.S.$ = 2.20 won[2]; 1 £ = 3.55 won.

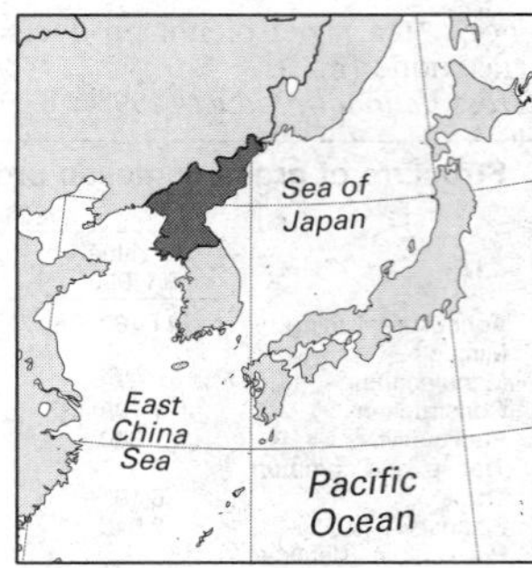

Area and population

		area		population[3]
Provinces	Capitals	sq mi	sq km	1987 estimate
Chagang-do	Kanggye	6,551	16,968	1,156,000
Kangwŏn-do	Wŏnsan	4,306	11,152	1,227,000
North Hamgyŏng (Hamgyŏng-pukto)	Ch'ŏngjin	6,784	17,570	2,003,000
North Hwanghae (Hwanghae-pukto)	Sariwŏn	3,091	8,007	1,409,000
North Pyŏngan (P'yŏngan-pukto)	Sinŭiju	4,707[4]	12,191[4]	2,380,000
South Hamgyŏng (Hamgyŏng-namdo)	Hamhŭng	7,324	18,970	2,547,000
South Hwanghae (Hwanghae-namdo)	Haeju	3,090	8,002	1,914,000
South Pyŏngan (P'yŏngan-namdo)	P'yŏngsan	4,470	11,577	2,653,000
Yanggang-do	Hyesan	5,528	14,317	628,000
Special cities				
Kaesŏng	—	485	1,255	331,000
Namp'o	—	291	753	715,000
P'yŏngyang	—	772	2,000	2,355,000
Special district				
Hyangsan-chigu	—	[4]	[4]	28,000
TOTAL		47,399	122,762	19,346,000

Demography

Population (1997): 24,317,000.
Density (1997): persons per sq mi 513.0, persons per sq km 198.1.
Urban-rural (1995): urban 61.3%; rural 38.7%.
Sex distribution (1997): male 48.83%; female 51.17%.
Age breakdown (1997): under 15, 26.5%; 15–29, 26.0%; 30–44, 21.9%; 45–59, 15.2%; 60–74, 8.7%; 75 and over, 1.7%.
Population projection: (2000) 25,491,000; (2010) 28,491,000.
Ethnic composition (1989): Korean 99.8%; Chinese 0.2%.
Religious affiliation (1980): atheist or nonreligious 67.9%; traditional beliefs 15.6%; Ch'ŏndogyo 13.9%; Buddhist 1.7%; Christian 0.9%.
Major cities (1987): P'yŏngyang 2,500,000[5]; Hamhŭng 701,000; Ch'ŏngjin 520,000; Namp'o 370,000; Sunch'ŏn 356,000.

Vital statistics

Birth rate per 1,000 population (1996): 22.5 (world avg. 25.0).
Death rate per 1,000 population (1996): 5.3 (world avg. 9.3).
Natural increase rate per 1,000 population (1996): 17.2 (world avg. 15.7).
Total fertility rate (avg. births per childbearing woman; 1996): 2.3.
Marriage rate per 1,000 population (1987): 9.3.
Divorce rate per 1,000 population (1987): 0.2.
Life expectancy at birth (1997): male 69.0 years; female 75.0 years.
Major causes of death per 100,000 population (1986): diseases of the circulatory system 224.9; malignant neoplasms (cancers) 69.0; diseases of the digestive system 51.6; diseases of the respiratory system 46.7; injuries and poisoning 38.2; infectious and parasitic diseases 19.4.

National economy

Budget (1994). Revenue: 41,525,200,000 won (1984; turnover tax 55.0%, payments by state enterprises 30.0%). Expenditures: 41,525,200,000 won (national economy 67.8%, social and cultural affairs 19.8%, defense 11.6%).
Public debt (external, outstanding; 1993): U.S.$10,300,000,000.
Population economically active (1994)[6]: total 12,486,000; activity rate of total population 53.2% (participation rates [1988–93]: ages 15–64, 49.5%; female 46.0%; unemployed, n.a.).
Production (metric tons except as noted). Agriculture, forestry, fishing (1997): rice 2,300,000, potatoes 1,550,000, corn (maize) 1,500,000, cabbages 700,000, apples 650,000, sweet potatoes 455,000, soybeans 420,000, pears 120,000, peaches and nectarines 110,000, watermelons 105,000, wheat 100,000, cucumbers and gherkins 65,000, tomatoes 65,000, tobacco leaves 63,000, barley 55,000, millet 10,000, oats 10,000; livestock (number of live animals) 3,100,000 pigs, 1,150,000 cattle, 355,000 sheep, 265,000 goats, 14,000,000 chickens; roundwood (1995) 4,923,000 cu m; fish catch (1995) 1,850,000. Mining and quarrying (1995): iron ore 11,000,000; magnesite (metal content) 1,600,000; phosphate rock 520,000; sulfur 250,000; zinc 200,000; lead (metal content) 80,000; fluorspar 40,000; graphite 40,000; copper 16,000; silver 50; gold 5,000 kg. Manufacturing (1995): cement 17,000,000; crude steel 8,100,000; pig iron 6,600,000; coke 3,000,000; steel semimanufactures 2,700,000[7]; chemical fertilizers 2,500,000[7]; meat 259,200[5]; gasoline 8,600,000 barrels; textile fabrics 350,000,000 sq m[7]. Construction: n.a. Energy production (consumption): electricity (kW-hr; 1994) 37,000,000 (37,000,000); coal (metric tons; 1994) 71,500,000 (73,425,000); crude petroleum (barrels; 1994) none (16,492,500); petroleum products (metric tons; 1994) 2,835,000 (4,346,000).

Household income and expenditure. Average household size (1987) 4.8; average annual income per household (1980) 3,677 won (U.S.$4,275); sources of income: n.a.; expenditure (1984)[8]: food 46.5%, clothing 29.9%, furniture 3.8%, energy 3.3%, housing 0.6%.
Gross national product (1995): U.S.$22,300,000,000 (U.S.$950 per capita).

Structure of gross domestic product and labour force

	1982		1990–92	
	in value '000,000 won	% of total value	labour force	% of labour force
Agriculture	...	...	4,987,000	43.0
Mining and manufacturing	...	...	3,479,000	30.0
Construction	...	...		
Public utilities	...	...		
Transp. and commun.	...	...	3,131,000	27.0
Trade	...	...		
Finance	...	...		
Pub. admin., defense	...	...		
Services	...	...		
Other	...	...		
TOTAL	11,800	100.0	11,597,000	100.0

Land use (1994): forested 61.2%; meadows and pastures 0.4%; agricultural and under permanent cultivation 16.6%; other 21.8%.

Foreign trade[9]

Balance of trade (current prices)

	1990	1991	1992	1993	1994	1995
U.S.$'000,000	−420.5	−764.7	−600.0	−600.0	−429.5	−880.0
% of total	21.0%	35.6%	18.8%	22.7%	20.4%	42.7%

Imports (1995): U.S.$1,470,000,000 (crude petroleum, coal and coke, industrial machinery and transport equipment [including trucks], industrial chemicals, textile yarn and fabrics, and grain are among the major imports). *Major import sources:* China 30.0%; Japan 15.8%; Austria 9.3%; Ukraine 5.9%.
Exports (1995): U.S.$590,000,000 (minerals [including lead, magnesite, zinc], metallurgical products [iron and steel, nonferrous metals], cement, agricultural products [including fish, grain, fruit and vegetables, tobacco], and manufactured goods [textile fabrics, clothing] are among the major exports). *Major export destinations:* Japan 31.4%; Austria 17.3%; India 6.9%.

Transport and communications

Transport. Railroads (1990): length 8,533 km. Roads (1992): total length 18,600 mi, 30,000 km (paved 6.2%). Vehicles (1990): passenger cars 248,000. Merchant marine (1992): vessels (100 gross tons and over) 100; total deadweight tonnage 951,222. Air transport (1994): passenger-mi 52,200,000, passenger-km 84,000,000; short ton-mi cargo 1,370,000, metric ton-km cargo 2,000,000; airports (1997) with scheduled flights 1.

Communications

Medium	date	unit	number	units per 1,000 persons
Daily newspapers	1994	circulation	5,000,000	213.0
Radio	1995	receivers	4,700,000	200.0
Television	1995	receivers	2,000,000	85.1
Telephones	1995	main lines	1,104,000	47.0

Education and health

Educational attainment (1987–88). Percentage of population age 16 and over having attended or graduated from postsecondary-level school: 13.7%. *Literacy* (1992): 95%.

Education (1987)

	schools	teachers	students	student/ teacher ratio
Primary (age 6–9)	6,122	138,945	1,543,000	11.1
Secondary (age 10–15)	...	111,000	2,468,000	22.2
Voc., teacher tr.	473[10]	...	220,000	...
Higher	281	27,000	390,000	14.4

Health (1989): physicians 57,690 (1 per 370 persons); hospital beds 290,590 (1 per 74 persons); infant mortality rate per 1,000 live births (1997) 52.0.
Food (1995)[11]: daily per capita caloric intake 2,360 (vegetable products 91%, animal products 9%); 109% of FAO recommended minimum requirement.

Military

Total active duty personnel (1997): 1,055,000 (army 87.5%, navy 4.4%, air force 8.1%). *Military expenditure as percentage of GNP* (1995): 28.6% (world 2.8%); per capita expenditure U.S.$255.

[1]Kim Jong Il (son of the previous president Kim Il Sung, who died on July 8, 1994) had not assumed the title of president as of mid-October 1997. [2]Transfer rate; the black market rate (June 1997) was about 200 won to 1 U.S.$. [3]Civilian population only; UN cites a 1993 census total of 21,123,376, but details are not available. [4]North P'yŏngan includes special district of Hyangsan-chigu. [5]1996 estimate. [6]The Democratic People's Republic of Korea categorizes economically active as including students in higher education, retirees, and heads of households, as well as those in the civilian labour force. [7]1994. [8]Workers and clerical workers only. [9]Imports are f.o.b. [10]1986. [11]Owing to famine in 1996 and 1997, daily per capita caloric intake was reduced to less than 1,000 calories.

Internet resources for further information:
- **Korean News http://www.kcna.co.jp**
- **United States Department of Energy http://www.eia.doe.gov/emeu/cabs/nkorea.html**

Korea, South

Official name: Taehan Min'guk (Republic of Korea).
Form of government: unitary multiparty republic with one legislative house (National Assembly [299]).
Head of state and government: President, assisted by Prime Minister.
Capital: Seoul.
Official language: Korean.
Official religion: none.
Monetary unit: 1 won (W) = 100 chon; valuation (Oct. 3, 1997) 1 U.S.$ = W 914; 1 £ = W 1,473.

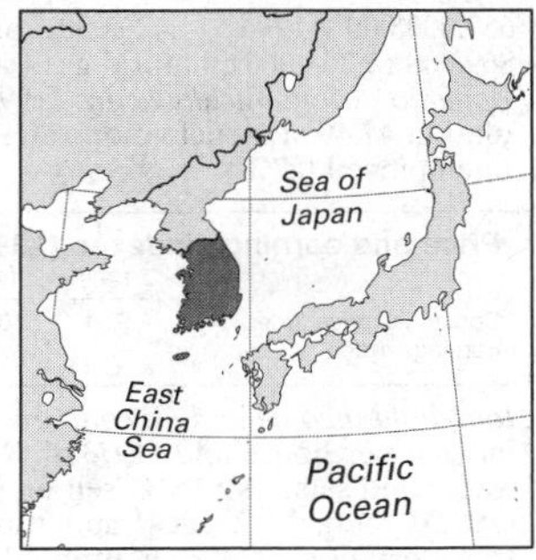

Area and population

Provinces	Capitals	area sq mi	area sq km	population 1995 census
Cheju-do	Cheju	712	1,845	505,442
Chŏlla-namdo	Kwangju	4,599	11,911	2,066,865
Chŏlla-pukto	Chŏnju	3,111	8,059	1,902,205
Ch'ungch'ŏng-namdo	Taejŏn	3,300	8,547	1,767,105
Ch'ungch'ŏng-pukto	Ch'ŏngju	2,870	7,433	1,396,481
Kangwŏn-do	Ch'unch'ŏn'	6,384	16,534	1,466,794
Kyŏnggi-do	Suwŏn	3,905	10,115	7,649,914
Kyŏngsang-namdo	Masan	4,466	11,566	3,845,569
Kyŏngsang-pukto	Taegu	7,345	19,022	2,676,344
Special cities				
Inch'ŏn-si	Inch'ŏn	369	955	2,307,618
Kwangju-si	Kwangju	193	501	1,257,504
Pusan-si	Pusan	289	749	3,813,814
Sŏul-t'ŭkpyŏlsi	Seoul	234	606	10,229,262
Taegu-si	Taegu	342	886	2,449,139
Taejŏn-si	Taejŏn	209	540	1,272,143
TOTAL		38,328	99,268	44,606,199

Demography

Population (1997): 45,628,000.
Density (1997): persons per sq mi 1,190.5, persons per sq km 459.6.
Urban-rural (1995): urban 81.0%; rural 19.0%.
Sex distribution (1996): male 50.34%; female 49.66%.
Age breakdown (1996): under 15, 22.6%; 15–29, 28.0%; 30–44, 25.5%; 45–59, 14.6%; 60–74, 7.5%; 75 and over, 1.8%.
Population projection: (2000) 46,789,000; (2010) 49,683,000.
Doubling time: 78 years.
Ethnic composition (1990): Korean 99.9%; other 0.1%.
Religious affiliation (1995): religious[1] 51.1%, of which Buddhist 23.3%, Protestant 19.8%, Roman Catholic 6.7%, Confucian 0.4%, Wonbulgyo 0.2%, Ch'ondogyo 0.1%, other 0.6%; nonreligious 48.9%.
Major cities (1995): Seoul 10,229,262; Pusan 3,813,814; Taegu 2,449,139; Inch'ŏn 2,307,618; Taejon 1,272,143.

Vital statistics

Birth rate per 1,000 population (1997): 15.1 (world avg. 25.0).
Death rate per 1,000 population (1997): 6.4 (world avg. 9.3).
Natural increase rate per 1,000 population (1997): 8.7 (world avg. 15.7).
Total fertility rate (avg. births per childbearing woman; 1997): 1.7.
Marriage rate per 1,000 population (1994): 6.8.
Divorce rate per 1,000 population (1994): 1.1.
Life expectancy at birth (1997): male 69.0 years; female 76.0 years.
Major causes of death per 100,000 population (1994): diseases of the circulatory system 155.0; malignant neoplasms (cancers) 111.3; accidents, poisoning, and violence 72.0; diseases of the digestive system 39.6.

National economy

Budget (1996). Revenue: W 81,581,000,000,000 (taxes on goods and services 32.8%, income taxes 29.1%, nontax revenue 11.9%, social security contributions 7.7%, taxes on international trade 6.2%). Expenditures: W 73,582,000,000,000 (education 21.1%, defense 16.8%, social security and welfare 10.5%, agriculture 8.9%, transportation and communications 9.0%, agriculture 8.2%, public order 5.9%, general public services 4.5%).
Public debt (external, outstanding; 1995): U.S.$24,095,000,000.
Production (metric tons except as noted). Agriculture, forestry, fishing (1996): rice 6,284,000, cabbages 3,200,000, apples 630,000, tangerines 600,000, dry onions 570,000; livestock (number of live animals) 6,950,000 pigs, 3,463,000 cattle, 88,000,000 chickens; roundwood (1995) 6,485,000 cu m; fish catch (1993) 2,648,977. Mining and quarrying (1995): copper ore 233,000; iron ore 184,443; zinc concentrate 15,494. Manufacturing (1995): cement 56,101,000; pig iron 22,344,000; newsprint 956,864; polyvinyl chloride resin 914,201; woolen fabrics 17,773,134 sq m; colour television receivers 18,555,000 units; passenger cars 1,999,000 units. Construction (permits authorized; 1996): residential 71,404,000 sq m; nonresidential 73,226,000 sq m. Energy production (consumption): electricity (kW-hr; 1995) 163,270,000,000 (163,270,000,000); coal (metric tons; 1994) 7,438,000 (42,660,000); crude petroleum (barrels; 1994) none (544,639,000); petroleum products (metric tons; 1994) 103,580,000 (84,788,000); natural gas (cu m; 1994) none (3,864,000,000).
Household income and expenditure (1995)[2]. Average household size 3.7; income per household W 39,390,000 (U.S.$51,070); sources of income: wages 50.0%, other 50.0%; expenditure: food and beverages 25.5%, education and recreation 13.4%, transportation and communications 9.8%, clothing and footwear 7.0%, health care 4.4%, household durable goods 4.3%, utilities 3.7%, housing 3.4%, other 28.5%.

Gross national product (1995): U.S.$435,137,000,000 (U.S.$9,700 per capita).

Structure of gross domestic product and labour force

	1996			
	in value W '000,000,000[3]	% of total value	labour force	% of labour force
Agriculture	17,582.9	6.4	2,405,000	11.3
Mining	825.0	0.3	24,000	0.1
Manufacturing	82,849.0	30.0	4,677,000	22.1
Construction	31,128.2	11.3	1,968,000	9.3
Public utilities	6,881.9	2.5		
Transp. and commun.	22,976.6	8.3		
Trade	34,282.2	12.4	11,689,000	55.2
Finance	47,366.8	17.2		
Pub. admin., defense	15,274.0	5.5		
Services	15,593.1	5.7		
Other	1,089.8[4]	0.4[4]	425,000[5]	2.0[5]
TOTAL	275,849.5	100.0	21,188,000	100.0

Population economically active (1996): total 21,188,000; activity rate 46.5% (participation rates: ages 15 and over, 62.0%; female [1994] 40.1%; unemployed 2.0%).

Price and earnings indexes (1990 = 100)

	1990	1991	1992	1993	1994	1995	1996
Consumer price index	100.0	109.3	116.1	121.7	129.3	135.1	141.8
Monthly earnings index	100.0	116.9	135.2	149.9	173.1	190.2	213.6

Tourism (1995): receipts from visitors U.S.$5,587,000,000; expenditures by nationals abroad U.S.$5,903,000,000.

Foreign trade

Balance of trade (current prices)

	1991	1992	1993	1994	1995	1996
U.S.$'000,000	−3,968	−588	+2,880	−729	−2,896	−12,411
% of total	3.6%	0.4%	1.8%	0.5%	1.1%	4.6%

Imports (1996): U.S.$150,339,100,000 (machinery and transport equipment 36.3%, mineral fuels and lubricants 16.2%, manufactured goods 13.9%, chemicals 8.8%, inedible crude materials 7.3%). *Major import sources:* U.S. 22.2%; Japan 20.9%; Germany 4.8%; Saudi Arabia 4.4%; Australia 4.2%.
Exports (1996): U.S.$129,715,100,000 (machinery and transport equipment 52.1%, manufactured goods 20.8%, chemicals 7.1%, mineral fuels 3.0%). *Major export destinations:* United States 16.7%; Japan 12.2%; Hong Kong 8.6%; Singapore 5.0%; Germany 3.6%.

Transport and communications

Transport. Railroads (1995): length 6,554 km; passenger-km 29,292,000,000; metric ton-km cargo 13,838,000,000. Roads (1995): total length 74,235 km (paved 76%). Vehicles (1995): passenger cars 6,006,290; trucks and buses 2,462,611. Air transport (1995): passenger-km 48,504,000,000; metric ton-km cargo 5,729,328,000; airports (1996) with scheduled flights 14.

Communications

Medium	date	unit	number	units per 1,000 persons
Daily newspapers	1994	circulation	18,000,000	405
Radio	1996	receivers	42,000,000	928
Television	1995	receivers	10,430,000	233
Telephones	1995	main lines	18,600,200	415
Cellular telephones	1995	subscribers	1,641,000	37
Facsimile machines	1995	units	375,000	8.4
Personal computers	1995	units	5,420,000	121

Education and health

Educational attainment (1995). Percentage of population age 25 and over having: no formal schooling 8.5%; primary education or less 17.7%; some secondary and secondary 53.1%; postsecondary 20.6%. *Literacy* (1990): total population age 15 and over literate 96.3%; males 99.1%; females 93.5%.

Education (1996)

	schools	teachers	students	student/teacher ratio
Primary (age 6–13)	5,732	137,912	3,800,540	27.6
Secondary (age 14–19)	3,790	157,731	3,683,857	23.4
Vocational	797	44,163	950,173	21.5
Higher	802	60,883	2,056,370	33.8

Health (1995): physicians 57,188 (1 per 784 persons); hospital beds 196,232 (1 per 229 persons); infant mortality rate per 1,000 live births (1996) 10.0.
Food (1995): daily per capita caloric intake 3,268 (vegetable products 84%, animal products 16%); 139% of FAO recommended minimum requirement.

Military

Total active duty personnel (1996): 660,000 (army 83.0%, navy 9.1%, air force 7.9%). *Military expenditure as percentage of GNP* (1994): 3.7% (world 3.0%); per capita expenditure U.S.$293.

[1]Refers to persons who have received commandments, accepted baptism, or entered a faith and who participate in a religious function regularly or put the religious idea into practice. [2]Excludes farm households. [3]At 1990 constant prices. [4]Import duties less imputed bank service charges. [5]Unemployed.

Internet resources for further information:
- **Korean Statistical Information System http://www.nso.go.kr/eindex.html**
- **KoreaNet http://www.iworld.net/Korea/**

Kuwait

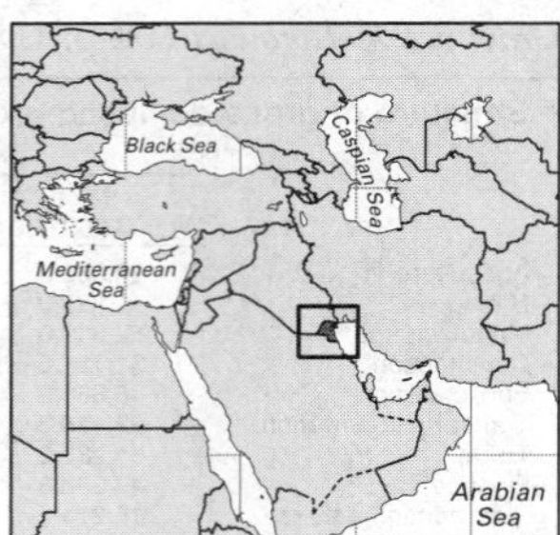

Official name: Dawlat al-Kuwayt (State of Kuwait).
Form of government: Constitutional monarchy with one legislative body (National Assembly [64[1]]).
Head of state and government: Emir[2].
Capital: Kuwait City.
Official language: Arabic.
Official religion: Islam.
Monetary unit: 1 Kuwaiti dinar (KD) = 1,000 fils; valuation (Oct. 3, 1997) 1 KD = U.S.$3.29 = £2.04.

Area and population[3]

Governorates[5]	Capitals	area sq mi	area sq km	population[4] 1997 estimate
Al-Aḥmadī	Al-Aḥmadī	1,984	5,138	303,769
Al-Farwānīyah	Al-Farwānīyah	...	...	483,501
Al-Jahrā'	Al-Jahrā'	4,372	11,324	244,552
Capital	Kuwait City	38	98	296,327
Ḥawallī	Ḥawallī	138	358	481,121
Islands[6]	—	347	900	...
TOTAL		6,880[7]	17,818	1,809,270[4]

Demography

Population (1997): 1,809,000.
Density (1997): persons per sq mi 262.9, persons per sq km 101.5.
Urban-rural (1995): urban 97.0%; rural 3.0%.
Sex distribution (1995): male 61.45%; female 38.55%.
Age breakdown (1994): under 15, 29.4%; 15–29, 28.3%; 30–44, 30.5%; 45–59, 9.5%; 60–74, 2.0%; 75 and over, 0.3%.
Population projection: (2000) 2,108,000; (2010) 2,753,000.
Doubling time: 22 years.
Ethnic composition (by nationality; 1995): Kuwaiti 41.1%; non-Kuwaiti (including other Arab, South Asian, Palestinian, and stateless persons) 58.9%.
Religious affiliation (1995): Muslim 85%, of which Sunnī 45%, Shī'ī 30%; other Muslim 10%; other (mostly Christian and Hindu) 15.0%.
Major cities (1995): As-Sālimīyah 130,215; Qalīb ash-Shuyūkh 102,178; Ḥawallī 82,238; Abraq Khīṭān 63,628; Kuwait City 28,859.

Vital statistics

Birth rate per 1,000 population (1995): 24.3 (world avg. 25.0).
Death rate per 1,000 population (1995): 2.2 (world avg. 9.3).
Natural increase rate per 1,000 population (1995): 22.1 (world avg. 15.7).
Total fertility rate (avg. births per childbearing woman; 1994): 3.7.
Marriage rate per 1,000 population (1993): 8.0[8].
Divorce rate per 1,000 population (1993): 1.9[8].
Life expectancy at birth (1994): male 74.4 years; female 79.0 years.
Major causes of death per 100,000 population (1995): circulatory diseases 87.5; accidents, poisoning, and violence 35.8; cancers 24.9; respiratory diseases 12.3; congenital anomalies 11.3; endocrine, nutritional, and metabolic diseases 8.2; infectious and parasitic diseases 6.7; genitourinary diseases 6.0.

National economy

Budget[9] (1996–97). Revenue: KD 3,000,000,000 (oil revenue 85.3%). Expenditures: KD 4,210,000,000 (current expenditures 67.7%, of which transfers 21.1%, defense 20.2%, education 7.6%, health 6.3%; development expenditure 10.5%).
Public debt (external, outstanding; 1991): U.S.$792,000,000[10].
Tourism (1995): receipts from visitors U.S.$107,000,000; expenditures by nationals abroad U.S.$2,322,000,000.
Gross national product (1995): U.S.$28,491,000,000 (U.S.$17,390 per capita).

Structure of gross domestic product and labour force

	1996 in value KD '000,000[11]	% of total value	labour force[12]	% of labour force[12]
Agriculture	37.9	0.4	23,400	1.9
Mining (oil sector)	4,127.4	44.5	8,600	0.7
Manufacturing	1,036.0	11.2	83,600	6.8
Construction	243.7	2.6	136,500	11.1
Public utilities	2.0	0.0	8,600	0.7
Transp. and commun.	397.1	4.3	44,300	3.6
Trade[13]	627.0	6.8	206,600	16.8
Finance and business services	950.6	10.3	43,100	3.5
Pub. admin., defense; Services	1,953.1	21.1	597,800	48.6
Other	−97.7[14]	−1.1[14]	77,500	6.3
TOTAL	9,277.1	100.0[7]	1,230,000	100.0

Production (metric tons except as noted). Agriculture, forestry, fishing (1997): cucumbers and gherkins 26,500, onions 20,500, tomatoes 20,500, eggplants 3,250, garlic 1,450; livestock (number of live animals) 320,000 sheep, 75,000 goats, 22,000 cattle, 8,600 camels; fish catch (1995) 8,706. Mining and quarrying (1994): sulfur 175,000; lime 35,000. Manufacturing (value added in KD '000; 1993): refined petroleum products 383,525; clothing and apparel 35,722; food products 35,610; fabricated metal products 33,343; cement, bricks, and tile 31,302; furniture and fixtures 15,103. Construction (floor area of new construction; 1995): residential 2,018,600 sq m; nonresidential 141,200 sq m. Energy production (consumption): electricity (kW-hr; 1994) 23,152,000,000 (23,152,000,000); coal, none (none); crude petroleum (barrels; 1995) 657,000,000 ([1994] 44,426,000); petroleum products (metric tons; 1994) 33,869,000 (5,268,000); natural gas (cu m; 1994) 5,970,000,000 (5,970,000,000).
Population economically active (1995): total 746,408; activity rate of total population 47.4% (participation rates: ages 15–59, 70.7%; female [1988] 18.8%; unemployed 0.7%).

Price and earnings indexes (1990 = 100)

	1989	1990	1991	1992	1993	1994	1995
Consumer price index	91.1	100.0	109.1	108.5	108.9	111.6	114.6
Earnings index	...	...	...	...	...	...	...

Household income and expenditure. Average household size (1986) 7.4; annual income per household (1973)[15] KD 4,246 (U.S.$12,907); sources of income: wages and salaries 53.8%, self-employment 20.8%, other 25.4%; expenditure (1992): food, beverages, and tobacco 37.0%, housing and energy 18.7%, transportation 15.3%, household appliances and services 11.1%, clothing and footwear 10.0%, education and health 2.5%.
Land use (1994): forest 0.1%; pasture 7.7%; agriculture 0.3%; other 91.9%.

Foreign trade

Balance of trade (current prices)

	1991	1992	1993	1994	1995	1996
KD '000,000	−1,135	−202	+962	+1,324	+1,635	+2,056
% of total	64.9%	5.0%	18.6%	25.1%	27.7%	30.5%

Imports (1996): KD 2,507,170,000 (machinery and transport equipment 41.6%, manufactured goods 19.8%, food and live animals 14.0%, miscellaneous manufactured articles 12.9%, chemical products 7.2%, beverages and tobacco 1.1%). *Major import sources:* U.S. 16.7%; Japan 12.1%; Germany 7.0%; Italy 6.9%; Saudi Arabia 6.7%; U.K. 6.1%; France 4.0%; India 3.2%.
Exports (1996)[16]: KD 4,449,700,000 (crude petroleum and petroleum products 94.9%). *Major export destinations:* India 18.6%; Saudi Arabia 16.9%; U.A.E. 15.0%; U.S. 5.7%; China 4.9%; Philippines 2.6%; Bahrain 2.3%; Egypt 2.3%.

Transport and communications

Transport. Railroads: none. Roads (1995): total length 2,709 mi, 4,360 km (paved 81%). Vehicles (1995): passenger cars 545,000; trucks and buses 155,000. Merchant marine (1992): vessels (100 gross tons and over) 209; total deadweight tonnage 3,188,526. Air transport (1995)[17]: passenger-mi 3,184,038,000, passenger-km 5,124,223,000; short ton-mi cargo 225,837,000, metric ton-km cargo 329,717,000; airports (1997) with scheduled flights 1.

Communications

Medium	date	unit	number	units per 1,000 persons
Daily newspapers	1995	circulation	671,672	397
Radio	1995	receivers	1,000,000	592
Television	1996	receivers	800,000	456
Telephones	1994	main lines	373,000	230
Cellular telephones	1995	subscribers	119,520	70.7
Facsimile machines	1995	units	35,500	21.0
Personal computers	1995	units	96,530	57.1

Education and health

Educational attainment (1988). Percentage of population age 25 and over having: no formal schooling 44.8%; primary education 8.6%; some secondary 15.1%; complete secondary 15.1%; higher 16.4%. *Literacy* (1995 est.): total population age 15 and over literate 78.6%; males literate 82.2%; females literate 74.9%.

Education (1995–96)

	schools	teachers	students	student/ teacher ratio
Primary (age 6–9)	251	9,414	140,979	15.0
Secondary (age 10–17)	409	18,700	204,194	10.9
Voc., teacher tr.	36	717	3,604	5.0
Higher[18]	1	960	16,767	17.5

Health (1995): physicians 3,642 (1 per 464 persons); hospital beds 4,093[19] (1 per 357 persons); infant mortality rate per 1,000 live births 11.1.
Food (1995): daily per capita caloric intake 3,160 (vegetable products 75%, animal products 25%); 131% of FAO recommended minimum requirement.

Military

Total active duty personnel (1997): 15,300 (army [including central staff] 71.9%, navy 11.8%, air force 16.3%). *Military expenditure as percentage of GNP* (1995): 11.6% (world 2.8%); per capita expenditure U.S.$1,919.

[1]50 elected seats include 4 elected Cabinet ministers; nonelected Cabinet ministers serving ex officio occupy the other 14 seats. [2]Assisted by prime minister. [3]Area of governorates reflects situation prior to Amiri Decree No. 156 of 1988, which established Al-Farwānīyah governorate; but population figures account for the reorganization. [4]Estimates based on census taken on April 23, 1995. [5]Governorates have no administrative function. [6]Bubian Island 333 sq mi (863 sq km) and Warba Island 14 sq mi (37 sq km). [7]Detail does not add to total given because of rounding. [8]Provisional. [9]Approved budget for 1996–97. [10]Includes external long-term debt not guaranteed by the government. [11]At purchaser's value. [12]Size of labour force and subtotal figures derived from percentages. [13]Trade includes restaurants and hotels. [14]Includes import duties and imputed bank service charges. [15]Kuwaiti households only. [16]Total exports and reexports include oil and non-oil, but breakdown by destination is derived from non-oil exports. [17]Kuwait Airways only. [18]1994–95. [19]1993; public hospitals only.

Internet resources for further information:
- **Central Bank of Kuwait http://www.cbk.gov.kw**
- **Kuwait Information Office (Washington, D.C.) http://www.kuwait.info.nw.dc.us/main.htm**

Kyrgyzstan

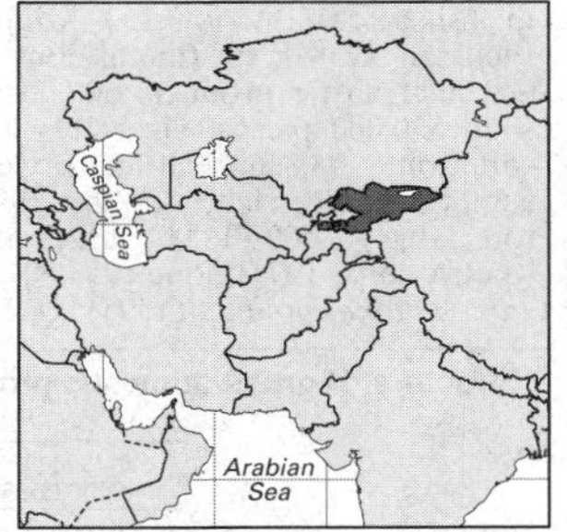

Official name: Kyrgyz Respublikasy (Kyrgyz Republic).
Form of government: unitary multiparty republic with two legislative houses (Assembly of People's Representatives [70]; Legislative Assembly [35]).
Head of state and government: President assisted by Prime Minister.
Capital: Bishkek (formerly Frunze).
Official languages: Kyrgyz; Russian.
Official religion: none.
Monetary unit: 1 som = 100 tyiyn; valuation (Jan. 29, 1997) free rate, 1 U.S.$ = 17.15 som.

Area and population

		area		population
Provinces	**Capitals**	sq mi	sq km	1993[1] estimate
Chüy (Chu)	Kara-Balta	7,200	18,700	774,000
Jalal-Abad (Dzhalal-Abad)	Jalal-Abad (Dzhalal-Abad)	15,200	39,500	812,800
Naryn	Naryn	18,300	47,300	267,900
Osh	Osh	14,700	38,100	1,360,900
Talas	Talas	4,400	11,400	203,000
Ysyk-Köl (Issyk-Kul)	Ysyk-Köl (Issyk-Kul)	16,800	43,500	429,300
City of republic subordination				
Bishkek (Frunze)	—	...	...	634,100
TOTAL		76,600[2]	198,500[2]	4,482,000

Demography

Population (1997): 4,595,000.
Density (1997): persons per sq mi 59.0, persons per sq km 23.1.
Urban-rural (1996): urban 34.7%; rural 65.3%.
Sex distribution (1996): male 49.35%; female 50.65%.
Age breakdown (1989): under 15, 37.5%; 15–29, 27.0%; 30–44, 16.3%; 45–59, 10.9%; 60–74, 6.2%; 75 and over, 2.1%.
Population projection: (2000) 4,697,000; (2010) 5,442,000.
Doubling time: 47 years.
Ethnic composition (1996[1]): Kyrgyz 59.7%; Russian 16.2%; Uzbek 14.1%; Ukrainian 1.7%; Tatar 1.2%; Kazak 0.9%; other 6.2%.
Religious affiliation (1997): Muslim (mostly Sunnī) 70.0%; Russian Orthodox 5.7%; other 24.3%.
Major cities (1991): Bishkek (Frunze) 631,300; Osh 218,700; Jalal-Abad 74,200; Tokmok 71,200; Kara-Köl 64,300.

Vital statistics

Birth rate per 1,000 population (1995): 25.9 (world avg. 25.0); (1994) legitimate 83.2%; illegitimate 16.8%.
Death rate per 1,000 population (1995): 8.1 (world avg. 9.3).
Natural increase rate per 1,000 population (1995): 17.8 (world avg. 15.7).
Total fertility rate (avg. births per childbearing woman; 1995): 3.3.
Marriage rate per 1,000 population (1994): 5.8.
Divorce rate per 1,000 population (1994): 1.2.
Life expectancy at birth (1994): male 64.0 years; female 72.0 years.
Major causes of death per 100,000 population (1993): diseases of the circulatory system 290.0; diseases of the respiratory system 125.0; accidents, poisoning, and violence 91.2; malignant neoplasms (cancers) 67.3; infectious and parasitic diseases 30.1; diseases of the digestive system 29.7.

National economy

Budget (1995). Revenue: 2,671,000,000 som (tax revenue 93.4%, of which value-added tax 27.7%, enterprise profits tax 15.5%, excise taxes 11.5%, personal income tax 10.8%, other 27.9%; nontax revenue 6.6%). Expenditures: 4,579,800,000 som (education 19.4%; social security 18.4%; health 10.9%; government services 7.4%; industrial expenditure 7.2%; public safety 6.8%; defense 4.9%).
Public debt (external, outstanding; 1995): U.S.$474,300,000.
Population economically active (1995): total 1,692,000; activity rate of total population 37.2% (1993; participation rates: ages 16–59 [male], 16–54 [female] 81.1%; female 49.0%; (1995) unemployed 1.1%).

Price and earnings indexes (1990 = 100)

	1988	1989	1990	1991	1992	1993	1994
Consumer price index	95.2	97.1	100.0	185.0	1,766	23,122	89,534
Monthly earnings index	84.5	90.9	100.0	166.9	1,179	12,559	...

Production (metric tons except as noted). Agriculture, forestry, fishing (1996): grain 1,419,000, potatoes 562,000, vegetables (other than potatoes) 369,000, fruit (other than grapes) 81,000, seed cotton 73,000, grapes 21,000; livestock (number of live animals) 4,279,000 sheep and goats, 869,000 cattle, 250,000 horses, 114,000 pigs; roundwood (1990) 6,000 cu m; fish catch (1995) 797. Mining and quarrying (1995): antimony 1,400; mercury 300; gold 850 kg. Manufacturing (value of production in '000,000 som; 1994): textiles 1,112; processed foods 729; ferrous and nonferrous metals 678; machinery and metalwork 650; construction materials 258; footwear and leather goods 89. Construction (1992): residential 1,232,000 sq m. Energy production (consumption): electricity (kW-hr; 1994) 12,932,000,000 (10,427,000,000); coal (metric tons; 1994) 298,000 (595,000); crude petroleum (barrels; 1994) 645,000 (154,000); petroleum products (metric tons; 1994) none (256,000); natural gas (cu m; 1994) 33,930,000 (1,008,000,000).
Household income and expenditure (1990). Average household size 4.7; income per household (1994) 4,359 som (U.S.$325.30); sources of income: wages and salaries 49.7%, pensions and stipends 11.1%, income from sale of agricultural products 3.5%, other 35.7%; expenditure: food and clothing 48.0%, health care 13.1%, housing 5.9%, cultural affairs 5.2%, appliances 4.4%.
Gross national product (at current market prices; 1995): U.S.$3,158,000,000 (U.S.$700 per capita)[3].

Structure of gross domestic product and labour force

	1994		1995	
	in value '000,000 som	% of total value	labour force	% of labour force
Agriculture	4,611	38.4	776,000	45.9
Mining, Manufacturing, Public utilities	2,462	20.5	205,000	12.1
Construction	409	3.4	66,000	3.9
Transp. and commun.	547	4.6	88,000	5.2
Trade	1,210	10.1	152,000	9.0
Finance	577	4.8	7,000	0.4
Public admin., defense	...	...	65,000	3.8
Services	1,443	12.0	278,000	16.4
Other	760	6.3	50,000	3.0
TOTAL	12,019	100.0[4]	1,692,000[4]	100.0[4]

Land use (1994): forest 3.7%; pasture 45.4%; agriculture 7.2%; other 43.7%.
Tourism (1995): receipts from visitors, U.S.$5,000,000; expenditures by nationals abroad, U.S.$6,000,000.

Foreign trade

Balance of trade (current prices)

	1993	1994	1995	1996
U.S.$'000,000	−166.3	−118.9	−263.4	−383.4
% of total	19.9%	14.9%	24.4%	27.4%

Imports (1996): U.S.$889,800,000 (1995; oil and gas 24.2%, machine-building equipment 15.4%, food products 14.4%, chemical products 4.5%, light industrial products 3.5%). *Major import sources:* Russian Federation 21.9%; Kazakstan 21.5%; Uzbekistan 17.0%; Turkey 7.3%; Cuba 4.3%.
Exports (1995): U.S.$506,400,000 (1995; food products 20.2%, light industrial products 20.1%, metals 17.7%, machinery 10.8%, oil and gas 9.9%). *Major export destinations:* Russian Federation 25.6%; Uzbekistan 17.1%; China 16.8%; Kazakstan 16.3%; U.K. 6.7%.

Transport and communications

Transport. Railroads (1995): length 249 mi, 400 km; (1992) passenger-mi 81,500,000, passenger-km 131,200,000; short ton-mi cargo 987,000,000, metric ton-km cargo 1,588,900,000. Roads (1995): total length 11,533 mi, 18,560 km (paved 91%). Vehicles (1995): passenger cars 164,000; trucks and buses, n.a. Merchant marine: vessels (100 gross tons and over) none; landlocked state. Air transport (1996): passenger-mi 2,738,000,000, passenger-km 4,408,000,000; short ton-mi cargo 40,512,000, metric ton-km cargo 65,199,000; airports (1997) with scheduled flights 2.

Communications

Medium	date	unit	number	units per 1,000 persons
Daily newspapers	1994	circulation	53,000	11
Television	1995	receivers	1,110,000	238
Telephones	1995	main lines	357,000	77

Education and health

Educational attainment (1989). Percentage of population age 19 and over having: primary education 4.7%; some secondary 20.9%; completed secondary 44.4%; some postsecondary 19.3%; higher 10.7%. *Literacy* (1989): total population age 15 and over literate 4,130,562 (97.0%); males literate 2,048,536 (98.6%); females literate 2,082,026 (95.5%).

Education (1995–96)

	schools	teachers	students	student/teacher ratio
Primary (age 6–13)	1,885	24,086	473,077	19.7
Secondary (age 14–17)	1,474[5]	38,915	498,849	12.8
Voc., teacher tr.	53[5]	3,371	32,005	9.5
Higher	23[5]	3,691	49,744	13.5

Health (1995): physicians 15,000 (1 per 303 persons); hospital beds 41,000 (1 per 111 persons); (1996) infant mortality rate per 1,000 live births 31.5.
Food (1995): daily per capita caloric intake 2,183 (vegetable products 76%, animal products 24%); 85% of FAO recommended minimum requirement.

Military

Total active duty personnel (1997): 12,200 (army 80%, air force 20%). *Military expenditure as percentage of GNP* (1994): 0.7% (world 3.0%); per capita expenditure U.S.$12.

[1]January. [2]Total area per more recent survey is 77,200 sq mi (199,900 sq km). [3]Ruble-area GNP and exchange-rate data are very speculative. [4]Detail does not add to total given because of rounding. [5]1993–94.

Internet resources for further information:
- **National Human Development Report of the Kyrgyz Republic 1997 http://www.undp.bishkek.su/hdre97.htm**
- **Welcome to the Kyrgyz Republic http://www.kyrgyzstan.org/**

Laos

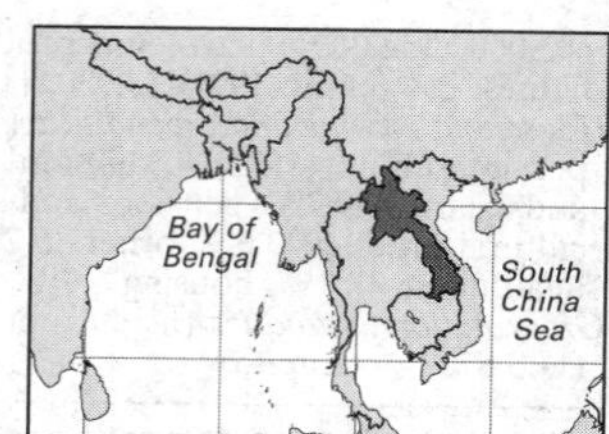

Official name: Sathalanalat Paxathipatai Paxaxôn Lao (Lao People's Democratic Republic).
Form of government: unitary single-party people's republic with one legislative house (National Assembly[1] [85]).
Chief of state: President.
Head of government: Prime Minister.
Capital: Vientiane (Viangchan).
Official language: Lao.
Official religion: none.
Monetary unit: 1 kip (KN) = 100 at; valuation (Oct. 3, 1997) 1 U.S.$ = KN 1,021; 1 £ = KN 1,646.

Area and population

Provinces	Capitals	area sq mi	area sq km	population 1995 estimate
Attapu	Attapu	3,985	10,320	87,700
Bokèo	Houayxay	2,392	6,196	114,900
Bolikhamxai	Pakxan	5,739	14,863	164,900
Champasak	Pakxé	5,952	15,415	503,300
Houaphan	Xam Nua	6,371	16,500	247,300
Khammouan	Thakhek	6,299	16,315	275,400
Louangnamtha	Louangnamtha	3,600	9,325	115,200
Louangphrabang	Louangphrabang	6,515	16,875	367,200
Oudomxay	Xay	5,934	15,370	211,300
Phôngsali	Phôngsali	6,282	16,270	153,400
Salavan	Salavan	4,128	10,691	258,300
Savannakhét	Savannakhét	8,407	21,774	674,900
Special Region	...	2,743	7,105	54,200
Viangchan	Muang Phôn-Hông	6,149	15,927	286,800
Xaignabouli	Xaignabouli	6,328	16,389	293,300
Xékong	Thong	2,959	7,665	64,200
Xiangkhoang	Phônsavan	6,131	15,880	201,200
Municipalities				
Viangchan	Vientiane (Viangchan)	1,514	3,920	531,800
TOTAL		91,429[2]	236,800	4,605,300

Demography

Population (1997): 5,117,000.
Density (1997): persons per sq mi 56.0, persons per sq km 21.6.
Urban-rural (1997): urban 23.0%; rural 77.0%.
Sex distribution (1995): male 49.46%; female 50.54%.
Age breakdown (1990): under 15, 43.7%; 15–29, 26.0%; 30–44, 16.2%; 45–59, 9.2%; 60–74, 4.2%; 75 and over, 0.7%.
Population projection: (2000) 5,557,000; (2010) 7,168,000.
Doubling time: 23 years.
Ethnic composition (1983): Lao-Lum (Lao) 67.0%; Lao-Theung (Mon-Khmer) 16.5%; Lao-Tai (Tai) 7.8%; Lao-Soung (Miao [Hmong] and Man [Yao]) 5.2%; other 3.5%.
Religious affiliation (1980): Buddhist 57.8%; tribal religionist 33.6%; Christian 1.8%, of which Roman Catholic 0.8%, Protestant 0.2%; Muslim 1.0%; atheist 1.0%; Chinese folk religionist 0.9%; none 3.8%; other 0.1%.
Major cities (1985): Vientiane (Viangchan) 178,203; Savannakhét 96,652; Louangphrabang 68,399; Pakxé 47,323.

Vital statistics

Birth rate per 1,000 population (1997): 44.3 (world avg. 25.0).
Death rate per 1,000 population (1997): 13.7 (world avg. 9.3).
Natural increase rate per 1,000 population (1997): 30.6 (world avg. 15.7).
Total fertility rate (avg. births per childbearing woman; 1997): 6.2.
Marriage rate per 1,000 population: n.a.
Divorce rate per 1,000 population: n.a.
Life expectancy at birth (1997): male 51.0 years; female 54.0 years.
Major causes of death per 100,000 population (incomplete, 1990): malaria 7.6; pneumonia 3.0; meningitis 1.5; diarrhea 1.2; tuberculosis 0.8.

National economy

Budget (1996–97). Revenue: KN 321,200,000,000 (taxes 66.2%, foreign grants 21.2%, nontax revenue 12.6%). Expenditures: KN 404,100,000,000 (current expenditure 47.9%, capital expenditure 52.1%).
Public debt (external, outstanding; 1995): U.S.$2,091,000,000.
Tourism (1995): receipts from visitors U.S.$51,000,000; expenditures by nationals abroad U.S.$30,000,000.
Population economically active (1989): total 1,888,000; activity rate of total population 49.0% (participation rates [1985]: ages 15–64, 84.2%; female 45.3%; unemployed [1994] 2.6%).

Price and earnings indexes (1990 = 100)

	1989	1990	1991	1992	1993	1994	1995
Consumer price index	73.7	100.0	113.4	124.6	132.4	141.4	169.1
Earnings index	...	...	...	...	...	...	...

Production (metric tons except as noted). Agriculture, forestry, fishing (1996): rice 1,414,000, sweet potatoes 111,000, sugarcane 87,000, corn (maize) 72,000, cassava 69,000, pineapples 35,000, melons 35,000, potatoes 31,000, oranges 25,000, bananas 22,000, seed cotton 20,000, coffee 10,000; livestock (number of live animals) 1,772,000 pigs, 1,212,000 water buffalo, 1,186,000 cattle, 159,000 goats, 26,000 horses, 11,656,000 chickens; roundwood (1995) 5,508,000 cu m; fish catch (1995) 40,250. Mining and quarrying (1995): gypsum 110,000; rock salt 12,000; tin (metal content) 687. Manufacturing (1995): detergent 800,000; plastic products 500,000; nails 58,000; clothing 11,495,000 pieces; soap 550,000 pieces; cigarettes 45,000,000 packs; beer 126,300 hectolitres; soft drinks 94,800 hectolitres. Construction: n.a. Energy production (consumption): electricity (kW-hr; 1994) 905,000,000 (294,000,000); coal (metric tons; 1994) 1,000 (1,000); crude petroleum, n.a. (n.a.); petroleum products (metric tons; 1994) none (95,000); natural gas, n.a. (n.a.).
Gross national product (1995): U.S.$1,694,000,000 (U.S.$350 per capita).

Structure of gross domestic product and labour force

	1996 in value KN '000,000[3]	1996 % of total value	1989 labour force	1989 % of labour force
Agriculture	463,900	52.0	1,359,000	72.0
Manufacturing	138,300	15.5		
Mining	2,400	0.3		
Construction	30,100	3.4		
Public utilities	12,900	1.4		
Transp. and commun.	50,200	5.6		
Trade	90,100	10.1	58,533	8.1
Finance	41,500	4.7		
Pub. admin., defense; Services	40,200	4.5		
Other	22,600	2.5		
TOTAL	892,200	100.0	1,888,000	100.0

Household income and expenditure. Average household size (1985) 6.0; average annual income per household KN 3,710 (U.S.$371); sources of income: n.a.; expenditure: n.a.
Land use (1994): forested 54.4%; meadows and pastures 3.5%; agricultural and under permanent cultivation 3.9%; other 38.2%.

Foreign trade[4]

Balance of trade (current prices)

	1990	1991	1992	1993	1994	1995
U.S.$'000,000	−127.8	−131.7	−133.0	−179.0	−263.7	−239.3
% of total	46.4%	45.8%	33.3%	27.8%	30.5%	25.6%

Imports (1996): U.S.$689,600,000 (consumption goods 44.7%; investment goods 40.2%, of which construction and electrical equipment 14.7%, motor vehicles 10.4%; machinery and equipment 10.3%, materials for garment assembly 10.2%). *Major import sources:* Thailand 45.0%; Japan 7.6%; Vietnam 3.7%; China 3.4%; Singapore 2.5%; Hong Kong 1.2%.
Exports (1996): U.S.$320,700,000 (wood products 38.9%; garments 20.0%; electricity 9.3%; coffee 7.8%). *Major export destinations:* Vietnam 49.1%; Thailand 30.2%; France 2.6%; United Kingdom 2.1%; Germany 1.5%.

Transport and communications

Transport. Railroads: none. Roads (1995): total length 11,280 mi, 18,153 km (paved 14%). Vehicles (1995): passenger cars 17,200; trucks and buses 6,020. Merchant marine (1992): vessels (100 gross tons and over) 1; total deadweight tonnage 1,469. Air transport (1993): passenger-mi 29,000,000, passenger-km 46,000,000; short ton-mi cargo 3,000,000, metric ton-km cargo 4,000,000; airports (1996) with scheduled flights 11.

Communications

Medium	date	unit	number	units per 1,000 persons
Daily newspapers	1994	circulation	14,000	3.0
Radio	1996	receivers	575,000	116
Television	1995	receivers	80,000	17
Telephones	1995	main lines	20,400	4.2
Cellular telephones	1995	subscribers	1,500	0.3
Facsimile machines	1995	units	500	0.1

Education and health

Educational attainment (1985). Percentage of population age 6 and over having: no schooling 49.3%; primary 41.2%; secondary 9.1%; higher 0.4%.
Literacy (1985): total population age 15 and over literate 83.9%; males literate 92.0%; females literate 75.8%.

Education (1995–96)

	schools	teachers	students	student/teacher ratio
Primary (age 6–10)	7,591	24,600	724,100	29.4
Secondary (age 11–16)	750[5]	35,100	886,500	25.3
Voc., teacher tr.	139[6]	1,600	9,400	5.9
Higher	9[5]	1,300	7,800	6.0

Health (1990): physicians 1,173 (1 per 3,555 persons); hospital beds 10,364 (1 per 402 persons); infant mortality rate per 1,000 live births (1997) 87.
Food (1995): daily per capita caloric intake 2,117 (vegetable products 94%, animal products 6%); 95% of FAO recommended minimum requirement.

Military

Total active duty personnel (1996): 37,000 (army 89.2%, navy 1.4%, air force 9.4%). *Military expenditure as percent of GNP* (1995): 4.2% (world 2.8%); per capita expenditure U.S.$15.

[1]Formerly known as the Supreme People's Assembly. [2]Detail does not add to total given because of rounding. [3]At constant 1990 prices. [4]Import figures are c.i.f. in balance of trade and commodities. [5]1989–90. [6]1988–89.

Internet resources for further information:
- **Discovering Laos http://www.laoembassy.com/discover/index.htm**

Latvia

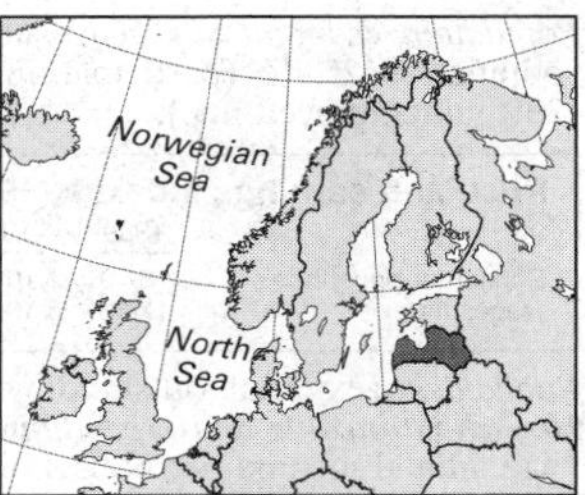

Official name: Latvijas Republika (Republic of Latvia).
Form of government: unitary multiparty republic with a single legislative body (Parliament, or Saeima [100]).
Chief of state: President.
Head of government: Prime Minister.
Capital: Riga.
Official language: Latvian.
Official religion: none.
Monetary unit: 1 lats (Ls; plural lati) = 100 santimi; valuation (Oct. 3, 1997) 1 U.S.$ = 0.58 lats; 1 £ = 0.94 lats.

Area and population

Cities	area sq km	population 1995 estimate[1]	Districts	area sq km	population 1995 estimate[1]
Daugavpils	72	120,152	Jelgava	1,613	37,473
Jelgava	60	71,129	Krāslava	2,288	39,438
Jūrmala	100	59,247	Kuldīga	2,503	41,047
Liepāja	60	100,271	Liepāja	3,589	51,677
Rēzekne	17	42,081	Limbaži	2,602	41,258
Riga	295	839,670	Ludza	2,566	40,128
Ventspils	46	47,005	Madona	3,348	48,725
			Ogre	1,816	63,870
Districts			Preiļi	2,042	43,656
Aizkraukle	2,558	44,046	Rēzekne	2,654	42,485
Alūksne	2,246	27,670	Rīga (Riga)	3,094	145,499
Balvi	2,384	32,715	Saldus	2,134	39,831
Bauska	1,884	53,890	Talsi	2,748	50,406
Cēsis	3,062	62,043	Tukums	2,457	56,748
Daugavpils	2,526	45,125	Valka	2,444	36,215
Dobele	1,680	41,513	Valmiera	2,377	61,901
Gulbene	1,876	29,797	Ventspils	2,471	14,363
Jēkabpils	2,998	58,469	TOTAL	64,610	2,529,543

Demography

Population (1997): 2,472,000.
Density (1997): persons per sq mi 99.1, persons per sq km 38.3.
Urban-rural (1996[1]): urban 69.0%; rural 31.0%.
Sex distribution (1996[1]): male 46.3%; female 53.7%.
Age breakdown (1996[1]): under 15, 20.4%; 15–29, 20.3%; 30–44, 21.5%; 45–59, 18.5%; 60–74, 14.3%; 75 and over, 5.0%.
Population projection: (2000) 2,426,000; (2010) 2,337,000.
Ethnic composition (1996): Latvian 55.1%; Russian 32.6%; Belarusian 4.0%; Ukrainian 2.9%; Polish 2.2%; Lithuanian 1.3%; other 1.9%.
Religious affiliation (1995): Christian 39.5%, of which Protestant 16.7% (of which Lutheran 14.6%), Roman Catholic 14.9%, Orthodox 8.0%; Jewish 0.6%; other (mostly nonreligious) 59.9%.
Major cities (1996[1]): Riga 826,508; Daugavpils 118,530; Liepāja 98,490; Jelgava 70,957; Jūrmala 59,002.

Vital statistics

Birth rate per 1,000 population (1996): 7.9 (world avg. 25.0); (1994) legitimate 73.6%; illegitimate 26.4%.
Death rate per 1,000 population (1996): 13.8 (world avg. 9.3).
Natural increase rate per 1,000 population (1996): −5.9 (world avg. 15.7).
Total fertility rate (avg. births per childbearing woman; 1996): 1.2.
Marriage rate per 1,000 population (1995): 4.4.
Divorce rate per 1,000 population (1995): 3.2.
Life expectancy at birth (1996): male 60.8 years; female 73.2 years.
Major causes of death per 100,000 population (1994): diseases of the circulatory system 917.0; accidents, poisoning, and violence 235.9; malignant neoplasms (cancers) 219.6; diseases of the respiratory system 52.8.

National economy

Budget (1995). Revenue: Ls 686,500,000 (social security contributions 34.1%, value-added taxes 32.0%, nontax revenue 13.0%, excises 7.5%, corporate income taxes 6.9%). Expenditures: Ls 756,390,000 (social security and welfare 41.3%, education 13.0%, health 6.8%, police 6.2%, defense 2.6%).
Production (metric tons except as noted). Agriculture, forestry, fishing (1996): potatoes 900,000, barley 384,000, wheat 306,000, sugar beets 245,000, vegetables and melons 232,000, fruits and berries 91,000; livestock (number of live animals) 553,000 pigs, 537,000 cattle, 72,100 sheep, 3,500,000 poultry; roundwood (1995) 6,907,000 cu m; fish catch (1995) 149,719. Mining and quarrying (1996): peat 462,700; gypsum 77,226. Manufacturing (value added in U.S.$'000,000; 1994): food products 193; beverages 76; transport equipment 59; wood and wood products 56; electrical machinery 42; textiles 41; nonelectrical machinery 39. Construction (1995): new residential 219,000,000 sq m. Energy production (consumption): electricity (kW-hr; 1995) 3,984,000,000 ([1994] 6,258,000,000); coal (1994) none (425,000); crude petroleum, n.a. (n.a.); petroleum products (1994) none (2,516,000); natural gas (cu m; 1994) none (886,000,000).
Household income and expenditure. Average household size (1989) 3.1; average annual income per household: n.a.; sources of income (1994): wages and salaries 67.0%, pensions and transfers 17.4%, self-employment 5.4%, other 10.2%; expenditure (1995): food and beverages 44.2%, housing and energy 14.1%, clothing and footwear 8.1%, transport and communications 7.8%, recreation and education 6.3%.
Gross national product (1995): U.S.$5,708,000,000 (U.S.$2,270 per capita).

Structure of gross domestic product and labour force

	1996 in value Ls '000,000	1996 % of total value	1995 labour force[2]	1995 % of labour force
Agriculture, forestry	218.9	7.9	220,000	17.2
Mining and quarrying	5.6	0.2	3,000	0.2
Manufacturing	529.9	19.1	208,000	16.3
Construction	117.0	4.2	71,000	5.6
Public utilities	134.5	4.9	17,000	1.3
Transp. and commun.			105,000	8.3
Trade			191,000	15.0
Finance	1,403.5	50.7	77,000	6.0
Pub. admin., defense			56,000	4.4
Services			241,000	18.9
Other	359.1[3]	13.0	87,000[4]	6.8
TOTAL	2,768.4[5]	100.0	1,276,000	100.0

Population economically active (1995): total 1,276,000; activity rate of total population 50.8% (participation rates: ages 15–64, n.a.; female 49.1%; unemployed [1997[6]] 7.5%).

Price and earnings indexes (1992 = 100)

	1992	1993	1994	1995	1996	1997
Consumer price index	100.0	208.8	283.8	354.7	417.1	452.4[6]
Annual earnings index	100.0	211.7	338.6	420.3	486.6	...

Land use (1994): forested 44.4%; meadows and pastures 12.4%; agricultural and permanent cultivation 27.0%; other 16.2%.

Foreign trade[7]

Balance of trade (current prices)

	1992	1993	1994	1995	1996
Ls '000,000	−158	+37	−142	−235	−428
% of total	11.4%	2.8%	11.4%	14.6%	21.2%

Imports (1996): Ls 1,278,000,000 (mineral products 22.2%, machinery and equipment 16.8%, chemicals and chemical products 11.0%, textiles 8.0%, base metals 6.4%). *Major import sources:* Russia 20.2%; Germany 13.8%; Finland 9.2%; Sweden 7.9%; Lithuania 6.3%.
Exports (1996): Ls 795,000,000 (forestry products 24.4%, textiles 16.9%, food and agricultural products 16.4%, machinery and apparatus 9.7%). *Major export destinations:* Russia 22.8%; Germany 13.8%; U.K. 11.1%; Lithuania 7.4%; Sweden 6.6%.

Transport and communications

Transport. Railroads (1996): length 2,413 km; passenger-km 1,182,000,000; metric-km cargo (1996) 12,412,000,000. Roads (1993): total length 64,693 km (paved 18.2%). Vehicles (1996): passenger cars 379,895; trucks and buses 90,184. Merchant marine (1992): cargo vessels 261; total deadweight tonnage 1,436,899. Air transport (1996): passenger-km 301,500,000; metric ton-km cargo 5,201,000; airports with scheduled flights (1996) 1.

Communications

Medium	date	unit	number	units per 1,000 persons
Daily newspapers	1995	circulation	590,000	235
Radio	1996	receivers	1,396,000	560
Television	1996	receivers	1,126,000	452
Telephones	1995	main lines	704,500	280
Cellular telephones	1995	subscribers	15,000	6.0
Facsimile machines	1995	units	900	0.4
Personal computers	1995	units	20,000	8.0

Education and health

Educational attainment (1988). Percentage of persons age 25 and over having: no formal schooling 0.6%; incomplete primary education 18.5%; complete primary 21.2%; secondary 46.3%; higher 13.4%. *Literacy* (1989): percentage of total population age 15 and over literate 99.5%.

Education (1996–97)

	schools	teachers	students	student/ teacher ratio
Primary	643	23,779[8]	98,694	...
Secondary	376	41,029[8]	235,952	...
Vocational[9]	128	9,576[8]	43,170	...
Higher	28	...	55,434	...

Health (1995): physicians 8,400 (1 per 298 persons); hospital beds 27,800 (1 per 90 persons); infant mortality rate per 1,000 live births (1996) 15.9.
Food (1995): daily per capita caloric intake 2,967 (vegetable products 73%, animal products 27%); 116% of FAO recommended minimum requirement.

Military

Total active duty personnel (1997): 8,100 (border guard 44.4%, army 42.0%, navy 12.1%, air force 1.5%). *Military expenditure as percentage of GNP* (1995): 0.9% (world 2.8%); per capita expenditure U.S.$29.

[1]January 1. [2]Annual average official estimate. [3]Indirect taxes less subsidies. [4]Includes 6,000 not adequately defined and 81,000 unemployed. [5]Detail does not add to total given because of rounding. [6]Average of 2nd and 3rd quarters. [7]Imports are f.o.b. in balance of trade and c.i.f. for commodities and trading partners. [8]1995–96. [9]Includes special secondary institutions.

Internet resources for further information:
- **Embassy of Latvia (Washington, D.C.) http://www.seas.gwu.edu/guest/latvia/**
- **Central Statistical Bureau of Latvia http://www.latnet.lv/ligumi/CSBL/**

Lebanon

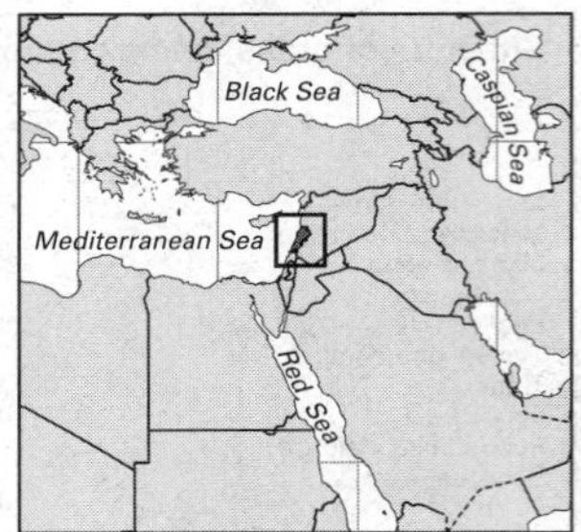

Official name: Al-Jumhūrīyah al-Lubnānīyah (Republic of Lebanon).
Form of government: unitary multiparty republic with one legislative house (National Assembly [128])[1].
Chief of state: President.
Head of government: Prime Minister.
Capital: Beirut.
Official language: Arabic.
Official religion: none.
Monetary unit: 1 Lebanese pound (£L) = 100 piastres; valuation (Oct. 3, 1997) 1 U.S.$ = £L 1,537; 1 £ = £L 2,478.

Area and population

		area		population
Governorates	Capitals	sq mi	sq km	1970 estimate
Bayrūt	Beirut (Bayrūt)	7	18	474,870
Al-Biqāʿ	Zaḥlah	1,653	4,280	203,520
Jabal Lubnān	Bʿabdā	753	1,950	833,055
Al-Janūb	Sidon (Ṣaydā)	772	2,001	249,945
An-Nabaṭīyah	...	...	...	...
Ash-Shamāl	Tripoli (Ṭarābulus)	765	1,981	364,935
TOTAL		4,016[2]	10,400[2]	2,126,325

Demography

Population (1997): 3,112,000.
Density (1997): persons per sq mi 774.9, persons per sq km 299.2.
Urban-rural (1995): urban 87.2%; rural 12.8%.
Sex distribution (1995): male 48.74%; female 51.26%.
Age breakdown (1994): under 15, 33.2%; 15–29, 29.3%; 30–44, 18.6%; 45–59, 11.1%; 60–74, 6.3%; 75 and over, 1.5%.
Population projection: (2000) 3,289,000; (2010) 3,742,000.
Doubling time: 35 years.
Ethnic composition (1996): Arab *c.* 93%, of which Lebanese *c.* 84%, Palestinian *c.* 9%; Armenian *c.* 6%, Kurd and other *c.* 1%.
Religious affiliation (1995): Muslim 55.3%, of which Shīʿī 34.0%, Sunnī 21.3%; Christian 37.6%, of which Catholic 25.1% (Maronite 19.0%, Greek Catholic or Melchite 4.6%), Orthodox 11.7% (Greek Orthodox 6.0%, Armenian Apostolic 5.2%), Protestant 0.5%; Druze 7.1%.
Major cities (1991): Beirut 1,100,000; Tripoli 240,000; Jūniyah 100,000; Zaḥlah 45,000[3]; Sidon (Ṣaydā) 38,000[3]; Tyre 14,000[3].

Vital statistics

Birth rate per 1,000 population (1990–95): 26.9 (world avg. 25.0).
Death rate per 1,000 population (1990–95): 7.1 (world avg. 9.3).
Natural increase rate per 1,000 population (1990–95): 19.8 (world avg. 15.7).
Total fertility rate (avg. births per childbearing woman; 1990–95): 3.1.
Life expectancy at birth (1990–95): male 66.6 years; female 70.5 years.
Major causes of death: n.a.

National economy

Budget (1996). Revenue: £L 4,022,000,000,000 (indirect taxes 46.7%, of which customs revenues 44.7%; direct taxes 14.3%, of which income tax 8.7%, property tax 3.1%; real estate fees 6.8%; miscellaneous taxes and fees 32.2%). Expenditures: £L 6,458,000,000,000 (current expenditures 86.0%, of which debt service 40.3%, salaries and wages 34.7%; capital expenditures 14.0%).
Production (metric tons except as noted). Agriculture, forestry, fishing (1997): grapes 350,000, potatoes 320,000, tomatoes 240,000, oranges 185,000, cucumbers and gherkins 162,000, apples 136,000, lemons and limes 99,500, olives 85,000, onions 72,000; livestock (number of live animals) 425,000 goats, 246,000 sheep, 80,000 cattle, 29,000,000 chickens; roundwood (1995) 515,000 cu m; fish catch (1995) 4,385. Mining and quarrying (1994): lime 15,000; salt 3,000; gypsum 2,000. Manufacturing (1993): cement 3,422,411[4]; distillate fuel 85,000; gasoline 70,000. Construction (1996): 13,499,868 sq m[5]. Energy production (consumption): electricity (kW-hr; 1995) 5,281,000,000 (5,005,000,000); coal, n.a. (none); crude petroleum (barrels; 1993) none (2,602,000); petroleum products (metric tons; 1993) 323,000 ([1994] 3,493,000).
Land use (1994): forested 7.8%; meadows and pastures 1.0%; agricultural and under permanent cultivation 29.9%; wasteland and other areas 61.3%.
Gross national product (1995): U.S.$10,673,000,000 (U.S.$2,660 per capita).

Structure of gross domestic product and labour force

	1995			
	in value U.S.$'000,000[6]	% of total value	labour force	% of labour force
Agriculture	380	4.0	143,900	14.0%
Mining	—	—		
Manufacturing	1,235	13.0	277,600	27.0%
Construction	950	10.0		
Public utilities / Transp. and commun.	2,375[7]	25.0[7]		
Trade	2,660	28.0	606,500	59.0%
Finance / Real estate and business services / Services	1,900	20.0		
Pub. admin., defense	[7]	[7]		
TOTAL	9,500	100.0	1,028,000	100.0

Population economically active (1995): total 1,028,000; activity rate of total population 25.4% (participation rates: over age 15 [1988] 44%; female *c.* 30%; unemployed n.a.).

Price and earnings indexes (1990 = 100)

	1989	1990	1991	1992	1993	1994	1995
Consumer price index	57.9	100.0	151.5	333.3	430.3	466.0	494.0
Wages index[8]	170.0	100.0	104.2	85.4	78.3	118.5	134.7

Public debt (external, outstanding; 1995): U.S.$1,551,000,000.
Household income and expenditure. Average household size (1987) 5.0; average annual income per household (1994) £L 2,400,000 (U.S.$1,430); sources of income (1974): wages 27.9%, transfers 3.0%, other 69.1%; expenditure (1966)[9]: food 42.8%, housing 16.8%, clothing 8.6%, health care 7.2%.
Tourism (1995): receipts from visitors U.S.$710,000,000.

Foreign trade[10]

Balance of trade (current prices)

	1991	1992	1993	1994	1995	1996
U.S.$'000,000	−3,202	−3,185	−4,222	−4,798	−5,770	−10,310
% of total	74.6%	72.6%	75.5%	76.4%	74.5%	76.4%

Imports (1995): U.S.$7,295,000,000 (machinery and transport equipment 27.0%, metals and metal products 9.8%, mineral products 8.8%, processed food 7.8%, chemicals 6.7%). *Major import sources:* Italy 13.0%; U.S. 10.6%; Germany 8.4%; France 7.6%; Switzerland 4.6%.
Exports (1995): U.S.$985,000,000 (reexports 27.7%, paper products 21.8%, food and live animals 14.5%, machinery and transport equipment 9.5%, fibres and fibre products 8.2%, pearls and semiprecious stones and metals 7.0%, metals and metal products 6.7%). *Major export destinations*[11]: U.A.E. 28.8%; Saudi Arabia 11.2%; Syria 8.5%; France 6.1%; Jordan 3.5%.

Transport and communications

Transport. Railroads (1996)[12]: length 222 km. Roads (1996): total length 6,359 km (paved 95%). Vehicles (1995): passenger cars 1,197,521; trucks and buses 84,736. Merchant marine (1992): vessels (100 gross tons and over) 163; total deadweight tonnage 438,165. Air transport (1996)[13]: passenger-km 1,889,000,000; metric ton-km cargo 46,274,000; airports (1997) with scheduled flights 1.

Communications

Medium	date	unit	number	units per 1,000 persons
Daily newspapers	1994	circulation	500,000	172
Radio	1995	receivers	2,247,000	608
Television	1995	receivers	1,075,000	291
Telephones	1995	main lines	330,000	89
Cellular telephones	1995	subscribers	120,000	32
Facsimile machines	1995	units	3,000	0.8
Personal computers	1995	units	50,000	14

Education and health

Educational attainment: n.a. *Literacy* (1995): total population age 15 and over literate 1,829,000 (92.4%); males literate 94.7%; females literate 90.3%.

Education (1994–95)

	schools	teachers	students	student/ teacher ratio
Primary (age 5–9)	2,100[14]	22,810[15]	365,174	...
Secondary (age 10–16)	1,405[15]	21,344[15]	277,646	...
Voc., teacher tr.	275	6,065	45,776	7.5
Higher	20	7,173	79,029	11.0

Health (1995): physicians 6,987 (1 per 529 persons); hospital beds 11,596 (1 per 319 persons); infant mortality rate per 1,000 live births (1990–95) 34.0.
Food (1995): daily per capita caloric intake 3,270 (vegetable products 85.6%, animal products 14.4%); 132% of FAO recommended minimum.

Military

Total active duty personnel (1997): Lebanese national armed forces 55,100 (army 96.7%, navy 1.8%, air force 1.5%). External regular military forces include: UN peacekeeping force in Lebanon 4,488; Syrian army 30,000. Two civilian militias remained active in 1997, though on a much-reduced scale[16]: Shīʿī Muslim (pro-Iran Hezbollah [Party of God]) 3,000; predominantly Maronite Christian and some Shīʿī and Druze (South Lebanese Army) 2,500. *Military expenditure as percentage of GDP* (1995): 3.7% (world 2.8%); per capita expenditure: U.S.$111.

[1]The current legislature was elected between August and October 1996; one-half of its membership is Christian and one-half Muslim/Druze. [2]Includes water area of 66 sq mi (170 sq km) not distributed by governorate. [3]1988 estimate. [4]1995. [5]Permits authorized. [6]Although the Lebanese pound continues to be the official currency, most financial transactions are done in U.S. dollars. By 1993, however, the pound had once again stabilized against the dollar. [7]Public utilities and transportation and communications includes public administration and defense. [8]Based on minimum wage, in real terms. [9]Weights based on consumer price index components. For capital city only. [10]Imports are f.o.b. in balance of trade and c.i.f. in commodities and trading partners. [11]Domestic exports only; reexports not included. [12]Apart from a 14-mi (23-km) section delivering oil from the Zahrani refinery to a thermal power station serving Beirut, no passenger or general cargo track is currently in use. [13]MEA-Airliban international flights only. [14]1991–92. [15]1981–82. [16]Active personnel.

Internet resources for further information:
- **U.S. Embassy of Lebanon http://www.erols.com/lebanon/stat.htm**
- **Bank of Lebanon http://www.bdl.gov.lb/**
- **United Nations Development Programme—Lebanon http://www.undp.org.lb**

Lesotho

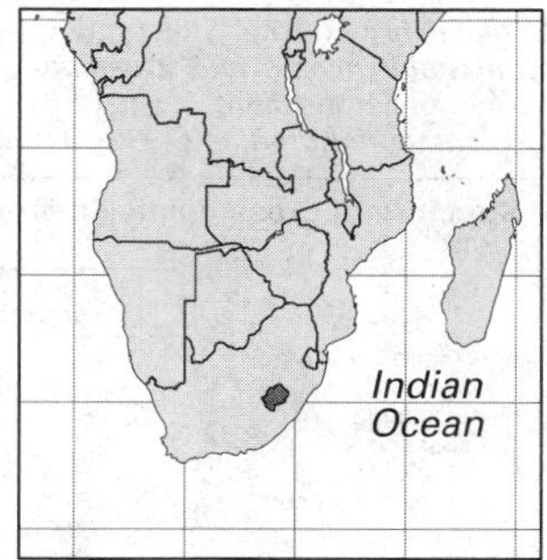

Official name: Lesotho (Sotho); Kingdom of Lesotho (English).
Form of government: multiparty republic[1] with 2 legislative houses (Senate [33[2]]; National Assembly [65]).
Chief of state: King.
Head of government: Prime Minister.
Capital: Maseru.
Official languages: Sotho; English.
Official religion: Christianity.
Monetary unit: 1 loti (plural maloti [M]) = 100 lisente; valuation (Oct. 3, 1997) 1 U.S.$ = M 4.67; 1 £ = M 7.53.

Area and population		area		population
				1995
Districts	Capitals	sq mi	sq km	estimate[3]
Berea	Teyateyaneng	858	2,222	206,200
Butha-Buthe	Butha-Buthe	682	1,767	135,400
Leribe	Hlotse	1,092	2,828	349,500
Mafeteng	Mafeteng	818	2,119	259,000
Maseru	Maseru	1,652	4,279	400,200
Mohale's Hoek	Mohale's Hoek	1,363	3,530	231,300
Mokhotlong	Mokhotlong	1,573	4,075	100,300
Qacha's Nek	Qacha's Nek	907	2,349	86,800
Quthing	Quthing	1,126	2,916	151,900
Thaba-Tseka	Thaba-Tseka	1,649	4,270	136,200
TOTAL		11,720	30,355	2,056,800

Demography

Population (1997): 2,008,000[4].
Density (1997)[4]: persons per sq mi 171.3, persons per sq km 66.2.
Urban-rural (1992): urban 20.9%; rural 79.1%.
Sex distribution (1995): male 49.23%; female 50.77%.
Age breakdown (1995): under 15, 41.3%; 15–29, 27.0%; 30–44, 16.0%; 45–59, 9.1%; 60–74, 5.0%; 75 and over, 1.6%.
Population projection[4]: (2000) 2,114,000; (2010) 2,428,000.
Doubling time: 28 years.
Ethnic composition (1986): Sotho 85.0%; Zulu 15.0%.
Religious affiliation (1992): Christian 93.0%, of which Roman Catholic 42.8%, Protestant (mostly Lesotho Evangelical) 29.1%, other Christian 21.1%; other (mostly traditional beliefs) 7.0%.
Major urban centres (1986): Maseru 109,382; Maputsoe 20,000; Teyateyaneng 14,251; Mafeteng 12,667; Hlotse 9,595.

Vital statistics

Birth rate per 1,000 population (1995–2000): 35.4 (world avg. 25.0); legitimate, n.a.; illegitimate, n.a.
Death rate per 1,000 population (1995–2000): 10.6 (world avg. 9.3).
Natural increase rate per 1,000 population (1995–2000): 24.8 (world avg. 15.7).
Total fertility rate (avg. births per childbearing woman; 1995–2000): 4.9.
Marriage rate per 1,000 population: n.a.
Divorce rate per 1,000 population: n.a.
Life expectancy at birth (1990–95): male 58.0 years; female 63.0 years.
Major causes of death per 100,000 population: n.a.; however, major diseases include malaria, typhoid fever, and infectious and parasitic diseases.

National economy

Budget (1995–96). Revenue: M 1,790,300,000 (1993–94; tax revenue 78.8%, of which customs receipts 53.5%, sales tax 10.1%, income tax 7.3%, company tax 4.6%; grants and nontax revenue 21.2%). Expenditures: M 1,608,800,000 (recurrent expenditure 67.5%, of which education 20.9%, public works [1994–95] 12.8%, health 6.7%, defense 6.4%; capital expenditure 32.5%).
Production (metric tons except as noted). Agriculture, forestry, fishing (1996): corn (maize) 199,000, roots and tubers 63,000, sorghum 31,000, wheat 20,000, vegetables 20,000, fruit 16,000, dry beans 4,500, dry peas 1,075; livestock (number of live animals) 1,200,000 sheep, 750,000 goats, 590,000 cattle, 152,000 asses, 120,000 horses, 70,000 pigs, 1,500,000 chickens; roundwood (1995) 709,000 cu m; fish catch (1994) 35. Mining and quarrying (1988): sand and gravel 50,000 cu m. Manufacturing (value added in U.S.$'000,000; 1994): food products 51; beverages 38; textiles 12; chemical products 8; metal products 4; wearing apparel 3. Construction (permits issued in M '000,000; 1996): residential 11.17; nonresidential 165.97. Energy production (consumption): electricity (kW-hr; 1988) 1,000,000 (n.a.); coal, none (n.a.); petroleum, none (n.a.); natural gas, none (n.a.).
Public debt (external, outstanding; 1995): U.S.$611,000,000.
Tourism (1994): receipts from visitors U.S.$17,000,000; expenditures by nationals abroad U.S.$7,000,000.
Population economically active (1993): total 617,871; activity rate of total population 45.1% (participation rates: ages 15–64 [1986] 79.8%; female 23.7%; unemployed [1992] 35.0%).

Price and earnings indexes (1990 = 100)							
	1990	1991	1992	1993	1994	1995	1996
Consumer price index	100.0	117.7	137.9	156.0	168.9	184.5	201.8
Annual earnings index[5]	100.0	112.7	123.5	132.7	144.6	166.9	...

Household income and expenditure. Average household size (1986) 4.8; average annual income per household (1986–87) M 2,832 (U.S.$1,297); sources of income (1986–87): transfer payments 44.7%, self-employment 27.8%, wages and salaries 22.4%, other 5.1%; expenditure (1989): food 48.0%, clothing 16.4%, household durable goods 11.9%, housing and energy 10.1%, transportation 4.7%.
Gross national product (at current market prices; 1995): U.S.$1,519,000,000 (U.S.$770 per capita).

Structure of gross domestic product and labour force	1995		1986	
	in value M '000,000	% of total value	labour force	% of labour force
Agriculture	395.5	10.5	474,171	66.2
Mining	2.7	0.1	6,446	0.9
Manufacturing	556.5	14.8	19,339	2.7
Construction	889.5	23.6	31,516	4.4
Public utilities	90.3	2.4	1,433	0.2
Transp. and commun.	122.8	3.3	5,014	0.7
Trade	332.9	8.9	22,204	3.1
Finance	440.9	11.7	3,581	0.5
Pub. admin., defense	467.4	12.4	17,907	2.5
Services	99.2	2.6	126,780	17.7
Other	366.4[6]	9.7[6]	7,879	1.1
TOTAL	3,764.1	100.0	716,270[7]	100.0[7]

Land use (1994): meadows and pastures 65.9%; agricultural and under permanent cultivation 10.5%; other 23.6%.

Foreign trade[8]

Balance of trade (current prices)						
	1990	1991	1992	1993	1994	1995
M '000,000	−1,523.0	−1,976.0	−2,374.7	−2,435.9	−2,384.0	−2,867.4
% of total	83.3%	84.2%	79.3%	73.8%	70.1%	71.2%

Imports (1995): M 2,880,930,000 (1990; manufactured goods [excluding chemicals, machinery, and transport equipment] 42.5%; food and live animals 19.1%; machinery and transport equipment 15.3%; petroleum products 8.6%). *Major import sources:* Customs Union of Southern Africa 90.0%; Asia 5.9%; Europe 3.3%, of which European Economic Community 2.3%; the Americas 0.8%.
Exports (1995): M 395,110,000 (1994; manufactured goods 87.5%, of which clothing 54.8%, furniture 8.0%, footwear 6.9%, machinery and transport equipment 2.0%; crude materials 6.3%, of which wool 4.5%, mohair 1.7%; food and live animals 5.5%, of which cereals 1.5%, cattle 1.2%, vegetables 0.7%; chemicals 0.5%; diamonds 0.2%). *Major export destinations:* Customs Union of Southern Africa 51.6%; the Americas 37.6%; Europe 9.4%, of which European Economic Community 9.3%; Asia 0.2%.

Transport and communications

Transport. Railroads (1996): length 1.6 mi, 2.6 km. Roads (1995): total length 3,079 mi, 4,955 km (paved 18%). Vehicles (1995): passenger cars 11,100; trucks and buses 22,200. Merchant marine: vessels (100 gross tons and over) none. Air transport (1996): passenger-mi 3,900,000, passenger-km 6,200,000; short ton-mi cargo 395,000, metric ton-km cargo 577,000; airports (1997) with scheduled flights 1.

Communications				units
Medium	date	unit	number	per 1,000 persons
Daily newspapers	1994	circulation	14,000	7.4
Radio	1996	receivers	1,100,000	558
Television	1995	receivers	13,000	6.7
Telephones	1995	main lines	17,800	9.2
Facsimile machines	1995	units	600	0.3

Education and health

Educational attainment (1986–87). Percentage of population age 10 and over having: no formal education 22.9%; primary 52.8%; secondary 23.2%; higher 0.6%. *Literacy* (1995): total population age 15 and over literate 849,700 (71.3%); males literate 468,000 (81.1%); females literate 381,700 (62.3%).

Education (1994–95)	schools	teachers	students	student/ teacher ratio
Primary (age 6–12)	1,234	7,433	366,935	49.4
Secondary (age 13–17)	187[9]	2,597	61,615	23.7
Voc., teacher tr.[9]	9	225	2,326	10.3
Higher[9]	1	492	4,001	8.1

Health (1993): physicians 136 (1 per 14,306 persons); hospital beds (1992) 2,400 (1 per 765 persons); infant mortality rate per 1,000 live births 71.5.
Food (1995): daily per capita caloric intake 1,972 (vegetable products 93%, animal products 7%); 86% of FAO recommended minimum requirement.

Military

Total active duty personnel (1997): 2,000[10]. *Military expenditure as percentage of GNP* (1995): 1.9% (world 2.8%); per capita expenditure U.S.$14.

[1]New constitution, effective April 1993, ended seven years of military rule. [2]Composed of 22 chiefs and 11 nominated members. [3]De jure population. [4]Excludes absentee miners working in South Africa. [5]Based on average annual wages, including overtime, of mine workers. [6]Indirect taxes less imputed bank service charges. [7]Approximately 117,600 persons (*c.* 40% of Lesotho's adult male labour force) were employed as mine workers in South Africa in 1993. [8]Import figures are f.o.b. in balance of trade and c.i.f. in commodities and trading partners. [9]1993–94. [10]Royal Lesotho Defence Force.

Liberia

Official name: Republic of Liberia.
Form of government: multiparty republic with two legislative houses (Senate [26]; House of Representatives [64]).
Head of state and government: President assisted by State Minister for Presidential Affairs.
Capital: Monrovia.
Official language: English.
Official religion: none.
Monetary unit: 1 Liberian dollar (L$) = 100 cents; valuation (Oct. 3, 1997) 1 U.S.$ = L$1.00[1]; 1 £ = L$1.61.

Area and population

		area		population
Counties	Capitals	sq mi	sq km	1986 estimate
Bomi	Tubmanburg	755	1,955	67,300
Bong	Gbarnga	3,127	8,099	268,100
Grand Bassa	Buchanan	3,382	8,759	166,900
Grand Cape Mount	Robertsport	2,250	5,827	83,900
Grand Gedeh	Zwedru	6,575	17,029	109,000
Grand Kru	Barclayville	[2]	[2]	[2]
Lofa	Voinjama	7,475	19,360	261,000
Margibi	Kakata	1,260	3,263	104,000
Maryland	Harper	2,066[2]	5,351[2]	137,700[2]
Montserrado	Bensonville	1,058	2,740	582,400
Nimba	Sanniquellie	4,650	12,043	325,700
Rivercess	Rivercess City	1,693	4,385	39,900
Sinoe	Greenville	3,959	10,254	65,400
TOTAL		38,250[3]	99,067[3,4]	2,221,300[5]

Demography

Population (1997): 2,602,000[6].
Density (1997): persons per sq mi 68.9[6], persons per sq km 26.6[6].
Urban-rural (1995): urban 44.9%; rural 55.1%.
Sex distribution (1995): male 50.69%; female 49.31%.
Age breakdown (1995): under 15, 44.5%; 15–29, 25.6%; 30–44, 15.6%; 45–59, 9.0%; 60–74, 3.9%; 75 and over, 1.4%.
Population projection: (2000) 3,089,000; (2010) 4,342,000.
Doubling time: 23 years.
Ethnic composition (1984): Kpelle 19.4%; Bassa 13.8%; Grebo 9.0%; Gio 7.8%; Kru 7.3%; Mano 7.1%; other 35.6%.
Religious affiliation (1995): traditional beliefs 63.0%[7]; Christian 21.0%, of which Protestant 13.5%, African Christian 5.1%, Roman Catholic 2.4%; Muslim 16.0%[7].
Major cities (1985): Monrovia 668,000[8]; Harbel 60,000; Gbarnga 30,000[9]; Buchanan 25,000; Yekepa 16,000.

Vital statistics

Birth rate per 1,000 population (1996): 42.8 (world avg. 25.0).
Death rate per 1,000 population (1996): 11.9 (world avg. 9.3).
Natural increase rate per 1,000 population (1996): 30.9 (world avg. 15.7).
Total fertility rate (avg. births per childbearing woman; 1996): 6.2.
Marriage rate per 1,000 population: n.a.
Divorce rate per 1,000 population: n.a.
Life expectancy at birth (1996): male 56.0 years; female 61.2 years.
Major causes of death per 100,000 population (1985)[10]: complications during pregnancy 632.6[11]; malaria 79.8; pneumonia 64.2; anemia 50.2; malnutrition 23.4; measles 12.7. Violence and acts of war were major causes of both morbidity and mortality from 1990 onward.

National economy

Budget (1993). Revenue: L$249,825,000 (1989; income and profits taxes 33.9%; import duties and consular fees 29.6%; excise tax 12.7%; property taxes 1.9%). Expenditures: L$273,930,000 (1988; current expenditure 91.1%, of which wages and salaries 34.1%, interest on public debt 13.1%, goods and services 7.8%, subsidies and grants 5.1%; development expenditure 8.9%).
Tourism: receipts from visitors (1986) U.S.$6,000,000; expenditures by nationals abroad, n.a.
Population economically active (1994): total 993,000; activity rate 43.5% (participation rates: ages 10–64, 64.0%; female 28.5%; unemployed [1996] 95%).

Price and earnings indexes (1990 = 100)

	1989	1990	1991	1992	1993	1994	1995
Consumer price index	79.8	100.0	110.0	121.0	133.1	146.4	161.0
Earnings index	...	...	...	...	...	...	...

Production (metric tons except as noted). Agriculture, forestry, fishing (1996): sugarcane 235,000, cassava 213,000, oil palm fruit 155,000, rice 94,000, bananas 85,000, plantains 35,000, natural rubber 25,000, yams 20,000, coffee 3,000, cacao beans 500; livestock (number of live animals) 220,000 goats, 210,000 sheep, 120,000 pigs, 36,000 cattle, 3,500,000 chickens; roundwood (1995) 5,436,000 cu m; fish catch (1995) 7,782. Mining and quarrying: iron ore[12]; diamonds 150,000 carats[13]; gold 16,000 troy oz[14]. Manufacturing (1996): palm oil 45,000; cement 8,300[13]; cigarettes 22,000,000 units[15]; soft drinks 171,000 hectolitres[16]; beer 158,000 hectolitres[16]. Construction: n.a. Energy production (consumption): electricity (kW-hr; 1994) 485,000,000 (485,000,000); coal, none (none); crude petroleum, none (none); petroleum products (metric tons; 1994) none (101,000); natural gas, none (none).

Public debt (external, outstanding; 1995): U.S.$1,161,000,000.
Household income and expenditure. Average household size (1983) 4.3; income per household: n.a.; sources of income: n.a.; expenditure: n.a.
Gross national product (1995): U.S.$890,000,000 (U.S.$390 per capita).

Structure of gross domestic product and labour force

	1989		1994	
	in value L$'000,000	% of total value	labour force	% of labour force
Agriculture	410.7	34.4	676,000	68.1
Mining	122.3	10.2		
Manufacturing	81.6	6.8		
Construction	26.3	2.2		
Public utilities	19.0	1.6		
Transp. and commun.	79.1	6.6	77,000	7.7
Trade	63.3	5.3		
Finance	141.8	11.9		
Pub. admin., defense	139.4	11.7		
Services	35.5	3.0		
Other	74.8[17]	6.3[17]	240,000	24.2
TOTAL	1,193.6[4]	100.0	993,000	100.0

Land use (1994): forested 47.8%; meadows and pastures 20.8%; agricultural and under permanent cultivation 3.8%; other 27.6%.

Foreign trade[18]

Balance of trade (current prices)

	1991	1992	1993	1994	1995	1996
U.S.$'000,000	−4,548	−4,987	−4,807	−5,393	−4,829	−2,718
% of total	82.3%	76.2%	86.9%	81.7%	71.7%	54.5%

Imports (1996): U.S.$3,854,000,000 (1990; machinery and transport equipment 26.9%, petroleum and petroleum products 23.5%, food and live animals 21.1%, basic manufactures 13.9%, chemicals 5.8%). *Major import sources* (1996): South Korea 25%; Japan 24%; France 9%; Singapore 9%; Croatia 8%.
Exports (1996): U.S.$1,136,000,000 (1988; iron ore 55.1%, rubber 28.0%, logs and timber 8.4%, diamonds 2.1%, gold 1.8%, coffee 1.5%). *Major export destinations* (1996): Belgium-Luxembourg 48%; Singapore 12%; Ukraine 11%; Norway 6%; Malaysia 5%.

Transport and communications

Transport. Railroads (1993)[12, 19]: route length 306 mi, 493 km; short ton-mi cargo 137,000,000, metric ton-km cargo 200,000,000. Roads (1995): total length 6,400 mi, 10,300 km (paved 6%). Vehicles (1995): passenger cars 10,300; trucks and buses 28,300. Merchant marine (1992): vessels (100 gross tons and over) 1,672; total deadweight tonnage 97,373,965. Air transport (1992): passenger-mi 4,300,000, passenger-km 7,000,000; short ton-mi cargo 68,000, metric ton-km cargo 100,000; airports (1997) with scheduled flights 1.

Communications

Medium	date	unit	number	units per 1,000 persons
Daily newspapers	1994	circulation	35,000	15
Radio	1995	receivers	600,000	263
Television	1995	receivers	45,000	20
Telephones	1995	main lines	4,500	2.0

Education and health

Educational attainment, n.a. *Literacy* (1995): total population age 15 and over literate 705,000 (38.3%); males literate 523,000 (53.9%); females literate 182,000 (22.4%).

Education (1980)

	schools	teachers	students	student/teacher ratio
Primary (age 6–12)	1,651	9,099	167,000[13]	...
Secondary (age 13–18)	419	1,129	51,666	45.8
Voc., teacher tr.	6	63	2,322	36.9
Higher	3	472[20]	5,716[13]	...

Health: physicians (1992) 257 (1 per 8,333 persons); hospital beds, n.a.; infant mortality rate (1996) 108.1.
Food (1992): daily per capita caloric intake 1,640 (vegetable products 96%, animal products 4%); 71% of FAO recommended minimum requirement.

Military

Total active duty personnel: All militias were formally disarmed by February 1997. The 10,000-member West African (ECOMOG) peacekeeping force was expected to depart Liberia in February 1998. *Military expenditure as percentage of GNP* (1995): 2.2% (world 2.8%); per capita expenditure U.S.$21.

[1]Officially at par with the U.S.$; the unofficial free/black market exchange rate (a truer value of the L$) was roughly L$60 = U.S.$1 in February 1997. [2]Figures for Grand Kru included in Maryland. [3]Total area per more recent survey is 37,743 sq mi (97,754 sq km). [4]Detail does not add to total given because of rounding. [5]Includes 10,000 persons not allocated by county. [6]Excludes about 650,000 Liberian refugees in surrounding countries. [7]Rough estimate. [8]1990 estimate; the 1996 population is estimated to be 850,000 (including many persons displaced because of war). [9]1986. [10]Hospital inpatient morbidity rates. [11]1984. [12]Mining ceased in late 1992. [13]1993. [14]1995 gold production taxed for export (including gold imported from Sierra Leone and Guinea). [15]1992. [16]1988. [17]Import duties less imputed bank service charges. [18]All balance of trade and trading partner data are based on estimates. [19]For iron-ore transport only. [20]1987.

Internet resources for further information:
- **Liberian Daily News Bulletin (link) http://www.africanews.org/west/liberia/**

Libya

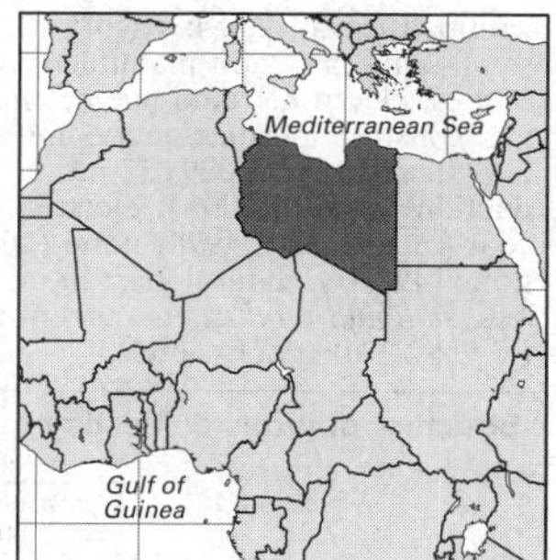

Official name: Al-Jamāhīrīyah al-ʿArabīyah al-Lībīyah ash-Shaʿbīyah al-Ishtirākīyah (Socialist People's Libyan Arab Jamahiriya).
Form of government: socialist state with one policy-making body (General People's Congress [760]).
Chief of state: Muammar al-Qaddafi (de facto)[1]; Secretary of General People's Congress (de jure).
Head of government: Secretary of the General People's Committee (prime minister).
Capital: Tripoli[2].
Official language: Arabic.
Official religion: Islam.
Monetary unit: 1 Libyan dinar (LD) = 1,000 dirhams; valuation[3] (Oct. 3, 1997) 1 Libyan dinar = U.S.$2.61 = £1.62.

Area and population

Baladīyāt	Capitals	area sq mi	area sq km	population 1988 estimate
Banghāzī	Banghāzī	5,800	15,000	512,200
Al-Jabal al-Akhḍar	Al-Bayḍā'	14,300	37,000	308,300
Al-Jabal al-Gharbī	Gharyān	33,600	87,000	204,300
Khalīj Surt	Surt	145,200	376,000	382,100
Al-Kufrah	Al-Kufrah	186,900	484,000	23,800
Margib	Al-Khums	11,200	29,000	408,900
Marzūq	Marzūq	135,100	350,000	45,200
Nikāt al-Khums	Zuwārah	39,000	101,000	196,000
Sabhā	Sabhā	31,700	82,000	121,700
Ṭarābulus	Tripoli (Ṭarābulus)	1,200	3,000	1,083,100
Ṭubruq	Ṭubruq	32,400	84,000	110,900
Wādī al-Ḥa'iṭ	Awbārī	40,500	105,000	49,600
Az-Zāwiyah	Az-Zāwiyah	1,500	4,000	326,500
TOTAL		678,400	1,757,000	3,772,600

Demography

Population (1997): 5,648,000.
Density (1997): persons per sq mi 8.3, persons per sq km 3.2.
Urban-rural (1995): urban 86.0%; rural 14.0%.
Sex distribution (1996): male 50.98%; female 49.02%.
Age breakdown (1995): under 15, 45.4%; 15–29, 26.4%; 30–44, 14.7%; 45–59, 9.1%; 60–74, 3.7%; 75 and over, 0.6%.
Population projection: (2000) 6,294,000; (2010) 8,913,000.
Doubling time: 19 years.
Ethnic composition (1995): Libyan Arab and Berber 79%; other 21% (mostly Egyptians, Sudanese, and Chadians).
Religious affiliation (1992): Sunnī Muslim 97.0%; other 3.0%.
Major cities (1995): Tripoli 1,682,000[4]; Banghāzī 804,000[4]; Miṣrātah 121,700[5]; Az-Zāwiyah 89,338[5].

Vital statistics

Birth rate per 1,000 population (1996): 44.4 (world avg. 25.0).
Death rate per 1,000 population (1996): 7.7 (world avg. 9.3).
Natural increase rate per 1,000 population (1996): 36.7 (world avg. 15.7).
Total fertility rate (avg. births per childbearing woman; 1996): 6.3.
Marriage rate per 1,000 population (1991): 5.1[6].
Divorce rate per 1,000 population (1988): 0.6[6].
Life expectancy at birth (1995): male 62.1 years; female 66.6 years.
Major causes of death per 100,000 population: n.a.; however, the main causes of hospital mortality in 1987 were injuries and poisoning 15.5%, diseases of the circulatory system 11.6%, conditions originating in the perinatal period 11.4%, diseases of the respiratory system 7.0%, neoplasms (cancers) 4.4%.

National economy

Budget (1991–92). Revenue: LD 2,655,000,000 (1990–91; current revenue 55.7%, of which oil revenues 17.7%, income taxes 13.7%, customs duties 9.7%, stamp duties 2.4%; capital revenue 44.3%). Expenditures: LD 2,846,000,000 (1990–91; current expenditures 55.7%, of which municipalities 39.4%, education and scientific research 4.3%, health 2.7%; capital expenditures 44.3%, of which agriculture and land reclamation 13.6%, industry 5.3%).
Production (metric tons except as noted). Agriculture, forestry, fishing (1997): watermelons 179,000, wheat 168,000, barley 150,000, tomatoes 134,000, potatoes 130,000, oranges 79,000, onions 74,500, dates 67,000, olives 55,000, almonds 29,000; livestock (number of live animals) 4,400,000 sheep, 800,000 goats, 129,000 camels, 100,000 cattle, 16,600,000 chickens; roundwood (1995) 660,000 cu m; fish catch (1994) 8,800. Mining and quarrying (1996): lime 260,000[7]; salt 30,000; gypsum 4,000. Manufacturing (1993): distillate fuel 4,470,000; cement 2,300,000[7]; gasoline 1,995,000; jet fuel 1,664,000; crude steel 920,000; fertilizer 347,000[7]. Construction (gross value in LD; 1982): residential 127,051,000; nonresidential 200,877,000. Energy production (consumption): electricity (kW-hr; 1994) 17,800,000,000 (17,800,000,000); coal (metric tons; 1994) none (5,000); crude petroleum (barrels; 1996) 525,600,000 ([1994] 112,725,000); petroleum products (metric tons; 1994) 13,260,000 (7,480,000); natural gas (cu m; 1996) 6,200,000,000 ([1994] 4,910,000,000).
Population economically active (1993): total 1,192,000; activity rate of total population 23.6% (participation rates: ages 10 and over, 35.2%; female 9.8%; unemployed, n.a.).

Price index (1990 = 100)

	1989	1990	1991	1992	1993	1994	1995
Consumer price index	88.5	100.0	111.7	128.5	154.1	200.4	260.5

Public debt (long-term debt; 1992): U.S.$2,592,000,000.
Gross domestic product (1994): U.S.$32,900,000,000 (U.S.$6,510 per capita).

Structure of gross domestic product and labour force

	1992 in value[8] LD '000,000	1992 % of total value	1993 labour force	1993 % of labour force
Agriculture	638	7.5	119,000	10.0
Mining and quarrying	2,173	25.4	381,000	32.0
Manufacturing	720	8.4		
Construction	1,070	12.5		
Public utilities	193	2.3		
Transp. and commun.	539	6.3	692,000	58.0
Trade	770	9.0		
Finance, insurance	986	11.5		
Pub. admin., defense	885	10.4		
Services	574	6.7		
TOTAL	8,548	100.0	1,192,000	100.0

Household income and expenditure. Average household size (1980) 5.1; income per household: n.a.; sources of income: n.a.; expenditure (1977): food 37.2%, housing and energy 32.2%, transportation 9.4%, education and recreation 8.5%, clothing 6.9%, health care 3.3%.
Land use (1994): forested 0.5%; meadows and pastures 7.6%; agricultural and under permanent cultivation 1.2%; desert and built-up areas 90.7%.
Tourism (1994): receipts U.S.$7,000,000; expenditures U.S.$210,000,000.

Foreign trade[9, 10]

Balance of trade (current prices)

	1991	1992	1993	1994	1995	1996
U.S.$'000,000	+5,873	+4,778	+2,165	+3,637	+3,615	+4,896
% of total	35.5%	31.6%	16.8%	30.5%	27.1%	32.3%

Imports (1996): U.S.$5,137,000,000 (1991; manufactured goods 78.3%, agricultural goods 20.3%). *Major import sources:* Italy 21.7%; Germany 13.9%; U.K. 8.4%; France 6.8%; Turkey 5.6%; Tunisia 4.2%; Spain 3.7%.
Exports (1996): U.S.$10,033,000,000 (1991; crude petroleum 99.8%). *Major export destinations:* Italy 41.0%; Germany 18.0%; Spain 10.0%; Turkey 4.1%; France 4.1%; Switzerland 3.0%; The Sudan 2.3%.

Transport and communications

Transport. Railroads: none. Roads (1995): total length 81,600 km (paved 56%). Vehicles (1995): passenger cars 904,000; trucks and buses 322,000. Merchant marine (1992): vessels (100 gross tons and over) 150; total deadweight tonnage 1,223,589. Air transport (1996)[11]: passenger-km 412,353,000; metric ton-km cargo 284,000; airports with scheduled flights: n.a.

Communications

Medium	date	unit	number	units per 1,000 persons
Daily newspapers	1992	circulation	71,000	15
Radio	1995	receivers	1,000,000	191
Television	1995	receivers	550,000	105
Telephones	1995	main lines	318,000	61

Education and health

Educational attainment (1984). Percentage of population age 25 and over having: no formal schooling (illiterate) 59.7%; incomplete primary education 15.4%; complete primary 8.5%; some secondary 5.2%; secondary 8.5%; higher 2.7%. *Literacy* (1995): percentage of total population age 15 and over literate 76.2%; males literate 87.9%; females literate 63.0%.

Education (1992–93)

	schools	teachers	students	student/ teacher ratio
Primary (age 6–12)	2,744[12]	103,791	1,254,242	12.1
Secondary (age 13–18)	1,555[12]	14,941[13]	181,368[13]	12.1[13]
Voc., teacher tr.	195[12]	7,072[13]	94,961	10.8[13]
Higher	10[14]	...	72,899[13]	...

Health: physicians (1989–91) 4,749 (1 per 948 persons); hospital beds (1990) 18,503[15] (1 per 246 persons); infant mortality rate (1995) 61.4.
Food (1995): daily per capita caloric intake 3,126 (vegetable products 90%, animal products 10%); 132% of FAO recommended minimum requirement.

Military

Total active duty personnel (1997): 65,000 (army 53.8%, navy 12.3%, air force 33.9%). *Military expenditure as percentage of GNP* (1995): 6.0% (world 2.8%); per capita expenditure U.S.$381.

[1]No formal titled office exists. [2]Policy-making body (General People's Congress) meets in Surt. [3]Official exchange rate. [4]Urban area. [5]1988. [6]Registered events; incomplete to some degree. [7]1994. [8]At factor cost. [9]Dollar values based on IMF Direction of Trade Statistics (DOTS), which are compiled from available reports of trading partners (not the subject country's reports) and may, thus, be substantially incomplete. [10]Import figures are f.o.b. [11]Jamahiriya Libyan Arab Airlines. [12]1982–83. [13]1991–92. [14]1988–89. [15]Includes beds in clinics.

Internet resources for further information:
- **CIA World Factbook—Libya**
http://www.odci.gov/cia/publications/nsolo/factbook/ly.htm

Liechtenstein

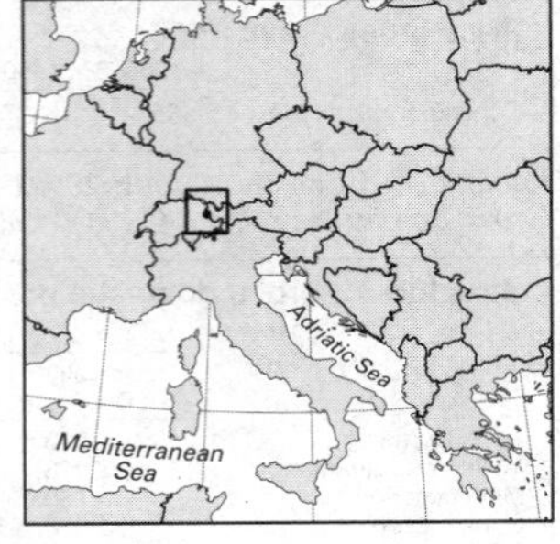

Official name: Fürstentum Liechtenstein (Principality of Liechtenstein).
Form of government: constitutional monarchy with one legislative house (Diet [25]).
Chief of state: Prince.
Head of government: Prime Minister.
Capital: Vaduz.
Official language: German.
Official religion: none.
Monetary unit: 1 Swiss franc (Sw F) = 100 centimes; valuation (Oct. 3, 1997) 1 U.S.$ = Sw F 1.45; 1 £ = Sw F 2.34.

Area and population

Regions / Communes	area sq mi	area sq km	population 1997[1] estimate
Oberland	48.3	125.2	20,907
Balzers	7.6	19.6	3,972
Planken	2.0	5.3	333
Schaan	10.3	26.8	5,130
Triesen	10.2	26.4	3,988
Triesenberg	11.5	29.8	2,467
Vaduz	6.7	17.3	5,017
Unterland	13.4[2]	34.8	10,236
Eschen	4.0	10.3	3,459
Gamprin	2.4	6.1	1,138
Mauren	2.9	7.5	3,088
Ruggell	2.9	7.4	1,642
Schellenberg	1.4	3.5	909
TOTAL	61.8[2]	160.0	31,143

Demography

Population (1997): 31,300.
Density (1997): persons per sq mi 506.5, persons per sq km 195.7.
Urban-rural: n.a.
Sex distribution (1997[1]): male 48.73%; female 51.27%.
Age breakdown (1997[1]): under 15, 18.8%; 15–29, 22.3%; 30–44, 25.4%; 45–59, 19.4%; 60–74, 9.6%; 75 and over, 4.5%.
Population projection: (2000) 32,300; (2010) 35,900.
Doubling time: n.a.; doubling time exceeds 100 years.
Ethnic composition (1997[1]): Liechtensteiner 62.4%; Swiss 14.8%; Austrian 6.9%; German 3.4%; Italian 2.8%; other 9.7%.
Religious affiliation (1997[1]): Roman Catholic 80.0%; Protestant 7.5%; Muslim 3.3%; Eastern Orthodox 0.7%; Atheist 0.6%; other 7.9%.
Major cities (1997[1]): Schaan 5,130; Vaduz 5,017.

Vital statistics

Birth rate per 1,000 population (1996): 13.0 (world avg. 25.0); (1995) legitimate 89.9%; illegitimate 10.1%.
Death rate per 1,000 population (1996): 7.4 (world avg. 9.3).
Natural increase rate per 1,000 population (1996): 5.6 (world avg. 15.7).
Total fertility rate (avg. births per childbearing woman; 1994): 1.5.
Marriage rate per 1,000 population (1996): 14.1.
Divorce rate per 1,000 population (1996): 1.4.
Life expectancy at birth (1996): male 66.5 years; female 77.8 years.
Major causes of death per 100,000 population (1996): diseases of the circulatory system 283.6; malignant neoplasms (cancers) 183.7; accidents, poisoning, and acts of violence 51.6; diseases of the respiratory system 51.6.

National economy

Budget (1996). Revenue: Sw F 579,500,000 (taxes and interest 71.3%, customs duties and repayments 17.9%, investment income 8.9%; other revenue sources include real estate capital-gains taxes and death and estate taxes). Expenditures: Sw F 530,900,000 (financial affairs 36.2%, education 15.3%, social affairs 14.9%, transportation 12.9%, general administration 7.9%).
Public debt: none.
Tourism (1996): 119,264 tourist overnight stays; receipts from visitors, n.a.; expenditures by nationals abroad, n.a.
Population economically active (1997[1]): total 16,181; activity rate of total population 52.0% (participation rates: ages 15–64, 71.3%; female 40.3%; unemployed 2.7%).

Price and earnings indexes (1990 = 100)

	1990	1991	1992	1993	1994	1995	1996
Consumer price index[3]	100.0	105.8	110.2	113.7	114.7	116.8	117.8
Earnings index	...	...	...	...	...	...	...

Household income and expenditure. Average household size (1990) 2.7; income per household: n.a.; sources of earned income (1987): wages and salaries 92.9%, self-employment 7.1%; expenditure (1990)[4]: rent 20.9%, food 17.7%, transportation 11.0%, education and self-improvement 9.7%, clothing 7.0%, health 4.7%.
Production (metric tons except as noted). Agriculture, forestry, fishing (1996): silo corn (maize) 27,880[5], milk 12,801, potatoes 1,040[5], wheat 460[5], barley 416[5], grapes 150; livestock (number of live animals) 5,905 cattle, 3,352 sheep, 2,392 pigs; commercial timber (1996) 18,087 cu m; fish catch, n.a. Mining and quarrying: n.a. Manufacturing (1995): processed milk 12,801; milk for whipped cream 2,654; yogurt 122; cheese 4; wine (1993) 635.2 hectolitres; small-scale precision manufacturing includes optical lenses, electron microscopes, electronic equipment, and high-vacuum pumps; metal manufacturing, construction machinery, and ceramics are also important. Construction (1995): residential 329,057 cu m; nonresidential 318,284 cu m. Energy production (consumption): electricity (kW-hr; 1996) 75,096,000 (259,303,000); coal (metric tons; 1995) none (26); petroleum products (metric tons; 1995) none (49,291); natural gas (cu m; 1994) none (19,350,000).
Gross national product (at current market prices; 1994): *c.* U.S.$1,130,000,000 (*c.* U.S.$37,000 per capita).

Structure of gross domestic product and labour force

	1988 in value Sw F '000	1988 % of total value	1997[1] labour force	1997[1] % of labour force
Agriculture	...	...	316	2.0
Manufacturing	...	...	4,724	29.2
Construction	...	...	1,134	7.0
Public utilities	...	...	164	1.0
Transportation and communications	...	...	514	3.2
Trade, public accommodation	...	...	2,064	12.8
Finance, insurance, real estate	...	...	1,233	7.6
Pub. admin., defense	...	...	1,029	6.4
Services	...	...	4,563	28.2
Other	...	...	440[6]	2.7[6]
TOTAL	1,700,000	100.0	16,181	100.0[2]

Land use (latest): forested 34.8%; meadows and pastures 15.7%; agricultural and under permanent cultivation 24.3%; other 25.2%.

Foreign trade

Balance of trade (current prices)

	1990	1991	1992	1993	1994	1995
Sw F '000,000	+757.1	+822.8	+947.1	+1,024.2	+1,043.3	+1,078.0
% of total	27.8%	31.4%	30.6%	33.8%	33.1%	33.5%

Imports (1995): Sw F 1,071,796,000 (machinery and transport equipment 33.9%; other finished goods 24.4%; metal products 14.1%; limestone, cement, and other building materials 11.9%; unrefined and semifabricated metal 5.8%; chemical products 4.6%). *Major import sources:* n.a.
Exports (1995): Sw F 2,149,796,000 (machinery and transport equipment 46.9%; metal products 16.9%; other finished goods 12.1%; limestone, cement, and other building materials 10.3%; chemical products 8.1%). *Major export destinations* (1994): European Economic Community countries 39.6%; Switzerland 14.0%; other European Free Trade Association countries 6.0%; other 40.4%.

Transport and communications

Transport. Railroads (1996): length 11.5 mi, 18.5 km; passenger and cargo traffic, n.a. Roads (1995): total length 201 mi, 323 km. Vehicles (1997): passenger cars 19,926; trucks and buses 2,684. Merchant marine: none. Air transport: none.

Communications

Medium	date	unit	number	units per 1,000 persons
Daily newspapers	1995	circulation	17,355	564
Radio	1995	receivers	11,808	384
Television	1995	receivers	11,421	371
Telephones	1995	main lines	19,632	638

Education and health

Educational attainment (1990). Percentage of population not of preschool age or in compulsory education having: no formal schooling 0.3%; primary and lower secondary education 39.3%; higher secondary and vocational 47.6%; some postsecondary 7.4%; university 4.2%; other and unknown 1.1%. *Literacy:* virtually 100%.

Education (1996–97)

	schools	teachers[7]	students	student/teacher ratio
Primary (age 7–12)	14	144	1,998	13.9
Secondary (age 13–19)	8	164	1,887	11.5
Vocational[8]	2	247	2,515	10.2

Health: physicians (1995) 32 (1 per 962 persons); hospital beds[9] (1985) 100 (1 per 269 persons); infant mortality rate per 1,000 live births (1996) 7.4.
Food (1996)[10]: daily per capita caloric intake 3,440 (vegetable products 69%, animal products 31%); 129% of FAO recommended minimum requirement.

Military

Total active duty personnel: none. *Military expenditure as percentage of GNP:* none.

[1]January 1. [2]Detail does not add to total given because of rounding. [3]The index is for Switzerland, which is united with Liechtenstein in a customs and monetary union. [4]Household expenditures are taken from a 1986 Swiss sample survey; a similarity of consumption patterns is assumed. [5]1987. [6]Unemployed. [7]Full-time teachers only. [8]1994–95. [9]Liechtenstein has one hospital. Agreements with the Swiss cantons of St. Gallen and Graubünden and the Austrian Federal State of Vorarlberg allow use of certain hospitals. [10]Figures are derived from statistics for Switzerland and Austria.

Internet resources for further information:
- **Principality of Liechtenstein http://hkreuzer.phys.dal.ca/fl.htm**

Lithuania

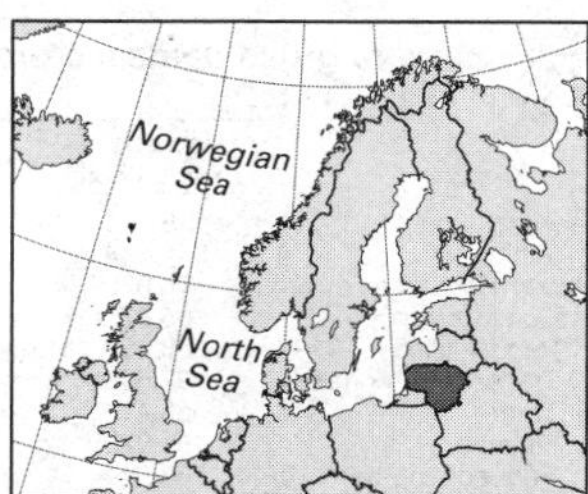

Official name: Lietuvos Respublika (Republic of Lithuania).
Form of government: unitary multiparty republic with a single legislative body, the Seimas (141).
Head of state: President.
Head of government: Prime Minister.
Capital: Vilnius.
Official language: Lithuanian.
Official religion: none.
Monetary unit: 1 litas (plural litai) = 100 centai; valuation (Oct. 3, 1997) 1 U.S.$ = 4.00 litai; 1 £ = 6.45 litai.

Area and population

		area		population
Provinces	**Capitals**	sq mi	sq km	1996 estimate
Alytus	Alytus	2,095	5,425	202,600
Kaunas	Kaunas	3,154	8,170	756,300
Klaipėda	Klaipėda	2,219	5,746	415,800
Marijampolė	Marijampolė	1,723	4,463	198,500
Panevėžys	Panevėžys	3,042	7,880	323,600
Šiauliai	Šiauliai	3,379	8,751	401,700
Tauragė	Tauragė	1,496	3,874	130,100
Telšiai	Telšiai	4,598	4,139	182,800
Utena	Utena	2,780	7,201	202,600
Vilnius	Vilnius	3,726	9,651	897,900
TOTAL		25,213[1, 2]	65,301[1, 2]	3,711,900

Demography

Population (1997): 3,706,000.
Density (1997): persons per sq mi 147.0, persons per sq km 56.8.
Urban-rural (1996): urban 67.8%; rural 32.2%.
Sex distribution (1996): male 47.22%; female 52.78%.
Age breakdown (1996): under 15, 21.6%; 15–29, 22.0%; 30–44, 22.1%; 45–59, 16.9%; 60–69, 9.7%; 70 and over, 7.7%.
Population projection: (2000) 3,699,000; (2010) 3,721,000.
Doubling time: not applicable.
Ethnic composition (1996): Lithuanian 81.4%; Russian 8.2%; Polish 7.0%; Belorusian 1.5%; Ukrainian 1.0%; other 0.9%.
Religious affiliation (1994): Roman Catholic 78.6%; Russian Orthodox, Old Believer, Evangelical Lutheran, and nonreligious minorities.
Major cities (1996): Vilnius 573,200; Kaunas 410,800; Klaipėda 201,500; Siauliai 146,500; Panevezys 132,300; Alytus 77,400.

Vital statistics

Birth rate per 1,000 population (1996): 10.6 (world avg. 25.0); (1995) legitimate 87.4%, illegitimate 12.6%.
Death rate per 1,000 population (1996): 11.6 (world avg. 9.3).
Natural increase rate per 1,000 population (1996): –1.0 (world avg. 15.7).
Total fertility rate (avg. births per childbearing woman; 1995): 1.5.
Marriage rate per 1,000 population (1995): 6.0.
Divorce rate per 1,000 population (1995): 2.8.
Life expectancy at birth (1995): male 63.6 years; female 75.2 years.
Major causes of death per 100,000 population (1995): circulatory diseases 654; malignant neoplasms (cancers) 203; accidents 176; respiratory diseases 49; digestive diseases 32.

National economy

Budget (1995). Revenue: 5,758,000,000 litai (value-added tax 34.3%, individual income tax 29.3%, excise taxes 10.7%, property tax 2.8%). Expenditures: 6,197,000,000 litai (economy 27.9%, education 21.8%, health 14.3%, social insurance 8.3%).
Production (metric tons except as noted). Agriculture, forestry, fishing (1996): potatoes 1,594,000, barley 1,000,000, wheat 550,000, sugar beets 650,000; livestock (number of live animals) 1,150,000 pigs, 1,100,000 cattle, 8,530,000 poultry; roundwood (1995) 4,495,000 cu m; fish catch (1993) 120,078. Mining and quarrying (1995): limestone 3,000,000; peat 214,000. Manufacturing (value of production in '000 litai; 1995): processed foods 4,781,421; textile and knitwear 1,748,812; chemicals 1,066,200; wood and wood products 630,334. Construction (1996): residential 2,000,900,000 litai. Energy production (consumption): electricity (kW-hr; 1994) 10,055,000,000 (11,199,000,000); coal (metric tons; 1994) none (482,000); crude petroleum (barrels; 1994) 682,000 (27,000,000); petroleum products (metric tons; 1994) 3,819,000 (3,606,000); natural gas (cu m; 1994) none (1,871,000,000).
Gross national product (1995): U.S.$7,070,000,000[3] (U.S.$1,900 per capita).

Structure of gross national product and labour force

	1995			
	in value '000,000 litai	% of total value	labour force	% of labour force
Agriculture, forestry	2,222.5	9.3	391,800	22.4
Manufacturing, mining	6,180.9	25.9	306,200	17.5
Construction	1,590.5	6.7	114,700	6.5
Public utilities	723.3	3.0	42,300	2.4
Transp. and commun.	1,813.8	7.6	95,100	5.4
Trade	5,698.0	23.9	229,600	13.1
Finance	751.9	3.2	57,400	3.3
Pub admin., defense	...	...	67,600	3.9
Services	...	...	244,900	14.0
Other	4,848.2	20.4	203,000[4]	11.6
TOTAL	23,829.0	100.0	1,752,600	100.0[2]

Population economically active (1995): total 1,753,000; activity rate of total population 47.2% (participation rates: ages 16–60/55[5], 83.0%; female [1993] 48.5%; unemployed 6.2%).

Price and earnings indexes (1994 = 100)

	1990	1991	1992	1993	1994	1995	1996
Consumer price index	0.76	1.65	11.4	58.1	100	139.7	174.0
Monthly earnings index	2.63	6.84	15.8	52.5	100	143.4	195.0

Household income and expenditure (1995). Average household size (1989) 3.2; sources of income: wages 71.4%, pensions and grants 14.0%, self-employment in agriculture 6.6%, other 7.0%; expenditure: food 45.1%, nonfood goods 17.6%, services 15.6%, taxes 14.4%, agricultural expenses 4.3%.
Land use (1994): forested 30.4%; meadows and pastures 7.6%; agricultural and under permanent cultivation 53.9%; other 8.1%.
Tourism (1995): receipts from visitors U.S.$124,000,000; expenditures by nationals abroad U.S.$138,000,000.

Foreign trade

Imports (1995): U.S.$3,083,000,000 (petroleum and gas 26.7%, machinery 16.5%, textiles 9.3%, chemicals 9.0%, transport equipment 7.5%, base metals 6.7%, prepared foods 4.5%). *Major import sources:* Russia 31.1%; Germany 15.2%; United Kingdom 4.3%; Poland 4.1%; Denmark 3.9%; Finland 3.6%.
Exports (1995): U.S.$2,707,000,000 (textiles 14.7%, chemicals 12.2%, mineral products 11.9%, machinery 10.8%, base metals 8.7%, live animals 8.4%, prepared foods 5.6%). *Major export destinations:* Russia 20.4%; Germany 14.4%; Belarus 10.7%; Ukraine 7.5%; Latvia 7.1%; The Netherlands 4.9%; Poland 3.9%.

Transport and communications

Transport. Railroads (1995): length 1,802 mi, 2,900 km; passenger-mi 702,000,000, passenger-km 1,130,000,000; short-ton mi cargo 5,264,000,000, metric-ton km cargo 7,685,000,000. Roads (1995): total length 38,178 mi, 61,442 km (paved 86%). Vehicles (1995): passenger cars 718,469; trucks and buses 110,696. Merchant marine (1995): vessels (100 gross tons and over) 95; total deadweight tonnage 569,288. Air transport (1996): passenger-mi 226,000,000, passenger-km 363,000,000; short-ton mi cargo 1,566,000, metric-ton km cargo 2,287,000; airports with scheduled flights (1996) 3.

Communications

Medium	date	unit	number	units per 1,000 persons
Daily newspapers	1994	circulation	506,000	136
Radio	1995	receivers	1,500,000	404
Television	1995	receivers	1,350,000	364
Telephones	1995	main lines	941,000	254
Cellular telephones	1995	subscribers	14,800	4.0
Facsimile machines	1995	units	500	0.13
Personal computers	1995	units	24,000	6.5

Education and health

Educational attainment (1989). Percentage of population age 25 and over having: no schooling 9.1%; complete primary 21.3%; incomplete secondary 57.0%; postsecondary 12.6%. *Literacy* (1995[6]): total population age 15 and over literate 99.5%; males literate 99.6%; females literate 99.3%.

Education (1995–96)

	schools	teachers	students	student/teacher ratio
Primary and secondary	2,361	47,000	562,000	12.0
Voc., teacher tr.	106	4,671	49,000	10.5
Higher	15	9,003[7]	54,000	7.3[7]

Health (1995): physicians 14,737 (1 per 252 persons); hospital beds 40,262 (1 per 92 persons); infant mortality rate per 1,000 live births (1995) 12.4.

Military

Total active duty personnel (1996): 5,100 (army 82.3%, navy 6.9%, air force 10.8%). *Military expenditure as percentage of GNP* (1995): 0.5% (world 2.8%); per capita expenditure U.S.$21.

[1]Total includes 12 sq mi (30 sq km) not distributed by administrative subdivision. [2]Detail does not add to total given because of rounding. [3]GNP estimate is preliminary. [4]Includes 109,000 undistributable unemployed and 94,000 undistributable employed. [5]Males retire at age 60, females at 55. [6]Estimate. [7]1987–88.

Internet resources for further information:
- **Lithuanian Department of Statistics http://www.std.lt**

Luxembourg

Official name: Groussherzogtum Lëtzebuerg (Luxemburgian); Grand-Duché de Luxembourg (French); Grossherzogtum Luxemburg (German) (Grand Duchy of Luxembourg).
Form of government: constitutional monarchy with two legislative houses (Council of State [21][1]; Chamber of Deputies [60]).
Chief of state: Grand Duke.
Head of government: Prime Minister.
Capital: Luxembourg.
Official language: none: Luxemburgian (national); French (used for most official purposes); German (lingua franca).
Official religion: none.
Monetary unit: 1 Luxembourg franc (Lux F) = 100 centimes; valuation (Oct. 3, 1997) 1 U.S.$ = Lux F 36.38; 1 £ = Lux F 58.64.

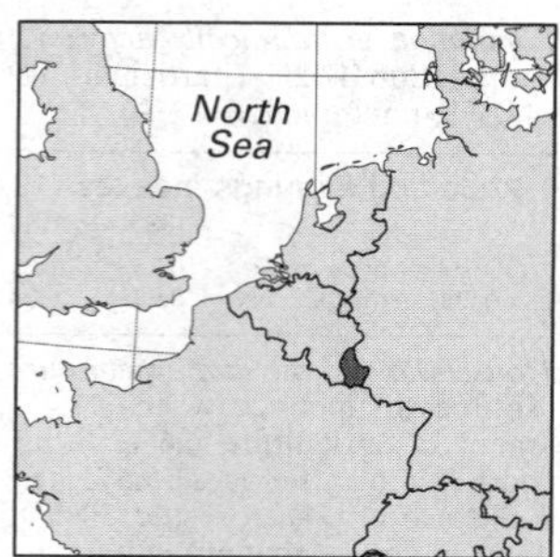

Area and population

Districts / Cantons	area sq mi	area sq km	population 1995[2] estimate
Diekirch	447	1,157	60,900
Clervaux	128	332	11,300
Diekirch	92	239	24,600
Redange	103	267	12,000
Vianden	21	54	2,900
Wiltz	102	265	10,100
Grevenmacher	203	525	46,700
Echternach	72	186	13,000
Grevenmacher	82	211	19,400
Remich	49	128	14,300
Luxembourg	349	904	298,000
Capellen	77	199	34,200
Esch	94	243	122,700
Luxembourg (Ville et Campagne)	92	238	120,500
Mersch	86	224	20,600
TOTAL	999	2,586	406,600[3]

Demography

Population (1997): 420,000.
Density (1997): persons per sq mi 420.4, persons per sq km 162.4.
Urban-rural (1993): urban 88.0%; rural 12.0%.
Sex distribution (1996[2]): male 49.08%; female 50.92%.
Age breakdown (1996): under 15, 18.5%; 15–29, 19.6%; 30–44, 24.8%; 45–59, 18.0%; 60–74, 13.5%; 75 and over, 5.6%.
Population projection: (2000) 433,000; (2010) 462,000.
Doubling time: not applicable; population stable.
Ethnic composition (nationality; 1996[2]): Luxemburger 66.6%; Portuguese 12.5%; Italian 4.8%; French 3.6%; Belgian 2.6%; German 2.3%; other 7.6%.
Religious affiliation (1990): Roman Catholic 94.9%; Protestant 1.1%; other 4.0%.
Major cities (1995[2]): Luxembourg 76,446; Esch-sur-Alzette 24,255; Differdange 16,196; Dudelange 15,833; Petange 13,066.

Vital statistics

Birth rate per 1,000 population (1996): 13.7 (world avg. 25.0); (1995) legitimate 86.9%; illegitimate 13.1%.
Death rate per 1,000 population (1996): 9.4 (world avg. 9.3).
Natural increase rate per 1,000 population (1996): 4.3 (world avg. 15.7).
Total fertility rate (avg. births per childbearing woman; 1995): 1.7.
Marriage rate per 1,000 population (1995): 5.1.
Divorce rate per 1,000 population (1995): 1.8.
Life expectancy at birth (1990–92): male 72.6 years; female 79.1 years.
Major causes of death per 100,000 population (1995): circulatory diseases 392.1, of which ischemic heart disease and myocardial infarction 125.8, cerebrovascular disease 119.4; malignant neoplasms (cancers) 253.1.

National economy

Budget (1996). Revenue: Lux F 155,837,400,000 (income and excise taxes 57.9%, customs taxes 15.9%). Expenditures: Lux F 156,604,200,000 (social security 20.5%, education 12.0%, transportation 9.1%, administration 7.3%, defense 2.4%, debt service 1.1%).
Public debt (1995): U.S.$541,240,000.
Tourism (1989): receipts from visitors U.S.$286,000,000.
Production (metric tons except as noted). Agriculture, forestry, fishing (1995): barley 63,300, wheat 52,800, potatoes 22,800, rye 16,800, oats 11,800, sugar beets 10,400, apples 5,595; livestock (number of live animals) 213,887 cattle, 76,640 pigs; roundwood (1993) 305,200 cu m. Mining and quarrying (1987): sand and gravel 956,810; gypsum 420,000; crushed stone 344,841. Manufacturing (1994): steel 3,073,268; pig iron 1,926,890; milk 261,600; beef and pork 23,120; wine 179,998 hectolitres. Construction (1995): residential 514,616 sq m; nonresidential 320,184 sq m. Energy production (consumption): electricity (kW-hr; 1994) 1,190,000,000 (5,645,000,000); coal (metric tons; 1994) none (323,000); crude petroleum, none (n.a.); petroleum products (metric tons; 1994) none (1,721,000); natural gas (cu m; 1994) none (582,040,000).
Gross national product (1995): U.S.$16,876,000,000 (U.S.$41,210 per capita).

Structure of gross domestic product and labour force

	1995 in value Lux F '000,000	% of total value	labour force	% of labour force
Agriculture	5,174	1.1	5,800	2.7
Mining	4	4	4	4
Manufacturing	78,920[4]	17.4[4]	32,800[4]	15.4[4]
Construction	35,875	7.9	23,900	11.2
Public utilities	8,099	1.8	1,400	0.6
Transp. and commun.	27,505	6.1	14,500	6.8
Trade	65,419	14.4	44,700	20.9
Finance	91,929	20.2	20,100	9.4
Pub. admin., defense	63,644	14.0	29,900	14.0
Services	142,200	31.3	40,300	18.9
Other	−64,572[5]	−14.2[5]	...	...
TOTAL	454,193	100.0	213,500[3]	100.0[3]

Population economically active (1995): total 213,500; activity rate of total population 52.2% (participation rates: ages 15–64, 61.6%[6]; female 35.9%[6]; unemployed 3.0%).

Price and earnings indexes (1990 = 100)

	1991	1992	1993	1994	1995	1996
Consumer price index	103.1	106.4	110.2	112.6	114.8	116.4
Hourly earnings index	105.3	112.0	116.5	121.8	127.7	...

Household income and expenditure. Average household size (1991) 2.6; income per household (1992) Lux F 1,438,000 (U.S.$44,700); sources of income (1992): wages and salaries 67.1%, transfer payments 28.1%; self-employment 4.8%, expenditure (1994): food, beverages, and tobacco 19.7%, housing 17.3%, transportation and communications 16.2%, household goods and furniture 9.9%, clothing and footwear 8.2%, health 7.9%.
Land use (1992): forested 34.2%; meadows and pastures 25.6%; agricultural and under permanent cultivation 23.2%; other 17.0%.

Foreign trade

Balance of trade (current prices)

	1990	1991	1992	1993	1994	1995
Lux F '000,000	−43,100	−60,500	−56,300	−62,300	−61,500	−62,400
% of total	9.3%	12.4%	11.9%	13.3%	12.3%	12.0%

Imports (1995): Lux F 290,717,000,000 (machinery and transport equipment 46.9%; food 11.4%; mineral products 9.5%; chemicals 8.3%). *Major import sources:* Belgium 38.1%; Germany 29.8%; France 12.0%; The Netherlands 4.7%; U.S. 3.3%; Italy 2.1%.
Exports (1995): Lux F 228,263,000,000 (machinery and transport equipment 55.1%; plastics and rubber products 14.1%; textiles 6.6%; food 6.6%; chemicals 4.6%). *Major export destinations:* Germany 28.3%; France 19.7%; Belgium 13.3%; U.K. 6.3%; The Netherlands 5.3%; Italy 5.0%; U.S. 3.1%.

Transport and communications

Transport. Railroads (1995): route length 171 mi, 275 km; passenger-mi 176,000,000[7], passenger-km 284,000,000[7]; short ton-mi cargo 387,687,000, metric ton-km cargo 566,013,000. Roads (1996[2]): total length 3,206 mi, 5,160 km (paved 99%). Vehicles (1996[2]): passenger cars 231,666; trucks and buses 25,529. Merchant marine (1992): vessels (100 gross tons and over) 54; total deadweight tonnage 2,603,611. Air transport (1995): passenger arrivals 617,809, departures 624,088; airports (1997) with scheduled flights 1.

Communications

Medium	date	unit	number	units per 1,000 persons
Daily newspapers	1994	circulation	154,000	381
Radio	1995	receivers	240,000	586
Television	1991	receivers	134,845	384
Telephones	1994	main lines	221,898	550

Education and health

Educational attainment: n.a. *Literacy* (1995): virtually 100% literate.

Education (1994–95)

	schools	teachers	students	student/ teacher ratio
Primary (age 6–11)[8]	...	1,732	26,867	15.5
Secondary (age 12–18)	...	1,686	9,012	5.3
Voc., teacher tr.	...	2,904[9]	16,909	5.7[9]
Higher	1	200	1,100	5.5

Health (1996[2]): physicians 908 (1 per 454 persons); hospital beds (1995[2]) 4,443 (1 per 92 persons); infant mortality rate per 1,000 live births 4.9.
Food (1995): daily per capita caloric intake 3,530 (vegetable products 68%, animal products 32%); 134% of FAO recommended minimum.

Military

Total active duty personnel (1996): 800 (army 100.0%). *Military expenditure as percentage of GNP* (1994): 0.8% (world 3.0%); per capita expenditure U.S.$313.

[1]Has limited legislative authority. [2]January 1. [3]Detail does not add to total given because of rounding. [4]Manufacturing includes mining. [5]Imputed bank service charges. [6]1991. [7]1992. [8]Public schools only. [9]Vocational schools only.

Internet resources for further information:
- **STATEC: Luxembourg in Figures**
http://statec.gouvernement.lu/home1.htm

Macedonia

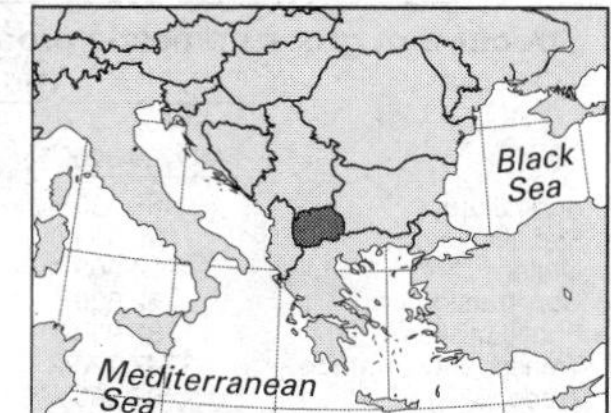

Official name[1]: Republika Makedonija (Republic of Macedonia).
Form of government: unitary multiparty republic with a unicameral legislature (Assembly [120]).
Head of state: President.
Head of government: Prime Minister.
Capital: Skopje.
Official language: Macedonian.
Official religion: none.
Monetary unit[2]: denar; valuation (Oct. 3, 1997) 1 U.S.$ = 54.69 denar; 1 £ = 88.15 denar.

Area and population (1994 census)

Municipalities	area sq km[3]	population	Municipalities	area sq km[3]	population
Berovo	806	19,737	Negotino	734	23,094
Bitola	1,798	106,012	Ohrid	1,069	60,841
Brod	924	10,912	Prilep	1,675	93,248
Debar	274	26,449	Probištip	326	16,373
Delčevo	589	25,052	Radoviš	735	30,378
Demir Hisar	443	10,321	Resen	739	17,467
Gevgelija	757	34,767	Skopje[4]	1,818	541,280
Gostivar	1,341	108,189	Štip	815	50,531
Kavadarci	1,132	41,801	Struga	507	62,305
Kičevo	854	53,044	Strumica	952	89,759
Kočani	570	48,105	Sveti Nikole	649	21,391
Kratovo	376	10,855	Tetovo	1,080	174,748
Kriva Palanka	720	25,112	Titov Veles	1,536	65,523
Kruševo	239	11,981	Valandovo	331	12,049
Kumanovo	1,212	126,543	Vinica	432	19,010
			TOTAL	25,713[5]	1,936,877

Demography

Population (1997): 1,984,000.
Density (1996): persons per sq mi 199.8, persons per sq km 77.2.
Urban-rural (1994): urban 58.7%; rural 41.3%.
Sex distribution (1994): male 50.39%; female 49.61%.
Age breakdown (1994): under 15, 24.8%; 15–29, 24.1%; 30–44, 22.3%; 45–59, 15.8%; 60–74, 10.6%; 75 and over, 2.4%.
Population projection: (2000) 2,033,000; (2010) 2,206,000.
Doubling time: 89 years.
Ethnic composition (1994): Macedonian 66.4%; Albanian 23.1%; Turkish 3.9%; Gypsy 2.3%; Serb 1.9%; other 2.4%.
Religious affiliation (1997): Serbian (Macedonian) Orthodox 53.8%; Sunnī Muslim 30.2%; other 16.0%.
Major cities (1994): Skopje 440,577; Bitola 75,386; Prilep 67,371; Kumanovo 66,237; Tetovo 50,376.

Vital statistics

Birth rate per 1,000 population (1995): 14.9 (world avg. 25.0); legitimate 91.5%; illegitimate 8.5%.
Death rate per 1,000 population (1995): 7.6 (world avg. 9.3).
Natural increase rate per 1,000 population (1995): 7.3 (world avg. 15.7).
Total fertility rate (avg. births per childbearing woman; 1995): 2.0.
Marriage rate per 1,000 population (1994): 7.6.
Divorce rate per 1,000 population (1994): 0.3.
Life expectancy at birth (1995): male 68.8 years; female 75.0 years.
Major causes of death per 100,000 population (1993): diseases of the circulatory system 385.8; accidents, violence, and poisoning 35.3; diseases of the respiratory system 34.5; diseases of the digestive system 14.8; infectious and parasitic diseases 12.9%; malignant neoplasms (cancers) 6.2.

National economy

Budget (1995). Revenue: 64,254,000,000 denar[2] (social security contributions 32.6%, excise taxes 19.1%, income and profits tax 17.3%, sales tax 12.3%). Expenditure: 66,032,000,000 denar[2] (pensions 24.1%, wages and salaries 22.7%, health 13.3%).
Tourism (1994): receipts from visitors U.S.$21,000,000; expenditures by nationals abroad U.S.$23,000,000.
Production (metric tons except as noted). Agriculture, forestry, fishing (1996): wheat 269,000, grapes 215,000, potatoes 157,000, corn (maize) 143,000; livestock (number of live animals) 2,320,000 sheep, 283,000 cattle, 175,000 pigs, 5,000,000 poultry; roundwood (1996) 774,000 cu m; fish catch (1995) 1,570 (all freshwater). Mining and quarrying (1995): copper ore 2,000,000; lead-zinc ore 430,000; refined silver 10,000 kilograms. Manufacturing (1995): cement 523,499; steel sheets 40,878; wool yarn 3,863; refrigerators 56,148 units; leather footwear 1,120,000 pairs; cotton fabric 15,525,000 sq m; cigarettes 10,615,000 units. Construction (residential, 1994): 348,004 sq m. Energy production (consumption): electricity (kW-hr; 1994) 5,924,000,000 (5,359,000,000); coal (metric tons; 1994) 6,900,000 (6,959,000); crude petroleum (barrels; 1993) none (8,063,000); petroleum products (metric tons; 1992) 556,000 (823,000); natural gas (cu m; 1993) none (269,100,000).
Population economically active (1995): total 596,600; activity rate 30.8% (participation rates: ages 15–64 [1991] 98.1%; [1994] female 25.5%; [1994] unemployed 32.0%).

Price and earnings indexes (1992 = 100)

	1992	1993	1994	1995	1996
Consumer price index	100.0	461.9	1,054	1,153	1,155
Earnings index[6]	100.0	595.7	1,221	1,352	1,388

External debt (1994): U.S.$924,000,000.
Gross national product (1995): U.S.$1,813,000,000 (U.S.$860 per capita).

Structure of gross domestic product and labour force

	1993		1995	
	in value '000,000 denar[2]	% of total value	labour force	% of labour force
Agriculture	5,795	10.0	53,700	9.0
Mining and manufacturing	15,019	25.8	136,600	22.9
Construction	2,977	5.1	31,400	5.3
Public utilities	1,195	2.1	8,100	1.4
Transp. and commun.	3,433	5.9	21,000	3.5
Trade	3,959	6.8	34,100	5.7
Finance	3,201	5.5	10,900	1.8
Public admin., defense	11,330	19.5	15,300	2.6
Services	1,871	3.2	69,300	11.6
Other	9,363[7]	16.1[7]	216,200[8]	36.2
TOTAL	58,143	100.0	596,600	100.0

Land use (1994): forested 38.9%; meadows and pastures 24.7%; agricultural and under permanent cultivation 25.7%; other 10.7%.
Household income and expenditure (1994). Average household size 3.8; income per household Din 49,635[2] (U.S.$1,223); sources of income: wages and salaries 59.9%, transfer payments 17.0%, transfers from abroad 13.4%, other 9.7%; expenditure: food 42.2%, fuel and lighting 7.5%, clothing and footwear 7.4%, transportation and communications 7.2%, drink and tobacco 7.0%, health care 4.7%, education and entertainment 3.2%.

Foreign trade

Balance of trade (current prices)

	1991	1992	1993	1994	1995
U.S.$'000,000	−225	−7	−172	−398	−232
% of total	8.9%	0.3%	7.5%	15.5%	8.7%

Imports (1995): U.S.$1,439,000,000 (machinery and transport equipment 19.0%, food products 17.0%, manufactured products 16.0%, chemical products 12.0%, petroleum products 12.0%). *Major import sources:* Germany 15.0%; Russia 8.0%; Bulgaria 7.0%; Italy 7.0%; U.K. 5.0%; Albania 4.0%.
Exports (1995): U.S.$1,204,000,000 (manufactured products 35.0%, machinery and transport equipment 13.0%, food products 11.0%, raw materials 8.0%, chemical products 6.0%). *Major export destinations:* Germany 13.0%; U.K. 7.0%; Italy 5.0%; Russia 4.0%.

Transport and communications

Transport. Railroads (1994): length 573 mi, 922 km; passenger-mi 41,632,000, passenger-km 67,000,000; short ton-mi cargo 103,426,000, metric ton-km cargo 151,000,000. Roads (1994): length 5,233 mi, 8,422 km (paved 62%). Vehicles (1994): passenger cars 263,181; trucks and buses 22,825. Merchant marine: n.a. Air transport (1993)[9]: passenger-mi 181,671,190, passenger-km 292,372,000; metric tons cargo transported 625; airports (1997) with scheduled flights 2.

Communications

Medium	date	unit	number	units per 1,000 persons
Daily newspapers	1995	circulation	44,000	21
Radio	1995	receivers	350,000	179
Television	1995	receivers	350,000	179
Telephones	1995	main lines	349,000	179

Education and health

Educational attainment (1981). Percentage of population age 15 and over having: less than full primary education 45.3%; primary 28.1%; secondary 21.2%; postsecondary and higher 5.1%; unknown 0.3%. *Literacy* (1981): total population age 10 and over literate 1,365,000 (89.1%); males literate 729,000 (94.2%); females literate 636,000 (83.8%).

Education (1994–95)

	schools	teachers	students	student/ teacher ratio
Primary (age 7–14)	1,050	13,102	258,955	19.9
Secondary (age 15–18)	95	4,520	77,754	16.5
Higher	27	1,122	26,959	24.0

Health (1994): physicians 4,505 (1 per 437 persons); hospital beds 10,664 (1 per 195 persons); (1995) infant mortality rate per 1,000 live births 27.3.

Military

Total active duty personnel (1997): 15,400 (army 100%). *Military expenditure as percentage of GNP* (1995): 3.3% (world 2.8%); per capita expenditure U.S.$30.

[1]Member of the United Nations under the name Former Yugoslav Republic of Macedonia. [2]Macedonia, as part of Yugoslavia, utilized the Yugoslav (old) dinar (Din) until Jan. 1, 1990, when it was replaced by the Yugoslav (new) dinar (Din) at a rate of 10,000 old for 1 new. Macedonia left the Yugoslav currency area in September 1991, utilizing a local coupon alone until May 1992, when a transitional local currency, the denar, was introduced. The denar (valued initially at denar 255 = 1 U.S.$) was established at par with the Yugoslav (new) dinar but circulated in parallel with the coupon until May 1993, when a differently defined denar was introduced, replacing both the transitional denar and the coupon. [3]One sq km is equal to approximately 0.3861 sq mi. [4]Skopje, a single administrative district, consists of 5 municipalities: Gazi Baba, Karpos, Kisela Voda, Centar, Cair. [5]Total includes 280 sq km of inland water not distributed by district. [6]Based on nominal net wages per worker. [7]Includes import duties, customs, imputed rents, and statistical discrepancy. [8]Registered unemployed. [9]Palair Macedonian airline only.

Madagascar

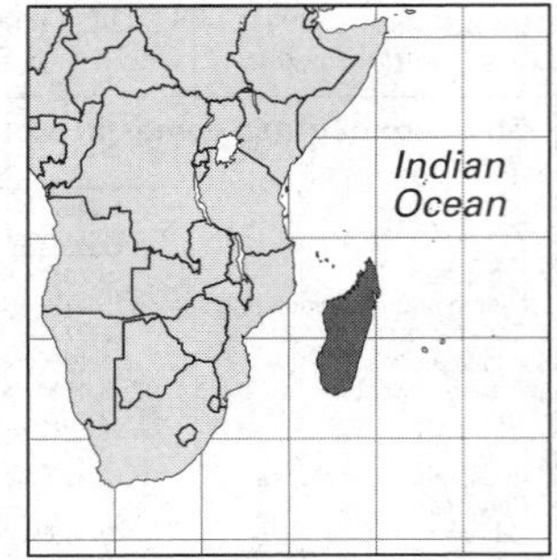

Official name: Repoblikan'i Madagasikara (Malagasy); République de Madagascar (French) (Republic of Madagascar).
Form of government: unitary multiparty republic with one legislative house (National Assembly [138]).
Chief of state: President.
Head of government: Prime Minister.
Capital: Antananarivo.
Official languages:[1].
Official religion: none.
Monetary unit: 1 Malagasy franc (FMG) = 100 centimes; valuation (Oct. 3, 1997) 1 U.S.$ = FMG 4,925; 1 £ = FMG 7,939.

Area and population

		area		population
Provinces	Capitals	sq mi	sq km	1993 census[2]
Antananarivo	Antananarivo	22,503	58,283	3,483,236
Antsirañana	Antsirañana	16,620	43,046	942,410
Fianarantsoa	Fianarantsoa	39,526	102,373	2,671,150
Mahajanga	Mahajanga	57,924	150,023	1,330,612
Toamasina	Toamasina	27,765	71,911	1,935,330
Toliary	Toliary	62,319	161,405	1,729,419
TOTAL		226,658	587,041	12,092,157

Demography

Population (1997): 14,062,000.
Density (1997): persons per sq mi 62.0, persons per sq km 24.0.
Urban-rural (1991): urban 24.4%; rural 75.6%.
Sex distribution (1993): male 49.55%; female 50.45%.
Age breakdown (1995): under 15, 46.1%; 15–29, 26.2%; 30–44, 15.2%; 45–59, 8.0%; 60–74, 3.8%; 75 and over, 0.7%.
Population projection: (2000) 15,295,000; (2010) 20,096,000.
Doubling time: 25 years.
Ethnic composition (1983): Malagasy 98.9%, of which Merina 26.6%, Betsimisaraka 14.9%, Betsileo 11.7%, Tsimihety 7.4%, Sakalava 6.4%, Antandroy 5.3%; Comorian 0.3%; Indian and Pakistani 0.2%; French 0.2%; Chinese 0.1%; other 0.3%.
Religious affiliation (1997): traditional beliefs 52.0%; Christian 41.0%, of which Roman Catholic 21.3%, Protestant 19.7%; Muslim 7.0%.
Major cities (1993): Antananarivo 1,052,835; Toamasina 127,441; Antsirabe 120,239; Mahajanga 100,807; Fianarantsoa 99,005.

Vital statistics

Birth rate per 1,000 population (1996): 42.6 (world avg. 25.0).
Death rate per 1,000 population (1996): 14.4 (world avg. 9.3).
Natural increase rate per 1,000 population (1996): 28.2 (world avg. 15.7).
Total fertility rate (avg. births per childbearing woman; 1996): 5.9.
Marriage rate per 1,000 population: n.a.
Divorce rate per 1,000 population: n.a.
Life expectancy at birth (1996): male 51.1 years; female 53.3 years.
Major causes of death per 100,000 population: n.a.; however, major causes of death in the early 1990s included maternal and perinatal diseases, malaria, infectious and parasitic diseases, malnutrition, diarrhea, and respiratory diseases.

National economy

Budget (1995). Revenue: FMG 1,138,300,000,000 (taxes 97.6%, of which duties on trade 55.7%, value-added tax 20.4%, income tax 14.4%; nontax receipts 2.4%). Expenditures: FMG 1,888,700,000,000 (current expenditure 79.7%, of which debt service 31.6%, education 10.0%, general administration 7.7%, defense 6.1%, health 3.9%, agriculture 0.7%; capital expenditure 20.3%).
Production (metric tons except as noted). Agriculture, forestry, fishing (1996): paddy rice 2,600,000, cassava 2,450,000, sugarcane 2,200,000, sweet potatoes 500,000, potatoes 280,000, bananas 230,000, mangoes 202,000, corn (maize) 180,000, taro 140,000, oranges 83,000, coconuts 83,000, coffee 72,000, dry beans 70,000, pineapples 50,000, peanuts (groundnuts) 37,000, seed cotton 30,000, livestock (number of live animals) 10,320,000 cattle, 1,629,000 pigs, 1,329,000 goats, 756,000 sheep, 16,000,000 chickens; roundwood (1994) 9,151,000 cu m; fish catch (1995) 120,140. Mining and quarrying (1995): salt 80,000; chromite ore 74,000; graphite 13,900; mica 387; gold 200 kg[3]; in addition, a wide variety of semiprecious stones and gemstones are produced. Manufacturing (1995): cotton cloth 25,000,000, refined sugar 89,474, cement 45,009, soap 15,000, tobacco products 1,936, beer 318,842 hectolitres, fuel oil 177,329 cu m, gas oil 129,227 cu m, kerosene 110,764 cu m, gasoline 87,905 cu m, shoes 972,000 pairs. Construction (1986)[4]: residential 19,700 sq m; nonresidential 5,700 sq m. Energy production (consumption): electricity (kW-hr; 1994) 605,000,000 (605,000,000); coal (metric tons; 1994) none (14,000); crude petroleum (barrels; 1994) none (1,450,000); petroleum products (metric tons; 1994) 185,000 (348,000); natural gas, none (n.a.).
Household income and expenditure. Average household size (1993) 4.6[4]; average annual income per household: n.a.; sources of income (1975)[5]: wages and salaries 58.8%, self-employment 14.1%, other 27.1%; expenditure (1983)[4, 6]: food 60.4%, fuel and light 9.1%, clothing and footwear 8.6%, household goods and utensils 2.4%.
Gross national product (1995): U.S.$3,178,000,000 (U.S.$230 per capita).

Structure of gross domestic product and labour force

	1991		1993	
	in value FMG '000,000[7]	% of total value	labour force	% of labour force
Agriculture	1,488,350	32.6	5,100,000	86.2
Manufacturing	530,560	11.6	86,000	1.5
Mining	14,800	0.3		
Construction	52,600	1.2	46,000	0.8
Public utilities	86,950	1.9		
Transp. and commun.	747,920	16.4	42,000	0.7
Trade	497,990	10.9	149,000	2.5
Finance	70,020	1.5		
Services[8]	791,890	17.4	243,000	4.1
Pub. admin., defense	284,430	6.2	208,000	3.5
Other	...	...	40,000	0.7
TOTAL	4,565,510	100.0	5,914,000	100.0

Population economically active (1993): total 5,914,000; activity rate of total population 48.9% (participation rates [1985]: ages 15–64, 74.9%; female 39.3%; unemployed [1982] 0.6%).

Price and earnings indexes (1990 = 100)

	1990	1991	1992	1993	1994	1995	1996
Consumer price index	100.0	108.5	124.4	136.8	190.1	283.3	339.3
Annual earnings index[9]	100.0	127.1	134.5	146.1	189.0	264.6	...

Public debt (external, outstanding; 1995): U.S.$3,691,000,000.
Land use (1994): forest 39.9%; pasture 41.3%; agriculture 5.3%; other 13.5%.
Tourism (1995): visitors U.S.$60,000,000; U.S.$59,000,000.

Foreign trade

Balance of trade

	1990	1991	1992	1993	1994	1995
FMG '000,000,000	−327.9	−93.0	−175.1	−244.3	−77.7	−2,082.3
% of total	25.6%	7.7%	14.5%	19.6%	3.2%	37.7%

Imports (1994): FMG 1,150,780,000,000 (capital equipment 20.2%; food 16.8%, of which rice 6.9%; raw materials and spare parts 15.8%; nonfood consumer goods 15.3%; crude petroleum 11.4%). *Major import sources* (1995): France 30.5%; Germany 10.3%; Iran 10.3%; South Africa 6.5%; Japan 6.1%.
Exports (1994): FMG 849,960,000,000 (coffee 18.0%; vanilla 16.7%; shrimp 13.2%; cotton fabrics 2.9%; cloves and clove oil 2.6%; sugar 2.2%). *Major export destinations* (1995): France 29.2%; U.S. 6.7%; Japan 6.4%; Réunion 6.1%; Italy 5.6%; Belgium-Luxembourg 5.0%.

Transport and communications

Transport. Railroads (1991): route length 640 mi, 1,030 km; passenger-mi 152,000,000, passenger-km 245,000,000; short ton-mi cargo 90,000,000, metric ton-km cargo 132,000,000. Roads (1995): total length 30,968 mi, 49,837 km (paved 15%). Vehicles (1992): passenger cars 47,711; trucks and buses 34,341. Merchant marine (1992): vessels (100 gross tons and over) 85; total deadweight tonnage 82,077. Air transport (1996): passenger-mi 409,440,000, passenger-km 658,913,000; short ton-mi cargo 12,122,000, metric ton-km cargo 17,697,000; airports (1994) with scheduled flights 44.

Communications

Medium	date	unit	number	units per 1,000 persons
Daily newspapers	1995	circulation	59,000	4.0
Radio	1995	receivers	2,850,000	193
Television	1995	receivers	295,000	20.0
Telephones	1995	main lines	32,600	2.2

Education and health

Educational attainment: n.a. *Literacy* (1995): percentage of total population age 15 and over literate 45.7%; males literate 59.8%; females literate 32.0%.

Education (1993–94)

	schools	teachers	students	student/ teacher ratio
Primary (age 6–13)	13,624	37,676	1,504,668	39.9
Secondary (14–18)	1,142[10]	15,118	298,241	19.7
Voc., teacher tr.	61[11]	1,484[12]	17,419[12]	11.7[12]
Higher	5[10]	855[13]	42,681[13]	49.9[13]

Health: physicians (1990) 1,392 (1 per 8,279 persons); hospital beds (1989) 10,900 (1 per 1,029 persons); infant mortality rate (1996) 93.3.
Food (1995): daily per capita caloric intake 2,009 (vegetable products 91%, animal products 9%); 89% of FAO recommended minimum requirement.

Military

Total active duty personnel (1997): 21,000 (army 95.2%, navy 2.4%, air force 2.4%). *Military expenditure as percentage of GNP* (1995): 0.9% (world 2.8%); per capita expenditure U.S.$2.

[1]The 1992 constitution identifies Malagasy as the "national" language, although neither Malagasy nor French, the languages of the two official texts of the constitution, is itself "official." [2]Preliminary. [3]1994. [4]Antananarivo only. [5]Malagasy households only. [6]Weights of consumer price index components; excludes housing. [7]At factor cost. [8]Includes artisans and servants. [9]Average salary, all public employees, including military. [10]1988–89. [11]1987–88. [12]1990–91. [13]1992.

Internet resources for further information:

- **Mission of Madagascar to the United Nations (Geneva; French, summary only in English) http://www3.itu.ch/MISSIONS/Madagascar**

Malaŵi

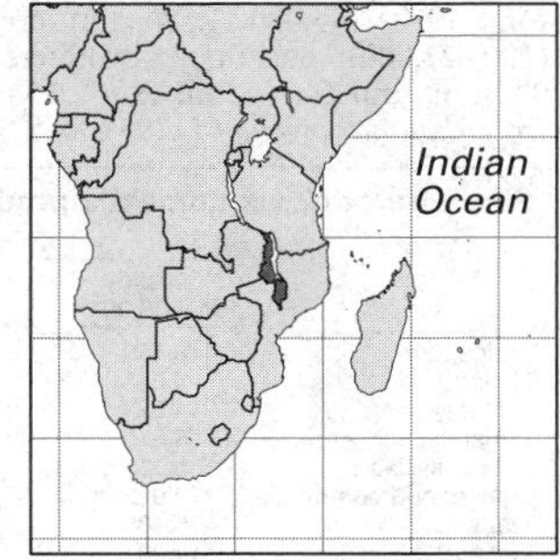

Official name: Republic of Malaŵi.
Form of government: multiparty republic with one legislative house (National Assembly [177]).
Head of state and government: President.
Capital:[1].
Official language: English.
Official religion: none.
Monetary unit: 1 Malaŵi kwacha (MK) = 100 tambala; valuation (Oct. 3, 1997) 1 U.S.$ = MK 17.37; 1 £ = MK 27.99.

Area and population		area		population
Regions				1987
Districts	**Capitals**	sq mi	sq km	census
Central	Lilongwe	13,742	35,592	3,110,986
Dedza	Dedza	1,399	3,624	411,787
Dowa	Dowa	1,174	3,041	322,432
Kasungu	Kasungu	3,042	7,878	323,453
Lilongwe	Lilongwe	2,378	6,159	976,627
Mchinji	Mchinji	1,296	3,356	249,843
Nkhotakota	Nkhotakota	1,644	4,259	158,044
Ntcheu	Ntcheu	1,322	3,424	358,767
Ntchisi	Ntchisi	639	1,655	120,860
Salima	Salima	848	2,196	189,173
Northern	Mzuzu	10,398	26,931	911,787
Chitipa	Chitipa	1,353	3,504	96,794
Karonga	Karonga	1,141	2,955	148,014
Mzimba	Mzimba	4,027	10,430	433,696
Nkhata Bay	Nkhata Bay	1,579	4,090	138,381
Rumphi	Rumphi	2,298	5,952	94,902
Southern	Blantyre	12,260	31,753	3,965,734
Blantyre	Blantyre	777	2,012	589,525
Chikwawa	Chikwawa	1,836	4,755	316,733
Chiradzulu	Chiradzulu	296	767	210,912
Machinga	Machinga	2,303	5,964	515,265
Mangochi	Mangochi	2,422	6,272	496,578
Mulanje	Mulanje	1,332	3,450	638,062
Mwanza	Mwanza	886	2,295	121,513
Nsanje	Nsanje	750	1,942	204,374
Thyolo	Thyolo	662	1,715	431,157
Zomba	Zomba	996	2,580	441,615
TOTAL LAND AREA		36,400	94,276[2]	
INLAND WATER		9,347	24,208	
TOTAL		45,747	118,484	7,988,507

Demography

Population (1997): 9,609,000.
Density (1997)[3]: persons per sq mi 264.0, persons per sq km 101.9.
Urban-rural (1987): urban 10.7%; rural 89.3%.
Sex distribution (1987): male 48.40%; female 51.60%.
Age breakdown (1987): under 15, 46.0%; 15–29, 25.4%; 30–44, 14.5%; 45–59, 8.1%; 60 and over, 6.0%.
Population projection: (2000) 10,011,000; (2010) 10,662,000.
Doubling time: 41 years.
Ethnic composition (1983): Maravi (including Nyanja, Chewa, Tonga, and Tumbuka) 58.3%; Lomwe 18.4%; Yao 13.2%; Ngoni 6.7%; other 3.4%.
Religious affiliation (1995): Christian 50.3%, of which Protestant 20.5%, Roman Catholic 18.0%; Muslim 20.0%; traditional beliefs 10.0%; other 19.7%.
Major cities (1994): Blantyre 446,800; Lilongwe 395,500[4]; Mzuzu 62,700.

Vital statistics

Birth rate per 1,000 population (1996): 41.6 (world avg. 25.0).
Death rate per 1,000 population (1996): 24.5 (world avg. 9.3).
Natural increase rate per 1,000 population (1996): 17.1 (world avg. 15.7).
Total fertility rate (avg. births per childbearing woman; 1996): 5.9.
Life expectancy at birth (1996): male 35.9 years; female 36.5 years.
Major causes of death per 100,000 population (1986)[5]: infectious and parasitic diseases 711, of which malaria 270, diarrheal diseases 148, measles 128; malnutrition 267; diseases of the respiratory system 265.

National economy

Budget (1995–96). Revenue: MK 4,436,000,000 (tax revenue 86.9%, nontax revenue 10.9%, other 2.2%). Expenditures: MK 7,738,000,000 (wages and salaries 21.5%, debt service 20.9%).
Public debt (external, outstanding; 1995): U.S.$1,978,000,000.
Production (metric tons except as noted). Agriculture (1996): sugarcane 1,860,000, corn (maize) 1,793,000, potatoes 380,000, cassava 220,000, plantains 200,000, tobacco 142,000, bananas 91,000, dry beans 80,000, sorghum 55,000, peanuts (groundnuts) 40,000, tea 37,000; livestock (number of live animals) 1,257,000 goats, 700,000 cattle, 220,000 pigs, 101,000 sheep; roundwood (1995) 10,475,000 cu m; fish catch (1995) 45,427. Mining and quarrying (1995): limestone 173,800[6]; rubies, sapphires, and aquamarines 550 kg. Manufacturing (value added in MK '000; 1986): chemicals 30,805; textiles 19,630; food products 11,988; beverages 11,988; tobacco 9,480. Construction (value in MK; 1994): 41,700,000[7]. Energy production (consumption): electricity (kW-hr; 1994) 802,000,000 (802,000,000); coal (metric tons; 1994) none (15,000); petroleum products (metric tons; 1994) none (190,000).
Tourism: receipts (1995) U.S.$6,000,000; expenditures (1994) U.S.$15,000,000.
Land use (1994): forested 39.3%; meadows and pastures 19.6%; agricultural and under permanent cultivation 18.1%; other 23.0%.
Gross national product (1995): U.S.$1,623,000,000 (U.S.$170 per capita).

Structure of gross domestic product and labour force	1996		1987	
	in value MK '000,000[8]	% of total value	labour force	% of labour force
Agriculture	493.3	43.4	2,967,933	85.8
Mining	...	...	7,164	0.2
Manufacturing	131.3	11.5	97,776	2.8
Construction	46.1	4.1	46,875	1.4
Public utilities	29.8	2.6	8,833	0.2
Transp. and commun.	57.2	5.0	24,863	0.7
Trade	128.8	11.3	94,445	2.7
Finance	119.5	10.5	5,590	0.3
Public administration	146.5	12.9	147,039	4.3
Services	48.4	4.3		
Other	−64.0[9]	−5.6[9]	57,235	1.6
TOTAL	1,136.8[2]	100.0	3,457,753	100.0

Population economically active (1987): total 3,457,753; activity rate 43.3% (participation rates: ages 15–64, 84.6%; female 51.5%; unemployed 5.4%).

Price and earnings indexes (1990 = 100)	1990	1991	1992	1993	1994	1995	1996
Consumer price index	100.0	112.6	138.2	163.7	222.6	408.2	561.6
Monthly earnings index	100.0	106.4	102.8	...	...	...	...

Household income and expenditure (1979–80). Average household size (1987) 4.3; income per household MK 1,934 (U.S.$2,419); sources of income: wages 83.3%, household enterprise 6.0%; expenditure (1990)[10]: food 55.5%, clothing and footwear 11.7%, housing 9.6%, household durable goods 8.4%.

Foreign trade[11]

Balance of trade (current prices)	1989	1990	1991	1992	1993	1994
MK '000,000	−96.1	+180.1	+140.9	−103.4	−29.0	+247.3
% of total	6.1%	8.7%	5.6%	3.4%	1.0%	4.6%

Imports (1995): MK 7,254,949,000 (1990; transport equipment 9.2%, petroleum products 8.3%, clothing 3.8%, pharmaceutical products 2.2%). *Major import sources:* South Africa 44.4%; Germany 4.5%; U.K. 4.3%; United States 3.7%.
Exports (1995): MK 6,192,563,000 (tobacco 63.2%, tea 6.7%, sugar 6.5%, cotton 0.9%). *Major export destinations:* South Africa 16.2%; Germany 14.7%; Japan 11.1%; U.S. 10.9%; Mozambique 7.6%.

Transport and communications

Transport. Railroads (1994): route length 490 mi, 789 km; passenger-km 18,995,000; metric ton-km cargo 56,778,000. Roads (1995): total length 17,324 mi, 27,880 km (paved 18%). Vehicles (1995): passenger cars 25,400; trucks and buses 28,900. Air transport (1994)[12]: passenger-km 289,000,000; metric ton-km cargo 28,000,000; airports (1997) 5.

Communications				units
Medium	date	unit	number	per 1,000 persons
Daily newspapers	1996	circulation	22,000[13]	2.3[13]
Radio	1996	receivers	1,060,000	112
Telephones	1995	main lines	34,300	3.5
Cellular telephones	1995	subscribers	400	—
Facsimile machines	1995	units	1,100	0.1

Education and health

Educational attainment (1987). Percentage of population age 25 and over having: no formal education 55.0%; primary education 39.8%; secondary and higher 5.2%. *Literacy* (1995): total population age 15 and over literate 56.4%; males literate 71.9%; females literate 41.8%.

Education (1989–90)	schools	teachers	students	student/ teacher ratio
Primary (age 6–13)[14]	3,425	45,775	2,860,819	62.5
Secondary (age 14–18)	94	1,096	48,332[14]	26.8
Teacher tr., voc.	13	250	1,080[14]	14.7
Higher	4	235	7,308[15]	11.4

Health: physicians (1989) 186 (1 per 47,634 persons); hospital beds (1987) 12,617 (1 per 627 persons); infant mortality rate per 1,000 live births (1996) 139.9.
Food (1995): daily per capita caloric intake 2,038 (vegetable products 97%, animal products 3%); 88% of FAO recommended minimum requirement.

Military

Total active duty personnel (1997): 5,000 (army 100%, marines none, air force, none). *Military expenditure as percentage of GNP* (1995): 1.6% (world 2.8%); per capita expenditure U.S.$2.

[1]A capital is not designated in the 1994 constitution. Current government operations are divided among Lilongwe (ministerial and financial); Blantyre (executive and judicial); and Zomba (legislative). [2]Detail does not add to total given because of rounding. [3]Based on land area. [4]Includes Limbe. [5]Estimates based on reported inpatient deaths in hospitals, constituting an estimated 8% of total deaths. [6]1994. [7]Cities of Blantyre, Lilongwe, and Mzuzu only. [8]At constant prices of 1978. [9]Less imputed bank service charges. [10]Weights of consumer price index components, cities of Blantyre and Lilongwe only. [11]Import figures are f.o.b. in balance of trade and c.i.f. in commodities and trading partners. Reexports included in balance of trade, excluded from commodities and trading partners. [12]Air Malaŵi only. [13]Circulation for one newspaper only. [14]1994–95. [15]1993–94.

Malaysia

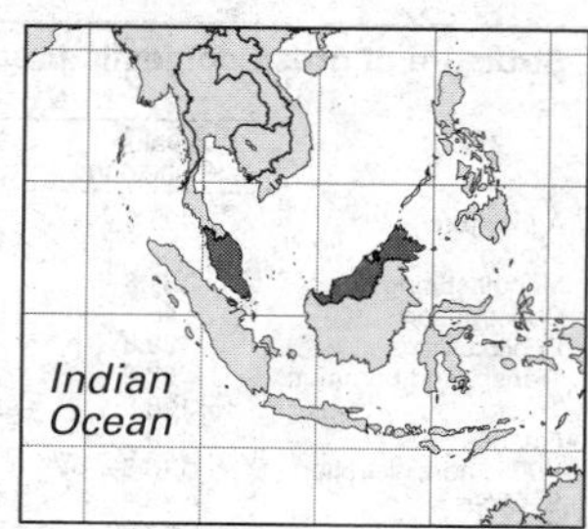

Official name: Malaysia.
Form of government: federal constitutional monarchy with two legislative houses (Senate [70[1]]; House of Representatives [192]).
Chief of state: Yang di-Pertuan Agong (Paramount Ruler).
Head of government: Prime Minister.
Capital: Kuala Lumpur.
Official language: Malay.
Official religion: Islam.
Monetary unit: 1 ringgit, or Malaysian dollar (RM) = 100 cents; valuation (Oct. 3, 1997) 1 U.S.$ = RM 3.36; 1 £ = RM 5.42.

Area and population

Regions / States	Capitals	area sq mi	area sq km	population 1991 census
East Malaysia				
Sabah	Kota Kinabalu	28,424	73,619	1,734,685
Sarawak	Kuching	48,050	124,449	1,642,771
West Malaysia				
Johor	Johor Baharu	7,331	18,986	2,069,740
Kedah	Alor Setar	3,639	9,426	1,302,241
Kelantan	Kota Baharu	5,761	14,920	1,181,315
Melaka	Melaka	637	1,651	506,321
Negeri Sembilan	Seremban	2,565	6,643	692,897
Pahang	Kuantan	13,886	35,964	1,045,003
Perak	Ipoh	8,110	21,005	1,877,471
Perlis	Kangar	307	795	183,824
Pulau Pinang	George Town	398	1,030	1,064,166
Selangor	Shah Alam	3,071	7,955	2,297,159
Terengganu	Kuala Terengganu	5,002	12,955	766,244
Federal Territories				
Kuala Lumpur	—	94	243	1,145,342
Labuan	—	36	92	54,241
TOTAL LAND AREA		127,311	329,733	
INLAND WATER		264	684	
TOTAL		127,575	330,417	17,563,420

Demography

Population (1997): 21,767,000.
Density (1997): persons per sq mi 171.0, persons per sq km 66.0.
Urban-rural (1997): urban 55.0%; rural 45.0%.
Sex distribution (1996): male 51.13%; female 48.87%.
Age breakdown (1996): under 15, 34.9%; 15–29, 28.0%; 30–44, 20.7%; 45–59, 10.6%; 60 and over, 5.8%.
Population projection: (2000) 22,270,000; (2010) 26,205,000.
Doubling time: 34 years.
Ethnic composition (1996): Malay and other indigenous 57.7%; Chinese 25.4%; Indian 7.2%; other nonindigenous 3.2%; noncitizen 6.5%.
Religious affiliation (1980): Muslim 52.9%; Buddhist 17.3%; Chinese folk-religionist 11.6%; Hindu 7.0%; Christian 6.4%; other 4.8%.
Major cities (1991): Kuala Lumpur 1,145,342; Ipoh 382,853; Johor Baharu 328,436; Melaka 296,897; Petaling Jaya 254,350.

Vital statistics

Birth rate per 1,000 population (1997): 25.6 (world avg. 25.0).
Death rate per 1,000 population (1997): 4.8 (world avg. 9.3).
Natural increase rate per 1,000 population (1997): 20.8 (world avg. 15.7).
Total fertility rate (avg. births per childbearing woman; 1997): 3.3.
Life expectancy at birth (1997): male 70.0 years; female 74.0 years.
Major causes of death per 100,000 population (1994): diseases of the circulatory system 54.0; accidents, homicide, and other violence 29.0; malignant neoplasms 20.4; birth injuries 18.5; infectious and parasitic diseases 15.4.

National economy

Budget (1997). Revenue: RM 60,778,000,000 (income tax 38.7%, taxes on goods and services 22.0%, nontax revenue 18.0%, taxes on international trade 12.6%). Expenditures: RM 41,413,000,000 (education 24.6%, defense and internal security 15.3%, general administration 12.3%, health 7.0%, trade and industry 3.0%, agriculture 3.0%).
Tourism (1995): receipts from visitors U.S.$3,910,000,000; expenditures by nationals abroad (1994) U.S.$1,737,000,000.
Population economically active (1996): total 8,398,200; activity rate 40.9% (participation rates: ages 15–64 66.9%; female [1990] 35.5%; unemployed 2.6%).

Price index (1990 = 100)

	1990	1991	1992	1993	1994	1995	1996
Consumer price index	100.0	104.4	109.3	113.2	117.4	123.6	128.0

Production (metric tons except as noted). Agriculture, forestry, fishing (1996): palm oil 8,386,000, rice 2,065,000, sugarcane 1,600,000, rubber 1,089,000, bananas 530,000, pineapples 200,000; livestock (number of live animals) 3,282,000 pigs, 720,000 cattle, 100,000,000 chickens; roundwood (1995) 45,573,000 cu m; fish catch (1995) 1,240,000. Mining and quarrying (1996): iron ore 325,114; bauxite 218,680; copper concentrates 87,580; tin concentrates 5,174. Manufacturing (1995): cement 10,713,000; refined sugar 1,052,000; fertilizer 269,000; plywood 3,506,000 cu m; radio receivers 38,767,000 units; automotive tires 11,368,000 units. Construction (completed; 1986)[2]: residential 8,809,100 sq m; nonresidential 959,900 sq m. Energy production (consumption): electricity (kW-hr; 1994) 39,975,000,000 (40,027,000,000); coal (metric tons; 1994) 174,000 (1,876,000); crude petroleum (barrels; 1994) 237,742,000 (100,021,000); petroleum products (metric tons; 1994) 11,406,000 (17,007,000); natural gas (cu m; 1994) 24,411,000,000 (13,166,000,000).
Gross national product (1995): U.S.$78,321,000,000 (U.S.$3,890 per capita).

Structure of gross domestic product and labour force

	1996 in value RM '000,000[3]	% of total value	labour force	% of labour force
Agriculture	16,489	12.7	1,375,900	16.4
Mining	9,257	7.1	41,800	0.5
Manufacturing	44,922	34.5	2,209,000	26.3
Construction	5,870	4.5	705,100	8.4
Public utilities	3,135	2.4	72,700	0.9
Transp. and commun.	10,022	7.7	420,400	5.0
Trade	16,185	12.4	1,353,700	16.1
Finance	14,231	10.9	394,500	4.7
Pub. admin., defense	11,907	9.2	876,600	10.4
Services	2,589	2.0	731,100	8.7
Other	−4,420[4]	−3.4[4]	217,400	2.6
TOTAL	130,187	100.0	8,398,200	100.0

Public debt (external, outstanding; 1995): U.S.$15,857,000,000.
Household income and expenditure. Average household size (1991) 4.9; annual income per household (1995) RM 24,080 (U.S.$9,620); sources of income: n.a.; expenditure (1983): food 28.7%, transportation 20.9%, recreation and education 11.0%, housing 10.2%, household durable goods 7.7%.

Foreign trade[5]

Balance of trade (current prices)

	1990	1991	1992	1993	1994	1995
RM '000,000	+7,947	+3,165	+11,446	+15,095	+12,628	+8,794
% of total	5.3%	1.7%	5.9%	6.6%	4.3%	2.4%

Imports (1995): RM 194,517,000,000 (machinery and transport equipment 60.6%, chemicals 6.9%, food 4.1%, inedible crude materials 2.4%, mineral fuels 2.3%). *Major import sources:* Japan 28.1%; U.S. 16.6%; Singapore 12.4%; Taiwan 5.1%; Germany 4.6%; South Korea 4.0%; Thailand 2.7%.
Exports (1995): RM 184,827,000,000 (machinery and transport equipment 55.1%, basic manufactures 8.9%, mineral fuels 7.0%, animal and vegetable oils 6.8%, inedible crude materials 6.4%, food 2.4%). *Major export destinations:* U.S. 20.7%; Singapore 20.3%; Japan 12.7%; Hong Kong 5.3%; U.K. 4.0%; Thailand 3.9%; Germany 3.2%.

Transport and communications

Transport. Railroads (1995): track length 1,791 km; passenger-km 1,284,000,000[6]; metric ton-km cargo 1,416,000,000[6]. Roads (1995): total length 93,975 km (paved 75%). Vehicles (1995): passenger cars 2,588,641; trucks and buses 465,940. Air transport (1995): passenger-km 22,558,000,000; metric ton-km cargo 1,160,036,000; airports (1997) 39.

Communications

Medium	date	unit	number	units per 1,000 persons
Daily newspapers	1994	circulation	2,800,000	139
Radio	1996	receivers	9,500,000	449
Television	1995	receivers	9,400,000	454
Telephones	1995	main lines	3,332,400	161
Cellular telephones	1995	subscribers	872,800	42
Facsimile machines	1995	units	58,100	2.8
Personal computers	1995	units	800,000	39

Education and health

Educational attainment (1980). Percentage of population age 25 and over having: no formal schooling 36.6%; primary education 42.1%; secondary 19.4%; higher 1.9%. *Literacy* (1995): total population age 15 and over literate 83.5%; males literate 89.1%; females literate 78.1%.

Education (1996)

	schools	teachers	students	student/teacher ratio
Primary (age 7–12)	7,049	144,937	2,843,663	19.6
Secondary (age 13–19)	1,427	86,891	1,694,243	19.5
Voc., teacher tr.	101	6,044	47,770	7.9
Higher	48	12,247	191,290	15.6

Health (1995): physicians 9,608 (1 per 2,153 persons); hospital beds 40,780 (1 per 507 persons); infant mortality rate per 1,000 live births (1997) 11.
Food (1995): daily per capita caloric intake 2,807 (vegetable products 82%, animal products 18%); 126% of FAO recommended minimum.

Military

Total active duty personnel (1997): 111,500 (army 76.2%, navy 12.6%, air force 11.2%). *Military expenditure as percentage of GDP* (1995): 3.0% (world 2.8%); per capita expenditure U.S.$122.

[1]Includes 40 appointees of the Paramount Ruler; the remaining 30 are indirectly elected at different times. [2]Results of the Central Bank Survey of four major towns: Kuala Lumpur, Shah Alam, Kelang, and Seberang Prai. [3]At constant prices of 1978. [4]Net bank service charges. [5]Import figures are f.o.b. in balance of trade. [6]Peninsular Malaysia and Singapore.

Internet resources for further information:
- **Department of Statistics http://spl.pnm.my/Qstat/**
- **Malaysia http://www.jaring.my/**
- **Malaysian Information Services (English) http://penerangan.gov.my/**

Maldives

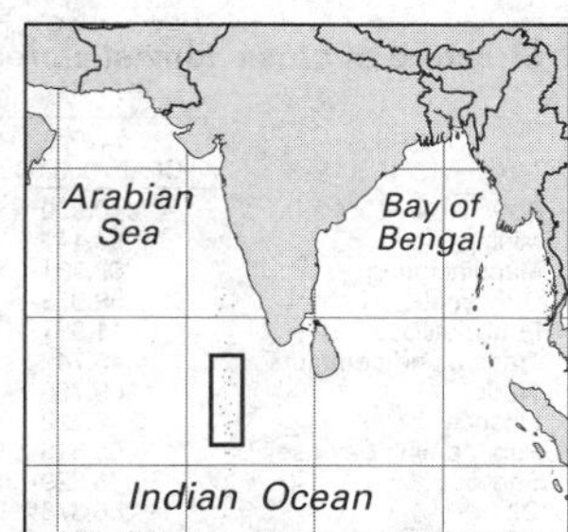

Official name: Divehi Jumhuriyya (Republic of Maldives).
Form of government: republic with one legislative house (Majlis[1] [48[2]]).
Head of state and government: President.
Capital: Male'.
Official language: Divehi.
Official religion: Islam.
Monetary unit: 1 Maldivian rufiyaa (Rf) = 100 laari; valuation (Oct. 3, 1997) 1 U.S.$ = Rf 11.77; 1 £ = Rf 18.97.

Area and population[3]

Administrative atolls	Capitals	area sq mi	area sq km	population 1995 census[4]
North Thiladhunmathi (Haa-Alifu)	Dhidhdhoo	...	...	13,657
South Thiladhunmathi (Haa-Dhaalu)	Nolhivaranfaru	...	...	14,769
North Miladhunmadulu (Shaviyani)	Farukolhu-funadhoo	...	...	10,462
South Miladhunmadulu (Noonu)	Manadhoo	...	...	10,096
North Maalhosmadulu (Raa)	Ugoofaaru	...	...	12,528
South Maalhosmadulu (Baa)	Eydhafushi	...	...	8,727
Faadhippolhu (Lhaviyani)	Naifaru	...	...	8,847
Male' (Kaafu)	Thulusdhoo	...	...	11,650
Ari Atoll Uthuru Gofi (Alifu)	Rasdhoo	...	...	5,340
Ari Atoll Dhekunu Gofi (Alifu)	Mahibadhoo	...	...	6,404
Felidhu Atoll (Vaavu)	Felidhoo	...	...	1,779
Mulakatholhu (Meemu)	Muli	...	...	4,810
North Nilandhe Atoll (Faafu)	Magoodhoo	...	...	3,167
South Nilandhe Atoll (Dhaalu)	Kudahuvadhoo	...	...	4,825
Kolhumadulu (Thaa)	Veymandoo	...	...	9,651
Hadhdhunmathi (Laamu)	Hithadhoo	...	...	10,192
North Huvadhu Atoll (Gaafu-Alifu)	Viligili	...	...	8,164
South Huvadhu Atoll (Gaafu-Dhaalu)	Thinadhoo	...	...	11,984
Foammulah (Gnyaviyani)	Foahmulah	...	...	6,971
Addu Atoll (Seenu)	Hithadhoo	...	...	17,648
Male'		...	...	62,973
TOTAL		115	298	244,644

Demography

Population (1997): 267,000.
Density (1997): persons per sq mi 2,322, persons per sq km 896.0.
Urban-rural (1997): urban 27.0%; rural 73.0%.
Sex distribution (1997): male 51.17%; female 48.83%.
Age breakdown (1997): under 15, 44.8%; 15–29, 27.7%; 30–44, 15.0%; 45–59, 7.3%; 60–74, 4.4%; 75 and over, 0.8%.
Population projection: (2000) 286,000; (2010) 349,000.
Doubling time: 21 years.
Ethnic composition: the majority is principally of Sinhalese and Dravidian extraction; Arab, African, and Negrito influences are also present.
Religious affiliation: virtually 100% Sunnī Muslim.
Major cities (1995): Male' 62,973.

Vital statistics

Birth rate per 1,000 population (1997): 41.8 (world avg. 25.0); legitimate, n.a.; illegitimate, n.a.
Death rate per 1,000 population (1997): 7.6 (world avg. 9.3).
Natural increase rate per 1,000 population (1997): 34.2 (world avg. 15.7).
Total fertility rate (avg. births per childbearing woman; 1997): 6.8.
Marriage rate per 1,000 population (1996): 9.6.
Divorce rate per 1,000 population (1996): 2.8.
Life expectancy at birth (1997): male 65.0 years; female 63.0 years.
Major causes of death per 100,000 population (1988): rheumatic fever 106.0; ischemic heart diseases 65.0; bronchitis, emphysema, and asthma 61.0; tetanus 23.5; tuberculosis 13.0; accidents and suicide 10.0.

National economy

Budget (1996). Revenue: Rf 1,968,900,000 (taxation 36.3%, nontax revenue 31.8%, loans for development 20.2%, foreign aid 11.1%). Expenditures: Rf 1,968,900,000 (social services 34.8%, social development 31.6%, economic development 23.9%).
Production (metric tons except as noted). Agriculture, forestry, fishing (1996): vegetables and melons 24,300, coconuts 13,000, fruits (excluding melons) 8,622, roots and tubers (including cassava, sweet potatoes, and yams) 7,731, copra (1994) 2,000; fish catch 105,413. Mining and quarrying: coral for construction materials. Manufacturing: details, n.a.; however, major industries include boat building and repairing, coir yarn and mat weaving, coconut and fish processing, lacquerwork, garment manufacturing, and handicrafts. Construction: n.a. Energy production (consumption): electricity (kW-hr; 1994) 46,000,000 (46,000,000); coal, none (n.a.); petroleum products (metric tons; 1994) none (35,000); natural gas, none (n.a.).
Tourism (1995): receipts from visitors U.S.$210,000,000; expenditures by nationals abroad (1994) U.S.$32,000,000.
Population economically active (1990): total 56,435; activity rate of total population 26.5% (participation rates: ages 15–64, 50.2%; female 19.9%; unemployed 0.9%).
Household income and expenditure (1990). Average household size 7.2; annual income per household Rf 2,616 (U.S.$274), sources of income: n.a.; expenditure (1981)[5]: food and beverages 61.8%, housing equipment 17.0%, clothing 8.0%, recreation and education 5.9%, transportation 2.6%, health 2.5%, rent 1.6%.
Public debt (external, outstanding; 1995): U.S.$151,900,000.
Gross national product (at current market prices; 1995): U.S.$251,000,000 (U.S.$990 per capita).

Structure of gross domestic product and labour force

	1996 in value Rf '000[6]	1996 % of total value	1990 labour force	1990 % of labour force
Agriculture[7]	263,300	18.2	14,117	25.0
Mining	24,400	1.7	496	0.9
Manufacturing	89,400	6.2	8,441	15.0
Public utilities			445	0.8
Construction	140,600	9.7	3,151	5.6
Transportation and communications	99,400	6.9	5,321	9.4
Trade	280,400	19.4	8,884	15.7
Finance	48,600	3.3	1,058	1.9
Public administration, defense	128,000	8.8	11,848	21.0
Services	97,000	6.7		
Other	276,900	19.1	2,674	4.7
TOTAL	1,448,000	100.0	56,435	100.0

Land use (1994): forested 3.3%; meadows and pastures 3.3%; agricultural and under permanent cultivation 10.0%; built-on, wasteland, and other 83.4%.

Foreign trade[9]

Balance of trade (current prices)

	1991	1992	1993	1994	1995	1996
U.S.$'000,000	−83.3	−126.6	−133.7	−149.2	−186.1	−206.3
% of total	43.7%	61.3%	65.9%	61.9%	65.3%	63.5%

Imports (1996): Rf 3,551,289,000 (machinery and transport equipment 27.9%, basic manufactures 23.7%, food and live animals 21.4%, petroleum products 9.1%). *Major import sources:* Singapore 32.0%; India 12.0%; Malaysia 8.5%; Sri Lanka 7.6%; United Kingdom 3.6%; Japan 3.5%.
Exports (1996): Rf 699,190,000 (canned fish 28.0%, yellowfin tuna 20.5%, apparel and clothing 17.4%, dried skipjack tuna 11.0%). *Major export destinations:* Sri Lanka 18.3%; United Kingdom 21.7%; United States 10.2%; Germany 10.8%; Japan 10.6%; Thailand 9.5%.

Transport and communications

Transport. Railroads: none. Roads: total length, n.a. Vehicles (1996): passenger cars 1,058; trucks and buses 1,244. Merchant marine (1992): vessels (100 gross tons and over) 44; total deadweight tonnage 78,994. Air transport (1994): passengers carried 38,000; passenger-km 7,000,000; airports (1997) with scheduled flights 5.

Communications

Medium	date	unit	number	units per 1,000 persons
Daily newspapers	1994	circulation	3,000	12
Radio	1996	receivers	25,000	96
Television	1995	receivers	4,750	19
Telephones	1995	main lines	13,900	55
Facsimile machines	1995	units	3,500	14
Personal computers	1995	units	3,000	12

Education and health

Educational attainment (1990). Percentage of population age 15 and over having: no standard passed 25.6%; primary standard 37.2%; middle standard 25.9%; secondary standard 6.3%; preuniversity 3.4%; higher 0.4%; not stated 1.2%. *Literacy* (1995): total population age 15 and over literate 93.2%; males literate 93.0%; females literate 93.3%.

Education (1992)

	schools	teachers	students	student/ teacher ratio
Primary (age 6–11)	134	1,138[10]	45,333	36.7[10]
Secondary (age 11–18)	9[10]	291[10]	15,933	12.3[10]
Voc., teacher tr.	10[10]	52[10]	452	8.9[10]
Higher	—	—	—	—

Health: physicians (1996) 99 (1 per 2,587 persons); hospital beds (1995) 305 (1 per 1,192 persons); infant mortality rate per 1,000 live births (1997) 50.
Food (1995): daily per capita caloric intake 2,485 (vegetable products 82%, animal products 18%); 112% of FAO recommended minimum requirement.

Military

Total active duty personnel: Maldives maintains a single security force numbering about 700–1,000; it performs both army and police functions.

[1]Also known or translated as Citizens' Majlis, Citizens' Council, or Citizens' Assembly. [2]Includes 8 nonelective seats. [3]Maldives is divided into 20 administrative districts corresponding to atoll groups; arrangement shown here is from north to south. Total area excludes 34,634 sq mi (89,702 sq km) of tidal waters. [4]Preliminary results. [5]Weights of consumer price index components. [6]At 1985 prices. [7]Primarily fishing. [8]Includes tourism. [9]Import figures are f.o.b. in balance of trade and c.i.f. for commodities and trading partners. [10]1986.

Internet resources for further information:
- **Maldives Mission to the United Nations**
http://www.undp.org:81/missions/maldives/maldives.htm

Mali

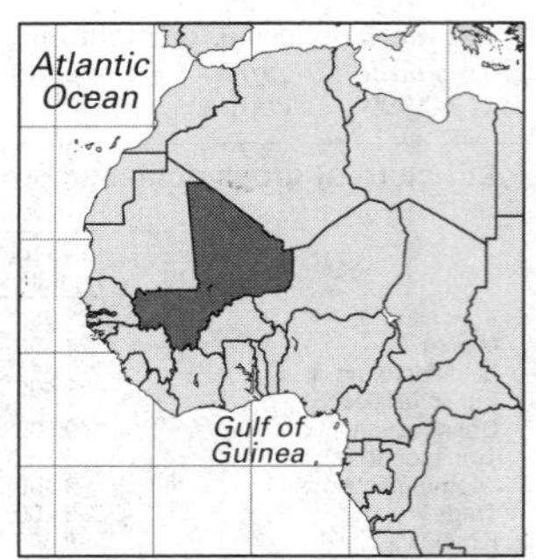

Official name: République du Mali (Republic of Mali).
Form of government: multiparty republic with one legislative house (National Assembly [147])[1].
Chief of state: President.
Head of government: Prime Minister.
Capital: Bamako.
Official language: French.
Official religion: none.
Monetary unit: 1 CFA franc (CFAF) = 100 centimes; valuation (Oct. 3, 1997) 1 U.S.$ = CFAF 592.29; 1 £ = CFAF 954.76.

Area and population

Regions	Capitals	area sq mi	area sq km	population 1995 estimate
Gao	Gao	65,858	170,572	408,000[2]
Kayes	Kayes	46,233	119,743	1,245,000
Kidal	Kidal	58,467	151,430	[2]
Koulikoro	Koulikoro	37,007	95,848	1,462,000
Mopti	Mopti	30,509	79,017	1,423,000
Ségou	Ségou	25,028	64,821	1,579,000
Sikasso	Sikasso	27,135	70,280	1,521,000
Tombouctou	Timbuktu (Tombouctou)	191,743	496,611	462,000
District				
Bamako	Bamako	97	252	913,000
TOTAL		482,077	1,248,574	9,013,000

Demography

Population (1997): 9,945,000.
Density (1997): persons per sq mi 20.6, persons per sq km 8.0.
Urban-rural (1995): urban 26.1%; rural 73.9%.
Sex distribution (1997): male 48.71%; female 51.29%.
Age breakdown (1997): under 15, 47.3%; 15–29, 26.1%; 30–44, 13.3%; 45–59, 8.2%; 60–74, 4.2%; 75 and over, 0.9%.
Population projection: (2000) 10,911,000; (2010) 14,966,000.
Doubling time: 23 years.
Linguistic composition (1987): Bambara-Malinké-Dyula (-Dioula) 50.3%; Fulani (Peulh-Foulfoulbe) 10.7%; Dogon-Kado 6.9%; Songhaï-Djerma 6.3%; Soninké-Marka 6.3%; Tamashek-Bella (Berber) 4.2%; Minianka 3.9%; Senufo 2.4%; Bwa- (Bobo-) Dafing 2.3%; Bozo-Somono 2.0%; other 4.7%.
Religious affiliation (1995): Muslim 90%; traditional beliefs 9%; Christian 1%.
Major cities (1987): Bamako 800,000[3]; Ségou 88,877; Mopti 73,979; Sikasso 73,050; Gao 54,874.

Vital statistics

Birth rate per 1,000 population (1997): 50.0 (world avg. 25.0).
Death rate per 1,000 population (1997): 20.0 (world avg. 9.3).
Natural increase rate per 1,000 population (1997): 30.0 (world avg. 15.7).
Total fertility rate (avg. births per childbearing woman; 1997): 7.1.
Life expectancy at birth (1995): male 44.7 years; female 48.1 years.
Major causes of death per 100,000 population: n.a.; morbidity ([notified cases of illness] by cause as a percentage of all reported infectious disease; 1985): malaria 62.1%; measles 10.3%; amebiasis 10.3%; syphilis and gonococcal infections 6.0%; influenza 4.9%.

National economy

Budget (1996). Revenue: CFAF 313,300,000,000 (fiscal receipts 55.2%, nonfiscal receipts 14.0%). Expenditures: CFAF 324,700,000,000 (current expenditure 50.2%, of which wages and salaries 15.6%, interest on public debt 4.5%; capital expenditure 49.8%).
Public debt (external, outstanding; 1995): U.S.$2,840,000,000.
Tourism (1995): receipts from visitors U.S.$17,000,000; expenditures by nationals abroad U.S.$56,000,000.
Population economically active (1987): total 3,437,489; activity rate of total population 44.7% (participation rates: ages 15–64, 67.4%; female 37.4%; unemployed 0.8%).

Price and earnings indexes (1990 = 100)

	1990	1991	1992	1993	1994	1995	1996
Consumer price index	100.0	101.8	95.4	95.2	117.3	133.0	142.1
Hourly earnings index[4]	100.0	100.0	100.0	100.0	100.0	...	...

Production (metric tons except as noted). Agriculture, forestry, fishing (1997): millet 1,030,000, sorghum 955,000, rice 623,000, seed cotton 500,000, corn (maize) 335,000, peanuts (groundnuts) 155,000, sweet potatoes 16,000; livestock (number of live animals) 14,500,000 goats and sheep, 5,725,000 cattle, 650,000 asses, 365,000 camels, 135,000 horses, 63,500 pigs; roundwood (1995) 6,539,800 cu m; fish catch (1994) 64,352. Mining and quarrying (1995): limestone 20,000; phosphate 3,000; iron oxide 708; gypsum 700[5]; gold 7,500 kg; silver 200 kg[5]. Manufacturing (1995): sugar 34,213; cement 11,197; soap 10,097; soft drinks 68,609 hectolitres; beer 41,690 hectolitres; shoes 111,000 pairs; cigarettes 114,928 cartons. Construction: n.a. Energy production (consumption): electricity (kW-hr; 1994) 289,000,000 (289,000,000); coal, none (n.a.); crude petroleum, none (n.a.); petroleum products (metric tons; 1994) none (149,000); natural gas, none (n.a.).
Gross national product (1995): U.S.$2,410,000,000 (U.S.$250 per capita).

Structure of gross domestic product and labour force

	1995 in value CFAF '000,000	1995 % of total value	1987 labour force	1987 % of labour force
Agriculture	440,950	40.5	2,802,722	82.2
Mining	34,143	3.1	1,524	—
Manufacturing	69,791	6.4	186,243	5.5
Construction	58,678	5.4	13,065	0.4
Public utilities	11,951	1.1	3,157	0.1
Transp. and commun.	45,742	4.2	6,174	0.2
Trade	209,765	19.3	158,892	4.7
Finance	9,222	0.9	320	—
Pub. admin., defense	62,515	5.8	158,704	4.6
Services	78,829	7.2	...	...
Other	66,378[6]	6.1[6]	78,470	2.3
TOTAL	1,087,964	100.0	3,409,271	100.0

Household income and expenditure. Average household size (1987) 5.6; average annual income per household: n.a.; sources of income: n.a.; expenditure (1986–87)[3, 7]: food 54.6%, clothing 14.2%, transportation and communications 11.9%, housing and energy 8.7%, household durable goods 4.2%.
Land use (1993): forested 5.7%; meadows and pastures 24.6%; agricultural and under permanent cultivation 2.0%; other 67.7%.

Foreign trade[8]

Balance of trade (current prices)

	1991	1992	1993	1994	1995	1996
CFAF '000,000,000	−41.8	−70.1	−80.5	−170.0	−156.4	−136.7
% of total	19.2%	27.9%	28.9%	35.1%	26.2%	22.1%

Imports (1995): CFAF 386,400,000,000 (machinery, appliances, and transport equipment 33.1%; food products 13.4%; construction products 10.2%; chemicals 9.2%; petroleum products 8.5%). *Major import sources:* Côte d'Ivoire 26.6%; France 17.3%; United Kingdom 3.8%; Belgium-Luxembourg 3.2%; China 2.5%; Germany 1.5%; Spain 1.1%.
Exports (1995): CFAF 234,700,000,000 (raw cotton and cotton products 55.5%; live animals 19.8%; gold 14.7%). *Major export destinations:* China 12.6%; Belgium-Luxembourg 8.7%; Spain 3.3%; France 2.9%; Côte d'Ivoire 2.1%; Germany 1.6%.

Transport and communications

Transport. Railroads (1994): route length 398 mi[9], 641 km[9]; passenger-mi 304,155,000, passenger-km 489,491,000; short ton-mi cargo 187,176,000, metric ton-km cargo 273,273,000. Roads (1995): total length 9,181 mi, 14,776 km (paved 12%). Vehicles (1995): passenger cars 24,700; trucks and buses 17,100. Merchant marine: vessels (100 gross tons and over) none. Air transport (1993)[10]: passenger-mi 139,675,000, passenger-km 224,736,000; short ton-mi cargo 11,247,000, metric ton-km cargo 16,420,000; airports (1997) with scheduled flights 9.

Communications

Medium	date	unit	number	units per 1,000 persons
Daily newspapers	1994	circulation	40,000	4.4
Radio	1995	receivers	1,575,000	168
Television	1995	receivers	110,000	12
Telephones	1995	main lines	17,000	1.8

Education and health

Educational attainment (1987). Percentage of population age 6 and over having: no formal schooling 86.0%; primary education 12.5%; secondary 1.2%; postsecondary and higher 0.3%. *Literacy* (1995): percentage of total population age 15 and over literate 1,760,000 (31.0%); males literate 1,084,000 (39.4%); females literate 676,000 (23.1%).

Education (1995–96)

	schools	teachers	students	student/ teacher ratio
Primary (age 6–14)	1,996	8,738	608,444	69.6
Secondary (age 15–17)[11]	307[12]	4,549	112,670	24.8
Higher[13]	7	701	6,703	9.6

Health: physicians (1993) 483 (1 per 18,376 persons); hospital beds (1987) 3,430 (1 per 2,253 persons); infant mortality rate (1997) 124.
Food (1995): daily per capita caloric intake 2,149 (vegetable products 91%, animal products 9%); 91% of FAO recommended minimum requirement.

Military

Total active duty personnel (1996): 7,350 (army 93.9%, navy 0.7%, air force 5.4%). *Military expenditure as percentage of GNP* (1995): 1.8% (world 2.8%); per capita expenditure U.S.$5.

[1]Multiparty legislative elections held in March 1997 were annulled by the constitutional court; new elections were held in July and August. [2]Population of Gao region includes Kidal region, established on May 15, 1991. Separate data not available. [3]1995 estimate. [4]Minimum hourly wages of industrial workers. [5]1994. [6]Less imputed bank service charges. [7]Weights of consumer price index components. [8]Import figures are f.o.b. in balance of trade and c.i.f. in commodities and trading partners. [9]1995. [10]Represents 1/11 of the traffic of Air Afrique, which is operated by 11 West African states. [11]Excludes vocational. [12]1991–92. [13]1990–91.

Internet resources for further information:
- **United Nations Development Program—Mali http://www.undp.org/undp/fomli/**
- **MaliNet http://www.malinet.ml/index2.html**

Malta

Official name: Malta (Maltese); Malta (English).
Form of government: unitary multiparty republic with one legislative house (House of Representatives [69[1]]).
Chief of state: President.
Head of government: Prime Minister.
Capital: Valletta.
Official languages: Maltese; English.
Official religion: Roman Catholicism.
Monetary unit: 1 Maltese lira (Lm) = 100 cents = 1,000 mils; valuation[2] (Oct. 3, 1997) 1 U.S.$ = Lm 0.39; 1 £ = Lm 0.63.

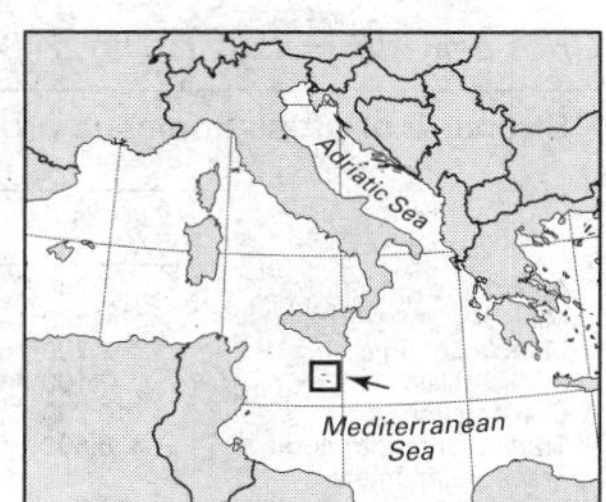

Area and population	area		population
			1996[3]
Census regions[4]	sq mi	sq km	estimate
Gozo and Comino	27	70	27,760
Inner Harbour	6	15	102,663
Northern	30	78	37,045
Outer Harbour	12	32	108,032
South Eastern	20	53	47,876
Western	27	69	48,754
TOTAL	122	316[5]	372,130

Demography

Population (1997): 375,000.
Density (1997): persons per sq mi 3,074, persons per sq km 1,187.
Urban-rural (1996): urban 89.7%; rural 10.3%.
Sex distribution (1996[3]): male 49.53%; female 50.47%.
Age breakdown (1996[3]): under 15, 21.6%; 15–29, 21.3%; 30–44, 22.7%; 45–59, 18.8%; 60–74, 11.5%; 75 and over, 4.1%.
Population projection: (2000) 380,000; (2010) 393,000.
Doubling time: 136 years.
Ethnic composition (by nationality; 1990): Maltese 95.7%; British 2.1%; other 2.2%.
Religious affiliation (1996): Roman Catholic 93.4%; other 6.6%.
Major cities (1996[3]): Birkirkara 22,055; Qormi 20,173; Hamrun 13,624; Sliema 13,470; Valletta 9,128.

Vital statistics

Birth rate per 1,000 population (1996): 12.2 (world avg. 25.0); (1995) legitimate 95.8%; illegitimate 4.2%.
Death rate per 1,000 population (1996): 7.5 (world avg. 9.3).
Natural increase rate per 1,000 population (1996): 4.7 (world avg. 15.7).
Total fertility rate (avg. births per childbearing woman; 1995): 1.8.
Marriage rate per 1,000 population (1995): 6.2.
Divorce rate per 1,000 population: n.a.
Life expectancy at birth (1995): male 74.9 years; female 79.5 years.
Major causes of death per 100,000 population (1995): diseases of the circulatory system 313.0; malignant neoplasms 197.1; diseases of the respiratory system 61.5; endocrine and metabolic diseases of the blood 28.3; diseases of the digestive system 26.4; accidents, poisoning, and violence 25.6.

National economy

Budget (1997). Revenue: Lm 476,945,000 (direct taxes 44.2%; indirect taxes 39.9%; nontax revenue 13.7%; foreign grants 2.2%). Expenditures: Lm 567,645,000 (recurrent expenditures 84.7%, of which social security 27.2%, education 10.4%, health 10.0%, debt service 4.9%, defense 4.2%; capital expenditure 15.3%).
Public debt (1996): U.S.$1,429,300,000.
Production (wholesale value in Lm except where noted). Agriculture, forestry, fishing (1995): vegetables 5,715,997 (of which tomatoes 845,855, melons 755,394, cauliflower 407,062, onions 422,676), fruits 758,040 (of which peaches 192,540, strawberries 188,281, grapes 71,124), potatoes 599,931; livestock (number of live animals; 1996) 69,000 pigs, 21,000 cattle, 16,000 sheep, 9,050 goats; fish catch 1,089,188. Quarrying (1993): 4,520,000. Manufacturing (value of sales in Lm; 1994–95): machinery and transport equipment 402,993,000; food 103,733,000; textiles and wearing apparel 80,813,000; paper and printing 40,610,000; chemicals 35,151,000. Construction (buildings completed; 1996): residential 3,360[6]; nonresidential 1,859. Energy production (consumption): electricity (kW-hr; 1994) 1,500,000,000 (1,500,000,000); coal (metric tons; 1994) none (300,000); crude petroleum, none (n.a.); petroleum products (metric tons; 1994) none (320,000).
Population economically active (1996): total 145,984; activity rate of total population 39.1% (participation rates: ages 15–64 [1985] 45.9%; female 27.5%; unemployed 3.6%).

Price and earnings indexes (1990 = 100)	1990	1991	1992	1993	1994	1995	1996
Consumer price index	100.0	102.5	104.2	108.5	113.0	117.5	120.5
Average weekly earnings	100.0	109.8	114.6	120.5	125.8	129.9	135.5

Household income and expenditure. Average household size (1985) 3.3; average annual income per household (1982) Lm 4,736 (U.S.$11,399); sources of income (1993): wages and salaries 63.8%, professional and unincorporated enterprises 19.3%, rents, dividends, and interest 16.9%; expenditure (1993): food and beverages 27.9%, transportation and communications 15.7%, household furnishings and operations 9.5%, recreation, entertainment, and education 7.2%, clothing and footwear 6.9%, housing 5.5%, health 3.3%, tobacco 2.6%.
Tourism (1995): receipts from visitors U.S.$606,000,000; expenditures by nationals abroad U.S.$184,000,000.
Gross domestic product (1995): U.S.$3,241,600,000 (U.S.$8,712 per capita).

Structure of gross domestic product and labour force	1995		1996	
	in value Lm '000	% of total value	labour force	% of labour force
Agriculture	28,600	2.9	2,846	1.9
Manufacturing	236,800	24.0 }	33,788	23.1
Mining }	37,400	3.8 }		
Construction }			6,938	4.8
Public utilities	60,800	6.2	...	...
Transp. and commun.	67,700	6.8	11,828	8.1
Trade	129,000	13.1	25,819[7]	17.7[7]
Finance	73,800	7.5	3,725	2.6
Pub. admin., defense	162,000	16.4	32,419	22.2
Services	101,700	10.3	18,779	12.9
Other	89,400	9.0	9,839[8]	6.7[8]
TOTAL	987,200	100.0	145,983[5]	100.0

Land use (1994): agricultural and under permanent cultivation 40.6%; other (infertile clay soil with underlying limestone) 59.4%.

Foreign trade[9]

Balance of trade (current prices)	1989	1990	1991	1992	1993	1994	1995
Lm '000,000	–169.0	–172.8	–214.5	–182.9	–229.5	–226.9	–747.5
% of total	22.3%	18.3%	21.1%	15.7%	18.2%	16.2%	16.2%

Imports (1996): Lm 1,010,254,000 (machinery and transport equipment 48.2%, manufactured and semimanufactured goods 25.9%, food 9.1%, chemicals 7.4%, mineral fuels 5.4%, beverages and tobacco 1.3%). *Major import sources:* Italy 19.6%; France 15.8%; U.K. 14.2%; Germany 9.4%; U.S. 6.9%.
Exports (1996): Lm 570,344,000 (machinery and transport equipment 62.1%, manufactured 32.6%, chemicals 2.5%, food and live animals 1.9%, beverages and tobacco 0.5%). *Major export destinations:* France 16.1%; Germany 15.1%; U.S. 14.7%; Italy 12.5%; U.K. 8.4%.

Transport and communications

Transport. Railroads: none. Roads (1994): total length 997 mi, 1,604 km (paved 94%). Vehicles (1995): passenger cars 173,259; trucks and buses 41,849. Merchant marine (1992): vessels (100 gross tons and over) 889; total deadweight tonnage 17,073,207. Air transport (1995): passenger-mi 1,070,479,000, passenger-km 1,722,772,000; short ton-mi cargo 9,404,000, metric ton-km cargo 13,729,000; airports (1996) with scheduled flights 1.

Communications Medium	date	unit	number	units per 1,000 persons
Daily newspapers	1996	circulation	54,000	145
Radio	1994	receivers	193,000	525
Television	1994	receivers	272,000	739
Telephones	1995	main lines	170,700	459
Cellular telephones	1995	subscribers	10,800	29
Facsimile machines	1995	units	3,200	300
Personal computers	1995	units	30,000	81

Education and health

Educational attainment (1967). Percentage of economically active population having: no formal schooling 10.8%; primary education 60.4%; lower secondary 3.4%; upper secondary 17.6%; technical secondary 3.9%; post-secondary and higher 3.9%. *Literacy* (1985): total population age 15 and over literate 250,419 (96.0%); males literate 121,899 (96.2%); females literate 128,520 (95.9%).

Education (1995–96)	schools	teachers	students	student/ teacher ratio
Primary (age 5–10)	111	1,990	35,479	17.8
Secondary (age 11–17)	59	2,679	29,907	20.9
Voc., teacher tr.	22	541	4,539	8.4
Higher[10]	1	284	3,679	13.0

Health (1996): physicians 925 (1 per 403 persons); hospital beds 2,140 (1 per 174 persons); infant mortality rate per 1,000 live births (1996) 10.5.
Food (1995): daily per capita caloric intake 3,387 (vegetable products 73%, animal products 27%); 136% of FAO recommended minimum requirement.

Military

Total active duty personnel (1996): 1,950 (army 100%). *Military expenditure as percentage of GNP* (1993): 0.9% (world 3.2%); per capita expenditure U.S.$63.

[1]Normally a 65-member body; however, in the elections of Oct. 26, 1996, 4 additional seats were awarded to the minority party (by seats won), which had obtained a majority of the popular vote. [2]The Maltese lira is tied to the currencies of several principal trading partners. [3]January 1. [4]Data are reported according to census regions as of January 1993; in late 1993 new administrative districts (Local Councils) were created. [5]Detail does not add to total given because of rounding. [6]Dwellings completed. [7]Includes hotels and catering. [8]Includes 5,328 unemployed. [9]Import figures are f.o.b. in balance of trade and c.i.f. for commodities and trading partners. [10]1992–93.

Internet resources for further information:
- **Central Office of Statistics http://www.magnet.mt/home/cos/**

Marshall Islands

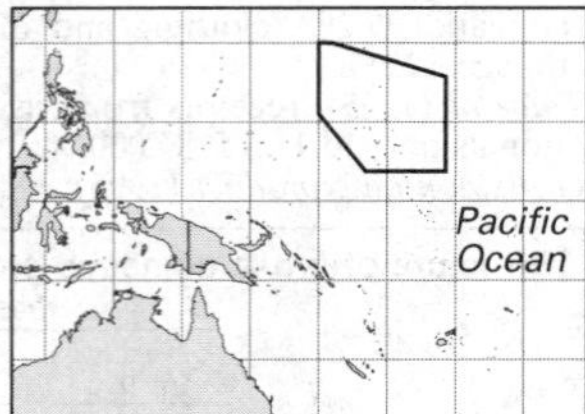

Official name: Majōl (Marshallese); Republic of the Marshall Islands (English).
Form of government: unitary republic with two legislative houses (Council of Iroij [12][1]; Nitijela [33]).
Head of state and government: President.
Capital: Majuro (Dalap-Uliga-Darrit).
Official languages: Marshallese (Kajin-Majōl); English.
Official religion: none.
Monetary unit: 1 U.S. dollar (U.S.$) = 100 cents; valuation (Oct. 3, 1997) 1 £ = U.S.$1.61.

Area and population

	area		population
Election districts	sq mi	sq km	1988 census
Ailinglaplap	5.67	14.68	1,715
Ailuk	2.07	5.36	488
Arno	5.00	12.95	1,656
Aur	2.17	5.62	438
Bikini	2.32	6.01	10
Ebon	2.22	5.75	741
Enewetak	2.26	5.85	715
Jabat	0.22	0.57	112
Jaluit	4.38	11.34	1,709
Kili	0.36	0.93	602
Kwajalein	6.33	16.39	9,311
Lae	0.56	1.45	319
Lib	0.36	0.93	115
Likiep	3.96	10.26	482
Majuro	3.75	9.71	19,664
Maloelap	3.75	9.71	796
Mejit	0.72	1.86	445
Mili	6.15	15.93	854
Namorik	1.07	2.77	814
Namu	2.42	6.27	801
Rongelap	3.07	7.95	0
Ujae	0.72	1.86	448
Ujelang	0.67	1.74	0
Utrik	0.94	2.43	409
Wotho	1.67	4.32	90
Wotje	3.16	8.18	646
Other atolls	4.10	10.62	0
TOTAL	70.07	181.48[2]	43,380

Demography

Population (1997): 60,300.
Density (1997): persons per sq mi 861.4, persons per sq km 333.1.
Urban-rural (1988): urban 64.5%; rural 35.5%.
Sex distribution (1997): male 51.02%; female 48.98%.
Age breakdown (1997): under 15, 50.2%; 15–29, 26.0%; 30–44, 13.9%; 45–59, 6.5%; 60–74, 2.6%; 75 and over, 0.8%.
Population projection: (2000) 68,100; (2010) 91,400.
Doubling time: 18 years.
Ethnic composition (nationality; 1988): Marshallese 96.9%; other Pacific islanders 1.7%; Filipino 0.5%; all other 0.9%.
Religious affiliation (1995): Protestant 62.8%; Roman Catholic 7.1%; Mormon 3.1%; Jehovah's Witness 1.0%; other (mostly nonreligious) 26.0%.
Major cities (1995): Majuro (Dalap-Uliga-Darrit) 28,000; Ebeye 8,324[3].

Vital statistics

Birth rate per 1,000 population (1997): 46.0 (world avg. 25.0).
Death rate per 1,000 population (1997): 7.0 (world avg. 9.3).
Natural increase rate per 1,000 population (1997): 39.0 (world avg. 15.7).
Total fertility rate (avg. births per childbearing woman; 1997): 6.8.
Life expectancy at birth (1997): male 62.6 years; female 65.8 years.
Major causes of death per 100,000 population (1990–93)[4]: infectious and parasitic diseases 169.9; circulatory diseases 155.1; respiratory diseases 105.1; malignant neoplasms (cancers) 68.4; digestive diseases 63.3; accidents, injuries, and violence 36.7.

National economy

Budget (1995–96). Revenue: U.S.$80,100,000 (U.S. government grants 59.7%, income tax 9.4%, import tax 8.5%, value-added and excise taxes 6.1%, fishing rights 3.0%, interest income 2.7%). Expenditures: U.S.$77,400,000 (debt service 10.2%, education 9.9%, health services 8.8%, public works and social programs 4.9%, internal security 2.1%).
Production (metric tons except as noted). Agriculture, forestry, fishing (1991): copra 5,545, fruits 1,809 (of which pandanus 836, breadfruit 645, bananas 264, papaya 64), tubers 1,500 (of which taro 1,300, sweet potatoes 182), vegetables 136 (of which cabbage 36, pumpkins 36); livestock (number of live animals; 1994) 12,352 pigs, 59,086 chickens; roundwood, n.a.; fish catch (1995) 260. Mining and quarrying: high-grade phosphate mining on Ailinglaplap Atoll, quarrying of sand and aggregate for local construction only. Manufacturing (1995): copra 7,728; coconut oil and processed (chilled or frozen) fish are important products; the manufacture of handicrafts and personal items (clothing, mats, boats, etc.) by individuals is also significant. Construction (1994): value added U.S.$9,300,000. Energy production (consumption): electricity (kW-hr; 1994) 57,891,000 (57,891,000); coal, none (n.a.); gasoline, oil, and lubricants (barrels; 1988)[5] n.a. (84,588).
Public debt (external, outstanding; 1994–95): U.S.$141,200,000.

Gross domestic product (1995): U.S.$105,300,000 (U.S.$1,870 per capita).

Structure of gross domestic product and labour force

	1995		1988	
	in value U.S.$'000	% of total value	labour force	% of labour force
Agriculture	15,700	14.9	2,150	18.7
Mining	300	0.3	2	—
Manufacturing	2,700	2.6	945	8.2
Public utilities	2,100	2.0	82	0.7
Construction	10,700	10.2	1,076	9.4
Transp. and commun.	6,500	6.2	537	4.7
Trade, restaurants, hotels	17,900	17.0	1,394	12.1
Finance, insurance, real estate	17,200	16.3	833	7.3
Public administration, Services	32,000	30.4	3,035	26.4
Other	200[6]	0.2[6]	1,434[7]	12.5[7]
TOTAL	105,300	100.0[2]	11,488	100.0

Land use (1989)[8]: forested 22.5%; meadows and pastures 13.5%; agricultural and under permanent cultivation 33.1%; other 30.9%.
Household income and expenditure. Average household size (1988) 8.7; income per household (1979) U.S.$3,366; sources of income: n.a.; expenditure (1982): food 57.7%, housing 15.6%, clothing 12.0%, personal effects and other 14.7%.
Population economically active (1988): total 11,488; activity rate of total population 26.5% (participation rates: over age 14, 54.1%; female 30.1%; unemployed 12.5%).

Price and earnings indexes (1990 = 100)

	1989	1990	1991	1992	1993	1994	1995
Consumer price index	99.4	100.0	103.4	116.8	119.5	125.6	134.4
Earnings index	...	...	...	...	...	...	...

Tourism (1994): receipts from visitors U.S.$2,000,000; expenditures by nationals abroad, n.a.

Foreign trade

Balance of trade (current prices)

	1990	1991	1992	1993	1994	1995
U.S.$'000,000	−53.9	−53.5	−52.6	−53.4	−49.3	−58.1
% of total	94.0%	90.3%	74.1%	77.7%	52.6%	27.2%

Imports (1995): U.S.$75,100,000 (food, beverages, and tobacco 28.2%, machinery and transport equipment 24.6%, mineral fuels and lubricants 24.0%, manufactured goods 8.9%, chemical products 2.5%). *Major import sources:* U.S. 51.0%; Guam 14.5%; Japan 7.5%; Australia 1.9%; Hong Kong 1.7%.
Exports (1995): U.S.$17,000,000 (chilled fish 38.8%, crude coconut oil 18.2%, pet fish 2.4%). *Major export destinations:* U.S. *c.* 80.0%; other *c.* 20.0%.

Transport and communications

Transport. Vehicles (1994): passenger cars 1,418; trucks and buses 193. Merchant marine (1992): vessels (100 gross tons and over) 35; total deadweight tonnage 4,182,356. Air transport (1994): passenger-km 49,000,000[9]; metric ton-km cargo 30,433; airports (1997) with scheduled flights 25.

Communications

Medium	date	unit	number	units per 1,000 persons
Telephones	1993	main lines	2,300	44.2

Education and health

Educational attainment (1988). Percentage of population age 25 and over having: no grade completed 5.1%; elementary education 43.2%; secondary 39.7%; higher 11.4%; not stated 0.6%. *Literacy* (latest): total population age 15 and over literate 19,377 (91.2%); males literate 9,993 (92.4%); females literate 9,384 (90.0%).

Education (1994–95)

	schools	teachers	students	student/ teacher ratio
Primary (age 6–14)	103	669	13,355	20.0
Secondary (age 15–18)	12	144	2,400	16.7
Voc., teacher tr.	...	...	...	...
Higher	...	...	...	...

Health (1995): physicians 17 (1 per 3,269 persons); hospital beds 108 (1 per 515 persons); infant mortality rate per 1,000 live births (1997) 45.7.

Military

Under the 1984 Compact of Free Association, the United States provides for the defense of the Republic of the Marshall Islands.

[1]Council of Iroij is an advisory body only. [2]Detail does not add to total given because of rounding. [3]1988. [4]Registered deaths only. [5]Imports only. [6]Import duties less imputed bank service charges. [7]Includes 1,432 unemployed. [8]Data are for the former Trust Territory of the Pacific Islands. [9]1993.

Internet resources for further information:
- **RMI Online, Internet Guide to the Republic of the Marshall Islands http://www.clark.net/pub/rmiemb/geninfo.html**
- **Bank of Hawaii-Republic of the Marshall Islands Economic Report http://www.boh.com/econ/pacific/rmiaer.html**

Martinique

Official name: Département de la Martinique (Department of Martinique).
Political status: overseas department (France) with two legislative houses (General Council [45]; Regional Council [41]).
Chief of state: President of France.
Heads of government: Prefect (for France); President of the General Council (for Martinique); President of the Regional Council (for Martinique).
Capital: Fort-de-France.
Official language: French.
Official religion: none.
Monetary unit: 1 French franc (F) = 100 centimes; valuation (Oct. 3, 1997) 1 U.S.$ = F 5.92; 1 £ = F 9.55.

Area and population

		area		population
				1990
Arrondissements	Capitals	sq mi	sq km	census
Fort-de-France	Fort-de-France	147	381	187,275
Le Marin	Le Marin	158	409	93,411
La Trinité	La Trinité	131	338	78,893
TOTAL		436	1,128	359,579

Demography

Population (1997): 399,000.
Density (1997): persons per sq mi 915.1, persons per sq km 353.7.
Urban-rural (1995): urban 93.4%; rural 6.6%.
Sex distribution (1995): male 48.55%; female 51.45%.
Age breakdown (1995): under 15, 24.0%; 15–29, 25.8%; 30–44, 22.2%; 45–59, 14.0%; 60–74, 9.8%; 75 and over, 4.2%.
Population projection: (2000) 415,000; (2010) 458,000.
Doubling time: 77 years.
Ethnic composition (1983): mulatto 93.7%; French (metropolitan and Martinique white) 2.6%; East Indian 1.7%; other 2.0%.
Religious affiliation (1997): Roman Catholic 86.5%; Protestant 8.0% (mostly Seventh-day Adventist); Jehovah's Witness 1.6%; other 3.9%, including Hindu, syncretist, and nonreligious.
Major urban areas (1990): Fort-de-France 100,080; Le Lamentin 30,028; Schoelcher 19,825; Sainte-Marie 19,682; Le Robert 17,713.

Vital statistics

Birth rate per 1,000 population (1994): 14.9 (world avg. 25.0); (1992) legitimate 34.1%; illegitimate 65.9%.
Death rate per 1,000 population (1994): 5.8 (world avg. 9.3).
Natural increase rate per 1,000 population (1994): 9.1 (world avg. 15.7).
Total fertility rate (avg. births per childbearing woman; 1993): 1.9.
Marriage rate per 1,000 population (1994): 3.9.
Divorce rate per 1,000 population (1993): 0.9.
Life expectancy at birth (1993): male 74.7 years; female 81.0 years.
Major causes of death per 100,000 population (1992): diseases of the circulatory system 192.7; malignant neoplasms (cancers) 137.7; accidents, poisoning, and violence 48.2; diseases of the digestive system 32.2; diseases of the respiratory system 30.1; endocrine and metabolic disorders 29.3.

National economy

Budget (1994). Revenue: F 1,816,000,000 (general receipts from French central government and local administrative bodies 45.0%; tax receipts 34.0%, of which indirect taxes 19.5%, direct taxes 14.5%). Expenditures: F 1,816,000,000 (health and social assistance 42.0%; wages and salaries 16.7%; other administrative services 7.2%; debt amortization 5.0%).
Public debt (1994): U.S.$186,700,000.
Production (metric tons except as noted). Agriculture, forestry, fishing (1996): sugarcane 212,000, bananas 210,000, pineapples 30,000, plantains 14,000, yams 7,000, tomatoes 4,000, cucumbers and gherkins 3,000, melons 3,000, sweet potatoes 1,000; livestock (number of live animals) 42,000 sheep, 33,000 pigs, 30,000 cattle, 22,000 goats; roundwood (1994) 12,000 cu m; fish catch (1995) 5,377. Mining and quarrying (1992): pumice 140,000; sand and gravel for local construction. Manufacturing (1996): cement 214,807; processed pineapples 15,715; sugar 7,722; rum 45,326 hectolitres; other products include clothing, fabricated metals, and yawls and sails. Construction (buildings authorized; 1994): residential permits 6,893; nonresidential 113,279 sq m. Energy production (consumption): electricity (kW-hr; 1996) 977,000,000 (856,000,000); coal, none (none); crude petroleum (barrels; 1994) none (5,805,000); petroleum products (metric tons; 1994) 718,000 (554,000); natural gas, none (none).
Household income and expenditure. Average household size (1990) 3.3; income per household (1989) F 147,150 (U.S.$24,525); sources of income (1989): wages and salaries 80%, other 20%; expenditure (1993): food and beverages 32.1%, transportation and communications 20.7%, housing and energy 10.6%, household durable goods 9.4%, clothing and footwear 8.0%, education and recreation 5.4%, health care 5.2%, other 8.6%.
Tourism (1995): receipts from visitors U.S.$384,000,000; expenditures by nationals abroad, n.a.

Gross domestic product (1991): U.S.$3,375,000,000 (U.S.$9,210 per capita).

Structure of gross domestic product and labour force

	1991		1990	
	in value F '000,000	% of total value	labour force	% of labour force
Agriculture, fishing	1,152.2	5.5	8,445	5.2
Mining, manufacturing	1,592.0	7.7	9,706	6.0
Construction	1,078.6	5.2	9,298	5.7
Public utilities	493.7	2.4		
Transp. and commun.	1,282.3	6.2	6,673	4.1
Trade, restaurants, hotels	4,556.1	21.9	13,965	8.6
Finance, real estate, insurance	1,017.6	4.9	26,489	16.2
Pub. admin. and defense	305.8	1.5	35,541	21.8
Services	3,424.5	16.4		
Other	5,883.2[1]	28.3[1]	52,900[2]	32.4[2]
TOTAL	20,786.0	100.0	163,017	100.0

Population economically active (1993): total 162,100[3]; activity rate of total population 43.0% (participation rates: ages 15–64, 73.8%; [1990] female 47.5%; unemployed [1996] 27.0%).

Price and earnings indexes (1990 = 100)

	1990	1991	1992	1993	1994	1995	1996
Consumer price index[4]	100.0	104.3	108.4	109.6	114.0	115.9	118.1
Monthly earnings index[5]	100.0	103.0	105.7	107.5	109.1	111.3	112.3

Land use (1994): forested 45.3%; meadows and pastures 13.2%; agricultural and under permanent cultivation 17.0%; other 24.5%.

Foreign trade[6]

Balance of trade (current prices)

	1990	1991	1992	1993	1994	1995
F '000,000	−7,970	−7,934	−7,982	−7,744	−7,877	−8,604
% of total	72.7%	78.4%	75.6%	78.0%	76.4%	78.2%

Imports (1996): F 10,072,400,000 (consumer goods 23.9%, goods for intermediate consumption [inputs to the manufacturing process changed or destroyed in the final product] 15.9%, automobiles 15.0%, professional equipment 15.2%, energy products 8.3%). *Major import sources* (1994): France 61.6%; United States 2.7%; Guadeloupe 1.1%; Venezuela 0.7%; other Caribbean 1.9%.
Exports (1996): F 1,086,000 ([1995] bananas 40.4%, refined petroleum 17.8%, rum 9.8%, melons 1.7%). *Major export destinations* (1994): France 47.5%; Guadeloupe 37.4%; French Guiana 3.3%.

Transport and communications

Transport. Railroads: none. Roads (1994): total length 1,299 mi, 2,091 km (paved [1988] 75%). Vehicles (1985): passenger cars 135,269; trucks and buses 7,328. Merchant marine (1992): vessels (100 gross tons and over) 6; total deadweight tonnage 1,121. Air transport (1996): passenger arrivals and departures 1,505,970; cargo handled 13,459 metric tons; airports (1997) with scheduled flights 1.

Communications

Medium	date	unit	number	units per 1,000 persons
Daily newspapers	1995	circulation	32,000	82.5
Radio	1995	receivers	77,000	198
Television	1995	receivers	65,000	168
Telephones	1995	main lines	155,200	400
Facsimile machines	1995	units	3,400	8.8

Education and health

Educational attainment (1990). Percentage of population age 25 and over having: incomplete primary, or no declaration 54.3%; primary education 18.0%; secondary 20.0%; higher 7.7%. *Literacy* (1982): total population age 15 and over literate 206,807 (92.5%); males literate 97,538 (91.8%); females literate 109,269 (93.2%).

Education (1993–94)

	schools	teachers	students	student/ teacher ratio
Primary (age 6–11)	276	3,251	33,532	10.3
Secondary (age 12–18) / Vocational	76	3,736	47,172	12.6
Higher	1	99	4,486	45.3

Health (1991): physicians 625 (1 per 584 persons); hospital beds 3,747 (1 per 97 persons); infant mortality rate per 1,000 live births (1993) 4.0.
Food (1995): daily per capita caloric intake 2,865 (vegetable products 75%, animal products 25%); 118% of FAO recommended minimum requirement.

Military

Total active duty personnel (1994): 1,542 French troops.

[1]Includes an estimated F 5,474,000,000 produced in the nonmoney economy. [2]Unemployed. [3]Includes military reserve personnel. [4]Figures are end-of-year unless otherwise footnoted. [5]Based on minimum-level wage of public employees. [6]Imports c.i.f.; exports f.o.b.

Internet resources for further information:

- **Martinique: Présentation générale (in French) http://www.outre-mer.gouv.fr/domtom/mar.htm**

Mauritania

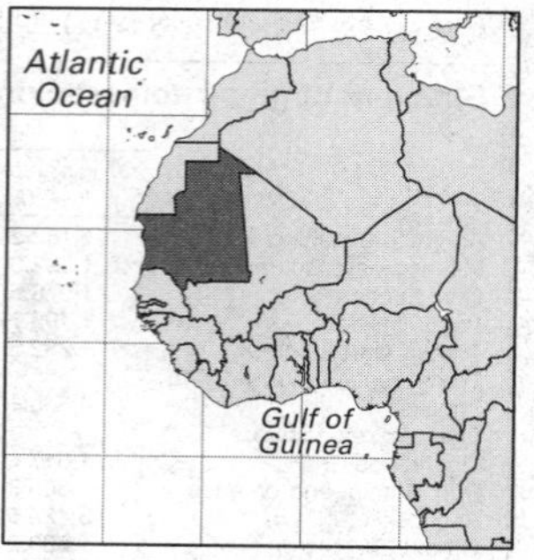

Official name: Al-Jumhūrīyah al-Islāmīyah al-Mūrītānīyah (Arabic) (Islamic Republic of Mauritania).
Form of government: unitary multiparty republic with two legislative houses (Senate [56]; National Assembly [79]).
Heads of state and government: President assisted by the Prime Minister.
Capital: Nouakchott.
Official language: Arabic[1].
Official religion: Islam.
Monetary unit: 1 ouguiya (UM) = 5 khoums; valuation (Oct. 3, 1997) 1 U.S.$ = UM 160.20; 1 £ = UM 258.24.

Area and population

		area		population
Regions	**Capitals**	sq mi	sq km	1992 estimate
El-'Açâba	Kiffa	14,100	36,600	185,574
Adrar	Atar	83,100	215,300	62,906
Brakna	Aleg	13,000	33,800	207,590
Dakhlet Nouadhibou	Nouadhibou	8,600	22,300	83,246
Gorgol	Kaédi	5,300	13,600	201,301
Guidimaka	Sélibaby	4,000	10,300	129,797
Hodh ech-Chargui	Néma	70,600	182,700	234,011
Hodh el-Gharbi	'Ayoûn el-'Atroûs	20,600	53,400	175,089
Inchiri	Akjoujt	18,100	46,800	13,630
Tagant	Tidjikdja	36,800	95,200	67,939
Tiris Zemmour	Zouérate	97,600	252,900	37,534
Trarza	Rosso	26,200	67,800	217,867
Capital District				
Nouakchott	Nouakchott	400	1,000	480,395
TOTAL		398,000[2]	1,030,700	2,096,879[3]

Demography

Population (1997): 2,411,000.
Density (1997): persons per sq mi 6.1, persons per sq km 2.3.
Urban-rural (1995): urban 53.8%; rural 46.2%.
Sex distribution (1995): male 49.52%; female 50.48%.
Age breakdown (1995): under 15, 43.1%; 15–29, 27.3%; 30–44, 16.1%; 45–59, 8.3%; 60–74, 4.3%; 75 and over, 0.9%.
Population projection: (2000) 2,653,000; (2010) 3,630,000.
Doubling time: 22 years.
Ethnic composition (1993)[4]: Moor 70% (of which about 40% "black" Moor [Ḥarāṭīn, or African Sudanic] and about 30% "white" Moor [Bidan, or Arab-Berber]); other black African 30% (mostly Wolof, Tukulor, Soninke, and Fulani).
Religious affiliation (1994): Sunnī Muslim 99.5%; Roman Catholic 0.2%; other 0.3%.
Major cities (1992): Nouakchott 735,000[5]; Nouadhibou 72,305; Kaédi 35,241; Kiffa 29,292[6]; Rosso 27,783[6].

Vital statistics

Birth rate per 1,000 population (1996): 46.9 (world avg. 25.0).
Death rate per 1,000 population (1996): 15.2 (world avg. 9.3).
Natural increase rate per 1,000 population (1996): 31.7 (world avg. 15.7).
Total fertility rate (avg. births per childbearing woman; 1996): 6.8.
Life expectancy at birth (1996): male 46.1 years; female 52.1 years.

National economy

Budget (1996). Revenue: UM 44,720,000,000 (tax revenue 59.0%, of which import taxes 12.6%, value-added taxes 10.8%, taxes on wages 8.4%; nontax revenue 39.1%, of which fishing royalties and penalties 31.6%). Expenditures: UM 36,740,000,000 (current expenditures 71.3%, of which interest on public debt 13.4%, defense 10.0%; development expenditures 22.5%; other 6.2%).
Land use (1994): forested 4.3%; meadows and pastures 38.3%; agricultural and under permanent cultivation 0.2%; desert 57.2%.
Production (metric tons except as noted). Agriculture, forestry, fishing (1996): sorghum 144,900, rice 52,800, dates 35,900, pulses 12,000, millet 7,500; livestock (number of live animals) 6,199,000 sheep, 4,133,000 goats, 1,312,000 cattle, 1,087,000 camels; roundwood (1995) 14,000 cu m; fish catch (metric tons; 1995) 90,000, of which octopuses 31,700[7]. Mining and quarrying (gross weight; 1996): iron ore 11,363,000; gold 57,900 troy oz[5]. Manufacturing (1994): cow's milk 91,000; goat's milk 77,000; meat 61,000, of which fresh beef and veal 18,000; hides and skins 4,318; cement, tiles, and bricks 5.9[8]; fabricated metal products 5.4[8]; paper and paper products 2.1[8]. Construction: n.a. Energy production (consumption): electricity (kW-hr; 1994) 148,000,000 (148,000,000); coal (metric tons; 1994) none (6,000); crude petroleum (barrels; 1994) none (6,905,000); petroleum products (metric tons; 1994) 835,000 (918,000); natural gas, none (none).
Population economically active (1994): total 687,000; activity rate of total population 31.3% (participation rates: over age 10 [1991] 45.5%; female 22.9%).

Price and earnings indexes (1990 = 100)

	1990	1991	1992	1993	1994	1995	1996
Consumer price index[9]	100.0	105.6	116.3	127.2	132.4	140.9	147.6
Monthly earnings index[10]	100.0	100.0	114.6	129.2	129.2	129.2	129.2

Household income and expenditure. Average household size, n.a.; expenditure (1990): food and beverages 73.1%, clothing and footwear 8.1%, energy and water 7.7%, transportation and communications 2.0%.
Gross national product (1995): U.S.$1,049,000,000 (U.S.$460 per capita).

Structure of gross domestic product and labour force

	1996		1988	
	in value UM '000,000	% of total value	labour force	% of labour force
Agriculture, livestock	33,232	22.1	225,238	38.5
Mining	13,440	9.0	6,322	1.1
Manufacturing	16,117	10.7	5,630	1.0
Public utilities }	12,766	8.5	1,326	0.2
Construction }			12,291	2.1
Transp. and commun.	10,282	6.9	8,378	1.4
Trade and finance	22,287	14.8	73,451	12.5
Services	10,210	6.8 }	86,807	14.8
Pub. admin., defense	15,684	10.5 }		
Other	16,124[11]	10.7[11]	166,366[12]	28.4[12]
TOTAL	150,142	100.0	585,809	100.0

Public debt (external, outstanding; 1995): U.S.$2,184,000,000.
Tourism (1996): receipts U.S.$2,000,000; expenditures U.S.$13,600,000.

Foreign trade

Balance of trade (current prices)

	1991	1992	1993	1994	1995	1996
U.S.$'000,000	+36.7	−54.5	+2.6	+41.7	+75.8	+49.8
% of total	4.4%	6.3%	0.3%	5.6%	8.3%	5.4%

Imports (1996): U.S.$435,400,000 (petroleum products 30.5%, private sector foodstuffs 22.4%, imports for National Industrial and Mining Company 20.8%, public sector food aid 12.7%). *Major import sources* (1995)[13]: France 24%; Spain 8%, United States 7%, Belgium 6%, China 5%.
Exports (1996): U.S.$485,200,000 (fish 57.0%, of which cephalopods 28.8%; iron ore 42.7%). *Major export destinations* (1995)[13]: Japan 27%; Italy 18%; France 12%; Spain 11%; Côte d'Ivoire 6%.

Transport and communications

Transport. Railroads (1995): route length 437 mi, 704 km; passenger-mi, negligible; passenger-km, negligible; (1993) short ton-mi cargo 4,719,000,000, metric ton-km cargo 6,890,000,000. Roads (1995): total length 4,700 mi, 7,600 km (paved 11%). Vehicles (1995): passenger cars 17,300; trucks and buses 9,210. Merchant marine (1992): vessels (100 gross tons and over) 126; total deadweight tonnage 23,875. Air transport (1996)[14]: passenger-mi 139,644,000, passenger-km 224,736,000; short ton-mi cargo 11,247,000, metric ton-km cargo 16,420,000; airports (1997) with scheduled flights 9.

Communications

Medium	date	unit	number	units per 1,000 persons
Daily newspapers	1994	circulation	1,000	0.05
Radio	1996	receivers	1,000,000	428
Television	1995	receivers	1,100	0.05
Telephones	1995	main lines	9,200	4.1
Facsimile machines	1995	units	300	0.01

Education and health

Educational attainment (1988). Percentage of population age 25 and over having: no formal schooling 60.8%; primary and incomplete secondary 34.1%; secondary 3.8%; higher 1.3%. *Literacy* (1995): percentage of total population age 15 and over literate 37.7%; males literate 49.6%; females literate 26.3%.

Education (1993–94)

	schools	teachers	students	student/ teacher ratio
Primary (age 6–11)	1,635	5,181[15]	268,216[15]	51.8[15]
Secondary (age 12–17)	56[16]	1,776	43,861	24.7
Voc., teacher tr.	5[16]	162	1,949	12.0
Higher	4	72[15, 17]	2,850[15, 17]	39.6[15, 17]

Health: physicians (1994) *c.* 200 (1 per 11,085 persons); hospital beds (1988) 1,556 (1 per 1,217 persons); infant mortality rate per 1,000 live births (1996) 81.7.
Food (1995): daily per capita caloric intake 2,592 (vegetable products 83%, animal products 17%); 112% of FAO recommended minimum requirement.

Military

Total active duty personnel (1996): 15,650 (army 95.8%, navy 3.2%, air force 1.0%). *Military expenditure as percentage of GNP* (1995): 3.2% (world 2.8%); per capita expenditure U.S.$15.

[1]The 1991 constitution names Arabic as the official language and the following as national languages: Arabic, Fulani, Soninke, and Wolof. [2]Detail does not add to total given because of rounding. [3]Official population projection based on 1988 census. [4]Estimated figures; 1988 census data for ethnicity/race not released by the government. [5]1995. [6]1988. [7]Fish catch (1995) including foreign fishing vessels equals 424,500 metric tons. [8]1993 value added of production in U.S.$'000,000. [9]Nouakchott only. [10]Statutory minimum wage rate of civil servants. [11]Indirect taxes. [12]Mostly unemployed. [13]Estimated figures. [14]Data represent 1/11th total scheduled traffic of Air Afrique. [15]1994–95. [16]1991–92. [17]University of Nouakchott only.

Internet resources for further information:
- **Embassy of Mauritania (Washington, D.C.)**
http://www.embassy.org/mauritania/

Mauritius

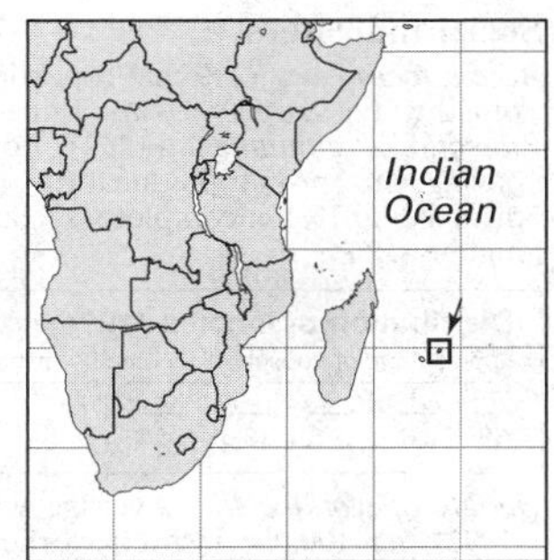

Official name: Republic of Mauritius.
Form of government: republic with one legislative house (National Assembly [66[1]]).
Chief of state: President.
Head of government: Prime Minister.
Capital: Port Louis.
Official language: English.
Official religion: none.
Monetary unit: 1 Mauritian rupee (Mau Re; plural Mau Rs) = 100 cents; valuation (Oct. 3, 1997) 1 U.S.$ = Mau Rs 21.78; 1 £ = Mau Rs 35.10.

Area and population

Islands Districts/Dependencies	area sq mi	area sq km	population 1996[2] estimate
Mauritius	720	1,865	1,094,430
Black River	100	259	49,819
Flacq	115	298	119,845
Grand Port	100	260	103,068
Moka	89	231	70,801
Pamplemousses	69	179	111,328
Plaines Wilhems	78	203	344,958
Port Louis	17	43	136,638
Rivière du Rempart	57	148	93,850
Savanne	95	245	64,123
Mauritian dependencies			
Agalega[3] Cargados Carajos Shoals (Saint Brandon)[3]	27	71	170
Rodrigues[4]	40	104	34,828
TOTAL	788[5]	2,040[5]	1,129,428

Demography

Population (1997): 1,143,000.
Density (1997): persons per sq mi 1,450.5, persons per sq km 560.3.
Urban-rural (1994): urban 43.6%; rural 56.4%.
Sex distribution (1995): male 50.02%; female 49.98%.
Age breakdown (1995)[6]: under 15, 27.3%; 15–29, 27.2%; 30–44, 24.6%; 45–59, 12.3%; 60–74, 6.8%; 75 and over, 1.8%.
Population projection: (2000) 1,270,000; (2010) 1,176,000.
Doubling time: 54 years.
Ethnic composition (1992): Indo-Pakistani 68.0%; Creole (mixed Caucasian, Indo-Pakistani, and African) 27.0%; Chinese 3.0%; white 2.0%.
Religious affiliation (1990): Hindu 50.6%; Roman Catholic 27.2%; Muslim 16.3%; Protestant 5.2%; Buddhist 0.3%; other 0.4%.
Major cities (1995): Port Louis 145,584; Beau Bassin–Rose Hill 98,014; Vacoas-Phoenix 95,600; Curepipe 77,765; Quatre Bornes 74,636.

Vital statistics

Birth rate per 1,000 population 18.3[6] (world avg. 25.0).
Death rate per 1,000 population (1995): 6.7[6] (world avg. 9.3).
Natural increase rate per 1,000 population (1995): 11.6[6] (world avg. 15.7).
Total fertility rate (avg. births per childbearing woman; 1995): 2.1[6].
Marriage rate per 1,000 population (1995): 9.5[6].
Life expectancy at birth (1993–95): male 66.5 years; female 74.0 years.
Major causes of death per 100,000 population (1995): diseases of the circulatory system 288.6; diseases of the respiratory system 63.4; malignant neoplasms (cancers) 60.2; homicide, suicide, and accidents 49.9.

National economy

Budget (1995–96). Revenue: Mau Rs 14,250,100,000 (tax revenue 86.3%, of which import duties 39.3%, income tax 14.3%, sales tax 10.2%, excise tax 8.0%). Expenditures: Mau Rs 15,900,000 (social services 36.1%, of which education, art, and culture 14.6%, social security 12.1%, health 8.0%.
Tourism (1995): receipts from visitors U.S.$430,000,000; expenditures by nationals abroad U.S.$159,000,000.
Public debt (external, outstanding; 1995): U.S.$1,182,000,000.
Gross national product (at current market prices; 1995): U.S.$3,815,000,000 (U.S.$3,380 per capita).

Structure of gross domestic product and labour force

	1996 in value Mau Rs '000,000	1996 % of total value	1995 labour force[7,8]	1995 % of labour force[7,8]
Agriculture	6,410	8.6	39,700	13.7
Mining	110	0.1	200	0.1
Manufacturing	15,490	20.8	103,800	35.8
Construction	4,300	5.8	10,800	3.7
Public utilities	1,550	2.1	3,500	1.2
Transp. and commun.	8,040	10.8	14,500	5.0
Trade	11,090	14.9	24,500	8.5
Finance	10,870	14.5	...	...
Pub. admin., defense	6,865	9.2	77,500	26.8
Services	4,250	5.7		
Other	5,625[9]	7.5[9]	15,100	5.2
TOTAL	74,600	100.0	289,600	100.0

Production (metric tons except as noted). Agriculture, forestry, fishing (1995): sugarcane 5,159,000, green tea 19,512, potatoes 15,718, tomatoes 13,486, bananas 9,437, cabbages 5,200, black tea 5,000, pineapples 4,199, onions 3,600, peanuts (groundnuts) 1,049; livestock (number of live animals) 98,000 goats, 34,000 cattle, 17,000 pigs, 7,000 sheep; roundwood 12,400 cu m; fish catch (1995) 16,023. Manufacturing (value added in Mau Rs '000; 1994): apparel 5,065,000; beverages and tobacco 1,995,800; food products 1,580,400; metal and metal products 882,900; textile yarn and fabrics 676,400; chemical products 505,600. Construction (1994): residential 1,097,858 sq m; nonresidential 210,755 sq m. Energy production (consumption): electricity (kW-hr; 1995) 922,100,000 (904,000,000); coal (metric tons; 1994) none (65,000); petroleum products (metric tons; 1994) none (476,000).
Population economically active (1994)[10]: total 503,346; activity rate of total population 46.5% (participation rates: ages 15–64, 67.0%; female 34.5%; unemployed 7.1%).

Price and earnings indexes (1990 = 100)

	1990	1991	1992	1993	1994	1995	1996
Consumer price index	100.0	107.0	112.0	123.7	132.8	140.8	150.0
Monthly earnings index[8]	100.0	115.8	128.5	135.6	164.2	...	...

Household income and expenditure. Average household size (1990) 4.5[10]; income per household (1979) Mau Rs 15,540 (U.S.$2,430); sources of income (1990): salaries and wages 48.4%, entrepreneurial income 41.2%, transfer payments 10.4%; expenditure (1986–87)[11]: food, beverages, and tobacco 49.1%, housing 13.5%, transportation 9.3%, clothing and footwear 8.4%, recreation, entertainment, education, and cultural services 6.0%.
Land use (1994): forested 21.7%; meadows and pastures 3.4%; agricultural and under permanent cultivation 52.2%; other 22.7%.

Foreign trade[12]

Balance of trade (current prices)

	1989	1990	1991	1992	1993	1994
U.S.$'000,000	−211.1	−280.0	−222.6	−170.8	−254.2	−392.8
% of total	9.6%	10.6%	8.4%	6.2%	8.9%	12.5%

Imports (1995): Mau Rs 34,363,000,000 (manufactured goods classified chiefly by material 34.4%, machinery and transport equipment 25.8%, food 13.6%, chemicals 7.8%, mineral fuels and lubricants 7.0%, inedible crude materials excluding fuels 3.5%, animal and vegetable oils and fats 1.3%). *Major import sources:* France 12.9%; South Africa 11.1%; India 8.4%; United Kingdom 6.6%; Japan 4.8%; Hong Kong 4.8%; Germany 4.5%; Malaysia 2.9%.
Exports (1995): Mau Rs 27,326,000,000 (clothing 54.2%, sugar 23.1%, yarn 3.8%, pearls and precious stones 1.7%). *Major export destinations:* United Kingdom 33.6%; France 20.7%; United States 14.5%; Germany 5.7%.

Transport and communications

Transport. Railroads: none. Roads (1991): total length 1,138 mi, 1,831 km (paved 93%). Vehicles (1995): passenger cars 37,766; trucks and buses 10,625. Air transport (1996)[13]: passenger-km 3,403,889,000; metric ton-km cargo 136,344,000; airports (1997) with scheduled flights 1.

Communications

Medium	date	unit	number	units per 1,000 persons
Daily newspapers	1995	circulation	55,000[14]	49[14]
Radio	1996	receivers	400,000	353
Television	1995	receivers	168,300	150
Telephones	1995	main lines	148,228	132
Cellular telephones	1995	subscribers	11,700	10
Facsimile machines	1995	units	20,000	18
Personal computers	1995	units	36,000	32

Education and health

Educational attainment (1990). Percentage of population age 25 and over having: no formal education 18.3%; incomplete primary 42.6%; primary 6.1%; incomplete secondary 18.0%; secondary 13.1%; higher 1.9%. *Literacy* (1995): percentage of total population age 15 and over literate 82.9%; males literate 87.1%; females literate 78.8%.

Education (1995)

	schools	teachers	students	student/teacher ratio
Primary (age 5–12)	279	6,381	122,895	19.3
Secondary (age 12–20)	123	4,375	91,104	20.8
Voc., teacher tr.	19[15]	69[16]	2,052[17]	...
Higher	2	526[18]	2,344	7.7[18]

Health (1995): physicians 960 (1 per 1,182 persons); hospital beds (1993) 3,330 (1 per 351 persons); infant mortality rate per 1,000 live births 19.7[6].
Food (1995): daily per capita caloric intake 2,943 (vegetable products 84%, animal products 16%); 130% of FAO recommended minimum requirement.

Military

Total active duty personnel: none; however, a special 1,300-person paramilitary force ensures internal security. *Military expenditure as percentage of GNP* (1994): 0.3% (world 3.0%); per capita expenditure U.S.$10.

[1]Includes 4 nonelective seats. [2]January 1. [3]Administered directly from Port Louis. [4]Administered by resident commissioner assisted by local council. [5]Detail does not add to total given because of rounding. [6]Excludes Agalega and Cargados Carajos Shoals. [7]Employed persons in establishments employing 10 or more persons. [8]March. [9]Indirect taxes less imputed bank service charges. [10]Island of Mauritius only. [11]Current weights of CPI components; Island of Mauritius only. [12]Import figures are f.o.b. in balance of trade and c.i.f. for commodities and trading partners. [13]Air Mauritius only. [14]Circulation for 5 newspapers only. [15]1992. [16]1982. [17]1993. [18]1991.

Mexico

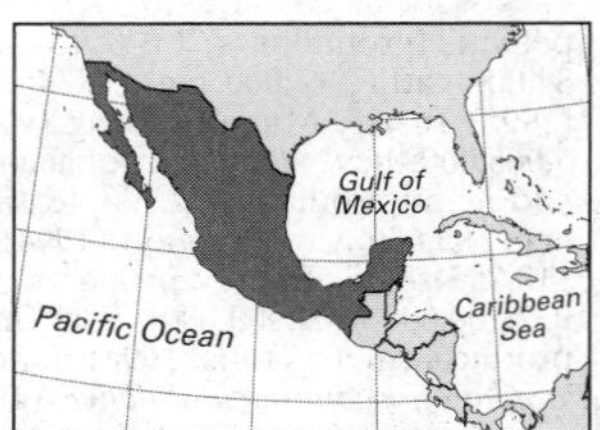

Official name: Estados Unidos Mexicanos (United Mexican States).
Form of government: federal republic with two legislative houses (Senate [128]; Chamber of Deputies [500]).
Chief of state and head of government: President.
Capital: Mexico City.
Official language: Spanish.
Official religion: none.
Monetary unit: 1 Mexican peso[1] (Mex$) = 100 centavos; valuation (Oct. 3, 1997) 1 U.S.$ = Mex$7.75; 1 £ = Mex$12.50.

Area and population

		area		population
States	Capitals	sq mi	sq km	1995 estimate
Aguascalientes	Aguascalientes	2,112	5,471	862,720
Baja California Norte	Mexicali	26,997	69,921	2,112,140
Baja California Sur	La Paz	28,369	73,475	375,494
Campeche	Campeche	19,619	50,812	642,516
Chiapas	Tuxtla Gutiérrez	28,653	74,211	3,584,786
Chihuahua	Chihuahua	94,571	244,938	2,793,537
Coahuila	Saltillo	57,908	149,982	2,173,775
Colima	Colima	2,004	5,191	488,028
Durango	Durango	47,560	123,181	1,431,748
Guanajuato	Guanajuato	11,773	30,491	4,406,568
Guerrero	Chilpancingo	24,819	64,281	2,916,567
Hidalgo	Pachuca	8,036	20,813	2,112,473
Jalisco	Guadalajara	31,211	80,836	5,991,176
México	Toluca	8,245	21,355	11,707,964
Michoacán	Morelia	23,138	59,928	3,870,604
Morelos	Cuernavaca	1,911	4,950	1,442,662
Nayarit	Tepic	10,417	26,979	896,702
Nuevo León	Monterrey	25,067	64,924	3,550,114
Oaxaca	Oaxaca	36,275	93,952	3,228,895
Puebla	Puebla	13,090	33,902	4,624,365
Querétaro	Querétaro	4,420	11,449	1,250,476
Quintana Roo	Chetumal	19,387	50,212	703,536
San Luis Potosí	San Luis Potosí	24,351	63,068	2,200,763
Sinaloa	Culiacán	22,521	58,328	2,425,675
Sonora	Hermosillo	70,291	182,052	2,085,536
Tabasco	Villahermosa	9,756	25,267	1,748,769
Tamaulipas	Ciudad Victoria	30,650	79,384	2,527,328
Tlaxcala	Tlaxcala	1,551	4,016	883,924
Veracruz	Xalapa (Jalapa)	27,683	71,699	6,737,324
Yucatán	Mérida	14,827	38,402	1,556,622
Zacatecas	Zacatecas	28,283	73,252	1,336,496
Federal District				
Distrito Federal	—	571	1,479	8,489,007
TOTAL		756,066	1,958,201	91,158,290

Demography

Population (1997): 94,275,000.
Density (1997): persons per sq mi 124.7, persons per sq km 48.1.
Urban-rural (1990): urban 71.3%; rural 28.7%.
Sex distribution (1995): male 49.88%; female 50.12%.
Age breakdown (1995): under 15, 35.9%; 15–29, 30.1%; 30–44, 18.2%; 45–59, 9.5%; 60–74, 4.8%; 75 and over, 1.5%.
Population projection: (2000) 98,881,000; (2010) 112,891,000.
Doubling time: 27 years.
Ethnic composition (1990): mestizo 60.0%; Amerindian 30.0%; Caucasian 9.0%; other 1.0%.
Religious affiliation (1990): Roman Catholic 89.7%; Protestant (including Evangelical) 4.9%; Jewish 0.1%; other 2.1%; none 3.2%.
Major cities (1990): Mexico City 9,815,795; Guadalajara 1,650,042; Ciudad Netzahualcóyotl 1,255,456; Monterrey 1,068,996; Puebla 1,007,170; Juarez 789,522; León 758,279; Tijuana 698,752; Mérida 523,422; Chihuahua 516,153.
Place of birth (1990): 93.1% native-born; 6.9% foreign-born and unknown.
Mobility (1990). Population 5 years and older living in the same state as in 1985: 94.3%; different state 4.9%; unspecified 0.8%.
Households. Total households (1992) 17,152,000; distribution by size (1990): 1 person 1.0%, 2 persons 4.3%, 3 persons 8.9%, 4 persons 14.9%, 5 persons 17.4%, 6 persons 15.3%, 7 or more persons 38.2%. Family households (1990): 17,064,507 (98.4%); nonfamily 1,039,738 (1.3%); unspecified 256,554 (0.3%).
Immigration (1987): permanent immigrants admitted 72,649.
Emigration (1995): legal immigrants into the United States 89,900.

Vital statistics

Birth rate per 1,000 population (1995): 30.4 (world avg. 25.0); (1983) legitimate 72.5%; illegitimate 27.5%.
Death rate per 1,000 population (1995): 4.8 (world avg. 9.3).
Natural increase rate per 1,000 population (1995): 25.6 (world avg. 15.7).
Total fertility rate (avg. births per childbearing woman; 1995): 3.1.
Marriage rate per 1,000 population (1994): 7.2.
Divorce rate per 1,000 population (1995): 0.4.
Life expectancy at birth (1994): male 66.5 years; female 73.1 years.
Major causes of death per 100,000 population (1995): heart diseases 69.8; malignant neoplasms (cancers) 52.9; accidents 39.0; diabetes mellitus 36.6; cerebrovascular diseases 25.7; cirrhosis of the liver 23.3; conditions originating in the perinatal period 22.5; pneumonia and influenza 21.6; homicide 17.1.

Social indicators

Access to services (1994). Proportion of dwellings having: electricity 91.1%; piped water supply 82.0%; drained sewage 67.7%.
Educational attainment (1992). Percentage of population age 15 and over having: no primary education 14.1%; some primary 22.3%; completed primary 20.7%; incomplete secondary 10.4%; complete secondary 24.2%; higher 8.3%.

Distribution of income (1994)

percentage of household income by quintile

1	2	3	4	5 (highest)
4.8	8.6	12.8	19.5	54.3

Quality of working life. Average workweek (1995) 43.4 hours[2]. Annual rate (1992) per 100,000 insured workers for: temporary disability 6,426; indemnification for permanent injury 239; death 18. Labour stoppages (1995): 96, involving 12,249 workers. Average duration of journey to work: n.a. Method of transport: n.a. Rate per 1,000 workers of discouraged (unemployed no longer seeking work): n.a.
Social participation. Eligible voters participating in last national election (1991): *c.* 60%. Population participating in voluntary work: n.a. Trade union membership in total workforce: n.a. Practicing religious population in total affiliated population: national average of weekly attendance (1993) 11%; (1970) weekly attendance 10% of urban dwellers, 25% of rural dwellers; yearly attendance 55% of urban dwellers, 73% of rural dwellers.
Social deviance (1991). Criminal cases tried by local authorities per 100,000 population for: murder 60.3; rape 22.4; other assault 301.0; theft 703.8. Incidence per 100,000 in general population of: alcoholism, n.a.; drug and substance abuse, n.a.[3]; suicide (1994) 2.47.
Leisure (1985). Favourite leisure activities (average daily paid attendance): cinema 582,416; sporting events 31,518; live theatre 16,400; museums and archaeological sites 12,169; bullfights 3,049.
Material well-being (1985). Households possessing: radio 96%; television 73%; washing machine 33%; automobile 29%; telephone 27%; refrigerator 23%.

National economy

Gross national product (1995): U.S.$304,596,000,000 (U.S.$3,320 per capita).

Structure of gross domestic product and labour force

	1996		1995[4]	
	in value Mex$'000,000[1]	% of total value	labour force	% of labour force
Agriculture	74,959.1	5.8	8,378,000	23.6
Mining	17,575.3	1.3	147,000	0.4
Manufacturing	241,487.3	18.7	5,168,000	14.5
Construction	51,196.9	4.0	1,819,000	5.1
Public utilities	20,492.1	1.6	80,000	0.2
Transp. and commun.	120,768.1	9.3	1,461,000	4.1
Trade	236,186.9	18.2	7,799,000	21.9
Finance	195,310.4	15.1	1,104,000	3.1
Pub. admin., defense } Services	263,675.3	20.4	7,765,000	21.8
Other	71,966.2[5]	5.6[5]	1,836,400[6]	5.2[6]
TOTAL	1,293,617.6	100.0	35,558,400[7]	100.0[7]

Budget (1994). Revenue: Mex$213,467,000,000[1] (petroleum revenues 24.8%). Expenditures: Mex$221,202,000,000[1] (transfers 53.7%, wages and salaries 19.1%, interest on public debt 12.2%).
Public debt (external, outstanding; 1995): U.S.$94,027,000,000.
Tourism (1995): receipts from visitors U.S.$6,164,000,000; expenditures by nationals abroad U.S.$3,153,000,000.

Manufacturing, mining, and construction enterprises (1993)

	no. of enterprises	no. of employees ('000)	yearly wages as a % of avg. of all wages[8]	value added (Mex$'000,000[1, 8])
Manufacturing	266,033	3,174.4	97.5	20,950,900
Metal products	46,667[9]	955.6[9]	114.2[9]	6,605,300[9]
Chemicals	7,321	371.2	152.3	4,228,000
Food, beverages, and tobacco	91,894	679.3	86.4	3,378,700
Textiles and apparel	44,071	530.6	80.0	2,414,800
Iron and steel	401	57.4	128.2	1,332,400
Nonmetallic mineral products	24,397	181.8	98.6	1,177,700
Paper and printing	15,022	193.2	100.0	1,127,900
Wood and wood products	31,549	162.6	62.8	497,000
Nonelectrical machinery and transport equipment	[9]	[9]	...[9]	[9]
Electrical machinery	[9]	[9]	...[9]	[9]
Other manufactures	4,711	42.7	...	189,200
Mining	2,845	95.6	161.0	1,643,800
Construction	5,308[8]	342.4[8]	62.1	1,414,800

Production (metric tons except as noted). Agriculture, forestry, fishing (1996): sugarcane 46,980,000, corn (maize) 17,300,000, sorghum 4,817,000, wheat 3,563,000, oranges 3,556,000, bananas 2,158,000, tomatoes 2,145,000, dry beans 1,495,000, mangoes 1,420,000, lemons and limes 1,001,000, apples 645,000, barley 616,000, cottonseed 596,000, grapes 535,000, rice 455,000, soybeans 350,000, pineapples 181,000, strawberries 85,000, walnuts 18,000; livestock (number of live animals) 28,141,000 cattle, 15,405,000 pigs, 10,500,000 goats, 6,250,000 horses, 5,987,000 sheep, 3,550,000 turkeys, 3,270,000 mules, 3,250,000 asses, 386,000,000 chickens; roundwood (1995) 22,034,000 cu m; fish catch (1995) 1,358,000. Mining and quarrying (value of production [metal content] in Mex$'000; 1993): copper 2,236,437; silver 1,339,057; zinc 1,321,759; gold 605,850; iron 530,658; lead 457,307; sulfur 219,833; gypsum 160,139; dolomite 119,728; fluorite 110,838; molybdenum 88,043; manganese 77,918; silica 68,956; bismuth 25,166; celestite 25,045. Manufacturing (gross value of production in Mex$'000[1]; 1994): machinery and equipment 82,169,495; food, beverages, and tobacco products 64,399,498; chemical products

50,455,651; metal products 25,363,292; mineral products 17,074,973; paper and paper products 9,209,617; textiles 8,555,146. Construction (gross value of new construction, in Mex$'000,000[1]; 1985): residential 154,835; nonresidential 168,096.

Trade and service enterprises (1993)

	no. of establishments	no. of employees	yearly wage as a % of avg. of all wages[10]	annual income (Mex$'000,000[1])
Trade	1,208,779	2,969,786	...	565,728,373
Wholesale	68,919	631,802	...	249,597,035
Retail	1,139,860	2,337,984	...	316,131,338
Boutiques (excluding food products)	422,299	922,890	...	108,507,889
Food and tobacco speciality stores	671,050	991,911	...	65,305,180
Automobile, tire, and auto parts dealers	32,138	152,821	...	47,888,576
Small supermarkets and grocery stores	8,719	168,752	...	48,769,283
Gasoline stations	3,042	35,340	...	32,517,091
Other	2,612	66,270	...	13,143,319
Services	711,843	2,766,750	85.2	200,001,682
Professional services	130,475	652,148	77.9	53,533,318
Food and beverage services	677	11,258	...	1,012,369
Transp. and travel agencies	9,967	62,767	133.4	11,858,406
Lodging	9,913	151,445	...	8,960,922
Automotive repair	112,293	252,950	...	7,263,560
Educational services (private)	20,622	247,086	134.3	10,815,238
Medical and social assistance	79,748	203,348	206.4	7,497,794
Amusement services (cinemas and theatres)	4,855	65,608	148.9	9,845,129
Recreation	20,973	65,936	...	3,065,672
Other repair	72,129	104,478	...	2,625,370
Commercial and professional organizations	1,946	11,946	77.9	264,770
Other	248,245	937,780	49.9	83,259,134

Energy production (consumption): electricity (kW-hr; 1994) 144,276,000,000 (143,447,000,000); coal (metric tons; 1994) 8,898,000 (9,188,000); crude petroleum (barrels; 1994) 972,000,000 (500,000,000); petroleum products (metric tons; 1994) 83,618,000 (89,164,000); natural gas (cu m; 1994) 26,378,000,000 (27,206,000,000).

Population economically active (1995): total 35,558,484; activity rate of total population 39.4% (participation rates: ages 15–64, 61.8%; female 32.6%; unemployed 4.7%[4]).

Price and earnings indexes (1990 = 100)

	1990	1991	1992	1993	1994	1995	1996
Consumer price index	100.0	122.7	141.7	155.5	166.3	224.5	301.7
Monthly earnings index	100.0	129.1	292.9	164.7	174.6	192.1	290.6[11]

Household income and expenditure. Average household size (1992) 4.8; income per household (1989) Mex$3,461[1] (U.S.$1,384); sources of income (1992): wages and salaries 61.5%, property and entrepreneurship 29.1%, transfer payments 7.8%, other 1.6%; expenditure (1992): food, beverages, and tobacco 36.9%, housing (includes household furnishings) 25.2%, transportation and communications 10.1%, clothing and footwear 8.5%, recreation and entertainment 5.5%, health and medical services 3.5%.

Financial aggregates[1, 12]

	1991	1992	1993	1994	1995	1996	1997 (7 mo.)
Exchange rate, Mex$ per:							
U.S. dollar	3.018	3.095	3.116	3.375	6.419	7.599	7.886
£	5.114	5.464	4.680	5.164	10.132	11.867	13.180
SDR	4.393	4.284	4.266	7.774	11.361	11.289	10.609
International reserves (U.S.$)							
Total (excl. gold; '000,000)	17,726	18,942	25,110	6,278	16,847	19,433	24,566
SDRs ('000,000)	586	548	223	177	1,597	257	568
Reserve pos. in IMF ('000,000)	—	—	—	—	—	—	—
Foreign exchange	17,140	18,394	24,886	6,101	15,250	17,217	19,176
Gold ('000,000 fine troy oz)	0.92	0.69	0.48	0.43	0.51	0.26	0.22
% world reserves	0.10	0.07	0.05	0.05	0.06	0.03	0.02
Interest and prices							
Treasury bill rate	19.28	15.62	15.03	14.10	48.44	31.39	18.80
Balance of payments (U.S.$'000,000)							
Balance of visible trade, of which:	−7,279	−15,934	−13,481	−18,464	+7,089	+6,531	...
Imports, f.o.b.	−49,966	−62,130	−65,366	−79,347	−72,454	−89,469	...
Exports, f.o.b.	42,687	46,196	51,885	60,882	79,543	96,000	...
Balance of invisibles	−7,609	−8,508	−9,919	−11,198	−8,665	−8,454	...
Balance of payments, current account	−14,888	−24,442	−23,400	−29,662	−1,576	−1,923	...

Land use (1994): forest 25.5%; pasture 39.0%; agriculture 13.0%; other 22.5%.

Foreign trade

Balance of trade (current prices)

	1990	1991	1992	1993	1994	1995
Mex$'000,000,000	−7,494.0	−27,746	−57,138	−53,615	−80,166	+19,923
% of total	4.7%	14.4%	25.1%	22.2%	25.6%	3.4%

Imports (1996): U.S.$89,468,800,000 (intermediate goods 80.4%; capital goods 12.2%; consumer goods 7.4%). *Major import sources:* U.S. 75.6%; Japan 4.4%; Germany 3.5%; Canada 1.9%; South Korea 1.3%; France 1.1%.

Exports (1996): U.S.$97,922,700,000 (manufacturing goods 82.1%; crude petroleum 10.9%; agricultural goods 3.7%). *Major export destinations:* U.S. 84.0%; Japan 1.4%; Canada 1.2%; Italy 1.2%; Spain 1.0%; Germany 0.7%.

Trade by commodity group (1995)

SITC group	imports U.S.$'000,000	imports %	exports U.S.$'000,000	exports %
00 Food and live animals	3,225	4.4	5,434	6.8
01 Beverages and tobacco	144	0.2	585	0.7
02 Crude materials, excluding fuels	3,213	4.4	2,007	2.5
03 Mineral fuels, lubricants, and related materials	1,585	2.1	8,186	10.3
04 Animal and vegetable oils, fats, and waxes	581	0.8	—	—
05 Chemicals and related products, n.e.s.	6,899	9.3	3,876	4.9
06 Basic manufactures	12,377	16.7	8,982	11.3
07 Machinery and transport equipment	31,693	42.8	41,634	52.4
08 Miscellaneous manufactured articles	9,318	12.6	8,507	10.7
09 Goods not classified by kind	4,958	6.7	218	0.3
TOTAL[13]	73,993	100.0	79,489[7]	100.0[7]

Direction of trade (1996)

	imports U.S.$'000,000	imports %	exports U.S.$'000,000	exports %
Western Hemisphere	71,590	80.0	87,742	91.4
United States	67,629	75.6	80,663	84.0
Latin America and the Caribbean	2,217	2.5	5,898	6.2
Canada	1,744	1.9	1,181	1.2
Europe	8,423	9.4	4,798	5.0
EU	7,733	8.7	4,190	4.4
EFTA	484	0.5	398	0.4
Russia	—	—	—	—
Other Europe	206	0.2	210	0.2
Asia	8,587	9.6	2,457	2.5
Japan	3,901	4.4	1,363	1.4
Africa	219	0.3	65	0.1
Other	645	0.7	929	1.0
TOTAL	89,464	100.0	95,991	100.0

Transport and communications

Transport. Railroads (1995): route length (1996) 16,543 mi, 26,623 km; passenger-mi 1,118,000,000, passenger-km 1,800,000,000; short ton-mi cargo 24,509,000,000, metric ton-km cargo 37,243,000,000. Roads (1996): total length 194,054 mi, 312,301 km (paved 36%[14]). Vehicles (1995): passenger cars 8,330,000; trucks and buses 4,221,000. Merchant marine (1992): vessels (100 gross tons and over) 635; total deadweight tonnage 1,495,311. Air transport (1996): passenger-mi 12,901,853,000, passenger-km 20,763,559,000; short ton-mi cargo 1,348,141,000, metric ton-km cargo 1,968,250,000; airports (1996) 83.

Communications

Medium	date	unit	number	units per 1,000 persons
Daily newspapers	1995	circulation	10,500,000	115
Radio	1996	receivers	21,000,000	227
Television	1995	receivers	17,600,000	192
Telephones	1995	main lines	8,736,000	96
Cellular telephones	1995	subscribers	642,000	7.0
Facsimile machines	1995	units	180,000	2.0
Personal computers	1995	units	2,400,000	26

Education and health

Literacy (1995): total population age 15 and over literate 89.6%; males literate 91.8%; females literate 87.4%.

Education (1994–95)

	schools	teachers	students	student/teacher ratio
Primary (age 6–12)	91,857	507,669	14,572,202	28.7
Secondary (age 12–18)	22,255	256,831	4,493,173	17.5
Voc., teacher tr.[15]	6,571	77,347	1,076,700	13.9
Higher	10,341	319,551	3,763,938	11.8

Health (1994): physicians 146,021 (1 per 613 persons); hospital beds 74,891 (1 per 1,196 persons); infant mortality rate per 1,000 live births (1995) 17.5.

Food (1995): daily per capita caloric intake 3,136 (vegetable products 84%, animal products 16%); 131% of FAO recommended minimum requirement.

Military

Total active duty personnel (1997): 175,000 (army 74.3%, navy 21.1%, air force 4.6%). *Military expenditure as percentage of GNP* (1995): 1.0% (world 2.8%); per capita expenditure U.S.$25.

[1]The Mexican new peso, equivalent to 1,000 old Mexican pesos, was introduced on Jan. 1, 1993. On Jan. 1, 1996, the name of the currency was changed to Mexican peso. [2]Manufacturing only. [3]Through 1982, cannabis remained the most abused drug. [4]2nd quarter. [5]Imputed bank service charge. [6]Includes 1,677,400 unemployed persons. [7]Detail does not add to total given because of rounding. [8]1988. [9]Metal products includes Nonelectrical machinery and transport equipment and Electrical machinery. [10]1984. [11]June. [12]Exchange rates and treasury bill rates are expressed in period averages; international reserves are expressed in end-of-period rates. [13]Totals include adjustments of unspecified nature. [14]1993. [15]1992–93.

Internet resources for further information:

- **National Institute of Statistics, Geography, and Informatics**
http://www.inegi.gob.mx/homeing/homeinegi/homeing.html

Micronesia, Federated States of

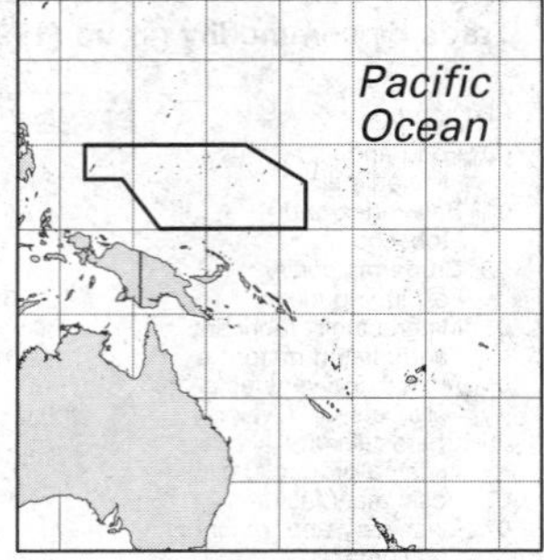

Official name: Federated States of Micronesia.
Political status: federal republic in free association with the United States with one legislative house (Congress [14])[1].
Head of state and government: President.
Capital: Palikir, on Pohnpei.
Official language: none.
Official religion: none.
Monetary unit: 1 U.S. dollar (U.S.$) = 100 cents; valuation (Oct. 3, 1997) 1 £ = U.S.$1.61.

Area and population

States / Major Islands	area sq mi	area sq km	population 1994 census
Chuuk (Truk)	49.1	127.2	53,319
Weno (Moen) Islands	7.0	18.1	16,121
Kosrae	42.3	109.6	7,317
Kosrae Island	42.3	109.6	7,317
Pohnpei	133.3	345.2	33,692
Pohnpei Island	129.0	334.1	31,540
Yap	45.9	118.9	11,178
Yap Island	38.7	100.2	6,919
TOTAL	270.8[2]	701.4[2]	105,506

Demography

Population (1997): 109,000.
Density (1997): persons per sq mi 402.5, persons per sq km 150.4.
Urban-rural (1992): urban 26.0%; rural 74.0%.
Sex distribution (1994): male 51.11%; female 48.89%.
Age breakdown (1994): under 15, 43.5%; 15–29, 26.7%; 30–44, 16.8%; 45–59, 7.5%; 60–74, 4.4%; 75 and over, 4.4%.
Population projection: (2000) 113,000; (2010) 127,000.
Doubling time: 36 years.
Ethnic composition (1994): Chuukese 46.7%; Pohnpeian 24.3%; Kosraean 6.8%; Yapese 5.4%; Mortlockese 4.9%; Filipino 0.8%; other 11.1%.
Religious affiliation (1996): Christianity is the predominant religious tradition; Catholic 52.9%, Protestant 47.1%; the Kosraeans, Pohnpeians, and Trukese are mostly Protestant and the Yapese mostly Roman Catholic.
Major cities (1994): Weno (Moen) 16,121; Tol 4,816; Kolonia 6,660.

Vital statistics

Birth rate per 1,000 population (1995): 23.7 (world avg. 25.0); legitimate, n.a.; illegitimate, n.a.
Death rate per 1,000 population (1995): 4.0 (world avg. 9.3).
Natural increase rate per 1,000 population (1995): 19.7 (world avg. 15.7).
Total fertility rate (avg. births per childbearing woman; 1994): 2.5.
Marriage rate per 1,000 population: n.a.
Divorce rate per 1,000 population: n.a.
Life expectancy at birth (1994): male 65.7 years; female 69.6 years.
Major causes of death per 100,000 population (1991)[3]: diseases of the cerebrovascular system 89.6; diseases of the respiratory system 42.8, of which tuberculosis 8.9; malignant neoplasms (cancers) 38.8; homicide, suicide, and accidents 30.8; infectious and parasitic diseases 22.9 (with especially high morbidity rates for tuberculosis and leprosy).

National economy

Budget (1994–95). Revenue: U.S.$172,500,000 (external grants 65.1%; tax revenue 12.2%; fishing rights fees 12.1%). Expenditures: U.S.$169,100,000 (current expenditures 82.6%, of which government services 74.4%, transfer payments 7.0%, debt services 3.0%; capital expenditure 17.4%).
Public debt (external, outstanding; 1994–95): U.S.$119,500,000.
Production (metric tons except as noted). Agriculture, forestry, fishing: n.a.; however, Micronesia's major crops include coconuts (which provide annually more than 4,000 tons of copra), breadfruit, cassava, sweet potatoes, peppers, and a variety of tropical fruits (including bananas); livestock comprises mostly pigs and poultry; fish catch (1995) 21,150, of which skipjack tuna 15,000, yellowfin tuna 5,000. Mining and quarrying: quarrying of sand and aggregate for local construction only. Manufacturing: n.a.; however, copra and coconut oil, traditionally important products, are being displaced by garment production; the manufacture of handicrafts and personal items (clothing, mats, boats, etc.) by individuals is also important. Construction: n.a. Energy production (consumption): electricity (kW-hr; 1990) 40,000,000 (40,000,000); coal, none (n.a.); crude petroleum, none (n.a.); petroleum products (metric tons; 1992) none (77,000); natural gas, none (n.a.).
Household income and expenditure. Average household size (1994) 6.8; annual income per household (1994) U.S.$8,645; sources of income (1994): wages and salaries 51.8%, operating surplus 23.0%, social security 2.1%; expenditure (1985): food and beverages 73.5%.
Land use (1984)[4]: forested 22.5%; meadows and pastures 13.5%; agricultural and under permanent cultivation 33.5%; other 30.5%.
Gross national product (at current market prices; 1995): U.S.$215,000,000 (U.S.$2,040 per capita).

Structure of gross domestic product and labour force

	1983 in value U.S.$'000,000	1983 % of total value	1994 labour force	1994 % of labour force
Agriculture and fishing	44.9	42.2	7,375[5]	26.7[5]
Mining	17.4 (Mining through Services)	16.3 (Mining through Services)	42	0.2
Manufacturing			656	2.4
Construction			1,171	4.2
Public utilities			279	1.0
Transp. and commun.			727	2.6
Finance			632	2.3
Services			2,125	7.7
Trade	12.7	11.9	2,258	8.2
Public administration	31.5	29.6	8,092	29.3
Other			4,216[6]	15.2[6]
TOTAL	106.5	100.0	27,573	100.0[2]

Population economically active (1994): total 27,573; activity rate of total population 26.3% (participation rates: ages 15–64, 60.6%[7]; female 33.8%; unemployed 15.3%).

Price and earnings indexes (1992 = 100)

	1990	1991	1992	1993	1994	1995
Price index	91.6	95.2	100.0	106.0	110.2	114.6
Annual wage index[8]	...	...	100.0	109.4	110.3	115.8

Tourism (1990): number of visitors 23,171.

Foreign trade

Balance of trade (current prices)

	1989	1990	1991	1992	1993	1994
U.S.$'000,000	−55.4	−62.2	−59.9	−57.3	−80.3	−50.5
% of total	61.6%	58.9%	51.0%	40.8%	57.9%	24.3%

Imports (1994): U.S.$129,060,000 (manufactured goods 32.0%; food, beverages, and tobacco 24.3%; machinery and transport equipment 23.5%; mineral fuels 14.3%; chemicals 4.4%). *Major import sources:* United States (including Guam) 56.1%; Japan 32.0%; Australia 3.5%.
Exports (1994): U.S.$78,570,000 (marine products 94.3%; clothing and textiles 2.8%; agricultural products 2.1%, of which bananas 0.6%, copra 0.5%). *Major export destinations* (1992): Japan 80.0%; United States 9.3%; Guam 8.3%; South Pacific Region 2.4%.

Transport and communications

Transport. Railroads: none. Roads (1990): total length 140 mi, 226 km (paved 17%). Vehicles: passenger cars, trucks, and buses, n.a. Merchant marine (1997[9]): vessels (100 gross tons and over) 19; deadweight tonnage 9,200. Air transport: n.a.; airports (1997) with scheduled flights 4.

Communications

Medium	date	unit	number	units per 1,000 persons
Radio	1995	receivers	70,000	664
Television	1995	receivers	2,000	19.0
Telephones	1995	main lines	7,900	74.9
Facsimile machines	1995	units	300	2.8

Education and health

Educational attainment (1994). Percentage of population age 25 and over having: no formal schooling 22.8%; some primary education 30.3%; some secondary 15.1%; secondary 13.6%; some college 13.6%; bachelors degree 3.1%; higher 1.6%. *Literacy* (1994): total population age 10 and over literate 69,779 (93.9%); males literate 35,688 (94.7%); females literate 34,091 (93.0%).

Education (1994)

	schools[10]	teachers	students	student/teacher ratio
Elementary (age 6–12)	177	1,051[11]	22,420	22.2[11]
Secondary (age 13–18)	16	314[11]	8,701	13.2[11]
College	1	...	1,461	...

Health (1993): physicians 50 (1 per 2,069 persons); hospital beds 325 (1 per 318 persons); infant mortality rate per 1,000 live births (1995) 20.4.
Food: daily per capita caloric intake, n.a.

Military

External security is provided by the United States.

[1]On Nov. 3, 1986, the United States unilaterally terminated the UN trusteeship it held over the Federated States of Micronesia (FSM), thus formally initiating their free-association political status. On Dec. 22, 1990, the United Nations Security Council joined the Trusteeship Council, which had endorsed the termination of the trusteeship in May 1986. [2]Detail does not add to total given because of rounding. [3]Based on registered deaths only. [4]Includes all areas formerly constituting the U.S. Trust Territory of the Pacific Islands. [5]Includes subsistence farming and fishing. [6]Unemployed. [7]1990. [8]Public sector only. [9]January 1. [10]1987–88. [11]1984–85.

Internet resources for further information:
- **General Information on The FSM http://fsmgov.org/info**

Moldova

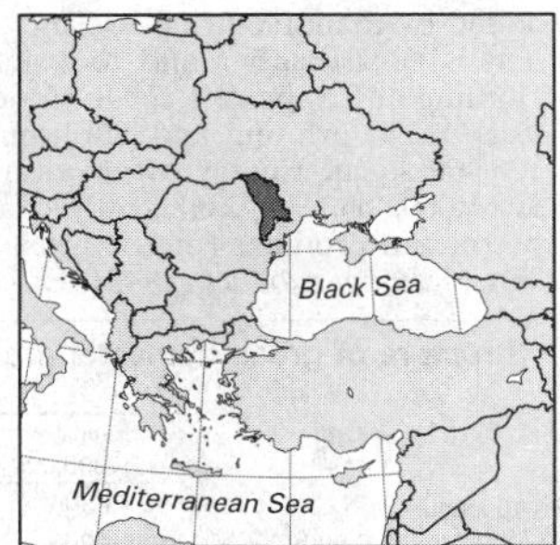

Official name: Republica Moldova (Republic of Moldova).
Form of government: unitary multiparty republic with a single legislative body (Parliament [104]).
Head of state: President.
Head of government: Prime Minister.
Capital: Chişinău.
Official language: Romanian.
Official religion: none.
Monetary unit: 1 Moldovan leu (plural lei) = 100 bani; valuation (Oct. 3, 1997) free rate, 1 U.S.$ = 4.61 Moldovan lei; 1 £ = 7.44 Moldovan lei.

Area and population

Administrative subdivisions[1]

Cities	area sq km[2]	population 1993	Rural districts	area sq km[2]	population 1993
Bălţi	...	159,420	Drochia	780	80,828
Cahul	...	43,259	Dubăsari	670	53,962
Chişinău	160	735,229	Edineţ	860	90,948
Dubăsari	...	24,243	Făleşti	1,070	95,025
Orhei	...	37,887	Floreşti	830	76,987
Râbniţa	...	61,824	Glodeni	760	65,781
Soroca	...	41,461	Grigoriopol	820	52,326
Tighina (Bendery)	...	137,423	Hânceşti	1,350	118,255
Tiraspol	...	203,865	Ialoveni	930	87,749
Ungheni	...	38,462	Leova	720	51,987
Rural districts			Nisporeni	760	81,626
			Ocniţa	660	63,073
Anenil Noi	830	77,468	Orhei	1,100	95,523
Basarabeasca	660	43,765	Râbniţa	850	32,793
Brinceni	810	83,340	Rezina	670	55,494
Cahul	800	44,489	Rişcani	1,000	83,456
Cainari	...	42,755	Sângerei	1,020	91,684
Călăraş	760	84,442	Slobozia	960	113,823
Camenca	820	59,356	Şoldăneşti	560	46,696
Cantemir	860	61,126	Soroca	870	58,097
Căuşeni	1,120	72,999	Ştefan-Vodă	1,030	76,702
Ciadâr-Lunga	720	68,698	Străşeni	760	96,107
Cimişlia	1,170	61,089	Taraclia	620	45,912
Comrat	840	71,273	Teleneşti	860	76,886
Criuleni	850	91,783	Ungheni	1,070	79,525
Donduşeni	890	66,483	Vulcăneşti	930	62,193
			TOTAL	33,700[3]	4,345,577

Demography

Population (1997): 4,362,000.
Density (1997): persons per sq mi 333.8, persons per sq km 128.9.
Urban-rural (1995): urban 46.8%; rural 53.2%.
Sex distribution (1995): male 47.76%; female 52.24%.
Age breakdown (1989): under 15, 27.9%; 15–29, 22.9%; 30–44, 21.0%; 45–59, 15.6%; 60–74, 9.7%; 75 and over, 2.9%.
Population projection: (2000) 4,420,000; (2010) 4,688,000.
Doubling time: not applicable; doubling time exceeds 100 years.
Ethnic composition (1989): Moldovan 64.5%; Ukrainian 13.8%; Russian 13.0%; Gagauz 3.5%; Jewish 2.0%; Bulgarian 1.5%; other 1.7%.
Religious affiliation: believers are predominantly Eastern Orthodox.
Major cities (1993): Chişinău 657,775; Tiraspol 184,852; Bălţi 156,081.

Vital statistics

Birth rate per 1,000 population (1997): 14.3 (world avg. 25.0); (1995) legitimate 87.7%; illegitimate 12.3%.
Death rate per 1,000 population (1997): 12.3 (world avg. 9.3).
Natural increase rate per 1,000 population (1997): 2.0 (world avg. 15.7).
Total fertility rate (avg. births per childbearing woman; 1997): 1.9.
Marriage rate per 1,000 population (1994): 7.8.
Divorce rate per 1,000 population (1994): 3.2.
Life expectancy at birth (1994): male 64.0 years; female 71.0 years.
Major causes of death per 100,000 population (1994): circulatory diseases 500.7; cancers 136.1; accidents and violence 113.3; digestive system diseases 110.4; respiratory diseases 75.1.

National economy

Budget (1995). Revenue: 1,916,000,000,000 lei (value-added tax 29.7%, enterprise profits tax 20.5%, income tax 10.5%, excise duties 9.7%, property tax 5.4%). Expenditures: 2,354,000,000,000 lei (education 24.1%, health care 15.6%, interest payments 11.3%).
Public debt (external, outstanding; 1995): U.S.$454,600,000.
Land use (1994): forest 10.6%; pasture 10.9%; agriculture 75.9%; other 2.6%.
Production (metric tons except as noted). Agriculture, forestry, fishing (1996): sugar beets 1,807,000, grapes 850,000, corn (maize) 750,000, wheat 614,000, potatoes 331,000, apples 330,000; livestock (number of live animals) 1,302,000 sheep, 1,015,000 pigs, 726,000 cattle, 14,000,000 poultry; roundwood (1991) 125,000 cu m; fish catch (1995) 4,700. Mining and quarrying (1995): sand and gravel 376,000; gypsum 13,600. Manufacturing ('000,000 lei; 1995): food processing 1,446,824; machinery and metalworking 383,153; construction materials 164,198; textiles 57,283. Construction (1994): 127,200,000 lei. Energy production (consumption): electricity (kW-hr; 1994) 8,228,000,000 (8,579,000,000); coal (metric tons; 1994) none (2,141,000); crude petroleum (barrels; 1990) none (51,625,000); petroleum products (metric tons; 1994) none (1,085,000); natural gas (cu m; 1994) none (2,611,000,000).
Gross national product (1995): U.S.$3,996,000,000 (U.S.$920 per capita).

Structure of gross domestic product and labour force

	1994			
	in value '000 lei	% of total value	labour force	% of labour force
Agriculture	1,877,607	43.3	767,000	45.1
Manufacturing, mining	1,402,883	32.3	232,000	13.7
Public utilities	...	...	39,000	2.2
Construction	429,551	9.9	91,000	5.4
Transp. and commun.	350,028	8.1	73,000	4.3
Trade	253,969	5.8	107,000	6.3
Finance	...	...	20,000	1.2
Pub. admin., defense	...	...	32,000	1.9
Services	8,176	0.2	305,000	18.0
Other	15,879	0.4	33,000	1.9
TOTAL	4,339,079[4]	100.0	1,699,000	100.0

Population economically active (1994): total (1995) 1,693,000; activity rate of total population 44.8% (participation rates: ages 16–59 [male], 16–54 [female] 85.2%; female 53.0%; unemployed 1.4%).

Price and earnings indexes (1990 = 100)

	1990	1991	1992	1993	1994	1995
Consumer price index	100.0	262.0	3,605	33,780	71,310	88,420
Earnings index	100.0	183.0	402.0	353.0	192.0	244.0

Household income and expenditure. Average household size (1989) 3.4; income per household: n.a.; sources of income (1994): wages and salaries 41.2%, social benefits 15.3%, agricultural income 10.4%, other 33.1%; expenditure (1995): food and drink 49.1%, clothing 9.7%, health 4.1%.

Foreign trade

Balance of trade (current prices)

	1992	1993	1994	1995
U.S.$'000,000	–37	–180	–54	–32
% of total	2.1%	16.6%	4.2%	2.1%

Imports (1995): U.S.$773,000,000 (mineral products 46.0%, machinery 16.0%, agricultural goods and foodstuffs 9.0%, chemical products 8.0%, textiles and textile products 5.0%, metal and metal products 4.0%, other 12.0%). *Major import sources* (1995): Russia 32.0%; Ukraine 26.0%; Romania 7.0%.
Exports (1995): U.S.$741,000,000 (food and agricultural goods 72.0%, machinery 8.0%, textile products 5.0%, metals and metal products 4.0%, chemical products 1.0%, mineral products 1.0%, other 9.0%). *Major export destinations* (1995): Russia 47.0%; Romania 14.0%; Ukraine 8.0%; Belarus 4.0%.

Transport and communications

Transport. Railroads (1995): length 1,200 km; passenger-km 1,019,000,000; metric ton-km cargo 3,133,600,000. Roads (1995): total length 12,259 km (paved 87.2%). Vehicles (1995): passenger cars 169,941; trucks and buses 69,069. Air transport (1994): passenger-km 225,000,000; metric ton-km cargo 1,000,000; airports (1997) 1.

Communications

Medium	date	unit	number	units per 1,000 persons
Daily newspapers	1994	circulation	106,000	24
Radio	1996	receivers	1,550,000	209
Television	1995	receivers	1,300	30
Telephones	1995	main lines	566,500	131
Facsimile machines	1995	units	600	0.1
Personal computers	1995	units	9,000	2.1

Education and health

Educational attainment (1989). Percentage of population age 15 and over having: no formal schooling or some primary education 24.5%; some secondary 20.4%; secondary or some postsecondary 46.4%; higher 8.7%.
Literacy (1989): percentage of total population age 15 and over literate 96.4%; males literate 98.6%; females literate 94.4%.

Education (1995–96)

	schools	teachers	students	student/ teacher ratio
Primary (age 7–13) } Secondary (age 14–17) }	1,700	48,000	733,000	15.3
Voc., teacher tr.	64		27,943	
Higher	20	8,846	87,700	9.9

Health (1995): physicians 17,200 (1 per 250 persons); hospital beds 53,000 (1 per 82 persons); infant mortality rate per 1,000 live births 22.6.
Food (1995): daily per capita caloric intake 2,525 (vegetable products 81%, animal products 19%); 99% of FAO recommended minimum requirement.

Military

Total active duty personnel (1997): 11,030 (army 84.3%, air force 15.7%). *Military expenditure as percentage of GNP* (1995): 0.1% (world 2.8%); per capita expenditure U.S.$3.

[1]Administrative subdivisions at independence in 1991. Area and population figures include the Gagauz autonomous region, recognized by the Moldovan government, and the separatist Transdniestrian republic, not recognized by the Moldovan government. Separate data for these regions is not available. [2]One sq km = 0.3861 sq mi. [3]Total includes approximately 320 sq km (125 sq mi) not distributed by administrative subdivision. [4]Detail does not add to total given because of rounding.

Internet resources for further information:
- **Moldova.Net http://www.moldova.net/**

Mongolia

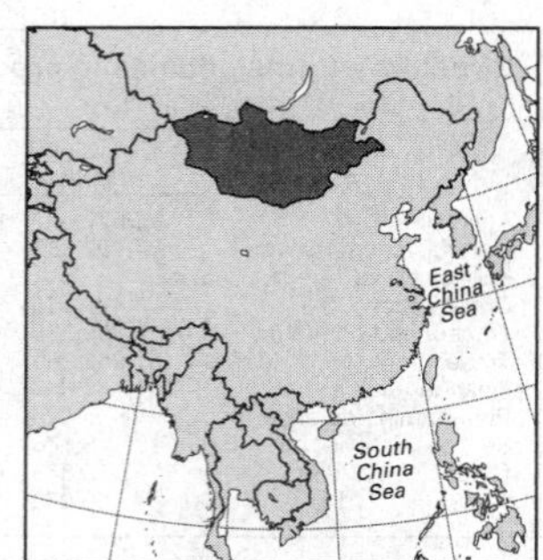

Official name: Mongol Uls (Mongolia).
Form of government: unitary multiparty republic with one legislative house (State Great Hural [76]).
Chief of state: President.
Head of government: Prime Minister.
Capital: Ulaanbaatar (Ulan Bator).
Official language: Khalkha Mongolian.
Official religion: none.
Monetary unit: 1 tugrik (Tug) = 100 möngö; valuation (Oct. 3, 1997) 1 U.S.$ = Tug 784.76; 1 £ = Tug 1,265.03.

Area and population

		area		population
Provinces	**Capitals**	sq mi	sq km	1997[1] estimate
Arhangay	Tsetserleg	21,000	55,000	105,000
Bayan-Ölgiy	Ölgiy	18,000	46,000	92,300
Bayanhongor	Bayanhongor	45,000	116,000	91,200
Bulgan	Bulgan	19,000	49,000	64,300
Darhan-Uul	Darhan	100	200	91,000
Dornod	Choybalsan	47,700	123,500	86,800
Dornogovĭ	Saynshand	43,000	111,000	48,900
Dundgovĭ	Mandalgovi	30,000[2]	78,000[2]	53,700
Dzavhan	Uliastay	32,000	82,000	107,600
Govĭ-Altay	Altay	55,000	142,000	75,400
Govĭ-Sümber	Choyr	[2]	[2]	12,600
Hentiy	Öndörhaan	32,000	82,000	76,500
Hovd	Hovd	29,000	76,000	92,700
Hövsgöl	Mörön	39,000	101,000	122,000
Ömnögovĭ	Dalandzadgad	64,000	165,000	45,800
Orhon	Erdenet	300	800	66,700
Övörhangay	Arvayheer	24,000	63,000	115,100
Selenge	Sühbaatar	16,000	42,000	104,400
Sühbaatar	Baruun-Urt	32,000	82,000	60,200
Töv	Dzüünmod	31,000	81,000	112,200
Uvs	Ulaangom	27,000	69,000	104,300
Autonomous municipality				
Ulaanbaatar	—	800	2,000	627,300
TOTAL		604,800[3]	1,566,500	2,356,000

Demography

Population (1997): 2,370,000.
Density (1997): persons per sq mi 3.9, persons per sq km 1.5.
Urban-rural (1995): urban 62.0%; rural 38.0%.
Sex distribution (1997): male 50.04%; female 49.96%.
Age breakdown (1997): under 15, 37.7%; 15–29, 29.7%; 30–44, 19.1%; 45–59, 7.9%; 60–69, 4.3%; 70 and over, 1.3%.
Population projection: (2000) 2,479,000; (2010) 2,879,000.
Doubling time: 47 years.
Ethnic composition (1989): Khalkha Mongol 78.8%; Kazak 5.9%; Dörbed Mongol 2.7%; Bayad 1.9%; Buryat Mongol 1.7%; Dariganga Mongol 1.4%; other 7.6%.
Religious affiliation (1995): Tantric Buddhist (Lamaism) 96.0%; Muslim 4.0%.
Major cities (1996): Ulaanbaatar (Ulan Bator) 627,300[4]; Darhan 87,100; Choybalsan 79,900; Erdenet 59,100; Ölgiy (1991) 29,400.

Vital statistics

Birth rate per 1,000 population (1997): 25.0 (world avg. 25.0).
Death rate per 1,000 population (1997): 8.0 (world avg. 9.3).
Natural increase rate per 1,000 population (1997): 17.0 (world avg. 15.7).
Total fertility rate (avg. births per childbearing woman; 1997): 2.9.
Marriage rate per 1,000 population (1989): 7.8.
Divorce rate per 1,000 population (1989): 0.5.
Life expectancy at birth (1996): male 64.0 years; female 67.0 years.
Major causes of death per 100,000 population: n.a.; however, in the early 1990s, major causes of mortality included diseases of the cardiovascular system, diseases of the respiratory system, and diseases of the cerebrovascular system.

National economy

Budget (1997). Revenue: Tug 157,802,100,000 (taxes 69.7%, of which income tax 18.9%, social security contribution 14.5%, customs duties 13.2%, sales tax 13.1%; nontax revenue 30.3%). Expenditures: Tug 184,105,800,000 (social and cultural services, education, and health 58.6%; capital investment 11.0%; defense 8.1%; salaries in state-run enterprises 7.3%).
Public debt (external; 1995): U.S.$451,700,000.
Population economically active (1995): total 868,200; activity rate of total population 37.7% (participation rates: ages 16–59 [1989] 77.9%; female [1992] 46.0%; unemployed 7.6%).

Price and earnings indexes (1990 = 100)

	1990	1991	1992	1993	1994	1995	1996
Consumer price index	100.0	220.2	523.9	1,928.6	3,616.9	5,670.7	7,451.1
Monthly earnings index	100.0	184.0	260.1	991.4	2,071.8	2,781.3	...

Production (metric tons except as noted). Agriculture, forestry, fishing (1997): wheat 198,060, potatoes 47,047, vegetables and melons 25,000; livestock (number of live animals) 13,606,000 sheep, 9,134,900 goats, 3,476,300 cattle, 2,400,000 horses, 390,000 camels, 19,085 pigs; roundwood (1995) 883,500 cu m; fish catch (1995) 130. Mining and quarrying (1996): fluorspar 565,100; copper 351,500; molybdenum 4,684; gold 5,242 kg. Manufacturing (value added by manufacturing in Tug '000,000; 1994): textiles 8,899.7; food products 8,055.2; leather and footwear 2,415.5; construction materials 1,863.0; clothing and apparel 1,259.8; wood products 1,209.4; beverages 944.5; chemicals 413.4; printing and publishing 339.9. Construction (1994): residential 120,400 sq m. Energy production (consumption): electricity (kW-hr; 1994) 3,265,000,000 (3,472,000,000); coal (metric tons; 1994) 635,000 (635,000); petroleum products (metric tons; 1994) none (595,000).
Gross national product (1995): U.S.$767,000,000 (U.S.$310 per capita).

Structure of gross domestic product and labour force

	1995			
	in value Tug '000,000[5]	% of total value	labour force	% of labour force
Agriculture	1,430	16.1	345,300	39.8
Manufacturing and mining	2,404	27.0	101,300	11.7
Construction	208	2.3	27,700	3.2
Transp. and commun.	366	4.1	32,000	3.7
Trade	1,569	17.6	85,800	9.9
Services[6]	2,931[7]	32.9[7]	110,800	12.8
Other			165,300[8]	19.0[8]
TOTAL	8,908	100.0	868,200	100.0[3]

Household income and expenditure. Average family size (1993) 4.4; income per household (1992)[9] Tug 5,500 (U.S.$140); sources of income (1993): wages and salaries 72.1%, transfer payments 9.7%, self-employment 9.5%[10], other 8.7%; expenditure (1991): food 48.6%, clothing 21.9%, housing 10.5%, transportation and communications 6.8%, household goods 4.1%.
Land use (1994): forest 8.8%; pasture 74.8%; agriculture 0.8%; other 15.6%.

Foreign trade

Balance of trade (current prices)

	1991	1992	1993	1994	1995	1996
U.S.$'000,000	−101	−29	−21	+106	−22	−15
% of total	12.7%	3.9%	3.0%	19.5%	2.4%	1.8%

Imports (1996): U.S.$438,283,000 (machinery and electronics 22.4%, mineral products 20.0%, motor vehicles and transport equipment 17.2%, food, beverages, and tobacco 13.1%, metals and finished products 7.3%). *Major import sources:* Russia 34.2%; Japan 17.5%; Germany 4.7%; South Korea 4.0%; Singapore 2.9%; U.S. 2.5%.
Exports (1996): U.S.$422,897,000 (mineral products 59.2%, textile products 23.5%, metals and finished products 3.5%, live animals 3.2%). *Major export destinations:* Switzerland 25.4%; Russia 20.6%; China 17.7%; Japan 8.5%; U.K. 4.4%.

Transport and communications

Transport. Railroads (1994): length 2,083 km; passenger-km 789,600,000; metric ton-km cargo 2,131,700. Roads (1996): total length 50,000 km (paved 3%). Vehicles (1996): passenger cars 28,000; trucks and buses 28,000. Air transport (1994): passenger-km 115,000,000; metric ton-km cargo 12,000,000; airports (1997) with scheduled flights 1.

Communications

Medium	date	unit	number	units per 1,000 persons
Daily newspapers	1995	circulation	211,830	92.0
Radio	1995	receivers	170,460	74.0
Television	1997	receivers	148,983	60.7
Telephones	1997	main lines	91,971	37.5
Cellular telephones	1997	subscribers	900	0.4
Facsimile machines	1995	units	2,072	0.9
Personal computers	1995	units	460	0.2

Education and health

Educational attainment (1989). Percentage of population age 10 and over having: primary education 33.7%; some secondary 31.9%; complete secondary 16.9%; vocational secondary 9.4%; some higher and complete higher 8.1%.
Literacy (1995): percentage of total population age 15 and over literate 82.9%; males literate 88.6%; females literate 77.2%.

Education (1995–96)

	schools	teachers	students	student/ teacher ratio
Primary (age 6–12)	650	7,088	176,036	24.8
Secondary (age 13–16)		12,323	227,811	18.5
Vocational (age 16–18)	...	495	7,987	16.1
Higher	12[11]	1,341[12]	13,800[11]	...

Health (1993): physicians 5,911 (1 per 401 persons); hospital beds 23,400 (1 per 101 persons); infant mortality rate per 1,000 live births (1997) 68.0.
Food (1995): daily per capita caloric intake 1,897 (vegetable products 60%, animal products 40%); 78% of FAO recommended minimum requirement.

Military

Total active duty personnel (1997): 14,900[13] (army 94%, air force 6%). *Military expenditure as percentage of GNP* (1995): 2.4% (world 2.8%); per capita expenditure U.S.$8.

[1]January. [2]Dundgovĭ includes Govĭ-Sümber. [3]Detail does not add to total given because of rounding. [4]1997 estimate. [5]At constant prices of 1986. [6]Services includes finance, public administration, and defense. [7]Includes depreciation of fixed capital. [8]Includes 66,000 unemployed. [9]Urban households. [10]Includes income from agricultural cooperatives. [11]1994–95. [12]1991–92. [13]Includes 5,900 paramilitary forces.

Internet resources for further information:
- **Mongolia Online http://www.MongoliaOnline.mn/english/**

Morocco[1]

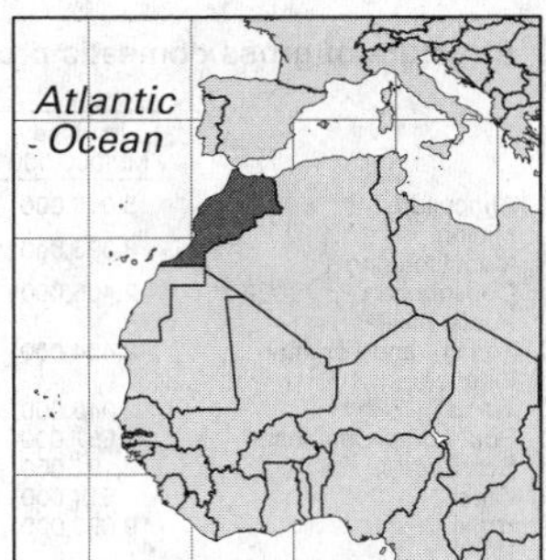

Official name: Al-Mamlakah al-Maghribīyah (Kingdom of Morocco).
Form of government: constitutional monarchy with one legislative house (House of Representatives [333]).
Chief of state and head of government: King assisted by Prime Minister.
Capital: Rabat.
Official language: Arabic.
Official religion: Islam.
Monetary unit: 1 Moroccan dirham (DH) = 100 Moroccan francs; valuation (Oct. 3, 1997) 1 U.S.$ = DH 9.68; 1 £ = DH 15.61.

Population (1994 census)

Region / Province/*Prefecture*	Population
Centre	
Azilal	454,914
Ben Slimane	213,398
Beni Mellal	869,748
El-Jadida	970,894
Khouribga	480,839
Settat	847,422
Prefecture	
Aïn Chok–Hay Hassani	516,261
Aïn Sebaâ–Hay Mohemmedi	520,993
Ben M'sik–Sidi Othmane	704,365
Casablanca-Anfa	523,279
Al Fida–Derb Sultan	386,700
Mechouar de Casablanca	3,956
Mohammedia	170,063
Sidi Bernoussi–Zenata	268,586
Centre-Nord	
Boulemane	161,622
Al-Hoceïma	382,972
Sefrou	237,095
Taounate	628,840
Taza	708,025
Prefecture	
Fès El-Jadid–Dar Dbibagh	256,340
Fès-Médina	284,822
Zouagha–Moulay Yacoub	382,594
Centre-Sud	
El-Hajeb	180,494
Ifrane	127,677
Khenifra	465,061
Er-Rachidia	522,117
Prefecture	
Al-Ismailia	314,916
Meknès–El-Menzeh	293,525
Nord-Ouest	
Chefchaouen	439,303
Kenitra	979,210
Khemisset	485,541
Larache	431,476
Sidi Kacem	645,872
Tanger	627,963
Tétouan	537,290
Prefecture	
Rabat	623,457
Salé	631,803
Skhirate-Témara	244,801
Oriental	
Berkane-Taourirt	399,017
Figuig	117,011
Jerada	149,686
Nador	683,914
Prefecture	
Oujda-Angad	419,063
Sud	
Assa-Zag	21,848
Chtouka–Aït Baha	240,092
Guelmim	147,124
Laâyoune[1]	8,251
Ouarzazate	694,884
Tan-Tan	58,079
Taroudannt	693,968
Tata	119,298
Tiznit	347,821
Prefecture	
Agadir–Ida-ou-Tanane	365,965
Inezgane–Aït Melloul	292,799
Tensift	
Chichaoua	311,800
Essaouira	433,681
Al-Haouz	435,090
El-Kelaâ des Sraghna	682,428
Safi	822,564
Prefecture	
Marrakech-Médina	189,367
Marrakech-Ménara	432,547
Sidi Youssef Ben Ali	239,291
TOTAL	25,829,822

Demography

Area: 177,117 sq mi, 458,730 sq km.
Population (1997): 27,225,000.
Density (1997): persons per sq mi 153.8, persons per sq km 59.4.
Urban-rural (1996): urban 48.9%; rural 51.1%.
Sex distribution (1996): male 50.06%; female 49.94%.
Age breakdown (1995): under 15, 36.1%; 15–29, 29.8%; 30–44, 18.9%; 45–59, 9.0%; 60–74, 5.0%; 75 and over, 1.2%.
Ethnic composition (1986): Arab 70%; Berber 30%; other, less than 1%.
Religious affiliation (1993): Muslim (mostly Sunnī) 98.7%; Christian 1.1%.
Major urban areas (1994): Casablanca 2,941,000; Rabat-Salé 1,386,000; Fès 510,000.

Vital statistics

Birth rate per 1,000 population (1995): 27.9 (world avg. 25.0).
Death rate per 1,000 population (1995): 6.0 (world avg. 9.3).
Natural increase rate per 1,000 population (1995): 21.9 (world avg. 15.7).
Life expectancy at birth (1995): male 67.0 years; female 71.0 years.
Major causes of death (1989)[2]: childhood diseases 22.9%; circulatory diseases 15.4%; accidents 7.3%; infectious and parasitic diseases 6.3%; cancers 5.6%.

National economy

Budget. Revenue (1995): DH 87,172,000,000 (current account taxes 69.8%, of which value-added taxes 5.5%; capital revenue 22.6%; customs and stamp duties 7.5%). Expenditures (1995): DH 82,015,000,000 (current expenditure 76.0%, of which administrative expenses 52.2%, debt payments 20.5%; capital expenditure 24.0%).
Public debt (external, outstanding; 1995): U.S.$21,347,000,000.
Tourism (1995): receipts U.S.$1,163,000,000; expenditures U.S.$302,000,000.
Production (metric tons except as noted). Agriculture, forestry, fishing (1997): sugar beets 2,595,000, wheat 2,316,500, barley 1,324,000, potatoes 1,145,000, sugar cane 900,000, tomatoes 895,000, oranges 794,800; livestock (number of live animals) 16,500,000 sheep, 5,500,000 goats, 2,550,000 cattle, 115,000,000 chickens; roundwood (1996) 2,371,000 cu m; fish catch (1995) 846,201. Mining and quarrying (value of production in DH '000,000; 1994): phosphate rock 3,600.0; zinc 276.9; lead 234.1; copper 140.6. Manufacturing (value added in DH '000,000; 1994) food 10,159; chemical products 5,951; textiles 4,108. Construction (authorized, urban areas; 1994): residential 7,069,557 sq m, nonresidential 998,424 sq m. Energy production (consumption): electricity (kW-hr; 1994) 10,773,000,000 (11,693,000,000); coal (metric tons; 1994) 650,000 (2,200,000); crude petroleum (barrels; 1994) 60,800 (50,030,800); petroleum products (metric tons; 1994) 5,659,000 (6,792,000); natural gas (cu m; 1994) 25,100,000 (25,100,000).
Gross national product (1995): U.S.$29,545,000,000 (U.S.$1,110 per capita).

Structure of gross domestic product and labour force

	1995		1993	
	in value DH '000,000	% of total value	labour force	% of labour force
Agriculture	39,723	14.4	2,906,000	34.0
Mining	4,904	1.8		
Manufacturing	51,629	18.6	2,650,000	31.0
Construction	12,199	4.4		
Public utilities	22,370	8.1		
Transp. and commun.	17,306	6.2		
Trade	54,934	19.8		
Finance	...	...	2,991,000	35.0
Pub. admin., defense	37,382	13.5		
Services / Other	36,431	13.2		
TOTAL	276,878	100.0	8,547,000	100.0

Population economically active (1994): total 8,694,000; activity rate 32.8% (participation rates [1993]: over age 15, 52.4%; unemployed 16.0%).

Price index (1990 = 100)

	1990	1991	1992	1993	1994	1995	1996
Consumer price index	100.0	108.0	114.2	120.1	126.3	134.0	138.0
Monthly earnings index[3]	100.0	110.0	130.0	130.0	140.0[4]	...	...

Household income and expenditure. Average household size (1994) 5.9; expenditure (1994)[5]: food 45.2%, housing 12.5%, transportation 7.6%.

Foreign trade[6]

Balance of trade (current prices)

	1991	1992	1993	1994	1995	1996
DH '000,000	–13,576	–23,192	–28,740	–23,353	–26,071	–16,856
% of total	15.4%	25.5%	31.1%	24.1%	24.5%	12.3%

Imports (1995): DH 72,869,000,000 (capital goods 22.3%; food, beverages, and tobacco 16.0%; energy products 13.8%; consumer goods 11.0%). *Major import sources:* France 21.8%; Spain 8.5%; U.S. 6.5%; Germany 6.3%.
Exports (1995): DH 40,240,000,000 (food 30.8%; consumer goods 23.7%; minerals 10.0%). *Major export destinations:* France 29.7%; Spain 9.4%; Japan 7.7%; India 5.4%; Italy 5.2%.

Transport and communications

Transport. Railroads (1994): route length 1,768 km; passenger-km 1,884,000,000; metric ton-km cargo 4,740,000,000. Roads (1995): total length 60,513 km (paved 50%). Vehicles (1995): passenger cars 1,030,000; trucks and buses 273,100. Air transport (1996)[7]: passenger-km 4,665,440,000; metric ton-km cargo 57,033,000; airports (1997) 11.

Communications

Medium	date	unit	number	units per 1,000 persons
Daily newspapers	1995	circulation	390,000	14.5
Radio	1995	receivers	6,000,000	222
Television	1995	receivers	2,500,000	92.7
Telephones	1995	main lines	1,158,000	42.9
Cellular telephones	1995	subscribers	29,500	1.1
Facsimile machines	1995	units	7,500	0.3
Personal computers	1995	units	45,000	1.7

Education and health

Educational attainment (1982). Percentage of population age 25 and over having: no formal education 47.8%; some primary education 47.8%; some secondary 3.8%; higher 0.6%. *Literacy* (1995): total population over age 15 literate 43.7%; males literate 56.6%; females literate 31.0%.

Education (1994–95)

	schools	teachers	students	student/ teacher ratio
Primary (age 7–12)	6,205	154,650	3,914,282	25.3
Secondary (age 13–17)	451	29,364	391,639	13.3
Vocational[8]	562[9]	2,951	17,585	6.0
Higher	13[10]	9,038	266,032	29.4

Health (1994): physicians 8,838 (1 per 2,923 persons); hospital beds 26,407 (1 per 978 persons); infant mortality rate (1995) 45.8.
Food (1995): daily per capita caloric intake 3,157 (vegetable products 93%, animal products 7%); 130% of FAO recommended minimum requirement.

Military

Total active duty personnel (1997): 196,300 (army 89.1%, navy 4.0%, air force 6.9%). *Military expenditure as percentage of GDP* (1995): 4.3% (world 2.8%); per capita expenditure U.S.$47.

[1]Excludes area and population of Western Sahara except population of northern Laâyoune province. [2]Registered deaths of urban population only. [3]Minimum wage. [4]July 1. [5]Weights of consumer price index components. [6]Import figures are f.o.b. in balance of trade and c.i.f. for commodities and trading partners. [7]Royal Air Maroc only. [8]Excludes teacher training. [9]1991–92. [10]Universities only.

Mozambique

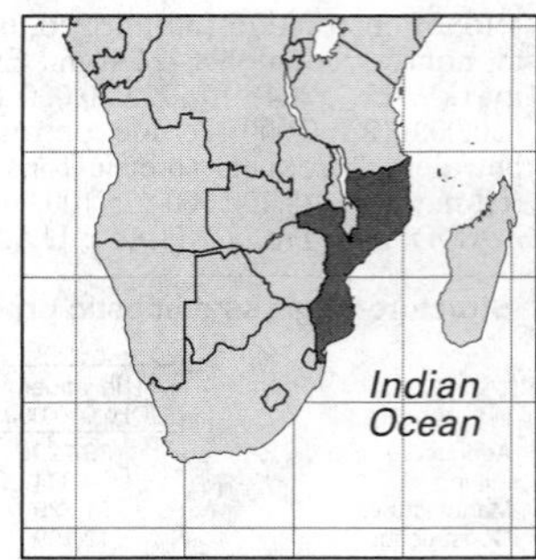

Official name: República de Moçambique (Republic of Mozambique).
Form of government: multiparty republic[1] with a single legislative house (Assembly of the Republic [250]).
Head of state and government: President assisted by the Prime Minister.
Capital: Maputo.
Official language: Portuguese.
Official religion: none.
Monetary unit: 1 metical (Mt; plural meticais) = 100 centavos; valuation (Oct. 3, 1997) 1 U.S.$ = Mt 11,495; 1 £ = Mt 18,530.

Area and population

		area		population
Provinces	Capitals	sq mi	sq km	1991 estimate
Cabo Delgado	Pemba	31,902	82,625	1,202,221
Gaza	Xai-Xai	29,231	75,709	1,401,485
Inhambane	Inhambane	26,492	68,615	1,156,958
Manica	Chimoio	23,807	61,661	609,512
Maputo	Maputo	9,944	25,756	840,757
Nampula	Nampula	31,508	81,606	2,841,416
Niassa	Lichinga	49,828	129,055	686,650
Sofala	Beira	26,262	68,018	1,427,493
Tete	Tete	38,890	100,724	734,561
Zambézia	Quelimane	40,544	105,008	2,619,281
City				
Maputo	—	232	602	931,591
TOTAL LAND AREA		308,642[2]	799,379	
INLAND WATER		5,019	13,000	
TOTAL		313,661	812,379	14,451,925[3, 4]

Demography

Population (1997): 18,165,000.
Density (1997)[5]: persons per sq mi 58.8, persons per sq km 22.7.
Urban-rural (1990–94): urban 32.7%; rural 67.3%.
Sex distribution (1997): male 48.85%; female 51.15%.
Age breakdown (1997): under 15, 44.9%; 15–29, 27.9%; 30–44, 15.1%; 45–59, 8.2%; 60–74, 3.3%; 75 and over, 0.6%.
Population projection: (2000) 19,614,000; (2010) 24,809,000.
Ethnolinguistic composition (1983): Makua 47.3%; Tsonga 23.3%; Malawi 12.0%; Shona 11.3%; Yao 3.8%; Swahili 0.8%; Makonde 0.6%; Portuguese 0.2%; other 0.7%.
Religious affiliation (1980): traditional beliefs 47.8%; Christian 38.9%, of which Roman Catholic 31.4%; Muslim 13.0%; other 0.3%.
Major cities (1991): Maputo 931,591; Beira 298,847; Nampula 250,473.

Vital statistics

Birth rate per 1,000 population (1997): 44.0 (world avg. 25.0).
Death rate per 1,000 population (1997): 18.0 (world avg. 9.3).
Natural increase rate per 1,000 population (1997): 26.0 (world avg. 15.7).
Total fertility rate (avg. births per childbearing woman; 1997): 6.1.
Marriage rate per 1,000 population (1974): 0.7.
Divorce rate per 1,000 population (1973): 0.01.
Life expectancy at birth (1995): male 46.8 years; female 49.5 years.

National economy

Budget (1997). Revenue: Mt 4,522,000,000 (1995; sales tax 47.8%, customs taxes 24.0%, individual income tax 16.6%). Expenditures: Mt 8,196,000,000 (current expenditure 52.2%, of which goods and services 23.6%, administrative salaries 22.3%, defense and security 19.4%; capital expenditure 47.8%).
Public debt (external, outstanding; 1995): U.S.$5,251,000,000.
Production (metric tons except as noted). Agriculture, forestry, fishing (1997): cassava 5,342,000, corn (maize) 1,153,000, sugarcane 500,000, coconuts 440,000, sorghum 263,000, peanuts (groundnuts) 127,000, bananas 86,000; livestock (number of live animals) 1,290,000 cattle, 386,000 goats, 175,000 pigs, 122,000 sheep, 23,000,000 chickens; roundwood (1995) 18,390,000 cu m; fish catch (1995) 26,870. Mining and quarrying (1994): marine salt 40,000; bauxite 9,620; copper 133[6, 7]; garnet 3,000 kg; gemstones 6,865 carats. Manufacturing (value in Mt '000,000; 1995): food processing 696,611; beverages and tobacco 395,871; textiles 207,378; nonmetallic mineral products 140,193; wood and cork products 134,951; chemical products 116,335; rubber products 87,827; clothing 82,123; machinery and transport equipment 72,507. Construction (value in Mt; 1994) 157,700,000. Energy production (consumption): electricity (kW-hr; 1994) 340,000,000 (728,000,000); coal (metric tons; 1994) 40,000 (60,000); crude petroleum (1993) none (none[8]); petroleum products (metric tons; 1994) none[8] (251,000); natural gas, none (none).
Population economically active (1980): total 5,671,290; activity rate 48.6% (participation rates: over age 15, 87.3%; female 52.4%; unemployed 1.7%).

Price and earnings indexes (1990 = 100)

	1990	1991	1992	1993	1994	1995	1996
Consumer price index	100.0	132.9	193.4	275.0	448.8	693.1	1,005.0
Monthly earnings index[9]	100.0	152.3	223.9	269.0	446.7	636.5	913.7

Gross national product (1995): U.S.$1,353,000,000 (U.S.$80 per capita).

Structure of gross domestic product and labour force

	1995		1980	
	in value Mt '000,000	% of total value	labour force	% of labour force
Agriculture	5,018,000	25.5	4,754,831	83.8
Mining	3,395,000[11]	17.2[11]	73,425	1.3
Manufacturing			273,369	4.8
Construction	2,405,000	12.2	42,121	0.7
Public utilities	[12]	[12]	[12]	[12]
Transp. and commun.	2,454,000	12.5	77,025	1.4
Finance	...	...	...	...
Trade	2,049,000	10.4	112,244	2.0
Pub. admin., defense	1,657,000	8.4	243,449[12]	4.3[12]
Services	2,191,000	11.1		
Other	514,000	2.6	94,826[13]	1.7[13]
TOTAL	19,685,000[2, 14]	100.0[2]	5,671,290	100.0

Household income and expenditure. Average family size (1992–93) 6.7[10]; income per household: n.a.; sources of income (1992–93)[10]: wages and salaries 51.6%, self-employment 12.5%, barter 11.5%, private farming 7.7%; expenditure (1992–93)[10]: food, beverages, and tobacco 74.6%; housing and energy 11.7%; transportation and communications 4.7%; clothing and footwear 3.7%; education and recreation 1.4%; health 0.8%.
Land use (1994): forested 22.1%; meadows and pastures 56.1%; agricultural and under permanent cultivation 4.0%; other 17.8%.

Foreign trade[15]

Balance of trade (current prices)

	1990	1991	1992	1993	1994	1995
U.S.$'000,000	−648	−737	−716	−823	−868	−615
% of total	71.8%	69.5%	72.0%	75.7%	74.4%	64.5%

Imports (1995): U.S.$783,600,000 (1990; foodstuffs 28.9%, capital equipment 22.9%, crude petroleum and derivatives 10.9%, machinery and spare parts 9.5%). *Major import sources* (1995): South Africa 37.6%; U.S. 6.7%; Japan 6.2%; Portugal 6.0%; U.K. 5.7%; France 5.6%.
Exports (1995): U.S.$168,900,000 (shrimp 43.3%, cotton 11.7%, cashew nuts 5.6%, sugar 4.3%, copra 3.6%, petroleum 1.9%). *Major export destinations:* South Africa 21.6%; Spain 21.6%; Japan 13.0%; Portugal 10.4%.

Transport and communications

Transport. Railroads (1995): route length 1,940 mi, 3,123 km; passenger-mi 194,000,000, passenger-km 312,000,000; short ton-mi cargo 612,000,000, metric ton-km cargo 893,000,000. Roads (1995): total length 18,523 mi, 29,810 km (paved 18.6%). Vehicles (1995): passenger cars 84,000; trucks and buses 26,800. Air transport (1995): passenger-mi 239,000,000, passenger-km 384,000,000; short ton-mi cargo 6,000,000, metric ton-km cargo 9,000,000; airports (1997) with scheduled flights 7.

Communications

Medium	date	unit	number	units per 1,000 persons
Daily newspapers	1995	circulation	130,000	8.0
Radio	1995	receivers	660,000	38.0
Television	1995	receivers	60,000	3.5
Telephones	1995	main lines	59,800	3.4
Facsimile machines	1995	units	...	0.4

Education and health

Literacy (1995): percentage of total population age 15 and over literate 40.1%; males literate 57.7%; females literate 23.3%.

Education (1995)

	schools	teachers	students	student/teacher ratio
Primary (age 5–9)	4,167	24,575	1,415,428	57.6
Secondary (age 10–16)[16]	239[17]	4,376	165,868	37.9
Voc., teacher tr.	31[17]	1,239	19,313	15.6
Higher	3[17]	833[17]	7,000	...

Health (1993): physicians 114[18] (1 per 131,991 persons); hospital beds 13,280 (1 per 1,133 persons); infant mortality rate per 1,000 live births (1997) 123.0.
Food (1995): daily per capita caloric intake 1,678 (vegetable products 97%, animal products 3%); 72% of FAO recommended minimum requirement.

Military

Total active duty personnel (1997): 5,100–6,100[19]. *Military expenditure as percentage of GNP* (1995): 5.4% (world 2.8%); per capita expenditure U.S.$4.

[1]Mozambique adopted a new multiparty constitution that became effective on Nov. 30, 1990, but was amended on Oct. 29, 1996, to create autonomous local governments. The first multiparty elections took place on Oct. 27–29, 1994. [2]Detail does not add to total given because of rounding. [3]Excludes refugees in neighbouring countries estimated at about 1,200,000 in 1991; most of these refugees were repatriated between June 1993 and the fall of 1994. [4]A census was taken Aug. 1–15, 1997, the detail of which was not available. [5]Based on land area. [6]1990. [7]Metal content only. [8]Internal disorder and a lack of foreign exchange have brought importation of crude petroleum and the production of refined petroleum products practically to a halt. [9]Agricultural workers only. [10]City of Maputo only. [11]Manufacturing includes fishing. [12]Services includes Public utilities. [13]Unemployed. [14]Reported as gross output. [15]Import figures are c.i.f. [16]Includes the two stages of secondary education and the upper-level primary stage. [17]1994. [18]Government personnel only. [19]Estimate; approximately 80% are in the army.

Internet resources for further information:
- **Mozambique http://www.hmnet.com/africa/mozambique/mz_tbl.html**
- **Mozambique Country Profile http://www.mbendi.co.za/cymzcy.htm**

Myanmar (Burma)

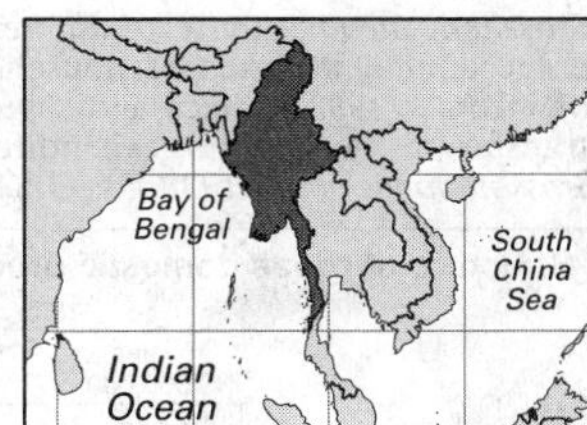

Official name: Pyidaungzu Myanma Naingngandaw (Union of Myanmar).
Form of government: military regime.
Head of state and government: Chairman of the State Peace and Development Council.
Capital: Yangôn (Rangoon).
Official language: Burmese.
Official religion: none.
Monetary unit: 1 Myanmar kyat (K) = 100 pyas; valuation (Oct. 3, 1997) 1 U.S.$ = K 6.25; 1 £ = K 10.08[1].

Area and population

Divisions	Capitals	area sq mi	area sq km	population 1994 estimate
Irrawaddy (Ayeyarwady)	Bassein (Pathein)	13,567	35,138	6,107,000
Magwe (Magway)	Magwe (Magway)	17,305	44,820	4,067,000
Mandalay	Mandalay	14,295	37,024	5,823,000
Pegu (Bago)	Pegu (Bago)	15,214	39,404	4,607,000
Sagaing	Sagaing	36,535	94,625	4,889,000
Tenasserim (Tanintharyi)	Tavoy (Dawei)	16,735	43,343	1,187,000
Yangôn	Yangôn (Rangoon)	3,927	10,171	5,037,000
States				
Chin	Hakha	13,907	36,019	438,000
Kachin	Myitkyinā	34,379	89,041	1,135,000
Karen	Pa-an (Hpa-an)	11,731	30,383	1,323,000
Kayah	Loi-kaw	4,530	11,733	228,000
Mon	Moulmein (Mawlamyine)	4,748	12,297	2,183,000
Rakhine (Arakan)	Sittwe (Akyab)	14,200	36,778	2,482,000
Shan	Taunggyi	60,155	155,801	4,416,000
TOTAL		261,228	676,577	43,922,000

Demography

Population (1997): 46,822,000.
Density (1997): persons per sq mi 179.2, persons per sq km 69.2.
Urban-rural (1997): urban 27.0%; rural 73.0%.
Sex distribution (1993): male 49.72%; female 50.28%.
Age breakdown (1990): under 15, 36.0%; 15–29, 29.7%; 30–44, 17.8%; 45–59, 10.1%; 60–74, 5.3%; 75 and over, 1.1%.
Population projection: (2000) 49,388,000; (2010) 58,236,000.
Doubling time: 40 years.
Ethnic composition (1983): Burman 69.0%; Shan 8.5%; Karen 6.2%; Rakhine 4.5%; Mon 2.4%; Chin 2.2%; Kachin 1.4%; other 5.8%.
Religious affiliation (1990): Buddhist 89.1%; Christian 4.9%; Muslim 3.8%; other 2.2%.
Major cities (1983): Yangôn (Rangoon) 2,513,023; Mandalay 532,949; Moulmein (Mawlamyine) 219,961; Pegu (Bago) 150,528; Bassein (Pathein) 144,096.

Vital statistics

Birth rate per 1,000 population (1997): 27.4 (world avg. 25.0).
Death rate per 1,000 population (1997): 9.9 (world avg. 9.3).
Natural increase rate per 1,000 population (1997): 17.5 (world avg. 15.7).
Total fertility rate (avg. births per childbearing woman; 1997): 3.3.
Marriage rate per 1,000 population: n.a.
Divorce rate per 1,000 population: n.a.
Life expectancy at birth (1997): male 58.0 years; female 62.0 years.
Major causes of death per 100,000 population (1987): infectious and parasitic diseases 29.5; respiratory diseases 14.8; circulatory diseases 10.0; malignant neoplasms (cancers) 7.9; malnutrition 2.2.

National economy

Budget (1994–95). Revenue: K 32,029,000,000 (revenue from taxes 62.7%, of which taxes on goods and services 28.5%, taxes on international trade 13.2%; nontax revenue 35.4%; capital revenue 1.9%). Expenditures: K 48,021,000,000 (defense 36.8%; transportation 13.5%; education 11.7%; agriculture 10.3%; health 4.0%; social security and welfare 3.6%).
Public debt (external, outstanding; 1995): U.S.$5,378,000,000.
Tourism: receipts from visitors (1995) U.S.$38,000,000; expenditures by nationals abroad (1992) U.S.$16,000,000.
Production (metric tons except as noted). Agriculture, forestry, fishing (1996): rice 20,865,000, sugarcane 3,132,000, pulses 1,289,000, peanuts (groundnuts) 568,000, sesame seeds 351,000, plantains 285,000, corn (maize) 247,000, seed cotton 214,000; livestock (number of live animals) 10,121,000 cattle, 4,710,000 ducks, 3,229,000 pigs, 2,266,000 buffalo, 1,492,000 sheep and goats, 27,600,000 chickens; roundwood (1995) 23,281,000 cu m; fish catch (1994) 824,468. Mining and quarrying (1995–96): gypsum 35,481; copper concentrates 19,060; refined lead 1,512; tin concentrates 473; jade 261; refined silver 112,270 troy oz. Manufacturing (1994): cement 469,582; urea 149,000; sugar 47,600; washing soap 36,431; noodles 25,065; stationery paper 14,315; cotton fabrics 10,804,000 metres; cigarettes 440,000,000 units; gunny-bags 26,769,000 units; glass bottles 16,268,000 units. Construction (units; 1987–88)[2]: residential 1,193; nonresidential 1,483. Energy production (consumption): electricity (kW-hr; 1994) 3,500,000,000 (3,500,000,000); coal (metric tons; 1994) 76,000 (78,000); crude petroleum (barrels; 1994) 4,817,000 (6,893,000); petroleum products (metric tons; 1994) 757,000 (921,000); natural gas (cu m; 1994) 1,359,000,000 (1,359,000,000).
Household income and expenditure. Average household size (1994) 5.6; average annual income per household: n.a.; sources of income: n.a.; expenditure (1994)[3]: food and beverages 67.1%, fuel and lighting 6.6%, transportation 4.0%, charitable contributions 3.1%, medical care 3.1%.

Gross national product (1995–96): U.S.$83,419,000,000 (U.S.$1,790 per capita).

Structure of gross domestic product and labour force

	1995–96 in value K '000,000	% of total value	labour force[4]	% of labour force[4]
Agriculture	295,200	62.2	11,848,000	67.4
Mining	2,784	0.6	116,000	0.7
Manufacturing	34,325	7.2	1,481,000	8.4
Construction	8,026	1.7	354,000	2.0
Public utilities	1,680	0.4	19,000	0.1
Transp. and commun.	8,238	1.7	441,000	2.5
Trade	106,595	22.4	1,715,000	9.7
Finance	788	0.2 }	1,339,000	7.6
Public admin., services	9,995	2.1 }		
Other	7,255	1.5	274,000	1.6
TOTAL	474,886	100.0	17,587,000	100.0

Population economically active (1995–96): total 18,766,000; activity rate of total population 41.2% (participation rates: ages 15–64 [1983] 64.2%; female [1987–88] 35.3%; unemployed 6.2%).

Price and earnings indexes (1990 = 100)

	1990	1991	1992	1993	1994	1995	1996
Consumer price index	100.0	132.3	161.3	212.6	263.8	330.3	384.0
Monthly earnings index[5]	100.0	92.8	129.4	144.8	...	...	...

Land use (1994): forested 49.3%; meadows and pastures 0.5%; agricultural and under permanent cultivation 15.3%; other 34.9%.

Foreign trade[6]

Balance of trade (current prices)

	1991	1992	1993	1994	1995	1996
K '000,000	−1,055.4	−338.1	−948.4	−195.8	−2,050.7	−3,231.5
% of total	16.7%	4.9%	11.6%	2.1%	17.5%	28.3%

Imports (1994–95): K 8,332,000,000 (machinery and transport equipment 31.8%; basic manufactures 17.5%; chemicals 7.3%; animal and vegetable oils 9.7%; food and live animals 5.6%). *Major import sources:* Japan 23.6%; Singapore 14.6%; China 12.2%; Thailand 10.0%; Malaysia 9.4%; South Korea 4.7%; Indonesia 3.9%.
Exports (1994–95): K 5,405,000,000 (food and live animals 50.6%; inedible crude materials 28.2%; basic manufactures 4.6%). *Major export destinations:* Singapore 16.4%; Indonesia 15.6%; India 12.9%; Thailand 10.0%; China 5.1%; Hong Kong 5.0%.

Transport and communications

Transport. Railroads (1995–96): track length (1994) 5,060 km; passenger-km 4,894,000,000; metric ton-km cargo 880,000,000. Roads (1995): total length 27,600 km (paved 12%). Vehicles (1995): passenger cars 44,000; trucks and buses 42,000. Air transport (1995–96): passenger-km 438,000,000; metric ton-km cargo 3,212,000; airports (1996) 19.

Communications

Medium	date	unit	number	units per 1,000 persons
Daily newspapers	1994	circulation	1,032,000	23
Radio	1996	receivers	3,300,000	72
Television	1995	receivers	1,000,000	22
Telephones	1995	main lines	146,700	3.3
Cellular telephones	1995	subscribers	2,100	0.05
Facsimile machines	1995	units	1,400	0.03

Education and health

Educational attainment (1983). Percentage of population age 25 and over having: no formal schooling 55.8%; primary education 39.4%; secondary 4.6%; religious 0.1%; postsecondary 0.1%. *Literacy* (1983): total population age 15 and over literate 16,472,494 (78.5%); males literate 8,816,031 (85.8%); females literate 7,656,463 (71.6%).

Education (1994–95)

	schools	teachers	students	student/teacher ratio
Primary (age 5–9)	35,856	169,748	5,711,202	33.6
Secondary (age 10–15)	2,916	71,904	1,779,503	24.7
Voc., teacher tr.	103	2,462	25,374	10.3
Higher	51	9,147	309,446	33.8

Health: physicians (1993–94) 12,245 (1 per 3,554 persons); hospital beds (1992–93) 27,830 (1 per 1,586 persons); infant mortality rate per 1,000 live births (1997) 79.
Food (1995): daily per capita caloric intake 2,752 (vegetable products 96%, animal products 4%); 127% of FAO recommended minimum requirement.

Military

Total active duty personnel (1996): 321,000 (army 93.5%, navy 3.7%, air force 2.8%). *Military expenditure as percentage of GNP* (1992): 4.0% (world 3.6%); per capita expenditure (1994) U.S.$57.

[1]Official exchange rate; black market exchange rate (July 15, 1997): 1 U.S.$ = K 125; 1 £ = K 211. [2]Construction Corporation activity only. [3]Yangôn only. [4]Employed only. [5]Wages in manufacturing. [6]Import figures are f.o.b. in balance of trade and c.i.f. in commodities and trading partners.

Internet resources for further information:
- **Myanmar Home Page http://www.myanmar.com/e-index.html**

Namibia

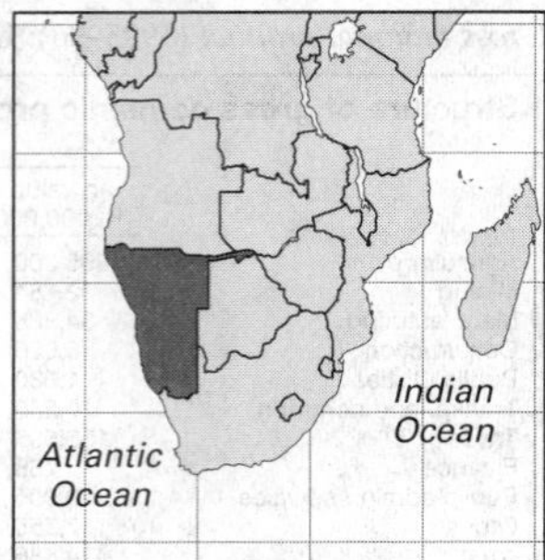

Official name: Republic of Namibia.
Form of government: republic with two legislative houses (National Council[1] [26]; National Assembly [72[2]]).
Head of state and government: President.
Capital: Windhoek.
Official language: English.
Official religion: none.
Monetary unit: 1 Namibian dollar (N$) = 100 cents; valuation (Oct. 3, 1997) 1 U.S.$ = N$4.70; 1 £ = N$7.53.

Area and population[3]

		area		population
Regions	Chief towns	sq mi	sq km	1992 estimate
Erongo[3]	Omaruru	24,602	63,719	98,500
Hardap	Mariental	42,428	109,888	80,000
Karas	Keetmanshoop	62,288	161,324	73,000
Khomas	Windhoek	14,210	36,804	161,000
Kunene	Opuwo	55,697	144,254	58,500
Liambezi	Katima Mulilo	7,541	19,532	92,000
Ohangwena	Oshikango	4,086	10,582	178,000
Okavango	Rundu	16,763	43,417	136,000
Omaheke	Gobabis	32,715	84,731	55,600
Omusati	Ongandjera	5,265	13,637	158,000
Oshana	Oshakati	2,042	5,290	159,000
Oshikoto	Tsumeb	10,273	26,607	176,000
Otjozondjupa	Grootfontein	40,667	105,327	85,000
Other		2	6	1,000
TOTAL		318,580[4]	825,118	1,511,600

Demography

Population (1997): 1,727,000.
Density (1997): persons per sq mi 5.4, persons per sq km 2.1.
Urban-rural (1996): urban 38.5%; rural 61.5%.
Sex distribution (1996): male 49.75%; female 50.25%.
Age breakdown (1991): under 15, 41.7%; 15–29, 28.8%; 30–44, 14.7%; 45–59, 7.8%; 60–74, 5.3%; 75 and over, 1.7%.
Population projection: (2000) 1,886,000; (2010) 2,513,000.
Doubling time: 27 years.
Ethnic composition (1991): Ovambo 50.7%; Nama 12.5%; Kavango 9.7%; Herero 8.0%; San (Bushman) 1.9%; Tswana 0.4%; other 16.8%.
Religious affiliation (1981): Lutheran 51.2%; Roman Catholic 19.8%; Dutch Reformed 6.1%; Anglican 5.0%; other 17.9%.
Major cities (1990): Windhoek 125,000; Swakopmund 15,500; Rundu 15,000; Rehoboth 15,000; Keetmanshoop 14,000.

Vital statistics

Birth rate per 1,000 population (1990–95): 37.5 (world avg. 25.0).
Death rate per 1,000 population (1990–95): 11.9 (world avg. 9.3).
Natural increase rate per 1,000 population (1990–95): 25.6 (world avg. 15.7).
Total fertility rate (avg. births per childbearing woman; 1990–95): 5.7.
Life expectancy at birth (1990–95): male 57.5 years; female 60.0 years.
Major causes of death per 100,000 population: n.a.; however, in the early 1990s, tuberculosis had become a serious problem (especially in the southern regions); AIDS cases, while few, were increasing exponentially.

National economy

Budget (1996–97). Revenue: N$4,459,400,000 (customs taxes 30.2%, individual income taxes 16.5%, general sales tax 14.3%, nontax revenues 10.5%, mining taxes 3.1%). Expenditures: N$5,072,600,000 (education 23.2%, health and welfare 10.3%, transportation 6.1%, defense 5.8%, social security 5.4%).
Tourism (1995): receipts from visitors U.S.$263,000,000; expenditures by nationals abroad U.S.$82,000,000.
Public debt (1993): U.S.$118,530,000.
Production (metric tons except as noted). Agriculture, forestry, fishing (1997): roots and tubers 230,000, cereals 168,000 (of which millet 107,000, corn [maize] 47,000, sorghum 10,000, wheat 4,100), fruits 10,000, vegetables and melons 9,000, pulses 8,000, wool 3,026[5], karakul pelts 770,627 units[6]; livestock (number of live animals; 1996) 2,136,545 sheep, 2,084,396 cattle, 1,670,822 goats; fish catch (1995) 285,980. Mining and quarrying (1996): diamonds 1,420,000 carats (mostly gem quality); zinc 69,689; copper 20,705; lead 18,845; uranium 2,886; silver 1,350,500 troy oz; gold 70,417 troy oz. Manufacturing: n.a.; products include cut gems (primarily diamonds), fur products (karakul), processed foods (fish, meats, and dairy products), textiles, carved wood products, refined metals (copper and lead). Construction (value of buildings completed in N$'000,000; 1994): residential 347.7; nonresidential 160.4. Energy production (consumption): electricity (kW-hr; 1992) 1,714,000,000 (1,714,000,000); coal, none (n.a.); crude petroleum, none (n.a.).
Population economically active: total (1991) 493,580; activity rate of total population, 34.9% (participation rates: ages 15–64, 61.3%; female 43.5%; unemployed 20.1%).

Price and earnings indexes (1990 = 100)

	1990	1991	1992	1993	1994	1995	1996
Consumer price index	100.0	111.9	131.7	143.0	158.4	174.2	188.2
Earnings index	...	...	...	...	...	...	...

Household income and expenditure. Average household size (1991) 5.2; average annual income per household (1980) R 3,223 (U.S.$4,143); sources of income (1992): wages and salaries 69.0%, income from property 25.6%, transfer payments 5.4%; expenditure: n.a.
Gross national product (1995): U.S.$3,098,000,000 (U.S.$2,000 per capita).

Structure of gross domestic product and labour force

	1995		1991	
	in value N$'000,000	% of total value	labour force[7]	% of labour force
Agriculture	1,502	15.4	189,929	38.5
Mining	1,097	11.2	14,686	3.0
Manufacturing	872	8.9	22,884	4.6
Construction	347	3.6	18,638	3.8
Public utilities	187	1.9	2,974	0.6
Transp. and commun.	566	5.8	9,322	1.9
Trade[8]	1,043	10.7	37,820	7.7
Finance	1,037	10.6	8,547	1.7
Services	135	1.4	89,541	18.1
Public administration and defense	2,697	27.7		
Other	267	2.7	99,239[9]	20.1[9]
TOTAL	9,750	100.0[4]	493,580	100.0

Land use (1994): forested 15.2%; meadows and pastures 46.2%; agricultural and under permanent cultivation 0.8%; other 37.8%.

Foreign trade

Balance of trade (current prices)

	1990	1991	1992	1993	1994	1995
U.S.$'000,000	−28	+102	+79	+122	+165	−98
% of total	0.8%	4.3%	3.0%	5.0%	6.6%	3.5%

Imports (1994): N$4,467,700,000 (machinery and transport equipment 27.1%, of which transport equipment 16.2%; food and live animals 22.3%; minerals and fuels 11.4%; chemical products 8.1%). *Major import sources* (1993): South Africa 87.0%[10]; Germany 3.0%; France 2.0%; Japan 2.0%.
Exports (1994): N$4,692,000,000 (minerals 50.1%, of which diamonds 31.4%; food and live animals 47.0%, of which fish and fish products 28.6%, cattle and meat products 12.6%; karakul pelts 0.2%). *Major export destinations* (1993): United Kingdom 34.0%; South Africa 27.0%; Japan 10.0%; Spain 6.0%.

Transport and communications

Transport. Railroads: length (1995) 1,480 mi, 2,382 km; passenger-km 34,700,000; metric ton-km 1,077,000,000. Roads (1995): total length 25,130 mi, 40,450 km (paved 12%). Vehicles (1995): passenger cars 62,500; trucks and buses 66,500. Merchant marine (1992): vessels (100 gross tons and over) 30; total deadweight tonnage 5,874. Air transport (1996)[11]: passenger-km 756,000,000; metric ton-km cargo 23,000,000; airports (1997) with scheduled flights 11.

Communications

Medium	date	unit	number	units per 1,000 persons
Daily newspapers	1994	circulation	43,300	27.4
Radio	1995	receivers	240,000	152
Television	1995	receivers	45,000	27.6
Telephones	1995	main lines	78,500	48.2
Cellular telephones	1995	subscribers	3,500	2.5

Education and health

Educational attainment (1991). Percentage of population age 25 and over having: no formal schooling 35.1%; primary education 31.9%; secondary 28.5%; higher 4.5%. *Literacy* (1991): total population age 15 and over literate 622,436 (75.8%); males literate 305,926 (77.7%); females literate 316,510 (73.9%).

Education (1994)

	schools	teachers	students	student/ teacher ratio
Primary (age 6–12)	933	10,912[12]	366,666	32.0[12]
Secondary (age 13–19)	114	2,534[13]	101,838	29.3[13]
Voc., teacher tr.	17	140[14]	1,503	11.9[14]
Higher	7	213[15]	6,523	11.8[15]

Health: physicians (1992) 324 (1 per 4,594 persons); hospital beds (1989) 6,997 (1 per 216 persons); infant mortality rate per 1,000 live births (1993) 63.8.
Food (1995): daily per capita caloric intake 2,107 (vegetable products 88%, animal products 12%); 92% of FAO recommended minimum requirement.

Military

Total active duty personnel (1997): 5,800 (army 98.3%, navy 1.7%[16]). *Military expenditure as percentage of GNP* (1995): 1.6% (world 2.8%); per capita expenditure U.S.$39.

[1]Mostly an advisory body. [2]72 elected and up to 6 appointed members. [3]Includes the 434 sq mi (1,124 sq km) district of Walvis Bay (1992 population estimate, 23,000) that was jointly administered with South Africa from November 1992 to March 1994. [4]Detail does not add to total given because of rounding. [5]1994. [6]1987. [7]Includes more than 140,000 nonwage (informal) workers. [8]Includes hotels. [9]Unemployed. [10]Includes goods from other countries shipped via South Africa. [11]Namib Air only. [12]1992. [13]1990. [14]1989. [15]1991. [16]Coast Guard for fishery protection.

Internet resources for further information:
- **Namibia Fact Sheet http://www.macroint.com/dhs/press/nm-fac.html**

Nepal

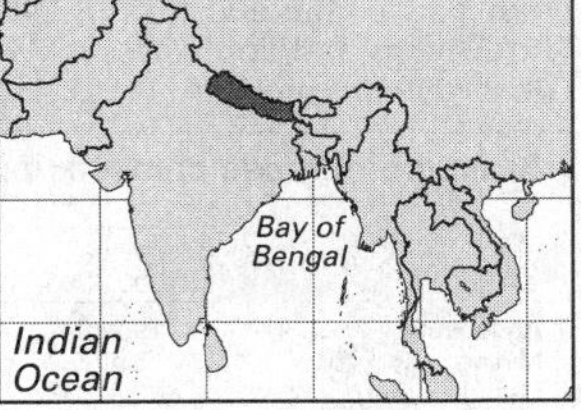

Official name: Nepāl Adhirājya (Kingdom of Nepal).
Form of government: constitutional monarchy with a bicameral parliament consisting of two legislative houses (National Council [60[1]]; House of Representatives [205]).
Chief of state: King.
Head of government: Prime Minister.
Capital: Kāthmāndu.
Official language: Nepālī.
Official religion: Hinduism.
Monetary unit: 1 Nepalese rupee (NRs) = 100 paisa (pice); valuation (Oct. 3, 1997) 1 U.S.$ = NRs 56.95; 1 £ = NRs 91.80.

Area and population

Development regions / Zones	Capitals	area sq mi	area sq km	population 1991 census
Eastern	Dhankūtā	10,987	28,456	4,446,749
Koshī	Dharān	3,733	9,669	1,728,247
Mechī	Ilam	3,165	8,196	1,118,210
Sāgarmāthā	Rājbiraj	4,089	10,591	1,600,292
Central	Kāthmāndu	10,583	27,410	6,183,955
Bāgmatī	Bhaktapur	3,640	9,428	2,250,805
Janakpur	Sindhulimādī	3,733	9,669	2,061,816
Nārāyanī	Hetaudā	3,210	8,313	1,871,334
Western	Pokharā	11,351	29,398	3,770,678
Dhawalāgiri	Bagluri	3,146	8,148	490,877
Gandakī	Chāme	4,740	12,275	1,266,128
Lumbinī	Butawal	3,465	8,975	2,013,673
Mid-western	Surkhet	16,362	42,378	2,410,414
Bherī	Nepālganj	4,071	10,545	1,103,043
Karnālī	Mānma	8,244	21,351	260,529
Rāptī	Tulsipur	4,047	10,482	1,046,842
Far-western	Dipāyal	7,544	19,539	1,679,301
Mahākālī	Dadeldhurā	2,698	6,989	664,952
Setī	Silgadhī	4,846	12,550	1,014,349
TOTAL		56,827	147,181	18,491,097

Demography

Population (1997): 21,424,000.
Density (1997): persons per sq mi 377.0, persons per sq km 145.6.
Urban-rural (1997): urban 15.0%; rural 85.0%.
Sex distribution (1997): male 50.20%; female 49.80%.
Age breakdown (1991): under 15, 42.3%; 15–29, 25.7%; 30–44, 16.7%; 45–59, 9.7%; 60–74, 4.7%; 75 and over, 0.9%.
Population projection: (2000) 23,042,000; (2010) 28,698,000.
Doubling time: 25 years.
Ethnic composition (1991): Nepalese 53.2%; Bihārī (including Maithilī and Bhojpurī) 18.4%; Tharu 4.8%; Tamang 4.7%; Newār 3.4%; Magar 2.2%; Abadhi 1.7%; other 11.6%.
Religious affiliation (1991): Hindu 86.5%; Buddhist 7.8%; Muslim 3.5%; Kirat 1.7%; Christian 0.2%; other 0.3%.
Major cities (1993 est.): Kāthmāndu 535,000; Lalitpur 190,000; Birātnagar 132,000; Bhaktapur 130,000.

Vital statistics

Birth rate per 1,000 population (1997): 36.6 (world avg. 25.0).
Death rate per 1,000 population (1997): 11.2 (world avg. 9.3).
Natural increase rate per 1,000 population (1997): 25.4 (world avg. 15.7).
Total fertility rate (avg. births per childbearing woman; 1996): 5.0.
Life expectancy at birth (1991): male 57.0 years; female 57.0 years.
Major causes of death per 100,000 population: n.a.; however, the leading causes of mortality are infectious and parasitic diseases, diseases of the respiratory system, and diseases of the nervous system.

National economy

Budget (1996). Revenue: NRs 30,303,000,000 (taxes on goods and services 39.7%, taxes on international trade 27.9%, income taxes 12.9%, state property revenues 7.9%, taxes on property 3.6%). Expenditures: NRs 49,485,000,000 (education 13.9%, transport and communications 11.9%, agriculture 7.7%, housing 6.2%, health 5.0%, defense 4.4%, public order 4.4%, general public services 3.2%).
Public debt (external, outstanding; 1995): U.S.$2,328,000,000.
Land use (1994): forested 42.0%; meadows and pastures 14.6%; agricultural and under permanent cultivation 17.2%; other 26.2%.
Tourism (1995): receipts from visitors U.S.$117,000,000; expenditures by nationals abroad U.S.$136,000,000.
Production (metric tons except as noted). Agriculture, forestry, fishing (1996): rice 3,578,830, sugarcane 1,568,700, corn (maize) 1,331,060, wheat 1,012,930, potatoes 898,350, millet 282,440, pulses 185,640; livestock (number of live animals) 7,008,420 cattle, 5,783,140 goats, 3,302,200 buffalo, 859,000 sheep, 670,340 pigs; roundwood (1995) 20,822,000 cu m; fish catch (1995) 21,148. Mining and quarrying (1995): limestone 350,000; salt 7,000; talc 1,500. Manufacturing (value added in U.S.$'000,000; 1994): food products 70; textiles 70; wearing apparel 50; tobacco products 37; nonmetal mineral products 32. Construction: n.a. Energy production (consumption): electricity (kW-hr; 1994) 908,000,000 (940,000,000); coal (metric tons; 1994) none (115,000); petroleum products (metric tons; 1994) none (343,000).
Gross national product (1995): U.S.$4,391,000,000 (U.S.$200 per capita).

Structure of gross domestic product and labour force

	1994–95 in value NRs '000,000[2]	1994–95 % of total value	1991 labour force	1991 % of labour force
Agriculture	87,072	41.9	5,961,788	81.2
Mining	1,268	0.6	2,367	—
Manufacturing	19,559	9.4	150,051	2.0
Construction	23,560	11.3	35,658	0.5
Public utilities	1,923	0.9	11,734	0.2
Transp. and commun.	15,252	7.3	50,808	0.7
Trade	9,735	4.7	256,012	3.5
Finance	20,673	10.0	20,847	0.3
Services	19,563	9.4	752,019	10.3
Other	9,265[3]	4.5[3]	98,302	1.3
TOTAL	207,870	100.0	7,339,586	100.0

Population economically active (1991): total 7,339,586; activity rate of total population 39.7% (participation rates: ages 10 years and over, 57.0%; female 45.5%; unemployed [1980] 5.5%).

Price and earnings indexes (1990 = 100)

	1990	1991	1992	1993	1994	1995	1996
Consumer price index	100.0	115.6	135.4	145.5	157.7	169.7	185.4
Monthly earnings index[4]	100.0	136.7	113.2	123.3	...	...	...

Household income and expenditure (1984–85). Average household size (1991) 5.6; income per household NRs 14,796 (U.S.$853); sources of income: self-employment 63.4%, wages and salaries 25.1%, rent 7.5%, other 4.0%; expenditure: food and beverages 61.2%, housing 17.3%, clothing 11.7%, health care 3.7%, education and recreation 2.9%, transportation and communications 1.2%, other 2.0%.

Foreign trade[5]

Balance of trade (current prices)

	1990	1991	1992	1993	1994	1995
NRs '000,000	−13,037	−17,059	−16,255	−21,781	−37,402	−49,843
% of total	51.4%	46.5%	33.7%	36.5%	51.0%	58.0%

Imports (1994–95): NRs 65,587,000,000 (basic manufactured goods 38.7%; machinery and transport equipment 19.7%; chemicals 11.6%; food and live animals, chiefly for food 7.9%; mineral fuels and lubricants 7.2%; crude materials except fuels 6.0%). *Major import sources:* other Asia 70.3%; European Economic Community 15.3%[6]; Oceania 5.3%.
Exports (1994–95): NRs 17,940,000,000 (basic manufactures 51.6%; miscellaneous manufactures 32.7%; food and live animals, chiefly for food 9.1%; crude materials except fuels 2.9%; chemicals and drugs 1.7%). *Major export destinations:* Germany 45.8%; U.S. 36.0%; India 13.3%[6]; Switzerland 3.3%.

Transport and communications

Transport. Railroads (1993–94): route length (1996) 101 km; passengers carried 653,000; freight handled 9,151 metric tons. Roads (1995): total length 7,550 km (paved 41%). Vehicles (1990–91): passenger cars 4,949; trucks and buses 3,363. Air transport (1993–94): passenger-km 769,000,000; metric ton-km cargo 93,126,000; airports (1996) with scheduled flights 24.

Communications

Medium	date	unit	number	units per 1,000 persons
Daily newspapers	1994	circulation	162,000	8.2
Radio	1996	receivers	625,000	30
Television	1995	receivers	250,000	12
Telephones	1995	main lines	77,300	3.8
Facsimile machines	1995	units	600	0.03

Education and health

Educational attainment (1981). Percentage of population age 25 and over having: no formal schooling 41.2%; primary education 29.4%; secondary 22.7%; higher 6.8%. *Literacy* (1991): total population age 15 and over literate 4,255,000 (37.7%); males literate 2,975,000 (51.7%); females literate 1,280,000 (23.3%).

Education (1995)

	schools	teachers	students	student/teacher ratio
Primary (age 6–10)	22,157	85,621	3,191,600	37.3
Secondary (age 11–15) } Vocational }	7,582	30,637	944,500	30.8
Higher	3[7]	4,925[8]	99,300	22.4[8]

Health (1995): physicians 1,478 (1 per 13,777 persons); hospital beds 3,188 (1 per 6,387 persons); infant mortality rate per 1,000 live births (1997) 83.
Food (1995): daily per capita caloric intake 2,367 (vegetable products 94%, animal products 6%); 108% of FAO recommended minimum requirement.

Military

Total active duty personnel (1996): 43,000 (army 99.5%, air force 0.5%). *Military expenditure as percentage of GNP* (1995): 0.9% (world 2.8%); per capita expenditure U.S.$2.

[1]Includes 10 members nominated by the king. [2]Tentative estimate. [3]Includes indirect taxes. [4]Real wage rates for unskilled industrial workers in Kāthmāndu. [5]Import figures are f.o.b. in balance of trade and c.i.f. for commodities and trading partners. [6]1993–94. [7]1993. [8]1991.

Internet resources for further information:
- **Nepal Home Page http://www.info-nepal.com/**

Netherlands, The

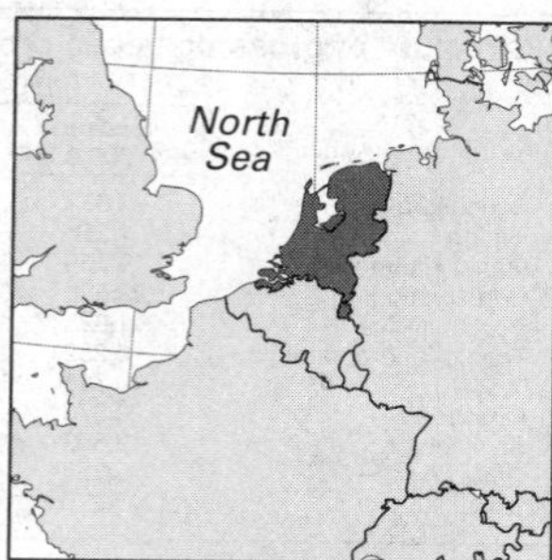

Official name: Koninkrijk der Nederlanden (Kingdom of The Netherlands).
Form of government: constitutional monarchy with a parliament (States General) comprising two legislative houses (First Chamber [75]; Second Chamber [150]).
Chief of state: Monarch.
Head of government: Prime Minister.
Seat of government: The Hague.
Capital: Amsterdam.
Official language: Dutch.
Official religion: none.
Monetary unit: 1 Netherlands guilder (f.) = 100 cents; valuation (Oct. 3, 1997) 1 U.S.$ = f. 1.99; 1 £ = f. 3.20.

Area and population

		area		population
Provinces	Capitals	sq mi	sq km	1996[1] estimate
Drenthe	Assen	1,024	2,652	457,300
Flevoland	Lelystad	551	1,426	272,800
Friesland	Leeuwarden	1,298	3,361	612,000
Gelderland	Arnhem	1,929	4,995	1,876,300
Groningen	Groningen	905	2,344	558,100
Limburg	Maastricht	837	2,167	1,133,700
Noord-Brabant	's-Hertogenbosch	1,907	4,938	2,290,400
Noord-Holland	Haarlem	1,027	2,660	2,468,400
Overijssel	Zwolle	1,288	3,337	1,054,000
Utrecht	Utrecht	524	1,356	1,070,600
Zeeland	Middelburg	692	1,792	367,400
Zuid-Holland	The Hague	1,104	2,860	3,332,900
TOTAL LAND AREA		13,085[2]	33,889[2]	
INLAND WATER		2,949	7,637	
TOTAL		16,033[2]	41,526[2]	15,493,900

Demography

Population (1997): 15,619,000.
Density (1997)[3]: persons per sq mi 1,193.6, persons per sq km 460.9.
Urban-rural (1996[1]): urban 91.0%; rural 9.0%.
Sex distribution (1996[1]): male 49.45%; female 50.55%.
Age breakdown (1996[1]): under 15, 18.4%; 15–29, 21.3%; 30–44, 23.9%; 45–59, 18.6%; 60–74, 12.1%; 75 and over, 5.7%.
Population projection: (2000) 15,921,000; (2010) 16,738,000.
Doubling time: not applicable; vital rates and net migration in near balance.
Ethnic composition (by nationality; 1996[1]): Netherlander 95.3%; Turkish 1.0%; Moroccan 1.0%; German 0.3%; other 2.4%.
Religious affiliation (1995): Roman Catholic 33.0%; Dutch Reformed Church 14.0%; Calvinist 7.0%; Muslim 4.1%; Hindu 0.5%; other 2.4%; no religion 39.0%.
Major cities (1996[1]): Amsterdam 718,119; Rotterdam 592,745; The Hague 442,503; Utrecht 234,254; Eindhoven 197,374.

Vital statistics

Birth rate per 1,000 population (1995): 12.3 (world avg. 25.0); legitimate 84.5%; illegitimate 15.5%.
Death rate per 1,000 population (1995): 8.8 (world avg. 9.3).
Natural increase rate per 1,000 population (1995): 3.5 (world avg. 15.7).
Total fertility rate (avg. births per childbearing woman; 1995): 1.5.
Marriage rate per 1,000 population (1995): 5.3.
Divorce rate per 1,000 population (1995): 2.2.
Life expectancy at birth (1995): male 74.6 years; female 80.4 years.
Major causes of death per 100,000 population (1995): malignant neoplasms (cancers) 233.1, of which lung cancer 55.3; ischemic heart diseases 132.5; cerebrovascular diseases 79.7; accidents, poisoning, and violence 31.8.

National economy

Budget (1995). Revenue: f. 168,474,000,000 (income and corporate taxes 42.3%; value-added and excise taxes 36.8%; property taxes 0.9%). Expenditures: f. 225,262,000,000 (social security and public health 18.3%; education, scientific research, and culture 15.7%; defense 5.9%; transportation 4.9%).
Public debt (1995): U.S.$249,208,000,000.
Tourism (1996): receipts U.S.$6,144,300,000; expenditures U.S.$11,112,000,000.
Production (metric tons except as noted). Agriculture, forestry, fishing (1996): sugar beets 7,600,000, potatoes 7,363,000, wheat 1,213,000, apples 570,000, tomatoes 525,000, cucumbers 500,000, onions 453,000, barley 218,000; livestock (number of live animals; 1995) 13,958,000 pigs, 4,557,000 cattle, 1,674,000 sheep; roundwood (1995) 1,103,000 cu m; fish catch (1995) 521,377. Manufacturing (value added in f. '000,000; 1994): foodstuffs 15,771; chemicals 14,968; machinery 10,284; electrical machinery 9,172; publishing 7,513. Construction (buildings completed by value in f. '000,000; 1995): residential 14,300; nonresidential 9,800. Energy production (consumption): electricity (kW-hr; 1994) 79,677,000,000 (90,239,000,000); coal (metric tons; 1994) none (14,240,000); crude petroleum (barrels; 1994) 23,554,000 (403,458,000); petroleum products (metric tons; 1994) 59,758,000 (29,130,000); natural gas (cu m; 1994) 87,810,000,000 (48,841,000,000).
Household income and expenditure (1994). Average household size 2.4; income per household f. 59,739 (U.S.$32,824); sources of income: wages 81.6%, profits 12.8%, property income 5.6%; expenditure: rent 26.2%; food, beverages, and tobacco 18.0%; education and recreation 16.2%; transportation and communications 13.4%; clothing and footwear 7.1%; household furnishings and appliances 6.6%; health care 5.7%; other 6.8%.
Gross national product (1995): U.S.$371,039,000,000 (U.S.$24,000 per capita).

Structure of gross domestic product and labour force

	1995			
	in value f. '000,000	% of total value	labour force	% of labour force
Agriculture	19,988	3.5	244,000	3.3
Mining	15,447	2.7	12,000	0.2
Manufacturing	102,849	18.0	1,079,000	14.8
Construction	31,459	5.5	406,000	5.6
Public utilities	10,738	1.9	43,000	0.6
Transp. and commun.	45,902	8.0	406,000	5.6
Trade	90,071	15.8	1,342,000	18.4
Finance	4	4	880,000	12.1
Pub. admin., defense	4	4	} 2,418,000	33.1
Services	277,437[4]	48.7[4]		
Other	−23,991[5]	−4.2[5]	467,000[6]	6.4[6]
TOTAL	569,910[2]	100.0[2]	7,297,000	100.0[2]

Population economically active (1995): total 7,297,000; activity rate of total population 47.2% (participation rates: ages 15–64, 70.1%; female 41.9%; unemployed 6.3%).

Price and earnings indexes (1990 = 100)

	1990	1991	1992	1993	1994	1995	1996
Consumer price index	100.0	103.1	106.4	109.2	112.2	114.4	116.8
Hourly earnings index	100.0	103.7	108.2	111.7	113.8	115.0	117.0

Land use (1994): forested 10.3%; meadows and pastures 31.0%; agricultural and under permanent cultivation 28.0%; other 30.7%.

Foreign trade

Balance of trade (current prices)

	1991	1992	1993	1994	1995	1996
f. '000,000	26,131	22,225	38,995	41,982	46,132	28,061
% of total	5.6%	4.7%	8.2%	8.0%	7.9%	4.4%

Imports (1995): f. 282,384,000,000 (machinery and transport equipment 29.5%, chemicals 11.9%, food 10.7%, petroleum 4.3%, clothing 2.8%). *Major import sources:* Germany 23.4%; Belgium-Luxembourg 11.8%; U.K. 10.1%; U.S. 8.0%.
Exports (1995): f. 313,545,000,000 (machinery and transport equipment 24.2%, food 17.2%, chemicals and chemical products 16.6%, petroleum products 4.1%, iron and steel 2.2%, clothing 1.4%). *Major export destinations:* Germany 28.6%; Belgium-Luxembourg 12.9%; France 11.1%.

Transport and communications

Transport. Railroads (1995): length 2,739 km; passenger-km 13,977,000,000; metric ton-km cargo 3,097,000,000. Roads (1996): total length 124,064 km (paved 91%). Vehicles (1996): passenger cars 5,740,000; trucks and buses 680,000. Merchant marine (1993): vessels (100 gross tons and over) 399; total deadweight tonnage 2,874,000. Air transport (1995–96): passenger-km 45,531,000,000; metric ton-km cargo 3,635,218,000; airports (1996) 6.

Communications

Medium	date	unit	number	units per 1,000 persons
Daily newspapers	1994	circulation	4,600,000	299
Radio	1993	receivers	13,400,000	877
Television	1995	receivers	7,660,000	495
Telephones	1995	main lines	8,120,000	525
Cellular telephones	1995	subscribers	513,000	33.2
Facsimile machines	1995	units	500,000	32.3
Personal computers	1995	units	3,100,000	200.5

Education and health

Educational attainment (1995). Percentage of population ages 15–64 having: primary education 14.9%; secondary 65.7%; higher 19.4%. *Literacy:* virtually 100% literate.

Education (1995–96)

	schools	teachers[7]	students	student/teacher ratio[7]
Primary (age 6–12)	7,411	99,031	1,477,000	15.7
Secondary (age 12–18)	1,124	89,370	868,000	7.7
Voc., teacher tr.	218	18,613	519,000	28.0
Higher	20	...	408,000	10.2

Health (1995[1]): physicians 37,493 (1 per 412 persons); hospital beds 85,579 (1 per 181 persons); infant mortality rate per 1,000 live births (1996) 5.1.
Food (1995): daily per capita caloric intake 3,230 (vegetable products 66%, animal products 34%); 120% of FAO recommended minimum requirement.

Military

Total active duty personnel (1996): 63,100 (army 51.3%, navy 22.2%, air force 19.6%, other[8] 6.9%). *Military expenditure as percentage of GNP* (1994): 2.2% (world 3.0%); per capita expenditure U.S.$464.

[1]January 1. [2]Detail does not add to total given because of rounding. [3]Based on land area only. [4]Services includes Finance and Pub. admin., defense. [5]Imputed bank service charge. [6]Includes 462,000 unemployed. [7]1990–91. [8]Includes 3,600 military police and 800 interservice personnel.

Internet resources for further information:
- **Statistics Netherlands http://www.cbs.nl/indexeng.htm**

New Zealand

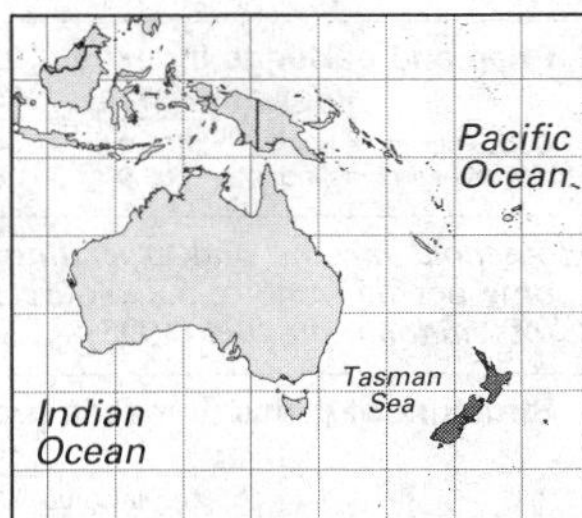

Official name: New Zealand (English); Aotearoa (Māori).
Form of government: constitutional monarchy with one legislative house (House of Representatives [120[1]]).
Chief of state: British Monarch, represented by Governor-General.
Head of government: Prime Minister.
Capital: Wellington.
Official languages: English; Māori.
Official religion: none.
Monetary unit: 1 New Zealand dollar ($NZ) = 100 cents; valuation (Oct. 3, 1997) 1 U.S.$ = $NZ 1.56; 1 £ = $NZ 2.51.

Area and population	area		population
Islands / **Regional Councils**	sq mi	sq km	1996 census
North Island	44,702	115,777	2,749,788
Auckland	...	...	1,077,205
Bay of Plenty	...	...	230,465
Gisborne[2]	...	...	46,089
Hawkes Bay	...	...	144,292
Manawatu-Wanganui	...	...	229,989
Northland	...	...	141,865
Taranaki	...	...	106,570
Waikato	...	...	357,294
Wellington	...	...	416,019
South Island	58,384	151,215	930,824
Canterbury	...	...	478,912
Marlborough[2]	...	...	40,242
Nelson[2]	...	...	42,073
Otago	...	...	193,132
Southland	...	...	100,758
Tasman[2]	...	...	40,036
West Coast	...	...	35,671
Offshore islands[3]	1,368	3,542	934
TOTAL	104,454	270,534	3,681,546

Demography

Population (1997): 3,653,000.
Density (1997): persons per sq mi 35.0, persons per sq km 13.5.
Urban-rural (1996): urban 85.0%; rural 15.0%.
Sex distribution (1996): male 49.15%; female 50.85%.
Age breakdown (1996): under 15, 23.0%; 15–29, 22.7%; 30–44, 23.1%; 45–59, 15.9%; 60–74, 10.6%; 75 and over, 4.7%.
Population projection: (2000) 3,749,000; (2010) 4,013,000.
Ethnic composition (1996)[4]: European 88.6%; Māori 15.1%; other Polynesian 5.8%; Asian 5.0%; other 0.5%.
Religious affiliation (1991): Anglican 21.4%; Presbyterian 16.0%; Roman Catholic 14.8%; Methodist 4.1%; nonreligious 19.7%; other 24.0%.
Major cities (1996): Auckland 353,670; Christchurch 313,969; Manukau 254,577; North Shore 170,913; Wellington 158,275.

Vital statistics

Birth rate per 1,000 population (1997): 15.4 (world avg. 25.0); (1996) legitimate 58.0%; illegitimate 42.0%.
Death rate per 1,000 population (1997): 7.6 (world avg. 9.3).
Natural increase rate per 1,000 population (1997): 7.8 (world avg. 15.7).
Total fertility rate (avg. births per childbearing woman; 1996): 2.0.
Life expectancy at birth (1996): male 74.0 years; female 80.0 years.
Major causes of death per 100,000 population (1994): diseases of the circulatory system 328.4, of which ischemic heart disease 188.7; malignant neoplasms (cancers) 204.3; diseases of the respiratory system 78.2.

National economy

Budget (1995–96). Revenue: $NZ 35,059,000,000 (income taxes 60.4%, taxes on goods and services 32.9%, nontax revenue 6.7%). Expenditures: $NZ 31,743,000,000 (social services 38.6%, health 16.5%, education 15.6%).
Public debt (year ending June 30, 1996): $NZ 31,747,000,000.
Tourism (1995): receipts U.S.$2,163,000,000; expenditures U.S.$1,283,000,000.
Land use (1994): forest 27.9%; pasture 50.4%; agriculture 14.2%; other 7.5%.
Production (metric tons except as noted). Agriculture, forestry, fishing (1997): apples 546,000, barley 377,998, wheat 255,316, corn (maize) 229,185; livestock (number of live animals) 47,394,000 sheep, 8,950,000 cattle, 400,000 pigs; roundwood (1995) 17,155,000 cu m; fish catch (1995) 612,243. Mining and quarrying (1995): limestone 3,930,000[5]; iron ore and sand concentrate 2,362,236; silver 27,800 kg; gold 12,100 kg. Manufacturing (1996–97): wood pulp 1,405,300; chemical fertilizers 1,365,000; yarn 21,302; beer 343,457,000 litres; footwear 2,840,000 pairs[6]; carpets 9,980,000 sq m. Energy production (consumption): electricity (kW-hr; 1994) 32,416,000,000 (32,416,000,000); coal (metric tons; 1994) 2,991,000 (2,191,000); crude petroleum (barrels; 1994) 14,401,000 (36,823,000); petroleum products (metric tons; 1994) 5,029,000 (4,504,000); natural gas (cu m; 1994) 4,442,300,000 (4,442,300,000).
Population economically active (1997[7]): total 1,806,000; activity rate 49.4% (participation rates: over age 15, 65.7%; female 44.6%; unemployed 6.4%).

Price and earnings indexes (1990 = 100)	1991	1992	1993	1994	1995	1996	1997
Consumer price index	102.6	103.6	105.0	106.8	110.8	113.4	114.3[8]
Weekly earnings index	103.0	104.8	105.5	108.5	111.8[9]	...	...

Gross national product (1995): U.S.$51,655,000,000 (U.S.$14,340 per capita).

Structure of gross domestic product and labour force	1993–94		1997[7]	
	in value $NZ '000,000	% of total value	labour force	% of labour force
Agriculture	6,673	8.3	149,900	8.3
Mining	1,121	1.4	4,500	0.2
Manufacturing	15,486	19.3	285,200	15.8
Construction	2,289	2.8	111,200	6.2
Public utilities	2,228	2.8	11,700	0.6
Transp. and commun.	6,433	8.0	101,600	5.6
Trade	12,675	15.8	355,200	19.7
Finance	17,791	22.2	205,400	11.4
Pub. admin., defense	8,716	10.8	458,600	25.4
Services	4,656	5.8		
Other	2,229[10]	2.8[10]	122,700[11]	6.8[11]
TOTAL	80,297	100.0	1,806,000	100.0

Household income and expenditure. Average household size (1995–96) 2.7; annual income per household[12] (1995–96) $NZ 46,282 (U.S.$32,140); sources of income (1994–95): wages and salaries 65.8%, transfer payments 15.2%, self-employment 9.8%, other 9.2%; expenditure (1996–97): housing 20.2%, transportation 18.2%, food 16.4%, household goods 13.7%, clothing 3.8%.

Foreign trade

Balance of trade (current prices)	1991	1992	1993	1994	1995	1996
$NZ '000,000	+443.3	+2,356.9	+1,638.5	+1,358.2	−337.6	−809.5
% of total	1.4%	7.1%	4.5%	3.5%	0.8%	1.9%

Imports (1996): $NZ 21,352,500,000 (machinery 26.0%; minerals, chemicals, and plastics 21.7%; transport equipment 13.6%; basic manufactures 7.5%; food, beverages, and tobacco 7.1%; metals and metal products 6.1%; textiles, clothing, and footwear 5.2%). *Major import sources:* Australia 21.8%; U.S. 16.0%; Japan 12.3%; U.K. 5.0%; Germany 4.6%.
Exports (1996): $NZ 20,543,000,000 (food and live animals 45.9%; basic manufactures 25.4%; minerals, chemicals, and plastics 10.2%; metals and metal products 7.0%). *Major export destinations:* Australia 20.5%; Japan 16.1%; U.S. 9.0%; U.K. 6.1%; South Korea 5.0%; Hong Kong 3.3%.

Transport and communications

Transport. Railroads (1996): length 3,915 km; passenger journeys 10,953,000; metric ton-km cargo 3,324,000,000. Roads (1996): total length 91,864 km (paved 73%). Vehicles (1996): passenger cars 1,650,112; trucks and buses 351,494. Merchant marine (1992): vessels (100 gross tons and over) 139; total deadweight tonnage 279,805. Air transport[13] (1996): passenger-km 17,848,000,000; metric ton-km cargo 648,092,000; airports (1997) 36.

Communications / **Medium**	date	unit	number	units per 1,000 persons
Daily newspapers	1995	circulation	850,000	239.0
Radio	1995	receivers	3,550,000	997.0
Television	1995	receivers	1,830,000	514.0
Telephones	1996	main lines	1,719,000	477.0
Cellular telephones	1995	subscribers	386,600	108.0
Facsimile machines	1995	units	64,800	18.1
Personal computers	1995	units	797,300	222.7

Education and health

Educational attainment (1991). Percentage of population age 25 and over having: primary and some secondary education 54.9%; secondary 31.1%; higher 6.9%; not specified 6.1%[6]. *Literacy:* virtually 100.0%.

Education (1996)	schools	teachers	students	student/ teacher ratio
Primary (age 5–12)[14]	2,397	23,379	455,671	19.5
Secondary (age 13–17)	339	15,246	227,934	14.9
Voc., teacher tr.	30	5,314	107,736	20.3
Higher[15]	7	5,982	105,690	17.7

Health (1996): physicians 11,557 (1 per 318 persons); hospital beds 22,488 (1 per 164 persons); infant mortality rate per 1,000 live births 6.7.
Food (1995): daily per capita caloric intake 3,379 (vegetable products 64%, animal products 36%); 128% of FAO recommended minimum requirement.

Military

Total active duty personnel (1997): 9,550 (army 46.1%, air force 31.9%, navy 22.0%). *Military expenditure as percentage of GNP* (1995): 1.3% (world 2.8%); per capita expenditure U.S.$211.

[1]Includes five elected seats allocated to Māoris. [2]Reorganized as a unitary authority that is administered by a district council with regional powers. [3]Includes Stewart, Chatham, Campbell, and Kermadec islands and persons on oil rigs. [4]Percentages add up to more than 100.0 as people specified more than one ethnic group on the 1996 census form. [5]1994. [6]1994–95. [7]March. [8]Second quarter. [9]May. [10]Includes import duties less imputed bank service charges. [11]Includes 116,000 unemployed. [12]Gross income. [13]Air New Zealand only. [14]Includes 96 composite schools that provide both primary and secondary education. [15]Universities only.

Internet resources for further information:
- **Statistics New Zealand Te Tari Tatau http://www.stats.govt.nz/statsweb.nsf**
- **New Zealand's Energy http://www.moc.govt.nz/energy/emsu**
- **Otago Daily Times Online Edition http://www.odt.co.nz**
- **The Press On-Line New Zealand News http://www.press.co.nz/**

Nicaragua

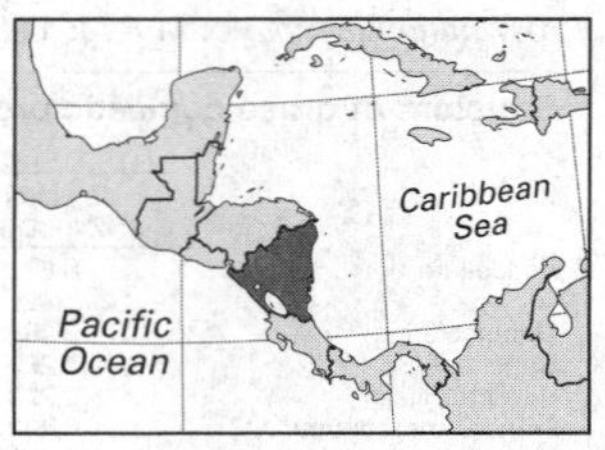

Official name: República de Nicaragua (Republic of Nicaragua).
Form of government: unitary multiparty republic with one legislative house (National Assembly [93[1]]).
Head of state and government: President.
Capital: Managua.
Official language: Spanish.
Official religion: none.
Monetary unit: 1 córdoba oro (C$)[2] = 100 centavos; valuation (Oct. 3, 1997) 1 U.S.$ = C$9.70; 1 £ = C$15.64.

Area and population

		area[3]		population
Departments	Capitals	sq mi	sq km	1995 census[4]
Boaco	Boaco	1,639	4,244	136,949
Carazo	Jinotepe	405	1,050	149,407
Chinandega	Chinandega	1,902	4,926	350,212
Chontales	Juigalpa	2,463	6,378	144,635
Estelí	Estelí	902	2,335	174,894
Granada	Granada	359	929	155,683
Jinotega	Jinotega	3,766	9,755	257,933
León	León	1,972	5,107	336,894
Madriz	Somoto	619	1,602	107,567
Managua	Managua	1,418	3,672	1,093,760
Masaya	Masaya	228	590	241,354
Matagalpa	Matagalpa	3,291	8,523	383,776
Nueva Segovia	Ocotal	1,206	3,123	148,492
Río San Juan	San Carlos	2,885	7,473	70,143
Rivas	Rivas	832	2,155	140,432
Autonomous regions				
North Atlantic	...	12,417	32,159	192,716
South Atlantic	Bluefields	10,582	27,407	272,252
TOTAL LAND AREA		46,884[5]	121,428	
INLAND WATER		4,009	10,384	
TOTAL		50,893	131,812	4,357,099

Demography

Population (1997): 4,632,000.
Density (1997)[6]: persons per sq mi 98.8, persons per sq km 38.1.
Urban-rural (1995): urban 54.4%; rural 45.6%.
Sex distribution (1995): male 49.28%; female 50.72%.
Age breakdown (1994): under 15, 44.2%; 15–29, 28.7%; 30–44, 15.5%; 45–59, 7.2%; 60–74, 3.6%; 75 and over, 0.8%.
Population projection: (2000) 4,993,000; (2010) 6,192,000.
Doubling time: 26 years.
Ethnic composition (1991): mestizo (Spanish/Indian) 69.0%; white 17.0%; black 9.0%; Amerindian 5.0%.
Religious affiliation (1995): Roman Catholic 76.7%; Protestant 15.2%, of which Pentecostal 10.0%; other 8.1%.
Major cities (1995)[4]: Managua 864,201; León 123,865; Chinandega 97,387; Masaya 88,971; Granada 71,783; Estelí 71,550.

Vital statistics

Birth rate per 1,000 population (1996): 33.8 (world avg. 25.0).
Death rate per 1,000 population (1996): 6.0 (world avg. 9.3).
Natural increase rate per 1,000 population (1996): 27.8 (world avg. 15.7).
Total fertility rate (avg. births per childbearing woman; 1996): 4.0.
Marriage rate per 1,000 population (1991): 3.3.
Divorce rate per 1,000 population (1991): 0.4.
Life expectancy at birth (1996): male 63.4 years; female 68.1 years.
Major causes of death per 100,000 population (1991)[7]: diseases of the circulatory system 142.0; infectious and parasitic diseases 100.0; accidents and violence 93.0; diseases of the respiratory system 73.0; malignant neoplasms (cancers) 56.0.

National economy

Budget (1995). Revenue: C$3,929,000,000 (tax revenue 74.6%, of which import duties 17.3%, excise taxes on petroleum products 14.6%; grants 20.2%). Expenditures: C$4,526,000,000 (current expenditure 62.8%, development expenditure 33.6%; net lending 3.6%).
Public debt (external, outstanding; 1995): U.S.$7,937,000,000.
Production (metric tons except as noted). Agriculture, forestry, fishing (1996): sugar cane 2,948,000, corn (maize) 332,600, rice 219,100, sorghum 127,300, dry beans 102,900, bananas 88,000, oranges 72,000, coffee 55,000, soybeans 24,100, sesame 14,800; livestock (number of live animals) 1,807,000 cattle, 410,000 pigs; roundwood (1995) 3,809,000 cu m; fish catch (1995) 13,503, of which shrimp 5,425. Mining and quarrying (1995): gold 42,300 troy oz. Manufacturing (value added in C$'000,000; 1995[8]): food, beverages, and tobacco 3,129; machinery and metal products 319; refined petroleum and rubber products 231; chemicals and chemical products 124. Construction (completed; 1991): 569 cu m. Energy production (consumption): electricity (kW-hr; 1995) 1,726,000,000 (1,130,000,000); coal, none (none); crude petroleum (barrels; 1994) none (4,178,000); petroleum products (metric tons; 1994) 540,000 (582,000); natural gas, none (none).
Tourism (in U.S.$'000,000; 1995): receipts 54.6; expenditures 40.
Population economically active (1994): total 1,407,700; activity rate of total population 34.8% (participation rates: over age 15 [1991] 62.0%; female [1991] 33.2%; unemployed [1996] 16.6%).

Price and earnings indexes (1992 = 100)

	1992	1993	1994	1995	1996	1997
Consumer price index	100.0	120.4	129.7	143.9	160.6	171.2[9]
Monthly earnings index[10]	100.0	111.8	126.7	142.9	...	...

Household income and expenditure. Average household size (1995) 5.8; income per household: n.a.; sources of income: n.a.; expenditure: n.a.
Gross national product (1995): U.S.$1,659,000,000 (U.S.$380 per capita).

Structure of gross domestic product and labour force

	1996		1994	
	in value C$'000,000	% of total value	labour force	% of labour force
Agriculture, forestry	5,981	34.9	415,400	29.5
Mining	133	0.8	7,300	0.5
Manufacturing	2,677	15.6	155,500	11.0
Construction	614	3.6	28,600	2.0
Public utilities	186	1.1	10,600	0.8
Transp. and commun.	612	3.6	30,000	2.1
Trade	4,184	24.4	189,000	13.4
Finance, real estate	859	5.0	16,200	1.2
Pub. admin., defense	928	5.4	81,900	5.8
Services	952	5.6	181,300	12.9
Other	—	—	291,900[11]	20.7[11]
TOTAL	17,126	100.0	1,407,700	100.0[5]

Land use (1994): forested 26.3%; meadows and pastures 45.3%; agricultural and under permanent cultivation 10.5%; other 17.9%.

Foreign trade[12]

Balance of trade (current prices)

	1991	1992	1993	1994	1995	1996
U.S.$'000,000	−396.4	−547.8	−402.8	−433.5	−263.8	−371.2
% of total	42.1%	55.1%	43.0%	38.2%	20.0%	22.6%

Imports (1996): U.S.$1,119,900,000 (capital goods 24.9%, consumer goods 24.7%, petroleum 14.1%). *Major import sources* (1995): U.S. 31.2%; CACM 23.9%; Venezuela 11.6%; Japan 5.2%.
Exports (1996): U.S.$634,800,000 (industrial products 24.4%, coffee 17.5%, crustaceans 10.9%, beef 6.9%, raw sugar 6.0%). *Major export destinations:* U.S. 38.1%; CACM 15.1%; Germany 10.4%; Spain 7.2%; The Netherlands 5.9%.

Transport and communications

Transport. Railroads: [13]. Roads (1995): total length 17,146 km (paved 10%). Vehicles (1995): passenger cars 72,413; trucks and buses 68,090. Air transport (1994)[14]: passenger-km 72,172,000; metric ton-km cargo 6,964,000; airports (1997) with scheduled flights 10.

Communications

Medium	date	unit	number	units per 1,000 persons
Daily newspapers	1994	circulation	130,000	31
Radio	1996	receivers	925,000	206
Television	1995	receivers	210,000	48
Telephones	1995	main lines	96,600	22
Cellular telephones	1995	subscribers	4,400	1.0

Education and health

Educational attainment: n.a. *Literacy* (1995): total population age 15 and over literate 1,574,000 (65.7%); males literate 727,000 (64.6%); females literate 847,000 (66.6%).

Education (1994)

	schools	teachers	students	student/ teacher ratio
Primary (age 7–12)	4,993	20,626	765,972	37.1
Secondary (age 13–18) / Voc., teacher tr.	451	5,356	211,606	39.5
Higher	10	2,005	22,120	11.0

Health (1994): physicians 2,577 (1 per 1,566 persons); hospital beds 4,413 (1 per 914 persons); infant mortality rate per 1,000 live births (1996) 45.8.
Food (1995): daily per capita caloric intake 2,311 (vegetable products 92%, animal products 8%); 103% of FAO recommended minimum requirement.

Military

Total active duty personnel (1996): 17,000 (army 88.2%, navy 4.7%, air force 7.1%). *Military expenditure as percentage of GNP* (1995): 2.2% (world 2.8%); per capita expenditure U.S.$8.

[1]Includes three unsuccessful 1996 presidential candidates meeting special conditions. [2]The córdoba oro (gold cordoba), introduced in August 1990, circulated simultaneously with the new córdoba until April 30, 1991, when the new córdoba ceased to be legal tender; on April 30, 1 córdoba oro equaled 5,000,000 new córdobas. The new córdoba had been introduced in February 1988 at the rate of 1 new córdoba to 1,000 (old) córdobas. [3]Lakes and lagoons are excluded from the areas of departments and autonomous regions. [4]Final figures. [5]Detail does not add to total given because of rounding. [6]Based on land area. [7]Projected rates based on about 45% of total deaths. [8]At prices of 1980. [9]April. [10]Base and all indexes are for December only. [11]Unemployed persons previously employed. [12]Imports f.o.b. in balance of trade and c.i.f. in commodities and trading partners. [13]Railroad service ended in January 1994. [14]Nica only.

Internet resources for further information:

- **Banco Central de Nicaragua: Informe Anual (Spanish language only) http://www.bcn.gob.ni/infanu/informes.html**

Niger

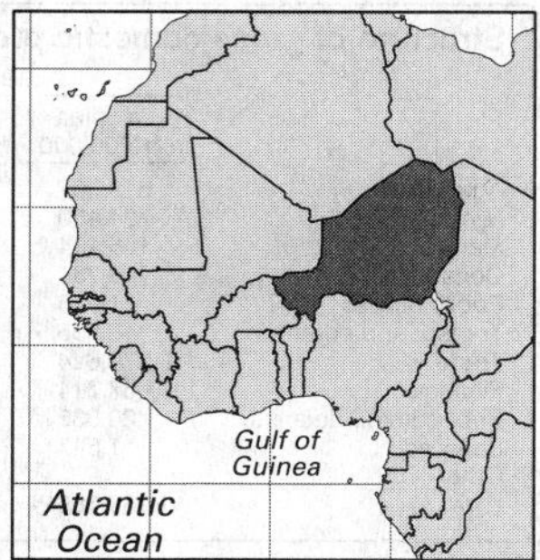

Official name: République du Niger (Republic of Niger).
Form of government: republic[1] with a single legislative body (National Assembly[2] [83[3]].
Head of state and government: President assisted by Prime Minister.
Capital: Niamey.
Official language: French.
Official religion: none.
Monetary unit: 1 CFA franc (CFAF) = 100 centimes; valuation (Oct. 3, 1997) 1 U.S.$ = CFAF 592.29; 1 £ = CFAF 954.76.

Area and population

		area[4]		population
Departments	Capitals	sq mi	sq km	1990 estimate
Agadez[5]	Agadez	244,869	634,209	189,000
Diffa	Diffa	54,138	140,216	227,000
Dosso	Dosso	11,970	31,002	982,000
Maradi	Maradi	14,896	38,581	1,415,000
Tahoua	Tahoua	41,188	106,677	1,373,000
Tillabéri[6]	Tillabéri	34,863[7]	90,293[7]	1,818,000[7]
Zinder	Zinder	56,151	145,430	1,467,000
City				
Niamey	Niamey	7	7	7
TOTAL		458,075	1,186,408	7,471,000

Demography

Population (1997): 9,389,000.
Density (1997)[4]: persons per sq mi 19.2, persons per sq km 7.4.
Urban-rural (1995): urban 17.0%; rural 83.0%.
Sex distribution (1995): male 49.40%; female 50.60%.
Age breakdown (1995): under 15, 48.4%; 15–29, 25.7%; 30–44, 14.4%; 45–59, 7.5%; 60–74, 3.4%; 75 and over, 0.6%.
Population projection: (2000) 10,260,000; (2010) 13,678,000.
Doubling time: 23 years.
Ethnic composition (1988): Hausa 53.0%; Zerma- (Djerma-) Songhai 21.2%; Tuareg 10.4%; Fulani (Peul) 9.8%; Kanuri-Nanga 4.4%; Teda 0.4%; Arab 0.3%; Gurma 0.3%; other 0.2%.
Religious affiliation (1995): Muslim, primarily Sunnī, *c.* 89%; traditional beliefs *c.* 11%.
Major cities (1988): Niamey 391,876; Zinder 119,827; Maradi 110,005; Tahoua 49,948; Agadez 32,272.

Vital statistics

Birth rate per 1,000 population (1996): 54.5 (world avg. 25.0).
Death rate per 1,000 population (1996): 24.6 (world avg. 9.3).
Natural increase rate per 1,000 population (1996): 29.9 (world avg. 15.7).
Total fertility rate (avg. births per childbearing woman; 1996): 7.4.
Marriage rate per 1,000 population: n.a.
Divorce rate per 1,000 population: n.a.
Life expectancy at birth (1996): male 41.1 years; female 40.2 years.
Major causes of death: n.a.; however, among selected major causes of infectious disease registered at medical facilities were malaria, measles, diarrhea, meningitis, pneumonia, diphtheria, tetanus, viral hepatitis, and poliomyelitis; malnutrition and shortages of trained medical personnel are widespread.

National economy

Budget (1996). Revenue: CFAF 123,500,000,000 (taxes 54.2%, external aid and gifts 38.8%, nontax revenue 7.0%). Expenditures: CFAF 120,200,000,000 (current expenditures 73.0%, development expenditures 27.0%).
Public debt (external, outstanding; 1995): U.S.$1,376,000,000.
Tourism (1995): receipts from visitors U.S.$15,000,000; expenditures by nationals abroad U.S.$21,000,000.
Gross national product (1995): U.S.$1,961,000,000 (U.S.$220 per capita).

Structure of gross domestic product and labour force

	1994		1988	
	in value CFAF '000,000	% of total value	labour force[8]	% of labour force
Agriculture	372,200	42.9	1,764,049	76.2
Mining	34,700	4.0	5,295	0.2
Manufacturing	56,900	6.6	65,793	2.8
Construction	16,100	1.9	13,742	0.6
Public utilities	18,400	2.1	1,778	0.1
Transp. and commun.	47,200	5.4	14,764	0.6
Trade and finance	130,000	15.0	210,354	9.1
Pub. admin., defense	94,700	10.9	59,271	2.6
Services	87,400	10.1	63,991	2.8
Other	10,300	1.2	116,657	5.0
TOTAL	867,800[9]	100.0[9]	2,315,694	100.0

Production (metric tons except as noted). Agriculture, forestry, fishing (1996): millet 1,832,000, cowpeas 430,000, sorghum 425,000, cassava (manioc) 225,000, onions 178,000, sugarcane 145,000, rice 70,000, peanuts (groundnuts) 57,000, tomatoes 47,000, tobacco leaf 930; livestock (number of live animals) 5,869,000 goats, 3,849,000 sheep, 1,987,000 cattle, 450,000 asses, 380,000 camels, 82,000 horses; roundwood (1995) 5,866,000 cu m; fish catch (1994) 2,200. Mining and quarrying (1996): salt 3,000[10]; uranium 3,326. Manufacturing (value added in CFAF '000,000; 1993): traditional-sector handicrafts 36,900; food and beverages 2,900; soaps and other chemical products 2,100; construction materials 600. Construction (value added in CFAF; 1994): 16,100,000,000. Energy production (consumption): electricity (kW-hr; 1994) 178,000,000 (375,000,000); coal (metric tons; 1994) 133,500 (174,000); crude petroleum, none (none); petroleum products (metric tons; 1994) none (211,000); natural gas, none (none).
Population economically active (1988)[8]: total 2,315,694; activity rate of total population 31.9% (participation rates: ages 15–64, 55.2%; female 20.4%).

Price and earnings indexes (1990 = 100)

	1991	1992	1993	1994	1995	1996	1997[11]
Consumer price index	92.2	88.1	87.0	118.4	130.9	137.8	141.4
Annual earnings index[12]	101.2	103.5	108.0	123.6	...	...	...

Household income and expenditure. Average household size (1988) 6.4; income per household: n.a.; expenditure (1987): food and beverages 43.1%, housing 22.8%, clothing 10.0%.
Land use (1994): forested 2.0%; meadows and pastures 8.2%; agricultural and under permanent cultivation 2.9%; other (largely desert) 86.9%.

Foreign trade

Balance of trade (current prices)

	1990	1991	1992	1993	1994	1995
CFAF '000,000	−39,900	−19,500	−12,700	−2,200	−11,000	+1,600
% of total	19.5%	10.8%	7.8%	1.5%	4.2%	0.7%

Imports (1994): CFAF 135,600,000,000 (consumer goods 72.3%, of which cereals 10.8%, petroleum products 7.7%; intermediate and capital goods 27.7%). *Major import sources*[13]: France 20%; Côte d'Ivoire 11%; China 4%; Belgium 4%; unspecified countries 14%.
Exports (1995): CFAF 143,000,000,000 (uranium 52.9%; livestock [mostly live cattle, sheep, and goats] 13.9%; cowpeas 5.2%). *Major export destinations* (1994)[13]: France 66%; Côte d'Ivoire 8%; United Kingdom 5%.

Transport and communications

Transport. Railroads: none. Roads (1995): total length 6,129 mi, 9,863 km (paved 9%). Vehicles (1995): passenger cars 37,500, trucks and buses 14,100. Air transport (1996)[14]: passenger-mi 139,644,000, passenger-km 224,736,000; short ton-mi cargo 11,247,000, metric ton-km cargo 16,420,000; airports (1996) with scheduled flights 6.

Communications

Medium	date	unit	number	units per 1,000 persons
Daily newspapers	1994	circulation	11,000	1.3
Radio	1996	receivers	440,000	48
Television	1995	receivers	25,000	2.8
Telephones	1995	main lines	13,300	1.5
Facsimile machines	1995	units	300	—

Education and health

Educational attainment (1988). Percentage of population age 25 and over having: no formal schooling 85.0%; Koranic education 11.2%; primary education 2.5%; secondary 1.1%; higher 0.2%. *Literacy* (1995): total population age 15 and over literate 641,000 (13.6%); males literate 482,000 (20.9%); females literate 159,000 (6.6%).

Education (1993–94)

	schools	teachers	students	student/ teacher ratio
Primary (age 7–12)	2,656	12,216	414,296	33.9
Secondary (age 13–19)	105[15]	2,219[16]	88,810	35.1[16]
Voc., teacher tr.	7[15]	175[16]	2,110	12.1[16]
Higher[17]	2	315	4,060	12.9

Health: physicians (1993) 242 (1 per 35,141 persons); hospital beds (1987) *c.* 3,500 (1 per 2,000 persons); infant mortality rate per 1,000 live births (1996) 117.6.
Food (1995): daily per capita caloric intake 2,136 (vegetable products 94%, animal products 6%); 91% of FAO recommended minimum requirement.

Military

Total active duty personnel (1996): 5,300 (army 98.1%, air force 1.9%). *Military expenditure as percentage of GNP* (1995): 1.2% (world 2.8%); per capita expenditure U.S.$2.

[1]Leader of military coup of January 1996 (now president) promulgated a new constitution on May 22, 1996; president approved dissolution of military ruling council in December 1996. [2]November 1996 elections to National Assembly were boycotted by major opposition parties. [3]Occupied seats only. [4]The departmental areas and total shown are obsolete. The total area, according to recent official estimates, is 489,000 sq mi (1,267,000 sq km); but subtotals distributing this total among the departments remain unpublished. [5]The peace accord signed in October 1994 provided for an eventual limited autonomy for the Tuaregs (a Berber-speaking people), who inhabit Agadez department. [6]Created 1992. [7]Tillabéri includes Niamey. [8]Excluding nomadic population. [9]Detail does not add to total given because of rounding. [10]1994. [11]April. [12]Public sector only. [13]Estimated figures. [14]Represents 1/11 of the traffic of Air Afrique, which is operated by 11 West African states. [15]1989–90. [16]1992–93. [17]Université de Niamey and École Nationale d'Administration du Niger only.

Internet resources for further information:

- **Welcome to the Delegation of Niger at UNESCO http://www.unesco.org/delegates/niger/welcome.htm**

Nigeria

Official name: Federal Republic of Nigeria.
Form of government: military regime[1].
Head of state and government: Chairman assisted by Provisional Ruling Council.
Capital: Abuja (Federal Capital Territory)[2].
Official language: English.
Official religion: none.
Monetary unit: 1 Nigerian naira (₦) = 100 kobo; valuation (Oct. 3, 1997) 1 U.S.$ = ₦21.89; 1 £ = ₦35.28.

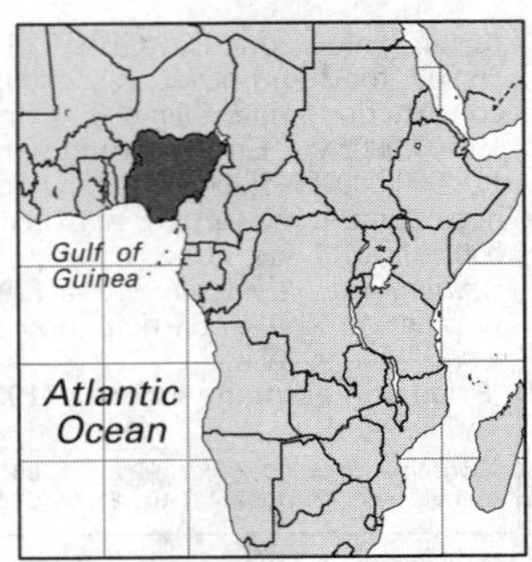

Area and population

States[3]	area sq km[2]	population 1995 estimate	States[3]	area sq km[2]	population 1995 estimate
Abia	6,320[4]	2,569,362[4]	Kebbi	36,800	2,305,768
Adamawa	36,917	2,374,892	Kogi	29,833	2,346,936
Akwa Ibom	7,081	2,638,413	Kwara	36,825	1,751,464
Anambra	4,844	3,094,783	Lagos	3,345	6,357,253
Bauchi	64,605[5]	4,801,569[5]	Niger	76,363	2,775,526
Bayelsa	[6]	[6]	Nassarawa	[8]	[8]
Benue	34,059	3,108,754	Ogun	16,762	2,614,747
Borno	70,898	2,903,238	Ondo	20,959[7]	4,343,230[7]
Cross River	20,156	2,085,926	Osun	9,251	2,463,185
Delta	17,698	2,873,711	Oyo	28,454	3,900,803
Ebonyi	[4]	[4]	Plateau	58,030[8]	3,671,498[8]
Edo	17,802	2,414,919	Rivers	21,850[6]	4,454,337[6]
Ekiti	[7]	[7]	Sokoto	65,735[9]	4,911,118[9]
Enugu	12,831[4]	3,534,633[4]	Taraba	54,473	1,655,443
Gombe	[5]	[5]	Yobe	45,502	1,578,172
Imo	5,530	2,779,028	Zamfara	[9]	[9]
Jigawa	23,154	3,164,134			
Kaduna	46,053	4,438,007	**Federal Capital**		
Kano	20,131	6,297,165	**Territory**		
Katsina	24,192	4,336,363	Abuja	7,315	423,391
			TOTAL	923,768	98,967,768

Demography

Population (1997): 103,460,000.
Density (1997): persons per sq mi 290.1, persons per sq km 112.0.
Urban-rural (1996): urban 40.1%; rural 59.9%.
Sex distribution (1996): male 49.57%; female 50.43%.
Age breakdown (1995): under 15, 45.6%; 15–29, 25.7%; 30–44, 15.7%; 45–59, 8.5%; 60–74, 3.8%; 75 and over, 0.7%.
Population projection: (2000) 112,500,000; (2010) 148,710,000.
Doubling time: 23 years.
Ethnic composition (1983): Hausa 21.3%; Yoruba 21.3%; Igbo (Ibo) 18.0%; Fulani 11.2%; Ibibio 5.6%; Kanuri 4.2%; Edo 3.4%; Tiv 2.2%; Ijaw 1.8%; Bura 1.7%; Nupe 1.2%; other 8.1%.
Religious affiliation (1995): Muslim 50.0%; Christian 40.0%, of which Protestant 21.4%, Roman Catholic 9.9%, African indigenous 8.7%; other 10.0%.
Major cities (1992): Lagos 1,347,000; Ibadan 1,295,000; Kano 699,900; Ogbomosho 660,600; Oshogbo 441,600; Ilorin 430,600.

Vital statistics

Birth rate per 1,000 population (1990–95): 45.4 (world avg. 25.0).
Death rate per 1,000 population (1990–95): 15.4 (world avg. 9.3).
Natural increase rate per 1,000 population (1990–95): 30.0 (world avg. 15.7).
Total fertility rate (avg. births per childbearing woman; 1990–95): 6.4.
Life expectancy at birth (1993): male 53.5 years; female 55.9 years.

National economy

Budget (1995). Revenue: ₦459,987,300,000 (petroleum royalties and rents 60.8%; import duties 8.1%; company income tax 4.8%; value-added tax 4.4%). Expenditures: ₦256,520,700,000 (recurrent expenditure 52.8%, of which debt service 19.9%, education 4.7%, health 1.8%, defense 0.5%; capital expenditure 47.2%).
Public debt (external, outstanding; 1995): U.S.$28,701,000,000.
Production (metric tons except as noted). Agriculture, forestry, fishing (1996): cassava 31,500,000, yams 23,264,000, sorghum 7,084,000, millet 5,681,000, corn (maize) 5,667,000, rice 3,122,000, peanuts (groundnuts) 1,723,000, plantains 1,712,000, taro 1,182,000, green peppers 970,000, palm oil 776,000; livestock (number of live animals) 24,500,000 goats, 18,115,000 cattle, 14,000,000 sheep; roundwood (1995) 111,049,000 cu m; fish catch (1995) 302,831. Mining and quarrying (1995): limestone 3,660,000; marble 22,460; tin 300[10, 11]. Manufacturing (value added in ₦'000,000; 1995): food and beverages 25,415; textiles 16,193; chemical products 11,181; machinery and transport equipment 5,639; paper products 2,828; wood products 996. Construction: n.a. Energy production (consumption): electricity (kW-hr; 1994) 14,790,000,000 (14,790,000,000); coal (metric tons; 1994) 50,000 (50,000); crude petroleum (barrels; 1994) 665,994,000 (84,452,000); petroleum products (metric tons; 1994) 5,234,000 (5,974,000); natural gas (cu m; 1994) 9,798,000,000 (9,798,000,000).
Tourism (1995): receipts U.S.$54,000,000; expenditures U.S.$144,000,000[12].
Household income and expenditure. Avg. household size (1995) 4.7; annual income per household (1992–93) ₦15,000 (U.S.$760): sources of income (1979): self-employment 49.4%, wages 30.2%, interest 5.4%, rent 4.7%, transfer payments 4.3%; expenditures (1979): food 53.0%, fuel and light 11.4%, clothing 6.0%, transportation 4.7%, household goods 3.8%, other 21.1%.
Gross national product (1995): U.S.$28,411,000,000 (U.S.$260 per capita).

Structure of gross domestic product and labour force

	1995		1986	
	in value ₦'000,000	% of total value	labour force	% of labour force
Agriculture	619,807	31.6	13,259,000	43.1
Mining[13]	794,450	40.5	6,800	0.1
Manufacturing	105,154	5.4	1,263,700	4.1
Construction	13,784	0.7	545,600	1.8
Public utilities	1,915	0.1	130,400	0.4
Transp. and commun.	48,855	2.5	1,111,900	3.6
Trade[14]	276,624	14.1	7,417,400	24.1
Finance	67,714	3.4	120,100	0.4
Pub. admin., defense	20,835	1.1	4,902,100	15.9
Services	11,547	0.6		
Other	...	...	2,008,500[15]	6.5[15]
TOTAL	1,960,686[16]	100.0	30,765,500	100.0

Population economically active (1993–94): total 29,000,000; activity rate 31.0% (participation rates: ages 15–59, 64.4%; female 44.0%; unemployed [1992] 4.0%).

Price and earnings indexes (1990 = 100)

	1990	1991	1992	1993	1994	1995	1996
Consumer price index	100.0	113.0	163.4	256.8	403.3	696.9	901.1
Earnings index	...	...	...	...	...	...	...

Land use (1994): forested 15.7%; pastures 43.9%; agricultural 35.9%; other 4.5%.

Foreign trade

Balance of trade (current prices)

	1990	1991	1992	1993	1994	1995
₦'000,000	+68,587	+40,696	+76,298	+69,145	+76,677	+91,796
% of total	45.4%	20.2%	22.8%	18.8%	22.8%	6.5%

Imports (1995): ₦111,728,000,000 (machinery and transport equipment 42.0%; manufactured goods [mostly iron and steel products, textiles, and paper products] 24.0%; chemicals 17.0%; food 8.4%). *Major import sources* (1992): Germany 18.9%; U.K. 17.8%; Belgium-Luxembourg 9.5%; U.S. 9.2%; France 7.4%.
Exports (1995): ₦220,408,900,000 (crude petroleum 94.8%; cocoa beans 0.7%; rubber 0.3%; other exports include cocoa products, textiles, and cashew nuts). *Major export destinations* (1992): U.S. 48.1%; Spain 16.6%; Italy 7.4%; Germany 7.2%; France 3.8%.

Transport and communications

Transport. Railroads (1993): length[17] 3,505 km; passenger-km 555,000,000; metric ton-km cargo 2,185,000. Roads (1995): total length 32,810 km (paved 83%). Vehicles (1995): passenger cars 663,000; trucks and buses 68,300. Merchant marine (1992): vessels (100 gross tons and over) 271; total deadweight tonnage 733,329. Air transport (1994): passenger-km 985,000,000; metric ton-km cargo 11,484,000[18]; airports (1996) 12.

Communications

Medium	date	unit	number	units per 1,000 persons
Daily newspapers	1995	circulation	1,760,000	18.0
Radio	1995	receivers	17,200,000	170.0
Television	1995	receivers	4,000,000	38.0
Telephones	1995	main lines	405,100	3.6
Cellular telephones	1995	subscribers	13,000	0.1
Personal computers	1995	units	440,000	4.1

Education and health

Literacy (1995): total population age 15 and over literate 34,969,000 (57.1%); males literate 20,027,000 (67.3%); females literate 14,669,000 (47.3%).

Education (1994–95)

	schools	teachers	students	student/teacher ratio
Primary (age 6–12)	38,649	435,210	16,191,000	37.2
Secondary (age 12–17)	6,074	152,596	4,451,000	29.2
Voc., teacher tr.	376[19]	15,738[20]	391,583[20]	24.9[20]
Higher	31	12,103	228,000	18.8

Health (1994): physicians 21,739 (1 per 4,496 persons); hospital beds 91,346 (1 per 1,070 persons); infant mortality rate (1990–95) 84.2.
Food (1995): daily per capita caloric intake 2,508 (vegetable products 97%, animal products 3%); 106% of FAO recommended minimum requirement.

Military

Total active duty personnel (1996): 77,100 (army 80.4%, navy 7.3%, air force 12.3%). *Military expenditure as percentage of GNP* (1994): 0.8% (world 3.0%); per capita expenditure U.S.$3.

[1]Assumed control on Sept. 14, 1995. [2]Statutory transfer of capital from Lagos to Abuja took place in December 1991. [3]In October 1996 six new states were created: Bayelsa, Ebonyi, Ekiti, Gombe, Nassarawa, and Zamfara. [4]Ebonyi is included partly in Abia and partly in Enugu. [5]Bauchi includes Gombe. [6]Rivers includes Bayelsa. [7]Ondo includes Ekiti. [8]Plateau includes Nassarawa. [9]Sokoto includes Zamfara. [10]Metal content. [11]1996. [12]1994. [13]Includes ₦792,372,000,000 from petroleum and natural gas. [14]Includes hotels. [15]Includes 1,263,000 unemployed. [16]Detail does not add to total given because of rounding. [17]1995. [18]1992. [19]1987–88. [20]1988–89.

Internet resources for further information:
- **Embassy of Nigeria (Washington, D.C.) http://tribeca.ios.com/Qn123**

Norway

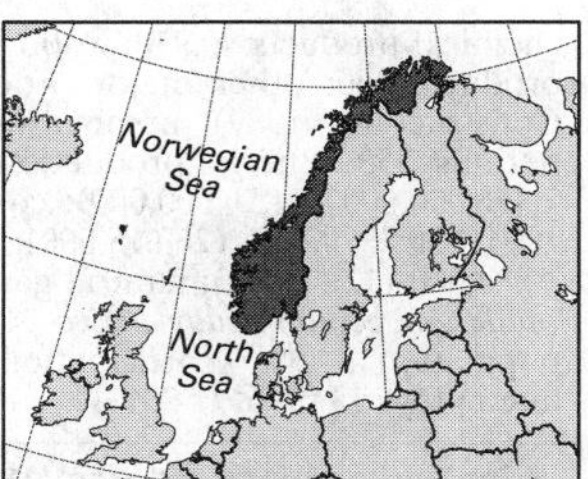

Official name: Kongeriket Norge (Kingdom of Norway).
Form of government: constitutional monarchy with one legislative house (Parliament [165]).
Chief of state: King.
Head of government: Prime Minister.
Capital: Oslo.
Official language: Norwegian.
Official religion: Evangelical Lutheran.
Monetary unit: 1 Norwegian krone (NKr) = 100 øre; valuation (Oct. 3, 1997) 1 U.S.$ = NKr 7.04; 1 £ = NKr 11.34.

Area and population

		area[1]		population
Counties	Capitals	sq mi	sq km	1997[2] estimate
Akershus	—	1,898	4,917	446,385
Aust-Agder	Arendal	3,557	9,212	100,602
Buskerud	Drammen	5,763	14,927	230,763
Finnmark	Vadsø	18,779	48,637	75,643
Hedmark	Hamar	10,575	27,388	186,021
Hordaland	Bergen	6,036	15,634	426,896
Møre og Romsdal	Molde	5,832	15,104	241,493
Nordland	Bodø	14,798	38,327	240,304
Nord-Trøndelag	Steinkjer	8,647	22,396	127,236
Oppland	Lillehammer	9,726	25,191	182,443
Oslo	Oslo	175	454	493,973
Østfold	Moss	1,615	4,183	241,206
Rogaland	Stavanger	3,529	9,141	360,380
Sogn og Fjordane	Leikanger	7,189	18,620	108,032
Sør-Trøndelag	Trondheim	7,271	18,838	258,246
Telemark	Skien	5,913	15,315	163,467
Troms	Tromsø	10,032	25,984	151,191
Vest-Agder	Kristiansand	2,811	7,281	151,577
Vestfold	Tønsberg	856	2,216	206,108
TOTAL		125,004[3]	323,758[3]	4,391,966[4]

Demography

Population (1997): 4,405,000.
Density (1997): persons per sq mi 35.2, persons per sq km 13.6.
Urban-rural (1990): urban 75.0%; rural 25.0%.
Sex distribution (1996): male 49.45%; female 50.55%.
Age breakdown (1996): under 15, 19.4%; 15–29, 21.6%; 30–44, 21.8%; 45–59, 17.0%; 60–74, 12.8%; 75 and over, 7.4%.
Population projection: (2000) 4,483,000; (2010) 4,681,000.
Ethnic composition (by country of citizenship; 1995): Norway 96.3%; Denmark 0.4%; Sweden 0.3%; United Kingdom 0.3%; Pakistan 0.2%; United States 0.2%; Yugoslavia 0.2%; Iran 0.1%; other 2.0%.
Major cities (1997)[5]: Oslo 493,973; Bergen 224,130; Trondheim 144,599.

Vital statistics

Birth rate per 1,000 population (1996): 13.9 (world avg. 25.0); (1995) legitimate 52.4%; illegitimate 47.6%.
Death rate per 1,000 population (1996): 10.1 (world avg. 9.3).
Natural increase rate per 1,000 population (1996): 3.8 (world avg. 15.7).
Total fertility rate (avg. births per childbearing woman; 1995): 1.9.
Marriage rate per 1,000 population (1994): 4.8.
Divorce rate per 1,000 population (1994): 2.5.
Life expectancy at birth (1994): male 74.9 years; female 80.6 years.
Major causes of death per 100,000 population (1993): ischemic heart disease 237.7; malignant neoplasms (cancers) 227.8; cerebrovascular disease 128.5.

National economy

Budget (1995). Revenue: NKr 339,237,000,000 (social security taxes 24.6%, value-added taxes 24.2%, taxes on interest and dividends 9.2%, taxes on petroleum income and activity 3.1%). Expenditures: NKr 339,144,000,000 (social security and welfare 25.2%, health 7.9%, debt service 6.0%).
Land use (1994): forested 27.2%; meadows and pastures 0.4%; agricultural and under permanent cultivation 2.9%; built-up and other 69.5%.
Tourism (1995): receipts from visitors U.S.$2,386,000,000.
Production (metric tons except as noted). Agriculture, forestry, fishing (1996): barley 645,000, potatoes 400,000, oats 380,000, wheat 295,000; livestock (number of live animals) 2,400,000 sheep, 1,326,700 cattle, 768,400 pigs; roundwood (1995) 9,035,000 cu m; fish catch 2,630,664, of which herring 758,210, cod 360,328, saithe 222,044, redfish 160,701. Mining and quarrying (1996)[6]: iron ore 1,554,599, ilmenite-titanium 758,711, copper 31,736, zinc 8,619. Manufacturing (value added in NKr '000,000; 1994): machinery and equipment 37,194; paper and paper products 19,748; food products 17,375; wood products 8,133; chemical products 6,851. Construction (1996): residential 2,907,000 sq m; nonresidential 3,545,000 sq m. Energy production (consumption): electricity (kW-hr; 1994) 113,389,000,000 (113,256,000,000); coal (metric tons; 1994) 301,000 (914,000); crude petroleum (barrels; 1994) 977,367,000 (110,386,000); petroleum products (metric tons; 1994) 14,512,000 (7,703,000); natural gas (cu m; 1994) 31,347,000,000 (4,051,000,000).
Household income and expenditure. Average household size (1994) 2.3; consumption expenditure per household (1994) NKr 269,620 (U.S.$38,203); expenditure (1994): housing 25.3%, transportation 20.1%, food 13.9%, recreation and education 11.0%, household furniture and equipment 8.4%, clothing and footwear 6.5%.
Gross national product (1995): U.S.$136,077,000,000 (U.S.$31,250 per capita).

Structure of gross domestic product and labour force

	1995			
	in value NKr '000,000	% of total value	labour force	% of labour force
Agriculture	22,029	2.4	106,000	4.8
Mining	1,532	0.2	23,000	1.1
Crude petroleum and natural gas	102,660	11.1	...	...
Manufacturing	116,608	12.6	308,000	14.1
Construction	33,897	3.7	126,000	5.8
Public utilities	23,938	2.6	22,000	1.0
Transp. and commun.	90,257	9.7	170,000	7.8
Trade	100,419[7]	10.8[7]	357,000	16.3
Finance	147,983	16.0	160,000	7.3
Pub. admin., defense	144,418	15.6	803,000	36.7
Services	45,442	4.9		
Other	96,682	10.4	107,000[8]	4.9[8]
TOTAL	925,866[3]	100.0	2,186,000[3]	100.0[3]

Population economically active (1995): total 2,186,000; activity rate of total population 50.0% (participation rates: ages 16–64 [1994] 79.6%; female 43.6%; unemployed 4.9%).

Price and earnings indexes (1990 = 100)

	1990	1991	1992	1993	1994	1995	1996
Consumer price index	100.0	103.4	105.8	108.2	109.8	112.5	113.9
Hourly earnings index	100.0	105.1	108.5	111.6	114.8	118.8	123.5

Public debt (1994): U.S.$39,044,000,000.

Foreign trade

Balance of trade (current prices)

	1990	1991	1992	1993	1994	1995
NKr '000,000	+48,231	+59,565	+61,730	+55,635	+51,512	+62,656
% of total	12.9%	15.9%	16.4%	14.0%	11.8%	11.9%

Imports (1996): NKr 229,720,000,000 (machinery and transport equipment 37.8%, of which road vehicles 10.0%, ships 2.6%; metals and metal products 10.8%, of which iron and steel 4.4%; food products 6.1%, of which fruits and vegetables 1.4%; petroleum products 4.5%). *Major import sources* (1995): Sweden 15.5%; Germany 14.0%; U.K. 9.8%; Denmark 7.6%.
Exports (1996): NKr 320,128,000,000 (fuels and fuel products 54.4%; machinery and transport equipment 11.1%; metals and metal products 10.7%; food products 7.6%, of which fish 6.7%). *Major export destinations* (1995): U.K. 20.3%; Germany 12.2%; Sweden 9.9%; The Netherlands 9.6%.

Transport and communications

Transport. Railroads (1995): route length 3,999 km; passenger-km 2,381,000,000; metric ton-km cargo 2,715,000,000. Roads (1996): total length 90,262 km (paved 74%). Vehicles (1995): passenger cars 1,684,664; trucks and buses 382,017. Merchant marine (1995): vessels (100 gross tons and over) 1,597; total deadweight tonnage 20,834,000. Air transport (1995): passenger-km 8,753,444,000; metric ton-km cargo 933,439,000; airports (1996) 50.

Communications

Medium	date	unit	number	units per 1,000 persons
Daily newspapers	1995	circulation	2,170,000	498
Radio	1996	receivers	3,342,000	763
Television	1995	receivers	2,000,000	459
Telephones	1995	main lines	2,431,271	558
Cellular telephones	1995	subscribers	1,013,358	232
Facsimile machines	1995	units	130,000	30
Personal computers	1995	units	1,193,000	273

Education and health

Educational attainment (1994). Percentage of population age 16 and over having: lower secondary education 28.7%; higher secondary 51.9%; higher 19.4%. *Literacy* (1995): virtually 100% literate.

Education (1994–95)

	schools	teachers	students	student/ teacher ratio
Primary (age 7–12)	3,308	37,640	470,936	12.5
Secondary (age 13–18) and vocational	746	21,197	226,983	10.7
Higher	86[9]	10,366	169,306	16.3

Health: physicians (1996) 15,368 (1 per 285 persons); hospital beds (1994) 21,967 (1 per 197 persons); infant mortality rate per 1,000 live births (1995) 4.1.
Food (1995): daily per capita caloric intake 3,274 (vegetable products 65%, animal products 35%); 122% of FAO recommended minimum requirement.

Military

Total active duty personnel (1996): 29,000 (army 50.7%, navy 22.1%, air force 27.2%). *Military expenditure as percentage of GNP* (1995): 2.7% (world avg. 2.8%); per capita expenditure U.S.$804.

[1]Excludes Svalbard and Jan Mayen (24,360 sq mi [63,080 sq km]). [2]January 1. [3]Detail does not add to total given because of rounding. [4]Includes the Norwegian population of Svalbard and Jan Mayen, registered as residents in municipalities on the mainland. [5]Population of municipalities. [6]Metal content of ore. [7]Includes hotels. [8]Unemployed. [9]The number of colleges is lower than in recent years because of reorganization.

Internet resources for further information:
- **Statistics Norway http://www.ssb.no/www-open/english**

Oman

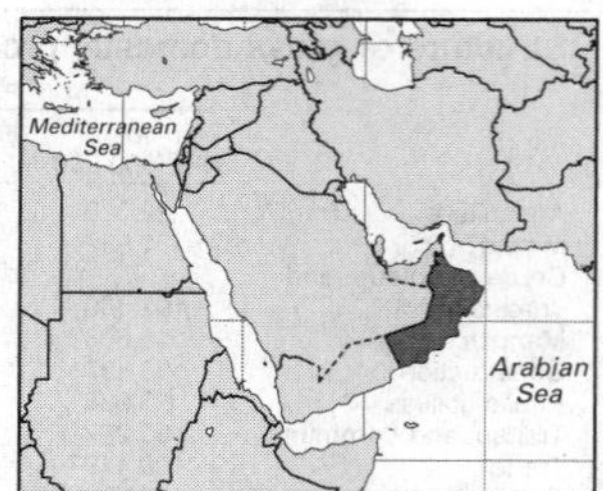

Official name: Salṭanat ʿUmān (Sultanate of Oman).
Form of government: monarchy[1].
Head of state and government: Sultan.
Capital: Muscat.
Official language: Arabic.
Official religion: Islam.
Monetary unit: 1 rial Omani (RO) = 1,000 baizas; valuation (Oct. 3, 1997) 1 RO = U.S.$2.60 = £1.61.

Area and population

		area[2]		population
				1993
Regions	**Centres**	sq mi	sq km	census
Al-Bāṭinah	Ar-Rustāq; Ṣuḥār	4,850	12,500	564,677
Ad-Dākhilīyah	Nizwā; Samā'il	12,300	31,900	229,791
Musandam	Khaṣab	700	1,800	28,727
Ash-Sharqīyah	Ibrā; Sūr	14,200	36,800	258,344
Al-Wusṭa	Haymā'	30,750	79,700	17,067
Aẓ-Ẓāhirah	Al-Buraymī; 'Ibri	17,000	44,000	181,224
Ẓufār (Dhofar)	Salālah	38,350	99,300	189,094
Governorate				
Masqaṭ	Muscat (Masqaṭ)	1,350	3,500	549,150
TOTAL		119,500	309,500	2,018,074

Demography

Population (1997): 2,265,000.
Density (1997): persons per sq mi 19.0, persons per sq km 7.3.
Urban-rural (1993): urban 71.7%; rural 28.3%.
Sex distribution (1993): male 58.37%; female 41.63%.
Age breakdown (1993): under 15, 41.0%; 15–29, 25.5%; 30–44, 21.9%; 45–59, 7.8%; 60–74, 2.9%; 75 and over, 0.9%.
Population projection: (2000) 2,512,000; (2010) 3,516,000.
Doubling time: 20 years.
Ethnic composition (1993): Omani Arab 73.5%; Indian 13.3%; Bangladeshi 4.3%; Pakistani (mostly Balochī) 3.1%; Egyptian 1.6%; other 4.2%.
Religious affiliation (1993): Muslim 87.7%, of which Ibāḍiyah Muslim *c.* 75% (principal minorities are Sunnī Muslim and Shīʿī Muslim); Hindu 7.4%; Christian 3.9%; Buddhist 0.5%; other 0.5%.
Major cities (1990): Muscat 51,969[3]; Nizwā 62,880; Samā'il 44,721; Salālah 10,000[4].

Vital statistics

Birth rate per 1,000 population (1990–95): 43.7 (world avg. 25.0).
Death rate per 1,000 population (1990–95): 4.8 (world avg. 9.3).
Natural increase rate per 1,000 population (1990–95): 38.9 (world avg. 15.7).
Total fertility rate (avg. births per childbearing woman; 1996): 6.9.
Life expectancy at birth (1990–95): male 67.7 years; female 71.8 years.
Major causes of death per 100,000 population: n.a.; however, the main causes of hospital deaths in 1989 were diseases of the circulatory system 25.7%, perinatal problems 11.4%, malignant neoplasms (cancers) 7.6%, diseases of the respiratory system 7.1%, and infectious and parasitic diseases 7.1%.

National economy

Budget (1997). Revenue: RO 2,003,000,000 (oil revenue 75.0%; other 25.0%). Expenditures: RO 2,266,000,000 (current expenditure 80.1%, of which civil ministries 39.6%, defense 30.8%, interest paid on loans 5.3%; capital development projects and subsidies 17.6%).
Public debt (external, outstanding; 1995): U.S.$2,563,000,000.
Gross national product (1995): U.S.$10,578,000,000 (U.S.$4,820 per capita).

Structure of gross domestic product and labour force

	1996		1993	
	in value RO '000,000[5]	% of total value	labour force	% of labour force
Agriculture[6]	133.9	2.3	64,161	9.1
Mining	2,496.6	42.7	14,393	2.0
Manufacturing	253.7	4.3	60,433	8.6
Construction	130.1	2.2	108,154	15.3
Public utilities	50.3	0.9	4,465	0.6
Transp. and commun.	359.1	6.1	24,770	3.5
Trade	767.3[7]	13.1[7]	104,066	14.8
Finance	448.6[8]	7.7[8]	17,372	2.5
Pub. admin., defense	714.3	12.2	165,602	23.5
Services	457.4[9]	7.8[9]	111,268	15.8
Other	43.1[10]	0.7[10]	30,114	4.3
TOTAL	5,854.4	100.0	704,798	100.0[11]

Tourism (1995): receipts U.S.$92,000,000; expenditures U.S.$47,000,000.
Household income and expenditure. Average household size (1993) 8.0; income per household: n.a.; sources of income: n.a.; expenditure (1990): housing and utilities 27.8%, food, beverages, and tobacco 26.4%, transportation 19.8%, clothing and shoes 7.8%, household goods and furniture 6.1%, education, health services, entertainment, and other 12.1%.
Production (metric tons except as noted). Agriculture, forestry, fishing (1996): vegetables and melons 167,000 (of which watermelons 30,000), dates 133,000, bananas 26,000, mangoes 11,000, onions 9,000, potatoes 6,000, papayas 3,000, tobacco leaf 2,000, wheat 1,000; livestock (number of live animals) 735,000 goats, 148,000 sheep, 142,000 cattle, 94,000 camels, 3,000,000 chickens; fish catch (1995) 139,864. Mining and quarrying (1994): copper 6,500; silver 3,300 kg; gold 75 kg. Manufacturing (value of production in RO '000; 1993): textiles and apparel 78,290; food products and beverages 72,930; chemical products 40,950; wood products 5,950; metal products 4,200; paper products 360; other major products include refined petroleum products. Construction (1989): number of residential permits 3,408; nonresidential permits 353. Energy production (consumption): electricity (kW-hr; 1994) 7,856,000,000 (7,856,000,000); coal, none (none); crude petroleum (barrels; 1994) 294,380,000 (26,615,000); petroleum products (metric tons; 1994) 3,884,000 (1,589,000); natural gas (cu m; 1994) 6,665,890,000 (6,665,890,000).
Population economically active (1993)[11]: total 704,798; activity rate of total population 34.9% (participation rates: over age 15, 60.9%; female 9.7%; unemployed [1996] *c.* 20%).

Price and earnings indexes (1990 = 100)

	1990	1991	1992	1993	1994	1995	1996
Consumer price index	100.0	104.6	105.6	106.9	106.1	104.7	105.0
Earnings index	...	...	...	...	...	...	...

Land use (1994): meadows and pastures 4.7%; agricultural and under permanent cultivation 0.3%; other (mostly desert and developed area) 95.0%.

Foreign trade[12]

Balance of trade (current prices)

	1990	1991	1992	1993	1994	1995
RO '000,000	+1,042	+594	+636	+411	+588	+648
% of total	32.6%	18.8%	17.5%	11.1%	16.0%	16.1%

Imports (1996): RO 1,760,200,000 (machinery and transport equipment 41.5%, basic manufactured goods 17.3%, food and live animals 12.9%, miscellaneous manufactured articles 9.0%, beverages and tobacco 4.2%). *Major import sources:* United Arab Emirates 23.7%; Japan 17.2%; United Kingdom 8.8%; United States 7.5%; Germany 5.2%; India 4.0%.
Exports (1996): RO 2,822,000,000 (domestic exports 86.3%, of which petroleum 80.2%, manufactured goods 2.7% [of which copper and copper products 0.9%], food and live animals 1.9%, mineral fuels and lubricants 0.5%; reexports 13.7%, of which machinery and transport equipment 8.9%). *Major export destinations*[13]: United Arab Emirates 41.6%; Iran 9.3%; Hong Kong 7.8%; United States 5.1%; Saudi Arabia 4.5%; Tanzania 4.4%.

Transport and communications

Transport. Railroads: none. Roads (1995): total length 19,160 mi, 30,830 km (paved *c.* 20%). Vehicles: automobiles (1995) 202,741, trucks and buses (1993) 108,600. Merchant marine (1992): vessels (100 gross tons and over) 26; total deadweight tonnage 11,727. Air transport (1996)[14]: passenger-mi 1,714,204,000, passenger-km 2,758,750,000; short ton-mi cargo 72,435,000, metric ton-km cargo 105,753,500; airports (1997) with scheduled flights 6.

Communications

Medium	date	unit	number	units per 1,000 persons
Daily newspapers	1994	circulation	63,000	31
Radio	1995	receivers	900,000	426
Television	1995	receivers	1,500,000	711
Telephones	1995	main lines	169,900	81
Cellular telephones	1995	subscribers	8,100	3.8
Facsimile machines	1995	units	1,600	0.8
Personal computers	1995	units	28,000	13.3

Education and health

Educational attainment (1993). Percentage of population age 15 and over having: no formal schooling (illiterate) 41.2%; no formal schooling (literate) 14.9%; primary 18.9%; secondary 21.1%; higher technical 2.0%; higher undergraduate 1.5%; higher graduate 0.1%; other 0.3%. *Literacy* (1993): total population age 15 and over literate 422,417 (58.8%); males literate 260,006 (71.1%); females literate 163,421 (46.2%).

Education (1993–94)

	schools	teachers	students	student/ teacher ratio
Primary (age 6–14)	415	11,158	297,209	26.6
Secondary (age 15–17)	128[15]	9,188	160,654	17.5
Voc., teacher tr.	25[15]	342	2,350	6.9
Higher	5[15]	732[16]	7,322[17]	...

Health (1995): physicians 2,476 (1 per 852 persons); hospital beds 4,411 (1 per 478 persons); infant mortality rate per 1,000 live births (1996) 28.2.
Food: daily per capita caloric intake, n.a.

Military

Total active duty personnel (1996): 43,500 (army 72.4%[18], navy 9.7%, air force 9.4%); foreign troops 3,700. *Military expenditure as percentage of GDP* (1995): 16.7% (world 2.8%); per capita expenditure U.S.$822.

[1]Appointed 82-member Consultative Council is an advisory body only. [2]Approximate; no comprehensive survey of surface area has ever been carried out in Oman. [3]1993 census. [4]1982. [5]In purchasers' values at current prices. [6]Agriculture includes fishing. [7]Trade includes restaurants and hotels. [8]Finance includes business services and real estate. [9]Services include education and health. [10]Other includes import taxes. [11]Non-Omani workers constitute 61.3% of the labour force. [12]Imports c.i.f.; exports f.o.b. [13]Non-oil exports only; includes reexports. [14]One-fourth apportionment of international flights of Gulf Air. [15]1989–90. [16]1990; universities and equivalent institutes. [17]1991–92. [18]Including personnel of Royal Household units not formally part of army table of organization.

Internet resources for further information:
- **Oman 95 Yearbook**
  http://www.brunet.bn/php/kharti/book95.htm

Pakistan

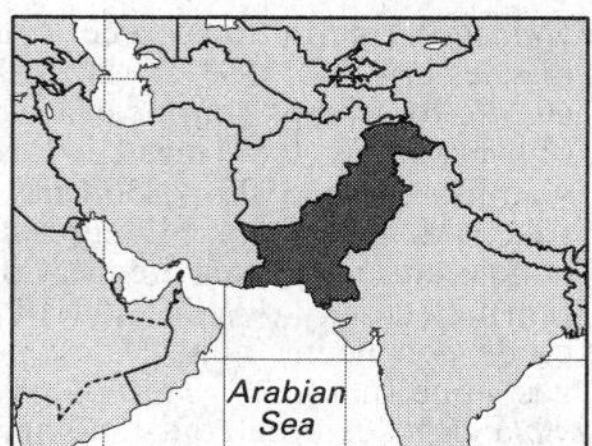

Official name: Islām-ī Jamhūrīya-e Pākistān (Islamic Republic of Pakistan).
Form of government: multiparty, federal Islamic republic with two legislative houses (Senate [87]; National Assembly [217]).
Chief of state: President.
Chief of government: Prime Minister.
Capital: Islāmābād.
Official language: Urdū.
Official religion: Islam.
Monetary unit: 1 Pakistan rupee (PRs) = 100 paisa; valuation (Oct. 3, 1997) 1 U.S.$ = PRs 40.48; 1 £ = PRs 65.25.

Area and population

		area[1]		population
Provinces	**Capitals**	sq mi	sq km	1983 estimate[2]
Balochistān	Quetta	134,051	347,190	4,611,000
North-West Frontier	Peshāwar	28,773	74,521	11,658,000
Punjab	Lahore	79,284	205,344	50,460,000
Sindh	Karāchi	54,407	140,914	20,312,000
Federally Administered Tribal Areas	...	10,509	27,220	2,329,000
Federal Capital Area				
Islāmābād	...	350	906	359,000
TOTAL		307,374	796,095	89,729,000

Demography

Population (1997)[3]: 136,183,000.
Density (1997)[4]: persons per sq mi 443.1, persons per sq km 171.1.
Urban-rural (1996): urban 32.4%; rural 67.6%.
Sex distribution (1996): male 52.50%; female 47.50%.
Age breakdown (1995): under 15, 41.3%; 15–29, 25.1%; 30–44, 17.1%; 45–59, 10.5%; 60–74, 4.9%; 75 and over, 1.1%.
Population projection: (2000) 144,560,000; (2010) 176,400,000.
Doubling time: 25 years.
Linguistic composition (1981): Punjābī 48.2%; Pashto 13.1%; Sindhī 11.8%; Saraiki 9.8%; Urdū 7.6%; other 9.5%.
Religious affiliation (1993): Muslim 95.0%[5]; Christian 2.0%; Hindu 1.8%; others (including Ahmadiyah) 1.2%.
Major cities (1981): Karāchi 5,208,132; Lahore 2,952,689; Faisalābād 1,104,209; Rāwalpindi 794,843; Islāmābād 204,364.

Vital statistics

Birth rate per 1,000 population (1997): 36.4 (world avg. 25.0).
Death rate per 1,000 population (1997): 7.9 (world avg. 9.3).
Natural increase rate per 1,000 population (1997): 28.5 (world avg. 15.7).
Total fertility rate (avg. births per childbearing woman; 1997): 5.1.
Marriage rate per 1,000 population (1975–80): 10.7.
Divorce rate per 1,000 population (1975–80): 0.3.
Life expectancy at birth (1997): male 63.0 years; female 65.0 years.
Major causes of death (percentage of total deaths; 1987): malaria 18.2%; childhood diseases 12.1%; diseases of digestive system 9.8%; diseases of respiratory system 9.2%; infection of intestinal tract 7.7%.

National economy

Budget (1995–96). Revenue: PRs 378,030,000,000 (customs duties 24.4%, nontax receipts 23.8%, income taxes 20.2%, excise taxes 13.6%, sales tax 13.4%). Expenditures: PRs 434,690,000,000 (public-debt service 36.2%, defense 26.5%, development 22.2%, general administration 3.9%).
Public debt (external, outstanding; 1995): U.S.$23,711,000,000.
Production (metric tons except as noted). Agriculture, forestry, fishing (1996): sugarcane 45,230,000, wheat 16,907,000, rice 5,551,000, seed cotton 4,597,000, cottonseed 3,065,000, corn (maize) 1,300,000, potatoes 1,064,000, chickpeas 638,000, rapeseed 246,000; livestock (number of live animals) 45,600,000 goats, 29,800,000 sheep, 20,200,000 buffalo, 17,900,000 cattle, 110,000,000 chickens; roundwood (1995) 29,665,000 cu m; fish catch (1994) 551,899. Mining and quarrying (1994–95): limestone 9,682,000; rock salt 890,000; gypsum 624,000; silica sand 152,000; chromite 13,513. Manufacturing (1994–95): cement 7,913,000; chemical fertilizers 3,826,000, of which urea 3,000,000; refined sugar 3,001,000; cotton yarn 1,370,000; vegetable products 678,000; industrial chemicals 377,000; paper and paperboard 215,000; jute textiles 67,300; cotton textiles 321,841,000 sq m; cigarettes 32,747,000,000 units; motor-vehicle tires 912,000 units; bicycles 475,000 units. Energy production (consumption): electricity (kW-hr; 1994) 57,147,000,000 (57,147,000,000); coal (metric tons; 1994) 3,534,000 (4,628,000); crude petroleum (barrels; 1994) 20,805,000 (50,063,000); petroleum products (metric tons; 1994) 5,778,000 (13,511,000); natural gas (cu m; 1994) 16,668,000,000 (16,668,000,000).
Population economically active (1995–96): total 36,700,000; activity rate of total population 27.9% (participation rates: ages 15–64 [1992–93] 50.4%; female [1992–93] 14.2%; unemployed 4.9%).

Price index (1990 = 100)

	1990	1991	1992	1993	1994	1995	1996
Consumer price index	100.0	111.8	122.4	134.6	151.3	170.0	187.6

Gross national product (1995): U.S.$59,991,000,000 (U.S.$460 per capita).

Structure of gross domestic product and labour force

	1995–96			
	in value PRs '000,000	% of total value	labour force	% of labour force
Agriculture	510,775	23.5	17,470,000	47.6
Mining	11,348	0.5		
Manufacturing	325,420	15.0	3,530,000	9.6
Construction	69,271	3.2	2,260,000	6.2
Public utilities	64,022	2.9	...	...
Transp. and commun.	190,409	8.8	1,730,000	4.7
Trade	324,364	14.9	4,460,000	12.1
Finance	144,007	6.6		
Pub. admin., defense	156,607	7.2	5,130,000	14.0
Services	155,407	7.1		
Other	223,277	10.3	2,120,000[6]	5.8[6]
TOTAL	2,174,907	100.0	36,700,000	100.0

Household income and expenditure (1988). Average household size 6.3; income per household PRs 25,572 (U.S.$1,420); sources of income: self-employment 56.0%, wages and salaries 22.0%, other 22.0%; expenditure: food 47.0%, housing 12.0%, clothing and footwear 8.0%, other 33.0%.
Tourism (1995): receipts U.S.$114,000,000; expenditures U.S.$449,000,000.
Land use (1994): forest 4.5%; pasture 6.5%; agriculture 27.7%; other 61.3%.

Foreign trade[7]

Balance of trade (current prices)

	1991	1992	1993	1994	1995	1996
PRs '000,000	−28,537	−31,283	−54,352	−22,968	−78,506	−64,476
% of total	8.4%	7.9%	12.6%	4.9%	13.4%	8.8%

Imports (1994–95): PRs 332,835,000,000 (petroleum products 15.3%, vegetable oil and fats 9.8%, specialized machinery 9.1%, power-generating machinery 4.9%, road vehicles 4.2%, organic chemicals 4.2%, wheat 4.0%, iron and steel manufactures 3.6%, industrial machinery 3.4%). *Major import sources:* Japan 9.2%; U.S. 9.0%; Malaysia 8.5%; Germany 6.5%; Kuwait 5.6%; Italy 5.0%; U.K. 4.9%; Saudi Arabia 4.8%; China 4.2%; South Korea 3.1%.
Exports (1994–95): PRs 260,522,000,000 (textile fabrics 52.8%, ready-made garments 20.5%, rice 5.6%, leather goods 3.5%, fresh fish 1.9%, cotton 1.8%). *Major export destinations:* U.S. 16.6%; Germany 6.8%; U.K. 6.8%; Japan 6.4%; Dubayy 3.9%; France 3.2%; S. Korea 3.2%; Netherlands 3.1%.

Transport and communications

Transport. Railroads (1994–95): route length 8,775 km; passenger-km 17,555,000,000; metric ton-km cargo 5,661,000,000. Roads (1994–95): total length 123,585 mi, 198,891 km (paved 55%). Vehicles (1994): passenger cars 955,098; trucks and buses 225,829. Merchant marine (1992): vessels (100 gross tons and over) 73; total deadweight tonnage 513,823. Air transport (1996): passenger-km 11,123,000,000; metric ton-km cargo 423,424,000; airports (1997) 35.

Communications

Medium	date	unit	number	units per 1,000 persons
Daily newspapers	1994	circulation	2,840,000	22
Radio	1996	receivers	10,200,000	76
Television	1995	receivers	2,080,000	16
Telephones	1995	main lines	2,127,000	16
Cellular telephones	1995	subscribers	43,000	0.3
Facsimile machines	1995	units	159,000	1.2
Personal computers	1995	units	155,000	1.2

Education and health

Educational attainment (1981). Percentage of population age 25 and over having: no formal schooling 78.9%; some primary education 8.7%; some secondary 10.5%; postsecondary 1.9%. *Literacy* (1993): total population age 15 and over literate 35.0%; males literate 47.3%; females literate 22.3%.

Education (1995–96)

	schools	teachers	students	student/ teacher ratio
Primary (age 5–9)	115,744	337,400	11,484,000	34.0
Secondary (age 10–14)	20,243	281,700	4,819,000	17.1
Voc., teacher tr.	687	7,459	94,000	12.6
Higher	888	33,654	953,659	28.3

Health (1995): physicians 69,694 (1 per 1,863 persons); hospital beds 85,552 (1 per 1,517 persons); infant mortality rate per 1,000 live births (1997) 75.
Food (1995): daily per capita caloric intake 2,475 (vegetable products 86%, animal products 14%); 107% of FAO recommended minimum requirement.

Military

Total active duty personnel (1996): 587,000 (army 88.6%, navy 3.7%, air force 7.7%). *Military expenditure as percentage of GNP* (1994): 6.0% (world 3.0%); per capita expenditure U.S.$24.

[1]Excludes 32,323 sq mi (83,716 sq km) area of Pakistani-administered Jammu and Kashmir (comprising both Azad Kashmir [AK] and the Northern Areas [NA]). [2]Excludes Afghan refugees and population (1981; 2,542,000) of AK/NA. [3]Excludes 1,200,000 Afghan refugees and the population (3,900,000) of AK/NA. [4]Excludes area and population of AK/NA. [5]Mostly Sunnī, with Shīʿī comprising about 20% of total population. [6]Includes unemployed. [7]Import figures are f.o.b. in balance of trade and c.i.f. for commodities and trading partners.

Internet resources for further information:
- **Government of Pakistan: http://www.pak.gov.pk/**

Palau

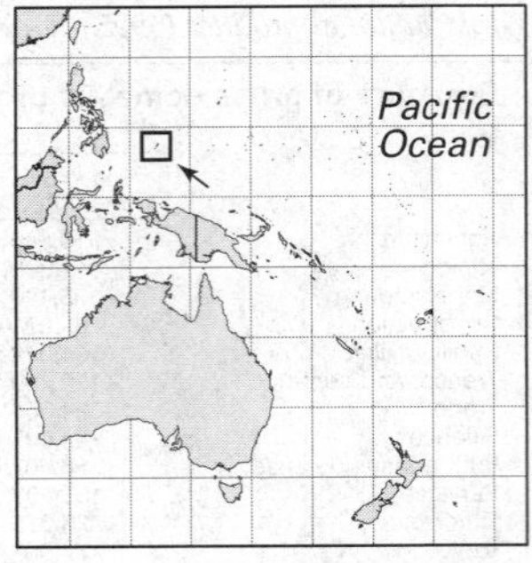

Official name: Belu'u er a Belau (Palauan); Republic of Palau (English).
Form of government: unitary republic with a national congress composed of two legislative houses (Senate [14]; House of Delegates [16]).
Head of state and government: President.
Capital: Koror[1].
Official languages[2]: Palauan; English.
Official religion: none.
Monetary unit: 1 U.S. dollar (U.S.$) = 100 cents; valuation (Oct. 3, 1997) 1 £ = U.S.$1.61.

Area and population

	area		population
States	sq mi	sq km	1995 census
Aimeliik	20	52	419
Airai	17	44	1,481
Angaur	3	8	193
Hatobohei	1	3	51
Kayangel	1	3	124
Koror	7	18	12,299
Melekeok	11	28	261
Ngaraard	14	36	421
Ngarchelong	4	10	253
Ngardmau	18	47	162
Ngatpang	18	47	221
Ngchesar	16	41	228
Ngeremlengui	25	65	281
Ngiwal	10	26	176
Peleliu	5	13	575
Sonsorol	1	3	80
Other			
Rock Islands	18	47	—
TOTAL	188[3]	488	17,225

Demography

Population (1997): 17,200.
Density (1997): persons per sq mi 91.5, persons per sq km 35.2.
Urban-rural (1990): urban 59.6%; rural 40.4%.
Sex distribution (1995): male 53.49%; female 46.51%.
Age breakdown (1990): under 15, 30.3%; 15–29, 27.8%; 30–44, 22.8%; 45–59, 10.5%; 60–74, 6.4%; 75 and over, 2.2%.
Population projection: (2000) 18,100; (2010) 19,700.
Doubling time: 35 years.
Ethnic composition (1995): Palauan 74.5%; Filipino 16.0%; Chinese 3.2%; other Micronesian and other 6.3%.
Religious affiliation (1995): Roman Catholic 38.4%; Protestant 24.7%; Modekne 26.5%; other 10.4%.
Major cities (1995): Koror 12,000.

Vital statistics

Birth rate per 1,000 population (1997): 21.0 (world avg. 25.0); legitimate, n.a.; illegitimate, n.a.
Death rate per 1,000 population (1997): 7.0 (world avg. 9.3).
Natural increase rate per 1,000 population (1997): 14.0 (world avg. 15.7).
Total fertility rate (avg. births per childbearing woman; 1997): 2.7.
Marriage rate per 1,000 population: n.a.
Divorce rate per 1,000 population: n.a.
Life expectancy at birth (1997): male 69.1 years; female 73.0 years.
Major causes of death per 100,000 population (1993): diseases of the circulatory system 192.9; malignant and benign neoplasms (cancers) 136.9; accidents, poisoning, and violence 112.0; diseases of the respiratory system 43.6; infectious and parasitic diseases 43.6.

National economy

Budget (1997). Revenue: U.S.$52,869,000 (grants from the U.S. 59.6%, tax revenue 33.7%). Expenditures: U.S.$59,867,000 (current expenditure 87.0%, of which wages and salaries 44.0%; capital expenditure 13.0%).
Gross national product (at current market prices; 1997)[4]: U.S.$159,800,000 (U.S.$8,806 per capita).

Structure of gross domestic product and labour force

	1996		1995	
	in value U.S.$'000	% of total value	labour force	% of labour force
Agriculture, fisheries	9,890	6.8	724	8.7
Mining Manufacturing	2,908	2.0	1,165[5]	14.0[5]
Public utilities	1,998	1.4	[6]	[6]
Construction	13,102	9.0	[5]	[5]
Transportation and communications	21,608	14.9	435[6]	5.2[6]
Trade	58,663	40.4	1,448	17.3
Finance	4,425	3.0	122	1.5
Public administration, defense	24,984	17.2	2,292	27.5
Services	6,430	4.4	1,573	18.8
Other	1,262[7]	0.9[7]	588[8]	7.0[8]
TOTAL	145,270	100.0	8,347	100.0

Production (metric tons except as noted). Agriculture, forestry, fishing (value of sales in U.S.$; 1993): eggs 262,701, fruit and vegetables 126,325, betel nuts 60,376, root crops (taro, cassava, sweet potatoes) 43,718; livestock (number of live animals; 1984) pigs 1,343, cows 82, goats 52, poultry 9,500; roundwood, n.a.; fish catch (1995) 1,450 (major species are parrot fish, snapper, unicorn fish, and rabbitfish). Mining and quarrying: n.a. Manufacturing: includes handicrafts and small items. Construction: Energy production (consumption): electricity (kW-hr; 1994) 203,000,000 (203,000,000); coal, none (n.a.); crude petroleum, none (n.a.); petroleum products, none (75,000); natural gas, none (n.a.).
Public debt (external, outstanding; 1993): U.S.$100,000,000.
Tourism (1996): receipts from visitors U.S.$67,900,000.
Population economically active (1995): total 8,347; activity rate of total population 48.5% (participation rates: over age 15, 66.2%; female (1990) 36.9%; unemployed 7.0%).
Land use: n.a.
Household income and expenditure. Average household size (1995) 4.9; income per household (1989) U.S.$8,882; sources of income (1989): wages 63.7%, social security 12.0%, self-employment 7.4%, retirement 5.5%, interest, dividend, or net rental 4.3%, remittance 4.1%, public assistance 1.0%, other 2.0%; expenditure: n.a.

Foreign trade[9]

Imports (1996): U.S.$72,400,000 (1984; food and agricultural raw materials 28.9%, machinery and transport equipment 24.5%, chemicals and related products 4.0%). *Major import sources* (1984): United States 41.8%; Japan 38.2%.
Exports (1996): U.S.$14,300,000 (1984; food and agricultural raw materials 69.1%, manufactured goods 30.9%). *Major export destinations* (1984): Japan 58.8%; United States 8.0%.

Transport and communications

Transport. Railroads: none. Roads (1993): total length 40 mi, 64 km (paved 59%). Vehicles (1994): passenger cars and trucks 4,271. Merchant marine (1991): vessels (100 gross tons and over) 4; total deadweight tonnage, n.a. Air transport (1993): passenger arrivals 50,366, passenger departures 49,376; airports (1997) with scheduled flights 1.

Communications

Medium	date	unit	number	units per 1,000 persons
Radio	1994	receivers	9,000	550.0
Television	1994	receivers	1,600	98.0
Telephones	1994	main lines	2,615	160.0

Education and health

Educational attainment (1990). Percentage of population age 25 and over having: no formal schooling 1.8%; some primary education 21.8%; completed primary 5.5%; some secondary 13.3%; completed secondary 26.6%; some postsecondary 11.1%; higher 19.9%. *Literacy* (1990): total population age 15 and over literate 10,288 (97.6%); males literate 5,677 (98.3%); females literate 4,611 (96.6%).

Education (1993)

	schools[10]	teachers[10]	students	student/teacher ratio
Primary (age 6–13)	26	289	2,635	...
Secondary (age 14–18)	6	[11]	1,021	...
Higher[12]	1	...	509	...

Health (1990): physicians[13] 10 (1 per 1,518 persons); hospital beds 70 (1 per 200 persons); infant mortality rate per 1,000 live births (1997) 25.1.
Food: daily per capita caloric intake, n.a.

Military

The United States is responsible for the external security of Palau, as specified in the Compact of Free Association of Oct. 1, 1994.

[1]A site on Babelthuap is to be the eventual permanent capital. [2]Sonsorolese-Tobian is also, according to official sources, considered an official language. [3]Detail does not add to total given because of rounding. [4]Gross national product comprises U.S. government spending only. [5]Manufacturing includes Construction. [6]Transportation and communications includes Public utilities. [7]Includes import duties and imputed bank service charge. [8]Includes unemployed. [9]Export and import figures are f.o.b. [10]1987. [11]Included with primary. [12]Palau Community College. [13]Government-employed health personnel only.

Internet resources for further information:
- **Republic of Palau Economic Report (Bank of Hawaii) http://www.boh.com/econ/pacific/pal/index.html**
- **U.S. Department of the Interior Office of Insular Affairs http://www.doi.gov/oia/index.html**
- **Palau Visitors Authority http://www.visit-palau.com**

Panama

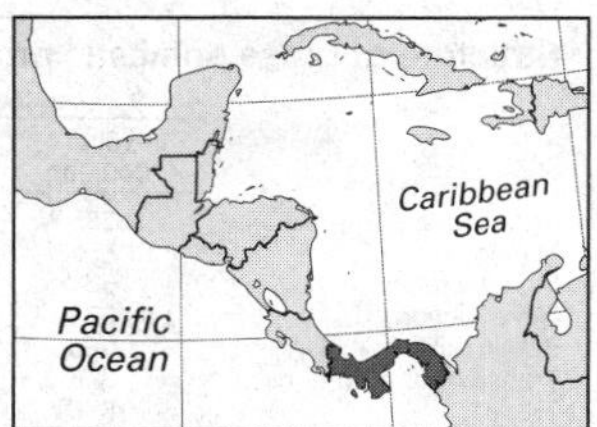

Official name: República de Panamá (Republic of Panama).
Form of government: multiparty republic with one legislative house (Legislative Assembly [72]).
Head of state and government: President assisted by Vice Presidents.
Capital: Panama City.
Official language: Spanish.
Official religion: none.
Monetary unit: 1 balboa (B) = 100 cents; valuation (Oct. 3, 1997) 1 U.S.$ = B 1.00; 1 £ = B 1.61.

Area and population

		area		population
Provinces	**Capitals**	sq mi	sq km	1996 estimate
Bocas del Toro	Bocas del Toro	3,376[1]	8,745[1]	123,655[1]
Chiriquí	David	3,341[1]	8,653[1]	412,981[1]
Coclé	Penonomé	1,902	4,927	191,677
Colón	Colón	1,888	4,890	190,697
Darién	La Palma	4,823[2]	12,491[2]	47,055[2]
Herrera	Chitré	904	2,341	101,775
Los Santos	Las Tablas	1,470	3,806	79,849
Panamá	Panama City	4,590	11,887	1,257,964
Veraguas	Santiago	4,339[1]	11,239[1]	220,110[1]
Indigenous districts				
Emberá		1,614[2]	4,180[2]	10,459[2]
Guaymí (Ngobe-Buglé)		[1]	[1]	[1]
Kuna Yala (San Blas)	El Porvenir	910	2,357	38,268
TOTAL		29,157	75,517[3]	2,674,490

Demography

Population (1997): 2,719,000.
Density (1997): persons per sq mi 93.3, persons per sq km 36.0.
Urban-rural (1995): urban 53.3%; rural 46.7%.
Sex distribution (1995): male 50.56%; female 49.44%.
Age breakdown (1995): under 15, 33.4%; 15–29, 28.4%; 30–44, 19.7%; 45–59, 11.0%; 60–74, 5.6%; 75 and over, 1.9%.
Population projection: (2000) 2,856,000; (2010) 3,266,000.
Doubling time: 40 years.
Ethnic composition (1992): mestizo 64.0%; black and mulatto 14.0%; white 10.0%; Amerindian 8.0%; Asian 4.0%.
Religious affiliation (1995): Roman Catholic 80.2%; Protestant 15.0%, of which Pentecostal 8.4%; other Christian 1.6%; other 3.2%.
Major cities (1990): Panama City 445,902[4]; San Miguelito 299,075[5, 6]; David 65,763[7]; Colón 54,654; Barú 46,093[7].

Vital statistics

Birth rate per 1,000 population (1996): 22.5 (world avg. 25.0).
Death rate per 1,000 population (1996): 5.2 (world avg. 9.3).
Natural increase rate per 1,000 population (1996): 17.3 (world avg. 15.7).
Total fertility rate (avg. births per childbearing woman; 1996): 2.6.
Marriage rate per 1,000 population (1994): 5.6[8].
Divorce rate per 1,000 population (1994): 0.9[8].
Life expectancy at birth (1996): male 71.4 years; female 76.9 years.
Major causes of death per 100,000 population (1994): diseases of the circulatory system 118.4; malignant neoplasms (cancers) 57.3; accidents 35.3; diseases of the respiratory system 24.0; homicide, suicide, and violence 22.7.

National economy

Budget (1996). Revenue: B 2,264,200,000 (current revenue 73.6%, of which nontax revenue 24.0%; development revenue 26.4%, of which foreign loans 17.9%). Expenditures: B 2,264,200,000 (current expenditure 79.1%, of which debt services 30.8%, education 10.4%, health 5.9%; development expenditure 20.9%).
Public debt (external, outstanding; 1995): U.S.$3,905,000,000.
Production (metric tons except as noted). Agriculture, forestry, fishing (1996): sugarcane 1,669,000, bananas 910,000, rice 230,000, plantains 106,000, corn (maize) 108,000, oranges 26,900, pineapples 14,300, coffee 12,400, tobacco 2,200; livestock (number of live animals; 1996) 1,456,000 cattle, 261,000 pigs; roundwood (1995) 1,069,800 cu m; fish catch (value of production in B '000,000; 1995): shrimps 38, fish 29. Mining and quarrying (1994): limestone 757,000; gold 7,900 troy oz. Manufacturing (value of production in B '000,000; 1995): food products 1,076, of which meat 276; refined petroleum 217; paper and paper products 145; beverages 139; plastic products 94. Construction (value of construction in B '000,000; 1995): residential 237; nonresidential 102. Energy production (consumption): electricity (kW-hr; 1995) 3,519,000,000 (2,870,000,000); coal (metric tons; 1994) none (52,000); crude petroleum (barrels; 1994) none (8,554,000); petroleum products (metric tons; 1994) 1,480,000 (1,842,000); natural gas (cu m; 1994) none (59,967,000).
Tourism (1996): receipts from visitors U.S.$343,100,000; expenditures by nationals abroad U.S.$135,800,000.
Household income and expenditure. Average household size (1990) 4.4; average annual income per household (1990) B 5,450 (U.S.$5,450); expenditure (1983–84)[9]: food and beverages 34.9%, transportation and communications 15.1%, housing and energy 12.6%, education and recreation 11.7%.
Population economically active (1995)[8]: total 1,006,147; activity rate of total population 42.0%[10] (participation rates: ages 15–69 [1993] 62.8%[10]; female [1993] 34.0%[10]; unemployed 13.7%).

Price and earnings indexes (1990 = 100)

	1991	1992	1993	1994	1995	1996	1997
Consumer price index	101.3	103.1	103.6	104.9	105.9	107.3	108.6[11]
Monthly earnings index[12]	100.3	101.6	105.8	108.9	111.7	...	...

Gross national product (1995): U.S.$7,235,000,000 (U.S.$2,750 per capita).

Structure of gross domestic product and labour force

	1996[13]		1995[8]	
	in value B '000,000	% of total value	labour force	% of labour force
Agriculture, fishing	515.6	8.5	185,231	18.4
Mining	8.1	0.1	2,618	0.3
Manufacturing	620.3	10.2	105,821	10.5
Construction	240.7	3.9	66,015	6.6
Public utilities	310.5	5.1	10,514	1.0
Transp. and commun.	782.2	12.8	68,210	6.8
Trade, restaurants	1,276.1	20.9	208,598	20.7
Finance, real estate	1,573.8	25.8	52,039	5.2
Pub. admin.	665.3	10.9	70,826	7.0
Services	357.6	5.9	197,479	19.6
Other	−251.8	−4.1	38,796	3.9
TOTAL	6,098.4	100.0	1,006,147	100.0

Land use (1994): forested 43.8%; meadows and pastures 19.8%; agricultural and under permanent cultivation 8.9%; other 27.5%.

Foreign trade[14, 15]

Balance of trade (current prices)

	1990	1991	1992	1993	1994	1995
B '000,000	−894	−1,071	−1,329	−1,426	−1,594	−1,655
% of total	50.1%	54.2%	57.0%	56.3%	57.7%	57.0%

Imports (1995): B 2,511,000,000 (machinery and apparatus 17.4%, mineral fuels 14.1%, transport equipment 11.6%, chemicals and chemical products 11.5%). *Major import sources:* U.S. 39.1%; Colón Free Zone 14.5%; Ecuador 5.3%; Japan 5.1%; Mexico 3.4%.
Exports (1995): B 571,000,000 (bananas 33.3%, shrimps 14.2%, coffee 5.7%, clothing 3.8%, fish products 3.4%). *Major export destinations:* U.S. 41.8%; Germany 12.5%; Costa Rica 7.2%; Sweden 4.9%; Belgium 4.8%.

Transport and communications

Transport. Railroads (1994): route length 220 mi, 354 km. Roads (1995): total length 6,706 mi, 10,792 km (paved 34%). Vehicles: passenger cars (1995) 140,900; trucks and buses 79,000. Panama Canal traffic (1994–95): oceangoing transits 13,459; cargo 193,357,000 metric tons. Air transport[16]: passenger-km (1996) 871,500,000; metric ton-km cargo 9,338,000; airports (1996) with scheduled flights 10.

Communications

Medium	date	unit	number	units per 1,000 persons
Daily newspapers	1994	circulation	160,000	62
Radio	1996	receivers	527,000	5.1
Television	1995	receivers	204,539	13
Telephones	1995	main lines	304,000	8.8

Education and health

Educational attainment (1990). Percentage of population age 25 and over having: no formal schooling 11.6%; incomplete primary education 20.0%; complete primary 21.6%; secondary 28.7%; incomplete undergraduate 5.4%; complete undergraduate 7.0%; graduate 0.7%; other/unknown 5.0%. *Literacy* (1995): total population age 15 and over literate 1,590,000 (90.8%).

Education (1995)

	schools	teachers	students	student/ teacher ratio
Primary (age 6–11)	2,845	14,998	362,142	24.1
Secondary (age 12–17) } Voc., teacher tr. }	399	11,627	216,217	18.6
Higher	9	4,689	76,839	16.4

Health (1995): physicians 3,074 (1 per 856 persons); hospital beds 7,138 (1 per 369 persons); infant mortality rate per 1,000 live births (1996) 25.3.
Food (1995): daily per capita caloric intake 2,490 (vegetable products 79%, animal products 21%); 108% of FAO recommended minimum requirement.

Military

Total active duty personnel (1996): military abolished in 1991 was replaced by an 11,000-member national police force; U.S. forces in former Canal Zone number 7,000.

[1]The 2,700 sq mi- (7,000 sq km-) Guaymí indigenous district (*comarca*) was created in December 1996 from parts of Bocas del Toro, Chiriquí, and Veraguas provinces. [2]Figures subject to change with announcement of official demarcation of Emberá boundaries. [3]Detail does not add to total given because of rounding. [4]1994. [5]1996. [6]Urban district adjacent to Panama City. [7]Population of the *cabecera* (county seat) of the municipality. [8]Excludes indigenous population. [9]Panama City only. [10]Estimated figure. [11]May. [12]Public sector only. [13]At prices of 1982. [14]Import figures are f.o.b. in balance of trade and c.i.f. in commodities and trading partners. [15]Excludes Colón Free Zone (1994 imports f.o.b. B 4,990,000,000; 1994 reexports f.o.b. B 5,735,000,000, of which textiles and clothing 25.8%, machinery and apparatus 22.3%). [16]COPA only.

Internet resources for further information:

- **Inter-American Development Bank: Basic Socio-Economic Data (Panama) http://database.iadb.org/int/basicrep/bapan.htm**

Papua New Guinea

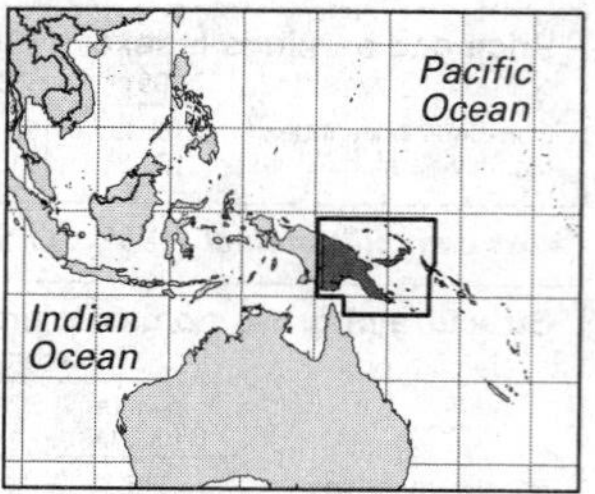

Official name: Independent State of Papua New Guinea.
Form of government: constitutional monarchy with one legislative house (National Parliament [109]).
Chief of state: British Monarch represented by Governor-General.
Head of government: Prime Minister.
Capital: Port Moresby.
Official language: English[1].
Official religion: none.
Monetary unit: 1 Papua New Guinea kina (K) = 100 toea; valuation (Oct. 3, 1997) 1 U.S.$ = K 1.43; 1 £ = K 2.31.

Area and population

		area		population
Provinces	Administrative centres	sq mi	sq km	1990 census[2]
Bougainville	Arawa (Buka)	3,600	9,300	3
Central	Port Moresby (Central)	11,400	29,500	140,584
East New Britain	Rabaul	6,000	15,500	184,408
East Sepik	Wewak	16,550	42,800	248,308
Eastern Highlands	Goroka	4,300	11,200	299,619
Enga	Wabag	4,950	12,800	238,357
Gulf	Kerema	13,300	34,500	68,060
Madang	Madang	11,200	29,000	270,299
Manus	Lorengau	800	2,100	32,830
Milne Bay	Alotau (Samarai)	5,400	14,000	157,288
Morobe	Lae	13,300	34,500	363,535
National Capital District	Port Moresby	100	240	193,242
New Ireland	Kavieng	3,700	9,600	87,194
Oro (Northern)	Popondetta	8,800	22,800	96,762
Sandaun (West Sepik)	Vanimo	14,000	36,300	135,185
Simbu (Chimbu)	Kundiawa	2,350	6,100	183,801
Southern Highlands	Mendi	9,200	23,800	302,724
West New Britain	Kimbe	8,100	21,000	127,547
Western	Daru	38,350	99,300	108,705
Western Highlands	Mount Hagen	3,300	8,500	291,090
TOTAL		178,704[4]	462,840	3,529,538[5]

Demography

Population (1997): 4,496,000.
Density (1997): persons per sq mi 25.2, persons per sq km 9.7.
Urban-rural (1997): urban 17.0%; rural 83.0%.
Sex distribution (1990)[2]: male 52.09%; female 47.91%.
Age breakdown (1990): under 15, 40.4%; 15–29, 28.8%; 30–44, 16.9%; 45–59, 9.3%; 60–74, 4.3%; 75 and over, 0.3%.
Population projection: (2000) 4,812,000; (2010) 5,925,000.
Doubling time: 31 years.
Ethnic composition (1983): New Guinea Papuan 84.0%; New Guinea Melanesian 15.0%; other 1.0%.
Religious affiliation (1980): Protestant 58.4%; Roman Catholic 32.8%; Anglican 5.4%; traditional beliefs 2.5%; Bahā'ī 0.6%; other 0.3%.
Major cities (1990)[2]: Port Moresby 193,242; Lae 80,655; Madang 27,057; Wewak 23,224; Goroka 17,855.

Vital statistics

Birth rate per 1,000 population (1997): 32.4 (world avg. 25.0).
Death rate per 1,000 population (1997): 10.0 (world avg. 9.3).
Natural increase rate per 1,000 population (1997): 22.4 (world avg. 15.7).
Total fertility rate (avg. births per childbearing woman; 1997): 4.7.
Life expectancy at birth (1997): male 57.0 years; female 59.0 years.
Major causes of death per 100,000 population (1993): acute respiratory infections 34.6; pneumonia 27.8; meningitis 7.6; conditions originating from perinatal period 6.2; malaria 3.8.

National economy

Budget (1997). Revenue: K 1,882,000,000 (direct taxes 46.4%, indirect taxes 36.3%, nontax revenue 10.6%, foreign grants 6.7%). Expenditures: K 2,001,000,000 (current expenditure 57.7%, transfers to provincial governments 28.4%, economic and infrastructure 13.9%).
Public debt (external, outstanding; 1995): U.S.$1,614,000,000.
Production (metric tons except as noted). Agriculture, forestry, fishing (1996): coconuts 700,000, bananas 650,000, sweet potatoes 450,000, sugarcane 300,000, palm oil 250,000, yams 222,000, taro 220,000, cassava 115,000, copra (1994) 100,000, palm kernels 62,000, coffee 60,000, cacao 30,000, pineapples 14,000, tea 9,000; livestock (number of live animals) 1,030,000 pigs, 110,000 cattle, 3,250,000 chickens; roundwood (1995) 8,772,000 cu m; fish catch (1995) 26,000. Mining and quarrying (1996): copper 186,715; silver 59,037 kg; gold 51,573 kg. Manufacturing (value added, in K; 1985): food, beverages, and tobacco 162,558,000; metals, metal products, machinery, and equipment 47,493,000; wood products 29,807,000. Construction (value in K; 1994)[6]: total 95,600,000. Energy production (consumption): electricity (kW-hr; 1994) 1,790,000,000 (1,790,000,000); coal (metric tons; 1994) none (1,000); petroleum products (metric tons; 1994) none (720,000).
Household income and expenditure. Average household size (1980) 4.6; income per household (1975–76) K 2,771 (U.S.$3,483); sources of income (1970): wages and salaries 57.3%, transfer payments 1.1%, self-employment and other 41.6%; expenditure (1987)[11]: food and beverages 40.9%, transportation and communications 13.0%, housing 12.5%, clothing and footwear 6.2%, heating and lighting 4.9%, services and other 22.5%.
Gross national product (1995): U.S.$4,976,000,000 (U.S.$1,160 per capita).

Structure of gross domestic product and labour force

	1996		1980	
	in value K '000,000	% of total value	labour force[7]	% of labour force[7]
Agriculture	1,785	26.5	564,500	77.0
Mining	1,851	27.5	4,300	0.6
Manufacturing	551	8.2	14,000	1.9
Construction	271	4.0	21,600	2.9
Public utilities	88	1.3	2,800	0.4
Transp. and commun.	348	5.2	17,400	2.4
Trade	576	8.6	25,100	3.4
Finance	64	0.9	4,500	0.6
Pub. admin., defense; Services	888	13.2	77,100	10.5
Other	310	4.6	1,500	0.2
TOTAL	6,732[8]	100.0	732,800	100.0[4]

Land use (1994): forested 92.8%; agricultural and under permanent cultivation 0.9%; meadows and pastures 0.2%; other 6.1%.
Population economically active (1980)[7]: total 732,800; activity rate 24.6% (participation rates: over age 10, 35.2%; female 39.8%; unemployed 12.8%[9]).

Price and earnings indexes (1990 = 100)

	1990	1991	1992	1993	1994	1995	1996
Consumer price index	100.0	107.0	111.6	117.1	120.5	141.3	157.7
Weekly earnings index[10]	100.0	106.1	110.9	110.9	110.9	110.9	110.9

Tourism (1995): receipts U.S.$60,000,000; expenditures U.S.$75,000,000.

Foreign trade[12]

Balance of trade (current prices)

	1991	1992	1993	1994	1995	1996
K '000,000	−52.7	+475.2	+1,318.9	+1,322.8	+1,769.9	+1,317.9
% of total	2.0%	15.7%	37.3%	33.1%	35.3%	24.8%

Imports (1996): K 1,996,000,000 (1990; machinery and transport equipment 38.7%; basic manufactures 20.4%; food and live animals 17.9%; chemicals 7.5%; mineral fuels, lubricants, and related materials 2.7%). *Major import sources* (1995): Australia 52.2%; U.S. 14.8%; Singapore 7.4%; Japan 5.6%; New Zealand 3.6%; Hong Kong 3.2%; U.K. 3.0%.
Exports (1996): K 3,313,900,000 (crude oil 32.4%; gold 23.3%; copper ore and timber 14.0%; concentrates 11.7%; coffee 5.7%; palm oil 5.5%; cocoa beans 1.4%). *Major export destinations* (1995): Australia 30.0%; Japan 24.3%; Germany 10.0%; U.K. 8.2%; South Korea 7.1%; U.S. 4.0%.

Transport and communications

Transport. Railroads: none. Roads (1986): total length 19,736 km (paved 6%). Vehicles (1994): passenger cars 13,000; trucks and buses 32,000. Merchant marine (1992): vessels (100 gross tons and over) 87; total deadweight tonnage 40,855. Air transport (1993): passenger-km 738,366,000; metric ton-km cargo 82,369,000; airports (1996) with scheduled flights 129.

Communications

Medium	date	unit	number	units per 1,000 persons
Daily newspapers	1994	circulation	65,000	15
Radio	1996	receivers	300,000	68
Television	1995	receivers	100,000	23
Telephones	1995	main lines	43,600	10
Facsimile machines	1995	units	800	0.2

Education and health

Educational attainment (1990). Percentage of population age 25 and over having: no formal schooling 82.6%; some primary education 8.2%; completed primary 5.0%; some secondary 4.2%. *Literacy* (1995 est.): total population age 15 and over literate 72.2%; males literate 81.0%; females literate 62.7%.

Education (1995)

	schools	teachers	students	student/teacher ratio
Primary (age 7–12)	2,790	13,652	525,995	38.5
Secondary (age 13–16)	135[13]	2,415[14]	68,818	24.1[14]
Voc., teacher tr.	117[13]	878[14]	9,941	12.9[14]
Higher	2[13]	902[15]	13,663	7.1[15]

Health: physicians (1993) 736 (1 per 5,584 persons); hospital beds (1989) 15,335 (1 per 234 persons); infant mortality rate (1997) 62.0.
Food (1992): daily per capita caloric intake 2,613 (vegetable products 91%, animal products 9%); 115% of FAO minimum.

Military

Total active duty personnel (1997): 4,300 (army 88.4%, navy 9.3%, air force 2.3%). *Military expenditure as percentage of GNP* (1995): 1.4% (world 2.8%); per capita expenditure U.S.$25.

[1]The national languages are English, Tok Pisin (English Creole), and Motu. [2]Preliminary results. [3]Data unavailable because of civil insurrection. [4]Detail does not add to total given because of rounding. [5]Excludes an estimated population of 160,000 in the North Solomons, 4,500 people in remote areas, and an estimated foreign population of about 20,000–30,000. [6]Construction starts. [7]Citizens of Papua New Guinea over age 10 involved in "money-raising activities" only. [8]International Monetary Fund estimate. [9]1977; in six urban centres. [10]Minimum wage of urban labourers; starting 1993, for whole country. [11]Weights of retail price index components. [12]Import figures are f.o.b. in balance of trade and c.i.f. for commodities and trading partners. [13]1990. [14]1992. [15]1986.

Paraguay

Official name: República del Paraguay (Spanish); Tetã Paraguáype (Guaraní) (Republic of Paraguay).
Form of government: multiparty republic with two legislative houses (Senate [45]; Chamber of Deputies [80]).
Head of state and government: President.
Capital: Asunción.
Official languages: Spanish; Guaraní.
Official religion: none[1].
Monetary unit: 1 Paraguayan Guaraní (₲) = 100 céntimos; valuation (Oct. 3, 1997) 1 U.S.$ = ₲2,194; 1 £ = ₲3,537.

Area and population

Regions / Departments	Capitals	area sq mi	area sq km	population 1992 census
Occidental		95,338	246,925	105,633
Alto Paraguay	Fuerte Olimpo	31,795	82,349	12,156
Boquerón	Filadelfia	35,393	91,669	29,060
Presidente Hayes	Pozo Colorado	28,150	72,907	64,417
Oriental		61,710	159,827	4,046,955
Alto Paraná	Ciudad del Este	5,751	14,895	406,584
Amambay	Pedro Juan Caballero	4,994	12,933	99,860
Asunción[2]	—	45	117	500,938
Caaguazú	Coronel Oviedo	4,430	11,474	386,412
Caazapá	Caazapá	3,666	9,496	129,352
Canindiyú	Salto del Guairá	5,663	14,667	103,785
Central	Asunción	952	2,465	866,856
Concepción	Concepción	6,970	18,051	167,289
Cordillera	Caacupé	1,910	4,948	198,701
Guairá	Villarrica	1,485	3,846	161,991
Itapúa	Encarnación	6,380	16,525	377,536
Misiones	San Juan Bautista	3,690	9,556	89,018
Ñeembucú	Pilar	4,690	12,147	69,770
Paraguarí	Paraguarí	3,361	8,705	208,527
San Pedro	San Pedro	7,723	20,002	280,336
TOTAL		157,048	406,752	4,152,588[3]

Demography

Population (1997): 5,089,000[3].
Density (1997): persons per sq mi 32.4, persons per sq km 12.5.
Urban-rural (1992): urban 50.3%; rural 49.7%.
Sex distribution (1992): male 50.23%; female 49.77%.
Age breakdown (1992): under 15, 40.1%; 15–29, 27.6%; 30–44, 18.7%; 45–59, 8.3%; 60–74, 4.2%; 75 and over, 1.1%.
Population projection: (2000) 5,480,000; (2010) 6,805,000.
Religious affiliation (1995): Roman Catholic 88.5%; Protestant 5.0%; other 6.5%.
Major cities (1992): Asunción 502,426; Ciudad del Este 133,893; San Lorenzo 133,311; Lambaré 99,681; Fernando de la Mora 95,287.

Vital statistics

Birth rate per 1,000 population (1995–2000): 31.3 (world avg. 25.0).
Death rate per 1,000 population (1995–2000): 5.4 (world avg. 9.3).
Natural increase rate per 1,000 population (1995–2000): 25.9 (world avg. 15.7).
Total fertility rate (avg. births per childbearing woman; 1995–2000): 4.2.
Marriage rate per 1,000 population (1992): 3.9[4].
Life expectancy at birth (1995–2000): male 67.5 years; female 72.0 years.
Major causes of death per 100,000 population (1993)[5]: diseases of the circulatory system 162.7; malignant neoplasms (cancers) 52.8; diseases of the respiratory system 38.1; infectious and parasitic diseases 32.7.

National economy

Budget (1996). Revenue: ₲2,937,992,000,000 (taxes on goods and services 46.5%, customs duties 15.1%, income on fixed assets 14.3%, royalty payments 12.6%, pension funds 7.2%, documentary tax 2.3%). Expenditures: ₲3,335,481,000,000 (education 21.3%, public works 11.4%, defense 8.1%, agriculture 8.2%, interior 7.2%, public health 7.2%, housing 5.2%).
Public debt (external, outstanding; 1995): U.S.$1,488,000,000.
Population economically active (1996): total 1,747,488; activity rate 35.3% (participation rates; 1992: ages 12 and over, 51.0%; female 23.8%; unemployed [1996] 9.8%).

Price and earnings indexes (1990 = 100)

	1990	1991	1992	1993	1994	1995	1996
Consumer price index	100.0	124.2	143.1	169.2	203.9	231.3	254.0
Earnings index	100.0	115.1	131.8	158.0	...	...	...

Production (metric tons except as noted). Agriculture, forestry, fishing (1996): cassava 2,770,000, sugarcane 2,736,000, soybeans 2,394,000, corn (maize) 654,000, seed cotton 330,000, oranges 175,000, lint cotton 115,000, bananas 67,000, sweet potatoes 67,000; livestock (number of live animals) 9,788,000 cattle, 2,525,000 pigs, 14,152,000 chickens; roundwood (1995) 10,401,000 cu m; fish catch (1995) 16,000. Mining and quarrying (1995): limestone 600,000; kaolin 74,000; gypsum 4,500. Manufacturing (value added in constant prices of 1982, ₲'000,000; 1995): food products 70,600; wood products and furniture 24,500; handicrafts 11,400; textiles 10,200; printing and publishing 7,800; nonmetal products 6,900; petroleum products 6,400; leather and hides 5,700.
Energy production (consumption): electricity (kW-hr; 1994) 35,862,000,000 (3,090,000,000); crude petroleum (barrels; 1994) none (1,986,000); petroleum products (metric tons; 1994) 293,000 (1,011,000).
Gross national product (1995): U.S.$8,158,000,000 (U.S.$1,690 per capita).

Structure of gross domestic product and labour force

	1996 in value ₲'000,000[6]	% of total value	labour force	% of labour force
Agriculture	291,745	26.5	559,042	32.0
Mining	5,133	0.5	2,568	0.1
Manufacturing	157,778	14.3	181,983	10.4
Construction	59,764	5.4	142,678	8.2
Public utilities	60,697	5.5	13,150	0.8
Transp. and commun.	52,180	4.8	55,972	3.2
Trade, Finance	279,758	25.4	224,210	12.8
Pub. admin., defense	60,671	5.5	330,697 (Pub. admin., defense; Services)	18.9
Services, Other	133,432	12.1		
Other			237,188[7]	13.6[7]
TOTAL	1,101,158	100.0	1,747,488	100.0

Household income and expenditure. Average household size (1992) 4.7; sources of income (1989): wages and salaries 33.9%, transfer payments 2.5%.
Tourism (1995): receipts U.S.$213,000,000; expenditures U.S.$181,000,000.

Foreign trade

Balance of trade (current prices)

	1990	1991	1992	1993	1994	1995
U.S.$'000,000	–234.7	–538.3	–580.6	–752.3	–1,323.6	–1,887.6
% of total	10.9%	26.7%	30.7%	34.2%	44.8%	50.5%

Imports (1996): U.S.$2,850,477,000[8] (machinery and transport equipment 33.5%, of which transport equipment 11.6%; fuels and lubricants 8.3%; chemicals and pharmaceuticals 4.6%). *Major import sources* (1996): Brazil 32.7%; Argentina 19.5%; U.S. 10.7%; Japan 6.2%; South Korea 3.4%.
Exports (1996): U.S.$1,043,446,000[8] (soybean flour 31.1%; cotton fibres 20.7%; timber 9.0%; oilseed cakes 8.2%; vegetable oil 7.4%, of which soybean oil 5.6%; processed meats 4.5%; hides and skins 4.2%). *Major export destinations* (1996): Brazil 49.9%; The Netherlands 16.5%; Argentina 9.2%; Uruguay 4.2%; United States 3.5%; Chile 2.4%; Italy 1.9%.

Transport and communications

Transport. Railroads (1994): route length 441 km; passenger-km 3,000,000; metric ton-km cargo 5,500,000. Roads (1995): total length 28,900 km (paved 9%). Vehicles (1993): passenger cars 174,212; trucks 76,565. Air transport (1994): passenger-km 1,235,000,000; metric ton-km cargo 11,700,000; airports (1997) 5.

Communications

Medium	date	unit	number	units per 1,000 persons
Daily newspapers	1995	circulation	194,000	40
Radio	1996	receivers	700,000	141
Television	1995	receivers	710,000	144
Telephones	1995	main lines	166,900	34
Cellular telephones	1995	subscribers	15,800	3.2
Facsimile machines	1995	units	1,700	0.4

Education and health

Educational attainment (1992). Percentage of population age 15 and over having: no formal schooling 7.0%; primary education 61.2%; secondary 23.2%; higher 6.6%; not stated 2.0%. *Literacy* (1995): percentage of total population age 15 and over literate 92.1%; males literate 93%; females literate 90.6%.

Education (1994–95)

	schools	teachers	students	student/ teacher ratio
Primary (age 7–12)	5,318	34,580	835,089	24.1
Secondary (age 13–18)[9]	1,102	20,793[10]	235,914	10.3[10]
Higher	2	742[10]	39,694	40.9[11]

Health (1993): physicians 3,341 (1 per 1,406 persons); hospital beds 5,435 (1 per 864 persons); infant mortality rate per 1,000 live births (1995–2000) 39.0.
Food (1995): daily per capita caloric intake 2,560 (vegetable products 77%, animal products 23%); 111% of FAO recommended minimum requirement.

Military

Total active duty personnel (1997): 20,200 (army 73.8%, navy 17.8%, air force 8.4%). *Military expenditure as percentage of GNP* (1995): 1.4% (world 2.8%); per capita expenditure U.S.$23.

[1]Roman Catholicism, although not official, enjoys special recognition in the 1992 constitution. [2]Asunción is the capital city, not a department. [3]The 1992 census figure is not adjusted for undercount. The 1997 population figure is adjusted for estimated undercount. [4]Civil Registry records only. [5]Reporting areas only (constituting about 75 percent of the total population). [6]1982 prices. [7]Includes 171,312 unemployed. [8]Preliminary. [9]Includes vocational and teacher training. [10]1993–94. [11]1992–93.

Internet resources for further information:
- **Presidency of the Republic (Spanish only)**
  http://www.presidencia.gov.py/home
- **Dirección de Censos y Estadísticas Agropecuarias (Spanish only)**
  http://www.una.py/sitios/mag/dcea/
- **UNDP Paraguay**
  http://www.undp.org.py/

Peru

Official name: República del Perú (Spanish) (Republic of Peru).
Form of government[1]: unitary multiparty republic with one legislative house (Congress [120]).
Head of state and government: President.
Capital: Lima.
Official languages: Spanish; Quechua; Aymara.
Official religion: Roman Catholicism.
Monetary unit[2]: 1 nuevo sol (S/.) = 100 céntimos; valuation (Oct. 3, 1997) 1 U.S.$ = S/. 2.64; 1 £ = S/. 4.25.

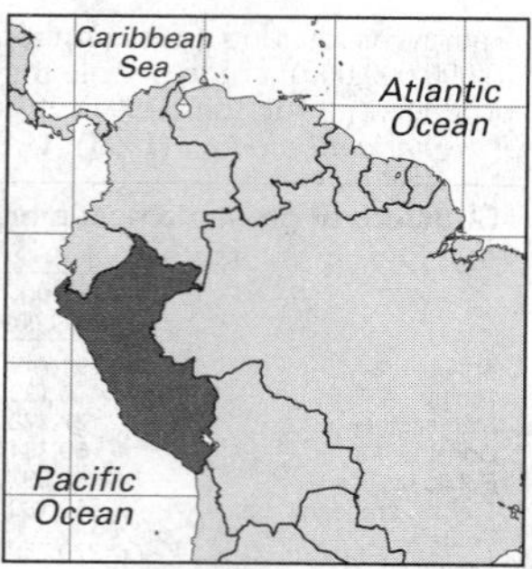

Area and population

Regions[3]	Capitals	area sq mi	area sq km	population 1997 estimate
Andres Avelino Cáceres	...	40,707	105,430	2,124,366
Arequipa	...	24,458	63,345	1,017,491
Chavín	...	15,686	40,627	1,035,321
Grau	...	15,661	40,562	1,665,555
Inca	...	66,696	172,741	1,607,279
José Carlos Mariátegui	...	40,081	103,809	1,551,264
La Libertad	...	9,873	25,570	1,390,568
Loreto	...	142,414	368,852	819,037
Los Libertadores-Wari	...	34,340	88,939	1,554,476
Nor Oriental del Marañón	...	33,486	86,728	2,773,098
San Martín	...	19,789	51,253	667,414
Ucayali	...	39,541	102,411	380,620
Department				
Lima	...	13,437	34,802	7,066,641
Constitutional Province				
Callao	Callao	57	147	717,913
TOTAL		496,225[4]	1,285,216	24,371,043

Demography

Population (1997): 24,371,000.
Density (1997): persons per sq mi 49.1, persons per sq km 19.0.
Urban-rural (1995): urban 71.2%; rural 28.8%.
Sex distribution (1995): male 49.67%; female 50.33%.
Age breakdown (1995): under 15, 35.9%; 15–29, 29.0%; 30–44, 18.2%; 45–59, 10.2%; 60–74, 5.3%; 75 and over, 1.4%.
Population projection: (2000) 25,662,000; (2010) 30,506,000.
Doubling time: 38 years.
Ethnic composition (1981): Quechua 47.1%; mestizo 32.0%; white 12.0%; Aymara 5.4%; other Amerindian 1.7%; other 1.8%.
Religious affiliation (1989): Roman Catholic 92.5%; Protestant 5.5%.
Major cities (1993): metropolitan Lima 5,706,127; Arequipa 619,156; Callao 615,046; Trujillo 509,312; Chiclayo 411,536.

Vital statistics

Birth rate per 1,000 population (1995–2000): 24.9 (world avg. 25.0); (1977) legitimate 57.8%; illegitimate 42.2%.
Death rate per 1,000 population (1995–2000): 6.4 (world avg. 9.3).
Natural increase rate per 1,000 population (1995–2000): 18.5 (world avg. 15.7).
Total fertility rate (avg. births per childbearing woman; 1995–2000): 3.0.
Marriage rate per 1,000 population (1993): 4.1[5].
Life expectancy at birth (1995–2000): male 65.9 years; female 70.9 years.
Major causes of death per 100,000 population (1989): diseases of the circulatory system 115.3; respiratory diseases 100.2; infectious diseases 84.5; malignant neoplasms 72.9; accidents, poisoning, and violence 53.6.

National economy

Budget (1995). Revenue: S/. 21,048,000,000 (taxes on goods and services 45.9%; income taxes 15.9%; nontax revenue 11.2%; social security contributions 10.1%; import duties 9.4%). Expenditures: S/. 24,649,000,000 (current expenditure 82.7%, of which transfer payments 35.7%, interest payments 15.4%, wages and salaries 15.0%; capital expenditure 17.3%).
Public debt (external, outstanding; 1995): U.S.$18,929,000,000.
Tourism (1995): receipts U.S.$520,000,000; expenditures U.S.$302,000,000.
Production (metric tons except as noted). Agriculture, forestry, fishing (1996): sugarcane 6,600,000, potatoes 2,265,000, rice 1,203,000, plantains 1,060,000, corn (maize) 1,054,000, cassava 547,000, seed cotton 269,000; livestock (number of live animals) 12,502,000 sheep, 4,629,000 cattle, 2,490,000 pigs, 79,089,000 chickens; roundwood (1995) 12,580,000 cu m; fish catch (1994) 11,587,339. Mining and quarrying (1995): iron ore 3,835,000; zinc 689,000; copper 405,000; lead 233,000; silver 1,908. Manufacturing (value in S/. '000,000[6]; 1995): processed foods 214.6; base metal products 164.6; industrial chemicals 114.2; wood products 77.6; textiles 71.8. Construction (value in S/. '000,000[6]; 1992): residential 22.4; nonresidential 14.6. Energy production (consumption): electricity (kW-hr; 1994) 15,163,000,000 (15,163,000,000); coal (metric tons; 1994) 109,000 (406,000); crude petroleum (barrels; 1994) 47,000,000 (54,000,000); petroleum products (metric tons; 1994) 7,227,000 (5,798,000); natural gas (cu m; 1994) 191,000,000 (191,000,000).
Household income and expenditure. Average household size (1993) 5.1; income per household (1988) I/. 1,086,620[2] (U.S.$2,173); sources of income (1988): business income 65.1%, wages 31.2%, transfers 3.7%; expenditure (1990): food 29.4%, recreation and education 13.2%, household durables 10.1%, clothing and footwear 8.5%, transportation 7.5%, health 7.0%, other 24.3%.
Gross national product (1995): U.S.$55,019,000,000 (U.S.$2,310 per capita).

Structure of gross domestic product and labour force

	1995 in value S/. [2]	1995 % of total value	1992 labour force	1992 % of labour force
Agriculture	608,488	14.4	2,658,000	33.0
Mining	355,344	8.4	198,000	2.4
Manufacturing	943,088	22.3	840,000	10.4
Construction	361,496	8.5	300,000	3.7
Public utilities	71,463	1.7	25,000	0.3
Transp. and commun.	291,992	6.9	355,000	4.4
Trade	762,261	18.0	1,297,000	16.1
Finance	608,070	14.4	192,000	2.4
Services	230,867[7]	5.4[7]	2,199,000[7]	27.3[7]
TOTAL	4,233,069	100.0	8,064,000	100.0

Population economically active (1995): total 8,906,009; activity rate of total population 37.8% (participation rates: over age 15, 59.1%; female 34.7%; unemployed [1993] 7.1%).

Price and earnings indexes (1990 = 100)

	1990	1991	1992	1993	1994	1995	1996
Consumer price index	100	510	884	1,314	1,626	1,806	2,015
Monthly earnings index[8]	100	706	1,163	2,059	...	...	...

Land use (1994): forest 66.3%; pasture 21.2%; agricultural 3.2%; other 9.3%.

Foreign trade

Balance of trade (current prices)

	1991	1992	1993	1994	1995	1996
U.S.$'000,000	−165.0	−566.7	−623.9	−1,095.2	−2,111.6	−1,996.5
% of total	2.4%	7.5%	8.2%	10.8%	15.9%	14.5%

Imports (1995): U.S.$7,583,860,000 (raw and intermediate materials 31.2%, machinery 22.7%, transport equipment 14.8%, consumer goods 12.1%). *Major import sources:* U.S. 25.2%; Colombia 8.1%; Japan 7.0%; Brazil 5.6%.
Exports (1995): U.S.$4,976,782,000 (copper and copper products 23.0%, fish meal fodder 13.3%, zinc products 6.9%, coffee 5.3%, petroleum and derivatives 4.9%, lead products 4.2%, clothing and accessories 3.7%, textile yarn and fabric 3.2%). *Major export destinations:* U.S. 18.7%; Japan 9.2%; China 7.0%; Germany 6.4%; The Netherlands 5.6%; Italy 5.0%; Brazil 4.0%.

Transport and communications

Transport. Railroads (1993): route length 2,121 km; passenger-km 165,304,000; metric ton-km cargo 884,352,000. Roads (1995): total length 71,400 km (paved 11%). Vehicles (1995): passenger cars 505,766; trucks and buses 338,871. Air transport (1995): passenger-km 2,470,000,000; metric ton-km cargo 259,000,000; airports (1996) 27.

Communications

Medium	date	unit	number	units per 1,000 persons
Daily newspapers	1994	circulation	2,000,000	87
Radio	1996	receivers	5,300,000	221
Television	1995	receivers	2,000,000	85
Telephones	1995	main lines	1,109,200	47
Cellular telephones	1995	subscribers	73,500	3.1
Facsimile machines	1995	units	15,000	0.6
Personal computers	1995	units	140,000	5.9

Education and health

Educational attainment (1993). Percentage of population age 15 and over having: no formal schooling 12.3%; less than primary education 0.3%; primary 31.5%; secondary 35.5%; higher 20.4%. *Literacy* (1993): total population age 15 and over literate 12,108,699 (87.2%); males 6,330,056 (92.9%); females 5,778,643 (81.7%).

Education (1995)

	schools	teachers	students	student/teacher ratio
Primary (age 6–11)	46,652	176,173	4,822,423	27.4
Secondary (age 12–16)	8,085	104,476	2,023,830	19.4
Voc., teacher tr.	2,425	12,293	270,576	22.0
Higher	886	49,249	714,512	14.5

Health (1992): physicians 20,124 (1 per 1,116 persons); hospital beds 44,100 (1 per 509 persons); infant mortality rate per 1,000 live births (1995–2000) 50.1.
Food (1995): daily per capita caloric intake 2,277 (vegetable products 83%, animal products 17%); 97% of FAO recommended minimum requirement.

Military

Total active duty personnel (1996): 125,000 (army 68.0%, navy 20.0%, air force 12.0%). *Military expenditure as percentage of GNP* (1995): 1.7% (world 2.8%); per capita expenditure U.S.$42.

[1]A new constitution promulgated in December 1993 replaced the 1980 constitution, which was suspended in April 1992. [2]A new currency, the nuevo sol, was introduced in January 1991, replacing the inti (abbrev.: I/.) at the rate of one million intis for one nuevo sol. [3]The regional administrative structure established in 1987 has been made functional only very slowly because of financing problems. [4]Detail does not add to total given because of rounding. [5]Excludes Indian jungle population; based on incomplete information. [6]At 1979 prices. [7]Includes public administration and other. [8]Estimate for Lima metropolitan area only.

Internet resources for further information:
- **Instituto Nacional de Estadística e Informática (Spanish) http://www.inei.gob.pe/**

Philippines

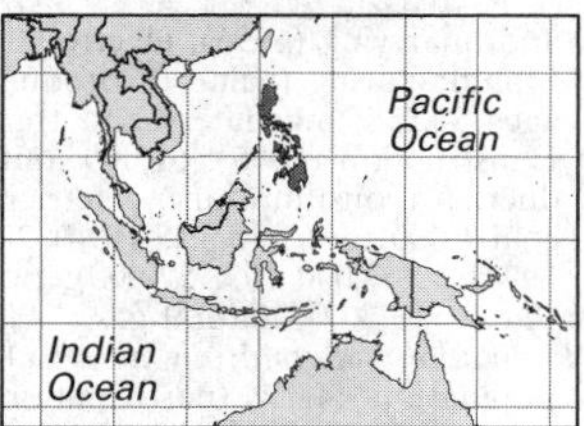

Official name: Republika ng Pilipinas (Pilipino); Republic of the Philippines (English).
Form of government: unitary republic with two legislative houses (Senate [24]; House of Representatives [221[1]]).
Chief of state and head of government: President.
Capital: Manila.
Official languages: Pilipino; English.
Official religion: none.
Monetary unit: 1 Philippine peso (₱) = 100 centavos; valuation (Oct. 3, 1997) 1 U.S.$ = ₱ 34.95; 1 £ = ₱ 56.34.

Area and population

	area		population
	sq mi	sq km	1995 census
Regions			
Bicol	6,808	17,633	4,325,307
Cagayan Valley	10,362	26,838	2,536,035
Caraga	7,277	18,847	1,942,687
Central Luzon	7,039	18,231	6,932,570
Central Mindanao	5,549	14,373	2,359,808
Central Visayas	5,773	14,951	5,014,588
Eastern Visayas	8,275	21,432	3,366,917
Ilocos	4,958	12,840	3,803,890
National Capital	246	636	9,454,040
Northern Mindanao	5,418	14,033	2,483,272
Southern Mindanao	10,479	27,141	4,604,158
Southern Tagalog	18,117	46,924	9,940,722
Western Mindanao	6,194	16,042	2,794,659
Western Visayas	7,808	20,223	5,776,938
Autonomous Regions			
Cordillera	7,063	18,294	1,254,838
Muslim Mindanao	4,493	11,638	2,020,903
TOTAL	115,860[2]	300,076	68,614,162[3]

Demography

Population (1997): 71,539,000.
Density (1997): persons per sq mi 617.5, persons per sq km 238.4.
Urban-rural (1997): urban 56.0%; rural 44.0%.
Sex distribution (1996): male 50.29%; female 49.71%.
Age breakdown (1996): under 15, 35.9%; 15–29, 28.8%; 30–44, 19.4%; 45–59, 10.2%; 60–74, 4.6%; 75 and over, 1.1%.
Population projection: (2000) 76,320,000; (2010) 86,423,000.
Doubling time: 30 years.
Ethnic composition (by mother tongue of households; 1995): Pilipino (Tagalog) 29.3%; Cebuano 23.3%; Ilocano 9.3%; Hiligaynon Ilongo 9.1%; Bicol 5.7%; Waray 3.8%; Pampango 3.0%; Pangasinan 1.8%; other 14.7%.
Religious affiliation (1996): Roman Catholic 82.9%; Protestant 5.4%; Muslim 4.6%; Aglipayan (Philippine Independent Church) 2.6%; other 4.5%.
Major cities (1995): Quezon City 1,989,419; Manila 1,654,761; Caloocan 1,023,159; Davao 960,910[4]; Cebu 688,196[4]; Zamboanga 464,466[4].

Vital statistics

Birth rate per 1,000 population (1997): 28.7 (world avg. 25.0); (1982) legitimate 93.9%; illegitimate 6.1%.
Death rate per 1,000 population (1997): 5.8 (world avg. 9.3).
Natural increase rate per 1,000 population (1997): 22.9 (world avg. 15.7).
Total fertility rate (avg. births per childbearing woman; 1997): 3.7.
Marriage rate per 1,000 population (1992): 6.9[5].
Life expectancy at birth (1997): male 66.0 years; female 70.0 years.
Major causes of death per 100,000 population (1992): heart diseases 64.3; pneumonia 57.9; tuberculosis 25.0; accidents 19.6.

National economy

Budget (1996). Revenue: ₱ 417,216,000,000 (taxes on goods and services 31.4%, income taxes 31.2%, international duties 24.7%, nontax revenues 12.7%). Expenditures: ₱ 415,557,000,000 (education 18.3%, general public administration 17.2%, debt service 16.7%, utilities and infrastructure 10.9%.
Public debt (external, outstanding; 1995): U.S.$29,908,000,000.
Production (metric tons except as noted). Agriculture, forestry, fishing (1996): sugarcane 26,000,000, rice 11,283,570, coconuts 10,000,000, corn (maize) 4,151,332, bananas 3,292,387, pineapples 1,476,879; livestock (number of live animals) 9,025,950 pigs, 6,400,000 goats, 2,841,277 buffalo, 115,782,000 chickens; roundwood (1995) 39,857,000 cu m; fish catch (1995) 2,259,234. Mining and quarrying (1996): coal 1,047,336; nickel ore 378,921; copper concentrate 188,442; silver 19,202 kg; gold 10,605 kg. Manufacturing (gross value added in ₱ '000,000; 1995)[6]: food products 176,200; petroleum and coal products 36,900; chemicals 35,700; footwear and clothing 30,400. Construction (private, authorized; 1996): residential ₱ 31,162,071,000; nonresidential ₱ 63,128,161,000. Energy production (consumption): electricity (kW-hr; 1994) 26,425,000,000 (26,425,000,000); coal (metric tons; 1994) 1,733,000 (2,503,000); crude petroleum (barrels; 1994) 2,186,000 (90,808,000); petroleum products (metric tons; 1994) 11,350,000 (12,559,000).
Household income and expenditure (1992). Average household size (1995) 5.1; income per family (1994) ₱ 83,160 (U.S.$3,150); sources of income: wages 45.7%, business profits 42.5%, self-employment 8.4%, transfers 3.4%; expenditure: food, beverages, and tobacco 57.7%, household furnishings and operations 13.5%, transportation 5.0%, fuel and power 4.1%, clothing 3.7%.
Gross national product (1995): U.S.$71,865,000,000 (U.S.$1,050 per capita).

Structure of gross domestic product and labour force

	1995			
	in value ₱ '000,000	% of total value	labour force	% of labour force
Agriculture	413,000	21.7	11,147,000	39.3
Mining	18,000	0.9	107,000	0.4
Manufacturing	438,000	23.0	2,617,000	9.2
Construction	107,000	5.6	1,302,000	4.6
Public utilities	49,000	2.6	114,000	0.4
Transp. and commun.	89,000	4.7	1,477,000	5.2
Trade	262,000	13.7	3,767,000	13.3
Finance	209,000	11.0	535,000	1.9
Services }	321,000	16.8	4,600,000	16.2
Other }			2,716,000[7]	9.5[7]
TOTAL	1,906,000	100.0	28,382,000	100.0

Population economically active (1995): total 28,382,000; activity rate 40.4% (participation rates: ages 15–64, 65.6%; female 37.4%; unemployed 9.5%).

Price and earnings indexes (1990 = 100)

	1990	1991	1992	1993	1994	1995	1996
Consumer price index	100.0	118.7	129.3	139.1	151.7	164.0	177.8
Daily earnings index[8]	100.0	128.5	128.5	147.0	155.2	157.9	...

Tourism (1995): receipts U.S.$2,450,000,000; expenditures U.S.$422,000,000.

Foreign trade[9]

Balance of trade (current prices)

	1991	1992	1993	1994	1995	1996
₱ '000,000	−89,465	−121,250	−76,298	−212,086	−229,214	−311,291
% of total	15.6%	19.6%	22.5%	23.2%	20.3%	22.5%

Imports (1996): U.S.$32,426,930,000 (machinery and transport equipment 29.8%, electronic materials and components 19.8%, mineral fuels and lubricants 9.3%, iron and steel 4.4%, textile yarns and fabrics 3.6%). *Major import sources:* Japan 22.0%; United States 19.6%; Singapore 5.4%; Saudi Arabia 5.2%; South Korea 5.2%.
Exports (1996): U.S.$20,542,550,000 (electronics 39.9%, garments 11.8%, coconut oil 2.8%, ignition wiring sets 2.3%, computer peripherals 2.3%, woodcraft and furniture 2.2%). *Major export destinations:* United States 33.9%; Japan 17.9%; Singapore 6.0%; The Netherlands 5.4%; Hong Kong 4.2%.

Transport and communications

Transport. Railroads (1996): route length 897 km; passenger-km 70,000,000; metric ton-km cargo 1,476,000. Roads (1994): total length 161,035 km (paved 17%). Vehicles (1995): passenger cars 609,000; trucks and buses 221,900. Air transport (1996)[10]: passenger-km 12,854,000,000; metric ton-km cargo 328,817,000; airports (1996) with scheduled flights 21.

Communications

Medium	date	unit	number	units per 1,000 persons
Daily newspapers	1994	circulation	4,286,000	65
Radio	1996	receivers	8,300,000	116
Television	1996	receivers	9,000,000	125
Telephones	1996	main lines	1,787,000	25
Cellular telephones	1995	subscribers	492,700	6.9
Facsimile machines	1995	units	35,000	0.5
Personal computers	1995	units	770,000	11

Education and health

Educational attainment (1990). Percentage of population age 25 and over having: no grade completed 6.7%; elementary education 46.9%; secondary 24.3%; postsecondary 11.0%; college 10.6%; not stated 0.5%. *Literacy* (1994): total population age 15 and over literate 34,215,672 (93.5%); males literate 17,080,157 (93.0%); females literate 17,135,515 (93.9%).

Education (1994–95)

	schools	teachers	students	student/ teacher ratio
Primary (age 7–12)	35,671	324,418	10,903,529	33.6
Secondary (age 13–16)	5,880[11] }	131,831	4,762,877	36.1
Voc., teacher tr.	1,261[12] }			
Higher	975[11]	56,880[13]	1,582,820[11]	23.7[13]

Health: physicians (1993) 78,445 (1 per 849 persons); hospital beds (1993) 77,434 (1 per 860 persons); infant mortality rate per 1,000 live births (1997) 36.
Food (1995): daily per capita caloric intake 2,395 (vegetable products 85%, animal products 15%); 106% of FAO recommended minimum requirement.

Military

Total active duty personnel (1996): 107,500 (army 63.3%, navy 21.4%, air force 15.3%). *Military expenditure as percentage of GNP* (1994): 1.9% (world 3.0%); per capita expenditure U.S.$19.

[1]Includes 17 members appointed by the President. [2]Detail does not add to total given because of rounding. [3]Includes 2,830 embassy employees abroad. [4]1994. [5]Estimate based on less than 90% of the total marriages. [6]Manufacturing firms with 10 or more workers. [7]Mostly unemployed. [8]Wages in nonagricultural activities in the National Capital Region. [9]Import figures are f.o.b. in balance of trade and c.i.f. for commodities and trading partners. [10]Philippines Airlines only. [11]1993–94. [12]1991–92. [13]1990–91.

Internet resources for further information:
- **National Statistics Office**
  http://www.census.gov.ph/
- **Government Website Directory**
  http://www.neda.gov.ph/html/government.html

Poland

Official name: Rzeczpospolita Polska (Republic of Poland).
Form of government: unitary multiparty republic with two legislative houses (Senate [100]; Diet [460]).
Chief of state: President.
Head of government: Prime Minister.
Capital: Warsaw.
Official language: Polish.
Official religion: none[1].
Monetary unit: 1 złoty (Zł)[2] = 100 groszy; valuation (Oct. 3, 1997) 1 U.S.$ = Zł 3.42; 1 £ = Zł 5.51.

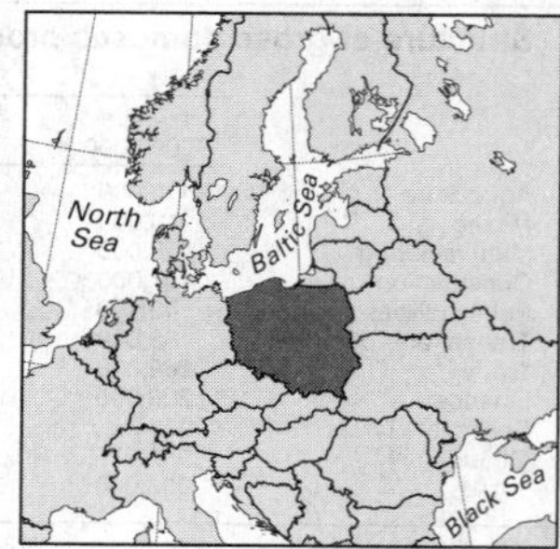

Area and population (1996[3] estimate)

Provinces	area sq km	population	Provinces	area sq km	population
Biała Podlaska	5,348	309,500	Opole	8,535	1,025,200
Białystok	10,055	700,700	Ostrołęka	6,498	408,400
Bielsko-Biała	3,704	918,600	Piła	8,205	494,000
Bydgoszcz	10,349	1,131,800	Piotrków	6,266	644,200
Chełm	3,866	249,900	Płock	5,117	522,000
Ciechanów	6,362	436,400	Poznań	8,151	1,353,700
Częstochowa	6,182	782,300	Przemyśl	4,437	414,600
Elbląg	6,103	491,400	Radom	7,294	763,800
Gdańsk	7,394	1,455,900	Rzeszów	4,397	746,300
Gorzów	8,484	510,800	Siedlce	8,499	661,700
Jelenia Góra	4,379	524,500	Sieradz	4,869	412,900
Kalisz	6,512	722,000	Skierniewice	3,960	424,000
Katowice	6,650	3,924,800	Słupsk	7,453	425,900
Kielce	9,211	1,136,600	Suwałki	10,490	485,500
Konin	5,139	479,700	Szczecin	9,982	990,500
Koszalin	8,470	521,900	Tarnobrzeg	6,283	609,300
Kraków	3,254	1,241,400	Tarnów	4,151	693,500
Krosno	5,702	506,600	Toruń	5,348	671,100
Legnica	4,037	523,600	Wałbrzych	4,168	739,400
Leszno	4,154	397,200	Warszawa	3,788	2,416,600
Łódź	1,523	1,116,200	Włocławek	4,402	435,000
Łomża	6,684	353,800	Wrocław	6,287	1,137,700
Lublin	6,792	1,026,800	Zamość	6,980	492,800
Nowy Sącz	5,576	733,100	Zielona Góra	8,868	674,100
Olsztyn	12,327	771,700	TOTAL	312,685	38,609,400

Demography

Population (1997): 38,802,000.
Density (1997): persons per sq mi 321.4, persons per sq km 124.1.
Urban-rural (1996): urban 61.8%; rural 38.2%.
Sex distribution (1997): male 48.63%; female 51.37%.
Age breakdown (1997): under 15, 21.4%; 15–29, 22.9%; 30–44, 22.6%; 45–59, 17.0%; 60–74, 12.2%; 75 and over, 3.9%.
Population projection: (2000) 39,055,000; (2010) 40,388,000.
Ethnic composition (1990): Polish 98.7%; Ukrainian 0.6%; other 0.7%.
Religious affiliation (1995): Roman Catholic 90.7%; Orthodox and other 9.3%.
Major cities (1996[3]): Warsaw 1,638,300; Łódź 825,600; Kraków 745,400.

Vital statistics

Birth rate per 1,000 population (1997): 10.0 (world avg. 25.0); (1985) legitimate 95.0%; illegitimate 5.0%.
Death rate per 1,000 population (1997): 10.0 (world avg. 9.3).
Natural increase rate per 1,000 population (1997): 0.0 (world avg. 15.7).
Total fertility rate (avg. births per childbearing woman; 1997): 1.4.
Marriage rate per 1,000 population (1996): 5.3.
Divorce rate per 1,000 population (1995): 1.0.
Life expectancy at birth (1997): male 68.3 years; female 76.9 years.
Major causes of death per 100,000 population (1994): diseases of the circulatory system 512.7; malignant neoplasms (cancers) 201.0; accidents, poisoning, and violence 75.4; diabetes mellitus 14.2; infectious and parasitic diseases 6.8.

National economy

Budget (1996). Revenue: Zł 100,171,200,000 (income tax 37.8%, value-added tax 25.7%, excise tax 18.1%). Expenditures: Zł 109,671,200,000 (current expenditure 50.6%, interest on debts 16.4%, social benefits 15.8%).
Public debt (external, outstanding; 1995): U.S.$41,073,000,000.
Gross national product (1995): U.S.$107,829,000,000 (U.S.$2,790 per capita).

Structure of gross domestic product and labour force

	1995			
	in value Zł '000,000[4]	% of total value	labour force	% of labour force
Agriculture	18,965.9	6.6	4,045,900	23.8
Mining and manufacturing	72,003.0	25.2	3,728,800	21.9
Public utilities	10,570.9	3.7		
Construction	14,806.5	5.2	827,400	4.9
Transp. and commun.	17,260.8	6.0	838,100	4.9
Trade	39,003.0	13.6	2,089,000	12.3
Finance	22,743.1	8.0	268,200	1.6
Public administration	13,875.9	4.8	381,300	2.2
Services	38,806.5	13.6	2,234,900	13.1
Other	37,990.0[5]	13.3[5]	2,590,400[6]	15.2[6]
TOTAL	286,025.6	100.0	17,004,000	100.0[7]

Production (metric tons except as noted). Agriculture, forestry, fishing (1995): (value of production in Zł '000,000) potatoes 6,606, wheat 3,055, rye 1,421, sugar beets 1,075; livestock (number of live animals; 1997) 18,152,000 pigs, 7,306,000 cattle; roundwood 19,334,000 cu m; fish catch 451,346. Mining and quarrying (1996): electrolytic copper 425,000; zinc 165,000; lead 66,000. Manufacturing (value of production in Zł '000,000; 1995): food and beverages 52,558; machinery and transport equipment 33,372; chemicals 16,360. Construction (1995): 61,000 units, of which residential 31,100. Energy production (consumption): electricity ('000,000 kW-hr; 1994) 135,347 (132,668); coal ('000 metric tons; 1994) 200,700 (171,000); crude petroleum (barrels; 1994) 2,107,000 (99,757,000); petroleum products ('000 metric tons; 1994) 12,625 (13,807); natural gas ('000,000 cu m; 1994) 4,079 (10,908).
Population economically active (1995): total 17,004,000; activity rate of total population 44.0% (participation rates: over age 15, 66.9%; female 45.9%; unemployed [1996] 14.3%).

Price and earnings indexes (1990 = 100)

	1991	1992	1993	1994	1995	1996	1997[8]
Consumer price index	176.7	256.8	351.5	468.4	593.9	713.5	827.8
Monthly earnings index	167.1	228.5	320.0	421.4	595.9	752.7	912.5

Household income and expenditure (1995). Average household size 3.1; average annual income Zł 8,431 (U.S.$2,990); sources of income: wages 55.7%, social security benefits 32.5% (of which pensions 26.6%), self-employment 6.9%, other 4.9%; expenditure: food 39.7%, housing 20.6%, clothing 7.0%.
Tourism (1995): receipts U.S.$6,700,000,000; expenditures U.S.$5,500,000,000.
Land use (1994): forest 28.8%; meadow 13.3%; agricultural and under permanent cultivation 47.0%; other 10.9%.

Foreign trade

Balance of trade (current prices)

	1991	1992	1993	1994	1995	1996
Zł '000,000	–654	–4,026	–8,262	–9,826	–14,987	–34,412
% of total	2.0%	10.1%	13.8%	11.1%	11.9%	20.7%

Imports (1996): Zł 100,231,000,000 (1995; machinery and transport equipment 29.9%, manufactured goods 21.6%, chemicals 15.0%, miscellaneous manufactured articles 9.3%, mineral fuels and lubricants 9.1%, food 8.0%). *Major import sources* (1995): Germany 26.6%; Italy 8.5%; Russia 6.7%; U.K. 5.2%.
Exports (1996): Zł 65,819,000,000 (1995; manufactured goods 27.6%, machinery and transport equipment 21.1%, miscellaneous manufactured articles 20.9%, food 9.2%, mineral fuels and lubricants 8.2%, chemicals 7.7%). *Major export destinations* (1995): Germany 38.3%; The Netherlands 5.6%.

Transport and communications

Transport. Railroads (1996): length 23,986 km; passenger-km 26,635,000,000; metric ton-km cargo 69,116,000,000. Roads (1995): total length 372,479 km (paved 65%). Vehicles (1995): passenger cars 7,517,300; trucks and buses 1,472,300. Merchant marine (1992): vessels (100 gross tons and over) 644; total deadweight tonnage 4,314,308. Air transport (1996): passenger-km 4,633,000,000; metric ton-km cargo 74,000,000; airports (1997) 8.

Communications

Medium	date	unit	number	units per 1,000 persons
Daily newspapers	1995	circulation	5,400,000	140.0
Radio	1996	receivers[9]	10,193,000	263.3
Television	1996	receivers[9]	9,677,000	249.9
Telephones	1996	main lines	5,728,000	147.9
Cellular telephones	1995	subscribers	73,400	1.9
Facsimile machines	1995	units	30,900	0.8
Personal computers	1995	units	1,101,000	28.5

Education and health

Educational attainment (1988). Percentage of population age 15 and over having: no formal schooling or less than full primary education 6.4%; primary 38.8%; secondary 48.3%; higher 6.5%. *Literacy* (1988): 98.7%.

Education (1995–96)

	schools	teachers	students	student/teacher ratio
Primary (age 7–14)	19,823	323,500	5,104,200	15.8
Secondary (age 15–18)	1,705	34,700	683,000	19.7
Voc., teacher tr.	8,887	88,700	1,729,300	19.5
Higher	179	71,300	794,600	11.1

Health (1996): physicians 88,523 (1 per 436 persons); hospital beds 213,969 (1 per 180 persons); infant mortality rate per 1,000 live births (1997) 14.0.
Food (1995): daily per capita caloric intake 3,307 (vegetable products 72%, animal products 28%); 126% of FAO recommended minimum.

Military

Total active duty personnel (1997): 241,750 (army 70%, navy 7%, air force 23%). *Military expenditure as percentage of GNP* (1995): 2.3% (world 2.8%); per capita expenditure U.S.$127.

[1]The 1997 Constitution of Poland specifies freedom of religion; the 1997 concordat with Vatican City (signed unilaterally by the Polish prime minister in May 1997), however, provides special recognition to Roman Catholicism. [2]On Jan. 1, 1995, the złoty was redenominated at a rate of 10,000 old złoty to 1 new złoty. [3]January 1. [4]In purchasers' values. [5]Includes import duties and value-added tax. [6]Includes 2,233,000 unemployed. [7]Detail does not add to total given because of rounding. [8]July. [9]Number of licenses issued.

Internet resources for further information:
- **Głównego Urzędu Statystycznego (Central Statistical Office) http://www.stsp.gov.pl/**
- **Polish World http://www.polishworld.com**

Portugal

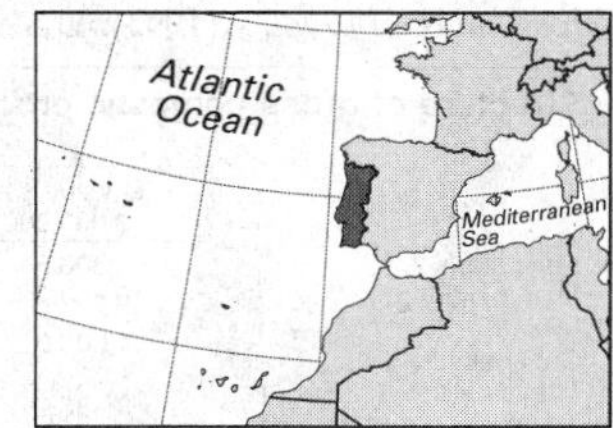

Official name: República Portuguesa (Portuguese Republic).
Form of government: republic with one legislative house (Assembly of the Republic [230]).
Chief of state: President.
Head of government: Prime Minister.
Capital: Lisbon.
Official language: Portuguese.
Official religion: none.
Monetary unit: 1 escudo (Esc) = 100 centavos; valuation (Oct. 3, 1997) 1 U.S.$ = Esc 179.56; 1 £ = Esc 289.44.

Area and population

		area		population
Continental Portugal Districts	**Capitals**	sq mi	sq km	1993[1] estimate
Aveiro	Aveiro	1,081	2,800	658,400
Beja	Beja	3,947	10,223	166,500
Braga	Braga	1,041	2,695	754,700
Bragança	Bragança	2,547	6,597	154,700
Castelo Branco	Castelo Branco	2,555	6,616	211,800
Çoimbra	Çoimbra	1,533	3,971	425,400
Évora	Évora	2,856	7,396	172,400
Faro	Faro	1,925	4,986	342,000
Guarda	Guarda	2,139	5,540	185,400
Leiria	Leiria	1,354	3,508	426,200
Lisboa	Lisbon (Lisboa)	1,065	2,758	2,048,000
Portalegre	Portalegre	2,341	6,064	132,400
Porto	Porto	904	2,341	1,652,000
Santarém	Santarém	2,590	6,707	441,900
Setúbal	Setúbal	1,955	5,064	716,200
Viana do Castelo	Viana do Castelo	853	2,210	248,300
Vila Real	Vila Real	1,662	4,305	233,100
Viseu	Viseu	1,934	5,009	398,800
Azores (Açores) Autonomous Region	Ponta Delgada	868	2,247	237,800
Madeira Autonomous Region	Funchal	306	794	253,800
TOTAL		35,456[2]	91,831[2]	9,859,600[3]

Demography

Population (1997): 9,943,000.
Density (1997): persons per sq mi 280.4, persons per sq km 108.3.
Urban-rural (1996): urban 36.0%; rural 64.0%.
Sex distribution (1996): male 48.16%; female 51.84%.
Age breakdown (1995): under 15, 18.9%; 15–29, 23.6%; 30–44, 21.6%; 45–59, 16.6%; 60–74, 13.9%; 75 and over, 5.4%.
Population projection: (2000) 9,995,000; (2010) 10,172,000.
Nationality (1996): Portuguese 98.2%; Cape Verdean 0.4%; other 1.4%.
Religious affiliation (1995): Christian 94.8%, of which Roman Catholic 92.2%, Protestant 1.5%, other Christian (Jehovah's Witness 0.7%; Mormon 0.4%) 1.1%; Muslim 0.1%; other and nonreligious 5.1%.
Major cities (1991): Lisbon 663,394; Porto 302,467; Amadora 181,774.

Vital statistics

Birth rate per 1,000 population (1996): 11.1 (world avg. 25.0); (1990) legitimate 85.5%; illegitimate 14.5%.
Death rate per 1,000 population (1996): 10.8 (world avg. 9.3).
Natural increase rate per 1,000 population (1996): 0.3 (world avg. 15.7).
Total fertility rate (avg. births per childbearing woman; 1995): 1.4.
Life expectancy at birth (1995–96): male 71.3 years; female 78.6 years.
Major causes of death per 100,000 population (1994): circulatory diseases 431.2, of which cerebrovascular diseases 231.0, ischemic heart disease 91.4; malignant neoplasms (cancers) 193.6; respiratory diseases 71.5.

National economy

Budget (1995). Revenue: Esc 6,110,600,000,000 (import duties and excise taxes 36.7%, social security taxes 29.0%, income and inheritance taxes 24.2%). Expenditures: Esc 6,332,900,000,000 (1988; education 12.4%, health 9.8%, defense 6.6%, administration 5.3%, public works 2.8%).
Production (metric tons except as noted). Agriculture, forestry, fishing (1997): potatoes 1,400,000, grapes 1,240,000, tomatoes 1,020,000, corn (maize) 867,000, olives 300,000, wheat 289,000, apples 200,000, oranges 160,000, cabbages 140,000, rice 140,000, cork 91,870[4], carrots 83,000; livestock (number of live animals) 6,200,000 sheep, 2,344,000 pigs, 1,311,000 cattle; roundwood (1996) 9,447,800 cu m; fish catch (1995) 265,508. Mining and quarrying (1996): salt 609,639; copper 111,459; kaolin 95,900[4]; tin 8,304; zinc 5,675[5]; tungsten 1,343. Manufacturing (value added in Esc '000,000; 1994): petroleum refining 361,511; machinery and transport equipment 356,941; wearing apparel and footwear 301,942; textiles 273,161; food and beverages 232,161; tobacco 132,614; printing and publishing 114,839. Construction (1993): residential 4,793,000 sq m; nonresidential 2,045,167 sq m[6]. Energy production (consumption): electricity (kW-hr; 1994) 31,380,000,000 (32,268,000,000); coal (metric tons; 1994) 147,000 (5,225,000); crude petroleum (barrels; 1994) none (99,069,000); petroleum products (metric tons; 1994) 12,251,000 (10,159,000).
Household income and expenditure. Average household size (1991) 3.1; income per household: n.a.; sources of income (1994–95): wages and salaries 45.8%, property and entrepreneurial income 32.4%, transfer payments 21.5%; expenditure (1994–95): food 23.9%, housing 20.6%, transportation and communications 18.9%, clothing and footwear 6.3%, health 4.6%, other 25.7%.
Gross national product (1995): U.S.$96,689,000,000 (U.S.$9,740 per capita).

Structure of gross domestic product and labour force

	1993		1994	
	in value Esc '000,000	% of total value	labour force	% of labour force
Agriculture	489,476	3.7	490,200	10.8
Mining	113,243	0.8 }	1,025,800	22.5
Manufacturing	3,417,963	25.8 }		
Construction	699,267	5.3	330,800	7.2
Public utilities	551,164	4.2	36,700	0.8
Trade	2,474,801	18.6 }	1,442,300	31.6
Finance	1,246,248	9.4 }		
Transp. and commun.	825,319	6.2 }		
Services	2,477,083	18.7 }		
Pub. admin., defense	976,901	7.4	925,600	20.3
Other	...	...	310,000[7]	6.8[7]
TOTAL	13,271,465	100.0[3]	4,561,400	100.0

Public debt (1992): U.S.$39,922,000,000.
Population economically active (1994): total 4,561,400; activity rate of total population 46.1% (participation rates: ages 15–64, 69.0%[5]; female 44.5%; unemployed 6.8%).

Price and earnings indexes (1990 = 100)

	1990	1991	1992	1993	1994	1995	1996
Consumer price index	100.0	111.4	121.3	129.6	136.0	141.5	146.0
Annual earnings index[8]	100.0	114.2	129.8	140.1	146.7	...	...

Tourism (1996): receipts U.S.$4,325,200,000; expenditures U.S.$2,321,500,000.
Land use (1994): forest 35.9%; pasture 10.9%; agriculture 31.5%; other 21.7%.

Foreign trade

Balance of trade (current prices)

	1991	1992	1993	1994	1995	1996
Esc '000,000	−1,067,800	−1,144.6	−1,051.8	−1,099.9	−1,011.4	−1,096.8
% of total	18.5%	18.8%	17.5%	15.9%	14.7%	13.0%

Imports (1994): Esc 4,595,200,000,000 (machinery and transport equipment 34.2%, of which road vehicles and parts 15.1%; food and live animals 11.6%; chemicals and chemical products 9.8%; mineral fuels 8.8%; textiles 6.1%; office machines 3.2%). *Major import sources:* Spain 19.8%; Germany 13.8%; France 12.8%; Italy 8.5%; United Kingdom 6.6%; The Netherlands 4.3%.
Exports (1994): Esc 3,057,600,000,000 (textiles and wearing apparel 25.9%; machinery and transport equipment 21.2%, of which transport equipment 6.0%; footwear 8.7%; cork and wood products 6.2%; chemicals and chemical products 4.7%). *Major export destinations:* Germany 18.7%; France 14.7%; Spain 14.4%; United Kingdom 11.7%; United States 5.2%.

Transport and communications

Transport. Railroads (1995): route length 3,072 km; passenger-km 4,869,000,000; metric ton-km cargo 2,018,000,000. Roads (1995): total length 68,732 km (paved 88%). Vehicles (1995): passenger cars 2,560,000; trucks and buses 219,696[9]. Merchant marine (1992): vessels (100 gross tons and over) 332; total deadweight tonnage 1,129,382. Air transport (1996): passenger-km 7,977,817,000; metric ton-km cargo 209,674,000; airports (1997) 16.

Communications

Medium	date	unit	number	units per 1,000 persons
Daily newspapers	1995	circulation	465,000	47
Radio	1995	receivers	2,776,000	280
Television	1995	receivers	3,300,000	333
Telephones	1995	main lines	3,586,000	362
Cellular telephones	1995	subscribers	340,800	34.4
Facsimile machines	1995	units	35,300	3.6
Personal computers	1995	units	600,000	60.5

Education and health

Educational attainment (1991). Percentage of population age 25 and over having: no formal schooling 16.1%; some primary education 61.5%; some secondary 10.6%; postsecondary 3.5%. *Literacy* (1995): total population age 15 and over literate 89.6%; males 92.5%; females 87.0%.

Education (1993–94)

	schools	teachers	students	student/ teacher ratio
Primary (age 5–11)	12,069	73,221	910,650	12.4
Secondary (age 12–19)	663	69,095[10]	749,838	11.3[10]
Vocational	214	[10]	28,627	[10]
Higher[11]	273	30,998[12]	236,537	6.9[12]

Health (1996): physicians 29,902 (1 per 332 persons); hospital beds 39,210 (1 per 253 persons); infant mortality rate per 1,000 live births (1996) 6.9.
Food (1996): daily per capita caloric intake 3,639 (vegetable products 74%, animal products 26%); 148% of FAO recommended minimum requirement.

Military

Total active duty personnel (1997): 59,300 (army 54.1%, navy 25.0%, air force 13.0%, paramilitary national guard 7.9%). *Military expenditure as percentage of GNP* (1995): 2.6% (world 2.8%); per capita expenditure U.S.$273.

[1]January 1. [2]Does not include 117 sq mi (304 sq km) of water areas comprising the Tagus and Sado estuaries and the Aveiro Lagoon. [3]Detail does not add to total given because of rounding. [4]1992. [5]1993. [6]1990. [7]Unemployed. [8]Based on average annual wage. [9]1994. [10]Secondary includes Vocational. [11]Includes teacher colleges. [12]1992–93.

Internet resources for further information:
- **Instituto Nacional de Estatística http://www.ine.pt/**

Puerto Rico

Official name: Estado Libre Asociado de Puerto Rico; Commonwealth of Puerto Rico.
Political status: self-governing commonwealth in association with the United States, having two legislative houses (Senate [29[1]]; House of Representatives [53[1]]).
Chief of state: President of the United States.
Head of government: Governor.
Capital: San Juan.
Official languages: Spanish; English.
Monetary unit: 1 U.S. dollar (U.S.$) = 100 cents; valuation (Oct. 3, 1997) 1 £ = U.S.$1.61.

Population (1995 estimate)

Municipio	population	Municipio	population	Municipio	population
Adjuntas	19,592	Fajardo	38,383	Naguabo	24,517
Aguada	37,651	Florida	8,434	Naranjito	29,016
Aguadilla	65,207	Guánica	21,596	Orocovis	24,075
Agunas Buenas	30,062	Guayama	41,994	Patillas	21,259
Aibonito	27,863	Guayanilla	27,316	Peñuelas	26,595
Añasco	27,007	Guaynabo	104,927	Ponce	189,988
Arecibo	100,755	Gurabo	32,003	Quebradillas	26,008
Arroyo	19,549	Hatillo	40,149	Rincón	13,589
Barceloneta	26,480	Hormigueros	16,121	Río Grande	48,997
Barranquitas	28,702	Humacao	57,643	Sabana Grande	23,244
Bayamón	231,845	Isabela	41,156	Salinas	29,962
Cabo Rojo	47,365	Jayuya	16,791	San Germán	36,925
Caguas	140,114	Juana Díaz	49,693	San Juan	433,705
Camuy	32,438	Juncos	41,424	San Lorenzo	36,435
Canóvanas	50,666	Lajas	26,704	San Sebastián	42,573
Carolina	188,427	Lares	32,282	Santa Isabel	19,546
Cataño	32,391	Las Marías	9,923	Toa Alta	58,240
Cayey	50,728	Las Piedras	30,111	Toa Baja	92,702
Ceiba	17,715	Loíza	27,904	Trujillo Alto	74,644
Ciales	19,447	Luquillo	18,407	Utuado	35,212
Cidra	49,326	Manatí	38,781	Vega Alta	35,828
Coamo	35,673	Maricao	5,979	Vega Baja	61,401
Comerío	20,914	Maunabo	13,503	Vieques	9,503
Corozal	36,304	Mayagüez	100,937	Villalba	22,695
Culebra	1,632	Moca	37,154	Yabucoa	40,602
Dorado	32,166	Morovis	33,388	Yauco	42,879
				TOTAL	3,782,862

Demography

Area: 3,515 sq mi, 9,104 sq km.
Population (1997): 3,809,000.
Density (1997): persons per sq mi 1,083.5, persons per sq km 418.3.
Urban-rural (1990): urban 71.2%; rural 28.8%.
Sex distribution (1992): male 48.43%; female 51.57%.
Age breakdown (1992): under 15, 27.2%; 15–29, 25.1%; 30–44, 20.4%; 45–59, 14.1%; 60–74, 9.2%; 75 and over, 4.0%.
Population projection: (2000) 3,945,000; (2010) 4,438,000.
Doubling time: 77 years.
Major cities (1990): San Juan 426,832; Ponce 159,151; Caguas 92,429; Mayagüez 83,010; Arecibo 49,545.

Vital statistics

Birth rate per 1,000 population (1996): 17.2 (world avg. 25.0).
Death rate per 1,000 population (1996): 7.9 (world avg. 9.3).
Natural increase rate per 1,000 population (1996): 9.3 (world avg. 15.7).
Total fertility rate (avg. births per childbearing woman; 1991): 2.2.
Marriage rate per 1,000 population (1992): 9.6.
Life expectancy at birth (1991): male 69.6 years; female 78.5 years.
Major causes of death per 100,000 population (1993): heart disease 142.6; cancers 95.4; diabetes 55.1; cerebrovascular disease 38.0; pneumonia and influenza 29.2.

National economy

Budget. Revenue (1995–96): U.S.$7,852,000,000 (income taxes 43.1%, excise taxes 17.3%, nontax revenue 5.0%, property taxes 1.0%, other receipts 33.6%). Expenditures (1992): U.S.$5,607,000,000 (education 30.3%, public safety and protection 11.4%, welfare 10.8%, health 10.7%.
Public debt (outstanding; 1995): U.S.$15,993,600,000.
Tourism (1995): receipts from visitors (1995) U.S.$1,826,100,000; expenditures by nationals abroad U.S.$833,000,000.
Production (in metric tons except as noted). Agriculture, forestry, fishing (1996): sugarcane 404,500; plantains 76,100; bananas 47,700; pineapples 18,500; oranges 16,700; pumpkins, squash, and gourds 16,300; coffee 12,800; mangoes 11,100; livestock (number of live animals) 326,000 cattle, 200,000 pigs; roundwood, n.a.; fish catch (1995) 2,629 metric tons. Mining (value of production in U.S.$'000; 1993): stone 50. Manufacturing (value added in U.S.$'000,000; 1995): chemicals, pharmaceuticals, and allied products 9,164; machinery and metal products 3,393; food products 2,269; clothing 510; printing and publishing 179; stone, clay, and glass products 171. Construction (authorized; 1985): residential 1,798,000 sq m; nonresidential 41,000 sq m. Energy production (consumption): electricity (kW-hr; 1994) 17,880,000,000 (17,880,000,000); coal (metric tons; 1994) none (172,000); crude petroleum (barrels; 1994) none (43,980,000); petroleum products (metric tons; 1994) 6,256,000 (7,540,000); natural gas, none (none).

Gross national product (1993): U.S.$25,317,000,000 (U.S.$6,700 per capita).

Structure of gross domestic product and labour force

	1995–96		1995	
	in value U.S.$'000,000	% of total value	labour force	% of labour force
Agriculture	306.5	0.7	42,000	3.4
Manufacturing	18,860.7	41.4	205,000	16.7
Mining	1,003.0	2.2	1,000	0.1
Construction			84,000	6.8
Public utilities	3,486.7	7.7	14,000	1.1
Transp. and commun.			42,000	3.4
Trade	6,224.4	13.7	250,000	20.4
Finance, real estate	5,877.8	12.9	34,000	2.8
Pub. admin., defense	4,871.4	10.7	550,000	44.8
Services	4,991.0	11.0		
Other	–116.5[2]	–0.3[2]	7,000	0.6
TOTAL	45,505.0	100.0	1,228,000[3]	100.0[3]

Population economically active (1995): total 1,228,000; activity rate 32.2% (participation rates: ages 16–64, 52.9%; female 39.4%; unemployed 13.8%).

Price and earnings indexes (1990 = 100)

	1989	1990	1991	1992	1993	1994	1995
Consumer price index	96.1	100.0	105.3	108.1	111.3	114.5	119.1
Hourly earnings index[4]	95.4	100.0	104.1	...	...	...	...

Household income and expenditure (1995). Average family size 3.6; income per family U.S.$27,017; sources of income: wages and salaries 56.3%, transfers 29.5%, self-employment 6.4%, rent 5.2%, other 2.6%; expenditure (1995): food and beverages 20.4%, transportation 13.6%, health care 13.4%, housing and energy 12.2%, household furnishings 12.0%, recreation 8.9%.

Foreign trade

Balance of trade (current prices)

	1990	1991	1992	1993	1994	1995
U.S.$'000,000	+3,584	+5,419	+5,857	+3,405	+5,098	+4,995
% of total	10.2%	14.6%	16.2%	9.4%	13.3%	11.7%

Imports (1995–96): U.S.$19,060,900,000 (chemicals [all forms] 21.8%, electrical machinery 12.8%, food 11.3%, transport equipment 9.3%, nonelectrical machinery 7.3%, petroleum and petroleum products 6.1%, professional and scientific instruments 4.5%, clothing and textiles 4.4%). *Major import sources:* U.S. 62.5%; Japan 6.4%; Dominican Republic 4.0%; U.K. 2.9%.
Exports (1995–96): U.S.$22,944,400,000 (chemicals and chemical products 43.3%, food 14.5%, nonelectrical machinery 14.2%, electrical machinery 9.6%). *Major export destinations:* U.S. 87.8%; Dominican Republic 2.9%; Germany 1.0%; Belgium 0.9%; Japan 0.8%; U.K. 0.7%.

Transport and communications

Transport. Railroads (1988)[5]: length 59 mi, 96 km. Roads (1994): total length 14,379 mi, 23,140 km (paved 87%). Vehicles (1994): passenger cars 1,432,000; trucks and buses 229,000. Merchant marine: n.a. Air transport (1990–91): passenger arrivals 4,245,137, passenger departures 4,262,164; cargo loaded and unloaded 222,172 metric tons[6]; airports (1997) with scheduled flights 7.

Communications

Medium	date	unit	number	units per 1,000 persons
Daily newspapers	1994	circulation	670,000	182
Radio	1996	receivers	2,480,000	659
Television	1995	receivers	1,160,000	322
Telephones	1995	main lines	1,195,900	329
Cellular telephones	1995	subscribers	171,200	48
Facsimile machines	1995	units	543,300	146

Education and health

Educational attainment (1990). Percentage of population age 25 and over having: primary education 26.8%; some secondary 23.5%; complete secondary 21.0%; higher 28.7%. *Literacy* (1990): total population age 18 and over literate 2,122,860 (89.7%); males literate 1,001,878 (89.6%); females literate 1,120,982 (89.7%).

Education (1985–86)

	schools	teachers	students	student/ teacher ratio
Primary (age 5–12)	1,542	18,359	427,582	23.3
Secondary (age 13–18)	395	13,612	334,661	24.6
Voc., teacher tr.	52	...	149,191	
Higher	45	9,045	156,818	17.3

Health: physicians (1988) 9,422 (1 per 349 persons); hospital beds (1993–94) 9,598 (1 per 381 persons); infant mortality rate (1994) 11.5.

Military

Total active duty personnel (1992): 3,518 U.S. personnel.

[1]Includes (each house) 2 special at-large seats above usual legally mandated membership of body that were created under a constitutional provision to limit majority party's control of either house to two-thirds. [2]Statistical discrepancy. [3]Detail does not add to total given because of rounding. [4]Manufacturing sector only. [5]Privately owned railway for sugarcane transport only. [6]Handled by the Luis Muñoz Marín International Airport only.

Internet resources for further information:
- **Puerto Rico, U.S.A. http://www.pr-eda.com/index.html**

Qatar

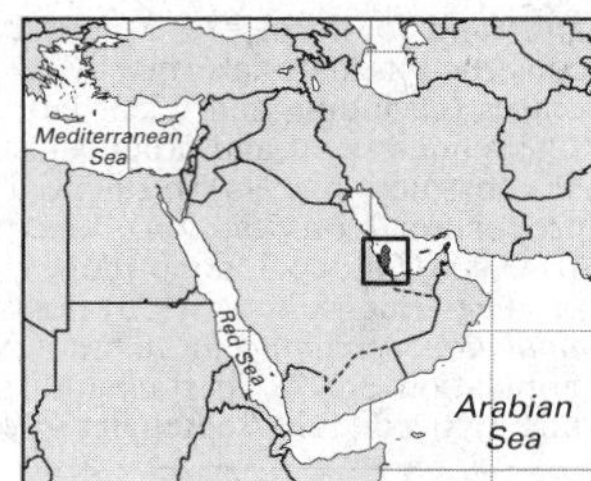

Official name: Dawlat Qaṭar (State of Qatar).
Form of government: monarchy (emirate)[1]; Islamic law is the basis of legislation in the state.
Heads of state and government: Emir assisted by Prime Minister.
Capital: Doha.
Official language: Arabic.
Official religion: Islam.
Monetary unit: 1 riyal (QR) = 100 dirhams; valuation (Oct. 3, 1997) 1 U.S.$ = QR 3.64; 1 £ = QR 5.87.

Area and population

Municipalities	Capitals	area sq mi	area sq km	population 1992 estimate
Ad-Dawḥah (Doha)	—	51	132	313,639
Al-Ghuwayrīyah	Al-Ghuwayrīyah	241	622	2,349
Jarayān al-Bāṭinah	Jarayān al-Bāṭinah	1,434	3,715	3,932
Al-Jumaylīyah	Al-Jumaylīyah	990[2]	2,565[2]	10,414
Al-Khawr	Al-Khawr	385	996	12,982
Ar-Rayyān	Ar-Rayyān	343	889	132,785
Ash-Shamāl	Madinat ash-Shamāl	348	901	6,323
Umm Ṣalāl	Umm Ṣalāl Muḥammad	190	493	16,110
Al-Wakrah	Al-Wakrah	430	1,114	34,185
TOTAL		4,416[3]	11,437[3]	532,719

Demography

Population (1997): 561,000.
Density (1997): persons per sq mi 127.0, persons per sq km 49.1.
Urban-rural (1995): urban 91.4%; rural 8.5%.
Sex distribution (1995): male 66.41%; female 33.59%.
Age breakdown (1994): under 15, 26.2%; 15–29, 21.5%; 30–44, 38.5%; 45–59, 11.7%; 60–74, 1.7%; 75 and over, 0.3%.
Population projection: (2000) 588,700; (2010) 691,300.
Doubling time: 42 years.
Ethnic composition (1995): Arab 40%; other (Pakistanis, Indians, and Iranians) 60%.
Religious affiliation (1995): Muslim (mostly Sunnī) 95%; other 5%.
Major cities (1993): Doha 339,471; Ar-Rayyān 143,046; Al-Wakrah 30,976; Umm Salal 16,785.

Vital statistics

Birth rate per 1,000 population (1990–95): 19.9 (world avg. 25.0).
Death rate per 1,000 population (1990–95): 3.4 (world avg. 9.3).
Natural increase rate per 1,000 population (1990–95): 16.5 (world avg. 15.7).
Total fertility rate (avg. births per childbearing woman; 1990–95): 4.1.
Marriage rate per 1,000 population (1994): 2.8.
Divorce rate per 1,000 population (1994): 1.0.
Life expectancy at birth (1990–95): male 68.8 years; female 74.2 years.
Major causes of death per 100,000 population (1992): diseases of the circulatory system 56.9; injuries and poisoning 36.0; neoplasms (including benign neoplasms) 21.4; certain conditions originating in the perinatal period 11.1; diseases of the respiratory system 7.5; endocrine, metabolic, and nutritional diseases and immunity disorders 7.3; diseases of the digestive system 3.4; signs, symptoms, and ill-defined conditions 10.9.

National economy

Budget (1996–97)[4]. Revenue: QR 10,797,000,000 (crude oil about 90%). Expenditures: QR 13,747,000,000 (1994–95; wages and salaries 44.4%, state capital-development projects 41.7%, social and health services 8.1%, education 2.7%).
Public debt (external, outstanding; 1995): U.S.$3,900,000,000.
Production (metric tons except as noted). Agriculture, forestry, fishing (value of production in QR '000; 1994): milk and dairy products 142,898, forage 93,293, vegetables and other crops (except cereals) 73,172, beef 47,854, fruits and dates 29,413, poultry meat 28,036, eggs 12,345, cereals 1,748; livestock (number of live animals; 1997) 199,682 sheep, 172,071 goats, 47,000 camels, 13,651 cattle; roundwood, n.a.; fish catch (1995) 4,271. Mining and quarrying (1993): limestone 900,000; sulfur 60,000; gypsum, sand and gravel, and clay are also produced. Manufacturing (value added in QR '000,000; 1994): refined petroleum 919; chemical products 887; iron and steel 319; pottery, china, and earthenware 219; textiles and apparel 193; food, beverages, and tobacco 99; metal products 89; wood products and furniture 79. Construction (1992): residential 12,420 units; nonresidential 1,416 units. Energy production (consumption): electricity (kW-hr; 1994) 5,850,000,000 (5,850,000,000); coal, none (n.a.); crude petroleum (barrels; 1996) 173,380,000 (1994; 21,450,000); petroleum products (metric tons; 1994) 5,219,000 (701,000); natural gas (cu m; 1996) 13,500,000,000 ([1994] 13,500,000,000).
Tourism (1994): receipts and expenditures, n.a.; total number of tourists staying in hotels 241,000.
Population economically active (1988): total 292,568; activity rate of total population 53.7% (participation rates: ages 15–64, 80.8%; female 11.2%; unemployed [1986] 0.5%).

Price and earnings indexes (1990 = 100)

	1989	1990	1991	1992	1993	1994	1995
Consumer price index	97.1	100.0	104.4	107.5	110.9	114.2	117.6
Earnings index	...	...	...	...	...	...	...

Gross national product (1995): U.S.$7,448,000,000 (U.S.$11,600 per capita).

Structure of gross domestic product and labour force

	1995[4] in value QR '000,000	1995[4] % of total value	1988 labour force	1988 % of labour force
Agriculture	290	1.1	4,544	1.6
Oil sector	8,900	32.5	7,657	2.6
Manufacturing	3,120	11.4	10,627	3.6
Construction	1,850	6.8	64,213	21.9
Public utilities	403	1.5	3,672	1.3
Transportation	1,045	3.8	11,877	4.1
Trade	2,050	7.5	34,246	11.7
Finance	3,070	11.2	6,172	2.1
Pub. admin., defense, Services, Other	6,627	24.2	149,560	51.1
TOTAL	27,355	100.0	292,568	100.0

Household income and expenditure. Average household size (1986) 6.4; income per household: n.a.; sources of income (1988): wages and salaries 80.8%, rents and royalties 10.6%, self-employment 5.6%, other 3.0%; expenditure (1993): food 28.7%, transportation 19.3%, housing 12.4%, clothing 10.6%, education 7.6%, health 1.2%.
Land use (1994): meadows and pastures 4.5%; agricultural and under permanent cultivation 0.7%; built-up, desert, and other 94.7%.

Foreign trade

Balance of trade (current prices)[5]

	1990	1991	1992	1993	1994	1995
QR '000,000	+7,992	+5,423	+6,644	+5,154	+4,729	+1,714
% of total	39.3%	30.2%	31.2%	29.6%	27.9%	8.1%

Imports (1994): QR 7,015,600,000 (machinery and transport equipment 39.7%, manufactured goods 21.8%, food and live animals 13.2%, chemicals and chemical products 7.0%, raw materials 3.4%). *Major import sources:* Japan 13.4%; United States 10.6%; United Kingdom 10.3%; United Arab Emirates 6.9%; Germany 6.6%; Saudi Arabia 5.0%; Italy 4.3%.
Exports (1994): QR 11,453,000,000 (mineral fuels and lubricants 81.2%, chemicals and chemical products 10.4%, manufactured goods 5.9%). *Major export destinations* (1989): Japan 54.4%; Thailand 5.0%; Singapore 4.0%; South Korea 3.6%; United Arab Emirates 3.4%; Italy 2.7%; India 2.7%.

Transport and communications

Transport. Railroads: none. Roads (1995): total length 752 mi, 1,210 km (paved 90%). Vehicles (1994): passenger cars 125,700; trucks and buses 63,800. Merchant marine (1992): vessels (100 gross tons and over) 65; total deadweight tonnage 635,580. Air transport (1995)[6]: passenger-mi 1,719,000,000, passenger-km 2,766,000,000; short ton-mi cargo 77,400,000, metric ton-km cargo 113,000,000; airports (1997) with scheduled flights 1.

Communications

Medium	date	unit	number	units per 1,000 persons
Daily newspapers	1994	circulation	80,000	143
Radio	1995	receivers	180,000	322
Television	1995	receivers	252,000	451
Telephones	1995	main lines	122,700	219
Cellular telephones	1995	subscribers	18,500	33
Facsimile machines	1995	units	9,400	17
Personal computers	1995	units	30,000	54

Education and health

Educational attainment (1986). Percentage of population age 25 and over having: no formal education 53.3%, of which illiterate 24.3%; primary 9.8%; preparatory (lower secondary) 10.1%; secondary 13.3%; postsecondary 13.3%; other 0.2%. *Literacy* (1995): total population age 15 and over literate 460,000 (79.4%); males literate 298,000 (79.2%); females literate 122,000 (79.9%).

Education (1994–95)[7]

	schools	teachers	students	student/ teacher ratio
Primary (age 6–11)	169	5,853	52,130	8.9
Secondary (age 12–17)	123[8]	3,738	36,964	9.9
Vocational	3[8]	120	671	5.6
Higher	1[8]	637	7,794	12.2

Health: (1994) physicians 718 (1 per 793 persons); hospital beds 1,118 (1 per 509 persons); (1990–95) infant mortality rate per 1,000 live births 20.0.
Food: daily per capita caloric intake, n.a.

Military

Total active duty personnel (1997): 11,800 (army 72.0%, navy 15.3%, air force 12.7%). *Military expenditure as percentage of GNP* (1995): 4.4% (world 2.8%); per capita expenditure U.S.$617.

[1]Provisional constitution of 1970 provided limited constitutional forms but has not been fully implemented. [2]Includes area of unpopulated Hawar Islands (also claimed by Bahrain). [3]Includes approximately 4 sq mi (10 sq km) of area not distributed by municipalities. [4]Preliminary estimates. [5]After 1992, balance based on f.o.b. valuation of imports. [6]One-fourth apportionment of international flights of Gulf Air. [7]Public schools only; available detail for private schools (1991–92) included 17,728 primary students, 1,695 secondary students, and 1,465 teachers. [8]1993–94.

Internet resources for further information:
- **Qatar Ministry of Foreign Affairs http://www.mofa.gov.qa/**

Réunion

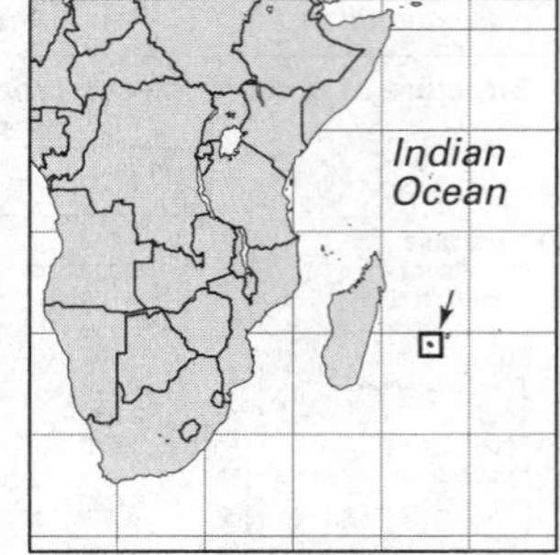

Official name: Département de la Réunion (Department of Réunion).
Political status: overseas department (France) with two legislative houses (General Council [47]; Regional Council [45]).
Chief of state: President of France.
Heads of government: Prefect (for France); President of General Council (for Réunion); President of Regional Council (for Réunion).
Capital: Saint-Denis.
Official language: French.
Official religion: none.
Monetary unit: 1 French franc (F) = 100 centimes; valuation (Oct. 3, 1997) 1 U.S.$ = F 5.92; 1 £ = F 9.55.

Area and population

		area		population
				1990
Arrondissements	Capitals	sq mi	sq km	census
Saint-Benoît	Saint-Benoît	285	737	85,132
Saint-Denis	Saint-Denis	163	421	207,158
Saint-Paul	Saint-Paul	180	467	113,071
Saint-Pierre	Saint-Pierre	341	883	192,462
TOTAL		968[1,2]	2,507[1,2]	597,823

Demography

Population (1997): 681,000.
Density (1997): persons per sq mi 703.5, persons per sq km 271.6.
Urban-rural (1995): urban 67.8%; rural 32.2%.
Sex distribution (1995): male 49.00%; female 51.00%.
Age breakdown (1995): under 15, 29.4%; 15–29, 27.7%; 30–44, 21.7%; 45–59, 12.2%; 60–74, 6.9%; 75 and over, 2.1%.
Population projection: (2000) 717,000; (2010) 851,000.
Doubling time: 49 years.
Ethnic composition (1983): mixed race 63.5%; East Indian 28.2%; Chinese 2.2%; white 1.9%; East African 1.1%; other 3.1%.
Religious affiliation (1995): Roman Catholic 89.4%; Pentecostal 2.7%; other Christian 1.8%; other (mostly Muslim) 6.1%.
Major cities (1990): Saint-Denis (1994) 104,454[3]; Le Port 29,190; Le Tampon 27,300; Saint-André 25,237; Saint-Pierre 23,899.

Vital statistics

Birth rate per 1,000 population (1996): 19.6 (world avg. 25.0); (1994) legitimate 44.1%; illegitimate 55.9%.
Death rate per 1,000 population (1996): 5.4 (world avg. 9.3).
Natural increase rate per 1,000 population (1996): 14.2 (world avg. 15.7).
Total fertility rate (avg. births per childbearing woman; 1996): 2.3.
Marriage rate per 1,000 population (1996): 4.9.
Divorce rate per 1,000 population (1995): 1.4.
Life expectancy at birth (1996): male 71.7 years; female 78.0 years.
Major causes of death per 100,000 population (1993): diseases of the circulatory system 170.1; malignant neoplasms (cancers) 99.7; accidents, suicide, and violence 65.3; diseases of the digestive system (including all deaths associated with alcoholism) 59.5; diseases of the respiratory system 41.5.

National economy

Budget (1995). Revenue: F 4,067,000,000 (receipts from the French central government and local administrative bodies 49.8%, subsidies and related receipts 12.8%, new loans 8.6%). Expenditures: F 4,066,000,000 (current expenditures 69.0%, development expenditures 31.0%).
Public debt (external, outstanding): n.a.
Tourism (1995): receipts U.S.$224,000,000; expenditures, n.a.
Gross national product (at current market prices; 1992): U.S.$5,500,000,000 (U.S.$8,800 per capita).

Structure of gross domestic product and labour force

	1992		1994	
	in value F '000,000	% of total value	labour force	% of labour force
Agriculture, fishing	1,200	3.6	12,015	5.0
Manufacturing	3,100	9.2	9,854	4.1
Construction	2,100	6.2	16,711	7.0
Public utilities	1,300	3.9	...	...
Transp. and commun.	2,000[4]	6.0[4]	5,495	2.3
Trade, restaurants	6,000[4]	17.9[4]	22,587	9.4
Finance, real estate, business services	7,200	21.4	11,148	4.7
Pub. admin., defense }	10,700	31.8	23,678	9.9
Services }			50,986	21.3
Other	—	—	86,905[5]	36.3[5]
TOTAL	33,600	100.0	239,379	100.0

Production (metric tons except as noted). Agriculture, forestry, fishing (1996): sugarcane 1,806,000, corn (maize) 18,000, cabbages 16,000, potatoes 15,000, pineapples 6,500, bananas 6,000, green onions and shallots 5,800, tomatoes 4,000, eggplants 3,200, pimento 430, ginger 95, tobacco 20, vanilla 6, geranium essence (1995) 5.2; livestock (number of live animals) 95,000 pigs, 32,000 goats, 26,500 cattle; roundwood (1995) 36,100 cu m; fish (value of catch in F '000,000; 1994) lobster 45[6], other 47. Mining and quarrying: gravel and sand for local use. Manufacturing (value added in F '000,000; 1994): construction materials (mostly cement) 345; alcoholic and nonalcoholic beverages (excluding milk) 253; fabricated metals 252; printing and publishing 129; refined sugar and other sugar products 123. Construction (value of public construction; 1994): residential F 741,600,000; nonresidential, n.a. Energy production (consumption): electricity (kW-hr; 1996) 1,386,000,000 ([1995] 1,143,000,000); coal, none (none); crude petroleum, none (none); petroleum products (metric tons; 1995) none (507,000); natural gas, none (none).
Population economically active (1993): total 234,576; activity rate of total population 36.9% (participation rates: ages 15–64, 56.7%; female 41.7%; unemployed [July–September 1996] 39.7%).

Price and earnings indexes (December 1992 = 100)[7]

	1991	1992	1993	1994	1995	1996	1997[8]
Consumer price index	97.3	100.0	102.4	105.0	107.1	109.2	110.2
Monthly earnings index[9]	97.4	100.0	101.7	104.1	106.8	106.8	...

Household income and expenditure. Average household size (1994) 3.5; income per household (1994) F 114,900 (U.S.$20,695); sources of income (1994): wages and salaries and self-employment 68.9%, transfer payments 16.0%, interest, dividends, and self-employment 15.1%; expenditure (1994–95): food and beverages 22.0%, transportation and communications 19.0%, housing and energy 10.0%, household furnishings 8.0%, recreation 6.0%.
Land use (1994): forested 35.2%; meadows and pastures 4.8%; agricultural and under permanent cultivation 19.6%; other 40.4%.

Foreign trade

Balance of trade (current prices)

	1991	1992	1993	1994	1995	1996
F '000,000	−11,975	−11,542	−10,859	−12,109	−12,458	−13,143
% of total	87.6%	83.9%	84.5%	86.4%	85.7%	86.0%

Imports (1995): F 13,494,000,000 (consumer goods 25.3%, food and agricultural products 20.1%, transport equipment 14.2%, fabricated metals 7.0%, mineral fuels 4.7%). *Major import sources:* France 66.3%; Italy 3.5%; Bahrain 3.1%.
Exports (1995): F 1,036,000,000 (sugar 63.0%, machinery and apparatus 9.9%, transport equipment 4.5%, lobster 4.2%, rum 2.4%). *Major export destinations:* France 71.4%; Japan 6.1%; Belgium 5.0%.

Transport and communications

Transport. Railroads:[10]. Roads (1994): total length 1,711 mi, 2,754 km (paved [1991] 79%). Vehicles (1995): passenger cars 157,700; trucks and buses 38,600. Merchant marine (1992): vessels (100 gross tons and over) 7; total deadweight tonnage 33,476. Air transport (1996): passenger arrivals 629,034, passenger departures 624,733; cargo unloaded 13,678 metric tons, cargo loaded 4,396 metric tons; airports (1996) with scheduled flights 1.

Communications

Medium	date	unit	number	units per 1,000 persons
Daily newspapers	1994	circulation	55,000	85
Radio	1996	receivers	170,000	254
Television	1995	receivers	90,500	137
Telephones	1995	main lines	218,723	332
Facsimile machines	1995	units	1,900	2.9

Education and health

Educational attainment (1986–87). Percentage of population age 25 and over having: no formal schooling 18.8%; primary education 44.3%; lower secondary 21.6%; upper secondary 11.0%; higher 4.3%. *Literacy* (1996): total population age 16–66 literate 373,487 (91.3%); males literate 179,154 (89.9%); females literate 194,333 (92.7%).

Education (1994–95)

	schools	teachers	students	student/ teacher ratio
Primary (age 6–10)	345	...	73,702[11]	...
Secondary (age 11–17) }	104	4,591[12]	71,694[11]	16.3[12]
Voc., teacher tr. }		1,108[12]	15,055	12.4[12]
Higher[13]	1	242	8,058	33.3

Health (1995): physicians (1996) 1,164 (1 per 571 persons); hospital beds 2,902 (1 per 225 persons); infant mortality rate per 1,000 live births 7.3.
Food (1995): daily per capita caloric intake 3,308 (vegetable products 79%, animal products 21%); 146% of FAO recommended minimum requirement.

Military

Total active duty personnel (1996): 4,000 French troops[14].

[1]Detail does not add to total given because of rounding. [2]Indian Ocean islets administered by France from Réunion are excluded from total. Areas of these islets, which have no permanent population, are: Îles Glorieuses 1.9 sq mi (5.0 sq km), Île Juan de Nova 1.7 sq mi (4.4 sq km), Île Tromelin 0.4 sq mi (1.0 sq km), Bassas da India 0.1 sq mi (0.2 sq km), Île Europa 7.8 sq mi (20.2 sq km). [3]Urban population. [4]Transportation and communications includes hotels and restaurants. [5]Includes 2,621 not adequately defined and 84,284 unemployed. [6]Lobster are trapped around the islands of Saint-Paul and Nouvelle Amsterdam in the overseas territory of French Southern and Antarctic Lands. [7]Indexes refer to December. [8]March. [9]Minimum monthly wage in public administration. [10]No public railways; railways in use are for sugar industry. [11]1995–96. [12]1993–94. [13]University only. [14]Includes troops stationed on Mayotte.

Internet resources for further information:
- **Ministère de l'Outre-mer (Paris)**
http://www.outre-mer.gouv.fr/domtom/reu.htm

Romania

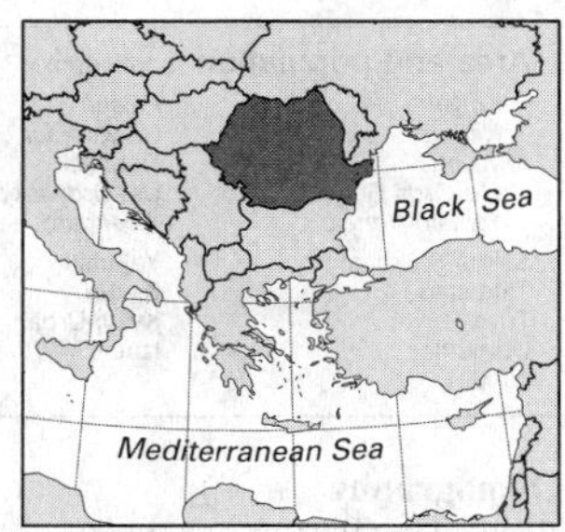

Official name: România (Romania).
Form of government: unitary republic with two legislative houses (Senate [143]; Assembly of Deputies [343[1]]).
Chief of state: President.
Head of government: Prime Minister.
Capital: Bucharest.
Official language: Romanian.
Official religion: none.
Monetary unit: 1 Romanian leu (plural lei) = 100 bani; valuation (Oct. 3, 1997) 1 U.S.$ = 7,698 lei; 1 £ = 12,408 lei.

Area and population

Counties	Capitals	area sq mi	area sq km	population 1994 estimate
Alba	Alba Iulia	2,406	6,231	408,457
Arad	Arad	2,954	7,652	482,144
Arges	Pitești	2,626	6,801	679,868
Bacău	Bacău	2,551	6,606	742,901
Bihor	Oradea	2,909	7,535	633,629
Bistrița-Năsăud	Bistrița	2,048	5,305	328,786
Botoșani	Botoșani	1,917	4,965	462,370
Brăila	Brăila	1,824	4,724	391,923
Brașov	Brașov	2,066	5,351	642,764
Buzău	Buzău	2,344	6,072	515,202
Călărași	Călărași	1,959	5,074	336,657
Caraș-Severin	Reșița	3,283	8,503	370,058
Cluj	Cluj-Napoca	2,568	6,650	727,033
Constanța	Constanța	2,724	7,055	747,441
Covasna	Sfântu Gheorghe	1,431	3,705	232,951
Dâmbovița	Târgoviște	1,558	4,036	558,518
Dolj	Craiova	2,862	7,413	758,895
Galați	Galați	1,709	4,425	642,983
Giurgiu	Giurgiu	1,356	3,511	305,661
Gorj	Târgu Jiu	2,178	5,641	397,927
Harghita	Miercurea-Ciuc	2,552	6,610	347,145
Hunedoara	Deva	2,709	7,016	547,180
Ialomița	Slobozia	1,718	4,449	305,454
Iași	Iași	2,112	5,469	815,368
Maramureș	Baia Mare	2,400	6,215	539,718
Mehedinți	Drobeta-Turnu Severin	1,892	4,900	330,017
Mureș	Târgu Mureș	2,585	6,696	607,355
Neamț	Piatra Neamț	2,274	5,890	584,364
Olt	Slatina	2,126	5,507	520,871
Prahova	Ploiești	1,812	4,694	874,219
Sălaj	Zalău	1,486	3,850	264,448
Satu Mare	Satu Mare	1,701	4,405	398,401
Sibiu	Sibiu	2,093	5,422	448,474
Suceava	Suceava	3,303	8,555	708,571
Teleorman	Alexandria	2,224	5,760	477,527
Timiș	Timișoara	3,356	8,692	691,797
Tulcea	Tulcea	3,255	8,430	269,311
Vâlcea	Râmnicu Vâlcea	2,203	5,705	436,989
Vaslui	Vaslui	2,045	5,297	463,832
Vrancea	Focșani	1,878	4,863	394,257
Municipality				
Bucharest	Bucharest	703	1,820	2,339,156
TOTAL		91,700	237,500	22,730,622

Demography

Population (1997): 22,572,000.
Density (1997): persons per sq mi 246.2, persons per sq km 95.0.
Urban-rural (1995): urban 55.4%; rural 44.6%.
Sex distribution (1995): male 49.27%; female 50.73%.
Age breakdown (1995): under 15, 20.4%; 15–29, 25.0%; 30–44, 20.5%; 45–59, 16.9%; 60–74, 13.6%; 75 and over, 3.6%.
Population projection: (2000) 22,464,000; (2010) 22,107,000.
Ethnic composition (1992): Romanian 89.4%; Hungarian 7.1%; other 3.5%.
Religious affiliation (1992): Romanian Orthodox 86.8%; Roman Catholic 5.0%; Greek Orthodox 3.5%; Pentecostal 1.0%; Muslim 0.2%; other 3.5%.
Major cities (1994): Bucharest 2,080,363; Constanța 348,575; Iași 339,889; Timișoara 327,830; Galați 326,728.

Vital statistics

Birth rate per 1,000 population (1995): 10.4 (world avg. 25.0).
Death rate per 1,000 population (1995): 12.0 (world avg. 9.3).
Natural increase rate per 1,000 population (1995): –1.6 (world avg. 15.7).
Total fertility rate (avg. births per childbearing woman; 1993): 1.5.
Marriage rate per 1,000 population (1994): 6.8.
Divorce rate per 1,000 population (1990): 1.4.
Life expectancy at birth (1995): male 69.3 years; female 75.4 years.
Major causes of death per 100,000 population (1992): circulatory disease 707.7; cancers 163.4; respiratory disease 94.0; diseases of the digestive system 57.9.

National economy

Budget ('000,000,000,000 lei; 1996). Revenue: 32.5 (social security 25.0%, personal income tax 20.5%, value-added tax 16.5%). Expenditures: 36.8 (social security 27.3%, education 10.5%, health 8.2%, housing 5.6%).
Tourism (1995): receipts U.S.$574,000,000; expenditures U.S.$695,000,000.
Production (metric tons). Agriculture (1997): corn (maize) 11,500,000, wheat 7,100,000, potatoes 2,800,000, sugar beets 2,800,000, barley 1,500,000; livestock (number of live animals) 9,663,000 sheep, 8,235,000 pigs, 3,435,000 cattle; roundwood (1996) 12,616,000 cu m; fish catch (1995) 85,101. Mining (1995): iron 184,000; bauxite 174,000; zinc 35,000; copper 24,000. Manufacturing (value in U.S.$'000,000; 1994): food products 1,415; beverages 499; textiles 472; iron and steel 387; pottery 370; metal products 366; electrical machinery 358. Construction (1995): 9,300 dwelling units. Energy production (consumption): electricity (kW-hr; 1994) 55,136,000,000 (55,861,000,000); coal (metric tons; 1994) 40,547,000 (44,893,000); crude petroleum (barrels; 1994) 50,568,000 (109,995,000); petroleum products (metric tons; 1994) 13,066,000 (10,291,000); natural gas (cu m; 1994) 15,868,000,000 (20,214,000,000).
Public debt (external, outstanding; 1995): U.S.$3,896,000,000.
Gross national product (1995): U.S.$33,488,000,000 (U.S.$1,480 per capita).

Structure of gross domestic product and labour force

	1994 in value '000,000,000 lei	1994 % of total value	1994 labour force	1994 % of labour force
Agriculture	10,001	20.1	3,653,000	32.5
Industry[2]	16,091	32.3	2,881,700	25.6
Construction	3,010	6.0	562,700	5.0
Transp. and commun.	4,934	9.9	556,000	4.9
Trade	5,806	11.7	772,300	6.9
Finance	} 8,263	} 16.6	59,100	0.5
Pub. admin. / Services			} 1,526,800	13.6
Other	1,690	3.4	1,237,400[3]	11.0[3]
TOTAL	49,795	100.0	11,249,000	100.0

Population economically active (1995): total 10,491,000; activity rate 46.2% (participation rates: ages 15–64, 67.2%[4]; female 44.2%[4]; unemployed 7.4%).

Price and earnings indexes (1990 = 100)

	1990	1991	1992	1993	1994	1995	1996
Consumer price index	100.0	274.4	854.0	3,033.1	7,181.2	9,496.6	13,184.1
Annual earnings index	100.0	221.3	597.4	1,804.8	4,142.0	...	...

Household income and expenditure. Average household size (1992) 3.1; income per household (1989) 73,500 lei (U.S.$4,940); sources of income (1982): wages 62.6%; expenditure (1989): food 51.1%, housing 16.4%.

Foreign trade

Balance of trade (current prices)

	1991	1992	1993	1994	1995	1996
U.S.$'000,000	–1,182	–1,420.5	–1,127.8	–411.1	–1,150.5	–2,130
% of total	12.5%	14.0%	10.3%	3.2%	7.1%	10.3%

Imports (1996): 10,368,000,000,000 lei (mineral fuels 25.4%, machinery and transport equipment 24.1%, textiles 12.0%, chemicals 8.4%). *Major import sources:* Germany 16.5%; Italy 15.6%; Russia 13.1%; France 4.8%.
Exports (1996): 10,272,827,000,000 lei (textiles 20.8%, mineral products 9.2%, chemicals 9.0%, machinery 8.0%, footwear 6.1%). *Major export destinations:* Germany 18.2%; Italy 16.6%; France 5.6%; U.K. 2.9%; U.S. 2.2%.

Transport and communications

Transport. Railroads (1995): length 11,365 km[5]; passenger-km 18,880,000,000; metric ton-km cargo 27,180,000,000. Roads (1992): length 153,014 km (paved 51%). Vehicles (1995): cars 2,197,777; trucks and buses 385,111. Merchant marine (1992): vessels (100 gross tons and over) 439; total deadweight tonnage 4,845,539. Air transport (1994): passenger-km 2,580,000,000; metric ton-km cargo 19,404,000; airports (1997) 8.

Communications

Medium	date	unit	number	units per 1,000 persons
Daily newspapers	1995	circulation	6,800,000	297
Radio	1996	receivers	4,500,000	198
Television	1995	receivers	4,580,000	201
Telephones	1995	main lines	2,968,000	131
Personal computers	1995	units	120,000	5.3

Education and health

Educational attainment (1992). Percentage of population age 25 and over having: no schooling 5.4%; some primary education 24.4%; some secondary 63.2%; postsecondary 6.9%. *Literacy* (1992): total population age 15 and over literate 96.7%; males 98.5%; females 95.0%.

Education (1994–95)

	schools	teachers	students	student/teacher ratio
Primary (age 6–9)[6]	13,963	168,702	2,532,169	15.0
Secondary (age 10–17)[7]	1,276	60,514	757,673	12.5
Voc., teacher tr.	1,530	9,360	345,394	36.9
Higher	63	20,452	255,162	12.5

Health: physicians (1993) 40,265 (1 per 565 persons); hospital beds (1992) 215,629 (1 per 105 persons); infant mortality rate (1995) 21.2.
Food (1995): daily per capita caloric intake 3,166 (vegetable products 78%, animal products 22%); 128% of FAO recommended minimum requirement.

Military

Total active duty personnel (1997): 227,000 (army 57.0%, navy 7.7%, air force 21.0%, other 14.3%). *Military expenditure as percentage of GNP* (1995): 2.5% (world 2.8%); per capita expenditure U.S.$115.

[1]Includes 15 nonelective seats. [2]Mining, manufacturing, and public utilities. [3]Unemployed. [4]1992. [5]1994. [6]Includes lower secondary. [7]Upper secondary only.

Internet resources for further information:
- **Embassy of Romania (Washington, D.C.) http://www.embassy.org/romania**
- **Romania Human Development Report 1997 http://www.undp.ro/ftop.html**

Russia

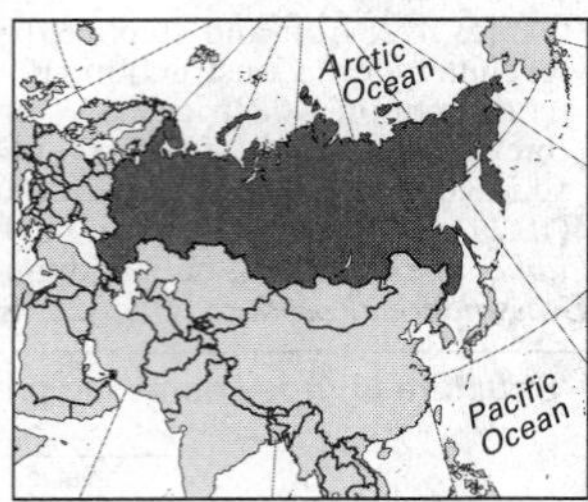

Official name: Rossiyskaya Federatsiya (Russian Federation).
Form of government: federal multiparty republic with a bicameral legislative body (Federal Assembly comprising a Federation Council [178] and a State Duma [450]).
Head of state: President.
Head of government: Prime Minister.
Capital: Moscow.
Official language: Russian.
Official religion: none.
Monetary unit: 1 ruble (Rub) = 100 kopecks; valuation (Oct. 3, 1997) market rate, 1 U.S.$ = Rub 5,878; 1 £ = Rub 9,476.

Area and population

Federal Republics / Other entities	Capitals	area sq mi	area sq km	population 1996[1] estimate
Adygea	Maykop	2,900	7,600	450,000
Bashkortostan	Ufa	55,400	143,600	4,097,000
Buryatia	Ulan-Ude	135,600	351,300	1,053,000
Chechnia (Chechnya)[2, 3]	...	[4]	[4]	[4]
Chuvashia	Cheboksary	7,100	18,300	1,361,000
Dagestan	Makhachkala	19,400	50,300	2,098,000
Gorno-Altay	Gorno-Altaisk	35,700	92,600	202,000
Ingushetia[2]	Grozny	7,400[4]	19,300[4]	1,165,000[4]
Kabardino-Balkaria	Nalchik	4,800	12,500	790,000
Kalmykia (Khalmg Tangch)	Elista	29,400	76,100	319,000
Karachay-Cherkessia	Cherkessk	5,400	14,100	436,000
Karelia	Petrozavodsk	66,600	172,400	785,000
Khakassia	Abakan	23,900	61,900	586,000
Komi	Syktyvkar	160,600	415,900	1,185,000
Mari El	Yoshkar-Ola	9,000	23,200	766,000
Mordvinia	Saransk	10,100	26,200	956,000
North Ossetia	Vladikavkaz	3,100	8,000	663,000
Russia	Moscow	4,709,800[5]	12,198,300	124,333,000
Regions (Oblasts)				
Amur[6]	Blagoveshchensk	140,400	363,700	1,038,000
Arkhangelsk	Arkhangelsk	226,800	587,400	1,521,000
Astrakhan	Astrakhan	17,000	44,100	1,029,000
Belgorod	Belgorod	10,500	27,100	1,469,000
Bryansk	Bryansk	13,500	34,900	1,480,000
Chelyabinsk	Chelyabinsk	33,900	87,900	3,689,000
Chita	Chita	166,600	431,500	1,295,000
Irkutsk	Irkutsk	296,500	767,900	2,795,000
Ivanovo	Ivanovo	9,200	23,900	1,266,000
Kaliningrad[6]	Kaliningrad	5,800	15,100	932,000
Kaluga	Kaluga	11,500	29,900	1,097,000
Kamchatka	Petropavlovsk-Kamchatsky	182,400	472,300	411,000
Kemerovo	Kemerovo	36,900	95,500	3,063,000
Kirov	Kirov	46,600	120,800	1,634,000
Kostroma	Kostroma	23,200	60,100	806,000
Kurgan	Kurgan	27,400	71,000	1,112,000
Kursk	Kursk	11,500	29,800	1,347,000
Leningrad	St. Petersburg	33,200[7]	85,900[7]	1,676,000
Lipetsk	Lipetsk	9,300	24,100	1,250,000
Magadan	Magadan	178,100	461,400	258,000
Moskva (Moscow)	Moscow	18,100[8]	47,000[8]	6,597,000
Murmansk	Murmansk	55,900	144,900	1,048,000
Nizhny Novgorod	Nizhny Novgorod	28,900	74,800	3,727,000
Novgorod	Novgorod	21,400	55,300	743,000
Novosibirsk	Novosibirsk	68,800	178,200	2,749,000
Omsk	Omsk	53,900	139,700	2,176,000
Orenburg	Orenburg	47,900	124,000	2,229,000
Oryol (Orel)	Oryol	9,500	24,700	914,000
Penza	Penza	16,700	43,200	1,562,000
Perm	Perm	62,000	160,600	3,009,000
Pskov	Pskov	21,400	55,300	832,000
Rostov	Rostov-na-Donu	38,900	100,800	4,425,000
Ryazan	Ryazan	15,300	39,600	1,325,000
Sakhalin	Yuzhno-Sakhalinsk	33,600	87,100	648,000
Samara	Samara	20,700	53,600	3,312,000
Saratov	Saratov	38,700	100,200	2,739,000
Smolensk	Smolensk	19,200	49,800	1,172,000
Sverdlovsk[6]	Yekaterinburg	75,200	194,800	4,686,000
Tambov	Tambov	13,200	34,300	1,310,000
Tomsk	Tomsk	122,400	316,900	1,078,000
Tula	Tula	9,900	25,700	1,815,000
Tver	Tver	32,500	84,100	1,651,000
Tyumen	Tyumen	554,100	1,435,200	3,170,000
Ulyanovsk (Simbirsk)	Simbirsk	14,400	37,300	1,495,000
Vladimir	Vladimir	11,200	29,000	1,645,000
Volgograd	Volgograd	44,000	113,900	2,704,000
Vologda[6]	Vologda	56,300	145,700	1,350,000
Voronezh	Voronezh	20,200	52,400	2,504,000
Yaroslavl	Yaroslavl	14,100	36,400	1,451,000
Autonomous Region				
Yevreyskaya (Jewish)	Birobidzhan	13,900	36,000	210,000
Territories (Krays)				
Altay	Barnaul	65,300	169,100	2,690,000
Khabarovsk	Khabarovsk	304,500	788,600	1,571,000
Krasnodar	Krasnodar	29,300	76,000	5,044,000
Krasnoyarsk	Krasnoyarsk	903,400	2,339,700	3,106,000
Primorye (Maritime)[6]	Vladivostok	64,100	165,900	2,255,000
Stavropol	Stavropol	25,700	66,500	2,667,000
Autonomous cities				
Moscow	—	[8]	[8]	8,664,000
St. Petersburg[6]	—	[7]	[7]	4,801,000
Autonomous districts (Okrugs)[9]				
Aga-Buryat	*Aginskoye*	*7,300*	*19,000*	79,000
Chukchi (Chukotka)	Anadyr	284,800	737,700	91,000
Evenk	*Tura*	*296,400*	*767,600*	20,000
Khanty-Mansi	*Khanty-Mansiysk*	*202,000*	*523,100*	1,331,000
Komi-Permyak	*Kudymkar*	*12,700*	*32,900*	157,000
Area and population (continued)				
Koryak	*Palana*	*116,400*	*301,500*	33,000
Nenets	*Naryan-Mar*	*68,100*	*176,400*	48,000
Taymyr	*Dudinka*	*332,900*	*862,100*	47,000
Ust-Orda Buryat	*Ust-Ordynsky*	*8,600*	*22,400*	143,000
Yamalo-Nenets	*Salekhard*	*289,700*	*750,300*	488,000
Sakha (Yakutia)	Yakutsk	1,198,200	3,103,200	1,023,000
Tatarstan	Kazan	26,300	68,000	3,760,000
Tuva (Tyva)	Kyzyl-Orda	65,800	170,500	309,000
Udmurtia	Izhevsk	16,300	42,100	1,639,000
TOTAL		6,592,800	17,075,400	147,976,000

Demography

Population (1997): 147,231,000.
Density (1997): persons per sq mi 22.3, persons per sq km 8.6.
Urban-rural (1996): urban 73.2%; rural 26.8%.
Sex distribution (1996): male 46.94%; female 53.06%.
Age breakdown (1996): under 15, 21.0%; 15–29, 20.8%; 30–44, 24.5%; 45–59, 17.0%; 60–74, 12.9%; 75 and over, 3.8%.
Population projection: (2000) 145,750,000; (2010) 140,579,000.
Doubling time: not applicable; population is declining.
Ethnic composition (1996): Russian 81.5%; Tatar 3.8%; Ukrainian 3.0%; Chuvash 1.2%; Bashkir 1.0%; Belorussian 0.8%; Mordovian 0.7%; Chechen 0.6%; other 7.4%.
Religious affiliation (1995): Russian Orthodox 16.3%; Muslim 10.0%; Protestant 0.9%; Jewish 0.4%; Roman Catholic 0.3%; other (mostly nonreligious) 72.1%.
Major cities (1996): Moscow 8,400,000; St. Petersburg 4,200,000; Nizhny Novgorod 1,400,000; Novosibirsk 1,400,000; Yekaterinburg 1,300,000; Samara 1,200,000; Omsk 1,200,000; Chelyabinsk 1,100,000; Kazan 1,100,000; Ufa 1,100,000; Perm 1,000,000; Rostov-na-Donu 1,000,000.

Other principal cities (1995)

	population		population		population
Astrakhan	486,000	Krasnoyarsk	868,800	Tolyatti	702,300
Barnaul	658,200	Naberezhnye Chelny	529,300	Tula	532,300
Irkutsk	585,000	Novokuznetsk	586,000	Ulyanovsk (Simbirsk)	699,300
Izhevsk	654,400	Orenburg	532,100	Vladivostok	631,800
Kemerovo	502,500	Penza	533,900	Volgograd	1,002,800
Khabarovsk	617,800	Ryazan	539,800	Voronezh	907,800
Krasnodar	645,700	Saratov	902,200	Yaroslavl	629,000

Mobility (1989). Population living in the same residence as in 1988: 78.8%; different residence, same oblast 11.5%; different republic 9.7%.
Households (1994). Total family households 52,930,000; average household size 2.8; 2 persons 26.2%; 3 persons 22.6%; 4 persons 20.5%; 5 persons or more 11.5%. Population in family households (1989): 128,787,000 (87.0%), nonfamily population 19,254,000 (13.0%).

Vital statistics

Birth rate per 1,000 population (1995): 9.3 (world avg. 25.0); (1994) legitimate 80.4%; illegitimate 19.6%.
Death rate per 1,000 population (1995): 15.0 (world avg. 9.3).
Natural increase rate per 1,000 population (1995): −5.7 (world avg. 15.7).
Total fertility rate (avg. births per childbearing woman; 1995): 1.3.
Marriage rate per 1,000 population (1995): 7.3.
Divorce rate per 1,000 population (1995): 4.5.
Life expectancy at birth (1996): male 58.3 years; female 71.7 years.
Major causes of death per 100,000 population (1995): circulatory diseases 790.1; accidents, poisoning, and violence 236.6, of which suicide 41.4, murder 30.7; malignant neoplasms (cancers) 200.8; respiratory diseases 73.9; digestive diseases 46.1; infectious and parasitic diseases 20.7.

Social indicators

Educational attainment (1994). Percentage of population age 15 and over having: primary or no formal education 10.0%; some secondary 20.2%; secondary and some postsecondary 77.8%; higher and postgraduate 15.1%.
Quality of working life (1990). Average workweek: 40 hours. Annual rate per 100,000 workers of: injury or accident 569; industrial illness 5.3; death 11.2. Proportion of labour force insured for damages or income loss resulting from: injury 100%; permanent disability 100%; death 100%. Average days lost to labour stoppages per 1,000 workdays (1992): 1.1.
Access to services (1990). Proportion of dwellings having access to: electricity, virtually 100%; safe public water supply 94%; public sewage collection 92%; central heating 92%; bathroom 87%; gas 72%; hot water 79%.
Social participation. Eligible voters participating in last national election (1996): 68.8%. Trade union membership in total workforce (1989): 100%. Practicing religious population in total affiliated population (1991): 32%.
Social deviance. Offense rate per 100,000 population (1995) for: murder 21.4; rape 8.5; serious injury 41.7; larceny-theft 1,020.0. Incidence per 100,000 population (1992) of: alcoholism 1,727.5; substance abuse 25.1; suicide 26.5.
Material well-being (1994). Durable goods possessed per 100 family households: automobile 25; radio receiver 103; television receiver 116; refrigerator or freezer 95; washing machine 81; camera 37; motorcycle 23; bicycle 54.

National economy

Budget (1996). Revenue: Rub 329,000,000,000,000 (tax revenue 84.5%, of which profit tax 19.5%, value-added tax 18.4%, individual income tax 15.7%, property tax 11.2%, other taxes 19.7%; nontax revenue 15.5%). Expenditures: Rub 410,800,000,000,000 (current expenditure 74.3%, of which economy 23.3%, defense 20.9%, education 5.8%, health 3.0%, interest on foreign debt 2.4%; development expenditure 25.7%).
Public debt (external, outstanding; 1996)[10]: U.S.$125,000,000,000.
Gross national product (1995): U.S.$331,948,000,000 (U.S.$2,240 per capita).

Structure of gross domestic product and labour force

	1995			
	in value Rub '000,000	% of total value	labour force	% of labour force
Agriculture	143,282,300	8.8	10,500,000	14.4
Mining } Manufacturing }	511,393,000	31.4 }	17,200,000	23.5
Public utilities	64,266,500	3.9 }		
Construction	107,525,800	6.6	6,500,000	8.9
Transp. and commun.	170,936,800	10.5	5,300,000	7.2
Trade	310,086,500	19.0	6,500,000	8.9
Finance	145,000,900	8.9	900,000	1.2
Services	122,601,300	7.5	17,100,000	23.4
Pub. admin., defense	55,863,300	3.4	1,700,000	2.3
Other	...	...	7,440,000	10.2
TOTAL	1,630,956,400	100.0	73,140,000	100.0

Production (metric tons except as noted). Agriculture, forestry, fishing (1996): potatoes 38,529,000, wheat 34,900,000, sugar beets 16,132,000, barley 15,900,000, vegetables (other than potatoes) 11,099,000, oats 8,570,000, rye 5,900,000, sunflower seeds 2,764,900, corn (maize) 1,700,000, peas 1,000,000, buckwheat 620,000, millet 500,000, rice 500,000; livestock (number of live animals) 39,696,000 cattle, 25,800,000 sheep, 22,631,000 pigs; roundwood 96,250,000 cu m; fish catch 4,374,000. Mining and quarrying (1995): nickel 251,000,000; chrome ore 107,700,000; iron ore 78,300,000; tin 10,000,000; molybdenum 8,800,000; antimony 7,000,000; gold 4,249,000 troy oz. Manufacturing (1995): crude steel 51,600,000; pig iron 39,800,000; rolled steel 39,000,000; cement 36,400,000; mineral fertilizers 9,600,000; sulfuric acid 6,900,000; cellulose 4,193,000; synthetic resins and plastics 1,794,000; cardboard 1,298,000; caustic soda 1,156,000; detergents 296,000; synthetic fibres 216,000; cotton fabrics 1,235,000,000 sq m; silk fabrics 197,000,000 sq m; linen fabrics 131,000,000 sq m; wool fabrics 72,000,000 sq m; cigarettes 141,000,000,000 units; watches 29,800,000 units; television receivers 1,888,000 units; refrigerators 1,766,000 units; washing machines 1,303,000 units; vacuum cleaners 911,000 units; passenger cars 835,000 units; bicycles 759,000 units; tape recorders 671,000 units; cameras 296,000 units; sewing machines 165,400 units; motorcycles 82,100 units; video recorders 20,900 units; leather footwear 67,300,000 pairs; beer 19,800,000 hectolitres; vodka and liquors 12,200,000 hectolitres; champagne 8,200,000 hectolitres; grape wine 1,460,000 hectolitres; brandy 171,400 hectolitres. Construction (1995): residential 14,600,000 sq m; nonresidential 26,400,000 sq m.

Manufacturing, mining, and construction enterprises (1995)

	no. of enter-prises	no. of employees	monthly wages as a % of avg. of all wages[11]	value added (Rub '000,000,000)
Manufacturing				
Machinery and metal products	48,905	4,842,000	98.2	27,234
Fuel and energy	1,758	1,554,000	133.3	44,211
Metallurgy	2,158	1,248,000	124.3	26,437
Chemicals	23,027	2,432,000	94.1	17,934
Light industry	23,007	1,368,000	80.0	2,931
Food	14,713	1,514,000	100.1	12,886
Other industries	19,073	2,085,000	...	4,685
Building materials	8,359	994,000	108.2	3,761

Energy production (consumption): electricity (kW-hr; 1994) 875,914,000,000 (855,418,000,000); coal (metric tons; 1994) 176,754,000 (180,988,000); crude petroleum (barrels; 1994) 2,265,000,000 (1,375,000,000); petroleum products (metric tons; 1994) 162,085,000 (126,758,000); natural gas (cu m; 1994) 498,995,000,000 (327,275,000,000); peat (metric tons; 1994) 2,928,000 (4,007,000); oil shale (metric tons; 1994) 2,000,000 (1993; 3,300,000).

Population economically active (1995): total 73,140,000; activity rate of total population 49.5% (participation rates: ages 16–59 [male], 16–54 [female] 72.6%; female 46.7%; unemployed [1996] 9.1%).

Price and earnings indexes (1990 = 100)

	1991	1992	1993	1994	1995	1996
Consumer price index	192.7	2,800	27,900	112,100	221,300	269,500
Monthly earnings index	180.9	1,978	19,361	71,494	101,700	264,000

Land use (1994): forest 44.9%; pasture 5.2%; agriculture 7.7%; other 42.2%.

Household income and expenditure. Average household size (1995) 2.8; income per household: Rub 6,395,000 (U.S.$1,176); sources of income (1995): wages 77.8%, pensions and stipends 12.0%, other 10.2%; expenditure (1994): food 46.8%, clothing 13.6%, taxes and other financial payments 10.1%, furniture and household appliances 8.7%, transportation 6.1%, culture 5.1%.

Foreign trade

Balance of trade (current prices; non-CIS)

	1991	1992	1993	1994	1995	1996
U.S.$'000,000	+6,438	+4,986	+17,490	+21,800	+32,879	+37,368
% of total	6.8%	6.7%	24.6%	27.9%	33.2%	37.3%

Imports (1996): U.S.$45,438,000,000 (machinery and transport equipment 27.0%, food 24.3%, chemicals 13.5%, ferrous and nonferrous metals 8.2%, textiles and clothing 4.3%, fuels and lubricants 3.7%). *Major import sources*[12]: Germany 11.8%; Italy 5.3%; U.S. 5.2%; Finland 3.8%; France 2.9%; U.K. 2.6%.

Exports (1996): U.S.$84,387,000,000 (fuels and lubricants 45.5%, ferrous and nonferrous metals 19.1%, machinery and transport equipment 8.9%, chemicals 8.2%, precious metals 4.3%, forestry products 4.1%). *Major export destinations*[12]: Germany 8.2%; China 5.7%; U.S. 5.6%; Italy 5.0%; Switzerland 4.8%; The Netherlands 4.1%; U.K. 3.8%.

Trade by commodity group (1996)

	imports		exports	
SITC group	U.S.$'000,000	%	U.S.$'000,000	%
00 Food and live animals	11,028	24.3	1,654	1.9
02 Raw materials, excl. fuels	5,614	12.4	20,843	24.7
03 Mineral fuels, lubricants	1,703	3.6	38,365	45.5
05 Chemicals	6,140	13.5	6,899	8.2
65 Textile yarn, fabrics	894	2.0	555	0.7
07 Machinery and transport equip.	11,859	26.1	7,477	8.8
08 Misc. manufactured articles	8,200	18.1	8,594	10.2
TOTAL	45,438	100.0	84,387	100.0

Direction of trade (1994)

	imports		exports	
	U.S.$'000,000	%	U.S.$'000,000	%
Africa	217	0.8	512	1.0
Asia	4,650	16.5	9,985	20.4
Japan	1,114	3.9	2,245	4.6
South America	791	2.8	1,021	2.1
North and Central America	2,263	8.0	3,619	7.4
United States	2,069	7.3	3,373	6.9
Europe	20,020	70.9	33,872	69.1
EU	15,278	54.1	22,211	45.3
EFTA	3,154	11.2	9,373	19.1
other Europe	1,588	5.6	2,288	4.7
Oceania	300	1.1	42	0.1
TOTAL	28,241	100.0[5]	49,051	100.0[5]

Transport and communications

Transport. Railroads (1995): length 151,000 km; passenger-km 192,200,000,000; metric ton-km cargo 1,213,000,000. Roads (1995): total length 949,000 km (paved 79%). Vehicles (1993): passenger cars 10,499,000; trucks and buses 407,000. Merchant marine (1993): vessels (100 gross tons and over) 24; total deadweight tonnage 91,000,000. Air transport (1995): passenger-km 71,700,000,000; metric ton-km cargo 1,800,000,000; airports (1996) 75.

Distribution of traffic (1995)

	cargo carried ('000,000 tons)	% of national total	passengers carried ('000,000)	% of national total
Intercity transport			26,549	56.2
Road	1,441	41.7	22,817	48.3
Rail	1,028	29.7	1,833	3.9
Sea and river	203	5.9	32	0.1
Air	1	...	34	0.1
Pipeline	783	22.7	—	—
Urban transport			20,684	43.8
Road	—	—	86	0.2
Rail	—	—	20,598	43.6
TOTAL	3,456	100.0	47,233	100.0

Communications

Medium	date	unit	number	units per 1,000 persons
Daily newspapers	1994	circulation	39,301,000	267
Radio	1995	receivers	50,600,000	341
Television	1995	receivers	56,244,000	379
Telephones	1995	main lines	25,019,000	170
Cellular telephones	1995	subscribers	88,500	0.6
Facsimile machines	1995	units	30,600	0.2
Personal computers	1995	units	2,600,000	18

Education and health

Health (1995): physicians 630,000 (1 per 235 persons); hospital beds 1,860,000 (1 per 80 persons); infant mortality rate per 1,000 live births (1995) 18.0.

Education (1995–96)

	schools	teachers	students	student/ teacher ratio
Primary (age 6–13) } Secondary (age 14–17) }	70,200	1,705,000	22,000,000	12.9
Voc., teacher tr.	2,612	...	1,923,000	...
Higher	569	...	2,655,000	...

Food (1995): daily per capita caloric intake 2,926 (vegetable products 74%; animal products 26%); 114% of FAO recommended minimum.

Military

Total active duty personnel (1997): 1,240,000 (army 71.8%, navy 17.7%, air force 10.5%). *Military expenditure as percentage of GNP* (1995): 11.4% (world 3.0%); per capita expenditure U.S.$513.

[1]January 1995. [2]The former Chechen-Ingush republic was split into two separate republics June 4, 1992; the final status of Chechnia was unresolved in December 1997. [3]Republic is not signatory to the March 31, 1992, treaty establishing the Russian Federation. [4]Ingushetia's area and population include Chechnia. [5]Detail does not add to total given because of rounding. [6]Entity has formally proclaimed itself a federal republic; final status remains undetermined. [7]Leningrad region includes area of autonomous city of St. Petersburg. [8]Moskva region includes area of autonomous city of Moscow. [9]With the exception of the Chukchi autonomous district (identified in Roman type), which has formally separated from Magadan region, all autonomous districts are administratively part of another national administrative subdivision, within which their area and population are included. [10]Total as of March 31, 1995; Russia has also assumed responsibility for the governmental and commercial debts of the former U.S.S.R., estimated to constitute a further U.S.$88,000,000,000. [11]1990. [12]Based on IMF Direction of Trade Statistics (DOTS), which values total trade with all known trading partners, rather than the customs statement of the subject country. Total DOTS valuation: imports U.S.$43,318,000,000, exports U.S.$81,438,000,000.

Internet resources for further information:

- **Permanent Mission of the Russian Federation to the United Nations http://www.undp.org/missions/russianfed**

Rwanda

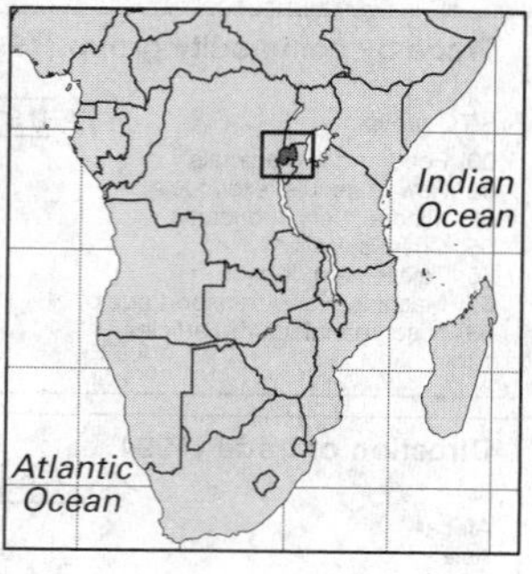

Official name: Repubulika y'u Rwanda (Rwanda); République Rwandaise (French); Republic of Rwanda (English).
Form of government: transitional regime with one legislative body (Transitional National Assembly[1] [70]).
Head of state and government: President in conjunction with Prime Minister and Vice President (Minister of Defense).
Capital: Kigali.
Official languages: Rwanda; French; English.
Official religion: none.
Monetary unit: 1 Rwanda franc (RF); valuation (Oct. 3, 1997) 1 U.S.$ = RF 300.82; 1 £ = RF 484.93.

Area and population

Prefectures	Capitals	area sq mi	area sq km	population 1991 census
Butare	Butare	709	1,837	766,839
Byumba	Byumba	1,838	4,761	783,350
Cyangugu	Cyangugu	712	1,845	515,129
Gikongoro	Gikongoro	794	2,057	464,585
Gisenyi	Gisenyi	791	2,050	734,697
Gitarama	Gitarama	845	2,189	851,516
Kibungo	Kibungo	1,562	4,046	655,368
Kibuye	Kibuye	658	1,705	470,747
Kigali	Kigali (city)	1,159	3,002	918,869
Kigali (city)	—	45	116	237,782
Ruhengeri	Ruhengeri	642	1,663	766,112
TOTAL LAND AREA		9,757[2]	25,271	
TOTAL		10,169	26,338	7,164,994[3]

Demography

Population (1997): 7,738,000[4].
Density (1997): persons per sq mi 760.9, persons per sq km 293.8.
Urban-rural (1991): urban 5.4%; rural 94.6%.
Sex distribution (1996): male 49.56%; female 50.44%.
Age breakdown (1996): under 15, 46.1%; 15–29, 27.9%; 30–44, 15.1%; 45–59, 6.6%; 60–74, 3.5%; 75 and over, 0.8%.
Population projection: (2000) 8,900,000; (2010) 10,080,000.
Doubling time: 33 years.
Ethnic composition (1991): Hutu 85.0%; Tutsi 14.0%; Twa 1.0%.
Religious affiliation: In 1991 the largest organized religion was the Roman Catholic church, representing approximately 44% of the population, followed by Muslims at about 8–9%, with the remainder consisting of indigenous African Protestant churches or traditional animist believers.
Major cities (1991): Kigali 237,782[3]; Ruhengeri 29,578[5]; Butare 28,645[5]; Gisenyi 21,918[5].

Vital statistics

Birth rate per 1,000 population (1996): 39.1 (world avg. 25.0); (1978) legitimate 94.9%; illegitimate 5.1%.
Death rate per 1,000 population (1996): 18.0 (world avg. 9.3).
Natural increase rate per 1,000 population (1996): 21.1 (world avg. 15.7).
Total fertility rate (avg. births per childbearing woman; 1996): 6.0.
Marriage rate per 1,000 population (1984)[6]: 2.5.
Life expectancy at birth (1996): male 42.9 years; female 43.6 years.
Major causes of death per 100,000 population: n.a.; however, principal causes in 1991 were malaria, bronchopneumonia, diarrhea, AIDS, pulmonary diseases, cerebrospinal meningitis, kwashiorkor, and road accidents.

National economy

Budget (1995). Revenue: RF 61,500,000,000 (grants 62.4%, taxes on goods and services 16.1%, import and export duties 14.5%, income tax 4.6%). Expenditures: RF 69,400,000,000 (capital expenditures 39.3%, goods and services 25.1%, wages 19.6%, debt payment 11.2%, transfers 4.8%).
Production (metric tons except as noted). Agriculture, forestry, fishing (1996): plantains 2,105,000, sweet potatoes 1,100,000, cassava 250,000, potatoes 150,000, sorghum 85,000, corn [maize] 71,000, coffee 21,000; livestock (number of live animals) 920,000 goats, 465,000 cattle, 250,000 sheep, 80,000 pigs; roundwood (1995) 5,660,000 cu m; fish catch (1995) 3,349. Mining and quarrying (1993): cassiterite (tin ore) 400; wolframite (tungsten ore) 175; gold 1,000 kg. Manufacturing (1994): cement 21,000; lye soap 2,200; sugar 600; beer 45,800,000 bottles; nonalcoholic beverages 21,900,000 bottles; textiles 2,800,000 metres. Energy production (consumption): electricity (kW-hr; 1994) 166,000,000 (177,000,000); petroleum products (metric tons; 1994) none (155,000); natural gas (cu m; 1994) 179,389 (179,389).
Population economically active (1991): total 3,649,000; activity rate of total population 50.2% (participation rates: ages 14–74 [1989] 46.3%; female 53.5%; unemployed, n.a.).

Price and earnings indexes (1990 = 100)

	1990	1991	1992	1993	1994	1995	1996
Consumer price index	100.0	119.6	131.1	147.3	...	293.0	314.7
Earnings index	100.0	100.0	100.0	100.0	100.0	100.0	120.0[7]

Public debt (external, outstanding; 1995): U.S.$949,000,000.
Gross national product (1995): U.S.$1,128,000,000 (U.S.$180 per capita).

Structure of gross domestic product and labour force

	1995 in value RF '000,000	1995 % of total value	1989 labour force	1989 % of labour force
Agriculture	114,622	35.0	2,832,557	90.1
Mining	81	—	4,691	0.2
Manufacturing	46,841	14.3	45,089	1.4
Construction	5,034	1.5	38,237	1.2
Public utilities	1,382	0.4	2,562	0.1
Transp. and commun.	17,055	5.2	7,333	0.2
Trade	58,251	17.8	80,026	2.6
Pub. admin., defense	16,508	5.0	123,147	3.9
Services	48,882	14.9		
Other	18,831[8]	5.8[8]	9,414	0.3
TOTAL	327,485[2]	100.0[2]	3,143,056	100.0

Tourism: receipts (1993) U.S.$2,000,000; expenditures (1992) U.S.$17,000,000.
Land use (1994): forested 10.1%; meadows and pastures 28.4%; agricultural and under permanent cultivation 47.4%; other 14.1%.
Household income and expenditure. Average household size (1991) 4.7; average annual income per household (1983) RF 122,870 (U.S.$1,300); sources of income (1977): self-employment 71.0%, salaries and wages 16.5%, transfers 9.5%; expenditure (1982)[9]: food 44.2%, housing 13.2%, clothing and footwear 11.4%, transportation 10.3%, household equipment 8.4%.

Foreign trade[10]

Balance of trade (current prices)

	1989	1990	1991	1992	1993	1994
RF '000,000	−10,918	−6,834	−15,181	−17,729	−23,934	−3,068
% of total	41.7%	27.0%	39.6%	49.9%	55.9%	14.6%

Imports (1995): U.S.$291,500,000 (food 35.2%, capital goods 17.6%, intermediate goods 11.1%, energy products 7.3%). *Major import sources* (1991): Belgium-Luxembourg 17.1%; Kenya 13.4%; France 6.8%; Germany 6.0%; Italy 2.8%; The Netherlands 2.7%; U.K. 2.1%; U.S. 1.0%; Zaire 0.7%.
Exports (1995): U.S.$51,200,000 (coffee 74.4%, tea 10.0%, hides and skins 4.9%). *Major export destinations* (1991): Germany 21.3%; The Netherlands 18.8%; Belgium-Luxembourg 11.8%; U.K. 6.4%; U.S. 5.8%; Italy 1.7%.

Transport and communications

Transport. Railroads: none. Roads (1995): total length 14,565 km (paved 10%). Vehicles (1995): passenger cars 11,900; trucks 15,900. Air transport: (1993) passenger-km 2,000,000; (1991) metric ton cargo loaded 2,674, metric ton cargo unloaded 4,794; airports (1997) with scheduled flights 2.

Communications

Medium	date	unit	number	units per 1,000 persons
Daily newspapers	1995	circulation	500	0.07
Radio	1995	receivers	525,000	78.4
Telephones	1995	main lines	15,000	2.2
Facsimile machines	1995	units	500	0.07

Education and health

Educational attainment (1978). Percentage of population age 25 and over having: no formal schooling 76.9%; some primary education 16.8%; complete primary education 4.0%; some secondary and complete secondary education 2.0%; some postsecondary vocational and higher education 0.3%.
Literacy (1995): percentage of total population age 15 and over literate 60.5%; males literate 69.8%; females literate 51.6%.

Education (1991–92)

	schools	teachers	students	student/teacher ratio
Primary (age 7–15)	1,710	18,937	1,104,902	58.3
Secondary (age 16–19)[11]	...	3,413	94,586	27.7
Higher[12]	3[13]	646	3,389	5.2

Health: physicians (1992) 150 (1 per 50,000 persons); hospital beds (1990) 12,152 (1 per 588 persons); infant mortality rate (1996) 114.2.
Food (1992): daily per capita caloric intake 1,821 (vegetable products 97%, animal products 3%); 78% of FAO recommended minimum requirement.

Military

Total active duty personnel (1997): 62,000 (army 100%). *Military expenditure as percentage of GNP* (1995): 5.2% (world 2.8%); per capita expenditure U.S.$20.

[1]Transitional National Assembly was appointed on Nov. 25, 1994, for an interim period of five years. [2]Detail does not add to total given because of rounding. [3]The population of Kigali decreased to about 100,000–120,000 because of the 1994 civil war. [4]Includes adjustments for (1) the death of an estimated 500,000 Tutsi killed during the events of 1994; (2) the return of 400,000–600,000 Tutsi herdsmen from surrounding countries who had been in exile since 1959; and (3) the loss of 2 million Hutu refugees in 1994 and the return of all but 370,000 of them by 1997. [5]De jure population only. [6]Excludes marriages not registered in court. [7]Minimum wage unchanged 1980–95; a 20% increase was made in 1996. [8]Indirect taxes plus statistical adjustments. [9]Weights of consumer price index components. [10]Imports f.o.b. in balance of trade and c.i.f. in commodities and trading partners. [11]Includes vocational and teacher training. [12]1989–90. [13]1985.

Internet resources for further information:

- **CIA World Factbook—Rwanda**
  http://www.odci.gov/cia/publications/nsolo/factbook/rw.htm

Saint Kitts and Nevis

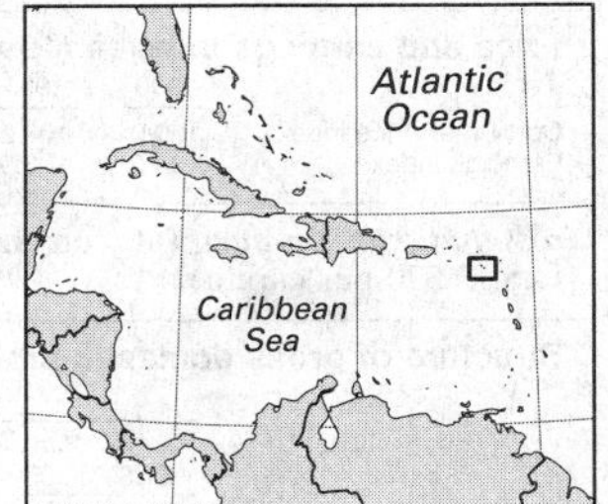

Official name: Federation of Saint Kitts and Nevis[1].
Form of government[2]: constitutional monarchy with one legislative house (National Assembly [15[3]]).
Chief of state: British Monarch represented by Governor-General.
Head of government: Prime Minister.
Capital: Basseterre.
Official language: English.
Official religion: none.
Monetary unit: 1 Eastern Caribbean dollar (EC$) = 100 cents; valuation (Oct. 3, 1997) 1 U.S.$ = EC$2.70; 1 £ = EC$4.35.

Area and population

		area		population
Islands	Capitals	sq mi	sq km	1995 estimate
Nevis[2, 4]	Charlestown	36.0	93.2	8,010
St. Kitts	Basseterre	68.0	176.2	35,340
TOTAL		104.0	269.4	43,350

Demography

Population (1997): 41,800.
Density (1997): persons per sq mi 401.9, persons per sq km 155.2.
Urban-rural (1995): urban 42.9%; rural 57.1%.
Sex distribution (1990): male 51.56%; female 48.44%.
Age breakdown (1990): under 15, 32.5%; 15–29, 25.6%; 30–44, 18.9%; 45–59, 10.1%; 60–74, 8.9%; 75 and over, 4.0%.
Population projection: (2000) 43,000; (2010) 50,000.
Doubling time: 67 years.
Ethnic composition (1991): black 94.9%; mixed/white/Indo-Pakistani 5.1%.
Religious affiliation (1995): Protestant 84.6%, of which Anglican 25.2%, Methodist 25.2%, Pentecostal 8.4%, Moravian 7.6%; Roman Catholic 6.7%; other 8.7%.
Major towns (1994): Basseterre 12,605; Charlestown 1,411.

Vital statistics

Birth rate per 1,000 population (1995): 20.2[5] (world avg. 25.0); (1983) legitimate 19.2%; illegitimate 80.8%.
Death rate per 1,000 population (1995): 9.8[5] (world avg. 9.3).
Natural increase rate per 1,000 population (1995): 10.4[5] (world avg. 15.7).
Total fertility rate (avg. births per childbearing woman; 1996): 2.5.
Marriage rate per 1,000 population: n.a.
Divorce rate per 1,000 population: n.a.
Life expectancy at birth (1996): male 63.8 years; female 70.1 years.
Major causes of death per 100,000 population (1985): diseases of the circulatory system 443.2, of which cerebrovascular disease 220.5, diseases of pulmonary circulation and other heart disease 122.7; malignant neoplasms (cancers) 95.5.

National economy

Budget (1996). Revenue: EC$208,300,000 (tax revenue 68.9%, of which taxes on international transactions 37.4%, income taxes 15.7%, consumption taxes 14.4%; nontax revenue 26.7%). Expenditures: EC$231,700,000 (current expenditure 85.9%; development expenditure 14.1%).
Production (metric tons except as noted). Agriculture, forestry, fishing (1996): sugarcane 203,740, coconuts 1,700, tropical fruit 1,500, sweet potatoes 250, onions 141; sea island cotton is grown on Nevis; livestock (number of live animals; 1996) 17,000 sheep, 13,000 goats, 3,000 pigs; roundwood, n.a.; fish catch (1995) 220. Mining and quarrying: excavation of sand for local use. Manufacturing (1996): raw sugar 20,249; molasses 6,000[6]; carbonated beverages 47,000 hectolitres[7]; beer 17,200 hectolitres[7]; other manufactures include electronic components, garments, footwear, and batik. Construction (value added; 1994): EC$57,000,000. Energy production (consumption): electricity (kW-hr; 1994) 86,000,000 (86,000,000); coal, none (none); crude petroleum, none (none); petroleum products (metric tons; 1994) none (32,000); natural gas, none (none).
Gross national product (1995): U.S.$212,000,000 (U.S.$5,170 per capita).

Structure of gross domestic product and labour force

	1995		1994	
	in value EC$'000,000	% of total value	labour force[8]	% of labour force[8]
Sugarcane	13.4	2.0	1,525[9]	9.2[9]
Other agriculture, forestry, fisheries	18.0	2.7	914	5.5
Mining	1.9	0.3	29	0.2
Manufacturing	59.7	8.9	1,290[10]	7.8[10]
Construction	67.0	10.0	1,745	10.5
Public utilities	9.3	1.4	416	2.5
Transportation and communications	87.4	13.1	534	3.2
Trade, restaurants	131.2	19.6	3,367	20.3
Finance, real estate	87.7	13.1	3,708[11]	22.3[11]
Pub. admin., defense	101.9	15.3	2,738	16.5
Services	24.1	3.6	[11]	[11]
Other	66.1[12]	9.9[12]	342	2.1
TOTAL	667.7	100.0[13]	16,608	100.0[13]

Household income and expenditure. Average household size (1980) 3.7; average annual income per wage earner (1994) EC$9,940 (U.S.$3,681); sources of income: n.a.; expenditure (1978)[14]: food, beverages, and tobacco 55.6%, household furnishings 9.4%, housing 7.6%, clothing and footwear 7.5%, fuel and light 6.6%, transportation 4.3%, other 9.0%.
Public debt (external, outstanding; 1995): U.S.$54,000,000.
Population economically active (1980): total 17,125; activity rate of total population 39.5% (participation rates: ages 15–64, 69.5%; female 41.0%; unemployed [1996] 4.5%).

Price and earnings indexes (1990 = 100)

	1990	1991	1992	1993	1994	1995	1996
Consumer price index	100.0	104.2	107.1	109.0	110.6	113.9	116.2
Earnings index	...	...	...	...	...	...	...

Land use (1994): forested 17%; meadows and pastures 3%; agricultural and under permanent cultivation 39%; other 41%.
Tourism (1995): receipts from visitors U.S.$63,000,000; expenditures by nationals abroad U.S.$5,100,000.

Foreign trade[15]

Balance of trade (current prices)

	1992	1993	1994	1995	1996
EC$'000,000	−120	−177	−211	−217	−242
% of total	36.1%	46.2%	53.3%	52.4%	55.8%

Imports (1995): EC$359,000,000 (basic and miscellaneous manufactures 35.3%, machinery 27.7%, food 17.1%, chemicals and chemical products 8.3%). *Major import sources:* United States 42.4%; Caricom countries 17.2%, of which Trinidad and Tobago 9.8%; United Kingdom 11.3%.
Exports (1995): EC$99,000,000 (machinery and transport equipment [mostly electronic goods] 47.1%, sugar 39.3%). *Major export destinations* (1994): United States 46.6%; United Kingdom 26.4%; Caricom countries 9.3%, of which Antigua and Barbuda 2.6%.

Transport and communications

Transport. Railroads (1995)[16]: length 22 mi, 36 km. Roads (1995): total length 193 mi, 310 km (paved 43%). Vehicles (1991): passenger cars 3,700; trucks and buses 2,200. Merchant marine (1992): vessels (100 gross tons and over) 1; total deadweight tonnage 550. Air transport: passenger arrivals (1992) 123,195[17]; passenger departures, n.a.; cargo handled, n.a.; airports (1997) with scheduled flights 2.

Communications

Medium	date	unit	number	units per 1,000 persons
Radio	1995	receivers	26,000	659
Television	1995	receivers	9,500	241
Telephones	1994	main lines	14,000	355

Education and health

Educational attainment (1980). Percentage of population age 25 and over having: no formal schooling 1.1%; primary education 29.6%; secondary 67.2%; higher 2.1%. *Literacy* (1990): total population age 15 and over literate 25,500 (90.0%); males literate 13,100 (90.0%); females literate 12,400 (90.0%).

Education (1994–95)

	schools	teachers	students	student/ teacher ratio
Primary (age 5–12)[18]	31	366	7,101	19.4
Secondary (age 13–17)	7	326	4,541	13.9
Higher[19]	1	51	394	7.7

Health (1995): physicians (1992) 39 (1 per 1,057 persons); hospital beds 276 (1 per 142 persons); infant mortality rate per 1,000 live births 25.1[5].
Food (1995): daily per capita caloric intake 2,234 (vegetable products 76%, animal products 24%); 92% of FAO recommended minimum requirement.

Military

Total active duty personnel: in July 1997 the National Assembly approved a bill creating a 50-member army.

[1]Both Saint Christopher and Nevis and the Federation of Saint Christopher and Nevis are officially acceptable, variant, short- and long-form names of the country. [2]Nevis was to hold a referendum (in late 1997 or early 1998) for possible secession from the federation. [3]Includes 4 nonelective seats. [4]Nevis has full internal self-government. The Nevis legislature is subordinate to the National Assembly only with regard to external affairs and defense. [5]Based on year of registration rather than year of occurrence. [6]1994. [7]1991. [8]Employed persons only. [9]Includes sugar manufacturing. [10]Excludes sugar manufacturing. [11]Finance, real estate includes Services. [12]Net of indirect taxes less imputed service charge. [13]Detail does not add to total given because of rounding. [14]Weights of consumer price index components. [15]Imports f.o.b. in balance of trade and c.i.f. in commodities and trading partners. [16]Light railway serving the sugar industry on Saint Kitts. [17]Saint Kitts airport only. [18]1993–94. [19]1992–93.

Internet resources for further information:

- **Official web-site of the Government of St. Kitts & Nevis http://www.stkittsnevis.net/**

Saint Lucia

Official name: Saint Lucia.
Form of government: constitutional monarchy with a Parliament consisting of two legislative chambers (Senate [11]; House of Assembly [17[1]]).
Chief of state: British Monarch represented by Governor-General.
Head of government: Prime Minister.
Capital: Castries.
Official language: English.
Official religion: none.
Monetary unit: 1 Eastern Caribbean dollar (EC$) = 100 cents; valuation (Oct. 3, 1997) 1 U.S.$ = EC$2.70; 1 £ = EC$4.35.

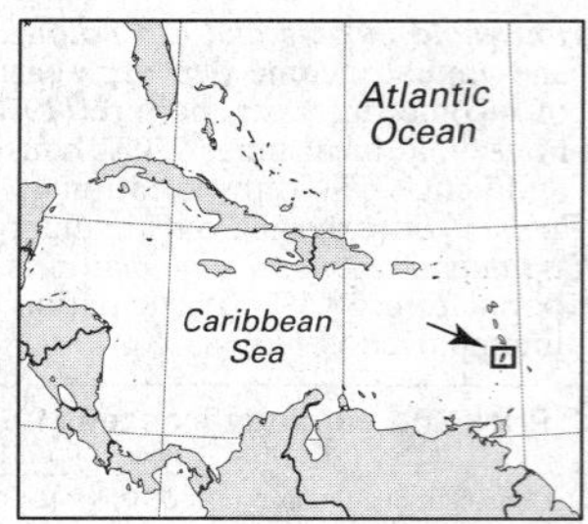

Area and population

Districts	Capitals	area sq mi	area sq km	population 1992 estimate
Anse-la-Raye	Anse-la-Raye	18	47	5,218
Canaries	Canaries			1,864
Castries	Castries	31	79	53,883
Choiseul	Choiseul	12	31	6,638
Dennery	Dennery	27	70	11,574
Gros Islet	Gros Islet	39	101	13,996
Laborie	Laborie	15	38	7,763
Micoud	Micoud	30	78	15,636
Soufrière	Soufrière	19	51	7,962
Vieux Fort	Vieux Fort	17	44	13,617
TOTAL		238[2]	617[2]	138,151

Demography

Population (1997): 148,000.
Density (1997): persons per sq mi 621.8, persons per sq km 239.9.
Urban-rural (1995): urban 48.1%; rural 51.9%.
Sex distribution (1992): male 48.49%; female 51.51%.
Age breakdown (1992): under 15, 36.7%; 15–29, 29.4%; 30–44, 16.3%; 45–59, 8.8%; 60–74, 6.3%; 75 and over, 2.5%.
Population projection: (2000) 153,000; (2010) 170,000.
Doubling time: 37 years.
Ethnic composition (1990): black 90.5%; mixed 5.5%; East Indian 3.2%; white 0.8%.
Religious affiliation (1995): Roman Catholic 79.2%; Protestant 19.4%, of which Pentecostal 5.4%, Seventh-day Adventist 5.2%; other 1.4%.
Major city (1992): Castries city proper 2,063 (urban area 13,615).

Vital statistics

Birth rate per 1,000 population (1995): 25.2 (world avg. 25.0); legitimate 14.2%; illegitimate 85.8%.
Death rate per 1,000 population (1995): 5.9 (world avg. 9.3).
Natural increase rate per 1,000 population (1995): 19.3 (world avg. 15.7).
Total fertility rate (avg. births per childbearing woman; 1996): 2.5.
Marriage rate per 1,000 population (1995): 3.4.
Divorce rate per 1,000 population (1995): 0.2.
Life expectancy at birth (1996): male 67.5 years; female 75.0 years.
Major causes of death per 100,000 population (1992): diseases of the circulatory system 205.6, of which ischemic heart diseases 133.2; malignant neoplasms (cancers) 64.4; diseases of the respiratory system 48.5; infectious and parasitic diseases 31.1; ill-defined conditions 130.3.

National economy

Budget (1996–97). Revenue: EC$418,600,000 (consumption duties on imported goods 24.3%; taxes on income and profits 23.3%; import duties 15.9%; nontax revenue 10.2%; grants 6.5%). Expenditures: EC$456,900,000 (current expenditures 69.7%; development expenditures and net lending 30.3%).
Public debt (external, outstanding; 1995): U.S.$111,000,000.
Tourism (1995): receipts from visitors (1994) U.S.$229,500,000; expenditures by nationals abroad U.S.$25,100,000.
Production (metric tons except as noted). Agriculture, forestry, fishing (1996): bananas 135,000, mangoes 27,000, coconuts 18,000, yams 4,300, pepper 160, ginger 60; livestock (number of live animals; 1996) 14,700 pigs, 12,500 sheep, 12,450 cattle; roundwood, n.a.; fish catch (1995) 1,023. Mining and quarrying: excavation of sand for local construction and pumice. Manufacturing (value of production in EC$'000; 1995): paper products and cardboard boxes 50,173; alcoholic beverages and tobacco 30,893; electrical and electronic components 14,125; garments 8,903; refined coconut oil 6,335; food products 4,165. Construction (buildings approved; 1992): residential 91,900 sq m; nonresidential 43,300 sq m. Energy production (consumption): electricity (kW-hr; 1994) 112,000,000 (112,000,000); coal, none (none); crude petroleum, none (none); petroleum products (metric tons; 1994) none (61,000); natural gas, none (none).
Household income and expenditure. Average household size (1991) 4.0; income per household: n.a.; sources of income: n.a.; expenditure (1982)[3]: food 46.8%, housing 13.5%, clothing and footwear 6.5%, transportation and communications 6.3%, household furnishings 5.8%, other 21.1%.
Population economically active (1992): total 57,797; activity rate of total population 41.8% (participation rates: ages 15–64, 72.7%; female 46.5%; unemployed [1995] 15%).

Price and earnings indexes (1990 = 100)

	1990	1991	1992	1993	1994	1995	1996
Consumer price index	100.0	106.2	112.1	113.0	116.1	122.9	126.8
Earnings index[4]	100.0	103.0	...	...	...	...	...

Gross national product (at current market prices; 1995): U.S.$532,000,000 (U.S.$3,370 per capita).

Structure of gross domestic product and labour force

	1995 in value EC$'000,000[5]	1995 % of total value[5]	1992 labour force[6]	1992 % of labour force[6]
Agriculture	135	10.5	2,824	8.9
Mining	7	0.5	...	...
Manufacturing	88	6.8	4,360	13.8
Construction	99	7.7	2,197	6.9
Public utilities	56	4.3	832	2.6
Transportation and communications	218	16.9	2,551	8.0
Trade, restaurants	334	25.9	8,714	27.5
Finance, real estate	212	16.5	3,488	11.0
Pub. admin., defense	180	14.0	6,758	21.3
Services	45	3.5	...	...
Other	–86[7]	–6.7[7]	—	—
TOTAL	1,288	100.0[8]	31,724	100.0

Land use (1994): forested 13%; meadows and pastures 5%; agricultural and under permanent cultivation 30%; other 52%.

Foreign trade[9]

Balance of trade (current prices)

	1991	1992	1993	1994	1995
U.S.$'000,000	–182	–179	–180	–202	–191
% of total	44.6%	41.0%	42.9%	50.2%	44.8%

Imports (1995): U.S.$306,000,000 (food 22.5%; machinery and transportation equipment 19.0%; chemicals and chemical products 9.5%; crude petroleum and petroleum products 7.5%). *Major import sources:* United States 36.2%; Caricom countries 22.3%, of which Trinidad and Tobago 12.4%; United Kingdom 11.1%; Japan 4.6%; Canada 3.9%.
Exports (1995): U.S.$115,000,000 (bananas 40.8%; clothing 12.1%; primarily paper and paperboard 6.2%; beer 3.8%). *Major export destinations:* United Kingdom 50.4%; United States 24.2%; Caricom countries 15.8%.

Transport and communications

Transport. Railroads: none. Roads (1994): total length 510 mi, 820 km (paved 88%). Vehicles (1993): passenger cars 10,000; trucks and buses 9,200. Merchant marine (1992): vessels (100 gross tons and over) 7; total deadweight tonnage 2,070. Air transport (1994)[10]: passenger arrivals 573,000, passenger departures 581,000; cargo unloaded 2,002 metric tons, cargo loaded 3,918 metric tons; airports (1997) with scheduled flights 2.

Communications

Medium	date	unit	number	units per 1,000 persons
Radio	1995	receivers	90,000	619
Television	1995	receivers	25,000	172
Telephones	1995	main lines	30,600	211
Cellular telephones	1995	subscribers	1,000	6.9

Education and health

Educational attainment (1980). Percentage of population age 25 and over having: no formal schooling 17.5%; primary education 74.4%; secondary 6.8%; higher 1.3%. *Literacy* (1995): about 82%.

Education (1992–93)

	schools	teachers	students	student/ teacher ratio
Primary (age 5–11)	88	1,204	32,545	27.0
Secondary (age 12–16)	14	524	9,550	18.2
Vocational	1	34	806	23.7
Higher	1	389	870	2.4

Health (1995): physicians (1992) 64 (1 per 2,159 persons); hospital beds 541 (1 per 269 persons); infant mortality rate per 1,000 live births 18.0.
Food (1995): daily per capita caloric intake 2,801 (vegetable products 73%, animal products 27%); 116% of FAO recommended minimum requirement.

Military

Total active duty personnel (1994): [11].

[1]Attorney general serves ex officio in House of Assembly if not elected (House of Assembly total 18). [2]Total includes the uninhabited 30 sq mi (78 sq km) Central Forest Reserve. [3]Castries area only. [4]Public sector only. [5]At factor cost in current prices. [6]Data exclude workers (all self-employed and many agricultural workers) not making contributions to the national insurance plan and all unemployed. [7]Less imputed bank service charges. [8]Detail does not add to total given because of rounding. [9]Imports c.i.f.; exports f.o.b. [10]Combined data for both Castries and Vieux Fort airports. [11]The more than 500-member police force includes a specially trained paramilitary unit and a coast guard unit.

Internet resources for further information:
- **The St. Lucia Mirror (unofficial weekly newspaper) http://www.stluciamirror.com/**

Saint Vincent and the Grenadines

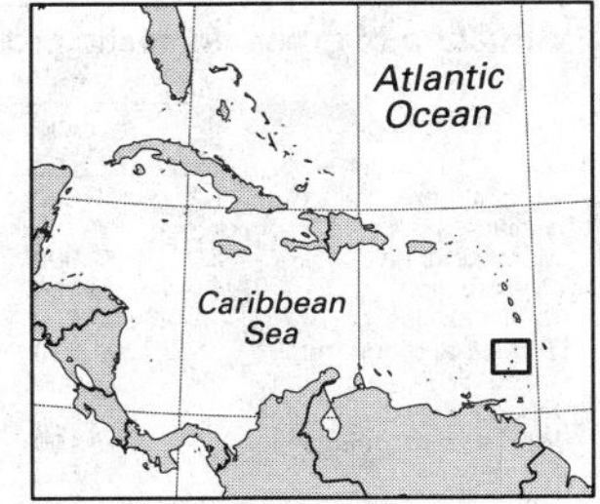

Official name: Saint Vincent and the Grenadines.
Form of government: constitutional monarchy with one legislative house (House of Assembly [21[1]]).
Chief of state: British Monarch represented by Governor-General.
Head of government: Prime Minister.
Capital: Kingstown.
Official language: English.
Official religion: none.
Monetary unit: 1 Eastern Caribbean dollar (EC$) = 100 cents; valuation (Oct. 3, 1997) 1 U.S.$ = EC$2.70; 1 £ = EC$4.35.

Area and population

	area		population
Constituencies[2]	sq mi	sq km	1995 estimate[3]
Island of Saint Vincent			
Barrouallie	14.2	36.8	5,346
Bridgetown	7.2	18.6	7,746
Calliaqua	11.8	30.6	20,868
Chateaubelair	30.9	80.0	6,217
Colonarie	13.4	34.7	8,115
Georgetown	22.2	57.5	7,511
Kingstown (city)	1.9	4.9	15,908
Kingstown (suburbs)	6.4	16.6	11,063
Layou	11.1	28.7	6,164
Marriaqua	9.4	24.3	9,117
Sandy Bay	5.3	13.7	2,873
Saint Vincent Grenadines			
Northern Grenadines	9.0	23.3	5,672
Southern Grenadines	7.5	19.4	2,934
TOTAL	150.3	389.3[4]	109,534

Demography

Population (1997): 112,000.
Density (1997): persons per sq mi 745.2, persons per sq km 287.7.
Urban-rural (1995)[5]: urban 24.6%; rural 75.4%.
Sex distribution (1995): male 49.90%; female 50.10%.
Age breakdown (1991): under 15, 37.2%; 15–29, 29.5%; 30–44, 16.1%; 45–59, 8.3%; 60–74, 6.4%; 75 and over, 2.5%.
Population projection: (2000) 115,000; (2010) 126,000.
Doubling time: 44 years.
Ethnic composition (1995): black 82.0%; mixed 13.9%; other 4.1%.
Religious affiliation (1995): Protestant 57.0%, of which Anglican 17.9%, Pentecostal 14.9%, Methodist 10.5%; Roman Catholic 10.7%; other/nonreligious 32.3%.
Major city (1995): Kingstown 15,908.

Vital statistics

Birth rate per 1,000 population (1995)[6]: 22.4 (world avg. 25.0); legitimate, n.a.; illegitimate, n.a.
Death rate per 1,000 population (1995)[6]: 6.6 (world avg. 9.3).
Natural increase rate per 1,000 population (1995)[6]: 15.9 (world avg. 15.7).
Total fertility rate (avg. births per childbearing woman; 1996): 2.0.
Marriage rate per 1,000 population (1994): 4.2.
Divorce rate per 1,000 population (1994): 0.8.
Life expectancy at birth (1996): male 71.4 years; female 74.5 years.
Major causes of death per 100,000 population (1994): diseases of the circulatory system 237.2, of which cerebrovascular diseases 75.7, ischemic heart disease 72.1; malignant neoplasms (cancers) 94.0; endocrine and metabolic disorders 68.4; infectious and parasitic diseases 44.7.

National economy

Budget (1995). Revenue: EC$194,800,000 (consumption duties on imports 28.9%, income taxes 24.6%, nontax revenue 12.4%, taxes on goods and services 11.7%, import duties 11.4%). Expenditures: EC$191,300,000 (current expenditure 87.0%; development expenditure 13.0%).
Public debt (external, outstanding; 1995): U.S.$85,700,000.
Land use (1994): forested 36%; meadows and pastures 5%; agricultural and under permanent cultivation 28%; other 31%.
Tourism (1995): receipts from visitors U.S.$47,200,000; expenditures by nationals abroad U.S.$5,600,000.
Production (metric tons except as noted). Agriculture, forestry, fishing (1996): bananas 55,000, coconuts 23,000, eddoes and dasheens[7] 6,252[8], sweet potatoes 1,700, mangoes 1,400, yams 1,100, oranges 960, lemons and limes 870, ginger 799[8], arrowroot starch 635[9], soursops, guavas, and papaws are other important fruits; livestock (number of live animals) 13,000 sheep, 9,400 pigs, 6,200 cattle; roundwood, n.a.; fish catch (1995) 1,480. Mining and quarrying: sand and gravel for local use. Manufacturing (export value of manufactures in U.S.$'000,000; 1995): packaged flour 8.7; packaged rice 6.4; other goods (mostly garments, sporting goods, and electronic goods) 8.1. Construction (gross floor area planned; 1994): 104,878 sq m. Energy production (consumption): electricity (kW-hr; 1995) 73,200,000 (64,100,000); coal, none (none); crude petroleum, none (none); petroleum products (metric tons; 1994) none (39,000); natural gas, none (none).
Gross national product (1995): U.S.$253,000,000 (U.S.$2,280 per capita).

Structure of gross domestic product and labour force

	1995		1991	
	in value EC$'000,000	% of total value	labour force	% of labour force
Agriculture, forestry, fishing	80.1	11.4	8,377	20.1
Mining	2.0	0.3	98	0.2
Manufacturing	50.5	7.2	2,822	6.8
Construction	67.9	9.7	3,535	8.5
Public utilities	29.7	4.2	586	1.4
Transportation and communications	120.9	17.2	2,279	5.5
Trade, restaurants	105.5	15.0	6,544	15.7
Finance, real estate	61.2	8.7	1,418	3.4
Pub. admin., defense	102.6	14.6 }	7,696	18.5
Services	10.3	1.5 }		
Other	71.0[10]	10.2[10]	8,327[11]	20.0[11]
TOTAL	702.0[4]	100.0	41,682	100.0[4]

Population economically active (1991): total 41,682; activity rate of total population 39.1% (participation rates: ages 15–64, 67.5%; female 35.9%; unemployed [1996] more than 30%).

Price and earnings indexes (1990 = 100)

	1989	1990	1991	1992	1993	1994	1995
Consumer price index	92.9	100.0	106.1	110.1	114.8	115.3	118.1
Daily earnings index[12]	100.0	100.0	100.0	100.0	100.0	100.0	100.0

Household income and expenditure. Average household size (1991) 3.9; income per household (1988) EC$4,579 (U.S.$1,696); sources of income: n.a.; expenditure (1975–76): food and beverages 59.8%, clothing 7.7%, household furnishings 6.6%, housing 6.3%, energy 6.2%, other 13.4%.

Foreign trade

Balance of trade (current prices)

	1990	1991	1992	1993	1994	1995
U.S.$'000,000	−82.7	−57.2	−42.9	−62.6	−64.2	−63.7
% of total	18.3%	30.3%	22.6%	36.0%	39.1%	36.3%

Imports (1995): U.S.$119,500,000 (basic manufactures 37.5%; food products 20.1%; machinery and transport equipment 17.6%; chemical products 13.8%). *Major import sources:* United States 36.5%; Caricom countries 27.9%, of which Trinidad and Tobago 17.0%; United Kingdom 12.9%.
Exports (1995): U.S.$55,800,000 (domestic exports 93.1%, of which bananas 39.2%, packaged flour 15.6%, packaged rice 11.5%, eddoes and dasheens[7] 2.7%; reexports 6.9%). *Major export destinations:* Caricom countries 48.6%, of which St. Lucia 12.7%, Trinidad and Tobago 9.0%; United Kingdom 16.1%; United States 9.7%.

Transport and communications

Transport. Railroads: none. Roads (1995): total length 634 mi, 1,020 km (paved 31%). Vehicles (1994): passenger cars 5,753; trucks and buses 3,042. Merchant marine (1992): vessels (100 gross tons and over) 881; total deadweight tonnage 7,044,189. Air transport (1994): passenger arrivals 111,234, passenger departures 116,536; airports (1997) with scheduled flights 5.

Communications

Medium	date	unit	number	units per 1,000 persons
Radio	1995	receivers	65,000	591
Television	1995	receivers	17,700	161
Telephones	1995	main lines	18,200	165
Cellular telephones	1995	subscribers	100	0.9
Facsimile machines	1995	units	700	6.4

Education and health

Educational attainment (1980). Percentage of population age 25 and over having: no formal schooling 2.4%; primary education 88.0%; secondary 8.2%; higher 1.4%. *Literacy* (1991): total population age 15 and over literate 64,000 (96.0%).

Education (1993–94)

	schools	teachers	students	student/teacher ratio
Primary (age 5–11)	65	1,080	21,386	19.8
Secondary (age 12–18)	21[13]	395	9,870	25.0
Voc., teacher tr.	2[13]	49	414	8.4

Health (1995): physicians (1992) 55 (1 per 2,000 persons); hospital beds 444 (1 per 248 persons); infant mortality rate per 1,000 live births 19.0[6].
Food (1995): daily per capita caloric intake 2,427 (vegetable products 83%, animal products 17%); 100% of FAO recommended minimum requirement.

Military

Total active duty personnel (1992): 634-member police force includes a coast guard and paramilitary unit.

[1]Includes 6 nonelective seats occupied by senators (rather than representatives); excludes speaker who may be elected from within or from outside of the House of Assembly membership. [2]For statistical purposes and the election of legislative representatives only. [3]January 1. [4]Detail does not add to total given because of rounding. [5]Urban defined as Kingstown and suburbs. [6]Based on year of registration rather than year of occurrence. [7]Varieties of taro roots. [8]1993. [9]1992–93. [10]Net of indirect taxes less imputed bank service charges. [11]Unemployed. [12]Minimum wage in private sector. [13]1991–92.

Internet resources for further information:
- **The Herald (unofficial daily newspaper) http://www.heraldsvg.com/**

Samoa[1]

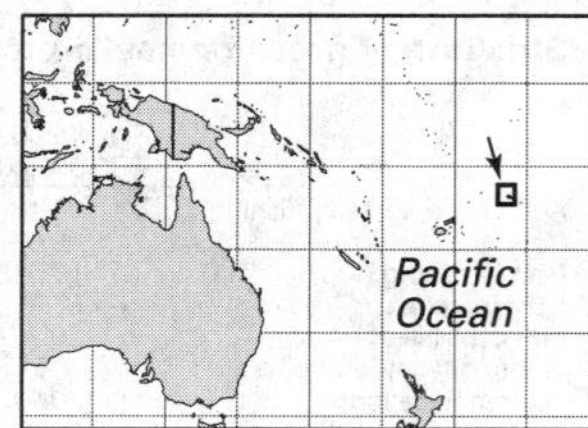

Official name: Malo Sa'oloto Tuto'atasi o Samoa (Samoan); Independent State of Samoa (English).
Form of government: constitutional monarchy[2] with one legislative house (Legislative Assembly [49]).
Chief of state: Head of State[3].
Head of government: Prime Minister.
Capital: Apia.
Official languages: Samoan; English.
Official religion: none.
Monetary unit: 1 tala (WS$, plural tala) = 100 sene; valuation (Oct. 3, 1997) 1 U.S.$ = WS$2.61; 1 £ = WS$4.21.

Area and population

Islands / Political Districts	area sq mi	area sq km	population 1991 census
Savaii	659	1,707	45,050
Fa'aseleleaga			...
Gaga'emauga			...
Gaga'ifomauga			...
Palauli			...
Satupa'itea			...
Vaisigano			...
Upolu	432	1,119	116,248
A'ana			...
Aiga-i-le-Tai			...
Atua			...
Tuamasaga			...
Vaa-o-Fonoti			...
TOTAL	1,093[4]	2,831[4]	161,298

Demography

Population (1997): 169,100.
Density (1997): persons per sq mi 154.7, persons per sq km 59.7.
Urban-rural (1997): urban 21.0%; rural 79.0%.
Sex distribution (1991): male 52.45%; female 47.55%.
Age breakdown (1991): under 15, 40.6%; 15–29, 29.9%; 30–44, 14.6%; 45–59, 8.8%; 60–74, 5.0%; 75 and over, 1.1%.
Population projection: (2000) 174,200; (2010) 192,500.
Doubling time: 34 years.
Ethnic composition (1982): Samoan (Polynesian) *c.* 88%; Euronesian *c.* 10%; European *c.* 2%.
Religious affiliation (1991): Congregational 43.0%; Roman Catholic 21.0%; Methodist 17.0%; Mormon 10.0%; Seventh-day Adventist 3.0%; other 6.0%.
Major city (1991): Apia 34,126.

Vital statistics

Birth rate per 1,000 population (1997): 26.7 (world avg. 25.0); (1978) legitimate 43.5%; illegitimate 56.5%.
Death rate per 1,000 population (1997): 6.0 (world avg. 9.3).
Natural increase rate per 1,000 population (1997): 20.7 (world avg. 15.7).
Total fertility rate (avg. births per childbearing woman; 1997): 3.8.
Marriage rate per 1,000 population (1989)[5]: 5.3.
Divorce rate per 1,000 population (1989)[5]: 0.2.
Life expectancy at birth (1997): male 67.0 years; female 71.0 years.
Major causes of death (percent distribution; 1992)[5]: congestive heart failure 14.0%; malignant neoplasms (cancers) 11.0%; cerebrovascular diseases 8.0%; injury and poisoning 8.0%; pneumonia 6.0%; septicemia 6.0%; diabetes mellitus 4.0%; intestinal infectious diseases 2.0%.

National economy

Budget (1996–97). Revenue: WS$230,700,000 (tax revenue 55.4%; grants 30.3%; nontax revenue 14.3%). Expenditures: WS$243,800,000 (current expenditure 62.2%, of which net lending 2.3%; development expenditure 37.8%).
Production (metric tons except as noted). Agriculture, forestry, fishing (1996): coconuts 130,000, taro 36,900, bananas 10,000, papayas 10,000, pineapples 5,700, mangoes 4,900, avocados 1,700, cacao beans 400; livestock (number of live animals) 178,800 pigs, 26,000 cattle, 350,000 chickens; roundwood (1995) 131,000 cu m; fish catch (1994) 1,500. Mining and quarrying: n.a. Manufacturing (in WS$'000; 1990): beer 8,708; cigarettes 6,551; coconut cream 5,576; sawn wood 3,662; coconut oil 3,442; corned meat 2,905; soap 1,487; paints 1,457. Construction (permits issued in WS$; 1995): residential 7,749,000; commercial, industrial, and other 30,867,000. Energy production (consumption): electricity (kW-hr; 1994) 64,000,000 (64,000,000); coal, none (n.a.); crude petroleum, none (n.a.); petroleum products (metric tons; 1994) none (40,000).
Household income and expenditure. Average household size (1981) 5.1; income per household (1972) WS$1,518 (U.S.$2,200); sources of income (1972): wages 49.4%, self-employment 22.8%, remittances, gifts, and other assistance 18.0%, land rent 8.7%, other 1.1%; expenditure (1987)[6]: food 58.8%, transportation 9.0%, housing and furnishings 5.1%, fuel and lighting 5.0%, clothing 4.2%, other goods and services 1.9%, other 16.0%.
Public debt (external, outstanding; 1995): U.S.$159,600,000.
Gross national product (at current market prices; 1995): U.S.$184,000,000 (U.S.$1,120 per capita).

Structure of gross domestic product and labour force

	1996 in value WS$'000	1996 % of total value	1986 labour force	1986 % of labour force
Agriculture	172,000	39.9	29,023	63.6
Mining	...	... }	1,587	3.5
Manufacturing	77,300	17.9 }		
Construction	8,300	1.9	62	0.1
Public utilities	27,500	6.4	855	1.9
Transp. and commun.	11,800	2.7	1,491	3.3
Trade	45,000	10.4	1,710	3.7
Finance	...	...	842	1.8
Pub. admin., defense	48,100	11.2 }	9,436	20.7
Services	41,500	9.6 }		
Other	...	...	629	1.4
TOTAL	431,500	100.0	45,635	100.0

Population economically active (1994): total 47,207; activity rate of total population 28.7% (participation rates: ages 15–64 [1981] 48.6%; female [1986] 18.8%).

Price and earnings indexes (1990 = 100)

	1990	1991	1992	1993	1994	1995	1996
Consumer price index	100.0	98.2	107.0	108.9	128.9	130.2	140.0
Earnings index	...	...	...	...	...	...	...

Tourism (1993): receipts from visitors U.S.$21,000,000; expenditures by nationals abroad U.S.$2,000,000.
Land use (1994): forested 47.3%; meadows and pastures 0.4%; agricultural and under permanent cultivation 43.1%; other 9.2%.

Foreign trade[7]

Balance of trade (current prices)

	1991	1992	1993	1994	1995	1996
WS$'000	–196,994	–238,965	–228,318	–178,638	–192,293	–199,996
% of total	83.9%	89.3%	87.4%	90.7%	81.5%	80.1%

Imports (1995): WS$235,353,000 (food 29.5%, industrial supplies 26.4%, machinery 21.6%, consumer goods 11.7%, petroleum products 10.1%). *Major import sources:* New Zealand 36.6%; Australia 20.9%; Fiji 12.0%; United States 11.9%; Japan 10.7%; Singapore 1.5%; Hong Kong 1.4%; Germany 1.0%.
Exports (1995): WS$21,859,000 (coconut oil 37.5%, coconut cream 22.6%, copra 10.2%, kava 6.7%, beer 5.3%, cigarettes 3.2%). *Major export destinations:* New Zealand 44.2%; Australia 22.2%; American Samoa 9.8%; Germany 4.3%; United States 1.7%.

Transport and communications

Transport. Railroads: none. Roads (1995): total length 485 mi, 781 km (paved 42%). Vehicles (1995): passenger cars 1,068; trucks and buses 1,169. Merchant marine (1997): vessels (100 gross tons and over) 7; total deadweight tonnage 6,501. Air transport: passengers, n.a.; cargo, n.a.; airports (1997) with scheduled flights 3.

Communications

Medium	date	unit	number	units per 1,000 persons
Radio	1996	receivers	75,000	448
Television	1995	receivers	5,000	30
Telephones	1995	main lines	7,800	47
Facsimile machines	1995	units	400	2.4

Education and health

Educational attainment (1981). Percentage of population age 25 and over having: some primary education 16.5%; complete primary 24.5%; some secondary 52.1%; complete secondary 3.1%; higher 2.0%; unknown 1.8%. *Literacy* (1981): virtually 100%.

Education (1986–87)

	schools	teachers	students	student/teacher ratio
Primary (age 5–11)	164[8]	1,511[9]	40,755	27.0
Secondary (age 12–18)	38[10]	492	11,395	23.2
Voc., teacher tr.	4[8]	37	228	6.2
Higher[8]	6	25	271	10.8

Health: physicians (1992) 60 (1 per 2,682 persons); hospital beds (1991) 863 (1 per 255 persons); infant mortality rate per 1,000 live births (1997) 59.
Food (1992): daily per capita caloric intake 2,828 (vegetable products 74%, animal products 26%); 124% of FAO recommended minimum requirement.

Military

No military forces are maintained; New Zealand is responsible for defense.

[1]In July 1997 the Legislative Assembly approved the removal of the word "western" from the country's name. The country will be officially known as Samoa as soon as the Head of State signs the amendment. [2]According to the constitution, the current Head of State, paramount chief HH Malietoa Tanumafili II, will hold office for life. Upon his death, the monarchy will functionally cease, and future Heads of State will be elected by the Legislative Assembly. [3]Official title is O le Ao o le Malo. [4]Total includes 2 sq mi (5 sq km) of uninhabited islands. [5]Registered only. [6]Consumer price index components. [7]Import figures are f.o.b. in balance of trade and c.i.f. in commodities and trading partners. [8]1983. [9]Includes some secondary teachers. [10]1982.

San Marino

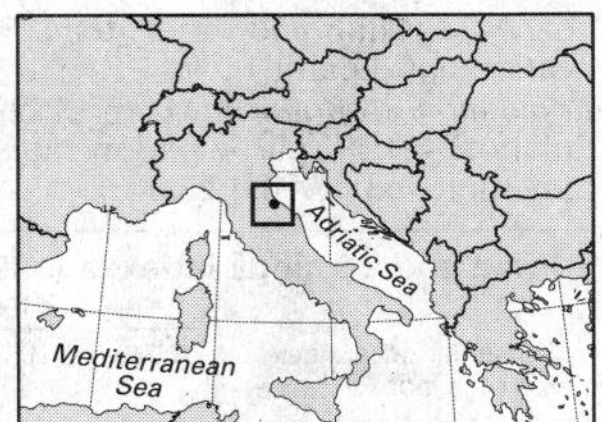

Official name: Serenissima Repubblica di San Marino (Most Serene Republic of San Marino).
Form of government: unitary multiparty republic with one legislative house (Great and General Council [60]).
Head of state and government: Captains-Regent (2).
Capital: San Marino.
Official language: Italian.
Official religion: none.
Monetary unit: 1 Italian lira (Lit; plural lire) = 100 centesimi; valuation (Oct. 3, 1997) 1 U.S.$ = Lit 1,726; 1 £ = Lit 2,783.

Area and population

		area		population
Castles	Capitals	sq mi	sq km	1997[1] estimate
Acquaviva	Acquaviva	1.88	4.86	1,264
Borgo Maggiore	Borgo	3.48	9.01	5,358
Chiesanuova	Chiesanuova	2.11	5.46	866
Città	San Marino	2.74	7.09	4,350
Domagnano	Domagnano	2.56	6.62	2,207
Faetano	Faetano	2.99	7.75	870
Fiorentino	Fiorentino	2.53	6.56	1,798
Montegiardino	Montegiardino	1.28	3.31	717
Serravalle/Dogano	Serravalle	4.07	10.53	8,085
TOTAL		23.63[2]	61.19	25,515

Demography

Population (1997): 25,600.
Density (1997): persons per sq mi 1,083.4, persons per sq km 418.4.
Urban-rural (1997[1]): urban 89.3%; rural 10.7%.
Sex distribution (1997[1]): male 48.70%; female 51.30%.
Age breakdown (1997[1]): under 15, 14.9%; 15–29, 20.9%; 30–44, 25.0%; 45–59, 18.8%; 60–74, 14.0%; 75 and over, 6.4%.
Population projection: (2000) 26,900; (2010) 31,500.
Doubling time: not applicable; natural population growth is negligible.
Ethnic composition (1997[1]): Sammarinesi 83.1%; Italian 12.0%; other 4.8%.
Religious affiliation (1980): Roman Catholic 95.2%; no religion 3.0%; other 1.8%.
Major cities (1997[1]): Serravalle/Dogano 4,802; Borgo Maggiore 2,394; San Marino 2,294; Murata 1,549; Domagnano 1,048.

Vital statistics

Birth rate per 1,000 population (1992–96): 10.5 (world avg. 25.0); (1985) legitimate 95.2%; illegitimate 4.8%.
Death rate per 1,000 population (1992–96): 7.1 (world avg. 9.3).
Natural increase rate per 1,000 population (1992–96): 3.4 (world avg. 15.7).
Total fertility rate (avg. births per childbearing woman; 1996): 1.2.
Marriage rate per 1,000 population (1992–96): 8.1.
Divorce rate per 1,000 population (1991–95): 1.0.
Life expectancy at birth (1995): male 77.2 years; female 85.3 years.
Major causes of death per 100,000 population (1991–95): diseases of the circulatory system 324.8; malignant neoplasms (cancers) 229.4; accidents, violence, and suicide 45.2; diseases of the respiratory system 10.7.

National economy

Budget (1995). Revenue: Lit 374,900,000,000 (indirect taxes 44.9%; direct taxes 28.9%; social security 17.8%). Expenditures: Lit 377,300,000,000 (current expenditures 46.8%, of which social security 39.9%, wages and salaries 30.8%; capital expenditures 6.7%; other 46.5%).
Public debt: n.a.
Tourism: number of tourist arrivals (1996) 3,345,381; receipts from visitors (1994) U.S.$252,500,000,000; expenditures by nationals abroad, n.a.
Population economically active (1996[1]): total 16,073; activity rate of total population 63.5% (participation rates: ages 15–64, 88.4%; female 40.2%; unemployed 3.1%).

Price and earnings indexes (1990 = 100)

	1989	1990	1991	1992	1993	1994	1995
Consumer price index	94.0	100.0	108.0	115.7	121.9	128.0	134.3
Earnings index	...	...	...	...	...	...	...

Household income and expenditure. Total number of households (1997[1]) 10,093; average household size 2.5; income per household: n.a.; sources of income: n.a.; expenditure (1991)[3]: food, beverages, and tobacco 22.1%, housing, fuel, and electrical energy 20.9%, transportation and communications 17.6%, clothing and footwear 8.0%, furniture, appliances, and goods and services for the home 7.2%, education 7.1%, health and sanitary services 2.6%, other goods and services 14.5%.
Production (metric tons except as noted). Agriculture, forestry, fishing[4]: wheat *c.* 4,400, grapes *c.* 700, barley *c.* 500; livestock (number of live animals; 1995) 954 cattle, 694 pigs. Manufacturing (1995): processed meats 366,177 kg, of which beef 273,515 kg, pork 85,688 kg, veal 6,902 kg; cheese 78,803 kg; butter 13,739 kg; milk 1,097,890 litres; yogurt 5,722 litres; other major products include electrical appliances, musical instruments, printing ink, paint, cosmetics, furniture, floor tiles, gold and silver jewelry, clothing, and postage stamps. Construction (new units completed; 1995): residential 145; nonresidential 123. Energy production (consumption): all electrical power is imported via electrical grid from Italy (consumption, n.a.); coal, none (n.a.); crude petroleum, none (n.a.); petroleum products, none (n.a.); natural gas, none (n.a.).
Gross national product (at current market prices; 1993): U.S.$380,000,000 (U.S.$15,800 per capita).

Structure of labour force (1996[1])

	labour force	% of labour force
Agriculture	249	1.6
Manufacturing	5,256	32.7
Construction and public utilities	1,440	9.0
Transportation and communications	311	1.9
Trade	2,641	16.4
Finance and insurance	417	2.6
Services	1,432	8.9
Public administration and defense	3,832	23.8
Other	495[5]	3.1[5]
TOTAL	16,073	100.0

Land use (1985): agricultural and under permanent cultivation 74%; meadows and pastures 22%; forested, built-on, wasteland, and other 4%.

Foreign trade

Balance of trade: n.a. San Marino and Italy form a single customs area; separate figures for San Marino are not available.
Imports (1995): manufactured goods of all kinds, oil, and gold. *Major import source:* Italy.
Exports (1995): wine, wheat, woolen goods, furniture, wood, ceramics, building stone, dairy products, meat, and postage stamps. *Major export destination:* Italy.

Transport and communications

Transport. Railroads: none (nearest rail terminal is at Rimini, Italy, 17 mi [27 km] northeast). Roads (1987): total length 147 mi, 237 km. Vehicles (1996[1]): passenger cars 23,561; trucks and buses 4,013. Merchant marine: vessels (100 gross tons and over) none. Air transport: airports with scheduled flights, none; there is, however, a heliport that provides passenger and cargo service between San Marino and Rimini, Italy, during the summer months.

Communications

Medium	date	unit	number	units per 1,000 persons
Daily newspapers	1995	circulation	2,000	82
Radio	1994	receivers	12,600	514
Television	1994	receivers	9,000	367
Telephones	1994	main lines	14,000	571

Education and health

Educational attainment (1997[1]). Percentage of population age 14 and over having: basic literacy[6] or primary education 35.6%; secondary 30.7%; some postsecondary 27.9%; higher degree 5.8%. *Literacy* (1997[1]): total population age 15 and over literate 21,885 (99.1%); males literate 10,546 (99.4%); females literate 11,339 (98.8%).

Education (1995–96)

	schools	teachers	students	student/ teacher ratio
Primary (age 6–10)	14	217	1,134	5.2
Secondary (age 11–18)	3	134	771	5.8
Voc., teacher tr.	...	44[6]	428	6.2[7]
Higher	...	...	...	...

Health (1987): physicians 60 (1 per 375 persons); hospital beds 149 (1 per 151 persons); infant mortality rate per 1,000 live births (1990–94) 7.1.
Food (1995)[8]: daily per capita caloric intake 3,458 (vegetable products 74%, animal products 26%); 137% of FAO recommended minimum requirement.

Military

Total active duty personnel (1995): none[9]. *Military expenditure as percentage of national budget* (1992): 1.0% (world 3.6%); per capita expenditure (1987) U.S.$155.

[1]January 1. [2]Detail does not add to total given because of rounding. [3]Weighting coefficients for component expenditures are those of the 1991 official Italian consumer price index for the North-Central region of Italy. [4]Early 1980s. [5]Unemployed. [6]Includes 0.9 percent illiterate population. [7]1993–94. [8]Figures are for Italy. [9]Defense is provided by a public security force of about 50; all fit males ages 16–55 constitute a militia.

Internet resources for further information:
- **San Marino http://www.intergo.com/Library/ref/atlas/europe/sm.htm**

São Tomé and Príncipe

Official name: República democrática de São Tomé e Príncipe (Democratic Republic of São Tomé and Príncipe).
Form of government: Multiparty republic with one legislative house (National Assembly [55]).
Chief of state: President.
Head of government: Prime Minister.
Capital: São Tomé.
Official language: Portuguese.
Official religion: none.
Monetary unit: 1 dobra (Db) = 100 cêntimos; valuation (Oct. 3, 1997) 1 U.S.$ = Db 2,390; 1 £ = Db 3,853.

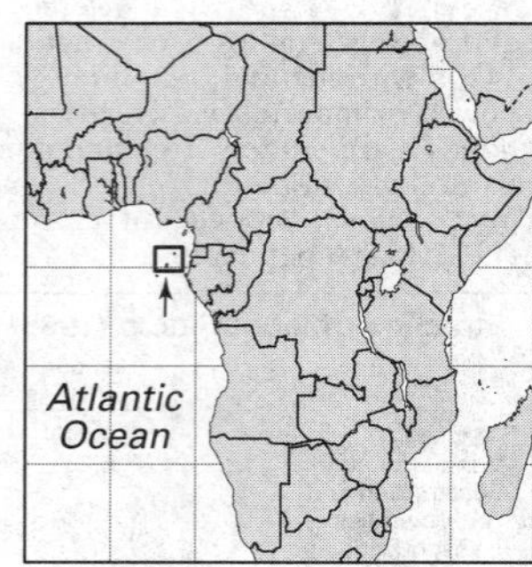

Area and population

Islands / Districts	Capitals	area sq mi	area sq km	population 1991 census[1]
São Tomé		332	859	114,507
Aqua Grande	São Tomé	7	17	43,420
Cantagalo	Santana	46	119	11,421
Caué	São João Angolares	103	267	5,541
Lemba	Neves	88	229	9,448
Lobata	Guadalupe	41	105	13,101
Mé-Zóchi	Trindade	47	122	31,576
Autonomous Island		55	142	5,639
Príncipe	Santo António	55	142	5,639
TOTAL		386	1,001	120,146

Demography

Population (1997): 137,000.
Density (1997): persons per sq mi 354.2, persons per sq km 136.6.
Urban-rural (1994): urban 44.1%; rural 55.9%.
Sex distribution (1997): male 49.24%; female 50.76%.
Age breakdown (1997): under 15, 47.5%; 15–29, 27.1%; 30–44, 12.5%; 45–59, 6.7%; 60–74, 4.9%; 75 and over, 1.3%.
Population projection: (2000) 146,000; (2010) 182,000.
Doubling time: 23 years.
Ethnolinguistic composition: mestiços, angolares (descendants of Angolan slaves), forros (descendants of freed slaves), serviçais (alien contract labourers), and tongas (children of serviçais) speak Portuguese; non-Portuguese-speaking Europeans speak French and Spanish.
Religious affiliation (1991): Roman Catholic, about 80.8%; remainder mostly Protestant, predominantly Seventh-day Adventist and an indigenous Evangelical Church.
Major cities (1991): São Tomé 43,420; Trindade 11,388[2]; Santana 6,190[2]; Neves 5,919[2]; Santo Amaro 5,878[2].

Vital statistics

Birth rate per 1,000 population (1995): 34.9 (world avg. 25.0); (1977) legitimate 9.8%; illegitimate 90.2%.
Death rate per 1,000 population (1995): 8.7 (world avg. 9.3).
Natural increase rate per 1,000 population (1995): 26.2 (world avg. 15.7).
Total fertility rate (avg. births per childbearing woman; 1995): 4.4.
Marriage rate per 1,000 population: n.a.
Divorce rate per 1,000 population: n.a.
Life expectancy at birth (1995): male 61.8 years; female 65.6 years.
Major causes of death per 100,000 population (1987): malaria 160.6; direct obstetric causes 76.7; pneumonia 74.0; influenza 61.5; anemias 47.3; hypertensive disease 32.1.

National economy

Budget (1996). Revenue: Db 36,547,000,000 (grants 63.6%; indirect taxes 16.7%, of which import taxes 7.0%, sales taxes 6.0%; nontax revenue 12.0%; direct taxes 7.7%). Expenditures: Db 68,387,000,000 (capital 60.8%; recurrent expenditure 39.2%, of which debt service 14.3%, personnel costs 6.1%, goods and services 5.0%).
Public debt (external, outstanding; 1995): U.S.$260,800,000.
Tourism (1990): receipts from visitors U.S.$2,000,000; expenditures by nationals abroad U.S.$2,000,000.
Production (metric tons except as noted). Agriculture, forestry, fishing (1996): coconuts 26,000, bananas 14,000, taro 7,000, vegetables and melons 3,300, corn (maize) 3,200, cacao 3,000, cereals 3,000, palm kernels 3,000, palmetto 3,000[3], cassava 2,600, fruits (other than melon) 1,900, copra 1,000[4]; livestock (number of live animals) 4,600 goats, 3,900 cattle, 2,400 sheep, 2,000 pigs; roundwood (1995) 9,000 cu m; fish catch (1995) 2,200, principally marine fish and shellfish. Mining and quarrying: some quarrying to support local construction industry. Manufacturing (value in Db; 1995): beer 880,000; clothing 679,000; lumber 369,000; bakery products 350,000; palm oil 228,000; soap 133,000; ceramics 87,000. Construction (1972): buildings authorized 44 (5,561 sq m, of which residential 3,698, mixed residential-commercial 1,361, commercial 502). Energy production (consumption): electricity (kW-hr; 1995) 18,664,000 (11,931,000); coal, none (n.a.); crude petroleum, none (n.a.); petroleum products (metric tons; 1994) none (25,000); natural gas, none (n.a.).
Household income and expenditure. Average household size (1981): 4.0; income per household: n.a.; sources of income: n.a.; expenditure (1995)[5]: food 71.9%, housing and energy 10.2%, transportation and communications 6.4%, clothing and other items 5.3%, household durable goods 2.8%, education and health 1.7%.
Population economically active (1991): total 49,216; activity rate of total population 41.0% (participation rates [1981]: ages 15–64, 61.1%; female 32.4%; unemployed [1994[6]] 22.0%).

Price and earnings indexes (1990 = 100)

	1990	1991	1992	1993	1994	1995
Consumer price index	100.0	152.7	194.4	236.8	326.2	406.3
Earnings index	...	...	...	...	...	...

Gross national product (at current market prices; 1995): U.S.$45,000,000 (U.S.$350 per capita).

Structure of gross domestic product and labour force

	1996 in value Db '000,000	1996 % of total value	1991 labour force	1991 % of labour force
Agriculture	24,583	24.9	13,592	27.6
Mining	...	...	...	...
Manufacturing	5,250	5.3	1,510	3.1
Public utilities			269	0.6
Construction	12,487	12.6	2,866	5.8
Transportation and communications	18,754	19.0	2,186	4.4
Trade			4,451	9.0
Finance	7,484	7.6	176	0.4
Pub. admin., defense	21,788	22.0	5,592	11.4
Services	8,554	8.6	2,369	4.8
Other	...	...	16,205[7]	32.9[7]
TOTAL	98,900	100.0	49,216	100.0

Land use (1994): meadows and pastures 1.3%; agricultural and under permanent cultivation 54.0%; forest, built-on, wasteland, and other 44.7%.

Foreign trade[8]

Balance of trade (current prices)

	1991	1992	1993	1994	1995	1996
U.S.$'000,000	−24.6	−22.7	−25.4	−23.9	−24.2	−19.9
% of total	67.2%	67.8%	65.8%	64.8%	70.3%	67.0%

Imports (1996): U.S.$24,800,000 (capital goods 29.8%, food and other agricultural products 23.8%, petroleum products 15.4%). *Major import sources* (1996): Portugal 29.0%; Angola 13.3%; Belgium 10.1%; Japan 10.1%; France 8.1%; United Kingdom 4.4%; Italy 2.8%; Germany 1.2%; The Netherlands 0.8%; Gabon 0.4%.
Exports (1996): U.S.$4,900,000 (cocoa 96.4%). *Major export destinations* (1996): The Netherlands 63.9%; Germany 20.9%; Portugal 2.0%.

Transport and communications

Transport. Railroads: none. Roads (1994): total length 236 mi, 380 km (paved 66%). Vehicles (1994): passenger cars 4,581; trucks and buses 561. Merchant marine (1992): vessels (100 gross tons and over) 4; total deadweight tonnage 2,277. Air transport (1994): passenger-mi 5,000,000, passenger-km 8,000,000; short ton-mi cargo 700,000, short ton-km cargo 1,000,000; airports (1997) with scheduled flights 2.

Communications

Medium	date	unit	number	units per 1,000 persons
Radio	1996	receivers	31,000	232
Television	1995	receivers	21,000	154
Telephones	1995	main lines	2,500	19
Facsimile machines	1995	units	200	1.5

Education and health

Educational attainment (1981). Percentage of population age 25 and over having: no formal schooling 56.6%; incomplete primary education 18.0%; primary 19.2%; incomplete secondary 4.6%; complete secondary 1.3%; postsecondary 0.3%. *Literacy* (1981): total population age 15 and over literate 28,114 (54.2%); males literate 17,689 (70.2%); females literate 10,425 (39.1%).

Education (1989)

	schools	teachers	students	student/ teacher ratio
Primary (age 6–13)	64	559	19,822	35.5
Secondary (age 14–18)	11[9]	318	7,446	23.4
Voc., teacher tr.	2[9]	18[10]	289	...
Higher	...	...	700[11]	...

Health: physicians (1989) 61 (1 per 1,881 persons); hospital beds (1983) 640 (1 per 158 persons); infant mortality rate per 1,000 live births (1995) 62.1.
Food (1995): daily per capita caloric intake 2,156 (vegetable products 96%, animal products 4%); 92% of FAO recommended minimum requirement.

Military

Total active duty personnel: a gendarmerie of about 900 men was to be established in the early 1990s. *Military expenditure as percentage of GNP* (1980): 1.6% (world 5.4%); per capita expenditure U.S.$6.

[1]Preliminary. [2]1981. [3]1988. [4]1994. [5]Weights based on CPI components. [6]First 10 months. [7]Includes 15,148 unemployed. [8]Import figures are c.i.f. [9]1984–85. [10]Vocational teachers only. [11]Students abroad, 1982–83.

Saudi Arabia

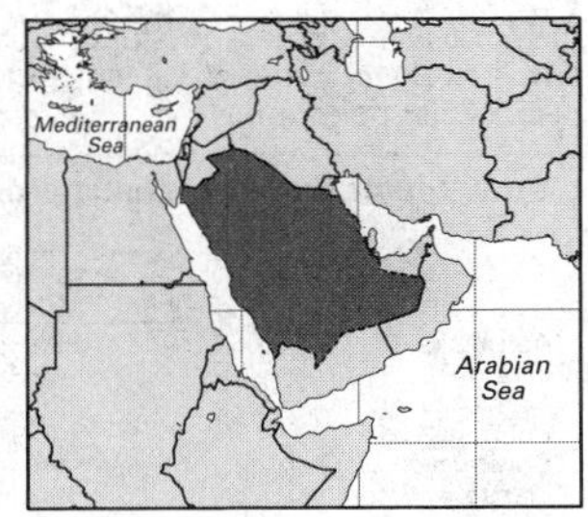

Official name: Al-Mamlakah al-ʿArabīyah as-Saʿūdīyah (Kingdom of Saudi Arabia).
Form of government: monarchy[1].
Head of state and government: King.
Capital: Riyadh.
Official language: Arabic.
Official religion: Islam.
Monetary unit: 1 Saudi riyal (SRls) = 100 halalah; valuation (Oct. 3, 1997) 1 U.S.$ = SRls 3.75; 1 £ = SRls 6.05.

Area and population

Geographic Regions / Administrative Regions[3]	Capitals	area[2] sq mi	area[2] sq km	population 1985 estimate
Al-Gharbīyah (Western)		—	—	3,043,189
Al-Bāḥah	Al-Bāḥah	6,000	15,000	...
Al-Madīnah al-Munawwarah	Medina (Al-Madīnah)	67,000	173,000	...
Makkah al-Mukarramah	Mecca (Makkah)	63,000	164,000	...
Al-Janūbīyah (Southern)		—	—	625,017
ʿAsīr	Abha	31,000	81,000	...
Jīzān	Jīzān	7,000	17,000	...
Najrān	Najrān	46,000	119,000	...
Ash-Shamālīyah (Northern)		—	—	679,476
Al-Ḥudūd ash-Shamālīyah (Northern Borders)	ʿArʿar	46,000	120,000	...
Al-Jawf	Sakākah	54,000	139,000	...
Tabūk	Tabūk	42,000	108,000	...
Ash-Sharqīyah (Eastern)		—	—	3,030,765
Ash-Sharqīyah (Eastern)	Ad-Dammām	274,000	710,000	...
Al-Wūsṭā (Central)		—	—	3,632,092
Ḥā'il	Ḥā'il	48,000	125,000	...
Al-Qaṣīm	Buraydah	25,000	65,000	...
Ar-Riyāḍ	Riyadh (Ar-Riyāḍ)	159,000	412,000	...
TOTAL		868,000	2,248,000	11,010,539[4]

Demography

Population (1997): 19,072,000.
Density (1997): persons per sq mi 22.1, persons per sq km 8.5.
Urban-rural (1995): urban 80.2%; rural 19.8%.
Sex distribution (1995): male 55.72%; female 44.28%.
Age breakdown (1995): under 15, 41.9%; 15–29, 24.5%; 30–44, 19.7%; 45–59, 9.5%; 60–74, 3.6%; 75 and over, 0.8%.
Population projection: (2000) 21,257,000; (2010) 28,880,000.
Doubling time: 23 years.
Ethnic composition (1983): Saudi 82.0%; Yemeni 9.6%; other 8.4%.
Religious affiliation (1980): Sunnī Muslim 95.5%; Shīʿī Muslim 3.3%; Christian 0.8%; other 0.4%.
Major cities (1991): Riyadh (Ar-Riyāḍ) 1,800,000; Jiddah 1,500,000; Mecca (Makkah) 630,000; Aṭ-Ṭā'if 410,000; Medina 400,000.

Vital statistics

Birth rate per 1,000 population (1990–95): 35.1 (world avg. 25.0).
Death rate per 1,000 population (1990–95): 4.7 (world avg. 9.3).
Natural increase rate per 1,000 population (1990–95): 30.4 (world avg. 15.7).
Total fertility rate (avg. births per childbearing woman; 1990–95): 6.4.
Life expectancy at birth (1990–95): male 68.4 years; female 71.4 years.
Major causes of death per 100,000 population: n.a.

National economy

Budget (1997). Revenue: SRls 164,000,000,000 (oil revenues [1996] 76.0%). Expenditures: SRls 181,000,000,000 (defense and security 37.6%, education 23.0%, health and social development 7.9%, transportation and communications 3.8%, municipal services 3.0%).
Public debt (external, outstanding; 1991): U.S.$2,893,000,000.
Production (metric tons except as noted). Agriculture, forestry, fishing (1997): wheat 1,500,000; barley 800,000; dates 597,000; tomatoes 500,000; potatoes 435,000; watermelons 410,000; grapes 135,000; cucumbers and gherkins 135,000; eggplants 70,000; pumpkins, squash, and gourds 70,000; carrots 30,000; millet 13,700; livestock (number of live animals) 7,800,000 sheep, 4,400,000 goats, 422,000 camels; fish catch (1994) 49,920. Mining and quarrying (1995): gypsum (1994) 337,573; gold 8,080 kg. Manufacturing (value added in U.S.$'000,000; 1994): industrial chemicals 2,663; cement, glass, and other nonmetal mineral products 875; refined petroleum 818; iron and steel 516; food, beverages, and tobacco 457; metal products 358; plastic products 206. Construction (1991): residential 16,077,677 sq m; nonresidential 2,204,894 sq m. Energy production (consumption): electricity (kW-hr; 1994) 66,760,000,000 (66,760,000,000); coal, n.a. (n.a.); crude petroleum (barrels; 1996) 2,993,000,000 ([1994] 588,700,000); petroleum products (metric tons; 1994) 87,769,000 (34,482,000); natural gas (cu m; 1994) 37,701,000,000 (37,701,000,000).
Land use (1994): forested 0.8%; meadows and pastures 55.8%; agricultural and under permanent cultivation 1.8%; built-on, waste, and other 41.6%.
Population economically active (1994): total 5,614,000; activity rate of total population 32.2% (participation rates [1988] ages 15–64, 59.1%; female 3.5%; unemployed [1997] *c.* 25%).

Price and earnings indexes (1990 = 100)

	1990	1991	1992	1993	1994	1995	1996
Consumer price index	100.0	104.6	104.2	105.0	105.7	111.1	112.0
Earnings index	...	...	...	...	...	...	...

Gross national product (1995): U.S.$133,540,000,000 (U.S.$7,040 per capita).

Structure of gross domestic product and labour force

	1996 in value[5] SRls '000,000	1996 % of total value	1990 labour force	1990 % of labour force
Agriculture	32,162	6.3	569,200	9.9
Mining }	185,190	36.4	3,500	0.1
Oil sector }			46,800	0.8
Manufacturing	47,652	9.4	374,900	6.5
Construction	44,447	8.7	944,100	16.4
Public utilities	853	0.2	126,900	2.2
Transp. and commun.	31,507	6.2	262,300	4.5
Trade	34,258	6.7	898,300	15.6
Finance	28,002[6]	5.5[6]	99,000	1.7
Pub. admin., defense	88,873	17.5	624,800	10.8
Services	13,800	2.7 }	1,822,000	31.6
Other	2,542[7]	0.5[7] }		
TOTAL	509,286	100.0[8]	5,771,800	100.0[8]

Household income and expenditure. Average household size (1992) 6.1; income per household: n.a.; sources of income: n.a.; expenditure (1988)[9]: food 37%, housing 21%, transportation and communications 15%, clothing 8%, household furnishings 7%, education and entertainment 2%.
Tourism (in U.S.$'000,000): receipts (1989) 2,050; expenditures (1988) 2,000.
Pilgrims to Mecca from abroad (1996): more than 2,000,000.

Foreign trade[10]

Balance of trade (current prices)

	1991	1992	1993	1994	1995	1996
U.S.$'000,000	+21,818	+20,039	+16,522	+21,289	+24,390	+31,345
% of total	29.6%	24.9%	24.2%	33.3%	32.2%	38.2%

Imports (1996): SRls 103,979,000,000 (machinery and appliances 21.0%, transport equipment 15.3%, metals and metal articles 10.0%, chemicals and chemical products 8.1%, vegetables 7.4%, textiles and clothing 7.3%, live animals and animal products 4.9%). *Major import sources:* U.S. 21.9%; U.K. 9.0%; Germany 7.5%; Japan 7.0%; Italy 4.7%; Switzerland 4.7%.
Exports (1996): SRls 212,353,000,000[11] (petroleum 88.6%, of which crude 72.3%; petrochemicals 4.9%). *Major export destinations*[12]: Japan 16.9%; U.S. 15.0%; S. Korea 10.6%; Singapore 7.9%; France 4.5%; India 3.3%.

Transport and communications

Transport. Railroads (1995): route length 1,390 km; (1993–94) passenger-km 139,000,000; (1993–94) metric ton-km cargo 816,000,000. Roads (1995): total length 159,000 km (paved 42.7%). Vehicles (1995): passenger cars 1,710,000; trucks and buses 1,172,600. Merchant marine (1992): vessels (100 gross tons and over) 301; total deadweight tonnage 1,381,651. Air transport (1995)[13]: passenger-km 18,501,400,000; metric ton-km cargo 894,900,000; airports (1997) with scheduled flights 25.

Communications

Medium	date	unit	number	units per 1,000 persons
Daily newspapers	1994	circulation	950,000	54
Radio	1995	receivers	3,800,000	213
Television	1995	receivers	4,600,000	257
Telephones	1995	main lines	1,719,400	96
Cellular telephones	1995	subscribers	16,000	0.9
Facsimile machines	1995	units	78,700	4.4
Personal computers	1995	units	600,000	34

Education and health

Educational attainment (1986). Percentage of population age 25 and over having: no formal schooling 31.8%; primary, secondary, or higher education 68.2%. *Literacy* (1995): percentage of population age 15 and over literate 62.8%; males literate 71.5%; females literate 50.2%.

Education (1995–96)

	schools	teachers	students	student/teacher ratio
Primary (age 6–12)	11,217	169,321	2,248,122	13.3
Secondary (age 13–18)	6,346[14]	105,056	1,375,753	13.1
Voc., teacher tr.	293[14, 15]	4,473	49,032	11.0
Higher[14]	77	18,039	233,710	13.0

Health (1995): physicians 30,306 (1 per 590 persons); hospital beds 41,916 (1 per 427 persons); infant mortality rate per 1,000 live births (1990–95) 29.0.
Food (1995): daily per capita caloric intake 2,746 (vegetable products 88%, animal products 12%); 113% of FAO recommended minimum requirement.

Military

Total active duty personnel (1997): 105,500 (army 66.4%, navy 12.8%, air force 20.9%). *Military expenditure as percentage of GDP* (1995): 13.5% (world 2.8%); per capita expenditure U.S.$919.

[1]The Consultative Council, which consists of 90 appointed members. [2]Estimated. [3]13 administrative regions created September 1993. [4]Preliminary 1992 census total 16,929,294; detail, n.a. [5]In producers' values at current prices. [6]Finance includes real estate and business services. [7]Other equals import duties less imputed bank services charge. [8]Detail does not add to total given because of rounding. [9]Urban middle-income households only. [10]Import figures are f.o.b. in balance of trade and c.i.f. in commodities and trading partners. [11]Includes re-exports. [12]Based on direction of trade statistics. [13]Domestic and international operation of Saudi Arabian Airlines. [14]1994–95. [15]Includes intermediate colleges.

Internet resources for further information:

- **Embassy of Saudi Arabia, U.S.A. http://www.saudi.net/mainpage.html**

Senegal

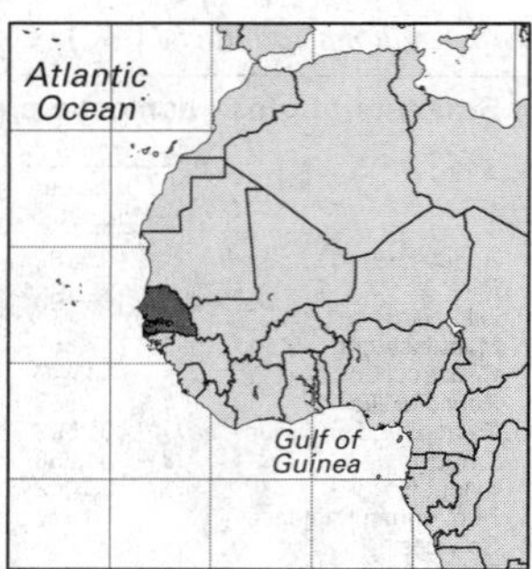

Official name: République du Sénégal (Republic of Senegal).
Form of government: multiparty republic with one legislative house (National Assembly [120]).
Chief of state: President.
Head of government: Prime Minister.
Capital: Dakar.
Official language: French.
Official religion: none.
Monetary unit: 1 CFA franc (CFAF) = 100 centimes; valuation (Oct. 3, 1997) 1 U.S.$ = CFAF 592.29; 1 £ = CFAF 954.76.

Area and population		area		population
				1994
Regions	Capitals	sq mi	sq km	estimate
Dakar	Dakar	212	550	1,869,000
Diourbel	Diourbel	1,683	4,359	750,000
Fatick	Fatick	3,064	7,935	569,000
Kaolack	Kaolack	6,181	16,010	948,000
Kolda	Kolda	8,112	21,011	689,000
Louga	Louga	11,270	29,188	525,000
Saint-Louis	Saint-Louis	17,034	44,117	749,000
Tambacounda	Tambacounda	23,012	59,602	449,000
Thiès	Thiès	2,549	6,601	1,115,000
Ziguinchor	Ziguinchor	2,834	7,339	467,000
TOTAL		75,951	196,712	8,127,000[1]

Demography

Population (1997): 9,404,000.
Density (1997): persons per sq mi 123.8, persons per sq km 47.8.
Urban-rural (1995): urban 42.3%; rural 57.7%.
Sex distribution (1995): male 50.05%; female 49.95%.
Age breakdown (1995): under 15, 44.6%; 15–29, 26.9%; 30–44, 15.5%; 45–59, 8.3%; 60–74, 3.9%; 75 and over, 0.8%.
Population projection: (2000) 10,390,000; (2010) 14,362,000.
Doubling time: 21 years.
Ethnic composition (1988): Wolof 42.7%; Serer 14.9%; Peul (Fulani) 14.4%; Tukulor 9.3%; Diola 5.3%; Malinke (Mandingo) 3.6%; other 9.8%.
Religious affiliation (1996): Sunnī Muslim 92.0%; traditional beliefs and other 6.0%; Christian (predominantly Roman Catholic) 2.0%.
Major cities (1994): Dakar 785,071 (urban agglomeration 1,869,323[2]); Thiès 216,381; Kaolack 193,115; Ziguinchor 161,680; Rufisque 138,837[3]; Saint-Louis 132,444.

Vital statistics

Birth rate per 1,000 population (1996): 45.5 (world avg. 25.0).
Death rate per 1,000 population (1996): 11.8 (world avg. 9.3).
Natural increase rate per 1,000 population (1996): 33.7 (world avg. 15.7).
Total fertility rate (avg. births per childbearing woman; 1996): 6.3.
Marriage rate per 1,000 population: n.a[4].
Divorce rate per 1,000 population: n.a.
Life expectancy at birth (1996): male 53.7 years; female 59.3 years.
Major causes of death (percentage of officially confirmed deaths from infectious diseases only; 1988): malaria 44.8%; tetanus 17.8%; meningitis 15.3%; tuberculosis of respiratory system 10.4%.

National economy

Budget (1996). Revenue: CFAF 452,600,000,000 (tax revenue 80.7%, grants 11.1%, nontax revenue 8.2%). Expenditures: CFAF 452,000,000,000 (current expenditures 71.8%, development expenditure 28.2%).
Production (metric tons except as noted). Agriculture, forestry, fishing (1996): sugarcane 883,000, peanuts (groundnuts) 816,000, millet 650,000, paddy rice 160,000, sorghum 125,000, corn (maize) 110,000, oil palm fruit 70,000, cassava 56,000, seed cotton 37,000; livestock (number of live animals) 4,800,000 sheep, 3,250,000 goats, 2,900,000 cattle, 502,000 horses; roundwood (1995) 5,220,000 cu m; fish catch (1995) 261,000. Mining and quarrying (1996): phosphate 1,376,000; salt (1994) 87,600. Manufacturing (1993): cement (1994) 590,000; phosphoric acid (1996) 258,000; fertilizers 147,900; wheat flour (1995) 110,000; sugar 46,100; soap 35,700; canned fish 22,476; cigarettes (1992) 3,350,000,000 units; plastic footwear 507,500 pairs. Construction (authorized; 1993)[5]: residential 357,000 sq m; nonresidential 235,000 sq m. Energy production (consumption): electricity (kW-hr; 1994) 769,000,000 (408,000,000); coal, none (none); crude petroleum (barrels; 1994) none (6,392,000); petroleum products (metric tons; 1994) 856,000,000 (903,000,000); natural gas, none (none).
Population economically active (1988): total 2,347,556; activity rate of total population 34.0% (participation rates: ages 15–60, 53.1%; female 25.6%; unemployed [1992] 24.4%).

Price and earnings indexes (1990 = 100)	1991	1992	1993	1994	1995	1996	1997
Consumer price index[5]	98.2	98.1	97.6	129.1	139.2	143.1	144.4
Hourly earnings index[6]	100.0	100.0	100.0	...	...	...	...

Household income and expenditure. Average household size (1991) 8.7; average annual income per household: n.a.; sources of income: n.a.; expenditure (early 1980s): food 49%, clothing and footwear 11%, housing 7%, education 6%.

Public debt (external, outstanding; 1995): U.S.$3,191,000,000.
Gross national product (at current market prices; 1995): U.S.$5,070,000,000 (U.S.$600 per capita).

Structure of gross domestic product and labour force	1996		1991	
	in value CFAF '000,000,000[7]	% of total value	labour force	% of labour force
Agriculture	360.8	21.4	1,789,467	65.3
Mining	2.6	0.2	1,998	0.1
Manufacturing	228.3	13.6	161,124	5.9
Public utilities	36.8	2.2	...	...
Construction	66.5	4.0	60,935	2.2
Transp. and commun.	159.0	9.4	58,081	2.1
Trade	355.4	21.1	378,241	13.8
Finance	...	...	4,623	0.2
Services	190.6	11.3	...	...
Pub. admin., defense	281.9	16.8	268,721	9.8
Other	—	—	16,286	0.6
TOTAL	1,681.9	100.0	2,739,476	100.0

Tourism (1995): receipts from visitors U.S.$130,000,000; expenditures by nationals abroad U.S.$75,000,000.
Land use (1994): forested 39.5%; meadows and pastures 29.6%; agricultural and under permanent cultivation 12.2%; other 18.7%.

Foreign trade[8]

Balance of trade (current prices)	1990	1991	1992	1993	1994	1995
U.S.$'000,000	−553	−447	−489	−630	−522	−664
% of total	27.1%	25.5%	26.4%	35.5%	29.2%	32.8%

Imports (1995): U.S.$1,344,000,000 (agricultural products 34.5%, of which rice 7.1%, fixed vegetable oils 5.2%; capital goods 15.0%[9]; refined petroleum 11.0%[9]. *Major import sources:* France 37.8%; Cameroon 7.9%; Nigeria 6.9%; Italy 5.4%; Thailand 4.6%.
Exports (1995): U.S.$680,000,000 ([9]fish and crustaceans 28.0%; chemical products 12.0%; peanut [groundnut] oil 11.0%; phosphates 3.0%). *Major export destinations*[9]: France 30.0%; Italy 13.0%; Mali 7.0%; Spain 5.0%; India 4.0%.

Transport and communications

Transport. Railroads: (1995) route length 562 mi, 904 km; (1993) passenger-mi 128,000,000, passenger-km 206,000,000; short ton-mi cargo 476,000,000, metric ton-km cargo 695,000,000. Roads (1995): total length 9,060 mi, 14,580 km (paved 29%). Vehicles (1995): passenger cars 80,600, trucks and buses 32,410. Merchant marine (1992): vessels (100 gross tons and over) 183; total deadweight tonnage 27,473. Air transport (1996)[10]: passenger-mi 139,644,000, passenger-km 224,736,000; short ton-mi cargo 11,247,000, metric ton-km cargo 16,420,000; airports (1996) with scheduled flights 7.

Communications Medium	date	unit	number	units per 1,000 persons
Daily newspapers	1994	circulation	50,000	5.9
Radio	1996	receivers	850,000	93
Television	1995	receivers	61,000	6.9
Telephones	1995	main lines	82,000	9.3
Cellular telephones	1995	subscribers	100	0.01
Personal computers	1995	units	60,000	6.8

Education and health

Educational attainment (1988). Percentage of population age 6–34 having: no formal schooling 62.6%; primary education 25.7%; secondary 8.4%; higher 0.8%; other 2.5%. *Literacy* (1995): percentage of total population age 15 and over literate 1,523,000 (33.1%); males literate 985,000 (43.0%); females literate 538,000 (23.2%).

Education (1992–93)	schools	teachers	students	student/ teacher ratio
Primary (age 6–12)	2,454	12,711	738,550	58.1
Secondary (age 13–18)	359	5,509	182,140	33.1
Vocational	19	182	7,301	40.1
Higher[11]	2	784	16,733	21.3

Health (1992): physicians 520 (1 per 14,825 persons); hospital beds 7,408 (1 per 1,041 persons); infant mortality rate per 1,000 live births (1996): 64.0.
Food (1995): daily per capita caloric intake 2,416 (vegetable products 91%, animal products 9%); 102% of FAO recommended minimum requirement.

Military

Total active duty personnel (1996): 13,400[12] (army 89.9%, navy 5.2%, air force 4.9%). *Military expenditure as percentage of GNP* (1995): 1.6% (world 2.8%); per capita expenditure U.S.$9.

[1]Detail does not add to total given because of rounding. [2]Urbanized area of Pikine (1994 population estimate 855,287) is within Dakar urban agglomeration. [3]Within Dakar urban agglomeration. [4]In 1996 about half of all women lived in polygynous unions. [5]Capital region only. [6]Index refers to the *S.M.I.G. (salaire minimum interprofessionnel garanti)*, a form of minimum professional wage. [7]At constant 1987 prices. [8]Imports f.o.b.; exports c.i.f. [9]Estimated figure(s). [10]Represents 1/11 of total international scheduled traffic of Air Afrique (government-supported airline of 11 West African countries). [11]Universities only; 1994–95. [12]Excludes 1,500 French troops.

Internet resources for further information:
- **République du Sénégal (French language only)**
http://www.primature.sn/

Seychelles

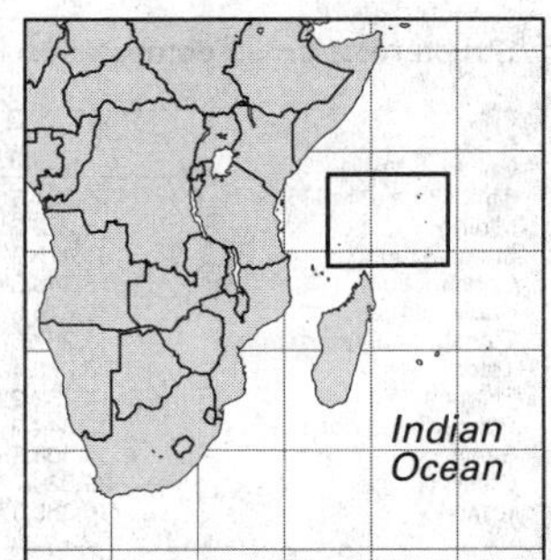

Official name: Repiblik Sesel (Creole); Republic of Seychelles (English); République des Seychelles (French).
Form of government: multiparty republic with one legislative house (National Assembly [33]).
Head of state and government: President.
Capital: Victoria.
Official languages: none[1].
Official religion: none.
Monetary unit: 1 Seychelles rupee (SR) = 100 cents; valuation (Oct. 3, 1997) 1 U.S.$ = SR 5.05; 1 £ = SR 8.14.

Area and population

		area		population
Island Groups	**Capital**	sq mi	sq km	1987 census
Central (Granitic) group				
La Digue and satellites	—	6	15	1,926
Mahé and satellites	Victoria	61	158	61,183
Praslin and satellites	—	16	42	5,002
Silhouette	—	8	20	191
Other islands	—	2	4	0
Outer (Coralline) islands	—	83	214	296
TOTAL		176	455[2]	68,598

Demography

Population (1997): 77,300.
Density (1997): persons per sq mi 439.2, persons per sq km 169.9.
Urban-rural (1990): urban 59.3%; rural 40.7%.
Sex distribution (1997): male 48.37%; female 51.63%.
Age breakdown (1997): under 15, 30.2%; 15–29, 31.1%; 30–44, 21.9%; 45–59, 8.2%; 60–74, 6.0%; 75 and over, 2.6%.
Population projection: (2000) 80,900; (2010) 94,100.
Doubling time: 47 years.
Ethnic composition (1983): Seychellois Creole (mixture of Asian, African, and European) 89.1%; Indian 4.7%; Malagasy 3.1%; Chinese 1.6%; English 1.5%.
Religious affiliation (1996): Roman Catholic 88.6%; other Christian (mostly Anglican) 7.7%; Hindu 0.7%; other 3.0%.
Major city (1993): Victoria 25,000.

Vital statistics

Birth rate per 1,000 population (1997): 20.0 (world avg. 25.0); (1993) legitimate 21.6%; illegitimate 78.4%.
Death rate per 1,000 population (1997): 7.0 (world avg. 9.3).
Natural increase rate per 1,000 population (1997): 13.0 (world avg. 15.7).
Total fertility rate (avg. births per childbearing woman; 1997): 2.0.
Marriage rate per 1,000 population (1993): 11.3.
Divorce rate per 1,000 population (1993): 1.1.
Life expectancy at birth (1997): male 65.7 years; female 75.6 years.
Major causes of death per 100,000 population (1993): diseases of the circulatory system 239.4, of which cerebrovascular disease 72.0; malignant neoplasms (cancers) 141.2; diseases of the respiratory system 87.2, of which pneumonia 23.5; infectious and parasitic diseases 49.8; diseases of the digestive system 47.1; accidents and adverse effects 45.7.

National economy

Budget (1997). Revenue: SR 1,377,900,000 (customs taxes and duties 40.9%, dividends and interest 10.8%, business taxes 10.6%, transfers from Social Security Fund 7.3%, administrative fees 7.0%, fees and fines 4.1%, grants 2.9%). Expenditures: SR 1,363,100,000 (debt service 18.6%, capital projects 11.0%, education 10.6%, health 8.6%, social security 7.3%, tourism and transport 6.7%, defense 3.7%).
Tourism (1996): receipts from visitors SR 531,400,000; expenditures by nationals abroad U.S.$24,000,000[3].
Land use (1994): forested 11.1%; agricultural and under permanent cultivation 15.6%; built-on, wasteland, and other 73.3%.
Gross national product (1995): U.S.$487,000,000 (U.S.$6,620 per capita).

Structure of gross domestic product and labour force

	1996			
	in value SR '000,000	% of total value	labour force[4]	% of labour force
Agriculture	104.0	4.1	1,717	6.5
Mining, manufacturing, and construction	571.0	22.5	5,153	19.6
Tourism	240.0	9.4	4,846	18.4
Transportation and communications	726.5	28.6	4,076	15.5
Finance	255.0	10.0		
Public admin., defense	351.9	13.8	10,484	39.9
Other	293.3	11.5		
TOTAL	2,541.7	100.0[2]	26,276	100.0[2]

Production (metric tons except as noted). Agriculture, forestry, fishing (1997): coconuts 3,600, bananas 1,850, copra 1,000[5], cinnamon 650, tea 250; livestock (number of live animals) 18,200 pigs, 4,900 goats, 2,100 cattle, 540,000 chickens; fish catch (1996) 4,508, of which (1989) jack 36.9%, snapper 20.8%, mackerel 6.7%, kawakawa 5.3%. Mining and quarrying (1994): guano 5,000. Manufacturing (1996): canned tuna 12,708; soft drinks 78,520 hectolitres; beer and stout 63,650 hectolitres; cigarettes 62,000,000 units. Energy production (consumption): electricity (kW-hr; 1994) 126,000,000 (126,000,000); coal, none (n.a.); crude petroleum, none (n.a.); petroleum products (metric tons; 1994) none (55,000); natural gas, none (n.a.).
Population economically active (1993): total 28,100; activity rate of total population 38.9% (participation rates: ages 15–64 [1989] 74.3%; female [1989] 42.5%; unemployed 11.5%).

Price and earnings indexes (1990 = 100)

	1991	1992	1993	1994	1995	1996	1997[6]
Consumer price index	102.0	105.3	106.7	106.7	108.4	107.2	107.4
Monthly earnings index	100.6	117.3	115.0	115.4	120.2	...	...

Public debt (external, outstanding; 1995): U.S.$151,100,000.
Household income and expenditure. Average household size (1987) 4.5; average annual income per household (1978) SR 18,480 (U.S.$2,658); sources of income: wages and salaries 77.2%, self-employment 3.8%, transfer payments 3.2%; expenditure (1991–92): food and beverages 47.6%, housing 15.1%, clothing and footwear 8.6%, transportation 8.0%, energy and water 7.4%, recreation 6.7%, household and personal goods 6.6%.

Foreign trade

Balance of trade (current prices)

	1991	1992	1993	1994	1995	1996
SR '000,000	−652.2	−735.2	−969.8	−786.7	−855.7	−1,188.7
% of total	55.8%	59.9%	64.7%	60.6%	62.8%	46.1%

Imports (1996): SR 1,882,419,000 (machinery and transport equipment 44.7%, of which aircraft and spare parts 24.6%, electrical machinery 7.9%, nuclear reactors, boilers, and other heavy machinery 6.9%; manufactured goods 18.7%, of which metal manufactures 5.0%, paper and wood products 3.6%; food, beverages, and tobacco 18.3%; mineral fuels [including petroleum], lubricants, and related materials 11.2%; chemicals 4.8%). *Major import sources*: United States 26.5%; United Kingdom 11.3%; Yemen 10.6%; South Africa 10.4%; Singapore 9.2%; France 7.0%; Italy 3.6%; India 2.4%; Japan 2.2%; Germany 2.1%; Spain 1.8%; Thailand 1.8%; The Netherlands 1.3%.
Exports (1996): SR 693,744,000[7] (canned tuna 24.5%; petroleum products 21.8%[8]; other fish, including dried shark fins 2.1%; frozen prawns 1.6%; cinnamon bark 0.7%). *Major export destinations* (1995)[9]: China 15.0%; United Kingdom 12.4%; Thailand 11.5%; India 3.5%; Germany 2.6%; United States 1.8%; Japan 1.8%.

Transport and communications

Transport. Railroads: none. Roads (1996): total length 214 mi, 345 km (paved 80%). Vehicles (1995): passenger cars 5,100; trucks and buses 2,000. Merchant marine (1992): vessels (100 gross tons and over) 9; total deadweight tonnage 3,337. Air transport (1996): passenger arrivals 151,000, passenger departures 151,000; metric ton cargo unloaded 3,390, metric ton cargo loaded 1,112; airports (1997) with scheduled flights 2.

Communications

Medium	date	unit	number	units per 1,000 persons
Daily newspapers	1995	circulation	3,000	41.0
Radio	1995	receivers	50,000	666.9
Television	1995	receivers	13,000	173.4
Telephones	1996	main lines	15,712	206.4
Cellular telephones	1996	subscribers	1,043	13.7
Facsimile machines	1996	units	650[10]	8.5

Education and health

Educational attainment (1987). Percentage of population age 12 and over having: no formal schooling 7.8%; primary education 51.5%; some secondary 12.2%; complete secondary 13.4%; vocational 9.9%; postsecondary 3.1%; unspecified 2.1%. *Literacy* (1987): total population age 15 and over literate 37,984 (84.2%); males literate 18,427 (82.9%); females literate 19,557 (85.7%).

Education (1997)

	schools	teachers	students	student/ teacher ratio
Primary (age 6–15)	27[3]	633	9,825	15.5
Secondary (age 16–18)	20[11]	440	6,548	14.9
Voc., teacher tr.	1[11]	134	1,338	10.0

Health[12] (1996): physicians 84 (1 per 906 persons); hospital beds 414 (1 per 184 persons); infant mortality rate per 1,000 live births (1997) 17.0.
Food (1995): daily per capita caloric intake 2,428 (vegetable products 83%, animal products 17%); 104% of FAO recommended minimum requirement.

Military

Total active duty personnel (1997): 400[13]. *Military expenditure as percentage of GNP* (1995): 3.9% (world 2.8%); per capita expenditure U.S.$192.

[1]Creole, English, and French are all national languages per 1993 constitution. [2]Detail does not add to total given because of rounding. [3]1995. [4]Excludes unemployed, self-employed, and domestic workers. [5]1993. [6]June. [7]Includes SR 488,711,000 of reexports. [8]Items reexported. [9]Domestic export only. [10]Number of subscribers. [11]1994. [12]Physicians and hospital beds in government hospitals only. [13]All services form part of the army.

Internet resources for further information:
- **UNDP Seychelles http://www.intnet.mu/undp/indexsey.htm**

Sierra Leone

Official name: Republic of Sierra Leone.
Form of government: military regime[1].
Head of state and government: President.
Capital: Freetown.
Official language: English.
Official religion: none.
Monetary unit: 1 leone (Le) = 100 cents; valuation (Oct. 3, 1997) 1 U.S.$ = Le 780; 1 £ = Le 1,257.

Area and population

Provinces / Districts	Capitals	area sq mi	area sq km	population 1985 census[2]
Eastern Province	Kenema	6,005	15,553	960,551
Kailahun	Kailahun	1,490	3,859	233,839
Kenema	Kenema	2,337	6,053	337,055
Kono	Sefadu	2,178	5,641	389,657
Northern Province	Makeni	13,875	35,936	1,259,641
Bombali	Makeni	3,083	7,985	317,729
Kambia	Kambia	1,200	3,108	186,231
Koinaduga	Kabala	4,680	12,121	183,286
Port Loko	Port Loko	2,208	5,719	329,344
Tonkolili	Magburaka	2,704	7,003	243,051
Southern Province	Bo	7,604	19,694	741,377
Bo	Bo	2,015	5,219	268,671
Bonthe (incl. Sherbro)	Bonthe	1,339	3,468	105,007
Moyamba	Moyamba	2,665	6,902	250,514
Pujehun	Pujehun	1,585	4,105	117,185
Western Area[3]	Freetown	215	557	554,243
TOTAL		27,699	71,740	3,515,812

Demography

Population (1997): 4,424,000.
Density (1997): persons per sq mi 159.7, persons per sq km 61.7.
Urban-rural (1996): urban 37.0%; rural 63.0%.
Sex distribution (1996): male 49.02%; female 50.98%.
Age breakdown (1995): under 15, 44.2%; 15–29, 26.2%; 30–44, 15.7%; 45–59, 9.0%; 60–74, 4.2%; 75 and over, 0.7%.
Population projection: (2000) 5,069,000; (2010) 6,366,000.
Doubling time: 29 years.
Ethnic composition (1983): Mende 34.6%; Temne 31.7%; Limba 8.4%; Kono 5.2%; Bullom-Sherbro 3.7%; Fulani 3.7%; Kuranko 3.5%; Yalunka 3.5%; Kissi 2.3%; other 3.4%.
Religious affiliation (1993): Sunnī Muslim 60.0%; traditional beliefs 30.0%; Christian 10.0%.
Major cities (1985): Freetown 469,776; Koidu–New Sembehun 80,000; Bo 26,000; Kenema 13,000; Makeni 12,000.

Vital statistics

Birth rate per 1,000 population (1990–95): 49.1 (world avg. 25.0); legitimate, n.a.; illegitimate, n.a.
Death rate per 1,000 population (1990–95): 25.1 (world avg. 9.3).
Natural increase rate per 1,000 population (1990–95): 24.0 (world avg. 15.7).
Total fertility rate (avg. births per childbearing woman; 1990–95): 6.5.
Marriage rate per 1,000 population: n.a.
Divorce rate per 1,000 population: n.a.
Life expectancy at birth (1990–95): male 41.4 years; female 44.6 years.
Major causes of death per 100,000 population: n.a.; however, the major diseases are malaria, tuberculosis, leprosy, whooping cough, measles, tetanus, and diarrhea.

National economy

Budget (1995–96). Revenue: Le 69,700,000,000 (customs duties 49.0%; excise taxes 20.2%; personal income tax 7.7%; corporate income tax 6.8%). Expenditures: Le 141,941,000,000 (recurrent expenditures 81.5%, of which defense 34.0%, debt service 11.3%, education 8.0%, health 4.3%, social security 1.6%; capital expenditures 18.5%).
Production (metric tons except as noted). Agriculture, forestry, fishing (1996): rice 391,700, cassava 281,400, sweet potatoes 46,400, peanuts (groundnuts) 35,800, tomatoes 32,000, palm kernels 29,160, plantains 26,000, coffee 25,000, sugarcane 21,000, millet 20,700, sorghum 20,500, cacao beans 10,000; livestock (number of live animals) 360,200 cattle, 301,900 sheep, 165,800 goats, 50,000 pigs, 6,000,000 chickens; roundwood (1995) 3,327,600 cu m; fish catch (1995) 62,568. Mining and quarrying (1995–96): bauxite 728,000[4]; rutile and ilmenite (titanium ores) 203,000[4]; diamonds 216,000 carats; gold 3,949 oz[5]. Manufacturing (value added in Le '000,000; 1993): food 36,117; chemicals 10,560; earthenware 1,844; printing and publishing 1,171; metal products 1,073; furniture 647. Construction (value added in Le; 1994–95): 15,788,200,000. Energy production (consumption): electricity (kW-hr; 1994) 237,000,000 (237,000,000); coal, none (n.a.); crude petroleum (barrels; 1994) none (2,148,000); petroleum products (metric tons; 1994) 168,000 (138,000); natural gas, none (n.a.).
Household income and expenditure. Average household size (1985) 6.6; average annual income per household (1984): U.S.$320; sources of income (1984): self-employment 61.6%, wages and salaries 27.9%, other 10.5%; expenditure (1989): food 66.2%, clothing 9.9%, housing 5.8%, transportation 4.4%, household goods 4.0%, recreation and education 3.8%, health 3.5%.
Gross national product (1995): U.S.$762,000,000 (U.S.$180 per capita).

Structure of gross domestic product and labour force

	1994–95 in value Le '000,000	1994–95 % of total value	1991 labour force	1991 % of labour force
Agriculture	275,327.5	38.8	945,000	61.7
Mining	119,229.2	16.8		
Manufacturing	61,475.3	8.6	275,000	18.0
Construction	15,788.2	2.2		
Public utilities	2,816.8	0.4		
Transp. and commun.	61,267.5	8.6		
Trade[6]	98,270.1	13.8		
Finance	14,732.2	2.1		
Pub. admin., defense	19,844.9	2.8	312,000	20.3
Services	12,308.9	1.7		
Other	29,329.7[7]	4.2[7]		
TOTAL	710,389.3[8]	100.0	1,532,000	100.0

Public debt (external, outstanding; 1995): U.S.$968,000,000.
Population economically active (1991): total 1,532,000; activity rate of total population 35.9% (participation rates: ages 10–64, 53.3%; female 32.4%; unemployed [registered; 1992] 10.6%).

Price index (1990 = 100)

	1990	1991	1992	1993	1994	1995	1996
Consumer price index	100.0	202.7	335.4	409.9	509.1	641.5	790.4

Tourism (1995): receipts U.S.$6,000,000; expenditures U.S.$2,000,000.
Land use (1994): forest 28.5%; pasture 30.7%; agriculture 7.5%; other 33.3%.

Foreign trade[9]

Balance of trade (current prices)

	1991	1992	1993	1994	1995	1996
Le '000,000	−1,542	+2,142	−16,553	−20,742	−85,743	−150,930
% of total	1.7%	1.4%	11.0%	13.3%	70.4%	63.7%

Imports (1995–96): Le 144,896,500,000 (food and live animals 51.6%; fuels and lubricants 11.6%; chemicals 10.2%; machinery and transport equipment 8.9%; beverages and tobacco 2.7%; crude minerals 2.5%). *Major import sources* (1994–95): United States 42.7%; The Netherlands 14.2%; United Kingdom 5.7%; Indonesia 3.7%; Germany 3.0%.
Exports (1995–96): Le 39,935,100,000 (mineral exports 56.4%, of which diamonds 50.6%, rutile [titanium ore] 5.7%; cocoa 5.0%; coffee 3.7%; reexports 4.8%). *Major export destinations* (1994–95): United States 44.8%; United Kingdom 17.3%; Belgium 16.8%; The Netherlands 4.1%; Germany 2.0%.

Transport and communications

Transport. Railroads (1990): length 52 mi, 84 km. Roads (1995): total length 7,254 mi, 11,674 km (paved 11%). Vehicles (1995): passenger cars 20,860; trucks and buses 11,014. Merchant marine (1992): vessels (100 gross tons and over) 62; total deadweight tonnage 18,384. Air transport (1985)[10]: passenger-mi 68,290,000, passenger-km 109,903,000; short ton-mi cargo 1,400,000, metric ton-km cargo 2,044,000; airports (1997) with scheduled flights 1.

Communications

Medium	date	unit	number	units per 1,000 persons
Daily newspapers	1995	circulation	9,200	2
Radio	1995	receivers	330,000	72
Television	1995	receivers	1,600	0.3
Telephones	1995	main lines	16,600	4

Education and health

Educational attainment (1985). Percentage of population age 5 and over having: no formal schooling 64.1%; primary education 18.7%; secondary 9.7%; higher 1.5%. *Literacy* (1995): total population age 15 and over literate 791,000 (31.4%); males literate 555,000 (45.4%); females literate 236,000 (18.2%).

Education (1992–93)

	schools	teachers	students	student/teacher ratio
Primary (age 5–11)	1,643	10,595	267,425	25.2
Secondary (age 12–18)	167	4,313	70,900	16.4
Voc., teacher tr.	44	709	7,756	10.9
Higher[11]	2	257	2,571	10.0

Health: physicians (1992) 404 (1 per 10,832 persons); hospital beds (1988) 4,025 (1 per 980 persons); infant mortality rate (1990–95) 166.
Food (1995): daily per capita caloric intake 2,029 (vegetable products 96%, animal products 4%); 88% of FAO recommended minimum requirement.

Military

Total active duty personnel (1996): 14,200 (army 98.6%, navy 1.4%, air force, none). *Military expenditure as percentage of GNP* (1995): 4.6% (world 2.8%); per capita expenditure U.S.$9.

[1]Military takeover from May 1997; constitution suspended. [2]Preliminary figures exclude adjustment for underenumeration; adjusted total is 3,760,000. [3]Not officially a province; the administration of the Western Area is split among Greater Freetown (the city and its suburbs) and other administrative bodies. [4]1994–95; production ceased January 1995 with seizure of mines by rebel forces. [5]1994–95. [6]Includes hotels. [7]Import duties less imputed bank service charges. [8]Detail does not add to total given because of rounding. [9]Import c.i.f.; exports f.o.b. [10]International flights only. [11]1990–91.

Internet resources for further information:
- **Sierra Leone http://www.Sierra-Leone.org**

Singapore

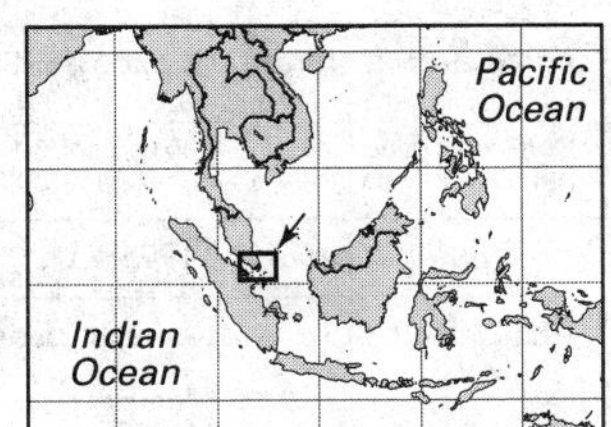

Official name: Hsin-chia-p'o Kung-ho-kuo (Mandarin Chinese); Republik Singapura (Malay); Singapore Kudiyarasu (Tamil); Republic of Singapore (English).
Form of government: unitary multiparty republic with one legislative house (Parliament [90[1]]).
Chief of state: President.
Head of government: Prime Minister.
Capital: Singapore.
Official languages: Chinese; Malay; Tamil; English.
Official religion: none.
Monetary unit: 1 Singapore dollar (S$) = 100 cents; valuation (Oct. 3, 1997) 1 U.S.$ = S$1.54; 1 £ = S$2.49.

Population (1990 census)

Census division[2]	population	Census division[2]	population	Census division[2]	population
Alexandra	27,245	Henderson	18,445	Nee Soon East	58,651
Aljunied	51,669	Hong Kah Central	48,379	Nee Soon South	49,771
Ang Mo Kio	35,814	Hong Kah North	33,265	Pasir Panjang	35,824
Ayer Rajah	44,977	Hong Kah South	37,900	Paya Lebar	41,903
Bedok	22,032	Hougang	36,774	Potong Pasir	32,992
Boon Lay	39,249	Jalan Besar	28,298	Punggol	68,270
Boon Teck	22,652	Jalan Kayu	34,907	Queenstown	19,676
Braddell Heights	47,738	Joo Chiat	35,777	Radin Mas	35,730
Brickworks	10,593	Jurong	74,696	Sembawang	28,039
Bukit Batok	44,918	Kaki Bukit	32,782	Serangoon Gardens	44,702
Bukit Gombak	46,149	Kallang	34,178	Siglap	36,022
Bukit Merah	18,666	Kampong Chai Chee	33,928	Tampines East	41,474
Bukit Panjang	95,827	Kampong Glam	29,481	Tampines North	73,634
Bukit Timah	47,056	Kampong Kembangan	33,510	Tampines West	38,833
Buona Vista	23,873	Kampong Ubi	40,682	Tanah Merah	32,314
Cairnhill	48,445	Kebun Baru	36,878	Tanglin	43,544
Changi	50,003	Kim Keat	28,538	Tanjong Pagar	29,217
Changkat	41,995	Kim Seng	23,683	Teck Ghee	26,622
Cheng San	27,821	Kolam Ayer	22,420	Telok Blangah	29,157
Chong Boon	32,174	Kreta Ayer	29,631	Thomson	71,345
Chong Pang	38,613	Kuo Chuan	26,968	Tiong Bahru	27,468
Chua Chu Kang	43,465	Leng Kee	28,886	Toa Payoh	22,811
Clementi	37,635	Macpherson	23,764	Ulu Pandan	42,923
Eunos	52,976	Marine Parade	31,003	West Coast	46,052
Fengshan	27,285	Moulmein	33,872	Whampoa	18,285
Geylang Serai	36,800	Mountbatten	23,891	Yio Chu Kang	28,589
Geylang West	34,560	Nee Soon Central	47,032	Yuhua	32,733
				TOTAL	3,016,379

Demography

Area: 249.5 sq mi, 646.1 sq km.
Population (1997)[3]: 3,104,000.
Density (1997): persons per sq mi 12,441, persons per sq km 4,804.
Urban-rural: urban 100.0%.
Sex distribution (1996): male 50.29%; female 49.71%.
Age breakdown (1996): under 15, 22.8%; 15–29, 22.8%; 30–44, 28.9%; 45–59, 15.5%; 60–74, 7.4%; 75 and over, 2.6%.
Population projection: (2000) 3,289,000; (2010) 3,988,000.
Doubling time: 64 years.
Ethnic composition (1996): Chinese 77.3%; Malay 14.1%; Indian 7.3%.
Religious affiliation (1995):[4] Buddhist 31.9%; Taoist 22.0%; Muslim 14.9%; Christian 12.9%; Hindu 3.3%; traditional beliefs 0.5%; nonreligious 14.5%.

Vital statistics

Birth rate per 1,000 population (1996): 16.0 (world avg. 25.0).
Death rate per 1,000 population (1996): 5.1 (world avg. 9.3).
Natural increase rate per 1,000 population (1996): 10.9 (world avg. 15.7).
Total fertility rate (avg. births per childbearing woman; 1996): 1.7.
Marriage rate per 1,000 population (1996): 7.9.
Divorce rate per 1,000 population (1994): 1.3.
Life expectancy at birth (1996): male 74.4 years; female 78.9 years.
Major causes of death per 100,000 population (1994): diseases of the circulatory system 185.3; malignant neoplasms (cancers) 128.9; diseases of the respiratory system 87.0; accidents, poisoning, and violence 32.5

National economy

Budget (1996). Revenue: S$28,038,000,000 (income tax 34.0%, nontax revenue 21.8%, motor vehicle taxes 8.7%, goods and services tax 6.4%, customs and excise duties 5.9%). Expenditures: S$19,175,000,000 (security 36.5%, education 18.2%, general services 9.1%, communications 5.6%, health 5.5%).
Production (metric tons except as noted). Agriculture, forestry, fishing (1996): vegetables and fruits 5,310; livestock (number of live animals) 2,000,000 chickens; fish catch 9,665. Mining and quarrying (value of output in S$; 1994): granite 75,800,000. Manufacturing (value added in S$'000,000; 1995): machinery and appliances 18,752.6; chemical products 3,113.2; fabricated metal products 2,355.4; transport equipment 2,322.4; paper products 2,064.1. Construction (completed; 1994): residential 3,999,000 sq m; nonresidential 2,213,000 sq m. Energy production (consumption): electricity (kW-hr; 1994) 20,676,000,000 (20,585,000,000); crude petroleum (barrels; 1994) none (408,800,000); petroleum products (metric tons; 1994) 47,760,000 (18,989,000).
Household income and expenditure. Average household size (1990) 4.2; income per household (1993) S$45,948 (U.S.$28,437); sources of income (1987–88): wages 81.2%, self-employment 16.8%, transfer payments and other 2.0%; expenditure (1992–93): food 30.0%, housing costs and furnishings 23.4%, transportation and communications 15.8%, recreation and education 9.0%, clothing and footwear 6.1%, health 2.8%, others 12.9%.
Gross national product (1995): U.S.$79,831,000,000 (U.S.$26,730 per capita).

Structure of gross domestic product and labour force

	1996			
	in value S$'000,000[5]	% of total value[5]	labour force[6]	% of labour force[6]
Agriculture	192.2	0.2 }	3,700	0.2
Quarrying	28.0	... }		
Manufacturing	29,485.5	26.9	406,300	23.2
Construction	8,982.8	8.2	115,000	6.6
Public utilities	1,868.6	1.7	7,200	0.4
Transp. and commun.	14,500.7	13.2	195,300	11.2
Trade	19,834.9	18.1	405,900	23.2
Finance	29,905.2	27.2	246,000	14.1
Services	11,454.6	10.4	367,700	21.0
Other	−6,465.4[7]	−5.9[7]	1,000[8]	0.1[8]
TOTAL	109,787.1	100.0	1,748,100	100.0

Population economically active (1995): total 1,748,200; activity rate of total population 58.5% (participation rates: ages 15 and over, 64.3%; female 38.7%; unemployed 2.7%).

Price and earnings indexes (1990 = 100)

	1990	1991	1992	1993	1994	1995	1996
Consumer price index	100.0	103.4	105.8	108.2	111.5	113.5	115.0
Monthly earnings index	100.0	109.2	118.1	125.5	136.5	144.8	153.2

Tourism (1995): receipts U.S.$8,212,000,000; expenditures U.S.$5,134,000,000.

Foreign trade[9]

Balance of trade (current prices)

	1991	1992	1993	1994	1995	1996
S$'000,000	−5,770	−7,490	−10,338	−216	+1,178	+1,631
% of total	2.7%	3.5%	4.1%	0.1%	0.4%	0.5%

Imports (1996): S$185,183,400,000 (office machines 11.7%, crude petroleum 6.1%, telecommunications apparatus 5.5%, electric power machinery 3.7%, petroleum products 3.3%, scientific instruments 3.0%, industrial machinery 2.5%). *Major import sources:* Japan 18.2%; U.S. 16.3%; Malaysia 15.0%; Thailand 5.5%; Taiwan 4.0%; Saudi Arabia 3.8%; Germany 3.7%.
Exports (1996): S$176,271,900,000 (office machines 26.5%, telecommunications apparatus 8.0%, petroleum products 7.7%, optical instruments 2.1%, electrical circuit apparatus 2.0%, industrial machinery 1.6%, clothing 1.1%). *Major export destinations:* U.S. 18.4%; Malaysia 18.0%; Hong Kong 8.9%; Japan 8.2%; Thailand 5.7%; Taiwan 4.0%; Germany 3.1%.

Transport and communications

Transport. Railroads (1996): length 83 km. Roads (1995): total length 3,035 km (paved [1994] 97%). Vehicles (1996): passenger cars 384,450; trucks and buses 139,113. Air transport (1996): passenger-km 53,640,000,000; metric ton-km cargo 4,191,000,000; airports (1997) 1.

Communications

Medium	date	unit	number	units per 1,000 persons
Daily newspapers	1995	circulation	1,015,100	340
Radio	1996	receivers	822,000	270
Television	1995	receivers	650,000	218
Telephones	1995	main lines	1,429,000	478
Cellular telephones	1995	subscribers	291,900	98
Facsimile machines	1995	units	55,600	19
Personal computers	1995	units	515,000	172

Education and health

Educational attainment (1990). Percentage of population age 25 and over having: no schooling 64.0%; primary education 31.3%; postsecondary 4.7%.
Literacy (1990): total population age 10 and over literate 90.7%; males literate 95.7%; females literate 85.6%.

Education (1995)

	schools	teachers	students	student/ teacher ratio
Primary (age 6–11)	199	10,356	261,648	25.3
Secondary (age 12–18)	178	9,777	203,662	20.8
Voc., teacher tr.	11	1,382	9,476	6.9
Higher	7	6,902	83,914	12.2

Health (1996): physicians 4,566 (1 per 667 persons); hospital beds 10,668 (1 per 285 persons); infant mortality rate per 1,000 live births 3.8.
Food (1988–90): daily per capita caloric intake 3,121 (vegetable products 76%, animal products 24%); 136% of FAO recommended minimum requirement.

Military

Total active duty personnel (1996): 53,900 (army 83.5%, navy 5.4%, air force 11.1%). *Military expenditure as percentage of GNP* (1995): 4.7% (world 2.8%); per capita expenditure U.S.$1,329.

[1]Includes 7 nonelective seats. [2]The census divisions have no administrative function. [3]De jure population. [4]De jure population aged 10 years and over. [5]At prices of 1990. [6]Employed only. [7]Imputed bank service charges. [8]Activities not adequately defined. [9]Import figures are f.o.b. in balance of trade.

Internet resources for further information:
- **Statistics Singapore http://www.singstat.gov.sg/**

Slovakia

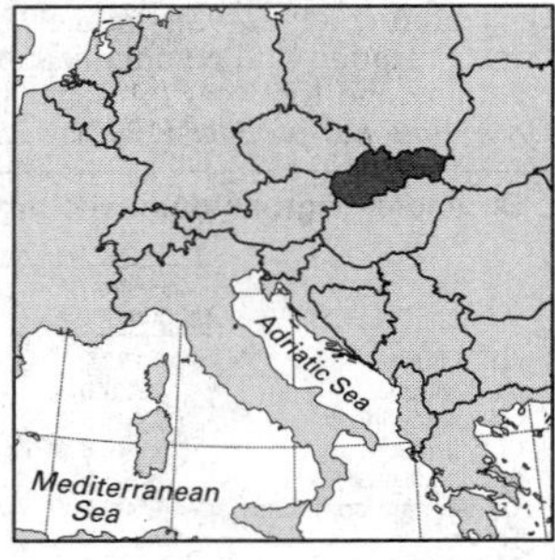

Official name: Slovenská Republika (Slovak Republic).
Form of government: unitary multiparty republic with one legislative house (National Council [150]).
Chief of state: President.
Head of government: Prime Minister.
Capital: Bratislava.
Official language: Slovak.
Official religion: none.
Monetary unit: 1 Slovak koruna (Sk) = 100 halura; valuation (Oct. 3, 1997) 1 U.S.$ = Sk 33.75; 1 £ = Sk 54.40.

Area and population

Districts[1]	area sq km[2]	population 1996 estimate	Districts[1]	area sq km[2]	population 1996 estimate
Banská Bystrica	2,075	178,992	Prievidza	960	141,184
Bardejov	1,014	82,527	Provažská Bystrica	1,196	173,566
Bratislava-vidiek	1,261	148,606	Rimavská Sobota	1,823	99,080
Čadca	934	125,008	Rožňava	1,621	87,625
Dolný Kubín	1,659	125,719	Senica	1,691	148,095
Dunajská Streda	1,075	111,100	Spišská Nová Ves	1,529	149,878
Galanta	965	144,023	Stará L'ubovňa	624	49,004
Humenné	1,909	114,657	Svidnik	862	45,010
Komárno	1,100	109,027	Topol'čany	1,361	161,399
Košice	244	240,915	Trebišov	1,322	119,390
Košice-vidiek	1,533	101,630	Trenčín	1,310	181,314
Levice	1,551	120,995	Trnava	1,390	236,007
Liptovský Mikuláš	1,968	134,187	Vel'ký Krtíš	848	46,876
Lučenec	1,304	95,741	Vranov nad Topl'ou	847	76,521
Martin	1,128	114,740	Žiar nad Hronom	1,264	94,475
Michalovce	1,310	113,434	Žilina	1,097	185,711
Nitra	1,443	212,879	Zvolen	1,721	123,558
Nové Zámky	1,347	152,380			
Poprad	1,963	161,192	**Capital city**		
Prešov	1,418	209,292	Bratislava	368	451,587
			TOTAL	49,036[3]	5,367,324

Demography

Population (1997): 5,404,000.
Density (1997): persons per sq mi 285.4, persons per sq km 110.2.
Urban-rural (1991): urban 56.8%; rural 43.2%.
Sex distribution (1995): male 48.69%; female 51.31%.
Age breakdown (1995): under 15, 22.3%; 15–29, 23.8%; 30–44, 22.9%; 45–59, 15.9%; 60–74, 11.5%; 75 and over, 3.6%.
Population projection: (2000) 5,466,000; (2010) 5,676,000.
Doubling time: not applicable; population growth is negligible.
Ethnic composition (1995): Slovak 85.7%; Hungarian 10.6%; Gypsy 1.6%; Czech 1.1%; Ruthenian 0.3%; Ukrainian 0.3%; German 0.1%; other 0.3%.
Religious affiliation (1995): Roman Catholic 60.3%; nonreligious and atheist 9.7%; Protestant 7.9%, of which Slovak Evangelical 6.2%, Reformed Christian 1.6%; Greek Catholic 3.4%; Eastern Orthodox 0.7%; other 18.0%.
Major cities (1996): Bratislava 452,053; Košice 240,915; Prešov 92,687.

Vital statistics

Birth rate per 1,000 population (1996): 11.2 (world avg. 25.0); legitimate 86.0%; illegitimate 14.0%.
Death rate per 1,000 population (1996): 9.5 (world avg. 9.3).
Natural increase rate per 1,000 population (1995): 1.6 (world avg. 15.7).
Total fertility rate (avg. births per childbearing woman; 1996): 1.5.
Marriage rate per 1,000 population (1996): 5.1.
Divorce rate per 1,000 population (1996): 1.8.
Life expectancy at birth (1996): male 68.8 years; female 76.7 years.
Major causes of death per 100,000 population (1995): diseases of the circulatory system 541.1; malignant neoplasms (cancers) 206.5.

National economy

Budget (1995). Revenue: Sk 163,138,000,000 (tax revenue 80.3%; nontax revenue 16.3%; customs 3.3%; insurance 0.1%). Expenditures: Sk 171,437,000,000 (education, health, and social welfare 39.7%; debt service 6.8%).
Public debt (external, outstanding; 1995): U.S.$3,570,000,000.
Production (metric tons except as noted). Agriculture, forestry, fishing (1996): cereals 3,941,000 (of which wheat 2,112,000, barley 960,000, corn [maize] 650,000, rye 105,600); livestock (number of live animals) 2,076,000 pigs, 929,000 cattle, 430,000 sheep; roundwood (1995) 4,887,000 cu m; fish catch (1993) 2,773. Mining and quarrying (1995): iron ore 820,000; lead-zinc ore 300,000; copper ore 280,000. Manufacturing (1995): crude steel 3,958,000; pig iron 3,207,000[4]; cement 2,981,000; plastic and resins 449,900; flour 375,000; nitrogenous fertilizers 229,300; cotton yarn 11,655; beer 4,369,000 hectolitres; refrigerators and freezers 330,200 units. Construction (1991): residential 1,147,000 sq m. Energy production (consumption): electricity (kW-hr; 1994) 24,740,000,000 (25,898,000,000[5]); coal (metric tons; 1995) 3,725,000 (14,390,000[5]); crude petroleum (barrels; 1994) 492,850 (32,866,000); petroleum products (metric tons; 1993) 3,603,000 (2,323,000); natural gas (cu m; 1994) 288,000,000 (5,037,986,000[5]).
Land use (1994): forested 40.6%; meadows and pastures 17.0%; agricultural and under permanent cultivation 32.9%; other 9.5%.
Population economically active (1995): total 2,586,300; activity rate of total population 48.2% (participation rates: ages 15–64, 76.4%; female 66.0%; unemployed 6.1%).

Price and earnings indexes (1990 = 100)

	1990	1991	1992	1993	1994	1995	1996
Consumer price index	100.0	156.1	171.7	218.5	247.7	272.3	288.1
Annual earnings index	100.0	115.0	136.5	161.1	190.8	228.3	261.7

Gross national product (1995): U.S.$15,848,000,000 (U.S.$2,950 per capita).

Structure of gross domestic product and labour force

	1995			
	in value Sk '000,000	% of total value	labour force[6]	% of labour force
Agriculture	32,634	6.3	208,000	9.7
Mining and manufacturing	140,378	27.1	582,000	27.2
Construction	26,418	5.1	158,000	7.4
Public utilities	24,346	4.7	51,000	2.4
Transp. and commun.	48,174	9.3	158,000	7.4
Trade	116,550	22.5	303,000	14.2
Finance	29,526	5.7	33,000	1.5
Pub. admin., defense	34,188	6.6	381,000	17.8
Services	65,786	12.7	184,000	8.6
Other	—	—	80,000	3.7
TOTAL	518,000	100.0	2,138,000	100.0[3]

Household income and expenditure. Average household size (1995) 4.0; income per household (1994) Sk 48,190[7] (U.S.$1,545[7]); sources of income (1995): wages and salaries 78.9%, transfer payments 8.1%, other 13.0%; expenditure (1995): food and beverages 26.4%, taxes 18.7%, clothing and footwear 8.7%, housing 7.7%, household durable goods 3.5%, other 35.0%.

Foreign trade

Balance of trade (current prices)

	1993	1994	1995
Sk '000,000	−27,310	+2,858	−5,695
% of total	7.5%	1.0%	1.1%

Imports (1995): Sk 260,791,000,000 (machinery and transport equipment 28.9%; semimanufactured products 17.8%; petroleum and petroleum products 17.5%; chemical products 13.6%; manufactured products 8.0%). *Major import sources:* Czech Republic 27.8%; Russian Federation 16.6%; Germany 14.3%; Austria 5.1%; Italy 4.6%; Poland 2.8%.
Exports (1995): Sk 255,096,000,000 (semimanufactured products 40.4%; machinery and transport equipment 18.8%; chemical products 13.2%; manufactured goods 12.2%; food, beverages, and tobacco 5.9%). *Major export destinations:* Czech Republic 35.3%; Germany 18.8%; Austria 5.0%.

Transport and communications

Transport. Railroads (1995): length 3,665 km; passenger-km 4,202,000,000; metric ton-km cargo 13,674,000,000. Roads (1995): total length 17,869 km (paved, n.a.). Vehicles (1995): passenger cars 1,015,794; trucks and buses 97,516. Merchant marine: n.a. Air transport (1994): passenger-km 60,283,000,000; metric ton-km cargo 5,557,000; airports (1996) with scheduled flights 2.

Communications

Medium	date	unit	number	units per 1,000 persons
Daily newspapers	1994	circulation	1,363,000	256[4]
Television	1995	receivers	1,157,000	216
Telephones	1995	main lines	1,119,000	208
Cellular telephones	1995	subscribers	12,300	2.3
Facsimile machines	1995	units	44,700	5.3

Education and health

Educational attainment (1991). Percentage of adult population having: incomplete primary education 0.5%; primary and incomplete secondary 30.6%; complete secondary 58.6%; higher 9.4%; unknown 0.9%. *Literacy* (1990): total population age 15 and over literate 3,980,202 (100%); males literate 1,916,410 (100%); females literate 2,063,792 (100%).

Education (1995–96)

	schools	teachers	students	student/teacher ratio
Primary (age 6–14)	2,485	39,224	661,082	16.7
Secondary (age 15–18)	190	5,457	76,380	14.0
Voc., teacher tr.	364	9,558	119,853	12.5
Higher	14	8,014	74,322	9.3

Health (1995): physicians 14,081 (1 per 381.2 persons); hospital beds 62,634 (1 per 86 persons); infant mortality rate per 1,000 live births (1996) 10.2.

Military

Total active duty personnel (1996): 47,000 (army 70.2%, air force 29.8%). *Military expenditure as percentage of GNP* (1994): 2.4% (world 3.0%); per capita expenditure U.S.$160.

[1]Districts have the same names as district seats. [2]One sq km is equal to approximately 0.3861 sq mi. [3]Detail does not add to total given because of rounding. [4]1995. [5]1993. [6]Excluding women on regular and additional maternity leave and including employees with a second job. [7]Households of employees with two children and wife not economically active.

Internet resources for further information:

- **Embassy of the Slovak Republic (Washington, D.C.) http://www.slovakemb.com/index.shtml**
- **Slovak Information Agency http://www.sia.gov.sk**

Slovenia

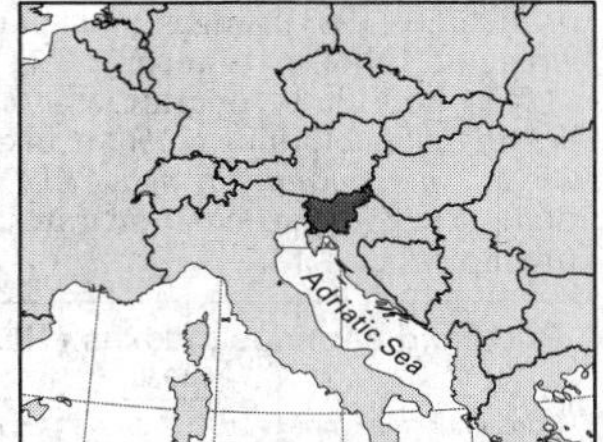

Official name: Republika Slovenija (Republic of Slovenia).
Form of government: unitary multiparty republic with two legislative houses (National Council [40]; National Assembly [90]).
Head of state: President.
Head of government: Prime Minister.
Capital: Ljubljana.
Official language[1]: Slovene.
Official religion: none.
Monetary unit: 1 Slovene tolar (SIT; plural tolarji) = 100 stotin; valuation (Oct. 3, 1997) 1 U.S.$ = 166.64 tolarji; 1 £ = 268.62 tolarji.

Area and population		area		population
				1995
Statistical regions	Capital	sq mi	sq km	estimate
Dolenjska	—	642	1,663	101,917
Gorenjska	—	824	2,135	192,523
Goriška	—	897	2,322	118,627
Koroška	—	401	1,041	73,715
Notranjsko-kraška	—	562	1,456	49,214
Obalno Kraško	—	403	1,043	100,193
Osrednjeslovenska	—	1,369	3,546	507,486
Podravska	—	837	2,168	324,156
Pomurska	—	516	1,336	128,923
Savinjska	—	919	2,380	256,076
Spodnjeposavska	—	349	905	73,750
Zasavska	—	102	263	45,820
TOTAL		7,821	20,258	1,972,400

Demography

Population (1997): 1,955,000.
Density (1997): persons per sq mi 251.7, persons per sq km 97.3.
Urban-rural (1991): urban 50.5%; rural 49.5%.
Sex distribution (1995): male 48.59%; female 51.41%.
Age breakdown (1995): under 15, 18.1%; 15–29, 22.3%; 30–44, 23.8%; 45–59, 17.9%; 60–74, 13.6%; 75 and over, 4.3%.
Population projection: (2000) 1,965,000; (2010) 2,004,000.
Doubling time: not applicable; population is static.
Ethnic composition (1991): Slovene 87.8%; Croat 2.8%; Serb 2.4%; Bosnian Muslim 1.4%; Hungarian (Magyar) 0.4%; other 5.2%.
Religious affiliation (1995): Roman Catholic 86.0%; other (predominantly Christian adherents of the Slovene Old Catholic Church and the Eastern Orthodox Church) 14.0%.
Major cities (1995): Ljubljana 269,621; Maribor 134,289; Novo Mesto 50,862; Kranj 50,791; Celje 49,459.

Vital statistics

Birth rate per 1,000 population (1996): 9.3 (world avg. 25.0); legitimate 70.2%; illegitimate 29.8%.
Death rate per 1,000 population (1996): 4.8 (world avg. 9.3).
Natural increase rate per 1,000 population (1996): 4.5 (world avg. 15.7).
Total fertility rate (avg. births per childbearing woman; 1995): 1.3.
Marriage rate per 1,000 population (1995): 4.2.
Divorce rate per 1,000 population (1995): 0.8.
Life expectancy at birth (1994–95): male 70.3 years; female 77.8 years.
Major causes of death per 100,000 population (1995): circulatory diseases 408.1; cancers 235.6; accidents 87.6; respiratory diseases 74.7; digestive diseases 56.7; endocrine and metabolic disorders 28.8.

National economy

Budget (1995). Revenue: SIT 1,006,794,900,000 (taxes 52.3%, of which value-added tax 28.1%, income tax 14.5%, duties 7.7%, other 2.0%; social security 40.2%; nontax revenue 5.9%; privatization 1.6%). Expenditures: SIT 1,016,005,400,000 (pensions 26.9%; work of provider organizations 15.6%; health services 12.9%; social transfers 7.4%; capital expenditure 5.8%; defense 3.1%).
Production (metric tons except as noted). Agriculture, forestry, fishing (1996): potatoes 407,000, corn (maize) 322,000, sugar beets 295,000, wheat 167,000, grapes 105,000; livestock (number of live animals) 592,000 pigs, 496,000 cattle, 9,320,000 poultry; roundwood (1995) 1,709,000 cu m; fish catch (1995) 2,929. Mining and quarrying (1995): glass sand 200,000; pumice 40,000; ferrosilico calcium 12,000. Manufacturing (1995): cement 991,000; crude steel 407,000; paper 278,000; glue 85,632; welded tubular steel 61,575; refrigerators 863,000 units; telephones 749,000 units; washing machines and dryers 242,000 units; motorcycles 56,198 units. Construction (in '000 sq m; 1994): residential 581; nonresidential 4,596. Energy production (consumption): electricity (kW-hr; 1994) 12,616,000,000 (9,376,000,000); coal (metric tons; 1994) 4,854,000 (4,915,000); crude petroleum (barrels; 1994) 12,578 (1993; 3,540,000); petroleum products (metric tons; 1993) 452,000 (1,966,000); natural gas (cu m; 1994) 12,595,000 (396,000,000).
Household income and expenditure. Average household size (1994) 3.1; income per household (1995) SIT 1,805,135 (1994; U.S.$10,191); sources of income (1995): wages 53.2%, transfers 24.6%, self-employment 9.7%, other 12.5%; expenditure (1995): food 23.1%, transportation 16.2%, clothing 7.3%, health care 6.7%, education and entertainment 6.7%, energy 5.8%, household durable goods 4.8%, housing 4.3%.
Gross national product (1995): U.S.$16,328,000,000 (U.S.$8,200 per capita).

Structure of gross domestic product and labour force				
	1995			
	in value SIT '000,000	% of total value	labour force	% of labour force
Agriculture	95,674	4.3	8,840	1.0
Mining	23,119	1.1	235,457	24.7
Manufacturing	538,351	24.5		
Construction	97,368	4.4	29,725	3.1
Public utilities	52,803	2.4	8,427	1.0
Transp. and commun.	140,221	6.4	29,893	3.1
Trade	225,478	10.2	55,855	5.9
Finance	305,324	13.9	36,509	3.8
Pub. admin., defense	101,747	4.6	40,146	4.2
Services	269,929	12.3	146,694	15.4
Other	352,007[2]	15.9[2]	360,454[3]	37.8[3]
TOTAL	2,202,021	100.0	952,000	100.0

Population economically active (1995): total 952,000; activity rate 58.7% (participation rates: ages 15–64, 83.0%; female 45.2%; unemployed 7.4%).

Price and earnings indexes (1990 = 100)	1990	1991	1992	1993	1994	1995	1996
Consumer price index	100	215	659	867	1,040	1,172	1,285
Monthly earnings index	100	165	546	826	1,059	1,256	1,442

Land use (1994): forest 53.2%; pasture 24.8%; agricultural 11.6%; other 10.4%.
Tourism (1995): receipts U.S.$1,079,000,000; expenditures U.S.$413,000,000.

Foreign trade

Balance of trade (current prices)	1991	1992	1993	1994	1995	1996
U.S.$'000,000	−257	+540	−410	−509	−1,166	−853
% of total	3.2%	4.2%	3.3%	3.6%	6.5%	4.9%

Imports (1995): U.S.$9,492,000,000 (machinery and transport equipment 33.8%, chemicals 12.1%, basic manufactures 10.6%, food 6.7%, mineral fuels 6.6%). *Major import sources:* Germany 23.2%; Italy 17.0%; Austria 9.7%; France 8.4%; Croatia 6.1%.
Exports (1995): U.S.$8,316,000,000 (machinery and transport equipment 31.4%, basic manufactures 28.5%, chemicals 10.5%, food 3.2%, mineral fuels 1.2%). *Major export destinations:* Germany 30.2%; Italy 14.6%; Croatia 10.7%; France 8.2%; Austria 6.4%.

Transport and communications

Transport. Railroads (1995): length 746 mi, 1,201 km; passenger-km 595,000,000; metric ton-km cargo 2,881,000,000. Roads (1994): total length 9,158 mi, 14,739 km (paved 79%). Vehicles (1995): passenger cars 698,211; trucks and buses 40,206. Merchant marine (1995): vessels (100 gross tons and over) 13; total deadweight tonnage 346,466. Air transport (1995): passenger-mi 382,000,000, passenger-km 614,000,000; short ton-mi cargo 2,271,000, metric ton-km cargo 3,655,000; airports (1996) 1.

Communications				units
				per 1,000
Medium	date	unit	number	persons
Daily newspapers	1994	circulation	360,000	181
Radio	1997	receivers	630,000	317
Television	1995	receivers	745,000	374
Telephones	1995	main lines	614,800	309
Cellular telephones	1995	subscribers	27,000	13.6
Facsimile machines	1995	units	15,500	7.8
Personal computers	1995	units	95,000	47.7

Education and health

Educational attainment (1991). Percentage of population age 15 and over having: less than full primary education 17.1%; primary 29.9%; secondary 42.8%; postsecondary and higher 8.8%. *Literacy* (1991): virtually 100%.

Education (1994–95)	schools	teachers	students	student/ teacher ratio
Primary (age 7–14)	850	15,471	210,989	13.6
Secondary (age 15–18)	224	9,748	102,117	10.5
Higher[4]	28	2,783	45,951[5]	14.5

Health (1995): physicians 2,298[6] (1 per 858 persons); hospital beds 11,411 (1 per 173 persons); infant mortality rate per 1,000 live births 5.5.

Military

Total active duty personnel (1997): 9,550 (army 100%). *Military expenditure as percentage of GNP* (1995): 1.5% (world 2.8%); per capita expenditure U.S.$175.

[1]Hungarian and Italian spoken in autochthonous Hungarian and Italian communities. [2]Includes taxes on production, imports, and subsidies. [3]Includes 70,000 unemployed and 290,454 nondistributable employed. [4]1993–94. [5]1995–96. [6]Physicians and dental physicians in hospitals only.

Internet resources for further information:
- **Statistical Office of the Republic of Slovenia http://www.sigov.si/zrs/indok_e.html**
- **Country Info/Economy and Government http://www.ijs.si/slo/country/economy/**
- **The National Assembly http://www.sigov.si/dz/edz-ds.html**

Solomon Islands

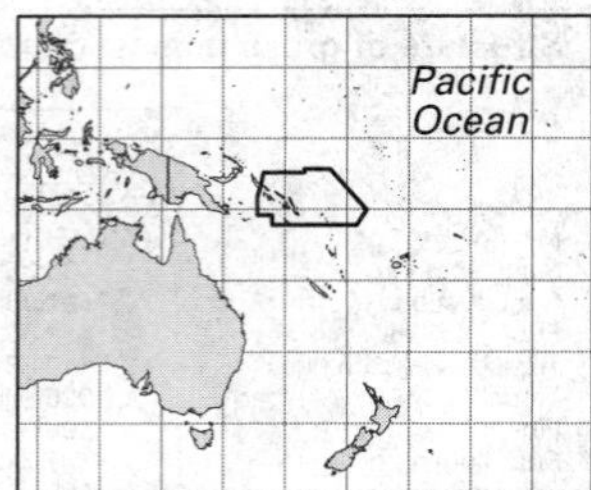

Official name: Solomon Islands.
Form of government: constitutional monarchy with one legislative house (National Parliament [50]).
Chief of state: British Monarch represented by Governor-General.
Head of government: Prime Minister.
Capital: Honiara.
Official language: English.
Official religion: none.
Monetary unit: 1 Solomon Islands dollar (SI$) = 100 cents; valuation (Oct. 3, 1997) 1 U.S.$ = SI$3.65; 1 £ = SI$5.88.

Area and population		area		population
				1997
Provinces	**Capitals**	sq mi	sq km	estimate
Central Islands	Tulagi	237	615	30,071[1]
Choiseul	Taro	1,481	3,837	[2]
Guadalcanal	Honiara	2,060	5,336	61,243
Isabel	Buala	1,597	4,136	22,653
Makira	Kira Kira	1,231	3,188	29,110
Malaita	Auki	1,631	4,225	105,882
Rennell and Bellona	Tigoa	259	671	[1]
Temotu	Santa Cruz	334	865	21,159
Western	Gizo	2,114	5,475	95,193[2]
Capital Territory				
Honiara	—	8	22	45,610
TOTAL		10,954[3]	28,370	410,921

Demography

Population (1997): 411,000.
Density (1997): persons per sq mi 37.5, persons per sq km 14.5.
Urban-rural (1997): urban 18.0%; rural 82.0%.
Sex distribution (1996): male 51.65%; female 48.35%.
Age breakdown (1996): under 15, 43.7%; 15–29, 28.7%; 30–44, 15.2%; 45–59, 8.1%; 60–74, 3.6%; 75 and over, 0.7%.
Population projection: (2000) 459,000; (2010) 600,000.
Doubling time: 22 years.
Ethnic composition (1986): Melanesian 94.2%; Polynesian 3.7%; other Pacific Islander 1.4%; European 0.4%; Asian 0.2%; other 0.1%.
Religious affiliation (1986): Christian 96.7%, of which Protestant 77.5%, Roman Catholic 19.2%; Bahāʾī 0.4%; traditional beliefs 0.2%; other and no religion 2.7%.
Major cities (1986)[4]: Honiara 43,643[5]; Gizo 3,727; Auki 3,262; Kira Kira 2,585; Buala 1,913.

Vital statistics

Birth rate per 1,000 population (1997): 36.2 (world avg. 25.0).
Death rate per 1,000 population (1997): 4.1 (world avg. 9.3).
Natural increase rate per 1,000 population (1997): 32.1 (world avg. 15.7).
Total fertility rate (avg. births per childbearing woman; 1997): 5.0.
Marriage rate per 1,000 population: n.a.
Divorce rate per 1,000 population: n.a.
Life expectancy at birth (1997): male 69.0 years; female 74.0 years.
Major causes of death per 100,000 population (1990): respiratory diseases 22.4; diarrheal diseases 13.6; malaria 10.0.

National economy

Budget (1996). Revenue: SI$484,900,000 (foreign grants 30.6%, taxes on goods and services 25.1%, taxes on foreign trade 20.5%, nontax revenue 15.1%, income taxes 8.7%). Expenditures: SI$540,100,000 (administrative 40.8%, capital expenditure 38.1%, interest payments 11.3%, subsidies and transfers 9.8%).
Tourism: receipts from visitors (1993) U.S.$6,000,000; expenditures by nationals abroad (1992) U.S.$11,000,000.
Land use (1994): forested 87.5%; meadows and pastures 1.4%; agricultural and under permanent cultivation 2.0%; other 9.1%.
Gross national product (at current market prices; 1995): U.S.$341,000,000 (U.S.$910 per capita).

Structure of gross domestic product and labour force	1995		1993	
	in value SI$'000[6]	% of total value	labour force[7]	% of labour force
Agriculture	115,600	35.6	8,106	27.4
Mining	200	0.1 }	2,844 }	9.6 }
Manufacturing	12,200	3.7 }		
Construction	7,600	2.3	977	3.3
Public utilities	4,800	1.5	245	0.8
Transportation and communications	18,800	5.8	1,723	5.8
Trade	27,200	8.4	3,390	11.5
Finance	13,500	4.1	1,144	3.9
Pub. admin., defense }	72,300 }	22.2 }	4,303	14.6
Services }			6,845	23.1
Other	52,900	16.3	...	...
TOTAL	325,100	100.0	29,577	100.0

Household income and expenditure. Average household size (1996) 5.8; average annual income per household[8] (1983) SI$1,010 (U.S.$1,160); sources of income (1983): wages and salaries 74.1%, self-employment, remittances, gifts, and other assistance 25.9%; expenditure (1992)[9]: food 46.8%, housing 11.0%, household operations 10.9%, transportation 9.9%, recreation and health 7.9%, clothing 5.7%, drinks and tobacco 5.0%.
Population economically active (1993): total 29,577[7]; activity rate of total population 8.3% (participation rates: ages 15–60 [1986] 98.6%; female 22.6%; unemployed, n.a.).

Price and earnings indexes (1990 = 100)	1990	1991	1992	1993	1994	1995	1996
Consumer price index	100.0	115.1	118.3	138.7	157.6	172.7	193.0
Annual earnings index[7]	100.0	121.2	140.5	142.8	...	...	...

Production (metric tons except as noted). Agriculture, forestry, fishing (1996): coconuts 225,000, sweet potatoes 63,000, palm oil and kernels 33,000, taro 27,000, yams 20,500, vegetables and melons 5,900, cacao beans 2,700; livestock (number of live animals) 55,000 pigs, 10,000 cattle, 145,000 chickens; roundwood (1995) 872,000 cu m; fish catch (1995) 46,462. Mining and quarrying (1994): gold 997 troy oz. Manufacturing (1993): processed fish 34,700; sawnwood 16,000 cu m; other major industries include beer brewing, soap and tobacco manufacturing, garment manufacturing, weaving, wood carving, fibreglass products, boatbuilding, and leatherworking. Construction (gross value in SI$ in Honiara; 1994): residential 9,508,000; nonresidential 11,151,000. Energy production (consumption): electricity (kW-hr; 1994) 30,000,000 (30,000,000); coal, none (n.a.); petroleum products (metric tons; 1994) none (50,000); natural gas, none (n.a.).
Public debt (external, outstanding; 1995): U.S.$99,000,000.

Foreign trade[10]

Balance of trade (current prices)	1989	1990	1991	1992	1993	1994
SI$'000	−47,300	−21,030	−23,770	+59,150	+33,520	−246
% of total	12.1%	5.6%	5.0%	11.0%	5.9%	0.0%

Imports (1994): SI$468,121,000 (machinery and transport equipment 38.0%, manufactured goods 19.9%, food 13.1%, mineral fuels and lubricants 8.2%). *Major import sources:* Australia 37.2%; Japan 17.1%; New Zealand 9.6%; Singapore 8.4%; United States 2.8%; Thailand 2.7%.
Exports (1994): SI$467,875,000 (timber products 59.2%, fish products 21.2%, palm oil products 9.5%, copra 4.2%, cacao beans 2.7%). *Major export destinations:* Japan 41.1%; South Korea 14.1%; United Kingdom 13.1%; The Netherlands 8.5%; Thailand 4.5%; Singapore 3.4%; Australia 1.5%.

Transport and communications

Transport. Railroads: none. Roads (1995): total length 826 mi, 1,330 km (paved 2%). Vehicles (1993): passenger cars 2,052; trucks and buses 2,574. Merchant marine (1992): vessels (100 gross tons and over) 33; total deadweight tonnage 4,985. Air transport (1994): passenger-mi 40,000,000, passenger-km 65,000,000; short ton-mi cargo 3,000,000, metric ton-km cargo 5,000,000; airports (1997) with scheduled flights 21.

Communications				units
Medium	date	unit	number	per 1,000 persons
Radio	1996	receivers	38,000	96
Television	1995	receivers	6,000	16
Telephones	1995	main lines	6,500	17
Cellular telephones	1995	subscribers	200	0.5
Facsimile machines	1995	units	800	2.1

Education and health

Educational attainment (1986)[11]. Percentage of population age 25 and over having: no schooling 44.4%; primary education 46.2%; secondary 6.8%; higher 2.6%. *Literacy* (1976): total population age 15 and over literate 55,500 (54.1%); males 33,600 (62.4%); females 21,900 (44.9%).

Education (1994)	schools	teachers	students	student/ teacher ratio
Primary (age 7–12)	520	2,510	73,120	29.1
Secondary (age 13–18)	23	618	7,981	12.9
Voc., teacher tr.[12]	1	...	...	...
Higher[12]	1	...	...	...

Health (1990): physicians 52 (1 per 6,154 persons); hospital beds 265 (1 per 1,208 persons); infant mortality rate per 1,000 live births (1997) 23.
Food (1995): daily per capita caloric intake 2,131 (vegetable products 93%, animal products 7%); 93% of FAO recommended minimum requirement.

Military

Total active duty personnel: no military forces are maintained, but a police force of 475 provides internal security.

[1]Central Islands includes Rennell and Bellona. [2]Western includes Choiseul. [3]Detail does not add to total given because of rounding. [4]Ward populations. [5]1996. [6]At 1985 factor cost. [7]Persons employed in the monetary sector only. [8]Public-service earnings. [9]Retail price index components. [10]Import figures are f.o.b. [11]Indigenous population only. [12]Vocational and teacher training are carried out at the College of Higher Education.

Somalia[1]

Official name: Soomaaliya (Somali)(Somalia).
Form of government: republic[2].
Head of state and government: [2].
Capital: Mogadishu.
Official languages: Somali; Arabic.
Official religion: Islam.
Monetary unit: 1 Somali shilling (So.Sh.) = 100 cents; valuation (Oct. 3, 1997) 1 U.S.$ = So.Sh. 2,620; 1 £ = So.Sh. 4,223.

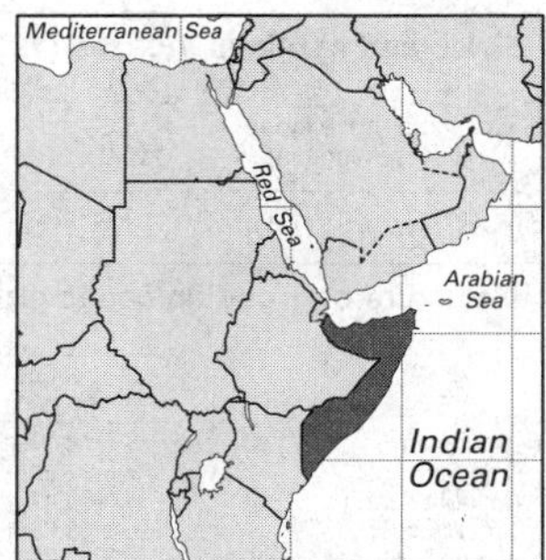

Area and population		area		population
				1980
Regions	Capitals	sq mi	sq km	estimate
Bakool	Xuddur	10,000	27,000	148,700
Banaadir	Mogadishu (Muqdisho)	400	1,000	520,100
Bari	Boosaaso	27,000	70,000	222,300
Bay	Baydhabo	15,000	39,000	451,000
Galguduud	Dhuusamarreeb	17,000	43,000	255,900
Gedo	Garbahaarrey	12,000	32,000	235,000
Hiiraan	Beledweyne	13,000	34,000	219,300
Jubbada Dhexe	Bu'aale	9,000	23,000	147,800
Jubbada Hoose	Kismaayo	24,000	61,000	272,400
Mudug	Gaalkacyo	27,000	70,000	311,200
Nugaal	Garoowe	19,000	50,000	112,200
Sanaag	Ceerigaabo	21,000	54,000	216,500
Shabeellaha Dhexe	Jawhar	8,000	22,000	352,000
Shabeellaha Hoose	Marka	10,000	25,000	570,700
Togdheer	Burao	16,000	41,000	383,900
Woqooyi Galbeed	Hargeysa	17,000	45,000	655,000
TOTAL		246,000[3]	637,000	5,074,000

Demography

Population (1997): 6,870,000[4].
Density (1997): persons per sq mi 27.9, persons per sq km 10.8.
Urban-rural (1991): urban 37.2%; rural 62.8%.
Sex distribution (1996): male 51.21%; female 48.79%.
Age breakdown (1996): under 15, 44.4%; 15–29, 27.1%; 30–44, 16.1%; 45–59, 6.9%; 60–74, 4.0%; 75 and over, 1.5%.
Population projection: (2000) 7,079,000; (2010) 7,823,000.
Doubling time: 27 years.
Ethnic composition (1983): Somali 98.3%[5]; Arab 1.2%; Bantu 0.4%; other 0.1%.
Religious affiliation (1995): Sunnī Muslim 99.9%; other 0.1%.
Major cities (1990): Mogadishu 900,000; Hargeysa 90,000; Kismaayo 90,000; Berbera 70,000; Marka 62,000.

Vital statistics

Birth rate per 1,000 population (1996): 44.3 (world avg. 25.0); legitimate, n.a.; illegitimate, n.a.
Death rate per 1,000 population (1996): 18.2 (world avg. 9.3).
Natural increase rate per 1,000 population (1996): 26.1 (world avg. 15.7).
Total fertility rate (avg. births per childbearing woman; 1996): 6.5.
Marriage rate per 1,000 population: n.a.
Divorce rate per 1,000 population: n.a.
Life expectancy at birth (1996): male 44.6 years; female 47.8 years.
Major causes of death per 100,000 population: n.a.; however, major diseases include leprosy, malaria, tetanus, and tuberculosis; civil violence, malnutrition, and poor health services remained epidemic in the mid-1990s.

National economy

Budget (1991). Revenue: So.Sh. 151,453,000,000 (domestic revenue sources, principally indirect taxes and import duties 60.4%; external grants and transfers 39.6%). Expenditures: So.Sh. 141,141,000,000 (general services 46.9%; economic and social services 31.2%; debt service 7.0%).
Public debt (external, outstanding; 1995): U.S.$1,961,000,000.
Production (metric tons except as noted). Agriculture, forestry, fishing (1996): fruits (excluding melons) 210,000, sugarcane 210,000, sorghum 145,000, corn (maize) 142,000, bananas 47,000, cassava 40,000, sesame seed 25,000, beans 14,000, dates 9,500, seed cotton 6,000, other forest products include khat, frankincense, and myrrh; livestock (number of live animals) 13,500,000 sheep, 12,500,000 goats, 6,100,000 camels, 5,200,000 cattle; roundwood (1995) 9,025,000 cu m; fish catch (1995) 14,850. Mining and quarrying (1992): sepiolite 2,000 kilograms. Manufacturing (value added in So.Sh. '000,000; 1988): food 794; cigarettes and matches 562; hides and skins 420; paper and printing 328; plastics 320; chemicals 202; beverages 144. Construction (value added in So.Sh.; 1991): 51,100,000,000. Energy production (consumption): electricity (kW-hr; 1994) 259,000,000 (259,000,000); coal, none (n.a.); crude petroleum (barrels; 1991) n.a. (806,000); petroleum products (metric tons; 1991) none (59,000); natural gas, none (n.a.).
Household income and expenditure. Average household size (1980) 4.9; income per household: n.a.; sources of income: n.a.; expenditure (1983)[6]: food and tobacco 62.3%, housing 15.3%, clothing 5.6%, energy 4.3%, other 12.5%.
Tourism: receipts from visitors (1986) U.S.$8,000,000; expenditures by nationals abroad (1983) U.S.$13,000,000.
Population economically active (1991): total 3,215,000; activity rate of total population 40.9% (participation rates [1987] over age 10, 63.1%; female 48.7%; unemployed, n.a.).

Price and earnings indexes (1989 = 100)	1989	1990	1991	1992	1993	1994	1995
Consumer price index[7]	100.0	240.0	372.2	507.4	630.7	749.8	872.1
Earnings index	...	...	...	...	...	...	...

Gross national product (1995): U.S.$1,010,000,000 (U.S.$150 per capita).

Structure of gross domestic product and labour force	1991			
	in value So.Sh. '000,000	% of total value	labour force	% of labour force
Agriculture	867,500	64.5	2,275,000	70.8
Mining	2,700	0.2	336,000	10.4
Manufacturing	59,200	4.4		
Construction	51,100	3.8		
Public utilities	9,400	0.7		
Transp. and commun.	80,700	6.0	604,000	18.8
Trade	125,000	9.3		
Finance	45,700	3.4		
Pub. admin., defense	80,700	6.0		
Services	30,900	2.3		
Other	−8,100	−0.6		
TOTAL	1,344,900[3]	100.0	3,215,000	100.0

Land use (1994): forest 25.5%; pasture 68.6%; agriculture 1.6%; other 4.3%.

Foreign trade[8]

Balance of trade (current prices)	1991	1992	1993	1994	1995	1996
U.S.$'000,000	−69	−99	−146	−133	−48	−95
% of total	27.5%	29.6%	38.4%	32.8%	14.2%	21.0%

Imports (1995): U.S.$193,000,000 (agricultural products 38.0%, of which raw sugar 16.1%, rice 7.8%, wheat 5.0%; unspecified 62.0%). *Major import sources* (1996)[9]: Kenya 28%; Djibouti 21%; Saudi Arabia 6%; Brazil 6%.
Exports (1995): U.S.$145,000,000 (agricultural products 51.4%, of which live sheep and goats 40.0%, bananas 6.9%, live camels and cattle 4.3%; other 48.6%). *Major export destinations* (1996)[9]: Saudi Arabia 55%; Yemen 19%; Italy 11%; United Arab Emirates 9%.

Transport and communications

Transport. Railroads: none. Roads (1995): total length 14,300 mi, 23,000 km (paved 12%). Vehicles (1995): passenger cars 11,800; trucks and buses 12,200. Merchant marine (1992): vessels (100 gross tons and over) 28; total deadweight tonnage 18,496. Air transport (1991): passenger-mi 81,000,000, passenger-km 131,000,000; short ton-mi cargo 3,000,000, metric ton-km cargo 5,000,000; airports (1997) with scheduled flights 1.

Communications Medium	date	unit	number	units per 1,000 persons
Radio	1995	receivers	300,000	45
Television	1995	receivers	118,000	18
Telephones	1995	main lines	15,000	2.2

Education and health

Educational attainment: n.a. *Literacy* (1995): percentage of total population age 15 and over literate 24%; males literate 36%; females literate 14%.

Education (1986–87)	schools	teachers	students	student/ teacher ratio
Primary (age 6–14)	1,125	8,208	171,830	20.9
Secondary (age 15–18)	82	2,109	42,764	20.3
Voc., teacher tr.	21	498	4,809	9.7
Higher	1	...	1,692	...

Health: physicians (1987) 323 (1 per 19,973 persons); hospital beds (1985) 5,536 (1 per 1,130 persons); infant mortality rate (1996) 126.
Food (1993–94 avg.): daily per capita caloric intake 1,545; 67% of FAO recommended minimum requirement.

Military

Total active duty personnel (1997): clan warfare since 1991. *Military expenditure as percentage of GNP* (1990): 0.9% (world 4.3%); per capita expenditure U.S.$1.

[1]Proclamation of a "Republic of Somaliland" by the Somali National Movement in May 1991 on territory corresponding to the former British Somaliland (which unified with the former Italian Trust Territory of Somalia to form Somalia in 1960) had received no international recognition by December 1997. This entity represented about a quarter of Somalia's territory and about 60% of its population. [2]No effective central government exists; however, a national reconciliation meeting aimed at establishing a central government for Somalia was scheduled for Dec. 20, 1997. [3]Detail does not add to total given because of rounding. [4]Includes 4.2 million residents of the "Republic of Somaliland"; excludes 450,000 refugees in neighbouring countries. [5]The Somali are divided into six major clans, of which four are predominantly pastoral (representing *c.* 70% of the population) and two are predominantly agricultural (representing *c.* 20% of the population); the remainder are urban dwellers with less clan identification. [6]Mogadishu only. [7]Reported inflation rate. [8]Imports c.i.f.; exports f.o.b. [9]Estimated figures.

Internet resources for further information:

- **USAID: Greater Horn Information Exchange: Somalia http://gaia.info.usaid.gov/horn/somalia/somalia.html**
- **CIA World Factbook: Somalia http://www.odci.gov/cia/publications/nsolo/factbook/so.htm**

South Africa

Official name: Republic of South Africa (English).
Form of government: multiparty republic with two legislative houses (National Council of Provinces [90]; National Assembly [400])[1].
Head of state and government: President[1].
Capitals (de facto): Pretoria (executive); Bloemfontein (judicial); Cape Town (legislative).
Official languages:[2].
Official religion: none.
Monetary unit: 1 rand (R) = 100 cents; valuation (Oct. 3, 1997) 1 U.S.$ = R 4.67; 1 £ = R 7.53.

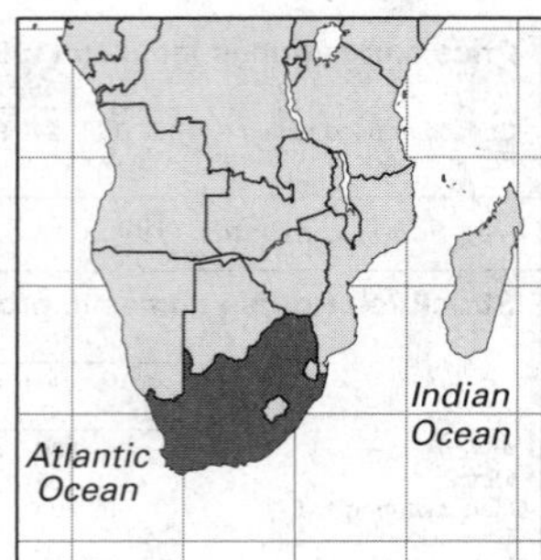

Area and population

		area		population
Provinces	Capitals	sq mi	sq km	1996 census[3]
Eastern Cape	Bisho	65,475	169,580	5,865,000
Free State	Bloemfontein	49,993	129,480	2,470,000
Gauteng	Johannesburg	6,568	17,010	7,171,000
KwaZulu/Natal	Ulundi	35,560	92,100	7,672,000
Mpumalanga	Nelspruit	30,691	79,490	2,646,000
Northern	Pietersburg	47,842	123,910	4,128,000
Northern Cape	Kimberley	139,703	361,830	746,000
North-West	Mafikeng (Mmabatho)	44,911	116,320	3,043,000
Western Cape	Cape Town	49,950	129,370	4,118,000
TOTAL		470,693	1,219,090	37,859,000

Demography

Population (1997)[4]: 42,446,000.
Density (1997): persons per sq mi 90.2, persons per sq km 34.8.
Urban-rural (1996): urban 55.4%; rural 44.6%.
Sex distribution (1996): male 47.98%; female 52.02%.
Age breakdown (1995): under 15, 37.3%; 15–29, 27.1%; 30–44, 18.5%; 45–59, 10.4%; 60–74, 5.2%; 75 and over, 1.5%.
Population projection[4]: (2000) 44,315,000; (2010) 46,038,000.
Doubling time: 43 years.
Ethnic composition (1995): black 76.3%, of which Zulu *c.* 22.0%, Xhosa *c.* 18.0%, Pedi *c.* 9.0%, Sotho *c.* 7.0%, Tswana *c.* 7.0%, Tsonga *c.* 3.5%, Swazi *c.* 3.0%; white 12.7%; Coloured 8.5%; Asian 2.5%.
Religious affiliation (1991)[5]: Christian 66.4%, of which Protestant 36.6%, black independent churches 22.2%, Roman Catholic 7.6%; Hindu 1.3%; Muslim 1.1%; nonreligious 1.2%; other/traditional beliefs 30.0%.
Major cities (1991)[6]: Cape Town 2,350,157; Johannesburg 1,916,063[7]; Durban 1,137,378; Pretoria 1,080,187; Port Elizabeth 853,204.

Vital statistics

Birth rate per 1,000 population (1996): 27.4 (world avg. 25.0).
Death rate per 1,000 population (1996): 11.1 (world avg. 9.3).
Natural increase rate per 1,000 population (1996): 16.3 (world avg. 15.7).
Marriage rate per 1,000 population (1995): 3.6.
Total fertility rate (avg. births per childbearing woman; 1996): 3.3.
Life expectancy at birth (1996): male 55.7 years; female 60.2 years.
Major causes of death per 100,000 population (1993–94): accidents and violence 221.9; diseases of the circulatory system 102.3; infectious and parasitic diseases 51.8; ill-defined conditions 424.0.

National economy

Budget (1995–96). Revenue: R 119,957,000,000 (personal income taxes 42.2%, value-added taxes 27.3%, company income taxes 13.8%). Expenditures: R 152,573,000,000 (education 21.9%, interest on public debt 19.3%, health 10.2%, defense 7.2%).
Public debt (external, December 1996): U.S.$3,053,000,000.
Production (in R '000,000 except as noted). Agriculture, forestry, fishing (in value of production; 1995): poultry 4,327, beef 3,080, corn (maize) 2,825, temperate fruits 1,964, wheat 1,955, sugarcane 1,657, milk 1,577, potatoes 1,081, citrus fruits 988, grapes 966, sheep and goat meat 824, swine 509; roundwood (1995) 25,332,000 cu m; fish catch (1995) 575,177 metric tons. Mining and quarrying (in value of sales; 1995): gold 23,335; rough diamonds 16,431; coal 12,586; platinum-group metals 6,573; copper 1,679; iron ore 1,658; lime and limestone 693. Manufacturing (in U.S.$'000,000 value added; 1994): food products 2,734; iron and steel 2,303; transport equipment 2,082; metal products 1,588; nonelectrical machinery 1,566; beverages 1,531; refined petroleum 1,281. Energy production (consumption): electricity (kW-hr; 1994) 182,448,000,000 ([1995] 172,039,000,000); coal (metric tons; 1994) 182,496,000 (140,581,000[8]); crude petroleum (barrels; 1996) 3,650,000 ([1994] 125,000,000[8]); petroleum products (metric tons; 1994) 16,425,000[8] (16,428,000[8]); natural gas (cu m; 1994): 1,896,000,000[8] (1,896,000,000[8]).
Tourism (1995): receipts U.S.$1,595,000,000; expenditures U.S.$1,749,000,000.
Household income and expenditure. Average household size (1994) 4.6; average annual income per household (1990–91)[5] R 16,814 (U.S.$6,500); expenditure (1992)[5]: food and beverages 35.8%, transportation 14.7%, household goods 10.0%, housing and energy 9.6%.
Population economically active (1994): total 14,297,048; activity rate of total population 35.3% (participation rates: over age 15, 55.6%; female 44.2%; unemployed [1997] *c.* 25%.

Price and earnings indexes (1990 = 100)

	1991	1992	1993	1994	1995	1996	1997[9]
Consumer price index	115.3	131.3	144.0	157.0	170.5	183.1	200.3
Monthly earnings index[10]	115.0	129.6	143.2	...	...	...	...

Gross national product (1995): U.S.$130,918,000,000 (U.S.$3,160 per capita).

Structure of gross domestic product and labour force

	1995		1994	
	in value R '000,000[11]	% of total value	labour force	% of labour force
Agriculture	18,779	4.4	1,277,346	8.9
Mining	33,305	7.7	277,176	1.9
Manufacturing	104,474	24.3	1,614,596	11.3
Construction	13,606	3.2	437,167	3.1
Public utilities	17,797	4.1	95,046	0.7
Transp. and commun.	32,691	7.6	520,789	3.6
Trade	70,094	16.3	1,675,448	11.7
Finance, real estate	56,877	13.2	587,331	4.1
Pub. admin., defense	65,463	15.2	3,055,753	21.4
Services	8,479	2.0		
Other	8,859	2.0	4,756,396[12]	33.3[12]
TOTAL	430,424	100.0	14,297,048	100.0

Land use (1994): forest 6.7%; pasture 66.7%; agriculture 10.8%; other 15.8%.

Foreign trade

Balance of trade (current prices)

	1991	1992	1993	1994	1995	1996
R '000,000	+16,146	+13,917	+20,500	+13,719	+2,783	+10,578
% of total	14.3%	11.6%	14.8%	8.3%	1.4%	4.4%

Imports (1995): R 98,614,000,000 (machinery and apparatus 31.9%, chemicals and chemical products 12.5%, motor vehicles 11.6%). *Major import sources:* Germany 15.9%; U.K. 11.5%; U.S. 10.9%; Japan 9.8%; Italy 4.5%.
Exports (1995): R 101,397,000,000 (gold 19.9%, base metals and metal products 15.4%, gem diamonds 9.8%, food 7.4%). *Major export destinations:* Italy 7.8%; Japan 7.3%; U.S. 6.6%; unspecified 27.9%.

Transport and communications

Transport. Railroads: route length (1995) 21,595 km; passenger-km (1992–93) 895,000,000[13]; metric ton-km cargo (1994–95) 95,260,000,000. Roads (1995): length 182,580 km (paved 33%). Vehicles (1995): passenger cars 3,810,000; trucks and buses 1,640,000. Air transport (1996)[14]: passenger-km 13,833,000,000; metric ton-km cargo 539,977,000; airports (1996) 24.

Communications

Medium	date	unit	number	units per 1,000 persons
Daily newspapers	1995	circulation	1,201,000	29
Radio	1996	receivers	11,200,000	268
Television	1995	receivers	3,485,000	84
Telephones	1995	main lines	3,919,100	95
Cellular telephones	1995	subscribers	535,000	13
Facsimile machines	1995	units	75,000	1.8
Personal computers	1995	units	1,100,000	27

Education and health

Educational attainment (1994). Percentage of population age 25 and over having: no formal schooling 14.5%; primary/incomplete secondary 61.6%; secondary/incomplete higher 20.4%; complete higher 3.1%; other/unknown 0.4%. *Literacy* (1995): total population age 15 and over literate: 81.8%.

Education (1994)

	schools	teachers	students	student/teacher ratio
Primary/Secondary	22,260	349,436	11,782,324	35.7
Voc., teacher tr.	187	10,807	140,531	13.0
Tertiary vocational	15	7,341[15]	151,410	18.7[15]
Higher	...	27,099	617,897	22.8

Health: physicians (1994) 26,452 (1 per 1,529 persons); hospital beds (1995) 172,292 (1 per 239 persons); infant mortality rate (1996) 52.4.
Food (1995): daily per capita caloric intake 2,890 (vegetable products 88%, animal products 12%); 118% of FAO recommended minimum.

Military

Total active duty personnel (1996): 137,900 (army 85.6%, navy 4.0%, air force 6.1%, intraservice medical service 4.3%). *Military expenditure as percentage of GNP* (1995): 2.2% (world 2.8%); per capita expenditure U.S.$71.

[1]All articles of permanent constitution announced in May 1996 were effective as of June 30, 1997. [2]Afrikaans; English; Ndebele; Pedi (North Sotho); Sotho (South Sotho); Swazi; Tsonga; Tswana (West Sotho); Venda; Xhosa; Zulu. [3]Adjusted preliminary figures. [4]Projection(s) based on 1991 census. [5]Excludes formerly nominally independent Transkei, Venda, Bophuthatswana, and Ciskei (TVBC). [6]Population of urban areas. [7]The 1991 population of the Witwatersrand (including East Rand [1,379,000], Far East Rand [701,000], and West Rand [870,000] urban areas) is 4,866,000. [8]Includes Botswana, Lesotho, Namibia, and Swaziland. [9]July. [10]Mining only. [11]At factor cost. [12]Includes 100,320 not adequately defined and 4,656,076 unemployed. [13]Excludes suburban traffic. [14]SAA only. [15]1993.

Internet resources for further information:
- **Central Statistical Service**
  http://www.css.gov.za/index.htm
- **South African High Commission in Canada**
  http://www.docuweb.ca/SouthAfrica/

Spain

Official name: Reino de España (Kingdom of Spain).
Form of government: constitutional monarchy with two legislative houses (Senate [257[1]]; Congress of Deputies [350]).
Chief of state: King.
Head of government: Prime Minister.
Capital: Madrid.
Official language: Castilian Spanish[2].
Monetary unit: 1 peseta (Pta) = 100 céntimos; valuation (Oct. 3, 1997) 1 U.S.$ = Ptas 148.84; 1 £ = Ptas 239.94.

Area and population

		area		population
Autonomous communities	Capitals	sq mi	sq km	1996[3] estimate
Andalucía	Seville	33,822	87,599	7,234,873
Aragón	Zaragoza	18,425	47,720	1,187,546
Asturias	Oviedo	4,094	10,604	1,087,885
Baleares (Balearic Islands)	Palma de Mallorca	1,927	4,992	760,379
Canarias (Canary Islands)	Santa Cruz de Tenerife	2,875	7,447	1,606,534
Cantabria	Santander	2,054	5,321	527,437
Castilla–La Mancha	Toledo	30,680	79,461	1,712,529
Castilla y León	Valladolid	36,380	94,224	2,508,496
Cataluña	Barcelona	12,399	32,113	6,090,040
Ceuta	—	8	20	68,796
Extremadura	Mérida	16,075	41,634	1,070,244
Galicia	Santiago de Compostela	11,419	29,575	2,742,622
La Rioja	Logroño	1,948	5,045	264,941
Madrid	Madrid	3,100	8,028	5,022,289
Melilla	—	5	12	59,576
Murcia	Murcia	4,368	11,314	1,097,249
Navarra	Pamplona	4,012	10,391	520,574
País Vasco (Basque Country)	Vitoria (Gasteiz)	2,793	7,234	2,098,055
Valencia	Valencia	8,979	23,255	4,009,329
TOTAL		195,364[4, 5]	505,990[5]	39,669,394

Demography

Population (1997): 39,323,000[6].
Density (1997): persons per sq mi 201.3, persons per sq km 77.7.
Urban-rural (1990): urban 78.4%; rural 21.6%.
Sex distribution (1997): male 48.92%; female 51.08%.
Age breakdown (1997): under 15, 15.8%; 15–29, 24.1%; 30–44, 22.1%; 45–59, 16.8%; 60–69, 10.4%; 70 and over, 10.8%.
Population projection: (2000) 39,466,000; (2010) 39,917,000.
Doubling time: not applicable; doubling time exceeds 100 years.
Ethnolinguistic composition (1991): Spanish 74.4%; Catalan 16.9%; Galician 6.4%; Basque 1.6%; other 0.7%.
Religious affiliation (1993): Roman Catholic 94.9%; Muslim 1.2%; Protestant 0.5%; other 3.4%.
Major cities (1996)[3, 7]: Madrid 2,866,850; Barcelona 1,508,805; Valencia 746,683; Seville 697,487; Zaragoza 601,674.

Vital statistics

Birth rate per 1,000 population (1995): 9.2 (world avg. 25.0).
Death rate per 1,000 population (1995): 8.7 (world avg. 9.3).
Natural increase rate per 1,000 population (1995): 0.5 (world avg. 15.7).
Total fertility rate (avg. births per childbearing woman; 1996): 1.3.
Life expectancy at birth (1996): male 74.9 years; female 81.8 years.
Major causes of death per 100,000 population (1994): circulatory diseases 334.2; malignant neoplasms (cancers) 224.3; respiratory diseases 78.8.

National economy

Budget (1996)[8]. Revenue: Ptas 16,090,900,000,000 (direct taxes 46.8%; indirect taxes 38.9%, of which value-added tax on products 24.1%; other taxes on production 14.3%). Expenditures: Ptas 18,099,200,000,000 (public debt 19.1%; health 18.2%; education 5.9%; pensions 5.0%; defense 4.8%).
Tourism (1995): receipts U.S.$25,701,000,000; expenditures U.S.$4,540,000,000.
Gross national product (1995): U.S.$532,347,000,000 (U.S.$13,580 per capita).

Structure of gross domestic product and labour force

	1996			
	in value Ptas '000,000	% of total value	labour force	% of labour force
Agriculture	2,582,800	3.5	1,310,600	8.2
Mining	} 17,468,000	} 23.7	78,900	0.5
Manufacturing			2,673,600	16.8
Public utilities			95,400	0.6
Construction	5,720,400	7.7	1,516,500	9.5
Transp. and commun.	...	...	803,900	5.0
Trade	} 43,505,100	} 59.1	3,307,100	20.8
Finance			1,217,900	7.6
Services			} 3,390,600	} 21.3
Pub. admin., defense				
Other	4,384,700[9]	6.0[9]	1,541,500[10]	9.7[10]
TOTAL	73,661,000	100.0	15,936,000	100.0

Production (metric tons except as noted). Agriculture, forestry, fishing (1996): barley 10,660,000, sugar beets 7,359,000, wheat 6,002,000, grapes 4,486,000, potatoes 4,032,000, corn (maize) 3,996,000, olives 2,856,000, tomatoes 2,780,000, oranges 2,154,000; livestock (number of live animals) 21,322,000 sheep, 18,000,000 pigs, 5,660,000 cattle, 2,465,000 goats; roundwood (1995) 15,121,000 cu m; fish catch (1995) 1,320,000. Mining and quarrying (metal content in metric tons; 1996): iron ore 1,269,000; zinc 140,000; lead 24,000. Manufacturing (value added in U.S.$'000; 1994): machinery and transport equipment 20,322,000; food products 11,072,000; chemical products 8,618,000; publishing products 6,082,000; wood products 3,208,000. Construction (1996): dwellings 311,038. Energy production (consumption): electricity (kW-hr; 1994) 161,502,000,000 (163,377,000,000); coal (metric tons; 1994) 29,556,000 (42,808,000); crude petroleum (barrels; 1994) 6,057,000 (407,793,000); petroleum products (metric tons; 1994) 47,227,000 (40,591,000); natural gas (cu m; 1994) 206,650,000 (7,754,694,000).
Public debt (1995): Ptas 38,697,700,000,000 (U.S.$312,000,000,000).
Population economically active (1996): total 15,936,000; activity rate of total population 40.6% (participation rates: ages [1995] 16–64, 60.7%; female 38.3%; unemployed 22.9%).

Price and earnings indexes (1990 = 100)

	1990	1991	1992	1993	1994	1995	1996
Consumer price index	100.0	105.9	112.2	117.3	122.9	128.6	133.2
Monthly earnings index	100.0	108.2	116.5	124.4	124.4	136.2	137.2[11]

Household income and expenditure. Average household size (1991) 3.4; income per household (1996) Ptas 2,964,843 (U.S.$23,408); expenditure (1995): housing 26.0%, food 24.0%, transportation 12.8%, clothing and footwear 7.4%, household goods and services 6.1%.

Foreign trade

Balance of trade (current prices)

	1991	1992	1993	1994	1995	1996
Ptas '000,000	−2,724.3	−3,022.5	−1,831.3	−1,853.9	−2,101.6	−1,630.8
% of total	19.6%	18.6%	10.2%	8.6%	8.4%	5.9%

Imports (1996): Ptas 15,435,699,000,000 (machinery 12.1%; energy products 9.1%, of which crude petroleum 9.0%; transportation equipment 8.5%; agricultural products 7.9%). *Major import sources:* France 17.8%; Germany 14.8%; Italy 9.5%; U.K. 8.3%; Japan 2.8%.
Exports (1996): Ptas 12,931,008,000,000 (transport equipment 20.2%; agricultural products 12.8%; machinery 8.3%). *Major export destinations:* France 20.1%; Germany 14.5%; Italy 8.7%; U.K. 8.5%.

Transport and communications

Transport. Railroads (1995): route length 13,280 km; passenger-km 15,330,000,000; metric ton-km cargo 9,671,000,000. Roads (1995): length 343,197 km (paved 99%). Vehicles (1995): cars 14,212,257; trucks and buses 2,984,140. Merchant marine (1992): vessels 2,190; deadweight tonnage 5,077,275. Air transport (1995): passenger-km 34,043,765,000; metric ton-km cargo 3,763,516,000; airports (1997) with scheduled flights 25.

Communications

Medium	date	unit	number	units per 1,000 persons
Daily newspapers	1994	circulation	4,100,000	104
Radio	1996	receivers	12,000,000	306
Television	1995	receivers	19,200,000	490
Telephones	1995	main lines	15,095,400	385
Cellular telephones	1995	subscribers	965,700	25
Facsimile machines	1995	units	215,000	5.2
Personal computers	1995	units	3,200,000	82

Education and health

Educational attainment (1996). Percentage of economically active population age 16 and over having: no formal schooling 6.9%[12]; primary 28.0%; secondary 57.2%; higher 7.9%.

Education (1994–95)

	schools	teachers	students	student/ teacher ratio
Primary (age 6–11)	16,540[13]	132,566	2,364,910	17.8
Secondary (age 12–18)[14]	25,775[15]	299,056	4,744,829	15.9
Higher	1,415[15]	80,563	1,398,113	17.3

Health (1995): physicians 162,650 (1 per 241 persons); hospital beds (1991) 168,514 (1 per 234 persons); infant mortality rate 5.6.
Food (1995): daily per capita caloric intake 3,338 (vegetable products 73%, animal products 27%); 136% of FAO recommended minimum requirement.

Military

Total active duty personnel (1997): 197,500 (army 65.1%, navy 19.7%, air force 15.2%). *Military expenditure as percentage of GNP* (1995): 1.6% (world 2.8%); per capita expenditure U.S.$221.

[1]At the March 1996 elections, 208 seats were directly elected and 49 indirectly elected by the parliaments of the autonomous communities. [2]The constitution states that "Castilian is the Spanish official language of the State," but that "all other Spanish languages will also be official in the corresponding Autonomous Communities." [3]January 1. [4]Detail does not add to total given because of rounding. [5]Includes other enclaves (*plazas de soberanía*). [6]Estimate based on 1991 census. [7]For municipios, which may contain rural population. [8]Preliminary. [9]Import taxes and value-added tax on products. [10]Includes 813,600 unemployed persons not previously employed. [11]June. [12]Includes illiterate. [13]1993–94. [14]Includes vocational. [15]1992–93.

Internet resources for further information:
- **"Sí Spain" (Embassy of Spain, Ottawa, Canada) http://www.DocuWeb.ca/SiSpain/**
- **National Institute of Statistics http://www.ine.es/**

Sri Lanka

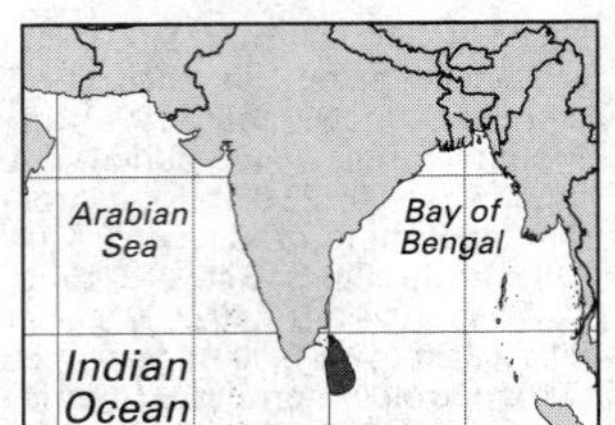

Official name: Śrī Lankā Prajātāntrika Samājavādī Janarajaya (Sinhala); Ilangai Jananayaka Socialisa Kudiarasu (Tamil) (Democratic Socialist Republic of Sri Lanka).
Form of government: unitary multiparty republic with one legislative house (Parliament [225]).
Head of state and government: President assisted by Prime Minister.
Capitals: Colombo (executive); Sri Jayewardenepura Kotte (Colombo suburb; legislative and judicial).
Official languages: Sinhala; Tamil.
Official religion: none.
Monetary unit: 1 Sri Lanka rupee (SL Rs) = 100 cents; valuation (Oct. 3, 1997) 1 U.S.$ = SL Rs 60.00; 1 £ = SL Rs 96.72.

Area and population

		area		population
				1994
Districts	Capitals	sq mi	sq km	estimate
Amparai	Amparai	1,705	4,415	512,000
Anuradhapura	Anuradhapura	2,772	7,179	750,000
Badulla	Badulla	1,104	2,861	735,000
Batticaloa	Batticaloa	1,102	2,854	443,000
Colombo	Colombo	270	699	2,062,000
Galle	Galle	638	1,652	983,000
Gampaha	Gampaha	536	1,387	1,568,000
Hambantota	Hambantota	1,007	2,609	537,000
Jaffna	Jaffna	396	1,025	896,000
Kalutara	Kalutara	617	1,598	969,000
Kandy	Kandy	749	1,940	1,286,000
Kegalle	Kegalle	654	1,693	763,000
Kilinochchi	Kilinochchi	494	1,279	110,000
Kurunegala	Kurunegala	1,859	4,816	1,481,000
Mannar	Mannar	771	1,996	140,000
Matale	Matale	770	1,993	434,000
Matara	Matara	495	1,283	810,000
Monaragala	Monaragala	2,177	5,639	367,000
Mullaitivu	Mullaitivu	1,010	2,617	98,000
Nuwara Eliya	Nuwara Eliya	672	1,741	541,000
Polonnaruwa	Polonnaruwa	1,271	3,293	336,000
Puttalam	Puttalam	1,186	3,072	626,000
Ratnapura	Ratnapura	1,264	3,275	972,000
Trincomalee	Trincomalee	1,053	2,727	327,000
Vavuniya	Vavuniya	759	1,967	119,000
TOTAL		25,332	65,610	17,865,000

Demography

Population (1997): 18,663,000.
Density (1997): persons per sq mi 736.7, persons per sq km 284.5.
Urban-rural (1997): urban 23.0%; rural 77.0%.
Sex distribution (1994): male 50.98%; female 49.02%.
Age breakdown (1994): under 15, 35.2%; 15–29, 29.7%; 30–44, 17.9%; 45–59, 10.6%; 60–74, 5.2%; 75 and over, 1.4%.
Population projection: (2000) 19,294,000; (2010) 21,414,000.
Doubling time: 58 years.
Ethnic composition (1991)[1]: Sinhalese 82.7%; Tamil 8.9%; Sri Lankan Moor 7.7%; other 0.7%.
Religious affiliation (1981): Buddhist 69.3%; Hindu 15.5%; Muslim 7.6%; Christian 7.5%; other 0.1%.
Major cities (1990): Colombo 615,000; Dehiwala–Mount Lavinia 196,000; Moratuwa 170,000; Jaffna 129,000; Sri Jayewardenepura Kotte 109,000.

Vital statistics

Birth rate per 1,000 population (1997): 17.9 (world avg. 25.0); (1986) legitimate 96.3%; illegitimate 3.7%.
Death rate per 1,000 population (1997): 5.9 (world avg. 9.3).
Natural increase rate per 1,000 population (1997): 12.0 (world avg. 15.7).
Total fertility rate (avg. births per childbearing woman; 1997): 2.1.
Marriage rate per 1,000 population (1992): 9.2.
Life expectancy at birth (1997): male 71.0 years; female 75.0 years.
Major causes of death per 100,000 population (1989): diseases of the circulatory system 47.8; violence and poisoning 38.6; malignant neoplasms 26.7.

National economy

Budget (1999). Revenue: SL Rs 148,206,000,000 (sales and turnover tax 27.5%, import duties 19.4%, excise taxes 14.8%, income taxes 11.6%, nontax revenue 10.5%). Expenditures: SL Rs 212,984,000,000 (current expenditure 79.7%, current expenditure 20.3%).
Public debt (external, outstanding; 1995): U.S.$7,010,000,000.
Tourism (1995): receipts U.S.$224,000,000; expenditures U.S.$186,000,000.
Production (metric tons except as noted). Agriculture, forestry, fishing (1996): rice 2,241,000, coconuts 2,000,000, sugarcane 1,273,000, plantains 560,000; livestock (number of live animals) 1,701,700 cattle, 764,200 buffalo, 591,100 goats; roundwood (1995) 9,624,700 cu m; fish catch (1995) 235,829. Mining and quarrying (1995): quartz stone 1,100,000; limestone 700,000; titanium concentrate 62,400; gemstones U.S.$61,000,000. Manufacturing (value added, in SL Rs '000,000; 1993): food, beverages, and tobacco 23,832; textiles and apparel 17,350; petrochemicals 5,264. Construction (units completed; 1993): residential 1,128; nonresidential 96. Energy production (consumption): electricity (kW-hr; 1994) 4,386,000,000 (4,386,000,000); crude petroleum (barrels; 1994) none (14,601,000); petroleum products (metric tons; 1994) 1,807,000 (1,647,000).
Gross national product (1995): U.S.$12,616,000,000 (U.S.$700 per capita).

Structure of gross domestic product and labour force

	1995			
	in value SL Rs '000,000	% of total value	labour force[1]	% of labour force[1]
Agriculture	124,854	18.8	1,985,300	32.7
Mining	8,042	1.2	56,400	0.9
Manufacturing	116,048	17.5	864,000	14.2
Construction	48,440	7.3	300,400	5.0
Public utilities	14,663	2.2	24,700	0.4
Transp. and commun.	62,325	9.4	244,700	4.0
Trade	142,836	21.6	557,100	9.2
Finance	47,383	7.2	91,500	1.5
Pub. admin., defense; Services	72,211	10.9	893,500	14.7
Other	25,562	3.9	1,057,500[2]	17.4[2]
TOTAL	662,364	100.0	6,075,100	100.0

Population economically active: total (1995) 6,102,154; activity rate 40.5% (participation rates: ages 15 and over, 54.9%; female 32.2%; unemployed 12.5%[1]).

Price and earnings indexes (1990 = 100)

	1990	1991	1992	1993	1994	1995	1996
Consumer price index	100.0	112.2	125.0	139.6	151.4	163.1	189.0
Average wage index[3]	100.0	111.7	128.4	155.4	158.8	160.7	175.6

Household income and expenditure (1992). Average household size (1994) 4.6[1]; income per household SL Rs 116,100 (U.S.$2,600); sources of income: wages 48.5%, property income and self-employment 41.8%, transfers 9.7%; expenditure: food 58.6%, transportation 16.0%, clothing 8.4%.

Foreign trade

Balance of trade (current prices)

	1991	1992	1993	1994	1995	1996
SL Rs '000,000	–29,612	–27,128	–36,037	–53,894	–44,594	–42,709
% of total	14.9%	11.0%	11.5%	14.5%	10.3%	8.6%

Imports (1995): SL Rs 272,201,000,000 (industrial supplies 54.6%, machinery and transport equipment 19.1%, food and live animals 11.1%, mineral fuels 7.9%). *Major import sources:* Japan 10.5%; India 9.8%; Singapore 5.2%.
Exports (1995): SL Rs 195,117,000,000 (clothing and accessories 48.6%, tea 12.6%, gems 6.3%, rubber products 4.0%, natural rubber 2.9%). *Major export destinations:* U.S. 35.5%; U.K. 9.1%; Germany 6.7%; Japan 5.3%.

Transport and communications

Transport. Railroads (1994): route length 1,493 km; passenger-km 3,264,000,000; metric ton-km cargo 144,000,000. Roads (1995): total length 102,600 km (paved 11%). Vehicles (1995): passenger cars 220,000; trucks and buses 248,900. Air transport (1996): passenger-km 3,868,000,000; metric ton-km cargo 159,054,000; airports (1996) 1.

Communications

Medium	date	unit	number	units per 1,000 persons
Daily newspapers	1994	circulation	450,000	25
Radio	1996	receivers	3,300,000	182
Television	1995	receivers	700,000	39
Telephones	1995	main lines	204,400	11
Cellular telephones	1995	subscribers	53,100	3.0
Facsimile machines	1995	units	11,000	0.6
Personal computers	1995	units	20,000	1.1

Education and health

Educational attainment (1981). Percentage of population age 25 and over having: no schooling 15.5%; less than complete primary education 12.1%; complete primary 52.3%; postprimary 14.7%; secondary 3.0%; higher 1.1%; unspecified 1.3%. *Literacy* (1991): percentage of population age 10 and over literate 86.9%; males literate 90.1%; females literate 83.8%.

Education (1994)

	schools	teachers	students	student/ teacher ratio
Primary (age 5–10)	9,648	70,108	1,960,495	28.0
Secondary (age 11–17)	5,771[4]	105,916	2,315,541	21.9
Voc., teacher tr.[5]	23	437	8,908	20.4
Higher	8[5]	1,937[5]	59,790	16.2[5]

Health (1993): physicians 3,713 (1 per 4,745 persons); hospital beds 48,963 (1 per 360 persons); infant mortality rate per 1,000 live births (1997) 15.
Food (1995): daily per capita caloric intake 2,334 (vegetable products 95%, animal products 5%); 102% of FAO recommended minimum.

Military

Total active duty personnel (1996): 112,300 (army 81.9%, navy 9.2%, air force 8.9%). *Military expenditure as percentage of GNP* (1994): 4.5% (world 3.0%); per capita expenditure U.S.$29.

[1]Excludes the Northern and Eastern provinces where Tamils are in the majority. [2]Mainly unemployed. [3]Agricultural minimum rates. [4]1992. [5]1991.

Internet resources for further information:
- **Central Bank of Sri Lanka http://www.lanka.net/centralbank**

Sudan, The

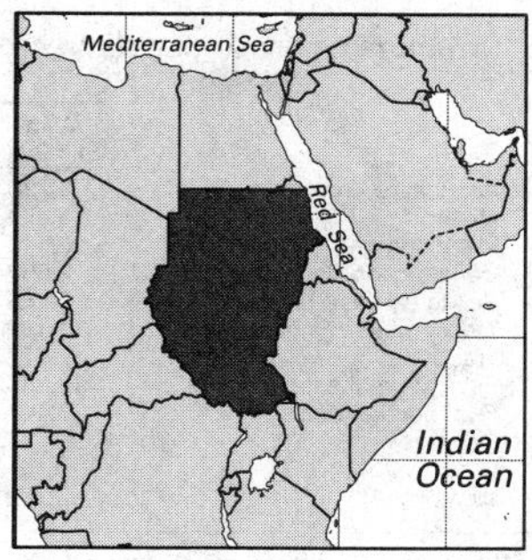

Official name: Jumhūrīyat as-Sūdān (Republic of the Sudan).
Form of government: Islamic military regime[1] with one legislative house (National Assembly [400][2]).
Head of state and government: President.
Capitals: Khartoum (executive); Omdurman (legislative).
Official language: Arabic.
Official religion: [3].
Monetary unit: 1 Sudanese dinar (Sd)[4]; valuation (Oct. 3, 1997) 1 U.S.$ = Sd 150.00; 1 £ = Sd 241.80.

Area and population

		area		population
States[5]	Capitals	sq mi	sq km	1983 census
A'ālī an-Nīl (Upper Nile)	Malakāl	92,198	238,792	1,599,605
Baḥr al-Ghazāl (Bahr el-Ghazal)	Wāw	77,566	200,894	2,265,510
Dārfūr (Darfur)	al-Fāshir	196,404	508,684	3,093,699
al-Istiwā'īyah (Equatoria)	Juba	76,436	197,969	1,406,181
al-Kharṭūm (Khartoum)	Khartoum	10,874	28,165	1,802,299
Kurdufān (Kordofan)	al-Ubayyiḍ	146,817	380,255	3,093,294
ash-Shamālīyah (Northern)	ad-Dāmir	183,800	476,040	1,083,024
ash-Sharqīyah (Eastern)	Kassalā	128,987	334,074	2,208,209
al-Wusṭā (Central)	Wad Madanī	53,675	139,017	4,012,543
TOTAL		966,757[6]	2,503,890[6]	20,564,364[7]

Demography

Population (1997): 32,594,000.
Density (1997): persons per sq mi 33.7, persons per sq km 13.0.
Urban-rural (1995): urban 24.6%; rural 75.4%.
Sex distribution (1995): male 50.20%; female 49.80%.
Age breakdown (1995): under 15, 43.9%; 15–29, 27.0%; 30–44, 15.6%; 45–59, 8.8%; 60–74, 3.9%; 75 and over, 0.8%.
Population projection: (2000) 35,530,000; (2010) 46,573,000.
Doubling time: 23 years.
Ethnic composition (1983): Sudanese Arab 49.1%; Dinka 11.5%; Nuba 8.1%; Beja 6.4%; Nuer 4.9%; Azande 2.7%; Bari 2.5%; Fur 2.1%; other 12.7%.
Religious affiliation (1992): Sunnī Muslim *c.* 72%; traditional beliefs *c.* 17%; Christian *c.* 11%, of which Roman Catholic *c.* 6%, Protestant *c.* 4%.
Major cities (1993): Omdurman 1,267,077; Khartoum 924,505; Khartoum North 879,105; Port Sudan 305,385; Kassalā 234,270; Nyala 228,778.

Vital statistics

Birth rate per 1,000 population (1996): 41.1 (world avg. 25.0).
Death rate per 1,000 population (1996): 11.5 (world avg. 9.3).
Natural increase rate per 1,000 population (1996): 29.6 (world avg. 15.7).
Total fertility rate (avg. births per childbearing woman; 1996): 5.9.
Life expectancy at birth (1996): male 54.2 years; female 56.1 years.
Major causes of death per 100,000 population: n.a.

National economy

Budget (1996). Revenue: LSd 679,600,000,000[4] (import duties 20.5%, taxes on business profits 19.1%, nontax revenue 17.4%, excise duties 16.7%). Expenditures: LSd 2,377,100,000,000[4] (interest on debt 58.5%, current expenditure 31.9%, development expenditure 4.1%).
Public debt (external, outstanding; 1995): U.S.$9,779,000,000.
Tourism (1994): receipts U.S.$3,000,000; expenditures U.S.$30,000,000.
Production (metric tons except as noted). Agriculture, forestry, fishing (1996): sugarcane 4,900,000, sorghum 4,104,000, wheat 550,000, millet 491,000, peanuts (groundnuts) 430,000, seed cotton 325,000, cottonseed 210,000, sesame seeds 160,000, dates 145,000, cotton lint 106,000, gum arabic 40,000[8]; livestock (number of live animals) 23,500,000 cattle, 23,400,000 sheep, 16,900,000 goats, 2,950,000 camels; roundwood (1995) 25,409,000 cu m; fish catch (1995) 45,000. Mining and quarrying: salt (1994) 75,000; gold (1996) 96,000 troy oz. Manufacturing (1995): raw sugar 450,000; wheat flour 350,000; cement 199,000; vegetable oils 70,000; cattlehides and horsehides 38,000[9]; shoes 6,000,000 pairs. Construction: n.a. Energy production (consumption): electricity (kW-hr; 1994) 1,333,000,000 (1,333,000,000); coal, none (none); crude petroleum (barrels; 1994) none (7,601,000); petroleum products (metric tons; 1994) 864,000 (1,051,000); natural gas, none (none).
Gross national product (1992): U.S.$8,176,000,000 (U.S.$300 per capita).

Structure of gross domestic product and labour force

	1996		1983	
	in value LSd '000,000[10]	% of total value	labour force[11]	% of labour force[11]
Agriculture	3,659	42.0	4,028,705	63.5
Mining	72	0.8	6,534	0.1
Manufacturing	698	8.0	266,693	4.2
Construction	548	6.3	139,282	2.2
Public utilities	206	2.4	43,728	0.7
Transportation and communications }	2,960	34.0	215,474	3.4
Trade and finance }			314,676	5.0
Services			550,409	8.7
Pub. admin., defense	571	6.5 }		
Other	—	—	777,480[12]	12.2[12]
TOTAL	8,714	100.0	6,342,981	100.0

Population economically active (1993): total 8,866,000; activity rate of total population 32.3% (participation rates: ages 15–64 [1983] 57.4%; female 22.3%; unemployed *c.* 30.0%).

Price and earnings indexes (1991–92 = 100)

	1991–92	1992–93	1993–94	1994–95	1995–96	1996–97
Consumer price index[13, 14]	100.0	218.3	448.7	511.7	832.3	1,609.1[15]
Earnings index	...	...	...	...	...	...

Household income and expenditure. Average household size: n.a.; income per household: n.a.[16]; expenditure (1983): food and beverages 63.6%, housing 11.5%, household goods 5.5%, clothing and footwear 5.3%.
Land use (1994): forested 18.1%; meadows and pastures 46.3%; agricultural and under permanent cultivation 5.5%; desert and other 30.1%.

Foreign trade

Balance of trade (current prices)

	1990–91	1991–92	1992–93	1993–94	1994–95	1995–96
U.S.$'000,000	−1,193	−941	−715	−463	−657	−673
% of total	63.6%	57.4%	50.3%	29.8%	42.5%	36.4

Imports (1994–95): U.S.$1,101,000,000 (petroleum products 17.2%; foodstuffs 17.0%, of which wheat flour 3.9%; electrical machinery 13.6%; chemicals and chemical products 10.0%; transport equipment 8.7%). *Major import sources:* Saudi Arabia 13.5%; U.K. 12.1%; Egypt 5.8%; Germany 4.4%; U.S. 3.6%.
Exports (1994–95): U.S.$444,000,000 (cotton 18.7%; sheep and lambs 14.0%; sesame seeds 12.8%; gum arabic 11.6%; gold 8.0%; peanuts [groundnuts] 5.1%). *Major export destinations:* Saudi Arabia 19.7%; U.K. 9.7%; Italy 9.0%; China 7.5%; Japan 5.3%; Switzerland 4.7%.

Transport and communications

Transport. Railroads: route length (1995) 4,764 km; (1993) passenger-km 1,183,000,000; (1993) metric ton-km cargo 2,240,000,000[17]. Roads (1995): total length 11,610 km (paved 36%). Vehicles (1995): passenger cars 263,000; trucks and buses 47,800[18]. Air transport (1996)[19]: passenger-km 650,049,000; metric ton-km cargo 30,706,000; airports (1997) with scheduled flights 3.

Communications

Medium	date	unit	number	units per 1,000 persons
Daily newspapers	1995	circulation	650,000	21
Radio	1996	receivers	5,755,000	182
Television	1995	receivers	250,000	8.2
Telephones	1995	main lines	75,000	2.5
Facsimile machines	1995	units	5,800	0.2

Education and health

Educational attainment (1983). Percentage of population age 25 and over having: no formal schooling 76.7%; complete secondary 2.0%; higher 0.8%.
Literacy (1995): total population age 15 and over literate 7,280,000 (46.1%); males 4,540,000 (57.7%); females 2,740,000 (34.6%).

Education (1994–95)

	schools	teachers	students	student/ teacher ratio
Primary (age 7–12)	12,187	83,306	3,023,955	36.3
Secondary (age 13–18)[20]	2,578	29,208	683,982	23.4
Vocational	...	621	15,443	24.9
Higher[20]	24	1,943	54,345	28.0

Health: physicians (1994) 2,600[21] (1 per 11,300 persons); hospital beds (1986) 18,571 (1 per 1,222 persons); infant mortality rate (1996) 76.0.
Food (1995): daily per capita caloric intake 2,313 (vegetable products 82%, animal products 18%); 98% of FAO recommended minimum.

Military

Total active duty personnel (1996): 89,000 (army 95.5%, navy 1.1%, air force 3.4%). *Military expenditure as percentage of GNP* (1994): 6.6% (world 3.0%); per capita expenditure U.S.$15.

[1]Main opposition parties boycotted the March 1996 executive elections; the president (and military general) who was elected in March 1996 appointed himself president in 1989 after overthrowing a democratically elected government in a military coup. [2]Includes 8 nonelected seats filled by head of state for 8 local administrative units controlled by opposition forces in extreme southern Sudan. [3]Islam was being imposed in 1997. [4]The Sudanese dinar (introduced May 1992 at a value equal to 10 Sudanese pounds [LSd]) circulates in tandem with the Sudanese pound. [5]Local administrative reorganization into 26 new states was officially announced in February 1994; area and population breakdown was not available in late 1997. [6]Including *c.* 50,000 sq mi (130,000 sq km) of inland water area. [7]Preliminary unadjusted 1993 census figure was 24,940,683, including an estimated 3,850,000 in the southern Sudan. [8]1994–95. [9]1992. [10]In constant prices of 1981–82 at factor cost. [11]Excludes nomads, the homeless, and institutionalized persons. [12]Includes 592,759 unemployed not previously employed. [13]Average of July 1–June 30 fiscal year. [14]For middle income residents of the Greater Khartoum area only. [15]September 1996 only. [16]Average annual income of paid worker (1992) U.S.$216. [17]Sections of the Sudan Railways were closed in 1995 because of insufficient funds. [18]Data unavailable for buses. [19]Sudan Airways only. [20]1991–92. [21]Estimated figure.

Internet resources for further information:
- **Republic of Sudan (university link)**
http://www.columbia.edu/Qtm146/sudan.html
- **The Sudan Page (unofficial link)**
http://www.sudan.net/

Suriname

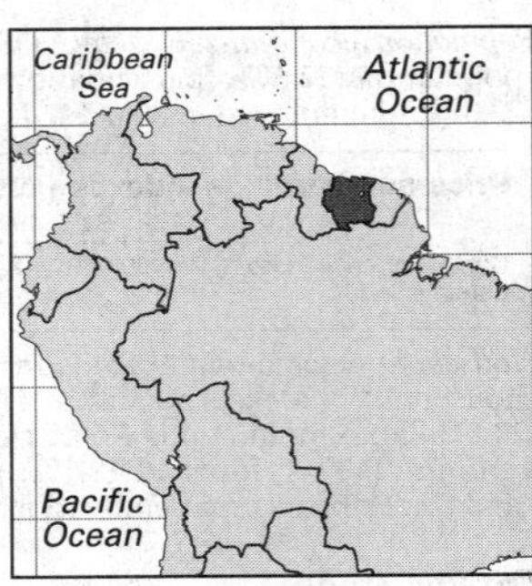

Official name: Republiek Suriname (Republic of Suriname).
Form of government: multiparty republic with one legislative house (National Assembly [51]).
Head of state and government: President.
Capital: Paramaribo.
Official language: Dutch.
Official religion: none.
Monetary unit: 1 Suriname guilder (Sf) = 100 cents; valuation (Oct. 3, 1997) 1 U.S.$ = Sf 401.00; 1 £ = Sf 646.41.

Area and population

Districts	Capitals	area sq mi	area sq km	population 1980 census
Brokopondo	Brokopondo	2,843	7,364	6,621
Commewijne	Nieuw Amsterdam	908	2,353	20,063
Coronie	Totness	1,507	3,902	2,777
Marowijne	Albina	1,786	4,627	16,125
Nickerie	Nieuw Nickerie	2,067	5,353	32,690
Para	Onverwacht	2,082	5,393	12,827
Saramacca	Groningen	1,404	3,636	10,808
Sipaliwini	...	50,412	130,566	23,226
Wanica	Lelydorp	171	443	60,725
Town district				
Paramaribo	Paramaribo	71	183	167,798
TOTAL		63,251[1]	163,820[1]	355,240[2]

Demography

Population (1997): 424,000.
Density (1997): persons per sq mi 6.7, persons per sq km 2.6.
Urban-rural (1996): urban 51.0%; rural 49.0%.
Sex distribution (1996): male 49.54%; female 50.46%.
Age breakdown (1995): under 15, 35.2%; 15–29, 29.7%; 30–44, 19.0%; 45–59, 8.8%; 60–74, 5.9%; 75 and over, 1.4%.
Population projection: (2000) 445,000; (2010) 511,000.
Doubling time: 47 years.
Ethnic composition (1991): Suriname Creole 35.0%; Indo-Pakistani 33.0%; Javanese 16.0%; Bush Negro 10.0%; Amerindian 3.0%; other 3.0%.
Religious affiliation (1986): Hindu 27.4%; Roman Catholic 22.8%; Muslim 19.6%; Protestant (mostly Moravian) 18.8%; other 11.4%.
Major cities (1980): Paramaribo 200,970[3]; Nieuw Nickerie 6,078; Meerzorg 5,355; Marienburg 3,633.

Vital statistics

Birth rate per 1,000 population (1995): 21.5 (world avg. 25.0); legitimate, n.a.; illegitimate, n.a.
Death rate per 1,000 population (1995): 6.6 (world avg. 9.3).
Natural increase rate per 1,000 population (1995): 14.9 (world avg. 15.7).
Total fertility rate (avg. births per childbearing woman; 1997): 2.6.
Marriage rate per 1,000 population (1991): 4.9.
Divorce rate per 1,000 population (1991): 2.5.
Life expectancy at birth (1990–95): male 67.8 years; female 72.8 years.
Major causes of death per 100,000 population (1992): noncommunicable diseases 769.0; external and other causes 608.1; communicable and perinatal diseases 232.8; ill-defined diseases 279.0.

National economy

Budget (1995). Revenue: Sf 94,096,600,000 (grants 29.2%; corporate income taxes 26.6%; custom duties 13.4%; individual income taxes 9.4%; value-added taxes 6.8%). Expenditures: Sf 88,973,500,000 (current expenditures 87.2%, of which welfare and social services 3.6%, defense 2.7%, education 2.1%, debt service 2.0%, health 1.9%; capital expenditures 12.8%).
Production (metric tons except as noted). Agriculture, forestry, fishing (1997): rice 218,000, sugarcane 84,500, bananas 41,000, plantains 19,000, oranges 14,200, coconuts 11,000, watermelons 6,000, cassava 6,000, cucumbers 5,500, tomatoes 1,700, cabbage 1,400, grapefruit 900; livestock (number of live animals) 104,000 cattle, 20,000 pigs; roundwood (1996) 122,000 cu m; fish catch (1995) 13,000. Mining and quarrying (1996): bauxite 3,708,000; gold 9,645 troy oz[3]. Manufacturing (value of production at factor cost in Sf; 1993): food products 992,000,000; beverages 558,000,000; tobacco 369,000,000; chemical products 291,000,000; pottery and earthenware 258,000,000; wood products 180,000,000. Construction (value of buildings authorized; 1985): residential Sf 46,500,000; nonresidential Sf 8,100,000. Energy production (consumption): electricity (kW-hr; 1994) 1,683,000,000 (1,683,000,000); hard coal (metric tons) none (n.a.); crude petroleum (barrels; 1994) 1,686,000 (1,370,000); petroleum products (metric tons; 1992) none (461,000); natural gas, none (none).
Household income and expenditure. Average household size (1980) 3.9; income per household: n.a.; sources of income (1975): wages and salaries 74.6%, transfer payments 3.2%, other 22.2%; expenditure (1968–69): food and beverages 40.0%, household furnishings 12.3%, clothing and footwear 11.0%, transportation and communications 9.5%, recreation and education 8.4%, energy 6.9%, housing 4.4%, other 7.5%.
Land use (1994): forested 96.2%; meadows and pastures 0.1%; agricultural and under permanent cultivation 0.4%; other 3.3%.
Gross national product (1994): U.S.$360,000,000 (U.S.$880 per capita).

Structure of gross domestic product and labour force

1994	in value Sf '000,000	% of total value	labour force	% of labour force
Agriculture, forestry	8,738.5	13.7	19,940[4]	20.3[4]
Mining	8,574.6	13.4	3,181	3.2
Manufacturing	6,548.9	10.3	4,432	4.5
Construction	2,360.3	3.7	1,656	1.7
Public utilities	2,885.2	4.5	1,288	1.3
Transp. and commun.	11,129.7	17.5	2,112	2.1
Trade[5]	12,877.3	20.2	4,383	4.5
Finance, real estate	13,257.3	20.8	1,954	2.0
Pub. admin., defense	3,441.7	5.4	38,552	39.2
Services	77.3	0.1	2,010	2.0
Other	−6,181.8[6]	−9.7[6]	18,732[7]	19.1[7]
TOTAL	63,709.1[8]	100.0[8]	98,240	100.0[8]

Public debt (external, outstanding; 1996): U.S.$216,500,000.
Population economically active (1994): total 98,240; activity rate of total population 24.3% (participation rates[9, 10]: ages 15–64, 56.0%; female 37.5%; unemployed 11.3%).

Price and earnings indexes (1990 = 100)

	1990	1991	1992	1993	1994	1995	1996
Consumer price index	100.0	126.0	181.0	440.7	2,064.5	6,927.7	6,878.1
Earnings index	...	...	...	...	...	...	...

Tourism (1995): receipts from visitors U.S.$14,000,000; expenditures by nationals abroad U.S.$3,000,000[11].

Foreign trade

Balance of trade (current prices)

	1991	1992	1993	1994	1995	1996
U.S.$'000,000	−117.9	−110.8	−77.2	−99.3	+38.3	+18.8
% of total	11.3%	10.2%	8.0%	20.4%	4.6%	2.2%

Imports (1994): U.S.$350,200,000 (fuels and lubricants 18.2%, machinery and transport equipment 13.3%, food and live animals 7.3%, home appliances 4.2%). *Major import sources:* United States 39.8%; The Netherlands 24.1%; Trinidad and Tobago 11.2%; Japan 3.3%; Brazil 3.0%.
Exports (1994): U.S.$339,800,000 (alumina 63.6%, shrimp and fish 9.7%, rice 9.6%, aluminum 9.3%, petroleum 3.0%, bananas 2.9%). *Major export destinations:* Norway 32.6%; The Netherlands 26.9%; United States 13.1%; Japan 6.6%; Brazil 6.3%; France 2.9%.

Transport and communications

Transport. Railroads (1991): length 187 mi, 301 km; passengers, not applicable; cargo, n.a. Roads (1995): total length 2,778 mi, 4,470 km (paved 26%). Vehicles (1995): passenger cars 44,300; trucks and buses 17,050. Merchant marine (1992): vessels (100 gross tons and over) 24; total deadweight tonnage 15,721. Air transport (1995)[12]: passenger-mi 548,885,000, passenger-km 883,347,000; short ton-mi cargo 17,684,000, metric ton-km cargo 25,818,000; airports (1997) with scheduled flights 3.

Communications

Medium	date	unit	number	units per 1,000 persons
Daily newspapers	1993	circulation	43,000	107
Radio	1993	receivers	290,300	719
Television	1994	receivers	59,000	146
Telephones	1995	main lines	53,200	130
Cellular telephones	1995	subscribers	3,700	9.0
Facsimile machines	1995	units	700	1.7

Education and health

Educational attainment: n.a. *Literacy* (1995): total population age 15 and over literate 271,000 (93.0%); males literate 137,000 (95.1%); females literate 134,000 (91.0%).

Education (1994–95)

	schools	teachers	students	student/teacher ratio
Primary (age 6–11)	280	3,447	62,613	18.2
Secondary (age 12–18)	100	2,056	29,554	14.4
Voc., teacher tr.	64[13]	...	12,307	...
Higher[14]	1	155	1,478	9.5

Health: physicians (1990) 331 (1 per 1,222 persons); hospital beds (1989) 1,901 (1 per 212 persons); infant mortality rate per 1,000 live births (1994) 27.9.
Food (1995): daily per capita caloric intake 2,556 (vegetable products 87%, animal products 13%); 113% of FAO recommended minimum requirement.

Military

Total active duty personnel (1997): 1,800[15] (army 77.8%, navy 13.3%, air force 8.9%). *Military expenditure as percentage of GNP* (1995): 3.0% (world 2.8%); per capita expenditure U.S.$90.

[1]Area excludes 6,809 sq mi (17,635 sq km) of territory disputed with Guyana. [2]Detail does not add to total given because of computational discrepancies. [3]1993. [4]Derived value. [5]Includes hotels. [6]Indirect taxes less subsidies and imputed bank service charges. [7]Includes 11,300 unemployed. [8]Detail does not add to total given because of rounding. [9]Districts of Wanica and Paramaribo only. [10]1992. [11]1994. [12]SLM (Suriname Airways) only. [13]1988–89. [14]1995–96. [15]All services are part of the army.

Internet resources for further information:

- **Suriname Home Page http://www.sesrtcic.org/DIR-SUR/SURHOME.HTM**

Swaziland

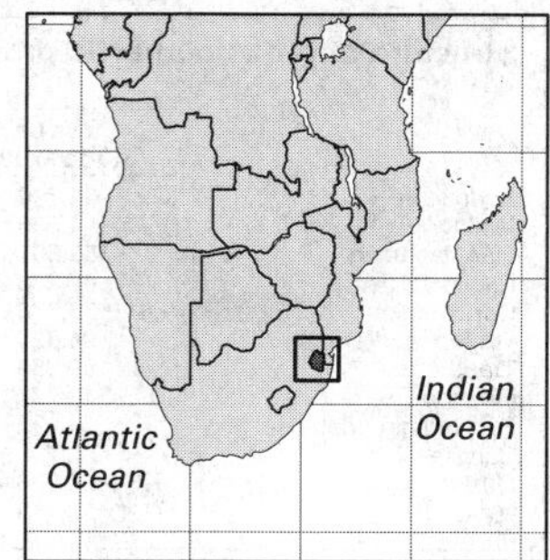

Official name: Umbuso weSwatini (Swazi); Kingdom of Swaziland (English).
Form of government[1]: monarchy with two legislative houses (Senate [30[2]]; House of Assembly [65[3]]).
Head of state and government: King, assisted by Prime Minister.
Capitals: Mbabane (administrative and judicial); Lozitha and Ludzidzini (royal); Lobamba (legislative).
Official languages: Swazi; English.
Official religion: none.
Monetary unit: 1 lilangeni[4] (plural emalangeni [E]) = 100 cents; valuation (Oct. 3, 1997) 1 U.S.$ = E 4.67; 1 £ = E 7.53.

Area and population		area		population
				1986
Districts	Capitals	sq mi	sq km	census[5]
Hhohho	Mbabane	1,378	3,569	178,936
Lubombo	Siteki	2,296	5,947	153,958
Manzini	Manzini	1,571	4,068	192,596
Shiselweni	Nhlangano	1,459	3,780	155,569
TOTAL		6,704	17,364	681,059

Demography

Population (1997): 1,032,000.
Density (1997): persons per sq mi 153.9, persons per sq km 59.3.
Urban-rural (1991): urban 34.3%; rural 65.7%.
Sex distribution (1996): male 48.53%; female 51.47%.
Age breakdown (1996): under 15, 45.7%; 15–29, 27.9%; 30–44, 14.9%; 45–59, 7.6%; 60–74, 3.3%; 75 and over, 0.6%.
Population projection: (2000) 1,137,000; (2010) 1,566,000.
Doubling time: 22 years.
Ethnic composition (1983): Swazi 84.3%; Zulu 9.9%; Tsonga 2.5%; Indian 0.8%; Pakistani 0.8%; Portuguese 0.2%; other 1.5%.
Religious affiliation (1980): Christian 77.0%, of which Protestant 37.3%, African indigenous 28.9%, Roman Catholic 10.8%; traditional beliefs 20.9%; other 2.1%.
Major cities (1986): Manzini 52,000; Mbabane 38,290; Nhlangano 4,107; Piggs Peak 3,223; Siteki 2,271.

Vital statistics

Birth rate per 1,000 population (1996): 42.9 (world avg. 25.0).
Death rate per 1,000 population (1996): 10.6 (world avg. 9.3).
Natural increase rate per 1,000 population (1996): 32.3 (world avg. 15.7).
Total fertility rate (avg. births per childbearing woman; 1996): 6.0.
Life expectancy at birth (1996): male 53.2 years; female 61.4 years.
Major causes of death (1992)[6]: accidents and injuries 15.8%; infectious intestinal diseases 13.3%; tuberculosis 10.3%; malnutrition 6.2%; respiratory diseases 5.3%; circulatory diseases 5.0%; digestive diseases 4.6%.

National economy

Budget (1996–97). Revenue: E 1,648,600,000 (receipts from Customs Union of Southern Africa 51.7%; tax on income and profits 26.1%; sales tax 12.1%; foreign-aid grants 2.3%; property income 1.1%; fees, services, and fines 0.8%). Expenditures: E 1,861,100,000 (recurrent expenditure 80.3%, of which general administration 24.3%, education 16.9%, economic services 13.2%, justice and police 7.7%, health 6.1%, defense 5.9%).
Tourism (1995): receipts U.S.$35,000,000; expenditures U.S.$37,000,000.
Gross national product (1995): U.S.$1,051,000,000 (U.S.$1,170 per capita).

Structure of gross domestic product and labour force	1995–96		1986	
	in value E '000	% of total value	labour force	% of labour force
Agriculture	383,800	9.2	30,197	18.8
Mining	45,200	1.1	5,245	3.3
Manufacturing	1,092,600	26.3	14,742	9.2
Construction	157,100	3.8	7,661	4.8
Public utilities	68,100	1.6	1,315	0.8
Transp. and commun.	209,800	5.0	7,526	4.7
Trade	316,600	7.6	12,348	7.7
Finance	250,800	6.0	1,931	1.2
Pub. admin., defense	704,600	16.9	32,309	20.1
Services	67,600	1.7		
Other	864,800[7]	20.8[7]	47,081[8]	29.4[8]
TOTAL	4,161,000	100.0	160,355	100.0

Population economically active (1986): total 160,355; activity rate of total population 23.5% (participation rates: ages 15 and over, 44.1%; female 34.2%; unemployed 27.0%).

Price and earnings indexes (1990 = 100)	1990	1991	1992	1993	1994	1995	1996
Consumer price index	100.0	110.8	119.9	140.3	160.4	184.0	207.1
Earnings index[9]	100.0	113.2	136.6	154.7	177.3	...	...

Public debt (external, outstanding; 1995): U.S.$236,800,000.

Production (metric tons except as noted). Agriculture, forestry, fishing (1996): sugarcane 3,846,000, corn (maize) 135,600, grapefruit and pomelo 35,100, oranges 32,874, seed cotton 14,000, pineapples 8,000, roots and tubers 8,000 (of which potatoes 6,000, sweet potatoes 2,000), lint cotton 5,000, peanuts (groundnuts) 5,000; livestock (number of live animals) 646,000 cattle, 438,000 goats, 31,000 pigs, 27,000 sheep, 1,000,000 chickens; roundwood 1,424,000 cu m; fish catch (1995) 115. Mining and quarrying (1996): asbestos 26,000; diamonds 64,000 carats[10]. Manufacturing (value added in U.S.$'000; 1994): food and beverages 244,000, of which beverage processing 153,000; paper and paper products 35,000; textiles 19,000; printing and publishing products 18,000; clothing 7,000; metal and metal products 7,000. Construction (value in E; 1996)[11]: residential 34,100,000; nonresidential 17,500,000. Energy production (consumption): electricity (kW-hr; 1991) 387,000,000 (815,000,000); coal (metric tons; 1992) 100,220 (1989; 28,454); crude petroleum, n.a. (n.a.).
Household income and expenditure. Average household size (1986) 5.7; annual income per household (1985) E 332 (U.S.$151); sources of income (1985): wages and salaries 44.4%, self-employment 22.2%, transfers 12.2%, other 21.2%; expenditure (1985): food and beverages 33.5%, rent and fuel 13.4%, household durable goods 12.8%, transportation and communications 8.8%, clothing and footwear 6.0%, recreation 3.3%.

Foreign trade

Balance of trade (current prices)	1991	1992	1993	1994	1995	1996
E '000,000	−98.6	−362.7	−406.9	−943.4	−55.6	−237.6
% of total	2.9%	9.1%	8.7%	16.8%	0.8%	3.2%

Imports (1995): U.S.$907,700,000 (machinery and transport equipment 25.1%; manufactured items 17.5%; foodstuffs 16.4%; chemicals 13.2%; minerals, fuels, and lubricants 5.1%). *Major import sources* (1993): South Africa 81.7%; U.K. 2.5%; The Netherlands 0.4%; Switzerland 0.3%; France 0.1%.
Exports (1995): U.S.$798,000,000 (wood and wood products 18.4%; sugar 15.3%; refrigerators 6.6%; cotton yarn 6.0%; paper and paper products 2.3%; canned fruits 2.0%; citrus fruits 1.9%; asbestos 1.6%). *Major export destinations* (1991): South Africa 47.0%; U.S. 3.6%; U.K. 3.3%; Mozambique 2.4%; South Korea 2.2%; Zimbabwe 2.2%.

Transport and communications

Transport. Railroads (1995): length 187 mi, 301 km; passenger-mi 752,000,000[12], passenger-km 1,210,000,000[12]; short ton-mi cargo 1,993,000,000[13], metric ton-km cargo 2,910,000,000[13]. Roads (1995): total length 2,377 mi, 3,825 km (paved 28%). Vehicles (1995): passenger cars 27,300; trucks and buses 26,340. Air transport (1995)[14]: passenger-mi 30,710,000, passenger-km 49,423,000; short ton-mi cargo 87,000, metric ton-km cargo 127,000; airports (1997) with scheduled flights 1.

Communications Medium	date	unit	number	units per 1,000 persons
Daily newspapers	1995	circulation	36,000	40
Radio	1995	receivers	117,000	129
Television	1995	receivers	90,000	96.0
Telephones	1995	main lines	19,800	21.0
Facsimile machines	1995	units	900	1.0

Education and health

Educational attainment (1986). Percentage of population age 25 and over having: no formal schooling 42.1%; some primary education 23.9%; complete primary 10.5%; some secondary 19.2%; complete secondary and higher 4.3%. *Literacy* (1995): total population age 15 and over literate 76.7%; males literate 78.0%; females literate 75.6%.

Education (1994)	schools	teachers	students	student/ teacher ratio
Primary (age 6–13)	535	5,887	192,599	32.7
Secondary (age 14–18)	165	2,872	52,571	18.3
Voc., teacher tr.[15]	5	228	2,958	13.0
Higher	1	190[15]	2,132	9.1[15]

Health: physicians (1990) 83 (1 per 9,265 persons); hospital beds (1984) 1,608 (1 per 396 persons); infant mortality rate per 1,000 live births (1996) 88.4.
Food (1995): daily per capita caloric intake 2,658 (vegetable products 90%, animal products 10%); 115% of FAO recommended minimum requirement.

Military

Total active duty personnel (1983): 2,657. *Military expenditure as percentage of GNP* (1995): 2.6% (world 2.8%); per capita expenditure U.S.$28.

[1]In July 1996 the king announced that a 30-member Constitutional Review committee had been formed to prepare proposals for a new draft constitution. [2]Includes 20 nonelective seats. [3]Includes 10 nonelective seats. [4]The lilangeni is at par with the South African rand. [5]Preliminary. [6]Percentage of deaths of known cause at government, mission, and private hospitals. [7]Includes indirect taxes less imputed bank service charges and subsidies. [8]Includes 43,925 unemployed. [9]Manufacturing sector only. [10]1994. [11]Urban areas under the jurisdiction of the Manzini and Mbabane town councils only. [12]1988. [13]1991. [14]Royal Swazi National Airways only; international flights only. [15]1993–94.

Internet resources for further information:
- **Central Bank of Swaziland**
  http://www.realnet.co.sz/cbs/cbs.html
- **Swaziland on the Internet**
  http://www.realnet.co.sz/

Sweden

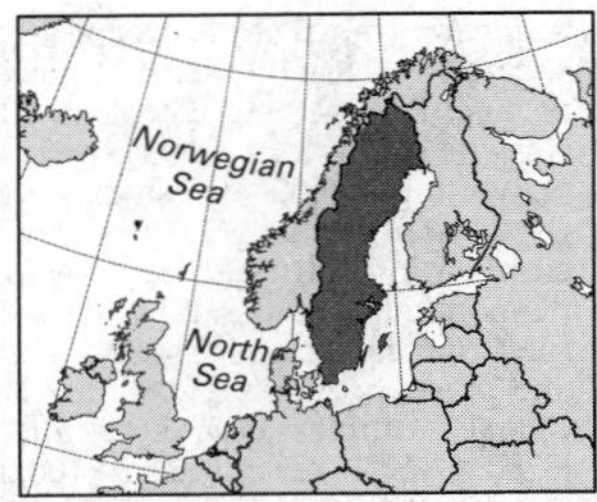

Official name: Konungariket Sverige (Kingdom of Sweden).
Form of government: constitutional monarchy and parliamentary state with one legislative house (Parliament [349]).
Chief of state: King.
Head of government: Prime Minister.
Capital: Stockholm.
Official language: Swedish.
Official religion: Church of Sweden (Lutheran).
Monetary unit: 1 Swedish krona (SKr) = 100 ore; valuation (Oct. 3, 1997 1 U.S.$ = SKr 7.53; 1 £ = SKr 12.14.

Area and population

		area		population
Counties	Capitals	sq mi	sq km	1997[1] estimate
Älvsborg	Vänersborg	4,400	11,395	448,074
Blekinge	Karlskrona	1,136	2,941	151,972
Dalarna	Falun	10,886	28,194	288,171
Gävleborg	Gävle	7,024	18,191	286,789
Göteborg och Bohus	Göteborg	1,985	5,141	775,638
Gotland	Visby	1,212	3,140	57,971
Halland	Halmstad	2,106	5,454	270,060
Jämtland	Östersund	19,090	49,443	134,561
Jönköping	Jönköping	3,839	9,944	311,765
Kalmar	Kalmar	4,313	11,170	241,896
Kronoberg	Växjö	3,266	8,458	179,655
Norrbotten	Luleå	38,191	98,913	264,320
Örebro	Örebro	3,289	8,519	275,855
Östergötland	Linköping	4,078	10,562	415,659
Skåne	Malmo	4,257	11,025	1,114,368
Skaraborg	Mariestad	3,065	7,937	278,263
Södermanland	Nyköping	2,340	6,060	257,383
Stockholm	Stockholm	2,505	6,488	1,744,330
Uppsala	Uppsala	2,698	6,989	289,153
Värmland	Karlstad	6,789	17,584	282,147
Västerbotten	Umeå	21,390	55,401	259,895
Västernorrland	Härnösand	8,370	21,678	256,587
Västmanland	Västerås	2,433	6,302	259,987
TOTAL LAND AREA		158,661[2]	410,929	
INLAND WATER		15,071	39,035	
TOTAL		173,732	449,964	8,844,499

Demography

Population (1997): 8,863,000.
Density (1997)[3]: persons per sq mi 55.9, persons per sq km 21.6.
Urban-rural (1996): urban 83.1%; rural 16.9%.
Sex distribution (1997[1]): male 49.41%; female 50.59%.
Age breakdown (1997[1]): under 15, 18.8%; 15–29, 19.0%; 30–44, 20.6%; 45–59, 19.6%; 60–74, 13.4%; 75 and over, 8.6%.
Population projection: (2000) 8,976,000; (2010) 9,243,000.
Ethnic composition (1997[1]): Swedish 89.3%; Finnish 2.3%; Yugoslavian 0.8%; Iranian 0.6%; Bosnian 0.5%; other 6.5%.
Religious affiliation (1995[1]): Church of Sweden 86.1% (nominally; about 30% nonpracticing); Roman Catholic 1.9%; Pentecostal 1.0%; other 11.0%.
Major cities (1997[1]): Stockholm 718,462; Göteborg 454,016; Malmö 248,007; Uppsala 184,507; Linköping 131,898.

Vital statistics

Birth rate per 1,000 population (1996): 10.8 (world avg. 25.0); (1995) legitimate 47.0%; illegitimate 53.0%.
Death rate per 1,000 population (1996): 10.6 (world avg. 9.3).
Natural increase rate per 1,000 population (1996): 0.2 (world avg. 15.7).
Total fertility rate (avg. births per childbearing woman; 1995): 1.7.
Marriage rate per 1,000 population (1996): 3.4.
Divorce rate per 1,000 population (1996): 2.4.
Life expectancy at birth (1991–95): male 75.6 years; female 81.0 years.
Major causes of death per 100,000 population (1994): heart disease 428.7; malignant neoplasms (cancers) 229.8; cerebrovascular disease 113.8.

National economy

Budget (1995–96). Revenue: SKr 816,978,000,000 (value-added and excise taxes 37.4%, social security 34.8%, income and capital gains taxes 15.1%, property taxes 3.2%). Expenditures: SKr 957,248,000,000 (health and social affairs 20.5%, debt service 12.9%, defense 4.7%, education 4.7%).
Public debt (1996): U.S.$108,500,000,000.
Production (metric tons except as noted). Agriculture, forestry, fishing (1996): sugar beets 2,430,000, barley 2,113,000, wheat 2,030,000, potatoes 1,211,000, oats 987,000; livestock (number of live animals) 2,348,800 pigs, 1,790,200 cattle, 469,000 sheep; roundwood (1995) 59,924,000 cu m; fish catch (1995) 395,721. Mining and quarrying (1996): iron ore 21,020,000; zinc 292,000; copper 269,000. Manufacturing (value added, in SKr '000,000; 1994): machinery and transport equipment 119,630; paper products 42,503; food 24,145; wood products 12,359; textiles and wearing apparel 3,767. Construction (dwellings completed; 1995): 12,678. Energy production (consumption): electricity (kW-hr; 1994) 142,889,000,000 (143,150,000,000); coal (metric tons; 1994) none (3,305,000); crude petroleum (barrels; 1994) 36,200 (128,773,000); petroleum products (metric tons; 1994) 16,616,000 (13,961,000); natural gas (cu m; 1994) none (763,223,000).
Gross national product (1995): U.S.$209,720,000,000 (U.S.$23,750 per capita).

Structure of gross domestic product and labour force

	1995			
	in value SKr '000,000	% of total value	labour force	% of labour force
Agriculture	34,770	2.4	124,000	2.9
Mining	4,525	0.3	8,000	0.2
Manufacturing	352,301	24.3	761,000	17.6
Public utilities	42,283	2.9	33,000	0.8
Construction	77,575	5.3	230,000	5.3
Transp. and commun.	94,824	6.5	261,000	6.0
Trade	169,339	11.6	609,000	14.1
Finance	343,791	23.6	415,000	9.6
Pub. admin., defense / Services }	392,817	27.0	1,506,000	34.9
Other	−58,806[4]	−4.0[4]	372,000[5]	8.6[5]
TOTAL	1,453,419	100.0[2]	4,319,000	100.0

Population economically active (1995): total 4,319,000; activity rate of total population 48.9% (participation rates: ages 16–64, 78.2%; female 47.9%; unemployed 7.7%).

Price and earnings indexes (1990 = 100)

	1990	1991	1992	1993	1994	1995	1996
Consumer price index	100.0	109.4	112.0	117.1	120.0	123.0	123.0
Hourly earnings index	100.0	105.0	110.0	113.0	118.0	123.0	132.0

Household income and expenditure. Average household size (1994) 2.1[6]; median income per household SKr 396,100 (U.S.$51,330); sources of income (1992): wages and salaries 58.9%, transfer payments 25.8%, self-employment 15.3%; expenditure (1995): housing and energy 29.6%, food 20.9%, transportation 16.1%, education and recreation 9.2%.
Tourism (1996): receipts U.S.$3,674,000,000; expenditures U.S.$6,236,800,000.
Land use (1994): forest 68.0%; pasture 1.4%; agriculture 6.8%; other 23.8%.

Foreign trade

Balance of trade (current prices)

	1991	1992	1993	1994	1995	1996
SKr '000,000	38,343	42,062	63,285	82,735	82,735	120,000
% of total	6.1%	6.9%	8.9%	9.6%	8.1%	11.8%

Imports (1996): SKr 447,600,000,000 (machinery and transport equipment 40.4%; chemicals 10.4%; food 6.6%). *Major import sources:* Germany 18.8%; U.K. 10.2%; Norway 7.8%; Denmark 7.5%; U.S. 5.8%.
Exports (1996): SKr 567,300,000,000 (machinery and transport equipment 47.4%, of which electrical machinery 17.2%; paper products 9.1%; chemicals 8.7%; iron and steel products 5.5%). *Major export destinations:* Germany 11.7%; U.K. 9.6%; Norway 8.4%; U.S. 8.3%; Denmark 6.3%.

Transport and communications

Transport. Railroads (1995): length 6,744 mi, 10,853 km; passenger-km 6,344,000,000; metric ton-km cargo 19,388,000,000. Roads (1996[1]): total length 84,419 mi, 136,223 km (paved 72%). Vehicles (1996[1]): passenger cars 3,630,760; trucks and buses 322,286. Merchant marine (1996[1]): vessels (100 gross tons and over) 430; total deadweight tonnage 2,881,000. Air transport (1994): passenger-km 8,426,647,000; metric ton-km cargo 249,528,000; airports (1995) 48.

Communications

Medium	date	unit	number	units per 1,000 persons
Daily newspapers	1995	circulation	4,544,000	515
Radio	1995	receivers	7,450,000	844
Television	1995	receivers	4,202,000	476
Telephones	1995	main lines	6,010,000	681
Cellular telephones	1995	subscribers	2,025,000	229.4
Facsimile machines	1995	units	329,000	37.3
Personal computers	1995	units	1,700,000	192.5

Education and health

Educational attainment (1995). Percentage of population age 16–64 having: primary education 30.7%; lower secondary education 32.2%; higher secondary 14.3%; some postsecondary 22.8%. *Literacy* (1995): virtually 100%.

Education (1994–95)

	schools	teachers	students	student/ teacher ratio
Primary (age 7–12)	4,900	89,275	916,661	10.3
Secondary (age 13–18)	629	29,563	309,952	10.5
Higher	...	29,487	268,448	9.1

Health: physicians (1995) 23,000 (1 per 384 persons); hospital beds 45,537 (1 per 194 persons); infant mortality rate per 1,000 live births (1996) 3.5.
Food (1995): daily per capita caloric intake 3,117 (vegetable 65%, animal 35%).

Military

Total active duty personnel (1996): 62,600 (army 68.8%, navy 16.0%, air force 15.2%). *Military expenditure as percentage of GNP* (1995): 2.8% (world 2.8%); per capita expenditure U.S.$683.

[1]January 1. [2]Detail does not add to total given because of rounding. [3]Density based on land area only. [4]Includes statistical discrepancies less imputed bank service charges. [5]Includes 333,000 unemployed. [6]1990.

Internet resources for further information:
- **Statistics Sweden http://www.scb.se/scbeng/keyeng.htm**

Switzerland

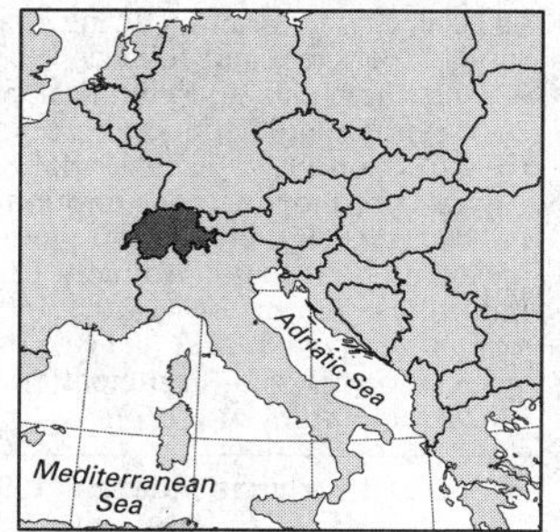

Official name: Confédération Suisse (French); Schweizerische Eidgenossenschaft (German); Confederazione Svizzera (Italian) (Swiss Confederation).
Form of government: federal state with two legislative houses (Council of States [46]; National Council [200]).
Head of state and government: President.
Capitals: Bern (administrative); Lausanne (judicial).
Official languages: French; German; Italian.
Official religion: none.
Monetary unit: 1 Swiss Franc (Sw F) = 100 centimes; valuation (Oct. 3, 1997) 1 U.S.$ = Sw F 1.45; 1 £ = Sw F 2.34.

Area and population

		area		population
Cantons	Capitals	sq mi	sq km	1996[1] estimate
Aargau	Aarau	542	1,404	528,887
Appenzell Ausser-Rhoden[2]	Herisau	94	243	54,104
Appenzell Inner-Rhoden[2]	Appenzell	67	173	14,750
Basel-Landschaft[2]	Liestal	200	517	252,331
Basel-Stadt[2]	Basel	14	37	195,759
Bern	Bern	2,302	5,961	941,952
Fribourg	Fribourg	645	1,671	224,552
Genève	Geneva	109	282	395,466
Glarus	Glarus	264	685	39,410
Graubünden	Chur	2,743	7,105	185,063
Jura	Delémont	323	836	69,188
Luzern	Luzern	576	1,493	340,536
Neuchâtel	Neuchâtel	310	803	165,258
Nidwalden[2]	Stans	107	276	36,466
Obwalden[2]	Sarnen	189	490	31,310
Sankt Gallen	Sankt Gallen	782	2,026	442,350
Schaffhausen	Schaffhausen	115	299	74,035
Schwyz	Schwyz	351	908	122,409
Solothurn	Solothurn	305	791	239,264
Thurgau	Frauenfeld	383	991	223,372
Ticino	Bellinzona	1,086	2,812	305,199
Uri	Altdorf	416	1,077	35,876
Valais	Sion	2,017	5,225	271,291
Vaud	Lausanne	1,240	3,212	605,677
Zug	Zug	92	239	92,392
Zürich	Zürich	668	1,729	1,175,457
TOTAL		15,940	41,285	7,062,354[3]

Demography

Population (1997): 7,116,000.
Density (1997): persons per sq mi 446.4, persons per sq km 172.4.
Urban-rural (1996): urban 67.7%; rural 32.3%.
Sex distribution (1996): male 48.83%; female 51.17%.
Age breakdown (1996): under 15, 17.6%; 15–29, 19.8%; 30–44, 23.9%; 45–59, 19.1%; 60–74, 12.9%; 75 and over, 6.7%.
Population projection: (2000) 7,225,000; (2010) 7,438,000.
Linguistic composition (1990): German 63.6%; French 19.2%; Italian 7.6%; Spanish 1.7%; Portuguese 1.4%; Romansch 0.6%; other 5.9%.
Religious affiliation (1990): Roman Catholic 46.2%; Protestant 40.0%; Muslim 2.2%; Orthodox Christian 1.0%; Jewish 0.3%; other 10.3%.
Major cities (1996[1]): Zürich 343,869 (928,696[4]); Basel 174,007 (404,262[4]); Geneva 173,559 (446,464[4]); Bern 127,469 (320,045[4]); Lausanne 115,878.

Vital statistics

Birth rate per 1,000 population (1996): 11.7 (world avg. 25.0); (1995) legitimate 93.2%; illegitimate 6.8%.
Death rate per 1,000 population (1996): 8.9 (world avg. 9.3).
Natural increase rate per 1,000 population (1996): 2.8 (world avg. 15.7).
Total fertility rate (avg. births per childbearing woman; 1995): 1.5.
Marriage rate per 1,000 population (1995): 5.8.
Life expectancy at birth (1994–95): male 75.3 years; female 81.7 years.
Major causes of death per 100,000 population (1994): heart disease 256.3, of which ischemic 146.8, other 109.5; malignant neoplasms (cancers) 238.7.

National economy

Budget (1996)[5]. Revenue: Sw F 39,924,000,000 (turnover taxes 29.1%, direct federal taxes 23.5%, motor fuel fees 11.5%). Expenditures: Sw F 43,972,000,000 (social services 27.3%, transportation 14.3%, defense 12.9%).
National debt (end of year; 1995): Sw F 82,152,000,000.
Tourism (1995): receipts from visitors U.S.$9,459,000,000; expenditures by nationals abroad U.S.$7,713,000,000.
Production (metric tons except as noted). Agriculture, forestry, fishing (1996): milk (1995) 3,900,000, sugar beets 1,000,000, wheat 626,000, potatoes 610,000, barley 362,000, apples 262,000, grapes 155,000; livestock (number of live animals) 1,755,000 cattle, 1,580,000 pigs; roundwood (1994) 4,974,000 cu m; fish catch (1994) 2,716. Mining (1995): salt 400,000. Manufacturing (value added in Sw F '000,000; 1994): nonelectrical machinery and transport vehicles 13,570; chemical products 13,088; electrical goods, electronics, and optics 12,306; base metals and metal products 8,241. Construction (in Sw F '000,000; 1995): residential 20,855; nonresidential 25,821. Energy production (consumption): electricity (kW-hr; 1995) 60,358,000,000 ([1994] 53,793,000,000); coal (metric tons; 1994) none (229,000); crude petroleum (barrels; 1994) none (34,796,000); petroleum products (metric tons; 1994) 4,694,000 (11,108,000); natural gas (cu m; 1994) 1,050,000 (2,374,000,000).
Gross national product (1995): U.S.$286,014,000,000 (U.S.$40,630 per capita).

Structure of gross domestic product and labour force

	1994		1995	
	in value Sw F '000,000	% of total value	labour force[6]	% of labour force
Agriculture	9,230	2.6	154,000	3.9
Manufacturing	80,997	23.0	782,000	19.9
Mining	...	...	27,000	0.7
Public utilities	7,741	2.2		
Construction	24,749	7.0	286,000	7.3
Transp. and commun.	22,173	6.3	227,000	5.8
Trade	61,092	17.3	733,000	18.6
Finance, insurance[7]	84,744	24.0	485,000	12.3
Pub. admin., defense	45,647	12.9	160,000	4.0
Services	27,769	7.9	928,000	23.6
Other	−11,218[8]	−3.2[8]	154,000[9]	3.9[9]
TOTAL	352,924	100.0	3,936,000[10]	100.0

Population economically active (1995): total 3,936,000; activity rate of total population 55.9% (participation rates: age 15 and over [1993] 60.8%; female 40.7%; unemployed [1996] 4.7%).

Price and earnings indexes (1990 = 100)

	1991	1992	1993	1994	1995	1996	1997
Consumer price index	105.8	110.1	113.8	114.7	116.8	117.8	118.6[11]
Annual earnings index	106.9	111.9	114.8	116.6	117.6	...	...

Household income and expenditure (1993). Average household size 2.2; average income per household Sw F 70,700 (U.S.$47,850); sources of income: wages 62.9%, transfer payments 17.9%; expenditure: food 18.8%, housing 16.4%, transportation 11.8%, health care 11.6%.
Land use (1994): forested 31.6%; meadows and pastures 29.0%; agricultural and under permanent cultivation 11.0%; other 28.4%.

Foreign trade[12]

Balance of trade (current prices)

	1991	1992	1993	1994	1995	1996
Sw F '000,000	−6,144	+268	+3,721	+3,798	+2,136	+3,118
% of total	3.4%	0.2%	3.2%	2.2%	1.2%	1.7%

Imports (1996): Sw F 91,967,000,000 (machinery and electronics 22.6%; chemical products 14.7%; vehicles 12.2%; food products 9.0%). *Major import sources:* Germany 32.7%; France 12.0%; Italy 11.2%; U.S. 6.6%; U.K. 4.9%.
Exports (1996): Sw F 94,137,000,000 (machinery and electronics 29.8%; chemical products 27.6%; precision instruments, watches, and jewelry 15.6%; base metals and finished products 8.7%). *Major export destinations:* Germany 23.3%; France 9.4%; U.S. 9.0%; Italy 7.7%; U.K. 5.7%.

Transport and communications

Transport. Railroads: length (1994) 3,125 mi, 5,030 km; passenger-km (1995) 11,400,000,000[13]; metric ton-km cargo (1995) 8,156,000,000[13]. Roads (1995): total length 44,151 mi, 71,055 km. Vehicles (1995): passenger cars 3,229,169; trucks and buses 277,399. Air transport (1995)[14]: passenger-km 19,725,000,000; metric ton-km cargo 1,508,000,000; airports (1996) with scheduled flights 5.

Communications

Medium	date	unit	number	units per 1,000 persons
Daily newspapers	1994	circulation	2,920,000	418
Radio	1996	receivers	5,600,000	791
Television	1995	receivers	2,602,000	370
Telephones	1995	main lines	4,318,500	613
Cellular telephones	1995	subscribers	447,200	64
Facsimile machines	1995	units	197,000	28
Personal computers	1995	units	2,450,000	348

Education and health

Educational attainment (1993). Percentage of resident Swiss and resident alien population age 25–64 having: lower secondary education or less 18%; vocational 50%; upper secondary 11%; higher technical 13%; university 8%.
Health (1994): physicians 11,814[15] (1 per 592 persons); hospital beds 48,539 (1 per 144 persons); infant mortality rate per 1,000 live births (1995) 5.0.
Food (1992): daily per capita caloric intake 3,379 (vegetable products 62%, animal products 38%); 126% of FAO recommended minimum.

Military

Total active duty personnel (1996): 3,300[16]. *Military expenditure as percentage of GNP* (1994): 1.9% (world 3.0%); per capita expenditure U.S.$712.

[1]January 1. [2]Demicanton; functions as a full canton. [3]Includes 1,363,590 resident aliens. [4]Urban agglomeration. [5]Confederation-level only. [6]Per revised official definition of June 1, 1995. [7]Includes consulting services. [8]Import duties less imputed bank charges. [9]Unemployed. [10]Labour force includes 976,000 foreign workers. [11]February. [12]Import figures are f.o.b. in balance of trade and c.i.f. in commodities and trading partners. [13]Swiss Federal Railways. [14]Swissair only. [15]Hospital-based physicians with private practice. [16]Excludes 396,000 reservists.

Internet resources for further information:
- **Embassy of Switzerland (London) http://www.swissembassy.org.uk**
- **Swiss Federal Statistical Office http://www.admin.ch/bfs/eindex.htm**

Syria

Official name: Al-Jumhūrīyah al-ʿArabīyah as-Sūrīyah (Syrian Arab Republic).
Form of government: unitary multiparty[1] republic with one legislative house (People's Council [250]).
Head of state and government: President.
Capital: Damascus.
Official language: Arabic.
Official religion: none[2].
Monetary unit: 1 Syrian pound (LS) = 100 piastres; valuation (official rate; Oct. 3, 1997) 1 U.S.$ = LS 40.00; 1 £ = LS 64.48[3].

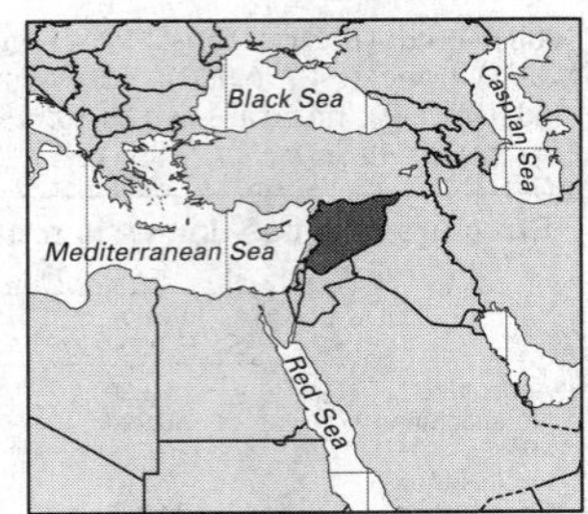

Area and population

Governorates	Capitals	area sq mi	area sq km	population 1995 estimate
Darʿā	Darʿā	1,440	3,730	623,000
Dayr az-Zawr	Dayr az-Zawr	12,765	33,060	722,000
Dimashq	Damascus	6,962	18,032	1,730,000
Ḥalab	Aleppo	7,143	18,500	3,035,000
Ḥamāh	Ḥamāh	3,430	8,883	1,120,000
Al-Ḥasakah	Al-Ḥasakah	9,009	23,334	1,050,000
Ḥimṣ	Homs	16,302	42,223	1,247,000
Idlib	Idlib	2,354	6,097	922,000
Al-Lādhiqīyah	Latakia	887	2,297	766,000
Al-Qunayṭirah	Al-Qunayṭirah	719[4]	1,861[4]	50,000
Ar-Raqqah	Ar-Raqqah	7,574	19,616	566,000
As-Suwaydāʾ	As-Suwaydāʾ	2,143	5,550	270,000
Ṭarṭūs	Ṭarṭūs	730	1,892	596,000
Municipality				
Damascus	—	41	105	1,489,000
TOTAL		71,498[4]	185,180[4]	14,186,000

Demography

Population (1997): 15,009,000.
Density (1997): persons per sq mi 209.9, persons per sq km 81.1.
Urban-rural (1995): urban 52.4%; rural 47.6%.
Sex distribution (1995): male 50.71%; female 49.29%.
Age breakdown (1995): under 15, 44.7%; 15–29, 28.2%; 30–44, 14.8%; 45–59, 7.3%; 60 and over, 5.0%.
Population projection: (2000) 16,392,000; (2010) 21,990,000.
Doubling time: 21 years.
Ethnic composition (1981): Arab 88.8%; Kurdish 6.3%; other 4.9%.
Religious affiliation (1992): Muslim 86.0%, of which Sunnī 74.0%, ʿAlawite (Shīʿī) 12.0%; Christian 8.9%; Druze 3.0%; other 2.1%.
Major cities (1994): Aleppo 1,591,400; Damascus 1,549,932; Homs 644,204; Latakia 306,535; Ḥamāh 229,000.

Vital statistics

Birth rate per 1,000 population (1995): 40.0 (world avg. 25.0).
Death rate per 1,000 population (1995): 6.0 (world avg. 9.3).
Natural increase rate per 1,000 population (1995): 34.0 (world avg. 15.7).
Total fertility rate (avg. births per childbearing woman; 1995): 6.1.
Marriage rate per 1,000 population (1995)[5]: 8.4.
Life expectancy at birth (1994): male 68.4 years; female 71.3 years.
Major causes of death per 100,000 population (1989): n.a.; however, the leading causes of mortality among the total population were diseases of the circulatory system 39.6%, injuries and poisoning 9.1%, diseases of the nervous system 7.4%, diseases of the respiratory system 7.4%.

National economy

Budget (1995). Revenue: LS 125,718,000,000 (current revenues 81.3%, capital [development] revenues 18.7%). Expenditures: LS 162,040,000,000 (current expenditures 54.3%, capital [development] expenditures 45.7%).
Public debt (external, outstanding; 1995): U.S.$16,757,000,000.
Gross national product (1995): U.S.$15,780,000,000 (U.S.$1,120 per capita).

Structure of gross domestic product and labour force

	1996[6] in value LS '000,000	1996[6] % of total value	1991 labour force	1991 % of labour force
Agriculture	171,354	27.7	916,952	26.3
Mining	43,780	7.1	6,651	0.2
Manufacturing	35,212	5.7	456,162	13.1
Construction	27,633	4.5	340,779	9.8
Public utilities	5,041	0.8	8,422	0.2
Transp. and commun.	65,873	10.6	166,965	4.8
Trade	157,816	25.5	378,250	10.9
Finance	28,206	4.6	24,651	0.7
Pub. admin.	62,838	10.2	951,104	27.3
Services	12,072	1.9		
Other	8,441[7]	1.4[7]	235,432[8]	6.8[8]
TOTAL	618,266	100.0	3,485,368	100.0[9]

Production (metric tons except as noted). Agriculture, forestry, fishing (1997): wheat 4,300,000, barley 1,800,000, seed cotton 765,000, grapes 455,000, tomatoes 425,000, apples 240,000, eggplants 160,000; livestock (number of live animals) 13,609,000 sheep, 1,137,000 goats, 818,000 cattle; roundwood (1995) 54,600 cu m; fish catch (1994) 7,500. Mining and quarrying (1994): phosphate rock 1,600,000; gypsum 235,000; salt 130,000; marble blocks 18,000,000 cu m. Manufacturing (value of production in LS '000,000; 1994): food, beverages, and tobacco 48,395; textiles, wearing apparel, and leather 47,372; chemicals and chemical products 35,300; fabricated metal products 20,558; nonmetallic mineral products 13,750; wood and wood products 9,116. Construction (1993): residential 628,000 sq m; nonresidential 209,000 sq m. Energy production (consumption): electricity (kW-hr; 1994) 14,800,000,000 (14,800,000,000); crude petroleum (barrels; 1996) 220,825,000 ([1994] 85,450,000); petroleum products (metric tons; 1994) 11,438,000 (10,044,000); natural gas (cu m; 1994) 2,050,160,000 (2,050,160,000).
Population economically active (1991): total 3,845,368; activity rate of total population 27.8% (participation rates: ages 15 and over, 49.0%; female 10.2%; unemployed 6.1%).

Price and earnings indexes (1990 = 100)

	1990	1991	1992	1993	1994	1995	1996
Consumer price index	100.0	109.0	121.0	137.0	158.0	170.6	184.7
Earnings index[10]	100.0	107.9	140.8	152.2	...	...	...

Average household size (1986): 5.7; income per household: n.a.; sources of income: n.a.; expenditure (1987)[11]: food 58.8%, rent, fuel, and light 16.0%, clothing 7.5%, household goods 5.8%, transportation 2.4%, education and recreation 2.1%.
Tourism (1995): receipts U.S.$1,325,000,000; expenditures U.S.$398,000,000.
Land use (1994): steppe and pasture 45.2%; cultivable 30.1%; forested 2.6%; other 22.1%.

Foreign trade[12]

Balance of trade (current prices)

	1991	1992	1993	1994	1995	1996
LS '000,000	+7,430	−4,458	−11,149	−21,550	−7,260	−13,970
% of total	10.7%	6.0%	13.6%	21.3%	7.5%	13.5%

Imports (1994): LS 61,370,000,000 (machinery and equipment 25.2%, food and beverages 15.7%, transportation equipment 12.0%, iron and steel 10.8%, chemicals and chemical products 8.5%, textiles 6.9%). *Major import sources:* Japan 10.1%; Italy 8.7%; Germany 8.5%; United States 5.8%; France 5.0%.
Exports (1994): LS 39,820,000,000 (crude petroleum and petroleum products 56.2%, fresh vegetables and fruits 10.7%, raw cotton 5.5%, textiles and fabrics 4.2%; live animals and meat 2.2%). *Major export destinations:* Italy 27.0%; France 12.4%; Lebanon 11.0%; Spain 6.8%; Saudi Arabia 5.5%.

Transport and communications

Transport. Railroads (1996): route length 1,766 km; passenger-km 498,000,000[13]; metric ton-km cargo 1,285,000,000[13]. Roads (1995): total length 39,243 km (paved 71%). Vehicles (1995): passenger cars 229,084; trucks and buses 218,900. Air transport (1996): passenger-km 1,113,614,000; metric ton-km cargo 117,638,000; airports (1997) with scheduled flights 5.

Communications

Medium	date	unit	number	units per 1,000 persons
Daily newspapers	1994	circulation	261,000	19
Radio	1995	receivers	3,000,000	211
Television	1995	receivers	700,000	49
Telephones	1995	main lines	930,000	66
Facsimile machines	1995	units	5,000	0.4
Personal computers	1995	units	10,000	0.7

Education and health

Educational attainment (1984). Percentage of population age 10 and over having: no schooling 20.1%; knowledge of reading and writing 26.3%; primary education 29.3%; secondary 18.4%; certificate 3.3%; higher 2.7%.
Literacy (1995): percentage of population age 15 and over literate 70.8%; males literate 85.7%; females literate 55.8%.

Education (1995–96)

	schools	teachers	students	student/ teacher ratio
Primary (age 6–11)	10,564	113,530	2,672,960	23.5
Secondary (age 12–18)	2,526[14]	51,483[15]	846,778	16.4
Voc., teacher tr.	292[14]	12,200[15]	94,204	7.7
Higher[16]	4[14, 17]	4,869[14]	161,185	46.6[18]

Health (1995): physicians 15,391 (1 per 953 persons); hospital beds 17,623 (1 per 832 persons); infant mortality rate per 1,000 live births (1994) 29.6.
Food (1995): daily per capita caloric intake 3,296 (vegetable products 90%, animal products 10%); 133% of FAO recommended minimum requirement.

Military

Total active duty personnel (1997): 320,000 (army 67.2%, navy 1.6%, air force 31.2%). *Military expenditure as percentage of GNP* (1995): 7.2% (world 2.8%); per capita expenditure U.S.$236.

[1]Parties ideologically compatible with the Baʿth Party. [2]Islam is required to be the religion of the head of state and is the basis of the legal system. [3]The primary rate used in foreign exchange is 1 U.S.$ = LS 41.95; 1 £ = LS 66.08. [4]Includes territory in the Golan Heights recognized internationally as part of Syria. [5]Syrian Arabs only. [6]UN estimates. [7]Import duties less imputed bank service charge. [8]Unemployed. [9]Detail does not add to total given because of rounding. [10]Annual wages index in manufacturing industries. [11]Weights of consumer price index components for Damascus only. [12]Import figures are c.i.f. [13]1995. [14]1994–95. [15]Estimated or provisional. [16]University-level institutions only. [17]Government schools only. [18]1993–94.

Internet resources for further information:
• **Syrian Official Homepage http://www.syria.org/**

Taiwan

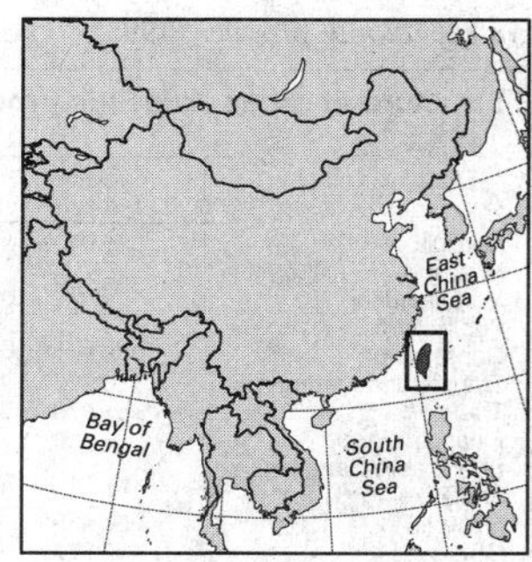

Official name: Chung-hua Min-kuo (Republic of China).
Form of government: multiparty republic with a National Assembly (334) and Legislative Yuan (164)[1].
Chief of state: President.
Head of government: Premier.
Capital: Taipei.
Official language: Mandarin Chinese.
Official religion: none.
Monetary unit: 1 New Taiwan dollar (NT$) = 100 cents; valuation (Oct. 3, 1997) 1 U.S.$ = NT$27.48; 1 £ = NT$46.10.

Area and population

		area		population
Taiwan area Counties	Capitals	sq mi	sq km	1996 estimate
Chang-hua	Chang-hua	415	1,074	1,289,554
Chia-i	Chia-i	734	1,902	565,099
Hsin-chu	Hsin-chu	551	1,428	410,985
Hua-lien	Hua-lien	1,787	4,629	358,679
I-lan	I-lan	825	2,137	464,793
Kao-hsiung	Feng-shan	1,078	2,793	1,199,876
Miao-li	Miao-li	703	1,820	559,674
Nan-t'ou	Nan-t'ou	1,585	4,106	545,370
P'eng-hu	Ma-kung	49	127	90,142
P'ing-tung	P'ing-tung	1,072	2,776	912,360
T'ai-chung	Feng-yuan	792	2,051	1,415,659
T'ai-nan	Hsin-ying	778	2,016	1,084,168
T'ai-pei	Pan-ch'iao	792	2,052	3,324,210
T'ai-tung	T'ai-tung	1,357	3,515	253,932
T'ao-yüan	T'ao-yüan	471	1,221	1,543,914
Yün-lin	Tou-liu	498	1,291	752,859
Municipalities				
Chia-i	—	23	60	262,300
Chi-lung	—	51	133	371,431
Hsin-chu	—	40	104	342,575
Kao-hsiung	—	59	154	1,428,694
T'ai-chung	—	63	163	864,363
T'ai-nan	—	68	176	709,440
Taipei	—	105	272	2,620,716
non-Taiwan area Counties[2]				
Kinmen (Quemoy) Lienchiang (Matsu)	—	69	179	53,286
TOTAL		13,969[3]	36,179	21,424,079

Demography

Population (1997)[4]: 21,616,000.
Density (1997)[4]: persons per sq mi 1,547.4, persons per sq km 597.5.
Urban-rural (1991)[5]: urban 74.7%; rural 25.3%.
Sex distribution (1997[6])[5]: male 51.40%; female 48.60%.
Age breakdown (1996)[5]: under 15, 23.8%; 15–29, 26.5%; 30–44, 25.7%; 45–59, 13.0%; 60–69, 6.5%; 70 and over, 4.5%.
Population projection: (2000) 22,183,000; (2010) 24,180,000.
Major cities (1997[6])[5]: Taipei 2,595,699; Kao-hsiung 1,434,907; T'ai-chung 881,870; T'ai-nan 712,172; Chi-lung 374,874.

Vital statistics

Birth rate per 1,000 population (1997[6]): 14.7 (world avg. 25.0).
Death rate per 1,000 population (1997[6]): 6.1 (world avg. 9.3).
Natural increase rate per 1,000 population (1997[6]): 8.6 (world avg. 15.7).
Total fertility rate (avg. births per childbearing woman; 1995)[5]: 1.8.
Life expectancy at birth (1994): male 71.8 years; female 77.7 years.
Major causes of death per 100,000 population (1996)[5]: malignant neoplasms 130.2; cerebrovascular diseases 64.9; accidents and suicide 57.8; heart disease 52.5; diabetes 35.0; liver diseases 21.5; kidney diseases 16.5; pneumonia 14.9.

National economy

Budget (1995)[7]. Revenue: NT$2,102,737,000,000 (income taxes 15.2%, land tax 11.9%, business tax 10.2%, commodity tax 7.4%, surplus of public enterprises 6.7%, customs duties 5.5%). Expenditures: NT$2,074,929,000,000 (administration and defense 23.7%, economic development 21.1%).
Population economically active (1990): total 10,236,324; activity rate 50.5% (participation rates: ages 15–64, 72.5%; female 38.5%; unemployed [1997] 2.7%).

Price and earnings indexes (1990 = 100)[5]

	1990	1991	1992	1993	1994	1995	1996[8]
Consumer price index	100.0	103.6	108.3	111.4	116.0	120.3	125.6
Monthly earnings index[9]	100.0	111.0	122.3	130.7	139.4	147.1	...

Production (metric tons except as noted). Agriculture, forestry, fishing (1996): sugarcane 4,190,000, rice 1,577,000, citrus fruits 463,710, corn (maize) 321,322[10], pineapples 274,113, sweet potatoes 204,000, bananas 140,997; livestock (number of live animals) 10,698,366 pigs, 318,404 goats, 164,825 cattle; timber 36,118 cu m; fish catch 1,231,834. Mining and quarrying (1990): silver 3,926 kg. Manufacturing (1996): cement 21,535,037; steel ingots 12,471,722; paperboard 3,209,458; fertilizers 2,197,742; polyester filament 1,199,470; polyvinyl chloride plastics 1,105,287; telephones 4,796,800 units; electronic calculators 2,951,086 units. Construction (1995): total residential and nonresidential 46,221,000 sq m. Energy production (consumption): electricity (kW-hr; 1996) 124,973,000,000 (111,140,000,000); coal (metric tons; 1993) 328,000 ([1992] 16,500,000); crude petroleum (barrels; 1993) 400,000 ([1992] 215,400); natural gas (cu m; 1992) 767,000,000 (n.a.).
Gross national product (1997): U.S.$298,368,000,000 (U.S.$13,819 per capita).

Structure of gross domestic product and labour force[5]

	1996			
	in value NT$'000,000	% of total value	labour force[11]	% of labour force[11]
Agriculture	246,538	3.3	918,000	9.9
Mining	20,483	0.3	14,000	0.1
Manufacturing	2,104,338	28.1	2,422,000	26.0
Construction	359,927	4.8	928,000	10.0
Public utilities	188,298	2.5	35,000	0.4
Transp. and commun.	509,259	6.8	472,000	5.1
Trade	1,218,045	16.2	1,976,000	21.2
Finance	1,627,624	21.7	567,000	6.1
Pub. admin., defense	790,389	10.5	1,736,000	18.6
Services	626,373	8.4		
Other	−193,597[12]	−2.6[12]	242,000[13]	2.6[13]
TOTAL	7,497,677	100.0	9,310,000	100.0

Tourism (1995): receipts from visitors U.S.$3,286,000,000.
Household income and expenditure (1995). Average household size (1996) 3.6; income per household NT$965,890 (U.S.$36,470[14]); expenditure: food 27.1%, rent, fuel, and power 19.7%, education 17.5%, transportation 11.6%, health care 7.6%, clothing 4.7%, furniture 2.9%.

Foreign trade

Balance of trade (current prices)

	1991	1992	1993	1994	1995	1996
NT$'000,000	350,013	231,668	199,604	194,360	206,730	361,505
% of total	9.4%	6.0%	4.7%	4.1%	3.6%	6.0%

Imports (1996): NT$2,815,720,000,000 (electronic machinery 15.8%, nonelectrical machinery 10.9%, chemicals 10.7%, iron and steel 5.6%, crude petroleum 4.7%, road motor vehicles 4.4%). *Major import sources:* Japan 26.8%; U.S. 19.5%; Germany 4.9%; South Korea 4.1%; Malaysia 3.5%; Singapore 2.7%.
Exports (1996): NT$3,176,625,000,000 (nonelectrical machinery 24.3%, electrical machinery 21.5%, plastic articles 6.6%, synthetic fibres 5.0%, transportation equipment 4.5%). *Major export destinations:* U.S. 23.2%; Hong Kong 23.1%; Japan 11.8%; Singapore 3.9%; Germany 3.1%.

Transport and communications

Transport. Railroads (1996): track length 3,879 km; passenger-km 8,975,200,000; metric ton-km cargo 1,584,800,000. Roads (1994): total length 19,038 km (paved 89%). Vehicles (1996): passenger cars 4,146,500; trucks and buses 799,600. Air transport (1996): passenger-km 40,603,500,000; metric ton-km cargo 3,567,900,000; airports (1996) 13.

Communications

Medium	date	unit	number	units per 1,000 persons
Daily newspapers	1988	circulation	4,000,000	202
Radio	1996	receivers	8,620,000	402
Television	1995	receivers	7,000,000	327
Telephones	1996	main lines	10,010,600	467
Cellular telephones	1996	subscribers	970,473	45.3
Facsimile machines	1995	units	430,000	20.2
Personal computers	1995	units	1,773,000	83.2

Education and health

Educational attainment (1995). Percentage of population age 25 and over having: no formal schooling 9.1%; less than complete primary education 6.9%; primary 23.9%; incomplete secondary 26.0%; secondary 20.5%; some college 8.2%; higher 5.4%. *Literacy* (1995): population age 15 and over literate 15,006,668 (93.7%); males 8,156,195 (97.6%); females 7,149,455 (90.2%).

Education (1995–96)

	schools	teachers	students	student/ teacher ratio
Primary (age 6–12)	2,523	87,934	1,971,439	22.4
Secondary (age 13–18)	920	76,562	1,412,201	18.4
Vocational	203	19,660	523,412	26.6
Higher	134	36,348	751,347	20.7

Health (1995): physicians 24,465 (1 per 867 persons); hospital beds 112,379 (1 per 189 persons); infant mortality rate per 1,000 live births 6.4.

Military

Total active duty personnel (1996): 376,000 (army 63.8%, navy 18.1%, air force 18.1%). *Military expenditure as percentage of GNP* (1995): 5.0% (world 2.8%); per capita expenditure U.S.$618.

[1]National Assembly functions as an electoral college or constituent body; the legislative branch is the formal lawmaking body. [2]The Nov. 7, 1992, constitutional reforms replaced the military administrations (established in 1949) on Quemoy and Matsu with civilian administrations. [3]Detail does not add to total given because of rounding. [4]Includes Quemoy and Matsu groups. [5]For Taiwan area only, excluding Quemoy and Matsu groups. [6]March. [7]General government. [8]October. [9]In manufacturing. [10]1991. [11]Civilian employed persons only. [12]Import duties less imputed bank service charge. [13]Unemployed. [14]Based on the average exchange rate.

Internet resources for further information:
- **The Republic of China Yearbook 1997**
  http://www.gio.gov.tw/info/yearbook/content.htm
- **Directorate-General of Budget, Accounting and Statistics (Taiwan)**
  http://www.dgbasey.gov.tw/english/english.htm

Tajikistan

Official name: Jumhurii Tojikiston (Republic of Tajikistan).
Form of government: parliamentary republic with one legislative house (Supreme Council [181]).
Chief of state: President.
Head of government: Prime Minister.
Capital: Dushanbe.
Official language: Tajik (Tojik).
Official religion: none.
Monetary unit: 1 Tajik ruble; valuation (Nov. 1, 1997) 1 U.S.$ = 750 Tajik rubles; 1 £ = 1,290 Tajik rubles.

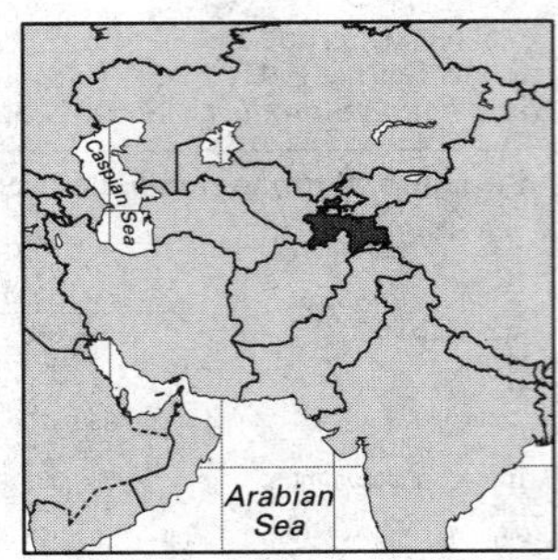

Area and population		area		population
		sq mi	sq km	1991 estimate
Autonomous republic	**Capitals**			
Badakhshoni Kuni (Gorno-Badakhshan)	Khorugh	24,600	63,700	167,100
Provinces				
Khujand	Khujand	10,100	26,100	1,635,900
Kŭlob	Kŭlob	4,600	12,000	668,100
Khatlon (Qŭrghonteppa)	Qŭrghonteppa	4,900	12,600	1,113,500
Regions under republican jurisdiction	—	11,000	28,400	1,181,800
City				
Dushanbe	—	100	300	591,900
TOTAL		55,300	143,100	5,358,300

Demography

Population (1997): 6,054,000.
Density (1997): persons per sq mi 109.5, persons per sq km 42.3.
Urban-rural (1995): urban 28.3%; rural 71.7%.
Sex distribution (1996): male 51.22%; female 48.78%.
Age breakdown (1989): under 15, 42.9%; 15–29, 28.1%; 30–44, 13.8%; 45–59, 9.0%; 60–74, 4.6%; 75 and over, 1.6%.
Population projection: (2000) 6,409,000; (2010) 8,051,000.
Doubling time: 35 years.
Ethnic composition (1991): Tajik 63.8%; Uzbek 24.0%; Russian 6.5%; Tatar 1.4%; Kyrgyz 1.3%; Ukrainian 0.7%; German 0.3%; other 2.0%.
Religious affiliation (1997): Sunnī Muslim 80.0%; Shīʿī Muslim 5.0%; Russian Orthodox 1.5%; Jewish 0.8%; other (mostly nonreligious) 12.7%.
Major cities (1989): Dushanbe 582,400; Khujand (formerly Leninabad) 164,500; Kŭlob 79,300; Qŭrghonteppa 58,400; Urateppa 47,700.

Vital statistics

Birth rate per 1,000 population (1996): 33.8 (1994; world avg. 25.0); (1994) legitimate 90.8%; illegitimate 9.2%.
Death rate per 1,000 population (1996): 8.4 (1994; world avg. 9.3).
Natural increase rate per 1,000 population (1996): 25.4 (1994; world avg. 15.7).
Total fertility rate (avg. births per childbearing woman; 1996): 4.4.
Marriage rate per 1,000 population (1994): 6.8.
Divorce rate per 1,000 population (1994): 0.8.
Life expectancy at birth (1995): male 64.4 years; female 70.4 years.
Major causes of death per 100,000 population (1993): diseases of the circulatory system 225.5; violence, poisoning, and accidents 184.0; diseases of the respiratory system 160.6; infectious and parasitic diseases 129.9; malignant neoplasms (cancers) 42.3; diseases of the digestive system 20.9.

National economy

Budget (1994). Revenue: 772,243,000,000 Tajik rubles (tax revenue 94.0%, of which domestic taxes 47.5%, income and profit taxes 35.8%, property taxes 8.7%, duties 7.5%; other 6.0%). Expenditures: 945,245,000,000 Tajik rubles (national economy 43.0%, social welfare and culture 30.0%, defense 4.0%).
Production (metric tons except as noted). Agriculture, forestry, fishing (1995): grain 206,200, vegetables 156,200, milk 76,100, eggs 31,100, potatoes 24,700; livestock (number of live animals) 2,930,000 sheep and goats, 1,147,000 cattle, 6,000 pigs, 1,200,000 poultry; roundwood, n.a.; fish catch (1995) 3,900. Mining and quarrying (1995): aluminum 500,000; lead 2,500; antimony 2,000. Manufacturing (value of production in '000,000 Tajik rubles; 1994): ferrous and nonferrous metals 604,705; textiles 496,481; energy 330,078; food products 163,559; machinery 77,331; chemical products 68,892; construction materials 66,306. Energy production (consumption): electricity (kW-hr; 1994) 17,000,000,000 (1993; 17,200,000,000); coal (metric tons; 1994) 150,000 (59,500); crude petroleum (barrels; 1994) 219,900 (1992; 279,000); petroleum products (metric tons; 1994) n.a. (305,500); natural gas (cu m; 1994) 40,000,000 (994,500).
Public debt (external, outstanding; 1995): U.S.$612,400,000.
Tourism: receipts from visitors, n.a.; expenditures by nationals abroad, n.a.
Population economically active (1995): total 1,783,000; activity rate of total population 30.7% (participation rates: ages 16–59 [male], 16–54 [female] 67.8%; female [1994] 38.0%; unemployed [1994] 27.0%).

Price and earnings indexes (1993 = 100)	1993	1994	1995
Consumer price index (Dec.)	100.0	107.2	1,428.8
Monthly earnings index	100.0	169.2	321.6

Gross national product (1995)[1]: U.S.$1,976,000,000 (U.S.$340 per capita).

Structure of gross domestic product and labour force	1994			
	in value '000,000 Russian rubles	% of total value	labour force	% of labour force
Agriculture	326,040	19.0	1,004,800	50.7
Mining Manufacturing	595,219	34.7	205,400	10.4
Public utilities	...	...	26,900	1.4
Construction	206,527	12.0	104,900	5.3
Transp. and commun.	58,393	3.4	63,000	3.2
Trade	51,979	3.0	112,000	5.7
Finance	...	...	...	...
Public administration, defense	...	...	21,000	1.1
Services	56,933	3.3	299,500	15.1
Other	422,877[2]	24.6	146,100	7.4
TOTAL	1,717,968	100.0	1,983,600	100.0[3]

Household income and expenditure. Average household size (1989) 6.1; (1995) income per household: 18,744 Tajik rubles (U.S.$114); sources of income (1995): wages and salaries 34.5%, self-employment 34.0%, borrowing 2.4%, pension 2.0%, other 27.1%; expenditure: food 81.5%, clothing 10.2%, transport 2.5%, fuel 2.1%, other 3.7%.
Land use (1994): forest 3.8%; pasture 24.8%; agriculture 6.0%; other 65.4%.

Foreign trade

Balance of trade (current prices)	1993	1994	1995
U.S.$'000,000	−100.0	−400.0	+29.0
% of total	14.3%	33.0%	2.3%

Imports (1995): U.S.$628,000,000 (alumina 29.0%, petroleum products 13.0%, agricultural products 12.0%, natural gas 11.0%). *Major import sources* (1993): Uzbekistan 33.5%; Russia 24.4%; Turkmenistan 15.9%; Kazakstan 13.2%; Lithuania 5.5%; Ukraine 5.5%.
Exports (1995): U.S.$657,000,000 (aluminum 59.0%, cotton fibre 32.0%). *Major export destinations* (1993): Russia 42.0%; Uzbekistan 20.6%; Lithuania 12.4%; Kazakstan 9.2%; Ukraine 4.6%; Latvia 3.1%.

Transport and communications

Transport. Railroads (1995): length 294.5 mi, 474.0 km; (1990) passenger-mi 6,094,400,000, passenger-km 9,808,000,000; short ton-mi cargo 7,617,000,000, metric ton-km cargo 11,121,000,000. Roads (1994): total length (state roads) 8,098 mi, 13,034 km (paved 28%). Vehicles (1994): passenger cars 184,900; trucks and buses, 3,600. Merchant marine: vessels (100 gross tons and over) n.a.; total deadweight tonnage, n.a. Air transport (1989): passenger-mi 3,214,600,000, passenger-km 5,173,400,000; short ton-mi cargo 22,124,000, metric ton-km cargo 32,300,000; airports (1997) with scheduled flights 1.

Communications Medium	date	unit	number	units per 1,000 persons
Daily newspapers	1994	circulation	80,000	13.7
Television	1995	receivers	1,500,000	259
Telephones	1995	main lines	262,700	45.3
Facsimile machines	1995	units	1,300	0.2

Education and health

Educational attainment (1989). Percentage of population age 25 and over having: primary education or no formal schooling 16.3%; some secondary 21.1%; completed secondary and some postsecondary 55.1%; higher 7.5%.
Literacy (1989): percentage of total population age 15 and over literate 97.7%; males literate 98.8%; females literate 96.6%.

Education (1994–95)	schools	teachers	students	student/ teacher ratio
Primary (age 6–13) Secondary (age 14–17)	3,400	84,000	1,289,000	15.3
Voc., teacher tr.	75	...	35,000	...
Higher	...	...	10,000	...

Health (1995): physicians 13,084 (1 per 443 persons); hospital beds 50,637 (1 per 115 persons); infant mortality rate per 1,000 live births (1994) 42.7.
Food: daily per capita caloric intake (mid-1990s) 1,400 (vegetable products 88%, animal products 12%); 55% of FAO recommended minimum requirement.

Military

Total active duty personnel (1997): 7,000 (army 100%); more than 6,000 Russian troops remained in Tajikistan in late 1997. *Military expenditure as percentage of GNP* (1995): 1.0% (world 2.8%); per capita expenditure U.S.$36.

[1]Preliminary estimates. [2]Includes 91,587,000,000 rubles in undistributed GDP and 331,300,000,000 rubles indirect taxes. [3]Detail does not add to total given because of rounding.

Internet resources for further information:
- **Tajikistan Human Development Report 1996**
  http://www.undp.org/undp/rbec/nhdr/1996/tajikistan/
- **Tajikistan Resource Page**
  http://www.soros.org/tajkstan.html
- **Interactive Central Asia Resource Project: Tajikistan**
  http://www.rockbridge.net/personal/bichel/tajik.htp

Tanzania

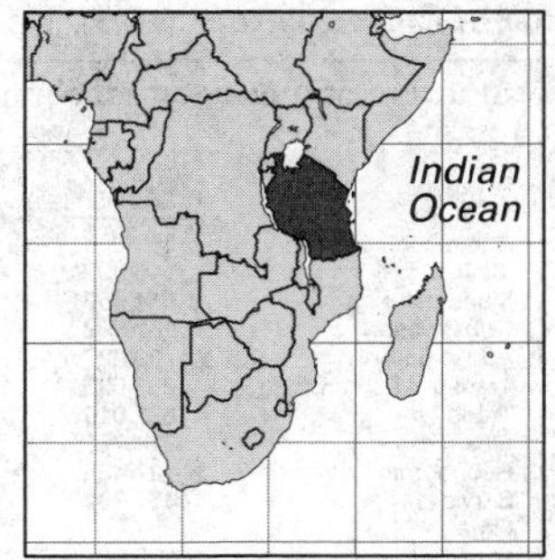

Official name: Jamhuri ya Muungano wa Tanzania (Swahili); United Republic of Tanzania (English).
Form of government: unitary multiparty republic with one legislative house (National Assembly [232[1]]).
Head of state and government: President.
Seat of government: Dar es Salaam[2] (Capital designate, Dodoma).
Official languages: Swahili; English.
Official religion: none.
Monetary unit: 1 Tanzania shilling (T Sh) = 100 cents; valuation (Oct. 3, 1997) 1 U.S.$ = T Sh 613.95; 1 £ = T Sh 989.69.

Area and population

Regions	Capitals	area sq mi	area sq km	population 1994 estimate
Arusha	Arusha	31,778	82,306	1,596,000
Coast	Dar es Salaam	12,512	32,407	753,000
Dar es Salaam	—	538	1,393	1,606,000
Dodoma	Dodoma	15,950	41,311	1,461,000
Iringa	Iringa	21,955	56,864	1,427,000
Kagera	Bukoba	10,961	28,388	1,607,000
Kigoma	Kigoma	14,300	37,037	1,015,000
Kilimanjaro	Moshi	5,139	13,309	1,308,000
Lindi	Lindi	25,501	66,046	763,000
Mara	Musoma	7,555	19,566	1,146,000
Mbeya	Mbeya	23,301	60,350	1,742,000
Morogoro	Morogoro	27,336	70,799	1,483,000
Mtwara	Mtwara	6,451	16,707	1,050,000
Mwanza	Mwanza	7,564	19,592	2,217,000
Pemba North	Wete	222	574	163,000
Pemba South	Chake Chake	128	332	151,000
Rukwa	Sumbawanga	26,500	68,635	820,000
Ruvuma	Songea	24,517	63,498	924,000
Shinyanga	Shinyanga	19,607	50,781	2,092,000
Singida	Singida	19,051	49,341	934,000
Tabora	Tabora	29,402	76,151	1,223,000
Tanga	Tanga	10,351	26,808	1,546,000
Unguja (Zanzibar) North	Mkokotoni	182	470	115,000
Unguja (Zanzibar) South and Central	Koani	330	854	83,000
Unguja (Zanzibar) West	Zanzibar	89	230	246,000
TOTAL LAND AREA		341,217[3]	883,749	
INLAND WATER		22,800	59,050	
TOTAL		364,017[4]	942,799[4]	27,471,000

Demography

Population (1997): 29,461,000.
Density (1997)[5]: persons per sq mi 80.7, persons per sq km 31.2.
Urban-rural (1995): urban 24.4%; rural 75.6%.
Sex distribution (1996): male 49.17%; female 50.83%.
Age breakdown (1996): under 15, 44.8%; 15–29, 28.6%; 30–44, 14.2%; 45–59, 7.8%; 60–74, 3.7%; 75 and over, 0.9%.
Population projection: (2000) 31,045,000; (2010) 36,076,000.
Doubling time: 29 years.
Ethnolinguistic composition (1987): Nyamwezi and Sukuma 26.3%; Swahili 8.8%; Haya 5.3%; Hehet and Bena 5.0%; Chagga 4.4%; Gogo 4.4%; Makonde 3.7%; other 42.1%.
Religious affiliation (1984): Muslim 35%; animist 35%; Christian 30%.
Major cities (1988): Dar es Salaam 1,360,850; Mwanza 223,013; Dodoma 203,833; Tanga 187,155; Zanzibar 157,634.

Vital statistics

Birth rate per 1,000 population (1996): 41.0 (world avg. 25.0).
Death rate per 1,000 population (1996): 17.0 (world avg. 9.3).
Natural increase rate per 1,000 population (1996): 24.0 (world avg. 15.7).
Total fertility rate (avg. births per childbearing woman; 1996): 5.6.
Life expectancy at birth (1995): male 41.5 years; female 45.0 years.
Major causes of death per 100,000 population: n.a.; however, the major diseases include malaria, bilharziasis, tuberculosis, and sleeping sickness.

National economy

Budget (1996–97). Revenue: T Sh 564,000,000,000 (import duties 29.7%, sales and excise tax 25.0%, income tax 24.1%). Expenditures: T Sh 673,000,000,000 (public administration 27.4%, interest payments on debt 14.8%, other 57.8%).
Public debt (external, outstanding; 1996): U.S.$8,164,000,000.
Tourism (1995): receipts from visitors U.S.$259,000,000; expenditures by nationals abroad U.S.$360,000,000[6].
Production (metric tons except as noted). Agriculture (1996): cassava 5,912,000, corn (maize) 2,638,000, sugarcane 1,560,000, rice 681,000, bananas 631,000, plantains 631,000, sorghum 609,000, coconuts 375,000, sweet potatoes 358,000, millet 338,000, potatoes 245,000; livestock (number of live animals) 13,360,000 cattle, 9,682,000 goats, 3,955,000 sheep, 335,000 pigs, 27,000,000 chickens; roundwood (1995) 35,577,000 cu m; fish catch (1993) 345,000. Mining and quarrying (1994): gemstones (including emeralds, sapphires, and rubies) 33,000 kg; gold 3,370 kg; diamonds 15,700 carats. Manufacturing (1995): cement 796,000; fresh meat and poultry 291,000[7]; sugar 88,000; hides and skins 48,325[6]; soap 20,000[7]; wheat flour 3,000[8]; textiles 12,000,000 m. Construction: n.a. Energy production (consumption): electricity (kW-hr; 1994) 912,000,000 (912,000,000); coal (metric tons; 1994) 4,000 (4,000); crude petroleum (barrels; 1994) none (4,288,000); petroleum products (metric tons; 1994) 579,000 (657,000).
Gross national product (1995)[9]: U.S.$3,703,000,000 (U.S.$120 per capita).

Structure of gross domestic product and labour force

	1995 in value T Sh '000,000	1995 % of total value	1991 labour force	1991 % of labour force
Agriculture	1,209,622	50.7	10,540,000	80.3
Mining	29,526	1.2		
Manufacturing	142,576	6.0	614,000	4.7
Construction	75,245	3.2		
Public utilities	46,365	1.9		
Transp. and commun.	153,690	6.4		
Trade	315,273	13.2		
Finance	51,901	2.2	1,969,000	15.0
Pub. admin., defense; Services	106,355	4.5		
Other	256,157	10.7	...	...
TOTAL	2,386,710	100.0	13,123,000	100.0

Population economically active (1994): total 13,852,000; activity rate 48.0% (participation rates [1991]: over age 10, 87.8%; female 40.0%).

Price index (1990 = 100)

	1990	1991	1992	1993	1994	1995	1996
Consumer price index	100.0	128.7	156.8	196.4	261.4	339.3	406.1

Household income and expenditure. Average household size (1988) 5.2; income per household: n.a.; sources of income: n.a.; expenditure (1994): food 64.2%, clothing 9.9%, housing 8.3%, energy 7.6%, transportation 4.1%.
Land use (1995): forested 37.0%; meadows and pastures 39.6%; agricultural and under permanent cultivation 4.2%; other 19.2%.

Foreign trade

Balance of trade (current prices)

	1991	1992	1993	1994	1995	1996
T Sh '000,000	−213,549	−258,245	−342,654	−385,977	−433,525	−363,605
% of total	58.8%	51.0%	48.6%	42.1%	35.7%	29.2%

Imports (1996): T Sh 804,949,000,000 (1995; machinery 31.3%, consumer goods 27.1%, chemicals 4.7%, food 2.3%). *Major import sources* (1995): U.K. 9.7%; Kenya 9.1%; Japan 7.2%; China 4.9%; India 4.7%.
Exports (1996): T Sh 441,344,000,000 (coffee 21.6%, cotton 18.2%, cashew nuts 9.7%, tobacco 4.1%). *Major export destinations* (1995): Germany 9.6%; Japan 8.5%; India 8.4%; U.K. 5.7%; Rwanda 5.0%; The Netherlands 5.2%.

Transport and communications

Transport. Railroads (1995): length 3,569 km; passenger-journeys 1,517,000[10]; metric ton-km cargo 1,160,000,000[10]. Roads (1995): length 88,100 km (paved 4.2%). Vehicles (1994): passenger cars 47,500; trucks and buses 38,000. Merchant marine (1992): vessels (100 gross tons and over) 43; deadweight tonnage 48,465. Air transport (1995)[11]: passenger-km 184,383,000; metric ton-km 2,904,000; airports (1997) with scheduled flights 11.

Communications

Medium	date	unit	number	units per 1,000 persons
Daily newspapers	1994	circulation	220,000	8.0
Radio	1995	receivers	565,200	20.0
Television	1995	receivers	80,000	2.8
Telephones	1995	main lines	90,300	3.2
Cellular telephones	1995	subscribers	3,500	0.1
Facsimile machines	1995	units	2,000	0.1

Education and health

Educational attainment (1978). Percentage of population age 10 and over having: no schooling 48.6%; some primary education 40.7%; completed primary 8.7%; secondary and higher 1.9%. *Literacy* (1995): percentage of population age 15 and over literate 67.8%; males 79.4%; females 56.8%.

Education (1994)[12]

	schools	teachers	students	student/ teacher ratio
Primary (age 7–13)	10,891	103,900	3,736,734[6]	...
Secondary (age 14–19)	491	10,612	180,899[6]	...
Teacher training	40	1,167[6]	15,824[6]	13.6
Higher	4[13]	1,206[13]	4,289	...

Health (1993): physicians 1,365 (1 per 20,511 persons); hospital beds 26,820 (1 per 1,000 persons); infant mortality rate (1995) 107.
Food (1995): daily per capita caloric intake 2,024 (vegetable products 93%, animal products 7%); 81% of FAO recommended minimum requirement.

Military

Total active duty personnel (1996): 34,600 (army 86.7%, navy 2.9%, air force 10.4%). *Military expenditure as percentage of GNP* (1995): 1.8% (world 3.0%); per capita expenditure U.S.$2.

[1]Includes 43 nonelective seats. [2]Government in process of being transferred from Dar es Salaam to Dodoma; legislative branch meets in Dodoma. [3]Detail does not add to total given because of rounding. [4]A recent survey indicates a total area of 364,901 sq mi (945,090 sq km). [5]Based on the total area of 364,901 sq mi. [6]1993. [7]1992. [8]1991. [9]Mainland Tanzania only. [10]Tanzanian Railways only; 1994. [11]Air Tanzania only. [12]Excludes Zanzibar and Pemba. [13]1989.

Thailand

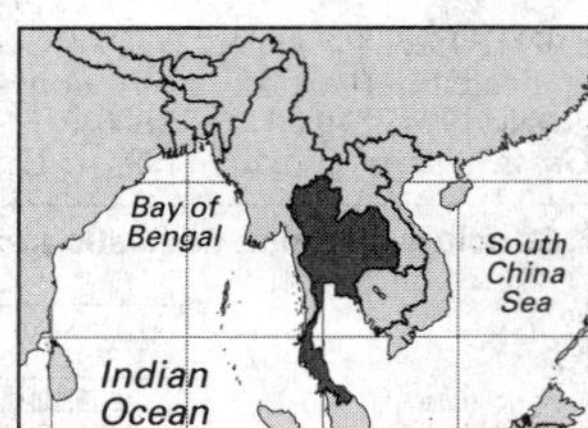

Official name: Muang Thai, or Prathet Thai (Kingdom of Thailand).
Form of government: constitutional monarchy with two legislative houses (Senate [260][1]; House of Representatives [393]).
Chief of state: King.
Head of government: Prime Minister.
Capital: Bangkok.
Official language: Thai.
Official religion: Buddhism.
Monetary unit: 1 Thai baht (B) = 100 stangs; valuation (Oct. 3, 1997) 1 U.S.$ = B 36.40; 1 £ = B 58.68.

Area and population

Regions[2]	area sq mi	area sq km	population 1995 estimate[3]
Bangkok Metropolis	2,995	7,758	8,896,506
Central	6,407	16,594	2,877,458
Eastern	14,094	36,503	3,922,078
Northeastern	65,195	168,854	20,663,191
Northern	65,500	169,644	11,896,331
Southern	27,303	70,715	7,706,208
Western	16,621	43,047	3,498,610
TOTAL	198,115	513,115	59,460,382

Demography

Population (1997): 60,602,000[4].
Density (1997): persons per sq mi 305.9, persons per sq km 118.1.
Urban-rural (1995): urban 18.3%; rural 81.7%.
Sex distribution (1995): male 49.91%; female 50.09%.
Age breakdown (1996): under 15, 27.4%; 15–29, 28.4%; 30–44, 22.8%; 45–59, 13.2%; 60–74, 6.6%; 75 and over, 1.6%.
Population projection: (2000) 62,405,000; (2010) 67,774,000.
Doubling time: 67 years.
Ethnic composition (1983): Thai 79.5%, of which Siamese 52.6%, Lao 26.9%; Chinese 12.1%; Malay 3.7%; Khmer 2.7%; other 2.0%.
Religious affiliation (1992): Buddhist 94.8%; Muslim 4.0%; Christian 0.6%; other 0.6%.
Major cities (1991)[3]: Bangkok 5,620,591; Nonthaburi 264,201; Nakhon Ratchasima 202,503; Chiang Mai 161,541; Khon Kaen 131,478.

Vital statistics

Birth rate per 1,000 population (1997): 17.8 (world avg. 25.0).
Death rate per 1,000 population (1997): 7.4 (world avg. 9.3).
Natural increase rate per 1,000 population (1997): 10.4 (world avg. 15.7).
Total fertility rate (avg. births per childbearing woman; 1997): 2.0.
Marriage rate per 1,000 population (1995): 7.9.
Divorce rate per 1,000 population (1995): 0.9.
Life expectancy at birth (1997): male 67.0 years; female 72.0 years.
Major causes of death per 100,000 population (1993)[5]: accidents, homicide, and poisonings 13.7; diseases of the heart 10.7; malignant neoplasms (cancers) 9.1; hypertension and cerebrovascular disease 3.3; pneumonia and other lung diseases 2.8; diseases of the liver and the pancreas 2.6.

National economy

Budget (1995). Revenue: B 760,755,000,000 (taxes 91.7%; state enterprises 4.9%; sale of property and services 1.0%). Expenditures: B 643,283,000,000 (current expenditure 67.7%, of which goods and services 58.1%, transfer payments 9.6%; capital expenditure 32.3%, of which government capital formation 29.8%, transfer payments 2.3%).
Public debt (external, outstanding; 1995): U.S.$17,231,000,000.
Production (metric tons except as noted). Agriculture, forestry, fishing (1996): sugarcane 62,422,000, rice 21,800,000, tapioca 17,340,000[6], cassava 16,000,000, corn (maize) 4,361,000, natural rubber 2,257,000, pineapples 2,031,000, bananas 1,750,000, soybean 412,000, palm oil 400,000, tobacco 69,900; livestock (number of live animals) 8,000,000 cattle, 4,807,000 buffalo, 4,023,000 pigs, 110,000,000 chickens; roundwood (1995) 39,288,000 cu m; fish catch (1994) 3,432,000. Mining and quarrying (1995): limestone 45,559,000; gypsum 8,533,000; kaolin clay 461,000; zinc ore 135,198; fluorite 24,114; lead ore 22,786; tin concentrates 2,201. Manufacturing (1995): cement 33,445,000; refined sugar 5,201,800; synthetic fibre 540,800; galvanized iron sheet 370,000; tin plate 250,500; jute products 76,000. Construction (1990): residential 16,343,000 sq m; nonresidential 13,449,000 sq m. Energy production (consumption): electricity (kW-hr; 1994) 74,452,000,000 (75,278,000,000); coal (metric tons; 1994) 17,095,000 (17,198,000); crude petroleum (barrels; 1994) 9,583,000 (137,883,000); petroleum products (metric tons; 1994) 21,291,000 (28,850,000); natural gas (cu m; 1994) 9,513,000,000 (9,513,000,000).
Land use (1994): forested 29.0%; meadows and pastures 1.6%; agricultural and under permanent cultivation 40.0%; other 29.4%.
Population economically active (1995): total 31,347,900; activity rate of total population 53.0% (participation rates: over age 13, 69.8%; female 44.1%; unemployed 2.3%).

Price and earnings indexes (1990 = 100)

	1990	1991	1992	1993	1994	1995	1996
Consumer price index	100.0	105.7	110.1	113.7	119.5	126.4	133.8
Monthly earnings index	100.0	116.8	132.8	144.7	133.8	...	...

Gross national product (1995): U.S.$159,630,000,000 (U.S.$2,740 per capita).

Structure of gross domestic product and labour force

	1994 in value B '000,000	1994 % of total value	1995 labour force[7]	1995 % of labour force[7]
Agriculture	369,053	10.2	13,418,100	42.8
Mining	48,599	1.5	64,000	0.2
Manufacturing	1,014,952	28.2	4,839,500	15.4
Construction	267,999	7.5	2,649,100	8.5
Public utilities	83,923	2.3	194,000	0.6
Transp. and commun.	267,933	7.4	1,025,800	3.3
Trade	592,016	16.4	4,274,500	13.6
Finance	374,795	10.4 }		
Pub. admin., defense	127,436	3.5 }	4,142,800	13.2
Services	454,201	12.6 }		
Other	...	...	740,100[8]	2.4[8]
TOTAL	3,600,907	100.0	31,347,900	100.0

Household income and expenditure (1994). Average household size 3.8; average annual income per household B 99,912 (U.S.$3,973); sources of income: wages and salaries 41.2%, self-employment 30.2%, transfer payments 7.1%, other 21.5%; expenditure: food, tobacco, and beverages 36.5%, housing 21.9%, transportation and communications 14.8%, medical and personal care 6.0%, clothing 5.4%, education and recreation 4.0%, other 11.4%.
Tourism (1995): receipts from visitors U.S.$7,664,000,000; expenditures by nationals abroad U.S.$3,372,000,000.

Foreign trade[9]

Balance of trade (current prices)

	1990	1991	1992	1993	1994	1995
U.S.$'000,000	−6,750	−5,990	−4,161	−4,297	−3,726	−7,968
% of total	12.9%	9.6%	6.1%	5.6%	4.0%	6.7%

Imports (1995): B 1,766,142,000,000 (electrical machinery 19.1%, nonelectrical machinery 18.9%, road vehicles 7.7%, iron and steel 7.1%, mineral fuels and lubricants 6.8%, organic chemicals 3.7%, plastics 3.4%). *Major import sources:* Japan 30.5%; U.S. 12.0%; Singapore 5.9%; Germany 5.3%; Taiwan 4.8%; Malaysia 4.6%; South Korea 3.5%.
Exports (1995): B 1,407,996,000,000 (electrical machinery 17.2%, nonelectrical machinery 14.0%, rubber products 5.8%, live fish 5.1%, garments 4.6%, plastics 4.4%, precious jewelry 3.9%, footwear 3.8%, cereals 3.5%). *Major export destinations:* U.S. 17.8%; Japan 16.8%; Singapore 14.0%; Hong Kong 5.2%; The Netherlands 3.2%; China 3.0%; Germany 2.9%.

Transport and communications

Transport. Railroads (1995[10]): route length 3,976 km; passenger-km 12,975,000,000; metric ton-km cargo 3,242,000,000. Roads (1995): total length 62,000 km (paved 97%). Vehicles (1995): passenger cars 1,440,000; trucks and buses 2,969,000. Air transport (1996): passenger-km 29,226,000,000; metric ton-km cargo 1,320,300,000; airports (1996) with scheduled flights 25.

Communications

Medium	date	unit	number	units per 1,000 persons
Daily newspapers	1994	circulation	2,766,000	47
Radio	1996	receivers	10,000,000	167
Television	1995	receivers	3,300,000	56
Telephones	1995	main lines	3,482,000	59
Cellular telephones	1995	subscribers	1,087,500	18
Facsimile machines	1995	units	60,000	1.0
Personal computers	1995	units	900,000	15

Education and health

Educational attainment (1990). Percentage of population age 25 and over having: no formal schooling 11.8%; primary education 71.3%; secondary 9.5%; postsecondary 6.6%; unknown 0.8%. *Literacy* (1990): total population age 15 and over literate 36,029,471 (93.3%); males literate 18,063,956 (95.6%); females literate 17,965,515 (91.2%).

Education (1993)

	schools	teachers	students	student/ teacher ratio
Primary (age 7–12)	34,412	445,542	8,583,525	19.3
Secondary (age 13–18)	2,318	107,025	2,118,767	19.8
Voc., teacher tr.	679	40,116	795,186	19.8
Higher	102	27,239	809,856	29.7

Health: physicians (1994) 14,098 (1 per 4,165 persons); hospital beds (1991) 93,852 (1 per 599 persons); infant mortality rate (1996) 32.0.
Food (1995): daily per capita caloric intake 2,296 (vegetable products 90%, animal products 10%); 103% of FAO recommended minimum requirement.

Military

Total active duty personnel (1996): 254,000 (army 59.1%, navy 25.2%, air force 15.7%). *Military expenditure as percentage of GNP* (1995): 2.5% (world 2.8%); per capita expenditure U.S.$68.

[1]All members are appointed by the prime minister. [2]Actual local administration is based on 76 provinces. [3]Based on registration records. [4]Based on 1990 census results, which are lower than the 1990 registration records estimate. [5]Percentage distribution. [6]1995. [7]February; economically active persons 13 years and over. [8]Mostly unemployed. [9]Import figures are f.o.b. in balance of trade and c.i.f. for commodities and trading partners. [10]Traffic data refer to fiscal year ending September 30.

Internet resources for further information:
- **National Statistical Office http://www.nectec.or.th/bureaux/nso/**

Togo

Official name: République Togolaise (Republic of Togo).
Form of government: multiparty republic[1] with one legislative body (National Assembly [81]).
Chief of state: President[1].
Head of government: Prime Minister.
Capital: Lomé.
Official language: French.
Official religion: none.
Monetary unit: 1 CFA franc (CFAF) = 100 centimes; valuation (Oct. 3, 1997) 1 U.S.$ = CFAF 592.29; 1 £ = CFAF 954.76.

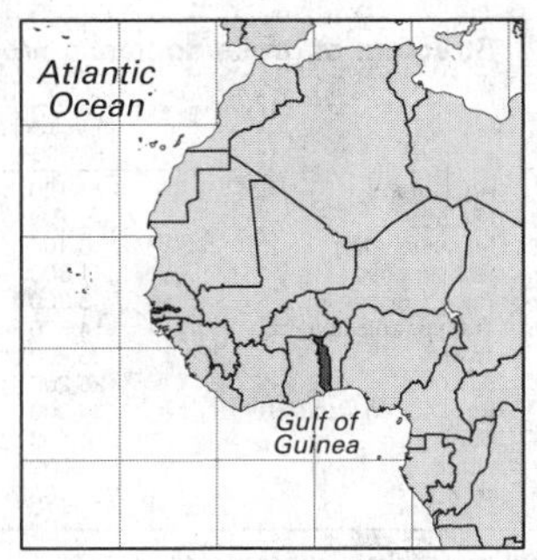

Area and population

Regions Prefectures	Capitals	area sq mi	area sq km	population 1989 estimate
Centrale	Sokodé			339,000
Sotouboua	Sotouboua	2,892	7,491	162,500
Tchamba	Tchamba	1,214	3,143	54,500
Tchaoudjo	Sokodé	984	2,549	122,000
De la Kara	Kara			531,500
Assoli	Bafilo	362	938	41,000
Bassar	Bassar	2,444	6,330	152,000
Binah	Pagouda	180	465	61,000
Doufelgou	Niamtougou	432	1,120	75,000
Kéran	Kandé	419	1,085	49,500
Kozah	Kara	653	1,692	153,000
Des Plateaux	Atakpamé			810,500
Amou	Amlamé	773	2,003	98,500
Haho	Notsé	1,406	3,641	139,000
Kloto	Kpalimé	1,072	2,777	233,500
Ogou	Atakpamé	2,349	6,083	204,000
Wawa	Badou	954	2,471	135,500
Des Savanes	Dapaong			410,500
Oti	Sansanné-Mango	1,453	3,762	98,500
Tône	Dapaong	1,869	4,840	312,000
Maritime	Lomé			1,300,000[2]
Golfe	Lomé	133	345	560,000
Lacs	Aného	275	713	172,500
Vo	Vogan	290	750	125,000
Yoto	Tabligbo	483	1,250	187,000
Zio	Tsévié	1,288	3,337	255,000
TOTAL		21,925	56,785	3,391,500

Demography

Population (1997): 4,736,000.
Density (1997): persons per sq mi 216.0, persons per sq km 83.4.
Urban-rural (1995): urban 30.8%; rural 69.2%.
Sex distribution (1995): male 49.54%; female 50.46%.
Age breakdown (1995): under 15, 45.7%; 15–29, 25.9%; 30–44, 14.9%; 45–59, 8.5%; 60–74, 4.1%; 75 and over, 0.9%.
Population projection: (2000) 5,263,000; (2010) 7,401,000.
Doubling time: 22 years.
Ethnic composition (1981): Ewe-Adja 43.1%; Tem-Kabre 26.7%; Gurma 16.1%; Kebu-Akposo 3.8%; Ana-Ife (Yoruba) 3.2%; non-African 0.3%; other 6.8%.
Religious affiliation (1993): traditional beliefs 50%; Christian 35%, of which Roman Catholic 23%; Muslim 15%.
Major cities (1983): Lomé 366,476; Sokodé 48,098[2]; Kpalimé 27,669[2].

Vital statistics

Birth rate per 1,000 population (1990–95): 44.5 (world avg. 25.0).
Death rate per 1,000 population (1990–95): 12.8 (world avg. 9.3).
Natural increase rate per 1,000 population (1990–95): 31.7 (world avg. 15.7).
Total fertility rate (avg. births per childbearing woman; 1990–95): 6.6.
Life expectancy at birth (1990–95): male 53.2 years; female 56.8 years.
Morbidity (reported cases of illness; 1989): malaria 730,162; injury and trauma 218,949; diarrheal diseases 153,074; diseases of the respiratory system 90,061.

National economy

Budget (1995). Revenue: CFAF 97,100,000,000 (tax revenue 91.4%, of which taxes on international trade 37.3%, public enterprise taxes 18.6%; nontax revenue 8.6%). Expenditures: CFAF 147,200,000,000 (current expenditure 70.6%, of which education 16.2%, defense 10.5%, health 4.0%; development/unclassified expenditures 15.6%; debt service 13.9%).
Public debt (external, outstanding; 1995): U.S.$1,297,000,000.
Production (metric tons except as noted). Agriculture, forestry, fishing (1996): cassava 469,000, corn (maize) 414,000, yams 375,000, sorghum 144,000, cottonseed 140,000, millet 78,000, rice 59,000, pulses 34,000, peanuts (groundnuts) 42,000, bananas 16,000, coffee 16,000, coconuts 14,000, palm oil 14,000; livestock (number of live animals) 1,900,000 goats, 1,200,000 sheep, 850,000 pigs, 202,000 cattle, 6,000,000 chickens; roundwood (1995) 2,387,000 cu m; fish catch (1995) 13,723. Mining and quarrying (1995): phosphate rock 2,650,000; limestone is quarried for cement manufacture. Manufacturing (value added in CFAF '000,000; 1995): food products, beverages, and tobacco manufactures 36,393; nonmetallic manufactures 6,099; textiles, clothing, and leather 3,833; chemical products 3,625; paper, printing, and publishing 3,125; wood products 3,020; steel 330. Construction (value added in CFAF; 1995): 19,958,000,000. Energy production (consumption): electricity (kW-hr; 1994) 93,000,000 (408,000,000); petroleum products (metric tons; 1994) none (184,000).
Gross national product (1995): U.S.$1,266,000,000 (U.S.$310 per capita).

Structure of gross domestic product and labour force

	1995 in value CFAF '000,000,000	1995 % of total value	1994 labour force	1994 % of labour force
Agriculture	210.5	33.9	1,041,000	67.7
Mining	36.6	5.9		
Manufacturing	62.6	10.1	177,000	11.5
Construction	20.0	3.2		
Public utilities	23.7	3.8		
Transp. and commun.	39.7	6.4		
Trade and finance	131.6	21.2	318,000	20.7
Pub. admin., defense	49.4	7.9		
Services	47.4	7.6		
TOTAL	630.3[3]	100.0	1,538,000[4]	100.0[4]

Population economically active (1994): total 1,538,000; activity rate of total population 33.8% (participation rates over age 10, 50.7%; female 35.6%; unemployed 16–18%).

Price and earnings indexes (1990 = 100)

	1990	1991	1992	1993	1994	1995
Consumer price index	100.0	100.4	101.8	101.8	137.7	159.3
Hourly earnings index[5]	100.0	100.0	100.0	100.0	100.0	...

Household income and expenditure. Average household size (1980) 5.6; average annual income per household CFAF 102,000 (U.S.$452); sources of income: n.a.; expenditure (1987): food and beverages 45.9%, household durable goods 13.9%, clothing 11.4%, housing 5.9%, services 20.5%.
Tourism: receipts (1995) U.S.$8,000,000; expenditures (1994) U.S.$23,000,000.
Land use (1994): forested 16.5%; meadows and pastures 3.7%; agricultural and under permanent cultivation 44.7%; other 35.1%.

Foreign trade[6]

Balance of trade (current prices)

	1991	1992	1993	1994	1995
CFAF '000,000,000	−16.7	−21.8	−10.2	+7.8	+8.8
% of total	7.0%	11.2%	7.7%	3.2%	2.6%

Imports (1995): CFAF 177,300,000,000 (consumer goods 45.3%; capital equipment 23.2%; intermediate goods 21.0%; energy products 10.4%). *Major import sources* (1994): France 24.0%; Germany 9.9%; Côte d'Ivoire 6.3%.
Exports (1995): CFAF 173,200,000,000 (domestic exports 73.3%, of which cotton 29.8%, phosphates 23.8%, coffee 5.5%; reexports 26.7%). *Major export destinations* (1994): Canada 17.0%; Bolivia 7.6%; Indonesia 5.7%.

Transport and communications

Transport. Railroads (1995): route length 395 km; (1994) passenger-km 14,000,000; metric ton-km cargo 5,600,000. Roads (1995): total length 12,040 km (paved 14%). Vehicles (1994): passenger cars 67,936; trucks and buses 31,986. Merchant marine (1992): vessels (100 gross tons and over) 8; total deadweight tonnage 20,633. Air transport (1996)[7]: passenger-km 224,736,000; metric ton-km cargo 16,420,000; airports (1997) 2.

Communications

Medium	date	unit	number	units per 1,000 persons
Daily newspapers	1995	circulation	10,000	2.4
Radio	1995	receivers	880,000	212
Television	1995	receivers	150,000	36
Telephones	1995	main lines	21,700	5.2
Facsimile machines	1995	units	10,000	2.4

Education and health

Educational attainment (1981). Percentage of population age 25 and over having: no formal schooling 76.5%; primary education 13.5%; secondary 8.7%; higher 1.3%. *Literacy* (1995): total population age 15 and over literate 51.7%; males 67.0%; females 37.0%.

Education (1995–96)

	schools	teachers	students	student/teacher ratio
Primary (age 6–11)	3,283	16,217	824,626	50.8
Secondary (age 12–18)	314[8]	4,736	161,672	34.1
Vocational	18[9]	586	7,631	13.0
Higher[10]	1	650	11,000	16.9

Health: physicians (1991) 319 (1 per 11,967 persons); hospital beds (1990) 5,307 (1 per 694 persons); infant mortality rate (1990–95) 85.
Food (1995): daily per capita caloric intake 1,754 (vegetable products 95%, animal products 5%); 76% of FAO recommended minimum requirement.

Military

Total active duty personnel (1997): 6,950 (army 93.5%, navy 2.9%, air force 3.6%). *Military expenditure as percentage of GNP* (1995): 2.3% (world 2.8%); per capita expenditure U.S.$6.

[1]Personal military-supported rule from 1967 continues under constitution approved by referendum in September 1992. [2]1981. [3]Total includes statistical discrepancy of CFAF 8,800,000,000. [4]Detail does not add to total given because of rounding. [5]January 1. [6]Import figures are f.o.b. in total and balance of trade and c.i.f. for commodities and trading partners. [7]Represents 1/11 of the traffic of Air Afrique, which is operated by 11 West African states. [8]1990. [9]1987. [10]University only; 1994–95.

Internet resources for further information:
- **CIA World Factbook—Togo**
http://www.odci.gov/cia/publications/nsolo/factbook/to.htm

Tonga

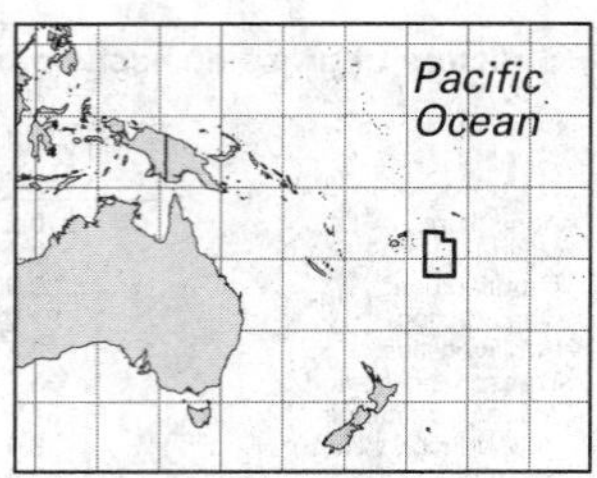

Official name: Pule'anga Fakatu'i 'o Tonga (Tongan); Kingdom of Tonga (English).
Form of government: constitutional monarchy with one legislative house (Legislative Assembly [30[1]]).
Head of state and government: King assisted by Privy Council.
Capital: Nuku'alofa.
Official languages: Tongan; English.
Official religion: none.
Monetary unit: 1 pa'anga[2] (T$) = 100 seniti; valuation (Oct. 3, 1997) 1 U.S.$ = T$1.37; 1 £ = T$2.21.

Area and population		area		population
Divisions				1986
Districts	Capitals	sq mi	sq km	census
'Eua	'Ohonua	33.7	87.4	4,393
'Eua Fo'ou		...	...	1,993
'Eua Motu'a		...	...	2,400
Ha'apai	Pangai	42.5	110.0	8,919
Foa		...	...	1,410
Ha'ano		...	...	891
Lulunga		...	...	1,584
Mu'omu'a		...	...	885
Pangai		...	...	2,850
'Uiha		...	...	1,299
Niuas	Hihifo	27.7	71.7	2,368
Niua Fo'ou		...	...	763
Niua Toputapu		...	...	1,605
Tongatapu	Nuku'alofa	100.6	260.5	63,794
Kolofo'ou		...	...	15,903
Kolomotu'a		...	...	13,115
Kolovai		...	...	4,031
Lapaha		...	...	7,005
Nukunuku		...	...	5,863
Tatakamotonga		...	...	6,773
Vaini		...	...	11,104
Vava'u	Neiafu	46.0	119.2	15,175
Hahake		...	...	2,299
Hihifo		...	...	2,093
Leimatu'a		...	...	2,884
Motu		...	...	1,384
Neiafu		...	...	5,268
Pangaimotu		...	...	1,247
TOTAL LAND AREA		278.1[3]	720.3[3]	
INLAND WATER		11.4	29.6	
TOTAL		289.5	749.9	94,649

Demography

Population (1997): 101,300.
Density (1997)[4]: persons per sq mi 364.3, persons per sq km 140.6.
Urban-rural (1997): urban 43.0%; rural 57.0%.
Sex distribution (1992): male 50.28%; female 49.72%.
Age breakdown (1986): under 15, 40.6%; 15–29, 29.0%; 30–44, 13.8%; 45–59, 10.2%; 60–74, 5.0%; 75 and over, 1.4%.
Population projection: (2000) 103,000; (2010) 105,000.
Doubling time: 33 years.
Ethnic composition (1986): Tongan 95.5%; part Tongan 2.8%; other 1.7%.
Religious affiliation (1996): Free Wesleyan 43.6%; Roman Catholic 15.8%.
Major cities (1986): Nuku'alofa 21,383; Neiafu 3,879; Haveluloto 3,070.

Vital statistics

Birth rate per 1,000 population (1997): 27.0 (world avg. 25.0).
Death rate per 1,000 population (1997): 5.8 (world avg. 9.3).
Natural increase rate per 1,000 population (1997): 21.2 (world avg. 15.7).
Total fertility rate (avg. births per childbearing woman; 1997): 3.4.
Marriage rate per 1,000 population (1992): 8.2.
Divorce rate per 1,000 population (1992): 1.1.
Life expectancy at birth (1997): male 68.0 years; female 72.0 years.
Major causes of death per 100,000 population (1993)[5]: circulatory diseases 58.1; nervous system diseases 51.0; senility 27.6; diabetes mellitus 17.3.

National economy

Budget (1996–97). Revenue: T$68,300,000 (foreign-trade taxes 41.6%, government services revenue 16.5%, direct taxes 12.0%, indirect taxes 10.7%, interest and rent 6.8%). Expenditures[6]: T$68,700,000 (education 17.8%, public works and communications 17.3%, general administration 14.4%, health 11.4%, law and order 10.5%, agriculture 9.0%).
Public debt (external, outstanding; 1995): U.S.$68,700,000.
Tourism (1995): receipts U.S.$11,000,000; expenditures (1993) U.S.$3,000,000.
Production (metric tons except as noted). Agriculture, forestry, fishing (1996): yams 31,000, cassava 28,000, taro 27,200, coconuts 24,500, fruits 12,500, vegetables 7,308, sweet potatoes 5,137, copra (1994) 2,000; livestock (number of live animals) 80,853 pigs, 13,939 goats, 11,400 horses, 9,318 cattle, 266,000 chickens; roundwood (1995) 4,600 cu m; fish catch (1995) 2,596. Mining and quarrying (1982): coral 150,000; sand 25,000. Manufacturing (output in T$'000,000; 1994): food products and beverages 7,766; chemical products 4,294; wood products 1,330; paper products 859; nonmetallic products 814; textile and wearing apparel 806. Construction (value in T$; 1984): residential 9,552,300; nonresidential 11,377,100. Energy production (consumption): electricity (kW-hr; 1994) 29,000,000 (29,000,000); petroleum (barrels; 1989) none (154,000); petroleum products (metric tons; 1994) n.a. (34,000).
Gross national product (1995): U.S.$170,000,000 (U.S.$1,630 per capita).

Structure of gross domestic product and labour force	1995–96		1990	
	in value T$'000	% of total value	labour force	% of labour force
Agriculture	71,100	31.7	11,682	36.5
Mining	700	0.3	4,665	14.6
Manufacturing	8,100	3.6		
Construction	11,300	5.0	1,257	3.9
Public utilities	3,200	1.4	408	1.3
Transp. and commun.	14,600	6.5	1,821	5.7
Trade	26,400	11.8	2,597	8.1
Finance	25,200	11.3	1,188	3.7
Pub. admin., defense	30,000	13.4	7,052	22.0
Services	10,500	4.7		
Other	23,000	10.3	1,343	4.2
TOTAL	224,100	100.0	32,013	100.0

Population economically active (1993–94): total 36,665; activity rate 36.9% (participation rates: ages 10 and over, 52.2%; female 42.9%; unemployed 11.8%).

Price and earnings indexes (1990 = 100)	1990	1991	1992	1993	1994	1995	1996
Consumer price index	100.0	110.6	119.4	120.5	121.8	123.5	127.2
Quarterly earnings index[7]	100.0	114.3	124.6	...	...	...	...

Household income and expenditure. Average household size (1986) 6.3; income per household: n.a.; sources of income: n.a.; expenditure (1984)[8]: food 49.3%, household operations 13.3%, housing 10.5%, tobacco and beverages 7.0%, transportation 5.8%, clothing and footwear 5.6%.
Land use (1994): forest 11.1%; pasture 5.6%; agriculture 66.7%; other 16.6%.

Foreign trade[9]

Balance of trade (current prices)	1990	1991	1992	1993	1994	1995
T$'000,000	−64.5	−59.4	−67.7	−61.5	−72.8	−79.6
% of total	69.0%	63.0%	67.1%	56.8%	66.5%	68.3%

Imports (1995–96): T$94,960,000 (food and live animals 28.7%, machinery and transport equipment 20.6%, basic manufactures 17.0%, mineral fuels 13.7%, chemicals 6.8%). *Major import sources:* New Zealand 36.1%; Australia 28.9%; U.S. 11.5%; Japan 8.0%; Fiji 7.2%.
Exports (1995–96): T$17,020,000 (squash 49.3%, fish 24.4%, vanilla beans 12.5%, root crops 5.5%). *Major export destinations:* Japan 51.8%; U.S. 27.7%; New Zealand 8.3%; Australia 4.0%; Fiji 1.5%.

Transport and communications

Transport. Railroads: none. Roads (1995): total length 674 km (paved 27%). Vehicles (1995): passenger cars 1,136, commercial vehicles 766. Merchant marine (1992): vessels (100 gross tons and over) 15; total deadweight tonnage 13,740. Air transport (1994): passenger-km 9,397,000; metric ton-km cargo 16,000; airports (1996) with scheduled flights 6.

Communications				units per 1,000
Medium	date	unit	number	persons
Daily newspapers	1994	circulation	7,000	70
Radio	1996	receivers	40,000	397
Television	1995	receivers	2,000	20
Telephones	1995	main lines	6,600	66

Education and health

Educational attainment (1986). Percentage of population age 25 and over having: complete primary 38.3%; lower secondary 30.3%; secondary 23.4%; postsecondary 4.9%; higher 1.0%; not stated 2.1%. *Literacy* (1976): total population age 15 and over literate 46,456 (92.8%); males 23,372 (92.9%); females 23,084 (92.8%).

Education (1994)	schools	teachers	students	student/ teacher ratio
Primary (age 6–11)	115	701	16,540	23.6
Secondary (age 12–18)	38	809	15,702	19.4
Voc., teacher tr.	9	65[10]	824	13.4[10]
Higher[11]	1	19	226	11.9

Health: physicians (1993) 45 (1 per 2,201 persons); hospital beds (1992) 307 (1 per 320 persons); infant mortality rate per 1,000 live births (1997) 15.
Food (1992): daily per capita caloric intake 2,946 (vegetable products 82%, animal products 18%); 129% of FAO recommended minimum requirement.

Military

Total active duty personnel (1991): Tonga has a national police (defense) force of about 300. *Military expenditure as percentage of GNP* (1989): 4.9% (world 4.9%); per capita expenditure U.S.$21.

[1]Includes 12 nonelective seats and 9 nobles elected by the 33 hereditary nobles of Tonga. [2]The pa'anga was pegged at par to the Australian dollar through Feb. 8, 1991, but beginning Feb. 11, 1991, it was linked to a weighted basket of foreign currencies. [3]Total includes 27.6 sq mi (71.5 sq km) of uninhabited islands. [4]Density is based on land area. [5]Reported inpatient deaths at all hospitals. [6]Excludes amortization of public debt and sinking funds. [7]In manufacturing. [8]Current weight of consumer price index components. [9]Import data used in computing balance of trade is c.i.f. [10]1990. [11]1992.

Internet resources for further information:
- **Tonga Page http://user.cs.tu-berlin.de/Qminibbjd/tonga/index.html**

Trinidad and Tobago

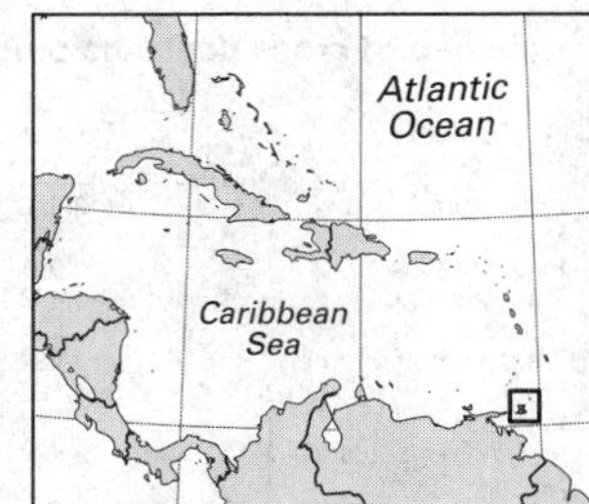

Official name: Republic of Trinidad and Tobago.
Form of government: multiparty republic with two legislative houses (Senate [31]; House of Representatives [36[1]]).
Chief of state: President.
Head of government: Prime Minister.
Capital: Port of Spain.
Official language: English.
Official religion: none.
Monetary unit: 1 Trinidad and Tobago dollar (TT$) = 100 cents; valuation (Oct. 3, 1997) 1 U.S.$ = TT$6.15; 1 £ = TT$9.91.

Area and population		area		population
				1990
Counties	**Capitals**	sq mi	sq km	census
Caroni	Chaguanas	191.0	494.7	120,508
Nariva/Mayaro	Rio Claro	349.0	903.9	36,781
St. Andrew/St. David	Sangre Grande	360.0	932.4	62,944
St. George	Tunapuna	354.0	916.9	445,620
St. Patrick	Siparia	252.0	652.7	120,129
Victoria	Princes Town	315.0	815.9	210,833
Unitary State				
Tobago	Scarborough	116.0	300.4	50,282
Cities				
Port of Spain	—	4.0	10.4	50,878
San Fernando	—	3.0	7.8	30,092
Boroughs				
Arima	—	4.0	10.4	29,695
Chaguanas	—	23.0	59.6	56,601
Point Fortin	—	9.0	23.3	20,025
TOTAL		1,980.1[2]	5,128.4	1,234,388

Demography

Population (1997): 1,276,000.
Density (1997): persons per sq mi 644.4, persons per sq km 248.8.
Urban-rural (1995): urban 71.8%; rural 28.2%.
Sex distribution (1995): male 49.46%; female 50.54%.
Age breakdown (1995): under 15, 31.7%; 15–29, 26.6%; 30–44, 22.1%; 45–59, 11.5%; 60–74, 6.0%; 75 and over, 2.1%.
Population projection: (2000) 1,297,000; (2010) 1,370,000.
Doubling time: 74 years.
Ethnic composition (1990): East Indian 40.3%; black 39.6%; mixed 18.4%; white 0.6%; Chinese 0.4%; other/not stated 0.7%.
Religious affiliation (1990): six largest Protestant bodies 29.7%; Roman Catholic 29.4%; Hindu 23.7%; Muslim 5.9%; other 11.3%.
Major cities (1990): Chaguanas 56,601; Port of Spain 46,222[3]; San Fernando 30,115[4]; Arima 29,483[4]; Point Fortin 20,025; Scarborough 4,000.

Vital statistics

Birth rate per 1,000 population (1996): 16.3 (world avg. 25.0).
Death rate per 1,000 population (1996): 6.9 (world avg. 9.3).
Natural increase rate per 1,000 population (1996): 9.4 (world avg. 15.7).
Total fertility rate (avg. births per childbearing woman; 1996): 2.0.
Marriage rate per 1,000 population (1993): 5.6.
Divorce rate per 1,000 population (1993): 0.9.
Life expectancy at birth (1996): male 67.9 years; female 72.8 years.
Major causes of death per 100,000 population (1993): diseases of the circulatory system 270.0; accidents, violence, and homicide 110.3; malignant neoplasms (cancers) 86.4; diabetes mellitus 83.5.

National economy

Budget (1996). Revenue: TT$9,570,000,000 (company taxes 28.8%, of which petroleum sector 19.2%; individual income taxes 18.9%; value-added taxes 15.3%; nontax revenues 7.9%). Expenditures: TT$9,123,000,000 (current expenditures 94.3%; development expenditures 5.7%).
Tourism (1994): receipts from visitors U.S.$80,000,000; expenditures by nationals abroad U.S.$90,000,000.
Production (metric tons except as noted). Agriculture, forestry, fishing (1996): sugarcane 1,404,000, coconuts 20,000, oranges (1995) 14,906, rice 9,539, grapefruit and pomelo (1995) 7,297, bananas 6,000, cocoa 2,540, coffee 353; livestock (number of live animals) 59,000 goats, 45,000 pigs, 9,500,000 chickens; roundwood (1995) 67,600 cu m; fish catch (1994) 11,000. Mining and quarrying (1994): natural asphalt 21,000. Manufacturing (1996): anhydrous ammonia and urea (nitrogenous fertilizers) 2,674,200; methanol 1,358,000; steel billets 643,600; cement 617,100; steel wire rods 575,400; refined sugar 42,100; beer and stout 418,800 hectolitres; rum 78,000 hectolitres. Construction (authorized; 1993): residential 207,900 sq m; nonresidential 46,900 sq m. Energy production (consumption): electricity (kW-hr; 1995) 4,229,000,000 (1994; 3,978,000,000); coal, none (none); crude petroleum (barrels; 1995) 41,493,000 (1994; 35,533,000); petroleum products (metric tons; 1994) 4,931,000 (1,268,000); natural gas (cu m; 1996) 9,033,000,000 (7,049,000,000).
Public debt (external, outstanding; 1995): U.S.$1,759,000,000.
Household income and expenditure. Average household size (1990) 4.1; average income per household (1988) TT$21,760 (U.S.$5,661); expenditure (1993): food, beverages, and tobacco 25.5%, housing 21.6%, transportation 15.2%, household furnishings 14.3%, clothing and footwear 10.4%.

Gross national product (1995): U.S.$4,851,000,000 (U.S.$3,840 per capita).

Structure of gross domestic product and labour force	1996		1995	
	in value TT$'000,000	% of total value	labour force	% of labour force
Agriculture	688	2.1	50,600	9.7
Petroleum[5], natural gas, quarrying	8,747	26.7	21,100	4.0
Manufacturing[6]	2,698	8.2	53,800	10.3
Construction	2,762	8.4	71,200	13.7
Public utilities	545	1.7	7,300	1.4
Transp. and commun.	2,760	8.4	34,100	6.5
Trade	4,979	15.2	93,600	18.0
Finance, real estate	3,882	11.8	35,000	6.7
Pub. admin., defense	3,264	9.9	154,100	29.6
Services	1,917	5.8		
Other	569[7]	1.7[7]	500	0.1
TOTAL	32,811	100.0[2]	521,000[2]	100.0

Population economically active (1995): total 521,000; activity rate of total population 41.3% (participation rates: ages 15–64, 65.4%; female 37.2%; unemployed [1996] 16.3%).

Price and earnings indexes (1990 = 100)	1990	1991	1992	1993	1994	1995	1996
Consumer price index	100.0	103.9	110.6	122.4	133.2	140.1	144.9
Weekly earnings index	100.0	100.1	103.0	104.6	109.9	111.1[8]	...

Land use (1994): forested 45.8%; meadows and pastures 2.1%; agricultural and under permanent cultivation 23.8%; other 28.3%.

Foreign trade[9]

Balance of trade (current prices)	1991	1992	1993	1994	1995	1996
TT$'000,000	+2,147	+4,720	+2,055	+5,426	+5,436	+3,433
% of total	16.6%	23.3%	13.2%	31.1%	22.9%	12.9%

Imports (1995): TT$9,452,000,000 (nonelectrical machinery 25.5%, of which general industrial machinery 17.3%; food and live animals 14.2%; chemicals and chemical products 13.8%). *Major import sources:* United States 50.4%; United Kingdom 6.8%; Germany 6.2%; Canada 5.2%; Brazil 4.3%.
Exports (1995): TT$14,303,000,000 (refined petroleum 29.9%; crude petroleum 16.2%; anhydrous ammonia 10.8%; iron and steel 10.2%; methanol 8.7%; urea 3.9%). *Major export destinations:* United States 43.3%; Jamaica 8.4%; Guyana 3.1%; Barbados 3.1%; France 2.9%.

Transport and communications

Transport. Railroads: none. Roads (1995): total length 8,160 km (paved 51%). Vehicles (1994): passenger cars 123,500; trucks and buses 24,500. Air transport (1994): passenger-km 4,084,000,000; metric ton-km cargo 404,000,000; airports (1996) with scheduled flights 2.

Communications				units
Medium	date	unit	number	per 1,000 persons
Daily newspapers	1994	circulation	175,000	139
Radio	1996	receivers	550,000	433
Television	1995	receivers	250,000	198
Telephones	1995	main lines	209,300	166
Cellular telephones	1995	subscribers	5,600	4.4
Facsimile machines	1995	units	2,000	1.6
Personal computers	1995	units	25,000	20

Education and health

Educational attainment (1990). Percentage of population age 25 and over having: no formal schooling 4.5%; primary education 56.4%; secondary 32.1%; higher 3.4%; other/not stated 3.6%. *Literacy* (1995): total population age 15 and over literate 886,000 (97.9%).

Education (1993–94)	schools	teachers	students	student/ teacher ratio
Primary (age 5–11)	475	7,210	195,013	27.0
Secondary (age 12–16)	101[10]	4,882[11]	100,609[11]	20.6[11]
Higher[12]	1	438	5,191	11.9

Health: physicians (1993) 1,051 (1 per 1,191 persons); hospital beds (1992) 3,653 (1 per 340 persons); infant mortality rate (1996) 18.2.
Food (1992): daily per capita caloric intake 2,585 (vegetable products 85%, animal products 15%); 107% of FAO recommended minimum requirement.

Military

Total active duty personnel (1996): 2,100 (army 66.7%, coast guard 33.3%). *Military expenditure as percentage of GNP* (1994): 1.7% (world 3.0%); per capita expenditure U.S.$60.

[1]Excludes speaker, who may be elected from outside the House of Representatives. [2]Detail does not add to total given because of rounding. [3]1994. [4]1991. [5]Includes refined petroleum. [6]Excludes refined petroleum. [7]Net of value-added taxes less imputed bank service charges. [8]Average of 2nd quarter. [9]Imports f.o.b. in balance of trade and c.i.f. in commodities and trading partners. [10]1992–93. [11]Excludes vocational. [12]University of the West Indies, St. Augustine campus only.

Internet resources for further information:
- **Inter-American Development Bank**
  http://database.iadb.org/int/basicrep/batto.htm

Tunisia

Official name: Al-Jumhūrīyah at-Tūnisīyah (Republic of Tunisia).
Form of government: multiparty republic with one legislative house (Chamber of Deputies [163]).
Chief of state: President.
Head of government: Prime Minister.
Capital: Tunis.
Official language: Arabic.
Official religion: Islam.
Monetary unit: 1 dinar (D) = 1,000 millimes; valuation (Oct. 3, 1997) D 1.00 = U.S.$1.12 = £0.55.

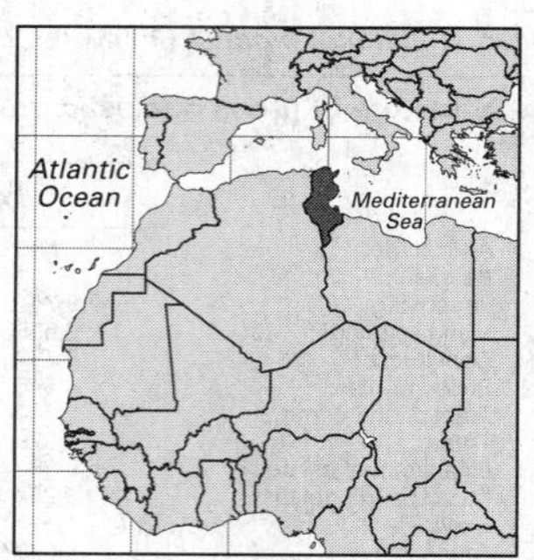

Area and population		area		population
Governorates	**Capitals**	sq mi	sq km	1994 census
Al-Ariānah	Al-Ariānah	602	1,558	570,700
Bājah	Bājah	1,374	3,558	306,500
Banzart	Bizerte (Banzart)	1,423	3,685	485,800
Bin ʿArūs	Bin ʿArūs	294	761	372,900
Jundūbah	Jundūbah	1,198	3,102	405,100
Al-Kāf	Al-Kāf	1,917	4,965	273,200
Madanīn	Madanīn	3,316	8,588	386,900
Al-Mahdīyah	Al-Mahdīyah	1,145	2,966	335,200
Al-Munastīr	Al-Munastīr	393	1,019	364,600
Nābul	Nābul	1,076	2,788	581,800
Qābis	Qābis	2,770	7,175	311,300
Qafṣah	Qafṣah	3,471	8,990	308,700
Al-Qaṣrayn	Al-Qaṣrayn	3,114	8,066	388,500
Al-Qayrawān	Al-Qayrawān	2,591	6,712	532,500
Qibilī	Qibilī	8,527	22,084	132,000
Ṣafāqis	Ṣafāqis	2,913	7,545	735,300
Sīdī Bū Zayd	Sīdī Bū Zayd	2,700	6,994	379,300
Siliānah	Siliānah	1,788	4,631	246,500
Sūsah	Sūsah	1,012	2,621	436,500
Tatāuīn	Tatāuīn	15,015	38,889	135,600
Tawzar	Tawzar	1,822	4,719	89,300
Tūnis	Tunis (Tūnis)	134	346	893,000
Zaghwān	Zaghwān	1,069	2,768	143,400
TOTAL		63,378[1]	164,150[1]	8,814,500[2]

Demography

Population (1997): 9,218,000.
Density (1997): persons per sq mi 144.0, persons per sq km 56.2.
Urban-rural (1994): urban 61.0%; rural 39.0%.
Sex distribution (1994): male 50.53%; female 49.47%.
Age breakdown (1994): under 15, 34.8%; 15–29, 28.5%; 30–44, 18.8%; 45–59, 9.6%; 60–74, 6.4%; 75 and over, 1.9%.
Ethnic composition (1983): Arab 98.2%; Berber 1.2%; French 0.2%; Italian 0.1%; other 0.3%.
Religious affiliation (1980): Sunnī Muslim 99.4%; Christian 0.3%; Jewish 0.1%; other 0.2%.
Major cities (commune; 1994): Tunis 674,100; Ṣafāqis 230,900; Aryānah 152,700; Ettadhamen 149,200; Sūsah 125,000.

Vital statistics

Birth rate per 1,000 population (1995–2000): 23.9 (world avg. 25.0).
Death rate per 1,000 population (1995–2000): 5.9 (world avg. 9.3).
Natural increase rate per 1,000 population (1995–2000): 18.0 (world avg. 15.7).
Total fertility rate (avg. births per childbearing woman; 1995–2000): 2.9.
Marriage rate per 1,000 population (1995): 6.0.
Divorce rate per 1,000 population (1993–94): 0.9.
Life expectancy at birth (1995–2000): male 68.4 years; female 70.7 years.
Major causes of death per 100,000 population: n.a.; however, of approximately 12,000 deaths[3] for which a cause was reported in 1992, complications of pregnancy and childbirth represented 31.6%, circulatory diseases 22.4%, accidents and poisoning 14.9%, respiratory diseases 7.2%.

National economy

Budget (1996). Revenue: D 5,710,000,000 (tax revenue 83.0%, of which goods and services 32.5%, social security 16.8%, income tax 15.6%, import duties 13.3%; nontax revenue 15.8%; grants 0.7%; capital revenue 0.5%). Expenditures: D 6,484,000,000 (education 15.8%; economic services 15.7%; social security 13.7%; general public services 7.3%; health 6.0%; public order 5.8%; defense 5.0%).
Public debt (external, outstanding; 1995): U.S.$8,814,000,000.
Production (metric tons except as noted). Agriculture, forestry, fishing (1996): wheat 2,018,000, olives 1,250,000, barley 834,000, tomatoes 700,000, watermelons 273,000, potatoes 270,000, sugar beets 306,000; livestock (number of live animals) 6,400,000 sheep, 1,250,000 goats, 700,000 cattle; roundwood (1995) 3,600,000 cu m; fish catch (1995) 84,000. Mining and quarrying (1995): phosphate rock 6,301,598; iron ore 224,949; zinc 80,446. Manufacturing (1995): cement 3,033,200; phosphoric acid 1,365,200; flour 473,600; crude steel 192,000[4]. Construction (1982): residential building authorized 2,679,000 sq m. Energy production (consumption): electricity (kW-hr; 1994) 6,714,000 (5,701,000); coal (metric tons; 1994) 9,000 (31,000); crude petroleum (barrels; 1994) 33,662,000 (12,994,000); petroleum products (metric tons; 1994) 1,591,000 (3,565,000); natural gas (cu m; 1994) 286,000,000 (786,000,000).
Land use (1994): forested 4.3%; meadows and pastures 20.0%; agricultural and under permanent cultivation 31.9%; other 43.8%.
Tourism (1995): receipts U.S.$1,325,000,000; expenditures U.S.$251,000,000.
Gross national product (1995): U.S.$16,369,000,000 (U.S.$1,820 per capita).

Structure of gross domestic product and labour force	1996		1994	
	in value D '000,000	% of total value	labour force	% of labour force
Agriculture	2,630	13.9	501,000	21.6
Mining	111	0.6	36,800	1.6
Public utilities	927[5]	4.9[5]		
Manufacturing	3,453	18.2	455,700	19.6
Construction	874	4.6	305,800	13.2
Transp. and commun.	1,424	7.5	[6]	[6]
Trade	4,588	24.2	315,600	13.6
Finance	2,624			
Pub. admin., defense		13.8	667,100[6]	28.7[6]
Services				
Other	2,340[7]	12.3[7]	38,600	1.7
TOTAL	18,971	100.0	2,320,600	100.0

Population economically active (1989): total 2,360,000; activity rate of total population 28.8% (participation rates: ages 15–64, 42.2%; female 20.9%; unemployed 13.4%).

Price and earnings indexes (1990 = 100)	1990	1991	1992	1993	1994	1995	1996
Consumer price index	100.0	107.8	113.8	118.7	124.7	132.5	137.4
Hourly earnings index[8]	100.0	101.6	105.5	113.3	...	...	...

Household income and expenditure. Average household size (1994) 5.2; income per household: n.a.; sources of income: n.a.; expenditure (1985): food and beverages 39.0%, household durable goods 11.2%, housing 10.7%, transportation 9.0%, recreation 7.1%, clothing and footwear 6.0%, energy 5.1%, health care 3.0%, education 1.8%, other 7.1%.

Foreign trade[9]

Balance of trade (current prices)	1991	1992	1993	1994	1995	1996
D '000,000	−1,371.9	−2,139.1	−2,419.1	−1,950.7	−914.2	−2,170.7
% of total	16.7%	23.2%	24.1%	17.2%	7.2%	12.9%

Imports (1996): D 7,542,700,000 (1995; machinery and electrical equipment 35.0%, textiles 25.2%, food products 12.8%, chemical products 9.4%). *Major import sources* (1995): France 25.6%; Italy 15.4%; Germany 12.5%.
Exports (1996): D 5,372,000,000 (clothing and accessories 49.9%, machinery and electrical products 13.7%, phosphate products 9.0%, energy 8.4%). *Major export destinations* (1995): France 28.1%; Italy 18.7%; Germany 15.7%.

Transport and communications

Transport. Railroads (1994): route length 2,152 km; passenger-km 1,038,000,000; metric ton-km cargo 2,225,000,000. Roads (1995): total length 22,490 km (paved 79%). Vehicles (1995): passenger cars 248,000; trucks and buses 283,000. Air transport (1996)[10]: passenger-km 2,120,989,000; metric ton-km cargo 18,352,000; airports (1997) 5.

Communications Medium	date	unit	number	units per 1,000 persons
Daily newspapers	1995	circulation	400,000	45
Radio	1996	receivers	1,700,000	188
Television	1995	receivers	1,400,000	156
Telephones	1995	main lines	521,700	58
Cellular telephones	1995	subscribers	3,200	0.4
Facsimile machines	1995	units	25,000	2.8
Personal computers	1995	units	60,000	6.7

Education and health

Educational attainment (1989). Percentage of population age 25 and over having: no formal schooling 54.9%; primary 26.9%; secondary 14.3%; higher 3.4%; unspecified 0.5%. *Literacy* (1995): total population age 15 and over literate 66.7%; males literate 78.6%; females literate 54.6%.

Education (1995–96)	schools	teachers	students	student/ teacher ratio
Primary (age 6–11)	4,384	59,887	1,468,998	24.5
Secondary (age 12–18)	712[11]	41,885	794,394	19.0
Teacher tr.[12, 13]	...	237	3,839	16.2
Higher[14]	...	5,655	96,101	17.0

Health (1994): physicians 5,344 (1 per 1,640 persons); hospital beds 15,759 (1 per 556 persons); infant mortality rate (1995–2000) 37.0.
Food (1995): daily per capita caloric intake 3,187 (vegetable products 91%, animal products 9%); 133% of FAO recommended minimum requirement.

Military

Total active duty personnel (1997): 35,000 (army 77.1%, navy 12.9%, air force 10.0%). *Military expenditure as percentage of GNP* (1995): 2.0% (world 2.8%); per capita expenditure U.S.$39.

[1]Total includes 3,714 sq mi (9,620 sq km) of territory that is not distributed by governorate. [2]Detail does not add to total given because of rounding. [3]Recorded deaths from urban areas only, including complete figures for Tunis. [4]1989. [5]Includes hydrocarbons. [6]Services includes transportation and communications. [7]Indirect taxes less subsidies. [8]Year-end; index refers to the *S.M.I.G.* (*salaire minimum interprofessionel garanti*), a form of minimum professional wage. [9]Imports c.i.f. in balance of trade. [10]Tunis Air only. [11]1994–95. [12]1987–88. [13]Teacher training only. [14]1993–94.

Internet resources for further information:
- **Tunisia Online http://www.tunisiaonline.com**

Turkey

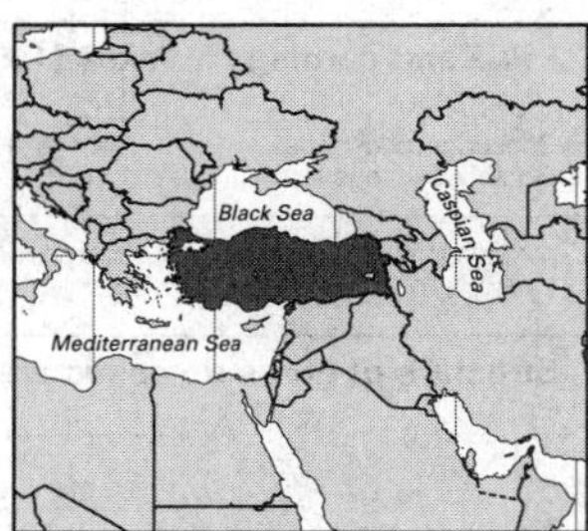

Official name: Türkiye Cumhuriyeti (Republic of Turkey).
Form of government: multiparty republic with one legislative house (Turkish Grand National Assembly [550]).
Chief of state: President.
Head of government: Prime Minister.
Capital: Ankara.
Official language: Turkish.
Official religion: none.
Monetary unit: 1 Turkish lira (LT) = 100 kurush; valuation (Oct. 3, 1997) 1 U.S.$ = LT 175,715; 1 £ = LT 283,253.

Area and population	area		population
			1990
Geographic regions[1]	sq mi	sq km	census
Akdeniz kıyısı (Mediterranean Coast)	22,933	59,395	5,443,867
Batı Anadolu (West Anatolia)	29,742	77,031	3,864,661
Doğu Anadolu (East Anatolia)	68,074	180,180	6,867,415
Güneydoğu Anadolu (Southeast Anatolia)	15,347	35,880	2,699,776
İç Anadolu (Central Anatolia)	91,254	236,347	13,096,179
Karadeniz kıyısı (Black Sea Coast)	31,388	81,295	6,827,304
Marmara ve Ege kıyıları (Marmara and Aegean coasts)	33,035	85,560	11,698,384
Trakya (Thrace)	9,175	23,764	5,975,449
TOTAL	300,948	779,452	56,473,035

Demography

Population (1997): 63,528,000.
Density (1997): persons per sq mi 211.1, persons per sq km 81.5.
Urban-rural (1995): urban 68.8%; rural 31.2%.
Sex distribution (1995): male 50.57%; female 49.43%.
Age breakdown (1995): under 15, 32.3%; 15–29, 28.8%; 30–44, 20.3%; 45–59, 11.0%; 60–74, 6.4%; 75 and over, 1.2%.
Population projection: (2000) 66,618,000; (2010) 76,570,000.
Doubling time: 44 years.
Ethnic composition (1994): Turks (including Turkmen) 80–88%; Kurds 10–20%; Arabs 1.5%; others 0.3%.
Religious affiliation (1994): Sunnī Muslim *c.* 80.0%; Shīʿī Muslim *c.* 19.8%, of which nonorthodox Alevi *c.* 14.0%; Christian *c.* 0.2%.
Major cities (1995): Istanbul 7,774,169; Ankara 2,837,937; İzmir 2,017,699; Adana 1,066,544; Bursa 1,016,760; Gaziantep 730,435; Konya 584,785.

Vital statistics

Birth rate per 1,000 population (1996): 22.3 (world avg. 25.0).
Death rate per 1,000 population (1996): 5.5 (world avg. 9.3).
Natural increase rate per 1,000 population (1996): 16.8 (world avg. 15.7).
Total fertility rate (avg. births per childbearing woman; 1996): 2.6.
Marriage rate per 1,000 population (1993): 7.7.
Divorce rate per 1,000 population (1993): 0.5.
Life expectancy at birth (1996): male 69.5 years; female 74.4 years.
Major causes of death per 100,000 population (1993)[2]: diseases of the circulatory system 369; malignant neoplasms (cancers) 80; accidents and violence 33; infectious and parasitic diseases 24; ill-defined conditions 60.

National economy

Budget (1996). Revenue: LT 2,738,148,000,000,000 (indirect taxes 49.8%, direct taxes 32.3%, nontax revenue 16.2%). Expenditures: LT 3,955,888,000,000,000 (interest payments 37.9%, personnel 24.6%, investments 6.5%).
Tourism (1996): receipts from visitors U.S.$5,650,000,000; expenditures by nationals abroad U.S.$1,265,000,000.
Production (in '000 metric tons except as noted). Agriculture, forestry, fishing (1996): wheat 18,515, sugar beets 14,455, barley 8,000, potatoes 4,950, grapes 3,550, apples 2,100, seed cotton 2,089, corn (maize) 2,000, olives 1,500, cottonseed 1,200, cotton lint 802, sunflower seeds 780, oranges 700, lentils 615, apricots 460, hazelnuts 410, pears 410, tobacco 230, sultana raisins 179[3], tea 124, honey 69[3], attar of roses 800 kg[4]; livestock (number of live animals) 33,791,000 sheep, 11,789,000 cattle; roundwood (1995) 19,279,000 cu m; fish catch (1995) 652,193. Mining (1995): boron (concentrate) 1,200[5]; chromite 800[5]; bauxite 440; copper ore (metal content) 34.2. Manufacturing (1993)[6]: refined petroleum 5,450; textiles 4,150; food products 4,150; motor vehicles 3,200; iron and steel 2,600; bricks, cement, and tiles 1,950. Construction (approved; 1996): residential 56,863,000 sq m; nonresidential 18,047,000 sq m.
Energy production (consumption): electricity (kW-hr; 1996) 94,863,000,000 (94,787,000,000); hard coal (metric tons; 1996) 2,424,000 ([1994] 8,192,000); lignite (metric tons; 1996) 52,503,000 ([1994] 52,167,000); crude petroleum (barrels; 1996) 25,018,000 ([1994] 180,663,000); petroleum products (metric tons; 1994) 22,219,000 (25,417,000); natural gas (cu m; 1994) 184,500,000 (4,815,100,000).
Land use (1994): forested 26.2%; meadows and pastures 16.1%; agricultural and under permanent cultivation 36.1%; other 21.6%.
Household income and expenditure. Average household size (1993) 4.5; income per household (1987) LT 3,680,500 (U.S.$4,294); expenditure (1994): food, tobacco, and café expenditures 38.5%, housing 22.8%, clothing 9.0%.
Population economically active (1995)[7]: total 22,899,000; activity rate of total population 37.1% (participation rates: ages 15–64, 57.8%; female 30.4%; unemployed [1996] 5.8%).

Price and earnings indexes (1990 = 100)	1991	1992	1993	1994	1995	1996	1997
Consumer price index	166.0	282.3	468.8	967.0	1,819.1	3,280.7	5,238.3[8]
Daily earnings index[9]	202.1	395.2	666.0	1,007	...	...	...

Gross national product (1995): U.S.$169,452,000,000 (U.S.$2,780 per capita).

Structure of gross domestic product and labour force	1996		1995	
	in value LT '000,000'000[10]	% of total value	labour force[7]	% of labour force[7]
Agriculture	2,408,532	18.0	10,227,000	44.7
Mining	160,096	1.2	131,000	0.6
Manufacturing	2,417,651	18.0	2,948,000	12.9
Construction	764,339	5.7	1,228,000	5.4
Public utilities	393,968	2.9	111,000	0.5
Transp. and commun.	1,955,042	14.6	854,000	3.7
Trade	2,539,687	19.0	2,612,000	11.4
Finance, real estate	987,244	7.4	487,000	2.1
Pub. admin., defense	1,238,527	9.2	2,779,000	12.1
Services	533,546	4.0		
Other	—	—	1,522,000[11]	6.6[11]
TOTAL	13,398,632	100.0	22,899,000	100.0

Public debt (external, outstanding; 1995): U.S.$50,128,000,000.

Foreign trade[12]

Balance of trade (current prices)	1991	1992	1993	1994	1995	1996
U.S.$'000,000	−7,454	−8,156	−14,080	−5,164	−14,073	−19,382
% of total	21.5%	21.7%	31.4%	12.5%	24.5%	29.6%

Imports (1996): U.S.$42,464,000,000 (nonelectrical machinery 19.3%; crude petroleum 8.1%; electrical and electronic equipment 7.0%; road vehicles and parts 6.2%; iron and steel 6.1%). *Major import sources:* Germany 17.6%; Italy 9.8%; United States 7.5%; France 6.3%; United Kingdom 5.8%.
Exports (1996): U.S.$23,082,000,000 (textiles and clothing 24.8%; iron and steel 7.6%; electrical and electronic machinery 5.7%; edible fruits 4.9%). *Major export destinations:* Germany 22.4%; United States 7.0%; Russia 6.4%; Italy 6.3%; United Kingdom 5.4%; France 4.5%.

Transport and communications

Transport. Railroads (1994): length 5,252 mi, 8,452 km; passenger-km 6,385,000,000; metric ton-km cargo 8,254,000,000. Roads (1995): total length 236,928 mi, 381,300 km (paved 23%). Vehicles (1995): passenger cars 3,231,562; trucks and buses 809,361. Air transport (1996)[13]: passenger-km 12,305,000,000; metric ton-km cargo 214,201,000; airports (1996) with scheduled flights 26.

Communications				units per 1,000
Medium	date	unit	number	persons
Daily newspapers	1994	circulation	2,679,000	44
Radio	1996	receivers	8,800,000	141
Television	1995	receivers	10,530,000	171
Telephones	1995	main lines	13,227,700	215
Cellular telephones	1995	subscribers	437,100	7.1
Facsimile machines	1995	units	99,100	1.6
Personal computers	1995	units	770,000	13

Education and health

Educational attainment (1993). Percentage of population age 25 and over having: no formal schooling 30.5%; incomplete primary education 6.6%; complete primary 40.4%; incomplete secondary 3.1%; complete secondary or higher 19.1%; unknown 0.3%. *Literacy* (1995): total population age 15 and over literate 33,605,000 (82.3%); males literate 19,191,000 (91.7%); females literate 14,414,000 (72.4%).

Education (1995–96)	schools	teachers	students	student/ teacher ratio
Primary (age 6–10)	49,240	232,000	6,403,000	27.6
Secondary (age 11–16)	10,689	138,000	3,498,000	25.3
Voc., teacher tr.	3,678	71,000	1,309,000	18.4
Higher	817	50,000	1,161,000	23.2

Health: physicians (1995) 51,000[14] (1 per 1,200 persons); hospital beds (1994) 134,665 (1 per 450 persons); infant mortality rate (1996) 43.2.
Food (1995): daily per capita caloric intake 3,593 (vegetable products 89%, animal products 11%); 143% of FAO recommended minimum requirement.

Military

Total active duty personnel (1996): 639,000 (army 82.2%, navy 8.0%, air force 9.8%). *Military expenditure as percentage of GNP* (1994): 4.1% (world 3.0%); per capita expenditure U.S.$87.

[1]Administratively divided into 76 provinces. [2]Projected rates based on about 35% of total deaths. [3]1995. [4]1993. [5]1994. [6]Value added in U.S.$'000,000. [7]Civilian population only. [8]April. [9]Based on June average. [10]At factor cost. [11]Unemployed. [12]Imports c.i.f.; exports f.o.b. [13]Turkish Airlines only. [14]Estimated figure.

Internet resources for further information:
- **Central Bank of the Republic of Turkey http://www.tcmb.gov.tr/**
- **Ministry of Foreign Affairs http://www.mfa.gov.tr/**
- **Republic of Turkey http://www.turkey.org/**
- **State Institute of Statistics http://www.die.gov.tr/**

Turkmenistan

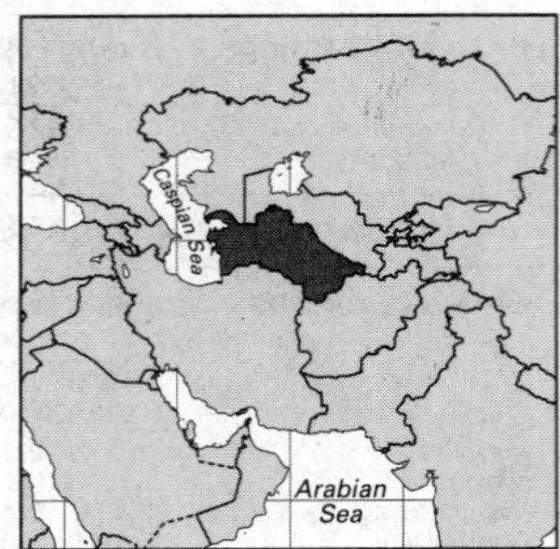

Official name: Türkmenistan Jumhuriyäti (Republic of Turkmenistan).
Form of government: unitary republic with one legislative body (Majlis [Parliament; 50]).
Head of state and government: President, assisted by the People's Council[1].
Capital: Ashgabat (formerly Ashkhabad).
Official language: Turkmen.
Official religion: none.
Monetary unit: manat; valuation (Nov. 1, 1997) 1 U.S.$ = 5,300 manat; 1 £ = 8,544 manat.

Area and population

		area		population
				1996
Provinces	**Capitals**	sq mi	sq km	estimate
Akhal	...	37,500	97,100	677,700
Balkan	Nebitdag	53,500	138,600	389,700
Dashhovuse	Dashhovuse	28,100	72,700	956,500
Leban	Leban	36,000	93,200	947,700
Mary	Mary	33,400	86,400	1,046,700
City				
Ashgabat	—	...	...	548,500
TOTAL		188,500[2]	488,100[2]	4,566,800

Demography

Population (1997): 4,695,000.
Density (1997): persons per sq mi 24.9, persons per sq km 9.6.
Urban-rural (1996): urban 44.8%; rural 55.2%.
Sex distribution (1996): male 49.59%; female 50.41%.
Age breakdown (1989): under 15, 40.5%; 15–29, 28.8%; 30–44, 15.5%; 45–59, 9.1%; 60–74, 4.7%; 75 and over, 1.4%.
Population projection: (2000) 4,961,000; (2010) 5,956,000.
Doubling time: 39 years.
Ethnic composition (1996): Turkmen 77.0%; Uzbek 9.2%; Russian 6.7%; Kazak 2.0%; Tatar 0.8%; other 4.3%.
Religious affiliation (1997): Muslim (mostly Sunnī) 87.0%; Russian Orthodox 6.4%; other 6.6%.
Major cities (1991): Ashgabat 416,400; Chärjew 166,400; Dashhovuse 117,000; Mary 94,900; Nebitdag 89,100.

Vital statistics

Birth rate per 1,000 population (1994): 32.1 (world avg. 25.0); legitimate 96.2%; illegitimate 3.8%.
Death rate per 1,000 population (1994): 7.9 (world avg. 9.3).
Natural increase rate per 1,000 population (1994): 24.2 (world avg. 15.7).
Total fertility rate (avg. births per childbearing woman; 1995): 4.0.
Marriage rate per 1,000 population (1994): 8.7.
Divorce rate per 1,000 population (1994): 1.5.
Life expectancy at birth (1994): male 61.5 years; female 68.5 years.
Major causes of death per 100,000 population (1994): diseases of the circulatory system 337.1; diseases of the respiratory system 150.3; infectious and parasitic diseases 75.7; accidents, poisoning, and violence 60.1; malignant neoplasms (cancers) 56.8; diseases of the digestive system 31.1.

National economy

Budget (1996). Revenue: 1,251,505,000,000 manat (value-added tax 35.0%, company profit tax 23.0%, social security tax 13.0%, natural resource tax 12.0%, other taxes 17.0%). Expenditures: 1,314,895,000,000 manat (capital investment 19.0%, social welfare 15.0%, education 13.0%, health 12.0%, defense 7.0%, price subsidies 4.0%, other expenditures 30.0%).
Public debt (external, outstanding; 1995): U.S.$374,700,000.
Production (metric tons except as noted). Agriculture, forestry, fishing (1996): vegetables 643,500, seed cotton 450,000, cereals 385,000, fruit 206,000; livestock (number of live animals) 6,574,000 sheep and goats, 1,199,000 cattle, 82,000 pigs, 3,500,000 poultry; roundwood (1990) 4,000,000 cu m; fish catch (1995) 40,013. Mining and quarrying (1995): sodium sulphate 400,000, sulfur 240,000. Manufacturing (value of production in '000,000 manat; 1994): ferrous and nonferrous metals 278; machinery and metalworks 223; food products 129; chemical products 90; construction materials 52; wood products 31. Construction (1994): 1,700,000 sq m. Energy production (consumption): electricity (kW-hr; 1994) 10,496,000,000 (7,846,000,000); coal (metric tons; 1994) none (none); crude petroleum (barrels; 1994) 30,053,000 (30,053,000); petroleum products (metric tons; 1994) 2,765,000 (2,765,000); natural gas (cu m; 1994) 30,891,000,000 (8,332,000,000).
Household income and expenditure. Average household size (1989) 5.6; income per household: 3,853 manat (U.S.$ equivalent, n.a.[3]); sources of income (1996): wages and salaries 70.6%, pensions and grants 20.9%, self-employment 2.3%[4], nonwage income of workers 1.1%; expenditure (1996): goods 26.8%, services 13.5%, taxes and other payments 9.4%.
Land use (1994): forested 8.2%; meadows and pastures 61.6%; agricultural and under permanent cultivation 3.0%; other 27.2%.
Population economically active (1996): total 1,680,000; activity rate of total population 36.8% (participation rates [1995]: ages 16–59 [male], 16–54 [female] 81.0%; female 41.0%; unemployed 3.0%[5]).

Price and earnings indexes (1994 = 100)[6]

	1994	1995	1996
Consumer price index	100	1,362	7,431
Monthly earnings index	100	739	6,334

Gross national product (at current market prices; 1994): U.S.$4,125,000,000 (U.S.$920 per capita)[3].

Structure of gross domestic product and labour force

	1995		1996	
	in value '000,000 manat	% of total value	labour force	% of labour force
Agriculture	325,156	30.3	746,000	44.4
Mining Manufacturing Public utilities	559,761	52.2	165,000	9.8
Construction	68,285	6.4	155,000	9.2
Transp. and commun.	26,199	2.4	83,000	4.9
Trade	31,796	3.0	106,700	6.4
Finance	...	...	8,000	0.5
Public administration, defense	...	...	25,000	1.5
Services	3,075	0.3	347,000	20.7
Other	57,639	5.4	44,000	2.6
TOTAL	1,071,911	100.0	1,680,000[2]	100.0

Tourism: n.a.

Foreign trade

Balance of trade (current prices)

	1994	1995	1996
U.S.$'000,000	+485	+536	+329
% of total	12.5%	15.4%	10.8%

Imports (1996): U.S.$1,532,000,000 (machinery and equipment 37.4%, food products 22.3%, chemicals 3.4%, medicines 2.5%). *Major import sources* (1995): U.S. 25.8%; Ukraine 17.4%; Turkey 13.1%; Russia 10.1%; Cyprus 3.9%.
Exports (1996): U.S.$1,691,000,000 (natural gas and oil products 69.2%, cotton 19.6%). *Major export destinations* (1995): Russia 62.5%; Switzerland 6.5%; Hong Kong 6.2%; Turkey 4.7%; Kazakstan 3.2%.

Transport and communications

Transport. Railroads (1995): length (1996) 1,317 mi, 2,120 km; passengers transported 1,773,000; short ton-mi cargo 6,004,000, metric ton-km cargo 8,766,000. Roads (1995): total length 8,451 mi, 13,600 km (paved 88.9%). Vehicles (1995): passenger cars 220,000; trucks and buses, 58,200. Merchant marine: vessels (100 gross tons and over) n.a.; total deadweight tonnage, n.a. Air transport (1989): passenger-mi 2,021,000,000, passenger-km 3,253,000,000; short ton-mi cargo 222,000,000, metric ton-km cargo 324,200,000; airports (1997) with scheduled flights 1.

Communications

Medium	date	unit	number	units per 1,000 persons
Radio	1995	receivers	850,000	189
Television	1995	receivers	850,000	189
Telephones	1995	main lines	320,000	71

Education and health

Educational attainment (1989). Percentage of population age 25 and over having: primary education or no formal schooling 13.6%; some secondary 21.3%; completed secondary and some postsecondary 56.8%; higher 8.3%.
Literacy (1989): total population age 15 and over literate 3,453,000 (97.7%); males literate 1,714,000 (98.8%); females literate 1,739,000 (96.6%).

Education (1994–95)

	schools	teachers	students	student/ teacher ratio
Primary (age 6–13) Secondary (age 14–17)	1,900	72,900	940,600	12.9
Voc., teacher tr.	78	...	26,000	...
Higher	15	...	29,435[7]	...

Health (1995): physicians 13,500 (1 per 330 persons); hospital beds 46,000 (1 per 97 persons); (1994) infant mortality rate per 1,000 live births 46.4.

Military

Total active duty personnel (1997): 18,000 (100% army). *Military expenditure as percentage of GNP* (1995): 1.7% (world 2.8%); per capita expenditure U.S.$48.

[1]The People's Council is the ultimate representative organ of governmental supervision and is composed of the president, membership of the Majlis, elected members, and a variety of ex officio members of national, provincial, and local government; its purpose is to consider and render decisions about the constitution, national development, and national boundaries and treaties. [2]Detail does not add to total given because of rounding. [3]Ruble-area GNP and exchange-rate data for this period are very speculative. [4]Mainly agricultural income. [5]Every Turkmen citizen is guaranteed employment, so that unemployment does not officially exist. However, the 1995 Household Survey indicates an unemployment rate of about 3 percent of the labour force (defined as those actively seeking employment but not employed as a proportion of the labour force). [6]December. [7]1995–96.

Internet resources for further information:

- **Turkmenistan Human Development Report 1996**
http://www.undp.org/undp/rbec/nhdr/1996/turkmenistan/

Tuvalu

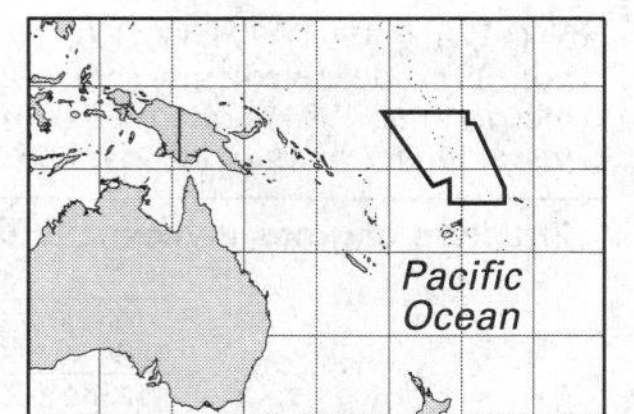

Official name: Tuvalu.
Form of government: constitutional monarchy with one legislative house (Parliament [12]).
Chief of state: British Monarch, represented by Governor-General.
Head of government: Prime Minister.
Capital: government offices are at Vaiaku, Fongafale islet, of Funafuti atoll.
Official language: none.
Official religion: none.
Monetary units[1]: 1 Tuvalu dollar = 1 Australian dollar ($T = $A) = 100 Tuvalu and Australian cents; valuation (Oct. 3, 1997) 1 U.S.$ = $A 1.37; 1 £ = $A 2.21.

Area and population

	area		population
Islands[2]	sq mi	sq km	1991 census
Funafuti	1.08	2.79	3,172
Nanumaga	1.07	2.78	717
Nanumea	1.49	3.87	901
Niulakita	0.16	0.42	74
Niutao	0.98	2.53	889
Nui	1.09	2.83	661
Nukufetau	1.15	2.99	831
Nukulaelae	0.70	1.82	359
Vaitupu	2.16	5.60	1,280
TOTAL	9.90[3, 4]	25.63	8,884[5]

Demography

Population (1997): 10,300.
Density (1997): persons per sq mi 1,040.4, persons per sq km 401.9.
Urban-rural (1995): urban 46.0%; rural 54.0%.
Sex distribution (1997): male 48.59%; female 51.41%.
Age breakdown (1997): under 15, 35.7%; 15–29, 23.2%; 30–44, 23.4%; 45–59, 10.5%; 60–74, 6.1%; 75 and over, 1.1%.
Population projection: (2000) 10,700; (2010) 12,400.
Doubling time: 43 years.
Ethnic composition (1979): Tuvaluan (Polynesian) 91.2%; mixed (Polynesian/Micronesian/other) 7.2%; European 1.0%; other 0.6%.
Religious affiliation (1995): Church of Tuvalu (Congregational) 85.4%; Seventh-day Adventist 3.6%; Roman Catholic 1.4%; Jehovah's Witness 1.1%; Bahā'ī 1.0%; other 7.5%.
Major locality (1995): Fongafale, on Funafuti atoll, 4,000.

Vital statistics

Birth rate per 1,000 population (1997): 23.0 (world avg. 25.0); (1989) legitimate 82.2%; illegitimate 17.8%.
Death rate per 1,000 population (1997): 9.0 (world avg. 9.3).
Natural increase rate per 1,000 population (1997): 14.0 (world avg. 15.7).
Total fertility rate (avg. births per childbearing woman; 1997): 3.1.
Marriage rate per 1,000 population: n.a.
Divorce rate per 1,000 population: n.a.
Life expectancy at birth (1997): male 62.4 years; female 64.8 years.
Major causes of death per 100,000 population (1985): diseases of the digestive system 170.0; diseases of the circulatory system 150.0; diseases of the respiratory system 120.0; diseases of the nervous system 120.0; malignant neoplasms (cancers) 70.0; infectious and parasitic diseases 40.0; endocrine and metabolic disorders 20.0; ill-defined conditions 430.0; in 1992 the leading causes of death included liver diseases, meningitis, tuberculosis, and still and perinatal deaths; other health problems included acute respiratory infections, diarrhea, filariasis, conjunctivitis, fish poisoning, diabetes, rheumatism, and hypertension.

National economy

Budget (1995)[6]. Revenue: $A 4,400,000 (government charges and grants 49.0%; indirect taxes 34.0%; direct taxes 10.0%). Expenditures: $A 7,300,000 (1987; capital [development] expenditures 68.9%, of which marine transport 20.7%, education 13.0%, fisheries 5.6%, health 3.1%; current expenditures 31.1%).
Public debt (external; 1993): U.S.$6,000,000.
Gross national product (1995): U.S.$7,800,000 (U.S.$800 per capita).

Structure of gross domestic product and labour force

	1995		1991	
	in value[7] $A	% of total value	labour force	% of labour force
Agriculture, fishing, forestry	3,152,000	22.2	4,020	68.0
Mining	317,000	2.2	—	—
Manufacturing[8]	452,000	3.2	60	1.0
Construction	1,963,000	13.9	240	4.0
Public utilities	345,000	2.4	—	—
Transp. and commun.	599,000	4.2	60	1.0
Trade, hotels, and restaurants	2,043,000	14.4	240	4.0
Finance	1,390,000	9.8	—	—
Pub. admin., defense / Services	3,922,000	27.7	1,290	22.0
TOTAL	14,183,000	100.0	5,910	100.0

Production (metric tons except as noted). Agriculture[9], forestry, fishing (1997): coconuts 1,800, fruits 860, hens' eggs 12, other agricultural products include breadfruit, pulaka (taro), bananas, pandanus fruit, sweet potatoes, and pawpaws; livestock (number of live animals) 12,600 pigs[10]; forestry, n.a.; fish catch (1995) 1,460, of which (1993) tuna 15.0%. Mining and quarrying: n.a.[11]. Manufacturing (1988): copra 90; handicrafts and baked goods are also important. Construction: n.a.; however, the main areas of construction activity are roadworks, coastal protection, government facilities, and water-related infrastructure projects. Energy production (consumption): electricity (kW-hr; 1992) 1,300,000 (1,300,000); coal, none (none); crude petroleum, none (n.a.); petroleum products, none (n.a.); natural gas, none (none).
Tourism (1993): receipts from visitors U.S.$300,000; expenditures by nationals abroad, n.a.
Population economically active (1991): total 5,910; activity rate of total population 65.3% (participation rates: ages 15–64, 85.5%; female [1979] 51.3%; unemployed [1979] 4.0%).

Price and earnings indexes (1990 = 100)

	1989	1990	1991	1992	1993	1994	1995
Consumer price index	96.4	100.0	106.4	108.7	110.3	111.9	113.6
Earnings index[12]	97.8	100.0	...	...	...	...	...

Household income and expenditure. Average household size (1979) 6.4; average annual income per household $A 2,575 (U.S.$2,044); sources of income (1987): agriculture and other 45.0%, cash economy only 38.0%, overseas remittances 17.0%; expenditure (1992)[13]: food 45.5%, housing and household operations 11.5%, transportation 10.5%, alcohol and tobacco 10.5%, clothing 7.5%, other 14.5%.
Land use (1987): agricultural and under permanent cultivation 73.6%[14]; scrub 16.1%; other 10.3%.

Foreign trade[15]

Balance of trade (current prices)

	1990	1991	1992	1993	1994	1995
$A '000	−5,909	−6,200	−6,595	−9,129	−9,498	−9,980
% of total	90.2%	86.8%	91.7%	93.3%	93.4%	93.5%

Imports (1995): U.S.$15,200,000 (1989; food 29.3%, manufactured goods 28.2%, petroleum and petroleum products 12.8%, machinery and transport equipment 12.2%, chemicals 7.1%, beverages and tobacco 3.9%). *Major import sources:* Fiji 65.8%; Australia 17.1%; New Zealand 3.9%; United Kingdom 3.3%; United States 2.0%; Germany 1.3%; The Netherlands 1.3%.
Exports (1995): U.S.$2,200,000 (1989; clothing and footwear 29.5%, copra 21.5%, fruits and vegetables 8.0%). *Major export destinations:* South Africa 63.6%; Colombia 9.1%; Belgium-Luxembourg 9.1%.

Transport and communications

Transport. Railroads: none. Roads (1995): total length 8 km (paved, none). Vehicles[16]: n.a. Merchant marine (1992): vessels (100 gross tons and over) 6; total deadweight tonnage 16,005. Air transport (1977): passenger arrivals (Funafuti) 1,443; cargo, n.a.; airports (1997) with scheduled flights 1.

Communications

Medium	date	unit	number	units per 1,000 persons
Radio	1995	receivers	3,000	320.0
Telephones	1994	main lines	113	11.5

Education and health

Educational attainment (1979). Percentage of population age 25 and over having: no formal schooling 0.4%; primary education 93.0%; secondary 6.1%; higher 0.5%. *Literacy* (1990): total population literate in Tuvaluan 8,593 (95.0%); literacy in English estimated at 45.0%.

Education (1991)

	schools	teachers[17]	students	student/ teacher ratio
Primary (age 5–11)	11	72	1,906[18]	...
Secondary (age 12–18)	1	21	314	...
Vocational	1	10	58	...
Higher	—	—	—	—

Health (1993): physicians 8 (1 per 1,152 persons); hospital beds (1990) 30 (1 per 302 persons); infant mortality rate per 1,000 live births (1997): 26.9.

Military

Total active duty personnel (1987): there is a police force numbering 32.

[1]The value of the Tuvalu dollar is pegged to the value of the Australian dollar, which is also legal currency in Tuvalu. [2]Local government councils have been established on all islands except Niulakita. [3]Another survey puts the area at 9.4 sq mi (24.4 sq km). [4]Detail does not add to total given because of rounding. [5]De facto population. [6]Estimated from 1995 gross national product. [7]At 1988 factor cost. [8]Including cottage industry. [9]Because of poor soil quality, only limited subsistence agriculture is possible on the islands. [10]Other livestock include goats. [11]Research into the mineral potential of Tuvalu's maritime exclusive economic zone (289,500 sq mi [750,000 sq km] of the Pacific Ocean) is currently being conducted by the South Pacific Geo-Science Commission. [12]Average minimum wage. [13]Weights of consumer price index components. [14]Capable of supporting coconut palms, pandanus, and breadfruit. [15]Exports and imports are f.o.b. [16]There are several cars, tractors, trailers, and light trucks on Funafuti; a few motorcycles are in use on most islands. [17]1990. [18]1994.

Internet resources for further information:

- **Tuvalu http://www.emulateme.com/tuvalu.htm**

Uganda

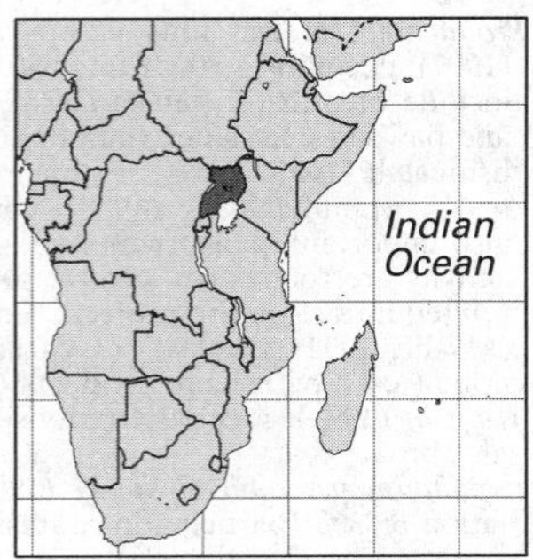

Official name: Republic of Uganda.
Form of government: republic with one legislative house (National Assembly [279[1]])[2].
Head of state and government: President.
Capital: Kampala.
Official language: English.
Official religion: none.
Monetary unit: 1 Uganda shilling (U Sh) = 100 cents; valuation (Oct. 3, 1997) 1 U.S.$ = U Sh 1,130; 1 £ = U Sh 1,822.

Area and population (1991 census)

Regions[3] Districts	area sq km	population	Regions[3] Districts	area sq km	population
Central			Arua	7,830	624,600
Kalangala	5,716	16,400	Gulu	11,735	338,700
Kampala	238	773,500	Kitgum	16,136	350,300
Kiboga	3,774	140,800	Kotido	13,208	190,700
Luwero	9,198	449,200	Lira	7,251	498,300
Masaka	10,611	831,300	Moroto	14,113	171,500
Mpigi	6,222	915,400	Moyo	5,006	178,500
Mubende	6,536	497,500	Nebbi	2,891	315,900
Mukono	14,242	816,200	Western		
Rakai	4,973	382,000	Bundibugyo	2,338	116,000
Eastern			Bushenyi	5,396	734,800
Iganga	13,113	944,000	Hoima	5,492	197,800
Jinja	734	284,900	Kabale	1,827	412,800
Kamuli	4,348	480,700	Kabarole	8,361	741,400
Kapchorwa	1,738	116,300	Kasese	3,205	343,000
Kumi	2,861	237,000	Kibaale	4,718	219,300
Mbale	2,546	706,600	Kisoro	662	184,900
Pallisa	1,919	356,000	Masindi	9,326	253,500
Soroti	10,060	430,900	Mbarara	10,839	929,600
Tororo	2,634	554,000	Ntungamo	...	...
Northern			Rukungiri	2,753	388,000
Apac	6,488	460,700	TOTAL	241,038[4]	16,582,700[5, 6]

Demography

Population (1997): 20,605,000.
Density (1997)[7]: persons per sq mi 270.8, persons per sq km 104.5.
Urban-rural (1995): urban 12.5%; rural 87.5%.
Sex distribution (1995): male 49.63%; female 50.37%.
Age breakdown (1995): under 15, 48.8%; 15–29, 26.5%; 30–44, 14.0%; 45–59, 6.9%; 60–74, 3.2%; 75 and over, 0.6%.
Population projection: (2000) 21,891,000; (2010) 26,355,000.
Doubling time: 24 years.
Ethnic composition (1983): Ganda 17.8%; Teso 8.9%; Nkole 8.2%; Soga 8.2%; Gisu 7.2%; Chiga 6.8%; Lango 6.0%; Rwanda 5.8%; other 31.1%.
Religious affiliation (1995): Christian 65%, of which Roman Catholic 39%, Protestant 26% (of which Anglican 22%); traditional beliefs 19%; Muslim 15%; other 1%.
Major cities (1991): Kampala 773,500; Jinja 61,000; Mbale 53,600; Masaka 49,100; Gulu 42,800; Entebbe 41,600.

Vital statistics

Birth rate per 1,000 population (1990–95): 50.8 (world avg. 25.0).
Death rate per 1,000 population (1990–95): 21.8 (world avg. 9.3).
Natural increase rate per 1,000 population (1990–95): 29.0 (world avg. 15.7).
Total fertility rate (avg. births per childbearing woman; 1990–95): 7.3.
Life expectancy at birth (1990–95): male 43.6 years; female 46.2 years.

National economy

Budget (1995–96). Revenue: U Sh 875,400,000,000 (taxes 71.7%, of which customs duties 36.0%, sales taxes 25.9%, income taxes 13.2%; grants 28.3%). Expenditures: U Sh 992,000,000,000 (1994–95; current expenditures 54.4%, of which security 13.9%, education 6.4%, health 2.4%; capital expenditures 44.3%).
Public debt (external, outstanding; 1995): U.S.$3,054,000,000.
Tourism (1995): receipts from visitors U.S.$79,000,000; expenditures by nationals abroad U.S.$93,000,000.
Land use (1994): forest 31.5%; pasture 9.1%; agriculture 34.0%; other 25.4%.
Population economically active (1991): total 8,365,000; activity rate of total population 49.6% (participation rates: ages 15–64, 78.9%[8]; female 35.2%).

Price index (1990 = 100)

	1990	1991	1992	1993	1994	1995	1996
Consumer price index	100.0	128.0	195.0	207.0	227.0	247.0	264.0
Earnings index	...	...	...	...	...	...	...

Production (metric tons except as noted). Agriculture, forestry, fishing (1996): plantains 9,550,000, cassava 2,650,000, sweet potatoes 2,250,000, sugarcane 1,450,000, corn (maize) 939,000, millet 640,000, sorghum 405,000, potatoes 390,000, coffee 257,000, peanuts (groundnuts) 144,000, rice 83,000; livestock (number of live animals) 5,200,000 cattle, 3,500,000 goats, 1,900,000 sheep; roundwood (1995) 17,226,000 cu m; fish catch (1996) 231,600. Mining and quarrying (1996): gold 162,900 troy oz[9]. Manufacturing (1996): cement 149,100; sugar 78,500; soap 58,300; metal products 31,300; footwear 1,786,000 pairs; beer 642,000 hectolitres. Energy production (consumption): electricity (kW-hr; 1994) 795,000,000 (681,000,000); coal (metric tons; 1994) none (none); crude petroleum (barrels; 1994) none (none); petroleum products (metric tons; 1994) none (319,000); natural gas (cu m; 1994) none (none).
Gross national product (1995): U.S.$4,668,000,000 (U.S.$240 per capita).

Structure of gross domestic product and labour force

	1995–96 in value U Sh '000,000	1995–96 % of total value	1991 labour force	1991 % of labour force
Agriculture	2,519,382	41.5	6,724,000	80.4
Mining	15,891	0.3	478,000	5.7
Manufacturing	397,874	6.5		
Construction	402,317	6.6		
Public utilities	65,167	1.1		
Transp. and commun.	213,856	3.5	1,163,000	13.9
Trade	742,024	12.2		
Finance	410,500	6.8		
Pub. admin., defense	248,231	4.1		
Services	293,394	4.8		
Other	768,398	12.6	...	...
TOTAL	6,077,035[5]	100.0	8,365,000	100.0

Household size. Average household size (1991) 4.8; income per household: n.a.; sources of income (1992–93)[10, 11]: wages and self-employment 86.4%; transfers 11.7%; rent 1.9%; expenditure (1992–93)[10]: food and beverages 64.0%; rent, energy, and services 18.3%; education 5.0%; health 4.2%.

Foreign trade

Balance of trade (current prices)

	1991	1992	1993	1994	1995	1996
U.S.$'000,000	−369.6	−278.6	−416.1	−463.8	−504.1	−627.7
% of total	51.3%	44.7%	57.0%	47.7%	31.9%	34.0%

Imports (1995–96): U.S.$1,218,000,000 (1995; machinery and transport equipment 32.3%, basic manufactures 11.0%, food and live animals 9.3%, chemicals 8.3%). *Major import sources* (1992): Kenya 22.6%; U.K. 10.0%; Japan 9.8%; Germany 5.5%; U.S. 4.8%.
Exports (1995–96): U.S.$590,300,000 (unroasted coffee 69.0%, cotton 2.2%, tea 2.1%). *Major export destinations* (1992): U.K. 20.7%; Belgium-Luxembourg 12.3%; Spain 9.2%; U.S. 8.1%; France 6.4%; Germany 4.3%.

Transport and communications

Transport. Railroads (1993): route length 1,241 km; passenger-km (1996) 28,000,000; metric ton-km cargo (1996) 187,000,000. Roads (1995): total length 26,800 km (paved 7.7%). Vehicles (1995): passenger cars 24,400; trucks and buses 25,300. Merchant marine (1992): vessels (100 gross tons and over) 2; total deadweight tonnage 8,600[12]. Air transport (1994): passenger-km 52,117,000; metric ton-km cargo 5,000,000; airports (1997) 1.

Communications

Medium	date	unit	number	units per 1,000 persons
Daily newspapers	1994	circulation	35,000	2.0
Radio	1997	receivers	10,000,000	485
Television	1995	receivers	500,000	27
Telephones	1995	main lines	43,200	2.3
Cellular telephones	1995	subscribers	1,700	0.1
Facsimile machines	1995	units	2,500	0.1
Personal computers	1995	units	10,000	0.5

Education and health

Educational attainment (1991). Percentage of population age 25 and over having: no formal schooling or less than one full year 46.9%; primary education 42.1%; secondary 10.5%; higher 0.5%. *Literacy* (1995): population age 15 and over literate 6,732,000 (61.8%); males literate 3,948,000 (73.7%); females literate 2,784,000 (50.2%).

Education (1995)

	schools	teachers	students	student/ teacher ratio
Primary (age 5–11)[13]	8,531	76,111	2,912,473	38.3
Secondary (age 12–15)[13]	...	14,447	256,258	17.7
Voc., teacher tr.[13]	...	1,788	36,063	20.2
Higher[14]	...	2,029	27,586	13.6

Health (1989): physicians 774 (1 per 20,720 persons); hospital beds 20,136 (1 per 817 persons); infant mortality rate (1990–95) 122.0.
Food (1995): daily per capita caloric intake 2,268 (vegetable products 93%, animal products 7%); 97% of FAO recommended minimum requirement.

Military

Total active duty personnel (1997): 40,000–55,000[15]. *Military expenditure as percentage of GNP* (1995): 2.3% (world 2.8%); per capita U.S.$6.

[1]62 of 276 elected seats are allocated to special interest groups; all government ministers not elected to the National Assembly (3 in 1996) serve ex officio. [2]New constitution promulgated on Oct. 8, 1995. [3]Regions are geographical areas with no administrative function. [4]Includes water area of 43,989 sq km; Uganda's portion of Lake Victoria comprises 30,960 sq km. [5]Detail does not add to total given because of rounding. [6]Preliminary figure; final census total equals 16,671,705. [7]Based on land area only. [8]1985. [9]Export production only. [10]Based on first nationally representative household survey. [11]Highest quartile only. [12]1988. [13]Public sector only. [14]1994–95. [15]Breakdown by branch of service is unavailable.

Internet resources for further information:

- **Uganda National Information Center (unofficial web site) http://www.nic.ug/**

Ukraine

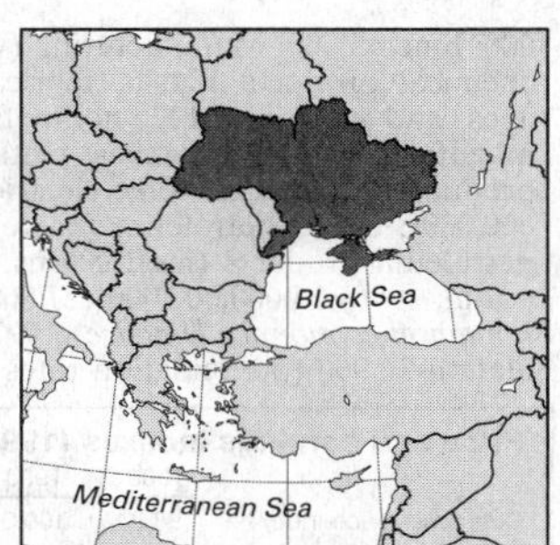

Official name: Ukrayina (Ukraine).
Form of government: unitary multiparty republic with a single legislative body (Supreme Council [450]).
Head of state: President.
Head of government: Prime Minister.
Capital: Kiev (Kyyiv).
Official language: Ukrainian.
Official religion: none.
Monetary unit: hryvnia (pl. hryvny)[1]; (no decimal unit); valuation (Oct. 3, 1997) free rate, 1 U.S.$ = 1.87 hryvny; 1 £ = 3.02 hryvny.

Area and population

		area		population
Autonomous republic	**Capitals**	sq mi	sq km	1996 estimate
Crimea (Krym)	Simferopol	10,400[2]	27,000[2]	2,205,600
Cities				
Kiev	—	[3]	[3]	2,638,700
Sevastopol	—	[2]	[2]	406,900
Provinces				
Cherkasy	Cherkasy	8,100	20,900	1,504,600
Chernihiv	Chernihiv	12,300	31,900	1,349,500
Chernivtsi	Chernivtsi	3,100	8,100	943,600
Dnipropetrovsk	Dnipropetrovsk	12,300	31,900	3,852,000
Donetsk	Donetsk	10,200	26,500	5,198,500
Ivano-Frankivsk	Ivano-Frankivsk	5,400	13,900	1,467,100
Kharkiv	Kharkiv	12,100	31,400	3,088,400
Kherson	Kherson	11,000	28,500	1,265,700
Khmelnytsky	Khmelnytsky	8,000	20,600	1,508,800
Kirovohrad	Kirovohrad	9,500	24,600	1,224,800
Kyyiv (Kiev)	Kiev	11,200[3]	28,900[3]	1,895,800
Luhansk	Luhansk	10,300	26,700	2,788,500
Lviv	Lviv	8,400	21,800	2,761,500
Mykolayiv	Mykolayiv	9,500	24,600	1,343,300
Odessa	Odessa	12,900	33,300	2,586,500
Poltava	Poltava	11,100	28,800	1,739,100
Rivne	Rivne	7,800	20,100	1,194,200
Sumy	Sumy	9,200	23,800	1,397,900
Ternopil	Ternopil	5,300	13,800	1,175,400
Vinnytsya	Vinnytsya	10,200	26,500	1,876,000
Volyn	Volodymyr-Volynsky	7,800	20,200	1,075,200
Zakarpatska	Uzhhorod	4,900	12,800	1,288,100
Zaporizhzhya	Zaporizhzhya	10,500	27,200	2,077,800
Zhytomyr	Zhytomyr	11,600	29,900	1,480,600
TOTAL		233,100	603,700	51,334,100

Demography

Population (1997): 50,668,000.
Density (1997): persons per sq mi 217.4, persons per sq km 83.9.
Urban-rural (1996): urban 67.9%; rural 32.1%.
Sex distribution (1994): male 46.45%; female 53.55%.
Age breakdown (1995): under 15, 19.5%; 15–29, 20.6%; 30–44, 22.3%; 45–59, 18.2%; 60–69, 10.3%; 70 and over, 9.1%.
Ethnic composition (1991): Ukrainian 72.6%; Russian 22.2%; Belarusian 0.9%; Jewish 0.7%; Moldovan 0.6%; Tatar 0.4%; other 2.6%.
Religious affiliation: Ukrainian Orthodox (Russian patriarchy) 30.7%; Ukrainian Orthodox (Kiev patriarchy) 19.5%; Ukrainian Autocephalous Orthodox 9.7%; Ukrainian Catholic (Uniate) 7.0%; Protestant 3.6%; Roman Catholic 1.2%; Jewish 1.0%; other (mostly nonreligious) 27.3%.
Major cities (1996): Kiev 2,630,200; Kharkiv 1,555,100; Dnipropetrovsk 1,147,200; Donetsk 1,088,200; Odessa 1,046,400.

Vital statistics

Birth rate per 1,000 population (1996): 9.1 (world avg. 25.0); (1993) legitimate 87.0%; illegitimate 13.0%.
Death rate per 1,000 population (1996): 15.2 (world avg. 9.3).
Natural increase rate per 1,000 population (1996): −6.1 (world avg. 15.7).
Marriage rate per 1,000 population (1995): 8.4.
Life expectancy at birth (1994): male 62.0 years; female 73.0 years.
Major causes of death per 100,000 population (1995): circulatory diseases 874.0; neoplasms (cancers) 199.0; accidents 160.0; respiratory diseases 89.0.

National economy

Budget (1996). Revenue: 19,633,000,000 hryvny (value-added tax 20.9%, corporate tax 18.1%, income tax 8.8%, excise tax 2.2%, other 50%). Expenditures: 23,258,000,000 hryvny (social-cultural spending and education 34.9%; national economy 10.2%; defense 3.6%).
Public debt (external; 1995): U.S.$6,585,000,000.
Production (metric tons except as noted). Agriculture, forestry, fishing (1996): sugar beets 23,009,000, potatoes 18,410,000, wheat 13,547,000, barley 5,726,000, corn (maize) 1,837,000; livestock (number of live animals) 17,557,000 cattle, 13,144,000 pigs, 4,098,000 sheep and goats; roundwood (1993) 4,888,200 cu m; fish catch (1995) 607,707. Mining and quarrying (1995): iron ore 51,000,000; manganese 3,200,000. Manufacturing (value in '000 hryvny; 1994): metals 2,783,065; machinery 2,225,093; processed foods 1,285,328; chemicals 898,635. Construction (1996): residential 6,500,000 sq m. Energy production (consumption): electricity (kW-hr; 1994) 209,100,000,000 (208,100,000,000); coal (metric tons; 1994) 91,800,000 (94,267,000); crude petroleum (barrels; 1994) 30,786,000 (137,900,000); petroleum products 10,678,000 (12,180,000); natural gas (cu m; 1994) 18,600,000,000 (18,800,000,000).
Gross national product (1995)[4]: U.S.$84,084,000,000 (U.S.$1,630 per capita).

Structure of gross domestic product and labour force

	1993		1995	
	in value '000,000 hryvny	% of total value	labour force	% of labour force
Agriculture	31,939	21.5	5,300,000	22.4
Mining } Manufacturing }	45,826	30.9 }	...	...
Public utilities	1,303	0.9 }	5,800,000	24.5
Construction	10,282	6.9	1,500,000	6.3
Transp. and commun.	17,425	11.8	1,400,000	5.9
Trade	16,482	11.1	1,600,000	6.8
Finance	17,784	12.0	200,000	0.8
Pub. admin., defense	5,304	3.6	700,000	3.0
Services	13,182	8.9	4,900,000	20.7
Other	−11,254[5]	−7.6[5]	2,427,000[6]	9.7[6]
TOTAL	148,273	100.0	23,627,000	100.0[7]

Population economically active (1995): total 23,627,000; activity rate of total population 46.0% (1993; participation rates: ages 16–59 [male], 16–54 [female] 82.4%; female [1994] 51.0%; unemployed [1997] 1.3%).

Price and earnings indexes (1993 = 100)

	1993	1994	1995	1996
Consumer price index	100.0	991.2	4,725	8,519
Monthly earnings index	100.0	886.6	4,736	...

Household income and expenditure (1996). Average household size 3.0; income per household 4,968 hryvny[1]; sources of income (1995): wages and salaries 66.4%, sales of agricultural products 9.3%, subsidies 6.9%, pensions 6.5%, remuneration from abroad 5.3%; expenditures (1995): food and beverages 43.1%, consumer goods 27.5%, services 7.2%, housing 6.7%, taxes 6.2%.

Foreign trade

Balance of trade (current prices)

	1993	1994	1995	1996
U.S.$'000,000	−2,519	−2,360	−2,105	−2,702
% of total	9.0%	9.1%	7.9%	8.7%

Imports (1996): U.S.$12,567,000,000 (1995; mineral commodities 55.2%; machinery 14.8%; chemicals 5.4%; nonferrous metals 4.8%; plastics, rubber, and products 3.6%). *Major import sources:* Russia 42.5%; Germany 6.7%.
Exports (1996): U.S.$13,413,000,000 (1995; ferrous metals 36.2%; machinery 11.8%; mineral commodities 10.6%; chemicals 9.7%; food 8.5%). *Major export destinations:* Russia 39.8%; China 5.3%.

Transport and communications

Transport. Railroads (1997): length 22,600 km; (1995) passenger-km 120,500,000,000; metric ton-km cargo 518,500,000,000. Roads (1995): total length 172,257 km (paved 94.8%). Vehicles (1995): passenger cars 4,510,000. Air transport (1996): passenger-km 2,014,000,000; metric ton-km cargo 44,205,000; airports (1997) with scheduled flights 12.

Communications

Medium	date	unit	number	units per 1,000 persons
Daily newspapers	1995	circulation	6,083,000	118
Radio	1996	receivers	18,000,000	346
Television	1995	receivers	12,000,000	233
Telephones	1995	main lines	8,311,000	161
Cellular telephones	1995	subscribers	14,000	0.3
Facsimile machines	1995	units	1,500	0.03
Personal computers	1995	units	290,000	5.6

Education and health

Educational attainment (1989). Percentage of population age 15 and over having: some primary education 6.8%; completed primary 13.8%; some secondary 18.4%; completed secondary 31.1%; some postsecondary 19.5%; higher 10.4%. *Literacy* (1989): percentage of total population age 15 and over literate 98.4%; males literate 99.5%; females literate 97.4%.

Education (1995–96)

	schools	teachers	students	student/ teacher ratio
Primary (age 6–13) } Secondary (age 14–17) }	21,900	576,000[8]	7,007,000	12.4[8]
Voc., teacher tr.	782	...	618,000	...
Higher	255	...	922,800	...

Health (1995): physicians 230,000 (1 per 224 persons); hospital beds 639,000 (1 per 81 persons); infant mortality rate per 1,000 live births 14.5.

Military

Total active duty personnel (1997): 387,400 (army 41.7%, air force 32.1%, navy 4.1%, other 22.1%). *Military expenditure as percentage of GNP* (1995) 2.9% (world 2.8%); per capita expenditure U.S.$70.

[1]On Sept. 2, 1996, the karbovanets, a transitional currency, was replaced by the hryvnia at a 100,000-to-1 ratio. [2]Crimea includes area of Sevastopol. [3]Kyyiv includes area of Kiev (city). [4]Ruble-area GNP and exchange-rate data are very speculative. [5]Less imputed bank service charges, net indirect taxes, and taxes on production. [6]Includes 126,900 unemployed. [7]Detail does not add to total given because of rounding. [8]1994–95.

Internet resources for further information:
- **Welcome to the Parliament of Ukraine http://www.rada.kiev.ua/**
- **United Nations Office in Ukraine WWW Service http://www.un.kiev.ua/**

United Arab Emirates

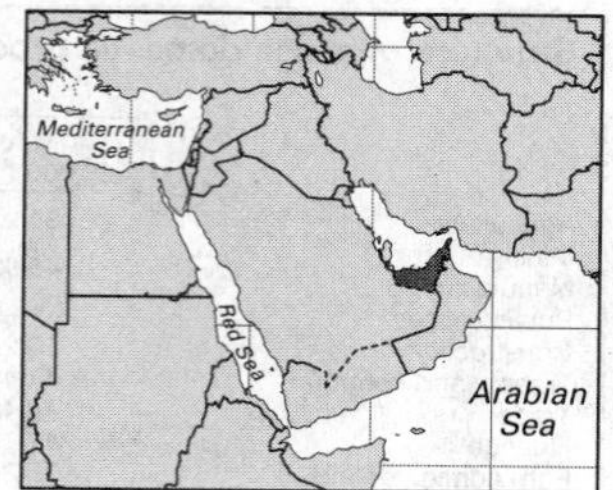

Official name: Al-Imārāt al-ʿArabīyah al-Muttaḥidah (United Arab Emirates).
Form of government: federation of seven emirates with one appointive advisory body (Federal National Council [40[1]]).
Chief of state: President.
Head of government: Prime Minister.
Capital: Abu Dhabi.
Official language: Arabic.
Official religion: Islam.
Monetary unit: 1 U.A.E. dirham (Dh) = 100 fils; valuation (Oct. 3, 1997) 1 U.S.$ = Dh 3.67; 1 £ = Dh 5.92.

Area and population

		area		population
Emirates	Capitals	sq mi	sq km	1995 census[2]
Abu Dhabi (Abū Ẓaby)	Abu Dhabi	28,210[3]	73,060[3]	928,360
ʿAjmān (Ajman)	ʿAjmān	100	260	118,812
Dubayy (Dubai)	Dubayy	1,510	3,900	674,101
Al-Fujayrah (Fujairah)	Al-Fujayrah	500	1,300	76,254
Raʾs al-Khaymah (Ras al-Khaimah)	Raʾs al-Khaymah	660	1,700	144,430
Ash-Shāriqah (Sharjah)	Ash-Shāriqah	1,000	2,600	400,339
Umm al-Qaywayn (Umm al-Qaiwain)	Umm al-Qaywayn	300	780	35,157
TOTAL		32,280	83,600	2,377,453

Demography

Population (1997): 2,580,000.
Density (1997): persons per sq mi 79.9, persons per sq km 30.9.
Urban-rural (1995): urban 84.0%; rural 16.0%.
Sex distribution (1995): male 66.45%; female 33.55%.
Age breakdown (1994): under 15, 34.3%; 15–29, 25.3%; 30–44, 30.6%; 45–59, 7.8%; 60–74, 1.5%; 75 and over, 0.5%.
Population projection: 2,722,000; (2010) 3,277,000.
Doubling time: 32 years.
Ethnic composition (1993): expatriates of Bangladesh, India, Pakistan, and Sri Lanka 45.0%; Arabs 25.0%, of which non-UAE Arabs (primarily Egyptians) 13.0%, UAE Arabs 12.0%; Iranians 17.0%; other Asians and Africans 8.0%; Europeans and North Americans 5.0%.
Religious affiliation (1995): Muslim 96.0% (Sunnī 80.0%, Shīʿī 16.0%); other (mostly Christian and Hindu) 4.0%.
Major cities (1989): Dubayy 585,189; Abu Dhabi 363,432; Al-ʿAyn 176,411; Ash-Shāriqah 125,000[4]; Raʾs al-Khaymah 42,000[4].

Vital statistics

Birth rate per 1,000 population (1994): 25.0 (world avg. 25.0).
Death rate per 1,000 population (1994): 3.4 (world avg. 9.3).
Natural increase rate per 1,000 population (1994): 21.6 (world avg. 15.7).
Total fertility rate (avg. births per childbearing woman; 1994): 3.5.
Marriage rate per 1,000 population (1994): 3.2.
Life expectancy at birth (1994): male 69.2 years; female 75.2 years.
Major causes of death per 100,000 population (1989)[5]: accidents and poisoning 43.7; diseases of the circulatory system 34.3; malignant neoplasms (cancers) 13.7; respiratory diseases 8.1.

National economy

Budget (1996). Revenue: Dh 17,396,000,000 (1994; current [domestic] grants 79.5%; other sources 20.5%, of which nontax revenue 15.3%, tax revenue 5.2%). Expenditures: Dh 18,254,000,000 (1994; current expenditures 95.3%, of which defense 37.1%, education 17.2%, public safety 12.9%, health 7.3%, economic services 5.3%; cultural and religious affairs 3.2%).
Gross national product (1995): U.S.$42,806,000,000 (U.S.$17,400 per capita).

Structure of gross domestic product and labour force

	1996		1990	
	in value[6] Dh '000,000	% of total value	labour force	% of labour force
Agriculture	3,703	2.4	43,100	6.3
Petroleum	53,572	34.7	10,000	1.5
Manufacturing	13,242	8.6	63,400	9.2
Construction	14,611	9.5	119,200	17.3
Public utilities	1,687	1.1	20,600	3.0
Transp. and commun.	8,696	5.6	71,700	10.4
Trade	19,323	12.5	101,400	14.7
Finance, real estate	20,357	13.2	18,800	2.7
Pub. admin., defense	17,547	11.4 }	241,300	35.0
Services	2,969[7]	1.9[7] }		
Other	–1,423[8]	–0.9[8]	—	—
TOTAL	154,284	100.0	689,500	100.0[9]

Public debt (external, outstanding; 1995): U.S.$3,900,000,000.
Tourism (1995): total number of tourist arrivals 2,200,000.
Production (metric tons except as noted). Agriculture, forestry, fishing (1997): tomatoes 545,000, dates 245,000, cabbages 45,000, lemons and limes 21,000, pumpkins and squash 20,000, eggplants 16,983, cucumbers and gherkins 13,612, mangoes 9,500; livestock (number of live animals) 990,000 goats, 385,000 sheep, 160,000 camels, 70,000 cattle, 10,700,000 chickens; fish catch (1994) 108,000. Mining and quarrying (1994): sulfur 144,000; gypsum 100,000; lime 45,000. Manufacturing (value of production in Dh '000,000; 1993): chemical products 13,086; fabricated metal products 2,234; food, beverages, and tobacco 2,122; nonmetallic mineral products 2,025; basic metal manufactures 1,992; textiles, clothing, and leather products 1,135. Energy production (consumption): electricity (kW-hr; 1994) 18,870,000,000 (18,870,000,000); crude petroleum (barrels; 1996) 803,000,000 ([1994] 73,722,000); petroleum products (metric tons; 1994) 14,710,000 (7,625,000); natural gas (cu m; 1996) 35,000,000,000 (27,800,000,000).
Population economically active (1992): total 733,500; activity rate of total population 36.9% (participation rates [1986]: ages 15–64, 76.7%; female 6.6%).

Price and earnings indexes (1990 = 100)

	1989	1990	1991	1992	1993	1994	1995
Consumer price index[10]	98.8	100.0	105.4	112.4	118.0	123.9	129.3
Earnings index	...	...	...	...	...	...	...

Household income and expenditure. Average household size (1986) 6.8; income per household: n.a.; sources of income: n.a.; expenditure (1991): rent, fuel, and light 23.9%, food 22.7%, transportation and communications 14.1%, durable household goods 11.6%, education, recreation, and entertainment 8.6%.
Land use (1994): forested, virtually none; meadows and pastures 2.4%; agricultural and under permanent cultivation 0.5%; built-on, wasteland, and other 97.1%.

Foreign trade

Balance of trade (current prices)

	1990	1991	1992	1993	1994	1995
U.S.$'000,000	+11,960	+10,471	+4,528	+3,755	–1,974	–1,000
% of total	34.1%	27.3%	10.1%	8.7%	4.9%	2.2%

Imports (1994): U.S.$23,883,000,000 (1993; machinery and transport equipment 38.4%, basic manufactures 24.8%, food and live animals 9.7%, chemicals 6.1%, crude minerals 1.6%, mineral fuels 1.4%). *Major import sources:* Japan 10.4%; United Kingdom 7.8%; Germany 7.5%; United States 7.3%; Italy 6.7%; South Korea 5.4%; India 4.9%; Hong Kong 4.5%; China 4.0%.
Exports (1994): U.S.$20,906,000,000 (1993; crude petroleum and refined petroleum 92.6%, manufactured goods 3.0%, machinery and transport equipment 0.8%, food and live animals 0.6%). *Major export destinations:* Japan 39.7%; India 5.3%; Oman 4.9%; South Korea 4.7%; Iran 4.6%; Singapore 3.8%; Thailand 2.7%; Hong Kong 2.4%; United States 2.1%.

Transport and communications

Transport. Railroads: none. Roads (1995): total length 2,952 mi, 4,750 km (paved 100%). Vehicles (1995): passenger cars 197,000; trucks and buses 49,150. Merchant marine (1992): vessels (100 gross tons and over) 276; total deadweight tonnage 1,491,728. Air transport (1996)[11]: passenger-mi 1,714,175,000, passenger-km 2,758,697,000; short ton-mi cargo 72,435,000, metric ton-km cargo 105,754,000; airports (1997) with scheduled flights 6.

Communications

Medium	date	unit	number	units per 1,000 persons
Daily newspapers	1994	circulation	300,000	135
Radio	1995	receivers	490,000	206
Television	1995	receivers	43,900	18
Telephones	1995	main lines	140,900	59
Cellular telephones	1995	subscribers	27,600	12
Facsimile machines	1995	units	5,700	2.4
Personal computers	1995	units	29,000	12

Education and health

Educational attainment (1975). Percentage of population age 25 and over having: no formal schooling 72.2%; primary education 5.2%; secondary 16.6%; higher 6.0%. *Literacy* (1995): total population age 15 and over literate 79.2%; males literate 78.9%; females literate 79.8%.

Education (1994–95)

	schools	teachers	students	student/teacher ratio
Primary (age 6–11) }	512[12]	15,449	262,628	17.0
Secondary (age 12–18) }		12,388	158,625	12.0
Vocational	9[13]	189	1,215	6.4
Higher	4	510[14]	13,900	19.2[14]

Health (1994): physicians 4,095 (1 per 545 persons); hospital beds 6,193 (1 per 360 persons); infant mortality rate per 1,000 live births (1995) 16.6.
Food (1995): daily per capita caloric intake 3,361 (vegetable products 75%, animal products 25%); 139% of FAO recommended minimum requirement.

Military

Total active duty personnel (1997): 64,500 (army 91.5%, navy 2.3%, air force 6.2%). *Military expenditure as percentage of GDP* (1995): 4.8% (world 2.8%); per capita expenditure U.S.$643.

[1]All appointed seats. [2]Preliminary. [3]Approximate, based on reported total and on reported partial areas for smaller emirates. [4]1980. [5]Registered; Abu Dhabi Emirate only. [6]At current prices. [7]Services include domestic help. [8]Import duties less imputed bank service charges. [9]Detail does not add to total given because of rounding. [10]Abu Dhabi only. [11]One-fourth apportionment of international flights of Gulf Air. [12]1991–92. [13]1990–91. [14]1992–93.

Internet resources for further information:
- **U.A.E. Ministry of Finance and Industry http://www.fedfin.gov.ae/engindex.htm**

United Kingdom

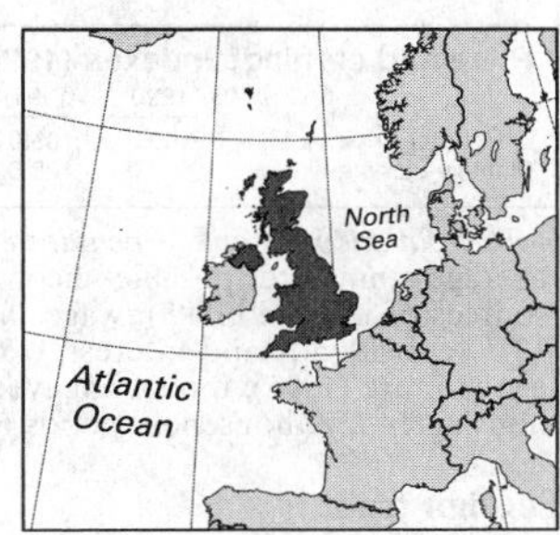

Official name: United Kingdom of Great Britain and Northern Ireland.
Form of government: constitutional monarchy with two legislative houses (House of Lords [1,197]; House of Commons [659]).
Chief of state: Sovereign.
Head of government: Prime Minister.
Capital: London.
Official language: English.
Official religion: Churches of England and Scotland "established" (protected by the state, but not "official") in their respective countries; no established church in Northern Ireland or Wales.
Monetary unit: 1 pound sterling (£) = 100 new pence; valuation (Oct. 3, 1997) 1 £ = U.S.$1.61; 1 U.S.$ = £0.62.

Area and population[1]

Countries	Capitals	area sq mi	area sq km	population 1995 estimate
England	London	50,363	130,439	48,903,400[2]
Counties				
Avon	Bristol	520	1,346	982,300
Bedfordshire	Bedford	477	1,235	545,700
Berkshire	Reading	486	1,259	783,200
Buckinghamshire	Aylesbury	727	1,883	665,900
Cambridgeshire	Cambridge	1,316	3,409	693,900
Cheshire	Chester	899	2,329	978,100
Cleveland	Middlesbrough	225	583	559,200
Cornwall[3]	Truro	1,376	3,564	482,700
Cumbria	Carlisle	2,629	6,810	490,300
Derbyshire	Matlock	1,016	2,631	957,900
Devon	Exeter	2,591	6,711	1,058,800
Dorset	Dorchester	1,025	2,654	678,700
Durham	Durham	941	2,436	607,700
East Sussex	Lewes	693	1,795	730,900
Essex	Chelmsford	1,418	3,672	1,577,500
Gloucestershire	Gloucester	1,020	2,643	552,700
Greater London	London	610	1,579	7,007,100
Greater Manchester	Manchester	497	1,287	2,578,300
Hampshire	Winchester	1,458	3,777	1,616,700
Hereford & Worcester	Worcester	1,516	3,927	694,300
Hertfordshire	Hertford	631	1,634	1,011,200
Humberside	Hull	1,356	3,512	889,200
Isle of Wight	Newport	147	381	125,100
Kent	Maidstone	1,441	3,731	1,551,300
Lancashire	Preston	1,183	3,064	1,426,000
Leicestershire	Leicester	986	2,553	923,000
Lincolnshire	Lincoln	2,284	5,915	611,800
Merseyside	Liverpool	252	652	1,427,200
Norfolk	Norwich	2,073	5,368	772,400
North Yorkshire	Northallerton	3,208	8,309	730,600
Northamptonshire	Northampton	914	2,367	599,300
Northumberland	Newcastle upon Tyne	1,943	5,032	307,300
Nottinghamshire	Nottingham	836	2,164	1,031,900
Oxfordshire	Oxford	1,007	2,608	598,400
Shropshire	Shrewsbury	1,347	3,490	419,900
Somerset	Taunton	1,332	3,451	481,000
South Yorkshire	Barnsley	602	1,560	1,303,900
Staffordshire	Stafford	1,049	2,716	1,056,400
Suffolk	Ipswich	1,466	3,797	656,800
Surrey	Kingston upon Thames	648	1,679	1,044,400
Tyne and Wear	Newcastle upon Tyne	208	540	1,131,000
Warwickshire	Warwick	765	1,981	498,700
West Midlands	Birmingham	347	899	2,637,200
West Sussex	Chichester	768	1,989	731,500
West Yorkshire	Wakefield	787	2,039	2,105,800
Wiltshire	Trowbridge	1,344	3,480	590,600
Northern Ireland[4]	Belfast	5,452	14,120	1,649,000
Scotland	Edinburgh	30,418	78,783	5,136,600
Regions				
Borders	Newton Saint Boswells	1,814	4,698	106,200
Central	Stirling	1,042	2,700	273,900
Dumfries and Galloway	Dumfries	2,481	6,425	147,900
Fife	Glenrothes	509	1,319	351,600
Grampian	Aberdeen	3,379	8,752	532,800
Highland	Inverness	10,092	26,137	208,300
Lothian	Edinburgh	683	1,770	764,600
Strathclyde	Glasgow	5,318	13,773	2,283,700
Tayside	Dundee	2,951	7,643	395,600
Island areas[5] (TOTAL)	—	2,149	5,566	72,000
Wales	Cardiff	8,019	20,768	2,916,800
Counties				
Clwyd	Mold	937	2,427	418,300
Dyfed	Carmarthen	2,227	5,768	353,300
Gwent	Newport	531	1,376	452,600
Gwynedd	Caernarvon	1,494	3,869	240,400
Mid Glamorgan	Cardiff	393	1,018	544,000
Powys	Llandrindod Wells	1,960	5,077	120,700
South Glamorgan	Cardiff	161	416	417,300
West Glamorgan	Swansea	316	817	370,200
TOTAL		94,251	244,110	58,605,800

Demography

Population (1997): 58,919,000.
Density (1997): persons per sq mi 625.1, persons per sq km 241.4.
Urban-rural (1996): urban 89.4%; rural 10.6%.
Sex distribution (1996): male 49.09%; female 50.91%.
Age breakdown (1996): under 15, 19.5%; 15–29, 20.1%; 30–44, 21.9%; 45–59, 18.0%; 60–74, 13.3%; 75 and over, 7.2%.
Population projection: (2000) 59,333,000; (2010) 60,395,000.
Ethnic composition (1992–94)[6]: white 93.7%; Asian Indian 1.8%; Pakistani 1.4%; Black 1.4%; other and not stated 1.6%.
Religious affiliation (1995): Christian 65.9%, of which Protestant 53.4% (Anglican 43.5%, Presbyterian 4.5%, Methodist 2.2%), Roman Catholic 9.8%, Orthodox 1.0%, other Christian 1.7%; Muslim 2.6%; Hindu 0.6%; Sikh 0.5%; Jewish 0.5%; other/nonreligious 29.9%.
Major cities (1995): Greater London 7,007,100; Birmingham 1,017,500; Leeds 725,000; Glasgow 674,800; Sheffield 528,500; Bradford 482,700; Liverpool 470,800; Edinburgh 447,600; Manchester 432,600; Bristol 400,700.
Place of birth (1991): U.K. 93.2% (52,721,000); foreign-born 6.8%, of which India 1.5%, Ireland 1.1%, Caribbean 0.9%, Pakistan 0.9%, other 2.2%.
Mobility (1991)[6]. Population living in the same residence as 1990: 90.1%; different residence, same country (of Great Britain) 8.1%; different residence, different country of Great Britain 1.2%; from outside Great Britain 0.6%.
Households (1994)[6]. Average household size 2.4; 1 person 27%, 2 persons 34%, 3 persons 16%, 4 persons 15%, 5 persons 6%, 6 or more persons 2%. Family households: 16,900,000 (72.0%), nonfamily 6,600,000 (28.0%, of which 1-person 12.0%).
Immigration (1995): permanent residents 245,000, from United States 11.0%, Australia 8.6%, Bangladesh, India, and Sri Lanka 4.5%, New Zealand 4.1%, South Africa 3.7%, Canada 3.3%, other 64.8%, of which EU 14.7%.

Vital statistics

Birth rate per 1,000 population (1996): 12.5 (world avg. 25.0); legitimate (1994) 68.0%; illegitimate 32.0%.
Death rate per 1,000 population (1996): 10.9 (world avg. 9.3).
Natural increase rate per 1,000 population (1996): 1.6 (world avg. 15.7).
Total fertility rate (avg. births per childbearing woman; 1994): 1.7.
Marriage rate per 1,000 population (1995): 5.5.
Divorce rate per 1,000 population (1995)[6]: 3.0.
Life expectancy at birth (1996): male 74.4 years; female 79.7 years.
Major causes of death per 100,000 population (1994): diseases of the circulatory system 473.3, of which ischemic heart disease 265.2, cerebrovascular disease 116.8; malignant neoplasms (cancers) 275.4; diseases of the respiratory system 155.6, of which pneumonia 92.9; diseases of the digestive system 36.4; diseases of the endocrine system 14.1, of which diabetes mellitus 11.2; diseases of the genitourinary system 13.4; suicide 7.5.

Social indicators

Educational attainment (1981). Percentage of population age 25 and over having: primary or secondary education only 89.7%; some postsecondary 4.8%; bachelor's or equivalent degree 4.9%; higher university degree 0.6%.

Distribution of disposable income (1994–95)

percentage of household income by quintile

1	2	3	4	5 (highest)
7.9	12.2	16.1	23.0	40.8

Quality of working life (1992). Average workweek (hours): male 43.3, female 30.2. Annual rate per 100,000 workers for: injury or accident 752.6; industrial diseases 1.3[7, 8]; death 1.5. Proportion of labour force (employed persons) insured for damages or income loss resulting from: injury 100%; permanent disability 100%; death 100%. Average days lost to labour stoppages per 1,000 employee workdays 1994: 0.05. Principal means of transport to work (1991; London only): public transportation 81%, private automobile 15%, motor or pedal cycle 2%, other 2%.
Access to services (1991)[6]. Proportion of households having access to: bath or shower 98.7%; toilet 99.8%; central heating 81.1%.
Social participation. Eligible voters participating in last national election (May 1997): 71.3%. Population age 16 and over participating in voluntary work (1987)[6]: 22%. Trade union membership in total workforce (1992) 32.0%.
Social deviance (1995)[6]. Offense rate per 100,000 population for: theft and handling stolen goods 4,944.2; burglary 2,431.0; violence against the person 406.2; fraud and forgery 277.8; robbery 135.8; sexual offense 58.5. Incidence per 100,000 population of: registered drug addicts 36.5[9]; suicide 7.5.
Leisure (1994). Favourite leisure activities (hours weekly): watching television 17.1; listening to radio 10.3; reading 8.8, of which books 3.8, newspapers 3.3; gardening 2.1.
Material well-being (1995). Households possessing: automobile 69.7%, telephone 92.4%, television receiver 98.3% (colour 95%)[10], refrigerator 98.5%, central heating 85.3%, washing machine 90.9%, video recorder 79.2%.

National economy

Budget (1996–97). Revenue: £280,900,000,000 (income tax 33.5%, value-added 16.9%, social security contributions 16.6%). Expenditures: £308,500,000,000 (social security 24.9%, health 11.0%, debt interest 7.2%, defense 7.2%).
Production (metric tons except as noted). Agriculture, forestry, fishing (1996): wheat 16,102,000, sugar beets 9,555,000, barley 7,784,000, potatoes 7,219,000, rapeseed 1,448,000, carrots 630,000, oats 590,000, cabbage 574,000; livestock (number of live animals) 41,530,000 sheep, 11,913,000 cattle, 7,496,000 pigs; roundwood (1995) 8,229,000 cu m; fish catch (1995) 1,003,740. Mining and quarrying (1996): limestone 97,000,000; tin 1,920; lead 1,080. Manufacturing (value added in £'000,000; 1996): electrical and optical equipment 18,270; food and beverages 17,622; paper, printing, and publishing 16,214; chemicals and chemical products 15,819; metals and metal products 15,199; transport equipment 13,914; machinery and equipment 12,196; textiles and leather products 7,186. Construction (value in £; 1995)[6]: residential 7,135,000,000; nonresidential 13,877,000,000.
Tourism (1996): receipts U.S.$20,019,700,000; expenditures U.S.$25,046,100,000.
Gross national product (1995): U.S.$1,094,734,000,000 (U.S.$18,700 per capita).

Structure of gross domestic product and labour force

	1996			
	in value £'000,000	% of total value	labour force	% of labour force
Agriculture	11,790	1.8	278,000	1.0
Mining[11]	18,068	2.8	268,000	1.0
Manufacturing	137,006	21.3	4,015,000	14.4
Construction	33,746	5.2	825,000	3.0
Public utilities	13,606	2.1	147,000	0.5
Transp. and commun.	54,056	8.4	1,315,000	4.7
Trade	93,091	14.5	3,749,000	13.4
Finance	164,282	25.6	984,000	3.5
Pub. admin., defense	120,120	18.7	5,798,000	20.7
Services	24,713	3.8	4,937,000	17.6
Other	−27,562[12]	−4.3[12]	5,653,000[13]	20.2[13]
TOTAL	642,916	100.0[1]	27,969,000	100.0

Total national debt: £337,733,000,000.

Financial aggregates

	1991	1992	1993	1994	1995	1996	1997[14]
Exchange rate:							
U.S. dollar per £	1.77	1.76	1.50	1.53	1.58	1.56	1.60
SDRs per £	1.31	1.10	1.08	1.07	1.04	1.18	1.19
International reserves (U.S.$)							
Total (excl. gold; '000,000,000)	41.89	36.64	36.78	41.01	42.02	39.90	35.18[15]
SDRs ('000,000,000)	1.31	0.54	0.29	0.49	0.41	0.34	0.44
Reserve pos. in IMF ('000,000,000)	1.85	2.01	1.86	1.99	2.42	2.43	2.18
Foreign exchange ('000,000,000)	38.73	34.09	34.63	38.53	39.18	37.12	32.65[15]
Gold ('000,000 fine troy oz)	18.89	18.61	18.45	18.44	18.43	18.43	18.42[15]
% world reserves	2.0	2.0	2.0	2.0	2.0	2.0	2.1[15]
Interest and prices							
Central bank discount (%)	...	...	...	...	...	...	...
Govt. bond yield (%) long term	9.92	9.12	7.87	8.05	8.26	8.10	6.97[16]
Industrial share prices (1990 = 100)	109.8	114.7	131.7	141.5	147.3	166.9	190.5[16]
Balance of payments (U.S.$'000,000)							
Balance of visible trade,	−17,990	−24,618	−20,570	−16,127	−18,266	−18,870	...
Imports, f.o.b.	201,081	212,058	201,802	222,263	259,154	278,400	...
Exports, f.o.b.	183,091	187,440	181,232	206,136	240,888	259,530	...
Balance of invisibles	6,768	3,904	4,179	13,736	7,697	19,110	...
Balance of payments, current account	−11,222	−20,714	−16,391	−2,391	−10,569	240	...

Manufacturing, mining, and construction enterprises (1993)

	no. of enter-prises[15]	no. of employees	annual wages as a % of avg. of all wages[16]	annual value added (£'000,000)
Manufacturing				
Food, beverages, and tobacco	9,463	554,700	...	16,559
Paper and paper products; printing and publishing	26,825	430,400	...	13,438
Electrical and data-processing equipment	13,902	512,800	...	13,209
Transport equipment	3,704	414,200	...	12,815
Chemical engineering	3,809	270,200	...	12,538
Machinery and equipment	11,636	387,500	...	9,391
Rubber and plastics	5,103	228,500	...	5,679
Metal manufacturing	3,524	144,400	...	4,197
Textiles	7,256	171,800	...	3,498
Clothing and footwear	8,119	211,800	...	2,716
Mineral-oil processing	148	13,100	...	1,618
Wood and wood products	7,767	73,600	...	1,292
Mining				
Extraction of coal, mineral oil, and natural gas	358	80,000[10]	...	10,261
Extraction of minerals other than fuels	921	30,200	...	1,090
Construction	199,363	1,016,000[10]	...	19,274

Land use (1994): forest 10.4%; pasture 45.9%; agriculture 24.8%; other 18.9%.

Retail trade enterprises (1992)

	no. of enter-prises	no. of employees	weekly wage as a % of all wages	annual turnover (£'000,000)[17]
Food and grocery, of which	60,119	854,000	...	51,462
large grocery	71	579,000	...	40,837
other grocery	18,557	95,000	...	4,086
meats	12,149	58,000	...	2,523
Household goods, of which	45,532	299,000	...	20,881
electrical and musical goods	10,887	87,000	...	7,270
furniture	11,927	60,000	...	4,575
Drink, confectionery, and tobacco, of which	46,671	254,000	...	13,810
tobacco and confectionery	41,502	215,000	...	10,880
Clothing and footwear, of which	24,923	264,000	...	12,428
women's, girls', and infants' wear	13,624	102,000	...	4,771
footwear	3,098	67,000	...	2,589
men's and boys' wear	3,751	37,000	...	2,063
Pharmaceuticals	7,560	87,000	...	5,231

Energy production (consumption): electricity (kW-hr; 1994) 325,383,000,000 (342,270,000,000); coal (metric tons; 1994) 47,717,000 (80,582,000); crude petroleum (barrels; 1994) 888,454,000 (629,354,000); petroleum products (metric tons; 1994) 86,184,000 (75,021,000); natural gas (cu m; 1994) 76,680,000,000 (79,391,000,000).

Population economically active (1996): total 27,969,000, activity rate of total population 47.6% (participation rates: ages 15–64, 76.2%[8]; female 44.3%; unemployed 7.7%).

Price and earnings indexes (1990 = 100)

	1990	1991	1992	1993	1994	1995	1996
Consumer price index	100.0	105.9	109.8	111.5	114.3	118.2	121.1
Monthly earnings index	100.0	108.0	114.6	118.5	123.3	127.4	132.3

Household income and expenditure (1994–95). Average household size 2.4; average annual disposable income per household £15,762 (U.S.$22,937); sources of income (1995): wages and salaries 64.3%, social security benefits 13.7%, dividends and interest 11.6%, income from self-employment 8.6%; expenditure (1995): food and beverages 17.8%, transport and vehicles 15.8%, housing 14.2%, household goods 6.9%, clothing 5.8%, energy 3.6%.

Foreign trade

Balance of trade (current prices)

	1991	1992	1993	1994	1995	1996
£'000,000	−17,990	−24,618	−20,570	−12,029	−10,621	−11,174
% of total	4.7%	6.2%	5.4%	4.3%	3.3%	3.2%

Imports (1996): £184,305,000,000 (machinery and transport equipment 42.2%, of which electrical equipment 19.8%, road vehicles 11.2%; chemicals 10.0%, of which organic chemicals 2.6%, plastics 2.4%; food 7.9%; clothing and footwear 4.3%; petroleum and petroleum products 3.1%; textiles 2.8%; paper and paperboard 2.7%). *Major import sources:* Germany 14.7%; U.S. 12.4%; France 9.6%; The Netherlands 6.8%; Japan 4.9%; Italy 4.8%; Belgium-Luxembourg 4.7%; Ireland 3.9%; Switzerland 2.9%; Spain 2.7%.

Exports (1996): £166,340,000,000 (machinery and transport equipment 44.1%, of which electrical equipment 19.8%, road vehicles 8.6%; chemicals 13.3%, of which organic chemicals 3.1%; petroleum and petroleum products 6.2%; food 4.2%; professional and scientific 4.0%; iron and steel products 2.4%). *Major export destinations:* Germany 12.3%; U.S. 11.8%; France 10.2%; The Netherlands 8.0%; Ireland 5.2%; Belgium-Luxembourg 5.1%; Italy 4.8%; Spain 4.0%; Sweden 2.6%; Japan 2.5%; Switzerland 1.9%.

Transport and communications

Transport. Railroads (1995–96)[18]: length 23,518 mi[19], 37,849 km[19]; passenger-mi 18,154,000,000, passenger-km 29,216,000,000; ton-mi cargo 2,026,000,000, metric ton-km cargo 2,916,000,000[20]. Roads (1995): total length 228,042 mi, 366,999 km (paved 100%). Vehicles (1995)[6]: passenger cars 20,505,000, trucks and buses 2,712,000. Merchant marine (1992): vessels (over 100 gross tons) 1,631; total deadweight tonnage 4,355,063. Air transport (1996): passenger-mi 77,575,900,000, passenger-km 124,846,500,000; short ton-mi cargo 2,662,600,000, metric ton-km cargo 3,831,900,000; airports (1997) 57.

Communications

Medium	date	unit	number	units per 1,000 persons
Daily newspapers	1995	circulation	22,450,000	383
Radio	1995	receivers	70,000,000	1,194
Television	1995	receivers	35,800,000	612
Telephones	1995	main lines	29,408,700	502
Cellular telephones	1995	subscribers	5,735,800	309
Facsimile machines	1995	units	1,800,000	30.7
Personal computers	1995	units	10,900,000	186

Education and health

Literacy (1990): total population literate, virtually 100%[21].

Education (1994–95)[22]

	schools	teachers	students	student/teacher ratio
Primary (age 5–10)	32,385	231,659	4,906,439	21.2
Secondary (age 11–19)		228,187	3,779,262	16.6
Voc., teacher tr.	...	...	586,000[23]	...
Higher[24]	70	c. 48,000	c. 810,000	c. 17.0

Health (1993)[6]: physicians 92,474 (1 per 629 persons); hospital beds 283,814 (1 per 205 persons); infant mortality rate (1995) 6.2.

Food (1995): daily per capita caloric intake 3,149 (vegetable products 67%, animal products 33%); 125% of FAO recommended minimum requirement.

Military

Total active duty personnel (1996): 213,800 (army 52.5%, navy 21.0%, air force 26.5%). *Military expenditure as percentage of GNP* (1995): 3.0% (world 2.8%); per capita expenditure U.S.$572.

[1]Breakdown does not reflect the U.K. administrative reorganization effective from April 1997 of which area and population data are unavailable. The first-order local government structure of England has changed to: the Greater London metropolitan area, 9 other metropolitan areas, 2 unitary councils (the City of York and the Isle of Wight), and 35 county councils; in Scotland the former 9 regions and 3 island councils have reorganized into 29 unitary councils; in Wales the former 8 county councils have reorganized into 22 unitary councils; Northern Island has not changed. [2]Detail does not add to total given because of rounding. [3]Includes separately administered Isles of Scilly (area 6 sq mi [16 sq km]; pop. 2,000). [4]Comprises 26 local government districts not shown separately. [5]Includes three separately administered island groups (Orkney 377 sq mi [976 sq km], pop. 19,900; Shetland 553 sq mi [1,432 sq km], pop. 23,100; Western Isles 1,119 sq mi [2,898 sq km], pop. 29,000). [6]Great Britain only. [7]Lung disease only. [8]1993. [9]1994. [10]1992. [11]Includes petroleum extraction. [12]Plus rent; less imputed bank service charges. [13]Includes 2,150,000 unemployed and 3,282,000 self-employed not distributed by sector and 221,000 military personnel. [14]August. [15]June. [16]July. [17]Includes value-added taxes. [18]British Rail only. [19]1990. [20]Much of British Rail's freight business was sold during 1996. [21]A survey in 1986–87, however, put the number of functional illiterates at 9–12% of the adult population. [22]Public sector only. [23]1992–93. [24]Universities only.

Internet resources for further information:

- **Office for National Statistics http://www.open.gov.uk/lmsd/lmsdhome.htm**

United States

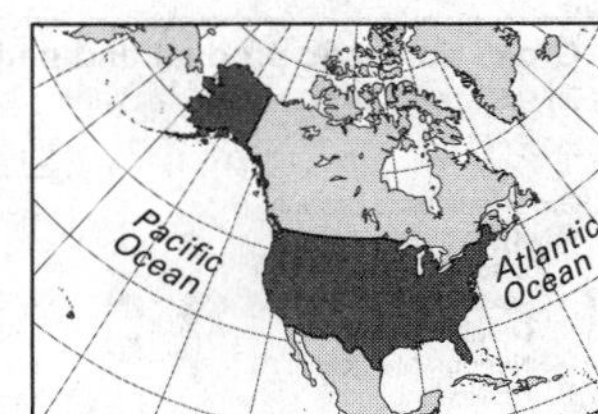

Official name: United States of America.
Form of government: federal republic with two legislative houses (Senate [100]; House of Representatives [435[1]]).
Head of state and government: President.
Capital: Washington, D.C.
Official language: none.
Official religion: none.
Monetary unit: 1 dollar (U.S.$) = 100 cents; valuation (Oct. 3, 1997) 1 U.S.$ = £0.62; 1 £ = U.S.$1.61.

Area and population

		area		population
States	Capitals	sq mi	sq km	1997 estimate
Alabama	Montgomery	51,718	133,950	4,319,154
Alaska	Juneau	587,875	1,522,595	609,311
Arizona	Phoenix	114,006	295,275	4,554,966
Arkansas	Little Rock	53,182	137,741	2,522,819
California	Sacramento	158,647	410,895	32,268,301
Colorado	Denver	104,100	269,619	3,892,644
Connecticut	Hartford	5,006	12,966	3,269,858
Delaware	Dover	2,026	5,247	731,581
Florida	Tallahassee	58,680	151,981	14,653,945
Georgia	Atlanta	58,930	152,629	7,486,242
Hawaii	Honolulu	6,459	16,729	1,186,602
Idaho	Boise	83,574	216,456	1,210,232
Illinois	Springfield	57,918	150,008	11,895,849
Indiana	Indianapolis	36,420	94,328	5,864,108
Iowa	Des Moines	56,276	145,755	2,852,423
Kansas	Topeka	82,282	213,110	2,594,840
Kentucky	Frankfort	40,411	104,664	3,908,124
Louisiana	Baton Rouge	47,719	123,592	4,351,769
Maine	Augusta	33,128	85,801	1,242,051
Maryland	Annapolis	10,455	27,078	5,094,289
Massachusetts	Boston	8,262	21,399	6,117,520
Michigan	Lansing	96,705	250,466	9,773,892
Minnesota	St. Paul	86,943	225,182	4,685,549
Mississippi	Jackson	47,695	123,530	2,730,501
Missouri	Jefferson City	69,709	180,546	5,402,058
Montana	Helena	147,046	380,849	878,810
Nebraska	Lincoln	77,359	200,360	1,656,870
Nevada	Carson City	110,567	286,368	1,676,809
New Hampshire	Concord	9,283	24,043	1,172,709
New Jersey	Trenton	7,790	20,176	8,052,849
New Mexico	Santa Fe	121,598	314,939	1,729,751
New York	Albany	53,013	137,304	18,137,226
North Carolina	Raleigh	52,672	136,420	7,425,183
North Dakota	Bismarck	70,704	183,123	640,883
Ohio	Columbus	44,828	116,104	11,186,331
Oklahoma	Oklahoma City	69,903	181,049	3,317,091
Oregon	Salem	97,052	251,364	3,243,487
Pennsylvania	Harrisburg	45,759	118,516	12,019,661
Rhode Island	Providence	1,213	3,142	987,429
South Carolina	Columbia	31,117	80,593	3,760,181
South Dakota	Pierre	77,121	199,743	737,973
Tennessee	Nashville	42,145	109,155	5,368,198
Texas	Austin	266,873	691,201	19,439,337
Utah	Salt Lake City	84,904	219,901	2,059,148
Vermont	Montpelier	9,615	24,903	588,978
Virginia	Richmond	40,598	105,149	6,733,996
Washington	Olympia	68,126	176,446	5,610,362
West Virginia	Charleston	24,232	62,761	1,815,787
Wisconsin	Madison	65,500	169,645	5,169,677
Wyoming	Cheyenne	97,819	253,351	479,743
District				
Dist. of Columbia	—	68	176	528,964
TOTAL		3,675,031[2]	9,518,323[2]	267,636,061[3]

Demography

Population (1997)[3]: 267,839,000.
Density (1997)[3]: persons per sq mi 72.9, persons per sq km 28.1.
Urban-rural (1996): urban 76.4%; rural 23.6%.
Sex distribution (1996): male 48.93%; female 51.07%.
Age breakdown (1996): under 15, 21.8%; 15–29, 20.8%; 30–44, 24.4%; 45–59, 16.5%; 60–74, 10.8%; 75 and over, 5.7%.
Population projection: (2000) 274,898,000; (2010) 297,980,000.
Doubling time: not applicable; doubling time exceeds 100 years.
Population by race and Hispanic[4] origin (1996): non-Hispanic white 73.1%; non-Hispanic black 12.0%; Hispanic 10.7%; Asian and Pacific Islander 3.5%; American Indian and Eskimo 0.7%.
Religious affiliation (1995): Christian 85.3%, of which Protestant 57.9%, Roman Catholic 21.0%, other Christian 6.4%; Jewish 2.1%; Muslim 1.9%; nonreligious 8.7%; other 2.0%.
Mobility (1996). Population living in the same residence as in 1995: 84.0%; different residence, same county 10.0%; different county, same state 3.0%; different state 3.0%; moved from abroad 1.0%.
Households (1996). Total households 99,627,000 (married-couple families 53,567,000 [53.8%]). Average household size (1995) 2.6; 1 person 25.0%, 2 persons 32.1%, 3 persons 17.0%, 4 persons 15.5%, 5 or more persons 10.4%. Family households: 69,594,000 (69.8%); nonfamily 30,033,000 (30.2%), of which 1-person 82.9%.
Immigration (1995[5]): permanent immigrants admitted 720,500, from Mexico 12.5%, Philippines 7.1%, Vietnam 5.8%, Dominican Republic 5.3%, China 4.9%, India 4.8%, Cuba 2.5%, Ukraine 2.4%, Jamaica 2.3%, South Korea 2.2%, Russia 2.0%, Poland 1.9%, Haiti 1.8%, Canada 1.8%, United Kingdom 1.7%, El Salvador 1.6%, Colombia 1.5%. Refugee arrivals (1995[5]): 114,664.

Major cities (1996): New York 7,380,906; Los Angeles 3,553,638; Chicago 2,721,547; Houston 1,744,058; Philadelphia 1,478,002; San Diego 1,171,121; Phoenix 1,159,014; San Antonio 1,067,816; Dallas 1,053,292; Detroit 1,000,272.

Other principal cities (1996)

	population		population		population
Akron	221,886	Fresno	396,011	Omaha	364,253
Albuquerque	419,681	Honolulu	423,475	Pittsburgh	350,363
Anaheim	288,945	Indianapolis	746,737	Portland (Ore.)	480,824
Anchorage	250,505	Jacksonville	679,792	Raleigh	243,835
Arlington (Tex.)	294,816	Jersey City	229,039	Riverside	255,069
Atlanta	401,907	Kansas City (Mo.)	441,259	Sacramento	376,243
Aurora (Colo.)	252,341	Las Vegas	376,906	St. Louis	351,565
Austin	541,278	Lexington (Ky.)	239,942	St. Paul	259,606
Baltimore	675,401	Long Beach	421,904	St. Petersburg	235,988
Birmingham	258,543	Louisville	260,689	San Francisco	735,315
Boston	558,394	Memphis	596,725	San Jose	838,744
Buffalo	310,548	Mesa	344,764	Santa Ana	302,419
Charlotte	441,297	Miami	365,127	Seattle	524,704
Cincinnati	345,818	Milwaukee	590,503	Stockton	232,660
Cleveland	498,246	Minneapolis	358,785	Tampa	285,206
Colorado Springs	345,127	Nashville	511,263	Toledo	317,606
Columbus	657,053	New Orleans	476,625	Tucson	449,002
Corpus Christi	280,260	Newark	268,510	Tulsa	378,491
Denver	497,840	Norfolk	233,430	Virginia Beach	430,385
El Paso	599,865	Oakland	367,230	Washington, D.C.	543,213
Fort Worth	479,716	Oklahoma City	469,852	Wichita	320,395

Place of birth (1990): native-born 227,078,000 (91.3%); foreign-born 21,632,000 (8.7%), of which Mexico 4,447,000, Germany (East and West) 1,163,000, Philippines 998,000, Canada 871,000, United Kingdom 765,000, Cuba 751,000, South Korea 663,000, Italy 640,000, Vietnam 556,000, China 543,000, India 463,000, Japan 422,000, Poland 397,000, U.S.S.R. 337,000.

Vital statistics

Birth rate per 1,000 population (1996): 14.9 (world avg. 25.0); (1994) legitimate 67.4%; illegitimate 32.6%.
Death rate per 1,000 population (1996): 9.2 (world avg. 9.3).
Natural increase rate per 1,000 population (1996): 5.7 (world avg. 15.7).
Total fertility rate (avg. births per childbearing woman; 1996): 2.1.
Marriage rate per 1,000 population (1996): 8.8; median age at first marriage (1991): men 26.3 years, women 24.1 years.
Divorce rate per 1,000 population (1996): 4.3.
Life expectancy at birth (1995): white male 73.4 years, black and other male 67.5[6] years; white female 79.6 years, black and other female 75.8[6] years.
Major causes of death per 100,000 population (1997[7]): cardiovascular diseases 353.9, of which ischemic heart disease 177.3, cerebrovascular diseases 60.0, atherosclerosis 10.0; malignant neoplasms (cancers) 202.4; diseases of the respiratory system 72.0, of which pneumonia 31.2; accidents and adverse effects 34.1, of which motor-vehicle accidents 16.5; diabetes mellitus 23.3; suicide 11.5; AIDS 10.6; chronic liver disease and cirrhosis 9.3.
Morbidity rates of infectious diseases per 100,000 population (1995): chlamydia 181.6; gonorrhea 149.3; chicken pox 45.8; AIDS 27.2; syphilis 26.2; salmonellosis 17.4; shigellosis 12.2; hepatitis A (infectious) 12.0; tuberculosis 8.7; lyme disease 4.4; hepatitis B (serum) 4.1; aseptic meningitis 3.4[6]; pertussis 1.9.
Incidence of chronic health conditions per 1,000 population (1994): chronic sinusitus 133.9; arthritis 128.3; deformities or orthopedic impairments 119.2; hypertension 108.3; hay fever 100.3; hearing impairment 85.9; heart conditions 85.5; asthma 55.9; chronic bronchitis 53.8; migraine 43.2.

Social indicators

Educational attainment (1996). Percentage of population age 25 and over having: some primary 9.3%; incomplete secondary 16.5%; secondary 35.1%; some postsecondary 25.5%; 4-year higher degree or more 13.6%. Number of earned degrees (1995): bachelor's degree 1,192,000; master's degree 405,000; doctor's degree 43,000; first-professional degrees (in fields such as medicine, theology, and law) 77,000.

Distribution of income (1995)

percentage of disposable household income by quintile

1	2	3	4	5 (highest)
4.8	10.4	16.0	23.0	46.5

Quality of working life (1996). Average workweek: 39.2 hours. Annual rate per 100,000 workers for (1995): injury or accident 2,720; death 4.0. Proportion of labour force insured for damages or income loss resulting from: injury, permanent disability, and death (1988) 56.6%. Average days per 1,000 workdays lost to labour stoppages (1996): 1.6. Average duration of journey to work (1990): 22.4 minutes (private automobile 94.7%, of which drive alone 80.0%, carpool 14.7%; take public transportation 5.3%). Rate per 1,000 employed workers of discouraged workers (unemployed no longer seeking work; 1992): 6.9.
Access to services (1995). Proportion of occupied dwellings having access to: electricity, virtually 100.0%; safe public water supply 99.4% (12.6% from wells); public sewage collection 77.0%; septic tanks 22.8%.
Social participation. Eligible voters participating in last presidential election (1996): 48.9%. Population age 18 and over participating in voluntary work (1995): 48.8%. Trade-union membership in total workforce (1996): 14.5%. Practicing religious population in total affiliated population (church attendance; 1987): once a week 47%; once in six months 67%; once a year 74%.
Social deviance (1995[7]). Offense rate per 100,000 population for: murder 8.2; rape 37.1; robbery 221.0; aggravated assault 418.0; motor-vehicle theft 561.0; burglary and housebreaking 988.0; larceny-theft 3,045.0; drug-abuse violation 434.2; drunkenness 200.2. Drug and substance users (population age 26 and over; 1994): alcohol 41.2%; tobacco (cigarettes) 33.5%; mari-

juana 16.0%; cocaine 0.4%; analgesics 1.3%; tranquilizers 0.2%; stimulants 0.4%; hallucinogens 1.2%; heroin, n.a. Rate per 100,000 population of suicide (1997): 11.5.

Crime rates per 100,000 population in metropolitan areas[8] (1995)

	violent crime				
	total	murder	rape	robbery	assault
Atlanta	3,646	45.5	109.1	1,301	2,191
Baltimore	3,018	45.6	95.9	1,594	1,282
Boston	1,738	17.4	68.8	653	998
Chicago	...	30.0	...	1,094	1,425
Dallas	1,532	26.5	81.8	566	858
Detroit	2,408	47.6	110.7	1,010	1,239
Houston	1,284	18.2	48.3	532	685
Los Angeles	2,034	24.5	45.9	840	1,124
Miami	3,413	29.0	52.3	1,499	1,833
Minneapolis	1,978	26.8	161.6	992	797
New York	1,573	16.1	32.4	810	715
Philadelphia	1,436	28.2	50.5	890	468
Pittsburgh	979	16.3	68.5	585	309
St. Louis	3,352	54.9	73.5	1,383	1,841
San Francisco	1,477	13.4	41.2	876	546
Washington, D.C.	2,662	65.2	52.7	1,239	1,305

	property crime			
	total	burglary	larceny	auto theft
Atlanta	13,421	2,898	8,464	2,066
Baltimore	10,300	2,326	6,405	1,569
Boston	7,755	1,211	4,722	1,822
Chicago	7,198	1,463	4,418	1,316
Dallas	7,932	1,603	4,709	1,620
Detroit	9,531	2,243	4,353	2,935
Houston	6,304	1,432	3,574	1,299
Los Angeles	5,646	1,192	3,120	1,333
Miami	12,210	2,607	7,271	2,332
Minneapolis	9,567	2,243	6,069	1,255
New York	4,503	1,010	2,501	993
Philadelphia	5,642	1,057	3,028	1,556
Pittsburgh	5,150	1,014	3,182	955
St. Louis	12,730	2,879	7,697	2,155
San Francisco	6,714	965	4,626	1,123
Washington, D.C.	9,505	1,838	5,827	1,840

Leisure (1992). Favourite leisure activities (percentage of total population age 18 and over that undertook activity at least once in the previous year): movie 59.0%, amusement park 50.0%, sports event 37.0%, live theatre 31.0%, art museum 27.0%; reading literature 54.0%, playing sports 39.0%.
Material well-being (1995). Occupied dwellings with householder possessing: automobile 84.9%[9]; telephone 93.9%; radio receiver 99.0%; television receiver 98.3%; air conditioner 68.4%[10]; washing machine 77.1%[10]; videocassette recorder 81.0%; cable television 63.4%.
Recreational expenditures (1995): U.S.$401,700,000,000 (television and radio receivers, computers, and video equipment 23.2%; sports supplies 10.9%; nondurable toys and sports equipment 10.6%; golfing, bowling, and other participatory activities 9.2%; magazines and newspapers 6.3%; books and maps 5.2%; spectator amusements 5.0%, of which theatre and opera 2.2%, movies 1.4%, spectator sports 1.3%; flowers, seeds, and potted plants 3.5%).

National economy

Budget (1997). Revenue: U.S.$1,577,700,000,000 (individual income tax 46.4%, social-insurance taxes and contributions 34.1%, corporation income tax 11.8%, other 7.7%). Expenditures: U.S.$1,615,000,000,000 (social security and medicare 34.5%, defense 16.6%, interest on debt 15.2%, income security 14.4%, health 7.8%, other 11.5%).
Total national debt (1997): U.S.$5,376,000,000,000.

Manufacturing, mining, and construction enterprises (1995)

	no. of enterprises[11]	no. of employees	hourly wage as a % of all wages	value added (U.S.$'000,000)
Manufacturing				
Chemical and related products	12,109	839,000	135.2	196,906
Food and related products	20,624	1,525,000	104.0	180,975
Electric and electronic machinery	15,962	1,534,000	101.1	173,920
Machinery, except electrical	52,135	1,926,000	114.9	172,945
Transportation equipment	10,500	1,523,000	144.7	172,926
Printing and publishing	...	1,534,000		125,936
Fabricated metal products	36,105	1,465,000	105.3	102,672
Instruments and related products	10,326	809,000	111.2	92,534
Paper and related products	6,342	630,000	125.5	79,836
Rubber and plastic products	14,515	1,018,000	95.8	73,023
Primary metals	6,771	688,000	127.8	69,594
Stone, clay, and glass products	16,166	503,000	108.4	42,424
Lumber and wood	33,982	741,000	88.9	40,937
Apparel and related products	22,872	950,100	66.3	39,519
Textile-mill products	6,412	606,800	81.8	32,705
Petroleum and coal products	2,254	110,000	167.5	31,580
Furniture and fixtures	11,613	514,000	85.6	26,238
Tobacco products	138	31,300	191.6	24,715
Leather and leather products	2,193	86,000	69.7	4,126
Miscellaneous manufacturing industries	16,544	397,000	87.2	25,672
Mining				
Oil and gas extraction	20,891[6]	320,700	127.9	79,700[6]
Coal mining	3,060[6]	105,300	159.9	17,283[6]
Nonmetallic, except fuels	5,804[6]	109,900	117.3	9,619[6]
Metal mining	1,023[6]	52,100	145.5	7,180[6]
Construction				
Special trade contractors	367,800[6]	3,383,500	134.6	122,422[6]
Heavy construction contractors	37,300[6]	814,200	129.5	49,066[6]
General contractors and operative builders	168,200[6]	1,251,100	123.4	63,743[6]

Gross national product (at current market prices; 1996): U.S.$7,567,100,000,000 (U.S.$28,495 per capita).

Gross domestic product and national income
(in U.S.$'000,000,000)

	1992	1993	1994	1995	1996
Gross domestic product	6,038.6	6,377.9	6,738.4	7,245.8	7,576.1
By type of expenditure					
Personal consumption expenditures	4,139.9	4,391.8	4,628.4	4,924.3	5,151.4
Durable goods	497.3	537.9	591.5	606.4	632.1
Nondurable goods	1,300.9	1,350.0	1,394.3	1,486.1	1,545.1
Services	2,341.6	2,503.9	2,642.7	2,831.6	2,974.3
Gross private domestic investment	796.5	891.7	1,032.9	1,066.3	1,117.0
Fixed investment	789.1	876.1	980.7	1,028.2	1,101.5
Changes in business inventories	7.3	15.6	52.2	33.7	15.4
Net exports of goods and services	−30.3	−65.3	−98.2	−114.2	−98.7
Exports	638.1	659.1	718.7	774.8	855.2
Imports	668.4	724.3	816.9	888.9	953.9
Government purchases of goods and services	1,131.8	1,158.1	1,175.3	1,260.7	1,406.4
Federal	448.8	443.4	437.3	472.7	523.1
State and local	313.8	714.6	738.0	788.8	...
By major type of product					
Goods output	2,312.8	2,421.9	2,584.7	2,697.4	2,799.8
Durable goods	977.9	1,047.9	1,153.6	1,179.8	1,232.3
Nondurable goods	1,334.9	1,374.0	1,431.1	1,517.6	1,567.5
Services	3,221.1	3,410.5	3,576.2	3,920.8	4,105.2
Structures	504.6	545.5	577.6	627.6	671.1
National income (incl. capital consumption adjustment)	4,836.6	5,140.3	5,458.4	5,799.2	6,164.2
By type of income					
Compensation of employees	3,582.0	3,772.2	4,004.6	4,209.1	4,448.5
Proprietors' income	414.3	321.0	473.7	478.3	3,630.1
Rental income of persons	−8.9	12.6	27.7	122.2	641.2
Corporate profits	407.2	466.6	542.7	588.6	670.2
Net interest	442.0	445.6	409.7	401.0	403.3
By industry division (excl. capital consumption adjustment)					
Agriculture, forestry, fishing	100.9	105.3	101.9	94.0	114.1
Mining and construction	251.3	268.1	278.5	301.2	325.9
Manufacturing	895.3	929.0	979.7	1,026.3	1,069.1
Durable	501.7	523.0	562.4	597.1	628.6
Nondurable	393.6	406.1	417.3	429.3	440.5
Transportation	151.0	161.8	177.5	189.4	196.5
Communications	103.7	107.4	113.4	136.6	148.5
Public utilities	101.5	106.9	116.5	125.0	126.5
Wholesale and retail trade	700.3	742.8	785.8	805.6	857.8
Finance, insurance, real estate	748.9	815.6	894.2	991.9	1,037.0
Services	1,085.8	1,171.0	1,254.4	1,335.9	1,444.1
Government and government enterprise	734.5	765.3	793.4	820.3	843.1
Other	7.3	0.2	−11.4	−7.0	−8.9

Structure of gross domestic product and labour force

	1994		1996	
	in value U.S.$'000,000,000	% of total value	labour force[12]	% of labour force[12]
Agriculture	117.3	1.7	3,443,000	2.6
Mining	90.1	1.3	569,000	0.4
Manufacturing	1,197.1	17.3	20,518,000	15.3
Construction	269.2	3.9	7,943,000	5.9
Public utilities	195.3	2.8	8,817,000	6.6
Transp. and commun.	411.1	5.9		
Trade	1,071.8	15.5	26,497,000	19.8
Finance	1,273.7	18.4	8,076,000	6.0
Public administration, defense	931.3	13.4	5,802,000	4.3
Services	1,342.7	19.4	45,043,000	33.6
Other	31.8[13]	0.4[13]	7,236,000[14]	5.4[14]
TOTAL	6,931.4	100.0	133,943,000[15]	100.0[15]

Business activity (1994): number of businesses 21,989,000 (sole proprietorships 73.5%, active corporations 19.7%, active partnerships 6.8%), of which services 9,488,000, wholesaling and retailing 4,213,000; business receipts $14,380,000,000,000 (active corporations 89.4%, sole proprietorships 5.5%, active partnerships 5.1%), of which wholesaling and retailing $4,343,000,000,000, services $1,602,000,000,000; net profit $827,000,000,000 (active corporations 69.8%, sole proprietorships 20.2%, partnerships 10.0%), of which services $167,700,000,000, wholesaling and retailing $88,600,000,000. New business starts and business failures (1995): total number of new business starts 168,158; total failures 71,194, of which commercial service 21,850, retail trade 12,952; failure rate per 10,000 concerns 90.0; current liabilities of failed concerns $37,507,000,000; average liability $526,830. Business expenditures for new plant and equipment (1995): total $594,465,000,000, of which trade, services, and communications $244,829,000,000, manufacturing businesses $172,308,000,000 (durable goods 53.0%, nondurable goods 47.0%), public utilities $42,816,000,000, transportation $37,021,000,000, mining and construction $35,985,000.
Production. Agriculture, forestry, fishing (value of production/catch in U.S.$'000,000 except as noted; 1996): corn (maize) 24,853, soybeans 16,276, wheat 9,764, cotton lint 6,524, tobacco 2,938, potatoes 2,515, grapes 2,242, sorghum 2,053, oranges 1,895, apples 1,840, rice 1,612, lettuce 1,423, barley 1,091, sugar beets 1,071, almonds 1,048, peanuts (groundnuts) 964, cotton seed 934, tomatoes 879, sugarcane 860, strawberries 770, dry beans 680, onions 590, bell peppers 461, sunflower seeds 405, cantaloupes 401, broccoli 396, peaches 378, carrots 347, grapefruit 310, oats 309, pears 297, watermelon 276, lemons 252, cabbage 245; livestock (number of live animals; 1997) 101,209,000 cattle, 56,171,000 pigs, 8,303,000 sheep, 6,150,000 horses, 1,553,000,000 chickens; roundwood (1996) 495,305,000 cu m; fish and shellfish catch (1995) 3,770, of which fish 2,136 (including salmon 527, Alaska pollack 266), shellfish 1,634 (including shrimp 570, crabs 512). Mining (metal content in metric tons except as noted; 1996): iron 39,342,000;

copper 1,910,000; zinc 620,000; lead 430,000; molybdenum 57,000; vanadium 2,700; mercury 550; silver 1,800,000 kg; gold 325,000 kg; helium 101,000,000 cu m. Quarrying (metric tons; 1996): crushed stone 1,300,000,000; sand and gravel 992,000,000; cement 75,000,000; clay 44,000,000; phosphate rock 43,000,000; common salt 40,000,000; gypsum 17,000,000; lime 18,900,000. Manufacturing (1995): motor vehicles 238,384; aircraft 104,858; meat products 94,072; industrial machinery 79,439; electronic components 73,642; pharmaceuticals 67,792; computer and office equipment 66,708; commercial printing 56,229; medical instruments 39,535; cigarettes 29,745; missiles and space vehicles 29,508; photographic equipment 22,119; household furniture 20,508; household appliances 18,633; ships and boats 15,249; toys and sporting goods 12,123; audio and video equipment 10,614. Construction (completed; 1996): private U.S.$427,776,000,000, of which residential U.S.$246,899,000,000, nonresidential U.S.$140,692,000,000; public U.S.$141,132,000,000.

Retail and wholesale trade and services (1996)

	no. of establishments[6]	no. of employees[16]	hourly wage as a % of all wages[16]	annual sales or receipts (U.S.$'000,000)
Retail trade	1,564,200	20,988,000	66.9	2,445,300
Automotive dealers	198,400	2,228,300	91.4	592,900
Food stores	182,500	3,376,600	70.5	423,300
General merchandise group stores	36,700	2,466,200	65.8	312,800
Eating and drinking places	449,100	7,432,500	46.6[17]	236,500
Gasoline service stations	99,300	647,100	60.5	155,000
Building materials, hardware, garden supply, and mobile home dealers	69,900	888,800	79.4	134,500
Furniture, home furnishings, equipment stores	114,500	937,900	88.4	133,500
Apparel and accessory stores	142,400	1,085,700	65.4	113,700
Drugstores and proprietary stores	45,700	607,800	77.5	90,700
Liquor stores	29,500	112,200	...	22,800
Wholesale trade	495,500[18]	6,367,000	107.7	2,420,700
Durable goods	313,500[18]	3,693,000	111.5	1,245,800
Professional and commercial equipment	46,800[18]	768,700	133.5	231,400
Motor vehicles, automotive equipment	47,300[18]	498,000	98.1	211,100
Machinery, equipment, and supplies	73,900[18]	774,300	112.5	187,300
Electrical goods	39,300[18]	477,400	116.2	173,800
Metals and minerals, except petroleum	11,200[18]	140,300	110.5	98,400
Lumber and other construction materials	19,500[18]	242,700	102.5	85,800
Hardware, plumbing, heating equipment and supplies	24,700[18]	290,600	105.8	70,500
Furniture and home furnishings	16,500[18]	149,600	97.7	43,600
Miscellaneous durable goods	34,300[18]	327,200	88.5	143,900
Nondurable goods	182,000[18]	2,674,000	102.3	1,174,900
Groceries and related products	42,900[18]	890,700	105.4	315,400
Petroleum and petroleum products	16,100[18]	166,400	96.6	177,800
Farm-products raw materials	11,600[18]	109,000	78.1	130,200
Drugs, drug proprietaries, and druggists' sundries	6,100[18]	197,100	128.2	102,900
Paper and paper products	19,700[18]	262,700	106.7	82,700
Apparel and accessories	19,600[18]	212,700	100.4	75,500
Beer, wine, and distilled alcoholic beverages	5,300[18]	155,900	116.3	56,400
Chemicals and allied products	14,200[18]	140,100	116.4	53,500
Miscellaneous nondurable goods	43,700[18]	539,800	84.5	180,500
Services[19]	2,342,300	33,106,000	98.4	1,826,200
Health	476,200	9,280,900	108.0	382,600
Business, except computer services	273,500	6,628,100	92.9	272,100
Computer and data-processing services	66,800	1,043,300	154.0	152,200
Legal services	161,600	946,200	140.0	114,400
Automotive repair, services, garages	178,400	1,031,200	86.4	98,300
Management and public relations	61,300	813,200	125.5	89,700
Hotels and motels	53,500	1,724,400	68.1	86,300
Amusement and recreation	90,800	1,720,600	73.2	77,400
Engineering services	42,600	579,000	154.7	76,600
Personal services	201,800	1,115,000	65.6	69,900
Motion pictures	42,700	601,700	121.8	58,100

Energy production (consumption): electricity (kW-hr; 1994) 3,268,250,000,000 (3,312,888,000,000); coal (metric tons; 1994) 937,580,000 (843,873,000); crude petroleum (barrels; 1994) 2,464,000,000 (5,024,000,000); petroleum products (metric tons; 1994) 704,201,000 (737,681,000); natural gas (cu m; 1994) 530,014,000,000 (592,209,000,000). Domestic production of energy by source (1994): coal 31.2%, natural gas 27.6%, crude petroleum 19.9%, other[20] 21.3%.

Energy consumption by source (1994): petroleum and petroleum products 38.8%, natural gas 24.0%, coal 22.0%, other[20] 15.2%; by end use: industrial 38.0%, residential and commercial 35.0%, transportation 26.5%.

Household income and expenditure. Average household size (1995) 2.6; average (median) annual income per household U.S.$34,076, of which average white household U.S.$35,766, average Hispanic[4] household U.S.$22,860, average black household U.S.$22,393; sources of income: wages and salaries 55.8%, transfer payments 16.5%, self-employment 7.9%, other 19.8%; expenditure: transportation 18.6%, housing 18.4%, food 14.0%, fuel and utilities 6.8%, household furnishings 5.9%, recreation 5.5%, health 5.4%, wearing apparel 5.3%, education 1.5%, other 18.6%.

Average annual expenditure of "consumer units" (households, plus individuals sharing households or budgets; 1995): total U.S.$32,277, of which housing U.S.$10,465, transportation U.S.$6,016, food U.S.$4,505, pensions and social security U.S.$2,593, health care U.S.$1,732, clothing U.S.$1,704, other U.S.$5,262.

Selected household characteristics (1996). Total number of households 99,627,000, of which (by race) white 84.8%, black 11.6%, other 3.6%; in central cities 31.4%[6], in suburbs 46.3%[6], outside metropolitan areas 22.3%[6]; (by tenure[6]) owned 64,045,000 (64.7%), rented 34,946,000 (35.3%); family households 69,594,000, of which married couple 76.9%, female head with own children[21] under age 18, 11.0%, female head without own children[21] under 18, 7.0%; nonfamily households 30,033,000, of which female living alone 48.6%, male living alone 34.2%, other 17.2%.

Financial aggregates

	1991	1992	1993	1994	1995	1996	1997[22]
Exchange rate, U.S.$ per:							
£[23]	1.77	1.76	1.50	1.53	1.58	1.56	1.61
SDR[23]	1.37	1.41	1.40	1.43	1.52	1.45	1.36
International reserves (U.S.$)[24]							
Total (excl. gold; '000,000,000)	66.66	60.27	62.35	63.28	74.78	64.04	56.10
SDRs ('000,000,000)	11.24	8.50	9.02	10.04	11.04	10.31	10.00
Reserve pos. in IMF ('000,000,000)	9.49	11.76	11.80	12.03	14.65	15.43	14.04
Foreign exchange ('000,000,000)	45.93	40.01	41.53	41.22	49.10	38.29	32.06
Gold ('000,000 fine troy oz)	261.91	261.84	261.79	261.73	261.70	261.66	261.72
% world reserves	27.86	28.13	28.67	28.70	29.00	28.86	29.34
Interest and prices							
Central bank discount (%)[24]	3.50	3.00	3.00	4.75	5.25	5.00	5.00
Govt. bond yield (%)[23]	6.81	5.31	4.44	6.26	6.26	6.44	6.21
Industrial share prices[23] (1990 = 100)	114.1	125.5	132.3	138.0	164.1	202.7	280.9
Balance of payments (U.S.$'000,000,000)							
Balance of visible trade	−73.44	−96.14	−112.74	−164.33	−158.78	−189.25	...
Imports, f.o.b.	−489.40	−536.28	−580.51	−668.87	−743.52	−803.23	...
Exports, f.o.b.	415.96	440.14	467.77	504.54	584.71	613.98	...
Balance of invisibles	69.75	29.84	3.49	162.83	10.55	40.52	...
Balance of payments, current account	−3.69	−66.30	−109.25	−1.50	−148.23	−148.73	...

Population economically active (1996): total 133,943,000[12]; activity rate of total population 50.4% (participation rates: ages 15–64, 79.4%; female 48.8%; unemployed 5.4%).

Price and earnings indexes (1990 = 100)

	1991	1992	1993	1994	1995	1996	1997[22]
Consumer price index	104.2	107.4	110.6	113.4	116.6	120.0	123.4
Hourly earnings index[25]	103.3	105.8	108.5	111.4	114.2	118.0	122.4

Average employee earnings

	average hourly earnings in U.S.$		average weekly earnings in U.S.$	
	July 1996	July 1997	July 1996	July 1997
Manufacturing				
Durable goods	13.35	13.63	556.70	571.10
Lumber and wood products	10.47	10.83	426.13	441.86
Furniture and fixtures	10.13	10.53	398.11	414.88
Stone, clay, and glass products	12.94	13.21	562.89	571.99
Primary metal industries	15.08	15.30	657.49	671.67
Fabricated metal products	12.51	12.68	520.42	528.76
Machinery, except electrical	13.55	14.01	574.52	599.63
Electrical and electronic equipment	12.26	12.70	497.78	524.51
Transportation equipment	17.29	17.26	738.28	730.10
Instruments and related products	13.18	13.55	540.38	556.91
Miscellaneous manufacturing	10.37	10.52	402.36	415.54
Nondurable goods	12.00	12.38	482.40	500.15
Food and kindred products	11.25	11.53	460.13	475.04
Tobacco manufactures	20.98	21.08	809.83	827.12[26]
Textile mill products	7.95	8.21	292.56	300.49
Apparel and other textile products	7.95	8.21	292.56	300.49
Paper and allied products	14.79	15.18	638.93	657.29
Printing and publishing	12.63	13.02	479.94	496.06
Chemicals and allied products	16.16	16.60	693.26	708.82
Petroleum and coal products	19.02	20.03	842.59	857.28
Rubber and miscellaneous plastics products	11.25	11.58	459.00	474.78
Leather and leather products	8.43	8.74	317.81	329.50
Nonmanufacturing				
Metal mining	17.28	17.71	753.41	782.78
Coal mining	18.65	19.00	813.14	830.30
Oil and gas extraction	14.80	15.47	651.20	685.32
Nonmetallic minerals, except fuels	13.88	14.34	673.18	698.36
Construction	15.51	15.59	617.30	641.20
Transportation and public utilities	17.67	17.78	848.16	878.33
Wholesale trade	12.82	13.36	488.44	513.02
Retail trade	7.93	8.26	233.14	244.50
Finance, insurance, and real estate	12.69	13.14	451.76	471.32
Hotels, motels, and tourist courts	7.96	8.38	249.15	261.46
Health services	12.84	13.25	418.58	438.58
Legal services	16.57	17.29	568.35	599.96
Miscellaneous services	15.99	16.50	574.04	570.90

Tourism (1996): receipts from visitors U.S.$84,133,000,000; expenditures by nationals abroad U.S.$68,976,000,000; number of foreign visitors (1995) 42,993,000 (13,668,000 from Canada, 9,610,000 from Mexico, 8,803,000 from Europe); number of nationals traveling abroad (1995) 47,419,000 (15,759,000 to Mexico, 12,920,000 to Canada).

Land use (1994): forested 32.3%; meadows and pastures 26.1%; agricultural and under permanent cultivation 20.5%; other 21.0%.

Foreign trade

Balance of trade (current prices)	1991	1992	1993	1994	1995	1996
U.S.$'000,000,000	−99.2	−84.5	−115.7	−151.3	−158.8	−189.2
% of total	9.8%	8.6%	11.1%	12.9%	12.0%	13.4%

Imports (1996): U.S.$803,239,000,000 (machinery and transport equipment 44.6%, of which motor vehicles and parts 16.0%; office and data-processing machines 15.8%; petroleum and petroleum products 9.0%; wearing apparel 5.8%; food and live animals 4.4%; chemicals and related products 3.3%). *Major import sources:* Canada 19.8%; Japan 14.3%; Mexico 9.4%; China 6.4%; Germany 4.8%; Taiwan 3.7%; United Kingdom 3.6%; South Korea 2.8%; Singapore 2.5%; France 2.3%; Malaysia 2.2%; Italy 2.2%; Thailand 1.4%; Hong Kong 1.2%; Brazil 1.1%.

Exports (1996): U.S.$612,069,000,000 (machinery and transport equipment 46.6%, of which motor vehicles and parts 11.9%; chemicals and related products 7.2%; food and live animals 6.9%; scientific and precision equipment 3.0%). *Major export destinations:* Canada 22.0%; Japan 10.8%; Mexico 9.3%; United Kingdom 4.9%; South Korea 4.2%; Germany 3.8%; Taiwan 2.9%; The Netherlands 2.7%; Singapore 2.6%; France 2.4%; Hong Kong 2.3%; Belgium 2.1%.

Trade by commodity group (1995)

	imports		exports	
SITC Group	U.S.$'000,000	%	U.S.$'000,000	%
00 Food and live animals	29,318[27]	3.8[27]	42,223[27]	7.3[27]
01 Beverages and tobacco	5,674	0.7	8,086	1.4
02 Crude materials, excluding fuels	22,311	2.9	34,758	6.0
03 Mineral fuels, lubricants, and related materials	63,052	8.2	10,720	1.8
04 Animal and vegetable oils, fat, and waxes	[27]	[27]	[27]	[27]
05 Chemicals and related products, n.e.s.	41,346	5.4	60,220	10.4
06 Basic manufactures	94,767	12.3	54,444	9.4
07 Machinery and transport equipment	357,625	46.5	281,184	48.4
08 Miscellaneous manufactured articles	129,077	16.8	62,106	10.7
09 Goods not classified by kind	26,204	3.4	26,793	4.6
TOTAL	770,822[28]	100.0	582,965[28]	100.0

Direction of trade (1996)

	imports		exports	
	U.S.$'000,000	%	U.S.$'000,000	%
Africa	19,460	2.4	10,584	1.7
South Africa	2,436	0.3	3,106	0.5
Other Africa	17,024	2.1	7,478	1.2
Americas	285,937	35.0	242,001	38.8
Canada	159,746	19.5	132,584	21.3
Caribbean countries and Central America	15,208	1.9	16,524	2.6
Mexico	74,111	9.1	56,761	9.1
South America	36,872	4.5	36,132	5.8
Asia	335,173	41.0[15]	208,383	33.4
China	54,409	6.6	11,978	1.9
Japan	117,963	14.4	67,536	10.8
Other Asia	162,801	19.9	128,869	20.7
Europe	171,713	21.0	149,085	23.9
EU	147,467	18.0	127,520	20.5
Russia	3,745	0.5	3,340	0.5
Other Europe	20,501	2.5	18,225	2.9
Oceania	5,916	0.7	13,872	2.2
Australia	4,127	0.5	11,992	1.9
Other Oceania	1,789	0.2	1,880	0.3
Other	−414	−0.1	−980	−0.2
TOTAL	817,785	100.0[15]	622,945	100.0[15]

Transport and communications

Transport. Railroads (1995): length[6] 137,900 mi, 222,000 km; passenger-mi 13,897,000,000, passenger-km 22,365,000,000; short ton-mi cargo 1,305,685,000,000, metric ton-km cargo 1,906,268,000,000. Roads (1995): total length 3,912,226 mi, 6,296,130 km (paved 91.0%). Vehicles (1995): passenger cars 134,803,000; trucks and buses 66,727,000. Merchant marine (1996): vessels (1,000 gross tons and over) 509; total deadweight tonnage 18,585,000. Air transport (1995): passenger-mi 540,400,000,000, passenger-km 869,700,000,000; short ton-mi cargo 14,568,400,000, metric ton-km cargo 21,269,500,000; localities (1996) with scheduled flights 834[29]. Certified route passenger/cargo air carriers (1992) 77; operating revenue (U.S.$'000,000; 1991) 74,942, of which domestic 56,119, international 18,823; operating expenses 76,669, of which domestic 56,596, international 20,073.

Intercity passenger and freight traffic by mode of transportation (1993)

	cargo traffic ('000,000,000 ton-mi)	% of nat'l total	passenger traffic ('000,000,000 passenger-mi)	% of nat'l total
Rail	1,183	38.1	14	0.7
Road	871	28.0	1,718	81.7
Inland water	467	15.1	—	—
Air	12	0.4	370	17.6
Petroleum pipeline	572	18.4	—	—
TOTAL	3,105	100.0	2,102	100.0

Communications

Medium	date	unit	number	units per 1,000 persons
Daily newspapers	1995	circulation	62,600,000	238
Radio	1994	receivers	558,440,000	2,122
Television	1995	receivers	204,100,000	776
Telephones	1995	main lines	164,624,400	626
Cellular telephones	1995	subscribers	33,785,700	128
Facsimile machines	1995	units	14,052,000	53
Personal computers	1995	units	23,012,250	87

Other communications media (1996)

	titles		titles
Print		General interest	181
Books (new)	46,898	History	151
of which		Home economics	90
Agriculture	443	Industrial arts	106
Art	1,511	Journalism and commun.	90
Biography	2,238	Labour and industrial relations	70
Business	1,266	Law	273
Education	1,215	Library and information sciences	118
Fiction	3,919	Literature and language	158
General works	2,061	Mathematics and science	238
History	2,466	Medicine	182
Home economics	1,027	Philosophy and religion	130
Juvenile	4,291	Physical education and recreation	151
Language	592	Political science	136
Law	764	Psychology	138
Literature	2,412	Sociology and anthropology	149
Medicine	2,866	Zoology	94
Music	322		
Philosophy, psychology	1,749	**Cinema**[16]	
Poetry, drama	1,119	Feature films	419
Religion	2,725		traffic
Science	2,576	**Cellular telephones**	
Sociology, economics	8,180	Number of subscribers	44,043,000
Sports, recreation	1,198		(pieces of mail)
Technology	1,572	**Post**	
Travel	386	Mail	182,661,000,000
Periodicals[9]	3,731	Domestic	181,662,000,000
of which		International	999,000,000
Agriculture	153		
Business and economics	262		
Chemistry and physics	170		
Children's periodicals	78		
Education	203		
Engineering	265		
Fine and applied arts	145		

Education and health

Literacy: studies in the late 1980s indicated that adult "functional" literacy may not exceed 85%.

Education (1995–96)

	schools	teachers	students	student/teacher ratio
Primary (age 5–13)[30]	85,393[31]	1,784,000	33,410,000	18.7
Secondary and vocational (age 14–17)		1,187,000	17,390,000	14.6
Higher, including teacher-training colleges	5,758[32]	833,000	14,210,000	17.1

Health (1995): doctors of medicine 720,300[33] (1 per 365 persons), of which office-based practice 427,300 (including specialties in internal medicine 17.0%, general and family practice 14.0%, pediatrics 7.9%, obstetrics and gynecology 6.8%, general surgery 5.6%, psychiatry 5.4%, anesthesiology 5.6%, orthopedics 4.0%, ophthalmology 4.3%); doctors of osteopathy 35,700; nurses 2,116,000 (1 per 124 persons); dentists 190,000 (1 per 1,385 persons); hospital beds 1,081,000 (1 per 243 persons), of which nonfederal 92.9% (community hospitals 80.8%, psychiatric 10.2%, long-term general and special 1.8%), federal 7.1%; infant mortality rate per 1,000 live births (1996) 7.2.

Food (1995): daily per capita caloric intake 3,603 (vegetable products 72%, animal products 28%); 136% of FAO recommended minimum requirement. Per capita consumption of major food groups (kilograms annually; 1995): milk 255.7; fresh fruits 123.2; cereal products 114.5; fresh vegetables 110.4; red meat 74.8; sweeteners 69.3; potatoes 58.7; poultry products 43.8; fats and oils 30.8; fish and shellfish 21.8.

Military

Total active duty personnel (1997): 1,447,600 (army 34.2%, navy 27.3%, air force 26.4%, marines 12.1%). *Military expenditure as percentage of GNP* (1995): 3.8% (world 2.8%); per capita expenditure U.S.$1,056. *Military aid* (1993): total $4,143,000,000 (Middle East 76.2%, of which Israel 43.4%, Egypt 31.4%; Europe 20.8%, of which Turkey 10.9%; Latin America 1.8%).

[1]Excludes 5 delegates having only committee voting privileges. [2]Total area per most recent official survey equals 3,675,267 sq mi (9,518,898 sq km); total area excluding U.S. share of Great Lakes is 3,615,215 sq mi (9,363,364 sq km). [3]Includes military personnel residing overseas. [4]Persons of Hispanic origin may be of any race. [5]Fiscal year ending September 30. [6]1994. [7]Data for 12-month period ending February 28. [8]Estimated crime rates include unreported crimes. [9]1988. [10]1993. [11]1987. [12]Excludes military personnel overseas. [13]Statistical discrepancy. [14]Unemployed. [15]Detail does not add to total given because of rounding. [16]1995. [17]Excludes tips. [18]1992. [19]Annual receipts for 1995. [20]Includes hydroelectric, nuclear, and geothermal power. [21]"Own children" includes adopted children and stepchildren. [22]September. [23]Period average. [24]End-of-year. [25]Manufacturing sector only. [26]June. [27]Animal and vegetable oils included in Food and live animals. [28]Detail does not add to total given because of statistical discrepancies in the data. [29]Includes 292 localities in Alaska. [30]Primary includes kindergarten. [31]1993–94. [32]1992–93. [33]646,000 professionally active.

Internet resources for further information:
- **U.S. Census Bureau http://www.census.gov**
- **1996 Statistical Abstract http://www.census.gov/prod/2/gen/96statab/96statab.html**

Uruguay

Official name: República Oriental del Uruguay (Oriental Republic of Uruguay).
Form of government: republic with two legislative houses (Senate [31][1]; Chamber of Representatives [99]).
Head of state and government: President.
Capital: Montevideo.
Official language: Spanish.
Official religion: none.
Monetary unit: 1 peso uruguayo (Uruguayan peso)[2]; valuation (Oct. 3, 1997) 1 U.S.$ = Ur$9.76; 1 £ = Ur$15.73.

Area and population

Departments	Capitals	area sq mi	area sq km	population 1996 census
Artigas	Artigas	4,605	11,928	75,786
Canelones	Canelones	1,751	4,536	410,524
Cerro Largo	Melo	5,270	13,648	81,218
Colonia	Colonia del Sacramento	2,358	6,106	117,380
Durazno	Durazno	4,495	11,643	56,986
Flores	Trinidad	1,986	5,144	25,348
Florida	Florida	4,022	10,417	68,257
Lavalleja	Minas	3,867	10,016	60,618
Maldonado	Maldonado	1,851	4,793	113,884
Montevideo	Montevideo	205	530	1,378,705
Paysandú	Paysandú	5,375	13,922	107,706
Río Negro	Fray Bentos	3,584	9,282	48,730
Rivera	Rivera	3,618	9,370	97,959
Rocha	Rocha	4,074	10,551	71,492
Salto	Salto	5,468	14,163	115,244
San José	San José de Mayo	1,927	4,992	91,874
Soriano	Mercedes	3,478	9,008	83,741
Tacuarembó	Tacuarembó	5,961	15,438	84,078
Treinta y Tres	Treinta y Tres	3,679	9,529	49,846
TOTAL LAND AREA		67,574	175,016	
INLAND WATER		463	1,199	
TOTAL		68,037	176,215	3,139,376

Demography

Population (1997): 3,185,000.
Density (1997): persons per sq mi 46.8, persons per sq km 18.6.
Urban-rural (1996): urban 88.7%; rural 11.3%.
Sex distribution (1996): male 48.47%; female 51.53%.
Age breakdown (1995): under 15, 24.5%; 15–29, 23.7%; 30–44, 19.5%; 45–59, 15.3%; 60–74, 12.2%; 75 and over, 4.8%.
Population projection: (2000) 3,278,000; (2010) 3,524,000.
Doubling time: 91 years.
Ethnic composition (1990): white (mostly Spanish, Italian, or mixed Spanish-Italian) 86.0%; mestizo 8.0%; mulatto or black 6.0%.
Religious affiliation (1997): Roman Catholic 78.5%[3]; Protestant 8.0%; Jewish 0.9%; other 12.6%.
Major cities (1985): Montevideo (1996) 1,378,707; Salto 80,823; Paysandú 76,191; Las Piedras 58,288; Rivera 57,316.

Vital statistics

Birth rate per 1,000 population (1995): 17.8 (world avg. 25.0).
Death rate per 1,000 population (1995): 10.0 (world avg. 9.3).
Natural increase rate per 1,000 population (1995): 7.8 (world avg. 15.7).
Total fertility rate (avg. births per childbearing woman; 1994): 2.4.
Marriage rate per 1,000 population (1992): 6.2.
Divorce rate per 1,000 population (1992): 2.7.
Life expectancy at birth (1994): male 70.9 years; female 77.5 years.
Major causes of death per 100,000 population (1990): diseases of the circulatory system 378.4; malignant neoplasms 222.8; respiratory diseases 76.3.

National economy

Budget (1996). Revenue: Ur$29,157,875,000 (direct taxes 78.0%, receipts from foreign trade 5.4%). Expenditures: Ur$32,151,841,000 (1995; social security and welfare 60.8%, general public services 14.3%, capital investments 7.7%).
Public debt (external, outstanding; 1995): U.S.$3,823,000,000.
Tourism (1994): receipts U.S.$632,000,000; expenditures U.S.$190,000,000.
Production (metric tons except as noted). Agriculture, forestry, fishing (1996): rice 868,000, wheat 628,000, barley 374,000, sugarcane 160,000, potatoes 145,000, oranges 133,000, corn (maize) 119,000, sunflower seed 112,000; livestock (number of live animals) 19,865,000 sheep, 10,677,000 cattle; roundwood (1995) 4,093,000 cu m; fish catch (1995) 120,737. Mining and quarrying (1995): hydraulic cement 1,000,000; gypsum 145,000. Manufacturing (value added in U.S.$'000,000; 1994): food products (excluding beverages) 792; beverages 393; chemicals and chemical products 313; textiles 253; tobacco products 170. Construction (approvals; 1994): residential 301,666 sq m; nonresidential 177,752 sq m. Energy production (consumption): electricity (kW-hr; 1994) 7,617,000,000 (5,957,000,000); crude petroleum, none (n.a.); petroleum products (metric tons; 1994) none (1,197,000).
Household income and expenditure. Avg. household size (1985) 3.3; avg. annual income per household (1985) NUr$266,261[2] (U.S.$2,625); sources of income[4]: wages 53.5%, self-employment 17.0%, transfer payments and other 29.5%; expenditure (1982–83)[5]: food 39.9%, housing 17.6%, transportation and communications 10.4%, health care 9.3%, clothing 7.0%.
Gross national product (1995): U.S.$16,458,000,000 (U.S.$5,170 per capita).

Structure of gross domestic product and labour force

	1996		1993	
	in value Ur$'000[2]	% of total value	labour force	% of labour force
Agriculture	15,057,460	10.0	47,700	3.8
Mining	248,752	0.2	2,100	0.2
Manufacturing	26,970,003	17.8	254,300	20.2
Construction	6,696,290	4.4	86,400	6.9
Public utilities	5,565,933	3.7	16,900	1.3
Transp. and commun.	10,401,852	6.9	67,900	5.4
Trade	18,695,930	12.4	231,300	18.3
Finance	13,000,875	8.6	68,400	5.4
Pub. admin., defense	14,706,486	9.7	455,800	36.1
Services	18,039,814	11.9		
Other	21,784,311[6]	14.4[6]	30,200[7]	2.4[7]
TOTAL	151,167,706	100.0	1,261,000	100.0

Population economically active (1994): total 1,307,600; activity rate 45.9% (participation rates: ages 14 and over, 58.1%; female 42.4%.

Price and earnings indexes (1990 = 100)

	1990	1991	1992	1993	1994	1995	1996
Consumer price index	100.0	202.0	340.2	524.3	758.9	1,079.5	1,385.4
Monthly earnings index[8]	100.0	212.0	363.7	588.1	858.3	1,185.5	1,364.5

Land use (1994): forested 5.3%; meadows and pastures 77.3%; agricultural and under permanent cultivation 7.5%; other 9.9%.

Foreign trade[9]

Balance of trade (current prices)

	1991	1992	1993	1994	1995	1996
U.S.$'000,000	+44.9	−248.9	−536.7	−732.2	−647.2	−773.4
% of total	1.4%	6.8%	14.0%	16.1%	13.4%	13.9%

Imports (1996): U.S.$3,322,798,000 (machinery and appliances 21.3%; chemical products 13.6%; mineral products 11.5%; transport equipment 11.2%; synthetic plastics, resins, and rubber 6.5%; processed foods 6.4%; textile products 5.8%). *Major import sources:* Brazil 22.4%; Argentina 20.8%; United States 12.0%; Italy 5.2%; France 3.5%; Spain 3.1%.
Exports (1996): U.S.$2,397,224,000 (live animals and live-animal products 26.3%; textiles and textile products 19.5%; vegetable products 17.0%; hides and skins 11.5%; processed foods 3.8%). *Major export destinations:* Brazil 34.7%; Argentina 11.3%; United States 7.0%; Germany 4.7%.

Transport and communications

Transport. Railroads: route length (1996) 2,073 km; metric ton-km cargo (1994) 189,000,000. Roads (1995): length 50,900 km (paved 14%). Vehicles (1995): passenger cars 444,835; trucks and buses 46,245. Air transport (1994): passenger-km 645,000,000; metric ton-km cargo 62,000,000; airports (1997) 1.

Communications

Medium	date	unit	number	units per 1,000 persons
Daily newspapers	1994	circulation	750,000	241
Radio	1996	receivers	1,850,000	586
Television	1995	receivers	600,000	191
Telephones	1995	main lines	622,000	198
Cellular telephones	1995	subscribers	40,000	13
Facsimile machines	1995	units	11,000	3.5
Personal computers	1995	units	70,000	22

Education and health

Educational attainment (1985). Percentage of population age 25 and over having: no formal schooling 7.5%; less than primary education 26.6%; primary 31.2%; secondary 19.9%; higher 14.8%. *Literacy* (1995 est.): population age 15 and over literate 97.3%; males 96.9%; females 97.7%.

Education (1994)

	schools	teachers	students	student/teacher ratio
Primary (age 6–11)	2,423	16,821	337,889	20.1
Secondary (age 12–17)	348	20,061	184,083	9.2
Vocational	104	...	56,879	...
Higher	2	7,157	61,367	8.6

Health: physicians (1994) 11,241 (1 per 282 persons); hospital beds (1987) 14,133 (1 per 215 persons); infant mortality rate (1995) 19.6.
Food (1992): daily per capita caloric intake 2,750 (vegetable products 63%, animal products 37%); 103% of FAO recommended minimum requirement.

Military

Total active duty personnel (1997): 25,600 (army 68.8%, navy 19.5%, air force 11.7%). *Military expenditure as percentage of GNP* (1995): 2.4% (world 2.8%); per capita expenditure U.S.$131.

[1]Includes the vice president, who serves as ex officio presiding officer. [2]The peso uruguayo (Uruguayan peso [Ur$]) replaced the new Uruguayan peso (Nur$) on March 1, 1993, at the rate of 1 Uruguayan peso = 1,000 new Uruguayan pesos. [3]About 30–40% of Roman Catholics are estimated to be nonreligious. [4]Salaried employees only. [5]Weights of consumer price index components in Montevideo. [6]Includes indirect taxes less subsidies. [7]Includes unemployed not previously employed. [8]From urban areas only. [9]Import figures are f.o.b. in balance of trade.

Internet resources for further information:
- **Embassy of Uruguay http://www.embassy.org/uruguay/**
- **Uruguay: Datos Estadisticos http://www.rau.edu.uy/web/rau/uruguay/generalidades/Uy.estad.htm**

Uzbekistan

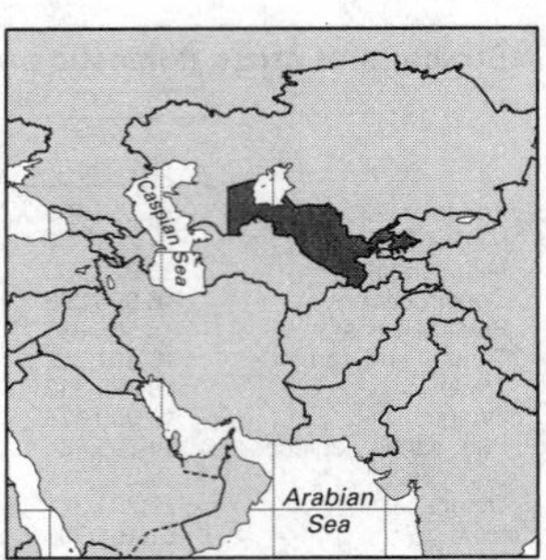

Official name: Ŭzbekiston Respublikasi (Republic of Uzbekistan).
Form of government: multiparty republic with a single legislative body (Supreme Assembly [250]).
Head of state: President.
Head of government: Prime Minister.
Capital: Tashkent (Toshkent).
Official language: Uzbek.
Official religion: none.
Monetary unit: sum[1] (plural sumy); valuation (Nov. 1, 1997) 1 U.S.$ = 75.30 sumy; 1 £ = 121.38 sumy.

Area and population

Autonomous Republic	Administrative centres	area sq mi	area sq km	population 1993 estimate
Qoraqalpoghiston	Nuqus	63,700	164,900	1,343,000
Provinces				
Andijon	Andijon	1,600	4,200	1,899,000
Bukhoro	Bukhara (Bukhoro)	15,200	39,400	1,262,000
Farghona	Fergana (Farghona)	2,700	7,100	2,338,000
Jizzakh	Jizzakh	7,900	20,500	831,000
Khorazm	Urganch	2,400	6,300	1,135,000
Namangan	Namangan	3,100	7,900	1,652,000
Nawoiy	Nawoiy	42,800	110,800	715,000
Qashqadaryo	Qarshi	11,000	28,400	1,812,000
Samarqand	Samarkand (Samarqand)	6,300	16,400	2,322,000
Sirdaryo	Guliston	2,000	5,100	600,000
Surkhondaryo	Termiz	8,000	20,800	1,437,000
Toshkent	Tashkent (Toshkent)	6,000	15,600	4,357,000
TOTAL		172,700	447,400	21,703,000

Demography

Population (1997): 23,664,000.
Density (1996): persons per sq mi 137.0, persons per sq km 56.0.
Urban-rural (1996): urban 38.38%; rural 61.62%.
Sex distribution (1995): male 49.50%; female 50.50%.
Age breakdown (1989): under 15, 40.8%; 15–29, 28.4%; 30–44, 15.0%; 45–59, 9.3%; 60–74, 4.7%; 75 and over, 1.8%.
Population projection: (2000) 25,035,000; (2010) 30,282,000.
Ethnic composition (1995): Uzbek 75.8%; Russian 6.0%; Tajik 4.8%; Kazak 4.1%; Kyrgyz 0.9%; Ukrainian 0.6%; Turkmen 0.6%; other 7.2%.
Religious affiliation (1997): Muslim (mostly Sunnī) 88.0%; Russian Orthodox 1.0%; other (mostly nonreligious) 11.0%.
Major cities (1995): Tashkent 2,107,000; Samarkand 362,000; Namangan 362,000; Andijon 313,000; Bukhara 238,000.

Vital statistics

Birth rate per 1,000 population (1994): 29.5 (world avg. 25.0); (1994) legitimate 96.5%; illegitimate 3.5%.
Death rate per 1,000 population (1994): 6.7 (world avg. 9.3).
Natural increase rate per 1,000 population (1994): 22.8 (world avg. 15.7).
Total fertility rate (avg. births per childbearing woman; 1993): 3.8.
Marriage rate per 1,000 population (1994): 7.9.
Divorce rate per 1,000 population (1994): 1.1.
Life expectancy at birth (1994): male 66.0 years; female 72.0 years.
Major causes of death per 100,000 population (1993): diseases of the circulatory system 303.6; diseases of the respiratory system 115.0; accidents, poisoning, and violence 50.0; cancers 48.7; infectious and parasitic diseases 38.4; diseases of the digestive system 31.8; diseases of the nervous system 10.3; endocrine and metabolic disorders 10.3.

National economy

Budget (1995). Revenue: 89,914,000,000 sumy (taxes on income and profits 38.1%, excise taxes 27.6%, value-added tax 19.2%, property and land taxes 4.7%, other 10.4%). Expenditures: 100,262,000,000 sumy (social and cultural affairs 36.9%, investments 18.8%, national economy 13.3%, payments on interest 4.9%, administration 3.0%, other 23.1%).
Household income and expenditure (1995). Average household size (1989) 5.5; income per household 35,165 sumy (U.S.$1,040); sources of income: wages and salaries 63.0%, subsidies, grants, and nonwage income 34.9%, other 2.1%; expenditure: food and beverages 71%, clothing and footwear 14%, recreation 6%, household durables 4%, housing 3%.
Public debt (external, outstanding; 1995): U.S.$1,260,000,000.
Production (metric tons except as noted). Agriculture, forestry, fishing (1996): seed cotton 3,300,000, vegetables 2,916,000, fruit (except grapes) and berries 1,165,000, grapes 580,000, potatoes 490,000, rice 480,000, barley 230,000; livestock (number of live animals) 8,352,000 sheep, 5,204,000 cattle, 208,000 pigs, 13,000,000 chickens; roundwood (1990) 15,000 cu m; fish catch (1995) 26,312. Mining and quarrying (1995): copper 100,000; zinc 80,000; gold 85. Manufacturing (value of production in '000,000 sumy; 1993): textiles 987; machine building and metalworking equipment 519; ferrous and nonferrous metals 484; processed foods 429; construction materials 294; chemical products 270. Construction (1992): residential 7,000,000,000 sq m. Energy production (consumption): electricity (kW-hr; 1994) 47,800,000,000 (47,400,000,000); coal (metric tons; 1995) 3,045,000 (1994; 4,200,000); crude petroleum (barrels; 1994) 25,655,000 (43,980,000); petroleum products (metric tons; 1994) 7,880,000 (7,880,000); natural gas (cu m; 1995) 48,600,000,000 (1994; 38,564,000,000).
Gross national product (1995): U.S.$21,979,000,000 (U.S.$970 per capita).

Structure of gross domestic product and labour force

	1995 in value '000,000 sumy	% of total value	labour force	% of labour force
Agriculture	85,070	28.5	3,735,000	44.8
Manufacturing and mining	49,068	16.4	1,010,000	12.1
Construction	23,228	7.8	493,000	5.9
Transp. and commun.	25,119	8.4	218,000	2.6
Trade	16,821	5.6	566,000	6.8
Finance Pub. admin., defense Services	58,864	19.7	2,135,000	25.6
Other	40,360[2]	13.5	188,000[3]	2.2
TOTAL	298,530	100.0[4]	8,345,000	100.0

Population economically active (1995): total 8,345,000; activity rate of total population 36.8% (participation rates: ages 16–59 [male], 16–54 [female] 74.5%; female [1994] 43.0%; unemployed 2.2%).

Price and earnings indexes (1992 = 100)

	1991	1992	1993	1994	1995
Consumer price index	13.4	100.0	634.1	5,219	11,724
Monthly earnings index	11.8	100.0	1,196	10,791	41,952

Land use (1994): forested 2.9%; meadows and pastures 46.5%; agricultural and under permanent cultivation 10.1%; other 40.5%.

Foreign trade

Balance of trade (current prices)

	1992	1993	1994	1995
U.S.$'000,000	−39.1	+314.8	+26.1	−103.7
% of total	13.7%	11.5%	0.8%	3.1%

Imports (1996): U.S.$4,763,000,000 (1995; machinery and metalworking products 29.1%, chemical products 13.6%, ferrous and nonferrous metal products 12.4%, food products 5.5%, forestry and paper products 4.0%, light industrial products 2.9%). *Major import sources:* Russia 24.9%; Korea 11.8%; Germany 11.0%; U.S. 8.1%; Turkey 5.4%.
Exports (1996): U.S.$2,649,000,000 (1995; light industrial products 34.7%, oil and gas 15.1%, machine-building equipment 5.9%, food products 5.8%, electricity 5.4%). *Major export destinations:* Russia 22.4%; Italy 8.8%; Tajikistan 6.8%; China 5.1%; Ukraine 5.1%.

Transport and communications

Transport. Railroads (1996): length 3,380 km; (1995) passenger-km 2,500,000,000; (1995) metric ton-km cargo 16,907,000,000. Roads (1995): total length 84,400 km (paved 86%). Vehicles (1994): passenger cars 865,300; buses 14,500. Air transport (1995): passenger-km 3,000,000,000; metric ton-km cargo 105,000,000; airports (1996) with scheduled flights 9.

Communications

Medium	date	unit	number	units per 1,000 persons
Daily newspapers	1995	circulation	160,000	7.0
Television	1995	receivers	4,000,000	176
Telephones	1995	main lines	1,738,000	76
Cellular telephones	1995	subscribers	3,700	0.2
Facsimile machines	1995	units	1,900	0.1

Education and health

Educational attainment (1989). Percentage of population age 25 and over having: primary education or no formal schooling 13.3%; some secondary 19.8%; completed secondary and some postsecondary 57.7%; higher 9.2%.
Literacy (1989): percentage of total population age 15 and over literate 97.2%; males literate 98.5%; females literate 96.0%.

Education (1995–96)

	schools	teachers	students	student/ teacher ratio
Primary (age 6–13) Secondary (age 14–17)	9,300	413,000	5,090,000	12.3
Voc., teacher tr.	252	22,164[5]	194,800	11.0[5]
Higher	58	...	192,100	...

Health (1995): physicians 76,000 (1 per 302 persons); hospital beds 192,000 (1 per 120 persons); infant mortality rate per 1,000 live births (1996) 25.7.

Military

Total active duty personnel (1997): 65,000 (army 69.2%, air force 6.2%, other 24.6%). *Military expenditure as percentage of GNP* (1995): 3.8% (world 2.8%); per capita expenditure U.S.$90.

[1]The sum was introduced on July 1, 1994, to replace the sum-coupon (an interim currency introduced in November 1993 to replace the Russian ruble) at a rate of 1 sum to 1,000 sum-coupons. The Russian ruble was banned from circulation in Uzbekistan from mid-April 1994. [2]Includes value-added taxes: excise taxes plus net import taxes minus subsidies. [3]Nondistributable unemployed. [4]Detail does not add to total given because of rounding. [5]1992–93.

Internet resources for further information:

- **Uzbekistan Human Development Report 1996**
  http://www.undp.org/undp/rbec/nhdr/1996/uzbekistan/
- **Welcome to Uzbekistan**
  http://www.gov.uz/
- **Republic of Uzbekistan**
  http://www.uzbekistan.org/

Vanuatu

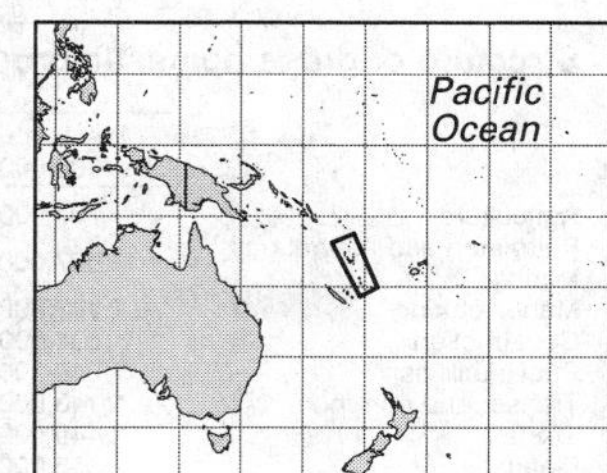

Official name: Ripablik blong Vanuatu (Bislama); République de Vanuatu (French); Republic of Vanuatu (English).
Form of government: republic with a single legislative house (Parliament [50]).
Chief of state: President.
Head of government: Prime Minister.
Capital: Vila.
Official languages: Bislama; French; English.
Official religion: none.
Monetary unit: vatu (VT); valuation (Oct. 3, 1997) 1 U.S.$ = VT 117.25; 1 £ = VT 189.01.

Area and population

		area		population
Local Government Regions	Capitals	sq mi	sq km	1989 census
Ambae/Maéwo	Longana	270	699	10,958
Ambrym	Eas	257	666	7,191
Banks/Torres	Sola	341	882	5,985
Éfaté	Vila	356	923	30,868
Épi	Ringdove	172	446	3,628
Malekula	Lakatoro	793	2,053	19,298
Paama	Liro	23	60	1,696
Pentecost	Loltong	193	499	11,341
Santo/Malo	Luganville	1,640	4,248	25,581
Shepherd	Morua	33	86	3,975
Taféa	Isangel	629	1,628	22,423
TOTAL		4,707	12,190	142,944

Demography

Population (1997): 176,300.
Density (1997): persons per sq mi 37.5, persons per sq km 14.5.
Urban-rural (1997): urban 20.0%; rural 80.0%.
Sex distribution (1989): male 51.60%; female 48.40%.
Age breakdown (1989)[1]: under 15, 45.5%; 15–29, 26.6%; 30–44, 15.2%; 45–59, 8.4%; 60–74, 3.7%; 75 and over, 0.6%.
Population projection: (2000) 189,000; (2010) 231,000.
Doubling time: 26 years.
Ethnic composition (1989): Ni-Vanuatu 97.9%; European 1.0%; other Pacific Islanders 0.4%; other 0.7%.
Religious affiliation (1989): Christian 77.2%, of which Presbyterian 35.8%, Roman Catholic 14.5%, Anglican 14.0%, Seventh-day Adventist 8.2%; Custom 4.6%; nonreligious 1.7%; unknown 4.0%; other 12.5%.
Major towns (1989): Vila (Port-Vila) 19,400; Luganville (Santo) 6,900; Port Olry 884[2]; Isangel 752[2].

Vital statistics

Birth rate per 1,000 population (1997): 33.0 (world avg. 25.0).
Death rate per 1,000 population (1997): 6.2 (world avg. 9.3).
Natural increase rate per 1,000 population (1997): 26.8 (world avg. 15.7).
Total fertility rate (avg. births per childbearing woman; 1997): 4.4.
Marriage rate per 1,000 population (1985): *c.* 7.4.
Divorce rate per 1,000 population (1985): less than 0.7.
Life expectancy at birth (1997): male 65.0 years; female 69.0 years.
Major causes of death per 100,000 population (1994)[3]: diseases of the circulatory system 39.0; diseases of the respiratory system 30.4; malignant neoplasms (cancers) 29.2; infectious and parasitic diseases 25.0; diseases of the digestive system 9.7.

National economy

Budget (1995). Revenue: VT 10,013,000,000 (foreign grants 35.5%, taxes on international trade 28.7%, taxes on goods and services 16.3%, nontax revenue 15.1%). Expenditures: VT 10,439,000,000 (current expenditure 67.4%, of which general public services 21.4%, education 12.7%, economic affairs and services 6.8%, health 5.7%, public order and safety 5.6%; development expenditure 32.6%).
Public debt (external, outstanding; 1995): U.S.$43,200,000.
Tourism (1994): receipts from visitors U.S.$55,000,000; expenditures by nationals abroad U.S.$1,000,000.
Production (metric tons except as noted). Agriculture, forestry, fishing (1996): coconuts 280,000, roots and tubers 50,000, copra (1994) 30,000, bananas 12,500, vegetables and melons 8,200, cacao beans 1,783, peanuts (groundnuts) 1,750, corn (maize) 700; livestock (number of live animals) 151,000 cattle, 60,000 pigs, 12,000 goats, 320,000 chickens; roundwood (1995) 63,200 cu m; fish catch (1995) 2,833. Mining and quarrying: small quantities of coral-reef limestone, crushed stone, sand, and gravel. Manufacturing (value added in VT '000,000; 1994): food, beverages, and tobacco 495; wood products 327; fabricated metal products 150; paper products 99; textiles, clothing, and leather 90; chemical, rubber, plastic, and nonmetallic products 83. Construction (approvals in Vila and Luganville; 1992): residential 20,386 sq m; nonresidential 19,876 sq m. Energy production (consumption): electricity (kW-hr; 1994) 29,000,000 (29,000,000); coal, none (none); crude petroleum, none (none); petroleum products (metric tons; 1994) none (20,000); natural gas, none (none).
Land use (1994): forested 75.0%; meadows and pastures 2.0%; agricultural 11.8%; other 11.2%.

Population economically active (1989): total 66,957; activity rate of total population 47.0% (participation rates: ages 15–64, 85.0%; female 46.3%; unemployed 0.5%).

Price and earnings indexes (1990 = 100)

	1990	1991	1992	1993	1994	1995	1996
Consumer price index	100.0	106.5	108.8	114.7	117.4	120.0	121.1
Earnings index	...	...	...	...	...	...	...

Gross national product (at current market prices; 1995): U.S.$202,000,000 (U.S.$1,200 per capita).

Structure of gross domestic product and labour force

	1995		1989	
	in value VT '000,000	% of total value	labour force	% of labour force
Agriculture	6,051	22.7	49,811	74.4
Mining	...	...	1	—
Manufacturing	1,386	5.2	891	1.3
Construction	1,721	6.4	1,302	1.9
Public utilities	462	1.7	109	0.2
Transportation and communications	2,247	8.4	1,031	1.5
Trade	8,611	32.2	2,713	4.1
Finance	1,918	7.2	646	1.0
Pub. admin., defense	3,089	11.6	7,892	11.8
Services	1,779	6.7		
Other	−550[4]	−2.1[4]	2,561	3.8
TOTAL	26,714	100.0	66,957	100.0

Household income and expenditure (1985)[5]. Average household size (1989) 5.1; income per household U.S.$11,299; sources of income: wages and salaries 59.0%, self-employment 33.7%; expenditure (1990)[5, 6]: food and nonalcoholic beverages 30.5%, housing 20.7%, transportation 13.2%, health and recreation 12.3%, tobacco and alcohol 10.4%.

Foreign trade[7]

Balance of trade (current prices)

	1991	1992	1993	1994	1995	1996
VT '000,000	−7,364	−6,689	−6,409	−7,493	−7,486	−7,520
% of total	67.0%	56.8%	53.7%	56.3%	54.1%	52.7%

Imports (1995): VT 10,659,000,000 (machinery and transport equipment 28.2%, basic manufactures 19.4%, food and live animals 15.0%, mineral fuels 8.0%, chemical products 6.6%, beverages and tobacco 3.5%). *Major import sources:* Australia 37.0%; New Zealand 12.0%; Japan 9.0%; France 6.0%; Fiji 6.0%.
Exports (1995): VT 3,173,000,000 (copra 34.7%, beef and veal 13.5%, timber 7.9%, squash and pumpkin 4.7%, cacao beans 4.0%). *Major export destinations*[8]: European Union 37.0%; Japan 24.0%; Australia 10.0%; Bangladesh 10.0%; New Caledonia 6.0%.

Transport and communications

Transport. Railroads: none. Roads (1995): total length 652 mi, 1,050 km (paved 24%). Vehicles (1994): passenger cars 4,000; trucks and buses 2,300. Merchant marine (1992): vessels (100 gross tons and over) 280; total deadweight tonnage 3,259,594. Air transport (1996): passenger-mi 93,000,000, passenger-km 150,000,000; short ton-mi cargo 845,000, metric ton-km 1,233,000; airports (1996) with scheduled flights 29.

Communications

Medium	date	unit	number	units per 1,000 persons
Radio	1996	receivers	55,000	319
Television	1993	receivers	2,000	13
Telephones	1995	main lines	4,200	25
Cellular telephones	1995	subscribers	100	0.6
Facsimile machines	1995	units	600	3.6

Education and health

Educational attainment (1989). Percentage of population age 6 and over having: no formal schooling or less than one year 22.3%; some primary education 52.6%; lower-level secondary 18.3%; upper-level secondary and higher 4.8%; not stated 2.0%. *Literacy* (1979): total population age 15 and over literate 32,120 (52.9%); males 18,550 (57.3%); females 13,570 (47.8%).

Education (1992)

	schools	teachers	students	student/ teacher ratio
Primary (age 6–11)[9]	272	852	26,267	30.8
Secondary (age 11–18)	21[10]	220	4,269	19.4
Voc., teacher tr.	...	...	444	...
Higher	1	...	124[11]	...

Health (1995): physicians 12 (1 per 14,025 persons); hospital beds 374 (1 per 450 persons); infant mortality rate per 1,000 live births (1997) 39.
Food (1995): daily per capita caloric intake 2,541 (vegetable products 85%, animal products 15%); 111% of FAO recommended minimum requirement.

Military

Total active duty personnel: Vanuatu has a paramilitary force of about 300.

[1]For indigenous population only. [2]1979. [3]Deaths reported to the Ministry of Health only. [4]Imputed bank service charges. [5]Vila and Luganville only. [6]Weights of consumer price index components. [7]Imports c.i.f.; exports f.o.b. [8]Destination of domestic exports only. [9]Excludes independent private schools. [10]1986. [11]1991.

Venezuela

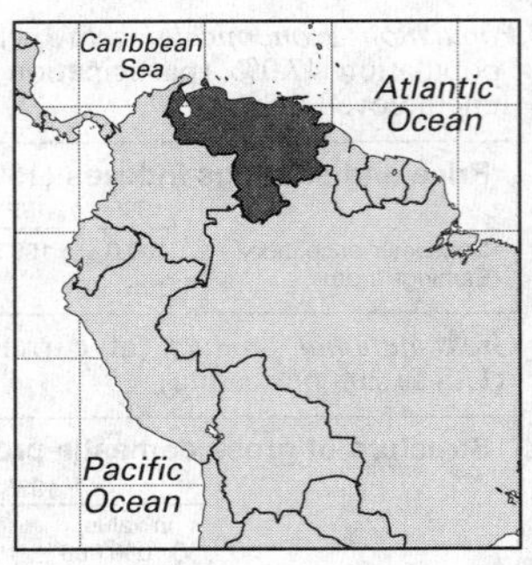

Official name: República de Venezuela (Republic of Venezuela).
Form of government: federal multiparty republic with two legislative houses (Senate [52[1]]; Chamber of Deputies [199]).
Head of state and government: President.
Capital: Caracas.
Official language: Spanish.
Official religion: none.
Monetary unit: 1 bolívar (B, plural Bs) = 100 céntimos; valuation (Oct. 3, 1997) 1 U.S.$ = Bs 497.35; 1 £ = Bs 801.73.

Area and population

		area		population
				1995
States	**Capitals**	sq mi	sq km	estimate
Amazonas	Puerto Ayacucho	67,900	175,750	66,668
Anzoátegui	Barcelona	16,700	43,300	1,028,097
Apure	San Fernando de Apure	29,500	76,500	376,220
Aragua	Maracay	2,708	7,014	1,335,303
Barinas	Barinas	13,600	35,200	516,789
Bolívar	Ciudad Bolívar	91,900	238,000	1,122,975
Carabobo	Valencia	1,795	4,650	1,807,542
Cojedes	San Carlos	5,700	14,800	226,684
Delta Amacuro	Tucupita	15,500	40,200	110,838
Falcón	Coro	9,600	24,800	684,062
Guárico	San Juan de Los Morros	25,091	64,986	585,418
Lara	Barquisimeto	7,600	19,800	1,423,683
Mérida	Mérida	4,400	11,300	686,709
Miranda	Los Teques	3,070	7,950	2,326,143
Monagas	Maturín	11,200	28,900	551,015
Nueva Esparta	La Asunción	440	1,150	325,909
Portuguesa	Guanare	5,900	15,200	719,473
Sucre	Cumaná	4,600	11,800	771,580
Táchira	San Cristóbal	4,300	11,100	944,259
Trujillo	Trujillo	2,900	7,400	549,878
Yaracuy	San Felipe	2,700	7,100	463,911
Zulia	Maracaibo	24,400	63,100	2,752,431
Other federal entities				
Dependencias Federales	—	50	120	...
Distrito Federal	Caracas	745	1,930	2,268,534
TOTAL		352,144[2]	912,050	21,644,121

Demography

Population (1997): 22,777,000.
Density (1997): persons per sq mi 64.7, persons per sq km 25.0.
Urban-rural (1992): urban 84.6%; rural 15.4%.
Sex distribution (1994): male 50.40%; female 49.60%.
Age breakdown (1992): under 15, 37.4%; 15–29, 28.0%; 30–44, 19.0%; 45–59, 9.7%; 60 and over, 5.9%.
Population projection: (2000) 24,170,000; (2010) 28,716,000.
Ethnic composition (1993): mestizo 67%; white 21%; black 10%; Indian 2%.
Religious affiliation (1996): Roman Catholic 92.7%; other 7.3%.
Major cities (1992): Caracas 1,964,846; Maracaibo (1990) 1,249,670; Valencia 1,034,033; Barquisimeto 692,599; Ciudad Guayana 523,578.

Vital statistics

Birth rate per 1,000 population (1996): 26.7 (world avg. 25.0); (1974) legitimate 47.0%; illegitimate 53.0%.
Death rate per 1,000 population (1996): 4.7 (world avg. 9.3).
Natural increase rate per 1,000 population (1996): 22.0 (world avg. 15.7).
Total fertility rate (avg. births per childbearing woman; 1996): 2.9.
Marriage rate per 1,000 population (1992): 5.4.
Divorce rate per 1,000 population (1992): 0.9.
Life expectancy at birth (1996): male 69.1 years; female 75.3 years.
Major causes of death per 100,000 population (1992): heart diseases 79.9; cancers 53.7; accidents 43.6; perinatal problems 33.0.

National economy

Budget (1994). Revenue: Bs 1,635,864,000,000 (tax revenues 78.3%, oil revenues 18.2%, nontax revenues 3.5%). Expenditures: Bs 1,627,732,000,000 (subsidies 32.0%, goods and services 29.9%, debt service 20.7%).
Public debt (external, outstanding; 1995): U.S.$28,494,000,000.
Tourism (1995): receipts U.S.$811,000,000; expenditures U.S.$1,865,000,000.
Land use (1994): forest 34.0%; pasture 20.2%; agriculture 4.4%; other 41.4%.
Production (metric tons except as noted). Agriculture, forestry, fishing (1996): sugarcane 6,844,000, bananas 1,365,000, corn (maize) 1,050,000, rice 733,000, plantains 516,086, oranges 493,028, sorghum 300,000, cassava 299,233; livestock (number of live animals) 14,584,500 cattle, 3,182,000 goats, 3,150,000 pigs, 100,000,000 chickens; roundwood (1995) 2,267,000 cu m; fish catch (1995) 504,791. Mining and quarrying (1996): iron ore 20,840,000; limestone 15,130,000; bauxite 5,600,000; gold 12,127 kg; diamonds 160,000 carats. Manufacturing (value added in 1990 U.S.$'000,000; 1994): petroleum refineries 2,718; food products 1,282; chemicals 1,163; beverages 760; transport equipment 691; iron and steel 458; nonferrous metals 386; metal products 382; tobacco 368; printing and publishing 294. Energy production (consumption): electricity (kW-hr; 1994) 73,116,000,000 (72,796,000,000); coal (metric tons; 1994) 4,741,000 (354,000); crude petroleum (barrels; 1994) 986,468,000 (380,-271,000); petroleum products (metric tons; 1994) 54,575,000 (24,229,000); natural gas (cu m; 1994) 24,675,000,000 (24,675,000,000).
Gross national product (1995): U.S.$65,382,000,000 (U.S.$3,020 per capita).

Structure of gross domestic product and labour force

	1995			
	in value Bs '000,000	% of total value	labour force	% of labour force
Agriculture	707,000	5.3	1,012,300	11.8
Petroleum and natural gas Mining	1,927,000	14.5	73,000	0.9
Manufacturing	2,282,000	17.2	1,046,800	12.3
Construction	534,000	4.0	623,900	7.3
Public utilities	340,000	2.6	66,000	0.8
Transp. and commun.	1,143,000	8.6	477,400	5.6
Trade	2,449,000	18.5	1,738,800	20.3
Finance	2,355,000	17.8	434,900	5.1
Pub. admin., defense	588,000	4.4	2,186,600	25.6
Services	150,000	1.1		
Other	791,000	6.0	885,000[3]	10.4[3]
TOTAL	13,266,000	100.0	8,544,600[2]	100.0[2]

Population economically active (1995): total 8,544,600; activity rate 39.1% (participation rates: over age 15 (1993) 57.9%; female (1993) 31.2%; unemployed 10.2%).

Price and earnings indexes (1990 = 100)

	1990	1991	1992	1993	1994	1995	1996
Consumer price index	100.0	134.2	176.4	243.6	391.8	626.5	1,252.3

Household income and expenditure. Average household size (1990) 5.1; average annual income per household (1981) Bs 42,492 (U.S.$9,899); expenditure (1990): food 37.1%, housing 9.4%, clothing 8.3%, transportation and communications 5.1%, education and recreation 4.9%.

Foreign trade

Balance of trade (current prices)

	1991	1992	1993	1994	1995	1996
Bs '000,000	+286,500	+154,700	+274,600	+1,159,400	+1,407.7	+5,996.8
% of total	20.1%	9.3%	12.1%	32.7%	27.2%	44.3%

Imports (1995): U.S.$10,791,261,000 (processed industrial supplies 34.9%, machinery 24.7%, transport equipment 12.4%, manufactured consumer goods 11.6%, food products 11.2%). *Major import sources:* U.S. 42.6%; Colombia 7.6%; Germany 4.8%; Japan 4.4%; Canada 4.2%; Brazil 3.9%; Mexico 3.3%.
Exports (1995): U.S.$18,814,219,000 (crude petroleum and petroleum products 76.8%, basic metal manufactures 8.2%). *Major export destinations:* U.S. 51.3%; Brazil 9.0%; Colombia 7.6%; Netherlands Antilles 4.9%; Suriname 2.1%; Germany 1.8%; The Netherlands 1.7%; Japan 1.6%.

Transport and communications

Transport. Railroads (1994): length 627 km; passenger-km 31,400,000; metric ton-km cargo 46,800,000. Roads (1995): total length 89,700 km (paved 39%). Vehicles (1995): passenger cars 1,485,221; trucks and buses 511,809. Merchant marine (1992): vessels (over 100 gross tons) 271; total deadweight tonnage 1,355,419. Air transport (1994): passenger-km 7,372,000,000; metric ton-km cargo 210,300,000; airports (1997) with scheduled flights 20.

Communications

Medium	date	unit	number	units per 1,000 persons
Daily newspapers	1994	circulation	4,600,000	215
Radio	1996	receivers	8,300,000	372
Television	1995	receivers	4,000,000	183
Telephones	1995	main lines	2,463,200	113
Cellular telephones	1995	subscribers	400,000	18
Facsimile machines	1995	units	16,000	0.7
Personal computers	1995	units	370,000	17

Education and health

Educational attainment (1990). Percentage of population age 25 and over having: no formal schooling 23.5%; primary education or less 47.2%; some secondary and secondary 22.3%; postsecondary 7.0%. *Literacy* (1995 est.): total population age 15 and over literate 91.1%; males 91.8%; females 90.3%.

Education (1993–94)

	schools	teachers	students	student/ teacher ratio
Primary (age 7–12)	15,984[4]	185,748	4,217,283	22.7
Secondary (age 13–17)[5]	1,621[6]	33,692	311,209	9.2
Higher	99[7]	43,833[6]	550,783[6]	12.6[6]

Health (1992): physicians (1989) 32,616 (1 per 576 persons); hospital beds 52,786 (1 per 382 persons); infant mortality rate (1996) 16.8.
Food (1995): daily per capita caloric intake 2,442 (vegetable products 83%, animal products 17%); 99% of FAO recommended minimum.

Military

Total active duty personnel (1997): 79,000 (army 72.1%, navy 19.0%, air force 8.9%). *Military expenditure as percentage of GNP* (1995): 1.1% (world 2.8%); per capita expenditure U.S.$39.

[1]Includes three former presidents holding lifetime membership. [2]Detail does not add to total given because of rounding. [3]Mostly unemployed. [4]1992–93. [5]Includes vocational and teacher training. [6]1991–92. [7]1990–91.

Internet resources for further information:
- **Central Office of Statistics and Informatics http://www.ocei.gov.ve/**
- **Embassy of the Republic of Venezuela http://www.embassy.org/embassies/ve.html**

Vietnam

Official name: Cong Hoa Xa Hoi Chu Nghia Viet Nam (Socialist Republic of Vietnam).
Form of government: socialist republic with one legislative house (National Assembly [450]).
Chief of state: President.
Head of government: Prime Minister.
Capital: Hanoi.
Official language: Vietnamese.
Monetary unit: 1 dong (D) = 10 hao = 100 xu; valuation (Oct. 3, 1997) 1 U.S.$ = D 11,724; 1 £ = D 18,900.

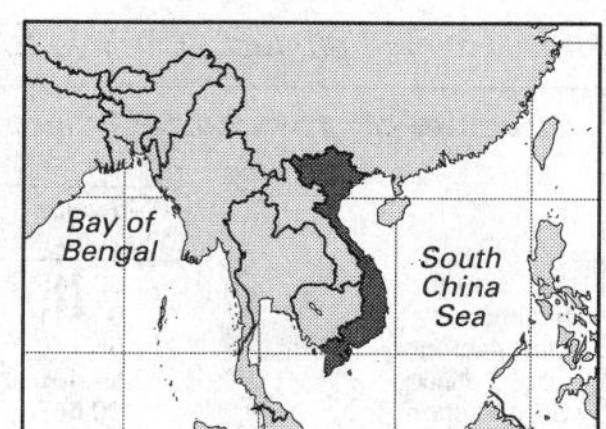

Area and population

Regions / Provinces	Capitals	area sq mi	area sq km	population 1993 estimate
Dong bang song Cuu Long		15,280	39,575[1]	15,531,600
An Giang	Long Xuyen	1,322	3,424	1,933,800
Ben Tre	Ben Tre	868	2,247	1,309,400
Can Tho	Can Tho	1,179	3,054	1,780,600
Dong Thap	Cao Lanh	1,265	3,276	1,462,900
Kien Giang	Rach Gia	2,410	6,243	1,326,600
Long An	Tan An	1,675	4,338	1,224,800
Minh Hai	Ca Mau	2,969	7,689	1,719,100
Soc Trang	Soc Trang	1,200	3,107	1,172,600
Tien Giang	My Tho	903	2,339	1,622,000
Tra Vinh	Tra Vinh	915	2,369	938,500
Vinh Long	Vinh Long	574	1,487	1,041,300
Dong bang song Hong		4,810[1]	12,457[1]	13,808,800
Ha Tay	Ha Dong	831	2,153	2,217,800
Hai Hung	Hai Duong	985	2,552	2,658,000
Haiphong (MUNICIPALITY)	—	580	1,503	1,583,900
Hanoi (CAPITAL)	—	355	920	2,154,900
Nam Ha	Nam Dinh	934	2,419	2,585,900
Ninh Binh	Ninh Binh	536	1,387	839,900
Thai Binh	Thai Binh	588	1,524	1,768,400
Dong Nam Bo		9,066[1]	23,481	8,692,900
Ba Ria–Vung Tau	Vung Tau	756	1,957	657,100
Dong Nai	Bien Hoa	2,264	5,864	1,762,900
Ho Chi Minh City (MUNICIPALITY)	—	807	2,090	4,322,300
Song Be	Thu Dau Mot	3,686	9,546	1,081,700
Tay Ninh	Tay Ninh	1,554	4,024	868,900
Duyen hai mien trung		17,692[1]	45,823	7,374,700
Binh Dinh	Quy Nhon	2,346	6,076	1,373,100
Binh Thuan	Phan Thiet	3,086	7,992	858,700
Khanh Hoa	Nha Trang	2,030	5,258	923,700
Ninh Thuan	Phan Rang Thap Cham	1,324	3,430	449,100
Phu Yen	Tuy Hoa	2,017	5,223	708,900
Quang Nam–Da Nang	Da Nang	4,629	11,988	1,911,700
Quang Ngai	Quang Ngai	2,261	5,856	1,149,500
Khu Bon cu		19,763	51,187	9,516,900
Ha Tinh	Ha Tinh	2,337	6,054	1,293,600
Nghe An	Vinh	6,325	16,381	2,680,600
Quang Binh	Dong Hoi	3,082	7,983	736,700
Quang Tri	Dong Ha	1,773	4,592	520,900
Thanh Hoa	Thanh Hoa	4,312	11,168	3,311,900
Thua Thien–Hue	Hue	1,934	5,009	973,200
Mien nui va trung du		39,749[1]	102,949	12,109,300
Bac Thai	Thai Nguyen	2,511	6,503	1,144,500
Cao Bang	Cao Bang	3,261	8,445	624,700
Ha Bac	Bac Giang	1,781	4,614	2,262,800
Ha Giang	Ha Giang	3,024	7,831	520,400
Hoa Binh	Hoa Binh	1,781	4,612	712,900
Lai Chau	Lai Chau	6,618	17,140	501,200
Lang Son	Lang Son	3,153	8,167	671,900
Lao Cai	Lao Cai	3,108	8,049	535,400
Quang Ninh	Hong Gai	2,293	5,939	889,600
Son La	Son La	5,487	14,210	776,000
Tuyen Quang	Tuyen Quang	2,240	5,801	628,500
Vinh Phu	Viet Tri	1,867	4,836	2,203,200
Yen Bai	Yen Bai	2,626	6,802	638,200
Tay Nguyen		21,455[1]	55,569	2,903,500
Dac Lac	Buon Ma Thuot	7,645	19,800	1,173,300
Gia Lai	Play Ku	6,047	15,662	737,700
Kon Tum	Kon Tum	3,835	9,934	249,600
Lam Dong	Da Lat	3,929	10,173	742,900
TOTAL		127,816[1]	331,041	70,982,500[2]

Demography

Population (1997): 75,124,000.
Density (1997): persons per sq mi 587.8, persons per sq km 226.9.
Urban-rural (1995): urban 20.8%; rural 79.2%.
Sex distribution (1997): male 49.03%; female 50.97%.
Age breakdown (1997): under 15, 35.5%; 15–29, 28.3%; 30–44, 20.2%; 45–59, 8.5%; 60–74, 5.8%; 75 and over, 1.7%.
Ethnic composition (1989): Vietnamese 87.1%; Tho (Tay) 1.8%; Chinese (Hoa) 1.5%; Tai 1.5%; Khmer 1.4%; Muong 1.4%; Nung 1.1%; other 4.2%.
Major cities (1996)[3]: Ho Chi Minh City 3,600,000; Hanoi 1,300,000.

Vital statistics

Birth rate per 1,000 population (1997): 22.0 (world avg. 25.0).
Death rate per 1,000 population (1997): 7.0 (world avg. 9.3).
Life expectancy at birth (1997): male 65.0 years; female 69.9 years.

National economy

Budget (1996). Revenue: D 60,500,000,000,000 (tax revenue 86.7%, nontax revenues 13.3%). Expenditures: D 66,417,000,000,000 (current expenditures 71.5%, of which social services 28.4%).
Public debt (external, outstanding; 1995): U.S.$22,962,000,000.
Gross national product (1995): U.S.$17,634,000,000[4] (U.S.$240 per capita[4]).

Structure of gross domestic product and labour force

	1995 in value D '000,000,000	% of total value	labour force	% of labour force
Agriculture, forestry, fishing	61,387	27.5	24,765,000	71.6
Mining, manufacturing }	67,075	30.1	3,395,000	9.8
Construction }			1,099,000	3.2
Transp. and commun.	8,747	3.9	568,000	1.6
Trade and restaurants	30,284	13.6	2,290,000	6.6
Finance, insurance	5,580	2.5 }	1,431,000	4.1
Pub. admin. } Services }	22,600	10.1 }		
Other	27,167[5]	12.2[5]	1,052,000	3.0
TOTAL	222,840	100.0[1]	34,600,000	100.0[1]

Tourism (1994): receipts from visitors U.S.$85,000,000.
Production (metric tons except as noted). Agriculture, forestry, fishing (1997): rice 26,396,700, sugarcane 9,000,000, cassava 2,067,300; livestock (number of live animals) 17,500,000 pigs, 3,700,000 cattle, 2,953,700 buffalo; roundwood (1995) 35,033,000 cu m; fish catch (1995) 1,200,000. Mining and quarrying (1994): phosphate rock 470,000; gold 10,000 kg. Manufacturing (1995): cement 5,731,000; fish sauce 131,700,000 litres[6]. Energy production (consumption): electricity (kW-hr; 1994) 12,020,000,000 (12,020,000,000); coal (metric tons; 1994) 5,600,000 (4,000,000); crude petroleum (barrels; 1994) 50,282,000 (283,300); petroleum products (metric tons; 1994) 38,000 (3,848,000).
Population economically active (1989): total 30,521,019; activity rate 47.4% (participation rates: ages 15–64, 79.9%; female 51.7%; unemployed 5.8%).
Household income and expenditure. Average household size (1989) 4.8; income per household (1990)[7] D 577,008 (U.S.$93); expenditure (1990): food 62.4%, clothing 5.0%, household goods 4.6%, education 2.9%, housing 2.5%.
Land use (1994): forest 29.6%; pasture 1.0%; agriculture 21.5%; other 47.9%.

Foreign trade

Balance of trade (current prices)

	1991	1992	1993	1994	1995	1996
U.S.$'000,000	−294	−109	−939	−1,772	−5,983	−6,735
% of total	6.3%	1.8%	13.6%	17.9%	34.4%	32.7%

Imports (1996): U.S.$13,668,000,000 (1995; machinery and spare parts 28.9%, petroleum products 8.6%, fertilizers 6.6%, steel 4.6%). *Major import sources* (1996): Singapore 13.8%; North and South Korea 12.9%; Taiwan 9.5%.
Exports (1996): U.S.$6,933,000,000 (1995; crude petroleum 19.7%, fish and fish products 11.9%, coffee 10.9%, rice 9.5%, rubber 3.1%). *Major export destinations* (1996): Japan 26.4%; Germany 8.1%; Singapore 5.7%.

Transport and communications

Transport. Railroads (1995): length 2,605 km; passenger-km 2,100,000,000[8]; metric ton-km cargo 1,062,000,000[8]. Roads (1995): total length 106,048 km (paved 26%). Vehicles (1994): passenger cars, trucks, and buses 200,000. Air transport (1994): passenger-km 209,000,000; metric ton-km cargo 19,000,000; airports (1997) with scheduled flights 12.

Communications

Medium	date	unit	number	units per 1,000 persons
Daily newspapers	1995	circulation	570,000	8.0
Radio	1995	receivers	7,800,000	106.0
Television	1995	receivers	3,200,000	43.0
Telephones	1996	main lines	1,050,000	14.2
Cellular telephones	1995	subscribers	14,600	0.2
Facsimile machines	1995	units	7,300	0.1
Personal computers	1996	units	100,000	1.4

Education and health

Educational attainment (1989). Percentage of population 25 and over having: no formal education (illiterate) 16.6%; some primary 46.6%; complete primary 23.5%; secondary 6.5%; postsecondary and higher 6.8%. *Literacy* (1995): persons 15 and over literate 93.7%; males 96.5%; females 91.2%.

Education (1995–96)

	schools	teachers	students	student/ teacher ratio
Primary (age 7–12)	13,092[9, 10]	298,856	10,228,800	34.2
Secondary (age 13–18)[11]	6,298[10]	193,814	5,332,400	27.5
Vocational	451[10]	9,425	197,500	21.0
Higher	104[10]	22,750	297,900	13.1

Health (1994): physicians 29,700 (1 per 2,444 persons); hospital beds 191,000 (1 per 380 persons); infant mortality rate (1997) 37.0.
Food (1995): daily per capita caloric intake 2,463 (vegetable products 91%, animal products 9%); 114% of FAO recommended minimum requirement.

Military

Total active duty personnel (1997): 492,000 (army 85.4%, navy 8.5%, air force 6.1%). *Military expenditure as percentage of GNP* (1995): 2.6%.

[1]Detail does not add to total given because of rounding. [2]Total includes 1,044,800 persons not distributed in province and region estimates. [3]Urban agglomeration. [4]Figure indicates the World Bank's nominal assessment of the Vietnamese economy. [5]Includes housing and tourism. [6]1992. [7]Wage workers and government officials only. [8]1994. [9]Includes 2,955 institutions that provide primary and first cycle of secondary education. [10]1993–94. [11]Includes first and second cycles of secondary education.

Internet resources for further information:
- **Vietnam Information http://www.batin.com.vn/**

Yemen

Official name: Al-Jumhūrīyah al-Yamanīyah (Republic of Yemen).
Form of government: multiparty republic with one legislative house (Council of Representatives [301]).
Head of state: President[1].
Head of government: Prime Minister.
Capital: Ṣan'ā'.
Official language: Arabic.
Official religion: Islam.
Monetary unit: 1 Yemeni Rial (YRls) = 100 fils; valuation (Oct. 3, 1997): 1 U.S.$ = YRls 137.00, 1 £ = YRls 220.84.

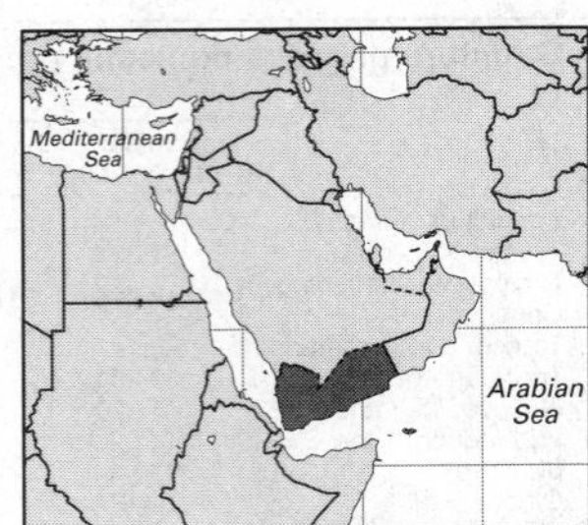

Area and population

Governorates	Capitals	area sq mi	area sq km	population 1994 census
Northern Yemen				
Al-Bayḍā'	Al-Bayḍā'	4,310	11,170	509,265
Dhamār	Dhamār	3,430	8,870	1,050,346
Ḥajjah	Ḥajjah	3,700	9,590	1,262,590
Al-Ḥudaydah	Al-Ḥudaydah	5,240	13,580	1,749,944
Ibb	Ibb	2,480	6,430	1,959,313
Al-Jawf	Al-Jawf	...	...	157,096
Al-Maḥwīt	Al-Maḥwīt	830	2,160	403,465
Ma'rib	Ma'rib	15,400	39,890	167,388
Ṣa'dah	Ṣa'dah	4,950	12,810	486,059
Ṣan'ā'	Ṣan'ā'	7,840	20,310	1,910,286
Ta'izz	Ta'izz	4,020	10,420	2,205,947
Southern Yemen				
Abyān	Zinjibār	8,297	21,489	414,543
'Adan	Aden	2,695	6,980	562,162
Ḥaḍramawt	Al-Mukallā	59,991	155,376	870,025
Laḥij	Laḥij	4,928	12,766	634,652
Al-Mahrah	Al-Ghayḍah	25,618	66,350	112,512
Shabwah	'Atāq	28,536	73,908	377,080
TOTAL		182,278[2, 3]	472,099[2]	14,832,673

Demography

Population (1997): 16,496,000.
Density (1997)[4]: persons per sq mi 77.0, persons per sq km 29.7.
Urban-rural (1994): urban 23.5%; rural 76.5%.
Sex distribution (1994): male 51.23%; female 48.77%.
Age breakdown (1994): under 15, 51.3%; 15–29, 22.9%; 30–44, 12.8%; 45–59, 7.7%; 60–74, 4.0%; 75 and over, 1.3%.
Population projection: (2000) 18,400,000; (2010) 25,800,000.
Doubling time: 21 years.
Ethnic composition (1986): predominantly Arab.
Religious affiliation (1980): Muslim 99.9%, of which Sunnī 53.0%, Shī'ī 46.9%; other 0.1%.
Major cities (1995): Ṣan'ā' 972,000; Aden 562,000; Ta'izz 290,107[5]; Al-Ḥudaydah 246,068[5]; Al-Mukallā 59,100[6].

Vital statistics

Birth rate per 1,000 population (1994): 45.1 (world avg. 25.0).
Death rate per 1,000 population (1994): 11.8 (world avg. 9.3).
Natural increase rate per 1,000 population (1994): 33.3 (world avg. 15.7).
Total fertility rate (avg. births per childbearing woman; 1994): 7.4.
Life expectancy at birth (1994): male 55.9 years; female 59.1 years.
Major causes of death per 100,000 population: n.a.; however, infant, child, and maternal mortality were very high (130, 190, and 100 per 1,000 live births, respectively).

National economy

Budget (1995). Revenue: YRls 87,951,000,000 (current revenue 75.7%, of which state property revenue 26.9%, international trade 18.4%, taxes on income and profits 15.6%; development revenue 19.7%; loans and grants 4.7%). Expenditures: YRls 124,140,409,000 (defense 25.2%; education 17.6%; public order and safety 8.1%; health 4.7%).
Production (metric tons except as noted). Agriculture, forestry, fishing (1997): sorghum 450,000, tomatoes 225,000, potatoes 185,000, wheat 170,000, grapes 153,000, watermelons 95,000, bananas 79,000, onions 68,000, papayas 57,500, millet 56,000; livestock (number of live animals) 4,000,000 sheep, 3,600,000 goats, 1,190,000 cattle, 500,000 asses, 180,000 camels, 3,000 horses, 21,900,000 chickens; roundwood (1995) 324,000 cu m; fish catch (1994) 86,811. Mining and quarrying (1994): salt 280,000; gypsum 80,000. Manufacturing (value of production in YRls '000,000; 1995): food, beverages, and tobacco 41,733.2; chemicals and chemical products 13,654.3; nonmetallic mineral products 7,539.6; paper products 2,601.8; basic metal industries 2,182.8; clothing, textiles, and leather 1,171.3; wood products 373.1. Construction: n.a. Energy production (consumption): electricity (kW-hr; 1994) 1,958,000,000 (1,958,000,000); coal, none (n.a.); crude petroleum (barrels; 1996) 135,050,000 ([1994] 25,945,000); petroleum products (metric tons; 1994) 3,330,000 (3,100,000).
Population economically active (1994): total 3,320,950; activity rate of total population 24.4% (participation rates: age 15 and over, 45.8%; female 18.2%; unemployed *c.* 50%).

Price index (1990 = 100)

	1990	1991	1992	1993	1994	1995
Consumer price index	100.0	174.9	223.2	295.0	412.5	654.0

Gross national product (1995): U.S.$4,044,000,000 (U.S.$260 per capita).

Structure of gross domestic product and labour force

	1996		1986	
	in value YRls '000,000[7]	% of total value	labour force	% of labour force
Agriculture	132,945	23.9	1,151,348	56.3
Mining	91,941	16.6	11,771	0.6
Manufacturing	56,778	10.2	94,913	4.6
Public utilities	11,488	2.1	160,952	7.9
Construction	20,647	3.7	32,852	1.6
Transp. and commun.	39,254	7.1	107,611	5.3
Trade	79,724	14.4	248,979	12.2
Finance, real estate	31,306	5.6	8,757	0.4
Pub. admin., defense	79,218	14.3	226,054	11.1
Services	12,515	2.2	...	...
Other	−475[8]	−0.1[8]	...	...
TOTAL	555,341	100.0	2,043,237	100.0

Household income and expenditure. Average household size (1994) 6.7.
Tourism (1995): receipts U.S.$38,000,000; expenditures U.S.$76,000,000.
Public debt (external, outstanding; 1995): U.S.$5,528,000,000.
Land use (1994): forest 3.8%; pasture 30.4%; agriculture 2.9%; other 62.9%.

Foreign trade[9]

Balance of trade

	1990	1991	1992	1993	1994	1995
U.S.$'000,000	−901.2	−1,517.3	−1,506.9	−1,508.7	−623.8	+242.8
% of total	38.8%	60.0%	77.4%	66.9%	25.1%	7.3%

Imports (1995): U.S.$1,537,800,000 (machinery and transport equipment 23.1%, basic manufactured goods 23.0%, food and live animals 22.1%, chemical products 8.2%, mineral fuels 7.9%, beverages and tobacco 2.1%). *Major import sources:* Arab countries 32.8%, of which Economic and Social Commission for Western Asia (ESCWA) countries 30.6%; Asia 28.1%, of which Japan 4.0%, India 1.6%; EC 23.2%; the Americas 11.6%, of which U.S. 7.7%.
Exports (1995): U.S.$1,780,600,000 (mineral fuels 95.3%, food and live animals 2.5%, crude minerals 1.2%). *Major export destinations:* Asia 85.4%, of which Japan 12.7%, India 0.1%; Arab countries 9.8%, of which ESCWA countries 9.1%; Africa 3.3%; EC 0.6%; the Americas 0.3%.

Transport and communications

Transport. Railroads: none. Roads (1995): total length 64,605 km (paved 7.9%). Vehicles (1995): passenger cars 229,084; trucks and buses 282,615. Merchant marine (1992): vessels (100 gross tons and over) 40; deadweight tonnage 13,653. Air transport (1994): passenger-km 1,183,000,000; metric ton-km cargo 119,000,000; airports (1997) with scheduled flights 11.

Communications

Medium	date	unit	number	units per 1,000 persons
Daily newspapers	1994	circulation	230,000	16
Radio	1995	receivers	665,000	43
Television	1995	receivers	100,000	6.5
Telephones	1995	main lines	187,000	12
Cellular telephones	1995	subscribers	8,300	0.5
Facsimile machines	1995	units	2,000	0.1

Education and health

Educational attainment (1986)[10]. Percentage of population age 10 and over having: no formal schooling 74.2%; reading and writing ability 19.8%; primary education 4.0%; secondary education 0.6%; higher 0.6%; not specified 0.8%. *Literacy* (1994): percentage of total population age 15 and over literate 43.2%; males literate 68.6%; females literate 23.1%.

Education (1994–95)

	schools	teachers	students	student/ teacher ratio
Primary (age 7–12)	11,013[11]	78,646[12]	2,493,017[12]	31.7[12]
Secondary (age 13–18)[12]	1,224	11,130	232,506	20.9
Voc., teacher tr.[12]	125	369	15,074	40.9
Higher[12]	2	1,991	90,826	45.6

Health (1995): physicians 3,220 (1 per 4,530 persons); hospital beds 9,169 (1 per 1,582 persons); infant mortality rate per 1,000 live births (1994) 80.9.
Food (1995): daily per capita caloric intake 2,025 (vegetable products 94%, animal products 6%); 84% of FAO recommended minimum requirement.

Military

Total active duty personnel (1997): 66,300 (army 92.0%, navy 2.7%, air force 5.3%). *Military expenditure as percentage of GNP* (1993): 15.7% (world 5.3%); per capita expenditure U.S.$100.

[1]Presidential Council assisting the President was abolished by a constitutional amendment of September 1994. [2]Yemeni territorial claims with regard to alignment of the long-undemarcated eastern boundary with Saudi Arabia (which increased Yemen's claimed total area to 214,300 sq mi [555,000 sq km]) were under negotiation with Saudi Arabia in 1996. [3]Detail does not add to total given because of rounding. [4]Based on the higher total area estimate of 214,300 sq mi (555,000 sq km). [5]1993. [6]1984. [7]In purchasers' value at current prices. [8]Includes import duties of 18.5 million Yemeni Rials less imputed bank service charges. [9]Imports are c.i.f. [10]Yemen Arab Republic only. [11]1993–94. [12]Public schools only, which comprise the vast majority of schools in Yemen.

Internet resources for further information:
- **The Yemen Times http://www.y.net.ye/yementimes/**
- **Embassy of Yemen http://www.nusacc.org/yemen/**

Yugoslavia

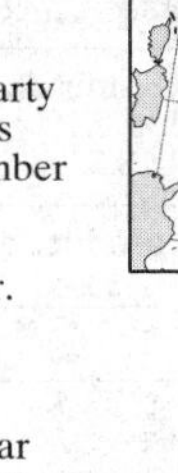

Official name: Savezna Republika Jugoslavija (Federal Republic of Yugoslavia).
Form of government: federal multiparty republic with two legislative houses (Chamber of Republics [40]; Chamber of Citizens [138]).
Chief of state: Federal President.
Head of government: Prime Minister.
Capital: Belgrade.
Official language: Serbo-Croatian.
Official religion[1]: none.
Monetary unit[2]: 1 Yugoslav new dinar (second) = 100 paras; valuation (Oct. 3, 1997) 1 U.S.$ = 5.71 Yugoslav new dinars; 1 £ = 9.20 Yugoslav new dinars.

Area and population

Republics	Capitals	area sq mi	area sq km	population 1996 estimate
Montenegro	Podgorica	5,333	13,812	640,000
Serbia	Belgrade	21,609	55,968	5,800,000
Autonomous provinces[3]				
Kosovo and Metohia	Priština	4,203	10,887	2,151,000
Vojvodina	Novi Sad	8,304	21,506	1,983,000
TOTAL		39,449	102,173	10,574,000

Demography

Population (1997): 10,632,000.
Density (1997): persons per sq mi 265.5, persons per sq km 104.1.
Urban-rural (1991): urban 51.2%; rural 48.8%.
Sex distribution (1996): male 49.53%; female 50.47%.
Age breakdown (1991): under 15, 22.8%; 15–29, 21.6%; 30–44, 21.7%; 45–59, 17.1%; 60–74, 12.2%; 75 and over, 3.5%; unknown, 1.1%.
Population projection: (2000) 10,808,000; (2010) 11,171,000.
Doubling time: not applicable; doubling time exceeds 100 years.
Ethnic composition (1991): Serb 62.6%; Albanian 16.5%; Montenegrin 5.0%; Yugoslav 3.4%; Hungarian 3.3%; Muslim 3.2%; Romany (Gypsy) 1.4%; Croat 1.1%; other 3.5%.
Religious affiliation (1996): Serbian Orthodox 64.0%; Muslim 19.3%; Roman Catholic 6.0%; other, mostly nonreligious 10.7%.
Major cities (1991): Belgrade 1,168,454; Novi Sad 179,626; Niš 175,391; Priština 155,499; Kragujevac 147,305; Podgorica 117,875.

Vital statistics

Birth rate per 1,000 population (1996): 12.9 (world avg. 25.0).
Death rate per 1,000 population (1996): 10.5 (world avg. 9.3).
Natural increase rate per 1,000 population (1996): 2.4 (world avg. 15.7).
Total fertility rate (avg. births per childbearing woman; 1995): 1.9.
Marriage rate per 1,000 population (1996): 5.4.
Divorce rate per 1,000 population (1996): 0.7.
Life expectancy at birth (1995): male 69.9 years; female 74.7 years.
Major causes of death per 100,000 population (1995): diseases of the circulatory system 573.6; malignant neoplasms (cancers) 167.6; accidents, violence, and poisoning 42.2; diseases of the respiratory system 40.9.

National economy

Budget (1997). Revenue: 28,745,000,000 Yugoslav new dinars (social security tax 39.1%, turnover tax 16.6%, income tax 16.5%). Expenditure: 28,745,000,000 Yugoslav new dinars (social security 39.1%, current transfers and other 60.9%).
Production (metric tons except as noted). Agriculture, forestry, fishing (1996): corn (maize) 5,367,000, sugar beets 2,418,000, wheat 1,507,000, grapes 433,000, sunflower seeds 390,000; livestock (number of live animals) 4,446,000 pigs, 2,656,000 sheep, 1,926,000 cattle, 26,457,000 poultry; roundwood 3,503,000 cu m; fish catch 7,461. Mining and quarrying: copper ore 20,206,000; lead-zinc ore 856,000; magnesite 89,000; aluminum and ingots 37,000; salt 21,646; asbestos ore 18,000; refined silver 69,000 kg. Manufacturing: wheat flour 798,000; crude steel 679,000; sulfuric acid 231,000; nitric acid 229,000; electrolytic copper 104,000; canned fruit 42,300; refined lead 30,000; welded pipes 25,000; rolled copper 16,800; medicines 14,600. Construction (residential units constructed; 1995): 11,847. Energy production (consumption): electricity (kW-hr; 1994) 35,328,000,000 (35,328,000,000); coal (metric tons; 1994) 38,351,000 (38,401,000); crude petroleum (barrels; 1994) 7,997,000 (10,222,000); petroleum products (metric tons; 1994) 781,000 (881,000); natural gas (cu m; 1994) 787,222,000 (1,630,200,000).
Population economically active (1996): total 3,232,000; activity rate 30.4% (1995; participation rates: over age 15, 59.0%; female 43.7%; (1996) unemployed 7.8%).

Price and earnings indexes (1991 = 100)

	1991	1992[4]	1993	1994	1995	1996
Consumer price index	100.0	9,026	222	103	179	192
Annual earnings index	100.0	151	211	158	205	187

Household income and expenditure. Average household size (1993) 3.9; income per household (1996) 20,073 Yugoslav new dinars (U.S.$3,515); sources of income (1996): wages and salaries 43.0%, pensions 15.7%, self-employment 13.5%, other 21.1%; expenditure (1996): food 47.1%, fuel and light 11.0%, beverages and tobacco 7.9%, clothing and footwear 6.5%, transportation and communications 5.3%, health care 4.7%, housing 2.7%.
Gross national product (1995): U.S.$15,910,000,000 (U.S.$1,510 per capita).

Structure of gross material product and labour force

	1996 in value '000,000 Yugoslav new dinars	% of total value	labour force	% of labour force
Agriculture	8,495.7	22.3	104,000	3.2
Mining / Manufacturing	14,806.3	38.9	848,000	26.2
Construction	2,124.3	5.6	130,000	4.0
Public utilities	498.6	1.3	55,000	1.7
Transp. and commun.	3,045.4	8.0	142,000	4.4
Trade	5,421.2	14.2	469,000	14.5
Finance	...	...	...	...
Pub. admin., defense / Services	2,045.5	5.4	665,000	20.6
Other	1,664.5	4.4	819,000[5]	25.3[5]
TOTAL	38,101.5[6]	100.0[6]	3,232,000	100.0[6]

Tourism (1994): receipts from visitors U.S.$31,000,000; expenditures, n.a.
Land use (1994): forested 17.3%; meadows and pastures 20.7%; agricultural and under permanent cultivation 40.0%; other 22.0%.

Foreign trade

Balance of trade (current prices)

	1987	1988	1989	1990	1991	1992
Din '000,000[7]	−1,431	−1,027	−1,716	−2,647	−1,356	−2,105
% of total	8.9%	6.3%	9.3%	12.3%	8.0%	20.8%

Imports (1996): Din 20,395,000,000 (manufactured goods 19.8%, machinery and transport equipment 19.4%, chemicals 14.3%, mineral fuels and lubricants 13.9%, food and live animals 12.2%). *Major import sources:* Germany 12.8%; Italy 10.6%; former U.S.S.R. 5.5%; Macedonia 5.2%.
Exports (1996): Din 9,156,000,000 (manufactured goods 33.1%, food and live animals 22.0%, machinery and transport equipment 12.2%, chemicals 9.1%). *Major export destinations:* Macedonia 11.5%; Russian Federation 8.5%; Germany 8.0%; Greece 5.1%; Switzerland 4.5%.

Transport and communications

Transport. Railroads (1996): length 4,031 km; (1996) passenger-km 1,830,000,000; metric ton-km cargo 2,062,000,000. Roads (1996): total length 49,620 km (paved 58.4%). Vehicles (1994): passenger cars 1,400,000; trucks and buses 132,000. Merchant marine (1992): fishing vessels 12. Air transport (1996): passenger-mi 598,000,000, passenger-km 963,000,000; short ton-mi cargo 3,371,000,000, metric ton-km cargo 4,921,000,000; airports (1997) 4.

Communications

Medium	date	unit	number	units per 1,000 persons
Daily newspapers	1995	circulation	1,363,000	256
Radio	1996	receivers	630,000	118
Television	1995	receivers	290,000	27
Telephones	1995	main lines	155,000	14
Facsimile machines	1995	units	10,000	0.9
Personal computers	1995	units	220,000	41

Education and health

Educational attainment (1991). Percentage of population age 15 and over having: less than full primary education 33.5%; primary 25.0%; secondary 32.2%; postsecondary and higher 9.3%. *Literacy* (1991): total population age 10 and over literate 93.0%; males literate 97.2%; females literate 88.9%.

Education (1995–96)

	schools	teachers	students	student/ teacher ratio
Primary (age 7–14)	4,441	51,728	914,532	17.7
Secondary (age 15–18)	570	26,954	352,346	13.1
Higher	93	10,544	131,689	12.5

Health (1995): physicians 21,313 (1 per 495 persons); hospital beds 56,107 (1 per 188 persons); infant mortality rate per 1,000 live births (1996) 14.3.
Food (1990)[8]: daily per capita caloric intake 3,545 (1988–90; vegetable products 93%, animal products 7%); 140% of FAO recommended minimum.

Military

Total active duty personnel (1997): 114,200 (army 78.8%, air force 14.6%, navy 6.6%). *Military expenditure as percentage of government expenditure* (1991): 3.9% (world 2.8%); per capita expenditure U.S.$167.

[1]Government gives "preferential treatment" to the Serbian Orthodox Church according to the U.S. Department of State, *Country Reports on Human Rights Practices for 1996.* [2]Yugoslavia experienced extreme hyperinflation between early 1993 and January 1994. The new dinar (second), or "super dinar," introduced on Jan. 24, 1994, was pegged to the Deutsche Mark at a rate of one-to-one and equaled 13,000,000,000,000,000,000,000 new dinars. The new dinar had been introduced Jan. 1, 1990, at the rate of 1 new dinar = 10,000 (old) dinars. Inflation was close to zero between January 1994 and September 1994. [3]The autonomous provinces are administratively part of the Republic of Serbia. [4]In new dinars after extreme hyperinflation. [5]Includes 819,000 unemployed. [6]Detail does not add to total given because of rounding. [7]In new dinars before extreme hyperinflation. [8]Data refer to Yugoslavia as constituted prior to 1991.

Internet resources for further information:
- **Federal Statistical Office of Yugoslavia http://www.szs.sv.gov.yu/homee.htm**
- **Federal Republic of Yugoslavia Official Web Site http://www.gov.yu**

Zambia

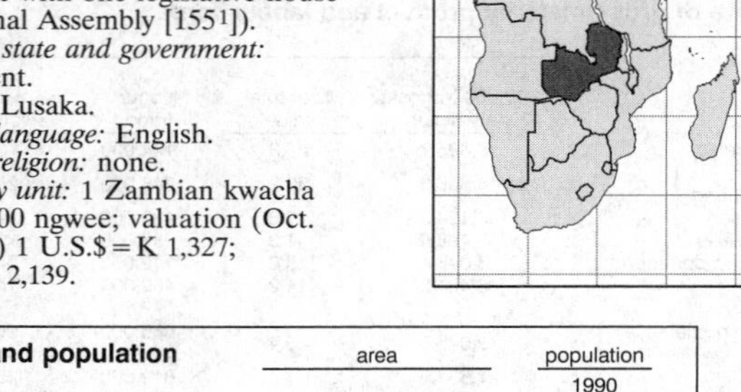

Official name: Republic of Zambia.
Form of government: multiparty republic with one legislative house (National Assembly [155[1]]).
Head of state and government: President.
Capital: Lusaka.
Official language: English.
Official religion: none.
Monetary unit: 1 Zambian kwacha (K) = 100 ngwee; valuation (Oct. 3, 1997) 1 U.S.$ = K 1,327; 1 £ = K 2,139.

Area and population

Provinces	Capitals	area sq mi	area sq km	population 1990 census
Central	Kabwe	36,446	94,395	725,611
Copperbelt	Ndola	12,096	31,328	1,579,542
Eastern	Chipata	26,682	69,106	973,818
Luapula	Mansa	19,524	50,567	526,705
Lusaka	Lusaka	8,454	21,896	1,207,980
North-Western	Solwezi	48,582	125,827	383,146
Northern	Kasama	57,076	147,826	867,795
Southern	Livingstone	32,928	85,283	946,353
Western	Mongu	48,798	126,386	607,497
TOTAL		290,586	752,614	7,818,447

Demography

Population (1997): 9,350,000.
Density (1997): persons per sq mi 32.2, persons per sq km 12.4.
Urban-rural (1995): urban 43.1%; rural 56.9%.
Sex distribution (1997): male 49.56%; female 50.44%.
Age breakdown (1997): under 15, 49.4%; 15–29, 28.0%; 30–44, 12.6%; 45–59, 6.2%; 60–74, 3.1%; 75 and over, 0.7%.
Population projection: (2000) 9,899,000; (2010) 11,471,000.
Doubling time: 24 years.
Ethnolinguistic composition (1980): Bemba peoples 36.2%; Maravi (Nyanja) peoples 17.6%; Tonga peoples 15.1%; North-Western peoples 10.1%; Barotze peoples 8.2%; Mambwe peoples 4.6%; Tumbuka peoples 4.6%; other 3.6%.
Religious affiliation (1980): Christian 72.0%, of which Protestant 34.2%, Roman Catholic 26.2%, African Christian 8.3%; traditional beliefs 27.0%; Muslim 0.3%; other 0.7%.
Major cities (1990): Lusaka 982,362 (metro. area, 1,400,000[2]); Ndola 376,311; Kitwe 348,571; Mufulira 175,025.

Vital statistics

Birth rate per 1,000 population (1997): 45.0 (world avg. 25.0); legitimate, n.a.; however, marriage is both early and universal, suggesting that legitimate births are a relatively high proportion of all births.
Death rate per 1,000 population (1997): 23.0 (world avg. 9.3).
Natural increase rate per 1,000 population (1997): 22.0 (world avg. 15.7).
Total fertility rate (avg. births per childbearing woman; 1997): 6.5.
Life expectancy at birth (1995): male 46.7 years; female 48.0 years.
Major causes of death per 100,000 population: n.a.; however, the major causes of morbidity are respiratory infections, diarrheal diseases, malaria, malnutrition, measles, AIDS, and accidents.

National economy

Budget (1997). Revenue: K 1,489,100,000,000 (1995; value-added and excise taxes 26.0%; customs duties 22.1%; grants 21.1%; personal income taxes 18.2%; company income taxes 5.2%). Expenditures: K 1,427,100,000,000 (1995; current expenditures 86.2%, of which debt service 34.7%, health 9.5%, education 9.4%, defense 5.3%; capital expenditures 13.8%).
Public debt (external, outstanding; 1995): U.S.$5,078,000,000.
Production (metric tons except as noted). Agriculture, forestry, fishing (1997): sugarcane 1,420,000, corn (maize) 963,000, cassava 540,000, fruits and vegetables 358,450 (of which onions 26,000, tomatoes 23,000, oranges 3,500), millet 61,000, wheat 60,000, sweet potatoes 52,000, peanuts (groundnuts) 50,000, seed cotton 35,000, sorghum 30,756, soybeans 29,292, sunflower seeds 7,983, tobacco 3,500; livestock (number of live animals) 2,600,000 cattle, 580,000 goats, 290,000 pigs, 65,000 sheep, 20,000,000 chickens; roundwood (1995) 14,613,000 cu m; fish catch (1995) 69,081. Mining and quarrying (1996)[3]: copper 307,071; cobalt 3,577; silver 8,676 kg; gold 2,926 troy oz. Manufacturing (value added in K '000,000; 1994): food products 39,765.1; beverages 36,596.5; chemicals and pharmaceuticals 32,141.5; textiles 15,358.5; tobacco 14,060.2; iron and steel, non-ferrous metals, and fabricated metal products 13,874.6. Construction (value added in K; 1995): 45,663,000,000. Energy production (consumption): electricity (kW-hr; 1994) 7,785,000,000 (6,305,000,000); coal (metric tons; 1994) 380,000 (375,000); crude petroleum (barrels; 1994) none (4,032,000); petroleum products (metric tons; 1994) 496,000 (435,000); natural gas, none (n.a.).
Household income and expenditure. Average household size (1990) 5.6; average annual income per household (1981) K 1,041 (U.S.$908); sources of income (1981): wages and salaries 94.0%, other 6.0%; expenditure (1977): food 37.7%, housing 11.0%, clothing 8.3%, transportation 4.3%, education 2.1%, health 1.0%.
Population economically active (1991): total 2,928,000; activity rate of total population 33.4% (participation rates: over age 10, 52.6%; female 29.6%; unemployed 17.4%[4]).

Price and earnings indexes (1990 = 100)

	1991	1992	1993	1994	1995	1996	1997[5]
Consumer price index	193.2	519.8	1,497.4	2,300.4	3,086.8	4,440.7	5,554.9
Earnings index	120.6	110.9	74.8	...	...	...	...

Land use (1994): forested 43.0%; meadows and pastures 40.4%; agricultural and under permanent cultivation 7.1%; other 9.5%.
Gross national product (1995): U.S.$3,605,000,000 (U.S.$400 per capita).

Structure of gross domestic product and labour force

	1995 in value K '000,000	1995 % of total value	1990 labour force	1990 % of labour force
Agriculture	581,164	16.5	1,872,000	68.9
Mining	318,438	9.0	56,800	2.1
Manufacturing	1,286,745	36.5	50,900	1.9
Construction	65,335	1.9	29,100	1.1
Public utilities	45,663	1.3	8,900	0.3
Transportation and communications	172,969	4.9	25,600	0.9
Trade	338,513	9.6	30,700	1.1
Finance	251,767	7.1	24,200	0.9
Public admin., defense; Services	371,801	10.6	111,600	4.1
Other	89,328[6]	2.5[6]	506,100	18.6
TOTAL	3,521,723	100.0[7]	2,716,000[7]	100.0[7]

Tourism (1995): receipts from visitors U.S.$47,000,000; expenditures by nationals abroad U.S.$56,000,000[8].

Foreign trade

Balance of trade (current prices)

	1991	1992	1993	1994	1995	1996
U.S.$'000,000	+420	−85	+202	+63	−88	+120
% of total	21.8%	5.3%	12.6%	3.0%	3.6%	6.3%

Imports (1996): U.S.$890,000,000 (1988; machinery and transport equipment 38.3%; basic manufactures 19.8%; chemicals 16.9%; mineral fuels, lubricants, and electricity 12.3%; food 3.8%). *Major import sources* (1995): South Africa 27.7%; United Kingdom 11.3%; Zimbabwe 9.2%; Japan 8.6%; United States 7.0%; India 4.9%; Germany 4.3%.
Exports (1996): U.S.$1,010,000,000 (1995; copper 70.6%; cobalt 11.3%). *Major export destinations* (1995): Japan 17.9%; Saudi Arabia 12.9%; Thailand 12.8%; Taiwan 7.2%; India 5.3%; Belgium-Luxembourg 5.0%; France 4.5%.

Transport and communications

Transport. Railroads (1995)[9]: length 791 mi, 1,273 km; passenger-mi 166,000,000, passenger-km 267,000,000; short ton-mi cargo 316,000,000, metric ton-km cargo 462,000,000. Roads (1995): total length 24,170 mi, 38,898 km (paved 18%). Vehicles (1995): passenger cars 142,000; trucks and buses 73,500. Merchant marine: vessels (100 gross tons and over) none. Air transport (1995)[10]: passenger arrivals and departures 294,000; metric ton cargo unloaded and loaded 6,900; airports (1997) with scheduled flights 4.

Communications

Medium	date	unit	number	units per 1,000 persons
Daily newspapers	1995	circulation	107,000	13.0
Radio	1995	receivers	800,000	99.0
Television	1995	receivers	260,000	32.0
Telephones	1995	main lines	76,800	8.2
Cellular telephones	1995	subscribers	1,800	0.2
Facsimile machines	1995	units	900	0.1

Education and health

Educational attainment (1993)[11]. Percentage of population age 14 and over having: no formal schooling 18.6%; some primary education 54.8%; some secondary 25.1%; higher 1.5%. *Literacy* (1995): population age 15 and over literate 3,890,000 (78.2%); males literate 2,060,000 (85.6%); females literate 1,830,000 (71.3%).

Education (1995)

	schools	teachers	students	student/ teacher ratio
Primary (age 7–13)	3,883	38,528	1,506,349	39.1
Secondary (age 14–18)	480[12]	5,786[13]	199,081[14]	...
Voc., teacher tr.	26[12]	846[12]	7,982[15]	...
Higher	2[12]	481[14]	5,270[14]	11.0

Health: physicians (1993) 786 (1 per 10,917 persons); hospital beds (1989) 22,461 (1 per 349 persons); infant mortality rate per 1,000 live births (1997) 93.
Food (1995): daily per capita caloric intake 1,931 (vegetable products 95%, animal products 5%); 84% of FAO recommended minimum requirement.

Military

Total active duty personnel (1997): 21,600 (army 92.6%; navy, none; air force 7.4%). *Military expenditure as percentage of GNP* (1995): 2.8% (world 2.8%); per capita expenditure U.S.$11.

[1]Includes 5 nonelective seats. [2]1996 estimate; urban agglomeration. [3]The lead and zinc mines at Kabwe were closed in 1994. [4]1987. [5]July. [6]Less imputed bank service charge. [7]Detail does not add to total given because of rounding. [8]1992. [9]Excludes Tanzania-Zambia Railway Authority (TAZARA) data. [10]Lusaka airport only. [11]Based on a sample survey of 35,502 persons. [12]1989. [13]1988. [14]1994. [15]1990.

Internet resources for further information:
- **Zambian National WWW Server (Zamnet) http://www.zamnet.zm/**

Zimbabwe

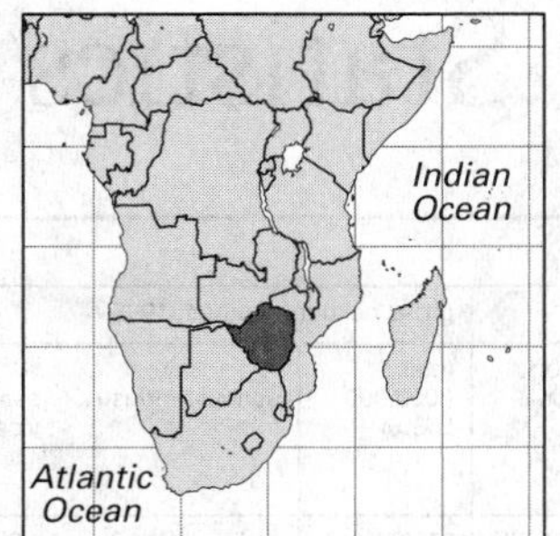

Official name: Republic of Zimbabwe.
Form of government: multiparty republic with one legislative house (House of Assembly [150[1]]).
Head of state and government: President.
Capital: Harare.
Official language: English.
Official religion: none.
Monetary unit: 1 Zimbabwe dollar (Z$) = 100 cents; valuation (Oct. 3, 1997) 1 U.S.$ = Z$12.30; 1 £ = Z$19.83.

Area and population		area		population
				1992
Provinces	Capitals	sq mi	sq km	census[2]
Bulawayo	—	185	479	620,936
Harare	—	337	872	1,478,810
Manicaland	Mutare	14,077	36,459	1,537,676
Mashonaland Central	Bindura	10,945	28,347	857,318
Mashonaland East	Marondera	12,444	32,230	1,033,336
Mashonaland West	Chinhoyi	22,178	57,441	1,116,928
Masvingo	Masvingo	21,840	56,566	1,221,845
Matabeleland North	...	28,967	75,025	640,957
Matabeleland South	Gwanda	20,916	54,172	591,747
Midlands	Gweru	18,983	49,166	1,302,214
TOTAL		150,872	390,757	10,401,767

Demography

Population (1997): 11,423,000.
Density (1997): persons per sq mi 75.7, persons per sq km 29.2.
Urban-rural (1988): urban 26.4%; rural 73.6%.
Sex distribution (1992): male 48.80%; female 51.20%.
Age breakdown (1997): under 15, 43.6%; 15–29, 31.5%; 30–44, 13.8%; 45–59, 6.8%; 60–74, 3.4%; 75 and over, 0.9%.
Population projection: (2000) 11,777,000; (2010) 11,905,000.
Doubling time: 50 years.
Ethnolinguistic composition (1982): African 97.6%, of which Shona-speaking Bantu 70.8%, Ndebele-speaking Bantu 15.8%; European 2.0%; Asian 0.1%; other 0.3%.
Religious affiliation (1980): Christian 44.8%, of which Protestant (including Anglican) 17.5%, African indigenous 13.6%, Roman Catholic 11.7%; animist 40.4%; other 14.8%.
Major cities (1992): Harare 1,184,169; Bulawayo 620,936; Chitungwiza 274,035; Mutare 131,808; Gweru 124,735.

Vital statistics

Birth rate per 1,000 population (1997): 31.6 (world avg. 25.0).
Death rate per 1,000 population (1997): 19.0 (world avg. 9.3).
Natural increase rate per 1,000 population (1997): 12.6 (world avg. 15.7).
Total fertility rate (avg. births per childbearing woman; 1997): 3.9.
Life expectancy at birth (1992): male 58.0 years; female 62.0 years.
Major causes of death per 100,000 population (1990): infectious and parasitic diseases 64.7; accidents and poisoning 44.4; diseases of the circulatory system 40.9; diseases of the respiratory system 39.5; malignant neoplasms (cancers) 28.4; diseases of the digestive system 12.1; diseases of the nervous system 9.4; endocrine and metabolic disorders 4.9.

National economy

Budget (1996–97). Revenue: Z$23,350,355,000 (income tax 36.4%; sales tax 20.5%; customs duties 16.5%; excise tax 4.8%; revenue from investments and property 4.2%; stamp duties 1.0%). Expenditures: Z$30,173,080,000 (recurrent expenditures 85.8%, of which goods and services 46.4%, transfer payments 39.4%).
Population economically active (1992): total 3,600,000; activity rate of total population 34.6% (participation rates: over age 15, 63.4%; female 39.8%; unemployed 7.2%[3]).

Price and earnings indexes (1990 = 100)	1990	1991	1992	1993	1994	1995	1996
Consumer price index	100.0	123.3	175.2	223.6	273.3	335.1	406.9
Earnings index	...	...	...	...	...	...	...

Production (metric tons except as noted). Agriculture, forestry, fishing (1996): sugarcane 2,826,000, corn (maize) 2,609,000, wheat 280,000, seed cotton 242,000, tobacco 209,000, cotton seed 153,000, cassava 150,000, vegetables (including melons) 147,000, millet 118,000, soybeans 110,000, sorghum 108,000, bananas 83,000, peanuts (groundnuts) 80,000; livestock (number of live animals) 5,436,000 cattle, 2,705,000 goats, 530,000 sheep, 267,000 pigs, 15,000,000 chickens; roundwood 8,102,000 cu m; fish catch (1993) 21,800 metric tons. Mining and quarrying (value of production in Z$; 1995): gold 2,567,100,000; nickel 738,900,000; asbestos 586,500,000; coal 557,100,000; chrome 197,400,000; copper 188,700,000. Manufacturing (value in Z$; 1993): foodstuffs 5,329,600,000; metals and metal products 4,107,100,000; chemicals and petroleum products 3,153,600,000; textiles 2,584,000,000; beverages and tobacco 2,523,400,000; clothing and footwear 1,394,600,000; transport equipment 1,387,500,000; paper, printing, and publishing 1,132,900,000; nonmetallic mineral products 740,200,000; wood and furniture 691,500,000; other manufactured goods 261,300,000. Construction (Z$; 1995): residential 794,054,000; commercial 248,794,000; industrial 136,358,000. Energy production (consumption): electricity (kW-hr; 1994) 7,334,000,000 (9,050,000,000); coal (metric tons; 1994) 5,469,000 (5,614,000); crude petroleum, none (none); petroleum products (metric tons; 1994) none (1,051,000); natural gas, none (none).
Public debt (external, outstanding; 1995): U.S.$3,360,000,000.
Household income and expenditure. Average household size (1992) 4.8; income per household Z$1,689 (U.S.$2,628); sources of income: n.a.; expenditure (1990[4]): food, beverages, and tobacco 39.1%, housing 18.7%, clothing and footwear 9.8%, transportation 8.4%, education 7.6%, household durable goods 7.2%, health 2.8%, recreation 2.0%, other 4.4%.
Gross national product (1994): U.S.$5,933,000,000 (U.S.$540 per capita).

Structure of gross domestic product and labour force	1994		1995	
	in value Z$'000,000	% of total value	labour force[5]	% of labour force[5]
Agriculture	4,004	10.1	334,000	26.9
Mining	2,739	6.9	59,000	4.7
Manufacturing	16,300	41.0	185,900	15.0
Construction	865	2.2	71,800	5.8
Public utilities	2,455	6.2	9,500	0.8
Transp. and commun.	2,125	5.3	50,900	4.1
Trade	4,357	10.9	100,600	8.2
Finance	1,973	5.0	21,100	1.7
Pub. admin., defense	902	2.3	406,800	32.8
Services	2,670	6.7		
Other	1,385[6]	3.4[6]	...	...
TOTAL	39,775	100.0	1,239,600	100.0

Tourism (1995): receipts U.S.$154,000,000; expenditures U.S.$106,000,000.

Foreign trade

Balance of trade (current prices)	1989	1990	1991	1992	1993	1994
Z$'000,000	277.6	−296.8	−1,867.4	−2,475.6	−95.3	−522.8
% of total	4.4%	3.4%	14.4%	14.4%	0.5%	1.7%

Imports (1996): Z$28,095,100,000 (machinery and transport equipment 38.7%, of which transport equipment 9.1%; manufactured goods 16.7%, of which textiles 2.6%, paper and paperboard 1.8%; fuels 10.4%, of which petroleum 9.7%). *Major import sources:* South Africa 38.3%; U.K. 7.9%; Japan 5.1%; U.S. 5.0%; Germany 4.9%; France 3.1%; Italy 2.5%; The Netherlands 1.8%.
Exports (1996)[7]: Z$24,209,300,000 (domestic exports 86.8%, of which tobacco 30.5%, gold sales 12.3%, ferroalloys 6.7%, nickel metal 3.2%, cotton 2.7%, asbestos 2.6%, cut flowers 1.4%, corn [maize] 1.2%). *Major export destinations:* U.K. 10.1%; South Africa 9.6%; Germany 7.9%; U.S. 6.7%; Japan 5.1%; Zambia 4.3%; Italy 4.3%; Botswana 4.0%; The Netherlands 3.8%.

Transport and communications

Transport. Railroads (1995): route length 1,714 mi, 2,759 km; passenger-mi 339,254,000, passenger-km 545,977,000; short ton-mi cargo 3,256,000, metric ton-km cargo 4,754,000. Roads (1995): total length 57,048 mi, 91,810 km (paved 19%). Vehicles (1995): passenger cars 492,000; trucks and buses 108,000. Merchant marine: none. Air transport (1995)[8]: passenger-mi 521,673,000, passenger-km 839,553,000; short ton-mi cargo 27,016,000, metric ton-km cargo 39,442,000; airports (1997) with scheduled flights 7.

Communications Medium	date	unit	number	units per 1,000 persons
Daily newspapers	1995	circulation	192,000	17
Radio	1996	receivers	1,300,000	113
Television	1995	receivers	137,090	12
Telephones	1995	main lines	154,600	14
Facsimile machines	1995	units	10,000	0.9
Personal computers	1995	units	33,000	3.0

Education and health

Educational attainment (1986–87). Percentage of employed population age 15 and over having: no formal schooling 24.5%; primary 42.9%; secondary and tertiary 31.7%. *Literacy* (1995): percentage of total population age 15 and over literate 85.1%; males literate 90.4%; females literate 79.9%.

Education (1995)	schools	teachers	students	student/ teacher ratio
Primary (age 7–13)	4,633	63,475	2,655,564	41.8
Secondary (age 14–19)	1,535	27,320	711,094	26.0
Voc., teacher tr.[9]	25	1,479	27,431	18.5
Higher[10]	28[9]	3,581	46,492	13.0

Health: physicians (1993) 1,551 (1 per 6,909 persons); hospital beds (1996) 22,975 (1 per 501 persons); infant mortality rate (1997) 72.6.
Food (1995): daily per capita caloric intake 1,965 (vegetable products 92%, animal products 8%); 82% of FAO recommended minimum requirement.

Military

Total active duty personnel (1997): 39,000 (army 89.7%, air force 10.3%). *Military expenditure as percentage of GNP* (1995): 4.0% (world 2.8%); per capita expenditure U.S.$21.

[1]Includes 30 nonelective seats. [2]Preliminary results. [3]Does not take into consideration seasonal unemployment of communal workers; 1986–87. [4]Based on consumer price index. [5]Wage-earning workers only. [6]Less imputed bank service charges. [7]Excludes gold sales and reexports. [8]Air Zimbabwe only. [9]1992. [10]Includes postsecondary vocational and teacher training at the higher level.

Comparative National Statistics

World and regional summaries

region/bloc	area and population, 1997						gross national product, 1995						labour force, 1990		
	area		population			population projection, 2010	total ('000,000 U.S.$)	% agriculture	% industry	% services	growth rate, 1990–95	GNP per capita (U.S.$)	total ('000)	% male	% female
	square miles	square kilometres	total	per sq mi	per sq km										
World	52,428,930	135,790,300	5,818,382,000	111.0	42.8	6,801,571,000	27,787,440	5	32	63	1.9	4,890	2,353,806	63.8	36.2
Africa	11,716,720	30,346,090	736,241,000	62.8	24.3	980,017,000	462,580	19	33	49	0.9	650	242,784	65.6	34.4
Central Africa	2,552,970	6,612,160	86,837,000	34.0	13.1	124,260,000	26,350	33	33	34	−3.5	320	26,428	64.7	35.3
East Africa	2,473,640	6,406,680	227,627,000	92.0	35.5	292,612,000	53,910	33	23	43	1.6	240	85,082	58.8	41.2
North Africa	3,287,810	8,515,370	166,579,000	50.7	19.6	215,873,000	173,120	15	34	50	1.1	1,140	40,016	84.6	15.4
Southern Africa	1,032,300	2,673,660	48,714,000	47.2	18.2	54,143,000	140,970	5	39	56	0.8	2,980	14,532	64.3	35.7
West Africa	2,370,000	6,138,220	206,484,000	87.1	33.6	293,129,000	68,230	37	23	40	1.8	330	76,726	63.8	36.2
Americas	16,247,310	42,080,380	784,284,000	48.3	18.6	908,088,000	9,269,180	3	27	70	2.7	12,010	293,723	66.5	33.5
Anglo-America[3]	8,304,760	21,509,250	298,251,000	35.9	13.9	333,180,000	7,676,610	2	26	72	2.5	26,210	135,438	58.7	41.3
Canada	3,849,670	9,970,610	30,287,000	7.9	3.1	35,065,000	573,700	3	32	66	1.8	19,380	13,360	60.2	39.8
United States	3,614,980	9,362,750	267,839,000	74.1	28.6	297,980,000	7,100,010	2	26	73	2.6	26,980	122,005	58.6	41.4
Latin America	7,942,550	20,571,130	486,033,000	61.2	23.6	574,908,000	1,592,570	10	33	57	3.2	3,320	158,285	73.1	26.9
Caribbean	90,740	234,980	35,624,000	392.6	151.6	40,787,000	85,780	8	36	57	2.0	2,390	13,813	66.9	33.1
Central America	202,240	523,820	33,774,000	167.0	64.5	44,841,000	45,240	19	21	60	4.9	1,380	9,520	78.5	21.5
Mexico	756,070	1,958,200	94,275,000	124.7	48.1	112,891,000	304,600	6	24	70	1.1	3,320	30,487	72.9	27.1
South America	6,893,500	17,854,130	322,360,000	46.8	18.1	376,389,000	1,156,950	11	35	54	3.9	3,630	104,465	73.6	26.4
Andean Group	2,110,450	5,466,100	117,635,000	55.7	21.5	143,789,000	271,720	9	35	56	4.6	2,360	34,715	75.6	24.4
Brazil	3,300,170	8,547,400	159,691,000	48.4	18.7	179,995,000	579,790	14	37	49	2.7	3,640	55,026	72.6	27.4
Other South America	1,482,880	3,840,630	45,034,000	30.4	11.7	52,605,000	305,440	7	31	63	5.5	6,930	14,724	72.4	27.6
Asia	12,312,440	31,888,980	3,539,603,000	287.5	111.0	4,125,315,000	8,463,060	8	39	53	2.9	2,460	1,464,452	64.5	35.5
Eastern Asia	4,546,960	11,776,530	1,454,696,000	319.9	123.5	1,593,702,000	6,580,200	5	41	55	2.7	4,620	775,590	57.4	42.6
China	3,696,120	9,572,900	1,227,740,000	332.2	128.3	1,348,957,000	744,890	21	48	31	12.8	620	669,693	56.7	43.3
Japan	145,880	377,820	126,110,000	864.5	333.8	130,344,000	4,963,590	2	40	58	1.0	39,640	62,202	62.1	37.9
South Korea	38,330	99,270	45,628,000	1,190.4	459.6	49,683,000	435,140	7	44	49	7.2	9,700	18,664	66.2	33.8
Other Eastern Asia	666,630	1,726,540	55,218,000	82.8	32.0	64,718,000	436,580	3	30	67	5.8	8,110	25,031	58.8	41.2
South Asia	1,938,850	5,021,590	1,294,088,000	667.5	257.7	1,571,113,000	439,410	29	28	43	4.4	350	411,136	77.4	22.6
India	1,222,240	3,165,600	967,613,000	791.7	305.7	1,155,830,000	319,660	29	29	41	4.6	340	322,944	74.8	25.2
Pakistan	307,370	796,100	136,183,000	443.1	171.1	176,400,000	59,990	23	23	54	4.6	460	33,698	87.5	12.5
Other South Asia	409,240	1,059,890	190,292,000	465.0	179.5	238,883,000	59,760	34	24	42	3.0	330	54,494	86.2	13.8
Southeast Asia	1,735,530	4,495,010	494,312,000	284.8	110.0	592,057,000	643,190	16	38	46	7.2	1,350	189,297	63.0	37.0
ASEAN	1,312,630	3,399,710	431,988,000	329.1	127.1	512,051,000	602,010	13	39	47	7.3	1,440	164,976	63.2	36.8
Non-ASEAN	422,900	1,095,300	62,324,000	147.4	56.9	80,006,000	41,180	60	10	30	5.8	690	24,321	62.2	37.8
Southwest Asia	4,091,100	10,595,850	296,507,000	72.5	28.0	385,443,000	800,260	14	36	49	1.1	2,770	88,429	69.4	30.6
Central Asia	1,545,720	4,003,400	55,562,000	35.9	13.9	66,912,000	53,390	21	32	47	−9.7	990	20,728	54.8	45.2
Gulf Cooperation Council	1,031,300	2,671,040	26,907,000	26.1	10.1	39,897,000	227,850	4	51	45	3.0	8,600	6,511	91.7	8.3
Iran	635,240	1,645,260	62,305,000	98.1	37.9	78,567,000	174,700	25	35	41	4.6	2,730	15,253	82.0	18.0
Other Southwest Asia	878,840	2,276,150	151,733,000	172.7	66.7	200,067,000	344,320	15	28	57	0.6	2,390	45,936	68.7	31.3
Europe	8,868,690	22,969,800	728,936,000	82.2	31.7	737,125,000	9,187,630	3	32	65	0.3	12,630	340,666	57.1	42.9
Eastern Europe	7,437,210	19,262,290	342,078,000	46.0	17.8	337,378,000	765,570	10	37	53	−7.9	2,230	171,080	50.6	49.4
Russia	6,592,850	17,075,400	147,231,000	22.3	8.6	140,579,000	331,950	7	36	57	−9.8	2,240	72,286	47.6	52.4
Ukraine	233,090	603,700	51,150,000	219.4	84.7	50,320,000	84,080	18	42	41	−14.3	1,630	25,401	48.0	52.0
Other Eastern Europe	611,270	1,538,190	143,697,000	235.1	90.8	146,479,000	349,540	11	36	53	−3.6	2,450	73,393	54.4	45.6
Western Europe	1,431,490	3,707,530	386,858,000	270.3	104.3	399,747,000	8,422,060	2	31	66	1.3	21,900	169,586	63.6	36.4
European Union (EU)	1,249,620	3,236,490	374,247,000	299.5	115.6	386,473,000	7,980,010	2	31	66	1.3	21,450	163,771	63.6	36.4
France	210,030	543,970	58,616,000	279.1	107.8	61,870,000	1,451,050	3	30	68	1.0	24,990	25,404	60.1	39.9
Germany	137,850	357,020	82,143,000	595.9	230.1	85,613,000	2,252,340	1	31	69	1.5	27,510	38,981	60.7	39.3
Italy	116,340	301,320	57,511,000	494.3	190.9	57,617,000	1,088,090	3	32	66	1.0	19,020	23,339	68.1	31.9
Spain	195,360	505,990	39,323,000	201.3	77.7	39,917,000	532,350	3	32	65	1.1	13,580	14,456	75.5	24.5
United Kingdom	94,250	244,110	58,919,000	625.1	241.4	60,395,000	1,094,730	2	32	66	1.4	18,700	27,766	61.4	38.6
Other EU	495,790	1,284,100	77,735,000	156.8	60.5	81,061,000	1,561,450	4	32	64	1.3	20,220	33,825	63.4	36.6
Non-EU	181,850	471,060	12,611,000	69.3	26.8	13,274,000	442,050	3	33	64	1.1	35,430	5,815	61.9	38.1
Oceania	3,283,800	8,505,070	29,318,000	8.9	3.4	34,026,000	404,990	4	29	66	3.6	14,190	12,181	63.0	37.0
Australia	2,966,150	7,682,300	18,508,000	6.2	2.4	20,830,000	337,910	3	30	67	3.5	18,720	7,963	61.9	38.1
Pacific Ocean Islands	317,650	822,770	10,810,000	34.0	13.1	13,196,000	67,080	10	26	64	3.9	6,400	4,218	65.0	35.0

[1]Refers only to the outstanding long-term external public and publicly guaranteed debt of the 136 countries that report under the World Bank's Debtor Reporting System (DRS). [2]World total contains

Africa

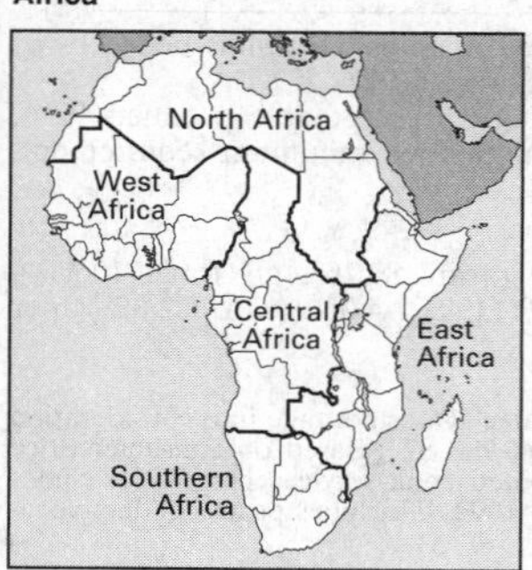

Americas

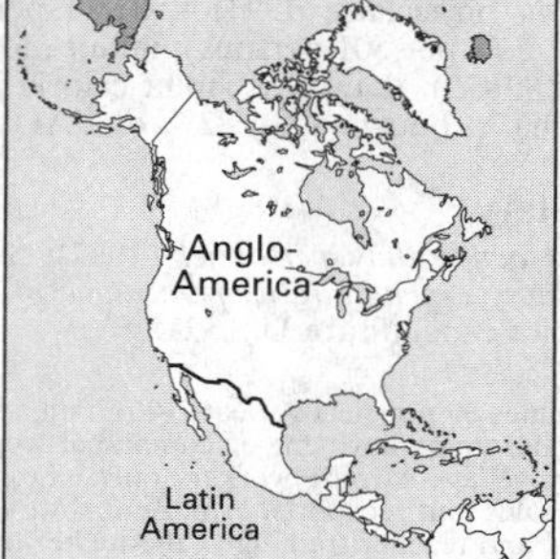

Asia

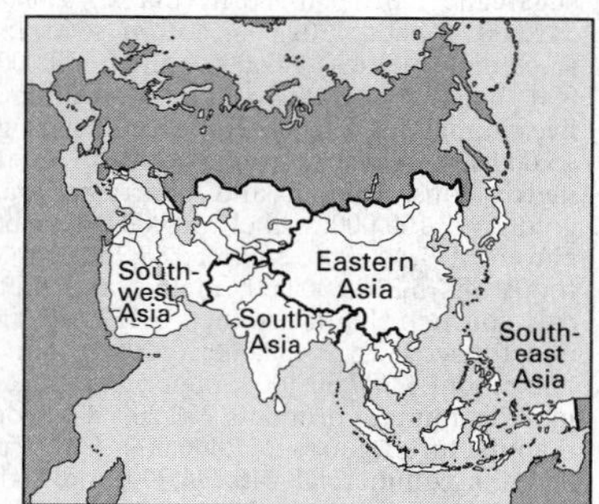

economic indicators							social indicators (latest)								region/bloc
pop. per 1,000 ha of arable land, 1995	electricity consump-tion (kW-hr per capita), 1995	trade ('000,000 U.S.$), 1995			debt ('000,000 U.S.$), 1995[1]		life expec-tancy (years)		health			food (% FAO recom-mended minimum), 1995	literacy (%)		
		imports (c.i.f.)	exports[2] (f.o.b.)	balance[2]	total	% of GNP	male	female	pop. per doctor	infant mor-tality per 1,000 births	pop. having safe water (%)		male	female	
4,160	2,296	5,432,210	5,265,800[2]	−166,410[2]	1,338,327	26.9	64.1	68.4	710	56.4	67	116	83.7	71.0	World
4,040	509	136,690	119,120	−17,570	252,041	81.0	53.2	56.2	2,570	85.5	53	104	65.9	45.5	Africa
3,720	135	7,490	6,930	−560	38,451	145.9	50.4	53.6	12,820	91.9	31	86	77.7	56.4	Central Africa
5,110	138	20,930	16,820	−4,110	45,126	91.9	47.9	50.7	12,340	98.9	42	86	65.4	44.1	East Africa
4,350	684	52,340	46,890	−5,450	101,707	63.4	63.2	66.1	880	55.8	76	125	64.8	40.1	North Africa
2,840	3,992	30,830	26,390	−4,440	1,530	22.0	61.3	66.9	1,690	68.0	68	115	81.6	80.0	Southern Africa
3,510	127	25,110	22,080	−3,020	65,228	95.6	49.9	52.9	6,300	89.6	52	103	58.4	37.5	West Africa
2,070	6,053	1,317,370	1,240,170	−77,200	377,972	24.7	67.7	74.6	510	31.1	86	125	91.3	89.9	Americas
1,270	13,095	1,005,870	968,590	−37,280	—	—	72.8	79.1	370	7.4	91	134	96.1	95.7	Anglo-America[3]
650	17,047	187,040	171,440	−15,600	—	—	74.6	81.0	470	6.1	100	116	96.6	96.6	Canada
1,420	12,663	817,790	796,040	−21,740	—	—	72.6	78.9	370	7.5	90	136	95.7	95.3	United States
3,420	1,671	311,500	271,570	−39,920	377,972	24.7	64.7	71.7	660	39.8	82	118	87.8	85.6	Latin America
5,750	1,485	29,740	22,450	−7,290	10,273	41.0	68.5	72.9	480	48.9	73	104	83.8	83.0	Caribbean
4,660	608	33,030	31,810	−1,220	23,721	52.5	67.3	72.3	1,170	43.2	69	109	73.6	68.1	Central America
3,550	1,646	98,410	73,770	−24,640	94,027	30.9	69.5	75.5	620	31.0	87	135	91.8	87.4	Mexico
3,160	1,802	150,320	143,540	−6,780	249,951	21.6	62.5	70.4	670	41.9	83	115	88.4	87.0	South America
6,850	1,562	58,030	54,300	−3,720	84,068	30.9	67.9	73.3	870	31.8	82	107	92.6	88.7	Andean Group
2,910	1,954	58,910	53,940	−4,970	96,609	16.7	56.7	66.8	680	55.3	92	119	83.3	83.2	Brazil
1,510	1,877	33,390	35,300	+1,910	69,274	22.8	69.2	76.0	410	25.2	56	127	96.0	95.7	Other South America
7,320	1,095	1,600,280	1,478,430	−121,850	491,956	20.8	64.5	67.6	970	55.8	60	114	81.2	63.7	Asia
14,060	1,702	943,290	872,880	−70,410	95,127	12.8	69.1	73.1	620	34.5	53	117	91.4	77.0	Eastern Asia
13,100	839	138,820	157,600	+18,770	94,675	12.7	68.2	71.7	630	38.0	46	116	89.9	72.7	China
31,540	7,915	349,510	316,590	−32,920	—	—	77.0	83.6	540	4.2	95	123	100.0	100.0	Japan
25,100	4,567	150,370	129,140	−21,230	—	—	68.8	76.0	780	10.0	89	139	99.3	96.7	South Korea
13,750	4,153	304,590	269,550	−35,030	452	58.9	70.8	76.6	510	17.2	97	108	95.9	91.4	Other Eastern Asia
6,020	398	65,410	60,710	−4,700	128,556	30.2	59.3	60.5	2,330	74.3	63	106	62.4	35.5	South Asia
5,640	448	40,090	37,770	−2,330	79,725	24.9	59.1	60.3	2,170	71.1	63	108	65.5	37.7	India
6,170	441	12,150	11,530	−620	23,711	39.5	62.9	65.1	1,860	75.0	60	107	50.0	24.4	Pakistan
8,960	104	13,170	11,420	−1,750	25,120	54.4	57.7	58.3	5,300	87.9	68	92	53.5	30.9	Other South Asia
7,800	573	380,630	354,670	−25,960	160,716	26.5	64.0	68.0	2,530	48.3	62	118	91.8	83.3	Southeast Asia
8,880	644	375,850	350,320	−25,520	151,305	29.2	65.0	69.2	2,480	41.0	66	117	92.6	84.9	ASEAN
4,200	71	4,790	4,350	−440	9,411	10.7	57.0	60.2	2,970	86.0	35	119	86.0	71.6	Non-ASEAN
2,780	2,062	210,950	190,170	−20,790	107,558	18.5	65.7	70.1	590	47.1	83	123	86.7	72.4	Southwest Asia
1,390	2,837	11,800	11,760	−40	5,554	10.4	63.5	71.1	300	35.0	80	...	98.8	96.1	Central Asia
6,690	6,352	85,180	76,800	−8,380	2,563	24.2	70.6	74.0	620	22.4	91	118	73.8	55.8	Gulf Cooperation Council
3,530	1,190	13,780	12,480	−1,300	17,078	5.6	66.1	68.7	1,600	52.7	89	123	78.4	65.8	Iran
3,400	1,415	100,190	89,130	−11,070	82,363	38.3	65.3	69.8	650	53.6	79	125	87.8	68.1	Other Southwest Asia
2,430	5,558	2,289,900	2,272,610	−17,290	214,203	27.8	68.7	77.0	290	10.5	99	125	99.0	97.5	Europe
1,550	4,440	220,220	223,490	+3,270	214,051	28.0	62.6	73.3	280	16.1	98	117	99.1	96.6	Eastern Europe
1,130	5,661	43,320	56,910	+13,590	100,279	30.2	58.0	71.5	240	18.0	...	114	99.5	96.8	Russia
1,550	3,694	24,240	16,210	−8,040	6,585	7.8	63.6	74.0	220	14.1	97	...	99.5	97.4	Ukraine
2,510	3,449	152,660	150,380	−2,280	107,187	30.7	66.8	74.9	380	15.3	99	121	98.7	96.1	Other Eastern Europe
4,960	6,561	2,069,680	2,049,120	−20,560	153	3.4	74.0	80.4	310	5.6	100	131	98.9	98.2	Western Europe
4,890	6,295	1,951,430	1,919,590	−31,840	—	—	73.9	80.4	310	5.6	100	131	98.8	98.1	European Union (EU)
3,180	7,282	275,970	269,070	−6,910	—	—	73.7	81.8	360	4.9	100	142	98.9	98.7	France
6,900	6,615	445,020	438,920	−6,100	—	—	73.0	79.5	300	5.6	100	123	100.0	100.0	Germany
7,070	4,867	207,000	187,110	−19,900	—	—	74.1	80.5	190	6.0	100	137	97.8	96.4	Italy
2,570	4,312	121,870	115,130	−6,740	—	—	74.9	81.8	240	5.6	99	136	98.1	95.1	Spain
9,890	6,016	283,590	271,920	−11,670	—	—	74.4	79.7	640	6.2	100	125	100.0	100.0	United Kingdom
4,630	7,503	617,990	637,450	+19,460	—	—	74.2	80.1	340	5.6	100	131	97.9	97.2	Other EU
8,810	14,651	118,240	129,530	+11,290	153	3.4	75.1	81.2	310	4.9	100	121	99.9	99.9	Non-EU
570	7,524	87,970	75,410	−12,550	2,154	27.4	71.8	76.9	470	23.5	85	116	96.3	94.0	Oceania
370	9,706	67,670	57,590	−10,080	—	—	75.4	81.1	400	5.7	95	115	99.5	99.5	Australia
5,150	3,887	20,300	17,820	−2,480	2,154	27.4	65.8	69.6	710	40.4	65	116	89.8	82.7	Pacific Ocean Islands

U.S.$80,060,000,000 undistributable by continent or region. [3]Anglo-America includes Canada, the United States, Greenland, Bermuda, and St. Pierre and Miquelon.

Europe

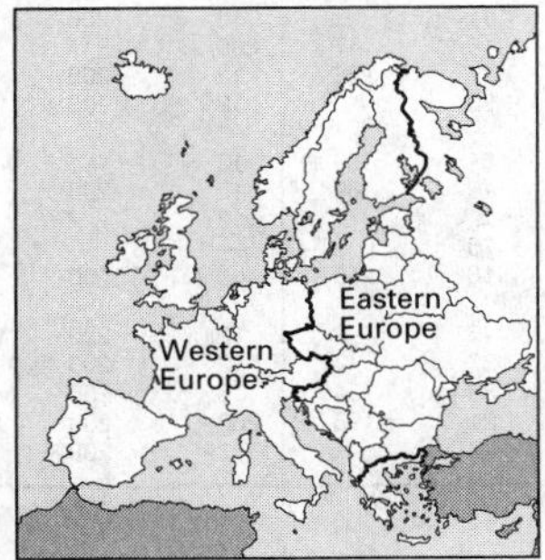

Eastern Europe

Oceania

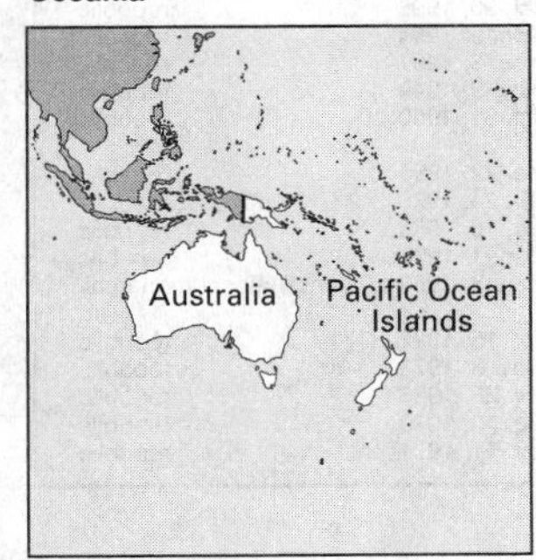

Government and international organizations

This table summarizes principal facts about the governments of the countries of the world, their branches and organs, the topmost layers of local government constituting each country's chief administrative subdivisions, and the participation of their central governments in the principal intergovernmental organizations of the world.

In this table "date of independence" may refer to a variety of circumstances. In the case of the newest countries, those that attained full independence after World War II, the date given is usually just what is implied by the heading—the date when the country, within its present borders, attained full sovereignty over both its internal and external affairs. In the case of longer established countries, the choice of a single date may be somewhat more complicated, and grounds for the use of several different dates often exist. The reader should refer to *Macropædia* and *Micropædia* articles on national histories and relevant historical acts. In cases of territorial annexation or dissolution, the date given here refers either to the final act of union of a state composed of smaller entities or to the final act of separation from a larger whole (*e.g.,* the separation of Bangladesh from Pakistan in 1971).

The date of the current, or last, constitution is in some ways a less complicated question, but governments sometimes do not, upon taking power, either adhere to existing constitutional forms or trouble to terminate the previous document and legitimize themselves by the installation of new constitutional forms. Often, however, the desire to legitimize extraconstitutional political activity by associating it with existing forms of long precedent leads to partial or incomplete modification, suspension, or abrogation of a constitution, so that the actual day-to-day conduct of government may be largely unrelated to the provisions of a constitution still theoretically in force. When a date in this column is given in italics, it refers to a document that has been suspended, abolished by extraconstitutional action, or modified extensively.

The characterizations adopted under "type of government" represent a compromise between the forms provided for by the national constitution and the more pragmatic language that a political scientist might adopt to describe these same systems. For an explanation of the application of these terms in the Britannica World Data, *see* the Glossary at page 533.

The positions denoted by the terms "chief of state" and "head of government" are usually those identified with those functions by the constitution. The duties of the chief of state may range from largely ceremonial responsibilities, with little or no authority over the day-to-day conduct of government, to complete executive authority as the effective head of government. In certain countries, an official of a political party or a revolutionary figure outside the constitutional structure may exercise the powers of both positions.

Membership in the legislative house(s) of each country as given here includes all elected or appointed members, as well as ex officio members (those who by virtue of some other office or title are members of the body), whether voting or nonvoting. The legislature of a country with a unicameral system is shown as the upper house in this table.

The number of administrative subdivisions for each country is listed down to the second level. A single country may, depending on its size, complexity, and historical antecedents, have as many as five levels of administrative subordination or it may have none at all. Each level of subordination may have several kinds of subdivisions.

Government and international organizations

country	date of independence[a]	date of current or last constitution[b]	type of government	executive branch[c]		legislative branch[d]		admin. subdivisions		seaward claims	
				chief of state	head of government	upper house (members)	lower house (members)	first-order (number)	second-order (number)	territorial (nautical miles)	fishing/economic (nautical miles)
Afghanistan	Aug. 19, 1919	—	Islamic emirate	leader of the faithful[1]		...	...	32	298	—	—
Albania	Nov. 28, 1912	April 29, 1991[2]	republic	president	prime minister	155	—	26	*c.* 200	12	[3]
Algeria	July 5, 1962	Dec. 7, 1996[5]	republic	president	prime minister	144[6]	380	48	1,541	12	[7]
American Samoa	—	July 1, 1967	territory (U.S.)	U.S. president	governor	18	21	3	14	12	200
Andorra	Dec. 6, 1288	May 4, 1993	parl. coprincipality	[8]	head of govt.	28	—	7	...	—	—
Angola	Nov. 11, 1975	Aug. 27, 1992	republic	president[9]		220	—	18	163	20	200
Antigua and Barbuda	Nov. 1, 1981	Nov. 1, 1981	constitutional monarchy	British monarch	prime minister	17	17	30	—	12[10]	200[10]
Argentina	July 9, 1816	Aug. 24, 1994[11]	federal republic	president[12]		72	257	24	503	12	200
Armenia	Sept. 23, 1991	July 5, 1995[13]	republic	president	prime minister	190	—	11	...	—	—
Aruba	—	Jan. 1, 1986	overseas territory (Neth.)	Dutch monarch	[14]	21	—	...	...	12	200
Australia	Jan. 1, 1901	July 9, 1900	federal parl. state[16]	British monarch	prime minister	76	148	8	*c.* 900	12	200
Austria	Oct. 30, 1918	Oct. 1, 1920	federal republic	president	chancellor	64	183	9	99	—	—
Azerbaijan	Aug. 30, 1991	Nov. 12, 1995[13]	republic	president[9]		124[17]	—	2	...	...	...
Bahamas, The	July 10, 1973	July 10, 1973	constitutional monarchy	British monarch	prime minister	16	40	—	21	12	200
Bahrain	Aug. 15, 1971	June 1973	monarchy (emirate)	emir	prime minister	40[18]	—	[19]	—	12	[20]
Bangladesh	March 26, 1971	Dec. 16, 1972	republic	president	prime minister	330	—	6	64	12	200
Barbados	Nov. 30, 1966	Nov. 30, 1966	constitutional monarchy	British monarch	prime minister	21	28	—	—	12	200
Belarus	Aug. 25, 1991	Nov. 27, 1996[21]	republic	president[9]		64[21]	110[21]	...	...	—	—
Belgium	Oct. 4, 1830	May 5, 1993	fed. const. monarchy	monarch	prime minister	71[22]	150	[23]	589	12	[20]
Belize	Sept. 21, 1981	Sept. 21, 1981	constitutional monarchy	British monarch	prime minister	8	29	6	...	12[24]	200
Benin	Aug. 1, 1960	Dec. 2, 1990	republic	president[9]		83	—	12	78	200	200
Bermuda	—	June 8, 1968	colony (U.K.)	British monarch	[25]	11	40	11	—	12	200
Bhutan	March 24, 1910	—	[26]	king		152	—	20	...	—	—
Bolivia	Aug. 6, 1825	Feb. 2, 1967	republic	president		27	130	9	112	—	—
Bosnia and Herzegovina	March 3, 1992	Dec. 14, 1995[27]	federal republic	[28]	[29]	15	42	2	...	...	...
Botswana	Sept. 30, 1966	Sept. 30, 1966	republic	president		15[18]	46	19	...	—	—
Brazil	Sept. 7, 1822	Oct. 5, 1988	federal republic	president		81	513	27	4,974	12	200
Brunei	Jan. 1, 1984	*Sept. 29, 1959*	monarchy (sultanate)	sultan		21[18]	—	4	...	12	200
Bulgaria	Oct. 5, 1908	July 12, 1991	republic	president	prime minister	240	—	9	278	12	200
Burkina Faso	Aug. 5, 1960	June 11, 1991	republic	president	prime minister	178[18]	111	30	109	—	—
Burundi	July 1, 1962	*March 13, 1992*	republic[31]	president[9]		81	—	15	122	—	—
Cambodia	Nov. 9, 1953	Sept. 24, 1993	constitutional monarchy	king	[32]	120	—	23	...	12	200
Cameroon	Jan. 1, 1960	Jan. 18, 1996	republic	president	prime minister	180	—	10	58	50	[3]
Canada	July 1, 1867	April 17, 1982	federal parl. state[16]	Canadian GG[33]	prime minister	104	301	12	...	12	200
Cape Verde	July 5, 1975	Sept. 25, 1992	republic	president	prime minister	72	—	16	...	12[10]	200[10]
Central African Republic	Aug. 13, 1960	Jan. 14, 1995	republic	president	prime minister	85	—	17	66	—	—
Chad	Aug. 11, 1960	April 1996	republic	president	prime minister	125	—	14	53	—	—
Chile	Sept. 18, 1810	March 11, 1981	republic	president		47	120	13	51	12	200
China	1523 BC	Dec. 4, 1982	people's republic	president	premier SC	2,978	—	31	334	12	[3]
Colombia	July 20, 1810	July 5, 1991	republic	president		102	165	26	1,011	12	200
Comoros	July 6, 1975	Oct. 20, 1996[13]	republic[31]	president		—	—	3[34]	7	12[10]	200[10]
Congo, Dem. Rep. of the	June 30, 1960	*April 9, 1994*	republic[31]	president		(738)	—	11	...	12	200
Congo, Rep. of the	Aug. 15, 1960	Nov. 3, 1997[2]	republic[31]	president		...	...	16	47	200	[3]
Costa Rica	Sept. 15, 1821	Nov. 9, 1949	republic	president		57	—	7	82	12	200
Côte d'Ivoire	Aug. 7, 1960	Oct. 31, 1960	republic	president	prime minister	175	—	50	...	12	200
Croatia	June 25, 1991	Dec. 22, 1990	republic	president	prime minister	68	127	21	489	12	...
Cuba	May 20, 1902	Feb. 24, 1976	socialist republic	president		589	—	15	169	12	200
Cyprus[36]	Aug. 16, 1960	Aug. 16, 1960	republic	president		56[37]	—	...	...	12	[3]
Czech Republic	Jan. 1, 1993	Jan. 1, 1993	republic	president	prime minister	81	200	75	...	—	—
Denmark	*c.* 800	June 5, 1953	constitutional monarchy	monarch	prime minister	179	—	16	275	3	200
Djibouti	June 27, 1977	Sept. 15, 1992	republic	president		65	—	5	9	12	200
Dominica	Nov. 3, 1978	Nov. 3, 1978	republic	president	prime minister	32	—	37	—	12	200
Dominican Republic	Feb. 27, 1844	Nov. 28, 1966	republic	president		30	120	30	154	6	200
Ecuador	May 24, 1822	Aug. 10, 1979	republic	president		82	—	21	193	200	200
Egypt	Feb. 28, 1922	Sept. 11, 1971	republic	president	prime minister	454	—	27	...	12[38]	200[38]

Finally, in the second half of the table are listed the memberships each country maintains in the principal international intergovernmental organizations of the world. This part of the table may also be utilized to provide a complete membership list for each of these organizations as of Dec. 1, 1997.

Notes for the column headings

a. The date may also be either that of the organization of the present form of government or the inception of the present administrative structure (federation, confederation, union, etc.).
b. Constitutions whose dates are in italic type had been wholly or substantially suspended or abolished as of late 1997.
c. For abbreviations used in this column see the list on the facing page.
d. When a legislative body has been adjourned or otherwise suspended, figures in parentheses indicate the number of members in the legislative body as provided for in constitution or law.
e. Vatican City also a member.
f. States contributing funds to or receiving aid from UNICEF in 1997.
g. Palestine (Liberation Organization) also a member.

International organizations, conventions

ACP	African, Caribbean, and Pacific (Lomé IV) convention
ADB	Asian Development Bank
APEC	Asia-Pacific Economic Cooperation Council
CARICOM	Caribbean Community and Common Market
EU	The European Union
ECOWAS	Economic Community of West African States
EEC	European Economic Community
FAO	Food and Agriculture Org.
GCC	Gulf Cooperation Council
I-ADB	Inter-American Development Bank
IAEA	International Atomic Energy Agency
IBRD	International Bank for Reconstruction and Development
ICAO	International Civil Aviation Org.
ICJ	International Court of Justice
IDA	International Development Association
IDB	Islamic Development Bank
IFC	International Finance Corporation
ILO	International Labour Org.
IMF	International Monetary Fund
IMO	International Maritime Org.
ITU	International Telecommunication Union
LAS	League of Arab States
OAS	Organization of American States
OAU	Organization of African Unity
OPEC	Organization of Petroleum Exporting Countries
SPC	South Pacific Commission
UNCTAD	United Nations Conference on Trade and Development
UNESCO	United Nations Educational Scientific and Cultural Org.
UNICEF	United Nations Children's Fund
UNIDO	United Nations Industrial Development Org.
UPU	Universal Postal Union
WHO	World Health Org.
WIPO	World Intellectual Property Org.
WMO	World Meteorological Org.
WTO	World Trade Org.

Abbreviations used in the executive-branch column

EC	Executive Council
FC	Federal Council
GG	Governor-General
GPC	General People's Committee
PC	People's Council
PNA	Palestine National Authority
PRC	Provisional Ruling Council
SC	State Council
SPDC	State Peace and Development Council

membership in international organizations																																					country
United Nations (date of admission)	UN organs★ and affiliated intergovernmental organizations																				Commonwealth of Nations	regional multipurpose						economic									
	UNCTAD★[e]	UNICEF★[f]	ICJ★	FAO	IAEA[e]	IBRD	ICAO	IDA	IFC	ILO	IMF	IMO	ITU[e]	UNESCO	UNIDO	UPU[e]	WHO	WIPO[e]	WMO	WTO		EU	GCC	LAS[g]	OAS	OAU	SPC	ACP	ADB	APEC	CARICOM	ECOWAS	EEC	I-ADB	IDB[g]	OPEC	
1946	●	●	●	●	●	●	●	●	●	●	●		●	●	●	●	●		●										●						●		Afghanistan
1955	●	●	●	●	●	●	●	●	●	●	●	●	●	●	●	●	●	●	●	●[4]															●		Albania
1962	●	●	●	●	●	●	●	●	●	●	●	●	●	●	●	●	●	●	●	●[4]				●		●									●	●	Algeria
—																●											●										American Samoa
1993	●												●	●			●	●		●[4]																	Andorra
1976	●	●	●	●		●	●	●	●	●	●	●	●	●	●	●	●	●	●	●						●		●									Angola
1981	●	●	●	●		●	●		●	●	●	●	●	●		●	●	●	●	●	●				●			●			●						Antigua and Barbuda
1945	●	●	●	●	●	●	●	●	●	●	●	●	●	●	●	●	●	●	●	●					●									●			Argentina
1992	●	●		●	●	●	●	●	●	●	●		●	●	●	●	●	●	●	●[4]																	Armenia
—														●[15]		●																					Aruba
1945	●	●	●	●	●	●	●	●	●	●	●	●	●	●	●	●	●	●	●	●	●						●		●	●							Australia
1955	●	●	●	●	●	●	●	●	●	●	●	●	●	●	●	●	●	●	●	●		●							●				●	●			Austria
1992	●	●		●		●	●	●	●	●	●	●	●	●	●	●	●	●	●	●[4]															●		Azerbaijan
1973	●	●	●	●		●	●		●	●	●	●	●	●	●	●	●	●	●		●				●			●			●			●			Bahamas, The
1971	●	●	●	●		●	●		●	●	●	●	●	●	●	●	●		●	●			●	●											●		Bahrain
1974	●	●	●	●	●	●	●	●	●	●	●	●	●	●	●	●	●	●	●	●	●								●						●		Bangladesh
1966	●	●	●	●		●	●		●	●	●	●	●	●	●	●	●	●	●	●	●				●			●			●			●			Barbados
1945	●	●			●	●	●		●	●	●		●	●	●	●	●	●	●	●[4]																	Belarus
1945	●	●	●	●	●	●	●	●	●	●	●	●	●	●	●	●	●	●	●	●		●							●				●	●			Belgium
1981	●	●	●	●		●	●	●	●	●	●	●	●	●	●	●	●		●	●	●				●			●			●			●			Belize
1960	●	●	●	●		●	●	●	●	●	●	●	●	●	●	●	●	●	●	●						●		●				●			●		Benin
—																●																					Bermuda
1971	●	●	●	●		●	●	●			●		●	●	●	●	●	●											●								Bhutan
1945	●	●	●	●	●	●	●	●	●	●	●	●	●	●	●	●	●	●	●	●					●									●			Bolivia
1992	●	●		●		●[30]	●			●	●	●	●	●	●	●	●	●																			Bosnia and Herzegovina
1966	●	●	●	●		●	●	●	●	●	●		●	●	●	●	●		●	●	●					●		●									Botswana
1945	●	●	●	●	●	●	●	●	●	●	●	●	●	●	●	●	●	●	●	●					●									●			Brazil
1984	●		●				●				●	●	●			●	●	●	●	●	●									●					●		Brunei
1955	●	●	●	●	●	●	●	●	●	●	●	●	●	●	●	●	●	●	●	●																	Bulgaria
1960	●	●	●	●		●	●	●	●	●	●	●	●	●	●	●	●	●	●	●						●		●				●			●		Burkina Faso
1962	●	●	●	●		●	●	●	●	●	●		●	●	●	●	●	●	●	●						●		●									Burundi
1955	●	●	●	●	●	●	●	●		●	●	●	●	●	●	●	●		●	●[4]									●								Cambodia
1960	●	●	●	●	●	●	●	●	●	●	●	●	●	●	●	●	●	●	●	●	●					●		●							●		Cameroon
1945	●	●	●	●	●	●	●	●	●	●	●	●	●	●	●	●	●	●	●	●	●				●				●	●				●			Canada
1975	●	●	●	●		●	●	●	●	●	●	●	●	●	●	●	●		●							●		●				●					Cape Verde
1960	●	●	●	●		●	●	●	●	●	●		●	●	●	●	●	●	●	●						●		●									Central African Republic
1960	●	●	●	●		●	●	●	●	●	●		●	●	●	●	●	●	●	●						●		●							●		Chad
1945	●	●	●	●	●	●	●	●	●	●	●	●	●	●	●	●	●	●	●	●					●					●				●			Chile
1945	●	●	●	●	●	●	●	●	●	●	●	●	●	●	●	●	●	●	●	●[4]								●	●	●							China
1945	●	●	●	●	●	●	●	●	●	●	●	●	●	●	●	●	●	●	●	●					●									●			Colombia
1975	●	●	●	●		●	●	●	●	●	●	●	●	●	●	●	●		●					●		●		●							●		Comoros
1960	●	●	●	●	●	●	●	●	●	●	[35]	●	●	●	●	●	●	●	●	●						●		●									Congo, Dem. Rep. of the
1960	●	●	●	●		●	●	●	●	●	●	●	●	●	●	●	●	●	●	●						●		●									Congo, Rep. of the
1945	●	●	●	●	●	●	●	●	●	●	●	●	●	●	●	●	●	●	●	●					●									●			Costa Rica
1960	●	●	●	●	●	●	●	●	●	●	●	●	●	●	●	●	●	●	●	●						●		●				●					Côte d'Ivoire
1992	●	●		●	●	●	●	●	●	●	●	●	●	●	●	●	●	●	●	●[4]														●			Croatia
1945	●	●	●	●	●		●			●		●	●	●	●	●	●	●	●	●					●[35]												Cuba
1960	●	●	●	●	●	●	●	●	●	●	●	●	●	●	●	●	●	●	●	●	●												●[15]				Cyprus[36]
1993	●	●		●	●	●	●	●	●	●	●	●	●	●	●	●	●	●	●	●																	Czech Republic
1945	●	●	●	●	●	●	●	●	●	●	●	●	●	●	●	●	●	●	●	●		●							●				●	●			Denmark
1977	●	●	●	●		●	●	●	●	●	●	●	●	●	●	●	●		●	●				●		●		●							●		Djibouti
1978	●	●	●	●		●	●	●	●	●	●	●		●	●	●	●		●	●	●				●			●			●						Dominica
1945	●	●	●	●	●	●	●	●	●	●	●	●	●	●	●	●	●		●	●					●			●			●[4]			●			Dominican Republic
1945	●	●	●	●	●	●	●	●	●	●	●	●	●	●	●	●	●	●	●	●					●									●			Ecuador
1945	●	●	●	●	●	●	●	●	●	●	●	●	●	●	●	●	●	●	●	●				●		●									●		Egypt

Government and international organizations (continued)

country	date of independence[a]	date of current or last constitution[b]	type of government	executive branch[c]		legislative branch[d]		admin. subdivisions		seaward claims	
				chief of state	head of government	upper house (members)	lower house (members)	first-order (number)	second-order (number)	territorial (nautical miles)	fishing/economic (nautical miles)
El Salvador	Jan. 30, 1841	Dec. 20, 1983	republic	—president—		84	—	14	262	200	200
Equatorial Guinea	Oct. 12, 1968	Nov. 16, 1991[13]	republic	president	prime minister	80	—	7	18	12	200
Eritrea	May 24, 1993	May 23, 1997[39]	republic[31]	—president—		150	—	6	...	...	...
Estonia	Aug. 20, 1991	July 3, 1992	republic	president	prime minister	101	—	15	198	12	...
Ethiopia	c. 1000 BC	Aug. 21, 1995[40]	republic	president	prime minister	117	548	10	...	—	—
Faroe Islands	—	April 1, 1948	part of Danish realm	Danish monarch	[41]	32	—	7	50	3	200
Fiji	Oct. 10, 1970	[42]	republic	president	prime minister	34	70	4	15	12[10]	200[10]
Finland	Dec. 6, 1917	July 17, 1919	republic	president	prime minister	200	—	6	20	12[43]	12
France	August 843	Oct. 4, 1958	republic	president	prime minister	321	577	22	96	12	200
French Guiana	—	Feb. 28, 1983	overseas dept. (Fr.)	French president	[44]	19	31	2	22	12	200
French Polynesia	—	Sept. 6, 1984	overseas territory (Fr.)	French president	[45]	41	—	5	48	12	200
Gabon	Aug. 17, 1960	March 26, 1991	republic	president	prime minister	91	120	9	37	12	200
Gambia, The	Feb. 18, 1965	Jan. 16, 1997	republic	—president—		49	—	7	45	12	200
Gaza Strip	—	May 4, 1994[46]	interim authority	—chairman PNA—		89	—	...	...	...	...
Georgia	April 9, 1991	Oct. 17, 1995	republic	—president—		235	—	13	67	...	...
Germany	May 5, 1955	May 23, 1949	federal republic	president	chancellor	68	672	16	29	12[38]	200
Ghana	March 6, 1957	Jan. 7, 1993	republic	—president—		200	—	110	...	12	200
Gibraltar	—	May 23, 1969	colony (U.K.)	British monarch	governor	18	—	—	—	...	...
Greece	Feb. 3, 1830	June 11, 1975	republic	president	prime minister	300	—	14	53	6/10	[3]
Greenland	—	May 1, 1979	part of Danish realm	Danish monarch	[41]	31	—	18	...	3	200
Grenada	Feb. 7, 1974	Feb. 7, 1974	constitutional monarchy	British monarch	prime minister	13	15	9	...	12	200
Guadeloupe	—	Feb. 28, 1983	overseas dept. (Fr.)	French president	[44]	43	41	3	34	12	200
Guam	—	Aug. 1, 1950	territory (U.S.)	U.S. president	governor	21	—	...	—	12	...
Guatemala	Sept. 15, 1821	Jan. 14, 1986	republic	—president—		80	—	22	330	12	200
Guernsey	—	Jan. 1, 1949[47]	crown dependency (U.K.)	British monarch[48]	bailiff	60	—	1	2	...	...
Guinea	Oct. 2, 1958	Dec. 23, 1990[2]	republic	—president[49]—		114	—	7	...	12	200
Guinea-Bissau	Sept. 10, 1974	May 11, 1991	republic	president	prime minister	100	—	9	37	12	200
Guyana	May 26, 1966	Oct. 6, 1980	cooperative republic	—president—		65	—	10	71	12	200
Haiti	Jan. 1, 1804	March 29, 1987	republic	president	prime minister	27	83	9	41	12	200
Honduras	Nov. 5, 1838	Jan. 20, 1982	republic	—president—		128	—	18	292	12	200
Hong Kong	[50]	April 4, 1990[51]	[52]	—chief executive EC—		60	—	...	...	12	[3]
Hungary	Nov. 16, 1918	Oct. 18, 1989[2]	republic	president	prime minister	386	—	20	184	—	—
Iceland	June 17, 1944	June 17, 1944	republic	president	prime minister	63	—	169	—	12	200
India	Aug. 15, 1947	Jan. 26, 1950	federal republic	president	prime minister	245	545	32	506	12	200
Indonesia	Aug. 17, 1945	Aug. 17, 1945	republic	—president—		1,000	500	27	303	12[10]	200[10]
Iran	Oct. 7, 1906	Dec. 2–3, 1979	Islamic republic	—president[53]—		270	—	26	255	12	50[54]
Iraq	Oct. 3, 1932	Sept. 22, 1968[55]	republic	—president—		250	—	19[56]	96	12	[3]
Ireland	Dec. 6, 1921	Dec. 29, 1937	republic	president	prime minister	60	166	32	86	12	200
Isle of Man	—	1961[47]	crown dependency (U.K.)	British monarch[48]	chief minister	11	24	...	—	12[57]	...
Israel	May 14, 1948	June 1950[47]	republic	president	prime minister	120	—	6	15	12	[3]
Italy	March 17, 1861	Jan. 1, 1948	republic	president	prime minister	325	630	20	102	12	[3]
Jamaica	Aug. 6, 1962	Aug. 6, 1962	constitutional monarchy	British monarch	prime minister	21	60	13	—	12	200
Japan	c. 660 BC	May 3, 1947	constitutional monarchy	emperor	prime minister	252	500	47	3,233	12[58]	200
Jersey	—	Jan. 1, 1949[47]	crown dependency (U.K.)	British monarch[48]	bailiff	58	—	—	—	3	...
Jordan	May 25, 1946	Jan. 8, 1952	constitutional monarchy	—king[9]—		40	80	12	...	3	[3]
Kazakstan	Dec. 16, 1991	Sept. 6, 1995	republic	—president[9]—		47	67	18	218	—	—
Kenya	Dec. 12, 1963	Dec. 12, 1963	republic	—president—		202	—	8	40	12	200
Kiribati	July 12, 1979	July 12, 1979	republic	—president—		41	—	21	—	12[10]	200[10]
Korea, North	Sept. 9, 1948	April 19, 1992[59]	socialist republic	supreme commander	premier	687	—	13	172	12	200
Korea, South	Aug. 15, 1948	Feb. 25, 1988	republic	—president[9]—		299	—	15	193	12[60]	12
Kuwait	June 19, 1961	Nov. 16, 1962	const. mon. (emirate)	—emir[9]—		64	—	—	—	12	[3]
Kyrgyzstan	Aug. 31, 1991	May 5, 1993	republic	—president[9]—		70	35	7	89	—	—
Laos	Oct. 23, 1953	Aug. 15, 1991	republic	president	prime minister	85	—	18	114	—	—
Latvia	Aug. 21, 1991	Nov. 7, 1922	republic	president	prime minister	100	—	33	...	12	...
Lebanon	Nov. 26, 1941	Sept. 21, 1990	republic	president	prime minister	128	—	6	26	12	[3]
Lesotho	Oct. 4, 1966	April 2, 1993	constitutional monarchy	king	prime minister	33[18]	65	10	...	—	—
Liberia	July 26, 1847	Aug. 20, 1995[61]	republic	—president[62]—		26	64	...	...	200	[3]
Libya	Dec. 24, 1951	March 2, 1977	socialist state[63]	rev. leader	sec. GPC	760	—	13	c. 1,500	12[64]	[3]
Liechtenstein	July 12, 1806	Oct. 5, 1921	constitutional monarchy	prince	head of govt.	25	—	11	—	—	—
Lithuania	Sept. 6, 1991	Nov. 6, 1992	republic	president	prime minister	141	—	10	56	12	...
Luxembourg	May 10, 1867	Oct. 17, 1868	constitutional monarchy	grand duke	prime minister	21[18]	60	3	12	—	—
Macau	—	May 10, 1990	special terr. (Port.)[65]	—governor—		23	—	...	...	6	12
Macedonia	Nov. 17, 1991	Nov. 17, 1991	republic	president	prime minister	120	—	30	...	—	—
Madagascar	June 26, 1960	Sept. 18, 1992	republic	president	prime minister	138	—	6	113	12	200
Malaŵi	July 6, 1964	May 18, 1994	republic	—president—		177	—	3	24	—	—
Malaysia	Aug. 31, 1957	Aug. 31, 1957	fed. const. monarchy	paramount ruler	prime minister	70	192	15	131	12	200
Maldives	July 26, 1965	Nov. 11, 1968	republic	—president—		48	—	21	201	12[10]	[38]
Mali	Sept. 22, 1960	Feb. 25, 1992	republic	president	prime minister	147	—	9	55	—	—
Malta	Sept. 21, 1964	Dec. 13, 1974	republic	president	prime minister	69	—	3	67	12	25
Marshall Islands	Dec. 22, 1990	May 1, 1979	republic	—president—		12[18]	33	24	—	12[10]	200
Martinique	—	Feb. 28, 1983	overseas dept. (Fr.)	French president	[44]	45	41	3	34	12	200
Mauritania	Nov. 28, 1960	July 21, 1991	republic	—president[9]—		56	79	13	53	12	200
Mauritius	March 12, 1968	March 12, 1992	republic	president	prime minister	66	—	11	105	12	200
Mayotte	—	Dec. 24, 1976	terr. collectivity (Fr.)	French president	[66]	19	—	19	—	12	200
Mexico	Sept. 16, 1810	Feb. 5, 1917	federal republic	—president—		128	500	32	2,378	12	200
Micronesia	Dec. 22, 1990	Jan. 1, 1981	federal republic	—president—		14	—	4	...	12	200
Moldova	Aug. 27, 1991	Aug. 27, 1994	republic	president	prime minister	104	—	2	50	—	—
Monaco	Feb. 2, 1861	Dec. 17, 1962	constitutional monarchy	prince	min. of state	18	—	1	—	12	[3]
Mongolia	March 13, 1921	Feb. 12, 1992	republic	president	prime minister	76	—	22	299	—	—
Morocco	March 2, 1956	Oct. 7, 1996	constitutional monarchy	—king[9]—		255	303	...	62[67]	12	200
Mozambique	June 25, 1975	Nov. 30, 1990	republic	—president—		250	—	11	112	12	200
Myanmar (Burma)	Jan. 4, 1948	*Jan. 4, 1974*	republic	—chairman SPDC—		(492)	—	14	58	12	200
Namibia	March 21, 1990	March 21, 1990	republic	—president—		26	78	13	—	12	200
Nauru	Jan. 31, 1968	Jan. 31, 1968	republic	—president—		18	—	1	—	12	200
Nepal	Nov. 13, 1769	Nov. 9, 1990	constitutional monarchy	king	prime minister	60	205	14	75	—	—

membership in international organizations																																					country
United Nations (date of admission)	UN organs★ and affiliated intergovernmental organizations																			Commonwealth of Nations	regional multipurpose						economic										
	UNCTAD★[e]	UNICEF★[f]	ICJ★	FAO	IAEA[e]	IBRD	ICAO	IDA	IFC	ILO	IMF	IMO	ITU[e]	UNESCO	UNIDO	UPU[e]	WHO	WIPO[e]	WMO	WTO		EU	GCC	LAS[g]	OAS	OAU	SPC	ACP	ADB	APEC	CARICOM	ECOWAS	EEC	I-ADB	IDB[g]	OPEC	
1945	•	•	•	•	•	•	•	•	•	•	•	•	•	•	•	•	•	•	•	•					•									•			El Salvador
1968	•	•	•	•		•	•	•	•	•	•	•	•	•	•	•	•									•		•									Equatorial Guinea
1993	•	•		•		•	•	•		•	•	•	•	•		•	•		•					•[30]		•											Eritrea
1991	•	•		•	•	•	•		•	•	•	•	•	•	•	•	•	•	•	•[4]																	Estonia
1945	•	•	•	•	•	•	•	•	•	•	•	•	•	•	•	•	•		•	•[4]						•		•									Ethiopia
—																•																					Faroe Islands
1970	•	•	•	•		•	•	•	•	•	•	•	•	•	•	•	•	•	•	•	•						•	•	•								Fiji
1955	•	•	•	•	•	•	•	•	•	•	•	•	•	•	•	•	•	•	•	•		•							•				•	•			Finland
1945	•	•	•	•	•	•	•	•	•	•	•	•	•	•	•	•	•	•	•	•		•					•		•				•	•			France
—																•																					French Guiana
—																•			•								•										French Polynesia
1960	•	•	•	•	•	•	•	•	•	•	•	•	•	•	•	•	•	•	•	•						•		•							•		Gabon
1965	•	•	•	•		•	•	•	•	•	•	•	•	•	•	•	•	•	•	•	•					•		•				•			•		Gambia, The
—		•														•																					Gaza Strip
1992	•	•		•		•	•	•	•	•	•	•	•	•	•	•	•			•[4]																	Georgia
1973	•	•	•	•	•	•	•	•	•	•	•	•	•	•	•	•	•	•	•	•		•							•				•	•			Germany
1957	•	•	•	•	•	•	•	•	•	•	•	•	•	•	•	•	•	•	•	•	•					•		•				•					Ghana
—		•														•																					Gibraltar
1945	•	•	•	•	•	•	•	•	•	•	•	•	•	•	•	•	•	•	•	•		•											•				Greece
—																•																					Greenland
1974	•	•	•	•		•	•	•	•	•	•		•	•	•	•	•			•	•				•			•			•						Grenada
—																•																					Guadeloupe
—																•											•										Guam
1945	•	•	•	•	•	•	•	•	•	•	•	•	•	•	•	•	•	•	•	•					•									•			Guatemala
—																•																					Guernsey
1958	•	•	•	•		•	•	•	•	•	•	•	•	•	•	•	•	•	•	•						•		•				•			•		Guinea
1974	•	•	•	•		•	•	•	•	•	•	•	•	•	•	•	•	•	•	•						•		•				•			•		Guinea-Bissau
1966	•	•	•	•		•	•	•	•	•	•	•	•	•	•	•	•	•	•	•	•				•			•			•			•			Guyana
1945	•	•	•	•	•	•	•	•	•	•	•	•	•	•	•	•	•	•	•	•					•			•			•			•			Haiti
1945	•	•	•	•		•	•	•	•	•	•	•	•	•	•	•	•	•	•	•					•									•			Honduras
—		•										•[15]				•			•	•									•	•							Hong Kong
1955	•	•	•	•	•	•	•	•	•	•	•	•	•	•	•	•	•	•	•	•																	Hungary
1946	•	•	•	•	•	•	•	•	•	•	•	•	•	•		•	•	•	•	•																	Iceland
1945	•	•	•	•	•	•	•	•	•	•	•	•	•	•	•	•	•	•	•	•	•								•								India
1950	•	•	•	•	•	•	•	•	•	•	•	•	•	•	•	•	•	•	•	•									•	•					•	•	Indonesia
1945	•	•	•	•	•	•	•	•	•	•	•	•	•	•	•	•	•		•																•	•	Iran
1945	•	•	•	•	•	•	•	•	•	•	•	•	•	•	•	•	•	•	•					•											•	•	Iraq
1955	•	•	•	•	•	•	•	•	•	•	•	•	•	•	•	•	•	•	•	•		•											•				Ireland
—																•																					Isle of Man
1949	•	•	•	•	•	•	•	•	•	•	•	•	•	•	•	•	•	•	•	•														•			Israel
1955	•	•	•	•	•	•	•	•	•	•	•	•	•	•	•	•	•	•	•	•		•							•				•	•			Italy
1962	•	•	•	•	•	•	•	•	•	•	•	•	•	•	•	•	•	•	•	•	•				•			•			•			•			Jamaica
1956	•	•	•	•	•	•	•	•	•	•	•	•	•	•	•	•	•	•	•	•									•	•				•			Japan
—																•																					Jersey
1955	•	•	•	•	•	•	•	•	•	•	•	•	•	•	•	•	•	•	•	•[4]				•											•		Jordan
1992	•	•			•	•	•	•	•	•	•	•	•	•		•	•	•	•	•[4]									•								Kazakstan
1963	•	•	•	•	•	•	•	•	•	•	•	•	•	•	•	•	•	•	•	•	•					•		•									Kenya
—		•				•	•	•	•		•		•	•		•	•				•						•	•	•								Kiribati
1991	•	•		•	•		•					•	•	•	•	•	•	•	•																		Korea, North
1991	•	•		•	•	•	•	•	•	•	•	•	•	•	•	•	•	•	•	•									•	•							Korea, South
1963	•	•	•	•	•	•	•	•	•	•	•	•	•	•	•	•	•		•	•			•	•											•	•	Kuwait
1992	•	•		•		•	•	•	•	•	•		•	•	•	•	•	•	•	•[4]									•						•		Kyrgyzstan
1955	•	•	•	•		•	•	•	•	•	•		•	•	•	•	•	•	•										•								Laos
1991	•	•		•		•	•	•	•	•	•	•	•	•		•	•	•	•	•[4]																	Latvia
1945	•	•	•	•	•	•	•	•	•	•	•	•	•	•	•	•	•	•	•					•											•		Lebanon
1966	•	•	•	•		•	•	•	•	•	•		•	•	•	•	•	•	•	•	•					•		•									Lesotho
1945	•	•	•	•	•	•	•	•	•	•	•	•	•	•	•	•	•	•	•							•		•				•					Liberia
1955	•	•	•	•	•	•	•	•	•	•	•	•	•	•	•	•	•	•	•					•		•									•	•	Libya
1990	•		•		•								•			•	•[4]	•		•																	Liechtenstein
1991	•	•		•	•	•	•		•	•	•		•	•	•	•	•	•	•	•[4]																	Lithuania
1945	•	•	•	•	•	•	•	•	•	•	•	•	•	•	•	•	•	•	•	•		•											•				Luxembourg
—				•								•[15]				•				•																	Macau
1993	•	•		•	•	•[30]	•	•	•	•	•	•	•	•	•	•	•	•	•	•[4]																	Macedonia
1960	•	•	•	•	•	•	•	•	•	•	•	•	•	•	•	•	•	•	•	•						•		•									Madagascar
1964	•	•	•	•		•	•	•	•	•	•	•	•	•	•	•	•	•	•	•	•					•		•									Malaŵi
1957	•	•	•	•	•	•	•	•	•	•	•	•	•	•	•	•	•	•	•	•	•								•	•					•		Malaysia
1965	•	•	•	•		•	•	•	•		•	•	•	•	•	•	•		•	•	•								•						•		Maldives
1960	•	•	•	•	•	•	•	•	•	•	•		•	•	•	•	•	•	•	•						•		•				•			•		Mali
1964	•	•	•	•		•	•			•	•	•	•	•	•	•	•	•	•	•	•												•[15]				Malta
1991	•	•		•		•	•	•	•		•					•[30]	•										•		•								Marshall Islands
—																•																					Martinique
1961	•	•	•	•		•	•	•	•	•	•	•	•	•	•	•	•	•	•	•				•		•		•				•			•		Mauritania
1968	•	•	•	•	•	•	•	•	•	•	•	•	•	•	•	•	•	•	•	•	•					•		•									Mauritius
—																•																					Mayotte
1945	•	•	•	•	•	•	•	•	•	•	•	•	•	•	•	•	•	•	•	•					•					•	•[4]			•			Mexico
1991	•	•				•	•	•	•		•		•			•[30]	•										•		•								Micronesia
1992	•	•	•	•		•	•	•		•	•		•	•	•	•	•	•		•[4]																	Moldova
1993	•	•			•		•				•	•	•	•		•	•	•																			Monaco
1961	•	•	•	•	•	•	•	•	•	•	•		•	•	•	•	•	•	•	•									•								Mongolia
1956	•	•	•	•	•	•	•	•	•	•	•	•	•	•	•	•	•	•	•	•				•											•		Morocco
1975	•	•	•	•		•	•	•	•	•	•	•	•	•	•	•	•		•	•	•					•		•									Mozambique
1948	•	•	•	•	•	•	•	•	•	•	•	•	•	•	•	•	•	•	•	•									•								Myanmar (Burma)
1990	•	•		•	•	•	•	•[30]	•	•	•		•	•	•	•	•	•	•	•	•					•		•									Namibia
—							•						•			•	•				•[68]						•		•								Nauru
1955	•	•	•	•		•	•	•	•	•	•	•	•	•	•	•	•		•	•[4]									•								Nepal

Government and international organizations (continued)

country	date of independence[a]	date of current or last constitution[b]	type of government	executive branch[c] chief of state	executive branch[c] head of government	legislative branch[d] upper house (members)	legislative branch[d] lower house (members)	admin. subdivisions first-order (number)	admin. subdivisions second-order (number)	seaward claims territorial (nautical miles)	seaward claims fishing/economic (nautical miles)
Netherlands, The	March 30, 1814	Feb. 17, 1983	constitutional monarchy	monarch	prime minister	75	150	12	633	12	200
Netherlands Antilles	—	Dec. 29, 1954	overseas territory (Neth.)	Dutch monarch	[14]	22	—	5	—	12	200
New Caledonia	—	Nov. 9, 1988	overseas territory (Fr.)	French president	[69]	54	—	3	33	12	200
New Zealand	Sept. 26, 1907	June 30, 1852[47]	constitutional monarchy	British monarch	prime minister	120	—	12	74	12	200
Nicaragua	April 30, 1838	Jan. 9, 1987	republic	president		93	—	17	145	200	200
Niger	Aug. 3, 1960	May 22, 1996	republic	president[9]		83	—	8	38	—	—
Nigeria	Oct. 1, 1960	*Oct. 1, 1979*	federal republic	chairman PRC		(91)	(593)	37	774	30	200
Northern Mariana Is.	—	Jan. 9, 1978	commonwealth (U.S.)	U.S. president	governor	9	18	4	—	12	200
Norway	June 7, 1905	May 17, 1814	constitutional monarchy	king	prime minister	165	—	19	435	4	200
Oman	Dec. 20, 1951	Nov. 6, 1996[70]	monarchy (sultanate)	sultan		82[18]	—	8	59	12	200
Pakistan	Aug. 14, 1947	Aug. 14, 1973	federal Islamic republic	president	prime minister	87	217	16[71]	...	12	200
Palau	Oct. 1, 1994	Jan. 1, 1981	republic	president		14	16	16	—	3	200
Panama	Nov. 3, 1903	May 20, 1983[72]	republic	president[73]		72	—	12	67	200	[3]
Papua New Guinea	Sept. 16, 1975	Sept. 16, 1975	constitutional monarchy	British monarch	prime minister	109	—	20	267	12[10]	200[10]
Paraguay	May 14, 1811	June 22, 1992	republic	president		45	80	18	217	—	—
Peru	July 28, 1821	Dec. 29, 1993	republic	president		120	—	[74]	...	200	200
Philippines	July 4, 1946	Feb. 11, 1987	republic	president		24	204[75]	16	77	...	200[10]
Poland	Nov. 10, 1918	Oct. 17, 1997	republic	president	prime minister	100	460	49	2,483	12	[76]
Portugal	c. 1140	April 25, 1976	republic	president	prime minister	230	—	20	305	12	200
Puerto Rico	—	July 25, 1952	commonwealth (U.S.)	U.S. president	governor	27[77]	51[77]	78	...	12	200
Qatar	Sept. 3, 1971	July 1970[55]	monarchy	emir[9]		35[18]	—	9	—	12	[78]
Réunion	—	Feb. 28, 1983	overseas dept. (Fr.)	French president	[44]	47	45	4	24	12	200
Romania	May 21, 1877	Dec. 13, 1991	republic	president	prime minister	143	343	41	...	12[38]	200[38]
Russia	Dec. 8, 1991	Dec. 24, 1993	federal republic	president	prime minister	178	450	89	1,863	12	...
Rwanda	July 1, 1962	May 5, 1995[79]	republic[31]	president[80]		70	—	11	...	—	—
St. Kitts and Nevis	Sept. 19, 1983	Sept. 19, 1983	constitutional monarchy	British monarch	prime minister	15	—	1	—	12	200
St. Lucia	Feb. 22, 1979	Feb. 22, 1979	constitutional monarchy	British monarch	prime minister	11	18	10	—	12	200
St. Vincent	Oct. 27, 1979	Oct. 27, 1979	constitutional monarchy	British monarch	prime minister	21	—	—	—	12	200
Samoa	Jan. 1, 1962	Oct. 28, 1960	[81]	head of state	prime minister	49	—	330[82]	—	12	200
San Marino	855	Oct. 8, 1600	republic	captains-regent (2)		60	—	9	—	—	—
São Tomé and Príncipe	July 12, 1975	Sept. 10, 1990	republic	president	prime minister	55	—	1	6	12[10]	200[10]
Saudi Arabia	Sept. 23, 1932	[83]	monarchy	king		90[18]	—	13	103	12	[3]
Senegal	Aug. 20, 1960	March 7, 1963	republic	president	prime minister	120	—	10	48	12[38]	200[38]
Seychelles	June 29, 1976	June 21, 1993	republic	president		33	—	...	...	12	200
Sierra Leone	April 27, 1961	*Oct. 1, 1991*	republic	president		(80)	—	4	12	200	[3]
Singapore	Aug. 9, 1965	June 3, 1959[47]	republic	president	prime minister	90	—	—	—	3	12
Slovakia	Jan. 1, 1993	Jan. 1, 1993	republic	president	prime minister	150	—	38	...	—	—
Slovenia	June 25, 1991	Dec. 23, 1991	republic	president	prime minister	40	90	147	...	...	...
Solomon Islands	July 7, 1978	July 7, 1978	constitutional monarchy	British monarch	prime minister	50	—	10	...	12[10]	200[10]
Somalia	July 1, 1960	July 1, 1960	republic	[84]		...	—	1	...	200	200
South Africa	May 31, 1910	Feb. 4, 1997	republic	president		90	400	9	360	12	200
Spain	1492	Dec. 29, 1978	constitutional monarchy	king	prime minister	257	350	19	50	12	200[85]
Sri Lanka	Feb. 4, 1948	Sept. 7, 1978	republic	president		225	—	...	...	12	200
Sudan, The	Jan. 1, 1956	*Oct. 10, 1985*	Islamic military regime	president		400	—	26	66	12	[3]
Suriname	Nov. 25, 1975	Nov. 25, 1987	republic	president		51	—	10	...	12	200
Swaziland	Sept. 6, 1968	*Sept. 6, 1968*	monarchy	king[9]		30[18]	65[18]	4	55	—	—
Sweden	before 836	Jan. 1, 1975	constitutional monarchy	king	prime minister	349	—	23	288	12	[20]
Switzerland	Sept. 22, 1499	May 29, 1874	federal state	president FC		46	200	26	2,973	—	—
Syria	April 17, 1946	March 14, 1973	republic	president		250	—	14	47	35	[3]
Taiwan	Oct. 25, 1945	Dec. 25, 1947[47]	republic	president	premier	334	164	2	25	24	200
Tajikistan	Sept. 9, 1991	Nov. 6, 1994	republic	president	prime minister	181	—	5	...	—	—
Tanzania	Dec. 9, 1961	April 25, 1977	republic	president		275	—	2	25	12	200
Thailand	1350	Oct. 11, 1997	constitutional monarchy	king	prime minister	260	393	76	711	12	200
Togo	April 27, 1960	Sept. 27, 1992[13]	republic	president	prime minister	81	—	5	21	30	200
Tonga	June 4, 1970	Nov. 4, 1875	constitutional monarchy[86]	monarch[87]		30	—	2	23	12	200
Trinidad and Tobago	Aug. 31, 1962	July 27, 1976	republic	president	prime minister	31	36	12	124	12[10]	200[10]
Tunisia	March 20, 1956	June 1, 1959	republic	president	prime minister	163	—	23	254	12	[3]
Turkey	Oct. 29, 1923	Nov. 7, 1982	republic	president	prime minister	550	—	76	829	12[88]	[20]
Turkmenistan	Oct. 27, 1991	May 18, 1992	republic	president PC		[50]	—	6	...	—	—
Tuvalu	Oct. 1, 1978	Oct. 1, 1986	constitutional monarchy	British monarch	prime minister	12	—	8	—	12[10]	200[10]
Uganda	Oct. 9, 1962	Oct. 8, 1995	republic[31]	president[9]		279	—	39	...	—	—
Ukraine	Aug. 24, 1991	June 28, 1996	republic	president	prime minister	450	—	27	485	12	200
United Arab Emirates	Dec. 2, 1971	Dec. 2, 1971	federation of emirates	president	prime minister	40[18]	—	7	—	12	200
United Kingdom	Oct. 14, 1066	[89]	constitutional monarchy	monarch	prime minister	1,197	659	...	...	12[57]	200
United States	July 4, 1776	March 4, 1789	federal republic	president		100	435	51	3,043	12	200
Uruguay	Aug. 25, 1828	Feb. 15, 1967	republic	president		31	99	19	...	200	200
Uzbekistan	Aug. 31, 1991	Dec. 8, 1992	republic	president	prime minister	250	—	13	...	...	...
Vanuatu	July 30, 1980	July 30, 1980	republic	president	prime minister	50	—	11	...	12[10]	200[10]
Venezuela	July 5, 1811	Jan. 23, 1961	federal republic	president		52	199	24	202	12	200
Vietnam	Sept. 2, 1945	April 15, 1992	socialist republic	president	prime minister	450	—	53	479	12	200
Virgin Islands (U.S.)	—	July 22, 1954	territory (U.S.)	U.S. president	governor	15	—	1	—	12	200
West Bank	—	May 4, 1994[46]	interim authority[90]	chairman PNA		89	—	...	...	—	—
Western Sahara	—	—	annexture of Morocco	—	—	—	—	5	...	12	200
Yemen	December 1918	Sept. 29, 1994[72]	republic	president	prime minister	301	—	18	...	12	200
Yugoslavia	Dec. 1, 1918	April 27, 1992	federal republic	federal president	prime minister	40	138	2	29	...	...
Zambia	Oct. 24, 1964	May 28, 1996[5]	republic	president		155	—	9	57	—	—
Zimbabwe	April 18, 1980	April 18, 1980	republic	president		150	—	10	80	—	—

[1]Title of the supreme leader of the Taleban. [2]Transitional constitution. [3]Territorial sea claim assumed to claim fishing/economic rights within the same zone. [4]Observer status. [5]Date president signed new constitution. [6]Pending elections in December 1997. [7]Varies between 32 and 52 nautical miles. [8]President of France and Bishop of Urgell, Spain. [9]Assisted by the prime minister. [10]Measured from claimed archipelagic baselines. [11]Promulgation date of significant amendments to July 9, 1853, constitution. [12]Assisted by the ministerial coordinator. [13]Date of referendum approving new constitution. [14]Executive responsibilities divided between (for The Netherlands) the governor and (locally) the prime minister. [15]Associate member. [16]Formally a constitutional monarchy. [17]Excludes one vacent seat reserved for Nagorno-Karabakh representative. [18]Body with limited or no legislative authority. [19]Creation of four administrative units began in 1997. [20]Defined by equidistant line. [21]Legal status is controversial. [22]Excludes certain members of the royal family. [23]10 provincial councils; 5 region/community councils. [24]3 nautical miles from the mouth of Sarstoon River (southern boundary with Guatemala) to Ranguana Caye. [25]Executive responsibilities divided between (for the U.K.) the governor and (locally) the premier of the Cabinet. [26]Resembles a constitutional monarchy without a formal constitution. [27]Date of international treaty confirming the existence of a single state. [28]Tripartite presidency. [29]Two co-chairmen assisted by the Council of Ministers. [30]Full membership pending. [31]Transitional government. [32]First prime minister assisted by second prime minister. [33]Govenor-general can exercise all the powers of the reigning monarch of the Commonwealth. [34]Unilateral independence was declared in August 1997 by 2 of 3 islands. [35]Suspended membership. [36]Republic of Cyprus only. [37]Occupied seats only. [38]Zone defined by geographic coordinates. [39]Date new constitution approved by constituent assembly. [40]Date new republic was formally established. [41]Executive responsibilities divided between (for Denmark) the high commissioner and (locally) the prime minister. [42]New constitution signed into law July 25, 1997, becomes effective in July 1998. [43]3 nautical miles in the Gulf of Finland. [44]Executive responsibilities divided among (for France) the prefect and (locally) the president of the General Council and the president of the Regional Council. [45]Executive responsibilities between (for France) the high commissioner and (locally) the president of the territorial government. [46]Date of agreement providing for Palestinian self-rule. [47]Evolving body of constitutional law. [48]Represented by

membership in international organizations																																					country
United Nations (date of admission)	UN organs★ and affiliated intergovernmental organizations																				Commonwealth of Nations	regional multipurpose							economic								
	UNCTAD★[e]	UNICEF★[f]	ICJ★	FAO	IAEA[e]	IBRD	ICAO	IDA	IFC	ILO	IMF	IMO	ITU[e]	UNESCO	UNIDO	UPU[e]	WHO	WIPO[e]	WMO	WTO		EU	GCC	LAS[g]	OAS	OAU	SPC	ACP	ADB	APEC	CARICOM	ECOWAS	EEC	I-ADB	IDB[g]	OPEC	
1945	•	•	•	•	•	•	•	•	•	•	•	•	•	•	•	•	•	•	•	•		•							•				•	•			Netherlands, The
—														•15		•			•	•											•4						Netherlands Antilles
—																•			•								•										New Caledonia
1945	•	•	•	•	•	•	•	•	•	•	•	•	•	•	•	•	•	•	•	•	•						•		•	•							New Zealand
1945	•	•	•	•	•	•	•	•	•	•	•	•	•	•	•	•	•	•	•	•					•									•			Nicaragua
1960	•	•	•	•	•	•	•	•	•	•	•		•	•	•	•	•	•	•	•						•		•				•			•		Niger
1960	•	•	•	•	•	•	•	•	•	•	•	•	•	•	•	•	•	•	•	•	•35					•		•				•				•	Nigeria
—																•											•										Northern Mariana Is.
1945	•	•	•	•	•	•	•	•	•	•	•	•	•	•	•	•	•	•	•	•									•					•			Norway
1971	•	•	•	•		•	•	•	•	•	•	•	•	•	•	•	•		•	•4			•	•											•		Oman
1947	•	•	•	•	•	•	•	•	•	•	•	•	•	•	•	•	•	•	•	•	•								•						•		Pakistan
1994		•														•											•										Palau
1945	•	•	•	•	•	•	•	•	•	•	•	•	•	•	•	•	•	•	•	•					•									•			Panama
1975	•	•	•	•		•	•	•	•	•	•	•	•	•	•	•	•		•	•	•						•	•	•	•							Papua New Guinea
1945	•	•	•	•	•	•	•	•	•	•	•	•	•	•	•	•	•	•	•	•					•									•			Paraguay
1945	•	•	•	•	•	•	•	•	•	•	•	•	•	•	•	•	•	•	•	•					•									•			Peru
1945	•	•	•	•	•	•	•	•	•	•	•	•	•	•	•	•	•	•	•	•									•	•							Philippines
1945	•	•	•	•	•	•	•	•	•	•	•	•	•	•	•	•	•	•	•	•																	Poland
1955	•	•	•	•	•	•	•	•	•	•	•	•	•	•	•	•	•	•	•	•		•											•	•			Portugal
—				•15												•	•15														•4						Puerto Rico
1971	•	•	•	•	•	•	•			•	•	•	•	•	•	•	•	•	•	•			•	•											•	•	Qatar
—																•																					Réunion
1955	•	•	•	•	•	•	•	•	•	•	•	•	•	•	•	•	•	•	•	•																	Romania
1991	•	•			•	•	•	•	•	•	•	•	•	•	•	•	•	•	•	•4																	Russia
1962	•	•	•	•		•	•	•	•	•	•		•	•	•	•	•	•	•	•						•		•									Rwanda
1983	•	•	•	•		•		•			•			•	•	•	•			•	•				•			•			•						St. Kitts and Nevis
1979	•	•	•	•		•	•	•	•	•	•	•		•	•	•	•	•	•	•	•				•			•			•						St. Lucia
1980	•	•	•	•		•	•	•			•	•	•	•	•	•	•			•	•				•			•			•						St. Vincent
1976	•	•	•	•		•		•	•		•		•	•		•	•				•						•	•	•								Samoa
1992	•	•	•				•			•	•		•	•		•	•	•	•																		San Marino
1975	•	•	•	•		•	•	•		•	•	•	•	•	•	•	•		•							•		•									São Tomé and Príncipe
1945	•	•	•	•	•	•	•	•	•	•	•	•	•	•	•	•	•	•	•	•4			•	•											•	•	Saudi Arabia
1960	•	•	•	•	•	•	•	•	•	•	•	•	•	•	•	•	•	•	•	•						•		•				•			•		Senegal
1976	•	•	•	•		•	•		•	•	•	•		•	•	•	•		•	•4	•					•		•									Seychelles
1961	•	•	•	•	•	•	•	•	•	•	•	•	•	•	•	•	•	•	•	•	•35					•		•				•			•		Sierra Leone
1965	•	•	•		•	•	•		•	•	•	•	•			•	•	•	•	•	•								•	•							Singapore
1993	•	•		•	•	•	•	•	•	•	•	•	•	•	•	•	•	•	•	•																	Slovakia
1992	•	•		•	•	•	•	•	•	•	•	•	•	•	•	•	•	•	•	•														•			Slovenia
1978	•	•	•	•		•	•	•	•	•	•	•	•	•		•	•		•	•	•						•	•	•								Solomon Islands
1960	•	•	•	•		•	•	•	•	•	•	•	•	•	•	•	•	•	•					•		•		•							•		Somalia
1945	•	•	•	•	•	•	•	•	•	•	•		•	•		•	•	•	•	•	•					•											South Africa
1955	•	•	•	•	•	•	•	•	•	•	•	•	•	•	•	•	•	•	•	•		•							•				•	•			Spain
1955	•	•	•	•	•	•	•	•	•	•	•	•	•	•	•	•	•	•	•	•	•								•								Sri Lanka
1956	•	•	•	•	•	•	•	•	•	•	•	•	•	•	•	•	•	•	•					•		•		•							•		Sudan, The
1975	•	•	•	•		•	•			•	•	•	•	•	•	•	•	•	•	•					•			•			•			•			Suriname
1968	•	•	•	•		•	•	•	•	•	•		•	•	•	•	•	•	•	•	•					•		•									Swaziland
1946	•	•	•	•	•	•	•	•	•	•	•	•	•	•	•	•	•	•	•	•		•							•				•	•			Sweden
—	•	•	•	•	•	•	•	•	•	•	•	•	•	•	•	•	•	•	•	•									•					•			Switzerland
1945	•	•	•	•	•	•	•	•	•	•	•	•	•	•	•	•	•		•					•											•		Syria
—																				•4									•	•							Taiwan
1992	•	•		•		•	•	•		•	•	•		•	•	•	•	•	•																		Tajikistan
1961	•	•	•	•	•	•	•	•	•	•	•	•	•	•	•	•	•	•	•	•	•					•		•									Tanzania
1946	•	•	•	•	•	•	•	•	•	•	•	•	•	•	•	•	•	•	•	•									•	•							Thailand
1960	•	•	•	•		•	•	•	•	•	•	•	•	•	•	•	•	•	•	•						•		•				•					Togo
—	•	•		•		•	•	•	•		•		•	•	•	•	•			•4	•						•	•	•								Tonga
1962	•	•	•	•		•	•	•	•	•	•	•	•	•	•	•	•	•	•	•	•				•			•			•			•			Trinidad and Tobago
1956	•	•	•	•	•	•	•	•	•	•	•	•	•	•	•	•	•	•	•	•				•		•									•		Tunisia
1945	•	•	•	•	•	•	•	•	•	•	•	•	•	•	•	•	•	•	•	•									•				•15		•		Turkey
1992	•	•		•		•	•	•30		•	•	•	•	•		•	•		•																•		Turkmenistan
—		•												•		•	•				•68						•	•	•								Tuvalu
1962	•	•	•	•	•	•	•	•	•	•	•		•	•	•	•	•	•	•	•	•					•		•							•		Uganda
1945	•	•			•	•	•	•30		•	•	•	•	•	•	•	•	•	•	•4																	Ukraine
1971	•	•	•	•	•	•	•	•	•	•	•	•	•	•	•	•	•	•	•	•			•	•											•	•	United Arab Emirates
1945	•	•	•	•	•	•	•	•	•	•	•	•	•	•4	•	•	•	•	•	•	•	•					•		•				•	•			United Kingdom
1945	•	•	•	•	•	•	•	•	•	•	•	•	•	•4	•	•	•	•	•	•					•		•		•	•				•			United States
1945	•	•	•	•	•	•	•		•	•	•	•	•	•	•	•	•	•	•	•					•									•			Uruguay
1992	•	•			•	•	•	•	•	•	•		•	•	•	•	•	•	•										•								Uzbekistan
1981	•	•	•	•		•	•	•	•		•	•	•	•	•	•	•		•	•4	•						•	•	•								Vanuatu
1945	•	•	•	•	•	•	•		•	•	•	•	•	•	•	•	•	•	•	•					•						•4			•		•	Venezuela
1977	•	•	•	•	•	•	•	•	•	•	•	•	•	•	•	•	•	•	•	•4									•								Vietnam
—																•															•						Virgin Islands (U.S.)
—		•																																			West Bank
—																										•91											Western Sahara
1947	•	•	•	•		•	•	•	•	•	•	•	•	•	•	•	•	•	•					•											•		Yemen
1945	•	•	•	•	•	•30	•30	•30	•	•	•	•	•	•	•	•	•	•	•	•																	Yugoslavia
1964	•	•	•	•	•	•	•	•	•	•	•		•	•	•	•	•	•	•	•	•					•		•									Zambia
1980	•	•	•	•	•	•	•	•	•	•	•		•	•	•	•	•	•	•	•	•					•		•									Zimbabwe

the lieutenant governor. [49]Assisted by extraconstitutional prime minister. [50]Reversion data to China in a semi-autonomous status. [51]Approval date for post-reversion Basic Law. [52]Special administrative region (China). [53]Shares coexecutive authority with spiritual leader. [54]Sea of Oman only; median line boundaries in Persian Gulf. [55]Provisional constitution. [56]Iraqi sovereignty in Kurdish areas is tenuous. [57]Median line between the Isle of Man and the United Kingdom. [58]3 nautical miles in 5 straits. [59]Approval date by legislature; made public Nov. 23, 1993. [60]3 nautical miles in Korea Strait. [61]Date of peace accord. [62]Assisted by State Minister for Presidential Affairs. [63]Formally a *jamahiriya*, translated as "the masses of people." [64]Based on Gulf of Sidra closing line (32° 30″ N), in part. [65]Macau will revert to Chinese sovereignty on Dec. 20, 1999. [66]Executive responsibilities divided between (for France) the prefect and (locally) the president of the General Council. [67]Excludes claims in the Western Sahara. [68]Special member. [69]Executive responsibilities divided between (for France) the high commissioner and (locally) the president of the General Council. [70]Basic law promulgated by sultan. [71]Includes 11 federally administered tribal areas, excludes Jammu and Kashmir. [72]Effective date of significant amendments. [73]Assisted by vice presidents. [74]Two concomitant administrative systems (14 regional units/25 departmental units). [75]Elective seats only. [76]Defined by international treaties. [77]Excludes additional seats for both houses of the legislature to meet ⅓ total representation requirements for minority parties per constitution. [78]Limits of continental shelf or median line boundaries. [79]Date constitution adopted by transitional legislature. [80]In conjunction with the vice president (minister of defense) and prime minister. [81]Mixed political system approximating a constitutional monarchy. [82]Number of villages. [83]Royal decrees since March 1, 1992, provide a formal description of the king's governance. [84]No central government in early December 1997. [85]Atlantic Ocean only. [86]In practice resembles a system of monarchical absolutism. [87]Assisted by Privy Council. [88]Black Sea and Mediterranean Sea; 6 nautical miles in Aegean Sea. [89]Based on evolving body of statutes and common law. [90]Urban areas only. [91]Membership held by the Sahrawi Arab Democratic Republic.

Area and population

This table provides the area and population for each of the countries of the world and for all but the smallest political dependencies having a permanent civilian population. The data represent the latest published and unpublished data for both the surveyed area of the countries and their populations, the latter both as of a single year (1997) to provide the best comparability and as of the most recent census to provide the fullest comparison of certain demographic measures that are not always available between successive national censuses. The 1997 midyear estimates represent a combination of national, United Nations (UN) or other international organizations, and *Encyclopædia Britannica* estimates so as to give the best fit to available published series, to take account of unpublished information received via Internet, facsimile, or correspondence, and to incorporate the results of very recent censuses for which published analyses are not yet available.

One principal point to bear in mind when studying these statistics is that all of them, whatever degree of precision may be implied by the exactness of the numbers, are estimates—all of varying, and some of suspect, accuracy—even when they *contain* a very full enumeration. The United States—which has a long tradition both of census taking and of the use of the most sophisticated analytical tools in processing the data—is unable to determine within 2.1% (the estimated 1990 undercount) its total population nationally. And that is an *average* underenumeration. In states and larger cities, where enumeration of particular populations, both legal and illegal, is most difficult, the accuracy of the enumerated count may be off as much as 4% at a state level and as much as 10% for a single city. The high accuracy attained by census operations in China may approach 0.25% of rigorously maintained civil population registers. Other national census operations not so based, however, are inherently less accurate. For example, Ethiopia's first-ever census in 1984 resulted in figures that were 30% or more above prevailing estimates; Nigeria's 1991 census corrected decades of miscounts and was well below prevailing estimates. An undercount of 2–8% is more typical, but even census operations offering results of 30% or more above or below prevailing estimates can still represent well-founded benchmarks from which future planning may proceed. The editors have tried to take account of the range of variation and accuracy in published data, but it is difficult to establish a value for many sources of inaccuracy unless some country or agency has made a conscientious effort to establish both the relative accuracy (precision) of its estimate and the absolute magnitude of the quantity it is trying to measure—for example, the number of people in Cambodia who died at the hands of the Khmer Rouge. If a figure of 2,000,000 is adopted, what is its accuracy: ± 1%, 10%, 50%? Are the original data documentary or evidentiary, complete or incomplete, analytically biased or unbiased, in good agreement with other published data?

Many similar problems exist and in endless variations: What is the extent of southern European immigration to western Europe in search of jobs? How many refugees from Afghanistan, Liberia, Rwanda, or Burundi are there in surrounding countries? How many undocumented aliens are there in the United States? How many Palestinians are there in the Middle East (they are politically inconvenient to enumerate everywhere)? How many Amerindians exist (remain, preserving their original language and a mode of life unassimilated by the larger national culture) in the countries of South America? How many people have died or emigrated as a result of the civil violence in Central America?

Area and population

country	area			population (latest estimate)					population (latest census)				
	square miles	square kilometres	rank	total midyear 1997	rank	density per sq mi	density per sq km	% annual growth rate 1992–97	census year	total	male (%)	female (%)	urban (%)
Afghanistan	251,825	652,225	41	23,738,000	40	94.3	36.4	7.4	1979	13,051,358[1]	51.4	48.6	15.1
Albania	11,100	28,748	142	2,393,000	127	296.7	114.5	0.7	1989	3,182,417	51.5	48.5	35.7
Algeria	919,595	2,381,741	11	29,476,000	34	32.1	12.4	2.3	1987	23,038,942	49.9	50.1	49.7
American Samoa	77	199	205	61,800	203	802.6	310.6	3.9	1990	46,773	51.4	48.6	33.4
Andorra	181	468	193	64,600	201	356.9	138.0	1.4	1992[2]	61,599	53.1	46.9	62.5[3]
Angola	481,354	1,246,700	24	10,624,000	68	22.1	8.5	3.2	1970	5,673,046	52.1	47.9	14.2
Antigua and Barbuda	171	442	195	64,500	202	377.2	145.9	0.2	1991	63,896	48.2	51.8	36.2
Argentina	1,073,400	2,780,092	8	35,409,000	31	33.0	12.7	1.2	1991	32,615,528	48.9	51.1	88.4
Armenia	11,484	29,743	141	3,773,000	120	328.5	126.9	0.5	1989	3,287,677	49.3	50.7	67.8
Aruba	75	193	206	84,200	196	1,122.7	436.3	3.9	1991	66,687	49.2	50.8	...
Australia	2,966,200	7,682,300	6	18,508,000	51	6.2	2.4	1.1	1996	17,892,423	49.5	50.5	85.3[4]
Austria	32,378	83,859	115	8,087,000	84	249.8	96.4	0.4	1991	7,795,786	48.2	51.8	64.5
Azerbaijan	33,400	86,600	113	7,617,000	88	228.1	88.0	0.8	1989	7,037,867	48.7	51.3	53.8
Bahamas, The	5,382	13,939	158	287,000	174	53.3	20.6	1.6	1990	255,095	49.0	51.0	64.3
Bahrain	268	694	186	620,000	161	2,313.4	893.4	3.6	1991	508,037	57.9	42.1	88.4
Bangladesh	56,977	147,570	93	125,340,000	9	2,199.8	849.4	1.9	1991	111,455,185	51.4	48.6	20.2
Barbados	166	430	196	265,000	178	1,596.4	616.3	0.2	1990[5]	257,083	47.7	52.3	37.9[6]
Belarus	80,153	207,595	85	10,360,000	71	129.3	49.9	0.1	1989	10,199,709	46.9	53.1	65.5
Belgium	11,787	30,528	139	10,189,000	73	864.4	333.8	0.3	1991	9,978,681	48.9	51.1	96.6[7]
Belize	8,867	22,965	150	228,000	179	25.7	9.9	2.8	1991	189,392	50.9	49.1	47.5
Benin	43,500	112,680	101	5,902,000	97	135.7	52.4	3.4	1992	4,855,349	48.7	51.3	39.6
Bermuda	21	54	212	61,700	204	2,938.1	1,142.6	0.6	1991[5]	58,460	48.5	51.5	100.0
Bhutan	18,150	47,000	131	860,000	156	47.4	18.3	2.3	...	...	50.6[6]	49.4[6]	5.3[6]
Bolivia	424,164	1,098,581	28	7,767,000	86	18.3	7.1	2.4	1992	6,420,792	49.4	50.6	57.5
Bosnia and Herzegovina	19,741	51,129	127	3,124,000	129	158.2	61.1	−7.9	1991	4,377,033	49.9	50.1	39.6
Botswana	224,607	581,730	47	1,501,000	146	6.7	2.6	1.9	1991	1,326,796	47.8	52.2	23.9
Brazil	3,300,171	8,547,404	5	159,691,000	5	47.4	18.3	1.3	1991	146,825,475	49.4	50.6	75.6
Brunei	2,226	5,765	167	308,000	173	138.4	53.4	2.7	1991	260,482	52.8	47.2	66.6
Bulgaria	42,855	110,994	103	8,329,000	83	194.4	75.0	−0.5	1992	8,487,317	49.1	50.9	67.2
Burkina Faso	105,946	274,400	73	10,891,000	66	102.8	39.7	2.7	1985[5]	7,964,705	48.1	51.9	11.7
Burundi	10,740	27,816	145	6,053,000	96	563.6	217.6	0.5	1990[5]	5,292,793	48.6	51.4	6.3
Cambodia	70,238	181,916	89	10,385,000	70	147.9	57.1	2.8	1993	9,307,597	48.3	51.7	21.0[9]
Cameroon	183,569	475,442	53	14,678,000	59	80.0	30.9	3.0	1987	10,516,232	49.0	51.0	38.3
Canada	3,849,674	9,970,610	2	30,287,000	33	7.9	3.0	1.2	1996	28,846,761	49.3[4]	50.7[4]	77.9
Cape Verde	1,557	4,033	169	394,000	171	253.1	97.7	1.7	1990	341,491	47.3	52.7	44.1
Central African Republic	240,324	622,436	43	3,342,000	126	13.9	5.4	2.4	1988	2,688,426	49.1	50.9	36.5
Chad	495,755	1,284,000	21	7,166,000	90	14.5	5.6	2.9	1993	6,279,931	47.9	52.1	21.4
Chile	292,135	756,626	38	14,583,000	60	49.9	19.3	1.4	1992	13,348,401	49.1	50.9	83.5
China	3,696,100	9,572,900	3	1,227,740,000	1	332.2	128.3	1.1	1990	1,133,682,501	51.6	48.4	26.4
Colombia	440,762	1,141,568	26	36,200,000	30	82.1	31.7	1.6	1993	33,109,840	49.2	50.8	70.3[6]
Comoros	719	1,862	175	514,000	163	714.9	276.0	2.4	1991	446,817	49.5	50.5	28.5
Congo, Dem. Rep of the	905,354	2,344,858	12	46,674,000	25	51.6	19.9	3.1	1984	29,671,407	49.2	50.8	29.1[9]
Congo, Rep. of the	132,047	342,000	63	2,583,000	133	19.6	7.6	2.3	1984[5]	1,909,248	48.7	51.3	52.0
Costa Rica	19,730	51,100	128	3,468,000	125	175.8	67.9	2.1	1984	2,416,809	50.0	50.0	43.9
Côte d'Ivoire	124,504	322,463	68	14,986,000	58	120.4	46.5	3.2	1988	10,815,694	51.1	48.9	39.0
Croatia	21,857	56,610	126	4,774,000	108	218.4	84.3	−0.0	1991	4,784,265	48.5	51.5	54.3
Cuba	42,804	110,861	104	11,190,000	65	261.4	100.9	0.7	1993	10,904,466	50.3	49.7	74.4
Cyprus[11]	3,572	9,251	164	860,000	155	240.8	93.0	1.7	1992[5, 12]	615,013	49.8	50.2	67.7
Czech Republic	30,450	78,866	117	10,307,000	72	338.5	130.7	−0.0	1991	10,302,215	48.5	51.5	75.2
Denmark	16,639	43,094	133	5,284,000	104	317.6	122.6	0.4	1996[2]	5,251,027	49.4	50.6	85.1[3]
Djibouti	8,950	23,200	149	622,000	160	69.5	26.8	3.2	1983	273,974	51.9	48.1	82.8[9]
Dominica	290	750	183	74,400	199	256.6	99.2	0.7	1991	71,183	49.8	50.2	...
Dominican Republic	18,792	48,671	130	7,802,000	85	415.2	160.3	1.8	1993	7,293,390	48.7	51.3	56.0
Ecuador	105,037	272,045	74	11,937,000	62	113.6	43.9	2.1	1990	9,648,189	49.7	50.3	55.4
Egypt	385,229	997,739	30	62,110,000	17	161.2	62.3	2.2	1996	61,452,382	51.2	48.8	44.6[9]

Still, much information is accurate, well founded, and updated regularly. The sources of these data are censuses; national population registers (cumulated periodically); registration of migration, births, deaths, and so on; sample surveys to establish demographic conditions; and the like.

The statistics provided for area and population by country are ranked, and the population densities based on those values are also provided. The population densities, for purposes of comparison within this table, are calculated on the bases of the 1997 midyear population estimate as shown and of total area of the country. Elsewhere in individual country presentations the reader may find densities calculated on more specific population figures and more specialized area bases: land area for Finland (because of its many lakes) or ice-free area for Greenland (most of which is ice cap). The data in this section conclude with the estimated average annual growth rate for the country (including both natural growth and net migration) during the five-year period, 1992–97.

In the section containing census data, information supplied includes the census total (usually de facto, the population actually present, rather than de jure, the population legally resident, who might be anywhere); the male-female breakdown; the proportion that is urban (according to the country's own definition); and finally an analysis of the age structure of the population by 15-year age groups. This last analysis may be particularly useful in distinguishing the type of population being recorded—young, fast-growing nations show a high proportion of people under 30 (most countries in sub-Saharan Africa and the Middle East have nearly one-half of their population under 15 years), while other nations (for example Sweden, which suffered no age-group losses in World War II) exhibit quite uniform proportions.

Finally, a section is provided giving the population of each country at 10-year intervals from 1940 to 2010. The data for years past represent the best available analysis of the published data by the country itself, by the demographers of the UN, or by the editors of Britannica. The projections for 2000 and 2010 similarly represent the best fit of available data through the mid-1990s with projected population structure and growth rates during the next two decades. The evidence of the last 25 years with respect to similar estimates published about 1970, however, shows how cloudy is the glass through which these numbers are read. In 1970 no respectable Western analyst would have imagined proposing that mainland China could achieve the degree of birth control that it apparently has since then (as evidenced by the results of 1982 and 1990 censuses); on the other hand, even the Chinese admit that their methods have been somewhat Draconian and that they have already seen some backlash in terms of higher birth rates among those who have so far postponed larger families. How much is "some" by 2000? Compound that problem with all the social, economic, political, and biological factors that can affect 217 countries' populations, and the difficulty facing the prospective compiler of such projections may be appreciated.

Specific data about the vital rates affecting the data in this table may be found in great detail in both the country statistical boxes in "The Nations of the World" section and in the *Vital statistics, marriage, family* table, beginning at page 778.

Percentages in this table for male and female population will always total 100.0, but percentages by age group may not, for reasons such as nonresponse on census forms, "don't know" responses (which are common in countries with poor birth registration systems), and the like.

age distribution (%)						population (by decade, '000s)								country
0–14	15–29	30–44	45–59	60–74	75 and over	1940	1950	1960	1970	1980	1990	2000 projection	2010 projection	
44.5	26.9	15.8	8.6	3.6	0.6	...	8,150	9,829	12,431	14,985	14,767	26,668	34,098	Afghanistan
33.0	28.9	18.5	11.7	5.9	1.9	1,088	1,227	1,623	2,157	2,699	3,273	3,427	3,858	Albania
43.9	28.0	13.9	8.4	4.2	1.6	7,688	8,956	10,800	14,330	18,666	25,022	31,410	38,479	Algeria
38.1	29.0	18.1	9.4	4.3	1.1	13	19	20	27	32	47	69	85	American Samoa
16.3	27.7	27.2	15.1	9.9	3.8	5	6	8	19	33	53	66	71	Andorra
41.7	23.2	17.0	7.4	3.8	1.0	3,738	4,118	4,797	5,606	6,794	8,430	11.513	14,982	Angola
30.4	27.8	20.5	10.2	7.7	3.4	34	45	55	66	69	64	65	66	Antigua and Barbuda
30.6	23.3	19.3	13.9	9.6	3.3	14,169	17,150	20,616	23,962	28,114	32,547	36,648	40,755	Argentina
30.3	25.7	20.8	13.6	6.4	3.2	1,320	1,354	1,867	2,520	3,067	3,545	3,787	3,892	Armenia
24.4	22.0	27.0	16.1	7.2	3.0	31	51	57	61	60	64	85	89	Aruba
22.1[4]	24.2[4]	23.4[4]	15.0[4]	11.1[4]	4.4[4]	7,079	8,219	10,315	12,552	14,741	17,065	19,058	20,830	Australia
17.4	23.7	21.6	17.2	13.4	6.7	6,684	6,935	7,048	7,447	7,549	7,718	8,149	8,283	Austria
32.8	29.7	16.8	12.8	5.7	2.2	3,274	2,896	3,895	5,172	6,165	7,159	7,784	8,285	Azerbaijan
32.2	30.8	19.7	10.6	5.0	1.8	70	79	110	170	210	256	295	321	Bahamas, The
31.7	28.4	28.2	8.0	3.1	0.6	90	110	149	210	334	503	660	780	Bahrain
41.5	25.2	16.2	8.1	4.3	1.1	41,259	45,646	54,622	67,403	88,077	110,118	132,081	153,195	Bangladesh
24.1	27.1	22.1	11.4	9.9	5.4	179	209	232	235	249	261	266	270	Barbados
23.0	22.4	20.6	18.0	11.5	4.5	9,046	7,745	8,190	9,040	9,650	10,260	10,456	10,831	Belarus
18.2	21.8	22.5	16.9	14.1	6.6	8,301	8,639	9,153	9,690	9,859	9,967	10,281	10,353	Belgium
43.9	27.9	14.9	7.2	4.4	1.6	56	68	90	120	146	189	248	307	Belize
48.3[8]	26.9[8]	13.3[8]	7.4[8]	3.2[8]	0.8[8]	...	1,673	2,055	2,620	3,444	4,676	6,517	8,955	Benin
19.5	24.0	26.8	16.4	—13.3—		31	37	43	53	55	59	63	67	Bermuda
40.6[6]	26.5[6]	17.1[6]	10.4[6]	4.6[6]	0.8[6]	...	...	...	...	600	737	916	1,129	Bhutan
41.2	26.2	16.8	8.9	—6.5—		2,508	2,714	3,351	4,212	5,355	6,573	8,329	10,229	Bolivia
23.5[7]	26.3[7]	22.6[7]	16.2[7]	8.9[7]	2.7[7]	...	2,662	3,240	3,703	4,107	4,308	3,012	3,328	Bosnia and Herzegovina
42.8	27.3	14.3	7.3	4.1	2.2	278	430	497	584	903	1,304	1,557	1,598	Botswana
34.7	28.1	19.3	10.6	5.7	1.6	41,525	53,444	72,594	95,847	118,563	144,723	164,163	179,995	Brazil
34.5	29.3	24.2	7.9	—4.1—		36	45	83	128	185	254	331	410	Brunei
20.5	19.2	—39.8—		—20.5—		6,344	7,251	7,867	8,490	8,862	8,718	8,218	7,898	Bulgaria
48.3	23.4	13.4	8.7	4.7	1.4	3,036	4,376	4,866	5,626	6,939	9,033	11,684	14,150	Burkina Faso
46.4	25.3	15.4	7.0	4.0	1.7	1,887	2,363	2,812	3,513	4,138	5,633	6,493	8,229	Burundi
47.0	—53.0—					3,400	4,346	5,433	6,938	6,400	8,592	11,267	14,602	Cambodia
46.4	24.5	14.6	8.7	4.1	1.6	...	4,888	5,609	6,727	8,761	11,905	15,996	20,630	Cameroon
20.9[4]	22.7[4]	25.1[4]	15.3[4]	11.3[4]	4.7[4]	11,693	13,737	17,909	21,324	24,593	27,791	31,472	35,065	Canada
45.0	27.3	11.4	8.0	5.5	2.9	181	146	197	269	296	349	411	464	Cape Verde
43.2	27.5	15.0	9.2	4.1	0.8	991	1,260	1,467	1,827	2,244	2,806	3,539	4,177	Central African Republic
48.1	24.6	14.7	7.2	4.2	1.3	2,351	2,608	3,042	3,733	4,507	5,889	7,760	10,055	Chad
29.4	27.3	21.2	12.2	7.2	2.5	5,063	6,082	7,608	9,496	11,147	13,100	15,086	16,480	Chile
27.7	31.0	20.7	12.1	6.9	1.7	530,000	556,613	667,070	818,316	981,242	1,133,683	1,261,480	1,348,957	China
33.1[10]	30.0[10]	20.6[10]	9.9[10]	5.2[10]	1.3[10]	9,097	11,268	15,321	20,884	26,906	32,300	37,822	42,959	Colombia
47.6[7]	27.0[7]	13.1[7]	7.7[7]	3.5[7]	1.0[7]	119	148	177	245	334	432	549	689	Comoros
47.3[9]	25.9[9]	14.1[9]	8.1[9]	3.8[9]	0.8[9]	10,370	13,055	16,151	21,368	27,009	37,460	51,136	68,876	Congo, Dem. Rep. of the
44.7	27.2	13.3	9.1	4.6	0.7	...	768	931	1,183	1,620	2,204	2,750	3,298	Congo, Rep. of the
37.9	31.5	15.8	9.2	4.4	1.2	619	862	1,236	1,731	2,246	2,994	3,687	4,401	Costa Rica
46.8	27.3	15.0	7.5	2.8	0.6	2,350	2,860	3,565	5,427	8,276	11,896	16,031	19,978	Côte d'Ivoire
19.4	20.7	22.7	18.3	12.9	4.5	...	3,851	4,140	4,411	4,588	4,778	4,771	4,761	Croatia
22.3	29.4	21.3	14.8	8.4	3.9	4,566	5,850	6,985	8,520	9,710	10,598	11,385	11,911	Cuba
25.4	22.0	22.3	15.4	10.2	4.7	413	494	573	615	631	757	895	1,023	Cyprus[11]
21.0	21.8	22.6	16.8	12.7	5.1	...	8,925	9,539	9,830	10,292	10,298	10,290	10,377	Czech Republic
17.5	20.8	22.0	19.9	12.7	7.0	3,832	4,271	4,581	4,929	5,123	5,141	5,348	5,504	Denmark
39.4	32.9	16.9	7.4	2.8	0.6	44	60	78	158	355	505	680	916	Djibouti
33.3	28.3	16.3	9.7	—11.8—		45	51	60	70	75	72	75	76	Dominica
36.5[10]	29.5[10]	18.4[10]	9.6[10]	4.8[10]	1.2[10]	1,759	2,353	3,231	4,423	5,697	6,698	8,187	9,414	Dominican Republic
38.8	28.5	17.3	9.0	4.7	1.7	2,546	3,307	4,421	5,958	8,123	10,264	12,646	14,899	Ecuador
36.9[13]	28.3[13]	18.4[13]	10.6[13]	4.9[13]	0.9[13]	16,942	20,461	26,085	33,329	40,546	53,051	65,604	77,349	Egypt

Area and population (continued)

country	area			population (latest estimate)					population (latest census)				
	square miles	square kilo-metres	rank	total midyear 1997	rank	density		% annual growth rate 1992–97	census year	total	male (%)	female (%)	urban (%)
						per sq mi	per sq km						
El Salvador	8,124	21,041	151	5,662,000	99	696.9	269.1	1.7	1992	5,118,599	48.6	51.4	50.4
Equatorial Guinea	10,831	28,051	144	443,000	164	40.9	15.8	2.6	1983	300,060	48.8	51.2	28.2
Eritrea	46,774	121,144	99	3,590,000	124	76.8	29.6	3.5	1984	2,703,998	49.9	50.1	15.1
Estonia	17,462	45,227	132	1,463,000	147	83.8	32.3	–1.1	1989	1,572,916	46.9	53.1	71.6
Ethiopia	437,794	1,133,882	27	58,733,000	20	134.2	51.8	2.9	1984	39,480,954	50.0	50.0	9.9
Faroe Islands	540	1,399	177	43,800	209	81.1	31.3	–1.4	1996[2]	43,495	51.6	48.4	...
Fiji	7,055	18,272	155	778,000	157	110.3	42.6	0.8	1996	772,655	50.7[14]	49.3[14]	46.4
Finland	130,559	338,145	64	5,145,000	105	39.4	15.2	0.4	1990	4,998,478	48.5	51.5	79.7
France	210,026	543,965	49	56,616,000	21	279.1	107.8	0.4	1990	56,625,026	48.7	51.3	74.0
French Guiana	33,399	86,504	114	152,000	186	4.6	1.8	2.6	1990	114,808	52.1	47.9	79.4
French Polynesia	1,544	4,000	170	227,000	180	147.0	56.8	1.9	1996	219,521	52.1[15]	47.9[15]	55.0[15]
Gabon	103,347	267,667	76	1,190,000	150	11.5	4.4	1.5	1993	1,011,710	49.3	50.7	73.2
Gambia, The	4,127	10,689	162	1,248,000	149	302.4	116.8	3.7	1993	1,038,145	50.1	49.9	36.7
Gaza Strip	140	363	199	1,028,000	154	7,342.9	2,832.0	7.0	1995[2, 16]	1,054,000	50.9	49.1	...
Georgia	26,831	69,492	121	5,377,000	103	200.4	77.4	–0.3	1989	5,443,359	47.2	52.8	55.7
Germany	137,830	356,978	62	82,143,000	12	596.0	230.1	0.4	1987[17]	61,077,042	48.0	52.0	85.3[6]
Ghana	92,098	238,533	81	18,101,000	53	196.5	75.9	2.4	1984	12,296,081	49.3	50.7	32.0
Gibraltar	2.2	5.8	216	27,100	213	12,318.2	4,672.4	–1.0	1991[18]	26,703	51.0	49.0	...
Greece	50,949	131,957	96	10,541,000	69	206.9	79.9	0.4	1991	10,264,156	49.3	50.7	58.9
Greenland	840,000	2,175,600	14	56,300	207	0.1	0.0	0.4	1996[2]	55,863	53.4	46.6	81.1
Grenada	133	344	201	98,400	193	739.8	286.0	0.5	1991	95,597	48.8	51.2	33.5
Guadeloupe	687	1,780	176	433,000	165	630.3	243.3	1.5	1990	387,034	48.9	51.1	48.4
Guam	209	541	190	156,000	185	746.4	288.4	2.3	1990	133,152	53.3	46.7	38.2
Guatemala	42,042	108,889	105	11,242,000	64	267.4	103.2	2.9	1994	8,331,874	49.3	50.7	35.0
Guernsey	30	78	210	61,700	205	2,056.7	791.0	–0.1	1996[19]	58,681	48.1[4]	51.9[4]	...
Guinea	94,926	245,857	78	7,405,000	89	78.0	30.1	2.3	1996	7,164,823	48.8	51.2	29.6
Guinea-Bissau	13,948	36,125	137	1,179,000	151	84.5	32.6	2.4	1991	983,367	48.4	51.6	20.3[7]
Guyana	83,044	215,083	84	773,000	158	9.3	3.6	0.3	1980	758,619	49.5	50.5	35.4[9]
Haiti	10,695	27,700	146	6,611,000	93	618.1	238.7	1.3	1982	5,053,792	48.5	51.5	20.6
Honduras	43,433	112,492	102	5,823,000	98	134.1	51.8	3.1	1988	4,376,839	49.6	50.4	39.4
Hong Kong	415	1,076	179	6,491,000	94	15,641.9	6,032.5	2.3	1996[5]	6,218,000	50.0	50.0	100.0
Hungary	35,919	93,030	110	10,157,000	74	282.8	109.2	–0.3	1990	10,375,323	48.1	51.9	61.8
Iceland	39,699	102,819	106	271,000	176	6.8	2.6	0.7	1996[2]	269,735	50.1	49.9	91.9
India	1,222,243	3,165,596	7	967,613,000	2	791.7	305.7	1.7	1991	846,302,688	51.9	48.1	25.7
Indonesia	741,052	1,919,317	16	199,544,000	4	269.3	104.0	1.6	1990	179,378,946	49.9	50.1	30.9
Iran	635,238	1,645,258	18	62,305,000	16	98.1	37.9	1.9	1991[5]	55,473,189	51.5	48.5	57.3
Iraq	167,975	435,052	58	22,219,000	44	132.3	51.1	3.8	1997	22,017,983	51.4[20]	48.6[20]	74.5[9]
Ireland	27,137	70,285	120	3,644,000	123	134.3	51.8	0.5	1996	3,626,087	49.6	50.4	57.0
Isle of Man	221	572	189	72,200	200	326.7	126.2	0.5	1996[5]	71,714	48.5	51.5	51.1[4]
Israel[21, 22]	7,876	20,400	152	5,652,000	100	717.6	277.1	2.4	1995[5, 23]	5,643,500	49.8[24]	50.2[24]	86.9[24]
Italy	116,341	301,323	71	57,511,000	22	494.3	190.9	0.2	1991	57,103,833	48.6	51.4	67.1
Jamaica	4,244	10,991	161	2,536,000	135	597.5	230.7	1.0	1991	2,374,193	49.0	51.0	50.4
Japan	145,877	377,819	61	126,110,000	8	864.5	333.8	0.3	1995	125,570,246	49.0	51.0	78.1[9]
Jersey	45	116	209	85,400	195	1,897.8	736.2	0.3	1996	85,150	48.6	51.4	...
Jordan[25]	34,489	89,326	112	4,522,000	113	131.1	50.6	3.7	1994	4,095,579	52.2	47.8	78.6
Kazakstan	1,052,090	2,724,900	9	16,554,000	54	15.7	6.1	–0.5	1989	16,536,511	48.5	51.5	57.2
Kenya	224,961	582,646	46	28,803,000	36	128.0	49.4	2.2	1989	21,443,636	49.6	50.4	23.6[6]
Kiribati	313	811	181	82,400	197	263.3	101.6	2.0	1990	72,335	49.2	50.8	35.1
Korea, North	47,399	122,762	98	24,317,000	39	513.0	198.1	1.8	1993	21,213,378	48.7	51.3	58.9
Korea, South	38,328	99,268	108	45,628,000	26	1,190.5	459.6	0.9	1995[5]	44,608,726	50.2	49.8	81.0[9]
Kuwait	6,880	17,818	156	1,809,000	143	262.9	101.5	4.9	1995	1,575,983	58.0	42.0	97.0[9]
Kyrgyzstan	77,200	199,900	86	4,595,000	112	59.5	23.0	0.4	1989	4,290,442	48.9	51.1	38.2
Laos	91,429	236,800	83	5,117,000	106	56.0	21.6	2.9	1995	4,581,258	49.5	50.5	20.7[9]
Latvia	24,946	64,610	124	2,472,000	136	99.1	38.3	–1.2	1989	2,680,029	46.6	53.4	71.1
Lebanon	4,016	10,400	163	3,859,000	118	960.9	371.1	2.0	1970	2,126,325	50.8	49.2	60.1
Lesotho	11,720	30,355	140	2,008,000	140	171.3	66.2	2.0	1986[5]	1,577,536	48.2	51.8	16.0
Liberia	37,743	97,754	109	2,602,000	132	68.9	26.6	3.9	1984	2,101,628	50.6	49.4	38.8
Libya	678,400	1,757,000	17	5,648,000	101	8.3	3.2	3.8	1995[5]	4,404,986	50.8	49.2	85.3[9]
Liechtenstein	62	160	208	31,300	212	504.8	195.6	1.1	1980	25,215	49.6	50.4	...
Lithuania	25,213	65,301	123	3,706,000	121	147.0	56.8	–0.2	1989	3,689,779	47.4	52.6	68.0
Luxembourg	999	2,586	172	420,000	168	420.4	162.4	1.4	1991	384,634	49.0	51.0	85.9[7]
Macau	8.1	21.0	215	421,000	167	52,039.6	20,085.9	2.6	1991	339,464	48.5	51.5	97.0
Macedonia	9,928	25,713	148	1,984,000	141	199.8	77.2	–0.1	1994	1,936,877	50.4	49.6	58.7
Madagascar	226,658	587,041	45	14,062,000	61	62.0	24.0	2.9	1993[5]	12,092,157	49.5	50.5	26.4[9]
Malaŵi	45,747	118,484	100	9,609,000	77	210.0	81.1	–0.2	1987	7,988,507	48.4	51.6	10.7
Malaysia	127,311	329,733	66	21,767,000	45	171.0	66.0	2.8	1991	17,566,982	50.5	49.5	50.6
Maldives	115	298	203	267,000	177	2,321.7	896.0	3.0	1995	244,644	51.1	48.9	25.9[26]
Mali	482,077	1,248,574	23	9,945,000	75	20.6	8.0	2.9	1987	7,696,348	48.9	51.1	22.0
Malta	122	316	202	375,000	172	3,073.8	1,186.7	0.7	1985	345,418	49.2	50.8	85.3
Marshall Islands	70	181	207	60,300	206	861.4	333.1	3.7	1988	43,380	51.1	48.9	64.5
Martinique	436	1,128	178	399,000	170	915.1	353.7	1.4	1990	359,579	48.4	51.6	80.5
Mauritania	398,000	1,030,700	29	2,411,000	137	6.1	2.3	3.2	1988	1,864,236	49.5	50.5	39.1
Mauritius	788	2,040	174	1,143,000	152	1,450.5	560.3	1.1	1990	1,056,827	49.9	50.1	39.3
Mayotte	145	375	198	128,000	189	882.8	341.3	5.0	1991	94,385	52.0	48.0	59.7[27]
Mexico	756,066	1,958,201	15	94,275,000	11	124.7	48.1	1.8	1990	81,249,645	49.1	50.9	71.3
Micronesia	271	701	185	107,000	191	394.8	152.6	0.9	1994	105,506	51.1	48.9	19.4[28]
Moldova	13,000	33,700	138	4,363,000	117	335.6	129.5	0.0	1989	4,337,592	47.5	52.5	46.9
Monaco	0.75	1.95	217	31,900	211	42,533.3	16,359.0	0.8	1990	29,972	47.5	52.5	100.0
Mongolia	604,800	1,566,500	19	2,373,000	138	3.9	1.5	1.6	1989	2,043,100	48.9	51.1	57.1
Morocco	177,117	458,730	55	27,225,000	37	153.7	59.3	1.9	1994	25,821,571	49.7	50.3	51.7
Mozambique	313,661	812,379	35	18,165,000	52	57.9	22.4	4.6	1980	11,673,725	48.6	51.4	13.2
Myanmar (Burma)	261,228	676,577	40	46,822,000	24	179.2	69.2	1.9	1983	35,307,913	49.6	50.4	24.0
Namibia	318,580	825,118	34	1,727,000	145	5.4	2.1	3.0	1991	1,401,711	48.6	51.4	32.8
Nauru	8.2	21.2	214	10,400	216	1,268.3	490.6	1.3	1992	9,919	51.2	48.8	100.0
Nepal	56,827	147,181	94	21,424,000	47	377.0	145.6	2.7	1991	18,491,097	49.9	50.1	9.6

age distribution (%) 0–14	15–29	30–44	45–59	60–74	75 and over	population (by decade, '000s) 1940	1950	1960	1970	1980	1990	2000 projection	2010 projection	country
38.7	28.7	16.0	9.2	5.4	1.9	1,550	1,940	2,574	3,583	4,527	5,041	5,931	6,850	El Salvador
41.7	25.1	15.7	11.2	5.3	1.0	...	211	244	270	256	369	478	615	Equatorial Guinea
46.1	23.0	15.9	8.9	4.4	1.6	...	1,403	1,612	2,153	2,555	2,896	4,461	5,956	Eritrea
22.2	21.4	21.0	18.5	11.7	5.1	1,054	1,101	1,216	1,365	1,473	1,571	1,430	1,401	Estonia
46.6	22.7	15.6	8.9	4.5	1.7	...	20,175	24,252	29,673	36,413	48,242	63,514	81,169	Ethiopia
24.4	—57.9—			—17.8—		27	31	35	39	43	48	44	44	Faroe Islands
38.2[14]	29.5[14]	17.8[14]	9.6[14]	3.8[14]	0.8[14]	218	289	394	520	634	739	796	860	Fiji
19.3	20.5	24.6	17.1	12.9	5.7	3,698	4,009	4,430	4,606	4,800	4,986	5,209	5,270	Finland
19.1	22.6	22.8	15.6	12.8	7.1	41,300	41,736	45,684	50,770	53,880	56,735	59,351	61,870	France
33.4	27.3	23.2	10.2	4.4	1.5	30	27	33	49	68	117	163	201	French Guiana
36.0[15]	29.7[15]	18.9[15]	10.4[15]	4.1[15]	0.9[15]	50	62	84	109	151	197	238	274	French Polynesia
33.8[10]	23.7[10]	17.0[10]	17.4[10]	6.9[10]	1.2[10]	...	416	446	514	808	1,078	1,244	1,445	Gabon
43.8	27.7	15.1	6.8	3.5	1.4	193	305	391	502	676	964	1,381	1,864	Gambia, The
50.3	25.8	13.1	6.2	3.7	0.9	...	...	...	370	456	630	1,175	1,781	Gaza Strip
24.8	24.1	19.2	17.5	10.8	3.6	3,612	3,527	4,160	4,708	5,075	5,460	5,309	5,367	Georgia
14.6	24.0	20.1	20.6	13.6	7.2	57,400	68,373	72,673	77,772	78,289	79,433	82,931	85,613	Germany
45.0	26.4	14.6	8.1	4.1	1.8	3,636	5,297	6,958	8,789	10,880	15,190	19,272	22,929	Ghana
19.6	21.3	22.6	18.2	12.9	5.3	14	23	24	26	30	31	27	27	Gibraltar
19.3	22.2	20.3	18.3	14.1	5.9	7,319	7,566	8,327	8,793	9,643	10,161	10,674	11,132	Greece
27.7	22.3	27.7	15.0	—7.4—		19	23	33	41	50	56	57	60	Greenland
42.5[7]	30.4[7]	12.9[7]	6.6[7]	5.5[7]	2.1[7]	71	76	90	95	89	95	100	104	Grenada
24.9	29.5	21.4	12.5	8.3	3.4	180	206	265	320	327	390	454	530	Guadeloupe
30.0	30.0	22.6	10.8	5.5	1.1	22	59	67	85	107	133	167	198	Guam
44.0	26.1	15.8	8.3	—5.8—		2,201	2,969	3,964	5,246	6,917	9,197	12,222	15,827	Guatemala
17.0[4]	23.3[4]	22.2[4]	16.8[4]	13.5[4]	7.2[4]	44	44	45	51	55	61	62	62	Guernsey
44.1[13]	26.5[13]	15.9[13]	9.0[13]	3.9[13]	0.6[13]	...	2,586	3,019	3,587	4,320	5,939	7,611	9,440	Guinea
43.9[7]	26.5[7]	16.1[7]	8.8[7]	3.7[7]	1.0[7]	341	573	617	620	789	998	1,263	1,579	Guinea-Bissau
40.8	30.5	14.0	8.8	4.4	1.2	344	428	571	715	759	759	780	807	Guyana
39.2	26.9	15.6	10.0	5.4	2.9	2,827	3,097	3,723	4,605	5,056	6,031	6,901	8,093	Haiti
46.8	25.8	14.4	7.9	3.8	1.4	1,146	1,390	1,873	2,553	3,316	4,681	6,323	7,998	Honduras
19.4[9]	22.7[9]	28.2[9]	14.7[9]	10.9[9]	4.1[9]	1,786	1,974	3,074	3,942	5,063	5,705	6,928	8,606	Hong Kong
21.3	19.4	22.5	17.9	13.4	5.6	9,280	9,338	9,984	10,337	10,693	10,365	10,056	9,727	Hungary
24.0	22.9	22.8	15.2	10.2	4.9	121	143	176	204	228	255	277	298	Iceland
36.0[7]	28.7[7]	18.5[7]	10.8[7]	5.1[7]	1.0[7]	317,000	369,880	445,857	555,042	692,394	855,591	1,012,909	1,155,830	India
36.6	28.3	18.1	10.6	5.2	1.1	70,500	75,449	92,701	119,467	146,449	178,302	208,706	237,653	Indonesia
44.3	26.6	15.1	8.2	4.8	0.8	14,000	16,913	21,554	28,359	38,783	54,051	65,730	78,567	Iran
45.2[20]	27.2[20]	14.2[20]	7.0[20]	3.7[20]	1.4[20]	3,745	5,163	6,822	9,413	13,233	18,425	24,731	34,545	Iraq
26.7	24.1	20.2	13.8	10.6	4.6	2,958	2,969	2,834	2,954	3,421	3,526	3,702	3,904	Ireland
17.3[4]	20.7[4]	20.4[4]	17.0[4]	15.3[4]	9.2[4]	52	55	49	52	64	69	72	72	Isle of Man
32.6[24]	26.4[24]	18.0[24]	12.3[24]	9.4[24]	3.1[24]	...	...	2,114	2,958	3,862	4,613	5,717	6,403	Israel[21, 22]
15.7[8]	23.6[8]	21.1[8]	18.5[8]	14.7[8]	6.4[8]	43,840	47,104	50,200	53,822	56,434	56,749	57,765	57,617	Italy
34.4	30.6	16.6	9.0	—9.4—		1,212	1,403	1,629	1,891	2,133	2,369	2,589	2,814	Jamaica
15.9	21.5	19.7	22.0	15.0	5.9	73,075	83,200	93,419	103,720	116,807	123,478	127,286	130,344	Japan
15.5[4]	24.9[4]	23.9[4]	17.0[4]	11.9[4]	6.8[4]	51	57	63	71	76	84	86	88	Jersey
42.2	31.4	13.8	8.1	—4.5—		...	1,095	1,384	1,795	2,183	3,306	5,039	6,734	Jordan[25]
31.9	26.3	19.4	13.2	6.9	2.3	6,148	6,703	9,996	13,110	14,940	16,742	16,573	17,181	Kazakstan
47.8	27.6	13.1	6.6	3.4	1.5	4,470	6,121	8,157	11,272	16,685	23,896	30,490	33,920	Kenya
40.3	27.5	17.3	9.2	4.8	0.9	29	33	41	49	58	72	87	95	Kiribati
29.5[10]	31.9[10]	21.3[10]	11.0[10]	5.0[10]	1.2[10]	...	9,740	10,568	14,388	17,999	21,412	25,491	28,491	Korea, North
23.0	27.6	25.7	14.5	7.4	1.9	...	21,147	25,142	32,976	38,124	42,869	46,789	49,683	Korea, South
40.4[9]	25.7[9]	22.5[9]	8.6[9]	2.2[9]	0.6[9]	...	145	292	748	1,358	2,141	2,108	2,753	Kuwait
37.5	27.0	16.3	10.9	6.2	2.1	1,528	1,740	2,173	2,965	3,631	4,395	4,697	5,442	Kyrgyzstan
45.4[9]	26.5[9]	14.9[9]	8.1[9]	4.2[9]	1.0[9]	1,075	1,886	2,309	2,845	3,293	4,191	5,557	7,168	Laos
21.4	21.7	20.3	19.2	12.0	5.3	1,886	1,949	2,129	2,374	2,544	2,671	2,426	2,337	Latvia
42.6	23.8	16.7	9.1	—7.7—		965	1,364	1,786	2,383	3,137	3,367	4,115	4,973	Lebanon
40.7	25.1	16.6	10.7	5.6	1.3	566	726	859	1,067	1,346	1,735	2,114	2,428	Lesotho
43.2	28.2	14.7	7.7	4.4	1.8	...	824	1,055	1,397	1,900	2,265	3,090	4,342	Liberia
45.4[9]	26.4[9]	14.7[9]	9.1[9]	3.7[9]	0.6[9]	900	961	1,338	2,056	3,119	4,355	6,294	8,913	Libya
23.0	26.5	24.1	14.1	9.2	3.1	11	14	16	21	26	29	32	36	Liechtenstein
22.6	23.8	20.0	17.9	10.9	4.8	2,925	2,567	2,779	3,148	3,439	3,722	3,699	3,721	Lithuania
17.3	21.5	23.8	17.5	12.8	7.1	296	296	314	339	364	382	433	462	Luxembourg
24.1	27.2	29.4	9.6	7.3	2.3	375	188	169	221	243	332	452	489	Macau
24.8	24.1	22.3	15.8	10.6	2.4	...	1,229	1,392	1,629	1,900	2,024	2,033	2,206	Macedonia
45.1[10]	26.8[10]	15.1[10]	7.7[10]	4.3[10]	1.0[10]	4,034	4,620	5,482	6,766	8,678	11,525	15,295	20,096	Madagascar
46.1	25.4	14.5	8.0	—6.0—		1,696	2,817	3,450	4,489	6,129	9,136	10,011	10,662	Malaŵi
36.7	27.6	20.0	9.9	4.6	1.2	...	6,187	7,908	10,466	13,764	17,857	23,116	27,201	Malaysia
46.9[26]	26.7[26]	12.3[26]	9.0[26]	4.0[26]	0.8[26]	81	82	106	128	155	213	286	349	Maldives
46.1	23.9	15.0	8.9	4.9	1.2	3,388	3,688	4,486	5,525	6,728	8,234	10,911	14,966	Mali
24.1	23.2	23.0	15.4	10.5	3.8	270	308	329	326	324	354	380	393	Malta
51.0	24.5	14.6	5.5	3.6	0.8	...	11	15	22	32	47	68	91	Marshall Islands
23.1	28.9	20.5	13.5	9.7	4.3	200	222	252	287	326	361	415	458	Martinique
44.1	26.6	15.0	8.1	4.7	1.4	666	960	1,057	1,227	1,456	1,935	2,653	3,630	Mauritania
29.7	28.9	22.3	10.9	6.6	1.6	428	479	662	829	966	1,059	1,176	1,270	Mauritius
47.0	27.4	15.0	6.5	3.0	1.2	16	17	25	35	52	89	148	241	Mayotte
38.3	29.4	16.6	8.9	4.5	1.7	19,815	27,737	36,945	50,596	67,570	83,226	98,881	112,891	Mexico
46.4[28]	26.8[28]	12.6[28]	8.5[28]	4.5[28]	1.1[28]	...	30	40	57	73	101	110	120	Micronesia
27.9	22.9	21.0	15.6	9.7	2.9	2,468	2,341	3,004	3,595	4,002	4,364	4,420	4,688	Moldova
12.3	16.7	21.2	20.4	17.9	10.8	20	18	21	24	27	30	32	33	Monaco
41.9	29.2	14.6	8.5	—5.8—		750	747	931	1,248	1,663	2,122	2,496	2,952	Mongolia
37.0[3]	29.6[3]	17.3[3]	9.2[3]	5.4[3]	1.5[3]	7,750	8,953	11,640	15,126	19,177	23,837	28,748	33,170	Morocco
46.4	23.9	15.6	8.6	4.0	1.2	...	6,250	7,472	9,304	12,103	14,056	19,614	24,809	Mozambique
38.6	28.7	15.5	10.9	5.2	1.1	...	19,488	22,836	27,386	33,766	41,078	49,388	58,236	Myanmar (Burma)
41.7	28.8	14.7	7.8	—6.9—		336	464	591	765	975	1,409	1,886	2,513	Namibia
41.8	25.0	20.7	8.2	—2.8—		3	3	4	7	8	9	11	11	Nauru
42.3	25.7	16.7	9.7	4.7	0.9	7,000	8,000	9,180	11,232	14,634	18,111	23,042	28,698	Nepal

Area and population (continued)

country	area			population (latest estimate)					population (latest census)				
	square miles	square kilometres	rank	total midyear 1997	rank	density per sq mi	density per sq km	% annual growth rate 1992–97	census year	total	male (%)	female (%)	urban (%)
Netherlands, The	16,033	41,526	134	15,619,000	56	974.2	376.1	0.6	1996[2]	15,493,889	49.5	50.5	91.0
Netherlands Antilles	308	800	182	214,000	181	694.8	267.5	2.3	1992	189,474	47.9	52.1	...
New Caledonia	7,172	18,576	154	201,000	182	28.0	10.8	2.6	1996	196,836	51.1[29]	48.9[29]	59.4[29]
New Zealand	104,454	270,534	75	3,653,000	122	35.0	13.5	1.2	1996	3,618,302	49.3[4]	50.7[4]	75.9[4]
Nicaragua	50,893	131,812	97	4,632,000	111	91.0	35.1	3.1	1995	4,357,099	49.3	50.7	62.1[9]
Niger	489,000	1,267,000	22	9,389,000	79	19.2	7.4	3.0	1988[5]	7,228,552	49.5	50.5	15.3
Nigeria	356,669	923,768	32	103,460,000	10	290.1	112.0	2.8	1991	88,514,501	50.3	49.7	35.0[6]
Northern Mariana Islands	184	477	192	53,600	208	291.3	112.4	2.6	1990	43,345	52.6	47.4	28.0
Norway	125,050	323,878	67	4,405,000	116	35.2	13.6	0.5	1990	4,247,546	49.4	50.6	72.0
Oman	119,500	309,500	70	2,265,000	139	19.0	7.3	3.7	1993	2,018,074	58.4	41.6	71.7
Pakistan[30]	307,374	796,095	36	136,183,000	7	443.1	171.1	2.7	1981	84,253,644	52.5	47.5	28.3
Palau	188	488	191	17,200	215	91.5	35.2	1.8	1990	15,122	53.8	46.2	69.4
Panama	29,157	75,517	118	2,719,000	131	93.3	36.0	1.8	1990	2,329,329	50.6	49.4	53.7
Papua New Guinea	178,704	462,840	54	4,496,000	114	25.2	9.7	2.3	1990[31]	3,607,954	52.7	47.3	15.2
Paraguay	157,048	406,752	59	5,089,000	107	32.4	12.5	2.7	1992	4,123,550	50.2	49.8	50.5
Peru	496,225	1,285,216	20	24,371,000	38	49.1	19.0	1.9	1993	22,639,443	49.7	50.3	70.1
Philippines	115,860	300,076	72	71,539,000	14	617.5	238.4	2.3	1995	68,614,162	50.4	49.6	48.6[26]
Poland	120,728	312,685	69	38,802,000	29	321.4	124.1	0.3	1988	37,878,641	48.7	51.3	61.2
Portugal	35,574	92,135	111	9,943,000	76	279.5	107.9	0.2	1991	9,862,540	48.2	51.8	48.2
Puerto Rico	3,515	9,104	165	3,809,000	119	1,083.6	418.4	1.3	1990	3,522,037	48.4	51.6	71.2
Qatar	4,412	11,427	160	561,000	162	127.2	49.1	1.6	1986	369,079	67.2	32.8	88.0[32]
Réunion	968	2,507	173	681,000	159	703.5	271.6	1.7	1990	597,828	49.2	50.8	73.4
Romania	91,699	237,500	82	22,572,000	43	246.2	95.0	−0.2	1992	22,760,449	49.1	50.9	54.4
Russia	6,592,800	17,075,400	1	147,231,000	6	22.3	8.6	−0.2	1989	147,400,537	46.9	53.1	73.6
Rwanda	10,169	26,338	147	7,738,000	87	760.9	293.8	0.6	1991	7,164,994	48.7	51.3	5.4
St. Kitts and Nevis	104	269	204	39,400	210	378.8	146.5	−0.9	1991	40,618	49.1	50.9	48.9[6]
St. Lucia	238	617	188	148,000	187	621.8	239.9	1.5	1991	133,308	48.5	51.5	44.1[6]
St. Vincent and the Grenadines	150	389	197	112,000	190	746.7	287.9	0.7	1991	106,499	49.9	50.1	24.6
Samoa	1,093	2,831	171	169,000	184	154.6	59.7	1.0	1991	161,298	52.5	47.5	21.2
San Marino	24	61	211	25,600	214	1,083.4	418.4	1.5	1976	19,149	50.4	49.6	90.1[7]
São Tomé and Príncipe	386	1,001	180	137,000	188	354.9	136.4	2.2	1991	117,504	49.4	50.6	44.1[8]
Saudi Arabia	865,000	2,248,000	13	19,072,000	49	22.0	8.5	2.6	1992	16,929,294	55.9	44.1	77.3[6]
Senegal	75,951	196,712	87	9,404,000	78	123.8	47.8	3.5	1988	6,928,405	48.7	51.3	38.6
Seychelles	176	455	194	77,300	198	439.2	169.9	1.8	1996	75,304	49.7[20]	50.3[20]	35.5[20]
Sierra Leone	27,699	71,740	119	4,424,000	115	159.7	61.7	0.3	1985	3,517,530	49.6	50.4	31.8
Singapore	249	646	187	3,104,000	130	12,465.9	4,805.0	1.9	1990[5]	2,705,115	50.6	49.4	100.0
Slovakia	18,933	49,036	129	5,404,000	102	285.4	110.2	0.4	1991	5,268,935	48.9	51.1	56.8
Slovenia	7,821	20,256	153	1,955,000	142	250.0	96.5	−0.4	1991	1,974,839	48.5	51.5	48.9
Solomon Islands	10,954	28,370	143	411,000	169	37.5	14.5	3.7	1986	285,176	51.9	48.1	15.7
Somalia	246,000	637,000	42	6,870,000	92	27.9	10.8	0.8	1975	4,089,203	50.1	49.9	25.4
South Africa	470,693	1,219,090	25	42,446,000	27	90.2	34.8	1.8	1996	37,859,000	48.0	52.0	60.3[4]
Spain	195,364	505,990	51	39,323,000	28	201.3	77.7	0.2	1991	38,999,181	49.1	50.9	75.3
Sri Lanka	25,332	65,610	122	18,663,000	50	736.7	284.5	1.4	1981	14,848,364	50.8	49.2	21.5
Sudan, The	966,757	2,503,890	10	32,594,000	32	33.7	13.0	2.9	1993	24,940,683	50.2	49.8	31.3[9]
Suriname	63,251	163,820	92	424,000	166	6.7	2.6	1.0	1980	354,860	49.5	50.5	49.1[9]
Swaziland	6,704	17,364	157	1,032,000	153	153.9	59.4	2.9	1986	681,059	47.2	52.8	22.8
Sweden	173,732	449,964	56	8,863,000	82	51.0	19.7	0.4	1996[2]	8,837,496	49.4	50.6	83.9
Switzerland	15,940	41,285	135	7,116,000	91	446.4	172.4	0.7	1990[33]	6,873,687	49.3	50.7	68.9
Syria	71,498	185,180	88	15,009,000	57	209.9	81.1	3.0	1994	13,812,000	51.1[3]	48.9[3]	52.2[9]
Taiwan	13,969	36,179	136	21,616,000	46	1,547.4	597.5	0.9	1990[5]	20,393,628	52.1	47.9	74.5
Tajikistan	55,300	143,100	95	6,054,000	95	109.5	42.3	1.7	1989	5,108,576	49.7	50.3	32.6
Tanzania	364,901	945,090	31	29,461,000	35	80.7	31.2	2.4	1988	23,174,336	48.9	51.1	18.5
Thailand	198,115	513,115	50	60,602,000	18	305.9	118.1	1.1	1990	54,532,300	49.6	50.4	18.7
Togo	21,925	56,785	125	4,736,000	109	216.0	83.4	3.6	1981	2,719,567	48.7	51.3	15.2
Tonga	290	750	184	101,000	192	348.3	134.7	0.6	1986[5]	94,649	50.3	49.7	30.7
Trinidad and Tobago	1,980	5,128	168	1,276,000	148	644.4	248.8	0.5	1990	1,234,388	50.1	49.9	64.8
Tunisia	63,378	164,150	91	9,245,000	81	145.9	56.3	1.6	1994	8,785,364	50.6	49.4	61.0
Turkey	300,948	779,452	37	63,528,000	15	211.1	81.5	1.7	1990	56,473,035	50.7	49.3	59.0
Turkmenistan	188,500	488,100	52	4,695,000	110	24.9	9.6	3.1	1995	4,483,251	49.6	50.4	46.0
Tuvalu	9.4	24.4	213	10,300	217	1,095.7	422.1	1.6	1991	9,043	48.4	51.6	42.5
Uganda	93,070	241,040	80	20,605,000	48	221.4	85.5	2.6	1991	16,671,705	49.1	50.9	11.3
Ukraine	233,100	603,700	44	51,150,000	23	219.4	84.7	−0.4	1989	51,706,746	46.3	53.7	66.9
United Arab Emirates	32,280	83,600	116	2,580,000	134	79.9	30.9	5.1	1995	2,377,000	66.4	33.6	84.0[9]
United Kingdom	94,251	244,110	79	58,919,000	19	625.1	241.4	0.3	1991[5]	56,467,000	48.4	51.6	89.1[6]
United States	3,679,192	9,529,063	4	267,839,000	3	74.1	28.6	1.0	1990[34]	248,709,873	48.7	51.3	75.2
Uruguay	68,037	176,215	90	3,185,000	128	46.8	18.1	0.7	1996	3,151,662	48.4	51.6	89.3
Uzbekistan	172,700	447,400	57	23,664,000	41	137.0	52.9	2.0	1989	19,905,158	49.3	50.7	40.7
Vanuatu	4,707	12,190	159	176,000	183	37.4	14.4	2.5	1989	142,630	51.6	48.4	17.7
Venezuela	352,144	912,050	33	22,777,000	42	64.7	25.0	2.2	1990	19,405,429	49.7	50.3	84.0
Vietnam	127,816	331,041	65	75,124,000	13	587.8	226.9	1.7	1989	64,411,713	48.7	51.3	20.1
Virgin Islands (U.S.)	136	352	200	97,200	194	714.7	276.1	−0.3	1990	101,809	48.3	51.7	37.2
West Bank[35]	2,270	5,900	166	1,793,000	144	789.9	303.9	4.8	1995[2, 16]	1,707,000	51.2	48.8	...
Western Sahara	97,344	252,120	77	281,000	175	2.9	1.1	3.9	1994	252,146	...	...	90.7
Yemen	214,300	555,000	48	16,496,000	55	77.0	29.7	3.7	1994	14,587,807	51.2	48.8	23.5
Yugoslavia	39,449	102,173	107	10,632,000	67	269.5	104.1	0.3	1991	10,394,026	49.6	50.4	53.2[6]
Zambia	290,586	752,614	39	9,350,000	80	32.2	12.4	2.1	1990	7,818,447	49.2	50.8	42.0
Zimbabwe	150,872	390,757	60	11,423,000	63	75.7	29.2	1.5	1992	10,412,548	48.8	51.2	30.6

[1]Settled population only. [2]Civil register; not a census. [3]1994 estimate. [4]1991 census. [5]Data are for de jure population. [6]1990 estimate. [7]1991 estimate. [8]1992 estimate. [9]1995 estimate. [10]1993 estimate. [11]Except census, data are for the island of Cyprus. [12]Republic of Cyprus only. [13]1996 estimate. [14]1986 census. [15]1988 census. [16]Projections from 1995 demographic survey. [17]Former West Germany only. [18]Excludes visitors, transients, and family members of British servicemen. [19]Data exclude Alderney (population 2,297) and Sark (population 604). [20]1987 census. [21]Area figures exclude the West Bank, East Jerusalem, Gaza Strip, and Golan Heights. [22]Population figures include the Golan Heights and East Jerusalem, and exclude Israelis in the West Bank and

age distribution (%) 0–14	15–29	30–44	45–59	60–74	75 and over	population (by decade, '000s) 1940	1950	1960	1970	1980	1990	2000 projection	2010 projection	country
18.4	21.3	23.9	18.6	12.1	5.7	8,834	10,027	11,417	12,958	14,150	14,952	15,921	16,738	Netherlands, The
26.0	23.9	25.5	14.3	7.3	3.0	77	112	136	163	174	188	230	288	Netherlands Antilles
32.6[29]	28.6[29]	19.8[29]	12.1[29]	5.4[29]	1.6[29]	53	59	79	110	140	170	211	251	New Caledonia
23.2[4]	24.6[4]	22.4[4]	14.4[4]	10.9[4]	4.5[4]	1,637	1,909	2,377	2,820	3,144	3,363	3,749	4,013	New Zealand
45.2[9]	28.4[9]	15.2[9]	7.1[9]	3.4[9]	0.7[9]	825	1,098	1,493	2,053	2,776	3,591	4,993	6,192	Nicaragua
48.7	24.8	14.6	6.8	3.6	1.5	1,700	2,482	3,168	4,182	5,629	7,644	10,260	13,678	Niger
47.9[6]	21.9[6]	14.3[6]	9.0[6]	5.2[6]	1.6[6]	...	31,797	39,230	49,309	65,699	85,103	112,500	148,710	Nigeria
23.8	33.5	30.7	9.1	2.3	0.5	48	6	9	10	17	44	57	71	Northern Mariana Islands
18.8	22.9	22.1	15.1	13.9	7.2	2,973	3,265	3,581	3,877	4,086	4,241	4,483	4,681	Norway
41.0	25.5	21.9	7.8	2.9	0.9	...	489	597	774	1,164	1,751	2,512	3,516	Oman
44.5	23.9	15.4	9.3	5.3	1.6	28,300	39,513	49,955	65,706	85,299	112,857	144,560	176,400	Pakistan[30]
30.3	27.8	22.8	10.5	6.4	2.2	25	7	9	12	13	15	18	20	Palau
34.8	29.2	18.2	10.2	5.5	2.0	620	893	1,148	1,531	1,950	2,398	2,856	3,266	Panama
41.9	28.5	16.6	8.7	—3.2—		1,308	1,412	1,747	2,288	2,991	3,823	4,812	5,925	Papua New Guinea
40.1	27.6	18.7	8.3	4.2	1.1	1,111	1,351	1,774	2,351	3,136	4,219	5,480	6,805	Paraguay
37.0	28.6	17.7	9.8	—7.0—		6,784	7,632	9,931	13,193	17,295	21,307	25,662	30,506	Peru
39.6[26]	28.7[26]	17.3[26]	9.2[26]	4.2[26]	1.1[26]	16,459	20,988	27,561	36,850	48,286	60,937	76,320	86,423	Philippines
25.4	21.2	23.3	15.5	10.4	4.2	31,500	24,824	29,561	32,526	35,578	38,057	39,055	40,388	Poland
19.9[7]	23.7[7]	20.3[7]	16.9[7]	13.7[7]	5.3[7]	7,696	8,405	8,826	9,040	9,766	9,896	9,995	10,172	Portugal
27.2	25.1	20.4	14.1	9.2	4.0	1,878	2,218	2,360	2,721	3,204	3,528	3,945	4,438	Puerto Rico
27.8	29.3	32.3	8.6	1.6	0.4	...	47	59	151	229	484	589	691	Qatar
29.5	29.8	20.3	11.7	6.5	2.1	221	244	338	447	507	602	717	851	Réunion
22.4	22.9	20.8	17.1	—16.8—		15,907	16,311	18,403	20,253	22,201	23,201	22,464	22,107	Romania
23.1	22.0	21.9	17.6	11.2	4.2	110,098	105,018	119,906	130,392	138,660	148,292	145,750	140,579	Russia
45.6	28.6	12.4	8.4	3.9	0.9	1,910	2,429	3,083	3,813	5,170	7,145	8,900	10,080	Rwanda
36.9[7]	31.8[7]	14.5[7]	6.0[7]	6.9[7]	3.8[7]	43	49	51	46	43	42	39	39	St. Kitts and Nevis
36.8	29.4	16.3	8.7	6.3	2.5	70	79	86	101	122	134	153	170	St. Lucia
37.2	29.5	16.1	8.3	6.4	2.5	61	67	80	86	99	105	115	126	St. Vincent and the Grenadines
40.5	30.0	14.6	8.7	—6.0—		61	82	111	143	155	159	174	192	Samoa
24.4	23.0	19.9	17.4	11.4	3.9	10	13	15	19	21	23	27	31	San Marino
46.9	26.2	12.2	8.0	—6.7—		60	60	64	74	94	117	146	182	São Tomé and Príncipe
42.1[8]	22.8[8]	21.6[8]	9.9[8]	3.0[8]	0.6[8]	...	3,201	4,075	5,745	9,604	16,048	21,257	28,880	Saudi Arabia
47.5	26.1	13.6	7.8	—5.0—		1,857	2,654	3,270	4,318	5,640	7,408	10,390	14,362	Senegal
33.6[20]	30.3[20]	15.3[20]	10.7[20]	7.1[20]	2.9[20]	32	34	42	54	63	70	81	94	Seychelles
43.9[32]	25.6[32]	15.7[32]	9.6[32]	4.5[32]	0.7[32]	1,700	2,087	2,396	2,789	3,333	4,283	4,983	6,674	Sierra Leone
23.2	27.3	27.7	12.7	6.9	2.2	751	1,022	1,639	2,075	2,282	2,705	3,289	3,988	Singapore
25.0	22.7	22.8	14.6	10.7	4.2	3,553	3,463	3,994	4,528	4,984	5,298	5,466	5,676	Slovakia
20.0	22.4	23.7	17.4	11.9	4.6	1,450	1,467	1,580	1,727	1,901	1,998	1,965	2,004	Slovenia
47.3	25.7	13.9	8.1	—4.9—		94	104	125	163	230	319	459	600	Solomon Islands
45.6	24.9	15.5	7.4	—5.4—		...	2,438	2,956	3,667	5,799	6,753	7,079	7,823	Somalia
34.6[4]	28.5[4]	19.6[4]	10.8[4]	5.1[4]	1.4[4]	10,353	13,596	17,417	22,783	29,208	37,164	44,315	46,038	South Africa
19.1[7]	24.9[7]	20.1[7]	16.5[7]	13.7[7]	5.7[7]	25,757	27,868	30,303	33,779	37,636	38,798	39,466	39,917	Spain
35.3	29.6	17.9	10.6	5.2	1.4	5,972	7,678	9,889	12,514	14,747	16,993	19,294	21,414	Sri Lanka
43.0	27.0	16.4	9.3	3.7	0.6	...	8,051	10,589	13,788	19,064	26,628	35,530	46,573	Sudan, The
39.3	29.5	13.8	10.0	4.5	2.8	193	208	285	373	355	402	445	511	Suriname
47.3	26.6	13.4	7.4	3.4	1.3	154	253	320	409	607	853	1,137	1,566	Swaziland
18.8	19.3	20.4	19.4	13.6	8.4	6,371	7,041	7,498	8,081	8,310	8,559	8,976	9,243	Sweden
16.8	22.8	23.2	18.0	12.5	6.7	4,234	4,715	5,429	6,270	6,362	6,712	7,225	7,438	Switzerland
47.3[3]	27.8[3]	13.8[3]	6.7[3]	3.7[3]	0.8[3]	2,597	3,495	4,561	6,305	8,704	12,116	16,392	21,990	Syria
27.1	27.8	23.1	12.3	7.9	1.8	5,987	7,619	10,668	14,583	17,705	20,279	22,183	24,180	Taiwan
42.9	28.1	13.8	9.0	4.6	1.6	1,525	1,532	2,083	2,942	3,968	5,303	6,409	8,051	Tajikistan
47.2[6]	26.7[6]	14.2[6]	7.8[6]	3.3[6]	0.7[6]	...	8,909	10,876	14,038	18,689	24,826	31,045	36,076	Tanzania
28.8	30.4	21.2	12.3	5.7	1.6	15,296	20,010	26,392	35,037	46,538	56,096	62,405	67,774	Thailand
49.8	24.8	13.1	6.8	3.3	2.0	834	1,329	1,514	2,020	2,596	3,680	5,263	7,401	Togo
40.6	29.0	13.8	10.1	5.0	1.4	37	50	65	80	92	97	103	105	Tonga
33.5	27.2	19.9	10.7	6.4	2.3	503	668	828	941	1,082	1,227	1,297	1,370	Trinidad and Tobago
34.8	28.5	18.8	9.6	6.4	1.9	2,887	3,157	4,149	5,099	6,443	8,207	9,645	10,960	Tunisia
35.0	28.6	18.4	10.9	5.6	1.6	17,723	20,809	27,509	35,321	44,438	56,123	66,618	76,570	Turkey
40.5[29]	28.8[29]	15.5[29]	9.1[29]	4.7[29]	1.4[29]	1,302	1,211	1,594	2,189	2,860	3,668	4,961	5,956	Turkmenistan
34.6	24.0	20.7	11.3	—9.2—		4	5	5	6	7	9	11	12	Tuvalu
47.3	27.7	13.1	6.9	3.7	1.3	4,233	5,522	7,262	9,724	12,252	17,040	21,891	26,355	Uganda
21.5	21.0	20.6	18.5	10.7	7.7	41,340	36,906	42,783	47,317	50,034	51,892	50,785	50,320	Ukraine
34.9[9]	18.7[9]	31.6[9]	12.7[9]	1.9[9]	0.2[9]	...	70	90	223	1,015	1,844	2,722	3,277	United Arab Emirates
19.1	21.9	21.2	16.7	14.1	7.0	48,226	50,290	52,372	55,632	56,330	57,561	59,333	60,395	United Kingdom
21.5	23.4	23.9	14.4	11.5	5.3	132,594	152,271	180,671	204,879	227,726	249,907	274,898	297,980	United States
24.4[13]	23.8[13]	19.3[13]	15.2[13]	12.3[13]	4.9[13]	1,974	2,194	2,531	2,824	2,914	3,041	3,278	3,524	Uruguay
40.8	28.4	15.0	9.3	4.7	1.8	6,551	6,314	8,559	11,973	15,977	20,515	25,035	30,282	Uzbekistan
45.5	26.6	15.2	8.4	3.7	0.6	43	52	65	86	115	147	189	231	Vanuatu
38.3	28.1	18.6	9.3	4.5	1.2	3,740	5,094	7,579	10,721	15,091	19,502	24,170	28,716	Venezuela
39.0	28.7	16.0	9.1	5.6	1.6	...	25,587	31,955	42,978	54,234	66,314	78,350	88,602	Vietnam
28.9	23.7	22.0	16.0	7.3	2.2	25	27	32	63	98	101	99	107	Virgin Islands (U.S.)
44.6	28.4	14.0	7.4	4.4	1.2	...	...	...	608	733	1,011	1,988	2,717	West Bank[35]
...	...	...	...	...	...	...	14	32	76	155	214	314	429	Western Sahara
47.6[3]	28.7[3]	11.9[3]	7.4[3]	3.6[3]	0.7[3]	...	4,316	5,247	6,332	8,219	11,230	18,355	25,787	Yemen
22.8	21.6	21.7	17.1	12.2	3.5	...	7,131	8,050	8,910	9,842	10,529	10,808	11,171	Yugoslavia
47.3	28.2	12.9	7.3	3.5	0.7	1,484	2,553	3,254	4,247	5,638	8,019	9,899	11,471	Zambia
45.1	28.3	14.0	7.2	3.9	1.2	1,940	2,853	4,011	5,515	7,298	10,121	11,777	11,905	Zimbabwe

Gaza Strip. [23]Includes East Jerusalem and Israelis in the West Bank, Gaza Strip, and Golan Heights. [24]1983 census. [25]Excludes the West Bank. [26]1990 census. [27]1985 census. [28]1980 census. [29]1989 census. [30]Excludes Afghan refugees (1997; 1.2 million) and the area (32,323 sq mi [83,716 sq km]) and population (1997; 3.9 million) of Pakistani-occupied Jammu and Kashmir. [31]Excludes an estimated 155,000 persons in North Solomons province and five remote census districts. [32]1985 estimate. [33]Includes resident aliens; excludes seasonal workers. [34]Excludes 515,000 armed forces overseas. [35]Excludes East Jerusalem.

Major cities and national capitals

The following table lists the principal cities or municipalities (those exceeding 100,000 in population [75,000 for Anglo-America]) of the countries of the world, together with figures for each national capital (indicated by a ★), regardless of size.

Most of the populations given refer to a so-called city proper, that is, a legally defined, incorporated, or chartered area defined by administrative boundaries and by national or state law. Some data, however, refer to the municipality, or commune, similar to the medieval city-state in that the city is governed together with its immediately adjoining, economically dependent areas, whether urban or rural in nature. Some countries define no other demographic or legal entities within such communes or municipalities, but many identify a centre, seat, head (*cabecera*), or locality that corresponds to the most densely populated, compact, contiguous core of the municipality. Because the amount of work involved in carefully defining these "centres" may be considerable, the necessary resources usually exist only at the time of a national census (generally 5 or 10 years apart). Between censuses, therefore, it may be possible only to track the growth of the municipality as a whole. Thus, in order to provide the most up-to-date data for cities in this table, figures referring to municipalities or communes may be given (identified by the abbreviation "MU"), even though the country itself may define a smaller, more closely knit city proper. Specific identification of municipalities is provided in this table *only* when the country also publishes data for a more narrowly defined city proper; it is *not* provided when the sole published figure is the municipality, whether or not this is the proper local administrative term for the entity.

Problems also exist in the identification of cities in terms of named legal entities. There is, for example, a single municipality (*commune*) named Brussel (Brussels) at the centre of the Brussels agglomeration in Belgium; the *commune* numbers only about 136,000 population, while the agglomeration, which is understood by most people to constitute the city, numbers nearly a million. Both are shown so as to apprise the reader of the existence of a problem.

For certain countries, more than one form of the name of the city is given, usually to permit recognition of recent place name changes or of *forms* of the place name likely to be encountered in press stories if the title of the city's entry in the *Encyclopædia Britannica* is spelled according to a different romanization or spelling policy. Chinese names, for example, are given first in their Wade-Giles spelling (the scholarly system used by Britannica) and then, parenthetically, in their Pinyin spelling, the official Chinese system now encountered in press reports, official documents and maps, and in the *Britannica Book of the Year*.

Sources for this data were usually the national census and statistical abstracts of the countries concerned, supplemented by the Internet and correspondence with most national statistical offices to solicit unpublished data.

Major cities and national capitals

country city	population
Afghanistan (early 1990s est.)	
Herāt	186,800
★ Kābul	700,000[1]
Kandahār (Qandahār)	237,500
Mazār-e Sharīf	127,800
Albania (1995 est.)	
★ Tiranë	270,000
Algeria (1987)	
★ Algiers	2,168,000[2]
Annaba	222,518
Batna	181,601
Béchar	107,311
Bejaïa	114,534
Biskra	128,280
Blida (el-Boulaida)	127,284
Constantine (Qacentina)	440,842
Mostaganem	114,037
Oran (Wahran)	609,823
Sétif	170,182
Sidi bel Abbès	152,778
Skikda	128,747
Tébessa	107,559
Tlemcen (Tilimsen)	107,632
American Samoa (1990)	
★ Fagatogo (legislative and judicial)	2,323[3]
★ Utulei (executive)	930[3]
Andorra (1995 est.)	
★ Andorra la Vella	21,984
Angola (1993 est.)	
Huambo	400,000
★ Luanda	2,081,000[2]
Lubango	105,000[4]
Antigua and Barbuda (1991)	
★ Saint John's	22,342
Argentina (1991)	
Avellaneda	346,620[5]
Bahía Blanca	260,096
★ Buenos Aires	2,988,006[2, 5]
Catamarca	110,269
Comodoro Rivadavia	124,104
Concordia	116,485
Córdoba	1,208,713[5]
Corrientes	258,103
Formosa	148,074
General San Martín	407,506[5]
La Matanza	1,111,811
La Plata	642,979[5]
La Rioja	103,727
Lanús	466,755[5]
Lomas de Zamora	572,769[5]
Mar del Plata	512,880
Mendoza	773,113[5]
Morón	641,541[5]
Neuquén	243,803[5]
Paraná	211,936[5]
Posadas	210,755[5]
Quilmes	509,445[5]
Resistencia	292,350[5]
Río Cuarto	138,853[5]
Rosario	1,118,984[5]
Salta	370,904[5]
San Fernando	132,626[5]
San Isidro	299,022[5]
San Juan	352,691[5]
San Luis	110,136
San Miguel de Tucumán	622,324[5]
San Nicolás de los Arroyos	119,302
San Salvador de Jujuy	180,102[5]
Santa Fe	406,388[5]
Santiago del Estero La Banda	263,471
Vicente López	289,142[5]
Armenia (1995 est.)	
Gyumri (Kumayri; Leninakan)	120,000[6]
★ Yerevan	1,248,700
Aruba (1996 est.)	
★ Oranjestad	21,000
Australia (1995 est.)	
Adelaide	1,081,000[7]
Bankstown	162,600[8]
Blacktown	228,400[8]
Brisbane	1,489,100[7]
Cairns	100,900
Campbelltown	149,100[8]
★ Canberra	303,700[7]
Canterbury	134,500[8]
Fairfield	186,100[8]
Geelong	152,600[9]
Gold Coast-Tweed	326,900[9]
Gosford	142,150[8]
Hobart	194,700[7]
Keilor	114,639[8]
Knox	132,686[8]
Lake Macquarie	175,510[8]
Liverpool	106,750[8]
Melbourne	3,218,100[7]
Moorabbin	100,389[8]
Newcastle	466,000[9]
Parramatta	137,450[8]
Penrith	163,500[8]
Perth	1,262,600[7]
Randwick	117,600[8]
Stirling	178,734[1]
Sydney	3,772,700[7]
Townsville	124,900[9]
Wanneroo	190,965[1]
Wollongong	253,600[9]
Austria (1991)	
Graz	237,810
Innsbruck	118,112
Linz	203,044
Salzburg	143,978
★ Vienna	1,560,471[10]
Azerbaijan (1995 est.)	
★ Baku (Baky)	1,739,900
Gäncä (Gyandzha)	292,500
Sumqayıt (Sumgait)	270,000
Bahamas, The (1990)	
★ Nassau	172,196[11]
Bahrain (1995 est.)	
★ Al-Manāmah	148,000
Bangladesh (1991)	
Barisāl	188,000
Bogra	130,000
Brāhmanbāria	125,000
Chittagong	1,599,000
Comilla	156,000
★ Dhākā (Dacca)	3,839,000
Dinājpur	138,000
Gāzipur	104,000
Jamālpur	111,000
Jessore	154,000
Khulna	731,000
Mymensingh	202,000
Naogaon	110,000
Nārāyanganj	296,000
Narsinghdi	106,000
Nawābganj (Nowābgonj)	141,000
Pābna	112,000
Rājshāhi	318,000
Rangpur	207,000
Saidpur	105,000
Savar	115,000
Sirājganj	108,000
Sylhet	109,000
Tangail	114,000
Tongi	181,000
Barbados (1990)	
★ Bridgetown	6,070
Belarus (1996 est.)	
Baranovichi (Baranavichy)	172,000
Bobruysk (Babrujsk)	227,100
Borisov (Barysau)	153,000
Brest (Bierascie)	293,000
Gomel (Homiel)	512,000
Grodno (Horadnia)	301,000
Lida	101,000
★ Minsk	1,700,000
Mogilyov (Mahilou)	367,000
Mozyr (Mazyr)	108,000
Orsha (Vorsha)	134,000
Pinsk	130,000
Soligorsk	101,000
Vitebsk (Viciebsk)	365,000
Belgium (1996 est.)	
Antwerp	455,852
Brugge (Bruges)	115,815
★ Brussels	136,424[12]
Agglomeration	948,122
Charleroi	205,591
Ghent	226,464
Liège (Luik)	190,525
Namur	105,059
Belize (1996 est.)	
★ Belmopan	6,490
Benin (1994 est.)	
Abomey-Calavi	125,565[13]
★ Cotonou (official)	750,000
Djougou	132,000
Parakou	120,000
★ Porto-Novo (de facto)	200,000
Bermuda (1995 est.)	
★ Hamilton	1,100
Bhutan (1993 est.)	
Paro	3,000[14]
★ Thimphu	30,340
Bolivia (1993 est.)	
Cochabamba	448,756
El Alto	446,189
★ La Paz (administrative)	784,976
Oruro	201,831
Potosí	123,327
Santa Cruz	767,260
★ Sucre (judicial)	144,994
Bosnia and Herzegovina (1991)	
Banja Luka	143,079
★ Sarajevo	250,000[2]
Botswana (1995 est.)	
★ Gaborone	182,000
Brazil (1991)	
Alvorada	132,582
Americana	153,592
Anápolis	222,400
Aracaju	401,676
Araçatuba	145,751
Arapiraca	124,790
Araraquara	101,302
Barra Mansa	145,112
Bauru	254,211
Belém	765,476
Belo Horizonte	1,529,566
Betim	152,846
Blumenau	185,200
Boa Vista	118,928
★ Brasília	1,492,542
Cachoeiro de Itapemirim	112,099
Campina Grande	298,331
Campinas	748,076
Campo Grande	516,403
Campos	275,508
Canoas	269,234
Carapicuíba	207,264
Caruaru	180,654
Cascavel	175,294
Caxias do Sul	262,983
Colombo	105,464
Contagem	195,705
Cuiabá	252,784
Curitiba	841,882
Diadema	305,068
Divinópolis	141,984
Dourados	116,754
Duque de Caxias	325,903
Embu	155,851
Feira de Santana	340,034
Florianópolis	191,664
Fortaleza	743,335
Foz do Iguaçu	186,362
Franca	227,613
Goiânia	912,136
Governador Valadares	210,396
Gravataí	166,954
Guarapuava	107,046
Guarulhos	544,698
Ilhéus	135,117
Imperatriz	209,970
Ipatinga	120,025
Itabuna	170,434
Itajaí	114,558
Itapevi	107,983
Itaquaquecetuba	164,665
Jaboatão	217,905
Jacareí	143,468
Jequié	114,542
João Pessoa	497,306
Joinville	326,208
Juàzeiro do Norte	163,527
Juiz de Fora	377,538
Jundiaí	253,177
Lages	137,169
Limeira	177,016
Londrina	355,062
Luziãnia	194,128
Macapá	146,523
Maceió	554,727
Manaus	1,005,634
Marabá	102,364
Maracanaú	133,206
Marília	144,906
Maringá	225,516
Mauá	294,631
Mogi das Cruzes	125,992
Montes Claros	223,046
Mossoró	117,020
Natal	459,827
Nilópolis	104,671
Niterói	400,586
Nova Friburgo	111,020
Nova Iguaçu	562,062
Novo Hamburgo	199,479
Olinda	341,059
Osasco	566,949
Parnaíba	105,131
Passo Fundo	135,158
Pelotas	260,510
Petrolina	123,857
Petrópolis	164,849
Piracicaba	223,170
Poços de Caldas	104,800
Ponta Grossa	219,648
Porto Alegre	1,237,223
Porto Velho	226,198
Presidente Prudente	157,618
Recife	1,296,995
Ribeirão Prêto	416,186
Rio Branco	167,457
Rio Claro	130,364
Rio de Janeiro	5,473,909
Rio Grande	157,608
Salvador	2,070,296
Santa Bárbara d'Oeste	140,208
Santa Maria	193,294
Santarém	168,153
Santo André	518,272
Santos	415,554
São Bernardo do Campo	550,030
São Caetano do Sul	149,203
São Carlos	100,502
São Gonçalo	296,021
São João de Meriti	220,742
São José do Rio Prêto	263,454
São José dos Campos	385,879
São Leopoldo	160,228
São Luís	164,334
São Paulo	9,393,753
São Vicente	268,467
Sapucaia do Sul	104,626
Sete Lagoas	137,537
Sorocaba	348,952
Susano (Suzano)	110,414
Taboão da Serra	159,894
Taubaté	185,790
Teresina	556,073
Uberaba	198,565
Uberlândia	354,710
Uruguaiana	103,160
Vila Velha	263,897
Vitória	258,243
Vitória da Conquista	179,868
Volta Redonda	219,988
Brunei (1991)	
★ Bandar Seri Begawan	21,484
Bulgaria (1996 est.)	
Burgas	199,470
Dobrich	103,532
Pleven	125,029
Plovdiv	344,326
Ruse	168,051
Sliven	107,011
★ Sofia	1,116,823
Stara Zagora	149,666
Varna	301,421

country city	population
Burkina Faso (1993 est.)	
Bobo Dioulasso	300,000
Koudougou	105,000
★ Ouagadougou	690,000
Burundi (1994 est.)	
★ Bujumbura	300,000
Gitega	101,827[15]
Cambodia (1994 est.)	
★ Phnom Penh	920,000
Cameroon (1992 est.)	
Bafoussam	120,000
Bamenda	110,690[16]
Douala	1,200,000
Garoua	160,000
Maroua	140,000
★ Yaoundé	800,000
Canada (1991)	
Brampton	234,445
Brantford	81,997
Burlington	129,575
Burnaby	158,858
Calgary	710,677
Cambridge	92,772
Coquitlam	84,021
Delta	88,978
East York	102,696
Edmonton	616,741
Etobicoke	309,993
Gatineau	92,284
Gloucester	101,677
Guelph	87,976
Halifax	114,455
Hamilton	318,499
Kelowna	75,950
Kitchener	168,282
Laval	314,398
London	303,165
Longueuil	129,874
Markham	153,811
Mississauga	463,388
Montreal	1,017,666
Montreal-Nord	85,516
Nepean	107,627
Niagara Falls	75,399
North York	562,564
Oakville	114,670
Oshawa	129,344
★ Ottawa	313,987
Quebec	167,517
Regina	179,178
Richmond	126,624
Richmond Hill	80,142
Saanich	95,577
Saint Catharines	129,300
Saint John's	95,770
Saskatoon	186,058
Sault Sainte Marie	81,476
Scarborough	524,598
Sherbrooke	76,429
Sudbury	92,884
Surrey	245,173
Thunder Bay	113,746
Toronto	635,395
Vancouver	471,844
Vaughan	111,359
Windsor	191,435
Winnipeg	616,790
York	140,525
Cape Verde (1995 est.)	
★ Praia	68,000
Central African Republic (1995 est.)	
★ Bangui	553,000
Chad (1993; MU)	
Abéché	187,936
Bongor	196,713
Doba	185,461
Moundou	282,103
★ N'Djamena	530,965
Sarh	193,753
Chile (1995 est.; MU)	
Antofagasta	236,730
Arica	173,336
Calama	120,602[1]
Chillán	157,083
Concepción	350,268
Copiapó	100,946[13]
Coquimbo	122,872[13]
Curicó	103,919[13]
Iquique	152,592
La Serena	117,983
Los Angeles	142,136[13]
Osorno	123,055
Puente Alto	318,898
Puerto Montt	122,399
Punta Arenas	117,206
Quilpué	110,340
Rancagua	193,755
San Bernardo	206,315
★ Santiago (administrative)	5,076,808
Talca	169,448
Talcahuano	260,915
Temuco	239,340
Valdívia	119,431
★ Valparaíso (legislative)	282,168
Viña del Mar	322,220
China (1990 est.)[17]	
A-ch'eng (Acheng)	197,595
A-k'o-su (Aksu)	164,092
An-ch'ing (Anqing)	250,718
An-k'ang (Ankang)	142,170
An-shan (Anshan)	1,500,000[18,19]
An-shun (Anshun)	174,142
An-ta (Anda)	136,446
An-yang (Anyang)	420,332
Canton (Guangzhou)	3,580,000[20]
Chan-chiang (Zhanjiang)	400,997
Ch'ang-chi (Changji)	132,260
Chang-chia-k'ou (Zhangjiakou)	529,136
Ch'ang-chih (Changzhi)	317,144
Ch'ang-chou (Changzhou)	531,470
Chang-chou (Zhangzhou)	181,424
Ch'ang-ch'un (Changchun)	2,110,000[20]
Ch'ang-sha (Changsha)	1,330,000[20]
Ch'ang-shu (Changshu)	181,805
Ch'ang-te (Changde)	301,276
Chao-ch'ing (Zhaoqing)	194,784
Ch'ao-chou (Chaozhou)	313,469
Ch'ao-hsien (Chaoxian)	123,676
Chao-tung (Zhaodong)	179,976
Ch'ao-yang (Chaoyang)	222,394
Chen-chiang (Zhenjiang)	368,316
Cheng-chou (Zhengzhou)	1,710,000[20]
Ch'eng-te (Chengde)	246,799
Ch'eng-tu (Chengdu)	2,810,000[20]
Chi-an (Ji'an)	148,583
Chi-hsi (Jixi)	683,885
Chi-lin (Jilin)	1,270,000[20]
Chi-nan (Jinan)	2,320,000[20]
Chi-ning (Jining) (*Inner Mongolia*)	163,552
Chi-ning (Jining) (*Shantung*)	265,248
Ch'i-t'ai-ho (Qitaihe)	214,957
Ch'i-tung (Qidong)	126,872
Chia-hsing (Jiaxing)	211,526
Chia-mu-ssu (Jiamusi)	493,409
Chiang-men (Jiangmen)	230,587
Chiang-yin (Jiangyin)	213,659
Chiang-yu (Jiangyou)	175,753
Chiao-hsien (Jiaoxian)	153,364
Chiao-nan (Jiaonan)	121,397
Chiao-tso (Jiaozuo)	409,100
Ch'ien-chiang (Qianjiang)	205,504
Ch'ih-feng (Chifeng)	350,077
Chin-ch'ang (Jinchang)	105,287
Chin-ch'eng (Jincheng)	136,396
Chin-chou (Jinzhou)	569,518
Ch'in-chou (Qinzhou)	114,586
Chin-hsi (Jinxi)	357,052
Chin-hua (Jinhua)	144,280
Ch'in-huang-tao (Qinhuangdao)	364,972
Ch'ing-chou (Qingzhou)	128,258
Ch'ing-tao (Qingdao)	2,060,000[20]
Ching-te-chen (Jingdezhen)	281,183
Ch'ing-yüan (Qingyuan)	164,641
Chiu-chiang (Jiujiang)	291,187
Chiu-t'ai (Jiutai)	180,130
Chou-k'ou (Zhoukou)	146,288
Chou-shan (Zhoushan)	156,317
Chu-ch'eng (Zhucheng)	102,134
Ch'ü-ching (Qujing)	178,669
Ch'u-chou (Quzhou)	112,373
Chu-chou (Zhuzhou)	409,924
Chu-hai (Zhuhai)	164,747
Ch'u-hsien (Chuxian)	125,341
Chu-ma-tien (Zhumadian)	123,232
Ch'üan-chou (Quanzhou)	185,154
Chung-shan (Zhongshan)	278,829
Chungking (Chongqing)	2,980,000[20]
Feng-ch'eng (Fengcheng)	193,784
Fo-shan (Foshan)	303,160
Fu-chin (Fujin)	103,104
Fu-chou (Fuzhou) (*Fukien*)	874,809
Fu-chou (Fuzhou) (*Kiangsi*)	1,290,000[20]
Fu-hsin (Fuxin)	635,473
Fu-ling (Fuling)	173,878
Fu-shun (Fushun)	1,350,000[20]
Fu-yang (Fuyang)	179,572
Fu-yü (Fuyu)	192,981
Ha-mi (Hami)	161,315
Hai-ch'eng (Haicheng)	205,560
Hai-k'ou (Haikou)	280,153
Hai-la-erh (Hailar)	180,650
Hai-lun (Kailun)	133,565
Hai-ning (Haining)	100,478
Han-chung (Hanzhong)	169,930
Han-tan (Handan)	1,110,000[20]
Hang-chou (Hangzhou)	1,340,000[20]
Harbin	2,830,000[20]
Heng-shui (Hengshui)	104,269
Heng-yang (Hengyang)	487,148
Ho-fei (Hefei)	1,000,000[20]
Ho-kang (Hegang)	522,747
Ho-pi (Hebi)	212,976
Ho-tse (Heze)	189,293
Ho-yuan (Heyuan)	120,101
Hsi-ch'ang (Xichang)	134,419
Hsi-ning (Xining)	551,776
Hsia-men (Xiamen)	368,786
Hsiang-fan (Xiangfan)	410,407
Hsiang-t'an (Xiangtan)	441,968
Hsiao-kan (Xiaogan)	166,280
Hsiao-shan (Xiaoshan)	162,930
Hsien-ning (Xianning)	136,811
Hsien-t'ao (Xiantao)	222,884
Hsien-yang (Xianyang)	352,125
Hsin-hsiang (Xinxiang)	473,762
Hsin-t'ai (Xintai)	281,248
Hsin-yang (Xinyang)	192,509
Hsin-yu (Xinyu)	173,524
Hsing-ch'eng (Xingcheng)	102,384
Hsing-hua (Xinghua)	161,910
Hsing-t'ai (Xingtai)	302,789
Hsü-ch'ang (Xuchang)	208,815
Hsü-chou (Xuzhou)	805,695
Hsuan-ch'eng (Xuancheng)	112,673
Hu-chou (Huzhou)	218,071
Hu-ho-hao-t'e (Hohhot)	652,534
Hua-tien (Huadian)	175,873
Huai-an (Huai'an)	131,149
Huai-hua (Huaihua)	126,785
Huai-nan (Huainan)	1,200,000[20]
Huai-pei (Huaibei)	366,549
Huai-yin (Huaiyin)	239,675
Huang-shan (Huangshan)	102,628
Huang-shih (Huangshi)	457,601
Hui-chou (Huizhou)	161,023
Hun-chiang (Hunjiang)	482,043
Hung-hu (Honghu)	190,772
I-ch'ang (Yichang)	371,601
I-cheng (Yizheng)	109,268
I-ch'un (Yichun)	795,789
I-ch'un (Yichun) (*Kiangsi*)	151,585
I-hsing (Yixing)	200,824
I-ning (Yining)	177,193
I-pin (Yibin)	241,019
I-yang (Yiyang)	185,818
Jen-ch'iu (Renqiu)	114,256
Jih-chao (Rizhao)	185,048
Jui-an (Rui'an)	156,468
K'ai-feng (Kaifeng)	507,763
K'ai-li (Kaili)	113,958
K'ai-yuan (Kaiyuan)	124,219
Kan-chou (Ganzhou)	220,129
Kashgar (Kashi)	174,570
Ko-chiu (Gejiu)	214,294
K'o-la-ma-i (Karamay)	197,602
K'u-erh-le (Korla)	159,344
Kuang-shui (Guangshui)	102,770
Kuang-yüan (Guangyuan)	182,241
Kuei-hsien (Guixian)	114,025
Kuei-lin (Guilin)	364,130
K'uei-t'un (Kuitun)	118,553
Kuei-yang (Guiyang)	1,530,000[20]
K'un-ming (Kunming)	1,520,000[20]
K'un-shan (Kunshan)	102,052
Kung-chu-ling (Gongzhuling)	226,569
Lai-chou (Laizhou)	198,664
Lai-wu (Laiwu)	246,833
Lai-yang (Laiyang)	137,080
Lan-chou (Lanzhou)	1,510,000[20]
Lang-fang (Langfang)	148,105
Lao-ho-k'ou (Laohekou)	123,366
Le-shan (Leshan)	341,128
Lei-yang (Leiyang)	130,115
Leng-shui-chiang (Lengshuijiang)	137,994
Lhasa	106,885
Li-ling (Liling)	108,504
Li-yang (Liyang)	109,520
Liang-ch'eng (Liangcheng)	156,307
Liao-ch'eng (Liaocheng)	207,844
Liao-yang (Liaoyang)	492,559
Liao-yüan (Liaoyuan)	354,141
Lien-yüan (Lianyuan)	118,858
Lien-yün-kang (Lianyungang)	354,139
Lin-ch'ing (Linqing)	123,958
Lin-fen (Linfen)	187,309
Lin-ho (Linhe)	133,183
Lin-i (Linyi)	324,720
Liu-chou (Liuzhou)	609,320
Liu-p'an-shui (Liupanshui)	363,954
Lo-ho (Luohe)	126,438
Lo-yang (Luoyang)	1,190,000[20]
Long-yen (Longyan)	134,481
Lou-ti (Loudi)	128,418
Lu-an (Lu'an)	144,248
Lu-chou (Luzhou)	262,892
Lung-ching (Longjing)	139,417
Lung-k'ou (Longkou)	148,362
Ma-an-shan (Ma'anshan)	305,421
Man-chou-li (Manzhouli)	120,023
Mao-ming (Maoming)	178,683
Mei-ho-k'ou (Meihekou)	209,038
Mei-hsien (Meixian)	132,156
Mi-shan (Mishan)	132,744
Mien-yang (Mianyang)	262,947
Mu-tan-chiang (Mudanjiang)	571,705
Nan-ch'ang (Nanchang)	1,350,000[20]
Nan-ch'ung (Nanchong)	180,273
Nan-ning (Nanning)	1,070,000[20]
Nan-p'ing (Nanping)	195,064
Nan-t'ung (Nantong)	343,341
Nan-yang (Nanyang)	243,303
Nanking (Nanjing)	2,500,000[20]
Nei-chiang (Neijiang)	256,012
Ning-po (Ningbo)	1,090,000[20]
O-ch'eng (Echeng)	190,123
Pai-ch'eng (Baicheng)	217,987
Pai-yin (Baiyin)	204,970
P'an-chih-hua (Panzhihua) (Tu-k'ou [Dukou])	415,466
P'an-shan (Panshan)	362,773
Pang-pu (Bengbu)	449,245
Pao-chi (Baoji)	337,765
Pao-ting (Baoding)	483,155
Pao-t'ou (Baotou)	1,200,000[20]
Pei-an (Bei'an)	204,899
Pei-hai (Beihai)	112,673
Pei-p'iao (Beipiao)	194,301
★ Peking (Beijing)	7,000,000[20]
Pen-hsi (Benxi)	768,778
Pin-chou (Binzhou)	133,555
P'ing-hsiang (Pingxiang)	425,579
P'ing-ting-shan (Pingdingshan)	410,775
P'ing-tu (Pingdu)	150,123
Po-chou (Bozhou)	106,346
P'u-ch'i (Puqi)	117,264
P'u-yang (Puyang)	175,988
San-men-hsia (Sanmenxia)	120,523
San-ming (Sanming)	160,691
San-ya (Sanya)	102,820
Sha-shih (Shashi)	281,352
Shan-t'ou (Shantou)	578,630
Shan-wei (Shanwei)	107,847
Shao-hsing (Shaoxing)	179,818
Shao-kuan (Shaoguan)	350,043
Shao-yang (Shaoyang)	247,227
Shang-chih (Shangzhi)	215,373
Shang-ch'iu (Shangqiu)	164,880
Shang-jao (Shangrao)	132,455
Shanghai	7,830,000[20]
Shen-chen (Shenzhen)	350,727
Shen-yang (Shenyang)	4,540,000[20]
Shih-chia-chuang (Shijiazhuang)	1,320,000[20]
Shih-ho-tzu (Shihezi)	299,676
Shih-shou (Shishou)	104,571
Shih-tsui-shan (Shizuishan)	257,862
Shih-yen (Shiyan)	273,786
Shuang-ch'eng (Shuangcheng)	142,659
Shuang-ya-shan (Shuangyashan)	386,081
Sian (Xi'an)	2,760,000[20]
Ssu-p'ing (Siping)	317,223
Su-ch'ien (Suqian)	105,021
Su-chou (Suzhou) (*Anhwei*)	151,862
Su-chou (Suzhou) (*Kiangsu*)	706,450
Sui-hua (Suihua)	227,881
Sui-ning (Suining)	146,086
Ta-an (Da'an)	138,963
Ta-ch'ing (Daqing)	657,297
Ta-hsien (Daxian)	188,101
Ta-li (Dali)	136,554
Ta-lien (Dalian)	2,400,000[20]
Ta-t'ung (Datong)	1,110,000[20]
T'ai-an (Tai'an)	350,696
T'ai-chou (Taizhou)	152,442
T'ai-yüan (Taiyuan)	1,960,000[20]
Tan-chiang (Danjiang)	103,211
Tan-tung (Dandong)	523,699
Tan-yang (Danyang)	169,603
T'ang-shan (Tangshan)	1,500,000
T'ao-nan (Taonan)	150,168
Te-chou (Dezhou)	195,485
Te-yang (Deyang)	182,488
T'eng-hsien (Tengxian)	315,083
T'ieh-fa (Tiefa)	131,807
T'ieh-li (Tieli)	265,683
T'ieh-ling (Tieling)	254,842
T'ien-men (Tianmen)	186,332
T'ien-shui (Tianshui)	244,974
Tientsin (Tianjin)	5,770,000[20]
Tsa-lan-t'un (Zalantun)	130,031
Ts'ang-chou (Cangzhou)	242,708
Tsao-chuang (Zaozhuang)	380,846
Tsao-yang (Zaoyang)	162,198
Tsitsihar (Qiqihar)	1,380,000[20]
Tsun-i (Zunyi)	261,862
Tu-chiang-yen (Dujiangyan)	123,357
Tu-yun (Duyun)	132,971
Tun-hua (Dunhua)	235,100
T'ung-ch'uan (Tongchuan)	280,657
T'ung-hua (Tonghua)	324,600
Tung-kuan (Dongguan)	308,669
T'ung-liao (Tongliao)	255,129
T'ung-ling (Tongling)	228,017
Tung-t'ai (Dongtai)	192,247
Tung-ying (Dongying)	281,728
Tz'u-hsi (Cixi)	107,329
Tzu-hsing (Zixing)	110,048
Tzu-kung (Zigong)	393,184
Tzu-po (Zibo)	2,460,000[20]
Wa-fang-tien (Wafangdian)	251,733
Wan-hsien (Wanxian)	156,823
Wei-fang (Weifang)	428,522
Wei-hai (Weihai)	128,888
Wei-nan (Weinan)	140,169
Wen-chou (Wenzhou)	401,871
Wen-teng (Wendeng)	133,910
Wu-chou (Wuzhou)	210,452
Wu-hai (Wuhai)	264,081
Wu-han (Wuhan)	3,750,000[20]
Wu-hsi (Wuxi)	826,833
Wu-hu (Wuhu)	425,740
Wu-lan-hao-t'e (Ulanhot)	159,538
Wu-lu-mu-ch'i (Ürümqi)	1,160,000[20]
Wu-wei (Wuwei)	133,101
Ya-k'o-she (Yakeshi)	377,869
Yang-chiang (Yangjiang)	215,196
Yang-chou (Yangzhou)	312,892
Yang-ch'üan (Yangquan)	362,268
Yen-an (Yan'an)	113,277
Yen-ch'eng (Yancheng)	296,831
Yen-chi (Yanji)	230,892
Yen-t'ai (Yantai)	452,127
Yin-ch'uan (Yinchuan)	356,652
Ying-k'ou (Yingkou)	421,589
Yü-lin (Yulin)	144,467
Yü-men (Yumen)	109,234
Yü-shu (Yushu)	131,861
Yü-tz'u (Yuci)	191,356
Yu-yao (Yuyao)	114,065
Yüan-chiang (Yuanjiang)	107,004
Yüeh-yang (Yueyang)	302,800
Yun-ch'eng (Yuncheng)	108,359
Yung-an (Yong'an)	111,762
Colombia (1997 est.)	
Armenia	283,842
Barrancabermeja	180,653[2]
Barranquilla	1,157,826
Bello	304,819[2]
Bucaramanga	508,240
Buenaventura	266,988[2]
Cali	1,985,906

Major cities and national capitals (continued)

country city	population
Cartagena	812,595
Cartago	117,166[2]
Ciénaga	144,340[2]
Cúcuta	589,196
Dosquebradas	163,599[2]
Envigado	109,240[2]
Florencia	114,848
Floridablanca	246,834[2]
Ibagué	419,883
Itagüí	169,374[2]
Magangué	104,496[2]
Malambo	112,289[2]
Manizales	358,194
Medellín	1,970,691
Montería	327,249
Neiva	305,625
Palmira	256,823[2]
Pasto	362,227
Pereira	434,267
Popayán	218,057
Quibdó	123,102
Ríohacha	114,608
Santa Marta	343,038
★ Santafé de Bogotá, D.C.	6,004,782
Sincelejo	213,916
Soacha	266,817[2]
Soledad	264,583[2]
Tuluá	138,124[2]
Tumaco	114,802[2]
Tunja	118,406
Turbo	127,045[2]
Valledupar	296,624
Villavicencio	299,296
Comoros (1991)	
★ Moroni	30,000
Congo, Dem. Rep. of the (1994 est.)	
Boma	135,284
Bukavu	201,569
Butembo	109,406
Goma	109,094
Kalemi	101,309
Kananga	393,030
Kikwit	182,142
★ Kinshasa	4,655,313
Kisangani	417,517
Kolwezi	417,810
Likasi	299,118
Lubumbashi	851,381
Matadi	172,730
Mbandaka	169,841
Mbuji-Mayi	806,475
Mwene-Ditu	137,459
Tshikapa	180,860
Uvira	115,590
Congo, Rep. of the (1992 est.)	
★ Brazzaville	937,579
Pointe-Noire	576,206
Costa Rica (1997 est.)	
★ San José	329,154[21]
Côte d'Ivoire (1995 est.)	
★ Abidjan (de facto; legislative)	2,500,000[18]
Bouaké	330,000
Daloa	123,000
Korhogo	109,445[22]
★ Yamoussoukro (de jure; administrative)	110,000
Croatia (1991)	
Osijek	129,792
Rijeka	167,964
Split	200,459
★ Zagreb	867,717
Cuba (1994 est.)	
Bayamo	137,663
Camagüey	293,961
Cienfuegos	132,038
Guantánamo	207,796
★ Havana	2,241,000[2]
Holguín	242,085
Las Tunas	126,930
Manzanillo	107,650[23]
Matanzas	123,843
Pinar del Río	128,570
Santa Clara	205,400
Santiago de Cuba	440,084
Cyprus (1994 est.)	
Limassol	143,400
★ Nicosia (Lefkosia)	186,400[24]
Czech Republic (1996 est.)	
Brno	388,899
Hradec Králové	100,528
Liberec	100,604
Olomouc	104,845
Ostrava	324,813
Plzen	171,249
★ Prague	1,209,855
Denmark (1996 est.; MU)	
Ålborg	159,980
Århus	279,759
★ Copenhagen	1,362,264[19]
Odense	183,564
Djibouti (1995 est.)	
★ Djibouti	383,000
Dominica (1991)	
★ Roseau	15,853
Dominican Republic (1993)	
La Romana	132,834
San Francisco de Macorís	129,943
San Pedro de Macorís	123,987
Santiago	364,859
★ Santo Domingo	1,555,656[25]
Ecuador (1997 est.)	
Ambato	160,302
Cuenca	255,028
Duran	135,675
Esmeraldas	117,722
Guayaquil	1,973,880
Ibarra	119,243
Loja	117,365
Machala	197,350
Manta	156,981
Milagro	119,371
Portoviejo	167,956
Quevedo	120,640
★ Quito	1,487,513
Riobamba	117,270
Santo Domingo	183,219
Egypt (1992 est.)	
Alexandria	3,700,000[18,19]
Aswān	220,000
Asyūṭ	321,000
Banhā	136,000
Banī Suwayf	179,000
Būr Saʿīd (Port Said)	460,000[8]
★ Cairo	9,900,000[18,19]
Damanhūr	222,000
al-Fayyūm	250,000
Hulwan (Helwan)	352,300[26]
Al-Ismāʿīlīyah	255,000
Al-Jīzah (Giza)	2,144,000
Kafr ad-Dawwar	226,000
Kafr ash-Shaykh	102,910[27]
Al-Maḥallah al-Kubrā	408,000
Al-Manṣūrah	371,000
Al-Minyā	208,000
Qinā	141,000
Sawhāj	156,000
Shibīn al-Kawm	158,000
Shubrā al-Khaymah	834,000
As-Suways (Suez)	388,000
Ṭanṭā	380,000
Al-Uqṣur (Luxor)	155,000[8]
Az-Zaqāzīq	287,000
El Salvador (1992; MU)	
Apopa	100,763
Delgado	104,790
Mejicanos	145,000[19]
Nueva San Salvador	116,575
San Miguel	182,817
★ San Salvador	422,570
Santa Ana	202,337
Soyapango	251,811[19]
Equatorial Guinea (1991 est.)	
★ Malabo	58,040
Eritrea (1995 est.)	
★ Asmara	431,000
Estonia (1996 est.)	
★ Tallinn	427,500
Tartu	103,400
Ethiopia (1994)	
★ Addis Ababa	2,112,737
Dire Dawa	164,851
Gonder	112,249
Harer	131,139
Nazret	127,842
Faroe Islands (1996 est.)	
★ Tórshavn	15,272
Fiji (1996)	
★ Suva	167,421[28]
Finland (1997 est.; MU)	
Espoo	196,260
★ Helsinki	532,053
Oulu	111,556
Tampere	186,026
Turku	166,929
Vantaa	168,778
France (1990)	
Aix-en-Provence	126,854
Amiens	136,234
Angers	146,163
Besançon	119,194
Bordeaux	213,274
Boulogne-Billancourt	101,971
Brest	153,099
Caen	115,624
Clermont-Ferrand	140,167
Dijon	151,636
Grenoble	153,973
Le Havre	197,219
Le Mans	148,465
Lille	178,301
Limoges	136,407
Lyon	422,444
Marseille	807,726
Metz	123,920
Montpellier	210,866
Mulhouse	109,905
Nancy	102,410
Nantes	252,029
Nice	345,674
Nîmes	133,607
Orléans	107,965
★ Paris	2,175,200
Perpignan	108,049
Reims	185,164
Rennes	203,533
Rouen	105,470
Saint-Étienne	201,569
Strasbourg	255,937
Toulon	170,167
Toulouse	365,933
Tours	133,403
Villeurbanne	119,848
French Guiana (1995 est.)	
★ Cayenne	45,000
French Polynesia (1988)	
★ Papeete	23,555
Gabon (1993)	
★ Libreville	362,386
Gambia, The (1993)	
★ Banjul	42,407
Serekunda	102,600[29]
Gaza Strip (early 1990s est.)	
Gaza (Ghazzah)	293,000
Khan Younis	160,463
Rafah	101,926
Georgia (1994 est.)	
Bat'umi (Batumi)	137,100
K'ut'aisi (Kutaisi)	240,600
Rust'avi (Rustavi)	155,500
Sukhumi	112,000[1]
★ T'bilisi (Tbilisi)	1,253,100
Germany (1996 est.)	
Aachen	247,923
Augsburg	259,699
Bergisch Gladbach	105,478
Berlin	3,471,418
Bielefeld	324,066
Bochum	400,395
★ Bonn	291,431
Bottrop	120,642
Braunschweig	252,544
Bremen	549,357
Bremerhaven	130,400
Chemnitz	266,737
Cologne (Köln)	965,697
Cottbus	123,214
Darmstadt	138,980
Dortmund	598,840
Dresden	469,110
Duisburg	535,250
Düsseldorf	571,030
Erfurt	211,108
Erlangen	101,406
Essen	614,861
Frankfurt am Main	650,055
Freiburg im Breisgau	199,273
Fürth	108,418
Gelsenkirchen	291,164
Gera	123,555
Göttingen	126,253
Hagen	212,003
Halle	282,784
Hamburg	1,707,901
Hamm	183,408
Hannover	523,147
Heidelberg	138,781
Heilbronn	121,509
Herne	179,897
Hildesheim	106,101
Ingolstadt	111,979
Jena	101,061
Kaiserslautern	102,002
Karlsruhe	275,690
Kassel	201,573
Kiel	246,033
Koblenz	109,219
Krefeld	249,606
Leipzig	470,778
Leverkusen	162,252
Lübeck	216,986
Ludwigshafen	167,369
Magdeburg	257,656
Mainz	183,720
Mannheim	311,292
Moers	107,095
Mönchengladbach	266,702
Mülheim an der Ruhr	176,530
Munich (München)	1,236,370
Münster	265,061
Neuss	148,796
Nürnberg	492,425
Oberhausen	224,397
Offenbach am Main	116,533
Oldenburg	151,382
Osnabrück	168,618
Paderborn	133,717
Pforzheim	118,763
Potsdam	136,619
Recklinghausen	127,216
Regensburg	125,836
Remscheid	122,260
Reutlingen	108,565
Rostock	227,535
Saarbrücken	187,032
Salzgitter	117,713
Schwerin	114,688
Siegen	111,398
Solingen	165,735
Stuttgart	585,604
Ulm	115,721
Wiesbaden	267,122
Witten	104,754
Wolfsburg	126,331
Wuppertal	381,884
Würzburg	127,295
Zwickau	102,563
Ghana (1988 est.)	
★ Accra	1,781,100[19, 23]
Kumasi	385,192
Sekondi-Takoradi	103,653
Tamale	151,069
Tema	109,975
Gibraltar (1997 est.)	
★ Gibraltar	27,100[30]
Greece (1991)	
★ Athens	748,110
Iráklion	117,167
Kallithéa	110,738
Larissa	113,426
Pátrai (Patras)	155,180
Peristérion	145,854
Piraiévs (Piraeus)	169,622
Thessaloníki	377,951
Greenland (1996 est.)	
★ Nuuk (Godthåb)	12,882
Grenada (1991)	
★ Saint George's	4,621
Guadeloupe (1990)	
★ Basse-Terre	14,107
Guam (1995 est.)	
★ Agana	2,000
Guatemala (1995 est.; MU)	
★ Guatemala City	1,167,495
Mixco	436,668
Villa Nueva	165,567
Guernsey (1991)	
★ St. Peter Port	16,648
Guinea (1995 est.)	
★ Conakry	1,508,000
Guinea-Bissau (1995 est.)	
★ Bissau	233,000
Guyana (1995 est.)	
★ Georgetown	254,000
Haiti (1995 est.)	
Cap-Haïtien	100,638
Carrefour	277,662
Delmas	232,142
★ Port-au-Prince	846,247
Honduras (1995 est.; MU)	
San Pedro Sula	383,900
★ Tegucigalpa	813,900[31]
Hong Kong (1997 est.)	
Hong Kong	6,491,000[30]
Hungary (1997 est.)	
★ Budapest	1,885,000
Debrecen	210,000
Györ	127,000
Kecskemét	105,000
Miskolc	178,000
Nyíregyháza	113,000
Pécs	161,000
Szeged	166,000
Székesfehérvár	106,000
Iceland (1996 est.)	
★ Reykjavík	105,487
India (1991)	
Abohar	107,163
Ādoni	136,182
Agartala	157,358
Āgra	891,790
Ahmadābād	2,876,710
Ahmadnagar	181,339
Āizawl	155,240
Ajmer	402,700
Akola	328,034
Alandur	125,244
Alappuzha (Alleppey)	174,666
Alībāg	328,640
Alīgarh	480,520
Allahābād	792,858
Alwar	205,086
Ambāla	119,338
Ambattur	215,424
Amrāvati	421,576
Amritsar	708,835
Amroha	137,061
Anand	110,266
Anantapur	174,924
Āra (Arrah)	157,082
Āsānsol	262,188
Āvadi	183,215
Baharampur	115,144
Bahraich	135,400
Bally	184,474
Bālurghāt	119,796
Bangalore	2,660,088
Bānkura	114,876
Barāhanagar	224,821
Bārāsat	102,660
Barddhamān (Burdwān)	245,079
Bareilly	587,211
Barrackpore	133,265
Basīrhāt	101,409
Bathinda (Bhatinda)	159,042
Beāwar	105,363
Belgaum	326,399
Bellary	245,391
Bhāgalpur	253,225
Bharatpur	148,519
Bharūch (Broach)	133,102
Bhātpāra	304,952
Bhāvnagar	402,338
Bhilainagar	395,360
Bhīlwāra	183,965
Bhīmavaram	121,314
Bhind	109,755
Bhiwandi	379,070
Bhiwāni	121,629
Bhopāl	1,062,771
Bhubaneshwar	411,542
Bhuj	102,176
Bhusāwal	145,143
Bīd (Bhīr)	112,434
Bīdar	108,016
Bidhān Nagar	100,048
Bihār Sharīf	201,323
Bijāpur	186,939
Bīkaner	416,289
Bilāspur	179,833
Bokāro	333,683
Brahmapur	210,418
Budaun	116,695
Bulandshahr	127,201
Burhānpur	172,710
Burnpur	174,933
Calcutta	4,399,819
Chāmpdānī	101,067
Chandannagar	120,378
Chandīgarh	504,094
Chandrapur	226,105
Chennai (Madras)	3,841,396
Chhapra	136,877
Chittoor	133,462
Coimbatore	816,321
Cuddalore	144,561
Cuddapah	121,463
Cuttack	403,418
Darbhanga	218,391
Dāvangere	266,082
Dehra Dūn	270,159
Delhi	7,206,704
Dewās	164,364
Dhānbād	151,789
Dhūle (Dhūlia)	278,317
Dibrugarh	120,127
Dindigul	182,447
Durg	150,645
Durgāpur	425,836
Elūru	212,866
Erode	159,232
Etāwah	124,072
Faizābād	124,437
Farīdābād	617,717
Farrukhābād-cum-Fatehgarh	194,567
Fatehpur	117,675
Fīrozābād	215,128
Gadag-Betigeri	134,051
Gāndhīdhām	104,585
Gāndhīnagar	123,359
Gangānagar	161,482
Gaya	291,675
Ghāziābād	454,156
Gondia	109,470
Gorakhpur	505,566
Gudivāda	101,656
Gulbarga	304,099
Guna	100,490
Guntakal	107,592
Guntūr	471,051
Gurgaon	121,486
Guwāhāti (Gauhāti)	584,342
Gwalior	690,765
Hābra	100,223

country city	population
Haldīa	100,347
Haldwāni-cum-Kāthgodam	104,195
Hālisahar	114,028
Hāora (Howrah)	950,435
Hāpur	146,262
Haridwār (Hardwār)	147,305
Hāthras	113,285
Hindupur	104,651
Hisār (Hissār)	172,677
Hoshiārpur	122,705
Hubli-Dhārwād	648,298
Hugli-Chunchura	151,806
Hyderābād	3,145,939
Ichalkaranji	214,950
Imphāl	198,535
Indore	1,091,674
Ingrāj Bāzār	139,204
Jabalpur	741,927
Jaipur	1,458,183
Jalandhar (Jullundur)	509,510
Jalgaon	242,193
Jālna	174,985
Jammu	206,135[14]
Jāmnagar	341,637
Jamshedpur	478,950
Jaunpur	136,062
Jhānsi	300,850
Jodhpur	666,279
Jūnāgadh	130,484
Kākināda	279,980
Kalyān	1,014,557
Kāmārhāti	266,889
Kānchipuram	144,955
Kānchrāpāra	100,194
Kānpur	1,874,409
Karīmnagar	148,583
Karnāl	173,751
Katihār	135,436
Khammam	127,992
Khandwa	143,133
Kharagpur	177,989
Kochi (Cochin)	564,589
Kolhāpur	406,370
Kollam (Quilon)	139,852
Kota	537,371
Kozhikode (Calicut)	419,831
Krishnanagar	121,110
Kukatpalle	186,963
Kulti-Barākar	108,518
Kumbakonam	139,483
Kurnool	236,800
Lālbāhādur Nagar	155,514
Lātūr	197,408
Lucknow	1,619,115
Ludhiāna	1,042,740
Machilīpatnam (Masulipatam)	159,110
Madurai	940,989
Mahbūbnagar	116,833
Mālegaon	342,595
Mālkājgiri	127,178
Mandya	120,265
Mangalore	273,304
Māngo	108,100
Mathura	226,691
Mauñāth Bhanjan	136,697
Medinīpur (Midnāpore)	125,498
Meerut	753,778
Mira-Bhayandar	175,605
Miraj	121,593
Mirzāpur-cum-Vindhyāchal	169,336
Modinagar	101,660
Moga	108,304
Morādābād	429,214
Morena	147,124
Mumbāi (Bombay)	9,925,891[19]
Munger (Monghyr)	150,112
Murwāra (Katni)	163,431
Muzaffarnagar	240,609
Muzaffarpur	241,107
Mysore	480,692
Nadiād	167,051
Nāgercoil	190,084
Nāgpur	1,624,752
Naihāti	132,701
Nānded (Nānder)	275,083
Nandyāl	119,813
Nāshik (Nāsik)	656,925
Navadwīp	125,037
Navsāri	126,089
Nellore	316,606
New Bombay	307,724
★ New Delhi	301,297
Neyveli	118,080
Nizāmābād	241,034
Noida	146,514
North Barrackpore	100,606
North Dum Dum	149,965
Ongole	100,836
Pālghāt (Palakkad)	123,289
Pāli	136,842
Pallavaram	111,866
Pānihāti	275,990
Pānīpat	191,212
Parbhani	190,255
Pathānkot	123,930
Patiāla	238,368
Patna	917,243
Pīlībhīt	106,605
Pimpri-Chinchwad	517,083
Pondicherry	203,065
Porbandar	116,671
Proddatūr	133,914
Pune	1,566,651
Puri	125,199
Pūrnia (Pūrnea)	114,912
Qutubullapur	106,591
Rāe Bareli	129,904
Rāichūr	157,551
Rāiganj	151,045
Raipur	438,639
Rāj Nāndgaon	125,371
Rājahmundry	324,851
Rājapālaiyam	114,202
Rājkot	559,407
Rāmagundam	214,384
Rāmpur	243,742
Rānchi	599,306
Ratlām	183,375
Raurkela Steel Township	215,509
Rewa	128,981
Rishra	102,815
Rohtak	216,096
Sāgar	195,346
Sahāranpur	374,945
Salem	366,712
Sambalpur	131,138
Sambhal	150,869
Sāngli	193,197
Satna	156,630
Shāhjahānpur	237,713
Shāmbājinagar (Aurangābād)	573,272
Shāntipur	109,956
Shiliguri (Silīguri)	216,950
Shillong	131,719
Shimoga	179,258
Shivpuri	108,277
Sholāpur (Solapur)	604,215
Shrīrāmpur	137,028
Sīkar	148,272
Silchar	115,483
Sirsa	112,841
Sitāpur	121,842
Sonīpat (Sonepat)	143,922
South Dum Dum	232,811
Srīnagar	586,038[14]
Sūrat	1,498,817
Surendranagar	106,110
Tāmbaram	107,187
Tenāli	143,726
Thalassery (Tellicherry)	103,579
Thāne (Thāna)	803,389
Thanjāvūr	202,013
Thiruvananthapuram (Trivandrum)	524,006
Tiruchchirāppalli	387,223
Tirunelveli	135,825
Tirupati	174,369
Tirupper (Tiruppūr)	235,661
Tiruvannāmalai	109,196
Tiruvottiyūr	168,642
Titāgarh	114,085
Tonk	100,079
Tumkūr	138,903
Tuticorin	199,854
Udaipur	308,571
Ujjain	362,266
Ulhāsnagar	369,077
Uluberia	155,172
Unnāo	107,425
Uttarpāra-Kotrung	101,268
Vadodara (Baroda)	1,031,346
Vārānasi (Benares)	929,270
Vellore	175,061
Vijayawāda	701,827
Vishākhapatnam	752,037
Vizianagaram	160,359
Warangal	447,657
Wardha	102,985
Yamunanagar	144,346
Yavatmāl (Yeotmāl)	108,578
Indonesia (1995 est.)	
Ambon	313,100
Balikpapan	416,200
Banda Aceh	291,300
Bandar Lampung	458,215[15]
Bandung	2,368,200
Banjarmasin	534,600
Batam	168,200
Bengkulu	262,100
Binjai	206,800
Blitar	122,600
Bitung	107,100
Bogor	285,000
Cilacap	113,893[32]
Cimahi	105,940[32]
Cirebon	262,300
Denpasar	435,000
Gorontalo	132,900
★ Jakarta	9,160,500
Jambi	410,400
Jayapura	180,400
Jember	140,105[32]
Kediri	261,300
Madiun	106,600
Magelang	123,100
Malang	763,400
Manado	398,900
Mataram	306,600
Medan	1,909,700
Mojokerto	170,900
Padang	721,500
Palangkaraya	148,700
Palembang	1,352,300
Pangkal Pinang	124,000
Pare Pare	109,700
Pasuruan	162,800
Pekalongan	341,400
Pekanbaru	558,200
Pematangsiantar	230,900
Pontianak	449,100
Probolinggo	190,100
Purwokerto	105,395[32]
Salatiga	103,000
Samarinda	536,100
Semarang	1,366,500
Sukabumi	125,400
Sumba	355,073[32]
Surabaya	2,701,300
Surakarta	516,500
Tangerang	1,198,300
Tanjung Balai	114,700
Tanjung Karang-Telukbetung	284,275[32]
Tasikmalaya	165,297[32]
Tebing Tinggi	129,300
Tegal	313,400
Ujung Pandang	1,091,800
Yogyakarta	419,500
Iran (1994 est.)	
Ahvāz	828,380
Āmol	154,796
Arāk	378,597
Ardabīl	329,869
Bābol	152,536
Bandar 'Abbās	383,515
Bandar-e Būshehr	140,615
Bīrjand	114,944
Bojnūrd	125,661
Borūjerd	212,056
Dezfūl	202,004
Eşfahān (Isfahan)	1,220,595
Gonbad-e Kavus	102,768[12]
Gorgān	178,080
Hamadān	406,070
Īlām	136,759
Islāmshahr (Eslāmshahr)	239,716
Karaj	588,287
Kāshān	166,080
Kermān	349,626
Kermānshāh (Bākhtarān)	665,636
Khomeynīshahr	127,415
Khorramābād	277,370
Khorramshahr	197,241[12]
Khvoy	153,473
Malāyer	149,774
Marāgheh	128,717
Mehrshahr	413,299
Mashhad (Meshed)	1,964,489
Masjed-e Soleymān	109,224
Najafābād	182,028
Neyshābūr	154,511
Orūmīyeh	396,392
Qā'emshahr	133,216
Qazvīn	298,705
Qom	780,453
Rājaishahr	192,912
Rasht	374,475
Sabzevār	160,755
Sanandaj	271,314
Sārī	185,899
Shīrāz	1,042,801
Sīrjān	120,224
Tabrīz	1,166,203
★ Tehrān	6,750,043
Yazd	306,268
Zāhedān	419,886
Zanjān	280,691
Iraq (1987)	
Al-'Amārah	208,797
★ Baghdad	4,400,000[18, 19]
Ba'qūbah	114,516[33]
Al-Başrah	406,296
Al-Ḥillah	268,834
Dīwānīyah	196,519
Irbīl	485,968
Karbalā'	296,705
Karkūk	418,624
Al-Kūt	183,183
Mosul	664,221
An-Najaf	309,010
An-Nāşirīyah	265,937
Ar-Ramādī	192,556
As-Sulaymānīyah	364,096
Ireland (1996)	
Cork	127,092[34]
★ Dublin	480,996[34]
Isle of Man (1996)	
★ Douglas	23,487
Israel (1997 est.)	
Ashdod	137,100
Bat Yam	140,800
Beersheba (Be'er Sheva')	156,500
Bene Beraq	130,500
Haifa (Ḥefa)	255,300
Ḥolon	163,900
★ Jerusalem (Yerushalayim, Al-Quds)	591,400
Netanya	148,400
Petaḥ Tiqwa	153,100
Ramat Gan	121,700
Rishon LeẒiyyon	165,300
Tel Aviv–Yafo	355,900
Italy (1996 est.; MU)	
Bari	336,560
Bergamo	116,990
Bologna	386,491
Brescia	190,208
Cagliari	174,543
Catania	341,623
Ferrara	135,135
Florence (Firenze)	383,594
Foggia	156,032
Forlì	108,017
Genoa (Genova)	659,116
Latina	110,233
Lecce	100,046
Livorno	164,569
Messina	263,092
Milan (Milano)	1,306,494
Modena	174,518
Monza	119,658
Naples (Napoli)	1,050,234
Novara	102,219
Padua (Padova)	212,731
Palermo	689,301
Parma	167,516
Perugia	151,118
Pescara	118,764
Prato	167,991
Ravenna	137,216
Reggio di Calabria	179,623
Reggio nell'Emilia	135,406
Rimini	129,598
★ Rome (Roma)	2,654,187
Salerno	143,863
Sassari	121,639
Siracusa (Syracuse)	127,448
Taranto	212,650
Terni	108,435
Trento	103,181
Trieste	223,611
Turin (Torino)	923,106
Venice (Venezia)	298,915
Verona	254,145
Vicenza	107,786
Jamaica (1991)	
★ Kingston	103,771[35]
Japan (1995)	
Abiko	124,255
Ageo	206,099
Aizuwakamatsu	119,632
Akashi	287,613
Akishima	107,289
Akita	312,035
Amagasaki	488,574
Anjō	149,459
Aomori	294,165
Asahikawa	360,569
Asaka	110,793
Ashikaga	165,830
Atsugi	208,622
Beppu	128,251
Chiba	856,882
Chigasaki	212,944
Chōfu	198,524
Daitō	128,840
Ebetsu	115,491
Ebina	113,416
Fuchu	216,202
Fuji	229,189
Fujieda	124,822
Fujinomiya	119,536
Fujisawa	368,636
Fukaya	100,271
Fukui	255,601
Fukuoka	1,284,741
Fukushima	285,745
Fukuyama	374,510
Funabashi	540,814
Gifu	407,145
Habikino	117,728
Hachinohe	242,657
Hachiōji	503,320
Hadano	164,703
Hakodate	298,868
Hamamatsu	561,568
Handa	106,451
Higashi-Hiroshima	113,935
Higashi-Kurume	111,076
Higashi-Murayama	135,115
Higashi-Ōsaka	517,228
Hikone	103,508
Himeji	470,986
Hino	166,429
Hirakata	400,130
Hiratsuka	253,818
Hirosaki	177,971
Hiroshima	1,108,868
Hitachi	199,241
Hōfu	118,802
Hoya	100,259
Ibaraki	258,237
Ichihara	277,080
Ichikawa	440,527
Ichinomiya	267,359
Iida	106,774
Ikeda	104,292
Ikoma	106,727
Imabari	120,215
Iruma	144,401
Ise	102,631
Isesaki	120,235
Ishinomaki	121,209
Itami	188,436
Iwaki	360,497
Iwakuni	107,386
Iwatsuki	109,551
Izumi	157,301
Joetsu	132,202
Kadoma	140,507
Kagoshima	546,294
Kakamigahara	131,955
Kakogawa	260,558
Kamakura	170,319
Kanazawa	453,977
Kariya	125,307
Kashihara	121,987
Kashiwa	317,752
Kasugai	277,579
Kasukabe	200,130
Kawachi-Nagano	117,082
Kawagoe	323,345
Kawaguchi	448,801
Kawanishi	144,539
Kawasaki	1,202,811
Kiryū	120,375
Kisarazu	123,499
Kishiwada	194,820
Kita-Kyūshū	1,019,562
Kitami	110,449
Kobe	1,423,830
Kochi	322,077
Kodaira	173,032
Kofu	201,123
Koganei	109,275
Kokubunji	105,781
Komaki	137,163
Komatsu	107,964
Koriyama	326,831
Koshigaya	298,285
Kumagaya	156,395
Kumamoto	650,322
Kurashiki	422,824
Kure	209,477
Kurume	234,433
Kusatsu	101,827
Kushiro	199,325
Kuwana	103,049
Kyōto	1,463,601
Machida	360,418
Maebashi	284,780
Matsubara	134,457
Matsudo	461,489
Matsue	147,414
Matsumoto	205,532
Matsusaka	122,449
Matsuyama	460,870
Minō	127,540
Misato	133,601
Mishima	107,890
Mitaka	165,739
Mito	246,350
Miyakonojō	132,712
Miyazaki	300,054
Moriguchi	157,290
Morioka	286,478
Muroran	109,767
Musashino	135,026
Nagano	358,512
Nagaoka	190,470
Nagareyama	146,250
Nagasaki	438,724
Nagoya	2,152,258
Naha	301,928
Nara	359,234
Narashino	152,884
Neyagawa	258,440
Niigata	494,785
Niihama	127,916
Niiza	144,735
Nishinomiya	390,388
Nobeoka	126,628
Noda	119,791
Numazu	212,245
Obihiro	171,714
Odawara	200,092
Ōgaki	149,758
Ōita	426,981
Okayama	616,056
Okazaki	322,615

Major cities and national capitals (continued)

country / city	population
Okinawa	115,342
Ōme	137,208
Ōmiya	433,768
Ōmuta	145,085
Ōsaka	2,602,352
Ōta	143,067
Otaru	157,024
Ōtsu	276,331
Oyama	150,114
Saga	171,219
Sagamihara	570,594
Sakai	802,965
Sakata	101,224
Sakura	162,624
Sapporo	1,756,968
Sasebo	244,879
Sayama	162,232
Sendai	971,263
Seto	129,396
Shimizu	240,172
Shimonoseki	259,791
Shizuoka	474,089
Sōka	217,912
Suita	342,794
Suzuka	179,795
Tachikawa	157,892
Tajimi	101,274
Takamatsu	330,997
Takaoka	173,612
Takarazuka	202,547
Takasaki	238,132
Takatsuki	362,259
Tama	148,127
Tokorozawa	320,448
Tokushima	268,712
Tokuyama	108,675
★ Tokyo	7,966,195
Tomakomai	169,324
Tondabayashi	121,690
Tottori	146,336
Toyama	325,303
Toyohashi	352,913
Toyokawa	114,379
Toyonaka	398,912
Toyota	341,038
Tsu	163,309
Tsuchiura	132,246
Tsukuba	156,009
Tsuruoka	100,538
Ube	175,113
Ueda	123,282
Uji	184,829
Urawa	453,300
Urayasu	123,660
Utsunomiya	435,446
Wakayama	393,951
Yachiyo	154,507
Yaizu	115,932
Yamagata	254,485
Yamaguchi	135,581
Yamato	203,920
Yao	276,658
Yatsushiro	107,708
Yokkaichi	285,777
Yokohama	3,307,408
Yokosuka	432,202
Yonago	134,769
Zama	118,146
Jersey (1996)	
★ St. Helier	27,523
Jordan (1994)	
★ Amman	963,490
Irbid	208,201
Al-Mafraq	109,841[19]
Ar-Ruṣayfah	131,130
As-Salṭ	187,014[19]
Az-Zarqāʾ	344,524
Kazakstan (1995 est.)	
★ Almaty (Alma-Ata)	1,150,500
★ Aqmola (Akmola; Tselinograd)	280,200
Aqtaū (Aktau; Shevchenko)	151,300
Aqtöbe (Aktyubinsk)	258,900
Atyraū (Guryev)	146,900
Auliye-Ata (Dzhambul)	310,600
Ekibastuz	141,100
Kökshetaū (Kokchetav)	141,400
Oral (Uralsk)	219,100
Öskemen (Ust-Kamenogorsk)	326,300
Pavlodar	340,700
Petropavl (Petropavlovsk)	239,000
Qaraghandy (Karaganda)	573,700
Qostanay (Kustanay)	232,100
Qyzylord (Kzyl-Orda)	162,000
Rūdny	125,700
Semey (Semipalatinsk)	320,200
Shymkent (Shimkent; Chimkent)	397,600
Taldyqorghan (Taldy-Kurgan)	116,100
Temirtaū	206,100
Zhezqazghan (Zhezkazgan; Dzhezkazgan)	108,700
Kenya (1991 est.)	
Kisumu	201,100
Mombasa	600,000
★ Nairobi	2,000,000
Nakuru	124,200
Kiribati (1990)	
★ Bairiki	2,226
Korea, North (1987 est.)	
Anju	186,000
Ch'ŏngjin	520,000
Haeju	195,000
Hamhŭng-Hungnam	701,000
Hŭich'ŏn	163,000
Kaesŏng	120,000
Kanggye	211,000
Kimch'aek (Songjin)	179,000
Kusŏng	177,000
Namp'o	370,000
★ P'yŏngyang	2,500,000[18,19]
Sinp'o	158,000
Sinŭiju	289,000
Sunch'ŏn	356,000
Tanch'ŏn	284,000
Tŏkch'ŏn	217,000
Wŏnsan	274,000
Korea, South (1995)	
Andong	188,452
Ansan	510,317
Anyang	590,996
Asan	154,635
Ch'angwŏn	481,678
Chech'ŏn	137,065
Cheju	258,509
Chinhae	125,997
Chinju	329,913
Ch'ŏnan	330,509
Ch'ŏngju	531,195
Chŏng-ŭp	139,084
Chŏnju	563,406
Ch'unch'ŏn	235,067
Ch'ungju	205,131
Hanam	115,805
Iksan	322,749
Inch'ŏn	2,307,618
Iri	203,382
Kangnŭng	220,430
Kimch'ŏn	146,996
Kimhae	256,270
Kimje	115,430
Kŏje	147,551
Kongju	131,220
Koyang	518,269
Kumi	311,488
Kunp'o	235,194
Kunsan	266,517
Kuri	142,299
Kwangju	1,257,504
Kwangmyŏng	350,902
Kwangyang	122,061
Kyŏngju	273,819
Kyŏngsan	173,762
Masan	441,358
Miryang	121,502
Mokp'o	247,524
Naju	107,831
Namwon	103,538
Namyangju	228,931
P'ohang	508,983
Poryŏng	122,631
Puch'ŏn	779,476
Pusan	3,813,814
P'yŏngt'aek	312,938
Sach'ŏn	113,492
Sangju	124,136
★ Seoul (Sŏul)	10,229,262
Shihŭng	133,411
Sŏngnam	869,243
Sŏsan	134,758
Sunch'ŏn	249,241
Suwŏn	755,502
Taegu	2,449,139
Taejŏn	1,272,143
Tongyŏng	131,716
Ŭijŏngbu	276,255
Ŭiwang	108,761
Ulsan	967,394
Wŏnju	237,423
Yŏngch'ŏn	113,510
Yŏngju	131,090
Yŏsu	183,557
Kuwait (1995)	
As-Sālimīyah	130,215
★ Kuwait (Al-Kuwayt)	28,859
Qalīb ash-Shuyūkh	102,178
Kyrgyzstan (1995 est.)	
★ Bishkek (Frunze)	589,800[18]
Osh	218,300
Laos (1996 est.; MU)	
★ Vientiane (Viangchan)	531,800
Latvia (1996 est.)	
Daugavpils	118,500
★ Rīga	826,100
Lebanon (1991 est.)	
★ Beirut (Bayrūt)	1,900,000[18,19]
Jūniyah	100,000
an-Nabaṭīyah	100,000[33]
Sidon (Ṣaydā)	100,000[33]
Tripoli (Ṭarābulus)	240,000
Zaḥlah	200,000[33]
Lesotho (1995 est.)	
★ Maseru	297,000[19]
Liberia (1995 est.)	
★ Monrovia	962,000[19]
Libya (1988 est.)	
Banghāzī	446,250
Misrātah	121,669
★ Tripoli (Ṭarābulus)	591,062
Liechtenstein (1997 est.)	
★ Vaduz	5,017
Lithuania (1996 est.)	
Kaunas	410,800
Klaipėda	201,500
Panevėžys	132,300
Šiauliai	146,500
★ Vilnius	573,200
Luxembourg (1997 est.)	
★ Luxembourg	78,300
Macau (1995 est.)	
★ Macau (Santo Nome de Deus)	424,000
Macedonia (1994; MU)	
Bitola	106,012
Giostivar	108,189
Kumanovo	126,543
★ Skopje (Skopije)	541,280
Tetovo	174,748
Madagascar (1993)	
★ Antananarivo	1,052,835
Antsirabe	120,239
Mahajanga	100,807
Toamasina	127,441
Malaŵi (1994 est.)	
★ Blantyre (executive; judicial)	446,800[36]
★ Lilongwe (ministerial; financial)	395,500
★ Zomba (legislative)	62,700
Malaysia (1991)	
Alor Setar	124,412
George Town (Pinang)	219,603
Ipoh	382,853
Johor Baharu	328,436
Kelang	243,355
Kota Baharu	219,582
Kota Kinabalu	208,484
★ Kuala Lumpur	1,145,342
Kuala Terengganu	228,119
Kuantan	199,484
Kuching	148,059
Melaka	296,897
Petaling Jaya	254,350
Port Kelang	192,080
Sandakan	125,841
Seloyang Baru	124,228
Seremban	182,869
Shah Alam	102,019
Sibu	126,381
Taiping	183,261
Tawau	244,765
Maldives (1995 est.)	
★ Male'	62,973
Mali (1995 est.)	
★ Bamako	800,000
Malta (1996 est.)	
★ Valletta	9,128
Marshall Is. (1995 est.)	
★ Majuro	28,000
Martinique (1995 est.)	
★ Fort-de-France	104,000
Mauritania (1995 est.)	
★ Nouakchott	735,000
Mauritius (1995 est.)	
★ Port Louis	145,584
Mayotte (1991; MU)	
★ Mamoudzou	20,274
★ Dzaoudzi	8,268
Mexico (1990)	
Acapulco	515,374
Aguascalientes	440,425
Atizapán de Zaragoza (Ciudad López Mateos)	315,059
Campeche	150,518
Cancún	167,730
Celaya	214,856
Chihuahua	516,153
Ciudad Apodaca	103,364
Ciudad Madero	160,331
Ciudad Obregón	219,980
Ciudad Santa Catarina	162,707
Ciudad Victoria	194,996
Coatzacoalcos	198,817
Colima	106,967
Córdoba	130,695
Cuautla	110,242
Cuernavaca	279,187
Culiacán	415,046
Durango	348,036
Ensenada	169,426
Gómez Palacio	164,092
Guadalajara	1,650,042
Guadalupe	535,332
Hermosillo	406,417
Heroica Nogales	105,873
Irapuato	265,042
Juárez	789,522
La Paz	137,641
León	758,279
Los Mochis	162,659
Matamoros	266,055
Mazatlán	262,705
Mérida	523,422
Mexicali	438,377
★ Mexico City	9,815,795
Minatitlán	142,060
Monclova	177,792
Monterrey	1,068,996
Morelia	428,486
Nezahualcóyotl	1,255,456
Nuevo Laredo	218,413
Oaxaca	212,818
Orizaba	114,216
Pachuca	174,013
Poza Rica	151,739
Puebla	1,007,170
Querétaro	385,503
Reynosa	265,663
Salamanca	123,190
Saltillo	420,947
San Luis Potosí	488,238
San Nicolás de los Garza	436,603
San Pedro Garza García	113,017
Soledad de Graciano Sanchez	123,943
Tampico	272,690
Tapachula	138,858
Tehuacán	139,450
Tepic	206,967
Tijuana	698,752
Tlaquepaque	328,031
Toluca	327,865
Tonala	151,190
Torreón	439,436
Tuxtla	289,626
Uruapan	187,623
Veracruz	438,821
Villahermosa	261,231
Xalapa (Jalapa) Enríquez	279,451
Zacatecas	100,051
Zamora de Hidalgo	109,751
Zapopan	668,323
Micronesia	
★ Palikir	—
Moldova (1993 est.)	
Bălţi (Beltsy)	156,081
★ Chişinău (Kishinyov)	657,775
Tighina (Bendery)	128,881
Tiraspol	184,852
Monaco (1997 est.)	
★ Monaco	31,900[30]
Mongolia (1997 est.)	
★ Ulaanbaatar (Ulan Bator)	627,300
Morocco (1994; MU)	
Agadir	155,244
Agdal	129,914
Ain-Chock	165,907
Ain-Sebaa	139,323
Al-Fida	109,565
Al-Idrissia	110,861
Al-Ismailia	117,989
Ben-Msick	195,753
Beni-Mellal	140,212
Bouchentouf	140,370
Casablanca	523,279[37]
El-Jadida	119,083
El-Youssoufia	195,208
Fes-Medina	263,828
Hay Mohammadi	174,635
Kenitra Saknia	150,113
Khouribga	152,090
Ksar el-Kebir	107,065
Marrakech	621,914[37]
Meknès	188,224[37]
Mohammedia	170,083
Moulay Rachid	167,909
Nador	112,450
Ouad Ennachef Sidi Maafa	112,840
Oujda Sidi Ziane	146,142
★ Rabat	623,457[38]
Safi	364,648[37]
Salé	504,420
Sidi Bernoussi	153,118
Sidi Moumen	107,825
Sidi Othmane	183,195
Sidi Youssef-Ben Ali	118,770
Tanger	521,735[37]
Temara	126,303
Tétouan	277,516
Zouagha	262,429
Mozambique (1991 est.)	
Beira	298,847
Chimoio	108,818
★ Maputo (Lourenço Marques)	931,591
Matala	337,239
Nacala	125,208
Nampula	250,473
Quelimane	146,206
Tete	112,221
Myanmar (Burma) (1983)	
Bassein (Pathein)	144,096
Mandalay	532,949
Monywa	106,843
Moulmein (Mawlamyine)	219,961
Pegu (Bago)	150,528
Sittwe (Akyab)	107,621
Taunggye	108,231
★ Yangôn (Rangoon)	4,000,000[18,19]
Namibia (1995 est.)	
★ Windhoek	190,000
Nauru (1983)	
★ Yaren	559
Nepal (1993 est.; MU)	
Bhaktapur (Bhādgāon)	130,000
Birātnagar	132,000
★ Kāthmāndu	535,000
Lalitpur (Patan)	190,000
Netherlands, The (1996 est.)	
Almere	112,704
Amersfoort	114,884
★ Amsterdam (capital)	718,119
Apeldoorn	150,915
Arnhem	135,026
Breda	130,033
Dordrecht	116,196
Eindhoven	197,374
Enschede	147,832
Groningen	169,627
Haarlem	147,617
Haarlemmermeer	106,095
Leiden	116,224
Maastricht	118,518
Nijmegen	147,600
Rotterdam	592,745
's-Hertogenbosch	125,044
★ The Hague (seat of government)	442,503
Tilburg	164,380
Utrecht	234,254
Zaanstad	133,817
Zoetermeer	106,581
Zwolle	100,835
Netherlands Antilles (1995 est.)	
★ Willemstad	119,000
New Caledonia (1989)	
★ Nouméa	65,110
New Zealand (1996)	
Auckland	353,670
Christchurch	313,969
Dunedin	121,100[2]
Hamilton	106,700[2]
Manukau	254,577
North Shore	170,913
Waitakere	147,500[2]
★ Wellington	158,275
Nicaragua (1995)	
León	123,865
★ Managua	864,201
Niger (1994 est.)	
★ Niamey	420,000
Zinder	100,000
Nigeria (1996 est.)[39]	
Aba	298,900
Abeokuta	427,400
★ Abuja (capital designate)	350,100[40]
Ado-Ekiti	359,400
Agege	105,000
Akure	162,300
Awka	111,200
Benin City	229,400
Bida	125,500
Calabar	174,400
Deba Habe	138,600
Ede	307,100
Effon-Alaiye	153,100
Ejigbo	105,900
Enugu	316,100
Epe	101,000
Gombe	107,800
Gusau	158,000
Ibadan	1,432,000
Ife	296,800
Igboho	106,800

country / city	population
Ijebu-Ode	156,400
Ikare	140,800
Ikerre	244,600
Ikire	123,300
Ikirun	181,400
Ikorodu	184,900
Ila	264,000
Ilawe-Ekiti	184,500
Ilegbo	101,600
Ilesha	378,400
Ilobu	199,000
Ilorin	475,800
Inisa	119,800
Ise-Ekiti	103,400
Iseyin	217,300
Iwo	362,000
Jos	206,300
Kaduna	342,200
Kano	674,100
Katsina	206,500
Kumo	148,000
Lafia	122,500
★ Lagos	1,518,000
Maiduguri	320,000
Makurdi	123,100
Minna	136,900
Mushin	333,200
Offa	197,200
Ogbomosho	730,000
Oka	142,900
Ondo	173,600
Onitsha	371,900
Oshogbo	476,800
Owo	183,500
Oyo	256,400
Port Harcourt	410,000
Sapele	139,200
Shagamu	117,200
Shaki	174,500
Shomolu	147,700
Sokoto	204,900
Ugep	102,600
Warri	126,100
Zaria	379,200
Northern Mariana Is. (1990)	
★ Saipan	38,896
Norway (1997 est.; MU)	
Bergen	224,130
★ Oslo	493,973
Stavanger	105,573
Trondheim	144,599
Oman (1993)	
★ Muscat	51,969
Pakistan (1981)	
Bahāwalpur	180,263
Chiniot	105,559
Dera Ghāzi Khān	102,007
Faisalābād (Lyallpur)	1,104,209
Gujrānwāla	658,753
Gujrāt	155,058
Hyderābād	751,529
★ Islamābād	204,364
Jhang	195,558
Jhelum	106,462
Karāchi	5,208,132
Kasūr	155,523
Lahore	2,952,689
Lahore Cantonment	237,000
Lārkāna	123,890
Mardān	147,977
Mīrpur Khās	124,371
Multān	730,070
Nawābshāh	102,139
Okāra	153,483
Peshāwar	566,248
Quetta	285,719
Rahīm Yār Khān	119,036
Rāwalpindi	794,843
Sāhiwāl	150,954
Sargodha	291,362
Sheikhūpura	141,168
Siālkot	302,009
Sukkur	190,551
Wāh Cantonment	122,335
Palau (1995 est.)	
Koror	12,000
Panama (1995 est.)	
Colón	137,825[10]
★ Panama City	452,041
San Miguelito	290,919
Papua New Guinea (1990)	
★ Port Moresby (National Capital District)	193,242
Paraguay (1992)	
★ Asunción	502,426
Ciudad del Este	133,893
San Lorenzo	133,311
Peru (1993)	
Arequipa	619,156
Ayacucho	105,918
Callao	615,046
Chiclayo	411,536
Chimbote	268,979
Chincha Alta	110,016
Cusco	255,568
Huancayo	258,209
Huánuco	118,814
Ica	161,406
Iquitos	274,759
Juliaca	142,576
★ Lima	421,570[23]
Metro Lima-Callao	5,706,127
Piura	277,964
Pucallpa	172,286
Sullana	147,361
Tacna	174,336
Trujillo	509,312
Philippines (1994 est.)	
Angeles	276,545
Bacolod	343,048
Bago	139,771
Baguio	169,565
Batangas	190,627
Butuan	244,900
Cabanatuan	185,728
Cadiz	143,299
Cagayan de Oro	413,689
Calbayog	130,321
Caloocan	642,670
Cavite	103,422
Cebu	688,196
Cotabato	112,934
Dagupan	116,936
Davao	960,910
General Santos	279,343
Gingoog	111,326
Iligan	209,639
Iloilo	302,200
Lapu-Lapu	141,009
Las Piñas	380,482
Legaspi	125,128
Lipa	159,769
Lucena	161,049
Makati	453,000[15]
Malabon	277,000[15]
Mandaluyong	247,000[15]
Mandaue	212,987
★ Manila	1,894,667[20]
Metro Manila	8,594,150
Marikina	308,000[15]
Muntilupa	275,056
Naga	102,545
Navotas	187,000[15]
Olongapo	208,633
Ormoc	142,092
Pagadian	113,905
Parañaque	308,000[15]
Pasay	388,129
Pasig	395,000[15]
★ Quezon City	1,676,644[41]
Roxas	111,649
San Carlos (*Negros Occidental*)	106,000[15]
San Carlos (*Pangasinan*)	123,473
San Juan del Monte	127,000[15]
San Pablo	163,297
Silay	140,175
Tacloban	153,068
Tagig	267,000[15]
Toledo	125,978
Valenzuela	340,000[15]
Zamboanga	464,466
Poland (1996 est.)	
Białystok	277,800
Bielsko-Biała	180,700
Bydgoszcz	386,100
Bytom	227,600
Chorzów	125,800
Czestochowa	259,500
Dąbrowa Górnicza	130,900
Elbląg	128,700
Gdańsk	462,800
Gdynia	251,400
Gliwice	214,000
Gorzów Wielkopolski	124,900
Grudziadz	102,900
Jastrzębie-Zdrój	103,500
Kalisz	106,800
Katowice	354,200
Kielce	213,700
Koszalin	111,700
Kraków	745,400
Legnica	108,000
Łódź	825,600
Lublin	353,300
Olsztyn	167,400
Opole	130,600
Płock	126,900
Poznań	581,800
Radom	232,300
Ruda Śląska	166,300
Rybnik	144,300
Rzeszów	160,300
Słupsk	102,700
Sosnowiec	249,000
Szczecin	419,300
Tarnów	121,500
Toruń	204,300
Tychy	133,900
Wałbrzych	139,600
★ Warsaw (Warszawa)	1,638,300
Włocławek	123,100
Wrocław	642,700
Zabrze	201,600
Zielona Góra	116,100
Portugal (1991)	
★ Lisbon	677,790
Porto	310,600
Puerto Rico (1996 est.; MU)	
Arecibo	100,755
Bayamón	231,845
Caguas	140,114
Carolina	188,427
Guaynabo	104,927
Mayaguez	100,937
Ponce	189,988
★ San Juan	433,705
Qatar (1993 est.)	
★ Doha	339,471
Réunion (1994 est.)	
★ Saint-Denis	104,454
Romania (1994 est.)	
Arad	187,876
Bacău	207,730
Baia Mare	149,975
Botoşani	128,322
Brăila	235,763
Braşov	324,210
★ Bucharest	2,060,551
Buzău	149,610
Cluj-Napoca	326,017
Constanţa	348,575
Craiova	306,825
Drobeta-Turnu Severin	118,383
Focşani	100,900
Galaţi	326,728
Iaşi	339,889
Oradea	221,885
Piatra Neamţ	125,622
Piteşti	184,171
Ploieşti	254,136
Râmnicu Vâlcea	114,286
Satu Mare	131,431
Sibiu	170,528
Suceava	117,314
Timişoara	327,830
Tirgu Mureş	166,315
Russia (1995 est.)	
Abakan	161,000
Achinsk	123,000
Almetyevsk	138,000
Angarsk	267,000
Anzhero-Sudzhensk	101,000
Arkhangelsk	374,000
Armavir	164,000
Arzamas	112,000
Astrakhan	486,000
Balakovo	206,000
Balashikha	136,000
Barnaul	596,000
Belgorod	322,000
Berezniki	184,000
Biysk	228,000
Blagoveshchensk	214,000
Bratsk	257,000
Bryansk	462,000
Cheboksary	450,000
Chelyabinsk	1,100,000[18]
Cherepovets	320,000
Cherkessk	119,000
Chita	322,000
Dimitrovgrad	135,000
Dzerzhinsk	285,000
Elektrostal	150,000
Engels	186,000
Glazov	107,000
Grozny (Dzhokhar)	364,000[1]
Irkutsk	585,000
Ivanovo	474,000
Izhevsk	654,000
Kaliningrad	419,000
Kaliningrad (*Moscow oblast*)	134,000
Kaluga	347,000
Kamensk-Uralsky	197,000
Kamyshin	128,000
Kansk	109,000
Kazan	1,100,000[18]
Kemerovo	503,000
Khabarovsk	618,000
Khimki	134,000
Kineshma	103,000
Kirov	464,000
Kiselyovsk	116,000
Kislovodsk	120,000
Kolomna	154,000
Kolpino	143,000
Komsomolsk-na-Amure	309,000
Kostroma	285,000
Kovrov	162,000
Krasnodar	646,000
Krasnoyarsk	869,000
Kurgan	363,000
Kursk	442,000
Kuznetsk	100,000
Leninsk-Kuznetsky	121,000
Lipetsk	474,000
Lyubertsy	166,000
Magadan	128,000
Magnitogorsk	427,000
Makhachkala	339,000
Maykop	165,000
Mezhdurechensk	105,000
Miass	167,000
Michurinsk	108,000
★ Moscow	8,400,000[18]
Murmansk	407,000
Murom	126,000
Mytishchi	152,000
Naberezhnye Chelny (Brezhnev)	526,000
Nakhodka	163,000
Nalchik	239,000
Neftekamsk	117,000
Nevinnomyssk	131,000
Nikolo-Beryozovka (Neftekamsk)	117,000
Nizhnekamsk	210,000
Nizhnevartovsk	238,000
Nizhny Novgorod (Gorky)	1,400,000[18]
Nizhny Tagil	409,000
Noginsk	119,000
Norilsk	159,000
Novgorod	233,000
Novocheboksarsk	123,000
Novocherkassk	190,000
Novokuybyshevsk	115,000
Novokuznetsk	572,000
Novomoskovsk (*Tula oblast*)	144,000
Novorossiysk	202,000
Novoshakhtinsk	107,000
Novosibirsk	1,400,000[18]
Novotroitsk	110,000
Obninsk	108,000
Odintsovo	129,000
Oktyabrsky	110,000
Omsk	1,200,000[18]
Orekhovo-Zuyevo	126,000
Orenburg	532,000
Orsk	275,000
Oryol	348,000
Penza	534,000
Perm	1,000,000[18]
Pervouralsk	137,000
Petropavlovsk-Kamchatsky	210,000
Petrozavodsk	280,000
Podolsk	202,000
Prokopyevsk	253,000
Pskov	207,000
Pyatigorsk	133,000
Rostov-na-Donu	1,000,000[18]
Rubtsovsk	170,000
Ryazan	536,000
Rybinsk (Andropov)	248,000
Saint Petersburg (Leningrad)	4,200,000[18]
Salavat	156,000
Samara (Kuybyshev)	1,200,000[18]
Saransk	320,000
Sarapul	109,000
Saratov	895,000
Sergiev Posad (Zagorsk)	114,000
Serov	100,000
Serpukhov	139,000
Severodvinsk	241,000
Seversk	110,000
Shakhty	230,000
Shchyolkovo	108,000
Simbirsk (Ulyanovsk)	678,000
Smolensk	355,000
Sochi	355,000
Solikamsk	108,000
Stary Oskol	198,000
Stavropol	342,000
Sterlitamak	259,000
Surgut	263,000
Syktyvkar	229,000
Syzran	177,000
Taganrog	292,000
Tambov	316,000
Tolyatti	702,000
Tomsk	470,000
Tula	532,000
Tver (Kalinin)	455,000
Tyumen	494,000
Ufa	1,100,000[18]
Ukhta	106,000
Ulan-Ude	366,000
Usolye-Sibirskoye	106,000
Ussuriysk	162,000
Ust-Ilimsk	110,000
Velikiye Luki	116,000
Vladikavkaz (Ordzhonikidze)	312,000
Vladimir	339,000
Vladivostok	632,000
Volgodonsk	183,000
Volgograd	1,003,000
Vologda	299,000
Volzhsky	288,000
Vorkuta	104,000
Voronezh	908,000
Votkinsk	104,000
Yakutsk	192,000
Yaroslavl	629,000
Yekaterinburg (Sverdlovsk)	1,300,000[18]
Yelets	119,000
Yoshkar-Ola	251,000
Yuzhno-Sakhalinsk	160,000
Zelenodolysk	101,000
Zelenograd	191,000
Zlatoust	203,000
Rwanda (1991)	
★ Kigali	232,733
St. Kitts and Nevis (1994 est.)	
★ Basseterre	12,605
St. Lucia (1992 est.)	
★ Castries	13,615[42]
St. Vincent and The Grenadines (1991)	
★ Kingstown	15,466
Samoa (1995 est.)	
★ Apia	33,000
San Marino (1996 est.)	
★ San Marino	2,316
São Tomé and Príncipe (1991)	
★ São Tomé	43,420
Saudi Arabia (1991 est.)	
Ad-Dammām	350,000
Jiddah	1,500,000
Mecca (Makkah)	630,000
Medina (Al-Madinah)	400,000
★ Riyadh (Ar-Riyad)	2,800,000[18,19]
Aṭ-Ṭā'if	410,000
Senegal (1995 est.)	
★ Dakar	1,500,000
Kaolack	181,000
Mboure	106,046[8]
Rufisque	138,837[8]
St.-Louis	179,000
Thiès	319,000
Ziguinchor	161,680[8]
Seychelles (1993 est.)	
★ Victoria	25,000
Sierra Leone (1990 est.)	
★ Freetown	669,000[19]
Singapore (1997 est.)[30]	
★ Singapore	3,104,000
Slovakia (1996 est.)	
★ Bratislava	452,053
Košice	240,915
Slovenia (1996 est.)	
★ Ljubljana	269,621
Maribor	134,289
Solomon Islands (1996 est.)	
★ Honiara	43,643
Somalia (1995 est.)	
★ Mogadishu	997,000
South Africa (1991)	
Alexandra	124,586
Benoni	113,501
★ Bloemfontein (judicial)	126,867
Boksburg	119,890
Botshabelo	177,926
★ Cape Town (legislative)	854,616
Carletonville	118,699
Daveyton	151,659
Diepmeadow	241,099
Durban	715,669
East London	102,325
Evaton	201,026
Germiston	134,005
Ibhayi	257,054
Johannesburg	712,507
Kathlehong (Katlehong)	201,785
Kempton Park	106,606
Khayelitsa	189,586
Kwamashu (Kwa Mashu)	156,679
Lekoa	217,582
Mamelodi	154,845
Manguang (Mangaung)	125,545
Mdantsane	242,823
Ntuzuma	102,310
Pietermaritzburg	156,473
Port Elizabeth	303,353
★ Pretoria (executive)	525,583
Roodepoort	162,632
Sandton	101,197
Soshanguve	146,334
Soweto	596,632
Tembisa	209,238
Umlazi	299,275

Major cities and national capitals (continued)

country city	population
Spain (1995 est.; MU)	
Albacete	143,779
Alcalá de Henares	166,925
Alcorcón	143,532
Algeciras	104,216
Alicante	276,526
Almería	169,509
Badajoz	132,154
Badalona	217,983
Barakaldo	102,561
Barcelona	1,614,571
Bilbao	370,997
Burgos	166,732
Cádiz	154,511
Cartagena	180,553
Castellón de la Plana	139,889
Córdoba	323,138
Coruña, La	254,822
Donostia (San Sebastián)	178,470
Elche (Elx)	192,424
Fuenlabrada	160,573
Getafe	144,662
Gijón	270,867
Granada	272,738
Hospitalet de Llobregat	262,501
Huelva	145,712
Jaén	113,141
Jerez de la Frontera	191,394
Laguna, La	127,743
Leganés	178,321
León	147,780
Lleida (Lérida)	114,367
Logroño	125,456
★ Madrid	3,029,734
Málaga	532,425
Mataró	102,137
Móstoles	199,411
Murcia	344,904
Ourense (Orense)	110,796
Oviedo	202,421
Palma (de Mallorca)	318,030
Palmas de Gran Canaria, Las (Is. Canarias)	373,772
Pamplona	181,776
Sabadell	188,386
Salamanca	167,316
Santa Coloma de Gramanet	129,751
Santa Cruz de Tenerife	204,948
Santander	194,837
Sevilla (Seville)	719,588
Tarragona	114,931
Terrassa	162,327
Valencia	763,299
Valladolid	334,820
Vigo	290,582
Vitoria (Gasteiz)	215,049
Zaragoza (Saragossa)	607,899
Sri Lanka (1990 est.)	
★ Colombo (administrative)	645,000[2]
Dehiwala-Mount Lavinia	196,000
Jaffna	129,000
Kandy	104,000
Moratuwa	170,000
★ Sri Jayawardenepura Kotte (legislative and judicial)	109,000[43]
Sudan, The (1993)	
Juba	114,980
Kassalā	234,270
★ Khartoum (executive)	924,505
Khartoum North	879,105
Nyala	228,778
★ Omdurman (legislative)	1,267,077
Port Sudan	305,385
al-Qaḍārif	189,384
al-Ubayyiḍ	228,096
Wad Madanī	218,714
Wāw	116,000[44]
Suriname (1993 est.)	
★ Paramaribo	200,970
Swaziland (1990 est.)	
★ Lobamba (legislative)	...
★ Lozitha (royal)	...
★ Ludzidzini (royal)	...
★ Mbabane (administrative)	47,000
Sweden (1997 est.; MU)	
Göteborg	454,016
Helsingborg	114,866
Jönköping	115,636
Linköping	131,898
Malmö	248,007
Norrköping	123,531
Örebro	120,774
★ Stockholm	718,462

country city	population
Umeå	102,487
Uppsala	184,507
Västerås	124,084
Switzerland (1996 est.)	
Basel (Bâle)	174,007
★ Bern (Berne)	127,469
Geneva (Genève)	173,549
Lausanne	115,878
Zürich	343,869
Syria (1994 est.)	
Aleppo (Ḥalab)	1,591,400
★ Damascus (Dimashq)	1,549,000
Dar'ā	180,093
Dayr az-Zawr	174,085
Dūmā	131,158
Ḥamāh	229,000[10]
Al-Ḥasakah	106,000[10]
Homs (Ḥims)	644,204
Jaramānah	138,469
Latakia (al-Ladhiqiyah)	306,535
Al-Qāmishlī	151,000[10]
Ar-Raqqah	219,016
Ṭarṭūs	136,812
Taiwan (1997 est.)	
Chang-hua	221,090[8]
Chi-lung (Keelung)	374,874
Chia-i	263,549
Chung-ho	387,123[2]
Chung-li	295,825[2]
Feng-shan (Kao-hsiung-hsien)	301,374[2]
Fēng-yüan	157,548[2]
Hsin-chu	346,979
Hsin-chuang	328,758[2]
Hsin-tien	248,822[2]
Hua-lien	107,824[2]
Kao-hsiung	1,434,907
Pan-ch'iao (T'ai-pei-hsien)	539,115[2]
P'ing-tung	214,728[2]
San-chu'ung	382,880[2]
T'ai-chung	881,870
T'ai-nan	712,172
T'ai-tung	109,189[2]
★ Taipei (T'ai-pei)	2,595,699
T'ao-yuan	260,680[2]
Yung-ho	241,104[2]
Tajikistan (1994 est.)	
★ Dushanbe	524,000
Khujand (Khudzhand; Leninabad)	164,500[20]
Tanzania (1988)	
Arusha	134,708
★ Dar es Salaam	1,360,850
★ Dodoma (legislative)	203,833
Mbeya	152,844
Morogoro	117,760
Mwanza	223,013
Shinyanga	100,724
Tanga	187,155
Zanzibar	157,634
Thailand (1993 est.)	
★ Bangkok	5,584,963[18]
Chiang Mai	170,397
Hat Yai	148,632
Nakhon Ratchasima	188,171
Nonthaburi	261,335
Ubon Ratchathani	105,936
Togo (1990 est.)	
★ Lomé	513,000[19]
Tonga (1990 est.)	
★ Nuku'alofa	34,000
Trinidad and Tobago (1995 est.)	
★ Port-of-Spain	52,000
Tunisia (1994)	
Aryānah	152,700
Ettadhamen	149,200
Kairouan	102,600
Ṣafāqis (Sfax)	230,900
Sūsah	125,000
★ Tunis	674,100
Turkey (1995 est.)	
Adana	1,066,544
Adapazari	186,000[8]
Adıyaman	129,919
Afyan	102,997
★ Ankara	2,837,937
Antakya	137,200[8]
Antalya	502,269
Aydın	123,163
Balıkesir	189,702
Batman	186,178
Bursa	1,016,760
Çorum	136,736
Denizli	239,698
Diyarbakır	448,145
Edirne	117,331

country city	population
Elazığ	224,781
Erzurum	247,585
Eskişehir	455,285
Gaziantep	730,435
Gebze	231,052
Hatay	138,998
İçel	532,774
İskenderun	153,871
Isparta	121,663
Istanbul	7,774,169
İzmir	2,017,699
İzmit	275,800[8]
Kahramanmaraş	242,491
Karabük	114,698
Kayseri	463,759
Kilis	107,605
Kırıkkale	154,764
Kocaeli	205,762
Konya	584,785
Kütahya	141,450
Malatya	314,539
Manisa	191,287
Mersin	523,000[8]
Ordu	123,782
Osmaniye	140,257
Sakarya	185,187
Samsun	330,360
Sivas	243,432
Sultanbeyli	169,999
Tarsus	229,518
Trabzon	143,573
Urfa (Şanlıurfa)	362,598
Uşak	121,972
Van	197,679
Zonguldak	113,627
Turkmenistan (1995 est.)	
★ Ashkhabad (Ashgabat)	536,000
Chärjew (Chardzhev; Chardzhou)	166,400[20]
Dashhowuz (Dashkhovuz; Tashauz)	117,000[20]
Tuvalu (1995 est.)	
★ Funafuti	4,000
Uganda (1995 est.)	
★ Kampala	954,000
Ukraine (1996 est.)	
Alchevsk	124,000
Berdyansk	135,000
Bila Tserkva (Belaya Tserkov)	216,000
Cherkasy (Cherkassy)	312,000
Chernihiv (Chernigov)	312,000
Chernivtsi (Chernovtsy)	261,000
Dniprodzerzhynsk (Dneprodzerzhinsk)	281,000
Dnipropetrovsk (Dnepropetrovsk)	1,147,000
Donetsk	1,088,000
Horlivka (Gorlovka)	322,000
Ivano-Frankivsk (Ivano-Frankovsk)	237,000
Kamyanets-Podilsky (Kamenets-Podolsky)	108,000
Kerch	175,000
Kharkiv (Kharkov)	1,555,000
Kherson	363,000
Khmelnytsky (Khmelnitsky)	259,000
★ Kiev (Kyyiv)	2,630,000
Kirovohrad	276,000
Kostyantynivka (Konstantinovka)	102,000
Kramatorsk	197,000
Krasny Luch	109,000
Kremenchuk (Kremenchug)	246,000
Kryvy Rih (Krivoy Rog)	720,000
Luhansk (Voroshilovgrad)	487,000
Lutsk	219,000
Lviv (Lvov)	802,000
Lysychansk (Lisichansk)	123,000
Makiyivka (Makeyevka)	409,000
Mariupol (Zhdanov)	510,000
Melitopol	174,000
Mykolayiv (Nikolayev)	508,000
Nikopol	157,000
Odesa (Odessa)	1,046,000
Oleksandriya (Aleksandriya)	103,000
Pavlohrad	134,000
Poltava	321,000
Rivne (Rovno)	246,000
Sevastopol	365,000
Severodonetsk	132,000
Simferopol	348,000

country city	population
Slovyansk (Slavyansk)	133,000
Stakhanov	109,000
Sumy	304,000
Ternopil (Ternopol)	235,000
Uzhhorod	126,000
Vinnytsya (Vinnitsa)	388,000
Yenakiyeve (Yenakiyevo)	114,000
Yevpatoriya	115,000
Zaporizhzhya (Zaporozhye)	882,000
Zhytomyr (Zhitomir)	301,000
United Arab Emirates (1989 est.)	
★ Abu Dhabi (Abū Ẓaby)	363,432
Al-'Ayn	176,441
Dubai (Dubayy)	585,189
Sharjah (Ash-Shāriqah)	125,123[25]
United Kingdom (1995 est.)[45]	
Aberdeen	219,100
Aylesbury	152,000[8]
Barnsley	226,700
Basildon	162,100[8]
Basingstoke/Deane	147,200[8]
Bedford	137,000[8]
Belfast	296,700
Beverley	118,000[8]
Birmingham	1,017,500
Blackburn	140,100[8]
Blackpool	154,000[8]
Bolton	265,400
Bournemouth	160,100[8]
Bracknell	104,600[8]
Bradford	482,700
Braintree	123,600[8]
Brighton	154,900[8]
Bristol	400,700
Bury	182,200[8]
Cambridge	113,000[8]
Canterbury	133,900[8]
Cardiff	302,700
Carlisle	103,300[8]
Chelmsford	155,800[8]
Cheltenham	106,800[8]
Chester	120,600[8]
Chesterfield	101,100[8]
Chichester	103,100[8]
Colchester	149,600[8]
Coventry	303,600
Crewe/Nantwich	111,400[8]
Darlington	100,600[8]
Derby	231,900
Doncaster	292,900
Dover	106,900[8]
Dudley	312,500
Dundee	167,600
Eastleigh	110,800[8]
Edinburgh	447,600
Elmbridge	119,700[8]
Epping Forest	118,900[8]
Exeter	104,500[8]
Fareham	101,800[8]
Gateshead	201,800
Glasgow	674,800
Gloucester	104,700[8]
Guildford	126,200[8]
Harrogate	148,400[8]
Havant	119,400[8]
Horsham	114,300[8]
Huntingdon	149,900[8]
Ipswich	114,100[8]
King's Lynn/West Norfolk	131,000[8]
Kingston upon Hull	268,600
Kirklees	387,700
Knowsley	154,000[8]
Lancaster	135,000[8]
Leeds	725,000
Leicester	295,700
Liverpool	470,800
★ London	7,007,100
Luton	180,800[8]
Macclesfield	151,500[8]
Maidstone	138,500[8]
Manchester	432,600
Mansfield	102,100[8]
Middlesbrough	146,900[8]
Milton Keynes	188,400[8]
Newbury	141,600[8]
Newcastle under Lyme	123,100[8]
Newcastle upon Tyne	283,100
Newport	137,400[8]
Northampton	187,600[8]
Norwich	127,800[8]
Nottingham	283,800
Nuneaton/Bedworth	119,100[8]
Oldham	220,000
Oxford	132,800[8]
Peterborough	158,700[8]
Plymouth	257,500
Poole	138,100[8]
Portsmouth	189,300[8]

country city	population
Preston	133,100[8]
Reading	138,500[8]
Reigate/Banstead	118,300[8]
Renfrew	203,100
Rhymney Valley	104,300[8]
Rochdale	207,600
Rochester upon Medway	145,500[8]
Rotherham	255,800
St. Albans	128,700[8]
St. Helens	181,000[8]
Salford	230,500
Salisbury	110,000[8]
Sandwell	293,700
Scarborough	108,700[8]
Sefton	291,000
Sevenoaks	109,900[8]
Sheffield	528,500
Slough	104,900[8]
Solihull	202,900
Southampton	213,500
Southend-on-Sea	169,900[8]
Stafford	122,500[8]
Stockport	290,600
Stockton-on-Tees	178,200[8]
Stoke-on-Trent	254,300
Stratford-on-Avon	109,500[8]
Stroud	106,300[8]
Sunderland	295,800
Swale	117,200[8]
Swansea	188,800[8]
Tameside	221,500
Tonbridge/Malling	102,800[8]
Trafford	218,300
Tunbridge Wells	102,700[8]
Wakefield	317,100
Walsall	262,800
Warrington	186,700[8]
Warwick	119,800[8]
Wigan	309,800
Winchester	101,800[8]
Windsor/Maidenhead	137,800[8]
Wirral	331,500
Wokingham	141,700[8]
Wolverhampton	244,300
Wrexham Maelor	117,400[8]
Wycombe	162,600[8]
York	104,100[8]
United States (1996 est.)	
Abilene (*Texas*)	108,476
Akron (*Ohio*)	216,882
Alameda (*Calif.*)	76,042
Albany (*Ga.*)	78,591
Albany (*N.Y.*)	103,564
Albuquerque (*N.M.*)	419,681
Alexandria (*Va.*)	117,586
Alhambra (*Calif.*)	83,644
Allentown (*Pa.*)	102,211
Amarillo (*Texas*)	169,588
Anaheim (*Calif.*)	288,945
Anchorage (*Alaska*)	250,505
Antioch (*Calif.*)	76,293
Ann Arbor (*Mich.*)	108,758
Arlington (*Texas*)	294,816
Arlington (*Va.*)	175,334[46]
Arlington Heights (*Ill.*)	76,740
Arvada (*Colo.*)	96,340
Atlanta (*Ga.*)	401,907
Aurora (*Colo.*)	252,341
Aurora (*Ill.*)	116,405
Austin (*Texas*)	541,278
Bakersfield (*Calif.*)	205,508
Baltimore (*Md.*)	675,401
Baton Rouge (*La.*)	215,882
Beaumont (*Texas*)	111,224
Bellevue (*Wash.*)	92,267
Berkeley (*Calif.*)	103,243
Billings (*Mont.*)	91,195
Birmingham (*Ala.*)	258,543
Bloomington (*Minn.*)	86,664
Boise City (*Idaho*)	152,737
Boston (*Mass.*)	558,394
Boulder (*Colo.*)	90,928
Bridgeport (*Conn.*)	137,990
Brockton (*Mass.*)	92,324
Brownsville (*Texas*)	132,091
Buffalo (*N.Y.*)	310,548
Burbank (*Calif.*)	96,579
Cambridge (*Mass.*)	93,707
Camden (*N.J.*)	84,844
Canton (*Ohio*)	81,079
Cape Coral (*Fla.*)	88,053
Carrollton (*Texas*)	96,757
Carson (*Calif.*)	86,516
Cedar Rapids (*Iowa*)	113,482
Chandler (*Ariz.*)	142,918
Charlotte (*N.C.*)	441,297
Chattanooga (*Tenn.*)	150,425
Chesapeake (*Va.*)	192,342
Chicago (*Ill.*)	2,721,547
Chula Vista (*Calif.*)	151,963
Cincinnati (*Ohio*)	345,818
Clarksville (*Tenn.*)	94,879
Clearwater (*Fla.*)	100,132

[1]1993 estimate. [2]1995 estimate. [3]Eight villages, including Fagatogo, Utulei, and Pago Pago, are collectively known as Pago Pago (1990 census pop. 10,559). [4]1984 estimate. [5]Population of municipality. [6]1989 census. [7]Population of the statistical division containing the city. [8]1994 estimate. [9]Statistical district. [10]1992 estimate. [11]Population cited is for New Providence Island. [12]1991 census. [13]1992 census. [14]1982 estimate. [15]1990 census. [16]1987 census. [17]Excludes the agricultural population of the named civil division. [18]1996 estimate. [19]Population refers to widest officially defined agglomeration or metropolitan area. [20]1991 estimate. [21]San José canton. [22]1988 census. [23]Mid-1990s estimate. [24]Excludes population of Lefkosia (Turkish-occupied Nicosia), estimated at 37,400 in 1985. [25]Population of the urban area of the National district. [26]1986 estimate. [27]1986 census. [28]Urban centre of Suva. [29]1983 census. [30]No separate areas within the state are

country city	population
Cleveland (*Ohio*)	498,246
Colorado Springs (*Colo.*)	345,127
Columbia (*Mo.*)	76,756
Columbia (*S.C.*)	112,773
Columbus (*Ga.*)	182,828
Columbus (*Ohio*)	657,053
Compton (*Calif.*)	91,700
Concord (*Calif.*)	114,850
Coral Springs (*Fla.*)	105,275
Corona (*Calif.*)	100,208
Corpus Christi (*Texas*)	280,260
Costa Mesa (*Calif.*)	100,938
Dallas (*Texas*)	1,053,292
Daly City (*Calif.*)	97,649
Davenport (*Iowa*)	97,010
Dayton (*Ohio*)	172,947
Dearborn (*Mich.*)	91,418
Decatur (*Ill.*)	81,369
Denver (*Colo.*)	497,840
Des Moines (*Iowa*)	193,422
Detroit (*Mich.*)	1,000,272
Downey (*Calif.*)	93,073
Duluth (*Minn.*)	83,699
Durham (*N.C.*)	149,799
El Cajon (*Calif.*)	92,057
El Monte (*Calif.*)	110,026
El Paso (*Texas*)	599,865
Elgin (*Ill.*)	86,034
Elizabeth (*N.J.*)	110,149
Erie (*Pa.*)	105,270
Escondido (*Calif.*)	116,184
Eugene (*Ore.*)	123,718
Evansville (*Ind.*)	123,456
Everett (*Wash.*)	81,028
Fairfield (*Calif.*)	85,610
Fall River (*Mass.*)	90,865
Fargo (*N.D.*)	83,778
Farmington Hills (*Mich.*)	79,918
Fayetteville (*N.C.*)	79,631
Flint (*Mich.*)	134,881
Fontana (*Calif.*)	104,124
Fort Collins (*Colo.*)	104,196
Fort Lauderdale (*Fla.*)	151,805
Fort Wayne (*Ind.*)	184,783
Fort Worth (*Texas*)	479,716
Fremont (*Calif.*)	187,800
Fresno (*Calif.*)	396,011
Fullerton (*Calif.*)	120,188
Gainesville (*Fla.*)	87,295
Garden Grove (*Calif.*)	149,208
Garland (*Texas*)	190,055
Gary (*Ind.*)	110,975
Glendale (*Ariz.*)	182,219
Glendale (*Calif.*)	184,321
Grand Prairie (*Texas*)	109,231
Grand Rapids (*Mich.*)	188,242
Green Bay (*Wis.*)	102,076
Greensboro (*N.C.*)	195,426
Gresham (*Ore.*)	81,583
Hammond (*Ind.*)	80,081
Hampton (*Va.*)	138,757
Hartford (*Conn.*)	133,086
Hayward (*Calif.*)	121,631
Henderson (*Nev.*)	122,339
Hialeah (*Fla.*)	204,684
Hollywood (*Fla.*)	127,894
Honolulu (*Ha.*)	423,475
Houston (*Texas*)	1,744,058
Huntington Beach (*Calif.*)	190,751
Huntsville (*Ala.*)	170,424
Independence (*Mo.*)	110,303
Indianapolis (*Ind.*)	746,737
Inglewood (*Calif.*)	111,040
Irvine (*Calif.*)	127,873
Irving (*Texas*)	176,993
Jackson (*Miss.*)	192,923
Jacksonville (*Fla.*)	679,792
Jersey City (*N.J.*)	229,039
Joliet (*Ill.*)	86,749
Kalamazoo (*Mich.*)	77,460
Kansas City (*Kan.*)	142,654
Kansas City (*Mo.*)	441,259
Kenosha (*Wis.*)	86,888
Killeen (*Texas*)	78,022
Knoxville (*Tenn.*)	167,535
Lafayette (*La.*)	104,899
Lakewood (*Calif.*)	75,462
Lakewood (*Colo.*)	134,999
Lancaster (*Calif.*)	115,675
Lansing (*Mich.*)	125,736
Laredo (*Texas*)	164,899
Las Vegas (*Nev.*)	376,906
Lawton (*Okla.*)	82,582
Lexington-Fayette (*Ky.*)	239,942
Lincoln (*Neb.*)	209,192
Little Rock (*Ark.*)	175,752
Livonia (*Mich.*)	105,099
Long Beach (*Calif.*)	421,904
Los Angeles (*Calif.*)	3,553,638
Louisville (*Ky.*)	260,689
Lowell (*Mass.*)	100,973
Lubbock (*Texas*)	193,565
Lynn (*Mass.*)	80,563
McAllen (*Texas*)	103,352
Macon (*Ga.*)	113,352
Madison (*Wis.*)	197,630
Manchester (*N.H.*)	100,967
Memphis (*Tenn.*)	596,725
Mesa (*Ariz.*)	344,764
Mesquite (*Texas*)	111,947
Miami (*Fla.*)	365,127
Miami Beach (*Fla.*)	94,540
Midland (*Texas*)	97,162
Milwaukee (*Wis.*)	590,503
Minneapolis (*Minn.*)	358,785
Mission Viejo (*Calif.*)	84,689
Mobile (*Ala.*)	202,581
Modesto (*Calif.*)	178,559
Montgomery (*Ala.*)	196,363
Moreno Valley (*Calif.*)	140,932
Naperville (*Ill.*)	107,001
Nashua (*N.H.*)	81,094
Nashville-Davidson (*Tenn.*)	511,263
New Bedford (*Mass.*)	96,903
New Haven (*Conn.*)	124,665
New Orleans (*La.*)	476,625
New York City (*N.Y.*)	7,380,906
Newark (*N.J.*)	268,510
Newport News (*Va.*)	176,122
Newton (*Mass.*)	80,238
Norfolk (*Va.*)	233,430
Norman (*Okla.*)	90,228
North Las Vegas (*Nev.*)	78,659
Norwalk (*Calif.*)	100,209
Norwalk (*Conn.*)	77,977
Oakland (*Calif.*)	367,230
Oceanside (*Calif.*)	145,941
Odessa (*Texas*)	90,883
Oklahoma City (*Okla.*)	469,852
Olathe (*Kan.*)	78,666
Omaha (*Neb.*)	364,253
Ontario (*Calif.*)	144,854
Orange (*Calif.*)	119,890
Orem (*Utah*)	79,736
Orlando (*Fla.*)	173,902
Overland Park (*Kan.*)	131,053
Oxnard (*Calif.*)	151,009
Palmdale (*Calif.*)	106,540
Parma (*Ohio*)	85,006
Pasadena (*Calif.*)	134,116
Pasadena (*Texas*)	131,620
Paterson (*N.J.*)	150,270
Pembroke Pines (*Fla.*)	100,662
Peoria (*Ariz.*)	76,045
Peoria (*Ill.*)	112,306
Philadelphia (*Pa.*)	1,478,002
Phoenix (*Ariz.*)	1,159,014
Pittsburgh (*Pa.*)	350,363
Plano (*Texas*)	192,280
Plantation (*Fla.*)	78,674
Pomona (*Calif.*)	134,706
Port St. Lucie (*Fla.*)	75,532
Portland (*Ore.*)	480,824
Portsmouth (*Va.*)	101,308
Providence (*R.I.*)	152,558
Provo (*Utah*)	99,606
Pueblo (*Colo.*)	99,406
Quincy (*Mass.*)	85,532
Racine (*Wis.*)	82,572
Raleigh (*N.C.*)	243,835
Rancho Cucamonga (*Calif.*)	116,613
Reading (*Pa.*)	75,723
Redding (*Calif.*)	76,616
Reno (*Nev.*)	155,499
Rialto (*Calif.*)	82,320
Richardson (*Texas*)	81,133
Richmond (*Calif.*)	91,018
Richmond (*Va.*)	198,267
Riverside (*Calif.*)	255,069
Roanoke (*Va.*)	95,548
Rochester (*Minn.*)	75,638
Rochester (*N.Y.*)	221,594
Rockford (*Ill.*)	143,531
Sacramento (*Calif.*)	376,243
St. Louis (*Mo.*)	351,565
St. Paul (*Minn.*)	259,606
St. Petersburg (*Fla.*)	235,988
Salem (*Ore.*)	122,566
Salinas (*Calif.*)	111,757
Salt Lake City (*Utah*)	172,575
San Angelo (*Texas*)	88,098
San Antonio (*Texas*)	1,067,816
San Bernardino (*Calif.*)	183,474
San Buenaventura (Ventura) (*Calif.*)	97,205
San Diego (*Calif.*)	1,171,121
San Francisco (*Calif.*)	735,315
San Jose (*Calif.*)	838,744
San Mateo (*Calif.*)	90,161
Sandy (*Utah*)	94,593
Santa Ana (*Calif.*)	302,419
Santa Barbara (*Calif.*)	86,154
Santa Clara (*Calif.*)	98,726
Santa Clarita (*Calif.*)	125,153
Santa Monica (*Calif.*)	88,471
Santa Rosa (*Calif.*)	121,879
Savannah (*Ga.*)	136,262
Scottsdale (*Ariz.*)	179,012
Scranton (*Pa.*)	77,189
Seattle (*Wash.*)	524,704
Shreveport (*La.*)	191,558
Simi Valley (*Calif.*)	106,974
Sioux City (*Iowa*)	83,791
Sioux Falls (*S.D.*)	113,223
South Bend (*Ind.*)	102,100
South Gate (*Calif.*)	88,125
Southfield (*Mich.*)	76,184
Spokane (*Wash.*)	186,562
Springfield (*Ill.*)	112,921
Springfield (*Mass.*)	149,948
Springfield (*Mo.*)	143,407
Stamford (*Conn.*)	110,056
Sterling Heights (*Mich.*)	118,698
Stockton (*Calif.*)	232,660
Sunnyvale (*Calif.*)	125,156
Sunrise (*Fla.*)	77,592
Syracuse (*N.Y.*)	155,865
Tacoma (*Wash.*)	179,114
Tallahassee (*Fla.*)	136,812
Tampa (*Fla.*)	285,206
Tempe (*Ariz.*)	162,701
Thousand Oaks (*Calif.*)	113,368
Toledo (*Ohio*)	317,606
Topeka (*Kan.*)	119,658
Torrance (*Calif.*)	136,183
Trenton (*N.J.*)	85,437
Troy (*Mich.*)	79,120
Tucson (*Ariz.*)	449,002
Tulsa (*Okla.*)	378,491
Tuscaloosa (*Ala.*)	82,379
Tyler (*Texas*)	82,185
Vacaville (*Calif.*)	81,355
Vallejo (*Calif.*)	109,593
Virginia Beach (*Va.*)	430,385
Visalia (*Calif.*)	87,737
Vista (*Calif.*)	78,494
Waco (*Texas*)	108,412
Warren (*Mich.*)	138,078
Warwick (*R.I.*)	84,514
★ Washington, D.C.	543,213
Waterbury (*Conn.*)	106,412
West Covina (*Calif.*)	101,526
West Palm Beach (*Fla.*)	79,305
West Valley City (*Utah*)	99,136
Westland (*Mich.*)	90,798
Westminster (*Calif.*)	82,425
Westminster (*Colo.*)	93,115
Whittier (*Calif.*)	78,740
Wichita (*Kan.*)	320,395
Wichita Falls (*Texas*)	100,138
Winston-Salem (*N.C.*)	153,541
Worcester (*Mass.*)	166,350
Yonkers (*N.Y.*)	190,316
Youngstown (*Ohio*)	87,405
Uruguay (1996)	
★ Montevideo	1,378,707
Uzbekistan (1993 est.)	
Andijon (Andizhan)	313,000
Angren	132,000[1]
Bukhoro (Bukhara)	238,000
Chirchiq (Chirchik)	156,000[1]
Farghona (Fergana)	191,000[1]
Jizzakh (Dzhizak)	116,000[1]
Marghilon (Margilan)	129,000[1]
Namangan	362,000
Nawoiy (Navoi)	115,000[1]
Nukus	185,000[1]
Olmaliq (Almalyk)	116,000[1]
Qarshi (Karshi)	177,000[1]
Quqon (Kokand)	184,000[1]
Samarqand (Samarkand)	362,000
★ Tashkent (Toshkent)	2,107,000
Urganch (Urgench)	135,000[1]
Vanuatu (1996 est.)	
★ Vila	31,800
Venezuela (1990)	
Acarigua	116,551
Barcelona	221,792
Barinas	153,630
Barquisimeto	625,450
Baruta	182,941[19]
Cabimas	165,755[19]
★ Caracas	1,822,465
Catia la Mar	100,104
Ciudad Bolívar	253,112[10]
Ciudad Guayana (San Felix de Guayana)	523,578[10]
Coro	137,040[10]
Cumaná	232,228[10]
Guacara	100,766
Guarenas	152,612[10]
Los Teques	162,145[10]
Maracaibo	1,249,670
Maracay	384,782[10]
Maturín	233,279[10]
Mérida	188,063[10]
Petare	379,338[10]
Puerto Cabello	143,765[10]
Puerto La Cruz	155,731
San Cristóbal	238,670[10]
Santa Ana de Coro	124,506
Turmero	195,711[10]
Valencia	1,034,033[10]
Valera	107,236[10]
Vietnam (1992 est.)	
Bien Hoa	97,094[6]
Buon Ma Thuot	282,095
Cam Pha	209,086
Cam Ranh	114,041[6]
Can Tho	215,587
Da Lat	106,409
Da Nang	382,674
Haiphong	783,133
★ Hanoi	2,154,900[1]
Ho Chi Minh City (Saigon)	4,322,300[1]
Hong Gai	127,484
Hue	219,149
Long Xuyen	132,681
My Tho	108,404
Nam Dinh	171,699
Nha Trang	221,331
Phan Thiet	114,236[6]
Qui Nhon	163,385
Rach Gia	141,132
Thai Nguyen	127,643
Vinh	112,455
Vung Tau	145,145
Virgin Islands (U.S.) (1990)	
★ Charlotte Amalie	12,331
West Bank (1987 est.)	
Nābulus	106,944
★ —	—
Western Sahara (1994)	
★ Laayoune (El Aaiún)	136,950
Yemen (1995 est.)[19]	
Aden	562,000
Al-Ḥudaydah	246,068[1]
Al-Mukallā	154,360
★ Ṣan'ā'	972,000
Ta'izz	290,107[1]
Yugoslavia (1991)	
★ Belgrade (Beograd)	1,168,454
Kragujevac	147,305
Niš	175,391
Novi Sad	179,626
Podgorica (Titograd)	117,875
Priština	155,499
Subotica	100,386
Zambia (1990)	
Chingola	167,954
Kabwe	166,519
Kitwe	338,207
Luanshya	146,275
★ Lusaka	982,362
Mufulira	152,944
Ndola	376,311
Zimbabwe (1992)	
Bulawayo	620,936
Chitungwiza	274,035
Gweru	124,735
★ Harare	1,184,169
Mount Darwin	164,362
Mutare	131,808

distinguished administratively as cities. [31]Population includes Comayagüela. [32]1980 census, adjusted for consistent bounding of localities. [33]1985 estimate. [34]County borough. [35]City of Kingston is coextensive with Kingston parish. [36]Population includes Limbe. [37]Includes adjoining municipalities. [38]Population of prefecture. [39]Projections based on a repudiated census taken in 1963. A 1991 census suggests that the 1963 census had overestimated Nigeria's population by as much as 70 percent. [40]Federal Capital territory. [41]National government centre. [42]Urban area. [43]Population refers to Kotte only. [44]1980 estimate. [45]Population of local authority areas. [46]Census-designated place (CDP).

Language

This table presents estimated data on the principal language communities of the countries of the world. The countries, and the principal languages (occasionally, language families) represented in each, are listed alphabetically. A bullet (●) indicates those languages that are official in each country. The sum of the estimates equals the 1997 population of the country given in the "Area and population" table.

The estimates represent, so far as national data collection systems permit, the distribution of mother tongues (a mother tongue being the language spoken first and, usually, most fluently by an individual). Many countries do not collect any official data whatever on language use, and published estimates not based on census or survey data usually span a substantial range of uncertainty. The editors have adopted the best-founded distribution in the published literature (indicating uncertainty by the degree of rounding shown) but have also adjusted or interpolated using data not part of the base estimate(s). Such adjustments have not been made to account for large-scale refugee movements, as these are of a temporary nature.

A variety of approaches have been used to approximate mother-tongue distribution when census data were unavailable. Some countries collect data on ethnic or "national" groups only; for such countries ethnic distribution often had to be assumed to conform roughly to the distribution of language communities. This approach, however, should be viewed with caution, because a minority population is not always free to educate its children in its own language and because better economic opportunities often draw minority group members into the majority-language community. For some countries, a given individual may be visible in national statistics only as a passport-holder of a foreign country, however long he may remain resident. Such persons, often guest workers, have sometimes had to be assumed to be speakers of the principal language of their home country. For other countries, the language mosaic may be so complex, the language communities so minute in size, scholarly study so inadequate, or the census base so obsolete that it was possible only to assign percentages to entire groups, or families, of related languages, despite their mutual unintelligibility (Papuan and Melanesian languages in Papua New Guinea, for instance). For some countries in the Americas, so few speakers of any single indigenous language remain that it was necessary to combine these groups as *Amerindian* so as to give a fair impression of their aggregate size within their respective countries.

No systematic attempt has been made to account for populations that may legitimately be described as bilingual, unless the country itself collects data on that basis, as does Bolivia or the Comoros, for example. Where a nonindigenous official or excolonial language constitutes a lingua franca of the country, however, speakers of the language as a second tongue are shown in italics, even though very few may speak it as a mother tongue. No comprehensive effort has been made to distinguish between dialect communities *usually* classified as belonging to the same language, though such distinctions were possible for some countries—*e.g.,* between French and Occitan (the dialect of southern France) or among the various dialects of Chinese.

In giving the names of Bantu languages, grammatical particles specific to a language's autonym (name for itself) have been omitted (the form *Rwanda* is used here, for example, rather than *kinyaRwanda,* and *Tswana* instead of *seTswana*). Parenthetical alternatives are given for a number of languages that differ markedly from the name of the people speaking them (such as Kurukh, spoken by the Oraon tribes of India) or that may be combined with other groups sometimes distinguishable in national data but appearing here under the name of the largest member—*e.g.,* "Tamil (and other Indian languages)" combining data on South Asian Indian populations in Singapore. The term *creole* as used here refers to distinguishable dialectal communities related to a national, official, or former colonial language (such as the French creole that survives in Mauritius from the end of French rule in 1810).

Internet resources for further information:

- *Ethnologue* (13th ed.; Summer Institute of Linguistics) http://www.sil.org/ethnologue
- Joshua Project 2000—People's List (Christian interfaith missionary database identifying some 2,000 ethnolinguistic groups) http://www.xc.org/Brigada/joshua/jp2000li.html

For additional detail in the Americas:

- (USA): http://www.census.gov/ftp/pub/ipc/www/idbconf.html (especially tables 57 and 59)
- Living Languages of the Americas (Summer Institute of Linguistics) http://www.sil.org/lla

Language

Major languages by country	Number of speakers
Afghanistan[1]	
Indo-Aryan languages	
Pashai	140,000
Iranian languages	
Balochi	220,000
● Dari (Persian)	
Chahar Aimak	670,000
Hazāra	2,090,000
Tajik	4,840,000
Nūristāni group	180,000
Pamir group	140,000
● Pashto	12,430,000
Turkic languages	
Turkmen	460,000
Uzbek	2,090,000
Other	450,000
Albania[1]	
● Albanian	3,226,000
Greek	61,000
Macedonian	5,000
Other	1,000
Algeria	
● Arabic	25,350,000
Berber	4,130,000
English	...
French	*13,000,000*
American Samoa	
● English	2,000
English (lingua franca)	*61,000*
● Samoan	56,000
Tongan	2,000
Other	2,000
Andorra[2]	
● Catalan (Andorran)	18,000
English	1,000
French	5,000
Portuguese	7,000
Spanish	30,000
Other	3,000
Angola[1]	
Ambo (Ovambo)	250,000
Chokwe	450,000
Herero	80,000
Kongo	1,400,000
Luchazi	250,000
Luimbe-Nganguela	570,000
Lunda	130,000
Luvale (Luena)	380,000
Mbunda	130,000
Mbundu	2,290,000
Nyaneka-Nkhumbi	570,000
Ovimbundu (Umbundu)	3,950,000
● Portuguese	*3,700,000*
Other	160,000
Antigua and Barbuda	
● English	*65,000*
English/English Creole	61,000
Other	3,000
Argentina	
Amerindian languages	110,000
Italian	620,000
● Spanish	34,290,000
Other	390,000
Armenia	
● Armenian	3,520,000
Azerbaijani (Azeri)	100,000
Other	150,000
Aruba	
● Dutch	5,000
English	8,000
Papiamento	64,000
Spanish	6,000
Other	1,000
Australia	
Aboriginal languages	49,000
Arabic	180,000
Cantonese	212,000
Dutch	45,000
● English	15,027,000
English (lingua franca)	*17,900,000*
French	42,000
German	108,000
Greek	288,000
Hungarian	29,000
Indonesian Malay	29,000
Italian	409,000
Macedonian	76,000
Mandarin	97,000
Maltese	50,000
Philippine languages	75,000
Polish	68,000
Portuguese	26,000
Russian	33,000
Serbo-Croatian	114,000
Spanish	97,000
Turkish	47,000
Vietnamese	149,000
Other/not stated	1,258,000
Austria	
Czech	19,000
● German	7,440,000
Hungarian	34,000
Polish	19,000
Romanian	17,000
Serbo-Croatian	175,000
Slovene	30,000
Turkish	123,000
Other	230,000
Azerbaijan	
Armenian	150,000
● Azerbaijani (Azeri)	6,780,000
Lezgi (Lezgian)	170,000
Russian	230,000
Other	290,000
Bahamas, The	
● English	...
English/English Creole	260,000
French (Haitian) Creole	30,000
Bahrain[2]	
● Arabic	410,000
English	...
Other	190,000
Bangladesh[1]	
● Bengali	122,490,000
Chakmā	460,000
● English	*3,300,000*
Gāro	110,000
Khāsī	100,000
Marma (Magh)	240,000
Mro	40,000
Santhālī	90,000
Tripurī	90,000
Other	1,720,000
Barbados	
Bajan (English Creole)	252,000
● English	...
Other	13,000
Belarus	
● Belarusian	6,800,000
Polish	60,000
● Russian	3,310,000
Ukrainian	130,000
Other	60,000
Belgium[2, 3]	
Arabic	160,000
● Dutch (Flemish; Netherlandic)	6,040,000
● French (Walloon)	3,330,000
● German	90,000
Italian	250,000
Spanish	50,000
Turkish	90,000
Other	180,000
Belize	
● English	115,000
English Creole (lingua franca)	*180,000*
Garifuna (Black Carib)	15,000
German	3,000
Mayan languages	22,000
Spanish	72,000
Spanish (lingua franca)	*130,000*
Benin[1]	
Adja	660,000
Aizo (Ouidah)	510,000
Bariba	510,000
Dendi	130,000
Djougou	180,000
Fon	2,350,000
● French	*910,000*
Fula (Fulani)	330,000
Somba (Ditamari)	390,000
Yoruba (Nago)	720,000
Other	140,000
Bermuda	
● English	62,000
Bhutan[1]	
Assamese	130,000
● Dzongkha (Bhutiā)	430,000
Nepālī (Hindī)	300,000
Bolivia	
● Aymara	250,000
Guaraní	10,000
● Quechua	630,000
● Spanish	3,240,000
Spanish-Amerindian (multilingual), of which	3,570,000
Spanish-Aymara	*1,503,000*
Spanish-Guaraní	*30,000*
Spanish-Quechua	*2,010,000*
Other	60,000
Bosnia and Herzegovina	
● Serbo-Croatian	3,100,000
Other	30,000
Botswana[1]	
● English (lingua franca)	*600,000*
Khoekhoe (Hottentot)	37,000
Ndebele	19,000
San (Bushman)	52,000
Shona	186,000
Tswana	1,133,000
Tswana (lingua franca)	*1,200,000*
Other	73,000
Brazil[1]	
Amerindian languages	270,000
German	880,000
Italian	670,000
Japanese	610,000
● Portuguese	155,780,000
Other	1,490,000
Brunei	
Chinese	29,000
English	10,000
● Malay	140,000
Malay-Chinese	3,000
Malay-English	89,000
English-Chinese	7,000
Malay-Chinese-English	12,000
Other	16,000
Bulgaria[1]	
● Bulgarian	6,930,000
French	*230,000*
Macedonian	210,000
Romany	310,000
Turkish	790,000
Other	100,000
Burkina Faso[4]	
Dogon	40,000
French	30,000
● French (lingua franca)	*650,000*
Fula (Fulani)	1,050,000
Gur (Voltaic) languages	
Bwamu	230,000
Gouin (Cerma)	60,000
Grusi (Gurunsi) group	
Ko	20,000
Lyele	260,000
Nuni	130,000
Sissala	10,000
Lobi	210,000
Mossi (Moore) group	
Dagara	340,000
Gurma	620,000
Kusaal	20,000
Mossi (Moore)	5,470,000
Senufo group	
Minianka	—
Senufo	150,000
Kru languages	
Seme (Siamou)	20,000
Mande languages	
Bobo	240,000
Busansi (Bisa)	390,000
Dyula (Jula)	290,000
Marka	180,000
Samo	250,000
Tamashek (Tuareg)	100,000
Other	780,000
Burundi[1]	
● French	*560,000*
● Rundi	5,930,000
Hutu	4,990,000
Tutsi	880,000
Twa	60,000
Other[5]	120,000

Major languages by country	Number of speakers
Cambodia[1]	
Cham	240,000
Chinese	320,000
● Khmer	9,200,000
Vietnamese	570,000
Other[6]	50,000
Cameroon[1]	
Chadic languages	
Buwal	290,000
Hausa	180,000
Kotoko	160,000
Mandara (Wandala)	830,000
Masana (Masa)	580,000
● English	*2,930,000*
● French	*2,210,000*
Niger-Congo languages	
Adamawa-Ubangi languages	
Baya (Gbaya)	180,000
Chamba	350,000
Mbum	190,000
Atlantic languages	
Fula (Fulani)	1,410,000
Benue-Congo languages	
Bamileke (Medumba)-Widikum (Moghamo)-Bamum (Mum)	2,720,000
Basa (Bassa)	160,000
Duala	1,600,000
Fang (Pangwe)-Beti-Bulu	2,880,000
Ibibio (Efik)	20,000
Igbo	80,000
Jukun	100,000
Lundu	400,000
Maka	720,000
Tikar	1,090,000
Tiv	380,000
Wute	50,000
Saharan languages	
Kanuri	50,000
Semitic languages	
Arabic	140,000
Other	110,000
Canada	
● English	18,448,000
● French	7,281,000
English-French	243,000
English-other	449,000
French-other	52,000
English-French-other	33,000
Aboriginal (Amerindian and Eskimo [Inuktitut]) languages	218,000
Arabic	49,000
Chinese	319,000
Czech	27,000
Danish	24,000
Dutch	149,000
Finnish	30,000
German	525,000
Greek	133,000
Hungarian	82,000
Italian	546,000
Pilipino (Filipino)	52,000
Polish	149,000
Portuguese	185,000
Punjābī	76,000
Russian	30,000
Serbo-Croatian	49,000
Spanish	100,000
Ukrainian	249,000
Vietnamese	49,000
Yiddish	27,000
Other	764,000
Cape Verde	
Crioulo (Portuguese Creole)	394,000
● Portuguese	...
Central African Republic	
Banda	780,000
Baya (Gbaya)	790,000
● French	*380,000*
Mandjia	490,000
Mbum	210,000
Ngbaka	250,000
Nzakara	50,000
● Sango (lingua franca)	*3,000,000*
Sara	220,000
Zande (Azande)	70,000
Other	470,000
Chad[1]	
● Arabic	1,870,000
Daju (Dagu)	160,000
● French	*930,000*
Hausa	160,000
Kanuri	160,000
Kotoko	150,000
Masa	160,000
Masalit, Maba, and Mimi	450,000
Mbum	460,000
Mubi	300,000
Sara, Bagirmi, and Kreish	2,180,000
Tama	450,000
Teda (Tubu)	520,000
Other	120,000
Chile[1]	
Araucanian (Mapuche)	1,400,000
Aymara	70,000
Rapa Nui	34,000
● Spanish	13,080,000
China[1]	
Achang	30,000
Bulang (Blang)	90,000
Ch'iang (Qiang)	210,000
Chinese (Han)	1,128,970,000
Cantonese (Yüeh [Yue])	*56,000,000*
Hakka	*42,000,000*
Hsiang (Xiang)	*54,000,000*
Kan (Gan)	*27,000,000*
● Mandarin	*807,000,000*
Min	*46,000,000*
Wu	*96,000,000*
Ching-p'o (Jingpo)	130,000
Chuang (Zhuang)	16,770,000
Daghur (Daur)	130,000
Evenk (Ewenki)	30,000
Gelo	470,000
Hani (Woni)	1,360,000
Hui	9,320,000
Kazak	1,200,000
Korean	2,080,000
Kyrgyz	150,000
Lahu	450,000
Li	1,200,000
Lisu	620,000
Manchu	10,640,000
Maonan	80,000
Miao	8,010,000
Mongol	5,210,000
Mulam	170,000
Na-hsi (Naxi)	300,000
Nu	30,000
Pai (Bai)	1,730,000
Pumi	30,000
Puyi (Chung-chia)	2,760,000
Salar	90,000
She	680,000
Shui	370,000
Sibo (Xibe)	190,000
Tai (Dai)	1,110,000
Tajik	40,000
Tibetan	4,970,000
Tu (Monguor)	210,000
T'u-chia (Tujia)	6,180,000
Tung (Dong)	2,720,000
Tung-hsiang (Dongxiang)	410,000
Uighur	7,810,000
Wa (Va)	380,000
Yao	2,310,000
Yi	7,120,000
Other	970,000
Colombia[1]	
Amerindian languages	310,000
Arawakan	40,000
Cariban	20,000
Chibchan	150,000
Other	100,000
English Creole	50,000
● Spanish	35,850,000
Comoros	
● Arabic	...
● Comorian	443,000
Comorian-French	76,000
Comorian-Malagasy	33,000
Comorian-Arabic	10,000
Comorian-Swahili	3,000
Comorian-French-other	23,000
● French	*30,000*
Other	3,000
Congo, Dem. Rep. of the[1]	
Azande (Zande)	2,850,000
Boa	1,090,000
Chokwe	850,000
● French	*3,600,000*
Kongo	7,490,000
Kongo (lingua franca)	*14,000,000*
Lingala (lingua franca)	*32,000,000*
Luba	8,390,000
Lugbara	750,000
Mongo	6,290,000
Ngala and Bangi	2,700,000
Rundi	1,800,000
Rwanda	4,790,000
Swahili (lingua franca)	*23,000,000*
Teke	1,270,000
Other	8,390,000
Congo, Rep. of the[1]	
Bobangi	30,000
● French	*750,000*
Kongo	1,330,000
Kota	20,000
Lingala (lingua franca)	...
Maka	50,000
Mbete	130,000
Mboshi	300,000
Monokutuba (lingua franca)	*1,500,000*
Punu	80,000
Sango	70,000
Teke	450,000
Other	130,000
Costa Rica	
Chibchan languages	10,000
Bribrí	6,000
Cabécar	4,000
Chinese	7,000
English Creole	69,000
● Spanish	3,382,000
Côte d'Ivoire[1]	
Akan (including Baule and Anyi)	4,500,000
● French	*5,200,000*
Gur ([Voltaic] including Senufo and Lobi)	1,750,000
Kru (including Bete)	1,580,000
Malinke (including Dyula and Bambara)	1,710,000
Southern Mande (including Dan and Guro)	1,150,000
Other (non-Ivoirian population)	4,290,000
Croatia	
● Serbo-Croatian	4,580,000
Other	190,000
Cuba	
● Spanish	11,190,000
Cyprus[1]	
● Greek	630,000
● Turkish	190,000
Other	30,000
Czech Republic[1]	
Bulgarian	3,000
● Czech	8,367,000
German	48,000
Greek	3,000
Hungarian	20,000
Moravian	1,327,000
Polish	60,000
Romanian	1,000
Romany	33,000
Russian	5,000
Ruthenian	2,000
Silesian	44,000
Slovak	315,000
Ukrainian	8,000
Other	70,000
Denmark[2]	
Arabic	24,000
● Danish	4,992,000
English	24,000
German	27,000
Iranian languages	10,000
Norwegian	15,000
South Slavic languages	24,000
Swedish	18,000
Turkish	26,000
Other	125,000
Djibouti[1]	
Afar	340,000
● Arabic	70,000
● French	*50,000*
Somali	210,000
Gadaboursi	...
Issa	...
Issaq	...
Dominica	
● English	...
English Creole	74,000
French Creole	*67,000*
Dominican Republic	
French (Haitian) Creole	160,000
● Spanish	7,650,000
Ecuador	
Quechuan (and other Amerindian languages)	840,000
● Spanish	11,100,000
Egypt[1]	
● Arabic	61,360,000
French	*280,000*
Other	750,000
El Salvador	
● Spanish	5,662,000
Equatorial Guinea[1]	
Bubi	40,000
Fang	370,000
● French	...
Krio (English Creole)	...
● Spanish	...
Other	30,000
Eritrea	
Cushitic languages	
Afar	150,000
Bilin	110,000
Hadareb (Beja)	140,000
Saho	110,000
Nilotic languages	
Kunama	100,000
Nara	70,000
Semitic languages	
Arabic (Rashaida)	10,000
Tigré	1,140,000
Tigrinya	1,760,000
Estonia[1]	
Belarusian	20,000
● Estonian	930,000
Finnish	10,000
Russian	420,000
Ukrainian	40,000
Other	30,000
Ethiopia[1]	
Amharic	17,640,000
Gurage	2,750,000
Oromo (Oromifa)	18,210,000
Sidamo	1,880,000
Somali	2,380,000
Tigrinya	4,220,000
Walaita	1,630,000
Other	10,010,000
Faroe Islands	
● Danish	...
● Faroese	44,000
Fiji[1]	
● English	*160,000*
Fijian	398,000
Hindī	339,000
Other	41,000
Finland	
Estonian	9,000
● Finnish	4,777,000
Russian	18,000
Sami (Lapp)	2,000
● Swedish	295,000
Other	44,000
France	
Arabic[7]	1,480,000
English[7]	80,000
● French[7, 8, 9]	54,890,000
Basque	*80,000*
Breton	*500,000*
Catalan (Rousillonais)	*260,000*
Corsican	*260,000*
Dutch (Flemish)	*90,000*
German (Alsatian)	*1,500,000*
Occitan	*910,000*
Italian[7]	260,000
Polish[7]	50,000
Portuguese[7]	670,000
Spanish[7]	220,000
Turkish[7]	200,000
Other[7]	740,000
French Guiana	
Amerindian languages	3,000
● French	...
French Creoles	143,000
Other	6,000
French Polynesia[10]	
Chinese	13,000
● French	183,000
Polynesian languages	207,000
● Tahitian	...
Other	44,000
Gabon[1]	
Fang	420,000
● French	*400,000*
Kota	40,000
Mbete	170,000
Mpongwe (Myene)	180,000
Punu, Sira, Nzebi	200,000
Teke	20,000
Other	160,000
Gambia, The	
● English	...
Gambians	
Aku (Krio)	7,000
Atlantic languages	
Diola (Jola)	115,000
Fula (Fulani)	202,000
Manjak	20,000
Serer	30,000
Wolof	157,000
Mande languages	
Bambara	9,000
Malinke	425,000
Soninke	96,000
Other	15,000
non-Gambians	172,000
Gaza Strip	
Arabic	1,023,000
Hebrew	5,000
Georgia	
Abkhaz	90,000
Armenian	370,000
Azerbaijani (Azeri)	300,000
● Georgian (Kartuli)	3,840,000
Ossetian	130,000
Russian	460,000
Other	170,000
Germany[2]	
● German	75,050,000
Greek	360,000
Italian	590,000
Polish	280,000
South Slavic languages	1,360,000
Turkish	2,020,000
Kurdish	*400,000*
Other	2,580,000
Ghana[1]	
Akan	9,490,000
● English	...
Ewe	2,150,000
Ga-Adangme	1,400,000
Gurma	600,000
Hausa (lingua franca)	*10,900,000*
Mole-Dagbani (Moore)	2,870,000
Yoruba	240,000
Other	1,340,000
Gibraltar[2]	
Arabic	2,000
● English	24,000
Spanish	...
Other	1,000
Greece	
● Greek	10,380,000
Turkish	90,000
Other	60,000
Greenland[2]	
● Danish	7,000
● Greenlandic	49,000
Grenada	
● English	...
English/English Creole	98,000
Guadeloupe	
French Creole/French	412,000
● French	...
Other	21,000
Guam	
● Chamorro	46,000
Chinese	2,000
Chuukese (Trukese)	2,000
● English	58,000
English (lingua franca)	*154,000*
Japanese	4,000
Korean	5,000
Palauan	2,000
Philippine languages	31,000
Other	6,000
Guatemala	
Garifuna (Black Carib)	30,000
Mayan languages	3,940,000
Cakchiquel	1,010,000
Kekchí	550,000
Mam	310,000
Quiché	1,140,000
● Spanish	7,270,000
Guernsey	
English	62,000
French	...
Guinea[1]	
Atlantic languages	
Basari-Konyagi	90,000
Fulani (Peul)	2,860,000
Kissi	440,000
Other	230,000
● French	*620,000*
Mande languages	
Kpelle	340,000
Loma	170,000
Malinke	1,720,000
Susu	820,000
Yalunka	210,000
Other	510,000
Other	10,000
Guinea-Bissau	
Balante	171,000
Crioulo (Portuguese Creole)	50,000
Crioulo-Portuguese	26,000
Crioulo-other (except Portuguese)	352,000
Fula (Fulani)	196,000
Malinke	81,000
Mandyako	58,000
Pepel	33,000
● Portuguese	—
Portuguese-other (except Crioulo)	95,000
Other	116,000
Guyana	
Amerindian languages	
Arawakan	11,000
Cariban	17,000
● English	...

Language (continued)

Major languages by country	Number of speakers
English/English Creoles	746,000
Haiti	
● French	*1,300,000*
French-Haitian (French) Creole	6,610,000
● Haitian (French) Creole	...
Honduras	
English Creole	12,000
Garifuna (Black Carib)	79,000
Miskito	11,000
● Spanish	5,718,000
Other	2,000
Hong Kong	
Chinese	
● Cantonese	5,756,000
Cantonese (lingua franca)	*6,220,000*
Chiu Chau	91,000
Fukien (Min)	123,000
Hakka	104,000
Putonghua (Mandarin)	72,000
Putonghua (lingua franca)	*1,170,000*
Sze Yap	26,000
● English	143,000
English (lingua franca)	*2,050,000*
Japanese	13,000
Pilipino (Filipino)	6,000
Other	156,000
Hungary	
German	40,000
● Hungarian	10,010,000
Romanian	10,000
Romany	50,000
Serbo-Croatian	20,000
Slovak	10,000
Other	20,000
Iceland[2]	
● Icelandic	260,000
Other	11,000
India	
Austroasiatic languages	
Ho	1,140,000
Khaṛiā	280,000
Khāsī	900,000
Korkū	520,000
Muṇḍā	500,000
Muṇḍārī	1,070,000
Santhālī	5,980,000
Savara (Sora)	330,000
Dravidian languages	
Goṇḍī	2,780,000
Kannaḍa	38,180,000
Khond	290,000
Koyā	340,000
Kui	720,000
Kurukh (Oraon)	1,800,000
Malayālam	36,850,000
Tamil	63,520,000
Telugu	77,000,000
Tuḷu	1,950,000
English	330,000
● English (lingua franca)	*31,000,000*
Indo-Iranian (Indo-Aryan) languages	
Assamese	15,840,000
Bengali	73,140,000
Bhīlī (Bhilodī)	6,320,000
Barel	*400,000*
Bhilalī	*400,000*
Dogrī	2,160,000
Gujarātī	47,130,000
Halabī	750,000
● Hindī	375,160,000
Aṅga (Aṅgikā)	*700,000*
Baghelkhaṇḍī	*400,000*
Bāgṛī	*1,900,000*
Banjārī	*800,000*
Bhojpurī	*25,400,000*
Bundelkhaṇḍī	*700,000*
Chhattīsgaṛhī	*11,800,000*
Gaṛhwālī	*2,300,000*
Gojrī	*600,000*
Hāṛautī	*600,000*
Khorthā (Khottā)	*900,000*
Kumaunī	*2,200,000*
Lamanī (Banjārī)	*2,100,000*
Magahī (Magadhī)	*11,700,000*
Maithilī	*10,800,000*
Mālvī	*1,100,000*
Maṇḍealī	*400,000*
Māṛwāṛī	*8,300,000*
Mewārī	*1,400,000*
Nagpurī	*600,000*
Nīmāḍī	*1,400,000*
Pahāṛī	*2,200,000*
Rājasthānī	*3,700,000*
Sadānī (Sadrī)	*1,400,000*
Surgujiā	*900,000*
Hindī (lingua franca)	*435,000,000*
Kashmīrī	4,510,000
Khandeshī	1,690,000
Kiṣan	220,000
Koṅkanī	2,250,000
Marāṭhī	70,470,000
Nepālī (Gorkhalī)	1,780,000
Oṛiyā	32,490,000
Punjābī	26,400,000
Sindhī	2,760,000
Kachchhī	*800,000*
Urdū	50,160,000
Sino-Tibetan languages	
Ādi	170,000
Āo	150,000
Gāro	580,000
Meithei (Manipurī)	1,280,000
Mizo (Lushai)	550,000
Nissī	200,000
Tripurī	700,000
Other	16,300,000
Indonesia	
Balinese	3,310,000
Banjarese	3,490,000
Batak	4,430,000
Buginese	4,390,000
● Indonesian Malay	24,160,000
Javanese	78,680,000
Madurese	8,640,000
Minangkabau	4,710,000
Sundanese	31,470,000
Other	36,260,000
Iran[1]	
Armenian	300,000
Iranian languages	
Bakhtyārī (Lurī)	1,050,000
Balochi	1,420,000
● Farsī (Persian)	28,430,000
Farsī (lingua franca)	*51,500,000*
Gīlakī	3,290,000
Kurdish	5,690,000
Lurī	2,690,000
Māzandarānī	2,240,000
Other	1,350,000
Semitic languages	
Arabic	1,350,000
Other	150,000
Turkic languages	
Afshari	700,000
Azerbaijani (Azeri)	10,470,000
Qashqa'i	790,000
Shahsavani	370,000
Turkish (mostly Pishagchi, Bayat, and Qajar)	450,000
Turkmen	970,000
Other	120,000
Other	460,000
Iraq[1]	
● Arabic	17,130,000
Assyrian	180,000
Azerbaijani (Azeri)	380,000
Kurdish	4,210,000
Persian	180,000
Other	130,000
Ireland	
● English	3,580,000
● Irish[11]	60,000
Irish	*1,190,000*
Isle of Man	
● English	72,000
Israel[12]	
● Arabic	1,020,000
● Hebrew	3,560,000
Russian	510,000
Other	570,000
Italy[1]	
Albanian	120,000
Catalan	30,000
French	300,000
German	300,000
Greek	40,000
● Italian	54,090,000
Rhaetian	740,000
Friulian	710,000
Ladin	30,000
Romany	110,000
Sardinian	1,520,000
Slovene	120,000
Other	130,000
Jamaica	
● English	...
English/English Creoles	2,380,000
Hindī and other Indian languages	50,000
Other	100,000
Japan[2]	
Ainu	15,000
Chinese	220,000
English	70,000
● Japanese	124,960,000
Korean	670,000
Philippine languages	70,000
Other	100,000
Jersey	
● English	85,000
French	...
Jersey Norman French	*6,000*
Jordan[1]	
● Arabic	4,430,000
Armenian	50,000
Kabardian (Circassian)	50,000
Kazakstan[1]	
Azerbaijani (Azeri)	100,000
Belarusian	170,000
German	510,000
● Kazak	7,610,000
Korean	100,000
Russian	5,750,000
Tatar	320,000
Uighur	190,000
Ukrainian	820,000
Uzbek	380,000
Other	610,000
Kenya[1]	
Bantu languages	
Bajun (Rajun)	70,000
Basuba	110,000
Embu	340,000
Gusii (Kisii)	1,770,000
Kamba	3,240,000
Kikuyu	6,020,000
Kuria	170,000
Luhya	3,980,000
Mbere	120,000
Meru	1,580,000
Nyika (Mijikenda)	1,380,000
Pokomo	70,000
Swahili	10,000
● Swahili (lingua franca)	*19,000,000*
Taita	290,000
Cushitic languages	
Oromo languages	
Boran	130,000
Gabbra	60,000
Gurreh	160,000
Orma	60,000
Somali languages	
Degodia	180,000
Ogaden	50,000
Somali	290,000
● English (lingua franca)	*2,200,000*
Nilotic languages	
Kalenjin	3,100,000
Luo	3,680,000
Masai	450,000
Sambur	140,000
Teso	250,000
Turkana	390,000
Semitic languages	
Arabic	70,000
Other	650,000
Kiribati[1]	
● English	...
Kiribati (Gilbertese)	81,500
Tuvaluan (Ellice)	400
Other	500
Korea, North[1]	
Chinese	40,000
● Korean	24,280,000
Korea, South[1]	
Chinese	50,000
● Korean	45,580,000
Kuwait	
● Arabic	1,710,000
Other	480,000
Kyrgyzstan[1]	
Azerbaijani (Azeri)	20,000
German	30,000
Kazak	40,000
● Kyrgyz	2,740,000
● Russian	740,000
Tajik	40,000
Tatar	60,000
Ukrainian	80,000
Uzbek	650,000
Other	200,000
Laos[1]	
● Lao-Lum (Lao)	3,430,000
Lao-Soung (Miao [Hmong] and Man [Yao])	270,000
Lao-Tai (Tai)	400,000
Lao-Theung (Mon-Khmer)	840,000
Other[13]	180,000
Latvia[1]	
Belarusian	100,000
● Latvian	1,360,000
Lithuanian	30,000
Polish	50,000
Russian	810,000
Ukrainian	70,000
Other	50,000
Lebanon[1]	
● Arabic	3,590,000
Armenian	230,000
French	*930,000*
Other	40,000
Lesotho[1]	
● English	*400,000*
● Sotho	1,710,000
Zulu	300,000
Liberia[1]	
Atlantic (Mel) languages	
Gola	103,000
Kissi	105,000
Other	129,000
● English	*520,000*
Krio (English Creole)	*2,300,000*
Kru languages	
Bassa	360,000
Belle	13,000
De (Dewoin, Dey)	9,000
Grebo	233,000
Krahn	98,000
Kru (Krumen)	191,000
Mande (Northern) languages	
Gbandi	73,000
Kpelle	505,000
Loma	147,000
Malinke (Mandingo)	133,000
Mende	20,000
Vai	93,000
Mande (Southern) languages	
Gio (Dan)	204,000
Mano	185,000
Libya	
● Arabic	5,420,000
Berber	60,000
Other[14]	170,000
Liechtenstein[2]	
● German	27,500
Italian	900
Turkish	800
Other	2,100
Lithuania[1]	
Belarusian	60,000
● Lithuanian	3,020,000
Polish	260,000
Russian	310,000
Ukrainian	40,000
Other	30,000
Luxembourg[2]	
Belgian	12,000
Danish	2,000
Dutch	4,000
English	5,000
French	15,000
German	10,000
Greek	1,000
Italian	20,000
Luxemburgian	283,000
Portuguese	51,000
Spanish	3,000
Other	14,000
Macau	
Chinese	
● Cantonese (Yüeh [Yue])	360,000
Mandarin	5,000
Other Chinese languages	40,000
English	2,000
● Portuguese	10,000
Other	5,000
Macedonia[1]	
Albanian	454,000
● Macedonian	1,320,000
Romany	45,000
Serbo-Croatian	40,000
Turkish	79,000
Vlach	9,000
Other	37,000
Madagascar[1]	
● French	*1,400,000*
● Malagasy	13,910,000
Other	150,000
Malaŵi[1]	
Chewa (Maravi)	5,600,000
● English	*480,000*
Lomwe	1,760,000
Ngoni	640,000
Yao	1,270,000
Other	330,000
Malaysia	
Bajau	130,000
Chinese	1,210,000
Chinese-others	690,000
Dusun	220,000
English	100,000
English-others	230,000
English (lingua franca)	*6,400,000*
Iban	500,000
Iban-others	80,000
● Malay	9,040,000
Malay-others	3,210,000
Tamil	810,000
Tamil-others	10,000
Other	4,720,000
Maldives	
● Divehi (Maldivian)	267,000
Mali[1]	
Afro-Asiatic languages	
Berber languages	
Tamashek (Tuareg)	730,000
Semitic languages	
Arabic (Mauri)	160,000
● French	*790,000*
Niger-Congo languages	
Atlantic languages	
Fula (Fulani) and Tukulor	1,390,000
Dogon	400,000
Gur (Voltaic) languages	
Bwa (Bobo)	240,000
Mossi (Moore)	40,000
Senufo and Minianka	1,190,000
Mande languages	
Bambara	3,170,000
Bambara (lingua franca)	*8,000,000*
Bobo Fing	10,000
Dyula (Jula)	290,000
Malinke, Khasonke, and Wasulunka	660,000
Samo (Duun)	70,000
Soninke	870,000
Nilo-Saharan languages	
Songhai	710,000
Other	20,000
Malta[1]	
● English	8,000
● Maltese	359,000
Other	8,000
Marshall Islands[2]	
● English	*60,300*
● Marshallese	58,400
Other	1,900
Martinique	
French Creole/French	386,000
● French	...
Other	13,000
Mauritania[1]	
● Arabic	...
French	*140,000*
Fula (Fulani)	30,000
Ḥassānīyah Arabic	1,970,000
Ṣoninke	70,000
Tukulor	130,000
Wolof	160,000
Zenaga	30,000
Other	30,000
Mauritius	
Bhojpurī	218,000
Bhojpurī-other	24,000
Chinese	4,000
● English	2,000
French	39,000
French Creole	705,000
French Creole-other	102,000
Hindī	14,000
Marāṭhī	8,000
Tamil	9,000
Telugu	7,000
Urdū	7,000
Other	3,000
Mayotte[15]	
● Arabic	...
Mahorais (local dialect of Comorian Swahili)	112,000
Other Comorian Swahili dialects	49,000
Malagasy	43,000
● French	54,000
Other	8,000
Mexico	
Amerindian languages	7,440,000
Amuzgo	40,000
Aztec (Nahuatl)	1,690,000
Chatino	40,000
Chinantec	150,000
Chocho	20,000
Chol	180,000
Chontal	50,000
Cora	20,000
Cuicatec	20,000
Huastec	170,000
Huave	20,000
Huichol	30,000
Kanjobal	20,000
Mame	20,000
Mayo	50,000
Mazahua	190,000
Mazatec	230,000
Mixe	130,000
Mixtec	540,000
Otomí	400,000

Major languages by country	Number of speakers
Popoluca	40,000
Purepecha	130,000
Tarahumara	80,000
Tepehua	10,000
Tepehuan	30,000
Tlapanec	100,000
Tojolabal	50,000
Totonac	290,000
Trique	20,000
Tzeltal	370,000
Tzotzil	330,000
Yaqui	10,000
Yucatec (Mayan)	1,000,000
Zapotec	550,000
Zoque	60,000
Other	330,000
● Spanish	86,840,000
Spanish-Amerindian languages	*6,050,000*
Micronesia	
Chuukese (Trukese)	44,500
● English	500
Kosraean	7,800
Mortlockese	8,100
Palauan	400
Pohnpeian	25,400
Woleaian	3,900
Yapese	6,200
Other	10,100
Moldova	
Bulgarian	70,000
Gagauz	140,000
● Romanian (Moldovan)	2,700,000
Russian	1,010,000
Ukrainian	370,000
Other	60,000
Monaco[2]	
English	2,000
● French	13,000
Italian	5,000
Monegasque	5,000
Other	6,000
Mongolia[1]	
Bayad	45,000
Buryat	40,000
Darhat	17,000
Dariganga	33,000
Dörbet	64,000
Dzakhchin	26,000
Kazak	140,000
● Khalkha (Mongolian)	1,868,000
Khalkha (lingua franca)	*2,130,000*
Ould	9,000
Torgut	12,000
Tuvan (Uryankhai)	24,000
Other	92,000
Morocco	
● Arabic	17,700,000
Berber	8,980,000
Other[16]	540,000
Mozambique	
Chopi	520,000
Chuabo	1,040,000
Koti	60,000
Kunda	10,000
Lomwe	1,420,000
Makonde	350,000
Makua	5,050,000
Marendje	630,000
Mwani	80,000
Ngulu	20,000
Nguni	
Swazi	20,000
Zulu	10,000
Nsenga	40,000
Nyanja	600,000
Nyungwe	410,000
Phimbi	20,000
● Portuguese	220,000
Ronga	660,000
Sena	1,700,000
Shona	1,190,000
Swahili	10,000
Tonga	350,000
Tsonga	2,250,000
Tswa	1,090,000
Yao	300,000
Other	120,000
Myanmar (Burma)[1]	
● Burmese	32,290,000
Burmese (lingua franca)	*37,500,000*
Chin	1,020,000
Kachin (Ching-p'o)	640,000
Karen	2,910,000
Kayah	190,000
Mon	1,130,000
Rakhine (Arakanese)	2,110,000
Shan	3,970,000
Other	2,570,000
Namibia	
Afrikaans	163,000
Caprivi	81,000
● English	13,000
English (lingua franca)	*144,000*
German	16,000
Herero	138,000
Kavango (Okavango)	167,000
Nama	215,000
Ovambo (Ambo [Kwanyama])	875,000
San (Bushman)	33,000
Tswana	7,000
Other	17,000
Nauru	
Chinese	900
English	800
English (lingua franca)	*10,300*
Kiribati (Gilbertese)	1,800
● Nauruan	6,000
Tuvaluan (Ellice)	900
Nepal	
Austroasiatic (Munda) languages	
Santhālī	40,000
Indo-Aryan languages	
Bengali	30,000
Bhojpurī	1,600,000
Dhanwar	30,000
Hindī	200,000
Hindī (Awadhī dialect)	430,000
Maithilī	2,540,000
● Nepālī (Eastern Pahāṛī)	10,780,000
Rājbanśī	100,000
Tharu	1,150,000
Urdū	230,000
Tibeto-Burman languages	
Bhutiā (Sherpa)	140,000
Chepang	30,000
Gurung	260,000
Limbū	290,000
Magar	500,000
Newārī	800,000
Rai and Kirāntī	510,000
Tamāng	1,050,000
Thakali	10,000
Thami	20,000
Other	680,000
Netherlands, The[2]	
Arabic	152,000
● Dutch	14,888,000
Dutch and Frisian	*590,000*
Turkish	155,000
Other	425,000
Netherlands Antilles	
● Dutch	...
English	17,000
Papiamento	184,000
Other	13,000
New Caledonia[1]	
● French	69,000
Indonesian	5,000
Melanesian languages	91,000
Polynesian languages (mostly Wallisian)	23,000
Vietnamese	3,000
Other	10,000
New Zealand	
● English	3,321,000
English-Maori	156,000
● Maori	52,000
Other	124,000
Nicaragua	
English Creole	40,000
Misumalpan languages	
Miskito	170,000
Sumo	10,000
● Spanish	4,050,000
Niger[1]	
Atlantic languages	
Fula (Fulani)	920,000
Berber languages	
Tamashek (Tuareg)	970,000
Chadic languages	
Hausa	4,970,000
Hausa (lingua franca)	*6,570,000*
● French	*1,410,000*
Gur (Voltaic) languages	
Gurma	30,000
Saharan languages	
Kanuri	420,000
Teda (Tubu)	40,000
Semitic languages	
Arabic	30,000
Songhai and Zerma	1,990,000
Other	20,000
Nigeria[1]	
Arabic	300,000
Bura	1,600,000
Edo	3,500,000
● English (lingua franca)	*16,000,000*
English Creole (lingua franca)[17]	*36,000,000*
Fula (Fulani)	11,600,000
Hausa	22,100,000
Hausa (lingua franca)	*52,000,000*
Ibibio	5,800,000
Igbo (Ibo)	18,600,000
Ijo (Ijaw)	1,900,000
Kanuri	4,300,000
Nupe	1,300,000
Tiv	2,300,000
Yoruba	22,100,000
Other	8,100,000
Northern Mariana Islands	
Carolinian	2,600
Chamorro	16,000
Chinese	3,800
Chuukese (Trukese)	1,200
● English	2,600
English (lingua franca)	*48,500*
Japanese	1,100
Korean	3,500
Palauan	1,800
Philippine languages	18,300
Other	2,700
Norway[2]	
Danish	18,000
English	24,000
● Norwegian	4,253,000
Swedish	12,000
Other	98,000
Oman	
● Arabic (Omani)	1,740,000
Other	530,000
Pakistan	
Balochī	4,100,000
Brāhūī	1,630,000
English (lingua franca)	*16,000,000*
Pashto	17,890,000
Punjābī	
Punjābī	65,600,000
Hindko	3,310,000
Sindhī	
Saraikī	13,390,000
Sindhī	16,030,000
● Urdū	10,350,000
Other	3,880,000
Palau	
Chinese	300
● English	500
English (lingua franca)	*17,100*
● Palauan	14,100
Philippine languages	1,600
Other	600
Panama	
Amerindian languages	
Bokotá	4,000
Chibchan	
Cuna	55,000
Guaymí	144,000
Teribe	2,000
Chocó	
Embera	17,000
Waunana	3,000
Chinese	8,000
English	...
English Creoles	381,000
● Spanish	2,088,000
Papua New Guinea[1]	
● English	*70,000*
Melanesian languages	900,000
Motu	*140,000*
Papuan languages	3,510,000
Tok Pisin (English Creole)	*2,980,000*
Other	90,000
Paraguay	
German	44,000
● Guaraní	2,042,000
Guaraní-Spanish	2,475,000
Portuguese	161,000
● Spanish	330,000
Other	37,000
Peru	
Amerindian languages	
● Aymara	560,000
● Quechua	4,010,000
Other	170,000
● Spanish	19,440,000
Other	190,000
Philippines	
Aklanon	520,000
Bantoanon	60,000
Bicol	4,070,000
Bilaan	40,000
Bontoc	60,000
Butuanon	70,000
Cebuano	16,650,000
Chavacano	440,000
Chinese	60,000
Davaweno (Mansaka)	490,000
● English (lingua franca)	*37,200,000*
Hiligaynon	6,520,000
Ibaloi (Nabaloi)	120,000
Ibanag	260,000
Ifugao	190,000
Ilocano	6,660,000
Ilongot	110,000
Kalinga	120,000
Kankanai	270,000
Kinaray-a (Hamtikanon)	450,000
Maguindanao	1,040,000
Manobo	480,000
Maranao	910,000
Masbateño	490,000
Palawano	80,000
Pampango	2,130,000
Pangasinan	1,290,000
● Pilipino (Filipino; Tagalog)	20,950,000
Romblon	220,000
Samal	450,000
Sambal	190,000
Subanon	290,000
Surigaonon	520,000
Tau Sug	820,000
Tboli	90,000
Tinggian	60,000
Tiruray	60,000
Waray-Waray	2,730,000
Yakan	140,000
Other	1,410,000
Poland	
Belarusian	190,000
German	500,000
● Polish	37,870,000
Ukrainian	230,000
Portugal[2]	
● Portuguese	9,850,000
Other	100,000
Puerto Rico	
● English	19,000
● Spanish	1,955,000
Spanish-English	1,786,000
Other	49,000
Qatar[2]	
● Arabic	250,000
Other[18]	370,000
Réunion	
Chinese	20,000
Comorian	20,000
● French	*200,000*
French Creole	620,000
Malagasy	10,000
Tamil	*130,000*
Other	10,000
Romania	
Bulgarian	9,000
Czech	5,000
German	98,000
Hungarian	1,622,000
Polish	3,000
● Romanian	20,468,000
Romany (Tigani)	165,000
Russian	31,000
Serbo-Croatian	33,000
Slovak	18,000
Tatar	23,000
Turkish	27,000
Ukrainian	63,000
Other	7,000
Russia	
Adyghian	120,000
Armenian	360,000
Avar	530,000
Azerbaijani (Azeri)	280,000
Bashkir	980,000
Belarusian	440,000
Buryat	360,000
Chechen	890,000
Chuvash	1,380,000
Dargin	350,000
Georgian (Kartuli)	90,000
German	350,000
Ingush	210,000
Kabardian	380,000
Kalmyk	150,000
Karachay	150,000
Kazak	560,000
Komi-Permyak	100,000
Komi-Zyryan	240,000
Kumyk	270,000
Lak	100,000
Lezgi (Lezgian)	240,000
Mari	530,000
Mordvin	740,000
Ossetian	380,000
Romanian	120,000
Romany	130,000
● Russian	127,490,000
Tabasaran	90,000
Tatar	4,730,000
Tuvan	200,000
Udmurt	510,000
Ukrainian	1,870,000
Uzbek	100,000
Yakut	360,000
Other	1,450,000
Rwanda	
● English	...
● French	*530,000*
● Rwanda	7,740,000
St. Kitts and Nevis	
● English	...
English/English Creole	39,000
St. Lucia	
● English	30,000
English/French Creole	115,000
St. Vincent and the Grenadines	
● English	...
English/English Creole	111,000
Other	1,000
Samoa	
● English	1,000
● Samoan	80,000
Samoan-English	88,000
San Marino[1]	
● Italian (Romagnolo)	26,000
São Tomé and Príncipe	
Crioulo (Portuguese Creole)	118,000
English	...
French	1,000
● Portuguese	...
Other	18,000
Saudi Arabia[1]	
● Arabic	18,120,000
Other	950,000
Senegal	
● French	*470,000*
Senegalese	
Bambara	90,000
Diola	470,000
Fula (Fulani)-Tukulor	2,040,000
Malinke (Mandingo)	350,000
Serer	1,180,000
Soninke	120,000
Wolof	4,520,000
Wolof (lingua franca)	*7,500,000*
Other	420,000
non-Senegalese	210,000
Seychelles	
English	2,000
English (lingua franca)	*30,000*
French	1,000
French (lingua franca)	*70,000*
● Seselwa (French Creole)	71,000
Other	3,000
Sierra Leone[1]	
Atlantic languages	
Bullom-Sherbro	180,000
Fula (Fulani)	180,000
Kissi	110,000
Limba	410,000
Temne	1,550,000
● English	*700,000*
Krio (English Creole [lingua franca])	*4,700,000*
Mande languages	
Kono-Vai	250,000
Kuranko	170,000
Mende	1,690,000
Susu	70,000
Yalunka	170,000
Other	90,000
Singapore[1]	
Chinese	2,399,000
● English	*1,161,000*
● Malay	439,000
● Mandarin Chinese	...
● Tamil (and other Indian languages)	226,000
Other	39,000
Slovakia[1]	
Czech, Moravian, and Silesian	58,000
German	5,000
Hungarian	574,000
Polish	3,000
Romany	85,000
Russian	2,000
Ruthenian and Ukrainian	32,000
● Slovak	4,631,000
Other	14,000
Slovenia	
Hungarian	9,000
Serbo-Croatian	154,000
● Slovene	1,718,000
Other	74,000

Language (continued)

Major languages by country	Number of speakers
Solomon Islands[1]	
● English	8,000
Melanesian languages	352,000
Papuan languages	35,000
Polynesian languages	15,000
Other[19]	9,000
Somalia[1]	
● Arabic	...
English	...
● Somali	6,750,000
Other	120,000
South Africa	
● Afrikaans	6,410,000
Afrikaans/English	80,000
● English	3,860,000
Nguni	
● Ndebele	640,000
● Swazi	1,100,000
● Xhosa	7,430,000
● Zulu	9,510,000
Sotho	
● North Sotho (Pedi)	4,160,000
● South Sotho	2,930,000
● Tswana (Western Sotho)	3,060,000
● Tsonga	1,780,000
● Venda	720,000
Other	760,000
Spain	
Basque (Euskera)	620,000
● Castilian Spanish	29,260,000
Catalan (Català)	6,640,000
Galician (Gallego)	2,510,000
Other	290,000
Sri Lanka	
English	10,000
English-Sinhala	990,000
English-Sinhala-Tamil	650,000
English-Tamil	210,000
● Sinhala	10,920,000
Sinhala-Tamil	1,690,000
● Tamil	3,550,000
Other	60,000
Sudan, The[1]	
● Arabic	16,090,000
Azande (Zande)	880,000
Bari	800,000
Beja	2,080,000
Dinka	3,760,000
Fur	670,000
Lotuko	480,000
Nubian languages	2,640,000
Nuer	1,600,000
Shilluk	560,000
Other	3,030,000
Suriname	
● Dutch	...
English	...
Sranantonga	170,000
Sranantonga-other	170,000
Other (mostly Hindī, Javanese, and Saramacca)	80,000
Swaziland[1]	
● English	...
● Swazi	930,000
Zulu	20,000
Other	80,000
Sweden[2]	
Arabic	68,000
Danish	41,000
English	32,000
Finnish	209,000
German	45,000
Iranian languages	49,000
Norwegian	46,000
Polish	39,000
South Slavic languages	116,000
Spanish	56,000
● Swedish	7,936,000
Turkish	29,000
Other	197,000
Switzerland	
● French	1,370,000
● German	4,530,000
● Italian	540,000
Romansch	40,000
Other	640,000
Syria[1]	
● Arabic	13,510,000
Kurdish	1,350,000
Other	150,000
Taiwan	
Austronesian languages	
Ami	135,000
Atayal	86,000
Bunun	41,000
Paiwan	66,000
Puyuma	10,000
Rukai	10,000
Saisiyat	6,000
Tsou	7,000
Yami	4,000
Chinese languages	
Hakka	2,380,000
● Mandarin	4,340,000
Min (South Fuklen)	14,420,000
Other	110,000
Tajikistan	
Russian	590,000
● Tajik	3,760,000
Uzbek	1,400,000
Other	300,000
Tanzania[1]	
Chaga (Chagga), Pare	1,450,000
● English	*900,000*
Gogo	1,160,000
Ha	1,010,000
Haya	1,740,000
Hehet	2,020,000
Iramba	840,000
Luguru	1,450,000
Luo	240,000
Makonde	1,740,000
Masai	290,000
Ngoni	390,000
Nyakyusa	1,590,000
Nyamwezi (Sukuma)	6,220,000
Shambala	1,260,000
● Swahili	2,600,000
Swahili (lingua franca)	*27,000,000*
Tatoga	220,000
Yao	720,000
Other	4,530,000
Thailand[1]	
Chinese	7,350,000
Karen	220,000
Malay	2,210,000
Mon-Khmer languages	
Khmer	770,000
Kuy	650,000
Other	210,000
Thai languages	
Lao	16,300,000
● Thai (Siamese)	31,860,000
Other	420,000
Other	620,000
Togo[1]	
Atlantic (Mel) languages	
Fula (Fulani)	64,000
Benue-Congo languages	
Ana (Ana-Ife)	119,000
Nago	12,000
Yoruba	9,000
Chadic languages	
Hausa	13,000
● French	*810,000*
Gur (Voltaic) languages	
Basari	83,000
Chakossi (Akan)	56,000
Chamba	46,000
Dye (Gangam)	45,000
Gurma	161,000
Kabre	653,000
Konkomba	67,000
Kotokoli (Tem)	272,000
Moba	254,000
Mossi (Moore)	12,000
Namba (Lamba)	144,000
Naudemba (Losso)	194,000
Tamberma	26,000
Yanga	14,000
Kwa languages	
Adja (Aja)	148,000
Adele	10,000
Ahlo	8,000
Akposo	127,000
Ane (Basila)	268,000
Anlo	4,000
Anyaga	10,000
Ewe	1,098,000
Fon	47,000
Hwe	6,000
Kebu	54,000
Kpessi	4,000
Peda-Hula (Pla)	19,000
Watyi (Ouatchi)	488,000
Other	200,000
Tonga	
● English	...
● Tongan	99,000
Other	2,000
Trinidad and Tobago	
● English	...
English Creole[20]	36,000
Hindī	44,000
Trinidad English	1,193,000
Other	3,000
Tunisia	
● Arabic	6,450,000
Arabic-French	2,420,000
Arabic-French-English	290,000
Arabic-other	10,000
Other-no Arabic	30,000
Other	30,000
Turkey[1]	
Arabic	870,000
Kurdish[21]	6,730,000
● Turkish	55,630,000
Other	290,000
Turkmenistan[1]	
Armenian	36,000
Azerbaijani (Azeri)	38,000
Balochi	38,000
Kazak	92,000
Russian	316,000
Tatar	38,000
● Turkmen	2,599,000
Ukrainian	24,000
Uzbek	431,000
Other	82,000
Tuvalu	
● English	...
Kiribati (Gilbertese)	700
Tuvaluan (Ellice)	8,800
Uganda[1]	
Bantu languages	
Amba	80,000
Ganda (Luganda)	3,730,000
Gisu (Masaba)	930,000
Gwere	340,000
Kiga (Chiga)	1,720,000
Konjo	450,000
Nkole (Nyankole and Hororo)	2,210,000
Nyole	280,000
Nyoro	610,000
Ruli	80,000
Rundi	130,000
Rwanda	660,000
Samia	280,000
Soga	1,690,000
Swahili (lingua franca)	*7,200,000*
Toro	600,000
Central Sudanic languages	
Lugbara	970,000
Madi	160,000
Ndo	210,000
● English	*2,100,000*
Nilotic languages	
Acholi	910,000
Alur	490,000
Kakwa	110,000
Karamojong	430,000
Kumam	140,000
Lango	1,210,000
Padhola	310,000
Sebei (Kupsabiny)	140,000
Teso	1,240,000
Other (mostly Gujarātī and Hindī)	520,000
Ukraine	
Belarusian	160,000
Bulgarian	160,000
Hungarian	160,000
Polish	30,000
Romanian	340,000
Russian	16,800,000
● Ukrainian	33,080,000
Other	440,000
United Arab Emirates[2]	
● Arabic	1,080,000
Other[18]	1,500,000
United Kingdom	
● English	57,320,000
Scots-Gaelic	80,000
Welsh	560,000
Other	960,000
United States	
Amharic	40,000
Arabic	410,000
Armenian	170,000
Bengali	40,000
Cajun	40,000
Chinese (including Formosan)	1,510,000
Czech	110,000
Danish	40,000
Dutch	170,000
● English	230,830,000
English (lingua franca)	*260,000,000*
Finnish	60,000
French	1,980,000
French Creole (mostly Haitian)	220,000
German	1,800,000
Greek	450,000
Gujarātī	120,000
Hebrew	170,000
Hindī (including Urdū)	390,000
Hungarian	170,000
Ilocano	50,000
Italian	1,520,000
Japanese	500,000
Korean	730,000
Kru (Gullah)	80,000
Lithuanian	60,000
Malayālam	40,000
Miao (Hmong)	100,000
Mon-Khmer (mostly Cambodian)	150,000
Navajo	170,000
Norwegian	90,000
Pennsylvania Dutch	100,000
Persian	230,000
Polish	840,000
Portuguese	500,000
Punjābī	60,000
Romanian	80,000
Russian	280,000
Samoan	40,000
Serbo-Croatian	140,000
Slovak	90,000
Spanish	20,150,000
Swedish	90,000
Syriac	40,000
Tagalog	980,000
Thai (including Laotian)	240,000
Turkish	50,000
Ukrainian	110,000
Vietnamese	590,000
Yiddish	250,000
Other	790,000
Uruguay	
● Spanish	3,050,000
Other	140,000
Uzbekistan	
Crimean Tatar	210,000
Karakalpak	470,000
Kazak	900,000
Korean	120,000
Kyrgyz	170,000
Russian	2,570,000
Tajik	1,050,000
Tatar	440,000
Turkish	120,000
Turkmen	130,000
Ukrainian	90,000
● Uzbek	16,880,000
Other	530,000
Vanuatu[22]	
● Bislama (English Creole)	120,000
● English	60,000
● French	30,000
Other	2,000
Venezuela	
Amerindian languages	
Goajiro	80,000
Warrau (Warao)	30,000
Other	110,000
● Spanish	22,060,000
Other	490,000
Vietnam[1]	
Bahnar	160,000
Cham	110,000
Chinese (Hoa)	1,050,000
French	*360,000*
Hre	110,000
Jarai	290,000
Khmer	1,040,000
Koho	110,000
Man (Mien, or Yao)	560,000
Miao (Meo, or Hmong)	650,000
Mnong	80,000
Muong	1,070,000
Nung	830,000
Rade (Rhadé)	230,000
Roglai	80,000
San Chay (Cao Lan)	140,000
San Diu	110,000
Sedang	110,000
Stieng	60,000
Tai	1,220,000
Tho (Tay)	1,390,000
● Vietnamese	65,230,000
Other	150,000
Virgin Islands (U.S.)	
● English	79,000
French	3,000
Spanish	13,000
Other	3,000
West Bank[23]	
Arabic	1,650,000
Hebrew	140,000
Western Sahara	
Arabic	281,000
Yemen[1]	
● Arabic	16,200,000
Other	300,000
Yugoslavia[1]	
Albanian	1,750,000
Hungarian	350,000
Macedonian	50,000
Romanian	40,000
Romany	150,000
● Serbo-Croatian	8,000,000
Serbo-Croatian (lingua franca)	*10,100,000*
Slovak	70,000
Vlach	20,000
Other	200,000
Zambia[24]	
Bemba group	
Bemba	2,780,000
Bemba (lingua franca)	*4,900,000*
Bisa	110,000
Lala	220,000
Lamba	210,000
Other	390,000
● English	100,000
English (lingua franca)	*1,800,000*
Lozi (Barotse) group	
Lozi (Barotse)	700,000
Other	100,000
Mambwe group	
Lungu	70,000
Mambwe	110,000
Mwanga (Winawanga)	130,000
Other	10,000
North-Western group	
Kaonde	220,000
Lunda	190,000
Luvale (Luena)	170,000
Other	250,000
Nyanja (Maravi) group	
Chewa	530,000
Ngoni	160,000
Nsenga	400,000
Nyanja (Maravi)	730,000
Nyanja (lingua franca)	*2,500,000*
Other	60,000
Tonga (Ila-Tonga) group	
Ila	80,000
Lenje	150,000
Tonga	1,030,000
Other	120,000
Tumbuka group	
Senga	70,000
Tumbuka	270,000
Other	10,000
Other	80,000
Zimbabwe	
● English	250,000
English (lingua franca)	*5,300,000*
Ndebele (Nguni)	1,850,000
Nyanja	260,000
Shona	8,240,000
Other	820,000

[1]Figures given represent ethnolinguistic groups. [2]Data refer to nationality (usually resident aliens holding foreign passports). [3]Data are partly based on place of residence. [4]Majority of population speak Moore (language of the Mossi); Dyula is language of commerce. [5]Swahili also spoken. [6]English and French also spoken. [7]Based on "nationality" at 1982 census. [8]Includes naturalized citizens. [9]French is the universal language throughout France; traditional dialects and minority languages are retained regionally in the approximate numbers shown, however. [10]Data reflect multi-lingualism; 1997 population estimate is 227,000. [11]Refers to Irish speakers in Gaeltacht areas. [12]Includes the population of the Golan Heights and East Jerusalem; excludes the Israeli population in the West Bank and Gaza Strip. [13]English and French also spoken. [14]English and Italian also spoken. [15]Data reflect ability to speak the language, not mother tongue; 1997 population estimate is 128,000. [16]French also spoken. [17]Includes speakers of standard English. [18]Mostly Pakistanis, Indians, and Iranians. [19]Solomon Islands Pidgin (English) is the lingua franca. [20]Spoken on Tobago only. [21]Other estimates of the Kurdish population range from 6 percent to 20–25 percent. [22]Data reflect multilingualism; 1997 population is 176,000. [23]Excludes East Jerusalem. [24]Groups are officially defined geographic divisions; elements comprising them are named by language.

Religion

The following table presents statistics on religious affiliation for each of the countries of the world. An assessment was made for each country of the available data on distribution of religious communities within the total population; the best available figures, whether originating as census data, membership figures of the churches concerned, or estimates by external analysts in the absence of reliable local data, were applied as percentages to the estimated 1997 midyear population of the country to obtain the data shown below.

Several concepts govern the nature of the available data, each useful separately but none the basis of any standard of international practice in the collection of such data. The word "affiliation" was used above to describe the nature of the relationship joining the religious bodies named and the populations shown. This term implies some sort of formal, usually documentary, connection between the religion and the individual (a baptismal certificate, a child being assigned the religion of its parents on a census form, maintenance of one's name on the tax rolls of a state religion, etc.) but says nothing about the nature of the individual's personal religious practice, in that the individual may have lapsed, never been confirmed as an adult, joined another religion, or may have joined an organization that is formally atheist.

The user of these statistics should be careful to note that not only does the nature of the affiliation (with an organized religion) differ greatly from country to country, but the social context of religious practice does also. A country in which a single religion has long been predominant will often show more than 90% of its population to be *affiliated,* while in actual fact, no more than 10% may actually *practice* that religion on a regular basis. Such a situation often leads to undercounting of minority religions (where someone [head of household, communicant, child] is counted at all), blurring of distinctions seen to be significant elsewhere (a Hindu country may not distinguish Protestant [or even Christian] denominations; a Christian country may not distinguish among its Muslim or Buddhist citizens), or double-counting in countries where an individual may conscientiously practice more than one "religion" at a time.

Until 1989 communist countries had for long consciously attempted to ignore, suppress, or render invisible religious practice within their borders. Countries with large numbers of adherents of traditional, often animist, religions and belief systems usually have little or no formal methodology for defining the nature of local religious practice. On the other hand, countries with strong missionary traditions, or good census organizations, or few religious sensitivities may have very good, detailed, and meaningful data.

The most comprehensive works available are DAVID B. BARRETT (ed.), *World Christian Encyclopedia* (1982); and PETER BRIERLEY, *World Churches Handbook* (1997).

Religion

Religious affiliation	1997 population
Afghanistan	
Sunnī Muslim	19,940,000
Shīʿī Muslim	3,560,000
other	240,000
Albania	
Muslim	2,310,000
Albanian Orthodox	240,000
Roman Catholic	170,000
other	570,000
Algeria	
Sunnī Muslim	29,340,000
Ibāḍīyah Muslim	110,000
other	20,000
American Samoa	
Congregational	35,000
Roman Catholic	12,000
other	14,000
Andorra	
Roman Catholic	59,000
other	5,000
Angola	
Roman Catholic	5,390,000
Protestant	1,560,000
African Christian	460,000
other (mostly traditional beliefs)	3,210,000
Antigua and Barbuda	
Protestant	27,000
Anglican	21,000
Roman Catholic	7,000
other	10,000
Argentina	
Roman Catholic	31,060,000
Protestant	2,660,000
Muslim	520,000
Jewish	260,000
other	910,000
Armenia	
Armenian Apostolic (Orthodox)	2,430,000
other	1,340,000
Aruba	
Roman Catholic	60,000
other	24,000
Australia	
Roman Catholic	5,060,000
Anglican	4,410,000
Uniting Church	1,530,000
Presbyterian	800,000
other Protestant	1,220,000
Orthodox	520,000
nonreligious	2,390,000
other	2,580,000
Austria	
Roman Catholic	6,310,000
Evangelical Lutheran	390,000
atheist and nonreligious	700,000
other	690,000
Azerbaijan	
Muslim (mostly Shīʿī)	7,110,000
Russian Orthodox	80,000
Armenian Apostolic (Orthodox)	80,000
other	350,000
Bahamas, The	
Protestant	158,000
Anglican	58,000
Roman Catholic	54,000
other	17,000
Bahrain	
Shīʿī Muslim	380,000
Sunnī Muslim	130,000
other	110,000
Bangladesh	
Muslim	110,680,000
Hindu	13,180,000
other	1,480,000
Barbados	
Anglican	87,000
Protestant	79,000
Roman Catholic	12,000
other	87,000
Belarus	
Belarusian Orthodox	3,270,000
Roman Catholic	1,840,000
other	5,250,000
Belgium	
Roman Catholic	8,960,000
other	1,230,000
Belize	
Roman Catholic	132,000
Protestant	62,000
Anglican	16,000
other	18,000
Benin	
Voodoo (traditional beliefs)	3,660,000
Roman Catholic	1,240,000
Muslim	710,000
other	290,000
Bermuda	
Anglican	23,000
Methodist	10,000
Roman Catholic	9,000
other	20,000
Bhutan	
Lamaistic Buddhist	650,000
Hindu	220,000
Bolivia	
Roman Catholic	6,870,000
Evangelical Protestant	700,000
other	200,000
Bosnia and Herzegovina	
Sunnī Muslim	1,250,000
Serbian Orthodox	890,000
Roman Catholic	420,000
other	560,000
Botswana	
African Christian	410,000
Protestant	190,000
Roman Catholic	60,000
other (mostly traditional beliefs)	840,000
Brazil	
Roman Catholic (including syncretic Afro-Catholic cults having Spiritist beliefs and rituals)	115,500,000
Evangelical Protestant	37,000,000
other	7,200,000
Brunei	
Muslim	207,000
other	101,000
Bulgaria	
Bulgarian Orthodox	3,040,000
Muslim (mostly Sunnī)	1,090,000
other	4,200,000
Burkina Faso	
Muslim	5,450,000
traditional beliefs	4,360,000
Christian	1,090,000
Burundi	
Roman Catholic	3,940,000
nonreligious	1,130,000
other (mostly Protestant)	980,000
Cambodia	
Buddhist	9,870,000
Muslim	220,000
other	300,000
Cameroon	
Roman Catholic	5,150,000
traditional beliefs	3,810,000
Muslim	3,200,000
Protestant	2,570,000
Canada	
Roman Catholic	13,690,000
Protestant	8,600,000
Anglican	2,430,000
Eastern Orthodox	430,000
Jewish	350,000
Muslim	280,000
Buddhist	180,000
Hindu	180,000
Sikh	160,000
nonreligious	3,790,000
other	200,000
Cape Verde	
Roman Catholic	378,000
Protestant	16,000
Central African Republic	
Protestant	850,000
traditional beliefs	800,000
Roman Catholic	570,000
Muslim	500,000
other	610,000
Chad	
Muslim	3,860,000
Roman Catholic	1,460,000
Protestant	1,030,000
traditional beliefs	530,000
other	270,000
Chile	
Roman Catholic	11,190,000
Evangelical Protestant	1,810,000
other	1,580,000
China	
nonreligious	637,000,000
Chinese folk-religionist	247,000,000
atheist	147,000,000
Buddhist	104,000,000
Christian	73,000,000
Muslim	18,000,000
traditional beliefs	1,000,000
Colombia	
Roman Catholic	33,270,000
other	2,930,000
Comoros	
Sunnī Muslim	586,000
Christian	4,000
Congo, Dem. Rep. of the	
Roman Catholic	19,140,000
Protestant	14,750,000
African Christian	6,240,000
traditional beliefs	4,990,000
Muslim	650,000
other	900,000
Congo, Rep. of the	
Roman Catholic	1,060,000
traditional beliefs	850,000
Protestant	630,000
Muslim	50,000
Costa Rica	
Roman Catholic	2,820,000
other	650,000
Côte d'Ivoire	
Muslim	5,800,000
Roman Catholic	3,110,000
traditional beliefs	2,550,000
nonreligious	2,010,000
Protestant	790,000
other	730,000
Croatia	
Roman Catholic	3,440,000
Serbian Orthodox	670,000
Sunnī Muslim	60,000
Protestant	30,000
other	570,000
Cuba	
Roman Catholic	4,420,000
other (mostly nonreligious and atheist)	6,770,000
Cyprus	
Greek Orthodox	630,000
Muslim (mostly Sunnī)	200,000
other (mostly Christian)	30,000
Czech Republic	
Roman Catholic	4,020,000
Evangelical Church of Czech Brethren	200,000
Czechoslovak Hussite	180,000
Silesian Evangelical	30,000
Eastern Orthodox	20,000
atheist and nonreligious	4,120,000
other	1,740,000
Denmark	
Evangelical Lutheran	4,600,000
other	680,000
Djibouti	
Sunnī Muslim	605,000
Christian	17,000
Dominica	
Roman Catholic	52,000
Protestant	12,000
other	10,000
Dominican Republic	
Roman Catholic	6,380,000
Protestant	500,000
other	920,000
Ecuador	
Roman Catholic	11,040,000
other	900,000
Egypt	
Sunnī Muslim	55,280,000
Coptic Orthodox[1]	6,210,000
Protestant	620,000
El Salvador	
Roman Catholic	4,430,000
Protestant	400,000
other	830,000
Equatorial Guinea	
Roman Catholic	410,000
other	30,000
Eritrea	
Muslim	2,490,000
Eritrean Orthodox	1,100,000
Estonia	
Estonian Orthodox	290,000
Evangelical Lutheran	200,000
other	970,000
Ethiopia	
Ethiopian Orthodox	20,060,000
other Christian	4,850,000
Muslim (mostly Sunnī)	17,670,000
traditional beliefs	7,170,000
other	8,980,000

Religion (continued)

Religious affiliation	1997 population
Faroe Islands	
Evangelical Lutheran	35,000
other	9,000
Fiji	
Christian (mostly Methodist and Roman Catholic)	412,000
Hindu	297,000
Muslim	61,000
other	8,000
Finland	
Evangelical Lutheran	4,420,000
other	730,000
France	
Roman Catholic	44,680,000
nonreligious	6,240,000
Muslim	3,220,000
atheist	2,000,000
Protestant	1,080,000
Jewish	610,000
other	790,000
French Guiana	
Roman Catholic	83,000
other	69,000
French Polynesia	
Protestant	114,000
Roman Catholic	90,000
other	23,000
Gabon	
Roman Catholic	600,000
traditional beliefs	230,000
Protestant	210,000
other	150,000
Gambia, The	
Muslim (mostly Sunnī)	1,190,000
other	60,000
Gaza Strip	
Muslim (mostly Sunnī)	1,015,000
other	13,000
Georgia	
Georgian Orthodox	1,970,000
Sunnī Muslim	590,000
Armenian Apostolic (Orthodox)	300,000
Russian Orthodox	140,000
other (mostly nonreligious)	2,380,000
Germany	
Protestant (mostly Evangelical Lutheran)	35,160,000
Roman Catholic	27,870,000
Muslim	1,750,000
other (mostly nonreligious)	17,360,000
Ghana	
African Christian	5,310,000
Protestant	3,630,000
traditional beliefs	3,180,000
Roman Catholic	2,660,000
Muslim	2,600,000
other	720,000
Gibraltar	
Roman Catholic	21,000
other	6,000
Greece	
Greek Orthodox	9,670,000
Muslim	140,000
other	730,000
Greenland	
Evangelical Lutheran	55,000
other	1,000
Grenada	
Roman Catholic	52,000
Anglican	14,000
other	32,000
Guadeloupe	
Roman Catholic	350,000
other	80,000
Guam	
Roman Catholic	116,000
Protestant	19,000
other	21,000
Guatemala	
Roman Catholic	8,540,000
Evangelical Protestant	2,450,000
other	250,000
Guernsey	
Anglican	40,000
other	22,000
Guinea	
Muslim	6,430,000
traditional beliefs	340,000
Christian	320,000
other	320,000
Guinea-Bissau	
traditional beliefs	770,000
Muslim	350,000
Christian	60,000
Guyana	
Hindu	263,000
Protestant	145,000
Roman Catholic	89,000
Muslim	70,000
Anglican	67,000
other	139,000
Haiti	
Roman Catholic	4,530,000
Protestant	1,510,000
other	570,000
Honduras	
Roman Catholic	5,050,000
Evangelical Protestant	600,000
other	170,000
Hong Kong	
Buddhist and Taoist	4,790,000
Protestant	280,000
Roman Catholic	270,000
other	1,150,000
Hungary	
Roman Catholic	6,410,000
Protestant	2,590,000
other (mostly nonreligious and atheist)	1,160,000
Iceland	
Evangelical Lutheran	245,000
other	26,000
India	
Hindu	777,000,000
Sunnī Muslim	80,000,000
Shīʿī Muslim	27,000,000
Sikh	19,000,000
Protestant	18,000,000
Roman Catholic	16,000,000
Buddhist	7,000,000
Jain	5,000,000
Zoroastrian (Parsi)	140,000
other	19,000,000
Indonesia	
Muslim	174,020,000
Protestant	12,050,000
Roman Catholic	7,140,000
Hindu	3,650,000
Buddhist	2,060,000
other	620,000
Iran	
Shīʿī Muslim	58,210,000
Sunnī Muslim	3,520,000
other	580,000
Iraq	
Shīʿī Muslim	13,890,000
Sunnī Muslim	7,670,000
other (mostly Christian)	670,000
Ireland	
Roman Catholic	3,340,000
other	300,000
Isle of Man	
Anglican	45,000
other	27,000
Israel	
Jewish[2]	4,550,000
Muslim (mostly Sunnī)	840,000
other	270,000
Italy	
Roman Catholic	47,000,000
Muslim	700,000
other (mostly nonreligious and atheist)	9,800,000
Jamaica	
Protestant	990,000
Roman Catholic	260,000
Anglican	90,000
other	1,200,000
Japan	
Shintoist[3]	118,270,000
Buddhist[3]	90,510,000
Christian	1,530,000
other	11,200,000
Jersey	
Anglican	53,000
Roman Catholic	20,000
other	13,000
Jordan	
Sunnī Muslim	4,360,000
Christian	160,000
Kazakstan	
Muslim (mostly Sunnī)	7,780,000
Russian Orthodox	1,350,000
Protestant	350,000
other (mostly nonreligious)	7,070,000
Kenya	
traditional beliefs	8,720,000
Protestant	8,130,000
Roman Catholic	5,630,000
African Christian	2,370,000
Muslim	1,730,000
Anglican	1,610,000
other	1,340,000
Kiribati	
Roman Catholic	44,000
Congregational	32,000
other	6,000
Korea, North	
atheist and nonreligious	16,610,000
traditional beliefs	3,790,000
Ch'ŏndogyo	3,380,000
other	540,000
Korea, South	
nonreligious	22,860,000
Buddhist	11,110,000
Protestant	8,290,000
Roman Catholic	2,690,000
Confucian	180,000
Wonbulgyo	140,000
Ch'ŏndogyo	50,000
other	310,000
Kuwait	
Sunnī Muslim	810,000
Shīʿī Muslim	540,000
other Muslim	180,000
other (mostly Christian and Hindu)	270,000
Kyrgyzstan	
Muslim (mostly Sunnī)	3,220,000
Russian Orthodox	260,000
other (mostly nonreligious)	1,120,000
Laos	
Buddhist	2,960,000
traditional beliefs	1,720,000
other	440,000
Latvia	
Roman Catholic	367,000
Evangelical Lutheran	362,000
Russian Orthodox	189,000
other (mostly nonreligious)	1,554,000
Lebanon	
Shīʿī Muslim	1,310,000
Sunnī Muslim	820,000
Maronite Catholic	730,000
Druze	270,000
Greek Orthodox	230,000
Armenian Apostolic (Orthodox)	200,000
Greek Catholic (Melchite)	180,000
other	120,000
Lesotho	
Roman Catholic	780,000
traditional beliefs	600,000
Protestant	280,000
African Christian	230,000
Anglican	110,000
Liberia	
Christian	1,760,000
traditional beliefs	480,000
Muslim	360,000
Libya	
Sunnī Muslim	5,480,000
other	170,000
Liechtenstein	
Roman Catholic	25,000
other	6,000
Lithuania	
Roman Catholic	2,670,000
Russian Orthodox	90,000
other (mostly nonreligious)	950,000
Luxembourg	
Roman Catholic	400,000
other	20,000
Macau	
nonreligious	256,000
Buddhist	71,000
other	94,000
Macedonia	
Serbian (Macedonian) Orthodox	1,070,000
Sunnī Muslim	600,000
other	320,000
Madagascar	
traditional beliefs	7,310,000
Roman Catholic	2,990,000
Protestant	2,770,000
Muslim	980,000
Malaŵi	
Protestant (mostly Presbyterian)	1,970,000
Muslim	1,920,000
Roman Catholic	1,730,000
traditional beliefs	960,000
African Christian	950,000
other	2,080,000
Malaysia	
Muslim	11,510,000
Buddhist	3,770,000
Chinese folk religionist	2,520,000
Hindu	1,520,000
Christian	1,390,000
other	1,040,000
Maldives	
Sunnī Muslim	267,000
Mali	
Muslim	8,950,000
traditional beliefs	900,000
Christian	100,000
Malta	
Roman Catholic	350,000
other	25,000
Marshall Islands	
Protestant	38,000
Roman Catholic	4,000
other	18,000
Martinique	
Roman Catholic	350,000
other	50,000
Mauritania	
Sunnī Muslim	2,400,000
other	10,000
Mauritius	
Hindu	580,000
Roman Catholic	310,000
Muslim	190,000
other	60,000
Mayotte	
Sunnī Muslim	124,000
Christian	4,000
Mexico	
Roman Catholic	85,220,000
Protestant	3,610,000
other Christian	1,710,000
other (mostly nonreligious)	3,740,000
Micronesia	
Roman Catholic	44,000
Protestant	39,000
other	24,000
Moldova	
Romanian Orthodox	1,530,000
Russian (Moldovan) Orthodox	410,000
other (mostly nonreligious)	2,420,000
Monaco	
Roman Catholic	26,000
other	6,000
Mongolia	
Tantric Buddhist (Lamaist)	2,280,000
Muslim	90,000
Morocco	
Muslim (mostly Sunnī)	27,180,000
other	50,000
Mozambique	
traditional beliefs	8,680,000
Protestant	2,410,000
Muslim	2,360,000
Roman Catholic	2,100,000
other	2,620,000
Myanmar (Burma)	
Buddhist	41,880,000
Christian	2,300,000
Muslim	1,790,000
traditional beliefs	540,000
Hindu	240,000
other	70,000
Namibia	
Protestant (mostly Lutheran and Dutch Reformed)	890,000
Roman Catholic	290,000
African Christian	120,000
Anglican	100,000
other	330,000
Nauru	
Protestant	5,300
Roman Catholic	2,900
other	2,200
Nepal	
Hindu	18,530,000
Buddhist	1,670,000
Muslim	760,000
other	470,000
Netherlands, The	
Roman Catholic	5,150,000
Dutch Reformed Church (NHK)	2,190,000
Reformed Churches	1,090,000
Muslim	640,000
nonreligious	6,250,000
other	300,000
Netherlands Antilles	
Roman Catholic	158,000
other	56,000
New Caledonia	
Roman Catholic	123,000
Protestant	29,000
other	49,000
New Zealand	
Anglican	790,000
Presbyterian	590,000
Roman Catholic	540,000
Methodist	150,000
Baptist	80,000
Ratana	50,000
Mormon	50,000
nonreligious	720,000
other	680,000
Nicaragua	
Roman Catholic	3,550,000
Protestant	700,000
other (mostly nonreligious)	380,000
Niger	
Sunnī Muslim	8,170,000
traditional beliefs	1,030,000
other	190,000

Religious affiliation	1997 population
Nigeria	
Muslim	44,500,000
traditional beliefs	19,700,000
Protestant	15,400,000
Roman Catholic	8,400,000
African Christian	6,900,000
Anglican	5,300,000
other	3,300,000
Northern Mariana Islands	
Roman Catholic	43,000
other	11,000
Norway	
Evangelical Lutheran (Church of Norway)	3,890,000
other	520,000
Oman	
Ibāḍīyāh Muslim	1,660,000
Sunnī Muslim	320,000
Hindu	170,000
Christian	90,000
other	20,000
Pakistan	
Sunnī Muslim	102,140,000
Shīʿī Muslim	27,240,000
Christian	2,720,000
Hindu	2,450,000
other	1,630,000
Palau	
Roman Catholic	7,000
Modekne	5,000
Protestant	4,000
other	1,000
Panama	
Roman Catholic	2,180,000
Protestant	390,000
other	150,000
Papua New Guinea	
Protestant	2,700,000
Roman Catholic	1,270,000
Anglican	180,000
other	350,000
Paraguay	
Roman Catholic	4,500,000
other (mostly Protestant)	590,000
Peru	
Roman Catholic	21,650,000
Protestant	1,620,000
other (mostly nonreligious)	1,100,000
Philippines	
Roman Catholic	59,320,000
Protestant	3,880,000
Muslim	3,270,000
Aglipayan	1,880,000
Church of Christ (Iglesia ni Cristo)	1,670,000
other	1,520,000
Poland	
Roman Catholic	35,190,000
Polish Orthodox	550,000
other (mostly nonreligious)	3,060,000
Portugal	
Roman Catholic	9,170,000
other	770,000
Puerto Rico	
Roman Catholic	2,470,000
Protestant	1,080,000
other	260,000
Qatar	
Muslim (mostly Sunnī)	533,000
other	28,000
Réunion	
Roman Catholic	600,000
other (mostly Muslim)	80,000
Romania	
Romanian Orthodox	19,600,000
Roman Catholic	1,130,000
other	1,840,000
Russia	
Russian Orthodox	24,040,000
Muslim	14,720,000
Protestant	1,340,000
Jewish	600,000
other (mostly nonreligious)	106,530,000
Rwanda	
Roman Catholic	5,030,000
traditional beliefs	1,930,000
Protestant	700,000
Muslim	80,000
St. Kitts and Nevis	
Anglican	13,000
Methodist	11,000
other	15,000
St. Lucia	
Roman Catholic	117,000
other	31,000
St. Vincent and the Grenadines	
Anglican	47,000
Methodist	23,000
Roman Catholic	13,000
other	29,000
Samoa	
Mormon	44,000
Congregational	42,000
Roman Catholic	36,000
Methodist	21,000
other	26,000
San Marino	
Roman Catholic	23,000
other	3,000
São Tomé and Príncipe	
Roman Catholic	123,000
Protestant	14,000
Saudi Arabia	
Sunnī Muslim	18,210,000
Shīʿī Muslim	640,000
other	230,000
Senegal	
Sunnī Muslim	8,650,000
traditional beliefs	560,000
Christian	190,000
Seychelles	
Roman Catholic	69,000
other	9,000
Sierra Leone	
Sunnī Muslim	2,940,000
traditional beliefs	1,470,000
Christian	490,000
Singapore	
Buddhist and Taoist	1,672,000
Muslim	463,000
Protestant	272,000
Roman Catholic	128,000
Hindu	102,000
nonreligious	449,000
other	18,000
Slovakia	
Roman Catholic	3,260,000
Slovak Evangelical	340,000
atheist	520,000
other	1,280,000
Slovenia	
Roman Catholic	1,620,000
other	340,000
Solomon Islands	
Protestant	172,000
Anglican	139,000
Roman Catholic	79,000
other	21,000
Somalia	
Sunnī Muslim	6,790,000
other	10,000
South Africa[4]	
Christian	22,870,000
Protestant	11,270,000
Dutch (Afrikaans) Reformed Churches	4,040,000
other Protestant	7,230,000
Methodist	2,010,000
Presbyterian	450,000
United Congregational	430,000
Lutheran	860,000
Apostolic Faith Mission of South Africa	450,000
New Apostolic Church	160,000
other Apostolic	470,000
Baptist	280,000
Pentecostal Protestant	80,000
African Protestant Church	30,000
Full Gospel	220,000
Pentecostal	20,000
Salvation Army	40,000
Seventh-day Adventist	90,000
Swiss	50,000
Assemblies of God	170,000
other	1,410,000
Roman Catholic	2,600,000
Anglican	1,300,000
Greek Orthodox	30,000
black independent churches	7,650,000
Zion Christian Church	1,690,000
other	5,960,000
Mormon	10,000
Hindu	430,000
Muslim	380,000
Jewish	80,000
other beliefs	30,000
nonreligious	410,000
not stated	10,220,000
Spain	
Roman Catholic	26,240,000
Muslim	450,000
other (mostly nonreligious)	12,630,000
Sri Lanka	
Buddhist	12,540,000
Hindu	2,800,000
Muslim	1,370,000
Roman Catholic	1,250,000
other	130,000
Sudan, The	
Sunnī Muslim	23,790,000
traditional beliefs	5,440,000
Christian[1]	2,970,000
other	390,000
Suriname	
Hindu	116,000
Roman Catholic	89,000
Muslim	83,000
Protestant	69,000
other	67,000
Swaziland	
Christian[1]	690,000
other (mostly traditional beliefs)	340,000
Sweden	
Church of Sweden (Lutheran)	7,660,000
other	1,200,000
Switzerland	
Roman Catholic	3,280,000
Protestant	2,850,000
other	990,000
Syria	
Sunnī Muslim	11,110,000
Shīʿī Muslim	1,800,000
Christian	830,000
Druze	450,000
other	830,000
Taiwan	
nonreligious	10,320,000
Buddhist	4,930,000
Taoist	3,910,000
I Kuan Tao	960,000
Protestant	430,000
Roman Catholic	310,000
Tien Te Chiao	200,000
Tien Ti Chiao	190,000
Confucianism (Li)	140,000
Hsuan Yuan Chiao	140,000
Muslim	50,000
Shinto (Tenrikyo)	20,000
Baha'i	20,000
Tajikistan	
Sunnī Muslim	4,840,000
Shīʿī Muslim	300,000
Russian Orthodox	90,000
other (mostly nonreligious)	820,000
Tanzania	
Muslim	10,310,000
traditional beliefs	10,310,000
Christian	8,840,000
Thailand	
Buddhist	57,450,000
Muslim	2,450,000
Christian	330,000
other	370,000
Togo	
traditional beliefs	2,780,000
Roman Catholic	1,020,000
Sunnī Muslim	570,000
Protestant	320,000
other	40,000
Tonga	
Free Wesleyan	44,000
Roman Catholic	16,000
other	41,000
Trinidad and Tobago	
Roman Catholic	375,000
Hindu	303,000
Protestant	240,000
Anglican	139,000
Muslim	75,000
other	144,000
Tunisia	
Sunnī Muslim	9,170,000
other	50,000
Turkey	
Muslim (mostly Sunnī)	63,380,000
other	150,000
Turkmenistan	
Muslim (mostly Sunnī)	4,090,000
Russian Orthodox	300,000
other (mostly nonreligious)	310,000
Tuvalu	
Congregational	8,800
other	1,500
Uganda	
Roman Catholic	8,000,000
Anglican	4,600,000
traditional beliefs	2,600,000
Muslim (mostly Sunnī)	1,360,000
other	4,040,000
Ukraine	
Ukrainian Orthodox (Russian patriarchy)	15,720,000
Ukrainian Orthodox (Kiev patriarchy)	9,960,000
Ukrainian Autocephalous Orthodox	4,980,000
Ukrainian Catholic (Uniate)	3,580,000
Protestant	1,820,000
Roman Catholic	600,000
Jewish	440,000
other (mostly nonreligious)	14,050,000
United Arab Emirates	
Sunnī Muslim	2,060,000
Shīʿī Muslim	410,000
other	100,000
United Kingdom	
Christian	38,850,000
Anglican	25,620,000
Protestant	5,870,000
Roman Catholic	5,750,000
Eastern Orthodox	580,000
other Christian	1,030,000
Muslim	830,000
Hindu	410,000
Jewish	300,000
Sikh	240,000
other (mostly nonreligious and atheist)	18,290,000
United States	
Christian (professing)	228,270,000
Christian (affiliated)	196,040,000
Protestant	120,420,000
Roman Catholic	59,510,000
Eastern Orthodox	5,640,000
Anglican	2,350,000
other Christian	11,420,000
multiply affiliated Christians	−3,310,000
Christian (unaffiliated)	32,230,000
nonreligious	23,420,000
Jewish	5,520,000
Muslim	3,770,000
Buddhist	1,870,000
atheist	870,000
Hindu	800,000
Baha'i	680,000
New-Religionist	600,000
Sikh	190,000
other	1,380,000
Uruguay	
Roman Catholic	2,500,000
other	680,000
Uzbekistan	
Muslim (mostly Sunnī)	20,820,000
Russian Orthodox	230,000
other (mostly nonreligious)	2,610,000
Vanuatu	
Presbyterian	63,000
Roman Catholic	25,000
Anglican	25,000
other	63,000
Venezuela	
Roman Catholic	19,920,000
Protestant	1,090,000
other	1,770,000
Vietnam	
Buddhist	50,080,000
Roman Catholic	6,520,000
New-Religionist	
Cao Dai	2,640,000
Hoa Hao	1,590,000
other	14,290,000
Virgin Islands (U.S.)	
Protestant	43,000
Roman Catholic	28,000
other	26,000
West Bank	
Muslim (mostly Sunnī)	1,470,000
Jewish[5]	180,000
Christian and other	140,000
Western Sahara	
Sunnī Muslim	281,000
Yemen	
Muslim (mostly Sunnī)	16,470,000
other	20,000
Yugoslavia	
Serbian Orthodox	6,650,000
Sunnī Muslim	2,020,000
Roman Catholic	620,000
other (mostly nonreligious)	1,340,000
Zambia	
traditional beliefs	2,520,000
Protestant	2,140,000
Roman Catholic	1,580,000
other	3,110,000
Zimbabwe	
traditional beliefs	4,630,000
Protestant	2,420,000
African Christian	1,540,000
Roman Catholic	800,000
other	2,030,000

[1]Official 1986 census figure is 5.9 percent. [2]Includes the Golan Heights and East Jerusalem; excludes the West Bank and Gaza Strip. [3]Many Japanese practice both Shintoism and Buddhism. [4]Excludes the former black independent states of Bophuthatswana, Ciskei, Transkei, and Venda, in which there are about 5,900,000 Christians and 2,100,000 practicers of traditional beliefs. [5]Excludes East Jerusalem.

Vital statistics, marriage, family

This table provides some of the basic measures of the factors that influence the size, direction, and rates of population change within a country. The accuracy of these data depends on the effectiveness of each respective national system for registering vital and civil events (birth, death, marriage, etc.) and on the sophistication of the analysis that can be brought to bear upon the data so compiled.

Data on birth rates, for example, depend not only on the completeness of registration of births in a particular country but also on the conditions under which those data are collected: Do all births take place in a hospital? Are the births reported comparably in all parts of the country? Are the records of the births tabulated at a central location in a timely way with an effort to eliminate inconsistent reporting of birth events, perinatal mortality, etc.? Similar difficulties attach to death rates but with the added need to identify "cause of death." Even in a developed country such identifications are often left to nonmedical personnel, and in a developing country with, say, only one physician for every 10,000 population, there will be too few physicians to perform autopsies to assess accurately the cause of death after the fact and also too few to provide ongoing care at a level where records would permit inference about cause of death based on prior condition or diagnosis.

Calculating natural increase, which at its most basic is simply the difference between the birth and death rates, may be affected by the differing degrees of completeness of birth and death registration for a given country. The total fertility rate may be understood as the average number of children that would be borne per woman if all childbearing women lived to the end of their childbearing years and bore children at each age at the average rate for that age. Calculating a meaningful fertility rate requires analysis of changing age structure of the female population over time, changing mortality rates among mothers and their infants, and changing medical practice at births, each improvement of natural survivorship or medical support leading to greater numbers of live-born children and greater numbers of children who survive their first year (the basis for measurement of infant mortality, another basic indicator of demographic conditions and trends within a population).

As indicated above, data for causes of death are not only particularly difficult to obtain, since many countries are not well equipped to collect the data, but also difficult to assess, as their accuracy may be suspect and their meaning may be subject to varying interpretation. Take the case of a citizen of a less developed country who dies of what is clearly a lung infection: Was the death complicated by chronic malnutrition, itself complicated by a parasitic infestation, these last two together so weakening the subject that he died of an infection that he might have survived had his general health been better? Similarly, in a developed country: Someone may die from what is identified in an autopsy as a cerebrovascular accident, but if that accident occurred in a vascular system that was weakened by diabetes, what was the actual cause of death? Statistics on causes of death seek to identify the "underlying" cause (that which sets the final train of events leading to death in motion) but often must settle for the most proximate cause or symptom. Even this kind of analysis may be misleading for those charged with interpreting the data with a view to ordering health-care priorities for a particular country. The eight groups of causes of death utilized here include most, but not all, of the detailed causes classified by the World Health Organization and would not, thus, aggregate to the country's crude death rate for the same year. Among the

Vital statistics, marriage, family

country	vital rates						causes of death (rate per 100,000 population)								
	year	birth rate per 1,000 population	death rate per 1,000 population	infant mortality rate per 1,000 live births	rate of natural increase per 1,000 population	total fertility rate	year	infectious and parasitic diseases	malignant neoplasms (cancers)	endocrine and metabolic disorders	diseases of the nervous system	diseases of the circulatory system	diseases of the respiratory system	diseases of the digestive system	accidents, poisoning, and violence
Afghanistan	1997	43.0	18.0	146.7	25.0	6.1	...	...	...	...	...	...	...	...	...
Albania	1996	16.6	4.7	32.0[2]	11.9	20.4	1993	10.8	53.8	5.1	24.1	187.0	84.5	16.5	41.7
Algeria	1996	28.5	5.9	48.7	22.6	3.6	...	...	...	...	...	...	...	...	...
American Samoa	1993	37.8	4.2	11.0	33.6	5.4[4]	1990	16.4[5]	46.8	16.4[6]	...	131.1[7]	65.6[8]	...	58.5
Andorra	1995	11.0	3.4	7.7	7.6	1.7	...	...	...	...	...	...	...	...	...
Angola	1995–2000	47.7	18.7	124.0	29.0	6.7	...	...	...	...	...	...	...	...	...
Antigua and Barbuda	1995	20.9	6.7	17.2[9]	14.2	1.7[9]	1988	14.0	44.5	25.4	7.6	237.5	44.5	15.2	5.1
Argentina	1995–2000	19.9	7.9	22.0	12.0	2.6	1991	27.3	143.0	26.3	13.7	337.3	49.0	33.5	51.6
Armenia	1995–2000	13.3	7.5	25.0	5.8	1.7	1993	11.0	93.8	21.6[12]	4.9[12]	369.7	51.4	27.8	62.8
Aruba	1995	17.4	6.2	9.6[13]	11.2	1.8[14]	1991	9.8	124.9	47.7	4.2	189.5	30.9	23.9	11.2
Australia	1996	14.1	6.9	5.7	7.2	1.8	1995	6.0	190.0	23.0	17.0	296.0	52.0	21.0	41.0
Austria	1996	10.8	9.9	5.0	0.9	1.5	1995	2.1	243.5	25.1	15.9	539.9	47.6	25.1	60.8
Azerbaijan	1995–2000	19.2	6.6	33.0	12.6	2.3	1994	28.8	67.4	12.8	12.0	336.3	98.8	8.1	106.4
Bahamas, The	1995	22.5	5.9	19.0	16.6	2.0	1990	18.0	80.4	72.2	11.0	126.3	52.2	29.0	40.8
Bahrain	1995–2000	21.0	3.6	18.0	17.4	3.0	1991	2.8	32.3	16.8	3.8	86.6	27.7	10.2	19.0
Bangladesh	1997	26.8	12.2	79.0	14.6	3.2	...	...	...	...	...	...	...	...	...
Barbados	1996	13.3	9.1	14.2	4.2	1.8	1992	19.0	178.5	120.2	17.1	366.8	39.9	28.9	40.3
Belarus	1996	9.3	13.0	12.6	−3.7	1.7[15]	1993	8.0	184.5	9.0[16]	14.7	624.7	69.7	8.9	132.6
Belgium	1996	11.4	10.4	5.6	1.0	1.6[17]	1990	11.1	270.1	23.1	38.0	398.9	88.1	38.8	65.1
Belize	1996	32.8	5.7	33.9	27.1	4.2	1990	...	52.4	37.0[6]	...	164.0	57.1	32.8	92.6[19]
Benin	1996	46.0	13.0	103.0	33.0	6.6	...	...	...	...	...	...	...	...	...
Bermuda	1992	15.1	7.4	8.8	7.7	1.8[13]	1990	...	181.5	...	...	344.4	25.2	...	38.6
Bhutan	1997	41.3	13.9	105.0	27.4	5.9	...	...	...	...	...	...	...	...	...
Bolivia	1995–2000	33.2	9.1	66.0	20.4	4.4	...	...	...	...	...	...	...	...	...
Bosnia and Herzegovina	1995	6.5	15.5	43.2	−9.0	1.0	1989	9.9	122.6[21]	12.6	11.9	344.1	29.0	29.2	47.1
Botswana	1991–95	37.1	6.6	39.0[15]	30.5	4.5[9]	...	...	...	...	...	...	...	...	...
Brazil	1996	20.8	9.2	55.3	11.6	2.3	1994[22]	*41*	*94*	*45*[16]	*9*	*238*	*79*	*36*	*104*
Brunei	1997	23.3	3.0	9.0	20.3	2.9	1986	5.3	27.0	...	...	80.0	23.4	...	39.8
Bulgaria	1996	8.6	14.0	15.6	−5.4	1.2[23]	1995	7.3	192.4	27.3	8.0	869.8	66.0	42.8	66.0
Burkina Faso	1996	47.0	20.0	117.8	27.0	6.8	...	...	...	...	...	...	...	...	...
Burundi	1996	42.7	17.8	104.8	24.9	6.5	...	...	...	...	...	...	...	...	...
Cambodia	1997	43.0	15.0	106.0	28.0	5.8	...	...	...	...	...	...	...	...	...
Cameroon	1995–2000	39.3	11.9	58.0	27.4	5.3	...	...	...	...	...	...	...	...	...
Canada	1996	12.5	7.2	6.1[23]	5.3	1.7[15]	1993	10.9	196.7	22.2	19.9	274.4	62.8	26.3	47.2
Cape Verde	1995–2000	31.9	7.1	41.0	24.8	3.6	1980	153.7	43.8	20.6	16.5	135.8	72.3	27.7	30.1
Central African Republic	1997	39.2	17.0	108.0	22.2	5.2	...	...	...	...	...	...	...	...	...
Chad	1995–2000	41.6	17.3	115.0	24.3	5.5	...	...	...	...	...	...	...	...	...
Chile	1995	19.7	5.5	11.1	14.2	2.3	1993	15.1	111.5	16.2	8.0	157.4	64.9	34.2	66.1
China	1995–2000	16.2	7.1	38	9.1	1.8	1994[24]	15.2	117.7	17.2[16]	4.4	206.4	125.3	25.3	56.6
Colombia	1996	25.9	5.9	26.9[23]	20.0	2.9	1991	18.3	62.9	12.5	7.4	144.7	37.9	16.7	132.3
Comoros	1996	45.8	10.3	75.3	35.5	6.7	...	...	...	...	...	...	...	...	...
Congo, Dem. Rep. of the	1995–2000	44.9	13.5	89.0	31.4	6.2	...	...	...	...	...	...	...	...	...
Congo, Rep. of the	1995–2000	42.5	14.6	90	27.9	5.9	...	...	...	...	...	...	...	...	...
Costa Rica	1995	23.8	4.2	13.3	19.6	2.8	1994	9.7	80.0	12.6	8.5	126.6	40.6	24.6	49.7
Côte d'Ivoire	1995–2000	37.2	13.8	86	23.4	5.1	...	...	...	...	...	...	...	...	...
Croatia	1995	10.5	10.6	8.9	−0.1	1.5[18]	1994	8.6	216.1	20.6	8.2	517.4	46.0	50.1	77.8
Cuba	1996	13.5	7.2	8.0	6.3	1.8[20]	1990	9.4	128.7	23.3	10.6	294.7	58.0	26.3	79.9
Cyprus	1995	15.4	7.7	4.9	7.7	2.1	...	...	...	...	...	...	...	...	...
Czech Republic	1996	8.8	10.9	6.0	−2.1	1.4[23]	1995	2.4	277.1	10.8	9.0	638.4	49.1	41.9	82.3
Denmark	1996	12.9	11.6	5.7	1.3	1.8	1994	9.8	296.6	21.3	14.5	471.3	95.6	50.3	70.8

lesser causes excluded by the present classification are: benign neoplasms; nutritional disorders; anemias; mental disorders; kidney and genitourinary diseases not classifiable under the main groups; maternal deaths (for which data *are* provided, however, in the "Health services" table); diseases of the skin and musculoskeletal systems; congenital and perinatal conditions; and general senility and other ill-defined (ill-diagnosed) conditions, a kind of "other" category.

Expectation of life is probably the most accurate single measure of the quality of life in a given society. It summarizes in a single number all of the natural and social stresses that operate upon individuals in that society. The number may range from as few as 40 years of life in the least developed countries to as much as 80 years for women in the most developed nations. The lost potential in the years separating those two numbers is prodigious, regardless of how the loss arises—wars and civil violence, poor public health services, or poor individual health practice in matters of nutrition, exercise, stress management, and so on.

Data on marriages and marriage rates probably are less meaningful in terms of international comparisons than some of the measures mentioned above because the number, timing, and kinds of social relationships that substitute for marriage depend on many kinds of social variables—income, degree of social control, heterogeneity of the society (race, class, language communities), or level of development of civil administration (if one must travel for a day or more to obtain a legal civil ceremony, one may forgo it). Nevertheless, the data for a single country say specific things about local practice in terms of the age at which a man or woman typically marries, and the overall rate will at least define the number of legal civil marriages, though it cannot say anything about other, less formal arrangements (here the figure for the legitimacy rate for children in the next section may identify some of the societies in which economics or social constraints may operate to limit the number of marriages that are actually confirmed on civil registers). The available data usually include both first marriages and remarriages after annulment, divorce, widowhood, or the like.

The data for families provide information about the average size of a family unit (individuals related by blood or civil register) and the average number of children under a specified age (set here at 15 to provide a consistent measure of social minority internationally, though legal minority depends on the laws of each country). When well-defined family data are not collected as part of a country's national census or vital statistics surveys, data for households have been substituted on the assumption that most households worldwide represent families in some conventional sense. But increasing numbers of households worldwide are composed of unrelated individuals (unmarried heterosexual couples, aged [or younger] groups sharing limited [often fixed] incomes for reasons of economy, or homosexual couples). Such arrangements do not yet represent great numbers overall. Increasing numbers of census programs, however, even in developing countries, are making more adequate provision for distinguishing these nontraditional, often nonfamily households.

Internet resources for further information:

- World Health Organization (World) http://www.who.ch/
- Pan American Health Organization (the Americas) http://www.paho.org
- National Center for Health Statistics (U.S.) http://www.cdc.gov/nchswww/nchshome.htm

expectation of life at birth (latest year)		nuptiality, family, and family planning															country
		marriages			age at marriage (latest)						families (F), households (H) (latest)						
		year	total number	rate per 1,000 population	groom (percent)			bride (percent)			families (households)		children		induced abortions		
male	female				19 and under	20–29	30 and over	19 and under	20–29	30 and over	total ('000)	size	number under age 15	percent legitimate	number	ratio per 100 live births	
46.4	45.2	...	...	...	...	...	...	...	...	...	H 2,110	H 6.2	H 2.8[1]	...	...	...	Afghanistan
68.0	74.0	1991	24,853	7.6	1.5	80.4	18.1	24.0	71.4	4.6	F 675	F 4.7	F 1.6	...	...	...	Albania
67.2	69.5	1993	153,137	5.7	0.7[3]	67.1[3]	32.2[3]	29.8[3]	61.4[3]	8.8[3]	H 3,824	H 6.9	H 3.0	...	...	...	Algeria
69.0	74.0	1990	370	7.8	...	...	...	...	...	...	H 7	H 7.0	H 2.7	72.0	...	...	American Samoa
75.6	81.7	1994	132	2.0	...	...	...	...	...	...	...	...	...	...	...	...	Andorra
44.9	48.1	...	...	...	...	...	...	...	...	...	...	H 4.8	...	...	...	...	Angola
71.5	75.8	1988	382	4.9	1.0[10]	37.4[11]	61.6	3.7[10]	52.4[11]	43.9	H 18	H 3.2	H 1.2	23.4	...	...	Antigua and Barbuda
69.6	76.8	1983	177,010	6.0	5.6	71.5	22.9	26.0	58.6	15.4	H 10,097	H 3.2	H 1.0	67.5	...	...	Argentina
67.2	74.0	1994	17,300	4.6	5.0	73.8	21.2	39.3	49.9	10.8	H 559	H 4.7	H 1.8	87.7	27,958	39.6	Armenia
71.1	77.1	1992	566	7.9	...	...	...	...	...	...	H 19	H 3.6	...	63.2	...	...	Aruba
75.4	81.1	1996	109,386	6.0	0.7	54.5	44.8	3.6	63.6	32.8	H 6,636	H 2.6	H 0.6	75.0	...	...	Australia
73.5	80.1	1994	43,284	5.4	1.2	55.1	43.7	5.3	64.9	29.8	H 3,131	H 2.5	H 0.5	75.2	...	...	Austria
66.5	74.5	1994	47,386	6.4	1.2[13]	80.4[13]	18.4[13]	24.8[13]	63.9[13]	11.3[13]	H 1,381	H 4.8	H 1.7	97.5	42,134	23.2	Azerbaijan
68.0	77.2	1994	2,506	9.2	19.0[12]	53.0[12]	27.7[12]	34.0[12]	48.3[12]	17.1[12]	H 68	H 3.9	...	44.7	...	...	Bahamas, The
71.1	75.3	1994	2,973	5.3	2.2	63.8	34.0	25.8	56.2	18.0	H 67	H 6.5	H 2.2	...	...	...	Bahrain
58.0	58.0	1995	1,320,000	10.2	...	...	...	...	...	...	H 19,980	H 5.6	...	...	...	...	Bangladesh
71.6	77.2	1993	2,310	8.5	0.1	40.2	59.7	1.4	53.6	44.9	H 67	H 3.5	H 1.5	26.9	723	19.6	Barbados
66.0	75.7	1993	82,326	7.9	6.5	71.5	22.0	30.7	51.3	18.0	H 2,796	H 3.2	H 0.8	91.0	85,685	73.0	Belarus
73.0	79.8	1994	51,962	5.1	0.7[18]	64.9[18]	34.4[18]	4.9[18]	69.5[18]	25.6[18]	F 3,613	F 2.7	F 0.5	88.7	...	...	Belgium
66.6	70.6	1994	1,347	6.3	6.5	57.2	36.3	24.2	51.6	24.2	H 38	H 4.9	H 2.2	41.6	990	15.1	Belize
50.7	54.7	1980–85	...	12.8	...	...	...	...	...	...	...	H 5.9	...	...	...	...	Benin
73.0	79.0	1992	909	15.1	0.2[20]	37.4[20]	62.4[20]	1.5[20]	49.4[20]	49.1[20]	H 22	H 2.6	H 0.5	63.9	92	11.0	Bermuda
51.0	53.0	...	...	...	...	...	...	...	...	...	...	H 5.4	...	...	...	...	Bhutan
59.8	63.2	1980	26,990	4.8	8.3	75.1	16.6	26.1	55.4	18.5	H 1,655	H 3.8	H 1.6	80.9	...	...	Bolivia
72.1	77.7	1990	31,449	7.0	2.1	75.2	22.7	28.5	59.2	12.3	H 1,203	H 3.6	H 1.1	...	...	...	Bosnia and Herzegovina
59.5	65.6	1986	1,638	1.5	—	33.0	67.0	5.0	69.2	25.8	H 125	H 5.7	H 2.0	28.8	17	0.1	Botswana
56.7	66.8	1994	763,129	5.0	7.5[12]	70.6[12]	21.9[12]	32.4[12]	54.7[12]	12.9[12]	F 39,768	F 3.7	1.2	...	...	...	Brazil
73.0	78.0	1993	1,971	7.1	10.6[12]	50.1[12]	39.3[12]	11.4[12]	54.7[12]	33.9[12]	H 45	H 5.8	H 2.0	99.6	...	...	Brunei
67.1	74.9	1996	...	4.3	4.8[18]	75.9[18]	19.3[18]	34.8[18]	54.5[18]	10.7[18]	H 2,795	H 3.0	...	74.3	107,416	127.3	Bulgaria
43.5	42.9	...	...	...	...	...	...	...	...	...	...	H 6.2	...	...	...	...	Burkina Faso
44.3	47.3	...	...	...	...	...	...	...	...	...	...	H 4.6	...	...	...	...	Burundi
52.0	55.0	...	...	...	...	...	...	...	...	...	...	H 5.6	...	...	...	...	Cambodia
54.5	57.2	...	...	...	...	...	...	...	...	...	...	H 5.2	...	...	...	...	Cameroon
74.7	81.7	1993	159,316	5.5	0.9	52.1	47.0	3.9	60.2	35.9	H 10,018	H 2.7	H 0.6	83.8	99,971	25.7	Canada
65.5	67.5	1992	1,360	3.8	2.3[14]	62.4[14]	35.3[14]	17.0[14]	61.1[14]	21.9[14]	F 59	F 5.1	...	55.2	...	...	Cape Verde
44.7	48.3	...	...	...	...	...	...	...	...	...	...	H 4.7	...	...	...	...	Central African Republic
46.3	49.3	...	...	...	...	...	...	...	...	...	...	H 3.9	...	...	...	...	Chad
71.8	77.8	1994	91,555	6.5	5.8	68.8	25.4	19.9	62.4	17.7	H 3,537	H 3.8	...	61.9	67	—	Chile
68.2	71.7	1994	9,290,027	7.8	...	...	...	...	...	...	H 278.6[25]	H 4.1	H 1.1	...	10,500,000	47.7	China
65.4	73.4	1986	70,350	2.3	4.0	64.1	31.5	22.3	58.5	19.0	F 4,772	F 5.4	F 2.5	75.2	...	...	Colombia
56.4	61.0	...	...	...	...	...	...	...	...	...	...	H 5.6	...	...	...	...	Comoros
51.3	54.5	...	...	...	...	...	...	...	...	...	...	H 6.0	...	...	...	...	Congo, Dem. Rep. of the
48.6	53.4	...	...	...	...	...	...	...	...	...	H 326	H 4.7	H 2.0	...	...	...	Congo, Rep. of the
71.9	77.5	1995	23,564	7.1	7.3[15]	61.5[15]	31.2[15]	26.6[15]	52.1[15]	21.3[15]	H 772	H 4.1	...	53.4	...	...	Costa Rica
50.0	52.2	...	...	...	...	...	...	...	...	...	...	H 5.4	...	...	...	...	Côte d'Ivoire
68.6	76.0	1994	23,966	5.0	1.4[15]	67.2[15]	31.4[15]	15.7[15]	66.2[15]	18.1[15]	H 1,544	H 3.1	H 0.6	...	...	...	Croatia
73.9	77.6	1991	161,160	15	6.3	54.1	39.6	18.8	51.0	30.2	F 2,860	F 3.7	H 1.6	...	124,059	71.3	Cuba
75.3	79.8	1994	6,097	9.6	0.6	61.0	38.4	11.0	64.7	24.3	H 160	H 3.5	H 1.1	99.6	...	...	Cyprus
70.0	76.9	1996	53,896	5.2	5.1	66.4	28.5	19.8	61.3	18.9	H 3,557	H 2.9	...	84.4	61,590	64.1	Czech Republic
72.6	77.8	1995	34,970	6.7	0.3[15]	37.4[15]	62.3[15]	1.9[15]	48.6[15]	49.5[15]	H 2,027	H 2.2	...	53.5	17,598	25.2	Denmark

Vital statistics, marriage, family (continued)

country	vital rates						causes of death (rate per 100,000 population)								
	year	birth rate per 1,000 population	death rate per 1,000 population	infant mortality rate per 1,000 live births	rate of natural increase per 1,000 population	total fertility rate	year	infectious and parasitic diseases	malignant neoplasms (cancers)	endocrine and metabolic disorders	diseases of the nervous system	diseases of the circulatory system	diseases of the respiratory system	diseases of the digestive system	accidents, poisoning, and violence
Djibouti	1996	38.6	15.0	106.0	23.6	5.4	...	...	...	...	...	...	...	...	...
Dominica	1996	18.4	5.3	9.6	13.1	1.9	1990	37.5	116.6	51.4	9.7	273.5	43.0	20.8	18.0
Dominican Republic	1996	23.5	5.7	47.7	17.8	2.7	1985[26]	85	45	15[6]	7[27]	165	41	25	*56*
Ecuador	1995	15.8	4.4	30.5	11.4	11.4[15]	1992	52.0	50.0	11.8[6]	1.9[27]	93.1	40.6	13.2	66.7
Egypt	1997	27.8	8.6	71.0	19.2	3.5	1987	98.9	22.0	9.1	13.6	314.4	140.7	45.8	39.1
El Salvador	1996	27.7	6.6	31.5	21.1	3.2	1991[29]	*43*	*49*	*17*	*12*	*120*	*43*	*38*	*140*
Equatorial Guinea	1995–2000	40.8	16.2	107.0	24.6	5.5	...	...	...	...	...	...	...	...	...
Eritrea	1995–2000	39.8	14.7	98.0	25.1	5.3	...	...	...	...	...	...	...	...	...
Estonia	1996	9.0	12.9	10.5	–3.9	1.3[23]	1994	11.3	218.1	10.1	13.6	815.7	44.3	34.5	233.1
Ethiopia	1995–2000	48.2	16.2	107.0	32.0	7.0	...	...	...	...	...	...	...	...	...
Faroe Islands	1996	15.4	9.0	8.5[4]	6.4	2.7[20]	1992	4.3	191.3	14.9[6]	—	352.8	59.5	14.9	57.4
Fiji	1997	22.7	4.6	20.0	18.1	2.8	1987	18.2	35.5	27.3[6]	2.4[27]	153.4	31.7	15.5	32.2
Finland	1996	11.8	9.6	3.9	2.2	1.7	1994	7.0	192.3	12.0	18.0	448.6	71.8	36.3	85.0
France	1996	12.6	9.2	4.9	3.4	1.7[23]	1993	12.6	247.5	27.6	20.1	302.0	70.0	45.4	81.0
French Guiana	1993	29.2	4.1	15.4	25.1	3.7[4]	1989	61.7	58.1	16.3	10.9	114.3	20.9	13.6	98.0
French Polynesia	1996	21.0	4.5	10.2	16.5	3.9[20]	1986–92	22.0	83.0	12.0	12.0	118.0	35.0	14.0	69.0
Gabon	1995–2000	37.6	14.3	85.0	23.3	5.4	...	...	...	...	...	...	...	...	...
Gambia, The	1995–2000	39.9	17.4	122.0	22.5	5.2	...	...	...	...	...	...	...	...	...
Gaza Strip	1995–2000	46.7	5.3	37.0	41.4	8.0	...	...	...	...	...	...	...	...	...
Georgia	1996	9.9	6.4	17.4	3.5	2.2[15]	1990	12.7	100.8	14.6	4.3	548.4	43.3	8.5	56.1
Germany	1995	9.3	10.7	5.6	–1.4	1.3[15]	1994	7.3	260.2	33.6	16.9	527.4	64.7	52.5	50.1
Ghana	1995–2000	38.2	10.4	73.0	27.8	5.3	...	...	...	...	...	...	...	...	...
Gibraltar	1996	16.5	8.3	5.7[4]	8.2	2.8[4]	1987	17.0	203.9	—	—	601.4	34.0	23.8	3.4
Greece	1996	9.7	9.6	8.1	0.1	1.4[18]	1994	6.4	206.7	10.3	11.7	478.5	52.0	24.3	42.4
Greenland	1994	20.7	8.0	13.0	12.7	2.9[12]	1993	27.1	186.3	...	...	188.2	47.0	12.7	152.0
Grenada	1996	21.3	7.9	14.3	13.4	3.8[23]	1987	9.6	82.8	57.3	7.4	264.3	45.6	38.2	...
Guadeloupe	1995–2000	18.5	6.5	8.0	12.0	2.1	1990	20.8[14]	121.2	23.0[14]	12.3[14]	186.8	30.5	29.7	72.9
Guam	1995	24.0	4.0	8.0	20.0	3.1	1994	1.4	60.0	26.5[6]	6.8	141.8	27.9	1.4	64.1
Guatemala	1994	35.4	7.5	53.9	27.9	4.8	1984	211.5	29.8	29.6	9.0	57.2	145.7	21.7	52.0
Guernsey	1996	11.2	10.4	7.6	0.8	1.6[13]	1996	5.3	282.3	15.9	15.9	441.1	150.0	49.4	24.7
Guinea	1995–2000	48.2	18.4	124.0	29.8	6.6	...	...	...	...	...	...	...	...	...
Guinea-Bissau	1995–2000	40.3	20.6	132.0	19.7	5.4	...	...	...	...	...	...	...	...	...
Guyana	1996	19.0	9.5	51.4	9.5	2.2	1984	19.3	37.1	33.3	11.6	202.5	39.8	74.0	56.5
Haiti	1996	33.5	15.5	105.1	18.0	4.8	...	...	...	...	...	...	...	...	...
Honduras	1993	35.8	6.4	47.2	29.4	4.9	1983	46.6	12.4	5.3	7.8	48.4	26.3	16.7	42.2
Hong Kong	1996	10.0	4.9	4.1	5.1	1.1[23]	1996	17.9	156.1	9.1	4.3	131.3	96.6	21.6	26.2
Hungary	1996	10.4	14.1	10.9	–3.7	1.6[23]	1994	8.2	318.7	20.6	12.3	722.9	67.0	117.6	115.6
Iceland	1995	16.0	7.2	4.6[33]	8.8	2.1	1994	4.1	166.5	5.3	14.7	300.4	80.1	15.8	35.7
India	1996	25.9	9.6	71.1	16.3	3.2	...	...	...	...	...	...	...	...	...
Indonesia	1997	22.4	7.9	51.0	14.5	2.6	...	...	...	...	...	...	...	...	...
Iran	1996	33.7	6.6	52.7	27.1	4.7	1990[35]	*34*	*61*	*12*[16]	*26*	*304*	*48*	*24*	*108*
Iraq	1994	34.1	9.8	91.9	24.3	4.9[9]	...	...	...	...	...	...	...	...	...
Ireland	1996	13.9	8.7	5.9[15]	5.2	1.8	1994	4.8	205.6	11.6	...	392.1	66.8	...	62.2
Isle of Man	1996	11.4	13.2	5.7[3]	–1.8	1.8[13]	1994	107.9	217.4	8.6[6]	—	552.7	204.4	20.2	95.0
Israel	1996	21.2	6.0	5.8	15.2	2.9	1993	9.6	137.6	20.3	10.0	268.8	32.0	18.9	36.7
Italy	1996	9.2	9.5	6.0	–0.3	1.2	1993	3.6	270.5	...	29.2	423.7	56.2	49.8	49.8
Jamaica	1995	23.2	5.0	28.6	18.2	3.0	1991	8.1	84.1	51.3	7.5	189.5	30.2	14.1	8.4
Japan	1995	9.5	7.4	4.2[15]	2.1	1.4	1994	12.7	196.4	11.5	6.2	239.1	94.7	32.1	49.1
Jersey	1991	12.5	9.9	6.0[13]	2.6	1.3[13]	...	...	...	...	...	...	...	...	...
Jordan	1995	32.9	3.0	34.0[15]	29.9	5.9[23]	...	...	...	...	...	...	...	...	...
Kazakstan	1995	16.7	10.2	27.9	6.5	2.5[15]	1994	30.3	133.5	10.6	9.0	456.6	87.4	30.3	125.0
Kenya	1996	32.4	10.8	55.2	21.6	4.3	...	...	...	...	...	...	...	...	...
Kiribati	1994	31.0	11.0	54.0[9]	20.0	3.3[36]	...	...	...	...	...	...	...	...	...
Korea, North	1996	22.5	5.3	23.0	17.2	2.3	1986	19.4	69.0	3.0[16]	6.5	224.9	46.7	51.6	38.2
Korea, South	1997	15.1	6.4	10.0[9]	8.7	1.7	1994	12.8	110.3	17.6	5.3	155.0	25.2	39.6	72.0
Kuwait	1995	24.3	2.2	11.1	22.1	3.7[15]	1994	5.8	22.6	6.6	6.0	76.5	11.9	3.8	35.2
Kyrgyzstan	1995	26.0	8.2	27.7	17.8	3.1[15]	1994	32.9	67.3	7.9	9.0	333.0	132.4	11.0	96.3
Laos	1997	44.3	13.7	87.0	30.6	6.2	...	...	...	...	...	...	...	...	...
Latvia	1996	7.9	13.8	15.9	–5.9	1.4[15]	1994	19.9	220.1	12.2	9.4	915.9	51.7	24.8	233.8
Lebanon	1994	24.9	4.3	28.0	20.6	2.9	...	...	...	...	...	...	...	...	...
Lesotho	1995–2000	35.4	10.6	72.0	24.8	4.9	...	...	...	...	...	...	...	...	...
Liberia	1995–2000	47.5	15.3	153.0	32.2	6.3	...	...	...	...	...	...	...	...	...
Libya	1995–2000	40.0	6.9	56.0	33.1	5.9	...	...	...	...	...	...	...	...	...
Liechtenstein	1995	11.7	6.7	5.5	5.0	1.5	1994	23.0	134.6	...	6.6	328.2	36.1	26.3	36.1
Lithuania	1996	10.6	11.6	10.1	–1.0	2.0[13]	1994	14.5	200.7	7.7	10.3	654.3	49.2	29.8	185.9
Luxembourg	1996	13.7	9.4	4.9	4.3	1.7	1994	8.9	234.5	18.8	13.6	391.1	68.4	44.8	62.7
Macau	1995	14.1	3.2	5.6	10.9	1.6[4]	1995	9.4	76.6	6.8	1.6	119.5	28.0	14.1	23.3
Macedonia	1995	14.9	7.6	22.7	7.3	2.2[15]	1993	12.9	6.2	16.4	4.7	385.8	34.5	14.8	35.3
Madagascar	1995–2000	41.1	9.9	77.0	31.2	5.7	...	...	...	...	...	...	...	...	...
Malaŵi	1996	41.6	24.5	139.9	17.1	5.9	1986[37]	*711*	*27*	*25*	*60*	*50*	*265*	*34*	*78*
Malaysia	1997	25.6	4.8	11.0	20.8	3.3	1994	15.4	20.4	4.2	1.0	54.0	7.9	7.5	29.0
Maldives	1997	41.8	7.6	50.0	34.2	6.8	1988	31.3	—	—	—	170.1	66.2	—	9.9
Mali	1995–2000	47.4	17.1	149.0	30.3	6.6	...	...	...	...	...	...	...	...	...
Malta	1996	12.2	7.5	10.5	4.7	1.8	1994	4.3	187.8	23.6	9.0	324.2	63.6	32.6	25.5
Marshall Islands	1996	26.1	4.0	26.0	22.1	7.0[18]	1993[38]	169.9	68.4	...	—	155.1	105.1	63.3	36.7
Martinique	1995–2000	16.8	7.1	7.0	9.7	2.0	1990	22.0	135.5	30.7	10.7[28]	208.0	34.2	31.3	54.8
Mauritania	1996	46.9	15.2	81.7	31.7	6.8	...	...	...	...	...	...	...	...	...
Mauritius	1995	18.3	6.7	19.7	11.6	2.1	1995	13.7	60.2	25.8	5.8	288.6	63.4	35.6	49.9
Mayotte	1991	43.7	6.0	38.0	37.7	6.8[13]	...	...	...	...	...	...	...	...	...
Mexico	1995	30.4	4.8	17.5	25.6	3.7[20]	1993	26.4	49.9	42.8	6.8	100.7	45.2	41.4	64.6
Micronesia	1997	35.0	8.0	49.0	27.0	5.1	1984	20.4	27.1	6.8	4.5	53.2	47.5	5.7	23.8
Moldova	1996	12.3	11.8	20.4	0.5	2.1[15]	1994	16.1	138.0	12.0	11.5	504.4	72.6	112.2	112.8
Monaco	1988	22.9	18.5	9.0[13]	4.4	1.2[13]	...	...	...	...	...	...	...	...	...
Mongolia	1996	22.0	7.6	40.5	14.4	4.5[15]	...	...	...	...	...	...	...	...	...
Morocco	1995–2000	25.3	6.7	51.0	18.6	3.1	1992	10.2	14.0	12.2	4.9	35.5	9.5	7.9	19.2

expectation of life at birth (latest year)		nuptiality, family, and family planning															country
		marriages			age at marriage (latest)						families (F), households (H) (latest)						
		year	total number	rate per 1,000 popu-lation	groom (percent)			bride (percent)			families (households)		children		induced abortions		
male	female				19 and under	20–29	30 and over	19 and under	20–29	30 and over	total ('000)	size	number under age 15	percent legiti-mate	number	ratio per 100 live births	
48.7	52.0	...	...	...	...	...	...	...	...	...	...	H 5.6	...	96.8	...	...	Djibouti
74.5	80.4	1990	228	3.3	—	41.2	58.8	3.1	58.3	38.6	H 19	H 3.6	H 2.2	...	...	...	Dominica
66.9	71.3	1992	25,351	3.6	8.0[28]	63.0[28]	29.0[28]	29.7[28]	51.0[28]	19.3[28]	H 1,804	H 3.9	...	32.8	562	0.5	Dominican Republic
67.5	72.6	1993	68,193	6.2	12.6	63.9	23.5	33.4	52.3	14.3	...	H 4.1	...	67.9	...	...	Ecuador
65.4	69.5	1993	479,000	8.3	3.8[20]	61.0[20]	35.2[20]	34.4[20]	52.9[20]	12.7[20]	H 9,733	H 4.9	H 2.1	100.0	...	...	Egypt
65.5	72.4	1992	23,084	4.2	6.6	54.8	38.6	21.5	51.4	27.1	H 1,092	H 4.8	...	30.6	...	...	El Salvador
48.4	51.6	...	...	...	...	...	...	...	...	...	...	H 4.5	...	...	...	...	Equatorial Guinea
49.1	52.1	1992	6.8	...	...	...	...	...	...	...	...	[30]	...	...	...	...	Eritrea
65.0	75.0	1995	6,852	4.5	5.3[15]	53.7[15]	41.0[15]	17.2[15]	47.8[15]	35.0[15]	H 427	H 3.1	H 0.8	66.1	28,403	157.7	Estonia
48.4	51.6	...	...	...	...	...	...	...	...	...	...	H 4.5[30]	...	...	...	...	Ethiopia
72.8	79.6	1990	203	4.3	1.0[31]	68.8[31]	30.2[31]	8.8[31]	70.7[31]	20.5[31]	F 14	F 3.0	F 0.9	57.5	26	3.3	Faroe Islands
70.0	75.0	1988	6,892	9.6	6.6[31]	68.7[31]	24.7[31]	31.0[31]	55.8[31]	13.2[31]	F 97	F 6.0	F 2.5	82.7	...	...	Fiji
72.8	80.2	1995	23,737	4.6	1.1[15]	52.7[15]	46.2[15]	4.0[15]	61.1[15]	34.9[15]	H 2,270	H 2.2	...	66.9	10,013	15.4	Finland
73.7	81.8	1996	279,690	4.8	0.2[15]	55.7[15]	44.1[15]	2.0[15]	66.0[15]	32.0[15]	H 20,899	H 2.6	H 1.0	63.9	162,902	21.5	France
63.4	69.7	1992	716	5.3	...	...	...	...	...	...	H 33	H 3.4	H 1.2	20.3	388	16.8	French Guiana
68.4	72.8	1994	1,263	5.9	11.3[31, 32]	75.8[31, 32]	12.9[31, 32]	41.5[31, 32]	52.5[31, 32]	6.0[31, 32]	H 40	H 4.7	H 1.7	37.2	...	...	French Polynesia
53.8	57.2	...	...	...	...	...	...	...	...	...	H 136	H 4.0	...	...	...	...	Gabon
45.4	48.7	...	...	...	...	...	...	...	...	...	...	H 8.3	...	...	...	...	Gambia, The
66.2	69.3	...	...	...	...	...	...	...	...	...	...	...	...	...	...	...	Gaza Strip
68.9	76.5	1993	24,105	4.9	5.7[13]	66.2[13]	28.1[13]	27.8[13]	55.7[13]	16.5[13]	H 1,244	H 4.1	H 1.1	82.3	68,883	75.6	Georgia
72.5	79.0	1995	428,650	5.2	0.6[15]	49.4[15]	50.0[15]	3.6[15]	60.8[15]	35.6[15]	H 36,230	H 2.2	H 0.3	86.6	103,586	13.5	Germany
56.2	59.9	...	...	...	...	...	...	...	...	...	H 2,355	H 4.9	H 2.2	...	...	...	Ghana
73.4	80.4	1994	697	5.2	...	...	...	...	...	...	H 8	H 3.2	H 0.7	97.1	...	...	Gibraltar
74.6	79.8	1995	62,000	5.9	1.0[15]	54.5[15]	44.5[15]	10.7[15]	68.7[15]	20.6[15]	H 2,990	H 3.3	H 0.7	97.1	11,977	11.5	Greece
60.7	68.4	1991	451	8.1	1.1	44.6	54.3	2.7	59.6	37.7	F 31	F 1.8	F 0.5	28.0	962	80.7	Greenland
68.2	73.2	1991	...	4.3	...	...	...	...	...	...	H 24	H 3.7	H 2.2	...	...	...	Grenada
72.1	78.8	1992	1,880	4.7	0.5[4]	51.4[4]	48.0[4]	7.2[4]	61.4[4]	31.4[4]	H 112	H 3.4	H 0.9	39.3	561	8.7	Guadeloupe
73.0	79.0	1994	1,596	10.9	3.0[12]	55.5[12]	41.5[12]	9.2[12]	59.3[12]	31.5[12]	H 31	H 4.0	H 1.3	41.3	...	...	Guam
61.9	67.1	1993	46,789	4.7	15.9[14]	55.7[14]	28.4[14]	41.5[14]	38.0[14]	20.5[14]	H 1,806	H 5.2	...	34.8	...	...	Guatemala
...	...	1996	340	5.8	...	...	...	...	...	...	H 21	H 2.6	H 0.5	73.2	...	...	Guernsey
46.0	47.0	...	...	...	...	...	...	...	...	...	H 1,064	H 4.7	...	...	...	...	Guinea
42.4	45.2	...	...	...	...	...	...	...	...	...	H 124	H 4.1	H 2.8	11.3	...	...	Guinea-Bissau
57.2	62.8	...	...	...	...	...	...	...	...	...	H 150	H 5.1	H 2.1	...	...	...	Guyana
47.3	51.3	...	...	...	...	...	...	...	...	...	H 1,147	H 4.4	H 1.8	...	...	...	Haiti
64.8	69.2	1983	19,875	4.9	7.7	65.1	27.2	27.9	58.5	13.6	H 463	H 5.7	H 2.8	...	...	...	Honduras
75.9	81.5	1996	37,045	5.9	0.9[15]	46.0[15]	53.1[15]	3.7[15]	66.3[15]	30.0[15]	H 1,840	H 3.2	...	94.5	17,600	25.2	Hong Kong
64.8	74.2	1995	54,000	5.3	4.2	65.2	24.6	19.6	64.3	16.1	F 3,058	F 2.9	F 0.8	81.5	74,491	64.4	Hungary
76.5	80.6	1995	1,238	4.6	0.2	44.3	56.5	2.3	55.5	42.2	H 85	H 2.9	H 1.3	39.1	775	17.4	Iceland
59.1	60.3	...	...	...	...	...	...	...	...	...	H 151,033	H 5.6	H 2.4	...	581,215	...	India
63.0	66.0	1992–93[34]	1,423,774	7.6	...	...	...	...	...	...	H 39,695	H 4.5	H 1.8	...	...	...	Indonesia
66.1	68.7	1993	460,888	7.9	...	...	...	...	...	...	H 9,759	H 5.1	H 2.2	...	...	...	Iran
57.3	60.4	1992	144,055	7.8	...	...	...	...	...	...	H 1,873	H 8.9	H 4.1	...	...	...	Iraq
72.3	77.9	1995	15,623	4.4	0.8[12]	67.4[12]	31.8[12]	2.4[12]	78.5[12]	19.1[12]	H 541	H 3.3	H 1.3	77.8	...	...	Ireland
...	...	1994	452	6.5	0.4	42.7	56.9	2.2	54.0	43.8	...	...	...	76.1	...	...	Isle of Man
75.1	78.5	1995	33,365	6.4	3.5[18]	73.7[18]	22.8[18]	22.0[18]	67.4[18]	10.6[18]	H 1,355	H 3.7	H 1.1	98.5	17,164	15.3	Israel
74.1	80.5	1996	274,621	4.7	0.6	62.6	36.8	6.2	74.6	19.2	F 19,766	F 2.6	F 0.5	90.2	124,334	23.6	Italy
74.4	75.8	1994	15,171	6.1	...	...	...	...	...	...	H 554	H 4.2	H 1.4	14.9	...	...	Jamaica
76.4	82.8	1995	...	6.4	1.3	61.7	37.0	3.1	78.6	18.3	H 43,447	H 2.8	...	99.0	364,350	29.4	Japan
...	...	...	...	...	...	...	...	...	...	...	H 29	H 2.6	H 0.4	88.1	313	29.2	Jersey
64.4	69.9	1992	37,216	8.0	5.2	72.4	22.4	39.2	54.3	6.5	H 11,891	H 6.1	H 3.4	...	...	...	Jordan
63.2	72.7	1993	146,161	8.6	7.7	74.1	18.2	35.6	51.3	13.1	H 3,824	H 4.0	H 1.4	87.6	206,877	65.4	Kazakstan
54.2	54.6	...	...	...	...	...	...	...	...	...	H 1,938	H 6.2	H 2.7	...	...	...	Kenya
62.0	67.0	1988	352	5.2	...	...	...	...	...	...	H 11	H 6.6	H 2.5	...	...	...	Kiribati
69.0	75.0	1987	188,007	9.3	...	...	...	...	...	...	H 4,054	H 4.8	H 1.7	...	...	...	Korea, North
69.0	76.0	1994	304,146	6.8	0.3	69.4	30.3	1.9	87.4	10.7	H 12,961	H 3.7	H 1.0	99.5	...	...	Korea, South
74.4	79.0	1993	11,418	7.8	6.1[12]	72.2[12]	21.7[12]	35.9[12]	53.3[12]	10.8[12]	H 246	H 7.4	H 1.6	100.0	...	...	Kuwait
63.9	72.6	1994	26,097	5.8	6.3	79.3	14.4	40.6	50.1	9.3	H 856	H 4.2	H 1.9	83.2	31,389	28.5	Kyrgyzstan
51.0	54.0	...	...	...	...	...	...	...	...	...	...	H 6.0	...	...	...	...	Laos
64.2	74.6	1995	11,072	4.4	6.5[15]	64.9[15]	28.8[15]	19.8[15]	56.1[15]	24.1[15]	H 732	H 3.1	H 0.8	73.6	26,795	110.5	Latvia
72.5	77.9	...	...	...	...	...	...	...	...	...	H 405	H 5.3	H 2.2	...	...	...	Lebanon
58.0	63.0	...	...	...	...	...	...	...	...	...	H 330	H 4.8	H 2.0	...	...	...	Lesotho
50.0	53.0	...	...	...	...	...	...	...	...	...	H 474	H 5.0	...	...	...	...	Liberia
63.9	67.5	...	...	...	...	...	...	...	...	...	F 383	F 5.4	F 2.9	...	...	...	Libya
66.5	79.5	1994	202	13.1	—	54.5	44.5	0.0	66.3	29.2	H 8	H 3.0	H 0.7	85.3	...	...	Liechtenstein
65.3	76.1	1995	22,150	6.0	8.4[18]	70.7[18]	20.9[18]	27.9[18]	55.0[18]	17.1[18]	H 1,000	H 3.2	H 0.8	93.3	42,023	89.9	Lithuania
72.6	79.1	1993	2,379	6.3	1.1	53.2	45.7	4.9	65.0	30.1	H 145	H 2.6	H 0.5	87.3	...	...	Luxembourg
68.1	71.8	1995	2,146	5.1	0.7	43.6	55.7	3.0	65.0	32.0	H 99	H 3.5	H 0.9	99.3	...	...	Macau
70.1	74.4	1994	15,736	7.6	5.1	75.4	19.5	27.7	62.5	9.8	H 468	H 3.8	H 1.3	91.5	18,754	57.9	Macedonia
57.0	60.0	...	...	...	...	...	...	...	...	...	H 1,709	H 4.7	H 2.0	...	...	...	Madagascar
35.9	36.5	...	...	...	...	...	...	...	...	...	...	H 4.3	...	...	...	...	Malaŵi
70.0	74.0	...	...	...	...	...	...	...	...	...	H 3,580	H 4.9	...	...	...	...	Malaysia
65.0	63.0	1995	4,998	19.7	13.7[18]	58.2[18]	29.1[18]	...	...	...	...	H 7.2	...	...	...	...	Maldives
46.4	49.7	1987	33,646	4.4	0.1	1.4	98.5	...	...	...	H 1,364	H 5.6	...	...	...	...	Mali
74.9	79.5	1995	2,203	6.2	2.3	73.4	24.3	9.4	76.3	14.3	H 76	H 3.3	H 1.2	95.8	...	...	Malta
61.9	65.0	...	...	...	...	...	...	...	...	...	H 5	H 8.7	...	...	...	...	Marshall Islands
73.7	80.3	1993	1,555	4.2	0.1[12]	46.8[12]	53.1[12]	3.3[12]	61.5[12]	35.2[12]	H 107	H 3.3	H 0.8	34.1	1,753	30.6	Martinique
46.1	52.1	...	...	...	...	...	...	...	...	...	H 246	H 5.0	...	...	...	...	Mauritania
66.5	74.0	1995	10,430	9.5	1.9[15]	59.9[15]	38.2[15]	25.5[15]	55.9[15]	18.6[15]	F 155	F 5.3	F 2.0	72.8	...	...	Mauritius
54.0	58.0	...	...	...	...	...	...	...	...	...	H 19	H 4.9	H 2.3	89.2	...	...	Mayotte
66.5	73.1	1994	671,640	7.2	15.7	65.2	19.1	34.6	53.7	11.7	H 17,152	H 5.1	H 2.0	72.5	...	...	Mexico
72.0	72.0	...	...	...	...	...	...	...	...	...	H 11	H 7.0	...	...	...	...	Micronesia
67.9	71.5	1993	39,469	9.1	5.9[4]	74.6[4]	19.5[4]	37.6[4]	46.9[4]	15.5[4]	H 1,144	H 3.4	H 1.1	89.6	52,003	74.7	Moldova
72.0	80.0	1987	...	7.5	...	...	...	...	...	...	H 14	H 2.2	H 0.3	96.8	...	...	Monaco
60.0	63.5	1989	16,100	7.8	...	...	...	...	...	...	F 428	F 4.8	...	...	...	...	Mongolia
64.8	68.5	...	...	...	...	...	...	...	...	...	H 2,819	H 5.8	H 2.5	...	...	...	Morocco

Vital statistics, marriage, family (continued)

country	vital rates						causes of death (rate per 100,000 population)								
	year	birth rate per 1,000 population	death rate per 1,000 population	infant mortality rate per 1,000 live births	rate of natural increase per 1,000 population	total fertility rate	year	infectious and parasitic diseases	malignant neoplasms (cancers)	endocrine and metabolic disorders	diseases of the nervous system	diseases of the circulatory system	diseases of the respiratory system	diseases of the digestive system	accidents, poisoning, and violence
Mozambique	1995–2000	42.5	17.5	110.0	25.0	6.1	...	...	...	...	...	...	...	...	...
Myanmar (Burma)	1997	27.4	9.9	79.0	17.5	3.3	...	...	...	...	...	...	...	...	...
Namibia	1995–2000	35.9	11.8	60.0	24.1	4.9	...	...	...	...	...	...	...	...	...
Nauru	1997	18.8	4.5	26.0[9]	14.3	2.5[13]	1976–81[39]	33.0	38.0	24.0	13.0	89.0	16.0	53.0	116.0
Nepal	1997	36.6	11.2	83.0	25.4	5.0	...	...	...	...	...	...	...	...	...
Netherlands, The	1995	12.3	8.8	5.1[9]	3.5	1.5	1994	6.7	237.1	28.9	14.6	335.9	73.7	32.6	34.3
Netherlands Antilles	1995	18.3	6.7	6.3[13]	12.5	2.2[12]	1995[40]	16.7	149.0	61.7	9.9	71.6	40.8	21.4	47.6
New Caledonia	1995	22.7	5.5	7.8	17.2	2.9[15]	1992	19.3	129.0	10.8	9.1	115.3	45.4	15.3	80.7
New Zealand	1995	16.3	7.9	6.7	8.4	2.0[15]	1993	4.1	205.1	19.5	13.0	346.7	78.2	21.2	50.3
Nicaragua	1996	33.8	6.0	45.8	27.8	4.0	1991[41]	*100*	*56*	*18*	*13*	*142*	*73*	*34*	*93*
Niger	1996	54.5	24.6	117.6	29.9	7.4	...	...	...	...	...	...	...	...	...
Nigeria	1990–95	45.4	15.4	84.2	30.0	6.4	...	...	...	...	...	...	...	...	...
Northern Mariana Islands	1992	29.0	3.0	9.0[2]	26.0	2.4[20]	1987	18.7	70.2[21]	23.4	14.0	135.7	70.2	9.4	145.1
Norway	1996	13.9	10.1	4.1[23]	3.5	1.9[23]	1993	7.4	237.0	17.0	17.6	483.7	125.8	29.8	56.5
Oman	1990–95	43.7	4.8	28.2[9]	38.9	6.9	...	...	...	...	...	...	...	...	...
Pakistan	1997	36.4	7.9	75.0	28.5	5.1	...	...	...	...	...	...	...	...	...
Palau	1997	22.0	8.0	21.0	14.0	3.2	1993	43.6	136.9	...	...	192.9	43.6	...	112.0
Panama	1996	22.5	5.2	25.3	17.3	2.6	1994	18.3	57.3[21]	14.2[6]	1.9[27]	118.4	24.0	7.5	58.0
Papua New Guinea	1997	32.4	10.0	62.0	22.4	4.7	...	...	...	...	...	...	...	...	...
Paraguay	1995–2000	31.3	5.4	39.0	25.9	4.2	1993[43]	*33*	*53*	*22*	*8*	*162*	*38*	*17*	*45*
Peru	1995–2000	24.9	6.4	50.1	18.5	3.0	1989[41]	*85*	*73*	*19*	*11*	*115*	*100*	*36*	*67*
Philippines	1997	28.7	5.8	36.0	22.9	3.7	1991	65.9	35.2	17.9	124.9	82.2	20.5	20.5	71.8
Poland	1995	12.0	10.1	14.0	1.9	2.1[4]	1994	6.8	198.2	15.2	7.9	512.7	32.7	32.8	75.4
Portugal	1996	11.5	10.8	6.9	0.3	1.4	1994	8.5	193.6	41.2	9.4	431.2	71.5	44.5	57.2
Puerto Rico	1996	17.2	7.9	11.5[15]	9.3	2.0[23]	1993	59.4	122.2	66.7	19.2	242.3	80.5	43.9	34.1
Qatar	1990–95	19.9	3.4	20.0	16.5	4.1	1992	3.4	21.4[21]	7.3[20]	2.6	59.9	7.5	3.4	36.0
Réunion	1996	19.6	5.4	7.3	14.2	2.3	1993	14.9	99.7	22.5	16.0	170.1	41.5	59.5[45]	65.3
Romania	1995	10.4	12.0	21.2	−1.6	2.2[13]	1992	12.4	163.4	11.7	8.2	707.7	94.0	57.9	74.3
Russia	1995	9.3	15.0	18.0	−5.7	1.4	1995	21.0	203.0	11.0[15]	10.9[15]	784.0	75.0	46.0	234.0
Rwanda	1995–2000	42.8	19.7	125.0	23.1	6.0	...	...	...	...	...	...	...	...	...
St. Kitts and Nevis	1995	19.4	9.4	25.1	10.0	2.6[15]	1985	50.0	95.5	20.5[6]	11.4	443.2	81.8	25.0	29.5
St. Lucia	1995	25.2	5.9	18.0	19.3	2.5[15]	1992	31.1	64.4	22.4	5.8	205.6	48.5	21.0	34.7
St. Vincent and the Grenadines	1994	23.3	6.7	14.1	16.6	2.1[12]	1994	44.7	94.0	68.5	14.6	239.2	44.7	21.0	39.3
Samoa	1997	26.7	6.0	60.0	20.7	3.8	1992[38]	3.1	11.2	9.9	3.1	24.2	9.9	6.8	2.5
San Marino	1996	11.1	6.8	7.1[46]	4.3	1.5[23]	1991–95	...	229.4	2.4[6]	...	324.8	10.7	...	45.2
São Tomé and Príncipe	1995	34.9	8.7	62.1	26.2	4.4	1987	240.7	19.6	5.3[6]	2.7[27]	143.5	86.5	15.2	14.3
Saudi Arabia	1995–2000	34.3	4.2	23.0	30.1	5.9	...	...	...	...	...	...	...	...	...
Senegal	1996	45.5	11.8	64.0	33.7	6.3	...	...	...	...	...	...	...	...	...
Seychelles	1997	20.0	7.0	17.0	13.0	2.0	1994	43.3	128.6	16.2	16.2	288.4	98.8	39.3	43.3
Sierra Leone	1990–95	49.1	25.1	166.0	24.0	6.5	...	...	...	...	...	...	...	...	...
Singapore	1996	16.0	5.1	3.8	10.9	1.7	1994	12.5	128.2	12.8	2.4	186.2	87.4	13.4	37.5
Slovakia	1996	11.2	9.5	10.2	1.6	1.5	1995	3.4	206.5	13.7	4.4	541.1	67.9	42.1	67.9
Slovenia	1996	9.3	4.8	5.5[23]	4.5	1.3[23]	1995	4.4	235.6	28.8	8.5	408.1	74.7	56.7	87.6
Solomon Islands	1997	36.2	4.1	23.0	32.1	5.0	...	...	...	...	...	...	...	...	...
Somalia	1995–2000	50.0	16.9	112.0	33.1	7.0	...	...	...	...	...	...	...	...	...
South Africa	1996	27.4	11.1	52.4	16.3	3.3	1993	42.4	48.0	19.1	7.7	91.2	38.2	12.4	99.3
Spain	1995	9.2	8.7	5.6	0.5	1.3	1994	10.3	224.3	39.1	15.1	334.2	78.8	47.0	41.1
Sri Lanka	1997	17.9	5.9	15.0	12.0	2.1	1989	26.0	26.7	8.4	36.9	101.4	31.1	17.4	135.7
Sudan, The	1995–2000	33.7	11.7	71.0	22.0	4.6	...	...	...	...	...	...	...	...	...
Suriname	1995	21.3	6.6	30.2	14.7	2.7	1992[47]	40	68	40	11	193	37	32	71
Swaziland	1996	42.9	10.6	88.4	32.3	6.0	...	...	...	...	...	...	...	...	...
Sweden	1996	10.8	10.6	3.5	0.2	1.7	1994	7.5	229.8	21.9	...	514.8	78.9	...	32.6
Switzerland	1997	11.7	8.9	5.0[23]	2.8	1.5[23]	1994	16.3	238.7	23.3[16]	18.1	381.5	64.2	27.1	69.3
Syria	1995	40.0	6.0	29.6	34.0	6.1	1981[29]	*22*	*12*	*7*	*13*	*86*	*19*	*8*	*27*
Taiwan	1997	14.7	6.1	6.4[23]	8.6	1.8[23]	1992	...	101.5	23.7[6]	...	140.1[18]	24.3[47]	18.2[48]	63.7[48]
Tajikistan	1994	28.2	7.0	42.4	21.2	4.5	1993	128.3	40.7	8.8[4, 16]	7.9[4]	222.8	158.7	20.7	181.3
Tanzania	1996	41.0	17.0	107.0	24.0	5.6	...	...	...	...	...	...	...	...	...
Thailand	1996	17.8	7.4	32.0	10.4	2.0	1991	...	162.0	...	...	250.0	55.0	73.0	104.0
Togo	1995–2000	41.2	14.9	86.0	26.3	6.1	...	...	...	...	...	...	...	...	...
Tonga	1997	27.0	5.8	15.0	21.2	3.4	1992	16.3	54.9	15.2	6.1	158.5	31.5	18.3	4.1
Trinidad and Tobago	1996	16.3	6.9	18.2	9.4	2.0	1993	31.1	86.4	83.5[6]	2.8[27]	270.0	34.3	12.3	56.1
Tunisia	1995–2000	23.9	5.9	37.0	18.0	2.9	...	...	...	...	...	...	...	...	...
Turkey	1996	22.3	5.5	43.2	16.8	2.6	1993[48]	24	80	9[6]	2[15]	369	19	10	33
Turkmenistan	1994	33.0	7.0	45.0	26.0	4.1	1994	75.7	55.4	11.2	7.6	337.2	150.3	7.6	60.1
Tuvalu	1997	27.0	9.0	41.0	18.0	5.3	1985	40.0	70.0	20.0	120.0	150.0	120.0	170.0	...
Uganda	1995–2000	51.1	21.0	113.0	30.1	7.1	...	...	...	...	...	...	...	...	...
Ukraine	1996	13.0	10.5	14.1	2.5	1.7[15]	1993	14.5	198.9	8.2[12, 16]	8.9[12]	782.6	81.3	38.3	131.2
United Arab Emirates	1995–2000	18.7	2.9	15.0	15.8	3.5	...	...	...	...	...	...	...	...	...
United Kingdom	1996	12.5	10.9	6.2[23]	1.6	1.7[15]	1994	6.2	275.4	14.1	17.2	473.3	155.6	36.4	32.8
United States	1996	14.7	8.8	7.5	5.9	2.0[4]	1996	25.1[49]	204.5	23.2[6]	0.2[27]	355.1	70.6[50]	13.6	54.4
Uruguay	1995	17.8	10.0	19.6	7.8	2.4[15]	1990	16.0	222.8	25.5	16.2	378.4	76.3	39.1	61.7
Uzbekistan	1994	33.0	6.0	35.0	27.0	4.0	1993	38.0	48.2	9.4[12]	8.9[12]	300.3	113.8	31.4	49.5
Vanuatu	1997	33.0	6.2	39.0	26.8	4.4	1994[38]	25.0	29.2	9.1	5.5	39.0	30.4	9.7	9.1
Venezuela	1996	26.7	4.7	16.8	22.0	3.1[15]	1989	30.0	51.1	18.6	7.4	115.0	29.0	18.8	61.4
Vietnam	1997	25.6	7.0	38.0	18.6	3.2	1979	48.0	54.0	...	...	123.8	...	...	...
Virgin Islands (U.S.)	1993	24.3	5.5	12.3	18.8	2.6[13]	1989	10.8	78.9	36.5[5]	—	232.7	14.8[50]	12.8	56.2
West Bank	1994	46.0	7.0	40.0	39.0	5.7	...	...	...	...	...	...	...	...	...
Western Sahara	1995–2000	31.4	8.6	64.0	22.8	4.0	...	...	...	...	...	...	...	...	...
Yemen	1995–2000	47.7	10.4	80.0	37.3	7.6	...	...	...	...	...	...	...	...	...
Yugoslavia	1996	13.0	10.5	14.1	2.5	1.9[23]	1995	9.0	167.7[21]	23.8	10.1	573.7	40.9	28.3	42.2
Zambia	1995–2000	42.4	18.0	103	24.4	5.5	...	...	...	...	...	...	...	...	...
Zimbabwe	1997	31.6	19.0	62.3	12.6	3.9	1990	64.7	28.4	4.9	9.4	40.8	39.5	12.1	44.9

[1]Excludes nomadic tribes. [2]1995–2000. [3]1986. [4]1991. [5]Septicemia only. [6]Diabetes mellitus only. [7]Cerebrovascular disease and heart disease only. [8]Chronic obstructive pulmonary diseases, pneumonia, and influenza only. [9]1996. [10]Under 21 years of age. [11]21–29 years of age. [12]1992. [13]1989. [14]1988. [15]1994. [16]Includes nutritional disorders. [17]1990–95. [18]1993. [19]Accidents only. [20]1990. [21]Includes benign neoplasms (cancers). [22]Projected rates based on about 67 percent of the total deaths. [23]1995. [24]Results based on a sample population of about 100,000. [25]Millions of households. [26]Projected rates based on about 60 percent of the total deaths. [27]Meningitis only. [28]1985. [29]Projected rates based on about 75 percent of the total deaths. [30]Ethiopia

expectation of life at birth (latest year)		nuptiality, family, and family planning																country
		marriages			age at marriage (latest)						families (F), households (H) (latest)							
					groom (percent)			bride (percent)			families (households)		children		induced abortions			
male	female	year	total number	rate per 1,000 popu-lation	19 and under	20–29	30 and over	19 and under	20–29	30 and over	total ('000)	size	number under age 15	percent legiti-mate	number	ratio per 100 live births		
45.5	48.4	...	...	...	...	...	...	...	...	...	F 1,860	F 4.4	F 2.0	73.1	...	...		Mozambique
58.0	62.0	...	...	...	...	...	...	...	...	...	...	H 5.6	...	...	...	...		Myanmar (Burma)
54.7	56.6	...	...	...	...	...	...	...	...	...	...	H 5.2	...	...	...	...		Namibia
64.0	69.0	1976	43	6.1	...	...	...	...	...	...	H 1	H 8.0	H 2.6	...	...	...		Nauru
57.0	57.0	...	...	...	...	...	...	...	...	...	H 3,345	H 5.6	H 2.3	...	...	...		Nepal
74.6	80.4	1995	81,469	5.3	0.3	51.8	47.9	1.9	64.5	33.6	H 6,185	H 2.4	H 0.4	84.5	20,811	10.6		Netherlands, The
71.8	77.7	1995	1,056	5.2	...	...	...	...	...	...	H 41	H 3.7	H 2.1	51.6	...	...		Netherlands Antilles
69.0	76.0	1993	896	5.0	0.1	45.4[14]	54.5[14]	5.0[14]	61.3[14]	33.7[14]	...	H 4.1	...	48.1	...	...		New Caledonia
73.4	79.1	1994	21,858	6.2	0.8	50.6	48.6	3.2	60.8	36.0	H 1,178	H 2.9	H 0.7	63.3	11,460	19.3		New Zealand
63.4	68.1	1991	13,122	3.3	18.1[10, 28]	—81.9[28, 42]—		48.2[10, 28]	—51.8[28, 42]—		H 752	H 5.8	...	...	...	...		Nicaragua
41.1	40.2	...	...	...	...	...	...	...	...	...	H 1,130	H 6.4	...	...	...	...		Niger
53.5	55.9	...	...	...	...	...	...	...	...	...	H 21,283	H 4.7	...	...	...	...		Nigeria
59.0	64.0	1987	685	31.2	2.5	50.2	47.3	5.7	70.4	23.9	H 7	H 4.6	H 1.5	53.9	...	...		Northern Mariana Islands
74.9	80.6	1994	20,605	4.8	0.6[12]	53.7[12]	45.7[12]	3.2[12]	67.6[12]	29.2[12]	H 1,864	H 2.3	...	52.4	14,909	25.0		Norway
67.7	71.8	...	...	...	...	...	...	...	...	...	...	H 8.0	...	...	...	...		Oman
63.0	65.0	...	...	...	...	...	...	...	...	...	...	H 6.3	...	...	...	...		Pakistan
69.1	73.0	...	...	...	...	...	...	...	...	...	...	...	...	...	...	...		Palau
71.0	76.5	1994	13,523	5.6	2.5[18]	52.0[18]	45.5[18]	11.9[18]	55.2[18]	32.9[18]	H 524	H 4.4	H 1.5	25.5	...	...		Panama
57.0	59.0	...	...	...	...	...	...	...	...	...	H 674	H 4.6	...	...	...	...		Papua New Guinea
67.5	72.0	1992	16,042	3.6	4.2	64.8	31.0	30.4	50.2	19.4	H 868	H 4.7	1.9	68.7	...	...		Paraguay
65.9	70.9	1993	90,000	4.1	5.5[44]	60.4[44]	34.1[44]	25.9[44]	51.4[44]	22.6[44]	H 3,099	H 5.1	...	57.8	...	...		Peru
66.0	70.0	1992	454,155	6.9	5.3	67.2	27.5	18.9	64.0	17.1	F 9,566	F 5.7	F 2.4	93.9	2,315	...		Philippines
67.5	76.1	1994	208,900	5.4	3.7	76.6	19.7	19.4	67.6	13.0	F 9,435	F 3.6	F 0.9	95.0	874	0.2		Poland
71.3	78.6	1996	63,700	6.4	4.0[18]	7.9[18]	17.0[18]	18.0[18]	71.0[18]	11.0[18]	H 3,150	H 3.1	H 0.8	85.5	...	...		Portugal
69.6	78.5	1994	33,200	9.0	9.9	54.5	35.6	21.1	50.3	28.6	H 1,005	H 3.6	H 1.0	59.6	...	...		Puerto Rico
68.8	74.2	1994	1,495	2.8	3.7	69.0	27.3	26.6	62.0	11.4	H 61	H 6.4	...	...	...	...		Qatar
71.7	78.0	1996	3,313	4.9	1.2[20]	65.2[20]	33.6[20]	12.5[20]	66.8[20]	20.7[20]	H 185	H 3.5	...	44.1	4,302	31.7		Réunion
69.3	75.4	1995	153,943	6.8	3.0[15]	76.2[15]	20.8[15]	29.4[15]	58.3[15]	12.3[15]	H 7,115	H 3.1	...	...	530,191	214.9		Romania
58.0	72.0	1995	1,074,900	7.3	9.7[15]	79.4[15]	10.9[15]	41.0[15]	51.6[15]	7.4[15]	H 40,426	H 3.2	H 0.8	85.4	2,481,493	176.2		Russia
40.8	43.4	1982	14,313	2.6	...	...	...	...	...	...	H 1,509	H 4.7	2.3	94.9	...	...		Rwanda
63.0	69.0	...	...	...	...	...	...	...	...	...	H 12	H 3.7	H 1.4	19.2	...	...		St. Kitts and Nevis
67.0	72.0	1992	436	3.2	0.8[13]	34.4[13]	64.8[13]	3.5[13]	45.1[13]	51.4[13]	H 33	H 4.0	H 2.0	14.2	...	...		St. Lucia
71.0	74.0	1994	458	4.2	1.0[12]	37.0[12]	62.0[12]	4.8[12]	46.3[12]	48.9[12]	H 27	H 3.9	H 2.0	...	...	...		St. Vincent and the Grenadines
67.0	71.0	1993	759	4.7	0.5	51.0	48.5	8.0	65.0	27.0	F 20	F 7.8	F 3.8	43.5	...	...		Samoa
77.2	85.3	1989	169	7.4	0.6	75.1	24.3	5.3	85.3	9.5	H 9	H 2.6	H 0.4	95.2	...	...		San Marino
61.8	65.6	...	...	...	...	...	...	...	...	...	...	H 4.0	...	9.8	...	...		São Tomé and Príncipe
69.9	73.4	...	...	...	...	...	...	...	...	...	H 1,513	H 6.6	...	...	...	...		Saudi Arabia
53.7	59.3	...	...	...	...	...	...	...	...	...	...	H 8.7	...	...	...	...		Senegal
66.0	73.0	1994	937	12.7	2.0	45.8	42.2	11.2	51.5	29.6	H 13	H 4.8	H 1.9	27.2	387	22.8		Seychelles
41.4	44.6	...	...	...	...	...	...	...	...	...	...	H 6.6	...	...	...	...		Sierra Leone
74.4	78.9	1996	24,106	7.9	0.5[23]	56.4[23]	43.1[23]	3.7[23]	74.7[23]	21.6[23]	H 662	H 4.2	H 1.3	...	15,690	31.7		Singapore
68.8	76.7	1996	27,489	5.1	6.9[15]	76.2[15]	16.9[15]	30.5[15]	59.5[15]	10.0[15]	...	H 4.0	...	86.0	34,883	52.6		Slovakia
70.3	77.8	1995	8,245	4.2	0.6	64.9	34.5	6.6	73.6	19.8	H 637	H 3.1	...	70.2	11,324	58.1		Slovenia
69.0	74.0	...	...	...	...	...	...	...	...	...	H ...	H 5.8	...	...	...	...		Solomon Islands
47.4	50.6	...	...	...	...	...	...	...	...	...	...	H 4.9	...	...	...	...		Somalia
55.7	60.2	1995	148,148	3.6	...	...	...	...	...	...	H 8,688	H 4.6	...	75.9	...	...		South Africa
74.9	81.8	1995	187,049	4.8	1.8[4]	71.5[4]	26.7[4]	8.2[4]	76.7[4]	15.1[4]	F 10,665	F 3.5	...	89.5	...	...		Spain
71.0	75.0	1992	152,154	9.2	0.6	67.0	32.4	15.7	70.9	13.4	H 3,282	H 4.6	...	96.3	...	...		Sri Lanka
53.6	56.4	...	...	...	...	...	...	...	...	...	H 3,471	H 5.3	...	...	...	...		Sudan, The
67.2	72.4	1993	1,944	4.7	...	...	...	...	...	...	...	H 3.9	...	...	...	...		Suriname
53.2	61.4	1989	...	4.3	...	...	...	...	...	...	H 122	H 5.7	...	...	1,145	...		Swaziland
75.6	81.0	1996	33,484	3.4	0.3	40.5	59.2	1.5	54.0	44.5	H 3,670	H 2.1	H 0.5	47.0	32,293	28.8		Sweden
75.3	81.7	1995	40,820	5.8	0.3	45.1	54.6	2.1	60.7	37.2	H 3,250	H 2.2	0.4	93.2	...	...		Switzerland
68.4	71.3	1993	114,979	8.6	...	...	...	...	...	...	F 1,151	H 6.2	F 2.4	...	...	...		Syria
71.8	77.7	1996	169,096	7.8	1.5[20]	62.3[20]	36.2[20]	6.0[20]	77.7[20]	16.3[20]	H 5,964	H 3.6	H 1.0	97.2	...	...		Taiwan
65.7	71.5	1993	53,946	9.6	2.1	86.8	11.1	39.0	54.3	6.7	H 799	H 6.1	H 2.7	93.0	40,078	21.5		Tajikistan
41.5	45.0	...	...	...	...	...	...	...	...	...	H 3,435	H 5.2	H 2.3	...	...	...		Tanzania
67.0	72.0	1995	470,751	7.9	...	...	...	...	...	...	H 15,551	H 3.8	...	...	...	...		Thailand
48.8	51.5	1979	...	2.3	...	...	...	...	...	...	H 479	H 5.6	...	...	...	...		Togo
68.0	72.0	1992	806	8.2	...	...	...	...	...	...	F 15	F 6.3	F 2.7	80.6	...	...		Tonga
67.9	72.8	1993	7,012	5.6	5.7	59.1	35.2	23.5	52.4	24.1	H 301	H 4.1	H 1.3	...	9	—		Trinidad and Tobago
68.4	70.7	1995	52,203	6.0	...	60.5[12]	39.5[12]	24.7[12]	62.7[12]	20.2[12]	H 1,703	H 5.1	H 1.9	99.8	23,300	10.9		Tunisia
69.5	74.4	1993	460,002	7.7	6.5	76.4	17.1	33.6	58.3	8.2	...	H 4.5	...	...	...	...		Turkey
61.4	68.6	1993	42,106	10.7	3.0[13]	87.4[13]	9.6[13]	16.1[13]	77.1[13]	6.8[13]	H 598	H 5.6	H 2.4	96.5	39,068	31.3		Turkmenistan
64.0	70.0	...	...	...	...	...	...	...	...	...	H 1	H 6.4	H 2.2	82.2	...	...		Tuvalu
40.4	42.3	...	...	...	...	...	...	...	...	...	H 2,766	H 4.8	...	...	...	...		Uganda
65.3	74.7	1993	427,882	8.2	8.3	67.5	24.2	37.2	43.2	19.6	H 14,507	H 3.2	H 0.8	89.2	957,022	159.5		Ukraine
73.9	76.5	1991	...	2.7	...	...	...	...	...	...	H 247	H 6.8	...	...	...	...		United Arab Emirates
74.4	79.7	1995	282,900	5.5	1.1[18]	53.9[18]	45.0[18]	4.1[18]	61.6[18]	34.3[18]	H 29,533	H 2.4	H 1.7	68.0	169,964	22.6		United Kingdom
72.0	78.9	1996	2,324,000	8.8	4.3[20]	51.8[20]	43.9[20]	10.9[20]	55.8[20]	35.3[20]	H 96,391	H 2.6	F 1.0	70.5	1,388,937	33.8		United States
70.9	77.5	1992	54,754	6.2	7.2[20]	59.8[20]	33.0[20]	23.6[20]	52.3[20]	24.1[20]	H 863	H 3.3	H 0.9	73.8	...	...		Uruguay
65.1	71.8	1994	176,300	7.8	2.3[18]	87.4[18]	10.3[18]	37.9[18]	55.2[18]	6.9[18]	H 3,415	H 5.5	H 2.4	95.8	226,276	33.8		Uzbekistan
65.0	69.0	...	...	...	...	...	...	...	...	...	H 28	H 5.1	H 2.2	...	113	2.4		Vanuatu
70.1	76.0	1992	108,955	5.4	10.7[4]	61.3[4]	28.0[4]	30.4[4]	51.7[4]	17.9[4]	H 2,707	H 5.3	H 2.2	47.0	...	...		Venezuela
66.0	69.0	...	...	...	...	...	...	...	...	...	H 12,958[51]	H 4.8[51]	H 1.9[51]	...	...	...		Vietnam
66.7	70.7	1993	3,646	35.1	0.4	33.6	66.0	1.9	45.9	52.2	H 32	H 3.1	H 1.0	38.4	...	...		Virgin Islands (U.S.)
65.7	67.5	...	...	...	...	...	...	...	...	...	...	...	...	...	...	...		West Bank
59.8	63.1	...	...	...	...	...	...	...	...	...	...	...	...	...	...	...		Western Sahara
57.4	58.4	...	...	...	...	...	...	...	...	...	H 1,848	H 5.6	...	...	...	...		Yemen
69.1	74.3	1995	60,325	5.7	2.3	64.5	33.2	18.7	63.5	17.8	H 2,870	H 3.6	H 0.9	...	...	...		Yugoslavia
42.2	43.7	...	...	...	...	...	...	...	...	...	H 1,370	H 4.4	H 2.1	...	...	...		Zambia
58.0	62.0	...	...	...	...	...	...	...	...	...	H 2,166	H 4.8	1.1	95.8	...	...		Zimbabwe

includes Eritrea. [31]1987. [32]First marriages only. [33]1993–95. [34]Muslims only. [35]Projected rates based on about 20 percent of the total deaths. [36]1997. [37]Projected rates based on about 10 percent of the total deaths. [38]Registered deaths only. [39]Average annual rates for the period. [40]Includes Aruba. [41]Projected rates based on about 45 percent of the total deaths. [42]Over 21 years of age. [43]Reporting areas only (constituting about 75 percent of the total population). [44]1982. [45]Includes all deaths associated with alcoholism. [46]1990–94. [47]Projected rates based on about 70 percent of the total deaths. [48]Projected rates based on about 35 percent of the total deaths. [49]Of which AIDS, 11.8. [50]Bronchitis, pneumonia, and influenza only. [51]Private households only.

National product and accounts

This table furnishes, for most of the countries of the world, breakdowns of (1) gross national product (GNP)—its global and per capita values, purchasing power parity (PPP), and growth rates (1985–94), (2) principal industrial and accounting components of gross domestic product (GDP), and (3) principal elements of each country's balance of payments, including international goods trade, invisibles, and tourism payments.

Measures of national output. The two most commonly used measures of national output are GDP and GNP. Each of these measures represents an aggregate value of goods and services produced by a specific country. The GDP, the more basic of these, is a measure of the total value of goods and services produced entirely within a given country. The GNP, the more comprehensive value, is composed of both domestic production (GDP) and the net income from current (short-term) transactions with other countries. When the income received from other countries is greater than payments to them, a country's GNP is greater than its GDP. In theory, if all national accounts could be equilibrated, the global summation of GDP would equal GNP.

In the first section of the table, data are provided for the nominal and real GNP. ("Nominal" refers to value in current prices for the year indicated and is distinguished from a "real" valuation, which is one adjusted to eliminate the effect of recent inflation [most often] or, occasionally, of deflation between two given dates.) Both the total and per capita values of this product are denominated in U.S. dollars for ease of comparison, as is a new value for GNP per capita adjusted for purchasing power parity. The latter is a concept that provides a better approximation of the ability of equivalent values of two (or more) national currencies to purchase comparable quantities of goods and services in their respective domestic markets and may differ substantially from two otherwise equal GNP per capita values based solely on currency exchange rates. Beside these are given figures for average annual growth of total and per capita real GNP. GNP per capita provides a rough measure of annual national income per person, but values should be compared cautiously, as they are subject to a number of distortions, notably of exchange rate, but also of purchasing power parity and in the existence of elements of national production that do not enter the monetary economy in such a way as to be visible to fiscal authorities (*e.g.,* food, clothing, or housing produced and consumed within families or communal groups or services exchanged). For reasons of comparability, the majority of the data in this section are taken from the World Bank's *The World Bank Atlas* (annual).

The internal structure of the national product. GDP/GNP values allow comparison of the relative size of national economies, but further information is provided when these aggregates are analyzed according to their industrial sectors of origin, component kinds of expenditure, and cost components.

The distribution of GDP for ten industrial sectors, usually compiled from national sources, is aggregated into three major industrial groups:

1. The primary sector, composed of agriculture (including forestry and fishing) and mineral production (including fossil fuels).

National product and accounts

country	gross national product (GNP), 1995						origin of gross domestic product (GDP) by economic sector, 1994 (%)										
	nominal ('000,000 U.S.$)	per capita		average annual growth rates, 1985–95			primary		secondary			tertiary					other
		nominal (U.S.$)	purchasing power parity (PPP; U.S.$)	real GNP (%)	population (%)	real GNP per capita (%)	agriculture	mining	manufacturing	construction	public utilities	transp., communications	trade	financial svcs.	other svcs.	government	
Afghanistan	13,598[1]	600[1]	...	...	...	...	48[2]	[3]	26[2, 3]	10[2]	[3]	4[2]	10[2]		—2[2]—		—
Albania	2,199	670	...	...	...	...	55	[3]	13[3]	9	[3]	3		—19—			—
Algeria	44,609	1,600	5,300	−0.1	2.5	−2.6	10	23	9	12	—		—33—			13	—
American Samoa	128[1, 6]	2,600[1, 6]	...	...	...	...	...	...	...	...	...	...	...	...	...	...	...
Andorra	760[1, 6]	16,200[1, 6]	...	...	...	...	...	...	...	...	...	...	...	...	...	...	...
Angola	4,422	410	...	−3.1	3.0	−6.1	12	51	3	2	—	2	10	—	—19—		—
Antigua and Barbuda	495[1]	7,690[1]	...	...	...	...	4	1	2	9	4	20	25	15	7	18	−5
Argentina	278,431	8,030	8,310	3.2	1.3	1.9	6[5]	2[5]	22[5]	5[5]	2[5]	5[5]	15[5]	17[5]	—26[5]—		—
Armenia	2,752	730	2,260	−13.9	1.2	−15.1	43	[3]	29[3]	7	[3]	1	4		—15—		—
Aruba	1,256[8]	15,890[8]	...	...	...	...	...	...	...	...	...	...	...	...	...	...	...
Australia	337,909	18,720	18,940	2.8	1.4	1.4	3	4	16	7	3	9	19	22	14	4	−1
Austria	216,547	26,890	21,250	2.5	0.6	1.9	2	[9]	24[9]	8	3	6	16	19	5	14	3
Azerbaijan	3,601	480	1,460	−15.1	1.2	−16.3	30	[3]	25[3]	4	[3]	7		—34—			—
Bahamas, The	3,297	11,940	14,710	0.7	1.7	−1.0	1	15	17	6	2	11	11	19	5	19	−6
Bahrain	4,525	7,840	13,400	3.7	3.1	0.6	1	15	15	6	3	11	8	22	5	20	−7
Bangladesh	28,599	240	1,380	4.1	2.0	2.1	30	[9]	10[9]	6	2	12	8	2	24	5	—
Barbados	1,745	6,560	10,620	0.3	0.5	−0.2	4	1	6	4	3	8	27	14	4	15	16
Belarus	21,356	2,070	4,220	−4.8	0.4	−5.2	16	[3]	45[3]	9	[3]	5	9	8	7	2	—
Belgium	250,710	24,710	21,660	2.5	0.3	2.2	2	—	22	5	2	8	13[10]	18	18[10]	7	5
Belize	568	2,630	5,400	7.0	2.6	4.4	19	—	14	7	4	11	17	11	6	13	−4
Benin	2,034	370	1,760	2.6	3.0	−0.4	33	[9]	8[9]	4	1	8	20	—11—		9	5
Bermuda	1,936	31,870	...	...	...	...	...	...	...	...	...	...	...	...	...	...	...
Bhutan	295	420	1,260	6.6	2.6	4.0	38	1	10	12	7	7	8	6	—9—		3
Bolivia	5,905	800	2,540	4.0	2.3	1.7	16[11]	10[11]	14[11]	4[11]	2[11]	11[11]	11[11]	11[11]	7[11]	9[11]	6[11]
Bosnia and Herzegovina	797[1]	300[1]	...	...	...	...	...	...	...	...	...	...	...	...	...	...	...
Botswana	4,381	3,020	5,580	9.0	3.0	6.0	5	35	4	5	3	3	16	5	3	22	—
Brazil	579,787	3,640	5,400	0.9	1.6	−0.7	14	1	23	8	6	6	7	9	25	10	−9
Brunei	4,618[1]	15,800[1]	...	...	...	...	3	[9]	41[9]	5	1	4	8	8	—32—		−3
Bulgaria	11,225	1,330	4,480	−2.8	−0.6	−2.2	12	[9]	29[9]	5	[12]	7	11	15[12]	—20—		2
Burkina Faso	2,417	230	780	2.7	2.8	−0.1	30	[9]	18[9]	5	1	4	18		—20—		4
Burundi	984	160	630	1.5	2.8	−1.3	47	1[13]	11	4	[13]	4	4	—2—		15	11
Cambodia	2,718	270	...	5.0	3.0	2.0	51	—	5	8	1	3	15	—13—		4	—
Cameroon	8,615	650	2,110	−4.1	2.9	−7.0	39	9	10	2	2		—24—			13	2
Canada	573,695	19,380	21,130	1.7	1.3	0.4	3[11]	4[11]	19[11]	5[11]	3[11]	9[11]	12[11]	16[11]	22[11]	6[11]	—
Cape Verde	366	960	1,870	4.1	2.0	2.1	18[2]	—	6[2]	18[2]	3[2]	11[2]	21[2]	3[2]	1[2]	7[2]	13[2]
Central African Republic	1,123	340	1,070	0.3	2.3	−2.0	53	6	7	4	—	3	12	—5—		10	—
Chad	1,144	180	700	3.0	2.5	0.5	21	—	6	1	—		—12—		—5—		55
Chile	59,151	4,160	9,520	7.7	1.6	6.1	8	8	17	6	3	8	17	17	7	3	7
China	744,890	620	2,920	9.3	1.3	8.0	21	[3]	41[3]	6	[3]	6	9		—17—		—
Colombia	70,263	1,910	6,130	4.6	1.8	2.8	13	4	19	6	3	10		—33—			—
Comoros	237	470	1,320	1.4	2.8	−1.4	39[11]	...	4[11]	7[11]	1[11]	4[11]	27[11]	[14]	3[11]	14[11, 14]	—
Congo, Dem. Rep. of the	5,313	120	490	−5.3	3.2	−8.5	58	5	5	2	2	3	16	—6—		3	1
Congo, Rep. of the	1,784	680	2,050	−0.1	3.1	−3.2	11	33	8	2	1	8	12	—8—		14	3
Costa Rica	8,884	2,610	5,850	5.4	2.5	2.9	16	[9]	19[9]	3	4	5	20	11	7	14	—
Côte d'Ivoire	9,248	660	1,580	−0.9	3.4	−4.3	31	—	18	—2—		8	18	—8—		10	5
Croatia	15,508	3,250	...	...	...	...	11	[9]	28[9]	2	—	4	16	8	—30—		—
Cuba	14,353[1]	1,300[1]	...	...	...	...	...	...	...	...	...	...	...	...	...	...	...
Cyprus[15]	8,616	13,420	...	6.7	2.1	4.6	5	—	13	9	2	8	19	16	7	13	7
Czech Republic	39,990	3,870	9,770	−1.8	0.0	−1.8	5[2]	[4]	28[2, 4]	4[2]	6[2]	6[2]	8[2]		—29[2]—		13[2]
Denmark	156,027	29,890	21,230	1.7	0.2	1.5	4	1	19	5	2	10	14	19	5	22	−2
Djibouti	495[1]	850[1]	...	...	...	...	3[11]	—	5[11]	5[11]	8[11]	15	15[11]	9[11]	4[11]	23[11]	12[11]
Dominica	218	2,990	...	3.9	−0.1	4.0	17	1	6	7	4	15	12	12	1	16	9
Dominican Republic	11,390	1,460	3,870	4.1	2.0	2.1	13	2	18	9	2	10	18	10	8	9	—
Ecuador	15,997	1,390	4,220	3.1	2.3	0.8	17	15	15	3	1	9	15	12	6	7	1
Egypt	45,507	790	3,820	3.3	2.2	1.1	15	[9]	25[9]	5	2	10	17	5	—7—		13

2. The secondary sector, composed of manufacturing, construction, and public utilities.
3. The tertiary sector, which includes transportation and communications, trade (wholesale and retail), restaurants and hotels, financial services (including banking, real estate, insurance, and business services), other services (community, social, and personal), and government services.

Percentages in this section of the table may not add to 100 because the value of each economic sector is calculated as a percentage of the total GDP, which may contain adjustments such as import duties and bank service charges that are not distributed by sector.

There are three major domestic components of GDP expenditure: private consumption (analyzed in greater detail in the "Household budgets and consumption" table), government spending, and gross domestic investment. The fourth, nondomestic, component of GDP expenditure is net foreign trade; values are given for both exports (a positive value) and imports (a negative value, representing obligations to other countries). The sum of these five percentages, excluding statistical discrepancies and rounding, should be 100% of the GDP.

The structure of GDP as accounted by cost components here comprises four general categories: indirect taxes (excise or value-added taxes), net of subsidies; consumption of fixed capital (depreciation); and two income categories: (a) compensation of employees (salaries, wages, etc.) and (b) net operating surplus ("profits," interests, rent, etc.).

Balance of payments (external account transactions). The external account records the sum (net) of all economic transactions of a current nature between one country and the rest of the world. The account shows a country's net of overseas receipts and obligations, including not only the trade of goods and merchandise but also such invisible items as services, interest and dividends, short- and long-term investments, tourism, transfers to or from overseas residents, etc. Each transaction gives rise either to a foreign claim for payment, recorded as a deficit (*e.g.,* from imports, capital outflows), or a foreign obligation to pay, recorded as a surplus (*e.g.,* from exports, capital inflows) or a domestic claim on another country. Any international transaction automatically creates a deficit in the balance of payments of one country and a surplus in that of another. Values are given in U.S. dollars for comparability.

Tourist trade. Net income or expenditure from tourism (in U.S. dollars for comparability) is often a significant element in a country's balance of payments. Receipts from foreign nationals reflect payments for goods and services from foreign currency resources by tourists in the given country. Expenditures by nationals abroad are also payments for goods and services, but in this case made by the residents of the given country as tourists abroad. The majority of the data in this section are compiled by the World Tourism Organization.

gross domestic product (GDP) by type of expenditure, 1994(%)					cost components of gross domestic product (GDP), 1994 (%)				balance of payments, 1995 (current external transactions; '000,000 U.S.$)			tourist trade, 1995 ('000,000 U.S.$)		country
consumption		gross domestic invest-ment	foreign trade		indirect taxes net of subsides	consump-tion of fixed capital	compen-sation of employ-ees	net operating surplus	net transfers		current balance of payments	receipts from foreign nationals	expendi-tures by nationals abroad	
private	govern-ment		exports	imports					goods, merchan-dise	invisibles				
...	...	...	...	...	...	...	...	...	...	...	...	1[4]	1[4]	Afghanistan
—170[5]—		10[5]	12[5]	−92[5]	...	13[4]	62[4]	25[4]	−474.8	463.3	−11.5	7	5	Albania
56	17	32	24	−28	...	...	...	...	60	−2,370	−2,310	27	135	Algeria
...	...	...	...	...	...	...	...	...	...	...	...	10[6]	...	American Samoa
...	...	...	...	...	...	...	...	...	...	...	...	...	...	Andorra
56	34	14	66	−70	7[4]	[7]	39[4]	54[4, 7]	1,369[8]	−2,241[8]	−872[8]	13[8]	66[3]	Angola
53	21	24	106	−104	15		—85—		−253.7[8]	235.7[8]	−18.0[8]	329	24[8]	Antigua and Barbuda
—82—		20	7	−9	...	...	...	...	2,237	−4,627	−2,390	4,306	2,067	Argentina
87[2]	16[2]	9[2]	44[2]	−57[2]	...	...	...	...	−179[8]	81[8]	−98[8]	...	...	Armenia
62	16	27	36	−41	...	...	...	...	−425.3	425.0	−0.3	521	73	Aruba
62	18	22	19	−20	12	15	49	24	−4,168	−15,892	−20,060	7,100	4,604	Australia
55	19	26	37	−37	14	13	52	22	−5,103	261	−4,842	14,618	11,687	Austria
69	24	21	58	−71	3	25	24	48	...	...	...	146	70	Azerbaijan
76[2]	15[2]	21[2]	44[2]	−56[2]	14[5]	[7]	52[5]	34[5, 7]	−901.4	689.2	−212.2	1,346	213	Bahamas, The
30	25	26	107	−88	3[2]	17[2]	44[2]	35[2]	768.6	−211.6	557.0	288	163	Bahrain
78	14	14	12	−18	7		—93—		−2,324.1	1,500.2	−823.9	23	229	Bangladesh
64	20	13	49	−47	16		—84—		−440.0	549.6	109.6	680	52[3]	Barbados
63	21	29	72	−85	9[2]	20[2]	49[2]	22[2]	−542[8]	−3[8]	−545[8]	...	...	Belarus
63	15	18	72	−67	10	9	53	27	10,206	4,807	15,013	5,719	9,215	Belgium
66	17	23	53	−59	15[5]	6[5]	—78[5]—		−66.1	48.9	−17.2	78	21	Belize
78	12	20	31	−41	...	...	...	...	−65[8]	101[8]	36[8]	27	6[8]	Benin
69	13	12	61	−55	...	...	...	...	−498	576	78	488	140[3]	Bermuda
53	18	45	31	−47	4	9	—87—		−26.7	−21.5	−48.2	5	...	Bhutan
75	14	16	23	−28	...	...	...	...	−182.3	−146.1	−328.4	146	148	Bolivia
...	...	...	...	...	...	...	...	...	...	...	...	...	...	Bosnia and Herzegovina
43	31	26	51	−51	10[2]	13[2]	31[2]	45[2]	585.7	−243.6	342.1	162	145	Botswana
63	15	21	9	−7	14		—86—		−3,157	−14,979	−18,136	2,171	4,245	Brazil
...	...	...	...	...	...	...	...	...	...	...	...	...	...	Brunei
71	16	13	43	−44	6[2]	13[2]	52[2]	27[2]	431.8	−137.9	293.9	473	195	Bulgaria
78	16	22	14	−30	4		—96—		−128.7[8]	143.6[8]	14.9[8]	22	23[8]	Burkina Faso
84	16	13	12	−25	11		—89—		−63.1	56.6	−6.5	1	25	Burundi
83	11	19	11	−25	...	...	...	...	−331.9	146.0	−185.9	100	8	Cambodia
72	8	16	28	−23	2		—98—		502.4[2]	−1,067.8[2]	−565.4[2]	47[2]	225[2]	Cameroon
60	20	19	33	−33	13	13	55	19	22,341	−31,034	−8,693	8,012	10,220	Canada
82	24	42	—−48—		13[2]		—87[2]—		−223.8	185.1	−38.8	10	12	Cape Verde
76	15	13	22	−27	6		—94—		15.3	−40.0	−24.7	6[2]	43[8]	Central African Republic
87	14	16	22	−39	...	...	...	...	−76.8[8]	39.1[8]	−37.7[8]	36[8]	26[8]	Chad
62	9	27	28	−27	...	...	...	...	1,383	−1,226	157	990	774	Chile
51[2]	9[2]	41[2]	24[2]	−25[2]	...	...	...	...	18,050	−16,432	1,618	8,733	3,688	China
69	13	22	16	−20	10[5]	[7]	39[5]	51[5, 7]	−2,548	−1,568	−4,116	851	822	Colombia
80	22	19	14	−35	...	...	...	...	−29[8]	20[8]	−9[8]	8[5]	6[5]	Comoros
86	8	3	13	−10	...	...	...	...	643[8]	−1,058[8]	−415[8]	6[2]	16[2]	Congo, Dem. Rep. of the
55	22	51	64	−93	...	...	...	...	522.5	−1,092.7	−570.2	4	39	Congo, Rep. of the
60	17	27	39	−43	13[2]	2[2]	50[2]	35[2]	−473.5	330.5	−143.0	660	312	Costa Rica
65	13	12	44	−33	...	...	...	...	1,470.5	−1,739.8	−269.3	72	159	Côte d'Ivoire
71	27	3	—−1—		11[4]	13[4]	62[4]	14[4]	−2,126.2	414.2	−1,712.0	1,584	771	Croatia
...	...	...	...	...	...	...	...	...	...	...	...	1,100	...	Cuba
60	17	24	49	−49	7	11	—83—		−2,085.5	1,872.9	−212.6	1,783	293	Cyprus[15]
58	22	20	52	−53	...	...	...	...	−3,685	2,311	−1,374	2,875	1,630	Czech Republic
54	26	15	35	−29	14[2]	10[2]	54[2]	23[2]	6,820	−5,213	1,607	3,672	4,280	Denmark
71	38	12	47	−67	13		—87—		−171.5	148.5	−23.0	13[2]	7[2]	Djibouti
71	23	24	—−17—		16		—84—		−51.9[8]	16.1[8]	−35.7[8]	33	5	Dominica
75	5	23	24	−27	12[2]	6[2]	—82[2]—		−1,792.0	1,666.8	−125.2	1,604	85	Dominican Republic
69	9	19	27	−24	12[2]	[7]	14[2]	74[2, 7]	267	−1,089	−822	255	235	Ecuador
75	10	20	23	−28	4[2]	4[2]	27[2]	64[2]	−7,597	7,343	−254	2,800	1,278	Egypt

National product and accounts

country	gross national product (GNP), 1995						origin of gross domestic product (GDP) by economic sector, 1994 (%)										
	nominal ('000,000 U.S.$)	per capita		average annual growth rates, 1985–95			primary		secondary			tertiary					other
		nominal (U.S.$)	purchasing power parity (PPP; U.S.$)	real GNP (%)	population (%)	real GNP per capita (%)	agriculture	mining	manufacturing	construction	public utilities	transp., communications	trade	financial svcs.	other svcs.	government	
El Salvador	9,057	1,610	2,610	4.7	1.8	2.9	14	—	21	4	1	18	17	12	18	6	—
Equatorial Guinea	152	380	...	4.8	2.5	2.3	47	[9]	21[9]	5	3	2	9	2	3	5	2
Eritrea	1,900[1]	570[1]	...	...	...	...	18	—	12	4	1	13	28	4	3	10	7
Estonia	4,252	2,860	...	−4.6	−0.3	−4.3	9	2	17	6	3	9	19	8	8	4	16
Ethiopia	5,722	100	450	2.1	2.6	−0.5	54	[4]	8[4]	3	1	5	10	8	4	7	—
Faroe Islands	670[1]	15,000[1]	...	...	...	...	15[2]	—	13[2]	4[2]	1[2]	9[2]	11[2]	7[2]	24[2]	16[2]	−10[2]
Fiji	1,985	2,440	5,780	3.4	1.1	2.3	22	—	12	3	1	15	21	12	—16—		−3
Finland	105,174	20,580	17,760	0.2	0.4	−0.2	5	—	25	5	3	9	11	19	3	20	−1
France	1,451,051	24,990	21,030	2.0	0.5	1.5	3	1	20	5	3	6	14[16]	6	18[16]	19	6
French Guiana	1,543	10,580	...	...	...	...	10[6]	[3]	11[3,6]	16[6]	[3]	17[6]	16[6]		—30[6]—		—
French Polynesia	3,699[1]	16,940[1]	...	...	...	...	5[4]	—	7[4]	6[4]	2[4]	[17]	23[4]	—29[4,17]—		29[4]	−1[4]
Gabon	3,759	3,490	...	1.3	2.9	−1.6	9	45	5	4	2	5	7	1	10	11	—
Gambia, The	354	320	930	4.3	4.0	0.3	21	—	6	4	1	18	17	6	4	11	13
Gaza Strip	979[8]	1,160[8]	...	...	...	...	13	—	10	8	2	5	15	23	8	16	—
Georgia	2,358	440	1,470	−16.8	0.2	−17.0	29	[3]	21[3]	5	[3]	9	6		—29—		—
Germany	2,252,343	27,510	20,070	...	...	...	1	2[13]	23	5	[13]	5	8	13	19	9	16
Ghana	6,719	390	1,990	4.5	3.0	1.5	47	2	9	3	2	4	19	4	—9—		—
Gibraltar	205[1,2]	6,600[1,2]	...	...	...	...	...	...	...	...	...	...	...	...	...	...	...
Greece	85,885	8,210	11,710	1.7	0.5	1.2	15	1	15	6	3	7	14	3	10	19	8
Greenland	893[1]	15,500[1]	...	...	...	...	...	...	...	...	...	...	...	...	...	...	...
Grenada	271	2,980	...	...	...	...	12	—	6	7	4	23	21	13	3	17	−6
Guadeloupe	3,706[1]	9,200[1]	...	...	...	...	...	...	...	...	...	...	...	...	...	...	...
Guam	3,033[8]	20,300[8]	...	...	...	...	...	...	...	...	...	...	...	...	...	...	...
Guatemala	14,255	1,340	3,340	3.2	2.9	0.3	24	—	14	2	3	9	24	9	6	8	—
Guernsey[18]	1,531[5]	26,000[5]	...	...	...	...	...	...	...	...	...	...	...	...	...	...	...
Guinea	3,593	550	...	4.2	2.8	1.4	24	19	5	7	—	5	—26—		6	5	3
Guinea-Bissau	265	250	790	3.7	1.9	1.8	52	[3]	11[3]	4	[3]	2	25	—1—		4	1
Guyana	493	590	2,420	1.4	0.6	0.8	31	18	10[19]	3	[19]	4	4	6	1	7	16
Haiti	1,777	250	910	−3.2	2.0	−5.2	41	—	11	2	1	1	11	—12—		20	1
Honduras	3,566	600	1,900	3.2	3.0	0.2	24	2	18	6	3	5	10	15	10	7	—
Hong Kong	142,332	22,990	22,950	6.1	1.3	4.8	—	—	9	5	2	9	26	25	—15—		10
Hungary	42,129	4,120	6,410	−1.3	−0.3	−1.0	6	[9]	20[9]	5	3	8	11	18	—19—		10
Iceland	6,686	24,950	20,460	1.4	1.1	0.3	9[11]	—	13[11]	6[11]	3[11]	6[11]	10[11]	15[11]	5[11]	14[11]	18[11]
India	319,660	340	1,400	5.0	1.9	3.1	31	2	17	6	3	8	13	9	6	5	—
Indonesia	190,105	980	3,800	7.7	1.7	6.0	17	8	24	7	1	7	17	7	6	5	—
Iran	303,740[1]	4,700[1]	...	...	...	...	21	19	13	3	1	6	15	9	2	10	−1
Iraq	41,288[1]	2,000[1]	...	...	...	...	35[5]	—	9[5]	4[5]	—	10[5]	26[5]	8[5]	—12[5]—		−5[5]
Ireland	52,765	14,710	15,680	5.3	0.1	5.2	9	[20]	38[20]	[20]	[20]	—16—		—31—		6	—
Isle of Man	780[5]	10,800[5]	...	...	...	...	2[6]	—	12[6]	8[6]	3[6]	9[6]	[21]	27[6]	33[6,21]	6[6]	—
Israel	87,875	15,920	16,490	5.2	2.7	2.5	3[5]	[9]	22[5,9]	8[5]	2[5]	8[5]	10[5]	25[5]	4[5]	23[5]	−5[5]
Italy	1,088,085	19,020	19,870	1.8	0.1	1.7	3	[9]	21[9]	5	6	6	18	14	14	12	1
Jamaica	3,803	1,510	3,540	4.6	0.9	3.7	10	8	20	13	2	9	25	14	5	4	−9
Japan	4,963,587	39,640	22,110	3.3	0.4	2.9	2[11]	—	25[11]	10[11]	3[11]	7[11]	13[10,11]	18[11]	19[10,11]	8[11]	−4[11]
Jersey	2,198[1,8]	25,920[1,8]	...	...	...	...	5[4]	—		—2[4]—				—93[4]—			—
Jordan	6,354	1,510	4,060	1.9	4.7	−2.8	8	3	14	7	2	16	10	17	4	19	−1
Kazakstan	22,143	1,330	3,010	−8.1	0.5	−8.6	12	[3]	26	9	[3]	8	8		—37—		—
Kenya	7,583	280	1,380	3.0	2.9	0.1	29	—	11	5	1	8	15	19	—12—		—
Kiribati	73	920	...	1.7	2.0	−0.3	23	—	1	2	2	12	16	4	—29—		12
Korea, North	22,300[1]	950[1]	...	...	...	...	...	...	...	...	...	...	...	...	...	...	...
Korea, South	435,137	9,700	11,450	8.5	0.9	7.6	7	—	29	11	2	8	13	17	6	6	—
Kuwait	28,941	17,390	23,790	0.6	−0.3	0.9	—	39	11	3	—	4	7	12	—25—		−1
Kyrgyzstan	3,158	700	1,800	−5.7	1.2	−6.9	38	[3]	21[3]	3	[3]	4	10	5	—12—		6
Laos	1,694	350	...	...	...	...	56	—	13	3	2	5	9	5	—5—		2
Latvia	5,708	2,270	3,370	−7.0	−0.4	−6.6	6	[9]	15[9]	5	3	15	7	5	33	10	—
Lebanon	10,673	2,660	...	5.0	2.3	2.7	8	—	12	5	5	3	26	13	8	18	—
Lesotho	1,519	770	1,780	3.9	2.4	1.5	11	—	14	22	2	3	9	12	3	12	14
Liberia	2,300[1,8]	770[1,8]	...	...	...	...	...	...	...	...	...	...	...	...	...	...	...
Libya	32,900[1,8]	6,510[1,8]	...	...	...	...	7[5]	25[5]	8[5]	13[5]	2[5]	6[5]	9[5]	12[5]	7[5]	10[5]	—
Liechtenstein	993[1,2]	33,000[1,2]	...	...	...	...	...	...	...	...	...	...	...	...	...	...	...
Lithuania	7,070	1,900	4,120	−11.2	0.5	−11.7	15[2]	[9]	26[2,9]	7[2]	5[2]	8[2]	17[2]	6[2]	5[2]	7[2]	5[2]
Luxembourg	16,876	41,210	37,930	2.1	1.1	1.0	1[6]	—	24[6]	7[6]	2[6]	7[6]	16[6]	14[6]	15[6]	15[6]	−2[6]
Macau	7,555[1]	18,100[1]	...	...	...	...	...	...	...	...	...	...	...	...	...	...	...
Macedonia	1,813	860	...	...	...	...	19	[9]	38[9]	6	—	4	25		—7—		—
Madagascar	3,178	230	640	1.1	3.1	−2.0	37	[9]		—13[9]—				—41—		5	5
Malaŵi	1,623	170	750	2.4	3.1	−0.7	31	—	14	4	3	5	12	11	5	16	−2
Malaysia	78,321	3,890	9,020	8.2	2.5	5.7	15	7	31	4	2	7	12	11	2	10	−2
Maldives	251	990	3,080	9.9	3.2	6.7	8	2	6[19]	9	[19]	7	19	40	—9—		—
Mali	2,410	250	550	3.4	2.8	0.6	41[11]	3[11]	6[11]	5[11]	1[11]	4[11]	19[11]	1[11]	7[11]	6[11]	6[11]
Malta	4,461[1]	12,000[1]	...	...	...	...	3	[22]	24	3[22]	8	7		—39—		16	—
Marshall Islands	106[1]	1,890[1]	...	...	...	...	16	—	1	10	2	5	19	17	—27—		2
Martinique	3,948[1]	10,000[1]	...	...	...	...	...	...	...	...	...	...	...	...	...	...	...
Mauritania	1,049	460	1,540	3.0	2.5	0.5	23	10	10	—8—		6	14	—7—		11	11
Mauritius	3,815	3,380	13,210	6.7	1.0	5.7	9	—	24	8	2	12	18	11	6	11	—
Mayotte	54[8]	600[8]	...	...	...	...	...	...	...	...	...	...	...	...	...	...	...
Mexico	304,596	3,320	6,400	2.2	2.1	0.1	7	3	22	6	2	8	25	12	—17—		−2
Micronesia	215	2,010	...	...	...	...	...	...	...	...	...	...	...	...	...	...	...
Moldova	3,996	920	...	−7.8	0.4	−8.2	48	[9]	24[9]	2	1	1	4		—20—		—
Monaco	788[1,8]	25,000[1,8]	...	...	...	...	...	...	...	...	...	...	...	...	...	...	...
Mongolia	767	310	1,950	−1.3	2.5	−3.8	34	[9]	32[9]	2	—	4	14		—13—		1
Morocco	29,545	1,110	3,340	2.8	2.0	0.8	19	2	17	4	8	6	20	...	12	12	—
Mozambique	1,353	80	810	5.4	1.8	3.6	31[2]	—	8[2]	11[2]	2[2]	15[2]	10[2]	—	—23[2]—		—
Myanmar (Burma)	83,419	1,790	...	...	...	...	61	1	8	1	—	2	22	—	—5—		—
Namibia	3,098	2,000	4,150	5.5	2.7	2.8	14	16	9	3	1	5	10	12	1	26	3
Nauru	81[8]	8,070[8]	...	...	...	...	...	...	...	...	...	...	...	...	...	...	...
Nepal	4,391	200	1,170	4.9	2.5	2.4	42	1	9	11	1	7	5	10	—9—		4

gross domestic product (GDP) by type of expenditure, 1994 (%)					cost components of gross domestic product (GDP), 1994 (%)				balance of payments, 1995 (current external transactions; '000,000 U.S.$)			tourist trade, 1995 ('000,000 U.S.$)		country
consumption		gross domestic investment	foreign trade		indirect taxes net of subsides	consumption of fixed capital	compensation of employees	net operating surplus	net transfers		current balance of payments	receipts from foreign nationals	expenditures by nationals abroad	
private	government		exports	imports					goods, merchandise	invisibles				
87	8	20	20	−35	6[5]	4[5]	90[5]		−1,523.2	1,201.0	−322.2	75	72	El Salvador
59	16	25	55	−55	...	...	...	...	30.7[8]	−32.4[8]	−1.7[8]	...	...	Equatorial Guinea
...	...	...	...	...	10		90		−131.7[8]	175.8[8]	44.1[8]	...	...	Eritrea
59	23	29	80	−91	12[2]	12[2]	50[2]	25[2]	−673.6	508.2	−165.4	353	90	Estonia
84	11	15	12	−22	...	...	...	...	−724.9	696.6	−28.3	36	25	Ethiopia
49[2]	34[2]	4[2]	44[2]	−32[2]	...	...	...	...	51.6	94.4	146.0	...	...	Faroe Islands
67[2]	20[2]	15[2]	56[2]	−59[2]	13[2]	7[2]	34[2]	46[2]	−246.0	246.1	0.1	312	55	Fiji
56	22	15	36	−29	11	17	51	20	12,346	−6,961	5,385	1,716	2,383	Finland
60	20	18	23	−21	13	13	52	23	11,175	5,268	16,443	27,527	16,328	France
...	...	...	...	...	8[5]	[7]	61[5]	31[5,7]	...	...		...	...	French Guiana
60[4]	40[4]	21[4]	9[4]	−31[4]	...	...	...	...	...	...	...	260	...	French Polynesia
31	17	27	65	−40	3		97		1,592.9[8]	1,273.2[8]	319.7[8]	4	112	Gabon
79	18	16	44	−57	16		84		−37.6	29.4	−8.2	23	16	Gambia, The
149[5]	16[5]	41[5]	19[5]	−84[5]	...	...	...	...	...	...	...	...	...	Gaza Strip
89[2]	9[2]	32[2]	36[2]	−66[2]	...	...	...	...	−363[8]	172[8]	−191[8]	...	...	Georgia
57	19	23	23	−22	12[2]	13[2]	54[2]	21[2]	66,270	−87,090	−20,820	16,221	50,675	Germany
85	11	16	27	−39	...	...	...	...	−353.1[8]	89.3[8]	−263.8[8]	233	20[8]	Ghana
...	...	...	...	...	...	...	...	...	...	...	...	90[2]	...	Gibraltar
74	14	21	17	−26	14[2]	9[2]	36[2]	41[2]	−14,425	11,561	−2,864	4,106	1,322	Greece
...	...	...	...	...	...	...	...	...	...	...	...	...	...	Greenland
50	19	36	50	−55	16		84		−99.3	66.5	−32.9	58	4	Grenada
...	...	...	...	...	11[5]	[7]	78[5]	11[5,7]	...	...	...	458	...	Guadeloupe
...	...	...	...	...	...	...	...	...	...	...	...	950[2]	...	Guam
86	6	16	18	−25	6[4]	2[4]	92[4]		−877.1	304.9	−572.2	277	174	Guatemala
...	...	...	...	...	...	...	...	...	...	...	...	146[2]	...	Guernsey[18]
82	9	14	20	−24	...	...	...	...	−39.0	−157.7	−196.7	1	21	Guinea
88	9	22	19	−38	...	...	...	...	−35.4	−6.0	−41.5	...	...	Guinea-Bissau
64	18	32	108	−122	16		84		−40.8	−94.0	−134.8	47	21	Guyana
101	6	2	4	−12	1		99		−414.7	348.1	−66.6	81	35	Haiti
63	10	38	39	−50	14[2]	6[2]	48[2]	32[2]	−141.4	−59.5	−200.9	80	57	Honduras
59	8	32	140	−138	6[2]	[7]	47[2]	46[2,7]	...	...	...	9,604	...	Hong Kong
72	13	21	29	−35	16[2]	[7]	54[2]	34[2,7]	−2,433	−102	−2,535	1,723	1,070	Hungary
59	21	15	36	−31	17[2]	13[2]	50[2]	14[2]	206.0	−155.0	51.0	167	282	Iceland
65[2]	12[2]	23[2]	12[2]	−12[2]	10[2]	10[2]	80[2]		−4,788	−775	−5,563	2,574	470[5]	India
57	8	32	26	−24	7[2]	5[2]	88[2]		5,710	−12,733	−7,023	5,228	2,172	Indonesia
56	13	24	25	−18	2[4]	15[4]	84[4]		5,697	−2,219	3,478	160	862[2]	Iran
48[6]	35[6]	19[6]	3[6]	−5[6]	−7[6]	10[6]	45[6]	52[6]	...	...	...	55[4]	...	Iraq
60	16	14	72	−63	10[2]	9[2]	50[2]	31[2]	13,125	−11,746	1,379	2,688	2,030	Ireland
...	...	...	...	...	...	...	...	...	...	...	...	...	...	Isle of Man
64	28	24	33	−48	17[2]	14[2]	49[2]	20[2]	−7,694	2,412	−5,282	2,784	3,148	Israel
63	17	17	23	−20	10[2]	12[2]	44[2]	34[2]	44,082	−18,376	25,706	27,451	12,419	Italy
64	12	31	58	−66	...	...	...	...	−813.2	568.0	−245.2	1,069	148	Jamaica
59	10	29	9	−7	7	16	56	21	131,790	−20,750	111,040	3,226	36,792	Japan
...	...	...	...	...	...	...	...	...	...	...	...	526[4]	...	Jersey
66	24	35	50	−74	16	11	38	35	−1,579.4[8]	1,181.4[8]	−398.0[8]	696	420	Jordan
43[2]	14[2]	49[2]	33[2]	−39[2]	...	...	...	...	−439[8]	100[8]	−339[8]	...	...	Kazakstan
62	15	20	38	−34	15[2]	[7]	35[2]	50[2,7]	−738.1	337.7	−400.4	454	135	Kenya
...	...	...	...	...	12		88		...	...	...	1	3[8]	Kiribati
...	...	...	...	...	...	...	...	...	...	...	...	...	...	Korea, North
54	11	36	30	−31	11[2]	10[2]	47[2]	31[2]	−4,746	−3,505	−8,251	5,587	5,903	Korea, South
41	34	16	51	−43	...	...	...	...	5,478	−1,280	4,198	107	2,322	Kuwait
66	20	20	33	−39	6		94		−95.7[8]	−21.8[8]	−117.5[8]	5	6	Kyrgyzstan
90[6]	10[6]	13[6]	13[6]	−25[6]	2		98		−199.2	−31.1	−230.3	51	30	Laos
52[2]	22[2]	9[2]	73[2]	−57[2]	13	12	46	29	−580	553	−27	20	24	Latvia
110[4]	44[4]	10[4]	32[4]	−96[4]	...	...	...	...	...	...	...	672[8]	...	Lebanon
89	19	84	21	−114	18		82		−666.7[8]	774.8[8]	108.1[8]	17[8]	7[8]	Lesotho
58[4]	13[4]	10[4]	42[4]	−23[4]	...	...	...	...	...	...	...	...	...	Liberia
34[6]	27[6]	22[6]	46[6]	−28[6]	...	...	...	...	3,777[4]	−1,576[4]	2,201[4]	7[8]	154[5]	Libya
...	...	...	...	...	...	...	...	...	...	...	...	...	...	Liechtenstein
76[2]	13[2]	18[2]	71[2]	−78[2]	10[5]	2[5]	39[5]	50[5]	−697.9	83.5	−614.4	124	138	Lithuania
49	11	19	94	−73	16[5]	11[5]	66[5]	8[5]	−1,599[8]	3,512[8]	1,913[8]	290[4]	...	Luxembourg
30	8	33	69	−39	...	...	...	...	...	...	...	3,117	117	Macau
57	6	42	44	−49	11[2]	[7]	67[2]	22[2,7]	−433[8]	106[8]	−327[8]	19	24[8]	Macedonia
90	7	11	22	−30	...	...	...	...	−122	−154	−276	60	59	Madagascar
69	23	13	30	−35	7		93		−276.4[8]	−173.2[8]	−449.2[8]	6	15[8]	Malawi
50	13	39	90	−91	14[5]		86[5]		−100	−7,262	−7,362	3,910	1,737[8]	Malaysia
49[4]	22[4]	19[4]	62[4]	−53[4]	...	...	...	...	−139.3[2]	91.7[2]	−47.6[2]	210	32[8]	Maldives
88	13	25	22	−48	4		96		−101.9[8]	−62.5[8]	−164.4[8]	17	56	Mali
61	21	30	97	−110	11	6	46	38	−747.6	345.7	−401.9	606	184	Malta
...	...	...	...	...	4[6]	4[6]	70[6]	22[6]	−50.7[8]	54.6[8]	3.9[8]	2[8]	...	Marshall Islands
...	...	...	...	...	10[5]	[7]	71[5]	19[5,7]	...	...	...	384	...	Martinique
83	10	16	42	−51	...	...	...	...	183.8	−161.7	22.1	15[4]	31[4]	Mauritania
64	12	32	57	−66	15	[7]	42	43[7]	−240.5	218.6	−21.9	430	159	Mauritius
47[4]	92[4]	3[4]	−42[4]		...	...	...	...	...	...	...	...	...	Mayotte
70	12	23	13	−18	9	11	29	50	7,089	−7,743	−654	6,164	3,153	Mexico
162		—	34	−96	...	...	...	...	−112.0[8]	109.5[8]	−2.5[8]	...	...	Micronesia
51	20	35	−6		...	...	...	...	−32.4	−62.3	−94.7	57	56	Moldova
...	...	...	...	...	...	...	...	...	...	...	...	...	...	Monaco
66[2]	18[2]	19[2]	63[2]	−66[2]	[23]	22[4]	39[4]	40[4,23]	25.3	13.6	38.9	...	...	Mongolia
67	17	21	21	−27	...	...	...	...	−2,397	876	−1,521	1,163	302	Morocco
66	20	70	23	−79	...	...	...	...	−869.0[8]	563.6[8]	−305.4[8]	...	...	Mozambique
88		12	1	−2	3	3	46	48	−737[8]	563[8]	−174[8]	38	16[5]	Myanmar (Burma)
49	31	24	54	−59	16[2]	[7]	46[2]	38[2,7]	−98.1	148.1	50.0	263	82	Namibia
...	...	...	...	...	...	...	...	...	...	...	...	...	...	Nauru
77	8	22	24	−32	6		94		−961.0	604.6	−356.4	117	136	Nepal

National product and accounts

country	gross national product (GNP), 1995						origin of gross domestic product (GDP) by economic sector, 1994 (%)										
	nominal ('000,000 U.S.$)	per capita		average annual growth rates, 1985–95			primary		secondary			tertiary					other
		nominal (U.S.$)	purchasing power parity (PPP; U.S.$)	real GNP (%)	popu-lation (%)	real GNP per capita (%)	agri-culture	mining	manu-factur-ing	con-struc-tion	public util-ities	transp., commu-nications	trade	finan-cial svcs.	other svcs.	govern-ment	
Netherlands, The	371,039	24,000	19,950	2.4	0.6	1.8	4	3	19	6	2	7	16	—48—			−4
Netherlands Antilles	2,127[1, 8]	10,400[1, 8]	...	...	...	...	...	...	...	...	...	...	...	...	...	...	...
New Caledonia	1,476[1]	8,000[1]	...	...	...	...	2[4]	4[4]	13[4]	6[4]	3[4]	6[4]	23[4]	—20[4]—		25[4]	−2[4]
New Zealand	51,655	14,340	16,360	1.6	1.0	0.6	9[2]	1[2]	18[2]	3[2]	3[2]	8[2]	15[2]	22[2]	6[2]	11[2]	4[2]
Nicaragua	1,659	380	2,000	−2.7	3.1	−5.8	33	1	16	3	1	4	24	5	6	7	—
Niger	1,961	220	750	1.1	3.2	−2.1	43	4	7	2	2	5	—15—		10	11	1
Nigeria	28,411	260	1,220	4.1	2.9	1.2	39	27	6	1	—	3	16	4	—	2	—
Northern Mariana Is.	524[1, 8]	10,500[1, 8]	...	...	...	...	...	...	...	...	...	...	...	...	...	...	...
Norway	136,077	31,250	21,940	2.1	0.5	1.6	3[6]	15[6]	13[6]	4[6]	4[6]	9[6]	11[6]	9[6]	10[6]	16[6]	6[6]
Oman	10,578	4,820	8,140	4.8	4.5	0.3	3	38	5	4	1	5	15	4	12	18	−6
Pakistan	59,991	460	2,230	4.2	3.0	1.2	23	—	16	3	3	9	14	7	7	7	10
Palau	82[1, 8]	5,000[1, 8]	...	...	...	...	...	...	...	...	...	...	...	...	...	...	...
Panama	7,235	2,750	5,980	1.5	1.9	−0.4	10[2]	—	8[2]	6[2]	4[2]	20[2]	13[2]	19[2]	9[2]	13[2]	−3[2]
Papua New Guinea	4,976	1,160	2,420	4.3	2.2	2.1	27	26	8	4	1	5	8	1	—15—		5
Paraguay	8,158	1,690	3,650	3.8	2.7	1.1	26	—	15	5	5	5	27	—13—		5	—
Peru	55,019	2,310	3,770	0.5	2.1	−1.6	14[11]	8[11]	22[11]	9[11]	2[11]	7[11]	18[11]	14[11]	—5[11]—		—
Philippines	71,865	1,050	2,850	3.8	2.3	1.5	22	1	25	6	3	6	15	10	—12—		—
Poland	107,829	2,790	5,400	0.0	0.4	−0.4	6	[9]	29[9]	6	4	6	14	7	13	4	11
Portugal	96,689	9,740	12,670	3.6	−0.1	3.7	6[4]	[9]	29[4, 9]	8[4]	3[4]	6[4]	17[4]	9[4]	8[4]	13[4]	—
Puerto Rico	29,016[1]	7,800[1]	...	...	...	...	1	[22]	42	2[22]	[24]	8[24]	14	13	11	10	−1
Qatar	7,448	11,600	17,690	3.2	5.8	−2.6	1	31	13	5	1	4	7	12	—27—		—
Réunion	2,864[1]	4,300[1]	...	...	...	...	4[5]	...	9[5]	6[5]	4[5]	6[5]	18[5]	21[5]	—32[5]—		—
Romania	33,488	1,480	4,360	−4.0	0.0	−4.0	20	[3]	32[3]	6	[3]	10	12	—17—			3
Russia	331,948	2,240	4,480	−4.8	0.3	−5.1	7	[3]	29[3]	8	[3]	13	16	14	10	5	—
Rwanda	1,128	180	540	−4.4	0.6	−5.0	40	[9]	14[9]	3	1	3	20	—8—		6	5
St. Kitts	212	5,170	9,410	4.2	−0.4	4.6	6	—	11	12	2	15	24	12	4	19	−5
St. Lucia	532	3,370	...	5.3	1.4	3.9	8	1	5	7	4	14	22	14	3	12	10
St. Vincent	253	2,280	...	4.7	0.8	3.9	9	—	8	10	4	18	15	9	2	15	11
Samoa	184	1,120	2,030	0.1	0.5	−0.4	42	...	12	2	7	3	11	...	11	13	—
San Marino	607[1, 8]	24,700[1, 8]	...	...	...	...	...	...	...	...	...	...	...	...	...	...	...
São Tomé and Príncipe	45	350	...	0.2	2.3	−2.1	25	—	5[19]	14	[19]	—19—		6	8	22	—
Saudi Arabia	133,540	7,040	...	2.4	4.3	−1.9	6[2]	35[2]	8[2]	8[2]	—	7[2]	7[2]	6[2]	2[2]	20[2]	2[2]
Senegal	5,070	600	1,780	1.6	2.8	−1.2	22	[9]	13[9]	3	2	10	—21—		—29—		—
Seychelles	487	6,620	...	5.4	1.2	4.2	4	[9]	11[9]	8	1	28	8	9	2	14	16
Sierra Leone	762	180	580	−1.8	1.6	−3.4	39	17	9	2	—	9	14	2	2	3	4
Singapore	79,831	26,730	22,770	8.0	1.8	6.2	—	—	28	7	2	15	18	27	—10—		−6
Slovakia	15,848	2,950	3,610	−2.3	0.3	−2.6	8	[9]	25[9]	5	6	10	16	9	10	11	—
Slovenia	16,328	8,200	...	...	...	...	5[5]	2[5]	30[5]	4[5]	2[5]	7[5]	13[5]	13[5]	14[5]	4[5]	7[5]
Solomon Islands	341	910	2,190	5.3	3.1	2.2	33	—	4	2	2	6	9	5	—24—		17
Somalia	4,582[1]	500[1]	...	...	...	...	65[6]	—	4[6]	4[6]	1[6]	6[6]	9[6]	3[6]	2[6]	6[6]	−1[6]
South Africa	130,918	3,160	5,030	1.3	2.3	−1.0	5	9	23	3	4	8	16	17	2	15	−2
Spain	532,347	13,580	14,520	2.8	0.2	2.6	3	[3]	23[3]	8	[3]	—60—					—
Sri Lanka	12,616	700	3,250	4.0	1.3	2.7	24	2	15	7	—	—52—					—
Sudan, The	24,445[1]	800[1]	...	...	...	...	37	—	9	5	2	—37—				8	—
Suriname	360	880	2,250	1.0	0.3	0.7	14	13	10	4	5	17	20	21	—	5	−10
Swaziland	1,051	1,170	2,880	3.7	3.1	0.6	10	2	29	3	1	5	7	5	5	18	16
Sweden	209,720	23,750	18,540	0.5	0.6	−0.1	2	—	22	6	3	7	11	25	—28—		−5
Switzerland	286,014	40,630	25,860	1.0	0.8	0.2	3[5]	[9]	23[5, 9]	7[5]	2[5]	6[5]	17[5]	25[5]	—21[5]—		−4[5]
Syria	15,780	1,120	5,320	4.1	3.1	1.0	29	7	5	4	1	9	29	4	2	10	1
Taiwan	263,624	12,400	...	7.8	1.0	6.8	4	—	29	5	3	7	15	21	7	11	−1
Tajikistan	1,976	340	920	−10.6	2.4	−13.0	19	[3]	35[3]	12	[3]	5	1	—9—			19
Tanzania	3,703	120	640	4.0	3.1	0.9	50	1	7	5	2	7	13	9	—4—		2
Thailand	159,630	2,740	7,540	9.7	1.3	8.4	10	1	28	7	2	7	16	10	—16—		—
Togo	1,266	310	1,130	0.2	3.0	−2.8	34	5	9	3	4	6	22	—7—		9	—
Tonga	170	1,630	...	1.1	0.9	0.2	33	[9]	4[9]	4	...	12	12	...	—12—		22
Trinidad and Tobago	4,851	3,770	8,610	−0.7	0.9	−1.6	2	27	9	7	2	9	14	13	6	10	1
Tunisia	16,369	1,820	5,000	3.9	2.1	1.8	13	4	18	4	2	8	27	—14—			10
Turkey	169,452	2,780	5,580	4.1	1.9	2.2	16	1	20	7	3	15	19	6	4	10	—
Turkmenistan	4,125	920	...	−6.3	3.3	−9.6	9	66	7	5	1	2	3	1	—2—		3
Tuvalu	8[1]	800[1]	...	...	...	...	22	2	3	14	2	4	14	10	—28—		—
Uganda	4,668	240	1,470	5.8	3.0	2.8	45	—	6	5	1	4	11	6	9	4	9
Ukraine	84,084	1,630	2,400	−9.1	0.1	−9.2	22[2]	[9]	31[2, 9]	7[2]	1[2]	12[2]	11[2]	12[2]	9[2]	4[2]	−8[2]
United Arab Emirates	42,806	17,400	16,470	2.3	5.8	−3.5	3	33	8	10	2	6	11	12	3	12	−2
United Kingdom	1,094,734	18,700	19,260	1.7	0.3	1.4	2	2	21	5	3	8	14	27	4	19	−5
United States	7,100,007	26,980	26,980	2.3	0.9	1.4	2[2]	1[2]	18[2]	4[2]	3[2]	6[2]	16[2]	19[2]	20[2]	12[2]	—
Uruguay	16,458	5,170	6,630	3.9	0.6	3.3	9	—	18	5	—	7	15	10	12	10	14
Uzbekistan	21,979	970	2,370	−1.6	2.3	−3.9	28[11]	[3]	16[3, 11]	8[11]	[3]	8[11]	6[11]	—20[11]—			14[11]
Vanuatu	202	1,200	2,290	1.6	2.7	−1.1	22	—	5	6	2	8	34	13	1	12	−2
Venezuela	65,382	3,020	7,900	2.9	2.4	0.5	5[2]	22[2]	16[2]	7[2]	2[2]	5[2]	14[2]	—19[2]—		8[2]	2[2]
Vietnam	17,634	240	...	6.4	2.2	4.2	29	[9]	—30[9]—			4	14	2	—11—		11
Virgin Islands (U.S.)	1,246[1, 25]	11,740[1, 25]	...	...	...	...	...	...	...	...	...	...	...	...	...	...	...
West Bank	2,552[8]	1,830[8]	...	...	...	...	14	1	14	10	—	8	17	18	7	11	—
Western Sahara	60[1, 6]	300[1, 6]	...	...	...	...	...	...	...	...	...	...	...	...	...	...	...
Yemen	4,044	260	...	...	...	...	18	10	13	3	1	11	14	6	1	20	3
Yugoslavia	19,881[1]	2,000[1]	...	...	...	...	23[11]	[9]	41[9, 11]	7[11]	—	7[11]	16[11]	—1[11]—			4[11]
Zambia	3,605	400	930	1.6	2.6	−1.0	26	8	30	3	1	4	12	6	—8—		3
Zimbabwe	5,933	540	2,030	2.2	−2.8	−0.6	10	7	41	2	6	5	11	5	7	2	3

[1]Gross domestic product (GDP). [2]1993. [3]Manufacturing includes mining and public utilities. [4]1990. [5]1992. [6]1991. [7]Net operating surplus includes consumption of fixed capital. [8]1994. [9]Manufacturing includes mining. [10]Services includes restaurants and hotels. [11]1995. [12]Finance includes public utilities. [13]Mining includes public utilities. [14]Government includes finance, insurance. [15]Republic of Cyprus only. [16]Services includes hotels. [17]Services includes transportation, communications. [18]Excludes Alderney and Sark. [19]Manufacturing includes public utilities.

gross domestic product (GDP) by type of expenditure, 1994 (%)					cost components of gross domestic product (GDP), 1994 (%)				balance of payments, 1995 (current external transactions; '000,000 U.S.$)			tourist trade, 1995 ('000,000 U.S.$)		country
consumption		gross domestic investment	foreign trade		indirect taxes net of subsides	consumption of fixed capital	compensation of employees	net operating surplus	net transfers		current balance of payments	receipts from foreign nationals	expenditures by nationals abroad	
private	government		exports	imports					goods, merchandise	invisibles				
60	14	20	51	−46	10	12	52	26	20,979	−2,981	17,998	5,762	11,455	Netherlands, The
...	...	...	...	...	...	...	...	...	−964.4	1,050.9	86.5	639[8]	...	Netherlands Antilles
...	...	...	...	...	8[5]	10[5]	51[5]	30[5]	...	...	...	102[8]	...	New Caledonia
62	15	21	32	−30	14	10	43	33	901	−4,679	−3,778	2,163	1,283	New Zealand
86	16	25	24	−52	...	...	...	...	−323.5	−382.5	−706.0	50	40	Nicaragua
82	16	10	16	−25	1		——99——		−44.5[8]	−81.6[8]	−126.1[8]	15	21	Niger
82	3	9	24	−19	1	2	9	88	2,948[8]	−5,076[8]	−2,128[8]	54	144[8]	Nigeria
...	...	...	...	...	...	...	...	...	...	...	...	655	...	Northern Mariana Is.
50	21	23	38	−32	11[2]	15[2]	51[2]	23[2]	8,321[8]	−4,676[8]	3,645[8]	2,386	4,221	Norway
42	31	17	49	−40	[23]	[7]	33[5]	67[5,7,23]	2,015	−2,994	−979	92	47	Oman
71	12	19	16	−19	10	6	——84——		−2,228[8]	−424[8]	−1,804[8]	114	449	Pakistan
...	...	...	...	...	...	...	...	...	...	...	...	...	...	Palau
60	15	28	100	−104	10	7	41	42	−575.0	−232.0	−343.0	310	128	Panama
52[2]	21[2]	19[2]	49[2]	−40[2]	11[6]	12[6]	37[6]	40[6]	1,408.0	−734.1	673.9	60	75	Papua New Guinea
88	7	23	34	−53	7[5]	8[5]	30[5]	56[5]	−1,276.7[8]	527.9[8]	−748.8[8]	213	181	Paraguay
74	7	22	11	−14	7[6]	4[6]	20[6]	69[6]	−2,111	−2,134	−4,245	520	302	Peru
72	10	23	33	−39	10	11	26	53	−8,944	6,964	−1,980	2,450	422	Philippines
64	19	16	24	−23	15	[7]	44	40[7]	−3,224	−1,021	−4,245	6,700	5,500	Poland
68	19	25	25	−36	12	4	48	36	−8,484	8,255	−229	4,402	2,155	Portugal
63	14	17	69	−63	5	7	40	49	1,730[6]	−5,131[6]	−3,401[6]	1,826	833	Puerto Rico
32[2]	34[2]	19[2]	46[2]	−31[2]	1[2]	12[2]	36[2]	52[2]	...	...	...	...	...	Qatar
79[5]	29[5]	27[5]	4[5]	−39[5]	9[5]	[7]	59[5]	31[5,7]	...	...	...	157[5]	...	Réunion
62	27	11	——1——		5[2]	[7]	36[2]	59[2,7]	−1,231	−111	−1,342	574	695	Romania
47	23	26	28	−23	11	20	38	30	22,309	−11,675	10,634	4,312	11,599	Russia
147	8	3	6	−64	5		——95——		−200.0[2]	71.1[2]	−128.9[2]	2[2]	17[5]	Rwanda
49[2]	25[2]	39[2]	——−13[2]——		13[5]		——87[5]——		−69.0[8]	42.5[8]	−26.5[8]	65	5	St. Kitts
67	15	24	65	−71	16		——84——		−165.7[8]	100.8[8]	−64.9[8]	268	23[8]	St. Lucia
71	20	33	41	−65	16		——84——		−63.5	27.5	−36.0	57	3	St. Vincent
...	...	...	...	...	...	...	...	...	−71.5	81.2	9.8	36	3	Samoa
61	17	25	275	−278	...	...	...	...	−235.9	288.9	53.0	...	...	San Marino
84	33	41	25	−83	...	...	...	...	−17.9[8]	3.4[8]	−14.5[8]	1[4]	2[4]	São Tomé and Príncipe
43	27	20	40	−30	2[2]	9[2]	30[2]	60[2]	24,390	−29,714	−5,324	1,884[4]	...	Saudi Arabia
78	12	15	35	−40	...	...	...	...	−203.2[8]	206.4[8]	3.2[8]	130	75	Senegal
53[2]	30[2]	29[2]	54[2]	−65[2]	22[6]	11[6]	38[6]	29[6]	−162.8	129.7	−33.1	100	24	Seychelles
70	11	8	31	−20	8[4]	6[4]	14[4]	73[4]	−72.7[8]	−16.4[8]	−89.1[8]	6	2	Sierra Leone
42	8	32	——17——		...	...	...	...	1,625	13,468	15,093	8,212	5,134	Singapore
50	22	23	65	−59	13[6]	14[6]	48[6]	25[6]	−229	619	390	620	330	Slovakia
54	20	21	61	−56	13[2]	17[2]	61[2]	9[2]	−953.5	917.0	−36.5	1,079	413	Slovenia
...	...	...	...	...	...	...	...	...	14.3[5]	−15.7[5]	−1.4[5]	6[5]	11[6]	Solomon Islands
75[4]	9[4]	20[4]	1[4]	−5[4]	...	...	...	...	...	...	...	...	...	Somalia
60	21	18	23	−22	11	14	54	22	1,610	−4,430	−2,820	1,595	1,749	South Africa
63	17	20	22	−22	8	12	45	36	−17,721	19,001	1,280	25,701	4,540	Spain
75	10	27	34	−46	14[2]	5[2]	44[2]	37[2]	−879.6	333.2	−546.4	224	186	Sri Lanka
71[6]	18[6]	17[6]	5[6]	−10[6]	...	...	...	...	−510.3	−10.4	−499.9	3[2]	33[5]	Sudan, The
61	23	21	120	−125	7[5]	11[5]	45[5]	36[5]	99.3[8]	−40.7[8]	58.6[8]	14	3[8]	Suriname
65	27	18	105	−115	...	...	...	...	−100.1	49.0	−51.1	35	37	Swaziland
54	27	14	37	−32	10[2]	14[2]	59[2]	16[2]	15,973	−11,340	4,633	3,447	5,422	Sweden
59	14	22	36	−32	5	10	63	22	3,237	18,385	21,622	9,364	7,636	Switzerland
70	14	30	30	−45	−9[2]	4[2]	——106[2]——		−143	583	440	1,325	398	Syria
59	15	24	44	−42	11	9	53	27	13,540	−8,716	4,824	3,286	8,457	Taiwan
...	...	...	...	...	19		——81——		−208.1[2]	4.4[2]	−203.7[2]	...	...	Tajikistan
92	7	28	25	−52	9	3	8	80	−657.5	28.3	629.2	259	360	Tanzania
53	9	42	37	−42	12[2]	11[2]	26[2]	51[2]	−7,968	−5,576	−13,544	7,664	3,372	Thailand
78	12	14	31	−35	...	...	...	...	−37.1[8]	−19.7[8]	−56.8[8]	8	23[8]	Togo
...	...	...	...	...	14		——86——		−40.5[2]	34.6[2]	−5.9[2]	11	1[2]	Tonga
57	15	13	44	−28	10[2]	11[2]	50[2]	29[2]	587.7	−293.9	293.8	73	79	Trinidad and Tobago
56	24	23	40	−43	...	...	...	...	−1,989	1,252	−737	1,325	251	Tunisia
66	12	21	21	−20	9	5	——86——		−13,212	10,873	−2,339	4,957	912	Turkey
44[2]	23[2]	46[2]	——−13[2]——		...	...	...	...	485[8]	−401[8]	84[8]	...	...	Turkmenistan
...	...	...	...	...	...	...	...	...	...	...	...	0.3[2]	...	Tuvalu
84	9	13	11	−17	9		——91——		−317.8	42.1	−275.7	79	93	Uganda
59	9	35	35	−39	−5[6]	15[6]	77[6]	13[6]	−2,702	1,550	−1,152	...	...	Ukraine
54	18	27	70	−68	−1[2]	15[2]	24[2]	62[2]	...	...	...	...	...	United Arab Emirates
64	21	15	26	−27	13[2]	10[2]	56[2]	20[2]	−18,390	12,160	−6,230	19,073	24,737	United Kingdom
68	16	17	10	−12	8[2]	12[2]	61[2]	19[2]	−171,990	23,760	−148,230	61,137	45,855	United States
74	13	15	21	−22	19[5]	[7]	44[5]	37[5,7]	−576.2	217.8	−358.4	611	236	Uruguay
58[2]	25[2]	15[2]	——3[2]——		−1[5]	3[5]	65[5]	33[5]	−378[2]	−51[2]	−429[2]	...	...	Uzbekistan
51	29	30	49	−60	...	...	...	...	−51.2	32.9	−18.3	58	5	Vanuatu
72	7	13	30	−22	7	8	34	51	7,290	−5,035	2,255	811	1,865	Venezuela
70[2]	16[2]	19[2]	28[2]	−33[2]	...	...	...	...	−900[8]	−66[8]	−966[8]	85[4]	...	Vietnam
...	...	...	...	...	...	...	...	...	...	...	...	821	...	Virgin Islands (U.S.)
...	...	...	...	...	...	...	...	...	...	...	...	...	...	West Bank
...	...	...	...	...	...	...	...	...	...	...	...	...	...	Western Sahara
68[2]	29[2]	20[2]	15[2]	−32[2]	11[2]	5[2]	——84[2]——		−11.0	193.7	182.7	38	76	Yemen
...	...	...	...	...	6	17	46	31	...	...	...	42	...	Yugoslavia
66	19	14	22	−20	7[4]	9[4]	57[4]	26[4]	−1[2]	−86[2]	−87[2]	47	56[5]	Zambia
63	18	18	40	−40	10[6]		——90[6]——		157.6[8]	−582.5[8]	−424.9[8]	154	106	Zimbabwe

[20]Manufacturing includes mining, construction, and public utilities. [21]Services includes trade. [22]Construction includes mining. [23]Net operating surplus includes indirect taxes net of subsidies. [24]Transportation includes public utilities. [25]1987.

Employment and labour

This table provides international comparisons of the world's national labour forces—giving their size; composition by demographic component and employment status; and structure by industry.

The table focuses on the concept of "economically active population," which the International Labour Organisation (ILO) defines as persons of all ages who are either employed or looking for work. In general, the economically active population does not include students, persons occupied solely in domestic duties, retired persons, persons living entirely on their own means, and persons wholly dependent on others. Persons engaged in illegal economic activities—smugglers, prostitutes, drug dealers, bootleggers, black marketeers, and others—also fall outside the purview of the ILO definition. Countries differ markedly in their treatment, as part of the labour force, of such groups as members of the armed forces, inmates of institutions, the unemployed (both persons seeking their first job and those previously employed), seasonal and international migrant workers, and persons engaged in informal, subsistence, or part-time economic activities. Some countries include all or most of these groups among the economically active, while others may treat the same groups as inactive.

Three principal structural comparisons of the economically active total are given in the first part of the table: (1) participation rate, or the proportion of the economically active who possess some particular characteristic, is given for women and for those of working age (usually ages 15 to 64), (2) activity rate, the proportion of the total population who *are* economically active, is given for both sexes and as a total, and (3) employment status, usually (and here) grouped as employers, self-employed, employees, family workers (usually unpaid), and others.

Each of these measures indicates certain characteristics in a given national labour market; none should be interpreted in isolation, however, as the meaning of each is influenced by a variety of factors—demographic structure and change, social or religious customs, educational opportunity, sexual differentiation in employment patterns, degree of technological development, and the like. Participation and activity rates, for example, may be high in a particular country because it possesses an older population with few children, hence a higher proportion of working age, or because, despite a young population with many below working age, the economy attracts eligible immigrant workers, themselves almost exclusively of working age. At the same time, low activity and participation rates might be characteristic of a country having a young population with poor employment possibilities or of a country with a good job market distorted by the presence of large numbers of "guest" or contract workers who are not part of the domestic labour force. An illiterate woman in a strongly sex-differentiated labour force is likely to begin and end as a family or

Employment and labour

country	year	economically active population										distribution by economic sector			
		total ('000)	participation rate (%)		activity rate (%)			employment status (%)				agriculture, forestry, fishing		manufacturing; mining, quarrying; public utilities	
			female	ages 15–64	total	male	female	employers, self-employed	employees	unpaid family workers	other	number ('000)	% of econ. active	number ('000)	% of econ. active
Afghanistan	1979	3,941	7.9	49.1	30.3	54.2	4.9	52.2	33.8	14.0	—	2,369	60.1	494	12.5
Albania	1994	1,340	47.0[3]	92.0[3, 4]	57.4[3]	60.8[3]	54.0[3]	...	...	...	...	534	39.9	84[5]	6.3[5]
Algeria	1987	5,341	9.2	44.3	23.6	42.4	4.4	16.8	61.7	2.6	18.9	725	13.6	622	11.6
American Samoa	1990	14.2	41.1	52.6[8]	30.4	34.8	25.7	2.1	92.6	0.2	5.1	0.3	2.3	4.8	33.7
Andorra	1989	25	45.6	74.3	55.1	...	...	...	...	...	...	0.3	1.2	2.7	11.0
Angola	1991	4,166	38.4	60.1[10]	40.3	50.4	30.4	...	...	...	...	2,892	69.4	438[11]	10.5[11]
Antigua and Barbuda	1991	26.8	45.6	69.7	45.1	50.9	39.6	12.1	82.8	0.7	4.4	1.0	3.9	1.9	7.3
Argentina	1995	14,345	36.7	64.5	41.5	53.5	29.9	28.0[13]	60.4[13]	5.0[13]	6.6[13]	1,201[14]	12.0[14]	2,136[14]	21.3[14]
Armenia	1994	1,618	...	74.5[16]	43.1	...	...	...	...	...	...	538	33.3	323	20.0
Aruba	1991	31.1	42.5	67.1	46.7	54.5	39.0	7.0	86.4	0.3	6.3	0.2	0.5	2.3	7.3
Australia	1995–96[18]	9,066	42.9	73.3[19]	49.9	57.2	42.6	13.4	77.2	0.8	8.6	422	4.7	1,278	14.1
Austria	1994[18]	3,881	42.8	70.8	48.3	57.0	40.1	9.7[20]	87.4[20]	3.0[20]	—	273	7.0	898	23.1
Azerbaijan	1994	2,698	...	64.4[16, 20]	36.2	...	...	...	...	...	...	1,011	37.5	466	17.3
Bahamas, The	1994	139	47.5	77.8	50.7	54.8	46.8	11.6[22]	85.1[22]	0.3[22]	3.0[22]	6.9	5.0	7.3	5.3
Bahrain	1991	226	17.5	66.8	44.6	63.5	18.5	5.1	88.5	0.1	6.3	5	2.3	33	14.6
Bangladesh	1990–91[18]	51,155	39.3	76.9	46.0	54.2	38.9	26.3	11.5	46.2	16.0	33,033	65.1	5,980	11.7
Barbados	1995[18]	137	49.5	79.9	51.8	54.6	49.1	8.8[24]	76.4[24]	0.2[24]	14.6[24]	6.3	4.6	15.6	11.4
Belarus	1994	4,798	...	77.7[16]	46.5	...	...	...	...	...	...	917	19.1	1,365	28.4
Belgium	1992	4,237	42.3	51.5[25]	42.2	49.8	34.9	12.7	72.4	3.4	11.5	95	2.2	788	18.6
Belize	1996	75.5	30.8	58.5[26]	34.1	47.2	21.0	26.2[20]	59.2[20]	4.9[20]	9.8[20]	18.3[13]	31.4[13]	7.0[13]	12.0[13]
Benin	1992	2,085	42.6	73.4	43.0	50.6	35.7	58.4	5.3	30.5	5.8	1,148	55.0	162	7.8
Bermuda	1995	34.1	50.0	63.5[13]	55.8	57.4	54.4	9.7[13]	84.0[13]	0.1[13]	6.2[13]	0.5	1.5	1.4	4.2
Bhutan	...	...	...	...	...	...	...	...	...	...	...	...	...	...	...
Bolivia	1992	2,530	38.2	64.0	39.4	48.7	30.4	41.2	31.5	7.1	20.2	984	38.9	281	11.1
Bosnia and Herzegovina	1990[5]	1,026	36.9	...	22.7	...	...	...	...	...	...	39	3.8	519	50.5
Botswana	1991[18]	441	38.5	59.4	33.3	42.8	24.5	6.5	62.5	17.1	13.9	98	22.1	47	10.7
Brazil	1993[18]	70,965	39.6	68.2[25]	47.9	59.2	37.1	26.3[22]	62.3[22]	7.7[22]	3.7[22]	18,254	25.7	9,486	13.4
Brunei	1991	112	32.9	67.6	43.0	54.6	30.0	3.5	91.4	0.4	4.7	2.2	1.9	11.6	10.4
Bulgaria	1995	3,738	48.4[28]	68.8[28]	46.3[28]	48.7[28]	44.1[28]	8.4	75.9	0.9	14.8	783	20.9	1,003	26.8
Burkina Faso	1991	4,679	49.4	83.9[25]	50.9	52.7	49.2	...	...	...	...	4,294	91.8	58	1.2
Burundi	1990	2,780	52.6	91.4	52.5	51.2	53.8	62.8	5.1	30.3	1.8	2,574	92.6	37	1.3
Cambodia	1993	4,010	55.8	86.2	43.1	39.5	46.4	...	...	...	...	2,454[14]	74.4[14]	220[11, 14]	6.7[11, 14]
Cameroon	1991	4,740	33.2	58.9[10]	40.0	53.9	26.3	60.2[22]	14.6[22]	18.0[22]	7.1[22]	2,856	60.3	628[11]	13.2[11]
Canada	1995[18]	14,928	45.1	74.7	50.4	55.9	45.0	9.6[20]	89.0[20]	0.5[20]	0.9[20]	554	3.7	2,375	15.9
Cape Verde	1990	121	37.1	64.3	35.3	46.9	24.9	24.7	53.7	2.0	19.6	29.9	24.8	6.8	5.7
Central African Republic	1988	1,187	46.8	78.3	48.2	52.2	44.3	75.3	8.0	8.1	8.6	881	74.2	31	2.6
Chad	1991	2,016	18.2	51.6[10]	35.3	56.5	14.7	...	...	...	...	1,489	73.9	149[11]	7.4[11]
Chile	1995[18]	5,274	32.4	58.6	37.8	52.1	24.0	26.4[19]	64.6[19]	3.2[19]	5.8[19]	810	15.4	983	18.6
China	1990	657,290	44.9	85.0	57.9	61.8	53.7	...	...	...	...	467,926	71.2	87,275	13.3
Colombia	1985	9,558	32.8	49.4[29]	34.3	46.6	22.3	...	...	...	...	2,412[14]	28.5[14]	1,231[14]	14.5[14]
Comoros	1991	215	40.0	57.8[10]	44.4	53.7	35.2	47.6[14]	25.6[14]	—26.8[14]—		171	79.4	14[11]	6.5[11]
Congo, Dem. Rep. of the	1991	13,848	35.2	64.2[10]	36.1	47.2	25.2	...	...	...	...	9,021	65.1	2,200[11]	15.9[11]
Congo, Rep. of the	1984	563	45.6	54.0	29.5	33.0	26.2	64.3	31.4	1.2	3.1	294	52.2	50	8.8
Costa Rica	1995	1,232	30.5	57.0[19, 25]	36.9	50.8	22.8	24.0[19]	72.2[19]	3.3[19]	0.6[19]	261	21.2	218	17.7
Côte d'Ivoire	1988	4,263	32.3	66.6	39.4	52.2	26.0	...	...	...	...	2,628	61.6	100	2.3
Croatia	1991	2,040	42.9	65.2	45.3	53.9	37.4	12.7	73.7	2.0	11.6	341	16.7	571	28.0
Cuba	1988	4,570	36.1	56.9[25]	44.2	56.2	32.1	5.7[30]	94.1[30]	0.2[30]	—	791[30]	22.3[30]	668[30]	18.9[30]
Cyprus[31, 32]	1995	303	38.6	71.5	47.0	57.8	36.2	18.7[28]	73.1[28]	6.1[28]	2.1[28]	31	10.1	48	15.9
Czech Republic	1995	5,283	46.2	77.9[13]	51.1	56.6	46.0	12.7	83.4	0.5	3.4	342	6.5	1,733	32.8
Denmark	1995	2,812	45.3	79.1	53.4	59.2	47.8	8.8	84.2	—	7.0	123	4.4	582	20.7
Djibouti	1991	282	40.8	70.4[10]	61.5	74.1	50.3	...	...	...	...	212	75.2	31[11]	11.0[11]
Dominica	1991	26.4	34.5	62.4	38.0	50.0	26.1	29.2[33]	50.6[33]	1.9[33]	18.3[33]	7.3	27.9	2.3	8.8
Dominican Republic	1981	1,915	28.9	53.6	33.9	48.1	19.7	36.5	51.3	3.3	8.9	420	22.0	243	12.7
Ecuador	1990	3,360	26.4	55.7	34.8	51.5	18.3	45.7	42.5	4.4	7.4	1,036	30.8	404	12.0
Egypt	1994[18]	17,572	23.0	50.9	30.4	45.9	14.2	24.7[28]	50.0[28]	16.4[28]	9.0[28]	5,365	30.5	2,274	12.9
El Salvador	1995	2,136	37.1	62.9	39.1	51.4	27.8	31.7	48.2	8.0	12.1	585	27.4	412	19.3
Equatorial Guinea	1983	103	35.7	66.7	39.2	52.5	26.9	29.0	16.0	29.9	25.1	59.4	57.9	1.8	1.8
Eritrea	...	...	...	...	...	...	...	...	...	...	...	...	...	...	...
Estonia	1994	730[34]	47.6[34]	71.8[34]	48.9[34]	54.9[34]	43.7[34]	4.8	85.2	0.8	9.2	92	12.9	182	25.5
Ethiopia	1995	24,606	41.1	72.2	43.3	50.3	36.5	58.5[35]	6.5[35]	34.0[35]	1.0[35]	21,605	87.8	419	1.7

traditional agricultural worker. Loss of working-age men to war, civil violence, or emigration for job opportunities may also affect the structure of a particular labour market.

The distribution of the economically active population by employment status reveals that a large percentage of economically active persons in some less developed countries falls under the heading "employers, self-employed." This occurs because the countries involved have poor, largely agrarian economies in which the average worker is a farmer who tills his own small plot of land. In countries with well-developed economies, "employees" will usually constitute the largest portion of the economically active.

Caution should be exercised when using the economically active data to make intercountry comparisons, as countries often differ in their choices of classification schemes, definitions, and coverage of groups and in their methods of collection and tabulation of data. The population base containing the economically active population, for example, may range, in developing countries, from age 9 or 10 with no upper limit to, in developed countries, age 18 or 19 upward to a usual retirement age of from 55 to 65, with sometimes a different range for each sex. Data on female labour-force participation, in particular, often lack comparability. In many less developed countries, particularly those dominated by the Islamic faith, a cultural bias favouring traditional roles for women results in the undercounting of economically active women. In other less developed countries, particularly those in which subsistence workers are deemed economically active, the role of women may be overstated.

The second major section of the table provides data on the distribution by economic (also conventionally called industrial) sector of the economically active population. The data usually include such groups as unpaid family workers, members of the armed forces, and the unemployed, the last distributed by industry as far as possible.

The categorization of industrial sectors is based on the divisions listed in the *International Standard Industrial Classification of All Economic Activities.* The "other" category includes persons whose activities were not adequately defined and the unemployed who were not distributable by industrial sector.

A substantial part of the data presented in this table is summarized from various issues of the ILO's *Year Book of Labour Statistics,* which compiles its statistics both from official publications and from information submitted directly by national census and labour authorities. The editors have supplemented and updated ILO statistical data with information from Britannica's holdings of relevant official publications and from direct correspondence with national authorities.

construction		transportation, communications		trade, hotels, restaurants		finance, real estate		public administration, defense		services		other		country
number ('000)	% of econ. active	number ('000)	% of econ. active	number ('000)	% of econ. active	number ('000)	% of econ. active	number ('000)	% of econ. active	number ('000)	% of econ. active	number ('000)	% of econ. active	
51	1.3	66	1.6	138	3.5	[1]	[1]	[1]	[1]	749[1]	19.0[1]	78[2]	2.0[2]	Afghanistan
33[5]	2.5[5]	19[5]	1.4[5]	3[5]	0.2[5]	3[5]	0.2[5]	16[5]	1.2[5]	145[5]	10.8[5]	505[6]	37.7[6]	Albania
690	12.9	216	4.1	391	7.3	143	2.7	[7]	[7]	1,180[7]	22.1[7]	1,374	25.7	Algeria
1.2	8.3	0.8	5.5	1.8	13.0	0.3	2.1	1.4	10.0	2.8	19.8	0.7[9]	5.1[9]	American Samoa
2.9	11.8	...	...	6.0	24.2	1.3	5.4	2.6	10.3	4.1	16.7	0.1	0.5	Andorra
[11]	[11]	[12]	[12]	[12]	[12]	[12]	[12]	[12]	[12]	836[12]	20.1[12]	—	—	Angola
3.1	11.6	2.4	9.0	8.5	31.9	1.5	5.4	[7]	[7]	6.4[7]	23.9[7]	1.9	7.0	Antigua and Barbuda
1,003[14]	10.0[14]	460[14]	4.6[14]	1,702[14]	17.0[14]	396[14]	3.9[14]	[7]	[7]	2,399[7, 14]	23.9[7, 14]	736[14, 15]	7.3[14, 15]	Argentina
108	6.7	49	30.0	65	4.0	29	1.8	30	1.9	350	21.6	126[17]	7.8[17]	Armenia
3.2	10.4	2.3	7.5	11.0	35.4	2.4	7.8	[7]	[7]	8.6[7]	27.7[7]	1.1[17]	3.5[17]	Aruba
600	6.6	547	6.0	2,107	23.2	1,111	12.3	379	4.2	1,844	20.3	779[17]	8.6[17]	Australia
372	9.6	251	6.5	810	20.9	355	9.1	[7]	[7]	912[7]	23.5[7]	10	0.3	Austria
200	7.4	180	6.7	169	6.3	11	0.4	[7]	[7]	589[7]	21.8[7]	71[21]	2.6[21]	Azerbaijan
11.6	8.3	11.2	8.1	44.2	31.8	12.9	9.3	10.7	7.7	29.7	21.4	4.5[23]	3.2[23]	Bahamas, The
27	11.8	14	6.1	30	13.2	17	7.6	41	18.1	43	19.0	16[17]	7.3[17]	Bahrain
525	1.0	1,611	3.1	4,285	8.4	296	0.6	[7]	[7]	1,909[7]	3.7[7]	3,245[21]	6.3[21]	Bangladesh
12.2	8.9	5.9	4.3	35.3	25.8	8.4	6.1	[7]	[7]	48.8[7]	35.7[7]	4.3[2]	3.1[2]	Barbados
370	7.7	318	6.6	459	9.6	97	2.0	90	1.9	952	19.8	230[21]	4.8[21]	Belarus
245	5.8	257	6.1	634	15.0	342	8.1	[7]	[7]	1,393[7]	32.9[7]	484[17]	11.4[17]	Belgium
4.1[13]	7.0[13]	2.9[13]	5.0[13]	10.0[13]	17.2[13]	1.8[13]	3.1[13]	5.4[13]	9.2[13]	6.0[13]	10.3[13]	2.8[13]	4.8[13]	Belize
52	2.5	53	2.5	433	20.7	3	0.1	[7]	[7]	165[7]	7.9[7]	71[21]	3.4[21]	Benin
1.7	5.0	2.2	6.4	10.8	31.6	5.2	15.3	[7]	[7]	12.3[7]	35.9[7]	—	—	Bermuda
...	...	...	...	...	...	...	...	...	...	...	...	...	...	Bhutan
129	5.1	117	4.6	232	9.2	54	2.1	59	2.3	350	13.8	323[15]	12.7[15]	Bolivia
75	7.3	69	6.7	131	12.8	39	3.8	[7]	[7]	155[7]	15.1[7]	—	—	Bosnia and Herzegovina
58	13.2	11	2.6	35	8.0	13	3.0	[7]	[7]	107[7]	24.2[7]	72[17]	16.2[17]	Botswana
4,289	6.0	2,284	3.2	8,475[27]	11.9[27]	1,389	2.0	[7]	[7]	22,392[7, 27]	31.6[7, 27]	4,395[9]	6.2[9]	Brazil
14.1	12.6	5.4	4.8	15.4	13.8	5.8	5.2	[7]	[7]	52.1[7]	46.6[7]	5.3[17]	4.7[17]	Brunei
188	5.0	251	6.7	357	9.5	51	1.4	76	2.0	532	14.2	497[17]	13.3[17]	Bulgaria
11	0.2	1.5	0.3	120	2.6	2	—	[7]	[7]	112[7]	2.4[7]	67[17]	1.4[17]	Burkina Faso
20	0.7	9	0.3	26	0.9	2.0	0.1	[7]	[7]	85[7]	3.1[7]	27[17]	1.0[17]	Burundi
[11]	[11]	[12]	[12]	[12]	[12]	[12]	[12]	[12]	[12]	625[12, 14]	18.9[12, 14]	—	—	Cambodia
[11]	[11]	[12]	[12]	[12]	[12]	[12]	[12]	[12]	[12]	1,256[12]	26.5[12]	—	—	Cameroon
724	4.9	890	6.0	3,168	21.2	1,676	11.2	810	5.4	3,308	22.2	1,422[9]	9.5[9]	Canada
22.7	18.8	6.1	5.1	12.7	10.6	0.8	0.7	[7]	[7]	17.4[7]	14.4[7]	24.1	20.0	Cape Verde
6	0.5	7	0.6	92	7.8	0.7	0.1	[7]	[7]	70[7]	5.9[7]	100[17]	8.5[17]	Central African Republic
[11]	[11]	[12]	[12]	[12]	[12]	[12]	[12]	[12]	[12]	377[12]	18.7[12]	—	—	Chad
411	7.8	401	7.6	974	18.5	340	6.4	[7]	[7]	1,323[7]	25.1[7]	34[15]	0.6[15]	Chile
11,890	1.8	11,814	1.8	25,631	3.9	8,268	1.3	[7]	[7]	34,053[7]	5.2[7]	10,434	1.6	China
242[14]	2.9[14]	353[14]	4.2[14]	1,262[14]	14.9[14]	278[14]	3.3[14]	[7]	[7]	1,998[7, 14]	23.6[7, 14]	691[14, 15]	8.2[14, 15]	Colombia
[11]	[11]	[12]	[12]	[12]	[12]	[12]	[12]	[12]	[12]	30[12]	14.1[12]	—	—	Comoros
[11]	[11]	[12]	[12]	[12]	[12]	[12]	[12]	[12]	[12]	2,627[12]	19.0[12]	—	—	Congo, Dem. Rep. of the
25	4.5	29	5.1	67	11.8	3	0.5	[7]	[7]	85[7]	15.1[7]	10	2.0	Congo, Rep. of the
80	6.5	64	5.2	239	19.4	52	4.2	[7]	[7]	298[7]	24.2[7]	19[15]	1.6[15]	Costa Rica
85	2.0	118	2.8	530	12.4	[1]	[1]	[1]	[1]	591[1]	13.9[1]	210[2]	4.9[2]	Côte d'Ivoire
93	4.5	112	5.5	223	10.9	58	2.8	104	5.1	204	10.0	329[17]	16.1[17]	Croatia
313[30]	8.8[30]	249[30]	7.0[30]	306[30]	8.6[30]	[1]	[1]	[1]	[1]	1,086[1, 30]	30.7[1, 30]	128[30]	3.6[30]	Cuba
26	8.7	19	6.2	77	25.4	23	7.6	[7]	[7]	65[7]	21.6[7]	13	4.4	Cyprus[30, 31]
479	9.1	396	7.5	835	15.8	353	6.7	277	5.2	823	15.6	44[23]	0.8[23]	Czech Republic
175	6.2	197	7.0	471	16.8	279	10.0	167	6.0	803	28.5	15[23]	0.5[23]	Denmark
[11]	[11]	[12]	[12]	[12]	[12]	[12]	[12]	[12]	[12]	39[12]	13.8[12]	—	—	Djibouti
2.8	10.7	1.2	4.6	3.7	13.9	0.8	3.1	1.5	5.8	3.4	13.1	3.2[17]	12.3[17]	Dominica
81	4.3	40	2.1	192	10.0	22	1.2	[7]	[7]	363[7]	18.9[7]	553[15]	28.9[15]	Dominican Republic
197	5.9	131	3.9	477	14.2	81	2.4	[7]	[7]	838[7]	24.9[7]	196[15]	5.8[15]	Ecuador
1,037	5.9	849	4.8	1,581	9.0	297	1.7	[7]	[7]	3.919[7]	22.3[7]	2,250[23]	12.8[23]	Egypt
147	6.9	86	4.0	414	19.4	28	1.3	[7]	[7]	433[7]	20.2[7]	32[2]	1.5[2]	El Salvador
1.9	1.9	1.8	1.7	3.1	3.0	0.4	0.4	[7]	[7]	8.4[7]	8.2[7]	25.8[17]	25.2[17]	Equatorial Guinea
...	...	...	...	...	...	...	...	...	...	...	...	...	...	Eritrea
53	7.5	63	8.8	114	16.0	39	5.5	38	5.3	124	17.4	9[23]	1.2[23]	Estonia
61	0.2	103	0.4	936	3.8	19	0.1	[7]	[7]	1,252[7]	5.1[7]	210[2]	0.9[2]	Ethiopia

Employment and labour (continued)

country	year	economically active population										distribution by economic sector			
		total ('000)	participation rate (%)		activity rate (%)			employment status (%)				agriculture, forestry, fishing		manufacturing; mining, quarrying; public utilities	
			female	ages 15–64	total	male	female	employers, self-employed	employees	unpaid family workers	other	number ('000)	% of econ. active	number ('000)	% of econ. active
Faroe Islands	1977	17.6	27.2	64.0	41.9	58.2	23.9	11.9	86.1	...	2.0	3.3	18.8	3.9	21.9
Fiji	1986	241	21.2	56.0	33.7	52.4	14.5	33.6	42.2	16.3	7.9	106	44.1	22	9.0
Finland	1995	2,521	47.0	73.5	49.4	53.7	45.2	12.7[19]	83.3[19]	0.6[19]	3.4[19]	176	7.0	517	20.5
France	1994[18]	25,871	44.9	67.7	44.8	50.6	39.2	10.2	77.4	—	12.4	1,048	4.1	4,432	17.4
French Guiana	1990	48.8	38.2	67.3	42.5	50.5	33.9	10.6	62.7	2.5	24.2	4.2	8.6	3.1	6.4
French Polynesia	1988	75	37.1	64.8	39.9	48.2	30.9	13.0	55.0	4.0	28.0	7.6	10.0	5.4	7.2
Gabon	1991	504	36.9	56.0[10]	43.9	53.9	30.7	...	...	...	...	338	67.1	71[11]	14.1[11]
Gambia, The	1983	326	46.3	78.2	47.3	51.1	43.6	0.5	78.0	14.3	7.1	240	73.7	9	2.9
Gaza Strip	1996	173	9.0	36.3[25]	18.0	32.0	3.2	15.7	46.8	6.7	30.8	9.0	5.2	17.0[36]	9.8[36]
Georgia	1993	1,920	...	58.1[16, 28]	35.7	...	...	...	...	...	...	562	29.3	303	15.8
Germany	1995	40,083	42.8	71.9	49.1	57.8	40.9	8.3	80.4	1.2	10.1	1,334	3.3	10,956	27.3
Ghana	1984	5,580	51.2	82.5[25]	45.4	44.9	45.8	67.7	15.7	12.2	4.4	3,311	59.3	631	11.3
Gibraltar	1994	12.9	38.0	66.9[13, 25]	47.5	58.7	36.2	6.6[30]	89.7[30]	...	3.6[30]	—	—	0.7	5.7
Greece	1995[18]	4,249	38.1	60.7	41.5	53.3	30.5	30.4	48.5	11.1	10.0	788	18.6	703	16.5
Greenland	1976	21.4	33.4	63.5[25]	43.1	53.0	31.4	12.6	82.5	0.4	4.5	3.2	15.1	3.3	15.3
Grenada	1988	38.9	48.6	72.7[35]	39.9	42.9	37.2	16.0[30]	64.2[30]	0.8[30]	19.0[30]	5.6	14.3	3.3	8.6
Guadeloupe	1990	172	45.5	66.4	44.5	49.6	39.7	13.2	53.7	2.0	31.1	8.4	4.9	9.6	5.6
Guam	1990	66.1	37.4	75.7[8]	49.7	58.4	39.7	2.4	94.4	0.1	3.1	0.5	0.8	3.5	5.3
Guatemala	1989[18]	2,898	25.5	59.1	33.5	50.8	16.7	32.7	47.6	16.2	3.5	1,416	48.9	405	14.0
Guernsey[38]	1991	30.2	43.2	74.2	51.2	60.6	42.6	13.7	86.3	—	—	2.4	7.8	2.4	7.9
Guinea	1983	1,823	39.4	63.5	39.1	48.7	30.1	36.2	15.6	37.6	10.6	1,424	78.1	27	1.5
Guinea-Bissau	1991	464	40.5	67.1[10]	45.9	56.2	36.1	...	...	...	...	362	78.0	21[11]	4.5[11]
Guyana	1992–93	278	34.1	61.8	38.8	51.9	26.0	14.3[14]	63.8[14]	1.9[14]	20.0[14]	50[14]	20.4[14]	41[14]	16.8[14]
Haiti	1990	2,679	40.0	64.8	41.1	50.3	32.3	59.1	16.5	10.4	14.0	1,535	57.3	178	6.6
Honduras	1995[18]	1,866	29.9	59.4[25]	35.0	49.7	20.7	36.5[28]	48.7[28]	10.7[28]	4.1[28]	680	36.5	346	18.6
Hong Kong	1995[18]	3,068	37.9	70.0	50.8	62.2	39.1	9.9[19]	87.4[19]	0.7[19]	1.9[19]	17	0.5	591	19.3
Hungary	1995[18]	4,095	43.6	58.6	40.1	47.3	33.5	10.6	76.8	1.0	11.5	336	8.2	1,100	26.9
Iceland	1995	149.0	46.7	81.9	55.6	59.2	52.1	17.2	76.6	1.1	4.8	14.1	9.5	26.7	17.9
India	1991	314,131	28.6	60.7[25, 30]	37.5	51.6	22.3	8.8[30]	16.3[30]	3.6[30]	71.3[30]	191,341	60.9	30,423	9.7
Indonesia	1995	86,361	38.2[28]	67.0[28]	42.9[28]	53.1[28]	32.7[28]	42.7	33.0	17.1	7.2	35,233	40.8	10,987	12.7
Iran	1991	14,737	11.1	46.8	26.4	45.6	6.0	39.7	45.4	2.3	12.6	3,205	21.8	2,243	15.2
Iraq	1988	4,127	12.0	45.3	24.7	42.3	6.1	25.4[39]	59.5[39]	11.4[39]	3.7[39]	477	11.6	439	10.6
Ireland	1995	1,443	37.8	61.6	40.3	50.6	30.2	18.1	68.5	1.2	12.1	150	10.4	293	20.3
Isle of Man	1991	33.2	42.3	73.2	47.6	56.9	38.9	15.8	80.1	—	4.1	1.2	3.7	3.9	11.6
Israel	1995[18]	2,100	43.2	53.8[25]	37.9	43.4	32.5	13.8	79.3	0.6	6.3	57	2.7	424	20.2
Italy	1994[18]	22,680	36.9	57.4	40.1	52.1	28.8	21.4	62.8	4.0	11.8	1,573	6.9	4,837	21.3
Jamaica	1994	1,091	47.4	72.0[40]	43.6	46.8	40.6	32.7	49.5	2.0	15.8	218	20.0	107	9.8
Japan	1995	66,660	40.5	71.5	53.2	64.6	42.3	12.0[19]	78.8[19]	6.1[19]	3.1[19]	3,670	5.5	15,330	23.0
Jersey	1991	47.5	43.2	66.9[25]	56.5	66.1	47.5	12.6	84.0	...	3.4	2.2	4.7	3.8	8.0
Jordan	1993	859	11.4[42]	43.2[42]	22.2	...	...	22.8[43]	67.2[43]	0.8[43]	9.2[43]	55	6.4	97	11.3
Kazakstan	1995	6,976	...	71.8[16, 20]	40.8	...	...	...	...	...	...	1,442	20.7	1,372	19.7
Kenya	1991	10,260	39.4	64.4[10]	39.0	47.4	30.7	...	...	...	...	7,857	76.6	816[11]	8.0[11]
Kiribati	1990	32.6	46.4	75.6[25]	45.1	48.9	41.4	71.9	25.3	...	2.8	23.1	71.0	0.9	2.8
Korea, North	1985	9,084	46.0	75.3	44.6	48.6	40.6	...	...	...	...	3,726[24]	44.1[24]	2,790[11, 24]	33.0[11, 24]
Korea, South	1995[18]	20,797	40.2	62.0[25]	46.4	55.2	37.5	27.4	61.2	9.3	2.0	2,544	12.2	4,937	23.7
Kuwait	1995	746	26.1	61.5[42]	47.4	60.4	29.4	3.9[42]	94.1[42]	0.1[42]	1.9[42]	9[42]	1.3[42]	69[42]	9.4[42]
Kyrgyzstan	1995	1,691	...	...	37.5	...	...	...	...	...	...	378	22.3	162	9.6
Laos	1985	2,014	45.3	84.2	48.9	53.1	44.6	...	...	...	...	1,393[14]	75.7[14]	130[11, 14]	7.1[11, 14]
Latvia	1995	1,272	49.1	...	50.8	...	...	...	...	...	...	220	17.3	228	17.9
Lebanon	1988	904	16.6	44.0	26.5	43.9	8.9	...	...	...	...	132[44]	19.1[44]	131[44]	18.9[44]
Lesotho	1986	504	27.0	44.0	31.6	47.3	16.7	16.8	55.7	20.5	7.0	131	25.9	142	28.2
Liberia	1984	704	41.0	56.3	33.5	39.1	27.8	59.1	21.6	14.4	5.0	481	68.3	31	4.4
Libya	1991	1,169	9.3	37.1[10]	24.8	42.9	4.9	...	...	...	...	129	11.0	372[11]	31.8[11]
Liechtenstein	1996	16.2	40.3	71.3	52.0	63.7	40.8	6.4	90.8	0.1	2.7	0.3	2.0	4.9	30.2
Lithuania	1994	1,937	...	81.8[16, 20]	52.1	...	...	...	...	...	...	390	20.1	378	19.5
Luxembourg	1991[45]	168	36.5	62.5	43.5	56.4	31.2	9.2	85.3	1.1	4.4	5	3.2	26	15.8
Macau	1995[18]	187.1	43.2	64.0	44.1	51.7	36.9	10.5	84.6	1.2	3.7	0.5	0.2	43.0	23.0
Macedonia	1993	937	...	...	45.2	...	...	...	...	...	...	215	22.9	168	17.9
Madagascar	1991	5,311	39.3	63.9[10]	42.8	52.4	33.0	...	...	...	...	4,043	76.1	632[11]	11.9[11]
Malaŵi	1987	3,458	51.0	89.4	43.3	43.9	42.8	4.9	16.2	77.6	1.3	2,968	85.8	114	3.3
Malaysia	1995[18]	7,869	33.9	57.3[13]	35.1[13]	47.3[13]	22.6[13]	21.1[20]	71.4[20]	7.5[20]	—	1,527	19.4	1,861	23.6
Maldives	1990	56.4	19.9	50.2	26.5	41.3	10.8	39.7	49.3	4.5	6.5	14.1	25.0	9.4	16.6
Mali	1987	3,438	37.4	67.4	44.7	57.2	32.7	35.4	5.2	57.6	1.8	2,803	81.5	191	5.6
Malta	1990	132	25.4	47.4[13]	37.2	56.1	18.7	14.1[48]	77.4[48]	...	8.5[48]	3	2.5	38	28.8
Marshall Islands	1988	11.5	30.1	54.1[28]	26.5	37.7	14.8	21.6	58.9	7.1	12.5	2.2	18.7	1.0	9.0
Martinique	1990	165	47.5	68.1	45.9	49.8	42.2	9.5	56.9	1.5	32.1	8.4	5.1	9.7	5.9
Mauritania	1991	638	22.3	45.5[10]	30.8	48.1	13.8	...	...	...	...	410	64.3	70[11]	11.0[11]
Mauritius[49]	1993	463	35.2	68.0	44.5	57.9	31.2	12.2[22]	80.1[22]	1.9[22]	5.9[22]	81	17.5	146	31.5
Mayotte	1991	27.3	29.4	56.4	28.9	39.2	17.7	12.0	42.9	7.3	37.8	3.1	11.4	1.3	4.7
Mexico	1995	35,558	32.1	61.8	39.4	54.5	24.9	30.1[20]	53.8[20]	13.6[20]	2.6[20]	8,453	23.8	5,628	15.8
Micronesia	1990	30.5	29.8[14]	60.6	30.3	...	...	2.7[14]	74.4[14]	0.1[14]	22.7[14]	12.7	41.5	1.6	5.2
Moldova	1994	1,699	...	68.7[16]	39.1	...	...	...	...	...	...	767	45.1	232	13.7
Monaco	1990	12.6	39.7	...	42.0	53.2	31.8	17.4	75.1	0.3	7.2	—	0.3	2.7	21.8
Mongolia	1993	845	47.2[33]	77.9[33, 51]	39.3[33]	41.6[33]	37.1[33]	...	...	...	...	300	35.5	124	14.7
Morocco	1982	5,999	19.7	48.9	29.3	47.1	11.6	27.1	40.5	17.6	14.8	2,352	39.2	1,016	16.9
Mozambique	1980	5,671	52.4	87.3[25]	48.6	47.6	49.5	...	...	...	...	4,755	83.8	347	6.1
Myanmar (Burma)	1994[18]	17,358	35.3[48]	64.2[48]	40.2[48]	52.4[48]	28.2[48]	41.4[48]	27.4[48]	30.2[48]	1.0[48]	11,551	66.5	1,354	7.8
Namibia	1991	494	43.6	61.3	35.2	39.9	30.5	17.8	49.1	17.9	15.2	190	38.5	41	8.2
Nauru	1977	2.2	...	...	30.5	...	...	...	...	...	...	...	...	...	...
Nepal	1991	7,340	40.4	57.0[10]	40.0	47.8	32.2	75.8	21.4	2.3	0.4	5,962	81.2	164	2.2
Netherlands, The	1995	7,358	41.5	70.1	47.5	56.2	39.0	9.9	81.8	1.1	7.1	244	3.3	1,134	15.4
Netherlands Antilles	1992	87.8	45.1	68.6	46.3	53.1	40.1	...	...	...	...	0.5	0.6	8.4	9.6
New Caledonia	1989	66	37.5	70.7[53]	40.2	49.1	30.8	16.3	64.3	1.6	17.8	7.8	11.8	6.2	9.3
New Zealand	1995[18]	1,742	44.1	74.7	48.7	55.2	42.1	18.2[20]	71.3[20]	1.0[20]	9.5[20]	169	9.7	330	18.9
Nicaragua	1995	1,459	33.2[13]	51.6[10, 20]	35.2	...	...	...	...	...	...	457	31.4	183	12.5

construction		transportation, communications		trade, hotels, restaurants		finance, real estate		public administration, defense		services		other		country
number ('000)	% of econ. active	number ('000)	% of econ. active	number ('000)	% of econ. active	number ('000)	% of econ. active	number ('000)	% of econ. active	number ('000)	% of econ. active	number ('000)	% of econ. active	
2.0	11.1	1.9	11.1	2.1	11.9	0.3	1.9	[7]	[7]	3.5[7]	20.1[7]	0.6	3.2	Faroe Islands
12	4.9	13	5.5	26	10.8	6	2.5	[7]	[7]	37[7]	15.2[7]	20[17]	8.2[17]	Fiji
174	6.9	177	7.0	353	14.0	198	7.9	[7]	[7]	832[7]	33.0[7]	96[23]	3.8[23]	Finland
1,443	5.7	1,397	5.5	3,716	14.6	2,340	9.2	[7]	[7]	7,733[7]	30.3[7]	3,376[17]	13.2[17]	France
4.4	9.1	1.9	3.8	4.2	8.5	1.7	3.5	[7]	[7]	17.5[7]	35.9[7]	11.8[9]	24.2[9]	French Guiana
5.5	7.4	2.8	3.7	10.3	13.7	1.2	1.5	[7]	[7]	21.5[7]	28.6[7]	21.1[17]	28.0[17]	French Polynesia
[11]	[11]	[12]	[12]	[12]	[12]	[12]	[12]	[12]	[12]	95[12]	18.8[12]	—	—	Gabon
4	1.3	8	2.5	17	5.1	5	1.4	8	2.5	9	2.9	25	7.7	Gambia, The
17.8	10.3	5.7	3.3	20.8	12.0	[1]	[1]	[1]	[1]	49.3[1, 36]	28.5[1, 36]	53.3[9]	30.8[9]	Gaza Strip
125	6.5	107	5.6	117	6.1	20	1.0	49	2.6	479	24.9	158[17]	8.2[17]	Georgia
3,756	9.4	2,218	5.5	6,916	17.3	3,685	9.2	3,362	8.4	7,623	19.0	235[2]	0.6[2]	Germany
65	1.2	123	2.2	792	14.2	27	0.5	98	1.7	376	6.7	158[9]	2.8[9]	Ghana
1.2	9.6	0.9	7.4	3.2	24.7	1.6	12.4	1.9	14.8	3.3	25.5	—	—	Gibraltar
273	6.4	266	6.3	906	21.3	250	5.9	279	6.6	573	13.5	210[23]	4.9[23]	Greece
3.1	14.6	1.8	8.6	2.7	12.6	0.3	1.6	[7]	[7]	6.3[7]	29.5[7]	0.6	2.8	Greenland
3.5	9.1	1.7	4.4	5.4	13.9	0.8	2.0	[7]	[7]	5.9[7]	15.3[7]	12.7[17]	32.5[17]	Grenada
14.0	8.1	7.0	4.0	15.0	8.7	2.8	1.6	[7]	[7]	60.8[7]	35.2[7]	54.9[17]	31.8[17]	Guadeloupe
8.0	12.1	4.5	6.8	11.5	17.5	3.9	6.0	17.7	26.7	14.5	21.9	2.0[9]	3.1[9]	Guam
114	3.9	72	2.5	375	12.9	38	1.3	[7]	[7]	417[7]	14.4[7]	60[17]	2.1[17]	Guatemala
3.2	10.5	1.4	4.5	7.4	24.6	5.8	19.3	1.9	6.4	5.3	17.7	0.4	1.3	Guernsey[38]
9	0.5	29	1.6	37	2.0	4	0.2	[7]	[7]	138[7]	7.5[7]	156	8.5	Guinea
[11]	[11]	[12]	[12]	[12]	[12]	[12]	[12]	[12]	[12]	81[12]	17.5[12]	—	—	Guinea-Bissau
7[14]	2.8[14]	9[14]	3.8[14]	15[14]	6.2[14]	3[14]	1.2[14]	30[14]	12.1[14]	29[14]	11.9[14]	61[14, 17]	24.7[14, 17]	Guyana
28	1.0	21	0.8	353	13.2	5	0.2	[7]	[7]	155[7]	5.8[7]	404[17]	15.1[17]	Haiti
107	5.7	60	3.2	300	16.1	37	2.0	[7]	[7]	317[7]	17.0[7]	18[17]	1.0[17]	Honduras
252	8.2	347	11.3	869	28.3	355	11.6	[7]	[7]	626[7]	20.4[7]	12[2]	0.4[2]	Hong Kong
261	6.4	342	8.4	637	15.6	225	5.5	334	8.2	793	19.4	68[23]	1.7[23]	Hungary
10.3	6.9	9.6	6.4	24.8	16.6	13.5	9.1	6.3	4.2	41.8	28.1	1.9[23]	1.3[23]	Iceland
5,543	1.8	8,108	2.6	21,296	6.8	[1]	[1]	[1]	[1]	29,312[1]	9.3[1]	28,199	9.0	India
3,768	4.4	3,458	4.0	13,884	16.1	658	0.8	[7]	[7]	12,122[7]	14.0[7]	6,251[9]	7.2[9]	Indonesia
1,372	9.3	762	5.2	1,238	8.4	195	1.3	[7]	[7]	3,518[7]	23.9[7]	2,203[17]	14.9[17]	Iran
461	11.2	266	6.4	282	6.8	42	1.0	[7]	[7]	2,160[7]	52.3[7]	—	—	Iraq
101	7.0	81	5.6	272	18.8	120	8.3	74	5.1	283	19.6	69[15]	4.8[15]	Ireland
3.4	10.3	2.4	7.3	6.1	18.4	4.4	13.1	[7]	[7]	10.4[7]	31.4[7]	1.4[9]	4.1[9]	Isle of Man
141	6.7	115	5.5	330	15.7	244	11.6	107	5.1	533	25.4	149[17]	7.1[17]	Israel
1,641	7.2	1,080	4.8	4,221	18.6	1,514	6.7	[7]	[7]	5,134[7]	22.6[7]	2,676[9]	11.8[9]	Italy
66	6.1	40	3.7	196	17.9	47	4.3	[7]	[7]	237[7]	21.7[7]	180[17]	16.5[17]	Jamaica
6,750	10.1	4,130	6.2	14,790[41]	22.2[41]	5,550	8.3	[7]	[7]	15,190[7, 41]	22.8[7, 41]	1,240[17]	1.9[17]	Japan
4.4	9.3	2.4	5.0	6.8	14.4	7.4	15.6	3.1	6.5	15.7	33.1	1.6[17]	3.4[17]	Jersey
60	7.0	58	6.7	130	15.1	25	2.9	[7]	[7]	435[7]	50.6[7]	—	—	Jordan
364	5.2	507	7.3	1,035	14.8	334	4.8	[7]	[7]	1,664[7]	23.9[7]	258[17]	3.7[17]	Kazakstan
[11]	[11]	[12]	[12]	[12]	[12]	[12]	[12]	[12]	[12]	1,587[12]	15.5[12]	—	—	Kenya
0.3	1.0	0.9	2.8	1.3	4.1	0.4	1.4	2.1	6.5	2.3	7.0	1.1[17]	3.4[17]	Kiribati
[11]	[11]	[12]	[12]	[12]	[12]	[12]	[12]	[12]	[12]	1,939[12, 24]	22.9[12, 24]	—	—	Korea, North
1,934	9.3	1,082	5.2	5,445	26.2	1,655	8.0	647	3.1	2,390	11.5	165[2]	0.8[2]	Korea, South
115[42]	15.7[42]	38[42]	5.2[42]	83[42]	11.4[42]	22[42]	3.0[42]	[7]	[7]	384[7, 42]	52.6[7, 42]	11[2, 42]	1.5[2, 42]	Kuwait
77	4.6	86	5.1	112	6.6	17	1.0	58	3.4	610	36.1	191[21]	11.3[21]	Kyrgyzstan
[11]	[11]	[12]	[12]	[12]	[12]	[12]	[12]	[12]	[12]	316[12, 14]	17.2[12, 14]	—	—	Laos
71	5.6	105	8.3	191	15.0	77	6.1	56	4.4	241	18.9	83	6.5	Latvia
43[44]	6.2[44]	48[44]	7.0[44]	115[44]	16.5[44]	24[44]	3.5[44]	[7]	[7]	200[7, 44]	28.8[7, 44]	—	—	Lebanon
28	5.5	8	1.6	24	4.7	2	0.5	[7]	[7]	157[7]	31.1[7]	13	2.6	Lesotho
4	0.6	14	2.0	47	6.7	[1]	[1]	[1]	[1]	63[1]	9.0[1]	64[17]	9.1[17]	Liberia
[11]	[11]	[12]	[12]	[12]	[12]	[12]	[12]	[12]	[12]	668[12]	57.1[12]	—	—	Libya
1.1	7.0	0.5	3.2	2.4	14.8	1.3	7.8	1.0	6.4	4.1	25.4	0.6[17]	3.4[17]	Liechtenstein
111	5.7	92	4.7	246	12.7	63	3.3	60	3.1	335	17.3	262[9]	13.5[9]	Lithuania
14	8.4	11	6.3	29	17.5	15	9.2	21	12.8	31	18.7	14[21]	8.1[21]	Luxembourg
18.6	9.9	10.4	5.6	47.3	25.3	11.4	6.1	[7]	[7]	55.4[7]	29.6[7]	0.3	0.1	Macau
37	3.9	21	2.3	54	5.8	20	2.2	15	1.6	69	7.4	338[46]	36.1[46]	Macedonia
[11]	[11]	[12]	[12]	[12]	[12]	[12]	[12]	[12]	[12]	636[12]	12.0[12]	—	—	Madagascar
46	1.4	25	0.7	94	2.7	6	0.2	[7]	[7]	147[7]	4.3[7]	57	1.7	Malaŵi
611	7.8	359	4.6	1,371	17.4	364	4.6	[7]	[7]	1,552[7]	19.7[7]	224[9]	2.8[9]	Malaysia
3.2	5.6	5.3	9.4	8.9	15.7	1.1	1.9	[7]	[7]	11.8[7]	21.0[7]	2.7[47]	4.7[47]	Maldives
13	0.4	6	0.2	159	4.6	0.3	—	75	2.2	84	2.4	107	3.1	Mali
6	4.4	9	6.9	13	9.8	5	3.7	[7]	[7]	53[7]	40.0[7]	5[9]	3.8[9]	Malta
1.1	9.4	0.5	4.7	1.4	12.1	0.8	7.3	[7]	[7]	3.1[7]	26.4[7]	1.4[17]	12.5[17]	Marshall Islands
9.3	5.6	6.7	4.0	14.0	8.5	3.0	1.8	[7]	[7]	59.1[7]	35.8[7]	54.8[17]	33.2[17]	Martinique
[11]	[11]	[12]	[12]	[12]	[12]	[12]	[12]	[12]	[12]	158[12]	24.8[12]	—	—	Mauritania
24	5.2	32	6.9	61	13.2	11	2.4	[7]	[7]	94[7]	20.3[7]	14[17]	3.1[17]	Mauritius[49]
3.1	11.4	1.5	5.4	2.0	7.2	0.1	0.4	[7]	[7]	5.7[7]	21.0[7]	10.5[17]	38.4[17]	Mayotte
2,033	5.7	1,528	4.3	8,015	22.5	1,183	3.3	[7]	[7]	8,030[7]	22.6[7]	688[17]	1.9[17]	Mexico
1.8	6.1	[50]	[50]	[50]	[50]	[50]	[50]	6.3	20.8	3.7[50]	12.1[50]	4.1[9]	13.5[9]	Micronesia
91	5.4	73	4.3	107	6.3	20	1.2	32	1.9	344	20.2	33[17]	1.9[17]	Moldova
0.7	5.3	...	...	2.5	20.2	1.0	8.0	2.8	22.4	1.9	14.9	0.9[21]	7.1[21]	Monaco
33	3.9	38	4.4	62	7.3	[1]	[1]	[1]	[1]	123[1]	14.5[1]	166[21]	19.7[21]	Mongolia
437	7.3	141	2.3	498	8.3	[52]	[52]	533	8.9	474[52]	7.9[52]	548[2]	9.1[2]	Morocco
42	0.7	7.7	1.4	112	2.0	[1]	[1]	[1]	[1]	243[1]	4.3[1]	95[9]	1.7[9]	Mozambique
292	1.7	420	2.4	1,450	8.4	1,264	7.3	[7]	[7]	486[7]	2.8[7]	541[9]	3.1[9]	Myanmar (Burma)
19	3.8	9	1.9	38	7.7	9	1.7	[7]	[7]	6[7]	1.2[7]	183[17]	37.1[17]	Namibia
...	...	...	...	...	...	...	...	...	...					Nauru
36	0.5	51	0.7	256	3.5	20	0.3	[7]	[7]	752[7]	10.3[7]	98	1.3	Nepal
406	5.5	406	5.5	1,342	18.2	880	12.0	529	7.2	1,650	22.4	762[17]	10.4[17]	Netherlands, The
6.5	7.4	5.0	5.7	20.9	23.8	8.2	9.3	[7]	[7]	24.8[7]	28.2[7]	13.4[9]	15.3[9]	Netherlands Antilles
4.5	6.8	3.1	4.7	9.5	14.3	2.5	3.8	[7]	[7]	22.0[7]	33.4[7]	13.5[9]	16.0[9]	New Caledonia
106	6.1	103	5.9	368	21.1	179	10.3	[7]	[7]	460[7]	26.4[7]	29[15]	1.7[15]	New Zealand
32	2.2	32	2.2	201	13.8	16	1.1	79	5.4	195	13.4	265[9]	18.2[9]	Nicaragua

Employment and labour (continued)

country	year	economically active population										distribution by economic sector			
		total ('000)	participation rate (%)		activity rate (%)			employment status (%)				agriculture, forestry, fishing		manufacturing; mining, quarrying; public utilities	
			female	ages 15–64	total	male	female	employers, self-employed	employees	unpaid family workers	other	number ('000)	% of econ. active	number ('000)	% of econ. active
Niger	1988[54]	2,316	20.4	55.2	31.9	51.1	13.0	51.4	5.0	40.3	3.3	1,764	76.2	73	3.1
Nigeria	1986[18]	30,766	33.3	58.8	31.1	41.1	20.9	64.6	18.8	10.7	5.9	13,259	43.1	1,401	4.6
Northern Mariana Islands	1990	26.6	43.2	83.6[8]	61.3	66.2	55.9	1.4	96.1	0.2	2.3	0.6	2.3	6.0	22.5
Norway	1995	2,186	45.7	77.3[8]	50.2	55.1	45.3	8.1[19]	85.3[19]	0.9[19]	5.7[19]	109	5.0	363	16.6
Oman	1993	705	9.7	60.9	34.9	54.0	8.1	5.2	91.0	0.1	3.7	64	9.1	79	11.3
Pakistan	1993–94[18]	34,726	15.4	50.2	27.9	45.7	8.9	41.2[55]	32.4[55]	20.2[55]	6.2[55]	16,535	47.6	3,677	10.6
Palau	1990	6.1	36.9	64.1[8]	40.2	47.1	32.1	2.5	89.5	0.2	7.8	0.4	7.1	0.2	3.0
Panama	1994	967	34.3	60.7[25]	37.5	48.6	26.0	24.1	59.1	2.8	14.0	171	17.7	115	11.9
Papua New Guinea	1980[56]	733	39.8	35.2[10]	24.6	28.3	20.5	72.7	26.4	—	0.9	564	77.0	21	2.9
Paraguay	1982	1,039	19.7	57.5	34.3	54.8	13.6	43.1	37.7	9.2	9.9	446	42.9	129	12.4
Peru	1995	8,906	34.7	60.9	37.8	49.8	26.1	39.8[30]	41.8[30]	8.4[30]	10.0[30]	2,693[20]	32.5[20]	1,091[20]	13.2[20]
Philippines	1995[18]	28,040	37.4	67.3	...	...	...	36.2[19]	41.7[19]	13.7[19]	8.4[19]	11,323	40.4	2,769	9.9
Poland	1995[18]	17,004	45.9	66.9	44.0	48.9	39.3	20.1	61.6	5.1	13.1	3,355	19.7	4,436	26.1
Portugal	1993[18]	4,806[19]	44.6[19]	67.8[19]	48.8[19]	56.4[19]	41.9[19]	23.1	74.2	1.8	0.9	528	11.2	1,173	24.9
Puerto Rico	1995[18]	1,228	39.4	52.9[8]	32.2	40.1	24.8	13.6	85.2	0.7	0.6	42	3.4	220	17.9
Qatar	1988	293	11.2	80.8	53.7	77.3	22.2	1.8[44]	97.7[44]	—	0.5[44]	4.5	1.6	22.0	7.5
Réunion	1990[18]	234	41.1	60.3	39.1	46.8	31.6	8.4	53.1	1.1	37.4	11	4.8	11	4.8
Romania	1995	12,120	46.3	72.6	53.4	58.5	48.5	22.8	55.8	13.4	8.0	4,581	37.8	3,302	27.2
Russia	1994	73,655	...	...	49.8	...	...	...	...	...	...	11,029	15.0	18,126	24.6
Rwanda	1991	3,649	47.5	79.1[10]	50.2	53.3	47.2	...	...	...	...	3,313	90.8	129[11]	3.5[11]
St. Kitts and Nevis	1980	17.1	41.0	69.5	39.5	48.4	31.2	9.7	78.5	0.4	11.4	4.5	26.1	3.8	22.3
St. Lucia	1991	53.1	40.3	67.6	39.9	49.1	31.2	21.0[14]	55.8[14]	1.6[14]	21.6[14]	11.6	21.8	7.5	14.0
St. Vincent	1991	41.7	35.9	67.5	39.1	50.3	28.0	18.2	59.6	2.1	20.1	8.4	20.1	3.5	8.4
Samoa	1986	45.6	18.8	48.6[30]	29.0	44.5	11.6	21.1[30]	43.5[30]	35.0[30]	0.4[30]	29.0	63.6	2.4	5.4
San Marino	1995	16.8	39.3	76.4	57.2	66.1	47.4	15.3	77.1	0.3	7.3	0.2	1.5	5.3	31.3
São Tomé and Príncipe	1991	35	33.6	59.1	30.1	40.5	20.0	25.8	68.6	0.7	4.9	13.6	38.4	1.8	5.0
Saudi Arabia	1988	5,369	3.6	59.1	36.3	54.9	3.6	...	...	...	...	192	3.6	595	11.1
Senegal	1991	3,249	39.1	64.2[10]	42.6	52.6	32.9	...	...	...	...	2,543	78.3	228[11]	7.0[11]
Seychelles	1993[57]	28.1	...	...	38.9	...	...	...	...	...	...	2.2	7.7	4.6[11]	16.4[11]
Sierra Leone	1991	1,532	32.4	53.3[10]	35.9	49.4	22.8	...	...	...	...	945	61.7	275[11]	18.0[11]
Singapore	1995[18]	1,748	38.7	68.7	58.5	71.4	45.5	10.6	85.5	1.2	2.7	4	0.2	414	23.7
Slovakia	1995[18]	2,481	44.9	68.9	46.2	52.3	40.5	5.6	80.4	0.1	13.9	224	9.0	692	27.9
Slovenia	1995	952	46.2	67.9	47.9	53.1	42.9	11.3	77.0	4.3	7.4	94	9.9	363	38.1
Solomon Islands	1993[58]	29.6	25.6[44]	24.9[44, 59]	13.7[44]	19.7[44]	7.3[44]	29.6[44]	68.6[44]	—	1.8[44]	8.1	27.4	3.1	10.4
Somalia	1991	3,215	40.5	64.3[10]	40.9	51.1	31.0	...	...	...	...	2,275	70.8	336[11]	10.5[11]
South Africa[60]	1991	11,624	39.4	69.3[53]	37.5	45.5	29.5	7.0	74.8	...	18.2	1,224	10.5	2,361	20.3
Spain	1995[18]	15,625	38.3	60.7[8]	40.2	50.7	30.1	16.7	57.2	2.9	23.1	1,351	8.6	2,864	18.3
Sri Lanka	1995	6,115	33.3	54.9[25]	40.5	54.8	26.6	24.9	54.2	7.8	13.1	1,985	32.5	945	15.5
Sudan, The	1983[54]	6,343	29.1	57.4	35.1	50.0	20.4	...	...	...	...	4,029	63.5	317	5.0
Suriname	1994[61]	89.8	35.1	52.3	45.2	59.4	31.4	...	...	...	...	4.8	5.3	10.7	11.9
Swaziland	1991	326	39.0	62.3[10]	39.8	49.5	30.3	...	...	...	...	215	66.0	39[11]	12.0[11]
Sweden	1995	4,319	47.9	78.2[8]	48.9	51.6	46.3	9.9	82.0	0.4	7.7	132	3.1	841	19.5
Switzerland	1995[18, 45]	3,860	43.2	66.7[25]	55.0	64.0	46.4	12.8[19]	84.3[19]	2.9[19]	—	154	4.0	809	21.0
Syria	1991[18]	3,485	18.0	46.7[44]	27.8	44.6	10.2	31.0	49.3	13.0	6.7	917	26.3	471	13.5
Taiwan	1996[18]	9,310	39.2	58.4[25]	43.4	51.3	35.0	21.7	67.5	8.1	2.6	918	9.9	2,471	26.5
Tajikistan	1994	1,984	...	63.5[16, 20]	34.4	...	...	...	...	...	...	1,005	50.7	205	10.4
Tanzania	1991	13,123	40.0	87.8[10]	46.0	48.9	43.2	...	...	...	...	10,540	80.3	614[11]	4.7[11]
Thailand	1995[18, 62]	33,002	45.6	74.4[25, 63]	55.5	60.5	50.5	31.2[63]	40.3[63]	19.5[63]	9.1[63]	16,991[64]	51.5[64]	4,365	13.2
Togo	1991	1,432	36.2	58.8[10]	40.0	51.8	28.5	70.3[30]	10.4[30]	11.3[30]	8.0[30]	991	69.2	161[11]	11.2[11]
Tonga	1990	32.0	33.0	57.0	33.6	45.2	22.0	33.7	45.4	16.8	4.1	11.7	36.5	5.1	15.8
Trinidad and Tobago	1995	521	37.2	65.4	41.3	52.4	30.4	17.8	61.3	2.7	18.3	51	9.7	82	15.8
Tunisia	1989	2,361	20.9	50.6	29.8	46.5	12.7	20.9	54.9	7.4	16.8	510	21.6	418	17.7
Turkey	1995[18]	22,899	30.4	57.0	37.1	51.0	23.0	27.6[20]	41.5[20]	27.7[20]	3.2[20]	10,477	45.8	3,397	14.8
Turkmenistan	1996	1,680	40.0	71.9[16]	36.1	43.9	28.5	...	...	...	...	746	44.4	165	9.8
Tuvalu	1991	5.9	51.3[43]	85.5	65.3	...	...	0.3[43]	22.2[43]	—77.5[43]—		4.2	68.0	0.1	2.0
Uganda	1991	8,365	40.8	67.3[10]	43.6	52.2	35.2	...	...	...	...	6,724	80.4	478[11]	5.7[11]
Ukraine	1994	22,270	...	...	43.5	...	...	...	...	...	...	4,821	21.6	6,249	28.1
United Arab Emirates	1990	690	10.4[42]	69.0[42]	47.0[42]	67.6[42]	12.9[42]	6.8[14]	92.7[14]	0.1[14]	0.5[14]	43	6.3	94	13.6
United Kingdom	1993	28,271	43.8	76.2	49.4	56.8	42.3	11.2	76.7	0.5	11.6	522	1.8	5,775	20.4
United States	1995[18]	132,304	46.0	79.1[53]	50.1	55.4	46.2	8.3[19]	91.0[19]	0.1[19]	0.5[19]	3,866	2.9	23,750	18.0
Uruguay	1995[65]	1,344	42.8	70.4[40]	46.8	57.0	37.8	22.9[28]	72.3[28]	2.3[28]	2.5[28]	62	4.6	261	19.4
Uzbekistan	1994	8,235	...	...	37.3	...	...	...	...	...	...	3,754	45.6	1,225	14.9
Vanuatu	1989	67.0	46.3	85.0	47.0	49.0	44.9	...	...	...	...	49.8	74.4	1.0	1.5
Venezuela	1995[18]	8,611	33.6	64.0	39.4	52.0	26.6	30.2[20]	61.8[20]	1.7[20]	6.3[20]	1,043	12.1	1,344	15.6
Vietnam	1989	30,521	51.7	79.9	47.4	47.0	47.7	...	...	...	...	20,471	67.1	3,390	11.1
Virgin Islands (U.S.)	1990[18]	47.4	47.8	70.3	46.6	50.3	43.1	7.6	85.5	0.2	6.7	0.6	1.2	3.7	7.8
West Bank	1996	356.9	16.1	42.2[25]	22.7	37.7	7.4	24.5	49.0	8.1	18.5	41.3	11.6	51.8[36]	14.5[36]
Western Sahara	...	...	...	...	...	...	...	...	...	...	...	...	...	...	...
Yemen	1988	3,029	31.6	52.6	26.4	36.8	16.4	...	...	...	...	2,152	71.1	129	4.3
Yugoslavia	1996	3,182	43.4[19]	58.7[25, 34]	30.1	...	...	...	...	...	...	104	3.3	903	28.4
Zambia	1991	2,928	29.6	52.6[10]	33.4	47.4	19.6	22.9[14]	42.5[14]	3.6[14]	31.0[14]	2,010	68.6	333[11]	11.4[11]
Zimbabwe	1992	3,601	39.6	63.4	34.6	42.8	26.7	24.1	43.9	9.2	22.8	2,110[67]	64.7[67]	179[67]	5.5[67]

[1]Services includes finance, real estate and public administration, defense. [2]Unemployed, not previously employed only. [3]Includes emigrant workers (352,000). [4]Ages 15–59 (male) and 15–54 (female). [5]State sector only. [6]Includes nonagricultural private sector (241,000) and unemployed (261,000). [7]Services includes public administration, defense. [8]Ages 16–64. [9]Unemployed only. [10]Over age 10. [11]Manufacturing; mining, quarrying; public utilities includes construction. [12]Services includes transportation, communications; trade, hotels, restaurants; finance, real estate; and public administration, defense. [13]1991. [14]1980. [15]Includes unemployed, not previously employed. [16]Ages 16–59 (male) and 16–54 (female). [17]Mostly unemployed. [18]Excludes all or some classes or elements of the military. [19]1994. [20]1993. [21]Includes unemployed. [22]1990. [23]Mostly unemployed, not previously employed. [24]1982. [25]Over age 15. [26]Ages 14–64. [27]Services includes restaurants and hotels. [28]1992. [29]Over age 12. [30]1981. [31]Republic of Cyprus only. [32]1993 population economically active for Turkish Republic of Northern Cyprus is 75,947. [33]1989. [34]1995.

construction		transportation, communications		trade, hotels, restaurants		finance, real estate		public administration, defense		services		other		country
number ('000)	% of econ. active	number ('000)	% of econ. active	number ('000)	% of econ. active	number ('000)	% of econ. active	number ('000)	% of econ. active	number ('000)	% of econ. active	number ('000)	% of econ. active	
14	0.6	15	0.6	209	9.0	2	0.1	[7]	[7]	123[7]	5.3[7]	117[21]	5.0[21]	Niger
546	1.8	1,112	3.6	7,417	24.1	120	0.4	[7]	[7]	4,902[7]	15.9[7]	2,009[17]	6.5[17]	Nigeria
5.8	21.7	1.4	5.3	5.3	19.8	1.0	3.8	1.4	5.3	4.5	16.9	0.6[9]	2.3[9]	Northern Mariana Islands
131	6.0	174	8.0	369	16.9	164	7.5	150	6.9	671	30.7	56[23]	2.6[23]	Norway
108	15.3	25	3.5	104	14.8	17	2.5	166	23.5	111	15.8	30[23]	4.3[23]	Oman
2,166	6.2	1,651	4.8	4,237	12.2	259	0.7	[7]	[7]	4,638[7]	13.4[7]	1,542[23]	4.4[23]	Pakistan
0.9	14.2	0.4	6.6	1.1	18.7	0.2	2.9	0.8	13.7	1.6	26.1	0.5[9]	7.8[9]	Palau
63	6.5	66	6.8	199	20.6	50	5.2	67	6.9	192	19.8	44[23]	4.6[23]	Panama
22	2.9	1.7	2.4	25	3.4	4	0.6	[7]	[7]	77[7]	10.5[7]	2	0.2	Papua New Guinea
70	6.7	31	2.9	86	8.3	18	1.7	[7]	[7]	174[7]	16.8[7]	86[15]	8.3[15]	Paraguay
308[20]	3.7[20]	364[20]	4.4[20]	1,352[20]	16.3[20]	197[20]	2.4[20]	[7]	[7]	2,287[7, 20]	27.6[7, 20]	—	—	Peru
1,239	4.4	1,489	5.3	3,745[27]	13.4[27]	551	2.0	[7]	[7]	4,559[7, 27]	16.3[7, 27]	2,363[17]	8.4[17]	Philippines
1,126	6.6	940	5.5	2,430	14.3	690	4.1	793	4.7	2,723	16.0	511[23]	3.0[23]	Poland
384	8.2	216	4.6	923	19.6	312	6.6	[7]	[7]	1,137[7]	24.1[7]	42[2]	0.9[2]	Portugal
84	6.8	42	3.4	250	20.4	34	2.8	[7]	[7]	550[7]	44.8[7]	7	0.6	Puerto Rico
64.2	22.0	11.9	4.1	34.2	11.7	6.2	2.1	[7]	[7]	149.6[7]	51.1[7]	—	—	Qatar
17	7.1	7	3.1	18	7.7	3	1.3	[7]	[7]	79[7]	33.9[7]	87[17]	37.4[17]	Réunion
521	4.3	584	4.8	807	6.7	249	2.1	572	4.7	1,018	8.4	486[23]	4.0[23]	Romania
6,274	8.5	5,354	7.3	5,788	7.9	3,755	5.1	1,450	2.0	16,688	22.7	5,171[9]	7.0[9]	Russia
[11]	[11]	[12]	[12]	[12]	[12]	[12]	[12]	[12]	[12]	207[12]	5.7[12]	—	—	Rwanda
0.4	2.5	0.3	1.6	1.3	7.3	0.8	4.7	1.0	5.7	2.9	17.0	2.2[17]	12.8[17]	St. Kitts and Nevis
5.0	9.3	2.7	5.0	11.1	20.8	1.9	3.6	[7]	[7]	9.2[7]	17.2[7]	4.3	8.2	St. Lucia
3.5	8.5	2.3	5.5	6.5	15.7	1.4	3.4	[7]	[7]	7.7[7]	18.5[7]	8.3[9]	20.0[9]	St. Vincent
0.1	0.1	1.5	3.3	1.7	3.7	0.8	1.8	[7]	[7]	9.4[7]	20.7[7]	0.6	1.4	Samoa
1.4	8.6	0.3	1.9	2.6	15.7	1.1	6.8	2.0	12.1	2.5	14.9	1.2[21]	7.2[21]	San Marino
2.9	8.1	2.2	6.2	4.5	12.6	0.2	0.5	[7]	[7]	8.0[7]	22.5[7]	2.4	6.7	São Tomé and Príncipe
1,181	22.0	321	6.0	964	18.0	151	2.8	[7]	[7]	1,965[7]	36.6[7]	—	—	Saudi Arabia
[11]	[11]	[12]	[12]	[12]	[12]	[12]	[12]	[12]	[12]	477[12]	14.7[12]	—	—	Senegal
[11]	[11]	3.4	12.2	5.2	18.6	1.0	3.4	2.6	9.1	5.6	20.0	3.6[17]	12.6[17]	Seychelles
[11]	[11]	[12]	[12]	[12]	[12]	[12]	[12]	[12]	[12]	312[12]	20.4[12]	—	—	Sierra Leone
113	6.4	183	10.5	344	19.7	253	14.5	100	5.7	289	16.5	47[9]	2.7[9]	Singapore
227	9.1	177	7.1	331	13.3	134	5.4	146	5.9	426	17.2	126[15]	5.1[15]	Slovakia
50	5.3	54	5.7	145	15.2	56	5.9	39	4.1	131	13.8	19[23]	2.0[23]	Slovenia
1.0	3.3	1.7	5.8	3.4	11.5	1.1	3.9	4.3	14.6	6.8	23.1	—	—	Solomon Islands
[11]	[11]	[12]	[12]	[12]	[12]	[12]	[12]	[12]	[12]	604[12]	18.8[12]	—	—	Somalia
526	4.5	497	4.3	1,358	11.7	504	4.3	[7]	[7]	2,641[7]	22.7[7]	2,513[17]	21.6[17]	South Africa[60]
1,474	9.4	797	5.1	3,289	21.1	1,119	7.2	844	5.4	2,374	15.2	1,514[23]	9.7[23]	Spain
300	4.9	245	4.0	557	9.1	92	1.5	[7]	[7]	894[7]	14.6[7]	1,098[17]	17.9[17]	Sri Lanka
139	2.2	215	3.4	294	4.6	21	0.3	[7]	[7]	550[7]	8.7[7]	777[23]	12.3[23]	Sudan, The
4.2	4.6	5.1	5.6	11.4	12.7	3.5	3.9	[7]	[7]	35.7[7]	39.7[7]	14.6[17]	16.3[17]	Suriname
[11]	[11]	[12]	[12]	[12]	[12]	[12]	[12]	[12]	[12]	72[12]	20.1[12]	—	—	Swaziland
266	6.2	272	6.3	639	14.8	471	10.9	205	4.7	1,330	30.8	21	0.5	Sweden
286	7.4	227	5.9	733	19.0	485	12.6	[7]	[7]	1,088[7]	28.2[7]	77	2.0	Switzerland
341	9.8	167	4.8	378	10.9	25	0.7	[7]	[7]	951[7]	27.3[7]	235[9]	6.8[9]	Syria
928	10.0	472	5.1	1,976	21.2	567	6.1	324	3.5	1,412	15.2	242[9]	2.6[9]	Taiwan
105	5.3	63	3.2	112	5.6	[52]	[52]	21	1.1	326[52]	16.5[52]	146[17]	7.4[17]	Tajikistan
[11]	[11]	[12]	[12]	[12]	[12]	[12]	[12]	[12]	[12]	1,969[12]	15.0[12]	—	—	Tanzania
1,857	5.6	977	3.0	4,104	12.4	[1]	[1]	[1]	[1]	4,104[1]	12.4[1]	603[17]	1.8[17]	Thailand
[11]	[11]	[12]	[12]	[12]	[12]	[12]	[12]	[12]	[12]	280[12]	19.6[12]	—	—	Togo
1.3	3.9	1.8	5.7	2.6	8.1	1.2	3.7	[7]	[7]	7.1[7]	22.0[7]	1.3[9]	4.2[9]	Tonga
71	13.7	44	8.4	84	16.1	35	6.7	[7]	[7]	154[7]	29.6[7]	1	0.1	Trinidad and Tobago
248	10.5	96	4.1	217	9.2	15	0.7	[7]	[7]	444[7]	18.8[7]	412[17]	17.5[17]	Tunisia
1,379	6.0	892	3.9	2,776	12.1	519	2.3	[7]	[7]	2,892[7]	12.6[7]	567[2]	2.5[2]	Turkey
155	9.2	83	4.9	107	6.4	55	3.3	25	1.5	300	17.9	44	2.6	Turkmenistan
0.2	4.0	0.1	1.0	0.2	4.0	—	—	[7]	[7]	1.3[7]	22.0[7]	—	—	Tuvalu
[11]	[11]	[12]	[12]	[12]	[12]	[12]	[12]	[12]	[12]	1,163[12]	13.9[12]	—	—	Uganda
1,640	7.4	1,491	6.7	1,629	7.3	176	0.8	681	3.1	5,023	22.6	560[21]	2.5[21]	Ukraine
119	17.3	72	10.4	101	14.7	19	2.7	[7]	[7]	241[7]	35.0[7]	—	—	United Arab Emirates
1,679	5.9	1,626	5.8	5,031	17.8	3,210	11.4	[7]	[7]	7,214[7]	25.5[7]	3,214[17]	11.4[17]	United Kingdom
8,478	6.4	7,527	5.7	27,804[41]	21.0[41]	14,462	10.9	[7]	[7]	45,805[7, 41]	34.6[7, 41]	612[23]	0.5[23]	United States
98	7.3	73	5.4	261	19.4	79	5.9	[7]	[7]	479[7]	35.7[7]	33[2]	2.4[2]	Uruguay
550	6.7	330	4.0	501	6.1	29	0.4	90	1.1	1,690	20.5	66	0.8	Uzbekistan
1.3	1.9	1.0	1.5	2.7	4.1	0.6	1.0	[7]	[7]	7.9[7]	11.8[7]	2.6	3.8	Vanuatu
753	8.7	524	6.1	1,894	22.0	488	5.7	[7]	[7]	2,353[7]	27.3[7]	220[23]	2.6[23]	Venezuela
581	1.9	576	1.9	1,880	6.2	90	0.3	305	1.0	1,374	4.5	1,854[17]	6.1[17]	Vietnam
5.7	12.0	3.7	7.8	10.3	21.8	3.6	7.7	5.1	10.8	7.8	16.4	6.9	14.6	Virgin Islands (U.S.)
60.8	17.0	15.7	4.4	52.6	14.8	[1]	[1]	[1]	[1]	68.6[1, 36]	19.2[1, 36]	66.0[9]	18.5[9]	West Bank
...	...	...	...	...	...	...	...	...	...	...	...	...	...	Western Sahara
178	5.9	90	3.0	84	2.8	4	0.1	[7]	[7]	391[7]	12.9[7]	—	—	Yemen
130	4.1	142	4.5	557[66]	17.5[66]	77	2.4	92	2.9	356	11.2	819[9]	25.7[9]	Yugoslavia
[11]	[11]	[12]	[12]	[12]	[12]	[12]	[12]	[12]	[12]	585[12]	20.0[12]	—	—	Zambia
51[67]	1.6[67]	76[67]	2.3[67]	128[67]	3.9[67]	24[67]	0.7[67]	[7]	[7]	397[7, 67]	12.2[7, 67]	277[17, 67]	8.5[17, 67]	Zimbabwe

[35]1984. [36]Services includes public utilities. [37]Ages 15–65. [38]Excludes Alderney and Sark. [39]1977. [40]Ages 14–64. [41]Services includes hotels. [42]1988. [43]1979. [44]1986. [45]Excludes foreign border workers. [46]Includes unemployed, emigrant workers, and employees in private nonagricultural sector. [47]Includes unemployed, previously employed. [48]1983. [49]Island of Mauritius only. [50]Services includes transportation, communications; trade, hotels, restaurants; and finance, real estate. [51]Ages 16–59. [52]Services includes finance, real estate. [53]Ages 20–64. [54]Excludes nomadic population. [55]1992–93. [56]Citizens over age 10 involved in money-raising activities only. [57]Excludes domestic workers (private households), self-employed, and family workers. [58]Wage earners only. [59]Over age 14. [60]Excludes the former black independent states of Bophuthatswana, Ciskei, Transkei, and Venda. [61]Districts of Wanica and Paramaribo only. [62]August survey. [63]1994; February survey. [64]Includes seasonally inactive labour force (51,600). [65]Urban areas only. [66]Includes arts and crafts and owners and employees of private shops. [67]1986–87.

Agriculture and land use

This table provides data on the structure of national agricultural sectors from the perspective of farms and farmland use. The data are taken mainly from national agricultural censuses and surveys, supplemented by reports of the United Nations Food and Agriculture Organization's (FAO's) *World Census of Agriculture* (WCA). Many of these national censuses, of course, are taken under guidelines established by the FAO for the *World Census of Agriculture* programs (the 1990 census was the fifth and included national censuses taken during the decade 1986–95). Some 120 countries participated in the 1990 census. WCA 2000 commenced in 1996 and represents a continuing cooperative effort by FAO member countries to collect agricultural data within a general framework that permits international harmonization of concepts and definitions; transfer of technical expertise; and increased effectiveness in the collection, analysis, publication, and policy-related use of such statistics.

All agricultural statistics are subject to methodological problems, including errors or biases arising from such factors as incomplete or inaccurate lists of holdings, ambiguous questions, respondents who inadvertently or willfully give inaccurate information, failure to record data for all parts of fragmented holdings, respondents' misunderstandings of the definitions of land use and cropping methods, or a failure to report livestock temporarily absent from the holding on public or common pasture land or in transit. Frequently, subjects studied, classificational schemes, and definitions vary from the FAO guidelines (economic planners need different information about a commercial, high-technology, multicrop agricultural sector than they do for a family-subsistence, low-technology, one-crop sector). When a complete census of agriculture is impossible, a sample survey may be taken. This is a limited census of a predetermined number of carefully screened holdings. From these results, nationwide projections may be prepared.

With respect to the first section of the table, number and size of farms, many countries impose a minimum size limit for holdings that may be covered in their census reports, and this cutoff, if not sufficiently low, can result in a substantial undercount of smaller holdings; conversely Soviet-bloc nations formerly published statistics only on state collective or cooperative farms and excluded production from privately held plots of land, even though these often represented a significant fraction of agricultural output.

The land tenure statistics classify farms (a single parcel of land, or holding, or a group of holdings operated as a single farm) according to the rights under which the farmer holds the land or operates the enterprise represented by the farm. Owner-operated includes two types of ownership: outright ownership in which the holder has title and has the right to determine use and transfer of the land; and ownerlike possession in which the holder lacks the legal title but uses it under perpetual lease, hereditary tenure, or leases of 30 years or more with nominal, or no, rent. Farms classed as owner-operated are divided into individual and family, corporate or state, and socialized or collective proprietorships. Rented includes sharecropping; communal/tribal includes types of customary or traditional

Agriculture and land use

country	farms (latest census of agriculture)[a]															
	year	number of farms ('000)	size of holding								tenure (% of farms)					
			average (ha)	size class (%)							owner-operated			rented (including share-croppers)	tribal/ com-munal	other[b]
				under 1 ha	1–5 ha	5–10 ha	10–20 ha	20–50 ha	50–200 ha	over 200 ha	individual/ family	corporate/ state	socialized/ collective			
Afghanistan	1994	126[1]	3.5[1]	44.8[1]	35.2[1]	20.0[1]					55.1[1]	—	—	25.1[1]	—	19.8[1]
Albania	1990	0.5[3]	1,182[2, 3]	...	...	...	...	...	...	...	100.0[4]	—	—	—	—	—
Algeria	1987	899[6]	6.2[6]	1.1[6]	12.7[6]	15.8[6]	21.7[6]	25.6[6]	18.0[6]	5.1[6]	...	...	...	...	...	...
American Samoa	1990	1.1	2.9	44.7[8]	40.0[9]	13.8[10]		1.5[11]			93.9	—	—	2.2	—	3.9
Andorra	—	...	...	...	...	...	...	...	...	...	...	...	...	...	...	...
Angola	1970–71	1,067	3.9	3.3	13.5	9.3	11.3	13.7	19.2	29.7	80.5	1.1	—	—	18.2	0.2
Antigua and Barbuda	1984	2.3	2.1	61.7	33.8	2.9	0.6	0.6	0.4	—	32.1[14]	22.9[14]		40.5[14]	—	4.5[14]
Argentina	1988	421	469	15.1		8.4	14.0[15]	12.0[16]	25.1	25.5	85.1[14]	—	—	8.3[14]	—	6.6[14]
Armenia	1996	316[18]	1[18]		...	...	...	...	...	...	...	...	...	...	...	...
Aruba	...	...	...	...	...	...	...	...	...	...	...	...	...	...	...	...
Australia	1994–95	150	3,710[7]	15.7					9.2[19]	75.1[20]	...	...	...	...	...	...
Austria	1993	267	26.4[24]	3.3[24]	32.2[24]	17.8[24]	20.0[24]	21.5[24]	4.6[24]	0.6[24]	38.9[24]	1.5[24]	—	59.5[24]	—	0.1[24]
Azerbaijan	1996	3.2[18]	19[18]	...	...	...	...	...	...	...	...	...	...	...	...	...
Bahamas, The	1994	1.8	8.5	43.6[25, 26]	34.5[27]	9.7	6.2	2.3	3.7		25.7	—	—	20.1	39.7	14.5
Bahrain	1980	0.8	4.4	19.4	52.9	17.4	8.2	2.0	0.1		37.9	0.1	—	62.0	—	—
Bangladesh	1983–84	10,045	0.9	70.3	27.0[28]	2.5[29]	0.2[30]				62.8	...	...	1.4	...	35.8
Barbados	1989	17.2	95.8[33]	95.0[25]	3.9	0.3	0.2	0.1	0.3	0.2	76.2[14]	—	—	7.5[14]	16.3[14]	
Belarus	1996	3.0[18]	20[18]	...	...	...	...	...	...	...	52.1	13.1	34.8	—	—	—
Belgium	1995	73	16.5	13.9	24.1	14.8	19.1	22.1	6.0		33.4[14]	...	...	65.7[14]	—	0.9[14]
Belize	1996	11.0[36]	26.7[36]	9.3[36]	15.2[36]	56.3[36]			19.2[36]		43.6[17]	56.4[17]	—	—	—	—
Benin	1992	408	...	...	...	...	...	...	...	...	...	...	...	...	...	...
Bermuda	1990	0.08[37]	3.1[37]	...	...	...	...	...	...	...	...	...	...	...	...	...
Bhutan	1984	160	0.8	51.3[8, 38]	42.9[9, 38]	5.8[38, 39]					...	...	...	...	...	...
Bolivia	1996	519	72.1	27.1	41.1	11.8	6.6	6.0	4.8	2.6	78.0	...	...	2.0	4.1	15.9
Bosnia and Herzegovina[18]	1981	540	...	34.5	48.9	13.7	2.3	0.6			100.0	—	—	—	—	—
Botswana	1990	90.3[40]	5.0	9.1	56.1	26.9	7.9				—	0.4	—	—	99.6	—
Brazil	1985	5,835	64.5	11.3	28.6	13.2	14.0	15.6	12.4	4.9	63.2	—	—	17.9	—	18.9[42]
Brunei	1964	6.3	2.6	44.1[8]	40.4[9]	15.5[39]					52.3	1.0	—	22.0	—	24.7
Bulgaria	1991	2.2[44, 45]	2,467[44, 45]	...	...	...	...	...	...	...	19.0[46]	40.0[46]	41.0[46, 47]	—	—	—
Burkina Faso	1984	1,860	4.8	...	...	...	...	...	...	...	...	...	...	...	...	...
Burundi	1983	...	...	...	...	...	...	...	...	...	...	...	...	...	...	...
Cambodia	1962[49]	840	3.6	30.7	54.9	10.4	3.4	0.6			...	...	...	...	...	...
Cameroon	1973	926	1.6	42.7	53.8	3.2	0.3	—	—	—	2.4	—	—	5.2	59.5	32.9
Canada	1996	277[50]	246[50]	1.4[8]	3.5[9]	24.2[51]			70.9[52]		63.5[14]			36.5[14]	—	—
Cape Verde	1988	32.2	1.3	...	...	...	...	...	...	...	...	...	...	...	...	...
Central African Republic	1980	283[17]	1.7[17]	32.2[17]	65.2[17]	2.6[17]	—	—	—	—	0.3[14]	—	—	0.1[14]	98.6[14]	1.0[14]
Chad	1973	366	2.6	19.7	69.5	10.0	0.8		—	—	...	...	...	...	...	...
Chile	1983–84	306[55]	94.1[55]	16.0[55]	32.5[55]	13.4[55]	12.3[55]	11.8[55]	9.2[55]	4.8[55]	84.0			7.2	8.8	
China	1987	1,650	...	...	...	...	...	...	...	...	—	10.0[57]	90.0[57]	—	—	—
Colombia	1988	1,548	26.3[57]	19.2[27]	32.4	15.0	11.8	10.8	8.8	2.0	77.6	—	—	5.6	3.7	13.1
Comoros	1982	...	...	...	...	...	...	...	...	...	...	...	...	...	...	...
Congo, Dem. Rep. of the	1990	4,480	2.3	86.7	13.3			—	—	—	19.7	...	—	2.7	69.5	8.1
Congo, Rep. of the	1986	143[6]	1.4[6]	37.3[6]	62.2[6]	0.5[6]	—	—	—	—	91.7[14]	8.3[14]	—	—	—	—
Costa Rica	1973	82	38.3	23.3	25.5	11.2	10.8	15.2	10.7	3.3	97.9	1.7	—	0.1	—	0.3
Côte d'Ivoire	1975	550	5.0	9.5	54.4	24.9	9.4	1.7	0.1	—	...	...	...	...	...	...
Croatia[58]	1981	569	...	31.6	51.1	14.7	2.3	0.3			100.0	—	—	—	—	—
Cuba	1988	1.8[45]	1,047[45]	...	...	...	...	...	...	...	...	...	...	...	...	...
Cyprus	1985	48.0	3.8	24.4	56.8	15.0	2.9	0.9			79.0			9.4	—	11.6[59]
Czech Republic[60]	1995	26.9[61]	...	31.0		19.0	18.0	13.6	8.2	10.2	51.2	—	45.1[47]	—	—	3.7
Denmark	1995[63]	68.8	35.9[64]	3.1		16.5	21.7	33.8	24.9		64.4[3]			35.6[3]		
Djibouti	1988–89	1.2	0.4	*c. 100*	...	...	...	...	...	...	...	...	...	...	...	...
Dominica	1995	10.1	2.5	72.2[65]	26.4[66]			1.4			76.0	...	...	5.6	5.6	12.8
Dominican Republic	1981	385	6.3	16.0	65.7	8.5	5.4	2.6	1.5	0.3	53.2	18.5	4.5	1.6	—	22.2
Ecuador[17]	1991	517	15.4	27.8	38.8	10.6	8.0	8.2	5.6	1.0	70.3	0.3	—	7.7	7.4	14.3
Egypt	1990	3,896	0.7[37]	95.8[67]	2.3[68]	1.9[69]					...	...	...	...	...	...

arrangements in which title or goods do not change hands. "Other" usually includes farms operated on several parcels of land and held under multiple forms of tenure.

Statistics on types of farms by commodities produced refer to FAO categories. The terms "mainly crops" and "mainly livestock" indicate that more than half of the for-sale production was that indicated.

The section on technology provides some measures of the role modern technology plays in the farm activities of each country (although, of course, irrigation may employ technology developed in ancient times). Ratios referred to area mean area of "arable" (cultivated and cultivable) land, roughly "cropland," less area of permanent crops (see below).

The classification of farmland by economic use is also subject to differing treatment internationally. For purposes of this table, "cropland" comprises: (1) land under temporary crops (those requiring replanting after each harvest), (2) land under permanent crops (those *not* requiring replanting, including tree, bush and shrub, and vine crops), and (3) land temporarily (less than five years) fallow (unused, but capable of being returned to cultivation with no special preparation). "Meadows and pastures" includes land (both permanent and temporary use) whose principal purpose is the raising of animal fodder or forage. "Woodland and forest" includes both natural and planted tracts of timber (*e.g.,* plantings of Christmas trees), whether harvested or not. "Other" comprises: (1) mixed and multiple use lands, (2) residue of farmland holdings not classifiable according to categories listed above (including areas of farm buildings, roads, ornamental gardens, watercourses and flooded land, wasteland, etc.), (3) land not classified by respondents in census, or (4) detail not distinguishable as one of the categories above by reason of its summarization in a published source. When "cropland" is indicated to compose 100 percent of farmland, it should usually be understood to mean only that woodland, pasture, etc., were not part of the published data, rather than that those classes of land use do not exist.

Measurements of area are given in hectares (ha; 1 hectare is equal to 2.471 acres). A kilogram (kg) is equal to 2.205 pounds (1 kg/ha = 0.89 lb/ac). The following notes further define the column headings:

a. All properties used wholly or partly for agricultural production. A property need not have agricultural land to be considered a farm; piggeries, hatcheries, and poultry batteries are farms because they engage in agricultural production, *i.e.,* raise livestock and produce livestock products.
b. All forms of tenure not included in the preceding categories. Includes land operated by schools, religious bodies, squatters, seasonally by nomads, and built-on, waste, and similar types of alienation.

... Not available, or no agricultural census or survey ever taken.
— None, less than half the smallest unit shown, or not applicable.

Internet resources for further information:

- Food and Agriculture Organization (Agricultural World Census Programme) gopher://faov02.FAO.ORG:70/11gopher_root:[fao]

							farmland use									country
activity (% of farms)			technology (latest)				land in farms		land use (%)							
mainly crops	mainly livestock	mixed/ other	tractors (per 1,000 ha)	electricity (% of farms having)	irrigation (% of land irrig.)	artificial fertilizer (kg/ha)	total ('000 ha)	% of total land area	cropland				meadows and pastures	woodland and forest	other	
									permanent crops	temporary crops	fallow	total cropland				
...	...	...	0.1	...	35	7	38,054[2]	58.4[2]	1.8	46.3	51.9	19.9	75.4	4.7	—	Afghanistan
48.9[5]	51.1[5]	—	15.6	...	61	158	1,126[2]	41.1[2]	17.8	—82.2—		24.0[4]	15.0[4]	36.0[4]	25.0[4]	Albania
...	...	...	13.2	...	7	13	39,640	16.6	6.9[7]	55.2[7]	37.9[7]	20.4[7]	77.2[7]	—	2.4[7]	Algeria
55.7[5]	44.3[5]	—	15.0	38.5	...	...	3.2	16.4	—88.7—		11.3	71.4	5.3	...	23.3	American Samoa
...	...	...	...	...	...	...	...	2.0	...	...	...	2.2	55.6	22.2	20.0	Andorra
...	...	...	3.4	...	89[12]	7	3,500[13]	2.8[13]	36.8	63.2	—	1.7	82.0	...	16.3	Angola
32.9	44.1	23.0	30.0	...	...	...	2.5	5.7	26.0	57.1	16.9	62.6	36.0	—1.4—		Antigua and Barbuda
10.6[17]	78.9[17]	10.5[17]	11.2	...	7	4	177,437	64.8	4.8	71.5	23.7	15.4	56.4	21.3	6.9	Argentina
...	...	...	33.1	...	59	...	1,261[2]	44.7[2]	12.6	84.3	3.1	30.8	61.5	—	7.7	Armenia
...	...	...	...	...	...	...	...	...	...	...	...	...	...	...	...	Aruba
26.7[21]	58.9	14.4[22]	6.8	...	5	28	463,100	60.3	1.1	—98.9—		4.0	8.0	...	88.0[23]	Australia
59.8[24]	—	40.2[24]	242	...	0.3	201	7,563	91.4	—100.0—			19.7	26.1	43.4	10.8	Austria
...	...	...	20.6	...	62	...	4,200[2]	48.5[2]	28.9	63.9	7.2	37.2	53.5	—	9.3	Azerbaijan
...	...	...	13.3	...	10[12]	...	20.3	2.0	50.0	17.8	32.2	38.5	11.0	28.3	22.2	Bahamas, The
...	...	...	...	21.3	100	333	3.5	5.2	50.7	49.3	—	45.9	...	...	54.1	Bahrain
91.3[31]	8.7[31]	—	0.6	...	35	98	9,137[32]	70.2[32]	—88.2[32]—		11.8[32]	89.5[32]	—10.5[32]—			Bangladesh
...	...	...	38.0	...	6	91	21.6	50.2	3.0	82.9	14.1	78.7	8.9	0.6	11.8	Barbados
73.2	26.8	—	19.9	...	2	119.0	9,346	45.0	...	...	...	64.5	33.3	—	2.2	Belarus
97.5[34]	2.5[35]	—	144	...	0.1	496	1,392	45.6	1.2	98.4	0.4	51.9	45.2	0.5	2.4	Belgium
...	...	...	25.6	...	4	88	233[17]	10.0[17]	13.1[17]	81.1[17]	5.8[17]	36.5[17]	11.5[17]	36.1[17]	11.5[17]	Belize
...	...	...	0.1	...	0.7	2	3,300	29.3	...	...	...	100.0	—	—	—	Benin
...	...	...	9.0	...	...	...	2.4	4.4	18.6	72.9	8.5	91.1	8.9	...	...	Bermuda
...	...	...	...	...	34	1	156	3.4	11.7	—88.3—		100.0	—	—	—	Bhutan
...	...	...	2.5	...	5	3	22,670	20.6	3.6	96.4	—	5.0	47.4	41.6	6.0	Bolivia
...	...	...	48.3	...	0.3	...	2,525[24]	49.4[24]	8.9[24]	70.9[24]	20.2[24]	44.2[24]	55.4[24]	—	0.4[24]	Bosnia and Herzegovina[18]
13.6[37]	27.9[37]	58.5[37]	14.3	...	0.2	1	343[41]	5.9[41]	—	100.0[41]	—	83.5[41]	...	...	16.5[41]	Botswana
80.0[43]	16.2[43]	3.8[43]	17.0	4.1[43]	7	43	376,287	44.5	18.2[41]	66.9[41]	14.9[41]	15.8[41]	47.8[41]	24.2[41]	12.2[41]	Brazil
...	...	...	24.0	...	33	57	16.4	2.8	78.0	22.0	—	54.8	0.1	16.4	28.7	Brunei
48.8[48]	46.9[48]	4.3[48]	9.2	...	20	195	6,164[2]	55.8[2]	4.3[48]	—95.7[48]—		76.1[48]	23.9[48]	...	...	Bulgaria
...	...	...	0.04	...	0.7	6	9,565[2]	35.0[2]	...	...	...	...	...	...	...	Burkina Faso
...	...	...	0.2	...	1.4	4	2,170[2]	84.5[2]	—73.8—		26.2	56.7	37.7	5.6	...	Burundi
...	...	...	0.4	...	4	1	2,984	16.5	94.9	3.5	1.6	96.1	—	3.9	—	Cambodia
...	...	...	0.1	...	0.3	6[3]	1,490	3.3	...	...	...	100.0	—	—	—	Cameroon
43.9	42.9	13.2	16.3	...	1.6	47	68,057	7.4	—82.1—		17.9	60.5	—39.5—			Canada
...	...	...	0.4	...	7	—	41	10.2	20.8[53]	79.2[53]	...	100.0[53]	—	—	—	Cape Verde
...	...	...	0.1	...	...	2	491	0.8	11.8	88.2	—	100.0	—	—	—	Central African Republic
...	...	...	0.05	...	0.4	2	23,877[54]	45.8[54]	50.0[54]	—50.0[54]—		23.7[54]	76.3[54]	...	...	Chad
...	...	...	10.4	...	32	69	8,746[56]	11.7[56]	26.5[56]	59.5[56]	14.0[56]	15.3[56]	52.4[56]	...	32.3[56]	Chile
...	...	...	7.7	...	53	261	166,902	17.4	4.1	—95.9—		100.0	—	—	—	China
...	...	...	9.4	...	19	101	36,034	34.7	47.3	34.6	18.1	14.7	48.5	14.0	22.8	Colombia
...	...	...	...	...	...	...	100	44.8	56.4	—43.6—		100.0	—	—	—	Comoros
92.3	—7.7—		0.3	...	0.1	1	7,900[13]	3.5[13]	7.7	—92.3—		70.6	20.1	2.0	7.3	Congo, Dem. Rep. of the
6.2[5]	93.8[5]	—	4.8	...	0.7	3	226	0.7	14.8	85.2	—	100.0	—	—	—	Congo, Rep. of the
...	...	...	24.6	...	44	203	2,870	56.2	42.2	57.8	—	15.7	49.9	22.9	11.5	Costa Rica
...	...	...	1.5	...	3	11	2,753	8.6	65.9	34.1	—	100.0	—	—	—	Côte d'Ivoire
...	...	...	3.6	...	0.3	...	3,220	57.0	8.8	81.8	9.4	50.4	48.5	—	1.1	Croatia[58]
...	...	...	30.0	...	35	199	8,679	78.3	...	...	...	33.9	32.1	31.9	2.1	Cuba
51.5[5, 46]	37.0[5, 46]	11.5[5, 46]	137	...	40	144	210	35.6	34.7	54.3	11.0	74.9	—	—25.1—		Cyprus
43.5[5]	56.5[5]	—	21.1	100.0	0.8	97	4,280[62]	55.4[62]	0.9[62]	—99.1[62]—		74.1[62]	21.1[62]	—4.8[62]—		Czech Republic[60]
49.1	27.9	23.0	61.8	...	19	255	2,726	64.2	...	92.7	7.3	70.7	29.3	...	...	Denmark
...	...	...	...	...	...	...	1	0.5	...	6.8	...	100.0	—	—	—	Djibouti
...	...	...	12.9	...	...	259	23[2]	30.7[2]	91.0	7.1	1.9	61.7	...	28.3	10.0	Dominica
44.0	56.0	—	2.4	60.0	25	50	2,412	49.8	38.0	40.2	21.8	34.1	51.6	13.0	1.3	Dominican Republic
67.8	12.4	19.8	5.5	...	34	29	7,954[30]	30.5[30]	50.1[30]	20.7[30]	29.2[30]	34.7[30]	62.0[30]	—3.3[30]—		Ecuador[17]
...	...	...	25.1	...	112	384	5,216[2, 4]	5.2[2, 4]	7.3[4]	92.7[4]	...	100.0[4]	—	—	—	Egypt

Agriculture and land use (continued)

country	farms (latest census of agriculture)[a]															
	year	number of farms ('000)	size of holding								tenure (% of farms)					
			average (ha)	size class (%)							owner-operated			rented (including share-croppers)	tribal/communal	other[b]
				under 1 ha	1–5 ha	5–10 ha	10–20 ha	20–50 ha	50–200 ha	over 200 ha	individual/family	corporate/state	socialized/collective			
El Salvador	1970–71	271	5.4	48.9	37.9	5.8	3.4	2.6	1.2	0.2	41.5	—	—	28.2	6.3	24.0
Equatorial Guinea	...	...	...	...	...	...	...	...	...	...	...	...	...	...	...	...
Eritrea	—	...	...	...	...	...	...	...	...	...	...	...	...	...	...	...
Estonia[18]	1994	10.4	...	8.0[4]		12.8[4]	27.8[4]	42.2[4]	9.2[4]		93.5[4]	6.5[4]		...	...	...
Ethiopia[70]	1994–95[71]	6,092[71]	1.3[71]	49.9[31]	46.5[31]	3.4[31]	0.2[31]	—	—	—	98.4[31]	1.6[31]	—	—	...	...
Faroe Islands	...	...	...	...	...	...	...	...	...	...	...	...	...	...	...	...
Fiji	1991	95	4.2[72]	43.3	31.4	13.3	6.6	3.3	1.5[19]	0.6[20]	15.8	0.4	—	49.5	32.2	2.1
Finland	1995[74]	170	12.8[24]	—	31.9	20.1	22.8	21.3	3.9			84.5[46]		15.5[46]	—	—
France	1995	735[48]	26.6[41]		36.7		25.7[75]	10.5[76]	27.1		45.0[35]	—	—	55.0[35]	—	—
French Guiana	1993	3.9	4.6	16.2	72.3	6.0	2.1		3.4	—	17.0[2]	—	—	57.2[2]	—	25.8[2]
French Polynesia	1987	5.6	...	37.7			62.3				36.5	...	...	6.3	...	57.2
Gabon	1975	71	1.0	68.0	32.0		—	...	...	...	81.8	—	—	0.3	5.3	12.6
Gambia, The	1989–90	...	...	...	...	...	...	...	...	...	...	...	...	...	...	...
Gaza Strip	1968	...	...	...	...	...	...	...	...	...	...	...	...	...	...	...
Georgia	1990	17.0[18, 56]	...	...	...	...	...	...	...	...	...	...	...	...	...	...
Germany	1995[74]	581	28.0[56]	15.8[65]	15.7[78]	15.2	18.2	23.0	12.1		89.1	—	—	10.9	—	...
Ghana	1970	805	3.2	36.6	48.7	9.0	3.9	1.8	—	—	...	...	...	...	...	...
Gibraltar	—	...	...	...	...	...	...	...	...	...	...	...	...	...	...	...
Greece	1991	862	0.8	26.8[79]	50.6	14.4	6.2		2.0		79.9	—	—	18.7	...	1.4
Greenland	—	...	...	...	...	...	...	...	...	...	...	...	...	...	...	...
Grenada	1995	8	1.7	88.3[65]	6.9[80]	3.3[81]	0.7	0.4[82]	0.4[83]			73.2		14.1	—	12.7
Guadeloupe	1993	14	2.8	34.6	52.1	10.0	2.4		0.9		57.7[2, 14]	—	—	18.8[2, 14]	—	23.5[2, 14]
Guam	1997	0.2[56]	4.0	58.8[8]	17.6[9]	19.6[10]			4.0[11]		53.8	—	—	30.1	—	16.1[84]
Guatemala	1979	600	6.8	39.7[85]	49.8[86]		8.2[87]		2.3[88]			74.0[89]		6.3[89]	5.8[89]	13.9[89]
Guernsey	1993	0.089	16.2[64]	6.7[17]	24.0[17]	23.1[17]	46.2[17]		—	—	32.4[3, 14]	—	—	67.6[3, 14]	—	—
Guinea	1989[2]	431	2.4[90]	95.4		4.0		0.6			9.0	...	...	12.4	73.3	5.3
Guinea-Bissau	1988	84	3.0[1]	13.4[1]	73.3[1]	10.0[1]	3.0[1]	0.3[1]	—	—	...	...	...	...	...	...
Guyana	1993	25[91]	...		90.0		10.0		—	—	...	90.0	—	...	...	10.0
Haiti	1987	667	1.4[57]	61.8	36.6	1.5	0.1	—	—	—	93.4	...	—	5.9	...	0.7
Honduras	1992–93	318	13.5	25.2	46.5	11.0	7.2	6.3	3.1	0.7	39.9	23.1	—	16.6	—	20.4
Hong Kong	1986	11	0.3	97.5	2.3	0.1	0.2		—	—		9.0		77.0	—	14.0
Hungary	1996	3.2[4, 47]	...	90.0[64]	9.9[64]			0.1[64]			51.9[48]	17.6[48]	30.5[48]	—	—	—
Iceland	1981	7.0	...	15.7	9.3	11.7	23.7	35.8	3.8		...	...	...	...	...	...
India	1990–91	105,300	1.6	59.0	32.2	7.2			1.6		94.1	—	—	0.5	—	5.4
Indonesia	1993	21,737	1.0	70.8	27.8	1.2		0.2			74.8[44]	—[6]	—[6]	3.2[6]	—[6]	22.0[6]
Iran	1988	3,326	...	26.8	39.3	17.1	10.9	4.8	1.0	0.1	...	...	...	...	...	...
Iraq	1979	470	13.3	25.9[93]	27.6[94]	23.2[95]	11.5[96]	9.4	1.9[97]	0.5[98]	52.5[12]	—	—	40.9[12]	—	6.6[12]
Ireland	1995	153	27.7	0.9	10.3	14.1	28.3	34.8	11.1	0.5	95.9	0.4	—	3.7	—	—
Isle of Man	1992	0.8	59.7		26.7[99]		16.2[100]	17.0[82]	12.4[101]	27.7[102]	72.4[44]	—	—	27.6[44]	—	—
Israel	1981	52	11.3	26.5	57.6	8.3	4.0	2.0	1.6		84.0	—	1.4	—	—	14.6
Italy	1990	2,941	7.5[32]	33.0[32]	43.0[32]	11.7[32]	6.7[32]	3.8[32]	1.8[32]		88.0	—	—	3.1	—	8.9
Jamaica	1978–79	184	2.9	32.5[103]	60.7[104]	4.8[81]	0.9	0.4[82]	0.3[101]	0.4[102]	99.5[35]	0.2[35]	—	—	—	0.3[35]
Japan	1995	3,444	1.2	24.5	53.5	13.9			8.1			76.5			23.5	
Jersey	1990	0.6	11.1	45.0[105]		16.4[106]	19.6[107]		19.0[108]		31.4[37]	—	—	68.6[37]	—	—
Jordan	1983	57	6.3	25.3	44.6	15.6	8.6	4.5	1.3	0.1	80.5	—	—	13.1	0.3	6.1
Kazakstan	1996	30.8[18]	412[18]								...	...	...	...	...	...
Kenya	1976–79[112]	2,750	2.5	65.5	27.3	2.7[113]			4.5[114]		...	...	...	...	...	...
Kiribati		...	...	...	...	...	...	...	...	...	...	...	...	...	...	...
Korea, North	...	...	...	...	...	...	...	...	...	...	...	...	...	...	...	...
Korea, South	1995[2]	1,500[91]	3.7[91]	59.2[25]			40.8				82.5[24, 43]	—	—	17.4[24, 43]	—	0.1[24, 43]
Kuwait	1994–95	2.6	2.4[115]	48.6[43]	25.4[43]	10.2[43]	8.7[43]	4.0[43]	3.1[43]	—	95.3[7]	...	...	...	...	4.7[7]
Kyrgyzstan	1996	23.2[18]	86[18]	...	...	...	...	...	...	...	100.0[46]	—	—	—	—	—
Laos	1983	...	...	...	...	...	...	...	...	...	...	...	...	...	...	...
Latvia	1993	64.3[18, 46]	16.5[18, 56]	...	...	...	...	...	...	...	64.0[46]	2.0[46]	17.0[46, 47]	...	...	17.0[46]
Lebanon	1970	143	4.3	47.7	44.5		6.5		1.2	0.1	...	...	...	...	...	...
Lesotho	1989–90	229	1.5	46.8	49.6	3.6		—	—	—	87.0	...	...	10.0	...	3.0
Liberia	1971[116]	122	3.0	52.8	31.0	12.0	3.7		0.5		40.0[14]	—	—	—	43.3[14]	16.7[14]
Libya	1987	176	14.0	8.2	37.5	24.7	17.3	9.8	2.5		...	...	...	...	...	...
Liechtenstein	1995	0.40	8.7[24]	63.1		5.0	12.2		19.7		31.7[24]	—	—	24.5[24]	—	43.8[24]
Lithuania	1994	5.9[18, 56]	16[18, 56]	...	...	...	...	...	...	...		57.2[4]			42.8[4]	
Luxembourg	1996	3.1	41.3	14.3[65]	10.2	8.3	8.3	20.7	38.2		50.1[24]	...	...	49.4[24]	...	0.5[24]
Macau	—	...	...	...	...	...	...	...	...	...	...	...	...	...	...	...
Macedonia[58]	1981	176	...	46.7	45.2	6.7	1.2		0.2		100.0	—	—	—	—	—
Madagascar	1984–85	1,453	1.3	54.4	44.2	1.0	0.2	0.1	0.1			87.3[14]		4.9[14]	...	7.8[14]
Malaŵi	1980–81[112]	1,136	1.2	54.9	40.1[119]			5.0[120]			...	...	...	...	...	...
Malaysia	1980[112, 121]	920	2.2	...	...	...	...	...	...	...	53.2[43]	18.2[43]	...	19.6[43]	...	9.0[43]
Maldives	1985	...	...	...	...	...	...	...	...	...	...	...	...	...	...	...
Mali	1982–83	562	4.0	20.1	54.1	17.4		8.4		—	96.8[123]	3.2	—	...	—	—
Malta	1982–83	12	1.1	67.8	30.0	2.0			0.2		16.0	—	—	70.4	—	13.6[59]
Marshall Islands	—	...	...	...	...	...	...	...	...	...	...	...	...	...	...	...
Martinique[2]	1993	10.2	2.3	54.1	37.0	4.9	2.0		2.0		65.3[14]	...	...	22.5[14]	...	12.2[14]
Mauritania	1984–85	100	2.0	49.2	41.0[28]	7.0[81]	2.0	0.5[82]	0.3[83]		68.4	...	...	4.4	10.4	16.8
Mauritius	1980	32.5	1.1	61.3	36.2	1.9	0.3	0.2	0.1		95.8	—	—	4.2	—	—
Mayotte	1987	5.9[117]	1.7[109]	...	...	...	...	...	...	...	...	...	...	...	...	...
Mexico	1991	4,408[125]	50	23.5[43]	39.4[43]	21.1[43]	8.8[43]	2.7[43]	2.9[43]	1.6[43]		95.8		1.1	—	3.1
Micronesia		...	...	...	...	...	...	...	...	...	...	...	...	...	...	...
Moldova	1996	16.1[18]	3[18, 48]	...	...	...	...	...	...	...	—	30.8	55.2	—	—	14.0
Monaco	...	...	...	...	...	...	...	...	...	...	...	...	...	...	...	...
Mongolia	1985	0.3	385,000	...	...	...	...	...	...	...	—	16.0	84.0	—	—	—
Morocco	1996	1,900[109]	3.9[109]	29.8[6]	44.0[6]	14.9[6]	7.7[6]	3.0[6]	0.6[6]		...	...	...	...	...	...
Mozambique	1973	1,605	3.1	...	...	...	...	...	...	...	0.2	0.1	—	—	99.7	—
Myanmar (Burma)	1992–93	2,925	2.3	53.6[65]	27.8[80]	15.2[127]	3.3[100]		0.1[11]		...	...	...	...	...	...
Namibia	1989	6.3[128]	...	...	...	...	...	...	...	...	45.0	—	—	55.0	—	—
Nauru	...	...	...	...	...	...	...	...	...	...	...	...	...	...	...	...
Nepal	1992	2,736	1.1[38]	69.8[25]	28.7	1.2			0.3		82.6	—	—	1.8	—	15.6

activity (% of farms)			technology (latest)				farmland use									country
							land in farms		land use (%)							
									cropland							
mainly crops	mainly live-stock	mixed/ other	tractors (per 1,000 ha)	electri-city (% of farms having)	irriga-tion (% of land irrig.)	artificial fertilizer (kg/ha)	total ('000 ha)	% of total land area	perma-nent crops	tempo-rary crops	fallow	total crop-land	mead-ows and pastures	wood-land and forest	other	
95.3	4.7	—	6.1	...	21	106	1,340[2]	64.7[2]	25.0	58.6	16.4	44.9	38.2	11.6	5.3	El Salvador
...	...	...	0.8	...	...	...	...	...	...	...	...	...	...	...	...	Equatorial Guinea
...	...	...	1.9	...	6	...	362	3.6	...	...	...	...	...	...	...	Eritrea
...	...	...	13.3	...	...	...	252.3	22.7	...	...	...	44.0	10.0	34.0	12.0	Estonia[18]
16.5[71]	2.0[71]	81.5[71]	0.3	...	2	7	7,042[71]	6.4[71]	6.9[71]	82.0[71]	11.1[71]	87.0[71]	8.7[71]	0.8[71]	3.5[71]	Ethiopia[70]
...	...	...	...	...	...	...	...	...	...	...	...	...	...	...	...	Faroe Islands
26.5	29.3	44.2[73]	38.9	...	2	96[72]	260[13]	14.2[13]	...	...	...	37.8	34.0	19.1	9.1	Fiji
52.3[46]	—47.6[46]—		88.7	100.0	3	210	12,966	42.6	1.4	78.5	20.1	19.4	0.8	60.1	19.7	Finland
37.3[24, 77]	38.7[24]	24.0[24]	78.6	...	8	319	30,059	54.7	7.6	81.3	11.1	51.5	35.1	—13.4—		France
...	...	...	35.0	...	20	64	23.8[2]	0.3[2]	9.1[2, 48]	80.7[2, 48]	10.2[2, 48]	43.5[2, 48]	46.8[2, 48]	—9.7[2, 48]—		French Guiana
...	...	...	31.2	...	19.4	33	36.8	10.4	90.0	7.1	2.9	62.0	8.5	1.9	27.6	French Polynesia
...	...	...	5.1	...	1	3	73.0	0.3	...	...	...	...	...	...	...	Gabon
...	...	...	0.3	...	1	11	172[13]	17.2[13]	...	100.0	...	100.0	...	...	...	Gambia, The
...	...	...	83.3	...	133	...	16.5[56]	50.0[56]	68.8[56]	31.2[56]	...	100.0	—	—	—	Gaza Strip
...	...	...	22.9	...	59	...	3,011	43.2	36.4	—63.6—		36.6	63.4	—	—	Georgia
...	...	...	110.1	...	4	384	17,344	49.7	1.7	—98.3—		68.2	30.4	—1.4—		Germany
...	...	...	1.5	...	0.2	3	2,574	10.8	61.4	38.6	—	100.0	—	—	—	Ghana
...	...	...	...	...	...	4	...	...	...	...	...	...	...	...	...	Gibraltar
69.2	1.1	29.7	93.8	...	55	175	3,351	26.0	32.5	63.5	4.0	90.1	9.9	...	...	Greece
...	c. 100	...	...	...	...	...	...	...	...	...	...	...	...	...	...	Greenland
...	...	...	6.0	...	...	...	12.5	36.8	...	...	...	...	...	...	...	Grenada
...	...	...	38.6	...	14	307	53.6[2]	31.7[2]	13.1[2, 48]	79.8[2, 48]	7.1[2, 48]	52.3[2, 48]	45.5[2, 48]	—2.2[2, 48]—		Guadeloupe
38.2	29.6	32.2	181.5	...	20.7	...	0.8	1.4	—51.0—		49.0	71.6	9.5	6.5	12.4	Guam
...	...	...	3.2	...	9	66	4,510[2]	41.6[2]	27.6	—72.4—		42.0	27.3	27.2	3.5	Guatemala
28.1[34]	71.9	...	...	...	...	...	2	27.6	—	100.0	—	12.3	87.7	...	...	Guernsey
...	...	...	0.5	...	15	1	727	3.0	...	...	...	...	...	...	...	Guinea
...	...	...	0.1	...	6	3	96[2]	3.4[2]	...	...	...	...	...	...	...	Guinea-Bissau
...	...	...	7.6	...	27	33	10,652	26.2	...	...	...	8.4	91.6	...	...	Guyana
...	...	...	0.4	...	13	4	1,405[2]	51.0[2]	...	...	...	33.5	18.0	1.5	47.0	Haiti
...	...	...	2.9	...	4	18	3,337	29.8	23.8	33.7	42.5	41.7	45.9	10.9	1.5	Honduras
56.3	37.3	6.4	0.7	...	33	100.0[37]	8.0[2]	8.1[2]	7.4	37.0	55.6	100.0	—	—	—	Hong Kong
55.0[5]	31.0[5]	14.0[5]	7.6	...	4	231	8,017	86.2	4.1	95.9	—	58.8	14.3	22.0	4.9	Hungary
...	...	...	1,667	87.0[53]	...	2,529	...	...	...	...	...	...	...	...	...	Iceland
...	...	...	7.6	...	29	75	165,600	55.7	—84.4[92]—		15.6[92]	97.9[92]	—2.1[92]—			India
86.8[6]	—[6]	13.2[6]	3.2	...	27	110	51,050	28.2	—77.8[46]—		22.2[46]	61.1[46]	3.7[46]	18.6[46]	16.6[46]	Indonesia
...	...	...	7.1	...	44	80	104,900[38]	63.8[38]	6.4	62.4	31.2	10.2	89.8	...	...	Iran
87.9	11.2	0.9	5.8	...	46	39	5,750[13]	13.1	3.0	62.4	34.6	87.2	0.7	0.2	11.9	Iraq
2.9	93.2	3.9	127	...	...	741	5,692	82.6	65.1[48]	—	34.9[48]	9.1[48]	—90.9[48]—			Ireland
...	...	...	...	...	...	...	47	81.4	3.4	—96.6—		11.3	88.7	...	...	Isle of Man
...	...	...	73.2	...	55	252	435[13]	21.1[13]	25.0[56]	—75.0[56]—		81.5[56]	—18.5[56]—			Israel
81.2	13.2	5.6	176	...	32	151	22,702	75.3	25.5	—74.5—		48.1	18.2	24.7	9.0	Italy
...	...	...	19.9	...	23	116	476[2]	44.0[2]	22.2[35]	72.2[35]	5.6[35]	41.3[35]	21.6[35]	13.5[35]	23.6[35]	Jamaica
90.0	1.9	8.1	513	...	70	414	5,038	13.4	10.3	—89.7—		82.6	9.9	—7.5—		Japan
85.1[109]	14.9[109]	—	...	...	...	...	6.5	56.2	—98.9—		1.1	63.4	—36.6—			Jersey
58.2[110, 111]	14.9[110, 111]	26.9[110, 111]	24.2	1.5	20	63	405	4.5	13.3	63.0	23.7	87.7	1.0	0.3	11.0	Jordan
...	...	...	6.0	...	6	19	179,800	66.2	1.2	—98.8—		19.3	80.6	—	0.1	Kazakstan
...	...	...	3.5	...	2	48	6,922	11.9	11.5	—88.5—		71.0	23.8	1.9	3.3	Kenya
...	...	...	...	...	...	...	...	...	...	...	...	...	...	...	...	Kiribati
...	...	...	44.2	...	86	407	...	...	...	...	...	...	...	...	...	Korea, North
75.0[5]	25.0[5]	—	42.6	...	71	454	1,985[2]	20.1[2]	6.7	—93.3—		100.0	—	—	—	Korea, South
38.9[7]	61.1[7]	—	20.0	100.0	100	167	7.9	0.4	20.6[7]	79.4[7]	—	70.0[7]	—30.0[7]—			Kuwait
...	...	...	16.4	...	71	...	10,100	50.9	6.1	90.9	3.0	13.9	86.1	—	—	Kyrgyzstan
...	...	...	1.1	...	18	2	1,700[2]	7.4[2]	2.3	—97.7—		52.4	47.6	...	...	Laos
...	...	...	32.5	...	...	...	2,540	39.3	...	...	...	68.5[48]	—31.5[48]—			Latvia
77.0[110]	8.1[110]	14.9[110]	13.9	...	41	79	316[2]	30.9[2]	36.7[41]	39.7[41]	23.6[41]	100.0[41]	—	—	—	Lebanon
56.0[5]	3.0[5]	41.0[5]	5.8	...	0.9	14	320[13]	10.5[13]	...	...	...	76.4	...	...	23.6	Lesotho
...	...	...	2.6	...	2	7	375	3.9	66.2[117]	33.8[117]	—	98.3[117]	...	1.7[117]	...	Liberia
...	...	...	18.7	...	26	39	15,470[2]	8.8[2]	—28.7—		71.3	49.5	11.7	...	38.8	Libya
23.9[37]	61.6[37]	14.5[37]	112	...	...	...	4.0[13]	24.0[13]	1.1[24]	—98.9[24]—		39.9[24]	57.5[24]	1.1[24]	1.5[24]	Liechtenstein
...	...	...	28.6	...	...	...	3,519	54.3	38.3	60.9	0.8	76.2	13.5	—10.3—		Lithuania
25.3[118]	57.7	17.0	134	...	...	...	136	53.3	—97.9—		2.1	42.9	48.9	6.3	1.9	Luxembourg
...	...	...	...	...	...	...	...	...	...	...	...	...	...	...	...	Macau
...	...	...	77.3	...	11	...	1,320	51.3	9.3	65.4	25.3	46.4	52.4	—	1.2	Macedonia[58]
...	...	...	1.1	...	42	2	3,105[13]	5.3[13]	15.4	84.6	—	100.0	—	—	—	Madagascar
22.1	...	77.9	0.8	...	2	23	1,700[13]	18.1[13]	0.2	99.8	—	94.8	...	5.2	...	Malawi
...	...	...	21.4[122]	...	33[122]	170[122]	7,604[13]	23.1[13]	84.8[37]	15.2[37]	—	100.0[37]	...	...	...	Malaysia
...	...	...	...	...	...	...	19	63.5	...	...	...	...	...	...	...	Maldives
...	...	...	0.3	...	3	9	2,503[13]	2.0[13]	—	100.0	—	100.0	—	—	—	Mali
...	...	...	37.5	...	8	39	13.0	40.6	5.0	—95.0—		87.5	—12.5—			Malta
...	...	...	...	...	...	...	...	...	...	...	...	...	...	...	...	Marshall Islands
...	...	...	117	...	50	945	32.3[2]	30.5[2]	59.9[2, 48]	36.5[2, 48]	3.6[2, 48]	54.4[2, 48]	37.4[2, 48]	—8.2[2, 48]—		Martinique[2]
...	...	...	1.6	...	24	12	208[2]	0.2[2]	—	56.2	43.8	100.0	—	—	—	Mauritania
...	...	...	3.7	...	19[46]	304	90[46]	44.3[46]	4.2[124]	95.8[124]	—	90.0[124]	—10.0[124]—			Mauritius
...	...	...	...	...	...	...	14.6	39.0	33.3	66.7	—	100.0	—	—	—	Mayotte
83.9	12.9	3.2	7.4	...	26	70	99,229[2]	52.0[2]	6.3	58.1	35.6	16.5	53.3	14.2	16.0	Mexico
61.4[5]	15.7[5]	22.9[5]	7.4	45	0	...	5.8	12.2	—9.3—		90.7	32.9	30.2	—36.9—		Micronesia
67.4[5, 46]	32.6[5, 46]	—	30.5	...	18	...	2,614[2]	79.3[2]	26.5[56]	—73.5[56]—		68.0[56]	12.0[56]	—	20.0[56]	Moldova
...	...	...	...	...	...	...	...	...	...	...	...	...	...	...	...	Monaco
13.6[5, 46]	86.4[5, 46]	—	8.4	...	6	12	118,470[2]	75.6[2]	—	66.8	33.2	0.9	99.1	...	...	Mongolia
...	...	...	4.9	...	15	36	9,291[65, 126]	20.8[65, 126]	7.2[65, 126]	73.3[65, 126]	19.5[65, 126]	100.0[65, 126]	—	—	—	Morocco
...	...	...	1.9	...	4	1	13,626	17.8	—44.9—		55.1	55.0	45.0	...	...	Mozambique
93.3	6.7	—	1.2	...	14	8	6,887	10.5	3.3	93.3	3.4	99.7	...	...	0.3	Myanmar (Burma)
1.3[5]	94.4[5]	4.3[5]	4.8	...	0.9	...	662[13]	0.8[13]	0.3	—99.7—		100.0	—	—	—	Namibia
...	...	...	...	...	...	...	...	...	...	...	...	...	...	...	...	Nauru
...	...	...	2.0	...	37	25	2,599	19.0	1.7	97.1	1.2	90.6	1.4	4.2	3.8	Nepal

Agriculture and land use (continued)

country	farms (latest census of agriculture)[a]															
	year	number of farms ('000)	size of holding								tenure (% of farms)					
			average (ha)	size class (%)							owner-operated			rented (including share-croppers)	tribal/ com-munal	other[b]
				under 1 ha	1–5 ha	5–10 ha	10–20 ha	20–50 ha	50–200 ha	over 200 ha	individual/ family	corporate/ state	socialized/ collective			
Netherlands, The	1996[63]	110[129]	15.5[35]	9.1	23.9	15.8	18.1	26.5	—6.6—		—31.5[14, 35]—		—	12.2[14, 35]	—	56.3[14, 35]
Netherlands Antilles	...	...	...	...	...	...	...	...	...	...	...	...	...	...	...	...
New Caledonia	1991	10.3	23[130]	71.2[65, 130]	13.8[78, 130]	3.7[130]	2.3[130]	2.5[130]	3.8[130]	2.7[130]	...	...	...	...	84.5	15.5
New Zealand	1995	68.8	241	—12.6—		9.1	8.8	14.8	31.2	23.5	85.7[37]	10.9[37]	—	—	—	3.4[37]
Nicaragua	1991	...	...	—26.2[90]—				—30.6[90]—		43.2[90]	64.4[14, 38]	—35.6[14, 38]—		—	—	—
Niger	1980[2]	699	4.9	3.8	54.1	37.8	—4.3—				...	...	...	...	...	...
Nigeria	1993–94	...	...	92.0	7.8	0.2	—	—	—	—	—56.0—			9.0	—35.0—	
Northern Mariana Is.	1997	0.1[24]	49.1	26.1[133]	35.3[134]	—24.4[10]—		—14.2—			56.3	...	...	23.5	...	20.2
Norway	1995[63]	83.2[135]	10.2[3]	—28.7—		24.2	29.7	16.0	—1.4—		—65.4[3]—			34.6[3]	—	—
Oman	1992–93	95	1.6	71.0	24.3	3.8	0.5	0.3	0.1	—	99.3	—	—	0.4	—	0.3
Pakistan	1990	5,071	9.3	27.0	54.0	12.2	4.7	—2.1—			68.8	—	—	—31.2—		
Palau[136]	1989	0.3	...	...	...	...	...	...	...	...	79.1[14]	—	—	12.7[14]	8.2[14]	—
Panama	1991	214	13.8	46.7	24.8	7.6	7.1	7.7	5.3	0.8	28.6	—	—	1.4	—	70.0[42]
Papua New Guinea	1985[137]	0.8	483	—26.8[63]—					28.3[87]	44.9[87]	26.9[14]	71.0[14]	—	2.1[14]	—	—
Paraguay	1991	307	88[117]	7.3	31.0	22.3	22.1	10.5	4.0	2.8	52.4	—	—	7.4	—	40.2[42]
Peru	1994	1,574	9.5	24.1	47.7	13.2	6.7	5.5	—2.8—		75.5	—	—	0.8	6.8	16.9
Philippines	1991	4,610	2.2	22.7	63.3	10.5	—3.5—				58.3	—	—	27.4	—	14.3
Poland[18]	1994	2,030	7.6	21.7[65]	32.8[78]	26.7	11.0[138]	—7.8[139]—			78.3[4, 14]	13.9[4, 14]	3.3[4, 14]	—	—	4.5[4, 14]
Portugal[4]	1995	489	10.5	24.9	53.2	—17.0—		3.0	—1.9—		92.0	—	—	—8.0—		
Puerto Rico	1997	22[56]	14.5	—5.1[140]—		7.5[141]	14.3[142]	14.2[143]	—58.9[83]—		—79.5—		—	10.6	—	9.9
Qatar	1990	0.8	7.0	20.5	41.8	18.0	12.6	5.8	—1.3—		...	...	...	...	...	...
Réunion[2]	1993	12.6	4.1	37.7	41.8	14.9	4.0	—1.6—			46.1[6]	—	—	22.5[6]	—	31.4[6]
Romania	1996	3.6[45]	3,900[45]	...	...	...	...	...	...	...	51.0[14]	14.0	35.0[47]	—	...	—
Russia	1996	280[18]	43[18]	...	...	...	...	...	...	...	45.0[48]	55.0[48]	—	—	...	—
Rwanda	1984	1,112	1.2	56.8	26.8[144]	—16.4[145]—					50.9	—	—	1.4	—	47.7[59]
St. Kitts and Nevis	1987	3.4	...	90.1[26]	8.7[27]	0.5[29]	—0.7—				82.0[14]	—	—	7.7[14]	—	10.3[42]
St. Lucia	1996	12	2.0	76.9[65]	11.4[80]	5.9[81]	1.9	1.3[82]	1.2[101]	1.4[102]	72.0	—	—	15.5	—	12.5
St. Vincent	1988	9	1.8[146]	78.4[25]	18.6[28]	2.0[81]	0.4[147]	—0.6—			53.8	—	—	12.3	—	33.9[42]
Samoa	1989	11	6.1	...	...	...	...	...	...	...	0.1	...	—	2.6[14]	94.2[14]	3.2[14]
San Marino	1975	0.7	7.0	21.3	47.8	—24.7—		5.1	—1.1—		39.9[14]	15.5[14]	—	29.9[14]	—	14.7[14]
São Tomé and Príncipe	1989	13.8	8.7[148]	88.5[148]	9.8[148]	0.7[148]	0.2[148]	0.2[148]	0.2[148]	0.4[148]	77.2[148]	—	—	20.5[148]	—	2.3[148]
Saudi Arabia	1982–83	212	10.1	36.6	35.8	11.3	8.2	5.0	2.6	0.5	85.9	—	—	2.6	—	11.5
Senegal	1976	362	7.0	—99.4—					—0.6—		...	...	0.6	...	...	99.4
Seychelles	1993	0.9[149]	...	...	...	...	...	...	...	...	98.9	—1.1—		—	—	—
Sierra Leone	1971	286	1.8	38.8	55.0	—6.1—		—0.1—			93.6	—	—	6.4	—	—
Singapore	1973	16	0.8	77.4	22.2	0.3	—0.1—				7.4	—	—	88.8	—	3.8
Slovakia	1994	10	245	—52.4—		12.6	9.8	6.8	—18.4—		77.6	2.2	9.9	—10.3—		
Slovenia	1991	157	...	28.4	36.0	18.0	—17.6—				93.0[14, 46]	7.0[14, 46]	—	—	—	—
Solomon Islands	1975[112]	92	1.0	...	...	...	...	...	...	...	—	—	—	—	100.0	—
Somalia	1984	198	3.6	...	...	...	...	...	...	...	99.9	0.1	—	—	—	—
South Africa[152]	1996	62[153]	1,319	—0.8[105]—		1.5	1.9	6.4	13.7	75.7	89.6[84]	...	...	...	...	10.4
Spain	1989	2,285	19.0	27.7	36.6	13.2	9.5	6.8	3.9	2.3	72.5	...	...	19.8	—7.7—	
Sri Lanka	1982	1,817	1.1	77.5[8]	—22.2[155]—		0.1[156]	0.1[82]	—0.1[83]—		59.0[157]	27.2[157]	—	8.2[157]	—	5.6[157]
Sudan, The	1982	...	...	...	...	...	...	...	...	...	22.3	2.2	—	28.0	42.0	5.5
Suriname	1981	22	7.5	21.9[33]	61.2[33]	11.1[33]	3.6[33]	1.6[33]	0.3[33]	0.3[33]	20.2[33]	0.9[33]	—	49.5[33]	—	29.4[33]
Swaziland[158]	1992–93	0.4	51	41.2	29.5	10.3	6.1	—12.9—			84.4[32]	—	—	—15.6[32]—		
Sweden	1996	90	29.5[24]	...	16.3	19.7	20.7	25.6	—17.7—		46.4	—	—	14.5	—	39.1[59]
Switzerland	1990	108	9.9	21.7	19.0	17.4	29.1	12.3	0.5	—	59.1[14, 160]	—	—	39.9[14, 160]	—	1.0[14, 160]
Syria	1994	444	8.9	16.7	36.8[28]	22.8[81]	13.1	8.5	2.0[161]	0.1[162]	65.8[14, 123]	1.8[14]	32.4[14]	...	—	—
Taiwan	1994	808[91]	1.1[91]	72.6[3]	27.4[3]	...	...	...	...	...	83.5	—	—	3.8	—	12.7
Tajikistan	1995	2.8[91]	7.0[91]	...	...	...	...	...	...	...	...	...	...	...	...	...
Tanzania	1993–94	5,440	0.5	70.1	28.8	1.0	—0.1—				49.0[163]	—	...	3.0	38.2	9.8
Thailand	1993	5,647	3.4	19.7	67.5[164]	—12.8[165]—					77.4	—	—	7.3	—	15.3[84]
Togo	1982–83	263	1.5	48.8	38.6[119]	—12.6[120]—					70.7[14]	—	—	21.1[14]	8.2[14]	—
Tonga	1985	10.1	3.3	18.9	67.9	12.7	—	0.5	—	—	—97.2—			—	—	2.8
Trinidad and Tobago	1987	30.6	4.3	35.1	50.7	9.6	4.1	—	0.4	0.1	52.1	—	—	36.5	—	11.4
Tunisia	1988	376	13.6	—45.7—		20.6	17.9	11.4	—4.4—		...	...	...	...	...	...
Turkey	1991	4,068	...	16.0[167]	51.1	18.0	9.7	4.4	—0.8—		95.9	—	—	1.1	—	3.0
Turkmenistan	1996	1.0[18]	6[18]	...	...	...	...	...	...	...	3.3[3, 48]	—96.7[3, 48]—		...	...	...
Tuvalu	1976	1.5	1.7	...	...	...	...	...	...	...	99.9	...	...	...	0.1	—
Uganda	1991	1,704	3.9	49.2	41.5	5.7	—3.6—				13.2[14]	—	—	—	17.3[14]	69.5[14, 42]
Ukraine	1996	34.8[18]	23[18]	...	...	...	...	...	...	...	...	...	...	...	...	...
United Arab Emirates	1986–87	17.9	2.3	45.4	38.8[168]	—15.8[169]—					...	...	...	...	...	...
United Kingdom	1995	242[56]	107.3[56, 170]	5.6[56, 65]	8.4[56, 66]	11.9[56]	15.2[56]	24.7[56]	28.0[56]	6.2[56]	—74.3[171]—		—	25.7[171]	—	—
United States	1992	2,073[172]	190[172]	—8.6[104]—		—20.1[10]—		30.3[173]	22.2[174]	18.8[175]	57.7	...	—	11.3	—	31.0[84]
Uruguay	1990	55	280.5[124]	—	8.2	12.1	13.2	16.5	23.3	26.7	—59.1[41]—		—	17.3[41]	—	23.6[41]
Uzbekistan[18]	1996	18.1	15	...	...	...	...	...	...	...	9.0	55.0	35.0	—1.0—		
Vanuatu[176]	1993	22	6.9[130]	...	...	...	...	...	...	...	65.3[41]	34.7[41]	—	...	...	...
Venezuela	1984–85	381	82.0	8.3	36.3	15.7	13.0	10.4	9.3	7.0	61.5[57]	...	—	6.1[57]	...	32.4[57]
Vietnam	1991	31[45]	28.0[2]	...	...	...	...	...	...	...	—	—100.0—		...	...	...
Virgin Islands (U.S.)	1997	0.3[44]	27.0[44]	30.0[44, 177]	30.3[44, 178]	12.0[44]	13.9[44]	6.0[44]	3.7[44, 179]	4.1[44, 180]	75.3[44]	...	—	8.6[44]	—	16.1[44]
West Bank	1965	55	3.4	49.8	34.4	10.6	4.0	1.0	0.2	0.0	71.6	—	—	6.4	—	22.0
Western Sahara	1983	...	...	...	...	...	...	...	...	...	...	...	...	...	...	...
Yemen[181]	1977–83	591	2.3	57.5	30.9	7.4	3.3	0.8	0.1	—	90.3[14]	—	—	9.4[14]	...	0.3[14]
Yugoslavia	1991	1,176	...	24.7	48.8	19.9	4.4	—2.2—			83.0	—17.0—		—	—	—
Zambia	1990	520	3.1[57]	—92.2—		—7.4—		—0.4—			99.9	0.1	—	—	—	—
Zimbabwe[184]	1996	1,000[48]	38.7[17]	—16.7[17, 99]—			—82.6[17, 185]—		—0.7[17, 20]—		—2.0[17]—		—	—	98.0[17]	—

[1]1967. [2]Cultivated area only. [3]1989. [4]1993. [5]Based on value of output by sector. [6]1973. [7]1991–92. [8]Less than 1.6 ha. [9]1.6 to 4.0 ha. [10]4.0 to 20 ha. [11]20 ha or more. [12]Percentage of farms having irrigation. [13]Arable and permanent crops only. [14]Based on area, not number, of holdings. [15]10 to 25 ha. [16]25 to 50 ha. [17]1974. [18]Private farms only. [19]50 to 100 ha. [20]100 ha or more. [21]Includes fruits and vegetables. [22]Includes houseplants and cut flowers. [23]Includes fallow and grazing lands. [24]1990. [25]Includes holdings without land. [26]Less than 1.2 ha. [27]1.2 to 4.0 ha. [28]1.0 to 4.0 ha. [29]4.0 to 10.1 ha. [30]10.1 ha or more. [31]1977. [32]1990–91. [33]1969. [34]Includes mixed/other activity. [35]1988. [36]1984–85. [37]1985. [38]1982. [39]4.0 ha or more. [40]Includes about 21,000 farms without land; distribution by size refers to traditional farms with land only. [41]1980. [42]More than one-half squatters. [43]1970. [44]1987. [45]State farms and cooperatives only. [46]1994. [47]Agricultural cooperatives only. [48]1995. [49]Precollectivization. [50]Includes Christmas tree farms, which were enumerated for the first time in the 1996 agricultural census. [51]4.0 to 52.2 ha. [52]52.2 ha and over. [53]Irrigated land only. [54]1968. [55]1975–76. [56]1992. [57]1971. [58]Holdings and tenure refer to private plots only; size and tenure 1990. [59]Owned and rented holdings. [60]Data for Czech Republic exclude Slovakia unless otherwise noted. [61]Number of units reported in the census. [62]1996. [63]Arable area only. [64]1991. [65]Less than 2.0 ha. [66]2.0 to 20 ha. [67]2.1 ha or less. [68]2.1 to 4.2 ha. [69]4.2 ha or more. [70]Data for Ethiopia include Eritrea, unless otherwise stated. [71]Excludes Eritrea, Tigray, Asab, Ogaden, and regions and nomadic areas. [72]1978–79. [73]Includes 28 percent under forests. [74]Excludes holdings of less than 1.0 ha. [75]10 to 35 ha. [76]35 to 50 ha. [77]Includes fruit-growing and viticulture. [78]2.0 to 5.0 ha. [79]Excludes 1.1 percent of holdings with no agricultural land. [80]2.0 to 4.0 ha. [81]4.0 to 10 ha. [82]20 to 40 ha. [83]40 ha or more. [84]Includes part-owners. [85]Less than 0.7 ha. [86]0.7 to 7.1 ha. [87]7.1 to 45 ha. [88]45 ha or more. [89]Excludes holdings of 0.04 ha (500 sq m) or less. [90]1984. [91]Farm households only. [92]1986–87. [93]Less than 2.5 ha. [94]2.5 to 7.5 ha. [95]7.5 to 12.5 ha. [96]12.5 to 20 ha. [97]50 to 250 ha. [98]250 ha or more. [99]Less than 8.0 ha. [100]8.0 to 20 ha. [101]40 to 61 ha. [102]61 ha or more. [103]Less than 0.4 ha. [104]0.4 to 4.0 ha. [105]Less than 4.5 ha. [106]4.5 to 9.0 ha. [107]9.0 to 18 ha.

activity (% of farms)			technology (latest)				farmland use: land in farms		farmland use: land use (%)							country
mainly crops	mainly livestock	mixed/other	tractors (per 1,000 ha)	electricity (% of farms having)	irrigation (% of land irrig.)	artificial fertilizer (kg/ha)	total ('000 ha)	% of total land area	cropland: permanent crops	cropland: temporary crops	cropland: fallow	cropland: total cropland	meadows and pastures	woodland and forest	other	
32.2	57.3	10.5	198	...	61	628	1,982	58.4	—99.4—		0.6	46.9	53.1	—	—	Netherlands, The
...	...	...	2.5	...	...	...	...	...	...	...	...	...	...	...	...	Netherlands Antilles
...	...	...	200	...	...	60	314	17.2	39.9	—60.1—		4.8	68.2	10.6	16.4	New Caledonia
25.3	73.6	1.1	197	...	74	741	16,578	61.9	—80.1[46]—		19.9[46]	1.9[46]	80.1[46]	9.0[46, 131]	9.0[46, 132]	New Zealand
52.7[5, 46]	38.0[5, 46]	9.3[5, 46]	2.4	...	8	28	5,651	47.7	...	...	...	...	...	...	...	Nicaragua
...	...	...	0.05	...	2	1	3,605[13]	2.8[13]	...	...	...	...	...	...	...	Niger
—94.0—		6.0	0.4	...	0.8	12	32,700[13]	35.9[13]	—20.0—		80.0	31.4	27.5	41.1	...	Nigeria
64.3[5]	35.7[5]	—	22	45	...	...	5.8	12.2	...	...	...	32.9	30.2	—36.9—		Northern Mariana Is.
24.3[5]	70.6[5]	5.1[5]	164	...	11	242	1,026[2]	3.3[2]	—95.7—		4.3	42.7	—57.3—			Norway
28.0	34.0	38.0	9.4	...	92	83	106	0.4	68.5	31.5	—	59.1	—40.9—			Oman
...	...	...	13.6	...	82	91	22,150	28.7	—76.9—		23.1	95.4	—4.6—			Pakistan
...	...	...	2.2	...	...	...	...	...	—78.5—		21.5	43.3	—56.7—			Palau[136]
88.1	11.9	—	10.1	0.5[57]	6	58	2,942	39.5	23.7	41.3	35.0	22.2	50.0	24.1	3.7	Panama
...	...	...	28.5	...	...	40	415[13]	0.9[13]	100.0	—	—	33.7	26.4	...	39.9	Papua New Guinea
33.0[117]	—67.0[117]—		7.5	...	3	9	23,818	59.9	1.9	85.5	12.6	19.1	43.1	32.8	5.0	Paraguay
4.9	93.0	2.1	3.5	6.5	45	41	14,893	11.6	24.1	75.9	—	27.1	47.5	19.8	5.6	Peru
98.2	1.5	0.3	2.1	...	29	67	9,190[13]	30.8[13]	57.5	42.5	—	86.3	6.8	—6.9—		Philippines
53.8[5]	46.2[5]	—	91.7	...	0.7	219	18,648	61.3	1.9	—98.1—		78.3	21.7	...	...	Poland[18]
66.7	19.4	13.9	68.2	...	29	73	4,822	52.4	28.0	50.1	21.9	56.0	18.9	18.3	6.8	Portugal[4]
61.0[5]	33.4[5]	5.6[5]	126.7	...	118	...	325	36.7	—78.9—		21.1	33.3	50.1	9.4	7.2	Puerto Rico
50.4[5]	49.6[5]	—	8.6	...	100	200	8.0[13]	0.7[13]	25.2	74.8	—	100.0	—	—	—	Qatar
...	...	...	38.9	...	27	282	59.7	23.9	3.8[48]	92.0[48]	4.2[48]	71.1[48]	21.5[48]	—7.4[48]—		Réunion[2]
...	...	...	17.3	...	33	133	14,797[2]	64.2[2]	6.0	94.0	—	67.2	32.8	—	—	Romania
52.1	47.9	—	8.8	...	4	17	209,600	12.4	—86.4[48]—		13.6[48]	60.9[48]	37.5[48]	—	1.6[48]	Russia
...	...	...	0.1	...	0.5	1	1,170[13]	47.4[13]	—85.6—		14.4	63.7	10.6	5.2	20.5	Rwanda
...	...	...	27.0	...	...	...	8.9	24.7	17.3	70.7	12.0	65.5	18.3	10.9	5.3	St. Kitts and Nevis
25.0[17]	—75.0[17]—		17.4	...	20	...	21	34.4	68.5[17]	—31.5[17]—		57.9[17]	10.2[17]	26.4[17]	5.5[17]	St. Lucia
...	...	...	20.0	...	25	...	12	30.8	64.3	16.1	19.6	84.2	...	12.3	3.5	St. Vincent
...	...	...	1.4	...	...	...	67	23.7	71.2[111]	28.8[111]	—	93.8[111]	6.2[111]	...	...	Samoa
...	...	...	...	...	...	...	4.7	76.5	60.9	6.5	32.6	69.2	6.0	8.2	16.6	San Marino
...	...	...	62.5	...	...	...	55	72.4	94.9	—5.1—		54.3	—45.7—			São Tomé and Príncipe
...	...	...	0.6	...	12	398	2,135	1.0	4.1	18.7	77.2	88.5	—11.5—			Saudi Arabia
...	...	...	0.2	...	3	2	8,050	41.8	0.1	—99.9—		22.4	77.6	...	...	Senegal
1.8[150]	32.4	65.8[151]	40.0	...	...	...	7.0[2]	15.6[2]	89.6	—10.4—		100.0	—	—	—	Seychelles
50.3	—49.7—		1.1	...	6	1	2,740[2]	38.3[2]	20.7	—79.3—		19.3	80.7	...	...	Sierra Leone
12.5	6.2	81.3	65.0	...	100	5,600	5.6[90]	9.0[90]	75.0	25.0	—	66.7	...	33.3	...	Singapore
50.0	28.4	21.6	22.1	...	5.4	45[48]	2,446	49.9	3.2	92.1	4.7	60.5[48]	34.2[48]	—5.3[48]—		Slovakia
50.7	11.9	37.4	214	...	0.8	270[48]	739	36.7	12.7[48]	54.6[48]	32.7[48]	21.2[48]	24.4[48]	54.2[48]	0.2[48]	Slovenia
43.4	—56.6—		...	...	...	...	96[2]	3.4[2]	40.0	45.2	14.8	100.0	—	—	—	Solomon Islands
20.0	60.0	20.0	1.8	...	20	3	...	...	...	...	...	...	...	...	...	Somalia
26.2	52.5	21.3[154]	10.2	...	10	59	94,557[2]	77.4[2]	...	...	...	12.5[35]	83.7[35]	2.1[35]	1.7[35]	South Africa[152]
...	...	...	50.6	...	23	101	30,816[2]	61.7[2]	—79.4—		20.6	48.9	34.3	16.8	—	Spain
...	...	...	36.3	...	61	111	2,323[2]	35.9[2]	56.4	43.6	—	86.0	1.0	2.7	10.3	Sri Lanka
...	...	...	0.8	...	15	4	31,500	13.3	0.8	88.7	10.5	23.8	76.2	...	...	Sudan, The
33.0[33]	12.5[33]	54.5[33]	23.3	...	105	26	165	1.0	15.0	53.0	32.0	40.4	23.1	19.1	17.4	Suriname
45.8[130]	25.3[130]	28.9[130, 131]	21.6	...	36	46	527	30.6	6.3	70.8	22.9	10.2	57.2	17.9	14.7	Swaziland[158]
15.3	39.0	45.7[159]	61.3	...	4	127	8,134	19.8	—90.4—		9.6	34.6	5.5	50.1	9.8	Sweden
58.0	—42.0—		278	...	6	430	1,071	27.1	6.2	93.8	—	31.2	68.1	—	0.7	Switzerland
...	...	...	16.1	...	22	46	5,527[13]	30.1[13]	—83.2[4]—		16.8[4]	32.1[4]	44.4[4]	3.2[4]	20.3[4]	Syria
41.9[3]	30.3[3]	27.8[3]	...	...	38	400[109]	2,827	78.5	27.5[3]	72.5[3]	—	31.7[3]	...	65.7[3]	2.4[3]	Taiwan
66.3[46]	33.7[46]	—	36.6	...	88	...	4,300	30.1	43.1	56.6	0.3	20.9	76.7	—	2.4	Tajikistan
65.0	0.4	35.0	2.2	...	5	9	7,545[146]	8.5[146]	19.1[146]	72.5[146]	8.4[146]	49.8[146]	10.2[146]	24.7[146]	15.3[146]	Tanzania
...	...	...	6.9	...	27	36	19,002	37.2	17.2	—82.8—		93.8	...	2.7	3.5	Thailand
...	...	...	0.2	...	0.3	8	406	7.1	17.3[31]	—82.7[31]—		71.0[31]	29.0[31]	...	...	Togo
...	—	...	6.8	...	...	2	48[13]	66.7[13]	—62.7—		37.3	81.2	6.7	10.2	1.9	Tonga
63.7[166]	—36.3[166]—		35.3	40.7	29	57	133[2]	25.9[2]	55.9	—44.1—		62.3	4.4	6.1	27.2	Trinidad and Tobago
...	...	...	9.2	...	13	20	10,040[56]	64.6[56]	—87.1[56]—		12.9[56]	74.5[56]	25.5[56]	...	...	Tunisia
—	3.6[24]	96.4[24]	30.9	...	17	64	23,896	31.0	11.1[46]	69.9[46]	19.0[46]	91.5	3.9	0.8	3.8	Turkey
...	...	...	35.7	...	93	...	35,200	74.9	...	...	...	3.7	96.0	—	0.3	Turkmenistan
...	...	...	...	...	...	...	...	...	...	...	...	...	...	...	...	Tuvalu
...	...	...	0.9	...	0.2	...	3,683	15.3	29.8[148]	70.2[148]	—	100.0[148]	—	—	—	Uganda
47.9[5, 46]	52.1[5, 46]	—	13.1	...	8	...	40,400	69.7	7.7	88.2	4.1	80.9	16.3	—	2.8	Ukraine
...	...	...	5.7	...	17	120	39.0[13]	0.5[13]	64.8[109]	18.2[109]	17.0[109]	97.6[109]	...	1.3[109]	1.1[109]	United Arab Emirates
...	...	...	84.1	...	2	376	18,406	76.2	0.8[46]	98.5[46]	0.7[46]	32.3[46]	60.0[46]	—7.7[46]—		United Kingdom
44.8	55.2	—	25.9	68.8	12	99	393,471[172]	41.1[172]	—88.5—		11.5	46.0	43.5	7.8	2.7	United States
37.1[41]	58.7[41]	4.2[41]	26.2	...	11	54	15,682	88.4	6.6	—93.4—		4.3	—95.7—			Uruguay
...	...	...	41.5	...	98	...	26,200	63.2	43.9	—56.1—		16.8	80.5	—	2.7	Uzbekistan[18]
92.2[130]	7.2[130]	0.6[130]	3.8	...	...	...	183	15.0	62.5[130]	3.0[130]	34.5[130]	84.9[130]	15.1[130]	...	...	Vanuatu[176]
27.6	9.0	63.4	15.2	...	6	138	31,278	34.3	19.0[57]	59.0[57]	22.0[57]	13.2[57]	57.0[57]	22.8[57]	7.0[57]	Venezuela
74.5[5]	25.5[5]	—	6.3	...	31	82	9,060	27.4	7.4	—92.6—		100.0	...	...	...	Vietnam
48.3[44]	40.8[44]	10.9[44]	15.6	15.6	...	...	7.2	21.2	18.3[44]	13.7[44]	68.0[44]	10.7[44]	75.3[44]	10.3[44]	3.7[44]	Virgin Islands (U.S.)
61.9[5, 46]	38.1[5, 46]	—	14.1[38]	...	5	...	185[41]	31.4[41]	62.2[41]	37.8[41]	—	100.0[41]	—	—	—	West Bank
...	...	...	...	...	...	...	5,002[2]	18.8[2]	—	—	—	—	100.0	...	...	Western Sahara
35.5[14, 182]	56.9[14, 182]	7.6[14, 182]	3.8	...	33	12	1,545[13]	2.9[13]	6.7	69.7	23.6	98.8	...	...	1.2	Yemen[181]
12.7[33, 183]	—87.3[33, 183]—		111	...	2	221	6,243	61.2	8.6[46]	88.8[46]	2.6[46]	65.4[46]	33.9[46]	—	0.7[46]	Yugoslavia
15.8[57]	9.7[57]	74.5[57]	1.1	...	0.9	15	938	1.3	4.5[57]	—95.5—		14.2[57]	38.1[57]	...	47.7[57]	Zambia
74.2[5, 48]	25.8[5, 48]	—	7.1	...	4	53	32,800	84.8	2.5[17]	—97.5—		34.5[17]	65.5[17]	...	...	Zimbabwe[184]

[108]18 ha or more. [109]1978. [110]Commercial farms only. [111]1975. [112]Excludes large commercial farms. [113]5.0 to 8.0 ha. [114]8.0 ha or more. [115]1985–86. [116]Excludes temporary rangeland available for agricultural use to subsistence farms. [117]1981. [118]Three-fourths under horticulture and viticulture. [119]1.0 to 3.0 ha. [120]3.0 ha or more. [121]West Malaysia except as noted. [122]Malaysia. [123]Includes some rented farms. [124]1986. [125]Farms in rural areas only. [126]1993–94. [127]4.0 to 8.0 ha. [128]Commercial farms owned mostly by whites. [129]Includes agricultural and horticultural farms. [130]1983–84. [131]Includes timber plantations. [132]Includes conservation planting and plantations of native trees. [133]Less than 0.8 ha. [134]0.8 to 4.0 ha. [135]Excludes holdings of less than 0.5 ha. [136]Partial data. [137]Large holdings only; tenure data 1983. [138]10 to 15 ha. [139]15 ha or more. [140]1.0 to 3.9 ha. [141]3.9 to 7.5 ha. [142]7.5 to 19.3 ha. [143]19.3 to 39 ha. [144]1.0 to 2.0 ha. [145]2.0 ha or more. [146]1972. [147]10.0 to 20.1 ha. [148]1964. [149]Includes 700 part-time farmers. [150]Includes root crops. [151]Includes fruits, vegetables, coconuts, and cinnamon. [152]Data excludes Transkei, Bophuthatswana, Venda, and Ciskei states. [153]Total indicates white commercial farmers, of which 60 percent have viable farming units. [154]Includes horticulture. [155]1.2 to 12 ha. [156]12 to 20 ha. [157]1988–89. [158]Includes individual-tenured farms and large estates. [159]Includes 38 percent of small farms not identified by activity. [160]Data excludes tenure of communal grazing lands. [161]50 to 300 ha. [162]300 ha or more. [163]Includes 5 percent multiple tenure. [164]1.0 to 6.4 ha. [165]6.4 ha or more. [166]1963. [167]Excludes approximately 102,000 holdings without land. [168]1.0 to 7.5 ha. [169]7.5 ha or more. [170]Full-time operations only. [171]Excludes Northern Ireland. [172]July 1995. [173]20 to 72 ha. [174]72 to 202 ha. [175]202 ha or more. [176]Tanna Island only. [177]Less than 3.0 ha. [178]3.0 to 10 ha. [179]100 to 260 ha. [180]260 ha or more. [181]Former Yemen Arab Republic only. [182]1976. [183]Data refer to Yugoslavia as constituted prior to 1991. [184]Total number of farms includes resettlement schemes and commercial land holdings. [185]8.0 to 100 ha.

Crops and livestock

This table provides comparative data for selected categories of agricultural production for the countries of the world. The data are taken mainly from the United Nations Food and Agriculture Organization's (FAO) annual *Production Yearbook.*

The FAO depends largely on questionnaires supplied to each country for its statistics, but, where no official or semiofficial responses are returned, the FAO makes estimates, using incomplete, unofficial, or other similarly limited data. And, although the FAO provides standardized guidelines upon which many nations have organized their data collection systems and methods, persistent, often traditional, variations in standards of coverage, methodology, and reporting periods reduce the comparability of statistics that *can* be supplied on such forms. FAO data are based on calendar-year periods; that is, data for any particular crop refer to the calendar year in which the harvest (or the bulk of the harvest) occurred.

In spite of the often tragic food shortages in a number of countries in recent years, worldwide agricultural production is probably more often underreported than overreported. Many countries do not report complete domestic production. Some countries, for example, report only crops that are sold commercially and ignore subsistence crops produced for family or communal consumption, or barter; others may limit reporting to production for export only, to holdings above a certain size, or represent a sampling only.

Methodological problems attach to much smaller elements of the agricultural whole, however. The FAO's cereals statistics relate, ideally, to weight or volume of crops harvested for dry grain (excluding cereal crops used for grazing, harvested for hay, or harvested green for food, feed, or silage). Some countries, however, collect the basic data they report to the FAO on sown or cultivated areas instead and calculate production statistics from estimates of yield. Millet and sorghum, which in many European and North American countries are used primarily as livestock or poultry feed, may be reportable by such countries as animal fodder only, while elsewhere many nations use the same grains for human consumption and report them as cereals. Statistics for tropical fruits are frequently not compiled by producing countries, and coverage is not uniform, with some countries reporting only commercial fruits and others including those consumed for subsistence as well. Figures on wild fruits and berries are seldom included

Crops and livestock

country	crops																	
	grains				roots and tubers[a]				pulses[b]				fruits[c]		vegetables[d]			
	production ('000 metric tons)		yield (kg/hectare)		production ('000 metric tons)		yield (kg/hectare)		production ('000 metric tons)		yield (kg/hectare)		production ('000 metric tons)		production ('000 metric tons)			
	1989–91 average	1996	1989–91 average	1996	1989–91 average	1996	1989–91 average	1996	1989–91 average	1996	1989–91 average	1996	1989–91 average	1996	1989–91 average	1996		
Afghanistan	2,754	2,562	1,200	1,156	217	235	16,291	16,786	32	35	913	946	647	615	466	492		
Albania	792	538	2,609	2,531	88	137	8,409	11,513	20	25	729	867	154	115	377	460		
Algeria	2,482	4,602	823	1,279	962	1,150	9,173	13,463	49	50	424	526	1,055	1,133	1,782	2,258		
American Samoa	...	...	...	...	2	2	3,721	3,361	...	...	...	...	1	1	—	—		
Andorra	...	...	...	...	...	...	...	...	...	...	...	...	...	...	...	...		
Angola	313	530	350	559	1,818	2,723	3,914	6,099	35	175	273	539	414	446	250	263		
Antigua and Barbuda	—	—	1,921	1,607	—	—	5,171	4,811	...	...	...	...	9	7	2	2		
Argentina	19,938	29,554	2,341	2,809	2,296	2,500	18,240	18,382	244	280	1,089	1,015	5,977	6,979	2,798	2,987		
Armenia	282[1]	288	1,500[1]	1,597	365[1]	423	12,080[1]	12,963	3[1]	5	1,714[1]	1,921	237[1]	335	444[1]	429		
Aruba	...	...	...	...	...	...	...	...	...	...	...	...	...	...	...	...		
Australia	21,390	34,602	1,665	2,109	1,127	1,129	28,301	29,611	1,530	2,186	1,025	1,116	2,361	2,717	1,525	1,772		
Austria	5,115	4,335	5,443	5,210	810	795	24,907	30,188	119	104	3,555	2,942	944	871	455	437		
Azerbaijan	1,130[1]	1,032	1,733[1]	1,689	153[1]	209	8,179[1]	13,933	...	...	...	...	803[1]	652	771[1]	886		
Bahamas, The	1	—	1,522	1,793	1	1	6,900	5,125	1	—	1,199	718	12	23	27	22		
Bahrain	...	...	...	...	—	—	14,112	12,222	—	—	836	1,091	20	25	10	16		
Bangladesh	28,032	29,445	2,530	2,720	1,643	1,877	9,744	10,569	512	527	699	751	1,331	1,386	1,332	1,517		
Barbados	2	2	2,656	2,500	6	9	9,271	9,049	1	1	1,261	1,254	3	3	7	17		
Belarus	6,749[1]	5,320	2,610[1]	2,174	9,623[1]	10,677	12,975[1]	14,850	235[1]	583	1,335[1]	1,756	561[1]	355	917[1]	1,176		
Belgium[2]	2,236	2,712	6,094	8,317	1,838	2,490	37,421	40,161	18	25	4,062	3,992	371	740	1,479	1,830		
Belize	28	38	1,640	1,824	4	4	21,838	21,765	3	3	763	811	134	243	5	5		
Benin	566	668	860	1,021	2,102	2,672	9,354	9,303	60	69	552	656	160	161	211	239		
Bermuda	...	...	...	...	1	1	20,985	20,706	...	...	...	...	—	—	3	3		
Bhutan	102	112	1,062	1,097	52	56	9,910	10,750	2	2	800	800	64	64	9	10		
Bolivia	882	1,166	1,416	1,646	1,219	1,123	6,192	5,969	31	26	1,079	1,014	782	802	374	402		
Bosnia and Herzegovina	1,176[1]	842	3,230[1]	2,904	230[1]	347	4,672[1]	7,700	19[1]	16	1,086[1]	1,223	130[1]	98	533[1]	599		
Botswana	60	83	308	358	7	9	5,385	6,000	17	14	556	467	11	11	16	16		
Brazil	37,705	46,101	1,868	2,352	27,247	28,156	12,574	12,724	2,471	2,862	473	563	30,184	35,928	5,590	6,165		
Brunei	1	1	1,793	2,667	1	2	3,344	4,437	...	...	...	...	5	5	8	9		
Bulgaria	8,872	3,495	4,121	1,982	495	302	11,987	7,550	89	27	1,021	485	1,576	830	1,754	1,575		
Burkina Faso	1,975	2,461	717	846	79	70	5,830	4,902	60	62	815	795	71	73	229	254		
Burundi	283	273	1,299	1,337	1,429	1,365	6,843	6,455	333	327	1,014	974	1,675	1,624	210	210		
Cambodia	2,591	3,450	1,431	1,730	105	143	5,366	6,492	13	20	500	784	239	299	472	455		
Cameroon	892	1,314	1,182	1,367	2,070	2,075	6,293	5,780	68	97	517	658	1,846	2,183	451	493		
Canada	53,016	59,407	2,467	2,811	2,903	3,800	24,683	26,162	628	1,852	1,587	1,654	751	814	1,993	2,099		
Cape Verde	10	9	287	327	17	6	9,102	12,041	5	—	380	250	14	15	8	8		
Central African Republic	103	109	845	826	816	801	3,551	3,199	16	26	941	963	196	222	60	71		
Chad	665	931	565	616	648	539	4,812	4,013	36	34	566	576	108	100	74	74		
Chile	2,997	2,578	3,862	4,265	858	835	14,315	13,776	128	97	1,141	1,191	2,596	3,589	1,943	2,963		
China	388,969	435,654	4,208	4,832	141,227	166,111	14,976	16,566	5,589	4,979	1,364	1,579	21,729	45,462	114,949	202,155		
Colombia	4,090	3,490	2,471	2,743	4,120	4,616	11,578	12,798	167	192	691	856	4,880	6,428	1,598	1,294		
Comoros	19	21	1,289	1,336	58	63	5,230	5,676	7	8	838	833	54	60	4	5		
Congo, Dem. Rep. of the	1,480	1,632	803	766	19,525	18,861	7,940	7,962	191	200	609	626	3,309	3,537	558	575		
Congo, Rep. of the	26	27	885	938	724	804	6,745	6,935	9	10	792	805	168	209	42	47		
Costa Rica	262	211	2,775	3,896	152	229	20,865	22,241	34	23	524	680	2,119	2,808	126	198		
Côte d'Ivoire	1,239	1,948	884	1,144	4,334	4,761	5,751	5,792	8	8	667	667	1,598	1,837	450	532		
Croatia	2,562[1]	2,759	4,128[1]	4,512	517[1]	665	8,085[1]	10,152	22[1]	24	1,914[1]	2,288	539[1]	545	259[1]	317		
Cuba	543	309	2,383	1,872	823	840	5,099	5,900	27	18	363	340	1,402	995	582	365		
Cyprus	107	144	1,901	2,337	187	223	22,328	23,189	2	2	967	1,096	368	311	125	132		
Czech Republic	6,622[3]	6,683	4,101[3]	4,217	1,652[3]	1,758	19,261[3]	20,315	175[3]	139	2,371[3]	2,463	496[3]	451	541[3]	569		
Denmark	9,211	9,545	5,887	6,060	1,394	1,674	36,010	37,254	481	285	4,303	3,239	88	61	304	291		
Djibouti	—	—	1,524	1,250	...	...	...	...	...	...	...	...	...	...	22	22		
Dominica	—	—	1,354	1,308	23	25	9,298	9,883	—	—	450	333	85	67	6	6		
Dominican Republic	523	641	3,737	4,224	310	275	7,262	6,676	92	92	974	1,134	1,561	1,352	252	206		
Ecuador	1,422	2,267	1,718	2,153	500	546	6,596	5,962	40	66	489	656	4,446	6,374	357	317		
Egypt	12,667	16,542	5,526	6,499	1,904	1,376	21,762	21,359	423	506	2,511	3,022	4,456	5,753	9,249	9,377		
El Salvador	785	889	1,840	2,027	38	107	15,090	18,388	55	51	802	834	290	222	146	155		
Equatorial Guinea	...	...	...	...	77	86	2,898	2,606	...	...	...	...	16	17	...	...		
Eritrea	175[3]	182	740[3]	611	109[3]	110	2,804[3]	2,828	36[3]	45	545[3]	604	4[3]	5	30[3]	35		
Estonia	638[1]	563	1,665[1]	1,987	590[1]	560	13,743[1]	15,669	1[1]	13	1,452[1]	2,326	33[1]	23	75[1]	58		
Ethiopia	7,783[3]	11,128	1,409[3]	1,167	2,000[3]	2,018	3,659[3]	3,679	978[3]	1,108	890[3]	892	228[3]	227	568[3]	565		

in national reports at all. FAO vegetable statistics include vegetables and melons grown for human consumption only. Some countries do not make this distinction in their reports, and some exclude the production of kitchen gardens and small family plots, although in certain countries, such small-scale production may account for 20 to 40 percent of total output.

Livestock statistics may be distorted by the timing of country reports. Ireland, for example, takes a livestock enumeration in December that is reported the following year and that appears low against data for otherwise comparable countries because of the slaughter and export of animals at the close of the grazing season. It balances this, however, with a June enumeration, when numbers tend to be high. Milk production as defined by the FAO includes whole fresh milk, excluding milk sucked by young animals but including amounts fed by farmers or ranchers to livestock, but national practices vary. Certain countries do not distinguish between milk cows and other cattle, so that yield per dairy cow must be estimated. Some countries do not report egg production statistics (here given in metric tons), and external estimates must be based on the numbers of chickens and reported or assumed egg-laying rates. Other countries report egg production by number, and this must be converted to weight, using conversion factors specific to the makeup by species of national poultry flocks.

Metric system units used in the table may be converted to English system units as follows:

metric tons × 1.1023 = short tons
kilograms × 2.2046 = pounds
kilograms per hectare × 0.8922 = pounds per acre.

The notes that follow, keyed by references in the table headings, provide further definitional information.

a. Includes such crops as potatoes and cassava.
b. Includes beans and peas harvested for dry grain only. Does not include green beans and green peas.
c. Excludes melons.
d. Includes melons, green beans, and green peas.
e. From milk cows only.
f. From chickens only.

livestock														country
cattle		sheep		hogs		chickens		milk[e]				eggs[f]		
stock ('000 head)		stock ('000 head)		stock ('000 head)		stock ('000 head)		production ('000 metric tons)		yield (kg/animal)		production (metric tons)		
1989–91 average	1996	1989–91 average	1996	1989–91 average	1996	1989–91 average	1996	1989–91 average	1996	1989–91 average	1995	1989–91 average	1996	
1,500	1,500	14,173	14,300	...	...	7,073	7,200	300	300	395	395	14,300	18,300	Afghanistan
657	850	1,645	2,500	183	110	4,864	4,300	403	893	1,384	1,628	15,033	16,560	Albania
1,366	1,228	17,302	17,565	5	6	73,000	90,000	595	530	940	946	120,000	150,000	Algeria
—	—	—	—	11	11	34	37	—	—	800	800	30	30	American Samoa
...	...	...	...	...	...	...	...	...	...	...	...	...	...	Andorra
3,117	3,309	240	245	802	810	6,117	6,500	151	162	483	488	3,900	4,200	Angola
16	16	13	12	2	2	87	90	6	6	935	968	173	160	Antigua and Barbuda
52,633	54,000	28,139	17,000	2,633	3,100	42,333	64,000	6,375	9,176	2,102	2,114	298,453	270,000	Argentina
522[1]	497	858[1]	548	130[1]	79	3,209[1]	2,700	394[1]	400	...	1,556	11,242[1]	11,000	Armenia
...	...	1	—	1	—	50	—	...	...	...	...	...	...	Aruba
23,086	26,952	165,046	126,320	2,617	2,663	55,991	65,000	6,514	8,986	3,945	4,783	186,667	155,000	Australia
2,546	2,272	284	381	3,762	3,564	13,738	12,215	3,344	3,100	3,805	3,902	94,284	95,000	Austria
1,726[1]	1,658	4,714[1]	4,390	84[1]	31	21,267[1]	13,000	798[1]	841	...	1,180	37,333[1]	26,000	Azerbaijan
4	1	39	6	12	5	1,733	3,200	1	1	1,000	1,000	500	850	Bahamas, The
14	17	21	29	...	...	553	660	19	20	2,602	2,564	2,800	3,500	Bahrain
23,173	24,340	871	1,155	...	...	90,253	123,000	741	782	206	206	56,936	82,000	Bangladesh
28	28	40	41	29	30	3,437	3,700	14	8	1,784	1,658	1,511	1,276	Barbados
6,216[1]	5,054	332[1]	264	4,397[1]	3,895	47,573[1]	39,145	5,660[1]	4,950	...	2,356	193,200[1]	192,000	Belarus
3,264	3,369	174	161	6,439	7,225	35,000	35,000	3,875	3,560	4,313	4,692	168,171	220,000	Belgium[2]
51	60	4	3	26	22	987	1,300	7	7	1,031	1,015	1,284	1,250	Belize
1,037	1,350	869	601	479	584	23,333	25,000	16	19	130	130	17,940	18,000	Benin
1	—	...	...	1	1	75	45	1	1	2,901	3,043	472	280	Bermuda
402	435	49	59	69	75	250	310	29	29	257	257	317	380	Bhutan
5,542	6,118	7,573	8,039	2,160	2,482	23,697	55,676	113	142	1,399	1,400	47,333	68,000	Bolivia
438[1]	314	518[1]	276	404[1]	165	5,167[1]	3,870	303[1]	292	...	1,392	17,833[1]	7,100	Bosnia and Herzegovina
2,694	1,950	317	250	16	7	2,080	1,900	113	82	350	350	1,860	1,710	Botswana
147,797	165,000	20,061	18,000	33,643	36,600	557,282	900,000	15,004	19,845	769	849	1,244,227	1,400,000	Brazil
2	2	...	...	17	4	2,254	2,500	...	...	...	...	3,083	3,200	Brunei
1,548	632	8,226	3,383	4,219	2,140	34,167	17,509	1,999	1,050	3,370	3,333	129,127	96,712	Bulgaria
3,937	4,350	5,049	5,800	510	560	17,028	19,000	101	121	156	175	15,283	17,000	Burkina Faso
431	390	352	320	92	72	4,000	3,900	33	30	350	350	3,040	2,964	Burundi
2,178	2,800	...	...	1,601	2,050	8,565	10,100	17	19	170	170	8,667	10,450	Cambodia
4,660	4,900	3,407	3,800	1,344	1,410	17,333	20,000	116	125	500	500	11,867	13,000	Cameroon
11,165	13,186	595	677	10,505	12,097	110,000	139,000	7,915	8,000	5,800	6,089	319,848	330,840	Canada
18	19	6	4	115	450	505	520	1	2	500	483	495	520	Cape Verde
2,589	2,800	134	170	430	550	2,772	3,500	46	50	224	229	1,314	1,377	Central African Republic
4,298	4,539	1,926	2,219	14	18	3,950	4,400	116	123	270	270	3,555	3,960	Chad
3,402	3,858	4,803	4,516	1,144	1,486	32,000	68,000	1,353	1,873	1,861	1,911	95,761	95,000	Chile
79,282	104,450	112,299	127,261	360,247	452,199	2,120,630	2,801,838	4,410	5,838	1,562	1,606	6,698,453	13,995,000	China
24,383	26,088	2,547	2,540	2,627	2,431	53,333	110,000	3,897	5,000	934	998	236,933	315,000	Colombia
47	50	13	15	...	...	392	430	4	4	500	500	632	680	Comoros
1,535	1,480	934	1,043	1,050	1,157	28,623	34,000	8	8	851	854	8,143	8,500	Congo, Dem. Rep. of the
65	70	104	114	49	59	1,650	1,950	1	1	500	500	1,170	1,170	Congo, Rep. of the
2,181	1,585	3	3	270	300	14,000	16,500	431	536	1,308	1,301	18,976	27,147	Costa Rica
1,101	1,277	1,137	1,314	361	290	24,333	27,337	18	23	150	166	12,693	16,470	Côte d'Ivoire
566[1]	462	502[1]	427	1,264[1]	1,196	11,665[1]	9,984	643[1]	590	...	1,818	51,167[1]	52,000	Croatia
4,922	4,650	385	310	2,184	1,500	27,876	19,000	1,100	920	1,866	1,604	109,506	63,670	Cuba
50	69	300	250	281	374	2,625	3,400	98	138	4,746	4,896	7,942	10,200	Cyprus
2,234[3]	1,989	205[3]	134	4,179[3]	4,016	25,574[3]	26,617	3,207[3]	2,960	...	4,245	154,226[3]	152,700	Czech Republic
2,227	2,052	103	145	9,390	11,079	15,808	18,673	4,710	4,695	6,227	6,471	82,800	87,800	Denmark
188	190	433	470	...	...	...	...	7	7	350	350	...	...	Djibouti
9	13	7	8	4	5	129	190	5	6	1,000	1,000	155	225	Dominica
2,283	2,435	115	135	543	950	31,227	42,952	345	437	1,701	1,714	38,864	42,611	Dominican Republic
4,351	5,105	1,417	1,708	2,213	2,621	51,901	63,105	1,529	1,848	2,092	2,376	51,471	55,000	Ecuador
2,771	2,700	3,310	3,491	24	27	34,555	42,000	974	1,000	689	678	143,817	160,000	Egypt
1,213	1,287	5	5	305	400	5,200	5,600	268	290	999	951	45,612	44,640	El Salvador
5	5	35	36	5	5	228	245	...	...	...	...	175	190	Equatorial Guinea
1,290[3]	1,320	1,520[3]	1,530	...	...	4,300[3]	4,300	30[3]	31	...	197	5,934[3]	5,934	Eritrea
595[1]	348	116[1]	42	588[1]	315	3,965[1]	2,860	834[1]	682	...	3,713	22,487[1]	18,800	Estonia
29,575[3]	29,900	21,700[3]	21,700	20[3]	20	54,200[3]	54,200	738[3]	740	...	209	73,370[3]	73,370	Ethiopia

Crops and livestock (continued)

country	crops															
	grains				roots and tubers[a]				pulses[b]				fruits[c]		vegetables[d]	
	production ('000 metric tons)		yield (kg/hectare)		production ('000 metric tons)		yield (kg/hectare)		production ('000 metric tons)		yield (kg/hectare)		production ('000 metric tons)		production ('000 metric tons)	
	1989–91 average	1996	1989–91 average	1996	1989–91 average	1996	1989–91 average	1996	1989–91 average	1996	1989–91 average	1996	1989–91 average	1996	1989–91 average	1996
Faroe Islands	...	...	...	...	1	2	13,677	13,636	...	...	...	...	...	...	...	...
Fiji	30	20	2,289	2,649	36	56	3,739	6,784	—	1	773	1,111	13	13	9	19
Finland	3,845	3,687	3,360	3,430	845	766	20,656	22,003	14	13	2,549	2,333	90	88	205	236
France	57,683	62,488	6,240	7,070	5,213	6,462	29,853	36,385	3,310	2,636	4,735	4,769	10,560	11,211	7,441	7,927
French Guiana	22	26	4,199	3,626	32	28	10,178	11,429	...	...	...	...	7	12	9	8
French Polynesia	...	...	...	...	13	13	12,273	12,547	...	...	...	...	8	7	7	6
Gabon	22	28	1,563	1,805	376	408	5,409	5,477	—	...	639	667	256	270	30	33
Gambia, The	99	105	1,076	1,120	6	6	3,000	3,000	4	4	267	267	4	4	8	8
Gaza Strip	1	1	510	529	23	35	22,624	21,875	...	...	...	...	168	137	140	158
Georgia	457[1]	645	1,823[1]	1,624	223[1]	360	10,300[1]	13,333	...	...	...	...	745[1]	600	1,205[1]	1,145
Germany	37,910	42,102	5,534	6,231	14,057	13,600	27,747	37,260	267	204	2,750	2,869	4,652	4,881	3,806	3,448
Ghana	1,155	1,793	1,074	1,444	5,504	10,493	7,000	11,295	18	20	102	100	1,149	1,789	416	511
Gibraltar	...	...	...	...	...	...	...	...	...	...	...	...	...	...	...	...
Greece	5,504	4,371	3,741	3,322	1,065	1,154	20,131	22,897	51	41	1,511	1,559	3,987	3,967	3,965	4,198
Greenland	...	...	...	...	...	...	...	...	...	...	...	...	...	...	...	...
Grenada	—	—	1,000	1,000	4	4	5,206	5,227	1	1	1,094	1,139	24	22	2	2
Guadeloupe	...	...	...	...	20	16	9,649	7,568	—	—	577	756	129	130	24	25
Guam	—	—	2,000	2,000	2	2	14,904	14,904	...	...	...	...	2	2	4	5
Guatemala	1,410	1,239	1,943	1,940	61	73	4,899	5,582	119	117	848	807	838	1,189	380	439
Guernsey	...	...	...	...	...	...	...	...	...	...	...	...	...	...	...	...
Guinea	632	864	1,052	1,353	578	691	7,320	7,351	60	60	857	857	856	990	420	420
Guinea-Bissau	165	173	1,556	1,360	67	60	6,953	6,977	2	2	960	600	64	60	20	20
Guyana	213	523	3,115	3,716	31	51	7,045	10,646	1	1	612	591	67	60	12	13
Haiti	405	388	996	917	770	770	3,785	3,802	92	82	634	675	1,005	868	283	214
Honduras	671	690	1,409	1,450	30	32	8,836	8,868	81	55	767	661	1,404	1,552	197	316
Hong Kong	—	—	1,667	—	—	—	22,000	33,750	...	...	...	...	4	4	116	88
Hungary	14,592	10,245	5,173	3,690	1,230	1,000	16,713	14,286	347	151	2,251	2,500	2,184	1,458	2,041	1,397
Iceland	...	...	...	...	9	7	9,553	9,155	...	...	...	...	—	—	2	2
India	195,478	214,082	1,911	2,141	21,280	25,070	15,906	16,917	13,427	15,414	567	602	30,505	39,197	59,320	64,672
Indonesia	51,258	60,090	3,814	3,977	19,150	19,014	11,616	11,806	455	812	1,322	1,579	6,493	7,430	4,558	5,783
Iran	12,973	17,108	1,377	1,772	2,387	3,200	17,383	20,644	398	660	584	648	7,088	9,774	7,630	9,900
Iraq	2,541	1,859	927	644	196	380	15,980	15,200	19	37	995	1,153	1,507	1,474	2,855	2,916
Ireland	1,950	2,142	6,374	7,360	577	733	25,060	30,542	8	19	4,798	4,524	24	20	235	243
Isle of Man	...	...	...	...	...	...	...	...	...	...	...	...	...	...	...	...
Israel	234	161	2,222	1,437	209	287	32,359	37,260	9	7	1,276	1,129	1,711	1,526	1,263	1,438
Italy	17,921	20,537	4,005	4,820	2,340	2,134	19,637	23,558	221	156	1,430	1,450	17,569	17,182	14,436	13,554
Jamaica	3	4	1,232	1,377	225	346	12,534	15,419	6	9	898	1,072	383	420	108	207
Japan	13,946	13,791	5,645	5,902	5,539	5,071	25,459	27,002	145	133	1,670	1,833	4,838	4,121	14,457	13,589
Jersey	...	...	...	...	...	...	...	...	...	...	...	...	...	...	...	...
Jordan	105	98	1,040	973	59	146	23,167	38,111	4	6	740	742	233	339	634	1,065
Kazakstan	22,521[1]	11,209	1,040[1]	651	2,303[1]	1,656	9,742[1]	8,746	96[1]	33	782[1]	692	160[1]	138	1,096[1]	1,031
Kenya	2,893	2,901	1,567	1,673	1,536	1,710	8,200	8,143	219	270	312	386	888	984	624	655
Kiribati	...	...	...	...	7	8	7,449	8,020	...	...	...	...	5	6	4	5
Korea, North	5,955	4,980	3,784	3,547	2,543	2,050	13,338	12,059	325	300	922	882	1,304	1,385	4,344	3,988
Korea, South	8,412	6,676	5,891	5,799	940	681	21,156	20,015	45	24	1,134	945	2,027	2,174	9,768	10,562
Kuwait	2	2	4,568	5,037	2	1	19,476	17,500	...	...	...	...	1	2	84	98
Kyrgyzstan	1,339[1]	1,423	2,271[1]	2,454	321[1]	562	12,190[1]	11,500	...	...	...	...	97[1]	102	291[1]	369
Laos	1,433	1,355	2,269	2,464	265	211	8,011	9,054	36	44	1,870	1,985	130	164	87	150
Latvia	1,072[1]	910	1,739[1]	2,035	1,161[1]	1,082	13,147[1]	13,226	6[1]	5	1,480[1]	1,444	73[1]	81	256[1]	180
Lebanon	82	74	1,995	1,850	249	322	18,708	22,519	28	39	1,631	1,910	1,222	1,247	798	958
Lesotho	170	252	805	1,600	45	63	15,319	14,651	9	6	481	756	18	16	24	20
Liberia	225	55	1,032	1,100	432	523	7,327	7,356	3	3	517	500	130	144	73	76
Libya	297	321	676	685	141	130	7,704	7,222	12	12	1,113	1,117	287	250	708	619
Liechtenstein	...	...	...	...	...	...	...	...	...	...	...	...	...	—	...	...
Lithuania	2,319[1]	2,519	1,974[1]	2,391	1,316[1]	2,023	11,213[1]	16,129	30[1]	35	1,239[1]	1,416	145[1]	134	306[1]	433
Luxembourg[2]	...	...	...	...	...	...	...	...	...	...	...	...	...	...	...	...
Macau	...	...	...	...	7	...	13,394	...	1	...	...	...	—	...	1	...
Macedonia	583[1]	546	2,453[1]	2,455	127[1]	156	9,534[1]	10,861	29[1]	27	1,348[1]	1,723	342[1]	332	462[1]	476
Madagascar	2,545	2,791	1,919	2,055	3,155	3,370	6,562	6,879	59	82	876	879	790	808	328	346
Malaŵi	1,560	1,943	1,104	1,391	506	600	4,294	4,691	268	271	589	586	485	511	252	260
Malaysia	2,014	2,110	2,890	3,080	497	530	9,683	9,701	...	...	...	...	1,115	1,140	334	510
Maldives	—	—	1,125	1,000	7	8	5,108	4,997	—	—	633	688	9	9	20	24
Mali	2,114	2,163	879	809	28	28	4,772	5,250	57	38	224	132	15	52	255	322
Malta	9	7	3,517	3,488	17	32	13,181	25,600	1	1	2,341	2,667	12	18	53	80
Marshall Islands	...	...	...	...	...	...	...	...	...	...	...	...	...	...	...	...
Martinique	...	...	...	...	23	22	11,540	10,675	...	...	...	...	273	256	24	24
Mauritania	131	220	831	810	6	5	1,933	2,000	28	17	385	321	19	38	9	9
Mauritius	2	2	3,885	4,339	19	20	18,733	16,778	1	2	708	714	8	11	42	57
Mayotte	...	...	...	...	...	...	...	...	...	...	...	...	...	...	...	...
Mexico	23,553	26,846	2,350	2,481	1,302	1,331	15,957	20,067	1,290	1,688	646	732	9,216	12,179	5,925	6,740
Micronesia	...	...	...	...	...	...	...	...	...	...	...	...	...	...	...	...
Moldova	2,274[1]	1,448	3,019[1]	2,846	504[1]	331	7,989[1]	5,517	107[1]	41	1,537[1]	751	1,562[1]	1,370	689[1]	339
Monaco	...	...	...	...	...	...	...	...	...	...	...	...	...	...	...	...
Mongolia	719	202	1,104	726	128	47	10,613	7,205	3	1	708	667	—	—	41	10
Morocco	7,457	10,100	1,346	1,680	975	1,134	17,347	17,439	386	231	790	647	2,306	2,568	2,942	3,225
Mozambique	629	1,380	403	825	3,944	4,869	4,136	4,794	87	140	301	378	368	360	197	167
Myanmar (Burma)	14,109	21,378	2,737	3,048	214	281	8,594	8,988	432	1,289	677	696	957	1,075	2,160	2,431
Namibia	103	87	745	268	197	230	8,194	8,519	7	8	1,062	1,096	10	10	8	9
Nauru	...	...	...	...	...	...	...	...	...	...	...	...	—	—	—	—
Nepal	5,685	6,247	1,887	1,927	826	1,043	7,401	7,672	168	186	597	609	457	565	962	1,250
Netherlands, The	1,327	1,659	6,909	8,293	6,947	8,081	40,168	43,681	85	24	4,109	3,000	506	658	3,455	3,732
Netherlands Antilles	...	...	...	...	...	...	...	...	...	...	...	...	...	...	...	...
New Caledonia	1	1	1,837	2,744	21	23	6,023	6,209	—	—	393	567	4	4	4	3
New Zealand	783	858	5,028	5,443	277	298	26,817	25,496	61	75	2,262	1,864	794	957	506	711
Nicaragua	453	679	1,483	1,702	77	81	11,790	11,518	69	103	621	696	304	270	54	59

livestock														country
cattle		sheep		hogs		chickens		milk[e]				eggs[f]		
stock ('000 head)		stock ('000 head)		stock ('000 head)		stock ('000 head)		production ('000 metric tons)		yield (kg/animal)		production (metric tons)		
1989–91 average	1996	1989–91 average	1996	1989–91 average	1996	1989–91 average	1996	1989–91 average	1996	1989–91 average	1995	1989–91 average	1996	
2	2	67	68	...	...	...	...	...	...	...	...	...	...	Faroe Islands
274	354	—	8	88	121	2,600	3,500	58	66	1,705	1,680	2,494	3,100	Fiji
1,352	1,179	59	115	1,322	1,394	5,583	5,543	2,712	2,450	5,666	6,188	72,967	70,000	Finland
21,407	20,661	11,196	10,556	12,233	14,800	198,306	221,421	26,334	25,668	4,797	5,437	903,413	1,017,600	France
15	8	4	3	9	9	202	190	—	—	2,411	2,526	250	423	French Guiana
8	7	—	—	33	42	100	100	2	2	2,207	1,778	1,347	1,250	French Polynesia
30	39	161	172	160	165	2,217	2,600	1	1	250	250	1,500	1,500	Gabon
333	323	127	159	11	14	558	750	7	7	175	175	820	1,138	Gambia, The
3	3	24	24	...	...	2,633	3,600	7	8	4,000	4,000	4,867	7,500	Gaza Strip
1,051[1]	980	1,160[1]	674	525[1]	353	15,113[1]	11,000	450[1]	530	...	753	12,717[1]	17,000	Georgia
20,048	15,890	3,824	2,437	33,350	23,737	116,263	104,000	30,976	28,621	4,931	5,356	989,467	836,000	Germany
1,159	1,200	2,199	2,400	495	440	9,682	12,900	23	24	130	130	12,278	13,780	Ghana
...	...	...	...	...	...	...	...	...	...	...	...	...	...	Gibraltar
651	640	8,684	9,500	1,002	1,070	27,213	28,000	646	690	2,739	3,416	132,343	126,000	Greece
...	...	21	22	...	...	...	...	...	...	...	...	...	...	Greenland
4	4	11	13	3	5	260	280	1	1	800	887	920	920	Grenada
70	60	4	3	28	14	311	280	1	—	506	500	1,412	1,656	Guadeloupe
—	—	...	...	4	4	170	200	...	...	...	...	367	700	Guam
2,052	2,291	432	551	602	950	14,633	21,000	312	321	752	732	66,051	73,580	Guatemala
...	...	...	...	...	...	...	...	9	...	4,202	...	...	...	Guernsey
1,491	2,212	429	618	24	45	5,800	7,000	42	50	185	185	14,035	7,350	Guinea
412	475	239	255	290	310	807	850	12	12	170	170	580	612	Guinea-Bissau
138	190	129	130	42	30	2,000	7,500	19	13	822	818	8,600	5,300	Guyana
1,067	1,246	86	184	330	500	5,167	6,000	25	37	247	248	3,583	3,750	Haiti
2,412	2,127	10	13	589	600	9,436	15,400	346	528	911	1,000	27,923	40,800	Honduras
2	2	—	—	296	109	5,678	3,290	2	—	2,190	2,688	1,497	900	Hong Kong
1,619	928	2,050	977	7,996	5,032	50,950	31,458	2,733	1,980	4,977	4,836	253,631	192,586	Hungary
75	73	540	450	18	42	450	430	112	105	3,509	3,500	2,647	2,195	Iceland
191,897	196,003	43,706	45,390	11,193	11,900	400,000	610,000	26,333	33,000	880	1,000	1,229,333	1,540,000	India
10,390	11,930	6,008	7,684	7,231	7,825	560,093	1,103,307	335	458	1,132	1,185	383,000	493,100	Indonesia
7,382	8,492	44,754	51,499	—	—	161,667	202,140	2,480	3,809	1,014	1,074	310,000	520,000	Iran
1,416	1,000	7,804	5,000	...	...	58,500	42,000	297	200	734	700	64,450	40,000	Iraq
5,923	6,532	5,523	5,772	1,125	1,542	8,697	11,221	5,376	5,690	3,864	4,483	32,733	31,700	Ireland
...	...	...	...	...	...	...	...	...	...	...	...	...	...	Isle of Man
340	379	383	352	122	105	22,733	23,000	964	1,136	8,783	9,105	104,663	98,450	Israel
8,541	7,018	11,088	10,531	9,150	7,964	133,000	130,000	10,893	10,674	3,724	4,925	686,867	680,000	Italy
382	420	2	2	192	180	7,167	7,500	51	53	1,000	1,000	25,833	28,000	Jamaica
4,772	4,880	30	25	11,673	9,900	337,667	310,000	8,169	8,290	5,825	6,334	2,446,228	2,562,000	Japan
...	...	...	...	...	...	...	...	...	...	...	...	...	...	Jersey
35	43	1,660	2,100	...	...	52,300	78,000	60	90	2,485	3,000	32,420	49,600	Jordan
9,336[1]	6,860	33,688[1]	18,725	2,610[1]	1,623	50,400[1]	19,500	5,327[1]	3,762	...	1,683	176,667[1]	72,000	Kazakstan
13,583	13,838	6,447	5,600	103	104	24,667	25,000	2,297	2,210	497	491	41,440	42,000	Kenya
...	...	...	...	9	10	259	300	...	...	...	...	124	140	Kiribati
1,293	1,350	385	395	3,215	3,350	20,767	22,500	88	90	2,379	2,250	144,333	150,000	Korea, North
2,149	3,463	3	1	4,792	6,950	70,336	88,000	1,752	2,070	6,467	6,620	398,578	468,000	Korea, South
14	25	197	350	...	...	16,982	22,000	21	35	1,506	1,667	6,390	9,250	Kuwait
1,124[1]	869	8,261[1]	4,075	257[1]	114	9,867[1]	3,300	918[1]	882	...	1,964	22,000[1]	8,800	Kyrgyzstan
853	1,200	...	...	1,397	1,680	8,165	11,500	9	11	200	200	32,500	35,000	Laos
1,068[1]	537	154[1]	72	865[1]	553	5,397[1]	3,300	1,212[1]	921	...	3,002	25,033[1]	26,000	Latvia
65	80	222	246	46	55	21,638	29,000	94	138	2,826	2,813	55,167	65,000	Lebanon
550	590	1,450	1,200	62	70	967	1,500	24	26	290	290	826	980	Lesotho
38	36	222	210	123	120	3,800	3,500	1	1	130	130	3,904	3,600	Liberia
238	100	5,100	4,400	...	...	15,867	16,500	99	85	1,202	1,214	33,917	33,000	Libya
6	6	3	3	3	3	...	...	13	12	4,645	4,444	...	...	Liechtenstein
1,761[1]	1,065	52[1]	32	1,579[1]	1,270	10,860[1]	8,000	2,128[1]	1,889	...	3,903	41,167[1]	41,500	Lithuania
...	...	...	...	...	...	...	...	...	...	...	...	...	...	Luxembourg[2]
...	...	...	...	...	...	450	430	...	...	...	...	638	635	Macau
282[1]	283	2,425[1]	2,320	176[1]	175	4,458[1]	4,880	127[1]	129	...	1,800	25,653[1]	25,500	Macedonia
10,254	10,320	719	756	1,431	1,629	13,062	16,229	476	484	273	276	15,050	12,800	Madagascar
862	700	179	101	236	220	11,500	14,000	37	32	460	460	11,203	18,300	Malaŵi
677	720	212	269	2,577	3,282	62,377	100,000	29	32	470	417	287,400	360,000	Malaysia
...	...	...	...	...	...	...	...	...	...	...	...	...	...	Maldives
5,007	5,708	6,072	5,431	59	63	22,000	22,000	123	140	245	245	11,880	11,880	Mali
21	21	6	16	101	69	867	820	24	41	3,850	4,667	6,800	6,450	Malta
...	...	...	...	...	...	...	...	...	...	...	...	...	...	Marshall Islands
37	30	46	42	39	33	347	250	2	2	756	750	1,214	1,500	Martinique
1,350	1,312	5,067	6,199	...	...	3,800	3,900	97	107	350	350	4,250	4,590	Mauritania
34	34	7	7	12	17	2,200	2,800	25	25	2,500	2,500	4,200	4,500	Mauritius
...	...	...	...	...	...	...	...	...	...	...	...	...	...	Mayotte
32,194	28,141	5,862	5,897	15,715	18,000	240,218	290,000	6,336	8,059	992	1,214	1,066,065	1,266,469	Mexico
...	...	...	...	...	...	...	...	...	...	...	...	...	...	Micronesia
962[1]	726	1,300[1]	1,302	1,468[1]	1,015	17,767[1]	14,000	998[1]	737	...	1,849	35,833[1]	32,000	Moldova
...	...	...	...	...	...	...	...	...	...	...	...	...	...	Monaco
2,694	3,476	14,266	13,606	166	19	351	58	271	366	352	296	1,669	280	Mongolia
3,284	2,420	13,528	16,267	9	10	71,200	115,000	955	850	536	553	170,800	195,000	Morocco
1,373	1,290	120	122	167	175	21,833	23,000	63	59	170	170	11,333	12,000	Mozambique
9,269	10,120	275	328	2,355	3,229	23,989	27,600	422	448	245	245	35,208	49,090	Myanmar (Burma)
2,104	2,084	3,289	2,137	18	20	1,717	2,300	70	74	411	412	1,306	1,730	Namibia
...	...	...	...	3	3	5	5	...	...	...	...	16	16	Nauru
6,274	7,008	903	859	571	670	8,233	9,500	252	297	366	377	16,133	19,000	Nepal
4,918	4,557	1,663	1,674	13,747	13,958	92,050	89,561	11,198	11,188	6,040	6,378	644,480	592,800	Netherlands, The
1	1	6	7	3	2	125	135	—	—	1,278	1,250	432	510	Netherlands Antilles
122	113	3	4	37	39	317	650	4	3	600	600	1,367	1,400	New Caledonia
7,987	9,204	57,861	48,816	404	429	9,067	12,000	7,572	9,934	2,845	3,166	45,507	37,000	New Zealand
1,693	1,807	4	4	565	410	4,533	8,000	162	187	797	798	25,500	28,658	Nicaragua

Crops and livestock (continued)

country	crops: grains, production ('000 metric tons), 1989–91 average	grains, production, 1996	grains, yield (kg/hectare), 1989–91 average	grains, yield, 1996	roots and tubers[a], production ('000 metric tons), 1989–91 average	roots and tubers, production, 1996	roots and tubers, yield (kg/hectare), 1989–91 average	roots and tubers, yield, 1996
Niger	1,902	2,344	310	342	248	263	7,689	7,405
Nigeria	18,100	21,653	1,139	1,221	34,383	56,085	10,031	10,527
Northern Mariana Islands	...	...	...	...	...	...	...	...
Norway	1,410	1,335	3,943	3,991	452	400	24,246	22,240
Oman	5	5	2,124	2,180	5	6	25,208	22,917
Pakistan	21,038	24,328	1,784	1,960	1,052	1,461	11,467	14,156
Palau	...	...	...	...	...	...	...	...
Panama	336	351	1,884	2,354	66	67	5,901	5,746
Papua New Guinea	3	3	1,761	1,698	1,254	1,267	7,224	7,073
Paraguay	859	1,340	1,844	2,200	3,471	2,839	15,074	14,170
Peru	2,003	2,582	2,492	3,208	2,302	3,266	8,112	9,327
Philippines	14,350	15,435	2,018	2,308	2,716	2,790	6,876	6,902
Poland	27,594	25,783	3,231	2,973	33,247	22,500	18,350	15,210
Portugal	1,673	1,599	2,012	2,441	1,258	1,332	10,097	15,112
Puerto Rico	—	1	7,462	8,000	28	11	6,499	4,864
Qatar	3	5	2,910	2,914	—	—	9,611	10,833
Réunion	12	18	5,590	5,947	15	17	11,006	12,058
Romania	18,286	14,242	3,084	2,455	3,159	3,200	10,517	12,456
Russia	92,890[1]	68,030	1,612[1]	1,323	36,603[1]	38,529	10,673[1]	11,801
Rwanda	299	168	1,234	1,640	1,631	1,543	6,275	6,906
St. Kitts and Nevis	...	...	...	...	1	1	3,688	3,075
St. Lucia	—	—	699	714	11	10	4,179	3,906
St. Vincent and the Grenadines	1	1	3,348	3,910	21	14	4,917	5,342
Samoa	...	...	...	...	41	41	5,002	6,164
San Marino	...	...	...	...	...	...	...	...
São Tomé and Príncipe	3	3	2,015	2,000	6	13	7,346	6,940
Saudi Arabia	4,214	1,880	4,177	3,506	59	435	19,157	19,773
Senegal	996	1,048	823	853	67	68	4,009	3,661
Seychelles	...	...	...	...	—	—	5,000	5,000
Sierra Leone	566	443	1,225	1,263	139	331	5,220	4,996
Singapore	...	...	...	...	—	—	13,933	10,000
Slovakia	3,494[3]	3,941	4,068[3]	4,489	566[3]	568	13,232[3]	13,457
Slovenia	486[1]	545	4,131[1]	5,025	379[1]	407	13,756[1]	18,535
Solomon Islands	...	...	...	...	107	112	17,595	16,986
Somalia	497	393	715	489	50	44	10,421	10,000
South Africa	12,237	13,815	1,956	2,174	1,334	1,538	16,535	21,662
Spain	19,306	22,517	2,489	3,354	5,337	4,055	19,448	19,629
Sri Lanka	2,370	2,278	2,924	2,722	547	433	8,845	8,928
Sudan, The	2,755	5,240	505	624	138	160	2,674	2,911
Suriname	229	220	3,770	3,661	3	7	11,900	11,853
Swaziland	127	138	1,401	2,167	9	8	1,665	1,930
Sweden	5,677	5,625	4,594	4,855	1,132	1,211	32,977	32,730
Switzerland	1,331	1,405	6,352	6,831	731	765	37,867	43,966
Syria	2,598	5,961	668	1,793	407	478	17,543	19,521
Taiwan	...	...	...	...	...	...	...	...
Tajikistan	256[1]	394	944[1]	1,539	151[1]	112	12,215[1]	28,000
Tanzania	4,142	4,330	1,390	1,342	8,167	6,613	8,824	7,416
Thailand	23,624	26,246	2,149	2,446	21,776	16,208	14,245	13,292
Togo	505	700	809	865	913	865	7,992	5,857
Tonga	...	...	...	...	99	91	6,551	10,008
Trinidad and Tobago	17	15	2,816	3,659	10	12	9,645	10,222
Tunisia	1,611	2,879	1,115	1,458	205	290	12,592	13,426
Turkey	28,283	29,342	2,065	2,106	4,321	4,950	22,388	23,569
Turkmenistan	1,038[1]	400	2,870[1]	682	32[1]	25	4,750[1]	6,250
Tuvalu	...	...	...	...	...	—	...	...
Uganda	1,597	2,076	1,483	1,572	5,360	5,290	6,335	5,852
Ukraine	37,208[1]	23,471	2,957[1]	1,997	19,129[1]	18,400	12,040[1]	11,885
United Arab Emirates	7	7	5,383	7,487	4	4	19,300	20,000
United Kingdom	22,644	24,496	6,168	7,298	6,333	7,219	35,916	40,785
United States	292,060	337,667	4,582	5,186	18,530	23,169	32,018	37,892
Uruguay	1,237	2,118	2,414	3,156	215	200	7,514	11,662
Uzbekistan	2,281[1]	2,494	1,714[1]	1,738	468[1]	490	10,083[1]	10,208
Vanuatu	1	1	515	539	49	50	10,072	10,000
Venezuela	1,989	2,083	2,423	2,668	682	819	8,686	10,245
Vietnam	20,013	27,296	3,060	3,487	4,758	4,142	7,432	6,788
Virgin Islands (U.S.)	...	...	...	...	...	...	...	...
West Bank	...	30	...	...	...	17	...	...
Western Sahara	...	2	...	774	...	...	...	...
Yemen	693	664	871	943	153	183	12,223	12,839
Yugoslavia	7,613[1]	7,519	3,102[1]	3,258	766[1]	720	6,928[1]	8,471
Zambia	1,467	1,574	1,569	2,554	573	594	5,388	5,415
Zimbabwe	2,391	3,124	1,488	1,518	127	183	4,792	4,495

country	pulses[b], production ('000 metric tons), 1989–91 average	pulses, production, 1996	pulses, yield (kg/hectare), 1989–91 average	pulses, yield, 1996	fruits[c], production ('000 metric tons), 1989–91 average	fruits, production, 1996	vegetables[d], production ('000 metric tons), 1989–91 average	vegetables, production, 1996
Niger	330	438	133	166	44	47	274	264
Nigeria	1,421	1,700	734	497	6,595	7,112	5,017	6,039
Northern Mariana Islands	...	...	...	...	...	...	...	...
Norway	—	—	...	...	122	114	182	173
Oman	...	...	...	...	184	202	155	187
Pakistan	719	883	483	561	3,931	5,438	3,165	4,314
Palau	...	...	...	...	...	...	...	...
Panama	9	12	526	463	1,225	1,089	65	94
Papua New Guinea	2	2	500	522	1,076	1,154	357	381
Paraguay	49	62	859	774	522	496	264	273
Peru	105	137	882	956	1,891	2,540	910	1,346
Philippines	36	40	792	786	6,250	7,388	4,143	5,014
Poland	635	276	1,857	1,857	1,793	2,491	5,797	5,808
Portugal	69	43	300	214	2,221	1,799	2,019	2,012
Puerto Rico	2	—	569	609	258	184	43	30
Qatar	...	...	...	...	8	14	30	42
Réunion	1	1	1,429	741	46	37	45	57
Romania	149	96	889	1,372	2,295	2,230	3,215	3,510
Russia	2,880[1]	1,300	1,383[1]	895	2,989[1]	3,386	10,411[1]	11,099
Rwanda	216	117	777	632	2,912	2,160	131	120
St. Kitts and Nevis	—	—	1,000	1,000	1	2	—	1
St. Lucia	—	—	2,133	2,500	176	170	1	1
St. Vincent and the Grenadines	—	—	1,000	1,000	78	61	3	4
Samoa	...	...	...	...	51	43	1	1
San Marino	...	...	...	...	...	...	...	...
São Tomé and Príncipe	...	...	...	...	10	16	3	3
Saudi Arabia	7	7	1,832	1,850	832	975	1,987	2,461
Senegal	19	35	337	455	105	122	129	135
Seychelles	...	...	...	...	2	2	2	2
Sierra Leone	38	42	652	676	163	151	189	187
Singapore	...	...	...	...	1	—	8	5
Slovakia	161[3]	178	2,313[3]	2,716	285[3]	255	528[3]	522
Slovenia	7[1]	11	777[1]	866	255[1]	217	77[1]	113
Solomon Islands	2	2	1,175	1,000	15	15	6	6
Somalia	13	13	312	236	284	212	65	74
South Africa	135	74	1,269	756	3,903	3,986	1,885	2,080
Spain	238	288	755	724	13,490	12,095	10,966	10,524
Sri Lanka	50	38	780	738	743	811	578	607
Sudan, The	103	119	1,064	1,126	758	831	903	990
Suriname	—	—	690	727	75	86	26	32
Swaziland	5	6	569	731	144	80	13	12
Sweden	91	78	2,494	2,378	188	102	261	237
Switzerland	8	10	4,267	4,077	625	503	308	290
Syria	131	252	577	1,012	1,353	1,684	1,691	1,977
Taiwan	...	...	...	...	...	...	...	...
Tajikistan	7[1]	6	742[1]	600	248[1]	234	623[1]	591
Tanzania	437	385	501	542	2,094	1,826	1,099	1,055
Thailand	476	370	794	819	6,164	6,577	2,514	2,712
Togo	22	34	202	215	48	48	152	159
Tonga	...	...	...	...	15	13	20	7
Trinidad and Tobago	3	2	1,458	1,662	62	75	16	18
Tunisia	73	105	663	826	670	806	1,477	1,657
Turkey	1,946	1,831	885	967	9,117	9,534	17,963	20,796
Turkmenistan	...	...	...	...	158[1]	206	539[1]	643
Tuvalu	...	...	...	...	1	1	—	—
Uganda	493	510	774	675	8,384	10,189	404	424
Ukraine	2,840[1]	1,845	2,300[1]	1,716	2,597[1]	2,467	5,750[1]	5,531
United Arab Emirates	...	...	...	...	205	298	270	744
United Kingdom	750	558	3,425	3,135	514	480	3,747	4,129
United States	1,621	1,431	1,832	1,734	25,392	28,841	30,808	34,393
Uruguay	6	6	986	981	391	464	117	148
Uzbekistan	...	...	...	...	985[1]	1,165	3,760[1]	2,901
Vanuatu	...	...	...	...	18	19	8	8
Venezuela	57	40	585	646	2,579	2,971	498	678
Vietnam	187	216	639	671	4,009	4,355	3,625	4,163
Virgin Islands (U.S.)	...	...	...	...	—	—	...	...
West Bank	...	2	...	...	...	153	...	228
Western Sahara	...	...	...	...	...	...	...	...
Yemen	64	67	1,424	1,246	314	391	536	520
Yugoslavia	100[1]	103	1,438[1]	1,624	1,391[1]	1,190	1,045[1]	1,223
Zambia	15	24	629	562	105	101	274	273
Zimbabwe	50	45	694	636	170	190	153	147

livestock														country
cattle		sheep		hogs		chickens		milk[e]				eggs[f]		
stock ('000 head)		stock ('000 head)		stock ('000 head)		stock ('000 head)		production ('000 metric tons)		yield (kg/animal)		production (metric tons)		
1989–91 average	1996	1989–91 average	1996	1989–91 average	1996	1989–91 average	1996	1989–91 average	1996	1989–91 average	1995	1989–91 average	1996	
1,712	1,987	3,100	3,849	37	39	17,833	20,000	140	168	393	400	8,500	9,180	Niger
14,650	18,115	12,477	14,000	3,558	6,926	122,120	125,000	350	380	239	233	313,000	325,000	Nigeria
...	...	...	...	...	...	...	...	...	...	...	...	...	...	Northern Mariana Islands
959	998	2,202	2,400	696	768	3,663	3,900	1,944	1,851	5,757	5,530	51,046	53,454	Norway
137	142	141	148	...	...	2,500	2,700	18	19	420	420	5,850	6,160	Oman
17,677	17,900	25,703	29,800	...	...	77,767	110,000	3,525	4,442	842	949	210,867	311,000	Pakistan
...	...	...	...	...	...	...	...	...	...	...	...	...	...	Palau
1,401	1,456	...	...	228	261	7,668	10,376	129	155	1,162	1,240	11,117	13,579	Panama
103	110	4	4	997	1,030	2,883	3,250	—	—	106	114	2,950	3,600	Papua New Guinea
7,985	9,788	422	390	2,443	2,525	15,065	14,152	224	300	1,904	2,204	34,883	47,000	Paraguay
4,126	4,629	12,484	12,502	2,417	2,490	62,406	79,089	788	905	1,323	1,521	103,800	130,000	Peru
1,644	2,128	30	30	7,968	9,026	76,853	115,782	14	18	1,036	1,029	276,000	305,000	Philippines
9,875	7,396	3,934	552	20,056	18,759	58,196	43,977	15,560	11,430	3,260	3,111	410,255	348,152	Poland
1,355	1,316	5,531	6,200	2,531	2,400	19,667	26,000	1,500	1,500	3,734	3,947	85,400	105,000	Portugal
595	326	7	8	204	101	11,241	14,000	396	363	4,233	4,101	16,690	17,950	Puerto Rico
10	13	126	187	...	...	2,932	3,550	3	4	1,490	1,500	3,270	3,350	Qatar
20	27	2	2	88	95	6,916	7,800	7	6	627	520	4,117	5,000	Réunion
6,029	3,496	15,236	10,381	12,675	7,960	120,969	80,524	3,450	4,615	1,867	2,053	354,367	262,000	Romania
51,939[1]	39,696	46,998[1]	25,800	31,820[1]	22,631	582,667[1]	415,000	45,088[1]	35,445	...	2,162	2,233,333[1]	1,747,000	Russia
592	465	387	250	117	80	1,292	1,400	85	80	579	727	1,787	2,000	Rwanda
4	2	14	17	2	3	56	60	...	...	...	...	347	123	St. Kitts and Nevis
12	12	16	12	12	15	223	250	1	1	1,396	1,563	528	530	St. Lucia
6	6	13	13	10	9	205	200	1	1	1,351	1,414	627	640	St. Vincent and the Grenadines
24	26	...	...	186	179	356	350	1	1	1,000	1,000	192	200	Samoa
...	...	...	...	...	...	...	...	...	...	...	...	...	...	San Marino
4	4	2	2	3	2	124	260	—	—	170	171	175	280	São Tomé and Príncipe
195	225	6,370	7,800	...	...	76,000	83,000	274	350	6,254	6,863	113,005	140,000	Saudi Arabia
2,616	2,900	3,500	4,800	295	320	19,667	40,000	98	103	360	360	14,767	31,500	Senegal
2	2	...	...	18	18	293	540	—	—	533	535	1,760	2,240	Seychelles
333	360	271	302	50	50	5,900	6,000	17	17	250	250	6,785	6,900	Sierra Leone
—	—	—	—	300	190	2,500	2,000	...	...	...	...	16,543	18,191	Singapore
1,030[3]	929	412[3]	430	2,162[3]	2,076	13,321[3]	13,000	1,206[3]	1,236	...	3,389	79,549[3]	89,000	Slovakia
488[1]	496	23[1]	28	574[1]	592	10,420[1]	8,550	569[1]	590	...	2,714	19,712[1]	18,000	Slovenia
11	10	...	...	53	55	144	145	1	1	783	920	288	300	Solomon Islands
3,967	5,200	12,117	13,500	9	9	2,833	3,000	435	560	403	412	2,267	2,400	Somalia
12,920	13,000	32,060	29,000	1,480	1,630	46,000	42,000	2,426	2,370	2,637	2,683	213,362	237,000	South Africa
5,125	5,660	23,800	21,323	16,720	18,000	75,000	83,000	6,100	6,000	3,728	4,511	649,413	696,000	Spain
1,690	1,702	25	19	88	87	8,630	10,500	172	214	271	316	46,033	49,000	Sri Lanka
20,593	23,500	20,179	23,400	...	...	32,371	38,000	2,252	2,880	480	480	33,212	38,500	Sudan, The
91	104	9	9	29	20	7,625	2,700	17	18	1,832	1,565	3,033	4,000	Suriname
712	646	24	27	23	31	1,133	980	42	37	269	272	315	340	Swaziland
1,704	1,790	408	469	2,243	2,349	11,433	12,724	3,401	3,300	6,097	6,784	116,333	105,000	Sweden
1,845	1,772	392	442	1,793	1,580	5,912	6,000	3,892	3,913	4,954	5,000	37,833	34,305	Switzerland
786	800	14,571	12,000	1	1	14,405	18,000	782	836	2,314	2,500	75,133	106,000	Syria
157	165[4]	...	...	8,813	10,509[4]	80,119	101,838[4]	204	318[4]	4,349	4,802	...	...	Taiwan
1,238[1]	1,147	2,110[1]	1,783	49[1]	6	4,029[1]	1,200	472[1]	340	...	968	14,667[1]	2,600	Tajikistan
13,047	13,360	3,551	3,955	320	335	20,567	27,000	516	585	169	182	41,167	54,080	Tanzania
5,513	8,000	161	130	4,766	4,023	107,858	110,000	137	265	1,659	2,208	430,033	432,000	Thailand
247	202	1,164	1,200	617	850	6,070	5,685	8	10	225	225	5,558	6,325	Togo
11	9	...	...	94	81	221	266	—	—	1,500	1,500	287	260	Tonga
55	36	14	12	53	45	9,500	9,500	11	9	1,609	1,434	9,167	9,500	Trinidad and Tobago
626	700	5,935	6,400	6	6	39,367	35,573	393	605	1,604	1,823	52,250	63,400	Tunisia
12,037	11,789	43,195	33,791	10	5	73,181	129,015	8,183	9,133	1,352	1,501	369,080	560,000	Turkey
962[1]	1,199	5,793[1]	6,150	203[1]	82	6,900[1]	3,200	565[1]	735	...	2,664	14,933[1]	14,300	Turkmenistan
...	...	...	...	12	13	29	27	...	...	...	...	12	12	Tuvalu
4,777	5,200	1,350	1,900	797	920	18,667	22,500	418	455	350	350	14,933	18,000	Uganda
22,597[1]	15,611	6,658[1]	2,144	16,437[1]	13,144	180,352[1]	127,960	18,363[1]	15,704	...	2,205	664,865[1]	496,000	Ukraine
49	70	255	360	...	...	6,733	10,550	5	7	210	206	9,877	12,500	United Arab Emirates
11,980	11,619	29,241	28,797	7,519	7,351	124,076	125,718	14,976	14,600	5,206	5,353	616,334	614,000	United Kingdom
96,316	103,487	11,384	8,457	54,557	58,264	1,333,000	1,553,000	66,423	69,975	6,673	7,462	4,004,766	4,501,000	United States
9,019	10,677	25,359	19,865	217	270	7,900	11,000	1,006	1,342	1,604	1,954	21,933	31,850	Uruguay
5,273[1]	5,204	8,681[1]	8,352	524[1]	208	26,867[1]	13,000	3,622[1]	3,088	...	2,168	96,833[1]	56,000	Uzbekistan
124	151	...	...	59	60	306	320	2	3	202	203	312	280	Vanuatu
13,311	14,585	551	1,200	2,801	3,150	59,890	95,000	1,518	1,417	1,285	1,268	118,562	153,650	Venezuela
3,153	3,700	...	...	12,225	16,903	77,228	95,000	38	43	800	800	97,133	136,000	Vietnam
8	8	3	3	3	3	30	35	2	2	2,725	2,703	120	160	Virgin Islands (U.S.)
...	12	...	352	...	...	...	...	...	27	...	...	...	14,800	West Bank
...	...	...	29	...	...	...	...	...	...	...	...	...	...	Western Sahara
1,154	1,181	3,682	3,922	...	...	16,385	21,700	152	154	600	608	17,612	18,600	Yemen
1925[1]	1,926	2,701[1]	2,656	3,876[1]	4,446	21,920[1]	24,287	1,841[1]	1,947	...	1,791	96,833[1]	82,500	Yugoslavia
2,845	2,600	59	65	296	288	16,033	20,000	77	70	300	300	25,653	32,000	Zambia
6,147	5,436	584	530	300	266	12,000	15,000	609	570	451	424	15,500	19,500	Zimbabwe

[1]1992–94 average. [2]Belgium includes Luxembourg. [3]1993–95 average. [4]1995.

Extractive industries

Extractive industries are generally defined as those exploiting in situ natural resources and include such activities as mining, forestry, fisheries, and agriculture; the definition is often confined, however, to nonrenewable resources only. For the purposes of this table, agriculture is excluded; it is covered in the two tables immediately preceding.

Extractive industries are divided here into three parts: mining, forestry, and fisheries. These major headings are each divided into two main subheadings, one that treats production and one that treats foreign trade. The production sections are presented in terms of volume except for mining, and the trade sections are presented in terms of U.S. dollars. Volume of production data usually imply output of primary (unprocessed) raw materials only, but, because of the way national statistical information is reported, the data may occasionally include some processed and manufactured materials as well, since these are often indistinguishably associated with the extractive process (sulfur from petroleum extraction, cured or treated lumber, or "processed" fish). This is also the case in the trade sections, where individual national trade nomenclatures may not distinguish some processed and manufactured goods from unprocessed raw materials.

Mining. In the absence of a single international source publication or standard of practice for reporting volume or value of mineral production, single-country sources predominantly have been used to compile mining production figures, supplemented by U.S. Bureau of Mines data, by the United Nations' *National Accounts Statistics* (annual; 2 parts), and by industry sources, especially *Mining Journal*'s *Mining Annual Review*. Each country has its own methods of classifying mining data, which do not always accord with the principal mineral production categories adopted in this table—namely, "metals," "nonmetals," and "energy." The available data have therefore been adjusted to accord better with the definition of each group. Included in the "metal" category are all ferrous and nonferrous metallic ores, concentrates, and scrap; the "nonmetal" group includes all nonmetallic minerals (stone, clay, precious gems, etc.) except the mineral fuels; the last group, "energy," is composed predominantly of the natural hydrocarbon fuels, though it may also include manufactured gas.

The contribution (value) of each national mineral sector to its country's gross domestic product is given, as is the distribution by group of that contribution (to gross domestic product and to foreign trade), although statistics regarding the value of mineral production are less readily available in country sources than those regarding trade or volume of minerals produced. Figures for value added by mineral output, though not always available, were sought first, as they provide the most consistent standard to compare the importance of minerals both within a particular national economy and among national mineral sectors worldwide. Where value added to the gross domestic product was not available, gross value of production or sales was substituted and the exception footnoted. Figures for value of production are reported here in millions of U.S. dollars to permit comparisons to be made from country to country. Comparisons can also be made as to the relative importance of each mineral group within a given country.

Extractive industries

country	mining														
	% of GDP, 1995	mineral production (value added)					trade (value)								
		year	total ('000,000 U.S.$)	by kind (%)			year	exports				imports			
				metals[a]	non-metals[b]	energy[c]		total ('000,000 U.S.$)	by kind (%)			total ('000,000 U.S.$)	by kind (%)		
									metals[a]	non-metals[b]	energy[c]		metals[a]	non-metals[b]	energy[c]
Afghanistan	...	1988[1]	16.2	—	17.7	82.3	1995	0.5	—	100.0	—	—	—	—	—
Albania	...	1994[1]	81.4	46.1	0.8	53.1	1995	8.6	99.7	0.3	—	—	—	—	—
Algeria	25.7	1995	10,628.8	—0.5—		99.5	1995	7,156.6	—	0.3	99.7	54.7	23.7	2.2	74.1
American Samoa	...	1995	...	—	100.0	—	...	...	...	...	...	...	...	...	...
Andorra	...	...	...	...	...	...	1992	0.3	—	100.0	—	7.8	—	100.0	—
Angola	52.1[2]	1994	2,610.9	—	2.0	98.0	1995	2,788.0	—	3.7	96.3	—	—	—	—
Antigua and Barbuda	1.5	1995	7.6	—	100.0	—	1991	—	—	—	—	—	—	—	—
Argentina	1.7[3]	1993	4,383.3	2.7[4]	3.9[4]	93.4[4]	1995	1,688.1	—	1.2	98.8	563.9	44.1	8.8	47.2
Armenia	...	1995	...	—100.0—		—	1993	5.4	—	100.0	—	—	—	—	—
Aruba	...	1995	...	—	100.0	—	1991	0.4	31.2	68.8	—	0.5	—	97.9	2.1
Australia	4.4[2]	1994–95	14,150.8	37.5[5]	7.1[5]	55.4[5]	1995	14,129.4	40.7	4.1	55.2	2,245.8	5.9	10.3	83.8
Austria	0.4	1994	515.1	—	39.3	60.7	1995	501.4	41.3	58.3	0.5	2,316.4[2]	18.7[2]	11.1[2]	70.2[2]
Azerbaijan	...	...	...	...	...	...	1995	24.5	100.0	—	—	—	—	—	—
Bahamas, The	...	1995	...	—	100.0	—	1995	252.7	8.1	79.1	12.8	10.8	62.2	—	37.8
Bahrain	15.1[2]	1994	763.8	—	3.9[6]	96.1[6]	1995	2,471.1	0.6	—	99.3	1,372.7	3.0	0.1	96.9
Bangladesh	—	1995	5.2[7]	—	—100.0[7]—		1995	0.6	100.0	—	—	207.0	0.9	9.1	90.0
Barbados	0.6	1995	10.4[7]	—	—100.0[8]—		1995	3.2	—	100.0	—	7.2	—	44.5	55.5
Belarus	0.1[6]	1992	2.0	—	—100.0—		1995	18.8	35.4	4.5	60.1	65.1	0.6	99.4	—
Belgium	0.2[2]	1994	541.0	—	—100.0—		1995[9]	12,480.1	6.6	91.2	2.1	19,724.5	15.1	56.8	28.1
Belize	0.6	1995	3.5	—	100.0	—	1995	—	—	—	—	3.1	—	21.5	78.5
Benin	0.7	1995	14.4[10]	—	—100.0[10]—		1995	—	—	—	—	—	—	—	—
Bermuda	...	...	...	...	...	...	1995	0.0	—	100.0	—	0.3	—	100.0	—
Bhutan	1.9	1995	6.0	—	—100.0—		1995	—	—	—	—	2.2[6]	—	39.7[6]	60.3[6]
Bolivia	5.3	1995	369.6	—58.1[3]—		41.9[3]	1995	336.0	71.5	1.0	27.5	26.6	82.7	17.3	—
Bosnia and Herzegovina	...	...	...	...	...	...	...	...	...	...	...	...	...	...	...
Botswana	35.5	1995	1,478.7	11.4[2]	88.0[2]	0.7[2]	11	...	...	...	...	...	...	...	...
Brazil	1.0	1995	7,171.9	...	...	...	1995	3,049.2	91.6	8.4	—	4,107.9[2]	12.0[2]	4.3[2]	83.8[2]
Brunei	57.9[2]	1994	1,437.7	—3.0—		97.0	1995	1,970.2	—	—	100.0	31.6[2]	—	100.0[2]	—
Bulgaria	...	1991[1]	582.1	24.6	28.2	47.2	1995	96.1	85.2	14.8	—	1,044.5	5.5	0.3	94.2
Burkina Faso	0.9[3]	1992	28.4	—100.0—		—	1991	0.6	—	100.0	—	3.2[4]	—	100.0[4]	—
Burundi	0.6	1994	5.4	...	...	...	1993	—	—	—	—	1.2	—	100.0	—
Cambodia	0.2	1995	4.4	—	100.0	—	...	...	...	...	...	...	...	...	...
Cameroon	7.3	1995	681.6	...	...	...	1995	303.4	—	—	100.0	153.9[12]	84.3[12]	8.6[12]	7.1[12]
Canada	4.4	1990	25,411.4	24.6	6.4	69.0	1995	18,899.6	19.4	4.8	75.8	7,688.7	32.4	7.2	60.5
Cape Verde	0.3[12]	1991	0.8	—	100.0	—	1994	0.0	—	100.0	—	1.5	—	—	100.0
Central African Republic	5.8	1995	65.5[13]	—100.0[13]—		—	1995	78.6	—	100.0	—	—	—	—	—
Chad	0.5[12]	1991	5.0	—	100.0	—	...	...	...	...	...	...	...	...	...
Chile	8.0[2]	1994	2,440.0	...	...	...	1995	2,564.2	97.5	2.5	—	1,315.1	12.2	2.9	84.9
China	2.7[12]	1991	9,885.2	10.7	11.8	77.5	1995	4,888.9	3.0	30.6	66.4	6,304.0	48.5	5.7	45.7
Colombia	5.1	1995	4,045.4	...	...	...	1995	2,685.0	0.1	17.0	82.9	85.7	31.9	68.1	—
Comoros	—	1995	...	—	100.0	—	1994	—	—	—	—	—	—	—	—
Congo, Dem. Rep. of the	4.3	1995	226.5	—100.0—		—	1995	302.7	—	84.5	15.5	3.4	—	100.0	—
Congo, Rep. of the	32.8[15]	1995	659.9[15]	...	...	...	1995	906.3	—	32.2	67.8	2.7	—	100.0	—
Costa Rica	...	1990	3.8	12.8	87.2	—	1995	6.9	100.0	—	—	73.9	—	13.1	86.9
Côte d'Ivoire	0.2[2]	1994	13.3	...	...	...	1995	73.8	—	100.0	—	2.6	—	—	100.0
Croatia	...	1991	119.7	1.3	71.3	27.4	1995	57.3	37.8	23.4	38.8	775.4	0.3	6.5	93.1
Cuba	...	...	...	...	...	...	1995	342.3	100.0	—	—	13.0	—	100.0	—
Cyprus	0.3[16]	1995[16]	23.7	—	100.0	—	1995[16]	14.7	62.7	37.3	—	116.8	—	13.8	86.2
Czech Republic	...	1995[1]	1,050.3	—8.4—		91.6	1995	739.9	21.3	11.8	67.0	1,927.7	15.2	5.4	79.5
Denmark	0.9	1995	1,289.7	—	14.5[6]	85.5[6]	1995	990.2	24.8	9.3	65.9	932.2	7.4	16.7	75.9
Djibouti	—	1995	...	—	100.0	—	1992	—	—	—	—	—	—	—	—
Dominica	0.7	1995	1.5	—	100.0	—	1991	0.2	—	100.0	—	1.6	—	21.1	78.9
Dominican Republic	2.8	1995	126.0	...	...	...	1994	2.6	—	100.0	—	0.0	—	100.0	—
Ecuador	10.5	1995	1,883.6	—6.8[3]—		93.2[3]	1995	1,247.0	0.3	0.1	99.7	92.4	—	15.2	84.8
Egypt	9.8[2]	1994	5,151.3	—1.0—		99.0	1995	738.4	—	2.6	97.4	264.3	46.6	15.7	37.7

Since the data for value of mineral production are obtained mostly from country sources, there is some variation (from a standard calendar year) in the time periods to which the data refer. In addition, the time period for which production data are available does not always correspond with the year for which mineral trade data are available.

The Standard International Trade Classification (SITC), Revision 3, was used to determine the commodity groupings for foreign trade statistics. The actual trade data for these groups is taken largely from the United Nations' *International Trade Statistics Yearbook* (2 vol.) and national sources.

Forestry. Data for the production and trade sections of forestry are based on the Food and Agriculture Organization (FAO) of the United Nations' *Yearbook of Forest Products.* Production of roundwood (all wood obtained in removals from forests) is the principal indicator of the volume of each country's forestry sector; this total is broken down further (as percentages of the roundwood total) into its principal components: fuelwood and charcoal, and industrial roundwood. The latter group was further divided to show its principal component, sawlogs and veneer; lesser categories of industrial roundwood could not be shown for reasons of space. These included pitprops (used in mining, a principal consumer of wood) and pulpwood (used in papermaking and plastics). Value of trade in forest products is given for both imports and exports, although exports alone tend to be the significant indicator for producing countries, while imports of wood are rarely a significant fraction of the trade of most importing countries.

Fisheries. Data for nominal (live weight) catches of fish, crustaceans, mollusks, etc., in all fishing areas (marine areas and inland waters) are taken from the FAO *Yearbook of Fishery Statistics* (*Catches and Landings*). Total catch figures are given in metric tons; the catches in inland waters and marine areas are given as percentages of the total catch, as are the main kinds of catch—fish, crustaceans, and mollusks. The total catch figures exclude marine mammals, such as whales and seals; and such aquatic animal products as corals, sponges, and pearls; but include frogs, turtles, and jellyfish. The subtotals by kind of catch, however, exclude the last group, which do not belong taxonomically to the fish, crustaceans, or mollusks.

Figures for trade in fishery products (including processed products and preparations like oils, meals, and animal feeding stuffs) are taken from the FAO's *Yearbook of Fishery Statistics* (*Commodities*). Value figures for trade in fish products are given for both imports and exports.

The following notes further define the column headings:

a. Includes ferrous and nonferrous metallic ores, concentrates, and scraps, such as iron ore, bauxite and alumina, copper, zinc, gold (except unwrought or semimanufactured), lead, or uranium.

b. Includes natural fertilizers; stone, sand, and aggregate; and pearls, precious and semiprecious stones, worked and unworked.

c. Includes hydrocarbon solids, liquids, and gases.

1 cubic metre = 35.3147 cubic feet

1 metric ton = 1.1023 short tons

forestry, 1995						fisheries, 1994								country
production of roundwood				trade (value, '000 U.S.$)		catch (nominal)						trade (value, '000 U.S.$)		
total ('000 cubic metres)	fuelwood, charcoal (%)	industrial roundwood (%)		exports	imports	total ('000 metric tons)	by source (%)		by kind of catch (%)			exports	imports	
		total	sawlogs, veneer				marine	inland	fish	crusta-ceans	mollusks			
7,680	78.0	22.0	11.1	234	240	1.3	—	100.0	100.0	—	—	—	...	Afghanistan
409	84.5	15.5	15.5	6,177	6,823	3.2	59.7	40.3	87.9	0.5	11.6	1,770	430	Albania
2,517	84.5	15.5	1.6	366	453,252	135.4	99.7	0.3	97.3	2.0	0.7	2,362	9,130	Algeria
...	...	...	...	—	302	0.04	100.0	—	100.0	—	—	...	...	American Samoa
...	...	...	...	444	6,383	—	—	100.0	100.0	—	—	...	...	Andorra
7,005	85.8	14.2	0.9	877	5,282	77.9	91.0	9.0	97.2	2.6	0.2	7,165	23,510	Angola
...	...	...	...	246	4,604	0.6	100.0	—	77.2	11.0	11.8	420	1,940	Antigua and Barbuda
11,792	45.5	54.5	20.9	280,956	575,009	949.3	98.7	1.3	76.9	1.7	21.4	728,091	66,805	Argentina
...	...	...	...	17	42	4.1	—	100.0	100.0	—	—	...	555	Armenia
...	...	...	...	6	7,321	0.3	100.0	—	100.0	—	—	20	7,430	Aruba
22,458	12.9	87.1	42.7	737,797	1,814,759	210.5	95.5	4.5	61.5	18.6	19.9	758,011	428,116	Australia
14,405	21.2	78.8	56.1	3,360,990	1,986,551	4.6	—	100.0	99.9	0.1	—	5,424	192,874	Austria
...	...	...	...	409	663	35.0	—	100.0	100.0	—	—	480	900	Azerbaijan
117	—	100.0	14.5	436	24,271	10.0	100.0	—	16.3	78.4	5.3	48,160	7,300	Bahamas, The
—	—	—	—	411	33,281	7.6	100.0	—	70.5	28.2	1.3	3,240	5,570	Bahrain
32,044	97.7	2.3	0.9	118	59,102	1,090.6	25.6	74.4	90.5	9.4	—	239,550	160	Bangladesh
5	—	100.0	100.0	2,033	18,433	2.6	100.0	—	100.0	—	—	349	6,891	Barbados
10,015	8.1	91.9	39.1	40,487	3,296	14.5	—	100.0	100.0	—	—	2,030	9,000	Belarus
4,185[9]	13.1[9]	86.9[9]	60.9[9]	2,790,723[9]	4,066,241[9]	34.6	97.6	2.4	92.7	5.1	2.2	320,421[9]	920,918[9]	Belgium
188	67.2	32.8	32.8	3,703	3,849	1.9	99.9	0.1	9.4	79.6	11.0	13,253	707	Belize
5,899	94.6	5.4	0.8	813	1,484	37.0	21.6	78.4	81.2	18.8	—	390	8,300	Benin
...	...	...	...	822	9,004	0.4	100.0	—	97.4	2.6	—	...	9,250	Bermuda
1,399	96.8	3.2	1.3	66	1,511	0.3	—	100.0	100.0	—	—	...	...	Bhutan
2,567	49.6	50.4	34.7	79,717	25,237	6.0	—	100.0	100.0	—	—	138	2,790	Bolivia
5,379[4]	...	...	...	366	336	2.4	—	100.0	100.0	—	—	...	4,700	Bosnia and Herzegovina
1,584	93.8	6.2	—	...	...	2.0	—	100.0	100.0	—	—	11	5,222	Botswana
285,295	70.3	29.7	16.7	3,547,061	1,217,981	820.0	73.2	26.8	89.6	9.7	0.7	178,548	261,453	Brazil
295	26.8	73.2	69.8	482	28,101	4.5	99.6	0.4	70.8	28.4	0.8	520	6,590	Brunei
2,856	31.0	69.0	30.7	38,522	43,116	22.0	56.1	43.9	95.5	—	4.5	12,175	9,890	Bulgaria
10,033	95.5	4.5	—	193	943	8.0	—	100.0	100.0	—	—	—	2,956	Burkina Faso
4,969	97.8	2.2	0.9	227	1,024	23.1	—	100.0	100.0	—	—	230	906	Burundi
7,765	86.6	13.4	5.3	171,139	1,827	103.2	29.6	70.4	90.7	7.9	1.4	14,225	...	Cambodia
15,710	78.8	21.2	15.6	329,114	24,117	66.0	65.2	34.8	99.2	0.8	—	2,060	20,600	Cameroon
186,195	3.2	96.8	75.8	27,786,860	2,952,518	1,010.6	96.4	3.6	69.1	16.0	14.8	2,182,078	913,404	Canada
...	...	...	...	77	3,619	5.9	100.0	—	99.2	0.8	—	2,350	350	Cape Verde
3,864	84.1	15.9	8.4	29,165	271	13.0	—	100.0	100.0	—	—	—	890	Central African Republic
4,531	85.6	14.4	0.3	573	4,895	80.0	—	100.0	100.0	—	—	...	...	Chad
31,365	31.8	68.2	31.9	2,060,239	136,535	7,841.0	99.7	0.3	97.7	0.4	1.4	1,303,974	27,574	Chile
300,360[14]	67.9[14]	32.1[14]	16.9[14]	1,499,458[14]	7,209,168[14]	20,718.9	56.3	43.7	73.9	9.2	16.4	2,320,125	855,706	China
20,491	86.8	13.2	8.3	30,415	286,103	122.7	57.9	42.1	90.1	9.7	0.2	259,259	95,962	Colombia
...	...	...	...	426	2,033	13.5	100.0	—	99.9	0.1	—	—	915	Comoros
47,189	92.9	7.1	0.6	54,904	4,169	194.0	2.1	97.9	100.0	—	—	...	33,820	Congo, Dem. Rep. of the
3,830	61.5	38.5	16.6	126,638	717	37.0	48.7	51.3	99.3	0.7	—	5,761	21,726	Congo, Rep. of the
4,806	69.9	30.1	25.0	20,409	148,114	20.8	80.2	19.8	70.3	28.4	0.8	104,864	23,985	Costa Rica
14,782	78.4	21.6	15.5	354,713	26,960	74.1	78.8	21.2	98.4	1.6	—	134,361	157,267	Côte d'Ivoire
2,670	33.7	66.3	47.7	248,365	176,564	21.4	77.8	22.0	90.3	3.5	6.2	50,256	25,199	Croatia
3,152	80.6	19.4	6.1	349	28,666	87.7	76.8	23.2	75.2	16.2	8.3	103,359	18,672	Cuba
54	31.4	68.6	46.0	1,662	122,883	3.1	97.2	2.8	77.4	0.2	22.4	2,319	30,243	Cyprus
12,906	6.6	93.4	45.3	731,059	410,900	21.8	—	100.0	100.0	—	—	24,478	69,636	Czech Republic
2,288	21.5	78.5	38.2	534,520	1,587,591	1,886.9	98.1	1.9	93.7	0.9	5.4	2,359,034	1,415,239	Denmark
—	—	—	—	992	1,190	0.3	100.0	—	100.0	—	—	100	1,130	Djibouti
...	...	...	...	41	3,077	0.9	99.7	0.3	99.8	0.2	—	...	1,470	Dominica
982	99.4	0.6	0.4	1,972	134,461	25.9	75.1	24.9	72.2	9.5	18.3	960	32,250	Dominican Republic
10,361	50.2	49.8	43.4	66,525	230,310	339.9	99.6	0.4	69.7	29.5	0.8	723,691	9,454	Ecuador
2,698	95.4	4.6	—	12,658	965,005	305.7	27.9	72.1	96.4	3.1	0.5	4,120	91,818	Egypt

Extractive industries (continued)

country	mining														
	% of GDP, 1995	mineral production (value added)					trade (value)								
		year	total ('000,000 U.S.$)	by kind (%)			year	exports				imports			
				metals[a]	non-metals[b]	energy[c]		total ('000,000 U.S.$)	by kind (%)			total ('000,000 U.S.$)	by kind (%)		
									metals[a]	non-metals[b]	energy[c]		metals[a]	non-metals[b]	energy[c]
El Salvador	0.4	1995	40.3	100.0	—	—	1995	—	—	—	—	135.5[2]	1.8[2]	5.4[2]	92.8[2]
Equatorial Guinea	20.2[2]	1994	26.0	—	—	100.0	1990	—	—	—	—	2.1	—	100.0	—
Eritrea	0.1	1995	0.3	—100.0—		—	...	...	...	...	...	...	...	...	...
Estonia	1.6	1995	58.3	—	—100.0—		1995	135.7	59.2	17.7	23.0	11.0	—	100.0	—
Ethiopia	0.3[2]	1994	13.9	—100.0—		—	1993	—	—	—	—	72.3	—	1.3	98.7
Faroe Islands	0.1[2]	1994	0.9	...	...	...	1994	—	—	—	—	1.5	—	100.0	—
Fiji	0.2[2]	1994	1.7	...	...	...	1994	0.8	100.0	—	—	5.8	—	41.4	58.6
Finland	0.3	1995	424.1	18.1[2]	81.9[2]	...	1995	209.1	49.1	47.3	3.7	2,900.1	25.8	10.2	64.0
France	0.8	1995	11,521.0	3.0[6]	21.2[6]	75.8[6]	1995	2,604.6	52.9	33.1	13.9	17,183.1	11.5	6.6	81.9
French Guiana	...	1995	...	—100.0—		—	1995	—	—	—	—	—	—	—	—
French Polynesia	...	...	...	...	...	...	1995	169.8	—	100.0	—	—	—	—	—
Gabon	37.4	1995	1,214.1	8.1	—	91.9	1995	2,224.1	7.8	—	92.2	3.8[2]	—	100.0[2]	—
Gambia, The	...	1995	...	—	100.0	—	1994	—	—	—	—	7.4	—	—	100.0
Gaza Strip	...	...	...	...	...	...	...	...	...	...	...	...	...	...	...
Georgia	...	...	...	...	...	...	1995	29.2	100.0	—	—	29.5[3]	—	100.0[3]	—
Germany	...	1989[17]	11,803.2	0.6	20.0	79.4	1995	5,194.2	51.7	28.4	19.9	27,778.6	18.4	7.3	74.3
Ghana	1.7	1995	109.8	—100.0—		—	1995	335.8	12.2	87.8	—	4.9	100.0	—	—
Gibraltar	...	...	...	...	...	...	...	...	...	...	...	...	...	...	...
Greece	1.0	1995	922.1	13.6[4]	34.6[4]	51.8[4]	1995	306.6	47.3	35.0	17.7	1,637.3[2]	3.1[2]	3.6[2]	93.3[2]
Greenland	—	1995	—	—	—	—	1995	—	—	—	—	1.2	—	100.0	—
Grenada	0.5	1995	1.4	—	100.0	—	1991	—	—	—	—	1.6	—	11.2	88.8
Guadeloupe	...	1995	...	—	100.0	—	1995	0.9	100.0	—	—	58.0	—	—	100.0
Guam	...	1995	...	—	100.0	—	...	...	...	...	...	...	...	...	...
Guatemala	0.4	...	...	...	...	...	1995	39.0	—	15.8	84.2	149.5	—	—	100.0
Guernsey	...	...	...	...	...	...	...	...	...	...	...	...	...	...	...
Guinea	19.1[2]	1994	336.5[19]	—100.0[19]—		—	1995	416.7	78.7	21.3	—	—	—	—	—
Guinea-Bissau	—	1995	...	—	100.0	—	...	...	...	...	...	...	...	...	...
Guyana	19.4	1995	105.8	—100.0—		—	1995	78.1	99.2	0.8	—	—	—	—	—
Haiti	—	1994	0.2	—	100.0	—	1994	—	—	—	—	—	—	—	—
Honduras	1.8	1995	69.2	—100.0—		—	1995	2.3	100.0	—	—	9.0	—	37.1	62.9
Hong Kong	—	1995	34.7	—	100.0	—	1995	2,256.6	28.4	71.0	0.6	4,923.7	14.3	77.9	7.7
Hungary	0.9[3]	1993	335.0	4.8[20]	4.3[20]	90.9[20]	1995	250.6	90.3	2.6	7.1	232.2	33.3	25.2	41.5
Iceland	...	1995	...	—	100.0	—	1995	26.7	24.9	75.1	—	71.0	75.5	16.4	8.1
India	1.8	1995	6,065.9	7.6[21]	12.9[21]	79.5[21]	1995	6,397.4	14.1	85.9	0.1	6,805.9[2]	11.0[2]	29.9[2]	59.1[2]
Indonesia	8.4	1995	16,919.4[8]	...	...	...	1995	12,212.9	15.4	1.1	83.5	2,193.5	24.7	13.8	61.5
Iran	19.2[22]	1994–95	14,341.5	—2.5—		97.5	1995	18,525.9	1.0	0.4	98.6	1,271.4	17.5	7.5	75.0
Iraq	0.4[6]	1992	739.9	...	...	...	1995	451.0	—	—	100.0	—	—	—	—
Ireland	...	1989	512.1[23]	30.3	68.7	1.0[23]	1995	502.6	74.3	13.4	12.3	700.3	19.3	13.3	67.4
Isle of Man	...	1995	...	—	100.0	—	...	...	...	...	...	...	...	...	...
Israel	...	1990	352.6	...	...	...	1995	6,122.1	0.5	98.0	1.6	6,823.9	—	77.3	22.7
Italy	...	1989	2,554.5	3.4	25.2	71.4	1995	501.2	56.1	32.5	11.5	14,946.6	19.4	9.7	70.9
Jamaica	6.4	1995	271.4	99.2[12]	0.8[12]	—	1995	539.5	100.0	—	—	—	—	—	—
Japan	0.2[2]	1994	10,047.9	...	...	...	1995	875.1	41.2	57.9	0.9	61,982.7	15.2	8.5	76.3
Jersey	...	...	...	...	...	...	...	...	...	...	...	...	...	...	...
Jordan	3.5	1995	194.7	—	100.0	—	1995	343.4	5.2	94.8	—	416.2	0.5	8.8	90.7
Kazakstan	...	...	...	...	...	...	1995	263.4	9.7	—	90.3	—	—	—	—
Kenya	0.2	1995	14.1	—100.0—		—	1995	7.1	—	100.0	—	17.8[3]	11.9[3]	21.1[3]	67.0[3]
Kiribati	—	1995	—	...	...	...	1992	—	—	—	—	—	—	—	—
Korea, North	...	...	...	...	...	...	1995	57.0	22.6	46.0	31.4	1,004.0	5.0	4.8	90.2
Korea, South	0.3	1995	1,103.6	2.5[2]	72.1[2]	25.4[2]	1995	236.0	20.7	56.6	22.7	18,969.2	17.1	3.7	79.3
Kuwait	39.5	1995	10,513.4	—	—	100.0	1995	12,258.4	0.3	—	99.7	30.6	—	100.0	—
Kyrgyzstan	...	...	...	...	...	...	1995	—	—	—	—	—	—	—	—
Laos	0.2	1995	3.6	—100.0—		—	...	...	...	...	...	...	...	...	...
Latvia	0.2	1991	30.9	—	—100.0—		1995	11.4	61.0	—	39.0	109.4	—	6.2	93.8
Lebanon	—	1995	...	—	100.0	—	1995	75.5	34.0	66.0	—	53.0	—	100.0	—
Lesotho	0.1[2]	1994	0.8	—	100.0	—	[11]	...	...	...	...	...	...	...	...
Liberia	3.0[4]	1989	122.3[24]	—100.0[24]—		—	1995	244.6	—	100.0	—	—	—	—	—
Libya	25.4[6]	1992	7,212.2[8]	—	—100.0[8]—		1995	9,451.2	—	—	100.0	70.4	80.2	19.8	—
Liechtenstein	...	...	...	...	...	...	...	...	...	...	...	...	...	...	...
Lithuania	...	...	...	...	...	...	1995	221.9	85.8	—	14.2	194.9[2]	—	13.4[2]	86.6[2]
Luxembourg	0.3[12]	1991	29.2	—	100.0	—	[9]	...	...	...	...	...	...	...	...
Macau	...	1991	1.8	—	100.0	—	1995	—	—	—	—	16.9	—	25.6	74.4
Macedonia	...	...	...	...	...	...	1994	20.9	69.1	30.9	—	151.2[3]	5.0[3]	9.1[3]	85.9[3]
Madagascar	0.3[12]	1991	8.1	—100.0—		—	1995	28.4	44.8	55.2	—	—	—	—	—
Malaŵi	1.0[2]	1994	12.8	...	...	...	1991	—	—	—	—	6.6	—	100.0	—
Malaysia	7.3	1995	6,103.8	2.1[4]	2.4[4]	95.5[4]	1995	4,473.0	3.6	3.1	93.3	1,284.1	41.8	31.3	26.8
Maldives	1.7	1995	3.3	—	100.0	—	1991	—	—	—	—	—	—	—	—
Mali	3.1	1995	68.4	—100.0—		—	1995	19.4	—	100.0	—	—	—	—	—
Malta	...	1992	6.7	—	100.0	—	1995	3.5	97.9	2.1	—	17.7[3]	—	52.1[3]	47.9[3]
Marshall Islands	0.3	1995	0.3	—	100.0	—	...	...	...	...	...	...	...	...	...
Martinique	...	1995	...	—	100.0	—	1995	4.1	19.4	38.3	42.3	102.5	—	—	100.0
Mauritania	10.1[2]	1994	104.1	—100.0—		—	1995	280.2	100.0	—	—	—	—	—	—
Mauritius	0.1	1995	4.9	—	100.0	—	1995	27.5	—	100.0	—	46.6	—	71.5	28.5
Mayotte	...	...	...	...	...	...	...	...	...	...	...	...	...	...	...
Mexico	1.7[26]	1996	5,526.5	...	...	...	1995	8,519.5	7.5	3.3	89.2	1,005.5	34.0	32.5	33.5
Micronesia	—	—	—	—	—	—	1994	—	—	—	—	—	—	—	—
Moldova	...	1995	...	—	100.0	—	1995	18.6	100.0	—	—	162.7	2.7	2.2	95.1
Monaco	...	...	...	...	...	...	...	...	...	...	...	...	...	...	...
Mongolia	...	...	...	...	...	...	1995	132.8	100.0	—	—	—	—	—	—
Morocco	1.8	1995	574.2	...	...	...	1995	473.6	30.9	69.1	—	1,248.1	—	17.0	83.0
Mozambique	0.4	1995[1]	8.2[1]	...	...	...	1994	2.4	100.0	—	—	—	—	—	—
Myanmar (Burma)	0.5	1995	497.4	...	...	...	1995	65.1	0.2	99.8	—	—	—	—	—
Namibia	11.2	1995	302.4	—100.0—		—	[11]	...	...	...	...	...	...	...	...
Nauru	...	1995	...	—	100.0	—	1995	140.8	—	100.0	—	—	—	—	—
Nepal	0.5	1995	20.6	—100.0—		—	1995	—	—	—	—	4.6	100.0	—	—

forestry, 1995						fisheries, 1994								country
production of roundwood				trade (value, '000 U.S.$)		catch (nominal)						trade (value, '000 U.S.$)		
total ('000 cubic metres)	fuelwood, charcoal (%)	industrial roundwood (%)		exports	imports	total ('000 metric tons)	by source (%)		by kind of catch (%)			exports	imports	
		total	sawlogs, veneer				marine	inland	fish	crusta-ceans	mollusks			
6,804	97.9	2.1	1.3	5,470	70,410	13.1	64.0	36.0	58.3	35.4	6.3	31,314	5,841	El Salvador
811	55.1	44.9	44.9	35,876	998	3.7	89.2	10.8	84.3	11.4	3.8	...	1,970	Equatorial Guinea
...	...	...	...	...	...	3.0	100.0	—	100.0	—	—	...	...	Eritrea
3,730	15.4	84.6	38.4	191,694	51,680	124.1	98.3	1.7	99.2	0.8	—	101,212	13,539	Estonia
47,337	96.4	3.6	0.1	800	3,444	5.3	—	100.0	100.0	—	—	—	200	Ethiopia
...	...	...	...	221	4,162	249.9	100.0	—	94.8	3.7	1.5	311,816	13,464	Faroe Islands
598	6.2	93.8	42.6	37,385	20,930	32.0	90.2	9.8	83.5	1.8	13.7	38,606	18,147	Fiji
50,217	8.2	91.8	45.5	11,967,800	981,472	167.2	69.8	30.2	99.9	0.1	—	20,129	140,725	Finland
46,345	22.6	77.4	46.8	5,850,807	8,197,550	838.3	93.0	7.0	65.3	2.5	32.2	909,734	2,796,719	France
132	54.4	45.6	38.8	2,581	2,424	7.5	100.0	—	43.8	56.2	—	36,255	4,502	French Guiana
...	...	...	...	3	16,541	8.6	99.9	0.1	99.2	0.8	—	732	8,689	French Polynesia
4,882	59.2	40.8	40.8	387,948	2,251	24.4	89.7	10.3	97.0	2.7	0.3	1,780	8,382	Gabon
1,221	90.8	9.2	8.7	212	682	22.3	89.2	10.8	97.0	2.7	0.3	3,061	202	Gambia, The
...	...	...	...	...	...	...	...	...	...	...	...	...	...	Gaza Strip
...	...	...	...	308	303	35.0	92.2	7.8	99.9	—	0.1	...	830	Georgia
38,970	9.7	90.3	53.1	7,716,631	10,857,540	270.8	82.1	17.9	91.6	6.2	2.2	772,731	2,580,349	Germany
26,473	95.2	4.8	4.5	275,773	11,132	336.3	83.7	16.3	98.6	0.7	0.7	30,738	10,986	Ghana
...	...	...	...	268	827	—	100.0	—	100.0	—	—	...	...	Gibraltar
2,306	57.2	42.8	32.3	50,315	414,230	223.1	92.8	7.2	83.6	2.0	14.4	148,276	167,645	Greece
—	—	—	—	141	7,179	112.6	100.0	—	27.2	71.0	1.8	267,058	3,455	Greenland
...	...	...	...	—	6,244	1.6	100.0	—	95.7	1.8	0.1	135	2,310	Grenada
15	98.0	2.0	2.0	153	40,069	8.7	99.7	0.3	92.1	2.0	5.8	230	25,182	Guadeloupe
...	...	...	...	14	2,378	0.7	70.6	29.4	96.9	3.1	—	...	...	Guam
14,123	94.4	5.6	5.3	26,781	131,704	11.6	61.0	39.0	45.6	54.2	0.2	31,365	7,954	Guatemala
...	...	...	...	...	...	[18]	[18]	[18]	[18]	[18]	[18]	...	...	Guernsey
4,788	86.7	13.3	3.6	4,236	2,506	44.0	90.0	10.0	96.1	1.4	2.5	8,110	4,800	Guinea
579	72.9	27.1	6.9	3,991	186	5.3	95.2	4.8	79.6	20.2	0.2	740	400	Guinea-Bissau
508	7.8	92.2	88.0	38,823	1,283	46.4	98.3	1.7	83.9	16.1	—	16,129	...	Guyana
6,417	96.3	3.7	3.5	18	16,099	5.2	90.4	9.6	75.6	17.1	7.3	1,970	3,350	Haiti
6,459	90.9	9.1	8.8	21,005	81,151	23.2	98.6	1.4	25.8	49.9	24.3	87,421	4,590	Honduras
19[2]	100.0[2]	—	—	784,330[2]	2,804,335[2]	220.1	99.9	0.1	87.6	4.3	8.1	677,371	1,642,105	Hong Kong
4,415	46.0	54.0	29.5	161,228	400,627	24.0	—	100.0	100.0	—	—	8,892	40,985	Hungary
—	—	—	—	1,907	58,593	1,560.2	99.9	0.1	94.4	5.0	0.5	1,264,615	25,209	Iceland
299,163	91.7	8.3	6.1	34,516	357,944	4,540.2	65.4	34.6	89.3	8.6	2.1	1,125,440	6,618	India
185,895	81.4	18.6	16.9	4,727,553	847,879	3,954.2	75.1	24.9	87.2	9.5	2.3	1,583,416	120,674	Indonesia
7,463	34.3	65.7	5.2	994	224,399	314.3	63.4	36.6	97.3	2.2	0.5	52,885	21,780	Iran
161	68.9	31.1	12.4	159	439	22.0	18.2	81.8	100.0	—	—	...	...	Iraq
2,204	2.9	97.1	62.2	223,590	729,008	314.1	98.6	1.4	88.9	4.3	6.8	286,050	76,661	Ireland
...	...	...	...	...	...	3.6	100.0	—	26.6	2.2	71.2	...	...	Isle of Man
113	11.5	88.5	31.9	18,337	508,219	20.4	18.5	81.5	98.7	1.0	0.3	9,246	112,923	Israel
9,802	54.4	45.6	25.9	2,874,407	8,637,262	547.3	89.5	10.5	59.8	4.8	35.3	289,873	2,257,462	Italy
577	92.6	7.4	7.2	859	102,116	11.0	68.2	31.8	98.2	1.6	0.2	13,340	31,560	Jamaica
23,257	1.5	98.5	70.9	1,781,177	19,485,870	7,363.3	97.7	2.3	75.9	2.2	20.2	742,972	16,140,465	Japan
...	...	...	...	...	...	4.3[18]	100.0[18]	—[18]	11.0[18]	49.8[18]	39.2[18]	...	...	Jersey
11	63.6	36.4	—	8,258	177,093	0.1	2.3	97.7	100.0	—	—	810	19,772	Jordan
...	...	...	...	390	2,997	45.6	—	100.0	100.0	—	—	8,175	2,950	Kazakstan
41,696	95.4	4.6	1.1	791	21,110	203.5	2.9	97.1	99.6	0.3	0.1	22,534	2,966	Kenya
...	...	...	...	...	769	29.0	100.0	—	85.3	0.7	14.0	1,329	338	Kiribati
4,923	87.8	12.2	12.2	6,406	46,597	1,800.0	93.7	6.3	96.2	0.7	3.1	62,390	1,430	Korea, North
6,485	69.3	30.7	16.4	1,210,245	4,972,032	2,700.0	98.9	1.1	63.9	5.2	28.6	1,411,052	718,451	Korea, South
...	...	...	...	1,846	78,115	7.8	100.0	—	73.0	27.0	—	3,011	15,270	Kuwait
...	...	...	...	18	66	0.3	—	100.0	100.0	—	—	...	425	Kyrgyzstan
5,508	81.9	18.1	15.9	70,427	1,108	35.0	—	100.0	100.0	—	—	...	170	Laos
6,907	17.6	82.4	42.0	277,228	105,647	138.7	99.2	0.8	95.3	0.2	4.5	54,288	12,058	Latvia
515	98.6	1.4	1.4	871	91,756	2.4	90.9	9.1	98.0	1.0	1.0	...	...	Lebanon
709	100.0	—	—	...	...	0.04	—	100.0	100.0	—	—	[11]	[11]	Lesotho
6,267	84.3	15.7	12.8	68,080	325	7.7	48.2	51.8	98.0	1.9	0.1	908	1,672	Liberia
651	82.3	17.7	9.7	177	45,083	8.5	98.9	1.1	99.5	0.5	—	31,260	13,680	Libya
...	...	...	...	...	...	...	...	...	...	...	...	[25]	[25]	Liechtenstein
5,499	18.3	81.7	38.9	170,809	62,960	51.0	94.0	6.0	91.9	1.7	6.4	18,157	22,571	Lithuania
[9]	[9]	[9]	[9]	[9]	[9]	...	...	...	...	...	...	[9]	[9]	Luxembourg
...	...	...	...	4,244	23,269	1.9	100.0	—	66.6	29.7	3.7	4,314	16,376	Macau
151	—	100.0	95.4	25,243	37,663	1.2	—	100.0	100.0	—	—	130	7,778	Macedonia
10,893	96.0	4.0	0.9	3,962	10,258	104.8	71.3	28.7	84.5	13.3	0.5	103,656	11,005	Madagascar
10,475	94.9	5.1	1.2	2,043	8,057	58.8	—	100.0	100.0	—	—	215	917	Malawi
45,573	21.5	78.5	75.0	4,225,865	987,386	1,173.5	97.9	2.1	76.8	9.6	12.7	324,857	304,258	Malaysia
...	...	...	...	28	4,220	104.1	100.0	—	99.8	—	0.1	36,503	...	Maldives
6,540	93.6	6.4	0.2	172	1,556	63.0	—	100.0	100.0	—	—	410	660	Mali
...	...	...	...	—	68,823	1.8	100.0	—	99.5	0.2	0.3	6,869	14,606	Malta
...	...	...	...	...	1,923	0.3	100.0	—	100.0	—	—	690	250	Marshall Islands
12	83.3	16.7	16.7	136	22,872	5.9	98.2	1.8	97.1	2.6	—	161	34,196	Martinique
14	57.1	42.9	7.1	137	711	85.0	94.1	5.9	54.7	0.6	44.7	154,528	800	Mauritania
12	50.0	50.0	33.3	291	50,145	19.0	99.5	0.5	97.6	0.5	1.9	30,391	29,329	Mauritius
...	...	...	...	...	...	0.5	100.0	—	100.0	—	—	...	...	Mayotte
22,474	73.0	27.0	21.0	230,102	1,366,614	1,260.0	86.1	13.9	85.7	7.7	6.5	480,872	158,627	Mexico
...	...	...	...	...	2,110	1.7	99.8	0.2	97.8	1.2	0.9	440	5,700	Micronesia
...	...	...	...	3,492	19,314	4.8	—	100.0	100.0	—	—	195	2,537	Moldova
...	...	...	...	...	...	0.003	100.0	—	100.0	—	—	...	...	Monaco
541	69.6	30.4	30.4	4,186	773	0.1	—	100.0	100.0	—	—	...	1,840	Mongolia
2,346	61.8	38.2	10.5	102,852	445,905	750.1	99.8	0.2	87.8	1.1	11.1	620,451	7,044	Morocco
18,390	94.2	5.8	0.4	2,968	4,033	30.0	84.3	15.7	59.0	40.2	0.8	74,040	11,682	Mozambique
23,281	87.8	12.2	6.2	307,303	11,366	824.5	72.8	27.2	99.2	0.8	—	102,710	...	Myanmar (Burma)
[27]	[27]	[27]	[27]	[27]	[27]	300.9	99.7	0.3	99.8	0.1	0.1	[11]	[11]	Namibia
...	...	...	...	50	205	0.5	100.0	—	100.0	—	—	...	...	Nauru
20,822	97.0	3.0	3.0	185	2,230	17.0	—	100.0	100.0	—	—	...	...	Nepal

Extractive industries (continued)

country	mining														
	% of GDP, 1995	mineral production (value added)					trade (value)								
		year	total ('000,000 U.S.$)	by kind (%)			year	exports				imports			
				metals[a]	non-metals[b]	energy[c]		total ('000,000 U.S.$)	by kind (%)			total ('000,000 U.S.$)	by kind (%)		
									metals[a]	non-metals[b]	energy[c]		metals[a]	non-metals[b]	energy[c]
Netherlands, The	2.7	1995	9,620.1	—	5.5[6]	94.5[6]	1995	6,350.8	22.5	8.1	69.5	11,696.7	14.3	7.4	78.3
Netherlands Antilles	...	1994	...	—	100.0	—	1995	283.3	—	55.3	44.7	840.2	—	0.4	99.6
New Caledonia	10.4[4]	1990	262.4	100.0	—	—	1995	175.3	100.0	—	—	5.0	—	—	100.0
New Zealand	1.4[28]	1993–94	621.0	——29.8——		70.2	1995	264.5	15.3	6.1	78.6	782.9	18.8	15.4	65.8
Nicaragua	0.6	1995	11.3	82.2[12]	17.8[12]	—	1995	3.8	100.0	—	—	140.3	—	—	100.0
Niger	3.5[2]	1994	62.5	——100.0——		—	1995	233.3[2]	100.0[2]	—	—	5.0	—	100.0	—
Nigeria	16.8	1995	11,361.0	—	0.8	99.2	1995	11,131.5	—	—	100.0	19.9	1.5	98.5	—
Northern Mariana Islands	—	—	—	—	—	—	...	...	...	...	...	...	...	...	...
Norway	11.3	1995	16,446.5	0.4[12]	1.2[12]	98.4[12]	1995	18,502.9	0.8	1.2	97.9	1,779.3	73.8	11.7	14.5
Oman	38.5	1995	5,300.9	—	0.7[2]	99.3[2]	1995	4,611.9	—	0.1	99.9	80.0	82.0	18.0	—
Pakistan	0.5	1995	284.4	...	...	...	1995	45.3	—	2.3	97.7	794.2	13.8	4.3	82.0
Palau	...	...	...	...	...	...	...	...	...	...	...	...	...	...	...
Panama	0.1	1995	8.6	——100.0——		—	1994	7.3	100.0	—	—	1,390.1	0.5	4.4	95.1
Papua New Guinea	19.5[3]	1993	944.9	100.0	—	—	1995	1,123.1	48.0	—	52.0	—	—	—	—
Paraguay	0.3	1995	25.6	—	100.0	—	1994	—	—	—	—	66.7	2.8	15.5	81.6
Peru	9.6[3]	1991	1,098.1	——52.9[30]——		47.1	1995	1,013.5	86.1	0.1	13.9	354.2	0.1	—	99.9
Philippines	0.9	1995	668.9	67.3[6]	29.1[6]	3.6[6]	1995	402.0	70.5	2.6	26.9	2,863.2	14.4	5.2	80.4
Poland	4.2	1995	4,964.0	17.9[4]	17.6[4]	64.5[4]	1995	1,519.7	6.2	12.8	81.0	2,636.2	14.8	7.1	78.0
Portugal	0.9[3]	1993	704.2	...	...	...	1995	450.1	72.3	27.7	—	2,294.3	1.4	6.4	92.2
Puerto Rico	0.1[21]	1992–93	31.0	—	100.0	—	...	...	...	...	...	...	...	...	...
Qatar	32.5	1995	2,445.1[8]	...	...	...	1995	3,000.3	—	0.1	99.9	51.3[2]	75.3[2]	24.7[2]	—
Réunion	...	1995	...	—	100.0	—	1995	0.9	100.0	—	—	15.0	—	—	100.0
Romania	...	1991	1,315.6	1.7	7.8	90.5	1994	44.0	64.9	35.1	—	1,723.1	9.7	3.7	86.6
Russia	...	...	...	...	...	...	1995	26,969.2	7.4	5.3	87.3	560.0	60.2	16.9	23.0
Rwanda	—	1995	0.3	...	...	...	...	...	...	...	...	...	...	...	...
St. Kitts and Nevis	0.3	1995	0.6	—	100.0	—	1991	—	—	—	—	—	—	—	—
St. Lucia	0.6	1995	3.1	—	100.0	—	1991	—	—	—	—	5.0	—	61.5	38.5
St. Vincent	0.3	1995	0.8	—	100.0	—	1993	—	—	—	—	1.7	—	19.3	80.7
Samoa	—	1995	—	—	—	—	...	...	...	...	...	...	...	...	...
San Marino	...	...	...	...	...	...	...	...	...	...	...	...	...	...	...
São Tomé and Príncipe	—	1995	—	—	100.0	—	...	...	...	...	...	...	...	...	...
Saudi Arabia	33.1[2]	1994	39,809.9	——1.4——		98.6	1995	32,557.4	0.4	0.4	99.2	96.4	79.9	20.1	—
Senegal	0.7[6]	1992	42.3	—	100.0	—	1995	51.5	—	100.0	—	21.8	—	100.0	—
Seychelles	...	1995	—	—	100.0	—	1994	—	—	—	—	0.7	—	100.0	—
Sierra Leone	16.8[22]	1994–95	117.7	——100.0——		—	1995	16.7	25.4	74.6	—	0.6	—	100.0	—
Singapore	—	1995	25.6	—	100.0	—	1995	669.7	42.8	35.0	22.2	7,248.2	1.6	8.8	89.5
Slovakia	...	...	...	...	...	...	1995	139.5	52.8	38.6	8.6	1,374.4[2]	10.9[2]	2.7[2]	86.4[2]
Slovenia	1.2	1995	195.1	0.7[12]	15.2[12]	84.1[12]	1995	0.2	—	—	100.0	381.8	30.5	17.1	52.4
Solomon Islands	0.1	1995	—	——100.0——		—	1994	—	—	—	—	—	—	—	—
Somalia	0.2[12]	1991	1.0	—	100.0	—	...	...	...	...	...	...	...	...	...
South Africa	7.7	1995	9,182.3	...	...	...	1995[11]	5,537.0	24.2	46.5	29.3	3,274.7	5.7	12.5	81.8
Spain	...	1990	3,786.9	8.6	32.3	59.1	1995	647.5	39.9	54.5	5.6	10,444.7	19.8	4.5	75.7
Sri Lanka	1.2	1995	157.3[33]	——100.0[33]——		—	1995	176.3	5.2	94.8	—	271.1	—	40.0	60.0
Sudan, The	0.8[26]	1996	95.4	...	...	...	...	...	...	...	...	...	...	...	...
Suriname	13.4	1994	63.9[34]	...	...	...	1995	449.5	100.0	—	—	14.5[6]	—	45.9[6]	54.1[6]
Swaziland	1.0[35]	1995–96	10.6	...	...	...	[11]	...	...	...	...	...	...	...	...
Sweden	0.3	1995	634.3	55.2[6]	44.8[6]	—	1995	1,046.0	80.2	15.6	4.2	2,836.6	14.9	8.5	76.6
Switzerland	...	1995	...	—	100.0	—	1995	2,297.2	12.0	87.5	0.4	3,264.2	2.0	65.4	32.5
Syria	6.6[2]	1994	2,594.1[10]	—	——100.0[10]——		1995	2,675.5	—	1.4	98.6	44.9[2]	30.9[2]	16.3[2]	52.9[2]
Taiwan	0.3	1995	791.6	—	79.6	20.4	1995	843.7	...	...	...	8,035.8	——35.8——		64.2
Tajikistan	...	...	...	...	...	...	1995	1.9	100.0	—	—	—	—	—	—
Tanzania	1.1[12]	1991	22.0	...	...	...	1995	—	—	—	—	3.4	—	100.0	—
Thailand	1.3	1995	2,231.6	1.3[12]	36.2[12]	62.5[12]	1995	1,553.6	3.5	86.7	9.9	4,536.3	7.0	27.9	65.1
Togo	5.9	1995	73.3	—	100.0	—	1995	62.4	—	100.0	—	—	—	—	—
Tonga	0.3	1995	0.4	—	100.0	—	1994	0.1	—	100.0	—	0.9	—	40.3	59.7
Trinidad and Tobago	26.8	1995	1,300.8[8]	—	——100.0[8]——		1995	452.3	—	—	100.0	75.8	86.4	13.6	—
Tunisia	4.1	1995	704.5	...	...	...	1995	457.9	7.7	9.8	82.5	466.7	0.2	31.3	68.5
Turkey	1.3	1995	1,882.4	10.6[4]	19.9[4]	69.5[4]	1995	453.1	42.7	54.9	2.3	5,548.5	22.0	2.1	75.9
Turkmenistan	...	1995	...	—	——100.0[8]——		1995	26.1	—	2.0	98.0	—	—	—	—
Tuvalu	0.9	1995	0.1	—	100.0	—	...	...	...	...	...	...	...	...	...
Uganda	0.3[35]	1995–96	15.8	——100.0——		—	1994	—	—	—	—	—	—	—	—
Ukraine	...	...	...	...	...	...	1995	1,311.8	70.7	9.2	20.1	473.5	27.3	17.8	55.0
United Arab Emirates	33.4[2]	1994	12,269.1	—	0.5[3]	99.5[3]	1995	13,815.3	0.8	0.5	98.6	214.3	38.2	61.8	—
United Kingdom	2.4	1995	23,006.6	...	...	...	1995	17,479.3	6.8	30.6	62.6	13,736.7	17.1	37.1	45.8
United States	1.4[3]	1993	89,400.0	6.2[12]	7.7[12]	86.1[12]	1995	13,962.7	40.1	29.0	31.0	63,642.5	6.8	12.8	80.4
Uruguay	0.2	1995	30.8	—	100.0	—	1995	—	—	—	—	195.8	—	4.1	95.9
Uzbekistan	...	...	...	...	...	...	1995	4.0	—	100.0	—	—	—	—	—
Vanuatu	...	1995	—	—	100.0	—	1993	—	—	—	—	0.6	—	—	100.0
Venezuela	14.5	1995	9,156.9	3.0[6]	1.5[6]	95.5[6]	1995	8,842.6	1.5	0.2	98.3	123.7	39.7	60.3	—
Vietnam	...	1989	1,062.9	...	...	...	1995	823.1	0.1	—	99.9	10.8	—	100.0	—
Virgin Islands (U.S.)	...	1995	...	—	100.0	—	...	...	...	...	...	...	...	...	...
West Bank	...	...	...	...	...	...	...	...	...	...	...	...	...	...	...
Western Sahara	...	...	...	...	...	...	...	...	...	...	...	...	...	...	...
Yemen	9.8[2]	1994	1,788.2[10]	—	——100.0[10]——		1995	1,502.8	—	—	100.0	208.4	—	—	100.0
Yugoslavia	9.5[2]	1994	981.7	12.0	3.1	84.9	1995	3.7	100.0	—	—	335.9	—	19.0	81.0
Zambia	9.0	1995	371.5	...	...	...	1995	12.9	—	100.0	—	1.7	100.0	—	—
Zimbabwe	6.9[2]	1994	336.1	...	...	...	1995	124.0	18.9	79.7	1.4	37.2	63.0	37.0	—

[1]Gross value of production (output). [2]1994. [3]1993. [4]1990. [5]1988–89. [6]1992. [7]Mostly natural gas. [8]Mostly crude petroleum and natural gas. [9]Belgium includes Luxembourg. [10]Mostly crude petroleum. [11]South Africa includes Botswana, Lesotho, Namibia, and Swaziland. [12]1991. [13]Mostly diamonds, some gold. [14]China includes Taiwan. [15]Petroleum sector only. [16]Republic of Cyprus only. [17]Data refer to former West Germany only. [18]Jersey includes Guernsey. [19]Mostly bauxite and diamonds. [20]1989. [21]1992–93. [22]1994–95. [23]Excludes crude petroleum and natural gas.

forestry, 1995: production of roundwood: total ('000 cubic metres)	fuelwood, charcoal (%)	industrial roundwood (%): total	industrial roundwood (%): sawlogs, veneer	trade (value, '000 U.S.$): exports	trade (value, '000 U.S.$): imports	fisheries, 1994: catch (nominal): total ('000 metric tons)	by source (%): marine	by source (%): inland	by kind of catch (%): fish	crusta-ceans	mollusks	trade (value, '000 U.S.$): exports	trade (value, '000 U.S.$): imports	country
1,103	15.3	84.7	46.9	3,017,387	5,163,185	526.1	99.7	0.3	70.5	1.9	27.6	1,614,368	1,430,696	Netherlands, The
...	...	...	...	256	21,052	1.1	100.0	—	100.0	—	—	148	7,672	Netherlands Antilles
5	—	100.0	58.3	47	10,925	3.9	100.0	—	58.1	18.7	2.5	8,179	6,275	New Caledonia
17,155	0.3	99.7	64.9	1,634,147	317,853	493.2	99.7	0.3	77.5	0.9	21.4	691,733	40,315	New Zealand
3,809	96.1	3.9	3.9	15,321	6,566	12.3	93.3	6.7	32.6	67.4	—	53,081	1,319	Nicaragua
5,866	93.8	6.2	—	258	696	2.2	—	100.0	100.0	—	—	740	1,830	Niger
111,049	92.6	7.4	5.4	12,134	50,961	282.1	58.3	41.7	95.5	4.5	—	26,420	159,378	Nigeria
...	...	...	...	...	51	0.1	100.0	—	99.3	0.7	—	20	...	Northern Mariana Islands
9,035	5.2	94.8	50.5	2,179,431	1,158,851	2,551.5	100.0	—	98.1	1.6	0.3	2,718,132	322,087	Norway
...	...	...	...	1,309	53,484	118.6	100.0	—	96.9	0.9	2.2	49,467	4,646	Oman
29,665	94.8	5.2	3.7	1,000	154,902	551.9	75.8	24.2	93.3	5.5	1.2	153,265	152	Pakistan
...	...	...	...	990	1,123	1.5	100.0	—	98.6	1.1	0.1	...	195	Palau
1,070	89.0	11.0	5.4	17,696	76,273	165.4	99.7	0.3	88.5	10.6	0.9	106,293[29]	11,161[29]	Panama
8,772	63.1	36.9	34.9	536,220	5,501	27.0	48.1	51.9	91.6	6.2	—	11,131	44,150	Papua New Guinea
10,401	62.7	37.3	32.8	98,071	27,536	13.9	—	100.0	100.0	—	—	519	2,505	Paraguay
12,580	84.9	15.1	15.0	23,430	140,552	11,587.3	99.6	0.4	98.1	0.1	1.8	979,502	2,201	Peru
39,857	91.7	8.3	1.2	91,323	983,218	2,276.2	74.2	25.8	82.5	6.9	10.5	533,087	108,193	Philippines
19,334	14.0	86.0	46.8	690,120	745,372	460.2	88.7	11.3	97.7	1.7	0.6	117,992	154,180	Poland
9,448	6.3	93.7	44.3	1,732,571	1,145,268	253.9	99.1	0.9	91.3	0.6	8.1	203,123	669,888	Portugal
...	...	...	...	...	...	2.2	85.9	14.1	77.8	15.9	6.3	[31]	[31]	Puerto Rico
...	...	...	...	192	10,333	5.1	100.0	—	98.3	1.0	0.7	35	3,980	Qatar
36	85.9	14.1	11.6	846	69,029	4.5	99.9	0.1	89.8	10.1	—	13,477	38,478	Réunion
12,856	22.1	77.9	33.2	276,616	127,614	42.7	27.3	72.7	100.0	—	—	1,847	21,848	Romania
109,552	26.3	73.7	44.8	3,230,725	150,569	3,780.5	92.2	7.8	96.6	1.3	2.0	1,191,192	61,225	Russia
5,660	95.3	4.7	1.1	239	1,003	3.5	—	100.0	100.0	—	—	...	270	Rwanda
...	...	...	...	33	1,797	0.2	100.0	—	90.1	—	9.9	180[32]	1,260[32]	St. Kitts and Nevis
...	...	...	...	—	11,692	0.9	100.0	—	98.3	1.7	—	5	3,290	St. Lucia
...	...	...	...	14	6,578	1.7	100.0	—	93.7	—	6.3	654	680	St. Vincent
131	53.4	46.6	44.3	158	1,724	1.5	100.0	—	98.0	0.5	1.5	35	3,960	Samoa
...	...	...	...	...	...	—	—	100.0	100.0	—	—	...	...	San Marino
9	—	100.0	100.0	189	144	3.0	100.0	—	99.2	0.1	0.7	...	240	São Tomé and Príncipe
...	...	...	...	21,400	880,421	58.0	94.2	5.8	89.9	9.5	0.6	2,485	52,135	Saudi Arabia
5,219	86.2	13.8	0.8	94	20,464	388.0	92.8	7.2	94.7	1.0	4.3	113,292	11,970	Senegal
...	...	...	...	99	1,416	5.4	100.0	—	95.4	3.3	1.3	21,694	7,954	Seychelles
3,328	96.3	3.7	0.1	400	895	63.9	76.5	23.5	96.4	2.0	1.6	14,000	3,420	Sierra Leone
120	100.0	—	—	746,738	1,234,403	13.7	99.8	0.2	68.4	11.6	20.0	563,502	619,595	Singapore
5,323	8.2	91.8	39.6	364,343	149,467	3.5	—	100.0	100.0	—	—	2,049	33,222	Slovakia
1,944	12.1	87.9	53.8	351,567	346,489	3.1	67.8	32.2	100.0	—	—	6,227	23,321	Slovenia
872	15.8	84.2	84.2	115,219	833	49.2	100.0	—	98.7	—	0.2	28,189	200	Solomon Islands
8,794	98.8	1.2	0.3	29	172	16.3	98.2	1.8	93.8	2.5	3.7	5,680	80	Somalia
25,332[27]	28.2[27]	71.8[27]	21.4[27]	991,506[27]	564,285[27]	521.1	99.6	0.4	97.7	0.4	1.9	255,996[11]	134,565[11]	South Africa
15,121	17.9	82.1	36.8	1,617,660	3,826,287	1,380.0	97.6	2.4	77.7	2.5	19.8	1,021,015	2,638,697	Spain
9,625	92.7	7.3	0.6	6,182	101,826	224.0	94.6	5.4	96.3	3.6	0.1	31,896	32,074	Sri Lanka
25,410	90.7	9.3	—	488	7,150	44.2	9.0	91.0	100.0	—	—	190	2,560	Sudan, The
122	15.6	84.4	81.1	2,893	2,406	14.5	99.0	1.0	98.4	1.6	—	3,470	500	Suriname
1,424	39.3	60.7	18.3	59,665	—	0.1	—	100.0	100.0	—	—	[11]	[11]	Swaziland
59,924	6.4	93.6	52.6	10,849,980	1,588,361	394.2	98.7	1.3	98.6	0.9	0.5	160,941	448,661	Sweden
4,748	17.5	82.5	69.6	1,912,101	2,856,728	2.7	—	100.0	100.0	—	—	5,536[25]	390,403[25]	Switzerland
55	36.8	63.2	29.3	182	97,049	7.3	21.2	78.8	98.9	1.1	—	105	1,452	Syria
48	25.3	74.7	...	...	...	1,286.8	80.3	19.7	...	...	...	...	...	Taiwan
...	...	...	...	24	101	3.8	—	100.0	100.0	—	—	...	150	Tajikistan
36,747	94.1	5.9	0.9	5,870	3,520	342.9	12.5	87.5	98.8	0.6	0.1	19,118	230	Tanzania
39,288	92.9	7.1	0.1	552,939	2,458,975	3,432.0	91.5	8.5	78.0	13.0	8.5	4,190,036	815,616	Thailand
2,401	90.0	10.0	1.5	390	4,158	13.2	91.3	8.7	99.9	—	0.1	600	13,550	Togo
5	—	100.0	100.0	—	1,953	2.5	100.0	—	96.8	3.2	—	2,987	542	Tonga
68	32.5	67.5	63.6	1,891	56,529	11.0	100.0	—	87.7	12.3	—	8,813	5,124	Trinidad and Tobago
3,562	94.2	5.8	0.6	17,824	239,453	86.6	97.7	0.3	87.2	3.2	9.6	80,048	7,619	Tunisia
19,279	44.3	55.7	28.4	103,735	891,085	604.1	91.3	8.7	91.2	0.7	7.8	70,705	38,149	Turkey
...	...	...	...	92	784	38.0	—	100.0	100.0	—	—	300	305	Turkmenistan
...	...	...	...	—	323	0.6	100.0	—	100.0	—	—	389	...	Tuvalu
17,226	86.7	13.3	0.9	33	3,317	213.1	—	100.0	100.0	—	—	12,263	...	Uganda
...	...	...	...	15,622	22,660	310.7	81.4	18.6	92.6	2.8	4.6	114,850	16,360	Ukraine
...	...	...	...	14,849	273,975	108.0	100.0	—	99.9	0.1	—	16,774	24,279	United Arab Emirates
8,299	3.1	96.9	48.1	1,713,905	8,083,620	953.9	98.1	1.9	88.6	4.9	6.5	1,180,158	1,880,350	United Kingdom
503,413	18.8	81.2	46.9	18,715,270	22,516,470	5,940.7	94.9	5.1	78.0	6.7	14.8	3,229,585[31]	7,043,431[31]	United States
4,093	74.5	25.5	19.2	41,799	60,480	120.7	99.2	0.8	97.3	0.7	2.0	82,445	6,815	Uruguay
...	...	...	...	166	654	17.7	—	100.0	100.0	—	—	500	...	Uzbekistan
63	38.0	62.0	62.0	1,785	368	2.8	100.0	—	63.8	13.6	21.2	60	1,150	Vanuatu
2,267	39.7	60.3	55.8	69,923	415,279	424.0	94.4	5.6	86.0	4.9	9.1	99,067	14,916	Venezuela
34,913	87.3	12.7	6.9	62,087	95,403	1,150.0	75.0	25.0	66.8	27.8	5.4	452,380	...	Vietnam
...	...	...	...	...	...	0.9	100.0	—	87.2	8.7	4.1	...	...	Virgin Islands (U.S.)
...	...	...	...	...	...	...	...	...	...	...	...	...	...	West Bank
...	...	...	...	...	...	—	—	—	—	—	—	...	...	Western Sahara
324	100.0	—	—	245	48,698	82.8	98.9	1.1	98.2	1.3	0.4	102,550	5,958	Yemen
1,320	3.8	96.2	82.6	20,892	8,843	6.8	3.9	96.1	99.6	0.1	0.3	...	...	Yugoslavia
14,613	92.1	7.9	4.1	2,198	4,483	70.1	—	100.0	100.0	—	—	66	1,561	Zambia
8,102	77.4	22.6	6.5	28,407	27,545	20.3	—	100.0	100.0	—	—	270	7,665	Zimbabwe

[24]Mostly iron ore. [25]Switzerland includes Liechtenstein. [26]1996. [27]South Africa includes Namibia. [28]1993–94. [29]Excludes the Free Zone of Colón and the Canal Zone. [30]Includes coal mining. [31]United States includes Puerto Rico. [32]Includes Anguilla. [33]Mostly precious and semiprecious stones. [34]Mostly bauxite. [35]1995–96.

Manufacturing industries

This table provides a summary of manufacturing activity by industrial sector for the countries of the world, providing figures for total manufacturing value added, as well as the percentage contribution of 29 major branches of manufacturing activity to the gross domestic product. U.S. dollar figures for total value added by manufacturing are given but should be used with caution because of uncertainties with respect to national accounting methods; purchasing power parities; preferential price structures and exchange rates; labour costs; and costs for material inputs influenced by "most favored" international trade agreements, barter, and the like.

Manufacturing activity is classified here according to a modification of the International Standard Industrial Classification (ISIC), revision 2, published by the United Nations. A summary of the 2-, 3-, and 4-digit ISIC codes (groups) defining these 29 sectors follows, providing definitional detail beyond that possible in the column headings.

The collection and publication of national manufacturing data is usually carried out by one of three methods: a full census of manufacturing (usually done every 5 to 10 years for a given country), a periodic survey of manufacturing (usually taken at annual or other regular intervals between censuses), and the onetime sample survey (often limited in geographic, sectoral, or size-of-enterprise coverage). The full census is, naturally, the most complete, but, since up to 10 years may elapse between such censuses, it has sometimes been necessary to substitute a survey of more recent date but less complete coverage. In addition to national sources, data published by the United Nations Industrial Development Organization (UNIDO), especially its *International Yearbook of Industrial Statistics* and *Industrial Development Global Report;* occasional publications of the International Monetary Fund (IMF); and other sources have been used.

ISIC code(s)		Products manufactured
31		Food, beverages, and tobacco
	311+312	food including prepared animal feeds
	313	alcoholic and nonalcoholic beverages
	314	tobacco manufactures
32		Textiles, wearing apparel, and leather goods
	321	spinning of textile fibres, weaving and finishing of textiles, knitted articles, carpets, rope, etc.
	322	wearing apparel (including leather clothing; excluding knitted articles and footwear)
	323+324	leather products (including footwear; excluding wearing apparel), leather substitutes, and fur products

Manufacturing industries

country	year	total manufacturing value added ('000,000 U.S.$)	(31) food (311+312)	beverages (313)	tobacco manufactures (314)	(32) textiles (exc. wearing apparel) (321)	wearing apparel (322)	leather and fur products (323+324)	(33) wood products (exc. furniture) (331)	wood furniture (332)	(34) paper, paper products (341)	printing and publishing (342)	(35) industrial chemicals (351)	paints, soaps, etc. (352 exc. 3522)	drugs and medicines (3522)
Afghanistan	1988–89[1]	435	18.3	1.9	—	8.0	0.4	16.7	—0.5—		0.9	4.9	4.8	0.2	2.7
Albania	1993[2]	224	42.5	0.9	3.7	4.6	2.0	2.3	2.1	1.3	0.2	1.3	1.7	0.9	—
Algeria	1994	4,084	16.8	3.5	4.5	3.2	2.7	1.0	1.9	0.9	2.3	0.3	0.3	—2.2—	
American Samoa	1993[3, 4]	326	99.5[5]	...	...	...	...	...	...	...	...	...	...	...	...
Andorra	1992[6]	38	2.3	9.0	0.1	0.3	30.2	0.9	—0.6—		2.6	5.9	1.0	1.8	0.1
Angola	1989	319	20.0	—12.2—			—11.6—		—3.7—		—0.3—		9.1[7]	[7]	[7]
Antigua and Barbuda	1995	8.4	...	...	...	...	...	...	...	...	...	...	...	...	...
Argentina	1993[9]	29,622	16.0	6.0	6.2	4.4	2.4	2.4	1.2	1.2[10]	2.0	5.1	2.2	3.6	3.8
Armenia	1994	368	4.1	15.7	2.2	12.4	18.6	...	1.6	1.9	0.3	0.3	5.4	—0.8—	
Aruba	...	...	...	...	...	...	...	...	...	...	...	...	...	...	...
Australia	1992–93	47,563	15.7	3.8	0.7	2.9	2.2	0.7	3.1	1.9	2.8	9.7	3.4	2.8	2.1
Austria	1994[9]	33,371	7.7	3.6	4.7	3.7	1.2	0.7	2.4	4.2	4.0	3.7	3.7	1.7	2.0
Azerbaijan	1994[2]	512	21.4	1.6	1.3	14.7	—	0.8	0.3	0.2	—	0.2	5.4	0.4	0.1
Bahamas, The	1992[3]	95	7.4	38.9	—	0.3	3.6	—	—	3.5	...	10.0	...	22.0	...
Bahrain	1992[2]	1,730	6.8	1.2	—	—	4.8	0.2	0.1	5.0	0.5	3.0	4.4	0.2	0.1
Bangladesh	1991–92[9, 11]	1,899	12.7	0.6	12.2	23.5	10.2	3.9	0.7	0.1	2.9	1.2	5.6	4.5	5.8
Barbados	1993[9]	95[12]	26.8[12]	—19.6—		0.6[13]	2.6	[13]	—0.6—		—11.0—		14.4[14]	—3.0—	
Belarus	1994[2, 3, 15]	3,006	16.2	...	...	7.0	2.1	2.6	—5.4[16]—		—[16]—		16.3[7]	[7]	[7]
Belgium	1994	44,163	14.9	1.6	0.8	4.7	2.4	0.5	1.0	3.7	2.1	4.5	10.8	—3.4—	
Belize	1992[9]	59	45.9	7.5	3.9		—3.8—		5.5	2.7	1.1	1.5		—14.1—	
Benin	1990	59	20.6	13.1	—	3.2	5.5	6.9	3.6	5.2	—	2.5	—	—9.5—	
Bermuda	1990	173	...	...	...	...	...	...	...	...	...	...	...	...	...
Bhutan	1989[9]	21	6.0	10.1	...		—5.6—		18.1	2.7	0.4	1.0	21.5	—1.7—	
Bolivia	1994[9, 19]	880	20.4	10.9	2.8	3.0	0.5	1.3	2.1	0.2	0.5	1.8	0.3	0.8	1.8
Bosnia and Herzegovina	1991	4,021	9.1	2.6	1.7	5.9	4.5	3.3	6.3	4.2	3.9	1.4	5.5	—4.1—	
Botswana	1994	186	32.8	12.9	—	11.2	2.2	2.7	1.6	1.6	2.7	2.7	1.1	—1.6—	
Brazil	1994	154,425	12.6	1.5	1.3	4.6	2.9	2.3	0.7	0.7	3.4	2.2	7.1	—10.1—	
Brunei	1991	305	...	...	...	...	...	...	...	...	...	...	...	...	...
Bulgaria	1994	5,889	6.6	2.3	2.1	4.1	2.4	2.2	1.1	0.9	0.8	1.3	34.1[20]	—3.8—	
Burkina Faso	1994	131	48.5	16.1	0.8	14.6	1.5	4.6	—	1.5	—	0.8	0.8	—	—
Burundi	1994	94	55.8	21.0	5.2	8.4	1.1	—	1.1	1.1	—	1.1	—	—1.1—	
Cambodia	1994	128	...	...	...	...	...	...	...	...	...	...	...	...	...
Cameroon	1994	470	11.5	18.9	1.1	7.6	0.2	0.2	16.4	0.6	1.5	0.6	1.9	—1.5—	
Canada	1993[9]	103,690	11.9	3.2	0.9	2.7	2.1	0.4	5.9	1.7	5.9	6.4	3.7	3.4	2.5
Cape Verde	1990	14	33.1	0.6	26.8	...	8.0	2.0	...	...	...	9.2	...	...	...
Central African Republic	1990	27	29.8	13.9	25.4	−25.0	−3.7	−0.5	25.6	1.9	—	5.9	4.1	—8.9—	
Chad	1994[3]	98	...	...	...	18.8[21]	—	—	—	—	—	—	—	...	—
Chile	1993[9, 22]	11,841	19.6	5.1	3.7	3.2	2.4	1.8	3.5	0.7	5.7	3.2	3.5	4.9	3.0
China	1995	146,612	5.8	2.9	5.0	7.3	2.8	1.6	1.5	0.5	1.9	1.0	—9.4—		2.2
Colombia	1994	10,846	19.1	10.8	0.5	7.0	3.6	1.9	0.7	0.4	3.8	3.1	6.4	—9.0—	
Comoros	1995	9.9	...	...	—	...	...	...	...	...	—	—	—	—	—
Congo, Dem. Rep. of the	1990	808	86.7	5.4	1.9	0.6	0.2	0.6	0.1	0.2	—	0.1	0.9	—0.1—	
Congo, Rep. of the	1994	75	27.4	26.0	6.8	1.4	1.4	1.4	4.1	2.7	1.4	1.4	4.1	—4.1—	
Costa Rica	1994[9]	1,285	29.5	14.4	2.0	2.3	3.7	1.1	1.9	1.3	3.2	3.8	3.5	4.4	4.4
Côte d'Ivoire	1994	1,022	28.3	4.1	0.4	10.2	0.7	0.8	7.2	—	0.3	1.2	2.5	—3.8—	
Croatia	1994	5,227	17.1	3.7	3.6	5.5	5.0	2.2	3.6	2.7	2.2	3.2	3.4	—6.9—	
Cuba	1994	5,560[23]	15.7	5.4	39.8	3.5	1.8	1.4	1.0	0.8	0.2	1.2	1.9	—7.9—	
Cyprus[24]	1994	899	15.1	9.3	7.0	3.5	10.0	3.6	5.4	4.7	2.3	4.9	0.6	3.7	1.4
Czech Republic	1995[25]	9,896		—13.9—		—6.2—		1.5	—1.6—		—5.3—			—6.8—	
Denmark	1994	26,633	18.6	3.6	1.0	2.4	1.0	0.4	2.0	2.7	2.7	6.6	5.3	—7.1—	
Djibouti	1995	23	...	...	—	—	...	...	...	...	—	—	...	...	—
Dominica	1995	13	...	...	—	—	...	—	...	...	—	—	—	...	—
Dominican Republic	1990	1,298	31.9	13.8	5.2	3.5	1.2	3.0	0.2	1.5	2.9	1.7	1.6	—3.4—	
Ecuador	1994[9, 11]	3,095	11.8	2.8	0.2	3.3	0.4	0.4	0.8	0.4	0.9	1.7	1.3	0.7	29.1
Egypt	1992–93[28, 29]	5,486	10.7	1.5	2.0	9.7	1.0	1.5	0.4	0.3	2.4	1.5	4.4	1.5	2.4
El Salvador	1994	521	15.9	4.0	5.0	8.6	5.4	1.9	—	1.1	4.2	5.2	2.9	—17.5—	
Equatorial Guinea	1990[2]	1.9	27.6	4.1	...	...	2.6	...	...	49.3	...	1.2	...	—13.8—	
Eritrea	1993[2]	58	16.7	22.7	1.3	—5.7—		9.8	—	—	—6.1—			—17.7—	
Estonia	1994[2, 3]	1,254	35.0[30]	6.7	[30]	5.6	3.9	1.7	5.7	5.4	0.8	3.0	9.2[31]	[31]	[31]
Ethiopia[32]	1992	529	18.3	24.6	8.5	10.8	1.5	4.7	0.9	0.7	0.7	1.9	0.2	—2.3—	

ISIC code(s)	Products manufactured
33	Wood and wood products
331	sawlogs, wood products (excluding furniture), cane products, and cork products
332	wood furniture
34	Paper and paper products, printing and publishing
341	wood pulp, paper, and paper products
342	printing, publishing, and bookbinding
35	Chemicals and chemical, petroleum, coal, rubber, and plastic products
351	basic industrial chemicals (including fertilizers, pesticides, and synthetic fibres)
352 minus 3522	chemical products not elsewhere specified (including paints, varnishes, and soaps and other toiletries)
3522	drugs and medicines
353+354	refined petroleum and derivatives of petroleum and coal
355	rubber products
356	plastic products (excluding synthetic fibres)
36	Glass, ceramic, and nonmetallic mineral products
361+362	pottery, china, glass, and glass products
369	bricks, tiles, cement, cement products, plaster products, etc.

ISIC code(s)	Products manufactured
37	Basic metals
371	iron and steel
372	nonferrous basic metals and processed nickel and cobalt
38	Fabricated metal products, machinery and equipment
381	fabricated metal products (including cutlery, hand tools, fixtures, and structural metal products)
382 minus 3825	nonelectrical machinery and apparatus not elsewhere specified
3825	office, computing, and accounting machinery
383 minus 3832	electrical machinery and apparatus not elsewhere specified
3832	radio, television, and communications equipment (including electronic parts)
384 minus 3843	transport equipment not elsewhere specified
3843	motor vehicles (excluding motorcycles)
385	professional and scientific equipment; photographic and optical goods; watches and clocks
39	Other manufactured goods
390	jewelry, musical instruments, sporting goods, artists' equipment, toys, etc.

			(36)		(37)		(38)								(39)	country
refined petroleum and products	rubber products	plastic products	pottery, china, and glass	bricks, tiles, cement, etc.	iron and steel	non-ferrous metals	fabricated metal products	nonelectrical machinery	office equip., computers	electrical equip.	radio, television	transport equip. exc. motor vehicles	motor vehicles	professional equip.	jewelry, musical instruments	
(353+354)	(355)	(356)	(361+362)	(369)	(371)	(372)	(381)	(382 exc. 3825)	(3825)	(383 exc. 3832)	(3832)	(384 exc. 3843)	(3843)	(385)	(390)	
—	—	2.1	1.1		0.4	—	—	—	—	—	—	—	0.1	—	37.1	Afghanistan
21.6	—	1.2	0.1	7.9	2.5	—	1.2	0.7	—	0.5	0.7	—	—	0.1	—	Albania
3.7	0.4	0.8	1.2	8.8	14.5	0.8	12.0	2.0		5.6		8.2		1.3	1.2	Algeria
...	...	...	...	...	...	...	...	...	...	...	...	...	...	...	...	American Samoa
—	0.3	0.4	0.6	0.3	1.7	0.2	0.5	3.8		4.3		—	21.1	9.1	2.9	Andorra
20.0	[7]	[7]	11.3		1.9		5.0					4.7		[8]	0.3[8]	Angola
...	...	...	...	...	...	...	...	...	...	...	...	...	...	...	...	Antigua and Barbuda
9.1	0.9	3.0	1.2	2.4	2.4	0.8	4.6	5.6	0.2	2.2	1.4	0.6	7.6	0.7	0.8	Argentina
0.5	0.3	1.1	0.5	2.2	0.3	3.2	0.5	3.2		10.5		0.3		3.2	10.8	Armenia
...	...	...	...	...	...	...	...	...	...	...	...	...	...	...	...	Aruba
2.5	0.9	3.5	2.0	3.3	4.4	4.2	7.8	4.1	0.6	3.8	1.9	2.5	4.8	1.1	0.8	Australia
1.8	1.0	2.2	2.2	5.2	4.7	1.1	8.5	9.8		10.4	2.7	0.9	4.7	0.7	0.8	Austria
34.9	0.5	1.1	0.4	2.2	1.1	1.8	2.2	4.4		4.1	—	0.5	—	—	0.5	Azerbaijan
...	...	...	...	7.0	2.6	—	—	—	—	...	...	—	—	...	...	Bahamas, The
11.2	—	1.1	—	5.7	2.4	36.0	2.4	—	—	6.0	—	3.6	—	0.1	5.2	Bahrain
0.4	0.5	0.4	1.0	1.7	3.6	0.1	1.2	0.4	—	1.2	0.5	0.8	3.7	—	0.6	Bangladesh
[14]	[14]	[14]	2.3		—	—	9.0	8.3				1.6			0.2	Barbados
7.6	[7]	[7]	5.5		3.0		26.8								...	Belarus
1.0	0.6	4.6	2.4	2.3	4.6	1.8	6.2	8.8		6.6		8.2		1.1	1.4	Belgium
—	0.3[17]		[17]	6.2	—	—	2.0	—	—	0.1		4.2		—	1.1	Belize
—	—	—	0.5	24.6	—	—	4.8	—	—	—	—	—	—	—	—	Benin
...	...	...	...	...	...	...	...	...	...	...	...	...	...	...	...	Bermuda
...	0.7	2.2	29.0		...	...	1.0[18]								[18]	Bhutan
38.1	—	0.8	0.5	6.0	0.2	3.0	0.9	0.1		0.3	0.1	—	0.3	0.1	3.2	Bolivia
2.3	0.3	1.3	0.5	3.2	5.5	3.4	10.8	5.0		3.3		8.6		2.6	0.7	Bosnia and Herzegovina
—	0.5	0.5	—	—	—	—	3.2	1.1		0.5		1.1		—	19.9	Botswana
3.2	1.1	2.2	1.0	3.7	5.7	1.7	3.9	7.5		8.0		10.4		0.8	1.4	Brazil
...	...	...	...	...	...	...	...	...	...	...	...	...	...	...	...	Brunei
[20]	0.7	0.8	2.1	1.6	12.1	2.5	3.6	3.8		3.3		3.3		0.1	4.4	Bulgaria
—	0.8	0.8	—	—	0.8	—	—	—	—	0.8		1.5		—	6.2	Burkina Faso
—	—	—	—	1.1	—	—	2.1	—	—	—	—	—	—	—	—	Burundi
...	...	...	...	...	...	...	...	...	...	...	...	...	...	...	...	Cambodia
6.8	0.8	14.0	1.1	1.5	8.1	3.2	0.6	0.2		0.6		—	—	—	1.1	Cameroon
1.9	1.6	2.8	0.6	2.0	3.2	2.6	4.7	5.8	1.0	2.5	3.9	3.7	10.8	0.8	1.4	Canada
...	...	...	...	...	...	...	...	...	...	...	...	20.1		...	0.2	Cape Verde
—	—	—	—	—	—	—	0.9	—	—	0.2		4.8		—	7.7	Central African Republic
—	—	—	—	—	—	—	—	...	—	—	—	...	—	—	...	Chad
8.2	1.1	2.7	0.9	4.1	2.4	10.3	4.1	1.8	—	1.4	0.2	1.0	1.1	0.2	0.2	Chile
4.6	1.1	1.8	7.3		8.6	2.5	3.1	9.1		4.9	5.2	6.6		1.0	2.2	China
3.2	1.7	3.5	2.3	4.7	4.1	0.5	3.2	1.7		3.3		3.8		0.7	1.0	Colombia
—	—	—	—	—	—	—	—	—	—	—	—	—	—	—	—	Comoros
0.1	—	—	—	0.2	...	...	0.4	0.3		0.2		0.5		—	1.5	Congo, Dem. Rep. of the
—	1.4	—	—	1.4	—	—	6.8	1.4		2.7		4.1		—	—	Congo, Rep. of the
2.6	1.5	4.0	1.2	3.3	...	0.1	2.4	1.7		1.3	4.3	1.2	0.5	...	0.4	Costa Rica
20.8	1.4	—	0.1	2.0	0.2	0.1	5.3	—	—	0.3		7.2		—	3.1	Côte d'Ivoire
3.6	0.4	1.6	1.6	3.9	2.7	0.9	4.7	5.8		6.9		8.1		0.4	0.3	Croatia
...	2.4	2.1	0.5	2.0	0.6	0.9	1.6	1.7		0.9		3.5		0.2	3.0	Cuba
1.1	0.4	3.2	0.5	9.4	—	—	6.5	2.9		1.3	—	0.4	0.7	0.1	2.0	Cyprus[24]
4.3	2.9		7.3		18.7[26]		[26]	12.1		7.2[27]		8.1		[27]	4.2	Czech Republic
1.5	0.4	2.9	0.7	3.6	1.1	0.3	8.2	12.9		4.9		4.9		2.6	2.6	Denmark
—	—	...	—	...	—	—	—	—	—	—	—	—	—	—	...	Djibouti
—	—	—	—	...	—	—	...	—	—	...	—	—	—	—	...	Dominica
16.2	0.8	1.6	0.7	3.5	1.8	0.2	3.7	0.5		0.8		0.1		0.2	0.2	Dominican Republic
32.3	0.9	1.8	0.6	3.2	1.1	0.2	2.4	0.1	—	1.7	0.2	—	1.3	0.2	0.2	Ecuador
32.1	0.3	1.5	0.8	6.8	3.5	1.4	5.6	1.7	—	2.8	0.8	1.4	1.6	0.2	0.2	Egypt
12.1	1.0	3.8	—	3.1	0.6	—	2.1	0.4		3.6		0.2		0.6	0.8	El Salvador
...	...	...	...	0.8	...	...	0.6	...	...	...	...	...	...	...	...	Equatorial Guinea
—	—	—	8.3		11.7[26]		[26]	—	—	—	—	—	—	—	—	Eritrea
[31]	1.3		5.7		...	...	3.8	3.1		2.2	0.3	5.0		0.9	0.3	Estonia
16.6	1.1	1.3	0.2	2.1	0.6	—	1.7	—	—	—	—	1.3		—	—	Ethiopia[32]

Manufacturing industries (continued)

country	year	total manufacturing value added ('000,000 U.S.$)	(31) food (311+312)	(31) beverages (313)	(31) tobacco manufactures (314)	(32) textiles (exc. wearing apparel) (321)	(32) wearing apparel (322)	(32) leather and fur products (323+324)	(33) wood products (exc. furniture) (331)	(33) wood furniture (332)	(34) paper, paper products (341)	(34) printing and publishing (342)	(35) industrial chemicals (351)	(35) paints, soaps, etc. (352 exc. 3522)	(35) drugs and medicines (3522)
Faroe Islands	1990[3, 28]	120	69.3[33]	...	...	...	...	...	...	...	...	...	...	...	...
Fiji	1992[9]	156	38.5	—10.1—		—13.6—		1.0	7.2	2.8	3.7	4.4	—	5.8	—
Finland	1994	20,972	9.2	1.7	0.5	1.5	1.0	0.5	6.6	1.3	18.1	6.5	4.2	2.0	1.1
France	1994[9]	254,935	10.4	2.4	1.2	2.6	2.0	0.9	1.7	1.6	2.3	6.0	3.3	—5.9—	
French Guiana	1991[11]	45	...	...	...	—[35]—			—38.2[35]—		...	...	...	...	...
French Polynesia	1993[3]	214	—27.2—		—	...	...	—	...	...	—	—	—	...	—
Gabon	1994	174	9.2	6.9	5.7	1.2	1.7	—	17.8	2.3	1.2	1.7	3.4	—1.7—	
Gambia, The	1990	22	58.1	5.3	—	4.1	—	0.1	—	6.3	—	3.8	—	—2.0—	
Gaza Strip	1994	50	...	...	...	...	...	...	...	...	...	...	...	...	...
Georgia	1992	150	...	...	...	...	...	...	...	...	...	...	...	...	...
Germany	1994[37]	596,225	—8.8—		2.5	1.6	1.1	0.3	—3.0—		2.5	2.1	—11.7—		
Ghana	1993[9, 37]	610	8.4	9.1	18.1	4.6	—0.5—		15.2	0.8	1.8	1.3	0.9	—8.9—	
Gibraltar	...	...	...	...	...	...	...	...	...	...	...	...	...	...	...
Greece	1992[11, 28]	10,660	17.0	5.9	3.6	10.2	5.3	1.7	1.8	1.0	3.0	3.2	2.2	4.9	2.4
Greenland	1991	27	...	...	...	...	...	...	...	...	...	...	...	...	...
Grenada	1995[2, 39]	19	29.1	55.2	2.4	—	...	—	...	...	7.0	—	—	6.3	...
Guadeloupe	1993[40]	77	...	...	...	...	...	...	...	...	...	...	...	...	...
Guam	1986	9.1	...	—	—	...	—	—	...	—	...	...	—	—	—
Guatemala	1993[2, 9, 37]	3,674	38.4	12.9	3.2	9.4	0.9	1.2	0.6	0.2	1.8	1.6	1.6	4.4	4.2
Guernsey	1993[4]	61	—5.1—		—	—1.5—		—	...	...	—	17.6	—	—	7.8
Guinea	1994	83	...	...	...	...	...	...	...	...	...	...	...	...	...
Guinea-Bissau	1991	16	...	...	...	...	...	...	...	...	...	...	...	...	...
Guyana	1995[41]	20	...	...	...	...	...	...	...	...	...	...	—	...	...
Haiti	1994–95[3]	73	40.0	4.7	5.8	—7.7—			...	...	...	...	—10.1—		
Honduras	1994[9, 42]	526	28.3	17.1	5.5	2.1	13.1	1.0	4.8	1.5	2.7	2.2	0.4	2.9	0.9
Hong Kong	1994	11,198	4.7	2.1	1.6	13.4	15.6	0.4	0.3	0.2	2.3	11.5	—2.4—		
Hungary	1994	8,062	—19.0—		0.7	3.0	4.4	1.9	2.8	2.8[43]	1.8	4.6	—10.5—		
Iceland	1993[9]	795	49.9	2.0	—	1.9	1.6	0.8	0.2	4.2	1.2	9.3	1.5	2.4	—
India	1992–93[28, 44]	22,176	8.3	1.0	2.1	10.1	1.6	0.9	0.3	—	1.9	1.7	10.4	4.2	3.8
Indonesia	1994[28, 37]	27,701	8.8	1.0	10.4	13.5	3.8	4.1	7.8	1.0	3.2	1.4	4.7	2.1	2.2
Iran	1994	5,839	12.9	2.2	0.9	10.9	0.3	1.0	0.7	0.3	1.6	0.9	4.8	—5.4—	
Iraq	1994	606	9.7	3.1	1.2	3.3	1.2	3.6	—	0.2	3.3	1.3	13.0	—1.0—	
Ireland	1990[45]	14,780	20.5	5.4	1.1	2.3	1.4	0.3	1.2	0.6	1.3	3.8	2.8	1.4	12.6
Isle of Man	1990–91[3, 28]	98	—15.7—		...	...	...	...	...	...	...	...	...	...	...
Israel	1993[9, 42]	10,624	10.3	—1.5—		3.4	4.5	0.7	1.3	1.5	2.2	5.3	5.0	—6.2—	
Italy	1991[37]	146,179	7.4	1.3	0.4	7.2	3.8	2.5	1.1	2.1	2.7	4.4	3.6	2.8	—
Jamaica	1995	819	20.1	15.4[46]	10.3	—6.6—		0.7	0.2	2.6	—3.8—		9.7[7]	[7]	[7]
Japan	1993[48]	1,140,051	8.7	1.2	0.3	2.8	1.3	0.3	1.6	0.9	2.6	5.7	4.3	2.7	3.1
Jersey	1991	45	...	...	...	...	...	...	...	...	...	...	...	...	...
Jordan	1994[9]	987	11.3	5.3	12.5	2.8	2.5	1.1	1.2	2.7	3.5	2.1	5.7	2.7	5.3
Kazakstan	1994[2, 3, 15]	6,867	14.9	...	...	3.1	1.0	0.6	—1.3[16]—		—[16]—		4.6[7]	[7]	[7]
Kenya	1994[28]	703[49]	32.4	9.7	1.5	5.7	1.8	1.4	1.8	0.8[10]	4.4	2.6	1.9	—6.6—	
Kiribati	1992	0.68	...	...	—	—	—	—	...	—	—	—	—	...	—
Korea, North	...	...	...	...	...	...	...	...	...	...	...	...	...	...	...
Korea, South	1994[9, 42]	161,226	—7.7—		1.7	6.3	3.3	1.8	0.9	2.5	2.4	2.7	—9.8—		
Kuwait	1993[9]	2,232	5.3	1.9	—	1.1	5.3	0.2	0.5	2.2	1.1	1.0	2.8	1.0	—
Kyrgyzstan	1994[2]	452	25.3	1.9	4.5	26.7	3.1	1.5	0.4	0.8	—	0.5	—	0.1	0.1
Laos	1990[2]	66	4.5	7.4	16.3	—	5.1	0.3	40.1	5.0	—	1.2	—4.0—		
Latvia	1994[28]	714	27.0	10.6	0.5	5.7	3.2	1.7	7.8	2.9	0.5	3.4	1.9	1.9	1.0
Lebanon	1994	870	...	...	...	...	...	...	...	...	...	...	...	...	...
Lesotho	1994[3]	128	—52.9—		...	—30.5—		2.0	—2.8—		...	3.0	—2.2—		
Liberia	1985[2, 9, 37]	64	10.8	42.7	...	—	—	0.3	—	4.5	0.6	1.3	0.4	—7.2—	
Libya	1994	784	4.6	2.3	9.8	3.8	0.6	8.8	0.9	0.3	0.4	1.0	6.9	—6.1—	
Liechtenstein	...	...	...	...	...	...	...	...	...	...	...	...	...	...	...
Lithuania	1994[2]	2,667	25.1	5.9	1.3	8.0	3.5	1.7	4.0	2.0	1.4	1.4	4.2	0.4	0.6
Luxembourg	1994	2,035	5.4	3.2	0.7	6.5	0.6	...	0.4	0.5	2.6	3.2	6.7	—4.8—	
Macau	1994[9]	448	2.2	0.6	0.3	18.9	52.1	2.4	0.2	0.8	0.5	3.1	—	0.5	0.4
Macedonia	1994	768	2.2	8.8	12.7	6.8	11.7	3.5	0.8	2.9	1.3	1.5	5.9	—3.7—	
Madagascar	1994	121	14.5	10.5	0.8	34.7	3.2	2.4	0.8	0.8	4.0	1.6	—	—6.5—	
Malaŵi	1994	92	20.9	7.7	5.5	13.2	1.1	2.2	1.1	1.1	—	6.6	5.5	—17.6—	
Malaysia	1993[28]	16,287	8.0	0.9	1.0	3.1	2.3	0.2	7.6	1.2	1.6	2.7	8.0	1.9	0.3
Maldives	1994	11[52]	...	...	—	—	...	—	—	...	—	—	—	...	—
Mali	1990	96	18.4	1.2	13.1	36.5	10.3	0.1	0.1	—	0.4	0.8	0.8	—0.7—	
Malta	1993	499	10.3	9.2	1.0	2.6	13.5	3.6	0.5	5.4	1.4	9.3	0.5	—3.6[53]—	
Marshall Islands	1995[3]	2.7	3.7[55]	...	...	...	...	...	...	...	...	...	...	...	...
Martinique	1993	145	...	...	...	...	...	...	...	...	...	...	...	...	...
Mauritania	1993	35	—42.9—		—	—		—	—	—	6.0	—	—18.8—		
Mauritius	1993[9, 57]	658	15.8	10.2	5.1	3.4	40.9	1.2	0.6	1.2	0.9	2.5	2.1	2.1	0.1
Mayotte	1992	...	...	...	—	—	—	—	—	—	—	—	—	—	—
Mexico	1994	49,208	14.8	6.5	1.7	4.6	1.9	1.5	1.2	0.9	2.7	2.9	6.4	—7.3—	
Micronesia	1992	2.2[4]	[58]	...	...	...	91.0	...	...	...	...	...	...	1.6[58]	...
Moldova	1995[2, 3, 59]	254	—58.1—			1.9	1.6	1.3	—3.3[16]—		—[16]—		0.3[7]	[7]	[7]
Monaco	...	...	...	...	...	...	...	...	...	...	...	...	...	...	...
Mongolia	1994[3, 9, 11]	86	22.6	2.7	—	25.0	3.5	6.8	3.4	0.1	—1.0—		...	—1.2—	
Morocco	1994	4,165	7.3	14.1	6.0	9.9	8.1	1.3	1.7	0.4	3.0	0.8	11.1	—0.5—	
Mozambique	1995[2]	238	32.5	16.2	2.2	9.7	3.8	0.1	6.3	0.2	1.5	...	—5.4—		
Myanmar (Burma)	1993	858[49]	14.8	20.4	4.6	26.4	...	...	1.9	0.7	5.7	...	0.2	2.0	1.6
Namibia	1994[3]	234	63.6[60]	...	...	...	...	...	...	...	...	...	...	...	...
Nauru	1989	—	—	—	—	—	—	—	—	—	—	—	...	...	...
Nepal	1993–94[3, 9, 11]	356	18.4	7.3	9.6	17.8	12.7	3.4	1.8	0.9	1.4	1.1	...	4.1	0.3
Netherlands, The	1993[9, 37]	43,948	15.0	3.8	4.7	2.1	0.5	0.3	1.1	0.9	3.5	8.3	7.8	3.3	2.3
Netherlands Antilles	1993	101	...	...	...	...	...	...	...	...	...	...	...	...	...
New Caledonia	1992[3]	341[3]	—15.4—			...	...	...	...	...	...	...	...	...	...
New Zealand	1994	8,251	25.6	3.0	0.6	3.0	2.3	1.2	4.8	1.9	7.6	7.7	3.5	—3.1—	
Nicaragua	1994	653	23.2	27.2	7.8	6.1	2.7	3.4	0.9	0.2	0.2	2.3	2.0	—6.9—	

refined petroleum and products (353+354)	rubber products (355)	plastic products (356)	(36) pottery, china, and glass (361+362)	bricks, tiles, cement, etc. (369)	(37) iron and steel (371)	non-ferrous metals (372)	(38) fabricated metal products (381)	nonelectrical machinery (382 exc. 3825)	office equip., computers (3825)	electrical equip. (383 exc. 3832)	radio, television (3832)	transport equip. exc. motor vehicles (384 exc. 3843)	motor vehicles (3843)	professional equip. (385)	(39) jewelry, musical instruments (390)	country
...	...	...	...	...	...	...	...	...	...	...	...	...	...	...	...	Faroe Islands
—	0.5	1.6	—	4.0[34]	[34]	—	4.3	0.8				0.6	0.4	—	0.7	Fiji
2.5	0.6	2.5	0.9	2.2	4.9	1.4	4.4	10.5	0.6	3.3	5.2	2.9	1.3	1.5	1.2	Finland
6.4	1.4	3.2	1.1	2.9	2.5	1.9	8.0	7.6		10.0		11.4		1.5	1.8	France
...	...	...	61.8[36]		[36]		[36]								...	French Guiana
—	...	...	...	...	—	—	35.4								...	French Polynesia
10.3	—	—	0.6	5.7	1.7	1.7	9.2	1.2		5.2		7.5		0.6	3.5	Gabon
—	1.3	—	—	0.9	—	—	3.5	—	—	—	—	—	—	—	14.6	Gambia, The
...	...	...	...	...	...	...	...	...	...	...	...	...	...	...	...	Gaza Strip
...	...	...	...	...	...	...	...	...	...	...	...	...	...	...	...	Georgia
5.2	1.1	3.5	1.3	3.5	3.1	1.0	7.5	11.4	1.2	13.2		1.2	11.2	1.5	0.6	Germany
8.1	0.6	2.6	4.4		0.7	8.2	3.4	0.3		1.5		0.6[38]		—	[38]	Ghana
...	...	...	...	...	...	...	...	...	...	...	...	...	...	...	...	Gibraltar
5.5	0.7	3.1	1.0	6.0	1.9	2.7	4.7	1.6	—	3.4	1.6	3.8	1.2	0.2	0.5	Greece
...	...	...	...	...	...	...	...	...	...	...	...	...	...	...	...	Greenland
—	...	—	—	—	—	—	—	—	—	...	...	—	—	—	...	Grenada
...	...	...	...	...	...	...	...	...	...	...	...	...	...	...	...	Guadeloupe
—	...	...	...	...	...	...	—	—	—	—	—	...	—	...	...	Guam
3.2	1.6	4.3	0.8	3.7	1.9	—	1.5	0.5	—	0.8	0.1	0.3	0.1	0.3	0.5	Guatemala
—	—	10.9	—	1.9	—	—	—	7.4		—	40.3	3.0	—	—	4.6	Guernsey
...	...	...	...	...	...	...	...	...	...	...	...	...	...	...	...	Guinea
...	...	...	...	...	...	...	...	...	...	...	...	...	...	...	...	Guinea-Bissau
—	—	—	—	—	—	—	—	...	—	...	—	—	—	—	...	Guyana
			...	3.6	...	...	20.0	...	...	...	...	...	...	...	...	Haiti
0.2	1.0	2.8	0.1	6.6	0.5	0.2	3.5	0.7	—	0.9	0.1	—	0.2	0.1	0.7	Honduras
0.1	0.1	2.9	1.7		0.8		5.6	7.6	4.1	1.1	9.4	4.1		4.1	3.9	Hong Kong
9.8	3.3		4.9		2.5		6.3	6.6	0.3	4.3	2.2	0.9	3.8	3.6	[43]	Hungary
—	—	3.2	0.5	3.8	1.7	2.2	7.4	—	—	—	—	2.5	—	—	3.7	Iceland
5.6	2.1	1.3	0.6	3.9	8.2	2.8	2.3	7.4	1.1	5.7	2.7	3.6	5.0	0.7	0.7	India
0.1	2.0	1.9	1.5	2.4	5.8	1.2	3.5	1.3	—	1.8	2.2	5.6	5.8	0.2	0.7	Indonesia
0.6	2.1	1.6	1.7	7.7	15.2	3.6	4.5	3.9		7.9		8.1		0.7	0.4	Iran
24.1	0.7	1.6	0.7	16.5	4.0	—	4.6	2.1		4.3		0.5		—	—	Iraq
0.2	0.8	2.2	1.2	3.8	0.6	0.1	3.2	2.6	11.2	2.9	9.5	1.5	0.6	4.1	0.9	Ireland
...	...	...	...	...	...	...	...	...	...	...	...	...	...	...	...	Isle of Man
—	0.7	5.4	0.6	3.7	1.3	0.6	11.4	3.0		22.9		6.0		1.3	1.2	Israel
1.8	1.6	3.4	3.1	3.1	4.9	1.2	5.9	13.0	1.0	7.5	2.9	3.1	6.1	1.2	1.0	Italy
9.5	[7]	[7]	5.9		[47]		15.0[47]								0.2	Jamaica
1.4	1.3	3.7	1.2	3.1	4.7	1.2	7.5	9.5	3.0	6.5	7.8	1.6	9.1	1.3	1.6	Japan
...	...	...	...	...	...	...	...	...	...	...	...	...	...	...	...	Jersey
4.4	0.1	3.9	0.2	16.9	2.4	1.8	4.6	2.0	—	2.1	—	—	2.3	0.1	0.5	Jordan
27.0	[7]	[7]	5.1		29.5		9.0								...	Kazakstan
0.8	2.9	3.3	0.5	3.7	...	...	6.4	0.6		5.7		3.7		[8]	1.8[8]	Kenya
—	—	—	—	—	—	—	...	—	—	—	—	...	—	—	...	Kiribati
...	...	...	...	...	...	...	...	...	...	...	...	...	...	...	...	Korea, North
3.1	3.8		5.0		6.8		5.2	8.0	1.0	3.1	12.4	3.7	7.8	[8]	1.1[8]	Korea, South
57.2	—	1.7	0.6	4.7	1.1	—	5.0	2.6	—	1.5	—	2.1	0.2	—	0.9	Kuwait
0.4	0.1	0.2	3.0	6.0	—	9.0	2.6	6.4	0.1	5.1	—	—	1.3	0.9	—	Kyrgyzstan
—	0.5		0.1	3.8	—	—	10.8	0.5		0.2		—	—	—	0.1	Laos
0.1	0.1	0.9	1.2	2.4	2.7	—	1.8	5.3	0.2	3.6	2.3	6.3	2.0	0.4	2.6[50]	Latvia
...	...	...	...	...	...	...	...	...	...	...	...	...	...	...	...	Lebanon
...	...	...	3.3		1.5	...	...	...	...	...	...	...	...	...	...	Lesotho
—	—	0.6	0.2	20.7	—	—	9.5	0.3		0.7		—	—	—	—	Liberia
26.1	—	0.9	0.3	22.6	—	—	0.5	—	—	—	—	—	—	—	4.1	Libya
...	...	...	...	...	...	...	...	...	...	...	...	...	...	...	...	Liechtenstein
19.7	—	0.4	0.5	4.1	0.4	—	1.3	5.0	0.2	1.1	3.3	2.3	0.2	1.1	0.9[50]	Lithuania
0.1	6.1	3.6	3.5	8.3	16.8	3.4	11.1	7.3		3.5		0.6		1.0	0.1	Luxembourg
—	[51]	0.5	[51]	4.3	—	—	2.0	0.1	—	2.3	—	0.8	—	—	7.9	Macau
4.7	0.1	1.9	1.7	1.0	3.4	0.8	6.8	1.8		7.3		7.0		0.3	1.4	Macedonia
7.3	0.8	1.6	0.8	2.4	—	—	3.2	—	—	1.6		1.6		—	0.8	Madagascar
—	—	4.4	—	6.6	—	—	3.3	2.2		—	—	1.1		—	—	Malaŵi
1.5	4.5	3.4	0.9	3.9	2.9	0.7	4.3	4.1	0.9	4.3	22.9	1.8	2.9	1.1	1.1	Malaysia
—	—	...	—	...	—	—	...	—	—	—	—	...	—	—	...	Maldives
0.7	0.3	0.4	—	1.3	—	—	6.2	0.5		1.7		6.5		—	—	Mali
[53]	3.4	2.6	0.5	3.4	—	[54]	4.0[54]	2.0		4.5	8.8	1.1	0.3	3.4	5.1	Malta
...	...	...	...	...	...	...	...	...	...	...	...	...	...	...	14.8[56]	Marshall Islands
...	...	...	...	...	...	...	...	...	...	...	...	...	...	...	...	Martinique
			—	16.8	—	—	15.5	—	—	—	—	—	—	—	—	Mauritania
—	0.3	1.2	0.1	3.5	1.0		2.4	0.2		0.8	0.2	0.1	0.2	1.3	2.7	Mauritius
—	—	—	—	...	—	—	—	—	—	—	—	—	—	—	—	Mayotte
10.8	2.0	1.8	1.9	1.8	4.2	0.8	4.1	3.3		3.2		10.1		1.7	1.9	Mexico
...	...	...	...	...	...	...	...	...	...	...	...	...	...	...	7.4	Micronesia
...	[7]	[7]	...	4.5	...	...	13.9								...	Moldova
...	...	...	...	...	...	...	...	...	...	...	...	...	...	...	...	Monaco
0.1	—	—	0.1	5.2	—	...	2.0	...	...	...	...	...	...	0.1	...	Mongolia
8.8	1.7	1.2	0.3	8.0	1.3	0.6	5.1	1.7		3.2		3.6		0.2	0.1	Morocco
3.0	4.1	0.6	6.8		2.4	0.3	1.3	0.2		1.1		2.1		—	0.2	Mozambique
...	0.5	0.2	...	0.5	6.1	7.0	0.2	...	...	0.7	—	...	1.5	...	5.0	Myanmar (Burma)
...	...	...	...	...	...	...	...	...	...	...	...	...	...	...	...	Namibia
—	—	—	—	—	—	—	—	—	—	—	—	—	—	—	—	Nauru
...	1.1	1.8	[51]	8.2	2.0	...	4.3	...	...	2.3	0.4	...	...	[51]	0.8	Nepal
2.3	0.6	3.1	1.6	2.4	3.9		6.7	8.3		11.4		4.8		0.9	0.4	Netherlands, The
...	...	...	...	...	...	...	...	...	...	...	...	...	...	...	...	Netherlands Antilles
...	...	...	...	...	...	43.2	...	...	...	...	...	...	...	...	...	New Caledonia
1.8	0.9	3.3	1.3	2.1	1.7	2.0	7.6	4.9		4.1		4.4		0.4	1.2	New Zealand
7.3	0.7	1.8	0.2	1.5	0.2	—	4.0	0.3		0.6		0.3		—	0.2	Nicaragua

Manufacturing industries (continued)

country	year	total manufacturing value added ('000,000 U.S.$)	(31) food (311+312)	(31) beverages (313)	(31) tobacco manufactures (314)	(32) textiles (exc. wearing apparel) (321)	(32) wearing apparel (322)	(32) leather and fur products (323+324)	(33) wood products (exc. furniture) (331)	(33) wood furniture (332)	(34) paper, paper products (341)	(34) printing and publishing (342)	(35) industrial chemicals (351)	(35) paints, soaps, etc. (352 exc. 3522)	(35) drugs and medicines (3522)
Niger	1993	153		—6.7—		—1.1—		...	—[61]—		...	0.9		—4.8—	
Nigeria	1994	3,165	16.9	15.3	1.8	11.2	—	2.9	0.5	0.8	3.4	3.2	0.3	—11.2—	
Northern Mariana Islands	1987[1, 3]	58		—3.3—		26.0	—62.7[62]—		...	...	...	1.3	...	...	...
Norway	1994[11]	13,472	12.3	—9.3—		1.3	0.4	0.2	3.9	2.1[10]	4.8	9.9	6.1	1.2	1.8
Oman	1993	669	—10.6—		...	1.9[13]	2.9	[13]	1.2	3.5[43]	1.0	1.5		—4.3—	
Pakistan	1994	5,719	16.7	1.9	10.1	16.8	2.0	1.4	0.3	0.1	1.0	0.9	6.9	—7.2—	
Palau	1992	12	...	...	...	...	...	...	...	...	...	...	...	...	...
Panama	1995	694	43.5	10.0	3.6	0.8	2.6	1.1	1.4	1.3	4.0	2.8	1.4	—5.5—	
Papua New Guinea	1989	451	48.4	13.1	4.9	—	0.4	—	11.6	2.0	1.1	2.4	1.1	—1.1—	
Paraguay	1994	782	30.9	9.7	0.8	7.3	0.3	5.5	18.2	1.7	—	4.4	0.8	—0.8—	
Peru	1994	6,895	14.9	12.0	0.9	7.9	1.1	0.6	0.6	0.5	1.1	2.9	2.8	—7.0—	
Philippines	1992[9]	10,548	17.2	9.1	5.0	3.5	5.8	0.6	1.3	0.8	2.4	1.4	3.6	6.3	5.1
Poland	1994	22,523	—20.6—		3.8	3.7	4.6	1.7	3.6	3.7	1.6	3.6		—18.1—	
Portugal	1994[9]	17,025	8.2	2.5	4.7	9.7	7.0	4.5	3.6	1.8	3.6	4.1	1.7	1.9	1.5
Puerto Rico	1992[3]	22,737	4.6	11.6	...	0.5	4.0	1.0	...	0.5	0.8	1.4	2.7	1.9	43.9
Qatar	1994[9]	810	3.4	0.5	...	0.3	—6.2—		0.9	1.8	0.1	3.2	29.6	—0.4—	
Réunion	1994	371	34.5	12.3	—	—0.5—		—	—3.8—		5.0[64]	6.3	...	—3.7—	
Romania	1993[65]	6,651	19.6	6.8	0.9	5.9	3.4	2.6	3.3	3.1	1.1	0.7	3.5	2.4	1.0
Russia	1994	54,512[49]	15.3	1.3	0.3	2.4	1.5	1.0	1.7	1.0	1.6	0.8	6.9	1.2	0.9
Rwanda	1990	178	29.1	18.1	11.2	...	...	...	4.4	0.9	1.0	1.3	9.0	—	—
St. Kitts and Nevis	1994[28]	19	...	...	...	...	...	...	...	...	...	...	...	...	...
St. Lucia	1995[2, 39]	46	10.0	—27.6—		2.4	7.2	...	...	...	40.8	...	...	...	...
St. Vincent	1988[3, 28]	14	24.9	—25.4—			—10.1—		—1.9—		—5.3—		...	...	...
Samoa	1990	15	36.0	25.5	19.2	—	...	—	10.7	—	—	—	—	8.6	...
San Marino	...	...	...	...	...	...	...	...	...	...	...	...	...	...	...
São Tomé and Príncipe	1993[2]	4.6	26.3	20.7	—	—	26.3	—	—15.1—		—	1.2	—	6.6	—
Saudi Arabia	1994	6,780	5.9	0.5	0.3	0.4	0.1	0.1	0.2	0.6	2.3	1.0	39.3	—1.9—	
Senegal	1994[9]	310[68]	41.7[68]	2.9	3.8	5.1	—	—	0.2	0.1	1.2	1.5	16.7	4.8	1.8
Seychelles	1989	26		—79.6—			—0.6—		—2.1—		—6.0—			—4.1—	
Sierra Leone	1993[9]	92	37.0	21.6	10.5	—	1.0	0.1	0.3	1.2	0.2	2.2		—20.2—	
Singapore	1994[11, 28]	20,593	2.5	1.0	0.7	0.3	1.2	0.2	0.2	0.6	1.5	4.7	3.7	1.4	3.5
Slovakia	1994[3]	2,720	9.7[49]	3.0	...	3.1[49]	3.5	2.1	2.3	1.7	4.5	2.5	5.1	1.2	2.4
Slovenia	1994[9]	4,837	12.6	2.1	0.5	3.6	4.0	3.8	3.0	5.1	6.2	3.9	8.1	—4.5—	
Solomon Islands	1994	7.8	...	...	...	—	...	—	...	...	—	...	—	—	—
Somalia	1990	36	21.6	6.3	37.5	10.5	0.8	2.0	—	7.3	−0.6	0.3	0.4	—5.1—	
South Africa	1994	25,669	10.6	6.0	0.4	3.4	2.9	1.3	1.4	1.1	4.8	3.5	4.9	—4.9—	
Spain	1992[28, 42]	94,549	13.2	4.4	1.2	3.3	2.7	1.3	2.3	1.9	2.3	5.3	3.3	3.4	3.4
Sri Lanka	1993[9, 42]	1,267	14.8	12.4	11.8	8.3	20.1	1.9	0.6	0.2	2.5	1.1	0.9	4.5	0.3
Sudan, The	1990	1,179	40.0	3.0	16.7	11.9	0.4	5.4	0.2	0.2	2.1	6.4	0.7	—2.2—	
Suriname	1992[2, 28, 39]	700	33.4	22.3	12.3	...	1.5	1.6	8.7	1.4	0.7	1.6	...	—8.3—	
Swaziland	1994	344	26.3	44.2	—	5.5	2.0	0.3	1.2	1.2	10.1	5.2	—	—0.3—	
Sweden	1994[11, 28]	35,125	7.2	1.2	0.5	1.0	0.2	0.1	4.9	1.1	9.8	5.8	3.9	1.8	5.4
Switzerland	1994	60,111	8.1	1.4	0.8	1.8	1.0	0.5	4.6	3.0	1.9	7.4	7.4	—5.9—	
Syria	1994	2,990	13.1	2.3	7.4	25.5	1.5	2.6	2.0	5.3	0.4	0.7	0.3	—2.0—	
Taiwan	1995	73,210	—7.3—		1.5	5.8	2.2	0.7	0.6	0.9	2.1	1.2	9.0	—2.0—	
Tajikistan	1994[2, 3]	862	19.4	1.0	1.1	27.5	1.8	0.3	0.3	0.2	...	0.2	3.4	0.2	...
Tanzania	1994	101	10.9	5.9	10.9	16.8	1.0	2.0	2.0	1.0	3.9	3.0	14.8	—2.0—	
Thailand	1991[9, 11]	65,413	4.1	2.3	2.9	3.1	5.0	1.4	0.6	0.4	0.2	33.9	1.5	0.7	0.6
Togo	1994[3]	90		—65.3—			—6.7—		—6.5—		—4.7—			—6.4—	
Tonga	1994[2, 9]	13		—45.1—		1.1	1.5	2.0	1.3	[69]	[69]	5.0	—	—24.9—	
Trinidad and Tobago	1993	593	17.3	9.6	6.2	0.3	1.4	0.3	0.5	0.7	2.3	3.6	21.1	3.0	0.1
Tunisia	1993[3, 9]	3,696	9.8	3.3	6.5	7.1	13.1	3.4	—5.1—		—2.2—		2.6	2.7	0.5
Turkey	1993[9, 72]	40,159	10.3	2.9	3.5	10.3	3.6	0.5	0.8	0.4	1.5	2.2	3.7	2.9	3.0
Turkmenistan	1992[2, 3, 15]	801	13.3	...	...	18.9	1.2	0.4	—0.3[16]—		—[16]—		3.2[7]	[7]	[7]
Tuvalu	1994[28]	0.31	...	—	—	—	...	—	—	...	—	—	—	...	—
Uganda	1989	155	42.8	11.9	8.9	8.0	1.3	1.5	0.1	4.0	0.9	1.4	0.3	0.7	5.1
Ukraine	1994[2, 3, 28]	28,630	24.3	1.8	0.1	3.2[49]	0.9	1.4	0.7	1.2	0.6	0.3	6.3[49]	1.0[49]	0.5
United Arab Emirates	1993[2]	6,621		—8.7—			—4.7—		—2.8—		—2.8—			—53.8—	
United Kingdom	1993[28]	169,348	11.0	2.6	1.1	3.1	1.9	0.8	1.1	2.1[10]	3.1	8.8	4.1	3.4	3.6
United States	1994	1,598,464	8.8	2.0	1.4	2.7	1.8	0.3	2.5	1.6	4.0	7.5	5.2	2.9	3.5
Uruguay	1993[9, 42]	2,962	24.0	12.6	5.6	8.3	3.7	2.6	0.6	0.6	2.1	4.9	1.9	—8.4—	
Uzbekistan	1992[2, 3, 15]	2,147	12.6	...	...	21.4	3.1	1.9	—1.3[16]—		—[16]—		5.4[7]	[7]	[7]
Vanuatu	1993[3]	10		—44.5—			—3.8—		—22.5—		5.3	...		—9.2[73]—	
Venezuela	1993[3, 42]	11,292	11.8	7.1	3.4	1.7	−1.3	2.1	0.3	0.8	2.3	2.8	5.1	3.6	2.4
Vietnam	1995[2, 3]	5,472		—33.4—		7.2	2.6	1.0	3.7	...	2.3	1.1	9.3[74]	[74]	[74]
Virgin Islands (U.S.)	...[51]	...	...	...	...	...	...	...	...	...	...	...	...	...	...
West Bank	1994	132	...	...	...	...	...	...	...	...	...	...	...	...	...
Western Sahara	...	...	...	...	...	...	...	...	...	...	...	...	...	...	...
Yemen	1994[2, 76]	3,541		—64.0—			—1.7—		—0.6—		—8.5—			—13.2—	
Yugoslavia	1994[3]	4,506	19.5	5.7	4.7	3.1	5.3	2.9	1.0	3.2	2.0	2.0	3.6	—9.2—	
Zambia	1994[9, 11]	305	19.5	18.0	6.9	7.5	1.2	0.8	3.4	1.1	1.0	2.4	5.0	9.0	1.8
Zimbabwe	1993–94[28]	1,479	20.3	13.0	4.7	8.4	3.1	2.9	2.3	1.0	2.5	3.5	4.0[77]	1.3	1.7

[1]Gross output in value of sales. [2]Gross output of production. [3]Complete ISIC detail is not available. [4]Value of manufactured exports. [5]Canned tuna and salmon. [6]Value of manufactured exports (excluding duty-free reexports). [7]351 includes 352, 355, and 356. [8]390 includes 385. [9]In producer's prices. [10]Includes metal furniture. [11]Establishments employing 10 or more persons. [12]Excludes sugar refining. [13]321 includes 323 + 324. [14]351 includes 353 + 354, 355, and 356. [15]Includes extraction of petroleum, natural gas, metals, and nonmetals. [16]33 includes 34. [17]355 and 356 includes 361 + 362. [18]38 includes 39. [19]Establishments employing 15 or more persons. [20]351 includes 353 + 354. [21]Cotton fibre only. [22]Establishments employing 50 or more persons. [23]Excludes petroleum refining. [24]Republic of Cyprus only. [25]Establishments employing 100 or more persons. [26]37 includes 381. [27]383 includes 385. [28]In factor values. [29]Private establishments employing 10 or more persons, and all public establishments. [30]311 + 312 includes 314. [31]351 includes 352, 353, and 354. [32]Ethiopia includes Eritrea. [33]Processed fish only. [34]369 includes 371. [35]33 includes 32. [36]36 includes 37 and 38. [37]Establishments employing 20 or more persons. [38]384 includes 390. [39]Selected industries only. [40]Establishments employing six or more persons; excludes food and beverages. [41]Excludes sugar and rice manufacturing; includes public utilities. [42]Establishments employing five or more persons. [43]332 includes 390. [44]Establishments with

			(36)		(37)		(38)								(39)	country
refined petroleum and products (353+354)	rubber products (355)	plastic products (356)	pottery, china, and glass (361+362)	bricks, tiles, cement, etc. (369)	iron and steel (371)	non-ferrous metals (372)	fabricated metal products (381)	nonelectrical machinery (382 exc. 3825)	office equip., computers (3825)	electrical equip. (383 exc. 3832)	radio, television (3832)	transport equip. exc. motor vehicles (384 exc. 3843)	motor vehicles (3843)	professional equip. (385)	jewelry, musical instruments (390)	
			...	1.3	0.2[61]			...	...	...		...	...	...	85.0[56]	Niger
1.1	1.8	2.7	0.4	5.6	1.1	1.8	5.0	1.1		2.0		9.6		—	0.3	Nigeria
...	62	62	4.9		...	...	...	...	...	...	...	...	...	...	...	Northern Mariana Islands
1.6	0.2	1.8	0.8	2.4	2.4	5.5	4.3	6.7	0.4	3.5	1.8	11.7[63]	1.1	1.7	0.8	Norway
34.8	1.8		15.4		3.8		5.4	11.1		...	...	0.1	0.7	...	43	Oman
6.7	0.8	0.5	1.0	8.6	7.2	—	0.9	1.8		3.1		3.5		0.3	0.3	Pakistan
...	...	...	...	...	...	...	...	...	...	...	...	...	...	...	...	Palau
5.8	0.2	4.1	0.6	4.8	1.2	0.4	2.2	...	—	0.9	—	1.2	0.2	0.1	0.3	Panama
—	—	0.4	0.7	1.6	...	—	6.7	1.3		0.7		2.4		...	...	Papua New Guinea
5.2	—	1.8	0.5	2.9	—	1.3	1.3	0.3		0.1		0.6		0.1	5.5	Paraguay
21.0	0.7	2.2	1.0	3.7	1.5	7.7	2.9	1.4		1.8		1.8		0.3	1.7	Peru
7.5	2.4	1.8	1.4	3.2	3.6	0.7	1.6	1.1	0.1	3.0	6.6	2.4	1.3	0.2	1.0	Philippines
			5.3		5.0		5.1	7.3	0.2	2.7	1.5	6.3		1.2	0.3	Poland
12.8	0.6	1.5	3.6	5.2	0.8	0.5	6.0	3.4	0.1	3.3	2.4	1.6	1.9	0.5	1.0	Portugal
0.5	0.1	1.0	0.3	1.1	...	...	1.4	1.1	2.1	3.2	4.3	—	0.4	5.7	0.9	Puerto Rico
31.3	...	0.9	7.4		10.8	...	3.0								0.2	Qatar
—	—	64	...	16.8	—	—	12.2	5.0							—	Réunion
5.7	1.9	1.5	6.6		5.2	0.5	4.7	8.9	0.2	1.3	1.9	2.7	3.0	1.1	0.5	Romania
5.1	1.2	0.5	0.9	6.1	8.6	7.9	1.7	12.1	0.6	2.6	51	3.0[66]	6.5	1.6	1.5	Russia
—	—	—	—	11.7	—	—	10.3	0.9		0.8		1.4		—	...	Rwanda
...	...	...	...	...	...	...	...	...	...	...	...	...	...	...	...	St. Kitts and Nevis
...	...	...	...	...	...	...	...	...	...	12.0		...	...	...	...	St. Lucia
...	...	0.4	...	...	...	...	6.6[67]	...	...	67	67	...	...	...	...	St. Vincent
—	—	—	—	—	—	—	—	—	—	—	—	—	—	—	—	Samoa
...	...	...	...	...	...	...	...	...	...	...	...	...	...	...	...	San Marino
—	—	—	3.8		—	—	—	—	—	—	—	—	—	—	—	São Tomé and Príncipe
13.9	0.1	3.0	0.6	12.3	7.6	0.4	5.3	1.1		1.9		0.6		—	0.6	Saudi Arabia
5.5	—	2.2	—	6.5	—	—	3.5	0.2	—	—	—	1.5	0.8	—	...	Senegal
			5.2		—	—	2.4								—	Seychelles
			3.5		...	—	2.1	...	...	...	...	...	...	...	0.1	Sierra Leone
6.1	0.3	2.8	0.4	1.6	0.5	0.3	6.5	5.6	20.7	4.0	20.1	7.0	0.3	1.8	0.5	Singapore
6.7	2.1	2.0	2.5	3.9	9.5[49]	1.5[49]	3.7[49]	5.9[49]	0.2	2.5	1.5	1.2[49]	1.3	1.7	0.6[49]	Slovakia
0.2	1.6	1.7	4.1		9.7	0.3	4.8	6.0		8.2		3.9		1.8	0.4	Slovenia
—	—	—	—	—	—	—	—	—	—	—	—	...	—	—	—	Solomon Islands
1.6	—	0.5	—	3.0	—	—	1.1	—	—	—	—	0.9		—	1.7	Somalia
5.8	1.4	2.6	1.5	3.4	9.0	3.4	6.2	6.1		4.6		8.1		1.0	1.7	South Africa
2.8	1.8	3.0	1.7	5.0	3.3	1.2	6.3	5.9	0.3	4.1	1.8	2.9	10.5	0.5	1.0	Spain
1.4	4.2	1.4	1.8	2.9	1.1	0.2	1.3	0.9	0.2	1.1	0.1	1.6	0.3	—	2.1	Sri Lanka
1.3	0.8	1.2	0.1	0.5	0.1	0.7	2.6	0.1		1.2		2.1		—	0.1	Sudan, The
...	0.7	0.6	5.3		...	...	...	...	...	...	...	0.9		0.2	0.5	Suriname
—	—	—	0.3	0.9	—	—	2.0	0.3		0.3		—	—	—	—	Swaziland
1.2	0.7	1.4	0.7	1.6	4.8	1.3	7.7	11.9	0.8	3.1	5.6	2.7	10.5	2.8	0.3	Sweden
2.0	0.8	2.3	1.7	2.7	1.2	1.9	6.4	12.8		16.9		1.7		5.4	0.4	Switzerland
7.0	1.3	1.0	2.1	6.8	—	1.9	10.9	2.3		2.7		0.4		—	0.5	Syria
8.2	1.1	5.1	4.3		7.8		6.8	4.5		18.7		7.5		0.9	1.8	Taiwan
...	0.1	—	0.3	5.0	...	31.8	0.2	1.0	...	1.0	...	...	0.6	...	0.1	Tajikistan
4.0	1.0	1.0	—	5.9	2.0	2.0	3.9	1.0		2.0		3.0		—	—	Tanzania
7.9	1.6	0.3	0.9	3.5	1.7	0.5	1.7	10.3	0.1	1.5	5.6	0.2	5.8	0.2	1.5	Thailand
			6.5		0.3	...	2.8	...	...	...	...	...	...	...	...	Togo
—	—	—	4.7		—	—	3.8	—	—	—	—	4.1		—	6.4[69]	Tonga
11.0	0.6	0.6	1.9	4.3	7.5	—	2.0	—	—	1.2	0.5	0.3	0.9	8	2.8[8]	Trinidad and Tobago
20.2	0.9	1.3[70]	2.9	6.4	1.6	3.3[71]	71	0.4		2.8	...	...	...	...	...	Tunisia
13.6	1.8	1.3	2.8	4.9	6.5	1.0	3.0	4.3	—	2.5	3.2	1.0	8.0	0.4	0.2	Turkey
55.7	7	7	4.0		0.1		0.8								...	Turkmenistan
—	—	—	—	...	—	—	—	—	—	—	—	—	—	—	...	Tuvalu
—	0.2	—	—	2.5	3.0	—	4.7	0.7	—	1.3	0.5	—	0.1	—	—	Uganda
7.5	1.1	0.2	0.9	5.1	18.5	1.3	4.6	5.7	0.2	2.1[49]		3.4[49]	2.0	0.7[49]	0.4[49]	Ukraine
			8.3		8.2		9.2								1.4	United Arab Emirates
2.1	1.2	3.8	1.5	1.7	2.1	1.7	6.7	8.3	1.9	3.7	3.0	5.1	6.3	3.1	1.1	United Kingdom
1.8	1.2	3.2	0.9	1.6	2.2	1.6	6.0	7.9	2.1	3.4	5.7	4.5	6.4	5.8	1.5	United States
3.0	1.2	2.9	1.6	2.3	0.9	0.4	3.6	1.2		2.8		3.5		0.7	0.6	Uruguay
12.4	7	7	5.4		12.2		13.2								...	Uzbekistan
			73		12.0[26]		26	...	...	...	...	...	...	...	...	Vanuatu
26.3	1.6	1.9	1.8	3.2	4.3	3.9	3.7	1.8	0.1	1.8	0.3	0.1	6.3	0.4	0.4	Venezuela
17.4[75]	74	...	1.2	8.7	1.5	0.7	1.8	...	...	...	2.1	...	...	...	...	Vietnam
...	...	...	...	...	...	...	...	...	...	...	...	...	...	...	...	Virgin Islands (U.S.)
...	...	...	...	...	...	...	...	...	...	...	...	...	...	...	...	West Bank
...	...	...	...	...	...	...	...	...	...	...	...	...	...	...	...	Western Sahara
			10.5		1.5		...	...	...	...	...	...	...	...	...	Yemen
—	2.8	...	5.1		2.0	2.7	8.6	3.9		6.3		5.7		...	...	Yugoslavia
3.8	1.8	1.3	−0.2	3.3	1.3	0.1	5.4	4.7				0.6		—	0.1	Zambia
77	2.3	1.3	0.6	2.5	9.5	0.6	5.1	1.0		2.9	0.3	0.4	4.2	0.1	0.5	Zimbabwe

electric power and employing 10 or more workers and all establishments employing 20 or more workers. [45]Establishments employing three or more persons. [46]Includes refined sugar and molasses. [47]38 includes 37. [48]Establishments employing four or more persons. [49]Sum of available data. [50]Includes recycled waste and scrap. [51]Data withheld for reasons of confidentiality. [52]Includes public utilities. [53]352 includes 353 + 354. [54]381 includes 372. [55]Processed copra only. [56]Traditional sector handicrafts. [57]All establishments employing 10 or more persons and smaller establishments with an annual output of production of more than U.S.$56,000. [58]Coconut soap includes coconut oil. [59]Excludes Transdniester area and city of Tighina (Bendery). [60]Fish and meat processing. [61]37 includes 33. [62]322 and 323 + 324 includes 355 + 356. [63]Includes petroleum platforms (6.5% of total). [64]341 includes 356. [65]State enterprises only; state enterprises account for about 80% of all industrial output. [66]Excludes shipbuilding and aircraft. [67]381 includes 383. [68]Excludes fish processing. [69]39 includes 332 and 341. [70]Includes synthetic fibres. [71]372 includes 381. [72]Private establishments employing 25 or more persons, and all public establishments. [73]35 includes 36. [74]351 includes 352 and 355. [75]Includes crude petroleum production. [76]Conversion to U.S. dollars based on official exchange rate. [77]351 includes 353 + 354.

Energy

This table provides data about the commercial energy supplies (reserves, production, consumption, and trade) of the various countries of the world, together with data about oil pipeline networks and traffic. Many of the data and concepts used in this table are adapted from the United Nations' *Energy Statistics Yearbook*.

Electricity. Total installed electrical power capacity comprises the sum of the rated power capacities of all main and auxiliary generators in a country. "Total installed capacity" (kW) is multiplied by 8,760 hours per year to yield "Total production capacity" (kW-hr).

Production of electricity comprises the total gross production of electricity by publicly or privately owned enterprises and also that generated by industrial establishments for their own use, but usually excludes consumption by the utility itself. Measured in millions of kilowatt-hours (kW-hr), annual production of electricity ranges generally between 50% and 60% of total production capacity. The data are further analyzed by type of generation: fossil fuels, hydroelectric power, and nuclear fuel.

The great majority of the world's electrical and other energy needs are met by the burning of fossil hydrocarbon solids, liquids, and gases, either for thermal generation of electricity or in internal combustion engines. Many renewable and nontraditional sources of energy are being developed worldwide (wood, biogenic gases and liquids, tidal, wave, and wind power, geothermal and photothermal [solar] energy, and so on), but collectively these sources are still negligible in the world's total energy consumption. For this reason only hydroelectric and nuclear generation are considered here separately with fossil fuels.

Trade in electrical energy refers to the transfer of generated electrical output via an international grid. Total electricity consumption (residential and nonresidential) is equal to total electricity requirements less transformation and distribution losses.

Coal. The term coal, as used in the table, comprises all grades of anthracite, bituminous, subbituminous, and lignite that have acquired or may in the future, by reason of new technology or changed market prices, acquire an economic value. These types of coal may be differentiated according to heat content (density) and content of impurities. Most coal reserve data are based on proven recoverable reserves only, of all grades of coal. Exceptions are footnoted, with proven in-place reserves reported only when recoverable reserves are unknown. Production figures include deposits removed from both surface and underground workings as well as quantities used by the producers themselves or issued to the miners. Wastes recovered from mines or nearby preparation plants are excluded from production figures.

Natural gas. This term refers to any combustible gas (usually chiefly methane) of natural origin from underground sources. The data for production cover, to the extent possible, gas obtained from gas fields,

Energy

country	electricity													coal		
	installed capacity, 1994 ('000 kW)	production, 1994		power source, 1994			trade, 1994		consumption					reserves, latest ('000,000 metric tons)	production, 1994 ('000 metric tons)	consumption, 1994 ('000 metric tons)
		capacity ('000,000 kW-hr)	amount ('000,000 kW-hr)	fossil fuel (%)	hydropower (%)	nuclear fuel (%)	exports ('000,000 kW-hr)	imports ('000,000 kW-hr)	amount, 1994 ('000,000 kW-hr)	per capita, 1994 (kW-hr)	residential, 1994 (%)	nonresidential, 1994 (%)				
Afghanistan	494	4,327	687	31.3	68.7	—	—	128	815	43	...	...		66	6	6
Albania	1,892	16,574	3,903	3.4	96.6	—	—	—	3,903	1,143	...	...		15[1]	179	179
Algeria	6,007	52,621	19,888	99.1	0.9	—	1,191	67	18,764	687	28.8	71.2		43	20	1,280
American Samoa	33	289	110	100.0	—	—	—	—	110	2,075	27.5[3]	72.5[3]		—	—	...
Andorra	...	...	...	...	...	...	...	...	...	...	...	...		—	—	...
Angola	617	5,405	1,865	26.0	74.0	—	—	—	1,865	175	27.5[2]	72.5[2]		...	—	—
Antigua and Barbuda	26	228	97	100.0	—	—	—	—	97	1,492	42.4[4]	57.6[4]		...	...	...
Argentina	19,610	171,784	66,196	46.0	41.4	12.6	11	977	67,162	1,965	41.4	58.6		130	348	1,596
Armenia	2,768	24,248	5,658	37.9	62.1	—	...	16	5,674	1,599	...	...		...	...	36
Aruba	90	788	355	100.0	—	—	—	—	355	5,145	...	...		...	...	...
Australia	38,829	340,142	167,151	89.9	10.1	—	—	—	167,151	9,363	30.1[2]	69.9[2]		90,940	226,058	102,658
Austria	17,426	152,652	53,359	30.9	69.1	—	9,042	8,219	52,536	6,635	23.1[2]	83.4[2]		31	1,391	4,397
Azerbaijan	5,239	45,894	17,600	89.8	10.2	—	300	500	17,800	2,382	...	...		...	...	8
Bahamas, The	401	3,513	985	100.0	—	—	—	—	985	3,621	33.6[4]	66.4[4]		...	—	—
Bahrain	1,050	9,198	4,550	100.0	—	—	—	—	4,550	8,288	...	...		...	...	...
Bangladesh	2,970	26,017	10,010	94.0	6.0	—	—	—	10,010	85	50.7	49.3		1,054[1]	—	198
Barbados	140	1,226	571	100.0	—	—	—	—	571	2,188	32.7	67.3		...	—	—
Belarus	7,205	63,116	31,397	99.9	0.1	—	3,944	7,764	35,217	3,465	...	...		...	—	1,199
Belgium	14,899	130,515	72,236	42.1	1.7	56.2	5,070	9,053	76,219	7,561	26.9[8]	73.1[8]		410	753	13,050
Belize	23	201	110	100.0	—	—	—	—	110	524	89.4	10.6		...	...	...
Benin	15	131	6	100.0	—	—	—	242	248	47	78.7	21.3		...	...	...
Bermuda	140	1,226	520	100.0	—	—	—	—	520	8,254	39.6[5]	60.4[5]		...	—	—
Bhutan	361	3,162	1,682	0.4	99.6	—	1,455	3	230	143	19.2[3]	69.8[3]		...	2	20
Bolivia	786	6,885	2,876	51.6	48.4	—	3	19	2,892	400	51.6	48.4		1	—	—
Bosnia and Herzegovina	2,327	20,385	1,921	34.9	65.1	—	412	572	2,081	590	21.8[5]	78.2[5]		...	1,400[6]	1,400[6]
Botswana	[10]	[10]	522[10, 11]	[10]	[10]	[10]	[10]	82[10, 11]	[10]	[10]	41.0	59.0		3,500	[10]	[10]
Brazil	57,640	504,926	260,682	6.8	93.2	0.0	—	31,657	292,339	1,837	47.2	52.8		2,845	5,194	16,434
Brunei	492	4,310	1,315	100.0	—	—	—	—	1,315	4,696	56.6	43.4		...	—	—
Bulgaria	12,087	105,882	38,133	55.9	3.9	40.2	1,245	1,173	38,061	4,316	50.4	49.6		2,710	28,757	32,540
Burkina Faso	78	683	216	66.2	33.8	—	—	—	216	22	...	...		...	...	...
Burundi	43	377	149	1.4	98.6	—	—	43	192	31	73.7	26.3		...	...	...
Cambodia	35	307	187	61.5	38.5	—	—	—	187	19	...	...		...	—	—
Cameroon	627	5,493	2,740	3.0	97.0	—	—	—	2,740	213	...	...		...	1	1
Canada	113,828	997,133	554,186	21.3	59.2	19.5	50,919	7,005	510,272	17,510	28.8[4]	71.2[4]		8,623	72,824	52,229
Cape Verde	7	61	39	100.0	—	—	—	—	39	102	...	...		...	—	—
Central African Republic	43	377	101	20.8	79.2	—	—	—	101	31	...	...		4	...	...
Chad	29	254	85	100.0	—	—	—	—	85	14	...	...		...	...	...
Chile	5,504	48,215	25,250	32.9	67.1	—	—	—	25,250	1,798	34.5	65.5		1,181	1,222	3,185
China	190,100	1,665,276	928,083	80.4	18.1	1.5	3,893	1,847	926,037	780	27.3	72.7		114,500	1,239,902	1,231,928
Colombia	10,781	94,442	43,474	25.7	74.3	—	—	143	43,617	1,263	71.9	28.1		4,539	22,527	6,476
Comoros	5	44	17	88.2	11.8	—	—	—	17	27	...	...		...	...	...
Congo, Dem. Rep. of the	2,831	24,800	5,545	0.4	99.6	—	1,077	55	4,523	106	24.6	75.4		88	93	136
Congo, Rep. of the	118	1,034	435	0.7	99.3	—	—	112	547	217	...	...		...	...	...
Costa Rica	1,094	9,583	4,772	25.2	74.8	—	6	...	4,766	1,424	77.6	22.4		...	...	...
Côte d'Ivoire	1,173	10,275	1,917	42.5	57.5	—	—	—	1,917	139	33.0	67.0		...	...	...
Croatia	3,593	31,475	8,275	40.4	59.6	—	982	4,547	11,840	2,629	62.6	37.4		39	103	640
Cuba	3,988	34,935	10,982	99.0	1.0	—	—	—	10,982	1,002	52.5	47.5		...	—	153
Cyprus	666	5,834	2,681	100.0	—	—	—	—	2,681	3,653	80.4	19.6		...	—	27
Czech Republic	13,852	121,344	58,705	74.9	3.0	22.1	5,860	5,415	58,260	5,659	23.6[3, 13]	76.4[3, 13]		5,142	76,944	67,244
Denmark	10,212	89,457	41,096	97.1	0.1	2.8[14]	6,623	1,779	36,252	7,008	32.5[8]	67.5[8]		63[5]	—	13,087
Djibouti	85	745	185	100.0	—	—	—	—	185	327	...	...		...	...	...
Dominica	8	70	34	50.0	50.0	—	—	—	34	479	53.5[4]	46.5[4]		...	...	...
Dominican Republic	1,447	12,676	6,182	69.7	30.3	—	—	—	6,182	805	74.3	25.7		...	—	104
Ecuador	2,278	19,955	8,163	21.9	78.1	—	—	—	8,163	728	71.6	28.4		24	...	...
Egypt	13,040	114,230	47,920	82.2	17.8	—	—	—	47,920	777	76.7	23.3		53	—	1,852

petroleum fields, or coal mines that is actually collected and marketed. (Much natural gas in Middle Eastern and North African oil fields is flared [burned] because it is often not economical to capture and market it.) Manufactured gas is generally a by-product of industrial operations such as gasworks, coke ovens, and blast furnaces. It is usually burned at the point of production and rarely enters the marketplace. Production of manufactured gas is, therefore, only reported as a percentage of domestic gas consumption.

Crude petroleum. Crude petroleum is the liquid product obtained from oil wells; the term also includes shale oil, tar sand extract, and field or lease condensate. Production and consumption data in the table refer, so far as possible, to the same year so that the relationship between national production and consumption patterns can be clearly seen; both are given in barrels.

Proven reserves are that oil remaining underground in known fields whose existence has been "proved" by the evaluation of nearby producing wells or by seismic tests in sedimentary strata known to contain crude petroleum, and that is judged recoverable within the limits of present technology and economic conditions (prices). The published proven reserve figures do not necessarily reflect the true reserves of a country, because government authorities or corporations often have political or economic motives for withholding or altering such data.

The estimated exhaustion rate of petroleum reserves is an extrapolated ratio of published proven reserves to the current rate of withdrawal/production. Present world published proven reserves will last about 40 to 45 years at the present rate of withdrawal, but there are large country-to-country variations above or below the average.

Data on petroleum and refined product pipelines are provided because of the great importance to both domestic and international energy markets of this means of bringing these energy sources from their production or transportation points to refineries, intermediate consumption and distribution points, and final consumers. Their traffic may represent a very significant fraction of the total movement of goods within a country. Available data for petroleum pipelines are often incomplete and their basis varies internationally, some countries reporting only international shipments, others reporting domestic shipments of 50 kilometres or more, and so on.

For data in the hydrocarbons portions of the table (coal, natural gas, and petroleum), extensive use has been made of a variety of international sources, such as those of the United Nations, the International Energy Agency (of the Organization for Economic Cooperation and Development), the World Energy Council (in its *World Energy Resources* [triennial]); the U.S. Department of Energy (especially its *International Energy Annual*); and of various industry surveys, such as those published by the *International Petroleum Encyclopedia* and *World Oil.*

natural gas						crude petroleum							country
published proven reserves, 1997 ('000,000,000 cu m)	production		consumption			reserves, 1997		production, 1996 ('000,000 barrels)	consumption, 1994 ('000,000 barrels)	refining capacity, 1997 ('000 barrels per day)	pipelines (latest)		
	natural gas, 1995 ('000,000 cu m)	manufactured gas, 1994 (% of total gas consumption)	amount, 1994 ('000,000 cu m)	residential, 1990 (%)	non-residential, 1990 (%)	published proven ('000,000 barrels)	years to exhaust proven reserves				length (km)	traffic ('000,000 metric ton-km)	
99	294	...	175	...	...	...	...	—	—	—	...	...	Afghanistan
2	136	...	77	...	...	165	55	3	3	40	200	...	Albania
3,690	51,817	27.6	19,208	26.8[2]	73.2[2]	9,200	31	298	160	465	6,910	...	Algeria
...	...	...	...	...	...	...	...	—	—	—	—	...	American Samoa
...	...	...	...	...	...	...	...	—	—	—	—	—	Andorra
48	561	10.9	167	...	...	5,412	21	258	12	32	179	...	Angola
...	...	...	...	...	...	...	...	—	—	—	—	—	Antigua and Barbuda
619	17,336	9.9	31,293	49.2	50.8	2,386	9	275	174	665	6,990	...	Argentina
...	170[5]	...	884	...	...	...	...	—	1	—	—	—	Armenia
...	...	...	...	...	...	...	...	—	2	...	—	—	Aruba
550	29,554	30.3	17,438	...	...	1,800	9	195	202	771	3,000	...	Australia
22	1,475	13.3	7,459	25.7[2]	74.3[2]	76	10	8	63	210	725	6,701	Austria
100	3,896	0.9	7,706	...	...	3,300[6]	38[6]	190	77	442	1,760	1,705	Azerbaijan
...	—	—	...	...	...	...	...	—	—	—	—	—	Bahamas, The
147	5,250	4.9	6,383	...	...	210	6	38	90	249	72	...	Bahrain
288	7,365	0.2	6,635	34.2	65.8	5	10	0.5	9	31	—	—	Bangladesh
0.1	17	6.9	22	62.6	37.4	2	5	0.4	2	4	—	—	Barbados
...	262[7]	1.5	13,061	...	...	...	...	37	94	473	2,570	...	Belarus
—	1.4[7]	20.4	14,141	43.4[8]	56.6[8]	...	...	—	207[9]	630	1,328	1,168	Belgium
...	...	...	...	...	...	...	...	—	—	—	—	—	Belize
1.2	...	...	...	...	...	29	41	0.7	0.04	—	—	—	Benin
...	...	...	...	...	...	...	...	—	—	—	—	—	Bermuda
...	...	...	...	...	...	...	...	—	—	—	—	—	Bhutan
128	3,279	18.7	1,159	—	100.0	132	12	11	9	48	2,380	...	Bolivia
...	—	7.4[6]	378	...	...	...	...	—	15[6]	...	174	—	Bosnia and Herzegovina
...	...	[10]	...	...	...	—	...	—	[10]	—	—	—	Botswana
154	2,880	62.5	4,103	—	100.0	4,800	17	285	467	1,256	5,804	...	Brazil
399	9,922	0.9	1,938	...	...	1,350	25	55	2	9	553	...	Brunei
4	11	16.2	4,554	...	...	15	38	0.4	51	300	718	259	Bulgaria
...	...	...	...	...	...	...	...	—	—	—	—	—	Burkina Faso
...	...	...	...	...	...	...	...	—	—	—	—	—	Burundi
...	...	...	...	...	...	...	...	—	—	—	—	—	Cambodia
110	—	100.0	...	...	...	400	12	33	8	42	—	—	Cameroon
1,929	175,897	22.8	78,223	20.6[2]	79.4[2]	4,894	7	664	508	1,852	23,564	99,908	Canada
...	...	...	...	...	...	...	...	—	—	—	—	—	Cape Verde
...	...	...	...	...	...	...	...	—	—	—	—	—	Central African Republic
...	...	...	...	...	...	...	...	—	—	—	—	—	Chad
102	1,164	34.1	1,865	23.4	76.6	300	100	3	54	192	1,540	...	Chile
1,171	17,300	51.0	17,540	12.2	87.8	24,000	21	1,141	1,024	2,867	10,800	61,200	China
234	4,437	25.0	5,111	12.8	87.2	2,800	12	227	94	249	4,935	...	Colombia
...	...	...	...	...	...	...	...	—	—	—	—	—	Comoros
1	—	7.8	—	—	—	187	17	11	3	17	390	...	Congo, Dem. Rep. of the
91	2[12]	47.6	5	...	...	1,506	20	74	8	21	25	...	Congo, Rep. of the
...	—	6.3	—	—	—	...	...	—	5	15	176	...	Costa Rica
23	—	56.7	—	—	—	100	14	7	25	64	—	—	Côte d'Ivoire
22	1,869	44.5	938	...	...	55	5	12	37	294	690	89	Croatia
3	31[5]	85.2	39	3.4	96.6	100	10	10	38	301	—	—	Cuba
—	—	74.8	—	—	—	...	...	—	6	26	—	—	Cyprus
4	290	25.4	7,339	...	...	6	9	0.7	45	187	—	—	Czech Republic
109	4,936	15.5	2,992	...	...	957	13	75	66	189	688	2,212	Denmark
...	...	...	...	...	...	...	...	—	—	—	—	—	Djibouti
...	...	...	...	...	...	—	—	—	—	—	—	—	Dominica
—	—	11.6	...	...	...	...	...	—	15	50	104	...	Dominican Republic
105	102	43.8	204	—	—	2,115	15	141	35	148	2,158	...	Ecuador
576	12,233	12.1	10,544	5.3	94.7	3,696	11	337	192	546	1,767	...	Egypt

Energy (continued)

country	electricity												coal		
	installed capacity, 1994 ('000 kW)	production, 1994		power source, 1994			trade, 1994		consumption				reserves, latest ('000,000 metric tons)	production, 1994 ('000 metric tons)	consumption, 1994 ('000 metric tons)
		capacity ('000,000 kW-hr)	amount ('000,000 kW-hr)	fossil fuel (%)	hydro-power (%)	nuclear fuel (%)	exports ('000,000 kW-hr)	imports ('000,000 kW-hr)	amount, 1994 ('000,000 kW-hr)	per capita, 1994 (kW-hr)	residential, 1994 (%)	non-residential, 1994 (%)			
El Salvador	751	6,579	3,324	22.8	62.2	15.0[14]	14	105	3,415	605	66.2	33.8	...	...	...
Equatorial Guinea	5	44	20	90.0	10.0	—	—	—	20	51	...	...	...	...	...
Eritrea	...	...	...	...	...	...	...	...	...	...	...	...	...	...	...
Estonia	3,287	28,794	9,151	99.9	0.1	—	2,146	3,874	10,879	7,060	53.4	46.6	...	14,530	16,395
Ethiopia	464	4,065	1,284	6.3	88.4	5.3[14]	—	—	1,284	24	34.9	65.1	11	...	—
Faroe Islands	91	797	199	57.8	42.2	—	—	—	199	4,234	...	...	...	...	—
Fiji	200	1,752	520	21.2	78.8	—	—	—	520	674	25.7	74.3	...	—	20
Finland	14,143	123,893	65,546	52.4	18.0	29.6	630	7,171	72,087	14,182	18.6[2]	81.3[2]	...	—	7,501
France	107,229[16]	939,326[16]	475,622[16]	7.3[16]	17.0[16]	75.7[16]	66,886[16]	3,718[16]	412,454[16]	7,139[16]	30.3[8]	69.7[8]	139	9,039[16]	21,809[16]
French Guiana	165	1,445	446	100.0	—	—	—	—	446	3,163	...	58.7[2, 17]	...	...	...
French Polynesia	79	692	335	71.0	29.0	—	—	—	335	1,558	...	...	...	...	...
Gabon	310	2,716	933	23.0	77.0	—	—	—	933	727	52.6	47.4	...	...	...
Gambia, The	29	254	75	100.0	—	—	—	—	75	69	...	...	...	...	...
Gaza Strip	...	...	...	...	...	...	...	...	...	...	...	...	...	...	...
Georgia	4,558	39,928	6,803	30.7	69.3	—	200	1,000	7,603	1,395	...	...	...	34	274
Germany	114,355	1,001,750	528,221	66.9	4.3	28.8	33,571	35,908	530,558	6,528	26.3[8, 18]	73.7[8, 18]	67,300	264,700	275,563
Ghana	1,187	10,398	6,167	0.7	99.3	—	310	...	5,857	346	45.0	55.0	...	—	3
Gibraltar	30	263	88	100.0	—	—	—	—	88	3,143	...	...	...	—	—
Greece	8,921	78,148	40,623	92.9	7.0	0.1	434	816	41,005	3,937	30.6[8]	69.4[8]	3,000	56,741	59,569
Greenland	106	929	255	100.0	—	—	—	—	255	4,397	35.3[19]	64.7[19]	183	...	...
Grenada	9	79	70	100.0	—	—	—	—	70	761	88.1	11.9	...	...	...
Guadeloupe	388	3,399	1,005	100.0	—	—	—	—	1,005	2,387	...	32.9[17, 19]	...	...	...
Guam	302	2,646	800	100.0	—	—	—	—	800	5,442	39.7[5]	60.3[5]	...	...	...
Guatemala	766	6,710	3,161	35.4	64.6	—	—	—	3,161	306	66.1	33.9	...	...	...
Guernsey	...	...	227[6]	100.0[6]	...	...	...	...	227[6]	4,997[6]	...	...	...	...	...
Guinea	176	1,542	530	66.0	34.0	—	—	—	530	82	...	...	...	...	...
Guinea-Bissau	11	96	45	100.0	—	—	—	—	45	43	...	...	...	...	...
Guyana	114	999	242	97.9	2.1	—	—	12	254	308	...	...	...	...	...
Haiti	153	1,340	362	54.4	45.6	—	—	—	362	51	56.9	43.1	13[1]	...	...
Honduras	305	2,672	2,655	7.8	92.2	—	...	17	2,672	486	64.3	35.7	21[1]	...	...
Hong Kong	10,323	90,429	26,741	100.0	—	—	1,758	8,253	33,236	5,490	70.8[5]	29.2[5]	...	—	8,450
Hungary	6,979	61,136	33,486	57.6	0.4	42.0	921	2,955	35,520	3,496	61.3	38.7	4,461	14,111	15,369
Iceland	1,083	9,487	4,780	0.1	94.5	5.4[14]	—	—	4,780	17,970	20.9[2]	79.1[2]	...	—	71
India	91,555	802,022	384,422	80.0	18.5	1.5	120	1,600	385,902	420	52.2	47.8	69,947	273,859	284,497
Indonesia	16,265	142,481	61,370	78.2	20.0	1.8[14]	—	—	61,370	315	37.7	62.3	32,063	28,549	3,461
Iran	25,117	220,025	79,128	90.6	9.4	—	—	—	79,128	1,122	21.1[11]	78.9[11]	193	980	1,280
Iraq	7,260	63,598	27,060	97.9	2.1	—	—	—	27,060	1,358	...	...	...	—	—
Ireland	3,910	34,252	17,105	92.9	7.0	0.1[14]	—	—	17,105	4,833	41.4[8]	58.6[8]	14	1	2,738
Isle of Man	...	...	188[4]	100.0	—	—	—	—	172[3]	2,530[3]	48.1[8]	51.9[8]	...	...	...
Israel	4,280	37,493	28,315	99.9	0.1	—	330	—	27,985	5,127	70.3	29.7	...	—	6,026
Italy	64,067[20]	561,227[20]	231,783[20]	77.9[20]	20.6[20]	1.5[4, 20]	1,096[20]	38,695[20]	269,382[20]	4,711[20]	25.0[8]	75.0[8]	34	267[20]	16,672[20]
Jamaica	1,182	10,354	3,927	98.0	2.0	—	—	—	3,927	1,617	56.3	43.7	...	—	64
Japan	220,743	1,933,709	964,328	64.0	7.8	28.2	—	—	964,328	7,281	20.8[2]	79.2[2]	821	6,933	123,099
Jersey	...	...	440[6]	...	...	...	...	...	440[6]	6,579[6]	...	...	...	...	...
Jordan	1,066	9,338	5,075	99.7	0.3	—	—	...	5,075	976	64.9	35.1	...	...	...
Kazakstan	18,900	165,564	66,777	85.7	13.7	0.6	54,000	65,500	78,277	4,597	...	...	25,000	109,257	81,257
Kenya	808	7,078	3,538	5.9	86.7	7.4[14]	—	264	3,802	139	39.0	61.0	...	—	109
Kiribati	2	18	7	100.0	—	—	—	—	7	91	...	...	...	...	...
Korea, North	9,500	83,220	37,000	36.5	63.5	—	—	—	37,000	1,576	...	...	600	98,000	99,925
Korea, South	31,665	277,385	185,993	66.3	2.2	31.5	—	—	185,993	4,174	37.0	63.0	183	7,438	43,892
Kuwait	6,988	61,215	23,152	100.0	—	—	—	—	23,152	14,178	93.2	6.8	...	...	...
Kyrgyzstan	3,632	31,816	12,932	9.4	90.6	—	8,227	5,722	10,427	2,234	...	...	812	848	1,145
Laos	256	2,243	905	4.8	95.2	—	637	26	294	62	...	...	...	1	1
Latvia	2,035	17,827	4,440	25.6	74.4	—	830	2,648	6,258	2,423	58.9	41.1	...	—	425
Lebanon	1,220	10,687	5,150	81.4	18.6	—	—	—	5,150	1,767	...	...	...	—	112
Lesotho	[10]	[10]	[10]	[10]	[10]	[10]	[10]	[10]	[10]	[10]	...	...	...	[10]	[10]
Liberia	332	2,908	485	63.3	36.7	—	—	—	485	165	...	...	...	...	...
Libya	4,600	40,296	17,800	100.0	—	—	—	—	17,800	3,407	...	...	—	—	5
Liechtenstein	[22]	[22]	[22]	[22]	[22]	[22]	[22]	[22]	[22]	[22]	...	...	...	—	[22]
Lithuania	5,463	47,856	10,055	16.2	7.2	76.6	6,015	7,159	11,199	3,022	...	...	...	...	482
Luxembourg	1,238	10,845	1,190	42.2	57.8	—	564	5,019	5,645	14,077	15.3[8]	84.7[8]	...	—	323
Macau	260	2,278	1,277	100.0	—	—	—	140	1,417	3,560	82.8	17.2	...	—	—
Macedonia	1,366	11,966	5,511	87.4	12.6	—	54	221	5,678	2,651	27.4[5]	72.6[5]	...	6,860	7,235
Madagascar	220	1,927	605	42.3	57.7	—	—	—	605	42	32.2	67.8	1,075[1]	—	14
Malawi	185	1,621	802	2.0	98.0	—	—	—	802	74	65.2	34.8	2	—	15
Malaysia	7,830	68,591	39,975	86.2	13.8	—	50	102	40,027	2,032	45.3	54.7	4	174	1,876
Maldives	14	123	46	100.0	—	—	—	—	46	187	50.9[3]	49.1[3]	...	...	...
Mali	87	762	289	22.5	77.5	—	—	—	289	28	...	...	—	...	...
Malta	250	2,190	1,500	100.0	—	—	—	—	1,500	4,121	25.1[11]	74.9[11]	...	—	300
Marshall Islands	99[8]	867[8]	...	...	...	—	—	—	...	...	...	...	...	...	...
Martinique	115	1,007	903	100.0	—	—	—	—	903	2,408	...	40.9[17, 19]	...	...	...
Mauritania	105	920	148	82.4	17.6	—	—	—	148	67	...	...	...	—	6
Mauritius	361	3,162	1,000	89.4	10.6	—	—	—	1,000	906	65.2	34.8	...	—	65
Mayotte	11	96	27	100.0	...	—	—	—	27	241	...	...	...	...	...
Mexico	35,466	310,682	144,276	74.5	18.4	7.1[14]	1,845	1,016	143,447	1,562	29.7	70.3	1,211	8,898	9,188
Micronesia	...	...	...	...	...	—	...	...	...	...	...	...	...	...	...
Moldova	2,635	23,083	8,228	96.6	3.4	—	5,003	5,354	8,579	1,941	...	...	...	—	2,141
Monaco	[16]	[16]	[16]	[16]	[16]	[16]	[16]	[16]	[16]	[16]	...	...	...	[16]	[16]
Mongolia	901	7,893	3,265	100.0	—	—	—	207	3,472	1,469	29.8[3]	70.2[3]	24,000[1]	7,585	7,075
Morocco	3,788	33,183	10,773	92.2	7.8	—	—	920	11,693	441	51.0	49.0	45	650	2,200
Mozambique	2,358	20,656	490	89.8	10.2	—	—	325	815	52	...	...	240	40	60
Myanmar (Burma)	1,212	10,617	3,500	54.8	45.2	—	—	—	3,500	77	59.6	40.4	2.3	76	78
Namibia	[10]	[10]	[10]	[10]	[10]	[10]	[10]	[10]	[10]	[10]	...	...	...	[10]	[10]
Nauru	10	88	30	100.0	—	—	—	—	30	2,727	...	...	...	...	...
Nepal	292	2,558	908	3.6	96.4	—	63	95	940	44	58.5	41.5	...	—	115

natural gas						crude petroleum							country
published proven reserves, 1997 ('000,000,000 cu m)	production		consumption			reserves, 1997		production, 1996 ('000,000 barrels)	consumption, 1994 ('000,000 barrels)	refining capacity, 1997 ('000 barrels per day)	pipelines (latest)		
	natural gas, 1995 ('000,000 cu m)	manufactured gas, 1994 (% of total gas consumption)	amount, 1994 ('000,000 cu m)	residential, 1990 (%)	non-residential, 1990 (%)	published proven ('000,000 barrels)	years to exhaust proven reserves				length (km)	traffic ('000,000 metric ton-km)	
—	—	49.4	—	—	—	...	...	—	7	21	—	—	El Salvador
37	...	...	...	...	...	12	4	3	...	—	—	—	Equatorial Guinea
...	...	...	...	...	...	...	...	...	...	18	—	—	Eritrea
...	...	4.1[15]	548	...	...	—	—	—	...	...	—	—	Estonia
25	—	100.0	—	...	...	0.4	...	—	6	—	—	—	Ethiopia
...	...	...	...	...	...	...	...	—	—	—	—	—	Faroe Islands
...	—	...	—	—	—	...	...	—	—	—	—	—	Fiji
—	—	30.6	3,433	0.6[8]	99.4[8]	...	...	—	67	200	—	—	Finland
19	3,395	20.6[16]	33,450[16]	32.4[8]	67.6[8]	117	7	16	563[16]	1,786	7,546	22,501	France
...	...	...	...	...	...	...	...	—	—	—	—	—	French Guiana
...	...	...	...	...	...	...	...	—	—	—	—	—	French Polynesia
14	102	9.7	88	19.7	80.3	1,340	10	135	12	17	284	...	Gabon
...	...	...	...	...	...	...	...	—	—	—	—	—	Gambia, The
...	...	...	...	...	...	...	...	—	—	—	—	—	Gaza Strip
...	45[12]	...	2,797	...	...	...	...	3.0	2	106	670	...	Georgia
329	18,998	18.3	92,770	36.6[8, 18]	63.4[8, 18]	385	18	21	784	2,108	7,590	13,872	Germany
6	—	94.8	—	—	—	17	9	2	7	27	—	—	Ghana
...	...	...	...	...	...	...	...	—	...	—	—	—	Gibraltar
8	119	106.6	55	...	...	12	4	3	101	396	573	...	Greece
...	...	...	...	...	...	...	...	—	—	—	—	—	Greenland
...	...	...	...	...	...	...	...	—	—	—	—	—	Grenada
...	...	...	...	...	...	...	...	—	—	—	—	—	Guadeloupe
...	—	100.0[5]	—	—	—	...	...	—	—	—	—	—	Guam
0.3	8	9.0	9	...	...	200	40	5	7	20	275	...	Guatemala
...	...	...	...	...	...	...	...	—	—	—	—	—	Guernsey
24[6]	...	...	...	...	...	...	...	—	—	—	—	—	Guinea
...	...	...	...	...	...	...	...	—	—	—	—	—	Guinea-Bissau
...	...	...	...	...	...	...	...	—	—	—	—	—	Guyana
...	...	...	...	...	...	...	...	—	—	—	—	—	Haiti
—	—	30.7[6]	—	—	—	...	...	—	3[6]	14	—	—	Honduras
...	—	81.5	—	—	—	...	...	—	—	—	—	—	Hong Kong
94	5,479	8.4	9,530	14.0[8]	86.0[8]	120	11	11	47	232	1,204	2,607	Hungary
...	...	...	...	...	...	...	...	—	—	—	—	—	Iceland
685	19,595	15.3	17,638	53.7	46.3	4,333	18	235	441	1,086	5,692	...	India
2,046	61,864	39.0	23,191	—	100.0	4,980	9	553	309	805	2,961	...	Indonesia
21,000	31,857	9.9	40,056	—	100.0[4]	93,000	69	1,341	343	1,242	9,800	...	Iran
3,341	3,426	29.4	3,170	...	...	112,000	511	219	207	348	5,075	...	Iraq
11	2,500	3.0	2,566	13.9[8]	86.1[8]	...	...	—	17	65	—	—	Ireland
...	—	...	...	...	...	...	...	—	...	—	—	—	Isle of Man
0.3	23	108.1	22	—	100.0	4	100	0.04	89	220	998	...	Israel
297	20,499	14.7[20]	49,513[20]	45.6[8]	54.4[8]	685	19	37	545[20]	2,262	3,851	11,348	Italy
—	—	36.5	—	—	—	...	...	—	6	36	10	...	Jamaica
30	2,192	40.8	58,029	61.3[8]	38.7[8]	50	10	5	1,637	4,989	406	...	Japan
...	...	...	...	...	...	...	...	—	—	—	—	—	Jersey
6	294	75.4	—	—	—	0.3	8	0.04	22	100	209	...	Jordan
1,800	5,500	...	9,588	...	...	...	...	169	87	427	4,350	22,300	Kazakstan
—	—	103.4	—	—	—	...	...	—	16	86	483	...	Kenya
...	...	...	...	...	...	...	...	—	—	—	—	—	Kiribati
...	...	...	...	...	...	...	...	—	16	71	37	...	Korea, North
—	—	31.2	8,013	...	...	...	...	—	562	2,211	455	...	Korea, South
1,498	5,975	59.1	5,970	25.0	75.0	96,500	128	752	44	824	917	...	Kuwait
...	34[7]	...	1,008	...	...	...	...	0.7	0.2	10	—	—	Kyrgyzstan
...	...	...	...	...	...	...	...	—	—	—	136	...	Laos
...	—	...	886	...	...	...	...	—	...	...	1,530	...	Latvia
—	—	2.7[15]	...	...	...	...	...	—	3[15]	38	72	...	Lebanon
—	—	[10]	—	...	...	...	...	—	[10]	—	—	—	Lesotho
—	—	50.5[21]	—	...	...	...	...	—	—	15	—	—	Liberia
1,311	6,298	13.1	4,910	...	...	29,500	58	512	113	348	4,826	...	Libya
—	—	[22]	[22]	...	...	...	...	—	[22]	—	—	—	Liechtenstein
...	...	9.0	1,871	...	...	...	...	1.2	27	240	105	...	Lithuania
...	—	33.1	570	48.0[8]	52.0[8]	...	...	—	[9]	—	48	...	Luxembourg
...	...	...	...	...	...	...	...	—	—	—	—	—	Macau
...	—	13.3	269[15]	...	...	...	...	—	1	51	—	—	Macedonia
2	—	33.6	—	...	...	...	...	—	1.5	15	—	—	Madagascar
...	—	—	—	—	—	...	...	—	—	—	—	—	Malaŵi
2,271	26,193	7.4	13,166	6.6	93.4	4,000	17	237	100	330	1,307	...	Malaysia
...	...	...	...	...	...	...	...	—	—	—	—	—	Maldives
...	...	...	...	...	...	...	...	—	—	—	—	—	Mali
—	...	—	...	...	...	...	...	—	—	—	—	—	Malta
...	...	...	...	...	...	...	...	—	—	...	—	—	Marshall Islands
—	—	153.9	...	...	...	...	...	—	6	16	—	—	Martinique
...	...	88.4	...	...	...	...	...	—	7	—	—	—	Mauritania
...	...	...	...	...	...	...	...	—	—	—	—	—	Mauritius
...	...	...	...	...	...	...	...	—	—	—	—	—	Mayotte
1,916	38,454	26.6	27,206	3.9[11]	96.1[11]	48,796	47	1,042	500	1,520	38,350	...	Mexico
...	...	...	...	...	...	...	...	—	—	...	—	—	Micronesia
...	—	...	2,612	...	...	...	...	—	52[5]	...	—	—	Moldova
...	...	[16]	[16]	...	...	...	...	—	[16]	—	—	—	Monaco
...	...	...	...	...	...	...	...	—	—	—	—	—	Mongolia
1.1	17	28.5	25	—	100.0	1.2	30	0.04	50	156	362	...	Morocco
57	—	—	—	...	...	...	...	—	—	...	595	...	Mozambique
311	1,430	0.9	1,359	—	100.0[4]	50	10	5	7	32	1,343	...	Myanmar (Burma)
85	—	[10]	—	...	...	...	...	—	[10]	—	—	—	Namibia
...	...	...	...	...	...	...	...	—	—	—	—	—	Nauru
...	—	—	—	—	—	...	...	—	—	—	—	—	Nepal

Energy (continued)

country	electricity												coal		
	installed capacity, 1994 ('000 kW)	production, 1994		power source, 1994			trade, 1994		consumption				reserves, latest ('000,000 metric tons)	pro-duction, 1994 ('000 metric tons)	con-sump-tion, 1994 ('000 metric tons)
		capacity ('000,000 kW-hr)	amount ('000,000 kW-hr)	fossil fuel (%)	hydro-power (%)	nuclear fuel (%)	exports ('000,000 kW-hr)	imports ('000,000 kW-hr)	amount, 1994 ('000,000 kW-hr)	per capita, 1994 (kW-hr)	resi-dential, 1994 (%)	non-resi-dential, 1994 (%)			
Netherlands, The	18,348	160,728	79,677	94.6	0.1	5.3	288	10,850	90,239	5,861	25.0[4]	75.0[4]	497	—	14,240
Netherlands Antilles	200	1,752	883	100.0	—	—	—	—	883	4,482	...	...	...	...	...
New Caledonia	253	2,216	1,170	70.5	29.5	—	—	—	1,170	6,573	...	...	2	—	165
New Zealand	7,520	65,875	32,416	24.7	71.8	3.5[14]	—	—	32,416	9,180	37.5[4]	62.5[4]	117	3,241	2,441
Nicaragua	457	4,003	1,740	51.4	18.7	29.9[14]	13	—	1,727	404	79.3	20.7	...	...	...
Niger	63	552	178	100.0	—	—	—	197	375	42	49.2	50.8	70	174	174
Nigeria	5,881	51,518	14,790	59.4	40.6	—	...	—	14,790	136	80.4[5]	19.6[5]	190	50	50
Northern Mariana Islands	114[6]	999[6]	...	...	...	—	...	...	...	...	...	...	...	...	...
Norway	27,498	240,882	113,389	0.5	99.5	—	4,968	4,835	113,256	26,205	27.0[2]	73.0[2]	4	301	914
Oman	1,744	15,277	7,856	100.0	—	—	—	—	7,856	3,782	...	...	...	...	...
Pakistan	13,169	115,360	57,147	65.1	34.0	0.9	—	—	57,147	418	66.1	33.9	734	3,534	4,628
Palau	62	543	203	85.2	14.8	—	—	—	203	857	...	...	—	—	—
Panama	957	8,383	3,500	31.7	68.3	—	—	33	3,533	1,367	83.2	16.8	...	—	52
Papua New Guinea	490	4,292	1,790	74.3	25.7	—	—	—	1,790	426	28.0	72.0	...	...	1
Paraguay	6,533	57,229	35,862	0.1	99.9	—	32,773	1	3,090	640	68.9	31.1	...	...	...
Peru	4,187	36,678	15,163	23.2	76.8	—	—	—	15,163	650	35.8[5]	64.2[5]	1,060	109	406
Philippines	7,640	66,926	26,425	53.9	24.1	22.0[14]	—	—	26,425	399	56.9	43.1	263	1,733	2,503
Poland	29,636	259,611	135,347	97.2	2.8	—	7,242	4,563	132,668	3,460	38.9	61.1	42,100	200,703	170,961
Portugal	8,831	77,360	31,380	65.7	34.1	0.2	1,369	2,257	32,268	3,283	36.4[2]	63.6[2]	36	147	5,225
Puerto Rico	4,465	39,113	17,880	98.2	1.8	—	—	—	17,880	4,904	31.0[11]	69.0[11]	...	—	172
Qatar	1,303	11,414	5,850	100.0	—	—	—	—	5,850	10,833	83.7	16.3	...	...	...
Réunion	299	2,619	1,137	55.9	44.1	—	—	—	1,137	1,766	...	...	...	...	...
Romania	22,060	193,246	55,136	76.3	23.7	—	1,065	1,790	55,861	2,437	25.7	74.3	3,118	40,547	44,893
Russia	214,687	1,880,658	875,914	68.6	20.2	11.2	44,147	23,651	855,418	5,805	37.7	62.3	241,000[23]	275,346	279,057
Rwanda	34	298	166	2.4	97.6	—	3	14	177	23	...	...	...	...	...
St. Kitts and Nevis	16	140	86	100.0	—	—	—	—	86	2,098	...	...	...	...	...
St. Lucia	22	193	112	100.0	—	—	—	—	112	794	26.6[3]	73.4[3]	...	...	...
St. Vincent and the Grenadines	14	123	64	67.2	32.8	—	—	—	64	577	45.3[4]	54.7[4]	...	...	...
Samoa	19	166	64	60.9	39.1	—	—	—	64	379	...	...	...	...	...
San Marino	[20]	[20]	[20]	[20]	[20]	[20]	[20]	[20]	[20]	[20]	...	...	...	[20]	[20]
São Tomé and Príncipe	6	53	16	50.0	50.0	—	—	—	16	123	...	...	...	...	...
Saudi Arabia	20,900	183,084	66,760	100.0	—	—	—	—	66,760	3,826	69.3[19]	30.7[19]	...	...	...
Senegal	231	2,024	769	100.0	—	—	—	—	769	95	...	...	...	...	...
Seychelles	28	245	126	100.0	—	—	—	—	126	1,726	32.0	68.0	...	...	...
Sierra Leone	126	1,104	237	100.0	—	—	—	—	237	54	...	...	...	—	—
Singapore	4,513	39,534	20,676	100.0	—	—	91	—	20,585	7,297	48.0[5]	52.0[5]	...	—	1
Slovakia	7,115	62,327	24,740	32.3	18.6	49.1	2,099	1,260	23,901	4,482	...	...	228	2,363	11,161
Slovenia	2,524	22,110	12,630	36.6	26.9	36.5	2,382	448	10,696	5,508	18.0[5]	82.0[5]	...	4,854	5,018
Solomon Islands	12	105	30	100.0	—	—	—	—	30	82	69.4[5]	30.6[5]	...	...	...
Somalia	70	613	259	100.0	—	—	—	—	259	29	...	...	...	...	...
South Africa	26,739[10]	234,234[10]	183,790[10]	94.3[10]	0.5[10]	5.2[10]	2,600[10]	100	181,290[10]	3,913[10]	49.1[10]	50.9[10]	55,333	183,581[10]	140,581[10]
Spain	44,444	389,329	161,502	47.7	18.1	34.2	3,251	5,106	163,357	4,129	16.7[2]	83.2[2]	1,450	29,556	42,808
Sri Lanka	1,557	13,639	4,386	6.8	93.2	—	—	—	4,386	242	60.2	39.8	...	—	1[6]
Sudan, The	500	4,380	1,333	29.4	70.6	—	—	—	1,333	49	...	...	...	—	—
Suriname	425	3,723	1,683	15.8	84.2	—	—	—	1,683	4,026	...	...	...	—	—
Swaziland	[10]	[10]	[10]	[10]	[10]	[10]	[10]	[10]	[10]	[10]	...	...	1,115	[10]	[10]
Sweden	35,889	314,388	142,889	7.2	41.5	51.3	6,419	6,680	143,150	16,382	26.4[2]	73.6[2]	1	...	3,305
Switzerland	16,405[22]	143,708[22]	65,636[22]	2.0[22]	60.9[22]	37.1[22]	28,093[22]	16,250[22]	53,793[22]	7,512[22]	26.6[8]	73.4[8]	...	—	229[22]
Syria	4,157	36,415	14,800	54.0	46.0	—	—	—	14,800	923	21.2[8]	78.8[8]	...	—	—
Taiwan	20,983	183,811	110,276	61.6	8.0	30.4	—	—	98,561	4,665	31.9[5]	68.1[5]	99	285	...
Tajikistan	4,443	38,921	17,000	3.5	96.5	...	5,800	4,900	16,100	2,714	...	...	...	140	140
Tanzania	439	3,846	912	31.1	68.9	—	—	—	912	32	...	...	200	4	4
Thailand	15,838	138,741	74,452	93.9	6.1	—	58	884	75,278	1,294	53.7	46.3	999	17,095	17,198
Togo	34	298	93	94.6	5.4	—	—	315	408	102	...	...	...	...	...
Tonga	7	61	29	100.0	—	—	—	—	29	296	...	...	...	...	...
Trinidad and Tobago	1,150	10,074	3,978	100.0	—	—	—	—	3,978	3,079	36.7	63.3	...	—	—
Tunisia	1,414	12,387	6,473	99.0	1.0	—	122	135	6,486	743	15.6	84.4	—	9	31
Turkey	20,858	182,716	78,322	60.8	39.1	0.1[14]	570	31	77,783	1,280	14.2[11]	85.8[11]	7,148	54,342	60,359
Turkmenistan	3,950	34,602	10,496	100.0	0.0	—	3,690	1,040	7,846	1,957	...	...	...	...	...
Tuvalu	...	...	...	...	...	...	...	...	...	...	...	...	...	...	...
Uganda	162	1,419	795	0.9	99.1	—	114	—	681	33	...	...	...	...	...
Ukraine	54,243	475,169	209,100	61.2	0.0	38.8	13,400	12,400	208,100	4,044	...	...	...	94,400	96,867
United Arab Emirates	5,290	46,340	18,870	100.0	—	—	—	—	18,870	10,140	...	...	...	...	...
United Kingdom	68,937	603,888	325,383	70.8	2.0	27.2	—	16,887	342,270	5,870	35.4[8]	64.6[8]	2,500	47,717	80,582
United States	769,989	6,745,104	3,268,250	71.1	8.6	20.3	7,592	52,230	3,312,888	12,711	34.9[8]	65.1[8]	240,558	937,580	843,873
Uruguay	2,055	18,002	7,617	2.0	98.0	—	1,675	15	5,957	1,881	67.2	32.8	...	—	—
Uzbekistan	11,422	100,057	47,800	85.0	15.0	...	15,200	14,800	47,400	2,121	...	...	...	3,800	4,200
Vanuatu	11	96	29	100.0	—	—	—	—	29	176	...	...	...	...	...
Venezuela	18,975	166,221	73,116	29.7	70.3	—	320	—	72,796	3,405	45.7	54.3	417	4,741	354
Vietnam	5,320	46,603	12,020	15.8	79.0	5.2[14]	—	—	12,020	165	36.4[3]	63.6[3]	150	5,600	4,000
Virgin Islands (U.S.)	316	2,768	1,057	100.0	—	—	—	—	1,057	10,163	40.2[4]	59.8[4]	...	—	245
West Bank	...	...	...	...	...	...	...	...	...	...	...	...	...	...	...
Western Sahara	56	491	87	100.0	—	—	—	—	87	320	...	...	...	...	...
Yemen	810	7,096	1,958	100.0	—	—	—	—	1,958	141	...	...	1[5]	...	...
Yugoslavia	11,779	103,184	35,328	68.5	31.5	—	—	—	35,328	3,282	26.0[5]	74.0[5]	16,570[24]	38,351	38,401
Zambia	2,436	21,339	7,785	0.5	99.5	—	1,500	20	6,305	686	31.7	68.3	55	380	375
Zimbabwe	2,148	18,816	7,334	67.7	32.3	—	...	1,716	9,050	823	52.8	47.2	734	5,469	5,614

natural gas						crude petroleum							country
published proven reserves, 1997 ('000,000,-000 cu m)	production		consumption			reserves, 1997		production, 1996 ('000,000 barrels)	consumption, 1994 ('000,000 barrels)	refining capacity, 1997 ('000 barrels per day)	pipelines (latest)		
	natural gas, 1995 ('000,000 cu m)	manufactured gas, 1994 (% of total gas consumption)	amount, 1994 ('000,000 cu m)	residential, 1990 (%)	nonresidential, 1990 (%)	published proven ('000,000 barrels)	years to exhaust proven reserves				length (km)	traffic ('000,000 metric ton-km)	
1,815	78,778	18.5	48,841	46.8[4]	53.4[4]	88	4	22	377	1,187	1,383	5,503	Netherlands, The
—	—	119.6	...	...	...	...	...	—	100	525	—	—	Netherlands Antilles
...	...	...	...	...	...	...	...	—	—	—	—	—	New Caledonia
68	4,763	9.0	4,442	4.8[4]	95.2[4]	135	10	13	37	91	160	...	New Zealand
—	—	83.9	—	—	—	...	...	—	4	17	56	...	Nicaragua
...	—	—	—	—	—	...	...	—	...	—	—	—	Niger
2,965	4,131	0.7	9,798	—	100.0	15,521	21	735	84	433	5,042	...	Nigeria
...	...	...	...	...	...	...	...	—	...	...	—	—	Northern Mariana Islands
1,352	27,663	36.3	4,051	...	...	11,234	10	1,126	110	307	53	11,019	Norway
850	4,361	1.0	6,666	...	...	5,138	16	322	27	85	1,300	...	Oman
623	17,840	0.6	16,668	41.5	58.5	208	10	20	50	137	1,135	...	Pakistan
—	—	—	...	...	...	—	—	—	...	...	—	—	Palau
—	—	25.6	60	—	—	...	...	—	9	60	130	...	Panama
42	99	...	79	—	—	275	7	39	—	—	—	—	Papua New Guinea
—	—	6.1	...	...	...	...	...	—	2	8	—	—	Paraguay
200	1,303	45.5	191	61.4	38.6	808	18	44	54	182	800	...	Peru
109	—	54.3	—	—	—	213	533	0.4	91	323	357	...	Philippines
149	4,593	31.3	10,908	...	...	40	20	2	100	352	2,346	11,932	Poland
—	—	61.5	...	...	...	...	...	—	99	304	80	...	Portugal
—	—	166.7	...	...	...	...	...	—	44	134	—	—	Puerto Rico
7,079	13,499	10.0	13,500	—	100.0	3,700	21	175	21	58	235	...	Qatar
...	...	...	...	...	...	...	...	—	...	—	—	—	Réunion
396	21,300	10.4	19,792	...	...	1,606	32	50	113	559	4,229	2,558	Romania
48,334	582,988	4.7	327,275	...	...	155,146	71	2,183	1,375	6,733	63,000	1,899,000	Russia
57	0.2[8]	—	0.2	...	...	...	...	—	—	—	—	—	Rwanda
...	...	...	...	...	...	...	...	—	—	—	—	—	St. Kitts and Nevis
...	...	...	...	...	...	...	...	—	—	—	—	—	St. Lucia
...	...	...	...	...	...	...	...	—	—	—	—	—	St. Vincent and the Grenadines
...	...	...	...	...	...	...	...	...	...	—	—	—	Samoa
...	...	[20]	[20]	...	...	...	...	—	[20]	—	—	—	San Marino
...	...	...	...	...	...	...	...	—	—	—	—	—	São Tomé and Príncipe
5,355	37,718	47.0	37,700	9.8[8]	90.2[8]	261,500	88	3,039	589	1,651	6,550	...	Saudi Arabia
—	—	14.3	...	...	...	...	...	—	6	17	—	—	Senegal
...	...	...	...	...	...	...	...	—	—	—	—	—	Seychelles
—	...	...	...	...	...	...	...	—	2	10	—	—	Sierra Leone
—	—	353.1	—	—	—	...	...	—	410	1,157	—	—	Singapore
15	241[7]	15.3	5,101	...	...	9	23	0.4	33	115	...	...	Slovakia
4	11[7]	...	644	...	...	7	700	0.01	3	12	290	128	Slovenia
...	—	—	—	—	—	...	...	—	—	—	—	—	Solomon Islands
6	—	...	...	...	...	...	...	—	...	10	15	...	Somalia
25	—	67.0[10]	1,896	...	...	27	7	4	125[10]	414	2,679	...	South Africa
17	178	35.0	7,755	...	...	30	5	6	408	1,296	2,059	5,266	Spain
—	—	54.0	—	—	—	...	...	—	15	48	62	...	Sri Lanka
85	—	54.5	...	...	...	300	600	0.5	8	22	815	...	Sudan, The
—	...	...	...	...	...	74	25	3	1.4	—	—	—	Suriname
...	...	[10]	...	...	...	...	...	...	[10]	—	—	—	Swaziland
—	—	38.8	763	...	...	...	...	—	127	427	—	—	Sweden
—	—	15.4[22]	2,432[22]	38.3[8]	61.7[8]	...	...	...	35[22]	132	314	1,265	Switzerland
235	4,412	11.7	2,050	...	...	2,500	11	220	85	246	1,819	...	Syria
76	841	...	...	...	...	4	10	0.4	...	770	615	...	Taiwan
...	34[7]	...	1,212	...	...	...	...	0.7	1	...	—	—	Tajikistan
21	—	100.0	—	...	...	...	...	...	4	16	982	...	Tanzania
202	10,477	13.7	9,513	—	100.0	295	13	22	138	558	67	...	Thailand
—	...	...	...	...	...	...	...	...	...	—	—	—	Togo
...	...	...	...	...	...	...	...	...	...	—	—	—	Tonga
350	6,071	3.5	5,962	1.8	98.2	551	12	47	36	245	1,051	...	Trinidad and Tobago
68	337	12.7	786	9.1	90.9	308	10	32	13	34	883	...	Tunisia
9	201	30.7	5,046	...	...	260	10	25	176	683	4,059	2,994	Turkey
2,900	30,100	...	8,332	...	...	3,000	94	32	30	237	250	...	Turkmenistan
...	...	...	...	...	...	...	...	...	...	—	—	—	Tuvalu
...	...	...	...	...	...	...	...	...	...	—	—	—	Uganda
1,100	16,900	0.6	75,467	...	...	...	...	25	138	1,246	3,930	38,402	Ukraine
5,686	25,429	22.3	21,017	...	...	93,800	116	809	74	213	830	...	United Arab Emirates
700	71,144	13.0	79,391	52.7[8]	47.3[8]	4,517	5	961	629	1,941	3,926	10,388	United Kingdom
4,676	559,261	16.9	591,754	33.4[11]	66.6[11]	22,351	9	2,364	5,024	15,459	276,000	843,586	United States
—	—	11.7	—	—	—	...	...	...	3[15]	40	—	—	Uruguay
1,900	45,300	...	38,564	...	...	...	...	63	44	175	290	200	Uzbekistan
...	...	...	...	...	...	...	...	...	...	—	—	—	Vanuatu
4,010	25,406	18.6	24,675	9.1	90.9	64,878	60	1,079	380	1,177	6,850	...	Venezuela
142	697	...	3	...	...	600	10	62	0.3	—	150	...	Vietnam
—	—	104.2	...	...	...	...	...	...	117	545	—	—	Virgin Islands (U.S.)
...	...	...	...	...	...	...	...	...	...	—	—	—	West Bank
...	...	...	...	...	...	...	...	...	...	—	—	—	Western Sahara
479	...	100.0	...	...	...	4,000	33	123	26	120	676	—	Yemen
45	765	0.9	1,630	...	...	78	11	7	10	167	545	...	Yugoslavia
—	—	100.0	—	—	—	...	...	...	4	25	1,724	...	Zambia
...	—	88.7	—	—	—	...	...	...	...	—	212	...	Zimbabwe

[1]Estimated reserves in place. [2]1981. [3]1985. [4]1984. [5]1990. [6]1992. [7]1994. [8]1983. [9]Belgium includes Luxembourg. [10]South Africa includes Botswana, Lesotho, Namibia, and Swaziland. [11]1982. [12]1991. [13]Data refer to former Czechoslovakia. [14]Geothermally generated electricity. [15]1993. [16]France includes Monaco. [17]Transportation and industry only; excludes agricultural, commercial, and public-service sectors. [18]Data refer to former West Germany only. [19]1988. [20]Italy includes San Marino. [21]1989. [22]Switzerland includes Liechtenstein. [23]Data refer to former U.S.S.R. [24]Data refer to Yugoslavia as constituted prior to 1991.

Transportation

This table presents data on the transportation infrastructure of the various countries and dependencies of the world and on their commercial passenger and cargo traffic. Most states have roads and airports, with services corresponding to the prevailing level of economic development. A number of states, however, lack railroads or inland waterways because of either geographic constraints or lack of development capital and technical expertise. Pipelines, one of the oldest means of bulk transport if aqueducts are considered, are today among the most narrowly developed transportation modes worldwide for shipment of bulk materials. Because the principal contemporary application of pipeline technology is to facilitate the shipment of hydrocarbon liquids and gases, coverage of pipelines will be found in the "Energy" table. It is, however, also true that pipelines now find increasing application for slurries of coal or other raw materials.

While the United Nations' *Statistical Yearbook* and *Monthly Bulletin of Statistics* provide much data on infrastructure and traffic and have established basic definitions and classifications for transportation statistics, the number of countries covered is limited. Several commercial publications maintain substantial databases and publishing programs for their particular areas of interest: highway and vehicle statistics are provided by the International Road Federation's annual *World Road Statistics;* the International Union of Railways' *International Railway Statistics* and Jane's *World Railways* provide similar data for railways; Lloyd's *Register of Shipping Statistical Tables* summarizes the world's merchant marine; the *Official Airline Guide,* the International Civil Aviation Organization's *Digest of Statistics: Commercial Air Carriers,* and the International Air Transport Association's *World Air Transport Statistics* have also been used to supplement and update data collected by the UN. Because several of these agencies are commercially or insurance-oriented, their data tend to be more complete, accurate, and timely than those of intergovernmental organizations, which depend on periodic responses to questionnaires or publication of results in official sources. All of these international sources have been extensively supplemented by national statistical sources to provide additional data. Such diversity of sources, however, imposes limitations on the comparability of the statistics from country to country because the basis and completeness of data collection and the frequency and timeliness of analysis and publication may vary greatly. Data shown in italic are from 1992 or earlier.

The categories adopted in the table also have special problems of comparability. Total road length is subject to wide international variation of interpretation, as "roads" can mean anything from mere tracks to highly developed highways. Each country also has individual classifications that differ according to climate, availability of road-building materials, traffic patterns, administrative responsibility, and so on. "Paved roads," by contrast, is a much more tightly definable category, but the proportion of paved to total roads may be distorted by the less comparable total road statistics. Automobile and truck and bus fleet statistics, which are usually

Transportation

country	roads and motor vehicles (latest)								railroads (latest)					
	roads			motor vehicles			cargo		track length		traffic			
	length		paved (per-cent)	auto-mobiles	trucks and buses	persons per vehicle	short ton-mi ('000,-000)	metric ton-km ('000,-000)	mi	km	passengers		cargo	
	mi	km									passen-ger-mi ('000,000)	passen-ger-km ('000,000)	short ton-mi ('000,000)	metric ton-km ('000,000)
Afghanistan	13,000	21,000	13	31,000	34,000	332	*1,993*	*2,910*	16	25	...	...	...	...
Albania	9,631	15,500	30	58,682	34,441	34	55	80	419	674	139	223	0.3	0.5
Algeria	63,643	102,424	69	871,000	566,000	20	*9,589*	*14,000*	2,965[2]	4,772[2]	1,568	2,524	1,644	2,400
American Samoa	217	350	43	4,628	489	11	...	...	—	—	—	—	—	—
Andorra	167	269	74	35,941	4,186	1.6	...	...	—	—	—	—	—	—
Angola	45,128	72,626	25	197,000	26,000	52	...	...	*1,739*[2]	*2,798*[2]	*203*	*326*	*1,178*	*1,720*
Antigua and Barbuda	721	1,161	33	13,588	1,342	4.3	...	...	—	—	—	—	—	—
Argentina	134,278	216,100	29	4,665,329	1,181,569	5.9	...	...	21,015[2]	33,821[2]	4,014	6,460	5,214	7,613
Armenia	4,797	7,720	97	1,590	5,950	499	53	78	515	829	196	316	3,345	4,884
Aruba	*236*	*380*	*100*	35,679	935	2.2	...	...	—	—	—	—	—	—
Australia	556,145	895,030	39	8,370,000	2,640,300	1.6	*60,416*	*88,206*	22,385[2, 8]	36,026[2, 8]	7,152	11,510	67,593	98,684
Austria	80,792	130,023	100	3,593,588	300,042	2.1	7,362	10,749	3,524	5,672	6,509[8]	10,476[8]	9,526[8]	13,908[8]
Azerbaijan	35,897	57,770	94	289,000	88,800	20	1,190	1,740	1,305	2,100	516	830	1,055	1,540
Bahamas, The	1,522	2,450	57	46,089	11,858	4.7	...	...	—	—	—	—	—	—
Bahrain	1,762	2,835	75	141,901	29,584	3.4	...	...	—	—	—	—	—	—
Bangladesh	104,709	168,513	9	82,198	104,860	634	...	...	1,681[2]	2,706[2]	2,508	4,037	521	760
Barbados	1,000	1,610	95	43,711	10,583	4.9	...	...	—	—	—	—	—	—
Belarus	32,030	51,547	99	955,526	9,289	11	6,534	9,539	3,480	5,600	7,770	12,505	17,473	25,510
Belgium	88,579	142,555	97	4,339,231	431,376	2.1	18,800	27,500	2,093[2]	3,368[2]	4,199	6,757	5,334	7,787
Belize	1,721	2,770	19	10,667	6,108	12	...	...	—	—	—	—	—	—
Benin	5,257	8,460	31	22,200	12,400	160	...	...	359	578	66	107	173	253
Bermuda	149	240	100	20,700	4,000	2.5	...	...	—	—	—	—	—	—
Bhutan	1,998	3,216	*79*	*2,590*	*1,367*	*348*	...	...	—	—	—	—	—	—
Bolivia	34,478	55,487	5	213,666	133,984	21	*1,133*	*1,654*	2,295[2]	3,694[2]	216.8	348.9	521.9	761.9
Bosnia and Herzegovina	*13,153*	*21,168*	*54*	*438,080*	*50,578*	*8.9*	*2,708*	*3,954*	*634*	*1,021*	*344*	*554*	*1,333*	*1,946*
Botswana	11,388	18,327	25	27,058	42,696	20	...	...	603	971	53	86	1,171	1,710
Brazil	1,205,000	1,939,000	9	12,000,000	3,160,689	10	*178,359*	*260,400*	18,578[2]	29,899[2]	9,009	14,498	93,455	136,442
Brunei	1,527	2,457	59	141,371	16,557	1.9	...	...	12[15]	19[15]	—	—	...	...
Bulgaria	23,190	37,320	92	1,647,571	204,950	4.5	6,510	9,510	4,043	6,507	3,147	5,065	5,171	7,549
Burkina Faso	7,771	12,506	16	16,800	17,222	304	...	...	386[2]	622[2]	126	202	31	45
Burundi	8,997	14,480	7	16,800	15,000	186	...	...	—	—	—	—	—	—
Cambodia	7,643	12,300	34	42,210	9,005	197	1,360	1,990	380	612	*33.6*	*54.0*	*6.9*	*10.0*
Cameroon	21,300	34,300	13	92,200	60,000	91	*175*	*255*	686[2]	1,104[2]	247	398	405	592
Canada	634,400	1,021,000	35	14,280,000	3,895,600	1.6	*29,033*	*42,388*	44,182	71,104	889	1,430	185,641	271,032
Cape Verde	680	1,095	78	6,479	2,099	43	...	...	—	—	—	—	—	—
Central African Republic	14,795	23,810	2	9,500	7,000	195	62	90	—	—	—	—	—	—
Chad	20,319	32,700	1	9,630	14,360	265	580	850	—	—	—	—	—	—
Chile	49,550	79,750	14	888,645	469,142	10	...	...	4,084[2]	6,572[2]	428	689	1,595	2,329
China	718,931	1,157,009	90	4,179,000	5,213,270	128	321,570	469,490	45,319	72,934	220,319	354,570	881,539	1,287,025
Colombia	66,238	106,600	12	1,150,000	550,000	21	*4,265*	*6,227*	*2,007*[2]	*3,230*[2]	*9.6*	*15.5*	*166.4*	*242.9*
Comoros	544	875	76	7,080	4,870	41	...	...	—	—	—	—	—	—
Congo, Dem. Rep. of the	95,708	154,027	...	762,000	550,000	33	...	...	*3,162*	*5,088*	*360*[16]	*580*[16]	1,258[16]	1,836[16]
Congo, Rep. of the	7,929	12,760	10	36,100	15,600	48	*46*	*67*	*494*	*795*	141	227	152	222
Costa Rica	22,121	35,600	17	259,000	132,940	8.5	2,000	2,900	590[2]	950[2]	3.7	5.9	45.8	66.8
Côte d'Ivoire	31,168	50,160	10	271,000	150,000	34	...	...	405[2]	651[2]	117[19]	189[19]	182[19]	266[19]
Croatia	16,732	26,928	81	710,910	77,394	6.0	394	575	1,676	2,699	598	962	1,071	1,563
Cuba	16,839	27,100	56	20,000	33,000	205	*2,482*	*3,623*	*3,033*	*4,881*	*1,880*	*3,025*	*937*	*1,368*
Cyprus	6,307	10,150	57	219,749	103,852	2.6	...	...	—	—	—	—	—	—
Czech Republic	77,528	124,770	13	3,113,476	204,238	3.1	14,167	20,684	5,860	9,430	4,985	8,023	17,439	25,468
Denmark	44,378	71,420	100	1,729,405	288,464	2.6	7,300	10,600	1,780	2,865	3,004	4,834	1,360	1,985
Djibouti	1,796	2,890	13	8,550	1,870	56	...	...	*66*	*106*	173	279	187	273
Dominica	475	765	50	2,770	2,839	13	...	...	—	—	—	—	—	—
Dominican Republic	7,643	12,300	49	209,000	141,400	21	...	...	1,083[2]	1,743[2]	...	...	...	...
Ecuador	26,785	43,106	18	395,000	58,650	25	2,315	3,380	600[2]	966[2]	17	27	6	9
Egypt	36,000[23]	58,000[23]	78[23]	1,280,000	423,300	35	21,500	31,400	2,989	4,810	29,821	47,992	1,600	2,336

based upon registration, are relatively accurate, though some countries round off figures, and unregistered vehicles may cause substantial undercount. There is also inconsistent classification of vehicle types; in some countries a vehicle may serve variously as an automobile, a truck, or a bus, or even as all three on certain occasions. Relatively few countries collect and maintain commercial road traffic statistics.

Data on national railway systems are generally given for railway track length rather than the length of routes, which may be multitracked. Siding tracks usually are not included, but some countries fail to distinguish them. The United States data include only class 1 railways, which account for about 94 percent of total track length. Passenger traffic is usually calculated from tickets sold to fare-paying passengers. Such statistics are subject to distortion if there are large numbers of nonpaying passengers, such as military personnel, or if season tickets are sold and not all the allowed journeys are utilized. Railway cargo traffic is calculated by weight hauled multiplied by the length of the journey. Changes in freight load during the journey should be accounted for but sometimes are not, leading to discrepancies.

Merchant fleet and tonnage statistics collected by Lloyd's registry service for vessels over 100 gross tons are quite accurate. Cargo statistics, however, reflect the port and customs requirements of each country and the reporting rules of each country's merchant marine authority (although these, increasingly, reflect the recommendations of the International Maritime Organization); often, however, they are only estimates based on customs declarations and the count of vessels entered and cleared. Even when these elements are reported consistently, further uncertainties may be introduced because of ballast, bunkers, ships' stores, or transshipped goods included in the data.

Airport data are based on scheduled flights reported in the commercial *Official Airline Guide* and are both reliable and current. The comparability of civil air traffic statistics suffers from differing characteristics of the air transportation systems of different countries; data for an entire country may be two to three years behind those for a single airport.

Outside of Europe, where standardization of data on inland waterways is necessitated by the volume of international traffic, comparability of national data declines markedly. Calculations as to both the length of a country's waterway system (or route length of river, lake, and coastal traffic) and the makeup of its stock of commercially significant vessels (those for which data will be collected) are largely determined by the nature and use of the country's hydrographic net—its seasonality, relief profile, depth, access to potential markets—and inevitably differ widely from country to country. Data for coastal or island states may refer to scheduled coastwise or interisland traffic.

merchant marine (latest)				air					canals and inland waterways (latest)				country
fleet (vessels over 100 gross tons)	total dead-weight tonnage ('000)	international cargo (latest)		airports with sched-uled flights, 1996	traffic (latest)				length		cargo		
					passengers		cargo		mi	km	short ton-mi ('000,000)	metric ton-km ('000,000)	
		loaded metric tons ('000)	off-loaded metric tons ('000)		passenger-mi ('000,000)	passenger-km ('000,000)	short ton-mi ('000,000)	metric ton-km ('000,000)					
—	—	—	—	3	122[1]	197[1]	7.5[1]	11[1]	750	1,200	...	...	Afghanistan
24	81.0	1,065	664	1	...	...	...	...	27	43	24	35	Albania
149	1,093.4	57,607	14,284	28	1,643[3]	2,644[3]	10.1[3]	14.8[3]	...	...	...	...	Algeria
3	0.1	380	581	3	...	...	...	...	...	...	...	...	American Samoa
—	—	—	—	—	—	—	—	—	—	—	—	—	Andorra
113	123.5	23,288	1,261	17[4]	589[5]	948[5]	77[5]	113[5]	805	1,295	...	...	Angola
292	997.4	28	113	2	140	225	14	20	...	...	...	...	Antigua and Barbuda
423	1,173.1	55,572	17,316	39[4]	7,323[6]	11,785[6]	911[6]	1,330[6]	6,800	11,000	19,326	28,215	Argentina
...	...	...	...	1[4]	3,453	5,557	34	49	...	...	...	...	Armenia
7	7	...	...	1	...	...	...	...	...	...	...	...	Aruba
695	3,857.3	13,536	22,740	400	44,687	71,917	1,257	1,836	5,200	8,368	66,439	97,000	Australia
26	208.5	1,311	5,122	6	4,701	7,566	120.3	175.6	277	446	1,247	1,820	Austria
...	...	...	...	1	1,259	2,026	34	49	...	...	3,600	5,300	Azerbaijan
1,061	33,081.7	5,920	5,705	23	119	191	0.01	0.02	...	...	...	...	Bahamas, The
87	192.5	13,285	3,512	1	1,714[9]	2,759[9]	72.5[9]	105.8[9]	...	...	...	...	Bahrain
301	566.8	1,848	10,608	8[4]	1,763	2,838	82	121	5,000	8,046	...	...	Bangladesh
37	84.0	206	538	1	93[10]	149[10]	0.8[11]	1.1[11]	...	...	...	...	Barbados
...	18,373.0	...	...	2	864	1,390	7	10	...	...	91	133	Belarus
232	218.5	291,540	292,476	2	5,599	9,011	221.9	323.9	1,269	2,043	14,600	21,300	Belgium
32	45.7	178	241	9[4]	...	...	...	...	513	825	...	...	Belize
12	0.2	339	1,738	1[4]	139.6[12]	224.7[12]	11.2[12]	16.4[12]	...	...	...	...	Benin
94	5,206.5	130	470	1	...	...	...	...	...	...	...	...	Bermuda
—	—	—	—	1[4]	29	46	...	...	—	—	—	—	Bhutan
1	15.8	...	...	14[4]	912	1,468	31.7	46.2	6,214	10,000	90	132	Bolivia
...	...	...	...	1	...	...	...	...	...	...	...	...	Bosnia and Herzegovina
—	—	—	—	4	36.3[13]	58.4[13]	0.3[13]	0.5[13]	...	...	...	...	Botswana
635	9,348.3	168,026	52,570	139[14]	22,471	36,164	1,118	1,632	31,069	50,000	56,030	81,803	Brazil
51	349.7	13,554	1,325	1	1,685	2,712	74	108	130	209	...	...	Brunei
222	1,938.2	5,290	20,080	3	1,765	2,840	24.1	35.2	292	470	502	733	Bulgaria
—	—	—	—	2	134.9	217.2	23.4	34.2	...	...	...	...	Burkina Faso
1	0.4	35	188	1[4]	1.2	2.0	...	...	...	...	...	...	Burundi
3	3.8	11	95	8[4]	...	...	...	...	2,300	3,700	51	75	Cambodia
47	39.8	1,260	2,328	5	196	315	27	39	1,299	2,090	...	...	Cameroon
1,185	2,896.8	176,667	83,287	301	35,364	56,913	4,824	7,043	1,860	3,000	...	...	Canada
42	30.9	144	299	9[4]	106	171	13.2	19.2	...	...	...	...	Cape Verde
—	—	53	126	1[4]	139.6[12]	224.7[12]	11.2[12]	16.4[12]	500	800	161	235	Central African Republic
—	—	—	—	4	138	223	10.5	15.3	1,240	2,000	...	...	Chad
392	854.9	21,768	13,464	23[4]	3,935	6,333	923	1,348	450	725	5,629	8,218	Chile
2,390	20,658.0	105,852	101,688	113	42,334	68,130	1,527	2,230	68,700	110,562	1,202,226	1,755,220	China
101	403.0	159,084	456,636	43[4]	2,837	4,565	662	966	8,900	14,300	7,038	10,276	Colombia
6	3.6	12	107	2[4]	1.9	3.0	...	...	...	...	...	...	Comoros
27	30.7	2,395	1,453	12	135[17]	218[17]	29[17]	42[17]	9,300	15,000	678	990	Congo, Dem. Rep. of the
22	10.8	8,987	736	5	139[12]	223[12]	10.5	15.3	696	1,120	...	...	Congo, Rep. of the
24	8.4	2,643	4,054	14	1,135[18]	1,827[18]	30.0[18]	43.8[18]	454	730	...	...	Costa Rica
51	98.6	4,173	7,228	11	139[20]	223[20]	10.5[20]	15.3[20]	609	980	...	...	Côte d'Ivoire
203	140.9	3,948	7,776	5	306	492	2.4	3.5	488	785	160	230	Croatia
393	924.6	8,092	15,440	14	1,648	2,652	31.2	45.6	149	240	2,085	3,044	Cuba
1,416	36,198.1	2,232	5,028	2	1,588	2,556	26	38	...	...	...	...	Cyprus
22[21]	446.2[21]	...	...	2	1,469	2,364	16.0	23.4	295	475	221	322	Czech Republic
456	7,589.1	20,284	37,314	13	3,340[22]	5,376[22]	117[22]	171[22]	259	417	1,100	1,600	Denmark
10	4.1	414	958	1	42	67	4	6	...	...	...	...	Djibouti
7	3.2	103	181	2	...	...	...	...	...	...	...	...	Dominica
28	10.4	2,550	4,182	7[4]	145	234	1.7	2.5	...	...	...	...	Dominican Republic
154	504.1	11,783	1,958	14	876	1,410	111	162	932	1,500	...	...	Ecuador
444	1,685.2	14,808	22,860	11[4]	5,432	8,742	136	198	2,175	3,500	580	850	Egypt

Transportation (continued)

country	roads and motor vehicles (latest)								railroads (latest)					
	roads			motor vehicles			cargo		track length		traffic			
	length		paved (per-cent)	auto-mobiles	trucks and buses	persons per vehicle	short ton-mi ('000,-000)	metric ton-km ('000,-000)	mi	km	passengers		cargo	
	mi	km									passen-ger-mi ('000,000)	passen-ger-km ('000,000)	short ton-mi ('000,000)	metric ton-km ('000,000)
El Salvador	7,655	12,320	14	102,000	159,700	21	...	...	349[2]	562[2]	3.4	5.5	20.3	29.6
Equatorial Guinea	1,667	2,682	19	6,500	4,000	37	...	...	—	—	—	—	—	—
Eritrea	2,442	3,930	21	5,350	...	...	...	...	...	...	...	...	...	...
Estonia	9,316	14,992	54	383,444	72,607	3.3	1,061	1,549	636	1,024	262	421	2,634	3,846
Ethiopia	17,622	28,360	15	45,559	20,462	842	...	...	*486*[24]	*782*[24]	172	277	86	126
Faroe Islands	285	458	...	11,528	2,895	3.0	...	...	—	—	—	—	—	—
Fiji	3,200	5,100	20	49,712	33,928	9.4	...	...	370[15]	595[15]	...	...	...	...
Finland	48,294	77,722	63	1,900,855	260,115	2.4	15,900	23,200	3,641[2]	5,859[2]	1,626	2,616	6,551	9,564
France	504,987	812,700	*92*	25,100,000	5,005,000	1.9	104,500	152,500	19,847[2]	31,940[2]	34,467	55,470	32,466	47,400
French Guiana	*706*	*1,137*	*40*	*27,700*	*10,400*	*3.5*	...	...	—	—	—	—	—	—
French Polynesia	584	940	42	*38,900*	*16,500*	*3.9*	...	...	—	—	—	—	—	—
Gabon	4,743	7,633	8	23,800	15,700	29	...	...	415	668	*21*	*34*	*126*	*184*
Gambia, The	1,640	2,640	35	7,950	8,240	72	...	...	—	—	—	—	—	—
Gaza Strip	...	...	...	21,206	4,639	29	...	...	—	—	—	—	—	—
Georgia	13,049	21,000	94	441,828	50,220	11	67	98	983	1,583	792	1,274	705	1,030
Germany	404,325	650,700	99	40,499,442	2,336,760	1.9	138,975	202,900	54,994	88,504	39,830	64,100	45,649	66,646
Ghana	23,339	37,561	25	86,200	130,000	80	*873*	*1,275*	592[2]	953[2]	73.1	117.7	93.9	137.1
Gibraltar	27	43	100	18,404	1,064	1.4	...	...	—	—	—	—	—	—
Greece	72,350	116,440	92	2,204,761	908,423	3.4	11,400	16,700	1,537[2]	2,474[2]	869	1,399	210	307
Greenland	50	80	...	1,944	1,039	19	...	...	—	—	—	—	—	—
Grenada	700	1,127	51	*4,739*	*3,068*	*12*	...	...	—	—	—	—	—	—
Guadeloupe	2,000	3,200	*80*	*94,700*	*36,000*	*3.1*	...	...	—	—	—	—	—	—
Guam	550	885	76	74,728	30,739	1.4	...	...	—	—	—	—	—	—
Guatemala	7,950	12,795	28	102,000	96,800	52	...	...	549[2]	884[2]	*7.8*	*12.5*	32.3	47.2
Guernsey	...	...	...	33,037	7,522	1.6	...	...	—	—	—	—	—	—
Guinea	18,809	30,270	16	13,700	19,300	217	...	...	411[2]	662[2]	25.8	41.5	5.0	7.3
Guinea-Bissau	2,703	4,350	10	6,300	4,900	100	...	...	—	—	—	—	—	—
Guyana	4,859	7,820	7	24,000	9,000	22	...	...	116[15]	187[15]	...	...	...	...
Haiti	2,535	4,080	24	32,000	21,000	121	...	...	—	—	—	—	—	—
Honduras	9,383	15,100	20	81,439	170,006	22	...	...	614	988	*4.8*	*7.7*	*20.7*	*30.2*
Hong Kong	1,083	1,743	100	325,131	142,446	13	...	...	21	34	2,231	3,591	68	99
Hungary	18,640	29,999	93	2,264,165	322,000	3.9	495	723	8,190	13,181	5,814	9,358	5,200	7,600
Iceland	7,691	12,378	25	124,909	16,623	1.9	*318*	*464*	—	—	—	—	—	—
India	1,248,700	2,009,600	50	2,720,000	2,207,000	190	*144,000*	*210,000*	38,935[2]	62,660[2]	198,500	319,400	173,268	252,967
Indonesia	234,900	372,414	47	2,107,299	2,024,702	47	*17,000*	*25,000*	4,090	6,583	9,895	15,924	2,679	3,912
Iran	98,200	158,000	59	1,630,000	609,000	26	*46,750*	*68,250*	4,527[2]	7,286[2]	3,990	6,422	6,249	9,124
Iraq	28,900	46,500	86	672,000	368,000	20	...	...	1,263[2]	2,032[2]	973	1,566	1,129	1,649
Ireland	57,377	92,340	94	990,384	155,153	3.1	3,519	5,138	1,210[2]	1,947[2]	828	1,332	392	573
Isle of Man	357	574	58	38,917	4,925	1.6	...	...	37[2]	59[2]	...	...	...	...
Israel	9,134	14,700	100	1,121,730	272,593	3.9	...	...	379[2]	610[2]	166	267	805	1,176
Italy	195,334	314,360	100	31,700,000	5,127,000	1.6	138,000	202,000	9,944	16,003	30,882	49,700	28,499	41,608
Jamaica	11,600	18,600	71	86,791	41,312	19	...	...	*129*[2]	*208*[2]	*12.1*	*19.5*	*1.7*	*2.5*
Japan	706,091	1,136,346	73	44,680,000	21,934,000	1.9	188,000	274,000	12,511	20,134	248,584	400,058	17,193	25,101
Jersey	...	...	...	58,491	9,922	1.3	...	...	—	—	—	—	—	—
Jordan	4,194	6,750	100	167,828	82,516	16	*19,133*	*27,934*	421[2]	677[2]	*3.7*	*6.0*	915	1,336
Kazakstan	98,583	158,655	68	1,030,000	516,000	11	9	13	13,422	21,600	1,355	2,180	661	965
Kenya	39,558	63,663	14	271,000	75,900	80	*134*	*196*	1,885[2]	3,034[2]	288	464	899	1,312
Kiribati	407	655	*5*	*307*	*130*	*147*	...	...	—	—	—	—	—	—
Korea, North	*18,600*	*30,000*	*6*	*248,000*	...	...	...	...	*5,302*	*8,533*	*2,100*	*3,400*	*6,200*	*9,100*
Korea, South	46,127	74,235	76	6,006,290	2,462,611	5.3	36,100	52,700	4,072	6,554	18,201	29,292	9,478	13,838
Kuwait	2,704	4,360	81	545,000	155,000	2.4	...	...	—	—	—	—	—	—
Kyrgyzstan	11,533	18,560	91	164,000	...	...	555	811	249	400	*81.5*	*131.2*	394	575
Laos	11,280	18,153	14	17,200	6,020	208	16	23	—	—	—	—	—	—
Latvia	40,198	64,693	18	379,895	90,184	5.3	1,200	1,700	1,499	2,413	734	1,182	8,502	12,412
Lebanon	3,951	6,359	95	1,197,521	84,736	2.9	...	...	138	222	*5.3*	*8.6*	*29*	*42*
Lesotho	3,079	4,955	18	11,100	22,200	58	...	...	1.6	2.6	...	...	...	...
Liberia	6,400	10,300	6	10,300	28,300	59	...	...	306[2]	493[2]	...	...	137[15]	200[15]
Libya	50,704	81,600	57	592,000	312,000	5.8	...	...	—	—	—	—	—	—
Liechtenstein	201	323	...	18,820	1,949	1.5	...	...	12	19	...	...	...	...
Lithuania	38,178	61,442	86	718,469	118,474	4.4	3,534	5,160	1,862	2,996	702	1,130	5,264	7,685
Luxembourg	3,206	5,160	99	231,666	25,529	1.6	*164*	*239*	171[2]	275[2]	176	284	388	566
Macau	80	130	100	41,403	3,803	9.2	...	...	—	—	—	—	—	—
Macedonia	5,302	8,532	63	285,907	29,197	6.2	807	1,178	573	922	40	65	116	170
Madagascar	30,967	49,837	12	58,100	15,340	181	*220*	*321*	*640*[2]	*1,030*[2]	29	46	64	93
Malawi	17,324	27,880	18	25,400	28,900	174	—	—	490[2]	789[2]	11.8	19.0	38.9	56.8
Malaysia	58,393	93,975	75	2,588,641	465,940	6.8	...	...	1,113	1,791	798[33]	1,284[33]	970[33]	1,416[33]
Maldives	...	...	...	938	1,117	123	...	...	—	—	—	—	—	—
Mali	9,181	14,776	12	24,700	17,100	224	...	...	398[2]	641[2]	304.2	489.5	187.2	273.3
Malta	997	1,604	94	173,259	41,849	1.7	...	...	—	—	—	—	—	—
Marshall Islands	...	...	...	1,418	193	34	...	...	—	—	—	—	—	—
Martinique	1,286	2,069	*75*	*135,269*	*7,328*	*2.3*	...	...	—	—	—	—	—	—
Mauritania	4,700	7,600	11	17,300	9,210	85	...	...	437[2]	704[2]	...	...	4,719	6,890
Mauritius	*1,138*	*1,831*	*93*	37,766	10,625	23	...	...	—	—	—	—	—	—
Mayotte	195	284	39	——*1,528*——		*40*	...	...	—	—	—	—	—	—
Mexico	188,886	303,983	36	8,449,969	3,950,456	7.2	107,000	156,000	16,432[2]	26,445[2]	2,382	3,833	24,042	35,100
Micronesia	*140*	*226*	*17*	...	...	...	...	...	—	—	—	—	—	—
Moldova	7,617	12,259	87	165,941	69,069	18	579	845	746	1,200	633	1,019	2,147	3,134
Monaco	27	43	100	20,715	2,702	1.3	...	...	1	2	...	...	...	...
Mongolia	6,947	11,180	11	21,200	33,420	42	*183.8*	*268.4*	1,294	2,083	516	830	1.4	2.1
Morocco	37,601	60,513	50	1,030,000	273,100	20	1,288	1,880	1,099[2]	1,768[2]	951	1,531	3,165	4,621
Mozambique	18,523	29,810	19	84,000	26,800	155	...	...	1,940	3,123	194	312	612	893
Myanmar (Burma)	17,100	27,600	12	44,000	42,000	525	*71*	*103.7*	3,144	5,060	3,041	4,894	603	880
Namibia	25,134	40,450	13	62,500	66,500	13	...	...	1,480	2,382	1,248	2,008	741	1,082
Nauru	17	28	79	——*1,448*——		*6.3*	...	...	3[15]	5[15]	...	...	*4.7*	*6.8*
Nepal	4,691	7,550	41	*4,949*	*3,363*	*2,259*	*984*	*1,437*	63[2]	101[2]	...	...	...	...

merchant marine (latest): fleet (vessels over 100 gross tons)	merchant marine: total dead-weight tonnage ('000)	international cargo (latest): loaded metric tons ('000)	international cargo: off-loaded metric tons ('000)	air: airports with sched-uled flights, 1996	air traffic (latest): passengers: passenger-mi ('000,000)	passengers: passenger-km ('000,000)	cargo: short ton-mi ('000,000)	cargo: metric ton-km ('000,000)	canals and inland waterways (latest): length mi	length km	cargo short ton-mi ('000,000)	cargo metric ton-km ('000,000)	country
15	...	221	1,023	1[4]	1,229	1,978	9.8	14.3	...	...	...	...	El Salvador
3	6.7	110	64	1[4]	4	7	0.7	1.0	...	...	...	...	Equatorial Guinea
...	...	...	...	2	...	...	...	...	...	...	...	...	Eritrea
234	680.4	11,460	3,996	3	67	108	0.4	0.6	311	500	0.7	1	Estonia
27	84.3	592	3,120	31	1,142	1,838	77	112	...	...	...	...	Ethiopia
191	59.8	130	367	1	...	...	...	...	...	...	...	...	Faroe Islands
64	60.4	568	625	13[4]	742	1,195	51.6	75.4	126	203	...	...	Fiji
263	989.3	33,336	36,948	24	6,654	10,709	165.3	241.3	4,148	6,675	2,500	3,600	Finland
729	4,981.0	55,296	177,696	61	41,942[25]	67,500[25]	7,740[25]	11,300[25]	9,278	14,932	3,800	5,600	France
7	0.7	69	481	8	...	...	...	...	286	460	...	...	French Guiana
41	16.5	15	666	36	...	...	...	...	...	...	...	...	French Polynesia
29	30.2	12,828	212	23	354	570	56	82	994	1,600	...	...	Gabon
11	2.0	185	240	1	31	50	3	5	250	400	...	...	Gambia, The
—	—	...	...	—	...	...	...	...	—	—	...	...	Gaza Strip
54	1,108	...	...	1[4]	3,291	5,296	...	...	...	...	17,561	25,638	Georgia
1,375	6,832.3	71,028	128,448	40	39,409	63,423	8,611	12,572	4,686	7,541	39,425	57,559	Germany
155	131.0	2,424	2,904	1	407	655	20	30	803	1,293	75	110	Ghana
49	1,136.1	5	400	1	...	...	...	...	—	—	...	...	Gibraltar
1,872	45,276.6	21,087	33,048	36[4]	4,937	7,945	80	117	50	80	585	854	Greece
82	17.2	298	288	5	16.3	26.3	0.23	0.34	...	...	...	...	Greenland
3	0.5	21	193	2[4]	...	...	...	...	...	...	...	...	Grenada
20	4.4	431	1,933	6	...	...	...	...	...	...	...	...	Guadeloupe
5	0.1	195	1,524	1	...	...	...	...	...	...	...	...	Guam
8	0.4	2,096	3,822	2	239	384	14	21	162	260	...	...	Guatemala
—	...	...	...	1[4]	...	...	...	...	...	...	...	...	Guernsey
23	1.7	16,760	734	2	20.4	32.8	0.9	1.2	805	1,295	...	...	Guinea
19	1.8	46	283	2[4]	3.7	6.0	0.7	1.0	...	...	...	...	Guinea-Bissau
82	13.5	1,730	673	1	139	224	16	23	3,700	6,000	...	...	Guyana
4	0.4	170	704	2[4]	...	...	...	...	60	100	...	...	Haiti
966	1,437.3	1,316	1,002	8	180[26]	289[26]	26[26]	38[26]	289	465	...	...	Honduras
387	11,688.6	41,512[27]	87,106[27]	1[4]	...	...	...	...	...	...	...	...	Hong Kong
15	93.2	...	...	1[4]	1,716	2,762	22.5	32.9	1,008	1,622	569	831	Hungary
394	114.9	1,162	1,733	24	1,850	2,977	36.2	52.9	...	...	58	84	Iceland
888	10,365.9	53,220	75,000	66	12,563	20,219	437.9	639.3	10,054	16,180	202,000	295,000	India
2,014	3,130.2	216,396	64,656	81	8,904	14,330	415.6	606.8	13,409	21,579	17,000	25,000	Indonesia
403	8,345.3	113,207	16,719	19	3,808	6,128	75.1	109.6	562	904	...	...	Iran
131	1,578.8	97,830	8,638	...	976	1,570	37.4	54.6	631	1,015	...	...	Iraq
189	208.6	6,367	17,637	9	3,186	5,127	70	102	...	...	...	...	Ireland
101	2,836.5	6	203	1	115.5	185.9	0.2	0.3	...	...	...	...	Isle of Man
58	723.4	10,656	19,608	7	7,430[28]	11,957[28]	815[28]	1,190[28]	...	...	...	...	Israel
1,966	7,149.5	51,420	222,060	34[4]	18,429[29]	29,659[29]	914.3[29]	1,335[29]	1,500	2,400	59	86	Italy
12	16.2	8,802	5,285	4[4]	1,204[30]	1,938[30]	136[30]	199[30]	...	...	...	...	Jamaica
7,165	22,000	114,756	782,916	73	80,959	130,292	4,487	6,551	1,100	1,770	155,000	227,000	Japan
—	—	...	...	1	...	...	...	...	...	...	...	...	Jersey
5	113.6	7,392	4,608	2[4]	2,731	4,395	181.6	265.2	...	...	19,202	28,035	Jordan
...	...	...	...	6	2,858	4,600	68	100	2,487	4,002	123	180	Kazakstan
29	11.6	1,596	3,228	13	1,142[31]	1,838[31]	32.7[31]	47.8[31]	...	...	...	...	Kenya
7	2.7	15	26	17	6	10	0.5	0.8	3	5	...	...	Kiribati
100	951.2	635	5,520	1[4]	52.2	84.0	1.4	2.0	1,400	2,253	...	...	Korea, North
2,138	11,724.9	74,736	273,672	14	30,139	48,504	3,924	5,729	1,000	1,609	48,600	70,900	Korea, South
209	3,188.5	51,400	4,522	1[4]	3,184	5,124	225.8	329.7	...	...	...	...	Kuwait
...	...	...	...	2[4]	2,739	4,408	44.7	65.2	...	...	6	9	Kyrgyzstan
1	1.5	—	—	11	29	46	3	5	2,850	4,587	68	99	Laos
261	1,436.9	36,012	2,448	1	187.3	301.5	3.6	5.2	186	300	311	454	Latvia
163	438.2	152	1,150	1[4]	1,174	1,889	32	46	...	...	...	...	Lebanon
—	—	—	—	1[4]	3.9	6.2	0.4	0.6	—	—	—	—	Lesotho
1,672	97,374.0	21,653	1,608	1	4.3	7.0	0.7	1.0	...	...	...	...	Liberia
150	1,223.6	62,491	7,808	12	247.6[32]	398.5[32]	0.3[32]	0.4[32]	—	—	...	...	Libya
—	—	—	—	—	—	—	—	—	...	...	...	...	Liechtenstein
52	373.9	10,092	2,628	3	219	352	23	34	373	600	12	18	Lithuania
54	2,603.6	—	—	1[4]	79.5	232	606.9	886.1	23	37	232	338	Luxembourg
6	0.1	755	3,935	—	—	—	—	—	...	...	...	...	Macau
...	...	...	...	2[4]	181.7	292.4	20	29	...	...	...	...	Macedonia
85	82.1	540	984	19	409	659	58	85	...	...	...	...	Madagascar
1	0.3	...	...	5[4]	180	289	19	28	891	1,434	0.5	0.7	Malawi
552	2,916.3	23,472	44,184	39[4]	14,017	22,558	795	1,160	4,534	7,296	...	...	Malaysia
44	79.0	27	78	5[4]	4.8	7.0	...	...	...	...	...	...	Maldives
—	—	—	—	9[4]	139.6	224.7	11.2	16.4	1,128	1,815	18	27	Mali
889	17,073.2	309	1,781	1	1,070	1,723	9.4	13.7	...	...	...	...	Malta
35	4,182.4	29	123	23	30	49	7	10	...	...	...	...	Marshall Islands
6	1.1	768	1,524	2	...	...	...	...	...	...	...	...	Martinique
126	23.9	10,400	724	9[4]	139.6	224.7	11.2	16.4	...	...	...	...	Mauritania
35	152.2	834	2,419	1[4]	2,115	3,404	93.4	136.3	...	...	...	...	Mauritius
1	1.1	—	—	1	...	...	...	...	...	...	...	...	Mayotte
635	1,495.3	139,776	61,956	83	12,902	20,764	1,348	1,968	1,800	2,900	...	...	Mexico
17	6.9	...	...	6	...	...	...	...	...	...	...	...	Micronesia
...	...	...	...	1	1,461	2,352	13.0	19.0	263	424	172	251	Moldova
1	...	...	...	1	—	—	...	...	...	...	...	...	Monaco
—	—	—	—	1	305	491	31	45	247	397	613	895	Mongolia
492	586.2	19,476	21,120	12	2,992	4,815	268	391	...	...	...	...	Morocco
107	31.6	2,800	3,400	7[4]	239	384	6	9	2,330	3,750	...	...	Mozambique
144	1,354.0	2,040	3,624	19	272	439	2.2	3.2	7,954	12,800	240	351	Myanmar (Burma)
30	5.9	1,132	644	13	470	756	16	23	...	...	...	...	Namibia
2	5.8	1,650	59	1	128[34]	206[34]	14[34]	20[34]	...	...	...	...	Nauru
—	—	—	—	24	478	769	63.8	93.1	...	...	...	...	Nepal

Transportation (continued)

country	roads and motor vehicles (latest)								railroads (latest)					
	roads			motor vehicles			cargo		track length		traffic			
	length		paved (per-cent)	auto-mobiles	trucks and buses	persons per vehicle	short ton-mi ('000,-000)	metric ton-km ('000,-000)	mi	km	passengers		cargo	
	mi	km									passen-ger-mi ('000,000)	passen-ger-km ('000,000)	short ton-mi ('000,000)	metric ton-km ('000,000)
Netherlands, The	77,090	124,064	91	5,740,000	680,000	2.4	16,000	24,000	1,702	2,739	8,685	13,977	2,121	3,097
Netherlands Antilles	368	592	51	69,321	21,194	2.2	...	...	—	—	—	—	—	—
New Caledonia	3,580	5,762	22	58,500	22,600	2.3	...	...	—	—	—	—	—	—
New Zealand	57,081	91,864	73	1,650,112	351,494	1.8	...	...	2,433	3,915	*285*	*458*	2,277	3,324
Nicaragua	10,654	17,146	10	72,413	68,090	31	...	...	—	—	—	—	—	—
Niger	6,129	9,863	9	37,500	14,100	171	*1,044*	*1,524*	—	—	—	—	—	—
Nigeria	20,387	32,810	83	663,000	68,300	134	...	...	2,178	3,505	345	555	1.5	2.2
Northern Mariana Islands	*307*	*494*	*27*	12,113	6,479	3.0	...	...	—	—	—	—	—	—
Norway	56,086	90,262	74	1,684,664	382,017	2.1	6,575	9,600	2,485[2]	3,999[2]	1,479	2,381	1,860	2,715
Oman	19,160	30,830	20	202,741	108,600	6.8	...	...	—	—	—	—	—	—
Pakistan	123,585	198,891	55	955,098	225,829	107	2,723	3,976	5,453[2]	8,775[2]	10,908	17,555	3,877	5,661
Palau	40	64	59	——4,271——		3.8	...	...	...	...	...	...	...	...
Panama	6,706	10,792	34	140,900	79,000	12	...	...	220[2]	354[2]	...	...	0.5	0.7
Papua New Guinea	*12,263*	*19,736*	*6*	13,000	32,000	93	...	...	—	—	—	—	—	—
Paraguay	17,956	28,900	9	174,212	76,565	18	...	...	274[2]	441[2]	1.9	3.0	3.8	5.5
Peru	44,400	71,400	11	505,766	338,871	28	...	...	1,318[2]	2,121[2]	102.7	165.3	605.8	884.4
Philippines	100,062	161,035	17	609,000	221,900	82	...	...	557[2]	897[2]	43	70	1.0	1.5
Poland	231,447	372,479	65	7,517,266	1,472,278	4.3	49,042	71,600	14,904	23,986	16,550	26,635	47,341	69,116
Portugal	42,708	68,732	88	2,560,000	219,696	3.6	7,665	11,190	1,909[2]	3,072[2]	3,025	4,869	1,382	2,018
Puerto Rico	14,379	23,140	87	1,432,000	229,000	2.2	...	...	—	—	—	—	—	—
Qatar	752	1,210	90	125,700	63,800	3.0	...	...	—	—	—	—	—	—
Réunion	1,711	2,754	*79*	157,700	38,600	3.4	...	...	—	—	—	—	—	—
Romania	95,175	153,170	51	2,197,477	385,111	8.8	13,526	19,748	7,062	11,365	11,731	18,880	18,617	27,180
Russia	590,000	949,000	79	10,499,000	407,000	14	987	1,441	94,400	152,000	163,900	263,800	704	1,028
Rwanda	9,050	14,565	10	11,900	15,900	216	*140*	*200*	—	—	—	—	—	—
St. Kitts and Nevis	193	310	43	*4,000*	*700*	*10*	...	...	—	—	—	—	—	—
St. Lucia	*500*	*805*	*56*	10,000	9,200	7.3	...	...	—	—	—	—	—	—
St. Vincent and the Grenadines	634	1,020	31	5,473	2,878	13	...	...	—	—	—	—	—	—
Samoa	485	781	42	1,068	1,169	74	...	...	—	—	—	—	—	—
San Marino	*147*	*237*	...	23,561	4,013	0.9	...	...	—	—	—	—	—	—
São Tomé and Príncipe	193	310	68	3,810	1,470	25	...	...	—	—	—	—	—	—
Saudi Arabia	98,798	159,000	43	1,710,000	1,172,600	6.2	57,859	84,473	864[2]	1,390[2]	86	139	559	816
Senegal	9,060	14,580	29	80,600	32,410	78	*375*	*547*	562	904	128	206	476	695
Seychelles	214	345	80	5,100	2,000	11	...	...	—	—	—	—	—	—
Sierra Leone	7,254	11,674	11	20,860	11,014	141	*36*	*53*	*52*	*84*	...	...	...	...
Singapore	1,886	3,035	97	384,450	139,113	5.8	...	...	52	83	[33]	[33]	[33]	[33]
Slovakia	11,103	17,869	...	1,015,794	97,516	4.8	3,533	5,158	2,277	3,665	2,611	4,202	9,366	13,674
Slovenia	9,158	14,739	79	698,211	40,206	2.7	1,190	1,740	746	1,201	370	595	1,973	2,881
Solomon Islands	826	1,330	2	2,052	2,574	75	...	...	—	—	—	—	—	—
Somalia	14,300	23,000	12	11,800	12,200	278	...	...	—	—	—	—	—	—
South Africa	113,450	182,580	33	3,810,000	1,640,000	7.6	*1,053*	*1,538*	13,418[2]	21,595[2]	556	895	65,248	95,260
Spain	213,252	343,197	99	14,212,257	2,984,140	2.3	53,914	78,713	8,252[2]	13,280[2]	9,526	15,330	6,624	9,671
Sri Lanka	63,753	102,600	11	220,000	248,900	39	2,617	3,821	928[2]	1,493[2]	2,028	3,264	99	144
Sudan, The	7,214	11,610	36	263,000	47,800	98	...	...	2,960[2]	4,764[2]	735	1,183	1,534	2,240
Suriname	2,778	4,470	26	44,300	17,050	7.0	...	...	*187*	*301*	...	...	...	...
Swaziland	2,377	3,825	28	27,300	26,340	18	...	...	187	301	*752*	*1,210*	*1,993*	*2,910*
Sweden	84,645	136,223	72	3,630,760	322,286	2.2	20,800	30,400	6,744	10,853	3,942	6,344	13,280	19,388
Switzerland	44,151	71,055	96	3,229,169	277,399	2.0	7,108	10,378	3,125	5,030	7,084	11,400	5,586	8,156
Syria	24,384	39,243	71	134,000	218,900	40	*1,075*	*1,570*	1,097[2]	1,766[2]	531	855	751	1,097
Taiwan	11,830	19,038	89	4,146,500	799,600	4.3	9,326	13,616	2,410	3,879	5,577	8,975	1,086	1,585
Tajikistan	8,000	13,000	*93*	184,900	3,600	30	*3,518*	*5,136*	300	500	*6,094*	*9,808*	*7,617*	*11,121*
Tanzania	54,743	88,100	4	47,500	38,000	323	...	...	2,218	3,569	*2,324*	*3,740*	*1,021*	*1,490*
Thailand	38,000	62,000	97	1,440,000	2,969,000	13	...	...	2,471[2]	3,976[2]	8,062	12,975	2,221	3,242
Togo	4,672	7,519	32	74,662	33,061	41	...	...	245[2]	395[2]	9	14	3.8	5.6
Tonga	419	674	27	1,136	766	53	...	...	—	—	—	—	—	—
Trinidad and Tobago	5,070	8,160	51	123,500	24,500	8.5	...	...	—	—	—	—	—	—
Tunisia	13,975	22,490	79	248,000	283,000	17	*678*	*990*	1,337[2]	2,152[2]	636	1,038	1,524	2,225
Turkey	236,928	381,300	23	3,231,562	809,361	15	*67,017*	*97,843*	5,252	8,452	3,967	6,385	5,654	8,254
Turkmenistan	14,600	23,500	81	*170,600*	...	...	*3,283*	*4,793*	1,359	2,187	1,300	2,100	13,600	19,800
Tuvalu	5	8	—	...	...	...	...	...	—	—	—	—	—	—
Uganda	16,653	26,800	8	24,400	25,300	397	...	...	771[2]	1,241[2]	17	28	128	187
Ukraine	107,035	172,257	95	4,510,000	...	...	15,800	23,100	14,100	22,700	42,900	69,100	85,600	125,000
United Arab Emirates	2,952	4,750	100	197,000	49,150	9.7	...	...	—	—	—	—	—	—
United Kingdom	228,042	366,999	100	20,505,000	2,712,000	2.5	105,000	153,000	23,518[46]	37,849[46]	18,154	29,216	1,997	2,916
United States	3,912,226	6,296,130	91	134,803,000	66,727,000	1.3	1,096,000	1,600,000	137,900	222,000	13,897	22,365	1,305,685	1,906,268
Uruguay	31,600	50,900	14	444,835	46,245	6.4	*500*	*730*	1,288[2]	2,073[2]	*87.4*	*140.6*	129	189
Uzbekistan	48,715	78,400	86	865,300	14,500	25	*15,037*	*21,954*	2,100	3,380	*3,300*	*5,200*	*48,400*	*70,600*
Vanuatu	652	1,050	24	4,000	2,300	26	...	...	—	—	—	—	—	—
Venezuela	55,737	89,700	39	1,485,221	511,809	11	...	...	390[2]	627[2]	19.5	31.4	32.1	46.8
Vietnam	65,895	106,048	26	...	...	...	1,462	2,134	1,619	2,605	1,305	2,100	727	1,062
Virgin Islands (U.S.)	532	856	100	47,255	14,868	1.6	...	...	—	—	—	—	—	—
West Bank	...	...	...	69,200	20,723	13	...	...	—	—	—	—	—	—
Western Sahara	*3,900*	*6,200*	*23*	*6,284*	*424*	*20*	...	...	...	...	...	...	...	...
Yemen	40,144	64,605	8	229,084	282,615	31	...	...	—	—	—	—	—	—
Yugoslavia	30,832	49,620	58	1,400,000	132,000	6.9	*14,929*[49]	*21,796*[49]	2,505	4,031	1,137	1,830	1,412	2,062
Zambia	24,170	38,898	18	142,000	73,500	44	...	...	791	1,273	166	267	316	462
Zimbabwe	57,048	91,810	19	492,000	108,000	19	...	...	1,714[2]	2,759[2]	339	546	3.2	4.7

[1]Ariana Afghan Airlines only. [2]Route length. [3]Air Algérie International flights only. [4]1997. [5]TAAG airline only. [6]Aerolineas Argentinas only. [7]Included in Netherlands Antilles. [8]Government railways only. [9]Portion of Gulf Air traffic. [10]Caribbean Airways only. [11]Caribbean Air Cargo only. [12]Air Afrique only. [13]Air Botswana only. [14]1995. [15]For industrial purposes only. [16]Zaire National Railways only. [17]Air Zaire only. [18]LASCA only. [19]Traffic between Ouagadougou, Burkina Faso, and Abidjan, Côte d'Ivoire. [20]Air Ivoire only. [21]Data refer to former Czechoslovakia. [22]Including SAS international and domestic traffic. [23]National roads only. [24]Includes 62 mi (100 km) of the Chemin de Fer Djibouti-Ethiopien (CDE) in Djibouti. [25]Air France and UTA only. [26]TAN and SAHSA

country	merchant marine (latest): fleet (vessels over 100 gross tons)	total deadweight tonnage ('000)	international cargo (latest): loaded metric tons ('000)	off-loaded metric tons ('000)	air: airports with scheduled flights, 1996	traffic (latest): passengers: passenger-mi ('000,000)	passenger-km ('000,000)	cargo: short ton-mi ('000,000)	metric ton-km ('000,000)	canals and inland waterways (latest): length: mi	km	cargo: short ton-mi ('000,000)	metric ton-km ('000,000)
Netherlands, The	399	2,874	84,816	293,304	6	28,292	45,531	2,490	3,635	3,939	6,340	5,100	7,500
Netherlands Antilles	154[35]	1,053.6[35]	18,560	18,715	5	234[36]	377[36]	1.2[36]	1.8[36]	...	...	...	...
New Caledonia	17	18.1	1,040	930	10	145[37]	233[37]	3.4[37]	4.9[37]	...	...	...	...
New Zealand	139	279.8	19,692	11,604	36[4]	11,090	17,848	444	648	1,000	1,609	1,503	2,195
Nicaragua	25	1.3	320	1,629	10[4]	44.8	72.2	4.8	7.0	1,379	2,220	...	...
Niger	—	—	—	—	6	139.6	224.7	11.2	16.4	186	300	13	19
Nigeria	271	733.3	86,993	11,346	12	612	985	7.9	11.5	5,328	8,575	...	...
Northern Mariana Islands	2	0.9	33	205	3	...	...	...	...	...	...	...	...
Norway	1,597	20,834	152,604	22,776	50	5,439[22]	8,753[22]	639[22]	933[22]	980	1,577	5,920	8,650
Oman	26	11.7	33,843	2,492	6[4]	1,714[9]	2,759[9]	72.4[9]	105.8[9]	...	...	...	...
Pakistan	73	513.8	5,625	17,526	34	6,911	11,123	290	423	...	...	...	...
Palau	4	...	...	64	1	...	...	...	...	...	...	...	...
Panama	5,217	79,255.6	116,844	84,312	10	542	872	6.4	9.3	497	800	...	...
Papua New Guinea	87	40.9	2,463	1,784	129	458.8	738.4	56.4	82.4	6,798	10,940	...	...
Paraguay	38	38.5	...	...	5[4]	767	1,235	8.0	11.7	1,900	3,100	...	...
Peru	623	615.6	10,197	5,077	27	1,535	2,470	177	259	5,300	8,600	...	...
Philippines	1,499	13,807.1	12,864	34,128	21	7,987[38]	12,854[38]	225.2[38]	328.8[38]	2,000	3,219	...	...
Poland	644	4,314.3	30,823	17,247	8[4]	2,879	4,633	51	74	2,484	3,997	600	876
Portugal	332	1,129.3	9,672	37,260	16[4]	4,957	7,978	143.6	209.7	510	820	...	...
Puerto Rico	13	...	...	...	7[4]	...	...	...	...	...	...	...	...
Qatar	65	635.6	18,145	2,588	1[4]	1,714[9]	2,759[9]	72.4[9]	105.8[9]	...	...	...	...
Réunion	7	33.5	399	1,975	1	...	...	...	...	...	...	...	...
Romania	439	4,845.5	14,676	21,684	12	1,126	1,812	10.8	15.7	1,071	1,724	2,128	3,107
Russia	4,543	16,592.3	14,124	1,428	58	44,600	71,700	1,200	1,800	62,800	101,000	96	140
Rwanda	—	—	—	—	3	1.2	2.0	...	...	...	...	...	...
St. Kitts and Nevis	1	0.6	24	36	2	...	...	...	...	...	...	...	...
St. Lucia	7	2.1	150	234	2	...	...	...	...	...	...	...	...
St. Vincent and the Grenadines	881	7,044.2	80	140	4	...	...	...	...	...	...	...	...
Samoa	7	6.5	12	192	3[4]	...	...	...	...	—	—	—	—
San Marino	—	—	—	—	—	—	—	—	—	—	—	—	—
São Tomé and Príncipe	4	2.3	16	45	2	5	8	0.7	1.0	...	...	...	...
Saudi Arabia	301	1,361.7	214,070	46,437	25[4]	11,500	18,501	613	895	...	...	...	...
Senegal	183	27.5	1,739	2,959	7	139.6[32]	224.7[32]	11.2[32]	16.4[32]	557	897	...	...
Seychelles	9	3.3	11	348	2[4]	389	626	48	70	...	...	...	...
Sierra Leone	62	18.4	2,310	589	1[4]	68[39]	110[39]	1.4[39]	2.0[39]	500	800	447	652
Singapore	946	14,929.2	134,592	179,568	1[4]	33,330	53,640	2,871	4,191	...	...	...	...
Slovakia	...	...	...	...	2	37.5	60.3	3.8	5.6	107	172	1,005	1,468
Slovenia	13	346.5	137	2,204	1	382	614	2.3	3.7	...	...	12,175	17,775
Solomon Islands	33	5.0	278	349	21[4]	40[40]	65[40]	3	5	...	...	...	...
Somalia	28	18.5	324	1,007	1[4]	81	131	3.0	5.0	...	...	...	...
South Africa	219	282.5	114,331	22,203	24	8,595[41]	13,833[41]	370[41]	540[41]	...	...	...	...
Spain	2,190	5,077.3	49,860	147,804	25	21,154	34,044	2,578	3,764	649	1,045	21,836[42]	31,880[42]
Sri Lanka	66	472.6	5,892	9,588	1	2,403	3,868	109	159	267	430	...	...
Sudan, The	16	62.2	1,543	4,300	3[4]	404[43]	650[43]	21[43]	31[43]	3,300	5,310	...	...
Suriname	24	15.7	1,595	1,265	3[4]	549[44]	883[44]	18[44]	26[44]	746	1,200	...	...
Swaziland	—	—	—	—	1	30.7	49.4	0.09	0.1	—	—	—	—
Sweden	430	2,881	52,812	63,912	48	5,236[22]	8,427[22]	171[22]	250[22]	1,275	2,052	5,600	8,200
Switzerland	24	602.8	...	...	5	12,257	19,725	1,033	1,508	40	65	127	186
Syria	94	210.4	1,788	4,512	5	692	1,114	81	118	541	870	...	...
Taiwan	649	9,241.3	156,230	263,938	13	25,230	40,604	2,444	3,568	...	...	234	341
Tajikistan	...	...	...	...	1[4]	1,386	2,231	140	205	...	...	...	...
Tanzania	43	48.5	1,249	2,721	11[4]	114	184	2.0	2.9	...	...	...	...
Thailand	351	1,194.5	21,192	40,152	25	18,160	29,226	904	1,320	2,300	3,701	...	...
Togo	8	20.6	148	709	1	134	215	23	34	31	50	...	...
Tonga	15	13.7	15	104	6	5.8	9.4	0.01	0.01	...	...	...	...
Trinidad and Tobago	53	17.5	9,622	10,961	2	2,538	4,084	277	404	...	...	...	...
Tunisia	77	443.3	6,888	11,136	5	1,338	2,154	139.5	203.6	...	...	...	...
Turkey	880	7,114.3	22,956	61,728	26	7,646[45]	12,305[45]	146.7[45]	214.2[45]	750	1,200	209	305
Turkmenistan	...	...	...	...	1	971	1,562	98	143	...	...	...	...
Tuvalu	6	16.0	...	...	1	...	...	...	...	...	...	...	...
Uganda	2	8.6	...	...	1[4]	32.4	52.1	3	5	...	...	...	...
Ukraine	...	...	34,200	...	20	1,775	2,857	210	306	1,039	1,672	2,658	3,880
United Arab Emirates	276	1,491.7	88,153	9,595	6	1,714[9]	2,759[9]	72.5[9]	105.8[9]	...	...	...	...
United Kingdom	1,631	4,355	177,228	178,572	57[4]	77,576	124,847	2,625	3,832	1,990	3,200	34,400	50,200
United States	509	18,585	388,716[47]	602,436[47]	834	540,400	869,700	14,568	21,270	25,482	41,009	807,700	1,179,000
Uruguay	93	172.5	710[48]	1,450[48]	1[4]	401	645	42	62	1,000	1,600	...	...
Uzbekistan	...	...	...	...	9	3,017	4,855	306	447	...	...	...	...
Vanuatu	280	3,259.6	80	55	29	93	150	0.8	1.2	...	...	...	...
Venezuela	271	1,355.4	101,435	17,932	20[4]	4,581	7,372	144	210	4,400	7,100	...	...
Vietnam	230	872.8	303	1,510	12	130	209	13	19	11,000	17,702	1,339	1,955
Virgin Islands (U.S.)	1	...	105.5	648.3	4	...	...	...	...	...	...	...	...
West Bank	—	—	...	...	—	—	—	—	—	...	...	...	...
Western Sahara	—	—	40	15	1	...	...	...	...	...	...	...	...
Yemen	40	13.7	1,936	7,829	11	735	1,183	82	119	...	...	...	...
Yugoslavia	462[49]	5,173.1[49]	288	1,212	4	598	963	3,371	4,921	1,616[49]	2,600[49]	3,430[49]	5,007[49]
Zambia	—	—	—	—	4	192	308	6.8	9.9	1,398	2,250	...	...
Zimbabwe	—	—	—	—	7	522	840	27	39	...	...	...	...

airlines only. [27]Includes transshipments. [28]El Al only. [29]Alitalia only. [30]Air Jamaica only. [31]Kenya Airways only. [32]International traffic only. [33]Peninsular Malaysia and Singapore. [34]Air Nauru only. [35]Includes Aruba. [36]Antillean Airlines only. [37]Air Caledonie only. [38]Philippine Air Lines only. [39]Sierra Leone Airlines international traffic only. [40]Solair only. [41]SAA only. [42]Coastal shipping only. [43]Sudan Airways only. [44]Suriname Airways only. [45]Turkish Airlines only. [46]British Railways only; excludes Northern Ireland. [47]Includes Puerto Rico. [48]Port of Montevideo only. [49]Data refer to Yugoslavia as constituted prior to 1991.

Communications

Virtually all the states of the world have a variety of communications media and services available to their citizens: book, periodical, and newspaper publishing (although only daily papers are included in this table); postal services; and telecommunication systems: radio and television broadcasting, telephones (fixed and mobile), facsimile (fax) machines, personal computers (PCs), and access to the Internet. Unfortunately, the availability of information about these services often runs behind the capabilities of the services themselves. Certain countries publish no official information; others publish data analyzed according to a variety of fiscal, calendar, religious, or other years; still others, while they possess such data almost simultaneously with the end of the business or calendar year, may not see them published except in company or parastatal reports of limited distribution. Even when such data are published in national statistical summaries, it may be only after a delay of up to several years.

The data also differ in their completeness and reliability. Figures for book production, for example, generally include all works published in separate bindings except advertising works, timetables, telephone directories, price lists, catalogs of businesses or exhibitions, musical scores, maps, atlases, and the like. The figures include government publications, school texts, theses, offprints, series works, and illustrated works, even those consisting principally of illustrations. Figures refer to works actually published during the year of survey, usually by a registered publisher, and deposited for copyright. A book is defined as a work of 49 or more pages; a work published simultaneously in more than one country is counted as having been published in each. A periodical is a publication issued at regular or stated intervals and, in Unesco's usage, directed to the general public. Newspaper statistics are especially difficult to collect and compare. Newspapers continually are founded, cease publication, merge, or change frequency of publication. Data on circulation are often incomplete, slow to be aggregated at the national level, or regarded as proprietary. In some countries no daily newspaper exists.

Post office statistics are compiled mainly from the Universal Postal Union's annual summary *Statistique des services postaux*. Postal services, unlike the other media discussed earlier, tend most often to be operated by a

Communications

country	publishing (latest)							postal services				telecommunications	
	books		periodicals		daily newspapers			post offices, 1995				radio, 1996	
	number of titles	number of copies ('000)	number of titles	number of copies ('000)	number	total circulation ('000)	circulation per 1,000 persons	number	persons per office	pieces of mail handled ('000,000)	pieces handled per person	receivers (all types; '000)	receivers per 1,000 persons
Afghanistan	—	—	...	...	15	216	11	352	61,300	...	...	...	...
Albania	...	...	143	3,477	3.0	185	54	698	4,600	3.5	1.0	550	157
Algeria	323	...	48	803	6.0	1,250	46	3,145	8,950	564	20	3,500	125
American Samoa	...	...	...	...	1.0	2.8	51	...	—	—	—	...	...
Andorra	57	...	...	...	3.0	4.0	63	...	...	...	...	10	5.7
Angola	...	...	...	...	4.0	117	11	62	162,000	2.6	0.2	450	39
Antigua and Barbuda	...	...	...	...	1.0	6.0	94	...	—	—	—	50	778
Argentina	9,065	48,882	...	...	187	4,705	138	5,676	6,100	420	12	21,500	637
Armenia	224	1,739	40	5,064	7.0	80	23	...	...	1.8	0.5	...	...
Aruba	...	...	...	...	14	52	757	4.0	20,500	...	...	40	571
Australia	10,835	...	...	...	69	4,600	255	3,954	4,560	4,556	252	21,000	1,152
Austria	7,987	...	2,481	...	23	3,736	465	2,634	3,050	3,627	425	4,710	584
Azerbaijan	375	5,557	49	801	3.0	210	28	1,857	4,040	7.5	1.0	...	...
Bahamas, The	...	...	...	...	3.0	35	126	136	2,040	61[1]	216[1]	80	282
Bahrain	...	...	26	73	3.0	70	128	12	48,100	72[2]	122[2]	320	542
Bangladesh	...	...	...	...	51	710	6.0	...	...	261	2.2	8,000	67
Barbados	...	...	...	...	2.0	41	159	17	15,500	18	68	300	1,132
Belarus	3,346	80,606	155	3,765	10	1,899	187	3,894[2]	2,650[2]	6.7[4]	0.7[4]	3,200	311
Belgium	...	...	13,706	...	32	3,231	321	1,635	6,200	3,557	352	5,000	500
Belize	70	—	...	...	4.0	23.5	0.5	113	1,900	3.8	18	30	140
Benin	84	42	...	...	1.0	12	2	159	34,700	8.4	1.5	400	73
Bermuda	...	...	...	...	1.0	16	254	14	4,350	15	240	80	1,311
Bhutan	...	...	...	...	...	...	...	103	7,990	1.9	1.2	23	28
Bolivia	...	...	...	...	11	500	69	159	46,600	21	2.8	4,250	553
Bosnia and Herzegovina	...	...	...	...	2.0	518	131	159	21,800	0.5	0.1	840	263
Botswana	...	...	14	177	...	42.1	29.0	193	7,520	36	25	300	206
Brazil	21,574	104,397	...	...	317	7,200	45	10,905	14,300	5,564[5]	36[5]	55,000	340
Brunei	45	...	15	132	1.0	20	71	6.0	48,700	13	45	125	417
Bulgaria	5,925	42,746	745	3,097	17	1,179	141	3,579	2,340	156	19[3, 5]	3,920	437
Burkina Faso	...	...	37	24	1.0	17[6]	1.6[6]	66[7]	157,000[7]	14[7]	1.5[7]	513	48
Burundi	...	...	...	...	1.0	20	3.0	27[2]	219,000[2]	7.6[2]	1.3[2]	300	47
Cambodia	...	...	...	...	...	...	...	30	328,000	11[8]	1.1[8]	1,500	150
Cameroon	...	...	...	...	1.0	50	4.0	261	53,100	5.3	0.4	1,500	115
Canada	22,208	...	1,400	37,108	107	5,500	189	18,607[2]	1,590[2]	10,715[5, 8]	370[5, 8]	22,600	803
Cape Verde	...	...	...	...	...	...	...	55	6,930	1.7	4.5	57	135
Central African Republic	...	...	...	...	1.0	2.0	1.0	31	104,000	...	...	180	55
Chad	...	...	...	...	1.0	2.0	0.4	34[2]	200,000[2]	7.9[2]	1.3[2]	1,310	240
Chile	1,820	...	417	3,450	32	1,411	99	587	24,200	294[2]	21[2]	4,400	317
China	100,951	5,945	6,486	205,060	38	27,790	23	69,003	17,500	7,955[9]	6.5[9]	215,950	178
Colombia	...	...	...	...	46	2,200	64	1,655	21,207	136	3.9	5,400	150
Comoros	...	...	...	...	...	...	...	36[8]	13,611[8]	0.9[8]	1.5[8]	61	97
Congo, Dem. Rep. of the	64	535	...	...	9.0	112	3.0	304	144,000	...	...	3,480	81
Congo, Rep. of the	...	...	3	34	6.0	19	8.0	114	2,170	1.8	0.7	240	95
Costa Rica	963	...	...	...	5.0	333	102	...	...	28[8]	8.5[9]	760	224
Côte d'Ivoire	...	...	...	...	1.0	90	7.0	364	38,900	46	3.2	1,600	110
Croatia	2,671	...	352	6,357	6.0	2,600	575	1,190	4,010	262	58	1,100	230
Cuba	932	4,610	160	2,797	17	1,315	120	1,545[8]	7,150[8]	28[8]	2.6[8]	...	...
Cyprus	1,040	1,530	37	167	15	81	110	738	1,130	58	79	210	288
Czech Republic	9,309	...	1,168	81,387	23	2,259	219	3,511	2,940	729	71	9,100	884
Denmark	11,973	...	205	7,838	51	1,610	308	64	81,800	1,828	350	5,200	988
Djibouti	...	...	7	6.0	...	...	...	10	58,600	16	28	35	61
Dominica	...	...	...	...	...	—	—	131[2]	566[2]	2.9[2]	42[2]	65	875
Dominican Republic	...	...	...	...	11	264	35	215	35,000	9.8[1]	1.3[1]	1,180	154
Ecuador	11	40	199	...	24	808	72	267	42,900	18	1.6	3,240	277
Egypt	3,108	108,042	266	1,815	17	3,949	64	7,197	8,280	309	5.2	16,450	265
El Salvador	...	...	...	...	6.0	284	53	297	18,500	21	3.6	2,080	373
Equatorial Guinea	...	...	...	...	...	1.0	2.5	23[2]	18,300[2]	...	...	200	488
Eritrea	106	420	...	...	...	...	...	35	95,300	1.8	0.5	...	...
Estonia	2,291	8,592	470	...	4.0	373	242	582	2,550	49	32	...	...
Ethiopia	...	...	...	...	4.0	81	10	570	97,500	29	0.5	9,000	167

single national service, to cover a country completely, and to record traffic data according to broadly similar schemes (although the details of *classes* of mail handled may differ). Some countries do not enumerate domestic traffic or may record only international traffic requiring handling charges.

Data for some kinds of telecommunications apparatus are relatively easy to collect; telephones, for example, must be installed, and service recorded so that it may be charged. But in most countries the other types of apparatus mentioned above may be purchased by anyone and used whenever desired. As a result, data on distribution and use of these types of apparatus may be collected in a variety of ways—on the basis of numbers of subscribers, licenses issued, periodic sample surveys, trade data, census or housing surveys, or private consumer surveys. Data on broadcast media refer to receivers; data on telephones to "main lines," or the lines connecting a subscriber's apparatus (fixed or mobile) to the public, switched net. Information on fax machines and PCs is estimated only, as noted above. Internet "hosts" refers to the number of computers directly connected to the worldwide network.

The *Statistical Yearbook* of Unesco contains extensive data on book, periodical, and newspaper publishing, and on radio and television broadcasting that have been collected from standardized questionnaires. The quality and recency of its data, however, depend on the completion and timely return of each questionnaire by national authorities. The commercially published annual *World Radio TV Handbook* (Andrew G. Sennitt, editor) is a valuable source of information on broadcast media and has complete and timely coverage. It depends on data received from broadcasters, but, because some do not respond, local correspondents and monitors are used in many countries, and some unconfirmed or unofficial data are included as estimates. The statistics on telecommunication apparatus and computers are derived mainly from the UN-affiliated International Telecommunication Union's *World Telecommunication Development Report* (annual).

... Not available.

—None, nil, or not applicable.

television, 1995		telephones, 1995		cellular phones, 1995		fax, 1995		personal computers, 1995		Internet hosts, 1995	country
receivers (all types; '000)	receivers per 1,000 persons	main lines ('000)	main lines per 1,000 persons	cellular subscriptions ('000)	subscriptions per 1,000 persons	receivers ('000)	receivers per 1,000 persons	units ('000)	units per 1,000 persons	connections per 1,000,000 persons	
180	10	29	1.4	—	—	...	...	...	...	—	Afghanistan
300	89	42	12	—	—	0.6	—	...	...	10	Albania
1,945	71	1,176	42	4.7	0.2	5.2	0.2	85	3.0	0.6	Algeria
...	...	...	...	...	...	...	...	...	...	...	American Samoa
22	360	30	438	2.8	42	1.3	20	...	...	147	Andorra
550	51	60	5.6	2.0	0.2	...	...	...	...	—	Angola
27	419	20	311	...	...	...	...	...	...	2,424	Antigua and Barbuda
12,000	347	5,532	160	341	9.9	50	1.4	850	25	154	Argentina
900	241	583	155	—	—	0.3	0.1	...	...	46	Armenia
33	471	27	390	1.7	25	0.5	6.9	...	...	—	Aruba
11,565	641	9,200	510	2,305	128	475	26	4,979	276	17,146	Australia
4,000	497	3,749	466	384	48	285	35	1,000	124	6,623	Austria
1,600	212	640	85	6.0	0.8	2.5	0.1	...	...	2.1	Azerbaijan
65	233	77	277	2.4	8.6	0.5	1.8	...	...	989	Bahamas, The
255	442	141	242	28	48	5.7	9.9	29	50	244	Bahrain
850	7.0	287	2.4	2.5	2.1	4.0	3.3	...	...	—	Bangladesh
75	284	90	345	4.6	18	1.8	6.8	15	58	7.7	Barbados
2,700	265	1,968	190	5.9	0.6	8.9	0.9	...	...	2.2	Belarus
4,700	464	4,632	458	235	23	165	16	1,400	138	3,024	Belgium
36	167	29	134	1.2	5.7	0.5	2.3	6.0	28	4.6	Belize
400	73	28	5.2	1.1	0.2	0.8	0.1	...	...	—	Benin
...	...	...	...	...	...	...	...	...	...	...	Bermuda
...	...	5.2	6.3	—	—	0.3	0.4	...	...	—	Bhutan
1,500	202	348	47	7.2	1.0	...	...	...	...	8.9	Bolivia
385	111	238	69	—	—	...	...	...	...	—	Bosnia and Herzegovina
35	24	60	41	—	—	3.1	2.1	...	...	—	Botswana
45,000	278	12,083	78	1,286	8.2	200	1.3	2,000	13	124	Brazil
173	609	68	240	36	126	2.0	6.8	8.0	29	549	Brunei
3,011	359	2,563	306	21	2.5	15	1.8	180	22	126	Bulgaria
46	4.4	30	2.9	...	...	...	...	...	...	—	Burkina Faso
40	7.0	17	2.7	0.3	0.1	0.1	0.02	...	...	—	Burundi
80	8.0	5.4	0.5	15	1.5	0.6	0.1	...	...	—	Cambodia
960	75	60	4.5	2.8	0.2	...	...	...	...	—	Cameroon
18,917	647	17,457	590	2,590	88	525	18	5,700	193	12,595	Canada
1.0	3.0	22	55	—	—	0.5	1.3	...	...	—	Cape Verde
17	5.0	7.8	2.3	0.1	—	0.2	0.1	...	...	—	Central African Republic
11	2.0	5.3	0.8	—	—	0.2	0.03	...	...	—	Chad
4,000	280	1,885	132	197	14	15	1.1	540	38	632	Chile
300,000	247	40,706	34	3,629	3.0	270	0.2	2,600	2.1	1.8	China
7,314	188	3,873	100	275	7.1	100	2.6	630	16	58	Colombia
2.0	5.0	4.5	8.2	—	—	0.1	0.2	...	...	324	Comoros
1,800	41	36	0.8	10	0.2	5.0	0.1	...	...	—	Congo, Dem. Rep. of the
42	17	21	8.1	—	—	0.1	0.04	...	...	...	Congo, Rep. of the
750	220	557	167	19	5.6	2.2	0.7	...	...	439	Costa Rica
790	59	116	8.1	—	—	...	...	...	...	0.2	Côte d'Ivoire
1,100	230	1,287	269	34	7.1	38	8.0	100	21	515	Croatia
2,200	200	353	32	1.9	0.2	0.4	0.04	...	...	0.1	Cuba
105	143	347	474	45	61	7.0	9.3	30	41	532	Cyprus
4,200	406	2,444	237	49	4.7	74	7.1	550	53	2,115	Czech Republic
2,800	536	3,203	612	822	157	250	48	1,416	270	9,670	Denmark
42	73	7.6	13	—	—	0.1	0.2	1.0	1.7	10	Djibouti
10	141	18	240	—	—	0.3	4.0	...	...	521	Dominica
680	87	569	76	33	4.4	2.5	0.3	...	...	18	Dominican Republic
1,700	148	748	65	50	4.3	30	2.6	45	3.9	44	Ecuador
7,400	126	2,716	46	14	0.2	3.5	0.05	235	4.1	10	Egypt
1,300	241	285	53	14	2.5	...	...	...	...	4.3	El Salvador
37	92	2.5	6.3	—	—	0.1	0.3	...	...	—	Equatorial Guinea
22	6.0	17	4.8	—	—	0.8	0.2	...	...	—	Eritrea
610	411	412	277	31	21	13	8.7	10	6.7	2,782	Estonia
230	4.2	143	2.5	—	—	1.4	0.02	...	...	0.02	Ethiopia

Communications (continued)

country	publishing (latest)							postal services				telecommunications	
	books		periodicals		daily newspapers			post offices, 1995				radio, 1996	
	number of titles	number of copies ('000)	number of titles	number of copies ('000)	number	total circulation ('000)	circulation per 1,000 persons	number	persons per office	pieces of mail handled ('000,000)	pieces handled per person	receivers (all types; '000)	receivers per 1,000 persons
Faroe Islands	...	...	...	...	...	...	...	43	1,010	10	198	21	447
Fiji	401	2,256	...	...	1.0	35	45	261	2,930	24[7]	31[7]	450	574
Finland	12,539	...	5,711	...	56	2,368	464	1,791	2,850	1,143[5]	224[5]	4,950	966
France	45,311	1,041	2,672	120,018	118	13,685	237	16,919[2]	3,440[2]	24,391	419	50,000	862
French Guiana	...	...	...	...	1.0	2.0	11	...	...	...	...	71	486
French Polynesia	...	...	...	...	4.0	24	112	97	2,250	21[2]	95[2]	105	488
Gabon	...	...	...	...	1.0	20	16	60	19,300	5.7	4.3	155	119
Gambia, The	21	20	10	885	2.0	2.0	2.0	...	...	...	...	150	125
Gaza Strip	...	...	...	...	...	...	...	...	...	...	...	...	...
Georgia	314	1,131	...	...	...	...	...	...	...	1,025[2, 4]	188[2, 4]	...	...
Germany	70,643	...	9,010	395,036	411	25,757	317	17,172	4,760	19,963	244	150,000	1,875
Ghana	28	...	121	774	4.0	310	18	1,001	17,300	121	6.9	1,300	76
Gibraltar	...	...	...	...	2.0	6.0	214	3.0	9,040	6.4	214	17	573
Greece	...	...	...	...	168	1,622	156	1,266	8,260	368[5]	35[5]	4,200	400
Greenland	...	...	...	...	...	...	...	75	744	7.2	120	22	374
Grenada	...	...	...	...	1.0[10]	4.0[10]	45[10]	58[2]	1,680[2]	...	...	45	489
Guadeloupe	...	...	...	...	1.0	35	83	...	...	...	...	85	208
Guam	...	...	...	...	1.0	25	170	...	...	...	...	274	1,827
Guatemala	...	...	...	...	5.0	240	23	540[2]	19,700[2]	79[2]	7.7[2]	570	52
Guernsey	...	...	...	...	...	...	...	15	4,120	15[9]	251[9]	...	...
Guinea	...	...	3	5.0	...	...	...	83	86,300	9.5	1.4	230	35
Guinea-Bissau	...	...	...	...	1.0	6.0	6.0	26	43,300	311[11]	0.3[11]	40	36
Guyana	33	508	...	...	2.0	45	63	85	8,950	4.4[4]	5.3[4]	380	454
Haiti	...	...	...	...	4.0	45	7.1	121	53,200	8.6[4]	1.2[4]	270	41
Honduras	22	80	...	...	5.0	240	44	435	12,700	35	5.9	1,910	354
Hong Kong	...	...	598	...	43	2,951[12]	479[12]	123	50,000	1,151	187	3,700	586
Hungary	10,108	75,645	1,203	14,927	27	2,321	228	3,230	3,170	1,187	116	6,250	590
Iceland	1,429	...	938	384	5.0	137	515	...	...	...	...	197	733
India	11,460	...	...	...	...	...	...	152,792	6,130	13,751	15	111,000	121
Indonesia	6,303	...	117	3,985	56	3,800	20	8,146	23,800	775	4.0	26,000	132
Iran	10,753	26,275	318	6,166	12	1,200	20	10,539	5,700	223	3.3	13,000	213
Iraq	...	...	...	...	4.0	532	27	...	...	62	3.1	13,000	630
Ireland	...	...	...	...	8.0	600	170	1,934	1,860	614	172	...	...
Isle of Man	...	...	...	...	...	...	...	35	2,040	20[5, 8]	281[5, 8]	...	...
Israel	4,608	9,368	...	...	34	1,534	281	663	8,160	505	92	2,250	481
Italy	32,673	289,100	9,951	80,469	74	5,985	105	14,142	4,050	5,691	100	46,350	801
Jamaica	...	...	...	...	3.0	160	66	793	3,140	70	28	1,859	747
Japan	35,496	316,725	2,926	...	121	71,924	576	24,587	5,090	24,651	197	100,000	801
Jersey	...	...	...	...	...	...	...	23[8]	3,700[8]	50[8]	594[8]	...	...
Jordan	500	...	31	43	4.0	250	48	1,007	4,190	61	11	980	234
Kazakstan	1,148	18,999	...	...	...	...	...	4,355	3,810	201	0.01	...	...
Kenya	...	...	...	...	5.0	358	13	1,061	26,000	386	12	3,000	103
Kiribati	...	...	...	...	...	...	...	24[7]	3,310[7]	353[7]	4.7[7]	6.4	79
Korea, North	...	...	...	...	11	5,000	213	...	...	...	...	4.7	0.2
Korea, South	34,204	160,305	...	...	62	18,000	405	3,437	13,000	3,432[9]	77[9]	42,000	928
Kuwait	196	...	...	...	9.0	655	387	...	...	99[8]	68[8]	1,000	591
Kyrgyzstan	328	1,875	...	...	3.0	53	11	918	4,920	52[5]	11[5]	...	...
Laos	64	136	...	...	3.0	14	3.0	417	11,600	1.4	0.3	575	121
Latvia	1,677	10,835	213	1,660	22	589	228	1,019	2,470	23	9.0	1,396	547
Lebanon	...	...	...	...	16	500	135	...	...	...	...	2,247	601
Lesotho	...	...	...	...	2.0	14	7.0	155	12,500	74	36	1,100	569
Liberia	...	...	...	...	8.0	35	14	...	...	...	...	600	275
Libya	...	...	...	...	4.0	70	13	383[2]	13,700[2]	28[2]	5.8[2]	1,000	190
Liechtenstein	...	...	...	...	2.0	18	581	...	...	17[7]	0.6[7]	...	...
Lithuania	2,885	19,627	269	...	16	506	136	1,009	3,680	39	10	1,420	381
Luxembourg	681	...	508	...	5.0	154	384	106	3,860	155	378	240	586
Macau	...	...	16	...	9.0	250	591	13	34,500	16	37	250	591
Macedonia	672	2,918	74	347	3.0	44	21	...	...	...	...	350	179
Madagascar	114	287	55	108	7.0	60	4.5	816	16,300	39	2.6	2,300	173
Malaŵi	243	10	...	...	1.0	25	2.6	307	30,800	96	10	1,060	112
Malaysia	4,050	17,424	25	996	44	2,800	142	1,475	14,000	1,051	52	9,500	476
Maldives	...	...	...	...	2.0	3.0	12	362	700	2.4	9.6	25	99
Mali	...	...	...	...	2.0	40	4.4	124	75,600	4.1	0.4	1,600	176
Malta	417	...	359	...	3.0	54	145	50[2]	7,420[2]	136[2]	373[2]	95	260
Marshall Islands	...	...	...	...	...	...	...	...	...	...	...	...	...
Martinique	...	...	...	...	1.0	32	84	...	...	...	...	71	187
Mauritania	...	...	...	...	1.0	1.0	0.5	60	37,700	617	0.3	1,000	444
Mauritius	84	100	62	...	6.0	75	68	103	10,900	43	38	400	353
Mayotte	...	...	...	...	...	...	...	...	...	...	...	50	427
Mexico	...	...	158	13,097	309	10,420	113	7,382	12,300	948	10	21,000	230
Micronesia	...	...	...	...	...	...	...	...	...	...	...	70	667
Moldova	797	5,850	76	196	4.0	106	24	1,307	3,320	57	13	1,556	358
Monaco	...	...	3	38	1.0	8.0	263	...	...	...	...	30	987
Mongolia	285	959	45	6,361	1.0	207	88	358[2]	6,430[2]	2.3[2]	1.8[2]	280	121
Morocco	354	1,380	...	...	13	344	13	...	...	...	...	5,100	194
Mozambique	...	...	...	...	2.0	81	5.0	425	40,400	8.8	0.5	620	36
Myanmar (Burma)	3,660	...	...	...	5.0	1,032	23	1,206	37,400	88	1.9	3,300	72
Namibia	...	...	...	...	4.0	153	93	86	18,900	29[2, 5]	18[2, 5]	230	136
Nauru	...	...	...	...	...	...	...	25	406	...	...	6.0	577
Nepal	...	...	...	...	28	162	8.0	2,874[2]	7,080[2]	104[2]	4.9[2]	625	29
Netherlands, The	34,067	...	367	19,283	46	4,600	299	2,009	7,690	...	...	12,000	775
Netherlands Antilles	...	...	...	...	6.0	53	260	...	...	...	...	206	1,009
New Caledonia	...	...	...	...	3.0	23	123	57	3,280	24	131	92	495
New Zealand	...	...	...	...	31	1,050	297	...	...	...	...	3,100	866
Nicaragua	...	...	...	...	4.0	130	30	202[2]	21,600[2]	11[2, 4]	2.6[2, 4]	925	222

television, 1995		telephones, 1995		cellular phones, 1995		fax, 1995		personal computers, 1995		Internet hosts, 1995	country
receivers (all types; '000)	receivers per 1,000 persons	main lines ('000)	main lines per 1,000 persons	cellular subscriptions ('000)	subscriptions per 1,000 persons	receivers ('000)	receivers per 1,000 persons	units ('000)	units per 1,000 persons	connections per 1,000,000 persons	
...	...	...	...	...	...	...	...	...	...	...	Faroe Islands
70	89	65	83	2.2	2.8	3.0	3.8	...	...	66	Fiji
2,650	519	2,796	547	1,018	199	132	26	930	182	42,229	Finland
33,600	579	32,400	558	1,379	24	1,900	33	7,800	134	2,604	France
25	170	41	288	—	—	...	...	...	...	—	French Guiana
39	177	47	219	—	—	0.9	4.1	...	...	—	French Polynesia
100	76	32	24	4.0	3.0	0.4	0.4	6.0	4.5	—	Gabon
...	...	19	17	1.4	1.3	1.0	0.6	...	...	—	Gambia, The
...	...	...	...	...	...	...	...	...	...	...	Gaza Strip
1,200	220	554	103	0.2	0.04	0.5	0.1	...	...	11	Georgia
45,000	550	40,400	494	3,750	46	1,447	18	13,500	165	5,794	Germany
265	16	60	3.5	6.2	0.4	4.5	0.3	20	1.2	0.4	Ghana
...	...	...	...	...	...	...	...	...	...	...	Gibraltar
4,630	442	5,163	493	273	26	15	1.5	350	33	740	Greece
...	...	...	...	...	...	...	...	...	...	...	Greenland
15	158	23	255	0.4	4.4	0.3	3.1	...	...	—	Grenada
112	262	159	378	...	...	3.4	8.1	...	...	—	Guadeloupe
95	648	69	461	5.0	33	...	...	...	...	367	Guam
1,300	122	290	27	30	2.8	10	0.9	30	2.8	2.5	Guatemala
...	...	42	689	2.4	39	0.7	11	...	...	—	Guernsey
500	76	11	1.6	1.0	0.1	0.2	0.03	1.0	0.2	0.3	Guinea
...	...	9.4	8.8	—	—	0.5	0.5	...	...	—	Guinea-Bissau
35	42	45	63	1.2	1.6	...	...	...	...	—	Guyana
35	5.0	60	8.4	—	—	—	...	—	...	—	Haiti
450	80	161	29	—	—	...	...	...	...	—	Honduras
2,092	359	3,508	556	798	129	285	46	720	116	2,858	Hong Kong
4,530	444	1,893	185	265	26	45	4.4	400	39	1,546	Hungary
120	447	149	556	31	116	4.1	15	55	206	31,007	Iceland
57,000	61	11,978	13	136	0.1	50	0.1	1,200	1.3	0.9	India
28,000	147	3,291	17	219	1.1	85	0.4	730	3.7	12	Indonesia
9,000	134	5,090	85	9.2	0.2	30	0.5	...	...	4.0	Iran
1,450	74	675	33	—	—	...	...	...	...	—	Iraq
1,370	382	1,310	365	158	44	80	22	520	145	3,747	Ireland
...	...	...	...	...	...	...	...	...	...	...	Isle of Man
1,700	303	2,343	418	300	54	140	25	540	100	5,260	Israel
25,000	436	24,854	433	3,864	67	202	3.5	4,800	84	1,280	Italy
773	306	292	116	45	18	0.6	...	...	...	65	Jamaica
77,500	619	61,106	488	10,204	82	8,000	64	19,100	153	2,151	Japan
...	...	59	687	4.4	51	0.7	8.0	...	...	—	Jersey
740	175	317	73	12	2.6	32	7.3	35	8.0	4.4	Jordan
4,578	275	1,963	118	4.6	0.3	2.9	0.2	...	...	11	Kazakstan
462	18	240	9.0	2.3	0.1	3.8	0.1	18	0.7	0.6	Kenya
2.0	25	2.0	26	—	—	0.2	2.5	...	...	—	Kiribati
2,700	115	1,100	46	—	—	3.0	0.1	...	...	—	Korea, North
14,400	321	18,600	415	1,641	37	375	8.4	5,420	121	653	Korea, South
630	373	382	226	118	70	35	21	95	56	729	Kuwait
1,110	247	357	77	—	—	...	...	...	...	—	Kyrgyzstan
35	7.0	20	4.1	1.5	0.3	0.5	0.1	...	...	—	Laos
1,213	482	705	280	15	6.0	0.9	0.3	20	7.9	525	Latvia
1,075	291	330	89	120	30	3.0	0.8	50	13	22	Lebanon
13	7.0	18	9.0	—	—	0.6	0.3	...	...	—	Lesotho
54	25	4.5	2.1	—	—	...	...	...	...	—	Liberia
720	138	318	59	—	—	...	...	...	...	—	Libya
...	...	...	...	...	...	...	...	...	...	...	Liechtenstein
1,350	364	941	254	15	4.0	3.8	1.0	24	6.5	123	Lithuania
242	593	222	550	—	—	—	—	—	—	4,608	Luxembourg
48	113	153	361	37	86	7.3	17	40	94	153	Macau
350	179	349	179	—	—	1.8	0.8	...	...	42	Macedonia
320	24	33	2.4	—	—	...	...	...	...	—	Madagascar
...	...	34	3.6	0.4	0.04	1.1	0.1	...	...	—	Malawi
4,500	226	3,332	166	873	43	58	3.0	800	40	...	Malaysia
10	40	14	57	—	—	3.5	14	3.0	12	—	Maldives
110	12	17	1.7	—	—	...	...	...	...	—	Mali
167	448	171	459	11	29	3.2	8.6	30	81	231	Malta
...	...	...	...	...	...	...	...	...	...	...	Marshall Islands
53	137	148	381	12	31	20	52	36	93	—	Martinique
132	58	9.2	4.1	—	—	0.3	0.1	...	...	—	Mauritania
210	187	148	131	12	10	20	18	36	32	—	Mauritius
...	0.6	5.3	48	—	—	...	...	...	...	—	Mayotte
17,600	192	8,801	96	642	7.0	180	2.1	2,400	26	...	Mexico
2.0	21	7.9	74	—	—	0.3	2.9	...	...	—	Micronesia
1,300	300	567	131	—	—	0.6	0.1	9.0	2.1	1.2	Moldova
...	...	...	...	...	...	...	...	...	...	...	Monaco
143	59	78	32	—	—	2.2	0.9	...	...	—	Mongolia
3,800	145	1,158	43	1.6	0.1	7.5	0.3	45	1.7	8.6	Morocco
51	3.0	60	3.4	—	—	7.2	0.4	...	...	—	Mozambique
3,450	76	147	3.3	2.1	0.04	1.4	0.03	...	...	—	Myanmar (Burma)
45	29	79	51	3.5	2.3	...	...	...	...	7.1	Namibia
...	...	...	...	...	...	...	...	...	...	...	Nauru
60	3.0	77	3.6	—	—	0.6	0.03	...	...	0.9	Nepal
7,650	495	8,120	525	513	33	500	32	3,100	200	11,110	Netherlands, The
65	325	75	374	12	59	...	...	...	...	—	Netherlands Antilles
71	380	44	236	0.8	4.5	2.2	12	...	...	5.4	New Caledonia
1,818	506	1,719	479	388	108	65	18	800	223	14,923	New Zealand
700	170	97	23	4.4	1.1	...	...	...	...	34	Nicaragua

Communications (continued)

country	publishing (latest)							postal services				telecommunications	
	books		periodicals		daily newspapers			post offices, 1995				radio, 1996	
	number of titles	number of copies ('000)	number of titles	number of copies ('000)	number	total circulation ('000)	circulation per 1,000 persons	number	persons per office	pieces of mail handled ('000,000)	pieces handled per person	receivers (all types; '000)	receivers per 1,000 persons
Niger	...	...	...	...	4.0	11	1.3	66	134,000	3.9	0.4	440	48
Nigeria	1,562	...	...	...	27	1,950	18	3,639	26,900	812	7.3	17,200[13]	170[13]
Northern Mariana Islands	...	...	...	...	...	...	...	...	...	...	...	11	190
Norway	6,846	...	8,017	...	83	2,170	498	2,356	1,850	2,176	499	3,342	767
Oman	24	25	15	...	4.0	63	30	90	23,400	32[2, 5]	15[2, 5]	900	416
Pakistan	124	714	...	...	273	2,840	22	13,320	9,750	257[5]	2.0[5]	10,200	76
Palau	...	...	...	...	...	...	...	...	...	...	...	9.0	536
Panama	...	...	...	...	7.0	160	62	343	7,670	10	3.9	527	200
Papua New Guinea	...	...	...	...	2.0	65	15	108[14]	39,800[14]	39[14]	10[14]	300	72
Paraguay	152	...	...	...	5.0	203	42	321	15,000	5.0	1.0	700	144
Peru	1,993	...	...	...	48	2,000	86	836[2]	28,100[2]	22	0.9	5,300	225
Philippines	1,233	...	1,570	9,468	42	4,286	65	3,023[2]	22,600[2]	1,108[2]	16[2]	8,300	116
Poland	10,874	98,612	3,999	77,735	66	5,404	141	7,853	4,920	1,217	32	16,300	421
Portugal	6,667	26,942	984	10,208	23	404	41	6,638	1,490	1,009[9]	93[9]	2,220	224
Puerto Rico	...	...	...	...	3.0	670	184	...	...	...	...	2,480	666
Qatar	371	184	12	157	4.0	80	138	30	18,600	20[4]	36[4]	180	311
Réunion	69	...	...	...	3.0	55	83	...	...	...	...	170	265
Romania	4,074	50,230	987	...	69	6,800	297	5,243	4,330	292	13	4,500	198
Russia	30,390	594,323	2,592	918,218	17	39,301	267	45,594	3,250	7,110[5]	48[5]	...	...
Rwanda	...	...	15	101	1.0	0.5	0.1	1.0[2]	6,018,000[2]	...	...	...	...
St. Kitts and Nevis	...	...	10	44	...	...	...	7.0	5,630	2.4	59	4.5	110
St. Lucia	...	...	...	...	...	...	...	...	...	...	...	100	699
St. Vincent	...	...	...	...	...	...	...	41	2,680	...	...	65	565
Samoa	...	...	...	...	...	...	...	38	4,360	998	5,871	...	...
San Marino	...	...	18	11	5.0	1.3	0.5	10	2,488	...	...	13	522
São Tomé and Príncipe	...	...	...	...	...	...	...	10[2]	13,100[2]	0.3	0.02	31	237
Saudi Arabia	...	...	471	...	19	950	54	1,282	13,900	896	50	3,800	213
Senegal	...	...	...	...	3.0	48	6.0	131	61,100	6.7[9]	0.7[9]	...	...
Seychelles	...	...	...	...	1.0	3.0	40	5.0	15,000	4.5	64	50	667
Sierra Leone	...	...	...	...	1.0	10	2.2	54	85,000	1.1	0.2	1,000	221
Singapore	...	...	...	...	8.0	1,015	340	1,163	2,570	646	216	822	275
Slovakia	3,481	6,139	424	8,725	21	1,363	256	1,731	3,100	526	98	630	118
Slovenia	2,906	...	784	...	6.0	360	183	515	3,860	267	135	630	320
Solomon Islands	...	...	...	...	...	...	...	140	2,730	4.3	11	45	117
Somalia	...	...	...	...	1.0	9.0	1.0	...	...	...	...	300	41
South Africa	4,574	37,561	11	2,149	17.0	1,346	33	...	...	2,452	59	11,200	273
Spain	44,261	180,081	...	...	148	4,100	104	4,527	8,660	4,295	110	12,000	304
Sri Lanka	2,929	15,337	...	...	9.0	450	25	4,138	4,440	486	26	3,300	182
Sudan, The	...	...	...	...	5.0	620	23	411	74,300	5.3[8]	0.2[8]	5,755	193
Suriname	...	...	...	...	3.0	43	103	...	...	...	...	262	609
Swaziland	...	...	...	...	3.0	12	14	65	14,900	25	27	500	550
Sweden	13,822	...	4,272	...	94	4,544	515	1,745	5,060	4,533	513	7,450	844
Switzerland	15,378	...	60	4,561	80	2,920	415	3,674	1,920	4,230[7]	601[7]	5,600	791
Syria	598	...	...	...	8.0	261	18	650	21,800	17	1.2	3,000	207
Taiwan	...	...	...	...	...	4,000	188	...	...	...	...	8,620	402
Tajikistan	231	2,561	22	50	2.0	80	13	736	7,930	9.2	1.6	...	...
Tanzania	...	...	...	...	3.0	220	8.0	525	54,400	22	0.2	3,500	123
Thailand	7,626	...	1,522	...	35	2,766	47	4,264[2]	13,900[2]	1,228	21	10,000	167
Togo	...	...	...	...	1.0	10	2.0	50	88,200	4.1	1.0	720	170
Tonga	...	...	...	...	1.0	7.0	73	1.8[8]	55,600[8]	4.0[8]	40[8]	40	400
Trinidad and Tobago	26	30	...	...	4.0	175	135	243	5,190	30	23	550	433
Tunisia	539	94	...	...	7.0	403	46	955	9,390	117	13	1,700	193
Turkey	4,473	...	3,554	...	57	2,679	44	31,122	1,970	1,482	24	8,800	141
Turkmenistan	565	6,604	...	...	...	...	...	...	...	...	...	850	189
Tuvalu	...	...	...	...	...	...	...	...	...	...	...	3.0	319
Uganda	314	2,229	26	158	2.0	35	2.0	306	64,500	18	1.0	10,000	507
Ukraine	5,002	87,567	321	3,491	90	6,083	118	16,421	3,140	591	11	18,000	346
United Arab Emirates	293	5,117	80	922	8.0	300	126	180	13,200	162	70	490	206
United Kingdom	95,015	...	...	...	103	20,372	351	...	...	...	...	65,400	1,109
United States	51,863	...	11,593	...	1,548	59,305	228	49,906	5,300	178,970	0.7	520,000	1,976
Uruguay	...	...	...	...	32	750	237	295	10,600	15	4.7	1,850	591
Uzbekistan	1,340	44,033	70	2,032	4.0	160	7.0	...	...	...	...	...	...
Vanuatu	...	...	...	...	...	...	...	...	...	...	...	55	327
Venezuela	3,660	8,180	...	...	89	4,600	215	444	49,200	93	4.3	8,300	383
Vietnam	5,581	83,000	...	...	4.0	570	8.0	...	...	...	...	7,000	95
Virgin Islands (U.S)	...	...	...	...	2.0	26	267	9[2]	10,800	3.6[4]	0.2[4]	100	1,029
West Bank	...	...	...	...	...	...	...	...	...	...	...	...	...
Western Sahara	...	...	...	...	...	...	...	...	...	...	...	...	...
Yemen	...	...	...	...	3.0	230	17	451	34,000	6.8	0.5	665	48
Yugoslavia	2,799	11,905	395	...	9.0	966	90	1,569[7]	6,722[7]	0.2[15]	0.02[15]	2,692	256
Zambia	...	...	...	...	...	...	...	203	44,200	26	2.8	1,300	139
Zimbabwe	232	...	28	680	2.0	192	17	280	39,900	298	26	1,300	113

television, 1995		telephones, 1995		cellular phones, 1995		fax, 1995		personal computers, 1995		Internet hosts, 1995	country
receivers (all types; '000)	receivers per 1,000 persons	main lines ('000)	main lines per 1,000 persons	cellular subscriptions ('000)	subscriptions per 1,000 persons	receivers ('000)	receivers per 1,000 persons	units ('000)	units per 1,000 persons	connections per 1,000,000 persons	
200	23	13	1.5	—	—	300	33	...	...	—	Niger
4,000	38	405	3.6	13	0.1	...	...	440	4.1	—	Nigeria
...	...	...	...	...	...	...	...	...	...	...	Northern Mariana Islands
2,450	561	2,431	558	1,013	232	130	30	1,193	273	19,289	Norway
132	61	170	79	8.1	3.7	1.6	0.7	28	13	...	Oman
2,800	22	2,127	16	43	0.3	159	1.2	155	1.2	0.1	Pakistan
...	...	...	...	...	...	...	...	...	...	...	Palau
610	229	304	116	—	—	—	—	...	...	56	Panama
700	163	44	10	—	—	0.8	0.2	...	...	—	Papua New Guinea
710	144	167	34	16	3.2	1.7	0.4	...	...	—	Paraguay
2,350	100	1,109	47	74	3.1	15	0.6	140	5.9	35	Peru
9,000	129	1,787	25	493	6.9	35	0.5	770	11	26	Philippines
15,765	408	5,729	148	75	1.9	55	1.4	1,100	29	598	Poland
...	...	3,586	362	341	34	35	3.4	600	61	1,187	Portugal
1,160	311	1,196	321	171	48	543	146	...	...	23	Puerto Rico
...	...	123	212	19	33	9.4	16	30	52	11	Qatar
135	205	219	329	...	...	1.9	2.9	...	...	—	Réunion
4,580	201	2,968	131	9.1	0.4	21	0.9	120	5.3	77	Romania
56,244	380	25,019	170	89	0.6	31	0.2	2,600	18	149	Russia
10	1.7	15	2.5	—	—	0.5	0.1	...	...	—	Rwanda
...	...	...	...	...	...	...	...	...	...	...	St. Kitts and Nevis
...	...	...	...	...	...	...	...	...	...	...	St. Lucia
...	...	...	...	...	...	...	...	...	...	—	St. Vincent
7.0	38	7.8	46	—	—	0.4	2.4	...	...	—	Samoa
...	...	...	...	...	...	...	...	...	...	...	San Marino
...	...	2.5	19	—	—	0.2	1.5	...	...	—	São Tomé and Príncipe
4,600	257	1,719	96	16	0.9	75	4.4	600	35	1.5	Saudi Arabia
290	37	82	9.8	0.1	0.01	...	...	60	7.2	0.7	Senegal
14	184	14	187	0.3	4.3	0.6	8.0	...	...	—	Seychelles
73	16	17	3.7	—	—	1.0	0.2	...	...	—	Sierra Leone
650	218	1,429	478	292	98	56	19	515	172	7.624	Singapore
1,157	216	1,119	208	12	2.3	45	8.4	220	41	543	Slovakia
745	374	615	309	157	14	80	41	95	48	2,948	Slovenia
6.0	16	6.5	17	0.2	0.6	0.8	2.1	...	...	24	Solomon Islands
118	13	15	1.7	—	—	...	118[1]	...	...	—	Somalia
4,200	101	3,919	95	535	13	75	1.8	1,100	27	1,165	South Africa
19,200	490	15,095	385	966	25	215	5.2	3,200	82	1,018	Spain
1,200	66	204	11	53	3.0	11	0.6	20	1.1	0.3	Sri Lanka
2,300	76	75	2.7	—	—	5.8	0.2	...	...	—	Sudan, The
80	186	53	123	3.7	8.6	0.3	0.7	...	...	—	Suriname
90	96	20	21	—	—	0.9	1.0	...	...	1.1	Swaziland
4,202	476	6,010	681	2,025	229	329	37	1,700	193	16,405	Sweden
2,602	370	4,319	613	447	64	197	28	2,450	348	11,383	Switzerland
1,300	89	930	63	—	—	5.0	0.3	10	0.7	—	Syria
7,000	327	10,011	467	970	45	430	20	1,773	83	1,207	Taiwan
1,500	258	263	45	—	—	1.3	0.2	...	...	—	Tajikistan
450	16	90	3.0	3.5	0.1	0.1	...	...	...	—	Tanzania
13,500	227	3,482	59	1,088	18	60	1.0	900	15	68	Thailand
50	12	22	5.2	—	—	10	2.4	...	...	—	Togo
2.0	20	6.6	67	0.1	1.2	0.2	2.0	...	...	10	Tonga
415	328	209	166	5.6	4.4	2.6	1.6	25	20	42	Trinidad and Tobago
1,400	156	523	58	3.2	0.4	25	2.8	60	6.7	8.8	Tunisia
15,000	240	13,228	215	437	7.1	99	1.6	770	13	85	Turkey
850	189	320	71	—	—	...	...	...	...	—	Turkmenistan
...	...	...	...	...	...	...	...	...	...	...	Tuvalu
500	26	43	2.3	1.7	0.1	2.5	—	10	0.5	3.1	Uganda
12,000	233	8,311	161	14	0.3	1.5	0.03	290	5.6	45	Ukraine
500	26	672	283	129	54	25	11	115	48	154	United Arab Emirates
35,800	61	29,409	502	5,736	98	1,800	31	10,900	186	7,513	United Kingdom
204,100	78	164,624	626	33,786	128	14,052	54	86,300	328	23,012	United States
970	310	622	199	40	13	11	3.5	70	22	346	Uruguay
4,000	176	1,738	76	3.7	0.2	1.9	0.1	...	...	1.5	Uzbekistan
2.0	12	42	250	0.1	0.7	0.6	3.6	...	...	—	Vanuatu
4,000	180	2,463	111	400	18	16	0.8	370	17	52	Venezuela
12,000	163	775	11	24	0.3	15	0.1	30	0.4	—	Vietnam
...	...	58	597	...	...	...	32	...	...	—	Virgin Islands (U.S.)
...	...	80	63	20	16	...	...	...	...	...	West Bank
...	...	...	...	...	...	...	...	...	...	—	Western Sahara
3,900	243	187	12	8.3	0.5	2.0	0.1	...	...	—	Yemen
1,800	170	2,017	192	—	—	15	1.4	125	12	—	Yugoslavia
600	64	77	8.2	1.5	0.2	0.6	0.1	...	...	7.3	Zambia
290	27	155	14	—	—	10	0.9	33	3.0	8.5	Zimbabwe

[1]1985. [2]1994. [3]Letters dispatched only. [4]Foreign-dispatched and foreign-received only. [5]Domestic only. [6]Circulation for 3 newspapers only. [7]1992. [8]1993. [9]Domestic and foreign-dispatched only. [10]1980. [11]Foreign-received only. [12]Circulation for 32 newspapers only. [13]1995. [14]1991. [15]Letters only.

Trade: external

The following table presents comparative data on the international, or foreign, trade of the countries of the world. The table analyzes data for both imports and exports in two ways: (1) into several major commodity groups defined in accordance with the United Nations system called the Standard International Trade Classification (SITC) and (2) by direction of trade for each country with major world trading blocs and partners. These commodity groupings are defined by the SITC code numbers beneath the column headings. The single-digit numbers represent broad SITC categories (in the SITC, called "sections"); the double-digit numbers represent subcategories ("divisions") of the single-digit categories (27 is a subcategory of 2); the three-digit number is a subcategory ("group") of the double-digit (667 is a subcategory of 66). Where a plus or minus sign is used before one of these SITC numbers, the SITC category or subcategory is being added to or subtracted from the aggregate implied by the total of the preceding sections. The SITC commodity aggregations used here are listed in the table at the end of this headnote. The full SITC commodity breakdown—some 3,118 basic headings—is presented in the 1986 United Nations publication *Standard International Trade Classification, Revision 3*.

The SITC was developed by the United Nations through its Statistical Commission as an outgrowth of the need for a standard system of aggregating commodities of external trade to provide international comparability of foreign trade statistics. The United Nations Statistical Commission has defined external merchandise trade as "all goods whose movement into or out of the customs area of a country compiling the statistics adds to or subtracts from the material resources of the country." Goods passing through a country for transport only are excluded, but goods entering for reexport, or deposited (as in a bonded warehouse, or free trade area) for reimport, are included. Statistics in this table refer only to goods and exclude purely financial transactions that are covered in the "Finance" and "National product and accounts" tables. Gold for fabrication (*e.g.,* as jewelry) is included; monetary and reserve gold are excluded.

For purposes of comparability of data, total value of imports and exports is given in this table in U.S. dollars. Conversions from currencies other than U.S. dollars are determined according to the average market rates for the year for which data are supplied; these are mainly as calculated by the International Monetary Fund (IMF) or other official sources. The commodity categories are given in terms of percentages of the total value of the country's import or export trade (with the exclusions noted above). Value is based on transaction value: for imports, the value at which the goods were purchased by the importer plus the cost of transportation and insurance to the frontier of the importing country (c.i.f. [cost, insurance,

Trade: external

country	year	imports												
		total value ('000,000 U.S.$)	Standard International Trade Classification (SITC) categories (%)							direction of trade (%)				
			food and agricultural raw materials (0+1+2 −27−28 +4)	mineral ores and concen-trates (27+28 +667)	fuels and other energy (3)	manufactured goods: total[a] (5+6 −667 +7+8 +9)	of which chemicals and related products (5)	of which machinery and transport equipment (7)	of which other[a] (6−667 +8+9)	from European Union (EU)[b]	from United States	from Eastern Europe[c]	from Japan	from all other[d]
Afghanistan	1991[1]	936.4	15.0	—[2]	0.4	84.6[3]	2.1	48.2	34.3[3]	4.8[4]	0.2[4]	59.9[4, 5]	7.9[4]	27.2[4]
Albania	1994	601.0	25.7[6]	——24.5[6]——		49.8[6]	9.3[6]	31.0[6]	9.5[6]	67.9[7]	0.2	9.9	—	22.0
Algeria	1995	9,830.6	32.6	0.3	1.1	66.0	11.3	30.5	24.1	59.3	13.2	2.5	3.4	21.6
American Samoa	1993[8]	427.5	63.1	...	8.1	28.8[3]	0.2	5.5	23.1	0.2[9]	73.4[9]	—[9]	8.5[9]	17.9[9]
Andorra	1995	1,055.5	30.6	0.9	3.5	65.0	10.0	21.9	33.1	85.7	4.2	0.1	3.4	6.6
Angola	1993	2,041.9	——32.4[2, 6]——		0.7[6]	66.9[3, 6]	10.6[6]	25.0[6]	31.3[3, 6]	79.7[4]	7.2	0.9[4]	2.2	10.0[4]
Antigua and Barbuda	1991	245.9	——17.8[2]——		9.9	72.3[3]	6.2	26.8	39.3[3]	41.3[11]	29.5[11]	—[11]	—[11]	29.2[11]
Argentina	1995	20,121.7	7.5	1.5	4.2	86.8	17.8	44.5	24.4	29.9	20.9	1.1	3.5	44.6
Armenia	1995	673.9	33.6	——42.6——		23.8	8.8	8.3	6.7	13.2	17.0	22.6	—	47.2
Aruba	1991	486.9	23.3	0.1	0.4	76.2	8.7	27.6	39.9	16.7	57.3	—	3.4	22.6
Australia	1996	65,427.0	6.3	0.4[2]	6.2	87.1[3]	11.6	47.0	28.6[3]	24.9	23.0	0.2	13.0	39.0
Austria	1995	65,662.5	9.3	1.5	4.5	84.6	10.6	36.7	37.4	75.5	3.1	6.4	1.7	13.3
Azerbaijan	1995	667.6	42.3	——15.1——		42.6	10.9	17.9	13.8	12.7	2.0	24.4	0.2	60.7
Bahamas, The	1990	2,919.9	8.6	—	65.2	26.2	5.3	8.3	12.7	5.9	36.2	0.2[5]	0.5	57.3
Bahrain	1995	3,624.8	——13.3[2]——		38.1	48.5[3]	8.7	16.2	23.6[3]	19.7	8.2	0.2	4.1	67.8
Bangladesh	1993[12]	2,708.8	40.6	4.6	9.6	45.3	9.2	13.6	22.5	11.1	5.2	1.3	6.7	75.8
Barbados	1995	766.0	20.6	0.5	8.5	70.4	12.2	26.8	31.4	17.1	40.7	0.2	6.7	35.2
Belarus	1995	5,563.6	11.8	——36.1——		52.1	14.8	17.0	20.3	16.7	1.7	74.8	0.4	6.4
Belgium[13]	1995	150,624.7	13.2	9.4	6.1	71.3	13.7	26.1	31.5	74.5	5.6	2.1	2.6	15.1
Belize	1995	258.3	19.4	0.3	11.5	68.9	10.7	25.8	32.3	15.5	54.1	—	1.3	29.0
Benin	1991	408.0	——32.9[2]——		11.6	55.5[3]	7.5	13.7	34.4[3]	30.6	4.5	0.7	2.4	61.8
Bermuda	1993	588.9	20.5	0.1[2]	5.8	73.6[3]	13.9	23.3	36.3[3]	10.1[7]	70.2	—	5.4	14.3
Bhutan	1992	128.0	15.0	0.7	8.1	76.2	4.9	46.2	25.1	25.5	0.8	—	10.8	62.9[17]
Bolivia	1995	1,396.3	11.2	1.9	4.5	82.4	13.7	46.3	22.4	19.6	22.3	0.5	12.3	45.3
Bosnia and Herzegovina	1996	1,879.0[4]	...	...	31.6[6]	...	...	...	...	35.8[4]	3.4[4]	8.6[4]	0.1[4]	52.2[4]
Botswana	1994	1,636.6	21.1	2.7	5.7	70.5	7.7	29.6	33.2	7.5	1.9	0.1	2.1	88.5[20]
Brazil	1995	53,736.7	13.4	1.6	12.1	72.9	15.2	39.2	18.6	27.9	23.7	1.0	5.1	42.3
Brunei	1993	1,820.5	9.9	0.5	0.8	88.8	4.4	49.6	34.8	25.7	25.1	17.1	9.4	22.7
Bulgaria	1995	5,125.0	11.0	2.7	27.0	59.3	12.8	19.3	27.2	37.2	2.1	36.2	0.8	23.7
Burkina Faso	1991	536.0	——25.6[2]——		11.6	62.8[3]	18.5	20.8	23.5[3]	40.4	4.9	0.3	4.2	50.1
Burundi	1993	204.5	13.0	0.6	12.4	74.0	14.1	21.3	38.6	45.4	1.8	0.4	9.2	43.3
Cambodia	1993	403.9	17.2[22]	...	11.7	...	6.5[22]	17.0[22]	...	9.2[4]	4.5[4]	2.5[4]	12.2[4]	71.6[4]
Cameroon	1996	1,204.3	16.2	3.2	15.7	64.9	14.6	27.6	22.7	53.4	8.5	1.8	5.0	31.3
Canada	1996	171,007.2	7.3	1.8	4.3	86.6	8.4	51.1	27.1	9.8	67.6	0.4	4.5	17.8
Cape Verde	1994	210.1	32.8	—	3.6	63.6	5.1	36.0	22.5	75.0	2.3	0.7	5.0	17.0
Central African Republic	1995	265.5	25.5	0.3	8.7	65.6	8.0	42.2	15.3	43.5	1.8	—	19.7	34.9
Chad	1992	243.0	25.1[25]	1.4[15, 25]	1.6[25]	71.8[16, 25]	15.1[25]	20.7[25]	36.0[16, 25]	46.5[4]	2.5[4]	0.4[4]	1.6[4]	49.0[4]
Chile	1995	14,903.1	8.4	1.3	9.0	81.3	12.2	42.3	26.8	15.9	25.5	0.2	6.8	51.6
China	1995	132,083.5	12.2	2.6	3.9	81.3	12.9	39.9	28.6	16.1	12.2	3.7	22.0	46.1
Colombia	1995	13,863.1	11.9	0.6	2.8	84.7	18.1	37.4	29.2	18.5	33.8	1.3	8.9	37.5
Comoros	1994	52.8	27.8[22]	...	11.6	60.6	1.4[22]	7.4[22]	51.9	40.0[7]	—[4]	1.9[4]	5.7[4]	52.4[4]
Congo, Dem. Rep. of the	1992	420.0	——20.0[11]——		13.8[11]	66.2[11]	4.4[11]	45.5[11]	16.3[11]	57.9[4]	4.9[4]	0.8[4]	2.7[4]	33.7[4]
Congo, Rep. of the	1994	408.4	27.1	0.7	1.2	71.0	13.8	28.5	28.7	54.0	10.0	0.2	2.6	33.3
Costa Rica	1994	3,029.7	11.6	0.3	9.1	79.0	18.2	29.4	31.4	11.3	44.3	0.5[5]	5.5	38.3
Côte d'Ivoire	1992	2,447.0[4]	——23.7[26]——		21.3[26]	55.0[26]	14.8[26]	16.4[26]	23.8[26]	56.0[4]	3.9[4]	0.1[4]	3.8[4]	36.2[4]
Croatia	1996	7,787.8	13.1	0.8	11.0	75.1	10.9	27.3	36.8	59.4	2.7	10.5	1.3	26.1
Cuba	1992	2,185.0	14.9[26]	0.5[2, 26]	32.4[26]	52.2[3, 26]	6.2[26]	27.5[26]	18.5[3, 26]	30.0[4]	—[4]	9.0[4]	1.0[4]	60.0[4]
Cyprus	1996	3,982.5	25.5	0.4	8.5	65.6	7.8	24.3	33.5	48.6	16.8	5.5	6.0	23.1
Czech Republic	1995	20,915.0	10.9	1.9	9.4	77.8	13.2	35.1	29.4	56.4	3.7	27.3	1.7	10.9
Denmark	1995	41,626.4	15.6	0.5	3.4	80.4	11.6	33.2	35.7	68.7	4.7	3.7	2.7	20.3
Djibouti	1991	214.4	38.3	0.2	9.1	52.3	6.0	15.5	30.8	46.6	3.7	0.7[5]	7.2	41.8
Dominica	1991	109.6	27.6	0.3	7.9	64.2	12.0	21.6	30.5	21.2	31.4	0.3	5.6	41.5
Dominican Republic	1994	2,626.4	13.7[27]	0.3[27]	35.2[27]	50.7[27]	11.7[27]	23.2[27]	15.9[27]	2.0[4]	37.4[4]	—[4]	1.5[4]	59.1[4]
Ecuador	1995	4,195.2	10.4	0.4	5.9	83.3	17.6	40.1	25.6	15.3	30.7	0.4	8.6	44.9
Egypt	1995	11,739.0	35.4	1.4	1.2	61.9	13.2	25.3	23.4	38.9	18.8	7.1	2.7	32.5

and freight] valuation); for exports, the value at which the goods were sold by the exporter, including the cost of transportation and insurance to bring the goods onto the transporting vehicle at the frontier of the exporting country (f.o.b. [free-on-board] valuation).

The largest part of the information presented here comes from the United Nations' *Commodity Trade Statistics* (microfiche format) and *International Trade Statistics Yearbook*. These sources, however, cannot always provide the most recent data for all countries listed in this table and must be supplemented by national and regional information. In some cases where the original data were only available for an alternative trade classification, an approximation has been made of the SITC commodity groupings.

The notes that follow further define the column headings.

a. Also includes any unallocated commodities.
b. EU of 15 countries (Austria, Belgium, Denmark, Finland, France, Germany, Greece, Ireland, Italy, Luxembourg, The Netherlands, Portugal, Spain, Sweden, and the United Kingdom).
c. Includes Albania, Bulgaria, Czech Republic, Hungary, Poland, Romania, Slovakia, and European republics of the former U.S.S.R. (Belarus, Estonia, Latvia, Lithuania, Moldova, Russia, and Ukraine).
d. May include value of trade shown as not available (...) in any of the four preceding columns. May include any unspecified areas or countries.

... Not available.
— None, less than 0.05%, or not applicable.
Detail may not add to 100.0 or indicated subtotals because of rounding.

SITC category codes

0	food and live animals
1	beverages and tobacco
2	crude materials, inedible, except fuels
27	crude fertilizers and crude minerals (excluding coal, petroleum, and precious stones)
28	metalliferous ores and metal scrap
3	mineral fuels, lubricants, and related materials (including coal, petroleum, natural gas, and electric current)
4	animal and vegetable oils, fats, and waxes
5	chemicals and related products not elsewhere specified
6	manufactured goods classified chiefly by material
667	pearls, precious and semiprecious stones, unworked or worked
7	machinery and transport equipment
8	miscellaneous manufactured articles
9	commodities and transactions not classified elsewhere

exports														country
total value ('000,000 U.S.$)	Standard International Trade Classification (SITC) categories (%)							direction of trade (%)						
	food and agricultural raw materials (0+1+2−27−28+4)	mineral ores and concentrates (27+28+667)	fuels and other energy (3)	manufactured goods				to European Union (EU)[b]	to United States	to Eastern Europe[c]	to Japan	to all other[d]		
				total[a] (5+6−667+7+8+9)	of which chemicals and related products (5)	of which machinery and transport equipment (7)	of which other[a] (6−667+8+9)							
235.1	—63.0[2]—		...	37.0[3]	...	...	...	7.3[4]	0.5[4]	70.2[4, 5]	0.3[4]	21.8[4]		Afghanistan
141.3	37.9[6]	—46.8[6]—		15.3[6]	1.5[6]	0.8[6]	13.0[6]	76.2[7]	11.1	1.3	1.4	10.0		Albania
8,555.5	1.2	0.4	95.2	3.2	1.2	0.4	1.6	64.8	16.7	2.7	0.7	15.1		Algeria
488.2	100.0	—	—	—	—	—	—	—[10]	100.0[10]	—[10]	—[10]	—[10]		American Samoa
48.9	8.1	1.1	0.2	90.6	5.5	40.2	44.9	99.6	—	0.1	—	0.3		Andorra
3,178.9	0.1	1.1	98.6	0.2[4]	—	—	0.2[4]	25.3[4]	64.4	0.5[4]	1.3	8.5[4]		Angola
39.8	—4.4[2]—		25.0	70.6[3]	7.1	30.2	33.3[3]	15.0[11]	15.4[11]	—[11]	—[11]	69.5[11]		Antigua and Barbuda
20,962.6	54.1	0.2	10.3	35.3	6.4	10.9	18.0	21.4	8.6	0.7	2.2	67.2		Argentina
270.9	5.1	—43.7—		51.2	9.3	18.6	23.2	17.8	0.2	33.3	—	48.7		Armenia
37.5	12.6	1.0	3.1	83.3	3.8	11.9	67.5	6.7	9.7	—	—	83.6		Aruba
60,534.0	29.3	11.8[2]	16.8	42.0[3]	3.9	12.8	25.3[3]	10.8	6.4	0.4	20.1	62.2		Australia
57,141.5	8.0	1.0	0.9	90.1	8.8	39.6	41.7	58.6	2.8	11.1	1.2	26.2		Austria
547.4	7.1	—51.8—		41.2	6.1	8.0	27.1	17.2	0.2	26.9	—	55.7		Azerbaijan
2,592.6	—4.9—		73.5	21.5	19.9	0.6	1.0	2.6	93.8	—	0.6	3.0		Bahamas, The
4,092.1	—2.4[2]—		60.0	37.6[3]	5.0	1.3	31.3[3]	4.0[4]	3.2[4]	—	8.2[4]	84.6[4]		Bahrain
2,137.6	16.0	0.1	0.9	83.1	2.4	0.1	80.6	37.4	35.0	1.6	2.6	23.4		Bangladesh
237.5	29.9	1.7	14.4	54.0	13.9	19.8	20.4	20.5	16.0	—	0.6	62.8		Barbados
4,706.8	8.9	—13.0—		78.1	19.1	29.3	29.7	12.2	1.2	75.1	—	11.5		Belarus
165,173.1	11.6	7.4	2.7	78.4	16.1	27.3	35.0	71.2	3.7	2.3	1.3	21.4		Belgium[13]
161.7	81.9	0.2	3.2	14.8	0.2	3.0	11.6	51.4	36.6	—	0.1	12.0		Belize
43.0	—63.5[2]—		29.0	7.5[3]	1.0	2.8	3.8[3]	18.6	18.7	—	0.4	62.3		Benin
35.3	5.6[14]	3.1[14, 15]	45.6[14]	45.8[14, 16]	9.5[14]	18.5[14]	17.8[14, 16]	27.0[14]	62.3[14]	—[14]	—[14]	10.6[14]		Bermuda
67.1	34.3	3.1	22.1[18]	40.5	21.5	—	18.9	0.1	—	—	—	99.9[19]		Bhutan
1,181.4	27.8	20.6	12.9	38.6	1.1	3.2	34.3	25.9	27.8	0.1	0.3	45.9		Bolivia
171.0[4]	...	...	...	...	9.4[6]	20.8[6]	...	45.6[4]	5.3[4]	2.3[4]	1.2[4]	45.6[4]		Bosnia and Herzegovina
1,848.8	7.1	75.8	—	17.1	1.0	7.4	8.7	28.8	0.7	—	—	70.5[21]		Botswana
46,505.4	33.7	6.6	0.9	58.9	6.6	19.0	33.3	27.8	18.9	2.1	6.7	44.5		Brazil
2,093.9	—	—	99.7	0.3	—	—	0.3	—	0.4	—	74.8	24.8		Brunei
5,184.4	24.4	1.4	6.1	68.2	16.9	11.3	39.9	37.7	3.0	19.5	0.3	39.5		Bulgaria
105.4	83.5	0.5	—	16.0	0.1	1.0	14.9	36.2	0.3	—	1.8	61.6		Burkina Faso
68.7	85.1	—	—	14.9	1.4	—	13.4	63.8[4]	2.0[4]	—[4]	0.7[4]	33.6[4]		Burundi
219.1[23]	88.9[24]	...	...	...	...	...	...	15.5[4]	0.5[4]	0.5[4]	37.6[4]	45.9[4]		Cambodia
1,757.9	49.5	0.1	36.2	14.3	1.1	1.1	12.1	77.4	2.3	0.2	0.8	19.3		Cameroon
201,573.7	15.6	2.2	10.2	72.0	5.7	39.0	27.3	5.7	81.6	0.3	3.8	8.6		Canada
5.0[24]	50.6	0.6	—	48.9	0.1	2.2	46.6	98.3	0.1	—	—	1.6		Cape Verde
119.5	24.0	63.5	0.8	11.7	0.4	8.8	2.5	90.7	0.2	—	0.8	8.3		Central African Republic
261.0	88.2	—	—	11.9	6.5	3.1	2.3	42.9	0.8	0.8	7.3	48.2		Chad
15,901.1	37.2	16.1	0.2	46.4	3.5	1.8	41.1	22.0	13.4	0.5	17.9	46.3		Chile
148,779.6	10.1	1.1	3.6	85.2	6.1	21.1	58.0	12.9	16.6	2.0	19.1	49.4		China
10,327.8	35.1	4.7	24.4	35.7	7.9	5.6	22.2	25.5	34.3	0.5	3.5	36.2		Colombia
11.4	70.2	—	—	29.8	19.9	—	10.0	52.5[7]	28.7	—	—	18.8		Comoros
506.0	13.1	58.5[2, 15]	11.1	17.3[3, 16]	0.2	1.2	15.9[3, 16]	58.7	15.7[4]	4.5	6.5	14.6[4]		Congo, Dem. Rep. of the
948.5	13.4	1.1	83.4	2.2	—	0.4	1.8	35.9	42.1	—	0.3	21.7		Congo, Rep. of the
2,217.5	66.3	0.3	0.6	32.8	6.3	3.3	23.2	28.2	43.4	0.2[5]	0.9	27.2		Costa Rica
3,105.0	68.2	0.3[2, 15]	15.4	16.1[3, 16]	3.3	2.0	10.9[3, 16]	56.6	5.7	8.0	1.1	28.6		Côte d'Ivoire
4,511.7	16.1	0.7	9.2	73.9	14.3	21.4	38.3	51.0	2.0	7.9	—	39.0		Croatia
3,860.0	82.2	8.4[2, 15]	4.8	4.6[3, 16]	2.7	0.6	1.3[3, 16]	11.0[4]	—	76.2[5]	2.7	10.1		Cuba
1,391.0	57.4	1.2	4.4	37.0	6.0	11.1	19.9	28.4	0.7	36.3	0.1	34.5		Cyprus
17,099.1	11.6	1.4	5.3	81.8	10.3	25.4	46.1	55.2	1.8	30.0	0.5	12.5		Czech Republic
47,221.8	27.8	0.7	2.7	68.9	10.0	26.0	32.9	59.9	3.7	4.3	3.5	28.6		Denmark
17.3	32.5	—	—	67.5	0.4	8.3	58.7	62.6	0.8	—	0.9	35.7		Djibouti
54.2	67.2	0.4	—	32.4	23.7	4.2	4.4	61.2	5.2	—	—	33.6		Dominica
2,007.8	20.7	0.1	—	79.2[28]	2.6	11.6	65.1[28]	8.6	83.6	—	0.8	6.9		Dominican Republic
4,361.5	54.8	0.2	35.1	10.0	1.2	2.0	6.8	19.3	42.5	2.7	2.7	32.7		Ecuador
3,444.1	16.0	0.6	37.3	46.1	5.8	0.6	39.6	45.8	15.2	2.7	1.3	35.0		Egypt

Trade: external (continued)

country	year	imports												
		total value ('000,000 U.S.$)	Standard International Trade Classification (SITC) categories (%)							direction of trade (%)				
			food and agricultural raw materials (0+1+2 −27−28 +4)	mineral ores and concen-trates (27+28 +667)	fuels and other energy (3)	manufactured goods				from European Union (EU)[b]	from United States	from Eastern Europe[c]	from Japan	from all other[d]
						total[a] (5+6 −667 +7+8 +9)	of which chemicals and related products (5)	of which machinery and transport equipment (7)	of which other[a] (6−667 +8+9)					
El Salvador	1994	2,261.8	17.8	0.7	9.5	72.1	16.9	30.8	24.4	10.6	41.5	0.5	6.3	41.1
Equatorial Guinea	1990	61.6	13.5	3.4	7.7	75.4	3.9	58.2	13.3	31.5	39.9	—	0.3[4]	28.3
Eritrea	1995	423.6	—21.3[2]—		1.9	76.8[3]	6.0	45.2	25.6[3]	27.2[7]	5.9	...	...	66.9
Estonia	1996	3,197.2	17.0	—10.0—		72.9	13.6	29.4	29.9	64.8	2.3	21.7	2.0	9.2
Ethiopia	1993	771.6	17.4	0.1	21.6	60.9	13.8	26.8	20.3	39.3	9.5	—	4.1	47.2
Faroe Islands	1994	238.2	30.7	0.6	11.8	56.8	8.5	19.8	28.5	67.5	1.4	3.6	2.0	25.5
Fiji	1994	830.5	15.9	0.3	11.2	72.5	7.3	30.9	34.3	3.9	14.8	0.1	8.0	73.3
Finland	1996	30,904.9	9.2	4.0	10.5	76.2	11.3	39.2	25.7	58.5	7.3	10.2	5.2	18.8
France[31]	1995	273,387.4	13.3	1.1	6.8	78.8	12.5	35.4	30.8	63.9	7.8	2.4	3.5	22.4
French Guiana	1995	783.3	18.8	0.1	5.3	75.8	8.0	42.2	25.6	76.9	3.3	0.5	1.4	17.9
French Polynesia	1994	880.7	20.4[32]	0.2[32]	5.4[32]	74.1[32]	6.4[32]	35.9[32]	31.8[32]	44.8[7]	13.9	—	4.0	37.3
Gabon	1994	680.8	17.9	0.5	2.3	79.2	10.2	44.5	24.5	67.6	11.8	0.3	5.3[4]	15.0
Gambia, The	1995[12]	141.3	—35.3[2]—		14.4	50.3[3]	5.6	20.3	24.5[3]	47.3	5.2	0.7	3.5	43.3
Gaza Strip	1994	339.3	...	...	...	...	...	...	...	...	...	...	...	100.0[33]
Georgia	1995	379.0	32.3	—52.7—		15.0	4.0	5.8	5.3	13.4	4.7	30.0	0.2	51.6
Germany	1995	443,223.8	12.5	1.6	6.4	79.5	9.4	34.4	35.7	54.7	7.1	8.3	5.5	24.4
Ghana	1992	2,145.4	12.5	3.1	17.4	66.9	11.1	33.6	22.2	43.6	10.2	1.4	6.6	38.2
Gibraltar	1995	436.0[37]	—24.4[2, 32]—		20.7[32]	54.9[3, 32]	4.3[32]	21.4[32]	29.2[3, 32]	75.7	...	...	1.9	22.4
Greece	1995	25,926.8	18.5	0.6	7.2	73.7	13.2	27.4	33.1	69.9	3.2	6.6	2.6	17.6
Greenland	1995	421.1	15.4	0.3	5.8	78.5	4.3	24.6	49.7	83.2	2.4	0.2	3.3	10.9
Grenada	1991	117.2	28.4	0.2	7.4	64.1	8.5	24.2	31.3	19.8	32.2	0.1	7.1	40.8
Guadeloupe	1995	1,901.3	22.6	0.3	5.8	71.3	9.5	32.0	29.8	77.8	3.3	0.3	2.2	16.5
Guam	1983	610.7	16.9	0.1	46.9	36.2	2.3	19.1	14.8	...	23.4	...	19.9	56.6
Guatemala	1995	3,292.5	13.4	0.3	12.4	73.9	17.2	31.5	25.2	10.4	44.9	1.0[5]	3.7	40.0
Guernsey[39]	...	...	...	...	...	...	...	...	...	...	...	...	...	...
Guinea	1994	687.0	10.8	...	9.9	...	...	22.3	...	54.3[4]	8.0[4]	0.7[4]	3.8[4]	33.2[4]
Guinea-Bissau	1994	63.5	31.7	...	9.9	58.4	...	33.1	...	44.8[4]	48.1[4]	—[4]	2.6[4]	4.5[4]
Guyana	1993	483.8	9.0	...	16.7	74.3	5.1	44.5	24.7	21.9[4]	27.9[4]	0.4[4]	18.2[4]	31.6[4]
Haiti	1993[8]	226.0	—46.6[2]—		28.4	25.1[3]	6.9	5.4	12.8	18.1[4]	57.9[4]	...	4.8[4]	19.3[4]
Honduras	1995	1,727.5	13.7	0.2	11.5	74.6	17.3	29.1	28.2	14.5	46.6	0.4[5]	3.4	35.0
Hong Kong	1996	201,164.5	7.1	2.1	2.2	88.6	6.8	36.5	45.3	11.0	7.8	0.4	13.4	67.5
Hungary	1995	15,466.3	8.8	0.9[2]	11.6	78.6[3]	14.3	30.7	33.6[3]	61.5	3.1	21.8	2.2	11.3
Iceland	1995	1,751.4	13.3	3.7	7.2	75.7	9.3	32.4	34.0	59.8	8.4	4.8	4.4	22.6
India	1995[1]	28,654.8	10.3	9.7	23.8	56.2	14.7	19.0	22.5	26.2	10.1	3.2	7.1	53.5
Indonesia	1995	40,628.7	15.0	2.1	7.4	75.5	15.4	40.1	20.0	20.1	11.7	1.6[5]	22.7	43.9
Iran	1992	30,712.1	—11.4[2]—		1.3	87.4[3]	9.8	50.3	27.3[3]	49.8	2.7	3.0[5]	12.0	32.5
Iraq	1990	4,833.9	—31.5[2]—		0.4	68.1[3]	8.8	30.3	28.9[3]	45.7[4]	10.8[4]	3.0[4]	4.6[4]	35.9[4]
Ireland	1996	35,767.7	9.5	0.6	3.7	86.2	12.3	42.1	31.9	56.5	15.5	0.7	5.4	21.9
Isle of Man[39]	...	...	...	...	...	...	...	...	...	...	...	...	...	...
Israel	1995	29,579.0	8.2	17.1	5.9	68.8	9.4	34.0	25.5	52.3	18.6	1.9	3.3	23.9
Italy[40]	1996	206,965.5	16.3	1.9	8.4	73.4	13.0	30.2	30.3	60.8	4.9	5.6	1.9	26.7
Jamaica	1996	2,916.4	16.2	0.2[2]	15.2	68.4[3]	10.1	26.7	31.7[3]	11.2	51.9	0.5	5.6	30.8
Japan	1996	349,186.1	21.0	3.8	17.4	57.9	6.5	24.4	26.9	14.1	22.8	1.3	—	61.7
Jersey	1980	537.1	23.9	0.4	9.3	66.5	6.5	24.8	35.2	84.9[41]	...	...	...	15.1
Jordan	1995	3,722.7	22.7	1.1	12.9	63.4	12.3	24.5	26.5	33.2	9.3	4.6	3.5	49.4
Kazakstan	1995	3,781.0	12.3	—29.3—		58.4	11.9	27.1	19.4	13.4	1.9	56.7	0.2	27.8
Kenya	1993	1,695.9	16.2	0.4	14.9	68.5	20.7	26.9	20.9	41.9	8.3	0.7[5]	8.4	40.7
Kiribati	1994	26.4	42.4	0.3	9.3	47.9	6.4	17.4	24.1	0.8	9.6	—	6.7	82.9
Korea, North	1996	2,238.0[4]	...	...	...	...	...	...	...	10.3[4]	—[4]	33.9[4]	11.1[4]	44.6[4]
Korea, South	1996	150,334.3	10.4	2.4	16.2	71.0	8.8	36.4	25.8	14.1	22.2	1.5	20.9	41.3
Kuwait	1995	7,789.8	16.6	0.4	0.5	82.4	7.3	41.2	33.9	38.1	16.1	0.9	9.4	35.6
Kyrgyzstan	1995	522.3	19.9	—37.5—		42.6	7.4	17.9	17.3	6.4	3.7	25.8	1.4	62.8
Laos	1994	564.1	18.6	8.3[22]	3.8	69.3	...	25.9	43.4	8.0[4]	0.9	0.3[4]	11.8	79.0
Latvia	1995	1,817.5	12.2	0.4	21.2	66.2	12.7	25.4	28.2	49.9	1.9	41.9	0.6	5.8
Lebanon	1994	5,990.0	21.7	—13.3—		65.0	10.2	27.0	27.8	49.1[4]	9.3	4.6[4]	4.2	32.8[4]
Lesotho	1992	977.0	23.2[43]	0.4[43]	8.7[43]	67.8[43]	7.4[43]	16.7[43]	43.7[43]	4.8	...	—[4]	—[4]	95.2[44]
Liberia	1992	5,760.0[4]	—19.8[2, 32]—		20.3[32]	59.9[3, 32]	5.6[32]	30.2[32]	24.1[3, 32]	22.6[4]	0.6[4]	0.8[4]	28.3[4]	47.7[4]
Libya	1991	5,357.5	25.7	0.3	0.4	73.7	7.6	33.8	32.2	62.6	1.3	0.9[5]	3.3	31.9
Liechtenstein	1995	906.4	3.8	0.3[2]	1.1	94.8[3]	4.6	33.9	56.3[3]	...	...	...	...	...
Lithuania	1996	4,558.8	15.6	1.9	18.0	64.5	12.2	25.8	26.6	39.8	2.6	46.1	1.2	10.4
Luxembourg	1995	9,861.5	12.6	—9.8—		77.6	14.2	28.1	35.3	91.1	3.3	...	1.2	4.3
Macau	1995	2,018.6	16.7	0.2	5.1	78.0	4.5	18.9	54.6	14.7	7.4	0.3	10.5	67.1
Macedonia	1994	1,484.1	24.4	1.5[2]	10.8	63.3[3]	13.3	19.7	30.4[3]	38.2	3.3	24.6	0.9	33.1
Madagascar	1995	549.5	18.1	0.3	14.0	67.7	13.0	25.7	28.9	50.6	3.8	0.7[5]	6.0	39.0
Malawi	1991	647.4	8.6	1.0	10.9	79.5	20.0	33.1	26.3	35.6	3.3	0.1	7.4	53.7
Malaysia	1995	77,292.3	6.0	1.2	2.2	90.5	7.1	59.9	23.5	15.3	16.4	0.5	27.5	40.3
Maldives	1993	191.4	31.5	2.8	12.8	52.9	7.5	22.2	23.2	7.9	1.0	0.4	3.9	86.9
Mali	1990	601.8	26.2	0.9	19.5	53.5	10.7	22.2	20.6	46.8	4.8	1.3[5]	4.3	42.9
Malta	1996	2,803.0	—12.0[2]—		5.4	82.6[3]	7.4	48.2	27.0[3]	68.5	6.9	1.3	3.2	20.1
Marshall Islands	1995	75.1	34.5	1.0[4]	30.0	34.5	2.6	12.8	19.2	...	51.1	...	7.4	41.5
Martinique	1995	1,969.8	20.4	0.2	7.5	71.9	10.3	32.4	29.2	76.8	2.9	0.2	2.2	17.9
Mauritania	1992	600.0[4]	30.6[32]	...	7.0[32]	62.4[32]	...	51.0[32]	11.4[32]	58.4[4]	11.2[4]	1.8[4]	3.8[4]	24.7[4]
Mauritius	1995	2,022.8	19.7	1.8	6.9	71.6	7.7	19.2	44.7	36.3	—	0.5	4.7	58.5
Mayotte	1996	144.3	—23.7—		4.6	71.7	11.0	35.1	25.6	74.0[14, 46]	...	...	3.3[14]	22.7[14]
Mexico	1995	73,993.0	8.8	0.9	2.1	88.2	10.0	42.9	35.3	9.4	74.3	0.2	5.0	11.0
Micronesia	1994	129.1	—24.7[2]—		14.3	61.0[3]	4.4	13.5	43.1[3]	...	32.9	...	32.0	35.1
Moldova	1995	840.7	10.7	1.0	45.9	42.4	9.2	15.2	17.9	13.7	1.3	80.2	0.2	4.7
Monaco[31]	...	...	...	...	...	...	...	...	...	...	...	...	...	...
Mongolia	1995	415.3	9.3	—20.0—		70.7	10.4	35.7	24.6	9.5	3.5	53.3	10.9	22.8
Morocco	1995	8,551.5	25.9	2.6	13.7	57.8	11.9	23.3	22.6	56.1	6.5	7.8	1.5	28.1
Mozambique	1994	544.0	19.2	0.3	14.1	66.4	13.5	35.5	17.4	33.0	4.1	—	8.4	54.5
Myanmar (Burma)	1995[1]	1,419.3	—16.2[2]—		3.4	80.4[3]	7.3	31.8	41.2[3]	4.4	1.2	0.3	23.6	70.6
Namibia	1994	1,374.3	23.8	1.1[2]	4.2	70.9[3]	7.1	31.4	32.5[3]	4.5	0.9	—	1.3	93.3[47]
Nauru	1991[48]	17.8	—24.2[2]—		4.8	70.9[3]	2.1	23.4[22]	45.4[3]	...	...	...	...	...
Nepal	1995[12]	855.9	14.1	0.5	13.7	71.6	8.1	13.4	50.1	10.6	1.0	1.0	7.5	79.9

exports													country
total value ('000,000 U.S.$)	Standard International Trade Classification (SITC) categories (%)							direction of trade (%)					
	food and agricultural raw materials (0+1+2 −27−28 +4)	mineral ores and concentrates (27+28 +667)	fuels and other energy (3)	manufactured goods: total[a] (5+6 −667 +7+8 +9)	of which chemicals and related products (5)	of which machinery and transport equipment (7)	of which other[a] (6−667 +8+9)	to European Union (EU)[b]	to United States	to Eastern Europe[c]	to Japan	to all other[d]	
812.7	52.2	0.1	0.5	47.1	12.3	3.0	31.8	25.0	22.6	—	0.8	51.6	El Salvador
61.7	48.6	—	—	51.4	0.1	39.8[29]	11.5	47.2	—	—	—	52.8	Equatorial Guinea
86.0	——59.8——		...	40.2	2.5	3.8	34.0	2.7[7]	...	...	...	97.3[30]	Eritrea
2,074.1	27.2	——7.5——		65.3	11.0	19.8	34.6	51.1	2.2	39.3	0.7	6.6	Estonia
201.7	95.3	—	4.0	0.7	0.1	—	0.6	41.6	9.2	0.3	19.0	29.9	Ethiopia
321.3	96.8	—	—	3.2	0.1	2.5	0.6	88.0	2.9	0.1	2.7	6.3	Faroe Islands
544.5	49.3	0.1	7.4	43.2	1.0	8.0	34.3	20.3	17.9	—	6.8	55.0	Fiji
40,556.5	9.9	0.6	3.1	86.4	6.2	38.4	41.9	52.7	7.9	12.8	2.6	24.1	Finland
284,045.7	15.6	0.8	2.3	81.3	12.8	39.7	28.8	63.5	5.9	2.2	2.0	26.5	France[31]
158.2	33.6	0.1	0.2	66.1	1.4	33.0	31.7	77.6	1.0	—	—	21.3	French Guiana
226.2	5.9[32]	31.3[32]	—[32]	62.8[32]	1.6[32]	38.6[32]	22.6[32]	32.7[7]	8.4	—	45.8	13.1	French Polynesia
1,040.9	19.8	7.5	70.4	2.3	0.8	0.5	1.0	49.4	6.5	—	8.0[4]	36.1	Gabon
21.5	——78.8[2]——		—	21.2[3]	1.6	2.5	17.1	57.1[4]	3.6[4]	—[4]	—[4]	39.3[4]	Gambia, The
49.4	...	...	...	...	...	...	...	...	...	...	...	100.0[34]	Gaza Strip
154.4	25.9	——14.5——		59.5	9.7	6.8	43.1	5.6	0.4	39.4	0.1	54.5	Georgia
508,508.5	6.1	0.8	0.9	92.1	13.5	49.6	29.1	57.1	7.5	7.4	2.6	25.5	Germany
1,234.4	37.7	6.2	5.4	50.6	0.2	1.2	49.3[35]	30.3	2.6	1.1	1.8	64.2[36]	Ghana
116.2[37]	——8.2[2, 32]——		51.5[32]	40.3[3, 32]	2.8[32]	18.1[32]	19.4[3, 32]	22.2[7, 32]	...	...	...	77.8[38]	Gibraltar
10,954.6	33.9	2.4	6.5	57.1	4.9	8.0	44.2	60.7	3.1	13.5	0.8	22.0	Greece
363.6	95.7	—	0.8	3.5	—	0.3	3.2	93.3	0.6	—	4.6	1.4	Greenland
20.1	77.0	—	—	23.0	4.5	2.1	16.4	44.1	14.2	—	2.6	39.2	Grenada
162.0	52.3	0.6	—	47.0	1.1	36.5	9.4	77.0	3.4	—	—	19.6	Guadeloupe
39.2	23.5	2.7	3.5	70.3	5.6	11.5	53.2	...	24.9	...	4.8	70.4	Guam
1,935.5	69.3	0.4	2.0	28.2	10.9	1.8	15.5	15.7	31.3	0.5[5]	2.8	49.7	Guatemala
...	...	...	...	...	...	...	...	...	...	...	...	...	Guernsey[39]
625.9	12.2[22]	66.3	—	21.5	...	...	...	63.4[4]	15.1[4]	8.3[4]	1.3[4]	11.9[4]	Guinea
33.2	95.2	...	—	4.8	...	...	...	52.2[4]	—[4]	—[4]	2.9[4]	44.9[4]	Guinea-Bissau
404.0	43.5[22]	47.3[22]	—	9.2	...	...	...	35.9[4]	22.8[4]	—[4]	2.1[4]	39.2[4]	Guyana
74.3	14.1	—	—	86.0	1.7	14.0	70.3	12.4[4]	78.8[4]	—[4]	0.8[4]	8.0[4]	Haiti
656.0	90.2	0.4	—	9.4	1.7	0.7	7.0	36.3	42.7	0.4	6.7	13.8	Honduras
180,801.9	4.3	1.2	1.1	93.4	5.9	32.2	55.3	14.8	21.2	0.6	6.5	56.8	Hong Kong
12,867.0	24.0	1.6[2]	3.2	71.1[3]	11.8	25.6	33.7[3]	62.8	3.2	19.2	0.6	14.2	Hungary
1,802.5	76.1	1.5	—	22.4	0.7	5.1	16.6	62.7	12.4	0.9	11.3	12.7	Iceland
26,330.0	16.7	18.5	1.9	62.8	8.2	7.2	47.5	27.9	19.1	3.9	7.7	41.5	India
45,418.0	18.0	4.4	25.3	52.2	3.4	8.4	40.4	14.9	13.9	0.7[5]	27.1	43.4	Indonesia
19,868.0	7.8	1.9[2, 15]	80.9	9.3[3, 16]	0.2	0.5	8.6[3, 16]	39.8	0.8	10.4[5]	13.5	35.5	Iran
6,659.0	0.8	0.3[15]	96.8	2.1[16]	1.2	0.2	0.7[16]	26.6[4]	33.6[4]	6.8[4, 5]	9.5[4]	23.5[4]	Iraq
48,153.2	16.6	1.0	0.4	82.1	22.3	34.8	25.0	68.6	9.4	1.8	2.9	17.4	Ireland
...	...	...	...	...	...	...	...	...	...	...	...	...	Isle of Man[39]
19,046.0	7.3	31.0	0.5	61.2	14.6	28.4	18.2	32.2	30.1	3.3	6.9	27.4	Israel
250,830.3	7.2	0.3	1.2	91.3	7.8	38.4	45.1	55.5	7.4	5.8	2.2	29.1	Italy[40]
1,386.9	23.7	49.7[2]	0.4	26.2[3]	3.4	2.3	20.5[3]	30.8	36.8	1.9	2.3	28.3	Jamaica
410,947.0	1.1	0.3	0.5	98.2	7.0	69.5	21.6	15.4	27.5	0.5	—	56.7	Japan
209.2	27.6	4.3[42]	—	68.0	1.2	31.1	35.7	67.3[41]	...	...	...	32.7	Jersey
1,782.0	24.1	19.4	—	56.5	27.0	13.1	16.4	8.0	3.9	1.3	1.1	85.7	Jordan
4,974.4	11.5	——28.0——		60.4	10.3	4.0	46.1	21.6	0.9	51.3	—	26.1	Kazakstan
1,391.9	58.1	2.7	9.3	30.0	4.3	1.4	24.3	36.2	3.5	0.1[5]	0.9	59.4	Kenya
5.2	91.8	—	—	8.2	—	—	8.2	4.4	12.1	—	0.1	83.4	Kiribati
1,095.0[4]	...	...	...	...	...	...	...	9.3[4]	—[4]	30.2[4]	24.2[4]	36.3[4]	Korea, North
129,714.6	3.4	0.1	3.0	93.5	7.1	52.1	34.3	11.9	16.9	3.0	12.2	56.0	Korea, South
12,944.4	0.3	0.3	94.7	4.7	2.0	1.4	1.3	11.7[4]	10.3[4]	—[4]	19.4[4]	58.5[4]	Kuwait
408.9	29.4	——11.8——		58.8	6.6	9.2	43.0	9.5	1.0	31.4	0.1	58.0	Kyrgyzstan
300.4	37.1	...	8.4	54.6	...	16.9	37.7	19.3[4]	3.2	3.2[4]	0.6	73.6	Laos
1,303.8	37.4	0.7	1.7	60.1	6.9	16.3	36.9	44.0	1.3	47.7	0.3	6.6	Latvia
572.7	19.6	——10.5——		69.9	9.1	11.5	49.3	17.0[4]	3.7	4.9[4]	0.7	73.7[4]	Lebanon
109.1	14.8	1.3	—	83.9	0.5	10.2	73.2	22.7	23.0[4]	—	—	54.3[4]	Lesotho
389.0	32.4	33.7[2, 15]	2.6	31.3[3, 16]	—	26.0	5.3[3, 16]	66.8	11.4[4]	1.5	—	20.3[4]	Liberia
11,211.7	0.7	—	95.4	3.9	3.4	—	0.5	86.2	—	1.6	—	12.2	Libya
1,817.7	4.4	—[2]	0.1	95.5[3]	8.1	46.9	40.5[3]	45.7[45]	...	...	...	54.3	Liechtenstein
3,354.9	22.5	2.3	14.9	60.4	12.8	19.0	28.7	32.9	0.8	58.3	0.5	7.5	Lithuania
7,743.0	7.2	——1.5——		91.3	18.6	19.8	52.9	85.5	3.1	...	0.6	10.8	Luxembourg
2,017.3	4.0	—	—	95.9	1.1	4.4	90.5	31.4	41.2	—	1.3	26.1	Macau
1,086.3	21.1	1.9[2]	0.1	76.8[3]	4.4	12.3	60.2[3]	33.6	3.6	35.0	0.1	27.7	Macedonia
359.9	73.5	7.9	4.0	14.6	2.1	0.9	11.6	59.9	6.6	0.9[5]	6.2	26.4	Madagascar
472.4	96.4	—	—	3.6	0.3	0.2	3.1	47.3	15.0	—	12.0	25.7	Malaŵi
74,120.1	15.7	0.4	7.0	76.9	3.1	55.1	18.7	14.2	20.7	0.3	12.7	52.1	Malaysia
34.4	83.7	0.2	—	16.1	0.1	—	16.0	31.3	11.3	—	4.1	53.3	Maldives
330.3	98.4	—	—	1.6	—	0.9	0.8	26.0	0.6[4]	—	0.9[4]	72.5	Mali
1,748.3	——3.5[2]——		2.7	93.8[3]	2.9	60.1	30.8[3]	57.1	13.3	1.0	2.9	25.7	Malta
23.1	71.0	—	—	29.0	—	—	29.0	...	80.0[4]	...	...	20.0[4]	Marshall Islands
241.9	62.3	1.0	17.8	18.9	2.1	13.0	3.8	78.0	2.6	—	—	19.3	Martinique
471.0	48.2	48.6[2, 15]	1.9	1.3[3, 16]	—	—	1.3[3, 16]	58.2	4.5	10.8[5]	20.4	6.1	Mauritania
1,555.8	29.6	2.0	—	68.4	0.8	2.3	65.3	87.3	—	0.1	0.6	12.0	Mauritius
8.2	21.3[24]	—[24]	—[24]	78.7[24]	78.7[24]	—[24]	—[24]	70.0[14, 46]	...	...	...	30.0[14]	Mayotte
79,488.6	9.0	1.2	10.3	79.5	4.9	52.4	22.2	4.2	83.7	...	1.2	10.8	Mexico
78.2	96.9	—	—	3.1	...	...	...	...	3.5	...	72.7	23.8	Micronesia
745.5	73.5	2.7	0.9	22.9	1.4	7.9	13.7	11.6	1.1	80.5	—	6.8	Moldova
...	...	...	...	...	...	...	...	...	...	...	...	...	Monaco[31]
473.3	4.8	——65.5——		29.7	0.3	3.1	26.2	12.9	5.5	16.6	9.9	55.2	Mongolia
4,728.1	34.8	10.0	2.2	53.0	20.8	3.2	28.9	62.1	3.4	1.5	7.7	25.4	Morocco
164.0	75.9	1.8	9.0	13.4	0.1	3.3	10.0	34.7	8.4	—	14.7	42.2	Mozambique
920.7	——78.9[2]——		0.9	20.2[3]	—	0.4	19.7[3]	1.9	5.1	0.7[4]	4.8	87.5	Myanmar (Burma)
1,321.4	47.0	50.1	—	2.8	—	...	...	...	3.0[4, 10]	...	—[4, 10]	97.0[4, 10]	Namibia
28.9	—	99.4	—	0.6	—	—	0.6	...	...	...	...	...	Nauru
286.3	1.1	—	—	98.9	—	0.2	98.6	57.1	36.0	0.1	0.5	6.2	Nepal

Trade: external (continued)

country	year	imports												
		total value ('000,000 U.S.$)	Standard International Trade Classification (SITC) categories (%)							direction of trade (%)				
			food and agricultural raw materials (0+1+2−27−28+4)	mineral ores and concentrates (27+28+667)	fuels and other energy (3)	manufactured goods				from European Union (EU)[b]	from United States	from Eastern Europe[c]	from Japan	from all other[d]
						total[a] (5+6−667+7+8+9)	of which chemicals and related products (5)	of which machinery and transport equipment (7)	of which other[a] (6−667+8+9)					
Netherlands, The	1996	160,896.3	15.8	1.4	8.9	73.9	11.7	34.4	27.8	58.8	8.4	2.9	3.8	26.1
Netherlands Antilles	1992	1,868.3	9.1	0.1	58.8	32.0	3.7	13.7	14.7	11.7	17.0	0.1	2.2	69.0
New Caledonia	1994	842.2	—21.0[2]—		10.2	68.7[3]	7.4	33.0	28.3[3]	43.7	4.6	—	4.8	47.0
New Zealand	1995	13,957.7	8.6	1.9	5.3	84.1	13.1	42.2	28.9	21.6	18.7	0.1	13.9	45.7
Nicaragua	1995	1,009.2	18.8	0.3	17.9	63.0	17.5	23.1	22.4	10.1	30.2	1.0	5.0	53.8
Niger	1991	355.3	25.7	2.1	9.4	62.7	9.6	13.6	39.5	39.6	5.1	0.3	6.6	48.4
Nigeria	1992	8,839.3	7.6	0.9	0.4	91.0	13.9	54.2	22.9	62.8	8.5	0.8[5]	6.3	21.7
Northern Mariana Islands	1991	392.2	19.3	—	20.9	59.8	2.3	22.2	35.3	...	18.2	...	16.6	65.2
Norway	1996	34,309.2	9.1	4.8	4.5	81.6	9.1	39.2	33.3	70.8	6.5	3.3	3.9	15.6
Oman	1995	4,248.6	20.6	1.9	1.5	76.0	6.8	39.4	29.8	27.9	6.5	0.4	15.8	49.5
Pakistan	1995	11,703.6	23.0	1.2	16.1	59.7	17.0	28.9	13.8	23.5	9.3	2.5	10.7	53.9
Palau	1984	25.1[50]	28.9	0.1[2]	0.9[50]	70.0[3]	4.0	24.5	41.5[3]	—	41.8	—	38.2	20.0
Panama[51]	1995	3,799.0	14.4	1.2	63.5	20.9	6.6	2.4	11.9	5.6	34.8	0.5	0.5	58.5
Papua New Guinea	1993	1,298.6	18.8[6]	0.3[6]	6.8[6]	74.1[6]	7.0[6]	38.3[6]	28.8[6]	4.0	3.9	0.9	14.5	76.7
Paraguay	1995	3,135.9	18.7	0.2	6.5	74.6	9.0	42.3	23.2	11.0	12.5	0.1	8.7	67.7
Peru	1995	9,224.0	15.4	0.4	8.8	75.4	13.2	39.2	23.1	17.9	25.2	0.7	7.0	49.3
Philippines	1995	28,487.4	10.5	2.0	9.2	78.3	9.2	32.5	36.6	10.7	18.9	1.9	22.1	46.4
Poland	1995	28,929.9	12.9	2.0	9.1	76.0	15.0	30.0	31.0	64.8	3.8	14.7	1.7	15.0
Portugal	1996	34,121.9	16.5	0.6	7.8	75.2	10.1	36.3	28.8	75.7	3.2	1.4	2.2	17.5
Puerto Rico	1992[12]	15,387.3	17.3	0.3	10.6	71.8	25.4	21.8	24.7	4.8	68.1	0.1	3.7	23.2
Qatar	1994	1,927.4	15.8	2.7	0.6	80.8	7.0	39.7	34.2	33.9	10.6	1.4[5]	13.4	40.8
Réunion	1995	2,711.1	21.5	0.2	4.7	73.6	10.7	29.8	33.1	80.1	0.6	0.1	2.1	17.2
Romania	1996	11,435.3	9.5	2.8	20.9	66.8	10.0	25.6	31.2	51.5	3.7	20.4	0.9	23.6
Russia	1995	46,680.0	28.8	—7.0—		64.2	10.9	29.5	23.8	37.9	5.7	30.1	1.6	24.7
Rwanda	1990	291.1	18.2	1.9	15.3	64.6	10.2	16.1	38.3	44.6	1.2	1.4[5]	7.7	45.1
St. Kitts and Nevis	1990	110.7	21.2	0.1	5.0	73.7	7.3	29.4	37.0	18.0	43.6	—	3.7	34.7
St. Lucia	1993	300.3	—26.8[2]—		7.6	65.6[3]	9.1	22.8	33.6[3]	19.1	37.3	—	5.6	38.0
St. Vincent and the Grenadines	1994	129.9	25.7	0.4[2]	6.3	67.6[3]	11.1	20.6	35.9[3]	24.8	35.1	0.3	2.8	37.1
Samoa	1993	130.9	21.6	0.6[2]	8.4	69.4[3]	5.0	37.0	27.4[3]	4.3	8.3	—	15.9	71.5
San Marino[40]	...	...	...	...	...	...	...	...	...	...	...	...	...	...
São Tomé and Príncipe	1994	30.4	21.5[22]	...	7.2	71.3	...	40.2	31.1	53.8[7]	25.0[4]	...	5.5	15.7[4]
Saudi Arabia	1994	23,343.5	14.0	0.9	0.2	84.8	8.7	40.1	36.1	34.7	21.3	0.6	11.7	31.6
Senegal	1993	1,139.2	35.3	1.4	9.1	54.2	11.8	22.2	20.3	57.1	5.2	1.5[5]	3.6	32.6
Seychelles	1994	206.5	22.7	0.3	15.6	61.4	6.9	23.2	31.4	35.1	3.8	—	3.3	57.8
Sierra Leone	1994	149.9	—41.7[2]—		18.5	39.8[3]	7.3	18.0	14.5[3]	47.0[4]	10.0[4]	2.2[4]	5.6[4]	35.2[4]
Singapore	1996	131,480.2	5.1	0.7	9.3	84.8	5.9	57.9	21.0	14.5	16.4	0.3	18.2	50.7
Slovakia	1994	6,611.0	11.0	2.8	19.3	66.9	13.2	27.8	25.9	33.5	2.8	54.2	1.2	8.3
Slovenia	1995	9,491.7	12.4	1.9	6.6	79.1	12.1	33.8	33.3	68.8	3.1	10.1	1.7	16.4
Solomon Islands	1994	170.6	—16.2[2]—		8.2	75.6[3]	5.2	38.0	32.5[3]	2.8	2.8	—	17.1	77.4
Somalia	1992	228.0[4]	30.3[43]	0.2[43]	4.6[43]	64.9[43]	5.1[43]	37.1[43]	22.7[43]	27.2[4]	10.1[4]	—[4]	0.7[4]	62.0[4]
South Africa[55]	1995	27,737.0	8.7	2.2	10.2	79.0	12.1	43.9	23.0	44.5	11.8	0.5	9.9	33.4
Spain	1996	121,255.4	14.9	2.1	9.1	73.9	11.8	37.3	24.8	66.3	6.2	2.2	2.8	22.5
Sri Lanka	1995	2,833.2	15.0	3.9	7.9	73.2	9.9	19.8	43.5	18.2	3.5	0.9	10.2	67.1
Sudan, The	1994	1,161.5	—22.4[2]—		20.6	57.0[3]	9.0	26.2	21.8[3]	32.8	3.5	3.7	2.1	57.8
Suriname	1992	639.8	8.5	1.0	13.5	76.9	12.8	38.7	25.4	22.5	39.7	—	15.6	22.2
Swaziland	1994	962.6	21.8[1]	0.4[1]	10.3[1]	67.4[1]	10.2[1]	26.7[1]	30.6[1]	7.6[1]	0.6[1]	—[1]	0.9[1]	90.9[1,57]
Sweden	1996	63,986.8	8.8	1.3	7.4	82.4	10.3	41.8	30.2	69.1	6.0	3.7	2.5	18.7
Switzerland[58]	1995	79,365.3	8.4	2.8	2.9	85.8	14.6	33.4	37.8	79.6	6.4	1.5	3.2	9.4
Syria	1995	4,708.8	20.0	0.5	1.1	78.4	10.2	31.6	36.7	34.4	6.8	10.8	4.4	43.7
Taiwan	1996	102,554.4	8.8	1.1	8.1	82.1	13.1	39.6	29.3	16.2	19.5	1.5	26.9	35.9
Tajikistan	1995	799.2	7.9	—74.6—		17.5	1.6	11.5	4.4	25.4	3.2	18.9	—	52.6
Tanzania	1990	1,021.5	5.4	1.5	10.3	82.8	9.8	45.6	27.4	58.2	1.6	0.8[5]	7.7	31.8
Thailand	1995	71,387.4	7.9	2.2	6.7	83.2	10.5	47.5	25.2	16.0	12.0	2.3	30.5	39.2
Togo	1994	222.0	24.4[10]	0.7[10]	9.8[10]	65.1[10]	11.9[10]	28.3[10]	25.0[10]	53.1	5.5	0.6	3.5	37.3
Tonga	1994	69.1	34.4	0.5	12.1	53.0	8.3	17.0	27.7	1.0	8.2	—	6.7	84.1
Trinidad and Tobago	1994	1,136.2	20.5	5.6	0.6	73.2	13.7	29.8	29.7	16.2	48.3	0.3	4.6	30.6
Tunisia	1996	7,698.2	13.1	1.7	8.4	76.8	9.2	27.3	40.3	72.4	4.2	3.3	2.1	18.1
Turkey	1995	35,707.5	12.6	3.8	12.9	70.7	15.0	32.2	23.6	47.2	10.4	11.4	3.9	27.0
Turkmenistan	1995	1,364.0	27.0	—6.3—		66.6	11.3	17.9	37.4	10.9	3.9	39.7	0.5	44.9
Tuvalu	1994	17.6	36.1[10]	0.1[2,10]	14.6[10]	49.2[3,10]	6.8[10]	13.9[10]	28.5[3,10]	...	0.6	...	1.7	97.7
Uganda	1992	524.4	13.0	1.5[2]	13.4	72.0[3]	8.3	32.2	31.5[3]	29.7	4.8	—	9.9	55.6
Ukraine	1995	11,335.5	4.9	—56.0—		39.1	9.1	17.4	12.6	16.4	2.6	61.4	0.1	19.5
United Arab Emirates	1992	17,410.0	11.6	0.7	1.7	86.1	5.5	35.1	45.4	33.5	8.9	0.5	16.6	40.5
United Kingdom[39]	1996	287,528.6	12.2	2.9	3.8	81.1	10.1	42.1	28.9	54.1	12.5	2.0	4.9	26.5
United States[59]	1996	817,627.2	7.0	1.6	9.4	82.0	5.7	45.2	31.1	18.0	—	0.9	14.4	66.7
Uruguay	1995	2,865.7	14.4	0.3	10.1	75.2	15.3	34.5	25.4	20.9	9.9	0.5	2.6	66.2
Uzbekistan	1995	2,892.7	19.3	—2.7—		78.0	9.0	43.1	25.9	17.7	1.1	36.9	1.5	42.8
Vanuatu	1993	73.5	22.2	0.2	9.3	68.3	6.6	29.8	31.9	8.5	1.1	—	8.1	82.3
Venezuela	1995	10,791.3	18.8	1.2	1.1	79.0	16.4	37.0	25.6	17.9	42.6	0.3	4.4	34.8
Vietnam	1993	3,924.0	—9.4[2,10]—		22.9[10]	67.8[3,10]	16.3[10]	26.1[10]	25.4[3,10]	10.4	0.1	4.8	11.5	73.2
Virgin Islands (U.S.)	1995	3,200.3	...	...	68.6[54]	...	...	...	...	...	32.7	...	...	...
West Bank	1994	102.5[61]	...	...	...	...	...	...	...	...	...	...	...	...
Western Sahara	...	...	...	...	...	...	...	...	...	...	...	...	...	...
Yemen	1994	2,087.4	39.3	0.3[2]	5.2	55.3[3]	7.7	20.5	27.0[3]	30.0	9.0	1.4[5]	4.5	55.1
Yugoslavia	1991	5,548.6	12.4	1.3	19.0	67.4	13.7	22.7	31.0	46.5[4]	4.2	24.5[5]	2.3	22.6
Zambia	1990	1,237.7	3.7	1.1[2]	15.2	79.9[3]	12.6	47.0	20.3[3]	38.7	10.1	0.1	6.7	44.4
Zimbabwe	1995	2,726.2	7.9	1.4	9.0	81.8	13.7	41.7	26.4	25.1	4.5	0.4	7.3	62.7

[1]Year ending March. [2]Excluding precious stones, etc. (667). [3]Including precious stones, etc. (667). [4]Estimate. [5]Including also Asian republics of the former U.S.S.R. [6]1990. [7]Main countries only. [8]Year ending September 30. [9]Percentage of the total excluding fish imports for the cannery (52.1% of the overall total), and government purchases (0.1%). [10]1991. [11]1987. [12]Year ending June 30. [13]Figures for Belgium-Luxembourg Economic Union (Luxembourg is also shown separately). [14]1992. [15]Including metals. [16]Excluding metals. [17]Includes 52.6% from India. [18]Mainly electricity. [19]Includes 83.8% to India. [20]Includes 77.7% from South Africa. [21]Includes 48.7% to Switzerland. [22]Main items only. [23]Includes 82.8% for reexports. [24]Domestic exports only. [25]1980. [26]1989. [27]1985. [28]Includes 9.1% for ferronickel. [29]Includes 38.7% for ships and boats. [30]Includes 63.3% for Ethiopia. [31]Figures for France include Monaco. [32]1988. [33]Includes 82.4% from Israel. [34]Includes 69.2% to Israel and 25.1% to Jordan. [35]Includes 42.5% for nonmonetary gold. [36]Includes 41.5% to Switzerland. [37]Excluding petroleum products. [38]Includes 51.5% for ships' bunkers. [39]Figures for United Kingdom include Guernsey, Isle of Man, and Jersey (data for Jersey is also shown separately). [40]Figures for Italy include San Marino. [41]United Kingdom only. [42]Including

exports													country
total value ('000,000 U.S.$)	Standard International Trade Classification (SITC) categories (%)							direction of trade (%)					
	food and agricultural raw materials (0+1+2 −27−28 +4)	mineral ores and concen- trates (27+28 +667)	fuels and other energy (3)	manufactured goods				to European Union (EU)[b]	to United States	to Eastern Europe[c]	to Japan	to all other[d]	
				total[a] (5+6 −667 +7+8 +9)	of which chemicals and related products (5)	of which machinery and transport equipment (7)	of which other[a] (6−667 +8+9)						
177,369.4	22.7	0.9	8.2	68.2	15.5	28.5	24.1	71.3	3.1	2.8	1.0	21.8	Netherlands, The
1,558.9	3.0	0.8	91.2	5.0	0.9	3.0	1.0	8.1	25.0	—	3.1	63.8	Netherlands Antilles
354.8	—	31.1	—	68.9	—	—	68.9[49]	45.0	4.8	—	27.1	23.1	New Caledonia
13,745.4	60.4	0.5	1.6	37.5	7.6	8.6	21.3	16.0	10.0	0.9	16.2	56.9	New Zealand
509.2	76.5	0.8	0.6	22.2	1.2	6.1	14.9	31.8	42.1	0.1	1.4	24.7	Nicaragua
311.9	22.4	74.8	0.8	2.0	0.1	1.2	0.7	56.4	0.1	—	18.8	24.7	Niger
11,886.5	1.8	—	97.6	0.7	—	—	0.6	46.9	44.1	—	—	9.0	Nigeria
263.0	—	—	—	100.0	—	—	100.0	—	100.0	—	—	—	Northern Mariana Islands
48,955.0	8.9	0.8	54.7	35.6	2.9	11.1	21.7	76.9	7.4	1.9	1.8	12.0	Norway
5,917.4	5.1	0.4	78.6	15.9	0.4	9.6	5.9	0.9	2.8	0.1	28.5	67.7	Oman
8,157.9	15.6	0.2	1.0	83.2	0.7	0.5	82.0	30.5	15.1	0.6	6.8	47.1	Pakistan
0.5	69.1	—	—	30.9	—	—	30.9	—	8.0	—	58.8	33.2	Palau
1,202.5	82.3	1.2	11.9	4.6	1.1	—	3.5	52.9	29.8	0.4	0.1	16.8	Panama[51]
2,624.6	26.8	19.5	30.6	23.1[52]	—	2.5	20.6[52]	12.1	4.0	—	21.4	62.5	Papua New Guinea
819.6	85.8	—	0.1	14.1	1.8	0.4	12.0	20.4	3.8	—	0.1	75.8	Paraguay
5,575.1	31.3	16.2	4.9	47.6	2.2	0.6	44.8	30.5	17.2	0.6	8.4	43.2	Peru
17,447.2	14.1	1.8	1.5	82.7	2.0	22.2	58.5	17.7	36.2	0.1	15.5	30.4	Philippines
22,863.3	13.3	1.3	8.1	77.4	7.8	21.1	48.5	70.1	2.7	17.0	0.2	9.9	Poland
23,185.6	10.6	1.5	2.4	85.5	4.6	30.6	50.3	79.5	4.7	1.2	0.8	13.8	Portugal
21,051.2	15.8	0.1	2.6	81.5	43.7	21.7	16.2	5.1	87.5	—	0.2	7.2	Puerto Rico
3,212.9	0.5	0.2	73.8	25.4	15.9	1.4	8.1	1.9[4]	2.5[4]	—[4]	55.6[4]	40.0[4]	Qatar
208.7	78.6	0.5	0.2	20.7	1.7	12.7	6.2	79.9	0.6	—	6.1	13.4	Réunion
8,084.5	12.0	0.3	7.4	80.3	9.8	13.6	56.9	56.6	2.4	8.7	0.5	31.9	Romania
79,910.0	6.1	——48.5——		45.5	9.8	9.9	25.8	32.6	5.7	27.2	4.5	30.0	Russia
131.9	72.8	3.9	—	23.3[53]	—	—	23.3[53]	64.1[4]	6.1[4]	—[4]	1.9[4]	27.9[4]	Rwanda
27.7	32.8	—	—	67.2	0.3	46.2	20.7	21.4	50.9	—	—	27.7	St. Kitts and Nevis
119.7	56.4	—	—	43.6	1.3	8.6	33.8	53.2	27.0	—	0.1	19.7	St. Lucia
50.4	75.0	0.2[2]	0.1	24.7[3]	0.8	12.3	11.7[3]	33.0	9.3	—	0.1	57.6	St. Vincent and the Grenadines
17.5	32.7	...	...	67.3	...	...	...	—	3.2	—	—	96.8	Samoa
...	...	...	...	...	...	...	...	...	...	...	...	...	San Marino[40]
6.5	76.9[22]	...	...	...	...	...	...	88.8[7]	1.9[4]	...	0.5[4]	8.8[4]	São Tomé and Príncipe
42,584.0	1.1[54]	0.3[54]	91.1[54]	7.5[54]	5.2[54]	0.9[54]	1.3[54]	22.6	18.5	—	16.0	42.9	Saudi Arabia
605.1	41.4	11.0	14.5	33.2	17.2	6.5	9.5	40.3	2.0	—	1.7	55.9	Senegal
51.8	46.7	0.1	45.9	7.3	0.1	2.7	4.4	42.5	4.0	—	0.6	53.0	Seychelles
115.8	4.8	84.2	...	11.0	...	...	...	51.0[4]	28.0[4]	1.1[4]	1.7[4]	18.2[4]	Sierra Leone
125,153.1	4.5	0.5	7.9	87.2	5.6	65.9	15.6	13.0	18.4	0.9	8.2	59.4	Singapore
6,690.2	9.3	1.5	4.6	84.6	12.9	19.0	52.6	35.0	1.6	52.8	0.1	10.5	Slovakia
8,315.8	5.7	0.2	1.2	92.9	10.5	31.4	51.0	67.0	3.1	9.7	0.3	19.9	Slovenia
142.2	——98.8[2]——		—	1.2[3]	—	—	1.2[3]	24.4	0.1	—	41.1	34.4	Solomon Islands
44.0	95.4	2.3	—	2.3	—	2.3	—	52.3	—	—	—	47.7	Somalia
27,339.9	12.3	14.3	8.1	65.4	7.7	8.8	48.9	28.3	6.6	0.7	5.8	58.6[56]	South Africa[55]
100,955.5	16.9	0.7	2.5	79.9	8.0	42.7	29.2	71.3	4.2	2.2	1.2	21.1	Spain
2,391.4	22.8	7.4	0.9	68.9	0.8	3.2	64.9	31.4	36.3	2.8	5.2	24.3	Sri Lanka
523.9	87.4[14]	5.3[14]	—[14]	7.2[14]	—[14]	—[14]	7.2[14]	29.8	3.4	0.1	4.5	62.2	Sudan, The
357.1	18.1	67.6	1.3	13.0	—	0.1	12.9	47.5	10.7	—	5.3	36.5	Suriname
751.8	69.1[24]	3.3[24]	0.9[24]	26.7[24]	1.4[24]	8.3[24]	17.1[24]	19.8[24]	3.1[24]	—[24]	0.7[24]	76.4[24]	Swaziland
82,880.5	7.6	1.2	2.1	89.1	6.8	44.4	37.9	56.1	8.5	4.0	3.3	28.1	Sweden
80,454.9	3.7	2.8	0.1	93.3	25.7	31.6	36.1	60.6	8.5	2.4	3.9	24.6	Switzerland[58]
3,969.9	18.6	0.6	62.5	18.2	0.6	0.8	16.8	57.0	0.9	6.1	0.2	35.8	Syria
115,724.0	4.1	0.1	0.9	94.9	8.6	50.8	35.5	13.6	23.2	0.5	11.8	50.9	Taiwan
748.6	0.6	——16.5——		82.9	—	0.6	82.2	46.3	2.0	21.3	1.1	29.4	Tajikistan
416.1	82.0	1.0	2.0	15.1	1.0	2.2	11.8	40.5	6.8	0.7[5]	3.9	48.2	Tanzania
56,743.2	24.6	2.5	0.7	72.1	4.4	33.7	34.0	15.1	17.9	2.1	16.8	48.1	Thailand
162.2	57.7[54]	32.8[54]	0.3[54]	9.2[54]	1.2[54]	3.4[54]	4.6[54]	19.6	0.1	2.5	—	77.7	Togo
14.0	93.0	0.4	—	6.6	0.4	1.8	4.4	0.4	23.7	—	50.8	25.1	Tonga
1,960.4	8.2	0.1	49.2	42.6	26.7	1.7	14.2	7.7	46.4	—	0.2	45.7	Trinidad and Tobago
5,517.4	8.1	1.5	10.5	79.9	12.7	9.8	57.4	80.1	1.4	0.5	0.3	17.7	Tunisia
21,598.7	21.0	2.1	1.3	75.6	4.1	11.1	60.4	51.3	7.0	11.8	0.8	29.1	Turkey
1,880.7	0.6	——72.6——		26.8	0.6	0.2	26.0	7.6	1.7	29.7	8.8	52.2	Turkmenistan
0.7	92.2[26]	—[26]	—[26]	7.8[26]	—[26]	—[26]	7.8[26]	42.9[7]	...	...	...	57.1	Tuvalu
171.4	95.2	—	3.0	1.8	—	0.9	0.9	63.8	8.1	—	0.6	27.5	Uganda
11,566.5	15.0	——11.2——		73.9	12.5	18.2	43.2	12.5	4.8	56.8	0.6	25.3	Ukraine
24,756.0	0.3	0.1	96.6	3.0	0.2	0.2	2.6	7.0[4]	3.2[4]	0.1[4]	35.7[4]	53.9[4]	United Arab Emirates
261,950.2	7.8	2.7	6.5	83.1	13.3	44.1	25.6	57.0	11.8	2.5	2.5	26.1	United Kingdom[39]
622,784.3	13.2	1.4	2.0	83.5	10.1	49.2	24.2	20.5	—	1.0	10.8	67.6	United States[59]
2,116.5	59.3	0.3	0.9	39.4	5.6	5.9	27.9	21.0	5.9	0.3	0.9	72.0	Uruguay
3,109.0	2.5	——14.8——		82.7	2.8	2.4	77.4	18.6	0.4	24.3	0.1	56.7	Uzbekistan
17.6	83.2	0.1	—	16.7	—	2.0	14.7	31.6	0.2	—	29.1	39.0	Vanuatu
18,914.2	3.0	0.8	77.0	19.2	4.2	2.8	12.2	9.1	51.0	0.2	1.5	38.1	Venezuela
2,985.2	——48.9[2, 10]——		35.6[10]	15.5[3, 10]	0.7[10]	0.1[10]	14.7[3, 10]	7.2	—	5.4	31.4	56.0	Vietnam
3,026.3	...	...	83.3[54, 60]	...	...	...	...	...	92.7	...	...	...	Virgin Islands (U.S.)
22.6[62]	...	...	...	...	...	...	...	...	...	...	...	...	West Bank
...	...	...	...	...	...	...	...	...	...	...	...	...	Western Sahara
933.9	9.6	0.2[2]	89.0	1.2[3]	0.5	—	0.7[3]	6.8	12.3	1.3[5]	13.3	66.4	Yemen
4,704.1	15.9	0.6	4.4	79.1	9.1	19.6	50.3	54.6[4]	4.5	29.1[5]	0.2	11.6	Yugoslavia
1,049.2	3.4	89.0[2, 15]	—	7.5[3, 16]	—	0.2	7.3[3, 16]	30.6	1.6	—	31.0	36.8	Zambia
1,895.5	50.2	6.1	1.3	42.4	2.6	2.7	37.2	40.3	4.7	1.6	7.9	45.4	Zimbabwe

coins. [43]1986. [44]Includes 83.8% from rest of Customs Union of Southern Africa. [45]Including also Iceland and Norway. [46]France only. [47]Includes 85.0% from South Africa. [48]Based on trade with Australia and New Zealand only. [49]Includes 58.8% for ferroalloys. [50]Excluding bulk imports of fuels. [51]Including trade with the former Canal Zone. [52]Includes 19.7% for nonmonetary gold. [53]Includes 19.8% for nonmonetary gold. [54]1993. [55]Figures for South Africa refer to the Customs Union of Southern Africa (includes South Africa, Botswana, Lesotho, Namibia, and Swaziland, also shown separately). [56]Including unspecified destinations of 21.2%. [57]Includes 87.7% from South Africa; these imports may have had their origin from other countries. [58]Figures for Switzerland include Liechtenstein also shown separately. [59]Figures for United States include American Samoa, Guam, Puerto Rico, and Virgin Islands (U.S.), also shown separately. [60]Exports of refined petroleum to United States only. [61]Excluding imports from Israel (90.9% in 1987). [62]Excluding exports to Israel (70.3% in 1987).

Trade: domestic

The following table presents data relating to domestic wholesale and retail trade for the countries of the world. The section on wholesale trade is based for the most part on establishments (service points from which a business enterprise operates [*see* note a]) engaged primarily in selling goods to retailers and distributors for resale or to purchasers who buy for business and farm uses. The retail trade section is based on businesses engaged in selling merchandise for personal or household consumption; restaurants are, when possible, included, hotels excluded.

The data presented here are based on information from a variety of country and international sources. The country sources include statistical abstracts, correspondence, annual reports, and censuses of business and trade.

Because there is no single published source or common international methodology for the compilation of data on wholesale and retail trade, nor a single current year on which, by common agreement, the various national reports would be based, allowance must be made for variations in the meaning and recency of the information provided for any single country and for its comparability internationally. Variations occur in part because of the ways in which countries define wholesale and retail trade; the conventional free-enterprise distinction between wholesale and retail activity (of a single enterprise or an entire national trade sector) may not exist in the business practice of some countries. Variations also exist in the kind and level of detail reported. For example, countries may design surveys differently according to the size (number of employees, sales, surface area) of establishments surveyed, their profitability, or other less direct criteria, such as ownership or location. The depth of analysis to which the data are subjected may also vary. The structure of a national trade sector is also affected by the degree of government involvement, which may range from total control of wholesale distribution in some socialist countries to partial involvement in some strategic sectors, or to relative noninvolvement in fully private trade sectors of capitalist countries. In some smaller countries data may refer to a single trading enterprise.

At the table's extreme left, preceding the year to which the trade data refer, the combined value of the country's wholesale and retail trade as a percentage of gross domestic product or net material product is given. Unless otherwise noted, GDP data include restaurants and exclude hotels.

Both the wholesale and retail sections of the table provide similar detail: establishments or outlets, employees, sales, and certain derived values for relationships among these measures; the retail section provides an additional breakdown of sales by an end-use classification of retail sales outlets.

Although all sales figures are given in U.S. dollars, the comparability of these dollar figures may differ considerably; for instance, the purchasing power of various national currencies in domestic transactions may bear only a distant relationship to the exchange rate of the same currency in international transactions, especially for countries having nonconvertible currencies. The price of goods may also vary, depending on the degree to which they are subject to direct subsidies and artificial cost controls such as tax, investment, or free-trade preferences by a central government seeking to influence social or economic conditions.

Trade: domestic

country	domestic trade as percentage of GDP, 1994	year	wholesale trade					retail trade		
			establishments[a]	employees[b]	sales[c] (U.S.$'000,000)	employees per establishment	sales per establishment (U.S.$'000)	outlets[a]	employees[b]	sales[c] (U.S.$'000,000)
Afghanistan	9.8	1981–82	...	[1]	...	...	...	...	126,100[1]	...
Albania	4.6[2]	1990	...	[1]	...	...	...	11,741[3]	62,000[1]	1,570[3]
Algeria	17.8[4]	1986	...	[1]	...	...	...	3,600[5,6]	390,990[1,7,8]	16,200
American Samoa	...	1990	177	255	...	1.4	...	583	1,495	...
Andorra	19.4[9]	1988	...	...	...	...	...	592[10]	7,227	...
Angola	6.1[11]	1973	[1]	...	...	...	...	29,138[1]	...	...
Antigua and Barbuda	24.7[7]	1980	25	350	...	14.0	...	199	1,000	23[12]
Argentina	15.4[13]	1985	54,452	351,087[14]	1,113	6.4[14]	20,435	500,342	1,055,071[14]	1,003
Armenia	2.2	1990	...	[1]	...	...	...	...	88,100[1]	...
Aruba	37.2[7,15]	1990	...	723	...	...	...	...	5,700	...
Australia	19.0[7,16]	1991–92	15,514	153,092	44,553	9.9	2,872	209,909	1,290,173	107,230
Austria	15.8	1995	17,149[4]	184,000	90,070	10.2[4]	3,526[4]	33,601[4]	252,000	47,912
Azerbaijan	2.2[17]	...	...	...	...	...	...	...	...	...
Bahamas, The[18]	23.0[13]	1980	23	1,066	143	46.3	6,235	132	4,059	460[19]
Bahrain	8.5	1983	[1]	[1]	...	[1]	...	255[1]	12,551[1]	1,601
Bangladesh	7.9[7,20]	1985	...	[1]	...	...	...	271,000	3,610,000[1]	5,500[19]
Barbados	26.8[7,9]	1990	...	[1]	...	...	...	1,911[21]	20,800[1]	264[12]
Belarus	12.6[9]	1994	[1]	[1]	[1]	...	...	30,300[1]	459,200[1]	654[1]
Belgium	14.1[17]	1984	60,589	160,600	65,110	2.6	1,075	135,534	193,500	20,957
Belize	17.2[7]	1983	...	[1]	...	...	...	...	4,558[1]	33[20]
Benin	20.0[22]	1979	...	...	...	...	...	170[5]	1,910[14,19]	150[12]
Bermuda	32.8[23]	1985	60[23]	820	...	...	...	310[5,23]	4,342[14]	116[24,25]
Bhutan	7.8[7]	1982	...	[1]	...	...	...	...	9,000[1,3,14]	...
Bolivia	10.7[9]	1992	4,820	21,814	...	4.5	...	64,136	122,892	1,570[19]
Bosnia and Herzegovina	13.9[4]	1990	...	[1]	18,469[4]	...	...	...	130,914[1]	18,065[4]
Botswana	15.7[16]	1983–84	205	3,500	494[12]	...	...	1,660	10,700	165[12]
Brazil	7.0	1990	45,278	652,054	22,706	14.1	501	680,634	4,102,638	39,312
Brunei	8.4[9]	1986	[1]	[1]	...	[1]	...	833[1,26]	4,261[1,26]	...
Bulgaria	10.6	1995	...	...	2,923	...	...	88,115	...	6,020
Burkina Faso	11.8	1975	...	[1]	...	...	...	...	19,354[1,14]	...
Burundi	3.3[9]	1986	...	...	...	...	...	...	...	210
Cambodia	14.8	...	...	...	...	...	...	...	...	...
Cameroon	11.7[11]	1980	...	...	...	...	...	1,312[5]	13,776[14,19]	1,430[19]
Canada	12.1[9]	1995	...	[1]	232,900[4]	...	...	...	2,428,000[1,2]	150,200
Cape Verde	28.0[11]	1980	...	[1]	...	...	...	...	3,930[1]	...
Central African Republic	11.6	1989	113	302	...	2.7	...	14,543	23,078	230
Chad	29.5[4]	1983	...	[1]	[1]	...	...	...	1,661[1,5,28]	497[1]
Chile	17.0	1983	561[5]	15,300[5]	2,312[5]	27.2[5]	4,121[5]	1,125[19,24]	21,700[19,24]	1,403[19,24]
China	9.0	1995	14,961,000	41,515,693[14]	196,241	2.8[14]	16	15,779,970[14]	37,051,765	246,905
Colombia	10.4	1985	...	...	...	...	...	1,110[31]	49,000[31]	8,600[19]
Comoros	27.0[7]	1980	...	[1]	...	...	...	...	1,873[1,5]	...
Congo, Dem. Rep. of the	16.7[9]	1981	...	...	...	...	...	3,036[5]	33,398[5]	3,300[12]
Congo, Rep. of the	11.9[9]	1984	...	[1]	...	...	...	...	13,240[1]	...
Costa Rica	20.3	1975	332[32]	4,073[32]	35[32]	12.3[32]	104[32]	9,713	26,486	475[33]
Côte d'Ivoire	27.1	1981	...	...	...	...	...	2,023[5]	16,720[5]	1,800[19]
Croatia	12.0	1994[34]	1,155	6,461	4,015	5.5	3,476	16,959	48,615	3,734
Cuba	20.1[4,35]	1989	...	...	15,174	...	...	56,916[36]	230,000[8,14]	8,124
Cyprus	19.4[1]	1993	1,559[25]	14,137	443	5.3[25]	720[25]	8,474[25]	39,676	1,102
Czech Republic	8.3[17]	1990[37]	63,110[36]	251,000[36]	40,083[36]	4.0[36]	635[36]	62,667[4]	258,127	21,235
Denmark	13.9	1992	32,432	176,205	73,937	5.4	2,280	40,733	210,015	32,145
Djibouti	15.5[9]	1985	28	371[15]	...	...	...	431	1,877[15]	...
Dominica	15.0[7,9]	1989	...	[1]	...	...	...	...	3,700[1]	790[19]
Dominican Republic	18.5[9]	1983	670	...	3,136	...	4,681	11,220[15]	...	1,259[15]
Ecuador	14.8	1990	426	18,014	139	42.3	326	554	20,168	102
Egypt	17.0[16]	1983–84	2,552	45,500[14]	4,492	18.0[14]	1,760	2,545	55,800[14]	29,700[19]

The data on distribution of retail sales by kind of consumer goods may have their origin in several different types of data or analysis. One country may aggregate sales data by kind of establishment only (this may be perfectly satisfactory in a country of small, independent outlets); another may aggregate data directly by kind of goods (most easily done in a country with well-developed statistical, tax-reporting, and commercial systems). Other countries may find it impolitic to publish data that reflect the poverty of their distribution network or their supply of consumer goods and may aggregate or publish data for only a few sectors: food or nonfood goods, for example. For countries with only a few trading enterprises in a particular sector, detail must often be withheld to preserve the confidentiality of individual businesses.

The notes that follow further define the column headings.

a. The number of establishments or outlets refers to economic units that operate at a single physical location in one principal kind of activity, whether singly owned or part of a multiunit firm. Such units are not necessarily identical with a company or enterprise.
b. Number of employees refers to full-time and part-time paid workers, including salaried managers and officers; it usually excludes owner-operators, partners, vendors, and unpaid relatives.
c. Total sales (also called turnover) includes the value of merchandise sold for cash or credit; amounts received from customers for layaway purchases; receipts from rental or leasing of vehicles, equipment, tools, instruments, etc.; receipts for delivery, installation, maintenance, repair, alteration, storage, and other services.
d. Outlets engaged primarily in the sale of food and nonalcoholic beverages, such as grocery stores, meat and fish markets, and bakeries.
e. Outlets engaged primarily in the sale of clothing and shoes; also includes outlets that sell accessory items, such as millinery, furs, and leather goods.
f. Outlets engaged primarily in the sale of home furnishings, including furniture, draperies, floor coverings, household appliances, and home entertainment equipment.
g. Outlets that primarily serve food and drink, including restaurants, lunchrooms, cafeterias, social caterers, refreshment places, contract feeders, ice cream parlors, and bars and taverns.
h. Outlets engaged primarily in the sale of pharmaceuticals, cosmetics, and perfumes.
i. Outlets engaged primarily in the sale of building materials, hardware, garden supplies, paint, electrical supplies, and farm equipment.
j. Outlets engaged primarily in the sale of motor vehicles, motorcycles, bicycles, and tires, batteries, and other automotive supplies and parts; includes service stations.
k. Outlets engaged in the sale of multiple lines of merchandise, such as department stores, variety stores, and rural general stores.
l. Miscellaneous specialized outlets such as those engaged primarily in the sale of liquors, sporting goods, books, jewelry, photographic and optical goods, gifts, flowers, tobacco products, home fuels, and newspapers.

retail trade (continued)

percentage breakdown of sales									employees per outlet	sales per outlet (U.S.$'000)	population per outlet	country
food[d]	clothing, shoes[e]	home furnishings[f]	eating, drinking[g]	drugs, pharma-ceuticals[h]	building materials[i]	automobile parts[j]	general merchandise[k]	other[l]				
...	...	...	...	...	...	...	...	...	...	...	...	Afghanistan
62.4				37.6					...	134[3]	277[3]	Albania
...	...	...	...	...	...	...	...	...	5.0[5, 6]	...	5,146[5, 6]	Algeria
...	...	...	...	...	...	...	...	...	...	...	81	American Samoa
...	...	...	...	...	...	...	...	...	3.8[10]	...	39[10]	Andorra
...	...	...	...	...	...	...	...	...	...	...	...	Angola
...	...	...	...	...	...	...	...	...	5.0	100	378	Antigua and Barbuda
15.5	13.3	7.1	5.4	4.3	7.8	13.7	10.1	22.8	2.1[14]	2,004	61	Argentina
...	...	...	...	...	...	...	...	...	...	...	...	Armenia
...	...	...	...	...	...	...	...	...	...	...	...	Aruba
28.9	3.6	8.9	3.7	2.9	2.4	31.9	7.9	10.7	6.1	511	82.8	Australia
31.0	12.2	6.9	...	6.7	1.9	17.3	4.3	19.7	7.1[4]	857[4]	227[4]	Austria
...	...	...	...	...	...	...	...	...	...	...	...	Azerbaijan
24.4[15]	7.7[15]	7.1[15]	—	3.7[15]	8.4[15]	30.1[15]	7.6[15]	11.0[15]	30.8	1,881	1,026	Bahamas, The[18]
...	...	...	...	...	...	...	...	...	49.2[1]	...	1,507[1]	Bahrain
...	...	...	...	...	...	...	...	...	...	...	...	Bangladesh
...	...	...	...	...	...	...	...	...	...	...	130[21]	Barbados
...	...	...	...	...	...	...	...	...	15.2[1]	2,157[1]	34[1]	Belarus
35.1				64.9					1.4	155	73	Belgium
...	...	...	...	...	...	...	...	...	...	...	...	Belize
...	...	...	...	...	...	...	...	...	11.3[14, 19]	...	19,871[19]	Benin
...	...	...	...	...	...	...	...	...	11.0[12, 24]	...	178[5, 23]	Bermuda
...	...	...	...	...	...	...	...	...	...	...	...	Bhutan
...	...	...	...	...	...	...	...	...	1.9	...	107	Bolivia
...	...	...	...	...	...	...	...	...	...	...	...	Bosnia and Herzegovina
...	...	...	...	...	...	...	...	...	6.4	99	604	Botswana
11.1	12.1	...	...	4.2	8.4	31.4	15.4	17.4	6.0	55	213	Brazil
...	...	...	...	...	...	...	...	...	5.1[1, 26]	...	279[1, 26]	Brunei
44.1	17.3	5.1	—	6.2	1.2	16.8	[27]	9.3[27]	...	68	...	Bulgaria
...	...	...	...	...	...	...	...	...	...	...	...	Burkina Faso
...	...	...	...	...	...	...	...	...	...	...	...	Burundi
...	...	...	...	...	...	...	...	...	...	...	...	Cambodia
...	...	...	...	...	...	...	...	...	10.5[5, 14]	...	6,481[5]	Cameroon
25.5	6.0	5.1	...	5.6	...	35.7	16.7	5.4	...	...	...	Canada
...	...	...	...	...	...	...	...	...	...	...	...	Cape Verde
...	...	...	...	...	...	...	...	...	1.6	16	187	Central African Republic
...	...	...	...	...	...	...	...	...	...	...	...	Chad
28.3[15]	[29]	5.0[15]	1.6[15]	5.4[15]	4.7[15]	18.0[15]	17.1[15, 29]	19.9[15]	19.3[19, 24]	1,247[19, 24]	10,210[19, 24]	Chile
57.3[30]	16.0[30]				26.7[30]				2.3[14]	16	76	China
...	...	...	...	...	...	...	...	...	44.1[31]	1,522[31]	...	Colombia
...	...	...	...	...	...	...	...	...	...	...	...	Comoros
...	...	...	...	...	...	...	...	...	11.0[5]	...	9,676[5]	Congo, Dem. Rep. of the
...	...	...	...	...	...	...	...	...	...	...	...	Congo, Rep. of the
37.7	13.5	6.9	...	8.2	7.0	15.1	5.9	5.7	2.7	59	202	Costa Rica
...	...	...	...	...	...	...	...	...	8.3[5]	...	4,257[5]	Côte d'Ivoire
25.2	5.5	1.6	...	—	3.2	19.1	28.5	16.9	2.9	220	282	Croatia
35.8	17.2	9.9	...	5.3	0.8	5.1	...	25.9	4.0[8, 14]	184[36]	177[36]	Cuba
10.2	8.2	...	43.7	2.4	3.1	14.9	...	17.5	1.0[25]	124[25]	77[25]	Cyprus
42.9	15.1	12.8	...	3.6	2.9	10.0	...	12.7	4.2[4]	362[4]	249[4]	Czech Republic
47.1	5.6	3.4	...	3.2	3.1	17.7	1.4	18.5	5.2	789	127	Denmark
...	...	...	...	...	...	...	...	...	...	...	998	Djibouti
...	...	...	...	...	...	...	...	...	...	...	...	Dominica
...	...	...	...	...	...	...	...	...	...	112[15]	519[15]	Dominican Republic
26.3	2.0	11.5	3.9	1.6	7.2	38.2	6.2	3.1	36.4	184	18,520	Ecuador
...	...	...	...	...	...	...	...	...	21.9[14]	1,278	17,756	Egypt

Trade: domestic (continued)

country	domestic trade as percentage of GDP, 1994	year	wholesale trade					retail trade		
			establishments[a]	employees[b]	sales[c] (U.S.$'000,000)	employees per establishment	sales per establishment (U.S.$'000)	outlets[a]	employees[b]	sales[c] (U.S.$'000,000)
El Salvador	16.5	1983	396	6,400	1,038	16.2	2,621	1,416	10,700	485
Equatorial Guinea	9.2	1983	...	36	...	...	...	...	2,701	...
Eritrea	19.7[9]	[39]	...	...	...	...	...	...	...	...
Estonia	18.6	1994	17,629	...	1,357	...	77	821	70,000[2]	807
Ethiopia	10.1[7, 20]	1984[39]	375[5, 42]	3,200[5, 42]	...	8.5[5, 42]	...	7,416[5, 42]	17,100[5, 42]	273
Faroe Islands	13.1[13]	1987	78	[1]	19	...	241	430	1,484[1, 7, 33]	38
Fiji	20.5[7]	1993	276	2,914	102	10.6	370	1,315	7,335	151
Finland	11.3	1995	9,367[43]	80,394[43]	49,376	8.6[43]	4,946[43]	37,303[13]	137,609[13]	31,842
France	14.3[1, 9]	1992	88,371	912,131	399,844	10.3	4,525	363,701	1,615,700	320,274
French Guiana	16.3[11]	1995	339	858	1,770	2.5	355	1,517	2,720	425
French Polynesia	17.7[17]	1986	[1]	[1]	...	...	...	947[1]	5,038[1]	...
Gabon	7.5	1982	...	[1]	...	...	...	...	12,683[1, 14, 23]	...
Gambia, The	16.6[16]	1983	...	[1]	...	...	...	...	16,551[1]	...
Gaza Strip	...	1986	...	[1]	...	...	...	...	13,400[1]	...
Georgia	2.7[13]	1988	...	[1]	...	...	...	...	172,400[1]	...
Germany	7.6	1993	194,381	1,544,085	674,247	7.9	3,469	487,320	2,727,312	406,188
Ghana	19.2	1983	460[44]	1,100[44]	115[44]	2.4[44]	250[44]	1,500	16,000	252[19]
Gibraltar	...	1991	...	737	...	...	...	...	1,835	...
Greece	13.5	1988	31,032	115,979	...	3.7	...	184,821	388,132	12,263[45]
Greenland	8.0[21]	1992	...	[1]	139	...	...	...	2,214[1, 8]	211
Grenada	21.1[7, 16]	1988	...	[1]	[1]	...	...	...	5,421[1]	6[1, 12]
Guadeloupe	19.6[4, 7]	1993	696	3,538	6,008	7.0	1,524	4,004	11,061	7,467
Guam	51.5[15]	1992	169	2,045	[1]	12.1	[1]	768	12,060	1,400[1]
Guatemala	24.3	1989	...	[1]	...	...	...	88,200[15]	374,690[1]	1,200[19]
Guernsey	...	1991	...	642	...	...	...	...	2,573	...
Guinea	26.0[22]	1979	...	[1]	...	...	...	...	12,808[44]	...
Guinea-Bissau	25.8[7, 11]	1979	[1]	[1]	...	...	...	685[1, 44]	5,085[1]	44[1, 26]
Guyana	4.4	1980	...	[1]	...	...	...	147[5]	14,690[1]	93[12]
Haiti	10.9[20]	1983	...	[1]	...	...	...	653[5, 46]	303,353[1]	500[19]
Honduras	10.3	1991	...	[1]	...	...	...	...	156,500[1]	401[12]
Hong Kong	25.5	1994	21,712	61,951	23,100	2.8	1,064	58,362	162,760	33,112
Hungary	11.4	1994	206[15]	122,600[15]	13,121[23]	595[23]	...	217,861	467,400	19,470
Iceland	10.4[9]	1992	1,509[12, 47]	5,132[23]	598[33, 47]	...	...	1,680	7,774[48]	825
India	13.4[16]	1980	[1]	[1]	...	...	...	3,132,000[1, 24]	3,615,000[1, 24]	108,300[12]
Indonesia	16.6	1980	[1]	[1]	[1]	[1]	[1]	54,632[1]	85,400[1]	3,451[1]
Iran	15.4[16]	1986–87	118,698	[1]	2,429[50]	...	133[50]	634,084	521,708[1, 51]	37,350
Iraq	25.6[13]	1987–88[26]	1,942	3,902	130	2.0	67	108,460	165,594	7,077
Ireland	17.1[7, 17]	1988	3,972	39,101	11,420	9.8	2,875	31,699	89,680	10,952
Isle of Man	10.5[52]	1991	...	851	...	...	...	...	2,993	...
Israel	10.4[13]	1988	17,967	67,300	16,875	3.8	939	43,844	103,100	10,763
Italy	18.4[7]	1983	...	[1]	...	...	...	1,033,725	1,369,200[1]	122,978
Jamaica	27.7[7, 9]	1991	...	[1]	...	...	...	10,150[33]	173,500[1]	1,457[12]
Japan	12.5	1994	429,302	4,581,372	5,272,000	10.7	12,280	1,499,948[24]	7,384,177[24]	1,321,000[24]
Jersey	...	1986	...	855	...	...	...	...	7,046	...
Jordan	10.5[9]	1993	508	3,292	405	6.5	798	35,866	81,656	1,766
Kazakstan	8.9[17]	1991	...	...	...	...	...	42,168	484,800	...
Kenya	14.9	1990	2,097	21,266	...	10.1	...	4,316	36,300	...
Kiribati	14.1[13]	1987	...	[1]	...	...	...	30	1,127[1, 36]	3.8
Korea, North	...	...	...	...	...	...	...	...	...	...
Korea, South	12.6	1994	118,471	603,093	91,480	5.1	772	758,953	1,548,297	79,850
Kuwait	7.6[7, 9]	1992	2,426	21,934	647	9.0	267	11,541	60,506	508
Kyrgyzstan	10.1	1992	...	[1]	...	...	...	...	92,900[1, 46]	138
Laos	8.2[9]	1990	...	...	...	...	...	15,000	...	576
Latvia	7.0	1994	...	...	...	...	...	7,214[11]	95,300[11]	986
Lebanon	25.6	1986	...	[1]	...	...	...	...	114,706[1]	1,662[14]
Lesotho	8.6	...	...	...	...	...	...	...	...	...
Liberia	5.3[4]	1984	...	[1]	...	...	...	...	46,850[1]	115[19]
Libya	9.0[13]	1973	1,126	4,148[14]	...	3.7[14]	...	26,825	44,605[14]	9,205[12]
Liechtenstein	...	1975	67	216	...	3.2	...	228	740	...
Lithuania	17.2[17]	1992	...	[1]	...	...	...	6,425	127,400[1]	236
Luxembourg	16.4[11]	1994	2,125	10,980	7,864	5.2	3,700	3,204	17,495	4,617
Macau	...	1991	...	[1]	...	...	...	...	47,706[1]	...
Macedonia	24.7	1990	...	[1]	9,522[4]	...	...	...	65,593[1, 4]	9,238[6]
Madagascar	10.9[11]	1976	1,104	...	...	...	...	1,570	...	696[23]
Malaŵi	11.5	1984	439	23,000	522	52	1,189	500	8,600	127
Malaysia	12.4	1980	19,663	116,200	15,461	5.9	786	95,993	73,000	8,200[19]
Maldives	19.1[7]	1990	...	[1]	...	...	...	...	8,884[1]	5[19]
Mali	19.3[7, 9]	1979	...	[1]	...	...	...	...	5,200[1]	...
Malta	14.3[7, 11]	1983	3	[1]	1.0	...	333	4[21]	11,936[1, 5]	2.3
Marshall Islands	19.2[7]	1988	...	[1]	...	...	...	...	1,394[1]	...
Martinique	21.9[7, 11]	1993	700	3,680	7,957	5.2	2,007	4,137	16,313	2,109
Mauritania	14.2[22]	1971[5]	23	100	102	4.3	4,445	59	700	103
Mauritius	17.8[7]	1986	[1]	[1]	...	[1]	...	207[1, 5, 7]	10,107[1, 5, 7]	164[1, 5, 7]
Mayotte	...	1983	[1]	[1]	[1]	...	[1]	41[1]	597[1, 8]	27[1]
Mexico	25.5	1988	36,512	[1]	23,506	...	644	713,315	3,875,100[1, 2]	39,810
Micronesia	12.7[17]	1980	...	348[14]	...	...	...	...	489[7, 14]	...
Moldova	5.8	1990	...	[1]	...	...	...	...	148,000[1]	...
Monaco	...	1975	...	273	...	...	...	...	1,439	...
Mongolia	17.6[9]	1983[1, 55]	...	...	...	...	...	4,828	21,100	1,235[36]
Morocco	19.8	1972	...	...	...	...	...	4,000[5]	20,000[5]	5,750[19]
Mozambique	10.4[17]	1980	...	[1]	...	...	...	...	63,058[1]	...
Myanmar (Burma)	22.3[20]	1983	...	[1]	...	...	...	...	1,405,000[1, 56]	2,116
Namibia	10.1[7]	1977	222	5,035	377	22.7	1,698	1,248	7,569	254
Nauru	...	...	...	...	...	...	...	...	...	...
Nepal	4.7[16]	1983	...	[1]	...	...	...	...	119,000[1, 14, 23]	736

retail trade (continued)												country
percentage breakdown of sales									employees per outlet	sales per outlet (U.S.$'000)	population per outlet	
food[d]	clothing, shoes[e]	home furnishings[f]	eating, drinking[g]	drugs, pharma-ceuticals[h]	building materials[i]	automobile parts[j]	general merchandise[k]	other[l]				
11.9[6,38]	7.6[6,38]	16.2[6,38]	...	7.9[6,38]	6.3[6,38]	12.4[6,38]	28.2[6,38]	9.5[6,38]	7.6	342	3,336	El Salvador
...	...	...	...	...	...	...	...	...	...	...	...	Equatorial Guinea
...	...	...	...	...	...	...	...	...	...	...	...	Eritrea
46.0	10.1	6.8[40]	...	[41]	[40]	13.1	18.2	5.8[41]	...	984	1,826	Estonia
15.9	45.2	...	...	...	7.9	9.8	10.5	10.7	2.3[5,42]	27[5,42]	55,200[5,42]	Ethiopia
...	...	...	...	...	...	...	...	...	...	89	109	Faroe Islands
11.9[11]	10.2[11]	7.6[11]	8.5[11]	2.6[11]	12.3[11]	9.6[11]	36.1[11]	1.2[11]	5.6	115	573	Fiji
31.6	6.0	6.0	...	4.6	5.4	27.9	11.2	7.3	3.7[13]	940[13]	135[13]	Finland
38.2	15.7	17.6	...	6.4	...	6.1	6.3	9.7	4.4	881	158	France
...	...	...	...	...	...	...	...	...	3.1	2,419	155	French Guiana
...	...	...	...	...	...	...	...	...	5.3[1]	...	188[1]	French Polynesia
50.5	9.6	...	...	...	33.8	6.1	...	...	...	...	...	Gabon
...	...	...	...	...	...	...	...	...	...	...	...	Gambia, The
...	...	...	...	...	...	...	...	...	...	...	...	Gaza Strip
...	...	...	...	...	...	...	...	...	...	...	...	Georgia
35.2	12.7	12.0	...	8.4	4.1	...	18.9	8.7	5.6	834	166	Germany
...	...	...	...	...	...	...	...	...	1.1	108[44]	7,993	Ghana
...	...	...	...	...	...	...	...	...	...	...	...	Gibraltar
60.0[45]	18.1[45]	9.5[45]	...	...	...	...	...	12.4[45]	2.1	...	54	Greece
...	...	...	...	...	...	...	...	...	...	...	...	Greenland
...	...	...	...	...	...	...	...	...	...	...	...	Grenada
44.8[11]	13.4[11]	19.6[11]	...	7.1[11]	...	...	...	15.1[11]	2.8	337	102	Guadeloupe
11.6[8]	10.9[8]	4.9[8]	8.0[8]	0.3[8]	5.2[8]	26.9[8]	3.3[8]	28.9[8]	15.7	1,494[1]	181	Guam
...	...	...	...	...	...	...	...	...	...	...	83[15]	Guatemala
...	...	...	...	...	...	...	...	...	...	...	...	Guernsey
...	...	...	...	...	...	...	...	...	...	...	...	Guinea
...	...	...	...	...	...	...	...	...	0.8[1,44]	...	1,080[1,44]	Guinea-Bissau
9.7	18.9	13.8	4.5	2.8	17.7	18.6	...	14.0	...	743	5,884	Guyana
...	...	...	...	...	...	...	...	...	...	...	7,034[5,46]	Haiti
...	...	...	...	...	...	...	...	...	...	...	...	Honduras
18.8[17]	13.6[17]	...	...	...	...	11.5[17]	...	56.1[17]	2.8	567	103	Hong Kong
11.4	5.2	7.6	6.8	2.1	13.6	19.1	23.4	10.8	2.1	89	47	Hungary
62.6[49]	8.8	...	...	...	...	...	[49]	28.6	4.6[48]	825	155	Iceland
...	...	...	...	...	...	...	...	...	1.2[1,24]	...	219[1,24]	India
...	...	...	...	...	...	...	...	...	1.6[1]	63[1]	2,681[1]	Indonesia
...	...	...	...	...	...	...	...	...	...	59	78	Iran
...	...	...	...	...	...	...	...	...	1.5	20	158	Iraq
40.6	9.1	1.4	10.4	2.9	5.1	21.6	2.8	6.1	2.8	345	112	Ireland
...	...	...	...	...	...	...	...	...	...	...	...	Isle of Man
35.4	12.2	20.0	...	...	...	...	6.2	26.2	2.4	245	103	Israel
50.8	15.1	...	...	3.4	...	...	...	30.7	...	119	55	Italy
...	...	...	...	...	...	...	...	...	...	...	214[33]	Jamaica
30.5	10.0	4.8	—	[53]	[53]	11.4	15.0	28.3[53]	4.9[24]	880[24]	83[24]	Japan
...	...	...	...	...	...	...	...	...	...	...	...	Jersey
23.5	12.6	11.2	—	1.5	9.2	22.9	12.5	6.6	2.3	49	109	Jordan
...	...	...	...	...	...	...	...	...	11.5	...	400	Kazakstan
...	...	...	...	...	...	...	...	...	8.4	...	6,003	Kenya
...	...	...	...	...	...	...	...	...	...	127	2,226	Kiribati
...	...	...	...	...	...	...	...	...	...	...	...	Korea, North
29.7	17.8	13.7	—	4.5	2.9	...	12.0	19.4	2.0	105	58	Korea, South
18.4[49]	14.5	17.3	...	2.6	6.5	16.4	[49]	24.3	5.2	150	123	Kuwait
...	...	...	...	...	...	...	...	...	...	...	...	Kyrgyzstan
...	...	...	...	...	...	...	...	...	...	38	278	Laos
53.9	9.1	2.1	8.1	...	1.2	...	...	25.6	13.2[11]	2,831[11]	373[11]	Latvia
...	...	...	...	...	...	...	...	...	...	...	...	Lebanon
...	...	...	...	...	...	...	...	...	...	...	...	Lesotho
...	...	...	...	...	...	...	...	...	...	...	...	Liberia
...	...	...	...	...	...	...	...	...	1.7[14]	...	84	Libya
...	...	...	...	...	...	...	...	...	3.2	...	105	Liechtenstein
59.2	10.9	3.7	...	...	1.3	0.8	...	24.1	19.8[1]	38	584	Lithuania
26.8	8.5	10.1	...	3.0	...	42.6	...	9.1	5.4	1,441	126	Luxembourg
...	...	...	...	...	...	...	...	...	...	...	...	Macau
...	...	...	...	...	...	...	...	...	...	...	...	Macedonia
...	...	...	...	...	...	...	...	...	...	...	4,977	Madagascar
...	...	...	...	...	...	...	...	...	17.2	254	14,196	Malaŵi
32.9[54]	7.3[54]	10.8[54]	...	2.5[54]	1.1[54]	33.3[54]	4.4[54]	7.7[54]	0.8	64	143	Malaysia
...	...	...	...	...	...	...	...	...	...	...	...	Maldives
...	...	...	...	...	...	...	...	...	...	...	...	Mali
...	...	...	...	...	...	...	...	...	...	578[5]	83,378[5]	Malta
...	...	...	...	...	...	...	...	...	...	...	...	Marshall Islands
...	...	...	...	...	...	...	...	...	3.9	510	91	Martinique
...	...	...	...	...	...	...	...	...	11.9	1,742	20,300	Mauritania
...	...	...	...	...	...	...	...	...	48.8[1,5,7]	792[1,5,7]	4,976[1,5,7]	Mauritius
...	...	...	...	...	...	...	...	...	...	652[1]	1,477[1]	Mayotte
33.8	...	...	...	...	37.0	23.7	...	5.8	...	59	113	Mexico
...	...	...	...	...	...	...	...	...	...	...	...	Micronesia
...	...	...	...	...	...	...	...	...	...	...	...	Moldova
...	...	...	...	...	...	...	...	...	...	...	...	Monaco
...	...	...	...	...	...	...	...	...	4.3	225	372	Mongolia
...	...	...	...	...	...	...	...	...	5.0[5]	...	*c.* 4,000[5]	Morocco
...	...	...	...	...	...	...	...	...	...	...	...	Mozambique
...	...	...	...	...	...	...	...	...	...	...	...	Myanmar (Burma)
31.4	11.9	5.3	...	2.8	1.7	...	41.9	5.0	5.9	196	713	Namibia
...	...	...	...	...	...	...	...	...	...	...	...	Nauru
...	...	...	...	...	...	...	...	...	...	...	...	Nepal

Trade: domestic (continued)

country	domestic trade as percentage of GDP, 1994	year	wholesale trade: establishments[a]	wholesale trade: employees[b]	wholesale trade: sales[c] (U.S.$'000,000)	wholesale trade: employees per establishment	wholesale trade: sales per establishment (U.S.$'000)	retail trade: outlets[a]	retail trade: employees[b]	retail trade: sales[c] (U.S.$'000,000)
Netherlands, The	15.6	1994	55,500	344,000[13]	180,165	6.8[13]	3,246	86,500	482,500[13]	64,121
Netherlands Antilles	21.8[2]	1988	...	[1]	...	...	...	...	15,890[1]	149[14]
New Caledonia	31.0[2]	1991	...	[1]	...	...	...	1,023	4,995[1]	...
New Zealand	14.7[7, 57]	1996	8,263[58]	76,664[58]	16,295[58]	9.3[58]	1,972[58]	29,961[24, 58]	116,301[24, 58]	6,399
Nicaragua	24.2	1987	...	[1]	...	...	...	20,610[15]	94,600[1]	790[19]
Niger	18.5[7, 17, 22]	...	...	...	...	...	...	...	...	...
Nigeria	16.4[7]	1983[5]	154	16,000	2,220	104	14,415	421	20,000	2,202
Northern Mariana Islands	...	1987	28	187	49	6.7	1,777	383	2,304	155
Norway	11.0[7, 11]	1992	18,390	101,385[48]	56,056	5.5[48]	3,048	40,154	121,677[48]	31,264
Oman	15.4[7]	1990	[1]	[1]	...	...	...	25,840[1, 4, 7]	87,500[1]	2,449[12]
Pakistan	14.4[7, 16]	1983	...	...	...	...	...	276,701[46]	501,773[14, 46]	12,848
Palau	20.0[36]	1984	...	124	...	...	...	...	133	...
Panama	12.7[17]	1982[60]	560	13,115	1,491	23.4	2,662	7,561	15,765[5]	1,334
Papua New Guinea	8.0[17]	1985	...	[1]	...	...	...	...	25,100[1, 33]	669[7]
Paraguay	30.4[7, 17]	1982	...	[1]	...	...	...	...	85,961[1]	2,645[19]
Peru	16.9[17]	1973	4,210	34,100	2,163	8.1	514	103,010	72,200	8,500[19]
Philippines	15.3	1981	20,642	122,717	4,538	5.9	220	279,968	241,872	4,836
Poland	14.1	1994	...	...	15,945[17]	...	...	785,000	984,883	57,467
Portugal	17.4[2]	1983	4,522	135,400[14]	9,260	29.9[14]	2,048	4,889	74,400[14]	3,057
Puerto Rico	14.5	1991	1,876	34,571	7,365[36]	18.4	3,165[36]	9,164	106,239	7,206[36]
Qatar	7.0	1990	134	3,801	85	28.4	636	4,956	18,238	1,048[43]
Réunion	17.9[7, 13]	1992	1,313	6,732	2,664	5.1	203	3,506	12,927	2,114
Romania	11.7	1989	...	...	...	...	...	82,035	465,200	19,926
Russia	15.7	1992	...	...	...	...	...	319,500	3,135,000	18,771
Rwanda	19.4[7]	1978	...	[1]	...	...	...	...	8,014[1, 7]	350[19]
St. Kitts and Nevis	23.9[7]	1984	...	[1]	...	...	...	...	940[1]	...
St. Lucia	24.6[17]	1980	...	[1]	...	...	...	...	4,770[1, 7, 14]	...
St. Vincent	17.5[7]	...	...	...	...	...	...	...	...	...
Samoa	8.3[17]	1986	...	[1]	...	...	...	...	842[1]	...
San Marino	...	1994	209	[1]	...	...	...	1,126	2,531[1]	...
São Tomé and Príncipe	10.0[4]	1981	...	[1]	...	...	...	...	1,994[1]	...
Saudi Arabia	7.0[17]	1991[24]	4,460	31,481[14]	1,354	7.1[14]	304	80,266	174,187[14]	2,292
Senegal	27.4[13]	1987	97[5]	1,843[5]	...	19[5]	...	289[5]	4,964[5]	664[12]
Seychelles	12.3[9]	1989	[1]	[1]	...	[1]	...	243[1]	1,301[1]	...
Sierra Leone	13.8[7, 20]	1983–84	...	[1]	...	...	...	...	7,211[1]	177[12]
Singapore	17.6[7]	1992	24,820	158,993	132,480	6.4	5,338	17,798[24]	78,152[24]	12,058[24]
Slovakia	16.2	1992	...	...	...	...	...	5,590	24,638	1,313
Slovenia	12.9[13]	1995	909	27,000	5,814	29.7	6,396	6,972	35,472	5,955
Solomon Islands	9.6[11]	1991	...	[1]	...	...	...	405[19]	2,849[1]	139[19]
Somalia	9.3[11]	...	...	...	...	...	...	...	...	...
South Africa	16.1	1991	...	...	46,541	...	...	58,100[33]	373,200[33]	35,592
Spain	20.5[7, 36]	1984	40,000[21]	...	...	...	...	710,865[21]	1,400,000[21]	54,777
Sri Lanka	21.4[7, 17]	1983[5]	190	15,000	[1]	78.9	...	1,348	44,300	1,116[1, 25]
Sudan, The	12.8[4]	1981	...	...	...	...	...	...	...	3,278
Suriname	20.2	1985	...	[1]	...	...	...	13,000[61]	12,840[1]	110[19]
Swaziland	6.7[7]	1984	67	1,000	...	14.9	...	656	3,700	23[21]
Sweden	11.1	1993	31,960[25]	167,800[25]	37,518[25]	5.2[25]	1,174[25]	58,497	248,208[13]	30,159
Switzerland	17.5[13]	1991	22,094	176,857	...	8.0	...	55,080	245,443	23,620[25]
Syria	28.7	1983	2,827[46]	...	...	...	...	75,865[46]	110,000[14, 46]	7,330[19]
Taiwan	16.1[7, 9]	1987	55,654[12]	169,100	7,572[36]	2.9[12]	101[12]	355,760[12]	181,200	14,291[36]
Tajikistan	4.0	...	...	[1]	...	...	...	...	145,400[1]	...
Tanzania	14.0[7]	1983	...	...	...	...	...	1,620[5]	16,524[5]	3,975[19]
Thailand	16.6[17]	1988	16,740	139,252	14,535	8.3	868	260,030	280,886	13,683
Togo	21.2[9, 22]	1980	...	...	...	...	...	181[5]	1,815[5]	112
Tonga	12.4[20]	1976	...	14[14]	...	...	...	...	654[14]	...
Trinidad and Tobago	14.3[7]	1977	124	6,786	509	54.7	4,102	370	15,986	1,670[19]
Tunisia	27.3[7]	1984	...	[1]	...	...	...	...	153,860[1, 36]	2,814
Turkey	18.5	1991	53,122	250,671	72,071	4.7	1,357	444,803	586,416	63,621
Turkmenistan	3.4	1990	...	[1]	...	...	...	...	90,000[1]	4,150
Tuvalu	14.2[7]	1979	...	[1]	...	...	...	...	113[1, 14]	...
Uganda	12.6[16]	1977	226	4,100	...	18.1	...	251	3,200	5,285[24]
Ukraine	11.1[17]	1991	...	[1]	...	...	...	...	1,753,000[1, 2]	70,800
United Arab Emirates	11.0	1983	[1]	[1]	...	[1]	...	13,906[1, 7, 44]	121,278[1, 44]	5,910[19]
United Kingdom	14.0[9]	1994[63]	117,771	800,000	382,905	6.8	3,251	289,996	2,379,000	202,030
United States	15.8[17]	1992	495,457	5,791,401	3,249,874	11.7	6,559	1,526,215	18,407,453	1,894,880
Uruguay	14.5	1988	...	[1]	...	...	...	52,954[1, 7]	161,285[1, 7]	5,397[24, 25]
Uzbekistan	5.6	1991	...	[1]	...	...	...	...	462,000[1]	...
Vanuatu	30.9[17]	1983[51]	18	187[14]	...	10.4[14]	...	256	1,439[14]	...
Venezuela	13.6[17]	1979	...	...	...	...	...	...	161,596	12,345[19]
Vietnam	13.6	1990	...	...	...	...	...	25,723	419,400	4,414
Virgin Islands (U.S.)	...	1987	84	1,322	211	15.7	2,509	1,311	8,529	703
West Bank	...	1986	...	[1]	...	...	...	...	23,000[1]	...
Western Sahara	...	...	...	...	...	...	...	...	...	...
Yemen[64]	14.3	1986	...	[1]	...	...	...	...	201,606[1]	2,195[13]
Yugoslavia	16.3[9, 35]	1992	5,723	17,693	8,671	3.1	1,515	51,159	125,348	8,958
Zambia	9.6[9]	1974	494[5]	15,500[5]	977[5]	31.4[5]	1,978[5]	1,636[5]	13,700[5]	768[12]
Zimbabwe	10.9	1990	...	[1]	...	...	...	...	95,400[1]	693[36]

[1]Retail-trade data include wholesale trade. [2]1990. [3]Excludes retail-trade network of the agricultural cooperatives. [4]1989. [5]Data refer to larger establishments only. [6]1971. [7]Includes hotels. [8]1987. [9]1995. [10]1972. [11]1991. [12]1983. [13]1992. [14]All persons engaged, including proprietors. [15]1982. [16]1994–95. [17]1993. [18]Data refer to New Providence Island only. [19]1986. [20]1993–94. [21]1979. [22]Includes finance. [23]1981. [24]Excludes restaurants (eating and drinking establishments). [25]1984. [26]Privately owned establishments only. [27]Other includes general merchandise. [28]1976. [29]General merchandise includes clothing and shoes. [30]1994. [31]For major cities only. [32]Wholesale selling directly to the public only. [33]1980. [34]Data exclude pharmacies. [35]Percentage of net material product. [36]1985. [37]Data refer to former Czechoslovakia. [38]Selected outlets in urban areas only. [39]Ethiopia includes Eritrea. [40]Home furnishings includes building materials. [41]Other

retail trade (continued)												country
percentage breakdown of sales									employees per outlet	sales per outlet (U.S.$'000)	population per outlet	
food[d]	clothing, shoes[e]	home furnishings[f]	eating, drinking[g]	drugs, pharma-ceuticals[h]	building materials[i]	automobile parts[j]	general merchandise[k]	other[l]				
40.3	11.4	6.8	...	3.2		——38.3——			5.9[12]	741	180	Netherlands, The
...	...	...	...	...	...	...	...	...	...	...	...	Netherlands Antilles
...	...	...	...	...	...	...	...	...	...	...	169	New Caledonia
20.8	4.3	6.2	14.9	2.8	1.9	32.3	4.9	11.9	3.9[24, 58]	346[24, 58]	106[24, 58]	New Zealand
...	...	...	...	...	...	...	...	...	...	...	143[15]	Nicaragua
...	...	...	...	...	...	...	...	...	...	...	...	Niger
...	...	...	...	...	...	...	...	...	47.5	5,230	226,615	Nigeria
27.0	[59]	2.3	8.8	...	7.2	[59]	4.7	50.0[59]	6.0	406	56	Northern Mariana Islands
34.9	9.9	7.3	...	...	4.8	27.0	4.0	12.1	3.0[48]	779	107	Norway
...	...	...	...	...	...	...	...	...	...	...	56[1, 4, 7]	Oman
64.0	12.0	4.0	...	...	...	...	...	20.0	1.8[14, 46]	...	273[46]	Pakistan
...	...	...	...	...	...	...	...	...	...	...	...	Palau
...	...	...	...	...	...	...	...	...	13.9[5]	176	270	Panama
...	...	...	7.1[7]	...	...	26.0	...	66.9	...	...	...	Papua New Guinea
...	...	...	...	...	...	...	...	...	...	...	...	Paraguay
...	...	...	...	...	...	...	...	...	0.7	20	145	Peru
25.4	12.3	6.7	...	...	11.3	29.5	...	14.8	0.9	17	177	Philippines
37.4	6.1	2.8	...	...	...	27.8	...	25.9	1.3	73	49	Poland
21.5[45]	14.1[45]	11.2[45]	...	3.3[45]	5.6[45]	35.2[45]	——9.1[45]——		15.3[14]	625	2,047	Portugal
30.5[15]	9.9[15]	4.5[15]	7.5[15]	4.3[15]	5.9[15]	23.2[15]	8.9[15]	5.3[15]	11.6	201[36]	387	Puerto Rico
9.0[43]	9.6[43]	13.2[43]	...	2.7[43]	7.2[43]	29.7[43]	9.1[43]	19.5[43]	3.7	177[10]	98	Qatar
54.4	11.5	17.8	...	6.9	...	...	...	9.4	3.7	603	178	Réunion
30.0[33]	10.0[33]	5.9[33]	25.0[33]	1.6[33]	0.8[33]	...	...	26.7[33]	5.7	243	282	Romania
...	...	...	...	...	...	...	...	...	9.8	59	563	Russia
...	...	...	...	...	...	...	...	...	...	...	...	Rwanda
...	...	...	...	...	...	...	...	...	...	...	...	St. Kitts and Nevis
...	...	...	...	...	...	...	...	...	...	...	...	St. Lucia
...	...	...	...	...	...	...	...	...	...	...	...	St. Vincent
...	...	...	...	...	...	...	...	...	...	...	...	Samoa
...	...	...	...	...	...	...	...	...	2.2[1]	...	21.8[1]	San Marino
...	...	...	...	...	...	...	...	...	...	...	...	São Tomé and Príncipe
...	...	...	...	...	...	...	...	...	2.2[14]	29	201	Saudi Arabia
...	...	...	...	...	...	...	...	...	17.2[5]	...	23,430[5]	Senegal
...	...	...	...	...	...	...	...	...	54[1]	...	285[1]	Seychelles
...	...	...	...	...	...	...	...	...	...	...	...	Sierra Leone
17.7[49]	20.4	11.6	...	...	...	24.2	[49]	26.1	4.4	677	158	Singapore
42.1	7.7	9.3	...	1.9	0.8	3.7	1.7	32.8	1.4	235	948	Slovakia
14.8	4.8	1.1	...	4.4	1.5	26.3	35.0	12.1	5.1	854	285	Slovenia
...	...	...	...	...	...	...	...	...	...	...	...	Solomon Islands
...	...	...	...	...	...	...	...	...	...	...	...	Somalia
35.0	13.9	8.1	...	3.3	...	18.7	4.5	16.5	6.4[33]	383[33]	*c.* 540[33]	South Africa
39.2	10.5	16.7	...	...	...	4.2	...	29.4	2.0[21]	119[21]	52[21]	Spain
...	...	...	...	...	...	...	...	...	32.9	...	11,436	Sri Lanka
...	...	...	...	...	...	...	...	...	...	...	...	Sudan, The
...	...	...	...	...	...	...	...	...	...	...	...	Suriname
52.5[21]	25.1[19]	22.4[19]	...	...	...	...	...	...	5.6	...	969	Swaziland
35.5[13]	——9.3[13]——		...	...	...	...	...	55.2[13]	3.5[13]	515	149	Sweden
46.4[25]	13.5[25]	...	...	4.0[25]	...	...	...	36.1[25]	4.5	...	123	Switzerland
16.0	2.5	...	...	3.5	12.3	39.5[62]	3.5	22.7	1.4[14, 46]	...	97[46]	Syria
21.5[23]	3.2[23]	8.8[23]	...	4.1[23]	3.1[23]	8.7[23]	3.1[23]	47.5[23]	0.3[12]	33[12]	52[12]	Taiwan
...	...	...	...	...	...	...	...	...	...	...	...	Tajikistan
...	...	...	...	...	...	...	...	...	10.0[5]	...	12,600[5]	Tanzania
10.5	3.4	4.6	...	1.0	7.2	43.2	12.4	17.7	1.1	53	209	Thailand
...	...	...	...	...	...	...	...	...	10.0[5]	...	15,600[5]	Togo
...	...	...	...	...	...	...	...	...	...	...	...	Tonga
18.6	...	8.5	2.7	...	10.7	28.2	15.3	15.9	43.2	1,467	2,798	Trinidad and Tobago
...	...	...	...	...	...	...	...	...	...	...	...	Tunisia
15.0[2]	10.6[2]	15.5[2]	3.8[2]	2.8[2]	2.9[2]	27.3[2]	10.6[2]	11.5[2]	1.3	143	129	Turkey
...	...	...	...	...	...	...	...	...	...	...	...	Turkmenistan
...	...	...	...	...	...	...	...	...	...	...	...	Tuvalu
...	...	...	...	...	...	...	...	...	12.7	...	47,200	Uganda
...	...	...	...	...	...	...	...	...	...	...	...	Ukraine
...	...	...	...	...	...	...	...	...	...	...	49[1, 7, 44]	United Arab Emirates
45.3	14.4	7.7	...	3.7	3.2	...	6.4	19.3	8.2	697	201	United Kingdom
19.5	5.4	4.9	10.3	4.1	5.2	28.0	12.9	9.7	12.1	1,242	165	United States
...	...	...	...	...	...	...	...	...	3.0[1, 7]	...	...	Uruguay
...	...	...	...	...	...	...	...	...	...	...	...	Uzbekistan
...	...	...	...	...	...	...	...	...	5.6[14]	...	484	Vanuatu
50.2	10.1	7.6	...	...	...	5.0	...	27.1	...	...	...	Venezuela
...	...	...	...	...	...	...	...	...	16.6	171	2,575	Vietnam
17.6	7.9	6.4	12.0	2.3	4.8	11.4	1.9	35.7	6.5	536	81	Virgin Islands (U.S.)
...	...	...	...	...	...	...	...	...	...	...	...	West Bank
...	...	...	...	...	...	...	...	...	...	...	...	Western Sahara
...	...	...	...	...	...	...	...	...	...	...	...	Yemen[64]
...	...	...	...	...	...	...	...	...	2.5	175	205	Yugoslavia
...	...	...	...	...	...	...	...	...	8.4[5]	359[5]	2,873[5]	Zambia
...	...	...	...	...	...	...	...	...	...	...	...	Zimbabwe

includes drugs, pharmaceuticals. [42]Excludes Addis Ababa and Asmera. [43]1988. [44]1977. [45]1978. [46]1975. [47]Excludes fuels, automobiles, alcohol and tobacco, and building materials. [48]Full-time equivalents. [49]Food includes general merchandise. [50]1972. [51]Urban establishments only. [52]1990–91. [53]Other includes drugs, pharmaceuticals, and building materials. [54]Peninsular Malaysia only. [55]State- and cooperative-owned establishments, including public catering. [56]1989–90. [57]1992–93. [58]1982–83. [59]Other includes clothing, shoes, and automobile parts. [60]Excludes Colón Free Zone. [61]1973. [62]Other includes machinery, transport equipment, and petroleum products. [63]Great Britain only. [64]Data refer to former Yemen Arab Republic only.

Finance

This table presents major statistical aggregates comprising national financial structure or constituting a basis for certain international financial comparisons. It includes such data as international reserves, money supply, central banking activity and discount rates, commercial (or "deposit money") banking activity, and external indebtedness of the central government. The country models are broadly similar and permit comparison of internal structure and external position at a high level of generalization.

One of the principal financial criteria of the relative economic position of a country is the size of its international reserves. International reserves as represented in this table comprise the sum of a country's (1) reserve position in the International Monetary Fund (IMF), a quota subscribed in the country's own currency, constituting a level up to which transactions may be effected within the IMF system, (2) holdings of foreign exchange, (3) holdings of gold, and (4) holdings of Special Drawing Rights (SDRs; an unconditional credit allocation, within a quota system set by the IMF, of currency needed by a country to maintain stability of foreign exchange transactions or markets). At appropriate accounting intervals these four elements are valued in a single unit of account (the SDR) and summed. The portion of this reserve total comprised by foreign exchange is very significant as an indication of the country's international liquidity (ability to pay its debts immediately in hard, or convertible, currencies). The ratio of external debt to total reserves, however, is less susceptible of interpretation in isolation: a low ratio, for example, may characterize the situation of a country with little need to borrow or of one with substantial debt but also the means to repay it. Much higher ratios, on the other hand, may be manageable, despite small reserves, if a country's export earnings are also high.

The section on money supply for the country, both as a total and as a per capita amount, refers to one particular measure of money in circulation: M1, the sum of money in private sector demand deposit accounts and outside banks in circulation; it is distinguished from a broader measure of supply, M2, which is roughly M1 plus "quasi-money" (the time, savings, and foreign-currency deposits of residents).

The section of the table outlining banking activity and the principal monetary aggregates encompasses both central bank authorities and commercial (deposit) banks. For both, the principal component aggregates are grouped under assets and liabilities. For certain countries, the four principal aggregates under assets and liabilities do not comprise the entire total, and the percentages shown, therefore, may add to less than 100% (occasionally more, when the net of other liabilities [capital, reserves, undistributed profits, checks, and other transit items] is negative, reducing the total against which these percentages are calculated). The items excluded by the choice of categories are the least significant worldwide but may be important locally; they include such items as quasi-money, money seasonally adjusted, unused bank overdrafts, and so on. In the case of the central bank authority, data are also provided for the central bank discount rate, generally the controlling interest rate for banking and commercial activity in the country.

Finance

country	international reserves, 1997[a]			money supply, 1996[b]		central bank authority, 1996[b]								
	total ('000,000 SDRs)	% foreign exchange	ratio of external debt to total reserves, 1995[b]	stock ('000,000,000 national currency)	M1 per capita	assets (%)				liabilities (%)				central bank discount rate, 1997[a]
						claims on government	claims on private sector	claims on banks	claims on foreign assets	reserve money	government deposits	foreign liabilities	capital accounts	
Afghanistan	...	...	...	...	...	...	...	...	...	...	...	...	...	...
Albania	202	98.0	2.3	90.4	27,600	46.7	—	3.0	50.3	54.2	2.9	32.5	13.5	36.0
Algeria	4,835	95.9	13.3	520.3[3]	18,300[3]	44.8[3]	—	34.7[3]	20.5[3]	46.9[3]	1.8[3]	17.7[3]	—	...
American Samoa	...	...	...	...	...	...	...	...	...	...	...	...	...	...
Andorra	...	...	...	...	...	...	...	...	...	...	...	...	...	...
Angola	...	...	...	...	...	...	...	...	...	...	...	...	...	...
Antigua and Barbuda	32	100.0	...	0.255	3,960	17.6	—	0.6	81.8	100.0	—	—	—	7.0[4]
Argentina	14,335	97.4	4.3	19.076	540	15.6	—	45.5	38.9	27.7	4.4	12.4	8.0	6.0[5]
Armenia	...	...	...	...	...	...	...	...	...	...	...	...	...	...
Aruba	135	97.0	...	0.447	5,330	—	—	—	100.0	63.9	23.2	—	15.4	9.5
Australia	10,511	94.0	...	95.650	5,200	57.5	—	—	42.5	75.7	7.9	0.1	—	5.28[6]
Austria	15,221	93.6	...	401.9	49,800	3.3	—	14.5	82.3	69.5	0.1	—	35.8	2.50
Azerbaijan	...	...	...	...	...	...	...	...	...	...	...	...	...	...
Bahamas, The	220	97.3	...	0.445	1,560	47.8	—	1.1	51.1	71.1	3.3	—	28.4	6.50
Bahrain	1,045	94.0	...	0.291	480	—	—	—	100.0	32.2	32.9	3.3	48.6	5.8[5]
Bangladesh	1,226	96.9	6.6	141.676	1,140	23.6[1]	—	27.8	48.6	72.2	—	5.9	4.4	7.00
Barbados	249	100.0	1.7	0.627	2,370	12.2	—	1.3	86.5	67.1	34.1	7.1	4.8	12.50
Belarus	...	...	...	15,708.4	1,519,000	37.6[1]	0.5	29.4	32.4	53.2	4.7	28.4	6.0	35.0[7]
Belgium	12,610	87.3	...	1,439.2	141,000	9.2	—	15.4	75.4	49.9	0.1	0.5	5.1	2.50
Belize	43	90.7	5.9	0.164	730	47.3	—	2.7	49.9	51.1	28.2	1.5	8.2	12.00
Benin	184	98.9	7.6	161.7[3]	28,800[3]	30.0	—	1.4	68.6	35.8	25.9	40.5	—	6.25
Bermuda	...	...	...	...	...	...	...	...	...	...	...	...	...	...
Bhutan	119	99.2	0.7	2.074	2,440	—	—	5.6	94.4	43.1	6.0	4.5	—	8.0[6,7]
Bolivia	781	91.2	6.3	4.759	620	27.6[1]	—	25.6	46.8	27.9	30.9	27.0	23.4	16.2[6]
Bosnia and Herzegovina	...	...	...	...	...	...	...	...	...	...	...	...	...	...
Botswana	3,961	98.8	0.1	0.951	640	—	—	—	100.0	12.5	39.6	—	33.3	12.50
Brazil	41,445	99.7	1.9	39.591	250	16.7[1]	—	41.0	42.3	30.1	15.2	2.1	2.5	21.1
Brunei	...	...	...	...	...	...	...	...	...	...	...	...	...	...
Bulgaria	...	...	...	...	...	...	...	...	...	...	...	...	...	...
Burkina Faso	238	96.2	3.3	213.7[3]	20,400[3]	25.7	—	1.9	72.4	62.7	16.2	19.5	—	6.25
Burundi	103	93.2	5.2	43.644	7,280	17.2[2]	2.2	13.8	66.8	36.4	10.1	9.1	24.2	...
Cambodia	...	...	...	328.926	32,100	22.6	—	1.0	76.4	47.7	8.7	19.9	21.3	...
Cameroon	2[7]	50.0[7]	1,355.7	319.2[3]	22,700[3]	92.1[3]	—	5.8[3]	2.1[3]	40.2[3]	15.4[3]	96.2[3]	0.7[3]	8.60[7]
Canada	15,315	88.6	...	155.8	5,170	9.3	—	—	90.7	97.3	—	—	—	3.25
Cape Verde	...	...	...	13.001	33,300	45.5[1]	9.8	5.1	39.6	93.0	—	0.5	24.8	5.00[6]
Central African Republic	165[7]	100.0[7]	3.6	111.2[3]	34,300[3]	23.8[3]	—	1.0[3]	75.1[3]	65.1[3]	1.0[3]	11.1[3]	0.5[3]	8.60[7]
Chad	123[7]	100.0[7]	5.9	85.3[3]	12,400[3]	39.4[3]	—	0.8[3]	59.8[3]	59.2[3]	8.5[3]	19.2[3]	1.3[3]	8.60[7]
Chile	11,928	99.2	0.5	2,686.7	185,000	28.2[1]	1.7	16.7	53.4	78.4	14.9	—	2.0	9.90[6]
China	88,926	98.0	1.2	3,066.3	2,510	6.0	2.5	55.4	36.2	101.7	4.6	—	1.5	9.00
Colombia	7,173	95.9	1.6	9,937.3	277,000	9.4[1]	—	3.9	86.7	62.8	2.1	3.0	27.4	30.2
Comoros	...	...	4.2	13.341	23,000	15.1	—	—	84.9	52.3	7.3	5.9	36.9	...
Congo, Dem. Rep. of the	45[7]	97.8[7]	64.7	1,889.0[3]	42,400[3]	5.4[1,3]	1.9[3]	24.7[3]	68.1[3]	47.6[3]	1.8[3]	326.2[3]	66.9[3]	221.0
Congo, Rep. of the	83[7]	98.8[7]	83.3	134.9[3]	52,800[3]	69.5[3]	—	3.7[3]	26.8[3]	80.1[3]	13.7[3]	8.8[3]	1.2[3]	8.60[7]
Costa Rica	825	98.9	3.0	166.9	48,600	55.2[1]	—	8.4	36.4	68.0	20.0	43.9	22.7	34.00
Côte d'Ivoire	634	99.7	22.4	944.5[3]	63,900[3]	48.6	—	15.5	35.9	61.8	5.5	29.4	—	6.25
Croatia	...	...	...	10.683	2,240	1.7	—	1.6	96.7	66.2	4.2	8.8	14.3	5.90
Cuba	...	...	...	...	...	...	...	...	...	...	...	...	...	...
Cyprus[8]	911	95.5	...	0.654	1,000	43.1	—	0.5	58.3	55.1	24.9	1.9	—	7.00
Czech Republic	8,659	99.2	0.7	451.6	43,800	0.8[1]	—	17.4	81.8	81.1	9.5	9.1	5.9	10.50
Denmark	11,301	94.5	...	325.5	61,700	9.1	3.6	36.5	50.8	56.3	18.6	1.0	—	3.25
Djibouti	52	100.0	3.0	35.925	58,600	—	—	0.3	99.7	72.8	2.1	—	12.6	...
Dominica	18	100.0	3.8	0.097	1,310	19.1	—	—	80.9	96.1	0.9	2.9	—	6.4[4]
Dominican Republic	263	99.6	9.7	20.884	2,760	22.3[1]	—	25.3	52.3	160.7	—	128.1	−25.1	...
Ecuador	1,662	98.0	7.3	5,349.5	453,000	6.8[1]	0.3	11.0	81.9	49.2	28.7	13.3	21.9	45.00
Egypt	13,260	98.2	1.9	44.521	720	37.4[1]	—	11.6	50.9	42.6	22.3	32.7	—	12.75

The largest share of assets in the case of both central and commercial banks is usually either claims on government and government agencies or foreign assets and holdings, though some of the latter, such as the large outstanding loans to socialist and less developed countries, have become the chief liabilities. The chief liability of a central bank is usually reserve money (the currency and notes issued by the bank). When government deposits represent a substantial share, budgetary surpluses have usually been deposited by the central government. Large foreign liabilities imply extensive foreign investment. Among the deposit money banks, loans to the private sector normally represent the largest share of assets and savings deposits the largest share of liabilities.

Because the majority of the world's countries are in the less developed bloc, and because their principal financial concern is often external debt and its service, data are given for outstanding external public and publicly guaranteed long-term debt rather than for total public debt, which is the major concern in the developed countries. For comparability, the data are given in U.S. dollars. The volume of debt by itself does not create external payment problems. If the country's external debt service (interest payments plus principal repayment) needs can be met by a strong, dependable export market, by export of services, or, occasionally, by direct remittances from abroad (by residents working abroad and sending wages home in foreign currencies, for example), no debt problem need exist. Countries whose debt service ratio (total debt service as a percent of exports of goods and services) is relatively high, however, must often base their external borrowing policy on maintenance of domestic conditions of strict efficiency and, sometimes, austerity. The failure to adhere to such policies may lead to eventual crises of financial liquidity, deflation, and slower growth.

Ideally, the data presented here should be obtained by utilizing a single international methodology to provide a universally comparable set of international statistics. No international agency, however, can collect such data for all countries because of differences, both overall and in detail, in national definitions of financial aggregates, in accounting methodology, and in the completeness with which it is possible to survey a country's financial activity. The greater part of the data presented in the table comes from the IMF's *International Financial Statistics* and the World Bank's *Global Development Finance* (formerly *World Debt Tables*). These sources are supplemented by other recent data from national, regional, or other international sources. In a few cases the desired data are negligible or unavailable, as noted.

Detailed percentages may not add to 100.0 because of rounding, statistical discrepancy, or nonaccounting of negligible quantities.

— None, less than half the last significant figure, or not applicable.

... Not available.

a. Latest month.

b. Year-end.

deposit money banks, 1996[b]									external public debt outstanding (long-term, disbursed only), 1995							country
assets (%)				liabilities					total ('000,000 U.S.$)	creditors (%)		debt service				
				deposits ('000,000,000 national currency)	composition (%)							total ('000,000 U.S.$)	repayment (%)		debt service ratio (%)	
loans to government	loans to private sector	reserves	foreign assets		demand depos.	savings depos.	govt. depos.	foreign liabilities		official	private		principal	interest		
...	...	...	...	...	...	...	...	...	...	...	...	...	...	...	...	Afghanistan
71.1[1]	5.3	6.3	17.3	205.2	20.8	31.3[2]	39.0	0.6	556.7	45.5	54.5	1.8	—	100.0	0.2	Albania
80.2[1,3]	14.4[3]	0.8[3]	4.6[3]	717.6[3]	29.4[3]	38.8[3]	8.1[3]	20.0[3]	30,442	50.8	49.2	4,112	57.8	42.2	33.3	Algeria
...	...	...	...	...	...	...	...	...	...	...	...	...	...	...	...	American Samoa
...	...	...	...	...	...	...	...	...	...	...	...	...	...	...	...	Andorra
...	...	...	...	...	...	...	...	...	9,533	24.2	75.8	406	81.0	19.0	11.1	Angola
14.6[1]	63.9	7.0	14.5	1.340	14.0	56.4[2]	5.3	15.4	...	...	...	...	...	...	...	Antigua and Barbuda
22.0[1]	63.4	2.8	11.8	84.950	8.6	50.2[2]	3.6	18.6	62,181	34.0	66.0	6,302	41.4	58.6	22.5	Argentina
...	...	...	...	...	...	...	...	...	300.4	100.0	—	7.3	8.9	91.1	2.3	Armenia
3.4	63.9	8.8	23.8	1.754	19.7	48.7	0.9	19.5	...	...	...	...	...	...	...	Aruba
7.6[1,3]	85.5[3]	1.4[3]	5.4[3]	415.513[3]	15.6[3]	52.1[3]	0.8[3]	16.0[3]	...	...	...	...	...	...	...	Australia
20.4[1,3]	54.7[3]	1.8[3]	23.0[3]	4,075.7[3]	6.0[3]	43.5[3]	1.9[3]	24.6[3]	...	...	...	...	...	...	...	Austria
...	...	...	...	...	...	...	...	...	206.1	100.0	—	8.7	—	100.0	...	Azerbaijan
17.8[1]	88.7	5.3	−11.9	2.219	15.7	71.2[2]	2.7	—	...	...	...	...	...	...	...	Bahamas, The
3.3	25.3	30.0	41.4	3.301	5.7	34.7	15.4	14.7	...	...	...	...	...	...	...	Bahrain
19.8[1]	61.9	11.4	7.0	468.212	15.7	74.0	7.9	3.6	15,543	98.4	1.6	656	73.5	26.5	11.9	Bangladesh
26.8	46.1	7.1	20.0	3.419	10.8	56.8[2]	7.2	23.5	369.6	51.3	48.7	86.5	68.3	31.7	...	Barbados
33.0[1]	36.1	16.3	14.6	34,919.9	26.5	33.2[2]	8.2	6.3	1,255	61.3	38.7	165	65.5	34.5	3.3	Belarus
29.6[1]	29.2	1.1	40.0	21,407.6	5.6	25.8[2]	0.3	43.9	...	...	...	...	...	...	...	Belgium
6.5[1]	73.3	8.4	11.8	0.652	15.2	64.6[2]	4.3	12.7	220.3	79.8	20.2	34.5	71.6	28.4	11.4	Belize
14.9[3]	30.0[3]	11.9[3]	43.2[3]	271.7[3]	39.7[3]	31.6[3]	12.5[3]	9.0[3]	1,514	99.7	0.3	45	53.3	46.7	7.8	Benin
...	...	...	...	8.475[3]	...	...	...	...	...	...	...	...	...	...	...	Bermuda
11.8[1]	15.1	42.0	31.1	4.962	33.3	29.5[2]	9.3	—	86.6	92.1	7.9	8.9	80.9	19.1	...	Bhutan
6.9	81.4	8.8	2.8	21.178	14.0	53.6[2]	0.5	13.7	4,452	98.4	1.6	291	53.1	46.9	22.7	Bolivia
...	...	...	...	...	...	...	...	...	—	—	—	—	—	—	...	Bosnia and Herzegovina
2.0[1]	47.7	37.8	12.5	3.621	19.4	60.6	1.1	4.2	682.1	93.1	6.9	92.0	70.1	29.9	3.2	Botswana
20.7[1]	61.1	12.3	5.9	327.431	3.7	50.4	4.8	15.8	96,609	29.8	70.2	13,838	47.9	52.1	23.5	Brazil
...	...	...	...	...	...	...	...	...	...	...	...	...	...	...	...	Brunei
...	...	...	...	...	...	...	...	...	9,574	37.0	63.0	936	44.3	55.7	14.0	Bulgaria
11.0[3]	31.8[3]	7.1[3]	50.1[3]	248.2[3]	32.9[3]	28.6[3]	24.7[3]	11.6[3]	1,136	99.6	0.4	46	62.0	38.0	12.6	Burkina Faso
18.2[1]	65.2	3.0	13.7	57.491	31.5	28.5	—	4.3	1,095	99.8	0.2	29	62.1	37.9	20.7	Burundi
0.5[1]	38.6	15.9	45.1	1,125.724	2.6	51.8[2]	0.4	14.4	1,942	99.3	0.7	5	80.0	20.0	0.5	Cambodia
32.3[1,3]	53.4[3]	5.3[3]	9.0[3]	711.9[3]	30.1[3]	46.3[3]	13.2[3]	5.6[3]	8,061	88.6	11.4	346	52.9	47.1	12.5	Cameroon
13.0[1]	73.0	0.7	13.3	728.7	17.4	47.8[2]	0.6	15.6	...	...	...	...	...	...	...	Canada
34.0[1]	37.1	18.8	10.2	27.806	35.8	50.7[2]	6.9	1.0	185.2	98.8	1.2	5.1	64.7	35.3	2.8	Cape Verde
29.7[1,3]	57.4[3]	5.1[3]	7.8[3]	40.4[3]	30.4[3]	22.2[3]	17.9[3]	9.6[3]	852.0	98.0	2.0	6.2	45.2	54.8	2.7	Central African Republic
26.5[1,3]	47.8[3]	17.3[3]	8.4[3]	58.2[3]	35.6[3]	13.5[3]	18.6[3]	14.6[3]	839.6	99.7	0.3	7.3	43.8	56.2	2.7	Chad
1.3[1]	93.1	4.3	1.3	17,298.8	10.6	53.9[2]	4.0	8.9	7,178	49.9	50.1	2,951	77.6	22.4	14.6	Chile
2.2	76.1	16.6	5.1	8,355.1	22.5	54.4	—	5.6	94,675	38.3	61.7	13,693	66.2	33.8	9.0	China
9.5[1]	77.7	10.9	1.9	25,156.9	20.8	36.4[2]	5.8	10.6	12,983	54.1	45.9	3,145	69.9	30.1	21.0	Colombia
3.4	54.0	41.5	1.0	12.238	38.0	50.4	−0.3	0.1	186.7	100.0	—	0.9	44.4	55.6	0.8	Comoros
1.7[1,3]	23.9[3]	4.4[3]	70.0[3]	1,466.0[3]	12.8[3]	43.0[2,3]	—	16.9[3]	9,621	90.9	9.1	—	—	—	—	Congo, Dem. Rep. of the
27.9[1,3]	56.6[3]	4.8[3]	10.6[3]	152.9[3]	32.2[3]	15.9[3]	7.2[3]	9.3[3]	4,955	81.4	18.6	142	57.4	42.6	11.3	Congo, Rep. of the
11.8[1]	41.4	40.0	6.9	796.9	9.3	76.6[2]	0.4	5.6	3,132	79.5	20.5	531	61.6	38.4	13.5	Costa Rica
23.2[3]	62.4[3]	3.6[3]	10.8[3]	1,600.8[3]	30.7[3]	30.3[3]	11.4[3]	12.3[3]	11,899	77.4	22.6	771	66.7	33.3	17.0	Côte d'Ivoire
27.9[1]	46.7	6.7	18.6	67.222	10.4	37.3[2]	2.6	18.5	1,693	88.8	11.2	158	62.0	38.0	2.1	Croatia
...	...	...	...	...	...	...	...	...	...	...	...	...	...	...	...	Cuba
11.3	57.3	7.5	24.0	6.403	6.0	54.5	0.6	31.7	...	...	...	...	...	...	...	Cyprus[8]
26.0[1]	54.4	9.8	9.8	1,615.1	19.7	41.1[2]	5.5	15.3	9,610	14.9	85.1	1,863	75.5	24.5	7.6	Czech Republic
8.6	49.0	5.2	37.2	996.6	28.8	29.7	—	24.0	...	...	...	...	...	...	...	Denmark
0.8[1]	54.8	0.9	43.5	70.864	26.4	32.7	0.8	22.4	218.0	99.9	0.1	6.3	77.0	23.0	3.0	Djibouti
16.2[1]	59.0	7.6	17.2	0.610	11.1	56.2[2]	7.9	15.6	84.6	100.0	—	5.6	67.9	32.1	5.0	Dominica
9.8[1]	68.9	16.5	4.8	51.177	21.9	53.1	5.1	7.7	3,550	81.6	18.4	346	53.5	46.5	10.4	Dominican Republic
3.4	79.4	8.3	8.9	22,319.4	13.3	65.2[2]	—	13.8	12,032	43.7	56.3	1,285	55.4	44.6	24.3	Ecuador
36.1[1]	36.6	11.9	15.4	235.802	7.6	57.6[2]	5.8	2.6	31,325	94.5	5.5	2,073	40.4	59.6	12.6	Egypt

Finance (continued)

country	international reserves, 1997[a]			money supply, 1996[b]		central bank authority, 1996[b]								
	total ('000,000 SDRs)	% foreign exchange	ratio of external debt to total reserves, 1995[b]	stock ('000,000,000 national currency)	M1 per capita	assets (%)				liabilities (%)				central bank discount rate, 1997[a]
						claims on government	claims on private sector	claims on banks	claims on foreign assets	reserve money	government deposits	foreign liabilities	capital accounts	
El Salvador	744	94.4	2.6	9.898	1,760	30.5[1]	—	18.4	51.0	69.9	6.4	10.0	10.4	11.25[6]
Equatorial Guinea	...	...	...	9.5[3]	22,300[3]	99.9[3]	—	—	0.1[3]	50.0[3]	0.4[3]	61.4[3]	1.7[3]	8.60[7]
Eritrea	...	...	...	...	...	...	...	...	...	...	...	...	...	...
Estonia	447	100.0	0.3	10.786	7,310	—	0.2	1.7	98.0	76.3	—	12.5	25.0	3.3[9]
Ethiopia	421	98.1	6.4	9.273	160	59.7	—	3.6	36.7	51.9	13.6	12.0	9.0	12.00[7]
Faroe Islands	...	...	...	...	...	...	...	...	...	...	...	...	...	...
Fiji	257	93.0	0.5	0.456	590	—	—	—	100.0	42.0	7.9	—	7.2	6.00
Finland	7,470	93.5	...	204.834	39,900	3.0	3.8	20.7	72.4	61.2	—	1.5	10.5	4.00
France	23,732	77.5	...	1,811.0	31,000	11.0	3.4	27.1	58.5	59.7	3.8	0.8	36.2	3.10[9]
French Guiana	...	...	...	4.621	30,700	...	...	...	...	...	...	...	...	...
French Polynesia	...	...	...	71.742	319,000	...	...	...	...	...	...	...	...	...
Gabon	105[7]	100.0[7]	27.6	219.1[3]	188,000[3]	56.4[3]	—	2.1[3]	41.5[3]	70.0[3]	6.9[3]	26.4[3]	0.7[3]	8.60[7]
Gambia, The	74	97.3	3.6	0.453	370	20.6[1]	—	—	79.4	30.6	53.0	15.9	6.4	14.00
Gaza Strip	...	...	...	...	...	...	...	...	...	...	...	...	...	...
Georgia	...	...	...	...	...	...	...	...	...	...	...	...	...	...
Germany	61,518	86.6	...	879.8	10,700	6.3	—	59.2	34.6	86.0	0.1	4.1	—	2.5
Ghana	640	95.3	6.4	1,215.7	67,900	50.8[1]	—	0.6	48.6	29.2	5.9	39.1	—	45.00
Gibraltar	...	...	...	...	...	...	...	...	...	...	...	...	...	...
Greece	11,205	97.9	...	3,839.8[3]	366,000[3]	40.2	—	3.6	56.2	44.3	6.7	24.6	—	14.5
Greenland	...	...	...	...	...	...	...	...	...	...	...	...	...	...
Grenada	27	100.0	2.6	0.148	1,510	17.6	—	—	82.4	99.5	0.5	—	—	6.5[4]
Guadeloupe	...	...	...	7.283	16,900	...	...	...	...	...	...	...	...	...
Guam	...	...	...	...	...	...	...	...	...	...	...	...	...	...
Guatemala	769	97.8	3.5	8.822	800	37.8[1]	—	10.5	51.6	347.5	101.4	15.5	7.3	5.5[6]
Guernsey	...	...	...	...	...	...	...	...	...	...	...	...	...	...
Guinea	...	...	...	274.125[3]	37,200[3]	62.0[1,3]	—	1.7[3]	36.3[3]	36.5[3]	46.0[3]	18.2[3]	10.2[3]	18.0[7]
Guinea-Bissau	12	100.0	40.8	709.3	609,000	48.8[1]	6.5	—	44.7	70.0	31.5	100.0	−164.6	35.0
Guyana	232	100.0	6.6	17.531	24,700	68.0[1]	—	—	32.0	14.3	20.8	60.0	1.8	11.5
Haiti	90	100.0	7.0	5.740	870	66.1[1]	1.6	0.7	31.6	64.3	16.1	13.4	8.0	...
Honduras	366	99.7	15.1	6.053	1,050	20.9[1]	0.9	20.3	57.9	77.0	32.5	106.2	30.7	23.7[6]
Hong Kong	...	...	...	217.840	34,000	...	...	...	...	...	...	...	...	5.13[9]
Hungary	6,173	99.0	2.0	1,030.5	101,000	36.2[3]	0.1[3]	9.7[3]	53.9[3]	48.6[3]	13.2[3]	99.8[3]	1.8[3]	27.0[7]
Iceland	299	96.0	...	42.472	157,000	26.6	0.9	3.6	68.9	36.3	18.0	27.7	—	6.5
India	18,963	96.5	4.3	2,124.5	2,210	58.1	—	5.6	36.2	81.3	—	2.4	6.8	11.00
Indonesia	14,759	97.3	4.7	51,652.0	261,000	...	...	...	...	...	...	...	...	10.63
Iran	...	...	...	45,865.0	743,000	74.0[1]	—	2.5	23.5	50.4	15.7	4.2	1.2	...
Iraq	...	...	...	...	...	...	...	...	...	...	...	...	...	...
Ireland	5,472	93.7	...	5.361[3]	1,480[3]	2.6	—	—	97.4	65.2	23.1	—	16.2	6.75
Isle of Man	...	...	...	...	...	...	...	...	...	...	...	...	...	...
Israel	12,868	100.0	...	16.716[3]	3,080[3]	26.5[3]	—	11.0[3]	62.5[3]	47.7[3]	47.3[3]	1.8[3]	—	14.2[4]
Italy	32,752	89.1	...	602,150.0	10,480,000	...	...	...	...	...	...	...	...	6.75
Jamaica	590	99.7	5.0	33.548	13,300	40.4	—	—	59.6	65.5	73.4	4.2	4.0	17.90[4]
Japan	160,146	95.6	...	181,150.0	1,440,000	53.3	—	16.9	29.8	98.5	13.0	—	—	0.50
Jersey	...	...	...	...	...	...	...	...	...	...	...	...	...	...
Jordan	1,198	96.9	3.4	1.533	340	29.2	—	—	70.8	68.0	10.2	—	—	8.50
Kazakstan	1,113	71.3	2.3	...	...	25.2[3]	0.2[3]	6.7[3]	67.9[3]	42.5[3]	9.4[3]	20.1[3]	40.1[3]	24.00
Kenya	668	97.8	16.5	78.999	2,770	54.8	—	—	45.2	79.3	26.2	17.8	1.8	25.25
Kiribati	...	...	...	...	...	...	...	...	...	...	...	...	...	...
Korea, North	...	...	...	...	...	...	...	...	...	...	...	...	...	...
Korea, South	24,555	97.7	...	39,542.0	870,000	4.2[1]	—	44.6	51.2	47.0	12.2	0.1	—	5.0
Kuwait	2,460	88.4	...	1.243	580	3.6	—	—	96.4	42.9	23.0	—	16.3	7.25
Kyrgyzstan	...	...	...	...	...	...	...	...	...	...	...	...	...	...
Laos	...	...	...	75.558	15,000	6.3[1]	5.8	21.8	66.1	43.5	27.0	26.1	10.5	35.00
Latvia	...	...	...	0.420	170	5.0	—	4.5	90.5	74.8	7.4	16.1	4.6	4.00
Lebanon	5,645	93.7	0.3	1,753.4	459,000	0.4	2.2	1.3	96.1	37.2	23.8	0.6	2.1	16.70
Lesotho	420	99.0	1.3	0.633	320	6.9	—	—	93.1	14.4	68.0	7.0	3.4	16.60
Liberia	...	...	...	...	...	94.7[1,10]	1.1[10]	3.8[10]	0.4[10]	39.0[10]	5.4[10]	45.7[10]	4.3[10]	...
Libya	...	...	...	6.324	1,140	59.2	8.1	—	32.6	63.0	10.5	—	—	...
Liechtenstein	...	...	...	...	...	...	...	...	...	...	...	...	...	...
Lithuania	...	...	...	3.643	980	—	—	4.2	95.8	71.8	1.9	31.5	—	9.5[9]
Luxembourg	59	30.5	...	111.4	267,000	36.1	—	7.5	56.4	42.9	24.8	6.8	32.3	3.50[6]
Macau	...	...	...	...	...	...	...	...	...	...	...	...	...	...
Macedonia	...	...	...	...	...	...	...	...	...	...	...	...	...	...
Madagascar	182	100.0	34.0	2,167.7	156,000	55.3[1]	—	4.9	39.8	65.7	23.2	24.6	1.3	...
Malaŵi	107	97.2	18.0	2.743	260	19.7[1]	—	3.4	76.8	74.2	20.0	14.8	10.9	27.00
Malaysia	18,946	96.5	0.7	63.594[3]	3,130[3]	2.9[3]	0.8[3]	9.2[3]	87.1[3]	65.5[3]	11.4[3]	—	—	7.25
Maldives	69	98.6	3.1	1.059	4,010	52.1[1]	—	0.1	47.8	63.6	7.8	10.0	5.5	6.80[5]
Mali	297	96.6	8.8	198.2[3]	31,900[3]	25.4	—	—	74.6	51.1	19.7	26.2	—	6.25
Malta	1,076	93.2	0.1	0.490	1,310	11.6	—	—	88.4	76.5	5.2	—	—	5.5
Marshall Islands	...	...	...	...	...	...	...	...	...	...	...	...	...	...
Martinique	...	...	...	6.937[3]	17,700[3]	...	...	...	...	...	...	...	...	...
Mauritania	118	99.2	25.3	16.227	6,840	41.5[1]	1.8	5.8	50.9	25.3	74.6	74.3	9.8	...
Mauritius	606	94.7	1.4	9.830	8,640	5.2	—	2.5	92.2	64.8	1.4	0.1	2.5	11.92
Mayotte	...	...	...	1.133	9,100	...	...	...	...	...	...	...	...	...
Mexico	17,135	98.7	5.6	206.166	2,210	−3.9	—	8.2	95.7	69.5	—	73.0	2.3	20.17[5]
Micronesia	...	...	...	...	...	...	...	...	...	...	...	...	...	...
Moldova	204	99.0	1.9	0.995	230	21.1	0.1	15.4	63.3	36.4	5.4	50.3	4.1	20.0[9]
Monaco	...	...	...	...	...	...	...	...	...	...	...	...	...	...
Mongolia	73	91.8	3.7	73.807	31,400	34.1	—	2.0	63.9	59.9	9.8	48.4	17.9	66.0
Morocco	2,993	98.1	5.9	143.818	5,330	29.5	14.0	1.9	54.5	88.5	1.3	0.9	—	8.00[5]
Mozambique	...	...	...	...	...	...	...	...	...	...	...	...	...	...
Myanmar (Burma)	136	93.4	9.4	...	...	...	...	...	...	...	...	...	...	12.50[6,7]
Namibia	...	...	...	2.800	1,640	48.3	—	—	51.7	28.4	9.1	46.0	—	17.75
Nauru	...	...	...	...	...	...	...	...	...	...	...	...	...	...
Nepal	...	...	3.9	35.540	1,680	40.3	1.5	2.9	55.3	56.1	12.2	5.6	26.3	11.00

deposit money banks, 1996[b]									external public debt outstanding (long-term, disbursed only), 1995							country
assets (%)				liabilities					total ('000,000 U.S.$)	creditors (%)		debt service				
loans to govern-ment	loans to private sector	re-serves	foreign assets	deposits ('000,000,000 national currency)	composition (%)					offi-cial	private	total ('000,000 U.S.$)	repayment (%)		debt service ratio (%)	
					demand depos.	savings depos.	govt. depos.	foreign liabilities					princi-pal	inter-est		
3.3	71.8	22.7	2.2	40.909	12.2	64.9[2]	3.9	8.5	2,025	95.1	4.9	256	60.5	39.5	8.1	El Salvador
11.0[1,3]	38.6[3]	22.1[3]	28.3[3]	8.8[3]	31.0[3]	23.3[3]	10.0[3]	19.8[3]	229.6	92.7	7.3	0.6	33.3	66.7	0.7	Equatorial Guinea
...	...	...	...	...	...	...	...	...	...	...	...	...	...	...	...	Eritrea
7.6[1]	60.9	10.2	21.3	18.855	34.5	17.9[2]	17.8	20.1	181.7	89.7	10.3	10.5	23.8	76.2	0.4	Estonia
16.9	57.4	7.9	17.8	15.467	25.0	43.3	4.8	9.5	4,958	91.9	8.1	153	60.1	39.9	13.4	Ethiopia
...	...	...	...	...	...	...	...	...	...	...	...	...	...	...	...	Faroe Islands
13.0[1]	67.6	13.1	6.3	1.724	19.1	59.9	1.2	10.0	169.9	99.6	0.4	42.5	74.8	25.2	3.7	Fiji
5.8	65.7	4.8	23.7	529.488	36.1	19.8	3.8	22.7	...	...	...	...	...	...	...	Finland
13.5	55.2	0.4	30.9	11,591.0	13.4	30.9	—	30.2	...	...	...	...	...	...	...	France
...	...	...	...	...	...	...	...	...	...	...	...	...	...	...	...	French Guiana
...	...	...	...	...	...	...	...	...	...	...	...	...	...	...	...	French Polynesia
38.6[1,3]	46.9[3]	6.1[3]	8.4[3]	442.0[3]	26.7[3]	31.6[3]	3.5[3]	8.9[3]	4,099	95.1	4.9	368	44.8	55.2	13.1	Gabon
39.8[1]	40.8	15.3	4.1	0.837	23.7	61.4	—	7.4	383.7	99.9	0.1	18.0	76.7	23.3	9.9	Gambia, The
...	...	...	...	...	...	...	...	...	...	...	...	...	...	...	...	Gaza Strip
...	...	...	...	...	...	...	...	...	988	89.1	10.9	17.0	—	100.0	...	Georgia
19.5[1]	63.0	1.5	16.0	5,893.5	10.7	25.1	4.2	12.9	...	...	...	...	...	...	...	Germany
6.0[1]	31.3	30.7	32.0	2,177.8	22.1	26.9	4.8	29.4	4,568	90.7	9.3	218	73.9	26.1	13.6	Ghana
...	...	...	...	...	...	...	...	...	...	...	...	...	...	...	...	Gibraltar
31.8[1,3]	31.9[3]	24.9[3]	11.4[3]	18,630.7[3]	8.4[3]	46.1[3]	—	36.5[3]	...	...	...	...	...	...	...	Greece
...	...	...	...	...	...	...	...	...	...	...	...	...	...	...	...	Greenland
9.0[1]	62.9	7.4	20.8	0.804	11.8	62.8[2]	5.1	17.0	98.4	92.6	7.4	6.9	76.8	23.2	...	Grenada
...	...	...	...	...	...	...	...	...	...	...	...	...	...	...	...	Guadeloupe
...	...	...	...	...	...	...	...	...	...	...	...	...	...	...	...	Guam
7.5	69.0	21.4	2.2	22.403	20.6	39.3	0.9	10.0	2,493	82.5	17.5	286	61.4	38.6	8.9	Guatemala
...	...	...	...	...	...	...	...	...	...	...	...	...	...	...	...	Guernsey
9.1[1,3]	54.9[3]	8.6[3]	27.4[3]	330.610[3]	31.5[3]	19.6[2,3]	5.0[3]	24.1[3]	2,975	97.2	2.8	167	75.1	24.9	23.4	Guinea
0.5[1]	31.2	15.4	52.9	1,104.1	26.5	37.2[2]	3.3	23.6	848.6	99.7	0.3	14.5	61.4	38.6	30.4	Guinea-Bissau
25.5[1]	53.3	15.7	5.5	68.529	11.0	65.2[2]	4.3	5.3	1,782	96.5	3.5	82	62.2	37.8	12.8	Guyana
0.1	50.5	34.5	14.9	11.483	19.1	78.4	0.5	0.6	751.8	100.0	—	55.3	55.0	45.0	26.5	Haiti
5.3[1]	66.4	11.9	16.3	16.547	18.6	52.7[2]	2.0	12.0	3,979	91.6	8.4	444	57.2	42.8	24.8	Honduras
...	...	...	...	7,906.0	...	...	...	...	...	...	...	...	...	...	...	Hong Kong
24.6[1,3]	38.5[3]	32.9[3]	4.0[3]	3,241.6[3]	17.9[3]	40.6[2,3]	0.4[3]	12.4[3]	23,572	17.7	82.3	4,791	64.3	35.7	26.7	Hungary
5.5	86.8	4.9	2.9	272.621	13.6	51.0	—	15.6	...	...	...	...	...	...	...	Iceland
30.0	58.9	11.1	—	5,056.1	15.3	78.2	—	—	79,725	71.6	28.4	10,150	65.3	34.7	21.8	India
...	...	...	...	...	...	...	...	...	65,347	78.4	21.6	9,491	60.2	39.8	17.9	Indonesia
2.3	51.8	36.4	9.5	79,286.0	42.4	62.3	—	5.9	17,078	...	...	...	...	...	...	Iran
...	...	...	...	...	...	...	...	...	...	...	...	...	...	...	...	Iraq
10.5[3]	61.5[3]	3.2[3]	24.9[3]	25.667[3]	11.3[3]	58.5[3]	0.6[3]	20.3[3]	...	...	...	...	...	...	...	Ireland
...	...	...	...	...	...	...	...	...	...	...	...	...	...	...	...	Isle of Man
21.7	61.5	5.1	11.8	357.555	3.4	60.7	7.7	13.7	...	...	...	...	...	...	...	Israel
...	...	...	...	...	...	...	...	...	...	...	...	...	...	...	...	Italy
20.8[1]	45.0	20.3	13.9	116.334	19.6	53.5	5.8	11.1	3,409	90.7	9.3	522	65.0	35.0	13.8	Jamaica
9.0[1]	76.1	1.2	13.8	756,960.0	18.4	49.3	—	10.6	...	...	...	...	...	...	...	Japan
...	...	...	...	...	...	...	...	...	...	...	...	...	...	...	...	Jersey
3.2	44.9	24.8	27.0	7.465	7.7	43.0	8.5	29.4	6,904	72.1	27.9	549	60.3	39.7	11.3	Jordan
4.3[3]	60.0[3]	12.3[3]	23.5[3]	120.060[3]	—53.2[3]—		4.5[3]	22.1[3]	2,833	80.8	19.2	202	47.8	52.2	3.3	Kazakstan
17.5[1]	58.2	15.4	8.9	275.670	15.6	57.9[2]	1.4	7.8	5,927	87.9	12.1	688	68.1	31.9	23.1	Kenya
...	...	...	...	...	...	...	...	...	...	...	...	...	...	...	...	Kiribati
...	...	...	...	...	...	...	...	...	...	...	...	...	...	...	...	Korea, North
2.4	69.6	14.0	14.0	204,487.0	11.8	19.0[2]	8.0	17.8	...	...	...	...	...	...	...	Korea, South
47.3	30.6	1.2	20.9	10.366	8.6	58.7	3.6	7.3	...	...	...	...	...	...	...	Kuwait
...	...	...	...	...	...	...	...	...	474.3	100.0	—	56.1	64.8	35.2	...	Kyrgyzstan
17.5[1]	37.9	15.9	28.8	373.746	8.7	45.3[2]	5.8	12.5	2,091	99.8	0.2	23	76.1	23.9	5.1	Laos
17.1[1]	20.0	7.1	55.9	1.016	15.4	22.7[2]	2.8	46.7	270.2	74.4	25.6	20.8	31.7	68.3	1.0	Latvia
33.6	35.4	12.2	18.7	35,844.1	1.6	75.1[2]	0.8	12.9	1,551	27.6	72.4	178	58.4	41.6	9.2	Lebanon
15.4[1]	47.6	17.5	19.5	1.403	39.1	49.4	2.8	4.3	611.0	95.4	4.6	37.0	59.3	40.7	6.1	Lesotho
13.3[1,10]	43.2[10]	41.7[10]	1.8[10]	0.516[10]	29.9[10]	62.9[10]	6.8[10]	9.0[10]	1,161	82.1	17.9	—	—	—	...	Liberia
—	53.2	43.2	3.6	6.062	57.9	33.5	5.6	1.3	...	...	...	...	...	...	...	Libya
...	...	...	...	...	...	...	...	...	...	...	...	...	...	...	...	Liechtenstein
15.6[1]	57.1	9.4	18.0	6.425	27.0	30.5[2]	19.8	12.5	491.3	64.8	35.2	29.9	42.1	57.9	0.9	Lithuania
0.1[1]	3.4	—	96.5	16,465.8	0.5	3.7	0.4	80.8	...	...	...	...	...	...	...	Luxembourg
...	...	...	...	...	...	...	...	...	...	...	...	...	...	...	...	Macau
...	...	...	...	...	...	...	...	...	773	79.9	20.1	28	67.9	32.1	1.8	Macedonia
6.3	48.1	27.3	18.3	3,270.6	40.9	26.8	5.0	4.9	3,691	97.9	2.1	52	54.8	45.2	6.8	Madagascar
36.2[1]	23.9	30.6	9.3	5.928	25.6	51.4[2]	7.9	2.7	1,978	99.3	0.7	94	62.2	37.8	22.0	Malaŵi
4.2[3]	83.3[3]	8.3[3]	4.2[3]	245.064[3]	14.8[3]	54.9[3]	1.7[3]	6.5[3]	15,857	31.4	68.6	3,043	74.3	25.7	3.6	Malaysia
7.4[1]	36.1	43.3	13.2	1.988	27.8	39.5	4.5	7.6	151.9	93.8	6.2	10.7	66.4	33.6	7.1	Maldives
7.8[3]	52.7[3]	6.9[3]	32.5[3]	247.0[3]	36.6[3]	22.8[3]	20.6[3]	20.3[3]	2,840	99.9	0.1	71	67.6	32.4	10.8	Mali
8.1	45.6	4.0	42.4	2.434	3.6	58.1	—	34.5	152.2	86.8	13.2	38.3	84.6	15.4	1.2	Malta
...	...	...	...	...	...	...	...	...	...	...	...	...	...	...	...	Marshall Islands
...	...	...	...	...	...	...	...	...	...	...	...	...	...	...	...	Martinique
5.9	74.3	11.5	8.3	46.584	23.6	18.2	7.4	10.8	2,184	99.6	0.4	101	68.3	31.7	18.8	Mauritania
23.7	57.8	10.5	7.9	59.892	8.0	80.8	0.5	1.8	1,182	57.7	42.3	134	61.9	38.1	5.6	Mauritius
...	...	...	...	...	...	...	...	...	...	...	...	...	...	...	...	Mayotte
2.4[1]	61.5	29.9	6.3	770.964	16.7	65.9[2]	−13.3	18.3	94,027	40.9	59.1	12,139	48.5	51.5	12.5	Mexico
...	...	...	...	...	...	...	...	...	...	...	...	...	...	...	...	Micronesia
51.2[1]	35.0	2.1	11.7	1.717	15.3	25.4[2]	1.6	14.2	454.6	96.7	3.3	59.2	66.6	33.4	6.8	Moldova
...	...	...	...	...	...	...	...	...	...	...	...	...	...	...	...	Monaco
14.2[1]	46.0	5.4	34.4	125.891	17.9	61.8[2]	17.9	6.8	451.7	82.7	17.3	35.7	77.6	22.4	7.0	Mongolia
32.0	58.3	6.0	3.7	156.494	55.8	35.1	—	2.9	21,347	74.6	25.4	3,405	60.5	39.5	30.9	Morocco
...	...	...	...	...	...	...	...	...	5,251	99.0	1.0	152	48.0	52.0	31.3	Mozambique
...	...	...	...	...	...	...	...	...	5,378	93.2	6.8	248	72.6	27.4	14.4[10]	Myanmar (Burma)
6.9	84.5	3.4	5.2	6.700	37.6	48.5[2]	1.2	4.4	...	...	...	...	...	...	...	Namibia
...	...	...	...	...	...	...	...	...	...	...	...	...	...	...	...	Nauru
10.4[1]	66.6	9.3	13.8	89.956	9.7	65.3	—	5.6	2,328	97.8	2.2	84	64.3	35.7	6.9	Nepal

Finance (continued)

country	international reserves, 1997[a]			money supply, 1996[b]		central bank authority, 1996[b]								
	total ('000,000 SDRs)	% foreign exchange	ratio of external debt to total reserves, 1995[b]	stock ('000,000,000 national currency)	M1 per capita	assets (%)				liabilities (%)				central bank discount rate, 1997[a]
						claims on government	claims on private sector	claims on banks	claims on foreign assets	reserve money	government deposits	foreign liabilities	capital accounts	
Netherlands, The	20,460	86.7	...	193.9	12,500	5.4	—	19.3	75.3	60.2	17.3	—	—	2.50[9]
Netherlands Antilles	138	86.2	...	0.893	4,210	10.6	—	—	89.4	63.0	5.7	3.1	30.3	6.00
New Caledonia	...	...	...	62.453[3]	325,000[3]	...	...	...	...	...	...	...	...	...
New Zealand	3,308	96.4	...	33.865	9,310	23.5	—	9.8	66.7	14.8	67.5	3.2	—	7.70
Nicaragua	...	...	...	1.330[3]	320[3]	89.9[1]	—	1.5	8.6	11.6	1.2	97.3	1.2	12.5[6]
Niger	66	83.3	14.5	100.2[3]	11,200[3]	50.7	—	4.1	45.2	65.9	7.2	22.3	—	6.25
Nigeria	5,564	99.6	19.4	200.325[3]	2,020[3]	86.1[1,3]	0.7[3]	5.9[3]	7.3[3]	30.4[3]	39.6[3]	12.1[3]	16.4[3]	13.50[7]
Northern Mariana Islands	...	...	...	...	...	...	...	...	...	...	...	...	...	...
Norway	20,538	95.7	...	392.7	89,400	5.2	—	0.1	94.7	29.8	55.1	—	—	5.25
Oman	1,211	95.7	2.2	0.503	230	5.7	—	—	94.3	39.4	3.8	—	32.4	6.41[6]
Pakistan	913	92.1	12.9	528.011	3,920	70.1	—	15.7	14.3	74.1	6.6	17.0	—	12.50[5]
Palau	...	...	...	...	...	...	...	...	...	...	...	...	...	...
Panama	1,337	98.8	5.0	0.841	310	52.3[1]	12.3	—	35.4	10.9	76.4	11.8	17.4	7.12[6]
Papua New Guinea	407	99.3	6.2	1.065	240	42.7	—	—	57.3	35.5	61.2	4.9	8.9	10.04[4]
Paraguay	595	84.9	1.4	1,715.6	342,000	29.0[1]	0.3	20.6	50.2	47.7	12.1	3.9	8.0	18.00
Peru	7,578	99.5	2.3	8.986	370	2.4[1]	—	−4.6	102.2	48.3	33.5	14.7	2.3	15.3
Philippines	7,600	96.8	4.6	233.1	3,210	42.8[1]	—	2.5	54.6	45.5	22.6	19.1	5.3	9.89
Poland	13,996	99.2	2.8	49.338	1,270	16.7[1]	—	14.7	68.6	44.8	8.0	0.9	0.5	22.0
Portugal	11,692	92.5	...	4,885.6	492,000	6.6[1]	—	7.3	86.1	35.9	13.9	0.2	8.2	6.00
Puerto Rico	...	...	...	...	...	...	...	...	...	...	...	...	...	...
Qatar	...	...	...	3.885	6,290	16.0	—	6.2	77.8	66.4	3.4	—	36.5	...
Réunion	...	...	...	11.497	17,000	...	...	...	...	...	...	...	...	...
Romania	1,747	90.8	2.3	10,747.5	476,000	25.0	—	45.7	29.3	46.7	17.8	40.5	—	50.0[9]
Russia	11,895	95.4	6.7	197,449.0	1,340,000	61.2[1]	0.3	3.7	34.8	54.1	5.0	23.3	23.1	17.5[9]
Rwanda	145	84.1	...	45.423	6,230	52.2[1]	0.4	0.2	47.2	48.7	22.9	24.8	19.1	13.00
St. Kitts and Nevis	28	100.0	1.6	0.089	2,250	4.3	—	—	95.7	97.3	2.7	—	—	6.5[4]
St. Lucia	43	97.7	1.8	0.246	1,660	13.5	—	—	86.4	97.3	2.7	—	—	7.0[4]
St. Vincent and the Grenadines	19	94.7	2.9	0.115	1,030	9.9	—	—	90.1	93.3	6.7	—	—	6.5[4]
Samoa	45	93.3	2.9	0.061	360	—	—	—	100.0	55.9	42.1	—	—	5.5[6]
San Marino	...	...	...	...	...	...	...	...	...	...	...	...	...	...
São Tomé and Príncipe	...	...	...	...	...	...	...	...	...	...	...	...	...	...
Saudi Arabia	6,826	82.6	...	132.9	7,090	...	...	...	...	...	...	...	...	...
Senegal	256	95.7	11.7	316.8[3]	35,400[3]	59.5	—	0.8	39.7	44.1	7.1	60.0	—	6.25
Seychelles	19	100.0	5.6	0.450	5,870	88.9	—	—	11.1	87.5	1.7	—	1.6	10.59[4]
Sierra Leone	24	79.2	28.3	53.208	11,100	93.3[1]	0.2	0.3	6.1	9.8	0.5	50.1	42.7	18.76[4]
Singapore	57,861	99.6	...	27.040	8,800	—	—	—	100.0	16.9	47.8	—	—	3.88[5]
Slovakia	2,181	97.4	1.0	173.350	32,100	16.6[1]	—	20.0	63.4	45.6	9.9	29.2	5.1	8.80
Slovenia	...	...	...	202.4	103,000	4.3	—	4.4	91.3	32.3	6.2	0.1	12.0	10.00
Solomon Islands	21	100.0	6.1	0.198	490	39.7[1]	—	—	60.3	50.6	1.9	1.2	35.3	12.75[4]
Somalia	...	...	...	...	...	...	...	...	...	...	...	...	...	...
South Africa	2,828	95.3	...	147.664	3,500	40.7	—	30.0	29.4	71.4	24.4	11.4	—	17.00
Spain	46,232	95.8	...	20,600.0	524,000	19.8	—	28.7	51.5	60.0	17.6	—	10.3	5.25
Sri Lanka	1,277	98.2	3.4	78.202	4,320	33.2	—	1.4	65.3	53.6	2.2	29.0	16.0	17.00
Sudan, The	75[7]	100.0[7]	59.8	404.6[3]	13,000[3]	78.7[1,3]	—	0.8[3]	20.4[3]	84.9[3]	—	534.4[3]	1.0[3]	...
Suriname	74	82.4	...	56.967	135,000	10.6	0.1	—	89.3	79.8	14.2	1.9	7.4	...
Swaziland	209	95.7	0.8	0.423	420	—	—	2.7	97.3	20.8	56.2	6.9	3.7	16.75
Sweden	10,431	92.0	...	...	...	28.3	—	4.6	67.1	54.7	—	2.0	—	2.50
Switzerland	28,130	85.7	...	128.2	18,100	7.4	—	4.0	88.6	56.6	1.5	—	—	1.00
Syria	...	...	...	...	...	...	...	...	...	...	...	...	...	...
Taiwan	...	...	...	3,426.1	159,000	0.1	—	14.6	85.4	51.0	4.6	—	—	5.00[7]
Tajikistan	...	...	...	...	...	...	...	...	...	...	...	...	...	...
Tanzania	331	97.0	22.5	462.1	15,800	52.6	—	1.0	46.5	59.0	14.5	89.4	—	11.60
Thailand	22,679	98.0	0.5	423.5	7,020	4.2	—	8.0	87.8	40.1	31.0	—	31.6	10.50
Togo	80	100.0	9.9	131.2[3]	29,200[3]	45.8	—	5.0	49.2	63.4	5.7	31.7	—	6.25
Tonga	22	90.9	2.4	0.023	230	14.1	—	—	85.9	56.2	4.1	—	6.4	5.58[6]
Trinidad and Tobago	386	99.2	4.9	4.161	3,270	12.6	—	5.5	82.0	50.0	19.8	5.1	32.7	13.00
Tunisia	1,121	97.2	5.5	4.109	450	4.7	—	8.1	87.2	103.2	11.6	11.4	6.1	7.88
Turkey	11,697	98.6	4.0	882,290.0	14,000,000	29.3[1]	—	2.5	68.3	32.7	7.6	46.9	3.8	66.30[9]
Turkmenistan	...	...	...	...	...	...	...	...	...	...	...	...	...	...
Tuvalu	...	...	...	...	...	...	...	...	...	...	...	...	...	...
Uganda	414	99.8	6.6	460.797	22,600	69.6[1]	0.1	0.4	29.9	18.4	73.4	24.1	7.8	14.80
Ukraine	1,364	97.6	6.3	6.316	120	57.3[1]	—	7.9	34.8	45.9	2.0	40.1	8.6	21.0
United Arab Emirates	6,455	95.6	...	22.266	8,870	—	—	0.2	99.8	65.9	28.1	0.2	5.6	...
United Kingdom	26,372	90.3	...	...	...	54.0	—	—	46.0	48.8	—	52.0	—	6.31[5]
United States	50,117	47.3	...	1,237.5	4,640	84.7	—	—	15.3	97.1	6.1	—	—	5.25
Uruguay	918	91.5	3.1	9.530	3,010	42.4[1]	0.3	16.0	41.3	45.2	31.8	21.5	—	147.4
Uzbekistan	...	...	...	...	...	...	...	...	...	...	...	...	...	...
Vanuatu	27	88.9	0.9	6.528	37,500	13.0[1]	1.9	1.7	83.4	60.0	29.8	0.3	11.2	...
Venezuela	9,921	92.6	4.1	3,349.4	149,000	16.1[1]	—	13.4	70.4	24.7	9.6	16.2	21.9	45.00
Vietnam	...	...	...	...	...	...	...	...	...	...	...	...	...	...
Virgin Islands (U.S.)	...	...	...	...	...	...	...	...	...	...	...	...	...	...
West Bank	...	...	...	...	...	...	...	...	...	...	...	...	...	...
Western Sahara	...	...	...	...	...	...	...	...	...	...	...	...	...	...
Yemen	786	96.8	8.9	156.579	9,300	60.7[1]	—	—	39.3	57.7	12.5	13.4	1.8	...
Yugoslavia	...	...	...	...	...	...	...	...	...	...	...	...	...	...
Zambia	...	...	...	227.9[3]	25,100[3]	90.1[3]	0.6[3]	—	9.3[3]	5.7[3]	25.8[3]	65.8[3]	—	29.00[4]
Zimbabwe	343	91.3	5.3	13.875	1,220	74.9[1]	—	—	25.1	20.1	74.4	16.4	—	25.50

deposit money banks, 1996[b]									external public debt outstanding (long-term, disbursed only), 1995							country
assets (%)				liabilities					total ('000,000 U.S.$)	creditors (%)		debt service				
loans to govern-ment	loans to private sector	re-serves	foreign assets	deposits ('000,000,000 national currency)	composition (%)					offi-cial	private	total ('000,000 U.S.$)	repayment (%)		debt service ratio (%)	
					demand depos.	savings depos.	govt. depos.	foreign liabilities					princi-pal	inter-est		
10.9[1]	55.7	0.3	33.2	1,254.9	12.4	29.7[2]	—	34.1	...	...	...	...	...	...	...	Netherlands, The
5.0[1]	68.3	5.0	21.7	3.296	20.4	50.7[2]	1.8	21.7	...	...	...	...	...	...	...	Netherlands Antilles
...	...	...	...	...	...	...	...	...	...	...	...	...	...	...	...	New Caledonia
2.6	90.3	3.1	4.1	97.868	33.0	48.5[2]	—	24.1	...	...	...	...	...	...	...	New Zealand
0.5[1,3]	77.0[3]	16.8[3]	5.7[3]	6.749[3]	7.0[3]	54.8[2,3]	9.3[3]	3.7[3]	7,937	87.8	12.2	260	70.0	30.0	35.6	Nicaragua
15.0[3]	50.5[3]	10.0[3]	24.5[3]	83.1[3]	46.3[3]	40.5[3]	23.2[3]	26.5[3]	1,376	100.0	—	16	50.0	50.0	5.6	Niger
8.4[1,3]	57.7[3]	8.8[3]	25.0[3]	305.420[3]	28.0[3]	36.4[2,3]	1.2[3]	1.0[3]	28,701	71.4	28.6	1,486	53.8	46.2	11.7	Nigeria
...	...	...	...	...	...	...	...	...	...	...	...	...	...	...	...	Northern Mariana Islands
12.3[1]	77.3	3.4	7.1	829.4	42.3	20.1[2]	4.5	15.4	...	...	...	...	...	...	...	Norway
8.2[1]	71.3	4.0	16.5	2.195	12.4	51.5	9.6	11.4	2,563	23.1	76.9	465	60.5	39.5	7.2	Oman
32.9	53.1	7.9	6.1	1,013.676	26.6	44.2	4.7	14.5	23,711	95.5	4.5	2,254	63.6	36.4	19.3	Pakistan
...	...	...	...	...	...	...	...	...	...	...	...	...	...	...	...	Palau
1.0	28.3	—	70.7	21.917	3.5	20.4	—	63.7	3,905	32.2	67.8	233	56.7	43.3	2.4	Panama
42.0	47.4	4.5	6.1	2.610	26.5	54.0	6.4	1.2	1,614	90.5	9.5	286	72.6	27.4	9.5	Papua New Guinea
1.3[1]	67.5	20.4	10.9	6,855.5	9.9	55.3	15.8	5.9	1,488	93.0	7.0	241	63.9	36.1	5.7	Paraguay
3.0[1]	62.7	22.5	11.8	45.510	12.4	55.1[2]	10.5	10.4	18,929	74.9	25.1	892	53.7	46.3	11.6	Peru
15.0[1]	64.5	8.2	12.3	1,743.0	5.5	54.5[2]	3.0	21.7	29,908	74.5	25.5	4,259	58.4	41.6	13.1	Philippines
43.0[1]	32.9	13.9	10.3	170.650	15.1	50.2[2]	4.6	4.5	41,073	78.5	21.5	2,274	26.9	73.1	6.8	Poland
18.8[1]	50.1	7.6	23.6	24,711.4	16.2	34.1	3.2	34.4	...	...	...	...	...	...	...	Portugal
...	...	...	...	...	...	...	...	...	...	...	...	...	...	...	...	Puerto Rico
38.9[1]	31.6	2.6	26.9	32.427	7.7	48.6[2]	11.7	11.5	...	...	...	...	...	...	...	Qatar
...	...	...	...	...	...	...	...	...	...	...	...	...	...	...	...	Réunion
74.7[1]	—	10.6	14.7	44,581.2	13.4	42.6[2]	5.0	11.2	3,896	76.9	23.1	393	55.2	44.8	4.3	Romania
45.2[1]	30.9	9.5	14.4	511,065.0	18.1	33.2[2]	2.4	11.9	100,279	56.6	43.4	6,009	54.5	45.5	6.3	Russia
7.6[1]	42.3	20.4	29.7	67.859	36.8	37.8	16.1	2.0	949	99.8	0.2	19	57.9	42.1	21.3	Rwanda
23.2[1]	46.9	5.8	24.1	0.995	5.7	39.7[2]	19.6	24.5	53.6	89.8	10.2	6.8	72.1	27.9	5.4[10]	St. Kitts and Nevis
8.6[1]	78.2	7.4	5.9	1.386	12.6	52.8[2]	15.4	15.6	111.0	100.0	—	11.0	57.3	42.7	2.9	St. Lucia
14.5[1]	60.3	7.4	17.8	0.684	12.8	47.0[2]	20.6	14.0	85.7	94.4	5.6	6.5	61.5	38.5	4.5	St. Vincent and the Grenadines
2.5[1]	61.4	29.0	7.0	0.187	21.3	61.7	4.4	4.4	159.6	100.0	—	4.5	64.4	35.6	4.2	Samoa
...	...	...	...	...	...	...	...	...	...	...	...	...	...	...	...	San Marino
...	...	...	...	...	...	...	...	...	260.8	100.0	—	1.5	40.0	60.0	11.7	São Tomé and Príncipe
25.4[1]	38.3	3.5	32.9	322.9	27.8	38.9[2]	—	11.9	...	...	...	...	...	...	...	Saudi Arabia
11.7[3]	67.5[3]	5.9[3]	14.9[3]	526.7[3]	30.4[3]	35.0[3]	25.9[3]	12.3[3]	3,191	97.4	2.6	192	70.8	29.2	11.2	Senegal
62.5[1]	14.3	32.4	5.1	1.890	15.0	49.7	4.7	4.5	151.1	85.4	14.6	19.9	68.6	31.4	6.8	Seychelles
29.0[1]	33.4	9.3	28.3	63.808	24.5	50.2	3.3	—	968	99.6	0.4	76	76.3	23.7	72.4	Sierra Leone
8.2	59.7	3.7	28.3	213.016	7.9	39.9	3.2	36.4	...	...	...	...	...	...	...	Singapore
35.4[1]	40.2	8.1	16.4	489.833	26.4	48.3[2]	5.2	14.1	3,570	37.3	62.7	742	82.1	17.9	6.6	Slovakia
19.9[1]	44.6	13.0	22.5	1,606.2	8.3	48.2[2]	9.1	12.1	1,491	48.8	51.2	296	74.3	25.7	2.8	Slovenia
47.5[1]	37.4	11.6	3.5	0.343	40.3	57.1	2.3	4.2	99.0	94.7	5.3	2.7	66.7	33.3	3.2[10]	Solomon Islands
...	...	...	...	...	...	...	...	...	1,961	98.1	1.9	—	—	—	—	Somalia
6.4	89.3	2.7	1.6	426.242	30.7	38.9	5.3	10.4	...	...	...	...	...	...	...	South Africa
24.2[1]	55.3	3.3	17.2	99,075.0	12.8	37.9	1.6	16.3	...	...	...	...	...	...	...	Spain
12.6[1]	64.2	13.7	9.5	300.672	11.8	58.2	4.3	17.8	7,010	92.5	7.5	348	62.1	37.9	5.9	Sri Lanka
0.4[3]	34.3[3]	21.0[3]	44.3[3]	381.2[3]	40.9[3]	67.5[3]	0.8[3]	7.4[3]	9,779	81.0	19.0	17	85.3	14.7	0.5[10]	Sudan, The
0.8	40.6	17.1	41.6	112.220	22.4	46.9	0.3	26.9	...	...	...	...	...	...	...	Suriname
3.9	55.8	11.4	28.9	1.743	19.1	54.6	5.8	13.6	236.8	99.9	0.1	22.2	74.3	25.7	2.1	Swaziland
7.4	57.0	0.7	34.9	1,639.4	—44.7[2]—		0.1	39.0	...	...	...	...	...	...	...	Sweden
5.1	59.3	1.1	34.5	1,025.0	9.1	36.5	—	29.4	...	...	...	...	...	...	...	Switzerland
55.6[1,3]	21.1[3]	9.8[3]	13.5[3]	297.516[3]	27.3[3]	27.1[3]	2.8[3]	0.9[3]	16,757	93.1	6.9	155	59.4	40.6	2.4	Syria
12.8[1,3]	75.4[3]	8.0[3]	3.8[3]	13,589.9[3]	19.5[3]	63.7[3]	5.0[3]	4.1[3]	...	...	...	...	...	...	...	Taiwan
...	...	...	...	...	...	...	...	...	612.4	100.0	—	—	—	—	—	Tajikistan
43.6[1]	17.7	11.1	27.6	657.6	31.1	57.3[2]	3.1	0.7	6,086	93.9	6.1	187	57.2	42.8	14.9	Tanzania
2.3[1]	91.3	3.1	3.4	5,369.2	2.0	61.5	3.3	23.3	17,231	64.0	36.0	2,820	68.5	31.5	3.8	Thailand
5.8[3]	62.2[3]	6.0[3]	26.0[3]	209.6[3]	26.9[3]	32.8[3]	17.8[3]	17.8[3]	1,297	95.9	4.1	15	50.0	50.0	4.7	Togo
8.5[1]	54.6	35.3	1.5	0.111	14.5	49.3	10.1	0.7	68.7	85.2	14.8	3.1	77.4	22.6	4.5[10]	Tonga
16.8[1]	59.0	13.9	10.4	17.104	17.5	55.4	2.6	3.6	1,759	54.1	45.9	324	55.2	44.8	11.1	Trinidad and Tobago
2.6	85.3	6.9	5.2	10.993	21.6	43.1	—	17.6	8,814	81.7	18.3	1,377	65.2	34.8	15.7	Tunisia
22.7[1]	50.8	10.7	15.8	6,439,550.0	8.7	70.0[2]	6.1	13.5	50,128	34.5	65.5	9,138	65.7	34.3	22.1	Turkey
...	...	...	...	...	...	...	...	...	374.7	57.1	42.9	97.4	77.5	22.5	...	Turkmenistan
...	...	...	...	...	...	...	...	...	...	...	...	...	...	...	...	Tuvalu
19.4[1]	42.7	16.2	21.7	677.602	33.9	30.2	7.1	20.7	3,045	97.2	2.8	104	67.3	32.7	16.2	Uganda
60.3[1]	12.0	9.0	18.8	9.469	23.8	30.5[2]	8.4	6.7	6,585	65.6	34.4	821	46.4	53.6	4.7	Ukraine
8.6[1]	45.1	7.4	38.9	180.199	8.6	35.9	5.6	20.5	...	...	...	...	...	...	...	United Arab Emirates
1.2[1]	51.3	0.4	47.1	1,775.7	—44.2[2]—		—	47.5	...	...	...	...	...	...	...	United Kingdom
10.5[1]	85.5	1.8	2.1	5,971.2	14.0	54.6	0.5	5.4	...	...	...	...	...	...	...	United States
6.4[1]	43.3	12.8	37.6	101.408	4.1	44.7[2]	2.6	34.1	3,823	41.8	58.2	764	61.6	38.4	20.8	Uruguay
...	...	...	...	...	...	...	...	...	1,260	78.4	21.6	208	72.1	27.9	4.5	Uzbekistan
1.5[1]	28.1	5.2	65.2	34.885	14.0	71.3[2]	—	9.0	43.2	99.1	0.9	1.6	56.3	43.7	1.2	Vanuatu
17.2[1]	41.5	34.9	6.4	5,856.2	33.6	42.4[2]	4.5	1.9	28,494	16.7	83.3	3,456	43.4	56.6	15.4	Venezuela
...	...	...	...	...	...	...	...	...	22,962	96.1	3.9	328	66.2	33.8	4.9	Vietnam
...	...	...	...	...	...	...	...	...	...	...	...	...	...	...	...	Virgin Islands (U.S.)
...	...	...	...	...	...	...	...	...	...	...	...	...	...	...	...	West Bank
...	...	...	...	...	...	...	...	...	...	...	...	...	...	...	...	Western Sahara
6.9[1]	16.7	44.7	31.7	133.914	20.4	66.2[2]	0.1	19.9	5,528	68.9	31.1	91	72.0	28.0	2.8	Yemen
...	...	...	...	...	...	...	...	...	8,725	52.6	47.4	...	...	...	...	Yugoslavia
30.5[1]	40.3	7.2	21.9	868.9	18.8	52.3[2]	5.7	1.7	5,078	96.8	3.2	369	65.2	34.8	28.5	Zambia
24.5[1]	54.8	10.9	9.8	33.100	34.1	24.6	3.3	27.1	3,360	82.9	17.1	485	65.8	34.2	18.6[1]	Zimbabwe

[1]Includes claims on nonfinancial government (public) enterprises and/or local governments. [2]Includes foreign currency deposits. [3]1995. [4]Treasury bill rate. [5]Money market rate. [6]Short-term deposit rate. [7]1996. [8]Republic of Cyprus only. [9]Interbank rate. [10]1994.

Housing and construction

The present table summarizes data about the housing stock and the construction industries of the countries of the world. The principal focus is on the elements that are most comparable internationally: the age of the housing (by decade, so far as possible), the legal tenure of the householder, construction of exterior walls, principal physical amenities, sanitary arrangements, and the amount of space both absolutely (total area of the average dwelling in square metres [1 square metre equals 1.20 square yards, or 10.76 square feet]) and relatively (persons per room). The data on construction characterize the industry in terms of: (1) the portion of national gross domestic product (GDP) represented by each country's construction industry, (2) the number of new dwelling units constructed annually, their area, and the rate (in years) required to replace the total national stock of dwellings shown on the extreme left of the table, and (3) for nonresidential construction, the number of buildings or portions of buildings built for nonresidential purposes and their area in square metres.

Because housing patterns differ greatly from country to country, the portion of each country's housing stock for which data are compared was defined as specifically as possible. In general, the numbers refer to permanent, private dwelling units that are usually occupied year-round, whether or not actually occupied on the date of the housing census or survey. That definition implies the exclusion of certain housing that is often part of national housing censuses: vacation homes, second homes occupied less than half the year, collective or communal dwellings, and so on. The housing unit to which the data on tenure refer may be either the individual dwelling or the household, according to the reporting practice of the country concerned.

The data are collected mostly from national housing censuses and surveys. The majority of countries combine the housing census with the population census at five- to ten-year intervals. Some countries, however, can conduct a meaningful housing census only in the capital city or in the few largest cities; others may be able to collect and process data for only a few of the most important housing characteristics even when national coverage is complete. These choices may be dictated by the lack of funding to collect data for the entire country or by the perception, particularly in a tropical, rural country where adequate dwellings can be built by hand, that no urgent housing problem exists. These choices may be complex, however, as

Housing and construction

country	housing stock														
	year	dwelling units[a]	median age[b] (years)	decade built (percent)					tenure[c] (percent)			construction of exterior walls (percent)			
				1949 or earlier	1950–59	1960–69	1970–79	1980 or later	owned	rented	collective, vacant, other	traditional materials	sawn/ framed wood	masonry or cement	other
Afghanistan	1979	2,260,000[1]	...	...	...	...	...	...	55.2	23.5	21.3	...	...	...	...
Albania	1989	674,633[3]	22.6	20.0[4]	14.3[5]	19.0[6]	24.3[7]	22.4[8]	91.2	8.8	—	...	...	...	...
Algeria	1987	3,050,812	...	—51.4[10]—		6.4[11]	18.6	23.6	64.1	22.6	13.3	...	...	...	...
American Samoa	1990	6,959	13.9	4.4	7.5	21.9	22.7	43.5	74.2	20.8	5.1	3.3	52.9	42.5	1.3
Andorra	1990	17,881	18.1	18.0	5.7	20.8	—55.5—		—86.0—		14.0	...	...	...	...
Angola	...	...	...	...	...	...	...	...	...	...	...	...	...	...	...
Antigua and Barbuda	1991	18,476	18.1	—39.6—		11.3	16.3	32.8	64.6	29.3	6.1	0.1	49.6	49.2	1.1
Argentina	1991	8,515,441[17]	21.6[18]	24.0[18]	17.3[18]	22.0[18]	18.3[18]	18.4[18]	78.0	16.0	6.0	6.1[18]	6.7[18]	84.2[18]	3.0[18]
Armenia	1989	559,000[19]	...	...	...	...	...	...	...	...	...	...	...	...	...
Aruba	1991	19,224	27.7	—46.8—		11.2	15.7	26.3	70.6	26.7	2.7	—	7.7	90.6	1.7
Australia	1994	6,677,900	26.1[20]	37.9[20]	10.4[20]	18.6[20]	—33.1[20]—		70.1	27.6	2.3	—	16.0	73.0	11.0
Austria	1991	3,393,271	33.8	33.0[28]	14.7[29]	18.1[6]	18.5[7]	15.7[8]	50.0	38.7	11.3	—	5.1[30]	81.9[30]	13.0[30]
Azerbaijan	1994	1,473,100	...	—15.0—			18.0	67.0	65.3	34.7	—	...	...	...	...
Bahamas, The	1980	54,308	30.7	—54.7—		25.6	—19.7—		51.4	37.4	11.2	4.0[32]	32.3	54.7	9.0
Bahrain	1991	83,470	15.2[20]	58.3[20]	14.5[20]	—27.2[20]—			51.3	38.2	10.5	—	—	93.6[20]	6.4[20]
Bangladesh	1991	19,020,489	...	...	...	...	...	...	86.3	6.5	7.2	78.9	2.4	8.0	10.7
Barbados	1990	75,211	19.1	—48.6—			22.9	28.5	76.1	20.4	3.5	0.2	61.2[34]	35.4	3.2
Belarus	1994	3,679,600	...	...	...	...	...	...	...	...	...	...	...	...	...
Belgium	1991	3,748,165	...	37.0[28]	21.5[35]	13.1[36]	18.5[7]	9.9[8]	64.5	34.2	1.3	...	...	...	...
Belize	1991	37,658	...	—26.3—			17.8	55.9	65.9	22.8	11.3	5.1	65.6	24.8	4.5
Benin	1992	832,526	...	...	...	...	...	...	76.8[37]	10.1[37]	13.1[37]	75.4	—24.6—		
Bermuda	1991	22,061	...	—56.0—		15.8	12.0	16.2	43.4	52.4	4.2	—	1.7[18, 34]	95.1[18]	3.2[18]
Bhutan	...	...	...	...	...	...	...	...	...	...	...	...	...	...	...
Bolivia	1992	1,614,995	...	...	...	...	...	...	65.5	19.8	14.7	72.3[38]	2.3[38]	21.1[38]	4.2[38]
Bosnia and Herzegovina	1991	1,203,000	...	...	...	...	...	...	...	...	...	...	...	...	...
Botswana	1991	276,209	...	...	...	...	...	...	59.2	22.9	17.9	48.7	—	49.3	2.0
Brazil	1991	34,734,715	...	...	...	...	...	...	69.8	16.4	13.8	...	...	...	...
Brunei	1991	40,351	...	...	...	...	...	...	83.8[20]	11.8[20]	4.4[20]	0.2[20]	54.8[20]	36.5[20]	8.5[20]
Bulgaria	1995	3,419,937	...	24.8[28, 33]	29.0[29, 33]	20.0[6, 33]	15.4[7, 33]	10.8[8, 33]	72.7[27]	16.4[27]	10.9[27]	...	...	...	...
Burkina Faso	1985	1,274,546	...	...	...	...	...	...	...	...	...	...	...	...	...
Burundi	1979	938,000[40]	...	...	...	...	...	...	98.7	1.1	0.2	...	...	...	...
Cambodia	...	...	...	...	...	...	...	...	...	...	...	...	...	...	...
Cameroon	1987	1,787,835[19]	...	...	...	...	...	...	74.0	18.0	8.0	66.0	13.0	17.0	4.0
Canada	1991	10,018,625	10.5	20.3[28]	20.0[29]	19.4[6]	—40.3[42]—		62.6	37.1	0.3	...	...	...	...
Cape Verde	1990	67,619	...	—73.6—				26.4	...	15.4[18]	...	36.1	—	60.1	3.8
Central African Republic	1988	519,314	...	...	...	...	...	...	88.2	—11.8—		71.7	—28.3—		
Chad	1993	1,228,862	...	...	...	...	...	...	85.0	8.4	6.6	88.6	—11.4—		
Chile	1992	3,369,849	20.4[41]	—46.2[41]—		21.1[41]	—32.7[41]—		68.3	24.6	7.1	14.0	53.1	31.9	1.0
China	1990	276,947,962	...	...	...	...	...	...	18.5[2, 41]	81.5[2, 41]	—	...	...	...	...
Colombia	1985	5,824,857	20.6[43]	54.6[43]	26.2[43]	19.2[43]	—	—	67.6	23.6	8.8	16.7	7.0	75.6	0.7
Comoros	1980	81,791	...	5.3	7.7	21.3	—63.7—		87.4	3.1	9.5	73.5	1.8	16.9	7.8
Congo, Dem. Rep. of the	1984	5,669,600[19]	...	...	...	...	...	...	47.4[43, 44]	38.3[43, 44]	14.3[43, 44]	52.4[43]	—45.5[43]—		2.1[43]
Congo, Rep. of the	1984	363,140[19]	...	...	...	...	...	...	61.4	24.1	14.5	10.5	15.9	54.9	18.7
Costa Rica	1984	500,788	...	...	...	...	...	...	65.8	20.7	13.5	1.1	60.1	35.6	3.2
Côte d'Ivoire	1985	1,798,799[19]	...	...	...	...	...	...	...	...	...	...	...	...	...
Croatia	1991	1,575,644	...	...	...	...	...	...	64.0	35.4	0.6	...	...	...	...
Cuba	1981	2,363,364	24.6	—44.5—		21.6	—25.6—		...	...	...	3.8	33.2	61.5	1.4
Cyprus	1992	185,459	22.8[41]	—39.9[41]—		15.4[41]	—44.7[41]—		60.0[41]	16.5[41]	23.5[41]	11.9[41]	—	87.6[41]	0.5[41]
Czech Republic	1991	3,705,691	42.4	41.7[28]	10.2[29]	14.5[6]	19.6[7]	14.0[8]	44.7[18]	41.7[18]	13.6[18]	—	32.0[47]	67.1	0.9
Denmark	1995	2,426,503	36.6[9]	43.2	9.8	16.1	17.8	13.1	52.4	45.4	2.2	...	...	...	...
Djibouti	1982	25,000[43]	27.6	...	...	...	...	...	...	...	...	—	73.0[48]	22.5	4.5
Dominica	1991	19,374[19]	18.6	—36.2—		11.6	12.8	31.8	71.9	19.7	8.4	—	50.5	48.4	1.1
Dominican Republic	1981	1,125,785[17]	...	...	...	...	...	...	72.0	17.0	11.0	31.1	31.3	31.4	6.2
Ecuador	1990	2,111,121	...	...	...	...	...	...	68.1	22.6	9.3	32.2	9.3	57.7	0.8
Egypt	1986	9,732,728	...	—37.1[2]—		—62.9[2]—			64.0	27.2	8.8	...	...	...	...
El Salvador	1992	1,236,866	...	...	...	...	...	...	69.6	17.9	12.5	39.8	2.9	52.6	4.7
Equatorial Guinea	...	...	...	...	...	...	...	...	...	...	...	...	...	...	...
Eritrea	...	...	...	...	...	...	...	...	...	...	...	...	...	...	...
Estonia	1995	618,300	24.5	15.0[28]	12.8[29]	22.9[6]	25.5[7]	23.8[8]	18.3[39]	81.5[39]	0.2[39]	—	18.2[39]	77.4[39]	4.4[39]
Ethiopia	1984	9,300,000	...	...	...	...	...	...	48.8[2]	47.2[2]	4.0[2]	89.5	...	5.9	4.6
Faroe Islands	1977	11,172[27]	32.5	—60.1—		21.8	—15.0—		84.5	9.9	5.6	—	43.9	53.5	2.6
Fiji	1986	124,098	...	...	...	...	...	...	75.5	11.1	13.4	9.0	26.4	29.8	34.8
Finland	1994	2,331,406	17.1	—25.5—		14.6	23.3	36.6	73.7	24.7	1.6	14.0[27, 30]	81.8[27, 30]	—4.2[27, 30]—	
France	1992	22,130,800	19.1[54]	36.8[55]	—19.8[56]—		28.8[57]	15.1[58]	53.8	39.2	7.0	...	...	...	...
French Guiana	1990	38,324	...	—38.7[60]—			21.5[61]	39.8[62]	41.3	—58.7—		29.4	—70.6—		

planners are always aware that much housing is physically inadequate to protect dwellers from the elements, is disadvantageously placed in relation to tainted or disease-infested water supply or to the outfall of unprocessed sewage, or is built of materials (mud, skins, thatch, etc.) that may harbour pests or disease. In the developed countries, median age and the distribution of physical amenities provide strong indicators of the quality and availability of housing.

The data for the construction industry refer to the most recent year in which a broad range of countries could be surveyed.

The broadest indication of total activity in a national construction industry is its contribution to the national gross domestic product, since that figure, in addition to construction of buildings, also includes civil engineering projects, such as dams, roads and other transportation infrastructure, recreational facilities, irrigation and land reclamation works, and the like. The scope of the data relating to construction of buildings may be limited in several respects. It may be confined to activity capable of being surveyed in the modern or urban sectors only, may be limited to private new construction only or to government and government-financed activity only, or may refer to construction mortgaged or financed through certain organizations only. Depending on national data-collection systems, it usually excludes remodeling of old premises but may include extensions or enlargements of existing buildings. The data for new construction are usually of two principal types: authorized new construction or certification after construction that newly built structures meet building and fire codes and the like. Data for construction completed are naturally more meaningful but are not available for every country, necessitating the substitution of authorized construction data, which are usually available only for areas regulated by certain types of governmental authorities.

The following notes further define the column headings:

a. Data refer to permanent, private dwelling units that are usually occupied year-round, whether or not occupied on the census date.
b. Data are estimates unless specifically provided by a country source.
c. Data may be either for dwellings or for households, depending on country reporting practice.
d. Data may be either for construction completed or for construction authorized, depending on country reporting practice.

physical amenities (percent)			sewage disposal (percent)			space[b]			construction industry (1994)						country
									percent of	new residential[d]			new nonresidential[d]		
piped water	electricity	inside toilet or WC	closed public sewer or septic tank	open public sewer	other	average area (sq m)	rooms per dwelling unit	persons per room	GDP	total no. of dwellings	floor area ('000 sq m)	years to replace nat'l stock	number of units	floor area ('000 sq m)	
25.3[2]	66.5[2]	5.5[2]	5.5	77.9	16.6	...	5.5	2.1	9.8	...	...	...	...	...	Afghanistan
44.6	...	29.9	...	...	...	35.7	1.8	2.6	9.5	12,428[9]	...	54.3	...	...	Albania
87.4	72.7	68.9	52.4	19.1	28.5	...	2.9	2.6	11.3[12]	71,433[13]	...	42.6	...	...	Algeria
96.2	94.4	93.4	68.5	—31.5—		...	4.5	1.6	...	223[14]	...	31.2	...	...	American Samoa
—	...	—	...	...	...	...	...	...	...	...	212[15]	...	...	[15]	Andorra
...	...	...	...	...	...	...	...	...	1.6	...	...	...	...	...	Angola
91.5	...	...	53.0	—	—	...	3.6	0.9	9.3	764[16]	...	20.2	...	...	Antigua and Barbuda
77.4	93.5	95.1[18]	77.1[18]	—22.9[18]—		...	3.9[18]	1.3[18]	6.7	37,272	7,091	228.4	10,405	3,942	Argentina
...	...	...	...	...	...	...	...	...	6.7	3,040	282	183.9	...	...	Armenia
97.9	98.7[20]	89.2[20]	...	...	...	...	5.2	0.7	8.2[21]	402[14]	...	47.8	...	...	Aruba
97.1[22]	98.4[23]	92.2[20]	99.0[20]	—1.0[20]—		...	5.1[20]	0.6[20]	6.9[24]	167,953[25]	11,170[26]	39.8	23,340[27]	13,727[26]	Australia
95.0[20]	...	88.7	94.3[20]	—	5.7[20]	85.0	4.3[16]	0.6[16]	7.9	48,851	4,616	69.5	...	...	Austria
88.4[31]	...	...	87.4[31]	...	...	...	...	...	3.5	9,400	779	156.7	...	...	Azerbaijan
83.0[33]	77.9	...	63.2	2.2	34.6	...	4.0	1.2	3.0[21]	733[15, 30]	...	...	[15]	...	Bahamas, The
92.8	97.1	78.2	99.8	...	0.2	...	4.2	1.4	6.0	3,066[14]	...	27.2	...	...	Bahrain
56.8[20]	14.3	12.5	1.5[20]	—98.5[20]—		...	2.0[20]	2.9[20]	5.9[25]	300,900[14]	...	49.1	...	...	Bangladesh
94.0	92.6	66.2	66.8	0.4	32.8	...	4.3	0.8	3.8	2,116[1]	...	...	...	...	Barbados
78.4[33]	...	76.7[33]	...	...	...	52.3	...	...	8.7	50,900	3,403	48.6	1,127	1,125	Belarus
99.6	100.0	91.9	...	...	...	86.3	4.3	0.6	5.3	35,600	32,600	105.3	8,323	7,915	Belgium
54.9	67.2	34.7	34.7	—65.3—		...	...	...	7.4	742[14]	...	40.0	...	...	Belize
...	...	...	...	...	...	...	3.2	1.0	4.5	17,011[14]	...	54.8	...	...	Benin
97.4[18]	...	96.7[18]	96.7[18]	—3.3[18]—		...	3.2[18]	0.7[18]	...	193	...	114.3	...	...	Bermuda
...	...	...	...	...	...	...	...	...	11.9	...	...	...	...	...	Bhutan
57.5	55.5	42.8	42.8	—57.2—		...	...	...	4.2	34,258[14]	...	47.1	...	...	Bolivia
66.2[39]	94.2[39]	53.2[39]	...	...	...	56.0[39]	4.0[20]	1.0[20]	...	26,568[9]	...	48.9	...	...	Bosnia and Herzegovina
77.0	5.4[20]	25.4[20]	8.6[20]	20.4[20]	71.0[20]	...	2.5	1.9	5.0[25]	...	...	...	...	...	Botswana
73.6	90.0[33]	...	58.7[33]	—41.3[33]—		...	5.1[18]	0.9[18]	7.7	865,825[14]	...	42.7	...	...	Brazil
90.3[20]	64.2[20]	94.2[20]	57.4[20]	—42.6[20]—		...	4.2[20]	1.6[20]	5.4	1,168[14]	...	34.6	...	...	Brunei
100	99.9[27]	...	90.4	—9.6—		63.7	2.9	0.9	6.4	8,669	727	394.5	7,024	2,217	Bulgaria
...	...	...	...	...	...	...	...	...	5.3	28,133[14]	...	45.3	...	...	Burkina Faso
11.0	0.6	...	1.6	—98.4—		37.2[41]	2.4[41]	0.6[41]	4.7	...	...	...	...	...	Burundi
...	...	...	...	...	...	...	...	1.2	7.6	...	...	...	...	...	Cambodia
32.0	22.0	7.0	2.2	70.4	27.6	...	4.1	1.2	5.3[9]	37,862[14]	...	47.2	...	...	Cameroon
99.9	100.0	99.5	98.9[29]	—1.1[17]—		...	5.7[17]	0.5[17]	5.3	205,391[14]	...	48.8	14,846[27]	...	Canada
16.2	24.9	25.1	—3.4[18]—		96.6[18]	...	1.8[18]	2.8[18]	20.0[9]	861	...	78.5	...	...	Cape Verde
...	...	...	...	...	...	...	...	...	4.1	...	...	...	...	...	Central African Republic
...	...	...	...	...	...	...	...	...	0.5	...	...	...	...	...	Chad
88.2	90.2	70.3	69.9	0.3	29.4	...	4.4	1.0	5.5	118,630	7,044	28.4	...	2,880	Chile
89.4[2, 13]	...	25.2[2, 13]	47.0[2, 13]	—53.0[2, 13]—		37.0[13]	2.2[13]	1.8[13]	6.4	...	323,830	...	...	...	China
70.5	78.5	77.9	69.6	—30.4—		...	3.3	1.6	6.3	10,705	9,436[33]	...	3,678	...	Colombia
12.9	5.7	...	2.1	—97.9—		33.7	2.5	2.1	6.3[12]	807[14]	...	89.2	...	...	Comoros
...	...	...	...	...	...	...	...	...	2.0	...	...	...	...	...	Congo, Dem. Rep. of the
30.5	8.8	16.6	—86.2[2]—		13.8[2]	...	3.7[2]	1.7[2]	1.7[12]	...	...	...	...	...	Congo, Rep. of the
86.9	97.3	...	66.5	—33.5—		...	4.0	1.4	2.7	...	1,914[39]	...	2,868[27]	178[27]	Costa Rica
23.0	39.6	23.9	—68.5—		31.5	88.0	...	...	1.9[12]	50,674[14]	...	35.5	...	...	Côte d'Ivoire
86.2	98.6	80.3	80.8	—19.2—		70.4	2.8	1.1	2.1	9,700	819	162.4	1,419	1,476	Croatia
74.1	82.9	45.2	60.9	9.3	30.1	...	4.1	1.0	9.3[39, 45]	25,344[38]	1,800[38]	93.2	469[27]	1,803[27]	Cuba
100.0[41]	98.1[41]	74.5[41]	95.6[41]	—4.4[41]—		...	4.6[41]	0.8[41]	9.1	8,400	1,496	22.1	...	1,632[46]	Cyprus
96.9	100.0	88.5	98.1	—1.9—		70.5	2.7	1.0	5.9	18,162	1,039	204.0	...	...	Czech Republic
100.0	100.0	97.1	98.6[20]	—1.4[20]—		107.8[9]	3.7	0.6	5.5	12,932	1,311	186.6	...	3,080	Denmark
45.0	58.0	82.0	26.0	23.0	51.0	...	1.9	6.9	4.8[12]	...	54[39]	...	26[13]	13.7[13]	Djibouti
87.4	...	36.8	36.8	—63.2—		...	3.3	1.1	6.7	188[14]	...	103.1	...	...	Dominica
64.4	...	14.1	...	...	...	...	...	...	9.5	3,234	1,225	—	...	...	Dominican Republic
62.7	77.7	49.6	39.5	25.1	35.4	...	2.8	1.7	2.5	42,204[14]	...	50.0	...	...	Ecuador
73.1	87.0	...	...	...	...	...	3.3	1.5	5.1[49]	160,613[26]	...	60.6	...	...	Egypt
46.4	69.3	39.7	39.7	—60.3—		...	1.5[50]	3.3[50]	3.7	694	341[27]	...	271	0.7[27]	El Salvador
...	...	...	...	...	...	...	...	...	4.7	...	...	...	...	...	Equatorial Guinea
...	...	...	...	...	...	...	...	...	5.5	...	...	...	...	...	Eritrea
93.8	99.9	89.6	...	...	...	34.5[39]	2.5[39]	0.9[39]	5.5	1,953	159.2	316.6	346	242	Estonia
67.9[2]	...	55.2[2]	...	...	...	...	1.9	2.4	2.9[49]	...	260[51]	...	92[52]	63.3[51]	Ethiopia
99.7	99.5	95.0	89.7	8.1	2.2	...	5.5	1.1	3.3	223[21]	...	50.1	...	...	Faroe Islands
73.7	48.5	56.0	35.4[53]	—64.6[53]—		...	3.3	1.8	3.3	1,356	108	91.5	...	60	Fiji
94.0	95.9[27, 30]	96.3	97.3	—2.7—		75.1	3.6	0.6	5.3	26,731	2,168	87.2	29,083	3,298	Finland
99.9	...	95.8	73.8[59]	—26.2[59]—		75.8[33]	3.8	0.7	4.9	356,000	...	60.5	...	34,548	France
77.0	86.7	62.0	34.3[41]	—65.7[41]—		...	2.8	1.2	9.3[39]	2,023	...	18.9	...	64	French Guiana

Housing and construction (continued)

country	housing stock														
	year	dwelling units[a]	median age[b] (years)	decade built (percent)					tenure[c] (percent)			construction of exterior walls (percent)			
				1949 or earlier	1950–59	1960–69	1970–79	1980 or later	owned	rented	collective, vacant, other	traditional materials	sawn/framed wood	masonry or cement	other
French Polynesia	1988	39,513	10.8	—11.3—		16.0	27.6	45.1	68.5	21.2	10.3	36.9	15.8	45.2	2.2
Gabon	1967	15,886[43]	...	...	...	...	...	...	—87.0—		13.0	...	...	...	...
Gambia, The	1983	202,199	...	...	...	...	...	...	63.9	21.9	14.2	82.9	—	12.9	4.2
Gaza Strip	1992	66,819[44]	23.0	4.7	31.2	14.3	25.8	23.9	89.1[27, 63]	7.6[27, 63]	3.3[27, 63]	—	—	96.0	4.0
Georgia	1989	1,244,000[19]	...	...	...	...	...	...	...	...	...	...	...	...	...
Germany	1993	34,988,753	39.4	32.9[55]	—62.4[64]—			4.7[65]	38.8	61.2	—	...	...	...	...
Ghana	1992	3,320,000[19]	...	...	...	...	...	...	37.0	19.6	43.4	62.6	1.3	33.6	2.5
Gibraltar	1991	7,604[17]	25.0	37.3[66]	16.7[67]	15.6[68]	23.0[69]	7.4[58]	15.2	84.8	—	...	...	...	...
Greece	1991	3,167,152	29.2[20]	30.2[20, 28]	27.4[20, 29]	20.7[6, 20]	—21.5[20]—		75.7	20.4	3.9	...	...	...	...
Greenland	1997	19,847	10.2	11.9[22]	18.8[22]	46.5[22]	—22.8[22]—		39.3[27]	—60.7[27]—		...	...	...	...
Grenada	1991	21,974	...	...	...	...	...	...	78.7	13.8	7.5	—	68.5	30.2	1.3
Guadeloupe	1990	112,478	...	—49.1[70]—			20.7[71]	30.2[58]	62.6	—37.4—		29.5	—70.5—		
Guam	1990	35,223	15.8	2.3	7.1	19.2	41.5	29.9	45.6	54.4	—	0.0	5.1	85.8	9.1
Guatemala	1981	1,259,598	12.5	—62.0—		10.0	—28.0—		64.7	11.3	24.0	55.6	21.1	19.3	4.0
Guernsey	1991	21,215[17]	...	...	...	...	...	...	68.4	31.6	—	...	...	...	...
Guinea	1983	716,378	...	...	...	...	...	...	81.3	10.6	8.1	26.2	...	12.7	61.1
Guinea-Bissau	1979	123,936	...	...	...	...	...	...	...	...	...	95.7	0.1	2.3	1.9
Guyana	1980	149,734[19]	17.6	—43.5—		19.4	—37.1—		57.2	27.3	15.5	1.8	85.6	6.6	6.0
Haiti	1987	1,164,136	...	—75.9—			—24.1—		73.2	4.5	22.3	37.0	57.4	5.4	0.2
Honduras	1988	809,263	12.1[72]	—38.9[72]—		37.8[72, 73]	—23.3[72, 74]—		71.8[72]	16.5[72]	12.7[72]	61.0[72]	26.4[72]	11.7[72]	0.9[72]
Hong Kong	1994	1,735,500	...	—48.1[20]—		13.6[20]	—38.3[20]—		45.1	50.1	4.8	...	...	...	...
Hungary	1995	3,971,000	16.4	32.9[1, 28]	11.8[1, 77]	14.9[1]	23.2[1]	17.2[1]	75.9	23.7	0.4	21.8	14.6	63.6	—
Iceland	1984	70,777	25.6	—46.0—		—54.1—			70.3[78]	—29.7[78]—		...	...	71.9[78]	...
India	1991	195,024,357	...	...	...	...	...	...	86.3	11.8	1.9	87.7	1.5	2.0	8.7
Indonesia	1993	42,016,761[24]	...	...	...	...	...	...	87.0[76]	5.0[76]	8.0[76]	...	...	...	...
Iran	1986	8,211,375	...	—82.5[22]—			—17.5[22]—		77.0	12.2	9.8	28.8	0.7	69.2	1.3
Iraq	1987	1,759,176	...	...	...	...	...	...	65.3[19]	18.1[19]	16.6[19]	...	...	...	...
Ireland	1991	1,006,506	47.2[20]	—48.2[80]—		11.7[6]	22.4[7]	18.2[8]	80.2	16.8	3.0	...	...	...	...
Isle of Man	1991	27,316	...	...	...	...	...	...	66.5	32.5	1.0	...	...	...	...
Israel	1983	1,104,270	...	9.5[81]	—90.5[82]—				74.3	23.1	2.6	...	...	...	...
Italy	1991	25,028,522	32.2	30.8[28]	19.7[35]	27.5[83]	—22.0[42]—		53.6	20.0	26.4	...	...	...	...
Jamaica	1982	517,297[19]	17.0	—33.6—		28.8	—39.6—		46.7	32.6	20.7	7.1	28.4	54.4	10.1
Japan	1993	40,835,000	16.5	5.4[85]	10.9[86]	13.4[6]	31.5[7]	38.8[8]	59.8	38.5	1.7	—	68.1	—31.9—	
Jersey	1991	32,463	...	...	...	...	...	...	49.6	48.0	2.4	...	...	...	...
Jordan	1994	683,000	...	...	...	...	...	...	59.7	38.8	1.5	...	...	...	...
Kazakstan	1993	4,410,000	...	...	...	...	...	...	...	...	...	...	...	...	...
Kenya	1989	4,352,751[19]	...	...	...	...	...	...	...	...	...	...	...	...	...
Kiribati	1990	11,301[19]	...	...	...	...	...	...	68.2[50]	17.9[50]	13.9[50]	64.4[50]	—35.6[50]—		
Korea, North	1987	4,054,027[19]	...	...	...	...	...	...	...	...	...	...	...	...	...
Korea, South	1995	9,204,929	13.1[1]	5.6	4.0	6.3	14.9	69.2	74.9	22.5	2.6	7.8[1]	18.9[1]	73.0[1]	0.3[1]
Kuwait	1995	251,682	14.5[18]	—12.2[18]—		38.8[18]	—34.5[18]—		38.2[27]	53.6[27]	8.2[27]	46.5[30]	—	36.5[30]	17.0[30]
Kyrgyzstan	1989	856,000[19]	...	...	...	...	...	...	...	...	...	...	...	...	...
Laos	1985	601,797[88]	...	...	...	...	...	...	...	...	...	...	...	...	...
Latvia	1994	953,000	...	—37.1[89]—		17.7[6]	22.0[7]	23.1[8]	40.8	59.2	—	...	...	...	...
Lebanon	1970	483,908[17]	...	30.1[90]	40.2[91]	29.4[6]	—	—	...	...	...	...	...	...	...
Lesotho	1986	312,655[19]	...	...	...	...	...	...	87.1	8.2	4.7	...	...	...	...
Liberia	1974[43]	263,333	...	...	...	...	...	...	...	...	...	...	...	...	...
Libya	1984	569,679	...	...	...	...	...	...	62.5[75]	28.0[75]	9.5[75]	...	...	...	...
Liechtenstein	1990	10,386[17]	29.4[30]	23.9[30]	14.4[30]	20.4[30]	—41.3[30]—		53.6	41.7	4.7	...	...	...	...
Lithuania	1994	1,225,800	...	...	...	...	...	...	87.1	12.9	—	...	...	...	...
Luxembourg	1991	144,683	33.1	34.5[28]	17.6[29]	12.5[6]	17.8[7]	17.6[8]	66.1	28.3	5.6	...	...	...	...
Macau	1991	89,193	...	...	...	...	...	...	65.9	32.0	2.1	—	0.5[92]	99.3[92]	0.2[92]
Macedonia	1991	511,300	...	6.9[28]	11.6[29]	21.2[6]	23.4[7]	41.8[8]	63.2	18.4	18.4	...	...	...	...
Madagascar	1993	2,688,951[19]	...	...	...	...	...	...	...	...	...	...	...	...	...
Malawi	1987	1,859,572[19]	...	...	...	...	...	...	39.6	—60.4—		51.6	3.1	44.4	0.9
Malaysia	1991	3,447,597	...	...	...	...	...	...	63.4[18]	25.0[18]	11.6[18]	...	...	...	...
Maldives	1990	37,114	11.6	15.1	7.9	13.7	21.7	41.6	96.4	3.6	—	53.8	2.7	41.1	2.4
Mali	1987	1,364,079[19]	...	...	...	...	...	...	84.2	8.5	7.3	75.9	8.5	10.3	5.3
Malta	1985	101,509	...	—81.8[94]—		18.2[95]	—	—	53.9	43.0	3.1	93.0[44]	...	92.9[44]	0.21[44]
Marshall Islands	1980[96]	4,923[38]	...	6.4	13.3	24.7	—55.5—		60.0	33.0	7.0	10.7	63.5	15.9	9.9
Martinique	1990	106,536	19.0	—54.5[60]—		17.9[61]	—27.6[58]—		60.9	32.5	6.6	20.4[41]	—79.6[41]—		
Mauritania	1977	246,462[19]	...	...	...	...	...	...	...	...	...	...	...	...	...
Mauritius	1990	236,885	...	—19.7[52]—		24.3[52, 97]	—56.0[52, 98]—		75.9	15.2	8.9	—	4.2[52]	66.8[52]	28.9[52]
Mayotte	1991	19,227	...	...	...	...	...	...	77.8	14.8	7.3	50.4	—48.2—		1.4
Mexico	1990	16,197,802	...	—51.4[18]—		15.4[18]	—33.2[18]—		77.9	14.6	7.5	19.0	8.1	69.5	3.4
Micronesia	1980	11,562	...	3.8	5.2	21.3	—69.7—		51.8	39.2	9.0	6.0	41.8	14.6	37.6
Moldova	1994	1,112,800	...	...	...	...	...	...	...	...	...	...	...	...	...
Monaco	1990	16,122	30.0	39.5[55]	13.0[99]	19.7[100]	27.8[61]	—	23.3	60.5	16.2	...	...	...	...
Mongolia	1969	242,000	...	...	...	...	...	...	100.0	—	—	...	...	...	...
Morocco	1994	4,444,271[19]	...	...	...	...	...	...	69.3[27]	22.1[27]	8.6[27]	24.5[47]	—	73.5[41]	1.8[41]
Mozambique	1980	2,712,439[19]	...	...	...	...	...	...	...	...	...	86.5	2.3	8.3	2.9
Myanmar (Burma)	1983	6,750,884	...	...	...	...	...	...	...	...	...	80.3	14.8	3.2	1.7
Namibia	1991	254,389	...	...	...	...	...	...	69.2	16.9	13.9	52.0	...	36.2	11.8
Nauru	1977	508[102]	...	—88.6[102]—			—11.4[102]—		11.0[103]	80.6[103]	8.4[103]	...	...	...	...
Nepal	1996	2,585,154[19]	...	...	...	...	...	...	93.8	2.2	4.0	—76.8—		10.7	12.6
Netherlands, The	1995	6,195,100	27.5	25.7	11.0	16.8	20.4	26.1	47.6[96]	52.4[96]	—	...	...	...	...
Netherlands Antilles	1992	57,608	14.0	—28.4—		13.6	21.3	36.7	59.8	36.7	—	—	18.3[20]	78.8[20]	2.9[20]
New Caledonia	1989	40,266	...	—19.3—		—80.7—			56.4	29.7	13.9	6.4	11.7	61.7	20.2
New Zealand	1991	1,185,396	...	—64.1[20]—		19.2[20]	—16.2[20]—		72.4	22.7	4.9	...	...	...	...
Nicaragua	1995	794,093	...	...	...	...	...	...	64.4[76]	20.3[76]	15.3[76]	30.8[76]	45.6[76]	21.8[76]	1.8[76]
Niger	1988	1,163,424[19]	...	...	...	...	...	...	77.3	6.3	16.4	83.0	—17.0—		
Nigeria	1982[43]	...	...	...	...	...	...	...	37.0	46.0	17.0	29.0	—	71.0	—
Northern Mariana Islands	1990	8,210	...	1.0	2.5	6.4	13.3	76.8	39.5	56.6	3.9	0.0	13.5	66.5	20.0
Norway	1990	1,769,000	25.3	44.1[28]	20.6[29]	17.8[6]	20.7[7]	16.0[8]	80.3	—19.7—		...	...	...	...
Oman	1993	344,846	...	...	...	...	...	...	61.6	21.7	16.7	...	...	...	...

physical amenities (percent)			sewage disposal (percent)			space[b]			construction industry (1994)						country
									percent of GDP	new residential[d]			new nonresidential[d]		
piped water	electricity	inside toilet or WC	closed public sewer or septic tank	open public sewer	other	average area (sq m)	rooms per dwelling unit	persons per room		total no. of dwellings	floor area ('000 sq m)	years to replace nat'l stock	number of units	floor area ('000 sq m)	
92.5	91.0	78.9	2.0[53]	67.0[53]	31.0[53]	...	3.8	1.3	6.1[1]	834	...	47.4	1,329	...	French Polynesia
...	50.5	...	...	...	...	...	3.0	1.3	3.9	...	...	...	...	...	Gabon
21.9	...	...	...	...	...	...	2.0	2.0	5.0	...	...	...	...	...	Gambia, The
97.2[27]	97.6	98.4	...	...	...	...	2.6[27]	2.5[27]	18.2[9]	1,247[13]	180[13]	53.6	...	31.1[13]	Gaza Strip
...	...	...	...	...	...	...	...	...	5.5	...	1,005[18]	...	...	...	Georgia
100.0	99.7	98.3	97.1[18]	—2.9[18]—		82.3	4.3	0.5	5.1	641,958	56,098	54.5	38,025	37,215	Germany
36.0	28.5	7.0	...	...	...	23.7	1.9[39]	2.4	3.3	...	...	...	...	...	Ghana
96.7[20]	100.0[20]	99.2	100.0[20]	—	—	...	3.3	1.1	...	66[14]	...	115.2	...	...	Gibraltar
96.4	99.2	87.5	56.6	—43.4—		138.4[17]	3.9	0.8	6.3	80,607	9,386	57.8	49,435	14,915	Greece
62.7[22]	84.2[22]	39.1[22]	39.1[22]	—60.9[22]—		64.7	2.9	1.1	8.5[21]	251	...	79.1	...	...	Greenland
88.1	...	36.1	36.1	—63.9—		...	2.9[20]	1.6[20]	7.0	...	...	...	...	...	Grenada
83.2	89.4	78.2	24.6[41]	—75.4[41]—		...	3.7	0.9	7.4[39]	676[39]	358	166.4	...	160	Guadeloupe
99.2	98.4	97.0	97.0	—3.0—		...	5.0	0.8	7.9[41]	697	...	50.5	500[13]	...	Guam
52.0	37.0	14.3	20.1	3.4	76.5	...	2.4	2.2	2.1	...	495[15, 39]	...	...	[15]	Guatemala
96.5[22]	...	98.3	68.9	—31.1—		...	5.5	0.5	...	311[14]	...	68.2	...	...	Guernsey
11.9	12.5	...	...	...	...	...	...	...	6.9	...	...	...	...	...	Guinea
3.7	3.9	...	4.2	—95.8—		...	1.4	4.5	4.1	...	...	...	...	...	Guinea-Bissau
38.1	69.0	29.0	10.4	—89.6—		...	2.9	1.8	3.6	...	...	...	...	...	Guyana
5.8	21.9	45.8	2.0[41]	—98.0[41]—		...	2.3	2.1	2.9	...	...	...	...	...	Haiti
55.0[18]	25.0[18]	13.0[18]	14.4[18]	—85.6[18]—		...	2.4[18]	2.3[18]	6.4	1,442[54]	214[16]	...	148[16]	98[16]	Honduras
85.7[20]	...	69.2[75]	65.4[75]	—34.6[75]—		53.2[76]	3.1[75]	2.8[75]	4.9	56,042	1,250	31.0	1,391	1,638	Hong Kong
84.1	98.8[23]	75.1	84.6	—15.4—		52.3	2.6	1.0	4.9	20,947	2,040	...	1,026[33]	1,590[33]	Hungary
99.1[23]	94.6[23]	93.6[23]	86.5[23]	—13.5[23]—		...	4.8[78]	0.9[78]	6.8	1,718	746	41.2	531	945[26]	Iceland
32.3	42.4	23.7	...	...	...	...	2.2	2.7	5.8[25]	5,206,944[14]	...	37.5	...	...	India
14.7	55.2	51.5	24.7	—75.3—		59.0	3.3	1.7[79]	7.4	107,269	...	...	...	...	Indonesia
74.6	84.1	43.6	...	...	...	60.0[22]	2.8	1.8	3.3[49]	129,181[79]	28,608[79]	—	...	...	Iran
...	...	90.3	...	...	...	...	5.9	1.5	2.8[9]	...	4,558[9]	...	11,799[27]	410[9]	Iraq
94.8[20]	94.7[76]	96.4	72.3[76]	—27.7[76]—		...	5.2	0.6	5.0[13]	25,735	2,913	36.3	5,344	1,735	Ireland
...	...	99.5	...	...	...	...	...	0.4[20]	9.8[13]	168[13]	...	162.6	...	...	Isle of Man
96.5[76]	96.5[76]	98.8	99.0[72]	—1.0[72]—		...	3.0	1.2	7.6[9]	33,820	4,880	32.7	...	1,464	Israel
99.1	99.0[20]	97.4	95.7[22]	—4.3[22]—		94.1	4.3	0.7	5.1	166,236	14,961	150.6	21,377	...	Italy
76.9	48.6	35.2	...	...	...	...	2.4[37]	4.3	12.6	7,950	...	65.1	...	6,989[84]	Jamaica
94.0[52]	...	74.7	61.2[52]	—38.8[52]—		89.2[38]	4.9[38]	0.7[38]	10.3	1,688,700	156,800	24.2	...	81,260	Japan
80.8	...	93.0[22]	98.0	—2.0—		...	4.7	0.5	...	354[13]	...	91.7	...	...	Jersey
95.8	93.9	55.4[23]	54.5	—84.3—		...	3.2	...	7.4	4,200	4,206[15]	—	820[16]	[15]	Jordan
50.0	...	...	...	—41.0—		...	...	...	9.6	65,000	3,432	67.8	...	...	Kazakstan
...	...	...	...	...	...	...	...	...	5.3	...	828[9, 15]	...	85[16]	[15]	Kenya
33.1	23.7[58]	53.3	...	...	...	...	...	...	2.2	190[14]	...	59.5	...	...	Kiribati
...	...	...	...	...	...	...	...	...	...	...	...	...	...	...	Korea, North
82.9[87]	49.9[23]	75.1	...	...	...	58.9	3.1	1.1	11.4	622,854	63,387	14.8	68,215	52,834	Korea, South
53.9[18]	99.5[18]	...	35.9[18]	—64.1[18]—		...	4.3[18]	1.8[18]	3.4	2,287[14]	713	110.0	1,459	102	Kuwait
...	...	...	...	...	...	...	...	...	3.4	5,000	405	171.2	...	...	Kyrgyzstan
...	...	...	...	...	...	...	...	...	3.4	...	...	...	...	...	Laos
78.3	100.0[9]	74.0	...	...	...	55.4	...	...	4.5	3,300	174	288.8	...	...	Latvia
...	93.4	82.9	...	...	...	...	...	...	5.2	...	...	...	...	...	Lebanon
31.9	2.2	2.5	2.5	—97.5—		...	2.2	2.4	21.9	7,081[14]	...	44.2	...	...	Lesotho
...	...	...	...	...	...	...	2.3[27]	1.7	2.2[39]	...	...	...	...	...	Liberia
70.1[75]	72.1[75]	40.6[75]	40.6[75]	—59.4[75]—		...	3.3[75]	1.8[75]	11.8[9]	...	...	...	...	...	Libya
96.5	96.6	86.7	90.2	—9.8—		102.0	4.5	0.6	...	197[14]	...	52.7	...	...	Liechtenstein
59.5	...	...	...	...	...	58.3	2.5	...	8.7	6,900	590	177.6	385	280	Lithuania
99.4	...	99.4	93.0[92]	—7.0[92]—		114.2	5.4[18]	0.5[18]	7.9	2,744	1,931[26]	52.7	282	1,964[26]	Luxembourg
98.0	99.8	97.9	...	...	...	...	3.1	1.3	...	9,553	1,141[15]	9.3	327	[15]	Macau
81.8	96.4[39]	61.4	...	...	...	68.6[39]	...	...	6.4	4,830	348	105.9	310	53	Macedonia
...	...	...	...	...	...	...	...	...	1.2[9]	...	...	...	...	...	Madagascar
23.6	22.8[18]	33.4[18]	33.0[44]	—67.0[44]—		...	1.9	1.7	4.2	...	...	...	...	...	Malawi
65.0[18]	64.4[18]	...	56.4[18]	4.4[18]	39.2[18]	...	2.3[92, 93]	2.6[92, 93]	4.1	...	8,809[16]	...	...	960[16]	Malaysia
...	53.4[27]	...	43.2	—56.8—		...	4.4	1.5	9.1	957[14]	...	34.5	...	...	Maldives
3.8	3.6	1.3	...	...	...	...	2.6	2.2	3.6[52]	10,025[14]	...	136.1	...	...	Mali
98.0	98.0	98.8	98.0	15.4[44]	6.1[44]	...	3.2[44]	1.3[44]	3.4	3,420	...	29.7	2,024[33]	...	Malta
49.8[38]	56.0[38]	43.7[38]	28.6	—71.4—		...	...	...	10.4	132	...	37.4	...	...	Marshall Islands
94.1	90.2	89.0	41.8[41]	—58.2[41]—		...	3.7	0.9	5.2[21]	6,893	113	15.5	...	...	Martinique
...	...	...	...	...	...	...	...	...	9.2[12]	...	...	...	...	...	Mauritania
94.7	96.2	63.3	63.3	—36.7—		...	3.6[52]	1.4[52]	7.6	4,592[14]	1,108	51.6	682	371	Mauritius
42.5	32.2	6.7	54.4	—45.6—		...	2.2	2.2	...	616[16]	...	21.3[16]	...	...	Mayotte
79.4	87.5	45.0[18]	60.9	2.7	36.4	...	3.4	1.5	5.5	412,319[14]	...	39.3	...	...	Mexico
40.0	28.3	...	8.0	—92.0—		...	...	...	...	...	...	...	...	...	Micronesia
74.9	100.0	71.6	46.0	—54.0—		61.7	...	...	9.9	7,500	...	148.4	158	86	Moldova
100.0	100.0	96.2	98.4[59]	—1.6[59]—		...	2.8	0.8	...	187[14]	...	86.2	...	...	Monaco
0.3	47.5	...	...	...	...	...	...	...	2.4[101]	...	112[9]	...	...	176[17]	Mongolia
32.1[27]	37.8[27]	52.5[27]	...	...	...	...	2.7[41]	2.2[41]	4.2	57,281	7,070	...	2,229	998	Morocco
12.7	4.2	...	...	...	...	...	...	...	10.6	...	...	...	...	...	Mozambique
...	...	...	...	...	...	...	...	...	1.7[49]	1,193[51]	...	...	1,483[51]	...	Myanmar (Burma)
49.8	24.2	30.9	...	...	...	...	3.6	1.4	2.7	...	...	...	...	...	Namibia
...	49.2	...	...	...	...	...	3.6[103]	1.6[103]	...	...	...	...	...	...	Nauru
32.8	14.1	21.6	9.2	—90.8—		56.1	3.0	1.9	10.4[49]	...	...	...	...	...	Nepal
100.0	98.0	100.0	90.0[13]	—10.0[13]—		...	4.1[27]	0.7[27]	5.7	87,369	...	70.9	13,034	13,625	Netherlands, The
79.6[20]	96.9[20]	82.0[20]	...	...	...	...	4.2[20]	1.0[20]	6.6[33]	547[9]	...	150.2[9]	361[33]	...	Netherlands Antilles
90.1	85.3	70.9	76.7	—23.3—		...	3.3	1.2	4.9[38]	942[33]	46[16]	46.8	1[54]	...	New Caledonia
92.7[76]	...	97.1[76]	...	...	...	...	5.6	0.5	3.1	22,540	3,700	52.6	...	2,568	New Zealand
27.9[76]	40.9[76]	19.3[76]	19.2[76]	—80.8[76]—		...	2.2[76]	2.1[76]	2.8	17,489[14]	...	41.3	...	...	Nicaragua
15.5	4.3	1.2	...	...	...	...	...	...	1.9	...	...	...	...	...	Niger
24.7	33.7	3.5	...	...	...	...	1.4	1.1	1.1	...	...	...	...	...	Nigeria
91.0	94.1[18]	79.5	81.7	—18.3—		...	3.6	1.1	...	469[14]	...	17.5	...	...	Northern Mariana Islands
97.5[92]	...	94.6	86.8[92]	—13.2[18]—		103.5	4.1	0.6	3.3	17,836	2,453	99.2	14,860	2,404	Norway
35.8	86.3	76.1	...	...	...	...	...	2.9	2.0	1,043[16]	...	...	266[16]	...	Oman

Housing and construction (continued)

country	housing stock			decade built (percent)					tenure[c] (percent)			construction of exterior walls (percent)			
	year	dwelling units[a]	median age[b] (years)	1949 or earlier	1950–59	1960–69	1970–79	1980 or later	owned	rented	collective, vacant, other	traditional materials	sawn/ framed wood	masonry or cement	other
Pakistan[104]	1980	12,597,000	17.2	17.1[90]	36.7[105]	24.9[106]	21.3[107]	—	78.4	7.7	13.9	49.2	2.4	41.4	7.1
Palau	1990	3,312	12.8	2.1	6.0	16.8	30.6	44.5	76.4	23.6	—	0.0	27.9	26.5	45.6
Panama	1990[108]	524,284[17]	18.0[18]	47.4[18]	12.8[18]	18.1[18]	—21.7[18]—		75.5	15.7	8.8	16.9	—81.2—		1.9
Papua New Guinea	1980	556,519[19]	...	...	...	...	...	...	40.0[59]	—60.0[59]—		...	...	...	...
Paraguay	1982	868,284[21]	21.1	—56.0—		17.0	—27.0—		80.4	10.5	9.1	21.5	29.7	47.6	1.2
Peru	1993	4,427,517	...	—30.9[20]—		—69.1[20]—			82.0	11.0	7.0	55.7	7.0	35.7	1.6
Philippines	1990	11,395,304	...	—78.5[92]—		—21.5[92]—			83.0	8.0	9.0	35.3	27.3	33.5	3.9
Poland	1988	11,967,021	...	35.0[85]	—33.7[110]—		—31.3[111]—		35.2	64.3	0.9	—14.1[50]—		—85.9[50]—	
Portugal	1991	3,059,300	33.7[20]	—38.3[80]—		16.9[6]	21.2[7]	22.6[8]	64.7	35.3	—	—	0.7[20]	61.0[20]	38.3[20]
Puerto Rico	1990	1,188,985	18.0	9.0	12.8	22.9	29.5	25.8	72.1	27.9	—	—	15.1	83.6	1.3
Qatar	1986	64,543	...	...	...	...	...	...	21.9	72.0	6.1	...	...	...	...
Réunion	1994	184,500[17]	14.3[1]	—47.6[60]—		19.9[61]	—32.5[58]—		50.3	38.9	10.8	23.9	12.5	—63.7—	
Romania	1992	7,632,000	...	...	...	19.9	14.2	...	78.6	20.8	0.6	...	...	...	...
Russia	1994	52,123,000	...	...	...	...	...	...	...	...	...	...	...	...	...
Rwanda	1978	1,055,950[19]	...	...	...	...	...	...	95.3	1.7	3.0	88.6	7.9	1.3	2.2
St. Kitts and Nevis	1980	11,615[19]	24.2	—63.5—		17.9	—14.7—		54.7	29.5	15.8	—	76.2	21.3	2.5
St. Lucia	1991	33,079	13.5	—17.0—		12.4	26.0	44.6	72.4	26.8	0.8	—	53.4	46.1	0.5
St. Vincent and the Grenadines	1980	27,110	...	—	...	...	...	...	72.1	16.0	11.9	—	53.8	42.9	3.3
Samoa	1981	33,402	...	...	...	...	...	...	80.1	2.0	17.9	62.3	24.4	8.6	4.7
San Marino	1991	8,518	...	...	...	...	...	...	73.5[37]	21.9[37]	4.6[37]	...	...	...	...
São Tomé and Príncipe	1981	27,449[19]	...	...	...	...	...	...	...	...	...	2.2	67.2	25.7	4.9
Saudi Arabia	...	...	...	...	...	...	...	...	...	...	...	...	...	...	...
Senegal	1955[43, 115]	13,000	...	...	...	...	...	...	—84.6—		15.4	...	...	...	...
Seychelles	1987	15,050	...	...	...	...	...	...	63.7	25.1	11.2	1.0	40.0	52.0	7.0
Sierra Leone	1985	486,550	...	...	...	...	...	...	75.2	20.7	4.1	64.6	...	26.2	9.2
Singapore	1990	744,203	...	—63.2[18]—		—36.8[18]—			87.5	—12.5—		4.7[18]	—95.3[18]—		
Slovakia	1991	1,617,829	26.9	17.1[28]	17.3[29]	20.3[6]	25.4[7]	19.9[8]	...	...	...	—	38.0[47]	61.4	0.6
Slovenia	1991	640,000	...	—35.3[80]—		18.2[6]	25.7[7]	19.4[8]	60.2	39.8	—	...	...	...	...
Solomon Islands	1986	43,842[19]	...	...	...	...	...	...	27.4[22]	43.0[22]	29.6[22]	...	...	...	...
Somalia	...	...	...	...	...	...	...	...	...	...	...	...	...	...	...
South Africa	1991	3,599,518	18.6[92]	40.6[92]	24.2[92]	35.2[92]	—	—	54.5	34.0	11.5	...	...	...	...
Spain	1991	11,736,000	39.4[16]	19.5[28]	14.3[29]	23.7[6]	27.2[7]	15.1[8]	67.5	14.9	17.6	...	...	...	...
Sri Lanka	1981	2,811,406	...	...	...	...	...	...	69.4	10.1	20.5	...	...	...	...
Sudan, The	1983	...	...	...	...	...	...	...	86.2	8.1	5.7	76.5	4.4	16.7	2.4
Suriname	1980	77,744	...	—52.4—		—47.6—			...	...	...	38.9[116]	—61.1[116]—		
Swaziland	1986	122,369	...	...	...	...	...	...	...	...	...	65.9	—34.1—		
Sweden	1990	3,830,037	20.0	33.2	14.2	22.4	22.2	10.6	55.9	40.0	4.1	...	...	...	...
Switzerland	1990	2,800,953	28.5	33.2[90]	15.9[91]	19.4[6]	17.2[7]	14.3[8]	31.3	66.5	2.2	...	...	...	...
Syria	1987	1,836,195	...	—91.3[92]—		—8.7[92]—			81.6[92]	15.5[92]	2.8[92]	...	...	...	...
Taiwan	1990	4,237,174[17]	17.2	6.1[28]	6.7[29]	15.8[6]	42.6[7]	28.8[8]	78.5	12.8	8.7	...	...	...	...
Tajikistan	1989	799,000[19]	...	...	...	...	...	...	...	...	...	...	...	...	...
Tanzania	1978	3,554,793	...	—17.0—		—83.0—			75.4	19.4	5.2	83.0	—	16.3	0.7
Thailand	1990	12,305,197[19]	...	22.0[92]	25.0[92]	53.0[92]	—	—	86.0	11.2	2.8	8.4	68.2	22.3	1.1
Togo	1981	462,694	...	...	...	...	...	...	...	...	...	...	...	...	...
Tonga	1986	15,091	22.5	—59.4[117]—		20.3[118]	—20.3[119]—		82.0	3.5	14.5	35.1[22]	45.4[22]	15.3[22]	4.2[22]
Trinidad and Tobago	1990	271,871	15.3	—41.6—			17.9	40.5	64.6[18]	34.0[18]	1.4[18]	1.0	28.1	70.0[34]	0.9
Tunisia	1984	1,703,279[96]	...	...	...	...	...	...	78.9	12.6	8.5	...	...	...	...
Turkey	1994	13,341,000	8.4[16]	16.2[117]	6.2[120]	19.6[106]	—58.0[108]—		77.2	12.0	10.8	—28.8—		—71.2—	
Turkmenistan	1989	598,000[19]	...	...	...	...	...	...	...	...	...	...	...	...	...
Tuvalu	1979	1,079	...	...	...	...	...	...	81.6	12.1	6.6	64.9	4.2	31.0	—
Uganda	1991	3,434,177	...	...	...	...	...	...	...	...	...	...	...	...	...
Ukraine	1989	14,057,000[19]	...	...	...	...	...	...	...	...	...	...	...	...	...
United Arab Emirates	1980	153,009	15.0	0.8	1.3	11.4	—86.5—		36.2	45.2	18.6	2.9	7.3	87.3	2.5
United Kingdom[122]	1991	21,897,322	32.6[20]	54.0[20]	13.0[20]	16.6[20]	—16.4[20]—		66.4	33.6	—	...	...	...	...
United States	1995	106,403,000	28.0	27.4	12.4	14.4	21.6	23.7	59.7	32.1	8.2	...	...	...	...
Uruguay	1985	852,400	...	...	...	...	...	...	57.6	23.2	19.2	...	...	...	...
Uzbekistan	1989	3,415,000[19]	...	...	...	...	...	...	...	...	...	...	...	...	...
Vanuatu	1979	28,252[19, 39]	...	...	...	...	...	...	40.9[43]	25.7[43]	33.4[43]	61.4	7.7	13.6	17.2
Venezuela	1990	3,534,507	...	...	...	...	...	...	75.8	13.9	10.3	14.6	0.5	84.9	—
Vietnam	1989	12,958,041[19]	...	...	...	...	...	...	...	...	...	...	...	...	...
Virgin Islands (U.S.)	1990	39,290	14.7	10.0[18]	8.9[18]	42.7[18]	—38.4[18]—		44.6	55.4	—	...	...	...	...
West Bank	1992	119,165[44]	12.2	8.0	12.7	24.6	26.2	28.6	86.2[63]	11.5[63]	2.3[63]	23.0	—	75.3	1.7
Western Sahara	1994	46,120	...	...	...	...	...	...	32.2[30]	62.3[30]	5.5[30]	...	...	...	...
Yemen[123]	1988[124]	1,701,203	...	...	...	...	...	...	83.9	5.2	10.9	...	...	...	...
Yugoslavia	1993	3,039,000	...	...	...	...	...	...	...	...	...	...	...	...	...
Zambia	1990	1,327,098[19]	...	...	...	...	...	...	78.8[125]	21.1[125]	...	...	...	...	...
Zimbabwe	1992	2,163,289[19]	...	...	...	...	...	...	58.3	39.1	2.6	55.9[125, 126]	—44.1[125, 126]—		

[1]1990. [2]Urban only. [3]Data refer to "apartments," approximately equal in numbers to families, or households. [4]1950 and earlier. [5]1951–60. [6]1961–70. [7]1971–80. [8]1981 and later. [9]1991. [10]1962 and earlier. [11]1963–69. [12]Includes public utilities. [13]1987. [14]Average annual gain in housing stock/households during intercensal interval ending year indicated at extreme left. [15]Residential includes nonresidential. [16]1986. [17]Occupied dwellings only. [18]1980. [19]Data refer to households. [20]1981. [21]1992. [22]1976. [23]Minimum. [24]1992–93. [25]1994–95. [26]1990–91. [27]1985. [28]1945 and earlier. [29]1946–60. [30]Data refer to buildings. [31]Public, state, and cooperative-owned dwellings only. [32]Stucco. [33]1993. [34]Includes wood and brick, and wood and concrete. [35]1946–61. [36]1962–70. [37]1979. [38]1988. [39]1989. [40]Data refer to compound dwellings. [41]1982. [42]1971 and later. [43]Capital city only. [44]1967. [45]Percentage of net material product. [46]Volume enclosed in cubic metres. [47]Includes prefabricated units. [48]Includes corrugated steel. [49]1993–94. [50]1978. [51]1987–88. [52]1983. [53]1977. [54]1984. [55]1948 and earlier. [56]1949–67. [57]1967–81. [58]1982 and later. [59]1975. [60]1974 and earlier. [61]1975–82. [62]1983 and later. [63]Excludes refugee camps. [64]1949–87. [65]1988 and later. [66]1952 and earlier. [67]1953–62. [68]1963–72. [69]1973–81. [70]1975 and earlier.

physical amenities (percent)			sewage disposal (percent)			space[b]			construction industry (1994)						country
									percent of GDP	new residential[d]			new nonresidential[d]		
piped water	electricity	inside toilet or WC	closed public sewer or septic tank	open public sewer	other	average area (sq m)	rooms per dwelling unit	persons per room		total no. of dwellings	floor area ('000 sq m)	years to replace nat'l stock	number of units	floor area ('000 sq m)	
20.3	30.6	25.1	...	...	...	...	1.9	3.3	3.5[49]	...	...	...	...	...	Pakistan[104]
87.9	87.5	46.3	44.3	—55.7—		...	2.6	1.8	7.5[21]	85[14]	...	33.8	...	...	Palau
80.7	72.8	74.3[18]	44.2	—55.8—		...	2.8	1.6	4.2	7,110	...	73.7	517	...	Panama
50.0	56.0	40.0	...	...	...	...	...	...	4.0	...	...	...	...	...	Papua New Guinea
...	...	26.4	...	...	...	...	2.2[109]	2.4[109]	5.4	...	61[27]	...	2,715[13]	365[13]	Paraguay
46.7	54.9	35.7	40.0	22.2	37.8	42.4[20]	2.6[20]	2.0[20]	8.5	97,533[14]	...	45.4	...	1,546	Peru
38.8	55.1	35.0[18]	67.6	14.4	18.0	...	2.4	2.3[109]	5.5	263,729[14]	3,862[33]	43.2	6,425[33]	3,693[33]	Philippines
84.3	96.2[50]	68.9	67.0[50]	—33.0[50]—		55.6[54]	3.2	1.0	6.3	76,100	6,735	157.5	30,949	...	Poland
90.6	99.4	91.8	75.5[20]	—24.5[20]—		...	5.0[34]	0.8	7.5[1]	62,000	...	49.3	4,292[33]	1,772[21]	Portugal
95.6	97.4[49]	94.7	95.7	—4.3—		...	4.8[18]	0.8[18]	2.2[112]	10,212[21]	1,872[21]	82.8	900[27]	41.0[27]	Puerto Rico
...	93.2	...	—50.5—		49.5	...	4.9	1.3	4.9	12,240[33]	391[16]	58.9	1,416[33]	168[16]	Qatar
95.0	98.0	80.0	52.4[41]	—47.6[41]—		86.0	3.7	0.9	6.2[1]	7,627	...	24.2	...	...	Réunion
51.4	48.6[113]	44.9	12.2[113]	—87.8[113]—		...	2.6	1.4	6.0	36,700	2,683	208.0	...	...	Romania
68.4	...	63.7	...	...	...	...	...	...	7.7	611,000	39,200	85.3	...	...	Russia
...	...	...	...	...	...	...	...	...	2.8	435[54]	60[20]	...	63[54]	34[20]	Rwanda
46.3	57.5	33.5	31.8[46]	—68.2[46]—		...	3.0	1.1	11.9	171[14]	...	68.0	...	...	St. Kitts and Nevis
64.7	72.9	35.7	35.7	—64.3—		...	3.4	1.2	8.2	752[14]	...	44.0	61[21]	41[21]	St. Lucia
95.0[52]	...	...	22.0[52]	—78.0[52]—		...	2.8	1.8	12.4	...	...	...	...	...	St. Vincent and the Grenadines
80.7	37.7	71.0	16.6	—83.4—		...	...	...	1.8	132[27]	...	...	118[27]	...	Samoa
100.0	100.0	100.0	98.3[37]	—1.7[37]—		...	3.8	0.7	...	145[114]	...	58.7	123[114]	...	San Marino
22.3	22.0	9.2	9.8	—90.2—		...	2.2	1.8	13.8	225[14]	...	122.0	...	...	São Tomé and Príncipe
...	...	...	...	...	...	...	...	...	8.6[21]	...	16,078[9]	...	2,205[9]	...	Saudi Arabia
44.1	23.1	...	...	...	...	...	2.3	1.5	3.4	584[21]	338[21]	...	22[21]	18[21]	Senegal
77.0	75.8	95.0	33.1[53]	—66.9[53]—		...	4.1	1.1	9.4	...	...	...	...	...	Seychelles
15.9	8.3	7.3	13.1	66.2	20.7	...	...	...	2.2[25]	...	...	...	...	...	Sierra Leone
90.6[92]	98.3[18]	63.6[92]	63.6[92]	—36.4[92]—		...	1.8[92]	2.5[92]	7.1	42,702[14]	4,303[33]	17.4	1,991[9]	2,730[33]	Singapore
91.8	...	80.1	87.6	—12.4—		71.7	2.9	1.1	5.2	6,710	760	241.1	...	...	Slovakia
97.4[21]	99.5[21]	89.9	...	...	...	103.1[33]	3.0	1.0	4.6[18]	5,500	589	116.4	1,571[33]	520[33]	Slovenia
92.7[22]	79.6[22]	89.2	89.2[22]	—10.8[22]—		10.8[22]	2.3[22]	2.0[22]	5.4	...	...	...	...	...	Solomon Islands
...	...	...	...	...	...	...	...	...	3.8[9]	...	...	...	...	...	Somalia
66.4	55.9	54.9	...	...	...	...	3.4[92]	...	3.2	29,587	4,266	...	1,686	2,437	South Africa
98.7	99.2	97.1	87.9[18]	—12.1[18]—		86.6	4.4[92]	...	8.0	219,511	...	53.5	...	...	Spain
18.2	14.9	4.7	4.7	—95.3—		18.6[92]	2.5	2.1	7.3	59,637[16]	...	47.2[16]	...	...	Sri Lanka
29.4	9.9	70.2[2, 113]	2.6[2, 113]	–97.4[2, 113]–		...	2.2[113]	2.5[113]	6.7	...	...	...	...	...	Sudan, The
62.9	82.0	40.4	19.6[116]	—80.4[116]—		...	2.1	1.9	3.7	...	355[27, 46]	...	161[27]	...	Suriname
42.5	11.6	21.4	...	...	...	...	...	...	2.7	...	...	...	...	...	Swaziland
99.0[27]	96.2[18]	98.0	96.3[18]	—3.7[18]—		...	3.4	0.6	5.8	21,630	...	177.1	...	3,818[54]	Sweden
100.0[18]	...	93.3[18]	92.2[16]	—	7.8[18]	93.0	3.7	0.6	7.0	47,107	...	59.5	8,109[16]	...	Switzerland
40.2[52]	41.7[52]	...	36.0[52]	—64.0[52]—		93.0	3.0	2.0	4.1	24,297[21]	2,977[21]	33.0[13]	...	1,147[21]	Syria
79.4[18]	99.7[18]	94.2[18]	69.3[18]	...	...	30.5	4.1	1.2	5.3	...	47,533[15, 33]	...	...	[15]	Taiwan
60[9, 87]	...	...	50	—50—		51.4	...	...	16.1	...	400[33]	...	...	...	Tajikistan
37.2	6.3	...	...	...	...	...	2.5	1.9	4.7	...	...	...	...	...	Tanzania
29.7	89.7	40.9[23]	40.9[22]	9.8[22]	49.3[22]	...	1.6	2.7	7.5	...	16,343[9]	...	...	13,499[9]	Thailand
4.1[78]	10.3[78]	...	—	—100.0[78]—		...	1.8	3.4	3.0	...	...	...	...	...	Togo
61.3[22]	20.9[22]	42.3[22]	11.2[22]	—88.8[22]—		...	...	...	5.1[49]	...	...	...	...	...	Tonga
64.3[18]	83.3[18]	41.1[18]	41.0[18]	—59.0[18]—		...	3.3[18]	1.4[18]	7.5	1,012	208	14.9	38	48	Trinidad and Tobago
26.4	63.4	43.3	69.2[39]	—30.8[39]—		...	1.9	2.4	4.1	34,566[13]	...	43.8	...	...	Tunisia
68.0	56.8	70.6	42.0	52.0	6.0	...	2.4[27]	2.2[92]	6.8	245,449	19,693	54.4	4,533	17,336	Turkey
...	...	...	...	...	...	...	...	...	4.7	...	20,754[15, 21]	...	...	[15]	Turkmenistan
65.4	7.4	37.3	...	...	...	...	...	...	13.9	...	...	...	...	...	Tuvalu
...	...	...	...	...	...	...	...	...	6.0[49]	...	...	...	65[109]	26.8[109]	Uganda
...	...	...	...	...	...	...	...	...	10.0[9]	...	14,454[9]	...	...	...	Ukraine
30.9[121]	24.2[121]	84.5	...	...	...	...	2.8	1.8	9.8	...	...	...	...	...	United Arab Emirates
...	...	99.8	...	...	...	...	5.0	0.5	5.4	182,438	...	120.0	...	...	United Kingdom[122]
86.8	96.9[1]	98.9[1]	99.8	—0.2—		156.7	5.5	0.5	5.8	1,284,000[33]	210,640	82.9	...	106,340	United States
89.3	84.7	73.3	...	92.0	...	...	3.4	1.7	5.3	...	274	...	84	70	Uruguay
...	...	...	...	...	...	...	...	...	7.2	...	7,000	...	...	...	Uzbekistan
39.2[39]	14.2	27.5[39]	...	...	...	...	...	...	5.6	574[14]	...	49.2	...	15.3[16]	Vanuatu
86.2	89.8	84.4[20]	80.2	—19.8—		...	4.2	1.3	4.9	91,666[16]	4,904[16]	29.5	678[16]	1,067[16]	Venezuela
...	...	...	...	...	...	...	...	...	6.8	298,073[14]	...	43.5	53[54]	59.3[54]	Vietnam
96.3[18]	98.1[18]	86.0[18]	93.6[18]	—6.4[18]—		...	4.3	0.6	...	574[14]	...	68.4	262[18]	...	Virgin Islands (U.S.)
75.2[27]	75.3	98.4	...	...	...	...	2.4[27]	2.7[27]	14.1[13]	5,740[9]	730[9]	20.8	...	175.8[9]	West Bank
78.5	95.3	...	...	...	...	...	4.5	1.2	4.4[39]	2,213[14]	...	20.8	...	...	Western Sahara
5.7[59]	4.6[59]	...	...	...	...	...	2.0[59]	2.8[59]	5.0[21]	...	1,988[27]	...	...	...	Yemen[123]
79.1	98.0	61.2	...	...	...	57.6[9]	2.8	1.3	7.8	17,442	...	179.1	40[33]	256	Yugoslavia
12.4[125]	27.5[78]	15.1[125]	...	...	82.3[125]	...	1.9[125]	2.6[125]	2.6	...	...	...	...	...	Zambia
39.1	28.2	37.0	...	...	...	...	2.8[125]	1.9[125]	2.2	...	...	...	...	...	Zimbabwe

[71]1976–81. [72]1974. [73]1969–78. [74]1979 and later. [75]1973. [76]1971. [77]1946–59. [78]1960. [79]Urban only. [80]1960 and earlier. [81]1947 and earlier. [82]1948–83. [83]1961–71. [84]Factory space only. [85]1944 and earlier. [86]1945–60. [87]Data refer to persons. [88]Data refer to families. [89]1960 and earlier. [90]1946 and earlier. [91]1947–60. [92]1970. [93]Peninsular Malaysia only. [94]1957 and earlier. [95]1958–67. [96]1994. [97]1960–68. [98]1969 and later. [99]1949–61. [100]1962–74. [101]Percentage of net material product. [102]Dwellings of indigenous population only. [103]1961. [104]Excludes Islāmābād, North-West Frontier, and federally administered tribal areas. [105]1947–65. [106]1966–75. [107]1976 and later. [108]Excludes areas under U.S. military control in the provinces of Colón and Panamá. [109]1972. [110]1945–70. [111]1971 and later. [112]Includes mining. [113]1966. [114]1995. [115]European-style dwellings only. [116]1964. [117]1955 and earlier. [118]1956–66. [119]1967 and later. [120]1956–65. [121]1968. [122]Excludes Northern Ireland. [123]Former Yemen Arab Republic only. [124]Total of 1986 and 1988 censuses. [125]1969. [126]Bantu dwellings only.

Household budgets and consumption

This table provides international data on household income, on the consumption expenditure of households for goods and services, and on the principal object of such expenditure (in most countries), food consumption (by kind). For purposes of this compilation, income comprises pretax monetary payments and payment in kind. The first part of the table provides data on distribution of income by households and by sources of income; the second part analyzes the largest portion of income use—consumption expenditure. Such expenditure is defined as the purchase of goods and services to satisfy current wants and needs. This definition excludes income expended on taxes, debts, savings and investments, and insurance policies. The third and last part of the table focuses on food, which usually, and often by a wide margin, represents the largest share of consumer spending worldwide. The data provided include daily available calories per capita and consumption of major food groups.

For both sources of income and consumption expenditure, the primary basis of analysis for most countries is the household, an economic unit that can be as small as a single person or as large as an extended family. For some of the countries that do not compile information by household, the table provides data on personal income and personal expenditure—*i.e.*, the income and expenditure of all the individuals constituting a society's households. When no expenditure data at all is available, the table reports the weights of each major class of goods and services making up a given country's consumer (or retail) price index (CPI). The weighting of the components of the CPI usually reflects household spending patterns within the country or its principal urban or rural areas.

The data on distribution of income show, collectively for an entire country, the proportion of total income earned (occasionally, expended) by households constituting the lowest quintile and highest decile (poorest 20% and wealthiest 10%) within the country. These figures show the degree to which either group represents a disproportionate share of poverty or wealth.

The data on sources of income illuminate patterns of economic structure in the gaining of an income. They indicate, for example, that in poor, agrarian countries income often derives largely from self-employment (usually farming) or that in industrial countries, with well-developed systems of salaried employment and social welfare, income derives mainly from wages and salaries and secondarily from transfer payments (*see* note a). Because household sizes and numbers of income earners vary so greatly internationally, and because the frequency and methodology of household and CPI surveys do not permit single-year comparisons for more than a few countries at once, no summary of total *household* income or expenditure was possible. Instead, U.S. dollar figures are supplied for *per capita* private final consumption expenditure (for a single, recent year) that are more comparable internationally and refer to the same date. The figures on distribution of consumption expenditure by end use reveal patterns of personal and family use of disposable income and indicate, inter alia, that in developing countries food may absorb 50% or more of disposable income, while in the larger household budgets of the developed countries, by contrast, food purchases may account for only 20–30% of spending. Each category of expenditure betrays similar complexities of local habit, necessity, and aspiration.

The reader should exercise caution when using these data to make inter-country comparisons. Most of the information comes from single-country surveys, which often differ markedly in their coverage of economically or demographically stratified groups, in sample design, or in the methods

Household budgets and consumption

country	income (latest)						consumption expenditure						
	percent received by		by source (percent)				per capita private final, U.S.$ 1995	by kind or end use (percent of household or personal budget; latest)					
	lowest 20% of households	highest 10% of households	wages, salaries	self-employment	transfer payments[a]	other[b]		food[c]	housing[d]	clothing[e]	health care	energy, water	education
Afghanistan	...	...	20.7	28.0	8.2	43.1	...	33.9	3.0	...	1.1	0.7	...
Albania	...	...	53.0	4.0	11.5	31.5	680	...	...	...	...	...	...
Algeria	6.9[1]	31.5[1]	43.1	38.3	18.6	1.8	810	52.3	6.7[2]	8.6	2.8	[2]	[3]
American Samoa	...	...	...	...	...	...	1,880[4]	32.9	20.4[5]	5.2	...	...	...
Andorra	...	...	...	...	...	...	...	...	...	...	...	...	...
Angola	...	...	...	...	...	...	370	74.1[6]	10.2[2, 6]	5.5[6]	1.8[6]	[2, 6]	2.7[6]
Antigua and Barbuda	...	...	...	...	...	...	4,050	*42.9*	*23.3*	*7.5*	...	5.5	...
Argentina	*4.4*	*35.2*	53.9	31.5	1.5	12.7	6,620	40.1	9.3	8.0	7.9	9.0	2.6
Armenia	...	...	24.5	13.6[7]	5.5	56.4	360	47.3	...	17.4	...	...	...
Aruba	...	...	...	...	...	...	11,190	26.9	9.9	8.4	2.9	8.5	1.9
Australia	3.8	28.0	72.7	7.5	13.0	6.8	12,040	18.7	18.5	5.6	7.1	2.2	1.6
Austria	*4.0*	*28.7*	55.7	[8]	24.4	19.9[8]	16,020	28.1	14.5	8.5	5.8	4.0	0.4
Azerbaijan	...	...	70.2	10.8[7]	19.0	—	460	42.2	—	13.6	4.8	—	—
Bahamas, The	3.6	32.1	...	...	...	...	3,950[9]	13.8	32.8	5.9	4.4	...	5.3
Bahrain	...	...	...	...	...	...	2,240	32.4	21.2	5.9	2.3	2.2	2.3
Bangladesh	9.4[1]	23.7[1]	18.7	48.3	7.5	25.5	170[10]	63.3	8.8	5.9	1.1	8.4	1.2
Barbados	*7.0*	*44.0*[11]	...	...	...	...	4,860	45.8	16.8	5.1	3.8	5.2	[3]
Belarus	11.1[12]	19.4[12]	47.1	7.3[9]	45.6	—	610	29.0	2.7	...	...	...	...
Belgium	*7.9*[13]	*21.5*[13]	49.6	10.9	20.7	18.8	16,550	18.3	11.4	7.0	10.5	6.2	[3]
Belize	...	...	*84.1*		*15.9*		1,780	34.0	9.0	8.8	1.6	9.1	2.3
Benin	*8.0*	*39.0*	26.3		73.7		240	37.0	10.0	14.0	5.0	2.0	4.0
Bermuda	7.2	24.7	65.3	9.0	3.3	22.4	12,690[14]	14.6	27.7	4.9	7.6	3.3	3.8
Bhutan	...	...	...	...	...	...	170	*72.3*	...	*21.2*	...	*3.7*	...
Bolivia	5.6[12]	31.7[12]	...	...	...	...	690	46.6	7.8	5.1	2.1	4.7	0.3
Bosnia and Herzegovina	...	...	53.2	12.0	18.2	16.6	1,890[15]	44.7	1.6	8.3	3.4	7.8	[3]
Botswana	3.7	42.9	73.3	15.4	10.8	0.4	1,030	39.5[16]	11.8	5.6	2.3	2.5	4.9
Brazil	2.1[12]	51.3[12]	62.4	14.7	10.9	12.0	4,420	25.3	21.3[2]	12.9	9.1	[2]	...
Brunei	...	...	...	...	...	...	...	*45.1*	*2.6*	*6.1*	...	*2.4*	[3]
Bulgaria	8.3[12]	24.7[12]	34.7	23.6[7]	14.8	—	1,470	47.0	4.1	7.4	3.2	4.3	[3]
Burkina Faso	...	...	...	...	...	...	220	38.7[6]	5.1[6]	4.4[6]	5.2[6]	13.7[6]	[3]
Burundi	...	...	...	...	...	...	190	59.6[6]	4.4[6]	11.1[6]	...	5.8[6]	...
Cambodia	...	...	...	...	...	...	280	...	...	...	...	...	...
Cameroon	...	...	41.4	52.6	3.0	3.0	570	49.1	18.0[2]	7.6	8.6	[2]	...
Canada	5.7	24.1	57.0	13.7	20.7	8.6	11,460	13.4	24.5[2]	5.3	4.7	[2]	3.1
Cape Verde	...	...	...	...	...	...	920	60.0	8.5	2.5	0.5	4.9	[19]
Central African Republic	...	...	...	...	...	...	350	70.5[6]	0.6[6]	9.5[6]	1.0[6]	6.5[6]	...
Chad	*8.0*	*30.0*	...	...	...	...	170	45.3[6]	...	3.5[6]	11.9[6]	5.8[6]	...
Chile	3.5[12]	46.1[12]	75.1		12.0	12.9	2,940	27.9	15.2	22.5	...	...	...
China	5.5[13]	30.9[13]	21.6	72.2	6.2		260	49.9[16, 20]	6.8[20]	13.7[20]	2.9[20]	...	2.3[20]
Colombia	3.6[12]	39.5[12]	45.1	35.4	14.2	5.3	1,540	45.0	7.8	4.5	6.4	2.2	1.7
Comoros	...	...	*25.6*	*64.5*	*8.7*	*1.2*	350	67.3	2.3	11.6	3.2	3.8	[3]
Congo, Dem. Rep. of the	...	...	...	...	...	...	190	61.7	11.5[2]	9.7	2.6	[2]	[3]
Congo, Rep. of the	*7.0*	*43.5*	...	...	...	...	870	37.0	6.0	6.0	6.0	3.0	8.0
Costa Rica	4.0[12]	34.1[12]	61.0	22.6	9.6	6.8	1,600	39.1	12.1[2]	9.4	3.7	[2]	[3]
Côte d'Ivoire	6.8[1]	28.5[1]	44.9	49.9	5.2		480	48.0	7.8	10.0	0.7	8.5	...
Croatia	...	...	40.2	40.8	12.1	6.9	3,790	37.8	2.9	8.6	4.3	7.6	[3]
Cuba	...	...	57.3		42.7		1,510[9]	26.7	...	...	...	2.5	...
Cyprus	*7.9*[20]	...	76.3	5.9	14.4	3.4	8,300	22.7	5.5	10.0	3.1	1.3	1.4
Czech Republic	10.5[12, 21]	23.5[12, 21]	66.7		27.6	5.7	2,620	26.1	5.5[2]	7.3	[22]	[2]	...
Denmark	3.5	25.6	63.3	14.6	25.9	−3.8	17,730	17.9	22.9	5.2	2.2	6.1	1.9
Djibouti	...	...	*51.6*	*36.0*	*10.5*	*1.9*	590	50.3	6.4	1.7	2.4	13.1	...
Dominica	...	...	...	...	...	...	2,110	43.1	16.1	6.5	...	5.4	...
Dominican Republic	4.2[12]	39.6[12]	*41.7*	*31.8*	*1.5*	*25.0*	1,150	46.0	10.0	3.0	8.0	5.0	3.0
Ecuador	5.4[1]	37.6[1]	17.4	76.9	3.6	2.1	1,040	36.1	9.0	10.1	4.2	3.3	[19]
Egypt	8.7[1]	26.7[1]	...	...	...	...	740	50.2	10.5[2]	10.9	2.7	[2]	[3]

employed for collection, classification, and tabulation of data. Further, the reference period of the data varies greatly; while a significant portion of the data is from 1980 or later, information for some countries dates from the 1970s. This older information is typeset in italic. Finally, intercountry comparisons of annual personal consumption expenditure may be misleading because of the distortions of price and purchasing power present when converting a national currency unit into U.S. dollars.

The table's food consumption data include total daily available calories per capita (food supply), which amounts to domestic production and imports minus exports, animal feed, and nonfood uses, and a percentage breakdown of the major food groups that make up food supply.

The data for daily available calories per capita provide a measure of the nutritional adequacy of each nation's food supply. The following list, based on estimates from the United Nations Food and Agriculture Organization (FAO), indicates the regional variation in recommended daily minimum nutritional requirements, which are defined by factors such as climatic ambience, physical activity, and average body weight: Africa (2,320 calories), formerly Centrally Planned Asia (2,300 calories), Far East (2,240 calories), Latin America (2,360 calories), Near East (2,440 calories).

The breakdown of diet by food groups describes the character of a nation's food supply. A typical breakdown for a low-income country might show a diet with heavy intake of vegetable foods, such as cereals, potatoes, or cassava. In the high-income countries, a relatively larger portion of total calories derives from animal products (meat, eggs, and milk). The reader should note that these data refer to total national *supply* and often do not reflect the differences that may exist within a single country.

In compiling this table, Britannica editors rely on both numerous national reports and principal secondary sources such as the World Bank's *World Development Report* (annual), the International Labour Organisation's *Sources and Methods: Labour Statistics vol. 1 Consumer Price Indices* (3rd ed.), the UN's *Yearbook of National Accounts Statistics* (annual) and *National Accounts Statistics: Compendium of Income Distribution Statistics,* and the FAO's *Food Balance Sheets 1995* and *Compendium of Food Consumption Statistics from Household Surveys in Developing Countries* (2 vol.).

The following terms further define the column headings:

a. Includes pensions, family allowances, unemployment payments, remittances from abroad, and social security and related benefits.
b. Includes interest and dividends, rents and royalties, and all other income not reported under the three preceding categories.
c. Includes alcoholic and nonalcoholic beverages and meals away from home when identifiable. Excludes tobacco except as noted.
d. Rent, maintenance of dwellings, and taxes only; excludes energy and water (heat, light, power, and water) and household durables (furniture, appliances, utensils, and household operations), shown separately.
e. Includes footwear.
f. Furniture, appliances, and utensils; usually includes expenditure on household operation.
g. Includes expenditure on cultural activities other than education.
h. May include data not shown separately in preceding categories, including meals away from home (*see* note c).
i. Represents pure fats and oils only.
j. Consists mainly of peas, beans, and lentils; spices; stimulants; alcoholic beverages (when combined with "other"); sugars and honey; and nuts and oilseeds.

transportation, communications	household durable goods[f]	recreation[g]	personal effects, other[h]	food consumption, 1995: daily available calories per capita	percent of total calories derived from: cereals	potatoes, cassava	meat, poultry	fish	eggs, milk	fruits, vegetables	fats, oils[i]	other[j]	country
...	...	...	61.3	...	...	...	...	...	...	...	...	...	Afghanistan
...	...	...	...	2,324	38.6	1.8	8.7	—	22.9	5.8	10.2	11.9	Albania
12.0	4.5	4.6[3]	8.5	3,042	59.3	1.5	3.0	0.3	5.1	3.8	16.9	10.3	Algeria
17.8	[5]	1.1	22.6	...	...	...	...	...	...	...	...	...	American Samoa
...	...	...	...	...	...	...	...	...	...	...	...	...	Andorra
3.9[6]	...	...	1.8[6]	1,927	28.1	35.3	3.6	1.2	1.7	3.3	10.8	15.9	Angola
10.0	...	...	*10.8*	2,406	26.7	1.0	14.5	4.4	11.0	7.2	16.0	19.2	Antigua and Barbuda
11.6	...	7.5	5.9	3,110	30.6	3.7	16.3	0.4	10.2	4.2	14.8	19.8	Argentina
...	6.6	...	28.7	...	...	...	...	...	...	...	...	...	Armenia
15.5	9.1	3.1	11.9	...	...	...	...	...	...	...	...	...	Aruba
15.1	7.0	7.5	16.7	3,068	24.6	3.0	15.3	1.0	14.2	5.5	11.9	24.4	Australia
16.3	7.8	7.1	7.5	3,417	22.2	3.3	13.4	0.7	12.0	6.0	20.7	21.6	Austria
5.1	6.5	0.7	27.1	...	...	...	...	...	...	...	...	...	Azerbaijan
14.8	8.9	4.9	9.2	2,498	29.0	1.5	17.5	1.7	7.3	7.9	9.6	25.5	Bahamas, The
8.5	9.8	6.4	9.0	...	...	...	...	...	...	...	...	...	Bahrain
0.9	...	...	10.4	2,017	82.4	1.4	0.8	0.8	1.4	1.1	5.8	6.2	Bangladesh
10.5	8.1	4.8[3]	—	3,207	28.1	4.2	13.7	1.8	6.3	4.6	13.7	27.5	Barbados
...	...	...	68.3	...	...	...	...	...	...	...	...	...	Belarus
13.4	10.6	6.8[3]	15.8	3,530	21.2	5.4	9.9	1.2	9.3	6.3	26.2	20.5	Belgium
13.7	8.0	...	9.4	2,791	31.2	1.6	8.2	0.4	8.8	7.5	11.1	31.2	Belize
14.0	5.0	...	9.0	2,405	35.1	37.2	2.3	0.8	0.9	2.8	5.4	15.6	Benin
7.3	16.6	10.8	3.4	3,050	27.0	1.8	13.9	2.0	7.6	10.3	14.7	22.8	Bermuda
...	*0.7*	...	*2.1*	...	...	...	...	...	...	...	...	...	Bhutan
17.7	9.7	2.7	3.3	2,192	44.4	7.0	10.4	0.1	3.1	7.5	9.9	17.5	Bolivia
6.0	4.1	3.5[3]	2.3	...	...	...	...	...	...	...	...	...	Bosnia and Herzegovina
13.1	13.8	3.1	3.4	2,153	52.9	1.6	5.9	0.6	8.1	2.6	7.5	20.9	Botswana
15.0	...	...	16.4	2,834	31.4	5.5	9.4	0.3	7.5	5.2	13.1	27.6	Brazil
17.2	*8.3*	*8.9*[3]	*9.4*	2,849	43.6	1.2	14.2	1.0	6.1	4.6	7.4	22.0	Brunei
6.6	4.0	3.0[3]	21.5[17]	2,907	40.3	1.9	9.0	0.1	9.6	6.3	15.6	17.2	Bulgaria
18.6[6]	3.0[6]	2.3[3, 6]	9.0[6]	2,250	75.6	0.7	2.4	0.1	1.4	1.0	4.1	14.7	Burkina Faso
...	6.0[6]	...	13.1[6, 18]	1,749	17.0	27.4	1.3	0.4	0.7	9.9	1.3	41.9	Burundi
...	...	...	...	2,012	81.2	1.7	4.2	0.8	0.6	2.9	3.9	4.6	Cambodia
13.0	...	2.4	1.3	2,214	42.4	16.0	3.3	0.7	1.4	13.7	7.9	14.5	Cameroon
14.3	8.8	8.0	17.9	3,093	22.1	3.5	11.5	1.1	9.7	6.7	19.8	25.6	Canada
8.8	6.9	[19]	7.9[19]	3,031	48.6	1.9	7.5	0.8	4.5	2.6	17.1	16.9	Cape Verde
4.1[6]	0.8[6]	1.3[6]	5.7[6]	1,885	21.3	31.5	6.3	0.4	1.5	6.5	16.1	16.4	Central African Republic
...	...	...	33.5[6]	1,913	54.0	12.1	2.7	0.6	2.5	1.9	6.2	20.0	Chad
6.4	...	...	28.0	2,769	39.4	3.6	11.8	2.0	7.0	6.0	10.8	19.3	Chile
4.7[20]	5.3[20]	2.4[20]	12.0[20]	2,741	57.6	5.5	13.6	0.8	2.4	4.9	6.3	8.9	China
18.5	5.7	...	8.2	2,758	32.5	7.4	6.8	0.3	7.7	7.6	10.8	26.9	Colombia
2.2	3.0	2.5[3]	4.1	1,850	44.3	15.4	1.9	3.0	1.1	8.3	9.4	16.6	Comoros
5.9	4.8	3.8[3]	—	1,879	16.6	55.3	1.9	0.5	0.1	7.8	6.7	11.2	Congo, Dem. Rep. of the
15.0	4.0	...	15.0	2,141	22.3	39.3	3.4	2.7	1.1	7.5	11.6	12.2	Congo, Rep. of the
11.6	10.9	4.4[3]	8.8	2,865	34.4	1.3	6.7	0.3	9.3	5.8	13.6	28.6	Costa Rica
12.2	3.4	...	9.4	2,517	41.5	26.1	2.0	1.0	0.8	10.0	7.4	11.3	Côte d'Ivoire
9.3	4.5	4.1[3]	1.5	2,413	30.2	7.0	5.9	0.2	12.0	6.8	12.8	24.9	Croatia
5.4	...	...	65.4	2,291	36.5	5.9	5.3	0.6	7.9	4.0	13.1	26.8	Cuba
15.6	10.5	6.3	23.6	3,708	24.1	2.1	20.6	0.8	12.5	6.4	15.3	18.2	Cyprus
3.1	4.5	0.8[22]	52.7	3,175	26.7	4.7	11.7	0.4	10.6	4.3	19.4	22.2	Czech Republic
15.5	6.1	8.3	13.9	3,704	21.7	3.2	22.5	2.1	9.1	3.8	15.4	22.2	Denmark
...	1.5	...	24.6	1,831	48.6	0.3	5.1	0.2	6.0	1.8	15.7	22.3	Djibouti
11.6	6.0	...	11.3	3,032	27.2	7.8	9.9	1.6	9.1	9.8	8.6	26.0	Dominica
4.0	8.0	...	13.0	2,323	31.4	3.2	7.3	0.7	6.4	10.2	16.0	24.8	Dominican Republic
12.8	5.5	[19]	19.0[19]	2,436	32.4	3.0	6.4	0.7	7.0	9.4	22.7	18.3	Ecuador
4.7	5.0	3.3[3]	12.7	3,327	66.3	1.6	2.4	0.4	1.8	6.2	7.7	13.7	Egypt

Household budgets and consumption (continued)

country	income (latest)						consumption expenditure						
	percent received by		by source (percent)				per capita private final, U.S.$ 1995	by kind or end use (percent of household or personal budget; latest)					
	lowest 20% of households	highest 10% of households	wages, salaries	self-employment	transfer payments[a]	other[b]		food[c]	housing[d]	clothing[e]	health care	energy, water	education
El Salvador	*5.5*[13]	*29.5*[13]	...	...	...	...	1,520	37.0[20]	12.1[20]	6.7[20]	4.2[20]	3.6[20]	3.7[20]
Equatorial Guinea	...	...	57.0[6]	42.0[6]	—	1.0[6]	310	62.0[6]	...	10.0[6]	6.0[6]	...	...
Eritrea[23]	...	...	...	...	...	...	170	...	...	...	...	...	...
Estonia	6.6[12]	31.3[12]	53.0	5.7	12.8	28.5	1,390	41.0	9.6	8.4	[22]	6.5	3.1
Ethiopia[23]	8.6[1]	27.5[1]	0.2	79.5	—	20.3	87	49.0	7.0	6.0	3.0	7.0	4.0
Faroe Islands	...	...	88.3	11.7	—	—	...	40.9	11.0	8.0	...	18.9	...
Fiji	*3.7*	*37.8*	*81.5*	*9.1*	—	*9.4*	1,430[11]	34.7	15.6[2]	9.3	2.4	[2]	[3]
Finland	3.7	26.9	70.3	7.4	9.7	12.6	13,260	22.5	16.9	5.0	4.8	4.6	[3]
France	5.6	26.1	51.1	14.1	27.5	7.3	15,810	17.4	16.2	6.1	9.8	3.8	0.7
French Guiana	...	...	74.6		—25.4—		...	30.0[16]	16.1[2]	6.7	4.4	[2]	[3]
French Polynesia	...	...	61.9	18.5	16.6	3.0	4,310[24]	39.6	9.7	6.3	1.0	8.1	1.0
Gabon	*3.3*	*54.4*	...	...	...	...	4,060	54.7[6, 16, 25]	13.0[6, 25]	17.5[6, 25]	1.9[6, 25]	...	...
Gambia, The	...	...	...	...	...	...	330	58.0[26]	5.1[26]	17.5[26]	...	5.4[26]	...
Gaza Strip	...	...	...	...	...	...	910[27]	...	...	...	...	...	...
Georgia	...	...	34.5	21.6[7]	21.7	22.0	430	38.3	...	14.8	...	0.3	...
Germany	7.0[28]	24.4[28]	57.9	[8]	21.3	20.8[8]	16,850	19.0	16.9	7.9	3.5	4.1	[3]
Ghana	7.9[1]	27.3[1]	41.6[29]	47.1[29]	—	11.3[29]	290	*57.4*	*11.5*[2]	*14.3*	*1.3*	[2]	[3]
Gibraltar	...	...	...	...	...	...	...	39.1[16]	12.6	11.0	...	...	...
Greece	...	...	34.0	22.8	17.0	26.2	8,140	29.9	14.1	6.5	3.1	3.3	0.5
Greenland	...	...	...	...	...	...	11,110	30.1	10.0	7.7	0.3	5.4	...
Grenada	...	...	...	...	...	...	1,650	40.7[16]	11.9	5.2	[30]	3.9	[3]
Guadeloupe	...	...	78.9	13.7	7.4	—	4,080[27]	31.6[16]	11.3[2]	9.3	4.6	[2]	[3]
Guam	...	...	...	...	...	...	...	*24.1*	*28.6*	*10.6*	*4.8*	...	...
Guatemala	2.1[12]	46.6[12]	...	...	...	...	1,180	64.4	16.0[2]	3.1	0.6	[2]	0.3
Guernsey	...	...	...	...	...	...	...	23.7	12.1	7.5	...	8.2	...
Guinea	3.0[1]	31.7[1]	...	...	...	...	510	*61.5*	*7.3*[2]	*7.9*	*11.1*	[2]	...
Guinea-Bissau	2.1[1]	42.4[1]	...	...	...	...	230	...	...	...	...	...	...
Guyana	4.0	40.0[11]	*73.0*	...	*6.3*	*20.7*	...	*42.5*[16]	*21.4*	*8.6*	...	*5.2*	[3]
Haiti	...	...	...	...	...	...	320	51.1[16]	4.3	8.7	2.2	...	[3]
Honduras	3.8[12]	41.9[12]	58.3	[8]	1.8	39.9[8]	450	44.4	22.4[2]	9.1	7.0	[2]	[3]
Hong Kong	5.4[21]	31.3[21]	...	...	...	...	13,880	15.1	15.7[2]	21.3	5.0	[2]	0.5
Hungary	9.5[1]	22.6[1]	—55.0—		19.2	5.8	4,270	38.1	5.7	7.4	1.5	6.1	0.7
Iceland	4.7	27.3	73.1	2.7	10.2	14.0	15,850	31.3	16.0	7.5	2.3	2.9	1.3
India	8.5[1]	28.4[1]	42.2	39.7	—18.1—		210	52.2	6.1[31]	10.0	2.4	4.7[31]	1.8
Indonesia	8.7[1]	25.6[1]	*42.1*	*41.5*	*2.5*	*13.9*	640	47.5[20]	20.1[2, 20]	5.5[20]	...	[2]	...
Iran	*3.8*	*41.7*	37.4[20]	30.5[20]	—32.1[20]—		1,040	42.6[16]	24.9[2]	11.8	3.9	[2]	[3]
Iraq	*2.1*	...	23.9	33.9	23.0	18.6	1,710[14]	50.2	19.9[2]	10.6	1.6	[2]	[3]
Ireland	4.6	26.5	58.6	13.3	19.9	8.2	9,650	30.5	7.1	7.4	3.2	6.1	2.4
Isle of Man	6.4	26.6	64.1	6.6	16.9	12.4	...	31.0	7.9	7.0	...	11.0	...
Israel	8.4	23.1	63.4[20, 25]	14.6[20, 25]	18.9[20, 25]	3.1[20, 25]	9,930	23.8	19.8	5.3	6.2	2.4	2.9
Italy	6.8	25.3	41.7	25.9	20.3	12.1	11,860	19.5	10.0	9.8	6.7	3.8	0.7
Jamaica	5.8[1]	31.9[1]	63.6	13.9	14.0	8.5	1,770	35.7	5.7	4.6	2.8	4.9	0.2
Japan	10.9	31.6[11]	59.3	11.1	19.5	10.1	24,670	22.6	6.7	6.0	2.7	5.6	5.3
Jersey	...	...	...	...	...	...	...	*28.3*	*14.9*	*8.3*	...	*6.5*	...
Jordan	5.9[1]	34.7[1]	51.4	11.1	13.7	23.8	1,020	40.6	15.8	6.7	2.2	5.0	3.5
Kazakstan	7.5[12]	24.9[12]	67.7	5.8[7]	16.9	9.6	1,290	29.6	2.6	...	...	...	...
Kenya	3.4	47.7	...	...	...	...	220	46.5	10.0	7.7	2.2	2.6	1.0
Kiribati	...	...	*69.7*	*21.4*	*6.0*	*2.9*	370[4]	50.0[16]	7.5[2, 5]	8.0	...	[2]	...
Korea, North	...	...	...	...	...	...	...	46.5[32]	0.6[32]	29.9[32]	...	3.3[32]	...
Korea, South	7.4	27.6	53.8	25.1	13.1	8.0	5,390	29.7	4.1	7.7	5.0	4.0	14.2
Kuwait	...	...	*53.8*	*20.8*	*—25.4—*		...	28.1[16]	15.5	8.1	0.7	9.6	[3]
Kyrgyzstan	3.0	57.0[11]	67.3		—32.7—		670	33.5	2.2	...	...	...	...
Laos	9.6[1]	26.4[1]	...	...	...	...	140[9]	...	...	...	...	...	...
Latvia	9.6[12]	22.1[12]	67.0	5.4[7]	17.4	10.2	2,400	51.6	...	...	...	...	...
Lebanon	*5.0*	*45.0*	*27.9*	...	*3.0*	*69.1*	3,010	*42.8*[6]	*16.8*[6]	*8.6*[6]	*7.2*[6]	*4.5*[6]	*3.9*[6]
Lesotho	2.8[1]	43.4[1]	22.4	27.8	44.7	5.1	530	48.0[20]	10.1	16.4	...	...	...
Liberia	5.0	73.0[11]	...	...	...	...	330[9]	*34.4*[6]	*14.9*[6]	*13.8*[6]	...	*5.0*[6]	...
Libya	*10.1*	...	...	...	...	...	2,330[9]	*37.2*[16]	*32.2*[2]	*6.9*	*3.3*	[2]	[3]
Liechtenstein	...	...	92.9[33]	7.1[33]	...	...	...	21.3[16]	18.0	6.6	7.7	4.4	[3]
Lithuania	8.1[12]	28.0[12]	66.4	9.7	18.7	5.2	1,910	50.3	...	...	...	...	...
Luxembourg	10.0	34.0[11]	67.1	4.8	28.1	—	15,140[34]	12.8	13.7	5.9	7.3	6.1	[3]
Macau	...	...	65.0	18.1	7.0	9.9	5,480	39.2[16]	17.5	6.8	4.0	5.2	[3]
Macedonia	...	...	57.7	17.2	16.2	9.0	1,010	40.6	1.9	7.8	3.0	7.8	[3]
Madagascar	5.8[1]	34.9[1]	*58.8*[6, 35]	*14.1*[6, 35]	—	*27.1*[6, 35]	220	59.0	6.0	6.0	2.0	6.0	4.0
Malaŵi	*10.4*	*40.1*	83.3	6.0	—	11.7	109	30.0	4.0	9.0	4.0	5.0	10.0
Malaysia	4.6[12]	37.9[12]	...	...	...	...	2,090	28.7	10.2[2]	4.3	2.5	[2]	0.6
Maldives	...	...	...	...	...	...	270[9]	57.4	1.6	8.0	2.5	...	[3]
Mali	...	...	...	...	...	...	200	57.0	2.0	6.0	2.0	6.0	4.0
Malta	...	...	63.8	19.3	—	16.9	5,380	31.2	3.5	7.6	3.5	2.0	0.4
Marshall Islands	...	...	...	...	...	...	...	57.7	15.6[2, 5]	12.0	...	[2]	...
Martinique	...	...	80.0	...	...	20.0	4,840[6]	32.1[16]	10.6[2]	8.0	5.2	[2]	[3]
Mauritania	3.6[1]	30.4[1]	...	...	...	...	470	73.1	2.5	8.1	0.9	7.7	0.4
Mauritius	4.0	46.7	51.7	29.0	11.2	8.1	2,290	41.9	8.8	8.4	3.0	6.4	2.9
Mayotte	...	...	...	...	...	...	...	42.2	...	31.5	...	6.8	...
Mexico	4.1[1]	39.2[1]	61.5	29.1	7.8	1.6	2,110	36.6[16]	13.3[2]	8.4	3.4	[2]	[3]
Micronesia	...	...	51.8	23.0	2.1	23.1	...	73.5	...	...	...	...	...
Moldova	6.9[12]	25.8[12]	41.2	10.4	15.3	33.1	220	...	...	...	...	...	...
Monaco	...	...	...	...	...	...	...	...	...	...	...	...	...
Mongolia	...	...	72.1	9.5[7]	9.7	8.7	230	39.1	5.9[2]	23.4	0.5	[2]	2.9
Morocco	6.6[1]	30.5[1]	...	...	...	...	900	38.0	7.0	11.0	5.0	2.0	8.0
Mozambique	...	...	51.6		—48.4—		57	74.6	11.7	3.7	0.8	...	[3]
Myanmar (Burma)	*8.0*	40.0[11]	...	...	...	...	750[34]	*49.1*[6]	*10.4*[6]	*15.3*[6]	*2.4*[6]	*4.0*[6]	*5.9*[6]
Namibia	...	...	67.1	27.5	5.4	...	1,050	...	...	...	...	...	...
Nauru	...	...	...	...	...	...	...	...	...	...	...	...	...
Nepal	7.6[1]	29.8[1]	25.1	63.4	—11.5—		170	61.2	17.3	11.7	3.7	...	[3]

				food consumption, 1995									country
				daily available calories per capita	percent of total calories derived from:								
transportation, communications	household durable goods[f]	recreation[g]	personal effects, other[h]		cereals	potatoes, cassava	meat, poultry	fish	eggs, milk	fruits, vegetables	fats, oils[i]	other[j]	
10.2[20]	5.7[20]	4.3[20]	12.5[20]	2,577	55.9	2.0	2.7	0.2	6.0	3.2	7.7	22.4	El Salvador
...	...	...	22.0[6]	...	...	...	...	...	...	...	...	...	Equatorial Guinea
...	...	...	...	...	...	...	...	...	...	...	...	...	Eritrea[23]
9.2	2.3	5.0[22]	15.0	...	...	...	...	...	...	...	...	...	Estonia
8.0	2.0	...	14.0	...	...	...	...	...	...	...	...	...	Ethiopia[23]
...	6.6	...	14.6	...	...	...	...	...	...	...	...	...	Faroe Islands
13.8	9.3	4.3[3]	10.6	3,078	38.1	5.6	8.8	2.0	3.9	1.7	17.2	22.7	Fiji
14.8	6.3	9.5[3]	15.6	3,022	21.2	4.3	16.4	2.1	16.1	4.1	14.2	21.4	Finland
16.1	7.7	6.9	15.3	3,588	23.7	3.6	15.9	1.1	12.7	5.3	19.4	18.2	France
17.5	7.9	6.2[3]	11.2	2,818	32.4	7.9	13.2	2.1	7.5	7.0	10.5	19.3	French Guiana
16.4	4.4	4.0	9.5	2,906	33.6	4.6	14.2	2.6	6.7	3.8	13.2	21.3	French Polynesia
6.3[6, 25]	...	...	6.6[6, 25]	2,511	26.0	20.3	8.2	2.7	2.1	16.3	7.6	16.8	Gabon
...	...	...	14.0[26]	2,157	53.5	0.8	1.4	1.6	1.5	1.3	13.0	26.9	Gambia, The
...	...	...	...	...	...	...	...	...	...	...	...	...	Gaza Strip
...	5.9	...	40.7	...	...	...	...	...	...	...	...	...	Georgia
17.8	9.4	10.6[3]	10.8	3,265	20.9	4.2	11.3	0.9	10.4	5.7	22.1	24.5	Germany
3.3	*3.8*	*3.9*[3]	*4.5*	2,622	28.4	45.6	1.4	1.9	0.2	8.9	5.6	8.0	Ghana
13.3	10.0	...	14.0	...	...	...	...	...	...	...	...	...	Gibraltar
17.5	6.9	5.2	13.0	3,561	29.0	4.2	8.7	1.1	10.8	9.1	20.4	16.7	Greece
8.0	9.2	15.5	13.8	...	...	...	...	...	...	...	...	...	Greenland
9.1	13.7	4.6[3]	10.9[30]	2,713	27.9	2.4	7.6	3.1	9.7	8.1	13.3	28.0	Grenada
20.5	9.3	4.7[3]	8.7	2,732	37.8	2.6	10.8	2.6	8.5	8.4	13.1	16.1	Guadeloupe
18.0	...	*5.1*	*8.8*	...	...	...	...	...	...	...	...	...	Guam
7.0	5.0	0.9	2.7	2,300	60.3	0.4	2.8	0.1	3.8	2.6	5.2	24.9	Guatemala
15.7	8.3	...	24.7	...	...	...	...	...	...	...	...	...	Guernsey
5.1	*2.9*	*4.1*	*0.1*	2,161	46.7	13.3	0.9	0.6	1.1	13.1	13.9	10.3	Guinea
...	...	...	...	2,433	63.2	6.2	4.5	0.4	1.4	3.7	14.7	5.8	Guinea-Bissau
4.8	*2.9*	*6.4*[3]	*8.2*	2,460	50.1	4.6	4.4	3.0	4.7	4.4	4.5	24.4	Guyana
7.6	9.2	5.3[3]	11.6	...	...	...	...	...	...	...	...	...	Haiti
3.0	8.3	2.4[3]	3.1	2,359	48.5	0.3	2.7	—	6.8	6.7	12.5	22.5	Honduras
8.4	17.5	8.1	8.4	3,285	31.1	1.6	20.3	3.0	5.2	4.7	17.9	16.2	Hong Kong
15.2	8.8	5.9	10.6	3,302	27.0	3.4	10.5	0.2	8.6	4.0	23.1	23.0	Hungary
14.5	7.6	9.6	7.0	3,159	24.1	3.0	14.4	6.1	13.9	4.0	10.4	24.3	Iceland
10.6	3.1	1.8	5.7	2,388	62.1	1.8	0.9	0.3	4.6	3.7	8.2	18.6	India
...	2.9[20]	...	24.0	2,732	63.7	6.2	2.3	1.2	0.7	2.5	8.4	15.0	Indonesia
5.0	6.4	1.7[3]	3.7	2,955	59.2	2.6	3.5	0.3	3.4	8.0	11.2	11.8	Iran
6.5	6.7	0.8[3]	3.7	2,268	51.2	1.4	1.6	0.1	1.6	8.6	27.4	8.1	Iraq
14.0	7.2	8.9	13.1	3,638	27.3	6.0	12.8	0.9	12.1	3.7	16.2	21.1	Ireland
14.9	5.7	...	22.5	...	...	...	...	...	...	...	...	...	Isle of Man
12.9	10.8	4.3	11.6	3,271	34.2	2.3	8.3	0.9	8.7	9.0	16.8	19.7	Israel
13.2	9.5	8.4	18.4	3,458	33.0	2.0	11.6	1.1	8.6	7.0	20.9	15.8	Italy
12.4	5.5	2.1	26.1	2,647	32.8	11.0	6.4	1.2	5.8	6.6	9.7	26.5	Jamaica
11.0	3.7	9.5	26.9	2,887	40.0	2.4	6.2	6.3	6.6	4.6	11.0	22.9	Japan
13.9	*7.1*	...	*21.0*	...	...	...	...	...	...	...	...	...	Jersey
11.2	6.1	4.0	4.9	2,734	47.0	1.5	5.4	0.3	4.6	5.5	16.1	19.6	Jordan
...	...	...	67.8	...	...	...	...	...	...	...	...	...	Kazakstan
8.4	9.4	3.1	9.1	1,991	52.9	7.7	3.8	0.5	7.0	3.1	9.3	15.6	Kenya
8.0	[5]	...	26.5	2,772	36.2	8.5	5.3	5.1	1.3	4.8	7.9	30.9	Kiribati
...	3.8[32]	...	15.9	2,360	62.1	5.4	3.7	3.3	1.2	6.2	5.7	12.4	Korea, North
11.3	5.0	——19.0——		3,268	47.6	0.9	8.6	2.8	2.0	6.7	10.3	21.1	Korea, South
13.7	11.2	5.2[3]	7.9	3,160	35.6	1.3	11.0	0.5	10.5	7.7	13.8	19.7	Kuwait
...	...	...	64.3	...	...	...	...	...	...	...	...	...	Kyrgyzstan
...	...	...	...	2,117	75.6	4.2	3.5	0.6	1.7	2.3	2.1	9.9	Laos
...	...	...	54.8	...	...	...	...	...	...	...	...	...	Latvia
5.4[6]	*2.6*[6]	*1.9*[6]	*6.3*[6]	3,270	34.6	3.6	4.6	—	5.8	14.2	15.7	21.3	Lebanon
4.7	11.9	...	8.8	1,972	73.2	4.8	4.4	0.4	1.4	1.6	3.7	10.5	Lesotho
...	*6.1*[6]	...	*25.8*[6]	...	...	...	...	...	...	...	...	...	Liberia
9.4	*4.6*	*8.5*[3]	*2.5*	3,126	47.8	1.5	4.0	0.3	4.6	5.5	23.2	13.1	Libya
13.3	5.8	16.3[3]	6.6	...	...	...	...	...	...	...	...	...	Liechtenstein
...	...	...	49.7	...	...	...	...	...	...	...	...	...	Lithuania
19.1	10.8	4.2[3]	20.1	3,530	21.2	5.4	9.9	1.2	9.3	6.3	26.2	20.5	Luxembourg
8.2	3.0	8.8[3]	7.3	3,094	37.7	0.6	14.8	2.0	4.6	4.8	17.7	17.8	Macau
6.5	4.2	3.3[3]	1.8	2,340	44.1	3.3	8.6	0.2	6.0	7.8	9.8	20.2	Macedonia
4.0	1.0	...	12.0	2,009	55.8	20.9	5.2	0.6	2.9	3.5	3.9	7.2	Madagascar
10.0	3.0	...	25.0	2,038	68.4	4.3	1.3	0.6	0.6	4.9	3.4	16.5	Malawi
20.9	7.7	11.0	14.1	2,807	40.3	2.4	9.6	1.5	6.2	3.8	13.1	23.1	Malaysia
2.6	17.0	5.9[3]	5.0	2,485	41.3	3.5	1.8	10.9	4.2	5.7	5.7	26.9	Maldives
10.0	1.0	...	12.0	2,149	76.1	0.3	3.8	0.6	4.1	0.8	7.4	7.0	Mali
16.4	9.9	7.1	18.4	3,387	29.0	3.7	8.9	1.2	11.0	7.9	13.7	24.5	Malta
...	[5]	...	14.7	...	...	...	...	...	...	...	...	...	Marshall Islands
20.7	9.4	5.4[3]	8.6	2,865	30.0	4.2	12.1	2.9	8.5	11.0	8.7	22.5	Martinique
2.0	1.2	4.0	0.1	2,592	53.6	0.4	4.2	0.9	11.1	2.4	11.9	15.4	Mauritania
10.0	6.4	—	12.2	2,943	45.8	1.3	4.6	2.0	7.6	2.5	16.7	19.5	Mauritius
5.1	8.8	...	5.6	...	...	...	...	...	...	...	...	...	Mayotte
10.0	11.8	5.5[3]	11.0	3,136	46.2	0.8	7.5	0.6	5.9	4.1	11.0	23.9	Mexico
...	...	...	26.5	...	...	...	...	...	...	...	...	...	Micronesia
...	...	...	...	...	...	...	...	...	...	...	...	...	Moldova
...	...	...	...	...	...	...	...	...	...	...	...	...	Monaco
3.5	8.0	0.4	16.2	1,897	46.4	1.2	26.3	0.1	9.0	0.5	5.9	10.6	Mongolia
8.0	5.0	...	16.0	3,157	62.6	1.2	2.7	0.5	2.0	4.3	12.3	14.4	Morocco
...	...	1.4[3]	7.9	1,678	41.8	35.6	1.7	0.2	0.7	1.5	9.7	8.8	Mozambique
3.8[6]	*0.5*[6]	*1.1*[6]	*7.5*[6]	2,752	77.6	0.4	1.8	0.9	1.1	2.3	8.9	7.2	Myanmar (Burma)
...	...	...	...	2,107	48.6	13.9	5.6	0.6	3.4	1.9	5.1	20.9	Namibia
...	...	...	...	...	...	...	...	...	...	...	...	...	Nauru
1.2	...	2.9[3]	2.0	2,367	77.9	2.9	1.4	—	3.2	2.6	5.5	6.5	Nepal

Household budgets and consumption (continued)

country	income (latest)						consumption expenditure						
	percent received by		by source (percent)				per capita private final, U.S.$ 1995	by kind or end use (percent of household or personal budget; latest)					
	lowest 20% of households	highest 10% of households	wages, salaries	self-employment	transfer payments[a]	other[b]		food[c]	housing[d]	clothing[e]	health care	energy, water	education
Netherlands, The	8.2	21.9	48.2	10.7	29.1	12.0	15,290	13.6	14.9	7.1	12.9	3.1	0.7
Netherlands Antilles	...	...	...	...	...	...	6,050[10]	24.4[36]	10.4[36]	8.7[36]	2.2[36]	8.3[36]	1.2[36]
New Caledonia	...	...	68.2	18.1	13.7	...	5,410[37]	25.9	23.3[2, 5]	3.5	3.2	[2]	...
New Zealand	5.1[21]	28.7[21]	65.8	9.8	15.2	9.1	10,300	20.0	19.4	4.4	2.9	3.2	1.5
Nicaragua	4.2[1, 38]	39.8[1, 11]	...	...	...	...	360	...	...	...	...	...	...
Niger	7.5[1]	29.3[1]	...	...	...	...	210	50.5	19.1[5]	7.3	...	...	...
Nigeria	4.0[1]	31.3[1, 11]	30.2[20]	46.3[20]	0.9[20]	22.6[20]	350[39]	48.0	3.0	5.0	3.0	1.0	4.0
Northern Mariana Islands	...	...	...	...	...	...	...	49.2[16]	19.5[2, 5]	9.1	[22]	[2]	...
Norway	2.6	26.6	58.8	9.9	24.2	7.1	16,570	23.5	13.7	7.0	5.4	6.2	0.6
Oman	...	...	...	...	...	...	3,000	40.6	24.6	5.1	2.4	3.2	[3]
Pakistan	8.4[1]	25.2[1]	22.0	56.0	——22.0——		300	37.0	11.0	6.0	1.0	5.0	1.0
Palau	...	...	63.7	7.4	18.5	10.4	...	...	...	...	...	...	...
Panama	2.0[12]	42.2[12]	60.8[6]	12.8[6]	13.2[6]	13.2[6]	1,570	34.9	12.6[2]	5.1	3.5	[2]	[3]
Papua New Guinea	...	...	*57.3*	[8]	*1.1*	*41.6*[8]	1,140	40.9	12.5[5]	6.2	...	4.9	...
Paraguay	6.0	46.0[11]	33.9	[8]	2.5	63.6[8]	1,590	48.7	16.4	9.7	3.4	—	1.5
Peru	4.9[1]	34.3[1]	31.2	65.1	3.7	...	1,820	44.1[16]	6.8[2]	10.1	2.7	[2]	[3]
Philippines	6.5[1]	32.1[1]	45.7	42.5	3.4	8.4	800	56.8	4.1[2]	3.9	...	[2]	...
Poland	9.3[1]	22.1[1]	34.0	4.3	20.7	41.0	1,940	41.2	2.8	10.9	8.1	1.0	[3]
Portugal	*5.2*	*33.4*	46.4	[8]	21.8	31.8[8]	6,860	34.8	2.0	10.3	4.5	3.0	1.4
Puerto Rico	*3.2*	*34.7*	56.3	6.4	29.5	7.8	5,640[10]	20.6	11.8[2]	7.4	11.6	[2]	3.1
Qatar	...	...	80.8	5.6	...	13.6	3,600[4]	24.5	35.1[5]	9.1	1.0	1.9	4.3
Réunion	*3.1*[21]	*51.4*[21]	68.9	[8]	16.0	15.1[8]	4,820[37]	22.4	11.8	7.9	2.2	2.2	[3]
Romania	9.2[12]	20.2[12]	62.6		——37.4——		1,570	51.1	16.4[2, 5]	15.7	1.2	[2]	[3]
Russia	3.7[1]	38.7[1]	68.5	6.4	15.7	12.1	1,180	34.8	2.7	22.3	...	...	...
Rwanda	9.7[1]	24.2[1]	10.4[38]	47.7[38]	13.9[38]	28.0[38]	130	32.1[38]	13.1[38]	9.4[38]	1.3[38]	1.2[38]	[38]
St. Kitts and Nevis	...	...	...	...	...	...	2,480[34]	*55.6*[16]	*7.6*	*7.5*	...	*6.6*	...
St. Lucia	...	...	...	...	...	...	...	49.6[16]	13.5	6.5	2.3	4.5	[3]
St. Vincent and the Grenadines	...	...	...	...	...	...	1,700	59.8	6.3	7.7	...	6.2	...
Samoa	...	...	*49.4*	*22.8*	...	*27.8*	710[1]	58.8	5.1[5]	4.2	...	5.0	...
San Marino	...	...	...	...	...	...	...	22.1	20.9[2]	8.0	2.6	[2]	[3]
São Tomé and Príncipe	...	...	...	...	...	...	270	...	...	...	...	...	...
Saudi Arabia	...	...	...	...	...	...	2,980	52.2[20, 40]	17.2[20, 40]	6.6[20, 40]	2.1[20, 40]	1.8[20, 40]	1.1[20, 40]
Senegal	3.5[1]	42.8[1]	51.6[6]		——48.4[6]——		380	49.0	7.0	11.0	2.0	4.0	6.0
Seychelles	4.1	35.6	*77.2*	*3.8*	*3.2*	*15.8*	3,410[39]	53.9	13.6	4.2	0.4	9.1	...
Sierra Leone	*5.6*	*37.8*	27.9	61.6	——10.5——		190	63.8	5.8[2]	7.3	4.5	[2]	[3]
Singapore	5.1	33.5	81.2	16.8	——2.0——		11,710	18.7	10.2[2]	7.1	4.6	[2]	1.4
Slovakia	11.9[12]	18.2[11, 12]	76.7	[8]	8.7	14.4[8]	1,580	26.8	7.6[2]	8.9	...	[2]	...
Slovenia	9.5[12]	23.8[12]	52.4	13.0	23.4	11.2	5,460	30.8	18.3	8.5	5.0	7.3	[3]
Solomon Islands	...	...	74.1		——25.9——		820[4]	46.8	21.9[2, 5]	5.7	[22]	[2]	...
Somalia	...	...	...	...	...	...	17[1]	62.3[6, 16]	15.3[6]	5.6[6]	...	4.3[6]	...
South Africa	3.3[1]	47.3[1, 11]	73.6	[8]	4.9	21.5[8]	1,970	29.3	12.6[2]	7.5	4.5	[2]	1.4
Spain	8.3[13]	21.8[13]	48.5	27.5	19.5	4.5	8,840	21.6[16]	12.6[2]	8.6	4.7	[2]	[3]
Sri Lanka	8.9[1]	25.2[1]	48.5	[8]	9.7	41.8[8]	520	48.0	1.9	10.1	1.8	3.3	0.8
Sudan, The	*4.0*	*34.6*	...	...	...	...	1,050[41]	63.6	11.5	5.3	4.1	3.8	[3]
Suriname	*9.3*	...	*74.6*	...	*3.2*	*22.2*	5,960[10]	*39.9*[6]	*4.4*[6]	*11.0*[6]	*3.6*[6]	*6.9*[6]	*2.6*[6]
Swaziland	*2.8*	*54.5*	44.4	22.2	12.2	21.2	500	33.5[16]	13.4[2]	6.0	1.8	[2]	[3]
Sweden	5.3	18.6	58.9	9.7	25.8	5.6	13,680	21.3	19.9	8.6	3.2	4.9	0.1
Switzerland	6.0[42]	27.0[42]	63.6	[8]	16.5	19.9[8]	26,060	27.0[16]	13.1	4.4	9.9	7.7	[3]
Syria	*6.0*	...	40.7	...	25.1	34.2	2,210	58.8[16]	16.0[2]	7.5	...	[2]	[3]
Taiwan	7.1	25.5	64.5	19.7	4.5	11.3	12,230	26.8	22.5	5.6	7.8	3.0	5.6
Tajikistan	...	...	64.3	5.6[9]	30.1	—	340	65.3	...	...	...	...	...
Tanzania	6.9[1]	30.2[1]	28.1	34.2	3.5	34.2	150	66.7	8.3	9.9	1.3	7.6	...
Thailand	5.6[1]	37.1[1]	36.4	45.0	0.9	17.7	1,540	29.0	6.3	11.6	8.0	1.7	0.5
Togo	*8.0*	*30.5*	...	...	...	...	210	42.5[6]	13.4[2, 6]	11.5[6]	5.0[6]	[2, 6]	[3, 6]
Tonga	...	...	...	...	...	...	...	49.3	10.5	5.6	0.3	2.7	...
Trinidad and Tobago	*2.6*	*33.6*	...	...	...	...	2,050	25.5[16]	21.6	10.4	[19]	...	1.5
Tunisia	5.9[1]	30.7[1]	...	...	...	...	1,260	39.0	10.7	6.0	3.0	5.1	1.8
Turkey	11.9	39.0[11]	24.1	51.4	10.8	13.7	1,940	38.5	22.8[2]	9.0	2.6	[2]	1.4
Turkmenistan	6.7[12]	26.9[12]	56.6	26.0[7]	14.4	3.0	570[10]	...	...	...	...	...	...
Tuvalu	...	...	*17.9*	*76.1*	...	*6.0*	...	45.5	11.5[5]	7.5	...	...	...
Uganda	6.8[1]	33.4[1]	...	...	...	...	260	57.1[6, 16]	...	5.5[6]	...	7.3[6]	...
Ukraine	9.5[12]	20.8[12]	66.4	9.3	13.4	10.9	490	41.3	1.7	...	...	...	[3]
United Arab Emirates	...	...	...	...	...	...	7,940	24.1	23.7	9.1	1.1	1.2	3.9
United Kingdom	4.6[13]	27.8[13]	66.2	9.8	13.9	11.0	12,020	17.1	21.7	6.0	...	4.6	...
United States	4.2	46.9[11]	64.4	9.0	19.3	7.3	18,840	15.4	14.9	6.9	17.0	3.5	2.2
Uruguay	6.0[13, 18]	29.3[13, 18]	53.5	17.0	——29.5——		4,140	39.9	17.6[2]	7.0	9.3	[2]	1.3
Uzbekistan	...	...	59.8	18.5	21.7	...	950	...	...	...	...	...	...
Vanuatu	...	...	59.0	33.7	——7.3——		680	30.5[16]	29.0[2, 5]	4.7	[22]	[2]	...
Venezuela	3.6[12]	42.7[12]	...	...	...	...	2,490	30.4	11.5	10.6	2.9	3.0	0.8
Vietnam	7.8[1]	29.0[1, 11]	17.2	64.6	17.6	0.5	280	62.4	2.5	5.0	...	...	2.9
Virgin Islands (U.S.)	...	...	65.7	2.6	13.0	12.7	...	25.3[43]	*24.9*[43]	*5.4*[43]	...	*6.5*[43]	...
West Bank	...	...	...	...	...	...	1,380[27]	...	...	...	...	...	...
Western Sahara	...	...	...	...	...	...	...	...	...	...	...	...	...
Yemen	...	...	...	...	...	...	310	61.0[44]	13.2[44]	...	1.1[44]	6.1[44]	...
Yugoslavia	5.3[12, 45]	27.4[12, 45]	41.7	15.8	12.7	29.8	2,480[41]	51.6	1.4	7.4	5.2	8.4	[3]
Zambia	3.9[1]	31.3[1]	79.9	17.8	1.3	1.0	220	36.0	7.0	10.0	8.0	4.0	14.0
Zimbabwe	4.0[1]	46.9[1]	92.0	1.0	...	7.0	580	30.1[16]	6.5	10.3	7.1	8.9	6.0

[1]Data refer to expenditure by fractiles of persons. [2]Housing includes energy, water. [3]Recreation includes education. [4]1988. [5]Housing includes household durable goods. [6]Capital city only. [7]Agricultural self-employment only. [8]Other includes self-employment. [9]1989. [10]1993. [11]Highest 20%. [12]Data refer to income shares by fractiles of persons. [13]Based on posttax income. [14]1985. [15]1990. [16]Includes tobacco. [17]1988–90. [18]Includes wage taxes. [19]Personal effects, other includes education and recreation. [20]Urban areas only. [21]Based on posttax per capita income. [22]Recreation includes health care. [23]Ethiopia includes Eritrea, except consumption expenditure. [24]1984. [25]Wage-earners only. [26]Low-income population in Banjul and Kombo St. Mary

transpor-tation, com-munications	household durable goods[f]	recrea-tion[g]	personal effects, other[h]	food consumption, 1995: daily available calories per capita	percent of total calories derived from: cereals	potatoes, cassava	meat, poultry	fish	eggs, milk	fruits, vegeta-bles	fats, oils[i]	other[j]	country
13.3	7.1	9.7	17.6	3,230	16.7	5.0	13.4	1.2	14.5	6.5	17.8	25.0	Netherlands, The
19.5[36]	10.0[36]	4.2[36]	10.1[36]	2,759	31.6	4.2	15.5	1.5	9.1	5.4	13.2	19.6	Netherlands Antilles
16.1	[5]	6.7	21.3	2,867	35.5	5.9	11.3	1.3	9.6	3.8	15.8	16.8	New Caledonia
17.1	10.9	—20.6—		3,379	23.2	3.0	15.9	0.8	10.5	6.9	14.6	25.0	New Zealand
...	...	...	...	2,311	50.7	1.5	2.6	0.1	4.3	2.4	11.3	27.0	Nicaragua
...	[5]	...	23.1	2,136	71.0	3.6	2.5	—	2.2	1.6	4.6	14.3	Niger
3.0	6.0	...	27.0	2,508	42.1	24.3	1.8	0.4	0.6	4.5	13.6	12.6	Nigeria
8.3	[5]	13.9[22]	—	...	...	...	...	...	...	...	...	...	Northern Mariana Islands
12.8	6.9	8.8	15.1	3,274	27.2	4.5	11.1	3.5	12.6	5.2	17.1	18.7	Norway
8.9	7.1	4.1[3]	4.0	...	...	...	...	...	...	...	...	...	Oman
13.0	5.0	...	21.0	2,475	55.2	0.8	2.7	0.2	8.0	2.9	15.6	14.7	Pakistan
...	...	...	...	...	...	...	...	...	...	...	...	...	Palau
15.1	8.4	11.7[3]	8.7	2,490	41.7	1.8	6.8	1.1	8.0	5.7	14.5	20.4	Panama
13.0	[5]	...	22.5	2,323	29.1	26.6	6.6	2.2	0.7	17.3	7.7	9.8	Papua New Guinea
4.5	6.2	2.3	7.3	2,560	26.5	15.5	13.2	0.3	6.2	4.7	11.0	22.6	Paraguay
7.3	7.5	7.6[3]	13.9	2,277	40.1	9.0	5.5	1.5	4.5	6.8	11.7	20.9	Peru
5.0	12.8	...	17.3	2,395	51.4	4.1	8.2	3.2	2.0	6.6	6.9	17.6	Philippines
8.9	8.3	15.0[3]	3.8	3,307	35.6	7.7	10.6	0.8	9.0	4.1	15.6	16.7	Poland
15.4	8.6	4.4	15.6	3,639	28.3	7.6	10.1	2.4	7.6	6.5	18.2	19.2	Portugal
11.8	11.2	7.9	14.7	...	...	...	...	...	...	...	...	...	Puerto Rico
13.0	[5]	—11.1—		...	...	...	...	...	...	...	...	...	Qatar
24.9	6.0	10.1[3]	12.5	3,308	41.4	1.7	11.9	1.5	5.2	5.0	9.8	23.5	Réunion
6.6	[5]	4.5[3]	4.5	3,166	49.1	4.1	7.0	0.2	11.2	4.8	9.7	13.8	Romania
...	9.4	...	30.8	2,926	42.2	7.6	9.3	1.3	9.2	3.2	10.5	16.6	Russia
1.7[38]	5.3[38]	0.4[38]	35.5[38]	...	...	...	...	...	...	...	...	...	Rwanda
4.3	*9.4*	...	*9.0*	2,234	27.7	2.4	11.2	3.5	7.9	3.4	14.7	29.2	St. Kitts and Nevis
6.3	5.8	3.2[3]	8.3	2,801	33.3	5.4	15.4	1.5	8.2	9.0	5.8	21.5	St. Lucia
3.7	6.6	...	9.7	2,427	34.4	8.0	10.1	1.3	4.6	5.1	8.1	28.5	St. Vincent and the Grenadines
9.0	[5]	...	17.9	...	...	...	...	...	...	...	...	...	Samoa
17.6	7.2	7.1[3]	14.5	...	...	...	...	...	...	...	...	...	San Marino
...	...	...	...	2,156	40.4	8.3	1.8	1.6	0.8	8.0	11.6	27.4	São Tomé and Príncipe
4.5[20, 40]	5.9[20, 40]	...	8.6[20, 40]	2,746	50.7	1.6	7.3	0.4	4.1	10.6	12.4	12.8	Saudi Arabia
5.0	2.0	...	12.0	2,416	55.2	1.0	3.6	2.1	2.3	1.1	16.8	17.8	Senegal
6.4	6.6	1.4	4.4	2,428	39.9	1.1	5.1	4.9	5.7	5.1	13.2	25.1	Seychelles
4.4	3.9	3.8[3]	4.8	2,029	53.5	8.9	1.1	1.8	0.7	3.2	18.1	12.8	Sierra Leone
13.8	8.9	13.1	23.3	...	...			...	...	...	...	...	Singapore
...	3.9	...	26.2	2,892	30.9	5.9	8.4	—	9.2	4.1	16.1	25.2	Slovakia
12.7	3.3	6.1[3]	8.0	3,396	32.2	7.8	11.8	0.3	10.0	5.0	17.5	15.4	Slovenia
9.9	[5]	[22]	15.7	2,131	35.9	34.4	3.2	2.2	0.7	2.7	3.2	17.8	Solomon Islands
...	...	...	12.1[6]	...	...	...	...	...	...	...	...	...	Somalia
16.7	10.0	6.3	11.7	2,890	54.3	1.9	7.1	0.5	3.8	2.3	12.8	17.3	South Africa
15.3	7.1	7.0[3]	23.1	3,338	22.8	5.5	13.4	2.1	9.4	6.6	22.1	18.2	Spain
17.0	3.9	2.4	10.8	2,334	58.7	2.0	0.9	1.4	2.8	4.2	1.8	28.3	Sri Lanka
1.5	5.5	0.7[3]	4.0	2,313	58.5	0.6	4.5	0.1	12.6	2.8	7.7	13.1	Sudan, The
9.5[6]	*12.3*[6]	*5.8*[6]	*4.0*[6]	2,556	51.1	2.3	5.2	1.4	5.9	7.2	7.9	19.0	Suriname
8.8	12.8	3.3[3]	20.4	2,658	47.0	1.2	5.8	—	3.8	2.4	5.6	34.3	Swaziland
15.7	6.6	10.9	8.8	3,117	23.9	3.8	9.3	2.4	15.1	4.7	20.6	20.1	Sweden
12.9	5.1	9.8[3]	10.1	3,220	22.0	3.0	15.5	0.8	12.8	5.6	18.0	22.4	Switzerland
2.4	5.8	2.1[3]	7.4	3,296	55.7	1.2	3.1	—	5.3	5.3	13.2	16.1	Syria
10.7	2.2	1.1[3]	4.7	...	...	...	...	...	...	...	...	...	Taiwan
...	...	...	34.7	...	...	...	...	...	...	...	...	...	Tajikistan
4.1	1.4	0.7	—	2,024	49.4	20.1	2.6	1.0	2.2	5.0	6.1	13.6	Tanzania
12.9	10.9	4.2	14.9	2,296	51.0	1.0	4.6	2.1	2.6	6.1	6.5	26.1	Thailand
9.5[6]	4.4[6]	5.1[3, 6]	8.6[6]	1,754	42.7	31.1	3.1	1.0	0.9	2.1	10.8	8.4	Togo
5.8	10.6	0.5	14.7	...	...	...	...	...	...	...	...	...	Tonga
15.2	14.3	[19]	6.2[19]	2,566	37.3	2.7	5.0	0.6	6.6	3.8	14.8	29.3	Trinidad and Tobago
9.0	11.2	7.1	7.1	3,187	50.3	1.7	2.9	0.5	4.9	6.0	19.4	14.4	Tunisia
8.8	9.0	5.6	2.3	3,593	49.5	3.3	2.4	0.4	7.4	8.2	13.8	14.9	Turkey
...	...	...	...	...	...	...	...	...	...	...	...	...	Turkmenistan
10.5	[5]	...	25.0	...	...	...	...	...	...	...	...	...	Tuvalu
5.9[6]	...	...	24.2[6]	2,268	21.0	22.0	3.1	0.8	1.8	24.2	2.9	24.3	Uganda
...	6.8	6.3[3]	43.9	...	...	...	...	...	...	...	...	...	Ukraine
14.1	11.6	4.7	6.5	3,361	34.1	1.6	12.0	1.0	9.3	14.1	10.6	17.5	United Arab Emirates
15.1	8.0	15.9	11.6	3,149	22.6	6.3	14.1	1.0	11.6	5.0	19.0	20.5	United Kingdom
13.9	1.5	5.8	18.9	3,603	23.5	2.8	12.0	0.8	11.6	5.2	18.4	25.6	United States
10.4	6.3	3.1	5.1	2,826	28.5	3.2	22.6	0.4	14.4	3.5	10.3	17.1	Uruguay
...	...	...	...	...	...	...	...	...	...	...	...	...	Uzbekistan
13.2	[5]	12.3[22]	10.3	2,542	17.9	28.0	9.5	1.5	1.8	7.0	12.2	22.0	Vanuatu
7.1	4.5	2.7	26.4	2,442	37.6	2.8	7.9	1.3	6.5	7.4	15.3	21.3	Venezuela
...	4.6	...	22.6	2,463	73.1	5.0	6.5	1.0	0.6	4.0	2.8	6.9	Vietnam
11.7[43]	*4.3*[43]	...	*21.9*[43]	...	...	...	...	...	...	...	...	...	Virgin Islands (U.S.)
...	...	...	...	...	...	...	...	...	...	...	...	...	West Bank
...	...	...	...	...	...	...	...	...	...	...	...	...	Western Sahara
1.9[44]	3.0[44]	...	13.7[44]	2,025	66.7	1.1	3.0	0.6	1.7	3.4	10.2	13.2	Yemen
5.7	1.6	2.4[3]	16.3	3,134	35.8	2.4	11.1	0.1	10.2	4.9	19.4	16.0	Yugoslavia
5.0	1.0	...	15.0	1,931	66.7	10.4	2.8	0.8	1.3	1.7	3.4	12.9	Zambia
1.1	12.9	0.6	16.5	1,965	58.9	2.2	1.8	0.2	2.3	1.1	11.9	21.5	Zimbabwe

only. [27]1986. [28]Former West Germany only. [29]Urban areas of Eastern region only. [30]Personal effects, other includes health care. [31]Housing includes water. [32]Workers and clerical workers only. [33]Earned income only. [34]1992. [35]Malagasy households only. [36]Curaçao only. [37]1987. [38]Rural areas only. [39]1994. [40]Middle-income population only. [41]1991. [42]Excludes transfer payments and property income. [43]St. Thomas only. [44]Data refer to former Yemen Arab Republic. [45]Data refer to former Socialist Federal Republic of Yugoslavia.

Health services

The provision of health services in most countries is both a principal determinant of the quality of life and a large and growing sector of the national economy. This table summarizes the basic indicators of health personnel; hospitals, by kind and utilization; mortality rates that are most indicative of general health services; external controls on health (adequacy of food supply and availability of safe drinking water); and sources and amounts of expenditure on health care. Each datum refers more or less directly to the availability or use of a particular health service in a country, and, while each may be a representative measure at a national level, each may also conceal considerable differences in availability of the particular service to different segments of a population or regions of a country. In the United States, for example, the availability of physicians ranges from about one per 730 persons in the least well-served states to one per 260 in the best-served, with a rate of one per 150 in the national capital. In addition, even when trained personnel exist and facilities have been created, limited financial resources at the national or local level may leave facilities underserved; or lack of good transportation may prevent those most in need from reaching a clinic or hospital that could help them.

Definitions and limits of data have been made as consistent as possible in the compilation of this table. For example, despite wide variation worldwide in the nature of the qualifying or certifying process that permits an individual to represent himself as a physician, organizations such as the World Health Organization (WHO) try to maintain more specific international standards for training and qualification. International statistics presented here for "physicians" refer to persons qualified according to WHO standards and exclude traditional health practitioners, whatever the local custom with regard to the designation "doctor." Statistics for health personnel in this table uniformly include all those actually working in the health service field, whether in the actual provision of services or in teaching, administration, research, or other tasks. One group of practitioners for whom this type of guideline works less well is that of midwives, whose training and qualifications vary enormously from country to country but who must be included, as they represent, after nurses, perhaps the largest and most important category of health auxiliary worldwide. The statistics here refer to those midwives working in some kind of institutional setting (a hospital, clinic, community health-care centre, or the like) and exclude rural noninstitutional midwives and traditional birth attendants.

Hospitals also differ considerably worldwide in terms of staffing and services. In this tabulation, the term hospital refers generally to a permanent facility offering inpatient services and/or nursing care and staffed by at least one physician. Establishments offering only outpatient or custodial care are excluded. These statistics are broken down into data for general hospitals (those providing care in more than one specialty), specialized facilities (with care in only one specialty), local medical centres, and rural health-care centres; the last two generally refer to institutions that provide a more limited range of medical or nursing care, often less than full-time. Hospital data are further analyzed into three categories of administrative classification: public, private nonprofit, and private for profit. Statistics on number of beds refer to beds that are maintained and staffed on a full-time basis for a succession of inpatients to whom care is provided.

Data on hospital utilization refer to institutions defined as above. Admission and discharge, the two principal points at which statistics are normally collected, are the basis for the data on the amount and distribution of care by kind of facility. The data on numbers of patients exclude babies born during a maternal confinement but include persons who die before being discharged. The bed-occupancy and average length-of-stay statistics depend on the concept of a "patient-day," which is the annual total of daily censuses of inpatients. The bed-occupancy rate is the ratio of total patient-days to potential days based on the number of beds; the average length-of-stay rate is the ratio of total patient-days to total admissions.

Health services

country	health personnel							hospitals									
	year	physicians	dentists	nurses	pharmacists	midwives	population per physician	year	number	kinds (%) general	kinds (%) specialized	kinds (%) medical centres	kinds (%) rural	ownership (%) government	ownership (%) private nonprofit	ownership (%) private for profit	hospital beds per 10,000 pop.
Afghanistan	1991	2,233	267	1,451	510	338	6,701	1988–93	...	...	...	...	...	...	...	...	3
Albania	1990	4,467	1,099	6,801[1]	772[2]	9,936[2]	729	1989	895	—17.9—		—82.1—		100.0	—	—	57
Algeria	1994	25,796	7,763	...	3,425	...	1,066	1990[3]	181	...	...	...	...	...	...	...	19[4]
American Samoa	1991	26	7[6]	140[6]	2[6]	1[6]	1,885	1990	1	100.0	—	—	—	100.0	—	—	27
Andorra	1994	132	...	...	...	...	491	1992	1	100.0	—	—	—	100.0	—	—	18[7]
Angola	1990	662	10	9,334	...	...	15,136	1990	58	...	...	...	...	...	...	...	12
Antigua and Barbuda	1992	59	13	179	13	...	1,083	1991	2	50.0	50.0	—	—	100.0	—	—	58[1]
Argentina	1992	88,800	21,900[10]	18,000[6]	...	...	376	1992	...	...	...	...	...	...	...	...	44
Armenia	1995	19,000[11]	[11]	34,900[4, 12]	...	[12]	198[11]	1994	183	...	...	...	...	100.0	...	...	82
Aruba	1992	74	19	515	13	3	936	1992	2	50.0	—	50.0	—	100.0	—	—	44
Australia	1995–96	45,800	9,100	160,500	12,900	...	400	1990	1,071[8]	...	...	...	...	65.5[8]	—34.5[8]—		89[7, 13]
Austria	1995	27,869	3,687	40,756	2,068[14]	1,030	289	1995	330	37.6	62.4	—	—	...	...	...	93
Azerbaijan	1995	29,300[11]	[11]	70,100[4, 12]	...	[12]	256[11]	1994	787	...	...	...	...	100.0	...	...	96
Bahamas, The	1992	373	58	1,067	52[15]	...	709	1995	5	60.0	20.0	20.0	—	60.0	—40.0—		40
Bahrain	1993	482	40	1,608	101	...	1,115	1991	12	58.3	42.7	—	—	75.0	16.7	8.3	28[7]
Bangladesh	1994	24,911	812	9,630	7,485[15]	7,713	4,759	1994	919	...	...	...	...	69.5	—30.5—		3
Barbados	1992	312	38	889	138	377	842	1992	10	70.0	30.0	—	—	80.0	—	20.0	75
Belarus	1995	45,000[11]	[11]	117,000[12]	...	[12]	222[11]	1995	880	...	...	...	...	100.0	...	...	122
Belgium	1996	38,363	6,983	...	13,926	...	264	1993	363	80.4	19.6	—	—	38.6	61.4	—	76
Belize	1995	139	12[7]	300[7]	17[7]	233[7]	1,546	1993	7	...	...	...	...	100.0	—	—	29
Benin	1993	363	16[6]	1,236	86[6]	453[6]	14,216	1993	...	...	...	...	...	...	...	...	2
Bermuda	1995	100	22	553	27	...	609	1995	2	50.0	50.0	—	—	...	...	...	43
Bhutan	1994	100	9[15]	233[15]	5[15]	70[15]	8,000	1996	27	...	...	...	...	...	...	...	12[4]
Bolivia	1993	3,392	1,643[1]	1,869	...	...	2,083	1995	336	10.7	8.9	23.5	56.8	...	...	...	10[7]
Bosnia and Herzegovina	1996	4,500	550	11,900	...	...	703	1989	...	...	...	...	...	...	...	...	46
Botswana	1994	339	...	3,329	...	...	4,395	1994	30	53.3	3.3	43.3	—	...	...	...	23
Brazil	1993	222,658	160,000	...	57,047[1]	...	681	1993	6,372	—100.0—		—	—	...	...	...	34
Brunei	1995	251	38	1,288	15	278	1,164	1995	10	90.0	—	—	10.0	90.0	—10.0—		33
Bulgaria	1996	29,529	5,467	51,269	1,736	6,576	283	1996	289	—79.2—		20.8	—	...	...	...	103
Burkina Faso	1991[16]	341	19	2,627	113	339	27,158	1993	78	—14.1—		85.9	—	100.0	—	—	5[10]
Burundi	1993	354	9[15]	1,270	55[15]	...	17,153	1993	...	...	...	...	...	...	...	...	7
Cambodia	1993	5,642	36[1]	9,950	262[1]	3,235	1,650	1988[3]	188	...	...	...	...	100.0	—	—	16
Cameroon	1989	945	55	6,053	206	...	11,848	1988	629	—27.0—		—73.0—		72.3	—27.7—		27
Canada	1995	63,700[13]	14,621[10]	262,288[10]	22,121[15]	...	465[13]	1989	1,079	81.8	16.6	1.6	—	95.8	—	4.2	54[4]
Cape Verde	1988	112	...	205	9	...	2,931	1987	75	6.7	—	93.3	—	100.0	—	—	15
Central African Republic	1992	157	8[15]	1,353[15]	22[15]	166[15]	18,660	1988	133	—21.1—		—78.9—		79.7	—20.3—		15
Chad	1993	217	5[6]	878	10	130	27,765	1993	...	...	...	...	...	...	...	...	7
Chile	1994	16,000	5,200[7]	5,653[7]	230[7, 16]	1,924[7, 16]	875	1994	198	...	...	...	...	89.4	—10.6—		31
China	1995	1,918,000[11, 17]	[11]	1,125,000	418,000	49,000	633[17]	1995	67,807	15.5	6.3	—78.2—		100.0	—	—	24
Colombia	1992	36,551	13,815	46,376	...	...	914	1989	947	...	...	...	...	...	...	...	14
Comoros	1993	77	6[15]	155[15]	6[15]	86[15]	6,600	1989	...	...	...	...	...	...	...	...	25
Congo, Dem. Rep. of the	1990	2,469	41	27,601	59	...	15,584	1986	400	...	...	...	...	52.5	—47.5—		21
Congo, Rep. of the	1990	613	35	1,624	175	498	4,028	1990	...	...	...	...	...	...	...	...	33
Costa Rica	1996	4,422	1,332	2,600	1,254	...	763	1996	33	...	...	...	...	87.9	—	12.1	18
Côte d'Ivoire	1990	2,020	219	3,691	135	1,533	5,931	1989	...	...	...	...	...	...	...	...	8
Croatia	1994	9,138	1,798	...	1,598	...	524	1994	84	38.1	61.9	—	—	...	...	...	59
Cuba	1992	46,860	8,057	73,943	...	...	231	1993	244	...	...	...	...	100.0	—	—	65[7]
Cyprus[18]	1993	1,455	498	2,536	423	120	433	1993[19]	110	39.1	58.2	—	2.7	10.0	0.9	89.1	52
Czech Republic	1995	32,195	6,267	...	4,032	...	321	1995	299	69.2	30.8	—	—	72.6	—27.4—		89
Denmark	1994	14,497	5,088	63,841	...	1,038	358	1992	163	42.9	57.1	—	—	42.9	57.1	—	35

Bed-occupancy rates may exceed 100% because stays of partial days are counted as full days.

Two measures that give health planners and policy makers an excellent indication of the level of ordinary health care are those for mortality of children under age five and for maternal mortality. The former reflects the probability of a newborn infant dying before age five. The latter refers to deaths attributable to delivery or complications of pregnancy, childbirth, the puerperium (the period immediately following birth), or abortion. A principal source for the former data was WHO's *The World Health Report* (annual) and for the latter, the UN Development Programme's *Human Development Report* (annual).

Levels of nutrition and access to safe drinking water are two of the most basic limitations imposed by the physical environment in which health-care activities take place. The nutritional data are based on reported levels of food supply (whether or not actually consumed), referred to the recommendations of the United Nations' Food and Agriculture Organization for the necessary daily intake (in calories) for a moderately active person of average size in a climate of a particular kind (fewer calories are needed in a hot climate) to remain in average *good* health. Excess intake in the many developed countries ranges to more than 40% above the minimum required to maintain health (the excess usually being construed to diminish, rather than raise, health). The range of deficiency is less dramatic numerically but far more critical to the countries in which deficiencies are chronic, because the deficiencies lead to overall poor health (raising health service needs and costs), to decreased productivity in nearly every area of national economic life, and to the loss of social and economic potential through early mortality. By "safe" water is meant only water that has no substantial quantities of chemical or biological pollutants—*i.e.*, quantities sufficient to cause "immediate" health problems. Data refer to the proportion of persons having "reasonable access" to an "adequate" supply of water within a "convenient" distance of the person's dwelling, as these concepts are interpreted locally.

The data on health care expenditure were excerpted from a joint effort by the WHO and the World Bank to create better analytical tools by which the interrelations among health policy, health care delivery systems, and human health might be examined against the more general frameworks of government operations, resource allocation, and development process. First published in the World Bank's *World Development Report 1993: Investing in Health* and, the following year, in the World Health Organization's *Global Comparative Assessments in the Health Sector* (edited by C.J.L. Murray and A.D. Lopez), the database and underlying methodology are expected to provide a continuing basis for international comparisons and policy analysis. The first two of ten volumes of the final results appeared in 1996 as *The Global Burden of Disease* and *Global Health Statistics* by the same editors.

Expenditures were tabulated for direct preventative and curative activities and for public health and public education programs having direct impact on health status—family planning, nutrition, and health education—but not more indirect programs like environmental, waste removal, or relief activities. Public, parastatal (semipublic, *e.g.,* social security institutions), international aid, and household expenditure reports and surveys were utilized to build up a comprehensive picture of national, regional, and world patterns of health care expenditures and investment that could not have been assembled from any single type of source. For reasons of space, public and parastatal are combined as the former.

Internet resources for further information:

- Most Recent Values of W.H.O. Global Health-For-All Indicators (for personnel and general indicators) http://www.who.ch/programmes/hst/hsp/a/country.htm

No comparable source exists for hospitals.

admissions or discharges					bed occupancy rate (%)	average length of stay (days)	mortality		population with access to safe water 1994–95 (%)	food supply (% of FAO requirement) 1995	total health expenditures, 1990					country
rate per 10,000 pop.	by kinds of hospital (%)						under age 5 per 1,000 live newborn 1996	maternal mortality per 100,000 live births 1990			as percent of GDP	per capita (U.S.$)	by source (percent)			
	general	specialized	medical centres	rural									public	private	international aid	
...	...	...	...	...	...	...	248	...	10	...	...	...	...	...	...	Afghanistan
...	...	...	...	...	...	...	38	65	...	96	4.00	26	84.0	16.0	—	Albania
400	...	...	...	...	49.3	5	54	160	78[5]	127	6.95	149	76.9	23.0	0.1	Algeria
965	100.0	—	—	—	38.4	4	...	...	...	...	...	...	...	...	...	American Samoa
...	...	...	...	...	...	...	...	...	...	...	...	...	...	...	...	Andorra
238	...	...	...	...	44.5[8]	16[8]	179	1,500	32	82	...	...	...	...	...	Angola
63[8]	...	...	...	...	49.9[8]	7[8]	22[9]	...	95	102	4.55	241	59.1	37.3	3.6	Antigua and Barbuda
520[3]	...	...	...	...	51.9[3]	8[3]	25	100	64	132	4.21	137	60.1	39.7	0.2	Argentina
...	...	...	...	...	...	...	23	50	...	...	4.17	152	59.8	40.2	—	Armenia
...	...	...	...	...	92.2	...	...	...	...	...	...	...	...	...	...	Aruba
...	...	...	...	...	...	14[7]	8	9	95	115	7.67	1,294	69.6	30.4	—	Australia
2,710	...	...	...	...	79.4	10	8	10	100[5]	130	8.38	1,711	66.4	33.6	—	Austria
...	...	...	...	...	...	...	37	22	...	...	4.27	99	61.2	38.8	—	Azerbaijan
822[3, 10]	...	...	...	...	83.7[3, 10]	8[3, 10]	24	...	97[5]	103	...	...	...	...	...	Bahamas, The
...	...	...	...	...	...	...	23	...	100[5]	...	4.62	324	63.0	36.9	0.1	Bahrain
853[2]	...	...	...	...	...	...	144	850	83	87	3.19	6	24.8	56.7	18.5	Bangladesh
810	93.5	6.5	—	—	88.3	32	15	...	100[5]	133	5.04	323	64.3	33.8	1.9	Barbados
...	...	...	...	...	...	...	19	37	...	...	3.19	157	68.7	31.3	—	Belarus
1,963	96.0	4.0	—	—	84.4	12	7	10	100[5]	134	7.50	1,449	82.5	17.5	—	Belgium
...	...	...	...	...	...	...	37	...	82	123	5.88	23	48.4	41.0	10.7	Belize
...	...	...	...	...	...	...	158	990	70	105	4.32	19	26.3	36.4	37.3	Benin
1,370	97.0	3.0	—	—	73.9	9	...	...	...	121	...	...	...	...	...	Bermuda
...	...	...	...	...	...	...	145	1,600	21	...	5.05	10	41.1	30.4	28.5	Bhutan
252[10]	...	...	...	...	45.9[10]	5[10]	88	650	60	92	4.01	25	39.9	39.6	20.5	Bolivia
529[8]	...	...	...	...	82.4[8]	11[8]	20	...	...	...	...	...	...	...	...	Bosnia and Herzegovina
...	...	...	...	...	93.1[6]	...	57	250	70	93	6.19	139	61.8	21.6	16.5	Botswana
970	...	...	...	...	...	7[4]	69	220	92	119	4.20	146	65.7	33.9	0.4	Brazil
...	...	...	...	...	...	...	13	...	90[5]	127	...	...	...	...	...	Brunei
...	...	...	...	...	...	...	18	27	99[5]	116	5.36	121	81.4	18.6	—	Bulgaria
...	...	...	...	...	...	...	186	930	78[5]	95	8.46	7	9.8	17.9	72.3	Burkina Faso
...	...	...	...	...	...	...	143	1,300	58	75	3.28	30	42.4	48.3	9.3	Burundi
...	...	...	...	...	...	...	137	900	13	91	...	...	...	...	...	Cambodia
...	...	...	...	...	...	...	109	550	41	95	2.62	27	26.4	61.7	11.9	Cameroon
...	...	...	...	...	...	14	8	6	100	116	9.05	1,945	74.1	25.9	—	Canada
...	...	...	...	...	...	...	60	...	51[5]	129	6.32	64	20.7	25.5	53.7	Cape Verde
...	...	...	...	...	...	...	149	700	18[5]	83	4.19	18	26.5	37.5	36.0	Central African Republic
...	...	...	...	...	...	...	172	1,500	29	80	6.22	12	27.6	24.7	47.7	Chad
749[3]	...	...	...	...	69.9[3]	7[3]	17	65	96	113	4.73	100	70.1	29.1	0.7	Chile
418	—60.4—		—39.6—		66.9	15	43	95	46	116	3.51	11	58.5	40.9	0.6	China
614	41.4	16.7	—41.9—		57.2	6	40	100	96	119	3.98	51	44.0	54.4	1.6	Colombia
...	...	...	...	...	...	...	111	...	48[5]	79	5.40	28	46.3	29.2	24.5	Comoros
...	...	...	...	...	...	...	131	870	25	85	2.38	5	8.5	64.8	26.7	Congo, Dem. Rep. of the
...	...	...	...	...	...	...	133	890	60	96	3.99	50	47.1	40.7	12.1	Congo, Rep. of the
958[10]	...	...	...	...	78.2[10]	6[10]	14	60	100	128	6.51	132	73.6	25.2	1.2	Costa Rica
...	...	...	...	...	...	...	137	810	82	109	3.35	28	48.7	47.9	3.4	Côte d'Ivoire
1,278	81.9	18.1	—	—	81.6	14	16	...	96	95	...	...	...	...	...	Croatia
1,376[10]	...	...	...	...	...	...	13	95	94	99	...	...	...	...	...	Cuba
747[3]	...	...	...	...	75.7[3]	7[3]	9	...	100[5]	150	3.96	64	62.9	26.8	10.3	Cyprus[18]
2,035	96.5	3.5	—	—	79.0	13	10	15	100[5]	129	5.94[20]	169[20]	84.9[20]	15.1[20]	—	Czech Republic
1,253	92.9	7.1	—	—	80.4	8	8	9	100	138	6.30	1,588	84.2	15.8	—	Denmark

Health services (continued)

country	health personnel							hospitals									
	year	physicians	dentists	nurses	pharma-cists	midwives	population per physician	year	number	kinds (%) general	kinds (%) specialized	kinds (%) medical centres	kinds (%) rural	ownership (%) government	ownership (%) private non-profit	ownership (%) private for profit	hospital beds per 10,000 pop.
Djibouti	1989	97	10	14	...		5,258	1993	8	—25.0—		—75.0—		100.0	...	...	27[6]
Dominica	1994	23	6	265	27	...	3,200	1994	53	1.9	—	—	98.1	100.0	—	—	25
Dominican Republic	1992	11,130	1,898	6,035	115[4]	...	671	1992[3]	723	—7.9—		—92.1—		...	...	...	12[4]
Ecuador	1993	12,149	1,524	4,215[1]	906	667[1]	904	1992	429	16.1	6.1	—77.8—		...	...	...	16
Egypt	1996	129,000	15,150[1]	...	34,700[1]	...	472	1991	6,418	5.1	—94.9—			...	...	...	19[4]
El Salvador	1993	4,525	1,182	5,094	...	1,940[10]	1,219	1993	78	...	...	...	...	61.5	1.3	37.2	17
Equatorial Guinea	1990	99	...	154	...	55	3,532	1988	...	...	...	...	...	...	...	...	29
Eritrea	1993	68	...	488	...	33	46,200	1993	10	...	...	...	...	...	...	...	9
Estonia	1994	4,680	820	7,302	930[10]	710	319	1994	107	...	...	...	...	96.3	—3.7—		84
Ethiopia	1988	1,466	...	3,496	364	...	30,195	1986–87	86	...	...	...	...	...	...	...	3
Faroe Islands	1994	81	40	385	10	19	550	1994	3	33.3	—	—	66.7	100.0	—	—	64
Fiji	1994	426	40	1,631	...	...	1,829	1994	25	...	...	...	...	...	...	...	22
Finland	1995	13,771	4,696	131,829	584[14]	3,975	371	1994[8]	380	...	...	...	...	...	...	...	98
France	1994	160,235	39,284	330,943	53,085	11,957	361	1993	3,810	—91.7—			8.3	27.7	—72.3—		118
French Guiana	1994	213	38	495	47	40	669	1993	...	...	...	...	...	...	...	...	56
French Polynesia	1993	353	81	586	47	54	595	1993	34[10]	...	...	...	...	...	...	...	48
Gabon	1989	448	32	759	71	240	2,504	1988	27	...	...	...	...	...	...	...	51
Gambia, The	1991	61	...	430[6]	...	...	14,536	1994	13	15.4		—84.6—		...	...	...	7[3]
Gaza Strip	1993[21]	...	...	...	...	...	...	1995	6	...	...	...	...	83.3	—16.7—		9
Georgia	1994	29,900[11]	[11]	64,100[12, 15]	...	[12]	182[11]	1994	422[15]	...	...	...	...	100.0[15]	...	...	105
Germany	1995	273,880	60,616	708,000[1, 12]	44,696	[12]	298	1993	2,354	...	...	...	...	49.2	36.0	14.8	77
Ghana	1995[16]	753	39[6]	11,808[6]	67[6]	1,736[6]	22,970	1991	121	90.9	9.1	—	—	60.3	—39.7—		16[4]
Gibraltar	1994	29	...	302[10]	...	...	951	1994	2	50.0	50.0	—	—	100.0	—	—	88
Greece	1994	40,487	10,865	34,314[7, 22]	8,147[14]	1,916[7, 22]	258	1993	368	47.8	52.2	—	—	...	...	...	50
Greenland	1995	83	31	539	10[10]	17[10]	672	1990	16	6.3	—	—	93.7	100.0	—	—	75
Grenada	1995	64	8	365	28[15]	36[15]	1,523	1991[8]	3	100.0	—	—	—	100.0	—	—	38
Guadeloupe	1993	590	119	1,470	206	108	692	1991	30[6]	...	...	...	...	56.7[6]	—43.3[6]—		80
Guam	1986	147	...	594[12]	...	[12]	823	...	...	...	...	...	...	...	...	...	...
Guatemala	1992	7,601	1,065[2]	14,401	...	...	1,282	1985	...	...	...	...	...	...	...	...	16[6]
Guernsey	1993	79	...	...	...	...	804	1993	1	100.0	—	—	—	100.0	—	—	...
Guinea	1991	920	...	...	197	371	6,448	1988	38	—100.0—		...	...	100.0	—	—	6
Guinea-Bissau	1986	274	13	...	12	...	3,245	1993	16	...	...	...	...	62.5	—37.5—		13
Guyana	1993	244	34	681	22	172[6]	3,148	1994	30	...	...	...	...	83.3	—16.7—		30
Haiti	1994	641	95	2,725	...	...	9,846	1994	50	...	...	...	...	...	...	...	10
Honduras	1993	3,803	622	6,288	975	...	1,358	1994	61	...	...	...	...	47.5	—52.5—		9
Hong Kong	1996	9,196	1,654	36,395	1,067	20	686	1995	88	...	...	...	...	78.4	—21.6—		47
Hungary	1995	37,420	5,069	54,792	2,024[14]	2,414	273	1995	...	...	...	...	...	...	...	...	91
Iceland	1995	797	273	1,952	176	194	335	1992	26	88.5	11.5	—	—	...	...	...	105
India	1993[23]	410,875[1]	19,523	449,351	...	...	2,173[1]	1991	15,067	...	...	...	...	55.0	—45.0—		7[7]
Indonesia	1994	28,989	...	138,816[12]	3,988[14]	[12]	6,570	1994	1,039	...	...	...	...	...	...	...	6
Iran	1994	37,000	6,080[7]	48,639[10, 12]	4,185[7]	[12]	1,600	1992	653	...	...	...	...	70.9	—29.1—		15[9]
Iraq	1993	8,787	1,656	13,206[10]	1,561	...	2,181	1993	185	...	...	...	...	...	...	...	14
Ireland	1995	6,200[13]	...	...	...	...	580[13]	1994[3, 8]	63	100.0	—	—	—	100.0	—	—	33
Isle of Man	1988	86	...	...	...	...	745	1986	3	33.3	33.3	—	33.3	100.0	—	—	...
Israel	1993	24,344	6,956	...	4,127	...	214	1995	259	18.5	81.5	—	—	12.0	51.7	36.3	61
Italy	1992	296,385	10,814[6]	170,409[6]	53,948[6]	...	193	1994	1,874	88.3	11.7	—	—	57.4	—42.6—		65
Jamaica	1995	1,589[1]	270[1]	1,836[16]	37[16]	250[16]	1,541[1]	1992	30	80.0	20.0	—	—	80.0	—20.0—		22[3]
Japan	1995	230,519	81,055	891,021	176,871	23,048	542	1993	9,844	88.9	11.1	—	—	73.4	—26.6—		135
Jersey	1995	95	...	...	...	...	895	1990	6	16.7	83.3	—	—	100.0	—	—	88
Jordan	1996	7,322	2,180	4,304[9]	3,265	861[9]	607	1994	63	...	...	...	...	42.9	—57.1—		18[24]
Kazakstan	1995	62,290	7,075[1]	213,320[1]	8,722[1]	16,280[1]	265	1996	1,805[10]	...	...	...	...	100.0[10]	...	...	86
Kenya	1994	4,558	630	27,143[7]	605[7]	...	5,954	1993	877	—35.1—		—64.9—		...	...	...	14
Kiribati	1993	10	...	147	...	...	7,687	1990	1	...	...	...	...	...	...	...	40
Korea, North	1993	61,200	...	...	...	...	370	1989	...	...	...	...	...	...	...	...	135
Korea, South	1995	57,188	13,681	120,415	43,269	8,352	784	1995[22]	...	63.6[25]	36.4[25]	—	—	...	...	...	34
Kuwait	1995	3,077	437	8,337	969	19	549	1995	24	...	...	...	...	66.7	—	33.3	31
Kyrgyzstan	1995	15,000	1,100	42,300	1,122[4]	3,414[4]	301	1994	396	89.1	—	10.9	—	100.0	—	—	99
Laos	1990	1,173	...	5,593[12]	...	[12]	3,555	1990	1,074	0.7	—99.3—			100.0	—	—	25
Latvia	1994	7,714	968	12,559	292	981	330	1994	170	51.2	4.1	28.8	15.9	97.6	2.4	—	121
Lebanon	1995	6,987	3,100	3,500	2,369	...	529	1995	153	...	...	...	...	10.5	—89.5—		22
Lesotho	1993	136	...	874[15]	60[15]	...	14,306	1987	22	90.9	9.1	—	—	54.5	45.5	—	15
Liberia	1985	89	5	908	...	443	24,600	1988	92	—37.0—		—63.0—		...	...	...	...
Libya	1989–91	4,749	686	13,849	...	...	690	1990	...	...	...	...	...	...	...	...	41
Liechtenstein	1995	32	12	...	2	...	966	1989	1	...	...	...	...	...	...	...	35
Lithuania	1995	14,737	1,742	29,259	3,203	1,829	252	1995	195	...	...	...	...	100.0	...	...	92
Luxembourg	1995	908	203[7]	...	336[7]	143[7]	454	1994	34	50.0	50.0	—	—	...	...	...	109
Macau	1995	467	22	861	41	...	876	1994	30	6.7	—	93.3	—	46.7	—53.3—		22
Macedonia	1995	4,516	1,087[4]	5,638[7]	357[4]	1,436[7]	432	1994	62	27.4	24.2	—48.4—		100.0	—	—	56
Madagascar	1990	1,392	89	3,124	19	1,703	8,628	1990	...	...	...	...	...	...	...	...	9
Malawi	1989	186	...	284	5	...	49,118	1987	395	12.2	0.8	—87.0—		59.2	—40.8—		16
Malaysia	1995	9,608	1,750	34,996[4]	...	5,500[4]	2,153	1995	315	...	...	...	...	37.5	—62.5—		20
Maldives	1995	100	...	281	134	461	2,533	1994	5	20.0	—	80.0	—	100.0	—	—	8
Mali	1993	483	13[27]	1,674	57[27]	321[27]	18,376	1987	...	...	...	...	...	...	...	...	4
Malta	1996	925	122	4,000	648	200	403	1996	7	...	...	...	...	71.4	—28.6—		57
Marshall Islands	1995	17	4	124	...	4[10]	3,269	1995	2	100.0	—	—	—	100.0	—	—	19
Martinique	1994	652	112	1,460	225	129	588	1993	...	...	...	...	...	...	...	...	77
Mauritania	1991	135	20	819	6	141	14,259	1990	16	...	...	...	...	100.0	—	—	7
Mauritius	1995	960	152	2,629[12, 16]	223	[12]	1,169	1994	23	73.9	17.4	8.7	—	60.9	4.3	34.8	28[3]
Mayotte	1985	9	1	51	1	2	7,427	1991	2	100.0	—	—	—	100.0	—	—	11
Mexico	1994	146,021	5,612[16]	166,644[16]	...	...	623	1993	1,539	...	...	...	...	53.9	—46.1—		10
Micronesia	1994	45	7[7]	230[7]	7[7]	...	2,311	1993	4	100.0	—	—	—	100.0	—	—	31
Moldova	1994	17,400[11]	[11]	48,400[12]	...	[12]	251[11]	1994	339	...	...	...	...	100.0	—	—	125
Monaco	1995	186	22	293[6]	64[6]	8[6]	169	1995	1	100.0	—	—	—	100.0	—	—	163
Mongolia	1993	5,911	299	9,183	1,113	...	376	1993	475	...	...	...	...	...	...	...	105
Morocco	1994	8,838	1,204	13,358[7]	2,470	87[15]	2,923	1993[28]	201	48.8	—	51.2	—	100.0	—	—	10

admissions or discharges: rate per 10,000 pop.	by kinds of hospital (%): general	by kinds of hospital (%): specialized	by kinds of hospital (%): medical centres	by kinds of hospital (%): rural	bed occupancy rate (%)	average length of stay (days)	mortality: under age 5 per 1,000 live newborn 1996	mortality: maternal mortality per 100,000 live births 1990	population with access to safe water 1994–95 (%)	food supply (% of FAO requirement) 1995	total health expenditures, 1990: as percent of GDP	total health expenditures, 1990: per capita (U.S.$)	by source (percent): public	by source (percent): private	by source (percent): international aid	country
...	...	...	...	...	...	...	164	...	90[5]	79	...	...	...	...	...	Djibouti
1,026	...	...	...	...	94.6	8	21[9]	...	77[5]	125	8.06	192	65.1	20.4	14.5	Dominica
470	...	...	...	...	...	...	46	110	79	103	3.72	38	52.7	43.3	4.0	Dominican Republic
518	...	...	...	...	57.5	7	57	150	70	106	4.14	44	55.9	37.3	6.8	Ecuador
...	...	...	...	...	...	...	70	170	84	133	2.61	28	30.3	62.0	7.7	Egypt
...	...	...	...	...	54.9[1, 3]	6[1, 3]	64	300	62	113	5.86	58	29.7	55.6	14.7	El Salvador
...	...	...	...	...	...	...	167	...	95[5]	...	7.60	28	36.6	20.7	42.7	Equatorial Guinea
...	...	...	...	...	...	...	146	1,400	...	...	...	...	...	...	...	Eritrea
1,773	76.7	21.5	—	1.8	83.7	14	19	41	...	...	3.62	228	53.0	47.0	—	Estonia
...	...	...	...	...	...	...	170	1,400	27	...	3.80	4	41.3	39.9	18.8	Ethiopia
...	...	...	...	...	86.4	...	...	...	...	...	...	...	...	...	...	Faroe Islands
...	...	...	...	...	...	...	23	...	77[5]	135	3.76	70	54.9	38.3	6.9	Fiji
2,322	...	...	...	...	70.9	11	6	11	100	112	7.82	2,046	83.3	16.7	—	Finland
2,345	...	...	...	...	...	...	9	15	100	142	9.40	1,869	74.2	25.8	—	France
1,714	...	...	...	...	70.3	8	...	...	...	125	...	...	...	...	...	French Guiana
...	...	...	...	...	...	...	...	...	...	127	...	...	...	...	...	French Polynesia
...	...	...	...	...	...	...	130	500	67	107	4.10	164	52.7	40.9	6.4	Gabon
...	...	...	...	...	...	...	190	1,100	61	91	7.53	22	28.3	20.7	51.0	Gambia, The
752	...	...	...	...	74.9	3	...	...	...	...	...	...	...	...	...	Gaza Strip
...	...	...	...	...	...	...	21	33	...	...	4.45	152	62.5	37.5	—	Georgia
1,812	...	...	...	...	82.8	13	7	22	100[5]	123	8.73	1,511	72.7	27.3	—	Germany
...	...	...	...	...	...	...	111	740	56	114	3.50	15	35.0	51.8	13.2	Ghana
1,730	...	...	...	...	40.6	8	...	...	...	...	...	...	...	...	...	Gibraltar
1,389	79.6	20.4	—	—	66.3	9	10	10	99[5]	142	5.39	359	76.0	24.0	—	Greece
2,450	29.2	—	—	70.8	69.4	8	...	...	...	...	...	...	...	...	...	Greenland
774	100.0	—	—	—	59.1	7	33[9]	...	85[5]	112	5.96	133	68.8	27.8	3.5	Grenada
2,136	...	...	...	...	82.3	11	...	...	...	113	...	...	...	...	...	Guadeloupe
...	...	...	...	...	...	...	...	...	...	...	...	...	...	...	...	Guam
284	...	...	...	...	57.7	9	67	200	64	105	3.70	27	44.2	43.2	12.6	Guatemala
1,100	100.0	—	—	—	...	...	...	...	...	...	...	...	...	...	...	Guernsey
...	...	...	...	...	...	...	196	1,600	49	94	3.90	17	39.7	40.3	20.0	Guinea
...	...	...	...	...	...	...	203	910	57	105	8.15	16	31.3	18.9	49.8	Guinea-Bissau
...	...	...	...	...	...	...	60	...	65[5]	108	10.37	42	40.7	15.1	44.2	Guyana
...	...	...	...	...	...	...	104	1,000	28	...	6.99	27	26.3	54.8	19.0	Haiti
459[7]	...	...	...	...	...	...	50	220	70	104	4.54	52	56.7	35.7	7.7	Honduras
1,811	...	...	...	...	...	...	6[9]	7	100[5]	143	5.69	687	19.5	80.5	0.0	Hong Kong
2,346	...	...	...	...	76.3	11	17	30	94	126	5.95	185	84.4	15.6	—	Hungary
2,828	94.0	6.0	—	—	86.5	12	4	...	100[5]	119	8.34	1,884	87.5	12.5	—	Iceland
...	...	...	...	...	...	...	99	570	63	108	6.00	21	20.0	78.4	1.6	India
...	...	...	...	...	...	...	63	650	63	126	2.01	12	25.6	66.7	7.7	Indonesia
...	...	...	...	...	...	...	59	120	89	123	2.54	244	56.9	43.1	0.0	Iran
645[15]	...	...	...	...	42.4[15]	4[15]	59	310	45	94	...	...	...	...	...	Iraq
1,465	100.0	—	—	—	79.8	7	7	10	100[5]	145	7.22	876	81.1	18.9	—	Ireland
...	...	...	...	...	...	...	...	...	...	...	...	...	...	...	...	Isle of Man
1,979	...	...	...	...	91.2	10	9	7	99	127	4.20	480	49.3	50.6	0.1	Israel
1,599	93.0	7.0	—	—	72.7	11	9	12	100[5]	137	7.54	1,449	77.7	22.3	—	Italy
550[3]	81.7[3]	18.3[3]	—	—	63.8[3, 8]	6[3, 8]	20	120	70	118	5.04	83	57.4	33.2	9.5	Jamaica
...	...	...	...	...	...	...	6	18	95	123	6.45	1,538	74.5	25.5	—	Japan
1,718	84.0	16.0	—	—	...	...	...	...	...	...	...	...	...	...	...	Jersey
478[3]	...	...	...	...	68.1[3]	4[3]	39	150	89	111	3.77	55	36.9	52.3	10.8	Jordan
...	...	...	...	...	...	...	31	80	...	...	4.44	154	62.3	37.7	—	Kazakstan
...	...	...	...	...	...	...	106	650	49	86	4.33	16	40.0	37.9	22.1	Kenya
...	...	...	...	...	...	...	78[4]	...	99[5]	122	...	...	...	...	...	Kiribati
...	...	...	...	...	...	...	26	70	100	101	...	...	...	...	...	Korea, North
629	97.5	2.5	—	—	65.5	13	13	130	89	139	6.61	365	40.9	58.9	0.2	Korea, South
950[3, 4]	72.2[3, 4]	27.8[3, 4]	—	—	64.9[3, 4]	7[3, 4]	16	29	100[5]	131	4.86	541	64.2	35.6	0.1	Kuwait
1,775	95.5	—	4.5	—	75.6	15	39	110	75	...	4.97	118	66.7	33.3	—	Kyrgyzstan
...	...	...	...	...	...	...	143	650	41	95	2.53	5	17.4	60.7	21.9	Laos
2,106	78.4	4.6	13.8	3.2	78.7	16	20	40	...	...	3.87	220	56.1	43.9	—	Latvia
...	...	...	...	...	...	...	36	300	100[5]	132	...	...	...	...	...	Lebanon
221[8]	...	...	...	...	...	...	81	610	57	86	8.32	26	38.3	26.5	35.2	Lesotho
...	...	...	...	...	...	...	151	...	40[5]	...	8.24	4	19.9	11.8	68.3	Liberia
...	...	...	...	...	...	...	80	220	30	132	...	...	...	...	...	Libya
...	...	...	...	...	...	...	...	...	...	...	...	...	...	...	...	Liechtenstein
2,001	...	...	...	...	74.4	15	17	36	...	...	3.58	159	72.0	28.0	—	Lithuania
1,941	94.6	5.4	—	—	75.0	16	8	...	100[5]	134	6.56	1,662	91.4	8.6	—	Luxembourg
329	...	...	...	...	64.4	16	...	...	...	135	...	...	...	...	...	Macau
995	67.2	6.1	—26.7—		68.5	14	37	...	...	92	...	...	...	...	...	Macedonia
...	...	...	...	...	...	...	121	490	32	89	2.56	7	29.0	49.6	21.4	Madagascar
...	...	...	...	...	...	...	212	560	54	88	4.98	11	35.0	41.7	23.3	Malaŵi
717[3, 6]	...	...	...	...	...	...	22	80	90	126	2.96	71	44.0	55.8	0.2	Malaysia
256[7, 26]	...	...	...	...	71.4[7, 26]	4[7, 26]	68	...	88[5]	112	...	...	...	...	...	Maldives
...	...	...	...	...	...	...	184	1,200	44	91	5.19	15	24.9	46.7	28.4	Mali
...	...	...	...	...	...	...	11	...	100[5]	137	5.38	349	68.3	31.7	0.0	Malta
...	...	...	...	...	...	...	92[4]	...	31[5]	...	...	...	...	...	...	Marshall Islands
2,092	...	...	...	...	73.7	10	...	...	...	118	...	...	...	...	...	Martinique
...	...	...	...	...	...	...	142	930	72	112	3.80	18	28.5	41.5	30.0	Mauritania
1,446[3]	...	...	...	...	74.6[3]	5[3]	17	120	100	130	4.40	100	47.8	39.0	13.3	Mauritius
...	...	...	...	...	...	...	...	...	...	...	...	...	...	...	...	Mayotte
403[3, 10]	...	...	...	...	64.7[3, 10]	5[3, 10]	40	110	87	135	3.17	89	49.3	49.8	0.9	Mexico
...	...	...	...	...	...	...	29[4]	...	100[5]	...	...	...	...	...	...	Micronesia
...	...	...	...	...	...	...	28	60	...	...	3.91	143	74.4	25.6	—	Moldova
...	...	...	...	...	...	...	...	...	...	...	...	...	...	...	...	Monaco
...	...	...	...	...	...	...	68	65	54	78	6.63	58	83.0	15.1	1.9	Mongolia
255	...	...	...	...	63.8	8	76	610	59	130	2.55	26	33.6	63.3	3.1	Morocco

Health services (continued)

country	health personnel							hospitals									
	year	physicians	dentists	nurses	pharma-cists	midwives	popu-lation per physi-cian	year	number	kinds (%)				ownership (%)			hos-pital beds per 10,000 pop.
										gen-eral	spe-cial-ized	medical centres	rural	govern-ment	private non-profit	private for profit	
Mozambique	1990	387	108	3,533	353	1,139	36,320	1990	238	4.2	0.8	—95.0—		100.0	—	—	8[7]
Myanmar (Burma)	1995	12,950	860	9,851	...	8,143	3,485	1995	710	...	...	...	...	...	...	...	6
Namibia	1992	324	51	4,471	91[10]	...	4,594	1992	47	...	...	...	...	91.5	—8.5—		45[10]
Nauru	...	...	...	...	...	...	...	...	...	...	...	...	...	...	...	...	...
Nepal	1995	1,478	45	5,015[12]	18	[12]	13,777	1995	84	...	...	...	...	...	...	...	2
Netherlands, The	1995	37,493	7,328	124,000[7]	2,484	1,276	412	1995	231	64.1	35.9	—	—	...	...	...	55
Netherlands Antilles	1996	314	67	1,441	37	10	669	1996	12	33.3	41.7	25.0	—	...	...	...	70
New Caledonia	1994	358	97	669	78	52	513	1990	8	12.5	12.5	75.0	—	62.5	—37.5—		62
New Zealand	1995	11,889	1,959	45,107[12]	3,532	[12]	301	1994	330	...	...	...	...	38.2	—61.8—		68
Nicaragua	1994	2,577	321	2,144	...	...	1,566	1994	56	46.4	7.1	46.4	—	...	...	...	11
Niger	1993	237	5[15]	2,213	29[15]	457[15]	35,141	1987	...	...	...	...	...	...	...	...	5
Nigeria	1993	21,739	1,335	80,186	6,474[1]	62,386	4,257	1985	11,588	6.6	0.5	—92.9—		81.4	—18.6—		7[9]
Northern Mariana Islands	1986	23	4	103	2	2	1,324	1988	1	100.0	—	—	—	100.0	—	—	19
Norway	1996	15,368	5,222	68,308	...	...	285	1994	...	...	...	...	...	...	...	...	51
Oman	1995[16]	2,476	152[7]	6,036	370	...	852	1995	53	...	...	...	...	...	...	...	21
Pakistan	1995	69,694	2,753	22,531	3,772[1]	20,869	1,863	1994	10,667	—7.6—		—92.4—		...	...	...	6
Palau	1990	10	...	84	...	...	1,518	1986	1	...	...	...	...	...	...	...	50
Panama	1995	3,074	656	2,823	115[6]	...	856	1995	59	...	...	...	...	...	...	...	27
Papua New Guinea	1993	736	...	2,614	...	...	5,584	1993	...	...	...	...	...	...	...	...	34
Paraguay	1993	3,341	1,160[1]	4,558[1]	...	...	1,406	1993	...	...	...	...	...	...	...	...	12
Peru	1992	23,771	7,945	15,026	5,940[10]	3,520[10]	944	1992	427	...	...	...	...	56.7	—43.3—		17
Philippines	1993	78,445	1,614[16]	14,853[16]	...	12,339[16]	849	1992	1,723	96.5	3.1	0.5	—	36.4	—63.6—		11
Poland	1996	88,523	17,619	210,425	19,450	24,445	436	1995	753	93.6	6.4	—	—	...	...	...	63
Portugal	1993	24,499	1,509	30,975	5,950	...	403	1993	335	43.0	18.8	38.2	—	74.3	14.7	11.0	42
Puerto Rico	1989	6,269	902	19,666	2,111	120	558	1994	72	83.3	8.3	8.3	—	36.1	30.6	33.3	26
Qatar	1995[16]	715	88	1,834	187	...	787	1995	4	25.0	75.0	—	—	100.0	—	—	18
Réunion	1996	1,164	295	2,785	266[14]	164	571	1995	...	...	...	...	...	69.6[25]	—30.4[25]—		44
Romania	1994[16]	41,827	6,163	...	6,432[6]	...	544	1994	...	...	...	...	...	...	...	...	77
Russia	1995	630,000	47,100[4]	1,008,800[4]	7,300[4]	117,200[4]	235	1994	12,265	37.4	17.2	—	45.4	99.8	—0.2—		119
Rwanda	1989	272	7	835	25	...	24,697	1985[3]	220	—13.6—		—86.4—		100.0	—	—	9[6]
St. Kitts and Nevis	1992	39	8	260	14	...	1,057	1992	4	50.0	—50.0—			...	...	...	67
St. Lucia	1992	64	6	256	...	...	2,235	1992	4	25.0	25.0	—	50.0	...	...	...	37
St. Vincent	1992	40	6	224	27[10]	...	2,708	1992	9	...	...	...	...	77.8	—22.2—		44
Samoa	1992	60	7	298	6	...	2,682	1992	36	2.8	—	—	97.2	100.0	—	—	34
San Marino	1987	60	...	...	...	...	375	1987	...	...	...	...	...	...	...	...	66
São Tomé and Príncipe	1989	61	5	223	1	54	1,881	...	...	...	...	...	...	...	...	...	...
Saudi Arabia	1995	29,227	...	61,246	...	...	612	1995	279	...	...	...	...	74.2	—25.8—		23
Senegal	1992	520	58[27]	...	200[27]	474[27]	14,825	1992	17	...	...	...	...	...	...	...	10
Seychelles	1996	84	9	346	4	...	906	1996	7	14.3	14.3	71.4	—	100.0	—	—	54
Sierra Leone	1992	404	...	...	...	...	10,832	1988	219	—25.6—		—74.4—		...	...	...	10
Singapore	1996	4,661	835	13,193	858	487	653	1996	24	...	...	...	...	41.7	—58.3—		35
Slovakia	1995	14,447	2,236[4]	...	322[14]	...	371	1991	111	72.1	27.9	—	—	100.0	—	—	92[9]
Slovenia	1990	4,086	1,194[9]	...	1,019	...	489	1995	24	54.2	45.8	—	—	...	...	...	57
Solomon Islands	1990	52	...	447	...	...	6,154	1986	8	100.0	—	—	—	75.0	25.0	—	53
Somalia	1986	450	2	1,834	180	556	13,315	1988	...	...	...	...	...	...	...	...	7
South Africa	1994	26,452	4,029	158,538	9,447	...	1,529	1995	698	...	...	...	...	66.8	—33.2—		42
Spain	1995	162,089	13,242	161,852	40,323	6,105	241	1991	813	...	...	...	...	42.4	—57.6—		42
Sri Lanka	1993[16]	3,713	333[6]	11,818	520[6]	5,030[6]	4,745	1993[3]	426	...	...	...	...	100.0	—	—	28
Sudan, The	1994	2,600	...	...	...	...	11,300	1986	...	...	...	...	...	...	...	...	8
Suriname	1994	251	...	995[1]	...	...	1,685	1989	...	...	...	...	...	...	...	...	33[4]
Swaziland	1990	83	7	1,264	13	...	9,265	1986	24	—41.7—		—58.3—		...	...	...	...
Sweden	1995	23,000	4,700	91,400[12]	5,945	[12]	382	1994	...	...	...	...	...	...	...	...	52
Switzerland	1994	21,680[13]	4,400[1]	...	1,591[14]	...	323[13]	1994	...	...	...	...	...	...	...	...	69
Syria	1995	15,391	8,025	23,151	5,919	6,063	922	1993	264	...	...	...	...	20.5	—79.5—		11
Taiwan	1996	27,782	7,332	61,494	19,667	774	775	1995	787	...	...	...	...	12.1	—87.9—		53
Tajikistan	1994	13,084	926	38,852	709	1,027	439	1994	449	...	...	...	...	98.2	—1.8—		88
Tanzania	1993	1,365	...	...	...	...	20,511	1993	173[10]	...	...	...	...	...	...	...	10
Thailand	1994	14,098	2,984	94,103	5,575	10,342	4,165	1992	1,097	92.9	7.1	—	—	73.7	—26.3—		17
Togo	1991	319	22	1,187	65	222	11,270	1990	...	...	...	...	...	...	...	...	16
Tonga	1993	45	9	292	...	...	2,139	1993	4	...	...	...	...	...	...	...	28
Trinidad and Tobago	1995	1,183	134	2,260[7, 12]	534	[12]	1,067	1992	...	...	...	...	...	...	...	...	29
Tunisia	1994	5,344	1,004	12,195	1,685	...	1,640	1994[3]	163	—13.5—		—86.5—		100.0	—	—	18
Turkey	1994	65,832	11,457	56,280	18,366	36,263[7]	917	1994	982	75.3	8.8	—15.9—		84.3	—15.7—		22
Turkmenistan	1994	14,100[11]	[11]	43,000[12]	...	[12]	320[11]	1994	398	...	...	...	...	100.0	...	...	115
Tuvalu	1993	8	2[1]	39	...	...	1,152	1985	8	11.1	—	—	88.9	100.0	—	—	36
Uganda	1993	840	...	2,782	...	...	22,399	1989	81	...	...	...	...	...	...	...	12
Ukraine	1995	230,000[11]	[11]	598,000[12]	...	[12]	224[11]	1995	3,900	...	...	...	...	100.0	...	...	130
United Arab Emirates	1994	4,095	563	8,506	686[10]	...	545	1994	47	...	...	...	...	70.2	—29.2—		28
United Kingdom	1994	91,100[13]	...	284,578[6]	37,832[15]	24,801[6]	641[13]	1994	...	...	...	...	...	...	...	...	49[13]
United States	1995	720,300	190,000[4]	2,044,000[4]	184,000	3,000	365	1995	6,580[7]	82.1[7]	17.9[7]	—	—	31.1[7]	51.2[7]	17.7[7]	41
Uruguay	1994	11,241	3,740	2,139	922	554	282	1993	112	...	...	...	...	61.6	—38.4—		45
Uzbekistan	1995	76,200	4,300[4]	249,600	1,700[4]	20,100[4]	299	1995	192	...	...	...	...	100.0	...	...	84
Vanuatu	1995	12	3	259	6	33	14,025	1995	90	5.6	—	21.1	73.3	100.0	—	—	22
Venezuela	1992	32,616	7,945	52,260	5,615	...	626	1992	610	...	...	...	...	37.0	—63.0—		26
Vietnam	1994	29,700	...	53,700[7]	6,500[7]	12,000[7]	2,411	1994	12,500	...	...	...	...	...	...	...	27
Virgin Islands (U.S.)	1985	167	...	...	...	...	622	1985	...	...	...	...	...	...	...	...	49
West Bank	1993[21]	1,344	445	2,279	149	56	1,536	1995	17	...	...	...	...	52.9	—47.1—		9
Western Sahara	1994	100	...	...	24	...	2,504	...	...	...	...	...	...	...	...	...	...
Yemen	1994	2,785	167	5,772	295	385	4,549	1994	81	...	...	...	...	...	...	...	7
Yugoslavia	1995	21,313	4,075	...	2,016	...	495	1995	...	...	...	...	...	...	...	...	52
Zambia	1990	713	26	1,503	24	311	11,414	1987	965	8.2	0.3	19.0	72.5	80.9	19.1	—	29[7]
Zimbabwe	1993	1,551	194	22,590	411	2,894	6,909	1993[3]	1,378	0.9	2.6	83.7	12.7	100.0	—	—	19[9]

[1]1992. [2]1987. [3]Government hospitals only. [4]1994. [5]Data refer to a period other than 1994–95, differ from the standard definition, or refer to only part of the country. [6]1989. [7]1993. [8]General hospitals only. [9]1995. [10]1991. [11]Physicians includes dentists. [12]Nurses includes midwives. [13]OECD estimate. [14]Number of pharmacies. [15]1990. [16]Government-employed health personnel only. [17]Includes doctors of traditional Chinese medicine (359,000 in 1995). [18]Republic of Cyprus only. [19]Excludes psychiatric hospitals. [20]Data refer to former Czechoslovakia. [21]West Bank includes Gaza Strip. [22]General and

admissions or discharges: rate per 10,000 pop.	by kinds of hospital (%): general	specialized	medical centres	rural	bed occupancy rate (%)	average length of stay (days)	mortality: under age 5 per 1,000 live newborn 1996	maternal mortality per 100,000 live births 1990	population with access to safe water 1994–95 (%)	food supply (% of FAO requirement) 1995	total health expenditures, 1990: as percent of GDP	per capita (U.S.$)	by source (percent): public	private	international aid	country
...	...	...	...	...	...	...	176	1,500	28	72	5.86	5	21.0	25.7	53.3	Mozambique
...	...	...	...	...	...	...	95	580	39	127	...	...	...	...	...	Myanmar (Burma)
...	...	...	...	...	...	...	91	370	57	92	3.92	45	47.8	41.3	10.9	Namibia
...	...	...	...	...	...	...	...	...	...	...	...	...	...	...	...	Nauru
...	...	...	...	...	...	...	122	1,500	48	108	4.54	7	23.0	51.7	25.4	Nepal
1,060	97.2	2.8	—	—	77.2	15	8	12	100	120	8.03	1,501	72.6	27.4	—	Netherlands, The
...	...	...	...	...	...	...	...	...	...	114	...	...	...	...	...	Netherlands Antilles
1,165[8]	...	...	...	...	84.8[8]	8[8]	...	...	...	126	...	...	...	...	...	New Caledonia
1,379[3]	...	...	...	...	60.7[3]	8[3]	10	25	100[5]	128	7.37	925	81.7	18.3	—	New Zealand
769	—76.2—		23.8	—	...	...	66	160	57	103	8.61	34	56.9	22.5	20.6	Nicaragua
...	...	...	...	...	...	...	182	1,200	57	91	4.98	16	24.5	31.3	34.1	Niger
...	...	...	...	...	...	...	146	1,000	43	106	2.72	10	36.5	57.4	6.1	Nigeria
1,550	100.0	—	—	—	54.7	4	...	...	...	...	...	...	...	...	...	Northern Mariana Islands
1,515	96.4	3.6	—	—	83.0	10	9	6	100	122	7.35	1,835	95.7	4.3	—	Norway
...	...	...	...	...	...	...	32	190	56	...	4.22	209	59.5	40.1	0.5	Oman
...	...	...	...	...	...	...	104	340	60	107	3.48	12	47.4	47.1	5.5	Pakistan
...	...	...	...	...	...	...	35[4]	...	...	...	...	...	...	...	...	Palau
1,112	...	...	...	...	61.8	6	28	55	82	108	7.13	142	72.6	23.1	4.3	Panama
...	...	...	...	...	...	...	82	930	31	102	4.44	37	59.1	36.1	4.8	Papua New Guinea
...	...	...	...	...	...	...	47	160	8	111	2.97	35	35.1	58.2	6.7	Paraguay
...	...	...	...	...	...	...	71	280	60	97	3.21	61	56.1	41.7	2.2	Peru
538	...	...	...	...	62.1	5	45	280	84	106	2.15	16	46.7	46.4	6.9	Philippines
1,288[1]	96.0[1]	4.0[1]	—	—	72.5[1]	14[1]	18	19	100[5]	126	5.07	84	80.3	19.7	—	Poland
1,146	86.3	10.5	3.2	—	74.5	10	11	15	100[5]	149	6.99	383	61.7	38.3	—	Portugal
1,101	94.0	4.3	1.7	—	63.1	5	...	...	...	...	...	...	...	...	...	Puerto Rico
...	...	...	...	...	71.7[1, 29]	7[1, 29]	23	...	100[5]	...	4.73	630	63.0	36.9	0.0	Qatar
1,951[4]	...	...	...	...	79.8[4]	7[4]	...	...	...	146	...	...	...	...	...	Réunion
...	...	...	...	...	...	...	30	130	100[5]	119	3.87	58	61.4	38.6	—	Romania
2,150	...	...	...	...	83.2	17	27	75	...	114	3.02	159	66.8	33.2	—	Russia
85	...	...	...	...	42.8[22]	7[22]	161	1,300	66[5]	...	3.44	10	15.0	45.2	39.8	Rwanda
1,068[8]	...	...	...	...	49.3[8]	9[8]	40[9]	...	100[5]	92	5.99	212	58.1	27.8	14.1	St. Kitts and Nevis
890[22]	...	...	...	...	...	...	22[9]	...	...	116	7.18	169	75.6	23.0	1.4	St. Lucia
776[8]	...	...	...	...	67.9[8]	6[8]	23[9]	...	...	100	5.69	102	68.5	28.8	2.7	St. Vincent
894	70.8	—	—	29.2	32.9	5	71	...	90[5]	...	2.94	20	6.1	54.2	39.7	Samoa
...	...	...	...	...	...	...	...	...	100[5]	...	...	...	...	...	...	San Marino
...	...	...	...	...	...	...	81[9]	...	70[5]	92	9.22	38	28.8	17.0	54.2	São Tomé and Príncipe
...	...	...	...	...	...	...	30	130	93	113	4.76	260	64.3	35.7	0.0	Saudi Arabia
...	...	...	...	...	...	...	157	1,200	50[5]	102	3.66	29	45.1	38.0	16.9	Senegal
1,744[30]	...	...	...	...	76.4[30]	6[30]	20[9]	...	97[5]	104	6.03	289	50.2	28.0	21.9	Seychelles
...	...	...	...	...	...	...	242	1,800	34[5]	88	2.43	4	19.6	30.9	49.5	Sierra Leone
1,127	...	...	...	...	73.1[4]	8[4]	9	10	100	...	1.87	215	58.3	41.6	0.1	Singapore
1,679	94.9	5.1	—	—	73.2	14	14	...	...	117	...	...	...	...	...	Slovakia
1,565	...	...	...	...	79.4	11	12	13	...	134	...	...	...	...	...	Slovenia
...	...	...	...	...	...	...	29	...	...	93	2.18	117	43.2	50.5	6.3	Solomon Islands
...	...	...	...	...	...	...	176	...	...	...	1.51	8	7.3	41.1	51.6	Somalia
...	...	...	...	...	...	...	73	230	70[5]	118	5.56	77	57.5	42.5	0.0	South Africa
997	...	...	...	...	76.7	12	8	7	99	136	6.59	831	78.4	21.6	—	Spain
1,464[15]	...	...	...	...	...	...	19	140	57	105	3.74	18	40.4	51.1	8.6	Sri Lanka
...	...	...	...	...	...	...	112	660	77	98	3.33	34	11.0	84.5	4.5	Sudan, The
766[31]	...	...	...	...	68.8[31]	10[31]	26	...	72[5]	113	2.88	93	37.9	58.0	4.1	Suriname
...	...	...	...	...	...	...	99	...	43[5]	115	7.22	64	43.6	22.2	34.2	Swaziland
1,906	...	...	...	...	82.2	8	6	7	100[5]	116	8.79	2,343	89.3	10.7	—	Sweden
...	...	...	...	...	...	...	7	6	100	120	7.52	2,520	68.5	31.5	—	Switzerland
352[3]	...	...	...	...	75.5[3]	3[3]	43	180	87	133	2.07	41	16.6	79.4	4.0	Syria
...	...	...	...	...	...	...	8[9]	8	...	...	4.30	323	53.0	47.0	0.0	Taiwan
1,492	...	...	...	...	70.2	15	56	130	...	...	5.98	100	72.6	27.4	—	Tajikistan
...	...	...	...	...	...	...	126	770	49	87	4.73	4	14.4	31.6	54.0	Tanzania
...	...	...	...	...	...	...	43	200	81	103	4.98	72	20.4	78.7	0.9	Thailand
...	...	...	...	...	...	...	118	640	67	76	4.10	18	40.4	38.5	21.2	Togo
622[1]	...	...	...	...	56.2[1]	10[1]	24[4]	...	100[5]	...	6.46	63	60.3	25.0	14.8	Tonga
1,114[3, 8]	...	...	...	...	70.7[3, 8]	6[3, 8]	17	90	82	106	4.54	180	62.4	36.9	0.6	Trinidad and Tobago
...	...	...	...	...	...	...	49	170	86	133	4.91	76	63.8	33.3	3.0	Tunisia
568[15]	...	...	...	...	...	...	65	180	92	143	3.94	76	36.2	63.3	0.5	Turkey
...	...	...	...	...	...	...	66	55	85	...	4.99	125	66.4	33.2	0.4	Turkmenistan
1,368	40.9	—	—	59.1	51.5[8]	12.2[8]	56[4]	...	100[5]	...	2.66	472	34.0	66.0	0.1	Tuvalu
...	...	...	...	...	...	...	172	1,200	42	97	3.40	8	13.3	53.0	33.7	Uganda
...	...	...	...	...	...	...	21	50	97	...	3.30	131	69.7	30.3	—	Ukraine
...	...	...	...	...	...	...	19	26	98	139	2.66	472	34.0	66.0	0.1	United Arab Emirates
...	...	...	...	...	...	...	8	9	100	125	6.11	1,039	84.9	15.1	—	United Kingdom
1,176[32]	...	...	...	...	62.8[32]	7[32]	9	12	90	136	12.71	2,765	44.1	55.9	—	United States
442[3, 4]	...	...	...	...	76.3[3, 4]	16[3, 4]	20	85	34	106	4.62	123	53.8	44.8	1.4	Uruguay
...	...	...	...	...	...	...	47	55	...	...	5.90	116	72.1	27.9	—	Uzbekistan
567	...	...	...	...	41.9	6	48	...	72[5]	111	5.68	67	51.5	25.7	22.8	Vanuatu
601[3]	...	...	...	...	69.7[3]	6[3]	25	120	88	99	3.60	88	54.2	45.6	0.1	Venezuela
...	...	...	...	...	...	...	56	160	38	114	2.11	3	39.3	47.4	13.3	Vietnam
...	...	...	...	...	...	...	...	...	...	...	...	...	...	...	...	Virgin Islands (U.S.)
711	...	...	...	...	80.9	4	...	...	...	...	...	...	...	...	...	West Bank
...	...	...	...	...	...	...	...	...	...	...	...	...	...	...	...	Western Sahara
...	...	...	...	...	...	...	155	1,400	52	84	3.19	20	34.7	54.1	11.3	Yemen
1,117	...	...	...	...	71.6	12	...	...	...	123	5.11[33]	264[33]	80.4[33]	19.6[33]	—	Yugoslavia
1,249	—75.7—		—24.3—		68.5	7	140	940	47	84	3.16	17	65.4	30.6	4.1	Zambia
546	...	...	...	...	69.8	7	103	570	74	82	6.23	39	40.3	48.7	11.0	Zimbabwe

specialized hospitals only. [23]Registered personnel; all may not be present and working in the country. [24]1996. [25]Based on bed ownership. [26]Central Hospital only. [27]1988. [28]Public sector only. [29]Hamad General Hospital only. [30]Victoria Hospital only. [31]Paramaribo hospitals (1,213 beds) only. [32]5,194 community hospitals only. [33]Data refer to the former Socialist Federal Republic of Yugoslavia.

Social protection

This table summarizes three principal areas of social protective activity for the countries of the world: social security, crime and law enforcement, and military affairs. Because the administrative structure, financing, manning, and scope of institutions and programmed tasks in these fields vary so greatly from country to country, no well-accepted or well-documented body of statistical comparisons exists in international convention to permit objective assessment of any of these subjects, either from the perspective of a single country or internationally. The data provided within any single subject area do, however, represent the most consistent approach to problems of international comparison found in the published literature for that field.

The provision of social security programs to answer specific social needs, for example, is summarized simply in terms of the existence or nonexistence of a specific type of benefit program because of the great complexity of national programs in terms of eligibility, coverage, term, age limits, financing, payments, and so on. Activities connected with a particular type of benefit often take place at more than one governmental level, through more than one agency at the same level, or through a mixture of public and private institutions. The data shown here are summarized from the U.S. Social Security Administration's *Social Security Programs Throughout the World* (biennial). A bullet symbol (●) indicates that a country has at least one program within the defined area; in some cases it may have several. A blank space indicates that no program existed providing the benefit shown; ellipses [...] indicate that no information was available as to whether a program existed.

Data given for social security expenditure as a percentage of total central governmental expenditure are taken from the International Monetary Fund's *Government Finance Statistics Yearbook,* which provides the most comparable analytic series on the consolidated accounts of central governments, governmentally administered social security funds, and independent national agencies, all usually separate accounting entities, through which these services may be provided in a given country.

Data on the finances of social security programs are taken in large part from the International Labour Office's *The Cost of Social Security* (triennial), supplemented by national data sources.

Figures for criminal offenses known to police, usually excluding civil offenses and minor traffic violations, are taken in part from Interpol's *International Crime Statistics* (annual) and a variety of national sources. Statistics are usually based on the number of offenses reported to police, not the number of offenders apprehended or tried in courts. Attempted offenses are counted as the offense that was attempted. A person identified as having committed multiple offenses is counted only under the most serious offense. Murder refers to all acts involving the voluntary taking of life, including infanticide, but excluding abortion, or involuntary acts such as those normally classified as manslaughter. Assault includes "serious," or aggravated, assault—that involving injury, endangering life, or perpetrated with the use of a dangerous instrument. Burglary involves theft from the premises of another; although Interpol statistics are reported as "breaking and entering," national data may not always distinguish cases of forcible

Social protection

country	social security															
	programs available, 1997					expenditures, 1994 (% of total central govt.)[f]	finances									
	old-age, invalidity, death[a]	sickness and maternity[b]	work injury[c]	unemployment[d]	family allowances[e]		year	receipts					expenditures			
								total ('000,000 natl. cur.)	insured persons (%)	employers (%)	government (%)	other (%)	total ('000,000 natl. cur.)	benefits (%)	administration (%)	other (%)
Afghanistan	●	●	●		●	...	...	...	...	...	...	...	...	...	...	...
Albania	●	●	●	●	●	21.7	1990	967.0	—	—	88.8	11.2	1,440.0	99.5	——0.5——	
Algeria	●	●	●	●	●	...	1990	27,700.0	...	...	...	...	28,748.0	61.8	30.6	7.6
American Samoa	●	...	...	...	...	...	1990	...	...	...	...	...	13.0	100.0	—	—
Andorra	●	●	●			...	1993	11,832.2	...	...	...	...	7,937.2	90.2	4.6	5.2
Angola	...	...	...	...	...	...	...	...	...	...	...	...	...	...	...	...
Antigua and Barbuda	●	●				...	1983	13.0	29.2	48.7	—	22.1	4.2	66.1	33.9	—
Argentina	●	●	●	●	●	50.7[9]	1989	1,015,837.0	28.8	45.0	16.6	9.6	989,009.0	95.0	5.0	—
Armenia	●	●	●	●	●	...	...	...	...	...	...	...	...	...	...	...
Aruba	●	...	●	...	...	[11]	1992	66.3	...	...	...	...	60.4	...	...	...
Australia	●	●	●	●	●	33.9	1989	28,525.6	1.9	7.8	88.4	1.9	28,880.4	98.7	1.0	0.3
Austria	●	●	●	●	●	46.4	1989	425,417.0	30.1	45.9	21.1	2.9	412,134.0	96.5	2.3	1.2
Azerbaijan	●	●	●	●	●	...	...	...	...	...	...	...	...	...	...	...
Bahamas, The	●	●	●			4.1[12]	1989	95.9	22.9	38.5	2.1	36.5	43.5	71.1	27.2	1.7
Bahrain	●		●			3.9	1989	39.6	12.3	40.2	—	47.5	9.7	69.8	20.9	9.3
Bangladesh		●	●	●		9.8[13]	1989	73.6	12.4	37.5	2.4	47.7	34.1	94.0	6.0	—
Barbados	●	●	●	●		19.8[6, 14]	1989	191.7	38.0	40.8	1.5	19.7	149.1	93.5	5.8	0.7
Belarus	●	●	●	●	●	11.0[9, 14]	1986	3,199.0	—	—	93.2	6.8	3,199.0	100.0	—	—
Belgium	●	●	●	●	●	42.3[6]	1986	1,347,070.0	24.4	39.7	31.6	4.3	1,322,636.0	94.5	4.3	1.2
Belize	●	●	●			4.6	1989	15.3	8.9	53.2	—	38.0	3.9	56.7	43.3	—
Benin	●		●		●	8.7[17]	1989	3,551.9	16.8	81.4	—	1.8	4,500.9	69.3	28.1	2.6
Bermuda	●		●			...	...	...	...	...	...	...	...	...	...	...
Bhutan	...	...	...	...	...	0.5[9]	1990	...	...	...	...	...	26.0[18]	...	...	...
Bolivia	●	●	●		●	14.6	1989	346.6	29.3	47.7	11.2	11.8	340.2	84.9	14.3	0.8
Bosnia and Herzegovina	●	●	●	●	●	...	...	...	...	...	...	...	...	...	...	...
Botswana			●			3.8[12]	1993	—	...	...	...	...	148.3[18]	...	...	...
Brazil	●	●	●	●	●	27.1[12]	1989	71,847.0	24.4	51.0	20.0	4.6	68,957.0	61.9	18.6	19.5
Brunei	●	...	...	...	...	...	1984	...	...	...	...	...	39.5	...	...	...
Bulgaria	●	●	●	●	●	28.0	1989	6,016.8	—	71.4	28.1	0.5	6,000.1	96.6	3.3	0.1
Burkina Faso	●		●		●	0.1[19]	1989	8,816.5	15.6	62.9	—	21.5	4,975.3	69.5	30.4	0.1
Burundi	●		●		●	0.7[14, 20]	1989	1,991.5	31.6	47.6	—	20.8	1,563.9	74.8	16.8	8.4
Cambodia	...	...	●	...	●	...	...	...	...	...	...	...	...	...	...	...
Cameroon	●		●		●	1.0[12]	1989	41,331.8	13.1	64.8	—	22.1	41,332.0	70.6	28.8	0.6
Canada	●	●	●	●	●	39.8	1989	130,306.6	9.9	15.6	64.4	10.1	115,764.2	96.9	2.5	0.6
Cape Verde	●	●	●		●	...	1989	697.7	26.5	58.5	—	15.0	316.7	82.4	16.1	1.5
Central African Republic	●		●		●	6.2[4]	1989	3,604.0	8.4	76.0	—	15.6	3,247.0	64.6	32.9	2.5
Chad	●		●		●	1.9[14, 21]	1989	1,172.8	12.6	77.6	—	9.8	634.5	43.0	51.4	5.6
Chile	●	●	●	●	●	33.3	1989	1,186,056.0	32.8	2.7	37.9	26.6	798,770.0	83.9	14.7	1.4
China	●	●	●	●		0.1	1989	57,446.2	—	99.4	—	0.6	54,654	98.4	0.6	1.0
Colombia	●	●	●		●	7.8	1989	294,438.0	24.8	56.0	0.2	19.0	257,455.0	85.5	11.5	3.0
Comoros	...	...	...	...	...	...	1983	40.7	100.0	—	—	—	54.3	17.4	62.3	20.3
Congo, Dem. Rep. of the	●		●		●	1.1[12]	1986	1,238.3	28.6	60.2	—	11.2	1,044.2	27.9	72.1	—
Congo, Rep. of the	●		●		●	0.4[14, 24]	1983	15,272.8	12.1	80.2	—	7.7	7,256.7	66.6	21.3	12.1
Costa Rica	●	●	●		●	17.7	1989	36,407.3	33.2	44.4	1.2	21.2	31,049.8	89.0	4.1	6.9
Côte d'Ivoire	●		●		●	3.6[4, 14]	1989	27,288.4	19.3	75.4	—	5.3	20,593.5	100.0	—	—
Croatia	●	●	●	●	●	30.5	...	...	...	...	...	...	...	...	...	...
Cuba	●	●	●			...	1989	2,284.8	—	37.4	62.6	—	2,284.8	96.7	—	3.3
Cyprus[25]	●	●	●	●	●	23.2	1989	217.5	24.7	40.3	17.3	17.7	117.7	98.4	1.6	—
Czech Republic	●	●	●	●	●	28.2	1989[26]	132,748.0	—	3.9	96.1	—	132,748.0	99.7	0.3	—
Denmark	●	●	●	●	●	43.2	1989	225,965.6	4.3	5.0	88.2	2.5	218,258.2	97.0	3.0	—
Djibouti	●	...	...	...	●	6.2[27]	1979	1,352.2	...	...	...	...	1,115.7	...	...	...
Dominica	●	●	●			1.4[14, 17]	1986	12.3	22.6	50.9	—	26.5	4.4	68.0	32.0	—
Dominican Republic	●	●	●			3.8	1986	77.9	20.1	72.9	—	6.8	74.3	75.9	24.1	—
Ecuador	●	●	●	●		1.9[3]	1988	71,286.0	37.0	50.0	—	13.0	52,032.4	86.0	14.0	—
Egypt	●	●	●	●		11.0[12]	1989	2,443.5	22.8	41.0	2.0	34.2	1,685.6	93.4	6.6	—

entry. Automobile theft excludes brief use of a car without the owner's permission, "joyriding," and implies intent to deprive the owner of the vehicle permanently. Criminal offense data for certain countries refer to cases disposed of in court, rather than to complaints. Police manpower figures refer, for the most part, to full-time, paid professional staff, excluding clerical support and volunteer staff. Personnel in military service who perform police functions are presumed to be employed in their principal activity, military service.

The figures for military manpower refer to full-time, active-duty military service and exclude reserve, militia, paramilitary, and similar organizations. Because of the difficulties attached to the analysis of data on military manpower and budgets (including problems such as data withheld on national security grounds, or the publication of budgetary data specifically intended to hide actual expenditure, or the complexity of long-term financing of purchases of military matériel [how much was actually spent as opposed to what was committed, offset by nonmilitary transfers, etc.]), extensive use is made of the principal international analytic tools: publications such as those of the International Institute for Strategic Studies (*The Military Balance* and *Strategic Survey*) and the U.S. Arms Control and Disarmament Agency (*World Military Expenditures and Arms Transfers*), both annuals.

The data on military expenditures are from the sources identified above, as well as from the IMF's *Government Finance Statistics Yearbook* and country statistical publications.

The following notes further define the column headings:

a. Programs providing cash payments for *each* of the three types of long-term benefit indicated to persons (1) exceeding a specified working age (usually 50–65, often 5 years earlier for women) who are qualified by a term of covered employment, (2) partially or fully incapacitated for their usual employment by injury or illness, and (3) qualified by their status as spouse, cohabitant, or dependent minor of a qualified person who dies.

b. Programs providing cash payments (jointly, or alternatively, medical services as well) to occupationally qualified persons for *both* of the short-term benefits indicated: (1) illness and (2) maternity.

c. Programs providing cash or medical services to employment-qualified persons who become temporarily or permanently incapacitated (fully or partially) by work-related injury or illness.

d. Programs providing term-limited cash compensation (usually 40–75% of average earnings) to persons qualified by previous employment (of six months minimum, typically) for periods of involuntary unemployment.

e. Programs providing cash payments to families or mothers to mitigate the cost of raising children and to encourage the formation of larger families.

f. Includes welfare.

g. A police officer is a full-time, paid professional, performing domestic security functions. Data include administrative staff but exclude clerical employees, volunteers, and members of paramilitary groups.

h. Includes all active-duty personnel, regular and conscript, performing national security functions. Excludes reserves, paramilitary forces, border patrols, and gendarmeries.

crime and law enforcement (latest)						military protection								country
offenses reported to the police per 100,000 population					population per police officer[g]	manpower, 1997[h]		expenditure, 1995				arms trade, 1995 ('000,000 U.S.$)		
total	personal		property			total ('000)	per 1,000 population	total '000,000	per capita	% of central government expenditure	% of GDP or GNP	imports	exports	
	murder	assault	burglary	automobile theft										
...	...	...	...	...	540[1]	[2]	[2]	408[3]	24[4]	64.4[4]	9.1[4]	20	0	Afghanistan
...	...	...	...	...	550	[5]	[5]	157[6]	56[6]	11.3[6]	4.1[6]	0	0	Albania
584	1.0	19.7	39.7	8.5	840	124.0	4.2	1,238	43	6.9	3.2	230	0	Algeria
3,006	8.0	494.0	588.0	6.0	460	—	[7]	—	—	—	—	...	...	American Samoa
2,795	1.6	36.5	796.8	111.1	220	—	—	...	...	...	...	...	...	Andorra
31	3.4	6.1	...	...	14[8]	110.5	10.4	225	22	...	3.0	90	0	Angola
4,977	4.7	475.0	1,984.4	35.9	120	0.2	2.3	...	...	...	...	...	...	Antigua and Barbuda
186.2	0.3	0.6	1.5	19.9	1,270	73.0	2.1	4,684	137	27.0[10]	1.7	40	70	Argentina
160.4	5.4	3.4	...	2.1	...	58.6	15.5	79	23	...	0.9	30	0	Armenia
5,461	1.2	180.0	451.3	202.5	...	—	[7]	—	—	—	—	...	...	Aruba
6,279	1.8	560.3	2,131.9	703	453	57.4	3.1	8,401	465	8.8	2.5	930	50	Australia
6,314	2.5	2.5	1,128.2	31.8	470	45.5	5.6	2,106	264	2.2[9]	0.9	120	0	Austria
247	8.1	5.6	8.4	4.1	...	66.7	8.8	304	40	3.8[9]	2.8	0	0	Azerbaijan
6,752	17.6	115.7	1,336.5	...	125	0.9	3.0	9[4]	40[4]	2.5[4]	0.5[4]	...	...	Bahamas, The
1,714	1.8	547.1	86.7	8.2	180	11.0	17.7	273	473	14.8	5.4	40	0	Bahrain
64	1.9	3.6	4.6	0.6	2,560	121.0	1.0	502	4.0	9.9[12]	1.7	60	0	Bangladesh
4,337	6.8	170.8	1,267.2	34.2	280	0.6	2.3	13	50	2.3	0.8	0	0	Barbados
650	2.9	7.0	...	...	...	80.0	7.7	...	...	...	...	0	170	Belarus
5,769	3.1	33.0	1,529.5	310.7	640	44.5	4.4	4,449	439	3.5[10]	1.7	340	130	Belgium
...	33.2[15]	275.6[16]	833.6	...	290	1.1	4.6	9	41	5.0	1.6	0	0	Belize
125	0.9	37.9	3.4	1.3	3,250	4.8	0.8	24	4	8.6[12]	1.2	0	0	Benin
8,871	5.1	221.7	1,949.2	...	370	—	[7]	—	—	—	—	...	...	Bermuda
...	...	...	...	...	...	4.0[13]	3.1[13]	...	...	...	...	0	0	Bhutan
...	...	...	...	...	...	33.5	4.3	132	19	9.5	2.3	10	0	Bolivia
402	2.5	2.6	...	...	...	40.0	12.8	...	...	...	...	270	0	Bosnia and Herzegovina
8,281	12.7	431.9	1.9	73.1	750	7.5	5.0	225	155	12.7	5.3	0	0	Botswana
116	...	...	...	...	...	314.7	2.0	10,900	68	3.9	1.7	170	10	Brazil
1,148	1.5	2.7	133.1	42.7	100	5.0	16.2	269	919	20.1[3]	6.0	5	0	Brunei
2,522	5.9	38.6	1,174.9	208.0	...	75.8	9.1	1,073	125	6.3	2.8	0	150	Bulgaria
41	0.2	4.1	—	—	...	10.0	0.9	68	7	12.0[12]	2.9	0	0	Burkina Faso
87	3.3	7.4	...	...	...	18.5	3.1	46	8	24.8	4.4	0	0	Burundi
...	...	...	...	...	1,980	140.5	13.5	90	9	16.7[10]	3.1	20	0	Cambodia
11	0.1	0.1	1.2	0.2	1,170	13.1	0.9	102[10]	8[10]	10.2[12]	1.9[10]	10	0	Cameroon
10,351	5.2	769.1	1,326.2	545.9	8,640	61.6	2.0	9,077	319	7.1[10]	1.7	210	280	Canada
...	...	...	...	...	110	1.1	2.8	4	9	1.3[12]	1.0	0	0	Cape Verde
135	1.6	22.8	2.7	...	2,740[1]	5.0	1.5	30[10]	10[10]	6.6[6]	3.2[10]	0	0	Central African Republic
...	...	...	...	...	990	25.4	3.5	34	5	9.7[9]	3.1	10	0	Chad
1,086	11.0	96.3	...	13.1	470	94.3	6.5	2,243	158	17.5	3.8	380	0	Chile
128	0.2	5.2	45.2	6.9	1,360[22]	2,840.0	2.3	63,510	53	18.5	2.3	725	625	China
641	81.9	110.5	...	32.4	420	146.3	4.0	2,000	55	16.2	2.6	60	0	Colombia
...	...	...	...	...	960	—	[23]	...	...	...	...	...	...	Comoros
...	...	...	...	...	910	—	—	17	0	3.7	0.3	0	0	Congo, Dem. Rep. of the
32	1.5	4.7	0.2	0.2	870	10.0	3.9	48	19	11.1[3]	2.9	10	0	Congo, Rep. of the
868	5.3	11.1	232.4	23.1	480	—	—	50	15	2.7	0.6	0	0	Costa Rica
67	2.5	73.1	19.5	11.9	4,640	8.4	0.6	98	7	4.2[12]	1.1	0	0	Côte d'Ivoire
1,334	7.4	23.2	379.8	20.9	...	58.0	12.1	...	...	...	...	110	0	Croatia
...	...	...	...	...	650	53.0	4.7	350	32	...	1.6	0	0	Cuba
689	1.9	17.7	203.3	3.0	180	10.0	13.0	495	672	17.1	5.8	50	0	Cyprus[25]
1,911[26]	2.0[26]	89.4[26]	621.5[26]	95.7[26]	640[26]	44.0	4.3	2,368	229	6.6	2.3	0	120	Czech Republic
10,525	4.9	190.1	2,046.3	663.3	600	32.9	6.2	3,118	596	4.1	1.8	80	20	Denmark
402	4.4	12.4	40.0	16.0	...	9.6	15.4	22	52	13.9[12]	4.5	0	0	Djibouti
1,956	4.2	25.2	1,078.1	33.6	300	[28]	[28]	...	...	...	...	...	...	Dominica
946	11.9	30.8	154.0	24.8	580	24.5	3.1	122	16	6.8	1.1	10	0	Dominican Republic
466	10.5	32.9	94.4	36.5	260	57.1	4.8	611	54	18.3	3.7	260	0	Ecuador
3,693	1.6	0.7	...	3.1	580	450.0	7.2	2,653	43	13.7	5.7	1,900	0	Egypt

Social protection (continued)

country	social security: programs available, 1997					social security: expenditures, 1994 (% of total central govt.)[f]	finances	receipts					expenditures			
	old-age, invalidity, death[a]	sickness and maternity[b]	work injury[c]	unemployment[d]	family allowances[e]		year	total ('000,000 natl. cur.)	insured persons (%)	employers (%)	government (%)	other (%)	total ('000,000 natl. cur.)	benefits (%)	administration (%)	other (%)
El Salvador	●	●	●			7.3[12]	1989	465.3	27.1	51.7	—	21.2	368.3	78.1	21.9	—
Equatorial Guinea	●	●	●		●	...	1989	141.0	7.1	92.9	—	—	134.0	49.3	50.7	—
Eritrea[30]	...	...	...	...	...	...	...	...	...	...	...	...	...	...	...	...
Estonia	●	●	●	●	●	30.0	...	90.1	...	...	...	...	...	...	...	...
Ethiopia[30]	●		●			6.9[9]	1989	190.9	32.8	65.3	—	1.9	153.7	98.3	1.7	—
Faroe Islands	●	...	...	...	●	...	...	...	...	...	...	...	...	...	...	...
Fiji	●	...	●	...	...	4.7	1989	153.5	20.9	33.8	0.8	44.5	75.47	95.3	4.7	—
Finland	●	●	●	●	●	44.4	1989	118,589.0	7.7	41.1	44.0	7.2	106,235	96.3	3.7	—
France	●	●	●	●	●	39.3[12]	1989	1,700,202.0	77.7	—	20.4	1.9	1,669,096.0	95.5	3.7	0.8
French Guiana	●	●	●		●	...	1991	1,071.5	...	...	...	...	997.1	...	...	...
French Polynesia	●	...	●	...	●	...	1990	19,268.0	...	...	...	...	17,832.0	...	...	...
Gabon	●		●		●	...	1989	3,415.0	—	44.3	29.3	26.4	2,737.0	55.2	44.8	—
Gambia, The	●		●			3.0[3]	1982	—	...	...	...	...	5.6	...	...	...
Gaza Strip	...	...	...	...	...	—	...	...	...	...	...	...	...	...	...	...
Georgia	●	●	●	●	●	...	...	...	...	...	...	...	...	...	...	...
Germany	●	●	●	●	●	45.3[19]	1989[33]	522,172.0	36.9	34.3	26.1	2.7	507,604.0	97.1	2.8	0.1
Ghana	●		●			7.1[12]	1989	17,920.8	21.1	52.9	—	26.0	4,147.7	13.3	64.0	22.7
Gibraltar	●	●	...	●	●	...	...	...	...	...	...	...	...	...	...	...
Greece	●	●	●	●	●	13.4[12]	1989	1,314,421.0	24.9	38.4	30.8	5.9	1,349,693.0	92.5	7.5	—
Greenland	●	...	...	...	●	...	...	...	...	...	...	...	...	...	...	...
Grenada	●	●				7.6	1989	24.1	20.1	60.3	3.2	16.3	13.5	93.1	6.9	—
Guadeloupe	●	...	...	...	●	...	1994	2,607.3	...	...	...	...	5,883.4	...	...	...
Guam	●	...	...	...	●	...	1989	...	...	...	...	...	7.3	...	...	...
Guatemala	●	●	●			5.2[6]	1989	348.5	29.1	54.8	—	16.1	279.7	82.7	14.6	2.7
Guernsey	●	●	●	●	●	...	1993	66,369	——44.3——		45.5	10.2	62,458	94.2	5.8	...
Guinea	●	●	●		●	...	1989	3,387.0	0.4	90.3	—	9.3	1,108.1	54.9	45.1	—
Guinea-Bissau	...	...	...	...	...	8.8[12]	1986	138.0	22.8	63.4	10.3	3.8	61.9	59.6	40.4	—
Guyana	●	●	●			3.7[14, 34]	1994	1,070.8	...	...	...	...	1,373.7	...	...	...
Haiti	●		●			5.1[4]	1977	60.5	——26.6——		69.9	3.5	52.4	92.7	7.3	—
Honduras	●	●	●			4.5[14, 17]	1986	166.2	23.9	40.8	3.3	32.0	76.8	84.6	15.4	—
Hong Kong	●	●	●	●	●	...	1995–96	...	...	...	...	...	13,267.7	74.9	25.1	—
Hungary	●	●	●	●	●	27.7[3]	1994	798,000.0	—	—	—	—	737,000.0	—	—	—
Iceland	●	●	●	●	[36]	22.5	1994	10,840	—	—	—	—	80,819.0	97.8	2.2	—
India	●	●	●			...	1989	43,913.8	23.8	27.7	5.3	43.2	13,775.8	90.0	8.2	1.8
Indonesia	●		●			5.3	1989	239,477.0	50.7	49.3	—	—	181,499.0	12.3	15.8	71.9
Iran	●	●	●	●	●	10.3	1986	346,460.0	83.2	0.1	8.2	8.5	167,879.0	43.4	6.3	50.0
Iraq	●	●	●			...	1977	107.8	9.9	55.6	21.9	12.6	71.0	94.0	2.4	3.6
Ireland	●	●	●	●	●	27.6[12]	1989	4,627.5	16.3	24.8	57.7	1.2	4,612.9	95.2	4.7	0.1
Isle of Man	●	●	●	●	●	37.0[14, 38]	1985	...	...	...	...	...	14.4	...	...	...
Israel	●	●	●	●	●	24.5	1989	13,851.1	31.1	27.7	35.0	6.2	13,593.3	81.7	15.4	2.9
Italy	●	●	●	●	●	38.0[14, 39]	1989	278,383.0	16.5	51.4	30.0	2.1	100,251.0	89.3	2.0	8.7
Jamaica	●		●			3.2[14, 20]	1989	374.3	11.5	13.6	43.8	31.1	273.6	92.6	7.4	—
Japan	●	●	●	●	●	36.8[12]	1989	59,571,299.0	27.4	31.6	24.4	16.6	46,684,159.0	94.3	1.7	4.0
Jersey	●	●	●	●	●	9.5[12, 14]	1991	60.9	——63.8——		23.4	12.8	52.8	...	...	...
Jordan	●		●			14.3	1986	53.6	28.7	55.3	—	16.0	9.5	77.4	14.0	8.6
Kazakstan	●	●	●	●	●	...	...	...	...	...	...	...	...	...	...	...
Kenya	●		●			0.1[12]	1989	4,262.0	18.2	13.7	10.0	58.1	1,857.8	53.8	46.1	0.1
Kiribati	●		●			...	...	...	...	...	...	...	...	...	...	...
Korea, North	...	...		...	...	...	...	...	...	...	...	...	...	...	...	...
Korea, South	●		●			9.9[12]	1995	4,981,400.0	60.3	—	—	—	7,862,000.0	...	...	...
Kuwait	●					16.6	1989	445.8	7.1	13.2	54.3	25.4	206.5	97.0	3.0	—
Kyrgyzstan	●	●	●	●	●	...	...	...	...	...	...	...	...	...	...	...
Laos	...	...	●	...	...	...	...	...	...	...	...	...	...	...	...	...
Latvia	●	●	●	●	●	36.7	...	...	...	...	...	...	...	...	...	...
Lebanon	●	●	●		●	...	...	...	...	...	...	...	...	...	...	...
Lesotho	...	...	...	...	...	1.1[9]	1992	—	...	...	...	...	12.0[18]	...	...	...
Liberia	●		●			1.0[14, 39]	1983	2.9	—	69.0	13.8	17.2	2.6	54.4	45.6	—
Libya	●	●	●			...	1989	314.3	21.6	25.4	50.2	2.8	260.0	77.5	19.5	3.0
Liechtenstein	●	●	●	●	●	...	...	...	...	...	...	...	...	...	...	...
Lithuania	●	●	●	●	●	35.6	...	...	...	...	...	...	24,981.7	...	...	...
Luxembourg	●	●	●	●	●	51.1	1989	72,471.8	24.2	34.6	34.4	6.8	65,214.4	97.2	2.4	0.4
Macau	●	...	...	...	●	...	1995	168.0	...	...	...	...	146.1	...	...	...
Macedonia	●	●	●	●	●	...	1995	20,785	...	...	...	...	...	...	...	...
Madagascar	●		●		●	1.9	1989	15,229.0	22.2	77.8	—	—	14,542.0	81.2	18.8	—
Malawi			●			0.1[39]	1986	—	...	...	...	...	5.4	...	...	...
Malaysia	●		●			6.6	1989	7,958.7	20.7	40.2	—	39.1	2,826.5	97.0	3.0	—
Maldives	...	...	...	...	...	3.2	1990	—	...	...	...	...	7.1	...	...	...
Mali	●		●		●	3.0[14, 39]	1986	8,128.8	16.6	74.3	—	9.1	7,924.6	63.7	34.7	1.6
Malta	●	●	●	●	●	33.6	1989	82.2	26.1	31.6	42.3	—	110.7	92.5	7.5	—
Marshall Islands	●					...	...	...	...	...	...	...	...	...	...	...
Martinique	●	...	...	...	●	...	1994	3,503.2	...	...	...	...	6,187.8	...	...	...
Mauritania	●		●		●	3.7[14, 17]	1989	808.4	1.5	90.4	—	8.1	735.2	63.5	31.2	5.3
Mauritius	●		●		●	16.6	1989	1,733.5	2.9	47.9	31.7	17.5	1,072.7	95.2	3.0	1.8
Mayotte	...	...	...	...	...	...	...	...	...	...	...	...	...	...	...	...
Mexico	●	●	●			22.8	1989	16,011,795.0	20.9	54.8	12.9	11.4	14,562,293.0	79.9	15.5	4.6
Micronesia	●					...	...	...	...	...	...	...	...	...	...	...
Moldova	●	●	●	●	●	...	...	...	...	...	...	...	...	...	...	...
Monaco	●	●			●	...	...	...	...	...	...	...	...	...	...	...
Mongolia	●	●	...	...	●	21.6	1989	2,431.6	—	—	20.8	79.2	2,304.6	100.0	—	—
Morocco	●	●	●		●	5.9[9]	1989	4,660.5	20.6	47.5	12.9	19.0	3,040.7	94.8	5.0	0.2
Mozambique	●	...	...	...	...	...	1986	228.2	—	86.2	13.7	0.1	145.0	100.0	—	—
Myanmar (Burma)		●	●			3.6	1986	44.3	19.9	59.6	18.5	2.0	35.9	51.5	15.6	32.9
Namibia	●	...	...	...	...	6.8[14, 19]	...	...	...	...	...	...	...	...	...	...
Nauru	●	●	●	...	●	...	...	...	...	...	...	...	...	...	...	...
Nepal	●		●			0.7[13, 14]	1985	—	...	...	...	...	59.3	...	...	...

crime and law enforcement (latest)						military protection								country
offenses reported to the police per 100,000 population					population per police officer[g]	manpower, 1997[h]		expenditure, 1995				arms trade, 1995 ('000,000 U.S.$)		
total	personal		property			total ('000)	per 1,000 population	total '000,000	per capita	% of central government expenditure	% of GDP or GNP	imports	exports	
	murder	assault	burglary	automobile theft										
...	...	...	...	...	1,000	28.4	5.0	101	18	7.4	1.1	20	0	El Salvador
...	...	...	...	...	190	1.3	3.0	2	6	21.0[29]	1.6	0	0	Equatorial Guinea
...	...	...	...	...	...	[31]	[31]	...	...	...	...	0	0	Eritrea[30]
2,383	24.3	29.3	1,160.7	169.1	...	3.5	2.4	118	80	2.9[10]	1.1	5	0	Estonia
263	16.4	49.9	6.3	2.3	1,100	[32]	[32]	118	2	9.2	2.2	0	0	Ethiopia[30]
...	...	...	...	...	...	—	[7]	—	—	—	—	...	...	Faroe Islands
2,518	11.5	51.3	463.7	51.7	407	3.6	4.6	32	42	6.0	1.7	20	0	Fiji
14,799	0.6	40.0	1,934.9	53.2	640	31.0	6.0	2,381	467	5.1	2.0	30	0	Finland
6,733	4.7	98.8	812.6	667.0	630	380.8	6.5	47,770	826	6.6	3.1	150	2,200	France
8,936	27.2	178.7	1,367.3	150.6	...	—	[7]	—	—	—	—	...	...	French Guiana
1,799	0.9	98.9	232.7	...	...	—	[7]	—	—	—	—	...	...	French Polynesia
114	1.4	17.9	2.3	7.5	1,290	4.7	3.9	104	90	9.6[12]	2.6	0	0	Gabon
89	0.4	10.6	5.6	...	3,310	0.8	0.6	15	13	16.2	4.6	0	0	Gambia, The
4,355	...	...	...	...	...	—	—	...	...	...	...	...	...	Gaza Strip
325	10.7	107.8	40.7	1.5	...	—	—	194	37	2.4[9]	2.4	10	0	Georgia
8,038	4.6	108.2	1,927.1	260.1	...	347.1	4.2	41,160	496	5.0	1.9	310	1,200	Germany
942	2.1	387.4	5.4	...	620	7.0	0.4	87	5	5.8[12]	1.4	0	0	Ghana
18,316	3.7[15]	3,213	5,250	...	170	—	[7]	—	—	—	—	...	...	Gibraltar
2,956	2.6	78.7	330.2	100.3	380	162.3	15.4	5,056	482	10.8	5.5	825	0	Greece
9,360	18.1	845.0	1,883.5	...	340	—	[7]	—	—	—	—	...	...	Greenland
8,543	7.8	98.9	582.2	...	230	[28]	[28]	...	...	...	...	...	...	Grenada
5,793	13.2	215.2	821.5	453.9	...	—	[7]	—	—	—	—	...	...	Guadeloupe
10,080	7.9	169.3	634.2	333.6	...	—	[7]	—	—	—	—	...	...	Guam
510	27.4	77.1	27.9	58.1	670	40.7	3.6	191	17	14.2	1.3	5	0	Guatemala
...	...	...	...	...	...	—	[7]	—	—	—	—	...	...	Guernsey
18.4	0.5	0.7	0.7	0.1	1,140	9.7	1.3	51	7	7.0[9]	1.5	5	0	Guinea
129	0.5	8.7	4.0	0.2	...	7.3	6.2	7	6	7.6[12]	2.8	0	0	Guinea-Bissau
3,682	4.5	40.2	242.6	32.2	190	1.6	2.1	7	10	3.0	1.3	0	0	Guyana
701	...	...	...	...	400	[35]	[35]	59	9	21.6	2.9	0	0	Haiti
...	9.4	7.7	...	3.3	1,040	18.8	3.2	51	9	8.7	1.4	10	0	Honduras
1,449	1.6	118.8	222.8	38.9	221	—	[7]	—	—	—	—	...	...	Hong Kong
3,789	4.3	79.3	767.4	51.1	710	49.1	4.8	961	95	4.6	1.5	30	20	Hungary
1,550	0.9	64.3	704.8	112.8	940	—	—	—	—	—	—	0	0	Iceland
594	4.6	...	15.6	...	820	1,145.0	1.2	7,831	8	12.7	2.4	410	5	India
60	0.8	5.1	24.8	8.0	1,119	284.0	1.4	3,398	17	8.9	1.8	170	10	Indonesia
76.6	0.5	47.7	...	...	...	518.0	8.3	4,191	65	13.6[10]	2.6	270	290	Iran
197	7.1	34.7	...	...	140	387.5	17.4	9,007[19]	528[19]	50.8[37]	74.9[19]	0	0	Iraq
2,834	1.2	13.3	859.7	44.3	310	12.7	3.5	689	193	3.4	1.3	0	0	Ireland
2,867	0.7	12.3	921.4	60.6	...	—	[7]	—	—	—	—	...	...	Isle of Man
5,191	2.1	267.2	817.2	479.5	210	175.0	31.0	8,734	1,646	21.1	9.6	340	775	Israel
3,828	4.7	36.8	...	532.8	680	325.2	5.7	19,380	338	3.9[10]	1.8	110	150	Italy
1,723	27.6	552.1	267.7	9.9	430	3.3	1.3	28	11	1.4	0.8	0	0	Jamaica
1,490	1.0	14.4	198.1	27.8	480	235.6	1.9	50,240	401	4.2[12]	1.0	625	20	Japan
...	...	...	...	...	...	—	[7]	—	—	—	—	...	...	Jersey
751	2.0	19.1	43.4	28.5	630	130.0	28.7	481	117	21.7	7.7	70	0	Jordan
815	...	...	...	...	...	35.1	2.1	426	25	...	0.9	280	20	Kazakstan
484	6.4	54.1	76.9	9.7	1,500	24.2	0.8	173	6	6.2	2.3	10	0	Kenya
261	5.1	11.6	38.6	...	330	—	—	...	...	...	...	...	...	Kiribati
...	...	...	...	...	460	1,055.0	43.4	6,000	255	40.7[39]	28.6	100	40	Korea, North
1,029	1.4	410.5	6.7	...	506	672.0	14.7	14,410	320	13.6	3.4	1,100	60	Korea, South
1,171	1.7	46.5	75.9	18.2	80	15.3	7.0	3,488	1,919	25.2	11.6	900	0	Kuwait
987	10.4[40]	12.6	482.4	...	...	12.2	2.7	57[10]	13[10]	1.1[9]	0.7[10]	0	10	Kyrgyzstan
...	...	...	...	...	280	29.0	5.7	72	15	21.3[4]	4.2	0	0	Laos
1,597	14.6	27.8	390.4	109.2	...	4.5	1.8	74	29	4.3[10]	0.9	5	0	Latvia
657	4.3	28.4	1.2	13.8	530	55.1	14.3	410	111	9.7[10]	3.7	40	0	Lebanon
1,885	33.9	170.6	221.5	...	1,130	2.0	1.0	28	15	2.5	1.9	0	0	Lesotho
...	...	...	...	...	1,570	[41]	[41]	45	21	13.3[6]	4.8[6]	0	0	Liberia
951	1.3	4.9	...	...	...	65.0	11.5	1,999	381	28.0[6]	6.0	0	0	Libya
...	...	114.3	614.3	153.6	660	—	[42]	—	—	—	—	...	...	Liechtenstein
1,199	6.9	9.1	325.2	28.1	...	5.3	1.4	78	21	2.1	0.5	5	0	Lithuania
6,933	13.2	291.7	855.2	275.5	829	0.8	1.9	142	348	1.9	0.7	0	0	Luxembourg
1,491	3.8	67.3	250.5	172.8	...	—	[7]	...	...	...	...	...	...	Macau
944	3.9	46.4	...	35.1	...	15.4	7.8	63	30	...	3.3	0	0	Macedonia
112	0.6	12.0	0.7	0.1	2,900	21.0	1.5	28	2	5.0	0.9	5	0	Madagascar
850	3.1	82.2	13.1	...	1,670	5.0	0.5	21	2	3.9[9]	1.6	0	0	Malaŵi
454	2.1	14.4	108.7	12.4	760	111.5	5.3	2,444	125	12.4	3.0	750	40	Malaysia
2,353	1.9	3.3	36.1	...	35,710	—	—	...	...	...	...	...	...	Maldives
33	—	1.1	3.9	—	160	7.4	0.7	43	5	9.4[9]	1.8	0	0	Mali
1,841	3.0	35.2	1,079.2	243.9	230	2.0	5.2	32	87	2.0[10]	1.1	0	0	Malta
2,273	...	...	...	...	400	—	[43]	—	—	—	—	...	...	Marshall Islands
6,305	5.8	184.9	641.2	192.8	...	—	[7]	—	—	—	—	...	...	Martinique
225	1.8	38	2.5	9.1	710	15.7	6.5	33	15	9.3[10]	3.2	5	0	Mauritania
3,430	3.2	11.2	85.9	...	240	—	—	14	12	1.6	0.4	0	0	Mauritius
...	...	...	...	...	...	—	[7]	—	—	—	—	...	...	Mayotte
108	7.3	30.2	...	...	...	175.0	1.9	2,321	25	5.1	1.0	20	20	Mexico
...	...	...	...	...	...	—	[43]	—	—	—	—	...	...	Micronesia
858	8.8	13.4	...	...	...	11.0	2.5	222	50	...	2.1	0	40	Moldova
4,277	...	63.4	407.1	126.8	...	—	—	...	...	...	...	...	...	Monaco
823	19.0	22.8	204.5	...	120	9.0	3.8	20	8	7.0	2.4	0	0	Mongolia
366	1.4	6.7	...	...	840	196.3	7.2	1,375	47	13.8[10]	4.3	50	0	Morocco
166	4.2	9.2	45.9	...	...	[44]	[44]	69	4	16.6[9]	5.4	0	0	Mozambique
309	4.1	31.2	0.1	0.1	650	429.0	9.2	1,833	41	37.5	3.9	140	0	Myanmar (Burma)
3,359	72.4	657.8	793.0	115.4	...	5.7	3.3	...	...	—	—	5	0	Namibia
...	25.0	400.0	100.0	...	110	—	—	...	...	...	...	...	...	Nauru
44	2.5	1.1	0.8	...	1,000	46.0	2.1	42	2	5.8	0.9	0	0	Nepal

Social protection (continued)

country	social security															
	programs available, 1997					expenditures, 1994 (% of total central govt.)[f]	finances									
							year	receipts					expenditures			
	old-age, invalidity, death[a]	sickness and maternity[b]	work injury[c]	unemployment[d]	family allowances[e]			total ('000,000 natl. cur.)	insured persons (%)	employers (%)	government (%)	other (%)	total ('000,000 natl. cur.)	benefits (%)	administration (%)	other (%)
Netherlands, The	●	●	●	●	●	37.2	1989	154,427.0	37.3	30.3	19.0	13.4	135,609.0	96.9	3.1	—
Netherlands Antilles		...	●	●	...	38.1[11]	1995	210.2	100.0	—	—	—	190.2	...	...	...
New Caledonia	...	...	...	...	●	...	1987	15,834.0	...	...	...	...	14,598.0	...	...	...
New Zealand	●	●	●	●	●	38.0	1989	14,266.0	1.0	4.7	92.5	1.8	14,372.3	95.6	2.8	1.6
Nicaragua	●	●	●		●	14.9	1989	647,454.8	13.5	49.1	7.6	29.8	452,038.6	82.4	17.6	—
Niger	●		●		●	1.7[29]	1989	5,634.9	9.4	90.6	—	—	3,804.2	62.5	—	37.5
Nigeria	●		●			2.5[47]	1989	54.0	50.0	50.0	—	—	22.6	42.5	57.5	—
Northern Mariana Islands	●	...	...	...	...	...	...	...	...	...	...	...	...	...	...	...
Norway	●	●	●	●	●	36.7	1989	158,105.0	18.3	31.4	46.6	3.7	131,578.2	98.7	1.3	—
Oman	●	...	●	...	...	3.2	1995	—	...	...	...	...	62.2[18]	...	...	...
Pakistan	●	●	●			0.2[14, 48]	1989	9,321.4	1.3	8.0	84.3	6.4	8,092.0	97.4	1.2	1.4
Palau	●					...	...	...	...	...	...	...	...	...	...	...
Panama	●	●	●			21.4	1989	496.7	31.0	39.5	7.1	22.4	452.8	94.0	4.8	1.2
Papua New Guinea	●		●			0.7	1983	45.0	40.5	32.1	8.0	19.4	9.4	82.3	9.7	8.0
Paraguay	●	●	●			16.2[12]	1993	49,272.0[39]	...	...	...	...	249,819.0	...	...	...
Peru	●	●	●			0.2[14, 34]	1989	1,363,280.6	30.2	65.1	4.7	—	1,435,134.1	78.5	21.5	—
Philippines	●	●	●			2.9[12]	1989	19,213.6	22.2	32.3	—	45.5	7,878.3	87.3	12.3	—
Poland	●	●	●	●	●	...	1989	11,572,248.0	2.1	70.2	25.1	2.6	11,452,165.0	98.8	1.2	—
Portugal	●	●	●	●	●	27.3[3]	1989	833,442.5	31.3	50.1	13.4	5.2	756,410.8	94.6	4.2	1.2
Puerto Rico	●	●	●	●	●	...	1980	...	...	...	...	...	1,041.3	100.0	—	—
Qatar	...	...	...	...	...	...	1986	80.0	—	—	100.0	—	80.0	100.0	—	—
Réunion	...	...	...	...	...	...	1994	...	...	...	...	...	11,030.7	...	...	...
Romania	●	●	●	●	●	28.8	1989	90,561.2	—	48.9	51.1	—	90,561.2	100.0	—	—
Russia	●	●	●	●	●	28.5	...	...	...	...	...	...	...	...	...	...
Rwanda	●		●			2.9[37]	1989	2,350.0	23.9	39.8	—	36.3	965.8	60.8	39.2	—
St. Kitts and Nevis	●	●	●			9.4[49]	1989	14.3	...	...	...	...	7.9	...	...	...
St. Lucia	●	●	●			...	1986	14.6	28.6	28.6	—	42.8	3.4	61.4	38.6	—
St. Vincent and the Grenadines	●	●	●			7.7	1989	—	...	...	...	...	—	...	...	...
Samoa	●		●			—	...	—	...	...	...	...	—	...	...	...
San Marino	●	...	...	●	...	...	1983	51,673.0	12.0	48.7	36.1	3.2	46,179.0	95.7	3.7	0.6
São Tomé and Príncipe	●	●	●			...	1986	46.4	37.7	56.3	—	6.0	23.7	100.0	—	—
Saudi Arabia	●		●			...	1989	1,761.4	26.8	73.2	—	—	4,292.9	100.0	—	—
Senegal	●		●		●	2.6[14, 19]	1989	17,202.0	—	47.6	51.4	1.0	15,371.0	84.6	11.1	4.3
Seychelles	●	●	●			12.8	1983	69.1	30.1	60.2	—	9.7	42.7	69.6	4.9	25.5
Sierra Leone			●			2.3[3]	1990	...	...	...	...	...	153.00	100.0	—	—
Singapore	●		●			2.9	1989	7,531.9	49.1	35.3	0.1	15.6	5,045.8	78.0	0.6	21.4
Slovakia	●	●	●	●	●	...	1995	44,603	18.5	66.4	10.6	0.5	28,673	...	...	...
Slovenia	●	●	●	●	●	...	...	...	...	...	...	...	...	...	...	...
Solomon Islands	●		●			0.7[14, 39]	1989	20.9	27.8	41.1	—	31.1	17.4	89.7	10.3	—
Somalia			●			1.7[47]	...	—	...	...	...	...	...	...	...	...
South Africa	●	●	●	●		...	1994	2,034	—	100.0	—	—	2,260.0	...	...	...
Spain	●	●	●	●	●	39.6[12]	1989	8,320,972.0	15.9	53.9	27.9	2.3	8,038,090.0	94.3	2.6	3.1
Sri Lanka	●		●		●	16.7	1989	15,399.9	22.0	24.4	29.1	24.5	5,819.0	98.5	1.3	0.2
Sudan, The	●		●			0.4[6, 14]	1989	62.0	24.9	0.5	—	74.6	14.7	37.5	62.5	—
Suriname	●	...	...	...	●	6.0[14, 48]	1989	73.0	24.7	75.3	—	—	70.6	100.0	—	—
Swaziland	●		●			0.4[12]	1986	10.7	31.4	31.4	—	37.2	3.9	45.8	54.2	—
Sweden	●	●	●	●	●	48.2	1989	446,909.7	2.8	37.9	50.8	8.5	439,997.3	93.7	3.3	3.0
Switzerland	●	●	●	●	●	48.2[12]	1989	45,800.1	45.6	22.6	25.9	5.9	41,745.7	91.5	3.0	5.5
Syria	●		●			2.1	1989	3,147.9	30.4	60.9	...	5.6	1,455.9	95.7	4.2	0.1
Taiwan	●	●	●			13.8[3]	...	...	...	...	...	...	...	...	...	...
Tajikistan	●	●	●	●	●	...	...	...	...	...	...	...	...	...	...	...
Tanzania	●		●			0.5[13]	1989	3,275.8	25.9	25.9	—	48.2	2,780.7	5.8	14.1	80.1
Thailand	●	●	●			3.5	1989	654.0	—	60.2	—	39.8	260.0	88.2	11.8	—
Togo	●		●		●	6.5[14, 49]	1989	10,162.0	8.1	61.5	—	30.4	5,844.0	77.5	22.5	—
Tonga	...	...	...	...	...	0.8[19]	...	...	...	...	...	...	...	...	...	...
Trinidad and Tobago	●	●	●			5.3[14, 27]	1989	584.9	12.0	24.1	39.7	24.2	438.4	85.6	11.1	3.3
Tunisia	●	●	●	●	●	14.3[13]	1989	325.3	36.9	63.1	—	—	358.3	90.0[20]	6.1[20]	3.9[20]
Turkey	●	●	●			3.9	1989	12,075,809.0	28.5	32.9	22.8	15.8	10,241,427.0	97.2	2.2	0.6
Turkmenistan	●	●	●	●	●	...	...	...	...	...	...	...	...	...	...	...
Tuvalu	●	...	...	...	...	...	1981	...	...	...	...	...	0.1	67.6	32.4	—
Uganda	●		●			2.1[14, 48]	1989	265.9	32.1	64.3	1.1	2.5	145.0	0.3	76.8	22.9
Ukraine	●	●	●	●	●	...	1989	20,350.0	—	—	—	—	20,350.0	100.0	—	—
United Arab Emirates	...	...	...	...	...	3.4	1989	182.2	17.3	6.2	0.5	76.0	182.2	100.0	...	...
United Kingdom	●	●	●	●	●	31.3	1989	92,157.0	18.1	24.9	52.9	4.1	88,294.0	93.8	3.3	2.9
United States	●		●	●		29.2	1989	804,909.0	25.5	33.9	28.8	11.8	627,653.0	95.5	3.3	1.2
Uruguay	●	●	●	●	●	60.6	1989	535,507.0	31.4	37.3	26.0	5.3	548,591.0	93.6	5.4	1.0
Uzbekistan	●	●	●	●	●	...	...	...	...	...	...	...	...	...	...	...
Vanuatu	●					0.9[14, 48]	...	—	...	...	...	...	—	...	...	...
Venezuela	●	●	●	●		6.9[48]	1986	7,457.6	21.3	40.7	12.7	25.3	6,355.7	86.1	14.9	—
Vietnam	●	●	●			...	...	...	...	...	...	...	...	...	...	...
Virgin Islands (U.S.)	●	...	...	●	●	...	...	...	...	...	...	...	...	...	...	...
West Bank	...	...	...	...	...	...	...	...	...	...	...	...	...	...	...	...
Western Sahara	...	...	...	...	...	...	...	...	...	...	...	...	...	...	...	...
Yemen	●	...	●	...	...	—	...	—	...	...	...	...	—	...	...	...
Yugoslavia	●	●	●	●	●	6.0[57]	1986[57]	2,777,651.0	63.3	32.2	3.4	1.1	2,732,679.0	90.3	1.9	7.8
Zambia	●		●			3.9	1986	179.2	28.4	28.4	—	43.2	67.7	40.6	59.4	—
Zimbabwe	●		●			3.4[6]	1983	167.0	25.9	7.6	64.2	2.3	112.2	93.7	6.2	0.1

[1]Rural areas only. [2]The bulk of the national armed forces disintegrated after the fall of the central government in April 1992, with only the northern corps retaining its integrity. [3]1990. [4]1984. [5]The Albanian forces have not been reconstituted since the civil unrest of early 1997. [6]1989. [7]Political dependency; defense is the responsibility of the administering country. [8]Includes civilian militia. [9]1992. [10]1994. [11]Netherlands Antilles includes Aruba. [12]1993. [13]1985. [14]Social security only. [15]Includes manslaughter. [16]Includes rape. [17]1979. [18]Includes welfare. [19]1991. [20]1977. [21]1976. [22]Local officers only. [23]Military defense is the responsibility of France. [24]1971. [25]Republic of Cyprus only. [26]Data refer to former Czechoslovakia. [27]1981. [28]Paramilitary unit of country participating in the U.S.-sponsored Regional Security System, a defense pact among eastern Caribbean countries. [29]1980. [30]Ethiopia includes Eritrea except in arms trade. [31]Demobilization of some Eritrean forces began in late 1993. Estimated strength of these forces is currently about 46,000. [32]Following the declaration of independence by Eritrea in May 1993, estimated strength of Ethiopian forces is currently about 100,000. [33]Former West Germany. [34]1983. [35]In 1994 the military government of Haiti was replaced by a civilian administration. Both the armed forces and police have been

crime and law enforcement (latest)						military protection								country
offenses reported to the police per 100,000 population					population per police officer[g]	manpower, 1997[h]		expenditure, 1995				arms trade, 1995 ('000,000 U.S.$)		
total	personal		property			total ('000)	per 1,000 population	total '000,000	per capita	% of central government expenditure	% of GDP or GNP	imports	exports	
	murder	assault	burglary	automobile theft										
10,181	24.9	191.8	3,803.0	316.8	510	52.8	3.4	8,012	518	4.4	2.1	220	230	Netherlands, The
5,574[45]	...	396	3,455	...	330	—	[7]	—	—	—	—	...	...	Netherlands Antilles
...	...	...	...	...	...	—	[7]	—	—	—	—	...	...	New Caledonia
13,854	3.9	546.3	2,352.9	788.6	630	9.6	2.6	740	211	3.3	1.3	40	5	New Zealand
1,069	25.6	203.8	110.7	...	90[8]	17.0	3.9	34	8	5.3	2.2	0	40	Nicaragua
32	0.2	2.5	1.0	0.1	2,350[46]	5.3	0.6	21	2	7.9	1.2	0	0	Niger
312	...	...	...	...	1,140	77.0	0.7	324[10]	3[10]	5.0[10]	0.8[10]	10	0	Nigeria
245	3.8	92.6	73.7	20.8	...	—	[7]	—	—	—	—	...	...	Northern Mariana Islands
9,187	1.0	—	95.0	516.6	660	33.6	7.6	3,508	804	6.5[10]	2.7	140	20	Norway
198	0.8	1.1	...	...	430	43.5	19.2	1,735	822	33.9	16.7	460	0	Oman
247	6.4	0.1	9.1	4.1	720	587.0	4.3	3,740	30	25.3	6.1	480	20	Pakistan
...	...	...	323.0	...	...	—	[43]	—	—	—	—	...	...	Palau
380	13.9	21.9	...	77.7	180	—	—	—	—	—	—	0	0	Panama
766	8.6	66.7	63	22.0	720	4.3	1.0	107	25	5.6	1.4	0	0	Papua New Guinea
313	15.6	62.2	105.1	50.3	310	20.2	4.0	121	23	7.3	1.4	0	0	Paraguay
1,178	9.3	104.3	87.0	22.7	730	125.0	5.1	989	41	9.3	1.7	280	0	Peru
230	30.1	41.8	...	1.2	1,160	110.5	1.5	1,151	16	8.5	1.5	90	0	Philippines
2,351	3.1	71.8	789.5	109.0	370	241.8	6.2	4,887	127	5.4	2.3	90	40	Poland
988	4.2	1.7	186.9	65.8	660	59.3	6.0	2,690	273	5.9[10]	2.6	90	0	Portugal
3,182	26.8	174.8	853.0	482.9	380	—	[7]	—	—	—	—	...	...	Puerto Rico
775	1.8	41.7	40.8	10.5	...	11.8	19.0	330	617	9.4	4.4	50	0	Qatar
2,097	7.8	123.1	181.3	137.9	220	—	[7]	—	—	—	—	...	...	Réunion
1,039	3.3	4.7	133.2	9.5	...	227.0	10.1	2,520	115	11.2	2.5	0	20	Romania
1,779	21.8	45.8	262.3	55.2	...	1,240.0	8.4	76,000	513	38.1[10]	11.4	0	3,300	Russia
14,550	12,500	25.0	12.5	12.5	4,650	55.0	7.1	118	20	23.3[12]	5.2	0	0	Rwanda
15,468	...	...	...	...	300	[28]	[28]	...	...	...	...	...	...	St. Kitts and Nevis
4,386	17.0	1,193.0	778.0	...	430	[28]	[28]	...	...	...	...	...	...	St. Lucia
3,977	10.3	986.9	...	...	250	[28]	[28]	...	...	...	...	...	...	St. Vincent and the Grenadines
...	...	...	...	...	...	—	[50]	—	—	—	—	...	...	Samoa
...	4.1	...	...	...	...	—	—	...	...	...	...	...	...	San Marino
558	4.0	...	...	...	400	—	—	1[29]	7[29]	2.5[29]	1.6[29]	0	0	São Tomé and Príncipe
131	0.9	17.2	...	28.5	280	105.5	5.5	17,210	919	41.5	13.5	8,600	40	Saudi Arabia
190	1.4	44.7	2.0	...	730	13.4	1.4	76	9	13.7[9]	1.6	5	0	Senegal
4,517	2.7	698.7	1,058.9	...	120	0.2	2.6	8[4]	124[4]	7.4[4]	5.6[4]	...	...	Seychelles
...	...	...	...	...	600	[51]	[51]	41	9	28.9	6.1	0	0	Sierra Leone
1,367	1.7	4.9	83.9	7.2	230	70.0	22.6	3,970	1,191	24.0	4.7	200	30	Singapore
2,571	2.4	158.1	629.8	170.6	...	35.8	6.6	577	108	6.8	3.0	290	70	Slovakia
2,210	4.9	20.9	526.4	25.1	...	9.6	4.9	344	176	3.5	1.5	30	5	Slovenia
...	...	...	...	...	620	—	—	...	...	...	...	0	0	Solomon Islands
144	1.5	8.0	31.2	...	540	[52]	[52]	8[12]	1[12]	30.0[48]	0.9[12]	0	0	Somalia
...	...	...	...	...	870	79.4	1.9	2,895	71	6.7	2.2	250	100	South Africa
2,287	2.6	23.5	555.4	253.0	580	197.5	5.0	8,652	221	5.6	1.6	675	80	Spain
280	8.2	10.8	54.7	...	860	115.3	6.3	585	32	15.7	4.6	160	0	Sri Lanka
1,565	4.2	40.5	0.4	3.4	740	79.7	2.4	882[9]	32[9]	175.4[9]	17.1[9]	100	0	Sudan, The
17,819	7.6	1,824.4	...	...	...	1.4	3.3	39	90	5.3[3]	3.0	0	0	Suriname
4,853	88.1	589.1	941.4	71.4	610	—	—	27	28	7.0	2.6	0	0	Swaziland
12,982	4.5	42.5	1,615.1	658.9	330	53.4	6.0	6,042	683	5.8	2.8	10	310	Sweden
4,326.8	2.3	52.9	973.0	1,247.4	640	3.3	0.5	5,034	703	6.0[12]	1.6	20	100	Switzerland
89	1.4	7.0	21.2	2.9	1,970	320.0	21.3	3,563	236	60.3[19]	7.2	20	0	Syria
799	8.2	...	...	124.9	720	376.0	17.4	13,140	618	34.9	5.0	1,200	10	Taiwan
317	2.5	4.6	...	...	...	7.0	1.2	209	36	...	3.7	0	10	Tajikistan
1,250	6.4	0.5	97.3	0.9	1,330	34.6	1.2	69	2	8.4	1.8	0	0	Tanzania
351	7.7	25.4	9.9	3.3	530	266.0	4.4	4,014	69	15.2	2.5	1,100	0	Thailand
11	...	...	...	...	1,970	7.0	1.5	28	7	10.2	2.3	0	0	Togo
2,100	...	...	...	...	330	—	[50]	—	—	—	—	...	...	Tonga
1,382	11.7	56.7	567.0	86.4	280	2.1	1.6	82	64	4.0[10]	1.7	0	0	Trinidad and Tobago
1,240	2.1	134.0	143.6	11.1	340	35.0	3.8	345	39	6.3[12]	2.0	40	0	Tunisia
339	3.6	24.2	...	17.0	1,570	639.0	10.0	6,606	108	17.6	4.0	700	60	Turkey
...	...	...	...	...	...	[53]	[53]	196	48	3.7[9]	4.1	30	0	Turkmenistan
...	...	...	...	—	290	—	—	...	...	...	...	...	...	Tuvalu
140	9.5	15.6	15.1	5.3	1,090	[54]	[54]	126	6	13.3	2.3	0	0	Uganda
1,096	8.8	32.3	...	42.3	...	387.4	7.6	3,588	70	7.8	2.9	0	0	Ukraine
1,496	1.1	1.7	10.5	...	140	35.0	13.6	1,880	643	38.4	4.8	875	10	United Arab Emirates
9,880[55]	2.5[55]	362.1[55]	2,404.4[55]	1,147.3[55]	350	213.8	3.6	33,400	572	7.2	3.0	190	5,200	United Kingdom
5,374	9.0	430.2	1,041.8	591.2	318	1,447.6	5.4	277,800	1,056	17.4	3.8	1,000	15.600	United States
6,806	4.1	169.6	56.9	...	170	25.6	8.0	410	127	7.3	2.4	5	0	Uruguay
334	5.5	4.5	40.9	5.9	...	49.0	2.1	2,062	90	...	3.8	0	10	Uzbekistan
...	...	...	...	...	450	—	—	...	...	...	...	...	...	Vanuatu
1,106	22.1	152.2	358.2	239.4	320	79.0	3.5	854	40	6.3	1.1	90	0	Venezuela
...	...	...	...	...	...	492.0	6.5	544	7	10.9	2.6	200	0	Vietnam
10,441	22.3	1,943.2	3,183.7	954	240	—	[7]	—	—	—	—	...	...	Virgin Islands (U.S.)
2,226	...	...	...	...	...	—	—	...	...	...	...	...	...	West Bank
...	...	...	...	...	...	—	[7]	—	—	—	—	...	...	Western Sahara
170[56]	...	...	...	...	1,940	66.3	4.0	2,082[10]	147[10]	14.5[10]	14.1[10]	140	0	Yemen
1,268	...	...	...	...	140[53]	114.2	10.7	3,608[19,57]	158[19,57]	55.0[3,57]	3.9[19,57]	0	0	Yugoslavia
666	9.8	9.5	153.5	9.6	540	21.6	2.3	102	11	12.6	2.8	0	0	Zambia
2,160	5.0	193.6	445.3	9.1	750	39.0	3.4	220	20	10.5[10]	3.9	0	0	Zimbabwe

disbanded and an Interim Public Security Force of about 3,000 has been formed. [36]Coverage is through tax system. [37]1982. [38]1988–89. [39]1988. [40]Includes attempted murders. [41]All militias agreed to disarm and demobilize under a transitional plan negotiated in 1996. [42]Military defense is the responsibility of Switzerland. [43]Military defense is the responsibility of the United States. [44]Forces are estimated between 5,100–6,100. [45]Curaçao only. [46]Includes paramilitary forces. [47]1978. [48]1986. [49]1987. [50]Military defense is the responsibility of New Zealand. [51]Following the civil war of May–June 1997, the armed forces were reorganized. An exact figure is not known. [52]Following the 1991 revolution, no national armed forces have yet been formed. [53]Forces estimated between 19,000–21,000. [54]Forces estimated between 40,000–50,000. [55]England and Wales. [56]Former Yemen Arab Republic. [57]Data refer to Yugoslavia as constituted prior to 1991.

Education

This table presents international data on education analyzed to provide maximum comparability among the different educational systems in use among the nations of the world. The principal data are, naturally, numbers of schools, teachers, and students, arranged by four principal levels of education—the first (primary); general second level (secondary); vocational second level; and third level (higher). Whenever possible, data referring to preprimary education programs have been excluded from this compilation. The ratio of students to teachers is calculated for each level. These data are supplemented at each level by a figure for enrollment ratio, an indicator of each country's achieved capability to educate the total number of children potentially educable in the age group usually represented by that level. At the first and second levels this is given as a net enrollment ratio and at the third level as a gross enrollment ratio. Two additional comparative measures are given at the third level: students per 100,000 population and proportion (percentage) of adults age 25 and over who have achieved some level of higher or postsecondary education. Data in this last group are confined as far as possible to those who have completed their educations and are no longer in school. No enrollment ratio is provided for vocational training at the second level because of the great variation worldwide in the academic level at which vocational training takes place, in the need of countries to encourage or direct students into vocational programs (to support national development), and, most particularly, in the age range of students who normally constitute a national vocational system (some will be as young as 14, having just completed a primary cycle; others will be much older).

At each level of education, differences in national statistical practice, in national educational structure, public-private institutional mix, training and deployment of teachers, and timing of cycles of enrollment or completion of particular grades or standards all contribute to the problems of comparability among national educational systems.

Reporting the number of schools in a country is not simply a matter of counting permanent red-brick buildings with classrooms in them. Often the resources of a less developed country are such that temporary or outdoor facilities are all that can be afforded, while in a developed but sparsely settled country students might have to travel 80 km (50 mi) a day to find a classroom with 20 students of the same age, leading to the institution of measures such as traveling teachers, radio or televisual instruction at home under the supervision of parents, or similar systems. According to UNESCO definitions, therefore, a "school" is defined only as "a body of students . . . organized to receive instruction."

Such difficulties also limit the comparability of statistics on numbers of teachers, with the further complications that many at any level must work part-time, or that the institutions in which they work may perform a mixture of functions that do not break down into the tidy categories required by a table of this sort. In certain countries teacher training is confined to higher education, in others as a vocational form of secondary training, and so on. For purposes of this table, teacher training at the secondary level has been treated as vocational education. At the higher level, teacher training is classified as one more specialization in higher education itself.

The number of students may conceal great variation in what each country defines as a particular educational "level." Many countries do, indeed, have a primary system composed of grades 1 through 6 (or 1 through 8) that passes students on to some kind of postprimary education. But the age of intake, the ability of parents to send their children or to permit

Education

country	year	first level (primary)					general second level (secondary)					vocational second level[a]	
		schools	teachers[c]	students[d]	student/ teacher ratio	net enroll-ment ratio[b]	schools	teachers[c]	students[d]	student/ teacher ratio	net enroll-ment ratio[b]	schools	teachers[c]
Afghanistan	1995	1,753[1]	20,055[2]	1,312,197	...	29	819[3]	17,548[2, 4]	512,815[4]	...	...	33[1]	[4]
Albania	1993	1,777	32,098	535,713	16.7	96	47[6]	4,149	73,259	17.7	...	466[6]	7,390[6]
Algeria	1996	17,186	169,010	4,617,000	27.3	95	3,954	150,397	2,544,864	16.9	56	...	...
American Samoa	1992	30	524	7,884	15.0	...	7[3]	245	3,483	14.2	...	1	21
Andorra	1997	12	...	5,424		...	6	...	2,655	...	...	...	...
Angola	1991	...	31,062	990,155	31.9	...	...	5,138[6]	166,812	30.2[6]	...	...	566[6]
Antigua and Barbuda	1995	43[8]	439	11,506	26.2	...	12[8]	277	4,294	15.5	...	1	16
Argentina	1995	25,448	286,885	5,126,307	17.9	...	7,239[4]	233,564[4]	2,238,091[4]	9.6[4]	...	[4]	[4]
Armenia	1995	1,400[9]	54,000[2, 9]	574,500[9]	11.0[2, 9]	...	[9]	[9]	[9]	[9]	...	69[2]	...
Aruba	1993	32	331	7,139	21.6	...	10	183	3,247	17.7	...	14	225
Australia	1995	9,865[9]	202,401[9]	3,109,337[9]	15.4[9]	98	[9]	[9]	[9]	[9]	89	...	...
Austria	1996	4,557[10]	65,977[10]	649,994[10]	9.9[10]	100	693[4]	39,553[4]	295,473[4]	7.5[4]	90	[4]	[4]
Azerbaijan	1995	4,502[9]	156,000[9]	1,486,000[9]	9.5[9]	...	[9]	[9]	[9]	[9]	...	78	...
Bahamas, The	1994	115	1,581	33,343	21.1	95	...	1,775	28,363	16.0	87	...	...
Bahrain	1995	124	3,536[12]	72,329	...	100	...	2,305[12]	48,944	...	85	...	820[12]
Bangladesh	1994	66,168	242,252	15,185,000	62.7	62	11,019	135,217	4,884,000	36.1	20	152	1,857
Barbados	1992	106	1,553	26,662	17.2	78	33[6]	1,406[6]	21,259[6]	15.1[6]	75	...	...
Belarus	1996	4,900[9]	127,000[9]	1,561,000[9]	12.3[9]	95	[9]	[9]	[9]	[9]	...	149	...
Belgium	1994	4,453	72,589[1, 13]	731,527	...	98	1,950	110,599[8]	796,914	...	98	304[1]	...
Belize	1997	245	1,939[7]	52,994	25.9[7]	99	30	740[7]	10,648	13.7[7]	36	...	...
Benin	1994	2,889	12,343	602,069	48.8	59	145	2,384	97,480	40.9	...	14	283
Bermuda	1995	24[6]	294	5,793	19.7	...	12[6]	198	3,610	18.2	...	...	...
Bhutan	1990	235[1]	1,859[1]	56,773[1]	30.5[1]	...	31	662	15,984	24.1	...	8	149
Bolivia	1991	...	51,763	1,278,775	24.7	91	...	12,434[4]	219,232[4]	17.6[4]	29	...	[4]
Bosnia and Herzegovina	1991	2,205	23,369	539,875	23.1	98	238	9,030	172,063	19.1	...	...	...
Botswana	1994	669	11,726	310,050	26.4	96	188	4,712	86,684	18.4	45	45	966
Brazil	1994	195,545	1,335,270	31,101,662	23.3	90	13,449	295,542	4,510,199	15.3	19	...	...
Brunei	1995	170[13]	3,380[13]	55,241[13]	16.3[13]	91	37	2,157	27,801	12.9	68	6	370
Bulgaria	1996	3,325[9]	70,763[9]	963,582[9]	13.6[9]	97	[9]	[9]	[9]	[9]	75	535	19,141
Burkina Faso	1994	2,971	10,300	600,032	58.2	31	173[8]	3,346	116,033	34.7	7	22[8]	639
Burundi	1993	1,418	10,400	651,086	62.6	52	113[14]	2,562	55,713	21.7	5	...	...
Cambodia	1995	4,539[1]	37,827	1,703,316	45.0	...	440[1]	16,349	297,555	18.2	...	65[1]	2,618[1]
Cameroon	1995	6,801	40,970	1,896,722	46.3	...	...	14,917	459,068	30.8	...	...	5,885
Canada	1995	12,700	148,724	2,413,126	16.2	95	3,324	133,358	2,469,552	18.5	92	...	...
Cape Verde	1994	370[14]	2,657	78,173	29.4	100	...	438	11,808	27.0	22	...	94[16]
Central African Republic	1991	930	4,004	308,409	77.0	54	46[4]	845[4]	46,989[4]	55.6[4]	...	[4]	[4]
Chad	1995	2,447	9,404[17]	591,784[17]	62.9[17]	...	66[3]	2,046	82,559	40.4	...	...	157
Chile	1994	8,323	78,813	2,119,737	26.9	86	...	50,187[4]	664,498[4]	13.2[4]	55	...	[4]
China	1995	849,123	6,539,000	159,064,000	24.3	99	81,020	3,334,000	53,710,000	16.1	...	14,196	549,000
Colombia	1994	46,707	170,526	4,327,507	25.4	85	8,161	141,484	2,879,681	20.3	50	...	...
Comoros	1994	275	1,737[12]	77,837	43.0[12]	53	...	613[8]	17,474	25.5[8]	...	...	...
Congo, Dem. Rep. of the	1995	14,885	121,054	5,417,506	44.8	61	4,276[1, 4]	59,325[1, 4]	640,298[2]	22.6[1, 4]	23	[4]	[4]
Congo, Rep. of the	1996	1,612	7,060	497,305	70.4	...	...	5,710	189,381	33.2	...	...	1,463
Costa Rica	1995	3,544	15,806[2]	508,923	31.4[2]	92	285	...	207,231	...	43	...	...
Côte d'Ivoire	1995	7,185	36,058	1,609,929	44.6	47	...	9,505	463,810	48.8	...	...	1,424
Croatia	1995	1,928	24,194	431,795	17.8	82	482	15,269	196,740	12.9	66	3	79
Cuba	1996	9,864	90,565	1,074,153	11.9	99	2,175[6]	46,722	460,438	9.8	59	618[6]	27,267
Cyprus[18]	1995	383	3,498	64,884	18.5	96	107	3,832	53,738	14.0	93	11	509
Czech Republic	1996	4,212	63,019	1,004,565	15.9	98	361	10,903	133,093	12.2	88	832	18,458
Denmark	1995	2,536	58,500[2]	605,798	10.4[2]	99	153	11,000[2]	75,793	6.8[2]	86	237	12,000[2]

them to finish that level, or the need to withdraw the children seasonally for agricultural work all make even a simple enrollment figure difficult to assess in isolation. All of these difficulties are compounded when a country has instruction in more than one language or when its educational establishment is so small that higher, sometimes even secondary, education cannot take place within the country. Enrollment figures in this table may, therefore, include students enrolled outside the country.

Student-teacher ratio, however, usually provides a good measure of the ratio of trained educators to the enrolled educable. In general, at each level of education both students and teachers have been counted on the basis of full-time enrollment or employment, or full-time equivalent when country statistics permit. At the primary and secondary levels, net enrollment ratio is the ratio of the number of children within the usual age group for a particular level who are actually enrolled to the total number of children in that age group (× 100). This ratio is usually less than (occasionally, equal to) 100 and is the most accurate measure of the completeness of enrollment at that particular level. It is not always, however, the best indication of utilization of teaching staff and facilities. Utilization, provided here for higher education only, is best seen in a gross enrollment ratio, which compares total enrollment (of all ages) to the population within the normal age limits for that level. For a country with substantial adult literacy or general educational programs, the difference may be striking: typically, for a less developed country, even one with a good net enrollment ratio of 90 to 95, the gross enrollment ratio may be 20%, 25%, even 30% higher, indicating the heavy use made by the country of facilities and teachers at that level.

Literacy data provided here have been compiled as far as possible from data for the population age 15 and over for the best comparability internationally. Standards as to what constitutes literacy may also differ markedly; sometimes completion of a certain number of years of school is taken to constitute literacy; elsewhere it may mean only the ability to read or write at a minimal level testable by a census taker; in other countries studies have been undertaken to distinguish among degrees of functional literacy. When a country reports an official 100% (or near) literacy rate, it should usually be viewed with caution, as separate studies of "functional" literacy for such a country may indicate 10%, 20%, or even higher rates of inability to read, or write, effectively. Substantial use has been made of UNESCO literacy estimates, both for some of the least developed countries (where the statistical base is poorest) and for some of the most fully developed, where literacy is no longer perceived as a problem, thus no longer in need of monitoring.

Finally, the data provided for public expenditure on education are complete in that they include all levels of public expenditure (national, state, local) but are incomplete for certain countries in that they do not include data for private expenditure; in some countries this fraction of the educational establishment may be of significant size. Occasionally data for external aid to education may be included in addition to domestic expenditure.

The following notes further define the column headings:

a. Usually includes teacher training at the second level.
b. Latest.
c. Full-time.
d. Full-time; may include students registered in foreign schools.

		third level (higher)							literacy[b]				public expenditure on education (percent of GNP)[b]	country
students[d]	student/ teacher ratio	institutions	teachers[c]	students[d]	student/ teacher ratio	gross enroll- ment ratio[b]	students per 100,000 popula- tion[b]	percent of population age 25 and over with post- secondary education[b]	over age	total (%)	male (%)	female (%)		
[4]	...	5[3, 5]	444[6]	9,367[6]	21.1[6]	1.8	165	...	15	31.5	47.2	15.0	...	Afghanistan
138,000[6]	18.7[6]	8[6]	1,774	30,185	17.0	9.6	899	...	10	91.8	95.5	88.0	3.4	Albania
...	...	...	14,475[7]	233,019[7]	16.1[7]	10.9	1,126	...	15	61.6	73.9	49.0	5.6	Algeria
160	7.6	2	...	...	...	...	...	22.6	15	95.9	95.6	96.3	...	American Samoa
...	...	—	—	—	—	...	...	...	15	100.0	100.0	100.0	...	Andorra
19,687	...	1	439	6,534	14.9	0.7	71	...	15	41.7	55.6	28.5	4.9	Angola
46	2.9	...	...	...	...	...	...	...	15	90.0	...	...	...	Antigua and Barbuda
[4]	[4]	1,705	118,695	926,793	7.8	38.1	3,116	12.0	15	96.2	96.2	96.2	4.5	Argentina
25,200[2]	...	14	...	36,500	...	41.8	3,225	...	15	98.8	99.4	98.1	7.2	Armenia
2,594	11.5	1	16	88	5.5	...	...	7.0	15	95.0	...	...	4.5	Aruba
917,801	...	95[3]	25,916[3]	604,177	...	71.7	5,401	...	15	99.5	...	...	5.6	Australia
[4]	[4]	44[7]	14,322[7]	222,095	15.9[7]	44.8	2,933	...	15	100.0	100.0	100.0	5.5	Austria
73,000	...	23	...	89,100	...	19.8	1,619	...	15	97.3	98.9	95.9	3.0	Azerbaijan
...	...	1[1, 11]	300[1, 11]	3,201[1, 11]	10.7[1, 11]	...	...	13.5	15	98.2	98.5	98.0	4.0	Bahamas, The
7,113	...	...	655[2]	7,676[2]	11.7[2]	20.2	1,445	10.3	15	85.2	89.1	79.4	4.8	Bahrain
29,923	16.1	1,268	36,000	1,032,635	28.7	4.4	399	...	15	38.1	49.4	26.1	2.3	Bangladesh
...	...	1[6]	153[6]	1,314[6]	8.6[6]	28.1	2,501	...	15	97.4	98.0	96.8	7.2	Barbados
122,400	...	59	16,900[2]	197,400	10.5[2]	42.6	3,031	...	15	97.9	99.4	96.6	5.6	Belarus
155,192[1]	...	21[1]	...	123,320[1]	...	49.1	3,206	...	15	100.0	100.0	100.0	5.7	Belgium
...	...	11	...	2,469	...	...	...	6.6	14	70.3	...	...	6.1	Belize
4,873	17.2	16	602	9,964	16.5	2.6	208	1.3	15	37.0	48.7	25.8	3.1	Benin
...	...	1	56[6]	512	8.9[6]	...	...	18.4	15	96.9	96.7	97.0	3.7	Bermuda
1,822	12.2	2	57	519	9.1	...	...	...	15	42.2	56.2	28.1	2.7	Bhutan
[4]	[4]	...	4,261[8]	109,503[8]	25.7[8]	22.2	2,154	9.9	15	83.1	90.5	76.0	6.6	Bolivia
...	...	44	2,802	37,541	13.4	...	...	...	10	85.5	96.5	76.6	...	Bosnia and Herzegovina
6,373	6.6	1	507	5,062	10.0	4.1	403	1.4	15	69.8	80.5	59.9	9.6	Botswana
...	...	851	155,776	1,661,034	10.7	11.3	1,094	...	15	83.3	83.3	83.2	4.6	Brazil
1,966	5.3	4	325	1,606	4.9	6.6	518	...	15	87.8	92.5	82.5	3.1	Brunei
213,337	11.1	88	25,339	248,571	9.8	39.4	2,942	15.0	15	97.9	98.7	97.1	4.2	Bulgaria
8,808	13.8	9[8]	571	8,815	15.4	1.1	93	...	15	19.2	29.5	9.2	3.6	Burkina Faso
...	...	8	556	4,256	7.6	0.9	74	0.6	15	35.3	49.3	22.5	2.8	Burundi
16,350	...	9[1]	784	11,652	14.9	1.6	119	...	15	65.3	79.7	53.4	...	Cambodia
91,779	15.6	...	1,086[14]	33,177[14]	30.5[14]	3.3	289	...	15	63.4	75.0	52.1	2.9	Cameroon
...	...	265[15]	64,100[2]	1,209,386[15]	14.4[2]	102.9	6,984	21.4	15	96.6	...	...	7.3	Canada
2,289	...	...	...	...	...	...	...	...	15	71.6	81.4	63.8	4.4	Cape Verde
[4]	[4]	1[5, 8]	139[5, 8]	2,923[5, 8]	21.0[5, 8]	1.4	131	2.0	15	60.0	68.5	52.4	2.5	Central African Republic
3,277	20.9	4[3]	311	3,049	9.8	0.8	70	...	15	48.1	62.1	34.7	2.2	Chad
[4]	[4]	...	18,084[1, 5]	315,653[1]	...	30.3	2,412	12.3	15	95.2	95.4	95.0	2.9	Chile
8,205,000	14.9	1,054	401,000	2,906,000	7.2	5.7	461	2.0	15	81.5	89.9	72.7	2.3	China
...	...	...	54,164[8]	510,649[8]	9.4[8]	17.2	1,643	...	15	91.3	91.2	91.4	3.5	Colombia
163	...	...	...	400	...	0.6	...	...	15	57.3	64.2	50.4	3.9	Comoros
701,148[2]	[4]	...	...	93,266	...	2.3	212	...	15	77.3	86.6	67.7	...	Congo, Dem. Rep. of the
25,269	17.3	...	656[8]	13,806[8]	21.0[8]	5.3	582	...	15	74.9	83.1	67.2	5.9	Congo, Rep. of the
...	...	29	...	79,959	...	31.9	2,919	...	15	94.8	94.7	95.0	4.5	Costa Rica
11,037	7.8	...	...	51,215[2]	...	4.4	396	8.7	15	40.1	49.9	30.0	4.7	Côte d'Ivoire
2,660	33.7	61	5,814	77,525	13.3	28.3	1,917	6.4	15	96.7	98.8	94.8	5.3	Croatia
244,253	9.0	35[6]	22,967	122,346	5.3	12.7	1,116	...	15	95.7	96.2	95.3	6.6	Cuba
4,066	8.0	32	648	7,765	12.0	20.0	1,069	17.0	15	95.2	97.8	92.8	4.4	Cyprus[18]
229,909	12.5	23	12,892	139,774	10.8	20.8	1,741	8.5	15	100.0	100.0	100.0	6.1	Czech Republic
168,417	13.6[2]	158	8,000[2]	155,661	19.5[2]	45.0	3,261	18.9	...	100.0	100.0	100.0	8.3	Denmark

Education (continued)

country	year	first level (primary)					general second level (secondary)					vocational second level[a]	
		schools	teachers[c]	students[d]	student/teacher ratio	net enroll-ment ratio[b]	schools	teachers[c]	students[d]	student/teacher ratio	net enroll-ment ratio[b]	schools	teachers[c]
Djibouti	1997	81[7]	1,005[7]	33,960	...	32	26[4, 14]	628[4, 7]	11,628[4]	...	...	[4]	[4]
Dominica	1995	64	641[1]	12,627	29.8[1]	...	13[1]	[1]	6,493	[1]	...	...	...
Dominican Republic	1995	4,001	42,135	1,462,722	34.7	81	...	10,757	240,441	22.4	22	...	1,297
Ecuador	1993	...	63,347	1,986,753	31.4	92	...	62,630[4]	813,557[4]	13.0[4]	...	...	[4]
Egypt	1996	16,188	302,916	7,470,437	24.7	89	7,307[2]	235,313	4,242,245	24.7	65	1,351[2]	133,794
El Salvador	1993	3,961	26,259[12]	1,042,256	39.7[12]	79	...	...	29,527	...	21	...	...
Equatorial Guinea	1994	781	1,381	75,751	54.9	...	...	466	14,511	31.1	...	...	122
Eritrea	1996	537	5,828	241,725	41.5	31	86[1]	2,031	78,902	38.8	15	41	133
Estonia	1995	741[9]	15,453[9]	218,600[9]	14.1[9]	94	[9]	[9]	[9]	[9]	77	84	1,585
Ethiopia	1995	9,276	83,113	2,722,192	32.8	24	...	22,779	747,142	32.8	...	...	826
Faroe Islands	1994	62[19]	...	6,895[19]	...	...	6[20]	...	1,017[20]	...	...	9	...
Fiji	1992	693	4,644	145,630	31.4	99	142	3,045	60,237	19.8	...	45	625
Finland	1996	4,474	...	588,162	...	99	477	...	134,851	...	93	520	21,245[7]
France	1995	41,244	301,699[13]	4,012,600	...	99	11,212[4]	454,000[2, 4]	5,737,458[2, 4]	12.6[2, 4]	92	[4]	[4]
French Guiana	1996	78[2]	802	17,006	21.2	...	22[14]	875	13,585	15.5	...	...	210
French Polynesia	1995	278	2,949	48,160	16.3	100	38	1,745	25,541	14.6	61	...	...
Gabon	1995	1,105	4,709	247,018	52.5	...	...	1,897	56,457	29.8	...	...	485
Gambia, The	1994	250	3,158	105,471	33.4	55	32[4]	1,126[4]	27,120[4]	24.1[4]	18	[4]	[4]
Gaza Strip	1997	339[9]	7,941[9]	281,255[9]	35.4[9]	...	[9]	[9]	[9]	[9]	...	...	...
Georgia	1994	3,378[9]	...	815,000[9]	...	82	[9]	...	[9]	...	71	...	...
Germany	1996	17,910	199,623	3,634,342	18.2	100	17,711	402,472	5,822,242	14	88	9,245	107,548
Ghana	1992	11,056	66,068	1,796,490	27.2	...	5,540	43,367	816,578	18.8	...	57[6]	422[6]
Gibraltar	1995	21[9]	305[9]	2,936	16.3[9]	...	[9]	[9]	1,805	[9]	...	1	29[3]
Greece	1993	7,634	37,549	745,666	19.9	98	2,988	45,794	700,488	15.3	85	695	14,349
Greenland	1997	88[9]	1,021[9]	9,056	10.5[9]	...	[9]	[9]	1,649	[9]	...	...	...
Grenada	1995	57	849	23,256	27.4	...	19	381	7,260	19.1	...	...	...
Guadeloupe	1994	344	3,167	38,092	12.0	...	84[4]	3,834[4]	51,366[4]	13.4[4]	...	[4]	[4]
Guam	1993	36[6]	898	16,816	18.7	...	24[6]	758	17,531	23.1	...	3[6]	370[6]
Guatemala	1993	10,770	44,220	1,393,921	31.5	...	1,274[14]	20,942[4]	334,383[4]	16.0[4]	...	626[14]	[4]
Guernsey	1993	22[8]	236	4,697	19.9	...	8[8]	276	3,642	13.2	...	...	...
Guinea	1996	3,237	11,875	584,161	49.2	37	...	4,690	127,517	27.2	...	...	1,302[1]
Guinea-Bissau	1988	...	...	100,369[7]	...	...	...	...	5,505	...	...	...	107
Guyana	1995	423[6]	3,453	100,806	29.2	90	93[6]	1,828	67,039	36.7	66	8[6]	176[6]
Haiti	1993	6,111[8]	27,607	787,553	28.5	26	630[4, 8]	10,174[4]	193,624[4]	19.0[4]	...	[4]	[4]
Honduras	1995	8,186	28,978	1,008,092	34.8	90	661[4]	12,480[4]	184,589[4]	14.8[4]	21	[4]	[4]
Hong Kong	1997	856	19,710[17]	466,507	23.7[17]	91	498	22,777[17]	477,708	21.2[17]	71	9	...
Hungary	1997	3,765	83,658	966,000	11.5	93	980	29,462	361,400	12.3	73	363	5,292
Iceland	1997	205	3,549	42,212	11.9	...	35	1,454	17,970	12.4	...	...	...
India	1996	590,421	1,740,736	109,734,292	63.0	...	265,869	2,657,985	63,521,637	23.9	...	...	...
Indonesia	1995	149,464	1,172,640	26,200,023	22.3	97	27,177	595,962	8,864,001	14.9	42	3,502[2]	102,114[2]
Iran	1995	61,889	311,531[2]	9,745,600	31.7[2]	...	18,445[6]	228,869	7,284,611	31.8	...	...	20,418
Iraq	1995	8,035	132,030	2,977,800	22.6	79	2,635	48,961	1,062,204	21.7	37	310	9,903
Ireland	1995	3,319	20,901	491,256	23.5	100	452	12,635	225,490	17.8	85	327	8,019
Isle of Man	1992	32[3]	...	5,550	...	...	7[3]	...	4,458	...	...	1[3]	...
Israel	1997	1,937[17]	57,618[17]	691,800	...	...	797[17]	39,093[1]	478,900	...	...	435[17]	17,141[1]
Italy	1996	20,442	289,055	2,825,838	9.8	97	9,278	214,861	1,907,024	8.9	...	7,888	313,001
Jamaica	1995	788[8]	11,283	319,298	28.3	100	126	8,377	207,035	24.7	64	18	950
Japan	1995	24,548	431,000	8,371,000	19.4	100	16,775	552,000	9,296,000	16.8	96	6,679[14]	53,000[14]
Jersey	1990	32	...	5,794	...	...	14	...	4,405	...	...	1	...
Jordan	1994	2,482	48,158	1,036,079	21.5	89	741	4,597	93,773	20.4	42	54	2,553
Kazakstan	1996	8,700[9]	262,000[9]	3,060,000[9]	11.7[9]	...	[9]	[9]	[9]	[9]	...	3,504[7]	...
Kenya	1993	15,804	173,002	5,428,600	31.4	...	2,639	31,657	517,577	16.3	...	63	...
Kiribati	1993	92	537	16,316	30.4	...	9[6]	179	3,152	17.6	...	6[6]	40
Korea, North	1987	6,122	138,945	1,543,000	11.1	...	...	111,000	2,468,000	22.2	...	...	...
Korea, South	1996	5,732	137,912	3,800,540	27.6	99	3,790	157,731	3,683,857	23.4	96	797	44,163
Kuwait	1996	251	9,414	140,979	15.0	65	409	18,700	204,194	10.9	54	36	717
Kyrgyzstan	1996	1,885	24,086	473,077	19.7	97	1,474[2]	38,915	498,849	12.8	...	53[2]	3,371
Laos	1996	7,591	24,600	724,100	29.4	68	750[6]	35,100	886,500	25.3	18	139[3]	1,600
Latvia	1997	643	23,779[17]	98,694	...	84	376	41,029[17]	235,952	...	78	128	9,576[17]
Lebanon	1995	2,100[8]	...	365,174	...	...	...	...	277,646	...	...	275	6,065
Lesotho	1995	1,234	7,433	366,935	49.4	65	187	2,597	61,615	23.7	16	9[2]	225[2]
Liberia	1987	...	...	...	...	...	...	...	...	...	...	...	...
Libya	1993	...	103,791	1,254,242	12.1	97	...	14,941[8]	181,368[8]	12.1[8]	...	...	7,072[8]
Liechtenstein	1997	14	144	1,998	13.9	...	8	164	1,887	11.5	...	2[7]	247[7]
Lithuania	1996	2,361[9]	47,000[9]	562,000[9]	12.0[9]	...	[9]	[9]	[9]	[9]	80	106	4,671
Luxembourg	1995	...	1,732[12]	26,867[12]	15.5[12]	...	...	1,686	9,012	5.3	...	...	2,904[16]
Macau	1995	61	1,482	45,153	30.5	81	25[4]	1,205[4]	21,813[4]	18.1[4]	53	[4]	[4]
Macedonia	1995	1,050	13,102[2]	258,955	19.9[2]	85	95	4,520[2, 4]	77,754[4]	16.5[2, 4]	51	...	[4]
Madagascar	1994	13,624	37,676	1,504,668	39.9	...	1,142[3]	15,118	298,241	19.7	...	...	1,484[14]
Malawi	1995	3,425	45,775	2,860,819	62.5	69	94[6]	1,096[6]	48,332	26.8[6]	2	13[6]	250[6]
Malaysia	1996	7,049	144,937	2,843,663	19.6	91	1,427	86,891	1,694,243	19.5	...	101	6,044
Maldives	1992	134	...	45,333	...	...	...	...	15,933	...	...	...	...
Mali	1996	1,996	8,738	608,444	69.6	25	307[8]	4,549	112,670	24.8	5	...	...
Malta	1996	111	1,990	35,479	17.8	100	59	2,679	29,907	20.9	84	22	541
Marshall Islands	1995	103	669	13,355	20.0	...	12	144	2,400	16.7	...	...	...
Martinique	1994	276	3,251	33,532	10.3	...	76[4]	3,736[4]	47,172[4]	12.6[4]	...	[4]	[4]
Mauritania	1994	1,635	5,181[7]	268,216[7]	51.8[7]	60	56[8]	1,776	43,861	24.7	...	5[8]	162
Mauritius	1995	279	6,381	122,895	19.3	96	123	4,375	91,401	20.8	...	19[8]	...
Mayotte	1993	88[6]	555	21,579	38.9	...	5	246	3,973	16.2	...	2[6]	17[6]
Mexico	1995	91,857	507,669	14,572,202	28.7	100	22,255	256,831	4,493,173	17.5	45	6,571[1]	77,347[1]
Micronesia	1988	177	...	25,139	...	...	16	...	5,385	...	...	...	...
Moldova	1996	1,700[9]	14,209	320,055	22.5	...	[9]	33,752[4]	412,679	...	...	64	[4]
Monaco	1996	7	102	1,893	18.6	...	...	196	2,387	12.2	...	...	91
Mongolia	1996	650[9]	7,088	176,036	24.8	80	[9]	12,323	227,811	18.5	...	...	495
Morocco	1995	4,740	102,163	2,895,737	28.3	72	1,172	73,726	1,247,608	16.9	57	562[8, 16]	2,951[16]

		third level (higher)							literacy[b]				public expenditure on education (percent of GNP)[b]	country
students[d]	student/ teacher ratio	institutions	teachers[c]	students[d]	student/ teacher ratio	gross enroll- ment ratio[b]	students per 100,000 popula- tion[b]	percent of population age 25 and over with post- secondary education[b]	over age	total (%)	male (%)	female (%)		
[4]	[4]	1[14]	13[14]	130[17]	...	0.2	22	...	15	46.2	60.3	32.7	3.8	Djibouti
...	...	2[1]	34[1]	484[1]	14.2[1]	...	...	...	15	90.0	...	...	5.5	Dominica
22,795	17.6	7[2, 5]	5,091[2, 5]	73,461[2, 5]	14.4[2, 5]	...	...	...	15	82.1	82.0	82.2	1.9	Dominican Republic
[4]	[4]	...	12,856[6]	206,541[6]	16.1[6]	20.0	2,012	12.7	15	90.1	92.0	88.2	3.4	Ecuador
1,900,406	14.2	12[5]	38,828[2, 5]	696,988[7]	...	18.1	1,674	4.6	15	51.4	63.6	38.8	5.6	Egypt
88,588	...	...	4,643[5]	77,359[5]	16.7[5]	17.7	2,031	6.3	15	74.1	77.4	71.3	2.2	El Salvador
2,105	17.3	...	58	578	10.0	...	164	...	15	78.5	89.6	68.1	1.8	Equatorial Guinea
1,246	9.4	1[2]	144[2]	2,032[2]	14.1[2]	1.1	102	...	...	20.0	...	...	1.9	Eritrea
27,806	17.5	22	...	23,169	...	38.1	2,670	13.7	15	99.7	99.9	99.6	6.9	Estonia
9,103	11.0	...	1,937	32,671	16.9	0.7	60	...	15	35.5	45.5	25.3	4.7	Ethiopia
2,090	...	1[14]	20[14]	91[14]	4.6[14]	...	...	...	15	99.0	99.0	99.0	...	Faroe Islands
7,283	11.6	...	277[14]	7,908[14]	28.5[14]	11.9	757	4.5	15	91.6	93.8	89.3	5.4	Fiji
199,200	9.5[7]	21	7,790[7]	133,359	16.4[7]	66.9	4,033	18.3	15	100.0	100.0	100.0	7.6	Finland
[4]	[4]	1,062[3]	52,663[2]	2,107,600	...	49.6	3,617	11.4	...	98.8	98.9	98.7	5.9	France
2,404	11.4	1[1]	...	324[1]	...	...	...	...	15	83.0	83.6	82.3	...	French Guiana
...	...	4[3]	70[3]	701[3]	10.0[3]	1.4	...	...	15	95.0	94.9	95.0	...	French Polynesia
9,261	19.1	2[5, 8]	299[5, 8]	3,000[5, 8]	10.0[5, 8]	...	449	...	15	63.2	73.7	53.3	3.2	Gabon
[4]	[4]	...	155	1,591	10.3	1.7	148	...	15	38.6	52.8	24.9	5.5	Gambia, The
...	...	5	717	20,153	28.1	...	...	...	...	...	...	...	...	Gaza Strip
29,300	...	19	...	93,000	...	38.1	2,845	...	15	99.5	99.7	99.4	5.2	Georgia
2,435,753	22.6	335	152,401	1,838,456	12.1	42.7	2,635	19.9[21]	15	100.0	100.0	100.0	4.7	Germany
13,232[6]	31.4[6]	16[6]	700[6]	9,274[6]	13.2[6]	1.4	127	...	15	64.5	75.9	53.5	3.1	Ghana
772	...	—	—	—	—	...	...	...	15	99.0	99.0	99.0	...	Gibraltar
190,443	13.3	17[8]	9,124[8]	115,284[8]	12.6[8]	38.1	2,846	8.7	15	95.2	97.7	93.0	3.7	Greece
...	...	...	...	...	...	...	...	...	15	100.0	100.0	100.0	...	Greenland
...	...	1[2]	66[2]	651[2]	9.9[2]	...	...	...	15	85.0	...	...	4.7	Grenada
[4]	[4]	1	121	4,673	38.6	...	...	...	15	90.1	89.7	90.5	...	Guadeloupe
3,788[6]	10.2[6]	1[3]	192[6]	2,385[6]	12.4[6]	...	...	39.9	15	99.0	99.0	99.0	...	Guam
[4]	[4]	5[3]	4,346[3]	69,532[3]	16.0[3]	8.1	755	...	15	55.6	62.5	48.6	1.7	Guatemala
...	...	—	—	—	—	...	...	...	15	100.0	100.0	100.0	...	Guernsey
9,278[1]	7.1[1]	...	805[1, 5]	6,245[1, 5]	7.8[1, 5]	1.1	93	...	15	35.9	49.9	21.9	1.8	Guinea
825	7.7	...	...	404	...	...	...	...	15	54.9	68.0	42.5	...	Guinea-Bissau
5,388[6]	30.6[6]	...	492[2]	8,257[2]	16.8[2]	8.6	846	...	15	98.1	98.6	97.5	4.1	Guyana
[4]	[4]	2[17, 22]	777[17, 22]	11,546[17, 22]	14.9[17, 22]	...	...	0.7	15	45.0	48.0	42.2	1.5	Haiti
[4]	[4]	8	3,676	54,293	14.8	10.0	985	...	15	72.7	72.6	72.7	3.9	Honduras
48,837	...	17	...	87,411	...	21.9	1,635	10.6	15	92.2	96.0	88.2	2.8	Hong Kong
143,800	27.2	89	19,426	141,900	7.3	19.1	1,522	10.1	15	98.9	99.2	98.6	6.6	Hungary
...	...	14	508	7,972	15.7	35.2	2,658	...	15	100.0	100.0	100.0	5.0	Iceland
...	...	8,407[2]	286,000[2]	5,007,000[2]	17.5[2]	6.4	601	...	15	52.0	65.5	37.7	3.5	India
1,405,220	13.8	1,236	150,607	2,229,796	14.8	11.1	1,167	2.3	15	83.8	89.6	78.0	...	Indonesia
368,218	18.0	...	36,366	478,455	13.2	14.8	1,533	...	15	72.1	78.4	65.8	4.0	Iran
135,711	13.7	12	11,847	201,984	17.0	...	...	...	15	58.0	70.7	45.0	...	Iraq
146,050	18.2	29	4,889	88,925	18.2	37.0	3,443	14.6	15	100.0	100.0	100.0	6.3	Ireland
425[14]	...	...	...	...	...	...	...	...	...	...	...	...	...	Isle of Man
142,900	...	7	7,829[7]	101,700[17]	...	41.1	3,598	...	15	95.6	97.7	93.6	6.6	Israel
2,661,760	8.5	48[5, 7]	58,874[5, 7]	1,601,873[5, 7]	27.2[5, 7]	40.6	3,134	...	15	97.1	97.8	96.4	4.9	Italy
15,898	16.7	15[3]	...	24,200	...	6.0	677	...	15	85.0	80.8	89.1	8.2	Jamaica
1,242,000[14]	23.4[14]	1,223	162,000	3,101,000	19.1	40.3	3,139	20.7	15	100.0	100.0	100.0	3.8	Japan
...	...	...	...	...	...	...	...	...	15	100.0	100.0	100.0	...	Jersey
30,052	11.8	55[3]	4,280	85,934	20.1	24.5	2,136	...	15	86.6	93.4	79.4	6.3	Jordan
984,300[7]	...	69[7]	...	267,000[7]	...	32.7	2,807	12.4	15	97.5	99.1	96.1	4.5	Kazakstan
29,593	...	14	4,392[5, 14]	88,180	8.1[5, 14]	1.6	143	...	15	78.1	86.3	70.0	7.4	Kenya
297	7.4	—	—	—	—	...	...	...	15	90.0	...	...	6.3	Kiribati
220,000	...	281	27,000	390,000	14.4	...	...	...	15	95.0	...	...	...	Korea, North
950,173	21.5	802	60,883	2,056,370	33.8	52.0	4,955	21.1	15	98.0	99.3	96.7	3.7	Korea, South
3,604	5.0	1	960	16,767	17.5	25.4	2,247	12.7	15	78.6	82.2	74.9	5.6	Kuwait
32,005	9.5	23[2]	3,691	49,744	13.5	12.2	1,115	...	15	97.0	98.6	95.5	6.8	Kyrgyzstan
9,400	5.9	9[6]	1,300	7,800	6.0	1.5	134	...	15	56.6	69.4	44.4	2.4	Laos
43,170	...	28	...	55,434	...	25.7	1,737	13.4	15	99.5	99.8	99.2	6.3	Latvia
45,776	7.5	20	7,173	79,029	11.0	27.0	2,712	...	15	92.4	94.7	90.3	2.0	Lebanon
2,326[2]	10.3[2]	1[2]	492[2]	4,001[2]	8.1[2]	2.4	221	...	15	71.3	81.1	62.3	5.9	Lesotho
...	...	...	472	5,095	10.8	...	...	...	15	38.3	53.9	22.4	...	Liberia
94,961[8]	10.8[8]	10[3]	...	72,899[8]	...	16.4	1,358	...	15	76.2	87.9	63.0	...	Libya
2,515[7]	10.2[7]	...	...	...	...	...	...	...	15	100.0	100.0	100.0	...	Liechtenstein
49,000	10.5	15	...	54,000	...	28.2	2,023	12.6	15	99.5	99.6	99.3	6.1	Lithuania
16,909	5.7[16]	1	200	1,100	5.5	...	...	10.8	15	100.0	100.0	100.0	...	Luxembourg
[4]	[4]	12	663	6,145	9.3	26.4	1,995	5.9	15	89.5	94.1	85.3	...	Macau
[4]	[4]	44	2,320[2]	27,340	11.8[2]	17.5	1,372	...	10	89.1	94.2	83.8	5.5	Macedonia
17,419[14]	11.7[14]	5[3]	855[8]	42,681[8]	49.9[8]	3.4	316	...	15	80.2	87.7	72.9	1.9	Madagascar
1,080	14.7[6]	4[6]	235[6]	7,308[2]	11.4[6]	0.8	76	0.4	15	56.4	71.9	41.8	5.7	Malaŵi
47,770	7.9	48	12,247	191,290	15.6	10.6	971	...	15	83.5	89.1	78.1	5.3	Malaysia
452	...	—	—	—	—	...	...	...	15	93.2	93.3	93.0	8.4	Maldives
...	...	7[14]	701[14]	6,703[14]	9.6[14]	0.8	73	...	15	31.0	39.4	23.1	2.2	Mali
4,539	8.4	1[1]	284[1]	3,679[1]	13.0[1]	21.8	1,595	...	15	96.0	96.2	95.9	5.2	Malta
...	...	...	...	...	...	...	...	...	15	91.2	92.4	90.0	...	Marshall Islands
[4]	[4]	1	99	4,486	45.3	...	...	...	15	92.5	91.8	93.2	...	Martinique
1,949	12.0	4	72[7, 23]	2,850[7, 23]	39.6[7, 23]	4.1	393	1.3	15	37.7	49.6	26.3	5.0	Mauritania
2,052[1]	...	2	526[14]	2,344	7.7[14]	6.3	564	1.9	15	82.9	87.1	78.8	4.3	Mauritius
839	23.1[6]	—	—	—	—	...	...	...	15	91.9	...	...	...	Mayotte
1,076,700[1]	13.9[1]	10,341	319,551	3,763,938	11.8	14.3	1,586	9.2	15	89.6	91.8	87.4	5.3	Mexico
...	...	...	...	...	...	...	...	...	15	76.7	67.0	87.2	...	Micronesia
27,943	...	20	8,846	87,700	9.9	25.0	1,976	11.3	15	96.4	98.6	94.4	6.1	Moldova
520	5.7	...	...	...	...	...	...	...	...	...	...	...	...	Monaco
7,987	16.1	12[7]	1,341[8]	13,800[7]	...	15.2	1,569	...	15	82.9	88.6	77.2	5.6	Mongolia
17,585[16]	6.0[16]	50[1]	6,877[1]	230,012[1]	33.4[1]	11.3	1,075	...	15	43.7	56.6	31.0	4.9	Morocco

Education (continued)

country	year	first level (primary)					general second level (secondary)					vocational second level[a]	
		schools	teachers[c]	students[d]	student/ teacher ratio	net enroll- ment ratio[b]	schools	teachers[c]	students[d]	student/ teacher ratio	net enroll- ment ratio[b]	schools	teachers[c]
Mozambique	1995	4,167	24,575	1,415,428	57.6	40	239[2]	4,376	165,868	37.9	6	31[2]	1,239
Myanmar (Burma)	1995	35,856	169,748	5,711,202	33.6	...	2,916	71,904	1,779,503	24.7	...	103	2,462
Namibia	1994	933	10,912[8]	366,666	32.0[8]	92	114	2,534[6]	101,838	29.3[6]	36	17	140[3]
Nauru	1989	3	61	1,367	22.4	...	2	34	629	18.5	...	1	3
Nepal	1995	22,157	85,621	3,191,600	37.3	...	7,582[4]	30,637[4]	944,500[4]	30.8[4]	...	[4]	[4]
Netherlands, The	1996	7,411	99,031[14]	1,477,000	15.7[14]	99	1,124	89,370[14]	868,000	7.7[14]	84	218	18,613[14]
Netherlands Antilles	1993	85	1,059	22,735	21.5	...	27	617	8,801	14.3	...	30	439
New Caledonia	1992	280	1,758	34,591	19.7	98	46	1,669[4, 14]	15,664	13.1[4, 14]	72	16	[4]
New Zealand	1996	2,397[24]	23,379[24]	455,671[24]	19.5[24]	100	339	15,246	227,934	14.9	93	30	5,314
Nicaragua	1994	4,993	20,626	765,972	37.1	83	451[4]	5,356[4]	211,606[4]	39.5[4]	27	[4]	[4]
Niger	1994	2,656	12,216	414,296	33.9	25	105[6]	2,219[1]	88,810	35.1[1]	6	7[6]	175[1]
Nigeria	1995	38,649	435,210	16,191,000	37.2	...	6,074	152,596	4,451,000	29.2	...	...	15,738[3]
Northern Mariana Islands	1989	18	240	4,882	20.3	...	9[4]	163[4]	2,075[4]	12.7[4]	...	[4]	[4]
Norway	1995	3,308	37,640	470,936	12.5	99	746[4]	21,197[4]	226,983[4]	10.7[4]	94	[4]	[4]
Oman	1994	415	11,158	297,209	26.6	71	128[6]	9,188	160,654	17.5	56	25[6]	342
Pakistan	1996	115,744	337,400	11,484,000	34.0	...	20,243	281,700	4,819,000	17.1	...	687	7,459
Palau	1993	...	...	2,635	...	...	...	...	1,021	...	...	...	...
Panama	1995	2,845	14,998	362,142	24.1	91	399[4]	11,627[4]	216,217[4]	18.6[4]	51	[4]	[4]
Papua New Guinea	1995	2,790	13,652	525,995	38.5	...	135[6]	2,415[8]	68,818	24.1[8]	...	117[6]	878[8]
Paraguay	1995	5,318	34,580	835,089	24.1	89	1,102[4]	20,793[2, 4]	235,914[4]	10.3[2, 4]	33	[4]	[4]
Peru	1995	46,652	176,173	4,822,423	27.4	91	8,085	104,476	2,023,830	19.4	53	2,425	12,293
Philippines	1995	35,671	324,418	10,903,529	33.6	100	5,880[2]	131,831[4]	4,762,877[4]	36.1[4]	60	1,261[8]	[4]
Poland	1996	19,823	323,500	5,104,200	15.8	97	1,705	34,700	683,000	19.7	83	8,887	88,700
Portugal	1994	12,069	73,221	910,650	12.4	100	663	69,095[4]	749,838	11.3[4]	78	214	[4]
Puerto Rico	1986	1,542	18,359	427,582	23.3	...	395	13,612	334,661	24.6	...	52	...
Qatar	1995[12]	169	5,853	52,130	8.9	80	123[2]	3,738	36,964	9.9	70	3[2]	120
Réunion	1995	345	...	73,702[17]	...	...	104[4]	4,591[2]	71,694[17]	16.3[2]	...	[4]	1,108[2]
Romania	1995	13,963[19]	168,702[19]	2,532,169[19]	15.0[19]	92	1,276[20]	60,514[20]	757,673[20]	12.5[20]	73	1,530	9,360
Russia	1996	70,200[9]	1,705,000[9]	22,000,000[9]	12.9[9]	100	[9]	[9]	[9]	[9]	...	2,612	...
Rwanda	1992	1,710	18,937	1,104,902	58.3	76	...	3,413[4]	94,586[4]	27.7[4]	8	...	[4]
St. Kitts and Nevis	1995	31[2]	366[2]	7,101[2]	19.4[2]	...	7	326	4,541	13.9	...	...	...
St. Lucia	1993	88	1,204	32,545	27.0	...	14	524	9,550	18.2	...	1	34
St. Vincent and the Grenadines	1994	65	1,080	21,386	19.8	...	21[8]	395	9,870	25.0	...	2[8]	49
Samoa	1989	...	...	37,833	...	99	...	...	...	...	45	...	...
San Marino	1996	14	217	1,134	5.2	...	3	134	771	5.8	...	...	44[2]
São Tomé and Príncipe	1989	64	559	19,822	35.5	...	...	318	7,446	23.4	...	...	...
Saudi Arabia	1996	11,217	169,321	2,248,122	13.3	62	6,346[7]	105,056	1,375,753	13.1	48	293[7]	4,473
Senegal	1993	2,454	12,711	738,550	58.1	54	359	5,509	182,140	33.1	...	19	182
Seychelles	1997	27[7]	633	9,825	15.5	...	20[2]	440	6,548	14.9	...	1[2]	134
Sierra Leone	1993	1,643	10,595	267,425	25.2	...	167	4,313	70,900	16.4	...	44	709
Singapore	1995	199	10,356	261,648	25.3	...	178	9,777	203,662	20.8	...	11	1,382
Slovakia	1996	2,485	39,224	661,082	16.7	...	190	5,457	76,380	14.0	...	364	9,558
Slovenia	1995	850	15,471	210,989	13.6	100	224	9,748	102,117	10.5	...	...	...
Solomon Islands	1994	520	2,510	73,120	29.1	...	23	618	7,981	12.9	...	1	...
Somalia	1987	1,125	8,208	171,830	20.9	...	82	2,109	42,764	20.3	...	21	498
South Africa	1994	22,260[9]	349,436[9]	11,782,324[9]	35.7[9]	96	[9]	[9]	[9]	[9]	52	187	10,807
Spain	1995	16,540[2]	132,566	2,364,910	17.8	100	25,775[1, 4]	299,056[4]	4,744,829[4]	15.9[4]	94	[4]	[4]
Sri Lanka	1994	9,648	70,108	1,960,495	28.0	...	5,771[8]	105,916	2,315,541	21.9	...	23[14]	437[14]
Sudan, The	1995	12,187	83,306	3,023,955	36.3	54	2,578[8]	29,208[8]	683,982[8]	23.4[8]	...	...	621
Suriname	1995	280	3,447	62,613	18.2	...	100	2,056	29,554	14.4	...	64[3]	...
Swaziland	1994	535	5,887	192,599	32.7	95	165	2,872	52,571	18.3	...	5	228
Sweden	1995	4,900	89,275	916,661	10.3	100	629	29,563	309,952	10.5	96	...	...
Switzerland	1996	...	...	452,789	...	100	...	...	369,036	...	79	...	...
Syria	1996	10,564	113,530	2,672,960	23.5	91	2,526[7]	51,483	846,778	16.4	39	292[7]	12,200
Taiwan	1996	2,523	87,934	1,971,439	22.4	...	920	76,562	1,412,201	18.4	...	203	19,660
Tajikistan	1995	3,400[9]	84,000[9]	1,289,000[9]	15.3[9]	...	[9]	[9]	[9]	[9]	...	75	...
Tanzania	1994[25]	10,892	101,816	3,736,734[1]	36.7[1]	48	491	10,612	180,899[1]	18.9[1]	...	40	1,167[1]
Thailand	1993	34,412	445,542	8,583,525	19.3	...	2,318	107,025	2,118,767	19.8	...	679	40,116
Togo	1996	3,283	16,217	824,626	50.8	85	...	4,736	161,672	34.1	18	...	586[7]
Tonga	1994	115	701	16,540	23.6	...	38	809	15,702	19.4	...	9	65[6]
Trinidad and Tobago	1994	475	7,210	195,013	27.0	88	...	4,844[4]	100,609[4]	20.6[4]	64	...	[4]
Tunisia	1996	4,384	59,887	1,468,998	24.5	97	712[7]	41,885	794,394	19.0	...	...	...
Turkey	1996	49,240	232,000	6,403,000	27.6	96	10,689	138,000	3,498,000	25.3	50	3,678	71,000
Turkmenistan	1995	1,900[9]	72,900[9]	940,600[9]	12.9[9]	...	[9]	[9]	[9]	[9]	...	78	...
Tuvalu	1991	11	72[6]	1,906[2]	...	...	1	21[6]	314	...	...	1	10[6]
Uganda	1995[12]	8,531	76,111	2,912,473	38.3	...	...	14,447	256,258	17.7	...	...	1,788
Ukraine	1996	21,900[9]	576,000[7, 9]	7,007,000[9]	12.4[7, 9]	...	[9]	[9]	[9]	[9]	...	782	...
United Arab Emirates	1995	512[8, 9]	15,449	262,628	17.0	83	[9]	12,388	158,625	12.0	71	9[14]	189
United Kingdom	1995	32,385[9]	231,659	4,906,439	21.2	100	[9]	228,187	3,779,262	16.6	92	...	...
United States	1996	85,393[2, 9]	1,784,000[26]	33,410,000[26]	18.7[26]	96	[9]	1,187,000	17,390,000	14.6	89	...	...
Uruguay	1994	2,423	16,821	337,889	20.1	95	348	20,061	184,083	9.2	...	104	...
Uzbekistan	1996	9,300[9]	413,000[9]	5,090,000[9]	12.3[9]	...	[9]	[9]	[9]	[9]	...	252	22,164[1]
Vanuatu	1992	272	852	26,267	30.8	...	...	220	4,269	19.4	17	...	...
Venezuela	1994	15,894[1]	185,748	4,217,283	22.7	88	1,621[4, 8]	33,692[4]	311,209[4]	9.2[4]	20	[4]	[4]
Vietnam	1996	13,092[2]	298,856	10,228,800	34.2	...	6,298[2]	193,814	5,332,400	27.5	...	451[2]	9,425
Virgin Islands (U.S.)	1993[12]	62	790	14,544	18.4	...	...	541[14]	12,502	17.2[14]	...	—	—
West Bank	1997	1,193[9]	15,912[9]	431,565[9]	27.1[9]	...	[9]	[9]	[9]	[9]	...	...	...
Western Sahara	1995[12]	40	925	32,257	34.9	...	13	1,267	10,541	8.3	...	...	...
Yemen	1995[12]	11,013[2]	78,646	2,493,017	31.7	...	1,224	11,130	232,506	20.9	...	125	369
Yugoslavia	1996	4,441	51,728	914,532	17.7	69	570	26,954	352,346	13.1	62	...	...
Zambia	1995	3,883	38,528	1,506,349	39.1	75	...	...	199,081[2]	...	16	...	...
Zimbabwe	1995	4,633	63,475	2,655,564	41.8	...	1,535	27,320	711,094	26.0	...	25[8]	1,479[8]

[1]1993. [2]1994. [3]1989. [4]General second level includes vocational second level. [5]Universities only. [6]1990. [7]1995. [8]1992. [9]First level includes general second level. [10]First level includes lower second level. [11]College of the Bahamas only. [12]Public schools only. [13]Includes preschool. [14]1991. [15]1997. [16]Excludes teacher training. [17]1996. [18]Republic of Cyprus only.

		third level (higher)							literacy[b]				public expenditure on education (percent of GNP)[b]	country
students[d]	student/ teacher ratio	institutions	teachers[c]	students[d]	student/ teacher ratio	gross enroll-ment ratio[b]	students per 100,000 popula-tion[b]	percent of population age 25 and over with post-secondary education[b]	over age	total (%)	male (%)	female (%)		
19,313	15.6	3[2]	833[2]	7,000	...	0.5	41	...	15	40.1	57.7	23.3	6.3	Mozambique
25,374	10.3	51	9,147	309,446	33.8	5.4	564	...	15	83.1	88.7	77.7	1.3	Myanmar (Burma)
1,503	11.9[3]	7	213[14]	6,523	11.8[14]	8.1	738	4.0	15	75.8	77.8	74.0	9.4	Namibia
30	10.0	1	...	200	...	...	...	...	15	99.0	...	...	...	Nauru
[4]	[4]	3[1]	4,925[14]	99,300	22.4[14]	5.2	501	2.5	15	27.5	40.9	14.0	2.9	Nepal
519,000	28.0[14]	20	...	408,000	...	48.9	3,485	...	15	100.0	100.0	100.0	5.3	Netherlands, The
5,817	13.3	2	51	734	14.4	...	...	8.8	15	93.8	94.2	93.4	...	Netherlands Antilles
7,543	[4]	6	141[3]	1,207[6]	9.9[3]	...	...	7.5	15	57.9	57.4	58.3	...	New Caledonia
107,736	20.3	7[5]	5,982[5]	105,690[5]	17.7[5]	58.2	4,603	39.1	15	100.0	100.0	100.0	6.7	New Zealand
[4]	[4]	10	2,005	22,120	11.0	9.4	947	...	15	65.7	64.6	66.6	3.9	Nicaragua
2,110	12.1[1]	2	315	4,060	12.9	...	55	...	15	13.6	20.9	6.6	3.1	Niger
391,583[3]	24.9[3]	31	12,103	228,000	18.8	4.1	367	...	15	57.1	67.3	47.3	...	Nigeria
[4]	[4]	1	102	1,097	10.8	...	...	...	15	96.3	96.9	95.6	...	Northern Mariana Islands
[4]	[4]	89	10,366	169,306	16.3	54.5	4,009	17.9	15	100.0	100.0	100.0	8.3	Norway
2,350	6.9	5[6]	732[6]	7,322[8]	...	4.7	334	...	15	58.8	71.1	46.2	4.4	Oman
94,000	12.6	888	33,654	953,659	28.3	3.0	291	2.5	15	37.8	50.0	24.4	2.7	Pakistan
...	...	...	...	509	...	...	...	...	15	97.6	98.3	96.6	...	Palau
[4]	[4]	9	4,689	76,839	16.4	30.0	2,921	13.2	15	90.8	91.4	90.2	5.2	Panama
9,941	12.9[8]	2[6]	...	13,663	...	3.2	318	...	15	72.2	81.0	62.7	...	Papua New Guinea
[4]	[4]	2	742[1]	39,694	40.9[1]	10.3	931	...	15	92.1	93.5	90.6	2.9	Paraguay
270,576	22.0	886	49,249	714,512	14.5	31.1	3,268	20.4	15	88.7	94.5	83.0	3.8	Peru
[4]	[4]	975[2]	56,880[14]	1,582,820[2]	23.7[14]	27.4	2,760	18.7	15	94.6	95.0	94.3	2.2	Philippines
1,729,300	19.5	179	71,300	794,600	11.1	27.4	1,946	7.9	15	98.7	99.2	98.3	4.6	Poland
28,627	[4]	273	30,998[1]	236,537	6.9[1]	34.0	3,003	7.7	15	89.6	92.5	87.0	5.4	Portugal
149,191	...	45	9,045	156,818	17.3	...	...	...	18	89.7	89.6	89.7	...	Puerto Rico
671	5.6	1	637	7,794	12.2	27.4	1,509	13.3	15	79.4	79.2	79.9	3.4	Qatar
15,055	12.4[2]	1[5]	242[5]	8,058[5]	33.3[5]	...	...	...	15	78.2	75.9	80.3	...	Réunion
345,394	36.9	63	20,452	255,162	12.5	18.3	1,483	6.9	15	96.7	98.5	95.0	3.0	Romania
1,923,000	...	569	...	2,655,000	...	42.9	2,998	15.1	15	98.0	99.5	96.8	4.1	Russia
[4]	[4]	...	646[3]	3,454	5.2[3]	0.6	...	...	15	60.5	69.8	51.6	3.7	Rwanda
...	...	1[1]	51[1]	394[1]	7.7[1]	...	...	...	15	90.0	90.0	90.0	3.3	St. Kitts and Nevis
808	23.7	1	389	870	2.4	...	...	...	15	82.0	...	...	9.9	St. Lucia
414	8.4	...	...	...	...	...	...	...	15	96.0	...	...	6.9	St. Vincent and the Grenadines
...	...	...	...	...	...	...	...	...	15	100.0	100.0	100.0	4.2	Samoa
428	6.2[2]	...	...	...	...	...	...	...	15	99.1	99.4	98.8	...	San Marino
289	...	...	...	...	...	...	...	...	15	54.2	70.2	39.1	...	São Tomé and Príncipe
49,032	11.0	77[7]	18,039[7]	233,710[7]	13.0[7]	15.3	1,316	...	15	62.8	71.5	50.2	5.5	Saudi Arabia
7,301	40.1	2[5, 7]	784[5, 7]	16,733[5, 7]	21.3[5, 7]	3.4	297	...	15	33.1	43.0	23.2	3.6	Senegal
1,338	10.0	...	...	...	...	...	...	4.6	15	84.2	82.9	85.7	7.5	Seychelles
7,756	10.9	2[14]	257[14]	2,571[14]	10.0[14]	1.3	119	...	15	31.4	45.4	18.2	0.9	Sierra Leone
9,476	6.9	7	6,902	83,914	12.2	33.7	2,522	4.7	15	89.1	95.1	83.0	3.0	Singapore
119,853	12.5	14	8,014	74,322	9.3	20.2	1,715	9.5	15	100.0	100.0	100.0	5.1	Slovakia
...	...	28	2,783[2]	45,951[17]	14.5[2]	31.9	2,387	10.4	15	100.0	100.0	100.0	5.8	Slovenia
...	...	1	...	...	...	...	...	...	15	54.1	62.4	44.9	3.8	Solomon Islands
4,809	9.7	1	...	1,692	...	...	...	...	15	24.0	36.0	14.0	...	Somalia
140,531	13.0	...	27,099	617,897	22.8	17.3	1,524	1.5	15	81.8	81.9	81.7	6.8	South Africa
[4]	[4]	1,415[8]	80,563	1,398,113	17.3	46.1	3,858	8.4	15	96.5	98.1	95.1	5.0	Spain
8,908[14]	20.4[14]	8[14]	1,937[14]	59,790	16.2[14]	5.1	474	...	15	90.2	93.4	87.2	3.1	Sri Lanka
15,443	24.9	24[8]	1,943[8]	54,345[8]	28.0[8]	3.0	272	...	15	46.1	57.7	34.6	...	Sudan, The
12,307[1]	...	1[1]	155[1]	1,478[1]	9.5[1]	...	1,124	...	15	93.0	95.1	91.0	3.5	Suriname
2,958	13.0	1	190	2,132	11.2	5.1	543	3.3	15	76.7	78.0	75.6	8.1	Swaziland
...	...	...	29,487	268,448	9.1	42.5	2,810	21.7	15	100.0	100.0	100.0	8.0	Sweden
191,696	...	...	...	148,024	...	31.8	2,085	...	15	100.0	100.0	100.0	5.5	Switzerland
94,204	7.7	...	4,869[5, 7]	161,185[5]	...	17.9	1,760	...	15	70.8	85.7	55.8	4.3	Syria
523,412	26.6	134	36,348	751,347	20.7	...	...	...	15	94.0	97.6	90.2	5.2	Taiwan
35,000	...	...	...	10,000	...	20.3	1,890	11.7	15	97.7	98.8	96.6	8.6	Tajikistan
15,824[1]	13.6[1]	4[3]	1,206[3]	4,289	4.4[3]	0.5	43	...	15	67.8	79.4	56.8	3.7	Tanzania
795,186	19.8	102	27,239	809,856	29.7	20.1	2,096	...	15	93.8	96.0	91.6	4.2	Thailand
7,631[7]	13.0[7]	1[5]	...	11,172	...	3.2	281	...	15	51.7	67.0	37.0	5.6	Togo
824	13.4[6]	1[8]	19[8]	226[8]	11.9[8]	...	...	2.8	15	92.8	92.9	92.8	4.7	Tonga
[4]	[4]	1	438	5,191	11.9	7.7	705	...	15	97.9	98.8	97.0	4.5	Trinidad and Tobago
...	...	...	5,655[2]	96,101[2]	17.0[2]	12.9	1,253	...	15	66.7	78.6	54.6	6.8	Tunisia
1,309,000	18.4	817	50,000	1,161,000	23.2	18.2	1,960	...	15	82.3	91.7	72.4	3.4	Turkey
26,000	...	15	...	29,435[17]	...	21.8	2,072	...	15	97.7	98.8	96.6	4.0	Turkmenistan
58	...	—	—	—	—	...	...	...	15	95.0	...	...	...	Tuvalu
36,063	20.2	...	2,029	27,586	13.6	1.5	142	0.5	15	61.8	73.7	50.2	1.9	Uganda
618,000	...	255	...	922,800	...	40.6	2,977	...	15	98.4	99.5	97.4	7.7	Ukraine
1,215	6.4	4	510[1]	13,900	19.2[1]	8.8	521	...	15	79.2	78.9	79.8	1.8	United Arab Emirates
586,000[1]	...	...	48,000[5]	810,000[5]	17.0[5]	48.3	3,126	...	15	100.0	100.0	100.0	5.5	United Kingdom
...	...	5,758[1]	833,000	14,210,000	17.1	81.1	5,398	46.5	15	95.5	95.7	95.3	5.3	United States
56,879	...	2	7,157	61,367	8.6	27.3	2,179	8.1	15	97.3	96.9	97.7	2.8	Uruguay
194,800	11.0[1]	58	...	192,100	...	31.7	2,938	...	15	97.2	98.5	96.0	9.5	Uzbekistan
444	...	1	...	124[14]	...	...	...	...	15	52.9	57.3	47.8	4.9	Vanuatu
[4]	[4]	99[14]	43,833[8]	550,783[8]	12.6[8]	28.5	2,820	11.8	15	91.1	91.8	90.3	5.2	Venezuela
197,500	21.0	104[2]	22,750	297,900	13.1	4.1	404	2.6	15	93.7	96.5	91.2	2.7	Vietnam
—	—	1	266	2,924	11.0	...	...	...	...	...	...	...	...	Virgin Islands (U.S.)
...	...	22	1,598	30,622	19.2	...	...	...	...	...	...	...	...	West Bank
1,222	...	—	...	...	...	...	...	...	...	...	...	...	...	Western Sahara
15,074	40.9	2	1,991	90,826	45.6	4.3	407	...	15	43.2	68.6	23.1	7.5	Yemen
...	...	93	10,544	131,689	12.5	21.1	1,556	...	15	93.3	97.6	89.2	...	Yugoslavia
7,982[14]	...	...	481[2]	5,270[2]	11.0[2]	2.5	241	1.5	15	78.2	85.6	71.3	1.8	Zambia
27,431[8]	18.5[8]	28[8]	3,581	46,492	13.0	6.9	679	4.9	15	85.1	90.4	79.9	8.5	Zimbabwe

[19]Includes lower second level. [20]Upper second level only. [21]Former West Germany only. [22]Port-au-Prince universities only. [23]University of Nouakchott only. [24]Includes schools that provide both first and second level education. [25]Mainland Tanzania only. [26]First level includes kindergarten.

BIBLIOGRAPHY AND SOURCES

The following list indicates the principal documentary sources used in the compilation of *Britannica World Data.* It is by no means a complete list, either for international or for national sources, but is indicative more of the range of materials to which reference has been made in preparing this compilation.

While *Britannica World Data* has long been based primarily on print sources, many rare in North American library collections, the burgeoning resources of the Internet can be accessed from any appropriately equipped personal computer (PC). At this writing, some 60 national statistical offices had Internet sites and there were also sites for central banks, national information offices, individual ministries, and the like.

Because of the relative ease of access to these sites for PC users, uniform resource locators (URLs) for mainly official sites have been added to both country statements (at the end, in boldface) and individual Comparative National Statistics tables (at the end of the headnote) when a source providing comparable international data existed. Many sites exist that are narrower in coverage or less official and that may also serve the reader (on-line newspapers; full texts of national constitutions; business and bank sites) but space permitted the listing of only the top national and intergovernmental sites. Sites that are wholly or predominantly in a language other than English are so identified.

International Statistical Sources

Asian Development Bank. *Asian Development Outlook* (annual); *Key Indicators of Developing Member Countries of ADB* (annual).

Billboard Books. *World Radio TV Handbook* (annual).

Caribbean Development Bank. *Annual Report.*

Christian Research. *World Churches Handbook* (1997).

Comité Monétaire de la Zone Franc. *La Zone Franc: Rapport* (annual).

Commonwealth of Independent States. *Demographic Yearbook; Sodruzhestvo Nezavizimykh Gosudarstv v 19** godu; Strany-Chleny SNG: Statistichesky Yezhegodnik* (*Member States of the CIS: Statistical Yearbook*).

Eastern Caribbean Central Bank. *Report and Statement of Accounts* (annual).

Europa Publications Ltd. *Africa South of the Sahara* (annual); *The Europa Year Book* (2 vol.); *The Far East and Australasia* (annual); *The Middle East and North Africa* (annual).

Food and Agriculture Organization. *Food Balance Sheets; Production Yearbook; Trade Yearbook; World Census of Agriculture* (decennial); *Yearbook of Fishery Statistics* (2 vol.); *Yearbook of Forest Products.*

Her Majesty's Stationery Office. *The Commonwealth Yearbook.*

Instituts d'Émission d'Outre-Mer et des Départements d'Outre-Mer (France). *Bulletin trimestriel* (quarterly); *Rapport annuel.*

Inter-American Development Bank. *Economic and Social Progress in Latin America* (annual).

Inter-Parliamentary Union. *Chronicle of Parliamentary Elections and Developments* (annual); *World Directory of Parliaments* (annual).

International Air Transport Association. *World Air Transport Statistics* (annual).

International Bank for Reconstruction and Development/The World Bank. *Statistical Handbook 19**: States of the Former USSR* (annual); *World Bank Atlas* (annual); *Global Development Finance* (2 vol.; annual); *World Development Report* (annual).

International Civil Aviation Organization. *Civil Aviation Statistics of the World* (annual); *Digest of Statistics.*

International Institute for Strategic Studies. *The Military Balance* (annual).

International Labour Organisation. *Year Book of Labour Statistics; The Cost of Social Security: Basic Tables* (triennial).

International Monetary Fund. *Annual Report on Exchange Arrangements and Exchange Restrictions; Direction of Trade Statistics Yearbook; Government Finance Statistics Yearbook; IMF Staff Country Reports* (irreg.); *International Financial Statistics* (monthly, with yearbook).

International Road Federation. *World Road Statistics* (annual).

International Telecommunication Union. *World Telecommunication Development Report* (irreg.).

Jane's Publishing Co., Ltd. *Jane's World Railways* (annual).

Keesing's Worldwide LLC. *Keesing's Record of World Events* (monthly except August).

Macmillan Press Ltd. *The Statesman's Year-Book.*

Middle East Economic Digest Ltd.; *Middle East Economic Digest* (semimonthly).

Mining Journal, Ltd. *Mining Annual Review* (2 vol.).

Organization for Economic Cooperation and Development. *Economic Surveys* (annual); *Financing and External Debt of Developing Countries* (annual).

Oxford University Press. *World Christian Encyclopedia* (David B. Barrett, ed. [1982]).

Pan American Health Organization. *Health Conditions in the Americas* (2 vol.; quadrennial).

PennWell Publishing Co. *International Petroleum Encyclopedia* (annual).

Reed Travel Group. *OAG Desktop Guide—Worldwide* (monthly).

René Moreux et Cie. *Marchés tropicaux & Méditerranéens* (weekly).

United Nations (UN). *Demographic Yearbook; Energy Balances and Electricity Profiles* (biennial); *Industrial Commodities Statistics Yearbook; Energy Statistics Yearbook; International Trade Statistics Yearbook* (2 vol.); *Monthly Bulletin of Statistics; Population Studies* (irreg.); *National Accounts Statistics* (2 parts; annual); *Population and Vital Statistics Report* (quarterly); *Statistical Yearbook; World Population Prospects 19*** (biennial).

UN: Economic Commission for Africa. *African Socio-Economic Indicators* (annual); *African Statistical Yearbook* (2 vol. in 4 parts); *Demographic and Related Socio-Economic Data Sheets for ECA Member States* (irreg.); *Economic and Social Survey of Africa* (annual).

UN: Economic Commission for Europe. *Annual Bulletin of Housing and Building Statistics for Europe; Annual Bulletin of Transport Statistics for Europe.*

UN: Economic Commission for Latin America. *Economic Survey of Latin America and the Caribbean* (2 vol.; annual); *Statistical Yearbook for Latin America and the Caribbean.*

UN: Economic and Social Commission for Asia and the Pacific. *Statistical Indicators for Asia and the Pacific* (quarterly); *Statistical Yearbook for Asia and the Pacific.*

UN: Economic and Social Commission for Western Asia. *Demographic and Related Socio-Economic Data Sheets* (irreg.); *National Accounts Studies of the ESCWA Region* (irreg.); *The Population Situation in the ESCWA Region* (irreg.); *Prices and Financial Statistics in the ESCWA Region* (irreg.); *Statistical Abstract of the Region of the Economic and Social Commission for Western Asia* (annual).

UN: Educational, Scientific, and Cultural Organization. *Statistical Yearbook.*

United Nations Development Programme. *Human Development Report* (annual); *National Human Development Report series* (irreg.).

United Nations Industrial Development Organization. *Industrial Development Review Series* (irreg.); *Industrial Development: Global Report* (annual); *International Yearbook of Industrial Statistics.*

United States: Central Intelligence Agency, *The World Factbook* (annual); Dept. of Commerce, *World Population Profile* (biennial); Dept. of Health and Human Services, *Social Security Programs Throughout the World* (biennial); Dept. of Interior, *Minerals Yearbook* (3 vol. in 6 parts); Dept. of State, *Background Notes* (irreg.).

World Energy Conference. *Survey of Energy Resources* (triennial).

World Health Organization. *World Health Statistics Annual; World Health Statistics Quarterly.*

World Tourism Organization. *Compendium of Tourism Statistics* (annual); *World Tourism Statistics* (2 vol.; annual).

National Statistical Sources

Afghanistan. *Afghanistan Rehabilitation Strategy: Action Plan* (6 vol.; 1993); *Preliminary Results of the First Afghan Population Census (1979).*

Albania. *Albanian Human Development Report 1996* (UNDP); *IMF Economic Reviews: Albania* (1994); *Population and Housing Census 1989; Statistical Yearbook of Albania.*

Algeria. *Annuaire statistique; Recensement général de la population et de l'habitat, 1987.*

American Samoa. *American Samoa Statistical Digest* (annual); *1990 Census of Population and Housing.*

Andorra. *Estadístiques* (annual); *Recull Estadístic General de la Població Andorra 90.*

Angola. *Angola—Recent Economic Developments* (IMF Staff Country Report [1995]); *Perfil estatístico de Angola* (annual).

Antigua. *Antigua and Barbuda—Statistical Annex* (IMF Staff Country Report [1996]); *Statistical Yearbook; 1991 Population and Housing Census.*

Argentina. *Anuario estadístico de la República Argentina; Censo nacional de población y vivienda, 1991; Encuesta permanente de hogares* (irreg.).

Armenia. *Armenia Human Development Report* (UNDP; 1996); *Economic Reviews: Armenia* (IMF [irreg.]); *Statisticheskii Yezhegodnik Armenii* (Statistical Yearbook of Armenia).

Aruba. *Statistical Yearbook; Third Population and Housing Census October 6, 1991.*

Australia. *Monthly Summary of Statistics, Australia; Social Indicators* (annual); *Year Book Australia; 1991 Census of Population and Housing.*

Austria. *Grosszählung 1991* (General Census 1991). *Sozialstatistische Daten* (irreg.); *Statistisches Jahrbuch für die Republik Österreich.*

Azerbaijan. *Azerbaijan—Recent Economic Developments* (IMF Staff Country Report [1997]); *Azerbaijan Human Development Report* (UNDP; 1996); *Statistical Yearbook of Azerbaijan.*

Bahamas, The. *Census of Population and Housing 1990; Statistical Abstract* (annual).

Bahrain. *Statistical Abstract* (annual); *The Population, Housing, Buildings and Establishments Census—1991.*

Bangladesh. *Bangladesh Population Census, 1991; Statistical Yearbook of Bangladesh.*

Barbados. *Barbados Economic Report* (annual); *Monthly Digest of Statistics; 1993–2000 Development Plan.*

Belarus. *Economic Reviews: Belarus* (IMF [irreg.]); *Narodnoye Khozyaystvo Respubliki Belarus: Statisticheskiy Yezhegodnik* (National Economy of the Republic of Belarus: Statistical Yearbook).

Belgium. *Annuaire statistique de la Belgique; Recensement de la population et des logements au 1er mars 1991.*

Belize. *Abstract of Statistics* (annual); *Belize Economic Survey* (annual); *Belize—Statistical Appendix* (IMF Staff Country Report [1997]); *Development*

Plan 1990–94; Labour Force Survey (1993); 1991 Population Census: Major Findings.

Benin. *Annuaire statistique; Recensement général de la population et de l'habitation* (1992).

Bermuda. *Bermuda Digest of Statistics* (annual); *Report of the Manpower Survey* (annual); *The 1991 Census of Population and Housing.*

Bhutan. *Bhutan—Selected Issues* (IMF Staff Country Report [1997]); *Statistical Yearbook of Bhutan.*

Bolivia. *Anuario Estadístico; Censo Nacional de población y vivienda 1992; Compendio Estadístico* (annual); *Estadísticas Socio-económicas* (annual); *Resumen estadístico* (annual).

Botswana. *National Development Plan 7, 1991–1997; 1991 Population and Housing Census.*

Brazil. *Anuário Estatístico do Brasil; Censo Demografico 1991.*

Brunei. *Brunei Statistical Yearbook; Summary Tables of the Population Census 1991.*

Bulgaria. *Prebroyavaneto na naselenìeto kŭm 4.12.1985 godina* (Census of Population of Dec. 4, 1985); *Naselenie* (Population; annual); *Statisticheskii godishnik na Republika Bŭlgariya* (Statistical Yearbook of the Republic of Bulgaria).

Burkina Faso. *Annuaire Statistique; Burkina Faso—Statistical Tables* (IMF Staff Country Report [1997]); *Recensement général de la population du 10 au 20 decembre 1985.*

Burundi. *Annuaire statistique; Recensement général de la population, 1990.*

Cambodia. *Cambodia: A Country Study* (1990); *Intersectoral Basic Needs Assessment Mission to Cambodia* (Unesco; 1991); *Report of the Kampuchea Needs Assessment Study* (UNDP; 1989).

Cameroon. *Cameroon—Selected Issues and Statistical Appendix* (IMF Staff Country Report [1996]); *Recensement général de la population et de l'habitat 1987.*

Canada. *Canada Year Book* (biennial); *Census Canada 1991: Population.*

Cape Verde. *Boletím Anual de Estatística; Cape Verde—Recent Economic Developments* (IMF Staff Country Report [1996]); *I.º Recenseamento Geral da População e Habitação—1990.*

Central African Republic. *Annuaire statistique; Central African Republic—Recent Economic Developments* (IMF Staff Country Report [1997]); *Recensement général de la population 1988.*

Chad. *Annuaire statistique; Chad: a Country Study* (1990); *Chad—Background Issues and Statistical Update (IMF Staff Country Report* [1995]).

Chile. *Chile XVI censo nacional de población y V de vivienda, 22 de abril 1992; Compendio estadístico* (annual).

China, People's Republic of. *People's Republic of China Year-Book; Statistical Yearbook of China; 10 Percent Sampling Tabulation on the 1990 Population Census of the People's Republic of China.*

Colombia. *Colombia estadística* (2 vol.; annual); *XV Censo nacional de población y IV de vivienda* (1985).

Comoros. *Comoros—Recent Economic Developments* (IMF Staff Country Report [1996]); *Recensement général de la population et de l'habitat 15 septembre 1980.*

Congo, Dem. Rep. of the (Zaire). *Annuaire statistique* (irreg.); *Recensement Scientifique de la Population du 1er juillet 1984.*

Congo, Rep. of the. *Annuaire statistique; Recensement Général de la Population et de l'Habitat de 1984.*

Costa Rica. *Anuario estadístico; Censo de Población 1984; Plan Nacional de Desarrollo, 1986–90* (2 vol.).

Côte d'Ivoire. *Côte d'Ivoire—Statistical Annex* (IMF Staff Country Report [1996]); *Recensement général de la population et de l'habitat 1988.*

Croatia. *Census of Population, Households, Dwellings and Farms 31st March 1991; Statistical Yearbook.*

Cuba. *Anuario estadístico; Censo de población y viviendas, 1981.*

Cyprus. *Census of Industrial Production* (annual); *Census of Population 1992; Economic Report* (annual); *Statistical Abstract* (annual).

Czech Republic. *Statistická ročenka České Republiky* (Statistical Yearbook of the Czech Republic).

Denmark. *Folke- og boligtaellingen, 1981* (Population and Housing Census); *Statistisk årbog* (Statistical Yearbook).

Djibouti. *Annuaire statistique de Djibouti.*

Dominica. *Dominica—Recent Economic Developments* (IMF Staff Country Report [1997]). *Population and Housing Census 1991; Statistical Digest* (irreg.).

Dominican Republic. *Cifras Dominicanas* (irreg.); *VI Censo nacional de población y vivienda, 1981.*

Ecuador. *Serie estadística* (quinquennial); *Censo de población (V) y de vivienda (IV) 1990.*

Egypt. *Population, Housing, and Establishment Census, 1986; Statistical Yearbook.*

El Salvador. *Censos Nacionales: V Censo de Población y IV de Vivienda (1992); El Salvador en cifras* (annual); *Indicadores Económicos y Sociales* (annual); *Plan de Desarrollo Economico y Social 1989–1994.*

Equatorial Guinea. *Censos Nacionales, I de Población y I de Vivienda—4 al 17 de Julio de 1983; Equatorial Guinea—Background Appendices* and *Recent Economic Developments* (IMF Staff Country Reports [1995 and 1996]); *Guinea en cifras* (irreg.).

Eritrea. *Eritrea—Recent Economic Developments* (IMF Staff Country Report [1996]); *Ethiopia and Eritrea: A Documentary Study* (1993).

Estonia. *Eesti Statistika Aastaraamat* (Estonia Statistical Yearbook); *Estonian Human Development Report* (annual).

Ethiopia. *Ethiopia 1984 Population and Housing Census; Ethiopia Statistical Abstract* (annual).

Faroe Islands. *Rigsombudsmanden på Færøerne: Beretning* (annual).

Fiji. *Annual Employment Survey; Census of Industries* (annual); *Current Economic Statistics* (quarterly); *1986 Census of the Population.*

Finland. *Annual Statistics of Agriculture; Economic Survey* (annual); *Population Census 1990; Statistical Yearbook of Finland.*

France. *Annuaire statistique de la France; Données sociales* (triennial); *Recensement général de la population de 1990; Tableaux de l'Economie Française* (annual).

French Guiana. *Recensement général de la population de 1990: logements-population-emplois, 973: Guyane; Tableaux economiques regionaux: Guyane* (biennial).

French Polynesia. *Résultats du Recensement Général de la Population de la Polynésie Française, du 6 Septembre 1988; Tableaux de l'economie polynesienne* (irreg.); *Te avei'a: Bulletin d'information statistique* (monthly).

Gabon. *Gabon: Poste d'Expansion Economique à Libreville* (1995); *Situation économique, financière et sociale de la République Gabonaise* (annual).

Gambia, The. *Statistical Abstract* (annual?); *The Gambia—Recent Economic Developments* (IMF Staff Country Report [1995]).

Gaza Strip. *Judaea, Samaria, and Gaza Area Statistics Quarterly; Palestinian Statistical Abstract* (annual).

Georgia. *Georgia—Recent Economic Developments* (IMF Staff Country Report [1997]); *Narodnoye Khozyaystvo Gruzinskoy SSR* (National Economy of the Georgian S.S.R. [annual]).

Germany. *Statistisches Jahrbuch für die Bundesrepublik Deutschland; Volkszählung vom 25. Mai 1987* (Census of Population).

Ghana. *Ghana—Selected Issues and Statistical Annex* (IMF [1996]); *Population Census of Ghana, 1984; Quarterly Digest of Statistics.*

Gibraltar. *Abstract of Statistics* (annual); *Census of Gibraltar, 1991.*

Greece. *Recensement de la population et des habitations, 1991; Statistical Yearbook of Greece.*

Greenland. *Grønland* (annual); *Grønlands befolkning* (Greenland Population [annual]).

Grenada. *Abstract of Statistics* (annual); *Grenada—Statistical Appendix* (IMF Staff Country Report [1996]). *1991 Population and Housing Census.*

Guadeloupe. *Recensement général de la population de 1990: logements-population-emplois, 971: Guadeloupe; Tableaux economiques regionaux: Guadeloupe* (biennial).

Guam. *Guam Annual Economic Review; Census '90: Guam.*

Guatemala. *Anuario Estadística; Censos nacionales, 1981: IX de población—IV de habitación.*

Guernsey. *Guernsey Census 1991; Statistical Digest* (annual).

Guinea. *Guinea—Background Paper* (IMF Staff Country Report [1996]).

Guinea-Bissau. *Guinea-Bissau—Recent Economic Developments* (IMF Staff Country Report [1996]); *Recenseamento Geral da População e da Habitação, 16 de Abril de 1979.*

Guyana. *Annual Statistical Abstract; Guyana: From Economic Recovery to Sustained Growth* (1993); *Guyana and Belize: Country Studies (1993).*

Haiti. *Dominican Republic and Haiti: Country Studies* (1991); *Haiti—Statistical Annex* (IMF Staff Country Report [1996]). *Résultats préliminaires du recensement général* (Septembre 1982).

Honduras. *Anuario estadístico; Censo nacional de Población y Vivienda, 1988; Honduras—Statistical Appendix* (IMF Staff Country Report [1997]); *Honduras en cifras* (annual).

Hong Kong. *Annual Digest of Statistics; Hong Kong* (annual); *Hong Kong 1991 Population Census; Hong Kong Social and Economic Trends* (biennial).

Hungary. *Statisztikai évkönyv* (Statistical Yearbook); *1990, Évi népszámlálás* (Census of Population).

Iceland. *Hagtidhindi* (monthly); *Landshagir* (Statistical Yearbook of Iceland [annual]); *Utanrikisverslun* (External Trade [annual]).

India. *Census of India, 1991; Economic Survey* (annual); *India: A Reference Annual; Statistical Abstract* (annual).

Indonesia. *Indonesia: An Official Handbook* (irreg.); *Hasil Sensus penduduk Indonesia, 1990* (Census of Population); *Statistical Yearbook of Indonesia.*

Iran. *Multi-Round Population Survey 1991; National Census of Population and Housing, October 1986; A Statistical Reflection of the Islamic Republic of Iran* (annual); *Iran Statistical Yearbook.*

Iraq. *Iraq: A Country Study* (1990); *Annual Abstract of Statistics.*

Ireland. *Census of Population of Ireland, 1991; National Income and Expenditure* (annual); *Statistical Abstract* (annual).

Isle of Man. *Census Report 1991; Isle of Man Digest of Economic and Social Statistics* (annual).

Israel. *1995 Census of Population and Housing; Statistical Abstract* (annual).

Italy. *Statistica agrarie; Statistiche demografiche* (4 parts); *Statistiche dell'istruzione; Annuario statistico Italiano; 13° Censimento generale della popolazione e delle Abitazioni 20 Ottobre 1991.*

Jamaica. *Economic and Social Survey* (annual); *Statistical Abstract* (annual); *Statistical Yearbook of Jamaica.*

Japan. *Japan Statistical Yearbook; Statistical Indicators on Social Life* (annual); *1995 Population Census of Japan.*

Jersey. *Report of the Census for 1991; Statistical Digest* (annual).

Jordan. *Population and Housing Census 1994; Family Expenditure Survey* (1980); *National Accounts* (irreg.); *Statistical Yearbook.*

Kazakstan. *Economic Reviews: Kazakhstan* (IMF [irreg.]); *Statistical Yearbook; Statistichesky Yezhegodnik* (Statistical Yearbook).

Kenya. *Economic Survey* (annual); *Population Census 1989; Statistical Abstract* (annual).

Kiribati. *Annual Abstract of Statistics; Kiribati Population Census 1990.*

Korea, North. *North Korea: A Country Study* (1994); *The Population of North Korea* (1990).

Korea, South. *Korea Statistical Yearbook; Social Indicators in Korea* (annual); *1995 Population and Housing Census.*

Kuwait. *Annual Statistical Abstract; General Census of Population and Housing and Buildings 1985.*

Kyrgyzstan. *Economic Reviews: Kyrgyz Republic* (IMF [irreg.]); *Statistichesky Yezhegodnik Kyrgyzstana* (Statistical Yearbook of Kyrgyzstan).

Laos. *Lao People's Democratic Republic—Recent Economic Developments* (IMF Staff Country Report [1996]).

Latvia. *Latvia: The Transition to a Market Economy* (1993); *Statistical Yearbook of Latvia.*

Lebanon. *Lebanon: A Country Study* (1989).

Lesotho. *Lesotho—Recent Economic Developments* (IMF Staff Country Report [1996]); *Statistical Yearbook; 1986 Population Census.*

Liberia. *Economic Survey* (annual); *1974 Census of Population and Housing.*

Libya. *The Five-Year Development Plan 1981–85; Libya Population Census, 1973.*

Liechtenstein. *Statistisches Jahrbuch; Volkszählung, 2 Dezember 1980* (Census of Population).

Lithuania. *Lietuvos Statistikos Metraštis* (Lithuanian Statistical Yearbook); *Lithuania: The Transition to a Market Economy* (1993).

Luxembourg. *Annuaire statistique; Bulletin du STATEC* (monthly); *Recensement général de la population du 31 mars 1991.*

Macau. *Anuário Estatístico; XIII Recenseamento Geral da População, 1991.*

Macedonia. *Former Yugoslav Republic of Macedonia—Statistical Appendix* (IMF Staff Country Report [1997]); *Statistical Yearbook of the Republic of Macedonia.*

Madagascar. *Madagascar—Selected Issues and Statistical Annex* (IMF Staff Country Report [1996]); *Recensement général de la population et de l'habitat, aout 1993; Situation économique* (annual).

Malaŵi. *Malaŵi Population and Housing Census, 1987; Malawi Statistical Yearbook; Malawi Yearbook.*

Malaysia. *Population and Housing Census of Malaysia 1991; Yearbook of Statistics.*

Maldives. *National Development Plan 1991–1993; Population and Housing Census of Maldives 1990; Statistical Year Book of Maldives.*

Mali. *Annuaire statistique du Mali; Recensement general de la population et de l'habitat (du 1er au 14 avril 1987).*

Malta. *Annual Abstract of Statistics; Quarterly Digest of Statistics.*
Marshall Islands. *Marshall Islands Statistical Abstract* (annual).
Martinique. *Recensement de la population de 1990: logements-population-emplois, 972: Martinique; Tableaux economiques regionaux: Martinique* (biennial).
Mauritania. *Annuaire Statistique; Mauritania—Statistical Appendix* (IMF Staff Country Report [1997]).
Mauritius. *Annual Digest of Statistics; 1990 Housing and Population Census of Mauritius.*
Mayotte. *Bulletin Trimestriel* (quarterly) and *Rapport Annuel* (Institut d'Emission, France); *Recensement général de la population de la Collectivité territoriale de Mayotte: août 1991.*
Mexico. *Anuario estadístico; XI Censo general de población y vivienda, 1990; Informe de Gobierno: Estadístico* (annual).
Micronesia. *Micronesia—Recent Economic Developments* (IMF Staff Country Report [1996]); *Second National Development Plan 1992–1996.*
Moldova. *Economic Reviews: Moldova* (IMF [irreg.]); *Republica Moldova in Cifre* (annual); *1996 National Human Development Report: Republic of Moldova* (UNDP).
Mongolia. *Mongolia—Background Material* (IMF Staff Country Report [1996]); *National Economy of the MPR for 70 years: 1921–91* (1991; quinquennial); *The Mongolian People's Republic: Towards a Market Economy* (1991).
Morocco. *Annuaire statistique du Maroc; Recensement général de la population et de l'habitat de 1994.*
Mozambique. *Anuário Estatístico; Mozambique—Recent Economic Developments* (IMF Staff Country Report [1996]); *1º Recenseamento Geral da População, 1980.*
Myanmar (Burma). *Myanmar—Recent Economic Developments* (IMF Staff Country Report [1997]); *Report to the Pyithu Hluttaw on the Financial, Social, and Economic Conditions for 19*** (annual); *Statistical Abstract* (irreg.); *1983 Population Census.*
Namibia. *1991 Population and Housing Census; Statistical/Economic Review* (annual).
Nepal. *Economic Survey* (annual); *Population Monograph of Nepal* (1995); *The Seventh Plan (1985–90); Statistical Pocket Book* (irreg.); *Statistical Yearbook of Nepal.*
Netherlands, The. *Statistical Yearbook of the Netherlands; 14e Algemene volkstelling, 28 februari 1971* (14th General Population Census).
Netherlands Antilles. *Netherlands Antilles—Recent Economic Developments* (IMF Staff Country Report [1997]); *Tweede Algemene Volks- en Woningtelling Nederlandse Antillen: toestand per 1 Februari 1981; Statistical Yearbook of the Netherlands Antilles.*
New Caledonia. *Annuaire statistique; Recensement de la population de la Nouvelle-Calédonie au 4 avril 1989; Tableaux de l'economie Caledonienne* (annual).
New Zealand. *1991 New Zealand Census of Population and Dwellings; New Zealand Official Yearbook.*
Nicaragua. *Censos Nacionales 1995; Compendio Estadístico* (annual); *Nicaragua—Recent Economic Developments* (IMF Staff Country Report [1996]).
Niger. *Annuaire statistique; Niger—Background Paper* (IMF Staff Country Report [1996]); *Plan de developpement economique et social du Niger 1987–91; 2ème Recensement général de la population 1988.*
Nigeria. *Annual Abstract of Statistics; Nigeria: A Country Study* (1992); *Nigeria—Statistical Appendix* (IMF Staff Country Report [1997]).
Norway. *Folke- og boligtelling 1990* (Population and Housing Census); *Industristatistikk* (annual); *Statistisk årbok* (Statistical Yearbook).
Oman. *General Census of Population, Housing, and Establishments* (1993); *Statistical Year Book; Fourth Five-Year Development Plan (1991–1995).*
Pakistan. *Economic Survey* (annual); *Eighth Five Year Plan* (1993–98); *Pakistan Statistical Yearbook; Population Census of Pakistan, 1981.*
Palau. *Abstract of Statistics* (annual); *Census '90.*
Panama. *Indicadores económicos y sociales* (annual); *Censos nacionales de 1990: IX de población y V de vivienda, 13 de mayo de 1990; Panama en cifras* (annual); *Situación económica: Cuentas nacionales* (annual); *Situación económica: Industria* (annual).
Papua New Guinea. *Papua New Guinea—Statistical Appendix* (IMF Staff Country Report [1997]); *Summary of Statistics* (annual); *1990 National Population Census.*
Paraguay. *Anuario estadístico del Paraguay; Censo nacional de población y viviendas, 1992.*
Peru. *Censos nacionales; IX de población: IV de vivienda, 11 de julio de 1993; Compendio estadístico* (3 vol.; annual); *Informe estadístico* (annual).
Philippines. *Philippine Statistical Yearbook; Philippine Yearbook; 1990 Census of Population and Housing.*
Poland. *Narodowy spis powszechny 1988* (Census of Population); *Rocznik statystyczny* (Statistical Yearbook).
Portugal. *Anuário Estatístico; XIII Recenseamento Geral da População: III Recenseamento Geral da Habitação, 1991.*
Puerto Rico. *Estadísticas socioeconomicas* (annual); *Informe económico al gobernador* (Economic Report to the Governor [annual]); *1990 Census of Population and Housing* (U.S.).
Qatar. *Annual Statistical Abstract; Economic Survey of Qatar* (annual); *Qatar Year Book.*
Réunion. *Recensement général de la population de 1990: logements-population-emploi, 974; Réunion; Tableau Economique de la Réunion* (biennial).
Romania. *Anuarul statistic al României; Population and Housing Census January 7, 1992.*
Russia. *Demograficheskiy Yezhegodnik Rossii* (Demographic Yearbook of Russia; [annual]); *Rossiysky Statistichesky Yezhegodnik* (Russian Statistical Yearbook).
Rwanda. *Bulletin de Statistique: Supplement Annuel; Recensement General de la Population et de l'Habitat 1991.*
St. Kitts and Nevis. *Annual Digest of Statistics; St. Christopher and Nevis—Recent Economic Developments* (IMF Staff Country Report [1995]).
St. Lucia. *Annual Statistical Digest; St. Lucia—Recent Economic Developments* (IMF Staff Country Report [1996]).
St. Vincent and the Grenadines. *Digest of Statistics* (annual); *Population and Housing Census 1991.*
Samoa (Western Samoa). *Annual Statistical Abstract; Census of Population and Housing,* 1981; *Seventh Development Plan 1992–1994; Western Samoa—Recent Economic Developments* (IMF Staff Country Report [1997]).
San Marino. *Bollettino di Statistica* (quarterly); *5 Censimento generale della popolazione* (1979).
São Tomé and Príncipe. *1° Recenseamento Geral da População e da Habitação 1981; Sao Tome—Select Issues and Statistical Appendix* (IMF Staff Country Report [1996]).
Saudi Arabia. *The Statistical Indicator* (annual); *Statistical Yearbook.*
Senegal. *Recensement de la Population et de l'Habitat 1988; Situation économique du Senegal* (annual).
Seychelles. *National Development Plan, 1990–94;* (2 vol.); *Statistical Abstract* (annual); *1987 Census Report.*
Sierra Leone. *Sierra Leone—Statistical Annex* (IMF Staff Country Report [1996]).
Singapore. *Census of Population, 1990; Singapore Yearbook; Yearbook of Statistics Singapore.*
Slovakia. *Sčítanie L'udu, Domov a Bytov 1991* (Census of Population, Housing, and Families 1991); *Statistical Yearbook of the Slovak Republic.*
Slovenia. *Statistični Letopis Republike Slovenija* (Statistical Yearbook of the Republic of Slovenia).
Solomon Islands. *Solomon Islands 1986 Population Census; Statistical Bulletin* (irreg.).
Somalia. *Statistical Abstract* (annual).
South Africa. *1991 Population Census; South Africa: Official Yearbook of the Republic of South Africa; South African Statistics* (biennial).
Spain. *Anuario estadístico; Censo de población de 1991.*
Sri Lanka. *Census of Population and Housing, 1981; Sri Lanka Year Book; Statistical Pocketbook of the Democratic Socialist Republic of Sri Lanka* (annual).
Sudan, The. *Sudan: A Country Study* (1992); *Third Population Census, 1983.*
Suriname. *General Population Census 1980; Statistisch Jaarboek van Suriname; Suriname—Statistical Annex* (IMF Staff Country Report [1996]).
Swaziland. *Annual Statistical Bulletin; Report on the 1986 Swaziland Population Census; Swaziland—Recent Economic Developments* (IMF Staff Country Report [1997]).
Sweden. *Folk- och bostadsräkningen, 1990* (Population and Housing Census); *Statistisk årsbok för Sverige* (Statistical Abstract of Sweden [annual]).
Switzerland. *Recensement fédéral de la population, 1990; Statistisches Jahrbuch* (Statistical Yearbook).
Syria. *General Census of Housing and Inhabitants, 1981; Statistical Abstract* (annual).
Taiwan. *Industry of Free China* (monthly); *The Republic of China Yearbook; Social Indicators of the Republic of China* (annual); *Statistical Abstract* (annual); *Statistical Yearbook of the Republic of China; Taiwan Statistical Data Book* (annual); *1990 Census of Population and Housing.*
Tajikistan. *Economic Reviews: Tajikistan* (IMF [irreg.]); *Narodnoye Khozyaystvo Tadzhikskoy SSR* (National Economy of the Tadzhik S.S.R. [annual]).
Tanzania. *Tanzania—Selected Issues and Statistical Appendix* (IMF Staff Country Report [1996]); *Tanzania in Figures* (annual); *Tanzania Statistical Abstract* (irreg.); *1978 Population Census.*
Thailand. *Report of the Industrial Survey, Whole Kingdom* (biennial); *Report of the Labor Force Survey: Whole Kingdom* (three issues annually); *Statistical Handbook of Thailand* (annual); *Statistical Yearbook; 1990 Population and Housing Census.*
Togo. *Annuaire statistique du Togo; Eurostat Country Profile: Togo* (1991); *Recensement Général de la Population et de l'Habitat 1981; Togo—Statistical Annex* (IMF Staff Country Report [1996]).
Tonga. *Population Census, 1986; Sixth Development Plan 1991–95; Tonga—Recent Economic Developments* (IMF Staff Country Report [1997]).
Trinidad and Tobago. *Annual Statistical Digest; 1990 Population and Housing Census.*
Tunisia. *Annuaire statistique de la Tunisie; Recensement général de la population et des logements, 30 mars 1984.*
Turkey. *1990 Genel Nüfus Sayımı* (1990 Census of Population); *Türkiye İstatistik Yilliği* (Statistical Yearbook of Turkey).
Turkmenistan. *Turkmenistan—Recent Economic Developments* (IMF Staff Country Report [1996]); *Turkmenistan Human Development Report* (UNDP [1996]); *Turkmenistan v tsifrakh* (Turkmenistan in figures [annual]).
Tuvalu. *1992–94 Medium-Term Economic Framework Programme.*
Uganda. *Uganda: A Country Study; Uganda—Background Paper (IMF Staff Country Report* [1995]).
Ukraine. *Statistichniy Shchorichnik Ukraini za 19*** *rik* (Statistical Yearbook of Ukraine for the year 19**); *Ukraine—Recent Economic Developments* (IMF Staff Country Report [1996]); *Ukraine Human Development Report* (UNDP [1996]).
United Arab Emirates. *Statistical Yearbook* (Abu Dhabi).
United Kingdom. *Annual Abstract of Statistics; Britain: An Official Handbook* (annual); *Census 1991; General Household Survey* series (individual titles vary; annual); *United Kingdom National Accounts.*
United States. *Agricultural Statistics* (annual); *Annual Energy Review; Current Population Reports; Digest of Education Statistics* (annual); *Minerals Yearbook* (3 vol. in 6 parts); *National Transportation Statistics* (annual); *Statistical Abstract* (annual); *U.S. Exports: SIC-Based Products* (annual); *U.S. Imports: SIC-Based Products* (annual); *Vital and Health Statistics* (series 1–20); *1992 Census of Agriculture; 1992 Census of Construction Industries; 1992 Census of Manufacturing; 1992 Census of Retail Trade; 1992 Census of Service Industries; 1992 Census of Wholesale Trade; 1990 Census of Population and Housing.*
Uruguay. *Anuario Estadístico; Censo General: VI de población: IV de viviendas, Octubre 1985.*
Uzbekistan. *Narodnoye Khozyaystvo Respubliki Uzbekistan v 19*** *g.* (National Economy of Uzbekistan in the Year 19** [annual]); *Republic of Uzbekistan; Uzbekistan—Selected Issues and Statistical Appendix* (IMF Staff Country Report [1996]).
Vanuatu. *National Population Census 1989; Second National Development Plan 1987–1991* (2 vol.); *Vanuatu Statistical Yearbook.*
Venezuela. *Anuario estadístico; Censo General de la Población y Vivienda 1990; Encuesta de hogares por muestreo* (annual); *Encuesta industrial* (annual).
Vietnam. *Nien Giam Thong Ke* (Statistical Yearbook); *Tong Dieu Tra Dan So Viet Nam—1989* (*Vietnam Population Census—1989*); *Vietnam—Recent Economic Developments* and *Selected Issues* (IMF Staff Country Reports [1996]).
Virgin Islands of the United States. *1990 Census of Population and Housing* (U.S.).
West Bank. *Judaea, Samaria, and Gaza Area Statistics Quarterly; Palestinian Statistical Abstract* (annual).
Western Sahara. *Recensement General de la Population et de l'Habitat* (1994 [Morocco]).
Yemen. *Country Presentation: Republic of Yemen* (1990); *The Yemens: Country Studies* (1986).
Yugoslavia. *Popis stanovištva, domaćinstava, stanova i poljoprivrednih gazdinstava 1991 godine* (Census of Population, Households, Housing, and Agricultural Holdings 1991); *Statistički godišnjak Jugoslavije* (Statistical Yearbook of Yugoslavia).
Zambia. *National Development Plan, 1989–93; Zambia—Statistical Annex* (IMF Staff Country Report [1996]); *1990 Census of Population, Housing, Agriculture.*
Zimbabwe. *Population Census 1992; Statistical Yearbook* (irreg.).

Index

This index covers both *Britannica Book of the Year* (cumulative for 10 years) and *Britannica World Data.*

Entries in dark type are titles of articles in the *Book of the Year;* **an accompanying year in dark type gives the year the reference appears, and the accompanying page number** in light type **shows where the article appears. References for previous years are preceded by the year in dark type. For example, "Architecture 98:**136; **97:**137; **96:**117; **95:**104; **94:**99; **93:**100; **92:**98; **91:**127; **90:**146; **89:**128**" indicates that the article "Architecture" appeared every year from 1989 through 1998. Other references that appear with a page number but without a year refer to references from the current yearbook.**

Indented entries in light type that follow dark-type article titles refer by page number to other places in the text where the subject of the article is discussed. Light-type entries that are not indented refer by page number to subjects that are not themselves article titles. Names of people covered in biographies and obituaries are followed by the abbreviation "(biog.)" or "(obit.)" with the year in dark type and a page number in light type, *e.g.,* Teresa, Mother, *or* Agnes Gonxha Bojaxhiu (obit.) 118, or Clinton, Bill, *or* William Jefferson Clinton (biogs.) **97:**70; **94:**37; **93:**37. In cases where a person has both a biography and an obituary, the words appear as subentries under the main entry and are alphabetized accordingly, *e.g.:*

Goldsmith, Sir James Michael
biography **90:**89
obituary **98:**101

References to illustrations are by page number and are preceded by the abbreviation *il.*

The index uses word-by-word alphabetization (treating a word as one or more characters separated by a space from the next word). Names beginning with "Mc" and "Mac" are alphabetized as "Mac"; "St." is treated as "Saint."

A

References with dark-type numbers refer to the previous years, *e.g.,* **97:**324 for the 1997 edition, page 324.

B

References with dark-type numbers refer to the previous years, *e.g.,* **97:**324 for the 1997 edition, page 324.

E

F

G

References with dark-type numbers refer to the previous years, *e.g.,* **97:**324 for the 1997 edition, page 324.

H

I

J

References with dark-type numbers refer to the previous years, *e.g.,* **97:**324 for the 1997 edition, page 324.

L

M

N

P

Q

R

S

References with dark-type numbers refer to the previous years, *e.g.,* **97:**324 for the 1997 edition, page 324.

T

U

Z